Accounting Standards

2013–14

Extant at 30 April 2013

General Editor
David Chopping

Moore Stephens LLP

CCH
a Wolters Kluwer business

Disclaimer

This publication is sold with the understanding that neither the publisher nor the authors, with regard to this publication, are engaged in rendering legal or professional services. The material contained in this publication neither purports, nor is intended to be, advice on any particular matter.

Although this publication incorporates a considerable degree of standardisation, subjective judgment by the user, based on individual circumstances, is indispensable. This publication is an 'aid' and cannot be expected to replace such judgment.

Neither the publisher nor the authors can accept any responsibility or liability to any person, whether a purchaser of this publication or not, in respect of anything done or omitted to be done by any such person in reliance, whether sole or partial, upon the whole or any part of the contents of this publication.

Telephone Helpline Disclaimer Notice

Where purchasers of this publication also have access to any Telephone Helpline Service operated by Wolters Kluwer (UK), then Wolters Kluwer's total liability to contract, tort (including negligence, or breach of statutory duty) misrepresentation, restitution or otherwise with respect to any claim arising out of its acts or alleged omissions in the provision of the Helpline Service shall be limited to the yearly subscription fee paid by the Claimant.

Wolters Kluwer (UK) Limited
145 London Road
Kingston upon Thames
KT2 6SR
Tel: 0844 561 8166
Fax: 0208 547 2638
E-mail: cch@wolterskluwer.co.uk
www.cch.co.uk

ISBN 978-1-84798-660-3

Financial Reporting Standards and UITF Abstracts are issued by the Financial Reporting Council in respect of their application in the United Kingdom and by the Institute of Chartered Accountants in Ireland in respect of their application in the Republic of Ireland.

British Library Cataloguing-in-Publication Data.
A catalogue record for this book is available from the British Library.

Typeset by YHT Ltd, London
Printed and bound by ROTÄBOOK, Ctra CM4001 Km26.600 45250 Añover de Tajo (TOLEDO)

Contents

	Page
Part One Introduction	
History of the Accounting Standards Committee	3
Report of the review committee on the making of Accounting Standards	3
The present standard-setting regime	4
ASB's Statement of Aims	7
Withdrawn standards	8
Part Two Statement of Principles	
Statement of Principles for Financial Reporting	13
Statement of Principles for Financial Reporting – Interpretation for public benefit entities	97
Part Three Accounting Standards	
Foreword to accounting standards	167
The true and fair requirement revisited	179
Statements of Standard Accounting Practice	
SSAP 4 Accounting for government grants	196
SSAP 5 Accounting for value added tax	205
SSAP 9 Stocks and long-term contracts	207
SSAP 13 Accounting for research and development	228
SSAP 19 Accounting for investment properties	238
SSAP 20 Foreign currency translation	242
SSAP 21 Accounting for leases and hire purchase contracts	255
Guidance Notes on SSAP 21	267
SSAP 25 Segmental reporting	307
Financial Reporting Standards	
FRS 1 Cash flow statements (revised 1996)	324
FRS 2 Accounting for subsidiary undertakings	366
FRS 3 Reporting financial performance	421
FRS 4 Capital instruments	453
FRS 5 Reporting the substance of transactions	461
FRS 6 Acquisitions and mergers	568
FRS 7 Fair values in acquisition accounting	603
FRS 8 Related party disclosures	636
FRS 9 Associates and joint ventures	661
FRS 10 Goodwill and intangible assets	705
FRS 11 Impairment of fixed assets and goodwill	748
FRS 12 Provisions, contingent liabilities and contingent assets	781
FRS 13 Derivatives and other financial instruments: disclosures	830
FRS 15 Tangible fixed assets	920
FRS 16 Current tax	966
FRS 17 Retirement benefits	983
FRS 18 Accounting policies	1026
FRS 19 Deferred tax	1062
FRS 20 (IFRS 2) Share-based payment	1119
FRS 21 (IAS 10) Events after the balance sheet date	1258
FRS 22 (IAS 33) Earnings per share	1274
FRS 23 (IAS 21) The effects of changes in foreign exchange rates	1338
FRS 24 (IAS 29) Financial reporting in hyperinflationary economies	1376

FRS 25 (IAS 32) Financial instruments: Presentation 1389
FRS 26 (IAS 39) Financial instruments: recognition and measurement 1484
FRS 27 Life Assurance 1865
FRS 28 Corresponding amounts 1948
FRS 29 (IFRS 7) Financial instruments: disclosures 1966
FRS 30 Heritage assets 2064
Financial Reporting Standard for Smaller Entities (effective April 2008) 2093
FRS 100 Application of Financial Reporting Requirements 2197
FRS 101 Reduced Disclosure Framework 2247
FRS 102 The Financial Reporting Standard applicable in the UK and Republic of Ireland 2294

Part Four Statements by the Accounting Standards Board
Reporting Statement: Operating and Financial review 2645
Reporting Statement: Retirement Benefits – Disclosures 2677
Statement: Half-Yearly Financial Reports 2696
Preliminary announcements 2716

Part Five UITF abstracts
Foreword to UITF abstracts 2729
UITF abstract 4: Presentation of long-term debtors in current assets 2737
UITF abstract 5: Transfers from current assets to fixed assets 2739
UITF abstract 9: Accounting for operations in hyper-inflationary economies 2741
UITF abstract 11: Capital instruments: issuer call options 2744
UITF abstract 15: (revised 1999) Disclosure of substantial acquisitions 2746
UITF abstract 19: Tax on gains and losses on foreign currency borrowings that hedge an investment in a foreign enterprise 2747
UITF abstract 21: Accounting issues arising from the proposed introduction of the euro 2749
UITF abstract 22: The acquisition of a Lloyd's business 2755
UITF abstract 23: Application of the transitional rules in FRS 15 2757
UITF abstract 24: Accounting for start-up costs 2760
UITF abstract 25: National Insurance contributions on share option gains 2762
UITF abstract 26: Barter transactions for advertising 2766
UITF abstract 27: Revision to estimates of the useful economic life of goodwill and intangible assets 2769
UITF abstract 28: Operating lease incentives 2771
UITF abstract 29: Website development costs 2775
UITF abstract 31: Exchanges of businesses or other non-monetary assets for an interest in a subsidiary, joint venture or associate 2778
UITF abstract 32: Employee benefit trusts and other intermediate payment arrangements 2781
UITF abstract 34: Pre-contract costs 2785
UITF abstract 35: Death-in-service and incapacity benefits 2789
UITF abstract 36: Contracts for sale of capacity 2791
UITF abstract 38: Accounting for ESOP trusts 2796
UITF abstract 39: (IFRIC Interpretation 2) Member's shares in co-operative entities and similar instruments 2804
UITF abstract 40: Revenue recognition and service contracts 2820
UITF abstract 41: Scope of FRS 20 (IFRS 2) 2825
UITF abstract 42: Reassessment of embedded derivatives 2833
UITF abstract 43: The interpretation of equivalence for the purposes of section 228A of the Companies Act 1985 2842

UITF abstract 44: (IFRIC Interpretation 11) FRS 20 (IFRS 2) Group and Treasury Share Transactions 2852
UITF abstract 45: (IFRIC Interpretation 6) Liabilities arising from participating in a specific market – Waste electrical and electronic equipment 2862
UITF abstract 46: (IFRIC Interpretation 16) Hedges of a net investment in a foreign operation 2867
UITF abstract 47: (IFRIC Intrepretation 19) Extinguishing Financial Liabilities with Equity Instruments 2889
UITF abstract 48: Accounting implications of the replacement of the retail prices index with the consumer prices index for retirement benefits 2900

Part Six Statements of Recommended Practice
Introductory note 2907
SORPs: Policy and Code of Practice 2910

Part Seven ICAEW Accounting Recommendations
[TECH 03/08] Guidance on materiality in financial reporting by UK entities 2919
[TECH 02/10] Guidance on the determination of realised profits and losses in the context of distributions under the Companies Act 2006 2931

Preface

This book presents, in one convenient bound volume, all UK accounting standards and UITF abstracts extant at 30 April 2013. These have been updated for amendments made since the documents were originally issued.

The main change in the year, and indeed for many years, is the publication of most of the new suite of accounting standards that will govern UK accounting practice from 2015. FRS 100 sets out the overall framework, including the various options that will be available. FRS 101 introduces a reduced disclosure framework which is based on the recognition and measurement requirements of IFRS (with a few changes to meet legal requirements) but which omits some of the extensive disclosure requirements that adoption of IFRS usually entails. FRS 102 replaces all current UK accounting standards and UITF abstracts for entities that are not applying IFRS (as adopted in the EU), FRS 101 or the FRSSE. One further standard is expected, FRS 103, which will deal with insurance contracts. An exposure draft of FRS 103 is expected later this year.

As a result of these changes, all of the other standards included in this volume have only a limited life. By 2015 every current accounting standard, other than the FRSSE, will have been removed. The FRSSE will also change in 2015. The changes to the FRSSE have been included, as footnotes, in the current volume.

The changes also mean that, for the first time, this volume no longer contains exposure drafts or other consultations since all such documents have been withdrawn.

As noted above, the text of standards and abstracts has been changed where later guidance amends the original documents. However, in the case of some of the changes made by FRSs 23 to 26, the changes apply to only some entities. In these cases, the original text has been left unaltered, but a footnote includes the text to be used in relevant cases.

FRSs 21 to 26 and 29 are all UK versions of international standards. The format in which they were originally published included all original text of the relevant IFRS or IAS, with deletions and additions made by the ASB clearly marked. In this volume, such changes have been made, and are not marked. The text as presented therefore represents the requirements applicable in the UK, without reference to how this differs from the IFRS or IAS on which those requirements are based.

As in previous years, footnotes have been added to refer to any major changes to legal or other references included in standards. However, these are not intended to provide a comprehensive summary. No attempt has been made to update any references to legislation in the Republic of Ireland.

Part One

Introduction

Introduction

HISTORY OF THE ACCOUNTING STANDARDS COMMITTEE

The Accounting Standards Committee ('ASC'), originally known as the Accounting Standards Steering Committee, was set up in January 1970 by the Council of The Institute of Chartered Accountants in England and Wales with the object of developing definitive standards for financial reporting.

The Institute of Chartered Accountants of Scotland and the Institute of Chartered Accountants in Ireland became members of the Committee in 1970, the Chartered Association of Certified Accountants and the Chartered Institute of Management Accountants joined in 1971 and the Chartered Institute of Public Finance and Accountancy in 1976.

From 1 February 1976 the ASC was reconstituted as a joint committee of the six member bodies who then acted collectively through the Consultative Committee of Accountancy Bodies ('CCAB'). On 1 January 1986, the CCAB was incorporated and the ASC became a Committee of CCAB Limited.

The Councils of the six major accountancy bodies in the United Kingdom and Ireland approved and issued accounting standards following proposals developed by the ASC.

On 1 August 1990 the ASC was replaced by the Accounting Standards Board ('ASB').

During its existence the ASC issued 55 EDs, 2 SORPs, 28 discussion papers and other documents and 65 technical releases. It also franked 14 industry SORPs. Thirty-four SSAPS or revised SSAPS were recommended to and approved by the Councils of the six member-bodies of CCAB.

The CCAB agreed that 'all statements (Exposure Drafts, Discussion Papers, Technical Releases and similar documents) issued by ASC and extant at 1 August 1990 will remain documents of record under the aegis of the CCAB. SORPs issued or franked by ASC will continue in force under the aegis of CCAB until formally withdrawn or superseded'.

REPORT OF THE REVIEW COMMITTEE ON THE MAKING OF ACCOUNTING STANDARDS

The Review Committee, under the Chairmanship of Sir Ron Dearing (now Lord Dearing) was appointed in November 1987 by the CCAB to review and make recommendations on the standard-setting process.

In September 1988 the Review Committee presented its report to the CCAB. The Report's recommendations included:

- Accounting standards should remain, as far as possible, the responsibility of auditors, preparers and users of accounts and there should not be a general move towards incorporating them into law.
- A Financial Reporting Council should be created covering at high level a wide constituency of interests, whose Chairman would be appointed jointly by the Secretary of State for Trade and Industry and the Governor of the Bank of England, to guide the standard-setting body on work programmes and issues of public concern; to see that the work on accounting standards is properly

financed; and to act as a powerful proactive public influence for securing good accounting practice.
- The task of devising accounting standards should be discharged by a newly constituted, expert Accounting Standards Board, with a full-time Chairman and Technical Director. Its total membership would not exceed nine. The Board would issue standards on its own authority. In the interests of clearly drawn standards avoiding compromise decisions, a majority of two thirds of the Board would suffice for approval of a standard. Government would have observer status.
- The Accounting Standards Board should establish a capability of high standing to publish authoritative, though non-mandatory, guidance on emerging issues.
- A Review Panel should be established to examine contentious departures from accounting standards by large companies.

THE PRESENT STANDARD-SETTING REGIME

General

In 1990 the Government announced the establishment of the Financial Reporting Council under the Chairmanship of Sir Ron Dearing. Sir Sydney Lipworth was appointed Chairman with effect from 1 January 1994. The present arrangements for setting accounting standards and enforcing compliance follow closely the recommendations of the Review Committee. The organisation is as shown in the diagram on page 5.

The ASB replaced the ASC on 1 August 1990. The Financial Reporting Council (FRC), of which the ASB previously formed part, was restructured in 2012. It is now the FRC that issues accounting standards in the UK. The funding for the present organisation is drawn from three broad sectors: the accountancy profession; the financial community; and the Government.

Accounting Standards

The Companies Act 1989 introduced into the Companies Act 1985 a definition of 'accounting standards' along with the requirement for directors of companies, other than most small or medium sized companies, to disclose whether the accounts have been prepared in accordance with applicable accounting standards, particulars of any material departure from those standards and the reasons for the departure.* Under section 245B of the Companies Act 1985 (now s. 456 of the Companies Act 2006), where the accounts of a company do not comply with the requirements of the Act, the court may order the preparation of revised accounts, and that all or part of the costs be borne by such of the directors as were party to the approval of the defective accounts.

At its first meeting the ASB unanimously agreed to adopt the 22 extant SSAPS issued by the ASC. Adoption by the ASB gives the SSAPS the status of accounting standards within the meaning of the Companies Act 1985.† In adopting the SSAPS the ASB noted that with the passage of time certain legal references in the SSAPS have become outdated. The preface to this volume explains the updating that has been carried out to the documents that have been included herein.

***Editor's note:** *This disclosure requirement is now contained in para 45 of Schedule 1 to the Large and Medium-sized Companies and Groups (Accounts and Reports) Regulations 2008 (SI 2008/410).*

†***Editor's note:*** *This should now be taken to refer to the Companies Act 2006.*

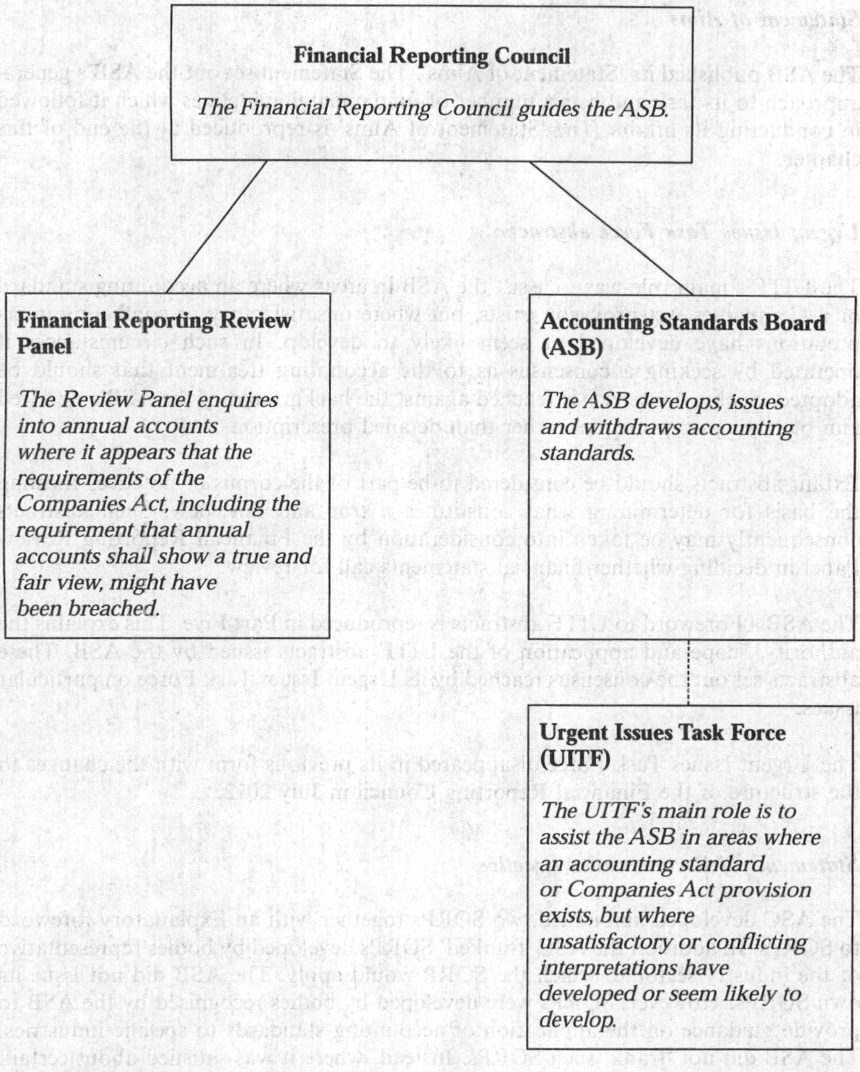

Financial Reporting Council
The Financial Reporting Council guides the ASB.
Financial Reporting Review Panel
The Review Panel enquires into annual accounts where it appears that the requirements of the Companies Act, including the requirement that annual accounts shall show a true and fair view, might have been breached.
Accounting Standards Board (ASB)
The ASB develops, issues and withdraws accounting standards.
Urgent Issues Task Force (UITF)
The UITF's main role is to assist the ASB in areas where an accounting standard or Companies Act provision exists, but where unsatisfactory or conflicting interpretations have developed or seem likely to develop.

The ASB announced that accounting standards that it develops and issues are to be known as Financial Reporting Standards (FRSs) and exposure drafts of FRSS are to be known as Financial Reporting Exposure Drafts (FREDs).

The ASB issued thirty Financial Reporting Standards (together with one for smaller entities updated as the need arises), certain amendments to earlier Standards and a number of Exposure Drafts and Discussion Documents. The FRC has issued three Financial Reporting Standards.

Statement of Principles

The ASB developed a Statement of Principles for Financial Reporting. This is not itself an accounting standard. It set out the principles that the ASB believed should underlie the preparation and presentation of company accounts.

The Statement was first published in December 1999 and is reproduced in Part Two.

Statement of Aims

The ASB published its 'Statement of Aims'. The Statement set out the ASB's general approach to its task and lists a number of fundamental guidelines which it followed in conducting its affairs. The 'Statement of Aims' is reproduced at the end of this chapter.

Urgent Issues Task Force abstracts

The UITF's main role was to assist the ASB in areas where an accounting standard or a Companies Act provision exists, but where unsatisfactory or conflicting interpretations have developed or seem likely to develop. In such circumstances it operated by seeking a consensus as to the accounting treatment that should be adopted. Such a consensus is reached against the background of the ASB's declared aim of relying on principles rather than detailed prescription.

Extant abstracts should be considered to be part of the corpus of practices forming the basis for determining what constitutes a true and fair view. Such abstracts consequently may be taken into consideration by the Financial Reporting Review Panel in deciding whether financial statements call for review.

The ASB's Foreword to UITF abstracts is reproduced in Part Five. This explains the authority, scope and application of the UITF abstracts issued by the ASB. These abstracts set out the consensus reached by its Urgent Issues Task Force on particular issues.

The Urgent Issues Task Force disappeared in its previous form with the changes to the structure of the Financial Reporting Council in July 2012.

Statements of Recommended Practice

The ASC developed and issued two SORPs together with an Explanatory foreword to SORPs. In addition the ASC 'franked' SORPs developed by bodies representative of the industry/sector to which the SORP would apply. The ASB did not issue its own SORPs. However, SORPs were developed by bodies recognised by the ASB to provide guidance on the application of accounting standards to specific industries. The ASB did not 'frank' such SORPs. Instead, where it was satisfied about certain particulars it required to be appended to the SORP a 'negative assurance statement'. Further details are contained in Part Seven.

SORPs will continue under the revised arrangements of the Financial Reporting Council.

International Financial Reporting Standards

Listed groups, and companies on AIM, are now required to comply with International Financial Reporting Standards (IFRS) rather than UK accounting standards. This option is also available to all UK companies, other than charities. IFRS are issued by the International Accounting Standards Board (IASB).

Financial Reporting Standards (and UITFs) continue to apply for those companies using UK GAAP, although the ASB and UITF both took into account international practice prior to issuing any guidance, and some standards are effectively UK versions of international standards.

The ASB issued proposals for significant change to UK GAAP. These proposals were finalised by the FRC and have resulted in FRSs 100, 100 and 102. FRS 103 will also be issued in due course. These standards involve the replacement on existing UK GAAP, other than for those entities using the FRSSE, with a completely new framework. As a result, all other current UK accounting standards will cease to be applicable in the next few years. The new framework is in force for accounting periods beginning on or after 1 January 2015, but may be adopted prior to this.

Aims & Objectives

(Issued July 2003)

AIMS

The Accounting Standards Board contributes to the achievement of the Financial Reporting Council's fundamental aim of supporting investor, market and public confidence in the financial and governance stewardship of listed and other entities by pursuing its own aims of establishing and improving standards of financial accounting and reporting, for the benefit of users, preparers, and auditors of financial information.

OBJECTIVES

The Board intends to achieve its aims by:

Developing principles to guide it in establishing standards and to provide a framework within which others can exercise judgement in resolving accounting issues. **1**

Issuing new accounting standards, or amending existing ones, in response to evolving business practices, new economic developments and deficiencies being identified in current practice. **2**

Addressing urgent issues promptly. **3**

Working with the International Accounting Standards Board (IASB), with national standards-setters and relevant European Union (EU) institutions to encourage high quality in the IASB's standards and their adoption in the EU. **4**

OPERATING GUIDELINES

In carrying out its work the Board will

Be objective and ensure that the information resulting from the application of accounting standards faithfully represents the underlying commercial activity. Such information should be neutral in the sense that it is free from any form of bias intended to influence users in a particular direction and should not be designed to favour any group of users or preparers. **1**

Ensure that accounting standards are clearly expressed and supported by a reasoned analysis of the issues. **2**

Determine what should be incorporated in accounting standards based on research, public consultation and careful deliberation about the usefulness of the resulting information. **3**

Ensure that there is consistency both from one accounting standard to another and between accounting standards and company law. **4**

Issue accounting standards only when the expected benefits exceed the perceived costs. The Board recognises that reliable cost/benefit calculations are seldom possible. However, it will always assess the need for standards in terms of the significance and extent of the problem being addressed and will choose the standard which appears to be most effective in cost/benefit terms. **5**

6 Take account of the desire of the financial community for evolutionary rather than revolutionary change in the reporting process where this is consistent with the objectives outlined above.

7 Follow best practice in its own governance and processes, deploy resources effectively and liaise with the Council's other Boards to promote and benefit from operating synergies wherever possible.

WITHDRAWN STANDARDS

Accounting Standards			
		Date issued	*Date withdrawn*
SSAP 1	Accounting for associated companies (revised April 1982) Superseded by FRS 9	January 1971	November 1997
SSAP 2	Disclosure of accounting policies Superseded by FRS 18	November 1971	December 2000
SSAP 3	Earnings per share Superseded by FRS 14	February 1972	October 1998
SSAP 6	Extraordinary items and prior year adjustments (revised August 1986) Superseded by FRS 3	April 1974	October 1992
SSAP 7	Accounting for changes in the purchasing power of money (Provisional)	May 1974	January 1978
SSAP 8	The treatment of taxation under the imputation system in the accounts of companies Superseded by FRS 16	August 1974	December 1999
SSAP 10	Statements of source and application of funds Superseded by FRS 1	July 1975	September 1991
SSAP 11	Accounting for deferred tax Superseded by SSAP 15	August 1975	October 1978
SSAP 12	Accounting for depreciation Superseded by FRS 15	December 1977	February 1999
SSAP 14	Group accounts Superseded by FRS 2	September 1978	July 1992
SSAP 15	Accounting for deferred tax Superseded by FRS 19	October 1978	December 2000
SSAP 16	Current cost accounting	March 1980	July 1988
SSAP 17	Accounting for post balance sheet events Superseded by FRS 21	August 1980	May 2004
SSAP 18	Accounting for contingencies Superseded by FRS 12	August 1980	September 1998

SSAP 20	Foreign currency translation Superseded by FRS 23, for entities applying that standard Remains in force for other companies	April 1983	December 2004
SSAP 22	Accounting for goodwill (revised July 1989) Superseded by FRS 10	December 1984	December 1997
SSAP 23	Accounting for acquisitions and mergers Superseded by FRS 6	April 1985	September 1994
SSAP 24	Accounting for pension costs Superseded by FRS 17	May 1988	November 2000
FRS 1	Cash flow statements Superseded by FRS 1 (revised 1996)	September 1991	October 1996
FRS 4	Capital instruments Partly superseded by FRS 25 Fully superseded where FRS 26 is applied	December 1993	December 2004
FRS 13	Derivatives and other financial instruments: disclosures Superseded by FRS 25 or 29, where entities are complying with the disclosure requirements of that standard	September 1998	December 2004
FRS 14	Earnings per share Superseded by FRS 22	October 1998	December 2004

UITF Abstracts		*Date issued*	*Date withdrawn*
UITF 1	Convertible bonds-supplemental interest/premium Superseded by FRS 4	July 1991	December 1993
UITF 2	Restructuring costs Superseded by FRS 3	October 1991	October 1992
UITF 3	Treatment of goodwill on disposal of a business Superseded by FRS 10	December 1991	December 1997
UITF 6	Accounting for post-retirement benefits other than pensions Superseded by FRS 17	November 1992	November 2000
UITF 7	True and fair override disclosures Superseded by FRS 18	December 1992	December 2000
UITF 8	Repurchase of own debt Superseded by FRS 4	March 1993	December 1993

UITF 9	Accounting for operations in hyper-inflationary economies Superseded by FRS 24, for companies complying with that standard	June 1993	December 2004
UITF 10	Disclosure of directors' share options. Withdrawn	September 1994	December 2002
UITF 11	Capital instruments: issuer call options Superseded by FRS 26, for companies complying with that standard	September 1994	December 2004
UITF 12	Lessee accounting for reverse lease premiums and similar incentives Superseded by UITF 28	December 1994	February 2001
UITF 13	Accounting for ESOP trusts Superseded by UITF 38	June 1995	June 2004
UITF 14	Disclosure of changes in accounting policy Superseded by FRS 18	November 1995	December 2000
UITF 15	Disclosure of substantial acquisitions Superseded by UITF 15 (revised 1999)	January 1996	February 1999
UITF 16	Income and expenses subject to non-standard rates of tax Superseded by FRS 16	February 1997	December 1999
UITF 17	Employee share schemes Superseded by FRS 20	October 2000, revised December 2003	April 2004
UITF 18	Pension costs following the 1997 tax changes in respect of dividend income Superseded by FRS 17	December 1997	November 2000
UITF 20	Year 2000 issue: accounting and disclosures Withdrawn	March 1998	July 2000
UITF 30	Date of award to employees of shares or rights to shares Superseded by FRS 20	March 2001	April 2004
UITF 33	Obligations in capital instruments Superseded by FRS 25	February 2002	December 2004
UITF 37	Purchases and sales of own shares Superseded by FRS 25	October 2003	December 2004

Part Two

Statement of Principles

Statement of principles for financial reporting

(Issued December 1999)

Contents

Paragraph

Detailed list of contents

Introduction 1–18

Chapters

1	The objective of financial statements	1.1–1.22
2	The reporting entity	2.1–2.20
3	The qualitative characteristics of financial information	3.1–3.37
4	The elements of financial statements	4.1–4.45
5	Recognition in financial statements	5.1–5.36
6	Measurement in financial statements	6.1–6.42
7	Presentation of financial information	7.1–7.21
8	Accounting for interests in other entities	8.1–8.16

Appendices

Contents of appendices

I	The Statement and the legal requirements concerning the form and content of financial statements	1–16
II	The Statement and IASC's 'Framework for the Preparation and Presentation of Financial Statements'	1–15
III	Background to issues dealt with in the Statement	1–64

Detailed list of contents

Introduction

Purpose 1–4

Status 5

Scope 6–9

Types of financial report 6–8

Types of entity 9

True and fair 10–13

The standard-setting process 14–17

Revisions to the statement 18

Chapter 1: The objective of financial statements

Principles

Explanation

The objective of financial statements 1.1–1.9

Useful to a wide range of users 1.1–1.2

Useful for making economic decisions 1.3–1.4

Information on financial performance and financial position 1.5–1.7

The limitations of financial statements 1.8–1.9

Investors as the defining class of user 1.10–1.12

The information required by investors 1.13–1.22
  Financial performance 1.13–1.14
  Financial position 1.15–1.16
  Generation and use of cash 1.17–1.18
  Financial adaptability 1.19–1.22

Chapter 2: The reporting entity

Principles

Explanation

Entities that should prepare and publish financial statements 2.1–2.3

The boundary of a reporting entity 2.4–2.7

What is control? 2.8–2.10

Controlling an entity 2.11–2.20
  When does one entity control another? 2.11–2.15
  Powers of veto and reserve powers 2.16
  Predetermined operating and financial policies 2.17
  Latent control 2.18
  Management but not control 2.19–2.20

Chapter 3: The qualitative characteristics of financial information

Principles

Explanation

Relevance 3.1–3.6

Reliability 3.7–3.20
  Faithful representation 3.9–3.14
  Neutrality 3.15
  Complete and free from material error 3.16–3.17
  Prudence 3.18–3.20

Comparability 3.21–3.25
  Consistency 3.23
  Disclosure of accounting policies 3.24–3.25

Understandability 3.26–3.27

Materiality 3.28–3.32

Constraints on the qualitative characteristics 3.33–3.37
  Relevance and reliability 3.34–3.35
  Neutrality and prudence 3.36
  Understandability 3.37

Chapter 4: The elements of financial statements

Principles

Explanation

The elements of financial statements 4.1–4.5
  Depicting the effects of transactions and other events 4.1–4.4
  Recognition 4.5

Assets 4.6–4.22
  Definition 4.6–4.7
  Rights or other access 4.8–4.12
  Future economic benefits 4.13–4.16

Controlled by the entity 4.17–4.21
Past transactions or events 4.22

Liabilities 4.23–4.32
Definition 4.23
Obligations 4.24–4.28
Transfer of economic benefits 4.29–4.30
Past transactions or events 4.31–4.32

Offsetting rights and obligations 4.33–4.36

Ownership interest 4.37–4.38

Gains and losses 4.39–4.41
Definitions 4.39–4.40
Offsetting gains and losses 4.41

Contributions from owners and distributions to owners 4.42–4.45
Definitions 4.42
In their capacity as owners 4.43
Contributions from owners 4.44
Distributions to owners 4.45

Chapter 5: Recognition in financial statements

Principles

Explanation

The recognition process 5.1–5.11
The stages of the recognition process 5.1
Transactions and events other than transactions 5.2–5.3
The effect of transactions and other events 5.4–5.7
Uncertainty and the recognition process 5.8–5.11

Initial recognition 5.12–5.21
Categories of uncertainty 5.12
Element uncertainty 5.13–5.15
Measurement uncertainty 5.16–5.17
Prudence 5.18–5.19
Unperformed contracts 5.20–5.21

Derecognition 5.22–5.25
Derecognition because the asset or liability has been eliminated 5.22–5.24
Derecognition because the criteria for recognition are no longer met 5.25

Revenue recognition 5.26–5.36
Matching 5.28–5.32
Critical event in the operating cycle 5.33–5.36

Chapter 6: Measurement in financial statements

Principles

Explanation

Alternative bases of measurement 6.1–6.5

Alternative measures of current value 6.6–6.9

The measurement process 6.10–6.22
Initial recognition 6.11–6.16
Subsequent remeasurement 6.17–6.22

Choosing a measurement basis and deciding whether to change it 6.23–6.29

Measurement issues 6.30–6.38
Going concern 6.30
Discounting 6.31–6.34
Arriving at a measure in the face of uncertainty 6.35–6.38

Capital maintenance adjustments and changing prices 6.39–6.42

Chapter 7: Presentation of financial information

Principles

Explanation

Presentation of information in financial statements 7.1–7.8
Clear, effective and simple communication 7.1
Highly structured and aggregated 7.2–7.5
Classification 7.6–7.8

Good presentation 7.9–7.14
Statement of financial performance 7.9–7.11
Balance sheet 7.12–7.13
Cash flow statement 7.14

Accompanying information 7.15–7.18

Highlights and summary indicators 7.19–7.21

Chapter 8: Accounting for interests in other entities

Principles

Explanation

Degree of influence 8.1–8.4

Reflecting the effects of interests in other entities 8.5–8.10
Consolidated financial statements and single entity financial statements 8.5–8.6
Interests involving control 8.7–8.8
Interests involving joint control or significant influence 8.9
Interests involving lesser or no influence 8.10

Consolidated financial statements 8.11–8.13

Accounting for business combinations 8.14–8.16

Statement of principles for financial reporting

Introduction

PURPOSE

This Statement of Principles for Financial Reporting sets out the principles that the Accounting Standards Board believes should underlie the preparation and presentation of general purpose financial statements.* 1

The primary purpose of articulating such principles is to provide a coherent frame of reference to be used by the Board in the development and review of accounting standards and by others who interact with the Board during the standard-setting process. 2

Such a frame of reference should clarify the conceptual underpinnings of proposed accounting standards and should enable standards to be developed on a consistent basis by reducing the need to debate fundamental issues each time a standard is developed or revised. As such, it will play an important role in the development of accounting standards. It is expected that it will play a similar role in the development of Statements of Recommended Practice. 3

The Statement is being published because knowledge of the principles should assist preparers and users of financial statements, as well as auditors and others, to understand the Board's approach to formulating accounting standards and the nature and function of information reported in general purpose financial statements. The principles will also help preparers and auditors faced with new or emerging issues to carry out an initial analysis of the issues involved in the absence of applicable accounting standards. 4

STATUS

The Statement of Principles is not an accounting standard, nor does it have a status that is equivalent to an accounting standard. It therefore does not contain requirements on how financial statements should be prepared or presented. 5

SCOPE

Types of financial report

Financial information takes many different forms. For the purposes of the Statement, it has been categorised: 6

(a) *special purpose financial reports*—Financial information prepared by the entity itself at the behest of, and in the form specified by, persons who have the authority to obtain the information they require to meet their needs. Regulatory returns, tax returns and financial reports prepared for bankers are examples of such reports.

(b) *general purpose financial reports*—Financial information that, although prepared by the entity itself, is not in the form of a special purpose financial report. Such reports comprise:

**The meaning of the term 'general purpose financial statements' is explained in paragraph 6(b)(i).*

(i) *general purpose financial statements*—for example, annual financial statements and the financial statements contained in interim reports, preliminary announcements and summary financial statements. General purpose financial statements are generally referred to in the Statement hereafter simply as 'financial statements'.

(ii) *other types of general purpose financial report*—for example, directors' reports, statements by the chairman, operating and financial reviews, historical summaries and trend information (such as five-year summaries), letters to shareholders and similar items.

(c) *other financial information*—Financial information that has not been prepared by the reporting entity itself, such as news articles and analysts' reports.

A diagram summarising and providing examples of the various categories of financial information is on the following page.

7 The primary focus of the Statement of Principles is on those financial statements that are required to give a true and fair view of the reporting entity's financial performance and financial position. For most entities, those statements will be their full annual financial statements. The Statement's principles will also be applicable to financial statements that are intended to be consistent with financial statements required to give a true and fair view (such as financial statements contained in interim reports, preliminary announcements and summary financial statements), although additional considerations are relevant in the context of such statements.

8 Whilst the Statement does not address to any significant extent other types of general purpose financial report, it will be relevant to such reports insofar as they provide financial information that is intended to be consistent with the financial statements.

Types of entity

9 The principles in the Statement are intended to be relevant to the financial statements of profit-oriented reporting entities, regardless of their size and whether they are private or public sector entities.* The Statement is, broadly speaking, also relevant to the financial statements of not-for-profit entities, although some of the principles need to be re-expressed and others need changes of emphasis before they can be applied to that sector.†

TRUE AND FAIR

10 The concept of a true and fair view lies at the heart of financial reporting in the UK and the Republic of Ireland. It is the ultimate test for financial statements and, as such, has a powerful, direct effect on accounting practice. No matter how skilled the standard-setters and law-makers are, it is the need to show a true and fair view that puts their requirements in perspective.

11 The true and fair view is, furthermore, a dynamic concept because its content evolves in response to changes in, inter alia, accounting and business practice. This dynamism pervades the whole system of financial reporting, affecting the interpretation of

**The application of accounting standards to the public sector is discussed more fully in the Foreword to Accounting Standards.*

†***Editor's note:*** *This has been dealt with by the ASB through the* Statements of Principles – Interpretation for Public Benefit Entities.

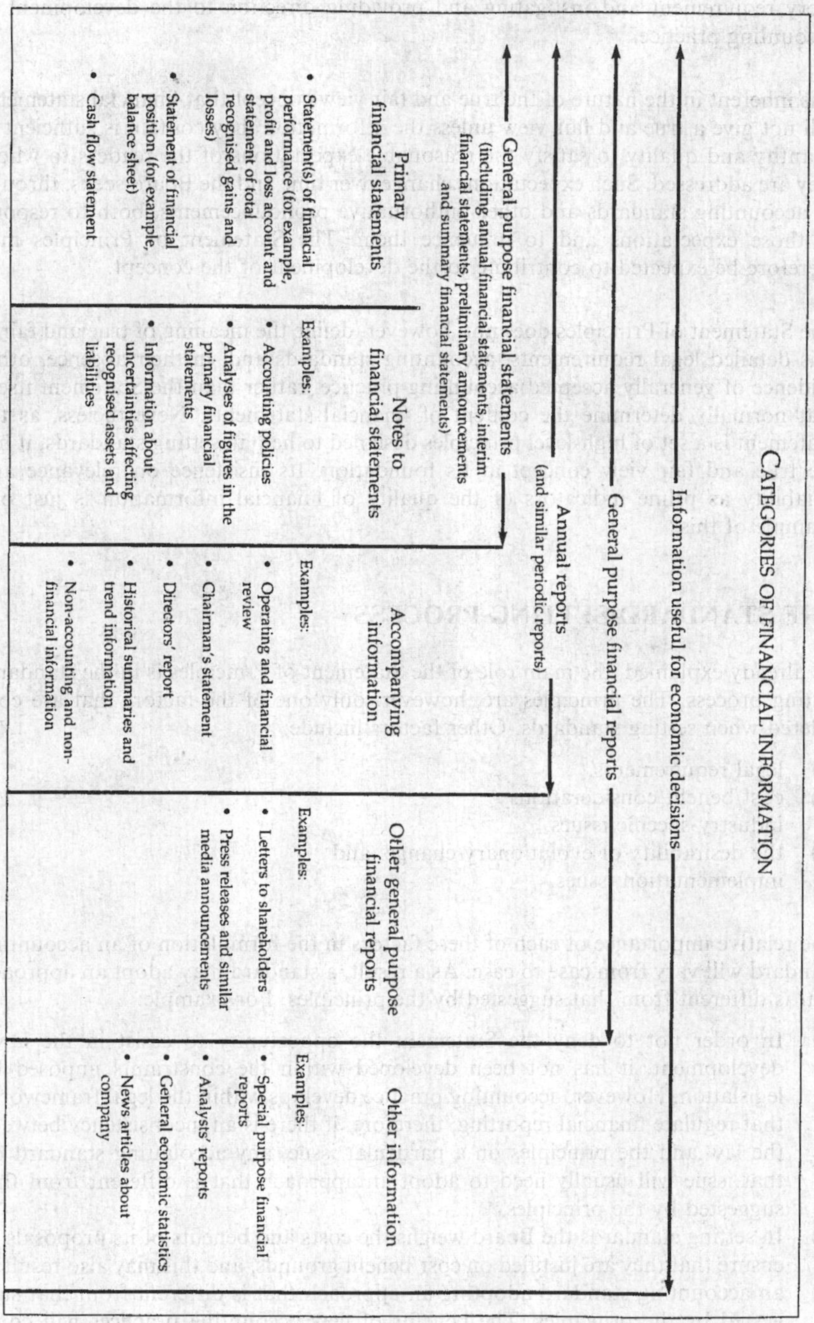
CATEGORIES OF FINANCIAL INFORMATION
Information useful for economic decisions
General purpose financial reports
Annual reports
(and similar periodic reports)
General purpose financial statements
(including annual financial statements, interim financial statements, preliminary announcements and summary financial statements)
Primary financial statements
• Statement(s) of financial performance (for example, profit and loss account and statement of total recognised gains and losses)
• Statement of financial position (for example, balance sheet)
• Cash flow statement
Notes to financial statements
Examples:
• Accounting policies
• Analyses of figures in the primary financial statements
• Information about uncertainties affecting recognised assets and liabilities
Accompanying information
Examples:
• Operating and financial review
• Chairman's statement
• Directors' report
• Historical summaries and trend information
• Non-accounting and non-financial information
Other general purpose financial reports
Examples:
• Letters to shareholders
• Press releases and similar media announcements
Other information
Examples:
• Special purpose financial reports
• Analysts' reports
• General economic statistics
• News articles about company

every requirement and instigating and providing direction to the development of accounting practice.

12 It is inherent in the nature of the true and fair view concept that financial statements will not give a true and fair view unless the information they contain is sufficient in quantity and quality to satisfy the reasonable expectations of the readers to whom they are addressed. Such expectations change over time and the Board seeks, through its accounting standards and other authoritative pronouncements, both to respond to those expectations and to influence them. The Statement of Principles may therefore be expected to contribute to the development of the concept.

13 The Statement of Principles does not, however, define the meaning of true and fair—it is detailed legal requirements, accounting standards and, in their absence, other evidence of generally accepted accounting practice, rather than the Statement itself, that normally determine the content of financial statements. Nevertheless, as the Statement is a set of high-level principles designed to help in setting standards, it has the true and fair view concept at its foundation. Its insistence on relevance and reliability as prime indicators of the quality of financial information is just one example of this.

THE STANDARD-SETTING PROCESS

14 As already explained, the main role of the Statement of Principles is in the standard-setting process. The principles are, however, only one of the factors that are considered when setting standards. Other factors include:

(a) legal requirements,
(b) cost/benefit considerations,
(c) industry-specific issues,
(d) the desirability of evolutionary change, and
(e) implementation issues.

15 The relative importance of each of these factors in the formulation of an accounting standard will vary from case to case. As a result, a standard may adopt an approach that is different from that suggested by the principles. For example:

(a) In order not to deny the Statement the opportunity to assist in the law's development, it has not been developed within the constraints imposed by legislation. However, accounting practice develops within the legal frameworks that regulate financial reporting; therefore, if there is an inconsistency between the law and the principles on a particular issue, any accounting standard on that issue will usually need to adopt an approach that is different from that suggested by the principles.*

(b) In setting standards the Board weighs the costs and benefits of its proposals to ensure that they are justified on cost/benefit grounds, and this may also result in an accounting standard adopting an approach that is different from that suggested by the principles. The benefits of new accounting practices will come from improvements in economic decision-making by users. The costs will include the costs of preparation and might also include, for example, the possible loss or diminution of competitive position.

**The relationship between the accounting requirements imposed by legislation and the Statement of Principles and the inconsistencies between the two are explained in Appendix I.*

As legal requirements, accounting techniques and markets evolve, the Board believes that it will be possible to reduce the number of conflicts between the Statement and accounting standards and that fewer new conflicts will emerge. 16

It will be made clear in each accounting standard how the standard relates to the Statement of Principles. 17

REVISIONS TO THE STATEMENT

The Statement may be revised from time to time in the light of the Board's experience of working with it and in response to developments in accounting thought. 18

Chapter 1: The objective of financial statements

Put simply, the objective of financial statements is to provide information that is useful to those for whom they are prepared. However, the objective needs to be expressed more precisely if it is to be of any use in determining the form and content of financial statements. This chapter does that by considering the persons for whom financial statements are prepared, the information needs of such persons and the role that financial statements play in meeting those needs.

PRINCIPLES

- The objective of financial statements is to provide information about the reporting entity's financial performance and financial position that is useful to a wide range of users for assessing the stewardship of the entity's management and for making economic decisions.
- That objective can usually be met by focusing exclusively on the information needs of present and potential investors, the defining class of user.
- Present and potential investors need information about the reporting entity's financial performance and financial position that is useful to them in evaluating the entity's ability to generate cash (including the timing and certainty of its generation) and in assessing the entity's financial adaptability.

EXPLANATION

The objective of financial statements

Useful to a wide range of users

1.1 Financial information about the activities and resources of an entity is typically of interest to many people. Although some of these people are able to command the preparation of special purpose financial reports in order to obtain the information they need, the rest—usually the vast majority—rely on general purpose financial reports, such as financial statements and other financial information. Many people are therefore potentially interested in an entity's financial statements.

1.2 It does not follow that financial statements are prepared specifically for all those interested persons. However, although there continues to be debate about for whom precisely they are prepared, there is no doubt that they are prepared for a range of persons that extends far beyond existing investors. These persons are referred to in the Statement as the 'users'.

Useful for making economic decisions

1.3 The persons potentially interested in an entity's financial statements need information on that entity for a variety of purposes.

(a) *Present and potential investors (hereafter generally referred to simply as 'investors').* In its stewardship role, management is accountable for the safekeeping of the entity's resources and for their proper, efficient and profitable use. Providers of risk capital are interested in information that helps them to assess how effectively management has fulfilled this role. They are also interested in information that is useful in taking decisions about their investment or potential investment in the entity. They are, as a result, concerned with the risk inherent in, and return provided by, their investments, and need information on the entity's financial performance and financial position that helps them to assess its cash-generation abilities and its financial adaptability.

(b) *Lenders*. Lenders are interested in information that helps them to assess whether their loans will be repaid, and related interest will be paid, when due. Similarly, potential lenders are interested in information that helps them to decide whether to lend to the entity and on what terms.

(c) *Suppliers and other trade creditors*. Suppliers and other trade creditors are interested in information that helps them to decide whether to sell to the entity and to assess the likelihood that amounts owing to them will be paid when due.

(d) *Employees*. Employees are interested in information on their employer's stability and profitability, with particular reference to that part (for example, the subsidiary or branch) of the entity in which they work. They are also interested in information that enables them to assess their employer's ability to provide remuneration, employment opportunities and retirement and other benefits.

(e) *Customers*. Customers are interested in information about the entity's continued existence. That is especially so when they have a long-term involvement with, or are dependent on, the entity, as will generally be the case if product warranties are involved or if specialised replacement parts may be needed.

(f) *Governments and their agencies*. Governments and their agencies are interested in the allocation of resources and, therefore, the activities of entities. They also require information that assists them in regulating the activities of entities, assessing taxation and providing a basis for national statistics. Although much of this information is obtained through special purpose financial reports, its consistency with published general purpose financial reports such as financial statements often needs to be demonstrated.

(g) *The public*. Entities affect members of the public in a variety of ways. For example, they may make a substantial contribution to a local economy by providing employment and using local suppliers. The public, including the local community, may therefore be interested in information that is useful in assessing the trends and recent developments in the entity's prosperity and the range of its activities.

This analysis illustrates that, although those potentially interested in an entity's financial statements need that information for a variety of purposes, all the purposes involve taking informed economic decisions. Even present investors assessing the stewardship of the entity's management do so in order to decide whether, amongst other things, to hold or sell their investment in the entity and to reappoint or replace the management. **1.4**

Information on financial performance and financial position

The economic decisions for which users need financial statements will not all be the same. Although different decisions usually require different information, there is, as can be seen from paragraph 1.3, some overlap in the information required: all potential users are interested, to varying degrees, in the financial performance and financial position of the entity as a whole. **1.5**

General purpose financial reports focus on this common interest of users. Their objective is therefore to provide information about the financial performance and financial position of an entity that is useful to a wide range of users for assessing the stewardship of management and for making economic decisions (including those based on assessments of the stewardship of management). **1.6**

As financial statements are the principal means of communicating accounting information on an entity to interested parties and are a central feature of general **1.7** purpose financial reporting, they carry much of the burden that is placed on general purpose financial reporting to meet this objective.

The limitations of financial statements

1.8 Financial statements do not seek to meet all the information needs of users: users will usually have to supplement the information they obtain from financial statements with information from other sources. Furthermore, financial statements have various inherent limitations that make them an imperfect vehicle for reflecting the full effects of transactions and other events on a reporting entity's financial performance and financial position. For example:

(a) they are a conventionalised representation of transactions and other events that involves a substantial degree of classification and aggregation and the allocation of the effects of continuous operations to discrete reporting periods.
(b) they focus on the financial effects of transactions and other events and do not focus to any significant extent on their non-financial effects or on non-financial information in general.
(c) they provide information that is largely historical and therefore do not reflect future events or transactions that may enhance or impair the entity's operations, nor do they anticipate the impact of potential changes in the economic environment.

1.9 These inherent limitations mean that some information on the financial performance and financial position of the reporting entity can be provided only by general purpose financial reports other than financial statements—or in some cases is better provided by such reports. For example, although a description of the business environment and markets in which a reporting entity operates and the strategies it has adopted is usually needed to put into context the numerical information provided by the financial statements, it is generally better to provide such information in the material accompanying the financial statements than in the financial statements themselves.*

Investors as the defining class of user

1.10 As explained in paragraph 1.3, the perspective from which investors view financial performance and financial position is one that focuses on the entity's cash-generation ability and financial adaptability. This perspective is also of fundamental importance to other users, because an entity's ability to generate cash and to respond to unexpected needs and opportunities ultimately determines its capacity over the medium to long term to repay loans, meet interest payments, pay employees and suppliers, and undertake investment. For example, although in origin the perspective of lenders and other creditors differs from that of investors, they require similar information to investors when their interests are long-term or the risk of loss is significant. That is because they will want to use that information as a frame of reference against which to evaluate the more specific information they obtain.

1.11 Therefore, in preparing financial statements, the rebuttable assumption is made that financial statements that focus on the interest that investors have in the reporting entity's financial performance and financial position will, in effect, also be focusing on the common interest that all users have in that entity's financial performance and financial position.

**Accompanying information is discussed in Chapter 7.*

It follows that, in determining which information to include in the financial statements and how to present that information, it can usually be presumed that: **1.12**

(a) information that is needed by investors will be given in either the financial statements or some other general purpose financial report; and
(b) information that is not needed by investors need not be given in the financial statements.

The information required by investors

Financial performance

The financial performance of an entity comprises the return it obtains on the resources it controls, the components of that return and the characteristics of those components. **1.13**

Investors require information on financial performance because such information: **1.14**

(a) provides an account of the stewardship of management and is useful in assessing the past and anticipated performance of the entity;
(b) is useful in assessing the entity's capacity to generate cash flows from its existing resource base and in forming judgements about the effectiveness with which the entity has employed its resources and might employ additional resources; and
(c) provides feedback on previous assessments of financial performance and can therefore assist users in modifying their assessments for, or in developing expectations about, future periods.

Financial position

An entity's financial position encompasses the economic resources it controls, its financial structure, its liquidity and solvency, its risk profile and risk management approach, and its capacity to adapt to changes in the environment in which it operates. **1.15**

Investors require information on financial position because: **1.16**

(a) information about the economic resources controlled and the use made of them in the past helps in assessing the stewardship of management and the entity's ability to generate cash in the future;
(b) information about financial structure is useful in assessing how future cash flows will be distributed among those with an interest in or claims on the entity. It is also useful in assessing how successful the entity has been in managing its resources, its requirements for future finance and its ability to raise that finance;
(c) information about liquidity and solvency helps in assessing the ability of the entity to meet its financial commitments as they fall due;
(d) information on an entity's risk profile and risk management approach is useful in evaluating its current performance and financial adaptability, and in assessing its ability to generate cash in the future; and
(e) information on an entity's capacity to adapt to changing circumstances (in other words, its financial adaptability) is useful in assessing the extent to which the entity is at risk, or able to benefit, from unexpected changes.

Generation and use of cash

Information about the ways in which an entity generates and uses cash in its operations, its investment activities and its financing activities provides an additional **1.17** perspective on its financial performance—one that is largely free from allocation and valuation issues.

1.18 Investors need such information because it is useful in assessing and reviewing previous assessments of:

(a) liquidity and solvency;
(b) the relationship between profits and cash flows;
(c) the implications that financial performance has for future cash flows; and
(d) other aspects of financial adaptability.

Financial adaptability

1.19 An entity's financial adaptability is its ability to take effective action to alter the amount and timing of its cash flows so that it can respond to unexpected needs or opportunities.

1.20 Financial adaptability is desirable for an entity because it helps it to mitigate the risks associated with operations, which in turn helps it to survive during a time of low (or possibly negative) cash flows from operations. It may also enable an entity to take advantage of unexpected investment opportunities. On the other hand, it also generally involves making sacrifices. For example, although holding assets that are readily marketable provides some financial adaptability, the rate of return involved may be lower than could be earned from holding less liquid assets.

1.21 The extent to which—and the ways in which—it is desirable for an entity to be financially adaptable will depend on the risks the entity faces and on the appetite for risk of its investors.

1.22 Financial adaptability comes from several sources, including the ability to:

(a) raise new capital, perhaps by issuing debt securities, at short notice;
(b) repay capital or debt at short notice;
(c) obtain cash by selling assets without disrupting continuing operations; and
(d) achieve a rapid improvement in the net cash inflows generated by operations.

Chapter 2: The reporting entity

It is important that entities that ought to prepare and publish financial statements do, in fact, do so and that those financial statements report on all relevant activities and resources. This chapter focuses on these issues—in other words, on identifying and circumscribing the reporting entity.

PRINCIPLES

- An entity should prepare and publish financial statements if there is a legitimate demand for the information that its financial statements would provide and it is a cohesive economic unit.
- The boundary of the reporting entity is determined by the scope of its control. For this purpose, first direct control and, secondly, direct plus indirect control are taken into account.

EXPLANATION

Entities that should prepare and publish financial statements

It is essential that entities that ought to prepare and publish financial statements do, in fact, do so. For similar reasons, if there is no justification for an entity to prepare and publish financial statements, it should not be required to do so. **2.1**

For the preparation of financial statements to be justified in any particular case, there needs to be a legitimate demand for the information that the financial statements would provide. This means, inter alia, that the information provided by the financial statements will need to be useful and that the benefits to be derived by providing the financial statements will need to exceed the costs of doing so. **2.2**

The financial statements of an entity will report on the entity's transactions and on other events that affect its financial performance and financial position. However, if the information provided by the financial statements is to be useful, the entity that is the subject of the financial statements (the reporting entity) needs to be a cohesive economic unit. This ensures accountability—the reporting entity is held to account for all the things it can control—and it gives the reporting entity a determinable boundary—because activities and resources are either within its control or outside its control. **2.3**

The boundary of a reporting entity

The control an entity exerts can be direct or indirect. **2.4**

(a) An entity has direct control of an asset if it has the ability in its own right to obtain the future economic benefits embodied in that asset and to restrict others' access to those benefits. An entity has direct control of its own activities and resources but does not have direct control of any other activities and resources.

(b) An entity indirectly controls an asset if it has control of an entity that has direct control of the asset.* A parent company therefore has indirect control of the activities and resources of its subsidiary.

2.5 If the boundary of the reporting entity is determined by reference to direct control only, when one entity controls another, there will be two reporting entities: the controlling entity and its activities and resources; and the controlled entity and its activities and resources. On the other hand, if the boundary is determined by reference to direct plus indirect control, there will in the same circumstances be a reporting entity that comprises the controlling entity, the controlled entity and all their activities and resources. This reporting entity is often referred to as 'the group'.

2.6 Both these approaches result in useful information being provided, and both are therefore used in the model described in the Statement.

(a) Direct control is used to determine the boundary of the reporting entity that prepares single entity financial statements. Those financial statements will therefore deal with the gains, losses, assets and liabilities directly controlled or borne by the entity but no other gains, losses, assets or liabilities.

(b) Direct plus indirect control is used to determine the boundary of the reporting entity that prepares consolidated financial statements. Those financial statements will deal with the gains, losses, assets and liabilities directly controlled or borne by the entity as well as those that are indirectly controlled or borne by that entity through its control of other entities.

2.7 It may be that, although an entity can influence another entity, it does not control it. Such entities do not comprise a single reporting entity.†

What is control?

2.8 Control has two aspects: the ability to deploy the economic resources involved and the ability to benefit (or to suffer) from their deployment. To have control, an entity must have both these abilities.

2.9 This can be contrasted with the position in a trusteeship or agency arrangement, where the abilities are held by different parties. For example, in a trusteeship, the trustee—unless required to act in a predetermined way—has the power to deploy the trust's resources whilst the beneficiaries benefit from their deployment.

2.10 Control in the context of assets and liabilities is considered in more detail in Chapter 4; indirect control—through control over other entities—is considered in the paragraphs below.

**For simplicity, the discussion in this chapter assumes that one entity (the parent) directly controls the other (the subsidiary). However, the discussion applies equally if the parent controls the subsidiary by controlling one or more other entities that themselves control the subsidiary. It also applies when a parent's control of its subsidiary is achieved through the combined influence of itself and other entities that it controls.*

†The accounting treatment of such relationships is addressed in Chapter 8.

Controlling an entity

When does one entity control another?

An entity will have control of a second entity if it has the ability to direct that entity's operating and financial policies with a view to gaining economic benefit from its activities. **2.11**

Control may be evidenced in a variety of ways depending on its basis (for example ownership or other rights) and the way in which it is exercised (interventionist or not). Although control of another entity has traditionally involved share ownership and voting rights, that need not be the case. Indeed, some forms of control do not involve an investment of any kind.* **2.12**

There is no single piece of evidence that is proof of an investor's control in all circumstances, although evidence that will help to determine whether control exists can be obtained by considering: **2.13**

(a) the respective rights held;
(b) the inflows and outflows of benefit; and
(c) exposure to risk—how and to what extent the investor suffers or gains from variability in outcome.

These sources of evidence are interrelated because the rights an investor holds in the investee usually determine its entitlement to benefits generated by the investee and therefore usually its exposure to risk from variations in the benefits that the investee generates. **2.14**

When determining whether the investor controls the investee, it is the relationship between the entities in practice, rather than the theoretical level of influence, that is important. The paragraphs below explain some of the factors that may need to be taken into account in determining whether control exists. **2.15**

Powers of veto and reserve powers

Control implies the ability to restrict others from directing the financial and operating policies of the controlled entity. Powers of veto and reserve powers may therefore form part of the rights by which an investor exercises control. However, such powers are unlikely to form the sole basis of control because they do not provide a basis for deploying the resources of the investee nor do they ensure the corresponding flows of benefit. **2.16**

Predetermined operating and financial policies

An investee whose operating and financial policies are predetermined will be controlled by the investor if the investor gains the benefits arising from the investee's net assets and is exposed to the risks inherent in them (ie the variability of outcome). **2.17**

Latent control

If an investor has the ability to control an investee, it is usually presumed to be exercising control, even if such control is not apparent. Generally speaking, the only **2.18**

**Although control need not involve an investment, for simplicity this chapter uses the term 'investor' to mean 'entity with the interest in the other entity' and 'investee' to mean 'entity in which the investor has an interest'.*

evidence that could rebut this presumption is evidence that a third entity is actually deploying the investee's resources on its own behalf and benefiting from them. It is, for example, not enough to show that the investee appears to be independent—it may be implementing the operating and financial policies desired by its investor without being given explicit instructions to do so.

Management but not control

2.19 Control needs to be distinguished from management. If an entity manages a second entity on its own behalf (ie it expects to benefit from the net assets of the second entity other than merely receiving a management fee) then it controls the second entity because it has the two abilities referred to in paragraph 2.8. A fee structure that in substance amounts to an interest in the net assets of an entity is treated as an ability to benefit (or to suffer) from the deployment of those net assets (sometimes referred to as an equity interest), whatever it is called.

2.20 On the other hand, if an entity manages the second entity on behalf of another party, it is not exposed to the benefits arising from, or risks inherent in, the activities of the second entity because the manager's interest in the managed entity is normally limited to its fee. As such, it does not have the second ability referred to in paragraph 2.8 and therefore does not have control of the second entity.

Chapter 3: The qualitative characteristics of financial information

In deciding which information to include in financial statements, when to include it and how to present it, the aim is to ensure that financial statements yield information that is useful. This chapter considers the qualities of financial information that make it useful.

PRINCIPLES

- Information provided by financial statements needs to be relevant and reliable and, if a choice exists between relevant and reliable approaches that are mutually exclusive, the approach chosen needs to be the one that results in the relevance of the information provided being maximised.
- Information is relevant if it has the ability to influence the economic decisions of users and is provided in time to influence those decisions.
- Information is reliable if:
  (a) it can be depended upon by users to represent faithfully what it either purports to represent or could reasonably be expected to represent, and therefore reflects the substance of the transactions and other events that have taken place;
  (b) it is free from deliberate or systematic bias and material error and is complete; and
  (c) in its preparation under conditions of uncertainty, a degree of caution has been applied in exercising the necessary judgements.
- Information in financial statements needs to be comparable.
- As an aid to comparability, information in financial statements needs to be prepared and presented in a way that enables users to discern and evaluate similarities in, and differences between, the nature and effects of transactions and other events over time and across different reporting entities.
- Information provided by financial statements needs to be understandable, although information should not be excluded from the financial statements simply because it would not be understood by some users.
- Information is understandable if its significance can be perceived by users that have a reasonable knowledge of business and economic activities and accounting and a willingness to study with reasonable diligence the information provided.
- Information that is material needs to be given in the financial statements and information that is not material need not be given.
- Information is material to the financial statements if its misstatement or omission might reasonably be expected to influence the economic decisions of users.

The relationship between these characteristics is portrayed in the diagram on the following page.

EXPLANATION

Relevance

Relevance is a general quality that is used as a selection criterion at all stages of the financial reporting process. Information provided by financial statements needs to be relevant. Furthermore, where choices have to be made between options that are relevant and reliable but mutually exclusive, the option selected should be the one that results in the relevance of the information package as a whole being maximised—in other words, the one that is reliable and would be of most use in taking economic decisions. 3.1

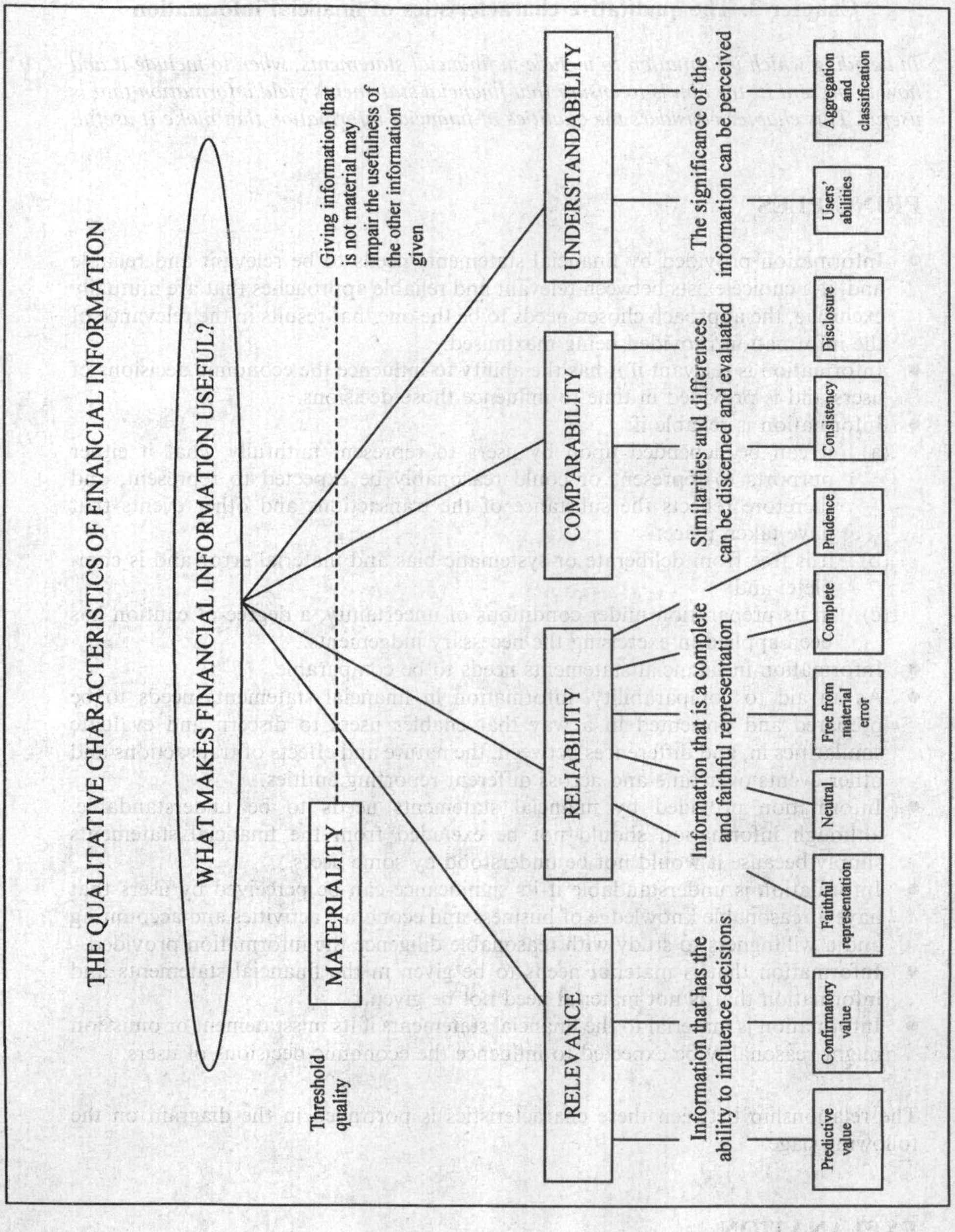
THE QUALITATIVE CHARACTERISTICS OF FINANCIAL INFORMATION
WHAT MAKES FINANCIAL INFORMATION USEFUL?
Threshold quality
MATERIALITY
Giving information that is not material may impair the usefulness of the other information given
RELEVANCE
RELIABILITY
COMPARABILITY
UNDERSTANDABILITY
Information that has the ability to influence decisions
Information that is a complete and faithful representation
Similarities and differences can be discerned and evaluated
The significance of the information can be perceived
Predictive value
Confirmatory value
Faithful representation
Neutral
Free from material error
Complete
Prudence
Consistency
Disclosure
Users' abilities
Aggregation and classification

Information is relevant if it has the ability to influence the economic decisions of users and is provided in time to influence those decisions. 3.2

Relevant information has predictive value or confirmatory value. It has predictive value if it helps users to evaluate or assess past, present or future events, and it does not need to be in the form of an explicit forecast to have predictive value. Information has confirmatory value if it helps users to confirm or correct their past evaluations and assessments. Information may have both predictive value and confirmatory value. For example, information about the current level and structure of asset holdings helps users to assess the entity's ability to exploit opportunities and react to adverse situations. The same information helps to confirm past assessments about the structure of the entity and the outcome of operations. 3.3

The ability to use information in financial statements to make assessments is enhanced by the way in which it is presented. For example, the predictive value of information provided by the financial performance statement is enhanced if unusual or infrequent items of gains or losses are disclosed and if information is provided that helps users to assess the likely incidence of similarly unusual or infrequent gains or losses in the future. In the same way, presentations that help users to understand the recurring/non-recurring nature of the various gains and losses also improve the predictive value of the performance statement. 3.4

Maximising the relevance of financial information involves maximising its predictive and confirmatory value. 3.5

There are a number of different perspectives from which an entity's financial performance and financial position could be viewed and the perspective adopted could have a significant effect on the assets and liabilities recognised and on their carrying amounts. In view of the objective of financial statements, the perspective that is usually most relevant is based on the assumption that the entity is to continue in operational existence for the foreseeable future. This perspective is commonly referred to as the going concern assumption. 3.6

Reliability

Information provided by financial statements needs to be reliable. 3.7

Information is reliable if: 3.8

(a) it can be depended upon by users to represent faithfully what it either purports to represent or could reasonably be expected to represent;
(b) it is free from deliberate or systematic bias (ie it is neutral);
(c) it is free from material error;
(d) it is complete within the bounds of materiality; and
(e) in its preparation under conditions of uncertainty, a degree of caution (ie prudence) has been applied in exercising judgement and making the necessary estimates.

Faithful representation

The portrayal of a transaction or other event in the financial statements depends, inter alia, on: 3.9

(a) the rights and obligations arising and the weight attached to each;
(b) how the rights and obligations to which most weight has been attached are characterised;

(c) which measurement basis (or bases) and presentation techniques are used to depict the rights and obligations; and
(d) the way in which the elements arising from the transaction or other event are presented in the financial statements.

3.10 A transaction or other event is faithfully represented in the financial statements if the way in which it is recognised, measured and presented in those statements corresponds closely to the effect of that transaction or event.

3.11 It needs to be borne in mind that most financial information is subject to some risk of being less than a faithful representation of what it purports to portray. This is partly due to inherent difficulties in identifying the transactions and other events to be dealt with and in identifying the consequences of such transactions and events that need to be measured. It reflects the difficulties in devising and applying measurement and presentation techniques that can convey messages that reflect those transactions and events. Furthermore, references to faithful representation need to be understood in the context of the Statement as a whole, which limits the kind of information that may properly be included in financial statements.

3.12 Faithful representation involves identifying *all* the rights and obligations arising from the transaction or event, giving greater weight to those that are likely to have a commercial effect in practice, then accounting for and presenting the transaction or other event in a way that reflects that commercial effect—in other words, in a way that reflects its substance.

3.13 The substance of a transaction or other event is not always consistent with that suggested by its legal form: although the effects of the legal characteristics of a transaction or other event are themselves a part of its substance and commercial effect, they have to be construed in the context of the transaction as a whole, including any related transactions. For example, an entity may pass legal ownership of an item of property to another party, yet, when the circumstances are looked at as a whole, it may be found that arrangements exist that ensure that the entity continues to have access to the future economic benefits embodied in that item of property. In such circumstances, the accounting needs to reflect this continuing interest.

3.14 A group or series of transactions that achieves an overall commercial effect will often need to be viewed as a whole in order to be accounted for in accordance with its substance.

Neutrality

3.15 The information provided by financial statements needs to be neutral—in other words, free from deliberate or systematic bias. Financial information is not neutral if it has been selected or presented in such a way as to influence the making of a decision or judgement in order to achieve a predetermined result or outcome.

Complete and free from material error

3.16 In requiring information provided by financial statements to represent faithfully what it purports to represent and to be neutral, there is an implication that the information is complete and free from error—at least within the bounds of materiality. Information that contains a material error or has been omitted for reasons other than materiality can cause the financial statements to be false or misleading and thus unreliable and deficient in terms of their relevance.

This reference to being complete within the bounds of materiality is important because completeness is relative: financial statements are a highly aggregated portrayal of an entity's financial performance and financial position and therefore cannot show everything. 3.17

Prudence

Uncertainty surrounds many of the events and circumstances that are reported on in the financial statements and it is dealt with in those statements by disclosing the nature and extent of the uncertainty involved and by exercising prudence. 3.18

Prudence is the inclusion of a degree of caution in the exercise of the judgements needed in making the estimates required under conditions of uncertainty, such that gains and assets are not overstated and losses and liabilities are not understated. In particular, under such conditions it requires more confirmatory evidence about the existence of, and a greater reliability of measurement for, assets and gains than is required for liabilities and losses. 3.19

However, it is not necessary to exercise prudence where there is no uncertainty. Nor is it appropriate to use prudence as a reason for, for example, creating hidden reserves or excessive provisions, deliberately understating assets or gains, or deliberately overstating liabilities or losses, because that would mean that the financial statements are not neutral and, therefore, are not reliable. 3.20

Comparability

Information in an entity's financial statements gains greatly in usefulness if it can be compared with similar information about the entity for some other period or point in time in order to identify trends in financial performance and financial position. Information about an entity is also much more useful if it can be compared with similar information about other entities in order to evaluate their relative financial performance and financial position. 3.21

Information in financial statements therefore needs to be comparable—at least as far as is possible. Furthermore, to help users to make comparisons, such information needs to be prepared and presented in a way that enables users to discern and evaluate similarities in, and differences between, the nature and effects of transactions and other events taking place over time and across different reporting entities. This can usually be achieved through a combination of consistency and disclosure of accounting policies. 3.22

Consistency

Comparability generally implies consistency throughout the reporting entity within each accounting period and from one period to the next. However, consistency is not an end in itself nor should it be allowed to become an impediment to the introduction of improved accounting practices. Consistency can also be useful in enhancing comparability between entities, although it should not be confused with a need for absolute uniformity. 3.23

Disclosure of accounting policies

In order to determine whether consistency exists or to assist in the making of comparisons despite inconsistencies, users need to be able to identify any differences between: 3.24

(a) the accounting policies adopted by an entity to account for like transactions and other events;
(b) the accounting policies adopted from period to period by an entity; and
(c) the accounting policies adopted by different entities.

3.25 Disclosure of the accounting policies employed in the preparation of the financial statements, of any changes in those policies and of the effects of such changes therefore enhances the usefulness of financial statements.

Understandability

3.26 Information provided by financial statements needs to be understandable—in other words, users need to be able to perceive its significance.

3.27 Whether financial information is understandable will depend on:

(a) the way in which the effects of transactions and other events are characterised, aggregated and classified. For example, information that does not properly reflect and communicate the substance of transactions and other events will not help users to understand the entity's financial performance or financial position.
(b) the way in which the information is presented. (This is considered further in Chapter 7.)
(c) the capabilities of users. Those preparing financial statements are entitled to assume that users have a reasonable knowledge of business and economic activities and accounting and a willingness to study with reasonable diligence the information provided.

Materiality

3.28 Materiality is the final test of what information should be given in a particular set of financial statements. While the paragraphs above describe the characteristics that, if present, will mean that the usefulness of the financial information has been maximised, the materiality test asks whether the resulting information content is of such significance as to require its inclusion in the financial statements.

3.29 Materiality is therefore a threshold quality that is demanded of all information given in the financial statements. Furthermore, when immaterial information is given in the financial statements, the resulting clutter can impair the understandability of the other information provided. In such circumstances, the immaterial information will need to be excluded.

3.30 An item of information is material to the financial statements if its misstatement or omission might reasonably be expected to influence the economic decisions of users of those financial statements, including their assessments of management's stewardship.

3.31 Whether information is material will depend on the size and nature of the item in question judged in the particular circumstances of the case. The principal factors to be taken into account are set out below. It will usually be a combination of these factors, rather than any one in particular, that will determine materiality.

(a) The item's size is judged in the context both of the financial statements as a whole and of the other information available to users that would affect their evaluation of the financial statements. This includes, for example, considering how the item affects the evaluation of trends and similar considerations.

(b) Consideration is given to the item's nature in relation to:
   (i) the transactions or other events giving rise to it;
   (ii) the legality, sensitivity, normality and potential consequences of the event or transaction;
   (iii) the identity of the parties involved; and
   (iv) the particular headings and disclosures that are affected.

If there are two or more similar items, the materiality of the items in aggregate as well as of the items individually needs to be considered. **3.32**

Constraints on the qualitative characteristics

On occasion, a conflict will arise between the characteristics of relevance, reliability, comparability and understandability. In such circumstances, a trade-off needs to be found that still enables the objective of financial statements to be met. **3.33**

Relevance and reliability

Sometimes the information that is the most relevant is not the most reliable and vice versa. Choosing the amount at which to measure an asset or liability will sometimes involve just such a conflict. In such circumstances, it will usually be appropriate to use the information that is the most relevant of whichever information is reliable.* **3.34**

Conflict between relevance and reliability can also arise over the timeliness of information. That is because a delay in providing information can make it out-of-date, which will affect its relevance, yet reporting on transactions and other events before all the uncertainties involved are resolved may affect the information's reliability. On the other hand, leaving information out of the financial statements because of reliability concerns may affect the completeness, and therefore reliability, of the information that *is* provided. Although financial information should generally be made available as soon as it is reliable and entities should do all that they reasonably can to speed up the process necessary to make information reliable, financial information should not be provided until it is reliable. **3.35**

Neutrality and prudence

There can also be tension between two aspects of reliability—neutrality and prudence—because, whilst neutrality involves freedom from deliberate or systematic bias, prudence is a potentially biased concept that seeks to ensure that, under conditions of uncertainty, gains and assets are not overstated and losses and liabilities are not understated. This tension exists only where there is uncertainty, because it is only then that prudence needs to be exercised. When there is uncertainty, the competing demands of neutrality and prudence are reconciled by finding a balance that ensures that the deliberate and systematic understatement of gains and assets and overstatement of losses and liabilities do not occur. **3.36**

Understandability

It may not always be possible to present a piece of relevant, reliable and comparable information in a way that can be understood by all the users with the capabilities **3.37**

**Choosing between alternative measurement bases is considered in Chapter 6.*

described in paragraph 3.27(c). However, information that is relevant and reliable should not be excluded from the financial statements simply because it is too difficult for some users to understand.

Chapter 4: The elements of financial statements

Elements of financial statements are the building blocks with which financial statements are constructed—the classes of items that financial statements comprise. This chapter identifies those elements and explains their attributes.

PRINCIPLES

- The elements of the financial statements are:
  - (a) assets
  - (b) liabilities
  - (c) ownership interest*
  - (d) gains†
  - (e) losses‡
  - (f) contributions from owners
  - (g) distributions to owners.

- Assets are rights or other access to future economic benefits controlled by an entity as a result of past transactions or events.
- Liabilities are obligations of an entity to transfer economic benefits as a result of past transactions or events.
- Ownership interest is the residual amount found by deducting all of the entity's liabilities from all of the entity's assets.
- Gains are increases in ownership interest not resulting from contributions from owners.
- Losses are decreases in ownership interest not resulting from distributions to owners.
- Contributions from owners are increases in ownership interest resulting from transfers from owners in their capacity as owners.
- Distributions to owners are decreases in ownership interest resulting from transfers to owners in their capacity as owners.

EXPLANATION

The elements of financial statements

Depicting the effects of transactions and other events

Financial statements need to reflect, in an appropriate manner and as far as is practicable, the effects of transactions and other events on the reporting entity's financial performance and financial position. This involves a high degree of classification and aggregation. Order is imposed on this process by specifying and defining the classes of items—the elements of financial statements—that encapsulate the key aspects of the effects of those transactions and other events. 4.1

The elements of financial statements are: 4.2

**This element is given various descriptions in financial statements including, for example, equity, owners' equity, shareholders' equity, equity capital, capital, capital and reserves, partners' capital, shareholders' funds, proprietorship and ownership.*

†This term incorporates all forms of income and revenue as well as all recognised gains (realised and unrealised) on non-revenue items.

‡This term incorporates all forms of expenses, sometimes referred to as revenue expenditure, and all recognised losses (realised and unrealised) on non-revenue items.

(a) in the case of the balance sheet (or statement of financial position)—assets, liabilities and ownership interest;
(b) in the case of the profit and loss account and any other statement of financial performance—gains and losses;
(c) contributions from owners; and
(d) distributions to owners.

4.3 Contributions from owners and distributions to owners are not the same as, and need to be distinguished from, other increases or decreases in ownership interest (in other words, gains and losses), which is why they are elements even though they are not identified with any particular primary financial statement.

4.4 Elements have been specified and defined to analyse comprehensively the way in which the financial effects of transactions and other events are represented in financial statements. However, as the cash flow statement represents only one type of financial effect—cash flows—analysis into elements is not relevant to that statement.

Recognition

4.5 Simply because a transaction or other event results, say, in a new asset being created, it does not follow that that new asset will be recognised. The criteria that need to be met before the effects of a transaction or other event on the elements will be recognised are considered in Chapter 5.

Assets

Definition

4.6 Assets are defined as follows:

Assets are rights or other access to future economic benefits controlled by an entity as a result of past transactions or events.

4.7 Although assets commonly have other features that help identify them—for example, they may be acquired at a cost and they may be tangible, exchangeable or legally enforceable—those features are not essential characteristics of an asset and their absence is not sufficient in itself to preclude an item from qualifying as an asset.

Rights or other access

4.8 An asset is not the item of property itself, but rather the rights or other access to some or all of the future economic benefits derived from the item of property.*

4.9 These rights or other access can be obtained in various ways. Often they are obtained by legal ownership of the underlying item of property. Such ownership usually gives the owner access to a number of future economic benefits, including the ability to use the item of property, to sell or exchange it or to exploit its value by, for example, pledging it as security for borrowing.

**The term 'item of property' has been used in this chapter to differentiate between the control of rights or other access to future economic benefits (the asset) and the thing from which those future economic benefits are derived (the item of property). It is recognised however that, in other contexts, the term may have a different meaning and could, for example, refer to the subdivided property rights.*

However, legal rights to future economic benefits derived from an item of property can be obtained without having legal ownership of the property itself, as is the case, for example, where property is leased. **4.10**

Other legal rights that give rise to assets include the right to require other parties to make payments or render services and the right to use a patent or trade mark. **4.11**

Access to future economic benefits—and therefore an asset—can also exist in the absence of legal rights. An example might be an unpatented invention. **4.12**

Future economic benefits

Capacity to obtain future economic benefits is the essence of an asset and is common to all assets irrespective of their form. Therefore, to be an asset, the right or other access must be capable, singly or in combination with other assets, of yielding economic benefits. **4.13**

This future economic benefit need not, however, be certain. Indeed, there is always some uncertainty whether expected future economic benefits will be obtained either to the extent expected or at all. In some cases, that uncertainty is so great that the asset is not recognised.* **4.14**

Future economic benefits eventually result in net cash inflows to the entity. Assets are not, however, always direct representations of cash flows: they are rights and other access to the future economic benefits that can generate or be used to generate future cash flows. In particular: **4.15**

(a) cash (including bank deposits) can be exchanged for virtually any good or service that is available or it can be saved and exchanged for them in the future. The command that cash gives over resources is the basis of its future economic benefits.
(b) debtors, investments and similar assets represent future economic benefits because they are direct claims to cash inflows that are expected to occur when customers pay their accounts, when investees pay interest or dividends, or when an investment is repaid or sold.
(c) payments made to external parties for services to be received from them in the future (such as prepayments) result in access to future economic benefits because they represent rights to receive services or to return of the payment.
(d) other assets provide access to future economic benefits through their ability to be:
    (i) exchanged for cash, claims to cash or other goods and services;
    (ii) used to provide goods or services; or
    (iii) used to settle liabilities.

As there does not need to be certainty that the economic benefits will arise, items that represent the right to exchange property on terms that will or may be favourable are also assets. For example, an option to acquire an asset will, subject to the other criteria being met, be an asset even if the price payable under the option is currently more than the market price of the asset. **4.16**

Controlled by the entity

The definition of an asset requires that the rights or other access to future economic benefits are controlled by the reporting entity. An entity will control the rights or other access if it has the ability both to obtain for itself any economic benefits that will arise and to prevent or limit the access of others to those benefits. **4.17**

**The recognition process is discussed in Chapter 5.*

4.18 This control does not need to be legally enforceable, which means that weight can be given to economic and social sanctions when these are effective in inducing entities to fulfil promises or to comply with widely accepted business practices or customs.

4.19 The requirement that the rights or other access should be controlled by the entity treating them as its asset means that a particular right or other access to future economic benefits will appear in only one set of single entity financial statements, because such rights or access can be directly controlled by only one entity. (As indirect control is important in determining the boundaries of reporting entities, a right that is directly controlled by one entity and indirectly controlled by a second—through its control of the first entity—will be an asset both of the first entity and of the reporting entity that comprises both entities, ie the group.*)

4.20 On the other hand, a single item of property may give rise to assets of more than one entity. If two entities control the rights to different future economic benefits from the same item of property, both entities will have an asset (subject to the other aspects of the definition being met). However, although the item of property underlying the asset will be the same, the assets will be different because the future economic benefits are different. For example, if an entity leases an item of property to another entity, both entities will recognise an asset based on rights relating to the leased item of property although, as the lessor's rights will not be identical to the lessee's, the assets will not be the same.

4.21 An item of property will be an asset of an entity even though that entity cannot dispose of it without fundamentally changing the nature of its business, as would be the case if, for example, a hotel company with one hotel sold its hotel or a television franchise company sold its franchise. In such cases, although the rights to future economic benefits derived from the hotel or television franchise are the essence of the entity's business, it controls those rights and is therefore still in a position to choose if and when to realise the economic benefits involved. On the other hand, it is generally not possible for an entity to choose if and when to realise the economic benefits derivable from factors such as its market share, superior management or good labour relations because the rights or other access to such benefits cannot be controlled independently of the business as a whole. The entity therefore does not have the control of these benefits envisaged by the Statement, which means that such factors are not assets of the entity.

Past transactions or events

4.22 If the reporting entity's control of the rights or other access to the future economic benefits involved is to represent an asset, it needs to be the result of *past* transactions or events. A reporting entity that has access to future economic benefits but did not, until after the balance sheet date, have the ability to restrict the access of others to those benefits, did not have an asset at the balance sheet date.

Liabilities

Definition

4.23 Liabilities are defined as follows:

> Liabilities are obligations of an entity to transfer economic benefits as a result of past transactions or events.

**Determining the boundaries of reporting entities is considered in Chapter 2.*

Obligations

For there to be a liability there must be an obligation that might result in the transfer of economic benefits. 4.24

The notion of an obligation implies that the entity is not free to avoid the outflow of resources. If an obligation exists, although an entity may offer inducements to its creditors to cancel or postpone settlement, it will not be able to insist that they accept such an offer. 4.25

Although many liabilities are based on legal obligations, a legal obligation is not a *necessary* condition: a liability can exist in the absence of legal obligations if commercial considerations create a constructive obligation. 4.26

A decision to transfer economic benefits does not, in itself, create a constructive obligation because the transfer can be avoided by changing the decision. On the other hand, a constructive obligation would be created if such a decision was coupled with an event that both created a valid expectation that the entity involved would implement that decision and meant that the entity could not realistically withdraw from it. For example, a constructive obligation may be created by communicating a decision to follow a particular course of action to another party. Such an obligation may also be created by an established pattern of past practice. 4.27

When preparing financial statements, it is usually most relevant to assume that the reporting entity is to continue in operational existence for the foreseeable future. It does not follow from this assumption, however, that, in preparing financial statements, the entity should be treated as being obliged to adopt a course of action that will enable it to continue in operational existence. Even if an obligation needs to be incurred to enable the entity to continue existing operations, until the entity ceases to be able to avoid the outflow of resources involved, there will be no obligation and, therefore, no liability. 4.28

Transfer of economic benefits

Certainty that the obligation *will* result in a transfer of future economic benefits is not necessary. Obligations that are not likely to result in a transfer of economic benefits—such as the guarantee of another entity's debt where that entity is expected to remain solvent—are liabilities, even though they may not be recognised in financial statements (or may be recognised with a carrying amount of nil). 4.29

Similarly, although many liabilities involve transfers of known amounts of cash, that need not be the case: a liability could involve an obligation to transfer an uncertain amount, and it could involve an obligation to transfer economic benefits other than cash—for example, by providing services or by undertaking to repair goods that are the subject of warranties. The recognition criteria described in Chapter 5 will filter out those liabilities that involve too much uncertainty to be recognised in the primary financial statements. 4.30

Past transactions or events

For a liability to exist at the balance sheet date, the obligation to transfer economic benefits must have resulted from a *past* transaction or event. For example, in the circumstances described in paragraph 4.27—where the event that gave rise to the obligation was the communication of the decision to transfer economic benefits—the 4.31

liability will have existed at the balance sheet date only if the communication took place on or before that date.

4.32 Sometimes a series of events must take place before the entity will have an obligation to transfer economic benefits. In such circumstances, whether the obligation exists depends on whether any of the events that have still to take place are under the entity's control. If they are, the entity retains discretion to avoid the transfer, so no obligation exists. For example, as long as it is possible to avoid a penalty clause in a contract by performing, a liability in respect of the penalty will not arise. In contrast, an obligation to repair goods subject to warranty cannot be avoided once the goods have been sold on terms that include the warranty, so the sale marks the inception of the liability.

Offsetting rights and obligations

4.33 When a transaction or other event gives rise to a number of rights and obligations, it is necessary to consider whether some or all of those rights and obligations need to be offset either with each other or with rights and obligations that arise from other transactions or events. This raises issues of:

(a) definition—when do rights and obligations represent separate assets and liabilities and when should some or all of them be aggregated or offset? This issue is considered in paragraphs 4.34-4.36.

(b) recognition—when should rights that represent an asset and obligations that represent a liability be combined and recognised as a single asset or liability? This Statement envisages no circumstances in which assets and liabilities will be treated in this way.

(c) presentation—when is it appropriate to present assets offset against liabilities (or vice versa) in the balance sheet? This issue is considered in Chapter 7.

4.34 If a right to receive future economic benefits and an obligation to transfer future economic benefits exist and the reporting entity has the ability—which is assured—to insist on net settlement of the balances, the right and obligation together form a single asset or liability regardless of how the parties intend to settle the balances.

4.35 When an entity enters into an agreement with another, it usually obtains certain rights and, in exchange, accepts certain obligations. Before any act of performance under the agreement has taken place, the entity does not have control of the future economic benefits arising from performance, nor does it have an obligation to transfer economic benefits that arise on performance. What it *does* have, however, is a contract that represents a net position comprising a combined right and obligation either to participate in the exchange or alternatively to be compensated (or to compensate) for the consequences of the exchange not taking place. Initially, the rights and obligations are likely to be exactly offsetting, although that will often not remain the case. The rights and obligations arising under such unperformed executory contracts together represent a single asset or liability.

4.36 It may be that the contract has been performed partially but is equally proportionately unperformed—in other words, that both parties to the contract have still to perform to an equal degree the actions promised by and required of them under the contract. In such a case, although the rights and obligations relating to the performed part of the contract may represent separate assets and liabilities, the rights and obligations relating to the unperformed part will together represent a single asset or liability.

Ownership interest

Ownership interest is defined as follows: **4.37**

> Ownership interest is the residual amount found by deducting all of the entity's liabilities from all of the entity's assets.

Since ownership interest is defined as a residual interest, the distinction between liabilities and ownership interest is highly significant. Owners invest in an entity in the hope of a return, at least part of which will usually be provided by the transfer to them from the entity of economic benefits (for example the payment of dividends). However, owners, unlike creditors, do not have the ability to insist that a transfer is made to them regardless of the circumstances: theirs is a residual interest in the assets of the entity after all the liabilities have been deducted. **4.38**

Gains and losses

Definitions

Financial statements draw a distinction between changes in ownership interest arising from transactions with owners in their capacity as owners and other changes. These latter changes are gains and losses and are defined as follows: **4.39**

> Gains are increases in ownership interest not resulting from contributions from owners.
>
> Losses are decreases in ownership interest not resulting from distributions to owners.

The terms 'gains' and 'losses' therefore include items that are often referred to as 'revenue' and 'expenses', as well as gains and losses arising from, for example, the disposal of fixed assets and the remeasurement of assets and liabilities. **4.40**

Offsetting gains and losses

Some transactions give rise to a gain (or a loss) that is the net of two amounts: the revenue or income arising from the transaction and the expenses or costs incurred in generating that revenue. For example, the profit that arises on selling an item of stock is the difference between the sale proceeds and the cost of the item sold. For the purpose of the Statement, the sale proceeds and cost of the item sold are separate items—the former being a gain and the latter a loss. Whether such gains and losses are shown separately in the financial statements is a presentation issue and is considered in Chapter 7. **4.41**

Contributions from owners and distributions to owners

Definitions

The remaining elements of financial statements relate to transactions with the owners in their capacity as owners and are defined as follows: **4.42**

> Contributions from owners are increases in ownership interest resulting from transfers from owners in their capacity as owners.
>
> Distributions to owners are decreases in ownership interest resulting from transfers to owners in their capacity as owners.

In their capacity as owners

4.43 Contributions from, and distributions to, owners include only those transactions to which owners are a party *in their capacity as owners*. Increases or decreases in ownership interest that result from transactions entered into with owners in other capacities (for example, as customers or suppliers) are gains or losses. In some cases a single transaction combines a transaction with owners in their capacity as owners and a transaction with them in some other capacity.

Contributions from owners

4.44 Contributions from owners involve the owners making a contribution to the entity by transferring assets, performing services, or accepting ownership interest in satisfaction of liabilities. Rights in the ownership interest are usually granted in return for a contribution from owners.

Distributions to owners

4.45 Distributions to owners include the payment of dividends and the return of capital. A purchase by a company of its own shares is an example of a return of capital and is therefore reflected in financial statements by reducing the amount of ownership interest.

Chapter 5: Recognition in financial statements

When the reporting entity undertakes a transaction or when some other relevant event occurs, the effect of that transaction or event on the elements of financial statements will need to be recognised in the financial statements if certain criteria are met. This chapter considers that recognition process.

PRINCIPLES

- If a transaction or other event has created a new asset or liability or added to an existing asset or liability, that effect will be recognised* if:
  - (a) sufficient evidence exists that the new asset or liability has been created or that there has been an addition to an existing asset or liability; and
  - (b) the new asset or liability or the addition to the existing asset or liability can be measured at a monetary amount with sufficient reliability.
- In a transaction involving the provision of services or goods for a net gain, the recognition criteria described above will be met on the occurrence of the critical event in the operating cycle involved.
- An asset or liability will be wholly or partly derecognised† if:
  - (a) sufficient evidence exists that a transaction or other past event has eliminated‡ all or part of a previously recognised asset or liability; or
  - (b) although the item continues to be an asset or a liability, the criteria for recognition are no longer met.

EXPLANATION

The recognition process

The stages of the recognition process

The objective of financial statements is achieved to a large extent through the recognition of elements in the primary financial statements—in other words, the depiction of elements both in words and by monetary amounts and the inclusion of those amounts in the primary financial statement totals. This recognition process has the following stages: 5.1

(a) initial recognition, which is where an item is depicted in the primary financial statements for the first time;
(b) subsequent remeasurement, which involves changing the amount at which an already recognised asset or liability is stated in the primary financial statements; and
(c) derecognition, which is where an item that was until then recognised ceases to be recognised.

**The term 'recognised' is used in the Statement to mean depicting an item both in words and by a monetary amount and including that amount in the primary financial statement totals.*

†The term 'derecognised' is used in the Statement to mean that an item ceases to be recognised.

‡To simplify the text, the word 'eliminated' is used in this chapter in place of the phrase 'consumed, transferred, disposed of, expired, settled or extinguished'.

Transactions and events other than transactions

5.2 The recognition process requires that all events that may have an effect on elements of the financial statements are, as far as is possible, identified and reflected in an appropriate manner in the financial statements.

5.3 Transactions are the most common form of such events and are therefore the most common reason for recognising and derecognising items. Events other than transactions may nevertheless also result in the recognition or derecognition of items. For example:

(a) events such as discovery, growth, extraction, processing or innovation may result in the creation of new assets that may meet the recognition criteria. Similarly, the imposition of a penalty by a court may create a new liability that meets the recognition criteria.
(b) events (such as a fire) that cause damage to an asset and events (such as the elapse of time) that result in an obligation expiring may result in a need to derecognise the asset or liability involved.

The effect of transactions and other events

5.4 No matter what element or change in element is being considered, the starting point for the recognition process is the effect that the transaction or other event involved has had on the reporting entity's assets and liabilities, because it is the assets and liabilities that demonstrate the lasting effect of changes in other elements. The interrelationship between the elements means that the recognition of one item as an element (or the recognition of a change in an element, including its derecognition) will inevitably result in the recognition of, or change in, another element. Thus, if a new asset is recognised, there will also be recognised a decrease in another asset, a new or increased liability, a gain, or a contribution from owners (or a combination of these).

5.5 A transaction or other event could have one of several effects on a reporting entity's assets and liabilities.

(a) It might create a new asset or liability or add to an existing asset or liability. When this is the case, it will be necessary to determine whether the new asset or liability (or the addition thereto) should be recognised, because not all assets and liabilities are recognised. Paragraphs 5.12-5.21 consider initial recognition in detail.
(b) It might provide additional evidence about an existing but unrecognised asset or liability and, as a result, enable that item to be recognised. This is also considered in paragraphs 5.12-5.21.
(c) It might change some aspect of an already recognised asset or liability. This change may involve:
    (i) the nature of the item. For example, an item of raw material may be converted through the production process into finished goods. Similarly, convertible debt may be converted into equity shares. A change in the nature of an item will usually require a change in description, possibly by reclassification from one balance sheet caption to another or by renaming within a balance sheet caption. The amount at which the item is stated in the financial statements may also need to be changed.
    (ii) a change to the flow of benefits associated with an already recognised asset or liability. For example, the market value of a property may change as a result of changes in its development or income potential. Doubts about the creditworthiness of a debtor may alter perceptions of the

collectability of the amount due from that debtor. Similarly, new information may cause the reporting entity to alter its estimate of the amount to be paid out to settle a liability of uncertain amount. A change in the flow of benefits associated with an item may require a change in the amount at which the item is stated. Changes in the amount at which an item is stated (in other words, subsequent remeasurements) are considered in Chapter 6.

(d) It might involve transferring, using up or consuming an asset or settling, extinguishing or transferring a liability. On the other hand, it might leave intact certain of the rights to future economic benefits inherent in an asset whilst transferring, using up or consuming others, or it might leave intact certain obligations inherent in a liability whilst settling, extinguishing or transferring others. In all such circumstances it will be necessary to consider whether the existing asset or liability that has been affected should be derecognised in whole or in part. Paragraphs 5.22-5.25 consider derecognition further.

The references in the definitions of assets and liabilities to past transactions or events ensure that the non-cash effects of transactions and other events will, as far as is possible, be reflected in the financial statements in the accounting period in which they occur and not, for example, in the period in which any cash involved is received or paid. This is commonly referred to as the 'accruals concept'. **5.6**

Whether the reporting entity is a going concern can play a significant role in the recognition process. For example, some contracts stipulate that the rights they give one party to the contract will lapse if that party discontinues its operations. Similarly, the reliability of measures—an important factor in the recognition process—may be affected if the reporting entity is not able to continue its operations. As explained in Chapter 3, the qualitative characteristic of relevance usually requires the going concern assumption to be applied. **5.7**

Uncertainty and the recognition process

Ideally, all assets, liabilities, gains, losses and other elements would be recognised immediately they arise. Similarly, in an ideal world an asset or liability would be derecognised as soon as it had ceased to exist or would be remeasured as soon as the need for remeasurement arose. In practice, however, entities operate in an uncertain environment and this uncertainty may sometimes make it necessary to delay the recognition process. **5.8**

If uncertainty exists, totally reliable information will become available only when the uncertainty has resolved itself. However, to defer a stage of the recognition process until the uncertainty has resolved itself will often reduce the relevance of the financial statements. It may also reduce their reliability because they will not represent faithfully the transactions and other events of the reporting period. Financial statements achieve a balance between these competing demands by seeking to provide information that has no more than an acceptable degree of uncertainty but not seeking to provide information that is totally free from uncertainty. **5.9**

In the business environment, uncertainty usually exists in a continuum, so the recognition process involves selecting the point on the continuum at which uncertainty becomes acceptable. The exact location of this point on the continuum will vary, depending on circumstances. For example, if additional information about the possible outcomes of an obligation is disclosed, it will usually be possible to recognise a liability despite this uncertainty. Furthermore, if a number of similar uncertain items are involved, it may be practicable to determine a sufficiently reliable measure **5.10** for the items taken as a whole despite the impracticality of determining a sufficiently reliable measure for each item individually.

5.11 There will nevertheless be circumstances in which it is not possible to reduce the uncertainty to an acceptable level. If that is the case, the recognition process will be deferred until such time as the uncertainty has been reduced to an acceptable level (and the effect of the transaction or other event will instead usually be reported in the notes to the financial statements).

Initial recognition

Categories of uncertainty

5.12 In the initial recognition process, there are two broad categories of uncertainty that could arise:

(a) element uncertainty, which involves uncertainty whether an item exists and meets the definitions of the elements of financial statements; and
(b) measurement uncertainty, which concerns the appropriate monetary amount at which to recognise the item.

Element uncertainty

5.13 Whether the rights or other access that underlie a potential asset exist, whether they are controlled by the reporting entity and whether they may yield future economic benefits may all be subject to uncertainty. Similarly, in the case of a potential liability there could be uncertainty whether the obligation exists and whether that obligation might require the reporting entity to transfer economic benefits.

5.14 Uncertainty of this kind (element uncertainty) is countered by evidence—the more evidence there is about an item and the better the quality of that evidence, the less uncertainty there will be over the item's existence and nature. To recognise an item it is necessary to have sufficient evidence, both in amount and quality, that the item exists and is an asset or liability of the reporting entity. This is reflected in the first of the two criteria for initial recognition, which requires that sufficient evidence must exist that a new asset or liability has been created or that there has been an addition to an existing asset or liability.

5.15 What constitutes sufficient evidence is a matter of judgement in the particular circumstances of each case although, while the evidence needs to be adequate, it need not be (and often cannot be) conclusive. The main source of evidence will be past or present experience with the item itself or with similar items, including:

(a) evidence provided by the event that has given rise to the possible asset or liability;
(b) past experience with similar items (for example, successful research and development in the past);
(c) current information directly relating to the possible asset or liability; and
(d) evidence provided by transactions of other entities in similar assets and liabilities.

Measurement uncertainty

5.16 To recognise an item, it is necessary to attribute a monetary amount to it. This involves two steps: selecting a suitable measurement basis (ie historical cost or current value) for the item and determining an appropriate monetary amount for the basis chosen.*

Uncertainty about the appropriate monetary amount at which to recognise the item (in other words, measurement uncertainty) is reflected in the second of the criteria for initial recognition, which requires that the new asset or liability or addition to an existing asset or liability can be measured at a monetary amount with sufficient reliability. **5.17**

Prudence

As explained earlier, in order to recognise a loss (or gain), it is necessary to consider whether there is sufficient evidence that a decrease (or increase) in ownership interest has occurred and whether the amount of the loss (or gain) can be measured with sufficient reliability. As explained in Chapter 3, if there is uncertainty prudence requires: **5.18**

(a) more confirmatory evidence about the existence of an asset or gain than about the existence of a liability or loss; and
(b) a greater reliability of measurement for assets and gains than for liabilities and losses.

However, the exercise of prudence does not justify the omission of assets or gains when there is sufficient evidence of occurrence and reliability of measurement or the inclusion of liabilities or losses when there is not. Nor does it justify any other deliberate and systematic overstatement of liabilities or losses or deliberate and systematic understatement of assets or gains. **5.19**

Unperformed contracts

As explained in Chapter 4, when an entity enters into an agreement with another party, it obtains certain rights and, in exchange, accepts certain obligations. Before any act of performance under the agreement has taken place, the entity will have only a net position comprising a combined right and obligation either to participate in the exchange or alternatively to be compensated (or to compensate) for the consequences of the exchange not taking place. Although this right and the obligation will usually be in balance initially, changing circumstances may cause an imbalance to arise, in which case the net position will be either an asset or a liability. **5.20**

This asset or liability will be recognised if the recognition criteria described in paragraphs 5.14 and 5.17 are met (and if the amount at which the asset or liability is to be measured is not nil). In particular: **5.21**

(a) the criterion that sufficient evidence must exist that the new asset or liability has been created will generally be met if it can be shown that the agreement is enforceable and, as a result, that a party to the agreement cannot cancel it (or otherwise fail to perform in accordance with it) without being obliged to compensate for such non-performance.
(b) the criterion that the new asset or liability must be capable of being measured at a monetary amount with sufficient reliability is dealt with in Chapter 6.
(c) if the historical cost basis of measurement is being used, the carrying amount will be the cost of entering into the agreement, which is usually nil. In effect, therefore, the contract is recognised at nil. An unperformed non-derivative

**The measurement process is described in Chapter 6.*

contract with no initial cost will nevertheless be recognised if it has become an onerous contract.

Derecognition

Derecognition because the asset or liability has been eliminated

5.22 Assets tend, in due course, to be consumed, transferred or otherwise disposed of, or they expire. For example, cash may be spent, debtors may be collected, raw materials may be consumed or processed, finished goods may be sold and the service potential of a machine may be fully used up. Similarly, liabilities tend to be settled, extinguished, transferred, or they expire. For example, creditors may be paid, a warranty attaching to goods sold may expire, long-term debt may be exchanged for other debt and obligations to perform in accordance with agreed contractual terms may be met. In all such circumstances, it may be necessary to derecognise some or all of the asset or liability involved.

5.23 It is usually relatively simple to determine whether and when a previously recognised asset or liability needs to be derecognised. For example, using the examples given in the previous paragraph, the cash will be derecognised when it is paid out, the raw materials as they are being used and so on (in other words, when the asset is eliminated). However, some transactions leave intact certain of the rights to future benefits inherent in an asset (or obligations inherent in a liability) while eliminating others. In such circumstances, analysis is required to ascertain whether the effect of the transaction should be reflected by derecognising some or all of the assets and liabilities involved. For example, if the reporting entity no longer has control of some of the rights that previously constituted an asset while retaining control of some of the other rights, the asset may need to be partially derecognised (or the existing asset completely derecognised and a new asset recognised instead).

5.24 Ideally, an asset or liability would be derecognised as soon as it has been eliminated. However, there will sometimes be uncertainty about an item's continued existence. In such circumstances, derecognition will not take place until sufficient evidence exists that the transaction or other event has resulted in the elimination of the item. When there is uncertainty, prudence usually requires more confirmatory evidence about the existence of, and a greater reliability of measurement for, assets than is required for liabilities. This tends to mean that, if there is any significant uncertainty about an asset's continued existence, it will be derecognised. However, in the case of a liability, more evidence of its elimination will be needed before it will be derecognised.

Derecognition because the criteria for recognition are no longer met

5.25 After initial recognition, an asset or liability will usually continue to be recognised until it has been eliminated, at which point it will be derecognised. It is possible, however, that, although there has been no significant change in the inherent nature of an already recognised asset or liability—in other words, although the asset or liability has not been eliminated—the criteria for recognition described in paragraphs 5.14 and 5.17 are no longer met. For example, an event may have occurred since initial recognition that has resulted in there no longer being sufficient evidence that the asset or liability concerned exists. Similarly, an event may have created additional uncertainty and, as a result, a previously recognised asset or liability can no longer be measured with sufficient reliability. On the rare occasions when this is the case, that asset or liability will be derecognised even though it has not been eliminated.

Revenue recognition

It was explained earlier in the chapter that, because of the interrelationship between the elements, the starting point for the recognition process is always the effect that the transaction or other event involved has had on the reporting entity's assets and liabilities. For example, assuming that no contribution from owners or transfer to owners is involved: 5.26

(a) if the effect of the transaction or other event is to increase the entity's recognised net assets, a gain will be recognised.
(b) a loss will be recognised if, and to the extent that, previously recognised assets have been reduced or eliminated or cease to qualify for recognition as assets without a commensurate increase in other assets or reduction in liabilities. Similarly, a loss will be recognised when and to the extent that a liability is incurred or increased without a commensurate increase in recognised assets or a reduction in other liabilities.

However, although the starting point for the recognition process may be the effect on assets and liabilities, the notions of matching and the critical event in the operating cycle will often help in identifying these effects. 5.27

Matching

Matching has two forms. 5.28

(a) Time matching involves the recognition of receipts (and payments) directly associated with the passage of time as gains (and losses) on a systematic basis over the course of the period involved. For example, rent paid at the beginning of a rental period is recognised as a loss over the course of the rental period, with amounts paid in advance of such recognition being recognised as an asset.
(b) Revenue/expenditure matching involves the recognition of expenditure directly associated with the generation of specific gains as a loss in the same period as the gains are recognised, rather than in the period in which the expenditure is incurred. For example, the cost incurred in obtaining or producing an item of stock is recognised in the performance statement as a loss in the same reporting period as the gain on selling that item, and in the meantime is recognised as an asset.

Almost all expenditure is undertaken with a view to acquiring some form of benefit in exchange. Consequently, if matching were used in an unrestricted way, it would be possible to delay the recognition in the performance statement of most items of expenditure insofar as the hoped-for benefits still lay in the future. The Statement imposes a degree of discipline on this process because only items that meet the definitions of, and relevant recognition criteria for, assets, liabilities or ownership interest are recognised in the balance sheet. 5.29

This means that the Statement does not use the notion of matching as the main driver of the recognition process. Nevertheless, the Statement envisages that: 5.30

(a) if the future economic benefits embodied in the asset are eliminated at a single point in time, it is at that point that the asset will be derecognised and a loss recognised; and
(b) if the future economic benefits are eliminated over several accounting periods—typically because they are being consumed over a period of time—the cost of the asset that comprises the future economic benefits will be recognised as a loss in the performance statement over those accounting periods.

5.31 When expenditure is being allocated to more than one accounting period, the amount allocated to each accounting period will depend on the circumstances involved, although the aim is always to recognise the expenditure as a loss on a systematic basis over the periods in which the asset delivers up its benefits. For example, if the association of the expenditure with the generation of specific gains can be only broadly or indirectly determined, it will often be necessary to assume that the asset declines in a systematic manner over its expected life.

5.32 Two implications of adopting the approach in the Statement, rather than using matching as a main driver of recognition, are that:

(a) expenditure or some other form of loss that cannot justifiably be shown to be associated with control of rights or other access to future economic benefits will be recognised in the performance statement as a loss in the period in which it is incurred; and

(b) expenditure incurred with a view to future economic benefits but whose relationship to such benefits is too uncertain to warrant recognition of an asset will be recognised immediately as a loss.

Critical event in the operating cycle

5.33 Sometimes it is easier to identify the appropriate point at which to recognise gains arising from the provision of services or goods—and therefore changes to the entity's assets and liabilities—by focusing on the operating cycle of the reporting entity and, in particular, on the critical event in that cycle.*

5.34 The critical event is the point in an operating cycle at which there will usually be sufficient evidence that the gain exists and it will usually be possible to measure that gain with sufficient reliability. In other words, it is the point at which the recognition criteria described earlier in the chapter will be met and the gain and related change to assets and liabilities will be recognised.

5.35 For many types of transaction, the critical event in the operating cycle is synonymous with full performance. In such cases a gain will be recognised when the entity providing the service or goods has fully performed. That need not, however, be the case: the critical event could occur at other times in the cycle and there could be more than one critical event in the cycle.

5.36 The identity of the critical event or events of an operating cycle will depend on the particular circumstances involved. For example:

(a) if the reporting entity has carried out all its obligations under an agreement except for a few minor acts of performance, the critical event will have occurred.

(b) if a sale is contingent upon acceptance by the buyer, the critical event will usually occur before acceptance unless the act of acceptance creates substantial uncertainty whether the contractual obligations will be met. The critical event will not usually have occurred if the likelihood of the goods or services not being accepted is significant.

(c) the operating cycle might involve a contract that is performed in stages, for each of which there is a critical event. (Contracts to build large buildings are

**In order to keep the explanation simple, it has been assumed in paragraphs 5.33-5.36 that the transaction being discussed is expected to generate a net profit and that the issue is therefore when to recognise that profit when using the historical cost basis of measurement. If the contract is expected to generate a loss the historical cost carrying amount will be adjusted immediately to reflect that expected loss.*

usually an example of such an operating cycle.) In such circumstances, the gain that is expected to be earned on the contract as a whole will need to be allocated among the critical events.

Chapter 6: Measurement in financial statements

Measuring an asset or liability entails deciding on the measurement basis to be used and determining the monetary amount that is appropriate for that basis. It may also involve revising the monetary amount when certain events occur. This chapter describes the measurement process and explains how a choice is made between the measurement bases available.

PRINCIPLES

- In drawing up financial statements, a measurement basis—either historical cost or current value*—needs to be selected for each category of assets or liabilities. The basis selected will be the one that best meets the objective of financial statements and the demands of the qualitative characteristics of financial information, bearing in mind the nature of the assets or liabilities concerned and the circumstances involved.
- An asset or liability being measured using the historical cost basis is recognised initially at transaction cost. An asset or liability being measured using the current value basis is recognised initially at its current value at the time it was acquired or assumed.
- Subsequent remeasurement will occur if it is necessary to ensure that:
  (a) assets measured at historical cost are carried at the lower of cost and recoverable amount;
  (b) monetary items denominated in foreign currency are carried at amounts based on up-to-date exchange rates; and
  (c) assets and liabilities measured on the current value basis are carried at up-to-date current values.
- Such remeasurements, however, will be recognised only if:
  (a) there is sufficient evidence that the monetary amount of the asset or liability has changed; and
  (b) the new amount of the asset or liability can be measured with sufficient reliability.

EXPLANATION

Alternative bases of measurement

6.1 Assets and liabilities have several different monetary attributes that could be represented in financial statements. Assets could, for example, be stated at historical cost, replacement cost or net realisable value and liabilities could, for example, be stated at historical cost, the cost of discharging the liability by the most economical means available or (in some cases) the amount that the entity could currently raise by issuing a similar debt security. The single most important characteristic that distinguishes these monetary attributes (which are known as measurement bases) is whether they are based on historical cost or current value. This chapter concentrates on that distinction.

6.2 These measurement bases could be used in financial statements in one of several ways. In particular:

(a) a single measurement basis could be used for all assets and liabilities. For example, all assets and liabilities could be measured using historical cost. This is

**The term 'historical cost' is, unless stated otherwise, used in the Statement to refer to the particular version of the historical cost basis described in paragraph 6.18. Similarly, the term 'current value' is used to refer to the value determined in accordance with paragraphs 6.7-6.9.*

known as the historical cost system. Alternatively, all assets and liabilities could be measured at current value. This is known as the current value system.

(b) some categories of assets or liabilities could be measured on a historical cost basis and some on a current value basis. This is known as the mixed measurement system. In reality there is not one mixed measurement system but many, each involving a different mix of historical cost and current value.

The mixed measurement system permits the measurement basis to be selected separately for each category of assets or liabilities. It also permits the use of historical cost (or current value) for all assets and liabilities if historical cost (or current value) is the most appropriate measure for each of those categories. Thus it can be adapted to fit the particular circumstances involved. **6.3**

The Statement therefore envisages that the mixed measurement system will be used and it focuses on the mix of historical cost and current value to be adopted. In doing so, it describes a framework that would guide the choice of basis for each category of assets or liabilities. **6.4**

One approach that is not appropriate is to remeasure a category of assets or liabilities at current value, then retain those assets or liabilities at that same amount indefinitely or for a long period of time. Such measures will usually soon cease to be up-to-date current values and will then be neither a historical cost nor a current value. As such, they disturb the comparability and consistency of accounting measurement and are not consistent with the principles contained in the Statement. **6.5**

Alternative measures of current value

The current value of an asset could be determined by reference to entry value (replacement cost), exit value (net realisable value) or value in use (discounted present value of the cash flows expected from continuing use and ultimate sale by the present owner). For some assets (for example investments in actively traded securities), these three alternative measures of current value produce very similar amounts, with only small differences due to transaction costs. However, for other assets (for example fixed assets specific to the business), differences between the alternative measures can be material. **6.6**

It is therefore necessary to select from these alternative measures of current value the measure that maximises the relevance of the current value basis. Current value is at its most relevant when it reflects the loss that the entity would suffer if it were deprived of the asset involved. That measure, which is often referred to as the 'deprival value' or the 'value to the business', will depend on the circumstances involved. **6.7**

(a) In most cases, as the entity will be putting the asset to profitable use, the asset's value in its most profitable use (in other words, its recoverable amount) will exceed its replacement cost. In such circumstances, the entity will, if deprived of the asset, replace it, and the current value of the asset will be its current replacement cost.

(b) An asset will not be replaced if the cost of replacing it exceeds its recoverable amount. In such circumstances, the asset's current value is that recoverable amount.

(i) When the most profitable use of an asset is to sell it, the asset's recoverable amount will be the amount that can be obtained by selling it, net of selling expenses; in other words, its net realisable value.

(ii) When the most profitable use of an asset is to consume it—for example by continuing to operate it—its recoverable amount will be the present value of the future cash flows obtainable and cash flows obviated as a result of the asset's continued use and ultimate disposal, net of any expenses that would need to be incurred; in other words, its value in use.

6.8 This can be portrayed diagrammatically as follows:

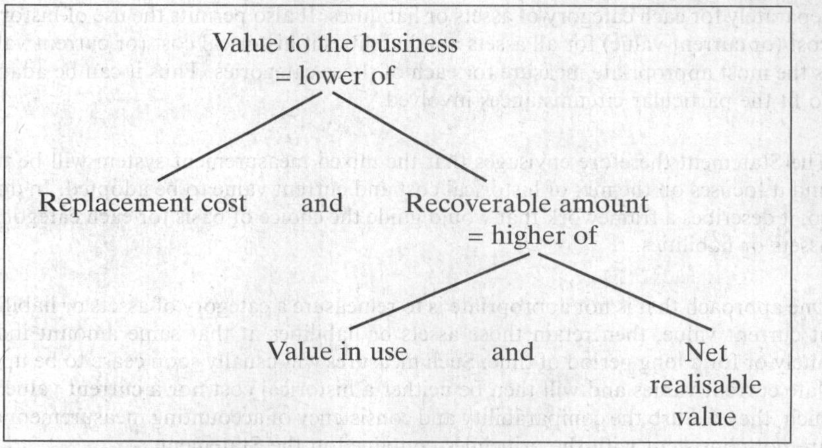

6.9 It is possible to select a current value for a liability in a similar manner (using the concept of 'relief value'). The relief value of a liability is the lowest amount at which the entity could divest itself of the obligation involved—in other words, the lowest amount at which the liability could, hypothetically, be settled.

The measurement process

6.10 It is not the function of financial statements to represent directly the total value that the reporting entity would fetch in an exchange transaction. Instead, the financial statements provide information designed to assist users to make judgements about the entity's financial performance and financial position and it is these judgements, in combination with other information, that enable, inter alia, a value for the entity to be assessed. The purpose of the measurement process is therefore to measure the effects of the transactions and events of the period on the financial performance and financial position of the entity.

Initial recognition

6.11 An asset or liability that is being measured using the historical cost basis will be recognised initially at transaction cost or, if an event other than a transaction is involved, at its fair value at the time it was acquired or assumed. The transaction cost of an asset acquired or liability assumed is the fair value of the consideration given or received in exchange for that asset or liability.

6.12 An asset or liability that is being measured using the current value basis will be recognised initially at its current value at the time it was acquired or assumed.

6.13 This means that, regardless of the measurement basis used, assets and liabilities that arise from transactions carried out at fair value—which is the vast majority of assets and liabilities—will be measured on initial recognition at their transaction cost. That is because, in the case of such a transaction, the fair value of the consideration paid or received (ie the transaction cost) is equal to the current value of the asset or liability at the time of acquisition.

It can generally be assumed that, in the absence of evidence to the contrary, a transaction has been carried out at fair value. In such circumstances, the transaction cost involved can be determined by reference to the fair value of either the asset (or liability) acquired or the consideration paid (or received); whichever fair value is easiest to measure will usually be used. For example (and assuming in both cases that there is no evidence suggesting that the transaction was not carried out at fair value): **6.14**

(a) if the reporting entity purchases mining rights in exchange for an immediate cash payment, those rights would usually be measured on initial recognition at the cash amount because that amount is easier to measure than the fair value of the rights.
(b) if the entity purchases an asset from an employee for an immediate cash payment, it may not be clear whether it also involves a payment for services provided by the employee. Where such uncertainty exists, it may be easier to measure the fair value of the asset purchased than the fair value of the services provided. If the former amount is, for example, less than the amount of the payment, the difference will be remuneration.

If an asset or liability arises from a transaction that was not carried out at fair value, it will often be more appropriate to measure the asset or liability at current value rather than historical cost. Choosing a measurement basis is considered in paragraphs 6.23-6.29. **6.15**

The initial recognition criteria described in Chapter 5 stipulate that, to be recognised, the asset or liability involved needs to be capable of being measured at a monetary amount with sufficient reliability. Whether a measure is sufficiently reliable for inclusion in primary financial statements depends on the quantity and quality of the evidence available to confirm that the measure has the attributes of reliability described in Chapter 3. A measure derived from a generally accepted valuation methodology and supported by a reasonable amount of confirmatory evidence will usually be a sufficiently reliable measure. **6.16**

Subsequent remeasurement

If a *pure* historical cost measurement basis is being used, the carrying amount of an asset or liability will always be the amount at which it was initially recognised; in other words, there is no subsequent remeasurement stage. The carrying amount of an asset or liability measured at historical cost may nevertheless need to be changed so that the item remains at cost. For example, as work is carried out on work-in-progress, so the carrying amount is changed to reflect the additional costs incurred. Similarly, in the case of assets that are consumed over more than one accounting period (such as fixed assets), the amount at which the asset was recognised initially will be reduced over the expected life of the asset so as to allocate the asset's cost over its expected life. Adjustments may also need to be made to the carrying amount of other assets and liabilities to reflect cost and income allocations. These adjustments are not remeasurements; they are adjustments to maintain the carrying amount at an amount based on historical cost. **6.17**

In practice, however, this 'pure historical cost basis' is rarely used. Instead, to make historical cost more relevant to the needs of users, a variation is used that involves a **6.18** limited amount of remeasurement. The purpose of this remeasurement is to ensure that:

(a) assets are not reported at amounts greater than their recoverable amount; and
(b) monetary assets and liabilities denominated in currencies other than the reporting currency are stated at an amount that is based on up-to-date exchange rates.

All references in the Statement to the historical cost basis are, unless stated otherwise, references to this version of the historical cost basis.

6.19 When the current value basis of measurement is being used, remeasurement takes place to ensure that the assets or liabilities involved are measured at an up-to-date current value. Such remeasurements will, however, be recognised in the financial statements only if:

(a) there is sufficient evidence that the amount of the asset or liability has changed. For example, if consideration is being given to writing down the carrying amount of an asset to its recoverable amount, there will need to be sufficient evidence that the asset's recoverable amount *is* lower than its carrying amount; and
(b) the new amount of the asset or liability is capable of being measured with sufficient reliability.

6.20 What constitutes sufficient evidence is a matter of judgement in the particular circumstances of each case although, whilst the evidence will need to be adequate, it need not (and often cannot) be conclusive. Relevant considerations as to whether the evidence is sufficient will include its persuasiveness and whether the change implies that a gain or a loss has occurred.*

6.21 Although the nature of the evidence will vary from item to item, its primary source will be past or present experience with the item itself or with similar items. This will include evidence provided by:

(a) current information directly relating to the item (eg the current physical condition of items of stock, their current selling price, and current levels of orders for them).
(b) other entities' transactions in similar assets and liabilities. If such transactions are frequent and the items traded are very similar to the item held by the reporting entity (ie there is an efficient market in homogeneous items), such evidence will often be sufficient. However, as the frequency of transactions decreases or differences between the items traded and the item held by the reporting entity increase, the evidence will become less persuasive and is less likely to be sufficient on its own.
(c) past experience with a group of similar items (eg the levels of losses arising in the past on stock of different ages).

6.22 The issues to be considered in deciding whether the new amount of the asset or liability is capable of being measured with sufficient reliability are identical to the reliability of measurement issues considered in the context of initial recognition (see paragraph 6.16).

**These factors, and the sources of evidence referred to in paragraph 6.21, are broadly similar to those that need to be taken into account when considering, in the initial recognition stage, whether there is sufficient evidence that an asset or liability itself has been changed (see paragraph 5.15).*

Choosing a measurement basis and deciding whether to change it

In choosing the measurement basis to be used for a particular category of assets or liabilities, the aim is to select the basis that is most appropriate bearing in mind: **6.23**

(a) the objective of financial statements and the qualitative characteristics of financial information, in particular relevance and reliability;
(b) the nature of the assets or liabilities concerned; and
(c) the particular circumstances involved.

Although these factors may not change, the measurement basis that best meets them may. For example, to the extent that markets develop, measurement bases that were once thought unreliable may become reliable. Similarly, to the extent that access to markets develops, so a measurement basis that was once thought insufficiently relevant may become the most relevant measure available. **6.24**

Although it is often difficult to make general statements about the appropriate measurement basis for any particular category of assets or liabilities, the observations set out in paragraphs 6.26-6.29 can be made. **6.25**

The need for financial information to be relevant means that, in selecting a measurement basis, the focus will be on providing information about financial performance and financial position that is useful in evaluating the reporting entity's cash-generation abilities and in assessing its financial adaptability. **6.26**

The carrying amounts of assets and liabilities need to be sufficiently reliable.* If only one of the measures available is reliable, it will be the one used provided that it is also relevant. On the other hand, if both the historical cost measure and the current value measure are reliable, the better measure to use will be the one that is the most relevant. **6.27**

Current value measures are sometimes characterised as less reliable than historical cost measures. Such a characterisation tends to assume, however, that all historical cost measures are transaction-based and involve little estimation, which is not the case. For example, adjustments made to the historical cost carrying value of debtors to make allowance for bad and doubtful debts involve a degree of estimation that is not dissimilar to that involved in estimating current values not derived from an active market—and the results are often of broadly similar reliability. There is a similar level of estimation involved in determining the cost of self-generated assets and by-products, and generally in all circumstances involving allocations of substantial amounts of indirect costs. The hurdle that a measure must clear to be deemed reliable is set at the same height for current value measures as for historical cost measures. **6.28**

Assessments of relevance and reliability need to take into account what the asset or liability represents. For example, if an entity 'stores' its spare cash by making an investment, that investment's relevance to the entity will be derived from the specific future cash flows that it represents rights to. The measure that will most faithfully represent those rights will generally be current value. Similarly, if an entity has a liability of uncertain amount, that liability's relevance to the entity will be derived from the most up-to-date information about those uncertainties. The measure that most faithfully represents those uncertainties will again generally be current value. **6.29**

**What the characteristic of reliability entails is considered in detail in Chapter 3 and is also dealt with in paragraphs 6.16 and 6.35-6.38.*

Measurement issues

Going concern

6.30 Financial statements are usually prepared—and measures are usually arrived at—on the basis that the reporting entity is a going concern because measures based on break-up values tend not to be relevant to users seeking to assess the entity's cash-generation ability and financial adaptability.

Discounting

6.31 Most transactions take place at fair value. Rational buyers and sellers will ensure that this fair value reflects the time value of money and the risk associated with the future expected cash flows, which means that market prices generally will reflect such factors.

6.32 This chapter has explained that assets will, depending on the circumstances, be carried in the financial statements at historical cost, replacement cost, net realisable value or value in use and that liabilities will, again depending on the circumstances, be carried at historical cost or the lowest amount at which the liability could be settled. Historical cost and replacement cost are both market prices and will therefore, for the reason set out in paragraph 6.31, take into account the time value of money and the risk associated with the future expected cash flows.

6.33 To be consistent, these factors need also to be reflected in the other measures that can be used to determine the carrying amount of assets (in other words, value in use and net realisable value) and the carrying amount of any liabilities measured by reference to expected future cash flows. It follows that, when basing carrying amounts on future cash flows, those cash flows will need to be discounted.

6.34 The discount rate used will reflect the risks associated with the future expected cash flows involved (unless those future expected cash flows are already risk-adjusted) and the time value of money. As such, it will reflect the risks specific to the item being measured but not the more general risks of the entity as a whole.*

Arriving at a measure in the face of uncertainty

6.35 It is quite common for there to be uncertainty about the appropriate monetary amount at which to measure an asset or liability. The existence of this uncertainty (measurement uncertainty) is acknowledged in the initial recognition and subsequent remeasurement criteria, both of which insist that the monetary amount at which an asset or liability is to be recognised is capable of being measured with sufficient reliability.

6.36 If uncertainty exists, the only way to determine an appropriate monetary amount for the asset or liability is through the use of estimates. As long as a generally accepted estimation method is used and the measure is supported by a reasonable amount of confirmatory evidence—prudence requires a greater reliability of measurement for assets (and gains) than for liabilities (and losses)—the use of estimates is acceptable and will not prevent the measure from being sufficiently reliable to be used in the financial statements.

**Discounting is discussed in greater detail in a Working Paper 'Discounting in Financial Reporting' published by the Board in April 1997.*

Estimating an appropriate carrying amount will often involve adopting one of the following approaches. 6.37

(a) If there is a reasonably efficient market for the item or for very similar items, a market-based measure such as a market price could be used as the carrying amount because the market consensus over the amount of the benefits inherent in the item is likely to mean that the measure will be reliable.
(b) If the entity has a group of homogeneous but not identical items, the expected value of the entire group could be used, provided the group is of a sufficient size and there is sufficient evidence of the various possible outcomes and their probabilities to permit an explicit calculation of expected value.*
(c) If neither of these approaches is practicable, a best estimate will need to be used. If there is a minimum amount that is reasonably assured, the item will be stated at no less than that minimum amount, and a higher amount will be used if that is a better estimate.

If the monetary amount at which an asset or liability is recognised is subject to significant uncertainty, the degree of uncertainty surrounding the estimate will usually be disclosed in order to avoid the impression that the outcome is certain. Such a disclosure might provide details of the significant assumptions and measurement basis used, the range of possible outcomes, and the principal factors that affect the outcome. 6.38

Capital maintenance adjustments and changing prices

Put simply, accounting profit is the return the reporting entity has earned on its capital. Therefore, in order to account properly for accounting profit, it is necessary to differentiate between return *on* capital and return *of* capital. This involves defining and measuring the capital of the entity. 6.39

Under the accounting model described by the Statement and adopted by almost all profit-making entities, the capital of the entity is defined as the monetary amount of ownership interest (the financial capital maintenance concept) and is measured in nominal amounts. 6.40

With this approach, the capital of the entity will be maintained if the amount of gains during a period is at least equal to the amount of losses in that period. This means that any surplus of gains over losses during a period represents a return *on* capital for that period. 6.41

Whilst this approach is satisfactory under conditions of stable prices, it is open to criticism when general or specific price changes are significant. 6.42

(a) General price changes can affect the significance of reported profits and of ownership interest. If this problem is acute, an approach will need to be adopted that involves recognising profit only after adjustments have been made to maintain the purchasing power of the entity's financial capital.

**Expected value is a weighted average of all possible outcomes, calculated using the probability of occurrence of an outcome as its weight. For a group of similar items, individual items will have different outcomes, and the number of items having a particular outcome will be related to the probability of that outcome. Hence, the expected value will represent a reasonable estimate of the monetary amount of the benefits associated with the entire group. For instance, in considering a large portfolio of non-interest bearing debts, it may be unlikely that any individual debt will prove to be bad, but some degree of non-payment is normally expected; hence a loss representing this expected reduction in economic benefits is recognised. If each debt were to be considered individually and measured at its most likely outcome, each debtor might be judged more likely than not to pay, and hence no bad debt provision would be made. However, this would not represent a reasonable measure of future economic benefits for the entire group.*

(b) Specific price changes can affect the significance of reported profits and financial position. If the problem is acute, it will be necessary to adopt a system of accounting that informs the user of the significance of specific price changes for the entity's financial performance and financial position.

Chapter 7: Presentation of financial information

Good presentation ensures that the essential messages of the financial statements are communicated clearly and effectively and in as simple and straightforward a manner as possible. This chapter explains what good presentation entails. It also considers the information that often accompanies financial statements and explains some of the roles fulfilled by such information.

PRINCIPLES

- Financial statements comprise primary financial statements and supporting notes that amplify and explain the primary financial statements. The primary financial statements themselves comprise the statement of financial performance,* the statement of financial position or balance sheet, and the cash flow statement.
- The presentation of information on financial performance focuses on the components of that performance and on the characteristics of those components.
- The presentation of information on financial position focuses on the types and functions of assets and liabilities held and on the relationships between them.
- The presentation of cash flow information will show the extent to which the entity's various activities generate and use cash, and will distinguish in particular between those cash flows that result from operations and those that result from other activities.
- Disclosure of information in the notes to the financial statements is not a substitute for recognition and does not correct or justify any misrepresentation or omission in the primary financial statements.

EXPLANATION

Presentation of information in financial statements

Clear, effective and simple communication

As financial statements are a means of communication, the objective of the presentation adopted is to communicate clearly and effectively and in as simple and straightforward a manner as is possible without loss of relevance or reliability and without unnecessarily increasing the length of the financial statements. **7.1**

Highly structured and aggregated

Even if it were practicable it would not be appropriate for financial statements to report every single aspect of every relevant transaction and event: the mass of detail would obscure the message. The presentation of information in financial statements therefore involves a high degree of interpretation, simplification, abstraction and aggregation—in other words, a loss of detailed information. Nevertheless, if this process is carried out in an orderly manner, greater knowledge will result because such a presentation will: **7.2**

(a) convey information that would otherwise have been obscured;
(b) highlight those items, and relationships between items, that are generally of most significance;

**Although many entities in the UK and the Republic of Ireland at present prepare two statements of financial performance, the number of statements prepared is a matter of convention and legal requirement; no significant financial reporting principle is involved. For simplicity, however, the Statement generally refers to 'the statement of financial performance'.*

(c) facilitate comparability between different entities' financial statements; and
(d) be more understandable to users.

7.3 The primary focus of financial statements is on the entity's cash generation and financial adaptability. This focus is met through a set of interrelated reports (known as the primary financial statements) on:

(a) financial performance (the profit and loss account and the statement of total recognised gains and losses are examples of financial performance statements);
(b) financial position (the balance sheet); and
(c) cash inflows and outflows (the cash flow statement),

and a series of supporting disclosures (the notes to the financial statements).

7.4 The notes and primary financial statements form an integrated whole, with the notes amplifying and explaining the statements by, for example, providing:

(a) more detailed information on items recognised in the primary financial statements. Good presentation strikes a balance between the detail provided on the face of the primary financial statements and that provided in the notes, thus avoiding cluttering up the former and obscuring their message.
(b) context for, or an alternative view of, items recognised in the primary financial statements. For instance, if a balance sheet includes a liability that is in dispute, the related note might disclose the range of possible outcomes. Similarly, the notes usually provide segmental information to supplement the primary financial statements, which focus on the reporting entity in aggregate.
(c) relevant information that it is not practicable to incorporate in the primary financial statements, for example because of pervasive uncertainty.

7.5 The notes to the financial statements therefore represent a very important part of the overall information package. Nevertheless, disclosure of information in the notes is not a substitute for recognition and does not correct or justify any misrepresentation in or omission from the primary financial statements.

Classification

7.6 In order to facilitate the analysis of the information provided, items that are similar are presented together in the financial statements and distinguished from dissimilar items.

7.7 The classifications used to achieve this also have regard to the additional insights that can be obtained by considering the relationships between different classes of items, for example the relative sizes of profits and capital employed or debtors and sales.

7.8 Classifications that are similar or related are presented in financial statements in a manner that highlights that similarity or relationship. For example, different kinds of current assets are shown adjacent to each other, and current liabilities are usually shown in a manner that highlights their relationship to current assets.

Good presentation

Statement of financial performance

7.9 The financial performance of a reporting entity is made up of components that exhibit differing characteristics in terms of, for example, nature, cause, function, relative continuity or recurrence, stability, risk, predictability and reliability. All these components are relevant to an assessment of financial performance and therefore need to be reported on in the statement of financial performance, although their individual characteristics mean that some will carry more weight in some assessments of financial performance than others.

Information on financial performance needs to be presented in a way that focuses attention on these components and on their key characteristics. Therefore, although it is not of fundamental importance whether one or more than one performance statement is provided, the presentation—including the headings used and the items that appear under each heading—is important. Good presentation of financial performance information typically involves: **7.10**

(a) recognising only gains and losses in the statement of financial performance.
(b) classifying components by reference to a combination of function (such as production, selling and administrative) and of the nature of the item (such as employment costs, interest payable and amounts written off investments).
(c) distinguishing amounts that are affected in different ways by changes in economic conditions or business activity (for example, by providing segmental information or by presenting income from continuing and discontinued operations as separate components).
(d) identifying separately:
    (i) items that are unusual in amount or incidence judged by the experience of previous periods or expectations of the future.
    (ii) items that have special characteristics, such as financing costs and taxation.
    (iii) items that are related primarily to the profits of future, rather than current, accounting periods, such as some research and development expenditure.

Gains and losses are generally not offset in presenting information on financial performance. For example, as explained in Chapter 4, if a transaction involves both a receipt and a cost (as is the case, for example, when an item of stock is sold), the transaction will usually be best presented by showing the gain (the receipt) separately from the loss (the cost). However, gains and losses will be offset if: **7.11**

(a) they relate to the same event or circumstance; and
(b) disclosing the gross components is not likely to be useful for an assessment of either future results or the effects of past transactions and events.

For example, if a profit is made on the disposal of a fixed asset, that profit is usually best presented by showing it as a gain rather than by showing the sales proceeds as a gain separately from the depreciated cost of the asset.

Balance sheet

In assessing the financial position of an entity, users are most interested in the types and amounts of assets and liabilities held and the relationship between them, and in the function of the various assets. Information on the reporting entity's financial position therefore needs to be presented in a way that focuses attention on these aspects. Good presentation typically involves: **7.12**

(a) recognising only assets, liabilities and ownership interest in the balance sheet;
(b) delineating the entity's resource structure (major classes and amounts of assets) and its financial structure (major classes and amounts of liabilities and ownership interest). The main basis for deciding the number of classes and the content of each is that the result will help users to assess the nature, amounts

and liquidity of available resources and the nature, amounts and timing of obligations that require or may require liquid resources for settlement.

(c) distinguishing assets by function. For example, assets held for sale will be reported separately from assets held on a continuing basis for use in the entity's activities.

7.13 In presenting information on the reporting entity's financial position, assets will not be offset against liabilities.*

Cash flow statement

7.14 Cash flow information will be of most use if it shows the extent to which the entity's activities generate and use cash, distinguishing in particular cash flows that are the result of operations from cash flows that result from other activities. This might include, for example, showing separately cash received from trading activities, cash used to repay debt, cash used to distribute dividends and cash reinvested.

Accompanying information

7.15 Financial statements are often accompanied and complemented by information that does not form part of the financial statements. Examples of such information include five-year trend information, operating and financial reviews, directors' reports and statements by the chairman. The Statement refers to such information as accompanying information.†

7.16 Although accompanying information generally has the same objective as financial statements, it usually comprises a different kind of information. For example, it often includes:

(a) narrative disclosures describing and explaining the entity's activities;
(b) historical summaries and trend information;
(c) non-accounting, and non-financial, information; and
(d) evolutionary or experimental disclosures that are not considered suitable for inclusion in the financial statements.

7.17 Some of the accompanying information therefore deals with matters that are not in the financial statements and some deals with matters that are in the financial statements, but from a different perspective. However, none of the accompanying information will be inconsistent with the information in the financial statements.

7.18 The more complex entities and their transactions become, the more users need an objective and comprehensive analysis and explanation of the main features underlying their financial performance and financial position. Such disclosures, which are typically included in the reporting entity's operating and financial review, are best presented in the context of a discussion of the entity's business as a whole and will be most useful if they discuss:

**The offsetting of rights and obligations to produce a single asset or liability is considered in paragraphs 4.33-4.36.*

†Such information is sometimes referred to as 'supplementary information'. However, the Statement avoids that term because it is also sometimes used to refer to certain information that is included within the financial statements.

(a) the main factors underlying the entity's financial performance, including the principal risks, uncertainties and trends involved in each of the main business areas and how the entity is responding to them;
(b) the dynamics of the entity's financial position, including the strategies being adopted on capital structure and treasury policy; and
(c) the activities and expenditure of the period that can be regarded as a form of investment in the future.

Highlights and summary indicators

Financial statements and accompanying information sometimes include amounts, ratios, and other computations that attempt to distil key information about the reporting entity's financial performance and financial position. Such highlights and summary indicators cannot, on their own, provide a basis for meaningful analysis or prudent decision-making. It is therefore essential that they are not presented in a way that exaggerates their importance. **7.19**

That having been said, well-presented highlights and summary indicators are useful to users who: **7.20**

(a) require only very basic information, such as the amount of sales or dividends; or
(b) will proceed to a detailed appraisal of all the financial information, since highlights and summary indicators may suggest particular aspects of the information that need to be analysed further.

As already mentioned, financial statements are a means of communication. Therefore, notwithstanding the limited usefulness of highlights and summary indicators, if such information is provided it needs to be presented in a manner and context that enable its meaning to be communicated to users. This will often entail explaining the reasons for changes in the relative or absolute size of the figures from one period to the next. **7.21**

Chapter 8: Accounting for interests in other entities

Financial statements need to reflect the effect on the reporting entity's financial performance and financial position of its interests in other entities. This involves various measurement and presentation issues. Rather than being dealt with in the relevant chapters and therefore in isolation from each other, they are dealt with together in this chapter. For similar reasons, various consolidation issues are dealt with in this chapter.

PRINCIPLES

- Single entity financial statements and consolidated financial statements present the interests the reporting entity may have in other entities from different perspectives.
- In single entity financial statements, interests in other entities are dealt with by focusing on the income and (depending on the measurement basis adopted) capital growth arising from those interests.
- In consolidated financial statements, the way in which interests in other entities are dealt with depends on the degree of influence involved.
  (a) An interest that involves control of another entity's operating and financial policies is dealt with by incorporating the controlled entity as part of the reporting entity.
  (b) An interest that involves joint control of, or significant influence over, another entity's operating and financial policies is dealt with by recognising the reporting entity's share of that other entity's results and resources in a way that does not involve showing those results and resources in the performance statement and balance sheet as if they were controlled by the reporting entity.
  (c) Other interests are dealt with in the same way as any other asset.
- Although consolidated financial statements are the financial statements of the group as a whole, they are prepared from the perspective of the parent's shareholders and, as a result, ultimately focus on the parent's ownership interest in its subsidiaries. The effect on benefit flows of any outside equity interest in the subsidiaries will therefore be separately identified.
- Consolidated financial statements reflect the whole of the parent's investment in its subsidiaries, including purchased goodwill.
- A transaction involving the amalgamation of two or more reporting entities is reflected in the consolidated financial statements in accordance with its character. Therefore, a transaction that is of the character of:
  (a) an acquisition is reflected in the consolidated financial statements as if the acquirer purchased the acquiree's assets and liabilities as a bundle of assets and liabilities on the open market.
  (b) a merger is reflected in the consolidated financial statements as if the new reporting entity, comprising all the parties to the transaction, had always existed.

EXPLANATION

Degree of influence

8.1 Although an entity's interest in a second entity may take many different forms, the key factor in determining its effect on the first entity's financial performance and financial position is the degree of influence it exerts over the operating and financial policies of the second entity involved.

The degree of influence exerted will depend on the facts of each particular case. Ownership of shares is usually the main basis of influence because owning voting rights confers influence. However, while the level of ownership of shares and voting rights is indicative of an entity's relationship with its investee,* it is not by itself sufficient to define the relationship because of the possible effect of other agreements, arrangements or working practices. Indeed, any mixture of share ownership, voting rights or agreements, formal or informal, can provide a means of influencing or controlling another entity. **8.2**

The highest degree of influence that an entity can have over an investee is control. As Chapter 2 explains, control comprises the ability to deploy the economic resources involved and to benefit (or to suffer) by their deployment. Other degrees of influence have these same aspects; in effect, the ability to influence the activities of the investee with a view to gaining economic benefits from that influence. **8.3**

Although it is possible to classify the degree of influence that an entity has over its investee in an almost infinite number of ways, it is sufficient for the purposes of the Statement to classify it as follows: **8.4**

(a) *Control*—where the entity controls the investee.
(b) *Joint control*—where the entity does not itself control the investee, but shares control through some form of arrangement jointly with others.
(c) *Significant influence*—where the entity has neither control nor joint control, but exerts a degree of influence over the investee's operating and financial policies that is at the least a significant influence and at the most just short of control.
(d) *Lesser or no influence*—where any influence that the entity has over the investee's operating and financial policies is less than a significant influence.

Reflecting the effects of interests in other entities

Consolidated financial statements and single entity financial statements

The effect on the entity's financial performance and financial position of an interest in an investee is reflected in the first entity's financial statements in different ways depending on the type of financial statements being prepared. **8.5**

(a) Financial statements of a reporting entity whose boundary has been drawn by reference to the scope of its direct control—in other words, single entity financial statements—take a narrow view of the reporting entity's interests in other entities and, as a result, reflect only the income and (depending on the measurement basis adopted) capital growth arising from those interests.
(b) Financial statements of a reporting entity whose boundary has been drawn by reference to the scope of the entity's control (both direct and indirect)—in other words, consolidated financial statements—present an expanded view of the reporting entity's interests in other entities that reflects the reporting entity's influence over, and its accountability for, the activities and resources of its investees.

Because of the narrow view taken in single entity financial statements, interests in other entities are treated like any other asset in those financial statements. On the other hand, the treatment of such interests in the consolidated financial statements will depend on the degree of influence involved, as explained more fully in paragraphs 8.7-8.10. **8.6**

**Although it is not necessary for an interest in another entity to involve an investment, that is the most common form. For simplicity, therefore, this chapter uses the term 'investee' to mean 'entity in which the first entity has an interest'.*

Interests involving control

8.7 As already explained in Chapter 2, if an entity controls* one or more other entities, the controlling entity (the parent) and the controlled entities (the subsidiaries) will be a reporting entity (the group). The group's financial statements (consolidated financial statements) are prepared by aggregating the gains, losses, assets, liabilities and cash flows of the parent and its subsidiaries. This ensures that the effects on the parent's financial performance and financial position of its interests in its subsidiaries are fully reflected in the financial statements.

8.8 Paragraphs 8.11-8.13 consider various issues relating to the preparation of consolidated financial statements.

Interests involving joint control or significant influence

8.9 If the reporting entity shares joint control of, or exercises significant influence over, another entity, it will be directly involved in and affected by that other entity's activities. Its interest in its investee is therefore reflected in the consolidated financial statements in a way that:

(a) recognises the reporting entity's share of the results and net assets of the investee; and

(b) does not misrepresent the extent of its influence over the investee—in other words, it does not treat activities and resources that are not controlled by the reporting entity as if they are controlled by the reporting entity. At present, the only commonly recognised method of accounting for investments that achieves this end is the equity method of accounting. This is where the reporting entity's share of the results and net assets of the investee are brought into its financial statements on a single line in the performance statement and balance sheet respectively. There are different types of equity method, usually involving the presentation of a greater or lesser degree of information than that just described, but in each case the reporting entity's share of the net results and of the position of the investee are not combined in the primary financial statements on a line-by-line basis with the reporting entity's own activities and resources.

Interests involving lesser or no influence

8.10 If the reporting entity's influence over its investee does not involve control, joint control or significant influence, the reporting entity will not be accountable for the investee's activities. In such circumstances, the only amounts recognised in the consolidated financial statements will be the investment (if any) and any income derived therefrom.

Consolidated financial statements

8.11 The gains, losses, assets, liabilities and cash flows of all subsidiaries are reflected in full in the consolidated financial statements, even if a subsidiary is not wholly-owned. This reflects the parent's ability, through its control, to deploy both its own economic resources and those of its subsidiaries even where it does not wholly own the subsidiaries.

**For simplicity, the discussion in the chapter assumes that the ultimate parent has 'direct' control of all its subsidiaries. However, it applies equally to situations in which the parent controls its subsidiary through its control of that subsidiary's parent. It also applies when the parent's control of its subsidiary is achieved through the combined influence of itself and other entities that it controls.*

However, the extent of outside ownership interests is an important factor in considering the parent's access and exposure to the results of its subsidiaries. Therefore, although consolidated financial statements are the financial statements of the group as a whole, they ultimately focus on the parent's ownership interest in the entities within its control. The effect of any outside equity interest (the minority interest) on benefit flows will therefore be separately identified in the financial statements. **8.12**

Purchased goodwill (sometimes referred to as goodwill arising on acquisition) is the part of a parent's investment in its subsidiary that has not been attributed to the separately identified assets and liabilities of the subsidiary. Although it is not an asset in itself, it is part of a larger asset (the investment). Furthermore, it does not represent a decrease in that larger asset's value and therefore a loss: it represents *part* of the asset's value. Therefore, if the parent's investment is to be fully reflected in the group's financial statements and the parent is to be held accountable for its investment in full, purchased goodwill needs to be recognised as if it were an asset. **8.13**

Accounting for business combinations

An amalgamation of two or more reporting entities—sometimes referred to as a business combination—can take a number of different forms. All these forms can be characterised as either: **8.14**

(a) a purchase—such transactions are commonly referred to as acquisitions; or
(b) a uniting of interests—such transactions are commonly referred to as mergers.

An acquisition is a business combination that is in the nature of an acquisition by one entity of another entity. The transaction therefore results in an existing reporting entity being enlarged and is reflected in the consolidated financial statements by treating the assets and liabilities of the entity acquired and the purchased goodwill as if the transaction was the purchase of a bundle of assets and liabilities on the open market. **8.15**

On the other hand, a merger is in the nature of a coming together of two entities to form a new reporting entity. This is reflected in the financial statements of the new reporting entity comprising all the parties to the transaction as if that entity had always existed. As a result, the assets and liabilities of each party to the transaction are treated as if they were acquired by the new reporting entity at the time that they were acquired by the party concerned: none of the assets or liabilities is treated as being purchased at the time of the business combination as part of a bundle of assets and liabilities on the open market. **8.16**

Contents of Appendices

Paragraphs

APPENDIX I — THE STATEMENT AND THE LEGAL REQUIREMENTS CONCERNING THE FORM AND CONTENT OF FINANCIAL STATEMENTS

Introduction 1
Why the statement was not developed within legal constraints 2–3
Main inconsistencies between the statement and the law 4–13
The reporting entity 4–5
The elements of financial statements 6
Recognition 7–8
Measurement 9–10
Presentation 11–13

The statement as a satisfactory frame of reference for standard-setters 14–15

Northern Ireland and the Republic of Ireland 16

APPENDIX II — THE STATEMENT AND IASC'S 'FRAMEWORK FOR THE PREPARATION AND PRESENTATION OF FINANCIAL STATEMENTS'

Introduction 5

Chapter 1: The objective of financial statements 6–7
Chapter 2: The reporting entity 8
Chapter 3: The qualitative characteristics of financial information 9
Chapter 4: The elements of financial statements 10
Chapter 5: Recognition in financial statements 11–12
Chapter 6: Measurement in financial statements 13
Chapter 7: Presentation of financial information 14
Chapter 8: Accounting for interests in other entities 15

APPENDIX III — BACKGROUND TO ISSUES DEALT WITH IN THE STATEMENT

Background to the statement of principles 1–6

Introduction 7–9
General purpose financial statements 7
Smaller entities and not-for-profit entities 8–9

Chapter 1: The objective of financial statements 10–13
A wide range of users 10–11
Investors as the defining class of user 12
Economic decisions and stewardship 13

Chapter 2: The reporting entity 14–19
Identifying a reporting entity 14
The boundary of the reporting entity 15–16
Single entity financial statements of parent companies 17–19

Chapter 3: The qualitative characteristics of financial information 20–26
Materiality and relevance 20

Prudence 21–23
Understandability 24–25
Relevance versus reliability 26

Chapter 4: The elements of financial statements 27–39
Identifying the elements 27
Should the definitions of the elements be interrelated and, if so, which definitions should be based on which? 28–29
How many elements should there be and how should they be defined? 30–34
Implications of the approach adopted to specifying and defining the elements 35–39

Chapter 5: Recognition in financial statements 40–50
The role of realisation in the Statement 40–50

Chapter 6: Measurement in financial statements 51–59
The mixed measurement system 51–55
Choosing a measurement basis 56–59

Chapter 7: Presentation of financial information 60–62
Presentation of gains and losses 60
Dividends paid and payable 61
Recycling 62

Chapter 8: Accounting for interests in other entities 63–64
Accounting for minority interests 63–64

Appendix I
The Statement and the legal requirements concerning the form and content of financial statements

INTRODUCTION

1 The Statement was not developed within the constraints imposed by the law. As a result, there was a risk that inconsistencies could arise between the Statement and the law that would invalidate the Statement as a frame of reference for standard-setting. The purpose of this appendix is to:

(a) explain why the approach was nevertheless adopted;
(b) describe the main respects in which legislation is inconsistent with the Statement; and
(c) explain why these inconsistencies do not prevent the Statement from being an acceptable framework to be used by standard-setters.

WHY THE STATEMENT WAS NOT DEVELOPED WITHIN LEGAL CONSTRAINTS

2 There are two main reasons why the Statement was developed without taking into account the legal frameworks that regulate financial reporting. First, on a practical level, the Statement is intended to be relevant to the financial statements of *all* profit-oriented organisations, and it would have been difficult to develop a set of principles that was both consistent in all respects with all the legal requirements relating to such financial statements and also sufficiently detailed for the Board's purposes. Secondly, there was a concern that, if the Statement of Principles was developed within the constraints imposed by the law, it would be denied the opportunity to assist in the development of that law. This would have been a pity because it is framework documents such as the Statement that provide direction to the development of such legal frameworks and help to ensure that such development takes place in a coherent way.

3 It is nevertheless recognised that the approach would not have been appropriate, despite these reasons, if there had been many significant differences between the Statement and the various legal frameworks involved. Paragraphs 4-13 describe briefly the main inconsistencies that exist at present between the principles in the Statement and the legal requirements that apply in Great Britain to the form and content of individual and group accounts prepared by companies that are not banks or insurance companies. Paragraph 14 concludes that these inconsistencies do not invalidate the Statement as a frame of reference to be used in the development of accounting standards for such entities. Although the paragraphs below deal with one type of entity only, the inconsistencies identified are believed to be typical of those that exist in the case of other entities. As a result, it is believed that the conclusion reached in paragraph 14 can be applied to all entities.

MAIN INCONSISTENCIES BETWEEN THE STATEMENT AND THE LAW

The reporting entity

4 Section 258 of the Companies Act 1985 identifies subsidiary undertakings by a list of tests. Although these tests are founded mainly on the concept of control, they may in

some cases either fail to identify as a subsidiary undertaking an entity that is controlled by another or they may identify as a subsidiary undertaking an entity that is not controlled. Hence those companies that are identified as subsidiary undertakings by applying the Companies Act tests may not always correspond to those the Statement would identify as subsidiaries.*

In practice, this difference tends not to be a problem because of other factors. For example, the Act's requirements concerning the treatment of subsidiaries that involve severe long-term restrictions on the rights of the parent reduce the practical effect of this difference in approach, as do the treatments of quasi-subsidiaries and jointly controlled entities required by FRS 5 'Reporting the Substance of Transactions' and FRS 9 'Associates and Joint Ventures'. **5**

The elements of financial statements

One implication of the Act is that proposed dividends are required to be recognised as liabilities, although they would not usually fall within the Statement's definition of a liability.† **6**

Recognition

The Act states that only profits realised at the balance sheet date can be included in the profit and loss account (Schedule 4, paragraph 12).‡ The Act defines realised profits, but does so in a way that allows the precise meaning of the term to be capable of development. The Statement adopts a different approach in which, rather than restrict the recognition of gains in the statement or statements of financial performance to those that are realised, it restricts their recognition to those that can be measured with sufficient reliability and for which sufficient evidence exists that they have actually arisen. **7**

Although the Statement and the Act clearly adopt different approaches, the way in which the Act defines a realised profit means that the exact effect of this difference is not clear. The potential inconsistency described in paragraph 12—concerning the number and format of the statement or statements of financial performance—makes the effect of the difference in approach even less clear. **8**

Measurement

The Statement envisages that, if the current value basis of measurement is regarded as the most appropriate measurement basis for a particular category of assets, all assets within that category will be recognised at their current value. That current value will, furthermore, be determined by reference to the value to the business rule. However, although the Act (Schedule 4, paragraph 31)§ permits: **9**

***Editor's note:** *While there were changes to the details of this section of CA 1985 after the Statement of Principles was published, and this has now been replaced by the Companies Act 2006, the point made in this paragraph remains broadly valid.*

†**Editor's note:** *This is no longer the case, as the Companies Act 1985 was amended with effect for accounting periods beginning on or after 1 January 2005. Therefore proposed dividends no longer fall to be treated as a liability under either the Companies Act 1985 or Companies Act 2006.*

‡**Editor's note:** *Now para. 13 (b) of Schedule 1 to the Large and Medium-sized Companies and Groups (Accounts and Reports) Regulations 2008 (SI 2008/410).*

§**Editor's note:** *Now para. 30 of Schedule 1 to the Large and Medium-sized Companies and Groups (Accounts and Reports) Regulations 2008 (SI 2008/410).*

(a) intangible fixed assets other than goodwill to be included at current cost;
(b) tangible fixed assets to be included at market value or current cost;
(c) fixed asset investments to be included at market value or directors' valuation; and
(d) current asset investments and stocks to be included at current cost,

current assets other than investments and stocks are required to be included in the balance sheet at the lower of cost and net realisable value (Schedule 4, paragraphs 22 and 23).* Thus, for some assets the Act requires the use of measurement bases that may differ from those suggested by the Statement. It also means that the Act does not permit the use of the range of current value measures that are envisaged by the Statement's value to the business rule.†‡

10 The Statement also envisages that some categories of liabilities could be measured at current value, whereas the Act does not specifically refer to this possibility.

Presentation

11 The balance sheet and profit and loss account of a company must be prepared in accordance with one of the statutory formats (although these formats may, subject to certain constraints, be adapted to suit the particular circumstances). Some specific items are also required to be shown in every profit and loss account (Schedule 4, paragraphs 1-3).§ These requirements may necessitate a presentation that differs in certain respects from what would be suggested by following the presentation principles set out in the Statement. These inconsistencies can, however, generally be overcome by providing additional disclosures.

12 The Act requires in most cases the preparation of, inter alia, a profit and loss account in one of the statutory formats and it makes no reference to any other performance statement. The Statement, on the other hand, is less specific about the format of any profit and loss account provided, and it acknowledges that entities may prepare more than one performance statement or may alternatively prepare a single statement that is more comprehensive than the profit and loss account the Act requires. As such, although the preparation of a profit and loss account in one of the statutory formats would meet the requirements of the Act *and* (subject to the point made in the preceding paragraph) be consistent with the Statement, other presentations possible under the Statement may not comply with the Act's requirements.

13 The Act requires the profit and loss account to show separately the aggregate amount of any dividends paid and proposed (Schedule 4, paragraph 3(7)).¶ The

***Editor's note:** Now paras. 23 and 24 of Schedule 1 to the Large and Medium-sized Companies and Groups (Accounts and Reports) Regulations 2008 (SI 2008/410).*

†Legislative proposals are being prepared by the European Commission to permit a wider use of current values in the measurement of financial instruments. This demonstrates both that the constraints of law are not immutable and that desirable change can be motivated by accounting developments guided by the framework described in the Statement.

*‡**Editor's note**: Changes to company law since the Statement of Principles was published now allow the use of fair values in more circumstances than are assumed in the Statement.*

*§**Editor's note:** Now paras,. 1 to 3 of Schedule 1 to the Large and Medium-sized Companies and Groups (Accounts and Reports) Regulations 2008 (SI 2008/410).*

*¶**Editor's note:** This has now changed, and dividends proposed are no longer shown in a profit and loss account. This is as a result of FRS 21 coming into force, with equivalent changes to the FRSSE, as well as the revision of Companies Act 1985 and its replacement by the Companies Act 2006.*

Statement envisages that, as dividends are a distribution to owners and not a gain or loss, they will *not* be reported in a performance statement but will instead be reported in the reconciliation of movements in shareholders' funds.

THE STATEMENT AS A SATISFACTORY FRAME OF REFERENCE FOR STANDARD-SETTERS

Of the inconsistencies identified above, probably the most significant is the one **14**
relating to the recognition of gains: the Act requires that only profits realised at the balance sheet date are to be recognised in the profit and loss account, whilst the Statement adopts an approach that is not based on the notion of realisation. Although, as already mentioned, the precise effect of this difference in approach is not clear, the Board does not believe that this difference in approach invalidates the statement as a satisfactory frame of reference for standard-setting. It notes, for example, that realised profits are defined in the Act in a way that is intended to enable its meaning to develop. It also notes that EU legislative proposals are being prepared which, if implemented, would permit the recognition in the profit and loss account of certain gains that might not be regarded by some as realised profits. This suggests that the legal requirements in this area are capable of evolving in response to the reasonable demands of accounting practice. In such circumstances, it seems appropriate that the Statement of Principles should try to give direction to, rather than merely follow, such changes.

As the Statement is expected to provide direction to the development of the legal **15**
requirements concerning the form and content of financial statements, the Board's expectation is that inconsistencies between the Statement and legal requirements will tend to be temporary and that the law will not be a permanent impediment to the adoption of approaches consistent with the Statement.

NORTHERN IRELAND AND THE REPUBLIC OF IRELAND

The following table gives the references to legislation in Northern Ireland and in the **16**
Republic of Ireland corresponding to the legislation in Great Britain referred to in this appendix.

Paragraph	***Great Britain***	***Northern Ireland***	***Republic of Ireland****
	Companies Act 1985	Companies (Northern Ireland) Order 1986	
4	Section 258	Article 266	GAR 1992, Regulation 4
7	Schedule 4, paragraph 12	Schedule 4, paragraph 12	CAA 1986, section 5
9	Schedule 4, paragraphs 22 and 23	Schedule 4, paragraphs 22 and 23	CAA 1986, Schedule, paragraphs 10 and 11
9	Schedule 4, paragraph 31	Schedule 4, paragraph 31	CAA 1986, Schedule, paragraph 19
11	Schedule 4, paragraphs 1-3	Schedule 4, paragraphs 1-3	CAA 1986, section 4
13	Schedule 4, paragraph 3(7)	Schedule 4, paragraph 3(7)	CAA 1986, section 4(15)

* CAA 1986 = Companies (Amendment) Act 1986
GAR 1992 = European Communities (Companies: Group Accounts) Regulations 1992

Appendix II
The Statement and IASC's 'Framework for the preparation and presentation of financial statements'

1 It is the Board's view that a common set of principles is necessary to achieve further harmonisation in international accounting practice. For that reason, the Statement of Principles is based on the International Accounting Standards Committee's 'Framework for the Preparation and Presentation of Financial Statements' (the IASC Framework), which was itself derived from the Statements of Financial Accounting Concepts issued in the USA by the Financial Accounting Standards Board.*

2 This appendix compares the Statement with the IASC Framework and highlights and explains the main differences. The appendix does not deal in detail with any other conceptual documents, although the principles and explanations in the Statement are similar to those set out in the conceptual statements issued by other leading accounting standard-setters, including those in Australia, Canada, New Zealand and the USA.

3 The Statement is much more detailed than the IASC Framework, which means that it deals with many issues on which the IASC Framework is silent. These differences in detail have not been treated as differences for the purposes of this appendix.

4 The commentary below follows the structure and order of the Statement and it uses the headings of that document.

INTRODUCTION

5 There are no significant differences between the two documents.

CHAPTER 1: THE OBJECTIVE OF FINANCIAL STATEMENTS

6 The objective of financial statements set out in the Statement is almost identical to that set out in the IASC Framework, although there are two minor differences.

(a) The Statement's description of the objective refers specifically to information that is useful for 'assessing the stewardship of management', while the IASC Framework's description does not. However, as both documents refer to providing information that is useful for making economic decisions and agree that the reason why the stewardship of management is assessed is to take economic decisions, this difference is of no practical effect.

(b) Although the objective in the IASC Framework refers to providing information about changes in financial position while the Statement's objective does not, it is clear from both documents that it is expected that such information will be provided.

7 Only the Statement refers to the notion of a defining class of user (the investor). This notion is used in the Statement to give a focus that would otherwise be lacking for the selection and presentation of financial information.

****Editor's note**: The IASC framework was adopted by the International Accounting Standards Board (IASB) in April 2001. The IASB is currently working on a revised conceptual framework.*

CHAPTER 2: THE REPORTING ENTITY

This chapter deals with two separate reporting entity issues: identifying a reporting entity and determining the boundary of a reporting entity. The two documents adopt a similar approach to the first issue, although neither deals with it in any detail. Only the Statement deals with the second issue. It was thought that the Statement would not be complete if it did not explain which activities and resources should be reported on in financial statements. **8**

CHAPTER 3: THE QUALITATIVE CHARACTERISTICS OF FINANCIAL INFORMATION

In most respects the two documents adopt the same approach to the desirable characteristics of financial information. For example, they both identify relevance, reliability, understandability and comparability as qualitative characteristics, and they describe those characteristics in very similar terms. There are however some differences: **9**

(a) Materiality is not treated in the same way in that, while the IASC Framework treats it as a subcategory of relevance and describes it as a *quantitative* characteristic, the Statement treats it as a separate characteristic and describes it as relating to both the nature and size of the item. However, the overall effect of the two documents will be the same because they agree that information should be included in the financial statements if it might reasonably be expected to influence the economic decisions of users and it can be excluded if it is not expected to have that effect.

(b) The IASC Framework describes the accruals basis and the going concern assumption as underlying assumptions. Although the Statement does not give them such a title, their role and the way in which they are described are, to all intents and purposes, the same.

These differences are minor and will have little effect in practice.

CHAPTER 4: THE ELEMENTS OF FINANCIAL STATEMENTS

The two documents adopt the same approach to this subject, although: **10**

(a) the elements that the Statement refers to as ownership interest, gains and losses are referred to by the IASC Framework as equity, income and expenses;

(b) the Statement defines as elements contributions by owners and distributions to owners while, in the IASC Framework, these are merely movements within owners' equity.

These differences are essentially concerned with nomenclature rather than principle.

CHAPTER 5: RECOGNITION IN FINANCIAL STATEMENTS

Both the IASC Framework and the Statement approach the initial recognition process by asking whether a new asset or liability has been created (or an existing one has been added to), then applying recognition criteria to that new (or increased) asset or liability to determine whether it should be recognised. Both documents also adopt similar recognition criteria, although they are described in slightly different terms in that, while the Statement's criteria require, inter alia, that sufficient evidence should exist that the new asset or liability has been created or that there has been an addition to an existing asset or liability, the IASC Framework refers to it needing to be probable that any future economic benefit associated with the item will flow to or **11** from the enterprise. The Board believes that this difference reflects a development in accounting thought since the publication of the IASC Framework.

12 The Statement deals with derecognition, a topic not covered in the IASC Framework. The Board believes that this reflects the fact that, as transactions and the instruments transacted have become more complex since the IASC Framework was published, greater emphasis than hitherto needs to be placed on the principles that underlie the derecognition process.

CHAPTER 6: MEASUREMENT IN FINANCIAL STATEMENTS

13 The Statement and the IASC Framework adopt different approaches to the subject of measurement. For example, while the IASC Framework briefly describes the measurement bases that might be used, the Statement goes on to develop a framework to guide the choice of measurement basis. It also discusses the measurement bases much more extensively than the IASC Framework and it uses the value to the business model to decide between alternative measures of current value. This material has been included in the Statement in order to help introduce a degree of consistency into the measurement process. For similar reasons, the Statement, unlike the IASC Framework, discusses subsequent remeasurement in detail.

CHAPTER 7: PRESENTATION OF FINANCIAL INFORMATION

14 The IASC Framework contains very little on this subject. The Statement nevertheless deals with it because the Board believes that good presentation is an essential element in effective financial reporting.

CHAPTER 8: ACCOUNTING FOR INTERESTS IN OTHER ENTITIES

15 Although the IASC Framework contains no material on this subject, the Statement deals with it because the Board believes it is an important issue.

Appendix III
Background to issues dealt with in the Statement

BACKGROUND TO THE STATEMENT OF PRINCIPLES

When the Board was formed in 1990, it recognised that, if it was to develop accounting standards that were consistent with each other, it needed to develop a coherent frame of reference to guide it in its work. Indeed, one of the recommendations of the committee that recommended that the Accounting Standards Board should be established was that further work on a conceptual framework should be undertaken.* 1

The frame of reference that the Board subsequently developed became the basis for a series of discussion drafts of individual chapters that were published in the early 1990s. Those drafts were revised and reissued together, in 1995, as an exposure draft of the complete Statement of Principles for Financial Reporting. A second exposure draft was published in March 1999. 2

The Board started to develop its frame of reference by looking to the accounting principles that, at that time, underpinned accounting practice in the UK. However, those principles were found wanting because: 3

(a) they were developed piecemeal at different times in response to particular problems and were not consistent with one another.
(b) some of them had not kept up with modern developments. For example, many had their origins in accounting solutions devised for manufacturing companies with an emphasis on accounting for stocks and fixed assets. Some of those principles are not as effective in coping with the more complex financial reporting issues of today, such as those arising from intangibles and complex contractual arrangements.
(c) some of them were out of line with developments internationally.

The Board therefore concluded that, although many of those principles continued to be relevant and appropriate, some would have to be modified and some additional principles were needed to produce a framework that was consistent, up-to-date and reasonably complete.

The main principles in this Statement are derived from that informal frame of reference. Many of them have been examined closely over the last nine years during the development of new accounting standards (and the revision of existing ones) and have benefited from that examination, with some of the principles being refined and some developed further as a result. Furthermore, a number of the principles now play significant roles in accounting standards and have found general acceptance. For example: 4

(a) FRS 2 'Accounting for Subsidiary Undertakings' uses the reporting entity concept described in Chapter 2 of the Statement;
(b) FRS 4 'Capital Instruments', FRS 5 'Reporting the Substance of Transactions', FRS 7 'Fair Values in Acquisition Accounting' and FRS 12 'Provisions, Contingent Liabilities and Contingent Assets' are based on the definitions of assets and liabilities set out in Chapter 4; and

**See 'The Making of Accounting Standards': Report of the Review Committee under the Chairmanship of Sir Ron Dearing CB (1988).*

(c) FRS 11 'Impairment of Fixed Assets and Goodwill' uses the recoverable amount notion described in Chapter 6.

Therefore, although in places the Statement may sound unfamiliar, it actually bears a close resemblance to much of existing practice.

5 The Board has in its work programme a number of projects that are exploring further some of the issues covered in the Statement. Although it is possible that this work may result in changes needing to be made to what is said in the Statement, that does not create a difficulty because the Board does not regard the Statement as its final word on the principles that underlie financial reporting. Accounting thought is continually evolving and it is only to be expected that the Statement will need to be revised from time to time.*

6 The remainder of this appendix discusses, and sets out the rationale behind, aspects of the Statement that would benefit from a fuller explanation. The discussion is organised by reference to the sections in the Statement (ie Introduction, Chapter 1 etc) to which they relate.

INTRODUCTION

General purpose financial statements

7 The Statement classifies financial information into special purpose financial reports, general purpose financial reports and other financial information, and explains that annual financial statements prepared to comply with companies legislation are examples of a general purpose financial report. Describing annual financial statements in this way is not intended to imply that such statements are all-purpose financial statements, because they are not. The term 'general purpose financial reports' has been used because it highlights the difference between special purpose financial reports and other financial reports.

Smaller entities and not-for-profit entities

8 Although the principles set out in the Statement are intended to be relevant to the financial statements of all profit-oriented entities, it has been prepared with large entities uppermost in mind: accounting issues are generally at their most complex where large entities are involved and it is only right that the Board should seek to prepare a Statement that will help it to address these issues. That does not mean, however, that the Statement would have been fundamentally different had it been prepared with smaller entities in mind. The principles in Chapters 2-8, for example, would have remained unchanged. As the financial statements of small entities probably have a narrower range of users and tend to be used for a narrower range of purposes, the objective of those financial statements might have needed to be expressed differently. This difference would, however, be one of application rather than principle.

9 The Statement explains that, although it is relevant to the financial statements of not-for-profit entities, some of the principles need to be re-expressed and others need

****Editor's note****: *The most obvious subsequent product of the Statement is FRS 18 'Accounting Policies' which is based on a number of the principles covered in the Statement.*

changes of emphasis before they can be applied to that sector. The Board has requested its Public Sector and Not-for-profit Committee to study the issue and make recommendations in due course.*

CHAPTER 1: THE OBJECTIVE OF FINANCIAL STATEMENTS

A wide range of users

Although it is sometimes suggested that the legal position is that a company's annual financial statements are prepared for its shareholders only, neither companies legislation nor, so far as the Board is aware, case law suggests that the courts should or would take such a view. Indeed, since companies legislation requires companies to put a copy of their annual financial statements on the public record, it is clear that the law envisages that those financial statements will be used by the public at large—a much wider range of people than existing shareholders. This position is reflected in the Statement. **10**

It is not reasonable to expect financial statements to meet the information needs of everyone who chooses to use them. They focus on the common interest that users have in the financial performance and financial position of the reporting entity as a whole. That means that they do not address the special interests that many users will have and they do not satisfy all users equally well. Users will therefore usually need to supplement the information they obtain from financial statements with information from other sources. **11**

Investors as the defining class of user

The Statement explains that investors are to be treated as the defining class of user. Investors are interested in financial information on the reporting entity as a whole. Other users require exactly the same information as a frame of reference against which to judge the more specialised information they obtain from other sources. For example, although potential lenders will gather specialised information from a range of sources to help them decide whether, and at what price, to lend to the reporting entity, they will also use information derived from the financial statements of the entity as a whole. **12**

Economic decisions and stewardship

The Statement explains that the financial statements provide information that is useful in assessing stewardship and for making economic decisions. At first sight these objectives—assessing stewardship and making economic decisions—seem mutually exclusive because stewardship reports are often thought to be limited to the use of historical cost whereas decision-useful reports are thought to require the comprehensive use of current values. The Board does not, however, believe that they are mutually exclusive. **13**

(a) Stewardship reports are limited to using historical cost only if a very narrow view is taken of what a stewardship report entails. However, the Statement takes a broad view in that it regards stewardship as being not merely about the safekeeping and proper use of an entity's resources but also about their efficient and profitable use.

****Editor's note**: This issue has now led the ASB to issue an interpretation of the Statement of Principles for Public Benefit Entities.*

(b) The need for financial statements to provide information that is relevant for making economic decisions seems to suggest that more assets and liabilities than hitherto should be measured at current value. However, it does not necessarily follow that there needs to be comprehensive use of current values: experience shows that much historical cost information can also have predictive value.

CHAPTER 2: THE REPORTING ENTITY

Identifying a reporting entity

14 Although those who are entrusted with resources by others are accountable to them for those resources and should therefore probably provide them with a set of accounts, when the Statement considers which entities should prepare financial statements it is considering a much wider issue: which entities should prepare financial statements and make them available to a wide range of users? This is a complex issue and, as it has been the practice in the UK and the Republic of Ireland for legislators to determine which profit-oriented entities should prepare financial statements, is an issue that the Statement discusses in general terms only.

The boundary of the reporting entity

15 There are two main approaches that can be used to determine the boundary of a reporting entity: one approach concentrates wholly on ownership (the proprietary view) and the other concentrates on the group as an entity, unified and encompassed by the parent's control (the entity view).

(a) The proprietary view regards ownership and the resulting access to benefits as of paramount interest to users. As a result, ownership is used to provide the basis of consolidated financial statements. On a strict proprietary view, the investor's ability to influence or even control its investee is irrelevant: consolidated financial statements will aggregate the parent's direct and indirect ownership interests in a proportional consolidation (the line-by-line consolidation of the investor's share of each item) as this shows the parent's access to benefit from all of its investments.

(b) On the entity view, the parent's ability to control its subsidiaries is all-important, regardless of the size of its ownership interest in the activities of the entity that it directs. The consolidated financial statements therefore consolidate in full the assets and liabilities of any entity that the parent controls—even if the entity is not a wholly-owned subsidiary—and the parent's ownership interest and any outside equity interest in a subsidiary are treated merely as part of an overall ownership interest.

16 The appropriate perspective to use depends on the relative usefulness of the information each provides. The Statement regards the entity view as providing the most useful information, and therefore uses control to determine the boundary of a reporting entity.

Single entity financial statements of parent companies

17 The Statement explains that, once a reporting entity has been identified, two boundaries will be drawn—one based on direct control and one based on direct plus indirect control. This means that, where a company is controlled by another company, both companies will be reporting entities as will the group of companies that they constitute.

Some commentators suggest that, because the activities and resources of a parent and its subsidiary are difficult to separate economically, it is inappropriate for an entity to report on the activities it carries out and the resources it holds in isolation from the activities and resources of its subsidiaries. This view suggests that companies preparing consolidated financial statements should not also be expected to prepare single entity financial statements. Some might argue that the present legal position—in which parent companies are not required to prepare profit and loss accounts—could be used to support this view. However, if it is inappropriate for a parent to report on the activities it carries out and the resources it holds in isolation from the activities and resources of its subsidiaries, it would seem to follow that it is also inappropriate for those subsidiaries to report in isolation from their parent; in other words, subsidiaries whose activities and resources are reported on in consolidated financial statements should not be required to prepare single entity financial statements. That is not the present legal position. **18**

The Board's view is that, although the usefulness of single entity financial statements has decreased as the structure of business organisations has become more complex, single entity financial statements—whether for parent companies or subsidiaries—still have a role to play, albeit a much narrower role than that of the financial statements of the group as a whole. Drawing a boundary by reference to direct control reflects this view. **19**

CHAPTER 3: THE QUALITATIVE CHARACTERISTICS OF FINANCIAL INFORMATION

Materiality and relevance

Although the Statement of Principles expects the financial information given in financial statements to be both material and relevant, it describes these two characteristics in similar ways. In particular, the tests of whether information is material and whether it is relevant are both based on influencing the economic decisions of users—although relevance involves *the ability* to influence decisions while materiality involves the reasonable expectation that decisions *will* be influenced. Similarly, both characteristics involve a consideration of the size and nature of the items or information involved. There are, however, important differences between the characteristics. **20**

(a) Materiality is a threshold characteristic—a discrete test—used to decide whether to include information in the financial statements. If an item of information is material, it will need to be included and if it is not, it need not be included. Relevance, on the other hand, is a 'continuous' quality; one item of information will be more relevant than another and the information given will (subject to other constraints) be that which is the most relevant.

(b) Put simply, characteristics such as relevance, reliability, comparability and understandability provide direction to the financial reporting selection process, thus enabling the usefulness of the information to be maximised. The materiality test, which recognises that some information has to be left out of financial statements, then asks whether the information is useful enough to be given.

Prudence

Accounting practice has evolved significantly over the last thirty years and, as a result, has become much more sophisticated in the way that it seeks to reflect the nuances of business activity. This is acknowledged in the Statement through its emphasis on specific principles rather than general notions and assumptions. In the **21** case of prudence, for example, the smoothing of reported profits has become as great a concern as their overstatement and, as a result, the deliberate understatement of assets and gains and the deliberate overstatement of liabilities and losses are no longer seen as a virtue. Indeed, it is now widely accepted that the use of prudence in this way can seriously affect the quality of the information provided.

22 This has been reflected in international practice for some time now. For example, the framework documents published by the International Accounting Standards Committee (IASC) and the accounting standard-setters in Canada and the USA describe prudence (sometimes referred to as conservatism) as involving a degree of caution in the exercise of the judgements needed in making the estimates required under conditions of uncertainty. The standard-setters in Australia and New Zealand have adopted a similar approach, although they have subsumed prudence within the notion of reliability.

23 The Statement's approach to prudence is consistent with the way in which accounting practice has evolved and with the approaches adopted internationally. It:

(a) treats prudence as one of the attributes that need to be present if financial information prepared under conditions of uncertainty is to be reliable;

(b) describes prudence as the inclusion of a degree of caution in the exercise of the judgements needed in making the estimates required under conditions of uncertainty; and

(c) makes it clear that prudence is a potentially biased concept and that care should therefore be taken to ensure that it does not result in the deliberate and systematic understatement of assets and gains and the overstatement of liabilities and losses.

Understandability

24 In an ideal world, financial statements would be prepared in a way that makes them intelligible to all users, regardless of their level of expertise or experience. However, as entities are increasingly complex and many of them enter into increasingly complex transactions, it can be difficult to represent their financial performance and financial position both faithfully and in a way that can be understood by all users. The Statement recognises this by explaining that the basis on which financial statements are to be prepared is that users have a reasonable knowledge of business and economic activities and accounting.

25 This means that financial statements will not always be capable of being understood by all users. Although this sounds an unsatisfactory state of affairs, it is, in fact, the present position. Users who do not have a reasonable knowledge of business and economic activities and accounting use the services of those who have that knowledge to help them derive information from the financial statements.

Relevance versus reliability

26 Although it is sometimes argued that the characteristics of relevance and reliability are often in conflict, such conflicts are exaggerated. As the Statement makes clear, reliability is a hurdle to be cleared (ie is the information sufficiently reliable?), not a competition that has to be won (ie is this information the most reliable?). This means that the approach to be adopted in preparing the financial statements will be the one that is the most relevant of those that are reliable. A conflict will therefore arise between the characteristics only in the rare circumstances in which the reliable approaches are not relevant and the relevant approaches are not reliable.

CHAPTER 4: THE ELEMENTS OF FINANCIAL STATEMENTS

Identifying the elements

In essence, the preparation of financial statements involves finding the best way to categorise financial information about the transactions and other events that affect a reporting entity's financial performance and financial position. It is generally accepted that the best way to report this information is to focus on what has happened to the entity over the reporting period (for example, revenues and expenses, gains and losses, cash flows, and capital transactions) and what is its position as a result (assets and liabilities). These effects will inevitably have to be reflected in the financial statements in a highly aggregated form, and the Statement envisages that order will be imposed on this process by specifying and defining the classes of items (elements) that encapsulate the key aspects of those effects. 27

Should the definitions of the elements be interrelated and, if so, which definitions should be based on which?

The performance statement elements and the balance sheet elements could, in theory, be defined independently of each other. However, such an approach risks leaving gaps or creating areas of overlap. It would also have been inconsistent with the notion that primary financial statements should articulate, a fundamental and long-accepted characteristic of such statements. The Statement therefore uses definitions that are interrelated. 28

It follows that either the balance sheet elements should be based on the definitions of the performance statement elements or vice versa. As the accounting process is essentially about allocating the effects of transactions and other events to reporting periods, it might seem more logical to define the performance statement elements and then base the balance sheet elements on those definitions. This approach requires the use of robust definitions of the performance statement elements in order to provide the unity, order and discipline needed for an effective framework. Those definitions need therefore to be precise and comprehensive, and they need to avoid placing reliance on management intent or referring to generally accepted accounting principles. However, accounting standard-setters around the world have carried out an exhaustive search for robust definitions of performance statement elements and have concluded that such definitions do not exist. On the other hand, robust definitions of balance sheet elements do exist. The Statement, like all the conceptual documents developed by all the leading accounting standard-setters around the world, therefore defines the balance sheet elements and bases the definitions of the performance statement elements on those definitions. 29

How many elements should there be and how should they be defined?

It is obviously both important and necessary to distinguish cash flows and capital transactions from other things that happen to an entity. It is, however, not immediately clear whether it is important or realistic to treat, say, all the credits in the performance statement as a single type of element and expect them to meet a single definition (and all the debits as a separate single element and expect them to meet a single definition). A similar question arises concerning the debits and credits in the balance sheet. 30

Reporting on the financial performance and financial position of an entity involves providing an account of the reporting entity's use of, and command over, economic resources. The Statement therefore bases its definitions on flows and prospective flows of future economic benefits embodied in economic resources. Thus, assets are 31 defined as 'rights or other access to future economic benefits controlled by an entity as a result of past transactions or events', liabilities as 'obligations of an entity to transfer economic benefits as a result of past transactions or events', and, apart from ownership interest, no other balance sheet elements are identified.

32 As the items in the profit and loss account are typically referred to as revenue, expenses, gains and losses, it would seem natural to use similar terminology in the Statement. Indeed, that is the approach adopted in the USA by the Financial Accounting Standards Board. However, as it has been decided that the definitions of the performance statement elements should be based on the definitions of the balance sheet elements, it is possible to define the credits in the performance statement in terms of increases in net assets not resulting from capital contributions and the debits in the performance statement as decreases in net assets not resulting from capital distributions. The issue the Board therefore had to consider was whether more comprehensive definitions should be used in order to differentiate between types of performance statement debits and credits.

33 At the moment, the Board is carrying out a review of FRS 3 'Reporting Financial Performance'. As part of this work, it is considering possible ways of restructuring the performance statements that are provided at present. It may be that, as a result of this work, it will conclude that gains and revenue should be differentiated from each other. Similarly, it may be concluded that losses and expenses should be differentiated from each other. However, until then, there does not appear to be sufficient reason for the Statement of Principles to distinguish revenue from gains and expenses from losses. It therefore identifies one credit performance statement element (gains) and one debit performance statement element (losses). IASC's 'Framework for the Preparation and Presentation of Financial Statements' adopts the same approach, except that it calls the two elements 'income' and 'expenses'.

34 It is recognised that, by not differentiating gains from revenue (and losses from expenses), items that are commonly referred to as 'revenue' (and 'expenses') have had to be referred to in the Statement as 'gains' (and 'losses') or vice versa. That is not ideal but is not regarded as sufficient reason to justify differentiation.

Implications of the approach adopted to specifying and defining the elements

35 Under the approach adopted in the Statement, if costs are to be carried forward (ie deferred) to a subsequent period to match income being earned in that period, they will need to meet the definition of an asset (and meet the relevant recognition criteria). This will mean, inter alia, asking whether the costs to be deferred constitute future economic benefits. It is recognised that the application of this approach in practice will result in some of the costs that are at present deferred and shown as assets being recognised as losses because they do not represent future economic benefits. Similarly, some of the credit items that are deferred at present in the balance sheet might, under the principles, need instead to be recognised as income because they do not qualify as liabilities. Nevertheless, the Board believes that the approach provides what is needed for an effective framework.

36 It is worth noting that the Statement's approach is almost identical to the approach adopted in the conceptual documents of IASC and the other leading accounting standard-setters around the world, including the standard-setters in Australia, Canada, New Zealand and the USA. It is also worth noting that the definitions of assets and liabilities set out in the Statement already provide the foundation for several UK accounting standards, including FRS 5 'Reporting the Substance of Transactions'. Indeed, through the Board's own work, the work of UK bodies preparing Statements of Recommended Practice, and the work of the aforementioned standard-setters, the elements and their definitions have for many years now been playing an important role in the standard-setting process throughout the world.

It has nevertheless been suggested by some that the approach means that the balance sheet will become the main accounting statement and the performance statement will be relegated to a statement of residual amounts. It means nothing of the kind. First, the Board accepts that the primary focus of users is on the performance statement and that this is likely to remain the case for the foreseeable future. Secondly, using definitions of assets and liabilities to define gains and losses is merely a means to an end—that end being to improve the quality of financial statements in general and, through the discipline that the definitions will impose on the recognition of gains and losses, performance statements in particular. **37**

It has also been suggested in the past that the approach means that the profit or loss for the period will be the difference between the opening and closing balance sheets, adjusted for capital contributions and distributions. Although it is correct to say that the amount of the difference is equal to the total of all the components of financial performance, it is an oversimplification to suggest that this means that the difference is regarded as the profit or loss for the period. The Board has spent much time and energy since its inception on improving the way in which financial performance is reported, and the focus of this work has been the need to move away from placing so much significance on any one line of the performance statement. FRS 3 —which was issued in 1992—makes it clear that the focus of performance reporting should be on the components of financial performance and on the characteristics of those components. This is also the approach adopted in the Statement. **38**

Finally, some commentators have suggested that, by defining the performance statement elements by reference to movements in assets and liabilities, the Statement will shift the focus of accounting away from transactions. The Board does not agree with this suggestion. Accounting is a process that is primarily concerned with allocating the effects of transactions to reporting periods, and the approach set out in the Statement will achieve exactly that. **39**

CHAPTER 5: RECOGNITION IN FINANCIAL STATEMENTS

The role of realisation in the Statement

The Statement envisages that all gains and losses will be recognised in a performance statement. Furthermore, as the Statement does not specify different recognition criteria for different performance statements (or for different parts of the same, single performance statement), realised profits may conceivably be shown alongside unrealised profits. **40**

An alternative approach might have been to base recognition on the notions of realisation and realised profit. For example, the Statement could have assumed that only realised gains would be recognised in the performance statements. It could, *alternatively*, have assumed that realised gains would be recognised in one performance statement (or in one part of a single performance statement) while unrealised gains would be recognised in a second performance statement (such as the statement of total recognised gains and losses) or in a separate part of the single performance statement. The main reasons that are usually put forward in support of this approach, and the counter-arguments, are set out below. **41**

Companies legislation

42 Companies legislation specifies that companies should include only profits realised at the balance sheet date in their profit and loss account. It could be argued that, for this reason alone, realisation should be acknowledged as a recognition criterion.

43 However, the development of the Statement has not been constrained by legal requirements because the Board believes that accounting practice evolves best if regard is had in documents such as the Statement of Principles to what is deemed to be right rather than what is required by law. The implications of this for the Statement of Principles are considered in Appendix I.

Distributable profits

44 Companies making distributions of income to their shareholders must make them from distributable profits. It is therefore sometimes argued that, if users are to have a proper understanding of the level of sustainable dividends and of the prospects of dividend growth, it is important that the level of distributable profits is reported and that dividends paid and payable are reported in the context of those distributable profits.

45 However, in practice—and particularly for a group—the potential for distributions, whether from profits or return of capital, is dependent on many factors, including companies legislation in the countries in which the operations are carried out, corporate structure, currency and dividend controls, and the entity's financial adaptability. In these circumstances it is unrealistic to suppose that distributability per se can serve as a primary focus of the presentation of financial performance.

Realisation as a criterion for determining what should be recognised

46 Regardless of the legal requirements, it is a desirable attribute of items included in the profit and loss account, particularly gains, that their existence should be reasonably certain. The realisation notion is one means of determining whether the existence of a gain is reasonably certain. However, in the Board's view, it is not necessarily the best way.

47 The realisation notion originally came into use in order to protect creditors from the uncertainties that arise in accruals accounting, and its purpose was to try to ensure that profits were not overstated and that there was sufficient cash available to distribute those profits without the company becoming insolvent. In this guise the notion was understood to involve the conversion into cash of non-cash resources and rights to cash.

48 As business practice developed, so the purpose of the notion changed and it came to be used to ensure that only gains that were reasonably certain and unlikely to reverse were included in the profit and loss account. Similarly, its meaning evolved to include conversion into claims to cash.

49 Developments since then have, however, made even this version of the notion irrelevant in some areas. For example, it is now often possible to be reasonably certain that a gain exists and to measure that gain reliably even if no disposal has occurred. Furthermore, the introduction of cash flow statements means that cash-based profit and loss accounts have largely been outgrown. A number of attempts have been made to update the notion to take account of these developments. For example, it has been suggested that changes in the market value of securities for which an active market exists are also realised, even though no claim to cash is involved. Similarly, some have suggested that the test should be extended to include gains that are realisable, in other words capable of being converted into cash or claims for cash.

However, in general it is not a good idea to bend a term so that it has a meaning other than its natural meaning. A better approach in this case would seem to be to focus on the underlying objective and then encapsulate that objective in the recognition criteria. It is the Board's view that the objective is to recognise a gain only if there is reasonable certainty that it exists and if it can be measured reliably. The initial recognition and subsequent remeasurement criteria set out in the Statement are designed to achieve that end. 50

CHAPTER 6: MEASUREMENT IN FINANCIAL STATEMENTS

The mixed measurement system

For many years entities carried all their assets and liabilities in their balance sheet at historical cost. However, the relevance of such measures in periods when prices have moved markedly has often been questioned and, to counteract this perceived fading relevance, the majority of larger UK listed companies now measure some of their assets at current values and some at cost. (According to Company Reporting No 80 (February 1997), more than 65 per cent of the companies in that journal's database had adopted this approach.) 51

Although this approach is commonly referred to as the modified historical cost basis, that term is something of a misnomer because it is a mixed measurement system. The Statement therefore uses this latter term. 52

The Statement explains that assets and liabilities have a number of different monetary attributes that could be represented in financial statements. It also explains that the single most important characteristic that distinguishes these monetary attributes is whether they are based on historical cost or current value. The remainder of its discussion is expressed in terms of this distinction. 53

In theory, the Statement could have adopted one of three broad approaches to measurement. 54

(a) It could have assumed strict adherence to historical cost in all circumstances. In view of existing practice, this would have been a revolutionary step. For example, when respondents to the Accounting Standards Committee's ED 51 'Accounting for fixed assets and revaluations' (1990) were asked whether it would be practicable to prohibit the carrying of selected fixed assets at revalued amounts, 96 per cent of those who answered the question believed it was not practicable.
(b) It could have assumed the adoption of a comprehensive current value system under which all assets and all liabilities, or at least the great majority of them, would be carried at current values. This too would have been a revolutionary step and it is not an approach that the Board has considered in the past nor is it one that it expects to consider in the foreseeable future.
(c) It could have assumed the continuance of the present, mixed measurement system. Previous consultations have shown that the majority of respondents favour this approach. For example, just over 70 per cent of those who responded to the Board's Discussion Paper 'The Role of Valuation in Financial Reporting' (1993) favoured continued use of the mixed measurement system.

55 In preparing the Statement, the Board has assumed the continued use of the mixed measurement system. This system has the advantage of requiring reporting entities to match the measurement basis used for a particular category of assets or liabilities to the circumstances relating to that category and, in so doing, acknowledges the different trade-offs between relevance and reliability in the measurement of different types of balance sheet item. The system is also flexible in that the mix of historical cost and current value can be changed as accounting thought develops and markets evolve.

Choosing a measurement basis

56 The main focus of the Statement's chapter on measurement is the measurement debate that is of most relevance today—what mix of historical cost and current value should be used. The Statement provides a framework to guide the choice of an appropriate measurement basis for each balance sheet category and thereby helps to apply some discipline and logic to the selection process. This should result in an improvement in the relevance and comparability of the information being provided.

57 The characteristic of relevance plays a major role in the framework described in the Statement. Current value information can be relevant in two rather different ways.

(a) For assets that generate cash flows indirectly through use—such as property, plant and equipment—a current value gives an up-to-date measure of the total resources invested and provides a basis for calculating the current cost of using the asset within the period.

(b) For assets and liabilities that represent rights to specific future cash flows—financial assets and financial liabilities—the market price gives the value of those cash flows at that time.

58 Whereas for the first type of balance sheet item some degree of choice may be appropriate for each entity in determining whether market values should be used as the basis of measure, the same flexibility may be less appropriate if extended to the second type because of their more direct relationship to future cash flows.

59 As the Statement explains, although the factors that should be used to determine the most appropriate measurement basis are unlikely to change, the measurement basis that best meets those factors may. Indeed, the Board expects that, if markets develop, greater use will probably be made of current value because measures that were once thought not relevant or unreliable may become both the most relevant measure and reliable. That having been said, it is unlikely that the framework set out in the Statement will suggest the use of current values other than for certain types of investments, commodity stocks and financial instruments. Under the framework, the practice of measuring some fixed assets at current value is also likely to continue.

CHAPTER 7: PRESENTATION OF FINANCIAL INFORMATION

Presentation of gains and losses

60 The way in which information on financial performance is presented is of fundamental importance to the quality of financial reporting. The Statement does not, however, deal with this matter in any detail, primarily because it is an issue that is being actively considered in the Board's review of FRS 3. If that review identifies principles about the presentation of gains and losses that could usefully be incorporated in the Statement, the Statement will be amended.

Dividends paid and payable

The Statement makes it clear that, regardless of the number of performance statements prepared, they will deal with gains and losses only and no items that are not gains and losses will be recognised in them. As dividends paid and payable are not gains and losses, the Statement envisages that they will not be included in the profit and loss account or other performance statement. Although that seems logical—dividends are not a component of financial performance—it is not consistent with how such dividends are dealt with at present. This issue is being considered as part of the review of FRS 3*. **61**

Recycling

The Statement explains that items that are not gains or losses are not included in the performance statement, which means that the notion of recycling† is not consistent with the principles. This is another matter that is being considered in the review of FRS 3. **62**

CHAPTER 8: ACCOUNTING FOR INTERESTS IN OTHER ENTITIES

Accounting for minority interests

As explained in paragraph 15, there are, in theory, two opposing perspectives from which minority interests could be viewed when preparing consolidated financial statements: one perspective concentrates wholly on ownership (the proprietary view) and the other on the group as an entity, unified and encompassed by the parent's control (the entity view). The Statement considers that the entity view provides the most useful information and therefore uses control to determine the boundary of a reporting entity. **63**

One implication of adopting the entity view is that all subsidiaries, even those that are not wholly-owned, will be fully consolidated. However, it is useful to show the extent of outside ownership interests since this is an important factor in determining the interest of investors in the reporting entity as a whole. This important feature—ownership—would be ignored if the focus was exclusively on the entity view. The Statement therefore envisages that any outside equity interests in entities within the parent's control will be identified in the primary financial statements. In this way the financial statements will reflect the parent's ownership interests in the entities within its control. **64**

Editor's note: *Dividends are no longer dealt with in a profit and loss account, and therefore the point made by the ASB no longer applies. The reconsideration of FRS 3, reflected in FRED 22, did not give rise to a new standard and is now extremely unlikely to do so.*

†*By 'recycling' the Statement means recognising a gain or loss in the performance statement in one period then, in a later period, recognising some or all of that gain or loss under a different heading in either the same or a different performance statement because the nature of the item is deemed to have changed in some way. Notwithstanding the ASB's comment that recycling is not consistent with the principles, it was introduced by FRS 26 in some situations.*

This Interpretation for Public Benefit Entities of the Statement of Principles for Financial Reporting was agreed by the Accounting Standards Board in May 2007. At that time, the Board comprised:

Ian Mackintosh	Chairman
David Loweth	Technical Director
Mike Ashley	
Edward Beale	
Marisa Cassoni	
Peter Elwin	
Roger Marshall	
Robert Overend	
Helen Weir	
Peter Westlake	
Geoffrey Whittington	

Statement of Principles for Financial Reporting

Interpretation for Public Benefit Entities

Contents

	Pages
Introduction	3 – 8
Chapter one: The objective of financial statements	9 – 17
Chapter two: The reporting entity	18 – 22
Chapter three: The qualitative characteristics of financial information	23 – 30
Chapter four: The elements of financial statements	31 – 46
Chapter five: Recognition in financial statements	47 – 58
Chapter six: Measurement in financial statements	59 – 68
Chapter seven: Presentation of financial information	69 – 76
Chapter eight: Accounting for interests in other entities	77 – 83
Appendix 1 – The principles that have been re-expressed	84 – 88
Appendix 2 – Comparison to material in the Statement	89 – 95
Appendix 3 – Decision Tree for commitments to provide public benefits	96
Appendix 4 – The Development of the Interpretation	97 – 108

Interpretation for Public Benefit Entities

INTRODUCTION

PURPOSE

1 This Interpretation for Public Benefit Entities of the Statement of Principles for Financial Reporting (this Interpretation) sets out the principles that the Accounting Standards Board (the Board) believes should underlie the preparation and presentation of general purpose financial statements of public benefit entities*.

2 The principles in this Interpretation are consistent with those relevant to profit-oriented entities, as set out in the Board's Statement of Principles for Financial Reporting (the Statement). The Statement is now almost ten years old and will need to be reviewed in the light of conceptual framework projects being taken forward by both the International Accounting Standards Board and the International Public Sector Accounting Standards Board. For this reason, the Board recognises this Interpretation may be superseded in the short to medium term. It should, however, make a useful contribution to the work that is being taken forward internationally as well as supporting the work of UK SORP making bodies until frameworks are agreed internationally.

3 Many of the principles are exactly the same as those that are relevant to profit-oriented entities. Any re-expression, change of emphasis or additions to the principles are designed to make them more relevant to public benefit entities and have been made only to clarify their application in situations specific to public benefit entities. Those principles that have been re-expressed in this Interpretation are detailed in Appendix 1, together with a brief explanation.

4 The primary purpose of articulating the application of the principles to public benefit entities is to provide a coherent frame of reference to be used in the development of Statements of Recommended Practice (SORPs)† or other sector specific guidance for public benefit entities and to assist preparers and auditors faced with new or emerging issues. Nothing in this Interpretation overrides the requirements of existing accounting standards or SORPs.

5 The prescription of accounting requirements for the public sector in the United Kingdom is carried out by the Government. Where entities in the public sector prepare annual reports and accounts on commercial lines, the Government's requirements may or may not refer specifically either to accounting standards or to the need for the financial statements concerned to give a true and fair view. However, when they do, the Government's requirements accord with the principles underlying the Board's pronouncements subject to such adaptations as are considered necessary in the public sector context.

* *The term 'public benefit entities' is explained in paragraph 11.*

† *SORPs are recommendations on accounting practices for specialised sectors. They supplement accounting standards and other legal and regulatory requirements in the light of the special factors prevailing or transactions undertaken in a particular sector. SORPs are not issued by the ASB, but by industry or sectoral bodies recognised for the purpose by the ASB. At present there are four SORPs relating to the public benefit sector addressing local authorities, education institutions, registered social landlords and charities.*

STATUS

This Interpretation is not an accounting standard, nor does it have a status that is equivalent to an accounting standard. It therefore does not contain requirements on how financial statements should be prepared or presented. Where there may be an inconsistency between the principles set out in this Interpretation and an extant standard, such as SSAP 4 'Accounting for government grants', the standard should be followed. **6**

Much of the wording in this Interpretation is based upon the Statement. This document is intended to supplement, not replace, the Statement and should therefore be read in conjunction with it. **7**

To ensure there is adequate context for the information on the application of the principles to public benefit entities some of the material in the Statement has been repeated in this Interpretation. However, it should not be assumed that where material has been omitted it is not relevant to public benefit entities. Appendix 2 provides a comparison of this Interpretation with the Statement highlighting the source of material and those paragraphs of the Statement that have not been repeated. **8**

SCOPE

Types of entity

The Statement is intended to be relevant to the financial statements of profit-oriented entities, regardless of whether they are private or public sector entities. **9**

The principles in this Interpretation are intended to be relevant to the financial statements of public benefit entities, regardless of their size, whether or not they aim to make a surplus and whether they are private or public sector entities*. **10**

Public benefit entities are reporting entities whose primary objective is to provide goods or services for the general public or social benefit and where any equity † has been provided with a view to supporting that primary objective rather than with a view to providing a financial return to equity shareholders. **11**

The term 'public benefit entities' does not necessarily imply that the purpose of the entity is to exist for the benefit of the public as a whole. For example, many public benefit entities exist for the direct benefit of a particular group of people, although it is possible that society as a whole also benefits indirectly. The important factor is what the primary purpose of such entities is, and that it does not exist primarily to provide economic benefit to its investors. Organisations such as mutual insurance companies, other mutual co-operative entities and clubs that provide dividends or other economic benefits directly and proportionately to their owners, members or participants are not public benefit entities. **12**

The use of the term does not mean that all entities that do not make a profit are for the public benefit. Neither does the term imply that all entities that make a profit (or surplus) are not for the public benefit. Furthermore, certain public benefit entities, such as housing associations or the trading arm of a charity, may aim to make a **13**

**Both the Statement and this Interpretation use the terms 'public' and 'private' in this context as mutually exclusive and to encompass between them all entities.*

†*Equity (for example, in the purchase of equity shares) is provided by investors.*

profit from some of their activities which is then utilised in furtherance of the entity's primary objective. It is possible that an entity could undertake some activities that are intended to make a surplus, without the entity as a whole being profit-oriented*.

14 Public benefit entities may have contributions in the form of equity, even though the entity does not have a primary profit motive. However, because of the fundamental nature of public benefit entities, any such contributions are made by the equity holders of the entity primarily for the provision of goods or services rather than with a view to a financial return for themselves†. This is different from the position of lenders; loans do not fall into the category of equity.

15 There is no exhaustive list of entities that are public benefit entities.

Types of financial report

16 Financial information takes many different forms. However, the Statement categorises financial information into three broad headings. These categories are:

- special purpose financial reports;
- general purpose financial reports; and
- other financial information.

17 General purpose financial reports include general purpose financial statements, for example the annual financial statements.

18 The primary focus of this Interpretation for public benefit entities is on those financial statements that are required to give a true and fair view of the reporting entity's financial performance and financial position. However, where the requirement to present a true and fair view is expressed in another form, for example 'presents fairly', this Interpretation still applies.

19 The principles in the Statement and this Interpretation have been developed in the context of entities that prepare accruals based financial statements. Accordingly, this Interpretation is not intended to be relevant to receipts and payments accounts and other non-accruals based general purpose financial statements, which would not give a true and fair view of the reporting entity's financial performance and financial position.

20 Whilst this Interpretation does not address to any significant extent other types of general purpose financial report, it will be relevant to such reports insofar as they provide financial information that is intended to be consistent with the financial statements.

Legal requirements

21 The financial statements of public benefit entities are subject to legal requirements. Such requirements may vary substantially between sub-sets of public benefit entities both in terms of the level of prescription (ie general or very specific) and in terms of quantity/sources. In order not to deny this Interpretation the opportunity to assist in

**Where a public benefit entity has a discrete division that is profit-oriented it may be useful to refer to the Statement in relation to that division, even though this Interpretation applies to the entity as a whole. Similarly, this Interpretation will not be directly relevant to any subsidiaries of public benefit entities that are not public benefit entities themselves.*

†It does not follow that all contributions from funders and financial supporters are in the form of risk capital.

the development of legal requirements, it has not been developed within the constraints imposed by legislation.

REVISIONS TO THE STATEMENT

The Statement may be revised from time to time in the light of the Board's experience of working with it and in response to developments in accounting thought. This Interpretation may also be revised from time to time. **22**

Chapter 1: the objective of financial statements

Put simply, the objective of financial statements is to provide information that is useful to those who use them. However, the objective needs to be expressed more precisely if it is to be of any use in determining the form and content of financial statements. This chapter does that by considering the persons for whom financial statements are prepared, the information needs of such persons and the role that financial statements play in meeting those needs.

PRINCIPLES

- The objective of financial statements is to provide information about the reporting entity's financial performance and financial position that is useful to a wide range of users for assessing the stewardship of the entity's management and for making economic decisions.
- That objective can usually be met by focusing exclusively on the information needs of funders and financial supporters, the defining class of user.
- Funders and financial supporters need information about the reporting entity's financial performance and financial position that is useful in helping them to evaluate the proper and efficient use of the entity's resources and in assessing the entity's future cash needs and its financial adaptability.

EXPLANATION

The main differences between the principles and explanation relevant to profit-orientated entities, as expressed in Chapter 1 of the Statement, and their interpretation for public benefit entities, are in the defining class of user and the role stewardship plays in the preparation of financial statements. Additional material specific to public benefit entities has therefore been added to this chapter of the Interpretation, although Chapter 1 of the Statement should also be referred to for a full understanding of the discussion that follows. Additional explanation specific to users of public benefit entities financial statements has also been added, including other groups of user that may be interested in the performance of a public benefit entity, for example beneficiaries and government agencies.

The objective of financial statements

Useful to a wide range of users

1.1 The Statement notes that many people may have an interest in the financial information of an entity. Certain bodies, such as regulators of public benefit entities, may have the power to insist on the preparation of special purpose financial reports. However, others will need to rely on general purpose financial reports, such as financial statements. These persons are referred to as the 'users'.

Useful for making economic decisions

1.2 The persons potentially interested in an entity's financial statements need information on that entity for a variety of purposes. For public benefit entities the groups of users that are interested in an entity's financial statements are largely consistent with those described in the Statement: some exceptions and clarifications are discussed below:

(a) *Present and potential investors*. Public benefit entities rarely have such investors; therefore this class of user has been replaced with *funders and financial supporters*.

(b) *Present and potential funders and financial supporters (hereafter generally referred to simply as 'funders and financial supporters')*. Providers of resources are interested in information that helps them to assess how effectively management has fulfilled their stewardship role. They are also interested in information about the utilisation of the resources they supplied to the entity that might be useful in taking decisions about resources they may choose, or be required, to supply in the future.

(c) *Lenders*. Lenders are interested in information that helps them to assess whether their loans and related interest will be paid, when due. Similarly, potential lenders are interested in information that helps them to decide whether to lend to the entity and on what terms.

(d) *Beneficiaries/customers*. Beneficiaries and customers are interested in information about the entity's continued existence. That is especially so when they have a long-term involvement with, or are dependent on, the entity. Beneficiaries and customers are also interested in how resources have been applied by the entity in meeting its objectives.

(e) *Governments and their agencies, including regulators*. Governments and their agencies are interested in the allocation of resources and, therefore, the activities of entities. They may also have specific regulatory (or intermediary) roles, through which they aim to give the public confidence in the operations of the entities they regulate, perhaps performing a scrutiny role on behalf of the funders and financial supporters, or the general public. They require information that assists them in regulating the activities of entities and for example, for providing a basis for national statistics. Some of this information is obtained through special purpose financial reports, which will often need to be able to demonstrate consistency with general purpose financial reports.

(f) *The public*. The interest the public may have in the financial statements of a public benefit entity will vary from that described in the Statement. For example, as part of the broad accountability of public benefit entities, the public may be interested in the quality of management's stewardship and in the relative allocation of resources between competing priorities. For a number of public benefit entities the public will be the funders and financial supporters of the entity.

Although those potentially interested in an entity's financial statements need that information for a variety of purposes, the Statement concludes that all the purposes involve taking economic decisions. The economic decisions made by users of the financial statements of profit-oriented entities may include whether to hold or sell their investments. They might also include whether to reappoint or replace the management of the entity. For public benefit entities, certain users will have the ability to make similar economic decisions. For example, funders and financial supporters may vary the level of financial support based on how effectively management have fulfilled their role. This might include a decision about whether to commence supporting an entity. **1.3**

Some users, such as members of the public and taxpayers in relation to a local authority, will not have the same ability to make direct economic decisions. They may however have the ability to vote at elections and this may indirectly influence the level of resources contributed to entities. **1.4**

Assessing stewardship

1.5 Stewardship plays an important role in the preparation of financial statements by public benefit entities. Accountability to a public benefit entity's stakeholders for the use of funds and the safekeeping of its resources is often of paramount importance and there may be a wide range of people having such an interest in the activities of the entity. For example, accountability to the public for the collection of taxation and its use in the provision of public goods and services is fundamental in public sector reporting. Therefore, a key objective of financial statements for public benefit entities is the provision of information to assist in a user's assessment of the efficient and effective use of funds and other resources.

1.6 To allow users to make a full assessment of the stewardship of an entity (perhaps including an assessment of the extent to which its public benefit objective has been met) additional information is likely to be required. Some of this information may accompany the financial statements but it will not form part of the financial statements. This is known as accompanying information and is discussed in Chapter 7.

Information on financial performance and financial position

1.7 There is overlap in the financial information that is required by users although all are interested in the financial performance and financial position of the entity as a whole. General purpose financial statements focus on this common interest of users and are the principal means of communicating accounting information of an entity to interested parties.

The limitations of financial statements

1.8 Financial statements do not seek to meet all the information needs of users: users will usually need to supplement the information they receive from financial statements with information from other sources. Financial statements have various inherent limitations* which means that some information on the financial performance and financial position of the reporting entity can be only provided by general purpose reports other than financial statements. For example, a description of the environment in which the reporting entity operates and the strategies it has adopted might be more appropriately included in the accompanying information. Those users with the authority to obtain special purpose financial reports might also utilise that authority to supplement the information in the financial statements.

1.9 The need to supplement the financial statements with other information is at least as important for public benefit entities as for profit-oriented entities. In assessing the efficient and effective use of resources, the user is likely to need information in addition to that reported in a conventional presentation of financial performance and financial position. For example, information in the material accompanying the financial statements, such as the management commentary, might be needed in order to put the numerical information in the financial statements into context. Such information might include qualitative and quantitative information on services provided by the entity during the year.

1.10 Many public benefit entities also utilise other forms of presentation, which may include financial information that may or may not be provided with the financial statements. One example might be a comparison of actual results to budget, which

**Including the degree of aggregation, the focus on the financial effects of transactions and events and the fact that they are largely historical.*

might provide information on whether an entity has spent according to plan. Public benefit entities might also use methods of communication other than the financial statements to provide financial information, particularly to classes of user other than the defining class.

Funders and financial supporters as the defining class of user

The Statement notes that, in preparing the financial statements of profit-oriented entities, the rebuttable assumption is that financial statements that focus on the interest that investors have in the reporting entity's financial performance and financial position will, in effect, also be focusing on the common interest that all users have in that entity's financial performance and financial position. **1.11**

However, public benefit entities often have no such investors (i.e. shareholders) and for those entities that do have shareholders, there may not be rights to participate in any surpluses or on winding-up*. For public benefit entities funders and financial supporters are similar to investors in profit-oriented entities in terms of their information requirements. **1.12**

The defining class of user for the financial statements of public benefit entities is funders and financial supporters. They provide a source of cash or other resources without the incentive of a direct return on their investment. Funders and financial supporters generally provide taxation, grants or donations to the entity. The defining class of user includes present and potential funders and financial supporters of the entity. Funders or financial supporters will also include an individual or entity that has made a contribution in the past if that contribution created an ongoing financial interest. **1.13**

There are differences between a 'financial supporter' and a 'funder'. A financial supporter is someone who has made a conscious decision to contribute, whereas this might not be true of a funder, such as a taxpayer. A lender, in his capacity as a provider of debt capital on which he receives a return, is neither a funder nor a financial supporter. **1.14**

Where a public benefit entity has 'members' who are required to make a financial contribution in order to be admitted to the membership, they should be considered as financial supporters where the value of the contribution is unlikely to represent the fair value of the benefits available from membership (ie it is at least partly a mechanism to provide financial support, not the purchase of goods or services). As a result, to the extent that contributions are financial support, they should be recognised as revenue when received. **1.15**

For many public benefit entities, funds are not received directly from their source, but are passed on through intermediaries (for example government entities providing grants). Often such intermediaries will be regulators that may have a statutory right to require certain information to be published in the financial statements. This information should be regarded as special purpose as it will not necessarily meet the information requirements of a general user of the financial statements (for example, where it relates to an amount of expenditure incurred under a specific piece of legislation). It is therefore necessary to look through intermediary financial supporters to the original source to ensure that financial statements are prepared to provide general purpose rather than special purpose information. **1.16**

**In the event of a winding-up any remaining net assets would often be dealt with in accordance with the governing instrument of the entity. Usually this would involve the transfer of the net assets to another public benefit entity with similar objectives.*

The information required by funders and financial supporters

Financial performance

1.17 Information on financial performance, amongst other things, provides an account of the stewardship of management and is useful in assessing the past and anticipated performance of the entity.

1.18 In the case of public benefit entities, stewardship is a particularly important part of reporting to users. Users require information to hold management to account for the safekeeping of the entity's resources and for their proper and efficient use.

Financial position

1.19 An entity's financial position encompasses the economic resources it controls, its financial structure, its liquidity and solvency, its risk profile and risk management approach, and its capacity to adapt to changes in the environment in which it operates. Information about the economic resources controlled and the use made of them in the past also helps in assessing the stewardship of management.

Cash needs

1.20 Information on the ways in which an entity uses cash provides an additional perspective on financial performance that is largely free from allocation and valuation issues and is relevant to an assessment of its future cash needs.

1.21 Information on the generation and use of cash is important for public benefit entities. In certain cases, the entity may have a limit imposed on the amount of cash that it has authority to spend each year. Where this is the case, information on the use of cash may be needed to demonstrate accountability and the effective use of funds.

1.22 An entity's financial adaptability is its ability to take effective action to alter the amount and timing of its cash flows so that it can respond to unexpected needs or opportunities.

1.23 Financial adaptability can help an entity mitigate the risks associated with activities, which in turn can help it survive during a time of low cash flows.

Chapter 2: the reporting entity

It is important that entities that ought to prepare and publish financial statements, do, in fact, do so and that those financial statements report on all relevant activities and resources. This chapter focuses on these issues – in other words, on identifying and circumscribing the reporting entity.

PRINCIPLES

- An entity should prepare and publish financial statements if there is a legitimate demand for the information that its financial statements would provide and it is a cohesive economic unit.
- The boundary of the reporting entity is determined by the scope of its control. For this purpose, first, direct control, and secondly, direct plus indirect control are taken into account.

EXPLANATION

There are few fundamental differences between the principles and explanation relevant to profit-oriented entities, as expressed in Chapter 2 of the Statement, and their interpretation for public benefit entities. Therefore much of what follows is a summary of the discussion in Chapter 2 of the Statement, which should be referred to for a full understanding.

Additional explanation specific to public benefit entities has been added covering assets held by an entity in a fiduciary capacity.

Entities that should prepare and publish financial statements

It is essential that entities that ought to prepare and publish financial statements, do so. For similar reasons, if there is no justification for an entity to prepare and publish financial statements, it should not be required to do so. 2.1

For the preparation of financial statements to be justified in any particular case, there needs to be a legitimate demand for the information that the financial statements would provide. This means, inter alia, that the information provided by the financial statements will need to be useful and that the benefits to be derived by providing the financial statements will need to exceed the costs of doing so. 2.2

The financial statements of an entity will report on the entity's transactions and on other events that affect its financial performance and financial position. However, if the information provided by the financial statements is to be useful, the entity that is the subject of the financial statements (the reporting entity) needs to be a cohesive economic unit. This ensures accountability – the reporting entity is held to account for all the things it can control – and it gives the reporting entity a determinable boundary – because activities and resources are either within its control or outside its control. 2.3

The boundary of a reporting entity

The control an entity exerts can be direct or indirect.

(a) An entity has direct control of an asset if it has the ability in its own right to obtain future economic benefits* embodied in that asset and to restrict others' access to those benefits.
(b) An entity indirectly controls an asset if it has control of an entity that has direct control of the asset.

2.5 Direct control is used to determine the boundary of the reporting entity that prepares single entity financial statements. Direct plus indirect control is used to determine the boundary of the reporting entity that prepares consolidated financial statements.

2.6 It may be that, although an entity can influence another entity, it does not control it. Such entities do not comprise a single reporting entity.

What is control?

2.7 Control has two aspects: the ability to deploy the economic resources involved and the ability to benefit (or to suffer) from their deployment. To have control, an entity must have both these abilities.

2.8 Control in the context of assets and liabilities is considered in more detail in Chapter 4, which provides further details on the interpretation of 'economic benefits' in the context of public benefit entities, in particular noting that access to future economic benefits includes the provision of goods and/or services to the benefit of the entity's beneficiaries.

Controlling an entity

When does one entity control another?

2.9 An entity will have control of a second entity if it has the ability to direct that entity's operating and financial policies with a view to gaining economic benefit from its activities (which might be achieved through concurrence of objectives) or being exposed to significant risks inherent in the activities. Control of another entity need not involve share ownership.

2.10 There is no single piece of evidence that is proof of an investor's control in all circumstances, although evidence that will help to determine whether control exists can be obtained by considering:

(a) the respective rights held;
(b) the inflows and outflows of benefit; and
(c) exposure to risk – how and to what extent the investor suffers or gains from variability of outcome.

2.11 In the absence of any other factors, an agreement to provide funding would not be expected to constitute control.

2.12 In some circumstances a public benefit entity may be the trustee of charitable funds. Depending on the circumstances of the case, the charitable funds may form part of the reporting entity, particularly if the trustee both controls the charitable funds and has objectives that are concurrent.

**The future economic benefits to which a public benefit entity might have access are discussed in Chapter 4.*

Powers of veto and reserve powers

Control implies the ability to restrict others from directing the financial and operating policies of the controlled entity. Powers of veto and reserve powers are unlikely to form the sole basis of control because they do not provide a basis for deploying the resources nor do they ensure the corresponding flows of benefit. **2.13**

Predetermined operating and financial policies

An entity whose operating and financial policies are predetermined will be controlled by another entity if that other entity gains the benefits arising from the former's net assets and is exposed to the risks inherent in them (ie the variability of outcome). **2.14**

Latent control

If an entity has the ability to control another entity, it is usually presumed to be exercising control, even if such control is not apparent. **2.15**

Management but not control

Control needs to be distinguished from management. If an entity manages a second entity on its own behalf, then it controls the second entity because it has the two abilities referred to in paragraph 2.7. On the other hand, if an entity manages the second entity on behalf of another party, it is not exposed to the benefits arising from, or risks inherent in, the activities of the second entity because the manager's interest in the managed entity is normally limited to its fee. As such, it does not have the second ability referred to in paragraph 2.7 and therefore does not have control of the second entity. **2.16**

Assets held in a fiduciary capacity

A number of public benefit entities have a fiduciary role for assets that they do not control, for example, residents' valuables held by a local authority care home or artwork on loan for an exhibition. Since the boundary of the reporting entity is based on control, such assets should not be reflected in the balance sheet of the reporting entity. Where a fiduciary arrangement does not pass the control test, appropriate disclosures should be provided to indicate the nature and extent of the entity's fiduciary responsibilities. In some circumstances an entity may also be required to prepare separate financial information relating to the assets held in a fiduciary capacity. **2.17**

Chapter 3: the qualitative characteristics of financial information

In deciding which information to include in financial statements, when to include it and how to present it, the aim is to ensure that financial statements yield information that is useful. This chapter considers the qualities of financial information that make it useful.

PRINCIPLES

- Information provided by financial statements needs to be relevant and reliable and, if a choice exists between relevant and reliable approaches that are mutually exclusive, the approach chosen needs to be the one that results in the relevance of the information provided being maximised.
- Information is relevant if it has the ability to influence the economic decisions of users, or their assessment of the effectiveness of the stewardship of management, and is provided in time to influence those decisions or assessments.
- Information is reliable if:
  - (a) it can be depended upon by users to represent faithfully what it either purports to represent or could reasonably be expected to represent, and therefore reflects the substance of the transactions and other events that have taken place;
  - (b) it is free from deliberate or systematic bias and material error and is complete; and
  - (c) in its preparation under conditions of uncertainty, a degree of caution has been applied in exercising the necessary judgements.
- Information in financial statements needs to be comparable. As an aid to comparability, information in financial statements needs to be prepared and presented in a way that enables users to discern and evaluate similarities in, and differences between, the nature and effects of transactions and other events over time and across different reporting entities.
- Information provided by financial statements needs to be understandable – that is its significance can be perceived by users that have a reasonable knowledge of business and economic activities and accounting and a willingness to study with reasonable diligence the information provided.
- Information that is material needs to be given in the financial statements and information that is not material need not be given. Information is material to the financial statements if its misstatement or omission might reasonably be expected to influence the economic decisions of users, or their assessment of the effectiveness of the stewardship of management.

EXPLANATION

There are few fundamental differences between the principles and explanation relevant to profit-oriented entities, as expressed in Chapter 3 of the Statement and their interpretation for public benefit entities. Therefore much of what follows is a summary of the discussion in Chapter 3 of the Statement, which should be referred to for a full understanding.

Additional explanation specific to public benefit entities has been added covering going concern, understandability and neutrality and prudence.

Relevance

3.1 Relevance is a general quality that is used as a selection criterion at all stages of the financial reporting process. Information is relevant if it has the ability to influence the economic decisions of users, or their assessment of the effectiveness of the stewardship of management, and is provided in time to influence those decisions.

Relevant information has predictive or confirmatory value. It has predictive value if it helps users to evaluate or assess past, present or future events. It has confirmatory value if it helps users to confirm or correct their past evaluations or assessments. Maximising the relevance of financial information involves maximising its predictive and confirmatory value. **3.2**

Going concern

There are a number of different perspectives from which an entity's financial performance and financial position could be viewed. The perspective that is usually most relevant is based on the assumption that the entity is to continue in operational existence for the foreseeable future. This perspective is commonly referred to as the going concern assumption. **3.3**

In determining whether a public benefit entity is a going concern some of the factors, including legal requirements, to be taken into account may vary from those that would be considered in relation to profit-oriented entities. For example, an entity may have tax raising powers that give it the ability to raise revenue as any liabilities fall due, regardless of whether at the time the assessment is undertaken it has sufficient assets to cover its future liabilities. **3.4**

Reliability

Information provided by financial statements needs to be reliable. Information is reliable if: **3.5**

(a) it can be depended upon by users to represent faithfully what it either purports to represent or could reasonably be expected to represent;
(b) it is free from deliberate or systematic bias (i.e. it is neutral);
(c) it is free from material error;
(d) it is complete within the bounds of materiality; and
(e) in its preparation under conditions of uncertainty, a degree of caution (i.e. prudence) has been applied in exercising judgement and making the necessary estimates.

Faithful representation involves identifying all the rights and obligations arising from the transaction or event, giving greater weight to those that are likely to have an economic effect in practice, then accounting for and presenting the transaction or other event in a way that reflects that economic effect – in other words, in a way that reflects its substance. **3.6**

The substance of a transaction or other event is not always consistent with that suggested by its legal form. A group or series of transactions that achieves an overall commercial effect will often need to be viewed as a whole in order to be accounted for in accordance with its substance. **3.7**

The information provided by financial statements needs to be neutral – in other words, free from deliberate or systematic bias. Financial information is not neutral if it has been selected or presented in such a way as to influence the making of a decision or judgement in order to achieve a predetermined result or outcome. **3.8**

Comparability

3.9 Information in an entity's financial statements gains greatly in usefulness if it can be compared with similar information about the entity for some other period. Information about an entity is also much more useful if it can be compared with similar information about other entities.

Consistency

3.10 Comparability generally implies consistency throughout the reporting entity within each accounting period and from one period to the next. Consistency can also be useful in enhancing comparability between entities, although this does not imply a need for absolute uniformity.

Disclosure of accounting policies

3.11 In order to determine whether consistency exists or to assist in making comparisons despite inconsistencies, users need information on accounting policies adopted by entities and of any changes in those policies and the effects of such changes.

Understandability

3.12 Information provided by financial statements needs to be understandable and users need to be able to perceive its significance. Whether financial information is understandable will depend on:

(a) the way in which the effects of transactions and other events are characterised, aggregated and classified;
(b) the way in which the information is presented; and
(c) the capabilities of users.

3.13 When considering the capabilities of users of the financial statements of public benefit entities, it may not always appear appropriate to assume that they will have a reasonable knowledge of business and economic activities and accounting, for example where the defining class of user is the taxpayer. However, if financial statements are to be useful to a wide range of users for general purposes, the preparers must be able to assume a reasonable knowledge*. In this regard an important role is played by intermediaries, such as oversight and regulatory bodies, who often work on behalf of users such as taxpayers and donors, in assessing the performance of an entity and its management. In these circumstances the capabilities of users might be determined by reference to the expected capabilities of the intermediary. However, the involvement of intermediaries in reviewing financial statements does not negate the need for a public benefit entity to communicate in an understandable way with other users, particularly its funders and financial supporters.

3.14 If there is to be informed public debate on the information provided by financial statements, then the basis on which it is prepared needs to be sound. Financial information will be more understandable to users if it is prepared on a true and fair basis (the concept of true and fair is discussed in the Statement).

**See also paragraph 3.25.*

Materiality

Materiality is the final test of what information should be given in a particular set of financial statements. The materiality test asks whether the information content is of such significance as to require inclusion in the financial statements. 3.15

When immaterial information is given in the financial statements, the resulting clutter can impair the understandability of the other information provided. In such circumstances, the immaterial information will need to be excluded. 3.16

An item of information is material to the financial statements if its misstatement or omission might reasonably be expected to influence the economic decisions of users of those financial statements, including their assessments of management's stewardship. 3.17

Whether information is material will depend on the size and nature of the item in question judged in the particular circumstances of the case. The principal factors to be taken into account are set out below. It will usually be a combination of these factors, rather than any one in particular, that will determine materiality. 3.18

(a) The item's size is judged in the context both of the financial statements as a whole and of other information available to users.
(b) Consideration is given to the item's nature in relation to:
    (i) the transactions or other events giving rise to it;
    (ii) the legality, sensitivity, normality and potential consequences of the transaction;
    (iii) the identity of the parties involved; and
    (iv) the particular headings and disclosures that are affected.

If there are two or more similar items, the materiality of the items in aggregate as well as of the items individually needs to be considered. 3.19

Constraints on the qualitative characteristics

On occasion, a conflict will arise between the characteristics of relevance, reliability, comparability and understandability. In such circumstances, a trade-off needs to be found that still enables the objective of financial statements to be met. 3.20

Relevance and reliability

Sometimes the information that is the most relevant is not the most reliable and vice versa. Choosing the amount at which to measure an asset or liability will sometimes involve just a conflict. In such circumstances, it will usually be appropriate to use the information that is the most relevant of whichever information is reliable. 3.21

Neutrality and prudence

There can also be tensions between two aspects of reliability – neutrality and prudence – as prudence is a potentially biased concept that seeks to ensure that, under conditions of uncertainty, gains and assets are not overstated and losses and liabilities are not understated. Where there is uncertainty, the competing demands are reconciled by finding a balance that ensures that the deliberate and systematic understatement of gains and assets and overstatement of losses and liabilities does not occur. 3.22

3.23 For public benefit entities there can also be tensions leading to the possibility of gains being understated and losses being overstated, for example where a certain level of spending must be achieved or to avoid the presentation of excessive surpluses.

3.24 As a result, neutrality must be the uppermost objective.

*Understandability**

3.25 It may not always be possible to present information in a way that can be understood by all users. However, information that is relevant and reliable should not be excluded because it is too difficult for some users to understand.

**Understandability is considered in more detail in paragraphs 3.12 to 3.14.*

Chapter 4: the elements of financial statements

Elements of financial statements are the building blocks with which financial statements are constructed – the classes of items that financial statements comprise. This chapter identifies those elements and explains their attributes.

PRINCIPLES

- The elements of the financial statements are:

  (a) assets
  (b) liabilities
  (c) residual interest
  (d) gains
  (e) losses
  (f) contributions establishing a financial interest in the residual interest
  (g) distributions to holders of a financial interest in the residual interest.

- Assets are rights or other access to future economic benefits controlled by an entity as a result of past transactions or events.
- Liabilities are obligations of an entity to transfer economic benefits as a result of past transactions or events.
- Residual interest is the amount found by deducting all of the entity's liabilities from all of the entity's assets*.
- Gains are increases in residual interest not resulting from contributions establishing a financial interest in the residual interest.
- Losses are decreases in residual interest not resulting from distributions to holders of a financial interest in the residual interest.
- Contributions establishing a financial interest in the residual interest are increases in residual interest resulting from transfers from parties that establish a financial interest in that residual interest.
- Distributions to holders of a financial interest in the residual interest are decreases in residual interest resulting from transfers to parties holding a financial interest in that residual interest in their capacity as holders of a financial interest.

EXPLANATION

Other than in relation to the service potential of assets and commitments to provide public benefits, there are few fundamental differences between the principles and explanation relevant to profit-oriented entities, as expressed in Chapter 4 of the Statement, and their interpretation for public benefit entities. Therefore much of what follows is a summary of the discussion in Chapter 4 of the Statement which should be referred to for a full understanding. Additional explanation specific to public benefit entities has been added covering the service potential of assets, control of economic benefits, commitments to provide public benefits, donated goods and services and designation of the residual interest.

The elements of financial statements

Depicting the effects of transactions and other events

Financial statements need to reflect, in an appropriate manner, and as far as possible, the effects of transactions and other events on the reporting entity's financial 4.1

**For profit-oriented entities this would be called the ownership interest.*

performance and financial position. This involves a high degree of classification and aggregation. Order is imposed on this process by specifying and defining the classes of items – the elements of financial statements – that encapsulate the key aspects of the effects of those transactions and other events.

4.2 The elements of financial statements are:

(a) in the case of the balance sheet (or statement of financial position) – assets, liabilities and residual interest;
(b) in the case of the statement of financial performance – gains and losses;
(c) contributions establishing a financial interest in the residual interest; and
(d) distributions to holders of a financial interest in the residual interest.

Recognition

4.3 The criteria that need to be met before the effects of a transaction or other event on the elements will be recognised are considered in Chapter 5.

Assets

Definition

Assets are rights or other access to future economic benefits controlled by an entity as a result of past transactions or events.

Rights or other access

4.4 An asset is not the item of property itself, but rather the rights or other access to some or all of the future economic benefits derived from the item of property*.

4.5 These rights can be obtained in various ways. Often they are obtained by legal ownership of the underlying item of property. However, legal rights to future economic benefit derived from an item of property can be obtained without having legal ownership of the property itself, for example, where property is leased.

4.6 Other legal rights that give rise to assets include the right to require other parties to make payments or render services and the right to use a patent or trademark.

Future economic benefits

4.7 Capacity to obtain future economic benefits is the essence of an asset. Therefore, to be an asset, the rights or other access must be capable, singly or in combination with other assets, of yielding economic benefits.

4.8 Many assets held by public benefit entities do not result in direct cash inflows for the entity. The economic benefits that arise from such assets are often in the form of services to the beneficiary or consumer. Furthermore, in many cases, assets are used to provide goods or services to the beneficiary or customer that are free or subsidised. An item can meet the definition of an asset if it is used either directly or indirectly to provide goods and/or services that are used in furtherance of an entity's objectives.

**The term 'item of property' is taken from the Statement. It is used to differentiate between the control of rights or other access to future economic benefits (the asset) and the thing from which those benefits are derived (the item of property).*

Therefore although the Statement notes that 'future economic benefits eventually result in net cash inflows to the entity,' this may not be the case for public benefit entities where access to future economic benefits includes: 4.9

- an eventual net inflow of cash to the entity; but also
- the provision of goods and/or services to the entity or for the benefit of the entity's beneficiaries.

This means that, for public benefit entities, an asset can embody service potential as well as, or instead of, cash flows. Service potential is the ability to be utilised to provide expected future goods and/or services (i.e. to fulfil a need or want of the identified customers/beneficiaries) in furtherance of the entity's objectives*. 4.10

In principle, all items meeting the definition of an asset should be recognised. These include heritage assets such as: 4.11

- Historic assets: which are of acknowledged historic, scientific or artistic importance, the continuing retention, preservation and use of which is in direct furtherance of an entity's objectives.
- Inalienable assets: which the entity is required by law to retain indefinitely for its own use in furtherance of its objectives and which therefore cannot be disposed of without external consent.

These items meet the definition of an asset because they provide future economic benefits; they are used to provide services to the benefit of the entity's beneficiaries. It is possible that even where, for example, such items are not on display, their preservation alone will meet the asset definition. 4.12

Controlled by the entity

The definition of an asset requires that the rights or other access to future economic benefits are controlled by the reporting entity. Control of economic benefits means the entity must have the ability both to obtain for itself any economic benefits that will arise and to prevent or limit the access of others to those benefits. 4.13

With public benefit entities, the economic benefits that arise from an asset need not flow to the entity itself. As noted above, the assets may instead be used to provide benefits for the beneficiaries of the entity. In the context of such assets, it is therefore the *capacity to provide* future economic benefits that must be controlled by the entity. 4.14

Accordingly, for the purposes of public benefit entities, control of economic benefits is reformulated as follows. An entity will control the rights or other access to future economic benefit if it has the ability: 4.15

- both to obtain for itself any economic benefits that will arise and to prevent or limit the access of others to those benefits; or
- to meet its objectives by determining the allocation to beneficiaries of future economic benefits (whether goods or services), including preventing or limiting the access to any future goods or services to be provided.

Public benefit entities that have custody of an asset may not have all the legal powers of ownership, such as the ability to sell the item. There may also be restrictions on the entity's use of the asset. However, this does not necessarily mean that the entity does not control access to future economic benefits. To satisfy the requirement for 4.16

**Measuring the replacement cost of the service potential of an asset is considered in paragraphs 6.7 to 6.10.*

control, the entity does not need unlimited power over the physical item. Instead, it is the rights or access to future economic benefits that need to be controlled.

4.17 The requirement that the rights or other access should be controlled by the entity treating them as its asset means that a particular right or other access to future economic benefits will appear in only one set of single entity financial statements. This is because such rights or access can be directly controlled by only one entity.

4.18 On the other hand, a single item of property may give rise to assets of more than one entity. If two entities control the rights to different future economic benefits from the same item of property, both entities will have an asset (subject to the other aspects of the definition being met).

Past transactions or events

4.19 If the reporting entity's control of the rights or other access to future economic benefits involved is to represent an asset, it needs to be the result of *past* transactions or events.

Liabilities*

Definition

Liabilities are obligations of an entity to transfer economic benefits as a result of past transactions or events.

Obligations

4.20 For there to be a liability there must be an obligation that might result in the transfer of economic benefits.

4.21 The notion of an obligation implies that the entity is not free to avoid the outflow of economic resources. If an obligation exists, although an entity may offer inducements to its creditors to cancel or postpone settlement, it will not be able to insist that they accept such an offer.

4.22 Although many liabilities are based on legal obligations, a legal obligation is not a *necessary* condition: a liability can exist in the absence of legal obligations if other considerations create a constructive obligation which leaves the entity with little, if any, discretion to avoid the transfer of economic benefits.

4.23 A decision to transfer economic benefits does not, in itself, create a constructive obligation, because the transfer can be avoided by changing the decision. On the other hand, a constructive obligation would be created if such a decision was coupled with an event that both created a valid expectation that the entity involved would implement the decision and meant that the entity could not realistically withdraw from it. For example, a constructive obligation may be created by communicating a decision to follow a particular course of action to another party. Such an obligation may also be created by an established pattern of past practice.

**There is a decision tree for commitments to provide public benefits at Appendix 3.*

Transfer of economic benefits

Certainty that the obligation *will* result in a transfer of economic benefits is not necessary. Obligations that are not likely to result in a transfer of economic benefits – such as a guarantee of another entity's debt where that entity is expected to remain solvent – are liabilities even though they may not be recognised in financial statements (or may be recognised with a carrying amount of nil). **4.24**

Similarly, although many liabilities involve transfers of known amounts of cash, that need not be the case: a liability could involve an obligation to transfer an uncertain amount, and it could involve an obligation to transfer economic benefits other than cash – for example, by providing services. **4.25**

Past transactions or events

For a liability to exist at the balance sheet date, the obligation to transfer economic benefits must have resulted from a *past* transaction or event. **4.26**

Sometimes a series of events must take place before the entity will have an obligation to transfer economic benefits. In such circumstances, whether the obligation exists depends on whether any of the events that have still to take place are under the entity's control. If they are, the entity retains discretion to avoid the transfer, so no obligation exists. For example, as long as it is possible to avoid a penalty clause in a contract by performing, a liability in respect of the penalty will not arise. **4.27**

An obligation to make an exchange in the future, which is still equally unperformed by both sides (often called an executory contract) does not usually result in the immediate recognition of a liability. An example is an order to purchase new office furniture: no liability is recognised by the purchaser until the furniture has been delivered **4.28**

General commitments

A general or policy statement that the entity intends to provide goods and services to certain classes of potential beneficiaries in accordance with its objectives will not necessarily give rise to a liability. Such statements do not of themselves create an obligation such that the entity cannot withdraw or amend the terms on which the goods and services will be provided. Potential beneficiaries of the goods and services may envisage they will receive them, but they do not have the ability to insist on their receipt. **4.29**

Examples of general commitments are political commitments made by governments, for example the announcement of a forthcoming new initiative to provide cash benefits to members of the public. Governments make, and amend, such promises and policies as part of their ongoing political processes to manage the economy and redistribute wealth within or between periods and generations. As such they do not give rise to constructive obligations. Equally a charity would not have a liability as a result of a general policy of providing grants and/or other services to certain classes *of people or entities.* **4.30**

Specific commitments

Where an entity has made a specific commitment that it will provide funding to another party, consideration of whether a liability exists depends on whether: **4.31**

(a) the obligation is such that the entity cannot realistically withdraw from it;
(b) the commitment has been communicated to the other party; and
(c) the commitment is performance-related.

4.32 A performance-related grant has the characteristics of a contract in that the terms of the grant require the performance of a specified service with payment being conditional on the service being provided. If the undertaking to pay is, in substance, performance-related, no liability would arise in advance of performance. Examples of such arrangements include a five-year grant to finance a meals-on-wheels service, where the amount is calculated based on the number of meals served.

4.33 Where there are service or performance conditions attached to a grant but they are insignificant in the context of the arrangement, the substance of the arrangement will be that it is not performance-related.

4.34 Where an entity has made a commitment that results in an obligation to transfer economic benefits and it is not performance-related, the financial consequences of that commitment will amount to a liability at the time the commitment is made.

Other matters

4.35 Where an entity has potential obligations that do not result in the recognition of liabilities it is appropriate to consider whether the disclosure of information relating to these potential obligations should be provided.

4.36 There may be circumstances in which a reporting entity is acting as an agent for another entity, where, for example, cash has been received by the entity to be passed on to persons meeting certain specific criteria specified by the other entity. Depending on the nature of the arrangement it is possible that a liability should be recognised to match the receipt of the cash prior to its dispersal. Such a liability would represent an obligation to the entity providing the cash, not to the ultimate recipient.

Offsetting rights and obligations

4.37 When a transaction or other event gives rise to a number of rights and obligations, it is necessary to consider whether some or all of those rights and obligations need to be offset either with each other or with rights and obligations that arise from other transactions or events.

4.38 If a right to receive future economic benefits and an obligation to transfer future economic benefits exists, and the reporting entity has the ability – which is assured – to insist on net settlement of the balances, the right and obligation together form a single asset or liability regardless of how the parties intend to settle the balances.

4.39 When an entity enters into an agreement with another, it usually obtains certain rights and, in exchange, accepts certain obligations. Before any act of performance under the agreement has taken place, the entity does not have control of the future economic benefits arising from performance, nor does it have an obligation to transfer economic benefits that arise on performance. What it *does* have, however, is a contract that represents a net position comprising a combined right and obligation either to participate in the exchange or alternatively to be compensated (or to compensate) for the consequences of the exchange not taking place. Initially, the rights and obligations are likely to be exactly offsetting, although that will often not remain the case. The rights and obligations arising under such unperformed executory contracts together represent a single asset or liability. Consistently with the discussion of restrictions in Chapter 5, the receipt of resources with restrictions attached does not usually delay their recognition as an asset and a gain.

It may be that the contract has been performed partially but is equally proportionately unperformed – in other words, that both parties to the contract have still to perform to an equal degree the actions promised by and required of them under the contract. In such a case, although the rights and obligations relating to the performed part of the contract may represent separate assets and liabilities, the rights and obligations relating to the unperformed part will together represent a single asset or liability. **4.40**

Residual interest

Residual interest is defined as follows: **4.41**

Residual interest is the amount found by deducting all of the entity's liabilities from all of the entity's assets.

The distinction between liabilities and residual interest is significant. Creditors have the ability to insist that a transfer of economic benefits is made to them regardless of the circumstances. In contrast, the residual interest represents resources that the entity retains for the provision of future benefits. In certain forms of entity, these resources may be held under trust, either to be retained for the generation of future income, or to be spent on particular restricted purposes. The nature of the residual interest should be clear from disclosure in the financial statements. Where, in the event of a winding-up, the ultimate interest would be required to be distributed in a particular way, that fact should be disclosed. **4.42**

In some cases, there may be more than one class of residual interest. The existence of different classes of residual interests requires disclosure within the financial statements. **4.43**

Where resources are held on trust for a particular purpose, this creates a separate class of residual interest in the balance sheet. Designation, reflecting no more than management intention, does not create a separate class of residual interest and should not lead to the recognition of a transaction in the financial statements. Such information could be disclosed in the notes to the accounts but would more normally be provided in the accompanying information (see paragraphs 7.15 to 7.20). **4.44**

Gains and losses

Definitions

Gains are increases in residual interest not resulting from contributions establishing a financial interest in the residual interest.

Losses are decreases in residual interest not resulting from distributions to holders of a financial interest in the residual interest.

The terms 'gains' and 'losses' therefore include items that are often referred to as 'revenue' or 'income' and 'expenses'. **4.45**

Chapter 5 provides guidance on the recognition process for transactions and events that have an effect on the financial statements. If neither a transaction nor an event **4.46** has occurred, there will be no change in the reporting entity's assets and liabilities and, consequently, no gain or loss to recognise.

Donated goods and services

4.47 Some public benefit entities receive donations of goods* or services.

4.48 Where a donation involves the receipt of cash or goods (for example works of art or furniture), it should be recognised based on the current value to the recipient (measures of current value are discussed in Chapter 6), provided it can be measured with sufficient reliability.

4.49 In contrast other donations involve the receipt of services that are immediately consumed (for example, volunteers' time, free occupation of premises and free professional services); these are events that potentially have an economic effect on the reporting entity. In principle, because such an event has an economic impact on a reporting entity it should be reflected in the financial statements. In practice, however, it may not be possible to measure some services with sufficient reliability for the financial statements and these services should not therefore be recognised.

4.50 Provided they can be reliably measured, donated services that would normally have otherwise been purchased should be recognised in the financial statements based on the estimated value to the recipient. Where donated services are recognised in the financial statements it would be as income and, usually, expenditure of an equal amount.

4.51 Where donated services are not recognised in the financial statements but disclosure of the nature and scale of the services received would help the user gain a better understanding of the entity's activities, this information could be disclosed in the notes to the accounts although, it will often be more practicable and appropriate for it to be provided in the accompanying information.

Contributions establishing a financial interest in the residual interest

Definition

Contributions establishing a financial interest in the residual interest (capital contributions†) are increases in residual interest resulting from transfers from parties that establish a financial interest in that residual interest.

4.52 Capital contributions include only those transactions that establish a financial interest in the residual interest. Transactions with the same parties that are not entered into in this capacity (for example those as customers, beneficiaries, donors or suppliers) result in gains and losses.

4.53 A financial interest in the residual interest is one that conveys a right to participate in the residual interest (either on an ongoing basis or in a winding-up).

4.54 Capital contributions involve parties making a contribution of economic benefits (which may, for example, be in the form of cash or assets providing service potential) to the entity. In practice, for public benefit entities, although capital contributions

**For this purpose 'goods' includes cash and financial instruments.*

†Here 'capital contribution' does not necessarily refer to the gift of an endowment.

establish a financial interest in the net assets of the entity, it may be that the contribution enables the entity to keep operating. The contribution may also have the effect of reducing the level of a potential future deficit to be met in the event of the entity being wound-up.

Some public benefit entities have a controlling party* (for example, as a result of powers to appoint the members of its governing body), although the controlling party may not be a legal 'owner' of the reporting entity. Contributions from a controlling party may or may not include capital contributions. However, due to the nature of the relationship between an entity and its controlling party the impact on the financial performance and financial position of a public benefit entity of any resources received that are not capital contributions should be clear. **4.55**

Distributions to holders of a financial interest in the residual interest

Definition

Distributions to holders of a financial interest in the residual interest (capital distributions) are decreases in residual interest resulting from transfers to parties holding a financial interest in that residual interest in their capacity as holders of a financial interest.

The Statement includes 'distributions to owners' as one of the elements of the financial statements. As noted above, most public benefit entities do not have owners, and those that do are often unable to make distributions (for example, it may be prohibited by the governing instrument). As a result, capital distributions are not likely to be common. **4.56**

Capital distributions include the payment of dividends and the return of capital. Where public benefit entities make capital distributions, achieving this financial return would not be their primary objective. **4.57**

**Consistent with Chapter 2, a controlling party is an individual or entity that has control of a second entity.*

Chapter 5: recognition in financial statements

When the reporting entity undertakes a transaction or when some other relevant event occurs, the effect of that transaction or event on the elements of financial statements will need to be recognised in the financial statements if certain criteria are met. This chapter considers that recognition process.

PRINCIPLES

- If a transaction or other event has created a new asset or liability or added to an existing asset or liability, that effect will be recognised if:

  (a) sufficient evidence exists that the new asset or liability has been created or that there has been an addition to an existing asset or liability; and
  (b) the new asset or liability or the addition to the existing asset or liability can be measured at a monetary amount with sufficient reliability.

- In a transaction involving the provision of goods or services for a net gain, the recognition criteria described above will be met on the occurrence of the critical event in the operating cycle involved.
- In a transaction involving the receipt of resources, other than for the provision of goods or services for a net gain, the recognition criteria described above will often be met when there is clear evidence of a right to receive the resources.
- An asset or liability will be wholly or partly derecognised if:

  (a) sufficient evidence exists that a transaction or other past event has eliminated all or part of a previously recognised asset or liability; or
  (b) although the item continues to be an asset or a liability, the criteria for recognition are no longer met.

EXPLANATION

Other than in relation to revenue recognition, there are few fundamental differences between the principles and explanation relevant to profit-oriented entities, as expressed in Chapter 5 of the Statement and their interpretation for public benefit entities. Therefore much of what follows is a summary of the discussion in Chapter 5 of the Statement, which should be referred to for a full understanding.

Additional explanation specific to public benefit entities has been added covering historic and inalienable assets and the various aspects of revenue recognition.

The recognition process

The stages of the recognition process

5.1 The objective of financial statements is achieved to a large extent through the recognition of elements in the primary financial statements – in other words, the depiction of elements both in words and by monetary amounts and the inclusion of those amounts in the primary financial statement totals. This recognition process has the following stages:

(a) initial recognition, which is where an item is depicted in the primary financial statements for the first time;
(b) subsequent remeasurement, which involves changing the amount at which an already recognised asset or liability is stated in the primary financial statements; and

(c) derecognition, which is where an item that was until then recognised ceases to be recognised.

Transactions and events other than transactions

The recognition process requires that all events that may have an effect on elements of the financial statements are, as far as is possible, identified and reflected in an appropriate manner in the financial statements. **5.2**

Transactions are the most common form of such events and are therefore the most common reason for recognising and derecognising items. Events other than transactions may nevertheless also result in the recognition or derecognition of items. For example, events such as discovery or innovation may result in the creation of new assets that may meet the recognition criteria. Events, such as a fire, that cause damage to an asset may result in a need to derecognise the asset or liability involved. **5.3**

The effect of transactions and other events

The starting point for the recognition process is the effect that the transaction or other event involved has had on the reporting entity's assets and liabilities. The interrelationship between the elements means that the recognition of one item as an element will inevitably result in the recognition of, or change in, another element. Thus, if a new asset is recognised, there will also be recognised a decrease in another asset, a new or increased liability, a gain, or a contribution from owners (or a combination of these). **5.4**

A transaction or other event could have one of several effects on a reporting entity's assets and liabilities. **5.5**

(a) It might create a new asset or liability or add to an existing asset or liability. When this is the case, it will be necessary to determine whether the new asset or liability (or the addition thereto) should be recognised, because not all assets and liabilities are recognised.
(b) It might provide additional evidence about an existing but unrecognised asset or liability and, as a result, enable that item to be recognised.
(c) It might change some aspect of an already recognised asset or liability.
(d) It might involve transferring, using up or consuming an asset or settling, extinguishing or transferring a liability. On the other hand, it might leave intact certain of the rights to future economic benefits inherent in an asset whilst transferring, using up or consuming others, or it might leave intact certain obligations inherent in a liability whilst settling, extinguishing or transferring others.

The non-cash effects of transactions and other events should, as far as is possible, be reflected in the financial statements in the accounting period in which they occur and not, for example, in the period in which any cash involved is received or paid. This is commonly referred to as the 'accruals concept'. **5.6**

Uncertainty and the recognition process

Entities operate in an uncertain environment and this uncertainty may sometimes make it necessary to delay the recognition process. **5.7**

If uncertainty exists, totally reliable information will become available only when the uncertainty has resolved itself. However, to defer recognition until the uncertainty **5.8** has resolved itself will often reduce the relevance of the financial statements. It may also reduce their reliability because they will not represent faithfully the transactions and other events of the reporting period. Financial statements achieve a balance between these competing demands by seeking to provide information that has no more than an acceptable degree of uncertainty but not seeking to provide information that is totally free from uncertainty.

5.9 There may be circumstances in which it is not possible to reduce the uncertainty to an acceptable level. If that is the case, the recognition process will be deferred until such time as the uncertainty has been reduced to an acceptable level (and the effect of the transaction or other event will instead usually be reported in the notes to the financial statements).

Initial recognition

Categories of uncertainty

5.10 In the initial recognition process, there are two broad categories of uncertainty that could arise:

(a) element uncertainty, which involves uncertainty whether an item exists and meets the definitions of the elements of financial statements; and

(b) measurement uncertainty, which concerns the appropriate monetary amount at which to recognise the item.

Element uncertainty

5.11 Element uncertainty is countered by evidence – the more evidence there is about an item and the better the quality of that evidence, the less uncertainty there will be over the item's existence and nature. To recognise an item it is necessary to have sufficient evidence, both in amount and quality, that the item exists and is an asset or liability of the reporting entity. One of the criteria for initial recognition is that sufficient evidence must exist that a new asset or liability has been created.

5.12 What constitutes sufficient evidence is a matter of judgement, although while the evidence needs to be adequate, it need not be (and often cannot be) conclusive. The main source of evidence will be past or present experience with the item itself or with similar items.

Measurement uncertainty

5.13 To recognise an item, it is necessary to attribute a monetary amount to it. This involves two steps: selecting a suitable measurement basis (i.e. historical cost or current value) for the item and determining an appropriate monetary amount for the basis chosen.

5.14 Uncertainty about the appropriate monetary amount at which to recognise the item (in other words, measurement uncertainty) is reflected in the second of the criteria for initial recognition, which requires that the new asset or liability or addition to an existing asset or liability can be measured at a monetary amount with sufficient reliability.

The purchase or receipt of an asset should be measured and included in the financial statements, provided it can be measured reliably. Thus where an historic or inalienable asset* is received, it should, in principle, be reflected in the financial statements. In some cases, sufficiently reliable information may not exist, but for assets that are newly acquired, reliable measurement information is likely to be available. **5.15**

Prudence

The exercise of prudence does not justify the omission of assets or gains when there is sufficient evidence of occurrence and reliability of measurement or the inclusion of liabilities or losses when there is not. Nor does it justify any other deliberate and systematic overstatement of liabilities or losses or deliberate and systematic understatement of assets or gains. **5.16**

Derecognition

Derecognition because the asset or liability has been eliminated

Assets tend, in due course, to be consumed, transferred or otherwise disposed of, or they expire. Similarly, liabilities tend to be settled, extinguished, transferred, or they expire. In such circumstances, it may be necessary to derecognise some or all of the asset or liability involved. **5.17**

It is usually relatively simple to determine whether and when a previously recognised asset or liability needs to be derecognised. However, some transactions leave intact certain of the rights to future benefits inherent in an asset (or obligations inherent in a liability) while eliminating others. In such circumstances, analysis is required to ascertain whether the effect of the transaction should be reflected by derecognising some or all of the assets and liabilities involved. **5.18**

Ideally, an asset or liability would be derecognised as soon as it has been eliminated. However, there will sometimes be uncertainty about an item's continued existence. In such circumstances, derecognition will not take place until sufficient evidence exists that the transaction or other event has resulted in the elimination of the item. When there is uncertainty, prudence usually requires more confirmatory evidence about the existence of, and a greater reliability of measurement for, assets than is required for liabilities. This tends to mean that, if there is any significant uncertainty about an asset's continued existence, it will be derecognised. However, in the case of a liability, more evidence of its elimination will be needed before it will be derecognised. **5.19**

Derecognition because the criteria for recognition are no longer met

It is possible that although there has been no significant change in the inherent nature of an already recognised asset or liability – in other words, although the asset or liability has not been eliminated – the criteria for recognition are no longer met. For example, an event may have created additional uncertainty and, as a result, a previously recognised asset or liability can no longer be measured with sufficient reliability. On the rare occasions when this is the case, that asset or liability will be derecognised even though it has not been eliminated. **5.20**

See also paragraphs 4.11 and 4.12.

Revenue recognition

5.21 Assuming that no capital contribution is involved:

(a) if the effect of a transaction or other event is to increase the entity's recognised net assets, a gain will be recognised.

(b) a loss will be recognised if, and to the extent that, previously recognised assets have been reduced or eliminated or cease to qualify for recognition as assets without a commensurate increase in other assets or reduction in liabilities. Similarly, a loss will be recognised when, and to the extent that, a liability is incurred or increased without a commensurate increase in recognised assets or a reduction in other liabilities.

5.22 However, although the starting point for the recognition process may be the effect on assets and liabilities, the notions of matching and the critical event in the operating cycle will often help in identifying these effects.

Matching

5.23 Matching has two forms.

(a) Time matching involves the recognition of receipts (and payments) directly associated with the passage of time as gains (and losses) on a systematic basis over the course of the period involved.

(b) Revenue/expenditure matching involves the recognition of expenditure directly associated with the generation of specific gains as a loss in the same period as the gains are recognised, rather than in the period in which the expenditure is incurred.

5.24 Almost all expenditure is undertaken with a view to acquiring some form of benefit in exchange. Consequently, if matching were used in an unrestricted way, it would be possible to delay the recognition in the performance statement of most items of expenditure insofar as the hoped-for benefits still lay in the future. The Statement imposes a degree of discipline on this process because only items that meet the definitions of, and relevant recognition criteria for, assets, liabilities or ownership interest (or residual interest for public benefit entities) are recognised in the balance sheet. This means that the Statement does not use the notion of matching as the main driver of the recognition process.

Critical event in the operating cycle

5.25 Sometimes it is easier to identify the appropriate point at which to recognise gains arising from the provision of services or goods – and therefore changes to the entity's assets and liabilities – by focusing on the operating cycle of the reporting entity and, in particular, on the critical event in that cycle.

5.26 The critical event is the point in an operating cycle at which there will usually be sufficient evidence that the gain exists and it will usually be possible to measure that gain with sufficient reliability.

5.27 For many types of transaction, the critical event in the operating cycle is synonymous with full performance. In such cases a gain will be recognised when the entity providing the service or goods has fully performed. That need not, however, be the case: the critical event could occur at other times in the cycle and there could be more than one critical event in the cycle.

The identity of the critical event or events of an operating cycle will depend on the particular circumstances involved. For certain public benefit entities the concept of the critical event has direct application to revenue arising from fees and charges and performance-related grants*. However, for other sources of revenue, such as taxation and donations, gains may occur that are unrelated to the provision of specific goods or services. There may therefore not be a need to look for a critical event in the operating cycle as part of the recognition process. Instead, the focus will be on whether an asset exists and whether or not it has led to a corresponding liability. As such the recognition criteria are likely to be met when the recipient has a right to receive the resources (in some cases this will not be prior to actual receipt of the resources). **5.28**

Should all gains be treated as revenue?

Fees and charges and performance-related grants that arise as a result of a critical event in the operating cycle of the entity should be classified as revenue. In this context revenue should be taken to mean 'turnover', or the revenue arising from the operating activities of the reporting entity. **5.29**

Gains† that arise, for example, from the raising of taxes, or through an appropriation or grant-in-aid, or donations, should also be classified as revenue, and be recognised when there is sufficient evidence that a gain exists and it can be measured with sufficient reliability. **5.30**

Other gains, such as those arising from the sale of fixed assets, do not normally give rise to revenue. **5.31**

Grants for financing capital projects

Some public benefit entities receive grants or donations intended to finance capital projects, such as the acquisition or construction of a fixed asset. Grants or donations for financing capital projects are often made because the asset will be used to provide goods or services that are provided at a subsidised rate or for free. Providing a subsidy for an asset that provides a service can be an alternative to an ongoing commitment to subsidise the revenue costs of providing the service. **5.32**

Transactions that establish an interest in the residual interest of an entity should be treated as capital contributions (even if that contribution is subsequently used to acquire a capital asset) and not as grants or donations. **5.33**

Conditions and restrictions attached to grants and donations

Grants and donations should be recognised as a gain unless there are conditions, in which case they should be recognised when any conditions are substantially met or are virtually certain to be met. For example, if the only condition attached to a grant is that the recipient must provide a copy of its annual report to the grantor, it would be appropriate to recognise the grant as a gain on receipt. **5.34**

**'Performance-related grants' is used in this context to refer to a grant that has the characteristics of a contract, where a specified amount of grant is receivable for a specific output.*

†*In accordance with the definition, gains exclude capital contributions.*

5.35 Where there are no conditions attached, the grant or donation should be recognised as a gain. In some cases, the conditions of the agreement are such that it amounts to a performance-related grant. Where this is the case, gains should usually be recognised as performance is delivered.

5.36 One common condition of capital grants to public benefit entities is that the grant must be repaid in the event of the recipient subsequently selling the asset. Where a decision on the sale of the asset is within the reporting entity's control, there is no liability and the grant should be recognised as a gain notwithstanding this condition.

5.37 Where grants and donations are subject to restrictions that limit their use, these restrictions do not affect the recognition of the asset or the grant. Restrictions should not therefore prevent recognition as a gain providing all conditions have been substantially met or are virtually certain to be met. Additional disclosure may be required to reflect the nature of any restrictions.

Chapter 6: measurement in financial statements

Measuring an asset or liability entails deciding on the measurement basis to be used and determining the monetary amount that is appropriate for that basis. It may also involve revising the monetary amount when certain events occur. This chapter describes the measurement process and explains how a choice is made between the measurement bases available.

PRINCIPLES

- In drawing up financial statements, a measurement basis – either historical cost or current value – needs to be selected for each category of assets or liabilities. The basis selected will be the one that best meets the objective of financial statements and the demands of the qualitative characteristics of financial information, bearing in mind the nature of the assets or liabilities concerned and the circumstances involved.
- An asset or liability being measured using the historical cost basis is recognised initially at transaction cost. An asset or liability being measured using the current value basis is recognised initially at its current value at the time it was acquired or assumed.
- Subsequent remeasurement will occur if it is necessary to ensure that:
  - (a) assets measured at historical cost are carried at the lower of cost and recoverable amount;
  - (b) monetary items denominated in foreign currency are carried at amounts based on up-to-date exchange rates; and
  - (c) assets and liabilities measured on the current value basis are carried at up-to-date current values.
- Such remeasurements, however, will be recognised only if:
  - (a) there is sufficient evidence that the monetary amount of the asset or liability has changed; and
  - (b) the new amount of the asset or liability can be measured with sufficient reliability.

EXPLANATION

There are few fundamental differences between the principles and explanation relevant to profit-oriented entities, as expressed in Chapter 6 of the Statement and their interpretation for public benefit entities. Therefore much of what follows is a summary of the discussion in Chapter 6 of the Statement, which should be referred to for a full understanding. Additional explanation specific to public benefit entities has been added covering alternative measures of current value.

Alternative bases of measurement

Assets and liabilities have several different monetary attributes that could be represented in financial statements. The single most important characteristic that distinguishes these monetary attributes (which are known as measurement bases) is whether they are based on historical cost or current value. This chapter concentrates on that distinction. **6.1**

The mixed measurement system permits the measurement basis to be selected separately for each category of assets or liabilities. It also permits the use of historical cost (or current value) for all assets and liabilities if historical cost (or current value) **6.2** is the most appropriate measure for each of those categories. Thus it can be adapted to fit the particular circumstances involved.

6.3 The Statement therefore envisages that the mixed measurement system will be used and it focuses on the mix of historical cost and current value to be adopted.

Alternative measures of current value

6.4 The current value of an asset could be determined by reference to entry value (replacement cost), exit value (net realisable value) or value in use (discounted present value of the cash flows expected from continuing use and ultimate sale by the present owner). For some assets, for example fixed assets specific to the entity's activities, differences between the alternative measures can be material.

Selection of a measure of current value

6.5 It is necessary to select from these alternative measures of current value the measure that maximises the relevance of the current value basis. Current value is at its most relevant when it reflects the loss that the entity would suffer if it were deprived of the asset involved. That measure, which is often referred to as the 'deprival value' or the 'value to the business', will depend on the circumstances.

(a) In most cases, the public benefit entity will be fully using the asset in order to further its objectives and therefore the entity will, if deprived of the asset, replace it, and the current value of the asset will be its current replacement cost.

(b) An asset will not be worth replacing if the cost of replacing it exceeds its recoverable amount. In such circumstances, the asset's current value is that recoverable amount. This will be either net realisable value or value in use, depending on the circumstances.

  (i) When the entity would further its objectives to the greatest extent by selling the asset, the asset's recoverable amount will be the amount that can be obtained by selling it, net of selling expenses; in other words, its net realisable value.

  (ii) When the entity would further its objectives to the greatest extent by consuming the asset – for example by continuing to operate it – its recoverable amount will be its value in use.

6.6 Many public benefit entities have assets that are specialised in nature, where there may be no viable market for the asset's sale. As a result, assets are infrequently valued on the basis of net realisable value because it is often difficult to estimate as a result of the lack of an active market.

Current values reflecting the service potential of an asset

6.7 Service potential was defined in paragraph 4.10. In the public sector, value in use may be difficult to calculate in practice. Many assets do not generate cash flows at a market rate because they are involved in the production of goods and services that are provided at a subsidised rate or for free. In such cases, assets should be stated at the replacement cost of the asset's service potential.

6.8 It is important that valuations properly reflect the asset's value to the entity and that reviews of asset values are carried out where there is evidence of impairment of service potential or, where relevant, cash flows. Such reviews should consider both the capacity of the asset to deliver services and the demand for these services and should be carried out regardless of how an asset is funded or whether the cost or valuation method has been used.

For example, if a hostel had been constructed to provide accommodation for fifty people, the fact that occupants are not charged a commercial rent would not in itself necessarily lead to an impairment. However, if at a later date it became clear that, because of changes in demographics, the hostel would in the future be occupied by no more than thirty people, even at periods of peak demand, then the capacity to deliver service potential would be diminished and the valuation of the hostel should be reviewed for impairment. This review might involve consideration of the replacement cost of a thirty-bed hostel. **6.9**

Since current value under this model represents the loss the entity would suffer if it were deprived of an asset, consideration needs to be given to the most efficient method of obtaining equivalent services to those derived from using the asset. If, for example, it is considered that the most efficient method, at present, would be to engage an external contractor rather than obtaining the services directly by using the asset owned by the reporting entity, then the asset's current value will be the higher of its net realisable value and the present value of the cash flows that would be incurred in obtaining equivalent services from the external contractor. **6.10**

Current value of liabilities

It is possible to select a current value for a liability in a similar manner to the 'deprival value' or 'value to the business' method used for assets (using the concept of 'relief value'). The relief value of a liability is the lowest amount at which the entity could divest itself of the obligation involved – in other words, the lowest amount at which the liability could, hypothetically, be settled*. **6.11**

The measurement process

It is not the function of financial statements to represent directly the total value that the reporting entity would fetch in an exchange transaction. Instead, the financial statements provide information designed to assist users to make judgements about the entity's financial performance and financial position. The purpose of the measurement process is therefore to measure the effects of the transactions and events of the period on the financial performance and financial position of the entity. **6.12**

Initial recognition

An asset or liability that is being measured using the historical cost basis will be recognised initially at transaction cost or, if an event other than a transaction is involved, at its fair value† at the time it was acquired or assumed. **6.13**

An asset or liability that is being measured using the current value basis will be recognised initially at its current value at the time it was acquired or assumed. **6.14**

**In October 2002 the ASB published 'Liabilities and how to account for them: an exploratory essay', which suggests that this definition could be expanded to be the higher of consideration and settlement amount (being the lower of the cost of performance and the cost of release).*

†The term 'fair value' has been repeated from the Statement and may not therefore reflect the sense in which it has been used in more recent work by standard setters.

6.15 This means that, regardless of the measurement basis used, assets and liabilities that arise from transactions carried out at fair value – which is the vast majority of assets and liabilities – will be measured on initial recognition at their transaction cost. That is because, in the case of such a transaction, the fair value of the consideration paid or received (i.e. the transaction cost) is equal to the current value of the asset or liability at the time of acquisition.

6.16 It can generally be assumed that, in the absence of evidence to the contrary, a transaction has been carried out at fair value. In such circumstances, the transaction cost involved can be determined by reference to the fair value of either the asset (or liability) acquired or the consideration paid (or received); whichever fair value is easiest to measure will usually be used.

6.17 If an asset or liability arises from a transaction that was not carried out at fair value, it will often be more appropriate to measure the asset or liability at current value rather than historical cost. For example, an asset might be received as a gift or donation, in which case it should be recognised at its current value to the entity on the date it is received. As discussed in paragraphs 6.5 and 6.7 to 6.9, the current value is likely to be the replacement cost of the service potential of the asset, which will reflect its expected utilisation.

Subsequent remeasurement

6.18 If a pure historical cost measurement basis is being used, the carrying amount of an asset or liability will always be the amount at which it was initially recognised; in other words, there is no subsequent remeasurement stage. The carrying amount of an asset or liability measured at historical cost may nevertheless need to be changed so that the item remains at cost. For example, in the case of assets that are consumed over more than one accounting period (such as fixed assets), the amount at which the asset was recognised initially will be reduced over the expected life of the asset so as to allocate the asset's cost over its expected life. These adjustments are not re-measurements; they are adjustments to maintain the carrying amount at an amount based on historical cost.

6.19 In practice, however, this 'pure historical cost basis' is rarely used. Instead, to make historical cost more relevant to the needs of users, a variation is used that involves a limited amount of remeasurement. The purpose of this remeasurement is to ensure that:

(a) assets are not reported at amounts greater than their recoverable amount*; and
(b) monetary assets and liabilities denominated in currencies other than the reporting currency are stated at an amount that is based on up-to-date exchange rates.

6.20 When the current value basis of measurement is being used, remeasurement takes place to ensure that the assets or liabilities involved are measured at an up-to-date current value. Such remeasurements will, however, be recognised in the financial statements only if:

(a) there is sufficient evidence that the amount of the asset or liability has changed; and
(b) the new amount of the asset or liability is capable of being measured with sufficient reliability.

**Recoverable amount might be determined by reference to the asset's service potential.*

What constitutes sufficient evidence is a matter of judgement in the particular circumstances, although whilst the evidence will need to be adequate, it need not be conclusive. Relevant considerations will include its persuasiveness and whether the change implies that a gain or loss has occurred. **6.21**

The issues to be considered in deciding whether the new amount of the asset or liability is capable of being measured with sufficient reliability are identical to the reliability of measurement issues considered in the context of initial recognition. **6.22**

Choosing a measurement basis and deciding whether to change it

In choosing the measurement basis to be used for a particular category of assets or liabilities, the aim is to select the basis that is most appropriate bearing in mind: **6.23**

(a) the objective of financial statements and the qualitative characteristics of financial information, in particular relevance and reliability;
(b) the nature of the assets or liabilities concerned; and
(c) the particular circumstances involved.

Although these factors may not change, the measurement basis that best meets them may. For example, measurement bases that were once thought unreliable may become reliable. **6.24**

Measurement issues

Going concern

Financial statements are usually prepared – and measures are usually arrived at – on the basis that the reporting entity is a going concern because measures based on break-up values tend not to be relevant to users seeking to assess the entity's financial performance. **6.25**

Discounting

Historical cost and replacement cost are both market prices and will therefore generally take into account the time value of money and the risk associated with the future expected cash flows. **6.26**

To be consistent, these factors need also to be reflected in the other measures that can be used to determine the carrying amount of assets (in other words, value in use and net realisable value) and the carrying amount of any liabilities measured by reference to expected future cash flows. It follows that, when basing carrying amounts on future cash flows, those cash flows will need to be discounted. **6.27**

The discount rate used will reflect the risks associated with the future expected cash flows involved (unless those future expected cash flows are already risk-adjusted) and the time value of money. As such it will reflect the risks specific to the item being measured but not the more general risks of the entity as a whole. **6.28**

Arriving at a measure in the face of uncertainty

If uncertainty exists, the only way to determine an appropriate monetary amount for the asset or liability is through the use of estimates. As long as a generally accepted estimation method is used and the measure is supported by a reasonable amount of confirmatory evidence – prudence requires a greater reliability of measurement for **6.29** assets (and gains) than for liabilities (and losses) – the use of estimates is acceptable and will not prevent the measure from being sufficiently reliable to be used in the financial statements.

6.30 If the monetary amount at which an asset or liability is recognised is subject to significant uncertainty, the degree of uncertainty surrounding the estimate will usually be disclosed in order to avoid the impression that the outcome is certain. Such a disclosure might provide details of the significant assumptions and measurement basis used, the range of possible outcomes, and the principal factors that affect the outcome.

Capital maintenance adjustments and changing prices

6.31 General price changes can affect the significance of reported surpluses/deficits and of residual interest. If this problem is acute, an approach will need to be adopted that involves recognising surpluses/deficits only after adjustments have been made to maintain the purchasing power of the entity's financial capital.

6.32 Specific price changes can affect the significance of reported surpluses/deficits and financial position. If the problem is acute, it will be necessary to adopt a system of accounting that informs the user of the significance of specific price changes for the entity's financial performance and financial position.

Chapter 7: presentation of financial information

Good presentation ensures that the essential messages of the financial statements are communicated clearly and effectively and in as simple and straightforward a manner as possible. This chapter explains what good presentation entails. It also considers the information that often accompanies financial statements and explains some of the roles fulfilled by such information.

PRINCIPLES

- Financial statements comprise primary financial statements and supporting notes that amplify and explain the primary financial statements. The primary financial statements themselves comprise the statement of financial performance*, the statement of financial position or balance sheet, and the cash flow statement.
- The presentation of information on financial performance focuses on the components of that performance and on the characteristics of those components.
- The presentation of information on financial position focuses on the types and functions of assets and liabilities held and on the relationships between them.
- The presentation of cash flow information will show the extent to which the entity's various activities generate and use cash, and will distinguish in particular between those cash flows that result from operations and those that result from other activities.
- Disclosure of information in the notes to the financial statements is not a substitute for recognition and does not correct or justify any misrepresentation or omission in the primary financial statements.

EXPLANATION

There are few fundamental differences between the principles and explanation relevant to profit-oriented entities, as expressed in Chapter 7 of the Statement and their interpretation for public benefit entities. Therefore much of what follows is a summary of the discussion in Chapter 7 of the Statement, which should be referred to for a full understanding. Additional explanation specific to public benefit entities has been added covering presentation in the balance sheet and accompanying information.

Presentation of information in financial statements

Clear, effective and simple communication

As financial statements are a means of communication, the objective of the presentation adopted is to communicate clearly and effectively and in as simple and straightforward a manner as is possible without loss of relevance or reliability and without unnecessarily increasing the length of the financial statements. **7.1**

Highly structured and aggregated

The presentation of information in financial statements involves a high degree of interpretation, simplification, abstraction and aggregation – in other words, a loss of detailed information. Nevertheless, if this process is carried out in an orderly manner, greater knowledge will result because such a presentation will: **7.2**

**Although many entities in the UK and the Republic of Ireland at present prepare two statements of financial performance, the number of statements prepared is a matter of convention and legal requirement; no significant financial reporting principle is involved. For simplicity, however, the Statement generally refers to 'the statement of financial performance'.*

(a) convey information that would otherwise have been obscured;
(b) highlight those items, and relationships between items, that are generally of most significance;
(c) facilitate comparability between different entities' financial statements; and
(d) be more understandable to users.

7.3 The primary focus of the financial statements of public benefit entities is to provide information to assist with accountability for the efficient and effective use of funds. This focus is met through a set of interrelated reports (known as the primary financial statements) on:

(a) financial performance (the operating cost statement and the statement of total recognised gains and losses are examples of financial performance statements);
(b) financial position (the balance sheet); and
(c) cash inflows and outflows (the cash flow statement),

and a series of supporting disclosures (the notes to the financial statements).

7.4 The notes and primary financial statements form an integrated whole, with the notes amplifying and explaining the statements by, for example, providing:

(a) more detailed information on items recognised in the primary financial statements;
(b) context for, or an alternative view of, items recognised in the primary financial statements; and
(c) relevant information that it is not practicable to incorporate in the primary financial statements, for example because of pervasive uncertainty.

7.5 The notes to the financial statements therefore represent a very important part of the overall information package. Nevertheless, disclosure of information in the notes is not a substitute for recognition and does not correct or justify any misrepresentation in or omission from the primary financial statements.

Classification

7.6 To facilitate the analysis of the information provided, items that are similar are presented together in the financial statements and distinguished from dissimilar items.

Good presentation

Statement of financial performance

7.7 The financial performance of a reporting entity is made up of components that exhibit differing characteristics in terms of, for example, nature, cause, function, relative continuity or recurrence, stability, risk, predictability and reliability. Information on financial performance needs to be presented in a way that focuses attention on these components and on their key characteristics.

7.8 Good presentation of financial performance information typically involves:

(a) recognising only gains and losses in the statement of financial performance;
(b) classifying components by reference to a combination of function (such as administrative) and of the nature of the item (such as employment costs);

(c) distinguishing amounts that are affected in different ways by changes in economic conditions or business activity (for example, by providing segmental information); and
(d) identifying separately:
- items that are unusual in amount or incidence judged by the experience of previous periods or expectations of the future;
- items that have special characteristics, such as financing costs and taxation; and
- items that are related primarily to the results of the future, rather than current, accounting periods, such as some research and development expenditure.

Gains and losses are generally not offset in presenting information on financial performance. However, gains and losses will be offset if: **7.9**

(a) they relate to the same event or circumstance; and
(b) disclosing the gross components is not likely to be useful for an assessment of either future results or the effects of past transactions and events.

Balance Sheet

In assessing the financial position of an entity, users are most interested in the types and amounts of assets and liabilities held and the relationship between them, and in the function of the various assets. Information on the reporting entity's financial position therefore needs to be presented in a way that focuses attention on these aspects. Good presentation typically involves: **7.10**

(a) recognising only assets, liabilities and residual interest in the balance sheet;
(b) delineating the entity's resource structure (major classes and amounts of assets) and its financial structure (major classes and amounts of liabilities and residual interest); and
(c) distinguishing assets by function. For example, assets held for sale will be reported separately from assets held on a continuing basis for use in the entity's activities.

In presenting information on the reporting entity's assets, it is necessary that the amount and nature of assets* that are subject to legal restrictions over their application are disclosed and explained. **7.11**

In presenting information on the reporting entity's financial position, assets will not be offset against liabilities. **7.12**

For some public benefit entities there may also be some focus on the presentation of different types of residual interest, for example of the extent to which restricted (including endowment) funds exist. Where, as noted in paragraph 7.11, legal restrictions exist over the application of assets, it should be clear how the relevant amount is reflected in the residual interest as well as in the assets themselves. **7.13**

Cash flow statement

Cash flow information will be of most use if it shows the extent to which the entity's activities generate and use cash, distinguishing in particular cash flows that are the result of operations from cash flows that result from other activities. **7.14**

**In some cases the assets might constitute a portfolio that at times includes liabilities. The disclosure requirements would also apply to any liabilities within such a portfolio.*

Accompanying information

7.15 Financial statements are often accompanied and complemented by information that does not form part of the financial statements. Examples of such information include trend information, operating and financial reviews, reports from the entity's governing body (eg directors' report, trustees' report), statements by the chief executive, key performance indicators, such as information on waiting lists, cost of refuse collection per household, and other indicators of a charity's performance. The Statement refers to such information as accompanying information.

7.16 The primary objective of public benefit entities is to provide goods or services for the general public or social benefit. Therefore, the accompanying information is often of high importance for users of such entities' financial statements in assessing the performance of the entity as a whole.

7.17 Although accompanying information generally has the same objective as financial statements, it usually comprises a different kind of information, some of which deals with matters that are not in the financial statements and some which deals with matters that are in the financial statements, but from a different perspective. For example, it often includes:

(a) narrative disclosures describing and explaining the entity's activities;
(b) historical summaries and trend information;
(c) non-accounting and non-financial information, including performance indicators; and
(d) evolutionary or experimental disclosures that are not considered suitable for inclusion in the financial statements.

7.18 The more complex entities become, the more users need an objective and comprehensive analysis and explanation of the main features underlying their financial performance and financial position. Such disclosures are best presented in the context of a discussion of the entity's business as a whole. This may include a discussion of what the residual interest represents and, where appropriate, management's future intentions regarding the net assets the residual interest represents.

Comparison to budget

7.19 Many funders and financial supporters will be interested in the extent to which actual expenditure compares to that forecast, for example where it is used to determine the extent of a compulsory levy. In addition, where a grant has been provided, the provider will be interested in the extent to which it covered the associated expenditure.

7.20 As a result it may be useful to provide information on a comparison to budget, or an outturn position for grants, within general purpose financial reports, as part of the accompanying information. However, in providing such information it is necessary to ensure that, for example:

(a) the information provided is of general use and not solely regulatory (or special purpose); and
(b) the information is provided at an appropriate level of detail or aggregation (such that it is useful, understandable and not so voluminous as to mask the key messages).

Highlights and summary indicators

Financial statements and accompanying information sometimes include amounts, ratios and other computations that attempt to distil key information about the reporting entity's financial performance and financial position. Such highlights and summary indicators cannot, on their own, provide a basis for meaningful analysis or prudent decision-making. It is therefore essential that they are not presented in a way that exaggerates their importance. **7.21**

However, well-presented highlights and summary indicators are useful to some users, who perhaps only require very basic information, or plan to use that information to identify areas to analyse further. **7.22**

Notwithstanding the limitations of highlights and summary indicators, if such information is provided it needs to be presented in a manner and context that enables its meaning to be communicated to users. This will often entail explaining the reasons for changes in the relative or absolute size of the figures from one period to the next. **7.23**

Chapter 8: accounting for interests in other entities

Financial statements need to reflect the effect on the reporting entity's financial performance and financial position of its interests in other entities. This involves various measurement and presentation issues. Rather than being dealt with in the relevant chapters and therefore in isolation from each other, they are dealt with together in this chapter. For similar reasons, various consolidation issues are dealt with in this chapter.

PRINCIPLES

- Single entity financial statements and consolidated financial statements present the interests the reporting entity may have in other entities from different perspectives.
- In single entity financial statements, interests in other entities are dealt with by focusing on the income and/or expenditure and (depending on the measurement basis adopted) capital growth arising from those interests.
- In consolidated financial statements, the way in which interests in other entities are dealt with depends on the degree of influence involved.

    (a) An interest that involves control of another entity's operating and financial policies is dealt with by incorporating the controlled entity as part of the reporting entity.
    (b) An interest that involves joint control of, or significant influence over, another entity's operating and financial policies is dealt with by recognising the reporting entity's share of that other entity's results and resources in a way that does not involve showing those results and resources in the performance statement and balance sheet as if they were controlled by the reporting entity.
    (c) Other interests are dealt with in the same way as any other asset.

- Although consolidated financial statements are the financial statements of the group as a whole, they are prepared from the perspective of the parent and, as a result, ultimately focus on the parent's interest in its subsidiaries. The effect on benefit flows of any outside interest in the subsidiaries will therefore be separately identified.
- Consolidated financial statements reflect the whole of the parent's investment in its subsidiaries, including, where applicable, purchased goodwill.
- A transaction involving the amalgamation of two or more reporting entities is reflected in the consolidated financial statements in accordance with its character. Therefore, a transaction that is of the character of:

    (a) an acquisition is reflected in the consolidated financial statements as if the acquirer purchased the acquiree's assets and liabilities as a bundle of assets and liabilities on the open market; and
    (b) a merger is reflected in the consolidated financial statements as if the new reporting entity, comprising all the parties to the transaction, had always existed.

EXPLANATION

There are few fundamental differences between the principles and explanation relevant to profit-oriented entities, as expressed in Chapter 8 of the Statement and their interpretation for public benefit entities. Therefore much of what follows is a summary of the discussion in Chapter 8 of the Statement, which should be referred to for a full understanding. Additional explanation specific to public benefit entities has been added covering business combinations.

Degree of influence

Although an entity's interest in a second entity may take many different forms, the key factor in determining its effect on the first entity's financial performance and financial position is the degree of influence it exerts over the operating and financial policies of the second entity involved. **8.1**

The highest degree of influence that an entity can have is control. As Chapter 2 explains, control comprises the ability to deploy the economic resources involved and to benefit (or to suffer) by their deployment. Other degrees of influence have these same aspects; in effect, the ability to influence the activities of the entity with a view to gaining economic benefits from that influence. **8.2**

Although it is possible to classify the degree of influence that an entity has over an entity in an almost infinite number of ways, it is sufficient for the purposes of the Statement and this Interpretation to classify it as follows: **8.3**

(a) *Control* – where one entity controls another entity.
(b) *Joint control* – where the entity does not itself control the other entity, but shares control through some form of arrangement jointly with others.
(c) *Significant influence* – where the entity has neither control nor joint control, but exerts a degree of influence over the entity's operating and financial policies that is at the least a significant influence and at the most just short of control.
(d) *Lesser or no influence* – where any influence that the entity has over the entity's operating and financial policies is less than a significant influence.

Reflecting the effects of interests in other entities

Consolidated financial statements and single entity financial statements

The effect on the entity's financial performance and financial position of an interest in an entity is reflected in the first entity's financial statements in different ways depending on the type of financial statements being prepared. **8.4**

(a) Financial statements of a reporting entity whose boundary has been drawn by reference to the scope of its direct control – single entity financial statements – take a narrow view of the reporting entity's interests in other entities and reflect only the income and capital growth arising from those interests.
(b) Financial statements of a reporting entity whose boundary has been drawn by reference to the scope of the entity's control (both direct and indirect) – consolidated financial statements – present an expanded view of the reporting entity's interests in other entities that reflects the reporting entity's influence over, and its accountability for, the activities and resources of these entities.

Interests involving control

If an entity controls one or more other entities, the controlling entity (the parent) and the controlled entities (the subsidiaries) will be a reporting entity (the group). The group financial statements (consolidated financial statements) are prepared by aggregating the gains, losses, assets, liabilities and cash flows of the parent and its subsidiaries. This ensures that the effects on the parent's financial performance and financial position of its interests in its subsidiaries are fully reflected in the financial statements. **8.5**

Interests involving joint control or significant influence

8.6 If the reporting entity shares joint control of, or exercises significant influence over, another entity, it will be directly involved in and affected by that other entity's activities. Its interest is therefore reflected in the consolidated financial statements in a way that:

(a) recognises the reporting entity's share of the results and net assets of the investee; and
(b) does not misrepresent the extent of its influence over the investee – in other words, it does not treat activities and resources that are not controlled by the reporting entity as if they are controlled by the reporting entity.

Interests involving lesser or no influence

8.7 If the reporting entity's influence does not involve control, joint control or significant influence, the reporting entity will not be accountable for the entity's activities. In such circumstances, the only amounts recognised in the consolidated financial statements will be the investment (if any) and any income derived therefrom.

Consolidated financial statements

8.8 The gains, losses, assets, liabilities and cash flows of all subsidiaries are reflected in full in the consolidated financial statements, even if a subsidiary is not wholly-owned. This reflects the parent's ability, through its control, to deploy both its own economic resources and those of its subsidiaries even where it does not wholly own the subsidiaries.

8.9 This Chapter separates general purpose financial statements into single entity financial statements and consolidated financial statements; such distinctions are not necessarily observed in regulatory requirements, which may require combined financial statements for a number of entities that do not meet the criteria for a reporting entity. An example would be financial statements showing the combined results of related initiatives where different elements may be carried out by different entities.

Accounting for business combinations

8.10 An amalgamation of two or more reporting entities – sometimes referred to as a business combination – can take a number of different forms. All these forms can be characterised as either:

(a) a purchase (for public benefit entities potentially at nil or nominal consideration) – such transactions are commonly referred to as acquisitions*; or
(b) a uniting of interests – such transactions are commonly referred to as mergers.

8.11 The fact that a business combination involves public benefit entities does not in itself influence whether the business combination is accounted for as an acquisition, representing the enlargement of a continuing entity, or as a merger, representing the creation of a new combined entity. It is important to consider the individual circumstances of each combination in determining the appropriate accounting.

**An acquisition is something that has been acquired by any means and therefore includes something that has been gifted as well as something that has been purchased.*

An acquisition is a business combination that is in the nature of an acquisition by one entity of another entity (ie one entity is the acquirer). The transaction therefore results in an existing reporting entity being enlarged and is reflected in the consolidated financial statements by treating the assets and liabilities of the entity acquired and any purchased goodwill as if the transaction was the purchase of a bundle of assets and liabilities on the open market. **8.12**

On the other hand, a merger is in the nature of a coming together of two entities to form a new reporting entity. This is reflected in the financial statements of the new reporting entity comprising all the parties to the transaction as if that entity had always existed. As a result, the assets and liabilities of each party to the transaction are treated as if they were acquired by the new reporting entity at the time that they were acquired by the party concerned* with none of the assets or liabilities treated as being purchased at the time of the business combination as part of a bundle of assets and liabilities on the open market. **8.13**

Where an acquisition is carried out at nil or nominal consideration: **8.14**

(a) the excess of the fair value of the assets acquired over the fair value of the liabilities assumed should be treated as a gain. The gain represents the gift of the value of one business to another and should be recognised as income;

(b) if the fair value of the liabilities assumed exceeds the fair value of the assets acquired, the deficit of the fair value of the liabilities in comparison to the assets should be treated as a loss. The loss represents the net obligations assumed, for which the acquiring entity has not received a financial reward, which will therefore result in a decrease in residual interest.

**This description of 'merger accounting' has been repeated from the Statement. However, although the Board continues to believe that there can be circumstances where a business combination does not have the characteristics of an acquisition, merger accounting has generally lost favour as a means of faithfully representing the economic substance of the combination that has occurred. In substance, it can be argued that a new entity has been created from the date of the business combination, which acquired the combined assets on that date. A more suitable presentation might be for all the assets and liabilities to be treated as if they were acquired on the open market on the date the combination took place.*

Appendix 1 – The principles that have been re-expressed

Many of the principles within this Interpretation are exactly the same as those that are relevant to profit-oriented entities. Those that have been amended or inserted are as follows:

Principle as expressed in the Statement of Principles for Financial Reporting	Principle as re-expressed in this Interpretation	Discussion
Chapter 1 • That objective can usually be met by focusing exclusively on the information needs of present and potential investors, the defining class of user.	• That objective can usually be met by focusing exclusively on the information needs of funders and financial supporters, the defining class of user.	Amended to reflect a different defining class of user.
Chapter 1 • Present and potential investors need information about the reporting entity's financial performance and financial position that is useful to them in evaluating the entity's ability to generate cash (including the timing and certainty of its generation) and in assessing the entity's financial adaptability.	• Funders and financial supporters need information about the reporting entity's financial performance and financial position that is useful to them in helping to evaluate the proper and efficient use of the entity's resources and in assessing the entity's cash needs and its financial adaptability.	Amended to reflect a different defining class of user and a slightly different emphasis on the use of the information.
Chapter 3 • Information is relevant if it has the ability to influence the economic decisions of users and is provided in time to influence those decisions.	• Information is relevant if it has the ability to influence the economic decisions of users, or their assessment of the effectiveness of the stewardship of management, and is provided in time to influence those decisions or assessments.	Amended to include reference to the use of information in assessing the effectiveness of the stewardship of management.

Principle as expressed in the Statement of Principles for Financial Reporting	Principle as re-expressed in this Interpretation	Discussion
Chapter 3 • Information is material to the financial statements if its misstatement or omission might reasonably be expected to influence the economic decisions of users.	• Information is material to the financial statements if its misstatement or omission might reasonably be expected to influence the economic decisions of users, or their assessment of the effectiveness of the stewardship of management.	Amended to include reference to the use of information in assessing the effectiveness of the stewardship of management.
Chapter 4 • The elements of the financial statements are: (a) assets; (b) liabilities; (c) ownership interest; (d) gains; (e) losses; (f) contributions from owners; (g) distributions to owners.	• The elements of the financial statements are: (a) assets; (b) liabilities; (c) residual interest; (d) gains; (e) losses; (f) contributions establishing a financial interest in the residual interest; (g) distributions to holders of a financial interest in the residual interest.	Amended due to the different nature of owners and financial interests in the context of public benefit entities.
Chapter 4 • Ownership interest is the residual amount found by deducting all of the entity's liabilities from all of the entity's assets.	• Residual interest is the amount found by deducting all of the entity's liabilities from all of the entity's assets.	Amended due to the different nature of owners in public benefit entities.
Chapter 4 • Gains are increases in ownership interest not resulting from contributions from owners.	• Gains are increases in residual interest not resulting from contributions establishing a financial interest in the residual interest.	Amended due to the different nature of owners and financial interests in the context of public benefit entities.

Principle as expressed in the Statement of Principles for Financial Reporting	**Principle as re-expressed in this Interpretation**	**Discussion**
Chapter 4 • Losses are decreases in ownership interest not resulting from distributions to owners.	• Losses are decreases in residual interest not resulting from distributions to holders of a financial interest in the residual interest.	Amended due to the different nature of owners and financial interests in the context of public benefit entities.
Chapter 4 • Contributions from owners are increases in ownership interest resulting from transfers from owners in their capacity as owners.	• Contributions establishing a financial interest in the residual interest are increases in residual interest resulting from transfers from parties that establish a financial interest in that residual interest.	Amended due to the different nature of owners and financial interests in the context of public benefit entities.
Chapter 4 • Distributions to owners are decreases in ownership interest resulting from transfers to owners in their capacity as owners.	• Distributions to holders of a financial interest in the residual interest are decreases in residual interest resulting from transfers to parties holding a financial interest in that residual interest in their capacity as holders of a financial interest.	Amended due to the different nature of owners and financial interests in the context of public benefit entities.
Chapter 5	• In a transaction involving the receipt of resources not related directly to the provision of goods or services, the recognition criteria described above will be met when there is clear evidence of a right to receive the resources.	New principle relating to the receipt of resources other than for net gain.

Principle as expressed in the Statement of Principles for Financial Reporting	Principle as re-expressed in this Interpretation	Discussion
Chapter 8 • In single entity financial statements, interests in other entities are dealt with by focusing on the income and (depending on the measurement basis adopted) capital growth arising from those interests.	• In single entity financial statements, interests in other entities are dealt with by focusing on the income and/or expenditure and (depending on the measurement basis adopted) capital growth arising from those interests.	Amended to include reference to expenditure, because the entity might be contributing to the interest, rather than receiving income from it.
Chapter 8 • Consolidated financial statements reflect the whole of the parent's investment in its subsidiaries, including purchased goodwill.	• Consolidated financial statements reflect the whole of the parent's investment in its subsidiaries, including, where applicable, purchased goodwill.	Amended because purchased goodwill may arise only rarely.

Appendix 2 – Comparison to material in the statement

The following table compares the material that is included in this Interpretation with that in the Statement in order to provide an indication of which material:

(a) is the same, or substantially the same, as the Statement;
(b) from the Statement has been omitted, but is equally relevant to public benefit entities;
(c) has been inserted specifically to address the circumstances of public benefit entities.

The table does not consider the principles themselves, which are addressed in Appendix 1.

Chapter	Comparison with the Statement
Introduction	*Purpose* Paragraphs 1 and 4 are substantially the same as paragraphs 1 to 4 of the Statement. Paragraphs 2, 3 and 5 are additional. *Status* Paragraph 6 is substantially the same as paragraph 5 of the Statement. Paragraphs 7 and 8 are additional. *Scope* Paragraphs 9 to 15 replace paragraph 9 of the Statement, although paragraphs 11 to 14 include a significant amount of new material. Paragraphs 16 to 20 are substantially the same as paragraphs 6 to 8 of the Statement, although paragraphs 18 and 19 include a significant amount of new material. *True and fair* Paragraphs 10 to 13 of the Statement have not been repeated. *The standard-setting process* Most of paragraphs 14 to 17 of the Statement have not been repeated, but paragraph 15(a) is reflected in paragraph 21 of this Interpretation. *Revisions to the statement* Paragraph 22 is substantially the same as paragraph 18 of the Statement.
Chapter 1	*The objective of financial statements* Paragraph 1.1 is a summarisation of paragraphs 1.1 and 1.2 of the Statement. Paragraphs 1.2 to 1.4 expand on paragraphs 1.3 and 1.4 of the Statement. Paragraphs 1.5 and 1.6 are additional. Paragraphs 1.5 to 1.7 of the Statement have not been repeated, although paragraph 1.7 provides a brief summary. Paragraph 1.8 summarises paragraphs 1.8 and 1.9 of the Statement. Paragraphs 1.9 and 1.10 are additional.

Chapter	Comparison with the Statement
	Defining class of user Paragraph 1.11 is substantially the same as paragraph 1.11 of the Statement. Paragraphs 1.10 and 1.12 of the Statement have not been repeated. Paragraphs 1.12 to 1.16 are additional. *Information required by funders and financial supporters* Paragraphs 1.17 to 1.23 summarise paragraphs 1.13 to 1.22 of the Statement with added public benefit entity context.
Chapter 2	*Entities that should prepare and publish financial statements* Paragraphs 2.1 to 2.3 are the same as the Statement. *The boundary of a reporting entity* Paragraphs 2.4 to 2.6 summarise paragraphs 2.4, 2.6 and 2.7 of the Statement; paragraph 2.5 has not been repeated. *What is control?* Paragraph 2.7 is the same as paragraph 2.8 in the Statement. Paragraph 2.8 repeats part of paragraph 2.10 in the Statement with added public sector context. Paragraph 2.9 has not been repeated. *Controlling an entity* Paragraphs 2.9 to 2.16 summarise paragraphs 2.11 to 2.20 of the Statement. *Assets held in a fiduciary capacity* Paragraph 2.17 is additional.
Chapter 3	*Relevance* Paragraph 3.1 is the first sentence of paragraph 3.1, and paragraph 3.2 of the Statement. Paragraph 3.2 is the first part of paragraph 3.3 and paragraph 3.5 of the Statement. The remainder of paragraphs 3.1 and 3.3 and paragraph 3.4 in the Statement are not repeated. Paragraph 3.3 is substantially the same as paragraph 3.6 in the Statement. Paragraph 3.4 is additional. *Reliability* Paragraph 3.5 is the same as paragraphs 3.7 and 3.8 in the Statement. Paragraph 3.6 is the same as paragraph 3.12 in the Statement. Paragraph 3.7 is the first sentence of paragraph 3.13 and paragraph 3.14 in the Statement. Paragraph 3.8 is the same as paragraph 3.15 in the Statement. Paragraphs 3.10, 3.11, the remainder of 3.13 and 3.16 to 3.20 of the Statement have not been repeated. *Comparability* Paragraph 3.9 is substantially the same as paragraph 3.21 in the Statement. Paragraphs 3.10 and 3.11 summarise paragraphs 3.23 to 3.25 in the Statement. Paragraph 3.22 of the Statement has not been repeated.

Chapter	Comparison with the Statement
	Understandability Paragraph 3.12 summarises paragraphs 3.26 and 3.27 in the Statement. Paragraphs 3.13 and 3.14 are additional. *Materiality* Paragraphs 3.15 to 3.19 are substantially the same as paragraphs 3.28 to 3.32 in the Statement. *Constraints on the qualitative characteristics* Paragraph 3.20 is the same as paragraph 3.33 in the Statement. Paragraphs 3.21, 3.22 and 3.25 summarise paragraphs 3.34, 3.36 and 3.37 in the Statement. Paragraph 3.35 of the Statement has not been repeated. Paragraphs 3.23 and 3.24 are additional.
Chapter 4	*The elements of financial statements* Paragraphs 4.1 and 4.2 are substantially the same as paragraphs 4.1 and 4.2 in the Statement. Paragraphs 4.3 and 4.4 of the Statement have not been repeated. Paragraph 4.3 is the same as the second sentence of paragraph 4.5 in the Statement. *Assets* The definition is the same as paragraph 4.6 in the Statement. Paragraph 4.4 is the same as paragraph 4.8 in the Statement. Paragraph 4.5 summarises paragraphs 4.9 and 4.10 in the Statement. Paragraph 4.6 is the same as paragraph 4.11 in the Statement. Paragraph 4.7 is substantially the same as paragraph 4.13 in the Statement. Paragraph 4.13 is substantially the same as paragraph 4.17 in the Statement. Paragraphs 4.17 and 4.18 summarise paragraphs 4.19 and 4.20 in the Statement. Paragraph 4.19 is the first sentence of paragraph 4.22 in the Statement. Paragraphs 4.8 to 4.12 and 4.14 to 4.16 are additional. Paragraphs 4.7, 4.12, 4.14 to 4.16, 4.18 and 4.21 of the Statement have not been repeated. *Liabilities* The definition is the same as paragraph 4.23 in the Statement. Paragraphs 4.20 to 4.22 are the same as paragraphs 4.24 to 4.25 in the Statement, except that paragraph 4.22 includes some additional material. Paragraph 4.23 is the same as paragraph 4.27 in the Statement. Paragraph 4.24 is the same as paragraph 4.29 in the Statement. Paragraphs 4.25 to 4.27 are the first part of paragraphs 4.30 to 4.32 in the Statement. Paragraphs 4.28 to 4.36 are additional. Paragraph 4.28 of the Statement has not been repeated. *Offsetting rights and obligations* Paragraphs 4.37 to 4.40 are essentially the same as paragraphs 4.33 to 4.36 in the Statement, except that the sub-paragraphs of 4.33 have not been repeated. *Residual interest (referred to as ownership interest in the Statement)* Paragraph 4.41 reflects the public benefit entity context of paragraph 4.37 in the Statement. Paragraph 4.42 includes much

Chapter	Comparison with the Statement
	of the material from paragraph 4.38 in the Statement. Paragraphs 4.43 and 4.44 are additional. *Gains and losses* The definition and paragraph 4.45 are substantially the same as paragraphs 4.39 and 4.40 in the Statement. Paragraph 4.46 is additional. Paragraphs 4.47 to 4.51, on donated goods and services, are also additional. Paragraph 4.41 in the Statement has not been repeated. *Contributions establishing a financial interest in the residual interest* Paragraph 4.52 relates to paragraph 4.43 in the Statement. Paragraph 4.54 builds on paragraph 4.44 in the Statement, providing additional public benefit entity context. Paragraphs 4.53 and 4. 55 are additional. *Distributions to holders of a financial interest in the residual interest* Paragraph 4.56 is additional. The first sentence of paragraph 4.57 is the first sentence of paragraph 4.45 in the Statement with additional public benefit entity context.
Chapter 5	*The recognition process* Paragraphs 5.1 and 5.2 are the same as paragraphs 5.1 and 5.2 in the Statement. Paragraphs 5.3 to 5.6 summarise paragraphs 5.3 to 5.6 in the Statement. Paragraphs 5.7 to 5.9 are substantially the same as paragraphs 5.8, 5.9 and 5.11 in the Statement. Paragraphs 5.7 and 5.10 of the Statement have not been repeated. *Initial recognition* Paragraph 5.10 is the same as paragraph 5.12 in the Statement. Paragraphs 5.11 and 5.12 summarise paragraphs 5.14 and 5.15 in the Statement. Paragraphs 5.13 and 5.14 are the same as paragraphs 5.16 and 5.17 in the Statement. Paragraph 5.16 is substantially the same as paragraph 5.19 in the Statement. Paragraph 5.15 is additional. Paragraphs 5.13 and 5.18 in the Statement have not been repeated. Paragraph 5..20 and 5.21 of the Statement have not been repeated. *Derecognition* Paragraphs 5.17 to 5.20 summarise paragraphs 5.22 to 5.25 in the Statement. *Revenue recognition* Paragraphs 5.21 to 5.24 summarise paragraphs 5.26 to 5.30 in the Statement. Paragraphs 5.25 to 5.27 are the same as paragraphs 5.33 to 5.35 in the Statement, except that the second sentence of paragraph 5.34 has not been repeated. Paragraphs 5.31 and 5.32 in the Statement have not been repeated. The first sentence of paragraph 5.28 is the same as the first sentence of paragraph 5.36 in the Statement, otherwise paragraphs 5.28 to 5.37 are additional.

Chapter	Comparison with the Statement
Chapter 6	*Alternative bases of measurement* Paragraph 6.1 summarises paragraph 6.1 in the Statement. Paragraph 6.2 is the same as paragraph 6.3 in the Statement. Paragraph 6.3 is substantially the same as the first sentence of paragraph 6.4 in the Statement. Paragraphs 6.2 and 6.5 of the Statement have not been repeated. *Alternative measures of current value* Paragraph 6.4 is substantially the same as paragraph 6.6 in the Statement. Paragraph 6.5 is based on paragraph 6.7 in the Statement. Paragraphs 6.6 to 6.10 are additional. Paragraph 6.11 is essentially the same as paragraph 6.9 in the Statement. The diagram in paragraph 6.8 of the Statement has not been repeated. *The measurement process* Paragraphs 6.12 to 6.17 are substantially the same as paragraphs 6.10 to 6.15 in the Statement, except that the sub-paragraphs of 6.14 have not been repeated and there is additional public benefit entity context in paragraph 6.17. Paragraph 6.16 of the Statement has not been repeated. Paragraphs 6.18 to 6.22 are substantially the same as paragraphs 6.17 to 6.22 in the Statement, except that paragraph 6.21 has not been repeated. *Choosing a measurement basis and deciding whether to change it* Paragraph 6.23 is the same as paragraph 6.23 in the Statement. Paragraph 6.24 is the same as the first part of paragraph 6.24 in the Statement. Paragraphs 6.25 to 6.29 of the Statement have not been repeated. *Measurement issues* Paragraph 6.25 is substantially the same as paragraph 6.30 in the Statement. Paragraph 6.26 is the same as part of paragraph 6.32 in the Statement. Paragraphs 6.27 and 6.28 are the same as paragraphs 6.33 and 6.34 in the Statement. Paragraph 6.29 is the same as paragraph 6.36 in the Statement. Paragraph 6.30 is the same as paragraph 6.38 in the Statement. Paragraphs 6.31, 6.35, 6.37 of the Statement have not been repeated. *Capital maintenance adjustments and changing prices* Paragraphs 6.31 and 6.32 are the same as the sub-paragraphs of 6.42 in the Statement. Paragraphs 6.39 to 6.41 of the Statement have not been repeated.
Chapter 7	*Presentation of information in financial statements* Paragraphs 7.1 to 7.6 are the same, or substantially the same, as paragraphs 7.1 to 7.6 in the Statement. Paragraphs 7.7 and 7.8 of the Statement have not been repeated. *Good presentation* Paragraphs 7.7 to 7.12 summarise paragraphs 7.9 to 7.13 in the Statement, except that paragraph 7.11 is additional. Paragraph

Chapter	Comparison with the Statement
	7.13 is additional. Paragraph 7.14 summarises paragraph 7.14 in the Statement. *Accompanying information* Paragraph 7.15 is substantially the same as paragraph 7.15 in the Statement. Paragraph 7.16 is additional. Paragraph 7.17 summarises paragraphs 7.16 and 7.17 of the Statement. Paragraph 7.18 summarises paragraph 7.18 in the Statement. Paragraphs 7.19 and 7.20 are additional. *Highlights and summary indicators* Paragraphs 7.21 to 7.23 are substantially the same as paragraphs 7.19 to 7.21 in the Statement.
Chapter 8	*Degree of influence* Paragraphs 8.1, 8.2 and 8.3 are the same as paragraphs 8.1, 8.3 and 8.4 in the Statement. Paragraph 8.2 has not been repeated. *Reflecting the effects of interests in other entities* Paragraphs 8.4 to 8.6 are substantially the same as paragraphs 8.5, 8.7 and 8.9 in the Statement. Paragraph 8.7 is substantially the same as paragraph 8.10 in the Statement. Paragraphs 8.6 and 8.8 of the Statement have not been repeated. *Consolidated financial statements* Paragraph 8.8 is the same as paragraph 8.11 in the Statement. Paragraph 8.9 is additional. Paragraphs 8.12 and 8.13 of the Statement are not repeated. *Accounting for business combinations* Paragraphs 8.10, 8.12 and 8.13 are substantially the same as paragraphs 8.14 to 8.16 in the Statement. Paragraphs 8.11 and 8.14 are additional.

Appendix 3 – Decision tree for commitments to provide public benefits

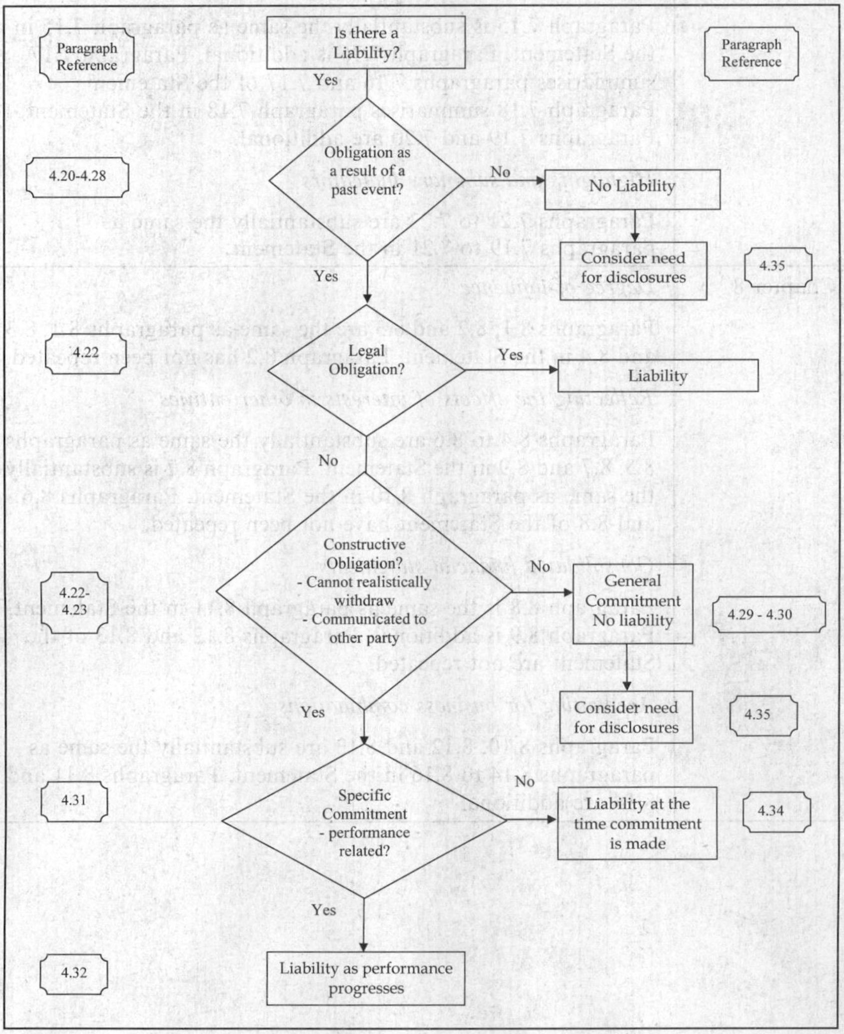

Appendix 4 – The development of the interpretation

Introduction

This Appendix explains the development of the Interpretation. It sets out the relationship between the Statement of Principles for Financial Reporting (the Statement) and this Interpretation. It also explains why the Accounting Standards Board (the Board) decided to publish an Interpretation of the Statement and sets out the main stages of its development and the main issues considered. 1

As with the Discussion Paper, the Board's Committee on Accounting for Public-benefit Entities (CAPE) played a leading role in the development of this Interpretation from preparing the Discussion Paper and the Exposure Draft through to publication of this final version. The Board gratefully acknowledges this significant and important contribution. 2

Statement of Principles for Financial Reporting

The Statement was issued by the Board in December 1999. It sets out the principles that the Board believes should underlie the preparation and presentation of general purpose financial statements. 3

The primary purpose of the Statement is to provide a coherent frame of reference to be used by the Board in the development and review of accounting standards and by others who interact with the Board during the standard-setting process. Publication of the Statement was also intended to assist preparers and users of financial statements, as well as auditors and others, to understand the Board's approach to formulating accounting standards and the nature and function of information reported in general purpose financial statements. 4

The Statement is primarily intended to be relevant to the financial statements of profit-oriented entities in the private and public sectors. However, the Board believes that a common set of principles should underlie financial reporting by all entities. This will assist users in understanding financial statements regardless of the nature of the entity producing them and allow comparability, where appropriate, between all entities. 5

Scope of Interpretation

The Interpretation is intended to be relevant to the financial statements of all public benefit entities, regardless of their size, whether or not they make a surplus and whether they are private or public sector entities. However, it does not apply to profit-oriented entities, including any in the public sector. 6

The Interpretation is intended to operate alongside the existing Statement, expanding on the common underlying principles for public benefit entities, and therefore, other than at the margin, there should be no difference in financial reporting resulting from applying the Statement or the Interpretation. As a result, the Board has decided not to produce a list of entities that it believes meet the definition of a public benefit entity. 7

International developments and convergence

8 An EU Regulation requires all listed companies in the EU to prepare their consolidated financial statements in accordance with EU-adopted international accounting standards from 2005. International Financial Reporting Standards (IFRSs), set by the International Accounting Standards Board (IASB), form the basis of these adopted standards. Other companies are permitted to adopt the same framework, unless they are charitable companies, in which case they must continue to report under UK accounting standards.

9 The government sector will continue to prepare accounts in accordance with the Financial Reporting Manual (FReM), as published by the Treasury based on UK standards. However, the Chancellor of the Exchequer announced in the 2007 Budget that the accounts of central government departments and entities in the wider public sector will be produced from 2008-09 using IFRS, as interpreted for the public sector in an IFRS based FReM.

10 Nonetheless, it is expected that many public benefit entities will, in the shorter term at least, continue to prepare their financial statements in accordance with UK accounting standards and, where applicable, Statements of Recommended Practice (SORPs) that have been developed to provide guidance on the application of UK accounting standards in the circumstances of particular sectors.

11 The ASB is pursuing a programme of convergence between UK accounting standards and IFRS and has issued new UK standards that are based on IFRS. The Board is continuing its consultations and has proposed that further standards will be introduced by the ASB with a common effective date, currently estimated to be financial years beginning on or after 1 January 2009. The expectation is that, over time, all entities will be preparing their financial statements in accordance with standards based on the same core set of IFRS.

12 The IASB has on its agenda a major project to revise its conceptual framework. It is a joint project with the Financial Accounting Standards Board (FASB) in the USA and aims to develop a framework that combines and improves upon the existing frameworks. The IASB plans to consider the impact of the framework on not-for-profit entities towards the end of its project. The ASB, in collaboration with other National Standards Setters, is closely monitoring the IASB project and contributing views as this work progresses. In the longer term, the ASB will reflect upon the implications of this work for the Statement and this Interpretation.

International Public Sector Accounting Standards Board (IPSASB)

13 IPSASB* continues with its programme to develop and maintain International Public Sector Accounting Standards (IPSASs) for accounting by governmental bodies. Most of the 24 standards currently in issue are based on International Accounting Standards extant at 31 August 1997, including the 11 revised accrual basis standards that were issued by IPSASB in January 2007 and are intended to increase the clarity and usability of IPSASs. The 11 revised IPSASs are effective for reporting periods beginning on or after 1 January 2008.†

**IPSASB was previously known as the Public Sector Committee (PSC) of the International Federation of Accountants (IFAC). IPSASBs aim is to converge IPSASs with IFRS, issued by the IASB, while at the same time also considering public sector specific issues and reflecting public sector emphasis within the IPSASs.*

*†**Editor's note:** There are now 31 IPSASs in issue, although some of these are not mandatory for some time to come, up to and including accounting periods beginning on or after 1 January 2013.*

The scope of this Interpretation, which includes all public benefit entities regardless of whether they are in the public or private sector, is wider than the work of the IPSASB, which covers only the public sector. 14

IPSASB's active work programme has recently seen it publish standards on public sector specific issues such as IPSAS 23 'Revenue from Non-Exchange Transactions (including Taxes and Transfers)' and IPSAS 24 'Presentation of Budget Information in Financial Statements'. IPSASB is also taking forward a project to develop a standard on accounting for the social policies of government and is aiming to publish an Exposure Draft in 2007 that will focus on the presentation and disclosure of social benefits. This approach will allow IPSASB to consider further recognition and measurement issues, on which it hopes to publish a Consultation Paper in 2007. 15

IPSASB, in conjunction with a number of participating National Standard Setters, has also just started a long-term project to establish a public sector conceptual framework which is intended to be applicable to the preparation and presentation of general purpose financial reports of public sector entities. 16

During the development of this Interpretation the Board has had regard to pronouncements and proposals issued by IPSASB. This is highlighted in the following discussion of the main issues debated in developing this Interpretation, with several of these issues including a comparison to IPSASB requirements or proposals. 17

Discussion Paper of Proposed Interpretation

In May 2003 the Board issued a Discussion Paper 'Statement of Principles for Financial Reporting: Proposed Interpretation for Public Benefit Entities'. The Discussion Paper sought comments on the Board's views of the application of the principles within the Statement to public benefit entities. 18

The Board received a number of helpful responses to the Discussion Paper. These showed there was a great deal of support for the project and allowed the Board to redebate and take forward its work on a number of issues. The results of these deliberations were explained in the Preface to the Exposure Draft of the proposed Interpretation. 19

Exposure Draft of Proposed Interpretation

In August 2005 the Board issued an Exposure Draft that built upon the consultation on the Discussion Paper. As a result of the Board's redeliberations, there were a number of areas where the Exposure Draft differed from the Discussion Paper, although neither the Discussion Paper, nor the Exposure Draft, attempted to redebate or update the Statement itself. 20

Main issues debated in developing the Interpretation

The ten main areas that were debated by the Board in developing the Exposure Draft from the Discussion Paper were highlighted in the Preface to the Exposure Draft. These included the following issues where respondents were generally supportive of the approach being taken by the Board: 21

- Funders and financial supporters as the defining class of user;
- Definitions of the elements of financial statements;
- Notional transactions;

- Capital contributions; and
- Budget reporting.

22 There were however five other main areas where respondents to the Exposure Draft raised a number of significant concerns. These issues, including the Board's further deliberations, are set out below.

Liabilities

23 Respondents to the Exposure Draft raised significant concerns with regard to the proposed Interpretation for commitments to provide public benefits. In particular, respondents disagreed with the executory contract analogy used in the Exposure Draft for non performance-related commitments. This stated that where resources are being provided in furtherance of the entity's objectives, the obligation to a particular recipient can be thought of as, in substance, an executory contract in which the provision of goods or services by the reporting entity is balanced by the achievement of its objectives.

24 Respondents argued this analogy was inappropriate on the grounds that no exchange was taking place. Respondents also felt that non-performance-related arrangements are adequately dealt with by Financial Reporting Standard (FRS) 12 which provides guidance on the circumstances in which constructive obligations should be recognised as liabilities.

25 Respondents did however agree that FRS 12 did not fully address the issue of possible liabilities in the public sector where there may be constructive obligations that are not recognised as liabilities. One respondent provided the example of patients with chronic conditions, such as diabetes, who would probably die if the National Health Service did not continue to prescribe insulin. In such cases, it could be argued that a constructive obligation has been created which leaves little scope for avoidance, yet such commitments are generally not currently provided for in the accounts of public benefit entities.

26 In considering liabilities further, the Board noted that respondents were content with the proposed treatment of general commitments and performance-related commitments. The Board also acknowledged concerns over the executory contract analogy for non-performance-related commitments and accepted that this was an area that was exercising the minds of standard setters internationally and where further work was being carried out. The Board therefore agreed that the proposed Interpretation should not seek to develop the executory contract analogy proposed in the Exposure Draft for non-performance related commitments. Instead, the Board agreed to revert back to an FRS 12 based approach on the grounds it is underpinned by principles which have, in general terms, been found to be robust and are logically derived from the definition and recognition criteria for liabilities in the Statement.

27 The Board does however acknowledge that further work is required in relation to governments and commitments to provide public benefits. It will therefore continue to consider these matters further in conjunction with other standard setters, particularly in the context of the IPSASB Conceptual Framework project. With this in mind, and working collaboratively with other National Standard Setters, the Board is involved in both contributing to the IPSASB project and in monitoring the IASB/FASB Conceptual Framework project, including the implications for public benefit entities.

The Board is also monitoring closely the IPSASB's project to develop an IPSAS on social policy obligations. Subject to the progress of these projects, and any other developments in terms of accounting for the social policy obligations of governments, the Board will consider further the need for an update to this Interpretation. 28

Grants for financing capital projects

The issue of capital grants generated more responses than any of the other questions raised in the Exposure Draft, particularly from Registered Social Landlords who were opposed to recognising capital grants as income (once any conditions attached to their receipt have been met). There were also respondents that did not support the need for an impairment test where the asset was fully or partially grant funded on the grounds that the manner in which an asset is funded should not influence the need for an impairment review. 29

In considering these comments, the Board agreed with the clarification requested by some respondents that where a capital grant meets the definition of a capital contribution it should be treated as such. However, the Board continues to feel that if a capital grant is not a capital contribution, and it results in an increase in net assets, then it should be recognised as a gain. Hence, in the case of a simple cash grant with no conditions attached, the Board's view is that there is clearly an increase in net assets; hence a gain should be recognised. 30

The Board acknowledges that the proposed approach for capital grants, whilst consistent with the principles in the Statement and IPSAS 23 'Revenue from Non-Exchange Transactions (Taxes and Transfers)', does differ from the two approaches set out in Statement of Standard Accounting Practice (SSAP) 4 'Government Grants'. However, the Board feels that it is important for the section on capital grants to remain consistent with the definitions of elements and other material in the Interpretation. The Board also feels that it would be neither possible nor appropriate for a principles document to attempt to provide solutions to issues facing a particular sector in how they account for capital grants. These are issues that will need to be addressed by the SORP-making bodies and by the Board in any future update of SSAP 4 or following any update by the IASB of IAS 20 'Accounting for Government Grants and Disclosure of Government Assistance'. 31

The Board therefore decided to remain faithful to the principle that, subject to not being a capital contribution, and once all conditions have been met, a capital grant which results in an increase in net assets should be recognised as a gain. The Board accepts that where capital grants are recognised as a gain, there is scope for explanatory material to be included in the information accompanying the financial statements. 32

Finally, the Board agreed with respondents that the manner in which an asset is funded should not influence the need for an impairment test. The section in the Interpretation on capital grants therefore focuses on initial recognition of the grant with valuation issues in relation to the asset funded being covered in section 6 of the Interpretation on Measurement. 33

Business combinations

Respondents disagreed with the emphasis in the Exposure Draft that the *majority* of business combinations would be acquisitions. There was also some concern from respondents with regard to the principle that where a business combination takes 34 place at nil consideration, the net assets should be recognised as a gain to the income and expenditure account (with net liabilities recognised as a loss).

35 The Board agreed with respondents that there should be no presumption in the Interpretation that whilst true mergers do occur it is likely that the majority of business combinations (other than those involving entities under common control) will be acquisitions. This presumption has therefore been removed with the emphasis now being on the need to consider the individual circumstances of each combination in determining whether it represents a merger or an acquisition.

36 The Board also decided to clarify that business combinations that are in substance a gift of one business to another are effectively acquisitions carried out at nil or nominal consideration – and that in these circumstances the principle should be that the net assets or liabilities should be treated as a gain or a loss in the income and expenditure account.

Donated goods and services

37 The Exposure Draft proposed the recognition of voluntary services based on the value to the recipient of those services that would have otherwise been purchased. The Exposure Draft also suggested these services would often be those which the provider would ordinarily carry out in the normal course of their usual trade or profession and for which they would ordinarily charge a fee commensurate to the services provided.

38 Just over half of respondents that commented on this issue disagreed with the proposal, albeit for differing reasons ranging from the view that no voluntary services should be recognised to recognising all voluntary services that can be reliably measured.

39 The IPSASB has adopted a high level principles based approach in IPSAS 23 'Revenue from Non-Exchange Transactions (Taxes and Transfers)'. This requires the recognition of goods in-kind when it is probable that future economic benefits will flow to the entity and when the fair value of the assets can be measured reliability. The IPSAS then adopts a permissive approach to the recognition of services in-kind in that *'an entity may, but is not required to recognise services in-kind as revenue and as an asset.'*

40 It is because of the many uncertainties surrounding services in-kind, including the ability to exercise control over the services and measuring the fair value of the services, that led to IPSASB not requiring recognition. The Board however remains of the view that where services in-kind can be reliably valued they should be recognised in the financial statements. The Board acknowledges that where it is not possible to measure some services in-kind with sufficient reliability for the financial statements, then these services in-kind should not be recognised.

41 Respondents were generally content with the Board's proposal that where donated services are not recognised in the financial statements, and where disclosure of this information would help the user gain a better understanding of the entity's activities, then this information could be disclosed in the notes to the accounts or in the accompanying information.

Residual interest

The Exposure Draft proposed that information on the designation of portions of the residual interest for specific purposes does not create a different class of residual interest and should not be reported as a transaction in the financial statements. Although all respondents agreed the designation of a portion of the residual interest did not represent a transaction, a significant number felt that careful designation by management can be informative and that it is unfair to place such a restriction on public benefit entities when profit-orientated entities are not prohibited from making such designations (albeit they are probably rare in practice). **42**

After further deliberation the Board agreed that where designations were made as a result of trust or other legal requirements then these should be shown on the face of the balance sheet. However other designations, such as those reflecting management's future intentions, should be reported either in the notes to the accounts or in the accompanying information. **43**

Other ASB projects

The ASB is undertaking a review of the accounting for heritage assets. The project aims to develop practical proposals that will result in greater consistency and transparency in the financial reporting of heritage assets. Following publication of a Discussion Paper in January 2006, the Board published an Exposure Draft (FRED 40) in December 2006 with the intention of issuing a Financial Reporting Standard in 2007 that will apply for accounting periods commencing on or after 1 April 2009.* **44**

The IPSASB, in collaboration with the UK ASB, published a Consultation Paper on heritage assets in February 2006 which included at its core the UK ASB Discussion Paper. Following an analysis of the responses to the Consultation Paper, IPSASB has signalled its intention to continue with this project. **45**

***Editor's note:** *This project resulted in FRS 30* Heritage Assets, *which was issued in June 2009 and is effective for accounting periods beginning on or after 1 April 2010.*

Part Three

Accounting Standards

Foreword to accounting standards

(Issued June 1993)

Contents

Paragraph

Introduction 1–5

Aims of the Accounting Standards Board 6

Authority of accounting standards 7–12

Scope and application of accounting standards 13– 15

Compliance with accounting standards 16–20

The public sector 21–22

The issue of a Financial Reporting Standard 23– 26

Applicability of an accounting standard to transactions entered into before the standard was issued 27–30

Early adoption of Financial Reporting Exposure Drafts 31–32

Reviews of Accounting Standards 33

Accounting standards and the legal framework 34–35

International Accounting Standards 36

Withdrawal of Explanatory Foreword to Statements of Standard Accounting Practice 37

Appendix
Opinion by Miss Mary Arden QC
'The true and fair requirement'

Foreword to accounting standards

INTRODUCTION

1 This foreword explains the authority, scope and application of accounting standards issued or adopted by the Accounting Standards Board (the Board).* The foreword also considers the procedure by which the Board issues accounting standards and their relationship to International Accounting Standards, issued by the International Accounting Standards Committee.

2 The Board at its meeting on 24 August 1990 agreed to adopt the 22 extant Statements of Standard Accounting Practice (SSAPs) issued by the Councils of the six major accountancy bodies following proposals developed by the Accounting Standards Committee (ASC).† Adoption by the Board gave these SSAPs the status of accounting standards within Part VII of the Companies Act 1985,‡ (the Act) and within Part VIII of the Companies (Northern Ireland) Order 1986§ (the Order). This status will apply until each SSAP is amended, rescinded or replaced by new accounting standards.

3 Accounting standards developed by the Board are designated Financial Reporting Standards (FRSs). Accounting standards developed by the ASC and adopted by the Board continue to be known as SSAPs.

4 FRSs are based on the Statement of Principles for Financial Reporting currently in issue, which addresses the concepts underlying the information presented in financial statements. The objective of this Statement of Principles is to provide a framework for the consistent and logical formulation of individual accounting standards. The framework also provides a basis on which others can exercise judgement in resolving accounting issues.

5 The Board may issue pronouncements other than FRSs, including the Urgent Issues Task Force 'Abstracts'. The Board will indicate the authority, scope and application of pronouncements other than FRSs as they are issued. UITF Abstracts are the subject of a separate foreword.

**The Accounting Standards Board is a committee of The Accounting Standards Board Limited. The Accounting Standards Board Limited is prescribed as a standard setting body for the purposes of Section 256(1) of the Companies Act 1985 with effect from 20 August 1990 by The Accounting Standards (Prescribed Body) Regulations 1990 (S.I. 1990 No. 1667). The Accounting Standards Board Limited is prescribed as a standard setting body for Northern Ireland for the purposes of Article 264(1) of the Companies (Northern Ireland) Order 1986 with effect from 15 October 1990, by the Accounting Standards (Prescribed Body) Regulations (Northern Ireland) 1990 (S.R. 1990 No. 338).*

†*Prior to 1 August 1990 accounting standards in the United Kingdom and Republic of Ireland were issued by the Councils of the six major accountancy bodies following proposals developed by the ASC. Since 1 August 1990 the Board has taken over the role of issuing accounting standards applicable in the United Kingdom. The Institute of Chartered Accountants in Ireland issues accounting standards applicable in the Republic of Ireland.*

‡*References to the Companies Act 1985 are to that Act as amended by, inter alia, the Companies Act 1989 and the Companies Act 1985 (Bank Accounts) Regulations 1991 (S.I. 1991 No. 2705).*
***Editor's Note**: With effect for accounting periods beginning on or after 6 April 2008, the accounting provisions of the Companies Act 1985 are replaced with the provisions of the Companies Act 2006.*

§*References to the Companies (Northern Ireland) Order 1986 (S.I. 1986 No. 1032 (N.I. 6)) are to that Order as amended by, inter alia, the Companies (Northern Ireland) Order 1990 (S.I. 1990 No. 593 (N.I. 5)), the Companies (No. 2) (Northern Ireland) Order 1990 (S.I. 1990 No. 1504 (N.I. 10)) and the Companies (1986 Order) (Bank Accounts) Regulations (Northern Ireland) Order (S.R. 1992 No. 258).*

AIMS OF THE ACCOUNTING STANDARDS BOARD

The aims of the Board are set out in the document 'The Accounting Standards Board – Statement of Aims'. 6

AUTHORITY OF ACCOUNTING STANDARDS

FRSs issued and SSAPs adopted by the Board are 'accounting standards' for the purposes of the Act, which requires accounts, other than those prepared by small or medium-sized companies (as defined by the Act), to state whether they have been prepared in accordance with applicable accounting standards and to give particulars of any material departure from those standards and the reasons for it. References to accounting standards in the Act are contained in paragraph 36A of Schedule 4, paragraph 49 of Part I of Schedule 9 and paragraph 18B of Part I of Schedule 9A.* The equivalent references in the Order are in paragraph 36A of Schedule 4, paragraph 49 of Part I of Schedule 9 and paragraph 18B of Part I of Schedule 9A. 7

Directors of companies incorporated under the Companies Acts are required by the Act to prepare accounts that give a true and fair view of the state of affairs of the company, and where applicable the group, at the end of the financial year and of the profit or loss of the company or the group for the financial year. 8

The Consultative Committee of Accountancy Bodies (CCAB) is committed to promoting and supporting compliance with accounting standards by its member bodies and by their members, whether as preparers or auditors of financial information. 9

The Councils of the CCAB bodies therefore expect their members who assume responsibilities in respect of financial statements to observe accounting standards. The Councils have agreed that: 10

(a) where this responsibility is evidenced by the association of members' names with such financial statements in the capacity of directors or other officers, other than auditors, the onus will be on them to ensure that the existence and purpose of accounting standards are fully understood by fellow directors and other officers. Members should also use their best endeavours to ensure that accounting standards are observed and that significant departures found to be necessary are adequately disclosed and explained in the financial statements.

(b) where members act as auditors or reporting accountants, they should be in a position to justify significant departures to the extent that their concurrence with the departures is stated or implied. They are not, however, required to refer in their report to departures with which they concur, provided that adequate disclosure has been made in the notes to the financial statements.

The CCAB bodies, through appropriate committees, may enquire into apparent failures by their members to observe accounting standards or to ensure adequate disclosure of significant departures. 11

The Board notes the continuing application of previously adopted SSAPs in the Republic of Ireland through their on-going promulgation by the Institute of Chartered Accountants in Ireland (ICAI). It further notes ICAI's intention of maintaining close liaison with the Board on promulgating, with appropriate modifications for legal differences, FRSs for application in the Republic of Ireland. The objective of the Board and ICAI is a regime of accounting standards common to both the United Kingdom and the Republic of Ireland. 12

****Editor's note****: *Also paragraph 56 of the new Schedule 9A inserted by the Companies Act 1985 (Insurance Companies Accounts) Regulations 1993 (S.I. 1993 No. 3246). Now paras. 45, 54 and 62 of Schedules 1, 2 and 3 to the Large and Medium-sized Companies and Groups (Accounts and Reports) Regulations 2008 (SI 2008/410) respectively.*

SCOPE AND APPLICATION OF ACCOUNTING STANDARDS

13 Accounting standards are applicable to financial statements of a reporting entity that are intended to give a true and fair view of its state of affairs at the balance sheet date and of its profit or loss (or income and expenditure) for the financial period ending on that date. Accounting standards need not be applied to immaterial items.

14 Accounting standards should be applied to United Kingdom and Republic of Ireland group financial statements (including any amounts relating to overseas entities that are included in those financial statements). Accounting standards are not intended to apply to financial statements of overseas entities prepared for local purposes.

15 Where accounting standards prescribe information to be contained in financial statements, such requirements do not override exemptions from disclosure given by law to, and utilised by, certain types of entity.

COMPLIANCE WITH ACCOUNTING STANDARDS

16 Accounting standards are authoritative statements of how particular types of transaction and other events should be reflected in financial statements and accordingly compliance with accounting standards will normally be necessary for financial statements to give a true and fair view.

17 In applying accounting standards it is important to be guided by the spirit and reasoning behind them. The spirit and reasoning are set out in the individual FRSs and are based on the Board's Statement of Principles for Financial Reporting.

18 The requirement to give a true and fair view may in special circumstances require a departure from accounting standards. However, because accounting standards are formulated with the objective of ensuring that the information resulting from their application faithfully represents the underlying commercial activity, the Board envisages that only in exceptional circumstances will departure from the requirements of an accounting standard be necessary in order for financial statements to give a true and fair view.

19 If in exceptional circumstances compliance with the requirements of an accounting standard is inconsistent with the requirement to give a true and fair view, the requirements of the accounting standard should be departed from to the extent necessary to give a true and fair view. In such cases informed and unbiased judgement should be used to devise an appropriate alternative treatment, which should be consistent with the economic and commercial characteristics of the circumstances concerned. Particulars of any material departure from an accounting standard, the reasons for it and its financial effects should be disclosed in the financial statements. The disclosure made should be equivalent to that given in respect of departures from specific accounting provisions of companies legislation.

20 The Financial Reporting Review Panel (the Review Panel) and the Department of Trade and Industry have procedures for receiving and investigating complaints regarding the annual accounts of companies in respect of apparent departures from the accounting requirements of the Act, including the requirement to give a true and fair view.* The Review Panel will be concerned with material departures from accounting standards, where as a result the accounts in question do not give a true

Similar provisions exist for receiving and investigating complaints regarding the annual accounts of companies in respect of apparent departure from the accounting requirements of the Order.* ***Editor's note:* *The Department of Trade and Industry is now the Department for Business, Innovation and Skills.*

and fair view, but it will also cover other departures from the accounting provisions of the Act. The Review Panel is empowered by regulations made under the Act to apply to the court for a declaration or declarator that the annual accounts of a company do not comply with the requirements of the Act and an order requiring the directors of the company to prepare revised accounts.* The Department of Trade and Industry has similar powers.

THE PUBLIC SECTOR

The prescription of accounting requirements for the public sector in the United Kingdom is a matter for the Government. Where public sector bodies prepare annual reports and accounts on commercial lines, the Government's requirements may or may not refer specifically either to accounting standards or to the need for the financial statements concerned to give a true and fair view. However, it can be expected that the Government's requirements in such cases will normally accord with the principles underlying the Board's pronouncements, except where in the particular circumstances of the public sector bodies concerned the Government considers these principles to be inappropriate or considers others to be more appropriate. **21**

In the Republic of Ireland accounting standards will normally be applicable to reporting entities in the public sector as such entities are either established under companies legislation or are established under special legislation which requires them to produce financial statements which give a true and fair view. **22**

THE ISSUE OF A FINANCIAL REPORTING STANDARD

Topics that become the subject of FRSs are identified by the Board either from its own research or from external sources, including submissions from interested parties. **23**

When a topic is identified by the Board as requiring the issue of an FRS the Board commissions its staff to undertake a programme of research and consultation. This programme involves consideration of and consultation on the relevant conceptual issues, existing pronouncements and practice in the United Kingdom, the Republic of Ireland and overseas and the economic, legal and practical implications of the introduction of particular accounting requirements. **24**

When the issues have been identified and debated by the Board a discussion draft is normally produced and circulated to parties who have registered their interest with the Board. When the issues require a more discursive treatment a discussion paper may be published instead. The purpose of either of these documents is to form a basis for discussion with parties particularly affected by, or having knowledge of, the issues raised in the proposals. An exposure draft of an accounting standard (a Financial Reporting Exposure Draft or FRED) is then published to allow an opportunity for all interested parties to comment on the proposals and for the Board to gauge the appropriateness and level of acceptance of those proposals. **25**

The exposure draft is refined in the light of feedback resulting from the period of public exposure. There may follow another period of public or selective exposure prior to the issue of an FRS. Although the Board weighs carefully the views of interested parties, the ultimate content of an FRS must be determined by the Board's own judgement based on research, public consultation and careful deliberation about the benefits and costs of providing the resulting information. **26**

**The Review Panel does not operate in the Republic of Ireland.*

APPLICABILITY OF AN ACCOUNTING STANDARD TO TRANSACTIONS ENTERED INTO BEFORE THE STANDARD WAS ISSUED

27 When a new accounting standard is issued the question arises whether its provisions should be applied to transactions which took place prior to the promulgation of the standard. The general policy of the Board is that the provisions of accounting standards should be applied to all material transactions irrespective of the date at which they are entered into. This is because exemption of certain transactions leads to similar transactions being accounted for differently in the same set of accounts, and can also hinder the comparison of the accounts of one entity with another.

28 In a few instances, application of the provisions of accounting standards to past transactions will entail a considerable amount of work and may result in information which is difficult for the user of accounts to interpret. In such a case, in drafting the standard, the Board will consider incorporating an exclusion for transactions which took place prior to the promulgation of the standard.

29 In some instances, a new standard may have unforeseen consequences where financial statements are used to monitor compliance with contracts and agreements. The most widespread example is the covenants contained in banking and loan agreements, which may impose limits on measures such as net worth or gearing as shown in the borrower's financial statements.

30 The Board considers that the developing nature of accounting requirements is a long-established fact that would be known to the parties when they entered into the agreement. It is up to the parties to determine whether the agreement should be insulated from the effects of a future accounting standard or, if not, the manner in which it might be renegotiated to reflect changes in reporting rather than changes in the underlying financial position.* The Board, therefore, has no general policy of exempting transactions occurring before a specific date from the requirements of new accounting standards.

EARLY ADOPTION OF FINANCIAL REPORTING EXPOSURE DRAFTS†

31 An exposure draft is issued for comment and is subject to revision. Until it is converted into an accounting standard the requirements of any existing accounting standards that would be affected by proposals in the exposure draft remain in force.

32 Some companies or other reporting entities may wish to provide additional information reflecting proposals in an exposure draft. In the Board's view there are two ways that this can be achieved:

(a) insofar as the information does not conflict with existing accounting standards, it could be incorporated in the financial statements. It should be remembered, however, that the proposals may change before forming part of an accounting standard and the consequences of a change to the proposals should be considered.

(b) the information could be provided in supplementary form.

**The British Bankers' Association has indicated that it does not believe that problems arising from breaches in covenants consequent upon changes in accounting policies will occur frequently in practice.*

†Similar conventions apply to discussion documents issued by the Board.

REVIEWS OF ACCOUNTING STANDARDS

Accounting standards are issued against the background of a business environment that evolves over time. The Board is, therefore, receptive to comments on accounting standards, recognising that, for some, a substantial period may be needed before their effectiveness can be judged, while in other cases there may be special reasons why an earlier review is necessary. However, the Board believes that it will normally be appropriate to allow new accounting standards a period in which to become established before commencing a process of formal post-issue review. **33**

ACCOUNTING STANDARDS AND THE LEGAL FRAMEWORK

In its debates on any accounting topic the Board initially develops its views by considering how its principles of accounting apply to the possible accounting options available for that topic. However, in deciding what is the most appropriate treatment the Board must also consider the environment in which its standards are to be applied. The legislation with which reporting entities must comply forms an important part of that environment. Accordingly, FRSs are drafted in the context of current United Kingdom and Republic of Ireland legislation and European Community Directives with the aim of ensuring consistency between accounting standards and the law. **34**

The status of accounting standards under United Kingdom legislation is addressed in the Opinion by Miss Mary Arden QC* 'The true and fair requirement', which is published as an appendix to this Foreword. **35**

INTERNATIONAL ACCOUNTING STANDARDS†

FRSs are formulated with due regard to international developments. The Board supports the International Accounting Standards Committee in its aim to harmonise international financial reporting. As part of this support an FRS contains a section explaining how it relates to the International Accounting Standard (IAS) dealing with the same topic. In most cases, compliance with an FRS automatically ensures compliance with the relevant IAS. Where the requirements of an accounting standard and an IAS differ, the accounting standard should be followed by entities reporting within the area of application of the Board's accounting standards. **36**

WITHDRAWAL OF EXPLANATORY FOREWORD TO STATEMENTS OF STANDARD ACCOUNTING PRACTICE

The 'Explanatory Foreword' to SSAPs, issued by the ASC in May 1975 and revised in May 1986, is superseded by this Foreword and is accordingly withdrawn. **37**

Now the Honourable Mrs Justice Arden.* ***Editor's note**: This note has now been supplemented by the opinion of Martin Moore QC which has been appended to this statement.*

†***Editor's note****: Now International Financial Reporting Standards.*

Appendix
Accounting Standards Board–
The true and fair requirement*

OPINION

1 This Opinion is concerned with the effect of recent changes in the law on the relationship between accounting standards and the requirement in Sections 226 and 227 of the Companies Act 1985 (as amended) that accounts drawn up in accordance with the Companies Act 1985 give a true and fair view of the state of affairs of the company, and where applicable the group, at the end of the financial year in question and of the profit or loss of the Company or group for that financial year. (I shall call this requirement 'the true and fair requirement'). As is well known, the true and fair requirement is overriding. Thus both sections provide that where in special circumstances compliance with the requirements of the Act as to the matters to be included in the accounts would be inconsistent with the true and fair requirement there must be a departure from those requirements to the extent necessary to give a true and fair view (sections 226(5) and 227(6)). The meaning of the true and fair requirement, as it appeared in earlier legislation, was discussed in detail in the Joint Opinions which I wrote in 1983 and 1984 with Leonard Hoffmann Q.C. (now the Right Hon. Lord Justice Hoffmann).

2 As stated in those Opinions, the question whether accounts satisfy the true and fair requirement is a question of law for the Court. However, while the true and fair view which the law requires to be given is not qualified in any way, the task of interpreting the true and fair requirement cannot be performed by the Court without evidence as to the practices and views of accountants. The more authoritative those practices and views, the more ready the Court will be to follow them. Those practices and views do not of course stand still. They respond to such matters as advances in accounting and changes in the economic climate and business practice. The law will not prevent the proper development of the practices and views of accountants but rather, through the process of interpretation, will reflect such development.

3 Up to August 1990 the responsibility for developing accounting standards was discharged by the Accounting Standards Committee ('the ASC'). Since August 1990 that responsibility has been discharged by the Accounting Standards Board ('the Board'). The Foreword to Accounting Standards approved by the Board describes in particular the circumstances in which accounts are expected to comply with accounting standards. For this purpose the key paragraph is paragraph 16, which provides

> 'Accounting standards are authoritative statements of how particular types of transaction and other events should be reflected in financial statements and accordingly compliance with accounting standards will normally be necessary for financial statements to give a true and fair view.'

The Foreword also describes the extensive process of investigation and consultation which precedes the issue of a standard and explains that the major accountancy bodies expect their members to observe accounting standards and may enquire into apparent failures by their members to observe standards or ensure adequate disclosure of departures from them.

Editor's note: *This opinion was given in the context of the Companies Act 1985. With effect for accounting periods beginning on or after 6 April 2008, the accounting provisions of the Act cease to apply, and are replaced with those of the Companies Act 2006. Therefore, all of the statutory references provided in this opinion will cease to be relevant. However, broadly the Companies Act 2006 requirements repeat those of the 1985 Act.*

What is the role of an accounting standard? The initial purpose is to identify proper accounting practice for the benefit of preparers and auditors of accounts. However, because accounts commonly comply with accounting standards, the effect of the issue of standards has also been to create a common understanding between users and preparers of accounts as to how particular items should be treated in accounts and accordingly an expectation that save where good reason exists accounts will comply with applicable accounting standards. **4**

The Companies Act 1989 now gives statutory recognition to the existence of accounting standards and by implication to their beneficial role in financial reporting. This recognition is achieved principally through the insertion of a new section (Section 256) into the Companies Act 1985 and of a new disclosure requirement into Schedule 4 to that Act. Section 256 provides: **5**

> '256. (1) In this Part 'accounting standards' means statements of standard accounting practice issued by such body or bodies as may be prescribed by regulations.
> (2) References in this Part to accounting standards applicable to a company's annual accounts are to such standards as are, in accordance with their terms, relevant to the company's circumstances and to the accounts.
> (3) The Secretary of State may make grants to or for the purposes of bodies concerned with –
> (a) issuing accounting standards,
> (b) overseeing and directing the issuing of such standards, or
> (c) investigating departures from such standards or from the accounting requirements of this Act and taking steps to secure compliance with them.
> (4) Regulations under this section may contain such transitional and other supplementary and incidental provisions as appear to the Secretary of State to be appropriate.'

In addition the notes to financial statements prepared under Schedule 4 must now comply with the following new requirement:*

> '36A. It shall be stated whether the accounts have been prepared in accordance with applicable accounting standards and particulars of any material departure from those standards and the reasons for it shall be given.'

Another significant change brought about by the 1989 Act is the introduction of a procedure whereby the Secretary of State or a person authorised by him may ask the Court to determine whether annual accounts comply with inter alia the true and fair requirement (Section 245B of the Companies Act 1985). The Financial Reporting Review Panel ('the Review Panel') has been authorised by the Secretary of State for this purpose. By agreement with the Department of Trade and Industry the ambit of the Review Panel is normally public and large private companies, with the Department exercising its powers in other cases. **6**

The changes brought about by the Companies Act 1989 will in my view affect the way in which the Court approaches the question whether compliance with an accounting standard is necessary to satisfy the true and fair view requirement. The Court will infer from Section 256 that statutory policy favours both the issue of accounting standards (by a body prescribed by regulation) and compliance with **7**

**This requirement also applies to group accounts drawn up under Schedule 4A. In addition the accounts of banking and insurance companies and groups drawn up under Schedules 9 and 9A must make the same disclosure. There is an exemption for small and medium-sized companies and for certain small and medium-sized groups.*

them: indeed Section 256(3)(c) additionally contemplates the investigation of departures from them and confers power to provide public funding for such purpose. The Court will also in my view infer from paragraph 36A of Schedule 4 that (since the requirement is to disclose particulars of non-compliance rather than of compliance) accounts which meet the true and fair requirement will in general follow rather than depart from standards and that departure is sufficiently abnormal to require to be justified. These factors increase the likelihood, to which the earlier Joint Opinions referred, that the Courts will hold that in general compliance with accounting standards is necessary to meet the true and fair requirement.

8 The status of accounting standards in legal proceedings has also in my view been enhanced by the changes in the standard-setting process since 1989. Prior to the Companies Act 1989 accounting standards were developed by the ASC, which was a committee established by the six professional accountancy bodies who form the Consultative Committee of Accountancy Bodies ('the CCAB') and funded by them. The standard-setting process was reviewed by a committee established by the CCAB under the chairmanship of Sir Ron Dearing CB. The report of that Committee (the Dearing Report), which was published in 1988 and is entitled The Making of Accounting Standards, contained a number of recommendations, including recommendations leading to what are now paragraph 36A and Section 245B and the further recommendation that the standard-setting body should be funded on a wider basis. As a result of the implementation of these recommendations the standard-setting body no longer represents simply the views of the accountancy profession. Its members are appointed by a committee drawn from the Council of the Financial Reporting Council Limited ('the FRC'). The Council includes representatives of the Government, representatives of the business and financial community and members of the accountancy profession. Moreover, the Board is now funded, via the FRC, jointly by the Government, the financial community and the accountancy profession.

9 The statements referred to in Section 256 are of standard accounting practice. Parliament has thus recognised the desirability of standardisation in the accountancy field. The discretion to determine the measure of standardisation is one of the matters left to the Board. By definition, standardisation may restrict the availability of particular accounting treatments. Moreover the Act does not require that the practices required by a standard should necessarily be those prevailing or generally accepted at the time.

10 As explained in the earlier Joint Opinions in relation to statements of standard accounting practice, the immediate effect of the issue of an accounting standard is to create a likelihood that the court will hold that compliance with that standard is necessary to meet the true and fair requirement. That likelihood is strengthened by the degree to which a standard is subsequently accepted in practice. Thus if a particular standard is generally followed, the court is very likely to find that accounts must comply with it in order to show a true and fair view. The converse of that proposition, that non-acceptance of a standard in practice would almost inevitably lead a court to the conclusion that compliance with it was not necessary to meet the true and fair requirement, is not however the case. Whenever a standard is issued by the Board, then, irrespective of the lack in some quarters of support for it, the court would be bound to give special weight to the opinion of the Board in view of its status as the standard-setting body, the process of investigation, discussion and consultation that it will have undertaken before adopting the standard and the evolving nature of accounting standards.

11 The fact that paragraph 36A envisages the possibility of a departure from an 'applicable accounting standard' (in essence, any relevant standard: see section 256(2), above) does not mean that the Companies Act permits a departure in any case where the disclosure is given. The departure must have been appropriate in the particular case. If the Court is satisfied that compliance with a standard is necessary to show a true and fair view in that case, a departure will result in a breach of the true and fair requirement even if the paragraph 36A disclosure is given.

Experience shows that from time to time and for varying reasons deficiencies in accounting standards appear. Following a recommendation in the Dearing Report, the Board has established a sub-committee called the Urgent Issues Task Force ('the UITF') to resolve such issues on an urgent basis in appropriate cases. The members of the UITF include leading members of the accountancy profession and of the business community. The agenda of the UITF is published in advance to allow for public debate. The UITF's consensus pronouncements (contained in abstracts) represent the considered views of a large majority of its members. When the UITF reaches its view, it is considered by the Board for compliance with the law and accounting standards and with the Board's future plans. If an abstract meets these criteria the Board expects to adopt it without further consideration. It will then be published by the Board. The expectation of the CCAB, the Board and the profession is that abstracts of the UITF will be observed. This expectation has been borne out in practice. Accordingly in my view, the Court is likely to treat UITF abstracts as of considerable standing even though they are not envisaged by the Companies Acts. This will lead to a readiness on the part of the Court to accept that compliance with abstracts of the UITF is also necessary to meet the true and fair requirement. **12**

The Joint Opinions were particularly concerned with the effect of standards on the concept of true and fair. The approach to standards taken in the Joint Opinions is consistent with the approach of the Court in Lloyd Cheyham v. Littlejohn [1987] BCLC 303 at 313. In that case Woolf J. (as he then was) held that standards of the ASC were 'very strong evidence as to what is the proper standard which should be adopted'. **13**

As regards the concept of true and fair, I would emphasise the point made in the Joint Opinions that the true and fair view is a dynamic concept. Thus what is required to show a true and fair view is subject to continuous rebirth and in determining whether the true and fair requirement is satisfied the Court will not in my view seek to find synonyms for the words 'true' and 'fair' but will seek to apply the concepts which those words imply. **14**

It is nearly a decade since the Joint Opinions were written. Experience and legislative history since then have both illustrated the subtlety and evolving nature of the relationship between law and accounting practice. Accounting standards are now assured as an authoritative source of the latter. In consequence it is now the norm for accounts to comply with accounting standards. I would add this. Just as a custom which is upheld by the courts may properly be regarded as a source of law, so too, in my view, does an accounting standard which the court holds must be complied with to meet the true and fair requirement become, in cases where it is applicable, a source of law in itself in the widest sense of that term. **15**

Mary Arden

Erskine Chambers
Lincoln's Inn
21st April 1993

True and Fair

The 'true and fair' concept has been a part of English law and central to accounting and auditing practice in the UK for many decades. There has been no statutory definition of 'true and fair'. The most authoritative statements as to the meaning of 'true and fair' have been legal opinions written by Lord Hoffmann and Dame Mary Arden in 1983 and 1984 and by Dame Mary Arden in 1993 ('the Opinions'). Since those Opinions were written, there have been some significant changes in accounting standards and company law which have led some to question whether the views expressed in those Opinions remain applicable.

In these circumstances, the FRC concluded that it would be helpful to its preparers, auditors and users of financial statements if it commissioned a further legal opinion to ascertain whether the approach to 'true and fair' taken in the Opinions requires to be revised. The FRC instructed Martin Moore QC and his Opinion is now published on the FRC website.

In his Opinion, Mr Moore has endorsed the analysis in the Opinions of Lord Hoffmann and Dame Mary Arden and confirmed the centrality of the true and fair requirement to the preparation of financial statements in the UK, whether they are prepared in accordance with international or UK accounting standards.

Directors must consider whether, taken in the round, the financial statements that they approve are appropriate. Similarly, auditors are required to exercise professional judgment before expressing an audit opinion. As a result, the Opinion confirms that it will not be sufficient for either directors or auditors to reach such conclusions solely because the financial statements were prepared in accordance with applicable accounting standards.

The FRC believes that this Opinion is an important confirmation of a key contributor to the integrity of financial reporting in the UK.

19 May 2008

THE TRUE AND FAIR REQUIREMENT REVISITED

Opinion

I am asked to advise whether: 1

(a) the provisions of the European Directives and Regulations governing the preparation and audit of financial statements and/or

(b) the requirements of the Companies Act 2006 and, in particular, Sections 393–397 and Section 495 of that Act

require any revision to the approach to be taken to the concept of "true and fair" as articulated in the opinions of Leonard Hoffmann QC and Mary Arden written in 1983 and 1984 and by Mary Arden QC written in 1993 ("the Opinions").

Parts 15 and 16 of the Companies Act 2006 ("the 2006 Act") which deal with Accounts and Reports and Audit came into force, almost entirely, on 6th April 2008 and apply, with some limited exceptions, to accounting periods commencing on or after that date. 2

In this Opinion I will refer to the provisions now in force but my conclusions are the same in relation to the former provisions of the Companies Act 1985 as amended. References to the provisions of the 2006 Act should be taken as references to the preceding equivalent provisions for the now limited period in which such provisions remain apposite. 3

In brief, and for the reasons which appear in this Opinion, my conclusions* are as follows: 4

(A) The central conclusions of the Opinions have been endorsed by the Courts in England, which will approach the true and fair requirement in the manner described in the Opinions (Paragraphs 11–17).

(B) The decisions of the European Court of Justice ("ECJ") do not show a different approach and indicate that the ECJ supports the superemacy of the concept of the true and fair requirement and will adopt interpretations of the relevant Directives which avoid formalism (Paragraphs 18–21).

(C) The requirement set out in applicable international accounting standards to present fairly is not a different requirement to that of showing a true and fair view, but is a different articulation of the same concept (Paragraphs 23–29).

(D) Although the routes by which the requirement to give a fair presentation or a true and fair view have become embedded in relation to the financial statements of UK companies differ slightly in each case that requirement remains paramount (Paragraphs 30–35).

(E) The ability to depart from accounting standards (whether international or domestic) has been preserved, albeit by slightly different routes, if the result would be so misleading as to conflict with the objective of the relevant financial statements (Paragraphs 36–37).

(F) The scope for arguing that financial statements which do not comply with relevant accounting standards nevertheless give a true and fair view, or a fair presentation, is very limited (Paragraph 38–40).

(G) The preparation of financial statements is not a mechanical process where compliance with relevant accounting standards will automatically ensure that those statements show a true and fair view, or a fair presentation. Such

**Save where expressly mentioned my conclusions are the same whether the accounts are single entity accounts or consolidated accounts.*

compliance may be highly likely to produce such an outcome; but it does not guarantee it (Paragraphs 41–45).

(H) The true and fair view, or fair presentation, concept is of an overarching nature. Any decision made or judgment reached by the preparer of financial statements is not made in a vacuum but is made against the requirement to give a true and fair view, or to achieve a fair presentation (Paragraph 46).

(I) The concept comes into play, for example,
- in the way in which a standard is applied,
- in consideration of whether a standard should be departed from in those "exceptional" or "extremely rare" cases in which departure is permitted,
- in the choices regarding the applicability of a particular standard, or
- in determining the closest analogy where the circumstances are not precisely covered by a standard. (Paragraph 46 (A) – (E))

(J) The Transparency Directive's requirement to produce half-yearly reports showing a true and fair view does not change the analysis. It provides an example of how the requirement to give a true and fair view, or achieve a fair presentation, is in part moulded by the expectations of the users of financial statements (Paragraphs 47–53).

(K) The provisions of the Companies Act 2006, which [I] have been asked to comment on particularly, have served to underline and reinforce the centrality of the true and fair requirement to the preparation of financial statements (Paragraphs 54–57).

5 Given the time which has elapsed since the Opinions were written and the considerable developments in the area which have occurred in that period, it will take a little time to explain my conclusion. The approach I propose to adopt in this Opinion is as follows:

(a) First, to describe shortly the central conclusions of those opinions.
(b) Second, to consider any recent authority which may bear upon the issue.
(c) Third, to consider the relevant European Directives and Regulations both in their European context and in so far as incorporated into domestic law.
(d) Fourth, to consider the specific provisions of the 2006 Act upon which I have been asked to comment.

6 It must be remembered, however, that the above categorisation should not disguise the considerable degree of overlap between community and domestic law; not least because of the principle that domestic legislation should be construed so far as possible in conformity with the provisions and objectives of applicable Community law: *Marleasing SA v La Commercial Internacional de Alimentacion Case* C-106/89 [1990] ECR I-4135 and see *It's a Wrap (UK) Ltd v. Gula* [2006] 2 BCLC 634 for an application of that principle.

THE OPINIONS

7 The Opinions have achieved almost iconic status in their sphere of operation. The Opinions are reproduced in many professional publications and what follows should not be taken as substitute for reading them. However, for the purposes of this Opinion, I must attempt a distillation of them.

8 It seems to me that the essence of the Opinions is that:

(A) The requirement to prepare accounts which show a true and fair view was a legal requirement derived from both domestic legislation, namely Section 149 the Companies Act 1948, and Article 2(3) the Fourth Council Directive (78/

660/EEC) which was incorporated into domestic law by the amendment of Section 149* of the 1948 Act.

(B) As a legal requirement, its satisfaction is a question of law for the Courts to determine.

(C) In determining that question, the Courts will rely very heavily upon the ordinary practices of professional accountants in determining whether accounts show a true and fair view. That is because those practices reflect the accumulation of experience and good professional practice and mould the expectations of the users of accounts as to the sufficiency and utility of the information in terms of quantity and quality.

(D) Compliance with generally accepted accounting principles as set out in relevant statements of standard accounting practice will be *prima facie* evidence of satisfaction of the true and fair standard and vice versa.

(E) The application of the concept involves judgment on questions of degree. Reasonable businessmen and accountants may differ over the degree of accuracy or comprehensiveness, there may be differences over the method used to adopt a true and fair view and there may be more than one view of a financial position, any of which could be described as true and fair.

(F) The concept is dynamic, evolving and subject to continuous rebirth. Accordingly, the detailed provisions of the Schedules to the Companies Act may have to yield to the overriding requirement to produce accounts which give a true and fair view.

(G) The provisions of the Companies Act 1989 which provides, amongst other things, for (a) the establishment and funding of the FRC, (b) a statutory definition of accounting standards, (c) the requirement to state that accounts have been prepared in accordance with applicable standards with departure to be particularised and justified and (d) the mandatory revision of defective accounts on the application by the Secretary of State or its authorised person, the FRRP, have served to underline the central importance and authority of accounting standards to the production of accounts showing a true and fair view.

(H) These factors, together with the more inclusive process of standard setting, all serve to increase the likelihood that a Court would hold that compliance with a standard is necessary to meet the true and fair requirement.

RECENT AUTHORITY

The Opinions remarked that there were no reported cases on the specific question of whether accounts show a true and fair view, although the issue had been adverted to in cases on other matters. The Opinions did, however, note that there had been discussion in revenue cases on whether a profit or loss has been calculated in accordance with "the correct principles of commercial accountancy"†, being those used when preparing accounts that show a true and fair view. **9**

As can be seen below, since the Opinions were written, there have been some cases of relevance on the topic, both before domestic tribunals and the European Court of Justice ("ECJ") which have followed the reasoning that the Opinions expected the courts to adopt. **10**

**This became section 226 and then 226A of the Companies Act 1985 and is now set out in section 396 of the 2006 Act.*

†*This approach was approved by the House of Lords in HMRC v William Grant & Sons Distillers Limited 28th March 2007 [2007] UKHL 15.*

The National Courts

11 The 1984 Opinion set out the approach of Pennycuick V-C in *Odeon Associated Theatres v Jones (Inspector of Taxes)* [1971] 1 W.L.R. 442 as an analogous guide to the approach a Court would take to the true and fair requirement. The approach of Pennycuick V-C was endorsed by the Court of Appeal in *Gallagher v Jones (Inspector of Taxes)* [1994] Ch. 107. Sir Thomas Bingham MR said at page 134:

> "*Despite the length of this judgment, the central issue is at root a very short one. The object is to determine, as accurately as possible, the profits or losses of the taxpayers' businesses for the accounting periods in question. Subject to any express or implied statutory rule, of which there is none here, the ordinary way to ascertain profits or losses of a business is to apply accepted principles of commercial accountancy. That is the very purpose for which such principles are formulated. As has often been pointed out, such principles are not static: they may be modified, refined and elaborated over time as circumstances change and accounting insights sharpen. But so long as such principles remain current and generally accepted they provide the surest answer to the question which the legislation requires to be answered. As Sir John Pennycuick V-C pointed out in Odeon Associated Theatres v Jones (Inspector of Taxes) [1971] 1 W.L.R. 442 different considerations arise where there is no accounting evidence or where there are two or more principles either or any of which is generally accepted. But these considerations do not apply here.*
>
> *The authorities do not persuade me that there is any rule of law such as that for which the taxpayers contend and that the judge found. Indeed, given the plain language of the legislation, I find it hard to understand how any judge-made rule could override the application of a generally accepted rule of commercial accountancy which (a) applied to the situation in question, (b) was not one of two or more rules applicable to the situation in question and (c) was not shown to be inconsistent with the true facts or otherwise inapt to determined the true profits of losses of the business*"

12 The House of Lords in *HMRC v William Grant & Sons Distillers Limited* 28th March 2007 [2007] UKHL 15 again adopted that approach and declined to find that some fundamental principle of accountancy demanded an answer different to that provided by that test.

13 In case Lord Bingham might be thought to be giving too much power to generally accepted principles of commercial accountancy, there has been a timely reminder in *Balloon Promotions Limited v. Wilson (Inspector of Taxes)* 3rd March 2006 SPC00524 (before a Special Commissioner) that the question of what constitutes compliance with the true and fair requirement remains a legal question. In that case the Special Commissioner was considering the meaning of goodwill for roll-over relief under section 152 of the Taxation of Capital Gains Act 1992. He was satisfied that the accountancy definition of goodwill was deficient. He said at p.35:

> "*The definition under SSAP 22 permits the possibility that intangible assets other than goodwill which cannot be separately identified and assessed to be categorised as goodwill. The central dispute in this appeal is about whether the consideration apportioned to goodwill should instead be apportioned to another intangible asset, namely compensation for the early termination of a franchise agreement. Thus goodwill should be construed in accordance with legal not accountancy principles.*"

14 There have been some cases where the question of true and fair has arisen in the context of breach of warranty claims. In some of the cases, the relevant accounts have been distorted by fraudulent entries. In those cases, it is easy to demonstrate that the accounts do not show a true and fair view. These cases therefore do not illuminate the approach of the Court.

The approach of the Opinions has been endorsed by the Court in *Bairstow v. Queen's Moat House PLC* (19th July 1999) by Nelson J where he says: 15

> "*In their joint opinion to the Accounting Standards Committee, Leonard Hoffmann QC and Mary H Arden (as they then were) expressed the view that the information contained in accounts must be accurate and comprehensive, that is, sufficient in quality and quantity to satisfy the reasonable expectations of the reader to whom they were addressed. They rightly anticipated that the courts would on this basis treat compliance with accepted accounting principles as prima facie evidence that the accounts were true and fair, and equally that deviation from accepted principles would be prima facie evidence that they were not (See Lloyd Cheyman v. Littlejohn [1987] BCLC 303). This view has now been strengthened by the Companies Act 1989 and subsequent regulation now make that more likely*"

An example of the acceptance by the Court of the points made in the Opinions, and summarised in paragraph 6(E) above, can be found in *Jeunique International Holdings Limited v. Foreshew* 2nd April 2001. This dispute concerned the valuation of fixed assets which were alleged to be overvalued such that the relevant warranty as to true and fair was wrong. It was found that certain assets should have been valued at net replacement cost but had been valued at gross replacement cost; in other words, not in accordance with the valuation rules in Part C of Schedule 4, Companies Act 1985. Nevertheless certain assets had been undervalued by at least as much as that overvaluation. Accordingly the line item in the audited accounts for Fixed Assets did give a true and fair view. 16

These authorities demonstrate that the approach to the true and fair requirement in the Opinions (as summarised at paragraph 6 above) has been affirmed by the English courts. 17

European Court of Justice

There have been two important cases before the ECJ on the compatibility with the Fourth Directive of, in both cases, German accounting rules. Both provide an insight into the approach that the ECJ takes to the requirement in the Fourth Directive that accounts should show a true and fair view. 18

The first, *Tomberger v. Gebruder von der Wettern* Case C-234/94 [1996] 2 BCLC 457, is instructive for the approach of the Court to the meaning of "true and fair view" in the Fourth Directive and the adoption by the Court of a flexible interpretation of the provisions of the Fourth Directive. 19

The second, *DE + ES Bauunternehmung GmbH v Finanzamt Bergeheim* Case C-275/97 [2000] BCC 757, construed the detailed provisions of the Directive against the yardstick of the true and fair requirement and, furthermore, subjected an exceptional case departure to a true and fair requirement. Both these cases are discussed in detail in the Appendix to this Opinion. 20

These decisions of the ECJ do not suggest that there is any reason to change the approach to the true and fair requirement articulated by the Opinions. On the contrary, they demonstrate that the ECJ will, in supporting the supermacy of the 21 concept, adopt interpretations of the relevant Directives in a manner which avoids formalism.

THE EUROPEAN DIRECTIVES AND REGULATIONS

22 Naturally, the Opinions were written against the backdrop of the Fourth and Seventh Company Law Directives and I do not, therefore, need to consider their impact, save to say that the decisions of the ECJ on the Directives have not shown that the approach is erroneous or that there is some divergence between the approach to the true and fair requirement between the domestic courts and the ECJ.

The IAS Regulation

'True and Fair' and 'Presents Fairly'

23 The Fourth and Seventh Directives stood for many years as the main harmonizing instruments in the accounting field. However, a further impetus to harmonisation has been given by the introduction of international accounting standards. The vehicle for such introduction on a community wide basis is Regulation 1606/2002 ("the IAS Regulation"), which provides for the procedure whereby International Accounting Standards ("IAS") are to be adopted and sets out the financial statements to which they must be applied. Broadly, the use of adopted IASs is mandatory for the consolidated accounts of listed companies whose securities are admitted to trading on a regulated market. It is important to note that the IAS Regulation provides that adoption of an IAS should not occur if to do so would be contrary to the true and fair requirements of the Fourth and Seventh Directives: see art 3(1).

24 This is significant because the IAS I does not use the term true and fair, but instead uses the adverb "fairly". Paragraph 13 of IAS 1 provides as follows:

> "*Financial statements shall present fairly the financial position, financial performance and cash flows of an entity. Fair presentation requires the faithful representation of the effects of the transactions, other events and conditions in accordance with the definitions and recognition criteria for assets, liabilities, income and expenses set out in the Framework. The application of IFRSs, with additional disclosure when necessary, is presumed to result in financial statements that achieve a fair presentation*"

25 The Framework referred to in IAS 1 is a document prepared by the International Accounting Standards Board (the IASB) entitled Framework for the Preparation and Presentation of Financial Statements ("the Framework"). The Framework is designed to set out the concepts which underlie the preparation and presentation of financial statements for external users and assist the IASB in setting international accounting standards.

26 The Framework is similar in scope in to the Statement of Principles of Financial Reporting made by the Accounting Standards Board in December 1999 ("the Statement").

27 The Statement is more explicit in its references to the true and fair requirement than the Framework. The Statement contains this passage:

> "12. *It is inherent in the nature of the true and fair concept that financial statements will not give a true and fair view unless the information they contain is sufficient in quantity and quality to satisfy the reasonable expectations of the*

readers to whom they are addressed. Such expectations change over time and the Board seeks, through its accounting standards and other authoritative pronouncements, both to respond to those expectations and to influence them. The Statement of Principles may therefore be expected to contribute to the development of the concept.

13. The Statement of Principles does not, however, define the meaning of true and fair – it is detailed legal requirements, accounting standards and, in their absence, other evidence of generally accepted accounting practice itself, that normally determine the content of financial statements. Nevertheless, as the Statement is a set of high level principles designed to help in setting standards, it has the true and fair view concept at its foundation. Its insistence on relevance and reliability as prime indicators of the quality of financial information is just one example of this"

In contrast, the Framework does not emphasise the true and fair concept in this way. It does, however, contain a passage which in my view makes it clear that "true and fair" and "present fairly" do not describe two different concepts, but are simply different articulations of the same concept. It says at Paragraph 46: **28**

"*Financial statements are frequently described as showing a true and fair view of, or as presenting fairly, the financial position, performance and changes in financial position of an entity. Although the Framework does not deal directly with such concepts, the application of the principal qualitative characteristics and of appropriate accounting standards normally results in financial statements that convey what is generally understood as true and fair view of, or as presenting fairly such information*"

I add that, given the similarity of the subject matter and scope of each of the Framework and the Statement dealing as they do with reliability, comparability, fundamental accounting concepts and principal elements of the financial statements in very similar ways, the conclusion would be that "true and fair" and "present fairly" were synonymous, even if it were left unexpressed in the Framework. It is noteworthy that "present fairly" is very similar to "quadro fedele" or "image fidele" which are respectively the Italian and French translations of true and fair in the Fourth and Seventh Directives. **29**

The manner in which accounting standards have been given legal effect

Pursuant to the IAS Regulation, the EC incorporated certain international accounting standards issued by the IASB (including IAS 1*) into European law by a series of regulations, each of which is binding on those preparing the consolidated accounts of listed companies whose securities are admitted to trading on a regulated market in the EC. **30**

The position in relation to the preparation of **31**

(i) the group accounts of companies whose securities are not admitted to trading on a regulated market in the EC ('non IAS group accounts'), and
(ii) the accounts of individual companies

was left to be addressed through national law.

**Adopted by EC 1725/2003.*

32 The changes to the Companies Act 1985 necessary to incorporate the IAS Regulation into domestic law were made by the Companies Act 1985 (International Accounting Standards and Other Accounting Amendments) Regulations 2004 (SI 2004/2947). The greater part of the changes were those necessary to implement the IAS Regulation, but additional changes were made to implement both the Directive 2001/65/EC (the Fair Value Directive) and Directive 2003/51/EEC (the Accounts Modernisation Directive) as they affected the annual and consolidated accounts of certain types of companies, banks and other financial institutions.

33 The 2006 Act sets out, by section 395, introduced two types of individual accounts for companies; Companies Act individual accounts (which are to be prepared in accordance with section 396) and IAS individual accounts (which, by virtue of section 397, are to be prepared in accordance with IAS). By section 403, save for those cases in which group accounts must be prepared in accordance with IAS, a similar choice is available for group accounts.

34 It is important to note that section 397 requires a company which prepares IAS individual accounts to state in the notes to the accounts that they have been prepared in accordance with international accounting standards. This is similar to Paragraph 45 in Part 3 of Schedule 1 to the Large and Medium-sized Companies and Groups (Accounts and Reports) Regulations 2008* as regards preparation in accordance with applicable UK accounting standards. The audit report must state clearly whether in the auditor's opinion the annual accounts have been properly prepared in accordance with the Act or Article 4 of the IAS regulation i.e. in accordance with IASs and whether the accounts give a true and fair view of, or present fairly, in accordance with the relevant accounting framework.

35 Thus the legislative route is slightly different for Companies Act Individual Accounts and IAS Individual Accounts in that the former have an express incorporation of the true and fair requirement in section 396 and the latter have, by virtue of section 397 the requirement to achieve a fair presentation incorporated by reference. Nevertheless, in each case the relevant requirement is embedded into domestic law.

The circumstances when departures from accounting standards are permitted

36 IAS 1 permits a departure from IFRS if a particular IFRS would be so misleading that it would conflict with the objective of the financial statements set out in the Framework. FRS18, provides for a departure from UK accounting standards in similar circumstances. Both IAS 1 and FRS 18 require disclosure and justification.

37 Just as the legal underpinning of the requirement to attain the relevant benchmark differs as between companies Act accounts and IAS accounts so does that of the ability to depart from the relevant accounting standards. In the case of Companies Act individual accounts that ability is expressly stated in section 396(5) whereas section 397 requires IAS individual accounts† to have been prepared in accordance with international accounting standards‡ IAS 1 was adopted by EC 1725/2003 and thus the ability to depart from an IFRS is incorporated by reference.

38 Although both accounting frameworks recognise that a departure from an accounting standard may be necessary where compliance with that standard would

**Formerly Paragraph 36A in Schedule 4 to the Companies Act 1985.*

†Section 406 for IAS group accounts.

‡Being those within the meaning of the IAS Regulation and adopted in accordance with it (section 474(1)).

produce a result so misleading that it would conflict with the objective of financial statements, the two frameworks use different terminology to describe the likelihood of such circumstances arising. IAS 1 states that the circumstances in which there should be such a conflict are "extremely rare". FRS 18 uses the word "exceptional".

Both these terms contemplate departures from a relevant standard in circumstances which are so removed from the contemplation of the relevant standard that compliance therewith would be inconsistent with the basic objective of fair presentation or true and fair view as the case may be. In my view, an English court dealing with words of such similar meaning as 'extremely rare' and 'exceptional' is most unlikely to discern any practical distinction between the circumstances which justify their use. 39

On any basis these words suggest that the circumstances in which departure from a relevant standard is appropriate are very limited indeed. 40

Mechanical application of standards.

Whilst the 1993 Opinion emphasised the central importance and authority of accounting standards in satisfaction of the requirement to give a true and fair view, it concluded that the true and fair requirement was the overarching concept to be used in the preparation of financial statements; a position which was emphasised by the express reference in the legislation of the true and fair override* 41

I am asked to consider whether there has been a subtle shift in the legal approach to fair presentation or indeed true and fair as a result of the statement in IAS 1 that the circumstances in which departure from a relevant international accounting standard could be justified are "extremely rare", coupled with the level of detail which is set out in the relevant standards, and the depth of expertise and consultation which is brought to bear in the standard setting process. Against this background, it may be said, that a preparer of financial statements in accordance with IAS can be certain that a fair presentation will always have been achieved if those standards are followed. 42

In my view a seeker after such certainty, whether in relation to IAS individual accounts or Companies Act individual accounts would be confusing outcome with process. In the case of IAS, any such suggestion is clearly contradicted by the fact that IAS 1 expressly provides for IFRS standards to be departed from and that the effect of the legislation is to require compliance with adopted IAS. In the case of individual accounts prepared under the Companies Act 2006, the same conclusion applies by virtue of section 396(5).. 43

It is no doubt true, as a practical matter, that, as accounting standards have become more detailed and departure from them has become harder to justify, the scope for persuading a Court that financial statements which do not comply with relevant accounting standards give a true and fair view, or achieve a fair presentation has become very limited and the scope for arguing that compliance with relevant accounting standards gives a true and fair view, or achieves a fair presentation, has correspondingly increased. 44

To make that observation, however, is only to comment on an historical trend which has been evident for some years and which, given the Court's approach to accounting 45

**The phrase 'legislative override' is used to describe a legislative provision which provides that the requirement to achieve a true and fair view when preparing accounts take precedence over some other specific legislative provision relating to the preparation of accounts.*

standards as the surest guide to the attainment of the true and fair view, is unsurprising. It does not follow from that observation that the preparation of financial statements can now be reduced to a mechanistic process of following the relevant standards without the application of objective professional judgment applied to ensure that those statements give a true and fair view, or achieve a fair presentation.

46 In my view, the true and fair, or fair presentation, concept, remains at the heart of the preparation of financial statements. It can aptly be described as an overarching concept which should inform all decisions made by the preparers of such statements. My view derives from the following factors:

(A) The appropriateness of a particular standard may be undeniable, yet there may well be difficult questions of judgment in the application of that statement which affect, perhaps critically, the resultant quantification or appearance of items in the financial statements. Such judgment is not exercised in a vacuum but in order to give a true and fair view, or achieve a fair presentation.

(B) A departure from a relevant standard may be "extremely rare" or "exceptional", but the preparers of financial statements will always have to ask themselves whether departure is nonetheless required in their particular circumstances. No doubt, in very many cases that will be a very easy question to answer, but it must always be asked. Again the question is not asked in a vacuum; it is answered in order to achieve a true and fair view, or fair presentation.

(C) It is possible that the treatment of a particular item could be justified by reference to the application of two different, but equally relevant, standards. A choice will have to be made. Again the question is not asked in a vacuum and is answered in order to give a true and fair view, or achieve a fair presentation.

(D) It is also possible that an undeniably appropriate treatment of another different item colours the judgments and questions referred to above.

(E) The greater detail in standards and the greater depth and length of the standard setting process may give rise to severe timing difficulties in that economic and financial circumstances can change at great speed. The pace of innovation in financial instruments, in particular, is relentless. The cost of the increased weight of the authority of a standard is in the length of time they take to be settled, still less generally used. This may cause particular difficulties in areas of swift change since the precise circumstances may not be covered by a relevant standard, or the instrument may be so new that there may be no standard at all. The question of how to present these transactions, whether by deciding upon the closest analogy or otherwise, can only be answered by reference to the need to give a true and fair view or achieve a fair presentation.

(F) Compliance with accounting standards is not an end in itself, but it is the means to an end. Hence the recognition in statute, so far as Companies Act individual accounts and the recognition in IAS 1 so far as IAS individual accounts are concerned, of the true and fair, or fair presentation, override.

The Transparency Directive

47 The last piece of European legislation which has impacted upon companies and their accounts has been the Directive 2004/109/EC ("the Transparency Directive") which has introduced, in relation to the companies to which it applies (broadly listed companies whose securities are admitted to trading on a regulated market), a requirement to produce half yearly reports.

48 The Transparency Directive, in so far as it refers to a true and fair view, is an example of the content of that concept being moulded by the expectations of the users of financial statements. The first reference is in Recital 9, which is in these terms:

> "*[The IAS Regulation] has already paved the way for a convergence of financial reporting standards throughout the community for issuers whose securities are admitted to trading on a regulated market and who are required to submit consolidated accounts. Thus, a specific regime for security issuers beyond the general system for all companies, as laid down in the Company Law Directives, is already established. This Directive builds on this approach with regard to annual and interim financial reporting, including the principle of providing a true and fair view of an issuer's assets, liabilities, financial position and profits or losses. A condensed set of financial statements, as part of a half – yearly financial report, also represents a sufficient basis for giving such a true and fair view of the first six months of an issuer's financial year*"

Article 5(2) prescribes what the half-yearly financial report should consist of. It is in these terms: **49**

> "*2. The half-yearly financial report shall comprise:*
>
> *(a) the condensed set of financial statements;*
> *(b) an interim management report;*
> *(c) statements made by the persons responsible within the issuer, ... to the effect that, to the best of their knowledge, the condensed set of financial statements which has been prepared in accordance with the applicable set of accounting standards gives a true and fair view of the assets, liabilities, financial position and profit and loss of the issuer, or the undertakings included in the consolidation as required under paragraph 3, and that the interim management report includes a fair review of the information required under paragraph 4.*"

The requirement to confirm that the condensed financial statements give a true and fair view would, if the true and fair requirement were not an elastic concept moulded in part by the expectations of users, give rise to a conundrum; namely, how could a standard which must be applied to audited accounts for a full year be complied with in relation to half-yearly accounts which not only do not require an audit report, but also are self-evidently not meant to be as detailed as accounts for a full year? **50**

As matter of principle the answer is supplied by remembering that any set of accounts is, of necessity, an exercise in distillation and summary so as to be generally and reasonably useful to their users. The extent of the summary is, in part, determined by the expectation of the users. In relation to interim financial statements, the user is likely to have or have had access to the full year accounts and, in the interests of timeliness, avoidance of repetition and cost, is likely to be looking for, in effect, an update and an appraisal of any new significant matters affecting the company. This is recognised by IAS 34 (Interim Financial Reporting) and ASB Statement "Half-yearly financial reports. Accordingly, one would expect that a set of half yearly accounts which complied with standards relevant to interim reporting to give a true and fair view, or achieve a fair presentation. **51**

And so it has proved. Part 43 of the Companies Act 2006 has implemented, as from 20th January 2006, the Transparency Directive by amending the Financial Services and Markets Act 2000. As the relevant authority, the Financial Services Authority has made Disclosure Rules and Transparency Rules which, by Rule 4.2.10, provide that the requirement to confirm that the condensed set of financial statements give a true and fair view will be satisfied by including a statement that the financial **52** statements have been prepared in accordance with IAS 34, or, for UK issuers not using IFRS, pronouncements on interim reporting issued by the ASB and for all other issuers not using IFRS, a national standard relating to interim reporting.

53 Accordingly, in my view the European Directives and Regulations have not required any change in the approach articulated in the Opinions.

SECTIONS 393 AND 495 OF THE 2006 ACT

54 I have been asked to comment in particular on Sections 393 and 495. Section 393 provides as follows:

> *(1) The directors of a company must not approve accounts for the purposes of this Chapter unless they are satisfied that they give a true and fair view of the assets, liabilities, financial position and profit or loss-*
>
> *(a) in the case of the company's individual accounts, of the company:*
> *(b) in the case of the company's group accounts, of the undertakings included in the consolidation as a whole, so far as concerns members of the company.*
>
> *(2) The auditor of a company in carrying out his functions under this Act in relation to the company's annual accounts must have regard to the directors' duty under subsection (1)*

Section 495 sets out the obligation upon the auditors to prepare a report and the required content of that report. It provides, relevantly, as follows:

> *(2) The auditor's report must include-*
>
> *(a) An introduction identifying the annual accounts that are the subject of the audit and the financial reporting framework that has been applied in their preparation, and*
> *(b) A description of the scope of the audit identifying the auditing standards in accordance with which the audit was conducted.*
>
> *(3) The report must state clearly whether, in the auditor's opinion, the annual accounts-*
> *(a) give a true and fair view-*
> *(i) in the case of an individual balance sheet, of the state of affairs of the company as at the end of the financial year,*
> *(ii) in the case of an individual profit and loss account, of the profit and loss of the company for the financial year,*
> *(iii) in the case of group accounts, of the state of affairs as at the end of the financial year and of the profit or loss for the financial year of the undertakings included in the consolidation as a whole, so far as concerns members of the company*
> *(b) have been properly prepared in accordance with the relevant financial reporting framework; and*
> *(c) have been prepared in accordance with the requirements of this Act (and, where applicable, Article 4 of the IAS Regulation).*

55 Section 393 makes no distinction between Companies Act individual accounts, IAS individual accounts or group accounts. Curiously, it is phrased as a negative obligation; directors are not to approve accounts unless they are satisfied that they give a true and fair view. Section 393 was not originally in the Companies Bill. It was added in November 2005. The ministerial statement on its introduction was to the effect that the clear primacy of the true and fair concept had become blurred as a result of a

combination of United Kingdom and Community law provisions and the opportunity was taken to express this principle more clearly in the legislation. The object of the inclusion of sub-section (2) was to "*underline the point that directors and auditors should approach the accounts with the same common sense objective of ensuring that accounts give a true and fair view of the company's financial position.* The approach necessary to achieve this objective is discussed in paragraphs 23 to 29 above.

In the light of the fact that the stated reason for the introduction of section 393(1), which applies to all types of accounts, was a desire to clarify an existing concept, which had perhaps become obscured by legislative changes, the inclusion of section 393 will not, in my view, be taken to have altered the central conclusion set out in the Opinions and affirmed by the Courts. At best, it provides support for the conclusion that there has been no shift of the type set out in paragraph 41 above to a more mechanistic approach to the preparation of financial statements. **56**

For the same reasons, the provisions of section 495 do not in my view require any change to the approach as articulated in the Opinions. Again, if anything the separation in sub-section (3) of the three matters which must be stated clearly in the auditor's report serves to emphasise the different elements required. In that respect the section is of a piece with Section 393 and points to Parliament's intention to maintain the primacy of the true and fair requirement as the overarching concept in the preparation of financial statements. It is not to be taken as undermining the approach to the attainment of that standard as described in the Opinions. **57**

Martin Moore QC

Appendix

Tomberger v. Gebruder von der Wettern

1 In *Tomberger v. Gebruder von der Wettern* Case C-234/94 [1996] 2 BCLC 457 the facts were that two wholly-owned subsidiaries of a holding company adopted accounts for the year to 31st December 1989 on 26th June 1990 which showed profits appropriated to the holding company. At the general meetings of the subsidiaries decisions were taken to distribute the profits to their shareholders, namely the holding company. The accounts for the holding company were also drawn to 31st December 1989, but were both audited and adopted by its shareholders after 26th June 1990. The holding company's accounts did not show the subsidiaries' profits as profits of the holding company. A shareholder commenced proceedings on the basis that such profits should have been shown in the holding company's accounts to 31st December 1989. The national court considered that the treatment contended for by the shareholder was compulsory, but referred the matter to the ECJ for a ruling on compatibility.

2 The relevant Article of the Fourth Directive was Article 31(1)(c) & (d) which provides as follows:

> "*(c) valuation must be made on a prudent basis, and in particular:*
>
> *i. (aa) only profits made at the balance sheet date may be included,*
>
> *ii. (bb) account must be taken of all foreseeable liabilities and potential; losses arising in the course of the financial year concerned or of a previous one, even if such liabilities or losses become apparent only between the date of the balance sheet and the date on which it is drawn up,*
>
> *iii. (cc) . . .*
>
> *(d) account must be taken of income and charges relating to the financial year, irrespective of the date of receipt or payment of such income or charges,*"

3 In his Opinion, the Advocate General referred to these provisions as incorporating the prudence concept and accruals concept. Tellingly, he went on to describe them in these terms:

> "*Both of these principles constitute a cogent enunciation of the more general principle of a true and fair view' (quadro fedele*), the actual guiding criterion of the Community rules as a whole, laid down in art 2 of the directive. That principle requires the balance sheet to be drawn up so as to give not only a true (even in the relative sense in which that adjective is traditionally and necessarily used as regards balance sheets) but also a fair (essentially with regard to the good faith of the persons drawing up the balance sheet) representation of the company's assets and liabilities, its financial position and its profit or loss*"

4 In his Opinion, the Advocate General noted that the German and United Kingdom governments ascribed importance to the sole control by the parent company and their argument that an approach which did not allow contemporaneous entry of profits in those circumstances would be excessively restrictive and formalistic. As a

**"In the French version, "image fidele"; in the German: den tatsachlichen Verhaltnissen entesprechendes Bild". I would note that the expression "rappresentazione veritiera e correcta" was preferred to "quadro fedele" when the Italian Civil Code was amended in order to implement the fourth directive (see art 2423 of the Italian Civil Code".*

result, the Governments contended that the parent company's right to a profit came into existence in financial terms, even if it had not been specified in legal terms.

However, the Advocate General took the view that the German rules were not compatible, essentially because the holding company could not be said to have made a profit as at 31st December 1989 when it had no legal entitlement to receive a dividend until the appropriation after the year end. The Advocate General did not accept that there was a wide discretion in defining "profits made" in art 31 (c)(aa). He relied on the fact that the article required member states to ensure that the items shown in the annual accounts are valued in according to the general principles there set out. He also went on to say: 5

> "*Secondly, the directive, as I have already pointed out, does not merely require prudence in general terms but also takes care to define its substance with various detailed provisions which implement it, including the possibility of including in the balance sheet only profits actually made at the end of the financial year. In those circumstances, it seems to me that the rationale on which the provision is based would be undermined if it were possible to interpret it in a way suggested by the German government*".

Furthermore, he considered that that whatever may be the position as to the interpretation of the phrase "profits made", it could not encompass a purely future profit. 6

The provisions of the Advocate General's opinion are important because of the discussion of the true and fair requirement in the Directive, and because the ECJ declined to follow his recommendation, which on purely linguistic grounds had considerable merit. 7

The ECJ's judgment affirmed the true and fair requirement as the primary object of the Fourth Directive, and adopted an approach to interpretation of the detailed provisions of the Fourth Directive which ensures the achievement of that objective. To put it in other words, it considered a purely literal or linguistic approach to construction of the relevant provisions was not appropriate. The ECJ disposed of the case in these terms: 8

> "*17. Article 31 of the fourth directive seeks to coordinate national provisions concerning the presentation of annual accounts of certain types of companies (see the first recital of the preamble). In order to coordinate the content of annual accounts, the directive lays down the principle of the "true and fair view", compliance with which is the primary objective of the directive. According to that principle, the annual accounts of companies to which the fourth directive applies must give a true and fair view of their assets and liabilities, financial position and profit and loss (see fourth recital in the preamble to the fourth directive and art 2(3) and (5) thereof).*
>
> *18. Application of that principle must, so far as possible, be guided by the general principles contained in art 31 of the fourth directive. In this case, the principles set out in art 31(1)(c)(aa) and (bb) and (d) are of particular importance.*
>
> *19. First, art 31(1)(c)(aa) provides that only profits made at the balance sheet date may be included in the balance sheet.*
>
> *20. Second, art 31(1)(d) provides that account must be taken in the balance sheet for a financial year of all income and charges relating to that year, irrespective of the date of receipt or payment of such income or charges.*

21. Third, in accordance with art 31(1)(c)(bb), account must be taken of liabilities and losses arising in the course of a financial year even if they become apparent only between the end of the financial year and the date on which the balance sheet for that year is drawn up.

22. It is clear from those provisions that taking account of all elements – profits made, charges, income, liabilities and losses – which actually relate to the financial year in question ensures observance of the requirement of a true and fair view.

23. In the present case, according to the subsidiary's annual accounts, the profits in question were made by that company during the financial year 1989 and were appropriated by it to the parent as at 31 December 1989, that is to say before the financial year. Before examining the parent company's accounts, the national court must be satisfied that there is no reason to question that that presentation of the subsidiary's financial position complies with the principle of the true and fair view.

24. It follows from all the foregoing that, if the subsidiaries accounts themselves comply with the principle of the true and fair view, it is not contrary to the rule laid down in art 31(1)(c)(aa) of the fourth directive for the national court to consider that, in the circumstances described, the profits in question must be entered in the parent company's balance sheet for the financial year in respect of which the subsidiary appropriated them."

9 The *Tomberger* case is important not only because it signifies a rejection by the ECJ of a formalistic or restrictive interpretation of the Directive in considering questions of compatibility, but also because of the insight it gives, in the Advocate General's opinion, of the meaning of true and fair. Thus, it seems that English law approaches "true and fair" as a blended concept, whereas the approach of Community law may be to regard it as a bifurcated concept, namely "true" and "fair".

10 This seems to me to be a distinction without a difference, in that both approaches are attempting to ascribe meaning to the same concept. This follows from the acceptance of the Advocate General that the adjective "true" is necessarily used in a relative sense and his references to "good faith". As a translation of "fidele" or "fedele" it might have been better rendered in English as "faithful" which is not the same thing as "good faith" so far as that term might be understood by an English lawyer.

ES Bauunternehmung GmbH v Finanzamt Bergeheim

11 The approach of the ECJ to the true and fair requirement in *Tomberger* was reiterated by the ECJ in the case of *DE + ES Bauunternehmung GmbH v Finanzamt Bergeheim* Case C-275/97 [2000] BCC 757. The ECJ again construed the detailed provisions of the Directive against the yardstick of the true and fair requirement and, furthermore, subjected an exceptional case departure to a true and fair requirement.

12 The case involved a German building company which sub-contracted some building works and made a global provision to cover the costs of remedying any defects in such work which were covered by warranties given by it. It did not specifically identify each claim because it could not identify whether such claims would require it to carry out repair work for no charge, to replace items, re-do certain works, reduce prices paid or pay damages. Instead it made a global provision calculated as percentage of annual turnover.

The articles in point were Arts 20(1) and 31(1)(e) which provide respectively as follows: 13

> "*20(1) – provisions are intended to cover losses or debts the nature of which is clearly defined and which at the date of the balance sheet are either likely to be incurred, or certain to be incurred but uncertain as to amount or as to the date on which they will arise*
>
> *31(1)(e) – the components of asset and liability items are to be valued separately*"

The ECJ accepted the argument of the German government that, even if only some of these liabilities materialised, these liabilities were inescapable even if it was not possible to say whether and to what extent the company would be obliged to bear them or to quantify them precisely. It held that any alternative interpretation of Art 20(1) would mean that such potential debts did not appear in the balance sheet and would be contrary to the principle of a true and fair view, compliance with which was the primary objective of the Directive. 14

In relation to the requirement that liability items should be separately valued, the ECJ invoked the true and fair override provided for in Art 2(5). A requirement which it described in the following terms: 15

> "*27. The principle of a true and fair view requires that the accounts reflect the activities and transactions which they are supposed to describe and that the accounting information be given in the form judged to be the soundest and most appropriate for satisfying third parties' needs for information, without harming the interests of the company*"

In a rather opaque passage the ECJ referred to the exceptional case exception in Art 31(2) in this way: 16

> "*31. Since the directive does not define what is meant by "exceptional cases", this expression must be interpreted in the light of the directive's aim, which, as indicated ... above, is that the annual accounts of the companies concerned must give a true and fair view of their assets, of their financial position and of their profit or loss.*
>
> *32 The exceptional cases referred to in art 31(2) are therefore those in which separate valuation would not give the truest and fairest possible view of the actual financial position of the company concerned*"

The reference to "truest and fairest" is puzzling, since it suggests that there is a hierarchy of true and fair, which gives rise to the difficulty that even the lowest place in the hierarchy would be *a* true and fair view and therefore have attained the necessary standard to comply with the requirement in the Directive. In my view, the ECJ was not seeking to suggest that there is such a hierarchy where compatibility requires achieving the top level, but rather to indicate that what might have been a true and fair view in one situation is not necessarily true and fair in another. 17

[SSAP 4]
Accounting for government grants*

(Issued April 1974; revised July 1990; amended October 1992 and December 2000)

Contents

	Paragraphs
Part 1 – Explanatory note	1–20
Part 2 – Definition of terms	21–22
Part 3 – Standard accounting practice	23–31
Part 4 – Legal requirements in Great Britain and Northern Ireland	32–35
Part 5 – Legal requirements in the Republic of Ireland	36–40
Part 6 – Compliance with International Accounting Standard No. 20 'Accounting for Government Grants and Disclosure of Government Assistance'	41

****Editor's note****: The areas covered in SSAP 4 are to be dealt with primarily in Section 24 of FRS 102.*

Accounting for government grants

The provisions of this statement of standard accounting practice should be read in conjunction with the Explanatory Foreword to Accounting Standards* *and need not be applied to immaterial items.*

Part 1 – Explanatory note

INTRODUCTION

Government assistance takes many forms, including grants, equity finance, subsidised loans and advisory assistance. This statement deals with the accounting treatment and disclosure of government grants and other forms of government assistance. It is also indicative of best practice for accounting for grants and assistance from other sources. 1

Government grants are made in order to persuade or assist enterprises to pursue courses of action which are deemed to be socially or economically desirable. The range of grants available is very wide and changes regularly, reflecting changes in government policy. More significantly different grants tend to be given on different terms as to the eligibility, manner of determination, manner of payment and conditions to be fulfilled. While this statement has been written in the context of grants available at the time of its preparation, it is intended that it will be equally applicable to other grants that may be created in the future. 2

For the purposes of this statement, the term 'government' is defined widely. Thus, it includes not only the national government and all of the various tiers of local and regional government of any country, but also government agencies and 'non-departmental public bodies' (or quangos). It also includes the Commission of the European Communities† and other EC bodies, together with other international bodies and agencies. 3

BASIC CONCEPTS

The 'accruals' concept requires that revenue and costs are accrued, matched with one another so far as their relationship can be established or justifiably assumed, and dealt with in the profit and loss account of the period to which they relate. Government grants should therefore be recognised in the profit and loss account so as to match them with the expenditure towards which they are intended to contribute.‡ 4

The 'prudence' concept requires that revenue and profits are not anticipated, but are recognised by inclusion in the profit and loss account only when realised in the form either of cash or of other assets the ultimate cash realisation of which can be established with reasonable certainty. Accordingly, government grants should not be recognised in the profit and loss account until the conditions for their receipt have been complied with and there is reasonable assurance that the grant will be received. 5

****Editor's note****: Now simply the* Foreword to Accounting Standards.

†***Editor's note****: Now the European Commission and the European Union.*

‡***Editor's note****: The explanation of the accruals concept in SSAP 4 is no longer entirely consistent with that included in FRS 18, having been based on that standard's predecessor SSAP 2.*

6 In many cases, the grant-making body has the right to recover all or part of a grant paid if the enterprise has not complied with the conditions under which the grant was made. On the assumption that the enterprise is a going concern, the application of the prudence concept does not normally require postponement of the recognition of the grant in the profit and loss account solely because there is a possibility that it might have to be repaid in the future. The enterprise should consider regularly whether there is a likelihood of a breach of the conditions on which the grant was made. If such a breach has occurred, or appears likely to occur, and it is probable that some grant will have to be repaid, provision should be made for the liability.

7 The treatment for taxation purposes of government grants varies according to the terms of the grant and the particular statute or regulation under which it is made. At one extreme, some grants are free of all tax; at the other, some are taxed as income on receipt. It is sometimes suggested that because grants are taxed as income on receipt they are intended to be regarded as income and should be credited to the profit and loss account as they are received. However, the treatment of an item for tax purposes does not necessarily determine its treatment for accounting purposes, and immediate recognition in the profit and loss account may result in an unacceptable departure from the principle that government grants should be matched with the expenditure towards which they are intended to contribute. Any timing differences that may arise between a tax charge and the recognition of the corresponding credit in the profit and loss account should be dealt with in accordance with FRS 19 'Deferred tax'.*

ESTABLISHING THE RELATIONSHIP BETWEEN GRANTS RECEIVED AND EXPENDITURE

8 The matching of grants received and expenditure is straightforward if the grant is made as a contribution towards specified items of expenditure (whether capital, revenue or a particular combination) and is described as such.

9 Difficulties arise where the terms of the grant do not specify precisely the expenditure it is intended to meet, but use such phrases as 'to assist with a project' or 'to encourage job creation', or where the basis of calculation is related to two or more criteria (for example the capital expenditure incurred and the number of jobs created). In these circumstances, it is usually appropriate to consider the circumstances which give rise to the payment of instalments of the grant. If the grant is paid when evidence is produced that certain expenditure has been incurred, the grant should be matched with that expenditure. If the grant is paid on a different basis, it will usually be paid on the achievement of a non-financial objective, such as the creation of a specified number of new jobs; in these circumstances, the grant should be matched with the identifiable costs of achieving that objective, for example the cost of creating and, if applicable, maintaining for the required period the specified new jobs.

10 In some cases, there may be persuasive evidence that the actual expenditure towards which the grant is intended to contribute differs from the expenditure that forms the basis of payment. Such evidence may be contained in the formal application for the grant and subsequent correspondence and negotiation with the grant-making body. Where such evidence exists and is sufficiently persuasive, it is appropriate to match the grant received with the identified expenditure and this approach should be preferred to that outlined in the previous paragraph. For example, a discretionary grant

**Editor's note: References to FRS 19 added with effect for accounting periods ending on or after 23 January 2002. Previously, the reference was to SSAP 15.*

might be given 'to assist with a project', with instalments of the grant being payable on the production of evidence that specific capital expenditure had been incurred; but it might be clear from correspondence that the grant had been made as a contribution to other costs as well, such as the provision of working capital or the meeting of initial training costs.

Where a grant is paid on the achievement of a non-financial objective, the costs of achieving that objective must be identified or estimated on a reasonable basis. For example, if a grant is given on condition that jobs are created and maintained for a minimum period, the grant should be matched with the cost of providing jobs for that period, taking due account of the incidence of the costs incurred. As the costs of job creation will often be higher in the early stages of a project, because of start-up costs and the fact that a significant element of wage costs will initially be non-productive, the matching principle may require that an equivalent, higher proportion of the grant should be recognised in the earlier periods. **11**

RECOGNITION OF GRANTS IN THE PROFIT AND LOSS ACCOUNT

Once the relationship between the grant and the related expenditure has been established, the recognition of the grant in the profit and loss account will follow. The grant should be recognised in the same period as the related expenditure. **12**

In certain circumstances, government grants may be given for the immediate financial support or assistance of an enterprise or for the reimbursement of costs previously incurred, without conditions regarding the enterprise's future actions or a requirement to incur further costs. Government grants may also be given to finance the general activities of an enterprise over a specified period or to compensate for a loss of income; in some instances, the extent of these grants may be such as to constitute a major source of income for the enterprise. Grants that are payable on this basis should be recognised in the profit and loss account of the period in respect of which they are paid or, if they are not stated to be paid in respect of a specified period, in the profit and loss account of the period in which they become receivable. **13**

Where an enterprise is required to repay a government grant, either in whole or in part, the full amount to be repaid, after taking into account any unamortised deferred income relating to the grant, should be charged to the profit and loss account immediately it becomes repayable. Where appropriate, the repayment should be dealt with in accordance with FRS 3 'Reporting Financial Performance' as an exceptional item. **14**

BALANCE SHEET TREATMENT OF GRANTS

The application of this statement may result in part or all of a grant that has been received not being recognised immediately in the profit and loss account. Any unrecognised amounts should normally be included in the balance sheet as deferred income. Where a grant is made as a contribution towards expenditure on fixed assets, there are two possible balance sheet treatments, both of which result in the grant being matched with the related expenditure in the profit and loss account. These are: **15**

(a) to treat the amount of the grant as deferred income which is credited to the profit and loss account by instalments over the expected useful economic life of the related asset on a basis consistent with the depreciation policy; or

(b) to deduct the amount of the grant from the purchase price or production cost of the related asset, with a consequent reduction in the annual charge for depreciation.

It is considered that both treatments are acceptable and are capable of giving a true and fair view. However, the CCAB has received Counsel's opinion that paragraphs 17 and 26 of Schedule 4 to the Companies Act 1985* have the effect of prohibiting enterprises to which the legislation applies from accounting for grants made as a contribution towards expenditure on fixed assets by deducting the amount of the grant from the purchase price or production cost of the related asset.

16 Where a government grant takes the form of a transfer of non-monetary assets, the amount of the grant is the fair value of the assets transferred.

DISCLOSURE

17 The financial statements should disclose the accounting policy adopted in respect of government grants in terms which make clear the method or methods adopted. The period or periods over which grants are credited to the profit and loss account should be disclosed insofar as this is practicable given the number and variety of grants that are being received. Normally, it will be sufficient to give a broad indication of the future periods in which grants already received will be recognised in the profit and loss account.

18 Where the results for the period have been affected materially by amounts credited in respect of government grants, and/or where the results of future periods are expected to be affected materially by the recognition in the profit and loss account of grants already received, it is important for an understanding of the financial statements that the effects on the results or the financial position of the enterprise should be disclosed.

19 Government assistance to an enterprise may also be given in a form other than grants, for example consultancy and advisory services, subsidised loans and credit guarantees. Where such assistance has had a material effect on the results for the period, the nature and, where measurable, the effects of the assistance should be disclosed.

20 Under SSAP 18 'Accounting for contingencies'† potential liabilities to repay grants should only be provided for to the extent that repayment is probable. A material contingent loss not so provided for should be disclosed, except where the possibility of repayment is remote.

Part 2 – Definition of terms

21 *Government* includes government and inter-governmental agencies and similar bodies whether local, national or international.

22 *Government grants* are assistance by government in the form of cash or transfers of assets to an enterprise in return for past or future compliance with certain conditions relating to the operating activities of the enterprise.

Editor's note: *Now paragraphs 17 and 27 of Schedule 1 to the Large and Medium-sized Companies and Groups (Accounts and Reports) Regulations 2008 (SI 2008/410).*

†***Editor's note:*** *SSAP 18 has been superseded by FRS 12 'Provisions, contingent liabilities and contingent assets'. However, the introduction of FRS 12 has not materially altered the accounting requirements in respect of potential liabilities to repay grants, and accordingly the point made in this paragraph remains valid.*

Part 3 – Standard accounting practice

23 Subject to paragraph 24 of this statement, government grants should be recognised in the profit and loss account so as to match them with the expenditure towards which they are intended to contribute. In the absence of persuasive evidence to the contrary, government grants should be assumed to contribute towards the expenditure that is the basis for their payment. To the extent that grants are made as a contribution towards specific expenditure on fixed assets, they should be recognised over the expected useful economic lives of the related assets. Grants made to give immediate financial support or assistance to an enterprise or to reimburse costs previously incurred should be recognised in the profit and loss account of the period in which they become receivable. Grants made to finance the general activities of an enterprise over a specific period or to compensate for a loss of current or future income should be recognised in the profit and loss account of the period in respect of which they are paid.

24 The foregoing requirements are subject to the proviso that a government grant should not be recognised in the profit and loss account until the conditions for its receipt have been complied with and there is reasonable assurance that the grant will be received.

25 Where the recognition in the profit and loss account of part or all of a grant that has been received is deferred, the amount so deferred should be treated as deferred income. To the extent that the grant is made as a contribution towards expenditure on a fixed asset, in principle it may be deducted from the purchase price or production cost of that asset. The CCAB has received Counsel's opinion, however, that the option to deduct government grants from the purchase price or production cost of fixed assets is not available to companies governed by the accounting and reporting requirements of the Companies Act 1985, as outlined in paragraph 34.*

26 Grants relating to leased assets in the accounts of lessors should be accounted for in accordance with the requirements of SSAP 21 'Accounting for leases and hire purchase contracts'.

27 Potential liabilities to repay grants either in whole or in part in specified circumstances should only be provided for to the extent that repayment is probable. The repayment of a government grant should be accounted for by setting off the repayment against any unamortised deferred income relating to the grant. Any excess should be charged immediately to the profit and loss account.

DISCLOSURE

28 The following information should be disclosed in the financial statements:

(a) the accounting policy adopted for government grants;
(b) the effects of government grants on the results for the period and/or the financial position of the enterprise;
(c) where the results of the period are affected materially by the receipt of forms of government assistance other than grants, the nature of that assistance and, to the extent that the effects on the financial statements can be measured, an estimate of those effects.

**Editor's note:* *The Companies Act 1985 is replaced by the Companies Act 2006 with effect for accounting periods beginning on or after 6 April 2008. The provisions of the Companies Act 1985 referred to here continue in place in Schedule 1 to the Large and Medium-sized Companies and Groups (Accounts and Reports) Regulations 2008 (SI 2008/410).*

29 Potential liabilities to repay grants in specified circumstances should, if necessary, be disclosed in accordance with paragraph 16 of SSAP 18 'Accounting for contingencies'.*

TRANSITIONAL PROVISIONS

30 Any adjustments arising as a result of a change in accounting policy to comply with the requirements of this statement should be accounted for as a prior year adjustment in accordance with FRS 3 'Reporting Financial Performance'.

APPLICATION TO SMALLER ENTITIES

30A Reporting entities applying the Financial Reporting Standard for Smaller Entities currently applicable are exempt from this accounting standard.

DATE FROM WHICH EFFECTIVE

31 The accounting practices set out in this statement should be adopted as soon as possible. They should be regarded as standard accounting practice in respect of financial statements relating to accounting periods beginning on or after 1 July 1990.

Part 4 – Legal requirements in Great Britain and Northern Ireland

References are to the Companies Act 1985 and the Companies (Northern Ireland) Order 1986.†

32 The balance sheet formats in Schedule 4 require that accruals and deferred income should be shown either under the heading 'Creditors' or separately as 'Accruals and deferred income'. This is relevant to the disclosure of deferred income in relation to government grants. (Standard paragraph 25)

33 Paragraph 12 of Schedule 4 requires that the amount of any item shall be determined on a prudent basis and, in particular, that only profits realised at the balance sheet date shall be included in the profit and loss account. (Paragraph 91 of the Schedule defines realised profits in relation to a company's accounts as 'such profits of the company as fall to be treated as realised profits for the purposes of those accounts in accordance with principles generally accepted with respect to the determination for accounting purposes of realised profits at the time when those accounts are prepared'.) (Standard paragraph 24)

****Editor's note:*** *SSAP 18 was superseded by FRS 12 'Provisions, contingent liabilities and contingent assets' September 1998. The reference should be read as paragraph 91 of FRS 12.*

†***Editor's note:*** *Schedule 4 to the Companies Act 1985 is replaced, with effect for accounting periods beginning on or after 6 April 2008 by Schedule 1 to the Large and Medium-sized Companies and Groups (Accounts and Reports) Regulations 2008 (SI 2008/410).*

The references change as follows:

Schedule 4 Paragraph Reference	***Schedule 1 SI 2008/410 Reference***
12	*13*
91	*s. 893 of the CA 2006.*
17	*17*
26 (1)	27
50 (2)	*63 (2)*

Paragraph 17 of Schedule 4 requires that, subject to any provision for depreciation or diminution in value, the amount to be included in the balance sheet in respect of any fixed asset shall be its purchase price or production cost. Paragraph 26(1) states that the purchase price of an asset shall be determined by adding to the actual price paid any expenses incidental to its acquisition. The CCAB has received Counsel's opinion that these paragraphs have the effect of prohibiting enterprises to which the legislation applies from accounting for grants made as a contribution towards expenditure on fixed assets by deducting the amount of the grant from the purchase price or production cost of the related asset. (Standard paragraph 25) **34**

Paragraph 50 (2) of Schedule 4 provides that 'The following information shall be given with respect to any other contingent liability not provided for: **35**

(a) the amount or estimated amount of that liability;
(b) its legal nature; and
(c) whether any valuable security has been provided by the company in connection with that liability and if so, what'. (Standard paragraph 29)

Part 5 – Legal requirements in the Republic of Ireland

References are to the Companies (Amendment) Act 1986 and the Schedule to that Act unless otherwise stated.

Note 8 to the balance sheet formats in the Schedule provides that government grants included in the item 'Accruals and deferred income' must be shown separately in a note to the accounts if not shown separately in the balance sheet. However, Note 8 does not impose an obligation to include government grants under 'Accruals and deferred income' and such grants may, therefore, be placed under a separate heading. This separate heading is often placed between liabilities and share capital/reserves. If a new heading is adopted (using Section 4(12)), the requirement under Note 8 to have a separate mention of the amount is not applicable. (Standard paragraph 25) **36**

Section 5(c) of the Act requires that the amount of any item shall be determined on a prudent basis and, in particular, that only profits realised at the balance sheet date shall be included in the profit and loss account. (Paragraph 72 of the Schedule defines realised profits in relation to a company's accounts as 'such profits of the company as fall to be treated as realised profits for the purposes of those accounts in accordance with principles generally accepted with respect to the determination for accounting purposes of realised profits at the time when those accounts are prepared'.) (Standard paragraph 24) **37**

Paragraph 5 of the Schedule requires that, subject to any provision for depreciation or diminution in value, the amount to be included in respect of any fixed asset shall be its purchase price or production cost. Paragraph 14(1) states that the purchase price of an asset shall be determined by adding to the actual price paid any expenses incidental to its acquisition. The CCAB has received legal opinion that the equivalent paragraphs in UK legislation have the effect of prohibiting enterprises to which the legislation applies from accounting for grants made as a contribution towards expenditure on fixed assets by deducting the amount of the grant from the purchase price or production cost of the related asset. (Standard paragraph 25) **38**

Paragraph 36(2) of the Schedule provides that 'The following information shall be given with respect to any other contingent liability not provided for: **39**

(a) the amount or estimated amount of that liability;

(b) its legal nature; and
(c) whether any valuable security has been provided by the company in connection with that liability and if so, what'. (Standard paragraph 29)

40 The Companies (Amendment) Act 1983, Section 40 requires the convening of an extraordinary general meeting not later than 28 days from the earliest day on which it is known to a director of the company that its net assets have fallen to half or less of the company's called-up share capital (that a 'financial situation' exists). The 1983 Act also extends the reporting duties of auditors by requiring auditors to state whether in their opinion there existed at the balance sheet date a 'financial situation' in the context of Section 40 which would require the convening of an extraordinary general meeting. For the purpose of calculating the net assets of the company, the term 'liability' should be taken to include not only creditors, but also provisions for liabilities and charges, accruals and deferred income. Government grants treated as deferred income should, therefore, be regarded as a liability for the purposes of calculating net assets under Section 40.

Part 6 – Compliance with International Accounting Standard No.20 'Accounting for Government Grants and Disclosure of Government Assistance'

41 The requirements of International Accounting Standard No.20 'Accounting for Government Grants and Disclosure of Government Assistance' accord very closely with the content of the United Kingdom and Irish Accounting Standard No.4 (Revised) 'Accounting for government grants' and accordingly compliance with SSAP 4 (Revised) will ensure compliance with IAS 20 in all material respects.*

***Editor's note**: Subsequent to the latest revision of SSAP 4, IAS 20 has been reformatted (in 1994) and an SIC has been issued, 'SIC 10 Government assistance — No specific relation to operating activities'. IAS 20 was also amended by IAS 10 'Events after the balance sheet date' and by IAS 41 'Agriculture'.*

The comment made in SSAP 4 remains basically true, but there are some differences between the standards. In particular, IAS 20 always allows capital grants to be treated as deferred income or deducted from the cost of the asset. While SSAP 4 also supports this treatment in principle, it is not allowed for UK companies as explained in paragraphs 15, 25 and 34 of SSAP 4.

[SSAP 5] Accounting for value added tax*

(Issued April 1974)

This statement seeks, by presenting a standard accounting practice, to achieve uniformity of accounting treatment of VAT in financial statements.

Part 1 – Explanatory note

GENERAL

VAT is a tax on the supply of goods and services which is eventually borne by the final consumer but collected at each stage of the production and distribution chain. As a general principle, therefore, the treatment of VAT in the accounts of a trader should reflect his role as a collector of the tax and VAT should not be included in income or in expenditure whether of a capital or of a revenue nature. There will however be circumstances, as noted below, in which a trader will himself bear VAT and in such circumstances the accounting treatment should reflect that fact. **1**

PERSONS NOT ACCOUNTABLE FOR VAT

Persons not accountable for VAT will suffer VAT on inputs. For them VAT will increase the cost of all goods and services to which it applies and should be included in such costs. In particular, the VAT on fixed assets should be added to the cost of the fixed assets concerned. **2**

ACCOUNTABLE PERSONS WHO ALSO CARRY ON EXEMPTED ACTIVITIES

In the case of persons who also carry on exempted activities there will be a residue of VAT, which will fall directly on the trader and which will normally be arrived at by division of his activities as between taxable outputs (including zero-rated) and those which are exempt. In such cases, the principle that such VAT will increase the costs to which it applies and should be included in such costs will be equally applicable. Hence the appropriate portion of the VAT allocable to fixed assets should, if irrecoverable, be added to the cost of the fixed assets concerned and the proportion allocable to other items should, if practicable and material, be included in such other items. In some cases, for example where financial and VAT accounting periods do not coincide, an estimate may be necessary. **3**

NON-DEDUCTIBLE INPUTS

All traders will bear tax in so far as it relates to non-deductible inputs (for example, motor-cars, other than for resale, and certain business entertaining expenses). Such tax should therefore be included as part of the cost of those items. A similar situation exists in the Republic of Ireland where traders dealing in products such as motor-cars, radios and television sets will bear some non-deductible VAT on the input cost of these items. **4**

**Editor's note*: *The matters covered in SSAP 5 are dealt with primarily in Section 29 of FRS 102, although the requirement to show turnover net of VAT is also mentioned in Section 23.*

AMOUNTS DUE TO OR FROM THE REVENUE AUTHORITIES

5 The net amount due to or from the revenue authorities in respect of VAT should be included as part of debtors or creditors and will not normally require separate disclosure.

CAPITAL COMMITMENTS

6 The estimated amount of capital commitments should include the appropriate amount, if any, of irrecoverable VAT.

COMPARISONS

7 Where it has been customary for purchase tax (or sales taxes in the Republic of Ireland) to be included in turnover, it may be desirable in the initial years of VAT to disclose the turnover of periods in which such tax applied both gross and net of tax so as to assist in comparisons. In some cases, for example retailers, it may not be possible to ascertain the amount of purchase tax (or sales taxes) included in turnover; in those cases an explanatory note will be desirable. Where customs or excise duties are included in turnover and such duties are reduced to take account of VAT, an explanatory note may be necessary.

Part 2 – Standard accounting practice

TURNOVER

8 Turnover shown in the profit and loss account should exclude VAT on taxable outputs*. If it is desired to show also the gross turnover, the VAT relevant to that turnover should be shown as a deduction in arriving at the turnover exclusive of VAT.

IRRECOVERABLE VAT

9 Irrecoverable VAT allocable to fixed assets and to other items disclosed separately in published accounts should be included in their cost where practicable and material.

APPLICATION TO SMALLER ENTITIES

9A Reporting entities applying the Financial Reporting Standard for Smaller Entities currently applicable are exempt from this accounting standard.

DATE FROM WHICH EFFECTIVE

10 The accounting practices set out in this statement should be adopted as soon as possible and regarded as standard in respect of accounting periods starting on or after 1st January 1974.

*****Editor's note****: Section 262(1) of the Companies Act 1985 defines 'turnover' in relation to a company. This is replaced by section 474 (1) of the Companies Act 2006.*

[SSAP 9]
Stocks and long-term contracts*

(Issued May 1975; Part 6 added August 1980; revised September 1988)

Contents

Paragraphs

Part 1 – Explanatory note 1–15

Part 2 – Definition of terms 16–25

Part 3 – Standard accounting practice 26–33

Part 4 – Note on legal requirements in Great Britain and Northern Ireland 34–44

Part 5 – Note on legal requirements in the Republic of Ireland 45

Part 6 – Compliance with International accounting Standard No. 2 'Valuation and presentation of inventories in the context of the historical cost system' and No. 11 'Accounting for construction contracts' 46

Appendices

1 – Further practical considerations

2 – Glossary of terms

3 – Long-term contracts; further consideration of financial statement presentation

****Editor's note**: The matters covered in SSAP 9 are dealt with in Sections 13 of FRS 102, in relation to stocks (inventories) and 23 in relation to long term work in progress (construction contracts).*

Stocks and long-term contracts

The provisions of this statement of standard accounting practice should be read in conjunction with the (Explanatory) Foreword to accounting standards *and need not be applied to immaterial items.*

Part 1 – Explanatory note

STOCKS

1 The determination of profit for an accounting year requires the matching of costs with related revenues. The cost of unsold or unconsumed stocks will have been incurred in the expectation of future revenue, and when this will not arise until a later year it is appropriate to carry forward this cost to be matched with the revenue when it arises; the applicable concept is the matching of cost and revenue in the year in which the revenue arises rather than in the year in which the cost is incurred. If there is no reasonable expectation of sufficient future revenue to cover cost incurred (e.g., as a result of deterioration, obsolescence or a change in demand) the irrecoverable cost should be charged to revenue in the year under review. Thus, stocks normally need to be stated at cost, or, if lower, at net realisable value.*

2 The comparison of cost and net realisable value needs to be made in respect of each item of stock separately. Where this is impracticable, groups or categories of stock items which are similar will need to be taken together. To compare the total realisable value of stocks with the total cost could result in an unacceptable setting off of foreseeable losses against unrealised profits.

3 In order to match costs and revenue, 'costs' of stocks should comprise that expenditure which has been incurred in the normal course of business in bringing the product or service to its present location and condition. Such costs will include all related production overheads, even though these may accrue on a time basis.

4 The methods used in allocating costs to stocks need to be selected with a view to providing the fairest possible approximation to the expenditure actually incurred in bringing the product to its present location and condition. For example, in the case of retail stores holding a large number of rapidly changing individual items, stock on the shelves has often been stated at current selling prices less the normal gross profit margin. In these particular circumstances this may be acceptable as being the only practical method of arriving at a figure which approximates to cost.

* ***Editor's note:*** *The introductory paragraph of SSAP 9 bases the accounting treatment for stock on the matching concept. Given the changes inroduced by FRS 18 'Accounting policies' this is somewhat at odds with the most fundamental current accounting requirements. FRS 18 stresses, however, that it has not eliminated the concept of matching, simply amended it. As paragraph 9 of Appendix IV to FRS 18 makes clear, the intention is that the definition of assets and liabilities of FRS 5, and the requirement that the non-cash effects of transactions be recorded when they occur, provide a discipline within which matching can operate. The practical import of this is limited, as the accounting treatment dictated by SSAP 9 can be as easily supported under FRS 18 as under SSAP 2. SSAP 9 has not been amended as a result of the issue of Application Note G* Revenue Recognition *to FRS 5. However, the guidance on the recognition of revenue on long-term contracts now needs to be read in the light of that Application Note.*

NET REALISABLE VALUE

Net realisable value is the estimated proceeds from the sale of items of stock less all further costs to completion and less all costs to be incurred in marketing, selling and distributing directly related to the items in question. **5**

REPLACEMENT COST

Items of stock have sometimes been stated in financial statements at estimated replacement cost where this is lower than net realisable value. Where the effect is to take account of a loss greater than that which is expected to be incurred, the use of replacement cost is not regarded as acceptable. However, in some circumstances (e.g., in the case of materials, the price of which has fluctuated considerably and which have not become the subject of firm sales contracts by the time the financial statements are prepared) replacement cost may be the best measure of net realisable value. Also, where a company adopts the alternative accounting rules of the Companies Act 1985, items of stock may be stated at the lower of current replacement cost and net realisable value.* **6**

LONG-TERM CONTRACTS

Separate consideration needs to be given to long-term contracts. Owing to the length of time taken to complete such contracts, to defer recording turnover and taking profit into account until completion may result in the profit and loss account reflecting not so much a fair view of the results of the activity of the company during the year but rather the results relating to contracts that have been completed in the year. It is therefore appropriate to take credit for ascertainable turnover and profit while contracts are in progress in accordance with paragraphs 8 to 11 below. **7**

Companies should ascertain turnover in a manner appropriate to the stage of completion of the contracts, the businesses and the industries in which they operate. **8**

Where the business carries out long-term contracts and it is considered that their outcome can be assessed with reasonable certainty before their conclusion, the attributable profit should be calculated on a prudent basis and included in the accounts for the period under review. The profit taken up needs to reflect the proportion of the work carried out at the accounting date and to take into account any known inequalities of profitability in the various stages of a contract. The procedure to recognise profit is to include an appropriate proportion of total contract value as turnover in the profit and loss account as the contract activity progresses. The costs incurred in reaching that stage of completion are matched with this turnover, resulting in the reporting of results that can be attributed to the proportion of work completed. **9**

Where the outcome of long-term contracts cannot be assessed with reasonable certainty before the conclusion of the contract, no profit should be reflected in the profit and loss account in respect of those contracts, although, in such circumstances, if no loss is expected it may be appropriate to show as turnover a proportion of the total contract value using a zero estimate of profit. **10**

If it is expected that there will be a loss on a contract as a whole, all of the loss should be recognised as soon as it is foreseen (in accordance with the prudence concept). **11**

****Editor's note**: Now included within Schedule 1 to the Large and Medium-sized Companies and Groups (Accounts and Reports) Regulations 2008 (SI 2008/410).*

Examples of how this can be achieved are given in Appendix 3. Initially, the foreseeable loss will be deducted from the work in progress figure of the particular contract, thus reducing it to net realisable value. Any loss in excess of the work in progress figure should be classified as an accrual within 'Creditors' or under 'Provisions for liabilities and charges'* depending upon the circumstances. Where unprofitable contracts are if such magnitude that they can be expected to utilise a considerable part of the company's capacity for a substantial period, related administration overheads to be incurred during the period to the completion of those contracts should also be included in the calculation of the provision for losses.

DISCLOSURE IN FINANCIAL STATEMENTS

12 A suitable description of the amount at which stocks (excluding long-term contract balances) are stated in financial statements would be 'at lower of cost and net realisable value.'

13 In the case of long-term contracts:

(a) long-term contract balances classified under the balance sheet heading of 'Stocks' are stated at total costs incurred, net of amounts transferred to the profit and loss account in respect of work carried out to date, less foreseeable losses and applicable payments on account. A suitable description in the financial statements would be 'at net cost, less foreseeable losses and payments on account.'

(b) cumulative turnover (i.e., the total turnover recorded in respect of the contract in the profit and loss accounts of all accounting periods since inception of the contract) is compared with total payments on account. If turnover exceeds payments on account an 'amount recoverable on contracts' is established and separately disclosed within debtors. If payments on account are greater than turnover to date, the excess is classified as a deduction from any balance on that contract in stocks, with any residual balance in excess of cost being classified with creditors.

14 In order to give an adequate explanation of the affairs of the company, the accounting policies followed in arriving at the amount at which stocks and long-term contracts are stated in the financial statements should be set out in a note. Where differing bases have been adopted for different types of stocks and long-term contracts, the amount included in the financial statements in respect of each type will need to be stated.

FURTHER PRACTICAL CONSIDERATIONS

15 The basic considerations which must be taken into account in determining cost and net realisable value in relation to stocks and long-term contracts are set out in Parts 2 and 3 of this statement. The majority of problems which arise in practice in determining these amounts result from considerations which are relevant to particular businesses and are not of such universal application that they can be the subject of a statement of standard accounting practice. Accordingly, Appendix 1 sets out in more detail some general guidelines which may be of assistance in determining cost and net realisable value and in identifying those situations in which net realisable value is likely to be less than cost. Appendix 1 also sets out considerations which need to be borne in mind in calculating the amount of profit to be taken into account in respect of long-term contracts.

**Editor's note*: *The statutory phrase is now "Provisions for liabilities".*

Part 2 – Definition of terms

Stocks comprise the following categories: **16**

(a) goods or other assets purchased for resale;
(b) consumable stores;
(c) raw materials and components purchased for incorporation into products for sale;
(d) products and services in intermediate stages of completion
(e) long-term contract balances; and
(f) finished goods.

Cost is defined in relation to the different categories of stocks as being that expenditure which has been incurred in the normal course of business in bringing the product or service to its present location and condition. This expenditure should include, in addition to cost of purchase (as defined in paragraph 18), such costs of conversion (as defined in paragraph 19) as are appropriate to that location and condition. **17**

Cost of purchase comprises purchase price including import duties, transport and handling costs and any other directly attributable costs, less trade discounts, rebates and subsidies. **18**

Cost of conversion comprises: **19**

(a) costs which are specifically attributable to units of production, eg direct labour, direct expenses and sub-contracted work;
(b) production overheads (as defined in paragraph 20);
(c) other overheads, if any, attributable in the particular circumstances of the business to bringing the product or service to its present location and condition.

Production overheads: Overheads incurred in respect of materials, labour or services for production, based on the normal level of activity, taking one year with another. For this purpose each overhead should be classified according to function (eg production, selling or administration) so as to ensure the inclusion, in cost of conversion, of those overheads (including depreciation) which relate to production, notwithstanding that these may accrue wholly or partly on a time basis. **20**

Net realisable value: The actual or estimated selling price (net of trade but before settlement discounts) less: **21**

(a) all further costs to completion; and
(b) all costs to be incurred in marketing, selling and distributing.

Long-term contract: A contract entered into for the design, manufacture or construction of a single substantial asset or the provision of a service (or of a combination of assets or services which together constitute a single project) where the time taken substantially to complete the contract is such that the contract activity falls into different accounting periods. A contract that is required to be accounted for as long-term by this accounting standard will usually extend for a period exceeding one year. However, a duration exceeding one year is not an essential feature of a long-term contract. Some contracts with a shorter duration than one year should be accounted for as long-term contracts if they are sufficiently material to the activity of the period that not to record turnover and attributable profit would lead to distortion of the period's turnover and results such that the financial statements would not give a true and fair view, provided that the policy is applied consistently within the reporting entity and from year to year. **22**

23 *Attributable profit:* That part of the total profit currently estimated to arise over the duration of the contract, after allowing for estimated remedial and maintenance costs and increases in costs so far as not recoverable under the terms of the contract, that fairly reflects the profit attributable to that part of the work performed at the accounting date. (There can be no attributable profit until the profitable outcome of the contract can be assessed with reasonable certainty.)

24 *Foreseeable losses:* Losses which are currently estimated to arise over the duration of the contract (after allowing for estimated remedial and maintenance costs and increases in costs so far as not recoverable under the terms of the contract). This estimate is required irrespective of:

(a) whether or not work has yet commenced on such contracts;
(b) the proportion of work carried out at the accounting date;
(c) the amount of profits expected to arise on other contracts.

25 *Payments on account:* All amounts received and receivable at the accounting date in respect of contracts in progress.

Part 3 – Standard accounting practice

STOCKS

26 The amount at which stocks are stated in periodic financial statements should be the total of the lower of cost and net realisable value of the separate items of stock or of groups of similar items.

27 Stocks should be sub-classified in the balance sheet or in the notes to the financial statements so as to indicate the amounts held in each of the main categories in the standard balance sheet formats (as adapted where appropriate) of Schedule 4 to the Companies Act 1985, Schedule 4 to the Companies (Northern Ireland) Order 1986 and, in the Republic of Ireland, the Schedule to the Companies (Amendment) Act 1986.*

LONG-TERM CONTRACTS

28 Long-term contracts should be assessed on a contract by contract basis and reflected in the profit and loss account by recording turnover and related costs as contract activity progresses. Turnover is ascertained in a manner appropriate to the stage of completion of the contract, the business and the industry in which it operates.

29 Where it is considered that the outcome of a long-term contract can be assessed with reasonable certainty before its conclusion, the prudently calculated attributable profit should be recognised in the profit and loss account as the difference between the reported turnover and related costs for that contract.

30 Long-term contracts should be disclosed in the balance sheet as follows:

(a) the amount by which recorded turnover is in excess of payments on account should be classified as 'amounts recoverable on contracts' and separately disclosed within debtors;

**Editor's note:* *For accounting periods beginning on or after 6 April 2008 Schedule 4 to the Companies Act 1985 is replaced by Schedule 1 to the Large and Medium-sized Companies and Groups (Accounts and Reports) Regulations 2008 (SI 2008/410) and Schedule 8 to the Companies Act 1985 is replaced by Schedule 1 to the Small Companies and Groups (Accounts and Directors' Report) Regulations 2008 (SI 2008/409).*

(b) the balance of payments on account (in excess of amounts (i) matched with turnover; and (ii) offset against long-term contract balances) should be classified as payments on account and separately disclosed within creditors;

(c) the amount of long-term contracts, at costs incurred, net of amounts transferred to costs of sales, after deducting foreseeable losses and payments on account not matched with turnover, should be classified as 'long-term contract balances' and separately disclosed within the balance sheet heading 'Stocks.' The balance sheet note should disclose separately the balances of:

  (i) net cost less foreseeable losses; and
  (ii) applicable payments on account;

(d) the amount by which the provision or accrual for foreseeable losses exceeds the costs incurred (after transfers to cost of sales) should be included within either provisions for liabilities and charges or creditors as appropriate.

Consequent upon the application of this revised standard, the corresponding amounts in the financial statements will need to be restated on a comparable basis. **31**

STATEMENT OF ACCOUNTING POLICIES

The accounting policies that have been applied to stocks and long-term contracts, in particular the method of ascertaining turnover and attributable profit, should be stated and applied consistently within the business and from year to year. **32**

APPLICATION TO SMALLER ENTITIES

Reporting entities applying the Financial Reporting Standard for Smaller Entities currently applicable are exempt from this accounting standard. **32A**

DATE FROM WHICH EFFECTIVE

The accounting practices set out in this statement should be adopted as soon as possible and regarded as standard in respect of financial statements relating to accounting periods beginning on or after 1 July 1988. **33**

Part 4 – Note on legal requirements in Great Britain and Northern Ireland

*All paragraph references unless otherwise indicated are to Schedule 4 to the Companies Act 1985 and Schedule 4 to the Companies (Northern Ireland) Order 1986.**

34 Paragraph 22 requires that, under the historical cost accounting rules, 'the amount to be included in respect of any current asset shall be its purchase price or production cost.' Paragraph 23(1) provides for the inclusion of the asset at net realisable value if lower than purchase price or production cost.

35 Paragraph 90 [paragraph 89 of Schedule 4 to the Companies (Northern Ireland) Order 1986] provides that 'the purchase price of any asset . . . includes any consideration (whether in cash or otherwise) given by the company in respect of that asset.' Counsel's opinion, obtained by the ASC, has indicated that one purpose of this paragraph is to enable debtors to be stated at face value, that is, at amounts which include a profit element, and that this does not conflict with paragraph 22.

36 Paragraph 26 requires expenses incidental to the acquisition of an asset to be included in the purchase price. It also requires the inclusion of directly attributable production overheads in the production cost of an asset and permits the inclusion of overheads which are only indirectly attributable to the production of an asset and interest on borrowed capital. In cases where interest is included the fact must be stated and the amount of interest included must be disclosed in a note to the financial statements. Paragraph 26 also prohibits the inclusion of distribution costs.

37 Paragraph 27 allows the following methods for valuation of stocks (but requires that the method chosen must be one which appears to the directors to be appropriate in the circumstances of the company):

(a) the method known as 'first in, first out' (FIFO);
(b) the method known as 'last in, first out' (LIFO);
(c) a weighted average price; and
(d) any other method similar to any of the methods mentioned above.

38 This standard requires the use of a method which provides a fair approximation to the expenditure actually incurred. The use of some of the methods allowed by paragraph 27 of the Schedule will not meet this requirement.

39 In particular, the use of the LIFO method can result in the reporting of current assets at amounts that bear little relationship to recent costs. This may result in not only a significant misstatement of balance sheet amounts but also a potential distortion of current and future results. This places a special responsibility on the directors to be

****Editor's note:*** *Schedule 4 to the Companies Act 1985 is replaced, with effect for accounting periods beginning on or after 6 April 2008 by Schedule 1 to the Large and Medium-sized Companies and Groups (Accounts and Reports) Regulations 2008 (SI 2008/410).*

The references change as follows:

Schedule 4 Paragraph Reference	***Schedule 1 SI 2008/410 Reference***
22	*23*
23 (1)	*24 (1)*
26	*27*
27	*28*
31 (5)	*32 (5)*

In addition, para. 89 of Schedule 4 now forms Part I of Schedule 9 to SI 2008/410, while s. 262 (3) to CA 1985 is now s. 853 CA 2006.

assured that the circumstances of the company require the adoption of such a valuation method in order for the accounts to give a true and fair view.

Paragraph 27(3) requires a company to state in a note to the accounts the difference between the replacement cost of stocks and their book amount – as determined by 37(a) to (d) above – where this difference is material. **40**

It is further provided in paragraph 27(5) that if the most recent actual purchase price or production cost before the balance sheet date appears to the directors of the company to constitute a more appropriate standard of comparison, then that amount may be used as a surrogate for replacement cost. **41**

Paragraph 31(5) provides that, where a company adopts the alternative accounting rules, 'stocks may be included at their current cost.' **42**

Paragraph 89 [paragraph 88 of Schedule 4 to the Companies (Northern Ireland) Order 1986] provides that provisions are amounts 'retained as reasonably necessary for the purpose of providing for any liability or loss which is either likely to be incurred, or certain to be incurred but uncertain as to amount or as to the date on which it will arise.' **43**

Paragraph 91 [paragraph 90 of Schedule 4 to the Companies (Northern Ireland) Order 1986] declares that realised profits are 'such profits of a company as fall to be treated as realised profits for the purposes of those accounts in accordance with principles generally accepted with respect to the determination for accounting purposes of realised profits.' It is a 'generally accepted principle' that it is appropriate to recognise profit on long-term contracts when the outcome can be assessed with 'reasonable certainty.' The principle of recognising profit on long-term contracts under this standard, therefore, does not contravene this paragraph. **44**

Part 5 – Note on legal requirements in the Republic of Ireland

The legal requirements in Great Britain and Northern Ireland are mirrored, in respect of the Republic of Ireland, in the Schedule to the Companies (Amendment) Act 1986. The following table indicates the corresponding paragraphs in respect of all the references contained in Part 4 of this statement. **45**

Schedule 4 to the Companies Act 1985	*Schedule 4 to the Companies (Northern Ireland) Order 1986*	*The Schedule to the Companies (Amendment) Act 1986*
Paragraph 22	Paragraph 22	Paragraph 10
Paragraph 23(1)	Paragraph 23(1)	Paragraph 11(1)
Paragraph 26	Paragraph 26	Paragraph 14
Paragraph 27	Paragraph 27	Paragraph 15*
Paragraph 27(4)	Paragraph 27(4)	Paragraph 15(4)
Paragraph 27(5)	Paragraph 27(5)	Paragraph 15(5)
Paragraph 31(5)	Paragraph 31(5)	Paragraph 19(5)
Paragraph 89	Paragraph 88	Paragraph 70
Paragraph 90	Paragraph 89	Paragraph 71
Paragraph 91	Paragraph 90	Paragraph 72

**There is no provision for the LIFO method of stock valuation in paragraph 15 of the Schedule to the Companies (Amendment) Act 1986.*

Part 6 – Compliance with International Accounting Standard No. 2 'Valuation and presentation of inventories in the context of the historical cost system' and No. 11 'Accounting for construction contracts'

46 The requirements of International Accounting Standard No. 2 'Valuation and presentation of inventories in the context of the historical cost system' and International Accounting Standard No. 11 'Accounting for construction contracts'* accord very closely with the content of the United Kingdom and Irish Accounting Standard No. 9 (Revised) 'Stocks and long-term contracts' and accordingly compliance with SSAP 9 will ensure compliance with both IAS 2 and IAS 11 in all material respects.

****Editor's note:*** *Revised versions of IAS 2 'Inventories' and IAS 11 'Construction contracts' were issued in November 1993. IAS 2 has subsequently been further revised, with the changes effective for periods beginning on or after 1 January 2005. As a result of the changes to IAS 2, there are no significant differences between the standards. There are no significant differences between IAS 11 and SSAP 9 in principle, but IAS 11 is far less prescriptive in terms of the precise accounting treatment to be adopted once attributable profits have been determined.*

Appendix 1

This appendix is for general guidance and does not form part of the statement of standard accounting practice.

Further practical considerations

Many of the problems involved in arriving at the amount at which stocks and long-term contracts are stated in financial statements are of a practical nature rather than resulting from matters of principle. This appendix discusses some particular areas in which difficulty may be encountered.

THE ALLOCATION OF OVERHEADS

Production overheads are included in cost of conversion (as defined in Part 2) together with direct labour, direct expenses and sub-contracted work. This inclusion is a necessary corollary of the principle that expenditure should be included to the extent to which it has been incurred in bringing the product 'to its present location and condition' (paragraph 17 of part 2). However, all abnormal conversion costs (such as exceptional spoilage, idle capacity and other losses) which are avoidable under normal operating conditions need for the same reason, to be excluded. 1

Where firm sales contracts have been entered into for the provision of goods or services to customer's specification, overheads relating to design, and marketing and selling costs incurred before manufacture, may be included in arriving at cost. 2

The costing methods adopted by a business are usually designed to ensure that all direct material, direct labour, direct expenses and sub-contracted work are identified and charged on a reasonable and consistent basis but problems arise on the allocation of overheads which must usually involve the exercise of personal judgement in the selection of an appropriate convention. 3

The classification of overheads necessary to achieve this allocation takes the function of the overhead as its distinguishing characteristic (e.g., whether it is a function of production, marketing, selling or administration), rather than whether the overhead tends to vary with time or with volume. 4

The costs of general management, as distinct from functional management, are not directly related to current production and are, therefore, excluded from cost of conversion and, hence, from the cost of stocks and long-term contracts. 5

In the case of smaller organisations whose management may be involved in the daily administration of each of the various functions, particular problems may arise in practice in distinguishing these general management overheads. In such organisations the cost of management may fairly be allocated on suitable bases to the functions of production, marketing, selling and administration. 6

Problems may also arise in allocating the costs of central service departments, the allocation of which should depend on the function or functions that the department is serving. For example the accounts department will normally support the following functions: 7

(a) production – by paying direct and indirect production wages and salaries, by controlling purchases and by preparing periodic financial statements for the production units;
(b) marketing and distribution – by analysing sales and by controlling the sales ledger;
(c) general administration – by preparing management accounts and annual financial statements and budgets, by controlling cash resources and by planning investments.

Only those costs of the accounts department that can reasonably be allocated to the production function fall to be included in the cost of conversion.

8 The allocation of overheads included in the valuation of stocks and long-term contracts needs to be based on the company's normal level of activity, taking one year with another. The governing factor is that the cost of unused capacity should be written off in the current year. In determining what constitutes 'normal' the following factors need to be considered:

(a) the volume of production which the production facilities are intended by their designers and by management to produce under the working conditions (eg single or double shift) prevailing during the year;
(b) the budgeted level of activity for the year under review and for the ensuing year;
(c) the level of activity achieved both in the year under review and in previous years.

Although temporary changes in the load of activity may be ignored, persistent variation should lead to revision of the previous norm.

9 Where management accounts are prepared on a marginal cost basis, it will be necessary to add to the figure of stocks so arrived at, the appropriate proportion of those production overheads not already included in the marginal cost.

10 The adoption of a conservative approach to the valuation of stocks and long-term contracts has sometimes been used as one of the reasons for omitting selected production overheads. In so far as the circumstances of the business require an element of prudence in determining the amount at which stocks and long-term contracts are stated, this needs to be taken into account in the determination of net realisable value and not by the exclusion from cost of selected overheads.

METHODS OF COSTING

11 It is frequently not practicable to relate expenditure to specific units of stocks and long-term contracts. The ascertainment of the nearest approximation to cost gives rise to two problems:

(a) the selection of an appropriate method for relating costs to stocks and long-term contracts (eg job costing, batch costing, process costing, standard costing);
(b) the selection of an appropriate method for calculating the related costs where a number of identical items have been purchased or made at different times (eg unit cost, average cost or FIFO).

12 In selecting the methods referred to in paragraphs 11(a) and (b) above, management must exercise judgement to ensure that the methods chosen provide the fairest practicable approximation to cost. Furthermore, where standard costs are used they need to be reviewed frequently to ensure that they bear a reasonable relationship to actual costs obtaining during the period. Methods such as base stock and LIFO are not usually appropriate methods of stock valuation because they often result in stocks being stated in the balance sheet at amounts that bear little relationship to recent cost levels. When this happens, not only is the presentation of current assets misleading, but there is potential distortion of subsequent results if stock levels reduce and out of date costs are drawn into the profit and loss account.

The method of arriving at cost by applying the latest purchase price to the total number of units in stock is unacceptable in principle because it is not necessarily the same as actual cost and, in times of rising prices, will result in the taking of a profit which has not been realised. **13**

One method of arriving at cost, in the absence of a satisfactory costing system, is the use of selling price less an estimated profit margin. This is acceptable only if it can be demonstrated that the method gives a reasonable approximation of the actual cost. **14**

In industries where the cost of minor by-products is not separable from the cost of the principal products, stocks of such by-products may be stated in accounts at their net realisable value. In this case the costs of the main products are calculated after deducting the net realisable value of the by-products. **15**

THE DETERMINATION OF NET REALISABLE VALUE

The initial calculation of provisions to reduce stocks from cost to net realisable value may often be made by the use of formulae based on predetermined criteria. The formulae normally take account of the age, movements in the past, expected future movements and estimated scrap values of the stock, as appropriate. Whilst the use of such formulae establishes a basis for making a provision which can be consistently applied, it is still necessary for the results to be reviewed in the light of any special circumstances which cannot be anticipated in the formulae, such as changes in the state of the order book. **16**

Where a provision is required to reduce the value of finished goods below cost, the stocks of the parts and sub-assemblies held for the purpose of the manufacture of such products, together with stocks on order, need to be reviewed to determine if provision is also required against such items. **17**

Where stocks of spares are held for sale, special consideration of the factors in paragraph 16 of this appendix will be required in the context of: **18**

(a) the number of units sold to which they are applicable;
(b) the estimated frequency with which a replacement spare is required;
(c) the expected useful life of the unit to which they are applicable.

Events occurring between the balance sheet date and the date of completion of the financial statements need to be considered in arriving at the net realisable value at the balance sheet date (eg a subsequent reduction in selling prices). However, no reduction falls to be made when the realisable value of material stocks is less than the purchase price, provided that the goods into which the materials are to be incorporated can still be sold at a profit after incorporating the materials at cost price. **19**

THE APPLICATION OF NET REALISABLE VALUE

The principal situations in which net realisable value is likely to be less than cost are where there has been: **20**

(a) an increase in costs or a fall in selling price;
(b) physical deterioration of stocks;
(c) obsolescence of products;
(d) a decision as part of a company's marketing strategy to manufacture and sell products at a loss;
(e) errors in production or purchasing.

Furthermore, when stocks are held which are unlikely to be sold within the turnover period normal in that company (ie excess stocks), the impending delay in realisation increases the risk that the situations outlined in (a) to (c) above may occur before the stocks are sold and needs to be taken into account in assessing net realisable value.

LONG-TERM CONTRACTS

21 In ascertaining costs of long-term contracts it is not normally appropriate to include interest payable on borrowed money. However, in circumstances where sums borrowed can be identified as financing specific long-term contracts, it may be appropriate to include such related interest in cost, in which circumstances the inclusion of interest and the amount of interest so included should be disclosed in a note to the financial statements.

22 In some businesses, long-term contracts for the supply of services or manufacture and supply of goods exist where the prices are determined and invoiced according to separate parts of the contract. In these businesses the most appropriate method of reflecting profits on each contract is usually to match costs against performance of the separable parts of the contract, treating each such separable part as a separate contract. In such instances, however, future revenues from the contract need to be compared with future estimated costs and provision made for any foreseen loss.

23 Turnover (ascertained in a manner appropriate to the industry, the nature of the contracts concerned and the contractual relationship with the customer) and related costs should be recorded in the profit and loss account as contract activity progresses. Turnover may sometimes be ascertained by reference to valuation of the work carried out to date. In other cases, there may be specific points during a contract at which individual elements of work done with separately ascertainable sales values and costs can be identified and appropriately recorded as turnover (eg because delivery or customer acceptance has taken place). This accounting standard does not provide a definition of turnover in view of the different methods of ascertaining it as outlined above. However, it does require disclosure of the means by which turnover is ascertained.

24 In determining whether the stage has been reached at which it is appropriate to recognise profit, account should be taken of the nature of the business concerned. It is necessary to define the earliest point for each particular contract before which no profit is taken up, the overriding principle being that there can be no attributable profit until the outcome of a contract can reasonably be foreseen. Of the profit which in the light of all the circumstances can be foreseen with a reasonable degree of certainty to arise on completion of the contract, there should be regarded as earned to date only that part which prudently reflects the amount of work performed to date. The method used for taking up such profit needs to be consistently applied.

25 In calculating the total estimated profit on the contract, it is necessary to take into account not only the total costs to date and the total estimated further costs to completion (calculated by reference to the same principles as were applied to cost to date) but also the estimated future costs of rectification and guarantee work, and any other future work to be undertaken under the terms of the contract. These are then compared with the total sales value of the contract. In considering future costs, it is necessary to have regard to likely increases in wages and salaries, to likely increases in the price of raw materials and to rises in general overheads, so far as these items are not recoverable from the customer under the terms of the contract.

Where approved variations have been made to a contract in the course of it and the amount to be received in respect of these variations has not yet been settled and is likely to be a material factor in the outcome, it is necessary to make a conservative estimate of the amount likely to be received and this is then treated as part of the total sales value. On the other hand, allowance needs to be made for foreseen claims or penalties payable arising out of delays in completion or from other causes. **26**

The settlement of claims arising from circumstances not envisaged in the contract or arising as an indirect consequence of approved variations is subject to a high level of uncertainty relating to the outcome of future negotiations. In view of this, it is generally prudent to recognise receipts in respect of such claims only when negotiations have reached an advanced stage and there is sufficient evidence of the acceptability of the claim in principle to the purchaser, with an indication of the amount involved also being available. **27**

The amounts to be included in the year's profit and loss account will be both the appropriate amount of turnover and the associated costs of achieving that turnover, to the extent that these amounts exceed corresponding amounts recognised in previous years. The estimated outcome of a contract which extends over several accounting years will nearly always vary in the light of changes in circumstances and for this reason the result of the year will not necessarily represent the proportion of the total profit on the contract which is appropriate to the amount of work carried out in the period; it may also reflect the effect of changes in circumstances during the year which affect the total profit estimated to accrue on completion. **28**

Appendix 2

This appendix is for general guidance and does not form part of the statement of standard accounting practice.

Glossary of terms

The use of the following terms in describing the accounting policies adopted in arriving at the amount at which stocks and long-term contracts are stated in financial statements should be restricted in conformity with the definitions given to each. Where these definitions are inapplicable, alternative expressions should be used and explained.

1 *Average cost:* The calculation of the cost of stocks on the basis of the application to the unit of stocks on hand of an average price computed by dividing the total cost of units by the total number of such units. This average price may be arrived at by means of a continuous calculation, a periodic calculation or a moving periodic calculation.

2 *Base stock:* The calculation of the cost of stocks on the basis that a fixed unit value is ascribed to a predetermined number of units of stock, any excess over this number being valued on the basis of some other method. If the number of units in stock is less than the predetermined minimum, the fixed unit value is applied to the number in stock.

3 *Completed long-term contract:* A long-term contract on which no further work, apart from maintenance work, is expected to take place.

4 *Current cost* of stock is the lower of:

(a) its net current replacement cost; and
(b) its net realisable value.

5 *FIFO (first in, first out):* The calculation of the cost of stocks on the basis that the quantities in hand represent the latest purchases or production.

6 *LIFO (last in, first out):* The calculation of the cost of stocks on the basis that the quantities in hand represent the earliest purchases or production.

7 *Replacement cost:* The cost at which an identical asset could be purchased or manufactured.

8 *Standard cost:* The calculation of the cost of stocks on the basis of periodically predetermined costs calculated from management's estimates of expected levels of costs and of operations and operational efficiency and the related expenditure.

9 *Unit cost:* The cost of purchasing or manufacturing identifiable units of stocks.

Appendix 3

This appendix is for general guidance and does not form part of the statement of standard accounting practice.

Long-term contracts: further consideration of financial statement presentation

The classification of an 'amount recoverable on contracts' within debtors is a somewhat unfamiliar concept which needs careful consideration. **1**

The determination of the point at which ownership of completed work passes from the contractor to the customer is a complex matter of legal form and industry practice. **2**

An 'amount recoverable on contracts' may not have the contractual status of a debtor in strict legal form. However, it is well established under the accruals concept of revenue and cost recognition that this should not preclude debtors and creditors from being recorded, where this is necessary to reflect the substance of a transaction. **3**

An essential test for an 'amount recoverable on contracts' to be recorded as an asset is that it should be realisable. This applies equally whether the balance is classified as a debtor or as an element of work in progress. **4**

An 'amount recoverable on contracts' represents an excess of the value of work carried out to date (which has been recorded as turnover) over cumulative payments on account. The amount and realisability of the balance therefore depend on the value of work carried out being ascertained appropriately. The balance arises as a derivative of this process of contract revenue recognition and is directly linked to turnover. In substance, it represents accrued revenue receivable and has the attributes of a debtor. **5**

Accordingly, the standard concludes that 'amounts recoverable on contracts' should be classified as debtors, although separate disclosure is prescribed. Counsel's opinion obtained by the ASC confirms that 'amounts recoverable on contracts' should be classified under 'Debtors' and cannot be classified under 'Stocks.' **6**

In determining the amounts at which long-term contracts should be included in the financial statements, contracting activity should be reviewed on an individual contract by contract basis. The following example illustrates the process of applying the principles set out in the standard to long-term contracts. **7**

Project Number

	1	*2*	*3*	*4*	*5*	*Balance Sheet Total*	*Profit & Loss Account*
Recorded as turnover – being value of work done	145	520	380	200	55		1,300
Cumulative payments on account	(100)	(600)	(400)	(150)	(80)		
Classified as amounts recoverable on contracts	45			50		95DR	
Balance (excess) of payments on account		(80)	(20)		(25)		
Applied as an offset against long-term contract balances – see below		60	20		15		
Residue classified as payments on account		(20)	–		(10)	(30)CR	
Total costs incurred	110	510	450	250	100		
Transferred to cost of sales	(110)	(450)	(350)	(250)	(55)		(1,215)
	–	60	100	–	45		
Provision/accrual for foreseeable losses charged to cost of sales				(40)	(30)		(70)
		60	100		15		
Classified as provision/accrual for losses				(40)		(40)CR	
Balance (excess) of payments on account applied as offset against long-term contract balances		(60)	20)		(15)		
Classified as long-term contract balances		–	80		–	80DR	
Gross profit or loss on long-term contracts	35	70	30	(90)	(30)		15

PROJECT 1

Profit and Loss Account – cumulative

Included in turnover	145
Included in cost of sales	(110)
Gross profit	35

Balance Sheet

The amount to be included in debtors under 'amounts recoverable on contracts' is calculated as follows:

Cumulative turnover	145
LESS: Cumulative payments on account	(100)
Included in debtors	45

In this case, all the costs incurred to date relate to the contract activity recorded as turnover and are transferred to cost of sales, leaving a zero balance in stocks.NB If the outcome of the contract could not be assessed with reasonable certainty, no profit would be recognised. If no loss is expected, it may be appropriate to show as turnover a proportion of the total contract value using a zero estimate of profit.

PROJECT 2

Profit and Loss Account – cumulative

Included in turnover	520
Included in cost of sales	(450)
Gross profit	70

Balance sheet

As cumulative payments on account are greater than turnover there is a credit balance, calculated as follows:

Cumulative turnover	520
LESS: Cumulative payments on account	(600)
Excess payments on account	(80)

This credit balance should firstly be offset against any debit balance on this contract included in stocks and then any residual amount should be classified under creditors as a payment received on account as follows:

Total cost incurred to date	510
LESS: Cumulative amounts recorded as cost of sales	(450)
	60
LESS: Excess payments on account (above)	(80)
Included in creditors	(20)

The amount to be included in stocks is zero and the credit balance of 20 is classified as a payment received on account and included in creditors.

The balance sheet note on stocks should disclose separately the net cost of 60 and the applicable payments on account of 60.

PROJECT 3
Profit and Loss Account – cumulative

Included in turnover	380
Included in the cost of sales	(350)
Gross profit	30

Balance sheet
As with Project 2, cumulative payments on account are greater than turnover and there is a credit balance calculated as follows:

Cumulative turnover	380
LESS: Cumulative payments on account	(400)
Excess payments on account	(20)

This credit balance should firstly be offset against any debit balance on this contract included in stocks and the residual amount, if any, should be classified under creditors as a payment received on account.

The amount to be included in stocks under long-term contract balances is calculated as follows:

Total costs incurred to date	450
LESS: Cumulative amounts recorded as costs of sales	(350)
	100
LESS: Excess payments on account (above)	(20)
Included in long-term contract balances	80

The balance sheet note on stocks should disclose separately the net cost of 100 and the applicable payments on account of 20.

PROJECT 4
Profit and Loss Account – cumulative

Included in turnover	200
Included in cost of sales	(290)
Gross loss	(90)

Balance sheet
The amount to be included in debtors under 'amounts recoverable on contracts' is calculated as follows:

Cumulative turnover	200
LESS: Cumulative payments on account	(150)
Included in debtors	50

The amount to be included as a provision/accrual for foreseeable losses is calculated as follows:

Total costs incurred to date		250
LESS: Transferred to cost of sales	(250)	
Foreseeable losses on contract as a whole	(40)	
		(290)
Classified as provision/accrual for foreseeable losses		(40)

Note that the credit balance of 40 is not offset against the debit balance of 50 included in debtors.

PROJECT 5
Profit and Loss Account – cumulative

Included in turnover	55
Included in cost of sales	(85)
Gross loss	(30)

Balance Sheet
As cumulative payments on account are greater than turnover there is a credit balance, calculated as follows:

Cumulative turnover	55
LESS: Cumulative payments on account	(80)
Excess payments on account	(25)

The credit balance should firstly be deducted from long-term contract balances (after having deducted foreseeable losses) and the residual balance included in creditors under payments received on account as follows:

Total costs incurred to date		100
LESS: Transferred to cost of sales	(55)	
Foreseeable losses on contract as a whole	(30)	
		(85)
		15
LESS: Excess payments on account (above)		(25)
Included in creditors		(10)

The balance sheet note on stocks should disclose separately the net cost of 15 and the applicable payments on account of 15.

[SSAP 13]
Accounting for research and development*

(Issued December 1977; revised January 1989)

Contents

	Paragraphs
Part 1 – Explanatory note	1–20
Part 2 – Definition of terms	21
Part 3 – Standard accounting practice	22–3
Part 4 – Note on legal requirements in Great Britain and Northern Ireland	34–42
Part 5 – Note on legal requirements in the Republic of Ireland	43–53
Part 6 – Compliance with International Accounting Standard No. 9 'Accounting for research and development activities'	54

***Editor's note**: The matters covered in SSAP 13 are dealt with primarily in Section 18 of FRS 102.*

Accounting for research and development

The provisions of this statement of standard accounting practice should be read in conjunction with the (Explanatory) Foreword to accounting standards *and need not be applied to immaterial items.*

Part 1 – Explanatory note

BASIC CONCEPTS

The accounting policies to be followed in respect of research and development expenditure must have regard to the fundamental accounting concepts including the 'accruals' concept by which revenue and costs are accrued, matched and dealt with in the period to which they relate and the 'prudence' concept by which revenue and profits are not anticipated but are recognised only when realised in the form either of cash or of other assets the ultimate cash realisation of which can be established with reasonable certainty. It is a corollary of the prudence concept that expenditure should be written off in the period in which it arises unless its relationship to the revenue of a future period can be established with reasonable certainty.* 1

THE DIFFERENT TYPES OF RESEARCH AND DEVELOPMENT EXPENDITURE

The term 'research and development' is currently used to cover a wide range of activities, including those in the services sector. The definitions of the different types of research and development used in this statement are based on those used by the Organisation for Economic Co-operation and Development for the purposes of collecting data world-wide. 2

Classification of expenditure is often dependent on the type of business and its organisation. However, it is generally possible to recognise three broad categories of activity, namely pure research, applied research and development. The definitions of the individual categories are set out in Part 2. 3

The dividing line between these categories of expenditure is often indistinct and particular expenditure may have characteristics of more than one category. This is especially so when new products or services are developed through research and development to production, when the activities may have characteristics of both development and production. 4

Research and development activity is distinguished from non-research activity by the presence or absence of an appreciable element of innovation. If the activity departs from routine and breaks new ground it should normally be included; if it follows an established pattern it should normally be excluded. 5

Examples of activities that would normally be included in research and development are: 6

(a) experimental, theoretical or other work aimed at the discovery of new knowledge, or the advancement of existing knowledge;
(b) searching for applications of that knowledge;

* ***Editor's note:*** *The glosses of the prudence and accruals concepts provided in this paragraph are no longer quite consistent with the terms as used in FRS 18 'Accounting policies.' This does not affect the accounting practices to be adopted.*

(c) formulation and design of possible applications for such work;
(d) testing in search for, or evaluation of, product, service or process alternatives;
(e) design, construction and testing of pre-production prototypes and models and development batches;
(f) design of products, services, processes or systems involving new technology or substantially improving those already produced or installed;
(g) construction and operation of pilot plants.

7 Examples of activities that would normally be excluded from research and development would include:

(a) testing analysis either of equipment or product for purposes of quality or quantity control;
(b) periodic alterations to existing products, services or processes even though these may represent some improvement;
(c) operational research not tied to a specific research and development activity;
(d) cost of corrective action in connection with break-downs during commercial production;
(e) legal and administrative work in connection with patent applications, records and litigation and the sale or licensing of patents;
(f) activity, including design and construction engineering, relating to the construction, relocation, rearrangement or start-up of facilities or equipment other than facilities or equipment whose sole use is for a particular research and development project;
(g) market research.

THE ACCOUNTING TREATMENT OF RESEARCH AND DEVELOPMENT

8 Expenditure incurred on pure and applied research can be regarded as part of a continuing operation required to maintain a company's business and its competitive position. In general, no one particular period rather than any other will be expected to benefit and therefore it is appropriate that these costs should be written off as they are incurred. Expenditure on pure or applied research may not be treated as an asset (Companies Act 1985, Schedule 4, paragraph 3(2)(c)).*

9 The development of new products or services is, however, distinguishable from pure and applied research. Expenditure on such development is normally undertaken with a reasonable expectation of specific commercial success and of future benefits arising from the work, either from increased revenue and related profits or from reduced costs. On these grounds it may be argued that such expenditure, to the extent that it is recoverable, should be deferred to be matched against the future revenue.

10 It will only be practicable to evaluate the potential future benefits of development expenditure if:

(a) there is a clearly defined project; and
(b) the related expenditure is separately identifiable.

11 The outcome of such a project would then need to be examined for:

(a) its technical feasibility; and
(b) its ultimate commercial viability considered in the light of factors such as:

    (i) likely market conditions (including competing products or services);

****Editor's note:*** *An identical provision is included in paragraph 3(2)(c) of Schedule 1 to the Large and Medium-sized Companies and Groups (Accounts and Reports) Regulations 2008 (SI 2008/410).*

(ii) public opinion;
(iii) consumer and environmental legislation.

Furthermore a project will be of value: **12**

(a) only if further development costs to be incurred on the same project, together with related production, selling and administrative costs, will be more than covered by related revenues; and
(b) adequate resources exist, or are reasonably expected to be available, to enable the project to be completed and to provide any consequential increases in working capital.

The elements of uncertainty inherent in the considerations set out in paragraphs 11 and 12 are considerable. There will be a need for different persons with different types of judgement to be involved in assessing the technical, commercial and financial viability of the project. Combinations of the possible differing assessments which they might validly make can produce different assessments of the existence and amounts of future benefits. **13**

If these uncertainties are viewed in the context of the concept of prudence, the future benefits of most development projects would be too uncertain to justify carrying the expenditure forward. Nevertheless, in certain industries it is considered that there are a number of major development projects that satisfy the stringent criteria set out in paragraphs 10 to 12. Accordingly, when the expenditure on development projects is judged on a prudent view of available evidence to satisfy these criteria, it may be carried forward and amortised over the period expected to benefit. **14**

At each accounting date the unamortised balance of development expenditure should be examined project by project to ensure that it still fulfils the criteria in paragraphs 10 to 12. Where any doubt exists as to the continuation of those circumstances the balance should be written off. **15**

Fixed assets may be acquired or constructed in order to provide facilities for research and/or development activities. The use of such fixed assets usually extends over a number of accounting periods and accordingly they should be capitalised and written off over their useful life. The depreciation so written off should be included as part of the expenditure on research and development and disclosed in accordance with SSAP 12.* **16**

EXCEPTIONS

Where companies enter into a firm contract: **17**

(a) to carry out development work on behalf of third parties on such terms that the related expenditure is to be fully reimbursed, or
(b) to develop and manufacture at an agreed price calculated to reimburse expenditure on development as well as on manufacture,

any such expenditure which has not been reimbursed at the balance sheet date should be dealt with as contract work-in-progress.

Expenditure incurred in locating and exploiting oil, gas and mineral deposits in the *extractive industries* does not fall within the definition of research and development used in this accounting standard. Development of new surveying methods and techniques as an integral part of research on geological phenomena should, however, be included in research and development. **18**

****Editor's note:*** *SSAP 12 has been superseded by FRS 15 'Tangible fixed assets'.*

DISCLOSURE

19 While there are uncertainties inherent in research and development projects, such activities are important in forming a view of a company's future prospects. Detailed disclosure raises considerable problems of definition and the disclosure requirements of this standard are therefore limited to:

(a) accounting policy as required by FRS 18 'Accounting policies';
(b) disclosure of the total amount of research and development expenditure charged in the profit and loss account, distinguishing between the current year's expenditure and amounts amortised from deferred expenditure;
(c) the movements on deferred development expenditure during the year.

20 Having regard to the problems of definition and disclosure referred to above, the scope of disclosure required under paragraph 19(b) is (except in the case of Republic of Ireland companies) restricted in effect to companies which are public limited companies, or special category companies*, or subsidiaries of such companies, or which exceed by a multiple of 10 the criteria for defining a medium-sized company under the Companies Act 1985.†

Part 2 – Definition of terms

The following definition is used for the purpose of this statement:

21 Research and development expenditure means expenditure falling into one or more of the following broad categories (except to the extent that it relates to locating or exploiting oil, gas or mineral deposits or is reimbursable by third parties either directly or under the terms of a firm contract to develop and manufacture at an agreed price calculated to reimburse both elements of expenditure):

(a) *pure (or basic) research:* Experimental or theoretical work undertaken primarily to acquire new scientific or technical knowledge for its own sake rather than directed towards any specific aim or application;
(b) *applied research:* Original or critical investigation undertaken in order to gain new scientific or technical knowledge and directed towards a specific practical aim or objective;
(c) *development:* Use of scientific or technical knowledge in order to produce new or substantially improved materials, devices, products or services, to install new processes or systems prior to the commencement of commercial production or commercial applications, or to improving substantially those already produced or installed.

Part 3 – Standard accounting practice

SCOPE

22 This standard applies to all financial statements intended to give a true and fair view of the financial position of profit or loss, but, except in the case of Republic of Ireland companies (see paragraphs 45 and 46), the provisions set out in paragraph 31 regarding the disclosure of the total amounts of research and development charged in the profit and loss account need not be applied by an entity that:

****Editor's note:*** *Now banking and insurance companies.*

†***Editor's note:*** *This also applies under the Companies Act 2006.*

(a) is not a public limited company or a special category company* (as defined by Section 257 of the Companies Act 1985)† or a holding company that has a public limited company or a special category company as a subsidiary; and
(b) satisfies the criteria, multiplied in each case by 10, for defining a medium-sized company under Section 248‡ of the Companies Act 1985, as amended from time to time by statutory instrument and applied in accordance with the provisions of Section 249‡ of the Act.§

APPLICATION TO SMALLER ENTITIES

Reporting entities applying the Financial Reporting Standard for Smaller Entities currently applicable are exempt from this accounting standard. **22A**

ACCOUNTING TREATMENT

The cost of fixed assets acquired or constructed in order to provide facilities for research and development activities over a number of accounting periods should be capitalised and written off over their useful lives through the profit and loss account. **23**

Expenditure on pure and applied research (other than that referred to in paragraph 23) should be written off in the year of expenditure through the profit and loss account. **24**

Development expenditure should be written off in the year of expenditure except in the following circumstances when it may be deferred to future periods: **25**

(a) there is a clearly defined project, and
(b) the related expenditure is separately identifiable, and
(c) the outcome of such a project has been assessed with reasonable certainty as to:
    (i) its technical feasibility, and
    (ii) its ultimate commercial viability considered in the light of factors such as likely market conditions (including competing products), public opinion, consumer and environmental legislation, and
(d) the aggregate of the deferred development costs, any further development costs, and related production, selling and administration costs is reasonably expected to be exceeded by related future sales or other revenues, and

**Editor's note:* *Now banking and insurance companies as defined in section 744 of the Companies Act 1985 and sections 1164 and 1165 of the Companies Act 2006.*

†*There is no exact equivalent of 'special category companies' in the Republic of Ireland. The Sixth Schedule to the 1963 Act refers to 'special classes of company' which include banking, discount and assurance companies but not shipping companies.*

‡***Editor's note:*** *Now section 247 of the Companies Act 1985 and section 465 of the Companies Act 2006.*

§**Equivalent legal references.**

Great Britain	Northern Ireland	Republic of Ireland
Companies Act 1985	*Companies (Northern Ireland) Order 1986*	*Companies (Amendment) Act 1986*
Section 248 (Now section 247)	Article 256 (as amended)	Section 8
Section 249 (Now section 247)	Article 257	Section 9
Section 257 (Now section 744)	Article 265	*Companies Act 1963* Sixth Schedule, paragraph 23

(e) adequate resources exist, or are reasonably expected to be available, to enable the project to be completed and to provide any consequential increases in working capital.

26 In the foregoing circumstances development expenditure may be deferred to the extent that its recovery can reasonably be regarded as assured.

27 If an accounting policy of deferral of development expenditure is adopted, it should be applied to all developmental projects that meet the criteria in paragraph 25.

28 If development costs are deferred to future periods, they should be amortised. The amortisation should commence with the commercial production or application of the product, service, process or system and should be allocated on a systematic basis to each accounting period, by reference to either the sale or use of the product, service, process or system or the period over which these are expected to be sold or used.

29 Deferred development expenditure for each project should be reviewed at the end of each accounting period and where the circumstances which have justified the deferral of the expenditure (paragraph 25) no longer apply, or are considered doubtful, the expenditure, to the extent to which it is considered to be irrecoverable, should be written off immediately project by project.

DISCLOSURE

30 The accounting policy on research and development expenditure should be stated and explained.

31 The total amount of research and development expenditure charged in the profit and loss account should be disclosed, analysed between the current year's expenditure and amounts amortised from deferred expenditure.

32 Movements on deferred development expenditure and the amount carried forward at the beginning and the end of the period should be disclosed under intangible fixed assets in the balance sheet.

DATE FROM WHICH EFFECTIVE

33 The accounting and disclosure requirements set out in this statement should be adopted as soon as possible and regarded as standard in respect of financial statements relating to accounting periods beginning on or after 1 January 1989.

Part 4 – Note on legal requirements in Great Britain and Northern Ireland

*All paragraph references unless otherwise indicated are to the Companies Act 1985 and the Companies (Northern Ireland) Order 1986.**

Paragraph 3(1) of Schedule 4 enables any items required to be shown in a company's balance sheet or profit and loss account to be shown in greater detail than required by the format adopted. **34**

Paragraph 3(2)(c) of Schedule 4 provides that a company's balance sheet or profit and loss account may include an item representing or covering the amount of any asset or liability, income or expenditure not otherwise covered by any of the items listed in the accounts format adopted. Cost of research shall not be treated as an asset in any company's balance sheet. **35**

Paragraph 19(1) of Schedule 4 does not allow provision to be made for a temporary diminution in value other than for a fixed asset investment. **36**

Paragraph 19(2) of Schedule 4 requires provision for diminution in value to be made in respect of any fixed asset which has diminished in value if the reduction is expected to be permanent (whether its useful economic life is limited or not) and the amount to be included in respect of it to be reduced accordingly. Any such provisions not shown in the profit and loss account shall be disclosed (either separately or in aggregate) in a note to the accounts. **37**

Paragraph 19(3) requires that where the reasons for which any provision was made have ceased to apply to any extent, then the provision shall be written back to the extent that it is no longer necessary. Any amounts written back in accordance with this subparagraph which are not shown in the profit and loss account shall be disclosed (either separately or in aggregate) in a note to the accounts. **38**

Paragraph 20(1) of Schedule 4 requires that notwithstanding that an item in respect of development costs is included under fixed assets in the balance sheet formats set out in Part 1 of Schedule 4, an amount may only be included in a company's balance sheet in respect of development costs in special circumstances. **39**

****Editor's note:*** *All of the references to Schedule 4 also apply to Schedule 8. Schedule 4 to the Companies Act 1985 is replaced, with effect for accounting periods beginning on or after 6 April 2008 by Schedule 1 to the Large and Medium-sized Companies and Groups (Accounts and Reports) Regulations 2008 (SI 2008/410).*

The references change as follows:

Schedule 4 Paragraph Reference	***Schedule 1 SI 2008/410 Reference***
3 (1)	*3 (1)*
3 (2)	*3 (2)*
19 (1)	*19 (1)*
19 (2)	*19 (2)*
19 (3)	*20 (1)*
20 (1)	*21 (1)*
20 (2)	*21 (2)*

The reference to paragraph 6 (c) of Schedule 7 to the Companies Act 1985 becomes a reference to paragraph 7 (1) (c) to Schedule 7 to The Large and Medium-sized Companies and Groups (Accounts and Reports) Regulations 2008 (SI 2008/410).

The reference to section 269 (2) (b) of the Companies Act 1985 becomes a reference to section 844 (3) of the Companies Act 2006.

40 Paragraph 20(2) of Schedule 4 requires that if any amount is included in a company's balance sheet in respect of development costs the following information shall be given in a note to the accounts:

(a) the period over which the amount of those costs originally capitalised is being or is to be written off; and

(b) the reasons for capitalising the development costs in question.

41 Paragraph 6(c) of Schedule 7 requires the Directors' Report to contain an indication of the activities (if any) of the company and its subsidiaries in the field of research and development.

42 Section 269(2)(b) of the Companies Act 1985 on the treatment of development costs requires that where the unamortised development expenditure carried forward is not treated as a realised loss when determining distributable reserves, the notes to the financial statements shall disclose:

(a) the fact that the amount of the unamortised development expenditure is not to be treated as a realised loss for the purposes of calculating distributable profits; and

(b) the circumstances that the directors relied upon to justify their decision not to treat the unamortised development expenditure as a realised loss.

Part 5 – Note on legal requirements in the Republic of Ireland

References are to the Companies (Amendment) Act 1986 and to the Schedule to that Act unless otherwise stated.

43 Section 4(5) of the Act enables any items required to be shown in a company's balance sheet or profit and loss account to be shown in greater detail than required by the format adopted.

44 Section 4(12) of the Act provides that the balance sheet, or profit and loss account, of a company may include an item representing or covering the amount of any asset or liability or income or expenditure not otherwise covered by any of the items listed in the format adopted but that costs of research shall not be treated as assets in the balance sheet of a company.

45 Paragraph 43(4) of the Schedule requires the amount expended on research and development in the financial year, and any amount committed in respect of research and development in subsequent years, to be stated.

46 Paragraph 43(5) of the Schedule provides that where, in the opinion of the directors, the disclosure of any information required by Paragraph 43(4) would be prejudicial to the interests of the company, that information need not be disclosed, but the fact that any such information has not been disclosed shall be stated.

47 Paragraph 7(1) of the Schedule does not allow provision to be made for a temporary diminution in value other than for a fixed asset investment.

48 Paragraph 7(2) of the Schedule requires provision for diminution in value to be made in respect of any fixed asset which has diminished in value if the reduction is expected to be permanent (whether its useful economic life is limited or not) and the amount to be included in respect of it shall be reduced accordingly. Any such provisions which are not shown in the profit and loss account shall be disclosed (either separately or in aggregate) in a note to the accounts.

49 Paragraph 7(3) of the Schedule requires that where the reasons for which any provision was made have ceased to apply to any extent, then the provision should be written back to the extent that it is no longer necessary. Any amounts written back in accordance with this sub-paragraph which are not shown in the profit and loss account shall be disclosed (either separately or in aggregate) in a note to the accounts.

Paragraph 8(1) of the Schedule requires that notwithstanding that an item in respect of development costs is included under fixed assets in the balance sheet formats set out in Part 1 of the Schedule, an amount may only be included in a company's balance sheet in respect of development costs in special circumstances. **50**

Paragraph 8(2) of the Schedule requires that if any amount is included in a company's balance sheet in respect of development costs, the following information shall be given in a note to the accounts: **51**

(a) the period over which the amount of those costs originally capitalised is being or is to be written off, and
(b) the reasons for capitalising the development costs in question.

Section 13(c) of the Act requires the Directors' Report to contain an indication of the activity, if any, of the company and its subsidiaries, if any, in the field of research and development. **52**

Section 45A of the Companies (Amendment) Act 1983 on the treatment of development costs, provides that where development costs are shown in a company's accounts any amount shown as an asset in respect of those costs shall be treated as a realised loss for the purpose of determining profits available for distribution. This provision does not apply to any part of that amount representing an unrealised profit made on revaluation of these costs; nor does it apply if: **53**

(a) there are special circumstances justifying the directors of the company concerned in deciding that the amount mentioned in respect thereof in the company's accounts shall not be treated as a realised loss, and
(b) the note to the accounts required by paragraph 8(2) of the Schedule states that the amount is not to be so treated and explains the circumstances relied upon to justify the decision of the directors to that effect.

Part 6 – Compliance with International Accounting Standard No. 9 'Accounting for research and development activities'

The requirements of International Accounting Standard No. 9 'Accounting for research and development activities'* accord very closely with the content of the United Kingdom and Irish Accounting Standard No. 13 (Revised) 'Accounting for research and development' and accordingly compliance with SSAP 13 (Revised) will ensure compliance with IAS 9 in all material aspects. **54**

*****Editor's note:** IAS 9 was superseded by IAS 38 'Intangible Assets' issued September 1998. There are two main differences between SSAP 13 and IAS 38:*

- *IAS 38 requires development costs to be capitalised where the recognition criteria are met. SSAP 13 allows, but does not require, this treatment;*
- *there is no equivalent in the IAS of paragraph 25(d) of SSAP 13. This paragraph requires that the aggregate costs are expected to be exceeded by aggregate revenues. This means that where any development project is likely to lead to a loss, however small, no asset may be recognised. Under the IAS, an asset could be recognised, although it would need to be written down to reflect any impairment.*

IAS 38 has subsequently been revised again, and a new version of the standard applies from 2005. It does not alter the main differences identified.

[SSAP 19] Accounting for investment properties*†

(Issued November 1981; amended October 1992 and July 1994)

Contents

	Paragraphs
Part 1 – Explanatory note	1–6
Part 2 – Definition of terms	7–8
Part 3 – Standard accounting practice	9–16
Part 4 – Legal requirements in UK and Ireland	17–19

****Editor's note:** The equivalent international accounting standard is IAS 40 'Investment Property'. There are some differences between the standards. In particular, IAS 40 allows companies to adopt either the fair value model (similar to the treatment under SSAP 19) or the cost model. The cost model is not allowed under SSAP 19. Under IAS 40, where a company adopts the fair value model then any changes in value are dealt with in the income statement.*

*†**Editor's note:** The matters dealt with in SSAP 19 are covered in Section 16 of FRS 102.*

Accounting for investment properties

The provisions of this Statement of Standard Accounting Practice should be read in conjunction with the (Explanatory) Foreword to Accounting Standards. *The provisions apply equally to financial statements prepared under the historical cost convention and to financial statements prepared under the current cost convention. They need not be applied to immaterial items.*

Part 1 – Explanatory note

Under the accounting requirements of SSAP 12 'Accounting for depreciation',* fixed assets are generally subject to annual depreciation charges to reflect on a systematic basis the wearing out, consumption or other loss of value whether arising from use, effluxion of time or obsolescence through technology and market changes. Under those requirements it is also accepted that an increase in the value of such a fixed asset does not generally remove the necessity to charge depreciation to reflect on a systematic basis the consumption of the asset. **1**

A different treatment is, however, required where a significant proportion of the fixed assets of an enterprise is held not for consumption in the business operations but as investments, the disposal of which would not materially affect any manufacturing or trading operations of the enterprise. In such a case the current value of these investments, and changes in that current value, are of prime importance rather than a calculation of systematic annual depreciation. Consequently, for the proper appreciation of financial position, a different accounting treatment is considered appropriate for fixed assets held as investments (called in this standard 'investment properties'). **2**

Investment properties may be held by a company which holds investments as part of its business such as an investment trust or a property investment company. **3**

Investment properties may be held by a company whose main business is not the holding of investments. **4**

Where an investment property is held on a lease with a relatively short unexpired term, it is necessary to recognise the annual depreciation in the financial statements to avoid the situation whereby a short lease is amortised against the investment revaluation reserve whilst the rentals are taken to the profit and loss account. **5**

This statement requires investment properties to be included in the balance sheet at open market value. The statement does not require the valuation to be made by qualified or independent valuers; but (in paragraph 12) calls for disclosure of the names or qualifications of the valuers, the bases used by them and whether the person making the valuation is an employee or officer of the company. However, where investment properties represent a substantial proportion of the total assets of a major enterprise (e.g., a listed company) the valuation thereof would normally be carried out: **6**

(a) annually by persons holding a recognised professional qualification and having recent post-qualification experience in the location and category of the properties concerned; and
(b) at least every five years by an external valuer.

***Editor's note:** *SSAP 12 has been superseded by FRS 15 'Tangible fixed assets'. There has been no material change to the accounting requirement mentioned in this paragraph.*

Part 2 – Definition of terms

7 For the purposes of this statement, but subject to the exceptions in paragraph 8 below, an *investment property* is an interest in land and/or buildings:

(a) in respect of which construction work and development have been completed; and
(b) which is held for its investment potential, any rental income being negotiated at arm's length.

8 The following are exceptions from the definition:

(a) A property which is owned and occupied by a company for its own purposes is not an investment property.
(b) A property let to and occupied by another group company is not an investment property for the purposes of its own accounts or the group accounts.

Part 3 – Standard accounting practice

9 [*Withdrawn by FRS 15*]

10 Investment properties should not be subject to periodic charges for depreciation on the basis set out in SSAP 12* except for properties held on lease which should be depreciated on the basis set out in SSAP 12* at least over the period when the unexpired term is 20 years or less.

11 Investment properties should be included in the balance sheet at their open market value.†

12 The names of the persons making the valuation, or particulars of their qualifications, should be disclosed together with the bases of valuation used by them. If a person making a valuation is an employee or officer of the company or group which owns the property this fact should be disclosed.

13 Subject to paragraph 14 below, changes in the market value of investment properties should not be taken to the profit and loss account but should be taken to the statement of total recognised gains and losses (being a movement on an investment revaluation reserve), unless a deficit (or its reversal) on an individual investment property is expected to be permanent, in which case it should be charged (or credited) in the profit and loss account of the period. In the special circumstances of investment companies as defined in companies legislation (as mentioned in paragraphs 31 and 66 of FRS 3 'Reporting Financial Performance') and of property unit trusts it may not be appropriate to deal with such deficits in the profit and loss account. In such cases they should be shown only in the statement of total recognised gains and losses.

14 Paragraph 13 does not apply to the financial statements of:

(a) insurance companies and groups (and consolidated financial statements incorporating such entities) where changes in the market value of investment properties (including those comprising assets of the long-term business) are included in the profit and loss account.
(b) pension funds where changes in the market value of investment properties are dealt with in the relevant fund account.

15 The carrying value of investment properties and the investment revaluation reserve should be displayed prominently in the financial statements.

****Editor's note:*** *SSAP 12 has been superseded by FRS 15 'Tangible fixed assets'.*

†***Editor's note:*** *See also UITF Abstract 28 'Operating lease incentives'.*

APPLICATION TO SMALLER ENTITIES

Reporting entities applying the Financial Reporting Standard for Smaller Entities currently applicable are exempt from this accounting standard. **15A**

DATE FROM WHICH EFFECTIVE

The accounting and disclosure requirements in this statement should be adopted as soon as possible and regarded as standard in respect of financial statements relating to accounting periods starting on or after 1 July 1981.* **16**

Part 4 – Legal requirements in UK and Ireland

The application of this standard will usually be a departure, for the overriding purpose of giving a true and fair view, from the otherwise specific requirement of the law to provide depreciation on any fixed asset which has a limited useful economic life. In this circumstance there will need to be given in the notes to the accounts 'particulars of that departure, the reasons for it, and its effect'. Paragraphs 62–65 of FRS 18 'Accounting policies' specify disclosures that should be made in connection with this statutory requirement.† **17**

In Great Britain paragraphs 19 and 32 of Schedule 4 (for banking companies and groups paragraphs 26 and 42 of Schedule 9) to the Companies Act 1985 set out the legal requirements relating to provisions for diminution in value that are expected to be permanent. In the case of insurance companies and groups reported under the amended Schedule 9A to the Companies Act 1985 (introduced by SI 1993/3246) note 9 on the profit and loss account format and paragraph 29(7) of the Schedule set out the relevant statutory requirements.‡ **18**

There are legal requirements similar to Schedule 4§ in Northern Ireland (the Companies (Northern Ireland) Order 1986 Schedule 4 paragraphs 19 and 32 and Schedule 9 paragraphs 26 and 42) and in the Republic of Ireland (the Companies (Amendment) Act 1986 (the Schedule paragraphs 7 and 20) and the European Communities (Credit Institutions: Accounts) Regulations 1992 (the Schedule paragraphs 26 and 42)). Requirements similar to the amended Schedule 9A are expected to be enacted in Northern Ireland and the Republic of Ireland. **19**

***Editor's note:** *The amendment in July 1994 (revised paragraphs 13 and 14) became standard in respect of financial statements relating to accounting periods ending on or after 22 September 1994. Earlier adoption was encouraged but not required. The amendment noted that 'if an enterprise changes its presentation of revaluation deficits as a result of this amendment, the classification of reserves and comparative figures should be restated in accordance with FRS 3 'Reporting financial performance'.*

†**Editor's note:** *Under Schedule 1 to the Large and Medium-sized Companies and Groups (Accounts and Reports) Regulations 2008 (SI 2008/410) investment properties may be stated at fair value if this would be allowed under IFRS, but in this case changes in fair value are taken to profit. There is therefore still a discrepancy between the statutory provisions and SSAP 19, even if the fair value rules are adopted.*

‡**Editor's note:** *Schedule 4 to the Companies Act 1985 is replaced, with effect for accounting periods beginning on or after 6 April 2008 by Schedule 1 to the Large and Medium-sized Companies and Groups (Accounts and Reports) Regulations 2008 (SI 2008/410). The paragraph references become references to paragraphs 19 and 33 to that Schedule.*

§**Editor's note:** *Also similar to Schedule 9.*

[SSAP 20]
Foreign currency translation*†

(Issued April 1983)

Contents

Paragraphs

Part 1 – Explanatory note 1–32

Part 2 – Definition of terms 33–44

Part 3 – Standard accounting practice 45–61

Individual companies 46–51
Consolidated financial statements 52–58
Disclosure 59–60
Application to smaller entities 60A
Date from which effective 61

Part 4 – Legal requirements in UK and Ireland 62–71

Part 5 – Compliance with International Accounting Standard No. 21 'Accounting for the effects of changes in foreign exchange rates' 72

****Editor's note:* SSAP 20 has been superseded by FRS 23, but only for entities which comply with that standard. In order to comply with FRS 23, entities must also comply with FRS 26. For other entities, SSAP 20 remains in force.*

*†**Editor's note:** The matters dealt with in SSAP 20 are covered primarily in Section 30 of FRS 102, although some of the matters covered in the SSAP, such as the treatment of instruments used for hedging exchange exposures, are within the scope of Section 12 of FRS 102.*

Foreign currency translation

The provisions of this statement of standard accounting practice should be read in conjunction with the (Explanatory) Foreword to accounting standards and need not be applied to immaterial items. The provisions apply to financial statements prepared under either the historical cost convention or the current cost convention.

This statement sets out the standard accounting practice for foreign currency translation, but does not deal with the method of calculating profits or losses arising from a company's normal currency dealing operations; neither does it deal specifically with the determination of distributable profits.

Part 1 – Explanatory note

BACKGROUND

A company may engage in foreign currency operations in two main ways: **1**

(a) Firstly, it may enter directly into business transactions which are denominated in foreign currencies; the results of these transactions will need to be translated into the currency in which the company reports.
(b) Secondly, foreign operations may be conducted through a foreign enterprise which maintains its accounting records in a currency other than that of the investing company; in order to prepare consolidated financial statements it will be necessary to translate the complete financial statements of the foreign enterprise into the currency used for reporting purposes by the investing company.

OBJECTIVES OF TRANSLATION

The translation of foreign currency transactions and financial statements should produce results which are generally compatible with the effects of rate changes on a company's cash flows and its equity and should ensure that the financial statements present a true and fair view of the results of management actions. Consolidated statements should reflect the financial results and relationships as measured in the foreign currency financial statements prior to translation. **2**

PROCEDURES

In this statement the procedures which should be adopted when accounting for foreign operations are considered in two stages, namely: **3**
(a) the preparation of the financial statements of an individual company; and
(b) the preparation of consolidated financial statements.

THE INDIVIDUAL COMPANY STAGE

During an accounting period, a company may enter into transactions which are denominated in a foreign currency. The result of each transaction should normally be translated into the company's local currency using the exchange rate in operation on the date on which the transaction occurred; however, if the rates do not fluctuate significantly, an average rate for a period may be used as an approximation. Where the transaction is to be settled at a contracted rate, that rate should be used; where a trading transaction is covered by a related or matching forward contract, the rate of exchange specified in that contract may be used. **4**

5 Once non-monetary assets, e.g., plant, machinery and equity investments, have been translated and recorded they should be carried in the company's local currency. Subject to the provisions of paragraph 30 concerning the treatment of foreign equity investments financed by foreign currency borrowings, no subsequent translations of these assets will normally need to be made.

6 At the balance sheet date monetary assets and liabilities denominated in a foreign currency, e.g., cash and bank balances, loans and amounts receivable and payable, should be translated by using the rate of exchange ruling at that date, or, where appropriate, the rates of exchange fixed under the terms of the relevant transactions. Where there are related or matching forward contracts in respect of trading transactions, the rates of exchange specified in those contracts may be used.

7 An exchange gain or loss will result during an accounting period if a business transaction is settled at an exchange rate which differs from that used when the transaction was initially recorded, or, where appropriate, that used at the last balance sheet date. An exchange gain or loss will also arise on unsettled transactions if the rate of exchange used at the balance sheet date differs from that used previously.

8 Exchange gains or losses arising on settled transactions in the context of an individual company's operations have already been reflected in cash flows, since a change in the exchange rate increases or decreases the local currency equivalent of amounts paid or received in cash settlement. Similarly, it is reasonably certain that exchange gains or losses on unsettled short-term monetary items will soon be reflected in cash flows. Therefore, it is normally appropriate, because of the cash flow effects, to recognise such gains and losses as part of the profit or loss for the year; they should be included in profit or loss from ordinary activities unless they arise from events which themselves would fall to be treated as extraordinary items, in which case they would be included as part of such items.

9 When dealing with long-term monetary items, additional considerations apply. Although it is not easy to predict what the exchange rate will be when a long-term liability or asset matures, it is necessary, when stating the liability or the asset in terms of the reporting currency, to make the best estimate possible in the light of the information available at the time; generally speaking translation at the year-end rate will provide the best estimate, particularly when the currency concerned is freely dealt in on the spot and forward exchange markets.

10 In order to give a true and fair view of results, exchange gains and losses on long-term monetary items should normally be reported as part of the profit or loss for the period in accordance with the accruals concept of accounting; treatment of these items on a simple cash movements basis would be inconsistent with that concept. Exchange gains on unsettled transactions can be determined at the balance sheet date no less objectively than exchange losses; deferring the gains whilst recognising the losses would not only be illogical by denying in effect that any favourable movement in exchange rates had occurred but would also inhibit fair measurement of the performance of the enterprise in the year. In particular, this symmetry of treatment recognises that there will probably be some interaction between currency movements and interest rates and reflects more accurately in the profit and loss account the true results of currency involvement.

11 For the special reasons outlined above, both exchange gains and losses on long-term monetary items should be recognised in the profit and loss account. However, it is necessary to consider on the grounds of prudence whether the amount of the gain, or the amount by which exchange gains exceed past exchange losses on the same items, to be recognised in the profit and loss account should be restricted in the exceptional cases where there are doubts as to the convertibility or marketability of the currency in question.

Gains or losses on exchange arising from transactions between a holding company and its subsidiaries, or from transactions between fellow subsidiaries, should normally be reported in the individual company's financial statements as part of the profit or loss for the year in the same way as gains or losses arising from transactions with third parties. 12

THE CONSOLIDATED FINANCIAL STATEMENTS STAGE

The method used to translate financial statements for consolidation purposes should reflect the financial and other operational relationships which exist between an investing company and its foreign enterprises. 13

In most circumstances the closing rate/net investment method, described in paragraphs 15 to 20, should be used and exchange differences accounted for on a net investment basis. However, in certain specified circumstances (see paragraphs 21 to 24) the temporal method should be used. 14

THE CLOSING RATE/NET INVESTMENT METHOD

This method recognises that the investment of a company is in the net worth of its foreign enterprise rather than a direct investment in the individual assets and liabilities of that enterprise. The foreign enterprise will normally have net current assets and fixed assets which may be financed partly by local currency borrowings. In its day-to-day operations the foreign enterprise is not normally dependent on the reporting currency of the investing company. The investing company may look forward to a stream of dividends but the net investment will remain until the business is liquidated or the investment disposed of. 15

Under this method the amounts in the balance sheet of a foreign enterprise should be translated into the reporting currency of the investing company using the rate of exchange ruling at the balance sheet date. Exchange differences will arise if this rate differs from that ruling at the previous balance sheet date or at the date of any subsequent capital injection (or reduction). 16

Amounts in the profit and loss account of a foreign enterprise should be translated at the closing rate or at an average rate for the accounting period. The use of the closing rate is more likely to achieve the objective of translation, stated in paragraph 2, of reflecting the financial results and relationships as measured in the foreign currency financial statements prior to translation. However, it can be argued that an average ate reflects more fairly the profits or losses and cash flows as they arise to the group hroughout an accounting period. The use of either method is therefore permitted, rovided that the one selected is applied consistently from period to period. 17

o definitive method of calculating the average rate had been prescribed, since the propriate method may justifiably vary as between individual companies. Factors will need to be considered include the company's internal accounting procedures the extent of seasonal trade variations; the use of a weighting procedure will in cases be desirable. Where the average rate used differs from the closing rate, a ence will arise which should be dealt with in reserves. 18

sults of the operations of a foreign enterprise are best reflected in the group and loss account by consolidating the net profit or loss shown in its local 19 currency financial statements without adjustment (other than for normal consolidation adjustments). If exchange differences arising from the retranslation of a company's net investment in its foreign enterprise were introduced into the profit and loss account, the results from trading operations, as shown in the local currency financial statements, would be distorted. Such differences may result from many factors unrelated to the trading performance or financial operations of the foreign enterprise; in particular, they do not represent or measure changes in actual or prospective cash flows. It is therefore inappropriate to regard them as profits or losses and they should be dealt with as adjustments to reserves.

20 Although equity investments in foreign enterprises will normally be made by the purchase of shares, investments may also be made by means of long-term loans and inter-company deferred trading balances. Where financing by such means is intended to be, for all practical purposes, as permanent as equity, such loans and inter-company balances should be treated as part of the investing company's net investment in the foreign enterprise; hence exchange differences arising on such loans and inter-company balances should be dealt with as adjustments to reserves.

THE TEMPORAL METHOD

21 For most investing companies in the UK and Ireland foreign operations are normally carried out through foreign enterprises which operate as separate or quasi-independent entities rather than as direct extensions of the trade of the investing company.

22 However, there are some cases in which the affairs of a foreign enterprise are so closely interlinked with those of the investing company that its results may be regarded as being more dependent on the economic environment of the investing company's currency than on that of its own reporting currency. In such a case the financial statements of the foreign enterprise should be included in the consolidated financial statements as if all its transactions had been entered into by the investing company itself in its own currency. For this purpose the temporal method of translation should be used; the mechanics of this method are identical with thos
used in preparing the accounts of an individual company, as stated in paragraphs
to 12.

23 It is not possible to select one factor which of itself will lead a company to con
that the temporal method should be adopted. All the available evidence sho
considered in determining whether the currency of the investing company
dominant currency in the economic environment in which the foreign e
operates. Amongst the factors to be taken into account will be:

(a) the extent to which the cash flows of the enterprise have a direct in
those of the investing company;

(b) the extent to which the functioning of the enterprise is dependent
the investing company;

(c) the currency in which the majority of the trading transactions ar

(d) the major currency to which the operation is exposed in its fina

24 Examples of situations where the temporal method may be approp
foreign enterprise:

(a) acts as a selling agency receiving stocks of goods from th
and remitting the proceeds back to the company;

(b) produces a raw material or manufactures parts or sub
then shipped to the investing company for inclusion ir

(c) is located overseas for tax, exchange control or similar reasons to act as a means of raising finance for other companies in the group.

THE TREATMENT OF FOREIGN BRANCHES

For the purpose of this statement, foreign operations which are conducted through a foreign branch should be accounted for in accordance with the nature of the business operations concerned. Where such a branch operates as a separate business with local finance, it should be accounted for using the closing rate/net investment method. Where the foreign branch operates as an extension of the company's trade and its cash flows have a direct impact upon those of the company, the temporal method should be used. **25**

AREAS OF HYPER-INFLATION*

Where a foreign enterprise operates in a country in which a very high rate of inflation exists it may not be possible to present fairly in historical cost accounts the financial position of a foreign enterprise simply by a translation process. In such circumstances the local currency financial statements should be adjusted where possible to reflect current price levels before the translation process is undertaken. **26**

THE SPECIAL CASE OF EQUITY INVESTMENTS FINANCED BY FOREIGN BORROWINGS

Under the procedures set out in this statement, exchange gains or losses on foreign currency borrowings taken up by an investing company or foreign enterprise would normally be reported as part of that company's profit or loss from ordinary activities and would flow through into the consolidated profit and loss account. **27**

Where an individual company has used borrowings in currencies other than its own to finance foreign equity investments, or where the purpose of such borrowings is to provide a hedge against the exchange risk associated with existing equity investments, the company may be covered in economic terms against any movement in exchange rates. It would be inappropriate in such cases to record an accounting profit or loss when exchange rates change. **28**

Therefore, provided the conditions set out in this paragraph apply, the company may denominate its foreign equity investments in the appropriate foreign currencies and translate the carrying amounts at the end of each accounting period at the closing rates of exchange. Where investments are treated in this way, any resulting exchange differences should be taken direct to reserves and the exchange gains or losses on the borrowings should then be offset, as a reserve movement, against these exchange differences. The conditions which must apply are as follows: **29**

(a) in any accounting period, exchange gains or losses arising on the borrowings may be offset only to the extent of exchange differences arising on the equity investments;

(b) the foreign currency borrowings, whose exchange gains or losses are used in the offset process, should not exceed, in the aggregate, the total amount of cash that the investments are expected to be able to generate, whether from profits or otherwise; and

****Editor's note:*** *See UITF Abstract 9 'Accounting for operations in hyper-inflationary economies'. This is also now covered by FRS 24. However, FRS 24 is applicable to the same entities as FRS 23, and therefore cannot apply to any entity applying SSAP 20.*

(c) the accounting treatment adopted should be applied consistently from period to period.

30 Similarly, within a group, foreign borrowings may have been used to finance group investments in foreign enterprises or to provide a hedge against the exchange risk associated with similar existing investments. Any increase or decrease in the amount outstanding on the borrowings arising from exchange movements will probably be covered by corresponding changes in the carrying amount of the net assets underlying the net investments (which would be reflected in reserves). Since in this case the group will be covered in economic terms against any movement in exchange rates, it would be inappropriate to record an accounting profit or loss when exchange rates change.

31 In the consolidated financial statements, therefore, subject to certain conditions, the exchange gains or losses on such foreign currency borrowings, which would otherwise have been taken to the group profit and loss account, may be offset as reserve movements against exchange differences on the retranslation of the net investments. The conditions which must apply are as follows:

(a) the relationship between the investing company and the foreign enterprises concerned should be such as to justify the use of the closing rate method for consolidation purposes;
(b) in any accounting period, exchange gains or losses arising on foreign currency borrowings may be offset only to the extent of the exchange differences arising on the net investments in foreign enterprises;
(c) the foreign currency borrowings, whose exchange gains or losses are used in the offset process, should not exceed, in the aggregate, the total amount of cash that the net investments are expected to be able to generate, whether from profits or otherwise; and
(d) the accounting treatment adopted should be applied consistently from period to period.

32 Where the provisions of paragraph 29 have been applied in the investing company's financial statements to a foreign equity investment which is neither a subsidiary nor an associated company, the same offset procedure may be applied in the consolidated financial statements.

Part 2 – Definition of terms

33 *Financial statements* are balance sheets, profit and loss accounts, statements of source and application of funds, notes and other statements, which collectively are intended to give a true and fair view of the financial position and profit or loss.*

34 *Company* includes any enterprise which comes within the scope of statements of standard accounting practice.

35 *An exempt company* is one which:

(a) is registered in Great Britain and does not prepare its accounts in accordance with either Sections 149 and 152 of the Companies Act 1948;† or

****Editor's note:*** *The reference to statements of source and application of funds should be read as a reference to cash flow statements for those companies required to prepare such a statement under FRS 1. The reference to other statements should be taken to include the statement of total recognised gains and losses.*

†***Editor's note:*** *Now sections 394 and 396 to the Companies Act 2006.*

(b) is registered in Northern Ireland and is exempted from full disclosure by Part 3 of Schedule 6A to the Companies Act (Northern Ireland) 1960 as amended by the Companies (Northern Ireland) Order 1982; or
(c) is registered in the Republic of Ireland and is exempted from full disclosure by Part 3 of Schedule 6 to the Companies Act 1963.

A foreign enterprise is a subsidiary, associated company or branch whose operations are based in a country other than that of the investing company or whose assets and liabilities are denominated mainly in a foreign currency. **36**

A foreign branch is either a legally constituted enterprise located overseas or a group of assets and liabilities which are accounted for in foreign currencies. **37**

Translation is the process whereby financial data denominated in one currency are expressed in terms of another currency. It includes both the expression of individual transactions in terms of another currency and the expression of a complete set of financial statements prepared in one currency in terms of another currency. **38**

A company's *local currency* is the currency of the primary economic environment in which it operates and generates net cash flows. **39**

An *exchange rate* is a rate at which two currencies may be exchanged for each other at a particular point in time; different rates apply for spot and forward transactions. **40**

The *closing rate* is the exchange rate for spot transactions ruling at the balance sheet date and is the mean of the buying and selling rates at the close of business on the day for which the rate is to be ascertained. **41**

A *forward contract* is an agreement to exchange different currencies at a specified future date and at a specified rate. The difference between the specified rate and the spot rate ruling on the date the contract was entered into is the discount or premium on the forward contract. **42**

The *net investment* which a company has in a foreign enterprise is its effective equity stake and comprises its proportion of such foreign enterprise's net assets; in appropriate circumstances, intra-group loans and other deferred balances may be regarded as part of the effective equity stake. **43**

Monetary items are money held and amounts to be received or paid in money and, where a company is not an exempt company, should be categorised as either short-term or long-term. Short-term monetary items are those which fall due within one year of the balance sheet date. **44**

Part 3 – Standard accounting practice

When preparing the financial statements of an individual company the procedures set out in paragraphs 46 to 51 should be followed. When preparing consolidated financial statements, the procedures set out in paragraphs 52 to 58 should be followed. **45**

INDIVIDUAL COMPANIES

Subject to the provisions of paragraphs 48 and 51 each asset, liability, revenue or cost arising from a transaction denominated in a foreign currency should be translated into the local currency at the exchange rate in operation on the date on which **46** the transaction occurred; if the rates do not fluctuate significantly, an average rate for a period may be used as an approximation. Where the transaction is to be settled at a contracted rate, that rate should be used. Where a trading transaction is covered by a related or matching forward contract, the rate of exchange specified in that contract may be used.

47 Subject to the special provisions of paragraph 51, which relate to the treatment of foreign equity investments financed by foreign currency borrowings, no subsequent translations should normally be made once non-monetary assets have been translated and recorded.

48 At each balance sheet date, monetary assets and liabilities denominated in a foreign currency should be translated by using the closing rate or, where appropriate, the rates of exchange fixed under the terms of the relevant transactions. Where there are related or matching forward contracts in respect of trading transactions, the rates of exchange specified in those contracts may be used.

49 All exchange gains or losses on settled transactions and unsettled short-term monetary items should be reported as part of the profit or loss for the year from ordinary activities (unless they result from transactions which themselves would fall to be treated as extraordinary items, in which case the exchange gains or losses should be included as part of such items).*

50 Exchange gains and losses on long-term monetary items should also be recognised in the profit and loss account; however, it is necessary to consider on the grounds of prudence whether, in the exceptional cases outlined in paragraph 11, the amount of the gain, or the amount by which exchange gains exceed past exchange losses on the same items to be recognised in the profit and loss account, should be restricted.

51 Where a company has used foreign currency borrowings to finance, or provide a hedge against, its foreign equity investments and the conditions set out in this paragraph apply, the equity investments may be denominated in the appropriate foreign currencies and the carrying amounts translated at the end of each accounting period at closing rates for inclusion in the investing company's financial statements. Where investments are treated in this way, any exchange differences arising should be taken to reserves and the exchange gains or losses on the foreign currency borrowings should then be offset, as a reserve movement, against these exchange differences. The conditions which must apply are as follows:

(a) in any accounting period, exchange gains or losses arising on the borrowings may be offset only to the extent of exchange differences arising on the equity investments;†

(b) the foreign currency borrowings, whose exchange gains or losses are used in the offset process, should not exceed, in the aggregate, the total amount of cash that the investments are expected to be able to generate, whether from profits or otherwise;* and

(c) the accounting treatment adopted should be applied consistently from period to period.

***Editor's note:** *This is of no practical relevance given the de facto abolition of extraordinary items by FRS 3.*

†**Editor's note:** *See also UITF Abstract 19 'Tax on gains and losses on foreign currency borrowings that hedge an investment in a foreign enterprise'.*

CONSOLIDATED FINANCIAL STATEMENTS

When preparing group accounts for a company and its foreign enterprises, which includes the incorporation of the results of associated companies or foreign branches into those of an investing company, the closing rate/net investment method of translating the local currency financial statements should normally be used. 52

Exchange differences arising from the retranslation of the opening net investment in a foreign enterprise at the closing rate should be recorded as a movement on reserves. 53

The profit and loss account of a foreign enterprise accounted for under the closing rate/net investment method should be translated at the closing rate or at an average rate for the period. Where an average rate is used, the difference between the profit and loss account translated at an average rate and at the closing rate should be recorded as a movement on reserves. The average rate used should be calculated by the method considered most appropriate for the circumstances of the foreign enterprise. 54

In those circumstances where the trade of the foreign enterprise is more dependent on the economic environment of the investing company's currency than that of its own reporting currency, the temporal method should be used. 55

The method used for translating the financial statements of each foreign enterprise should be applied consistently from period to period unless its financial and other operational relationships with the investing company change. 56

Where foreign currency borrowings have been used to finance, or provide a hedge against, group equity investments in foreign enterprises, exchange gains or losses on the borrowings, which would otherwise have been taken to the profit and loss account, may be offset as reserve movements against exchange differences arising on the retranslation of the net investments provided that: 57

(a) the relationships between the investing company and the foreign enterprises concerned justify the use of the closing rate method for consolidation purposes;
(b) in any accounting period, the exchange gains and losses arising on foreign currency borrowings are offset only to the extent of the exchange differences arising on the net investments in foreign enterprises;*
(c) the foreign currency borrowings, whose exchange gains or losses are used in the offset process, should not exceed, in the aggregate, the total amount of cash that the net investments are expected to be able to generate, whether from profits or otherwise;* and
(d) the accounting treatment is applied consistently from period to period.

Where the provisions of paragraph 51 have been applied in the investing company's financial statements to a foreign equity investment which is neither a subsidiary nor an associated company, the same offset procedure may be applied in the consolidated financial statements. 58

DISCLOSURE

The methods used in the translation of the financial statements of foreign enterprises and the treatment accorded to exchange differences should be disclosed in the financial statements. 59

**Editor's note:* *See also UITF Abstract 19 'Tax on gains and losses on foreign currency borrowings that hedge an investment in a foreign enterprise'.*

60 The following information should also be disclosed in the financial statements:

(a) for all companies, or groups of companies, which are not exempt companies, the net amount of exchange gains and losses on foreign currency borrowings less deposits, identifying separately:
   (i) the amount offset in reserves under the provisions of paragraphs 51, 57 and 58; and
   (ii) the net amount charged/credited to the profit and loss account;

(b) for all companies, or groups of companies, the net movement on reserves arising from exchange differences.*

APPLICATION TO SMALLER ENTITIES

60A Reporting entities applying the Financial Reporting Standard for Smaller Entities currently applicable are exempt from this accounting standard.

DATE FROM WHICH EFFECTIVE

61 The accounting and disclosure requirements set out in this statement should be adopted as soon as possible. They should be regarded as standard in respect of financial statements relating to accounting periods beginning on or after 1 April 1983.

Part 4 – Legal requirements in UK and Ireland

62 Paragraphs 63 to 69 below apply to companies preparing accounts in compliance with Sections 149 and 152* of the Companies Act 1948 or with Sections 143 and 146 of the Companies Act (Northern Ireland) 1960. The references to the Schedule which follow are to Schedule 8† to the Companies Act 1948 (as inserted by Section 1 of the Companies Act 1981). References to the Schedule will also be to Schedule 6 to the Companies Act (Northern Ireland) 1960, as inserted by Article 3 of the Companies (Northern Ireland) Order 1982, when this is brought into operation on 1 July 1983.

63 Paragraph 12 of the Schedule requires that the amount of any item shall be determined on a prudent basis and, in particular, that only profits realised at the balance sheet date shall be included in the profit and loss account. (Paragraph 90 of the Schedule‡ defines realised profits in relation to a company's accounts as 'such profits of the company as fall to be treated as realised profits for the purposes of those accounts in accordance with principles generally accepted with respect to the determination for accounting purposes of realised profits at the time when those accounts are prepared').

64 Paragraph 15 of the Schedule permits a departure from paragraph 12 of the Schedule if it appears to the directors that there are special reasons for such a departure.

****Editor's note:*** *Now sections 394 and 396 of the Companies Act 2006.*

†***Editor's note:*** *Now Schedule 1 to the Large and Medium-sized Companies and Groups (Accounts and Reports) Regulations 2008 (SI 2008/410). The reference becomes one to paragraph 13 of that Schedule.*

‡***Editor's note:*** *Now section 853 to the Companies Act 2006.*

Particulars of any departure, the reasons for it and its effect must be given in a note to the accounts.*

For companies other than exempt companies, all exchange gains taken through the profit and loss account, other than those arising on unsettled long-term monetary items, are realised. For such companies the application of paragraph 50 of this statement may result in unrealised exchange gains on unsettled long-term monetary items being taken to the profit and loss account. In this statement the need to show a true and fair view of results, referred to in paragraph 10 above, is considered to constitute a special reason for departure from the principle under paragraph 15 of the Schedule. **65**

This statement is based on the assumption that the process of translation at closing rates for the purposes of this statement does not constitute a departure from the historical cost rules under Section C of the Schedule nor does it give rise to a diminution in value of an asset under Section B of the Schedule. **66**

Paragraph 58 (1) of the Schedule requires that, where sums originally denominated in foreign currencies are brought into the balance sheet or profit and loss account, the basis on which those sums have been translated into sterling shall be stated.† **67**

Part I of the Schedule lays down the choice of formats permitted for the presentation of accounts. Distinction is drawn between operating and other income and expense. For this reason it is necessary to consider the nature of each foreign exchange gain or loss and to allocate each accordingly. Gains or losses arising from trading transactions should normally be included under 'Other operating income or expense' while those arising from arrangements which may be considered as financing should be disclosed separately as part of 'Other interest receivable/payable and similar income/expense'. Exchange gains or losses which arise from events which themselves fall to be treated as extraordinary items should be included as part of such items. **68**

Paragraph 46 of the Schedule requires the following information to be disclosed about movements on any reserve: **69**

(a) the amount of the reserve at the date of the beginning of the financial year and as at the balance sheet date respectively;
(b) any amounts transferred to or from the reserve during that year; and
(c) the source and application respectively of any amounts so transferred.‡

Paragraphs 1 and 2 of Schedule 2 to the Companies Act 1981 permit certain companies to prepare accounts in compliance with Sections 149A and 152A of and Schedule 8A to the Companies Act 1948 instead of Sections 149 and 152 and Schedule 8.§ Paragraph 11 (9) of Schedule 8A requires disclosure of the basis on which foreign currencies have been converted into sterling. Schedule 2 to the Companies (Northern Ireland) Order 1982 will permit similar companies registered in Northern Ireland to prepare accounts in accordance with Sections 143A and 146A **70**

Editor's note: *The reference to paragraph 15 is to paragraph 10 (2) of SI 2008/410, see note † on page 234.*

†***Editor's note:*** *The reference to paragraph 58 (1) becomes a reference to paragraph 70 of SI 2008/410, see note † on page 234.*

‡***Editor's note:*** *The reference to paragraph 46 becomes a reference to paragraph 59 of SI 2008/410, see note † on page 234.*

§***Editor's note:*** *These requirements have been replaced by the special provisions for banking companies and groups in Schedules 2 and 3 to SI 2008/410, see note † on page 234.*

of and Schedule 6A to the Companies Act (Northern Ireland) 1960 which require the same disclosure.

71 Similar legal requirements are expected to be enacted in the Republic of Ireland.

Part 5 – Compliance with International Accounting Standard No. 21 'Accounting for the effects of changes in foreign exchange rates'

72 Compliance with the requirements of Statement of Standard Accounting Practice No. 20 'Foreign currency translation' will automatically ensure compliance with International Accounting Standard No. 21 'Accounting for the effects of changes in foreign exchange rates.'*

***Editor's note:** *A revised version of IAS 21 was issued in November 1993. A further revision was issued in December 2003, which came into force in 2005. There are few differences between SSAP 20 and IAS 21 when dealing with the recording of transactions in company financial statements. In terms of consolidated financial statements, the major current difference is that IAS 21 prohibits the use of the closing rate for the translation of transactions during the year. SIC 19 and 30 also affect the currency in which transactions should be measured and presented, whilst SIC 11 affects capitalisation of losses resulting from severe currency devaluations. The revised version of IAS 21 differs materially from SSAP 20. It deals with the functional and therefore measurement currency of entities and with the presentation currency, the currency in which amounts are actually reported. Given that functional currency is crucial under IAS 21, the revised version draws no distinction between entities which are integral and entities which are not. In addition, IAS 32 requires certain currency disclosures not included in SSAP 20, whilst IAS 39 affects the treatment of foreign currency derivatives, and foreign currency items against which the reporting entity has hedged. IAS 21 has now been implemented in the UK as FRS 23. However, SSAP 20 continues to apply to those companies that have not adopted FRS 26.*

[SSAP 21]
Accounting for leases and hire purchase contracts*

(Issued August 1984; amended February 1997)

Foreword

Over the past few years, leasing has grown in importance such that it is now a major source of finance for industry in the UK. In consequence, the question of how to account for various types of lease has itself become important. SSAP 21 distinguishes finance leases from operating leases and sets out standard practice for each. It codifies accepted practice for some aspects of lease accounting and introduces a requirement for lessees to capitalise material finance leases – which a significant number of companies are doing already.

Why is a capitalisation requirement necessary? When a company is leasing a substantial amount of assets instead of buying them, the effect is that, unless the leased assets and obligations are capitalised, potentially large liabilities build up off balance sheet; equally, the leased assets employed are not reflected on the balance sheet. These omissions may mislead users of a company's accounts – both external users and the company's own management. SSAP 21 therefore requires assets held under finance leases and the related leasing obligations to be capitalised on a company's balance sheet.

Capitalisation of finance leases will be helpful in at least two respects: to external users of companies' accounts and for internal management purposes. External users may use a company's accounts when making investment or credit decisions. Capitalisation of assets held under finance leases results in a company's assets and obligations being more readily apparent than if leased assets and obligations are not recognised. The information provided by SSAP 21 should in this way enhance the usefulness of the accounts for decision-making purposes.

In the latter context, divisional managers may in some cases not be aware of or involved in the choice of finance for the assets which they use. Without capitalisation, the choice to lease instead of buy could result in a divisional manager's performance being assessed by reference to a misleading figure of capital employed, whilst at the group level assets (and obligations, and thus gearing) would be similarly understated. SSAP 21 removes these anomalies by requiring recognition on a balance sheet of the leased assets and related obligations.

It is sometimes argued that leased assets should not be recognised on a company's balance sheet as the company does not have legal title to the asset. Whilst it is true that a lessee does not have legal ownership of the leased asset, however, he has the right to use the asset for substantially the whole of its useful economic life. These rights are for most practical purposes equivalent to legal ownership. It has long been accepted that assets held under hire purchase contracts should be recognised on the balance sheet of the hirer of the asset. SSAP 21 extends this treatment to finance leasing; it recognises that whether an asset is owned, leased or held under a hire purchase contract, it represents an economic resource which is needed in the business and which the accounts ought to reflect in a consistent manner.

***Editor's note**: The matters dealt with in SSAP 21 are covered in Section 20 of FRS 102.*

Detailed guidance notes are published separately from the attached standard. They are non-mandatory and their primary purpose is to recommend practical methods which will assist companies to comply with the standard.

Finally I would stress that the standard, like all accounting standards, need not be applied to immaterial items. Hence, it is only of relevance to companies engaged in a significant amount of leasing.

Ian Hay Davison, *Chairman*

Accounting Standards Committee

[SSAP 21]
Accounting for leases and hire purchase contracts

Contents

Paragraphs

Part 1 – Explanatory note	1–12
Part 2 – Definition of terms	13–30
Part 3 – Standard accounting practice	31–62
Hire purchase and leasing	31
Accounting by lessees	32–37
Accounting by lessors	38–44
Manufacturer/dealer lessor	45
Sale and leaseback transactions	46–48
Disclosure by lessees	49–57
Disclosure by lessors	58–60
Application to smaller entities	60A
Date from which effective for lessors and finance companies	61
Date from which effective for lessees and hirers	62
Part 4 – Legal requirements in Great Britain	63–66
Part 5 – Legal requirements in Ireland	67–68
Northern Ireland	67
Republic of Ireland	68
Part 6 – Compliance with International Accounting Standard No. 17 'Accounting for leases'	69

Accounting for leases and hire purchase contracts

The provisions of this Statement of Standard Accounting Practice should be read in conjunction with the (Explanatory) Foreword to Accounting Standards *and need not be applied to immaterial items. The provisions apply equally to financial statements prepared under the historical cost convention and to financial statements prepared under the current cost convention.This statement does not apply to lease contracts concerning the rights to explore for or to exploit natural resources such as oil, gas, timber, metals and other minerals. Nor does it apply to licensing agreements for items such as motion picture films, video recordings, plays, manuscripts, patents and copyrights.*

Part 1 – Explanatory note

BACKGROUND

1 Leases and hire purchase contracts are means by which companies obtain the right to use or purchase assets. In the UK there is normally no provision in a lease contract for legal title to the leased asset to pass to the lessee.

2 A hire purchase contract has similar features to a lease except that under a hire purchase contract the hirer may acquire legal title by exercising an option to purchase the asset upon fulfilment of certain conditions (normally the payment of an agreed number of instalments).

3 Current tax legislation provides that in the normal situation capital allowances can be claimed by the lessor under a lease contract but by the hirer under a hire purchase contract.

4 Lessors fall into three broad categories. They may be companies, including banks and finance houses, which provide finance under lease contracts to enable a single customer to acquire the use of an asset for the greater part of its useful life; they may operate a business which involves the renting out of assets for varying periods of time probably to more than one customer; or they may be manufacturer or dealer lessors who use leasing as a means of marketing their products, which may involve leasing a product to one customer or to several customers.

5 As a lessor and lessee are both parties to the same transaction it is appropriate that the same definitions should be used and the accounting treatment recommended should ideally be complementary. However, this will not mean that the recorded balances in both financial statements will be the same because the taxation consequences and hence the pattern of cash flows will be different.

FORMS OF LEASE

6 Leases can appropriately be classified into finance leases and operating leases. The distinction between a finance lease and an operating lease will usually be evident from the terms of the contract between the lessor and the lessee.

7 An operating lease involves the lessee paying a rental for the hire of an asset for a period of time which is normally substantially less than its useful economic life. The lessor retains most of the risks and rewards of ownership of an asset in the case of an operating lease.

A finance lease usually involves payment by a lessee to a lessor of the full cost of the asset together with a return on the finance provided by the lessor. The lessee has substantially all the risks and rewards associated with the ownership of the asset, other than the legal title. In practice all leases transfer some of the risks and rewards of ownership to the lessee, and the distinction between a finance lease and an operating lease is essentially one of degree. **8**

Sometimes, the lessor may receive part of his return in the form of a guarantee from an independent third party, in which case the lease may be a finance lease as far as the lessor is concerned, but not from the lessee's point of view. **9**

Briefly, this standard requires that a finance lease should be capitalised by the lessee, that is, accounted for as the purchase of rights to the use and enjoyment of the asset with simultaneous recognition of the obligation to make future payments. A hire purchase is normally accounted for in a similar way. Under an operating lease, only the rental will be taken into account by a lessee. **10**

The effect of a lease is to create a set of rights and obligations related to the use and enjoyment by the lessee of a leased asset for the term of the lease. Such rights constitute the rewards of ownership transferred under the lease to the lessee whilst the obligations, including in particular the obligation to continue paying rent for the period specified in the lease, constitute the risks of ownership so transferred. Where the rights and obligations of the lessee are such that his corresponding rewards and risks are, despite the absence of the ability to obtain legal title, substantially similar to those of an outright purchaser of the asset in question, the lease will be a finance lease. **11**

Conceptually, what is capitalised in the lessee's accounts is not the asset itself but his rights in the asset (together with his obligation to pay rentals). However, the definition of a finance lease is such that a lessee's rights are for the practical purposes little different from those of an outright purchaser. Hence, it is appropriate that lessees should include these assets in their financial statements, but they should describe them as 'leased assets' to distinguish them from owned assets. **12**

Part 2 – Definition of terms

Company includes any enterprise which comes within the scope of statements of standard accounting practice. **13**

A *lease* is a contract between a lessor and a lessee for the hire of a specific asset. The lessor retains ownership of the asset but conveys the right to the use of the asset to the lessee for an agreed period of time in return for the payment of specified rentals. The term 'lease' as used in this statement also applies to other arrangements in which one party retains ownership of an asset but conveys the right to the use of the asset to another party for an agreed period of time in return for specified payments. **14**

A *finance lease* is a lease that transfers substantially all the risks and rewards of ownership of an asset to the lessee. It should be presumed that such a transfer of risks and rewards occurs if at the inception of a lease the present value of the minimum lease payments including any initial payment, amounts to substantially all (normally 90 per cent or more) of the fair value of the leased asset. The present value should be calculated by using the interest rate implicit in the lease (as defined in paragraph 24). If the fair value of the asset is not determinable, an estimate thereof should be used. **15**

16 Notwithstanding the fact that a lease meets the conditions in paragraph 15, the presumption that it should be classified as a finance lease may in exceptional circumstances be rebutted if it can be clearly demonstrated that the lease in question does not transfer substantially all the risks and rewards of ownership (other than legal title) to the lessee. Correspondingly, the presumption that a lease which fails to meet the conditions in paragraph 15 is not a finance lease may in exceptional circumstances be rebutted.

17 An *operating lease* is a lease other than a finance lease.

18 A *hire purchase contract* is a contract for the hire of an asset which contains a provision giving the hirer an option to acquire legal title to the asset upon the fulfilment of certain conditions stated in the contract.

19 The *lease term* is the period for which the lessee has contracted to lease the asset and any further terms for which the lessee has the option to continue to lease the asset, with or without further payment, which option it is reasonably certain at the inception of the lease that the lessee will exercise.

20 The *minimum lease payments* are the minimum payments over the remaining part of the lease term (excluding charges for services and taxes to be paid by the lessor) and:

(a) in the case of the lessee, any residual amounts guaranteed by him or by a party related to him; or
(b) in the case of the lessor, any residual amounts guaranteed by the lessee or by an independent third party.

21 The *gross investment* in a lease at a point in time is the total of the minimum lease payments and any unguaranteed residual value accruing to the lessor.

22 The *net investment* in a lease at a point in time comprises:

(a) the gross investment in a lease (as defined in paragraph 21): *less*
(b) gross earnings allocated to future periods.

23 The *net cash investment* in a lease at a point in time is the amount of funds invested in a lease by a lessor, and comprises the cost of the asset plus or minus the following related payments or receipts:

(a) government or other grants receivable towards the purchase or use of the asset;
(b) rentals received;
(c) taxation payments and receipts, including the effect of capital allowances;
(d) residual values, if any, at the end of the lease term;
(e) interest payments (where applicable);
(f) interest received on cash surplus;
(g) profit taken out of the lease.

24 The *interest rate implicit in a lease* is the discount rate that at the inception of a lease, when applied to the amounts which the lessor expects to receive and retain produces an amount (the present value) equal to the fair value of the leased asset. The amounts which the lessor expects to receive and retain comprise (a) the minimum lease payments to the lessor (as defined in paragraph 20), plus (b) any unguaranteed residual value, less (c) any part of (a) and (b) for which the lessor will be accountable to the lessee. If the interest rate implicit in the lease is not determinable, it should be estimated by reference to the rate which a lessee would be expected to pay on a similar lease.

Fair value is the price at which an asset could be exchanged in an arm's length transaction less, where applicable, any grants receivable towards the purchase or use of the asset. 25

Unguaranteed residual value is that portion of the residual value of the leased asset (estimated at the inception of the lease), the realisation of which by the lessor is not assured or is guaranteed solely by a party related to the lessor. 26

Finance charge is the amount borne by the lessee over the lease term, representing the difference between the total of the minimum lease payments (including any residual amounts guaranteed by him) and the amount at which he records the leased asset at the inception of the lease. 27

Gross earnings comprise the lessor's gross finance income over the lease term, representing the difference between his gross investment in the lease (as defined in paragraph 21) and the cost of the leased asset less any grants receivable towards the purchase or use of the asset. 28

The *inception of a lease* is the earlier of the time the asset is brought into use and the date from which rentals first accrue. 29

Initial direct costs are those costs incurred by the lessor that are directly associated with negotiating and consummating leasing transactions, such as commissions, legal fees, costs of credit investigations and costs of preparing and processing documents for new leases acquired. 30

Part 3 – Standard accounting practice

HIRE PURCHASE AND LEASING

Those hire purchase contracts which are of a financing nature should be accounted for on a basis similar to that set out below for finance leases. Conversely, other hire purchase contracts should be accounted for on a basis similar to that set out below for operating leases. 31

ACCOUNTING BY LESSEES

A finance lease should be recorded in the balance sheet of a lessee as an asset and as an obligation to pay future rentals. At the inception of the lease the sum to be recorded both as an asset and as a liability should be the present value of the minimum lease payments, derived by discounting them at the interest rate implicit in the lease. 32

In practice in the case of a finance lease the fair value of the asset will often be a sufficiently close approximation to the present value of the minimum lease payments and may in these circumstances be substituted for it. 33

The combined benefit to a lessor of regional development and other grants together with capital allowances, which reduce tax liabilities, may enable the minimum lease payments under a finance lease to be reduced to a total which is less than the fair value of the asset. In these circumstances, the amount to be capitalised and depreciated should be restricted to the minimum lease payments. A negative finance charge should not be shown. 34

35 Rentals payable should be apportioned between the finance charge and a reduction of the outstanding obligation for future amounts payable. The total finance charge under a finance lease should be allocated to accounting periods during the lease term so as to produce a constant periodic rate of charge on the remaining balance of the obligation for each accounting period, or a reasonable approximation thereto.

36 An asset leased under a finance lease should be depreciated over the shorter of the lease term (as defined in paragraph 19) and its useful life. However, in the case of a hire purchase contract which has the characteristics of a finance lease, the asset should be depreciated over its useful life.

37 The rental under an operating lease should be charged on a straight-line basis over the lease term, even if the payments are not made on such a basis, unless another systematic and rational basis is more appropriate.*

ACCOUNTING BY LESSORS

38 The amount due from the lessee under a finance lease should be recorded in the balance sheet of a lessor as a debtor at the amount of the net investment in the lease after making provisions for items such as bad and doubtful rentals receivable.

39 The total gross earnings under a finance lease should normally be allocated to accounting periods to give a constant periodic rate of return to the lessor's **net cash investment** in the lease in each period. In the case of a hire purchase contract which has characteristics similar to a finance lease, allocation of gross earnings so as to give a constant periodic rate of return on the finance company's **net investment** will in most cases be a suitable approximation to allocation based on the net cash investment. In arriving at the constant periodic rate of return, a reasonable approximation may be made.

40 As an alternative to paragraph 39, an allocation may first be made out of gross earnings of an amount equal to the lessor's estimated cost of finance included in the net cash investment calculation, with the balance being recognised on a systematic basis.

41 Tax free grants that are available to the lessor against the purchase price of assets acquired for leasing should be spread over the period of the lease and dealt with by treating the grant as non-taxable income.

42 An asset held for use in operating leases by a lessor should be recorded as a fixed asset and depreciated over its useful life.

43 Rental income from an operating lease, excluding charges for services such as insurance and maintenance, should be recognised on a straight-line basis over the period of the lease, even if the payments are not made on such a basis, unless another systematic and rational basis is more representative of the time pattern in which the benefit from the leased asset is receivable.†

44 Initial direct costs incurred by a lessor in arranging a lease may be apportioned over the period of the lease on a systematic and rational basis.

****Editor's note:*** *See also UITF Abstract 28 'Operating lease incentives'.*

†***Editor's note:*** *See also UITF Abstract 28 'Operating lease incentives'.*

MANUFACTURER/DEALER LESSOR

A manufacturer or dealer lessor should not recognise a selling profit under an operating lease. The selling profit under a finance lease should be restricted to the excess of the fair value of the asset over the manufacturer's or dealer's cost less any grants receivable by the manufacturer or dealer towards the purchase, construction or use of the asset. **45**

SALE AND LEASEBACK TRANSACTIONS Accounting by the seller/lessee

In a sale and leaseback transaction which results in a finance lease any apparent profit or loss (that is, the difference between the sale price and the previous carrying value) should be deferred and amortised in the financial statements of the seller/lessee over the shorter of the lease term and the useful life of the asset. **46**

If the leaseback is an operating lease: **47**

(a) any profit or loss should be recognised immediately, provided it is clear that the transaction is established at fair value;
(b) if the sale price is below fair value, any profit or loss should be recognised immediately except that if the apparent loss is compensated by future rentals at below market price it should to that extent be deferred and amortised over the remainder of the lease term (or, if shorter, the period during which the reduced rentals are chargeable);
(c) if the sale price is above fair value, the excess over fair value should be deferred and amortised over the shorter of the remainder of the lease term and the period to the next rent review (if any).

Accounting by the buyer/lessor

A buyer/lessor should account for a sale and leaseback in the same way as he accounts for other leases, that is, using methods set out in paragraphs 38 to 45 above. **48**

DISCLOSURE BY LESSEES

The gross amounts of assets which are held under finance leases* together with the related accumulated depreciation should be disclosed by each major class of asset. The total depreciation allocated for the period in respect of assets held under finance leases should be disclosed by each major class of asset. **49**

The information required by paragraph 49 may, as an alternative to being shown separately from that in respect of owned fixed assets, be integrated with it such that the totals of gross amount, accumulated depreciation, net amount and depreciation allocated for the period for each major class of asset are included with similar amounts in respect of owned fixed assets. Where this alternative treatment is adopted, the net amount of assets held under finance leases* included in the overall total should be disclosed. The amount of depreciation allocated for the period in respect of assets held under finance leases* included in the overall total should also be disclosed. **50**

**Including the equivalent information in respect of hire purchase contracts which have characteristics similar to that type of lease (see paragraph 31).*

51 The amounts of obligations related to finance leases* (net of finance charges allocated to future periods) should be disclosed separately from other obligations and liabilities, either on the face of the balance sheet or in the notes to the accounts.

52 These net obligations under finance leases* should be analysed between amounts payable in the next year, amounts payable in the second to fifth years inclusive from the balance sheet date, and the aggregate amounts payable thereafter. This analysis may be presented either (a) separately for obligations under finance leases* or (b) where the total of these items is combined on the balance sheet with other obligations and liabilities, by giving the equivalent analysis of the total in which it is included. If the analysis is presented according to (a) above, a lessee may, as an alternative to analysing the net obligations, analyse the gross obligations, with future finance charges being separately deducted from the total.

53 The aggregate finance charges allocated for the period in respect of finance leases* should be disclosed.

54 Disclosure should be made of the amount of any commitments existing at the balance sheet date in respect of finance leases* which have been entered into but whose inception occurs after the year end.

55 The total of operating lease rentals* charged as an expense in the profit and loss account should be disclosed, analysed between amounts payable in respect of hire of plant and machinery and in respect of other operating leases.*

56 In respect of operating leases,* the lessee should disclose the payments which he is committed to make during the next year, analysed between those in which the commitment expires within that year, in the second to fifth years inclusive and over five years from the balance sheet date, showing separately the commitments in respect of leases of land and buildings and other operating leases.*

57 Disclosure should be made of the policies adopted for accounting for operating leases* and finance leases.*

DISCLOSURE BY LESSORS

58 The net investment in (i) finance leases and (ii) hire purchase contracts at each balance sheet date should be disclosed.

59 The gross amounts of assets held for use in operating leases,* and the related accumulated depreciation charges, should be disclosed.

60 Disclosure should be made of:

(a) the policy adopted for accounting for operating leases* and finance leases* and, in detail, the policy for accounting for finance lease income;*

(b) the aggregate rentals receivable in respect of an accounting period in relation to (i) finance leases* and (ii) operating leases;* and

(c) the cost of assets acquired, whether by purchase or finance lease,* for the purpose of letting under finance leases.*

**Including the equivalent information in respect of hire purchase contracts which have characteristics similar to that type of lease (see paragraph 31).*

APPLICATION TO SMALLER ENTITIES

Reporting entities applying the Financial Reporting Standard for Smaller Entities currently applicable are exempt from this accounting standard. **60A**

DATE FROM WHICH EFFECTIVE FOR LESSORS AND FINANCE COMPANIES

The accounting practices set out in this statement should be adopted as soon as possible and regarded as standard for financial statements relating to accounting periods beginning on or after 1 July 1984 in respect of leases and hire purchase contracts (a) entered into on or after 1 July 1984 or (b) which have five years or more to run on 1 July 1984. If the provisions of this statement are not applied retroactively to all leases and hire purchase contracts existing at 1 July 1984, lessors and finance companies should disclose the amounts of gross earnings from finance leases and hire purchase contracts for the current year and the comparative period which have arisen under each of the principal bases used.* **61**

DATE FROM WHICH EFFECTIVE FOR LESSEES AND HIRERS

The accounting practices set out in this statement should be adopted by lessees and hirers as soon as possible and regarded as standard in respect of financial statements relating to accounting periods beginning on or after 1 July 1987. However, the disclosure requirements in paragraphs 52 and 54 to 57 should be regarded as standard in respect of financial statements relating to accounting periods beginning on or after 1 July 1984. **62**

Part 4 – Legal requirements in Great Britain

Paragraph 50 (5) of Schedule 8† provides that 'Particulars shall also be given of any other financial commitments which: **63**

(a) have not been provided for; and
(b) are relevant to assessing the company's state of affairs.'

Insofar as finance leases are capitalised by lessees, the obligations under finance leases are provided for in the accounts. This will not be the case to the extent that lessees take advantage of the delayed implementation of capitalisation as set out in paragraph 62.

Paragraph 53(6)‡ of Schedule 8† requires disclosure of the 'amount charged to revenue in respect of sums payable in respect of the hire of plant and machinery' (Standard, paragraphs 49, 50, 53 and 55 and guidance notes). **64**

* ***Editor's note:*** *The amendment in February 1997 (the removal of the option in paragraph 41 to gross up tax free grants) became standard in respect of financial statements relating to accounting periods ending on or after 22 June 1997. Earlier adoption was encouraged but not required.*

† ***Editor's note:*** *The reference to paragraph 50 (5) becomes a reference to paragraph 63 (5) of Schedule 1 to the Large and Medium-sized Companies and Groups (Accounts and Reports) Regulations 2008 (SI 2008/410).*

‡ ***Editor's note:*** *Paragraph 53(6) was repealed by S.I. 1996 No.189.*

65 The balance sheet formats in Schedule 8* require that creditors falling due within one year should be shown separately from creditors falling due after more than one year (Standard, paragraph 52 and guidance notes).

66 The balance sheet formats in Schedule 8* provide that the 'amount falling due after more than one year shall be shown separately for each item included under debtors'. This is relevant to the disclosure of amounts receivable by a lessor (Standard, paragraph 58 and guidance notes).

Part 5 – Legal requirements in Ireland

NORTHERN IRELAND

67 The Schedule references in Part 4 (paragraphs 63 to 66) apply equally to Schedule 6 of the Companies Act (Northern Ireland) 1960, as inserted by Article 3 of the Companies (Northern Ireland) Order 1982.

REPUBLIC OF IRELAND

68 General provisions as to accounts are set out in the Sixth Schedule to the Companies Act 1963. There are no legal requirements in the Republic of Ireland similar to those outlined in Part 4.

Part 6 – Compliance with International Accounting Standard No. 17 'Accounting for leases'

69 The requirements of International Accounting Standard No. 17 'Accounting for leases'† accord very closely with the content of the United Kingdom and Irish Accounting Standard No. 21 'Accounting for leases and hire purchase contracts' and accordingly compliance with SSAP 21 will ensure compliance with IAS 17 in all material respects.

****Editor's note:*** *Schedule 4 to the Companies Act 1985 is replaced, with effect for accounting periods beginning on or after 6 April 2008 by Schedule 1 to the Large and Medium-sized Companies and Groups (Accounts and Reports) Regulations 2008 (SI 2008/410), while Schedule 8 to the Companies Act 1985 is replaced by Schedule 1 to the Small Companies and Groups (Accounts and Directors' Report) Regulations 2008 (SI 2008/409).*

†***Editor's note:*** *A revised version of IAS 17 was issued in December 1997. This eliminated the previous option of using the net cash investment method required by SSAP 21 for allocating finance lease payments received by the lessor. In addition, there are some differences between the tests for the classification of a lease between the two standards, and IAS 17 now requires rather more disclosure than is required by SSAP 21. SIC 27 has also been issued 'Evaluating the substance of transactions in the legal form of a lease,' as well as SIC 15 'Operating leases – incentives'. A further revised version of IAS 17 was issued in December 2003. This draws a distinction between inception and commencement of a lease, and makes some changes to the treatment of initial costs. However, the main aim of the change was to deal with operating leases over properties held as investment properties.*

Guidance Notes on SSAP 21: Accounting for leases and hire purchase contracts

(Issued August 1984)

These notes are for guidance only and do not form part of the statement of standard accounting practice.

Contents

	Paragraphs
Introduction	1–13
Part I – Lessee accounting	14–68
A – General principles	15–19
B – The arithmetic of capitalising finance leases	20– 47
C – Balance sheet presentation, note disclosure and legal requirements for lessees	48–63
D – Initial recording of the leased asset	64–68
Part II – Lessor accounting	69–131
A – General principles	70–73
B – Finance leases – background considerations	74– 87
C – The arithmetic of lessor accounting for finance leases	88–122
D – Balance sheet presentation, note disclosure and legal requirements for lessors	123–131
Part III – Problem areas	132–185
A – Lease definition and classification	133–138
B – Land and buildings	139–144
C – Leasing by manufacturers or dealers	145–149
D – Sale and leaseback transactions	150–160
E – Sub-leases and back-to-back leases	161–169
F – Deferred taxation	170–175
G – Regional development grants	176–181
H – Bad debts	182–185
Part IV – Leased assets and current cost accounting	186–194

INTRODUCTION

General

1 The statement of Standard Accounting Practice on Accounting for Leases and Hire Purchase Contracts sets out objectives and disclosure requirements. The primary purpose of the guidance notes is to recommend practical methods which will assist companies to comply with the standard. The guidance notes are not mandatory.

2 The aim in writing the guidance notes has been to cover the most common situations which will be met in practice. It is not possible to lay down methods which will cover all situations.

3 The guidance notes do not recognise the effect of the transitional provisions set out in paragraphs 61 and 62 of the standard. In the periods affected by these provisions different methods and disclosures may be required.

4 All references in the guidance notes to legal requirements are to the UK Companies Acts; the examples assume that companies are subject to Schedule 8, Companies Act 1948.*

5 The definitions of terms in the standard apply also to the guidance notes.

6 The effects of value added tax have been ignored in the guidance notes.

Materiality

7 The standard, in common with all standards, need not be applied to immaterial items. In this context, the relevant criterion is the size of the lease (or leases in aggregate, if more than one) in the context of the size of the lessee or lessor.

8 In deciding whether or not a lease is material, regard should be had to the effect which treating the lease according to the main requirements of the standard (e.g., capitalising it) would have on the financial statements as a whole. Thus, it may be necessary to consider the effect of (in this example) capitalisation on (a) total fixed assets, (b) total borrowings and obligations, (c) the gearing ratio and (d) the profit or loss for the year (as a result of the difference between charging the lease payment and charging the total of depreciation plus finance charge). If capitalisation of the lease would not have a material effect on any of these items, the lease need not be capitalised.

The simplified approach to accounting for small leases

9 Where a lease is material, the main provisions of the standard will need to be applied. Thus, a finance lease will need to be capitalised by a lessee. Similarly, a finance lease should be shown as a receivable by a lessor.

10 However, Part I of these guidance notes describes the use of simplified methods for leases and suggests when they may be used. In particular, paragraphs 32 to 36 describe the simplified approach to lessee accounting whereby a lessee may use the straight-line method to write off finance charges under a finance lease. Part II

****Editor's note:*** *Now Schedule 1 to the Large and Medium-sized Companies and Groups (Accounts and Reports) Regulations 2008 (SI 2008/410).*

discusses a number of methods of lessors' income recognition, including simplified methods (see, for example paragraphs 81, 95, 119 and 122).

Hire purchase and leasing

It is not intended that this standard should change the existing best practice for accounting for hire purchase contracts by either finance companies or hirers. **11**

Most hire purchase contracts are of a financing nature. Generally, the option to purchase the asset is exercisable at below market value – often at a nominal amount – such that the hirer can be expected from the outset to take up the option. The standard therefore provides that such hire purchase contracts should be accounted for on a basis similar to that set out for finance leases. **12**

Less commonly, there are found hire purchase contracts which are not of a financing nature. For example, the option to purchase may be exercisable at a relatively high price such that the hirer may not take it up. The standard therefore provides that such hire purchase contracts should be accounted for on a similar basis to that set out for operating leases. **13**

Part I – Lessee accounting

INTRODUCTION

Part I explains the accounting requirements for lessees in the following sections: **14**

	Paragraphs
A – General principles	15–19
B – The arithmetic of capitalising finance leases	20–47
C – Balance sheet presentation, note disclosure and legal requirements for lessees	48–63
D – Initial recording of the leased asset	64–68

A – GENERAL PRINCIPLES

A lessee should classify his leases in (a) operating leases and (b) finance leases, according to the definitions in paragraphs 15 to 17 of the standard. Additional guidance on lease classification may be found in paragraphs 133 to 138. **15**

Operating leases

The right to use an asset or the obligation to pay rentals under an operating lease should not be recorded in the balance sheet but a lessee should disclose certain information by way of note to the financial statements (see paragraphs 57 to 63). The rentals under an operating lease should be charged on a straight-line basis over the lease term, even if the payments are not made on such a basis, unless another systematic and rational basis is more appropriate. Thus, in situations such as rental holidays in which a lease has been arranged so that, for example, no payment is made in the first year (although the asset is in use during that year), the total rentals should be charged over the period in which the asset is in use.* **16**

* ***Editor's note:*** *The last sentence was superseded by UITF Abstract 12 'Lessee accounting for reverse premiums and similar incentives' which has itself now been superseded by UITF Abstract 28 'Operating lease incentives'.*

Finance leases

17 Under a finance lease the lessee acquires substantially all the benefits of the use of an asset for the greater part of its useful economic life and takes on substantially all of the risks associated with ownership. In economic substance it is similar to the purchase of an asset even though legal title to the asset remains with the lessor.

18 The risks of ownership of an asset include unsatisfactory performance, obsolescence and idle capacity. The benefits include the right to the unencumbered use of the asset over most of its useful economic life.

19 The two aspects of a finance lease should be recorded in the lessee's balance sheet. The right to use the asset should be capitalised and shown as a fixed asset. The obligation to pay rentals should be shown as a liability.

B – THE ARITHMETIC OF CAPITALISING FINANCE LEASES

20 The capitalisation of finance leases is now illustrated by means of numerical examples. Three methods of writing off finance charges are shown:

(a) the actuarial method;
(b) the 'Rule of 78' (or 'Sum of the Digits') method; and
(c) the straight-line method.

The standard (paragraph 35) provides that the 'total finance charge under a finance lease should be allocated to accounting periods during the lease term so as to produce a constant periodic rate of charge on the remaining balance of the obligation for each accounting period, or a reasonable approximation thereto'. Of the above three methods, the actuarial method gives the most accurate result.

Terms of the lease

21 The examples illustrated are based on the following lease:

> A lessee leases an asset on a non-cancellable lease contract with a primary term of five years from 1 January 1987. The rental is £650 per quarter payable in advance. The lessee has the right to continue to lease the asset after the end of the primary period for as long as he wishes at a peppercorn rent. In addition the lessee is required to pay all maintenance and insurance costs as they arise. The leased asset could have been purchased for cash at the start of the lease for £10,000.

22 A lessee should, strictly, record a finance lease at the present value of the minimum lease payments (Standard, paragraph 32). However, for most practical purposes, it will be acceptable to record the leased asset at its fair value (Standard, paragraph 33). (The present value of the minimum lease payments in a finance lease will normally be at least 90% of the fair value of the leased asset.) The two approaches would produce different results where the lessor expects to benefit from a residual value which is not guaranteed by the lessee. In this example it is assumed for simplicity that the asset has no residual value at the end of the lease term. At the start of the lease, therefore, the lessee should capitalise the asset in his balance sheet at a cost of £10,000 and also record the obligation under the finance lease of £10,000 as a liability. Guidance on a more rigorous determination of the amount to be capitalised in respect of a leased asset is given in paragraphs 64 to 68.

The minimum lease payments amount to 20 × £650 = £13,000. The total finance charges under the lease are therefore £3,000. 23

The total finance charges should be allocated to accounting periods during the lease so as to produce a constant periodic rate of charge on the remaining balance of the obligation for each accounting period. This calculation is shown in Table 1. 24

The actuarial method

TABLE 1 25

CALCULATION OF THE PERIODIC FINANCE CHARGE IN THE LEASE

Period	*Capital sum at start of period*	*Rental paid*	*Capital sum during period*	*Finance charge (2.95% per quarter)**	*Capital sum at end of period*
	£	£	£	£	£
1/87	10,000	650	9,350	276	9,626
2/87	9,626	650	8,976	265	9,241
3/87	9,241	650	8,591	254	8,845
4/87	8,845	650	8,195	242	8,437
				1,037	
1/88	8,437	650	7,787	230	8,017
2/88	8,017	650	7,367	217	7,584
3/88	7,584	650	6,934	205	7,139
4/88	7,139	650	6,489	191	6,680
				843	
1/89	6,680	650	6,030	178	6,208
2/89	6,208	650	5,558	164	5,722
3/89	5,722	650	5,072	150	5,222
4/89	5,222	650	4,572	135	4,707
				627	
1/90	4,707	650	4,057	120	4,177
2/90	4,177	650	3,527	104	3,631
3/90	3,631	650	2,981	88	3,069
4/90	3,069	650	2,419	71	2,490
				383	
1/91	2,490	650	1,840	54	1,894
2/91	1,894	650	1,244	37	1,281
3/91	1,281	650	631	19	650
4/91	650	650	–	–	–
				110	
		£13,000		£3,000	

**The quarterly finance charge of 2.95% may be calculated in a number of ways: (a) by trial and error, (b) by financial pocket calculator or computer program, (c) by a mathematical formula, or (d) by reference to present value tables.*

26 The annual rental may therefore be apportioned between a finance charge and a capital repayment based on the figures in Table 1:

TABLE 2

APPORTIONMENT OF ANNUAL RENTALS – ACTUARIAL METHOD

	Finance charge	*Capital Repayment*	*Total rental*
	£	£	£
1987	1,037	1,563	2,600
1988	843	1,757	2,600
1989	627	1,973	2,600
1990	383	2,217	2,600
1991	110	2,490	2,600
	£3,000	£10,000	£13,000

27 The allocation of the finance charge to accounting periods by the actuarial method in Table 1 is not easy to calculate manually and it may be appropriate to use the rule of 78 or the straight-line method as an approximation. These are discussed in turn.

Rule of 78

28 The rule of 78 may normally be regarded as an acceptable approximation to the actuarial method; it works well provided that the lease term is not very long (say, not more than seven years) and interest rates are not very high. The calculations using the rule of 78 are as follows:

TABLE 3

'RULE OF 78' CALCULATIONS

Period	*Number of rentals not yet due*		£	*Finance charge per annum* £
1/87	19		= 300	
2/87	18		= 284	
3/87	17		= 268	
4/87	16		= 253	
				1,105
1/88	15		= 237	
2/88	14		= 221	
3/88	13		= 205	
4/88	12		= 190	
				853
1/89	11		= 174	
2/89	10	÷ 190 × 3000	= 158	
3/89	9		= 142	
4/89	8		= 126	
				600
1/90	7		= 110	
2/90	6		= 95	
3/90	5		= 79	
4/90	4		= 63	
				347
1/91	3		= 47	
2/91	2		= 32	
3/91	1		= 16	
4/91	–		= –	
				95
	190*		£3,000	£3,000

**This total may be calculated using the formula*

$\frac{n(n+1)}{2}$ *where n is the number of periods in question.*

Hence in this case $n = 19$ *and* $\frac{19 \times 20}{2} = 190.$

The term 'Rule of 78' arose because, if finance charges are allocated over a one year period, months 1 to 12 when added together add up to 78. Here, the weights add up to 190. **29**

In this example rentals are payable in advance. Hence the final payment is made on the first day of period 4/91, and no interest should be allocated to that period. If the rentals had been payable in arrears, then one unit of interest would have been chargeable to that period, and 20 units to period 1/87, with corresponding changes to the other periods. **30**

Having calculated the finance charge as in paragraph 28 using the rule of 78, all the other calculations are continued in the same way as for the actuarial method. **31**

The straight-line method

32 As noted above, and as can be seen in Table 5 below, the use of the rule of 78 results in a close approximation to the actuarial method. However, it may be appropriate in certain cases to use the straight-line method. This is the simplest of the methods illustrated. It does not attempt to produce a constant periodic rate of change, but if used in connection with a relatively small lease it may produce figures which in any year are not significantly different from those which would be produced by one of the other methods. What is a small lease will depend on the size of the company.

33 The calculations using the straight-line method are as follows. The finance charges under the lease should be apportioned on a straight-line basis over the period of the lease in which rentals are being paid:

£3,000 ÷ 5 = £600 per annum

34 The annual rental may be apportioned between the finance charge and the capital repayment as follows:

TABLE 4

APPORTIONMENT OF ANNUAL RENTALS – STRAIGHT-LINE METHOD

	Finance charge	*Capital repayment*	*Total rental*
	£	£	£
1987	600	2,000	2,600
1988	600	2,000	2,600
1989	600	2,000	2,600
1990	600	2,000	2,600
1991	600	2,000	2,600
	£3,000	£10,000	£13,000

35 The finance charges as calculated under the actuarial method, the rule of 78 and the straight-line method are compared below:

TABLE 5

COMPARISON OF FINANCE CHARGES

	Actuarial		*Rule of 78*		*Straight-line*	
	£	%	£	%	£	%
1987	1,037	34	1,105	37	600	20
1988	843	28	853	28	600	20
1989	627	21	600	20	600	20
1990	383	13	347	12	600	20
1991	110	4	95	3	600	20
	£3,000	100	£3,000	100	£3,000	100

Whether the straight-line method (or the rule of 78) provides a reasonable approximation to an accurate method depends on the facts of each case. Where a lease is small in relation to the size of the lessee, the difference between the methods may not be material.

36 It is sometimes argued that, in order to establish whether the straight-line method provides a reasonable approximation, it is necessary to calculate the finance charge

allocation on two or more bases. This is not necessarily so. In some cases the *total* finance charges may not be material in which case the straight-line method may be used: there will be no need to compare the allocation under the straight-line method with that under any other method.

Variation clauses

Where a lease contains an interest variation clause which adjusts the rental by reference to movements in Finance House base rate, or some other indicator, no adjustment need normally be made to the calculations, such as those in Table 1, which are carried out at the start of the lease. Any increase or reduction in rentals should be accounted for as an increase or reduction in finance charges in the period in which it arises. **37**

Where a lease contains a tax variation clause which adjusts the rental in order to protect the parties from the effects of tax changes, any increase or reduction in rentals should be accounted for as an increase or reduction in finance charges. Where the reduction in rentals exceeds the future finance charges, the excess should be applied to reduce future depreciation charges. **38**

Depreciation

The leased asset should be depreciated on a basis compatible with that adopted for assets which are owned. SSAP 12 'Accounting for depreciation'* requires an asset to be depreciated by allocating the cost less estimated residual value of the asset as fairly as possible to the periods expected to benefit from its use. **39**

The period over which a leased asset should be depreciated is the shorter of (a) the lease term and (b) the asset's useful life. The lease term is the primary period of the lease (i.e., the non-cancellable part) together with any secondary periods during which the lessee has the contractual right to continue to use the asset and which right, at the start of the lease, it is reasonable to expect him to exercise. **40**

In this example the lessee estimates that the lease will be continued for a further two years after the end of the primary period so that he should depreciate the leased asset over seven years. This is the period over which he depreciates similar assets which he owns. **41**

In most cases the residual value of leased assets at the end of the lease is likely to be small so that even where the lessee has the right to share in the ultimate residual value it is usual to assume for the purposes of establishing an appropriate depreciation charge that it will be nil. This will be the case whether the residual value takes the form of sale proceeds or a rebate of rentals. **42**

In this example the lessee estimates that the asset will have a useful life of seven years and that the residual value will be nil. The annual depreciation charge on a straight-line basis is therefore: **43**

$$£10,000 \div 7 = £1,429$$

In the case of a hire purchase contract which has the characteristics of a finance lease, it is expected from the outset that the hirer will take up the option to purchase. **44**

Editor's note: *Superseded by FRS 15 'Tangible fixed assets' published February 1999.*

Hence, the asset should be depreciated over its useful life, regardless of the term of the hire contract.

Calculation of balance sheet values

45 The leased asset should be described in the balance sheet as 'Assets held under finance leases'. The liability should be described as 'Obligations under finance leases'. The net book value of the asset at the end of each year, if straight-line depreciation is used, will be:

TABLE 6

BALANCE SHEET VALUES – LEASED ASSETS

	Cost		*Accumulated depreciation*		*Net book value of assets held under finance lease*
	£		£		£
31.12.87	10,000	–	1,429	=	8,571
31.12.88	10,000	–	2,858	=	7,142
31.12.89	10,000	–	4,287	=	5,713
31.12.90	10,000	–	5,716	=	4,284
31.12.91	10,000	–	7,145	=	2,855
31.12.92	10,000	–	8,574	=	1,426
31.12.93	10,000	–	10,000	=	–

46 The obligations under finance leases (i.e., the capital element of future rentals payable) will be calculated as follows:

TABLE 7

BALANCE SHEET VALUES – LEASING OBLIGATIONS

	Obligations under finance leases outstanding at start of year		*Capital repayment*		*Obligations under finance leases outstanding at year end*
	£		£		£
31.12.87	10,000	–	1,563	=	8,437
31.12.88	8,437	–	1,757	=	6,680
31.12.89	6,680	–	1,973	=	4,707
31.12.90	4,707	–	2,217	=	2,490
31.12.91	2,490	–	2,490	=	–
31.12.92					
31.12.93					

(These figures assume that the actuarial method is being used. The capital repayments are taken from Table 2.)

Comparison of the balance sheet amounts of the capitalised leased asset

47 The figures in Tables 6 and 7 are compared below:

TABLE 8

LEASED ASSETS AND OBLIGATIONS

	NBV of assets held under finance leases		*Obligations under finance leases outstanding at year end*		*Difference*
	£		£		£
31.12.87	8,571	–	8,437	=	134
31.12.88	7,142	–	6,680	=	462
31.12.89	5,713	–	4,707	=	1,006
31.12.90	4,284	–	2,490	=	1,794
31.12.91	2,855	–	–	=	2,855
31.12.92	1,426	–	–	=	1,426
31.12.93	–	–	–	=	–

The differences shown in the third column do not appear separately on a balance sheet. They are timing differences which result from capitalising a lease, and are needed for the calculation of deferred tax (see paragraphs 171 to 173*). Charging the total of depreciation and interest to the profit and loss account is likely to result in recognition of the total costs of a finance lease in a different pattern from that in which the rentals are paid and the tax allowances are received. In this example, the costs are recognised later because the asset is depreciated over seven years whereas the instalments are paid over five years. Hence the timing differences cause a temporary, reversing, increase in equity, which is reflected in the above table by asset values being temporarily higher than the obligations.

C – BALANCE SHEET PRESENTATION, NOTE DISCLOSURE AND LEGAL REQUIREMENTS FOR LESSEES

A finance lease will be shown in a lessee's balance sheet both as an asset and as an obligation. At the start of the lease the amount of the asset and the obligation will be the same but they are unlikely to be so in subsequent years. The obligation under the lease may be paid off before the asset is fully depreciated. **48**

Schedule 8 to the Companies Act 1948† contains, inter alia, formats which must be followed by companies (except those subject to Schedule 8A‡) in the presentation of their accounts. Leased assets and leasing obligations are not specifically mentioned in the formats, but paragraphs 3(1) and (2) of the 8th Schedule provide that items may be shown in greater detail than required by the formats and that new items may be inserted for items not covered by the formats. **49**

Assets held under finance leases are not legally owned by the lessee. (The same applies to assets subject to hire purchase contracts, until the purchase option is exercised.) The lessee's right is to use the asset, not to own it. Similarly, a lessee's obligations under a finance lease are not, from a legal point of view, debt but rather obligations under a bailment to hire. Therefore, in order to reflect this legal **50**

***Editor's note:** *The ASB noted in FRS 19 'Deferred tax' that it would be consistent with that FRS if paragraphs 170 and 173–175 of these Guidance Notes, and the references to them, were deemed to be deleted.*

†**Editor's note:** *Now Schedule 1 to the Large and Medium-sized Companies and Groups (Accounts and Reports) Regulations 2008 (SI 2008/410). The reference to paragraphs 3 (1) and (2) are to paragraphs with the same numbers in that Schedule.*

‡**Editor's note:** *Now Schedules 2 and 3 to the Large and Medium-sized Companies and Groups (Accounts and Reports) Regulations 2008 (SI 2008/410).*

difference, assets held under finance leases and the related obligations should be described in such a way as to be distinguishable from owned assets and debt respectively.

51 The standard permits a company to aggregate the amounts which are required to be presented on a balance sheet or disclosed in notes in respect of (i) finance leases and (ii) hire purchase contracts which have characteristics similar to finance leases. It is expected that most companies will choose to combine the amounts.

52 Assets held under finance leases and hire purchase contracts should generally be integrated with owned fixed assets on a balance sheet. The analysis of fixed assets may be in one of two forms: either

(a) the notes to the accounts should contain details of the assets held under finance leases and hire purchase contracts, by class of asset; or
(b) the fixed assets note should analyse, by class of asset, the combined total of owned assets and assets held under finance leases and hire purchase contracts. In order to distinguish owned assets from non-owned assets, a note similar to the following should be shown:

'The net book value of fixed assets of £x includes an amount of £8,571 in respect of assets held under finance leases and hire purchase contracts'.

53 Obligations under finance leases and hire purchase contracts should be analysed between those amounts payable within one year and those amounts payable in more than one year. These two amounts should be described, either on the face of the balance sheet or in the notes to the accounts, as 'Obligations under finance leases and hire purchase contracts' under the headings of 'Creditors: amounts falling due within one year' and 'Creditors: amounts falling due after more than one year' respectively.

54 Alternatively, obligations under finance leases and hire purchase contracts may be combined with other items (for example, bank loans and overdrafts) under each of the 'Creditors' headings referred to in the preceding paragraph.

55 The standard requires the amount of obligations under finance leases and hire purchase contracts falling due after more than one year, or the total in which it is included, to be further analysed as to amounts due in the second to fifth years inclusive from the balance sheet date and the aggregate amounts payable thereafter.

56 Where the treatment in paragraph 54 is adopted, a note such as the following will comply with the disclosure requirements and with company law:

Bank loans, overdrafts, obligations under finance leases and hire purchase contracts

These comprise:

Bank loans and overdrafts		20,000
Obligations under finance leases and hire purchase contracts (see paragraph 47)		8,437
		£28,437

The maturity of the above amounts is as follows:

Under one year		10,000
Over one year		
In the second to fifth years inclusive	12,500	
Over five years	5,937	
		18,437
		£28,437

The £10,000 should be included under the heading 'Creditors: amounts falling due within one year'; the £18,437 should be included under the heading 'Creditors: amounts falling due after more than one year'. (The Stock Exchange additionally requires listed companies to disclose the amount payable in the second year after the balance sheet date.)*

Note disclosure – profit and loss account

Paragraph 53(6) of Schedule 8† to the Companies Act 1948 requires disclosure of the amount, if material, charged to revenue in respect of sums payable in respect of the hire of plant and machinery. To comply with this requirement it is necessary to disclose the amounts charged to revenue for operating leases and finance leases and hire purchase contracts. In the latter cases this would consist of depreciation and finance charges. 57

The following is an example of an appropriate note which combines these legal requirements with those of the standard (assuming that the company has a charge for each item):

Profit is stated after charging:	£
Depreciation of owned assets	a
Depreciation of assets held under finance leases and hire purchase contracts	b
Interest payable – bank loans and overdrafts and other loans repayable within five years	c
Finance charges payable – finance leases and hire purchase contracts	d
Hire of plant and machinery – operating leases	e
Hire of other assets – operating leases	f

(Note: amounts charged to revenue in respect of finance leases and hire purchase contracts are shown separately under the headings of depreciation (£b) and finance charges (£d) (total, £g.))

Notes:

1. This amount is required to be disclosed by paragraphs 49 and 50 of the standard as well as in compliance with paragraph 53(6) of Schedule 8.†
2. This amount is required to be disclosed by paragraph 53 of the standard as well as in compliance with paragraph 53(6) of Schedule 8.†
3. This amount is required to be disclosed by paragraph 55 of the standard as well as in compliance with paragraph 53(6) of Schedule 8.†
4. This is required to be disclosed by paragraph 55 of the standard. When added to the amount in the above line for hire of plant and machinery, it gives the total charge in respect of operating leases.

Disclosure of commitments under operating leases

In the case of operating leases, the standard requires a lessee to disclose, in addition to the amount charged in the year, the yearly amount of the payments to which he is committed at the year end (the annual commitment). This will not necessarily be the same as the amount paid in the year then ending as it will include a full year's rental for leases which have been taken out during the year and it will exclude rentals in respect of leases which terminated during the year. The annual payments to which he 58

Editor's note: *The reference to Stock Exchange requirements is no longer relevant.*

†***Editor's note:*** *Became para 53(6) of Schedule 4 to the Companies Act 1985, but repealed by S.I. 1996 No. 89.*

is committed should be analysed between those in which the commitment expires within that year, in the second to fifth years inclusive and over five years from the balance sheet date. Leases of land and buildings are to be shown separately from other operating leases.

59 In the case of these disclosure requirements, materiality should be borne in mind. Thus if either the amounts for leases of land and buildings or for other leases are not material, the two categories may be aggregated. If the total is immaterial, no disclosure needs to be made.

60 A suggested note is set out below:

At 31 December 1987 the company had annual commitments under non-cancellable operating leases as set out below.

£000's	1987 *Land and Buildings*	*Other*	1986 *Land and Buildings*	*Other*
Operating leases which expire:				
within one year	30	100	25	90
in the second to fifth years inclusive	80	50	75	40
over five years	120	20	110	10
	230	170	210	140

The majority of leases of land and buildings are subject to rent reviews.

Other disclosures

61 SSAP 2 'Disclosure of accounting policies'* already requires disclosure of the accounting policies followed for dealing with items which are judged material or critical in determining profit or loss for the year and in stating the financial position. The present standard does not change the need to give such information and therefore disclosure should be made of the policies adopted for capitalisation and depreciation of leased assets and for the recognition of finance charges, where material.

62 It may also be necessary, in order to show a true and fair view, to disclose information relevant to lease contracts or hire purchase contracts which is of particular significance to users of financial statements. This may include such items as:

(a) the nature of any contingent rentals such as those based on usage or sales;
(b) the nature of any contingent liability, for example costs which may arise at the end of the lease term.

Further, as with any other form of financing, it may be appropriate to disclose financial restrictions imposed by the lease or hire purchase agreement such as limitations on additional borrowing or further leasing.

63 The standard (paragraph 54) requires disclosure of the amount of any material commitments in respect of finance leases which have been entered into but whose inception occurs after the year end. This is analogous to the legal requirement in

*****Editor's note:*** *SSAP 2 has now been superseded by FRS 18 'Accounting policies'.*

respect of capital commitments in paragraph 50(3)(a) of Schedule 8* to the Companies Act 1948.

D – INITIAL RECORDING OF THE LEASED ASSET

As noted in paragraph 22 above, strictly, a lessee should record a finance lease at the present value of the minimum lease payments. (The minimum lease payments comprise all payments guaranteed by the lessee including rentals and any residual value guaranteed by him.) However, the present value of the minimum lease payments in a finance lease will normally be at least 90% of the fair value of the leased asset. For most practical purposes therefore it will be acceptable to record the leased asset at its fair value. **64**

There are two occasions on which the leased asset would not be recorded at fair value. The first is where both the fair value and the present value of the minimum lease payments are known and the fair value is found to be not a sufficiently close approximation to the present value. Such cases are likely to be rare, as, by definition, the two figures are likely to be within 10% of each other. **65**

The second possibility would be where the fair value of the asset is not known. Whilst this would be unusual in the UK, it may occur, for example where the asset can be obtained from only one manufacturer and he will make it available only by way of a finance lease. In such a case, a lessee should follow the rule in paragraph 32 of the standard and record the finance lease at the present value of the minimum lease payments. The present value should be determined by reference to the interest rate implicit in a lease. This is defined in paragraph 24 of the standard; it should be noted in particular that if the interest rate implicit in a lease is not determinable, it should be estimated by reference to the rate which a lessee would be expected to pay on a lease of similar term and in respect of the same class of asset. **66**

Set out below is an example of the procedure to be followed in the circumstances described in paragraph 66. Assume that a lessee has entered into a finance lease for an asset whose fair value he does not know. The minimum lease payments are five annual instalments of £2,500 each, payable in advance. **67**

The lessee establishes that a typical implicit rate of interest for leases of this type is 11%. He therefore discounts the payments as follows:

TABLE 9
PRESENT VALUE CALCULATION

Year	*Discount factor*	*Payment*	*Present value*
0	1.000	2,500	2,500
1	0.901	2,500	2,252
2	0.812	2,500	2,030
3	0.731	2,500	1,828
4	0.659	2,500	1,647
	4.103		10,257

The asset should be recorded at £10,257, the balance of £2,243 (12,500 – 10,257) representing finance charges.

**Editor's note:* *Now paragraph 63 (3) of Schedule 1 to the Large and Medium-sized Companies and Groups (Accounts and Reports) Regulations 2008 (SI 2008/410).*

68 In some cases, there may be difficulties in deciding whether or not a lease is a finance lease, for example where the fair value of the asset is not known. Additional guidance on this and similar problems is given in paragraphs 133 to 138 and 180 to 181.

Part II – Lessor accounting

INTRODUCTION

69 Part II explains the accounting requirements for lessors in the following sections:

	Paragraphs
A – General principles	70–73
B – Finance leases – background considerations	74–87
C – The arithmetic of lessor accounting for finance leases	88–122
D – Balance sheet presentation, note disclosure and legal requirements for lessors	123–131

A – GENERAL PRINCIPLES

70 A lessor should classify his leases into (a) finance leases, and (b) operating leases.

71 Under a finance lease a lessor retains legal title to an asset but passes substantially all the risks and rewards of ownership to the lessee in return for a stream of rentals. In substance, under a finance lease, the lessor provides finance and expects a return thereon.

72 In the case of an operating lease the lessor retains both the legal title and the risks and rewards of ownership of the asset. It may not be possible to predict with certainty the future rentals and expenses, as they may be received and incurred under successive lease agreements with one or more parties; furthermore, the equipment may become obsolete, and changes in the level of economic activity may affect demand. In substance, under an operating lease the lessor is trading with the assets he leases.

73 The lessor should account for leases in accordance with their economic substance. Hence, a finance lease should be accounted for on a basis similar to that for a loan, rather than as a fixed asset subject to depreciation. Conversely, an operating lease should be accounted for by capitalising and depreciating the leased asset.

B – FINANCE LEASES – BACKGROUND CONSIDERATIONS

74 The standard deals, inter alia, with calculation of the carrying value of the finance lease receivables and with lessors' profit recognition. It requires the receivables to be carried on a balance sheet at an amount based on the net investment in the lease. Conversely, it requires that profit recognition should normally be based on the lessor's net *cash* investment.

75 The net investment in a lease is initially the cost of the asset to the lessor, less any government or other grants receivable (i.e., the fair value).

76 The rentals paid by the lessee should be apportioned by the lessor between (a) gross earnings (i.e., the lessor's interest earned) and (b) a repayment of capital.

Over the period of the lease the net investment in the lease (i.e., the carrying value of the receivables) will therefore be the fair value of the asset less those portions of the rentals which are apportioned as a repayment of capital. 77

For the purposes of profit recognition, however, the total gross earnings should normally be allocated to accounting periods to give a constant periodic rate of return on the lessor's net *cash* investment (NCI) in the lease in each period. (Paragraph 40 of the standard allows an alternative method, which is also partly based on NCI. This is described in paragraph 94 below.) The NCI is based on the funds which the lessor has invested in the lease. The amount of funds invested in a lease by a lessor is different from the net investment in the lease because there are a number of other cash flows which affect the lessor, in addition to those which affect net investment. In particular, tax cash flows are an important component of the NCI. The components of the NCI are listed in paragraph 23 of the standard. 78

Sometimes a lessor receives an amount which takes the form of a deposit or of non-recourse indebtedness. This amount may be received from the lessee and may in economic substance have the nature of an advance rental. It may be appropriate for the lessor to include such receipts and any repayments thereof in computing the net cash investment for the purpose of allocating gross earnings to accounting periods. 79

In the case of hire purchase, profit recognition should also, in principle, be based on net cash investment. However, since the capital allowances under a hire purchase contract accrue to the lessee, the finance company's net cash investment is often not significantly different from its net investment; hence allocation of gross earnings (i.e., finance charges) based on net investment will in most cases be a suitable approximation to allocation based on net cash investment. 80

The standard permits a reasonable approximation to be made in arriving at the constant periodic rate of return. Hence there are a number of different methods of profit recognition which may comply with the standard. Some of these methods are illustrated in the next section. However, other methods may be appropriate for use by lessors of any size where they provide a reasonable approximation to the methods described below. It may be appropriate for a lessor to use one of the methods specifically described for its large leases and a simplified method for other leases. What is a large lease will depend on the size of the company. 81

Initial direct costs are costs such as commissions and legal fees which are often incurred by lessors in negotiating and arranging a lease. The definition (standard, paragraph 30) is not intended to exclude salesperson's costs. Initial direct costs may be apportioned over the lease term on a systematic basis (or may be written off immediately). The same effect as apportioning the costs over the lease term may be achieved by either (a) treating the costs as a deduction from the total gross earnings before the latter are allocated to accounting periods or (b) recognising sufficient gross earnings in the first year to cover the costs. In the case of an operating lease initial direct costs may also either be written off immediately or be deferred and amortised over the lease term. 82

In most finance leases the estimated residual values of leased assets will be small. They are usually left out of calculations to apportion income from the lease and are accounted for as they arise. Where estimated residual values are used in assessing the lessor's investment in a lease, the estimate should be reviewed regularly and any permanent reduction in the estimated residual value (net of any profits to be recognised later in the lease) should be recognised immediately by an appropriate charge in the profit and loss account. 83

84 Where individual finance leases are for relatively small amounts, the administration costs in collecting the rentals may be significant. It may therefore be necessary to take them into account when determining an appropriate method of allocating the gross earnings. Failure to take administration costs into account in that manner could result in the recognition in a particular period of costs relating to a lease which exceed the gross earnings recognised in respect of the lease in that period.

85 There will always be a degree of uncertainty about cash flows which are predicted for a number of years ahead. Factors about which there may be uncertainties include:

(a) doubts about the ability of the lessee to fulfil his obligations under the lease;
(b) any term in the lease which suggests that the lease is cancellable without appropriate compensation for the lessor;
(c) doubts about the ability of the lessor to utilise capital allowances at the time he anticipated being able to do so at the start of the lease;
(d) material uncertainty about interest rates where the lessor is dependent on borrowed funds and the lease rentals are fixed;
(e) uncertainty concerning future tax changes in the territory where the lease is operative.

86 The treatment to be followed by the lessor will depend on the degree of uncertainty relating to cash flows. If the degree of uncertainty is not great, such that (a) collectibility of the minimum lease payments is reasonably assured and (b) there are no important uncertainties surrounding the amount of unreimbursable costs yet to be incurred by the lessor under the lease, then it will normally be appropriate to classify the lease as a finance lease. The necessity to make a provision for bad debts based on experience of similar finance lease receivables would not preclude a lessor from classifying a lease as a finance lease. In such circumstances the lessor should in general not change the way in which he recognises gross earnings, but should make specific provisions for those cash flows about which the uncertainty exists, such as a provision for bad debts.

87 The degree of uncertainty of cash flows may however be such as to indicate that the lease does not have the characteristics of a finance lease and should more appropriately be accounted for as an operating lease.

C – THE ARITHMETIC OF LESSOR ACCOUNTING FOR FINANCE LEASES

88 There will in most cases be a close relationship between the initial evaluation of a lease and the way in which it is subsequently accounted for. Many lessors evaluate leases by using a method similar to that shown in Table 13 (see paragraph 109). In such an evaluation, the pricing of the rental determines the rate of return in each period. Hence, the manner in which the income is recognised is related to the original lease evaluation.

89 The general approach in the standard is to regard each rental receivable as partly gross earnings and partly a return of capital. A method has to be determined for making this allocation of each rental between the gross earnings and the capital repayment.

90 The total rentals receivable will be known in advance from the terms of the contract and the fair value of the asset will generally be known so that the gross earnings may be calculated.

The numerical examples are based on rates of tax and allowances which, according to indications at the time of writing (August 1984), will be in force from April 1986 onwards, that is, a 35% rate of corporation tax and 25% writing down allowances. **91**

As already noted, the standard requires that gross earnings should normally be allocated to accounting periods so as to give a constant periodic rate of return (or a reasonable approximation thereto) on the lessor's net cash investment (NCI) in the lease in each period. This implies the use of a so-called 'after-tax' method such as: **92**

(a) the actuarial method after tax; or
(b) the investment period method (IPM).

These methods are illustrated below. However, as shown in paragraphs 120 to 122 below, other methods may yield acceptable results.

The fact that these methods are known as 'after-tax' methods does not mean that they seek to allocate the profit after tax to accounting periods. Rather, the term means that the gross earnings are being allocated on a basis which takes into account the tax effect on cash flows – that is, the allocation is based on the NCI. **93**

The standard (paragraph 40) also allows a lessor to adopt a method which involves making an allocation out of gross earnings of an amount equal to the lessor's estimated cost of finance included in the net cash investment calculation; the balance remaining after this allocation is then recognised on a systematic basis. For example, allocation of the profit after estimated finance costs on the rule of 78 basis has the merit, in the case of a lease providing for equal rentals at equal intervals, of relating profit recognition to the amount of outstanding future rentals, non-payment of which is one of the principal risks for the lessor. Since the cost of finance allocation is taken from the NCI calculation, it reflects the tax effects of cash flows, hence this method is also an 'after-tax' method. **94**

The concept of earning a constant periodic rate of return on the net cash investment is commonly known as the investment period principle (IPP), of which the actuarial method after tax and the IPM are two of the most common methods. The actuarial method after tax is the most accurate method. The IPM is based on similar principles. Other methods have also been developed which attempt to produce the same constant periodic rate of return. They are not all illustrated here. If they come close to producing the constant periodic rate of return, then they can be used. **95**

The examples are based on a lease as follows: **96**

> The terms of the lease used in this example are the same as those set out in paragraph 21 and used in the lessee examples in Part 1. A lessor leases an asset to a lessee on a non-cancellable finance lease for five years from 1 January 1987. The rental is £650 per quarter payable in advance. The lessee pays all the maintenance and insurance costs as they arise. The cost of the asset is £10,000.

The lessor obtains writing down allowances on the leased asset at the rate of 25%. The rate of corporation tax is 35%. The lessor's year end is 31 December and he pays or recovers tax nine months after the year end.

In the examples which follow, the lessor always needs funds to support the lease, that is, the lease does not generate a cash surplus. In other cases, a cash surplus may arise in certain periods, for example if the lessor buys the asset later in his accounting year, or where for other reasons tax allowances are receivable earlier in the lease. In these circumstances the lessor would use the surplus cash to invest and earn a return which would be attributed to the lease. Competition may force the lessor to take any **97** interest earnings on surplus cash into account when fixing the rental. Any cash surplus would tend to arise late in the lease and so the estimate of interest earnings should be made on a conservative basis. It should be treated in the lease evaluations as set out in Tables 10 and 13 as the converse of interest paid.

The actuarial method after tax

98 The actuarial method after tax is a method which recognises all significant cash flows which affect a lease. It apportions the gross earnings over the period of the lease to give a constant periodic rate of return on the net cash investment. The net cash investment in a lease at a point in time is the amount of funds invested in a lease by the lessor, and comprises the cost of the asset plus or minus the following related payments or receipts:

(a) government or other grants receivable towards the purchase or use of the asset;
(b) rentals received;
(c) taxation payments and receipts including the effect of capital allowances;
(d) residual values, if any, at the end of the lease term less any estimated rebate of rental arising therefrom;
(e) interest payments (where applicable);
(f) interest received on cash surplus (if any);
(g) profit taken out of the lease.

It is sometimes argued that the net cash investment need not be adjusted for profit taken out of the lease, but this assumes that all cash received is used to reduce the investment and ignores the fact that some of the cash will be used, for example, to meet indirect costs and pay dividends. Even if the surplus is not distributed or used to pay indirect costs, it should be regarded as unconnected with the lease. If the profit is not taken out of the lease, the level of cash needed to finance the lease and the interest charges are understated.

99 The calculations are illustrated in Tables 10 and 13. In Table 10, it is assumed for simplicity of illustration that the lessor has no interest cost. A more realistic way of making the allocation, where interest payable is introduced into the calculation, is illustrated in Table 13 (paragraph 109).

TABLE 10

ACTUARIAL METHOD AFTER TAX – NO INTEREST PAYMENTS

Period (3 months)	*Net cash investment at start of period*	*Cash flows in period (Note 1)*	*(Note 2)*	*Average net cash investment in period*	*Profit taken out of lease (2.06% Note 3)*	*Net cash investment at end of period*
	£	£	£	£	£	£
1/87	–	(10,000)	650	(9,350)	(193)	(9,543)
2/87	(9,543)		650	(8,893)	(183)	(9,076)
3/87	(9,076)		650	(8,426)	(174)	(8,600)
4/87	(8,600)		650	(7,950)	(164)	(8,114)
			2,600		(714)	
1/88	(8,114)		650	(7,464)	(154)	(7,618)
2/88	(7,618)		650	(6,968)	(143)	(7,111)
3/88	(7,111)		650	(6,461)	(133)	(6,594)
4/88	(6,594)	(35)	650	(5,979)	(123)	(6,102)
			2,600		(553)	

Period (3 months)	*Net cash investment at start of period*	*Cash flows in period (Note 1)*	*Cash flows in period (Note 2)*	*Average net cash investment in period*	*Profit taken out of lease (2.06% Note 3)*	*Net cash investment at end of period*
	£	£	£	£	£	£
1/89	(6,102)		650	(5,452)	(112)	(5,564)
2/89	(5,564)		650	(4,914)	(101)	(5,015)
3/89	(5,015)		650	(4,365)	(90)	(4,455)
4/89	(4,455)	(254)	650	(4,059)	(84)	(4,143)
			2,600		(387)	
1/90	(4,143)		650	(3,493)	(72)	(3,565)
2/90	(3,565)		650	(2,915)	(60)	(2,975)
3/90	(2,975)		650	(2,325)	(48)	(2,373)
4/90	(2,373	(418)	650	(2,141)	(44)	(2,185)
			2,600		(224)	
1/91	(2,185)		650	(1,535)	(31)	(1,566)
2/91	(1,566)		650	(916)	(19)	(935)
3/91	(935)		650	(285)	(6)	(291)
4/91	(291)	(541)	650	(182)	(4)	(186)
			2,600		(60)	
1/92	(186)			(186)	(4)	(190)
2/92	(190)			(190)	(4)	(194)
3/92	(194)			(194)	(4)	(198)
4/92	(198)	198		–	–	–
					(12)	
		(10,000) (1,050)	13,000		(1,950)	

Notes*: 100

1. (a) The fair value of the asset is £10,000.
   (b) Tax at the rate of 35% is payable at the beginning of period 4 in each year. It is calculated on rentals less capital allowances. (Interest received which arises on any cash surplus would also be taxable.) The figure of £(1,050) is the total of tax payments less recoveries.
   (c) In arriving at the figure of £198 of tax recoverable in period 4/92, it has been assumed that the lessor receives an allowance of the amount of expenditure – £2,372 – which is unrelieved after five years' writing down allowances have been claimed. This will be the case where the lessor sells the asset for its tax written down value and passes the proceeds to the lessee as a rebate of rentals; in this instance the allowance of £2,372 will take the form of tax relief on the rebate of rentals rather than a balancing allowance. (The sales proceeds and the rebate of rentals are not shown in the Table, as their net cash flow effect is nil.) In other circumstances, such as where the lessor continues to hold the asset, the tax written down value of £2,372 will remain part of a pool and will continue to attract a stream of allowances totalling £2,372 on a reducing balance basis into the indefinite future. In such circumstances, it may be appropriate for the lessor to make an adjustment in respect of the delay in receiving the allowances.
2. Rentals of £650 are payable in advance.
3. The profit taken out of the lease is calculated at 2.06% on the average net cash invested in each period until period 3/92, after which point the lessor no longer

****Editor's note:** to table 10.*

has funds invested in the lease. The calculations made to arrive at 2.06% will normally be carried out by financial institutions by computer program, but it can be attained by trial and error. The calculation is, initially, carried out ignoring the profit taken out of the lease and this will then leave a balance of surplus cash left over at the end which represents the approximate profit on the transaction.

By dividing the total profit by the total average net cash investment in the period, an approximate percentage is obtained. As the profit taken out of the lease each quarter affects the average net cash investment in the following quarter, the net cash investment at the end of the whole transaction will not be zero until the percentage used is refined as in the above example to 2.06%.

101 The profit and loss accounts resulting from the cash flows in paragraph 100 are:

TABLE 11

PROFIT AND LOSS ACCOUNTS – NO INTEREST PAYMENTS

	1987	*1988*	*1989*	*1990*	*1991*	*1992*	*Total*
	£	£	£	£	£	£	£
Rental	2,600	2,600	2,600	2,600	2,600	–	13,000
Less capital repayment	(1,502)	(1,749)	(2,005)	(2,255)	(2,508)	19	(10,000)
Profit before tax (= gross earnings)	1,098	851	595	345	92	19	3,000
	£	£	£	£	£	£	£
Taxation	(35)	(254)	(418)	(541)	198	–	(1,050)
	1,063	597	177	(196)	290	19	1,950
Deferred tax (see para. 174‡)	(349)	(44)	210	420	(230)	(7)	–
Net profit	£714	£553	£387	£224	£60	£12	£1,950
Average net cash investment in the period:*	8,655	6,718	4,697	2,718	729	142	
Gross earnings expressed as a % return on the average net cash investment in the period:	12.7%	12.7%	12.7%	12.7%	12.6%†	13.4%†	

102 Table 11 is constructed from the bottom line upwards. The net profit for each year is taken from Table 10. The rentals and tax payments and recoveries are also found in Table 10. The net profit figures should then be grossed up by the rate of tax of 35%, giving the profit before tax (e.g., £714 ÷ 0.65 = £1,098). The figures for deferred tax and capital repayments may then be found.

**These amounts may be derived from the column 'Average net cash investment in period' in Table 10, for example £(9,350 + 8,893 + 8,426 + 7,950) ÷ 4 = £8,655.*

†Rounding error.

*‡**Editor's note:** the ASB noted in FRS 19 'Deferred tax' that it would be consistent with that FRS if paragraphs 170 and 173–175 of these Guidance Notes, and the references to them, were deemed to be deleted.*

Table 11 is used to arrive at one figure only, namely the capital repayment in each year. In practice none of the other figures in the table will be used, as when financial statements are being drawn up actual figures will be used, i.e., it is not necessary to accumulate individual figures lease by lease for interest and tax; these will be calculated in total for a company. 103

In Table 11 the effects of the five year lease contract spread over into six financial years. In fact the capital repayments for 1991 and 1992 may be added together for all practical purposes. 104

The capital repayments may be expressed in percentage terms: 105

1987	*1988*	*1989*	*1990*	*1991/92*	*Total*
£1,502	£1,749	£2,005	£2,255	£2,489	£10,000
15%	17%	20%	23%	25%	100%

Using the method set out above, the percentages of the capital repayment by year may be calculated for any lease and, as long as tax and interest rates remain unchanged, the percentages so calculated may be applied to any other lease which possesses the same ratio of capital to rental payments and whose inception date is the same. Thus it is not always necessary to undertake a separate calculation for each individual lease. 106

The lessor's balance sheets would include the amounts shown below. The relevant disclosure requirements are described in paragraphs 123 to 131. 107

TABLE 12

BALANCE SHEETS – EXTRACTS

	1987	*1988*	*1989*	*1990*	*1991*	*1992*
	£	£	£	£	£	£
Assets: Net Investment in finance leases	8,498	6,749	4,744	2,489	(19)	–
Tax recoverable	–	–	–	–	198	–
Deferred tax	–	–	–	237	7	–
	£8,498	£6,749	£4,744	£2,726	£186	–
Liabilities:						
Deferred tax	349	393	183	–	–	–
Current tax	35	254	418	541	–	–
Cash deficit*	8,114	6,102	4,143	2,185	186	–
	£8,498	£6,749	£4,744	£2,726	£186	–

The actuarial method after tax – building in interest payments

Where a lessor borrows funds to finance his leases a more realistic reflection of his cash flows may be obtained by building into the cash flows in Table 10 payments of interest on his borrowings. The tax charges will of course alter as will the amount required to finance the lease in each period. 108

Table 10 may thus be re-stated as follows: 109

**These amounts represent the net cash investment (as referred to in paragraph 98 above). The cash deficits will not in practice appear as separate items on a balance sheet, but they represent the amount of funds invested in a lease by the lessor; this may be equity or debt or a mixture of the two.*

TABLE 13

ACTUARIAL METHOD AFTER TAX – BUILDING IN INTEREST PAYMENTS

Period (3 months)	*Net cash investment at start of period*	*Cash flows in period (Note 1)*	*(Note 2)*	*Average cash investment in period*	*Interest paid (Note 3)*	*Profit taken out of lease (Note 4)*	*Net cash investment at end of period*
	£	£	£	£	£	£	£
1/87	–	(10,000)	650	(9,350)	(234)	(33)	(9,617)
2/87	(9,617)		650	(8,967)	(224)	(32)	(9,223)
3/87	(9,223)		650	(8,573)	(214)	(30)	(8,817)
4/87	(8,817)		650	(8,167)	(204)	(29)	(8,400)
			2,600		(876)	(124)	
1/88	(8,400)		650	(7,750)	(194)	(28)	(7,972)
2/88	(7,972)		650	(7,322)	(183)	(26)	(7,531)
3/88	(7,531)		650	(6,881)	(172)	(25)	(7,078)
4/88	(7,078)	272	650	(6,156)	(154)	(22)	(6,332)
			2,600		(703)	(101)	
1/89	(6,332)		650	(5,682)	(142)	(20)	(5,844)
2/89	(5,844)		650	(5,194)	(130)	(18)	(5,342)
3/89	(5,342)		650	(4,692)	(117)	(17)	(4,826)
4/89	(4,826)	(8)	650	(4,184)	(105)	(15)	(4,304)
			2,600		(494)	(70)	
1/90	(4,304)		650	(3,654)	(91)	(13)	(3,758)
2/90	(3,758)		650	(3,108)	(78)	(11)	(3,197)
3/90	(3,197)		650	(2,547)	(64)	(9)	(2,620)
4/90	(2,620)	(245)	650	(2,215)	(55)	(8)	(2,278)
			2,600		(288)	(41)	
1/91	(2,278)		650	(1,628)	(41)	(6)	(1,675)
2/91	(1,675)		650	(1,025)	(26)	(4)	(1,055)
3/91	(1,055)		650	(405)	(10)	(1)	(416)
4/91	(416)	(440)	650	(206)	(5)	(1)	(212)
			2,600		(82)	(12)	
1/92	(212)			(212)	(5)	(1)	(218)
2/92	(218)			(218)	(5)	(1)	(224)
3/92	(224)			(224)	(6)	(1)	(231)
4/92	(231)	226		1	(1)	–	–
		6			(17)	(3)	
		(10,000)	13,000		(2,460)	(351)	
		(189)					

Notes:

1.
   (a) The fair value of the asset is £10,000.
   (b) Tax is payable at the beginning of period 4 in each year. It is calculated on rentals, interest paid and capital allowances. (Interest received which arises on any cash surplus would also be taxable.) In period 4/92 the £6 is tax recoverable in 1993. The figure of £(189) is the total of tax payments less recoveries.
   (c) See note 1(c) to Table 10.
2. Rentals of £650 are payable in advance.
3. Interest paid is calculated at 2.5% per quarter on the average net cash investment in each period.
4. The profit taken out of the lease is calculated at 0.36% on the average net cash invested in each period until period 3/92. (For an explanation of how this is calculated, see note 3 to Table 10.)

Similarly, profit and loss accounts resulting from the cash flows in Table 13 are: **110**

TABLE 14

PROFIT AND LOSS ACCOUNTS – BUILDING IN INTEREST PAYMENTS

	1987	*1988*	*1989*	*1990*	*1991*	*1992*	*Total*
	£	£	£	£	£	£	£
Rental	2,600	2,600	2,600	2,600	2,600	–	13,000
Less capital repayment	(1,533)	(1,742)	(1,998)	(2,249)	(2,500)	22	(10,000)
Gross earnings	1,067	858	602	351	100	22	3,000
Interest	(876)	(703)	(494)	(288)	(82)	(17)	(2,460)
Profit before tax	191	155	108	63	18	5	540
Taxation	272	(8)	(245)	(440)	226	6	(189)
	463	147	(137)	(377)	244	11	351
Deferred tax (see para. 174*)	(339)	(46)	207	418	(232)	(8)	–
Net profit	£124	£101	£70	£41	£12	£3	£351

This table is constructed in a manner similar to Table 11, as described in paragraph 102.

Where a lease contains interest variation clauses which adjust the rental by reference to movements in Finance House base rate, or some other indicator, no adjustment need normally be made to the calculations in paragraphs 109 and 110. Any increase or reduction in rentals should be accounted for as an increase or reduction in gross earnings in the period in which it arises; this treatment will compensate for the additional finance cost incurred in the same period. **111**

The investment period method

As referred to above, the investment period method is used by some leasing companies as an alternative to the actuarial method after tax. **112**

The investment period method of accounting for finance leases allocates the gross earnings over that part of the lease in which the lessor has a net cash investment in proportion to the net cash investment at each interval. **113**

Using the cash flows set out in paragraph 109 the allocation of gross earnings becomes: **114**

*****Editor's note:*** *the ASB noted in FRS 19 'Deferred tax' that it would be consistent with that FRS if paragraphs 170 and 173–175 of these Guidance Notes, and the references to them, were deemed to be deleted.*

TABLE 15

ALLOCATION OF GROSS EARNINGS UNDER IPM

Period	*Net cash investment at end of period**	*Gross earnings allocation*	*Total gross earnings for year*
	£	£	£
1/87	9,617	285	
2/87	9,223	274	1,070
3/87	8,817	262	
4/87	8,400	249	
1/88	7,972	236	
2/88	7,531	223	
3/88	7,078	210	857
4/88	6,332	188	
1/89	5,844	173	
2/89	5,342	158	
3/89	4,826	143	602
4/89	4,304	128	
1/90	3,758	111	
2/90	3,197	95	
3/90	2,620	78	352
4/90	2,278	68	
1/91	1,675	50	
2/91	1,055	31	
3/91	416	12	99
4/91	212	6	
1/92	218	6	
2/92	224	7	
3/92	231	7	20
4/92	–	–	
	£101,170	£3,000	£3,000

The allocation of gross earnings is calculated as follows:

1/87 $£9{,}617 \times \dfrac{3{,}000}{101{,}170} = £285$

The same calculation is repeated for each period.

115 The profit and loss accounts resulting from Table 15 are as follows:

**Use of the average net cash investment figures from Table 13 would yield the same result as use of the end-of-period figures. The reason for this is that the interest paid and the profit taken out of the lease are both proportional to the average NCI; hence the closing NCI figures are also proportional to the average NCI.*

TABLE 16

PROFIT AND LOSS ACCOUNTS – INVESTMENT PERIOD METHOD

	1987	*1988*	*1989*	*1990*	*1991*	*1992*	*Total*
	£	£	£	£	£	£	£
Rental	2,600	2,600	2,600	2,600	2,600	–	13,000
Less capital repayment	(1,530)	(1,743)	(1,998)	(2,248)	(2,501)	20	(10,000)
Gross earnings	1,070	857	602	352	99	20	3,000
Interest	(876)	(703)	(494)	(288)	(82)	(17)	(2,460)
Profit before tax	194	154	108	64	17	3	540
Taxation	272	(8)	(245)	(440)	226	6	(189)
	466	146	(137)	(376)	243	9	351
Deferred tax	(340)	(46)	207	418	(232)	(7)	–
Net profit	£126	£100	£70	£41	£11	£2	£351

This table is constructed differently from Tables 11 and 14. Under the IPM, the allocation of the gross earnings is calculated as shown in Table 15. The capital repayment may therefore be found by subtraction. The figures for interest are the same as those in Tables 13 and 14. The profit before tax may be found by subtraction; note that the total is the same as in Table 14 but the allocation among the years is slightly different. The tax payable figures are the same as in Tables 13 and 14. The net profit is calculated as 65% of the profit before tax, and the deferred tax line is calculated as a balancing figure.

Hire purchase

116 As noted in paragraph 80, for hire purchase contracts, allocation of finance charges to accounting periods based on the net investment will in most cases be a suitable alternative to allocation based on net cash investment. The following two methods are therefore illustrated, using the rentals and other details set out in paragraph 21:

(a) the actuarial method before tax;
(b) the rule of 78.

The actuarial method before tax

117 In this example the finance charges of £3,000 on the hire purchase contract (i.e., total rentals receivable minus the cost of the asset) are apportioned over the period of the contract to give a constant periodic rate of return on the net investment. In this method, the effects of taxation are ignored in apportioning the finance charges (hence the description 'before tax'). Interest on borrowed funds is usually ignored in this method but may be taken into account.

118 The calculations are the same as in Tables 1 and 2 in paragraphs 25 and 26. The results are as follows:

TABLE 17

ACTUARIAL METHOD BEFORE TAX

	1987	*1988*	*1989*	*1990*	*1991*	*Total*
	£	£	£	£	£	£
Rentals receiveable	2,600	2,600	2,600	2,600	2,600	13,000
Less capital repayments	1,563	1,757	1,973	2,217	2,490	10,000
Finance charges	£1,037	£843	£627	£383	£110	£3,000
Average sum outstanding in the period	8,778	7,144	5,308	3,246	929	
Finance charges expressed as a % return on the average net investment in the period:	11.8%	11.8%	11.8%	11.8%	11.8%	

The rule of 78

119 The calculations for apportioning the finance charge on the basis of the rule of 78 are the same as those shown in Table 3 in paragraph 28. For a hire purchase company it is particularly important to be aware that the rule of 78 has a tendency to front-load income, which tendency becomes more pronounced the higher finance charges are relative to the amount financed. Therefore, in the case of longer contracts (say, over seven years) the actuarial method before tax is preferred.

Comparison of methods

120 The allocation of gross earnings (or finance charges) under the methods described above may be compared as follows:

TABLE 18

COMPARISON OF GROSS EARNINGS ALLOCATION

	1987	*1988*	*1989*	*1990*	*1991*	*1992*	*Total*
	£	£	£	£	£	£	£
Actuarial method after tax (para. 110)	1,067	858	602	351	100	22	3,000
IPM (para. 115)	1,070	857	602	352	99	20	3,000
Actuarial method before tax (para. 118)	1,037	843	627	383	110	–	3,000
Rule of 78 (paras. 119 and 28)	1,105	853	600	347	95	–	3,000

121 A number of points may be noted from the above table. Under the assumption of 35% tax and 25% writing down allowances, the two after-tax methods give very similar results. The reason for this is that the lease never goes into surplus (see paragraph 109). If different assumptions are made about rates of tax and allowances, cash surpluses may arise in certain periods and in these circumstances the actuarial method after tax and the IPM yield different results. In the former method, the interest received on the cash surplus (the re-investment income) is brought back and recognised in the periods when the lessor has funds invested in the lease, rather than taken to income when it arises. Thus no profit is recognised in the periods when the lease is in surplus. Because of this effect, the lessor may be in an exposed position in this period in the event, for example, of early termination of the lease by the lessee. If

this method is used, it may therefore be necessary to make an appropriate provision for early termination losses so that the net investment in the lease does not exceed the termination value at any time. Under the IPM, any re-investment income is recognised when it arises, that is, it is not brought back and recognised in the periods in which the lessor has funds invested in the lease. Thus, where cash surpluses arise, the IPM is more conservative than the actuarial method after tax.

Depending on the materiality of the amounts involved, it may be appropriate under assumptions such as those used in the above numerical examples to use the actuarial method before tax and the rule of 78 to allocate gross earnings from finance leases, although these methods are primarily intended for use in allocating finance charges from hire purchase contracts. **122**

D – BALANCE SHEET PRESENTATION, NOTE DISCLOSURE AND LEGAL REQUIREMENTS FOR LESSORS

The standard requires disclosure of the net investment in (a) finance leases and (b) hire purchase contracts at each balance sheet date. The amounts should be described as receivables. Whereas in lessee accounting the figures in respect of leases and hire purchase contracts may be aggregated, in the case of lessors and finance companies the amounts in respect of each should be shown separately. **123**

For companies subject to Schedule 8* of the Companies Act 1948, the net investment in finance leases and hire purchase contracts should be included in current assets under the heading 'Debtors' and described as 'finance lease receivables' and/or 'hire purchase receivables' as appropriate. It should be analysed in the notes to the accounts between those amounts receivable within one year and those amounts receivable thereafter. **124**

A suitable form of disclosure would be: **125**

BALANCE SHEET AS AT 31 DECEMBER 1987

Current assets		*1986*
Finance lease and hire purchase receivables	£1200	£1100

Note to the accounts:

1. The amounts receivable under finance leases and hire purchase contracts comprise:

Finance leases	900	820
Hire purchase contracts	300	280
	£1200	£1100

Included in the totals receivable is £900 (1986 £850) which falls due after more than one year.

The standard requires that the gross amounts (i.e., original cost or revaluation) and accumulated depreciation of assets held for use in operating leases should be disclosed. This information could be incorporated into tables showing the amounts for other fixed assets or could be shown as a separate table. It is recognised that, for **126**

* ***Editor's note:*** *Now Schedule 1 to the Large and Medium-sized Companies and Groups (Accounts and Reports) Regulations 2008 (SI 2008/410).*

banks, assets held for use in operating leases are different in nature from a bank's infrastructure (e.g., its own premises). Hence it may not be appropriate to combine assets held for use in operating leases with a bank's infrastructure for capital adequacy purposes.

127 Details of the accounting policies followed by lessors in respect of both operating leases and finance leases are required by the standard, as well as by SSAP 2, 'Disclosure of accounting policies'. This would include information on the depreciation policy for assets leased on operating leases. The standard places particular emphasis on detailed disclosure of the policy adopted for recognition of finance lease income by lessors. This might include items such as the basic method of income recognition (e.g., investment period method); the policies followed in respect of initial direct costs; and assumptions about tax rates and payment dates.

128 It may also be necessary in order to show a true and fair view to disclose information relating to leases and hire purchase contracts which is of particular significance to users of accounts. This may include: contingent liabilities; contingent rentals payable or receivable (e.g., rentals receivable on a hotel may be related to its profits and therefore the income in future years may fluctuate); or new-for-old guarantees given (e.g. on computer leases).

Lessors' turnover

129 In the case of operating leases, a lessor's turnover should be the aggregate rentals receivable in respect of the accounting period.

130 In the case of finance leases, a lessor should disclose gross earnings as turnover. (This is analogous to 'interest receivable' in the case of a bank.) However, as this provides an incomplete measure of a lessor's activity, disclosure should also be made in the notes of the aggregate rentals receivable under finance leases and of the cost of assets acquired for letting under finance leases.

131 The term 'turnover', although used in the Companies Act formats, is not normally used in the leasing industry. Paragraph 3(3) of Schedule 8* to the Companies Act 1948 requires directors to adapt the headings used in the formats in any case where the special nature of a company's business requires such adaptation. It may therefore be appropriate to use a term such as 'gross earnings under finance leases'.

Part III – Problem areas

INTRODUCTION

132 Part III gives guidance on problem areas in accounting for leases as follows:

	Paragraphs
A – Lease definition and classification	133–138
B – Land and buildings	139–144
C – Leasing by manufacturers or dealers	145–149
D – Sale and leaseback transactions	150–160
E – Sub-leases and back-to-back leases	161–169
F – Deferred taxation	170–175
G – Regional development grants	176–181
H – Bad debts	182–185

* ***Editor's note:*** *Now Schedule 1 to the Large and Medium-sized Companies and Groups (Accounts and Reports) Regulations 2008 (SI 2008/410).*

A – LEASE DEFINITION AND CLASSIFICATION

The definition of a lease is contained in paragraph 14 of the standard. However, in practice there are a number of arrangements which may in substance be leases even though different terms are used to describe them. Whether such an arrangement falls within the definition of a lease is a question to be decided in the light of the facts of each case. For example, a bare-boat charter (a charter of a boat without a crew) will generally have the characteristics of a lease, and the terms of the charter will enable the parties to determine whether it is a finance lease or an operating lease. There are also other arrangements which would not normally be lease contracts (although in exceptional cases they could in substance be leases). An example of these other arrangements is where company A builds a plant on the basis that company B is obliged to buy sufficient of the output of the plant (whether or not B requires it) in order to give a full payout on the cost of the assets involved, together with a normal profit margin: such arrangements are sometimes called take-or-pay contracts or through-put agreements. In many cases such arrangements will in substance be more in the nature of long-term purchase/supply contracts than contracts 'for the hire of a specific asset . . . (under which) the lessor retains ownership of the asset but conveys the right to the use of the asset to the lessee for an agreed period of time in return for the payment of specified rentals' (standard, paragraph 14). **133**

A finance lease is defined in paragraphs 15 and 16 of the standard. The definition in paragraph 15 involves considering whether substantially all the risks and rewards of ownership are transferred to the lessee; the presumption is that this transfer occurs if at the inception of the lease the present value of the minimum lease payments amounts to (normally) 90% or more of the fair value of the leased asset. An alternative way of considering whether substantially all the risks and rewards are transferred to the lessee and whether therefore the lease is a finance lease is to consider whether the present value of any amounts excluded from the minimum lease payments exceeds 10% of the fair value. The amounts excluded from the minimum lease payments are (a) in the case of a lessee, amounts (usually residual amounts) which are unguaranteed or which are guaranteed by a third party, and (b) in the case of a lessor, any unguaranteed residual value. Hence, if these amounts are (or are anticipated to be) insignificant, a finance lease may be indicated. **134**

Exceptionally, it may not be practicable to determine the lease classification based on consideration of whether the present value of the minimum lease payments amounts to (normally) 90% or more of the fair value of the leased asset; equally, it may not be practicable to use the '10% approach' suggested above. In such a case, there may be other means of determining whether or not substantially all the risks and rewards of ownership of an asset are transferred to the lessee. For example, if a lessee has the use of an asset for the period in which substantially all the economic benefits can be derived from the asset, then a finance lease is indicated. **135**

In considering the classification of leases, especially in difficult and marginal cases, the role of residual values is particularly important. Of the residual value of a leased asset (i.e., its value at the end of the lease term), some or the whole (a) may be guaranteed by the lessee to the lessor or (b) may be guaranteed to the lessor by a third party or (c) may be unguaranteed. That part of the residual value which is guaranteed by the lessee (or by a party related to him) is included in the lessee's minimum lease payments. As far as the lessor is concerned his minimum lease payments include any residual amounts guaranteed by the lessee or by an independent third party. Thus the amounts which a lessor expects to receive in relation to the lease may exceed the minimum lease payments which a lessee expects to make to the extent of (a) residual amounts guaranteed by a third party and/or (b) unguaranteed residual amounts. (Insuring residual values is equivalent to obtaining a third party **136** guarantee.) Two examples may illustrate the effect of residual values on lease classification.

137 Consider first a lease of an asset which has a fair value of £3,900. The lessee is required to make three annual payments of £1,000 in advance. The lessor estimates that the asset will have a residual value of £1,500 at the end of the three years; the manufacturer guarantees to buy it back for £1,200.

The minimum lease payments as far as the lessee is concerned are £3,000; from the lessor's point of view they are £4,200. The unguaranteed residual value (URV) is £300 (£1,500–£1,200). The interest rate implicit in the lease is that rate which equates the lessor's minimum lease payments (£4,200) and the URV (£300) to the fair value of £3,900. The expected cash flows are therefore:

	Lessee	Lessor
T = 0	1,000	1,000
T = 1	1,000	1,000
T = 2	1,000	1,000
T = 3	–	1,500
	£3,000	£4,500

In this instance it is clear even without performing any calculations that the lease is an operating lease for the lessee, because, even with a zero rate of interest, the minimum lease payments are less than 90% of the fair value. Similarly, the lease is a finance lease from the lessor's point of view because the URV is less than 10% of the fair value of the asset before discounting; when discounted the URV would be even smaller. The presence of a third party guarantee means that the two parties to the lease classify it in different ways. (This is recognised in paragraph 9 of the standard.) If there had been no third party guarantee the lease would have been an operating lease for both lessor and lessee.

Where the figures are different and the classification is not as obvious as in the above example, the implicit rate of interest should be calculated using one of the methods suggested in paragraph 24 of the standard.

138 A slightly different problem relating to residual values may be illustrated by means of a further example.

> A lessee takes out a lease under which the total of his minimum lease payments approximately equals the fair value of the asset. The present value of the minimum lease payments will therefore be a smaller amount and the classification of the lease may appear borderline. In such a case the lessee should consider the substance of the transaction rather than the precise arithmetic of the 90% test. For example, the minimum lease payments may include a residual value which is guaranteed by the lessee. If this guaranteed value is in fact considerably less than the probable residual value of the leased asset, then it is likely that the lessor will sell the asset in the open market and the lessee will not be called on to pay the amount which he guaranteed. This would suggest that the lessor is trading in the asset rather than providing finance, and that the lease is an operating lease.

B – LAND AND BUILDINGS

Land and buildings which are subject to lease agreements should be accounted for using the same criteria as other assets. **139**

Many leases of land and buildings are for only a small part of the useful life of the building and the lessee does not obtain the economic benefits of ownership arising, for example, from any increase in value. Moreover, since the leases usually provide for regular rent reviews, the rent payable is regularly brought up to current market rates and the lease thereby has the characteristics not of a financing arrangement but of the provision of a service. Most leases involving land and buildings would therefore be classified as operating leases. **140**

There may, however, be instances when a lease of land and buildings has the characteristics of a financing arrangement and in such cases the lease would normally be classified as a finance lease. Examples might be: (a) a lease of a building with a relatively short useful life, for example a warehouse built to a customer's specification or a building with a specific use such as a battery house; or (b) certain leasebacks of office buildings in a sale and leaseback arrangement (see paragraphs 150 to 160). **141**

As with all types of lease, it is important in deciding whether a lease of land and buildings is a finance lease or an operating lease to consider its characteristics, in particular to consider whether or not substantially all the risks and rewards of ownership of the land and buildings in question are transferred to the lessee. It should be noted that under the definition of a finance lease set out in paragraphs 15 and 16 of the standard, the classification which results from the application of the '90% formula' to the lease may be rebutted if the lease in question does not transfer substantially all the risks and rewards of ownership to the lessee; this may occur for example because of rent reviews which revert the principal rewards of ownership to the lessor. **142**

In the context of land and buildings the term 'open market value' is commonly used for what is described elsewhere in this standard as 'fair value'. **143**

Nothing in the standard precludes the recognition as a fixed asset of an amount paid in the form of a premium as consideration for a leasehold interest. **144**

C – LEASING BY MANUFACTURERS OR DEALERS

Manufacturers or dealers may offer customers the choice of either buying or leasing an asset. The leases offered may be either finance leases or operating leases, and may be described by a variety of terms, including hire or rental agreements. **145**

Where a manufacturer or dealer enters into an operating lease, no sale has been made and it is therefore not appropriate to recognise a selling profit when the asset is first leased. A manufacturer or dealer lessor should account for an operating lease in the same way as any other lessor. **146**

When a manufacturer or dealer enters into a finance lease such transactions give rise to two types of income: (a) the initial profit or loss at the start of the lease which is equivalent to the profit or loss resulting from an outright sale of the asset being leased, and (b) the finance charges (or gross earnings) over the period of the lease. **147**

As the offer of a lease agreement is often influenced by a manufacturer's or dealer's marketing considerations, the pricing of the lease may not necessarily be based on **148** the normal outright sale price. Hence the initial selling profit on a lease should be restricted to an amount which will enable the finance charges under the lease to be based on the rate of interest which, in the absence of such marketing considerations, the lessor would expect to charge the lessee. The rate of interest should take into account any tax benefits accruing to the lessor.

149 Consider the following example. A manufacturer makes a machine which costs him £10,000. He normally sells the machine for £12,500 giving him a profit on the sale of £2,500.

The manufacturer offers the machine on a five year finance lease with a rental of £687.50 payable quarterly in advance. Using the figures in Table 1, paragraph 25, this rental would justify a capital cost of £10,577 for the cost of the asset. (Using the implicit rate in Table 1 of 2.95% per quarter, a quarterly rental of £650 is equivalent to a capital cost of £10,000. Therefore a quarterly rental of £687.50 is equivalent to a capital cost of:

$$£10{,}000 \times \frac{687.50}{650.00} = £10{,}577).$$

That is, where the implicit rate is not known, an estimate thereof has to be used in order to calculate the capital cost. The manufacturer should therefore restrict his selling profit to £577 at the start of the lease. The balance of the profit arises as gross earnings over the period of the lease.

D – SALE AND LEASEBACK TRANSACTIONS

150 A sale and leaseback transaction takes place when an owner sells an asset and immediately re-acquires the right to use the asset by entering into a lease with the purchaser.

151 Before dealing with the accounting for the sale and leaseback transaction itself, the carrying value of the asset in question should be reviewed. If the asset has suffered an impairment it should be written down to its recoverable amount. This is nothing to do with sale and leaseback specifically, but it is a step which should be taken so that the sale and leaseback accounting is not distorted.

152 Once that first step has been taken, the asset will be carried at fair value, or less. It is then necessary to determine whether the leaseback is an operating lease or a finance lease. This should be decided according to the criteria for all leases as set out in paragraphs 15 to 17 of the standard.

Finance leaseback

153 If the leaseback is a finance lease, the seller-lessee is in effect re-acquiring substantially all the risks and rewards of ownership of the asset. In other words, he never disposes of his ownership interest in the asset, and so it would not be correct to recognise a profit or loss in relation to an asset which (in substance) never was disposed of.

154 However, it is possible that a sale and leaseback resulting in a finance lease may be arranged on terms reflecting a higher or lower capital value than the book value of the asset (i.e., so as to reflect an *apparent* profit or loss). For example, an asset which has a carrying value of £70 may be sold at £120 and leased back on a finance lease. In such a case, the lease payments would (other things being equal) be higher than if the sale and leaseback had been arranged at carrying value. The standard therefore provides that the £50 apparent profit should be deferred and amortised (i.e., credited to income) over the lease term: this will have the effect of reducing the rentals – which are shown as interest and depreciation of the leased-back asset – to a level consistent with the previous carrying value of the asset. Where the asset is carried at below fair value, it may be appropriate to revalue it. If, in the same example, the fair value of the asset were £100, the asset could be revalued to that amount, and there would remain only £20 of apparent profit to be deferred and amortised over the lease term. The effect would then be to reduce the rentals to a level consistent with the fair value of the asset.

As an alternative to calculating the apparent profit and deferring and amortising that amount, the same result can be achieved by leaving the previous carrying value unchanged, setting up the amount received on sale as a creditor, and treating the lease payments partly as principal and partly as a finance charge. This treatment will reflect the substance of the transaction, namely that it represents the raising of finance secured on an asset which is held and not disposed of. **155**

Operating leaseback

Conversely, if the leaseback is an operating lease, the seller-lessee has disposed of substantially all the risks and rewards of ownership of the asset, and so has realised a profit or loss on the disposal. Provided that the transaction is established at fair value, the profit or loss should be recognised. However, it is possible that a sale and leaseback transaction can be arranged at other than fair value. If the sale price is above fair value (paragraph 47(c) of the standard), the excess will not be genuine profit, but will arise solely because the operating lease rentals payable in the ensuing years will also be at above fair value. The standard therefore provides that the excess of sale price over fair value should not be recognised as profit in the year but should be credited to income, over the shorter of the remainder of the lease term and the period to the next rent review (if any), so as to reduce the rentals payable to a level consistent with the fair value of the asset. **156**

This may be illustrated as follows: **157**

Carrying value of asset	£70	
Fair value of asset	£100	Recognise profit
Sale price	£120	on sale of £30
Annual rental (for 5 years)	£28	

The excess of the sale price over fair value should be deferred and amortised (credited to income) over the non-cancellable period, i.e.:

$$\frac{120-100}{5} = £4 \text{ p.a.}$$

This credit will in effect reduce the rentals from £28 p.a. to £24 p.a.

The converse situation may also arise, namely that the sale price is below fair value (standard, paragraph 47(b)). This could arise for two reasons. First, the sale could simply be a bad bargain, for example because the seller-lessee needed to raise cash quickly. In that case any profit or loss should be recognised immediately. Second, the price may be artificially low so as to compensate for future rentals at below market price. Depending on the previous carrying value, either a profit or loss may arise. These cases are considered in turn. **158**

159 The following figures illustrate the case where a profit arises, even though the price is artificially low so as to compensate for future rentals at below market price:

Carrying value	£70	
Sale price	£80	Profit £10
Fair value	£100	
Annual rental (5 years)	£20	

The profit of £10 should be recognised immediately, but the difference between £80 and £100 should not be recognised.

160 Conversely, an apparent loss may arise if the sale price is below the carrying value as well as being below fair value. This is illustrated as follows:

Carrying value	£95	
Sale price	£80	Apparent loss £15
Fair value	£100	
Annual rental (5 years)	£20	

In such a case, provided the apparent loss is compensated by below market rentals, the loss should not be recognised but should be deferred and amortised so as to give the effect of increasing the rentals to a level consistent with a selling price of £95. The loss should be deferred and amortised (i.e., debited to income) over the remainder of the lease term (or, if shorter, the period during which the reduced rentals are chargeable).

E – SUB-LEASES AND BACK-TO-BACK LEASES

161 The main provisions of the standard and the other sections of these guidance notes deal principally with leases in which only two parties, the lessor and the lessee, are involved. However, some lease arrangements are more complex and involve three (or more) parties. There are many different types of arrangement and it is not possible to give guidance on all of them. In addition, there are variations in the terms used to describe the leases and the parties to the lease. The notes in this section are intended therefore to give guidance on the general principles of three-party lease arrangements.

162 The three parties may be termed (a) the original lessor, (b) the intermediate party and (c) the ultimate lessee. In effect, the intermediate party may be both a lessee in the original lease and a lessor as regards the sub-lease.

163 Unless the original lease agreement is replaced by a new agreement, the accounting by the original lessor should not be affected by the fact that the intermediate party enters into a sub-lease.

164 The accounting by the intermediate party will depend on the structure of his arrangements with the original lessor and the ultimate lessee.

165 If the intermediate party's role is in substance that of a broker or an agent for transactions between the original lessor and the ultimate lessee such that there is no recourse to the intermediate party in the event of default, then the intermediate party should not include the asset or obligation in his balance sheet and should account for any income due to him on a systematic and rational basis. For example, a pure commission might be recognised immediately, whilst a guarantee fee might be spread over the period of risk. For both operating and finance leases, he should treat any contingent loss as required by SSAP 18.*

Conversely, the intermediate party may enter into a lease with the original lessor, the terms of which require him to make payments to the lessor regardless of whether the ultimate lessee completes his payments. That is, the asset would be sub-leased by the intermediate party to the ultimate lessee, but the lease agreement between the original lessor and the intermediate party would remain in effect. If the original lease is a finance lease, the intermediate party should record his obligation thereunder. If the sub-lease is also a finance lease, the intermediate party should account for it as such; this will result in his showing an obligation under the original lease and a receivable under the sub-lease. If the sub-lease is an operating lease, the leased asset remains as a fixed asset. The principal differences which arise if the sub-lease is a finance lease as opposed to an operating lease are that the intermediate party (a) treats the asset as a receivable instead of a fixed asset and (b) recognises income according to finance lease principles. **166**

The ultimate lessee should classify the sub-lease according to paragraphs 15 to 17 of the standard and account for it accordingly. **167**

In the context of complex multi-party leases, paragraph 16 of the standard is particularly important. This paragraph permits the presumption that a lease should be classified as a finance lease to be rebutted if it can be clearly demonstrated that in the circumstances in question the lease does not transfer substantially all the risks and rewards of ownership to the lessee. This rebuttal can be relevant, for example, where there is a series of sub-leases which results in a series of partial interests in an asset with each party carrying a percentage of the total risks in return for a percentage of the total rewards. **168**

Where the intermediate party is not relieved of his primary obligation under the original lease and where the sub-lease is a finance lease, it is sometimes thought that this results in the leased asset's being capitalised in the accounts of two companies. This is not the case. The asset is capitalised only in the books of the ultimate lessee. The remaining balances are in the nature of indebtedness between the parties. **169**

F – DEFERRED TAXATION

The accounting requirements for dealing with deferred tax are set out in SSAP 15 'Accounting for deferred taxation'. The present standard in no way changes these requirements. It should be noted, however, that at the time of writing SSAP 15 is under review.† **170**

Lessee's deferred taxation

Where a lessee charges the full rental he pays as a tax expense in the year of payment, timing differences may arise. These differences may be either (a) to the extent that the depreciation and finance charge exceed or fall short of the rental on a finance lease or (b) to the extent of any deferral or accrual of the rental on an operating lease. The lessee should consider whether deferred tax needs to be provided on these timing differences. **171**

****Editor's note:*** *SSAP 18 has been superseded by FRS 12.*

†***Editor's note:*** *See note to paragraph 173.*

172 The amounts in question in the example in Part 1 are those shown in column three of Table 8 in paragraph 47.

173* The timing difference described above will need to be considered together with all other timing differences which a lessee may experience and, unless the conditions set out in paragraphs 27 to 30 of SSAP 15 are met, a provision for deferred tax will be required.

Lessor's deferred taxation

174* It will be seen from paragraph 101 that capital allowances have a material impact on a lessor's position. If deferred tax were not provided by a lessor he would report profits in some periods and losses in others.

175* SSAP 15 requires that the total position of a company must be looked at and not just one contract. A lessor therefore needs to consider the likely pattern of future timing differences. For example, he may be able to decide not to provide for deferred tax because any reduction in leasing may be offset by increases of tax allowances in other areas.

G – REGIONAL DEVELOPMENT GRANTS

Lessors and RDGs

176 Leases which involve equipment on which a regional development grant (RDG) may be claimed need special consideration. The lessor may claim a grant (currently of 15% or 22%) towards the cost of purchasing an asset. The grant is not taxable and the lessor may also claim capital allowances on the full purchase price of the asset. The rentals charged to the lessee will reflect the benefit the lessor has obtained from both the RDG and the capital allowances. Unless any adjustments are made, the lessor's profit and loss account may show a loss before tax and a profit after tax from such a lease.

177 Some consider that presentation of a loss before tax and a profit after tax leads to difficulties in interpreting the accounts, and therefore prefer to adjust the profit and loss account by 'grossing up' the RDG by the rate of taxation to show it as a gross amount as if tax were payable on the grant.

178 The difference between the two approaches is illustrated in the following example. The figure shown represent the aggregate profit and loss accounts for all the years affected by the lease and, for simplicity, ignore interest.

***Editor's note:** The ASB noted in FRS 19 'Deferred tax' that it would be consistent with that FRS if paragraphs 170 and 173–175 of these Guidance Notes, and the references to them, were deemed to be deleted.*

TABLE 19

REGIONAL DEVELOPMENT GRANT PRESENTATION

	Actual transaction		*Adjusted presentation*	
	£	£	£	£
Rentals receivableover the lease term		750		750
Cost of asset	1,000		1,000	
Less RDG	220		338	
		780		662
Profit/(Loss) before tax		(30)		88
Taxation recoverable (payable)		87		(31)
Profit after tax		£57		£57

The standard permits either approach to be followed.* If a company grosses up its RDGs, it should disclose the amount by which the profit before tax and the tax charge have been increased as a result of grossing up such grants. **179**

Lessees and RDGs

In cases where the asset which is leased qualifies for an RDG the position of the lessee also calls for attention. In the example in paragraph 178 the net cost of the asset after allowing for the RDG is £780. The total rentals payable amount to £750 which is less than the net cost of the asset. **180**

In these circumstances an appropriate way of dealing with the situation is to capitalise the asset at £750 and to assume that no finance charge is payable. The £750 would then be depreciated over the shorter of the lease term or the useful life of the asset. It is not considered appropriate to show a negative finance charge. **181**

H – BAD DEBTS

Since a lessor's profit on a finance lease is assessed on the basis of the whole of the lease period, it is essential that bad debts resulting from the failure of the lessee to pay rentals throughout the period are taken into consideration. **182**

The level of bad debts will depend upon the type of business the lessor writes. In many instances bad debts will not be significant; in other instances they may be. **183**

As noted in paragraph 86, where a pattern of bad debt experience can be established, a lessor should make a provision for bad debts but this should not in general change the way in which he recognises gross earnings. **184**

Where there is a significant risk of bad debts, the carrying value of the leasing receivable should be determined having regard to the amount expected to be realised from the leased asset. For example, if it is likely that the asset will be re-possessed, the lessor may need to consider the amount which he will be able to recover through that route. As explained in paragraph 87 the bad debt risk may be sufficient to render classification as a finance lease inappropriate. **185**

* ***Editor's note:*** *The amendment to SSAP 21 in February 1997 removed the option to gross up tax free grants.*

Part IV – Leased assets and current cost accounting

INTRODUCTION

186 Part IV gives guidance on the procedures to be used for accounting for leased assets under SSAP 16 'Current cost accounting'. At the time of writing these guidance notes, SSAP 16 is under review*. However it remains in force until replaced.

ACCOUNTING BY LESSEES

187 A lessee should record a finance lease in his balance sheet as an asset and as an obligation to pay future rentals. For CCA purposes the asset and the obligation should be considered separately. The lessee's asset forms part of his operating capability which should be maintained.

188 The asset, which will be included amongst fixed assets in the lessee's balance sheet, should be restated at its value to the business on the basis suggested in the Guidance Notes on SSAP 16 'Current cost accounting'. The depreciation charge in each period should be based on current costs.

189 The obligation to pay future rentals is equivalent to a borrowing and should be included in the calculation of the gearing adjustment for CCA purposes.

190 In the example of lessee accounting given in Part I the amounts which have to be restated for CCA purposes in respect of the asset are shown in paragraph 45 and the obligations under finance leases which are to be taken into account in calculating the gearing adjustment are listed in paragraph 46.

191 The part of the rental under a lease which is apportioned as a finance charge should be included as part of the interest costs in the CCA profit and loss account. These amounts are given in paragraphs 26, 28, 34 and 35.

192 Rentals under an operating lease are charged to the profit and loss account and would not normally require adjustment for CCA purposes.

ACCOUNTING BY LESSORS

193 Assets held by lessors for use in operating leases should be restated for CCA purposes on the same basis as any other fixed asset. The lessor is trading in assets and it is appropriate that he maintains his operating capability in terms of the particular fixed assets he is using.

194 Where a lessor is engaged in finance leasing, the rentals he will receive will be fixed in money terms and he therefore has a monetary asset rather than a physical asset in his balance sheet. A monetary working capital adjustment relating to the finance lease receivables should therefore be made for CCA purposes.

***Editor's note:** *SSAP 16 was suspended in June 1985 and withdrawn in July 1988.*

[SSAP 25]
Segmental reporting*†

(Issued June 1990)

Contents

	Paragraphs
Part 1 – Explanatory note	1–29
Part 2 – Definition of terms	30–33
Part 3 – Standard accounting practice	34–45
Part 4 – Legal and International Stock Exchange requirements in Great Britain and Northern Ireland	46–55
Part 5 – Legal and International Stock Exchange requirements in the Republic of Ireland	56–63
Part 6 – Compliance with International Accounting Standard No. 14 'Reporting Financial Information by Segment'	64

Appendix
Illustrative segmental report

***Editor's note:** IFRS 8 Operating Segments *was issued by the IASB and came into force for accounting periods beginning on or after 1 January 2009. At the time it was issued the ASB indicated that it would consider any changes required to the UK standard. In the light of the ASB's plans for the development of UK GAAP any changes to SSAP 25 are now highly unlikely. However, SSAP 25 has been amended so that entities whose parents prepare segmental information that complies with IFRS 8 are now outside the scope of SSAP 25.*

†***Editor's note:** FRS 102 does not contain segmental reporting requirements in relation to most entities within its scope. Entities within the scope of FRS 102, but which have debt or equity instruments that are publicly traded, file or are in the process of filing financial statements with a securities commission or other regulatory organisation for the purpose of issuing any class of instruments in a public market, or which choose to provide information described as segment information, will be required to comply with IFRS 8* Operating Segments *(as adopted in the EU).*

Segmental reporting

The provisions of this statement of accounting practice should be read in conjunction with the (Explanatory) Foreword to accounting standards *and need not be applied to immaterial items.*

Part 1 – Explanatory note

PURPOSE OF SEGMENTAL INFORMATION

1 Many entities carry on several classes of business or operate in several geographical areas, with different rates of profitability, different opportunities for growth and different degrees of risk. It is not usually possible for the user of the financial statements of such an entity to make judgements about either the nature of the entity's different activities or their contribution to the entity's overall financial results unless the financial statements provide some segmental analysis of the information they contain. The purpose of segmental information is, therefore, to provide information to assist the users of financial statements:

(a) to appreciate more thoroughly the results and financial position of the entity by permitting a better understanding of the entity's past performance and thus a better assessment of its future prospects; and
(b) to be aware of the impact that changes in significant components of a business may have on the business as a whole.

2 This accounting standard should ensure as far as possible that the segmental information reported by an entity is disclosed on a consistent basis, year by year. However, caution should be exercised if comparing similar segments in different entities, because, in addition to any differences in accounting policies adopted, the basis of accounting for inter-segment sales or the treatment of common costs may not be consistent between entities.

SCOPE AND APPLICABILITY

3 This accounting standard contains provisions relating to the statutory segmental disclosure requirements contained in companies legislation in the United Kingdom and the Republic of Ireland. All companies are required to comply with these provisions.

4 This accounting standard also contains provisions relating to the disclosure of inter-segment turnover, geographical segment result, segment net assets, origin of turnover, and segmental information about associated undertakings, which are not required by companies legislation. These provisions apply to any entity that:

(a) is a public limited company or has a public limited company as a subsidiary; or
(b) is a banking or insurance company or group (as defined for the purposes of Sections 1164 and 1165 of the Companies Act 2006); or
(c) exceeds the criteria, multiplied in each case by 10, for defining a medium-sized company under Section 465 of the Companies Act 2006, as amended from time to time by statutory instrument.

However, a subsidiary that is not a public limited company or a banking or insurance company need not comply with these provisions if its parent provides segmental information in compliance with this accounting standard or provides segment information in accordance with International Accounting Standards as defined by Section 474(1) of the Companies Act 2006 or International Financial Reporting Standards as issued by the International Accounting Standards Board.*

All entities are encouraged to apply the provisions of this accounting standard in all financial statements intended to give a true and fair view of the financial position and profit or loss. **5**

Where, in the opinion of the directors, the disclosure of any information required by this accounting standard would be seriously prejudicial to the interests of the reporting entity, that information need not be disclosed; but the fact that any such information has not been disclosed must be stated. This repeats the exemption contained in paragraph 55(5) of Schedule 4 to the Companies Act 1985† in the wider context of this accounting standard.‡ **6**

DETERMINING REPORTABLE SEGMENTS

Information contained in financial statements can be segmented in two principal ways – by class of business and geographically. The Companies Act 1985 recognises both of these bases in paragraph 55 of Schedule 4, referring to the geographical areas as 'markets'. Paragraph 55 states that in analysing the source (in terms of either business or market) of turnover or profit or loss the directors should have regard to the manner in which the company's activities are organised. Paragraph 55 also states that it is for the directors to determine whether the company has carried on business of two or more classes or has supplied markets that differ substantially from each other and that where, in the opinion of the directors, the classes of business or the markets do not differ substantially from each other they may be treated as one.† **7**

In identifying separate reportable segments, the directors should have regard to the overall purpose of presenting segmental information (as set out in paragraph 1) and the need of the user of the financial statements to be informed where an entity carries on operations in different classes of business or in different geographical areas that: **8**

(a) earn a return on investment that is out of line with the remainder of the business; or
(b) are subject to different degrees of risk; or
(c) have experienced different rates of growth; or
(d) have different potentials for future development.

Each class of business or geographical segment that is significant to an entity as a whole should be identified as a reportable segment. For the purposes of this accounting standard a segment should normally be regarded as significant if: **9**

(a) its third party turnover is ten per cent or more of the total third party turnover of the entity; or

Editor's note: *Amended with effect for accounting periods beginning on or after 1 January 2011.*

†*Throughout this statement of standard accounting practice, references to paragraph 55 of Schedule 4 to the Companies Act 1985 should be read in the Republic of Ireland as references to paragraph 41 of the Schedule to the Companies (Amendment) Act 1986.*

‡***Editor's note:*** *Schedule 4 to the Companies Act 1985 is replaced, with effect for accounting periods beginning on or after 6 April 2008 by Schedule 1 to the Large and Medium-sized Companies and Groups (Accounts and Reports) Regulations 2008 (SI 2008/410). The reference to paragraph 55 should be taken as a reference to paragraph 68 of that Schedule.*

(b) its segment result, whether profit or loss, is ten per cent or more of the combined result of all segments in profit or of all segments in loss, whichever combined result is the greater; or
(c) its net assets are ten per cent or more of the total net assets of the entity.

10 The directors should review the definitions of the segments annually and re-define them when appropriate. In doing so the directors should have regard to the fundamental objective of this accounting standard, which is to achieve, as far as possible, consistency and comparability between years.

CLASSES OF BUSINESS

11 A separate class of business is a distinguishable component of an entity that provides a separate product or service or a separate group of related products or services.

12 When deciding whether or not an entity operates in different classes of business, the directors should take into account the following factors:

(a) the nature of the products or services;
(b) the nature of the production processes;
(c) the markets in which the products or services are sold;
(d) the distribution channels for the products;
(e) the manner in which the entity's activities are organised;
(f) any separate legislative framework relating to part of the business, for example, a bank or an insurance company.

13 Although it is possible to identify certain characteristics that differentiate between classes of business, no single set of characteristics is universally applicable nor is any single characteristic determinative in all cases. Consequently, determination of an entity's classes of business must depend on the judgement of the directors.

GEOGRAPHICAL SEGMENTS

14 A geographical segment is a geographical area comprising an individual country or a group of countries in which an entity operates, or to which it supplies products or services.

15 A geographical analysis should help the user of the financial statements to assess the extent to which an entity's operations are subject to factors such as the following:
(a) expansionist or restrictive economic climates;
(b) stable or unstable political regimes;
(c) exchange control regulations;
(d) exchange rate fluctuations.

16 It is not practicable to define a method of grouping that will reflect all the differences between international business environments and that would apply to all entities. The selected grouping should reflect the purpose of presenting segmental information (as set out in paragraph 1) and the factors noted in paragraphs 8 and 15. Although geographical proximity may indicate similar economic trends and risks, this will not necessarily be the case.

INFORMATION TO BE DISCLOSED

General

The entity should define in its financial statements each reported class of business and geographical segment. 17

Turnover

The factors listed in paragraph 15 apply both to the geographical locations of the entity's operations and to the geographical locations of its markets. The user of the financial statements gains a fuller understanding of the entity's exposure to these factors, if turnover is disclosed according to both location of operations and location of markets. For the purposes of this accounting standard, origin of turnover is the geographical area *from* which products or services are supplied to a third party or another segment. Destination of turnover is the geographical area *to* which goods or services are supplied. Because disclosure relating to segment results and net assets will generally be based on location of operations, an analysis of turnover on the same basis will enable the user to match turnover, result and net assets on a consistent basis, and to relate all three to the perceived risks and opportunities of the segments. For these reasons this accounting standard requires the disclosure of sales by origin, but reporting entities should also disclose turnover by destination unless there is no material difference between the two. If there is no material difference, a statement to that effect is required. 18

Inter-segment sales and transfers are often a material part of the total turnover of the reportable segments and in such cases they should be analysed segmentally and shown separately. The geographical analysis of inter-segment turnover should be disclosed by origin. Analysis by destination usually has little or no value and would not normally be provided. 19

The Companies Act 1985 and the Companies (Northern Ireland) Order 1986 contain provisions exempting banking and insurance companies and groups from the requirement to disclose turnover in certain circumstances.* In the Republic of Ireland, similar exemptions are extended to special classes of companies (banking, discount and insurance companies) under the Companies Act 1963. Certain other entities – for example, building societies – are subject to different statutory rules from those applied to companies. Where turnover is not required by statute to be disclosed, it is not required by this accounting standard to be disclosed segmentally. The fact that such turnover has not been disclosed segmentally should be stated. 20

Segment result

The entity should disclose the result of each reportable segment before accounting for taxation, minority interests and extraordinary items. The geographical analysis of segment result should normally be based on the areas from which products or services are supplied. 21

In the majority of entities, different classes of business or geographical segments are financed by different proportions of interest-bearing debt and equity. The interest earned or incurred by individual segments is therefore a result of the entity's overall financial policy rather than a proper reflection of the results of the various segments. Consequently, comparisons of profit between segments or between different years for 22

***Editor's note:** *Similar exemptions may be available under the Companies Act 2006.*

the same segment are likely to be meaningless if interest is included in arriving at the result. For these reasons, it will normally be appropriate for segment results to be disclosed before taking account of interest. However, where all or part of the entity's business is to earn and/or incur interest (as in the financial sector, for example), or where interest income or expense is central to the business (as in the contracting or travel businesses, for example), interest should normally be included in arriving at the segment result.

Common costs

23 Common costs are costs relating to more than one segment. They should be treated in the way that the directors deem most appropriate in pursuance of the objectives of segmental reporting. Entities may apportion some common costs for the purpose of internal reporting and, in such cases, it may be reasonable for such costs to be similarly apportioned for external reporting purposes. If the apportionment would be misleading, common costs should not be apportioned in the segmental disclosures but should be deducted from the total of the segment results. Costs that are directly attributable to individual reportable segments are not common costs for the purposes of this accounting standard and therefore should be allocated to those segments, irrespective of the fact that they may have been borne by a different segment or by the Head Office.

Segment net assets

24 The net assets of each reportable segment should be disclosed. In most cases these will be the non-interest bearing operating assets less the non-interest bearing operating liabilities. However, to the extent that the segment result is disclosed after accounting for interest as described in paragraph 22, the corresponding interest-bearing operating assets and liabilities should also be included.

25 Segment operating assets and liabilities may include assets and liabilities relating exclusively to one segment and also an allocated portion of assets and liabilities that relate jointly to more than one segment. Assets and liabilities used jointly by more than one segment should be allocated to the segments on a reasonable basis. Assets and liabilities that are not used in the operations of any segment should not be allocated to segments. Operating assets of a segment should not normally include loans or advances to, or investments in, another segment unless interest therefrom has been included in arriving at the segment result on the basis set out in paragraph 22.

Associated undertakings

26 Sometimes associated undertakings form a significant part of a reporting entity's results or assets. In such circumstances the following information should be analysed segmentally and shown separately in the segmental report:

(a) the reporting entity's share of the profits or losses of associated undertakings before accounting for taxation, minority interests and extraordinary items; and
(b) the reporting entity's share of the net assets of associated undertakings (including goodwill to the extent that it has not been written off) stated, where possible, after attributing fair values to the net assets at the date of acquisition of the interest in each associated undertaking.

However, it is recognised that this information might be unobtainable or publication might be prejudicial to the business of the associate. In such circumstances the disclosure is not required but the reason for non-disclosure should be stated by way of note, together with a brief description of the omitted business or businesses.

For the purposes of this accounting standard, associated companies form a significant part of the reporting entity's results or assets if, in total, they account for at least 20% of the total result or 20% of the total net assets of the reporting entity. 27

General

The total of the amounts disclosed by segment should agree with the related total in the financial statements. If it does not, the reporting entity should provide a reconciliation between the two figures. Reconciling items should be properly identified and explained. 28

Comparative figures for the previous accounting period should be provided. If a change is made to the definitions of the segments or to the accounting policies that are adopted for reporting segmental information, the nature of the change should be disclosed. The reason for the change and the effect of the change should be stated. The previous year's figures should be restated to reflect the change. 29

Part 2 – Definition of terms

A *class of business* is a distinguishable component of an entity that provides a separate product or service or a separate group of related products or services. 30

A *geographical segment* is a geographical area comprising an individual country or group of countries in which an entity operates, or to which it supplies products or services. 31

Origin of turnover is the geographical segment from which products or services are supplied to a third party or to another segment. 32

Destination of turnover is the geographical segment to which products or services are supplied. 33

Part 3 – Standard accounting practice

If an entity has two or more classes of business, or operates in two or more geographical segments which differ substantially from each other, it should define its classes of business and geographical segments in its financial statements, and it should report with respect to each class of business and geographical segment the following financial information: 34

(a) turnover, distinguishing between (i) turnover derived from external customers and (ii) turnover derived from other segments;
(b) result, before accounting for taxation, minority interests and extraordinary items; and
(c) net assets.

The reporting entity should disclose the geographical segmentation of turnover by origin. It should also disclose turnover to third parties by destination or state where appropriate that this amount is not materially different from turnover to third parties by origin. Segment result will normally be disclosed before taking account of interest. However, where all or part of the entity's business is to earn and/or incur interest, or where interest income or expense is central to the business, interest should normally be included in arriving at the segment result. Net assets will normally be non-interest bearing operating assets less the non-interest bearing operating liabilities, but to the extent that the segment result is disclosed after accounting for interest the corresponding interest-bearing assets or liabilities should also be included.

35 When both parent and consolidated financial statements are presented, segmental information should be presented on the basis of the consolidated financial statements.

36 The reporting entity should disclose the following information segmentally in relation to its associated undertakings if these account for at least 20% of its total result or 20% of its total net assets:

(a) the entity's share of the results of associated undertakings before accounting for taxation, minority interests and extraordinary items; and
(b) the entity's share of the net assets of associated undertakings (including goodwill to the extent it has not been written off) stated, where possible, after attributing fair values to the net assets at the date of acquisition of the interest in each undertaking.

The segmental disclosure should be of the aggregate amounts of all associated undertakings for which the information is available and should be shown separately in the segmental report. However, this information need not be disclosed if it is unobtainable or publication would be prejudicial to the business of the associate. In such circumstances, the reason for non-disclosure should be stated by way of note, together with a brief description of the omitted business or businesses.

37 The total of the amounts disclosed by segment should agree with the related total in the financial statements. If it does not, the reporting entity should provide a reconciliation between the two amounts. Reconciling items should be properly identified and explained.

38 Comparative figures for the previous accounting period should be provided. If, however, on the first occasion on which an entity provides a segmental report the necessary information is not readily available, comparative figures need not be provided.

39 The directors should re-define the segments when appropriate. If a change is made to the definitions of the segments or to the accounting policies that are adopted for reporting segmental information, the nature of the change should be disclosed. The reason for the change and its effect should be stated. The previous year's figures should be re-stated to reflect the change.

40 This accounting standard contains provisions relating to the statutory segmental disclosure requirements contained in companies legislation in the United Kingdom and the Republic of Ireland. All companies are required to comply with these provisions.

This accounting standard also contains provisions relating to segmental disclosures which are not required by companies legislation.* These provisions apply to any entity that: 41

(a) is a public limited company or that has a public limited company as a subsidiary; or
(b) is a banking or insurance company or group (as defined for the purposes of Part VII of the Companies Act 1985); or
(c) exceeds the criteria, multiplied in each case by 10, for defining a medium-sized company under section 247† of the Companies Act 1985,‡ as amended from time to time by statutory instrument.

However, a subsidiary that is not a public limited company or a banking or insurance company need not comply with these provisions if its parent provides segmental disclosures in compliance with this accounting standard.

All other entities are encouraged to apply the provisions of this accounting standard in all financial statements intended to give a true and fair view of the financial position and profit or loss. 42

Where, in the opinion of the directors, the disclosure of any information required by this accounting standard would be seriously prejudicial to the interests of the reporting entity, that information need not be disclosed. The fact that any such information has not been disclosed must be stated. 43

Entities that are not required by statute to disclose turnover in their financial statements are not required by this accounting standard to disclose turnover segmentally. The fact that turnover has not been disclosed segmentally should be stated in the financial statements. 44

APPLICATION TO SMALLER ENTITIES

Reporting entities applying the Financial Reporting Standard for Smaller Entities currently applicable are exempt from this accounting standard. 44A

DATE FROM WHICH EFFECTIVE

The provisions of this statement of standard accounting practice should be adopted as soon as possible and regarded as standard in respect of financial statements relating to accounting periods beginning on or after 1 July 1990. 45

******Disclosures not required by the Companies Act 1985 are those set out in paragraphs 34(a)ii, 34(b) insofar as it relates to geographical segment result, 34(c), 34 insofar as it relates to origin of turnover, and 36. (**Editor's note:** Also, as from February 1996, paragraph 34(b) insofar as it relates to business segment result. This continues to be valid under the Companies Act 2006.)*

†Equivalent legal references:

Great Britain	Northern Ireland	Republic of Ireland
Companies Act 1985	*Companies (Northern Ireland) Order 1986*	*Companies (Amendment) Act*
Section 247	Article 256 (as amended)	Section 8

‡The reference to section 247 of the Companies Act 1985 is replaced by section 465 of the Companies Act 2006. The previous reference to banking and insurance companies is also amended to refer to sections 1164 and 1165 of the Companies Act 2006.

45A 'Improvements to Financial Reporting Standards 2010' issued in November 2010 amended paragraph 4. An entity shall apply this amendment for annual periods beginning on or after 1 January 2011. Earlier application is permitted. If an entity applies the amendment for an earlier period, it shall disclose that fact.

Part 4 – Legal and International Stock Exchange requirements in Great Britain and Northern Ireland

COMPANY LAW

*All paragraph references, unless otherwise indicated, are to the Schedules to the Companies Act 1985 and the Companies (Northern Ireland) Order 1986.**

46 Paragraph 55(1) of Schedule 4 requires all companies that, in the course of the financial year, have carried on business of two or more classes that (in the opinion of the directors) differ substantially from each other to state:

(a) a description of each class of business;
(b) the amount of turnover attributable to each class of business; and
(c) the amount of the profit or loss of the company before taxation that is, in the opinion of the directors, attributable to each class of business.†

47 Paragraph 55(2) of Schedule 4 requires all companies that, in the course of the financial year, have supplied geographical markets that (in the opinion of the directors) differ substantially from each other to state the amount of the turnover attributable to each market.

48 Paragraph 55(3) of Schedule 4 provides that, in analysing the source (in terms of either classes of business or markets) of turnover or profit or loss for the purposes of paragraph 55, the directors of the company shall have regard to the manner in which the company's activities are organised.

49 Paragraph 55(4) of Schedule 4 provides that, for the purposes of paragraph 55:

(a) classes of business which, in the opinion of the directors, do not differ substantially from each other shall be treated as one class;
(b) markets which, in the opinion of the directors, do not differ substantially from each other shall be treated as one market; and
(c) any amounts properly attributable to one class of business or to one market which are not material may be included in the amount stated in respect of another.

50 Paragraph 55(5) of Schedule 4 states that where, in the opinion of the directors, the disclosure of any information required by paragraph 55 would be seriously

**Under the Companies Act 2006:*

- *all references to paragraph 55 of Schedule 4 to the Companies Act 1985 should be taken to refer to Schedule 1 to the Large and Medium-sized Companies and Groups (Accounts and Reports) Regulations 2008 (SI 2008/410);*
- *all references to Schedule 9 should be taken to refer to Schedules 2 and 3 to SI 2008/410.*

†***Editor's note:*** *The parts of paragraph 55(1) and (3) relating to profit or loss were repealed in February 1996 (S.I. 1996 No. 189). In the case of small companies, paragraph 49 of Schedule 8 to the Companies Act 1985 requires that companies disclose only the percentage of turnover attributable to markets outside the United Kingdom. This requirement has been carried over into Schedule 1 to the Small Companies and Group (Accounts and Reports) Regulations 2008 (SI 2008/409).*

prejudicial to the interests of the company, that information need not be disclosed but the fact that any such information has not been disclosed must be stated.

Schedule 9 deals with the special provisions for banking and insurance companies and groups.* Paragraph 17 of Schedule 9 requires the following matters to be stated by way of note, if not otherwise shown: 51

(a) the turnover for the financial year, except in so far as it is attributable to the business of banking or discounting;
(b) if some or all of the turnover is omitted by reason of its being attributable to the business of banking or discounting, the fact that it is so omitted; and
(c) the method by which turnover stated is arrived at.

Paragraph 17(5) of Schedule 9 provides that a company should not be subject to the requirements of paragraph 17 if it is neither a parent company nor a subsidiary undertaking and the turnover which, apart from sub-paragraph 17(5), would be required to be stated does not exceed £1 million. 52

Schedule 10 deals with the directors' report where accounts are prepared in accordance with the special provisions for banking or insurance companies or groups.† Paragraph 2 provides that where a company prepares group accounts in accordance with the special provisions and, in the course of the financial year to which the accounts relate, the group has carried on business of two or more classes (other than banking or discounting of a class prescribed for the purpose of paragraph 17(2) of that Schedule) that in the opinion of the directors differ substantially from each other, there shall be contained in the directors' report a statement of: 53

(a) the proportions in which the turnover for the financial year (so far as stated in the consolidated accounts) is divided amongst those classes (describing them); and
(b) as regards business of each class, the extent or approximate extent (expressed in money terms) to which, in the opinion of the directors, the carrying on of business of that class contributed to, or restricted, the profit or loss of the company for that year (before taxation).

Classes of business which, in the opinion of the directors, do not differ substantially from each other, are to be treated as one class.

INTERNATIONAL STOCK EXCHANGE

The International Stock Exchange of the United Kingdom and the Republic of Ireland Ltd‡ sets out its requirements for segmental information in the 'Admission of Securities to Listing'.§ Section 5, Chapter 2, paragraph 21(c) of that publication requires: 54

> 'a geographical analysis of both net turnover and contribution to trading results of those trading operations carried on by the company (or group) outside the United Kingdom and the Republic of Ireland'.

Editor's note: *Schedule 9 as amended dealt with banking companies and groups; paragraph 76 required analysis of specified income items by geographical market. Schedule 9A dealt with insurance companies and groups; paragraph 75 required certain analysis by class of business.*

†***Editor's note:*** *Now repealed.*

‡***Editor's note:*** *The London and Republic of Ireland stock exchanges are now separate. In the UK, listing rules are now issued by the Financial Conduct Authority.*

§***Editor's note:*** *These requirements have been deleted as they are covered by SSAP 25.*

55 No analysis of the contribution to trading results is required unless the contribution to profit or loss from a specific area is 'abnormal' in nature. 'Abnormal' is defined as substantially out of line with the normal ratio of profit to turnover.

Part 5 – Legal and International Stock Exchange requirements in the Republic of Ireland

COMPANY LAW

All paragraph references, unless otherwise indicated, are to the Schedule to the Companies (Amendment) Act 1986.

56 Paragraph 41(1) requires all companies that, in the course of the financial year, have carried on business of two or more classes that (in the opinion of the directors) differ substantially from each other to state:

(a) a description of each class of business; and
(b) the amount of turnover attributable to each class of business.

57 Paragraph 41(2) requires all companies that, in the course of the financial year, have supplied geographical markets that (in the opinion of the directors) differ substantially from each other, to state the amount of the turnover attributable to each market.

58 Paragraph 41(3) provides that, in analysing the source (in terms of either classes of business or markets) of turnover, the directors of the company shall have regard to the manner in which the company's activities are organised.

59 Paragraph 41(4) provides that, for the purposes of paragraph 41:

(a) classes of business which, in the opinion of the directors, do not differ substantially from each other shall be treated as one class;
(b) markets which, in the opinion of the directors, do not differ substantially from each other shall be treated as one market; and
(c) any amounts properly attributable to one class of business or to one market which are not material may be included in the amount stated in respect of another.

60 Paragraph 41(5) states that where, in the opinion of the directors, the disclosure of any information required by paragraph 41 would be seriously prejudicial to the interests of the company, that information need not be disclosed but the fact that any such information has not been disclosed must be stated.

61 Banking, discount and insurance companies are regarded as special classes of companies and as such come within Part III of the Sixth Schedule to the Companies Act 1963 which exempts them from the disclosure requirements of the Schedule to the Companies (Amendment) Act 1986.

62 The International Stock Exchange of the United Kingdom and the Republic of Ireland Ltd* sets out its requirements for segmental information in the 'Admission of Securities to Listing'. Section 5, Chapter 2, paragraph 21(c) of that publication requires:

> 'a geographical analysis of both net turnover and contribution to trading results of those trading operations carried on by the company (or group) outside the United Kingdom and the Republic of Ireland'.

***Editor's note:** The London and Republic of Ireland stock exchanges are now separate. In the UK, the listing rules are now issued by the Financial Conduct Authority.*

No analysis of the contribution to trading results is required unless the contribution to profit or loss from a specific area is 'abnormal' in nature. 'Abnormal' is defined as substantially out of line with the normal ratio of profit to turnover. **63**

Paragraph 4(b) makes reference to Section 1164 of the Companies Act 2006. In Irish law, the equivalent reference is to 'section 2(2) company', as defined in Regulation 2(1) of the European Communities (Credit Institutions: Accounts) Regulations, 1992 (SI 1992/294).* **63A**

Paragraph 4(b) makes reference to Section 1165 of the Companies Act 2006. In Irish law, insurance companies are subject to the European Communities (Insurance Undertakings: Accounts) Regulations, 1996 (SI 1996/23); see Regulation 3. **63B**

Paragraph 4(c) makes reference to Section 465 of the Companies Act 2006. For the Irish law equivalent, please refer to section 8 of the Companies (Amendment) Act, 1986 (as amended by Regulation 4 of the European Communities (Accounts) Regulations, 1993 (SI 1993/396), Regulation 5 of the European Communities (International Financial Reporting Standards and Miscellaneous Amendments) Regulations 2005 (SI 2005/116) and Regulation 4 of the European Communities (Directive 2006/46/EC) Regulations 2009 (SI 2009/450)). **63C**

Paragraph 4 makes reference to Section 474(1) of the Companies Act 2006. In Irish law, the equivalent definition is provided in section 2(1) of the Companies Act, 1963 (No. 33 of 1963) as inserted by Regulation 9 and Schedule 1 to the European Communities (International Financial Reporting Standards and Miscellaneous Amendments) Regulations 2005 (SI 2005/116). **63D**

Part 6 – Compliance with International Accounting Standard No.14 'Reporting Financial Information by Segment'†

Compliance with the requirements of this accounting standard will ensure compliance with IAS 14 in all material respects, except in the following circumstances. **64**

(a) This accounting standard does not require the basis of inter-segment pricing to be disclosed. This information must be disclosed in order to comply with IAS 14.
(b) This accounting standard requires the disclosure of segment 'net assets', whereas IAS 14 refers to 'assets employed'. However, as stated in paragraph 34, net assets will normally be the non-interest bearing operating assets less the non-interest bearing operating liabilities, and in those cases net assets will not be materially different from assets employed.
(c) This accounting standard gives the following exemptions which do not appear in IAS 14.

    (i) An entity need not disclose segmental information if disclosure would be seriously prejudicial to its interests.

***Editor's note**: Paragraphs 63A to 63D added in November 2010.*

†***Editor's note:** With effect for accounting periods beginning on or after 1 January 2009, IAS 14 is replaced by IFRS 8* Operating Segments. *This standard takes a very different approach to that which underpins both IAS 14 and SSAP 25. In particular the segmentation required is based primarily on the internal reporting structure used within the entity, and the basis on which information is presented to the chief operating decision maker. Given the emphasis on internal reporting, the specific disclosures required (for example, the measure of profit to be analysed) are also based on the nature of the information that is used internally. IFRS 8 applies to companies and groups with traded securities, or in the process of a public listing, although the IASB has stated that it will reconsider this in the near future.*

(ii) An entity that is not required by statute to disclose turnover is not required to disclose turnover segmentally.

(iii) A subsidiary that is not a public limited company or a banking or insurance company need not make the segmental disclosures required by this accounting standard if its parent does so.

Appendix: Illustrative segmental report

This Appendix is for general guidance only and does not form part of the Statement of Standard Accounting Practice

	CLASSES OF BUSINESS							
	Industry A		Industry B		Other industries		Group	
	1990 £000	1989 £000	1990 £000	1989 £000	1990 £000	1989 £000	1990 £000	1989 £000
TURNOVER								
Total sales	33,000	30,000	42,000	38,000	26,000	23,000	101,000	91,000
Inter-segment sales	(4,000)	–	–	–	(12,000)	(14,000)	(16,000)	(14,000)
Sales to third parties	29,000	30,000	42,000	38,000	14,000	9,000	85,000	77,000
PROFIT BEFORE TAXATION								
Segment profit	3,000	2,500	4,500	4,000	1,800	1,500	9,300	8,000
Common costs							300	300
Operating profit							9,000	7,700
Net interest							(400)	(500)
							8,600	7,200
Group share of the profits before taxation of associated undertakings	1,000	1,000	1,400	1,200	–	–	2,400	2,200
Group profit before taxation							11,000	9,400
NET ASSETS								
Segment net assets	17,600	15,000	24,000	25,000	19,400	19,000	61,000	59,000
Unallocated assets							3,000	3,000
							64,000	62,000
Group share of the net assets of associated undertakings	10,200	8,000	8,800	9,000	–	–	19,000	17,000
Total net assets							83,000	79,000

GEOGRAPHICAL SEGMENTS

	United Kingdom		North America		Far East		Other		Group	
	1990 £000	1989 £000	1990 £000	1989 £000	1990 £000	1989 £000	1990 £000	1989 £000	1990 £000	1989 £000
TURNOVER										
Turnover by destination										
Sales to third parties	34,000	31,000	16,000	14,500	25,000	23,000	10,000	8,500	85,000	77,000
Turnover by origin										
Total sales	38,000	34,000	29,000	27,500	23,000	23,000	12,000	10,500	102,000	95,000
Inter-segment sales	–	–	(8,000)	(9,000)	(9,000)	(9,000)	–	–	(17,000)	(18,000)
Sale to third parties	38,000	34,000	21,000	18,500	14,000	14,000	12,000	10,500	85,000	77,000
PROFIT BEFORE TAXATION										
Segment profit	4,400	2,900	2,500	2,300	1,800	1,900	1,000	900	9,300	8,000
Common costs									300	300
Operating profit									9,000	7,700
Net interest									(400)	(500)
									8,600	7,200
Group share of the profit before taxation of associated undertakings	950	1,000	1,450	1,200	–	–	–	–	2,400	2,200
Group profit before taxation									11,000	9,400
NET ASSETS										
Segment net assets	16,000	15,000	25,000	26,000	16,000	15,000	4,000	3,000	61,000	59,000
Unallocated assets									3,000	3,000
									64,000	62,000
Group share of the net assets of associated undertakings	8,500	7,000	10,500	10,000	–	–	–	–	19,000	17,000
Total net assets									83,000	79,000

Unallocated assets consist of assets at the Group's head office in London amounting to £2.4 million (1989 £2.5 million) and at the Group's regional office in Hong Kong amounting to £0.6 million (1989 £0.5 million).

Financial Reporting Standard 1 (Revised 1996) is set out in paragraphs 1–50.

The Statement of Standard Accounting Practice set out in paragraphs 4–50 should be read in the context of the Objective as stated in paragraph 1 and the definitions set out in paragraphs 2 and 3 and also of the Foreword to Accounting Standards and the Statement of Principles for Financial Reporting currently in issue.

The Explanation set out in paragraphs 51–68 shall be regarded as part of the Statement of Standard Accounting Practice insofar as it assists in interpreting that statement.

Appendix III 'The development of the FRS' reviews considerations and arguments that were thought significant by members of the Board in reaching the conclusions on FRS 1 (Revised 1996).

[FRS 1]
Cash flow statements (revised 1996)*†

(Issued October 1996)

Contents

	Paragraphs
Summary	
Financial Reporting Standard 1 (Revised 1996)	
Objective	1
Definitions	2–3
Statement of Standard Accounting Practice	4–50
Scope	5
Preparation of cash flow statements	6
Format for cash flow statements	7
Classification of cash flows	8–10
Classification of cash flows by standard heading	11–32
Operating activities	11–12
Returns on investments and servicing of finance	13–15
Taxation	16–18
Capital expenditure and financial investment	19–21
Acquisitions and disposals	22–24
Equity dividends paid	25
Management of liquid resources	26–28
Financing	29–32
Reconciliation to net debt	33
Banks	34
Insurance companies and groups	35–36
Exceptional and extraordinary items and cash flows	37–38
Value Added Tax and other taxes	39–40
Foreign currencies	41
Hedging transactions	42
Groups	43–44
Acquisitions and disposals of subsidiary undertakings	45
Material non-cash transations	46
Restrictions on remittability	47
Comparative figures	48
Date from which effective	49
Withdrawal of FRS 1 (issued September 1991)	50
Explanation	51–68
Definitions	51–53
Cash flow	51

****Editor's note:*** *FRS 1 has been revised by FRS 25. The various changes to FRS 1 have been included in the text, with footnotes showing where the changes have been made. The changes are effective for accounting periods beginning on or after 1 January 2005.*

†***Editor's note:*** *The matters covered in FRS 1 are dealt with in Section 7 of FRS 102.*

Liquid resources	52
Net debt	53
Scope	54
Classification of cash flows	55–57
Classification of cash flows by standard heading	58–61
Operating activities	58–59
Returns on investments and servicing of finance	60
Taxation	61
Insurance companies and groups	62
Exceptional and extraordinary items and cash flows	63
Value Added Tax	64
Foriegn currencies	65
Hedging transactions	66
Material non-cash transations	67
Restrictions on remittability	68

Adoption of FRS 1 (Revised 1996) by the Board

Appendices

I Examples of cash flow statements – for an individual company, a group, a bank and an insurance group

II Compliance with International Accounting Standards

III The development of the FRS

Cash flow statements (revised 1996)

Summary

GENERAL

a Financial Reporting Standard 1 (Revised 1996) 'Cash Flow Statements' requires reporting entities within its scope to prepare a cash flow statement in the manner set out in the FRS. Cash flows are increases or decreases in amounts of cash, and cash is cash in hand and deposits repayable on demand at any qualifying institution less overdrafts from any qualifying institution repayable on demand.

SCOPE

The FRS applies to all financial statements intended to give a true and fair view of the financial position and profit or loss (or income and expenditure) except those of:

(i) subsidiary undertakings where 90 per cent or more of the voting rights are controlled within the group, provided that consolidated financial statements in which those subsidiary undertakings are included are publicly available;
(ii) mutual life assurance companies;
(iii) pension funds;
(iv) open-ended investment funds, subject to certain further conditions;
(v) for two years from the effective date of the FRS, building societies that, as required by law, prepare a statement of source and application of funds in a prescribed format; and
(vi) small entities (based on the small companies exemption in companies legislation).

FORMAT FOR THE CASH FLOW STATEMENT

c An entity's cash flow statement should list its cash flows for the period classified under the following standard headings:

- operating activities (using either the direct or indirect method)
- returns on investments and servicing of finance
- taxation
- capital expenditure and financial investment
- acquisitions and disposals
- equity dividends paid
- management of liquid resources
- financing.

The last two headings can be shown in a single section provided a subtotal ... for each heading.

d Individual categories of inflows and outflows under the standard headin... disclosed separately either in the cash flow statement or in a note to it u... allowed to be shown net. Cash inflows and outflows may be shown n... to the management of liquid resources or financing and the inflov... either:

(i) relate in substance to a single financing transaction; or*
(ii) are due to short maturities and high turnover occurring from rollover or reissue (for example, short-term deposits or a commercial paper programme).

The requirement to show cash inflows and outflows separately does not apply to cash flows relating to operating activities.

LINKS TO OTHER PRIMARY STATEMENTS

Because the information given by a cash flow statement is best appreciated in the context of the information given by the other primary statements, the FRS requires two reconciliations, between: **e**

(i) operating profit and the net cash flow from operating activities; and
(ii) the movement in cash in the period and the movement in net debt.

Neither reconciliation forms part of the cash flow statement but each may be given either adjoining the statement or in a separate note.

The movement in net debt should identify the following components and reconcile these to the opening and closing balance sheet amounts: **f**

- the cash flows of the entity
- the acquisition or disposal of subsidiary undertakings (excluding cash balances)
- other non-cash changes
- the recognition of changes in market value and exchange rate movements.

INSURANCE COMPANIES AND GROUPS

Insurance companies and groups should include the cash flows of their long-term business only to the extent of cash transferred to, and available to meet the obligations of, the company or group as a whole. The cash flow statement of an insurance company or group should include a section for cash flows relating to portfolio investments rather than a section for cash flows relating to the management of liquid resources. **g**

BANKS

The cash flow statement of an entity qualifying as a bank should include under operating activities cash flows relating to investments held for trading. A bank need not include a section on the management of liquid resources or the reconciliation of cash flows to the movement in net debt. **h**

OTHER DISCLOSURES

Material transactions not resulting in movements of cash should be disclosed in the notes to the cash flow statement, if the disclosure is necessary for an understanding of the underlying transactions. A consolidated cash flow statement should identify and explain the circumstances and effect of restrictions preventing the transfer of cash from one part of the group to meet obligations of another. **i**

**Editor's note*: *Amended by FRS 25.*

Financial Reporting Standard 1 (Revised 1996)

Objective

1 The objective of this FRS is to ensure that reporting entities falling within its scope:

(a) report their cash generation and cash absorption for a period by highlighting the significant components of cash flow in a way that facilitates comparison of the cash flow performance of different businesses; and

(b) provide information that assists in the assessment of their liquidity, solvency and financial adaptability.

Definitions

2 The following definitions shall apply in this FRS and in particular in the Statement of Standard Accounting Practice set out in paragraphs 4–50.

Active market:-
A market of sufficient depth to absorb the investment held without a significant effect on the price.

Bank:-
An entity whose business is to receive deposits or other repayable funds from the public and to grant credits for its own account.*

Cash:-
Cash in hand and deposits repayable on demand with any qualifying financial institution, less overdrafts from any qualifying financial institution repayable on demand. Deposits are repayable on demand if they can be withdrawn at any time without notice and without penalty or if a maturity or period of notice of not more than 24 hours or one working day has been agreed. Cash includes cash in hand and deposits denominated in foreign currencies.

Cash flow:-
An increase or decrease in an amount of cash.

Equity dividends:-
Dividends relating to instruments classified as equity in accordance with FRS 25 '(IAS 32) Financial Instruments: Disclosure and Presentation'.†

**This definition is based on:*

(a) in Great Britain, section 262 of the Companies Act 1985, itself based on the definition in the Banking Act 1987;

(b) in Northern Ireland, Article 270 of the Companies (Northern Ireland) Order 1986;

(c) in the Republic of Ireland, section (2)(2) (other than paragraph (b)) of the Companies (Amendment) Act 1986.

***Editor's Note:** The definition of a banking company is now included in section 1164 of the Companies Act 2006.*

†***Editor's note:** The definition of equity dividends has been changed by FRS 25 with effect for accounting periods beginning on or after 1 January 2005.*

Insurance company or group:-
A company that carries on an insurance business and is regulated accordingly or an insurance group as defined in the relevant legislation.*

Investment fund:-†
An entity:
(a) whose business consists of investing its funds mainly in securities, with the aim of spreading investment risk and giving members the benefit of the results of the management of its funds;
(b) none of whose holdings in other entities (except those in other investment funds) represents more than 15 per cent by value of the investing entity's investments; and
(c) that has not retained more than 15 per cent of the income it derives from securities.

Liquid resources:-
Current asset investments held as readily disposable stores of value. A readily disposable investment is one that:
(a) is disposable by the reporting entity without curtailing or disrupting its business;
and is either:
(b)(i) readily convertible into known amounts of cash at or close to its carrying amount, or
(b)(ii) traded in an active market.

Net debt:–
The borrowings of the reporting entity (comprising capital instruments classified as liabilities in accordance with FRS 25 '(IAS 32) Financial Instruments: Disclosure and Presentation', together with related derivatives, and obligations under finance leases) less cash and liquid resources. Where cash and liquid resources exceed the borrowings of the entity reference should be to 'net funds' rather than to 'net debt'.‡

Non-equity dividends:-
Dividends relating to instruments classified as liabilities in accordance with FRS 25 '(IAS 32) Financial Instruments: Disclosure and Presentation'.§

**In the UK an insurance company is one to which Part II of the Insurance Companies Act 1982 applies. The equivalent reference in the Republic of Ireland is the Companies (Amendment) Act 1986 section 2(3). In the UK an insurance group is defined in section 255A of the Companies Act 1985. In the Republic of Ireland an insurance company or group is one to which Regulation 3 of the European Community (Insurance Undertakings: Accounts) Regulations 1996 applies.*
***Editor's note:** The definition of an insurance company and insurance group is now included in section 1164 of the Companies Act 2006.*

†This definition is based on three of the four conditions defining an investment company in companies legislation– in Great Britain section 266 of the Companies Act 1985; in Northern Ireland, Article 274 of the Companies (Northern Ireland) Order 1986; and in the Republic of Ireland, section 47 of the Companies (Amendment) Act 1983. Under the definition above, investment companies as defined in companies legislation will qualify as investment funds but so should certain investment entities that are not companies or do not qualify under companies legislation because they distribute capital.
***Editor's note:** The definition of an investment company is now included in section 833 of the Companies Act 2006.*

*‡**Editor's note:** The definition of net debt has been changed by FRS 25 with effect for accounting periods beginning on or after 1 January 2005.*

*§**Editor's note:** The definition of non-equity dividends has been changed by FRS 25 with effect for accounting periods beginning on or after 1 January 2005.*

Overdraft:-
A borrowing facility repayable on demand that is used by drawing on a current account with a qualifying financial institution.

Qualifying financial institution:-
An entity that as part of its business receives deposits or other repayable funds and grants credits for its own account.

3 References to companies legislation mean:

(a) in Great Britain, the Companies Act 1985;*
(b) in Northern Ireland, the Companies (Northern Ireland) Order 1986; and
(c) in the Republic of Ireland, the Companies Acts 1963-90 and the European Communities (Companies: Group Accounts) Regulations 1992.

Statement of Standard Accounting Practice

4 Reporting entities falling within the scope of paragraph 5 of Financial Reporting Standard 1 (Revised 1996) are required to provide as a primary statement within the reporting entity's financial statements a cash flow statement drawn up in accordance with the standard accounting principles set out in paragraphs 6-48 of the FRS.

SCOPE

5 The FRS applies to all financial statements intended to give a true and fair view of the financial position and profit or loss (or income and expenditure) except those of:
(a) subsidiary undertakings where 90 per cent or more of the voting rights are controlled within the group, provided that consolidated financial statements in which the subsidiary undertakings are included are publicly available.
(b) mutual life assurance companies.
(c) pension funds.
(d) open-ended investment funds that meet all the following conditions:

(i) substantially all of the entity's investments are highly liquid;
(ii) substantially all of the entity's investments are carried at market value; and
(iii) the entity provides a statement of changes in net assets.

(e) for two years from the effective date of the FRS, building societies, as defined by the Building Societies Act 1986 in the UK and by the Building Societies Act 1989 in the Republic of Ireland, that prepare, as required by law, a statement of source and application of funds in a prescribed format.
(f) companies incorporated under companies legislation and entitled to the exemptions available in the legislation for small companies when filing accounts with the Registrar of Companies.
(g) entities that would have been in category (f) above if they were companies incorporated under companies legislation.

PREPARATION OF CASH FLOW STATEMENTS

6 The cash flow statement should include all the reporting entity's inflows and outflows of cash. Transactions that do not result in cash flows of the reporting entity should not be reported in the cash flow statement.

***Editor's note:** *This should now be read as though it also referred to the Companies Act 2006.*

Format for cash flow statements

An entity's cash flow statement should list its cash flows for the period classified under the following standard headings: 7

- operating activities
- dividends from joint ventures and associates
- returns on investments and servicing of finance
- taxation
- capital expenditure and financial investment
- acquisitions and disposals
- equity dividends paid
- management of liquid resources
- financing.

The first seven headings should be in the sequence set out above. Operating cash flows can be presented by either the direct method (showing the relevant constituent cash flows) or the indirect method (calculating operating cash flows by adjustment to the operating profit reported in the profit and loss account). The cash flows relating to the management of liquid resources and financing can be combined under a single heading provided that the cash flows relating to each are shown separately and separate subtotals are given. Appendix I of the FRS contains examples of cash flow statements for an individual company, a group, a bank and an insurance group.

CLASSIFICATION OF CASH FLOWS

Except for cash inflows and outflows that are shown net (as permitted by paragraph 9), the individual categories of inflows and outflows under the standard headings set out in paragraphs 11-32 should be disclosed separately, where material, in the cash flow statement or in a note. The cash flow classifications may be subdivided further to give a fuller description of the activities of the reporting entity or to provide segmental information. 8

The requirement to show cash inflows and outflows separately does not apply to cash flows relating to operating activities. Cash inflows and outflows within the management of liquid resources or financing may also be netted against each other if they either: 9

(a) relate in substance to a single financing transaction, or*
(b) are due to short maturities and high turnover occurring from rollover or reissue (for example, short-term deposits or a commercial paper programme).

Each cash flow should be classified according to the substance of the transaction giving rise to it. That substance should be used to determine the most appropriate standard heading under which to report any cash flows that are not specified in the categories set out in paragraphs 11-32 below. However, cash flows relating to interest paid should always be classified under 'returns on investments and servicing of finance' even if the interest has been capitalised in the other primary statements. 10

**Editor's note:* *This paragraph has been amended by FRS 25. For accounting periods beginning on or after 1 January 2005 it no longer makes reference to FRS 4.*

CLASSIFICATION OF CASH FLOWS BY STANDARD HEADING

Operating activities

11 Cash flows from operating activities are in general the cash effects of transactions and other events relating to operating or trading activities, normally shown in the profit and loss account in arriving at operating profit. They include cash flows in respect of operating items relating to provisions, whether or not the provision was included in operating profit.

12 A reconciliation between the operating profit reported in the profit and loss account and the net cash flow from operating activities should be given either adjoining the cash flow statement or as a note. The reconciliation is not part of the cash flow statement: if adjoining the cash flow statement, it should be clearly labelled and kept separate. The reconciliation should disclose separately the movements in stocks, debtors and creditors related to operating activities and other differences between cash flows and profits.

12A Dividends received from joint ventures and associates should be included as separate items between operating activities and returns on investment and servicing of finance.

Returns on investments and servicing of finance

13 'Returns on investments and servicing of finance' are receipts resulting from the ownership of an investment and payments to providers of finance, non-equity shareholders (eg the holders of preference shares) and minority interests, excluding those items required by paragraphs 11-32 to be classified under another heading.

14 Cash inflows from returns on investments and servicing of finance include:

(a) interest received, including any related tax recovered; and
(b) dividends received, net of any tax credits (except dividends from equity accounted entities).

15 Cash outflows from returns on investments and servicing of finance include:

(a) interest paid (even if capitalised), including any tax deducted and paid to the relevant tax authority;
(b) cash flows that are treated as finance costs (this will include issue costs on debt and non-equity share capital);*
(c) the interest element of finance lease rental payments;
(d) dividends paid on non-equity shares of the entity; and
(e) dividends paid to minority interests.

Taxation

16 The cash flows included under the heading 'taxation' are cash flows to or from taxation authorities in respect of the reporting entity's revenue and capital profits. For a subsidiary undertaking, cash flows relating to group relief should be included in this section. Cash flows in respect of other taxation, including payments and receipts in respect of Value Added Tax, other sales taxes, property taxes and other taxes not assessed on the profits of the reporting entity, should be dealt with as set out in paragraphs 39-40 of the FRS.

**Editor's note:* *This paragraph has been amended by FRS 25. For accounting periods beginning on or after 1 January 2005 it no longer makes reference to FRS 4.*

Taxation cash inflows include cash receipts from the relevant tax authority of tax rebates, claims or returns of overpayments. For a subsidiary undertaking, payments received from other members of the group for group relief should be included as cash inflows. 17

Taxation cash outflows include cash payments to the relevant tax authority of tax, including payments of advance corporation tax. For a subsidiary undertaking, payments made to other members of the group for group relief should be included as cash outflows. 18

Capital expenditure and financial investment

The cash flows included in 'capital expenditure and financial investment' are those related to the acquisition or disposal of any fixed asset other than one required to be classified under 'acquisitions and disposals' as specified in paragraphs 22-24 of the FRS and any current asset investment not included in liquid resources dealt with in paragraphs 26-28. If no cash flows relating to financial investment fall to be included under this heading the caption may be reduced to 'capital expenditure'. 19

Cash inflows from 'capital expenditure and financial investment' include: 20

(a) receipts from sales or disposals of property, plant or equipment; and
(b) receipts from the repayment of the reporting entity's loans to other entities or sales of debt instruments of other entities other than receipts forming part of an acquisition or disposal or a movement in liquid resources, as specified respectively in paragraphs 22-24 and 26-28 of the FRS.

Cash outflows from 'capital expenditure and financial investment' include: 21

(a) payments to acquire property, plant or equipment; and
(b) loans made by the reporting entity and payments to acquire debt instruments of other entities other than payments forming part of an acquisition or disposal or a movement in liquid resources, as specified respectively in paragraphs 22-24 and 26-28 of the FRS.

Acquisitions and disposals

The cash flows included in 'acquisitions and disposals' are those related to the acquisition or disposal of any trade or business, or of an investment in an entity that is or, as a result of the transaction, becomes or ceases to be either an associate, a joint venture, or a subsidiary undertaking. 22

Cash inflows from 'acquisitions and disposals' include: 23

(a) receipts from sales of investments in subsidiary undertakings, showing separately any balances of cash and overdrafts transferred as part of the sale;
(b) receipts from sales of investments in associates or joint ventures; and
(c) receipts from sales of trades or businesses.

Cash outflows from 'acquisitions and disposals' include: 24

(a) payments to acquire investments in subsidiary undertakings, showing separately any balances of cash and overdrafts acquired;
(b) payments to acquire investments in associates and joint ventures; and
(c) payments to acquire trades or businesses.

Equity dividends paid

25 The cash outflows included in 'equity dividends paid' are dividends paid on the reporting entity's, or, in a group, the parent's, equity shares, excluding any advance corporation tax.

Management of liquid resources

26 The 'management of liquid resources' section should include cash flows in respect of liquid resources as defined in paragraph 2. Each entity should explain what it includes as liquid resources and any changes in its policy. The cash flows in this section can be shown in a single section with those under 'financing' provided that separate subtotals for each are given.

27 Cash inflows in management of liquid resources include:

(a) withdrawals from short-term deposits not qualifying as cash in so far as not netted under paragraph 9(b); and
(b) inflows from disposal or redemption of any other investments held as liquid resources.

28 Cash outflows in management of liquid resources include :

(a) payments into short-term deposits not qualifying as cash in so far as not netted under paragraph 9(b); and
(b) outflows to acquire any other investments held as liquid resources.

Financing

29 Financing cash flows comprise receipts or repayments of principal from or to external providers of finance. The cash flows in this section can be shown in a single section with those under 'management of liquid resources' provided that separate subtotals for each are given.

30 Financing cash inflows include:

(a) receipts from issuing shares or other equity instruments; and
(b) receipts from issuing debentures, loans, notes, and bonds and from other long-term and short-term borrowings (other than overdrafts).

31 Financing cash outflows include:

(a) repayments of amounts borrowed (other than overdrafts);
(b) the capital element of finance lease rental payments;
(c) payments to reacquire or redeem the entity's shares; and
(d) payments of expenses or commissions on any issue of equity shares.

32 The amounts of any financing cash flows received from or paid to equity accounted entities should be disclosed separately.

RECONCILIATION TO NET DEBT

33 A note reconciling the movement of cash in the period with the movement in net debt should be given either adjoining the cash flow statement or in a note. The reconciliation is not part of the cash flow statement: if adjoining the cash flow statement, it should be clearly labelled and kept separate. The changes in net debt should be

analysed from the opening to the closing component amounts showing separately, where material, changes resulting from:

(a) the cash flows of the entity;
(b) the acquisition or disposal of subsidiary undertakings;
(c) other non-cash changes; and
(d) the recognition of changes in market value and exchange rate movements.

Where several balance sheet amounts or parts thereof have to be combined to form the components of opening and closing net debt, sufficient detail should be shown to enable the cash and other components of net debt to be respectively traced back to the amounts shown under the equivalent captions in the balance sheet. A possible format for the analysis of net debt is provided in the examples in Appendix I.

BANKS

Banks should include as cash only cash and balances at central banks and loans and advances to banks repayable on demand. The cash flow statement of a bank should include under operating activities receipts and payments relating to loans made to other entities and cash flows relating to investments held for trading. A bank need not include a section on the management of liquid resources nor the reconciliation of cash flows to the movement in net debt. Appendix I contains an example of a cash flow statement for a bank. **34**

INSURANCE COMPANIES AND GROUPS

The cash flow statement of an entity qualifying as an insurance company or group should include a section for cash flows relating to 'portfolio investments' rather than a section for cash flows relating to the 'management of liquid resources'. Instead of the analysis of the movement in net debt that is generally required, insurance companies and groups should provide an analysis of the movement in portfolio investments less financing, either adjoining the cash flow statement or in a note. The reconciliation is not part of the cash flow statement: if adjoining the cash flow statement, it should be clearly labelled and kept separate. The reconciliation of operating profit to net cash flow from operating activities should normally take profit or loss on ordinary activities before tax as its starting point. Appendix I contains an example of a cash flow statement for an insurance group. **35**

Insurance companies and groups, other than mutual life assurance companies to which the FRS does not apply, should include the cash flows of their long-term business—long-term life, pensions and annuity businesses or their equivalents in relation to overseas operations—only to the extent of cash transferred and available to meet the obligations of the company or group as a whole. The note analysing the movements in the balance sheet amounts of portfolio investments and financing during the period should distinguish movements relating to the long-term business to the extent that these are included in the balance sheet amounts. **36**

EXCEPTIONAL AND EXTRAORDINARY ITEMS AND CASH FLOWS*

Where cash flows relate to items that are classified as exceptional or extraordinary in the profit and loss account they should be shown under the appropriate standard **37**

**Editor's note:* *Notwithstanding the comments in this section, there are no extraordinary items in the UK since the introduction of FRS 3.*

headings, according to the nature of each item. The cash flows relating to exceptional or extraordinary items should be identified in the cash flow statement or a note to it and the relationship between the cash flows and the originating exceptional or extraordinary item should be explained.

38 Where cash flows are exceptional because of their size or incidence but are not related to items that are treated as exceptional or extraordinary in the profit and loss account, sufficient disclosure should be given to explain their cause and nature.

VALUE ADDED TAX AND OTHER TAXES

39 Cash flows should be shown net of any attributable Value Added Tax or other sales tax unless the tax is irrecoverable by the reporting entity. The net movement on the amount payable to, or receivable from, the taxing authority should be allocated to cash flows from operating activities unless a different treatment is more appropriate in the particular circumstances concerned. Where restrictions apply to the recoverability of such taxes, the irrecoverable amount should be allocated to those expenditures affected by the restrictions. If this is impracticable, the irrecoverable tax should be included under the most appropriate standard heading.

40 Taxation cash flows other than those in respect of the reporting entity's revenue and capital profits and Value Added Tax, or other sales tax, should be included within the cash flow statement under the same standard heading as the cash flow that gave rise to the taxation cash flow, unless a different treatment is more appropriate in the particular circumstances concerned.

FOREIGN CURRENCIES

41 Where a portion of a reporting entity's business is undertaken by a foreign entity, the cash flows of that entity are to be included in the cash flow statement on the basis used for translating the results of those activities in the profit and loss account of the reporting entity. The same basis should be used in presenting the movements in stocks, debtors and creditors in the reconciliation between operating profit and cash from operating activities. Where intragroup cash flows are separately identifiable and the actual rate of exchange at which they took place is known, that rate, or an approximation thereto, may be used to translate the cash flows in order to ensure that they cancel on consolidation. If the rate used to translate intragroup cash flows is not the actual rate, any exchange rate differences arising should be included in the effect of exchange rate movements shown as part of the reconciliation to net debt.

HEDGING TRANSACTIONS

42 When a futures contract, forward contract, option contract or swap contract is accounted for as a hedge, the cash flows of the contract should be reported under the same standard heading as the transaction that is the subject of the hedge.

GROUPS

43 Cash flows that are internal to the group should be eliminated in the preparation of a consolidated cash flow statement. Where a subsidiary undertaking joins or leaves a group during a financial year the cash flows of the group should include the cash flows of the subsidiary undertaking concerned for the same period as that for which the group's profit and loss account includes the results of the subsidiary undertaking.

The cash flows of any equity accounted entity should be included in the group cash flow statement only to the extent of the actual cash flows between the group and the entity concerned, for example dividends received in cash and loans made or repaid. 44

ACQUISITIONS AND DISPOSALS OF SUBSIDIARY UNDERTAKINGS

A note to the cash flow statement should show a summary of the effects of acquisitions and disposals of subsidiary undertakings indicating how much of the consideration comprised cash. Material effects on amounts reported under each of the standard headings reflecting the cash flows of a subsidiary undertaking acquired or disposed of in the period should be disclosed, as far as practicable. This information could be given by dividing cash flows between continuing and discontinued operations and acquisitions. 45

MATERIAL NON-CASH TRANSACTIONS

Material transactions not resulting in movements of cash of the reporting entity should be disclosed in the notes to the cash flow statement if disclosure is necessary for an understanding of the underlying transactions. 46

RESTRICTIONS ON REMITTABILITY

A note to the cash flow statement should identify the amounts and explain the circumstances where restrictions prevent the transfer of cash from one part of the business or group to another. 47

COMPARATIVE FIGURES

Comparative figures should be given for all items in the cash flow statement and such notes thereto as are required by the FRS with the exception of the note to the statement that analyses changes in the balance sheet amounts making up net debt (or the equivalent note for insurance companies and groups) and the note of the material effects of acquisitions and disposals of subsidiary undertakings on each of the standard headings. 48

DATE FROM WHICH EFFECTIVE

The accounting practices set out in the FRS should be regarded as standard in respect of financial statements relating to accounting periods ending on or after 23 March 1997. Earlier adoption is encouraged but not required.* 49

WITHDRAWAL OF FRS 1 (ISSUED SEPTEMBER 1991)

The FRS supersedes FRS 1 issued in September 1991. 50

Editor's note: The changes introduced by FRS 25 are effective for accounting periods beginning on or after 1 January 2005.

Explanation

DEFINITIONS

Cash flows

51 Cash flows are defined as increases or decreases in cash. Cash includes cash in hand, deposits repayable on demand and overdrafts. Deposits are repayable on demand if they are in practice available within 24 hours without penalty. No investments, however liquid or near maturity, are included as cash. Overdrafts are included as cash because of their role as negative cash balances—a cheque drawn on an account can either reduce the cash balance or increase the overdraft. Although banks take large volumes of short-term and demand deposits, they do not usually have borrowings with the characteristics of an overdraft.

Liquid resources

52 The definition of liquid resources is expressed in general terms, emphasising the liquidity of the investment and its function as a readily disposable store of value rather than setting out a narrow range of investment instruments. Depending on the entity's policy (which should be disclosed), term deposits, government securities, loan stock, equities and derivatives may each form part of that entity's liquid resources, provided they meet the definition. Short-term deposits would also fall within the definition, though the requirement that they should be readily convertible into known amounts of cash at or close to their carrying amounts would tend to exclude any that are more than one year from maturity on acquisition.

Net debt

53 The objective of the reconciliation of cash flows to the movement in net debt is to provide information that assists in the assessment of liquidity, solvency and financial adaptability. Net debt is defined to include borrowings less liquid resources because movements in net debt so defined are widely used as indicating changes in liquidity, and therefore assist in assessing the financial strength of the entity. The definition excludes non-equity shares of the entity because, although these have features that may be similar to those of borrowings, they are not actually liabilities of the entity. The definition also excludes debtors and creditors because, while these are short-term claims on and sources of finance to the entity, their main role is as part of the entity's trading activities.

SCOPE

54 Most small reporting entities are exempt from the requirement to include a cash flow statement as part of their financial statements. This exemption does not extend to public companies or to banking companies, insurance companies, authorised persons under the Financial Services Act 1986,* or members of a group containing one or more of the above-mentioned entities. The scope of this exemption is currently being re-examined as part of a wider examination of the reporting requirements for small entities. However, the Board encourages small reporting entities to include a cash flow statement as part of their financial statements, if it would provide useful

**In the UK. The equivalent reference in the Republic of Ireland is the Investment Intermediaries Act 1995.*
Editor's note*: This should now be read as a reference to the Financial Services and Markets Act 2000.*

information to users of those financial statements and the benefits of the exercise outweigh the costs.*

CLASSIFICATION OF CASH FLOWS

In setting the conditions for netting cash flows, paragraph 9 permits the cash flows over the period of a single financing transaction to be reported net.† **55**

In order to improve the comparability of cash flow statements of different entities, paragraphs 11-31 give examples of certain standard subdivisions that should be separately disclosed, if material. Reporting entities are encouraged, however, to disclose additional information relevant to their particular circumstances. One form of segmentation that may often be useful is a division of cash flows from operating activities into those relating to continuing and to discontinued operations (as defined in FRS 3 'Reporting Financial Performance'). In some circumstances it may also be useful to divide cash flows in a way that reflects different degrees of access to the underlying cash balances—this may be of especial relevance in regulated industries such as the insurance industry. **56**

Certain accounting standards, such as SSAP 13 'Accounting for research and development', SSAP 21 'Accounting for leases and hire purchase contracts' and FRS 5 'Reporting the Substance of Transactions', specify how certain transactions are to be recognised and classified for financial reporting on the basis of the substance of the transaction. In order to achieve consistent treatment in the cash flow statement this FRS requires cash flows, too, to be classified according to the substance of the transaction giving rise to them. For example, cash flows relating to development costs that are capitalised would be included under 'capital expenditure'. Cash flows relating to finance leases are to be divided into the part relating to interest, to be classified under 'servicing of finance', and the part making up repayment of the capital amount, to be classified under 'financing'. Similarly, the cash flows relating to finance costs are to be classified under 'returns on investments and servicing of finance'. However, the Board believes that it is important to show the total of cash flows relating to interest paid in the cash flow statement. The FRS therefore requires interest paid to be included as servicing of finance, regardless of whether it is capitalised.‡ **57**

CLASSIFICATION OF CASH FLOWS BY STANDARD HEADING

Operating activities

The FRS allows operating cash flows to be presented using either the direct or the indirect method. A cash flow statement presented under the direct method shows operating cash receipts and payments (including, in particular, cash receipts from customers, cash payments to suppliers and cash payments to and on behalf of employees), aggregating to the net cash flow from operating activities. Rather than reporting the individual component cash flows to arrive at the net cash inflow or outflow from operating activities, the cash flow statement under the indirect method derives the net cash inflow or outflow by means of a reconciliation from operating profit. The FRS requires the reconciliation even if the direct method is used. The **58**

***Editor's note:** *See also section D of the Financial Reporting Standard for Smaller Entities.*

†***Editor's note:*** *The original final sentence of this paragraph, which referred to FRS 4, has been removed by FRS 25.*

‡***Editor's note:*** *Two references to FRS 4 in this paragraph have been removed by FRS 25.*

reconciliation adjusts operating profit for non-cash charges and credits and brings in operating item cash flows relating to provisions, whether or not the provision was deducted in arriving at operating profit. Examples of such cash flows are redundancy payments falling under a provision for the termination of an operation or for a fundamental reorganisation or restructuring (paragraph 20a and b of FRS 3 'Reporting Financial Performance'), also operating item cash flows provided for on an acquisition.

59 In some businesses material debtors and creditors may arise in relation to the purchase and sale of investments, including investments forming part of liquid resources. The changes in such debtors and creditors should be included in the reconciliation of operating profit to the net cash flow from operating activities only to the extent that the purchase and sale of the investments giving rise to them form part of the operating activities of the entity.

Returns on investments and servicing of finance

60 Interest paid and received and dividends received may result from investing activities, the management of liquid resources, financing or in some cases operating activities. To the extent that entities such as banks, insurance companies or investment companies show interest received or paid and dividends received in their profit and loss accounts as part of their operating profit they should include related cash flows as part of their operating cash flows, unless the interest paid clearly relates to financing—for example, relating to a bank's subordinated loans—in which case it should be included under 'returns on investments and servicing of finance'.

Taxation

61 The taxation cash flows of a reporting entity in relation to revenue and capital profits may result from complex computations that are affected by the operating, investing and financing activities of an entity. The Board believes that it is not useful to divide taxation cash flows into constituent parts relating to the activities that gave rise to them because the apportionment will, in many cases, have to be made on an arbitrary basis. As taxation cash flows generally arise from activities in an earlier period, apportioning the taxation cash flows would in any event not necessarily report the taxation cash flows along with the transactions that gave rise to them. Accordingly, the Board believes that taxation cash flows in relation to revenue and capital profits should be disclosed in a separate section within the cash flow statement entitled 'taxation'.

INSURANCE COMPANIES AND GROUPS

62 One purpose of a cash flow statement is to provide information that assists in the assessment of the liquidity, solvency and financial adaptability of an entity. This objective, however, is of only limited application to an insurance company or group. In interpreting the information given by the cash flow statement of an insurance company or group, users should bear in mind that cash inflows of premiums to insurance companies may not increase their liquidity in the same way as cash received for interest or dividends because the receipt of premiums engenders provision requirements for future claims and reserve requirements for solvency.

EXCEPTIONAL AND EXTRAORDINARY ITEMS AND CASH FLOWS*

The FRS requires cash flows relating to exceptional or extraordinary items to be identified and explained, to allow a user to gain an understanding of the effect of the underlying transactions on the cash flows. This requirement means that cash flows relating to reorganisation charges that are exceptional must be disclosed separately and explained. The FRS also requires identification of cash flows that are exceptional because of their size or incidence but are not related to items that are treated as exceptional or extraordinary in the profit and loss account. For a cash flow to be exceptional on the grounds of its size alone, it must be exceptional in relation to cash flows of a similar nature. A large prepayment against a pension liability is an example of a possible exceptional cash flow unrelated to an exceptional or extraordinary item in the profit and loss account. **63**

VALUE ADDED TAX

The cash flows of an entity include Value Added Tax (VAT) where appropriate and thus strictly the various elements of the cash flow statement should include VAT. However, this treatment does not take into account the fact that normally VAT is a short-term timing difference as far as the entity's overall cash flows are concerned and the inclusion of VAT in the cash flows may distort the allocation of cash flows to standard headings. The Board believes that, in order to avoid this distortion and to show cash flows attributable to the reporting entity's activities, cash flows should be shown net of sales taxes and the net movement on the amount payable to, or receivable from, the taxing authority should be allocated to cash flows from operating activities unless a different treatment is more appropriate in the particular circumstances concerned. **64**

FOREIGN CURRENCIES

Because of the complementary nature of the profit and loss account and the cash flow statement in reflecting different but related aspects of an entity's performance in the period, the standard requires the cash flow statement to be translated using the same rate as the profit and loss account, unless the actual rate at the date of the transaction is used. Cash flows between members of a group should not be included in the consolidated cash flow statement. However, these cash flows may not cancel unless the actual rate at the date of transfer is used for translation. The FRS allows the actual rate to be used where intragroup cash flows are separately identifiable and the actual rate is known. **65**

HEDGING TRANSACTIONS

Entities may undertake hedging transactions that result in cash flows. The Board is considering as part of its project on derivatives and other financial instruments the way in which such transactions should be reflected in financial statements. As an interim measure it has decided to confine the recognition of hedges in cash flow statements. An example of the presentation of a hedging transaction in accordance with the FRS would be the inclusion under 'returns on investments and servicing of **66**

*****Editor's note**: Notwithstanding the comments in this paragraph, there are no extraordinary items in the UK since the introduction of FRS 3.*

finance' of the cash flows of interest rate swaps held as a hedge of an entity's own debt.*

MATERIAL NON-CASH TRANSACTIONS

67 Consideration for transactions may be in a form other than cash. Since the purpose of a cash flow statement is to report cash flows, non-cash transactions should not be reported in a cash flow statement. However, to obtain a full picture of the alterations in financial position caused by the transactions for the period, separate disclosure of material non-cash transactions (such as shares issued for the acquisition of a subsidiary, the exchange of major assets or the inception of a finance lease contract) is also necessary.

RESTRICTIONS ON REMITTABILITY

68 The note identifying the amounts and explaining the circumstances where restrictions prevent the transfer of cash from one part of the business or group to another should refer only to circumstances where access is severely restricted by external factors such as strict exchange control rather than where the sole constraint is a special purpose designated by the reporting entity itself. Depending on the regulatory environment, cash balances in escrow, deposited with a regulator or held within an employee share ownership trust may be subject to restrictions on remittability that should be disclosed.

* ***Editor's note**: The project on derivatives and other financial instruments gave rise to FRS 25 and FRS 26.*

Adoption of FRS 1 (revised 1996) by the Board

Financial Reporting Standard 1 (Revised 1996) – 'Cash Flow Statements' was approved for issue by the nine members of the Accounting Standards Board.

Sir David Tweedie (Chairman)
Allan Cook (Technical Director)
David Allvey
Ian Brindle
John Coombe
Raymond Hinton
Huw Jones
Professor Geoffrey Whittington
Ken Wild

Appendix I – Examples of cash flow statements

EXAMPLE 1 A CASH FLOW STATEMENT FOR AN INDIVIDUAL COMPANY – XYZ LIMITED
CASH FLOW STATEMENT FOR THE YEAR ENDED 31 DECEMBER 1996

Reconciliation of operating profit to net cash inflow from operating activities

	£000	£000
Operating profit		6,022
Depreciation charges		899
Increase in stocks		(194)
Increase in debtors		(72)
Increase in creditors		234
Net cash inflow from operating activities		6,889

CASH FLOW STATEMENT

Net cash inflow from operating activities		6,889
Returns on investments and servicing of finance (note 1)		2,999
Taxation		(2,922)
Capital Expenditure		(1,525)
		5,441
Equity dividends paid		(2,417)
		3,024
Management of liquid resources (note 1)		(450)
Financing (note 1)		57
Increase in cash		**2,631**

Reconciliation of net cash flow to movement in net debt (note 2)

Increase in cash in the period	**2,631**	
Cash to repurchase debenture	149	
Cash used to increase liquid resources	450	
Change in net debt*		**3,230**
Net debt at 1.1.96		**(2,903)**
Net funds at 31.12.96		**327**

**In this example all changes in net debt are cash flows.*

NOTES TO THE CASH FLOW STATEMENT

Note 1 – GROSS CASH FLOWS

	£000	£000
Returns on investments and servicing of finance		
Interest received	3,011	
Interest paid	(12)	
		2,999
Capital expenditure		
Payments to acquire intangible fixed assets	(71)	
Payments to acquire tangible fixed assets	(1,496)	
Receipts from sales of tangible fixed assets	42	
		(1,525)
Management of liquid resources		
Purchase of treasury bills	(650)	
Sale of treasury bills	200	
		(450)
Financing		
Issuing of ordinary share capital	211	
Repurchase of debenture loan	(149)	
Expenses paid in connection with share issues	(5)	
		57

Note 2 – ANALYSIS OF CHANGES IN NET DEBT

	At 1 Jan 1996 £000	Cash flows £000	Other changes £000	At 31 Dec 1996 £000
Cash in hand, at bank	42	847		889
Overdrafts	(1,784)	1,784		
		2,631		
Debt due within 1 year	(149)	149	(230)	(230)
Debt due after 1 year	(1,262)		230	(1,032)
Current asset investments	250	450		700
TOTAL	(2,903)	3,230	–	327

EXAMPLE 2 A CASH FLOW STATEMENT FOR A GROUP – XYZ GROUP PLC

CASH FLOW STATEMENT FOR THE YEAR ENDED 31 DECEMBER 1996

	£000	£000
Cash flow from operating activities (note 1)		15,672
Dividends received from associates		350
Returns on investments and servicing of finance*(note 2)		(2,239)
Taxation		(2,887)
Capital expenditure and financial investment (note 2)		(865)
Acquisitions and disposals (note 2)		(17,824)
Equity dividends paid		(2,606)
Cash outflow before use of liquid resources and financing		**(10,399)**
Management of liquid resources (note 2)		700
Financing (note 2) - Issue of shares	600	
Increase in debt	2,347	
		2,947
Decrease in cash in the period		**(6,752)**

Reconciliation of net cash flow to movement in net debt (note 3)

	£000	£000
Decrease in cash in the period	**(6,752)**	
Cash inflow from increase in debt and lease financing	(2,347)	
Cash inflow from decrease in liquid resources	(700)	
Change in net debt resulting from cash flows		(9,799)
Loans and finance leases acquired with subsidiary		(3,817)
New finance leases		(2,845)
Translation difference		643
Movement in net debt in the period		**(15,818)**
Net debt at 1.1.96		**(15,215)**
Net debt at 31.12.96		**(31,033)**

**This heading would include any dividends received other than those from equity accounted entities included in operating activities.*

NOTES TO THE CASH FLOW STATEMENT

Note 1 – RECONCILIATION OF OPERATING PROFIT TO OPERATING CASH FLOWS

	Continuing	Discontinued	Total
	£000	£000	£000
Operating Profit	18,829	(1,616)	17,213
Depreciation charges	3,108	380	3,488
Cash flow relating to previous year restructuring provision (note 4)		(560)	(560)
Increase in stocks	(11,193)	(87)	(11,280)
Increase in debtors	(3,754)	(20)	(3,774)
Increase in creditors	9,672	913	10,585
Net cash inflow from continuing operating activities	16,662		
Net cash outflow in respect of discontinued activities		(990)	
Net cash inflow from operating activities			15,672

Note 2 – ANALYSIS OF CASH FLOWS FOR HEADINGS NETTED IN THE CASH FLOW STATEMENT

	£000	£000
Returns on investments and servicing of finance		
Interest received	508	
Interest paid	(1,939)	
Preference dividend paid	(450)	
Interest element of finance lease rental payments	(358)	
Net cash outflow for returns on investments and servicing of finance		(2,239)
Capital Expenditure and financial investment		
Purchase of tangible fixed assets	(3,512)	
Sale of trade investment	1,595	
Sale of plant and machinery	1,052	
Net cash outflow for capital expenditure and financial investment		(865)
Acquisitions and disposals		
Purchase of subsidiary undertaking	(12,705)	
Net overdrafts acquired with subsidiary	(5,516)	
Sale of business	4,208	
Purchase of interest in a joint venture	(3,811)	
Net cash outflow for acquisitions and disposals		(17,824)

Management of liquid resources*		
Cash withdrawn from 7 day deposit	200	
Purchase of government securities	(5,000)	
Sale of government securities	4,300	
Sale of corporate bonds	1,200	
Net cash outflow from management of liquid resources		700
Financing		
Issue of ordinary share capital		600
Debt due with a year:		
increase in short-term borrowings	2,006	
repayment of secured loan	(850)	
Debt due beyond a year:		
new secured loan repayable in 2000	1,091	
new unsecured loan repayable in 1998	1,442	
Capital element of finance lease rental payments	(1,342)	
		2,347
Net cash inflow from financing		2,947

Note 3 – ANALYSIS OF NET DEBT

	At 1 Jan 1996	Cash Flow	Acquisition† (excl. cash and overdrafts)	Other non-cash changes	Exchange movement	At 31 Dec 1996
	£000	£000	£000	£000	£000	£000
Cash in hand, at bank	235	(1,250)			1,392	377
Overdrafts	(2,528)	(5,502)			(1,422)	(9,452)
		(6,752)				
Debt due after 1 year	(9,640)	(2,533)	(1,749)	2,560	(792)	(12,154)
Debt due within 1 yr	(352)	(1,156)	(837)	(2,560)	1,465	(3,440)
Finance leases	(4,170)	1,342	(1,231)	(2,845)		(6,904)
		(2,347)				
Current asset investments	1,240	(700)				540
TOTAL	(15,215)	(9,799)	(3,817)	(2,845)	643	(31,033)

**XYZ Group PLC includes resources term deposits of less than a year, government securities and AA rated corporate bonds.*

†This column would include any net debt (excluding cash and overdrafts) disposed of with a subsidiary undertaking.

Note 4 – CASH FLOW RELATING TO EXCEPTIONAL ITEMS

The operating cash outflows include under discontinued activities an outflow of £560,000, which relates to the £1,600,000 exceptional provision for a fundamental restructuring made in the 1995 accounts.

Note 5 - MAJOR NON-CASH TRANSACTIONS

a. During the year the group entered into finance lease arrangements in respect of assets with a total capital value at the inception of the leases of £2,845,000.

b. Part of the consideration for the purchases of subsidiary undertakings and the sale of a business that occurred during the year comprised shares and loan notes respectively. Further details of the acquisitions and the disposal are set out below.

Note 6 – PURCHASE OF SUBSIDIARY UNDERTAKINGS

	£000
Net assets acquired	
Tangible fixed assets	12,194
Investments	1
Stocks	9,384
Debtors	13,856
Taxation recoverable	1,309
Cash at bank and in hand	1,439
Creditors	(21,715)
Bank overdrafts	(6,955)
Loans and finance leases	(3,817)
Deferred taxation	(165)
Minority shareholders' interests	(9)
	5,522
Goodwill	16,702
	22,224
Satisfied by	
Shares allotted	9,519
Cash	12,705
	22,224

The subsidiary undertakings acquired during the year contributed £1,502,000 to the group's net operating cash flows, paid £1,308,000 in respect of net returns on investments and servicing of finance, paid £522,000 in respect of taxation and utilised £2,208,000 for capital expenditure.

Note 7 – SALE OF BUSINESS

	£000
Net assets disposed of	
Fixed assets	775
Stocks	5,386
Debtors	474
	6,635
Loss on disposal	(1,227)
	5,408
Satisfied by	
Loan notes	1,200
Cash	4,208
	5,408

The business sold during the year contributed £200,000 to the group's net operating cash flows, paid £252,000 in respect of net returns on investments and servicing of finance, paid £145,000 in respect of taxation and utilised £209,000 for capital expenditure.

EXAMPLE 3 **A CASH FLOW STATEMENT FOR A BANK – XYZ INTERNATIONAL BANK PLC**
CASH FLOW STATEMENT FOR THE YEAR ENDED 31 DECEMBER 1996

Reconciliation of operating profit to net operating cash flows

	£m	£m
Operating profits		223.6
Increase in accrued income and prepayments		(161.2)
Increase in accruals and deferred income		118.1
Provision for bad and doubtful debts		20.8
Loans and advances written off net of recoveries		(50.7)
Depreciation and amortisation		42.4
Interest on subordinated loan added back		9.9
Profits on sale of investment debt and equity securities		(1.1)
Provisions for liabilities and charges		3.4
Other non-cash movements		6.3
Net cash flow from trading activities		211.5
Net increase in collections/transmissions	(81.1)	
Net increase in loans and advances to banks and customers	(1,419.1)	
Net increase in deposits by banks and customer accounts	2,542.8	
Net increase in debt securities in issue	39.9	
Net increase in non-investment debt and equity securities	(197.3)	
Net increase in other assets	(18.7)	
Net increase in other liabilities	18.6	
		885.1
Net cash inflow from operating activities		1,096.6

CASH FLOW STATEMENT	
Net cash inflow from operating activities	**1,096.6**
Dividends from associates	10.3
Returns on investments and servicing of finance (note 1)	(20.5)
Taxation	(88.0)
Capital expenditure and financial investment (note 1)	(90.3)
	908.1
Acquisitions and disposals (note 1)	15.1
Equity dividends paid	(57.2)
	866.0
Financing (note 1)	6.0
Increase in cash	**872.0**

NOTES TO THE CASH FLOW STATEMENT

Note 1 – GROSS CASH FLOWS

Returns on investments and servicing of finance	£m	£m
Interest paid on loan capital	(9.9)	
Preference dividends paid	(10.4)	
Dividends paid to minority shareholders in subsidiary undertaking	(0.2)	
		(20.5)
Capital expenditure and financial investment		
Purchase of investment securities	(14.7)	
Sale and maturity of investment securities	5.7	
Purchase of tangible fixed assets	(121.4)	
Sales of tangible fixed assets	40.1	
		(90.3)
Acquisitions and disposals		
Investment in associated undertaking	(56.1)	
Sale of investment in associated undertaking	71.2	
		15.1
Financing		
Issue of ordinary share capital	18.3	
Repayments of loan capital	(12.3)	
		6.0

Note 2 – ANALYSIS OF THE BALANCES OF CASH AS SHOWN IN THE BALANCE SHEET

	At 1.1.96	Cash flow	At 31.12.96
	£m	£m	£m
Cash and balances at central banks	1,342.9	148.5	1491.4
Loans and advances to other banks repayable on demand	23,743.6	723.5	24,467.1
	25,086.5	872.0	25,958.5

The group is required to maintain balances with the Bank of England which, at 31 December 1996, amounted to £54.0 million (1995 - £43.3 million).

Certain subsidiary undertakings of the group are required by law to maintain reserve balances with the Federal Reserve Bank in the United States of America. Such reserve balances amounted to $30.4 million at 31 December 1996 (1995 - $28.6 million).

Note 3 – ANALYSIS OF CHANGES IN FINANCING DURING THE YEAR

	Share capital	Loan capital
	£m	£m
Balance at 1 January 1996	435.3	1,248.1
Effect of foreign exchange differences		(115.7)
Cash inflow/(outflow) from financing	18.3	(12.3)
Other movements	(0.1)	
Balances at 31 December 1996	453.5	1,120.1

***EXAMPLE 4* A CASH FLOW STATEMENT FOR AN INSURANCE GROUP – XYZ INSURANCE GROUP PLC**
CASH FLOW STATEMENT FOR THE YEAR ENDED 31 DECEMBER 1996

Profit on ordinary activities before tax

	£m	£m
Operating profit before taxation after interest		300.2
Depreciation of tangible fixed assets	31.6	
Increase in general insurance technical provisions	198.5	
Decrease in amounts owed by agents	18.1	
Profits relating to long-term business	(135.3)	
Cash received from long-term business (note 1)	74.0	
Loan interest expense	38.7	
		225.6
Net cash inflow from operating activities		525.8

CASH FLOW STATEMENT

Net cash inflow from general business	484.4	
Shareholders' net cash inflow from long-term business	74.0	
Other operating cash flows attributable to shareholders	(32.6)	
Net cash inflow from operating activities		**525.8**
Dividends from associates		22.1
Interest paid (note 2)		(41.9)
Taxation paid		(54.2)
Capital expenditure		(52.1)
Acquisitions and disposals (note 2)		(313.5)
Equity dividends paid		(135.3)
Financing (note 2)		424.6
		375.5

CASH FLOWS WERE INVESTED AS FOLLOWS:

Increase in cash holdings		**22.8**
Net portfolio investment (not including long-term business) (note 2)		
Ordinary shares (note 2)	127.2	
Fixed income securities (note 2)	27.9	
Investment properties (note 2)	197.6	
		352.7
Net investment of cash flows		**375.5**

Movement in opening and closing portfolio investments net of financing (note 3)

	£m	£m	£m
Net cash inflow for the period	**22.8**		
Cash flow			
Portfolio investments	352.7		
Increase in loans	(213.9)		
Movement arising from cash flows		161.6	
Movement in long-term business		82.8	
Acquired with subsidiary		145.1	
Changes in market values and exchange rate effects		142.6	
Total movement in portfolio investments net of financing			532.1
Portfolio investments net of financing at 1.1.96			**2,692.3**
Portfolio investments net of financing at 31.12.96			**3,224.4**

NOTES TO THE CASH FLOW STATEMENT

Note 1 – CASH FLOWS OF THE LONG-TERM BUSINESS (OPTIONAL)

	£m
Premiums received	497.3
Claims paid	(326.1)
Net portfolio investments	(66.9)
Other net cash flows	(14.4)
Net cash inflow before retention and transfers	89.9
Transferred to general fund	(74.0)
Cash retained in long-term business	15.9

Note 2 – ANALYSIS OF CASH FLOWS FOR HEADINGS NETTED IN THE CASH FLOW STATEMENT

	£m	£m
Interest paid		
Interest paid	(35.2)	
Interest element of finance lease rental payments	(6.7)	
		(41.9)
Acquisitions and disposals		
Acquisition of subsidiary	(330.4)	
Net cash acquired with subsidiary	16.9	
		(313.5)
Financing		
Issue of ordinary share capital	210.7	
Repayment of long-term loan	(232.7)	
New fixed rate loan repayable 2000	446.6	
Net cash inflow from financing		424.6
Portfolio investments		
Purchase of ordinary shares	(869.5)	
Purchase of fixed income securities	(1,325.3)	
Purchase of investment property	(197.6)	
Sale of ordinary shares	742.3	
Sale of fixed income securities	1,297.4	
Net cash outflow on portfolio investments		(352.7)

Note 3 – MOVEMENT IN CASH, PORTFOLIO INVESTMENTS AND FINANCING

	At 1 Jan 1996*	Cash Flow	Changes in long-term business	Acquired with subsidiary (excl. cash)	Changes to market value and currencies	Other changes	At 31 Dec 1996*
	£m	£m	£m	£m	£m	£m	£m
Cash in hand, at bank	15.3	22.8	15.9		(2.3)		51.7
Ordinary shares	1,258.1	127.2	25.1	128.4	77.2		1,616.0
Fixed income securities	2,246.7	27.9	41.8	122.8	36.4		2,475.6
Investment properties	390.5	197.6			(12.4)		575.7
		352.7					
Loans due within 1 year	(325.7)	232.7		(19.7)	16.1	(31.2)	(127.8)
Loans due after 1 year	(892.6)	(446.6)		(86.4)	27.6	31.2	(1,366.8)
		(213.9)					
TOTAL	2,692.3	161.6	82.8	145.1	142.6	–	3,224.4

Note 4 - PURCHASE OF SUBSIDIARY UNDERTAKING

	£m	£m
Net cash acquired with subsidiary undertaking	16.9	
Portfolio investments less financing acquired with subsidiary undertaking	145.1	
Other net assets	108.1	
		270.1
Goodwill		60.3
		330.4
Settled by:		
Payment of cash		330.4

The subsidiary undertakings acquired during the year contributed £57.4m to the group's net operating cash flows, paid £6.2m in respect of interest, paid £4.9m in respect of taxation and utilised £13.2m for capital expenditure.

**These amounts are the same as the balance sheet amounts reported by the insurance group and include amounts relating to long-term business which are required by the EC Insurance Accounts Directive to be consolidated.*

Appendix II – Compliance With International Accounting Standards

1 The International Accounting Standard on cash flows is IAS 7 'Cash Flow Statements'. IAS 7 requires an entity to present its cash flows from operating, investing and financing activities. The cash flows to be reported are inflows and outflows of cash and cash equivalents leading to the reporting of the change in cash and cash equivalents for the period. For the reasons set out in Appendix III the FRS has modified the original FRS 1, which required a cash flow statement similar to that prepared under IAS 7.

The main difference between the standards

2 The FRS defines cash flows to include only movements in cash (cash in hand and deposits repayable on demand, less overdrafts). IAS 7 defines cash flows as movements in both cash and cash equivalents. Cash equivalents are defined as short-term, highly liquid investments that are readily convertible to known amounts of cash and subject to insignificant risk of changes in value. In the FRS cash flows relating to cash equivalents are to be included in the new 'management of liquid resources' section. The narrower definition of cash in the FRS is consistent with the definition of 'cash' in IAS 7.

Minor differences between the standards

3 The requirements of the FRS also differ from IAS 7 in the following ways:

- IAS 7 does not have any exemptions from its scope. The FRS gives exemption to small entities, subsidiary undertakings 90 per cent of whose voting rights are controlled within the group, mutual life assurance companies, pension funds and certain open-ended investment funds. Building societies that prepare a statement of source and application of funds in the prescribed format are permitted two years' exemption from the effective date of the FRS.
- IAS 7 (paragraph 22) allows the following cash flows to be reported net:

  (a) cash receipts and payments on behalf of customers when the cash flows reflect the activities of the customer rather than those of the entity; and

  (b) cash receipts and payments for items in which the turnover is quick, the amounts are large, and the maturities are short.

Cash flows fulfilling the conditions for net reporting in paragraph 9 of the FRS would also fulfil the conditions in paragraph 22(b) of IAS 7. The FRS has no equivalent permission for cash flows relating to customers to be shown net, since for some businesses the cash flows relating to customers can be an important source of finance.

- IAS 7 classifies cash flows under three headings: 'cash flows from operating activities', 'cash flows from investing activities', and 'cash flows from financing activities'. The FRS specifies a fuller analysis using eight headings.
- Unlike the FRS, IAS 7 does not require a reconciliation of the movement in cash flows to the movement in net debt.
- IAS 7 requires cash flows of a foreign subsidiary to be translated at the exchange rates prevailing at the dates of the cash flows. A weighted average exchange rate may be used that approximates to the actual rate. The FRS states that cash flows should be translated at the same rate as the profit and loss account but allows the use of actual rates or an approximation thereto for intragroup transactions.

Appendix III The development of the FRS

HISTORY

In September 1991 the Board issued FRS 1 'Cash Flow Statements' to replace SSAP 10 'Statements of source and application of funds'. The requirement for a cash flow statement instead of a statement of source and application of funds represented a radical change in financial reporting. In March 1994, when companies had had two years' practical experience with FRS 1, the Board called for comment on the functioning of the standard. The revised FRS is based on the subsequent proposals in FRED 10 'Revision of FRS 1 "Cash Flow Statements"' and the comments received on them. 1

THE FUNCTION OF A CASH FLOW STATEMENT

A cash flow statement has increasingly come to be recognised as a useful addition to the balance sheet and profit and loss account in their portrayal of financial position, performance and financial adaptability. Historical cash flow information gives an indication of the relationship between profitability and cash-generating ability, and thus of the quality of the profit earned. In addition, analysts and other users of financial information often, formally or informally, develop models to assess and compare the present value of the future cash flows of entities. Historical cash flow information could be useful to check the accuracy of past assessments and indicate the relationship between the entity's activities and its receipts and payments. 2

Assessing the opportunities and risks of an entity's business and the stewardship of its management requires an understanding of the nature of its business, which includes the way it generates and uses cash. A cash flow statement in conjunction with a profit and loss account and balance sheet provides information on financial position and performance as well as liquidity, solvency and financial adaptability. It is, therefore, important that the cash flow statement should cross-refer to the information given in the other primary statements. For this reason FRS 1 required a reconciliation of operating profit to cash flow from operating activities and some reconciliation with balance sheet figures. The revised FRS clarifies the link between cash flows and balance sheet movements by requiring a reconciliation between the cash flow statement and components of 'net debt', a widely used tool of financial analysis. 3

Although a cash flow statement shows information about the reporting entity's cash flows in the reporting period, it provides incomplete information for assessing future cash flows. Some cash flows result from transactions that took place in an earlier period and some cash flows are expected to result in further cash flows in a future period. Accordingly, cash flow statements should normally be used in conjunction with profit and loss accounts and balance sheets when making an assessment of future cash flows. 4

The Board specified a cash flow statement in FRS 1 rather than continue with a funds flow statement, which was usually based on changes in working capital, for the reasons given below. 5

(a) Funds flow data based on movements in working capital can obscure movements relevant to the liquidity and solvency of an entity. For example, a significant decrease in cash available may be masked by an increase in stock or debtors. Entities may, therefore, run out of cash while reporting increases in working capital. Similarly, a decrease in working capital does not necessarily indicate a cash shortage and a danger of failure.

(b) As cash flow monitoring is a normal feature of business life and not a specialised accounting technique, cash flow is a concept that is more widely understood than are changes in working capital.
(c) Cash flows can be a direct input into a business valuation model and, therefore, historical cash flows may be relevant in a way not possible for funds flow data.
(d) A funds flow statement is based largely on the difference between two balance sheets. It reorganises such data, but does not provide new data. The cash flow statement and associated notes required by the FRS may include data not disclosed in a funds flow statement.

CHANGES IMPLEMENTED BY THE REVISED FRS

General comments

6 The comments received on the functioning of FRS 1 indicated widespread support for a cash flow statement but also a belief that the statements produced by applying FRS 1 fell short in a number of respects from what could be achieved. The Board concluded that FRS 1 could be improved to make the cash flow statement a better means of communication between preparers and users of financial statements. FRED 10's proposals for amending the cash flow standard were generally well received by the commentators and have largely been taken up in the revised FRS.

Definition of cash flows and introduction of 'management of liquid resources' section

7 The issue most often raised in the comments on FRS 1 was its definition of cash equivalents, although there was no consensus on an alternative. The definition was criticised as not reflecting the way in which businesses were managed: in particular, the requirement that to be a cash equivalent an investment had to be within three months of maturity when acquired was considered unrealistic. The definition of cash equivalents had also been a controversial issue in the comments on ED 54, the exposure draft preceding FRS 1. As a result of these comments the Board proposed to omit cash equivalents from cash flows and use only cash (cash in hand and deposits repayable on demand, less overdrafts) as the basis of the cash flows reported in a cash flow statement. The proposal received widespread support and the revised FRS is based on a similar definition of cash.

8 To reflect better the way that entities manage their cash and similar assets and to distinguish cash flows in relation to this activity from other investment decisions, the revised FRS has a section dealing separately with the cash flows arising from the management of liquid resources. Liquid resources are to be identified by each reporting entity according to its policy (which should be disclosed) with the proviso that they include only current asset investments. Cash flows relating to items such as short-term deposits and other cash equivalents under the original standard are to be reported as cash flows under 'management of liquid resources'. The comments supported the FRED's proposal to introduce a section for cash flows relating to the management of liquid resources.

9 The adoption of a strict cash approach and introduction of the section for cash flows relating to the management of liquid resources have the following advantages. The approach:

(a) avoids an arbitrary cut-off point in the definition of cash equivalents;
(b) distinguishes cash flows arising from accumulating or using liquid resources from those for other investing activities; and

(c) provides information about an entity's treasury activities that was not previously available to the extent that the instruments dealt in fell within the definition of cash equivalents.

INFORMATION ABOUT LIQUIDITY

The FRS sets out in its objective the twin purposes of a cash flow statement: to report the cash generation and cash absorption of an entity; and to provide information to assist users to assess its liquidity, solvency and financial adaptability. The majority of those commenting on FRED 10 accepted this objective but a minority believed that a cash flow statement cannot reflect appropriately changes in an entity's liquidity because it focuses only on changes in an entity's cash. Those expressing this concern usually supported a change in focus to the movement in an entity's net debt or net funds. **10**

The FRS retains the focus on cash rather than using a broader measure such as net debt because the focus on cash: **11**

- highlights the significant components of cash that make up a cash flow statement;
- shows as cash flow movements transactions that would not be captured by a broader measure such as net debt in any case where the transaction involved an exchange of items that both fell within that broader measure;
- facilitates comparison of the cash flow performances of different entities; and
- is in line with the international focus on cash.

Recognising that movements in net debt can also provide information on an entity's liquidity, solvency and financial adaptability and are often used in discussions of performance, the revised FRS requires an analysis of the movement in net debt or net funds in the period to be given adjoining the cash flow statement or as a note to it.

SCOPE

In developing the FRS the Board has considered the comments on the scope of FRS 1 and FRED 10. Almost one-third of those commenting on FRS 1 mentioned aspects of its scope. **12**

(a) Small entities

At the date of issuing the revised FRS the Board has in hand a separate project reviewing the application of accounting standards to small entities. It will decide in the course of that project whether to continue the exemption of small companies from the requirement to provide a cash flow statement.*

(b) Subsidiary undertakings

The FRS exempts wholly-owned subsidiary undertakings and those where 90 per cent of the voting rights in the subsidiary undertaking are controlled within its group. Where the parent group holds 90 per cent of the voting rights in a subsidiary undertaking it is likely that the liquidity, solvency and financial adaptability of the subsidiary undertaking will essentially depend on the group rather than its own cash flows. The exemption is conditional on consolidated financial statements in which the subsidiary undertaking is included being publicly available. The original standard exempted wholly-owned subsidiary undertakings from the requirement to provide a

****Editor's note:*** *See now section D of the Financial Reporting Standard for Smaller Entities.*

cash flow statement subject to a number of further conditions and the extension and simplification of the exemption was generally supported when proposed by the FRED.

(c) Pension funds

The FRS makes it clear that pension funds are exempt from preparing a cash flow statement because such a statement would add little to the information already available from the fund account and net assets statement.

(d) Investment funds

The FRS exempts open-ended investment funds from preparing a cash flow statement if three conditions are fulfilled, relating to the liquidity of investments held, whether they are held at market value and whether a statement of changes in net assets is provided. Where these conditions are met a cash flow statement for an open-ended investment fund would be of very limited additional use. Investment funds are defined in paragraph 2 of the FRS using three of the conditions for qualifying as an investment company in companies legislation. A fourth condition in the legislation requires that capital profits should not be distributed. The Board agreed with those who commented that this condition was not relevant to the exemption and that its inclusion in the standard would have unreasonably excluded unauthorised investment companies that complied with all the relevant conditions.

FORMAT OF CASH FLOW STATEMENT

13 The Board believes that, to achieve the objectives of cash flow reporting by presenting the information in a way that is useful and easy to understand, individual cash flows should be classified according to the activity that gave rise to them. To promote comparability amongst different entities, the FRS prescribes the following standard headings: 'operating activities', 'returns on investments and servicing of finance', 'taxation', 'capital expenditure and financial investment', 'acquisitions and disposals', 'equity dividends paid', 'management of liquid resources' and 'financing'. In general the commentators supported proposals in FRED 10 to split 'investing activities' into 'capital expenditure' and 'acquisitions and disposals' and reporting dividends paid after these (in the FRS only equity dividends are included below acquisitions and disposals because the Board accepted the arguments of some commentators that non-equity dividends should be reported alongside interest paid). Except for insurance companies, the examples use a format that results in a residual amount of the increase or decrease in cash during the period. This format was preferred by those consulted on this issue, although they did not want the presentation to be mandatory. The FRS therefore follows FRED 10 in allowing reporting entities to choose the format of their cash flow statements, provided these comply with the requirements for classification and order.

14 Both in the consultation on the original cash flow standard and in that on the proposals in FRED 10 some commentators requested that the format of the cash flow statement should be changed to highlight the free cash flows of an entity. There were several interpretations of the exact composition of 'free cash flows'—indeed the commentators themselves suggested several different definitions—but a key issue was to distinguish cash flows for investing to maintain the business from cash flows for investing to expand the business. The Board believes that it is not feasible for an accounting standard to set out how to distinguish expenditure for expansion from expenditure for maintenance. As proposed in FRED 10, the FRS requires cash flows to be analysed into those relating to capital expenditure and those relating to

acquisitions and disposals. This distinction should not be interpreted as reflecting on the one hand maintenance expenditure and on the other expenditure for expansion because, depending on the circumstances, these may be included under either heading.

GROSS OR NET CASH FLOWS

To allow preparers flexibility to emphasise the relevant information for their entities as they wish, the FRS allows the gross cash flows to be shown either in the cash flow statement or in a note. The FRS also allows net reporting for cash flows relating to the management of liquid resources and financing: 15

(a) where there is in substance a single financing transaction that fulfils the conditions in paragraph 35 of FRS 4 'Capital Instruments' (determining when committed facilities can be taken into account in determining the maturity of debt); or
(b) where the inflows and outflows are due to short maturities and high turnover occurring from rollover or reissue.

Condition (b) would allow the netting of inflows and outflows relating to a constantly renewed short-term facility or a commercial paper programme.

Several commentators on the original cash flow standard were concerned about whether gross presentation was appropriate for all cash flows because the volume of some investing or financing transactions was so large that their disproportionate size tended to swamp the other cash flows reported. Other commentators noted that the costs of collecting information on gross cash flows could be high while they doubted the value of that information. FRED 10 proposed that the gross amounts should be shown, in a note if preferred, for all cash flows (other than operating cash flows under the indirect method). A minority of those commenting on FRED 10 also raised concerns with the requirement for gross cash flows even in the notes. However, the Board consulted users, who confirmed that they valued the disclosure of gross amounts. The requirement for gross cash flows therefore is retained in the FRS, except that only net amounts need be shown in relation to rollover and reissue transactions. The international standard allows cash flows to be shown net where turnover is quick, amounts large and maturities short. 16

CLASSIFICATION OF CASH FLOWS

The FRS requires that a cash flow should be classified according to the substance of the transaction or event that gave rise to it. The substance of a transaction may be determined by applying an accounting standard (for example, SSAP 21 'Accounting for leases and hire purchase contracts', FRS 4 'Capital Instruments' or FRS 5 'Reporting the Substance of Transactions'). The approach based on substance should result in transactions and events being treated on the same basis in cash flow statements as in the other primary statements where treatment is also determined by substance. However, to give a complete picture of interest cash flows in a period, the FRS requires all interest cash flows to be reported under servicing of finance, even if some interest is capitalised in the other financial statements. 17

DIRECT OR INDIRECT CASH FLOWS

In developing FRS 1 the Board considered the respective merits of the so-called 'direct' and 'indirect' methods for reporting net cash flow from operating activities. The principal advantage of the direct method is that it shows operating cash receipts 18 and payments. Knowledge of the specific sources of cash receipts and the purposes for which cash payments were made in past periods may be useful in assessing future cash flows. However, the Board noted that it did not believe that in all cases the benefits to users of this information outweighed the costs to the reporting entity of providing it and, therefore, did not require the information to be given. The Board remains of this view, and the FRS continues to encourage the direct method only where the potential benefits to users outweigh the costs of providing it.

RECONCILIATION OF OPERATING PROFIT TO OPERATING CASH FLOWS

19 The FRS permits the reconciliation of operating profit to operating cash flows to be shown either adjoining the cash flow statement, if it is separately identified and clearly labelled, or as a note. Although many commentators welcomed the proposal in FRED 10 to allow the reconciliation to appear above the cash flow statement, others believed the effect would be to detract from the emphasis on cash flows by wedging the statement itself between two reconciliations—one to operating profit, the other to net debt—neither of which represented cash flows. While not prohibiting such a presentation, the wording in the FRS would also permit both reconciliations to follow the primary statement. Some commentators were concerned about how cash flows in relation to provisions should be classified in cash flow statements. The FRS makes it clear that cash flows from operating activities should include cash flows in respect of operating items in relation to any provision, whether on acquisitions, or on termination or for a fundamental reorganisation or restructuring (under paragraph 20a and b of FRS 3).

BANKS

20 The Board has discussed the application of the requirement for a cash flow statement with representatives of the banking industry. The banks had argued for exemption during the development of FRS 1 on the basis that a bank's cash is its stock-in-trade and that more useful information would be given by a statement dealing with the capital resources available to the bank. The Board agreed that capital resources were an important indicator of the solvency and financial adaptability of financial institutions, but also believed that a cash flow statement could provide users of financial statements published by banks with useful information on the sources of cash and how it had been utilised. The Board remains of the view that cash flow statements for banks contain information on their generation and use of cash that may be useful to the users of their financial statements, and the FRS contains no exemption for banks.

21 Example 3 in Appendix I shows a cash flow statement for a bank. The special nature of banking and its regulation is recognised in the format headings and by splitting the cash flows from operating activities to show separately the cash flows from trading. A bank may hold a wide range of investments of different maturities for trading or investment and manage its liquidity in relation to all its assets and liabilities. It is therefore difficult to make a meaningful distinction by attempting to identify cash flows that relate to the management of a bank's liquid resources. Banking entities are not required to provide a reconciliation to net debt because, given the nature of their business, changes in net debt have limited meaning. Other measures, such as regulatory capital ratios, may give a better appreciation of a bank's solvency and financial adaptability.

BUILDING SOCIETIES

FRED 10 proposed that building societies should prepare cash flow statements on the same basis as banks and that their existing exemption should be ended. The proposal depended on changes in the legislation on financial reporting by building societies to make it effective. The Board still believes that the proposals in FRED 10 were correct, given the similarity and competition between the banks and building societies. However, the FRS has extended the existing exemption for building societies for a further two years to develop a consensus on cash flow statements and related aspects of financial reporting for banks and building societies. 22

INSURANCE COMPANIES AND GROUPS

In developing the FRS the Board considered the application of FRS 1 to insurance companies and groups. Comments from the insurance industry had raised several issues that were believed to arise because of the special nature of the business. A general issue raised was the meaning of a cash flow statement for an insurance company. The special implications of cash flow statements for insurance companies are discussed in paragraph 62 of the Explanation. The FRS encourages segmentation of the cash flows to assist users to understand the nature of the reporting entity's cash flows and the relationship between them. One suggestion is to use segmentation to reflect different degrees of access to cash balances. This would allow insurance companies to divide their businesses into segments to reflect the degree of access that shareholders had to cash balances. 23

The Board believes that cash flows arising from the long-term business of an insurance company or group should be dealt with in the cash flow statement only to the extent of cash transferred to, and available to meet the obligations of, the company or group as a whole. The internal cash flows of the long-term business may be shown in a note to the cash flow statement. The Board takes this approach because the shareholders of an insurance company generally have restricted rights to any profits, and associated cash surpluses, made by the long-term business. Because insurance companies and groups are now required by companies legislation to consolidate the long-term business, these funds need to be included in the note to the cash flow statement analysing the changes in the balance sheet amounts for portfolio investments net of financing. 24

Appendix I contains an example of a cash flow statement for an insurance group. By including a section showing the cash flows relating to portfolio investments, this format recognises the special nature of an insurance business, in particular the importance of generating resources for investment to meet provision requirements for future claims and reserve requirements for solvency. The example for insurance companies contains an analysis of the movement in portfolio investments less financing rather than an analysis of net debt as generally required. Presenting information on portfolio investments less financing recognises that the required balance sheet format for insurance companies does not distinguish between fixed and current financial assets. 25

EXCEPTIONAL AND EXTRAORDINARY ITEMS AND CASH FLOWS

To reflect the changes introduced by FRS 3 'Reporting Financial Performance', the text now acknowledges the extreme rarity of extraordinary items post-FRS 3. The FRS also explicitly recognises the possibility that cash flows can be exceptional of themselves because of their size or incidence without relating to an exceptional item 26 in the profit and loss account. Sufficient disclosure should be made to explain their cause and nature.

VALUE ADDED TAX AND OTHER TAXES

27 The existence of Value Added Tax (VAT), and other sales taxes, raises the question whether the relevant cash flows should be reported gross or net of the tax element and how the balance of tax paid to, or repaid by, the taxing authorities should be reported. Generally, sales taxes, including VAT, are payable by the ultimate consumer of the goods or services concerned. A business providing goods or services on which VAT is payable (even if at a zero rate) is generally able to reclaim the VAT incurred by it in providing those goods or services. However, businesses that make exempt supplies are unable to reclaim VAT. Between these two categories are partially exempt businesses that can reclaim part of the VAT incurred by them.

28 The cash flows of an entity include VAT where appropriate and thus strictly the various elements of the cash flow statement should include VAT. However, this treatment does not take into account the fact that normally VAT is a short-term timing difference as far as the entity's overall cash flows are concerned and the inclusion of VAT in the cash flows may distort the allocation of cash flows to standard headings. In order to avoid this distortion and to show cash flows attributable to the reporting entity's activities, the Board believes that cash flows should be shown net of sales taxes and the net movement on the amount payable to, or receivable from, the taxing authority should be allocated to cash flows from operating activities unless a different treatment is more appropriate in the particular circumstances concerned.

FOREIGN EXCHANGE

29 To meet the concern that intragroup cash inflows and outflows might not cancel each other out if average or closing rates are used to translate them for preparing consolidated cash flow statements, the FRS permits entities to use actual rates for intragroup cash flows envisaging that these will be applied where there are large single cash flows at rates significantly different from the average or closing rate used for the other cash flows. Several commentators had raised the treatment of foreign currency in cash flow statements. Because of the various approximations that may be required in particular cases, the Board has not sought to specify in detail the methods to be used to deal with foreign exchange differences. It has, however, set out the principle that in translating the cash flows of foreign entities the same basis should be used as for the translation of the profit and loss account. The FRS now clarifies that this principle applies also to the presentation of stocks, debtors and creditors in the reconciliation from operating profits and cash flow from operating activities.

HEDGING

30 FRS 1 required cash flows that result from transactions undertaken to hedge another transaction to be reported under the same standard heading as the transaction that is the subject of the hedge. Several commentators expressed concern that the FRS 1 requirement relating to hedging was too broad, for example it could justify cash flows relating to loans taken out to finance overseas investment being classified under 'investing' rather than 'financing'. To meet these concerns the FRS requires that the effect of hedging should be reflected in the cash flow statement only where hedging is by futures contracts, forward contracts, option contracts or swap contracts. This is a pragmatic position that follows the US cash flow standard while awaiting the

outcome of the Board's project on derivatives and other financial instruments, which will consider all aspects of hedging and its recognition.*

FRS 3 'REPORTING FINANCIAL PERFORMANCE'

The FRS encourages entities to analyse cash flows on the same basis as that required by FRS 3 in the profit and loss account and to show separately cash flows relating to continuing and discontinued operations. There was widespread support for such analyses when proposed by FRED 10 but commentators did not support a requirement for them. 31

RESTRICTIONS ON REMITTABILITY

Several of the comments received on FRS 1 had indicated that disclosures of restricted cash balances would be useful. FRED 10 proposed the disclosure of cash not available for use elsewhere in the group. The FRS requires disclosure for both businesses and groups of the circumstances and effect of restrictions preventing the transfer of cash from one part to another. Paragraph 68 of the Explanation gives examples of items that, depending on the regulatory environment, might be required to be disclosed. 32

***Editor's note:** *This project resulted in FRSs 25, 26 and 29. The requirements in respect of hedge accounting are in FRS 26. However, companies not adopting FRS 26 will find some guidance on hedge accounting, albeit only in respect of foreign currencies, in SSAP 20.*

[FRS 2]
Accounting for subsidiary undertakings*

(Issued June 2009)

Summary

a Financial Reporting Standard No. 2 – 'Accounting for Subsidiary Undertakings' (the FRS) sets out the conditions under which an undertaking that is the parent undertaking of other undertakings (its subsidiary undertakings) should prepare consolidated financial statements. The FRS also sets out the manner in which consolidated financial statements are to be prepared. The purpose of consolidated financial statements is to provide financial information about the economic activities of a group. The Companies Act 2006 defines a parent undertaking and its subsidiary undertakings that together make up a group. The FRS adopts these definitions.

b Withdrawn.

c The FRS applies to all parent undertakings that are required or opt to prepare consolidated financial statements. A parent undertaking that does not report under the Act should comply with the requirements of the FRS except to the extent that these are not permitted by any statutory framework under which the undertaking reports.

d A parent undertaking which is not subject to the small companies regime in the UK or which cannot take advantage of the size exemption set out in Irish Law†, should prepare consolidated financial statements for its group in accordance with standard accounting practice set out in the FRS unless it uses one of the exemptions permitted by the Act and set out in paragraph 21 of the FRS.

e The Act and the FRS exempt a parent undertaking (which is not subject to the small companies regime or which cannot take advantage of the size exemption set out in Irish law) from preparing consolidated financial statements if:

(i) it is a wholly-owned or majority-owned subsidiary undertaking and its immediate parent undertaking is established under the law of an EEA State. Exemption is conditional on compliance with certain further conditions in section 400; or

(ii) it is a wholly-owned or majority-owned subsidiary undertaking and its parent undertaking is not established under the law of an EEA State. Exemption is conditional on compliance with certain further conditions in section 401; or

(iii) all of its subsidiary undertakings are permitted or required to be excluded from consolidation by section 402.

f The consolidated financial statements should be prepared by consolidating financial information for the parent undertaking and all its subsidiary undertakings, except

****Editor's note****: *The matters covered in FRS 2 are dealt with in Section 9 of FRS 102.*

†*An Irish parent company within the scope of the European Communities (Companies: Group Accounts) Regulations 1992 is exempt from the requirement to prepare group accounts if it meets the size and other criteria set out in Regulation 7 of those Regulations. The size criteria in summary require that the parent and subsidiaries together meet two of the following three conditions (i) balance sheet total does not exceed €7,618,428; (ii) turnover does not exceed €15,236,858 and (iii) average number of employees does not exceed 250.*

for any subsidiary undertakings that are to be excluded from consolidation by virtue of the requirements of the Act and the FRS.

A subsidiary undertaking is to be excluded from consolidation if: **g**

(i) severe long-term restrictions substantially hinder the exercise of the parent undertaking's rights over the subsidiary undertaking's assets or management; or

(ii) the group's interest in the subsidiary undertaking is held exclusively with a view to subsequent resale and the subsidiary undertaking has not previously been consolidated.

The Act permits rather than requires exclusion in cases (i) and (ii) above. The FRS requires exclusion in these circumstances because the same conditions that justify permitting exclusion also make consolidation inappropriate. In addition, the FRS requires the circumstances in which subsidiary undertakings are to be excluded from consolidation to be interpreted strictly. It is important that only those subsidiary undertakings whose consolidation would be inappropriate are excluded from consolidation so that consolidated financial statements reflect in full the resources, obligations and results of the group.

The FRS requires additional disclosures for subsidiary undertakings excluded from consolidation and requires them to be accounted for as follows. **h**

(i) Subsidiary undertakings excluded from consolidation because of severe long-term restrictions are to be treated as fixed asset investments. They are to be included at their carrying amount when the restrictions came into force, subject to any write-down for impairment, and no further accruals are to be made for profits or losses of those subsidiary undertakings, unless the parent undertaking still exercises significant influence. In the latter case they are to be treated as associated undertakings.

(ii) Subsidiary undertakings excluded from consolidation because they are held exclusively for resale and have not previously been consolidated are to be included as current assets at the lower of cost and net realisable value.

Minority interests in total should be reported separately in the consolidated balance sheet and profit and loss account. When an entity becomes a subsidiary undertaking the assets and liabilities attributable to its minority interest should be included on the same basis as those attributable to the interest held by the parent and other subsidiary undertakings. The effect of this for an acquisition is that all the subsidiary undertaking's identifiable assets and liabilities are included at fair value as required by the Act. No goodwill should be attributed to the minority interest. **i**

Intra-group transactions may result in profits or losses being included in the book value of assets to be included in the consolidation; the FRS requires the elimination in full of any such profits or losses because, for the group as a whole, no profits or losses have arisen. **j**

Uniform group accounting policies should generally be used in preparing the consolidated financial statements; in exceptional cases different policies may be used with disclosure. **k**

The financial statements of all subsidiary undertakings to be used in preparing consolidated financial statements should have the same financial year end and be for the same accounting period as those of the parent undertaking of the group. Where the financial year of a subsidiary undertaking differs from that of the parent undertaking of the group, interim financial statements for that subsidiary **l** undertaking prepared to the parent undertaking's accounting date should be used. If this is impracticable, earlier financial statements of the subsidiary undertaking may be used, provided they are prepared for a financial year that ended not more than three months earlier.

m Changes in membership of a group occur on the date control passes, whether by a transaction or other event. Changes in the membership of the group during the period should be disclosed.

n When a subsidiary undertaking is acquired the FRS requires its identifiable assets and liabilities to be brought into the consolidation at their fair values at the date that undertaking becomes a subsidiary undertaking, even if the acquisition has been made in stages. When a group increases its interest in an undertaking that is already its subsidiary undertaking, the identifiable assets and liabilities of that subsidiary undertaking should be revalued to fair value and goodwill arising on the increase in interest should be calculated by reference to that fair value. This revaluation is not required if the difference between fair values and carrying amounts of the identifiable assets and liabilities attributable to the increase in stake is not material.

o The effect of consolidating the parent and its subsidiary undertakings may be that aggregation obscures useful information about the different undertakings and activities included in the consolidated financial statements. Parent undertakings are encouraged to give segmental analysis to provide readers of consolidated financial statements with useful information on the different risks and rewards, growth and prospects of the different parts of the group. The specification of such analysis, however, falls outside the scope of the FRS.

p The amendments to the FRS made in June 2009 take effect for accounting periods beginning on and/or after 6 April 2008, or when the provisions of the Act/or the Regulations are applied to other entities (eg limited liability partnerships), if later.

Objective

The objective of this FRS is to require parent undertakings to provide financial information about the economic activities of their groups by preparing consolidated financial statements*. These statements are intended to present financial information about a parent undertaking and its subsidiary undertakings as a single economic entity to show the economic resources controlled by the group, the obligations of the group and the results the group achieves with its resources. 1

Definitions

The following definitions apply for the purposes of the FRS and in particular the statement of standard accounting practice set out in paragraphs 18 to 56.

The terms defined below, which are also defined in the Act or the Regulations, have the same meaning in the FRS as in the Act or the Regulations, notwithstanding that in some cases the FRS definition is a summary or explanation rather than a repetition of the definition in the Act or the Regulations. The definitions should therefore be interpreted by reference to the full provisions of the Act or the Regulations. The marginal notes give the main references in the Act or the Regulations. References to sections and schedules are to those of the Act unless otherwise stated.

The Act:- 2
References in the FRS refer to the Companies Act 2006 unless otherwise specified.

Withdrawn. 3

Consolidated financial statements:- 4
The financial statements of a group prepared by consolidation.

Consolidation:- 5
The process of adjusting and combining financial information from the individual financial statements of a parent undertaking and its subsidiary undertakings to prepare consolidated financial statements that present financial information for the group as a single economic entity.

Control:- 6
The ability of an undertaking to direct the financial and operating policies of another undertaking with a view to gaining economic benefits from its activities.

[FRS defining phrase used in s1162(4)(a)]

Dominant influence:- 7
Influence that can be exercised to achieve the operating and financial policies desired by the holder of the influence, notwithstanding the rights or influence of any other party.

'Financial statements' is the term used in the FRS to mean the same as the term 'accounts' used in the Companies Act.

[From 7Sch 4(1)]

(a) In the context of paragraph 14(c) and section 1162(2)(c) *the right to exercise a dominant influence* means that the holder has a right to give directions with respect to the operating and financial policies of another undertaking with which its directors are obliged to comply, whether or not they are for the benefit of that undertaking.

[FRS defining phrase used in s1162(4)(a]

(b) *The actual exercise of dominant influence* is the exercise of an influence that achieves the result that the operating and financial policies of the undertaking influenced are set in accordance with the wishes of the holder of the influence and for the holder's benefit whether or not those wishes are explicit. The actual exercise of dominant influence is identified by its effect in practice rather than by the way in which it is exercised.

(c) *The power to exercise dominant influence* is a power that, if exercised, would give rise to the actual exercise of dominant influence as defined in paragraph 7b.

8 *Equity method*:-

A method of accounting for an investment that brings into the consolidated profit and loss account the investor's share of the investment undertaking's results and that records the investment in the consolidated balance sheet at the investor's share of the investment undertaking's net assets including any goodwill arising to the extent that it has not previously been written off.

9 *Group:-*

[From s474(1)]

A parent undertaking and its subsidiary undertakings.

10 *[FRS defining phrase used in 10Sch 11: The Large and Medium sized Companies and Groups (Accounts and Reports) Regulations 2008]*

Interest held on a long-term basis:-

An interest which is held other than *exclusively with a view to subsequent resale.*

11 *Interest held exclusively with a view to subsequent resale:-*

[FRS defining phrase used in 405(3)(c)]

(a) an interest for which a purchaser has been identified or is being sought, and which is reasonably expected to be disposed of within approximately one year of its date of acquisition; or

(b) an interest that was acquired as a result of the enforcement of a security, unless the interest has become part of the continuing activities of the group or the holder acts as if it intends the interest to become so.

Managed on a unified basis:- 12
Two or more undertakings are managed on a unified basis if the whole of the operations of the undertakings are integrated and they are managed as a single unit. Unified management does not arise solely because one undertaking manages another.
[FRS defining phrase used in s1162(4)(b)]

Minority interest in a subsidiary undertaking:- 13
The interest in a subsidiary undertaking included in the consolidation that is attributable to the shares held by or on behalf of persons other than the parent undertaking and its subsidiary undertakings.
[From 6Sch 17 The Large and Medium sized Companies and Group (Accounts and Reports) Regulations 2008]

Parent undertaking and subsidiary undertaking:- 14
An undertaking is the parent undertaking of another undertaking (a subsidiary undertaking) if any of the following apply.
[From s1162 and 7Sch]

(a) It holds a majority of the voting rights in the undertaking.
[From s1162(2)(a)]

(b) It is a member of the undertaking and has the right to appoint or remove directors holding a majority of the voting rights at meetings of the board on all, or substantially all, matters.
[From s1162(2)(b) and 7Sch 3]

(c) It has the right to exercise a dominant influence over the undertaking:

(i) by virtue of provisions contained in the undertaking's memorandum or articles; or
[From s1162(2)(c) and 7Sch 4]

(ii) by virtue of a control contract. The control contract must be in writing and be of a kind authorised by the memorandum or articles of the controlled undertaking. It must also be permitted by the law under which that undertaking is established.
[From 7Sch 4(2)]

(d) It is a member of the undertaking and controls alone, pursuant to an agreement with other shareholders or members, a majority of the voting rights in the undertaking.
[From s1162(2)(d)]

(e) (i) it has the power to exercise, or actually exercises, dominant influence or control over the undertaking; or
[From s1162(4)(a)]

(ii) it and the undertaking are managed on a unified basis.
[From s1162(4)(b)]

(f) A parent undertaking is also treated as the parent undertaking of the subsidiary undertakings of its subsidiary undertakings.
[From s1162(5)]

[From s1162(3)] For the purpose of section 1162 [parent and subsidiary undertakings] an undertaking shall be treated as a member of another undertaking:

(i) if any of its subsidiary undertakings is a member of that undertaking; or

(ii) if any shares in that other undertaking are held by a person acting on behalf of the parent undertaking or any of its subsidiary undertakings.

[From 7Sch 9] Any shares held, or powers exercisable, by a subsidiary undertaking should be treated as held or exercisable by its parent undertaking.

15 *The Regulations:-*

The Large and Medium-sized Companies and Groups (Accounts and Reports) Regulations 2008 (SI 2008 No 410)*.

16 *[From s1161]* *Undertaking:-*

A body corporate, a partnership or an unincorporated association carrying on a trade or business with or without a view to profit.

17 *Voting rights in an undertaking:-*

[From 7Sch 2(1)] Rights conferred on shareholders in respect of their shares or, in the case of an undertaking not having a share capital, on members, to vote at general meetings of the undertaking on all, or substantially all, matters. Schedule 7 deals with the attribution of voting rights in certain circumstances.

**The requirements for small companies are set out in the Companies Act 2006 and in 'The Small Companies and Groups (Accounts and Directors' Reports) Regulations 2008 (SI 2008 No.409).*

Statement of standard accounting practice

The statement of standard accounting practice set out in paragraphs 18 to 56 of the FRS should be read in the context of the Objective of the FRS as stated in paragraph 1, the definitions set out in paragraphs 2 to 17 and also of the Foreword to Accounting Standards and the Statement of Principles for Financial Reporting currently in issue.

In the statement of standard accounting practice, marginal notes give the main references to the Act and the Regulations. If no marginal reference is given the requirement is that of the FRS alone. The statement of standard accounting practice should be interpreted by reference to the full provisions of the Act and the Regulations notwithstanding that the statement summarises certain provisions of the Act and the Regulations. References to sections, regulations and schedules are to those of the Act and Regulations unless otherwise stated.

The Explanation section of the FRS, set out in paragraphs 59 to 94, shall be regarded as part of the statement of standard accounting practice in so far as it assists in interpreting that statement.

SCOPE

This standard applies to all parent undertakings that prepare the financial statements described below, whether or not they report under the Act. Parent undertakings that prepare consolidated financial statements intended to give a true and fair view of the financial position and profit or loss (or income and expenditure) of their group should prepare such statements in accordance with the requirements of the FRS. A parent undertaking that uses one of the exemptions from preparing consolidated financial statements (described in paragraph 21) but prepares individual financial statements intended to give a true and fair view of its own financial position and profit or loss (or income and expenditure) should include the statement required by paragraph 22. The FRS does not otherwise deal with the individual financial statements of a parent undertaking. **18**

Parent undertakings that do not report under the Act should comply with the requirements of the FRS, and of the Act where referred to in the FRS, except to the extent that these requirements are not permitted by any statutory framework under which such undertakings report. **19**

This Standard does not apply to retirement benefit schemes, which are within the scope of FRS 17 'Retirement Benefits'. **19A**

APPLICATION TO SMALLER ENTITIES

Reporting entities applying the Financial Reporting Standard for Smaller Entities (FRSSE) currently applicable are exempt from the **19B**

FRS unless preparing consolidated financial statements, in which case they should apply the FRS to such statements as required by the FRSSE*.

CONSOLIDATED FINANCIAL STATEMENTS

Preparation of consolidated financial statements

20 *[From s399, s403 and s398]* A parent undertaking, which is not subject to the small companies regime in the UK or which cannot take advantage of the size exemption set out in Irish Law†, should prepare consolidated financial statements for its group unless it uses one of the exemptions set out in paragraph 21. A parent undertaking subject to the small companies regime in the UK or which can take advantage of the size exemption set out in Irish Law† may opt to prepare consolidated financial statements.

Exempt parent undertakings

21 A parent undertaking is exempt from preparing consolidated financial statements for its group on any one of the following grounds.

[s400] (a) The parent undertaking is a wholly-owned subsidiary undertaking and its immediate parent undertaking is established under the law of an EEA State. Exemption is conditional on compliance with certain further conditions set out in section 400(2). A parent undertaking is not exempt if any of its securities are admitted to trading on a regulated market of any EEA State.

[s400] (b) The parent undertaking is a majority-owned subsidiary undertaking and meets all the conditions for exemption as a wholly-owned subsidiary undertaking set out in section 400(2) as well as the additional conditions set out in section 400(1)(b).

[s401] (c) The parent undertaking is a wholly-owned subsidiary of another undertaking and that parent undertaking is not established under the law of an EEA State. Exemption is conditional on compliance with certain further conditions set out in section 401(2). The exemption does not apply to a parent undertaking if any of its securities are admitted to trading on a regulated market of any EEA State.

(d) The parent undertaking is a majority-owned subsidiary undertaking and meets all of the conditions for exemption as a wholly-owned subsidiary undertaking set out in section

**The requirements for small companies are set out in the Companies Act 2006 and in 'The Small Companies and Groups (Accounts and Directors' Reports) Regulations 2008 (SI 2008 No.409).*

†An Irish parent company within the scope of the European Communities (Companies: Group Accounts) Regulations 1992 is exempt from the requirement to prepare group accounts if it meets the size and other criteria set out in Regulation 7 of those Regulations. The size criteria in summary require that the parent and subsidiaries together meet two of the following three conditions (i) balance sheet total does not exceed €7,618,428; (ii) turnover does not exceed €15,236,858 and (iii) average number of employees does not exceed 250.

401(2) as well as the additional conditions set out in section 401(1)(b).

(e) All of the parent undertaking's subsidiary undertakings are permitted or required to be excluded from consolidation by section 405. (The conditions of exclusion of section 405 are more fully described in paragraph 25 and are elaborated on in paragraphs 76 to 78.) *[s402]*

The Act and the Regulations set out disclosure requirements for parent companies not required to prepare consolidated financial statements. In addition to providing this information, a parent undertaking making use of an exemption from preparing consolidated financial statements should state that its financial statements present information about it as an individual undertaking and not about its group. This statement should include or refer to a note giving the grounds on which the parent undertaking is exempt from preparing consolidated financial statements, as required by Schedule 4 10(1) of the Regulations. *[s409, s410, regulation 7 and 4Sch Part 2 of the Regulations]* **22**

Undertakings to be included in the consolidation

As required by the Act, the consolidated financial statements should include the parent undertaking and all its subsidiary undertakings, except those that are required to be excluded under the conditions set out in paragraph 25 below. *[s405(1)]* **23**

Disproportionate expense and undue delay

Neither disproportionate expense nor undue delay in obtaining the information necessary for the preparation of consolidated financial statements can justify excluding from consolidation subsidiary undertakings that are individually or collectively material in the context of the group. *[FRS allows s405(3)(b) exclusion only where the undertaking is not material]* **24**

Subsidiary undertakings to be excluded from consolidation

The exclusions required by this paragraph are based on the exclusions permitted by section 405(3). A subsidiary undertaking should be excluded from consolidation where: *[s405(3)]* **25**

(a) severe long-term restrictions substantially hinder the exercise of the rights of the parent undertaking over the assets or management of the subsidiary undertaking. The rights referred to are those by reason of which the parent undertaking is defined as such under section 1162 and in the absence of which it would not be the parent undertaking; or *[FRS requires exclusion permitted by s405(3)(a)]*

(b) the interest in the subsidiary undertaking is held exclusively with a view to subsequent resale (as defined in paragraph 11) and the subsidiary undertaking has not previously been consolidated in group accounts prepared by the parent undertaking. *[FRS restricts exclusion permitted by s405(3)(c)]*

26 *[s409, regulation 7 and 4Sch 16(1) of the Regulations]* As required by the Act and the Regulations, subject to the conditions and exemptions of section 409 and regulation 7 and Schedule 4 16(1) of the Regulations the names of any subsidiary undertakings excluded from the consolidation and the reasons why they have been excluded should be given.

Accounting for excluded subsidiary undertakings

Severe long-term restrictions

27 A subsidiary undertaking excluded on the grounds set out in paragraph 25(a) [severe long-term restrictions] should be treated as a fixed asset investment. If restrictions were in force at its acquisition date, the subsidiary undertaking should be carried initially at cost; if restrictions came into force at a later date, the subsidiary undertaking should be carried at a fixed amount calculated using the equity method at that date. While the restrictions are in force, no further accruals should be made for the profits or losses of that subsidiary undertaking, unless the parent undertaking still exercises a significant influence over it. If this is the case, it should treat the subsidiary undertaking as an associated undertaking using the equity method. The carrying amount of subsidiary undertakings subject to severe long-term restrictions should be reviewed and written down for any impairment in value. When impairment is assessed, each subsidiary undertaking should be considered individually. Any intra-group amounts due from subsidiary undertakings excluded on the grounds of severe long-term restrictions should also be reviewed and written down, if necessary.

28 When the severe restrictions cease and the parent undertaking's rights are restored, the amount of the unrecognised profit or loss that accrued during the period of restriction for that subsidiary undertaking should be separately disclosed in the consolidated profit and loss account of the period in which control is resumed. Similarly, any amount previously charged for impairment that needs to be written back as a result of restrictions ceasing should be separately disclosed.

Held exclusively with a view to subsequent resale

29 A subsidiary undertaking that is excluded from consolidation on the grounds set out in paragraph 25(b) [held exclusively with a view to subsequent resale] should be recorded in the consolidated financial statements as a current asset at the lower of cost and net realisable value.

30 Withdrawn

DISCLOSURES FOR SUBSIDIARY UNDERTAKINGS EXCLUDED FROM CONSOLIDATION

[s409 of the Act and 4Sch 16 of the Regulations]

[4Sch 2, 3, 16 and 17 of the Regulations]

31 In addition to the disclosures required by virtue of section 409 of the Act and regulation 7 Schedule 4 Parts 1 and 3 of the Regulations, the following information should be given in the consolidated financial statements for subsidiary undertakings not included in the consolidation:

(a) particulars of the balances between the excluded subsidiary undertakings and the rest of the group;

(b) the nature and extent of transactions of the excluded subsidiary undertakings with the rest of the group;

(c) for an excluded subsidiary undertaking carried other than by the equity method, any amounts included in the consolidated financial statements in respect of:

(i) dividends received and receivable from that undertaking; and

(ii) any write-down in the period in respect of the investment in that undertaking or amounts due from that undertaking.

32 Disclosures for excluded subsidiary undertakings in general apply to individual excluded subsidiary undertakings. However, if the information about excluded subsidiary undertakings is more appropriately presented for a sub-unit of the group comprising more than one excluded subsidiary undertaking, the disclosures may be made on an aggregate basis. Any individual sub-unit for these disclosures is to include only subsidiary undertakings excluded under the same sub-paragraph of section 405(3). Individual disclosures should be made for any excluded subsidiary undertaking, including its sub-group where relevant, that alone accounts for more than 20% of any one or more of operating profits, turnover or net assets of the group. The group amounts should be measured by including all excluded subsidiary undertakings.

Disclosures for principal subsidiary undertakings

[4Sch of the Regulations]

33 In addition to the disclosures required by Schedule 4 of the Regulations, the following should be shown for each subsidiary undertaking whose results or financial position principally affects the figures in the consolidated financial statements:

(a) the proportion of voting rights held by the parent and its subsidiary undertakings; and

(b) an indication of the nature of its business.

Disclosure of the basis of dominant influence

34 Where an undertaking is a subsidiary undertaking only because its parent undertaking has the power to exercise, or actually exercises, dominant influence or control over it, the consolidated financial

[4Sch of the Regulations] statements should disclose the basis of the parent undertaking's dominant influence or control in addition to the disclosures required, by virtue of section 409 of the Act and, by Schedule 4 paragraph 1 and paragraph 16 of the Regulations.

Minority interests

35 *[6Sch 17 (2) of the Regulations]* The consolidated balance sheet should show separately the aggregate of the capital and reserves attributable to minority interests at the end of the period under 'Minority interests' in accordance with Schedule 6 paragraph 17(2) of the Regulations. This amount represents the aggregate share of net assets or liabilities of subsidiary undertakings included in the consolidation that are attributable to the minority interests.

36 *[6Sch 17(3) of the Regulations]* The consolidated profit and loss account should show separately the aggregate of profit or loss on ordinary activities for the period attributable to the minority interests under 'Minority interests' in accordance with Schedule 6 paragraph 17(3)(a) of the Regulations. Any extraordinary profit or loss attributable to minority interests should be shown separately in accordance with Schedule 6 paragraph 17(3)(b) of the Regulations.

37 Profits or losses arising in a subsidiary undertaking should be apportioned between the controlling and minority interests in proportion to their respective interests held over the period in which the profits or losses arose. Where the losses in a subsidiary undertaking attributable to the minority interest result in its interest being one in net liabilities rather than net assets, the group should make provision to the extent that it has any commercial or legal obligation (whether formal or implied) to provide finance that may not be recoverable in respect of the accumulated losses attributable to the minority interest.

38 Whether the assets and liabilities of a subsidiary undertaking are included at fair values or adjusted carrying amounts*, those attributable to the minority interest should be included on the same basis as those attributable to the interests held by the parent and its other subsidiary undertakings. However, goodwill arising on acquisition should only be recognised with respect to the part of the subsidiary undertaking that is attributable to the interest held by the parent and its other subsidiary undertakings. No goodwill should be attributed to the minority interest.

**Where the acquisition method of accounting is to be used in consolidating a subsidiary undertaking, Schedule 6 paragraph 9 of the Regulations requires the identifiable assets and liabilities of the undertaking acquired to be included in the consolidation at their fair values as at the date of acquisition.*

Where the merger method of accounting is to be used, Schedule 6 paragraph 11 of the Regulations requires the assets and liabilities of the subsidiary undertaking to be consolidated at the amounts at which they stand in that undertaking's financial statements, subject to any adjustments authorised or required by the Act.

CONSOLIDATION ADJUSTMENTS

Intra-group transactions

To the extent that they are reflected in the book value of assets to be included in the consolidation, profits or losses on any intra-group transactions should be eliminated in full. Amounts in relation to debts and claims between undertakings included in the consolida-tion should also be eliminated. The elimination of profits or losses relating to intra-group transactions should be set against the interests held by the group and the minority interest in respective proportion to their holdings in the undertaking whose individual financial statements recorded the eliminated profits or losses. *[FRS requirement in relation to 6Sch of the Regulations. The Regulations allow partial elimination but the FRS requires elimination in full]* 39

Accounting policies

Subject to paragraph 41 below, uniform group accounting policies should be used for determining the amounts to be included in the consolidated financial statements, if necessary by adjusting for consolidation the amounts which have been reported by subsidiary undertakings in their individual financial statements. *[6Sch 3(1) of the Regulations]* 40

In exceptional cases, different accounting policies may be used. Where the directors of the parent undertaking depart from the Regulations general requirement to use the same group accounting rules to value or otherwise determine the assets and liabilities to be included in the consolidated financial statements, Schedule 6 paragraph 3(2) of the Regulations requires disclosure of the parti-culars, which should include the different accounting policies used. *[6Sch 3(2) of the Regulations]* 41

Accounting periods and dates

The financial statements of all subsidiary undertakings to be used in preparing the consolidated financial statements should, wherever practicable, be prepared to the same financial year end and for the same accounting period as those of the parent undertaking of the group. 42

Where the financial year of a subsidiary undertaking differs from that of the parent undertaking of the group, interim financial statements should be prepared to the same date as those of the parent undertaking of the group for use in the preparation of the consolidated financial statements. If it is not practicable to use such interim financial statements, the financial statements of the sub-sidiary undertaking for its last financial year should be used, providing that year ended not more than three months before the relevant year end of the parent undertaking of the group. In this case any changes that have taken place in the intervening period that materially affect the view given by the group's financial statements should be taken into account by adjustments in the preparation of the consolidated financial statements. *[FRS preference of alternatives permitted by 6Sch 2(2) of the Regulations]* 43

44 The following information should be given for each subsidiary undertaking which is included in the consolidated financial statements on the basis of information prepared to a different date or for a different accounting period from that of the parent undertaking of the group:

(a) the name of the subsidiary undertaking;

(b) the accounting date or period of the subsidiary undertaking; and

(c) the reason for using a different accounting date or period for the subsidiary undertaking.

CHANGES IN COMPOSITION OF A GROUP

Date of changes in group membership

45 The date for accounting for an undertaking becoming a subsidiary undertaking is the date on which control of that undertaking passes to its new parent undertaking. This date is the date of acquisition for Schedule 6 paragraph 9 of the Regulations or the date of merger. The date for accounting for an undertaking ceasing to be a subsidiary undertaking is the date on which its former parent undertaking relinquishes its control over that undertaking.

Ceasing to be a subsidiary undertaking

46 When an undertaking ceases to be a subsidiary undertaking during a period, the consolidated financial statements for that period should include the results of that subsidiary undertaking up to the date that it ceases to be a subsidiary undertaking and any gain or loss arising on that cessation, to the extent that these have not been already provided for in the consolidated financial statements.

47 The gain or loss directly arising for the group on an undertaking ceasing to be its subsidiary undertaking is calculated by comparing the carrying amount of the net assets of that subsidiary undertaking attributable to the group's interest before the cessation with any remaining carrying amount attributable to the group's interest after the cessation together with any proceeds received. The net assets compared should include any related goodwill that has not previously been either written off through the profit and loss account or attributed to prior period amortisation or impairment on applying paragraph 70 of FRS 10 *Goodwill and Intangible Assets*. This calculation of gain or loss applies whether the cause of the undertaking ceasing to be a subsidiary undertaking is a direct disposal, a deemed disposal or other event.

48 *[6Sch 15 of the Regulations]* In addition to the disclosures required by Schedule 6 paragraph 15 of the Regulations, the consolidated financial statements should give the name of any material undertaking that has ceased to be a subsidiary undertaking in the period, showing any ownership interest retained. Where any material undertaking has ceased to be a subsidiary undertaking other than by the disposal of at least part of the interest held by the group, the circumstances should be explained.

Becoming or ceasing to be a subsidiary undertaking other than by a purchase or exchange of shares

Where an undertaking has become or ceased to be a subsidiary undertaking other than as a result of a purchase or exchange of shares, the circumstances should be explained in a note to the consolidated financial statements. **49**

CHANGES IN STAKE

Acquiring a subsidiary undertaking in stages

Schedule 6 paragraph 9 of the Regulations requires that the identifiable assets and liabilities of a subsidiary undertaking be included in the consolidation at fair value at the date of its acquisition, that is, the date it becomes a subsidiary undertaking. This requirement is also applicable where the group's interest in the undertaking that becomes a subsidiary undertaking is acquired in stages. *[6Sch 9 of the Regulations]* **50**

Increasing an interest held in a subsidiary undertaking

When a group increases its interest in an undertaking that is already its subsidiary undertaking, the identifiable assets and liabilities of that subsidiary undertaking should be revalued to fair value and goodwill arising on the increase in interest should be calculated by reference to those fair values. This revaluation is not required if the difference between net fair values and carrying amounts of the assets and liabilities attributable to the increase in stake is not material. **51**

Reducing an interest held in a subsidiary undertaking

Where a group reduces its interest in a subsidiary undertaking, it should record any profit or loss arising calculated as the difference between the carrying amount of the net assets of that subsidiary undertaking attributable to the group's interest before the reduction and the carrying amount attributable to the group's interest after the reduction together with any proceeds received. The net assets compared should include any related goodwill not previously written off through the profit and loss account. Where the undertaking remains a subsidiary undertaking after the disposal, the minority interest in that subsidiary undertaking should be increased by the carrying amount of the net identifiable assets that are now attributable to the minority interest because of the decrease in the group's interest. No amount for goodwill that arose on acquisition of the group's interest in that subsidiary undertaking should be attributed to the minority interest. **52**

DISTRIBUTIONS

Restrictions on distribution

Where significant statutory, contractual or exchange control restrictions on distributions by subsidiary undertakings materially limit the parent undertaking's access to distributable profits, the nature and extent of the restrictions should be disclosed. **53**

Tax on the accumulated reserves of overseas subsidiary undertakings

54 Withdrawn.

DATE FROM WHICH EFFECTIVE

55 The accounting practices set out in this statement should be adopted as soon as possible and regarded as standard in respect of consolidated financial statements relating to periods ending on or after 23 December 1992 except for those companies considered below. The accounting practices in this statement should be adopted by Republic of Ireland companies as soon as possible after the enactment of the Irish legislation implementing the European Community Seventh Directive and regarded as standard in respect of consolidated financial statements for periods specified in the date of application of that legislation

55A In 2009* the FRS was amended to update the legal references following the introduction of the Companies Act 2006 and The Large and Medium-sized Companies and Groups (Accounts and Report) Regulations 2000 (SI 2008 No. 410). The amendments take effect for accounting periods beginning on or after 6 April 2008 or when the provisions of the Act and/or the Regulations are applied to other entities (eg limited liability partnerships), if later.

WITHDRAWAL OF SSAP 14 'GROUP ACCOUNTS' AND 'INTERIM STATEMENT: CONSOLIDATED ACCOUNTS'

56 [Not reproduced]

**The FRS was also amended in December 2004 to reflect changes to the Companies Act 1985 introduced by the Companies Act 1985 (International Accounting Standards and Other Accounting Amendments) Regulations 2004 (SI 2004 No. 2947). The amendments took effect for accounting periods beginning on or after 1 January 2005.*

Financial Reporting Standard No. 2 'Accounting for Subsidiary Undertakings' was adopted by the unanimous vote of the nine members of the Accounting Standards Board

Members of the Accounting Standards Board

David Tweedie (Chairman)
Allan Cook (Technical Director)
Robert Bradfield
Sir Bryan Carsberg
Elwyn Eilledge
Michael Garner
Donald Main
Roger Munson
Graham Stacy

ADOPTION OF AMENDMENT TO FRS 2 BY THE ACCOUNTING STANDARDS BOARD (DECEMBER 2004)

Amendment to Financial Reporting Standard 2 'Accounting for Subsidiary Undertakings: Legal Changes' was approved for issue by the ten members of the Accounting Standards Board.

Ian Mackintosh (Chairman)
Andrew Lennard (Technical Director)
Michael Ashley
Douglas Flint
Anthony Good
Roger Marshall
Isobel Sharp
John Smith
Jonathan Symonds
Peter Westlake

ADOPTION OF AMENDMENT TO FRS 2 BY THE ACCOUNTING STANDARDS BOARD (JUNE 2009)

Amendment to Financial Reporting Standard 2 'Accounting for Subsidiary Undertakings: Legal Changes' was approved for issue by the eleven members of the Accounting Standards Board.

Ian Mackintosh (Chairman)
David Loweth (Technical Director)
Nick Anderson
Michael Ashley
Edward Beale
Marisa Cassoni
Peter Elwin
Ken Lever
Robert Overend
Andy Simmonds
Professor Geoffrey Whittington CBE

COMPLIANCE WITH INTERNATIONAL ACCOUNTING STANDARDS

57 Compliance with the amended FRS ensures substantial compliance with the relevant provisions of International Accounting Standard 27 *Consolidated and Separate Financial Statements* (IAS 27). However, IAS 27;

(a) does not include an exemption from consolidation for subsidiaries where severe long-term restrictions exist;
(b) does not exempt subsidiaries that are held exclusively with a view to resale. International Financial Reporting Standard (IFRS) 5 *Non-current Assets Held for Sale and Discounted Operations* requires newly acquired subsidiaries held for sale to be measured at the lower of carrying value and fair value less costs to sell; the assets and liabilities of the subsidiary may not be offset and should be presented separately from other assets and liabilities in the balance sheet*;
(c) specifies that changes in a parent's ownership interest in a subsidiary that do not result in a loss of control are accounted for as equity transactions (i.e. transactions with owners in their capacity as owners);
(d) does not require assets and liabilities of a subsidiary undertaking to be revalued to fair value when a group increases its interest in an undertaking that is already a subsidiary undertaking;
(e) specifies any investment retained in the former subsidiary be recognised at its fair value at the date when control is lost; and
(f) does not provide exemption from producing consolidated financial statements except where the ultimate or any immediate parent of the parent produces consolidated financial statements available for public use that comply with International Financial Reporting Standards.

58 Withdrawn.†

Explanation

The legal references in the Explanation of the FRS have been amended to take account of the Companies Act 2006 and The Large and Medium-sized Companies and Groups (Accounts and Reports) Regulations 2008. References are to the Companies Act 2006 unless otherwise specified.

The purpose of consolidated financial statements

59 For a variety of legal, tax and other reasons, undertakings generally choose to conduct their activities not through a single legal entity but through several undertakings under the ultimate control of the parent undertaking of that group. For this reason the financial statements of a parent undertaking by itself do not present a full picture of its economic activities or financial position. Consolidated financial statements are required in order to reflect the extended business unit that conducts activities under the control of the parent undertaking.

**The assets and liabilities of the newly acquired subsidiary held for sale may be presented together with the assets and liabilities of any other assets or disposal groups held for sale by the entity.*

†***Editor's note:*** *From 2013 IAS 27 deals only with separate financial statements, and group accounts are dealt with by IFRS 11.*

The legal background to the FRS

In the United Kingdom the preparation of consolidated financial statements for companies is governed by the Act. This implements the provisions of the European Community Seventh Directive. The FRS is drafted to be consistent with the Act, supplementing it with guidance on its application and additional requirements where necessary. The definitions and statement of standard accounting practice contain marginal notes that give references to the Act where these are relevant. The application of the FRS in the Republic of Ireland is explained in the section on the legal requirements in the Republic of Ireland (paragraph 98). **60**

Parent undertakings not subject to the Act

The FRS is drafted in terms derived from the Act but applies to all parent undertakings that prepare financial statements intended to give a true and fair view. A parent undertaking not subject to the Act should comply with the requirements of the FRS, and of the Act where referred to in the FRS, except to the extent that these requirements are not permitted by any statutory framework under which the undertaking reports. By reference to the Act, which in most cases accords with requirements the FRS might otherwise introduce itself in respect of such undertakings, the FRS achieves a single set of requirements relating to the preparation of consolidated financial statements both for companies that report under the Act and for other undertakings. **61**

The relationship between the legal background and accounting principles

The accounting concept that underlies the presentation of consolidated financial statements for a group as a single economic entity is summarised in the definition of control in paragraph 6. Although the definitions of parent and subsidiary undertakings in the Act are founded mainly on the accounting concept of control, section 1162 uses a list of tests, including control, to determine which undertakings are parent and subsidiary undertakings. In the main, the effect of applying the tests in the Act is the same as using a criterion based solely on the accounting concept of control. There may, however, be cases where section 1162 identifies more than one undertaking as the parent undertaking of the same subsidiary undertaking. Where more than one undertaking is thereby identified as a parent of one subsidiary undertaking, not more than one of those parents can have control as defined in paragraph 6. **62**

In practice, such apparent differences between the effects of applying the Act and the Standard can generally be resolved by taking into account the following factors: **63**

(a) the existence of a quasi-subsidiary (paragraph 64); or
(b) the existence of severe long-term restrictions on the rights of the parent undertaking (paragraph 65); or
(c) the existence of a joint venture agreement, whether formal or informal (paragraphs 66 and 67).

Undertakings that are directly or indirectly controlled by another undertaking and are sources of benefit to that other, but do not qualify according to the tests in the Act as subsidiary undertakings, are described as 'quasi-subsidiaries'. The definition and treatment of quasi-subsidiaries are not dealt with in this Standard*. **64**

**See FRS 5 'Reporting the Substance of Transactions'.*

65 The Act allows a subsidiary undertaking to be excluded from consolidation if the parent undertaking suffers severe long-term restrictions that substantially hinder the exercise of its rights over the assets or management of the subsidiary undertaking. Paragraph 78(c) discusses severe long-term restrictions further.

66 The control that identifies undertakings as parent and subsidiary undertakings should be distinguished from shared control, for example, as in a joint venture. It is the parent undertaking's sole control of its subsidiary undertakings that gives it access to its subsidiary undertakings' resources. The parent undertaking extends its economic activities through its subsidiary undertakings using their assets and liabilities in a similar way to its own. The ability of an undertaking that shares control to direct the operating and financial policies of the undertaking in which control is shared is circumscribed by the need to take account of the wishes of the other parties that share control. An undertaking identified as a parent by section 1162 that shares control over its subsidiary undertaking may be suffering from severe long-term restrictions, as discussed in paragraph 78(c), in relation to the undertaking in which it shares control.

67 Where the tests of the Act identify more than one undertaking as the parent of one subsidiary undertaking it is likely that they have shared control and, therefore, their interests in the subsidiary undertaking are in effect interests in a joint venture and should be treated accordingly. Alternatively, one or more of the undertakings identified under the Act as a parent undertaking may exercise a non-controlling but significant influence over its subsidiary undertaking, in which case it would be more appropriate to treat that subsidiary undertaking in the same way as an associated undertaking rather than to include it in the consolidation.

Identifying parent and subsidiary undertakings

68 Parent and subsidiary undertakings are defined in the FRS by applying the provisions of section 1162, which are repeated in an abbreviated form in paragraph 14 of the FRS. In addition, the FRS defines some of the phrases that are used in the Act to define undertakings that are parent or subsidiary undertakings. Paragraphs 69-74 below consider some of the terms used.

Dominant influence

69 The Act uses 'dominant influence' as a key phrase in two of the conditions of section 1162 that identify parent and subsidiary undertakings.

70 Section 1162(2)(c) identifies an undertaking as a parent undertaking if it has the right to exercise a dominant influence over another undertaking:

(a) by virtue of provisions contained in the undertaking's memorandum or articles; or

(b) by virtue of a control contract.

Schedule 7 paragraph 4(1) states that for the purposes of section 1162(2)(c) 'an undertaking shall not be regarded as having the right to exercise a dominant influence over another undertaking unless it has a right to give directions with respect to the operating and financial policies of that other undertaking which its directors are obliged to comply with whether or not they are for the benefit of that other undertaking'. This forms the basis of the definition set out in paragraph 7(a) of the FRS. In the United Kingdom, directors are bound by a duty to promote the success of the company for the benefit of its members as a whole (section 172 of the Act). For this reason there may, in some cases, be a risk that accepting a right to exercise dominant influence, as here defined, would be in breach of the above duty.

In a second reference to dominant influence, section 1162(4)(a) identifies an undertaking as the subsidiary undertaking of another (its parent undertaking) if that other has the power to exercise, or actually exercises, dominant influence over it. Schedule 7 paragraph 4(3) provides that the definition of the 'right to exercise a dominant influence' for the purposes of section 1162(2)(c) shall not affect the construction of 'actually exercises a dominant influence' in section 1162(4)(a). The FRS defines the 'actual exercise of dominant influence' as the exercise of an influence that achieves the result that the operating and financial policies of the undertaking influenced are set in accordance with the wishes of the holder of the influence and for its benefit (whether or not those wishes are explicit). The FRS defines 'the power to exercise dominant influence' as a power that, if exercised, would give rise to the actual exercise of dominant influence. **71**

As indicated in paragraph 7(b) of the FRS, the actual exercise of dominant influence is identified by its effect in practice rather than the means by which it is exercised. The effect of the exercise of dominant influence is that the undertaking under influence implements the operating and financial policies that the holder of the influence desires. Thus, a power of veto, or any other reserve power that has the necessary effect in practice, can form the basis whereby one undertaking actually exercises a dominant influence over another. However, such powers are likely to lead to the holder actually exercising a dominant influence over an undertaking only if they are held in conjunction with other rights or powers or if they relate to the day-to-day activities of that undertaking and no similar veto is held by other parties unconnected to the holder. The full circumstances of each case should be considered, including the effect of any formal or informal agreements between the undertakings, to decide whether or not one undertaking actually exercises a dominant influence over another. Commercial relationships such as that of supplier, customer or lender do not of themselves constitute dominant influence. **72**

A parent undertaking may actually exercise its dominant influence in an interventionist or non-interventionist way. For example, a parent undertaking may set directly and in detail the operating and financial policies of its subsidiary undertaking or it may prefer to influence these by setting out in outline the kind of results it wants achieved without being involved regularly or on a day-to-day basis. Because of the variety of ways that dominant influence may be exercised, evidence of continuous intervention is not necessary to support the view that dominant influence is actually exercised. Sufficient evidence might be provided by a rare intervention on a critical matter. Once there has been evidence that one undertaking has exercised a dominant influence over another, then the dominant undertaking should be assumed to continue to exercise its influence until there is evidence to the contrary. However, it is still necessary for the preparation of the consolidated financial statements to examine the relationship between the undertakings each year to assess any evidence of change in status that may have arisen. **73**

Managed on a unified basis

Section 1162(4)(b) identifies an undertaking as a parent undertaking of another undertaking (its subsidiary undertaking) if it and that other undertaking are managed on a unified basis. Undertakings are managed on a unified basis if the whole of the operations of the undertakings are integrated and they are managed as a single unit. Unified management does not arise solely because one undertaking manages **74** another because this may not fulfil the condition that the operations of the undertakings are integrated.

Preparation of consolidated financial statements

75 The requirements of the FRS apply to all parent undertakings that prepare consolidated financial statements intended to give a true and fair view of the financial position and profit or loss of the group. In giving such a view, the same accounting principles apply in general to consolidated financial statements as would apply to the financial statements of a single entity. Parent undertakings should comply with the requirements of the FRS in preparing consolidated financial statements giving a true and fair view, even if the parent undertaking is not specifically required to prepare consolidated financial statements.

Exclusion of subsidiary undertakings from consolidation

76 The Act requires that all the subsidiary undertakings of a parent undertaking are to be included in the consolidated financial statements for that group, subject to the exemptions permitted by section 405(2) and (3). The circumstances in which the Act permits a subsidiary undertaking to be excluded from consolidation are the following:

(a) 'if its inclusion is not material for the purpose of giving a true and fair view (but two or more undertakings may be excluded only if they are not material taken together)'; or

(b) 'where the information necessary for the preparation of group accounts cannot be obtained without disproportionate expense or undue delay'; or

(c) 'where severe long-term restrictions substantially hinder the exercise of the rights of the parent company over the assets or management of that undertaking'; or

(d) 'where the interest of the parent company is held exclusively with a view to subsequent resale'.

77 Within this statutory framework, the FRS elaborates on the conditions for exclusion set out in the Act so that these identify, as far as possible, only those undertakings, defined as subsidiary undertakings by section 1162, that are not controlled by their parent undertaking in a way that would in principle justify consolidation. This gives effect to the Board's view that a parent undertaking should consolidate all those undertakings that are its subsidiary undertakings unless there are circumstances that make consolidation inappropriate. Under the circumstances set out in paragraph 78(c) and (d) below, the FRS requires the parent undertaking to exclude a subsidiary undertaking because the same conditions that justify permitting exclusion of a subsidiary undertaking also make consolidation of that undertaking inappropriate. Exclusion from consolidation is not the only way of clarifying the effect on the group of the circumstances affecting some of its subsidiary undertakings; exclusion should only be used exceptionally. In many cases, circumstances such as restrictions or activities with special risks are better dealt with by disclosure, for example, by giving additional segmental information rather than by exclusion from consolidation of the subsidiary undertakings concerned.

78 In order to help preparers identify the exceptional circumstances where it is inappropriate to consolidate a subsidiary undertaking, the exclusions allowed by section 405(2) and (3) are discussed below.

Materiality

(a) The FRS deals only with material items. Thus, this ground for exclusion requires no special mention in the FRS. The Act only allows exclusion for two or more subsidiary undertakings if they are not material taken together.

Disproportionate expense and undue delay

(b) In principle, neither expense nor delay can justify excluding from consolidation subsidiary undertakings that are individually or collectively material in the context of the group.

Severe long-term restrictions

(c) Restrictions are only relevant to justify the exclusion of a subsidiary undertaking from consolidation if the restrictions substantially hinder the exercise of the rights of the parent undertaking over the assets or management of the subsidiary undertaking. The rights affected must be those by reason of which the undertaking holding them is the parent undertaking and without which it would not be the parent undertaking. Severe long-term restrictions justify excluding a subsidiary undertaking from consolidation only where the effect of those restrictions is that the parent undertaking does not control its subsidiary undertaking. Severe long-term restrictions are identified by their effect in practice rather than by the way in which the restrictions are imposed. For example, a subsidiary undertaking should not be excluded because restrictions are threatened or because another party has the power to impose them, unless such threats or the existence of such a power has a severe and restricting effect in practice in the long-term on the rights of the parent undertaking. Generally, restrictions are dealt with better by disclosure than by non-consolidation. However, the loss of the parent undertaking's control over its subsidiary undertaking resulting from severe long-term restrictions would make it misleading to include that subsidiary undertaking in the consolidation. Where a subsidiary undertaking is subject to an insolvency procedure in the United Kingdom, control over that undertaking may have passed to a designated official (for example, an administrator, administrative receiver or liquidator) with the effect that severe long-term restrictions are in force. A company voluntary arrangement does not necessarily lead to loss of control. In some overseas jurisdictions even formal insolvency procedures may not amount to loss of control.

Interest held exclusively with a view to subsequent resale

(d) This exclusion applies only to those undertakings that have never formed a continuing part of group activities and have not previously been included in consolidated financial statements prepared by the parent undertaking. Paragraph 11 defines the two sets of circumstances in which an interest in a subsidiary undertaking is considered to be held exclusively with a view to subsequent resale. The first set of circumstances (paragraph 11(a)) depends on an immediate intention to sell and the expectation of a sale within approximately one year. An interest for which a sale is not completed within a year of its acquisition may still fulfil the conditions of paragraph 11(a) if, at the date the accounts are signed, the terms of the sale have been agreed and the process of disposing of that interest is substantially complete. The second set of circumstances (paragraph 11(b)) depends on the way in which the interest was acquired, that is, whether it was acquired as a result of the enforcement of a security. The provisions of Schedule 7 paragraph 8(b) may be relevant in determining whether such an interest has been acquired. This paragraph provides that rights attached to shares held as a security are to be treated as held by the person providing the security, where the shares are held in connection with the granting of loans as part of normal business activities and, apart from the right to exercise them to preserve the value of the security or to realise it, the rights are exercisable only in the interests of the provider of the security.

79 ***Treatment of excluded subsidiary undertakings***

Severe long-term restrictions

(a) Where severe long-term restrictions are in force so that a subsidiary undertaking is no longer under the control of its parent undertaking, that subsidiary undertaking should not be consolidated. From the date severe long-term restrictions come into force and until they are lifted, the subsidiary undertaking subject to the restrictions should be excluded from consolidation and treated instead as a fixed asset investment. If restrictions are in force when the subsidiary undertaking is acquired, it should be carried initially at cost; if restrictions came into force at a later date, the subsidiary undertaking should be carried at a fixed amount calculated using the equity method as at the date the restrictions came into force. If, in spite of severe long-term restrictions, the parent undertaking retains significant influence over a subsidiary undertaking, the investment should be treated as an associated undertaking using the equity method. Because severe long-term restrictions may give rise to impairment, the FRS requires the value of the excluded subsidiary undertaking to be reviewed to assess whether any impairment has occurred. Any intra-group amounts due from such excluded subsidiary undertakings may also be affected by severe long-term restrictions, particularly if the restrictions extend to remittances. These balances should also be reviewed and provision made as necessary.

Held exclusively for resale

(b) A subsidiary undertaking held exclusively for resale and not previously included in the consolidated financial statements of the parent undertaking does not form part of the continuing activities of the group. Although the parent undertaking (as identified by section 1162 and paragraph 14 of the FRS) may control such a subsidiary undertaking, its control is temporary and is not used to deploy the underlying assets and liabilities of that subsidiary undertaking as part of the continuing group's activities for the benefit of the parent undertaking of the group. The subsidiary undertaking is therefore excluded from consolidation and the temporary nature of the parent undertaking's interest is recognised by carrying it as a current asset at the lower of cost and net realisable value.

(c) Withdrawn.

Intra-group guarantees re excluded subsidiary undertakings

(d) Liabilities to third parties of one group member guaranteed by another are themselves included in the consolidated financial statements so that intra-group guarantees do not normally require disclosure. Guarantees in respect of subsidiary undertakings excluded from consolidation have to be treated in the same way as guarantees given by members of the group to third parties because, in these cases, the intra-group guarantees relate to liabilities that are not included gross in the consolidated financial statements.

Minority interests

80 Despite the title 'Minority interests', there is, in principle, no upper limit to the proportion of shares in a subsidiary undertaking which may be held as a minority interest while the parent undertaking still qualifies as such under section 1162 of the Act (described in paragraph 14 of the FRS). The amounts reported in the consolidated balance sheet and profit and loss account for the minority interests indicate the extent to which the assets and liabilities and profits and losses of subsidiary undertakings included in the consolidation are attributable to shareholders other than the parent or its other subsidiary undertakings. The effect of the existence of minority interests on the returns to investors in the parent undertaking is best reflected by presenting the net identifiable assets attributable to minority interests on the same basis as those attributable to group interests. Using the same basis for including group assets and liabilities, irrespective of the extent to which they are attributable to the minority interest, presents the assets and liabilities on a consistent basis for the group as a whole.

The FRS requires that losses be attributed to the minority interest in a loss making subsidiary undertaking, regardless of whether or not this leads to a debit balance for the minority interest; to do otherwise would obscure the comparison between the assets and liabilities and results attributable to the minority interest and those attributable to the group interests both during the periods when the accumulated losses accrue and afterwards, if these are then made good by later profits. Accumulated losses of subsidiary undertakings do not of themselves necessarily require funding by the parent undertaking and a debit balance for minority interests represents net liabilities attributable to the shares held by the minorities in that subsidiary undertaking rather than a debt due from them. The group should provide for any commercial or legal obligation (whether formal or implied) to provide finance that may not be recoverable in respect of the accumulated losses attributable to the minority interests. Provisions of this sort would include the minorities' share of any liability guaranteed by the group, or any liability that the group itself would be likely to settle for commercial or other reasons, if the subsidiary undertaking could not do so itself. Any provision made with respect to minority debit balances should be set directly against the minority interest amount in the profit and loss account and the balance sheet. **81**

The FRS requires that the goodwill arising on acquisition of a subsidiary undertaking that is not wholly owned should be recognised only in relation to the group's interest and that none should be attributed to the minority interest. Although it might be possible to estimate by extrapolation or valuation an amount of goodwill attributable to the minority when a subsidiary undertaking is acquired, this would in effect recognise an amount for goodwill that is hypothetical because the minority is not a party to the transaction by which the subsidiary undertaking is acquired. **82**

Consolidation adjustments and intra-group transactions

Presenting information about the economic activities of the group as a single economic entity in consolidated financial statements requires adjustment for intra-group transactions of the amounts reported in the individual financial statements of the parent and its subsidiary undertakings. Intra-group transactions may result in a profit or loss that is included at least temporarily in the book value of group assets. To the extent that such assets are still held in the undertakings included in the consolidation at the balance sheet date, the related profits or losses recorded in the individual financial statements have not arisen for the group as a whole and must therefore be eliminated from group results and asset values. The elimination should be in full, even where the transactions involve subsidiary undertakings with minority interests. Transactions between undertakings included in the consolidation deal with the assets and liabilities that are wholly within the group's control, even if they are not wholly owned. From the perspective of the group as a single entity no profit or loss arises on intra-group transactions because no increase or decrease in the group's net assets has occurred. Profits or losses arising on transactions with undertakings excluded from consolidation because they are held exclusively with a view to subsequent re-sale or because of severe long-term restrictions need not be eliminated, **83** except to the extent appropriate where significant influence is retained and the subsidiary undertaking is treated as an associated undertaking. However, it is important to consider whether it is prudent to record any profit arising from transactions with subsidiary undertakings excluded on these grounds.

Changes in composition of a group

84 The date on which an undertaking becomes or ceases to be another undertaking's subsidiary undertaking marks the point at which a new accounting treatment for that undertaking is applied. The relevant date is the date on which control passes and paragraph 45 of the FRS is framed in these terms. This date should also be the one on which an undertaking begins or ceases to qualify as a parent or subsidiary undertaking under section 1162. The date on which control passes is a matter of fact and cannot be backdated or otherwise altered.

85 Where control is transferred by a public offer, the date control is transferred is the date the offer becomes unconditional, usually as a result of a sufficient number of acceptances being received. For private treaties, the date control is transferred is generally the date an unconditional offer is accepted. Where an undertaking becomes or ceases to be a subsidiary undertaking as a result of the issue or cancellation of shares, the date control is transferred is the date of issue or cancellation. The date that control passes may be indicated by the acquiring party commencing its direction of the operating and financial policies of the acquired undertaking or by changes in the flow of economic benefits. The date on which the consideration for the transfer of control is paid is often an important indication of the date on which a subsidiary undertaking is acquired or disposed of. However, the date the consideration passes is not conclusive evidence of the date of the transfer of control because this date can be set to fall on a date other than that on which control is transferred, with compensation for any lead or lag included in the consideration. Consideration may also paid in instalments.

86 An undertaking may cease to be a subsidiary undertaking as a result of the parent undertaking losing control over it because of changes in the rights it holds or in those held by another party in that subsidiary undertaking. A parent undertaking may also lose control of its subsidiary undertaking because of changes in some other arrangement that gave it control without there being any change in the former parent undertaking's holding in its former subsidiary undertaking. For example, control may pass if there is a change in voting rights or in how these are allocated. In these circumstances neither a gain nor a loss accrues in the consolidated financial statements, unless there is a payment for the transfer of control, because there is no change in the net assets attributable to the group's holding in the former subsidiary undertaking. The assets and liabilities of the former subsidiary undertaking should cease to be consolidated but should be shown instead as an associated undertaking or investment as appropriate.

87 An undertaking usually ceases to be a subsidiary undertaking because the group reduces its proportional interest in that undertaking. The reduction of the group's interest may result from its directly disposing of part of the interest it holds or from a deemed disposal. Any reduction in the group's proportional interest other than by a direct disposal is a deemed disposal. Disposals and deemed disposals may give rise to profits or losses for the group, which should be calculated as set out in paragraph 47. There may be other losses or gains that arise for the group as a result of an undertaking ceasing to be a subsidiary undertaking. These are not part of the direct gain or loss described here, but may need to be provided for if they are quantifiable or otherwise disclosed to show the full effect of the cessation. Deemed disposals may arise where the group's interest in a subsidiary undertaking is reduced, inter alia:

(a) because the parent undertaking and its group do not take up their full allocation of rights in a rights issue; or
(b) because the parent undertaking and its group do not take up their full share of scrip dividends while other equity holders in that subsidiary undertaking take up some, at least, of their share; or
(c) because another party has exercised its options or warrants; or
(d) because the subsidiary undertaking has issued shares to parties other than the parent undertaking and its group.

Changes in stake

When an undertaking is first consolidated, its identifiable assets and liabilities are initially brought into the consolidation at their fair values at the date of its acquisition as a subsidiary undertaking (the acquisition method of accounting as provided by Schedule 6 paragraph 9 of the Regulations). Where a subsidiary undertaking is acquired in stages, its net identifiable assets and liabilities are to be included in the consolidation at their fair values on the date it becomes a subsidiary undertaking, rather than at the date of the earlier purchases. Using other methods to compute the amounts to be included in the consolidation would fail to give a full picture of the assets and liabilities acquired that now comprise part of the group's resources. **88**

The effect of the Schedule 6 paragraph 9 of the Regulations' method of acquisition accounting is to treat as goodwill, or negative goodwill, the whole of the difference between, on the one hand, the fair value at the date an undertaking becomes a subsidiary undertaking of the group's share of its identifiable assets and liabilities and, on the other hand, the total acquisition cost of the interests held by the group in that subsidiary undertaking. This applies even where part of the acquisition cost arises from purchases of interests at earlier dates. In the generality of cases this method provides a practical means of applying acquisition accounting because it does not require retrospective assessments of the fair values of the identifiable assets and liabilities of the acquired undertaking. In special circumstances, however, not using fair values at the dates of earlier purchases while using an acquisition cost part of which relates to earlier purchases, may result in accounting that is inconsistent with the way the investment has been treated previously and, for that reason, may fail to give a true and fair view. For example, an undertaking that has been treated as an associated undertaking by a group may then be acquired by that group as a subsidiary undertaking. Using the method required by Schedule 6 paragraph 9 of the Regulations to calculate goodwill on such an acquisition has the effect that the group's share of profits or losses and reserve movements of its associated undertaking becomes reclassified as goodwill (usually negative goodwill). A similar problem may arise where the group has substantially restated its investment in an undertaking that subsequently becomes its subsidiary undertaking. For example, where such an investment has been written down because it is impaired, the effect of applying the Schedule 6 paragraph 9 of the Regulations' method of acquisition accounting would be to increase reserves and create an asset (goodwill). In the rare cases where the Schedule 6 paragraph 9 of the Regulations' calculation of goodwill would be misleading, goodwill should be calculated as the sum of goodwill arising from each purchase of an interest in the relevant undertaking adjusted as necessary for any subsequent impairment. Goodwill arising on each purchase should be calculated as the difference between the cost of that purchase and the fair value at the date of that purchase of the identifiable assets and liabilities attributable to the interest purchased. The difference between the goodwill calculated on this method and that calculated on the method provided by the Act is shown in reserves. Section **89**

404(5) sets out the disclosures required in cases where the statutory requirement is not applied.

90 Where a group increases its stake in an undertaking that is already its subsidiary undertaking, the consideration paid may not be equal to the fair value of the identifiable assets and liabilities previously attributed to the minority and now acquired from the minority. If the assets and liabilities were not revalued to fair values before calculating the goodwill arising on the change in stake, then the difference between the consideration paid and the relevant proportion of the carrying value of net assets acquired would be made up in part of goodwill and in part of changes in value. The FRS requires that the assets and liabilities of the subsidiary undertaking be revalued to fair value at the date of the increase in stake unless the difference between the fair values and the carrying amounts of the share of net assets acquired is not material.

91 Where the group decreases its stake in an undertaking whether or not it continues to be a subsidiary undertaking, a profit or loss generally arises. Consolidated financial statements are prepared from the perspective of investors in the parent undertaking of the group. Where the group disposes of part of its interest in a subsidiary undertaking, it transacts directly with third parties and a profit or loss for the group arises and is reported in the consolidated financial statements. This can be contrasted with the treatment of intra-group transactions where no profit or loss arises for the group as a whole because the transaction involves only undertakings included in the consolidation and under common control and does not directly involve any third party.

Distributions

92 Withdrawn.

Disclosures

93 The FRS refers to the disclosure requirements of the Act and the Regulations and, where appropriate, adds further disclosure requirements of its own. By referring to certain of the disclosure requirements in the Act and the Regulations in the text of the statement of standard accounting practice, the FRS extends these disclosure requirements to parent undertakings not subject to the Act. Requirements of the Act and the Regulations are identified by section, regulation or schedule numbers; reference to the Act and the Regulations is necessary to ascertain the full disclosures required.

Segmental information

94 Segmental information has a particular importance in group financial reporting. The aggregation and adjustments required to consolidate financial information for the parent undertaking and its subsidiary undertakings may obscure information about the different undertakings and activities included in the consolidated financial statements. The information about the separate group activities that may be obscured by consolidation can be restored by giving information about the group on a segmental basis. Parent undertakings should consider how to provide segmental information for their group, indicating the different risks and rewards, growth and prospects of the different parts of the group and treating the requirements of SSAP 25 'Segmental reporting' as a minimum rather than a limit to disclosure. Two examples of how segmental information could supplement consolidated financial statements are given below.

Segmentation rather than exclusion for certain subsidiary undertakings

(a) Where the FRS discusses excluding subsidiary undertakings from consolidation, it stresses the importance of the completeness of the information presented in the consolidated financial statements. Thus, where subsidiary undertakings engage in different activities or are subject to certain restrictions that are not such as to require exclusion from consolidation under the FRS, the most complete picture is presented by consolidating the subsidiary undertakings concerned and giving additional information or by identifying the assets, liabilities and results attributable to undertakings engaging in those activities or subject to those restrictions.

Minority interests

(b) Users of consolidated financial statements who are interested in assessing the effect of the existence of minority interests in certain parts of the group on the expected returns to investors in the parent undertaking may find it helpful to have information showing the amounts attributable to the minority interest in different group segments.

Note of legal requirements

Legal requirements in United Kingdom

Readers should refer to the Act or the Regulations themselves for an understanding of the relevant points of law. This section lists only the main sections in the Act or the Regulations containing provisions in relation to subsidiary undertakings. The provisions of the Act and the Regulations are not considered further here because they are dealt with in the many references to the Act and the Regulations in the other sections of the FRS.

Main sections of the Companies Act 2006

The main sections of the Companies Act 2006 containing provisions relating to the preparation of consolidated financial statements are the following: **95**

Section	**Topic**
398	Option to prepare group accounts
399	Duty to prepare group accounts
400	Exemption for company included in EEA group accounts of larger group
401	Exemption for company included in non-EEA group accounts of larger group
402	Exemption if no subsidiary undertakings need be included in the consolidation
403	Group accounts; applicable accounting framework
404	Companies Act group accounts
405	Companies Act group accounts: subsidiary undertakings included in the consolidation
409	Information about related undertakings
410	Information about related undertakings: alternative compliance
1161	Meaning of 'undertaking' and related expressions
1162	Parent and subsidiary undertakings

95A The main sections of The Large and Medium-sized Companies and Groups (Accounts and Reports) Regulations 2008 containing provisions relating to the preparation of consolidated financial statements are the following:

Section	**Topic**
Regulation 7 and Schedule 4	Information on related undertakings required whether preparing Companies Act or IAS Accounts
Schedule 6	Companies Act Group Accounts

95B The main sections of The Small Companies and Groups (Accounts and Directors' Report) Regulations 2008 containing provisions relating to the preparation of consolidated financial statements are the following:

Section		**Topic**
Regulation 8 to 11 and Schedule 6		
	Part 1	Form and Content of Companies Act Group Accounts
	Part 2	Information about related undertakings where company preparing group accounts (Companies Act or IAS Group Accounts)

Disclosure requirements

96 The following sections and paragraphs give the main disclosure requirements of the Act and the Regulations with respect to consolidated financial statements.

Section 404(4) and (5)
Sections 400(2) and 401(2)
Section 409
Schedule 6 to the Regulations – 'Companies Act Group Accounts' – Paragraphs 3, 4, 13, 14, 15 and 17

Regulation 7 and Schedule 4 to the Regulations – 'Information on Related Undertakings required whether preparing Companies Act or IAS Accounts'

97 Withdrawn.

Legal Requirements in the Republic of Ireland

98 The following table shows the provisions in the Companies Acts 1963-2006 and various Regulations implementing EC Accounting Directives, corresponding to the provisions of the UK Companies Act 2006 ('the 2006 Act') and the Schedules to the Large and Medium-sized Companies and Groups (Accounts and Reports) Regulations 2008 ('the 2008 Regulations') referred to in the Standard. The principal pieces of Irish legislation referred to in the table below are:

- The Companies Act 1963 ('1963 Act');
- The Companies (Amendment) Act 1986 ('1986 Act');
- The European Communities (Companies: Group Accounts) Regulations 1992 – SI 201 of 1992 ('Group Accounts Regulations 1992' or 'GAR 1992');

- The European Communities (Credit Institutions: Accounts) Regulations 1992 – SI 294 of 1992 – ('Credit Institutions Regulations 1992' or 'CIR 1992');
- The European Communities (Insurance Undertakings: Accounts) Regulations 1996, SI 23 of 1996 – ('Insurance Undertakings Regulations 1996' or 'IUR 1996').

This section is intended as a reference guide to the corresponding provisions in Irish company law and does not purport to be comprehensive. Readers are advised to refer to the Irish legislation for an understanding of relevant legal points.

Paragraph of FRS 2	UK References	ROI References				
	2006 Act and the 2008 Regulations	**1963 Act / 1986 Act**	**GAR 1992**	**CIR 1992**	**IUR 1996**	**Comments**
Summary						
Para a	Companies Act 2006 ('the 2006 Act')	Companies Act 1963 ('1963 Act'); Companies (Amendment) Act 1986 ('1986 Act')	European Communities (Companies: Group Accounts) Regulations 1992 ('GAR 1992')	European Communities (Credit Institutions: Accounts) Regulations 1992 ('CIR 1992')	European Communities (Insurance Undertakings: Accounts) Regulations 1996 ('IUR 1996')	Companies Acts 1963-2006
Para e	Section 400		Regulations 8 and 9	Regulation 8	Regulation 12	
Para e	Section 401		Regulation 9A	Regulation 8A	Regulation 12A	
Para e	Section 402			Paragraph 2(8) of Part II of the Schedule		No explicit equivalent to paragraph 2(8) in the Group Accounts Regulations 1992 (GAR 1992) or the Insurance Undertakings Regulations 1996 (IUR 1996).
Statement of Standard Accounting Practice						
Para 7a	Section 1162(2)(c)		Regulation 4(1)(b)	Regulation 2(1)	Regulation 11(1)(b)	
Para 14	Section 1162	Section 155 (1963 Act)	Regulation 4	Regulation 2(1)	Regulation 11	

Paragraph of FRS 2	UK References	ROI References				
	2006 Act and the 2008 Regulations	1963 Act / 1986 Act	GAR 1992	CIR 1992	IUR 1996	Comments
Para 15	The Large and Medium-sized Companies and Group (Accounts and Reports) Regulations 2008 – SI 2008 No 410 – ('the 2008 Regulations')		Schedule	Schedule	Schedule	
Para 17	Schedule 7 of the 2006 Act	Section 155 (1963 Act)	Regulation 4	Regulation 2(1)	Regulation 11	No explicit equivalent in Irish company law; the provisions noted deal with various aspects of holding and subsidiary undertakings.
Para 21a	Section 400(2)		Regulation 8(3)	Regulations 8(1) and 8(3)	Regulations 12(1) and 12(3)	
Para 21b	Sections 400(2) and 400(1)(b)		Regulations 8(1)-(3) and 9	Regulations 8(1)-(3) and 8(6)	Regulations 12(1)-(3) and 12(6)	
Para 21c	Section 401(2)		Regulations 9A(1) and 9A(3)	Regulations 8A(1) and 8A(3)	Regulations 12A(1) and 12A(3)	
Para 21d	Sections 401(2) and 401(1)(b)		Regulations 9A(3) and 9A(1)(b)	Regulations 8A(3) and 8A(1)(b)	Regulations 12A(3) and 12A(1)(b)	

Paragraph of FRS 2	UK References	ROI References				
	2006 Act and the 2008 Regulations	1963 Act / 1986 Act	GAR 1992	CIR 1992	IUR 1996	Comments
Para 21e	Section 405		Regulations 10 and 11	Paragraph 2 of Part II of the Schedule	Paragraph 2 of Part IV of the Schedule	
Para 22	Schedule 4 10(1) of the Regulations	Paragraph 54(2)(a) of the Schedule (1986 Act)	Regulations 8(3)(d), 9(2) and 9A(3)(d)	Regulations 8(3)(d) and 8A(3)(d)	Regulations 12(3)(d) and 12A(3)(d)	
Para 25	Section 405(3)		Regulation 11	Paragraph 2(3) of Part II of the Schedule	Paragraph 2(3) of Part IV of the Schedule	
Para 25a	Section 1162	Section 155 (1963 Act)	Regulation 4	Regulation 2(1)	Regulation 11	
Para 26	Section 409 and regulation 7 and Schedule 4 16(1) of the Regulations	Section 16(1) and paragraph 54(2)(a) of the Schedule (1986 Act)	Paragraph 18(2) of the Schedule	Paragraph 11 of Part III of the Schedule	Paragraphs 32 and 33 of Part IV of the Schedule	
Para 31	Section 409 and regulation 7 Schedule 4 Parts 1 and 3 of the Regulations	Section 16, Paragraphs 45, 45A, 46, 46A, 54 and 55 of the Schedule (1986 Act).	Paragraphs 18-22 of the Schedule	Regulation 10; Part III of the Schedule	Paragraphs 32-36 of Part IV of the Schedule	The provisions noted set out the requirements of Irish company law with regard to information on related undertaking

Paragraph of FRS 2	UK References	ROI References				
	2006 Act and the 2008 Regulations	**1963 Act / 1986 Act**	**GAR 1992**	**CIR 1992**	**IUR 1996**	**Comments**
Para 32	Section 405(3)		Regulation 11	Paragraph 2(3) of Part II of the Schedule	Paragraph 2(3) of Part IV of the Schedule	
Para 33	Schedule 4 of the Regulations	Section 16, Paragraphs 45, 45A, 46, 46A, 54 and 55 of the Schedule (1986 Act)	Paragraphs 18-22 of the Schedule	Regulation 10; Part III of the Schedule	Paragraphs 32-36 of Part IV of the Schedule	The provisions noted set out the requirements of Irish company law with regard to information on related undertakings.
Para 34	Section 409 and paragraphs 1 and 16 of Schedule 4 of the Regulations	Section 16(1) and paragraph 54(2)(a) of the Schedule (1986 Act)	Paragraph 18(2) of the Schedule	Paragraphs 1 and 11 of Part III of the Schedule	Paragraphs 32 and 33 of Part IV of the Schedule	The provisions noted set out the requirements of Irish company law with regard to information on related undertakings.
Para 35	Paragraph 17(2) of Schedule 6 of the Regulations		Paragraph 8(2) of the Schedule	Paragraph 18(2) of Part II of the Schedule	Paragraph 19(2) of Part IV of the Schedule	
Para 36	Paragraphs 17(3)(a) and 17(3)(b) of Schedule 6 of the Regulations		Paragraph 9 of the Schedule	Paragraphs 18(3) and 18(4) of Part II of the Schedule	Paragraphs 19(3) and 19(4) of Part IV of the Schedule	

Paragraph of FRS 2	UK References	ROI References				
	2006 Act and the 2008 Regulations	1963 Act / 1986 Act	GAR 1992	CIR 1992	IUR 1996	Comments
Para 41	Paragraph 3(2) of Schedule 6 of the Regulations		Regulation 30(3)	Paragraph 4(2) of Part II of the Schedule	Paragraph 15(2) of Part IV of the Schedule	
Para 45	Paragraph 9 of Schedule 6 of the Regulations		Regulation 19	Paragraph 10 of Part II of the Schedule	Paragraph 9 of Part IV of the Schedule	
Para 48	Paragraph 15 of Schedule 6 of the Regulations		Regulation 27	Paragraph 16 of Part II of the Schedule	Paragraph 6 of Part IV of the Schedule	Irish company law requires that where the composition of the undertakings dealt with in the group accounts has changed significantly, information must be provided to make the comparison of successive sets of group accounts meaningful.
Para 50	Paragraph 9 of Schedule 6 of the Regulations		Regulation 19	Paragraph 10 of Part II of the Schedule	Paragraph 9 of Part IV of the Schedule	
Explanation						
Para 62	Section 1162	Section 155 (1963 Act)	Regulation 4	Regulation 2(1)	Regulation 11	
Para 66	Section 1162	Section 155 (1963 Act)	Regulation 4	Regulation 2(1)	Regulation 11	

Paragraph of FRS 2	UK References	ROI References				
	2006 Act and the 2008 Regulations	1963 Act / 1986 Act	GAR 1992	CIR 1992	IUR 1996	Comments
Para 68	Section 1162	Section 155 (1963 Act)	Regulation 4	Regulation 2(1)	Regulation 11	
Para 69	Section 1162	Section 155 (1963 Act)	Regulation 4	Regulation 2(1)	Regulation 11	
Para 70	Section 1162(2)(c)		Regulation 4(1)(b)	Regulation 2(1)	Regulation 11(1)(b)	
Para 70	Paragraph 4(1) of Schedule 7 of the 2006 Act		Regulation 4(5)	Regulation 2(1)	Regulation 11(5)	
Para 70	Section 172					No corresponding Irish provision.
Para 71	Section 1162(4)(a)		Regulation 4(1)(c)	Regulation 2(1)	Regulation 11(1)(c)	
Para 71	Paragraph 4(3) of Schedule 7 of the 2006 Act		Regulation 4(7)	Regulation 2(1)	Regulation 11(7)	
Para 71	Section 1162(2)(c)		Regulation 4(1)(b)	Regulation 2(1)	Regulation 11(1)(b)	
Para 74	Section 1162(4)(b)		Regulation 4(1)(ca)	Regulation 2(1)	Regulation 11(1)(ca)	
Para 76	Section 405(2) and 405(3)		Regulations 10 and 11	Paragraph 2 of Part II of the Schedule	Paragraph 2 of Part IV of the Schedule	

Paragraph of FRS 2	UK References	ROI References				
	2006 Act and the 2008 Regulations	1963 Act / 1986 Act	GAR 1992	CIR 1992	IUR 1996	Comments
Para 77	Section 1162	Section 155 (1963 Act)	Regulation 4	Regulation 2(1)	Regulation 11	
Para 78	Section 405(2) and 405(3)		Regulations 10 and 11	Paragraph 2 of Part II of the Schedule	Paragraph 2 of Part IV of the Schedule	
Para 78d	Paragraph 8(b) of Schedule 7 of the 2006 Act		Regulation 4(3)(c)	Regulation 2(1)	Regulation 11(3)(c)	
Para 79b	Section 1162	Section 155 (1963 Act)	Regulation 4	Regulation 2(1)	Regulation 11	
Para 80	Section 1162	Section 155 (1963 Act)	Regulation 4	Regulation 2(1)	Regulation 11	
Para 84	Section 1162	Section 155 (1963 Act)	Regulation 4	Regulation 2(1)	Regulation 11	
Para 88	Paragraph 9 of Schedule 6 of the Regulations		Regulation 19	Paragraph 10 of Part II of the Schedule	Paragraph 9 of Part IV of the Schedule	
Para 89	Paragraph 9 of Schedule 6 of the Regulations		Regulation 19	Paragraph 10 of Part II of the Schedule	Paragraph 9 of Part IV of the Schedule	
Para 89	Section 404(5)		Regulations 14(3) and 14(4)	Regulations 7(7)(d) and 7(7)(e)	Regulations 10(7)(d) and 10(7)(e)	

Paragraph of FRS 2	UK References	ROI References				
	2006 Act and the 2008 Regulations	1963 Act / 1986 Act	GAR 1992	CIR 1992	IUR 1996	Comments
References in footnotes						
Para 38	Paragraph 9 of Schedule 6 of the Regulations		Regulation 19	Paragraph 10 of Part II of the Schedule	Paragraph 9 of Part IV of the Schedule	
Para 38	Paragraph 11 of Schedule 6 of the Regulations		Regulation 22	Paragraph 12 of Part II of the Schedule	Paragraph 11 of Part IV of the Schedule	
References in margins						
Para 6	FRS defining phrase used in s1162(4)(a)		Regulation 4(1)(c)	Regulation 2(1)	Regulation 11(1)(c)	
Para 7a	From 7Sch 4(1) of the 2006 Act		Regulation 4(5)	Regulation 2(1)	Regulation 11(5)	
Para 7b	FRS defining phrase used in s1162(4)(a)		Regulation 4(1)(c)	Regulation 2(1)	Regulation 11(1)(c)	
Para 9	s474(1)	Section 155 (1963 Act)	Regulation 4	Regulation 2(1)	Regulation 11	Irish company law does not define a group. Constituent elements of a group are defined in the provisions noted.

Paragraph of FRS 2	UK References	ROI References				
	2006 Act and the 2008 Regulations	1963 Act / 1986 Act	GAR 1992	CIR 1992	IUR 1996	Comments
Para 10	FRS defining phrase used in 10Sch 11 of the Regulations		Regulation 35(1)	Paragraph 1 of Part IV of the Schedule	Paragraph 23 of Part IV of the Schedule	
Para 11	FRS defining phrase used in s405(3)(c)		Regulation 11(c)	Paragraph 2(3)(c) of Part II of the Schedule	Paragraph 2(3)(c) of Part IV of the Schedule	
Para 12	FRS defining phrase used in s1162(4)(b)		Regulation 4(1)(ca)	Regulation 2(1)	Regulation 11(1)(ca)	
Para 13	From 6Sch 17 of the Regulations		Paragraphs 8 and 9 of the Schedule	Paragraph 18 of Part II of the Schedule	Paragraph 19 of Part IV of the Schedule	
Para 14	From s1162 and 7Sch of the 2006 Act	Section 155 (1963 Act)	Regulation 4	Regulation 2(1)	Regulation 11	
Para 14a	From s1162(2)(a)		Regulation 4(1)(a)(i)	Regulation 2(1)	Regulation 11(1)(a)(i)	
Para 14b	From s1162(2)(b) and 7Sch 3 of the 2006 Act		Regulations 4(1)(a)(ii) and 4(2)	Regulation 2(1)	Regulations 11(1)(a)(ii) and 11(2)	

Paragraph of FRS 2	UK References	ROI References				
	2006 Act and the 2008 Regulations	1963 Act / 1986 Act	GAR 1992	CIR 1992	IUR 1996	Comments
Para 14c(i)	From s1162(2)(c) and 7Sch 4 of the 2006 Act		Regulation 4(1)(b)(i)	Regulation 2(1)	Regulation 11(1)(b)(i)	
Para 14c(ii)	From 7Sch 4(2) of the 2006 Act		Regulations 4(1)(b)(ii) and 4(6)	Regulation 2(1)	Regulations 11(1)(b)(ii) and 11(6)	
Para 14d	From s1162(2)(d)		Regulation 4(1)(a)(iii)	Regulation 2(1)	Regulation 11(1)(a)(iii)	
Para 14e(i)	From s1162(4)(a)		Regulation 4(1)(c)	Regulation 2(1)	Regulation 11(1)(c)	
Para 14e(ii)	From s1162(4)(b)		Regulation 4(1)(ca)	Regulation 2(1)	Regulation 11(1)(ca)	
Para 14f	From s1162(5)		Regulation 4(1)(d)	Regulation 2(1)	Regulation 11(1)(d)	The Irish company law provisions noted define subsidiaries in detail. A parent undertaking is defined as an undertaking with one or more subsidiary undertakings.

Paragraph of FRS 2	UK References	ROI References				
	2006 Act and the 2008 Regulations	1963 Act / 1986 Act	GAR 1992	CIR 1992	IUR 1996	Comments
Para 14f	From s1162(3)		Regulations 4(3) and 4(4)	Regulation 2(1)	Regulations 11(3) and 11(4)	The Irish company law provisions noted define subsidiaries in detail. A parent undertaking is defined as an undertaking with one or more subsidiary undertakings.
Para 14f	From 7Sch 9 of the 2006 Act		Regulations 4(3) and 4(4)	Regulation 2(1)	Regulations 11(3) and 11(4)	The Irish company law provisions noted define subsidiaries in detail. A parent undertaking is defined as an undertaking with one or more subsidiary undertakings.
Para 16	From s1161		Regulation 3(1)	Regulation 2(1)	Regulation 2(1)	
Para 17	From 7Sch 2(1) of the 2006 Act		Regulation 3(4)	Regulation 2(5)(ii)	Regulation 11(4)	

Paragraph of FRS 2	UK References	ROI References				
	2006 Act and the 2008 Regulations	1963 Act / 1986 Act	GAR 1992	CIR 1992	IUR 1996	Comments
Para 20	From s399, s403 and s398	Sections 150, 150A and 150B (1963 Act)	Regulations 5(1), 7, 8, 9, 9A, 10 and 11	Regulations 7(3), 8, 8A, Schedule Part II paragraphs 2(2) and 2(3)	Regulations 10(3), 12, 12A, Schedule Part IV paragraphs 2(2) and 2(3)	Irish company law does not have an equivalent to the UK's "small companies' regime". An Irish parent company within the scope of the Group Accounts Regulations 1992 (GAR 1992) is exempt from the requirement to prepare group accounts if it meets the size and other criteria set out in Regulation 7 of those regulations.
Para 21a	s400		Regulations 8 and 9	Regulation 8	Regulation 12	
Para 21b	s400		Regulations 8 and 9	Regulation 8	Regulation 12	
Para 21c	s401		Regulation 9A	Regulation 8A	Regulation 12A	

Paragraph of FRS 2	UK References	ROI References				
	2006 Act and the 2008 Regulations	1963 Act / 1986 Act	GAR 1992	CIR 1992	IUR 1996	Comments
Para 21e	s402			Paragraph 2(8) of Part II of the Schedule		No explicit equivalent to paragraph 2(8) in the Group Accounts Regulations 1992 (GAR 1992) or the Insurance Undertakings Regulations 1996 (IUR 1996).
Para 22	s409, s410, regulation 7 and 4Sch Part 2 of the Regulations	Section 16 (1986 Act)		Regulation 10; Part III A of the Schedule	Paragraph 19 of Part III of the Schedule	The provisions noted set out the requirements of Irish company law with regard to information on related undertakings.
Para 23	s405(1)		Regulation 5(2)	Paragraph 2 of Part II of the Schedule	Paragraph 2 of Part IV of the Schedule	
Para 24	FRS allows s405(3)(b) exclusion only where the undertaking is not material		Regulation 11(b)	Paragraph 2(3)(b) of Part II of the Schedule	Paragraph 2(3) (b) of Part IV of the Schedule	
Para 25	s405(3)		Regulation 11	Paragraph 2(3) of Part II of the Schedule	Paragraph 2(3) of Part IV of the Schedule	

Paragraph of FRS 2	UK References			ROI References		
	2006 Act and the 2008 Regulations	1963 Act / 1986 Act	GAR 1992	CIR 1992	IUR 1996	Comments
Para 25a	FRS requires exclusion permitted by s405(3)(a)		Regulation 11(a)	Paragraph 2(3)(a) of Part II of the Schedule	Paragraph 2(3)(a) of Part IV of the Schedule	
Para 25b	FRS restricts exclusion permitted by s405(3)(c)		Regulation 11(c) (FRS restricts the exclusion permitted)	Paragraph 2(3)(c) of Part II of the Schedule (Exclusion restricted in same manner as per FRS)	Paragraph 2(3)(c) of Part IV of the Schedule (Exclusion restricted in same manner as per FRS)	
Para 26	s409, regulation 7 and 4Sch 16(1) of the Regulations	Section 16(1) and paragraph 54(2)(a) of the Schedule (1986 Act)	Paragraph 18(2) of the Schedule	Paragraph 11 of Part III of the Schedule	Paragraphs 32 and 33 of Part IV of the Schedule	
Para 31	s409 and 4Sch 16 of the Regulations	Section 16(1) and paragraph 54(2)(a) of the Schedule (1986 Act)	Paragraphs 18(2) and 19 of the Schedule	Paragraph 11 of Part III of the Schedule	Paragraph 32 and 33 of Part IV of the Schedule	

Paragraph of FRS 2	UK References	ROI References				
	2006 Act and the 2008 Regulations	**1963 Act / 1986 Act**	**GAR 1992**	**CIR 1992**	**IUR 1996**	**Comments**
Para 31	4Sch 2, 3, 16 and 17 of the Regulations	Section 16; Paragraphs 45, 45A, 46, 46A, 54 and 55 of the Schedule (1986 Act)	Paragraphs 18 and 19 of the Schedule	Regulation 10; Paragraphs 11-13 and 16 of Part III of the Schedule	Paragraphs 32 and 33 of Part IV of the Schedule	
Para 33	4Sch of the Regulations	Section 16; Paragraphs 45, 45A, 46, 46A, 54 and 55 of the Schedule (1986 Act)	Paragraphs 18-22 of the Schedule	Regulation 10; Part III of the Schedule	Paragraphs 32-36 of Part IV of the Schedule	The provisions noted set out the requirements of Irish company law with regard to information on related undertakings.
Para 34	4Sch of the Regulations	Section 16; Paragraphs 45, 45A, 46, 46A, 54 and 55 of the Schedule (1986 Act)	Paragraphs 18-22 of the Schedule	Regulation 10; Part III of the Schedule	Paragraphs 32-36 of Part IV of the Schedule	The provisions noted set out the requirements of Irish company law with regard to information on related undertakings.
Para 35	6Sch 17(2) of the Regulations		Paragraph 8(2) of the Schedule	Paragraph 18(2) of Part II of the Schedule	Paragraph 19(2) of Part IV of the Schedule	
Para 36	6Sch 17(3) of the Regulations		Paragraph 9 of the Schedule	Paragraphs 18(3) and 18(4) of Part II of the Schedule	Paragraphs 19(3) and 19(4) of Part IV of the Schedule	

Paragraph of FRS 2	UK References	ROI References				
	2006 Act and the 2008 Regulations	1963 Act / 1986 Act	GAR 1992	CIR 1992	IUR 1996	Comments
Para 39	FRS requirement in relation to 6Sch of the Regulations. The Act allows partial elimination but the FRS requires elimination in full		Regulation 25 does not provide for partial elimination	Paragraph 7 of Part II of the Schedule does not provide for partial elimination	Paragraph 5 of Part IV of the Schedule does not provide for partial elimination	
Para 40	6Sch 3(1) of the Regulations		Regulation 30(1)	Paragraph 4(1) of Part II of the Schedule	Paragraph 15(1) of Part IV of the Schedule	
Para 41	6Sch 3(2) of the Regulations		Regulation 30(3)	Paragraphs 4(2) of Part II of the Schedule	Paragraph 15(2) of Part IV of the Schedule	
Para 43	FRS preference of alternatives permitted by 6Sch 2(2) of the Regulations		Regulation 26(2)	Paragraph 3(3) of Part II of the Schedule	Paragraph 3(3) of Part IV of the Schedule	

Paragraph of FRS 2	UK References	ROI References				
	2006 Act and the 2008 Regulations	1963 Act / 1986 Act	GAR 1992	CIR 1992	IUR 1996	Comments
Para 48	6Sch 15 of the Regulations		Regulation 27	Paragraph 16 of Part II of the Schedule	Paragraph 6 of Part IV of the Schedule	Irish company law requires that where the composition of the undertakings dealt with in the group accounts has changed significantly, information must be provided to make the comparison of successive sets of group accounts meaningful.
Para 50	6Sch 9 of the Regulations		Regulation 19	Paragraph 10 of Part II of the Schedule	Paragraph 9 of Part IV of the Schedule	

The development of the standard

This section does not form part of the Financial Reporting Standard.

ASB Note: The ASB has retained this section from the original version of FRS 2 and (paragraph xxv) the amendment to FRS 2 issued in 2004.

History of the FRS

Statement of Standard Accounting Practice No. 14 (SSAP 14) 'Group Accounts', issued September 1978, dealt with the presentation of group accounts for a group of companies. The practice of preparing group accounts for companies and their subsidiaries had been well established in the United Kingdom and Ireland since 1947. However, the issue of International Accounting Standard No. 3 'Consolidated Financial Statements' made it desirable for there to be a domestic standard on the subject. **i**

SSAP 14 was drafted to accord with relevant provisions of the Companies Acts then in force. At that time the Companies Acts did not include detailed rules regarding the preparation of group accounts. **ii**

SSAP 14 defined a holding company and a subsidiary company by reference to the legal definitions current at that time. The terms now used are 'parent undertaking' and 'subsidiary undertaking' which are defined in the Companies Act 1985, as amended by the Companies Act 1989 (the Act). The Act now contains new provisions on group accounts to implement the European Community Seventh Company Law Directive with the result that the requirements of SSAP 14 are no longer entirely consistent with current legislation. **iii**

The need to revise SSAP 14 for changes in the law has provided an opportunity to conduct a thorough review of the Standard. This was undertaken initially by the Accounting Standards Committee whose proposals were issued as ED 50 'Consolidated accounts' in June 1990. The Accounting Standards Board issued the 'Interim Statement: Consolidated Accounts' in December 1990, to give timely guidance on how certain provisions of the Act were to be interpreted in the preparation of consolidated accounts. The Interim Statement also made the changes to SSAP 14 'Group Accounts' that were required as a consequence of the statutory changes. The issue of the FRS by the Accounting Standards Board completes the review process. **iv**

Summary of the principal changes from Statement of Standard Accounting Practice NO. 14 – 'Group Accounts'

SSAP 14 defined a company as a subsidiary of another 'if, but only if, **v**

(a) that other either:

(i) is a member of it and controls the composition of its board of directors; or
(ii) holds more than half in nominal value of its equity share capital; or

(b) the first mentioned company is a subsidiary of any company which is that other's subsidiary, and it otherwise comes within the terms of Section 154 of the Companies Act 1948' (now repealed).

The FRS defines a parent undertaking and a subsidiary undertaking in the same way as the Act using a set of conditions that are based on whether one undertaking controls another. These are set out in paragraph 14 of the FRS.

vi The FRS requires a parent undertaking not making use of an exemption to prepare consolidated financial statements for its group. SSAP 14 exceptionally allowed alternative forms of group reporting if the resulting group accounts were considered to give a fairer view of the financial position of the group as a whole than would consolidated financial statements.

vii SSAP 14 exempted from the obligation to prepare group accounts only holding companies that were wholly-owned subsidiaries not otherwise required by law to prepare group accounts. The FRS follows the Act in allowing other exemptions from preparing consolidated financial statements. A parent undertaking is in general exempt from the requirement to prepare consolidated financial statements if its group is a small or medium-sized one*; or if it is wholly or majority-owned by an undertaking established under the law of a member state of the European Community; or if all its subsidiary undertakings fall within the exclusions from consolidation.

viii The circumstances in which subsidiary undertakings are to be excluded from the consolidation have changed in certain respects from those in SSAP 14.

(a) SSAP 14 required a subsidiary to be excluded from consolidation if its activities were so dissimilar from those of other companies within the group that its consolidation would be misleading and information would be better provided by presenting financial statements for the excluded subsidiary separate from the financial statements for the rest of the group. The FRS requires a subsidiary undertaking to be excluded from consolidation if, exceptionally, its activities are so different from other subsidiary undertakings included in the consolidation that its inclusion in the consolidation would be incompatible with the obligation to give a true and fair view.

(b) SSAP 14 required a subsidiary to be excluded from consolidation if the holding company held more than half of the subsidiary's equity share capital but either: (a) it did not own share capital carrying more than half the votes; or (b) contractual or other restrictions were imposed on its ability to appoint the majority of the board of directors. Although the FRS does not have the same exclusion, the FRS will in most cases have the same practical effect because (a) an undertaking is a subsidiary undertaking if another undertaking holds a majority of its voting rights and (b) exclusion is required where severe long-term restrictions substantially hinder the rights of the parent undertaking over the assets or management of its subsidiary undertaking.

(c) SSAP 14 required exclusion from consolidation of a subsidiary where control was intended to be temporary. The FRS requires consolidation where one undertaking controls another and, therefore, has not based exclusion on control being temporary. However, it does require exclusion from consolidation of a subsidiary undertaking held exclusively with a view to resale which has not previously been consolidated. This condition for exclusion is more restrictive than the temporary control test.

**The Companies Act 2006 paragraph 399 applies to all companies that are not subject to the small companies regime. Consequently, a parent undertaking in the UK is no longer exempt from the requirement to prepare consolidated financial statements if its group is a medium-sized one. Irish company law continues to exempt medium-sized groups from the requirements to prepare consolidated financial statements under Regulation 7 of the European Communities (Companies: Group Accounts) Regulations 1992 (SI 201 of 1992) for parent undertakings within the scope of those Regulations.*

SSAP 14 required that the consolidated financial statements should contain sufficient information about material subsidiaries acquired or sold to enable shareholders to appreciate the effect on the consolidated results. There are now specific disclosure requirements in the law, as well as in accounting standards in respect of acquisitions, and the general SSAP 14 requirement is not repeated in the FRS. In addition FRS 1 'Cash Flow Statements' contains a requirement to show the cash flow effects of acquisitions and disposals. **ix**

SSAP 14 sets out the effective date of acquisition or disposal as the earlier of the date on which consideration passes or the date on which an offer becomes, or is declared, unconditional. This is replaced in the FRS by a single triggering date which is the date control of the undertaking passes. This date is a matter of fact and cannot be backdated or otherwise altered. **x**

SSAP 14 required that debit balances for the minority interests should only be recognised in the balance sheet if there was a binding obligation on minority shareholders to make good losses incurred which they were able to meet. The FRS requires minority interests to be debited in full with their share of any loss whether or not this results in a debit balance, subject to the need for a provision discussed below. A debit for minority interests does not represent a liability of the minority shareholders and it may be misleading to refer to their being obliged to make good losses. The group should make provision to the extent that it has any commercial or legal obligation (whether formal or implied) to provide finance that may not be recoverable in respect of the accumulated losses attributable to minority interests. **xi**

Summary of the principal changes from the Board's 'Interim Statement: Consolidated Accounts'

In December 1990, the Board issued the 'Interim Statement: Consolidated Accounts' to give timely guidance on the application of certain provisions of the new Act to the preparation of consolidated financial statements. The Interim Statement dealt mainly with the interpretation of the new phrases used in the conditions that identified parent and subsidiary undertakings and with the exclusions from consolidation permitted or required by the Act for certain subsidiary undertakings. Although the drafting has changed to fit the format of an accounting standard, the FRS incorporates the guidance given by the Interim Statement except in the following areas: **xii**

(a) Dominant influence is now defined without explicit reference to control although the effect of dominant influence is the same as control.

(b) The explanation dealing with subsidiary undertakings whose activities are so different that consolidation is incompatible with the obligation to give a true and fair view now states explicitly that the contrast between Schedule 9 and 9A companies and other companies, or between profit and not-for-profit undertakings, is not sufficient of itself to justify non consolidation.

(c) The Interim Statement defined a joint venture. The FRS deals only with accounting for subsidiary undertakings leaving joint ventures as a separate project.

Summary of the principal changes from Exposure Draft No. 50 – 'Consolidated accounts'

Exposure Draft No. 50 (ED 50) 'Consolidated accounts' was issued in June 1990 by the Accounting Standards Committee. It proposed standard accounting practice for the preparation of consolidated accounts covering both accounting for subsidiary undertakings and accounting for associated undertakings and joint ventures. The **xiii**

FRS deals only with accounting for subsidiary undertakings in consolidated financial statements. The Board is engaged in another project considering accounting for associated undertakings and joint ventures.

xiv The Explanatory Note in ED 50 considered the purpose of consolidated accounts, the basis of consolidation and the meaning of control. The FRS deals only briefly in its explanation section with the conceptual background to financial reporting for groups. The conceptual basis of consolidated financial statements and consideration of the group as a reporting entity are to be considered by the Board in the chapter of its Statement of Principles dealing with the boundaries of the reporting entity.

xv ED 50 used the terms 'subsidiary', 'parent' and 'enterprise' in line with earlier accounting standards. Commentators on its proposals considered that it would be more appropriate to use the terminology of the Act on which the FRS is based. The FRS now refers to 'subsidiary undertaking', 'parent undertaking' and 'undertaking'. However, in line with the Board's other published work, the FRS uses 'financial statements' instead of 'accounts' as used in the Act.

xvi ED 50 proposed definitions for the phrases used in the Act in the criteria for identifying parent and subsidiary undertakings. The FRS elaborates on these definitions in the light of the comments received on the ED. The general thrust of the definitions remains the same but the following changes are worth noting:

(a) 'Dominant influence' is no longer defined in terms of control but by its ability to achieve the operating and financial policies desired by the holder of the influence, notwithstanding the rights or influence of any other party. The actual exercise of dominant influence is identified by its effect in practice rather than the way in which it is exercised. The effect of dominant influence is the same as the effect of control.

(b) The role of reserve powers and powers of veto in the actual exercise of dominant influence has been clarified.

xvii ED 50 proposed that a parent undertaking using an exemption from preparing consolidated accounts should make additional disclosures if its individual financial statements alone were not sufficient to give a true and fair view of its financial position. ED 50 noted that in some cases such additional information might better be presented by providing consolidated financial statements for the whole group. This proposal attracted adverse comment because, in certain circumstances, its effect would be to take away an exemption given by the Act. The FRS requires a parent undertaking using an exemption to state that its financial statements present information about it as an individual undertaking and not about its group. Parent undertakings using any of the exemptions should also make the disclosures set out in Schedule 5 Part 1 of the Companies Act.

xviii ED 50 proposed definitions for the phrases used in the Act to set the conditions under which a subsidiary undertaking was permitted or required to be excluded from consolidation. As a result of the comments received the guidance of the FRS on how these conditions are to be interpreted has changed slightly from that given in ED 50 although the emphasis remains on interpreting these conditions restrictively. The main changes are set out below.

(a) *Interests held exclusively with a view to subsequent resale.* A second part has been added bringing acquisitions as a result of the enforcement of a security within the definition of interests held exclusively with a view to subsequent resale unless the subsidiary undertaking has become part of the continuing activities of the group or the holder acts as if it intends the interest to become so.

(b) *Activities so different that consolidation would be incompatible with the obligation to give a true and fair view*. ED 50 proposed that such an incompatibility could arise only from consolidating a Schedule 9 or 9A company with non Schedule 9 or 9A companies. Several commentators considered that a requirement not to consolidate Schedule 9 and 9A companies with others might result in a loss of useful and comparable information on group activities as a whole. Linking incompatibility with the true and fair view to issues relating to the format in which financial statements were presented was considered unsatisfactory. The FRS, therefore, stresses that the key feature of this exclusion is that including a given subsidiary undertaking in the consolidation is incompatible with the obligation to give a true and fair view. The FRS notes that this incompatibility will be so exceptional in practice that it would be misleading to associate it with any particular contrast of activities. For example, the contrasts between Schedule 9 or 9A companies and other companies or between profit and not-for-profit undertakings would not be sufficient to justify non-consolidation.

ED 50 followed SSAP 14 and proposed that losses should only be debited to minority interests where they resulted in a debit balance if there was a binding and reliable obligation on the minority to make good any such losses. The FRS's treatment for the minority's share of losses is explained in paragraph xi above. **xix**

ED 50 proposed dropping the requirement of SSAP 14 (paragraph 18) that appropriate adjustments should be made to the consolidated financial statements for any abnormal transactions in the intervening period between the end of the period of a subsidiary and the later one of the group. Commentators considered that some disclosure of this sort would be useful. The FRS requires that, where a subsidiary undertaking's financial year end differs from that of the parent undertaking, the consolidated financial statements should be prepared using interim financial statements or, only if this is impracticable, its financial statements for its last financial year ending not more than three months before that of the group's parent undertaking. In this latter case, adjustment is required for changes in the intervening period that materially affect the view given by the consolidated financial statements. **xx**

ED 50 proposed that the effective date of acquisition or disposal be the earlier of: **xxi**

(a) the date on which the consideration passes; or
(b) the date at which an offer becomes, or is declared, unconditional; or
(c) the date of such other event at which control is gained or ceases to exist.

The FRS now sets the date of changes in membership of the group as the date that control passes. The Explanation (paragraphs 84 and 85) considers the transactions and events that indicate when control passes.

ED 50 proposed that its requirement to include the appropriate proportion of the results of a subsidiary undertaking that has been disposed of should be subject to the requirements of SSAP 6 'Extraordinary items and prior year adjustments' (paragraphs 11-14) dealing with the disposal of a segment. The FRS does not refer to SSAP 6 and requires that the consolidated profit and loss account should include the results of a subsidiary undertaking up to the date of its disposal. The Board is proposing to supersede SSAP 6 with an FRS developed from FRED 1 'The Structure of Financial Statements – Reporting of Financial Performance'*. **xxii**

The FRS has dropped the proposed requirement of ED 50 in respect of disposals to disclose the amount of purchased goodwill attributable to business or business **xxiii**

**Subsequently issued as FRS 3 'Reporting Financial Performance'.*

segments disposed of, and how that goodwill has been treated in determining the profit or loss on disposal. These disclosures are still required by paragraph 52(b) of SSAP 22 'Accounting for goodwill'. The treatment of goodwill on disposal is set out in paragraph 47, which requires that the net assets disposed of include any related goodwill not previously written off through the profit and loss account.

xxiv In response to criticism of the ED 50 proposals, the FRS changes the treatment for increases in stake in a subsidiary undertaking. ED 50 did not propose to require a revaluation to fair value on an increase in stake, and, consequently, the goodwill balance arising could have consisted of an amount relating to revaluation of net identifiable assets as well as goodwill. The FRS requires that the goodwill should be calculated by revaluing the subsidiary undertaking's assets and liabilities to fair value at the date of the change in stake, unless the difference between fair values and carrying amounts is not material.

xxv In 2004, FRS 2 was amended to reflect changes to the Act that were introduced by the Companies Act 1985 (International Accounting Standards and Other Accounting Amendments) Regulations 2004 (SI 2004 No. 2947).

xxvi In 2009, FRS 2 was amended to update the legal references following the introduction of the Companies Act 2006 and The Large and Medium-sized Companies and Groups (Accounts and Reports) Regulations 2008 (SI 2008 No. 410) and The Small Companies and Groups (Accounts and Directors' Report) Regulations 2008 (SI 2008 No. 409).

[FRS 3]
Reporting financial performance*†

(Issued October 1992; amended June 1993 and June 1999)

Contents

	Paragraph
Summary	a–i
Objective	1
Definitions	2–11
Statement of standard accounting practice	12–33
Scope	12
Application to smaller entities	12A
Profit and loss account	13–24
Earnings per share	25
Note of historical cost profits and losses	26
Statement of total recognised gains and losses	27
Reconciliation of movements in shareholders' funds	28
Prior period adjustments	29
Comparative figures	30
Investment companies	31
Insurance businesses	31A
Date from which effective	32
Withdrawal of SSAP 6 and amendment of other statements	33
Compliance with international accounting standards	34
Explanation	35–66
Components of financial performance	35–37
Profit and loss account	38–51
Earnings per share	52
Segmental reporting	53
Note of historical cost profits and losses	54–55
Statement of total recognised gains and losses	56–58
Reconciliation of movements in shareholders' funds	59
Prior period adjustments	60–63
Comparative figures	64
Investment companies	65–66
Note on legal requirements	67–79
Illustrative examples	
Dissenting view	
The development of the standard	i–xii

***Editor's note:** *FRS 3 has been further amended by FRS 22 and FRS 25, with effect for accounting periods beginning on or after 1 January 2005 and separately with effect for accounting periods beginning on or after 1 January 2007.*

†***Editor's note:** *The matters covered in FRS 3 are dealt with in various sections of FRS 102. Presentational matters related to profits and other gains are covered in Section 5, movements in shareholders' funds in Section 6 and prior period adjustments in Section 10.*

Reporting financial performance

Summary

a Financial Reporting Standard No. 3 'Reporting Financial Performance' (the FRS) introduces: changes to the format of the profit and loss account; a note of historical cost profits and losses; a statement of total recognised gains and losses; and a reconciliation of movements in shareholders' funds. The FRS supersedes Statement of Standard Accounting Practice No. 6 (Revised) 'Extraordinary items and prior year adjustments' (SSAP 6), amends SSAP 3 'Earnings per share' and makes consequential changes to a number of other accounting standards.

b A layered format is to be used for the profit and loss account to highlight a number of important components of financial performance:

(i) results of continuing operations (including the results of acquisitions);
(ii) results of discontinued operations;
(iii) profits or losses on the sale or termination of an operation, costs of a fundamental reorganisation or restructuring and profits or losses on the disposal of fixed assets; and
(iv) extraordinary items.

The thrust of this approach can be illustrated diagrammatically.

Continuing	*Discontinued*
Normal operations	Normal operations
The items listed in b(iii) above	The items listed in b(iii) above

Extraordinary items — being unusual items outside ordinary activies

c In presenting the profit and loss account the following requirements should be observed:

(i) The analysis between continuing operations, acquisitions (as a component of continuing operations) and discontinued operations should be disclosed to the level of operating profit (which for non-financial reporting entities is normally profit before income from shares in group undertakings). The analysis of turnover and operating profit is the minimum disclosure required in this respect on the face of the profit and loss account.
(ii) All exceptional items, other than those in (iii) below, should be included under the statutory format headings to which they relate. They should be separately disclosed by way of note or, where it is necessary in order that the financial statements give a true and fair view, on the face of the profit and loss account.
(iii) The following items, including provisions in respect of such items, should be shown separately on the face of the profit and loss account after operating profit and before interest:
– profits or losses on the sale or termination of an operation;
– costs of a fundamental reorganisation or restructuring; and
– profits or losses on the disposal of fixed assets.

(iv) Extraordinary items should be disclosed.

[Withdrawn]* **d**

The note of historical cost profits and losses is a memorandum item, the primary purpose of which is to present the profits or losses of reporting entities that have revalued assets on a more comparable basis with those of entities that have not. It is an abbreviated restatement of the profit and loss account which adjusts the reported profit or loss, if necessary, so as to show it as if no asset revaluations had been made. Unless the historical cost information is unavailable, the note is required whenever there is a material difference between the result as disclosed in the profit and loss account and the result on an unmodified historical cost basis; it should be presented immediately following the profit and loss account or the statement of total recognised gains and losses. **e**

The statement of total recognised gains and losses is a primary financial statement that enables users to consider all recognised gains and losses of a reporting entity in assessing its overall performance. It, therefore, includes the profit or loss for the period together with all other movements on reserves reflecting recognised gains and losses attributable to shareholders. The statement is not intended to reflect the realisation of gains recognised in previous periods nor does it deal with transfers between reserves, which should continue to be shown in the notes to the financial statements. **f**

The reconciliation of movements in shareholders' funds brings together the performance of the period, as shown in the statement of total recognised gains and losses, with all the other changes in shareholders' funds in the period, including capital contributed by or repaid to shareholders. **g**

Prior period adjustments should be accounted for by restating the comparative figures for the preceding period in the primary statements and notes and adjusting the opening balance of reserves for the cumulative effect. The cumulative effect of the adjustments should also be noted at the foot of the statement of total recognised gains and losses of the current period. The effect of prior period adjustments on the results for the preceding period should be disclosed where practicable. **h**

The accounting practices set out in the FRS should be adopted as soon as possible and regarded as standard in respect of financial statements relating to accounting periods ending on or after 22 June 1993. **i**

Objective

The objective of the FRS is to require reporting entities falling within its scope to highlight a range of important components of financial performance to aid users in understanding the performance achieved by a reporting entity in a period and to assist them in forming a basis for their assessment of future results and cash flows. **1**

***Editor's note:** *Paragraph withdrawn by FRS 22. The paragraph referred to calculation and disclosure of earnings per share.*

Definitions

The following definitions apply for the purposes of the FRS and in particular the statement of standard accounting practice set out in paragraphs 12 to 33.

2 *Ordinary activities:-*
Any activities which are undertaken by a reporting entity as part of its business and such related activities in which the reporting entity engages in furtherance of, incidental to, or arising from, these activities. Ordinary activities include the effects on the reporting entity of any event in the various environments in which it operates, including the political, regulatory, economic and geographical environments, irrespective of the frequency or unusual nature of the events.

3 *Acquisitions:-*
Operations of the reporting entity that are acquired in the period.

4 *Discontinued operations:-*
Operations of the reporting entity that are sold or terminated and that satisfy all of the following conditions.

(a) The sale or termination is completed either in the period or before the earlier of three months after the commencement of the subsequent period and the date on which the financial statements are approved.
(b) If a termination, the former activities have ceased permanently.
(c) The sale or termination has a material effect on the nature and focus of the reporting entity's operations and represents a material reduction in its operating facilities resulting either from its withdrawal from a particular market (whether class of business or geographical) or from a material reduction in turnover in the reporting entity's continuing markets.
(d) The assets, liabilities, results of operations and activities are clearly distinguishable, physically, operationally and for financial reporting purposes.

Operations not satisfying all these conditions are classified as continuing.

5 *Exceptional items:-*
Material items which derive from events or transactions that fall within the ordinary activities of the reporting entity and which individually or, if of a similar type, in aggregate, need to be disclosed by virtue of their size or incidence if the financial statements are to give a true and fair view.

6 *Extraordinary items:-*
Material items possessing a high degree of abnormality which arise from events or transactions that fall outside the ordinary activities of the reporting entity and which are not expected to recur. They do not include exceptional items nor do they include prior period items merely because they relate to a prior period.

7 *Prior period adjustments:-*
Material adjustments applicable to prior periods arising from changes in accounting policies or from the correction of fundamental errors. They do not include normal recurring adjustments or corrections of accounting estimates made in prior periods.

8 *Total recognised gains and losses:-*
The total of all gains and losses of the reporting entity that are recognised in a period and are attributable to shareholders.

Companies Act 1985:- 9
The Companies Act 1985 as amended by the Companies Act 1989.*

Companies (Northern Ireland) Order 1986:- 10
The Companies (Northern Ireland) Order 1986 as amended by the Companies (Northern Ireland) Order 1990 and the Companies (No. 2) (Northern Ireland) Order 1990.

Companies (Amendment) Act 1986:- 11
The Republic of Ireland Companies (Amendment) Act 1986 as amended by the Companies Act 1990 and by the European Communities (Companies: Group Accounts) Regulations 1992 (*the* 1992 *Regulations*).

Statement of Standard Accounting Practice

The statement of standard accounting practice set out in paragraphs 12 to 33 of the FRS should be read in the context of the Objective of the FRS as stated in paragraph 1, the definitions set out in paragraphs 2 to 11 and also of the foreword to Accounting Standards and the Statement of Principles for Financial Reporting currently in issue.

The Explanation section of the FRS, set out in paragraphs 35 to 66, shall be regarded as part of the statement of standard accounting practice insofar as it assists in interpreting that statement

SCOPE

Subject to paragraphs 12A and 12B the FRS applies to all financial statements intended to give a true and fair view of a reporting entity's financial position and profit or loss (or income and expenditure). Every such reporting entity should apply the requirements of the FRS except to the extent that these requirements are not permitted by the statutory framework (if any) under which the entity reports.† 12

APPLICATION TO SMALLER ENTITIES

Reporting entities applying the Financial Reporting Standard for Smaller Entities currently applicable are exempt from this accounting standard. 12A

Paragraph 21 and the last sentence of paragraph 31A of the FRS do not apply to entities adopting FRS 26 (IAS 39) Financial Instruments: Recognition and Measurement, in relation to: 12B

a. financial instruments accounted for in accordance with FRS 26; and
b. foreign exchange differences on disposal of a foreign operation in accordance with FRS 23 (IAS 21) *The effects of changes in foreign exchange rates.*‡

PROFIT AND LOSS ACCOUNT

All gains and losses recognised in the financial statements for the period should be included in the profit and loss account or the statement of total recognised gains and 13

***Editor's note:** The Companies Act 1985 has been replaced by the Companies Act 2006.*

*†**Editor's note:** Paragraph amended with effect for accounting periods beginning on or after 1 January 2007.*

*‡**Editor's note:** Paragraph added with effect for accounting periods beginning on or after 1 January 2007.*

losses. Gains and losses may be excluded from the profit and loss account only if they are specifically permitted or required to be taken directly to reserves by this or other accounting standards or, in the absence of a relevant accounting standard, by law.

Continuing and discontinued operations

14 The aggregate results of each of continuing operations, acquisitions (as a component of continuing operations) and discontinued operations should be disclosed separately. The results of acquisitions included in continuing operations should not include those that are also discontinued in the same period. The minimum disclosure required down to the operating profit level on the face of the profit and loss account in respect of continuing operations, acquisitions and discontinued operations is the analysis of turnover and operating profit (which for non-financial reporting entities is normally profit before income from shares in group undertakings). The analysis between continuing operations, acquisitions (as a component of continuing operations) and discontinued operations of each of the other statutory profit and loss account format items between turnover and operating profit should be given by way of note where not shown on the face of the profit and loss account. In those circumstances where a reporting entity presents allocations of interest or tax between continuing and discontinued operations, the method and underlying assumptions used in making the allocations should be disclosed.

15 Where an acquisition, or a sale or a termination, has a material impact on a major business segment this should be disclosed and explained.

Acquisitions

16 Where it is not practicable to determine the post-acquisition results of an operation to the end of the current period, an indication should be given of the contribution of the acquisition to the turnover and operating profit of the continuing operations in addition to the information required by the Companies Act 1985*. If an indication of the contribution of an acquisition to the results of the period cannot be given, this fact and the reason should be explained.

Discontinued operations

17 Only income and costs directly related to discontinued operations should appear under the heading of discontinued operations. Reorganisation or restructuring of continuing operations resulting from a sale or termination should be treated as part of continuing operations.

The consequences of a decision to sell or terminate an operation

18 If a decision has been made to sell or terminate an operation, any consequential provisions should reflect the extent to which obligations have been incurred that are not expected to be covered by the future profits of the operation. This principle requires that the reporting entity should be demonstrably committed to the sale or

Companies Act 1985 Schedule 4A paragraph 13. The equivalent reference in Northern Ireland legislation is the Companies (Northern Ireland) Order 1986 Schedule 4A paragraph 13.* ***Editor's note:* *Reference should now be to para. 13 of Schedule 6 to the Large and Medium-sized Companies and Groups (Accounts and Reports) Regulations 2008 (SI 2008/410).*

The nearest equivalent reference in the Republic of Ireland is the 1992 Regulations section 27 which sets out a general requirement for disclosure in the case of changes in the composition of a group.

termination. This should be evidenced, in the former case, by a binding sale agreement and, in the latter, by a detailed formal plan for termination from which the reporting entity cannot realistically withdraw. The provision should cover only (a) the direct costs of the sale or termination and (b) any operating losses of the operation up to the date of sale or termination, in both cases, after taking into account the aggregate profit, if any, to be recognised in the profit and loss account from the future profits of the operation. Unless the operation qualifies as a discontinued operation in the period under review, the write down of assets and any provisions should appear in the continuing operations category. In the subsequent period when the operation does qualify as discontinued, the provisions should be used to offset the results of the operation in the discontinued category. The related disclosure in that subsequent period, however, should be to show the results of the discontinued operation under each of the statutory format headings with the utilisation of the provision analysed as necessary between the operating loss and the loss on sale or termination of the discontinued operation and disclosed on the face of the profit and loss account immediately below the relevant items.

Exceptional items

All exceptional items, other than those included in the items listed in paragraph 20, should be credited or charged in arriving at the profit or loss on ordinary activities by inclusion under the statutory format headings to which they relate. They should be attributed to continuing or discontinued operations as appropriate. The amount of each exceptional item, either individually or as an aggregate of items of a similar type, should be disclosed separately by way of note, or on the face of the profit and loss account if that degree of prominence is necessary in order to give a true and fair view. An adequate description of each exceptional item should be given to enable its nature to be understood. **19**

The following items, including provisions in respect of such items, should be shown separately on the face of the profit and loss account after operating profit and before interest, and included under the appropriate heading of continuing or discontinued operations: **20**

(a) profits or losses on the sale or termination of an operation;
(b) costs of a fundamental reorganisation or restructuring having a material effect on the nature and focus of the reporting entity's operations; and
(c) profits or losses on the disposal of fixed assets. In calculating the profit or loss in respect of the above items consideration should only be given to revenue and costs directly related to the items in question.

When the net amount of (a) or (c) above is not material, but the gross profits or losses are material, the relevant heading should still appear on the face of the profit and loss account with a reference to a related note analysing the profits and losses. Relevant information regarding the effect of these items on the taxation charge and, in the case of consolidated financial statements, any minority interests should both be shown in a note to the profit and loss account. As a minimum the related tax and the minority interest should both be shown in aggregate, but if the effect of the tax and minority interests differs for the various categories of items further information should be given, where practicable, to assist users in assessing the impact of the different items on the net profit or loss attributable to shareholders. The taxation effects of these items are also referred to in paragraphs 23 and 24.

Profit or loss on the disposal of an asset

21 The profit or loss on the disposal of an asset should be accounted for in the profit and loss account of the period in which the disposal occurs as the difference between the net sale proceeds and the net carrying amount, whether carried at historical cost (less any provisions made) or at a valuation.

Extraordinary items

22 Any extraordinary profit or loss should be shown separately on the face of the profit and loss account, after the profit or loss on ordinary activities after taxation but before deducting any appropriations such as dividends paid or payable and, in the case of consolidated financial statements, after the figure for minority interests. The amount of each extraordinary item should be shown individually either on the face of the profit and loss account or in a note and an adequate description of each extraordinary item should be given to enable its nature to be understood. The tax on extraordinary profit or loss and, in the case of consolidated financial statements, the extraordinary profit or loss attributable to minority shareholders should be shown separately as a part of the extraordinary item either on the face of the profit and loss account or in a note. Any subsequent adjustments to the tax on extraordinary profit or loss in future periods should be shown as an extraordinary item.

Taxation

23 Any special circumstances that affect the overall tax charge or credit for the period, or that may affect those of future periods, should be disclosed by way of note to the profit and loss account and their individual effects quantified. Such disclosures should include any special circumstances affecting the tax attributable to the items specified in paragraph 20. The effects of a fundamental change in the basis of taxation should be included in the tax charge or credit for the period and separately disclosed on the face of the profit and loss account.

24 The tax on items of the type listed in paragraph 20 or on an extraordinary profit or loss should be determined by computing the tax on the profit or loss on ordinary activities as if the items did not exist, and comparing this notional tax charge with the tax charge on the profit or loss for the period (after extraordinary items). Any additional tax charge or credit (including deferred tax) arising should be attributed to the items. If there are items in both groups in the same period, the tax on the items combined should be calculated then apportioned between the two groups in relation to their respective amounts, unless a more appropriate basis of apportionment is available. If a more appropriate basis is adopted the method of apportionment should be disclosed.

EARNINGS PER SHARE

25 [Withdrawn]*

NOTE OF HISTORICAL COST PROFITS AND LOSSES

26 Where there is a material difference between the result as disclosed in the profit and loss account and the result on an unmodified historical cost basis, a note of the historical cost profit or loss for the period should be presented. Where full historical

Editor's note: *Paragraph withdrawn by FRS 22.*

cost information is unavailable or cannot be obtained without unreasonable expense or delay, the earliest available values should be used. The note of the historical cost profit or loss should include a reconciliation of the reported profit on ordinary activities before taxation to the equivalent historical cost amount and should also show the retained profit for the financial year reported on the historical cost basis. The effects of fair value accounting under FRS 26 and hyperinflation adjustments under FRS 24 (IAS 29) *Financial Reporting in Hyperinflationary economies* and UITF Abstract 9 Accounting for Operations in Hyper-inflationary Economies are not required to be included in this reconciliation, but this omission should be noted. The note should be presented immediately following the profit and loss account or the statement of total recognised gains and losses.*

STATEMENT OF TOTAL RECOGNISED GAINS AND LOSSES

A primary statement should be presented, with the same prominence as the other primary statements, showing the total of recognised gains and losses and its components. The components should be the gains and losses that are recognised in the period insofar as they are attributable to shareholders.† **27**

RECONCILIATION OF MOVEMENTS IN SHAREHOLDERS' FUNDS

A note should be presented reconciling the opening and closing totals of shareholders' funds of the period. **28**

PRIOR PERIOD ADJUSTMENTS

Prior period adjustments should be accounted for by restating the comparative figures for the preceding period in the primary statements and notes and adjusting the opening balance of reserves for the cumulative effect. The cumulative effect of the adjustments should also be noted at the foot of the statement of total recognised gains and losses of the current period. Where practicable, the effect of a prior period adjustment on the results for the preceding period should be disclosed. Where it is not practicable to make this disclosure, that fact, together with the reasons, should be stated. **29**

COMPARATIVE FIGURES

Comparative figures should be given for all items in the primary statements and such notes thereto as are required by the FRS. The comparative figures in respect of the profit and loss account should include in the continuing category only the results of those operations included in the current period's continuing operations. **30**

INVESTMENT COMPANIES

[Withdrawn]‡ **31**

****Editor's note:*** *Paragraph amended with effect for accounting periods beginning on or after 1 January 2007.*

†*As explained in UITF Abstract 3 and paragraphs 6 and 7 of SSAP 22 'Accounting for Goodwill', the immediate write-off to reserves of purchased goodwill is not a recognised loss. (****Editor's note:*** *UITF 3 and SSAP 22 have been superseded by FRS 10 'Goodwill and Intangible Assets'.)*

‡***Editor's note:*** *Paragraph withdrawn by FRS 25.*

INSURANCE BUSINESSES

31A The requirements of paragraphs 21 and 26 do not apply to the financial statements of insurance companies or insurance groups as defined in companies legislation* for the gains or losses arising on the holding or disposal of investments. Additionally, the requirements of paragraphs 21 and 26 do not apply to consolidated financial statements to the extent they include insurance companies or insurance groups. However, for insurance companies and insurance groups both realised and unrealised gains and losses on investments held as part of their investment portfolios should be included as part of the investment return in the profit and loss account.

DATE FROM WHICH EFFECTIVE

32 The accounting practices set out in the FRS should be adopted as soon as possible and regarded as standard in respect of financial statements relating to accounting periods ending on or after 22 June 1993.†

WITHDRAWAL OF SSAP 6 AND AMENDMENT OF OTHER STATEMENTS

[Not reproduced as all changes have been reflected in the material reproduced in this volume.]

Financial Reporting Standard No. 3 'Reporting Financial Performance' was adopted by a vote of eight of the nine members of the Accounting Standards Board. Mr Bradfield dissented. His dissenting view is set out after the illustrative examples.

Members of the Accounting Standards Board

David Tweedie (Chairman)
Allan Cook (Technical Director)
Robert Bradfield
Sir Bryan Carsberg
Elwyn Eilledge
Michael Garner
Donald Main
Roger Munson
Graham Stacy

**Companies Act 1985 Section 744 and Section 255a(5).*

The equivalent legislation in Northern Ireland is the Companies (Northern Ireland) Order 1986 Article 2 and Article 263A(5). The equivalent legislation in the Republic of Ireland is the Companies (Amendment) Act 1986 Section 2(3) and the European Communities (Companies: Group Accounts) Regulations 1992 regulation 6(2)(g). ***Editor's note:*** *Section 744 is replaced by section 1164 of the Companies Act 2006.*

†***Editor's note:*** *The amendment to paragraph 31A in June 1999 was effective for financial statements relating to accounting periods ending on or after 23 August 1999.*

Compliance with International Accounting Standards

The requirements of the FRS are consistent with International Accounting Standard 5 'Information to be Disclosed in Financial Statements'* and International Accounting Standard 8 'Unusual and Prior Period Items and Changes in Accounting Policies'. The FRS is also consistent with the exposure draft of a proposed revised International Accounting Standard—'Extraordinary Items, Fundamental Errors and Changes in Accounting Policies' issued by the International Accounting Standards Committee in July 1992.† 34

Explanation

COMPONENTS OF FINANCIAL PERFORMANCE

The many parts of a reporting entity's activities exhibit features which differ in stability, risk and predictability, indicating a need for the separate disclosure of components of financial performance in the profit and loss account and in the statement of total recognised gains and losses. The disclosure of these components is designed to facilitate understanding of the performance achieved in a period and to assist users in deciding on the extent to which past results are useful in helping to assess potential future results. A component, of whatever nature, should be shown separately if it has a special significance for the assessment of some aspect of performance. 35

The total of all recognised gains and losses attributable to shareholders of a reporting entity includes the following components: 36

(a) profit or loss before the deduction of dividends;
(b) adjustments to the valuation of assets; and
(c) differences in the net investment in foreign enterprises arising from changes in foreign currency exchange rates.

The profit and loss account and statement of total recognised gains and losses are intended to present all the entity's gains and losses recognised in a particular period. Profit or loss of a period focuses on what a reporting entity earns for its output 37

****Editor's note:*** *This was replaced in August 1997 by a revised version of IAS 1, now titled 'Presentation of Financial Statements'. A further revised version of IAS 1 is effective for accounting periods beginning on or after 1 January 2009.*

†***Editor's note:*** *A revised version of IAS 8, now titled 'Net profit or loss for the period, fundamental errors and changes in accounting policies', was issued in November 1993.*

There are a number of differences between FRS 3 and its various international equivalents.

- *IAS 1 requires a second performance statement, which can either be similar to a statement of total recognised gains and losses or closer to a reconciliation of movements in shareholders' funds;*
- *there is no international equivalent of the requirement to disclose amounts in respect of acquisitions separately, although IAS 27 suggests that this might be useful;*
- *FRS 3 is more specific than IAS 8 when dealing with exceptional items (a term not used in IAS) in terms of allocation to a statutory heading and those items which can be shown after operating profit;*
- *IFRS 5 now deals with the treatment of discontinued operations, on a basis very different to that in FRS 3, with less disclosure and a test based on actual disposal or allocation to a disposal group.*
- *IAS 8 has been revised further, with a new version of the standard brought out in December 2003. This abolishes extraordinary items and treating prior period adjustments in the current year. It also requires prior period adjustments for all material errors, not just fundamental ones. IFRS 5 deals with discontinued operations, and replaces IAS 35. The proposals were published in the UK as FRED 32.*

The current version of IAS 8 is that issued in 2003, and effective since 2005, whilst discontinued operations are now covered by IFRS 5.

(revenue) and what it sacrifices to obtain that output (expenses). Gains and losses may be excluded from the profit and loss account only if they are specifically permitted or required to be taken directly to reserves by this or other accounting standards or, in the absence of a relevant accounting standard, by law. For example, a gain on the revaluation of a fixed asset should be reflected directly in the statement of total recognised gains and losses of the period in which the revaluation takes place. The realisation, or part realisation, of such a gain on the sale of the asset in a subsequent period is not itself a gain of that later period but, rather, confirmation of a gain that had already occurred by the time of the revaluation. Consequently, the gain or loss on the disposal of the asset is to be calculated as the difference between the net sale proceeds and the net carrying amount.

PROFIT AND LOSS ACCOUNT

Continuing and discontinued operations

38 The objective of reporting separately the results of continuing operations, acquisitions (as a component of continuing operations) and discontinued operations is to assist users, first, in assessing the financial performance of these aspects of a reporting entity's operations and, secondly, in forming a basis for the assessment of future income. Separate presentation assists analysis of the significance of the part of a reporting entity's operations that has ceased and of new operations that have been acquired. The various aspects of the definition and requirements regarding discontinued operations are explained in paragraphs 41 to 44. In respect of acquisitions, the requirement is to disclose their post-acquisition results for the period in which the acquisition occurs. In some circumstances it may also be useful to users for the results of acquisitions for the first full financial year for which they are a part of the reporting entity to be disclosed in the notes.

39 The FRS requires each of the statutory profit and loss account headings between turnover and operating profit to be analysed between continuing operations, acquisitions (as a component of continuing operations) and discontinued operations. For non-financial reporting entities operating profit is normally profit before income from shares in group undertakings, although in certain cases income from associated undertakings or from other participating interests may be considered to be part of operating profit. In order to avoid too much data on the face of the profit and loss account, the minimum disclosure required there in respect of continuing operations, acquisitions and discontinued operations is the analysis of turnover and operating profit. A similar analysis is required between continuing and discontinued operations for the items specifically required to be disclosed by paragraph 20; where practicable this analysis should identify, either on the face of the profit and loss account or in the notes, the amounts arising in respect of acquisitions.

40 The analysis in respect of continuing operations, acquisitions and discontinued operations is required only to the profit before interest level because interest payable is often a reflection of a reporting entity's overall financing policy, involving both equity and debt funding considerations on a group wide basis, rather than an aggregation of the particular types of finance allocated to individual segments of the reporting entity's operations. Any allocation of interest would involve a considerable degree of subjectivity, that could leave the user uncertain as to the relevance and reliability of the information. If a reporting entity wishes to provide such an allocation, the FRS requires that the method and underlying assumptions used in making the allocation be disclosed.

Discontinued operations

The FRS requires operations to be classified as discontinued when the sale or termination is completed either in the period or before the earlier of three months after the commencement of the subsequent period and the date on which the financial statements are approved. Only the results of operations up to the balance sheet date should be included; operations in the subsequent period should be included in the results of that period, separately classified as discontinued if material. Any income and costs associated with a sale or termination that has not been completed are to be included in the continuing category. In some cases it may be appropriate to disclose separately in a note to the profit and loss account the results of operations which although not discontinued are in the process of discontinuing, but they should not be classified as discontinued. **41**

To be included in the category of discontinued operations, a sale or termination must have a material effect on the nature and focus of the reporting entity's operations and represent a material reduction in its operating facilities resulting either from its withdrawal from a particular market (whether class of business or geographical) or from a material reduction in turnover in its continuing markets. The nature and focus of a reporting entity's operations refers to the positioning of its products or services in their markets including the aspects of both quality and location. For example, if a hotel company which had traditionally served the lower end of the hotel market sold its existing chain and bought luxury hotels then, while remaining in the business of managing hotels, the group would be changing the nature and focus of its operations. A similar situation would arise if the same company were to sell its hotels in, say, the United States of America and buy hotels in Europe. The regular sales and replacements of material assets which are undertaken by a reporting entity as part of the routine maintenance of its portfolio of assets should not be classified as discontinuances and acquisitions. In the example, the sale of hotels and the purchase of others within the same market sector and similar locations would be treated as wholly within continuing operations. **42**

To be classified as discontinued a sale or termination should have resulted from a strategic decision by the reporting entity either to withdraw from a particular market (whether class of business or geographical) or to curtail materially its presence in a continuing market (i.e. 'downsizing'). The sale or termination of a component of a reporting entity's operations which is undertaken primarily in order to achieve productivity improvements or other cost savings is a part of that entity's continuing operations and the effects of the sale or termination should be included under that heading. **43**

To be classified as discontinued, the assets, liabilities, results of operations and activities of an operation must be clearly distinguishable, physically, operationally and for financial reporting purposes. If the financial results of a sold or terminated operation are not identifiable separately from the accounting records or to a material extent can only be derived through making allocations of income or expenses, then the operation cannot be classified as a discontinued operation. For example, a manufacturing facility that is closed down but which lacks an external market price for its output cannot be classified as a discontinued operation. **44**

The consequences of a decision to sell or terminate an operation

Paragraph 18 sets out the principle underlying the establishment of provisions as a consequence of a decision to sell or terminate an operation. This principle focuses on the fact that an obligation arises at the point when the reporting entity becomes **45** demonstrably committed to the sale or termination. Evidence of the commitment might be the public announcement of specific plans, the commencement of implementation, or other circumstances effectively obliging the reporting entity to complete the sale or termination. A binding contract entered into after the balance sheet date may provide additional evidence of asset values and commitments at the balance sheet date. In the case of an intended sale for which no legally binding sale agreement exists, no obligation has been entered into by the reporting entity; accordingly, provisions for the direct costs of the decision to sell and for future operating losses should not be made. In accordance with normal practice, however, any impairments in asset values should be recorded.

Exceptional items

46 Exceptional items are defined in paragraph 5. They are an inherent part of the normal activities of a reporting entity and are included in the computation of profit or loss on ordinary activities but, because of their exceptional size or incidence, require separate disclosure to explain the performance of a period. Exceptional items may arise from a variety of sources and for larger or more complex businesses they are likely to occur in one form or another in most periods. They should not be aggregated on the face of the profit and loss account under one heading of exceptional items but, rather, each should be included within its natural statutory format heading or paragraph 20 category and separately disclosed in accordance with the requirements of paragraphs 19 and 20. The nature of exceptional items makes it necessary to distinguish exceptional profits from exceptional losses, in the notes if not on the face of the profit and loss account. The profits or losses on the disposal of fixed assets in paragraph 20 (c) are not intended to include profits and losses that are in effect no more than marginal adjustments to depreciation previously charged. In any references to profit or loss as including or excluding exceptional items, an explanation should be given of the relevance of their inclusion or exclusion (as the case may be) in the context of considering the results of the period or assessing maintainable earnings.

47 Exceptional items may occur in either continuing or discontinued operations and need to be identified individually as belonging to one or other category. In showing the amount of each exceptional item, individual items or groups of a similar type of item should not be combined if separately they relate to continuing and to discontinued operations.

Extraordinary items

48 Extraordinary items are defined in paragraph 6. Extraordinary items should be shown on the face of the profit and loss account before deducting any appropriations such as dividends paid or payable and, in the case of consolidated financial statements, after the figure for minority interests. Extraordinary items are extremely rare as they relate to highly abnormal events or transactions that fall outside the ordinary activities of a reporting entity and which are not expected to recur. In view of the extreme rarity of such items no examples are provided. Items falling into the category of exceptional in accordance with the terms of the FRS cannot, by definition, be extraordinary.

49 The FRS follows companies legislation in requiring the tax on extraordinary profit or loss and, in the case of consolidated financial statements, the minority shareholders' interest in an extraordinary profit or loss, to be shown separately.

Taxation

Companies legislation requires disclosure in the notes of the details of any special circumstances that affect any liability to taxation, whether for the financial year in question or for future years, and whether in respect of profits, income or capital gains. Such special circumstances could include, for example, the effect on the tax charge of losses whether utilised or carried forward. This disclosure can be useful in understanding the period's charge or credit in respect of taxation, particularly when there are items of the type specified in paragraph 20. It is recognised that analysing an entity's total taxation charge between component parts of its result for a period can involve arbitrary allocations that tend to become less meaningful the more components there are. However, in respect of items such as disposal profits or losses the tax can often be identified with the exceptional item concerned and the relationship between the profit or loss and the attributable tax may be significantly different from that in respect of operating profits or losses. In such circumstances it is relevant to identify the tax charge or credit more specifically. Disclosure of special circumstances can also be useful in assessing likely future amounts of taxation. Therefore, the FRS requires that the notes should not only disclose the existence of any special circumstances but should also quantify their individual effects. **50**

The application of the accounting concept of consistency requires that the tax effects of an extraordinary item should themselves be treated as extraordinary. This principle would apply even where an extraordinary item and its tax effects are recognised in different periods, such as where the tax relief in respect of an extraordinary loss is not recognised until it is utilised in a subsequent period. **51**

EARNINGS PER SHARE

[Withdrawn]* **52**

SEGMENTAL REPORTING

It is important for a thorough understanding of the results and financial position of a reporting entity that the impact of changes on material components of the business should be highlighted. To assist in this objective, if an acquisition, a sale or a termination has a material impact on a major business segment the FRS requires that this impact should be disclosed and explained. **53**

NOTE OF HISTORICAL COST PROFITS AND LOSSES

The note of historical cost profits and losses is a memorandum item that is an abbreviated restatement of the profit and loss account adjusting the reported profit or loss, if necessary, so as to show it as if no asset revaluations had been made. Adjustments are made for such items as: **54**

(a) gains recognised in prior periods in the statement of total recognised gains and losses and realised in the current period; for example, the difference between the profit on the disposal of an asset calculated on depreciated historical cost and that calculated on a revalued amount; and

(b) the difference between an historical cost depreciation charge and the depreciation charge calculated on the revalued amount included in the profit and loss account of the period.

***Editor's note:** *Paragraph withdrawn by FRS 22.*

55 Two reasons for disclosing the profit or loss for a period on the unmodified historical cost basis of accounting are commonly cited. The first is, that for as long as discretion exists on the timing or scale of revaluations included in financial statements, the unmodified historical cost basis will give the reported profits or losses of different reporting entities on a more comparable basis. The second is the wish of certain users to assess the profit or loss on sale of assets based on their historical cost, rather than, as the FRS requires, on their revalued carrying amount. In acknowledgement of these concerns, the Board has made the provision of a note of historical cost profits and losses a requirement of the FRS in those circumstances where there is a material difference between the result as disclosed in the profit and loss account and the result on an unmodified historical cost basis. Where full historical cost information is unavailable or cannot be obtained without unreasonable expense or delay, the earliest available values should be used. The note of historical cost profits and losses should be presented immediately following the profit and loss account or the statement of total recognised gains and losses. In consolidated financial statements, the profit and loss account figure for minority interests should be amended for the purposes of this note to reflect the adjustments made where they affect subsidiary companies with minority interest. For the purpose of paragraph 26 the fair value accounting adjustments necessary under FRS 26 and hyperinflation adjustments under FRS 24 and UITF Abstract 9 are not required to be included in the Reconciliation, but this omission should be noted.*

STATEMENT OF TOTAL RECOGNISED GAINS AND LOSSES

56 The range of important components of financial performance which the FRS requires reporting entities to highlight would often be incomplete if it stopped short at the profit and loss account, since certain gains and losses are specifically permitted or required by law or an accounting standard to be taken directly to reserves. An example is an unrealised gain, such as a revaluation surplus on fixed assets. It is necessary to consider all gains and losses recognised in a period when assessing the financial performance of a reporting entity during that period. Accordingly, the FRS requires, as a primary statement, a statement of total recognised gains and losses to show the extent to which shareholders' funds have increased or decreased from all the various gains and losses recognised in the period. It follows from this perspective that the same gains and losses should not be recognised twice (for example, a holding gain recognised when a fixed asset is revalued should not be recognised a second time when the revalued asset is sold).†

57 Statements of total recognised gains and losses contribute further to the purposes of financial reporting by:

(a) combining information about operating and related performance with other aspects of a reporting entity's financial performance; and
(b) providing information (jointly with the other primary statements) that is useful for assessing the return on investment in a reporting entity.

***Editor's note:** Paragraph amended with effect for accounting periods beginning on or after 1 January 2007.*

†ASB Footnote:

However, for entities applying FRS 23 based on the International Accounting Standard 21 The Effect of Changes in Foreign Exchange Rates *and FRS 26, based on the International Accounting Standard 39* Financial Instruments: Recognition and Measurement, *exchange differences and gains and losses (and the tax thereon) on remeasurement of certain categories of financial instruments are initially recognised in the STRGL and the related cumulative gain or loss recognised in the profit and loss account at a different date e.g. when the instrument is derecognised.*

If a reporting entity has no recognised gains or losses other than the profit or loss for the period a statement to this effect immediately below the profit and loss account will satisfy the requirement of paragraph 27.

Where there is a material recognised movement between the amount attributable to different classes of shareholders which does not affect total shareholders' funds an explanatory footnote to the statement may be appropriate. An example might be an appropriation of profit to accrue a premium on redemption of preference shares. 58

RECONCILIATION OF MOVEMENTS IN SHAREHOLDERS' FUNDS

The profit and loss account and the statement of total recognised gains and losses reflect the performance of a reporting entity in a period. There are, however, other changes in shareholders' funds that can also be important in understanding the change in the financial position of the entity. The purpose of the reconciliation of movements in shareholders' funds is to highlight those other changes. If included as a primary statement, the reconciliation should be shown separately from the statement of total recognised gains and losses. 59

PRIOR PERIOD ADJUSTMENTS

The majority of items relating to prior periods arise mainly from the corrections and adjustments which are the natural result of estimates inherent in accounting and more particularly in the periodic preparation of financial statements. They are dealt with in the profit and loss account of the period in which they are identified and their effect is stated where material. They are not exceptional or extraordinary merely because they relate to a prior period; their nature will determine their classification. Prior period adjustments, that is prior period items which should be adjusted against the opening balance of retained profits or reserves, are rare and limited to items arising from changes in accounting policies or from the correction of fundamental errors. 60

Estimating future events and their effects requires the exercise of judgement and will require reappraisal as new events occur, as more experience is acquired or as additional information is obtained. Because a change in estimate arises from new information or developments, it should not be given retrospective effect by a restatement of prior periods. Sometimes a change in estimate may have the appearance of a change of accounting policy and care is necessary to avoid confusing the two. 61

Where possible, the objective of comparability requires, *inter alia*, that there is consistency of accounting treatment within each accounting period and from one period to the next. FRS 18 'Accounting policies' requires an entity to adopt those accounting policies that are most appropriate to its particular circumstances. Accordingly, a change in accounting policy will be made only where a new policy is judged more appropriate. Where transactions or events that are clearly different in substance from those previously occurring necessitate the introduction of an accounting policy in circumstances where no policy previously existed, that is not a change in accounting policy. Following a change in accounting policy, the amounts for the current and corresponding periods should be restated on the basis of the new policies. The cumulative adjustments should also be noted at the foot of the statement of total recognised gains and losses of the current period and included in the reconciliation of movements in shareholders' funds of the corresponding period in order to highlight for users the effect of the adjustments. 62

63 In exceptional circumstances it may be found that financial statements of prior periods have been issued containing errors which are of such significance as to destroy the true and fair view and hence the validity of those financial statements. The corrections of such fundamental errors and the cumulative adjustments applicable to prior periods have no bearing on the results of the current period and they are therefore not included in arriving at the profit or loss for the current period. They are accounted for by restating prior periods, with the result that the opening balance of retained profits will be adjusted accordingly, and highlighted in the reconciliation of movements in shareholders' funds. As the cumulative adjustments are recognised in the current period, they should also be noted at the foot of the statement of total recognised gains and losses of the current period.

COMPARATIVE FIGURES

64 Comparative figures should be given for all items in the primary statements and such notes thereto as are required by the FRS. To aid comparison, the comparative figures in respect of the profit and loss account should be based on the status of an operation in the financial statements of the period under review and should, therefore, include in the continuing category only the results of those operations included in the current period's continuing operations. The comparative figures appearing under the heading 'continuing operations' may include figures which were shown under the heading of acquisitions in that previous period; no reference need be made to the results of those acquisitions, since they are not required to be presented separately in the current year. Where, however, information on acquisitions is provided voluntarily in respect of the first full year, it may be helpful to provide comparative figures for those acquisitions. Similarly, the comparative figures for discontinued operations will include both amounts relating to operations discontinued in the previous period and amounts relating to operations discontinued in the period under review, which in the previous period would have been included as part of continuing operations. The analysis of comparative figures between continuing and discontinued operations is not required on the face of the profit and loss account.

INVESTMENT COMPANIES

65 [Withdrawn]*

66 [Withdrawn]*

***Editor's note:** *Paragraphs withdrawn by FRS 25.*

Note on legal requirements

GREAT BRITAIN*

General

The requirements of Schedules 4 and 4A to the Companies Act 1985† relating to the form and content of company and group financial statements set out formats for the profit and loss account allowing some flexibility in certain circumstances in the manner in which the information is presented. The provisions of the FRS supplement those legal requirements, while remaining within their bounds. 67

Disclosure

Companies Act 1985 Schedule 4 paragraph 54 68

'(1) The basis on which the charge for United Kingdom corporation tax and United Kingdom income tax is computed shall be stated‡.
(2) Particulars shall be given of any special circumstances which affect liability in respect of taxation of profits, income or capital gains for the financial year or liability in respect of taxation of profits, income or capital gains for succeeding financial years.'

Companies Act 1985 Schedule 4A paragraph 13 69

'(1) The following information with respect to acquisitions taking place in the financial year shall be given in a note to the accounts.'
'(4) The profit or loss of the undertaking or group acquired shall be stated—
(a) for the period from the beginning of the financial year of the undertaking or, as the case may be, of the parent undertaking of the group, up to the date of the acquisition, and
(b) for the previous financial year of that undertaking or parent undertaking;

*****Editor's note:** The various statutory references change with the introduction of the Companies Act 2006, which affects accounting for periods beginning on or after 6 April 2008. The various statutory references have changed as follows:*

Companies Act 1985 reference	***Companies Act 2006 reference***
Schedule 4	*Schedule 1 to The Large and Medium-sized Companies and Groups (Accounts and Reports) Regulations 2008 (SI 2008/410)*
Schedule 4A	*Schedule 6 to SI 2008/410*
Para. 54 Schedule 4	*Para 67 Schedule 1 SI 2008/410 (but altered from version quoted)*
Para. 13 Schedule 4A	*Relevant part repealed.*
Para 15 Schedule 4A	*Para 15 Schedule 6 SI 2008/410*
Para 16 Schedule 4A	*Para 16 Schedule 6 SI 2008/410*
Section 266	*Section 833*
Section 265	*Section 832*

†*The requirements relating to banking and insurance companies and groups are set out in Schedule 9 to the Companies Act 1985.* (***Editor's note:*** *Insurance companies are now Schedule 9A. Small companies are covered by Schedule 8.*)

‡***Editor's note:*** *Paragraph 54(1) was repealed February 1996.*

and there shall also be stated the date on which the financial year referred to in paragraph (a) began.'*

70 Companies Act 1985 Schedule 4A paragraphs 15 and 16

'15 Where during the financial year there has been a disposal of an undertaking or group which significantly affects the figures shown in the group accounts, there shall be stated in a note to the accounts—

(a) the name of that undertaking or, as the case may be, of the parent undertaking of that group, and
(b) the extent to which the profit or loss shown in the group accounts is attributable to profit or loss of that undertaking or group.

16 The information required by paragraph 13, or . . . 15 above need not be disclosed with respect to an undertaking which—

(a) is established under the law of a country outside the United Kingdom, or
(b) carries on business outside the United Kingdom,

if in the opinion of the directors of the parent company the disclosure would be seriously prejudicial to the business of that undertaking or to the business of the parent company or any of its subsidiary undertakings and the Secretary of State agrees that the information should not be disclosed.'

Definition

71 Companies Act 1985 section 266

'(1) In section 265 "investment company" means a public company which has given notice in the prescribed form (which has not been revoked) to the registrar of companies of its intention to carry on business as an investment company, and has since the date of that notice complied with the requirements specified below.

(2) Those requirements are—

(a) that the business of the company consists of investing its funds mainly in securities, with the aim of spreading investment risk and giving members of the company the benefit of the results of the management of its funds,
(b) that none of the company's holdings in companies (other than those which are for the time being in investment companies) represents more than 15 per cent. by value of the investing company's investments,
(c) that distribution of the company's capital profits is prohibited by its memorandum or articles of association,
(d) that the company has not retained, otherwise than in compliance with this Part, in respect of any accounting reference period more than 15 per cent. of the income it derives from securities.'

NORTHERN IRELAND

72 Schedules 4 and 4A of the Companies (Northern Ireland) Order 1986 are similar to Schedules 4 and 4A of the Companies Act 1985 as referred to in paragraph 67.

73 Paragraph 54 of Schedule 4 of the Companies (Northern Ireland) Order 1986 is similar to paragraph 54 of Schedule 4 of the Companies Act 1985 as set out in paragraph 68.

***Editor's note:** *Paragraph 13(4) was repealed February 1996.*

Paragraphs 13, 15 and 16 of Schedule 4A of the Companies (Northern Ireland) Order 1986 are similar to paragraphs 13, 15 and 16 of Schedule 4A of the Companies Act 1985 as set out in paragraphs 69 and 70. **74**

Article 274 of the Companies (Northern Ireland) Order 1986 is similar to section 266 of the Companies Act 1985 as set out in paragraph 71. **75**

REPUBLIC OF IRELAND

The Schedule of the Companies (Amendment) Act 1986 is similar to Schedule 4 of the Companies Act 1985 as referred to paragraph 67. **76**

Paragraph 40 of the Schedule of the Companies (Amendment) Act 1986 is similar to paragraph 54 of Schedule 4 of the Companies Act 1985 as set out in paragraph 68. **77**

Section 27 of the 1992 Regulations sets out a general requirement for disclosure in the case of changes in the composition of a group. There are no specific equivalents to paragraphs 13(4) 15 and 16 of Schedule 4A of the Companies Act 1985 as set out in paragraphs 69 and 70. **78**

Section 47 of the Companies (Amendment) Act 1983 is similar to section 266 of the Companies Act 1985 as set out in paragraph 71. **79**

Illustrative examples

These illustrative examples are for general guidance and do not form part of the Financial Reporting Standard. The best form of the disclosure will depend on individual circumstances.

The example on pages 400 to 404 includes two profit and loss accounts along with a statement of total recognised gains and losses, a note of historical cost profits and losses, a reconciliation of movements in shareholders' funds and certain related notes. The following matters should also be noted:

The entity is a group of companies.

The group has made acquisitions and disposals of operations during the year under review.

In this example there is no extraordinary item. However, the positioning of such an item on the face of the profit and loss account is shown although in practice the caption would not appear if no extraordinary items existed.

The profit and loss account examples include the disclosure of earnings per share numbers and a pro forma reconciliation statement for adjusted earnings per share numbers is also shown.

The profit and loss account examples have been prepared using Format 1* as contained in Schedule 4 of the Companies Act 1985. Equivalent information should be shown if any of the other statutory formats are used.

The example on page 405 is one of a Companies Act investment company.

**The equivalent legislation in Northern Ireland is Format 1 in Schedule 4 of the Companies (Northern Ireland) Order 1986.*

The equivalent legislation in the Republic of Ireland is Format 1 in the Schedule to the Companies (Amendment) Act 1983.

Profit and loss account example 1

	1993	1993	1992 as restated
	£million	*£million*	*£million*
Turnover			
Continuing operations	550		500
Acquisitions	50		
	600		
Discontinued operations	175		190
		775	690
Cost of sales		(620)	(555)
Gross profit		155	135
Net operating expenses		(104)	(83)
Operating profit			
Continuing operations	50		40
Acquisitions	6		
	56		
Discontinued operations	(15)		12
Less 1992 provision	10		
		51	52
Profit on sale of properties in continuing operations		9	6
Provision for loss on operations to be discontinued			(30)
Loss on disposal of discontinued operations	(17)		
Less 1992 provision	20		
		3	
Profit on ordinary activities before interest		63	28
Interest payable		(18)	(15)
Profit on ordinary activities before taxation		45	13
Tax on profit on ordinary activities		(14)	(4)
Profit on ordinary activities after taxation		31	9
Minority interests		(2)	(2)
[Profit before extraordinary items]		29	7
[Extraordinary items] (included only to show positioning)			–
Profit for the financial year		29	7*

***Editor's note:** *Example of disclosure of earnings per share withdrawn by FRS 22 and amended with effect for accounting periods beginning on or after 1 January 2007.*

Profit and loss example 2

	Continuing operations 1993	Acquisitions 1993	Discontinued operations 1993	Total 1993	Total 1992 as restated
	£million	*£million*	*£million*	*£million*	*£million*
Turnover	550	50	175	775	690
Cost of sales	(415)	(40)	(165)	(620)	(555)
Gross profit	135	10	10	155	135
Net operating expenses	(85)	(4)	(25)	(114)	(83)
Less 1992 provision			10	10	
Operating profit	50	6	(5)	51	52
Profit on sale of properties	9			9	6
Provision for loss on operations to be discontinued					(30)
Loss on disposal of discontinued operations			(17)	(17)	
Less 1992 provision			20	20	
Profit on ordinary activities before interest	59	6	(2)	63	28
Interest payable				(18)	(15)
Profit on ordinary activities before taxation				45	13
Tax on profit on ordinary activities				(14)	(4)
Profit on ordinary activities after taxation				31	9
Minority interests				(2)	(2)
[Profit before extraordinary items]				29	7
[Extraordinary items] (included only to show positioning)				–	–
Profit for the financial year				29	7*

**Editor's note:* *Example of disclosure of earnings per share withdrawn by FRS 22 and amended with effect for accounting periods beginning on or after 1 January 2007.*

Statement of total recognised gains and losses

	1993	1992 as restated
	£million	*£million*
Profit for the financial year	29	7
Unrealised surplus on revaluation of properties	4	6
Unrealised (loss) /gain on trade investment	(3)	7
	30	20
Currency translation differences on foreign currency net investments	(2)	5
Total recognised gains and losses relating to the year	28	25
Prior year adjustment (as explained in note x)	(10)	
Total gains and losses recognised since last annual report	18	

Note of historical cost profits and losses

	1993	1992 as restated
	£million	*£million*
Reported profit on ordinary activities before taxation	45	13
Realisation of property revaluation gains of previous years	9	10
Difference between a historical cost depreciation charge and the actual depreciation charge of the year calculated on the revalued amount	5	4
Historical cost profit on ordinary activities before taxation	59	27
Historical cost profit for the year retained after taxation, minority interests, extraordinary items and dividends	35	20

Notes to the financial statements

Note required in respect of profit and loss account example 1

	1993			1992 (as restated)		
	Continuing	**Discontinued**	**Total**	**Continuing**	**Discontinued**	**Total**
	£million	*£million*	*£million*	*£million*	*£million*	*£million*
Cost of sales	455	165	620	385	170	555
Net operating expenses						
Distribution costs	56	13	69	46	5	51
Administrative expenses	41	12	53	34	3	37
Other operating income	(8)	0	(8)	(5)	0	(5)
	89	25	114	75	8	83
Less 1992 provision	0	(10)	(10)			
	89	15	104			

The total figures for continuing operations in 1993 include the following amounts relating to acquisitions: cost of sales £40 million and net operating expenses £4 million (namely distribution costs £3 million, administrative expenses £3 million and other operating income £2 million).

Note required in respect of profit and loss account example 2

	1993			1992		
	Continuing	**Discontinued**	**Total**	**Continuing**	**Discontinued**	**Total**
	£million	*£million*	*£million*	*£million*	*£million*	*£million*
Turnover				500	190	690
Cost of sales				385	170	555
Net operating expenses						
Distribution costs	56	13	69	46	5	51
Administrative expenses	41	12	53	34	3	37
Other operating income	(8)	0	(8)	(5)	0	(5)
	89	25	114	75	8	83
Operating profit				40	12	52

The total figure of net operating expenses for continuing operations in 1993 includes £4 million in respect of acquisitions (namely distribution costs £3 million, administrative expenses £3 million and other operating income £2 million).

Reconciliation of movements in shareholders' funds

	1993	**1992 as restated**
	£million	*£million*
Profit for the financial year	29	7
Dividends	(8)	(1)
	21	6
Other recognised gains and losses relating to the year (net)	(1)	18
New share capital subscribed	20	1
Goodwill written-off*	(25)	
Net addition to shareholders' funds	15	25
Opening shareholders' funds (originally £375 million before deducting prior year adjustment of £10 million)	365	340
Closing shareholders' funds	380	365

Reserves

	Share premium account	**Revaluation reserve**	**Profit and loss account**	**Total**
	£million	*£million*	*£million*	*£million*
At beginning of year as previously stated	44	200	120	364
Prior year adjustment			(10)	(10)
At beginning of year as restated	44	200	110	354
Premium on issue of shares (nominal value £7 million)	13			13
Goodwill written-off*			(25)	(25)
Transfer from profit and loss account of the year			21	21
Transfer of realised profits		(14)	14	0
Decrease in value of trade investment		(3)		(3)
Currency translation differences on foreign currency net investments			(2)	(2)
Surplus on property revaluations		4		4
At end of year	57	187	118	362

Note: Nominal share capital at end of year £18million (1992 £11 million).

**Editor's note:* *FRS 10 does not now permit goodwill to be written off directly to reserves, but it did not require prior year figures (such as 1993) to be restated.*

Dissenting view

Mr Bradfield dissents from the FRS because he fears that it could frequently produce misleading measures of performance. He notes that it emphasises the components of pre-tax profit, which are now to include the results of business disposals. Shareholders will attach a different level of significance to each of these components – profits from trading being the most important in assessing the underlying performance. However, the FRS ignores, so far as the face of the profit and loss account is concerned, the often material impact in the eyes of shareholders of tax, minority interests and the issue of further shares on each of these components. Here, he believes, the FRS meets neither its own objective nor the intent of many passages in the Board's Statement of Principles.

Under the FRS, the results from trading and business disposals are shown as separate components of profit before tax but are combined thereafter. Information on the tax and minority interests relating to disposals is required, where practicable, to be given in the notes. However, there is no requirement to identify the disposals component of 'profit before tax', 'profit after tax and minorities' or 'earnings per share'. Under SSAP 6, which the FRS replaces, business disposal profits were excluded from all these measures.

Business disposal profits reflect internally generated goodwill often accrued over many years, together with an element of inflation; they are different in kind from the trading results of the year. Pending realisation, they constitute a hidden reserve. They may attract little tax and rarely contain a minority interest. By contrast, Mr Bradfield notes, it is the magnitude and quality of the earnings from trading, after tax and minority interests, that are the focus of attention for the shareholder as he uses the financial statements to assess the continuity of the source of dividends.

Mr Bradfield believes it imperative that users should clearly see the effects of tax and minorities on trading results attributable to shareholders. If, in an international group of companies, the pre-tax trading profits in a low tax regime were to fall and those in a high tax regime were to rise by an identical amount, the shareholder would be materially worse off. SSAP 6 clearly displayed this decline; the FRS serves only to mask it.

Mr Bradfield notes that increasing tax and minority interests can convert an improvement in trading profit, from one year to the next, into a decline in profit attributable to shareholders. Also, where both disposal profits and losses arise, a modest pre-tax result from disposals can be transformed into a substantial after-tax result. Superimposing these elements of profit, as opposed to displaying them separately, may create a reassuring facade which will hide the underlying trend from many users of accounts. If, in addition, there has been a rights issue or an acquisition for shares, users will be left without a single indicator of whether the entity has done well or badly. SSAP 6, when faithfully applied, coped with all these situations.

In Mr Bradfield's view, such outcomes conflict with many of the qualities of financial statements referred to in chapter 2 of the draft Statement of Principles ('The Objective of Financial Statements and Qualitative Characteristics of Financial Information'). These qualities include:

> 'comparability', whereby 'users must be able to compare the financial statements of an enterprise over time to identify trends in its financial . . . performance' (paragraph 34); and 'understandability', whereby information should be 'readily understandable by users' (paragraph 38).

Furthermore, Mr Bradfield believes that the main sub-totals from 'profit before taxation on ordinary activities' downwards impart no useful information to the user. They therefore conflict with the twin primary characteristics of 'relevance' (paragraph 23) and 'reliability' (paragraph 26); in the latter case because of failure to 'represent faithfully the effect of the transactions and other events' (paragraph 28). Mr Bradfield therefore believes that the FRS will fail to meet the reasonable expectations of users of financial statements.

Mr Bradfield has suggested some alternative routes for the FRS. One would require each of the headings 'profit before tax', 'profit after tax and minorities' and 'earnings per share' to be analysed into two parts: one from trading and one from disposals. This remains an option open to preparers. He believes that it would enable individual profit and loss accounts, five year summaries and summary financial statements to present helpful and realistic pictures that accord with users' expectations of financial reporting.

The development of the Standard

GENERAL

SSAP 6, which is superseded by FRS 3, was originally issued in 1974 and was based on the 'all-inclusive' concept of profit. It was revised as recently as 1986, but, in spite of a number of improvements that were included, there remained significant problems with its interpretation in practice, particularly in respect of the variety of treatments of apparently similar events as either ordinary or extraordinary items in the profit and loss account. The 1986 revision had not achieved the objective of narrowing the differences and variety of accounting practice in this area and calls for change had been heard from users of financial statements as well as from many preparers and auditors involved with the problem. i

The Board responded by proposing a major change to the presentation of financial performance both in the profit and loss account itself and for items passing through reserves. Its initial proposals were issued in a discussion draft in April 1991 and these were developed in Financial Reporting Exposure Draft 1 'The Structure of Financial Statements – Reporting of Financial Performance' (FRED 1) published in December 1991. ii

The FRS has retained the essential features of FRED 1, in particular the shift of emphasis from a single performance indicator. The Board believes that the performance of complex organisations cannot be summarised in a single number and has therefore adopted an 'information set' approach that highlights a range of important components of performance. This approach inevitably means that financial statements will sometimes appear more complex than under the former standard. However, it is widely accepted that certain totals in the profit and loss account, such as profit before tax and earnings per share, have been used too simplistically and have obscured the significance of relevant underlying components of financial performance. The presentation and disclosure requirements of the FRS should provide a framework which will facilitate the analysis and interpretation of the various aspects of performance. iii

Under the previous SSAP 6 approach, the inconsistencies underlying earnings per share (calculated before extraordinary items) were not clearly evident to users of financial statements and automatic reliance was often placed on the resultant numbers without there being sufficient awareness of the subjective judgements of the preparers in what was included or excluded. In future earnings per share will be all-inclusive with the result that significant variations from one period to another or the absence of expected variations, whatever the cause, will demand some explanation. Earnings per share will tend to be more volatile than under SSAP 6, because, for example, they will include all business disposal profits and losses, but, as indicated above, there was, in any event, significant inconsistency in how SSAP 6 was applied in practice. Moreover, the FRS permits preparers of financial statements to present additional versions of earnings per share provided that (a) the assumptions on which they are based are explicitly disclosed, (b) the reasons for presenting the additional versions are explained and (c) there is consistency in the approach adopted. It is recognised that users may develop methods to calculate and publish an adjusted earnings per share of individual reporting entities on the basis of an independent assessment of financial statements. The FRS should facilitate such assessments by requiring the provision of a range of relevant information. iv

It will be for users to identify particular components that they consider of significance in varying circumstances. This is a feature of the information set approach. For the reasons stated above, it will not be appropriate under FRS 3 (any more than it v was in practice under SSAP 6) for users to pay particular attention to any 'headline' number on the face of the profit and loss account or statement of total recognised gains and losses without considering the number's composition. Using the information required by the FRS either on the face of the financial statements or in the notes, users should adapt any headline number to give the performance measure required. The Board considers that the FRS is an important step forward in providing the requisite information to users in a form designed to assist a more mature understanding and analysis of financial performance. Where summarised or highlighted information is presented, (such as a preliminary announcement) it will be the responsibility of the presenters of such information to emphasise the particular components of performance which are of significance in their specific circumstances.

PRINCIPAL CHANGES FROM FRED 1

The consequences of a decision to sell or terminate an operation

vi FRED 1 did not address the making of provisions in respect of operations that are to be discontinued in future periods. In response to comments received, this issue has been addressed in the FRS.

Exceptional items

vii In the light of the proposed severe restrictions on what should be categorised as extraordinary, FRED 1 proposed that a material profit or loss on the sale or termination of an operation should always be shown on the face of the profit and loss account. The FRS has extended this disclosure to two other items – costs of a fundamental reorganisation or restructuring having a material effect on the nature and focus of the reporting entity's operations and profits or losses on the disposal of fixed assets. FRED 1 also proposed that the tax and minority interest attributable to a profit or loss on sale or termination should be shown in a note. In view of the additional items required to be shown on the face of the profit and loss account by the FRS, the Board has given further thought to the question of attributable tax and minority interests and has added paragraphs requiring as a minimum that the aggregate tax and minority interest related to these three items should be disclosed. Preparers should provide further information, where practicable and relevant, identifying the tax and minority interest related to individual categories of these items, in order to assist users in assessing the impact of individual items on the net profit or loss attributable to shareholders.

viii A concern was expressed by respondents to FRED 1 about exceptional items and the prominence they were to be given. In summary, the view was that exceptional items should not be transferred to a single heading of 'exceptional', because profit before exceptional items could then become the focus of financial statement presentations, with the implication that no exceptional items are expected in the future. To meet this concern the FRS requires all exceptional items (other than three specific types of item) to be included in the income or expense heading to which they relate.

Revenue investment (discretionary expenditure)

ix The discussion draft introduced the concept of discretionary expenditure. Users of financial statements had encouraged the Board to require disclosure of expenses that are incurred largely for the benefit of future periods and that can therefore be varied by material amounts without affecting current revenues. The draft sought to do this by including a definition along these lines and amplifying it by reference to common examples of such expenses, viz., research and development expense, training, advertising and major maintenance.

In FRED 1 the concept of discretionary expenditure was developed and in the process the name 'discretionary expenditure' was changed to 'revenue investment'. More detailed guidance was given as to what should be included under this heading and a minimum disclosure requirement was proposed. This was for the disclosure, where material, of the charges to the profit and loss account of the period in respect of research and development, training, advertising and major maintenance and refurbishment. A requirement for an explanation of all material changes between the current and prior period in the level of revenue investment was also proposed. **x**

These revenue investment proposals failed to attract support in the context of the proposed accounting standard, and the Board therefore concluded that they should not be pursued by that means. The Board remains of the view that appropriate disclosures of this kind can be of assistance to users of financial statements but in the light of the responses to FRED 1 concluded that the concept can best be developed within the Board's proposals for an Operating and Financial Review to support a company's annual report – i.e. as part of a wider discussion of a company's performance.* The Board's decision on the FRED 1 proposal on revenue investment does not in any way affect the existing requirements of SSAP 13 – 'Accounting for research and development' and the Companies Act 1985 regarding the disclosure of research and development activities. **xi**

Reconciliation of movements in shareholders' funds

Several respondents to FRED 1, in commenting on the statement of total recognised gains and losses, suggested it should be extended to provide a complete reconciliation of the movements in shareholders' funds. The Board agreed that changes in shareholders' funds other than those included in the statement of total recognised gains and losses can also be important in understanding the change in the financial position of a reporting entity and concluded that this additional information should be required in a reconciliation of movements in shareholders' funds. In order not to divert attention from the components of performance of the total of recognised gains and losses for the period, it specified that if included as a primary statement, the reconciliation should be shown separately from the statement of total recognised gains and losses. **xii**

2007 Amendment

During 2007 the ASB set out to clarify the relationship between FRS 3 requirements and those contained in FRS 23 and FRS 26. FRS 26 specifies the treatment of gains and losses on remeasurement and derecognition of financial instruments. Paragraphs 21, 26 and 31A of FRS 3 specify the treatment of such gains or losses for all assets and liabilities, including financial instruments. Similarly, entities complying with FRS 23 are required by paragraph 48 of the standard to recycle the cumulative amount of exchange differences relating to a foreign operation, recognised in the STRGL, through the profit and loss on the disposal of that foreign operation. In contrast, although FRS 3 does not specifically prohibit recycling of these gains and losses through the profit and loss account, it appears to do so by analogy to the treatment of other gains and losses recognised in the STRGL which are not permitted to be recycled. Whilst FRS 23 and FRS 26 are the latter and more specific standards the ASB decided to clarify the situation by amending the scope of FRS 3. **xiii**

***Editor's note:** *See paragraphs 16 to 18 of the ASB Statement 'Operating and financial review'.*

Financial Reporting Standard 4 is set out in paragraphs 1–67.

The Statement of Standard Accounting Practice set out in paragraphs 18–67 should be read in the context of the Objective as stated in paragraph 1 and the definitions set out in paragraphs 2–17 and also of the Foreword to Accounting Standards and the Statement of Principles for Financial Reporting currently in issue.

The Application Notes specify how some of the requirements of FRS 4 are to be applied to transactions that have certain features.

The Explanation set out in paragraphs 68–102 and the Application Notes shall be regarded as part of the Statement of Standard Accounting Practice insofar as they assist in interpreting that statement.

Appendix III 'The development of the FRS' reviews considerations and arguments that were thought significant by members of the Board in reaching the conclusions on FRS 4. The Board adopted the FRS on the basis of the overall considerations; individual members gave greater weight to some factors than to others.

[FRS 4]
Capital instruments*†

(Issued December 1993)

Contents

	Paragraph
Summary	a–f
Financial Reporting Standard 4	
Objective	1
Definitions	2–17
Statement of standard accounting practice	18–67
Scope	18–22
Application to smaller entities	22A
Classification of capital instruments	23–24
Debt	25–36
Shares and warrants	37–48
Shares issued by subsidiaries	49–51
Investment companies	52
Disclosures	53–65
Date from which effective	66
Withdrawal of UITF Abstract 1 and Abstract 8	67
Explanation	68–102
Capital instruments	68
Identification of distinct capital instruments	69
The classification of capital instruments	70–72
The term of debt	73–74
Finance costs	75–76
The maturity of debt	77–81
Shares and warrants	82–87
Shares issued by subsidiaries	88–91
Issue costs	92–97
Investment companies	98
Scrip dividends	99
Disclosure requirements	100–102
Application notes	

****Editor's note:*** *FRS 4 has been substantially amended by FRS 25, with effect for accounting periods beginning on or after 1 January 2005. Given the number of changes, specific reference has not been made in the notes to the withdrawal of specific paragraphs of the standard. Reference has been made to paragraphs amended by FRS 25. The contents list has not been amended.*

Those parts of FRS 4 which remain are applicable only to companies which are not complying with FRS 26, as explained in paragraph 18 of FRS 4.

†***Editor's note:*** *The matters covered in FRS 4 are, broadly, dealt with in Section 11 of FRS 102.*

Adoption of FRS 4 by the Board

Appendix I – Note on legal requirements

Appendix II – Compliance with international accounting standards

Appendix III – The development of the FRS

Capital instruments

Summary

[Withdrawn]

Objective

The objective of this FRS is to ensure that costs associated with capital instruments that are classified as liabilities are allocated to accounting periods on a fair basis over the period the instrument is in issue; and that the financial statements provide relevant information concerning the nature and amount of the entity's source of finance.* 1

Definitions

The following definitions shall apply in this FRS and in particular in the Statement of Standard Accounting Practice set out in paragraphs 18-67.

Capital instruments:- 2
All instruments that are issued by reporting entities as a means of raising finance, including shares, debentures, loans and debt instruments, options and warrants that give the holder the right to subscribe for or obtain capital instruments. In the case of consolidated financial statements the term includes capital instruments issued by subsidiaries except those that are held by another member of the group included in the consolidation.

[Deleted] 3-5

Debt:- 6
Capital instruments that are classified as liabilities.

[Deleted] 7

Finance costs:- 8
The difference between the net proceeds of an instrument and the total amount of the payments (or other transfers of economic benefits) that the issuer may be required to make in respect of the instrument.

[Deleted] 9

Issue costs:- 10
The costs that are incurred directly in connection with the issue of a capital instrument, that is, those costs that would not have been incurred had the specific instrument in question not been issued.

Net proceeds:- 11
The fair value of the consideration received on the issue of a capital instrument after deduction of issue costs.

***Editor's note:** Amended by FRS 25.*

12-15 [Deleted]

16 *Term (of a capital instrument):-*
The period from the date of issue of the capital instrument to the date at which it will expire, be redeemed, or be cancelled.

If either party has the option to require the instrument to be redeemed or cancelled and, under the terms of the instrument, it is uncertain whether such an option will be exercised, the term should be taken to end on the earliest date at which the instrument would be redeemed or cancelled on exercise of such an option.

If either party has the right to extend the period of an instrument, the term should not include the period of the extension if there is a genuine commercial possibility that the period will not be extended.

17 [Deleted]

Statement of standard accounting practice

SCOPE

18 Financial Reporting Standard 4 applies to all financial statements intended to give a true and fair view of a reporting entity's financial position and profit or loss (or income and expenditure) for a period, but does not apply to entities applying FRS 26 (IAS 39) 'Financial Instruments: Measurement'. The terminology used in this statement will be appropriate for those reporting entities that are companies. Entities other than companies should adapt the terminology as appropriate.*

19 The FRS applies to accounting for capital instruments by entities that issue them. It does not address accounting for investments in capital instruments issued by other entities.

20 The scope of the FRS includes capital instruments denominated in a foreign currency. However, the FRS does not address the translation of foreign currency amounts relating to such instruments into the reporting currency or the accounting for foreign exchange differences arising from such translations.

21 The requirements of the FRS apply to all capital instruments with the following exceptions:

(a) warrants issued to employees under employee share schemes;
(b) leases, which should be accounted for in accordance with SSAP 21;
(c) equity shares issued as part of a business combination that is accounted for as a merger.

22 In applying the requirements of the FRS, capital instruments that are issued at the same time in a composite transaction should be considered together. They should be accounted for as a single instrument unless they are capable of being transferred, cancelled or redeemed independently of each other.

****Editor's note:*** *Amended by FRS 25. In addition, FRS 26 is now entitled Financial Instruments: Recognition and Measurement.*

APPLICATION TO SMALLER ENTITIES

Reporting entities applying the Financial Reporting Standard for Smaller Entities currently applicable are exempt from this accounting standard. **22a**

[Deleted] **23-26**

DEBT

Carrying amount and allocation of finance costs

Immediately after issue, debt should be stated at the amount of the net proceeds. **27**

The finance costs of debt should be allocated to periods over the term of the debt at a constant rate on the carrying amount. All finance costs should be charged in the profit and loss account, except in the case of investment companies, which are addressed in paragraph 52. **28**

The carrying amount of debt should be increased by the finance cost in respect of the reporting period and reduced by payments made in respect of the debt in that period. **29**

Accrued finance costs may be included in accruals rather than in the carrying amount of debt to the extent that the finance costs have accrued in one accounting period and will be paid in cash in the next. Any such accrual should be included in the carrying amount of the debt for the purposes of calculating finance costs and gains and losses arising on repurchase or early settlement. **30**

Where the amount of payments required by a debt instrument is contingent on uncertain future events such as changes in an index, those events should be taken into account in the calculation of the finance costs and the carrying amount once they have occurred. **31**

Repurchase of debt

Gains and losses arising on the repurchase or early settlement of debt should be recognised in the profit and loss account in the period during which the repurchase or early settlement is made. **32**

[Deleted] **33-67**

Explanation

CAPITAL INSTRUMENTS

The definition of capital instruments, given in paragraph 2, includes all kinds of shares and debt instruments as well as options and warrants to obtain such instruments. It characterises capital instruments as a means of raising finance: an instrument may be within the definition whether or not the consideration given for its issue takes the form of cash. Capital instruments may take the form of contracts between two parties (for example a borrower and its bank) as well as an issue of transferable securities. **68**

IDENTIFICATION OF DISTINCT CAPITAL INSTRUMENTS

69 In order to apply the requirements of the FRS it is necessary to determine whether instruments issued at the same time should be accounted for individually or not. Accounting for the individual instruments is required by paragraph 22 if (and only if) the instruments are capable of being transferred, cancelled or redeemed independently of each other. For example, if debt and warrants are issued simultaneously and the warrants can be transferred, cancelled or redeemed independently of the debt, the two components should be accounted for separately. It would be necessary in such a case to apportion the proceeds of the issue to each component.

70-72 [Deleted]

THE TERM OF DEBT

73 The FRS requires debt to be accounted for by allocating finance costs over the term of the instrument at a constant rate. The term of the instrument is usually self-evident but where either party has the option to extend the term, or to require the instrument to be redeemed early, such options should be carefully evaluated. If there is an option for early redemption, the term should be taken to end on the earliest date the option could be exercised, unless there is no genuine commercial possibility that the option will be exercised. The term should not include any period for which the instrument might be extended unless such an extension is virtually certain at the time the instrument is issued: that is, there is no genuine commercial possibility that the period will not be extended.*

74 In evaluating the commercial possibilities of options, it should be assumed that the parties will act in accordance with their economic interests. A severe deterioration in the creditworthiness of the issuer should not be anticipated, but should be taken into account when it occurs. For example, in the case of a zero coupon bond, the return to the lender consists entirely of the amount received at maturity. If the lender under such an instrument had the right to require early redemption, but on exercise of that right he would receive only the original issue price, it would be unrealistic to assume that he would exercise it unless the issuer's creditworthiness deteriorated to a significant extent. The term of such a bond would therefore normally be taken to extend to its final maturity.

FINANCE COSTS

75 The FRS requires finance costs to be recognised at a constant rate on the carrying amount of debt. In some instances the nominal yield on the debt will not be materially different from the amount required by the FRS to be recognised and in these circumstances calculations will not be necessary in order to derive the information required by the FRS.

76 The FRS also requires all finance costs to be charged in the profit and loss account. However, the FRS does not prohibit the capitalisation of finance costs as part of the cost of an asset by way of a simultaneous transfer from the profit and loss account that is separately disclosed.

77-91 [Deleted]

***Editor's note:** *Reference to non-equity interests removed by FRS 25.*

ISSUE COSTS

The FRS requires issue costs, as defined, to be accounted for as a reduction in the proceeds of a capital instrument. Such costs are not assets as defined in the Board's draft Statement of Principles because they do not provide access to any future economic benefits. **92**

[Deleted] **93**

In the case of most debt instruments, the issuer has the use of funds during the life of the instrument, and in return pays interest. The benefit obtained from the issue costs is reflected in the interest expense: indeed, issue costs are in some cases economically indistinguishable from a discount on issue. Issue costs are therefore appropriately accounted for as an adjustment to the amount of the liability, which effectively results in their being charged over the life of the instrument. If it became clear that the instrument would be redeemed early, then the amortisation of the issue costs and any discount on issue would have to be accelerated. **94**

Where the life of an instrument is indeterminate, the benefit of the issue costs is reflected in terms of the financing indefinitely. In such a case, the issue costs are therefore not taken to the profit and loss account until such time as the instrument is redeemed or cancelled. **95**

Care should be taken in the determination of the amount that falls to be treated as issue costs to avoid the danger of overstating finance costs over the life of the instrument in question. For this reason, the definition of issue costs is deliberately restrictive. The definition does not admit costs of researching and negotiating sources of finance or of ascertaining the suitability or feasibility of particular instruments, nor allocations of internal costs that would have been incurred had the instrument not been issued: for example management remuneration. The costs incurred in connection with a financial restructuring or renegotiation also do not qualify as issue costs; such costs relate to previous sources of finance and not to any instrument that may be issued following the restructuring or renegotiation. Costs that do not qualify as issue costs should be written off to the profit and loss account as incurred. **96**

The requirement of the FRS that issue costs are reflected in the amounts charged to the profit and loss account over the term of a capital instrument is not intended to prohibit the subsequent charging of issue costs to the share premium account by means of a transfer between reserves. The amounts that may be charged to the share premium account are determined by the requirements of companies legislation. **97**

[Deleted] **98-102**

Application notes

[Deleted]

Appendices I - III

[Deleted]

Financial Reporting Standard 5 is set out in paragraphs 1–39.

The Statement of Standard Accounting Practice set out in paragraphs 11–39 should be read in the context of the Objective as stated in paragraph 1 and the definitions set out in paragraphs 2–10 and also of the Foreword to Accounting Standards and the Statement of Principles for Financial Reporting currently in issue.

The Application Notes specify how some of the requirements of FRS 5 are to be applied to transactions that have certain features.

The Explanation set out in paragraphs 40–103 and the Application Notes shall be regarded as part of the Statement of Standard Accounting Practice insofar as they assist in interpreting that statement.

Appendix III 'The development of the FRS' reviews considerations and arguments that were thought significant by members of the Board in reaching the conclusions on FRS 5.

[FRS 5]
Reporting the substance of transactions*

(Issued April 1994, amended December 1994, September 1998 and November 2003)†

Contents

	Paragraph
Summary	a–n
Financial Reporting Standard 5	
Objective	1
Definitions	2–10
Statement of Standard Accounting Practice	11–39
Scope	11–13
Application to smaller entities	13A
General	14–15
The substance of transactions	14
Quasi-subsidiaries	15
The substance of transactions	16–31
Identifying assets and liabilities	16–19
Recognition of asset and liabilities	20
Transactions in previously recognised assets	21–25
Continued recognition of an asset in its entirety	21
Ceasing to recognise an asset in its entirety	22
Special cases	23–24
The meaning of 'significant'	25
Linked presentation for certain non-recourse finance arrangements	26–28
Offset	29
Disclosure of the substance of transactions	30–31
Quasi-subsidiaries	32–38
Identification of quasi-subsidiaries	32–34
Accounting for quasi-subsidiaries	35–37
Disclosure of quasi-subsidiaries	38
Date from which effective	39
Explanation	40–103
Scope	40–45
Exclusions from the FRS	42
Other standards	43–45

***Editor's note:** *The matters covered in FRS 5 itself are primarily dealt with in Section 2 of FRS 102. Most of the Application Notes are covered in Sections 11 and 12 of FRS 102 (where covered at all) whilst revenue recognition is covered in Section 23.*

†***Editor's note:** FRS 5 has been amended by FRS 25 with effect for accounting periods beginning on or after 1 January 2005 and by the amendments to FRS 26 with effect for accounting periods beginning on or after 1 January 2007.*

The substance of transactions 46–94
General principles 46–52
Features of more complex transactions 47–50
(a) Separation of legal title from benefits and risks 48
(b) Linking of transactions 49
(c) Inclusion of options 50
Assessing commercial effect by considering the position of other parties 51–52
Identifying assets and liabilities 53–63
Assets – control of access to benefits 54
Assets – risk 55–56
Liabilities – obligations to transfer benefits 57–58
Options 59–62
Guarantees and conditional provisions 63
Recognition of assets and liabilities 64–65
Transactions in previously recognised assets 66–75
Continued recognition of an asset in its entirety 67–68
Ceasing to recognise an asset in its entirety 69
Special cases 70–74
(a) Transfer of only part of an item 71
(b) Transfer of an item for only part of its life 72
(c) Transfer of an item for all of its life with some benefit or risk retained 73
Measurement and profit recognition 74
The meaning of 'significant' 75
Linked presentation for certain non-recourse finance arrangements 76–88
General principles 76–80
Separate presentation of an asset and liability 77
Linked presentation 78–80
Detailed conditions for use of a linked presentation 81–86
Profit or loss recognition and presentation 87– 88
Offset 89–91
Disclosure of the substance of transactions 92–94
Quasi-subsidiaries 95–103
Identification of quasi-subsidiaries 95–98
Benefits 96
Control 97–98
Accounting for quasi-subsidiaries 99–102
Disclosure of quasi-subsidiaries 103

Application notes
A CONSIGNMENT STOCK
B SALE AND REPURCHASE AGREEMENTS
C FACTORING OF DEBTS
D SECURITISED ASSETS
E LOAN TRANSFERS
F PRIVATE FINANCE INITIATIVE AND SIMILAR CONTRACTS
G REVENUE RECOGNITION

Adoption of FRS 5 by the Board

Appendices
I Note on legal requirements
II Compliance with International Accounting Standards
III The development of the FRS

Reporting the substance of transactions

Summary

GENERAL

Financial Reporting Standard 5 'Reporting the Substance of Transactions' requires an entity's financial statements to report the substance of the transactions into which it has entered. The FRS sets out how to determine the substance of a transaction (including how to identify its effect on the assets and liabilities of the entity), whether any resulting assets and liabilities should be included in the balance sheet, and what disclosures are appropriate. The FRS also contains some provisions in respect of how transactions should be reported in the profit and loss account and the cash flow statement. **a**

The FRS will not change the accounting treatment and disclosure of the vast majority of transactions. It will mainly affect those more complex transactions whose substance may not be readily apparent. The true commercial effect of such transactions may not be adequately expressed by their legal form and, where this is the case, it will not be sufficient to account for them merely by recording that form. **b**

Transactions requiring particularly careful analysis will often include features such as – **c**

(i) the party that gains the principal benefits generated by an item is not the legal owner of the item,

(ii) a transaction is linked with others in such a way that the commercial effect can be understood only by considering the series as a whole, or

(iii) an option is included on terms that make its exercise highly likely.

The FRS sets out principles that will apply to all transactions. In addition, there are five Application Notes that describe the application of the FRS to transactions with certain features: consignment stock; sale and repurchase agreements; factoring; securitised assets; and loan transfers. The Application Notes need not be referred to in all cases. At the start of each Note there is a 'Features' section that may serve as a quick reference point to determine whether further study is required. In addition, each Note concludes with a table summarising its main provisions. **d**

Identification and recognition of the substance of transactions

A key step in determining the substance of any transaction is to identify whether it has given rise to new assets or liabilities for the entity and whether it has increased or decreased the entity's existing assets or liabilities. Assets are, broadly, rights or other access to future economic benefits controlled by an entity; liabilities are, broadly, an entity's obligations to transfer economic benefits. **e**

The future economic benefits inherent in an asset are never completely certain in amount; there is always some risk that the benefits will turn out to be greater or less than expected. Whether the entity gains or suffers from such variations in benefits is evidence of whether it has an asset. **f**

The definition of a liability requires an obligation to transfer benefits. Evidence that an entity has such an obligation is given if there is some circumstance in which the entity is unable to avoid an outflow of benefits. **g**

h Once identified, an asset or liability should be recognised (ie included) in the balance sheet, provided that there is sufficient evidence that an asset or liability exists, and the asset or liability can be measured at a monetary amount with sufficient reliability.

i Following its recognition, an asset may be affected by a subsequent transaction. Where the transaction does not significantly alter the entity's rights to benefits or its exposure to risks, the entire asset should continue to be recognised. Conversely, where the transaction transfers to others all significant rights to benefits and all significant exposure to risks, the entity should cease to recognise the asset in its entirety. Finally, in other cases where not all significant benefits and risks have been transferred, it may be appropriate to amend the description or monetary amount of an asset and, where necessary, recognise a liability for any obligations it has assumed.

Linked presentation for certain non-recourse finance arrangements

j A special form of presentation, termed a 'linked presentation', should be used for certain non-recourse finance arrangements. This presentation shows, on the face of the balance sheet, the finance deducted from the gross amount of the item it finances. It should be used where, although the entity has significant rights to benefits and exposure to risks relating to a specific item, the item is financed in such a way that the maximum loss the entity can suffer is limited to a fixed monetary amount. For use of a linked presentation it is necessary that both –

(i) the finance will be repaid only from proceeds generated by the specific item it finances (or by transfer of the item itself) and there is no possibility whatsoever of a claim on the entity being established other than against funds generated by that item (or the item itself), and

(ii) there is no provision whatsoever whereby the entity may either keep the item on repayment of the finance or re-acquire it at any time.

Disclosure of the substance of transactions

k Adequate disclosure of a transaction is important to an understanding of its commercial effect. For most transactions, the disclosures currently required will be sufficient for this purpose. However, where the nature of any recognised asset or liability differs from that of items usually found under the relevant balance sheet heading, the differences should be explained. Furthermore, to the extent that a transaction has not resulted in the recognition of assets or liabilities, disclosure may nevertheless be required in order to give an understanding of its commercial effect.

Quasi-subsidiaries*

l Sometimes assets and liabilities are placed in an entity (a 'vehicle') that is in effect controlled by the reporting entity but does not meet the legal definition of a subsidiary. Where the commercial effect for the reporting entity is no different from that which would result were the vehicle a subsidiary, the vehicle will be a 'quasi-subsidiary'.

****Editor's note**: While not amended by the changes to FRS 2, it is the ASB's view that the relevance of the section of FRS 5 dealing with quasi-subsidiaries has declined with the changes to FRS 2 effective from 2005 since some entities which might previously have been classified as quasi-subsidiaries will now fall within the amended definition of a subsidiary.*

The FRS requires the assets, liabilities, profits, losses and cash flows of any quasi-subsidiary to be included in the consolidated financial statements of the group that controls it in the same way as if they were those of a subsidiary. However, where a quasi-subsidiary is used to finance a specific item in such a way that the provisions of paragraph j above are met from the point of view of the group, the assets and liabilities of the quasi-subsidiary should be included in consolidated financial statements using the linked presentation described in paragraph j. **m**

Disclosure is required, in summary form, of the financial statements of quasi-subsidiaries. **n**

Financial Reporting Standard 5

Objective

The objective of this FRS is to ensure that the substance of an entity's transactions is reported in its financial statements. The commercial effect of the entity's transactions, and any resulting assets, liabilities, gains or losses, should be faithfully represented in its financial statements. **1**

Definitions

The following definitions shall apply in this FRS and in particular in the Statement of Standard Accounting Practice set out in paragraphs 11–39.

Assets:- **2**
Rights or other access to future economic benefits controlled by an entity as a result of past transactions or events.

*Control in the context of an asset:-*The ability to obtain the future economic benefits relating to an asset and to restrict the access of others to those benefits. **3**

Liabilities:- **4**
An entity's obligations to transfer economic benefits as a result of past transactions or events.

Risk:- **5**
Uncertainty as to the amount of benefits. The term includes both potential for gain and exposure to loss.

Recognition:- **6**
The process of incorporating an item into the primary financial statements under the appropriate heading. It involves depiction of the item in words and by a monetary amount and inclusion of that amount in the statement totals.

Quasi-subsidiary:- **7**
A quasi-subsidiary of a reporting entity is a company, trust, partnership or other vehicle that, though not fulfilling the definition of a subsidiary, is directly or indirectly controlled by the reporting entity and gives rise to benefits for that entity that are in substance no different from those that would arise were the vehicle a subsidiary.

8 *Control of another entity:-*
The ability to direct the financial and operating policies of that entity with a view to gaining economic benefit from its activities.

9 *Subsidiary:-*
A subsidiary undertaking as defined by companies legislation.

10 *Companies legislation:-*
(a) In Great Britain, the Companies Act 1985;*
(b) in Northern Ireland, the Companies (Northern Ireland) Order 1986; and
(c) in the Republic of Ireland, the Republic of Ireland Companies Acts 1963–1990 and the European Communities (Companies: Group Accounts) Regulations 1992.

Statement of Standard Accounting Practice

SCOPE

11 Subject to paragraph 12, Financial Reporting Standard 5 applies to all transactions of a reporting entity whose financial statements are intended to give a true and fair view of its financial position and profit or loss (or income and expenditure) for a period. In the FRS, the term 'transaction' includes both a single transaction or arrangement and also a group or series of transactions that achieves or is designed to achieve an overall commercial effect.

12 The following are excluded from the scope of the FRS, unless they are a part of a transaction that falls within the scope of the FRS:
(a) forward contracts and futures (such as those for foreign currencies or commodities);
(b) foreign exchange and interest rate swaps;
(c) contracts where a net amount will be paid or received based on the movement in a price or an index (sometimes referred to as 'contracts for differences');
(d) expenditure commitments (such as purchase commitments) and orders placed, until the earlier of delivery or payment; and
(e) employment contracts.

13 Where the substance of a transaction or the treatment of any resulting asset or liability falls not only within the scope of this FRS but also directly within the scope of another FRS, a Statement of Standard Accounting Practice ('SSAP'), or a specific statutory requirement governing the recognition of assets or liabilities, the standard or statute that contains the more specific provision(s) should be applied.

APPLICATION TO SMALLER ENTITIES

13A Reporting entities applying the Financial Reporting Standard for Smaller Entities currently applicable are exempt from this accounting standard unless preparing consolidated financial statements, in which case they should apply the FRS to such statements as required by the FRSSE.

***Editor's note:** *This should now be taken to refer to the Companies Act 2006.*

Paragraphs 14 to 31 of the FRS do not apply to the recognition and derecognition of financial assets and financial liabilities within the scope of paragraphs 14 to 42 of FRS 26 (IAS 39) 'Financial Instruments: Recognition and Measurement'.* **13B**

GENERAL

The substance of transactions

A reporting entity's financial statements should report the substance of the transactions into which it has entered. In determining the substance of a transaction, all its aspects and implications should be identified and greater weight given to those more likely to have a commercial effect in practice. A group or series of transactions that achieves or is designed to achieve an overall commercial effect should be viewed as a whole. **14**

Quasi-subsidiaries

Where the entity has a quasi-subsidiary, the substance of the transactions entered into by the quasi-subsidiary should be reported in consolidated financial statements. **15**

THE SUBSTANCE OF TRANSACTIONS

Identifying assets and liabilities

To determine the substance of a transaction it is necessary to identify whether the transaction has given rise to new assets or liabilities for the reporting entity and whether it has changed the entity's existing assets or liabilities. **16**

Evidence that an entity has rights or other access to benefits (and hence has an asset) is given if the entity is exposed to the risks inherent in the benefits, taking into account the likelihood of those risks having a commercial effect in practice. **17**

Evidence that an entity has an obligation to transfer benefits (and hence has a liability) is given if there is some circumstance in which the entity is unable to avoid, legally or commercially, an outflow of benefits. **18**

Where a transaction incorporates one or more options, guarantees or conditional provisions, their commercial effect should be assessed in the context of all the aspects and implications of the transaction in order to determine what assets and liabilities exist. **19**

Recognition of assets and liabilities

Where a transaction results in an item that meets the definition of an asset or liability, that item should be recognised in the balance sheet if – **20**

(a) there is sufficient evidence of the existence of the item (including, where appropriate, evidence that a future inflow or outflow of benefit will occur), and
(b) the item can be measured at a monetary amount with sufficient reliability.

***Editor's note:** *Added by amendments to FRS 26, with effect for accounting periods beginning on or after 1 January 2007. While this paragraph has been placed under a heading dealing with smaller entities, it applies to entities that are not small.*

Transactions in previously recognised assets

Continued recognition of an asset in its entirety

21 Where a transaction involving a previously recognised asset results in no significant change in –

(a) the entity's rights or other access to benefits relating to that asset, or
(b) its exposure to the risks inherent in those benefits,

the entire asset should continue to be recognised and a financial liability recognised for the consideration received*. In particular this will be the case for any transaction that is in substance a financing of a previously recognised asset, unless the conditions for a linked presentation given in paragraphs 26 and 27 are met, in which case such a presentation should be used.

Ceasing to recognise an asset in its entirety

22 Where a transaction involving a previously recognised asset transfers to others –

(a) all significant rights or other access to benefits relating to that asset, and
(b) all significant exposure to the risks inherent in those benefits,

the entire asset should cease to be recognised.

Special cases

23 Paragraphs 21 and 22 deal with most transactions affecting items previously recognised as assets. In other cases where there is a significant change in the entity's rights to benefits and exposure to risks but the provisions of paragraph 22 are not met, the description or monetary amount relating to an asset should, where necessary, be changed and a liability recognised for any obligations to transfer benefits that are assumed. These cases arise where the transaction takes one or more of the following forms:

(a) a transfer of only part of the item in question;
(b) a transfer of all of the item for only part of its life; and
(c) a transfer of all of the item for all of its life but where the entity retains some significant right to benefits or exposure to risk.

24 In the special cases referred to in paragraph 23, where the amount of any resulting gain or loss is uncertain, full provision should be made for any probable loss but recognition of any gain, to the extent it is in doubt, should be deferred. In addition, where the uncertainty could have a material effect on the financial statements, this fact should be disclosed in the notes to the financial statements.

The meaning of 'significant'

25 In applying paragraphs 21–23 above and paragraph 26 below, 'significant' should be judged in relation to those benefits and risks that are likely to occur in practice, and not in relation to the total possible benefits and risks.

****Editor's note:*** *Amended by FRS 26, with effect for accounting periods beginning on or after 1 January 2007.*

Linked presentation for certain non-recourse finance arrangements

Where a transaction involving an item previously recognised as an asset is in substance a financing – and therefore meets the condition of paragraph 21 regarding no significant change in the entity's access to benefits or exposure to risks – but the financing 'ring-fences' the item such that – **26**

(a) the finance will be repaid only from proceeds generated by the specific item it finances (or by transfer of the item itself) and there is no possibility whatsoever of a claim on the entity being established other than against funds generated by that item (or the item itself),
(b) there is no provision whatsoever whereby the entity may either keep the item on repayment of the finance or re-acquire it at any time, and
(c) all of the conditions given in paragraph 27 are met,

the finance should be shown deducted from the gross amount of the item it finances on the face of the balance sheet within a single asset caption (a 'linked presentation'). The gross amounts of the item and the finance should be shown on the face of the balance sheet and not merely disclosed in the notes to the financial statements. A linked presentation should also be used where an item that is financed in such a way that all of the above three conditions are met has not been recognised previously as an asset.

A linked presentation should be used only where all of the following are met: **27**

(a) the finance relates to a specific item (or portfolio of similar items) and, in the case of a loan, is secured on that item but not on any other asset of the entity;
(b) the provider of the finance has no recourse whatsoever, either explicit or implicit, to the other assets of the entity for losses and the entity has no obligation whatsoever to repay the provider of finance;
(c) the directors of the entity state explicitly in each set of financial statements where a linked presentation is used that the entity is not obliged to support any losses, nor does it intend to do so;
(d) the provider of the finance has agreed in writing (in the finance documentation or otherwise) that it will seek repayment of the finance, as to both principal and interest, only to the extent that sufficient funds are generated by the specific item it has financed and that it will not seek recourse in any other form, and such agreement is noted in each set of financial statements where a linked presentation is used;
(e) if the funds generated by the item are insufficient to pay off the provider of the finance, this does not constitute an event of default for the entity; and
(f) there is no provision whatsoever, either in the financing arrangement or otherwise, whereby the entity has a right or an obligation either to keep the item upon repayment of the finance or (where title to the item has been transferred) to re-acquire it at any time. Accordingly:
    (i) where the item is one (such as a monetary receivable) that directly generates cash, the provider of the finance will be repaid out of the resulting cash receipts (to the extent these are sufficient); or
    (ii) where the item is one (such as a physical asset) that does not directly generate cash, there is a definite point at which either the item will be sold to a third party and the provider of the finance repaid from the proceeds (to the extent these are sufficient) or the item will be transferred to the provider of the finance in full and final settlement.

Where all of these conditions hold for only part of the finance, a linked presentation should be used for only that part. In such cases, the maximum future payment that the reporting entity could make (other than from funds generated by the specific item being financed) should be excluded from the amount deducted on the face of the balance sheet.

28 In respect of an arrangement for which a linked presentation is used, profit should be recognised on entering into the arrangement only to the extent that the non-returnable proceeds received exceed the previous carrying value of the item. Thereafter, any profit or loss deriving from the item should be recognised in the period in which it arises. The net profit or loss recognised in each period should be included in the profit and loss account and separate disclosure of its gross components should be given in the notes to the financial statements.

Offset

29 Assets and liabilities should not be offset. Debit and credit balances should be aggregated into a single net item where, and only where, they do not constitute separate assets and liabilities. For offset of financial assets and financial liabilities, FRS 25 'Financial Instruments: Disclosure and Presentation' applies.*

Disclosure of the substance of transactions

30 Disclosure of a transaction in the financial statements, whether or not it has resulted in assets or liabilities being recognised or ceasing to be recognised, should be sufficient to enable the user of the financial statements to understand its commercial effect.

31 Where a transaction has resulted in the recognition of assets or liabilities whose nature differs from that of items usually included under the relevant balance sheet heading, the differences should be explained.

QUASI-SUBSIDIARIES†

Identification of quasi-subsidiaries

32 In determining whether another entity (a 'vehicle') gives rise to benefits for the reporting entity that are in substance no different from those that would arise were the vehicle a subsidiary, regard should be had to the benefits arising from the net assets of the vehicle. Evidence of which party gains these benefits is given by which party is exposed to the risks inherent in them.

33 In determining whether the reporting entity controls a vehicle regard should be had to who, in practice, directs the financial and operating policies of the vehicle. The ability to prevent others from directing those policies is evidence of control, as is the ability to prevent others from enjoying the benefits arising from the vehicle's net assets.

34 Where the financial and operating policies of a vehicle are in substance predetermined, contractually or otherwise, the party possessing control will be the one that gains the benefits arising from the net assets of the vehicle. Evidence of which

***Editor's note:** *Amended by FRS 25.*

†***Editor's note:** While the amendment to FRS 2 has not strictly changed FRS 5, the preface to the amendment notes that many entities previously considered to be quasi-subsidiaries are likely to be subsidiaries in the future.*

party gains these benefits is given by which party is exposed to the risks inherent in them.

Accounting for quasi-subsidiaries

Subject to paragraph 37, the assets, liabilities, profits, losses and cash flows of a quasi-subsidiary should be included in the group financial statements of the group that controls it in the same way as if they were those of a subsidiary. Where an entity has a quasi-subsidiary but no subsidiaries and therefore does not prepare group financial statements, it should provide in its financial statements consolidated financial statements of itself and the quasi-subsidiary, presented with equal prominence to the reporting entity's individual financial statements.* **35**

Paragraph 35 should be applied by following the requirements regarding the preparation of consolidated financial statements set out in companies legislation and in FRS 2 'Accounting for Subsidiary Undertakings'. However, quasi-subsidiaries should be excluded from consolidation only where the interest in the quasi-subsidiary is held exclusively with a view to subsequent resale† and the quasi-subsidiary has not previously been included in the reporting entity's consolidated financial statements. **36**

Where a quasi-subsidiary holds a single item or a single portfolio of similar items and the effect of the arrangement is to finance the item in such a way that the provisions of paragraphs 26 and 27 are met from the point of view of the group, the quasi-subsidiary should be included in consolidated financial statements using a linked presentation. **37**

Disclosure of quasi-subsidiaries

Where one or more quasi-subsidiaries are included in consolidated financial statements, this fact should be disclosed. A summary of the financial statements of each quasi-subsidiary should be provided in the notes to the financial statements, unless the reporting entity has more than one quasi-subsidiary of a similar nature, in which case the summary may be given on a combined basis. These summarised financial statements should show separately each main heading in the balance sheet, profit and loss account, statement of total recognised gains and losses and cash flow statement for which there is a material item, together with comparative figures. **38**

DATE FROM WHICH EFFECTIVE

Subject to paragraph 39A, the accounting practices set out in the FRS should be regarded as standard in respect of financial statements relating to accounting periods ending on or after 22 September 1994.‡ Earlier adoption is encouraged but not required. **39**

****Editor's note:*** *Since FRS 5 was issued, FRS 2 has been revised. Some investments that would previously have fallen within the definition of a quasi-subsidiary under FRS 5 may now fall within the definition of a subsidiary under FRS 2.*

†*As defined in FRS 2, paragraph 11.*

‡***Editor's note:*** *The effective date for Application Note F Private Finance Initiative and Similar Contracts is accounting periods ending on or after 10 September 1998. The effective date for Application Note G Revenue Recognition is accounting periods ending on or after 23 December 2003.*

39A (a) The requirements of paragraph 29 in so far as they relate to balances arising either from insurance broking transactions or, for insurers (including Lloyd's syndicates), from insurance transactions placed through brokers, and

(b) the accounting practices set out in the FRS, in so far as they relate to financial reinsurance accounted for by Lloyd's syndicates as at 31 December 1993,

should be regarded as standard in respect of financial statements relating to accounting periods ending on or after 22 September 1996. Where, in accordance with the previous sentence, the accounting practices set out in the FRS are not applied for accounting periods ending on or after 22 September 1994, this fact and, where available, a quantification of the effect should be disclosed.'

Explanation

SCOPE

40 The scope of the FRS, as set out in paragraph 11, extends to all kinds of transactions, subject only to the exclusions given in paragraph 12 and 13B.* Most transactions are straightforward, giving rise to a number of standard rights and obligations with the result that their substance and commercial effect are readily apparent. Applying established accounting practices will be sufficient to ensure that the substance of such transactions is properly reported in the financial statements, without the need to refer to the FRS.

41 Conversely, applying established accounting practices may not be sufficient to portray the substance of more complex transactions whose commercial effect may not be readily apparent. For such transactions it will be necessary to refer to the FRS in order to ensure that their substance is correctly identified and properly reported.

Exclusions from the FRS

42 Paragraph 12 excludes from the FRS certain contracts for future performance except where they are merely a part of a transaction (or of a group or series of transactions) that falls within the FRS.†

42A Paragraph 13B excludes from the requirements in paragraphs 14 to 31 of the FRS those transactions in financial instruments that fall within the scope of the derecognition requirements of FRS 26 (IAS 39) 'Financial Instruments: Recognition and Measurement'.‡

Other standards

43 The FRS sets out general principles relevant to reporting the substance of all transactions. Other accounting standards, the Application Notes of the FRS and companies legislation apply general principles to particular transactions or events. It follows that where a transaction falls within the scope of both the FRS and another accounting standard or statute, whichever contains the more specific provisions should be applied. Nevertheless, the specific provisions of any standard or statute

* ***Editor's note:*** *Amended by FRS 26 with effect for accounting periods beginning on or after 1 January 2007.*

† ***Editor's note:*** *Amended by FRS 26 with effect for accounting periods beginning on or after 1 January 2007.*

‡ ***Editor's note:*** *Inserted by FRS 26 with effect for accounting periods beginning on or after 1 January 2007.*

should be applied to the substance of the transaction and not merely to its legal form and, for this purpose, the general principles set out in FRS 5 will be relevant.

Pension obligations are an example of an item falling within the scope of both FRS 5 and another standard, the latter being FRS 17 'Retirement benefits'. As FRS 17 contains the more specific provisions on accounting for pension obligations and does not require consolidation of pension funds, such funds should not be consolidated as quasi-subsidiaries. FRS 5, however, contains the more specific provisions in respect of certain other transactions that may take place between an entity and its pension fund, for example a sale and repurchase agreement relating to one of the entity's properties. 44

The relationship between SSAP 21 'Accounting for lease and hire purchase contracts' and FRS 5 is particularly close. In general, SSAP 21 contains the more specific provisions governing accounting for stand-alone leases that fall wholly within its parameters, although the general principles of the FRS will also be relevant in ensuring that leases are classified as finance or operating leases in accordance with their substance. However, for some lease arrangements, and particularly for those that are merely one element of a larger arrangement, the FRS will contain the more specific provisions. An example is a sale and leaseback arrangement where there is also an option for the seller/lessee to repurchase the asset; in this case the provisions of Application Note B are more specific than those of SSAP 21. 45

THE SUBSTANCE OF TRANSACTIONS

General principles

Paragraph 14 of the FRS sets out general principles for reporting the substance of a transaction. Particularly for more complex transactions, it will not be sufficient merely to record the transaction's legal form, as to do so may not adequately express the commercial effect of the arrangements. Notwithstanding this caveat, the FRS is not intended to affect the legal characterisation of a transaction, or to change the situation at law achieved by the parties to it. 46

Features of more complex transactions

Transactions requiring particularly careful analysis will often include features such as – 47

(a) the separation of legal title to an item from rights or other access to the principal future economic benefits associated with it and exposure to the principal risks inherent in those benefits,*
(b) the linking of a transaction with others in such a way that the commercial effect can be understood only by considering the series as a whole, or
(c) the inclusion of options or conditions on terms that make it highly likely that the option will be exercised or the condition fulfilled.

(a) Separation of legal title from benefits and risks

A familiar example of the separation of legal title from benefits and risks is a finance lease. Another is goods sold under reservation of title. In both cases, the location of legal title will not normally be expected to have a commercial effect in practice. Thus the party having the benefits and risks relating to the underlying property should 48

**For ease of reading, 'rights or other access to future economic benefits' are frequently referred to hereafter as 'rights to benefits' or 'benefits', and 'exposure to the risks inherent in those benefits' is frequently referred to hereafter as 'exposure to risks' or 'risks'.*

recognise an asset in its balance sheet even though it does not have legal title. Arrangements involving the separation of legal title from benefits and risks are dealt with in detail in Application Note B.

(b) Linking of transactions

49 The linking of two or more transactions extends the possibilities for separating legal title from benefits and risks. A sale of goods linked with a commitment to repurchase may leave the original owner with the principal benefits and risks relating to the goods if the repurchase price is set at the costs, including interest, incurred by the other party in holding the goods. In such a case, application of the FRS will result in the transaction being accounted for as a financing rather than a sale, showing the asset and a corresponding liability on the balance sheet of the original owner.

(c) Inclusion of options

50 Some sale transactions are accompanied by an option, rather than a commitment, for either the original owner to repurchase or the buyer to resell. Often the commercial effect of such an arrangement is that an economic penalty (such as the forgoing of a profit) would be suffered by the party having the option if it failed to exercise it. Some transactions incorporate both a put option for the buyer and a call option for the original owner, in such a way that it will almost certainly be in the commercial interests of one of the parties to exercise its option (as for example where both options have the same exercise price and are exercisable on the same date). In such cases, there will be no genuine commercial possibility that the original owner will fail to repurchase the item and application of the FRS will again result in the transaction being accounted for as a financing rather than a sale.

Assessing commercial effect by considering the position of other parties

51 Whatever the substance of a transaction, it will normally have commercial logic for each of the parties to it. If a transaction appears to lack such logic from the point of view of one or more parties, this may indicate that not all related parts of the transaction have been identified or that the commercial effect of some element of the transaction has been incorrectly assessed.

52 It follows that in assessing the commercial effect of a transaction, it will be important to consider the position of all of the parties to it, including their apparent expectations and motives for agreeing to its various terms. In particular, where one party to the transaction receives a lender's return but no more (comprising interest on its investment perhaps together with a relatively small fee), this indicates that the substance of the transaction is that of a financing. This is because the party that receives a lender's return is not compensated for assuming any significant exposure to loss other than that associated with the creditworthiness of the other party, nor is the other party compensated for giving up any significant potential for gain.

Identifying assets and liabilities

53 In accounting terms, the substance of a transaction is portrayed through the assets and liabilities, including contingent assets and liabilities, resulting from or altered by the transaction. A key step in reporting the substance of any transaction is therefore to identify its effect on the assets and liabilities of the entity.

Assets – control of access to benefits

The definition of an asset requires that access to future economic benefits is controlled by the entity. Access to future economic benefits will normally rest on a foundation of legal rights, although legally enforceable rights are not essential to secure access. Control is the means by which the entity ensures that the benefits accrue to itself and not to others. Control can be distinguished from management (ie the ability to direct the use of an item that generates the benefits) and, although the two often go together, this need not be so. For example, the manager of a portfolio of securities does not have control of the securities, as he does not have the ability to obtain the economic benefits associated with them. Such control rests with his appointer who has delegated to the manager the right to take day-to-day decisions about the composition of the portfolio. **54**

Assets – risk

The future economic benefits inherent in an asset are never completely certain in amount; there is always the possibility that the actual benefits will be greater or less than those expected, or will arise sooner or later than expected. For instance, the value of stocks may rise or fall as market conditions change; foreign currency balances may become worth more or less because of exchange rate movements; debtors may default or be slow in paying. This uncertainty regarding the eventual benefit is referred to as 'risk', with the term encompassing both an upside element of potential for gain and a downside element of exposure to loss. **55**

The entity that has access to the benefits will usually also be the one to suffer or gain if these benefits turn out to be different from those expected. Hence, evidence of whether an entity has access to benefits (and hence has an asset) is given by whether it has the risks inherent in those benefits. **56**

Liabilities – obligations to transfer benefits

The definition of liabilities requires an obligation to transfer economic benefits. Whilst most obligations are legally enforceable, a legal obligation is not a necessary condition for a liability. An entity may be commercially obliged to adopt a certain course of action that is in its long-term best interests in the widest sense, even if no third party can legally enforce that course. As illustrated in paragraph 50 above, the prospect of a commercial or economic penalty if a certain action is not taken may negate a legal right to refrain from taking that action. **57**

The notion of obligation implies that the entity is not free to avoid an outflow of resources. Where there is some circumstance in which the entity is unable to avoid such an outflow whether for legal or commercial reasons, it will have a liability. However, in accordance with SSAP 18 'Accounting for contingencies'* if the entity's obligation is contingent on the occurrence of one or more uncertain future events (as under a stand-alone guarantee given by the entity) its liability may not be recognised.† **58**

****Editor's note:*** *SSAP 18 has been superseded by FRS 12 'Provisions, contingent liabilities and contingent assets'.*

*†**Editor's note**: The accounting treatment mentioned in respect of guarantees may no longer quite apply to an entity which complies with FRS 26. As a result of the changes to FRS 26 (in respect of financial guarantees) such companies will normally have to record financial guarantees initially at their fair value, and thereafter at the higher of the unamortised balance of the initially recorded fair value and the amount that would be recognised under FRS 12.*

Options

59 On its own, an option to acquire an item of property in the future represents a different asset from ownership of the property itself. For example, when an option to purchase shares at a future date is acquired, the only asset is the option itself; the asset 'shares' will be acquired only on exercise of the option. Similarly, an unconditional obligation is not the same as a contingent commitment to assume such an obligation at another party's option. Although both are liabilities, they are different liabilities and if recognised in the balance sheet their descriptions will be different.

60 Where an option is part of a more complex transaction, it may not necessarily represent a separate asset or liability of the type discussed in paragraph 59. For example, an option may serve, in conjunction with the other aspects of the transaction, to give one party access to the future benefits arising from an item of property without legal ownership. Alternatively the terms of an option, together with other aspects of the overall transaction, may in effect create an unconditional obligation even though the legal obligation is expressed as being conditional on the exercise of the option. Options of this kind should be accounted for by considering the substance of the transaction as a whole.

61 In determining the substance of a transaction incorporating options, in accordance with paragraph 14, greater weight must be given to those aspects and implications more likely to have a commercial effect in practice. This will involve considering the extent to which there is a genuine commercial possibility that the option will be exercised or, alternatively, that it will not be exercised. In extreme cases, there will be no genuine commercial possibility that the option will be exercised, in which case the existence of that option should be ignored; alternatively, there will be no genuine commercial possibility that an option will fail to be exercised, in which case its future exercise should be assumed. For example, a transaction may be structured in such a way that the cost of exercising an option will almost inevitably be lower (or, alternatively, higher) than the benefits obtained from its exercise. As another example, there may be a combination of put and call options such that it will almost certainly be in the commercial interests of one or other party to exercise its option. In both these cases, the substance of the overall transaction is that the parties have outright, and not optional or conditional, obligations and access to benefits. In less extreme cases, further analysis will be required. It may be necessary to consider the true commercial objectives of the parties and the commercial rationale for the inclusion of such options in the transaction. This may reveal either that the parties in substance have outright obligations and access to benefits, or, alternatively, that the parties' obligations and access to benefits are genuinely optional or conditional.

62 In assessing the commercial effect of an option, all the terms of the transaction and the circumstances of the parties that are likely to be relevant during the exercise period of the option should be taken into account. It should be assumed that each of the parties will act in accordance with its economic interests. Any actions that the parties would take only in the event of a severe deterioration in liquidity or creditworthiness should not be anticipated but should be taken into account only when such a deterioration occurs (for example, when creditworthiness has declined because of the prospect of imminent cash flow difficulties).

Guarantees and conditional provisions

63 Paragraphs 59–62 should also be applied to guarantees and other conditional provisions. The commercial effect of such provisions should in all cases be determined in the context of the overall transaction.

Recognition of assets and liabilities

Once it appears from analysis of a transaction that an asset or liability has been acquired or assumed by an entity, it is necessary to apply various recognition tests to determine whether the asset or liability should be included in the balance sheet. **64**

The general criteria set out in paragraph 20* require that an asset or liability should be recognised only where it can be measured with 'sufficient' reliability. The effect of prudence is that less reliability of measurement is acceptable when recognising items that involve decreases in equity (eg increases in liabilities) than when recognising items that do not (eg increases in assets). It follows that, particularly for liabilities, where a reasonable estimate of the amount of an item is available, the item should be recognised. **65**

Transactions in previously recognised assets

Following its recognition, an asset may be affected by a subsequent transaction and it will be necessary to consider whether, as a result of the transaction, the description or monetary amount of the asset needs to be changed. In this regard paragraphs 21–28 and 67–88 will apply. **66**

Continued recognition of an asset in its entirety

Paragraph 21 requires that where there is no significant change in the entity's rights to benefits, its previously recognised asset should continue to be recognised. In the same way, the entity will continue to have an asset where its exposure to the risks inherent in the benefits of the asset is not significantly altered. Even if the proceeds generated by the asset are directed in the first instance to another party, provided the entity gains or suffers from all significant changes in those proceeds it should be regarded as having the benefits of the asset and should continue to recognise it.† **67**

Thus, under paragraph 21, it will not be appropriate to cease to recognise any part of an asset where the transaction entered into is in substance a financing of that asset, even if the financing is without recourse. Such financing transactions leave the entity with those rights to benefits and exposures to risks (including potential for gain) that are likely to have a commercial effect in practice, as well as creating a liability to repay the finance. The only exception to this is non-recourse finance arrangements that meet the conditions for a linked presentation given in paragraphs 26–27. Although such arrangements are in substance financings, their particular features are such that a linked presentation is required to portray all the effects of the arrangement. This is explained further in paragraphs 76–80 below. **68**

Ceasing to recognise an asset in its entirety

Conversely, paragraph 22 requires that where a transaction transfers to others all significant rights to benefits and all significant exposure to risks that relate to a previously recognised asset, the entire asset should cease to be recognised.‡ **69**

These criteria are drawn from Chapter 4 of the Board's draft Statement of Principles. (Editor's note:** Similar in final Statement published December 1999 Chapter 5.)*

†***Editor's note:*** *Amended by FRS 26 with effect for accounting periods beginning on or after 1 January 2007.*

‡***Editor's note:*** *Amended by FRS 26 with effect for accounting periods beginning on or after 1 January 2007.*

Special Cases

70 Paragraphs 21 and 22 deal with the great majority of transactions affecting previously recognised assets. However, in other cases there may be a significant change in the entity's rights to benefits and exposure to risks but not a complete transfer of all significant benefits and risks. In such cases, it will be necessary to consider whether the description or monetary amount of the asset needs to be changed and also whether a liability needs to be recognised for any obligations assumed or risks retained. These special cases arise where the transaction takes one or more of the following forms:

(a) a transfer of only part of the item in question;
(b) a transfer of all of the item for only part of its life; and
(c) a transfer of all of the item for all of its life but where the entity retains some significant right to benefits or exposure to risk.

(a) Transfer of only part of an item

71 Transfer of part of an item that generates benefits may occur in one of two ways. The most straightforward is where a proportionate share of the item is transferred. A second, less straightforward way of transferring a part of an item arises where the item comprises rights to two or more separate benefit streams, each with its own risks. A part of the item will be transferred where all significant rights to one or more of those benefit streams and associated exposure to risks are transferred whilst all significant rights to the other(s) are retained. In both these cases, the entity would cease to recognise the part of the original asset that has been transferred by the transaction, but would continue to recognise the remainder. A change in the description of the asset might also be required.*

(b) Transfer of an item for only part of its life

72 Paragraph 23 also applies to a transaction that transfers all of an item that generates benefits for only part of its life. Provided that the entity's access to benefits and exposure to risks following the transaction are both significantly different from those it had before the transaction, the description or monetary amount of the asset previously recognised would need to be changed. For example, an entity may sell an item of property but agree to repurchase it in a substantially depreciated form (as for example where the item will be used for most of its life by the buyer). In this case the entity's original asset has changed from being the original item of property to a residual interest in that item and, in addition, the entity has assumed a liability of its obligation to pay the repurchase price. Sale and repurchase agreements are dealt with further in Application Note B.

(c) Transfer of an item for all of its life with some benefit or risk retained

73 Finally, paragraph 23 applies to a transaction that transfers an item that generates benefits for all of its life, but leaves the entity with significant rights to benefits or exposure to risks relating to that item. Whilst control has passed to the transferee, the retention of significant rights to benefits or exposure to risks has the result that the transaction fails to meet the conditions in paragraph 22 for ceasing to recognise an asset in its entirety. For example, an entity may sell an investment in a subsidiary with the consideration including an element of deferred performance-related consideration. Provided that significant rights to benefits and exposure to risks

Editor's note: *Amended by FRS 26 with effect for accounting periods beginning on or after 1 January 2007.*

associated with the subsidiary have passed to the buyer (as will be the case where the deferred consideration is only a portion of the subsidiary's profits arising in only a limited period), both the description and the monetary amount of the asset will need to be changed. This reflects the fact that the asset is no longer an investment in a subsidiary but rather is a debtor for the performance-related consideration (although, under the provisions of SSAP 18*, the debtor may be measured at nil and therefore not recognised but merely disclosed). As another example, an entity may sell equipment subject to a warranty in respect of the condition of the equipment at the time of sale, or subject to a guarantee of its residual value. This would normally transfer all significant rights to benefits and some significant exposure to risks to the buyer (these being those arising from the equipment's future use and resale), but leave the seller with some significant risk in the form of obligations relating to the equipment's future performance or residual value. The seller would therefore cease to recognise the equipment as an asset, but would recognise a liability for its warranty obligation or guarantee (with the liability being accounted for in accordance with the provisions of SSAP 18†).

Measurement and profit recognition

In any of the above three classes of transaction, there arises the issue of how to measure the change in the entity's assets or liabilities and any resulting profit or loss. This measurement process requires that the previous carrying value of the asset is apportioned into an amount relating to those benefits and risks disposed of and an amount relating to those retained. In some cases, measurement will be relatively easy; for instance this might be the case where a proportionate share of the original asset is retained as described in paragraph 71 above or where there are similar and frequent transactions in liquid and freely accessible markets. In other cases, measurement may be more difficult with the result that the amount of any gain or loss is uncertain. In such cases, in accordance with the provisions of SSAP 18*, paragraph 24 requires a prudent approach to be adopted, with full provision being made for any probable loss but recognition of any gain, to the extent it is in doubt, being deferred. **74**

The meaning of 'significant'

In applying paragraphs 21–23 and 26 it may be necessary to determine whether certain rights to benefits or exposure to risks are 'significant'. When this is done, greater weight should be given to what is likely to have a commercial effect in practice. In particular, whether any retained risk is 'significant' should be judged not against the total possible variation in benefits, but against that variation which is likely to occur in practice.‡ **75**

Linked presentation for certain non-recourse finance arrangements

General principles

Sometimes an entity finances an item on terms that the provider of the finance has recourse to only the item it has financed and not to the entity's other assets. It is sometimes argued that the effect of such arrangements is that the entity no longer has **76**

***Editor's note:** *SSAP 18 has been superseded by FRS 12 'Provisions, contingent liabilities and contingent assets'.*

†**Editor's note:** *SSAP 18 was superseded by FRS 12 'Provisions, contingent liabilities and contingent assets'.*

‡**Editor's note:** *Amended by FRS 26 with effect for accounting periods beginning on or after 1 January 2007.*

an asset in respect of the item, nor does it have a liability for the finance. For the purpose of determining the appropriate accounting treatment, non-recourse finance arrangements can be classified into two types.

Separate presentation of an asset and liability

77 The first type of arrangement is where, although in the event of default the provider of the finance can obtain repayment only by enforcing its rights against the specified item, the entity retains rights to all the benefits generated by the item and can repay the finance from its general resources in order to preserve those rights. In such a case the entity has both an asset (its access to all the benefits generated by the item) and a liability (its obligation to repay the finance) and they should be included in the balance sheet in the normal way.

Linked presentation

78 The second type of non-recourse finance arrangement is where the finance will be repaid only from benefits generated by the specified item. Although the entity has rights to any surplus benefits remaining after repayment of the finance, it has no right or obligation to keep the item or to repay the finance from its general resources. In these cases the entity does not have an asset equal to the gross amount of the item (as it does not have access to all the future benefits generated by it), nor a liability for the full amount of the finance (as the financier will be repaid only from benefits generated by the specific item and not from benefits generated by any other assets of the entity). However, the entity does retain rights to those benefits and exposure to those risks that are likely to have a commercial effect in practice – ie the significant benefits and risks. It is retention of the significant benefits and risks that distinguishes this type of non-recourse financing from the transactions described in paragraph 23 that transfer a part of an asset. Where there is no transfer of significant benefits and risks the transaction is in substance a financing arrangement and the other party would usually receive a lender's return and no more. Conversely, the transactions described in paragraph 23 involve a transfer of significant benefits and risks. Indications of such transactions are where the other party has rights to benefits greater than those associated with a lender's return and has corresponding exposure to some significant risk.

79-80 [Withdrawn]*

Detailed conditions for use of a linked presentation

81 A linked presentation is appropriate only where the commercial effect for the entity is that the item is being sold but the sale process is not yet complete. Thus there must be no doubt whatsoever that the claim of the provider of the finance is limited strictly to funds generated by the specific item it finances. It must be clear that there is no legal, commercial or other obligation under which the entity may fund any losses (from whatever cause) on the items being financed or transfer any economic benefits (apart from those generated by the item). In addition, the entity must have no right or obligation to repay the finance from its general resources, to keep the item on repayment of the finance or to re-acquire it in the future. These principles are reflected in the detailed conditions for use of a linked presentation set out in paragraph 27.

Editor's note: *Paragraphs 79 and 80 deleted by amendments to FRS 26 with effect for accounting periods beginning on or after 1 January 2007.*

Condition 27(a) requires that the finance relates to a specific item or group of similar items. A linked presentation should not be used where the finance relates to two or more items that are not part of a portfolio, or to a portfolio containing items that would otherwise be shown under different balance sheet captions. Similarly, a linked presentation should not be used where the finance relates to any kind of business unit, or for items that generate the funds required to repay the finance only by being used in conjunction with other assets of the entity. The item must generate the funds required to repay the finance either by unwinding directly into cash or by its sale to a third party.* **82**

Conditions 27(b)–(e) require that there is no recourse and no other condition (legal, commercial or other) that could result in the entity supporting losses, from whatever cause, on the items being financed (or, as discussed in the next paragraph, supporting such losses beyond a fixed monetary ceiling). Recourse could take a number of forms, for instance: an agreement to repurchase non-performing items or to substitute good items for bad ones; a guarantee given to the provider of the finance or any other party (of performance, proceeds or other support); a put option under which items can be transferred back to the entity; a swap of some or all of the amounts generated by the item for a separately determined payment; or a penalty on cancelling an ongoing arrangement such that the entity bears the cost of any items that turn out to be bad. Normal warranties given in respect of the condition of the item at the time the non-recourse finance arrangement is entered into would not breach this condition; however, warranties relating to the condition of the item in the future or to its future performance would do so. **83**

If there is partial recourse for losses up to a fixed monetary ceiling, a linked presentation may still be appropriate in respect of that part of the finance for which there is no recourse. However, where the entity provides any kind of open-ended guarantee (ie one that does not have a fixed monetary ceiling) a linked presentation should not be used. An example of such an open-ended guarantee would be a guarantee of completion provided by a property developer. **84**

[Withdrawn]† **85**

Condition 27(f) requires there to be no provision for the entity to repurchase the item being financed. For instance, where legal title to the item has been transferred, a linked presentation should not be used to the extent that one party has a put or a call option to effect repurchase, or where there is an understanding between the parties that the item will be re-acquired in the future. **86**

Profit or loss recognition and presentation

Where a linked presentation is used, profits or losses should be recognised in the period in which they arise so as to reflect the fact that the entity continues to gain or suffer from the performance of the underlying gross item. For example, on entering into the arrangement, a gain will arise only to the extent that the non-returnable proceeds received exceed the previous carrying value of the item. In subsequent periods, a gain (or loss) will arise to the extent that the income from the item exceeds (or falls short of) the amounts due to the provider of finance in respect of that period. **87**

****Editor's note:** Amended by FRS 26 with effect for accounting periods beginning on or after 1 January 2007.*

*†**Editor's note:** Paragraph deleted by amendments to FRS 26 with effect for accounting periods beginning on or after 1 January 2007.*

Finally, any gain resulting from an onward sale of the item to a third party will arise only in the period in which the onward sale occurs.

88 Where a linked presentation is adopted in the balance sheet, normally it will be sufficient for only the net amount of any income or expense recognised in each period to be included in the profit and loss account, with the gross components being disclosed by way of note. However, the gross components should be shown on the face of the profit and loss account by using a linked presentation where the effect of the arrangement on the performance of the entity is so significant that to include merely the net amount of income or expense within the captions shown on the face of the profit and loss account would not be sufficient to give a true and fair view.

Offset

89-91 [Withdrawn]*

Disclosure of the substance of transactions

92 Paragraph 30 requires that disclosure of a transaction should be sufficient to enable the user of the financial statements to understand its commercial effect. For the vast majority of transactions this involves no more than those disclosures currently required. However, this may not be sufficient to portray fully the commercial effect of more complex transactions, in which case further information will need to be disclosed.

93 Assets and liabilities resulting from more complex transactions will not necessarily be exactly the same as those resulting from more straightforward transactions. The greater the differences the greater the need for disclosure. For example, certain assets may not be available for use as security for liabilities of the entity; or certain liabilities, whilst not qualifying for the linked presentation set out in paragraphs 26–27 may, in the event of default, be repayable only to the extent that the assets on which they are secured yield sufficient benefits.

94 Even where a transaction does not result in any items being recognised in the balance sheet, the need for disclosure should still be considered. The transaction may give rise to guarantees, commitments or other rights and obligations which, although not sufficient to require recognition of an asset or liability, require disclosure in order that the financial statements give a true and fair view.

QUASI-SUBSIDIARIES

Identification of quasi-subsidiaries

95 An entity may directly control access to future economic benefits or may control such access through the medium of another entity, normally a subsidiary. Control through the medium of another entity is of such widespread significance that it underlies the statutory definition of a subsidiary undertaking and is reflected in the requirement for the preparation of consolidated accounts. However, such control is not confined to cases where another entity is a subsidiary as defined in statute. 'Quasi-subsidiaries' are sometimes established by arrangements that give as much effective control over another entity as if that entity were a subsidiary.

****Editor's note:*** *Deleted by FRS 25.*

Benefits

In deciding whether or not an entity is a quasi-subsidiary, access to the whole of the benefit inflows arising from its gross assets and responsibility for the whole of the benefit outflows associated with its liabilities are not the key considerations. In practice, many subsidiaries do not give rise to a possible benefit outflow for their parent of an amount equal to their gross liabilities – indeed, the limiting of benefit outflows in the event of losses occurring may have been a factor for the parent in establishing a subsidiary. In addition, as the liabilities of a subsidiary have a prior claim on its assets, the parent will not have access to benefit inflows of an amount equal to those gross assets. For this reason, it is necessary to focus on the benefit flows associated with the net assets of the entity. Often evidence of where these benefits lie is given by which party stands to suffer or gain from the financial performance of the entity – ie which party has the risks inherent in the benefits. **96**

Control

Control is the means by which one entity determines how the assets of another entity are employed and by which the controlling entity ensures that the resulting benefits accrue to itself and not to others. Control may be evidenced in a variety of ways depending on its basis (eg ownership or other rights) and the way in which it is exercised (interventionist or not). Control includes the ability to restrict others from directing major policies, but a power of veto will not of itself constitute control unless its effect is that major policy decisions are taken in accordance with the wishes of the party holding that power. One entity will not control another where there is a third party that has the ability to determine all major issues of policy. **97**

In some cases, arrangements are made for allocating the benefits arising from the activities of an entity such that active exercise of control is not necessary. The party or parties who will gain the benefits (and bear their inherent risks) are irreversibly specified in advance. No party has direct control in the sense of day-to-day direction of the entity's financial and operating policies, since all such matters are predetermined. In such cases, control will be exercised indirectly via the arrangements for allocating the benefits and it will be necessary to look at the effects of those arrangements to establish which party has control. It follows that, for the reasons set out in paragraph 96 above, the party possessing control will be the one that gains the benefits arising from the net assets of the entity. **98**

Accounting for quasi-subsidiaries

In essence, consolidation is founded on the principle that all the entities under the control of the reporting entity should be incorporated into a single set of financial statements. Applying this principle has the result that the assets, liabilities, profits, losses and cash flows of any entity that is a quasi-subsidiary should be included in group financial statements in the same way as if they were those of a member of the statutory group (this is referred to below as 'inclusion of a quasi-subsidiary in group financial statements'). **99**

The entities that constitute a group are determined by companies legislation. Companies legislation also requires that where compliance with its provisions would not be sufficient to give a true and fair view, the necessary additional information shall be given in the accounts or in a note to them*. Inclusion of a quasi-subsidiary in group **100**

**In Great Britain section 227(5) of the Companies Act 1985. Equivalent references for Northern Ireland and the Republic of Ireland are given in paragraphs 5 and 6 respectively of Appendix I 'Note on legal requirements'.*
Editor's note: *The reference to section 227 changes to section 404 of the Companies Act 2006.*

financial statements is necessary in order to give a true and fair view of the group as legally defined and thus constitutes provision of such additional information.

101 Companies legislation and FRS 2 'Accounting for Subsidiary Undertakings' permit or require subsidiaries to be excluded from consolidation in certain circumstances. However, as inclusion of a quasi-subsidiary in group financial statements is required in order that those financial statements give a true and fair view of the group, these exclusions are generally not appropriate for a quasi-subsidiary. The following considerations are relevant.

(a) An immaterial quasi-subsidiary is outside the scope of this FRS, which need not be applied to immaterial items.

(b) Where severe long-term restrictions substantially hinder the exercise of the rights of the reporting entity over the assets or management of another entity, the reporting entity will not have the control necessary for the definition of a quasi-subsidiary to be met. Where the financial and operating policies of another entity are predetermined, this affects the manner in which control of that entity is exercised, but does not preclude the entity from being a quasi-subsidiary.

(c) Disproportionate expense or undue delay in obtaining information justifies excluding a quasi-subsidiary only if it is immaterial.

(d) Where there are significant differences between the activities of a quasi-subsidiary and those of the group that controls it, these should be disclosed. However, the quasi-subsidiary should nevertheless be included in the consolidation in order that the group financial statements present a true picture of the extent of the group's activities.

It is appropriate to exclude a quasi-subsidiary from consolidation only where the interest in the quasi-subsidiary is held exclusively with a view to subsequent resale and the quasi-subsidiary has not previously been included in the reporting entity's consolidated financial statements. In determining if this exclusion is appropriate in a particular instance, reference should be made to FRS 2.

102 Some arrangements for financing an item on a non-recourse basis involve placing the item and its finance in a quasi-subsidiary as a means of 'ring-fencing' them. Where, as a result, the conditions of paragraphs 26 and 27 are met from the point of view of the group as legally defined, the item and its finance should be included in the group financial statements by using a linked presentation. As noted above, the inclusion of a quasi-subsidiary in group financial statements forms additional information, necessary in order to give a true and fair view of the group as legally defined – the quasi-subsidiary is not part of that group. Where an item and its finance are effectively ring-fenced in a quasi-subsidiary, a true and fair view of the position of the group is given by presenting them under a linked presentation. In this situation, the group does not have an asset equal to the gross amount of the item, nor a liability for the full amount of the finance. However, where the item and its finance are similarly ring-fenced in a subsidiary, a linked presentation may not be used. This is because the subsidiary is part of the group as legally defined – hence the item and its finance, being an asset and a liability of the subsidiary, are respectively an asset and liability of the group. The subsidiary would be consolidated in the normal way in accordance with companies legislation and a linked presentation would not be used (unless a linked presentation were appropriate in the subsidiary's individual financial statements).

Disclosure of quasi-subsidiaries

When one or more quasi-subsidiaries are included in the consolidated financial statements of a statutory group, companies legislation requires the fact that such additional information has been included, and the effect of its inclusion, to be clearly disclosed.* **103**

**In Great Britain section 227 of the Companies Act 1985. Equivalent references for Northern Ireland and the Republic of Ireland are given in paragraphs 5 and 6 respectively of Appendix I 'Note on legal requirements'.*

Application notes

These Application Notes specify how the requirements of FRS 5 are to be applied to transactions that have certain features. For such transactions, observance of the Notes will normally be sufficient to ensure compliance with the requirements of FRS 5.

The tables, flow chart and illustrations shown in the shaded areas are provided as an aid to understanding and shall not be regarded as part of the Statement of Standard Accounting Practice.

It is not intended that the accounting treatment determined by FRS 5 or the terminology used in the Application Notes should change the situation at law achieved by the parties. Accordingly, it is not intended that the legal effectiveness of any transfer should be affected.

Contents

A CONSIGNMENT STOCK
B SALE AND REPURCHASE AGREEMENTS
C FACTORING OF DEBTS
D SECURITISED ASSETS
E LOAN TRANSFERS
F PRIVATE FINANCE INITIATIVE AND SIMILAR CONTRACTS
G REVENUE RECOGNITION

APPLICATION NOTE A – CONSIGNMENT STOCK

NB: Although this Application Note is drafted in terms of the motor trade it applies equally to similar arrangements in other industries.

Features

A1 Consignment stock is stock held by one party (the 'dealer') but legally owned by another (the 'manufacturer'), on terms that give the dealer the right to sell the stock in the normal course of its business or, at its option, to return it unsold to the legal owner. The stock may be physically located on the premises of the dealer, or held at a car compound or other site nearby. The arrangement has a number of commercial advantages for both parties: the dealer is able to hold or have faster access to a wider range of stock than might otherwise be practicable; the manufacturer can avoid a build-up of stock on its premises by moving it closer to the point of sale; and both benefit from the greater sales potential of the arrangement.

A2 The main features of a consignment stock arrangement are as follows:

(a) The manufacturer delivers goods to the dealer, but legal title does not pass until one of a number of events takes place, eg the dealer has held the goods for a specified period, adopts them by using them as demonstration models, or sells them to a third party. Until such a crystallising event, the dealer is entitled to return the goods to the manufacturer or the manufacturer is able to require their return or insist that they are passed to another dealer.

(b) Once legal title passes, the transfer price becomes payable by the dealer. This price may be fixed at the date goods are delivered to the dealer, it may vary with the period between delivery and transfer of title, or it may be the manufacturer's list price at the date of transfer of title.

FRS 5 APPLICATION NOTES

(c) The dealer may also be required to pay a deposit to the manufacturer, or to pay the latter a display or financing charge. This deposit or charge may be fixed for a period (eg one year) or may fluctuate. Its amount is usually set with reference to the dealer's past sales of the manufacturer's goods or to average or actual holdings of consignment stock. It may (or may not) bear interest. In some cases, a finance company will pay the deposit or charge to the manufacturer and will charge interest thereon to the dealer.

(d) Other terms of the arrangement will usually cover items such as inspection and access rights of the manufacturer, and responsibility for damage, loss or theft and related insurance. These are usually of minor importance in determining the accounting treatment.

Analysis

The purpose of the analysis below is to determine whether, at any particular time, the dealer has an asset in the stock and a corresponding liability to pay the manufacturer for it. To this end, it is necessary to identify whether the dealer has access to the benefits of the stock and exposure to the risks inherent in those benefits. From the dealer's perspective, the principal benefits and risks of consignment stock are as follows: A3

Benefits:

(i) the future cash flows from sale to a third party and the right to retain items of stock in order to achieve such a sale;

(ii) insulation from changes to the transfer price charged by the manufacturer for its stock (eg because the manufacturer has increased its list price); and

(iii) the right to use the stock (eg as a demonstration model) by adopting it.

Risks:

(i) the risk of being compelled to retain stock that is not readily saleable or is obsolete, resulting in no sale or a sale at a reduced price; and

(ii) the risk of slow movement, resulting in increased costs of financing and holding the stock and an increased risk of obsolescence.

Paragraphs A5–A10 show how the various features of a consignment stock agreement will determine where the above benefits and risks lie. The stock should be included on the dealer's balance sheet where the dealer has access to its principal benefits and bears the principal risks inherent in those benefits.

In determining the substance of an agreement, it will be necessary to look at all its features and give greater weight to those that are more likely to have a commercial effect in practice. In addition, it will be necessary to consider the interaction between the features and to evaluate the arrangement as a whole. A4

Manufacturer's right of return (benefit (i))

The dealer's access to the benefits of the stock will be constrained by any right of the manufacturer to require goods to be returned or transferred to another dealer. The likely commercial effect of this constraint should be assessed. For instance, if a high proportion of the consignment stock is returned or transferred without compensation, this indicates that the stock is not an asset of the dealer. Conversely, if the dealer is able to resist requests made by the manufacturer for transfers and in practice actually does so, or in practice the manufacturer compensates the dealer for agreeing to transfer stock in accordance with the manufacturer's wishes, this indicates that the stock is an asset of the dealer. A5

Dealer's right of return (risk (i))

A6 If the dealer has a right to return stock without payment of a penalty, it will not bear obsolescence risk. This indicates that the dealer has neither the asset 'stock', nor a liability to pay the manufacturer for it. Again, the likely commercial effect of any such right of return and the significance of obsolescence risk should be considered. If the right of return is exercised frequently or the manufacturer regularly provides a significant incentive (such as a price discount or a free extension to the consignment period) to persuade the dealer not to return stock where it would otherwise do so, this indicates that the stock is not an asset of the dealer. Conversely, if the dealer either has no right to return stock, or in practice does not exercise its right or is charged a significant penalty for doing so, this indicates that the dealer bears the principal risks relating to the stock and the stock is an asset for it. In such cases the dealer will also have a corresponding liability (legal or commercial) to pay for the stock.

Stock transfer price and deposits (benefit (ii), risk (ii))

A7 Whether the dealer is insulated from changes in the prices charged by the manufacturer for its stock depends on how the stock transfer price is determined. Where the price is based on the manufacturer's list price at delivery, then the manufacturer is unable to pass on any subsequent price changes, which indicates that the stock became an asset of the dealer at the date of delivery. Conversely, if the price charged to the dealer is the manufacturer's list price at the date of the transfer of legal title, this indicates that the stock remains an asset of the manufacturer until legal title is transferred.

A8 The stock transfer price will also affect the incidence of slow movement risk and who bears the variable cost of financing the stock until sold. In a simple arrangement where there is no deposit and stock is supplied for a fixed price that is payable by the dealer only when legal title is transferred it will be clear that the manufacturer bears the slow movement risk. The manufacturer will bear the slow movement risk wherever the transfer price is not determined by reference to the length of time for which stock is held (such as where the transfer price is the manufacturer's list price at either delivery or transfer of legal title). Conversely, if in the same basic arrangement, the price to be paid by the dealer increases by a factor that varies with the time the stock is held and approximates to commercial interest rates, then it will be equally clear that the dealer bears the slow movement risk. This may be so even where the financing element of the price charged to the dealer is based on average past movements of stocks held by that dealer (eg for administrative convenience), or is levied in another form (eg a display charge).

A9 The existence of a deposit complicates the analysis. The main question to be answered is whether the effect of the deposit is that the dealer, rather than the manufacturer, bears variations in the stock financing costs that are due to slow movement. For example, this could be achieved by a substantial, interest-free deposit whose amount is related to levels of stock held by the dealer. Alternatively, a finance company might advance the deposit to the manufacturer and charge interest thereon (in whatever form) to the dealer.

Dealer's right to use the stock (benefit (iii))

A10 Whilst a right for the dealer to use the stock in its business will not, of itself, be sufficient to make the stock an asset of the dealer, the exercise of the right will usually have this effect. Such exercise will usually cause the transfer of legal title to the dealer and give rise to an unconditional obligation for it to pay the manufacturer.

Required accounting

Substance of the transaction is that the stock is an asset of the dealer

Where it is concluded that the stock is in substance an asset of the dealer, the stock should be recognised as such on the dealer's balance sheet, together with a corresponding liability to the manufacturer. Any deposit should be deducted from the liability and the excess classified as a trade creditor. The notes to the financial statements should explain the nature of the arrangement, the amount of consignment stock included in the balance sheet and the main terms under which it is held, including the terms of any deposit. **A11**

Substance of the transaction is that the stock is not an asset of the dealer

Where it is concluded that the stock is not in substance an asset of the dealer, the stock should not be included on the dealer's balance sheet until the transfer of title has crystallised. Any deposit should be included under 'other debtors'. The notes to the financial statements should explain the nature of the arrangement, the amount of consignment stock held at the year-end, and the main terms under which it is held, including the terms of any deposit. **A12**

Table

Indications that the stock is not an asset of the dealer at delivery	Indications that the stock is an asset of the dealer at delivery
Manufacturer can require the dealer to return stock (or transfer stock to another dealer) without compensation, or Penalty paid by the dealer to prevent returns/transfers of stock at the manufacturers request.	Manufacturer cannot require dealer to return or transfer stock, or Financial incentives given to persuade dealer to transfer stock at manufacturer's request.
Dealer has unfettered right to return stock to the manufacturer without penalty and actually exercises the right in practice.	Dealer has no right to return stock or is commercially compelled not to exercise its right of return.
Manufacturer bears obsolescence risk, eg: - obsolete stock is returned to the manufacturer without penalty; or - financial incentives given by manufacturers to prevent stock being returned to it (eg on a model change or if it become obsolete).	Dealer bears obsolescence risk, eg: - penalty charged if dealer returns stock to manufacturer; or - obsolete stock cannot be returned to the manufacturer and no compensation is paid by manufacturer for losses due to obsolescence.
Stock transfer price charged by manufacturer is based on manufacturer's list price at date of transfer of legal title.	Stock transfer price charged by manufacturer is based on manufacturer's list price at date of delivery.

Manufacturer bears slow movement risk, eg; - transfer price set independently of time for which dealer holds stock, and there is no deposit.	Dealer bears slow movement risk, eg: - dealer is effectively charged interest as transfer price or other payments to manufacturer vary with time for which dealer holds stock; or - dealer makes substantial interest-free deposit that varies with the levels of stock held.

APPLICATION NOTE B – SALE AND REPURCHASE AGREEMENTS

The principles in this Application Note apply only to those transactions falling within the scope of paragraphs 14 to 31 of FRS 5, and not to those falling within the scope of paragraphs 14 to 42 of FRS 26 'Financial Instruments: Recognition and Measurement'.*

NB: For ease of reading the parties to a sale and repurchase agreement are referred to below as 'seller' and 'buyer', notwithstanding that analysis of the transaction in accordance with this Application Note may result in the seller continuing to show an asset on its balance sheet.

Features

B1 Sale and repurchase agreements are arrangements under which assets are sold by one party to another on terms that provide for the seller to repurchase the asset in certain circumstances. A similar commercial effect may be achieved by arrangements under which one party holds an asset on behalf of another: although such arrangements are not sale and repurchase agreements, a similar analysis is appropriate and these are therefore covered by this Application Note.

B2 The main features of a sale and repurchase agreement will usually be:

(a) the sale price – this may be market value or another agreed price (analysed in paragraph B9);

(b) the nature of the repurchase provision – this may be: an unconditional commitment for both parties; an option for the seller to repurchase (a call option); an option for the buyer to resell to the seller (a put option); or a combination of put and call options; (analysed in paragraphs B10–B12);

(c) the repurchase price – this may: be fixed at the outset; vary with the period for which the asset is held by the buyer; or be the market price at the time of repurchase. It may also be designed to permit the buyer to recover incidental holding costs (eg insurance) if these do not in fact continue to be met by the seller; (analysed in paragraphs B13–B14); and

(d) other provisions, including where appropriate: for the seller to use the asset whilst it is owned by the buyer; for determining the time of repurchase; or for remarketing the asset if it is to be sold to a third party; (analysed in paragraphs B15–B18).

***Editor's Note:** *Paragraph added by amendments to FRS 26 with effect for accounting periods beginning on or after 1 January 2007.*

Analysis

Overview of basic principles

The purpose of the analysis is to determine both whether the seller has an asset (and what is the nature of that asset), and whether the seller has a liability to repay the buyer some or all of the amounts received from the latter. **B3**

In a straightforward case, the substance of a sale and repurchase agreement will be that of a secured loan – ie the seller will retain all significant rights to benefits relating to the original asset and all significant exposure to the risks inherent in those benefits and will have a liability to the buyer for the whole of the proceeds received. For example, this would be the case where the seller has in effect an unconditional commitment to repurchase the original asset from the buyer at the sale price plus interest. The seller should account for this type of arrangement by showing the original asset on its balance sheet together with a liability for the amounts received from the buyer. **B4**

In certain more complex cases, it may be determined that a sale and repurchase agreement is not in substance a financing transaction and that the seller retains access to only some of the benefits of the original asset and retains only some of their inherent risks. Where this is so, in accordance with paragraph 23, the description or monetary amount of the original asset should be changed and a liability recognised for any obligation to transfer benefits that is assumed. It will also be necessary to give full disclosure of these more complex arrangements in the notes to the financial statements. **B5**

The substance of the arrangement may be more readily apparent if the position of both buyer and seller are considered, together with their apparent expectations and motives for agreeing to its various terms. In particular, where the substance is that of a secured loan, the buyer will require that it is assured of a lender's return on its investment and the seller will require that the buyer earns no more than this return. Thus whether or not the buyer earns such a return is an important indicator of the substance of the transaction. **B6**

Benefits and risks

The analysis that follows shows how the features set out in paragraph B2 may result in the seller having a liability to the buyer or in the seller retaining rights to some or all of the benefits of the original asset and exposure to some or all of the risks inherent in those benefits. These benefits and risks will usually include some or all of the following: **B7**

Benefits:

(i) the benefit of any expected increase in the value of the asset; and

(ii) benefits arising from use or development of the asset.

Risks:

(i) the risk of an unexpected variation (adverse or favourable) in the value of the asset;

(ii) the risk of obsolescence; and

(iii) where repurchase is not at a set date, the risk of a variation in the cost of financing the asset because of the variable period between sale and repurchase.

In analysing any specific agreement in practice, it will be necessary to look at all the features of the agreement and give greater weight to those that are more likely to have a commercial effect in practice. In addition, it will be necessary to consider the **B8** interaction between the features in order to determine the substance of the arrangement as a whole.

Feature (a) – Sale price

B9 A sale price of other than the market value of the asset at the time of sale indicates that some benefit and risk have been retained by the seller, such that the seller has an asset (either the original asset or a new one) or a liability to the buyer. Even where the sale price is the asset's market value, the seller may nevertheless have an asset or a liability since the other terms of the arrangement may result in the seller retaining significant benefits and risks.

Feature (b) – Nature of repurchase provision

1. Commitment

B10 Any type of unconditional commitment for the seller to repurchase will give rise to both a liability and an asset for the seller: the liability being the seller's commitment to pay the repurchase price; and the asset being continued access to some or all of the benefits of the original asset that forms the subject of the sale and repurchase agreement. The price at which repurchase will occur and the other provisions of the arrangement will determine the exact nature of the seller's asset; these are dealt with in paragraphs B13–B18 below.

B11 There may in effect be a commitment to repurchase even without a strict legal obligation. In particular, this will be the case where there is an option (or a combination of options) on terms that leave no genuine commercial possibility that the option will fail to be exercised. For example, the exercise price of a call option may be set at a significant discount to expected market value, the seller may need the asset to use on an ongoing basis in its business, or the asset may provide in effect the only source of the seller's future sales. Unwritten understandings between the parties may also result in a commercial commitment for the seller to repurchase even in the absence of a strict legal obligation. Such a commitment is more likely to exist where the buyer's business does not usually involve it in taking on risks of a kind associated with the asset.

2. Put and call options

B12 In some cases the seller may have a call option to repurchase the asset but have no commitment to do so, or the buyer may have a put option to transfer the asset back to the seller without the seller having an equivalent right to insist on repurchase. It will be important to determine why the parties have agreed to such a one-sided option and to assess the commercial effect of the option with regard to all aspects of the arrangement, including whether the seller has a commercial need to repurchase the asset. This analysis may reveal that, in substance, there is a commitment to repurchase as discussed above. Conversely, such an analysis may reveal that the buyer assumes significant benefits and risks relating to the original asset, indicating that the seller has neither the original asset, nor a liability for the option's exercise price. In such a case, where the seller holds a call option it will have a new asset in the form of the option itself; where the buyer has a put option, the seller will have a contingent liability to the buyer for the exercise price of the option (contingent on the buyer exercising its option). In both cases, the seller's new asset or liability should be recognised or disclosed, on a prudent basis, following the principles set out in SSAP 18 'Accounting for contingencies'.*

****Editor's note:** *SSAP 18 has been superseded by FRS 12 'Provisions, contingent liabilities and contingent assets'.*

Feature (c) – Repurchase price and provision for a lender's return

In the most straightforward case, the repurchase price will be the sum of the original sale price, plus any major costs incurred by the buyer and a lender's return (comprising interest on the sale price and costs incurred by the buyer, perhaps with a relatively small fee), but no more. In this case, even if the repurchase provision takes the form of an option, the repurchase price indicates that the substance of the transaction is that of a secured loan, with the benefits and risks of the asset remaining with the seller. This is because the buyer is not compensated for assuming any significant exposure to loss, nor is the seller compensated for giving up any significant potential for gain, thus indicating that the transaction is, in substance, a financing. It will be necessary to look at the arrangement as a whole to establish whether the buyer receives a lender's return since the means of providing it will vary. For example, it may be achieved by lease or other regular payments, licence fees, adjustment to the original sales price or the calculation of the repurchase price. **B13**

Conversely, if the buyer is not assured of a lender's return, this indicates that some benefit and risk have been passed to the buyer such that the seller has not retained the original asset. The seller may, nevertheless, have a different asset (and a corresponding liability). For example, if a manufacturer sells equipment but agrees to repurchase it in a substantially different form towards the end of its economic life, the manufacturer has both a liability (to pay the repurchase price) and an asset (the equipment as at the repurchase date). **B14**

Feature (d) – Other provisions

1. Ability to use the asset

Whilst the ability of the seller to determine the use of the original asset does not, of itself, result in the substance of the transaction being that of a secured loan, it will usually indicate this is so. Continued use of the asset by the seller may indicate that it has a commercial obligation to repurchase even if it has no legal obligation to do so, for instance if there is a commercial need for the seller to repurchase or an expectation that it will do so. **B15**

Where the seller continues to use the asset in its business by entering into a sale and leaseback transaction, the provisions of both SSAP 21 'Accounting for leases and hire purchase contracts' and this Application Note will be relevant. Where, in the terms of this Application Note, the substance of the transaction is that of a secured loan, it will be structured so that no significant benefits or risks are passed to the buyer, with the rentals and other lease payments providing the buyer with a lender's return. Thus, in the terms of SSAP 21, 'substantially all the risks and rewards of ownership' of the asset will remain with the seller, the leaseback will be classified as a finance lease, and the transaction will be accounted for as the raising of finance secured on the asset. If, on the other hand, the leaseback is in substance an operating lease, the transaction will be accounted for as a sale of the original asset. **B16**

2. Profits or losses on a sale of the asset to a third party

In some cases, the seller may retain access to any increase in the value of the asset via provisions that pass to it substantially all of any profit arising on a sale by the first buyer to a third party (subject to the buyer receiving a lender's return). In addition the buyer may be protected from risk of loss, for instance by the seller being obliged to reimburse the whole or part of any loss on a sale to a third party, or the original sale price being such that losses are unlikely to occur in practice. The substance of such an arrangement is that of a secured loan. **B17**

3. Use of special entities ('vehicles')

B18 Some cases may involve a sale to a special entity (a 'vehicle') that is partly or wholly financed by a party other than the seller (eg a financial institution). In such a case, the seller will usually retain access to any increase in the value of the asset and, where relevant, the benefits from its use, via a right either to repurchase the asset or, in the event that the seller does not repurchase, to receive the majority of any profits from a future sale to a third party. In addition, the seller may provide protection against loss to the other investors in the vehicle, eg by providing a subordinated loan to the vehicle that acts as a cushion to absorb any losses or by guaranteeing the value of the asset in the event that it is sold on to a third party. Such provisions are clear indications that the substance of the transaction is that of a secured loan. Where the terms of the arrangement taken as a whole mean that the investors in the vehicle are reasonably assured of recovering their original investment and earning a lender's return (but no more) thereon, the substance of the transaction will be that of a secured loan.

Required accounting

Substance of the transaction is that of a secured loan

B19 Where the substance of the transaction is that of a secured loan, the seller should continue to recognise the original asset and record the proceeds received from the buyer as a liability. Interest – however designated – should be accrued. The carrying amount of the asset should be reviewed and provided against if necessary. The notes to the financial statements should describe the principal features of the arrangement, including the status of the asset and the relationship between the asset and liability.

B20 Where the transaction is a sale and leaseback, no profit should be recognised on entering into the arrangement and no adjustment made to the carrying value of the asset. As stated in the guidance notes to SSAP 21, this represents the substance of the transaction, "namely the raising of finance secured on an asset that continues to be held and that is not disposed of".

Substance of the transaction is that the seller has a different asset

B21 Where the seller has a new asset or liability (for example, merely a call option to repurchase the original asset), it should recognise or disclose that new asset or liability on a prudent basis in accordance with the provisions of SSAP 18.* In particular, the seller should recognise (and not merely disclose) a liability for any kind of unconditional obligation it has entered into. Where doubts exist regarding the amount of any gain or loss arising, full provision should be made for any expected loss but recognition of any gain, to the extent that it is in doubt, should be deferred until it is realised. The notes to the financial statements should describe the main features of the arrangement, including: the status of the asset; the relationship between the asset and the liability; and the terms of any provision for repurchase (including any options) and of any guarantees.

***Editor's note:** *SSAP 18 has been superseded by FRS 12 'Provisions, contingent liabilities and contingent assets'.*

Table

Indications of sale of original asset to buyer (nevertheless, the seller may retain a different asset)	Indications of no sale of original asset to buyer (secured loan)
	Sale price does not equal market value at date of sale.
No commitment for seller to repurchase asset, eg: - call option where there is a real possibility the option will fail to be exercised.	Commitment for seller to repurchase asset, eg: - put and call option with the same exercise price; - either a put or a call option with no genuine commercial possibility that the option will fail to be exercised; or - seller requires asset back to use in its business, or asset is in effect the only source of seller's future sales.
Risk of changes in asset value borne by buyer such that buyer does not receive solely a lender's return, eg: - both sale and repurchase price equal market value at date of sale/purchase.	Risk of changes in asset value borne by seller such that buyer receives solely a lender's return, eg: - repurchase price equals sale price plus costs plus interest; - original purchase price adjusted retrospectively to pass variations in the value of the asset to the seller; - seller provides residual value guarantee to buyer or subordinated debt to protect buyer from falls in the value of the asset.
Nature of the asset is such that it will be used over the life of the agreement, and the seller has no rights to determine its use. Seller has no rights to determine asset's development or future sale.	Seller retains right to determine asset's use, development or sale, or rights to profits therefrom.

Illustrations

Illustration 1

A, a house-builder, agrees with B, a bank, to sell to B some of the land within its land bank. The arrangements surrounding the sale are as follows:

(a) the sales price will be open market value as determined by an independent surveyor;

(b) B grants A the right to develop the land at any time during B's ownership, subject to its approval of the development plans, which approval shall not be unreasonably withheld; for this right, A pays all the outgoings on the land plus an annual fee of 5 per cent of the purchase price;

(c) B will maintain a memorandum account in respect of the land for the purpose of determining the price to be paid by A should A ever re-acquire the land or any adjustments necessary to the original purchase price. In this account will be entered the purchase price, any expenses incurred by B in relation to the transaction, a sum added quarterly (or on the sale by B of the land) calculated by reference to B's base lending rate plus 2 per cent applied to the daily balance on the account; and from the account will be deduced any annual fees paid by A to B;

(d) B grants A an option to acquire the land at any time within the next five years; the acquisition price is to be the balance on the memorandum account at the time of exercising the option;

(e) A grants B an option to require it to repurchase the land at any time within the next five years, the price to be the balance on the memorandum account at that time;

(f) on the expiry of five years from the date of acquiring the land, B will offer it for sale generally; and at any time prior to that it may with the consent of A offer the land for sale; and

(g) in the event of B selling the land to a third party, the proceeds of sale shall be deducted from the memorandum account maintained by B and the balance on the account shall be settled between A and B in cash, as a retrospective adjustment of the price at which B originally purchased the land from A.

The commercial effect of the above arrangement is that of a secured loan. A continues to bear all significant benefits and risks relating to the land, retains control of its development, and bears all resulting gains and losses (via either exercise of its call option, or adjust to the purchase price on sale of the land to a third party). This latter feature also gives rise to a liability for A to repay the whole of the sale proceeds received from B. In addition, B is assured of a lender's return (and no more): whilst the regular payments by A to B to secure the right to develop the land are not sufficient to provide this, B's return is guaranteed through the operation of the memorandum account and its role in determining the option price on a resale.

Illustration 2

This illustration is similar to the first but makes use of V, a vehicle company, and a subordinated loan to effect the purchase. A agrees with B (the bank) and V to sell land within its land bank to V. Relevant terms are as follows:

(a) the sale price is open market value;

(b) B grants V a loan of 60 per cent of the market value to effect the purchase, with A providing V with a subordinated loan of the balance of the consideration. B's loan bears interest at the bank's base rate plus 2 per cent: A's loan bears interest at 10 per cent. All payments of interest and capital on A's loan are subordinated to all sums due to B in any period;

(c) V grants A the right to develop the land at any time during V's ownership, subject to its approval. For this right, A pays V a market rental on the land. If this is less than the interest payable on V's loan from B, then A will advance the amount of the shortfall as an addition to its subordinated loan;

(d) V grants A an option to acquire the land at any time within the next five years, at a price equal to the original sales price plus any incidental costs incurred by V;

(e) on the expiry of five years from the date of acquiring the land, V will offer it for sale generally, and at any time before then may with the consent of A offer the land for sale; and

(f) in the event of V selling the land, to the extent that the proceeds of sale and any other cash accumulated in V exceed any sums due to B and A under the terms of their respective loans, an immediate payment shall be made to A as a retrospective adjustment of the price at which V originally purchased the land from A.

In this illustration, the substance of the transaction is that of a secured loan. A continues to bear all significant benefits and risks relating to the land, it continues to have the ability to develop it and access to the whole of any profits from its future sale. In addition, the subordinated loan from A provides a cushion to absorb losses on the disposal of the land by the vehicle; this ensures that all foreseeable losses accrue to A and thus protects the position of the bank. In practice, such subordinated loans are often sufficiently large to make any loss by the bank through a loss in value of the land extremely remote. Where this is not the case or there is no subordinated loan, the necessary protection may be provided through put options – such as are incorporated within Illustration 1 – which enable the buyer to require the seller to repurchase the asset. Where the substance of the transaction is that of a secured loan, the buyer will require that the terms of the arrangement taken as a whole mean it is reasonably assured of receiving return of the purchase price and any costs it incurs plus a lender's return (but no more) on its investment.

APPLICATION NOTE C – FACTORING OF DEBTS*

NB: For ease of reading the parties to a factoring agreement are referred to in this Application Note as 'seller' and 'factor', notwithstanding that analysis of the transaction in accordance with this Application Note may result in the seller continuing to show the factored debts as an asset on its balance sheet.

Features

Factoring of debts is a well established method of obtaining finance, sales ledger administration services, or protection from bad debts. The principal features of a factoring arrangement are as follows: C1

(a) Specified debts are transferred to the factor (usually by assignment). The transfer may be of complete debtor balances or of all invoices relating to named debtors (perhaps subject to restrictions on the amount that will be accepted from any one debtor).
(b) The factor offers a credit facility that permits the seller to draw up to a fixed percentage of the face value of the debts transferred. Normally these advances are repaid as and when the underlying debts are collected, often by paying the money that is collected into a specially nominated bank account for the benefit of the factor.
(c) The factor may also offer a credit protection facility (or insurance cover). This will limit or eliminate the extent to which the factor has recourse to the seller for debts that are in default.
(d) The factor may administer the sales ledger of the seller. Where such a service is provided, the factor becomes responsible for collecting money from debtors and pursuing those that are slow in paying. In such cases the fact that debts have been factored is likely to be disclosed to the seller's customers; this may not be necessary in other circumstances.

On the transfer of debts, the factoring charges levied on the seller will be set by the factor with reference to expected collections from the debtors and any credit C2

**Editor's note:* This Application Note is deleted in its entirety by amendments to FRS 26, for those entities complying with that standard, with effect for accounting periods beginning on or after 1 January 2007.*

protection services provided (sales ledger administration services are usually invoiced separately). These charges may be fixed at the outset or subject to adjustment at a later date to reflect actual collections; they may be payable immediately or on some future date.

Analysis

Overview of basic principles

C3 The purpose of the analysis below is to determine the appropriate accounting treatment in the seller's financial statements. There are three possible treatments:

(a) to remove the factored debts from the balance sheet and show no liability in respect of any proceeds received from the factor ('derecognition');
(b) to show the proceeds received from the factor deducted from the factored debts on the face of the balance sheet within a single asset caption (a 'linked presentation'); or
(c) to continue to show the factored debts as an asset, and show a corresponding liability within creditors in respect of the proceeds received from the factor (a 'separate presentation').

C4 In order to determine the appropriate accounting treatment, it is necessary to answer two questions:

(a) whether the seller has access to the benefits of the factored debts and exposure to the risks inherent in those benefits (referred to below as 'benefits and risks'); and
(b) whether the seller has a liability to repay amounts received from the factor.

Where the seller has transferred all significant benefits and all significant risks relating to the debts, and has no obligation to repay the factor, derecognition is appropriate; where the seller has retained significant benefits and risks relating to the debts but there is absolutely no doubt that its downside exposure to loss is limited, a linked presentation should be used; and in all other cases a separate presentation should be adopted.

Benefits and risks

C5 The main benefits and risks relating to debts are as follows:

Benefits:
(i) the future cash flows from payment by the debtors.

Risks:
(i) slow payment risk; and
(ii) credit risk (the risk of bad debts).

Analysis of benefits

C6 At first glance it may appear that the factor has access to the cash flows from payments by debtors. This may be particularly so if the money that is collected is to be paid direct to the factor (or into a specially nominated bank account for its benefit). However, it may actually be the seller that benefits from payments by debtors, these payments merely representing the primary source from which the factor will be repaid. In particular, where the seller has an obligation to repay any sums received from the factor on or before a set date regardless of the level of collections from the underlying debts, it is clear that the seller has the benefit of payments by debtors, exposure to their inherent risks and a liability to the factor. Such an arrangement should be accounted for by using a separate presentation. Conversely, where the seller receives a single non-returnable cash payment from the factor and the only future payments to be made are by the seller passing to the factor all and any payments from debtors as and when paid, the seller will both have transferred the benefits and risks of the factored debts and have no obligation to repay amounts received from the factor.

This latter arrangement would qualify for derecognition.

Considering the benefits in isolation will not normally enable a clear decision to be made on the appropriate accounting treatment for a factoring. The cash flows may appear similar in both of the above arrangements – an initial cash inflow for the seller followed by a later cash outflow (or a sacrifice of a cash inflow that would otherwise occur). For this reason, the risks (both upside potential for gain and downside exposure to loss) are more significant than the benefits. C7

Slow payment risk: credit facility

The first main risk associated with non-interest bearing debts is slow payment risk (including the upside potential from prompt payment by debtors). Where the finance cost charged by the factor is essentially a fixed sum determined at the time the transfer is made, the factor will bear the risk of slow payment; where it varies to reflect the speed of collection of the debts subsequently, the seller will bear that risk. Close attention to the arrangements and to their commercial effect in practice may be necessary to determine whether a variable finance cost falls upon the seller since it may take various forms, including a bonus for early settlement, or a retrospective adjustment to the purchase price. C8

Credit risk: credit protection facility

Credit risk is the other main risk associated with trade debts. If there is no recourse to the seller for bad debts, the factor will bear this risk; if there is full recourse, the seller will bear it. Furthermore, as non-payment is merely the ultimate form of slow payment, where credit risk is retained by the seller, the latter will normally also bear at least some risk of slow payment. For example, where the arrangement takes the form of the seller repurchasing debts that remain outstanding after a given time, the seller bears the slow payment risk beyond this time as well as bearing the credit risk. C9

Administration arrangements and service-only factoring

For the purpose of deciding upon the appropriate accounting treatment, the administration arrangements will not be directly significant (provided they are on an arm's length basis, and for a fee that is commensurate with the service provided). In a service-only factoring arrangement, where the factor administers the sales ledger but cash is received no earlier than if the debts had not been factored, the seller retains access to the benefits of the debts and exposure to their inherent risks. Thus such an arrangement should be accounted for by using a separate presentation. C10

Derecognition

C11 Derecognition (ie ceasing to recognise the factored debts in their entirety) is appropriate only where the seller retains no significant benefits and no significant risks relating to the factored debts.

C12 Whilst the commercial effect of any particular transaction should be assessed taking into account all its aspects and implications, the presence of all of the following indicates that the seller has not retained significant benefits and risks, and derecognition is appropriate:

(a) the transaction takes place at an arm's length price for an outright sale;
(b) the transaction is for a fixed amount of consideration and there is no recourse whatsoever, either implicit or explicit, to the seller for losses from either slow payment or non-payment. Normal warranties given in respect of the condition of the debts at the time of the transfer (eg a warranty that goods have been delivered or that the borrower's credit limit had not been breached at the time of granting him credit) would not breach this condition. However, warranties relating to the condition of the debts in the future or to their future performance (eg that debtors will not move into arrears in the future) would breach the condition. Other possible forms of recourse are set out in paragraph 83; and
(c) the seller will not benefit or suffer in any way if the debts perform better or worse than expected. This will not be the case where the seller has a right to further sums from the factor which vary according to the future performance of the debts (ie according to whether or when the debtors pay). Such sums might take the form of deferred consideration, a retrospective adjustment to the purchase price, or rebates of certain charges; they include all forms of variable finance cost.

C13 Where any of the above three features is not present, this indicates that the seller has retained benefits and risks relating to the factored debts and, unless these are insignificant, either a separate presentation or a linked presentation should be adopted.

C14 Whether any benefit and risk retained are 'significant' should be judged in relation to those benefits and risks that are likely to occur in practice, and not in relation to the total possible benefits and risks. For example, if for a portfolio of factored debts of 100, expected bad debts are 5 and there is recourse to the seller for credit losses of up to 10, significant risk will have been retained (as the seller would bear losses of up to twice those expected to occur). Accordingly, in this example, derecognition would not be appropriate and either a linked presentation or a separate presentation should be used. The terms of any roll-over provisions and their effect in practice require careful consideration since these may result in the seller continuing to bear significant risk where, at first sight, it appears that the arrangements do not have this effect. For example, the pricing of future transfers may be adjusted to reflect recent slow payment or bad debt experience and there may be a significant disincentive (eg a penalty) for the seller to cancel the arrangement. This may result in the seller continuing to bear significant risk, albeit disguised as revised charges for debts factored subsequently.

Linked presentation

C15 A linked presentation will be appropriate where, although the seller has retained significant benefits and risks relating to the factored debts, there is absolutely no doubt that its downside exposure to loss is limited to a fixed monetary amount. A linked presentation should be used only to the extent that there is both absolutely no doubt that the factor's claim extends solely to collections from the factored debts, and no provision for the seller to re-acquire the debts in the future. The conditions that need to be met in order for this to be the case are set out in paragraph 27 and explained in paragraphs 81–86. When interpreting these conditions in the context of a factoring arrangement the following points apply:

condition (a) (specified assets) –
  a linked presentation should not be used where the debts that have been factored cannot be separately identified.

condition (d) (that the factor agrees in writing there is no recourse, and such agreement is noted in the financial statements) –
  the inclusion of an appropriate statement in the factoring agreement will meet the first part of this condition.

Where debts are factored on an ongoing basis, the arrangements for terminating the agreement must be carefully analysed in order to ensure that the conditions for a linked presentation are met. It will be necessary that, although the factor does not take on any new debts, it continues to bear losses on debts already factored and is not able to transfer them back to the seller. Where this is not the case, there remains the possibility that the factor will return debts that it suspects to be bad by terminating the arrangement. In such a case the seller's exposure to loss is not limited, and a separate presentation should be adopted. **C16**

Separate presentation

Where the seller has retained significant benefits and risks relating to the debts and the conditions for a linked presentation are not met, a separate presentation should be adopted. **C17**

Required accounting

Derecognition

Where the seller has retained no significant benefits and risks relating to the debts and has no obligation to repay amounts received from the factor, the debts should be removed from its balance sheet and no liability shown in respect of the proceeds received from the factor. A profit or loss should be recognised, calculated as the difference between the carrying amount of the debts and the proceeds received. **C18**

Linked presentation

Where the conditions for a linked presentation are met, the proceeds received, to the extent they are non-returnable, should be shown deducted from the gross amount of the factored debts (after providing for bad debts, credit protection charges and any accrued interest) on the face of the balance sheet. An example is given in illustration 2 below. The interest element of the factor's charges should be recognised as it accrues and included in the profit and loss account with other interest charges. The notes to the financial statements should disclose: the main terms of the arrangement; the gross amount of factored debts outstanding at the balance sheet date; the factoring charges recognised in the period, analysed as appropriate (eg between interest and other charges); and the disclosures required by conditions (c) and (d) in paragraph 27. **C19**

Separate presentation

C20 Where neither derecognition nor a linked presentation is appropriate, a separate presentation should be adopted, ie a gross asset (equivalent in amount to the gross amount of the debts) should be shown on the balance sheet of the seller within assets, and a corresponding liability in respect of the proceeds received from the factor should be shown within liabilities. The interest element of the factor's charges should be recognised as it accrues and included in the profit and loss account with other interest charges. Other factoring costs should be similarly accrued and included in the profit and loss account within the appropriate caption. The notes to the financial statements should disclose the amount of factored debts outstanding at the balance sheet date.

Table

Indications that derecognition is appropriate (debts are not an asset of the seller)	**Indications that a linked presentation is appropriate**	**Indications that a separate presentation is appropriate (debts are an asset of the seller)**
Transfer is for a single, non-returnable fixed sum.	Some non-returnable proceeds received, but seller has rights to further sums from the factor (or vice versa) whose amount depends on whether or when debtors pay.	Finance cost varies with speed of collection of debts, eg: - by adjustment to consideration for original transfer; or - subsequent transfers priced to recover costs of earlier transfers
There is no recourse to the seller for losses.	There is either no recourse for losses, or such recourse has a fixed monetary ceiling.	There is full recourse to the seller for losses.
Factor is paid all amounts received from the factored debts (and no more). Seller has no rights to further sums from the factor.	Factor is paid only out of the amounts collected from the factored debts, and sell has no right or obligation to repurchase debts.	Seller is required to repay amounts received from the factor on or before a set date, regardless of timing or amounts of collections from debtors.

Illustrations

Illustration 1 – Factoring with recourse (separate presentation)

Company S enters into a factoring arrangement with F, with the following principal terms:

(a) S will transfer (by assignment) all its trade debts to F, subject only to credit approval by F and a limit placed on the proportion of the total that may be due from any one debtor;

(b) F administers S's sales ledger and handles all aspects of collection of the debts in return for an administration charge at an annual rate of 1 per cent, payable monthly, based upon the total debts factored at each month-end;

(c) S may draw up to 70 per cent of the gross amount of debts factored and outstanding at any time, such drawings being debited in the books of F to a factoring account operated by F for S;
(d) weekly, S assigns and sends copy invoices to F as they are raised. F sends statements to debtors, following up all overdue invoices by telephone or letter;
(e) F credits collections from debtors to the factoring account, and debits the account monthly with interest calculated on the basis of the daily balances on the account using a rate of base rate plus 2 per cent. Thus this interest charge varies with the amount of finance drawn by S under the finance facility from F, the speed of payment of the debtors and the base rate;
(f) any debts not recovered after 90 days are reassigned to S for an immediate cash payment, which is credited to the factoring account;
(g) F pays for all other debts, less any advances and interest charges made, 90 days after the date of their assignment to F, and debits the payment to the factoring account; and
(h) on termination of the agreement the balance on the factoring account is settled in cash.

The commercial effect of the above arrangements is that, although the debts have been legally transferred to F, the benefits and risks are retained by S. S continues to bear the slow payment risk as the interest charged by F varies with the speed of payment by the debtors; S continues to bear all of the credit risk as it must pay for any debts not recovered after 90 days, and it therefore has unlimited exposure to loss. In addition, S in effect has an obligation to repay amounts received from F on or before a set date regardless of the levels of collections from the factored debts – either out of collections from debtors on the day they pay, or from its general resources after 90 days, whichever is the earlier. Thus a separate presentation should be adopted.

Illustration 2 – Factoring without recourse (linked presentation)

S enters into an agreement with F with the following principal terms:

(a) S will transfer (by assignment) to F such trade debts as S shall determine, subject only to credit approval by F and a limit placed on the proportion of the total that may be due from any one debtor. F levies a charge of 0.15 per cent of turnover, payable monthly, for this facility;
(b) S continues to administer the sales ledger and handle all aspects of collection of the debts;
(c) S may draw up to 80 per cent of the gross amount of debts assigned at any time, such drawings being debited in the books of F to a factoring account operated by F for S;
(d) weekly, S assigns and sends copy invoices to F as they are raised;
(e) S is required to bank the gross amounts of all payments received from debts assigned to F direct into an account in the name of F. Credit transfers made by debtors direct into S's own bank account must immediately be paid to F;
(f) F credits such collections from debtors to the factoring account, and debits the account monthly with interest calculated on the basis of the daily balances on the account using a rate of base rate plus 2.5 per cent. Thus this interest charge varies with the amount of finance drawn by S under the finance facility from F, the speed of payment of the debtors and base rate;
(g) F provides protection from bad debts. Any debts not recovered after 90 days are credited to the factoring account, and responsibility for their collection is passed to F. A charge of 1 per cent of the gross value of all debts factored is levied by F for this service and debited to the factoring account;

(h) F pays for the debts, less any advances, interest charges and credit protection charges, 90 days after the date of purchase, and debits the payment to the factoring account; and

(i) on either party giving 90 days' notice to the other, the arrangement will be terminated. In such an event, S will transfer no further debts to F, and the balance remaining on the factoring account at the end of the notice period will be settled in cash in the normal way.

The commercial effect of this arrangement is that, although the debts have been legally transferred to F, S continues to bear significant benefits and risks relating to them. S continues to bear slow payment risk as the interest charged by F varies with the speed of collections of the debts. Hence, the gross amount of the debts should continue to be shown on its balance sheet until the earlier of collection and transfer of all risks to F (ie 90 days). However, S's maximum downside loss is limited since any debts not recovered after 90 days are in effect paid for by F, which then assumes all slow payment and credit risk beyond this time. Thus, even for debts that prove to be bad, S receives some proceeds.* Hence, assuming the conditions given in paragraphs 26 and 27 are met, a linked presentation should be adopted. The amount deducted on the face of the balance sheet should be the lower of the proceeds received and the gross amount of the debts less all charges to the factor in respect of them. In the above example, for a debt of 100 this latter amount would be calculated at 100 less the credit protection fee of 1 and the maximum finance charge (calculated for 90 days at base rate plus 2.5 per cent). Assuming the proceeds received of 80 are lower than this, and accrued interest charges at the year-end are 2, the arrangement would be shown as follows:

Current Assets

Stock		x
Debts factored without recourse:		
Gross debts (after providing for credit protection fee and accrued interest)	97	
less: non-returnable proceeds	(80)	
		17
Other debtors		x

In addition, the non-returnable proceeds of 80 would be included within cash and the profit and loss account would include both the credit protection expense of 1 and the accrued interest charges of 2.

APPLICATION NOTE D – SECURITISED ASSETS†

Features

D1 Securitisation is a means by which providers of finance fund a specific block of assets rather than the general business of a company. The assets that have been most commonly securitised in the UK are household mortgages. Other receivables such as

**For a debt of 100 that subsequently proves to be bad, the proceeds received would be 100, less the credit protection fee of 1, less an interest charge calculated for 90 days at base rate plus 2.5%.*

†***Editor's note:*** *This Application Note is deleted in its entirety by amendments to FRS 26, for entities complying with that standard, with effect for accounting periods beginning on or after 1 January 2007.*

credit card balances, hire purchase loans and trade debts are sometimes securitised, as are non-monetary assets such as property and stocks. This Application Note applies to all kinds of assets.

The main features are generally as follows: D2

(a) The assets to be securitised are transferred by a company (the 'originator') to a special purpose vehicle (the 'issuer') in return for an immediate cash payment. Additional deferred consideration may also be payable.

(b) The issuer finances the transfer by the issue of debt, usually tradeable loan notes or commercial paper (referred to below as 'loan notes'). The issuer is usually thinly capitalised and its shares placed with a party other than the originator – charitable trusts have often been used for this purpose – with the result that the issuer is not classified as a subsidiary of the originator under companies legislation. In addition, the major financial and operating policies of the issuer are usually predetermined by the agreements that constitute the securitisation, such that neither the owner of its share capital nor the originator has any significant continuing discretion over how it is run.

(c) Arrangements are made to protect the loan noteholders from losses occurring on the assets by a process termed 'credit enhancement'. This may take the form of third party insurance, a third party guarantee of the issuer's obligations or an issue of subordinated debt (perhaps to the originator); all provide a cushion against losses up to a fixed amount.

(d) The originator is granted rights to surplus income (and, where relevant, capital profits) from the assets – ie to cash remaining after payment of amounts due on the loan notes and other expenses of the issuer. The mechanisms used to achieve this include: servicing or other fees; deferred sale consideration; 'super interest' on amounts owed to the originator (eg subordinated debt); dividend payments; and swap payments.

(e) In the case of securitised debts, the originator may continue to service the debts (ie to collect amounts due from borrowers, set interest rates etc). In this capacity it is referred to as the 'servicer' and receives a servicing fee.

(f) Cash accumulations from the assets (eg from mortgage redemptions) are reinvested by the issuer until loan notes are repaid. Any difference between the interest rate obtained on reinvestments and that payable on the loan notes will normally affect the originator's surplus under (d) above. The terms of the loan notes may provide for them to be redeemed as assets are realised, thus minimising this reinvestment period. Alternatively, cash accumulations may be invested in a 'guaranteed investment contract' that pays a guaranteed rate of interest (which may be determined by reference to a variable benchmark rate such as LIBOR) sufficient to meet interest payments on the loan notes. Another alternative, used particularly for short-term debts arising under a facility (eg credit card balances), is a provision for cash receipts (here from card repayments) to be reinvested in similar assets (eg new balances on the same credit card accounts). This reinvestment in similar assets will occur for a specified period only, after which time cash accumulations will either be used to redeem loan notes or be reinvested in other more liquid assets until loan notes are repaid.

(g) In certain circumstances, for example if tax changes affect the payment of interest to the noteholders or if the principal amount of loan notes outstanding declines to a specified level, the issuer may have an option to buy back the notes. Such repurchase may be funded by the originator, in which case the originator will re-acquire the securitised assets.

From the originator's standpoint, the effect of the arrangement is usually that it continues to obtain the benefit of surplus income (and, where relevant, capital profits) from the securitised assets and bears losses up to a set amount. Usually, D3 however, the originator is protected from losses beyond a limited amount and has transferred catastrophe risk to the issuer.

Analysis

D4 The purpose of the analysis is to determine the following:

(a) the appropriate accounting treatment in the originator's individual company financial statements. There are three possible treatments:

(i) to remove the securitised assets from the balance sheet and show no liability in respect of the note issue, merely retaining the net amount (if any) of the securitised assets less the loan notes as a single item ('derecognition');

(ii) to show the proceeds of the note issue deducted from the securitised assets on the face of the balance sheet within a single asset caption (a 'linked presentation'); or

(iii) to show an asset equivalent in amount to the gross securitised assets within assets, and a corresponding liability in respect of the proceeds of the note issue within creditors (a 'separate presentation');

(b) the appropriate accounting treatment in the issuer's financial statements. Again there are three possible treatments: derecognition, a linked presentation or a separate presentation; and

(c) the appropriate accounting treatment in the originator's group accounts. This involves issues of:

(i) whether the issuer is a subsidiary or (more usually) a quasi-subsidiary of the originator such that it should be included in the originator's group accounts; and

(ii) where the issuer is a quasi-subsidiary, whether a linked presentation should be adopted in the originator's consolidated accounts.

Each of these is considered in more detail below.

(a) Originator's individual accounts

Overview of basic principles

D5 The principles for determining the appropriate accounting treatment in the originator's individual company financial statements are similar to those applied in both Application Note C – 'Factoring of debts' and in Application Note E – 'Loan transfers'. It is necessary to establish what asset and liability (if any) the originator now has, by answering two questions:

(a) whether the originator has access to the benefits of the securitised assets and exposure to the risks inherent in those benefits (referred to below as 'benefits and risks') and

(b) whether the originator has a liability to repay the proceeds of the note issue.

Where the originator has transferred all significant benefits and risks relating to the securitised assets and has no obligation to repay the proceeds of the note issue, derecognition is appropriate; where the originator has retained significant benefits and risks relating to the securitised assets but there is absolutely no doubt that its downside exposure to loss is limited, a linked presentation should be used; and in all other cases a separate presentation should be adopted.

The benefits and risks relating to securitised assets will depend on the nature of the particular assets involved. In the case of interest bearing loans, the benefits and risks are described in paragraph E6 of Application Note E – 'Loan transfers'. D6

Derecognition

Derecognition (ie ceasing to recognise the securitised assets in their entirety) is appropriate only where the originator retains no significant benefits and no significant risks relating to the securitised assets. D7

Whilst the commercial effect of any particular transaction should be assessed taking into account all its aspects and implications, the presence of all of the following indicates that the originator has not retained significant benefits and risks, and derecognition is appropriate: D8

(a) the transaction takes place at an arm's length price for an outright sale;
(b) the transaction is for a fixed amount of consideration and there is no recourse whatsoever, either implicit or explicit, to the originator for losses from whatever cause. Normal warranties given in respect of the condition of the assets at the time of the transfer (eg in a mortgage securitisation, a warranty that no mortgages are in arrears at the time of transfer, or that the income of the borrower at the time of granting the mortgage was above a specified amount) would not breach this condition. However, warranties relating to the condition of the assets in the future or to their future performance (eg that mortgages will not move into arrears in the future) would breach the condition. Other possible forms of recourse are set out in paragraph 83; and
(c) the originator will not benefit or suffer if the securitised assets perform better or worse than expected. This will not be the case where the originator has a right to further sums from the vehicle that vary according to the eventual value realised for the securitised assets. Such sums could take a number of forms, for instance deferred consideration, a performance-related servicing fee, payments under a swap, dividends from the vehicle, or payments from a reserve fund.

Where any of these three features is not present, this indicates that the originator has retained benefits and risks relating to the securitised assets and, unless these are insignificant, either a separate presentation or a linked presentation should be adopted.

Whether any benefit and risk retained are 'significant' should be judged in relation to those benefits and risks that are likely to occur in practice, and not in relation to the total possible benefits and risks. Where the profits or losses accruing to the originator are material in relation to those likely to occur in practice, significant benefit and risk will be retained. For example, if for a portfolio of securitised assets of 100, expected losses are 0.5 and there is recourse to the originator for losses of up to 5, the originator will have retained all but an insignificant part of the downside risk relating to the assets (as the originator bears losses of up to ten times those expected to occur). Accordingly, in this example, derecognition will not be appropriate and either a linked presentation or a separate presentation should be used. D9

Linked presentation

A linked presentation will be appropriate where, although the originator has retained significant benefits and risks relating to the securitised assets, there is absolutely no doubt that its downside exposure to loss is limited to a fixed monetary amount. A linked presentation should be used only to the extent that there is both absolutely no D10 doubt that the noteholders' claim extends solely to the proceeds generated by the securitised assets, and there is no provision for the originator to re-acquire the securitised assets in the future. The conditions that need to be met in order for this to be the case are set out in paragraph 27 and explained in paragraphs 81–86. When interpreting these conditions in the context of a securitisation the following points apply:

condition (a) (specified assets) –

a linked presentation should not be used where the assets that have been securitised cannot be separately identified. Nor should a linked presentation be used for assets that generate the funds required to repay the finance only by being used in conjunction with other assets of the originator;

condition (d) (agreement in writing that there is no recourse; such agreement noted in the financial statements) –

where the noteholders have subscribed to a prospectus or offering circular that clearly states that the originator will not support any losses of either the issuer or the noteholders, the first part of this condition will be met. Provisions that give the noteholders recourse to funds generated by both the securitised assets themselves and third party credit enhancement of those assets would also not breach this condition;

condition (f) (no provision for the originator to repurchase assets) –

where there is provision for the originator to repurchase only part of the securitised assets (or otherwise to fund the redemption of loan notes by the issuer), the maximum payment that could result should be excluded from the amount deducted on the face of the balance sheet. Where there is provision for the issuer (but not the originator) to redeem loan notes before an equivalent amount has been realised in cash from the securitised assets, a linked presentation may still be appropriate provided there is no obligation (legal, commercial or other) for the originator to fund the redemption (eg by repurchasing the securitised assets).

D11 These conditions should be regarded as met notwithstanding the existence of an interest rate swap agreement between the originator and the issuer, provided all the following conditions are met:

(a) the swap is on arm's length market-related terms and the obligations of the issuer under the swap are not subordinated to any of its obligations under the loan notes;

(b) the variable interest rate(s) that are swapped are determined by reference to publicly quoted rates that are not under the control of the originator;

(c) at the time of transfer of the assets to the issuer, the originator had hedged exposures relating to these assets (either individually or as part of a larger portfolio) and entering into the swap effectively restores the hedge position left open by their transfer. Thereafter, where the hedging of the originator's exposure under the swap requires continuing management, any necessary adjustments to the hedging position are made on an ongoing basis. This latter requirement will be particularly relevant where any prepayment risk involved cannot be hedged exactly.

The conditions for a linked presentation should also be regarded as met notwithstanding the existence of an interest rate cap agreement between the originator and the issuer provided that, in addition to all the above conditions being met, the securitisation was entered into before 22 September 1994.

D12 In the case of securitisations of revolving assets that arise under a facility (eg credit card balances), a careful analysis of the mechanism for repaying the loan notes is required in order to establish whether or not conditions (b) and (f) in paragraph 27 are met. For such assets, the loan notes are usually repaid from proceeds received during a period of time (referred to as the 'repayment period'). The proceeds received in the repayment period will typically comprise both repayments of securitised balances existing at the start of the repayment period and repayments of balances arising subsequently (for example arising from new borrowings in the repayment period on the credit card accounts securitised). In order that the conditions for a linked presentation are met, it is necessary that loan notes are repaid only to the extent that there have been, in total, cash collections from securitised balances existing at the start of the repayment period equal to the amount repaid on the loan notes. This is necessary in order to ensure that the issuer is allocated its proper share of any losses.

It will also be necessary to analyse carefully any provisions that enable the originator to transfer additional assets to the issuer in order to establish whether or not conditions (b) and (f) in paragraph 27 are met. To the extent that the originator is obliged to replace poorly performing assets with good ones, there is recourse to the originator and a linked presentation should not be used. However, where there is merely provision for the originator to add new assets to replace those that have been repaid earlier than expected (and thus to 'top up' the pool in order to extend the life of the securitisation), the conditions for a linked presentation may still be met. For a linked presentation to be used, it is necessary that the addition of new assets does not result in either the originator being exposed to losses on the new or the old assets, or in the originator re-acquiring assets. Provided these features are present, the effect is the same as if the noteholders were repaid in cash and they immediately reinvested that cash in new assets, and a linked presentation may be appropriate. **D13**

Separate presentation

Where the originator has retained significant benefits and risks relating to the securitised assets and the conditions for a linked presentation are not met, the originator should adopt a separate presentation. **D14**

Multi-originator programmes

There are some arrangements where one issuer serves several originators. The arrangement may be structured such that each originator receives future benefits based on the performance of a defined portfolio of assets (typically those it has transferred to the issuer and continues to service or use). For instance, in a mortgage securitisation, the benefits accruing to any particular originator may be calculated as the interest payments received from a defined portfolio of mortgages, less costs specific to that portfolio (eg insurance premiums, payments for credit facilities), less an appropriate share of the funding costs of the issuer. The effect is that each originator bears significant benefits and risks of a defined pool of mortgages, whilst being insulated from the benefits and risks of other mortgages held by the issuer. Thus each originator should show that pool of mortgages for which it has significant benefits and risks on the face of its balance sheet, using either a linked presentation (if the conditions for its use are met) or a separate presentation. **D15**

(b) Issuer's accounts

The principles set out in paragraphs D5–D15 for the originator's individual financial statements also apply to the issuer's financial statements. In a securitisation, the issuer usually has access to all future benefits from the securitised assets (in the case of mortgages, to all cash collected from mortgagors) and is exposed to all their inherent risks. Hence, derecognition will not be appropriate. In addition, the **D16** noteholders usually have recourse to all the assets of the issuer (these may include the securitised assets themselves, the benefit of any related insurance policies or credit enhancement, and a small amount of cash). In this situation, the issuer's exposure to loss is not limited, and use of a linked presentation will not be appropriate. Thus the issuer should usually adopt a separate presentation.

(c) Originator's group financial statements

D17 Assuming a separate presentation is used in the issuer's financial statements but not in those of the originator, the question arises whether the relationship between the issuer and the originator is such that the issuer should be included in the originator's group financial statements. The following considerations are relevant:

(a) Where the issuer meets the definition of a subsidiary, it should be consolidated in the normal way by applying the relevant provisions of companies legislation and FRS 2. Where the issuer is not a subsidiary, the provisions of this FRS regarding quasi-subsidiaries are relevant.

(b) In order to meet the definition of a quasi- subsidiary, the issuer must give rise to benefits for the originator that are in substance no different from those that would arise were the entity a subsidiary. This will be the case where the originator receives the future benefits arising from the net assets of the issuer (principally the securitised assets less the loan notes). It is not necessary that the originator could face a possible benefit outflow equal in amount to the issuer's gross liabilities. Strong evidence of whether this part of the definition is met is whether the originator stands to suffer or gain from the financial performance of the issuer.

(c) The definition of a quasi-subsidiary also requires that the issuer is directly or indirectly controlled by the originator. Usually securitisations exemplify the situation described in paragraphs 34 and 98, in that the issuer's financial and operating policies are in substance predetermined (in this case under the various agreements that constitute the securitisation). Where this is so, the party possessing control will be the one that has the future benefits arising from the issuer's net assets.

D18 It follows that it should be presumed that the issuer is a quasi-subsidiary where either of the following is present:

(a) the originator has rights to the benefits arising from the issuer's net assets, ie to those benefits generated by the securitised assets that remain after meeting the claims of noteholders and other expenses of the issuer. These benefits may be transferred to the originator in a number of forms, as described in paragraph D2(d); or

(b) the originator has the risks inherent in these benefits. This will be the case where, if the benefits are greater or less than expected (eg because of the securitised assets realising more or less than expected), the originator gains or suffers.

D19 In general, where an issuer's activities comprise holding securitised assets and the benefits of its net assets accrue to the originator, the issuer will be a quasi-subsidiary of the originator. Conversely, the issuer will not be a quasi-subsidiary of the originator where the owner of the issuer is an independent third party that has made a substantial capital investment in the issuer, has control of the issuer, and has the benefits and risks of its net assets.

D20 Where the issuer is a quasi-subsidiary of the originator, the question arises whether a linked presentation should be adopted in the originator's group financial statements. It follows from paragraph 37 that where the issuer holds a single portfolio of similar assets, and the effect of the arrangement is to ring-fence the assets and their related finance in such a way that the provisions of paragraphs 26 and 27 are met from the point of view of the group, a linked presentation should be used.

Required accounting

Originator's individual financial statements

Derecognition

Where the originator has retained no significant benefits and risks relating to the securitised assets and has no obligation to repay the proceeds of the note issue, the assets should be removed from its balance sheet, and no liability shown in respect of the proceeds of the note issue. A profit or loss should be recognised, calculated as the difference between the carrying amount of the assets and the proceeds received. **D21**

Linked presentation

Where the conditions for a linked presentation are met, the proceeds of the note issue (to the extent they are non-returnable) should be shown deducted from the securitised assets on the face of the balance sheet within a single asset caption. Profit should be recognised and presented in the manner set out in paragraphs 28 and 87–88. The following disclosures should be given: **D22**

(a) a description of the assets securitised;
(b) the amount of any income or expense recognised in the period, analysed as appropriate;
(c) the terms of any options for the originator to repurchase assets or to transfer additional assets to the issuer;
(d) the terms of any interest rate swap or interest rate cap agreements between the issuer and the originator that meet the conditions set out in paragraph D11;
(e) a description of the priority and amount of claims on the proceeds generated by the assets, including any rights of the originator to proceeds from the assets in addition to the non-recourse amounts already received;
(f) the ownership of the issuer; and
(g) the disclosures required by conditions (c) and (d) in paragraph 27.

Where an originator uses a linked presentation for several different securitisations that all relate to a single type of asset (ie all the assets, if not securitised, would be shown within the same balance sheet caption), these may be aggregated on the face of the balance sheet. However, securitisations of different types of asset should be shown separately. In addition, details of each material arrangement should be provided in the notes to the financial statements, unless they are on similar terms and relate to a single type of asset, in which case they may be disclosed in aggregate. **D23**

Separate presentation

Where neither derecognition nor a linked presentation is appropriate, a separate presentation should be adopted, ie a gross asset (equal in amount to the gross amount of the securitised assets) should be shown on the balance sheet of the originator within assets, and a corresponding liability in respect of the proceeds of the note issue shown within liabilities. No gain or loss should be recognised at the time the securitisation is entered into (unless adjustment to the carrying value of the assets independent of the securitisation is required). Disclosure should be given in the notes **D24** to the financial statements of the gross amount of assets securitised at the balance sheet date.

Issuer's financial statements

D25 The requirements set out in paragraphs D21–D24 for the originator's individual financial statements also apply to the issuer's financial statements. For the reasons set out in paragraph D16, in most cases the issuer will be required to adopt a separate presentation, in which case the provisions of paragraph D24 will apply.

Originator's consolidated financial statements

D26 Where the issuer is a quasi-subsidiary of the originator, its assets, liabilities, profits, losses and cash flows should be included in the originating group's consolidated financial statements. Where the provisions of paragraph D20 are met, a linked presentation should be applied in the consolidated financial statements and the disclosures required by paragraphs D22 and D23 should be given; in all other cases a separate presentation should be used and the disclosure required by paragraph D24 should be given.

Indications that derecognition is appropriate (securitised assets are not assets of the originator)	**Indications that a linked presentation is appropriate**	**Indications that a separate presentation is appropriate (securitiesed assets are assets of the originator)**
	Originator's individual financial statements	
Transaction price is arm's length price for an outright sale.	Transaction price is not arm's length price for an outright sale.	Transaction price is not arm's length for an outright sale.
Transfer is for a single, non-returnable fixed sum.	Some non-returnable proceeds received, but originator has rights to further sums from the issuer, the amount of which depends on the performance of the securitised assets.	Proceeds received are returnable, or there is a provision whereby the originator may keep the securitiesed assets on repayment of the loan notes or re-acquire them.
There is no recourse to the originator for losses.	There is either no recourse for losses, or such recourse has a fixed monetary ceiling.	There is or may be full recourse to the originator for losses, eg: - originator's directors are unable to unwilling to state that it is not obliged to fund any losses; - noteholders have not agreed in writing that they will seek repayment only from funds generated by the securitised assets.

Originator's consolidated financial statements		
Issuer is owned by an independent third party that made a substantial capital investment, has control of the issuer, and has the benefits and risks of its net assets.	Issuer is a quasi-subsidiary of the originator, but the conditions for a linked presentation are met from the point of view of the group.	Issuer is a subsidiary of the originator.

APPLICATION NOTE E – LOAN TRANSFERS*

NB: In this Application Note, the following terminology is used:

(a) the 'lender' is the party that has rights to principal and interest under the original loan agreement, and is purporting to transfer them;

(b) the 'transferee' is the party purporting to acquire the loan, and includes a new lender (in a novation), an assignee and a sub-participant;

(c) the 'borrower' is the party that has obligations to make payments of principal and interest under the original loan agreement; and

(d) references to the transfer of a 'loan' or 'loans' apply equally to the transfer of both a single loan and a portfolio of loans.

Features

This Application Note deals with the transfer of interest-bearing loans to an entity other than a special purpose vehicle. The main features of a loan transfer are as follows: E1

(a) Specified loans are transferred from a lender to a transferee by one of the methods set out in paragraph E2 below, in return for an immediate cash payment. The transfer may be of the whole of a single loan, part of a loan, or of all or part of a portfolio of similar loans.

(b) Payments of principal and interest collected from borrowers are passed to the transferee (either direct or via the lender). In some cases, there may be a difference between amounts received from borrowers and those passed to the transferee (the lender retaining or making up the difference), or if a borrower fails to make payments when due, the lender may nevertheless make payments to the transferee.

Loans cannot be 'sold' in the same way as tangible assets. However, there are three methods by which the benefits and risks of a loan can be transferred: E2

Novation: The rights and obligations under the loan agreement are cancelled and replaced by new ones whose main effect is to change the identity of the lender. Although rights can be transferred by other means, novation is the only method of transferring obligations (eg to supply funds under an undrawn loan facility) with the consequent release of the lender.

Assignment: Rights (to principal and interest), but not obligations, are transferred to a third party (the 'assignee'). There are two types of assignment: statutory assignment, which must relate to the whole of the loan and where notice in writing must be given to the borrower and other obligors (eg a guarantor); and equitable assignment, which may relate to only part of a loan and which does not require notice to the borrower. Both types are subject to equitable rights arising before

****Editor's note:*** *This Application Note is deleted in its entirety by amendments to FRS 26, for entities complying with that standard, with effect for accounting periods beginning on or after 1 January 2007.*

FRS 5 APPLICATION NOTES

notice is received. For example, a right of set-off held by the borrower against the lender will be good against the assignee for any transactions undertaken before the borrower receives notice of the assignment.

Sub-participation: Rights and obligations are not formally transferred but the lender enters into a non-recourse back-to-back agreement with a third party, the 'sub participant', under which the latter deposits with the lender an amount equal to the whole or part of the loan and in return receives from the lender a share of the cash flows arising on the loan.

E3 The terms of a loan transfer will usually not be identical to those of the original loan, and a gain or loss will arise for the lender. This gain or loss may occur in one of two ways: first, if all future payments made by the borrower (and only such payments) are to be passed to the transferee, the consideration for the transfer will differ from the carrying amount of the loan and the lender's gain or loss will be realised in cash immediately. Alternatively, the consideration for the transfer may be set equal to the carrying amount of the loan, and the amounts to be paid by the borrower and those to be passed on to the transferee will differ. In this case, the lender's gain or loss will be the net present value of this difference and will be realised in cash over the term of the loan.

Analysis

Overview of basic principles

E4 The purpose of the analysis is to determine the appropriate accounting treatment in the financial statements of the lender. There are three possible treatments:

(a) to remove the loan (or a part of it) from the balance sheet and show no liability in respect of the amounts received from the transferee ('derecognition');

(b) to show the amounts received from the transferee deducted from the loan on the face of the balance sheet within a single asset caption (a 'linked presentation'); or

(c) to continue to show the loan as an asset, and show a corresponding liability within creditors in respect of the amounts received from the transferee (a 'separate presentation').

E5 The principles to be applied to determine the appropriate accounting treatment are similar to those applied in both Application Note D – 'Securitised assets' relating to individual (rather than consolidated) financial statements and in Application Note C – 'Factoring of debts'. It is necessary to answer two questions:

(a) whether the lender has access to the benefits of the loans and exposure to the risks inherent in those benefits (referred to below as 'benefits and risks'); and

(b) whether the lender has a liability to repay the transferee.

Where the lender has transferred all significant benefits and risks relating to the loans and has no obligation to repay the transferee, derecognition is appropriate (this would be the case where all future cash flows from borrowers – but only those cash flows – are passed to the transferee as and when received). Where the lender has retained significant benefits and risks relating to the loans but there is absolutely no doubt that its downside exposure to loss is limited, a linked presentation should be used (this is likely to be rare for a loan transfer). In all other cases a separate presentation should be adopted.

Benefits and risks

The main benefits and risks relating to loans are as follows: E6

Benefits:

(i) the future cash flows from payments of principal and interest.

Risks:

(i) credit risk (the risk of bad debts);
(ii) slow payment risk;
(iii) interest rate risk (the risk of a change in the interest rate paid by the borrower. Included in this risk is a form of basis risk, ie the risk of a change in the interest rate paid by the borrower not being matched by a change in the interest rate paid to the transferee);
(iv) reinvestment/early redemption risk (the risk that, where payments from the loans are reinvested by the lender before being paid to the transferee, the rate of interest obtained on the reinvested amounts is above or below that payable to the transferee); and
(v) moral risk (the risk that the lender will feel obliged, because of its continued association with the loans, to fund any losses arising on them).

Analysis of benefits

At first sight it may appear that the transferee has access to the cash collected from borrowers. However, as set out in more detail in paragraphs C6 and C7, the cash flows may appear similar even where different accounting treatments are appropriate and considering the benefits in isolation will not normally enable a clear decision to be made. Rather, it is necessary to determine which party is exposed to the risks relating to the loans (both upside potential for gain and downside exposure to loss). E7

Analysis of risks

The benefit of cash payments of principal and interest are subject to the five risks outlined in paragraph E6. The first of these, credit risk, will be borne by the lender to the extent there is recourse to it for bad debts; if there is no such recourse, the transferee will bear the credit risk. E8

The second risk, slow payment, will be borne by the party that suffers (or benefits) if borrowers pay later (or earlier) than expected. If amounts are passed to the transferee only when received from the borrower, the transferee will bear this risk; if the lender pays amounts to the transferee regardless of whether it has received an equivalent payment from the borrower, the lender will bear it. E9

Interest rate risk will be borne by the lender where the interest it receives from the borrower and payments it makes to the transferee are not directly related*. Where any changes in the interest rate charged to the borrower are passed on to the transferee after a short administrative delay, the lender may not bear significant interest rate risk; however, where any delays are significant the lender will bear significant risk. E10

The lender will bear reinvestment risk where payments received from the borrower are not immediately passed on to the transferee but are reinvested by the lender for a E11

* *'Directly related' in this context means that either the interest rates paid and received are both fixed, or the two rates are tied to the same external rate eg LIBOR.*

period. An exception would be where the transferee is entitled to all of any interest actually earned (but no more) on the amounts reinvested by the lender.

E12 The final risk is moral risk. For either derecognition or a linked presentation to be appropriate, the lender must have taken all reasonable precautions to eliminate this risk such that it will not feel obliged to fund any losses. This will include ensuring that the arrangements for servicing the loans reflect the standards of commercial behaviour expected of the lender.

Derecognition

E13 Derecognition (ie ceasing to recognise the loans in their entirety) is appropriate only where the lender retains no significant benefits and no significant risks relating to the loans. In determining whether any benefit and risk retained are 'significant', greater weight should be given to what is more likely to have a commercial effect in practice.

E14 The three possible methods of transferring the benefits and risks relating to a loan are described in paragraph E2; each may result in derecognition in appropriate cases:

(a) A novation (ie the replacement of the original loan by a new one with the consequent release of the lender) will usually transfer all significant benefits and risks, provided that there are no side agreements that leave benefits and risks with the lender.

(b) An assignment (ie the transfer of the rights to principal and interest that constitute the original loan, whilst not transferring any obligations) may also transfer all significant benefits and risks, provided that, in addition to there being no side agreements that leave benefits and risks with the lender, there are no unfulfilled obligations (eg to supply additional funds in the event of a restructuring of the loan) and any doubts regarding intervening equitable rights are satisfied.

(c) A sub-participation (ie the entering into an additional non-recourse back-to-back agreement with the sub-participant rather than the transfer of any of the rights or obligations that constitute the original loan itself) may also transfer all significant benefits and risks, provided that the lender's obligation to pay amounts to the transferee eliminates its access to benefits from the loans but extends only to those benefits. Thus the sub-participant must have a claim on all specified payments from the loans but on only those payments, and there must be no possibility that the lender could be required to pay amounts to the sub-participant where it has not received equivalent payments from the borrower.* Where this is the case, the loans no longer constitute an asset of the lender, nor does the deposit placed by the sub-participant represent a liability; it will therefore be appropriate to derecognise the loans. Particular attention should be paid to the effect of the borrower asking for a rescheduling. The lender may, for commercial reasons, wish to agree to a rescheduling plan, whereas the sub participant may simply look to the lender for compensation if it is not repaid. Where the lender has an obligation (legal, commercial or other) to provide such compensation, derecognition will not be appropriate.

E15 Whilst the commercial effect of any particular transaction should be assessed taking into account all its aspects and implications, the presence of all of the following indicates that the lender has not retained significant benefits and risks, and derecognition is appropriate:

* *Where only part of the payments due under the original loan are eliminated in this way, it may be appropriate to derecognise only part of the original loan. This is addressed in paragraphs E19 and E20 below.*

(a) the transaction takes place at an arm's length price for an outright sale;
(b) the transaction is for a fixed amount of consideration and there is no recourse whatsoever, either implicit or explicit, to the lender for losses from whatever cause. Normal warranties given in respect of the condition of the loans at the time of the transfer (eg a warranty that no loan was in arrears at the time of transfer) would not breach this condition. However, warranties relating to the condition of the loans in the future or to their future performance (eg that loans will not move into arrears in the future) would breach the condition. Other possible forms of recourse are set out in paragraph 83; and
(c) the lender will not benefit or suffer in any way if the loans perform better or worse than expected. This will not be the case where the lender has a right to further sums that vary according to the future performance of the loans (ie according to whether or when borrowers pay, or according to the amounts borrowers pay). Such sums might take the form of an interest differential, deferred consideration, a performance-related servicing fee or payments under a swap.

Where any of these three features is not present, this indicates that the lender has retained benefits and risks relating to the loan and, unless these are insignificant, either a separate presentation or a linked presentation should be adopted.

Whether any benefit and risk retained are 'significant' should be judged in relation to those benefits and risks that are likely to occur in practice, and not in relation to the total possible benefits and risks. Where the profits or losses accruing to the lender are material in relation to those likely to occur in practice, significant benefit and risk will be retained, such that derecognition will not be appropriate and either a linked presentation or a separate presentation should be used. E16

Linked presentation

A linked presentation will be appropriate where, although the lender has retained significant benefits and risks relating to the loans, there is absolutely no doubt that its downside exposure to loss is limited to a fixed monetary amount. A linked presentation should be used only to the extent that there is both absolutely no doubt that the transferee's claim extends solely to cash collected from the loans, and no provision for the lender to keep or re-acquire the loans by repaying the transferee. The conditions that need to be met in order for this to be the case are set out in paragraph 27 and explained in paragraphs 81–86. E17

Separate presentation

Where the lender retains significant benefits and risks relating to the loans and the conditions for a linked presentation are not met, a separate presentation should be adopted. E18

Transfers of part of a loan

In some cases the amount received by the lender from the transferee represents only part of the original loan. As explained in paragraph 71, where the effect of the arrangement is that a part of the loan is transferred, derecognition of that part will be appropriate. This will be the case where each party has a proportionate share of all future cash collected from the loan (and of related profits and losses). For example, were the transferee to be entitled to 40 per cent of any cash flows from payments of both principal and interest as and when paid by the borrower (ie it does not receive cash if such payments are not made), the lender should cease to recognise 40 per cent of the loan. Conversely, if the lender bears losses in preference to the transferee and thus retains significant risk relating to the loans, derecognition of any part of them is E19 not appropriate. For example, were the transferee to have first claim on any cash flows arising from a portfolio of loans with the lender's share acting as a cushion to absorb any losses, the lender should continue to show the gross amount of the whole portfolio on the face of its balance sheet (although if the conditions for a linked presentation are met, it should be used).

E20 In other cases, the entire principal amount of a loan may be funded by the transferee, but there may be a difference between the interest payments due from the borrower and those the lender has agreed to pass on to the transferee. In such cases derecognition of a part of the original loan may still be appropriate provided that the lender's interest differential does not result in it bearing significant risks relating to the loan. For instance, if the lender's interest differential is fixed and is in substance no more than a fee for originating or administering the loan, derecognition will be appropriate. Conversely, if the lender's interest differential varies depending on the performance of the loan (as where it acts as a cushion to absorb losses or the lender bears interest rate risk), either a separate presentation or a linked presentation should be used. A linked presentation should be used only where the lender's maximum loss is capped, as might be the case where a variable rate loan is funded by a fixed rate one (if the lender's maximum loss is capped at the fixed interest payments due to the transferee). However, a linked presentation should not be used where the lender's maximum loss is not capped, as will be the case where a fixed rate loan is funded by a variable rate one, or where a loan in one currency is funded by a loan in another. The principles in this paragraph apply equally where the transferee funds only part of the principal amount of the original loan.

Administration arrangements

E21 Whether or not the lender continues to administer the loans is not, of itself, relevant to deciding upon the appropriate accounting treatment. However, the administration arrangements may affect where certain benefits and risks lie. For instance, where the lender's servicing fee is not an arm's length fee for the services provided, this indicates it has retained significant benefits and risks relating to the loans.

Required accounting

Derecognition

E22 Where the lender has retained no significant benefits and risks relating to the loans and has no obligation to repay the transferee, the loans should be removed from its balance sheet and no liability shown in respect of the amounts received from the transferee. A profit or loss may arise for the lender in the two ways set out in paragraph E3. Where the profit or loss is realised in cash it should be recognised, calculated as the difference between the carrying amount of the loans and the cash proceeds received. Where, however, the lender's profit or loss is not realised in cash and there are doubts as to its amount, full provision should be made for any expected loss but recognition of any gain, to the extent it is in doubt, should be deferred until cash has been received.

Linked presentation

E23 Where the conditions for a linked presentation are met, the proceeds received, to the extent they are non-returnable, should be shown deducted from the gross amount of the loans on the face of the balance sheet. Profit should be recognised and presented as set out in paragraphs 28 and 87–88. The notes to the financial statements should disclose: the main terms of the arrangement; the gross amount of loans transferred and outstanding at the balance sheet date; the profit or loss recognised in the period, analysed as appropriate; and the disclosures required by conditions (c) and (d) in paragraph 27.

Separate presentation

Where neither derecognition nor a linked presentation is appropriate, a separate presentation should be adopted, ie a gross asset (equivalent in amount to the gross amount of the loans) should be shown on the balance sheet of the lender within assets, and a corresponding liability in respect of the amounts received from the transferee should be shown within creditors. No gain or loss should be recognised at the time of the transfer (unless adjustment to the carrying value of the loan independent of the transfer is required). The notes to the financial statements should disclose the amount of loans subject to loan transfer arrangements that are outstanding at the balance sheet date. **E24**

Table

Indications that derecognition is appropriate (off lender's balance sheet)	**Indications that a linked presentation is appropriate**	**Indications that a separate presentation is appropriate (on lender's balance sheet)**
Transfer is for a single, non-returnable fixed sum.	Some non-returnable proceeds received, but lender has rights to further sums whose amount depends on whether or when the borrowers pay.	The proceeds received are returnable in the event of losses occurring on the loans.
There is no recourse to the lender for losses from any cause.	There is either no recourse for losses, or such recourse has a fixed monetary ceiling.	There is full recourse to the lender for losses.
Transferee is paid all amounts received from the loans (and no more), as and when received. Lender has no rights to further sums from the loans or the transferee.	Transferee is paid only out of amounts received from the loans, and lender has no right or obligation to repurchase them.	Lender is required to repay amounts received from the transferee on or before a set date, regardless of the timing or amounts of payments by the borrowers.

APPLICATION NOTE F – PRIVATE FINANCE INITIATIVE AND SIMILAR CONTRACTS

NB *In this Application Note the following terminology is used:*

(a) the entity (usually a public sector body) that acquires services under the Private Finance Initiative (PFI) contract is referred to as the 'purchaser'.

(b) the entity (usually a private sector body) that provides services under the PFI contract in return for payments from the purchaser is referred to as the 'operator'.

(c) the road, hospital, prison etc that is the subject of the PFI contract is referred to as the 'property'. The word 'asset' is reserved for items that are recognised in the balance sheet.

FEATURES

F1 Under a PFI contract, the private sector is responsible for supplying services that traditionally have been provided by the public sector. It is integral to most PFI contracts that the operator designs, builds, finances and operates a property in order to provide the contracted service. Examples of such properties are roads, bridges, hospitals, prisons, offices, information technology systems and educational establishments.

F2 The main features of a PFI contract are as follows:

(a) A contract to provide services is awarded by the purchaser (a public sector entity) to the operator (a private sector entity). The contract will specify the level of service required over the period of the contract. Usually, the contract also provides for a single ('unitary') payment to be made in each period, linked to factors such as availability, performance and levels of usage.

(b) A property, which is legally owned by or leased to the operator, will usually be necessary to perform the contracted service. Such properties include buildings (eg a prison or hospital), roads, railways, bridges, vehicles, and computer systems. Under the PFI contract, the operator will typically design, build, finance and operate the property. The contract may specify features or standards required of the property, for example, in order to satisfy statutory obligations of the purchaser. The property may or may not have potential for third-party use during the term of the PFI contract.

(c) The PFI contract will specify arrangements for the property at the end of the contract term (which may include various options available to one or both parties). Legal title to the property may pass to the purchaser for a fixed, perhaps nominal, price. Alternatively, or in addition, there may be provision to re-tender the PFI contract for a further term and for the property to pass to the successful new operator. In either of these cases the PFI contract may require the property to be maintained to a minimum standard or to have a stated remaining useful economic life at the end of the contract term. Further possibilities are that the operator retains legal title to the asset at the end of the PFI contract or that the purchaser acquires legal title to the property for its market value at the time.

(d) As a public sector body, the purchaser is required to demonstrate that the involvement of the private sector offers value for money when compared with alternative ways of providing the services. This is generally achieved by a transfer of risk from the public to the private sector.

F3 Contracts of a similar nature to PFI contracts exist between entities in the private sector, for example some contracts for warehousing and distribution services, where a property is necessary to perform the contracted service. This Application Note is relevant to such contracts.

ANALYSIS

Overview of basic principles

F4 Present practice is not to capitalise contracts for services. However, where a property is needed to fulfil a contract for services, present practice may require the property to be recognised as the purchaser's asset. (For example, this is the case for some take-

or-pay contracts where the operator builds a specialist property with little alternative use.) The purpose of the analysis below is to determine:

(a) whether the purchaser in a PFI contract has an asset of the property used to provide the contracted services together with a corresponding liability to pay the operator for it or, alternatively, has a contract only for services; and
(b) whether the operator has an asset of the property used to provide the contracted services or, alternatively, a financial asset being a debt due from the purchaser.

Under the general principles of the FRS, a party will have an asset of the property where that party has access to the benefits of the property and exposure to the risks inherent in those benefits. If that party is the purchaser, it will have a corresponding liability to pay the operator for the property where the commercial effect of the PFI contract is to require the purchaser to pay amounts to the operator that cover the cost of the property. F5

In some cases the contract may be separable, ie the commercial effect will be that elements of the PFI payments operate independently of each other. 'Operate independently' means that the elements behave differently and can therefore be separately identified. Where this is the case, and where some elements relate only to services (such as cleaning, laundry, catering etc) rather than to the property, any such service elements are not relevant to determining whether each party has an asset of the property and should be ignored. A contract may be separable in various circumstances (see paragraph F10). F6

Once any separable service elements have been excluded, PFI contracts can be classed into: F7

(a) those where the only remaining elements are payments for the property. These will be akin to a lease and SSAP 21 'Accounting for leases and hire purchase contracts' (interpreted in the light of the FRS) should be applied.
(b) other contracts (ie where the remaining elements include some services). These contracts will fall directly within the FRS rather than SSAP 21.

For those contracts that fall directly within the FRS, the question of whether a party has an asset of the property should be determined by looking at the extent to which each party would bear any variations in property profits (or losses). There are three important principles to be considered when undertaking such an analysis: F8

(a) A range of factors will be relevant in determining the extent to which each party would bear any variations in property profits (or losses) and it will be necessary to look at the overall effect of these factors when taken together.
(b) However, any potential variations in profits (or losses) that relate purely to a service should be excluded since it is only the property that may be included on the balance sheet of one of the parties, not the capitalised value of the whole service contract. Consequently, potential variations relating to the provision of services are not relevant to determining whether each party has an asset of the property.
(c) Paragraph 14 requires that, in determining the appropriate accounting treatment, greater weight should be given to those features that are more likely to have a commercial effect in practice. Where there is no genuine commercial possibility of a particular scenario or cash flow occurring, this scenario/cash flow should be ignored.

The principles outlined above are considered in more detail below, under the following headings: F9

- Separation of the contract
- Should SSAP 21 or the FRS be applied?
- How to apply SSAP 21
- How to apply the FRS

Subsequently, the required accounting is explained.

Separation of the contract

F10 In some cases the contract may be separable, ie the commercial effect will be that elements of the PFI payments operate independently of each other. 'Operate independently' means that the elements behave differently and can therefore be separately identified. Any such separable elements that relate solely to services should be excluded when determining whether each party has an asset of the property. In establishing whether the contract is separable, regard should be had to the terms of the contract and how the payments vary under different scenarios: it will not be relevant that the contract designates the payments as 'unitary' or, indeed, what labels they are given. In particular, where the PFI contract includes ancillary services, such as catering and cleaning, the payments for these services may be separable. A contract may be separable in a variety of circumstances, including but not limited to the following.

(a) The contract identifies an element of a payment stream that varies according to the availability of the property itself and another element that varies according to usage or performance of certain services.
(b) Different parts of the contract run for different periods or can be terminated separately. For example, an individual service element can be terminated without affecting the continuation of the rest of the contract.
(c) Different parts of the contract can be renegotiated separately. For example, a service element is market tested and some or all of the cost increases or reductions are passed on to the purchaser in such a way that the part of the payment by the purchaser that relates specifically to that service can be identified.

Should SSAP 21 or the FRS be applied?

F11 Paragraph 13 requires that where a transaction falls within the scope of both this FRS and another FRS or a SSAP, the standard that contains the more specific provision(s) should be applied. As explained in paragraph 45, for transactions that contain a stand-alone lease, SSAP 21 will be the relevant standard. Other transactions, in particular those containing a lease as an element of a larger arrangement, will fall within the FRS.

F12 A PFI contract will contain a stand-alone lease (so that SSAP 21, interpreted in the light of the FRS, should be applied) where the only elements remaining after excluding any separable service elements are payments for the property.

F13 Other PFI contracts, ie those where there are some non-separable service elements, will fall directly within the FRS.

FRS 5 APPLICATION NOTES

How to apply* SSAP *21

In applying SSAP 21, the key question is whether the lease is a finance lease, ie one that "transfers substantially all the risks and rewards of ownership of an asset to the lessee.* One indication of this is given by comparing the present value of the minimum lease payments with the fair value of the asset (often referred to as the '90 per cent test'). However, in many cases such a numerical test will not be required. The principal risks and rewards of ownership in a leasing context are usually demand and residual value. Where substantially all of the risks and rewards associated with these lie with the purchaser, it will be clear, without performing any calculations, that the lease is a finance lease (ie that the property is an asset of the purchaser). Only where there is a sharing of risk will a 90 per cent test be required. **F14**

Even where a 90 per cent test is used, it is important neither to apply this as the only test nor to apply a 90 per cent cut-off in a mechanistic way. The overriding principle is to establish whether the purchaser has substantially all of the risks and rewards of ownership. **F15**

Where a 90 per cent test is used, the question arises what rate should be used to discount the minimum lease payments. The principles underlying SSAP 21 require a discount rate that relates only to the property. A rate based in some way on the return from the entire PFI contract may **not** be a suitable rate to use since it will include an allowance for the risk relating to the service element of the contract. Where the service element is perceived as being riskier, relative to the property, this will give rise to a rate that is too high. Since a prerequisite for using SSAP 21 is that the payments for the property have been separated from those for services, it will usually be possible to derive such a property-specific rate from the PFI contract. Where sufficient information is not available, the rate should be estimated by reference to the rate that would be expected on a similar lease (ie a lease of a similar property in a similar location and for a similar term). The estimate of the rate should be reviewed together with (i) the present value of the lease payments, (ii) the assumed fair value of the property, and (iii) the assumed residual value, to ensure that all figures are reasonable and mutually consistent. **F16**

In determining what are the minimum lease payments, regard should be had to what is likely to have a commercial effect in practice. It follows that the minimum lease payments will comprise the expected PFI payments for the property, less any amount for which there is genuine possibility of non-payment. **F17**

A further factor to be taken into account is residual value risk. Where this risk both is significant and lies with the purchaser, it is normally evidence that the PFI contract in substance contains a finance lease and the property is an asset of the purchaser. An example is where the property has a material remaining useful economic life at the end of the PFI contract and is passed to the purchaser for a nominal or substantially fixed amount. **F18**

***How to apply the* FRS**

What variations are relevant?

For those contracts that fall directly within the FRS, whether a party has an asset of the property will depend on whether it has access to the benefits of the property and exposure to the associated risks. This will be reflected in the extent to which each **F19**

**SSAP 21, paragraph 15.*

FRS 5 APPLICATION NOTES

party bears the potential variations in property profits (or losses). The principle here is to distinguish potential variations in costs and revenues that flow from features of the property—which are relevant to determining who has an asset of the property (see paragraphs F22-F50) – from those that do not—and which are therefore not relevant to determining who has an asset of the property (see paragraph F20).

F20 There may be features that could lead directly to profit variations for reasons that relate purely to a service. Such variations may take the form of potential penalties for underperformance, or potential variations in revenues or in operating costs. These should be ignored when assessing who has an asset of the property, irrespective of their size. For example, a penalty may arise in a PFI contract for a prison because the security staff have not been trained satisfactorily, or in a PFI contract involving a catering facility because the food purchased is not up to standard. Similarly, potential variations in operating costs may relate purely to a service, for example the cost of raw materials and consumables in a catering facility. Such potential variations are irrelevant to determining which party has an asset of the property.

F21 There may be a significant number of property factors (for example, those listed in paragraph F22). It will be important to assess the effect of all relevant factors and the interaction between them, giving greater weight to those that are more likely to have a commercial effect in practice. It will not be appropriate to focus on one feature in isolation. It will be necessary to consider both the probability of any future profit variation arising from a property factor and its likely financial effect. Additional costs may be incurred to correct a problem rather than risking the imposition of a much greater penalty, in which case the relevant variation to consider is the likely increase in costs rather than the possible penalty. Similarly, a possible increase in future costs may be avoided by altering some feature of the property at a lower net cost, in which case the variation to consider is the cost of altering the property.

Factors relevant to the property

F22 As noted in paragraph F19, in applying the FRS the key test is to establish who will bear any variations in property profits (or losses). Depending on the particular circumstances, a range of factors may be relevant to this assessment of profit variation. The principal factors that, depending on the particular circumstances, may be relevant are:

- graphs F32–F34)
- who determines the nature of the property (see paragraphs F35–F37)
- penalties for underperformance or non-availability (see paragraphs F38 and F39)
- potential changes in relevant costs (see paragraphs F40 and F41)
- obsolescence, including the effects of changes in technology (see paragraphs F42 and F43)
- the arrangements at the end of the contract and residual value risk (see paragraphs F44–F48).

F23 The above list of the factors to be considered should be applied only with reference to the analysis given in paragraphs F24-F50. The key features of the analysis are summarised and illustrated in the table at the end of this Application Note.

Demand risk

F24 Demand risk is the risk that demand for the property will be greater or less than predicted or expected. Where demand risk is significant, it will normally give the clearest evidence of who should record an asset of the property. Demand risk is imposed by the economic conditions of the market in which the PFI contract is written. Its existence and significance cannot be altered by the terms of the contract; the contract can only allocate demand risk between the parties to the contract, for example by allowing renegotiation of the contract at certain demand levels.

The first step is to identify whether demand is a significant risk. There may be instances where there is little genuine uncertainty about the level of future demand for the services provided by the property. For example, in a short-term IT contract there may be very little likelihood of demand varying greatly from the levels predicted under the contract. In such a case, demand risk is not significant and little weight should be given to this test. In other cases there may be much genuine uncertainty over the extent to which a property will be used – for example, a new road to be built in a newly developed area. In these cases demand risk will be significant and who bears it will be highly relevant to determining the appropriate accounting treatment. **F25**

The length of the contract may influence the significance of demand risk. In general, demand risk will be greater the longer the term of the contract, since it is usually more difficult to forecast for later periods. **F26**

It is also important to distinguish where demand risk is insignificant from where the terms of the contract are such that it is passed to one or other party. For example, there may be much uncertainty over the demand for a certain type of property in the long term. However, the terms of a long-term PFI contract for such a property may be such that the purchaser would fill the PFI property in preference to properties not subject to PFI, with the effect that it is very unlikely that the PFI property will not be full. In such a case, the purchaser has retained demand risk. **F27**

Where it is established that demand risk is significant, it is necessary to determine who will bear it, ie who will bear the effects of reasonably likely changes in demand. This will depend on the answers to two interrelated questions: **F28**

(a) Will the payments between the operator and the purchaser reflect the usage of the property or does the purchaser have to pay the operator regardless of the level of usage (paragraphs F29 and F30)?
(b) Who will gain if demand is greater than expected (paragraph F31)?

Where the PFI payments do not vary substantially with demand or usage of the property (although they may vary with other factors), the purchaser will be obliged to pay for the output or capacity of the property (eg prison places, hospital beds) whether or not it is needed (ie whether or not there are sufficient prisoners or patients). This is evidence that the property is the purchaser's asset and the purchaser has a liability to pay for it. In particular, if the purchaser, in substance, is obliged to pay a minimum amount (ie there is no genuine commercial possibility of non-payment) whether or not it will need the property, and the minimum amount more than covers the cost of the property, this is evidence that the property is an asset of the purchaser. In making this assessment of demand risk, any penalties or reductions in payments for non-availability of the property should be ignored: these relate to whether the property is in a state fit for use and do not affect the incidence of demand risk. **F29**

Conversely, where the PFI payments will vary proportionately over all reasonably likely levels of demand, the purchaser will not be obliged to pay for the property to the extent it is not needed, which is evidence that the property is the operator's asset. **F30**

F31 In addition, the party that bears demand risk will gain if demand is greater than expected. If the purchaser bears demand risk, it will benefit from additional usage of the property at little or no extra property cost (for example, if payment for a hospital outpatients facility is largely independent of its usage, the purchaser will benefit from additional patients being treated when usage is high at little or no extra cost). This is evidence that the property is an asset of the purchaser. Conversely, if the operator bears demand risk, it will benefit from the increased payments that result from any additional usage of the property (for example, if payment for a hospital outpatients facility is based on throughput, the operator will benefit from additional usage payments when usage is high, although it may bear little or no extra cost). This is evidence that the property is an asset of the operator.

The presence, if any, of third-party revenues

F32 A feature of some PFI contracts is that the property is expected to be used by third parties. Where the operator relies on revenues from third parties to cover its property costs, this is evidence that the property is an asset of the operator.

F33 Conversely, where third-party usage is minimal or merely a future possibility, it is more likely that the property is an asset of the purchaser. This would particularly be the case where the purchaser in some way guarantees the operator's income from the property or where there is genuine scope for significant third-party use of the property but the purchaser significantly restricts such use.

F34 The existence of third-party revenues may be linked to the incidence of demand risk. For example, the purchaser may have the option to reduce its usage of the property, in which case the operator will attempt to find third parties to use the resulting spare capacity. If the purchaser's option is a genuine one with a real possibility of exercise, and if the operator bears a significant risk of a large fall in property income as a result, this is evidence that the property is an asset of the operator.

Who determines the nature of the property

F35 This factor relates to who determines how the PFI contract is to be fulfilled and, in particular, what kind of property (road, hospital etc) is to be built. Where in essence the purchaser determines the key features of the property and how it is to be operated, bearing the cost implications of any changes to the method of operation, this is evidence that the property is its asset. The purchaser may determine the key features of the property explicitly by agreeing them as terms of the PFI contract or, for example, through a contractual acceptance provision at the end of the construction phase. Alternatively, the purchaser may implicitly determine the key features of the property. For example, a contract for a road may specify that the road will revert to the purchaser in a predefined state after a relatively short period: this may have the effect that the operator has little discretion over the standard of road to build in the first instance or how it is maintained subsequently.

F36 Conversely, where the operator has significant and ongoing discretion over how to fulfil the PFI contract and makes the key decisions on what property is built and how it is operated, bearing the consequent costs and risks, this is an indication that the property is the operator's asset. For example, this would be the case if the operator is free to redesign the property extensively during the term of the contract (perhaps even to scrap the original property and build a replacement), in the hope of reducing its costs. Similarly, in a PFI contract to design, build and operate a road, the operator may have complete discretion over the balance between the quality of the original road built and the consequent level of maintenance costs.

Design risk is the risk that the design of the property is such that, even if it is constructed satisfactorily, it will not fully meet the requirements of the contract. This is part of the question of who determines the nature of the property, discussed above. In contrast, construction risk refers to who bears the financial implications of cost and time overruns during the construction period (and related warranty repairs caused by poor building work after the asset has been completed). Construction risk is not generally relevant to determining which party has an asset of the property once construction is completed, because such risk normally has no impact during the property's operational life. However, construction risk may be relevant where it calls into question the other evidence. In particular, if the purchaser is bearing construction risk in a project in which the property is claimed to be that of the operator, it will be necessary to look closely at the other terms of the transaction to determine whether the property really is the operator's asset and is not actually an asset of the purchaser. **F37**

Penalties for underperformance or non-availability

Many PFI contracts provide for penalties if the property is below a specified standard or is unavailable because of operator fault. (Penalties relating purely to services, however, are not relevant and should not be brought into the assessment.) These penalties may take the form of either cash payments or reductions in revenue. It will be important to assess both the likelihood of the penalty occurring in practice and whether the likely payments are significant. For example, a penalty may have little impact in practice because the contract gives the operator ample time to rectify the fault or the penalty is invoked only if the property is completely unavailable. Where, as in this example, potential penalties are either not significant or are unlikely to occur, this is evidence that the property is an asset of the purchaser. **F38**

Conversely, the penalty mechanism may have the effect that the operator's profits associated with the property are genuinely subject to significant potential variation. For example, a PFI contract for a road may contain penalty clauses if lanes are closed for more than a minimal period for maintenance, with the penalty being significant and having a reasonable possibility of occurring. This would be evidence that the property is an asset of the operator. **F39**

Potential changes in relevant costs

Potential changes in relevant costs may be dealt with in different ways under a PFI contract. (Only changes in property costs are relevant; changes in service costs are not relevant and should not be brought into the assessment.) The contract may have the effect that any significant future cost increases can be passed on to the purchaser, which would be evidence that the property is an asset of the purchaser. For example, this would be the case where the PFI payments will vary with specific indices so as to reflect the operator's costs. **F40**

Conversely, where the operator's costs are both significant and highly uncertain, and there is no provision for cost variations to be passed on to the purchaser, this is evidence that the property is an asset of the operator. For example, this would be the case where the payments are fixed or vary in relation to a general inflation index such as the Retail Prices Index. Similar considerations apply to any cost savings and how they are shared between the parties. **F41**

Obsolescence, including the effects of changes in technology

F42 Whether obsolescence or changes in technology are relevant will depend on the nature of the contract. In contracts for the introduction of information technology systems, it will be of great significance who bears the future costs and any benefits associated with obsolescence or changes in technology: in other cases (eg a roads contract) it is likely to be of much less significance.

F43 Where the potential for obsolescence or changes in technology are significant, the party that bears the costs and any associated benefits will be the one for whom there is evidence that the property is its asset.

The arrangements at the end of the contract and residual value risk

F44 Residual value risk is the risk that the actual residual value of the property at the end of the contract will be different from that expected. This risk is more significant the shorter the PFI contract is in relation to the useful economic life of the property. Where it is significant, residual value risk will normally give clear evidence of who should record an asset of the property. In part, residual value risk stems directly from the economic conditions of the market for the property, ie the rise or fall of prices relevant to the property. The price aspects of residual value risk cannot be reduced or increased by the contract. The contract can only influence those aspects of residual value risk relating to the condition of the property at the end of the contract.

F45 Where this risk is significant, who bears it will depend on the arrangements at the end of the contract. For example, the purchaser will bear residual value risk (providing evidence that the property is its asset) where:

(a) it will purchase the property for a substantially fixed or nominal amount at the end of the contract;
(b) the property will be transferred to a new operator, selected by the purchaser, for a substantially fixed or nominal amount; or
(c) payments over the term of the PFI contract are sufficiently large for the operator not to rely on an uncertain residual value for its return.

F46 Where the purchaser has an option to purchase the property or, alternatively, an option to 'walk' and leave the property with the operator, the practical effect of the option should be carefully analysed. In particular, where there is no genuine possibility that a purchase option will not be exercised (or, alternatively, that a 'walk' option will be exercised), the option will not transfer residual value risk to the operator.

F47 The significance of a minimal payment for the residual interest at the end of the contract depends on other features of the contract. If the property has a significant remaining useful economic life, such minimal payment will be evidence, in the absence of evidence to the contrary, that the purchaser paid for the property over the term of the PFI contract. This in turn is evidence that the property was an asset of the purchaser throughout.

F48 Conversely, the operator will bear residual value risk (providing evidence that the property is its asset) where:

(a) it will retain the property at the end of the PFI contract; or
(b) the property will be transferred to the purchaser or another operator at the prevailing market price.

Assessment of relevant factors

In determining whether each party has an asset of the property, it will not be appropriate to focus on one feature in isolation. Rather, the combined effect of all relevant factors should be considered for a range of reasonably possible scenarios, with greater weight being given to those outcomes that are more likely to occur in practice. **F49**

In addition, it will often be useful in weighing all the evidence to consider the position of the various parties to the transaction, including their apparent expectations and motives for agreeing to its various terms. For example, an assessment of the operator's financing* may indicate a level of debt funding that could be credible only if another party stood behind the operator. In such circumstances the PFI contract would be deemed a financing arrangement and thus indicate that the property is an asset of the purchaser. Similarly, a financing arrangement would be indicated where, in the event that the contract is terminated early, the bank financing will be fully paid out by the purchaser under all events of default, including operator default. **F50**

REQUIRED ACCOUNTING

Purchaser has an asset of the property

Where it is concluded that the purchaser has an asset of the property and a liability to pay for it, these should be recorded in its balance sheet. The initial amount recorded for each should be the fair value of the property.† Subsequently, the asset should be depreciated over its useful economic life and the liability should be reduced as payments for the property are made. In addition, an imputed finance charge on the liability should be recorded in subsequent years using a property-specific rate (paragraph F16 discusses how to determine such a rate). The remainder of the PFI payments (ie the full payments, less the capital repayment and the imputed financing charge) should be recorded as an operating cost. If the purchaser has any other obligations in relation to the PFI contract, these should be accounted for in accordance with FRS 12 'Provisions, Contingent Liabilities and Contingent Assets'‡ **F51**

Generally, the purchaser should recognise each property when it comes into use. An exception is where the purchaser bears significant construction risk, in which case it should recognise the property as it is constructed. **F52**

Purchaser does not have an asset of the property

Where it is concluded that the purchaser does not have an asset of the property, there may nevertheless be other assets or liabilities that require recognition. These can arise in respect of contributions, acquisition of the residual and other obligations of the purchaser. **F53**

**All aspects of the financing arrangements should be taken into account, eg the use of senior or subordinated debt and the presence of any guarantees.*

†*For a lease the sum to be recorded both as an asset and as a liability is the present value of the minimum lease payments, derived by discounting them at the interest rate implicit in the lease.*

‡*FRS 12 will be issued in September 1998 and it will be effective for accounting periods ending on or after 23 March 1999. (**Editor's note:** FRS 12 has now been issued.)*

FRS 5 APPLICATION NOTES

Contributions

F54 Contributions to a PFI contract by the purchaser may take a number of forms, including an up-front cash payment or the contribution of existing assets for development by the operator. The accounting treatment of such contributions depends on whether they give rise to future benefits for the purchaser. For example:

- If the contribution of an existing property results in lower service payments, the carrying amount of the property should be reclassified as a prepayment (current asset) and subsequently charged as an operating cost over the period of reduced PFI payments. If there is in effect a sale of part of the contributed asset (for example, a parcel of surplus land that is not used in the PFI contract), any profit should be recognised in accordance with paragraphs 23 and 24 (as explained in paragraphs 70–74).
- If the contribution does not give rise to a future benefit for the purchaser, it should be charged as an expense when the contribution is made. For example, a capital grant might be given for which the operator would have qualified even if the transaction had not been part of the PFI, or short-life assets might be donated to the contract for no value.

Acquisition of the residual

F55 In some PFI transactions, all or part of the property (eg the land element) will pass to the purchaser at the end of the contract. Where the contract specifies that this transaction should take place at market value at the date of transfer, no accounting is required until the date of transfer, as this represents future capital expenditure for the purchaser.

F56 Where the contract specifies the amount (including zero) at which the property will be transferred to the purchaser at the end of the contract, the specified amount will not necessarily correspond with the expected fair value of the residual estimated at the start of the contract. Any difference must be built up over the life of the contract in order to ensure a proper allocation of payments made between the cost of services under the contract and the acquisition of the residual. At the end of the contract the accumulated balance (whether positive or negative), together with any final payment, should exactly match the originally estimated fair value of the residual. For example, if the expected residual value at the end of a 30-year contact is £20 million, but the contract specifies that £30 million should be paid by the purchaser for that residual at that date, then a credit balance of £10 million should be accrued over the life of the contract, with the corresponding charge each year being included in the service expense. The payment of £30 million at the end of the contract will extinguish the balance of £10 million and establish an asset of £20 million, representing the value of the residual.

F57 If, during the life of the contract, expectations change so that the expected value of the residual falls (but there are no changes to the payments scheduled under the contract), then consideration should be given to whether there has been an impairment. Ultimately, a positive difference may become negative, in which case a provision is required. Using the example in paragraph F56, if the expected residual value fell to zero after five years, then an expense and a liability of £20 million would be recorded immediately. The remaining £10 million is still accrued over the life of the contract, giving a final liability of £30 million which is paid at the end of the contract.

Other obligations of the purchaser

If the purchaser has any other obligations in relation to the PFI contract, these should be accounted for in accordance with FRS 12 'Provisions, Contingent Liabilities and Contingent Assets'.* **F58**

Operator has an asset of the property

Where it is concluded that the operator has an asset of the property, it should record this asset in its balance sheet. The asset should initially be recorded at its cost and then depreciated to its expected residual value over its useful economic life (which, unless the property is to be retained by the operator on the expiry of the PFI contract, will be constrained by the term of the PFI contract). Where the contract specifies a sum for which the residual value will be transferred to the purchaser, the difference between the amount payable and the expected residual value should be accounted for in a similar way to the accounting treatment adopted by the purchaser (see paragraph F56), on the assumption that the difference is accounted for by higher or lower PFI payments during the life of the contract. If the operator is obliged to meet any liabilities as a result of the contract (eg environmental clean-up costs), these should be recorded separately, within liabilities. **F59**

Operator does not have an asset of the property

Where it is concluded that the operator does not have an asset of the physical property, it will, instead, have a financial asset, being a debt due from the purchaser for the fair value of the property. This asset should be recorded at the outset and reduced in subsequent years as payments are received from the purchaser. In addition, finance income on this financial asset should be recorded in subsequent years using a property-specific rate (paragraph F16 discusses how to determine such a rate). The remainder of the PFI payments (ie the full payments, less the capital repayment and the imputed financing charge) should be recorded within operating profit. **F60**

FRS 12 will be issued in September 1998 and it will be effective for accounting periods ending on or after 23 March 1999. (Editor's note:** FRS 12 has now been issued.)*

FLOW CHART

This flow chart summarises the decision route set out in this Application Note.

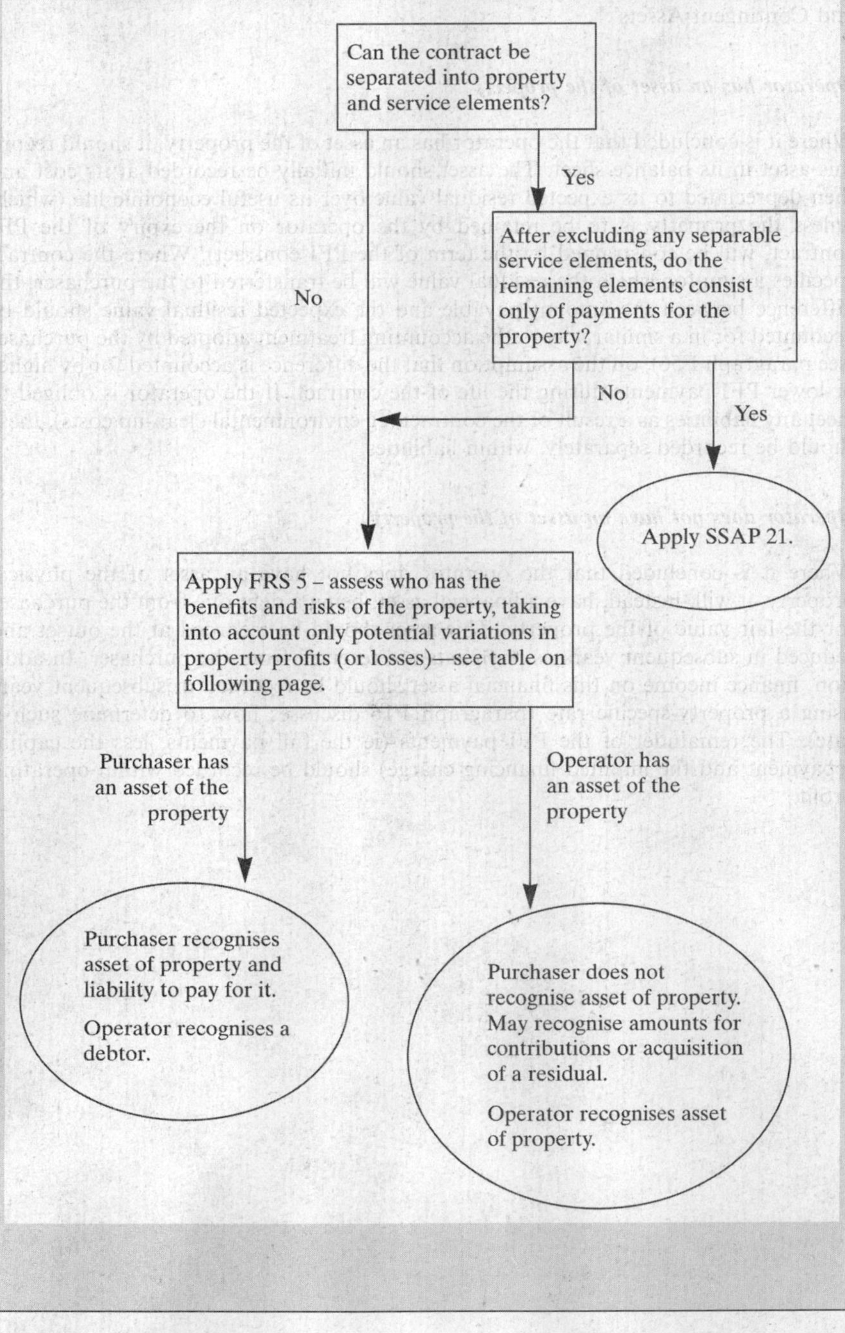
Can the contract be separated into property and service elements?
Yes
No
After excluding any separable service elements, do the remaining elements consist only of payments for the property?
No
Yes
Apply SSAP 21.
Apply FRS 5 – assess who has the benefits and risks of the property, taking into account only potential variations in property profits (or losses)—see table on following page.
Purchaser has an asset of the property
Operator has an asset of the property
Purchaser recognises asset of property and liability to pay for it.
Operator recognises a debtor.
Purchaser does not recognise asset of property. May recognise amounts for contributions or acquisition of a residual.
Operator recognises asset of property.

TABLE

Variations in profits/losses for the property, intransactions falling directly within the FRS rather than SSAP 21 Three principles govern the assessment of the indications set out below: • only variations in property profits/losses are relevant. • the overall effect of all of the factors taken together must be considered. • greater weight should be given to those factors that are more likely to have a commercial effect in practice	
Indications that the property is an asset of the purchaser	**Indications that the property is an asset of the operator**
Demand risk is significant and borne by the purchaser, eg (a) the payments between the operator and the purchaser will not reflect usage of the property so that the purchaser will have to pay the operator for the property whether or not it is used (b) the purchaser gains where future demand is greater than expected.	Demand risk is significant and borne out by the operator, eg (a) the payments between the operator and the purchaser will vary proportionately to reflect usage of the property over all reasonably likely levels of demand so that the purchaser will not have to pay the operator for the property to the extent it is not used (b) the operator gains where future demand is greater than expected.
There is genuine scope for significant third-party use of the property by the purchaser significantly restricts such use. The purchase in some way guarantees the operator's property income.	The property can be used, and paid for, to a significant extent by third parties and such revenues are necessary for the operator to cover its costs. The purchaser does not guaranteed the operator's property income.
The purchaser determines the key features of the property and how it will be operated.	The operator has significant ongoing discretion over what property is to e built and how it will be operated.f
Potential penalties for underperformance or non-availability of the property are either not significant or are unlikely to occur.	Potential penalties for underperformance or non-availability of the property are significant and have a reasonable possibility of occurring.
Relevant costs are both significant and highly uncertain, and all potential material cost variations will be passed on to the purchaser.	Relevant costs are both significant and highly uncertain, and all potential material cost variations will be borne by the operator.
Obsolescence or changes in technology are significant, and the purchaser will bear the costs and any associated benefits.	Obsolescence or changes in technology are significant, and the operator will bear the costs and any associated benefits.
Residual value risk is significant (the term of the PFI contract is materially less than the useful economic life of the property) and borne by the purchaser.	Residual value risk is significant (the term of the PFI contract is materially less than the useful economic life of the property) and borne by the operator.

Indications that the property is an asset of the purchaser	Indications that the property is an asset of the operator
The position of the parties to the transaction is consistent with the property being an asset of the purchaser, eg (a) the operator's debt funding is such that it implies the contract is in effect a financing arrangement (b) the bank financing would be fully paid out by the purchaser if the contract is terminated under all events of default including operator default.	The position of the parties to the transaction is consistent with the property being an asset of the operator, eg (a) the operator's funding includes a significant amount of equity (b) the bank financing would be fully paid out by the purchaser only in the event of purchaser default or limited force majeure circumstances.

APPENDIX APPLICATION NOTE G – REVENUE RECOGNITION

Introduction

G1 This Application Note deals with revenue recognition from the supply of goods or services by a seller to its customers. It sets out basic principles of revenue recognition which should be applied in all cases. It also provides specific guidance for:

- long-term contractual performance;
- separation and linking of contractual arrangements;
- bill and hold arrangements;
- sales with rights of return; and
- presentation of turnover as principal or as agent.

G2 The Application Note does not apply to the following arrangements:

- those resulting from transactions in financial instruments;
- those arising from insurance contracts; and
- those which are dealt with more specifically elsewhere in this, and other, accounting standards.

Definitions

G3 The following additional definitions apply in the Application Note:

Fair value

The amount at which goods or services could be exchanged in an arm's length transaction between informed and willing parties, other than in a forced or liquidation sale.

Performance

The fulfilment of the seller's contractual obligations to a customer through the supply of goods and services.

Right to consideration

A seller's right to the amount received or receivable in exchange for its performance. This right does not necessarily correspond to amounts falling due in accordance with a schedule of stage payments which may be specified in a contractual arrangement. Whilst stage payments will often be timed to coincide with performance, they may not correspond exactly. Stage payments reflect only the agreed timing of payment, whereas a right to consideration arises through the seller's performance.

Basic Principles

A seller recognises revenue under an exchange transaction with a customer, when, and to the extent that, it obtains the right to consideration in exchange for its performance. At the same time, it typically recognises a new asset, usually a debtor. G4

When a seller receives payment from a customer in advance of performance, it recognises a liability equal to the amount received, representing its obligation under the contract. When the seller obtains the right to consideration through its performance, that liability is reduced and the amount of the reduction in the liability is simultaneously reported as revenue. G5

A seller may obtain a right to consideration when some, but not all, of its contractual obligations have been fulfilled. Where a seller has partially performed its contractual obligations, it recognises revenue to the extent that it has obtained the right to consideration through its performance. G6

Revenue should be measured at the fair value of the right to consideration. Subject to paragraphs G8 - G9 or other evidence to the contrary, this will normally be the price specified in the contractual arrangement, net of discounts, value added tax and similar sales taxes. G7

Where the effect of the time value of money is material to reported revenue, the amount of revenue recognised should be the present value of the cash inflows expected to be received from the customer in settlement. The unwinding of the discount should be credited to finance income as this represents a gain from a financing transaction. G8

Where at the time revenue is recognised on a transaction there is a significant risk that there will be default on the amount of consideration due and the effect is material to reported revenue, an adjustment to the price specified in the contractual arrangement will be necessary to arrive at the amount of revenue to be recognised. G9

Subsequent adjustments to a debtor as a result of changes in the time value of money and credit risk should not be included within revenue. G10

Turnover

Turnover (which may be described as 'sales' in a seller's financial statements) is the revenue resulting from exchange transactions under which a seller supplies to customers the goods or services that it is in business to provide.* G11

**These transactions are often referred to as being part of the seller's 'operating activities'.*

FRS 5 APPLICATION NOTES

G12 A seller may enter into other exchange transactions such as the sale of fixed assets. Such transactions do not normally give rise to turnover, as they do not normally fall within the class of transactions set out in paragraph G11.*

Areas of specific guidance

G13 Although revenue recognition is normally straightforward, in a number of areas inconsistencies have arisen in practice. In addition to the basic principles outlined above, which should be applied in all cases, the Application Note addresses a number of specific types of transaction. These are confined to transactions that are generally regarded as giving rise to turnover.

Long-term contractual performance

G14 Statement of Standard Accounting Practice 9 'Stocks and long-term contracts' (SSAP 9) sets out requirements for accounting and disclosure under a long-term contract. The Application Note provides additional guidance on the recognition of turnover derived from such contracts, but does not amend the requirements of that accounting standard.

Features

G15 A seller's performance under a contractual arrangement with a customer for the design, manufacture or construction of a single substantial asset or the provision of a service may be significant in the context of the seller's overall business activities and fall into different financial periods.

G16 Recognition of turnover arising from these contractual arrangements on their completion, and not at interim stages, would result in the seller's financial statements reflecting the results relating to contracts that had been completed during the financial period, rather than its performance during the period. Therefore, in accordance with SSAP 9, the seller should recognise changes in its assets or liabilities, and related turnover, that represent the accrual, over the course of the contract, of its right to consideration.

Analysis

G17 The purpose of the analysis below is to assess how changes in a seller's assets or liabilities, and related turnover, that arise from its performance under an incomplete long-term contract should be recorded in its financial statements.

G18 A seller should recognise turnover in respect of its performance under a long-term contract when, and to the extent that, it obtains the right to consideration. This should be derived from an assessment of the fair value of the goods or services provided to its reporting date as a proportion of the total fair value of the contract. In some contracts, this proportion will correspond with the proportion of expenditure incurred in comparison with total expenditure; however, this will not always be the case. For all contracts, the guiding principle is to consider the stage of completion of the contractual obligations, which reflects the extent to which the seller has obtained the right to consideration (as defined in paragraph G3). As a result, different stages of contracts may vary in their relative profitability.

**For example, paragraph 20 of FRS 3 requires material profits or losses on the sale of fixed assets to be shown after operating profit.*

The fair values used should represent those applicable on inception of the contract, unless the contractual terms specify that changes in prices will be passed on to the customer. Paragraphs G22 - G42 may be relevant when attributing fair values to the goods or services which have been provided up to the seller's reporting date. G19

Required accounting

The application of SSAP 9 to the recording of a seller's long–term contractual performance results in the seller recognising turnover as contract activity progresses, to the extent that the outcome of the contract can be assessed with reasonable certainty. G20

The seller should recognise changes in its assets or liabilities, and turnover, in accordance with the stage of completion of its contractual obligations, which reflects the extent to which it has obtained the right to consideration. The amount of turnover recognised should be derived from the proportion of costs incurred only where these provide evidence of the seller's performance and hence the extent to which it has obtained the right to consideration. G21

Separation and linking of contractual arrangements

Features

A single contractual arrangement may require a seller to provide a number of different goods or services (or 'components') to its customers. These components may be unrelated and capable of being sold individually; alternatively, two or more components may be so closely related that their individual sale is not commercially feasible from either the seller's or the customer's perspective. G22

A seller may provide a number of goods or services to customers as a package, in which the amount payable is set below the price at which these items would be sold individually. G23

Analysis

The purpose of the analysis below is to determine whether, as a result of its performance: G24

(a) the seller should recognise a change in its assets or liabilities, and turnover, in respect of its right to consideration for each component on an individual basis; or

(b) two or more components should be combined and turnover recognised on that basis.

A contractual arrangement should be accounted for as two or more separate transactions only where the commercial substance is that the individual components operate independently of each other. 'Operate independently' means that each component represents a separable good or service that the seller can provide to customers, either on a stand alone basis or as an optional extra. Alternatively, one or more component(s) may be capable of being provided by another supplier. This separation for accounting purposes is frequently referred to as the 'unbundling' of a contractual arrangement. G25

G26 Conversely, the commercial substance of two or more separate contracts may require them to be accounted for as a single transaction. This is frequently referred to as the 'bundling' of a contractual arrangement.

G27 Where various components are to be unbundled, the seller should normally be capable of attributing a reliable fair value to each of them by reference to individual transactions. If various components are combined and sold at a price less than the total fair values of the individual components, the reduction should be allocated to each component pro rata to their fair values.

G28 Where it is not possible to attribute reliable fair values to every component, the seller may be able to unbundle the arrangement where reliable fair values can be obtained for either the completed or the uncompleted component(s). For example, where reliable fair values can be obtained only for the uncompleted components, the seller may be able to calculate by deduction a value for the completed components. Where a reliable fair value cannot be obtained for the uncompleted component(s), particular care must be taken to ensure that turnover is not overstated for the completed components. That is because the contract price may be set at a discount from the total amount at which the components would be sold individually.

Required accounting

Components operate independently of each other

G29 Where a contractual arrangement consists of various components that operate independently of each other and a reliable fair value can be attributed to every component, the seller should recognise changes in its assets or liabilities, and related turnover, in respect of its right to consideration for each component as if it were an individual contractual arrangement.

G30 Where reliable fair values can be attributed only to the uncompleted component(s), the fair value of the uncompleted component(s) should be deducted from the total fair value of the contract to derive the amount of turnover attributable to the completed component(s). Where reliable fair values cannot be attributed to the uncompleted component(s), particular care must be taken to ensure that turnover is not overstated for the completed components.

G31 Where reliable fair values cannot be attributed to individual completed or uncompleted components, the seller should recognise changes in its assets or liabilities, and turnover, for those components as a single, bundled, contractual arrangement. For example, where a contractual arrangement consists of three components and a reliable fair value can be attributed only to the second and third components combined, and not to any components individually, a fair value should be attributed to the first component in accordance with paragraph G30. The second and third components are then viewed together in accordance with paragraph G32 when determining the point at which changes in its assets or liabilities, and turnover, attributable to those components should be recognised by the seller.

Components do not operate independently of each other

G32 Where a contractual arrangement consists of various components that do not operate independently of each other, the seller should account for them together to reflect the seller's performance of its obligations as a whole in obtaining the right to consideration. Where the contractual arrangement meets the definition of a long-term contract in SSAP 9, it should be accounted for in accordance with that standard and paragraphs G14 - G21 of this Application Note.

Illustrations

Sales of software and related maintenance services

A customer may purchase 'off the shelf' packaged software from a seller, which also offers separately a support service that provides helpline assistance and advice about the package's operation. An analysis of the arrangement shows that the customer has no commercial obligation or requirement to purchase the support service; it is not needed for the software package to operate satisfactorily. The seller's performance is made up of two components and it should recognise turnover separately for each. **G33**

Conversely, a seller may enter into a contractual arrangement for the supply of bespoke software, together with its maintenance and the customer's right to future upgrades for a period of three years. An analysis of the arrangement shows that the maintenance and upgrades are required in order to ensure that the software continues to operate satisfactorily throughout the three year period and that these services are offered only by the supplier of the software. The commercial substance of the arrangement is therefore that the customer is paying for a three year service agreement. The seller should treat all three components (the software, the upgrades and the maintenance) as linked, and recognise turnover on a long-term contractual basis. **G34**

Inception fees

A contractual arrangement may require the payment of a fee at inception which permits the customer to purchase goods or services over a period of time. In determining when the seller should recognise turnover attributable to the fee, it should determine whether or not the fee and the charges for goods or services operate independently of each other. **G35**

The fee and the charges for goods or services may often together provide the seller's return on the contract as a whole. This may be the case, for example, where payment of the fee entitles the customer to purchase goods or services at lower prices than would otherwise be payable. In these circumstances the seller should record the fee as turnover on a systematic basis over the average period in which goods or services are expected to be provided to the customer. Before the seller has provided goods or services, it should report a liability for the fee to the extent that this has not been included in turnover. **G36**

Where it can be demonstrated that the seller has no further obligations to the customer in respect of the fee, the seller should record the fee as turnover on the date on which it becomes entitled to it. This may be the case, for example, where, notwithstanding payment of the fee, the customer is required to pay for all goods or services supplied under the arrangement at the current commercial rate. **G37**

Vouchers

A seller may, in a single transaction, sell goods or services and vouchers, where the vouchers are redeemable against future purchases from the seller. Where the fair value of the voucher is significant in the context of the transaction, revenue should be reported at the amount of consideration received or receivable less the fair value of the voucher issued. The latter represents a liability for future performance, which is **G38** extinguished and recognised in revenue when the voucher is tendered as part of the consideration on a future transaction.

G39 The fair value of a voucher will often be less than its face value. In determining the fair value of a voucher, regard should be paid to the terms of the voucher, including:

(a) the range of the goods or services which the customer can obtain on redemption of the vouchers;
(b) the discount the customer obtains when redeeming the voucher compared with the discount which might be obtained by customers who do not redeem vouchers;
(c) the length of time before which the right to use the voucher expires; and
(d) the extent to which the voucher is similar to other vouchers that are distributed to customers free of charge.

Regard should also be paid to the proportion of vouchers that are expected to be redeemed.

G40 An analysis of the above factors may indicate that the fair value of a voucher is not significant; in effect the issue of the voucher is an inducement to undertake a future transaction rather than being a separable component of the original transaction. In such circumstances, no adjustment is required to revenue at the time the voucher is issued.

G41 At each reporting date, the seller should review its estimated liability for outstanding vouchers having regard to experience of the proportion that are redeemed and expire. Adjustments to the estimate should be included within revenue.

G42 Vouchers distributed free of charge, independently of another transaction, do not give rise to a liability except where redemption of the voucher will result in products being sold at a loss. Where this is the case, the seller has entered into an onerous contract and provision will need to be made in accordance with FRS 12 'Provisions, Contingent Liabilities and Contingent Assets'. When the vouchers are redeemed, the seller should recognise revenue at the amount received for the product, ie after deducting the discount obtained for the vouchers.

Bill and hold arrangements

Features

G43 Under a bill and hold arrangement, a seller enters into a contractual arrangement with a customer for the supply of goods where there is transfer of title but physical delivery is deferred to a later date.

Analysis

G44 The purpose of the analysis below is to determine whether, in the circumstances described in paragraph G43, the seller should:

(a) recognise turnover and a right to consideration; or
(b) continue to recognise the goods as stock.

G45 In accordance with the general principles of the FRS the goods cease to be assets of the seller and become assets of the customer (and in exchange the seller obtains the right to consideration) when the seller transfers to the customer access to the significant benefits relating to the goods and exposure to the risks inherent in those benefits. From the customer's perspective, the principal benefits and risks include:

Benefits

(a) the right to obtain the goods as and when required;
(b) the sole right to the goods for their sale to a third party and the future cash flows from such a sale; and
(c) insulation from changes in prices charged by the seller (eg because the seller has revised its standard price list).

Risks

(a) slow movement, resulting in increased costs of financing and holding of the goods, and an increased risk of obsolescence; and
(b) being compelled to take delivery of goods that have become obsolete or not readily saleable, resulting in no onward sale or a sale at a reduced price.

In order for the seller to have the right to recognise changes in its assets or liabilities, and turnover, arising from its right to consideration in respect of the bill and hold arrangement, the terms of the contractual arrangement between the seller and the customer should include all of the following characteristics: **G46**

(a) the goods should be complete and ready for delivery;
(b) the seller should not have retained any significant performance obligations other than the safekeeping of the goods and their shipment when the customer requests this;
(c) subject to any rights of return, the seller should have obtained the right to consideration regardless of whether the goods are shipped, at the customer's request, to its delivery address. Where rights of return are granted, particular consideration is required of the commercial substance of the related sales, especially the transfer of risk. Rights of return are addressed at paragraphs G49-G59 below;
(d) the goods should be identified separately from the seller's other stock and should not be capable of being used to fill other orders that are received between the date of the bill and hold sale and shipment of the goods to the customer; and
(e) the bill and hold terms should be in accordance with the commercial objectives of the customer and not the seller. For example, where the delay in the delivery of the goods is to meet the customer's need for flexibility in the timing and location of delivery, and the conditions set out in paragraphs (a) to (d) above are met, it will be appropriate for the seller to recognise changes in assets or liabilities, and turnover.

Required accounting

Substance of the transaction is that the goods represent an asset of the customer

Where it is concluded that the stock is an asset of the customer, resulting in the seller having a right to consideration, the seller should recognise the related changes in its assets or liabilities, and turnover. **G47**

Substance of the transaction is that the goods represent an asset of the seller

G48 Where it is concluded that the stock remains an asset of the seller, it should be retained on the seller's balance sheet. Any amounts received from the customer should be included within creditors in accordance with paragraph G5.

Sales with rights of return

Features

G49 The terms of contractual arrangements may allow customers to return goods that they have purchased and obtain a refund or release from the obligation to pay.

G50 Rights of return may be included explicitly or implicitly within contractual arrangements. Alternatively, they may arise through statutory requirements.

Analysis

G51 The purpose of the analysis below is to determine the effect of rights of return on a seller's recognition of changes in its assets or liabilities, and turnover.

G52 The inclusion of rights of return in a contractual arrangement may affect both the quantification of the seller's right to consideration, compared to an otherwise identical arrangement which does not have these rights, and the point at which the seller should recognise that right. This is because rights of return give rise to a contractual obligation on the part of the seller to transfer economic benefits to its customer and in some cases oblige the seller to defer recognition of the sales transaction so long as substantially all of the risks associated with the goods are retained.

G53 The seller's recognition of its right to consideration and contractual obligation to transfer economic benefits to its customer in respect of rights of return are linked transactions. In consequence, changes in the seller's assets or liabilities should reflect the loss expected to arise from the rights of return. Turnover should exclude the sales value of estimated returns.

G54 A seller will generally be able to estimate reliably the sales value of returns, having regard to risk, which may be less than its maximum potential obligation. It will generally be possible to derive a reliable estimate from historical experience of the amount of comparable goods returned as a proportion of comparable sales.

G55 If a seller is unable to estimate reliably the expected value of returns, the maximum potential amount should be calculated in accordance with the terms of its contractual arrangement with the customer and excluded from turnover.

G56 In some cases, the risk of return may be so significant that substantially all of the risks associated with the goods are retained by the seller and accordingly the seller does not have the right to consideration. In such circumstances the seller should not recognise any changes in its assets or liabilities, and turnover, from the transaction. Any amounts received from the customer should be accounted for as a payment in advance, in accordance with paragraph G5.

Required accounting

A seller should record changes in its assets or liabilities, and turnover, to the extent that its performance has earned it the right to consideration, taking account of the expected loss in accordance with paragraphs 23 and 73. The amount recorded as turnover should exclude the sales value of estimated returns from the total sales value of the goods supplied to customers. G57

At each reporting date, the seller should review its estimate of returns, having regard to changes in expectations and the expiry of contractual rights of return. Subsequent adjustments to the estimate should be recorded within revenue. G58

Where a seller has been precluded from recognising changes in its assets or liabilities, and turnover, because substantially all of the risks associated with the goods are retained and so has not earned the right to consideration, it should recognise these changes and turnover on the earlier of the dates on which: G59

(a) it is capable of estimating the level of returns with reliability; and
(b) the right of return expires or is surrendered.

Presentation of turnover as principal or as agent

Features

A seller may act on its own account when contracting with its customers for the supply of goods in return for the right to consideration. In such transactions the seller is frequently referred to as a principal. G60

Alternatively, a seller may act as an intermediary, earning a fee or commission in return for arranging the provision of goods or services on behalf of a principal. In such transactions, the seller is frequently referred to as an agent. G61

Analysis

The purpose of the analysis below is to determine whether a seller obtains the right to consideration by performing its contractual obligations: G62

(a) as principal in an exchange transaction with its customer; or
(b) as agent in relation to a transaction between its principal and the principal's customer.

The general principles of the standard require that, in order for a seller to account for exchange transactions as principal, it should normally have exposure to all significant benefits and risks associated with at least one of the following: G63

(a) Selling price: the ability, within economic constraints, to establish the selling price with the customer, either directly or, where the selling price of an item is fixed, indirectly by providing additional goods or services or adjusting the terms of a linked transaction; or
(b) Stock: exposure to the risks of damage, slow movement and obsolescence, and changes in suppliers' prices.

Where the seller has not disclosed that it is acting as agent, there is a rebuttable presumption that it is acting as principal. G64

Additional factors which indicate that a seller may be acting as principal include: G65

(a) performance of part of the services, or modification to the goods supplied;
(b) assumption of credit risk; and
(c) discretion in supplier selection.

G66 In contrast, where a seller acts as agent it will not normally be exposed to the majority of the benefits and risks associated with the exchange transaction. Agency arrangements will typically include the following characteristics:

(a) the seller has disclosed the fact that it is acting as agent;
(b) once the seller has confirmed its customer's order with a third party, the seller will normally have no further involvement in the performance of the ultimate supplier's contractual obligations;
(c) the amount that the seller earns is predetermined, being either a fixed fee per transaction or a stated percentage of the amount billed to the customer; and
(d) the seller bears no stock or credit risk, other than in circumstances where it receives additional consideration from the ultimate supplier in return for its assumption of this risk.

Required accounting

Seller acts as principal

G67 Where the substance of a transaction is that the seller acts as principal, it should report turnover based on the gross amount received or receivable in return for its performance under the contractual arrangement.

Seller acts as agent

G68 Where the substance of a transaction is that the seller acts as agent, it should report as turnover the commission or other amounts received or receivable in return for its performance under the contractual arrangement. Any amounts received or receivable from the customer that are payable to the principal should not be included in the agent's turnover.

Illustrations

G69 A seller acts as a building contractor for the construction of a new office block. An analysis of the arrangement shows that the terms of the seller's contract with its customer include a negotiated selling price, credit risk for amounts due from the customer, primary responsibility for the construction and quality of the new building and discretion as to whether it carries out the work itself or employs subcontractors. The seller is acting as principal and should account for the gross amount of turnover, regardless of whether it carries out the work itself or employs subcontractors to carry out part or all of the construction activities.

G70 A seller acts as an online retailer from a website, where it advertises holidays. An analysis of the arrangement shows that it acts as an intermediary between its customers and the ultimate sellers of the holidays and that it does not set the selling price. Its contractual terms of business include an exclusion of any liability to its customers once they have been put in touch with the ultimate sellers. The seller is paid a fee for each customer that purchases a holiday from an ultimate seller and has no involvement in the transaction after it has put the customer in touch with the ultimate seller. The seller is acting as agent and its turnover should include only the fees it receives from the ultimate seller.

A department store provides space for concessionaires to sell products and receives a fixed amount of rental income from the concessionaire. An analysis of the factors discussed in paragraphs G63 - G66 shows that the concessionaire is acting as principal in an exchange transaction with its customers and is entitled to the amounts received from the sale of the goods and services. In these circumstances, the concessionaire should include within its turnover the amounts received or receivable in respect of the sale of the goods and services. The department store should not include within its turnover the value of the concessionaire's sales. **G71**

Disclosure - seller acts as agent

Where a seller acts as agent, it is encouraged, where practicable, to disclose the gross value of sales throughput as additional, non-statutory information. Where such disclosure is given, a brief explanation of the relationship of recognised turnover to the gross value of sales throughput should be given. **G72**

Adoption of FRS 5 by the Board

Financial Reporting Standard 5 – 'Reporting the Substance of Transactions' was approved for issue by the nine members of the Accounting Standards Board.

David Tweedie	(Chairman)
Allan Cook	(Technical Director)
Robert Bradfield	
Ian Brindle	
Sir Bryan Carsberg	
Michael Garner	
Raymond Hinton	
Donald Main	
Graham Stacy	

'Amendment to FRS 5 "Reporting the Substance of Transactions": Private Finance Initiative and Similar Contracts – September 1998' (Application Note F) was approved for issue by the ten members of the Accounting Standards Board.

Sir David Tweedie	Chairman
Allan Cook	Technical Director
David Allvey	
Ian Brindle	
Dr John Buchanan	
John Coombe	
Raymond Hinton	
Huw Jones	
Professor Geoffrey Whittington	
Ken Wild	

'Amendment to FRS 5 "Reporting the Substance of Transactions": Revenue Recognition – November 2003' was approved for issue by a vote of eight of the nine members of the Accounting Standards Board. Mr Wild dissented.

Members of the Accounting Standards Board

Mary Keegan	Chairman
Allan Cook CBE	Technical Director
Douglas Flint	
Huw Jones	
Roger Marshall	
Isobel Sharp	
John Smith	
Jonathan Symonds	
Ken Wild	

Appendix I
Note on legal requirements

GREAT BRITAIN

References are to the Companies Act 1985*

Group accounts

Definitions of 'parent undertaking' and 'subsidiary undertaking' are set out and explained in section 258 and Schedule 10A. 1

Other provisions of the Companies Act relevant to the preparation of consolidated accounts are given in paragraphs 95 and 96 of FRS 2 'Accounting for Subsidiary Undertakings'. 2

The requirement to show a true and fair view 3

Section 227 provides the following:

"(1) If at the end of a financial year a company is a parent company the directors shall, as well as preparing individual accounts for the year, prepare group accounts.

(2) Group accounts shall be consolidated accounts comprising –

(a) a consolidated balance sheet dealing with the state of affairs of the parent company and its subsidiary undertakings, and

(b) a consolidated profit and loss account dealing with the profit or loss of the parent undertaking and its subsidiary undertakings.

(3) The accounts shall give a true and fair view of the state of affairs as at the end of the financial year, and the profit or loss for the financial year, of the undertakings included in the consolidation as a whole, so far as concerns members of the company.

(4) A company's group accounts shall comply with the provisions of Schedule 4A as to the form and content of the consolidated balance sheet and consolidated profit and loss account and additional information to be provided by way of notes to the accounts.

(5) Where compliance with the provisions of that Schedule, and the other provisions of this Act, as to the matters to be included in a company's group accounts or in the notes to those accounts, would not be sufficient to give a true and fair view, the necessary additional information shall be given in the accounts or in a note to them.

***Editor's note:** *The various statutory references change with the introduction of the Companies Act 2006, which affects accounting for periods beginning on or after 6 April 2008. The various statutory references have changed as follows:*

Companies Act 1985 reference	***Companies Act 2006 reference***
Section 258	*Section 1162*
Schedule 10A	*Schedule 7*
Section 227	*Sections 399, 403 and 404, although these are substantially different as noted below*
Paragraph 5 Schedule 4	*Paragraph 8 of Schedule 1 to the Large and Medium-sized Companies and Groups (Accounts and Reports) Regulations 2008 (SI 2008/410)*
Paragraph 14 Schedule 4	*Paragraph 15 of Schedule 1 to the Large and Medium-sized Companies and Groups (Accounts and Reports) Regulations 2008 (SI 2008/410)*

(6) If in special circumstances compliance with any of those provisions is inconsistent with the requirement to give a true and fair view, the directors shall depart from that provision to the extent necessary to give a true and fair view.

Particulars of any such departure, the reasons for it and its effect shall be given in a note to the accounts."*

Section 255A(6) states that, in the case of a banking or insurance company, the references to the provisions of Schedule 4A in section 227(5) and (6) shall be read as references to those provisions as modified by Part II of Schedule 9.

Offset

4 The Companies Act contains the following provisions relating to offset:

Schedule 4 paragraph 5 (an identical requirement for banking companies and groups is contained in Schedule 9 paragraph 5)

> 'Amounts in respect of items representing assets or income may not be offset against amounts in respect of items representing liabilities or expenditure (as the case may be), or vice versa.'

Schedule 4 paragraph 14 (an identical requirement for banking companies and groups is contained in Schedule 9 paragraph 21)

> 'In determining the aggregate amount of any item the amount of each individual asset or liability that falls to be taken into account shall be determined separately.'†

NORTHERN IRELAND

5 The legal requirements in Northern Ireland are identical to those in Great Britain. In particular:

Article 266 of and Schedule 10A to the Companies (Northern Ireland) Order 1986 are identical to section 258 of and Schedule 10A to the Companies Act 1985 as referred to in paragraph 1 above.

Other provisions of companies legislation relevant to the preparation of consolidated accounts, as referred to in paragraph 2 above, are given in paragraph 97 of FRS 2 'Accounting for Subsidiary Undertakings'.

Articles 235 and 263A(5) of the Companies (Northern Ireland) Order 1986 are identical to sections 227 and 255A(5) respectively of the Companies Act 1985 as referred to in paragraph 3 above.

Paragraphs 5 and 14 of Schedule 4 to the Companies (Northern Ireland) Order 1986 are identical to paragraphs 5 and 14 of Schedule 4 to the Companies Act 1985 as referred to in paragraph 4 above.

***Editor's note:** *Section 227 was substantially redrafted, to reflect the fact that the Companies Act 1985 was amended to allow companies to produce financial statements under IFRS as well as UK GAAP. The changes have been carried over into sections 399, 403 and 404 of the Companies Act 2006.*

†**Editor's note:** *The requirements for banking companies are now reflected in Schedule 2 to the Large and Medium-sized Companies and Groups (Accounts and Reports) Regulations 2008 (SI 2008/410), whilst those for insurance companies are reflected in Schedule 3 to the same statutory instrument.*

REPUBLIC OF IRELAND

The legal requirements in the Republic of Ireland are similar to those in Great Britain. In particular: **6**

Regulation 4 of the European Communities (Companies: Group Accounts) Regulations 1992 is similar to section 258 of and Schedule 10A to the Companies Act 1985 as referred to in paragraph 1 above.

Other provisions of companies legislation relevant to the preparation of consolidated accounts, as referred to in paragraph 2 above, are given in the insert replacing paragraph 98 of FRS 2 'Accounting for Subsidiary Undertakings'.

Regulations 5, 13 and 14 of the European Communities (Companies: Group Accounts) Regulations 1992 are similar to section 227 of the Companies Act 1985 as referred to in paragraph 3 above. As regards banks, section 5(1) of the European Communities (Credit Institutions: Accounts) Regulations 1992 is similar to section 255A(5) of the Companies Act 1985 as referred to in paragraph 3 above. Pending implementation of the EC Insurance Accounts Directive (91/674 EC) there is no legislation similar to section 255A(5) for insurance companies.

Sections 4(11) and 5(e) of the Companies (Amendment) Act 1986 are similar to paragraphs 5 and 14 of Schedule 4 to the Companies Act 1985 as referred to in paragraph 4 above.

Appendix II
Compliance with International Accounting Standards

There is no International Accounting Standard on this subject. The International Accounting Standards Committee (IASC) has issued a 'Framework for the Preparation and Presentation of Financial Statements'. The definitions of assets and liabilities set out in the FRS and the principles underlying it are similar in all material respects to those set out in the IASC's Framework. However, neither International Accounting Standards nor the Framework currently envisage use of a linked presentation for certain non-recourse finance as required by paragraphs 26–28 of the FRS.*

* ***Editor's note:*** *IAS 18 Revenue deals with revenue recognition and is now covered by Application Note G to FRS 5. IFRIC 12 now deals with service concessions, covering similar areas to those included in Application Note F.*

Appendix III
The development of the FRS

GENERAL

The problems of what is commonly referred to as 'off balance sheet financing' became evident during the 1980s. In that period, a number of complex arrangements were developed that, if accounted for in accordance with their legal form, resulted in accounts that did not report the commercial effect of the arrangement. In particular, concern grew over arrangements for financing a company's operations in such a way that, if the arrangement were accounted for merely by recording its legal form, the finance would not be shown as a liability on the balance sheet. 1

At the same time, there was rapid innovation in financial markets. New arrangements for financing assets were developed, the accounting for which was not immediately obvious. An example of one such arrangement is securitisation, whereby an asset and its non-recourse finance are tightly ring-fenced using a separate vehicle company. 2

These developments raised fundamental questions about the nature of assets and liabilities and when they should be included in the balance sheet. Questions were also raised about the accounting for some transactions that had been used by businesses for many years. For example, some queried whether factoring should be accounted for as a secured loan rather than as a sale of debts. 3

The FRS has been developed to address these issues and to deal with the problems caused by the misleading effects that 'off balance sheet financing' can have on the accounts. As that term indicates, the most widely recognised effect is the omission of liabilities from the balance sheet. However, the assets being financed, as well as the finance itself, are excluded, with the result that both the resources of the entity and its financing are understated. There may also be important effects on the profit and loss account. For instance, a profit may be reported on a 'sale' that is, in substance, a secured loan. As another example, what is in substance a finance charge may be either omitted from the profit and loss account altogether or described as some other kind of expense. All of these effects make it harder for the reader of the accounts to assess the true economic position of the reporting entity because they obscure the true extent and nature of its borrowings, its assets and the results of its activities. 4

The Board believes that financial statements should represent faithfully the commercial effects of the transactions and other events they purport to represent. This requires transactions to be accounted for in accordance with their substance and not merely their legal form, since the latter may not fully indicate the commercial effect of the arrangements entered into. 5

HISTORY OF DOCUMENTS ISSUED

TR 603

The first authoritative document to address this issue was Technical Release 603 (TR 603) – 'Off Balance Sheet Financing and Window Dressing', issued in December 1985 by the Institute of Chartered Accountants in England and Wales. The main provision of this short, preliminary document was that, in determining the accounting treatment of transactions, their economic substance rather than their mere legal form should be considered. 6

ED 42

7 TR 603 was followed by ED 42 'Accounting for special purpose transactions', which was issued in March 1988 by the Accounting Standards Committee (ASC). ED 42 took a general approach, providing guidance that could be applied to a variety of situations, rather than specifying detailed rules for specific transactions. It proposed that assets and liabilities arising from off balance sheet transactions be included in the balance sheet rather than merely disclosed in the notes. For this purpose, ED 42 described the essential characteristics of assets and liabilities. It also proposed that 'controlled non-subsidiaries' should be consolidated as if they were subsidiaries as legally defined. The definition of a controlled non-subsidiary was substantially the same as that of a quasi-subsidiary given in FRS 5.

ED 49

8 ED 49 'Reflecting the substance of transactions in assets and liabilities' was issued by the ASC in May 1990. ED 49 responded to the comments received on ED 42 as well as certain changes in the law. The ED continued to take a general approach, proposing analysis of the substance of transactions by reference to the essential characteristics of assets and liabilities. It also continued to propose that controlled non-subsidiaries should be consolidated in group accounts, although these vehicle entities were renamed 'quasi subsidiaries'. The main changes from ED 42 were: the inclusion, for the first time, of general recognition tests; the inclusion of Application Notes specifying how the draft standard was to be applied to five specific transaction types (including securitisation and factoring) – these were included at the specific request of commentators to ED 42 and their inclusion was later supported by the majority of commentators to ED 49; and the addition of guidance on identifying control.

Bulletin 15

9 Respondents to ED 49 raised, inter alia, the concern that the treatment it proposed for factoring was inconsistent with that proposed for securitisation. This led the Accounting Standards Board to review the accounting for securitisation and, in October 1991, to issue proposals (in Bulletin 15) under which most securitised assets would be shown on the balance sheet, the arrangement being accounted for as a secured loan. This was on the grounds that, in most securitisations, the originating entity retains significantly all of the profits from the securitised assets. Although the entity has strictly limited its exposure to losses on those assets, the same is true for other non-recourse finance arrangements and for limited liability subsidiaries, where it is accepted that assets and liabilities should be reported gross.

10 The respondents to Bulletin 15 were divided on whether securitisations should be accounted for on balance sheet as a secured loan, or off balance sheet as a sale. Views on both sides of the argument were strongly held, reflecting different beliefs about the primary purpose of the balance sheet. Those who favoured securitisations being accounted for on balance sheet believed that the primary use of the balance sheet is in assessing the amounts, timing and certainty of future cash flows. In their view, the total resources that underlie these future cash flows (and on which income will be earned in the future) should be shown on one side of the balance sheet, and the means by which they are financed should be shown on the other. They also pointed out that typically, the originating entity continues to gain significantly all the profits from the securitised assets and to be exposed to all those losses likely to occur in practice.

Those respondents who favoured securitisations being accounted for as a sale and therefore off balance sheet believed that the primary use of the balance sheet is in assessing the maximum possible loss to which the entity is exposed. They thought that the accounting treatment of securitisations (and perhaps other forms of non-recourse finance) should concentrate on showing that the originating entity has a limited downside exposure to loss, and that only a net asset of the amount to which the entity is exposed should be presented. **11**

The Board debated in detail the issues raised by the respondents and also consulted numerous interested parties. It concluded that users of accounts need to know both the entity's gross resources and finance (as these determine the size of its future income) and the net amount of these (as this is the maximum loss the entity can suffer). Hence the Board developed a new kind of presentation – a 'linked presentation' – under which the finance is deducted from the gross securitised assets on the face of the balance sheet. This presentation shows the gross resources that underlie the business (and on which income will be earned in the future), yet highlights that the entity has a strictly limited exposure to loss. **12**

FRED 4

Finally, in February 1993, the Board issued FRED 4 'Reporting the Substance of Transactions'. This carried through the general principles set out in ED 49 with only two major changes. The first was the introduction of proposals for a linked presentation for certain forms of non-recourse finance (including securitisations), as described above. These proposals attracted general support and are retained in the FRS with only one minor change which is described in paragraphs 29–32 below. **13**

The only other major change from ED 49 was the inclusion of detailed criteria for when items may be offset in accounts. These prohibited offset of amounts denominated in different currencies or bearing interest on different bases, on the grounds that, for two items to be offset, they must exactly eliminate one another. Such elimination would not be present where the items were in different currencies or bore interest on different bases, because of the currency or interest rate risk that was present. It was therefore proposed that the two items should not be offset but should be reported as separate assets and liabilities. This proposal has been modified in the FRS, in the light of comments received, as described below. **14**

Other, less significant changes from ED 49 were: the inclusion of definitions of assets and liabilities as opposed to a description of their 'essential characteristics' (these definitions are drawn from the Board's draft Statement of Principles); the provision of more guidance on accounting for transactions with options; the inclusion, for the first time, of criteria for when assets should cease to be recognised; the introduction of a distinction between control of an asset and control of another entity; and changes to some of ED 49's recognition tests, including removing the proposal that recognition be based on a 'reasonable accounting analogy'. **15**

Matters considered in the light of responses to FRED 4

Most of the respondents to FRED 4 agreed with its principal proposals and these have been largely retained in the FRS. The following paragraphs describe those points on which respondents expressed concern and, where appropriate, explain, with reasons, the changes the Board has made to the proposals of FRED 4 or the Board's reasons for not adopting a change. **16**

Complexity of the FRS

17 Several respondents expressed concern that FRED 4 was complex and difficult to understand. In part, this complexity stemmed from the inclusion of proposals for a linked presentation as set out above. Another reason for the FRED being difficult to understand was its general approach of specifying principles applicable to all transactions rather than detailed rules for specific situations. Whilst this general approach was supported, there was concern that the resulting principles appeared somewhat abstract and difficult to comprehend on a first reading.

18 To meet these concerns, the structure and drafting of the FRED have been reviewed and, where possible, simplified. In addition, the Explanation section to the FRS gives examples where appropriate. However, the Board believes this is a complex area that cannot be reduced to a few simple rules without the danger of over-simplification. Indeed, simple rules, mechanically applied, would result in accounts that do not report substance.

Offset

19 As noted above, FRED 4 proposed prohibiting offset of amounts denominated in different currencies or bearing interest on different bases but asked for comments on this prohibition. The majority of those who commented favoured either allowing or requiring offset of such items. Their reasons included: that the balance sheet does not, in general, show currency or interest rate exposures, hence grossing up the items does not necessarily allow a better assessment of these risks; that the currency or interest rate risk may be hedged such that the risk portrayed by grossing up may, in fact, no longer exist; that given freely accessible and liquid foreign exchange markets, monetary items in different currencies can be regarded as being freely convertible, and essentially a single item; and that the balance sheet should focus on portraying credit risk since users expect to get information about credit risk from the balance sheet, but not about currency or interest rate risks. A majority of the Board is persuaded by these arguments and, accordingly, the FRS requires offset of amounts denominated in different currencies or bearing interest on different bases provided that certain criteria are met.

20 The Board also considered whether it should require disclosure of amounts in different currencies or bearing interest on different bases that have been offset. Such disclosure would allow the user to draw up a balance sheet incorporating all items that do not exactly eliminate one another. However, such a balance sheet would give only part of the information needed to assess the entity's exposure to currency and interest rate risk. For a full assessment, it would be necessary to disclose the currency and interest rate profile of all recognised assets and liabilities as well as the effects of 'off balance sheet' instruments such as swaps and options. The Board decided that it was not yet in a position to specify comprehensive disclosure of such risks and that to require disclosures that gave only partial information on currency and interest rate risk would be potentially misleading. Accordingly, the FRS does not require disclosure of amounts that have been offset.

21 FRED 4 also proposed prohibiting offset where the right to settle net was contingent (for example on the counterparty going into liquidation). This was on the basis that as such contingent rights could not have been exercised at the balance sheet date, they should not be reflected in the assets and liabilities reported at that date. After reviewing the comments on this issue, the Board decided that provided: (a) the right to settle net can be invoked in all situations of default; and (b) the entity's debit balance matures no later than its credit balance, the amounts should be offset. This is

because in such a situation there is no possibility that the entity could be required to pay out its credit balance without first having recovered its debit balance.

Finally, FRED 4 did not propose the approach taken in US and certain other overseas accounting standards that require for offset that the reporting entity intends to settle net; FRED 4 required merely that the reporting entity has the ability to do so. The reason FRED 4 did not propose this approach is that the intended manner of settlement is essentially a matter of administrative convenience and does not affect the economic position of the parties. This reasoning was supported by commentators and, accordingly, the conditions given in the FRS for offset are not based on the intent of the reporting entity. **22**

Ceasing to recognise assets

FRED 4 contained criteria for when assets should cease to be recognised. These required both that no significant access to benefits was retained and that any risk retained was immaterial. Commentators were particularly concerned over the second of these conditions: for instance that it might require continued recognition of an asset sold with a residual value guarantee or of a subsidiary sold with deferred performance-related consideration. **23**

As a result, the FRS distinguishes three types of transactions. The first is transactions that transfer all significant rights to benefits relating to an asset and all significant exposures to the risks inherent in those benefits. For such transactions, the asset should cease to be recognised in its entirety. Conversely, where a transaction transfers no significant rights to benefits relating to an asset or no significant exposures to their inherent risks, the asset should continue to be recognised in its entirety. The third type of transaction comprises those special cases where not all significant benefits and risks have been transferred, but it is necessary to amend the description or monetary amount of the original asset or to recognise a new liability for any obligations assumed. Examples of this third type of transaction are given in paragraphs 71–73. **24**

Contracts for future performance

For the avoidance of doubt, the Board decided that contracts for future performance, such as swaps, forward contracts and purchase commitments, should be removed from the scope of the FRS, except where they are merely a part of a transaction (or of a connected series of transactions) that falls within the FRS. The accounting for such contracts is a complex area that requires further research and consultation before an FRS dealing with their accounting could be issued. **25**

Options

FRED 4's approach to options and the new guidance it contained were generally supported. However, the comments revealed some uncertainty over the approach to be taken to options for which there is a genuine commercial possibility both that the option will be exercised and that it will not be exercised, but the transaction is structured such that one or other outcome is significantly more likely. The FRS provides that the commercial effect of an option should be assessed in the context of all the aspects and implications of the transaction. It also explains that it may be necessary to consider the true commercial objectives of the parties and the commercial rationale for the inclusion of the option in the transaction in order to **26** establish whether the parties' rights and obligations are, in substance, optional or conditional or, alternatively, outright.

27 Finally, for the avoidance of doubt, the FRS emphasises that, in assessing the commercial effect of an option, all the terms of the transaction and the circumstances of the parties that are likely to be relevant during the exercise period of the option should be taken into account – and not just conditions existing at the balance sheet date.

Linked presentation for subsidiaries

28 The FRS carries through the proposal in FRED 4 that where an item and its non-recourse finance are 'ring-fenced' in a quasi-subsidiary in such a way that the conditions for a linked presentation are met from the point of view of the group, the quasi-subsidiary should be included in consolidated financial statements using a linked presentation. However, if in a similar arrangement the item and its finance are held by a subsidiary, a linked presentation may not be used. In this case, the subsidiary is part of the group as legally defined: hence the item and its finance, being an asset and liability of the subsidiary, are respectively an asset and a liability of the group and companies legislation requires them to be shown in consolidated accounts in the normal way. Some respondents argued that the commercial effect is the same regardless of whether the vehicle is a subsidiary or a quasi-subsidiary, and hence the same accounting treatment should be adopted. However, companies legislation does not permit this. In legal terms, the inclusion of a quasi-subsidiary constitutes the provision of *additional* information about the group as legally defined and thus a quasi-subsidiary may be included in any way necessary to give a true and fair view of that group. However, a subsidiary is *part of* the group as legally defined and companies legislation requires the subsidiary to be consolidated in the normal way.

The use of swaps in securitisations

29 The Board was asked to clarify whether, in a securitisation, an interest rate swap or an interest rate cap between an originator and an issuer would restrict use of a linked presentation. FRED 4 required, as does the FRS, that, for a linked presentation, there must be 'no recourse whatsoever' to the originator and 'no possibility whatsoever of a claim being established on the entity [ie the originator] other than against funds generated by that item [ie the securitised assets]'. These provisions would prohibit use of a linked presentation where there is an interest rate swap or an interest rate cap between the originator and the issuer.

30 However, the argument was put to the Board that an exception to this principle was appropriate because the risks are often hedged by the originator as part of its normal hedging activities and thus payments to the issuer under the swap or cap would not represent a net loss to the originator. In many cases, the originator will have hedged any interest rate (and related) risks relating to the securitised assets prior to the securitisation, with the result that the securitisation opens up a gap in the originator's hedging portfolio by removing a hedged asset without removing its hedge. The most natural way to close this gap is for the issuer and the originator to enter into an interest rate swap or cap. Such a swap or cap will also be advantageous to the issuer by providing it with a hedge of the difference in the interest rate received on its newly acquired assets and that paid on its loan notes. It was also stated that, in the case of an interest rate swap (although not in the case of an interest rate cap), the issuer is currently unable to enter into a suitable swap with a third party as there is currently no market for such swaps in the UK (principally because the swap would require an amortising amount of principal to reflect actual repayments of the securitised assets).

The Board believes, as a matter of principle, that a linked presentation should be permitted only where there is no recourse whatsoever to the originator and accordingly should not be permitted where there is an interest rate swap or cap between the originator and the issuer. However, it decided with reluctance and as a pragmatic and provisional response to the issue, to permit use of a linked presentation in the originator's accounts notwithstanding the presence of an interest rate swap between the originator and the issuer in a securitisation provided certain strict criteria are met. (These are set out in paragraph D11.) In reaching this decision, the Board took into account the interaction of its decision with the present framework for regulating banks. The Board was also swayed by the fact that there is currently no market for such swaps in the UK and hence the issuer is unable to enter into a suitable swap with anyone other than the originator. For interest rate caps, the Board decided to give a similar concession but to resctrict it to those securitisations in existence prior to 22 September 1994 since the availability of a suitable market for interest rate caps means there is no need for future transactions of this kind to be undertaken with the originator and the issuer where a linked presentation is used. **31**

The Board's decision with respect to interest rate swaps represents an interim measure and will be reviewed in the light of developments in securitisations and of progress made in the Board's forthcoming project on derivatives. **32**

Disclosures of derecognised assets

Three of the Application Notes to FRED 4 contained specific disclosure requirements in respect of derecognised assets. Commentators generally thought these requirements were excessive, they have not been retained in the FRS. **33**

AMENDMENT TO FRS 5 – INSERTION OF APPLICATION NOTE F 'PRIVATE FINANCE INITIATIVE AND SIMILAR CONTRACTS'

The Preface to this amendment issued September 1998 stated the following:The Application Note has been prepared in response to the need for clarification of how the principles and requirements of FRS 5 should apply to transactions conducted under the UK Government's Private Finance Initiative (PFI). The Note will also be appropriate for other contracts of a similar nature.

The amendment was published as an Exposure Draft in December 1997 for public comment. In finalising this document the Accounting Standards Board has taken into consideration the comments received in response to the Exposure Draft and has consulted interested parties. In particular, in the final version of the Note the Board has clarified the question of separability and which variations in profits (or losses) should be taken into account when determining who has an asset of the property in a PFI contract.

The development of the Application Note

The need for guidance on revenue recognition

The absence of a UK standard dealing explicitly with revenue recognition has been a source of muted but continuing criticism for some time. Different entities and industries have followed practices that are in some respects inconsistent with one another. More generally, there are different views of what revenue is or represents, and of how financial statements should portray a business's operating activities. **1**

2 In practice, those seeking guidance on whether or when to recognise revenue have turned to International Accounting Standards (IAS) or accounting standards adopted in the United States. The international standard, IAS 18 'Revenue', was originally issued in 1982 and substantially revised in 1993. US requirements on the subject are to be found in various standards issued by the Financial Accounting Standards Board (FASB) and pronouncements of its Emerging Issues Task Force; the US Securities and Exchange Commission has also issued a relevant Staff Accounting Bulletin (SAB 101 'Revenue Recognition in Financial Statements' issued in 1999).

3 In recent years it has become common for investors in certain industries and start-up businesses to focus on revenue growth as an important indicator of a company's ability to meet its targets and achieve (or regain) profitability. This has led to, or highlighted, certain divergences in accounting treatments, some of which have been eliminated by pronouncements of the Urgent Issues Task Force, addressing specific issues. The Board therefore took the subject of revenue recognition on to its agenda and in July 2001 issued a Discussion Paper 'Revenue Recognition'.

4 A challenge for all standard setters in addressing this subject has been the need to tie in the principles of revenue recognition with other development work in progress. In September 2002 the International Accounting Standards Board and the FASB agreed to combine their work on this subject into a joint project that focused on the recognition of revenue based on the recognition of changes in assets and liabilities.

5 The Board considered whether it should develop its Discussion Paper into a new Financial Reporting Standard. It decided against this course of action for two reasons. First, in accordance with its convergence policy the Board intends to issue full standards on major topics of concern only after consultation with the Board's international partners. Secondly, at this stage the principles underlying the international project on revenue recognition have not yet been determined.

6 Nevertheless, questions continue to arise on accounting practices in this area. The Board has therefore issued this Application Note to promote the consistent treatment of exchange transactions that are reported as turnover.

The rationale of the application note

7 The Application Note contains basic principles of revenue recognition which set out the general approach and should be applied in all cases. These are accompanied by specific guidance for five types of transactions which give rise to turnover and have been subject to differing interpretations in practice.

8 The Application Note is based on the principle that a seller generates revenue by performing its contractual obligations and in exchange obtains the right to consideration. This entitles the seller to recognise either:

(a) an increase in assets (such as a debtor); or
(b) a decrease in liabilities (normally the release from an obligation arising from receipt of a payment in advance of performance).

The principle that a seller generates revenue by performing its contractual obligations to the customer is consistent with the idea of performance under the law of contract.* 9

The intention of the Application Note is to codify existing good practice and ensure that entities report turnover in accordance with the substance of their contractual arrangements with customers. 10

Matters considered in the light of responses to the Exposure Draft

This Application Note is based on an Exposure Draft which was published in February 2003. The following paragraphs give further details of the Board's reasoning for the requirements of the Application Note and explain changes made to the Exposure Draft. 11

The basic principles

The right to consideration

The Exposure Draft contained the basic principle that the seller obtains 'the right to be paid' in return for its performance of its obligations under a contractual arrangement. Some respondents were unclear as to what was meant by this right and how the proposals were linked to the seller's performance of its contractual obligations. The Exposure Draft stressed that the right to be paid does not necessarily correspond to the falling due of stage payments. Nevertheless, a number of respondents queried what else this right might represent. 12

In agreeing a contract, the seller and the customer will wish to ensure that they minimise the risk of losses arising from default by the other party. One way in which this is achieved is through the specification of stage payments. Often these stage payments will reflect the seller's performance of its contractual obligations in providing something of value to the customer. However, an exact correspondence is not necessarily obtained with a claim for stage payments; stage payments may fall short of or exceed the right to consideration that the seller has obtained through its performance. 13

The right to consideration does not represent a contractual right to demand stage payments from the customer. Rather, a seller obtains the right to consideration in exchange for the performance of its obligations under a contractual arrangement with a customer. This approach avoids the recognition of revenue being distorted by the timing of payment; to do so would move towards cash accounting. This would lead to a lack of comparability and allow wide discretion in reporting revenue. 14

The Application Note contains a definition of performance to emphasise the importance of the seller's performance. Furthermore, in the interests of clarity, the Application Note uses the term 'the right to consideration' in place of 'the right to be paid' to emphasise that this right does not necessarily correspond to stage payments. The Application Note stresses that a seller recognises revenue when, and to the extent that, it obtains this right as a result of its performance of its contractual obligations. 15

**Sir Guenter Treitel, in 'The Law of Contract' makes the point as follows: "A party who performs a contract in accordance with its terms is thereby discharged from his obligations under it. Such performance also normally entitles him to enforce the other party's undertakings." (Tenth edition), 1999, (page 697).*

The measurement of revenue

16 The Exposure Draft proposed that revenue should be measured at the fair value of the consideration receivable. It noted that this would normally be the amount specified in the contractual arrangement, with adjustments made, where material, for the time value of money and risk. A number of respondents suggested that this requirement would result in widespread changes to current practice.

17 The difficulty stems from the fact that, while the great majority of transactions are conducted at fair value, the amounts at which these are reported in financial statements depart, to some degree at least, from a strict representation of fair value. If the seller's right to consideration were to be stated at fair value, strictly, it should reflect both a discount in respect of any interest free period and an allowance for possible default by the debtors.

18 The Board is concerned that adjustments should be made to the price specified in the contractual arrangement in those cases where revenue would otherwise be materially overstated. This might be the case where the buyer makes payments on interest free credit over a number of years, or where at the time of the sale, the seller knows that there is a significant risk about the customer's ability to pay. This is made clear in paragraphs G8 and G9.

19 The Board believes that the Application Note achieves a reasonable accommodation between the principle that revenue should be recognised at fair value, which it asserts, and the present state of international practice in this area. It notes that this is consistent with the requirements of IAS 18 (paragraphs 9 - 12).

Payment received in advance of performance

20 A contract may require the customer to make payment in advance of the seller's performance. In such situations the seller recognises a liability equal to the amount of consideration received, representing its obligation under the contract. The seller is released from its obligation when its performance under the contract earns it the right to consideration.

21 The Application Note requires that liabilities relating to payments received in advance are reported at the amount the seller has received, for taking them on, which is their entry value. Some respondents to the Exposure Draft observed that the use of entry value reflected a fundamental assumption in this area which required debate.

22 The Board agrees that the measurement of assets and liabilities is a fundamental issue and is participating in various initiatives which it is hoped will develop thinking in the UK and elsewhere on these issues. The Application Note is not intended to pre-empt the outcome of this work. The Board notes, however, that this requirement of the Application Note reflects the prevailing practice in the UK and the Republic of Ireland.

23 In the Board's view there are also conceptual reasons for reporting liabilities for payments in advance at the amount received. In the normal case of a profitable contract the amount received will be greater than the expected cost of performance. On making a payment in advance, the customer will have a claim on the entity to receive value for the amount paid. If the liability were reported at the cost of performance, the financial statements would not faithfully report the entity's obligation to its customer. Reducing the liability would also give rise to a reported gain, which

might suggest that the success of the business in a particular period depended on obtaining orders rather than satisfying customers.*

Partial performance

Some respondents requested further clarification as to how the principles in the Exposure Draft should be applied to situations where the seller's contractual performance is incomplete. **24**

The final Application Note contains additional guidance on this issue. It states that there will be some arrangements where the seller obtains a right to consideration when some, but not all, of its contractual obligations have been fulfilled. Where a seller has partially performed its contractual obligations, the Application Note stresses that it recognises revenue to the extent that it has obtained the right to consideration through the performance of its contractual obligations in supplying goods and services. **25**

Obtaining the right to consideration does not necessarily involve delivery or the transfer of title. For example, if a seller is constructing a building to a customer's design, the customer may gain neither title nor physical custody until construction is complete. Nevertheless, the seller obtains the right to consideration through its performance as construction activity progresses, reflecting the value of the work performed to date. **26**

Sales tax

The current treatment of sales tax is well established and is set out in both legal requirements and in other accounting standards. **27**

(a) Section 262 (1) of the Companies Act 1985† defines turnover in relation to a company as the amounts derived from the provision of goods and services falling within the company's ordinary activities, after deduction of:

   (i) trade discounts,
   (ii) value added tax, and
   (iii) any other taxes based on the amounts so derived.

(b) SSAP 5 'Accounting for value added tax' requires that turnover should exclude VAT on taxable outputs.

The final Application Note contains guidance on the treatment of sales taxes which is consistent with the requirements noted in paragraph 27 above. **28**

Specific guidance

As well as setting out basic principles of revenue recognition, the Application Note also provides specific guidance in areas that have given rise to either inconsistency in practice or inappropriate accounting. **29**

**This issue is explored in greater depth in 'Liabilities and how to account for them: an exploratory essay', which is available at wwwfiasbfiorgfiuk/public/downloadsficfm.*

†*The corresponding provision in Northern Ireland is Article 270(1) The Companies (NI) Order 1986, inserted by The Companies (NI) Order 1990 (SI 1990/593) (NI 5) Article 24; and in the Republic of Ireland, Paragraph 75, Schedule to Companies (Amendment) Act 1986.* ***Editor's note****: Now 474 (1) of the Companies Act 2006.*

Long-term contractual performance

30 SSAP 9 contains guidance for the accounting and disclosure by a seller of its performance under a long–term contract. The Application Note also contains guidance for the recognition of turnover on such contracts and does not amend the requirements of SSAP 9.

31 Some respondents to the Exposure Draft commented that SSAP 9 was already adequate in prescribing the treatment in this area. It was also suggested that the guidance in the Exposure Draft could change existing practices as set out in SSAP 9, on the grounds that the Exposure Draft advocated a move away from measuring performance as the proportion of costs incurred to date in comparison with total expenditure.

32 SSAP 9 does not require costs incurred to date to be used in measuring turnover in a long-term contract. Paragraph 9 notes that the profit taken up needs to reflect the proportion of work carried out at the accounting date. There will be contracts where costs incurred to date do reflect the work performed and in such circumstances it would be appropriate to use the proportion of costs incurred in comparison with total expenditure in measuring revenue; however, this will not always be the case. The incurrence of costs by a seller, does not, in itself, justify the recognition of revenue. The Application Note therefore re-emphasises that the key principle in recognising revenue is the seller's performance of its contractual obligations.

Separation and linking of contractual arrangements

33 Most respondents were supportive of the proposals in the Exposure Draft which provided guidance on when the seller should combine or unbundle any separate components contained in a single contractual arrangement.

34 The Exposure Draft noted that one of the requirements for the unbundling of a contractual arrangement was whether or not reliable fair values could be attributed to at least the uncompleted components. Some respondents were unsure as to the degree of reliability that was required.

35 The existence of measurement uncertainty is acknowledged in the criteria for the recognition of an asset. This requires that the monetary amount at which an asset is to be measured is capable of being measured with sufficient reliability. As discussed in the Board's Statement of Principles, if uncertainty exists, the only way to determine an appropriate monetary amount is through the use of estimates.

36 However, in order for the seller to account for a contractual arrangement as separate transactions, the Application Note requires that the individual components operate independently and represent goods or services that the seller can provide on a stand alone basis or as an optional extra. Therefore, if the components do operate independently, the seller should be able to arrive at a measure that is sufficiently reliable to meet the asset recognition criteria.

Separation and linking of contractual arrangements - vouchers

37 The Board received requests from respondents to clarify the accounting treatment of points schemes and money-off coupons. The final Application Note therefore contains additional guidance in respect of revenue recognition in this area. It uses the term 'vouchers' which is intended to encompass all types of arrangements where the seller is committed to perform in the future at a reduced price.

The Board notes that issues might also arise as to whether the seller might have an onerous contract, for example if the exercise of the vouchers would result in products being sold at a loss. Where this is the case, it will be necessary to consider whether the vouchers give rise to an obligation on the part of the seller. Where an entity is obliged to supply goods or services at a loss, that is an onerous contract and provision will need to be made in accordance with FRS 12 'Provisions, Contingent Liabilities and Contingent Assets'. **38**

Separation and linking of contractual arrangements - inception fees

The Exposure Draft contained proposals on when the seller should record turnover in respect of non-refundable fees. In the final Application Note, the term 'inception fees' has been used in place of non-refundable fees. That is because the principle as to when the seller should recognise turnover in respect of a fee does not necessarily depend on whether or not a fee is refundable. Whilst the fact that a fee is stated to be non-refundable may suggest that the seller has no further performance obligations in respect of that fee, in some cases an obligation to provide goods or services may remain. **39**

Bill and hold arrangements

Most respondents agreed with the guidance in the Exposure Draft on bill and hold arrangements. Some, however, disagreed with the condition that the goods should be identified separately from the seller's other stock in order for the seller to recognise revenue. It was suggested that the separate identification of the goods should not be necessary where the item is fungible. **40**

The Board reconsidered this point when finalising the Application Note. It concluded that the buyer would not have the principal benefits and risks until the goods have been identified separately from the seller's other goods; the seller would continue to bear these benefits and risks until that time. This condition was therefore retained in the final Application Note. The Board also noted that this requirement is consistent with both IAS 18 and SAB 101. **41**

Sales with rights of return

Most respondents agreed with the proposals in the Exposure Draft which required the seller to exclude from turnover the sales value of estimated returns. However, some respondents were concerned that the proposals would require extensive changes to 'point of sale' systems in order to capture the required information on returns. **42**

The Board's subsequent research has indicated that a seller will generally be able to estimate reliably the level of returns without the need for extensive systems changes. The final Application Note stresses that a seller will generally be able to derive a reliable estimate from historical experience of the proportion of comparable goods returned as a proportion of comparable sales. **43**

Some respondents suggested that the proposals on sales with rights of return were inconsistent with the derecognition principles of the FRS. The Board debated this issue during the development of the Exposure Draft and, for the reasons outlined below, believes that the provisions are consistent with the FRS. **44**

45 The Board noted that the FRS requires that an entire asset should be derecognised when a transaction transfers all significant rights or other access to benefits and all significant exposure to the risks inherent in those benefits. The FRS also contains requirements (paragraph 23) which cover transactions that have resulted in a significant change in the entity's rights to benefits and exposure to risk, but where the provisions for full derecognition are not met. This might be where a transaction involves a transfer of all of the item for all of its life, but where the entity retains some significant right to benefits or exposure to risk. In such circumstances, the FRS requires the description or monetary amount to be changed and a liability recognised for any obligations to transfer benefits that are assumed.

46 A particular issue raised by some respondents was a perceived inconsistency between the requirements of the FRS in respect of receivables "sold" or securitised with full recourse to the seller (Application Notes C and D) and the treatment proposed in the Exposure Draft for expected returns of goods sold. No sale recognition was given to the former, to the extent that there was any possibility that the receivables could be put back to the transferor; for goods sold, however, the Exposure Draft proposed, and the final Application Note confirms, that revenue should generally be recognised after making an estimate of future returns.

47 The Board concluded that a different approach was needed to reflect a fundamental difference in the effect of the two transactions. A "sale" of receivables with full recourse does not change in the slightest the exposure of the seller to the benefits and risks attaching to the receivables: the speed of collection and the incidence of defaults are both borne by the seller to the same extent as if no transaction had taken place. The only effect is a cash advance, which should be recognised as a liability. By contrast, a normal sale of goods with rights of return is a significant event for the seller in that it transfers the great majority of the benefits and risks relating to the goods (for example, the purchaser is able to use the goods as it wishes and is exposed to the risk of subsequent damage). For the seller, subject to a provision for the return of some portion, the sale crystallises the profit from the production/sale process.

48 The objective of the FRS is to ensure that the substance of an entity's transactions are reported in its financial statements and that the commercial effect should be faithfully represented. The Board believes that the requirements on sales with rights of return are consistent with this objective and with the provisions of the FRS.

Presentation of turnover as principal or as agent

49 Respondents were generally supportive of the proposals in the Exposure Draft which provided guidance as to whether the seller should be regarded as acting as principal or agent in an exchange transaction with a customer.

50 In determining whether the seller is acting as principal or agent, the final Application Note gives greater prominence to the question of whether the agency relationship is disclosed. It states that where the seller has not disclosed that it is acting as agent, there is a rebuttable presumption that it is acting as principal.

51 The Board received requests to clarify the application of the principles in the Exposure Draft to trading concessions operated in department stores. The Board recognises that there are a wide variety of potential arrangements between department stores and concessionaires. However, where the department store is not acting as principal in an exchange transaction with the concessionaire's customers, it would be inappropriate for the department store to include within its own revenue the value of the concessionaire's sales. The final Application Note makes this clear.

Disclosure of accounting policies

The Board believes that preparers should provide disclosures that will help users understand the entity's adopted accounting policies and how they have been applied. This is one of the objectives of FRS 18 'Accounting Policies', which stresses that sufficient information should be provided in the financial statements to meet this objective. Entities should therefore have regard to the requirements of that standard when considering the disclosures required in respect of accounting policies. The Board's statement on the 'Operating and Financial Review' also contains guidance on accounting policies. It stresses the fact that the Operating and Financial Review should highlight accounting policies that are key to an understanding of the entity's performance and financial position. **52**

Implementation

The Board considered whether or not special transitional arrangements should be included in the final Application Note and concluded that they were not required. Accordingly, on implementation an entity should compare its current accounting for revenue with the requirements of this Application Note. If any change is required, it should consider whether this represents a change of accounting policy or of estimation technique in accordance with FRS 18 'Accounting Policies'. **53**

Dissenting view

Mr Wild dissents from the issue of this Amendment to FRS 5 because he believes that the Application Note it inserts, rather than significantly improving the quality of UK financial reporting, could introduce sufficient confusion over the principles to be adopted to have a detrimental effect on such reporting.

Internationally, revenue recognition is the subject of a joint project by the International Accounting Standards Board (IASB) and the Financial Accounting Standards Board (FASB) in the US. Mr Wild agrees that the ASB should not seek to issue a comprehensive revenue standard until the IASB and FASB have completed their review and accepts that the Application Note is intended to be an interim measure. However, he believes the Application Note is an inadequate compromise between a desire to establish principles and a desire to avoid major changes to existing practice for the majority of transactions. As a result, to the extent that current practice is open to abuse, the requirements of the Application Note are not sufficiently precise or clear to prevent it. Moreover, the inconsistent application of underlying principles, in favour of the status quo, may create confusion and, perhaps, extend opportunities for abuse.

Examples of aspects of the Application Note which particularly concern Mr Wild in this way are set out below.

- The requirement to measure revenue at the fair value of the right to consideration means, in principle, that account has to be taken of both the time value of money and the risk of default. While Mr Wild acknowledges that this principle may well be appropriate in the context of a full revenue standard, and is indeed set out in the international standard on revenue, he notes that it is not consistently applied in practice either in the UK or elsewhere. The Application Note attempts to reconcile this theory with practice by suggesting that existing practice is adopted merely on the grounds of materiality. Mr Wild thinks this leaves the position unhelpfully ambiguous for many entities.

- Mr Wild believes the treatment of sales with rights of return contradicts principles set out in other Application Notes to FRS 5. While in his view the treatment of sales with rights of return is appropriate to the current state of development of principles for revenue recognition, it is inconsistent with the existing requirements for the derecognition of items as a result of arrangements carried out other than as part of the normal business operating cycle. Consequently the various Application Notes seem to specify different treatments depending on the intent of the directors on any particular occasion. He thinks the confusion resulting from such an apparently self evident contradiction between the requirements of different Application Notes to the same standard could lead to those Application Notes being undermined, and could be exploited by those seeking to construct complex financial arrangements.

Financial Reporting Standard 6 is set out in paragraphs 1–39

The Statement of Standard Accounting Practice set out in paragraphs 4–39 should be read in the context of the Objective as stated in paragraph 1 and the definitions set out in paragraphs 2–3 and also of the Foreword to Accounting Standards and the Statement of Principles for Financial Reporting currently in issue.

The Explanation set out in paragraphs 40–89 shall be regarded as part of the Statement of Standard Accounting Practice insofar as it assists in interpreting that statement.

Appendix III 'The development of the FRS' reviews considerations and arguments that were thought significant by members of the Board in reaching the conclusions on FRS 6.

[FRS 6]
Acquisitions and mergers*†

(Issued September 1994)

Contents

	Paragraph
Summary	a–i
Financial Reporting Standard 6	
Objective	1
Definitions	2–3
Statement of Standard Accounting Practice	4–39
Scope	4
Application to smaller entities	4A
Use of merger accounting	5–15
Criteria for determining whether the definition of a merger is met	6–12
Group reconstructions	13
Combination effected by using a new parent company	14
Applicability to various structures of business combination	15
Merger accounting	16–19
Acquisition accounting	20
Disclosure	21–37
Acquisitions and mergers	21
Mergers	22
Acquisitions	23–35
Substantial acquisitions	36–37
Date from which effective	38
Withdrawal of SSAP 23 and amendment of SSAP 22	39
Explanation	40–89
Introduction	40–43
Definition of a merger and an acquisition	44–46
Rationale for merger accounting	47–51
Rationale for acquisition accounting	52–53
Deciding whether a business combination is a merger or an acquisition	54–77
Parties to the combination	57–59
Criterion 1 – role of the parties	60–62
Criterion 2 – dominance of management	63–66
Criterion 3 – relative size of the parties	67–68
Criterion 4 – non-equity consideration	69–74

****Editor's note:*** *FRS 6 was amended by FRS 25 with effect for accounting periods beginning on or after 1 January 2005. The statutory references have also been substantially amended by the ASB to reflect the introduction of the Companies Act 2006, without amendment to the substantive requirements.*

†***Editor's note:*** *The matters covered in FRS 6 are dealt with in Sections 9 and 19 of FRS 102.*

Criterion 5 – minorities etc 75–77
Group reconstructions 78–79
Disclosure 80–89
Mergers 81–82
Acquisitions 83–87
Substantial acquisitions 88–89

Adoption of FRS 6 by the Board

Appendices
I Note on legal requirements
II Compliance with international accounting standards
III The development of the FRS
IV Illustrative example of disclosure of reorganisation and integration costs

Acquisitions and mergers

Summary

a Financial Reporting Standard 6 'Acquisitions and Mergers' sets out the circumstances in which the two methods of accounting for a business combination—acquisition accounting and merger accounting—are to be used.

b Acquisition accounting regards the business combination as the acquisition of one company by another; the identifiable assets and liabilities of the company acquired are included in the consolidated balance sheet at their fair value at the date of acquisition, and its results included in the profit and loss account from the date of acquisition. The difference between the fair value of the consideration given and the fair values of the net assets of the entity acquired is accounted for as goodwill.

c Merger accounting, on the other hand, treats two or more parties as combining on an equal footing. It is normally applied without any restatement of net assets to fair value, and includes the results of each for the whole of the accounting period. Correspondingly, it does not reflect the issue of shares as an application of resources at fair value. The difference that arises on consolidation does not represent goodwill but is deducted from, or added to, reserves.

d The FRS requires acquisition accounting to be used for any business combination where a party can be identified as having the role of an acquirer, since this method of accounting reflects the application of resources by the acquirer and the net assets acquired.

e Merger accounting is restricted to, and required for, those business combinations where the use of acquisition accounting would not properly reflect the true nature of the combination. A merger is a business combination in which, rather than one party acquiring control of another, the parties come together to share in the future risks and benefits of the combined entity. It is not the augmentation of one entity by the addition of another, but the creation of what is effectively a new reporting entity from the parties to the combination.

f A combination meets the definition of a merger only if it satisfies the five criteria set out in paragraphs 6 – 11 of the FRS. These criteria relate to:

1 the way the roles of each party to the combination are portrayed;
2 the involvement of each party to the combination in the selection of the management of the combined entity;
3 the relative sizes of the parties to the combination;
4 whether shareholders of the combining entities receive any consideration other than equity shares in the combined entity;
5 whether shareholders of the combining entities retain an interest in the performance of only part of the combined entity.

g Where a combination meets these criteria, acquisition accounting is not permitted as this method would not fairly present the effect of the combination.

h The FRS also contains provisions for applying merger accounting to mergers effected by the creation of a new holding company, and also to certain group reconstructions where acquisition accounting may not be appropriate.

The FRS contains disclosure requirements applying to business combinations accounted for by using merger accounting so that the transition from separate entities to the merged entity can be understood; and further disclosure requirements, replacing those in SSAP 22 'Accounting for goodwill', for business combinations accounted for by using acquisition accounting, so that the effect of the acquisition can be understood.* i

Financial Reporting Standard 6

Objective

The objective of this FRS is: to ensure that merger accounting is used only for those business combinations that are not, in substance, the acquisition of one entity by another but the formation of a new reporting entity as a substantially equal partnership where no party is dominant; to ensure the use of acquisition accounting for all other business combinations; and to ensure that in either case the financial statements provide relevant information concerning the effect of the combination. 1

Definitions

The following definitions shall apply in this FRS and in particular in the Statement of Standard Accounting Practice set out in paragraphs 4 – 39. 2

Acquisition:-
A business combination that is not a merger.

Business combination:-
The bringing together of separate entities into one economic entity as a result of one entity uniting with, or obtaining control over the net assets and operations of, another.

Equity shares:-
Shares classified as equity in accordance with FRS 25 '(IAS 32) Financial Instruments: Disclosure and Presentation'.†

Group reconstruction:-
Any of the following arrangements:

(a) the transfer of a shareholding in a subsidiary undertaking from one group company to another;
(b) the addition of a new parent company to a group;
(c) the transfer of shares in one or more subsidiary undertakings of a group to a new company that is not a group company but whose shareholders are the same as those of the group's parent;
(d) the combination into a group of two or more companies that before the combination had the same shareholders.

Merger:-
A business combination that results in the creation of a new reporting entity formed

***Editor's note:** *Subsequent to the issue of FRS 6, SSAP 22 has itself been replaced by FRS 10 'Goodwill and Intangible Assets'.*

†***Editor's note:** *Definition amended by FRS 25.*

from the combining parties, in which the shareholders of the combining entities come together in a partnership for the mutual sharing of the risks and benefits of the combined entity, and in which no party to the combination in substance obtains control over any other, or is otherwise seen to be dominant, whether by virtue of the proportion of its shareholders' rights in the combined entity, the influence of its directors or otherwise.

Non-equity shares:-
Shares classified as liabilities in accordance with FRS 25 '(IAS 32) Financial Instruments: Disclosure and Presentation.'*

3 References to companies legislation mean:

(a) in the United Kingdom, the Companies Act 2006 (The Act); the Large and Medium-sized Companies and Groups (Accounts and Reports) Regulations 2008 ('The Regulations'); and the Small Companies and Groups (Accounts and Directors' Report Regulations 2008) i.e. for those small parent companies that opt to prepare group accounts.
(b) in the Republic of Ireland, the Companies Acts 1963–2006, the European Communities (Companies: Group Accounts) Regulations 1992, the European Communities (Credit Institutions: Accounts) Regulations 1992 and the European Communities (Insurance Undertakings: Accounts) Regulations 1996.†

Statement of Standard Accounting Practice

The marginal notes give the main reference to the Companies Act 2006 and Large and Medium-sized Companies and Groups (Accounts and Reports) Regulations 2008 in the United Kingdom. For the equivalent references in companies legislation in the Republic of Ireland see Appendix I.†

SCOPE

4 Financial Reporting Standard 6 applies to all financial statements that are intended to give a true and fair view of a reporting entity's financial position and profit or loss (or income and expenditure) for a period. Although the FRS is framed in terms of an entity becoming a subsidiary undertaking of a parent company that prepares consolidated financial statements, it also applies where an individual company or other reporting entity combines with a business other than a subsidiary undertaking.

APPLICATION TO SMALLER ENTITIES

4A Reporting entities applying the Financial Reporting Standard for Smaller Entities currently applicable are exempt from this accounting standard unless preparing consolidated financial statements, in which case they should apply the FRS to such statements as required by the FRSSE.

***Editor's note:** *Definition amended by FRS 25.*

†**Editor's note**: *Paragraphs amended by "Amendments to Financial Reporting Standards: FRS 2 'Accounting for Subsidiary Undertakings'; FRS 6 'Acquisitions and Mergers' and FRS 28 'Corresponding Amounts' Legal Changes" issued in June 2009.*

USE OF MERGER ACCOUNTING

A business combination should be accounted for by using merger accounting if: 5

(a) the use of merger accounting for the combination is not prohibited by companies legislation; and *[6 Sch 10, of the Regulations]**
(b) the combination meets all the specific criteria set out in paragraphs 6–11 below and thus falls within the definition of a merger.

Acquisition accounting should be used for all other business combinations, except as provided in paragraphs 13 and 14

Criteria for determining whether the definition of a merger is met

Criterion 1 – No party to the combination is portrayed as either acquirer or acquired, either by its own board or management or by that of another party to the combination. 6

Criterion 2 – All parties to the combination, as represented by the boards of directors or their appointees, participate in establishing the management structure for the combined entity and in selecting the management personnel, and such decisions are made on the basis of a consensus between the parties to the combination rather than purely by exercise of voting rights. 7

Criterion 3 – The relative sizes of the combining entities are not so disparate that one party dominates the combined entity by virtue of its relative size. 8

Criterion 4 – Under the terms of the combination or related arrangements, the consideration received by equity shareholders of each party to the combination, in relation to their equity shareholding, comprises primarily equity shares in the combined entity; and any non-equity consideration, or equity shares carrying substantially reduced voting or distribution rights, represents an immaterial proportion of the fair value of the consideration received by the equity shareholders of that party. Where one of the combining entities has, within the period of two years before the combination, acquired equity shares in another of the combining entities, the consideration for this acquisition should be taken into account in determining whether this criterion has been met. 9

For the purpose of paragraph 9, the consideration should not be taken to include the distribution to shareholders of: 10

(a) an interest in a peripheral part of the business of the entity in which they were shareholders and which does not form part of the combined entity; or
(b) the proceeds of the sale of such a business, or loan stock representing such proceeds.

A peripheral part of the business is one that can be disposed of without having a material effect on the nature and focus of the entity's operations.

****Editor's note****: Reference amended by "Amendments to Financial Reporting Standards: FRS 2 'Accounting for Subsidiary Undertakings'; FRS 6 'Acquisitions and Mergers' and FRS 28 'Corresponding Amounts' Legal Changes" issued in June 2009. All other marginal references have also been amended, but have not been marked as changed.*

11 *Criterion 5* – No equity shareholders of any of the combining entities retain any material interest in the future performance of only part of the combined entity.

12 For the purposes of paragraphs 6–11 above any convertible share or loan stock should be regarded as equity to the extent that it is converted into equity as a result of the business combination.

Group reconstructions

13 A group reconstruction may be accounted for by using merger accounting, even though there is no business combination meeting the definition of a merger, provided:

[*6 Sch 10, of the Regulations*]

(a) the use of merger accounting is not prohibited by companies legislation;

(b) the ultimate shareholders remain the same, and the rights of each such shareholder, relative to the others, are unchanged; and

(c) no minority's interest in the net assets of the group is altered by the transfer.

Combination effected by using a new parent company

14 Where a combination is effected by using a newly formed parent company to hold the shares of each of the other parties to a combination, the accounting treatment depends on the substance of the business combination being effected: that is, whether a combination of the entities other than the new parent company would have been an acquisition or a merger. If the combination would have been an acquisition, one entity can be identified as having the role of an acquirer. This acquirer and the new parent company should first be combined by using merger accounting; then the other parties to the business combination should be treated as acquired by this combined company by using the acquisition method of accounting. On the other hand, where the substance of the business combination effected by a new parent company is a merger, the new parent company and the other parties should all be combined by using merger accounting.

Applicability to various structures of business combination

15 The provisions of the FRS, which are explained by reference to an acquirer or issuing entity that issues shares as consideration for the transfer to it of shares in the other parties to the combination, should also be read so as to apply to other arrangements that achieve similar results.

MERGER ACCOUNTING

16[*6 Sch 11, of the Regulations*] With merger accounting the carrying values of the assets and liabilities of the parties to the combination are not required to be adjusted to fair value on consolidation, although appropriate adjustments should be made to achieve uniformity of accounting policies in the combining entities.

17 The results and cash flows of all the combining entities should be brought into the financial statements of the combined entity from the beginning of the financial year in which the combination occurred, adjusted so as to achieve uniformity of accounting policies. The corresponding figures should be restated by including the results for

all the combining entities for the previous period and their balance sheets for the previous balance sheet date, adjusted as necessary to achieve uniformity of accounting policies.

The difference, if any, between the nominal value of the shares issued plus the fair value of any other consideration given, and the nominal value of the shares received in exchange should be shown as a movement on other reserves in the consolidated financial statements. Any existing balance on the share premium account or capital redemption reserve of the new subsidiary undertaking should be brought in by being shown as a movement on other reserves. These movements should be shown in the reconciliation of movements in shareholders' funds. **18**

Merger expenses are not to be included as part of this adjustment, but should be charged to the profit and loss account of the combined entity at the effective date of the merger, as reorganisation or restructuring expenses, in accordance with paragraph 20 of FRS 3 'Reporting Financial Performance'. **19**

ACQUISITION ACCOUNTING

Business combinations not accounted for by merger accounting should be accounted for by acquisition accounting. Under acquisition accounting, the identifiable assets and liabilities of the companies acquired should be included in the acquirer's consolidated balance sheet at their fair value at the date of acquisition. The results and cash flows of the acquired companies should be brought into the group accounts only from the date of acquisition. The figures for the previous period for the reporting entity should not be adjusted. The difference between the fair value of the net identifiable assets acquired and the fair value of the purchase consideration is goodwill, positive or negative.* [*6 Sch 9, of the Regulations*] **20**

DISCLOSURE

Acquisitions and mergers

The following information in respect of all business combinations occurring in the financial year, whether accounted for as acquisitions or mergers, should be disclosed in the financial statements of the acquiring entity or, in the case of a merger, the entity issuing shares: [*6 Sch 13 (2), of the Regulations*] **21**

(a) the names of the combining entities (other than the reporting entity);
(b) whether the combination has been accounted for as an acquisition or a merger;
(c) the date of the combination.

Mergers

In respect of each business combination accounted for as a merger, other than group reconstructions falling within paragraph 13, the following information should be disclosed in the financial statements of the combined entity for the period in which the merger took place: **22**

**The date of acquisition and the acquisition of a subsidiary undertaking in stages are dealt with in FRS 2, paragraphs 45, 50, 84–85, 88–89.*

(a) an analysis of the principal components of the current year's profit and loss account and statement of total recognised gains and losses into
   (i) amounts relating to the merged entity for the period after the date of the merger, and
   (ii) for each party to the merger, amounts relating to that party for the period up to the date of the merger.

(b) an analysis between the parties to the merger of the principal components of the profit and loss account and statement of total recognised gains and losses for the previous financial year;

[*6 Sch 13 (3), of the Regulations*]

(c) the composition and fair value of the consideration given by the issuing company and its subsidiary undertakings;

(d) the aggregate book value of the net assets of each party to the merger at the date of the merger;

(e) the nature and amount of significant accounting adjustments made to the net assets of any party to the merger to achieve consistency of accounting policies, and an explanation of any other significant adjustments made to the net assets of any party to the merger as a consequence of the merger; and

(f) a statement of the adjustments to consolidated reserves resulting from the merger.

The analysis of the profit and loss account in (a) and (b) above should show as a minimum the turnover, operating profit and exceptional items, split between continuing operations, discontinued operations and acquisitions; profit before taxation; taxation and minority interests; and extraordinary items.

Acquisitions

23 The disclosure requirements for business combinations accounted for as acquisitions apply as follows:

(a) those in paragraphs 24–35 are required for each material acquisition; and, with the exception of those in paragraph 35, should also be given for other acquisitions in aggregate;

(b) the additional disclosure requirements in paragraph 36 apply to substantial acquisitions as defined in paragraph 37.

24 [*6 Sch 13 (3), of the Regulations*] The composition and fair value of the consideration given by the acquiring company and its subsidiary undertakings should be disclosed. The nature of any deferred or contingent purchase consideration should be stated, including, for contingent consideration, the range of possible outcomes and the principal factors that affect the outcome.

25 [*6 Sch 13 (4), of the Regulations*] A table should be provided showing, for each class of assets and liabilities of the acquired entity:

(a) the book values, as recorded in the acquired entity's books immediately before the acquisition and before any fair value adjustments;

(b) the fair value adjustments, analysed into
   (i) revaluations
   (ii) adjustments to achieve consistency of accounting policies, and
   (iii) any other significant adjustments,

   giving the reasons for the adjustments; and

(c) the fair values at the date of acquisition.

The table should include a statement of the amount of purchased goodwill or negative goodwill arising on the acquisition.

In the table required by paragraph 25, provisions for reorganisation and restructuring costs that are included in the liabilities of the acquired entity, and related asset write-downs, made in the twelve months up to the date of acquisition should be identified separately. **26**

Where the fair values of the identifiable assets or liabilities, or the purchase consideration, can be determined only on a provisional basis at the end of the accounting period in which the acquisition took place, this should be stated and the reasons given. Any subsequent material adjustments to such provisional fair values, with corresponding adjustments to goodwill, should be disclosed and explained. **27**

As required by FRS 3, in the period of acquisition the post-acquisition results of the acquired entity should be shown as a component of continuing operations in the profit and loss account, other than those that are also discontinued in the same period; and where an acquisition has a material impact on a major business segment this should be disclosed and explained. **28**

Where it is not practicable to determine the post-acquisition results of an operation to the end of the period of acquisition, an indication should be given of the contribution of the acquired entity to the turnover and operating profit of the continuing operations. If an indication of the contribution of an acquired entity to the results of the period cannot be given, this fact and the reason should be explained. **29**

Any exceptional profit or loss in periods following the acquisition that is determined using the fair values recognised on acquisition should be disclosed in accordance with the requirements of FRS 3, and identified as relating to the acquisition. **30**

The profit and loss account or notes to the financial statements of periods following the acquisition should show the costs incurred in those periods in reorganising, restructuring and integrating the acquisition. Such costs are those that: **31**

(a) would not have been incurred had the acquisition not taken place; and
(b) relate to a project identified and controlled by management as part of a reorganisation or integration programme set up at the time of acquisition or as a direct consequence of an immediate post-acquisition review.

Movements on provisions or accruals for costs related to an acquisition should be disclosed and analysed between the amounts used for the specific purpose for which they were created and the amounts released unused. **32**

In accordance with FRS 1, the cash flow statement should show the amounts of cash and cash equivalents paid in respect of the consideration, net of any cash and cash equivalents balances transferred as part of the acquisition. In addition, a note to the cash flow **33** statement should show a summary of the effects of acquisitions indicating how much of the consideration comprised cash and cash equivalents and the amounts of cash and cash equivalents transferred as a result of the acquisition.

34 In accordance with FRS 1, material effects on amounts reported under each of the standard headings reflecting the cash flows of the acquired entity in the period should be disclosed, as far as is practicable, as a note to the cash flow statement. This information need be given only in the financial statements for the period in which the acquisition occurs.

35 For a material acquisition, the profit after taxation and minority interests of the acquired entity should be given for:

(a) the period from the beginning of the acquired entity's financial year to the date of acquisition, giving the date on which this period began; and
(b) its previous financial year.

Substantial acquisitions

36 For acquisitions meeting the conditions set out in the next paragraph, the following information should be disclosed in the financial statements of the combined entity for the period in which the acquisition took place:

(a) the summarised profit and loss account and statement of total recognised gains and losses of the acquired entity for the period from the beginning of its financial year to the effective date of acquisition, giving the date on which this period began; this summarised profit and loss account should show as a minimum the turnover, operating profit and those exceptional items falling within paragraph 20 of FRS 3; profit before taxation; taxation and minority interests; and extraordinary items;
(b) the profit after tax and minority interests for the acquired entity's previous financial year.

This information should be shown on the basis of the acquired entity's accounting policies prior to the acquisition.

37 The disclosures in paragraph 36 should be given for each business combination accounted for by using acquisition accounting where:

(a) for listed companies, the combination is a Class I* or Super Class I transaction under the Stock Exchange Listing Rules†;
(b) for other entities, either
    (i) the net assets or operating profits of the acquired entity exceed 15 per cent of those of the acquiring entity, or
    (ii) the fair value of the consideration given exceeds 15 per cent of the net assets of the acquiring entity;

and should also be made in other exceptional cases where an acquisition is of such significance that the disclosure is necessary in order to give a true and fair view. For

****Editor's note:*** *See UITF Abstract 15 (revised 1999) 'Disclosure of Substantial Acquisitions'.*

†***Editor's Note:*** *The Listing Rules are now issued by the Financial Conduct Authority in its capacity as the UK Listing Authority.*

the purposes of (b) above, net assets and profits should be those shown in the financial statements

for the last financial year before the date of the acquisition; and the net assets should be augmented by any purchased goodwill eliminated against reserves as a matter of accounting policy and not charged to the profit and loss account.

DATE FROM WHICH EFFECTIVE

The accounting practices set out in the FRS should be regarded as standard in respect of business combinations first accounted for in financial statements relating to accounting periods commencing on or after 23 December 1994. Earlier adoption is encouraged but not required. **38**

In 2009 the FRS was amended to update the legal references following the introduction of the Companies Act 2006 and The Large and Medium-sized Companies and Groups (Accounts and Report) Regulations 2008 (SI 2008 No. 410) (equivalent provisions for small parent companies that opt to prepare group accounts are contained in the Small Companies and Groups (Accounts and Directors' Report) Regulations 2008 (SI 2008 No. 409). The amendments take effect for accounting periods beginning on or after 6 April 2008 or when the provisions of the Act and/or the Regulations are applied to other entities (eg limited liability partnerships), if later.* **38A**

WITHDRAWAL OF SSAP 23 AND AMENDMENT OF SSAP 22

The FRS supersedes SSAP 23 'Accounting for acquisitions and mergers' and paragraphs 48 – 51 of SSAP 22 'Accounting for goodwill'. **39**

Explanation

INTRODUCTION

Two different methods have been used to account for business combinations: merger accounting and acquisition accounting. **40**

In merger accounting the financial statements of the parties to the combination are aggregated, and presented as though the combining entities had always been part of the same reporting entity. Accordingly, although the merger may have taken place part of the way through the financial year, the results of the combining entities for the full financial year are reflected in the group accounts for the period and corresponding amounts are presented on the same basis. The accounting policies of the combining entities are adjusted to achieve uniformity, but the assets and liabilities need not be adjusted to reflect fair values at the date of the combination. Under merger accounting, a difference may arise on consolidation between the nominal value of the shares issued, taken together with the fair value of any other consideration, and the aggregate of the nominal values of the shares received in exchange. Such difference is not goodwill, as it does not result from the difference between the fair value of the consideration and the fair value of the identifiable net assets. It should be shown as a movement on consolidated reserves. Any share **41**

**Editor's note*: *Paragraph added by "Amendments to Financial Reporting Standards: FRS 2 'Accounting for Subsidiary Undertakings'; FRS 6 'Acquisitions and Mergers' and FRS 28 'Corresponding Amounts' Legal Changes" issued in June 2009.*

premium accounts and capital redemption reserves of the new subsidiary undertaking are not preserved as such in the consolidated accounts, since they do not relate to the share capital of the reporting entity, but are brought in by being shown as a movement on other reserves.

42 In acquisition accounting the results of the acquired company are brought into the group accounts only from the date of acquisition. The identifiable assets and liabilities acquired are included at fair value in the consolidated accounts and are therefore stated at their cost to the acquiring group. The fair value of the consideration given is set against the aggregate fair value of the net identifiable assets acquired and any resulting balance is goodwill, if positive, or else a negative consolidation difference called negative goodwill.*

43 The fact that a particular business combination does not meet the criteria for merger accounting, and is thus accounted for by using acquisition accounting, does not preclude the acquirer from obtaining merger relief in its individual accounts under the provisions of section 612 of the Companies Act 2006† if the requirements of that section are met. In such cases, in the consolidated accounts, acquisition accounting is applied in the normal way: goodwill is still calculated by comparing the fair value of the shares issued, rather than their nominal or recorded value, with the fair value of the net assets acquired; and any resulting excess over the nominal value of the shares issued, taken together with the fair value of any other consideration, is shown, not as share premium, but as a separate reserve.

DEFINITION OF A MERGER AND AN ACQUISITION

44 A merger is a rare type of business combination in which two or more parties come together for the mutual sharing of benefits and risks arising from the combined businesses, in what is in substance an equal partnership, each sharing influence in the new entity. No party can be regarded as acquiring control over another, or becoming controlled by another; and the reporting entity formed by the combination must be regarded as a new entity rather than the continuation of one of the combining entities, enlarged by its having obtained control over the others.

45 An acquisition is defined as any business combination that is not a merger. In many acquisitions, the shareholders of the acquired party do not have a continuing interest in the combined entity, but instead sell their shareholdings for cash or other non-equity consideration. Even where all parties in an acquisition retain an interest in the combined entity, the parties do not come together on equal terms; one party has a greater degree of influence than the others, and is seen as acquiring the other entities in exchange for a share in the combined entity. An acquisition is therefore a transaction that is, in substance, the application of resources by the acquiring entity to obtain control of one or more other entities, by the payment of cash, transfer of other assets, the incurring of a liability or the issue of shares.

46 The legal form of a business combination will normally be for one company to acquire shares in one or more others. This fact does not make that company an acquirer in the sense discussed above. Similarly, the question of whether the

The treatment of such balances is dealt with in SSAP 22 'Accounting for Goodwill' and is the subject of a current ASB project see FRED 12. (Editor's note:** See now FRS 10 'Goodwill and Intangible Assets'.)*

†***Editor's note**: Reference amended with effect from 1 October 2009 by "Amendments to Financial Reporting Standards: FRS 2 'Accounting for Subsidiary Undertakings'; FRS 6 'Acquisitions and Mergers' and FRS 28 'Corresponding Amounts' Legal Changes" issued in June 2009.*

combined entity should be regarded as a new reporting entity is not affected by whether or not a new legal entity has been formed to acquire shares in others.

RATIONALE FOR MERGER ACCOUNTING

In a merger, no party to the combination can be properly regarded as obtaining control over the other; rather, the parties to the combination join together on an equal footing to form a combined enterprise for their mutual benefit. **47**

For such mergers it is misleading to account for the combination as the application of resources by one party to obtain control over the other, since this assumes a distinction in the roles of the parties that does not reflect reality. Furthermore, it is only the legal structure of the combination that would determine which party would be treated under acquisition accounting as the acquirer, and thus determine the party whose net assets would be treated as being acquired and whose goodwill would be recognised. **48**

A merger is a true mutual sharing of the benefits and risks of the combined entity. Therefore the joint history of the entities that have combined will be relevant to the combined group's shareholders. This record will be provided by merger accounting because it treats the separate businesses as though they were continuing as before, only now jointly owned and managed. If acquisition accounting were to be used, it would focus artificially on only one of the parties to the combination, which would lead to a discontinuity in information reported on the combined entity. **49**

Thus the concept of a merger is of a partnership or pooling of interests, where all the parties to the combination participate in the combined businesses of the merged entity on substantially equal terms; and where the substance of the arrangement is such that the reporting entity cannot be regarded as merely being enlarged by the acquisition of the other entities, but must be considered as effectively a new reporting entity. **50**

In a business combination that qualifies as a merger, expenses of the combination are similar in nature to expenses of a fundamental reorganisation or restructuring, and should be charged to the profit and loss account for the period in which the merger occurred, shown as an exceptional item in accordance with paragraph 20 of FRS 3. This is not intended to prohibit the subsequent charging of issue costs to the share premium account by means of a transfer between reserves. **51**

RATIONALE FOR ACQUISITION ACCOUNTING

The acquisition of another entity is a transaction by which an entity seeks to increase the assets under its control. Acquisition accounting is appropriate for most business combinations since it reflects in the financial statements the application of resources by one party to the combination in order to obtain control of the other, represented by the fair value of the net assets over which control is obtained together with goodwill. **52**

The profits of the acquired company are brought into account only from the date of the combination and the history of the group is seen as the history of the acquirer with occasional additions when it acquires other entities. **53**

DECIDING WHETHER A BUSINESS COMBINATION IS A MERGER OR AN ACQUISITION

54 The FRS requires that to determine whether a business combination meets the definition of a merger, it should be assessed against certain specified criteria; failure to meet any of these criteria indicates that the definition was not met and thus that merger accounting is not to be used for the combination.

55 Individually these tests are insufficient to define the intangible quality of a true merger, and may appear arbitrary. Nevertheless, taken as a whole, they provide a reasonable basis for determining whether a particular business combination meets the definition of a merger and thus should be accounted for by using merger accounting.

56 In applying the criteria, it is necessary to consider the substance and not just the form of the arrangements, and to take account of all relevant information related to the combination. It is important to have regard to the transaction as a whole, including any related arrangements that are connected with the business combination either because they are entered into in contemplation of that combination or because they are part of the process by which that combination is effected. The vast majority of business combinations will be acquisitions and only in rare circumstances will a combination fulfil all the detailed conditions for it to be treated as a merger.

Parties to the combination

57 For the purposes of assessing whether a combination is a merger meeting the criteria, the parties to the combination are considered as comprising not solely the business of each entity that is combining but also the management of the entity and the body of its shareholders.

58 Merger accounting is not appropriate for a combination where one of the parties results from a recent divestment by a larger entity, because the divested business will not have been independent for a sufficient period to establish itself as being a party separate from its previous owner. Only once the divested business has established a track record of its own can it be considered as a party to a merger. However, a party to a combination may divest itself of a peripheral part of its business before the combination (or as part of the arrangements for the combination) and still meet the criteria for merger accounting.

59 Where a party to the combination is not a company with share capital, the conditions applying to equity shares should be interpreted as applying to those elements of its capital structure that allocate rights to profits and control.

Criterion 1 – role of the parties

60 An essential feature of a merger is that it represents a genuine combining of the interests of the parties; such a genuine combination of interests cannot exist if one party portrays itself, or another party, as having a dominant role as an acquirer or the subservient role of being acquired.

61 Where the terms of a share-for-share exchange indicate that one party has paid a premium over the market value of the shares acquired, this is evidence that that party has taken the role of an acquirer unless there is a clear explanation for this apparent premium other than its being a premium paid to acquire control.

The circumstances surrounding the transaction may provide evidence to indicate the nature of a business combination. The following, while not individually conclusive, would need to be considered: the form by which the combination was achieved, the plans for the combined entity's future operations (for example, whether any closures or disposals related more to one party than another), and the proposed corporate image (such as the name, logo and the location of the headquarters and principal operations). Where a publicly quoted company is a party to a business combination, the content of communications with its shareholders is likely also to be relevant in determining the substance of the transaction. **62**

Criterion 2 – dominance of management

An essential feature of the genuine combination of interests underlying the definition of a merger is that all parties to the combination are involved in determining the management of the combined entity and reach a consensus on the appropriate structure and personnel; if decisions can be reached only by the exercise of majority voting rights against the wishes of one of the parties to the merger, or if one party clearly dominates this process, this indicates that the combination is not a genuine pooling of interests. However, this does not preclude the possibility of all, or most, of the management team of the combined entity coming from only one of the parties, provided that this clearly reflects the wishes of the others. **63**

In applying this test, it is necessary to consider not only the formal management structure of the combined entity, but also the identity of all persons involved in the main financial and operating decisions and the way in which the decision-making process operates in practice within the combined entity. **64**

Normally the management of the combined entity would contain representatives of each of the combining parties. Where the senior management structure and personnel of the combined entity are essentially those of one of the combining parties, this criterion will not have been met unless it is clear that all the parties to the merger genuinely participated in the decision. **65**

In applying this test it is necessary to consider only the decisions made in the period of initial integration and restructuring at the time of the combination; but both the short-term effects and expected long-term consequences of decisions made in this period need to be considered. **66**

Criterion 3 – relative size of the parties

Where one party is substantially larger than the other parties it would be presumed that the larger party can or will dominate the combined undertaking. This will not be consistent with treating such a business combination as a merger as the combined entity will not be a substantially equal partnership. **67**

A party would be presumed to dominate if it is more than 50 per cent larger than each of the other parties to the combination, judged by reference to the ownership interests; that is, by considering the proportion of the equity of the combined entity attributable to the shareholders of each of the combining parties. However, this presumption may be rebutted if it can be clearly shown that there is no such dominance; other factors, such as voting or share agreements, blocking powers or other arrangements, can mean that a party to the combination has more influence, or conversely less influence, than is indicated by its relative size. Circumstances that rebut the presumption of dominant influence based on relative sizes would need to be disclosed and explained. **68**

Criterion 4 – non-equity consideration

69 Criterion 4 is concerned with the extent to which equity shareholders of the combining entities receive any consideration other than equity shares (as defined in paragraph 2 above) in the combined entity. Cash, other assets, loan stock and preference shares are all examples of non-equity consideration.

70 As stated in the note on legal requirements (Appendix I), companies legislation provides that one of the conditions for merger accounting is that the fair value of any consideration other than the issue of equity shares (as defined in companies legislation) did not exceed 10 per cent of the nominal value of the equity shares issued. Criterion 4 requires a further condition to be met, that all but an immaterial proportion of the fair value of the consideration received must be in the form of equity shares (as defined in paragraph 2); this definition of equity, which is that adopted in FRS 25 '(IAS 32) Financial Instruments: Disclosure and Presentation', is narrower than that of companies legislation, and is used to avoid the possibility of criterion 4 being met by the use of shares that, although within the statutory definition of equity, have characteristics that are closer to non-equity.*

71 The FRS requires that all arrangements made in conjunction with the combination must be taken into account. Equity shareholders will be considered to have disposed of their shareholding for cash where any arrangement is made in connection with the combination that enabled them to exchange or redeem the shares they received in the combination for cash (or other non-equity consideration); for example, a vendor placing or similar arrangement should be treated as giving rise to non-equity consideration. However, a normal market selling transaction, or privately arranged sale, entered into by a shareholder is not made in conjunction with the combination and does not prevent the criterion being met.

72 A business combination may not be accounted for as a merger if a material part of the consideration that the issuing entity offers the equity shareholders in the other parties is in the form of shares with substantially reduced rights. Such an offer would be contrary to the concept that a merger is the mutual sharing in risks and rewards of the combined entity. Some adjustment to the rights attaching to the shares held by the non-issuing entities' shareholders may be compatible with the combination being a merger, as business combinations result from a negotiating process where different pre-existing rights have to be reconciled. Whether any change in the rights of one group of shareholders is sufficient to prevent that business combination being treated as a merger will depend on the facts in any individual case, taking into account such matters as what rights shareholders originally had, the total arrangement negotiated, time limits and whether any new restrictions apply equally to all sets of shareholders. In determining whether equity shares with reduced rights have been issued, both rights to vote and rights to distributions attaching to the shares would need to be taken into account. If any of these individual rights were significantly reduced or circumscribed the combination would fail to fulfil this condition.

73 If one entity has acquired an interest in another in exchange for non-equity consideration, or equity shares with significantly reduced rights, within the two years before those entities combined, such consideration should be regarded as part of the consideration for the combination for the purpose of determining whether this criterion is met.

74 Sometimes a peripheral part of the business of one of the combining parties will be excluded from the combined entity. The FRS states that shares in the peripheral

***Editor's note:** *Reference to FRS 4 removed, and replaced by reference to FRS 25 by FRS 25.*

business, or the proceeds of sale of the business, that are distributed to the shareholders of that party to the combination as part of the arrangements for the combination are not to be counted as part of the consideration for the purposes of this criterion.

Criterion 5 – minorities etc

Criterion 5 is concerned with a party retaining an interest in only part of the combined entity. The concept of a merger is that the participants enter into a mutual sharing of the risks and rewards of the whole of the new entity, including the pooled future results of the combined entity. This concept is incompatible with certain participants having a preferential interest in one part of the combined entity. This criterion would not, therefore, be met if the share of the equity in the combined entity allocated to the shareholders of one of the parties to the combination depended to any material extent on the post-combination performance of the business, or any part of it, formerly controlled by that party. **75**

This criterion would similarly not be met where earn-outs or similar performance-related schemes are included in the arrangements to effect a merger. The test is also failed if there is any material minority (defined by companies legislation as 10 per cent) of shareholders left in one of the combining parties that have not accepted the terms of the combination offer. **76**

However, the criterion would not necessarily be invalidated by an arrangement whereby the allocation of consideration between the shareholders of the combining parties depended on the determination of the eventual value of a specific liability or asset contributed by one of the parties—such as the eventual outcome of a claim against one of the parties, or the eventual sales value of a specific asset owned by one of the parties—as opposed to the future operating performance of that party. **77**

GROUP RECONSTRUCTIONS

In addition to mergers as defined above, merger accounting may also be appropriate for a group reconstruction, provided that the relative rights of the ultimate shareholders are not altered. Such reconstructions include not only the transfer of shares in a subsidiary undertaking within a group, but also arrangements such as the introduction of a new holding company, the splitting off of one or more subsidiary undertakings, as in some demergers, where a separate group is formed, and the bringing together into a new group of two or more companies that were previously under common ownership. Acquisition accounting would require the restatement at fair value of the assets and liabilities of the company transferred, and the recognising of goodwill, which is likely to be inappropriate in the case of a transaction that does not alter the relative rights of the ultimate shareholders. **78**

Where a minority interest exists, merger accounting is permitted only for those group reconstructions that do not change the interest of the minority in the net assets of the group. Thus the transfer of a subsidiary undertaking within a subgroup that has a minority shareholder may qualify for merger accounting; but acquisition accounting must be used for the transfer of a subsidiary undertaking out of, or into, such a subgroup. If a minority has effectively acquired, or disposed of, rights to part of the net assets of the group, the FRS requires the transfer to be accounted for by using acquisition accounting rather than merger accounting. **79**

DISCLOSURE

80 The disclosure requirements in the FRS cover and supplement those in companies legislation.

Mergers

81 With merger accounting the financial statements of the combined entity are drawn up by combining the results of the combining entities for the whole of the financial year in which the merger occurred. Users, particularly those who have been assessing the parties to the combination as separate businesses, may require information on the financial performance of the individual parties. The FRS therefore requires an analysis of the profit and loss account and statement of total recognised gains and losses into pre- and post-merger amounts; and a further analysis of the pre-merger amounts between each of the parties to the merger. An analysis between the parties of the preceding financial year is also required. However, it is not necessary, where revaluation gains or losses have been recognised as a result of a valuation at the year-end, to obtain further valuations at the date of the merger in order to apportion the gains or losses between pre- and post-merger periods.

82 Group reconstructions that are accounted for by using merger accounting are exempted from the disclosure requirements in the FRS, but must still give the information required by companies legislation.

Acquisitions

83 The disclosure requirements of the FRS provide information about the resources applied in acquisitions, the net assets acquired and the effects on the consolidated financial statements of the acquiring group. Separate presentation of the results of acquisitions assists analysis of the significance of new operations that have been acquired. In some circumstances it may also be useful to users for the results of acquisitions for the first full financial year for which they are a part of the reporting entity to be disclosed in the notes.

84 Paragraph 23 of the FRS requires the disclosures in paragraphs 24–35 to be given for each material acquisition, and those in paragraphs 24–34 to be given for other acquisitions in aggregate. Materiality must be judged by whether the information relating to the acquisition might reasonably be expected to influence decisions made by the users of general purpose financial statements. Paragraph 36 applies further disclosure requirements to certain substantial acquisitions.

85 In order to give a true and fair view of post-acquisition financial performance, paragraph 30 of the FRS requires disclosure of exceptional profits or losses determined using fair values recognised on an acquisition. Examples include profits or losses on the disposal of acquired stocks where the fair values of stocks sold lead to abnormal trading margins after the acquisition; the release of provisions in respect of an acquired loss-making long-term contract that the acquirer makes profitable; and the realisation of contingent assets or liabilities at amounts materially different from their attributed fair values. In accordance with the requirements of FRS 3, exceptional items would be included in the profit and loss account format headings to which they relate, and would be disclosed by way of note, or on the face of the profit and loss account if necessary to give a true and fair view.

86 FRS 3 requires the profits or losses on the post-acquisition sale or termination of an operation, or on the disposal of fixed assets, to be shown in the profit and loss

account below operating profit. Post-acquisition integration, reorganisation and restructuring costs, including provisions in respect of them, would, if material, be reported as exceptional items; but only if the restructuring is fundamental, having a material effect on the nature and focus of the enlarged group's operations, would the costs be shown below operating profit as an item falling under paragraph 20 of FRS 3. Paragraph 31 of FRS 6 requires that costs of reorganising, restructuring and integration that relate to an acquisition, whether relating to a fundamental restructuring or not, should be shown separately from other exceptional items.

The costs of reorganising, restructuring and integrating an acquired entity may extend over more than one period. For major acquisitions, therefore, management may wish to state in the notes to the financial statements the nature and amount of such costs expected to be incurred in relation to the acquisition (including asset write-downs), indicating the extent to which they have been charged to the profit and loss account. If part of these costs relate to asset write-downs (beyond any impairments recognised in adjusting to fair values on the acquisition) it may be useful to distinguish these from cash expenditure. An illustrative example of how such information might be shown is included as Appendix IV to the FRS. **87**

Substantial acquisitions

Where an acquisition has been made that has a substantial effect on the consolidated results of the acquiring entity, additional disclosures are required to enable the user to assess the effect of the acquisition on the consolidated results. Although control over the acquired entity is obtained only at the date of acquisition, in most cases it is a continuing business that is acquired, and information on the results for the period up to the date of acquisition is relevant to the user. For acquisitions that meet the size tests in paragraph 37, the FRS therefore requires the disclosure of the results of the acquired entity for the part of its financial year up to the date of the acquisition, and for its previous financial year. Since neither of these periods will necessarily be twelve months, their commencing dates should also be indicated. **88**

Several components of the pre-acquisition results are required to be shown for the part of the acquired entity's financial year up to the date of acquisition, since this period may be particularly relevant to an understanding of the post-acquisition results and may not otherwise be publicly reported. Equivalent information for the preceding financial year is likely to be of less relevance, and the disclosure requirement is limited to profit after tax and minority interests. The FRS requires this information to be given on the basis of the acquired entity's accounting policies before the acquisition; in some cases, the management of the acquiring entity may consider it helpful in explaining the impact of the acquisition to give, in addition, the same information restated onto the basis of the acquiring entity's accounting policies. **89**

Adoption of FRS 6 by the board

Financial Reporting Standard 6 – 'Acquisitions and Mergers' was approved for issue by the eight members of the Accounting Standards Board.

Sir David Tweedie	(Chairman)
Allan Cook	(Technical Director)
Robert Bradfield	
Ian Brindle	
Michael Garner	
Raymond Hinton	
Donald Main	
Graham Stacy	

Adoption of Amendment to FRS 6 by the Accounting Standards Board (June 2009)

Amendment to Financial Reporting Standard 6 'Acquisitions and Mergers' was approved for issue by the eleven members of the Accounting Standards Board.

Ian Mackintosh	(Chairman)
David Loweth	(Technical Director)
Nick Anderson	
Michael Ashley	
Edward Beale	
Marisa Cassoni	
Peter Elwin	
Ken Lever	
Robert Overend	
Andy Simmonds	
Professor Geoffrey Whittington CBE	

Appendix I
Note on legal requirements

UNITED KINGDOM

References are to the Companies Act 2006 and The Large and Medium-sized Companies and Groups (Accounts and Reports) Regulations 2008 (SI 2008 No. 410).

The requirements for small companies and groups that opt to prepare group accounts are set out in Schedule 6 of The Small Companies and Groups (Accounts and Directors' Report) Regulations 2008 (SI 2008 No. 409).

Merger accounting

The Large and Medium-sized Companies and Groups (Accounts and Reports) Regulations 2008 ('the Regulations') describe the acquisition method of accounting (Schedule 6 paragraph 9 of the Regulations) and the merger method of accounting (Schedule 6 paragraph 11 of the Regulations). 1

Schedule 6 paragraph 10 of the regulations lays down the conditions that must be met if a business combination is to be accounted for as a merger. The conditions are:

(a) that at least 90% of the nominal value of the relevant shares in the undertaking acquired (excluding any shares in the undertaking held as treasury shares) is held by or on behalf of the parent company and its subsidiary undertakings;
(b) that the proportion referred to in (a) was attained pursuant to an arrangement providing for the issue of equity shares by the parent company or one or more of its subsidiary undertakings;
(c) that the fair value of any consideration other than the issue of equity shares given pursuant to the arrangement by the parent company and its subsidiary undertakings did not exceed 10 per cent of the nominal value of the equity shares issued; and
(d) that adoption of the merger method of accounting accords with generally accepted accounting principles or practice.*

Where a group is acquired, the Companies Act requirements described in the previous paragraph also apply. References to shares of the undertaking acquired are to be construed as references to the shares of the acquired group's parent and references to the assets and liabilities, income and expenditure, and capital and reserves of the undertaking acquired are to be construed as references to the same elements of the group acquired, after making the necessary set-off and adjustments required for the consolidated accounts (Schedule 6 paragraph 12 of the Regulations). 2

Disclosures

The following information shall be given in a note to the accounts for all business combinations taking place in the financial year: 3

(a) the names of the entities involved;

***Editor's note**: Paragraph amended by "Amendments to Financial Reporting Standards: FRS 2 'Accounting for Subsidiary Undertakings'; FRS 6 'Acquisitions and Mergers' and FRS 28 'Corresponding Amounts' Legal Changes" issued in June 2009. These amendments also changed all of the other statutory references included in this Appendix. These changes have not been individually noted.*

(b) whether the combination has been accounted for by the acquisition or merger method of accounting (Schedule 6 paragraph 13 (2) (b) of the Regulations).

4 In addition, for any business combination that significantly affects the figures shown in the group accounts, the following further information shall be given:

(a) the composition and fair value of the consideration for the acquisition given by the parent and its subsidiary undertakings (Schedule 6 paragraph 13 (3) of the Regulations).

5 Where the acquisition method of accounting has been adopted, the book values immediately prior to acquisition and fair values at the date of acquisition of each class of assets and liabilities of the acquired entity shall be stated in tabular form, including a statement of the amount of any goodwill or negative consolidation difference arising on the acquisition, together with an explanation of any significant adjustments made (Schedule 6 paragraph 13 (4) of the Regulations).

6 [Paragraph withdrawn]

7 None of the information required by paragraph 13 of Schedule 6 of the Regulations need be disclosed for an undertaking which:

(a) is established under the law of a country outside the United Kingdom; or
(b) carries on business outside the United Kingdom if, in the opinion of the directors of the parent company, the disclosure would be seriously prejudicial to the business of that undertaking or to the business of the parent company or any of its subsidiary undertakings and the Secretary of State agrees that the information should not be disclosed (Schedule 6 paragraph 16 of the Regulations).

Share premium and merger relief

8 Section 610(1) of the Companies Act provides that if a company issues shares at a premium, whether for cash or otherwise, a sum equal to the aggregate amount or value of the premiums on those shares should be transferred to an account called the share premium account. The provisions of the Companies Act relating to the reduction of a company's share capital apply, with exceptions, as if the share premium account were part of its paid-up share capital.

9 Limited relief from the above ('merger relief') is given by sections 611–615.

10 Section 612 of the Companies Act provides, inter alia, that, subject to specified conditions, where an issuing company has secured at least a 90 per cent equity holding in another company, section 610 does not apply to the premium on shares issued in the transaction which takes the holding in that other company to at least 90 per cent.

11 Section 615 provides that the premium on any shares to which the relief in sections 611 and 612 of the Companies Act applies may also be disregarded in determining the amount at which any shares, or other consideration provided for the shares issued, are to be included in the offeror company's balance sheet.

12–14 [Withdrawn]

Accounts of the parent company

The FRS deals only with the method of accounting to be used in group accounts; it does not deal with the form of accounting to be used in the acquiring or issuing company's own accounts and in particular does not restrict the reliefs available under sections 611, 612 and 615 of the Companies Act. **15**

Where a dividend is paid to the acquiring or issuing company out of pre-combination profits, it would appear that it need not necessarily be applied as a reduction in the carrying value of the investment in the subsidiary undertaking. Such a dividend received should be applied to reduce the carrying value of the investment to the extent necessary to provide for a diminution in value of the investment in the subsidiary undertaking as stated in the accounts of the parent company. To the extent that this is not necessary, it appears that the amount received will be a realised profit in the hands of the parent company. **16**

[Withdrawn] **17**

The following table shows the provisions in the Companies Acts 1963–2006 and various Regulations implementing EC Accounting Directives, corresponding to the provisions of the UK Companies Act 2006 ('the 2006 Act') and the Schedules to the Large and Medium-sized Companies and Groups (Accounts and Reports) Regulations 2008 ('the 2008 Regulations') referred to in the Standard. The principal pieces of Irish legislation referred to in the table below are: **18**

- The Companies Act 1963 ('1963 Act');
- The European Communities (Companies: Group Accounts) Regulations 1992 – SI 201 of 1992 ('Group Accounts Regulations 1992' or 'GAR 1992');
- The European Communities (Credit Institutions: Accounts) Regulations 1992 – SI 294 of 1992 – ('Credit Institutions Regulations 1992' or 'CIR 1992');
- The European Communities (Insurance Undertakings: Accounts) Regulations 1996, SI 23 of 1996 – ('Insurance Undertakings Regulations 1996' or 'IUR 1996').

This section is intended as a reference guide to the corresponding provisions in Irish company law and does not purport to be comprehensive. Readers are advised to refer to the Irish legislation for an understanding of relevant legal points.

Merger relief in the Republic of Ireland

As there is currently no legislation equivalent to merger relief in the Republic of Ireland, no explicit relief from the requirement of section 62(1) of the Companies Act 1963 to establish a share premium account is available. **19**

However, section 149(5) of the Companies Act 1963 provides that, whilst, in general, pre-acquisition profits of acquired subsidiaries may not be treated in the holding company's accounts as revenue profit, an exemption from that provision is available in that, where the directors and auditors are satisfied and so certify that it would be fair and reasonable and would not prejudice the rights and interests of any person, the profits or losses attributable to any shares in a subsidiary may be treated in a manner otherwise than in accordance with that subsection. **20**

The possible need for legal advice in relation to the application of section 149(5) to merger accounting should be considered before merger accounting is applied to Republic of Ireland companies. **21**

UK References	ROI References				
2006 Act and the 2008 Regulations	**1963 Act**	**GAR 1992**	**CIR 1992**	**IUR 1996**	**Comments**
Acquisition accounting					
Schedule 6 paragraph 9 of the Regulations		Regulation 19	Paragraph 10 of Part II of the Schedule	Paragraph 9 of Part IV of the Schedule	
Merger accounting					
Schedule 6 paragraph 10 of the Regulations		Regulation 21	Paragraph 11 of Part II of the Schedule	Paragraph 10 of Part IV of the Schedule	
Schedule 6 paragraph 11 of the Regulations		Regulation 22	Paragraph 12 of Part II of the Schedule	Paragraph 11 of Part IV of the Schedule	
Schedule 6 paragraph 12 of the Regulations		Regulation 23	Paragraph 13 of Part II of the Schedule	Paragraph 12 of Part IV of the Schedule	
Disclosures					
Schedule 6 paragraph 13(2)(b) of the Regulations		Paragraph 12(2)(b) of the Schedule	Paragraph 14(2)(b) of Part II of the Schedule	Paragraph 26(2)(b) of Part IV of the Schedule	

UK References	ROI References				
2006 Act and the 2008 Regulations	**1963 Act**	**GAR 1992**	**CIR 1992**	**IUR 1996**	**Comments**
Schedule 6 paragraphs 13(3)-13(5) of the Regulations		Regulation 27	Paragraph 16 of Part II of the Schedule	Paragraph 6 of Part IV of the Schedule	Irish company law requires that where the composition of the undertakings dealt with in the group accounts has changed significantly, information must be provided to make the comparison of successive sets of group accounts meaningful.
Schedule 6 paragraph 16 of the Regulations					No corresponding Irish provision
Share premium and merger relief – Appendix 1					
Section 610	Section 62				
Sections 611-615					No group reconstruction or merger relief in Irish company law.

Appendix II
Compliance with International Accounting Standards

The requirements of the FRS are consistent with International Accounting Standard 22 'Business Combinations' (revised 1993),* except for the provision in paragraph 13 of that standard relating to reverse acquisitions, which is incompatible with companies legislation in the UK and the Republic of Ireland.†

****Editor's note:*** *IAS 22 has now been replaced by IFRS 3. This eliminates merger accounting and requires acquisition accounting for all business combinations within its scope. A further revised version of IFRS 3 was issued in January 2008, which takes effect for accounting periods beginning on or after 1 July 2009.*

†***Editor's note:*** *UITF Information Sheet No 17 (issued 31 July 1996) noted that there could be some instances where it would be right and proper to invoke the true and fair override and apply reverse acquisition accounting, although each case should be considered on its merits.*

Appendix III
The development of the FRS

HISTORY

Before the Companies Act 1981

Although some use was made of merger accounting in the UK before the Companies Act 1981, and indeed an exposure draft of an accounting standard, ED 3, was published (in 1971), there was concern that the share premium provisions of the Companies Act 1948 might be interpreted so as to prohibit the use of merger accounting. This view was confirmed by the decision in *Shearer v Bercain* in 1980. **1**

The Companies Act 1981 and SSAP 23

The Companies Act 1981 introduced the concept of merger relief, removing the legal obstacle to merger accounting. Following this, the Accounting Standards Committee (ASC) issued an exposure draft, ED 31, converted into an accounting standard, SSAP 23 'Accounting for acquisitions and mergers', in 1985. **2**

SSAP 23 based its concept of a merger on whether or not the arrangements for the combination resulted in material resources leaving the group. This concept was supported by four criteria defining the circumstances in which merger accounting was permitted: **3**

(a) the business combination results from an offer to the holders of all equity shares and the holders of all voting shares that are not already held by the offeror; and
(b) the offeror has secured, as a result of the offer, a holding of (i) at least 90 per cent of all equity shares (taking each class of equity separately) and (ii) the shares carrying at least 90 per cent of the votes of the offeree; and
(c) immediately prior to the offer, the offeror does not hold (i) 20 per cent or more of all equity shares of the offeree (taking each class of equity separately) or (ii) shares carrying 20 per cent or more of the votes of the offeree; and
(d) not less than 90 per cent of the fair value of the total consideration given for the equity share capital (including that given for shares already held) is in the form of equity share capital; not less than 90 per cent of the fair value of the total consideration given for voting non-equity share capital (including that given for shares already held) is in the form of equity and/or voting non-equity share capital.

Note, however, that merger accounting remained optional even if these criteria were met. **4**

The EC Seventh Directive and the Companies Act 1989

The EC Seventh Company Law Directive introduced more stringent requirements to be met before merger accounting was permitted. The conditions of the Directive were implemented in Great Britain, with some additional provisions, by the Companies Act 1989, as amendments to the Companies Act 1985. These conditions are: **5**

(a) that at least 90 per cent of the nominal value of the relevant shares (those with unrestricted rights to participate both in distributions and in the assets on liquidation) in the undertaking acquired is held by or on behalf of the parent company and its subsidiary undertakings;

(b) that the proportion referred to in (a) was attained pursuant to an arrangement providing for the issue of equity shares by the parent company or one or more of its subsidiary undertakings;

(c) that the fair value of any consideration other than the issue of equity shares given pursuant to the arrangement by the parent company and its subsidiary undertakings did not exceed 10 per cent of the nominal value of the equity shares issued; and

(d) that adoption of the merger method of accounting accords with generally accepted accounting principles or practice.

6 In requiring compliance with generally accepted accounting principles, the Companies Act clearly acknowledged that merger accounting would not be appropriate for all business combinations that met the first three conditions.

7 The comparison, in condition (c), with the nominal value of shares issued is also noteworthy. The nominal value is of no economic significance. In contrast, the corresponding condition (d) of SSAP 23 refers to the fair value of the equity shares issued.

Limiting the use of merger accounting—the ED 48 proposals

8 ED 48 was issued by the ASC in February 1990 in response to widespread concern that the SSAP 23 conditions were too readily circumvented. It proposed to limit the use of merger accounting to a very restricted class of combinations that could be regarded as 'true' mergers. These were to be defined as a combination that was effectively an equal partnership between the combining parties, where no party saw itself as either an acquirer or an acquiree. In addition, there had to be continuing involvement from the management of each of the parties in the combined entity; and the parties were to be of broadly equal size. Any minority not accepting the merger offer was not to exceed 10 per cent, and no material consideration other than equity shares was permitted.

9 ED 48 then proposed that merger accounting would be required, and not merely permitted, for all combinations meeting these conditions (although, as a practical matter, it has been suggested that it would be relatively easy for merging parties to ensure that one of the conditions was not met, without fundamentally altering the commercial substance of the transaction, if they did not wish to use merger accounting—and thus for practical purposes the option to use acquisition accounting might be seen to remain).

10 Although respondents to ED 48 were generally in agreement with its proposals, there was criticism of the conditions for merger accounting, in particular of their subjective nature, which, it was expected, would give rise to difficulties in applying them consistently.

International Accounting Standards

11 The merger concept underlying ED 48 is similar to that proposed for a 'uniting of interests' in the International Accounting Standard 22, revised in 1993,* although that standard does not develop tests for identifying when a combination is a merger. IAS 22 defines a uniting of interests as:

****Editor's note:*** *IAS 22 was further revised in 1998 and has now been replaced by IFRS 3.*

'a business combination in which the shareholders of the combining enterprises combine control over the whole, or effectively the whole, of their net assets and operations to achieve a continuing mutual sharing in the risks and benefits attaching to the combined entity such that neither party can be identified as the acquirer.'

FRED 6

In considering the application of merger accounting, the Board was concerned by the apparent choice available in many cases between acquisition and merger accounting, and that two business combinations with very similar economic substance could be accounted for in different ways, with substantial differences in reported results and balance sheets not only for the financial year in which the combination occurred but for several years thereafter. The Board also found it difficult to identify any theoretical basis to justify the use of merger accounting for the wide range of business combinations for which it was then permissible. **12**

In issuing FRED 6, the Board therefore adopted the intention of ED 48, of narrowing the use of merger accounting. **13**

No major changes were proposed, but the Board sought to remove subjectivity where possible. The approach of the FRED was based on the belief that merger accounting should be applied to only a few rare instances of business combinations that were properly regarded as mergers, and that the vast majority of business combinations were more appropriately accounted for as acquisitions. **14**

The definition of a merger was redrafted, but its intent was unchanged. The definition of an acquisition was amended to make it clear that all combinations were either mergers or acquisitions. **15**

The six conditions under which merger accounting would have been permitted by ED 48 were redrafted as five criteria, as follows: **16**

Criterion 1 – redrafted form of ED 48 condition (a).

Criterion 2 – amended form of ED 48 condition (b), acknowledging that to require the board of a merged entity to have equal participation from each of the parties to the merger might prevent the parties to the merger from choosing the management they considered most appropriate; and might lead to too much focus on the numerical representation of each party on the new board at the expense of considering where the real decision taking influence lay.

Criterion 3 – redrafted form of ED 48 condition (e).

Criterion 4 – redrafted form of ED 48 condition (c).

Criterion 5 – redrafted form of ED 48 conditions (d) and (f), reducing these to a more general principle.

Disclosure

The disclosure requirements proposed by ED 48 were extended to require analysis into pre-combination and post-combination periods of several items in the profit and loss account, and the statement of total recognised gains and losses, rather than focusing solely on profit after tax and extraordinary items. **17**

MATTERS CONSIDERED IN THE LIGHT OF RESPONSES TO FRED 6

18 A large majority of the respondents to FRED 6 agreed with the proposals it contained, and these are accordingly unchanged. The following paragraphs describe those points on which respondents expressed concern and explain whether or not a change was made and the Board's reasoning for its decision.

Disclosure requirements on an acquisition

19 The full disclosure requirements proposed in the FRED relating to the pre-combination results of the parties to a merger, and the acquired entity in an acquisition, were supported by a majority of respondents, and particularly by users of accounts. Concern was expressed, however, at the practical difficulties in obtaining this information relating to acquisitions, and many preparers of financial statements questioned whether such disclosures were, in practice, of value to users.

20 The Board has therefore reconsidered the extent of the disclosures required in respect of the acquired company, and has made three main relaxations in the requirements:

(a) less detailed analysis of the results of the acquired company up to the date of acquisition is now required;
(b) only the profit after tax and minority interests for its previous financial year is now required to be shown; and
(c) fuller disclosure is now required only for substantial acquisitions, defined as being 'Class I'* or 'Super Class I' where the acquirer is a listed company, or in excess of 15 per cent of net assets or profits for others.

The FRS now states that this information is to be given using the accounting policies of the acquired company, instead of being restated using the acquirer's accounting policies.

21 Some respondents suggested that it would be more helpful for all disclosure requirements relating to acquisitions to be consolidated into one standard. The Board has accordingly included in this FRS the proposed disclosure requirements set out in FRED 7 (which were based on those in SSAP 22), amended to take account of responses made to that FRED. It has also incorporated references to the disclosure requirements relating to acquisitions in FRS 1 and FRS 3, unchanged other than to make it clear that the disclosures should be made separately for each material acquisition, and for other acquisitions in aggregate.

Disclosure requirements on a merger

22 The Board concluded that, in the case of a merger, no relaxation of the proposed disclosures was appropriate. Because of the continuing involvement of management of both parties to the merger, the practical difficulties would be less, and the likely significance of the merger to the shareholders would make it desirable to provide fuller information. Although it was argued that analysing pre-merger results among the parties was in some sense contrary to the concept of merger accounting, in that the financial statements were drawn up on the basis that the parties had always been merged, the Board took the view that full information on the combining parties separately was important to an understanding of the combined entity.

***Editor's note:** *See UITF Abstract 15 (revised 1999) 'Disclosure of substantial acquisitions'.*

Definitions and criteria for merger accounting

The definitions of mergers and acquisitions, and the criteria for merger accounting, were generally agreed as appropriate by respondents, and only minor drafting changes have been made. Criterion 4 has been amended to make clear the effect of an entity disposing of part of its business prior to the combination. **23**

Group reconstructions

There was general agreement with the proposed use of merger accounting in group reconstructions, but some respondents requested that this should be more widely available. The Board has therefore agreed to widen the definition of group reconstructions, provided minority rights are unaffected, to include situations where a new holding company is created; where a 'horizontal group' of companies under common ownership become a group under the companies legislation definition; and where a part of a group is transferred to a new company, not part of the group but owned by the same shareholders as the group. **24**

Merger expenses

The FRED proposed that merger expenses should be charged to the profit and loss account. Although a majority of respondents supported this proposal, there was significant support for deducting such costs from reserves, in a way similar to the costs of issuing an equity instrument under FRS 4. The Board believes, however, that there is a fundamental difference between the costs of issue of an equity instrument, which raises new capital, from which the costs may sensibly be deducted, and the costs of a merger, which does not raise new capital, but which requires an expenditure of resources that should therefore be charged to the profit and loss account. The Board has clarified that these costs should be shown as an exceptional item in accordance with paragraph 20 of FRS 3. **25**

Demergers

Several respondents suggested that the FRS should deal with the accounting issues arising on demergers as well. However, the Board took the view that such issues as arise on a demerger are unrelated to those of business combinations, and should not be dealt with in the same FRS (although the restructuring that takes place on a demerger may fall within the group restructuring provisions of this FRS). **26**

Alternative view – prohibiting the use of merger accounting

The Preface to the FRED set out an alternative view, that the use of merger accounting should be prohibited (other than for certain group reconstructions). This alternative view attracted little support; most commentators thought that mergers, although rare, were a separate class of business combination for which merger accounting should be available. The Board has, accordingly, not proceeded with that proposal. **27**

Legal Changes: 2009

In 2009 the legal references in FRS 6 were updated following the introduction of the Companies Act 2006 and The Large and Medium-sized Companies and Groups (Accounts and Reports) Regulations 2008 (SI 2008 No. 410). **28**

Appendix IV
Illustrative example of disclosure of reorganisation and integration costs

This example is provided as an aid to understanding and does not form part of the Financial Reporting Standard.

Paragraph 87 of the Explanation suggests that, for major acquisitions, management may wish to include in the notes to the financial statements the amount of reorganisation and other costs to be incurred in relation to the acquisition. The following example indicates one way in which this optional information might be presented. The best form of the disclosure will depend on individual circumstances.

COSTS OF REORGANISING AND INTEGRATING ACQUISITIONS

	Acquisition of European business (note (a)) £ million	Other acquisitions £ million	TOTAL £ million
Announced but not charged as at the previous year-end	–	25	25
Announced in relation to acquisitions during the year	170	–	170
Adjustments to previous years' estimates	–	(5)	(5)
	170	20	190
Charged in the year			
– operating profit	55	12	67
– elsewhere	65	–	65
	120	12	132
Announced but still to be charged at 31 December 1995	50	8	58

Note (a): Acquisition of European business

		£ million
Cost of acquisition		400
Reorganisation and integration expenditure announced		
Fundamental restructuring:		
–withdrawal from existing US business and related redundancies	65	
Other items (to be charged to operating profit):		
–other redundancy costs	75	
– re-branding and redesign costs	30	
Announced reorganisation and integration costs as shown in above table		170
Total investment		570

In addition to the £120 million expenditure shown in the above table, reorganisation and integration costs charged during the year include £30 million in respect of write-downs to fixed assets consequent on the closure of the XYZ plant.

Financial Reporting Standard 7 is set out in paragraphs 1–31.

The Statement of Standard Accounting Practice set out in paragraphs 4–31 should be read in the context of the Objective as stated in paragraph 1 and the definitions set out in paragraphs 2–3 and also of the Foreword to Accounting Standards and the Statement of Principles for Financial Reporting currently in issue.

The Explanation set out in paragraphs 32–85 shall be regarded as part of the Statement of Standard Accounting Practice insofar as it assists in interpreting that statement.

Appendix III 'The development of the FRS' reviews considerations and arguments that were thought significant by members of the Board in reaching the conclusions on FRS 7. The views of the member who dissented are set out in Appendix IV.

[FRS 7]
Fair values in acquisition accounting*†

(Issued September 1994)

Contents

	Paragraph
Summary	a–h
Financial Reporting Standard 7	
Objective	1
Definitions	2–3
Statement of Standard Accounting Practice	4–31
Scope	4
Application of smaller entities	4A
Determining the fair values of identifiable assets and liabilities acquired	5–25
Principles of recognition and measurement on an acquisition	5–6
Application of the principles	7–8
Tangible fixed assets	9
Intangible assets	10
Stocks and work-in-progress	11–12
Quoted investments	13
Monetary assets and liabilities	14
Contingencies	15
Business sold or held exclusively with a view to subsequent resale	16–18
Pensions and other post-retirement benefits	19–20
Deferred taxation	21–22
Investigation period and goodwill adjustments	23–25
Determining the cost of acquisition	26–28
Disclosures	29
Date from which effective	30
Amendment of SSAP 22	31
Explanation	32–85
Introduction	32–33
Determining the fair values of identifiable assets and liabilities acquired	34–75
Existing assets and liabilities of the acquired entity	34–38
Exclusion of post-acquisition costs	39–40
Measurement of identifiable assets and liabilities	41–46
Impaired assets	47–49
Tangible fixed assets	50–51

****Editor's note:*** *FRS 7 has been amended by FRS 25 with effect for accounting periods beginning on or after 1 January 2005 and by the 2008 improvements to Financial Reporting Standards.*

†***Editor's note:*** *The matters covered in FRS 7 are dealt with in Section 9 and 19 of FRS 102.*

Stocks and work-in-progress	52–57
Quoted investments	58
Monetary assets and liabilities	59–63
Contingencies	64
Business sold or held exclusively with a view to subsequent resale	65–69
Pensions and other post-retirement benefits	70–73
Deferred taxation	74–75
Determining the cost of acquisition	76–85
Fair values of the components of the purchase consideration	76
Cash and other monetary consideration	77
Capital instruments	78–79
Non-monetary consideration	80
Contingent consideration	81–84
Acquisition expenses	85

Adoption of FRS 7 by the Board

Appendices

I Note on legal requirements
II Compliance with International Accounting Standards
III The development of the FRS
IV Dissenting view

Fair values in acquisition accounting

Summary

GENERAL

Financial Reporting Standard 7 'Fair Values in Acquisition Accounting' sets out the principles of accounting for a business combination under the acquisition method of accounting. Companies legislation requires the identifiable assets and liabilities of the acquired entity to be included in the consolidated financial statements of the acquirer at their fair values at the date of acquisition. The difference between these and the cost of acquisition is recognised as goodwill or negative goodwill. The results of the acquired entity are included in the profit and loss account of the acquiring group from the date of acquisition. **a**

FAIR VALUES OF IDENTIFIABLE ASSETS AND LIABILITIES

The assets and liabilities recognised in the allocation of fair values should be those of the acquired entity that existed at the date of acquisition. They should be measured at fair values that reflect the conditions at the date of the acquisition. **b**

The liabilities of the acquired entity should not include provisions for future operating losses. Changes in the assets and liabilities resulting from the acquirer's intentions or from events after the acquisition should be dealt with as post-acquisition items. Similarly, costs of reorganisation and integrating the business acquired, whether they relate to the acquired entity or the acquiring group, should be dealt with as post-acquisition costs and do not affect the fair values at the date of acquisition. **c**

Fair values should be based on the value at which an asset or liability could be exchanged in an arm's length transaction. The fair value of monetary items should take into account the amounts expected to be received or paid and their timing. **d**

Unless they can be measured at market value, the fair values of non-monetary assets will normally be based on replacement cost, but should not exceed their recoverable amount as at the date of acquisition. The recoverable amount reflects the condition of the assets on acquisition but not any impairments resulting from subsequent events. The FRS specifies the methods for determining fair values of individual categories of assets and liabilities. **e**

INVESTIGATION PERIOD AND GOODWILL ADJUSTMENTS

The identification and valuation of assets and liabilities acquired should be completed, if possible, by the date on which the first post-acquisition financial statements of the acquirer are approved by the directors. If it has not been possible to complete the investigation of fair values by that date, provisional valuations should be made; these should be amended if necessary in the next financial statements with a corresponding adjustment to goodwill. **f**

COST OF ACQUISITION

The cost of acquisition is the amount of cash or cash equivalents paid and the fair value of other purchase consideration given by the acquirer, together with the **g** expenses of the acquisition. The FRS explains the methods used to determine the amounts to be ascribed to constituent parts of the purchase consideration.

h Where the payment of consideration for an acquisition is to be made after the date of acquisition, reasonable estimates of the amounts expected to be paid should be included in the cost of acquisition at their present values.

Financial Reporting Standard 7

Objective

1 The objective of this FRS is to ensure that when a business entity is acquired by another, all the assets and liabilities that existed in the acquired entity at the date of acquisition are recorded at fair values reflecting their condition at that date; and that all changes to the acquired assets and liabilities, and the resulting gains and losses, that arise after control of the acquired entity has passed to the acquirer are reported as part of the post-acquisition financial performance of the acquiring group.

Definitions

2 The following definitions shall apply in this FRS and in particular in the Statement of Standard Accounting Practice set out in paragraphs 4–31.

Acquisition:-
A business combination that is accounted for by using the acquisition method of accounting.

Business combination:-
The bringing together of separate entities into one economic entity as a result of one entity uniting with, or obtaining control over the net assets and operations of, another.

Date of acquisition:-
The date on which control of the acquired entity passes to the acquirer. This is the date from which the acquired entity is accounted for by the acquirer as a subsidiary undertaking under FRS 2 'Accounting for Subsidiary Undertakings'.

Fair value:-
The amount at which an asset or liability could be exchanged in an arm's length transaction between informed and willing parties, other than in a forced or liquidation sale.

Identifiable assets and liabilities:-
The assets and liabilities of the acquired entity that are capable of being disposed of or settled separately, without disposing of a business of the entity.

Recoverable amount:-
The greater of the net realisable value of an asset and, where appropriate, the value in use.

Value in use:-
The present value of the future cash flows obtainable as a result of an asset's continued use, including those resulting from the ultimate disposal of the asset.

References to companies legislation mean: 3

(a) in Great Britain, the Companies Act 1985;*
(b) in Northern Ireland, the Companies (Northern Ireland) Order 1986; and
(c) in the Republic of Ireland, the Companies Acts 1963–90 and the European Communities (Companies: Group Accounts) Regulations 1992.

Statement of Standard Accounting Practice

SCOPE

Financial Reporting Standard 7 applies to all financial statements that are intended to give a true and fair view of a reporting entity's financial position and profit or loss (or income and expenditure) for a period. Although the FRS is framed in terms of the acquisition of a subsidiary undertaking by a parent company that prepares consolidated financial statements, it also applies where an individual company or other reporting entity acquires a business other than a subsidiary undertaking. 4

APPLICATION TO SMALLER ENTITIES

Reporting entities applying the Financial Reporting Standard for Smaller Entities currently applicable are exempt from this accounting standard unless preparing consolidated financial statements, in which case they should apply the FRS to such statements as required by the FRSSE. 4A

DETERMINING THE FAIR VALUES OF IDENTIFIABLE ASSETS AND LIABILITIES ACQUIRED

Principles of recognition and measurement on an acquisition

The identifiable assets and liabilities to be recognised should be those of the acquired entity that existed at the date of the acquisition. 5

The recognised assets and liabilities should be measured at fair values that reflect the conditions at the date of the acquisition. 6

Application of the principles

As a consequence of the above principles, the following do not affect fair values at the date of acquisition and therefore fall to be treated as post-acquisition items: 7

(a) changes resulting from the acquirer's intentions or future actions;
(b) impairments, or other changes, resulting from events subsequent to the acquisition;
(c) provisions or accruals for future operating losses or for reorganisation and integration costs expected to be incurred as a result of the acquisition, whether they relate to the acquired entity or to the acquirer.

The application of these principles to specific classes of asset and liability is detailed in paragraphs 9–22 below. Subject to those paragraphs, fair values should be determined in accordance with the acquirer's accounting policies for similar assets and liabilities. 8

***Editor's note:** *This should now be taken to refer to the Companies Act 2006 as well.*

Tangible fixed assets

9 The fair value of a tangible fixed asset should be based on:

(a) market value, if assets similar in type and condition are bought and sold on an open market; or
(b) depreciated replacement cost, reflecting the acquired business's normal buying process and the sources of supply and prices available to it.

The fair value should not exceed the recoverable amount of the asset.

Intangible assets

10 Where an intangible asset is recognised, its fair value should be based on its replacement cost, which is normally its estimated market value.

Stocks and work-in-progress

11 Stocks, including commodity stocks, that the acquired entity trades on a market in which it participates as both a buyer and a seller should be valued at current market prices.

12 Other stocks, and work-in-progress, should be valued at the lower of replacement cost and net realisable value. Replacement cost is for this purpose the cost at which the stocks would have been replaced by the acquired entity, reflecting its normal buying process and the sources of supply and prices available to it—that is, the current cost of bringing the stocks to their present location and condition.

Quoted investments

13 Quoted investments should be valued at market price, adjusted if necessary for unusual price fluctuations or for the size of the holding.

Monetary assets and liabilities

14 The fair value of monetary assets and liabilities, including accruals and provisions, should take into account the amounts expected to be received or paid and their timing. Fair value should be determined by reference to market prices, where available, by reference to the current price at which the business could acquire similar assets or enter into similar obligations, or by discounting to present value.

Contingencies

15 Contingent assets and liabilities should be measured at fair values where these can be determined. For this purpose reasonable estimates of the expected outcome may be used.

Business sold or held exclusively with a view to subsequent resale

16 Where an interest in a separate business of the acquired entity is sold as a single unit within approximately one year of the date of acquisition, the investment in that business should be treated as a single asset for the purposes of determining fair values. Its fair value should be based on the net proceeds of the sale, adjusted for the

fair value of any assets or liabilities transferred into or out of the business, unless such adjusted net proceeds are demonstrably different from the fair value at the date of acquisition as a result of a post-acquisition event. This treatment should be applied to any business operation, whether a separate subsidiary undertaking or not, provided that its assets, liabilities, results of operations and activities are clearly distinguishable, physically, operationally and for financial reporting purposes, from the other assets, liabilities, results of operations and activities of the acquired entity.

Where the business has not been sold by the time of approval of the first financial statements after the date of acquisition, the fair value of the interest in the business should be based on the estimated net proceeds of the sale, provided: **17**

(a) a purchaser has been identified or is being sought; and
(b) the disposal is reasonably expected to occur within approximately one year of the date of the acquisition. The interest in the business or, if it is not a separate subsidiary undertaking, in the assets of the business, should be shown within current assets. When the sale price is subsequently determined, the original estimate of fair value should be adjusted to reflect the actual sale proceeds.

If the subsidiary undertaking or business operation is not, in fact, sold within approximately one year of the acquisition, it should be consolidated normally with fair values attributed to the individual assets and liabilities as at the date of acquisition, and corresponding adjustments to goodwill. **18**

Pensions and other post-retirement benefits

The fair value of a deficiency or, to the extent that it can be recovered through reduced contributions or through refunds from the scheme, a surplus in a funded pension or other post-retirement benefits scheme, or accrued obligations in an unfunded scheme, should be recognised as a liability or an asset of the acquiring group. **19***

Changes in pension or other post-retirement arrangements following an acquisition should be accounted for as post-acquisition items and should be dealt with in accordance with the requirements of the standard concerned with pension costs. **20**

Deferred taxation

Deferred tax on adjustments to record assets and liabilities at their fair values should be recognised in accordance with the requirements of FRS 19 'Deferred tax'. **21**

Deferred tax assets that were not regarded as recoverable and hence were not recognised before the acquisition may, as a consequence of the acquisition, satisfy the recognition criteria of FRS 19. Assets of the acquired entity should be recognised in the fair value exercise. Those of the acquirer or other entities within the acquiring group should be recognised as a credit to the tax charge in the post-acquisition period. **22**

Investigation period and goodwill adjustments

The recognition and measurement of assets and liabilities acquired should be completed, if possible, by the date on which the first post-acquisition financial statements of the acquirer are approved by the directors. **23**

***Editor's note:** *Amended by FRS 17 'Retirement benefits' with effect from 2005.*

24 If it has not been possible to complete the investigation for determining fair values by the date on which the first post-acquisition financial statements are approved, provisional valuations should be made; these should be amended, if necessary, in the next financial statements with a corresponding adjustment to goodwill.

25 Any necessary adjustments to those provisional fair values and the corresponding adjustment to purchased goodwill should be incorporated in the financial statements for the first full financial year following the acquisition. Thereafter, any adjustments, except for the correction of fundamental errors, which should be accounted for as prior period adjustments, should be recognised as profits or losses when they are identified.

DETERMINING THE COST OF ACQUISITION

26 The cost of acquisition is the amount of cash paid and the fair value of other purchase consideration given by the acquirer, together with the expenses of the acquisition as described in paragraph 28. Where a subsidiary undertaking is acquired in stages, the cost of acquisition is the total of the costs of the interests acquired, determined as at the date of each transaction.

27 Where the amount of purchase consideration is contingent on one or more future events, the cost of acquisition should include a reasonable estimate of the fair value of amounts expected to be payable in the future. The cost of acquisition should be adjusted when revised estimates are made, with consequential corresponding adjustments continuing to be made to goodwill until the ultimate amount is known.

28 Fees and similar incremental costs incurred directly in making an acquisition should, except for the issue costs of shares or other securities that are required by FRS 25 '(IAS 32) Financial Instruments: Disclosure and Presentation' to be accounted for as a reduction in the proceeds of a capital instrument, be included in the cost of acquisition. Internal costs, and other expenses that cannot be directly attributed to the acquisition, should be charged to the profit and loss account.*

DISCLOSURES

29 The disclosures that should be made relating to an acquisition are set out in paragraphs 21 and 23–37 of FRS 6 'Acquisitions and Mergers'.

DATE FROM WHICH EFFECTIVE

30 The accounting practices set out in the FRS should be regarded as standard in respect of business combinations first accounted for in financial statements relating to accounting periods commencing on or after 23 December 1994. Earlier adoption is encouraged but not required.

AMENDMENT OF SSAP 22

31 [*Not reproduced as SSAP 22 has now been superseded.*]

**Editor's note:* *Reference to FRS 25 added by that standard, and reference to FRS 4 removed.*

Explanation

INTRODUCTION

The FRS is consistent with the requirements of companies legislation regarding the acquisition method of accounting. It sets out principles for identifying the assets and liabilities of an acquired entity and determining their fair values, and for determining the cost of acquisition. 32

Under the acquisition method of accounting, the identifiable assets and liabilities acquired are recognised at their fair values as at the date of acquisition, and the difference between these and the cost of acquisition is accounted for as goodwill or negative goodwill. 33

DETERMINING THE FAIR VALUES OF IDENTIFIABLE ASSETS AND LIABILITIES ACQUIRED

Existing assets and liabilities of the acquired entity

The identifiable assets and liabilities over which the acquirer obtains control are those representing rights to future economic benefits and obligations to transfer economic benefits, including contingent rights and obligations, of the acquired entity that were in existence before the date of acquisition. 34

The identifiable assets and liabilities may include items that were not previously recognised in the financial statements of the acquired entity. These include assets and liabilities that are not normally recognised in accounts where no acquisition is involved, because other accounting standards preclude their immediate recognition. Examples are: 35

(a) pension surpluses or deficiencies identified on an acquisition that are otherwise recognised over several financial years in an entity's financial statements, in accordance with the requirements of SSAP 24 'Accounting for pension costs'*;
(b) contingent assets that may be assigned a value on acquisition, but cannot otherwise be recognised in financial statements because SSAP 18 'Accounting for contingencies'† precludes the recognition of a contingent gain until realisation becomes reasonably certain.

The examples given above are included in the identifiable assets and liabilities because when an acquisition is made it is necessary to identify and recognise, so far as possible, all assets and liabilities acquired, provided they can be reliably valued. If this is not done, the reporting of post-acquisition performance is distorted by changes in assets and liabilities not being recognised in the correct period. The usual accounting practice, for example, of deferring recognition of contingent assets, does not apply, because the recognition of an acquired asset represents the expectation that the amounts expended on its acquisition will be recovered; it does not anticipate a future gain. It is, however, necessary to review the recoverable amounts of such assets to ensure that provision is made for any probable losses. 36

Certain contingent assets and liabilities that crystallise as a result of the acquisition would also be recognised, provided that the underlying contingency was in existence 37

* ***Editor's note:*** *SSAP 24 has been superseded by FRS 17 'Retirement benefits'.*

† ***Editor's note:*** *SSAP 18 has been superseded by FRS 12 'Provisions, contingent liabilities and contingent assets'.*

before the acquisition. An example is where the acquired entity has previously entered into a contract that contains a clause under which obligations are triggered in the event of a change of ownership.

38 Identifiable liabilities include items such as onerous contracts and commitments that existed at the time of acquisition, whether or not the corresponding obligations were recognised as liabilities in the financial statements of the acquired entity. When an acquisition is made, provisions for liabilities would be recognised as identifiable liabilities only if such commitments had been made by the acquired entity before the date of acquisition. In the case of business closure decisions made by the acquired entity before the date of acquisition, the principles for recognising consequential provisions are set out in FRS 3 'Reporting Financial Performance', which states that obligations are incurred when there is a detailed formal plan for termination from which the entity cannot realistically withdraw.*

Exclusion of post-acquisition costs

39 The FRS does not permit provisions for future losses or for reorganisation costs expected to be incurred as a result of the acquisition to be included as liabilities acquired: they are not liabilities of the acquired entity as at the date of acquisition. As an example, if the acquirer decides to close a factory of the acquired entity as a measure to integrate the combined operations, this is a post-acquisition event. Only if the acquired entity was already committed to this course of action, and unable realistically to withdraw from it, would it be regarded as pre-acquisition. Similarly, if the acquirer undertakes a reorganisation to integrate the acquired operation or to improve its efficiency, this is also a post-acquisition event.

40 Where provisions for future costs were made by an acquired entity shortly before an acquisition took place, for example during the course of negotiations with the acquirer, it would be necessary to pay particular attention to the circumstances in order to determine whether obligations were incurred by the acquired entity before the acquisition. Only if the acquired entity was demonstrably committed to the expenditure whether or not the acquisition was completed would it have a liability at the date of acquisition. If obligations were incurred by the acquired entity as a result of the influence of the acquirer, it would be necessary to consider whether control of the acquired entity had been transferred at an earlier date and, consequently, whether the date of acquisition under the requirements of FRS 2 'Accounting for Subsidiary Undertakings' pre-dated such commitments.† Under paragraph 26 of FRS 6 'Acquisitions and Mergers', disclosure is required of provisions made by the acquired entity within the twelve months preceding the date of acquisition.

Measurement of identifiable assets and liabilities

41 Most acquisitions are not made on the basis of individual transactions in assets and liabilities. The acquisition transaction does not itself determine the values attributed to each asset and liability acquired and for this reason companies legislation and accounting standards require a fair value exercise to determine initial carrying amounts of assets and liabilities on an acquisition.

**FRS 3, paragraph 18.*

†*Under paragraph 45 of FRS 2 the date of acquisition may be indicated by the acquiring entity commencing its direction of the operating and financial policies of the acquired undertaking or by changes in flow of economic benefits.*

Although the FRS contains specific requirements for determining fair values of different classes of assets and liabilities, the concept of fair value underlying the specific rules is the value at which the asset, or liability, could be exchanged in an arm's length transaction between informed and willing parties. **42**

Where similar assets are bought and sold on a readily accessible market, the market price will represent the fair value. Where quoted market prices are not available, market prices can often be estimated, either by independent valuations, or valuation techniques such as discounting estimated future cash flows to their present values. In some cases, where quoted market prices are not available, subsequent sales of acquired assets may provide the most reliable evidence of fair value at the time of the acquisition. **43**

Where a fair value is based on a market price, it is important to ensure that such price is appropriate to the circumstances of the acquired business. For example, it may be possible to obtain a price for secondhand plant and machinery of the type used in the business, but the secondhand market may deal in very small volumes; or the items may not be identical in terms of the ability to obtain maintenance or technical support from the manufacturer or for the machinery to be customised to the requirements of the business. In general, unless the acquired business is genuinely able to consider the purchase of secondhand equipment as a viable alternative to purchasing direct from the manufacturer, the fair value of plant and machinery is more appropriately determined from the replacement cost of an equivalent new asset, depreciated where appropriate to reflect its age and condition. **44**

The fair value attributed to an asset should not exceed the value the business is able to recover from the asset, either from its disposal or, in the case of a fixed asset, by continuing to use the asset. Where the fair value is based on a market price, the net realisable value will be similar to the fair value, differing only by costs of realisation and the dealer's margin. However, where the fair value is based on depreciated replacement cost or cost of manufacture, the net realisable value and, in the case of a fixed asset, the value in use will also need to be considered. **45**

Both net realisable value and value in use at the time of the acquisition are unaffected by the acquirer's intentions for the future use of the asset. Net realisable value represents the amount for which the business would be able to sell the asset, whether or not such sale is intended. Similarly, the value in use of a fixed asset at the time of the acquisition depends, not on the intended use, but on the most profitable possible use of the asset. **46**

Impaired assets

Where the replacement cost of an acquired asset is not recoverable in full (owing, for example, to lack of profitability, under-utilisation or obsolescence), the fair value is the estimated recoverable amount. The FRS requires that a valuation at recoverable amount should reflect the condition of the asset on acquisition but not any impairments resulting from subsequent events. **47**

Where acquired assets that had not been impaired before acquisition are disposed of after acquisition for a reduced price (for example, as part of a post-acquisition reorganisation of the enlarged group), any losses resulting from their disposal would be treated as post-acquisition losses, ie attributed to the reorganisation, and would not reduce the fair values as at the date of acquisition. **48**

49 In some cases recoverable amount can be determined only by considering as a whole a group of assets that are used jointly, rather than by attempting to determine the recoverable amount of each identifiable asset in that group. Aggregation in such cases serves to facilitate the attribution of cash flows to the assets that help to generate them.

Tangible fixed assets

50 Where reliable market values are obtainable—for example, for quoted investments and certain types of property—fair value would be based on current market values of similar assets. As explained in paragraph 44 above, for many types of fixed asset—for example most plant and machinery, and specialised properties specific to the business—fair value is represented by gross replacement cost reduced by depreciation to take account of the age and condition of the asset. Depreciation rates need to reflect estimated asset lives and residual amounts used by the acquirer for similar types of asset; otherwise, without there being any change in the asset's use or intended use, the first post-acquisition profit and loss account would reflect the adjustment from the previous management's depreciation rate to the acquirer's depreciation rate.

51 For certain assets it is not easy to determine current replacement cost; neither is it possible to estimate the value of the future services that an asset can provide through its continued use, because of the inherent subjectivity of such a valuation. In such circumstances the historical cost of the asset updated by the use of price indices may be the most reliable means of estimating replacement cost. Where prices have not changed materially it would be acceptable to use a carrying value based on historical cost as a reasonable proxy for fair value.

Stocks and work-in-progress

52 Where stocks are replaced by purchasing in a ready market—for example, commodities and dealing stocks—to which the acquired entity has access, fair value is represented by market value. Where there is no ready market for a category of stocks—for example, most manufactured stocks—fair value is represented by the current cost to the acquired company of reproducing the stocks.

53 The FRS requires account to be taken of the way the acquired business purchased or manufactured the stocks. For example, for a business purchasing in wholesale markets the replacement cost would be the wholesale price; and the replacement cost of finished goods of a manufacturer will be the current cost of manufacture, not the cost of buying in finished goods from another manufacturer. Although this replacement cost takes account of the effects of input price changes during the period the stocks are held, no addition would be made for unrealised profit that would not normally be recognised in the acquired entity until the stocks are sold.

54 The current cost of manufacture for finished goods and work-in-progress would be based on current standard costs where these are employed. In practice, where there is a short manufacturing cycle, replacement cost may not be materially different from historical cost.

55 For long-term, maturing stocks, replacement cost would be based on market values if stocks at similar stages of completion are regularly traded in the market. In other cases, where such market transactions do not occur because either there is no market or the market is very thin, and where it is difficult to find replacement cost because replacement would be impossible in the short term, a surrogate for replacement cost

may be found in the historical cost of bringing the stocks to their present location and condition, including an amount representing an interest cost in respect of holding the stock.

For long-term contracts, SSAP 9 'Stocks and long-term contracts' requires turnover and cost of sales to be recognised as the contract progresses, and attributable profit to be recognised prudently as it is earned. For this reason, no adjustments to book values would be required to such contracts, other than adjustments that would normally result from assessing the outcome of the contract under SSAP 9, or reflecting the changeover to the acquirer's accounting policies.* 56

In estimating the net realisable value of stocks, an acquirer may reach a judgement about the value of slow-moving or redundant stocks that differs from that of the management of the acquired entity. However, any material write-down of the carrying value of stocks in the acquired entity's books before or at the time of the acquisition would need to be justified by the circumstances of the acquired entity before acquisition. If exceptional profits appear to have been earned on the realisation of stocks after the date of the acquisition, it will be necessary to re-examine the fair values determined on acquisition as required by paragraphs 23–25 of the FRS and, if necessary, to make an adjustment to these values and a corresponding adjustment to goodwill. If, alternatively, the profit is attributable to post-acquisition events it should be disclosed as an exceptional item as required by paragraph 30 of FRS 6. 57

Quoted investments

The fair value of quoted investments will normally be their market price. However, it may be necessary to adjust the market price to allow for short-term fluctuations or, in the case of large holdings, to reflect either a lower realisable value representing the difficulties of disposal or a higher value for a holding representing a substantial voting block. 58

Monetary assets and liabilities

Most short-term monetary assets and liabilities, including trade debtors and creditors, would be recognised at amounts expected to be received or paid on settlement or redemption. 59

The fair values of certain long-term monetary items may, however, be materially different from their book values. One example is where an acquired entity is carrying material amounts of long-term debt at fixed rates that do not reflect current borrowing rates. The fair value will be greater or lower than book value depending on the direction of changes in interest rates since the debt was issued. Another example is a material long-term debtor where the delay in settlement is not compensated by an interest charge reflecting current market rates. 60

The FRS requires monetary items to be stated at fair values where these are materially different from book values. Where the monetary item is a quoted security, its fair value is normally its market price. The fair values of other monetary items may be determined by considering the current terms on which a similar monetary asset or liability could be acquired or assumed, or by discounting to their present values the 61

**Editor's note:* *Account may also need to be taken of Application Note G to FRS 5 to the extent that this may affect the valuation of long-term contracts.*

total amounts expected to be received or paid. The choice of interest rate to be applied to long-term borrowings would be affected by current lending rates for an equivalent term, the credit standing of the issuer and the nature of any security. For long-term debtors (after any necessary provisions have been made) the interest rate would be based on current lending rates.

62 The differences between fair values arrived at by discounting and the total amounts receivable or payable in respect of the relevant items represent discounts or premiums on acquisition that would be dealt with in the financial statements of the acquiring group as interest income or expense—that is, by allocation to accounting periods over the term of the monetary items at a constant rate based on their carrying amounts.

63 Where debt instruments issued by the acquired company are quoted, market values at the date of acquisition would be used instead of present values. However, in cases where a reduced pre-acquisition market value of an acquired entity's debt reflected the market's perception that it was at risk of being unable to fulfil its repayment obligations, the reduction would not be recognised in the fair value allocation if the debt was expected to be repaid at its full amount.

Contingencies

64 The value attributed to a contingent asset or liability needs to reflect the best estimate of the likely outcome; otherwise the post-acquisition profit and loss account will reflect the change from the previous management's estimate to the acquirer's estimate, without any related event or change in circumstances. In rare cases where a commitment or a contingent asset is of a kind that is normally assumed or acquired in an arm's length transaction (for example, underwriting commitments), its fair value would reflect the market price for such transactions.

Business sold or held exclusively with a view to subsequent resale

65 Where the acquisition of a group of companies includes a subsidiary undertaking or a discrete business operation that has been sold, or is expected to be sold, as a single unit within approximately a year of the acquisition it is appropriate to treat the investment in this business as a single asset, and to assign a single fair value to the whole investment rather than assign individual fair values to the various assets and liabilities that are included in the operation to be sold. The asset the group acquires is regarded as the investment in the subsidiary undertaking or business operation, rather than the individual items; and the actual net realised value will normally provide the most reliable evidence of fair value at the date of acquisition. One effect of this treatment is that goodwill is effectively apportioned between the part of the acquired group that is to be kept and the part sold, with the result that no further adjustment to write off the goodwill relating to the business disposed of, to comply with UITF Abstract 3 'Treatment of goodwill on disposal of a business',* would be necessary. Where the effect is material, the net proceeds would be discounted to obtain their present value at the date of acquisition (taking into account any distribution of profits from the business). The principle explained in paragraph 85 below for attributing expenses to the cost of an acquisition would also apply to the costs of disposals.

66 Where the disposal has not been completed at the time of the first financial statements after the acquisition, the fair value is based on the estimated sales proceeds.

*****Editor's note:*** *UITF 3 has been superseded by FRS 10 'Goodwill and intangible assets'.*

Any initial estimate of fair value would normally be adjusted to actual net realised value within the period allowed for completing the investigation of fair values, with the change being adjusted against goodwill.

Such intended disposals would neither have been previously consolidated by the acquirer, nor have formed a continuing part of the activities of the acquiring group. In these circumstances, for an interest in a subsidiary undertaking, companies legislation* permits, and FRS 2 requires, the interest to be recognised as a current asset in the acquirer's consolidated accounts. The results of its operations during the holding period are excluded from the profit and loss account of the acquiring group. **67**

The FRS requires the same principles of valuation to be applied to disposals of other business operations that are not subsidiary undertakings. Therefore, for example, the assets of a division held for resale would be shown as a single separately described current asset. **68**

In the following circumstances it would be appropriate to estimate separately fair values at the acquisition date and to record a post-acquisition profit or loss on disposal: **69**

(a) the acquirer has made a material change to the acquired business before disposal;
(b) specific post-acquisition events occur during the holding period that materially change the fair value of the business from the fair value estimated at the date of acquisition; or
(c) the disposal is completed at a reduced price for a quick sale.

Pensions and other post-retirement benefits

The FRS requires that where an acquired entity sponsors a defined-benefit pension scheme, or a defined-benefit post-retirement scheme other than a pension scheme, the allocation of fair values should include an asset in respect of a surplus in a funded scheme and a liability in respect of a deficiency in a funded scheme or accrued obligations relating to an unfunded scheme.† **70**

The fair value of the deficiency or surplus should be measured in accordance with the requirements of FRS 17 'Retirement Benefits'. The extent to which a surplus can be recovered should also be determined in accordance with the requirements of FRS 17. **71‡**

[Withdrawn] **72§**

The valuation of the pension fund surplus or deficit depends on several assumptions: interest rates, inflation and investment returns; the likely turnover of staff; and future salary increases; and the acquirer would apply its own judgement in determining these assumptions. However, the FRS requires changes in pension or other post-retirement arrangements following an acquisition to be accounted for as post-acquisition items. An example is the cost of improvements to benefits granted to **73**

In Great Britain, the Companies Act 1985, section 229(3)(c); in Northern Ireland, the Companies (Northern Ireland) Order 1986, Article 237(3)(c); and in the Republic of Ireland the European Communities (Companies:Group Accounts) Regulations 1992, Regulation 11(c). (Editor's note:** For accounting periods beginning on or after 6 April 2008 this changes to section 405 (3) and (4) of the Companies Act 2006.)*

†***Editor's note:*** *The final sentence of this paragraph was deleted by FRS 17 'Retirement benefits'.*

‡***Editor's note:*** *The text was amended by FRS 17 'Retirement benefits'.*

§***Editor's note:*** *Deleted by FRS 17 'Retirement benefits'.*

members of an acquired scheme as part of a policy of harmonising remuneration packages in the enlarged group. This treatment is consistent with accounting for any changes stemming from the acquisition that affect the pension arrangements of the acquirer's own workforce, and has the effect of treating changes in pension arrangements on the same basis as the realignment of any other aspects of remuneration. The cost of post-acquisition changes to pension and other post-retirement arrangements would be dealt with in accordance with the requirements of FRS 17 relating to variations in pension cost.

Deferred taxation

74 Adjustments to record assets and liabilities of the acquired entity at their fair values are treated in the same way as they would be if they were timing differences arising in the entity's own accounts. For example, a non-monetary asset, such as a building, would be valued on acquisition at its market value. Any tax that would become payable if the asset were sold at that value would be provided for only if, before the acquisition, the acquired entity had entered into a binding agreement to sell the asset and rollover relief was not available.

75 There might be deferred tax assets, typically unrelieved tax losses, that were not recognised before the acquisition because there was insufficient evidence that they would be recoverable. The acquisition might make the recovery of the losses sufficiently likely to enable them to be recognised as assets in accordance with the criteria set out in FRS 19 'Deferred tax'. If the losses had arisen in the acquired entity, they would be regarded as contingent assets that had crystallised as a result of the acquisition and hence, consistently with paragraph 37, would be recognised as assets in the fair value exercise. If the losses had arisen in the acquiring group, they would not be assets of the acquired entity and hence would not be recognised in the fair value exercise.

DETERMINING THE COST OF ACQUISITION

Fair values of the components of the purchase consideration

76 In order to apply the requirements of the FRS, it is necessary to determine the fair values of the constituent parts of the purchase consideration. The purchase consideration may comprise:

(a) cash or other monetary items, including the assumption of liabilities by the acquirer;
(b) capital instruments issued by the acquirer, including shares, debentures, loans and debt instruments, share warrants and other options relating to the securities of the acquirer; or
(c) non-monetary assets, including securities of another entity.

Cash and other monetary consideration

77 Where the purchase consideration is in the form of cash or other monetary assets given or liabilities assumed, its fair value is normally readily determinable as the amount paid or payable in respect of the item. When settlement of cash consideration is deferred, fair values are obtained by discounting to their present value the amounts expected to be payable in the future. The appropriate discount rate is the rate at which the acquirer could obtain a similar borrowing, taking into account its credit standing and any security given.

Capital instruments

Where shares (and other capital instruments) issued by the acquirer are quoted on a ready market, the market price on the date of acquisition would normally provide the most reliable measure of fair value. Where control is transferred by a public offer, the relevant date is the date on which the offer or, where there is a series of revised offers, the successful offer becomes unconditional, usually as a result of a sufficient number of acceptances being received. Where, owing to unusual fluctuations, the market price on one particular date is an unreliable measure of fair value, market prices for a reasonable period before the date of acquisition, during which acceptances could be made, would need to be considered. **78**

Where securities issued by the acquirer are not quoted or, if they are quoted, the market price is unreliable owing, for example, to the lack of an active market in the quantities involved, it would be necessary to make a valuation of those securities. The fair value would be estimated by taking into account items such as: **79**

(a) the value of similar securities that are quoted;
(b) the present value of the future cash flows of the instrument issued;
(c) any cash alternative to the issue of securities; and
(d) the value of any underlying security into which there is an option to convert.

Where it is not possible to value the consideration given by any of the above methods, the best estimate of its value may be given by valuing the entity acquired.

Non-monetary consideration

Where the purchase consideration takes the form of non-monetary assets, fair values would be determined by reference to market prices, estimated realisable values, independent valuations, or other available evidence. **80**

Contingent consideration

The terms of an acquisition may provide that the value of the purchase consideration, which may be payable in cash, shares or other securities at a future date, depends on uncertain future events, such as the future performance of the acquired company. An example is an 'earn-out', where consideration payable to the vendor takes the form of an initial payment, together with further payments based on a multiple of future profits of the acquired company. By its nature, the fair value of such contingent consideration cannot be determined precisely at the date of acquisition. The FRS requires that the cost of acquisition should include a reasonable estimate of its fair value. Where it is not possible to estimate the total amounts payable with any degree of certainty, at least those amounts that are reasonably expected to be payable would be recognised. Initial estimates would be revised as further and more certain information becomes available. **81**

Where contingent consideration is to be satisfied by the issue of shares, amounts attributable to that consideration will need to be allocated between equity and liabilities in accordance with the classification principles in FRS 25 'Financial Instruments: Presentation'.* **82**

****Editor's note:*** *Paragraph amended by FRS 25, with effect for accounting periods beginning on or after 1 January 2009.*

83 [Withdrawn]*

84 Acquisition agreements may require payments to be made in various forms, for example as non-competition payments or as bonuses to the vendors who continue to work for the acquired company. In such circumstances, it is necessary to determine whether the substance of the agreement is payment for the business acquired, or an expense such as compensation for services or profit sharing. In the first case the expected payments would be accounted for as contingent purchase consideration; in the other case the payments would be treated as expenses of the period to which they relate.

Acquisition expenses

85 Acquisition expenses to be treated as part of the cost of acquisition include incremental costs such as professional fees paid to merchant banks, accountants, legal advisers, valuers and other consultants. Such expenses exclude any allocation of costs that would still have been incurred had the acquisition not been entered into—for example, the costs of maintaining an acquisitions department or management remuneration; such costs would be charged to the profit and loss account as incurred. Expenses of issuing shares and other capital instruments that qualify as issue costs are not added to the cost of acquisition.†

Adoption of FRS 7 by the Board

Financial Reporting Standard 7 – 'Fair Values in Acquisition Accounting' was approved for issue by a vote of seven of the eight members of the Accounting Standards Board. Mr Main dissented. His dissenting view is set out in Appendix IV.

Members of the Accounting Standards Board

Sir David Tweedie (Chairman)
Allan Cook (Technical Director)
Robert Bradfield
Ian Brindle
Michael Garner
Raymond Hinton
Donald Main
Graham Stacy

****Editor's note:*** *Paragraph deleted by FRS 25.*

†***Editor's note:*** *Paragraph amended by FRS 25.*

Appendix I
Note on legal requirements

GREAT BRITAIN

References are to the Companies Act 1985*

The Companies Act describes the acquisition method of accounting in Schedule 4A paragraph 9: 1

(a) The identifiable assets and liabilities of the undertaking acquired shall be included in the consolidated balance sheet at their fair values as at the date of acquisition. The 'identifiable' assets or liabilities of the undertaking acquired mean the assets or liabilities that are capable of being disposed of or discharged separately, without disposing of a business of the undertaking (Schedule 4A paragraph 9(2)).

(b) The income and expenditure of the undertaking acquired shall be brought into the group accounts only as from the date of the acquisition (Schedule 4A paragraph 9(3)).

(c) There shall be set off against the acquisition cost of the interest in the shares of the undertaking held by the parent company and its subsidiary undertakings the interest of the parent company and its subsidiary undertakings in the adjusted capital and reserves of the undertaking acquired. The resulting amount if positive shall be treated as goodwill, and if negative as a negative consolidation difference (Schedule 4A paragraph 9(4)-(5)).

(d) The 'acquisition cost' is defined as the amount of any cash consideration and the fair value of any other consideration, together with such amount (if any) in respect of fees and other expenses of the acquisition as the company may determine; and 'the adjusted capital and reserves' of the undertaking acquired are defined as the capital and reserves at the date of the acquisition after adjusting the identifiable assets and liabilities of the undertaking to fair values as at that date (Schedule 4A paragraph 9(4)).

Share premium and merger relief

Section 130(1) of the Act provides that if a company issues shares at a premium, whether for cash or otherwise, a sum equal to the aggregate amount or value of the premiums on those shares should be transferred to an account called the share premium account. The provisions of the Act relating to the reduction of a company's share capital apply, with exceptions, as if the share premium account were part of its paid-up share capital. 2

Limited relief from the above ('merger relief') is given by sections 131-134. 3

***Editor's note:** The various statutory references change with the introduction of the Companies Act 2006, which affects accounting for periods beginning on or after 6 April 2008. The various statutory references have changed as follows:*

Companies Act 1985 reference	***Companies Act 2006 reference***
Paragraphs 9 of Schedule 4A	*Paragraph 9 of Schedule 6 to the Large and Medium-sized Companies and Groups (Accounts and Reports) Regulations 2008 (SI 2008/410)*
Section 130	*Section 610*
Sections 131 to 134	*Sections 611 to 616*

4 Section 131 provides, inter alia, that, subject to specified conditions, where an issuing company has secured at least a 90 per cent equity holding in another company, section 130 does not apply to the premium on shares issued in the transaction that takes the holding in that other company to at least 90 per cent.

5 Section 133(1) provides that the premium on any shares to which the relief in sections 131 and 132 applies may also be disregarded in determining the amount at which any shares or other consideration provided for the shares issued is to be included in the offeror company's balance sheet.

Share premium and fair value

6 Shares forming part of the consideration are valued at their fair value for the purposes of computing acquisition cost and goodwill under paragraph 9(4) of Schedule 4A. By contrast, the value of the share premiums arising on the shares issued, for the purposes of section 130, is based on the value to the issuing company of the consideration it has received. Where these values are different, or where (if the merger relief provisions apply) the premiums are disregarded, the cost of investment in the parent company's books will be different from the cost of acquisition for the purposes of paragraph 9(4). In such circumstances the difference should form a separate element of consolidated reserves, and does not form part of goodwill.

NORTHERN IRELAND

7 The legal requirements in Northern Ireland are very similar to those in Great Britain. The following table shows the references to the Companies (Northern Ireland) Order 1986 that correspond to the legal references in paragraphs 1-6 above.

Great Britain	*Northern Ireland*
Schedule 4A paragraph 9	Schedule 4A paragraph 9
Sections 130-134	Articles 140-144

REPUBLIC OF IRELAND

8 The following table shows the references to the European Communities (Companies: Group Accounts) Regulations 1992 and the Companies Act 1963 that correspond to the legal references in paragraphs 1-6 above.

Great Britain	*Republic of Ireland*
Schedule 4A paragraph 9	Regulation 19
Section 130	Companies Act 1963 section 62
Sections 131–134	No equivalent

Appendix II
Compliance with International Accounting Standards

The International Accounting Standards Committee (IASC) has issued a revised standard IAS 22 'Business Combinations'.* The principal areas where the revised IAS 22 and the FRS are at variance† are as follows. First, the revised IAS 22 requires that fair values of identifiable assets and liabilities acquired in an acquisition should be determined by reference to their intended use by the acquirer. The FRS requires the identifiable assets and liabilities to be recorded at their fair values as at the date of acquisition. Secondly, certain adjustments that would be treated as fair value adjustments under the revised IAS 22, for example those for additional liabilities recognised to reflect an acquirer's different intentions regarding an acquisition, would be accounted for as post-acquisition items under the FRS.

***Editor's note:** *IAS 22 has now been replaced by IFRS 3. This potentially requires the identification of a greater number of intangible assets than FRS 7.*

†*The Board's reasons for adopting proposals that differ from those of the IASC's revised IAS 22 are set out in Appendix III, at paragraphs 15-16 and 27-28.*

Appendix III
The development of the FRS

GENERAL AND HISTORY

1 The principle of attributing fair values in consolidated financial statements to the assets and liabilities of newly acquired subsidiaries has been recognised in UK accounting standards for many years and, since 1989, in companies legislation.

SSAP 14

2 SSAP 14 'Group accounts', which was published in 1978, required the purchase consideration for the acquisition of a subsidiary to be allocated between the underlying net tangible and intangible assets other than goodwill on the basis of the fair value to the acquiring company. The standard gave no guidance on how to determine fair values.

SSAP 22

3 SSAP 22 'Accounting for goodwill', issued in 1984, gave limited guidance on how to identify the assets and liabilities of an acquired business that should be regarded as separable from the purchased goodwill arising on the acquisition. It also sanctioned the practice that had evolved of adjusting the fair values ascribed to the separable net assets acquired to include provisions for anticipated future losses or costs of reorganisation. Such provisions were permitted to be recognised in the fair value exercise if the future losses or costs were taken into account in arriving at the purchase price.

4 Subsequently, however, concern among users began to emerge over the extent to which the use of provisions could potentially be hidden or abused. The Accounting Standards Committee (ASC) took action to address these concerns by amending SSAP 22 to include some specific disclosure requirements relating to the fair value exercise. The revised SSAP 22, published in 1989, required disclosure of adjustments made to the book values of the assets and liabilities of an acquired business, analysed into revaluations and provisions. It also required disclosure of movements on provisions related to acquisitions, analysed into the amounts used and the amounts released unused or applied for another purpose. At the same time as SSAP 22 was being amended, the ASC was developing an accounting standard on fair value accounting (see paragraph 6 below).*

Companies Act 1989

5 The Companies Act 1989 introduced a new Schedule 4A to the Companies Act 1985, which set out rules regarding the form and content of consolidated financial statements. The Act requires that, in accounting for the acquisition of a subsidiary, the subsidiary's identifiable assets and liabilities must be included in the consolidated balance sheet at their fair values as at the date of acquisition. There is no guidance in the Act on how to determine the fair values of assets and liabilities acquired.

***Editor's note:** *SSAP 22 has been replaced by FRS 10 'Goodwill and Intangible Assets'.*

ED 53

The ASC issued a discussion paper in 1988, followed in 1990 by an exposure draft, ED 53 'Fair value in the context of acquisition accounting'. ED 53 contained proposals for determining fair values of assets and liabilities identified in an acquisition, for dealing with anticipated reorganisation costs and for valuing the consideration given for an acquisition. **6**

ED 53 proposed that fair values should be determined from the perspective of the acquiring company, based on circumstances at the date of acquisition. Its proposals for dealing with acquisition provisions did not permit provision to be made for future trading losses of acquired businesses but did, however, continue to permit provisions for reorganisation costs to be made as fair value adjustments if there was a clearly defined programme of reorganisation that had been costed in reasonable detail and there was evidence that the acquirer took account of the plans and costs in formulating the offer. **7**

ASB Discussion Paper

In April 1993, the Board published a Discussion Paper, 'Fair values in acquisition accounting'. The Board adopted much of the work of the ASC in framing its proposals, but concluded that a different approach to the recognition of liabilities was necessary to address a number of issues, including those raised in responses to ED 53. A theme common to several of the commentators' responses had been that the basic principles underlying ED 53's approach had not been properly developed and in particular that the exposure draft had failed to rationalise its conclusions on key issues such as the recognition of reorganisation and future loss provisions. **8**

The Discussion Paper contained proposals that attempted to draw a clear distinction of principle between recording the elements of the purchase transaction, including accounting for the pre-acquisition assets and liabilities of the acquired business, and the items that should fall into the post-acquisition period. The proposals would have precluded provisions both for future losses in acquired businesses and, as a departure from ED 53, for reorganisation costs following an acquisition from being included as fair value adjustments. The principal reasons for proposing such a radical change to existing practices were threefold: **9**

(a) the proposals for dealing with the recognition of anticipated future losses and reorganisation costs were consistent with the Board's draft Statement of Principles regarding the recognition of liabilities;
(b) the proposals were consistent with the philosophy behind the 'information set' approach in FRS 3 'Reporting Financial Performance' in respect of presenting the financial effects of post-acquisition activities, including reorganisation of acquired businesses;
(c) to meet users' concerns on perceived scope for abuse; it was doubtful whether an alternative approach of developing a standard founded on enhanced disclosure of acquisition provisions, supplemented by specific and probably arbitrary rules on cut-off between pre- and post- acquisition items would prove as effective in the long term as an approach built on the Board's draft Statement of Principles.

FRED 7

10 FRED 7 was published in December 1993. It retained the essential features of the proposals in the Discussion Paper, while refining and clarifying them to take account of the comments received.

11 Views on the proposal in the Discussion Paper that all costs of reorganising acquired businesses should be treated as charges to post-acquisition profits had been divided, with a small majority in favour of the proposed treatment. Support had been strongest among user groups, who generally welcomed the transparency of the proposals in providing a proper basis for analysing the financial consequences of acquisition activities. Opposition had been voiced by many—although by no means all—preparers, who argued that the proposals belied the reality of the way acquisitions are handled because they failed to reflect the fact that the cost of an acquisition and subsequent, directly related expenditure are the product of a single investment decision. As an example, many commentators had argued that the costs incurred in the immediate post-acquisition period to implement a business plan to reorganise an acquisition were probably discrete and significant and were an integral part of the investment appraisal process; such costs, they contended, should not be reported in the group's trading results. The purchase and integration of a subsidiary, in their eyes, was in substance a single capital transaction, despite the fact that some elements might be revenue in form.

12 The Board set out in FRED 7 the basis for its conclusions on the proposed treatment of post-acquisition reorganisation costs. The main arguments, which are equally applicable to the FRS, are summarised as follows.

(a) The proposals were made in the context of the fundamental changes to the disclosure of financial performance that were introduced by FRS 3. If a company incurs material revenue expenditure to improve future profitability, the costs are normally charged to the profit and loss account. FRS 3 and the Operating and Financial Review both provide the facility for proper disclosure and explanation of the resulting volatility in the reported results. The Board believed that all such expenditure should be treated similarly, whether it related to a reorganisation following an acquisition or to a reorganisation of an ongoing business. It would be left to investment analysis to assess the benefit to an entity of a reorganisation.

(b) The proposals in respect of the recognition of liabilities were consistent with the Board's draft Statement of Principles. The approach rested on whether there was an obligation in the acquired entity at the acquisition date. The Board recognised that, where an acquisition was made, the acquirer might have taken into account additional costs to reorganise the operations of the combining entities and such costs might have been factored into the investment decision and the amount of purchase consideration to be offered. However, it did not follow that these costs should be deemed to increase the liabilities of the acquired entity existing at the acquisition date.

(c) The proposals, which required reorganisations related to acquisitions to be treated on the same footing as any other reorganisations, set out principles that avoided the need to define cutoff points between items to be included in the fair value exercise and items to be recognised in the post-acquisition period, which would have been difficult to achieve. Framing an alternative approach on the basis of the acquirer's intentions at the time of the acquisition would, in the Board's opinion, have led to artificial distinctions being drawn not only between the treatment of reorganisations affecting the acquired business and consequential changes in the existing business of the acquirer, but also between reorganisations that were planned at the time of acquisition and those that occurred later.

Many commentators had argued that the 'acquirer's perspective' should be retained as a principle for attributing fair values to the assets and liabilities acquired. They had contended that because the purchase consideration was based on the acquirer's assessment of the fair value of the acquired entity and its underlying assets and liabilities, it followed that the allocation of the purchase consideration should also be based on the acquirer's perspective. **13**

The Board is of the view that under its draft Statement of Principles, management intent is not a sufficient basis for recognising changes to an entity's assets and liabilities. It is events, not intentions for future actions, that increase or decrease an entity's assets or liabilities. When intentions are translated into actions that commit the entity to particular courses of action, the accounting should then reflect any obligations or changes in assets that arise from those actions. In relation to acquisition accounting, the Board concluded that events of a post-acquisition period that resulted in the recognition of additional liabilities or the impairment of existing assets of an acquired entity should be reported as events of that period rather than of the pre-acquisition period. **14**

Some commentators expressed concern that the proposals for precluding any reorganisation provisions as fair value adjustments were more restrictive than the requirements in the USA or International Accounting Standards. They urged the Board to go no further than to achieve consistency with US GAAP which, although not permitting provisions for future losses of acquired companies to be recognised as fair value adjustments, would allow adjustments to be made to take account of management intentions in the valuation of acquired assets, including, for example, provisions in respect of the intended closure of facilities in the acquired entity that are duplicated in the enlarged group. **15**

In developing FRED 7, the Board took into account the fact that US GAAP in this area considerably pre-dates the development of the present framework of general accounting concepts in the USA, as well as the IASC framework and the UK draft Statement of Principles, which are similar. The Board took the view that its proposals were consistent with the conceptual frameworks that had been developed elsewhere and, in particular, noted that the principle of accounting for obligations rather than management intentions was gaining greater acceptance internationally. **16**

MATTERS CONSIDERED IN THE LIGHT OF RESPONSES TO FRED 7

The following paragraphs refer to comments made by respondents to FRED 7, and explain with reasons the changes the Board has made to the proposals of the FRED or the Board's reasons for rejecting arguments for changes. Individual Board members gave greater weight to some factors than to others. **17**

Reorganisation provisions

FRED 7 proposed that the identifiable assets and liabilities recognised in the fair value exercise should be those of the acquired entity that existed at the date of acquisition, and should include provisions neither for future operating losses nor for reorganisation and integration costs expected to be incurred as a result of the acquisition. **18**

19 This proposal met with outright support from institutional investors, analysts and users of accounts; substantial support from accountancy firms and accountancy bodies; and strong, though not unanimous, opposition from preparers of accounts.

20 The main arguments raised by respondents opposed to the proposals in the FRED are summarised below, together with the Board's response to the arguments.

Commercial reality

21 It was argued that the FRED ignored the commercial reality of the transaction, namely that the acquirer's management takes the reorganisation and integration costs into account in its 'project plan' for the acquisition, and regards these costs as part of the 'investment'; they should therefore be treated as akin to additional consideration. Furthermore, it was argued, under the FRED's proposals the acquisition of a poorly organised business that is then reorganised by the acquirer gives a different accounting result from the acquisition of an equivalent but well-organised business that is not in need of reorganisation.

22 Of those who preferred the status quo on reorganisation provisions, most agreed that the existing situation was unsatisfactory and that tighter definitions and controls were needed; in particular, there was little support for continuing to allow provisions to be made for future losses of the acquired business, and most agreed that there should be rules to restrict the use of reorganisation provisions made as fair value adjustments.

23 The Board has carefully reconsidered the arguments against its proposals, which reiterated the arguments raised by a majority of preparers against the proposals in the Discussion Paper. The Board recognises the strength of feeling held in some quarters against this aspect of its proposals, which changes long-standing accounting practice. It has also balanced these views with those of user and other groups who supported the proposals. While not discounting the reasons or rationale underlying the position of those opposed to its proposals, the Board decided that it should develop an FRS on the basis of the proposals in FRED 7. It believes that this FRS will lead to clearer and more consistent reporting than has been the case under existing practices. Furthermore, the Board remains of the view that the approach adopted in the FRS is more soundly based on principle than would be an alternative approach that sought to improve existing standards by addressing disclosure issues and developing detailed rules that had the principal objective of constraining reorganisation provisions solely in order to prevent abuse.

24 Without repeating all the arguments underlying the Board's position as set out in FRED 7, the Board reaffirms that the principles in the FRS for determining the fair values of the assets and liabilities of the acquired entity adhere closely to the Board's draft Statement of Principles in respect of the recognition of assets and liabilities, and to the philosophy behind FRS 3 (complemented by the Operating and Financial Review) for reporting financial performance and other gains and losses.

25 The FRS, therefore, follows the principle (as set out in the draft Statement of Principles) that identifiable liabilities are limited to obligations of the acquired entity that existed at the date of acquisition and, consequently, other changes should fall into the post-acquisition period. The Board recognises that rationalisation expenditures, whether to improve or to integrate part of the business following an acquisition, are undertaken because they are expected to result in lasting and long-term benefits. However, in the Board's view this does not justify the effective capitalisation of that expenditure as goodwill, irrespective of whether it was planned at the time of the acquisition or whether the plans were formulated after the acquisition took place.

The Board also takes the view that the acquisition of a well-organised company is a different transaction from the acquisition of a company in need of reorganisation, and there is no reason why the two transactions should result in the same accounting outcome. In one case the acquirer is reporting the acquisition of a business whose previous management ran it efficiently; in the other, the acquirer is reporting the acquisition of a less efficient business and the subsequent expenditure intended to improve it. In the first case, the success of the business was apparent before the acquirer agreed to buy it; in the second, the value of the reorganisation expenditure will be judged subsequently by the increase in profitability of the acquired business that is achieved. **26**

International competitiveness and international GAAP

It was suggested by some respondents that the FRED's approach, by being stricter in some respects than the corresponding provisions of accounting standards in other countries (in particular, US GAAP and the International Accounting Standard) would damage the competitiveness of UK companies. Conversely, others have argued that the existing flexible accounting practices in the UK have encouraged UK companies to overpay for acquisitions compared with foreign companies. The Board takes the view that accounting standards should be neutral as to economic effect. Therefore, the FRS seeks to provide greater clarity in the reporting of acquisition activities. The more transparent accounting resulting from the FRS and from other accounting reforms that the Board has undertaken should contribute to sound economic decisions. **27**

The Board carefully considered the international harmonisation issue during the development of FRED 7. As noted in paragraph 16 above, the Board believes that the FRS is consistent with the conceptual frameworks that have been adopted by various standard-setting bodies. **28**

'Socio-economic' consequences

Some respondents also claimed that acquirers will be less willing to acquire companies in need of reorganisation, thus allowing inefficient management to remain and preventing rationalisation that is beneficial to the economy as a whole. However, the Board notes that the cash flow effect of a transaction is the same whichever accounting treatment is adopted. **29**

Understandability of financial statements

Several preparers of accounts suggested that the reporting of acquisitions would be more difficult to understand, because the full cost to the acquirer will not be clear and the post-acquisition results will be distorted by reorganisation and integration costs. However, users who responded were unanimous that the FRED's proposals would provide them with clearer and more informative information on acquisitions. **30**

In response to those commentators who argued that the financial statements should be capable of showing the full cost of the investment in an acquisition, including the intended costs of post-acquisition reorganisation, the FRS has introduced a recommendation that the planned reorganisation expenditure relating to the acquisition should be disclosed in the notes to the financial statements (see paragraph 40 below). **31**

Anti-avoidance measures

32 There was concern that the requirements of the FRS could be circumvented by collusion between the vendor and the acquirer, resulting for example in the vendor entering into obligations to restructure the business on the instructions of the acquirer before the formal transfer of control.

33 The Discussion Paper had proposed that any reorganisation provisions made by the vendor in the six months before the acquisition should be treated as post-acquisition; however, this was generally regarded as unnecessarily draconian and was omitted from the FRED.

34 The FRS deals with the issue in three ways. First, it emphasises that provisions should be included in the balance sheet of the acquired company at the date of acquisition only if that entity had a commitment from which it could not realistically withdraw whether or not the acquisition had been completed. Secondly, it draws attention to the possibility that the effective transfer of control took place at an earlier date than the formal transfer of shares. Thirdly, there is an additional disclosure requirement (included in FRS 6) for any provisions for reorganisation made by the acquired company within 12 months before the date of acquisition to be shown separately in the 'fair value table'.

Conclusion

35 The Board gave careful consideration to the arguments of those opposed to the proposals in the FRED, and acknowledged the strength of feeling particularly among many preparers of accounts. However, it concluded that the arguments put forward were essentially those it had already addressed in coming to its initial views expressed in the Discussion Paper and FRED 7. Moreover, where the arguments concern the understandability of financial statements, due regard must be given to the views of the professional users of accounts—in particular, the institutional investors and analysts, who were fully in support of the proposals.

Other issues

'Acquirer's perspective'

36 Several respondents (including both some of those who supported the FRED's approach to reorganisation provisions as well as some of those who opposed it) argued that the fair values should be determined from the 'acquirer's perspective'. However, the Board took the view that this term had no single clear meaning, and might be interpreted to indicate that fair values should take into account the decisions of the acquirer taken after the acquisition. For this reason, the Board has avoided using the term in the FRS, but has added more specific descriptions of the extent to which the acquirer's estimates and perceptions are taken into account in determining fair values. The concept of fair value underlying these specific rules remains, however, the value at which the asset, or liability, could be exchanged in an arm's length transaction between informed and willing parties. This concept is independent of the particular circumstances of either the acquirer or the acquired business.

Disclosure of provisions for reorganisation costs

Several respondents were concerned that, if reorganisation and similar costs relating to an acquisition were reported in the profit and loss account in accordance with the provisions of FRS 3, such costs might be reported as a deduction from the results of acquisitions, or as part of continuing activities; or, if they related to a fundamental reorganisation of the acquiring entity, as an exceptional item outside operating profit. Users might therefore find it difficult to ascertain the total costs relating to acquisitions. Instead, they proposed that a new category of exceptional item should be defined, to include all costs of reorganisation, restructuring and integration relating to an acquisition, that would not form part of operating profit. **37**

The Board concluded that this alternative proposal would confuse different kinds of costs relating to acquisitions, some of which might properly be excluded from operating profit but others of which were just as much an operating cost as the costs of routinely reorganising an existing part of the business. Furthermore, the introduction of a new class of exceptional item would lead to considerable difficulties of definition, as in many cases it was difficult to draw a clear distinction between costs relating to the acquisition, and similar costs relating to the acquirer's existing business that might well still have been incurred had the acquisition not taken place. **38**

The Board therefore decided against introducing a new class of exceptional item. FRS 6, which now includes all disclosure requirements relating to acquisitions, sets out in paragraph 86 how the requirements of FRS 3 apply to costs relating to acquisitions. **39**

In addition, paragraph 87 of FRS 6 suggests that management may wish to show, in a note to the financial statements, the total expenditure announced in relation to reorganisation and integration of acquisitions, together with the expenditures charged in the profit and loss account in the period and the further amount expected to be incurred. This would provide users with a clear statement of the total costs involved with the acquisition, and companies would be able to add what further explanation and discussion of the figures they think appropriate. **40**

Pension surpluses

The FRED proposed that an actuarial surplus or deficit on a pension scheme operated by the acquired company should be recognised as an asset or liability on acquisition. Many respondents thought it imprudent to carry such a surplus as an asset, as it was often uncertain whether it could be realised. They therefore proposed that, whilst provision should still be made for a deficit, a surplus should not be recognised as an asset. **41**

The Board has reconsidered the issue, and concluded that, although recognition of a surplus is consistent with the principles on which the FRS is based, it is important that the fair value attributed to such a surplus is justified. The FRS therefore requires the fair value of a surplus to be determined taking into account the extent to which, and timescale over which, the surplus is reasonably expected to be realised, normally in the form of reductions in future contributions This requirement was amended by FRS 17 so that a surplus is recognised to the extent that it can be recovered through reduced contributions or through refunds from the scheme. **42**

The Board is currently reviewing the existing accounting standard on pension costs, SSAP 24*. However, the Board decided that to omit reference to pension surpluses and **43**

**SSAP 24 was superseded by FRS 17.*

deficits in the FRS, or to require fair values to be based on the assets or liabilities recognised by the acquired company in its own accounts under SSAP 24, might result in the omission of significant assets and liabilities and subsequent misstatement of profits of the enlarged group.

Acquisition expenses

44 The FRED proposed that the amount of incidental expenses that fall to be treated as an addition to the cost of acquisition should be restricted to incremental costs that would not have been incurred had the acquisition not taken place, and did not permit the capitalisation of internal costs even where they might be directly related to the acquisition. This proposal was consistent with the revised IAS 22 and US GAAP, and took a deliberately restrictive view to avoid the danger of overstating the cost of acquisition.

45 An alternative view is that the incremental cost approach is anomalous where the equivalent services, such as legal advice or acquisition search and investigation services, are provided by in-house departments rather than by external advisers or consultants.

46 There was substantial support from respondents for each view. The Board concluded that the difficulty of defining 'incremental' for in-house facilities might lead to excessive costs being capitalised, with the resulting overstatement of profits. This outweighed the possible anomalies that might arise. The proposals in the FRED have accordingly been carried through to the FRS.

Discounting

47 The FRED proposed that monetary assets and liabilities should be discounted to present value where they were materially different from nominal amounts. Although this was supported, a substantial minority of respondents were concerned over the introduction of discounting on a piecemeal basis, applying only to assets and liabilities of an acquisition, rather than as part of a more general application of discounting to all assets and liabilities.

48 The Board has reaffirmed its view that monetary assets and liabilities acquired in an acquisition should be included at their fair value at the time of the acquisition; this fair value will depend on the estimated amounts and timing of payments, and, in the case of long-term items not bearing interest at current market rates, may be materially different from their face value or nominal value. Significant distortions to reported profits may arise if such items are not included at their fair value. Discounting is an established and widely used valuation technique, and is one method of arriving at an estimate of fair value. The Board notes that this treatment is also consistent with the revised IAS 22 and with US GAAP.

Appendix IV
Dissenting view

Mr Main dissents from the FRS because of its treatment of the costs an acquiring company incurs to convert an acquired entity into the business unit it envisaged when making the acquisition. He was content at the exposure draft stage to let the proposal go forward in order to elicit a public response. However, he has found his concern reinforced by comments received and therefore feels unable to vote for the FRS. 1

Mr Main believes that it is very rare for a company to acquire another without intending to make changes to the acquired business to enable it to operate efficiently. Such changes may include, on the one hand, investment in, and reorganisation of, the assets being acquired to enable products or services to be provided efficiently, and, on the other hand, reductions of excessive manpower, buildings or equipment to enable an adequate profit to be earned. 2

Mr Main believes that the need for such changes and the likely cost of executing them are invariably known to the acquirer at the time the acquisition is made, and that the normal practice of management when considering a proposed acquisition for approval is to aggregate the acquisition price with these costs of bringing the acquired entity into a state acceptable to the buyer, in order to arrive at the investment total against which the expected earnings are judged. 3

The requirements of the FRS will prevent a company from recognising in the financial statements at the time of acquisition the costs of the intended changes. It is only when such costs are committed irrevocably that they are to be included in the financial statements, and even then, to the extent that these costs are not capital expenditure, they cannot be included as part of the investment cost of the acquisition. 4

For these reasons the financial statements will, in his view, be misleading and fail to provide accountability for the transactions that have taken place. 5

Mr Main supports the view expressed by many commentators on the Discussion Paper and exposure draft, as set out in paragraphs 11 and 21 of 'The development of the FRS' (Appendix III), that the costs of an acquisition and subsequent directly related expenditure are the product of a single investment decision; and that the purchase and integration of a subsidiary are in substance a single capital transaction. He believes that the opposition to this view by certain commentators reflected less an endorsement of the principles underlying the FRS than a reaction to perceived abuses in previous practice, including the making of excessive acquisition provisions to cover future trading losses and types of expenditure whose relationship to the acquisition was remote. He would summarise the responses to the exposure draft on this point as follows: 6

(a) from preparers of accounts: overwhelming opposition;

(b) from users: acceptance, because they want to know the amount of post-acquisition provisions (which he considers to be a valid point), but a view that they would ignore the amounts charged against profits (indicating that they do not

	regard such charges as a proper reduction of profit);
(c) from auditors:	acceptance, because it can be very difficult at times to pass judgement on directors' decisions as to the proper capital provision for post-acquisition costs.

7 Mr Main believes that the concerns over past abuses could be met, without over-turning long-standing practice, by a standard that provided a stricter definition of what costs should be permitted to be included in acquisition provisions, together with more detailed note disclosure of the provisions made. Provisions would be restricted to costs to be incurred within twelve months of the acquisition, and would exclude any costs relating to the acquiring entity's own activities. Provisions for future losses would also be prohibited. Notes to the financial statements would be required to disclose the separate elements of the provisions involved and the actual expenditure subsequently charged against the provisions. Surplus provisions would be required to be adjusted against goodwill rather than be released to the profit and loss account. He believes that the disclosure requirements in the related FRS 6 would provide sufficient information on the effects of an acquisition without the need for the radical change in practice introduced in FRS 7.

8 Mr Main believes that his alternative would ensure that:

(a) the total cost of the acquisition investment decision would be reflected clearly in the financial statements;
(b) accountability could be measured; and
(c) the potential for abuse would be removed and auditors would have a clear standard against which the contents of the provision could be judged.

Financial Reporting Standard 8 is set out in paragraphs 1–7.

The Statement of Standard Accounting Practice set out in paragraphs 3–7 should be read in the context of the Objective as stated in paragraph 1 and the definitions set out in paragraph 2 and also of the Foreword to Accounting Standards and the Statement of Principles for Financial Reporting currently in issue.

The Explanation set out in paragraphs 8–23 shall be regarded as part of the Statement of Standard Accounting Practice insofar as it assists in interpreting that statement.

Appendix IV 'The development of the FRS' reviews considerations and arguments that were thought significant by members of the Board in reaching the conclusions on FRS 8.

[FRS 8]
Related party disclosures*

(Issued October 1995 Amended December 2008)

Contents

	Paragraph
Summary	
Financial Reporting Standard 8	
Objective	1
Definitions	2
Statement of Standard Accounting Practice	3–7
Scope	3–4
Application to smaller entities	4A
Disclosure of control	5
Disclosure of transactions and balances	6
Date from which effective	7
Explanation	8–23
The effect of related parties	8–10
Applying the definition of 'related party'	11–15
Party	11
Relationship	12
Common control	13
Common influence	14
Pension funds	15
Scope	16–17
Exempt subsidiary undertakings	17
Disclosure of control	18
Disclosure of transactions	19–22
Transactions	19
Materiality	20
Aggregation	21
Other elements of the transaction	22
Relationship with statutory and London Stock Exchange requirements	23
Adoption of FRS 8 by the Board	

Appendices
I Note on legal requirements
II Note on London Stock Exchange requirements
III Compliance with International Accounting Standards
IV The development of the FRS

****Editor's note****: The matters covered in FRS 8 are dealt with in Section 33 of FRS 102.*

Related party disclosures

Summary

Financial Reporting Standard 8 'Related Party Disclosures' requires the disclosure of: a

(i) information on related party transactions and (ii)the name of the party controlling the reporting entity and, if different, that of the ultimate controlling party whether or not any transactions between the reporting entity and those parties have taken place.

Aggregated disclosures are allowed subject to certain restrictions.

Financial Reporting Standard 8

Objective

The objective of this FRS is to ensure that financial statements contain the disclosures necessary to draw attention to the possibility that the reported financial position and results may have been affected by the existence of related parties and by material transactions with them. 1

Definitions

The following definitions shall apply in this FRS and in particular in the Statement of Standard Accounting Practice set out in paragraphs 3-7. 2

2.1 Close members of the family of a person:-

Close members of the family of an individual are those family members, or members of the same household, who may be expected to influence, or be influenced by, that person in their dealings with the reporting entity and include:

(a) that person's children and spouse or domestic partner;
(b) children of that person's spouse or domestic partner; and
(c) dependants of that person or that person's spouse or domestic partner.*

2.2 Control:-

The ability to direct the financial and operating policies of an entity with a view to gaining economic benefits from its activities.

2.3 Key management personnel:-

Those persons having authority and responsibility for planning, directing, and controlling the activities of the entity, directly or indirectly, including any director (whether executive or otherwise) of that entity.†

***Editor's note:** Amended with effect for accounting periods beginning on or after 1 January 2011.*

†***Editor's note:** Amended in December 2008, with effect for accounting periods beginning on or after 6 April 2008.*

2.4 [Withdrawn].*

2.5 Related party:-

A related party is a person or entity that is related to the entity that is preparing its financial statements (in this Standard referred to as the 'reporting entity').

(a) A person or a close member of that person's family is related to a reporting entity if that person:

- (i) has control or joint control over the reporting entity;
- (ii) has significant influence over the reporting entity; or
- (iii) is a member of the key management personnel of the reporting entity or of a parent of the reporting entity.

(b) An entity is related to a reporting entity if any of the following conditions apply:

- (i) The entity and the reporting entity are members of the same group (which means that each parent, subsidiary and fellow subsidiary is related to the others).
- (ii) One entity is an associate or joint venture of the other entity (or an associate or joint venture of a member of a group of which the other entity is a member).
- (iii) Both entities are joint ventures of the same third party.
- (iv) One entity is a joint venture of a third entity and the other entity is an associate of the third entity.
- (v) The entity is a retirement benefit scheme† for the benefit of employees of either the reporting entity or an entity related to the reporting entity. If the reporting entity is itself such a scheme, the sponsoring employers are also related to the reporting entity.
- (vi) The entity is controlled or jointly controlled by a person identified in (a).
- (vii) A person identified in (a)(i) has significant influence over the entity or is a member of the key management personnel of the entity (or of a parent of the entity).‡

2.6 Related party transaction:-

The transfer of assets or liabilities or the performance of services by, to or for a related party irrespective of whether a price is charged.

Statement of Standard Accounting Practice

SCOPE

3 Financial Reporting Standard 8 applies to all financial statements that are intended to give a true and fair view of a reporting entity's financial position and profit or loss (or income and expenditure) for a period. The FRS does not, however, require disclosure:

****Editor's note:*** *Withdrawn with effect for accounting periods beginning on or after 1 January 2011.*

†IAS 24 refers to a 'post-employment benefit plan', but the term 'retirement benefit scheme' has been retained in FRS 8 so as to ensure consistency with other FRS.

*‡**Editor's note:*** *Amended with effect for accounting periods beginning on or after 1 January 2011.*

(a) in consolidated financial statements, of any transactions or balances between group entities that have been eliminated on consolidation;
(b) [Withdrawn]*
(c) of transactions entered into between two or more members of a group, provided that any subsidiary undertaking which is a party to the transaction is wholly owned by a member of that group;†
(d) of pension contributions paid to a pension fund; and
(e) of emoluments in respect of services as an employee of the reporting entity.

Reporting entities taking advantage of the exemption in (c) above are required to state that fact.

[Deleted].‡ 4

APPLICATION TO SMALLER ENTITIES

Reporting entities applying the Financial Reporting Standard for Smaller Entities currently applicable are exempt from this accounting standard. 4A

DISCLOSURE OF CONTROL

When the reporting entity is controlled by another party, there should be disclosure of the related party relationship and the name of that party and, if different, that of the ultimate controlling party. If the controlling party or ultimate controlling party of the reporting entity is not known, that fact should be disclosed. This information should be disclosed irrespective of whether any transactions have taken place between the controlling parties and the reporting entity. 5

DISCLOSURE OF TRANSACTIONS AND BALANCES

Financial statements should disclose material transactions undertaken by the reporting entity with a related party. Disclosure should be made irrespective of whether a price is charged. The disclosure should include: 6

(a) the names of the transacting related parties;
(b) a description of the relationship between the parties;
(c) a description of the transactions;
(d) the amounts involved;
(e) any other elements of the transactions necessary for an understanding of the financial statements;
(f) the amounts due to or from related parties at the balance sheet date and provisions for doubtful debts due from such parties at that date; and
(g) amounts written off in the period in respect of debts due to or from related parties.

Transactions with related parties may be disclosed on an aggregated basis (aggregation of similar transactions by type of related party) unless disclosure of an individual transaction, or connected transactions, is necessary for an understanding

****Editor's note:*** *Withdrawn in December 2008 with effect for accounting periods beginning on or after 6 April 2008.*

†***Editor's note:*** *Amended in December 2008, with effect for accounting periods beginning on or after 6 April 2008.*

‡***Editor's note:*** *Paragraph deleted with effect for accounting periods beginning on or after 1 January 2011.*

of the impact of the transactions on the financial statements of the reporting entity or is required by law.

DATE FROM WHICH EFFECTIVE

7 The accounting practices set out in the FRS should be regarded as standard in respect of financial statements relating to accounting periods commencing on or after 23 December 1995. Earlier adoption is encouraged but not required.

7A In December 2008 the Accounting Standards Board amended paragraphs 2.3, 2.5, 3(b) and 3(c). An entity shall apply the amendment set out in these paragraphs for accounting periods beginning on or after 6 April 2008.

7B In December 2008 the ASB withdrew paragraph 3(b) and amended paragraph 3(c) to comply with certain changes to the law introduced by 'The Large and Medium-sized Companies and Groups (Accounts and Reports) Regulations' (Statutory Instrument, SI 2008/410) (the Regulations). As a consequence, there is no longer an exemption from providing disclosure in the financial statements of subsidiaries where 90 per cent or more of the voting rights are controlled within the group. Instead, exemption is only available for wholly owned subsidiaries. FRS 28 'Corresponding Amounts' requires corresponding amounts in respect of every item stated in the notes to the financial statements. Entities, which previously took advantage of the exemption provided by FRS 8, and did not provide information for 90 per cent subsidiary undertakings may be unable to provide corresponding amounts in the first year of adopting this amendment. Corresponding amounts need not be provided where this information cannot be obtained in the first year of adopting this amendment. Entities that do not provide corresponding amounts should provide an explanation in the notes to the financial statements.*

7C 'Improvements to Financial Reporting Standards 2010' issued in November 2010 amended paragraphs 2.1, 2.5, 11, 12 and 13, and it deleted paragraphs 2.4, 4 and 14. An entity shall apply this amendment for annual periods beginning on or after 1 January 2011. Earlier application is permitted. If an entity applies the amendment for an earlier period, it shall disclose that fact.

Explanation

THE EFFECT OF RELATED PARTIES

8 In the absence of information to the contrary, it is assumed that a reporting entity has independent discretionary power over its resources and transactions and pursues its activities independently of the interests of its individual owners, managers and others. Transactions are presumed to have been undertaken on an arm's length basis, ie on terms such as could have obtained in a transaction with an external party, in which each side bargained knowledgeably and freely, unaffected by any relationship between them.

9 These assumptions may not be justified when related party relationships exist, because the requisite conditions for competitive, free market dealings may not be present. Whilst the parties may endeavour to achieve arm's length bargaining the very nature of the relationship may preclude this occurring. Sometimes the nature of the relationship between the parties is such that the disclosure of the relationship

****Editor's note:*** *Paragraphs 7A and 7B added in December 2008.*

alone will be sufficient to make users aware of the possible implications of related party transactions.*

Even when terms are arm's length, the reporting of material related party transactions is useful information, because the terms of future transactions are more susceptible to alteration as a result of the nature of the relationship than they would be in transactions with an unrelated party. Although the existence of a related party relationship sometimes precludes arm's length transactions, non-independent parties can deal with each other at arm's length, as in the situation where a parent undertaking places no restrictions on two subsidiaries, giving them complete freedom in deciding whether to deal with each other and on what terms. However, assertions in financial statements about transactions with related parties should not imply that the related party transactions were effected on terms equivalent to those that prevail in arm's length transactions unless the parties have conducted the transactions in an independent manner. **10**

APPLYING THE DEFINITION OF 'RELATED PARTY'

In considering each possible related party relationship, attention is directed to the substance of the relationship and not merely the legal form.† **11**

In the context of this FRS, the following are not related parties: **12**

(a) two entities simply because they have a director or other member of key management personnel in common or because a member of key management personnel of one entity has significant influence over the other entity.

(b) two venturers simply because they share joint control over a joint venture.

(c) (i) providers of finance,

(ii) trade unions,

(iii) public utilities, and

(iv) departments and agencies of a government that do not control, jointly control or significantly influence the reporting entity, simply by virtue of their normal dealings with an entity (even though they may affect the freedom of action of an entity or participate in its decision-making process).

(d) a customer, supplier, franchisor, distributor or general agent with whom an entity transacts a significant volume of business, simply by virtue of the resulting economic dependence.‡

In the definition of a related party, an associate includes subsidiaries of the associate and a joint venture includes subsidiaries of the joint venture. Therefore, for example, an associate's subsidiary and the investor that has significant influence over the associate are related to each other.§ **13**

**Editor's note:* *Amended in December 2008, with effect for accounting periods beginning on or after 6 April 2008.*

†***Editor's note:*** *Amended with effect for accounting periods beginning on or after 1 January 2011.*

‡***Editor's note:*** *Amended with effect for accounting periods beginning on or after 1 January 2011.*

§***Editor's note:*** *Amended with effect for accounting periods beginning on or after 1 January 2011.*

Common influence

14 [Deleted].*

Pension funds

15 The fact that certain pension funds are related parties of the reporting entity is not intended to call into question the independence of the trustees with regard to their fiduciary obligations to the members of the pension scheme. Transactions between the reporting entity and the pension fund may be in the interest of members but nevertheless need to be reported in the accounts of the reporting entity.

SCOPE

16 Related party disclosure provisions do not apply in circumstances where to comply with them conflicts with the reporting entity's duties of confidentiality arising by operation of law (although operation of law would not include the effects of terms stipulated in a contract). For example, banks are obliged by law to observe a strict duty of confidentiality in respect of their customers' affairs and the FRS would not override the obligation to preserve the confidentiality of customers' dealings.

Exempt subsidiary undertakings

17 In December 2008 the ASB amended paragraph 3(c) to provide exemption only for transactions entered into between two or more members of a group, provided that any subsidiary undertaking which is a party to the transaction is wholly owned by a member of that group. Disclosure would be required, however, of transactions with related parties of the reporting subsidiary other than those that are excluded by the exemption.†

DISCLOSURE OF CONTROL

18 If the reporting entity is controlled by another party, that fact is relevant information, irrespective of whether transactions have taken place with that party, because the control relationship prevents the reporting entity from being independent in the sense described in paragraph 8. Indeed, the existence and identity of the controlling party may sometimes be at least as relevant in appraising an entity's prospects as are the performance and financial position presented in its financial statements. The controlling party may establish the entity's credit standing, determine the source and price of its raw materials, determine the products it sells, to whom and at what price, and may affect the source, calibre and even the primary concern and allegiance of its management.

DISCLOSURE OF TRANSACTIONS

Transactions

19 Disclosure is required of all material related party transactions. As transactions include donations to or by the entity, related party transactions are required to be disclosed whether or not a price is charged. The following are examples of related party transactions that require disclosure by a reporting entity in the period in which they occur:

* ***Editor's note:*** *Paragraph deleted with effect for accounting periods beginning on or after 1 January 2011.*

† ***Editor's note:*** *Amended in December 2008, with effect for accounting periods beginning on or after 6 April 2008.*

- purchases or sales of goods (finished or unfinished);
- purchases or sales of property and other assets;
- rendering or receiving of services;
- agency arrangements;
- leasing arrangements;
- transfer of research and development;
- licence agreements;
- provision of finance (including loans and equity contributions in cash or in kind);
- guarantees and the provision of collateral security; and
- management contracts.

Materiality

Transactions are material when their disclosure might reasonably be expected to influence decisions made by the users of general purpose financial statements. The materiality of related party transactions is to be judged, not only in terms of their significance to the reporting entity, but also in relation to the other related party when that party is: **20**

(a) a director, key manager or other individual in a position to influence, or accountable for stewardship of, the reporting entity; or
(b) a member of the close family of any individual mentioned in (a) above; or
(c) an entity controlled by any individual mentioned in (a) or (b) above.

Aggregation

Disclosure of details of particular transactions with individual related parties would frequently be too voluminous to be easily understood. Accordingly, similar transactions may be aggregated by type of related party. For example, in the individual accounts of a group company, purchases or sales with other group companies can be aggregated and described as such. However, this should not be done in such a way as to obscure the importance of significant transactions. Hence purchases or sales of goods should not be aggregated with purchases or sales of fixed assets. Nor should a material related party transaction with an individual be concealed in an aggregated disclosure. **21**

Other elements of the transaction

Paragraph 6(e) requires disclosure of 'any other elements of the [related party] transactions necessary for an understanding of the financial statements'. An example falling within this requirement would be the need to give an indication that the transfer of a major asset had taken place at an amount materially different from that obtainable on normal commercial terms. **22**

RELATIONSHIP WITH STATUTORY AND LONDON STOCK EXCHANGE REQUIREMENTS*

There are extensive statutory and London Stock Exchange requirements and reliefs regarding disclosure of related party transactions and relationships. In certain instances, the FRS will extend existing disclosure requirements; in other instances, the statutory and London Stock Exchange disclosure requirements go beyond those of the FRS. The location of the principal statutory and London Stock Exchange requirements is given in Appendices I and II respectively. **23**

***Editor's note:** *Requirements in relation to listed companies are now issued by the Financial Conduct Authority in its capacity as UK Listing Authority.*

Adoption of FRS 8 by the board

Financial Reporting Standard 8 – 'Related Party Disclosures' was approved for issue by the ten members of the Accounting Standards Board.

Sir David Tweedie	(Chairman)
Allan Cook	(Technical Director)
David Allvey	
Ian Brindle	
Michael Garner	
Richard Goeltz	
Raymond Hinton	
Huw Jones	
Professor Geoffrey Whittington	
Ken Wild	

Adoption of Amendment to FRS 8 by the Accounting Standards Board

This amendment to FRS 8 'Related Party Disclosures' was issued for approval by the eleven members of the Accounting Standards Board.

Members of the Accounting Standards Board

Ian Mackintosh	(Chairman)
David Loweth	(Technical Director)
Nick Anderson	
Michael Ashley	
Edward Beale	
Marisa Cassoni	
Peter Elwin	
Ken Lever	
Robert Overend	
Andy Simmonds	
Professor Geoffrey Whittington CBE	

Appendix I
Note on legal requirements*

Readers should refer to the Act itself for an understanding of the relevant points of law. This section lists only the main sections in the Act containing provisions in relation to related party disclosures.

Legal requirements in the United Kingdom 1

Companies Act 2006	
Sections 409 and 410	Information about related undertakings
Section 412	Information about directors' benefits: remuneration
Section 413	Information about directors' benefits: advances, credit and guarantees
Sections 250 and 251	'Director' and 'shadow director'
Section 415	Duty to prepare the directors' report
Large and Medium-sized Companies and Groups (Accounts and Reports) 2008 Regulations (SI 2008/410)	
Regulation 4(2)(b) Schedule 1 Part 1 Part 3 Paragraph 72	Exemption for medium-sized companies from disclosing related party transactions Companies Act Individual Accounts: Companies which are not banking or insurance companies Form and content of company accounts Notes to the accounts Related party transactions
Schedule 2 (paragraph 92) and Schedule 3 (paragraph 90)	Provisions relating to banking and insurance companies: disclosure in notes to accounts of related party transactions
Schedule 4	Information on related undertakings whether preparing Companies Act or IAS Accounts
Schedule 5	Information about benefits of directors
Schedule 6 (paragraph 22)	Companies Act group accounts Related party transactions
Schedule 7	Matters to be dealt with in directors' report

Legal requirements in the Republic of Ireland 2

The following table shows the provisions in the Companies Acts 1963 -2006 and various Regulations implementing EC Accounting Directives, corresponding to the provisions of the Companies Act 2006 and the Schedules to the Large and Medium-sized Companies and Groups (Accounts and Reports) Regulations 2008 (see paragraph 1 above). The principal pieces of legislation referred to in the table below are:

- The Companies Act 1963 – ('1963 Act');
- The Companies (Amendment) Act 1986 – ('1986 Act');

****Editor's note***: *Appendix replaced in December 2008.*

- The Companies Act 1990 – ('1990 Act');
- The European Communities (Companies: Group Accounts) Regulations 1992 – SI No. 201 of 1992 – ('Group Accounts Regulations 1992');
- The European Communities (Credit Institutions: Accounts) Regulations 1992 – SI No. 294 of 1992 – ('Credit Institutions Regulations 1992');
- The European Communities (Insurance Undertakings: Accounts) Regulations 1996 – SI No. 23 of 1996 – ('Insurance Undertakings Regulations 1996');
- The European Communities (Takeover Bids (Directive 2004/25/EC)) Regulations 2006 – SI No. 255 of 2006 – ('Takeover Bids Regulations 2006').

This section is intended as a guide to the corresponding provisions in Irish company law and does not purport to be comprehensive. Readers should note that the provisions of Irish company law referred to in the following table are not necessarily identical to the relevant UK provisions. Readers are advised to refer to the Irish legislation for an understanding of relevant legal points.

Table of corresponding legal references in the Republic of Ireland:

United Kingdom	Republic of Ireland
Companies Act 2006	
Sections 409 and 410 *(Information about related undertakings)*	**1986 Act:** Section 16 and paragraphs 45, 45A, 46, 46A, 54 and 55 of the Schedule **Group Accounts Regulations 1992:** Paragraphs 18–22 of the Schedule **Credit Institutions Regulations 1992:** Regulation 10 and Part III of the Schedule **Insurance Undertakings Regulations 1996:** Part IV, Paragraphs 32–36 of the Schedule
Section 412 *(Information about directors' benefits: remuneration)*	**1963 and 1990 Acts:** Section 191, 1963 Act; Section 63, 1990 Act **Group Accounts Regulations 1992:** Paragraph 16 of the Schedule **Credit Institutions Regulations 1992:** Regulations 5 and 7; paragraphs 66(2) and 74(4) of Part I and paragraph 4 of Part IV of the Schedule **Insurance Undertakings Regulations 1996:** Regulations 5 and 10; paragraphs 18(4) and 21(e) of Part III and paragraph 30(1)of Part IV of the Schedule
Section 413 *(Information about directors' benefits: advances, credit and guarantees)*	**1990 Act:** Sections 41–45 **Group Accounts Regulations 1992:** Paragraph 17 of the Schedule **Credit Institutions Regulations 1992:** Regulations 5 and 7 **Insurance Undertakings Regulations 1996:** Regulations 5 and 10 and paragraph 31(2) of Part IV of the Schedule
Sections 250 and 251 *('Director' and 'shadow director')*	Section 2, 1963 Act; Section 27, 1990 Act
Section 415 *(Duty to prepare the directors' report)*	**1963 and 1986 Acts:** Section 158, 1963 Act; Section 13 1986 Act **Group Accounts Regulations 1992:** Regulations 37 and 39 **Credit Institutions Regulations 1992:** Regulation 11 **Insurance Undertakings Regulations 1996:** Regulation 14

United Kingdom	Republic of Ireland
Large and Medium-sized Companies and Groups (Accounts and Reports) 2008 Regulations (SI 2008/410)†*	
Regulation 4 (2) (b) *(Exemption for medium-sized companies from disclosing related party transactions)* Schedule 1 *(Companies Act Individual Accounts: Companies which are not banking or insurance companies)*	Exemption not taken up in European Communities (Directive 2006/46/EC) Regulations 2009 (SI 2009/450)
Part 1 *(Form and content of company accounts)*	Section 4, 1986 Act; Schedule to the 1986 Act, Part 1
Part 3 (*Notes to the accounts)*	Section 4, 1986 Act,; Schedule to the 1986 Act, Part IV
Paragraph 72 *Related party transactions)*	**1986 Act:** Paragraph 36B of Part IV of the Schedule (as inserted by Regulation 6 of the European Communities (Directive 2006/46/EC) Regulations 2009 (SI 2009/450))
Schedule 2 (paragraph 92) and Schedule 3 (paragraph 90) *(Provisions relating to banking and insurance companies: disclosure in notes to accounts of related party transactions)*	**Credit Institutions Regulations 1992:** Paragraph 66B of Part I of the Schedule (as inserted by Regulation 18 of the European Communities (Directive 2006/46/EC) Regulations 2009 (SI 2009/450)) **Insurance Undertakings Regulations 1996:** Paragraph 19B of Part III of the Schedule (as inserted by Regulation 24 of the European Communities (Directive 2006/46/EC) Regulations 2009 (SI 2009/450))

**There are no regulations in Ireland equivalent to the Large and Medium-sized Companies and Groups (Accounts and Reports) Regulations 2008 – SI 2008/410. The corresponding financial reporting requirements are contained within the Companies Acts, as discussed above. In transposing the provisions of Directive 2006/46/EC (SI 2009/450) into Irish law, Ireland chose not to take up the Member State option to exempt small and medium sized companies from the related party disclosures required by the Directive. Thus the legal references included below apply to companies in Ireland regardless of size.*

†In Ireland, there is an exemption from the preparation of group accounts for medium sized groups under the Group Accounts Regulations 1992. An Irish parent company within the scope of these Regulations is exempt from the requirement to prepare group accounts if it meets the size and other criteria set out in Regulation 7. The size criteria in summary require that the parent and subsidiaries together meet two of the following three conditions:

(i) balance sheet total does not exceed €7,618,428;
(ii) turnover does not exceed €15,236,858; and
(iii) average number of employees does not exceed 250.

United Kingdom	Republic of Ireland
Schedule 4 *(Information on related undertakings whether preparing Companies Act or IAS Accounts)*	**1986 Act:** Section 16 and paragraphs 45, 45A, 46, 46A, 54 and 55 of the Schedule **Group Accounts Regulations 1992:** Paragraphs 18–22 of the Schedule **Credit Institutions Regulations 1992:** Regulations 5, 7 and 10 and Part III of the Schedule **Insurance Undertakings Regulations 1996:** Regulations 5 and 10 and paragraphs 32–36 of Part IV of the Schedule
Schedule 5 *(Information about benefits of directors)*	**1963 and 1990 Acts:** Section 191, 1963 Act; Section 63, 1990 Act **Group Accounts Regulations 1992:** Paragraph 16 of the Schedule **Credit Institutions Regulations 1992:** Regulations 5 and 7; paragraphs 66(2) and 74(4) of Part I and paragraph 4 of Part IV of the Schedule **Insurance Undertakings Regulations 1996:** Regulations 5 and 10; paragraphs 18(4) and 21(e) of Part III and paragraph 30(1) of Part IV of the Schedule
Schedule 6* *(Companies Act group accounts)*	**Group Accounts Regulations 1992:** All regulations and the Schedule **Credit Institutions Regulations 1992:** Regulation 7 and Parts II and II of the Schedule **Insurance Undertakings Regulations 1996:** Regulation 10 and Part IV of the Schedule
(paragraph 22) *(Related party transactions)*	**Group Accounts Regulations 1992:** Regulation 15(1) **Credit Institutions Regulations 1992:** Paragraph 66B of Part I of the Schedule (as inserted by Regulation 18 of the European Communities (Directive 2006/46/EC) Regulations 2009 (SI 2009/450)) **Insurance Undertakings Regulations 1996:** Paragraph 19B of Part III of the Schedule (as inserted by Regulation 24 of the European Communities (Directive 2006/46/EC) Regulations 2009 (SI 2009/450))

**In Ireland, there is an exemption from the preparation of group accounts for medium sized groups under the Group Accounts Regulations 1992. An Irish parent company within the scope of these Regulations is exempt from the requirement to prepare group accounts if it meets the size and other criteria set out in Regulation 7. The size criteria in summary require that the parent and subsidiaries together meet two of the following three conditions:*

(i) balance sheet total does not exceed €7,618,428;

(ii) turnover does not exceed €15,236,858; and

(iii) average number of employees does not exceed 250.

United Kingdom	Republic of Ireland
Schedule 7 *(Matters to be dealt with in directors' report)*	**1963, 1986 and 1990 Acts:** Section 158, 1963 Act; Sections 13, 14 & 16, 1986 Act; Section 63, 1990 Act **Group Accounts Regulations 1992:** Regulation 37 **Credit Institutions Regulations 1992:** Regulation 11 **Insurance Undertakings Regulations 1996:** Regulation 14 **Other legislation:** Section 26 of the Electoral Act 1997; Section 21 of the Takeover Bids Regulations 2006

The Transparency (Directive 2004/109/EC) Regulations 2007 (SI No. 277 of 2007) require certain related party disclosures to be included in half-yearly financial reports.

Appendix II*
Note on Financial Services Authority requirements

The Financial Services Authority (FSA) UK Listing Authority requirements are set out in the FSA Handbook. Chapter 11 'Related Party Transactions' defines related parties and sets out the requirements for disclosure of transactions with related parties. Chapter 9 'Continuing Obligations' contains further disclosure requirements in respect of related parties.

***Editor's Note**: Appendix replaced in December 2008. The Financial Services Authority has been replaced by the Financial Conduct Authority in relation to the Listing Rules.*

Appendix III*
Compliance with International Accounting Standards

Compliance with the FRS will ensure compliance with International Accounting Standard (IAS) 24 'Related Party Disclosures' in all material respects except for the following:

(i) This FRS provides that particulars need not be given of transactions entered into between two or more members of a group, provided that any subsidiary undertaking which is a party to the transaction is wholly owned by a member of that group. IAS 24 does not provide relief from disclosure of transactions entered into between wholly owned subsidiaries; and

(ii) IAS 24 requires disclosure of key management compensation, whereas this FRS does not contain such provision.

**Editor's Note*: *Appendix replaced in December 2008.*

Appendix IV
The development of the FRS

HISTORY OF DOCUMENTS ISSUED

ED 46

ED 46 'Disclosure of related party transactions' was issued by the Accounting Standards Committee in April 1989. The major disclosure proposal was to report abnormal related party transactions. Detail required included the name and relationship of the transacting parties as well as the basis on which the transaction price had been determined. Aggregated disclosures were permitted subject to certain restrictions. Other proposals were: disclosure of the existence and nature of controlling related party relationships, whether or not any transactions had taken place between the parties; and disclosure of economic dependence. Economic dependence was deemed to exist where the transactions between an entity and another party, or other facts arising from a relationship with another party, had a pervasive influence on the entity. 1

FRED 8

FRED 8 'Related Party Disclosures' was published in March 1994. There were two main differences between ED 46 and FRED 8. First, FRED 8 proposed that *all* material related party transactions should be disclosed because reporting control relationships and related party transactions drew attention to the possibility that the financial statements might have been affected by the relationship. The provision in ED 46 allowing aggregated disclosures by aggregating similar transactions by type of related party was retained. The other major change from ED 46 was that FRED 8 did not require the disclosure of economic dependence. The Board believes that disclosure of any such dependence, if required, should not be in a standard dealing with related party transactions since a customer or supplier is not normally regarded as a related party. 2

International and overseas accounting standards

The International Accounting Standard, IAS 24 'Related Party Disclosures', requires the disclosure of all material related party transactions. This approach is also adopted in the US standard FAS 57 'Related Party Disclosures', and the Australian, Canadian and New Zealand related party standards. In all material respects the definition of a related party and the disclosure requirements are the same in those standards as in FRS 8. 3

Statutory and London Stock Exchange requirements

There are extensive statutory and London Stock Exchange requirements regarding disclosure of related party transactions. The requirements principally concern transactions between companies and their directors and principal shareholders and their connected parties. Both sets of requirements are designed to focus on the stewardship aspect of directors' duties, whilst the FRS concentrates on the relevance of the information to users of accounts. 4

MATTERS CONSIDERED IN THE LIGHT OF RESPONSES TO FRED 8

5 The following paragraphs refer to comments made by respondents to FRED 8, and explain, with reasons, the changes made by the Board to the proposals of the FRED or the Board's reasons for rejecting arguments for change.

Definition of a related party

Influence

6 Several respondents remarked that the phrase in the definition section of the FRED that described influence was too vague and should specify the level of influence that would trigger related party status. The description of the level of influence has therefore been strengthened so as to include the notion of the possible restriction on the ability of one of the parties to pursue at all times its own separate interests.

Common influence

7 In FRED 8, two or more parties were related parties when, *inter alia*, for all or part of the financial period one of the parties was subject to control and the other to influence from the same source. It was pointed out to the Board that, for those subsidiaries that are part of a large group, this could impose a reporting burden in their individual financial statements. A subsidiary not qualifying for an exemption from disclosure of transactions with other group companies and investees of the group qualifying as related parties might be unaware that it had had transactions with a related party being an associate of the group where the investment in that associate was held by another group company. In acknowledgement of this difficulty and that for two parties to be related parties there has to be a relationship between them, the Board has changed this part of the definition to include only transacting parties subject to influence from the same source to such an extent that one of the parties has subordinated its own separate interests.

Deemed/presumed

8 In the FRED, the definition of a related party was followed by two lists of types of related party:

(a) those deemed to be related parties; and
(b) those presumed to be related parties.

A number of respondents commented that, in some cases, the nature of the relationship of some parties classed as 'deemed' in the FRED did not justify this classification. Hence, in the standard, close families of directors have been moved to the 'presumed' list. This meets the criticism that those parties may not always have the requisite level of influence to qualify as a related party.

Immediate family

9 The immediate family of directors, substantial shareholders and key employees was stated in the FRED to be a possible type of related party. Several commentators asked for 'immediate family' to be more closely defined, some querying the use of the phrase 'members of the same household' and some the references to certain relatives and not others. The Board, in recognition of the fact that the emphasis should be on

influence rather than on the immediacy of the family relationship, decided to substitute 'close family' for 'immediate family', in line with IAS 24. 'Close family' is defined as 'those family members or members of the same household who may be expected to influence, or be influenced by, that person in their dealings with the reporting entity.' The phrase 'members of the same household' has been retained to accommodate the view of the Board that related parties in this context are not necessarily confined to the individual's legal family.

10 per cent shareholding threshold

FRED 8 included the presumption that a shareholder owning 10 per cent or more of the voting rights of the reporting entity was a related party. Twenty-eight out of the forty-six respondents addressing this issue wanted the threshold to be raised (the most common figure mentioned being 20 per cent). Subsequent research indicated that the presumption of related party status at 10 per cent would capture many situations where the requisite level of influence was not present but rebuttal of the presumption would be necessary nonetheless. The Board accordingly decided to raise the threshold to 20 per cent. **10**

Scope

Wholly-owned subsidiary exemption

Disclosure of transactions with entities that are part of the group or associates or joint ventures of the group was not required by the FRED in the financial statements of wholly-owned subsidiaries. The Board's reasons for granting this exemption were that the ultimate holding company is named in the notes to the financial statements and those wishing to find out more information about the group could do so provided that consolidated financial statements were 'publicly available'. **11**

Those who supported the wholly-owned subsidiary exemption in general terms wished to extend its scope by: **12**

(a) describing the wholly-owned subsidiary as a 'wholly-owned subsidiary undertaking';
(b) reducing the threshold to 90 per cent owned subsidiaries; and
(c) widening the definition to take into account preference shares held by a third party and small numbers of shares held by employees, in what would otherwise be a wholly-owned subsidiary, as part of an employee share scheme.

In response to the above comments, the Board decided to widen the exemption with the effect that disclosure is not required in the financial statements of subsidiary undertakings, 90 per cent or more of whose voting rights are controlled within the group, of transactions with entities that are part of the group or investees of the group qualifying as related parties.

Several commentators remarked that disclosure of transactions with group companies is not available in the consolidated financial statements as such transactions are eliminated on consolidation and disclosure should therefore be made in the individual financial statements of the subsidiary. The Board, however, believes that in the case of a subsidiary undertaking, 90 per cent or more of whose voting rights are controlled within the group, the nature of the relationship is such that disclosure of the fact that the exemption has been invoked is sufficient to alert the reader of the financial statements to the possible existence of related party transactions. **13**

Small company exemption

14 A majority of those who responded to the question of whether small companies should be granted an exemption from the disclosure of related party transactions considered that no exemption should be granted. The reason given was that these transactions were likely to be of greater significance in small than in larger companies. The minority who would have preferred the granting of an exemption cited as their main reason the fact that the costs of providing the additional disclosures would outweigh the benefits of reporting them. Subsequent to the receipt of comments on FRED 8, further consultation was undertaken. Representations from those auditing and using the accounts of small companies reinforced the view that appropriate related party disclosure is particularly important and relevant information in their financial statements, since transactions with related parties are more likely to be material in small companies.

15 The Board noted that Parts II and III of Schedule 6 to the Companies Act 1985, which applies equally to companies of all sizes and is concerned mainly with dealings in favour of directors and connected persons, overlapped in many respects with the disclosure requirements of the FRS; however, the FRS was broader in scope and, in particular, expressed more clearly than the statute the spirit of Schedule 6; it also clarified, to the benefit of both preparers and auditors, the disclosures necessary to meet the fundamental requirement that accounts should give a true and fair view.

16 In considering this question, the Board was aware of the work, which it had itself commissioned, of a working party of the Consultative Committee of Accountancy Bodies (CCAB) investigating possible bases for exempting small companies from some of the requirements of accounting standards. Concern was expressed that if small companies were to be exempt from the requirements of the FRS in advance of the outcome of this work, some transactions which would normally be disclosed could be hidden using the exemption as justification. Accordingly, the Board decided that the FRS should apply to all financial statements that are intended to give a true and fair view, with no exemption for small companies. For the reasons given above, the Board believes that the FRS essentially clarifies existing requirements applicable to small companies, rather than extends them to a significant degree. Its decision on the FRS should not be taken as an indication of how it might react to the eventual final report of the CCAB working party in relation to this or other accounting standards.*

Banker/client confidentiality

17 Concern was expressed by banking entities and associations that disclosure of all material related party transactions in the accounts of banks could result in a breach of the confidentiality of the relationship between banker and client. The confidentiality of this relationship is part of the common law and is also a provision of the 'Good Banking' code of practice. Consequently the Board agreed to include a further paragraph in the Explanation section of the FRS to recognise the legal obligation borne by banks in this respect.

Disclosure of all material related party transactions

18 FRED 8 proposed disclosure of all material related party transactions. This proposal was supported by the majority of respondents. Those who suggested a return to the ED 46 proposal that the disclosure requirement should be confined to abnormal

****Editor's note:*** *Following the final report the Board issued the Financial Reporting Standard for Smaller Entities.*

transactions with related parties argued that reporting all related party transactions did not provide useful information. The Board's view is that, when transactions with related parties are material in aggregate, they are of interest whatever their nature.

Materiality

A number of commentators noted that the area of materiality was one on which further guidance was required in addition to that given by the FRED. In response to this concern, further explanation has been given to address the perspective that needs to be considered when a related party transaction has been undertaken directly or indirectly with an individual in a position to influence, or accountable for stewardship of, the reporting entity (for example, a director or a substantial shareholder). **19**

Fair value

FRED 8 required 'any other elements of the [related party] transactions necessary for an understanding of the financial statements' to be disclosed and suggested, as an example, a material difference between the fair value and the transacted amount where material transfers of assets, liabilities or services had taken place. Commentators addressing this issue were evenly divided in their views. Those in favour of the disclosure endorsed the Board's view that such information is useful because there is more scope for transactions between related parties to be at artificial prices as a result of the relationship. Those who opposed the disclosure argued that ascertaining a fair value for these transactions would be unduly burdensome and impracticable, since in many cases a fair value could not be obtained, particularly within groups. Whilst retaining its original view that this disclosure is relevant for an understanding of the financial statements, the Board acknowledged the observations of commentators. The Explanation has been amended to suggest as an example of 'any other elements of the [related party] transactions necessary for an understanding of the financial statements' an indication that the transfer of a major asset has taken place at an amount materially different from that obtainable on normal commercial terms. The Board believes that the absence of this information could reasonably be expected to influence decisions made by users of general purpose financial statements. **20**

AMENDMENT TO FRS 8: LEGAL CHANGES 2008*

In 2008 FRS 8 was amended to reflect certain changes to the law introduced by 'The Large and Medium-sized Companies and Groups (Accounts and Reports) Regulations' (Statutory Instrument, SI 2008/410) (the Regulations). **21**

The Regulations include a requirement for particulars to be given in the notes to the accounts of transactions which the company has entered into with related parties, and which must be given if such transactions are material and have not been concluded under normal market conditions. This introduces into UK law a provision of Directive 2006/46/EC of the European Parliament and of the Council. **22**

The particulars of transactions required to be disclosed must include: **23**

(a) the amount of such transactions;
(b) the nature of the related party relationship; and
(c) other information about the transactions necessary for an understanding of the financial position of the company.

**Editor's Note: Paragraphs 21 to 37 added in December 2008.*

24 Information about individual transactions may be aggregated according to their nature, except where separate information is necessary for an understanding of the effects of related party transactions on the financial position of the company.

25 The Directive provides that Member States may exempt transactions entered into between two or more members of a group, provided that any subsidiary undertaking which is a party to the transaction is wholly owned by such a member. The Regulations provide for such an exemption in the UK.

26 The Regulations require that 'related party' has the same meaning as in international accounting standards. The Companies Act 2006 (Section 474(1)) provides that international accounting standards are those that have been adopted by the European Commission in accordance with Commission Regulation (EC) 1606/2002. The version of International Accounting Standard (IAS) 24 'Related Party Disclosures' that has been adopted by the European Commission is that published by the International Accounting Standards Board (IASB) in December 2003, which was adopted for use in the EU by Commission Regulation (EC) 2238/2004 of 29 December 2004.

27 The Regulations require compliance with the definition of 'related party' contained in that version of IAS 24 for financial years beginning on or after 6 April 2008.

28 The ASB had consulted on a number of occasions prior to making the Amendment to FRS 8 in 2008. In May 2002 the ASB issued for comment FRED 25, which sought to converge the UK standard with IAS 24 as it stood at that time. FRED 25 was not issued as an FRS and, as noted above, in December 2003 the IASB issued a revised IAS 24. In February 2007 the IASB issued an exposure draft of proposed amendments to IAS 24 'State-controlled Entities and the Definition of a Related Party'. In July 2007 the ASB, aware of the forthcoming requirement arising from Directive 2006/46/EC, decided to issue a revised FRED (FRED 41), based on the IASB's proposals, in order to:

- ensure compliance with the law; and
- increase convergence with International Financial Reporting Standards (IFRS).

29 At the time of issuing FRED 41, it was expected that the IASB would issue a revised version of IAS 24, which would be adopted by the European Commission in time to align with the legal requirements.

30 At its September 2008 meeting, however, the IASB decided to re-expose amendments to IAS 24. The re-exposure of the amendments to IAS 24 will entail a further comment period and will delay the issue of a revised version IAS 24, which will then have to be adopted by the European Commission. As a result of the delay, FRED 41 was not issued as an FRS.

31 If the ASB takes no action before the revised version of IAS 24 is available, there would be a significant interim period during which the definition of a 'related party' in FRS 8 is inconsistent with the law.

32 In view of this, the ASB considered that its most appropriate course of action was to issue an amendment to FRS 8 to ensure compliance with the legal definition of a 'related party', including a reference to 'key management personnel', which is more specific than the reference to 'key management' included in the FRS 8 definition. As the definition of related parties had already been proposed and consulted upon in the UK in FRED 25, the ASB considered that, in the light of this consultation and the fact that constituents were supportive of the proposal, a further exposure period was not necessary for this amendment.

Similarly, in FRED 41, the ASB consulted on the proposal referred to in paragraph 25 above, in order to align the proposed standard with the law. This was a change from FRS 8, which did not require disclosure in the financial statements of subsidiary undertakings 90 per cent or more of whose voting rights were controlled within the group, of transactions with entities that were part of the group or investees of the group qualifying as related parties, provided that the consolidated financial statements in which that subsidiary was included were publicly available. **33**

In withdrawing the relief for disclosure of transactions with 90 per cent subsidiary undertakings, the ASB has considered how to address the requirement in FRS 28 'Corresponding Amounts' that requires corresponding amounts for all amounts disclosed in the notes to the financial statements*, even though this is not a legal requirement. Entities that have previously taken advantage of the 90 per cent scope exclusion may not have the necessary information to provide corresponding amounts – i.e. entities may not have details of transactions with subsidiary undertakings where ownership is between 90 and 100 per cent. The Amendment provides relief from the requirement in FRS 28 by not requiring, in the first year of adopting the amendment, corresponding amounts where the information cannot be obtained. **34**

The Amendment was issued to take effect for accounting periods beginning on or after 6 April 2008. **35**

In FRED 41, the ASB noted that the law requires the disclosure of transactions that are material and have not been concluded under normal market conditions. The ASB stated its belief that the intention of Directive 2006/46/EC was to introduce minimum disclosure requirements in default of disclosure under IAS 24, not to add to those requirements. The European Commission has clarified that this is the case. The summary minutes of the meeting of the Accounting Regulatory Committee (ARC) of 20 November 2007 recorded the following: **36**

'IV. Directive 2006/46/EC and IAS 24 – Related Party Transactions

A question had arisen on whether the transposition of the material content of IAS 24 directly or indirectly into national law would be compliant with the requirements of the 4th Directive. The issue arises because the 4th Directive requires information about "material" transactions and transactions not concluded "under normal market conditions" whereas IAS 24 is silent on these elements. The Commission view is that the use of IAS 24 on a national level for companies not within the scope of the IAS Regulation would still be compliant with the requirements of the 4th Directive'.

FRS 8, as amended in December 2008, is not completely converged with IAS 24 but provides for equivalent disclosures about related party transactions. Therefore, compliance with the amended standard will ensure compliance with the requirements of the Directive. **37**

The wording used in paragraph 3(c) of FRS 8, as amended in December 2008, was derived from the Regulations. The exemption set out in that paragraph should only be applied where all subsidiary undertakings which are a party to the transaction are wholly owned, directly or indirectly, by the ultimate controlling entity of the group.† **38**

**Paragraph 10 FRS 28 'Corresponding Amounts'.*

†***Editor's note***: *Paragraph added in November 2010.*

Financial Reporting Standard 9 is set out in paragraphs 1-61.

The Statement of Standard Accounting Practice, which comprises the paragraphs set in bold type, should be read in the context of the Objective as stated in paragraph 1 and the definitions set out in paragraphs 4 and 5 and also of the Foreword to Accounting Standards and the Statement of Principles for Financial Reporting currently in issue.

The explanatory paragraphs contained in the FRS shall be regarded as part of the Statement of Standard Accounting Practice insofar as they assist in interpreting that statement.

Appendix III 'The development of the FRS' reviews considerations and arguments that were thought significant by members of the Board in reaching the conclusions on the FRS.

[FRS 9]
Associates and joint ventures*

(Issued November 1997)

Contents

Paragraphs

Summary

Financial Reporting Standard 9

Objective 1

Scope 2-3

Definitions 4-5

Applying the key definitions in practice 6-17

A joint arrangement that is not an entity 8-9
A joint venture 10-12
An associate 13-17

Treatment of a joint arrangement that is not an entity 18-19

Accounting for joint ventures 20-23

A structure with the form but not the substance of a joint venture 24-25

Accounting for associates 26-30

The investor's consolidated profit and loss account 27
The investor's consolidated statement of total recognised gains and losses 28
The investor's consolidated balance sheet 29
The investor's consolidated cash flow statement 30

Applying the equity method and the gross equity method 31-37

Impairment 38-39

Commencement or cessation of an associate or joint venture relationship 40-43

The treatment of losses and interests in net liabilities 44-45

Non-corporate associates and joint ventures 46–47

An investor that does not prepare consolidated financial statements 48

Investment funds 49–50

****Editor's note**: The matters covered in FRS 9 are dealt with in Sections 14 and 15 of FRS 102 for associates and joint ventures respectively.*

Disclosures 51–58

For all associates and joint ventures 52-56
Additional disclosures at 15 and 25 per cent thresholds 57-58

Date from which effective 59

Withdrawal of SSAP 1 and Interim Statement and amendment of FRS 1 (Revised 1996) 60–61

Appendices

I Note on legal requirements
II Compliance with international accounting standards
III The development of the FRS
IV Examples of alternative ways of giving information on joint ventures

Associates and joint ventures

Summary

Financial Reporting Standard 9 'Associates and Joint Ventures' sets out the definitions and accounting treatments for associates and joint ventures, two types of interests that a reporting entity may have in other entities. The FRS also deals with joint arrangements that are not entities. The definitions and treatments prescribed have been developed to be consistent with the Accounting Standards Board's approach to accounting for subsidiaries (dealt with in FRS 2 'Accounting for Subsidiary Undertakings'). The requirements are consistent with companies legislation.* **a**

The table below describes the different sorts of interests that a reporting entity may have in other entities or arrangements – the shaded sections indicate those covered by the FRS. The defining relationships described in the table form the basis for the definitions used in the FRS. **b**

**The relationship between companies legislation and the standard is discussed in Appendix I.*

Entity/ arrangement	Nature of relationship	Description of the defining relationship – the full definitions are given in paragraph 4 of the FRS
Subsidiary	Investor controls its investee.	Control is the ability of an entity to direct the operating and financial policies of another entity with a view to gaining economic benefits from its activities. To have control an entity must have both: (i) the ability to deploy the economic resources of the investee or to direct it; and (ii) the ability to ensure that any resulting benefits accrue to itself (with corresponding exposure to losses) and to restrict the access of others to those benefits.
Joint arrangement that is not an entity	Entities participate in an arrangement to carry on part of their own trades or businesses.	A joint arrangement, whether or not subject to joint control, does not constitute an entity unless it carries on a trade or business of its own.
Joint venture	Investor holds a long-term interest and shares control under a contractual arrangement.	The joint venture agreement can override the rights normally conferred by ownership interests with the effect that: • acting together, the venturers can control the venture and there are procedures for such joint action • each venturer has (implicitly or explicitly) a veto over strategic policy decisions. There is usually a procedure for settling disputes between venturers and, possibly, for terminating the joint venture.
Associate	Investor holds a participating interest and exercises significant influence.	The investor has a long-term interest and is actively involved, and influential, in the direction of its investee through its participation in policy decisions covering the aspects of policy relevant to the investor, including decisions on strategic issues such as: (i) the expansion or contraction of the business, participation in other entities or changes in products, markets and activities of its investee; and (ii) determining the balance between dividend and reinvestment.
Simple investment		The investor's interest does not qualify the investee as an associate, a joint venture or a subsidiary because the investor has limited influence or its interest is not long-term.

The investor's consolidated financial statements

The table below sets out the treatments in consolidated financial statements for the different interests that a reporting entity may have in other entities and for joint arrangements that are not entities – the shaded sections indicate the treatments covered by the FRS. **c**

Type of investment	Treatment in consolidated financial statements
Subsidiaries	The investor should consolidate the assets, liabilities, results and cash flows of its subsidiaries.
Joint arrangements that are not entities	Each party should account for its own share of the assets, liabilities and cash flows in the joint arrangement, measured according to the terms of that arrangement, for example pro rata to their respective interests.
Joint ventures	The venturer should use the gross equity method showing in addition to the amounts included under the equity method,* on the face of the balance sheet, the venturer's share of the gross assets and liabilities of its joint ventures, and, in the profit and loss account, the venturer's share of their turnover distinguished from that of the group. Where the venturer conducts a major part of its business through joint ventures, it may show fuller information provided all amounts are distinguished from those of the group. Appendix IV sets out an optional columnar presentation.
Associates	The investor should include its associates in its consolidated financial statements using the equity method. In the investor's consolidated profit and loss account the investor's share of its associates' operating result should be included immediately after group operating result. From the level of profit before tax, the investor's share of the relevant amounts for associates should be included within the amounts for the group. In the consolidated statement of total recognised gains and losses the investor's share of the total recognised gains and losses of its associates should be included, shown separately under each heading, if material. In the balance sheet the investor's share of the net assets of its associates should be included and separately disclosed. The cash flow statement should include the cash flows between the investor and its associates. Goodwill arising on the investor's acquisition of its associates, less any amortisation or write-down, should be included in the carrying amount for the associates but should be disclosed separately. In the profit and loss account the amortisation or write down of such goodwill should be separately disclosed as part of the investor's share of its associates' results.
Simple investments	The investor includes its interests as investments at either cost or valuation.

**The treatment under the equity method required by the FRS is set out in paragraph 4 and summarised under Associates in the above table.*

The investor's own financial statements

d In the investor's own financial statements associates and joint ventures should be treated as fixed asset investments, at cost less any amounts written off, or at a valuation.

Disclosures

e The FRS requires the following disclosures separately for associates and joint ventures that exceed certain thresholds.

(i) Where an investor's aggregate share in its associates exceeds 15 per cent of any of the gross assets, gross liabilities, turnover or, on a three-year average, operating result of the investing group, the investor's aggregate share of each of the following should be shown:
- turnover (unless it is already included as a memorandum item)
- fixed assets, current assets, liabilities due within one year and liabilities due after one year or more.

(ii) Where an investor's aggregate share in its joint ventures exceeds 15 per cent of any of the gross assets, gross liabilities, turnover or, on a three-year average, operating result of the investing group, the investor's aggregate share of each of the following should be shown:
- fixed assets, current assets, liabilities due within one year and liabilities due after one year or more.

(iii) For any associate or joint venture where the investor's share of that individual entity exceeds 25 per cent of any of the gross assets, gross liabilities, turnover or, on a three-year average, operating result of the investing group, the investor's share of the following items for that entity should be shown:
- turnover
- profit before tax
- taxation
- profit after tax
- fixed assets
- current assets
- liabilities due within one year
- liabilities due after one year or more.

Financial Reporting Standard 9

Objective

1 The objective of this FRS is to reflect the effect on an investor's financial position and performance of its interests in two special kinds of investments – associates and joint ventures – for whose activities it is partly accountable because of the closeness of its involvement:

- in associates, as a result of its participating interest and significant influence
- in joint ventures, as a result of its long-term interest and joint control. The FRS also deals with joint arrangements that do not qualify as associates or joint ventures because they are not entities.

Scope

2 **Subject to the provisions of paragraph 3, the FRS applies to all financial statements that are intended to give a true and fair view of a reporting entity's financial position and profit or loss (or income and expenditure) for a period.**

3 **Reporting entities applying the Financial Reporting Standard for Smaller Entities (FRSSE) currently applicable are exempt from the FRS unless preparing consolidated financial statements, in which case they should apply the FRS to such statements as required by the FRSSE.**

Definitions

4 The following definitions shall apply in the FRS and in particular in the Statement of Standard Accounting Practice set out **in bold type**.

*Associate:–**
An entity (other than a subsidiary) in which another entity (the investor) has a PARTICIPATING INTEREST and over whose operating and financial policies the investor EXERCISES A SIGNIFICANT INFLUENCE.

PARTICIPATING INTEREST:–
An interest held in the shares† of another entity on a long-term basis for the purpose of securing a contribution to the investor's activities by the exercise of

**This definition is consistent with the definition of an associated undertaking in companies legislation:*
(a) in Great Britain, paragraph 20 of Schedule 4A to the Companies Act 1985 (For accounting periods beginning on or after 6 April 2008 this changes to paragraph 19 of Schedule 6 to The Large and Medium-sized Companies and Groups (Accounts and Reports) Regulations 2008 (SI 2008/410));
(b) in Northern Ireland, paragraph 20 of Schedule 4A to the Companies (Northern Ireland) Order 1986; and
(c) in the Republic of Ireland, Regulation 34 of the European Communities (Companies: Group Accounts) Regulations 1992.
The statutory definitions in Great Britain and Northern Ireland specifically exclude non-corporate joint ventures that are proportionally consolidated. The full definitions are given in Appendix I.

†The reference to shares is to allotted shares in an entity with a share capital, to rights to share in the capital in an entity with capital but no share capital, and to interests conferring any right to share in the profits, or imposing a liability to contribute to the losses or giving an obligation to contribute to debts or expenses in a winding up for an entity without capital.

control or influence arising from or related to that interest. The investor's interest must, therefore, be a beneficial one and the benefits expected to arise* must be linked to the exercise of its significant influence over the investee's operating and financial policies. An interest in the shares of another entity includes an interest convertible into an interest in shares or an option to acquire shares.

Companies legislation provides that a holding of 20 per cent or more of the shares of an entity is to be presumed to be a participating interest unless the contrary is shown.† The presumption is rebutted if the interest is either not long-term or not beneficial.

EXERCISE OF SIGNIFICANT INFLUENCE:–
The investor is actively involved and is influential in the direction of its investee through its participation in policy decisions covering aspects of policy relevant to the investor, including decisions on strategic issues such as:

(a) the expansion or contraction of the business, participation in other entities or changes in products, markets and activities of its investee; and
(b) determining the balance between dividend and reinvestment.

Companies legislation provides that an entity holding 20 per cent or more of the voting rights in another entity should be presumed to exercise a significant influence over that other entity unless the contrary is shown.‡ For the purpose of applying this presumption, the shares held by the parent and its subsidiaries in that entity should be aggregated.§ The presumption is rebutted if the investor does not fulfil the criteria for the exercise of significant influence set out above.

Further guidance on how to apply the definition of an 'associate' in practice is given in paragraphs 13–17 with 'participating interest' considered in paragraph 13 and 'exercise of significant influence' in paragraphs 14–17.

Control:–
See definition under *subsidiary*.

**Dividends are not the only way a beneficial interest can be enjoyed: there are other ways of extracting benefit, for example, through a management contract with a fee based on performance (making the receiver of the fee more than just a manager).*

†*In Great Britain, section 260 of the Companies Act 1985. (**Editor's note:** For accounting periods beginning on or after 6 April 2008 this changes to paragraph 11 of Sch. 10 to the Large and Medium-sized Companies and Groups (Accounts and Reports) Regulations 2008 (SI 2008/410).)*
In Northern Ireland, Article 268 of the Companies (Northern Ireland) Order 1986.
In the Republic of Ireland, Regulation 35 of the European Communities (Companies: Group Accounts) Regulations 1992.

‡*In Great Britain, paragraph 20 of Schedule 4A to the Companies Act 1985. (**Editor's note:** For accounting periods beginning on or after 6 April 2008 this changes to paragraph 19 of Schedule 6 to SI 2008/410.)*
In Northern Ireland, paragraph 20 of Schedule 4A to the Companies (Northern Ireland) Order 1986.
In the Republic of Ireland, Regulation 34 of the European Communities (Companies: Group Accounts) Regulations 1992.

§*The provisions in companies legislation that deal with the voting rights to be taken into account in applying the rebuttable presumption are:*
*(a) in Great Britain, paragraphs 5-11 of Schedule 10A to the Companies Act 1985 (**Editor's note:** For accounting periods beginning on or after 6 April 2008 this changes to paragraphs 5 to 11 of Schedule 7 to the Companies Act 2006.);*
(b) in Northern Ireland, paragraphs 5-11 of Schedule 10A to the Companies (Northern Ireland) Order 1986; and
(c) in the Republic of Ireland, Regulation 4 of the European Communities (Companies: Group Accounts) Regulations 1992.

*Entity:–**
A body corporate, partnership, or unincorporated association carrying on a trade or business with or without a view to profit. The reference to carrying on a trade or business means a trade or business of its own and not just part of the trades or businesses of entities that have interests in it.

Equity method:–
A method of accounting that brings an investment into its investor's financial statements initially at its cost, identifying any goodwill arising. The carrying amount of the investment is adjusted in each period by the investor's share of the results of its investee less any amortisation or write-off for goodwill, the investor's share of any relevant gains or losses, and any other changes in the investee's net assets including distributions to its owners, for example by dividend. The investor's share of its investee's results is recognised in its profit and loss account. The investor's cash flow statement includes the cash flows between the investor and its investee, for example relating to dividends and loans.

Gross equity method:–
A form of equity method under which the investor's share of the aggregate gross assets and liabilities underlying the net amount included for the investment is shown on the face of the balance sheet and, in the profit and loss account, the investor's share of the investee's turnover is noted.

Interest held on a long-term basis:–
An interest that is held other than exclusively with a view to subsequent resale. An interest held exclusively with a view to subsequent resale is:

(a) an interest for which a purchaser has been identified or is being sought, and which is reasonably expected to be disposed of within approximately one year of its date of acquisition; or
(b) an interest that was acquired as a result of the enforcement of a security†, unless the interest has become part of the continuing activities of the group or the holder acts as if it intends the interest to become so.

Investee:–
An entity in which the investor has invested.

Joint arrangement that is not an entity:–
A contractual arrangement under which the participants engage in joint activities that do not create an entity because it would not be carrying on a trade or business of its own. A contractual arrangement where all significant matters of operating and financial policy are predetermined does not create an entity because the policies are those of its participants not of a separate entity.‡

**The first sentence of this definition is the same as the definition of 'undertaking' in companies legislation:*
*(a) in Great Britain, section 259 of the Companies Act 1985 (**Editor's note:** For accounting periods beginning on or after 6 April 2008 this changes to Section 1161 of the Companies Act 2006.);*
(b) in Northern Ireland, Article 267 of the Companies (Northern Ireland) Order 1986; and
(c) in the Republic of Ireland, Regulation 3 of the European Communities (Companies: Group Accounts) Regulations 1992.

†"Enforcement of a security" should be interpreted to include any other arrangement that has in substance the same effect.

‡Under FRS 5 'Reporting the substance of transactions', where all significant matters of operating and financial policy are predetermined in a contractual arrangement, if one party gains the benefits arising from the net assets of that arrangement and is exposed to the risks inherent in them, then that party possesses control and the arrangement is that party's quasi-subsidiary.

Further guidance on how to apply this definition in practice is given in paragraphs 8 and 9.

Joint venture:–
An entity in which the reporting entity holds an interest on a long-term basis and is JOINTLY CONTROLLED by the reporting entity and one or more other venturers under a contractual arrangement.

JOINT CONTROL:–
A reporting entity jointly controls a venture with one or more other entities if none of the entities alone can control that entity but all together can do so and decisions on financial and operating policy essential to the activities, economic performance and financial position of that venture require each venturer's consent.

Further guidance on how to apply this definition in practice is given in paragraphs 10–12 with 'joint control' considered in paragraphs 11 and 12.

Subsidiary:–
A subsidiary undertaking as defined by paragraph 14 of FRS 2 'Accounting for Subsidiary Undertakings', which is consistent with companies legislation.* In principle, a subsidiary is an entity over which another entity (the investor) has CONTROL.

CONTROL:–
The ability of an entity to direct the operating and financial policies of another entity with a view to gaining economic benefits from its activities.

5 References to companies legislation mean:

(a) in Great Britain, the Companies Act 1985;
(b) in Northern Ireland, the Companies (Northern Ireland) Order 1986; and
(c) in the Republic of Ireland, the Companies Acts 1963–90 and the European Communities (Companies: Group Accounts) Regulations 1992.

APPLYING THE KEY DEFINITIONS IN PRACTICE

6 The definitions set out in paragraph 4 identify five ways in which entities further their economic activities through investments or joint arrangements. Four of those involve interests in other entities – subsidiaries, joint ventures, associates and other investments. The basis for the classification of the interests in other entities is the relationship in practice between the investor and its investee. The fifth way involves joint arrangements that do not amount to entities. Subsidiaries are dealt with in FRS 2 and are not specifically addressed in this FRS. The FRS does not provide any guidance on the treatment of investments that are not associates or joint ventures. The paragraphs below deal with joint arrangements that are not entities, and with joint ventures and associates in that order because it reflects the decreasing degree of the reporting entity's direct involvement.

**Paragraph 14 of FRS 2 is based on the following:*
*(a) in Great Britain, section 258 of and Schedule 10A to the Companies Act 1985 (**Editor's note:** For accounting periods beginning on or after 6 April 2008 this changes to Section 1162 of the Companies Act 2006 and Schedule 7 to the Companies Act 2006.);*
(b) in Northern Ireland, Article 266 of and Schedule 10A to the Companies (Northern Ireland) Order 1986; and
(c) in the Republic of Ireland, Regulation 4 of the European Communities (Companies: Group Accounts) Regulations 1992.

Both associates (through the holding of a participating interest) and joint ventures are defined by reference to long-term interests. Whether any investee qualifies as an associate or joint venture should therefore be judged on long-term factors and, once an investee has qualified as an associate or joint venture, minor or temporary changes in the relationship between investor and investee should not affect its status. In particular, the status of an entity as an associate or joint venture does not change according to whether it is profitable or has net assets or is loss-making or has net liabilities or, once it has been accounted for as an associate or joint venture, whether the investor intends to keep its interest or dispose of it. 7

A joint arrangement that is not an entity

A reporting entity may enter a variety of commercial arrangements but not all of these result in the creation of entities. Even if the participants have a long-term interest and have joint control within an arrangement, that arrangement is not a joint venture as defined in the FRS unless it constitutes an entity. For a joint arrangement to amount to an entity, it must carry on a trade or business, meaning a trade or business of its own and not just part of its participants' trades or businesses. In its activities the joint arrangement must therefore have some independence (within the objectives set by the agreement governing the joint arrangement) to pursue its own commercial strategy in its buying and selling; it must either have access to the market in its own right for its main inputs and outputs or, at least, be able to obtain them from the participants or sell them to the participants on generally the same terms as are available in the market. The following indicate that the joint activities undertaken in a joint arrangement do not amount to its carrying on a trade or business of its own – and therefore that the joint arrangement is not an entity: 8

(a) the participants derive their benefit from product or services taken in kind rather than by receiving a share in the results of trading;* or
(b) each participant's share of the output or result of the joint activity is determined by its supply of key inputs to the process producing that output or result.

In practice, a joint arrangement will not be an entity if, rather than its activities amounting to its carrying on a trade or business of its own, it is no more than a cost- or risk-sharing means of carrying out a process in the participants' trades or businesses – for example a joint marketing or distribution network or a shared production facility. Carrying on a trade or business normally denotes a continuing activity with repetition of the buying and selling activities and, therefore, a joint arrangement carrying out a single project (as, for example, occurs in the construction industry) is unlikely to be carrying on a trade or business of its own, being instead a facility or agent in its participants' trades or businesses. The nature of a joint arrangement may change over time – for example, a pipeline operated as a joint arrangement that initially provided a service only directly to the participants may develop into a pipeline business providing services to others, where access to the pipeline is sold in the market. Changes in the nature of a joint arrangement should be reflected in its accounting treatment. 9

A joint venture

An entity is a joint venture only with respect to an investor that shares control in it. An investor may have an interest in an entity that is a joint venture to some of its 10

**This condition includes the possibility of a venturer taking in cash its share of the joint venture's product if the commodity is actively traded.*

other investors. However, if that investor does not share control of the entity, the entity for that investor is merely an investment and should be accounted for as such.

Joint control

11 Joint control, like control itself, is a relationship that has a benefit aspect.* The venturers exercise their joint control for their mutual benefit, each conducting its part of the contractual arrangement with a view to its own benefit. Each venturer that shares control should play an active role in setting the operating and financial policies of the joint venture, at least at a general strategy level. This does not preclude one venturer managing the joint venture provided that the venture's principal operating and financial policies are collectively agreed by the venturers and the venturers have the power to ensure that those policies are followed. In some cases an investor may qualify as the parent of an entity under the definition of a subsidiary in FRS 2 (for example by holding a majority of the voting rights in that entity) but contractual arrangements with the other shareholder mean that in practice the shareholders share control over their investee. In such a case the interests of the minority shareholder amount to "severe long-term restrictions" that "substantially hinder the exercise of the rights of the parent undertaking over the assets or management of the subsidiary undertaking".† The subsidiary therefore should not be consolidated but should instead be treated as a joint venture according to the requirements of this FRS.

12 The effect of the requirement in the definition for consent to high-level strategic decisions of joint control is to give each venturer a veto on such decisions. This veto is what distinguishes a joint venturer from a minority holder of the shares in a joint stock company because the latter, having no veto, is subject to majority rule (except for the limited statutory protection for the minority). The requirement for each venturer's consent to high-level strategic decisions does not have to be set out in the joint venture agreement, provided that the joint venture works in practice on the basis of securing such consent.

An associate

Participating interest

13 One of the conditions for an investment to qualify as an associate is that its investor should have a participating interest. A participating interest includes an interest convertible into an interest in shares or an option to acquire shares. Start-up situations, or other operations in which an investor holds convertibles or options rather than the shares themselves, may therefore qualify as associates if an entity initially has a close involvement in the strategic operating and financial policies, despite only a limited equity interest (for example, by a management contract rather than a holding of shares), and has an option to purchase shares later.

Exercise of significant influence

14 For an investment to be an associate, its investor must exercise significant influence over the investee's operating and financial policies. The relationship between an

**Control is defined in FRS 2 and FRS 5 to include a benefit aspect, ie the ability to direct is with a view to gaining economic benefits.*

†Subsidiary undertakings where there are severe long-term restrictions of this sort are required by paragraph 25 of FRS 2 to be excluded from consolidation.

investor and its associate can be contrasted with an interest in an ordinary fixed asset investment. The investor needs an agreement or understanding, formal or informal, with its associate to provide the basis for its significant influence. An investor exercising significant influence will be directly involved in the operating and financial policies of its associate. Rather than passively awaiting the outcome of its investee's policies, the investor uses its associate as a medium through which it conducts a part of its activities (although the associate need not be in the same business as the investor). Over time, the associate will generally implement policies that are consistent with the strategy of the investor and avoid implementing policies that are contrary to the investor's interests. Therefore, if an investee persistently implements policies that are inconsistent with its investor's strategy, that investor does not exercise significant influence over its investee.

The investor's active involvement in the operating and financial policies of its associate requires inter alia that it should have a voice in decisions on strategic issues such as determining the balance between dividend and reinvestment. The investor's long-term interest in the future cash flows of its investee is compatible with a policy of reinvestment by the investee; the investor may not, therefore, always press its investee to follow a strategy of paying high dividends. The investor's participation in policy decisions is with a view to gaining economic benefits from the activities of the investee; its expectation of gain through such participation exposes it to the risks relating to the investee's activities, including the possibility of losses being sustained. **15**

The investor's involvement in its associate is usually achieved through nomination to the board of directors (or its equivalent) but may result from any arrangement that allows the investor to participate effectively in policy-making decisions. It is unlikely that an investor can exercise significant influence unless it has a substantial basis of voting power. A holding of 20 per cent or more of the voting rights in another entity suggests, but does not ensure, that the investor exercises significant influence over that entity. **16**

The decisive feature in identifying investments that are associates is the actual relationship between investor and investee. The actual relationship usually becomes clear soon after an investment is acquired but arrangements (such as the number of board members the investor may nominate and the proposed decision-taking process) may be used to evaluate the relationship before its record is established. If the actual relationship develops differently from that assumed from the arrangements on acquisition, it may be necessary to modify the treatment originally adopted in the financial statements. Once the actual relationship has been established and the investor has qualified as exercising significant influence over an entity, it should be regarded as continuing to exercise such influence until an event or transaction removes the investor's ability to do so. **17**

TREATMENT OF A JOINT ARRANGEMENT THAT IS NOT AN ENTITY

Participants in a joint arrangement that is not an entity should account for their own assets, liabilities and cash flows, measured according to the terms of the agreement governing the arrangement. **18**

A joint arrangement that is not an entity includes any contractual arrangement between the participants to conduct certain activities jointly where those activities do not amount to the joint arrangement carrying on a trade or business of its own. Paragraphs 8 and 9 give guidance on determining when activities constitute the carrying on of a trade or business by the joint arrangement and when, therefore, a **19** joint arrangement is an entity. Those paragraphs also describe certain activities that are unlikely to constitute an entity.

ACCOUNTING FOR JOINT VENTURES

20 **In consolidated financial statements an investor should include its joint ventures using the gross equity method in all its primary financial statements. In the investor's individual financial statements, investments in joint ventures should be treated as fixed asset investments and shown either at cost, less any amounts written off, or at valuation.**

21 **Under the gross equity method the joint ventures should receive the same treatment as set out for associates in paragraphs 27–30 except that:**

- **in the consolidated profit and loss account the investor's share of its joint ventures' turnover should also be shown – but not as part of group turnover. In the segmental analysis too, the investor's share of its joint ventures' turnover should be clearly distinguished from the turnover for the group itself.**
- **in the consolidated balance sheet the investor's share of the gross assets and liabilities underlying the net equity amount included for joint ventures should be shown in amplification of that net amount.**

22 **Except for items below profit before tax in the profit and loss account, any supplemental information given for joint ventures, either in the balance sheet or in the profit and loss account, must be shown clearly separate from amounts for the group and must not be included in the group totals.**

23 Because an investor's joint control of its joint venture is a more direct form of influence than the significant influence exercised over associates, a reporting entity that conducts a major part of its business through joint ventures may wish to give more detailed supplementary information about them. One option for including supplementary information about joint ventures is the columnar presentation based on the gross equity method included as an example in Appendix IV.

A STRUCTURE WITH THE FORM BUT NOT THE SUBSTANCE OF A JOINT VENTURE

24 **A participant in a structure with the appearance of a joint venture but used only as a means for each participant to carry on its own business should account directly for its part of the assets, liabilities and cash flows held within that structure.**

25 Joint ventures are to be included using the gross equity method. However, sometimes a reporting entity operates through a structure that has the appearance of a joint venture, being a separate entity in which the participants hold a long-term interest and exercise joint management, but which confers extremely limited commonality of interest between the venturers because each venturer, in effect, operates its own business independently of the other venturers within that structure. The nature of such a structure means that the framework entity acts merely as an agent for the venturers, with each venturer able to identify and control its share of the assets, liabilities and cash flows within that framework. In these cases, to reflect the substance of its operations each venturer should account directly for its share of the assets, liabilities and cash flows arising within the entity.

ACCOUNTING FOR ASSOCIATES

A reporting entity that prepares consolidated financial statements should include its associates in those statements using the equity method in all the primary statements. In the investor's individual financial statements, its interests in associates should be treated as fixed asset investments and shown either at cost, less any amounts written off, or at valuation. 26

The investor's consolidated profit and loss account

In the investor's consolidated profit and loss account the investor's share of its associates' operating results should be included immediately after group operating result (but after the investor's share of the results of its joint ventures, if any). Any amortisation or write-down of goodwill arising on acquiring the associates should be charged at this point and disclosed. The investor's share of any exceptional items included after operating profit (paragraph 20 of FRS 3) or of interest should be shown separately from the amounts for the group. At and below the level of profit before tax, the investor's share of the relevant amounts for associates should be included within the amounts for the group, although for items below this level, such as taxation, the amounts relating to associates should be disclosed. Where it is helpful to give an indication of the size of the business as a whole, a total combining the investor's share of its associates' turnover with group turnover may be shown as a memorandum item in the profit and loss account but the investor's share of its associates' turnover should be clearly distinguished from group turnover. Similarly, the segmental analysis of turnover and operating profit (if given) should clearly distinguish between that of the group and that of associates. 27

The investor's consolidated statement of total recognised gains and losses

In the consolidated statement of total recognised gains and losses the investor's share of the total recognised gains and losses of its associates should be included, shown separately under each heading, if the amounts included are material, either in the statement or in a note that is referred to in the statement. 28

The investor's consolidated balance sheet

The investor's consolidated balance sheet should include as a fixed asset investment the investor's share of the net assets of its associates shown as a separate item. Goodwill arising on the investor's acquisition of its associates, less any amortisation or write-down, should be included in the carrying amount for the associates but should be disclosed separately. 29

The investor's consolidated cash flow statement

The investor's consolidated cash flow statement should include dividends received from associates as a separate item between operating activities and returns on investments and servicing of finance. Any other cash flows between the investor and its associates should be included under the appropriate cash flow heading for the activity giving rise to the cash flow. None of the other cash flows of the associates should be included. 30

APPLYING THE EQUITY METHOD AND THE GROSS EQUITY METHOD

31 **In calculating the amounts to be included in the investor's consolidated financial statements by the equity method for associates and the gross equity method for joint ventures, the same principles should be applied as are applied in the consolidation of subsidiaries.**

(a) When an entity acquires an associate or joint venture, fair values should be attributed to the investee's underlying assets and liabilities, identified using the investor's accounting policies, and these fair values should provide the basis for subsequent depreciation. Both the consideration paid in the acquisition and the goodwill arising should be calculated in the same way as on the acquisition of a subsidiary. The investee's assets used in calculating the goodwill arising on its acquisition should not include any goodwill carried in the balance sheet of the investee itself. Subject to the presentation requirement in paragraph 29 of the FRS, the goodwill balance should be treated in accordance with the provisions of FRS 10 'Goodwill and Intangible Assets'.

(b) Where profits and losses resulting from transactions between the investor and its associate or joint venture are included in the carrying amount of assets in either entity, the part relating to the investor's share should be eliminated. Where the transaction provides evidence of the impairment of those assets or any similar assets, this should be taken into account.

(c) In arriving at the amounts to be included by the equity method, the same accounting policies as those of the investor should be applied.

(d) Where the period-end of an associate or joint venture differs from that of the investor, the entity should be included on the basis of financial statements prepared to the investor's period-end. Where this is not practicable, the entity should be included on the basis of financial statements prepared for a period ending not more than three months before the investor's period-end. Where using these financial statements would release restricted, price-sensitive information, financial statements prepared for a period that ended not more than six months before the investor's period-end may be used. Any changes after the period-end of the associate or joint venture and before that of its investor that would materially affect the view given by the investor's financial statements should be taken into account by adjustment.

32 **Where the investor is a group, its share of its associate or joint venture is the aggregate of the holdings of the parent and its subsidiaries in that entity. The holdings of any of the group's other associates or joint ventures should be ignored for this purpose. Where an associate or joint venture itself has subsidiaries, associates or joint ventures, the results and net assets to be taken into account by the equity method are those reported in that investee's consolidated financial statements (including the investee's share of the results and net assets of its associates and joint ventures), after any adjustment necessary to give effect to the investor's accounting policies.**

33 **The investor may hold options, convertibles or non-equity shares in its associate or joint venture. In certain circumstances, the conditions attaching to such holdings are such that the investor should take them into account in reflecting its interest in its investee under the equity or gross equity method. In such cases, the costs of exercising the options or converting the convertibles, or future payments in relation to the non-equity shares, should also be taken into account. The necessary calculation depends on the relevant circumstances in any particular case but care should be taken not to count any interest twice – for example, by including a greater share of the investee under the equity method than that which would arise on the basis of the investor's existing equity**

holding while simultaneously writing up the value of options held in the investee to reflect an increase in market value.

To apply either the equity method or the gross equity method, the investor's share in its investee needs to be calculated. Where the investee is corporate, the investor's share is usually calculated at its proportional holding of ordinary shares in that entity because this is the basis of its entitlement to dividends and other distributions. In some cases the arrangements for sharing dividends and other distributions may be more complicated; for example, they may depend on the nature of the distribution to be made or the way that the underlying cash flows arise. In these cases the substance of the respective rights held needs to be assessed to establish the most appropriate measure of the investor's share. **34**

Paragraph 31 requires procedures in applying the equity methods for associates and joint ventures that are similar to those used in the consolidation of subsidiaries. However, an investor controls its subsidiaries, thus providing access to the information necessary for these procedures, but it exercises only significant influence over its associates or jointly controls its joint ventures. Where access to information is limited, estimates may be used. However, if the information available to the investor is extremely limited, the investor's relationship with its investee will need to be reassessed because there may be doubt in such instances whether its influence is significant or whether it jointly controls its investment. **35**

Among the adjustments required by paragraph 31 is the elimination of the investor's share of any profits or losses from transactions between the investor and its investee that are included in the carrying amount of assets in either entity. This adjustment applies only in the investor's consolidated financial statements. The adjustment required applies to transfers of assets or liabilities to set up a joint venture or to acquire an initial stake in an associate as well as to all other transactions during the life of the associate or joint venture. Because associates and joint ventures are not part of the group, balances between the investor and its associates or joint ventures are not eliminated and therefore unsettled normal trading transactions should be included as current assets or liabilities. **36**

Regulations on the dissemination of information may restrict the extent to which the financial statements of an investor may contain information about its associates and joint ventures unless such information is available to other interested parties at the same time. An investor should plan how to satisfy any regulations on the publishing of information about its associates and joint ventures. **37**

IMPAIRMENT

Where there has been an impairment in any goodwill attributable to an associate or joint venture, the goodwill should be written down. The amount written off in the accounting period should be separately disclosed. **38**

Any impairment in the underlying net assets of an associate or joint venture would normally be reflected at the level of the entity itself (ie by writing down the relevant assets) or in the adjustments made to apply the equity or gross equity method; accordingly, no further provision against the investor's share of these net assets should usually be necessary. **39**

COMMENCEMENT OR CESSATION OF AN ASSOCIATE OR JOINT VENTURE RELATIONSHIP

40 **The date on which an investment becomes an associate is the date on which the investor begins to fulfil the two essential elements of the definition of an associated undertaking: the holding of a participating interest and the exercise of significant influence. The date on which an investment ceases to be an associate is the date on which it ceases to fulfil either element. The date on which an investment becomes a joint venture is the date on which the investor begins to control that entity jointly with other venturers, provided it has a long-term interest. The date on which an investment ceases to be a joint venture is the date on which the investor ceases to have joint control.* When an interest in an associate or joint venture is disposed of, the profit or loss arising on disposal should be calculated after taking into account any related goodwill that has not previously been either written off through the profit and loss account or attributed to prior period amortisation or impairment on applying the transitional arrangements of FRS 10 'Goodwill and Intangible Assets'.**

41 **Where an investment in an associate or joint venture is acquired or disposed of in stages, processes similar to those set out for subsidiaries in FRS 2 (paragraphs 50–52) should be followed.**

42 **When an entity ceases to be either an associate or joint venture, the initial carrying amount of any interest retained in the entity is based on the percentage retained of the final carrying amount for the former associate or joint venture at the date the entity ceased to qualify as such, including any related goodwill as required by paragraph 40. The initial carrying amount calculated on this basis should be reviewed and written down, if necessary, to its recoverable amount.**

43 When an entity ceases to be either an associate or joint venture, the investor may retain all or some of its interest in that entity as a simple investment. An interest in another entity that ceases to be a joint venture may still qualify as an associate. Once an interest qualifies as long-term it should continue to be treated as long-term, whether the investor intends to keep its interest or dispose of it. The initial carrying amount of any interest retained in a former associate or joint venture is a surrogate cost derived from the former carrying amount rather than any consideration paid. In applying the requirement to review and write down that initial amount, if necessary, to its recoverable amount, it should be noted that the recoverable amount may be affected by the amount that has been paid in dividend or by other distributions to owners. The treatment required for remaining investments in former associates and joint ventures is similar to that applied to any remaining interest in an entity that has ceased to be a subsidiary (paragraph 47 of FRS 2).

THE TREATMENT OF LOSSES AND INTERESTS IN NET LIABILITIES

44 **The investor should continue to record changes in the carrying amount for each associate and joint venture even if application of the equity method or gross equity method results in an interest in net liabilities rather than net assets. The only exception is where there is sufficient evidence that an event has irrevocably changed the relationship between the investor and its investee, marking its irreversible withdrawal from its investee as its associate or joint venture.**

**Paragraph 7 of the FRS is relevant in determining the date on which an investment ceases to be an associate or joint venture.*

Evidence that the necessary irrevocable change has taken place includes a public statement by the investor that it is withdrawing, with a demonstrable commitment to the process of withdrawal, or evidence that the direction of the operating and financing policies of the investee is to become the responsibility of the investee's creditors, including its bankers, rather than its equity shareholders. Where an interest in net liabilities arises, the amount recorded is shown as a provision or liability. 45

NON-CORPORATE ASSOCIATES AND JOINT VENTURES

Where an investor has an interest in a non-corporate associate or joint venture, the investor should ensure that all its liabilities with respect to that entity are reflected appropriately in its financial statements. 46

Where an investor has an interest in an unincorporated entity, a liability could arise – for example as a result of joint and several liability in a partnership – that would exceed the amount resulting from taking into account only the investor's share of net assets. In such circumstances it may be necessary either to include an additional amount for that liability or to report it as a contingent liability. 47

AN INVESTOR THAT DOES NOT PREPARE CONSOLIDATED FINANCIAL STATEMENTS

Where an investor does not prepare consolidated financial statements, it should present the relevant amounts for associates and joint ventures, as appropriate, by preparing a separate set of financial statements or by showing the relevant amounts, together with the effects of including them, as additional information to its own financial statements. Investing entities that are exempt from preparing consolidated financial statements, or would be exempt if they had subsidiaries, are exempt from this requirement. 48

INVESTMENT FUNDS

Investment funds, such as those in the venture capital and investment trust industry, should include all investments that are held as part of their investment portfolio in the same way (ie at cost or market value), even those over which the investor has significant influence or joint control. Investments are held as part of an investment portfolio if their value to the investor is through their marketable value as part of a basket of investments rather than as media through which the investor carries out its business. 49

In the venture capital and investment trust industry, the business of the investor is to provide capital to other entities, often accompanied by advice and guidance. The stake taken by the investor and the rights attributable to that stake vary according to circumstances but the investor's relationship to its investment tends to be that of a portfolio investor. In these circumstances, for consistency, the stake is properly accounted for as an investment according to the method of accounting applied to other investments within that investment portfolio rather than as an associate or joint venture, even if the investor has significant influence or joint control. Outside their investment portfolio, venture capital funds and investment trusts may hold investments that qualify as associates or joint ventures. Such investments should be included using the equity method or the gross equity method, whatever the nature of their investor's business. For investment funds, investments that are associates or joint ventures often arise in a field of activity that is closely related or complementary to that of the investor. 50

DISCLOSURES

51 **The following disclosures should be made in addition to the amounts required on the face of the primary financial statements under the equity method or the gross equity method.**

For all associates and joint ventures

52 **The names of the principal associates and joint ventures should be disclosed in the financial statements of the investing group, showing for each associate and joint venture:**

(a) the proportion of the issued shares in each class held by the investing group, indicating any special rights or constraints attaching to them;

(b) the accounting period or date of the financial statements used if they differ from those of the investing group; and

(c) an indication of the nature of its business.

53 **Any notes relating to the financial statements of associates and joint ventures, or matters that should have been noted had the investor's accounting policies been applied, that are material to understanding the effect on the investor of its investments should be disclosed, in particular noting the investor's share in contingent liabilities incurred jointly with other venturers or investors and its share of the capital commitments of the associates and joint ventures themselves.**

54 **If there are significant statutory, contractual or exchange control restrictions on the ability of an associate or joint venture to distribute its reserves (other than those shown as non-distributable), the extent of the restrictions should be indicated.**

55 **The amounts owing and owed between an investor and its associates or its joint ventures should be analysed into amounts relating to loans and amounts relating to trading balances. This disclosure may be combined with those required by FRS 8 'Related Party Disclosures'.**

56 **A note should explain why the facts of any particular case rebut either the presumption that an investor holding 20 per cent or more of the voting rights of another entity exercises significant influence over the operating and financial policies of that entity or the presumption that an investor holding 20 per cent or more of the shares of another entity has a participating interest.**

Additional disclosures at 15 and 25 per cent thresholds

57 **The disclosures required for all associates and joint ventures should be supplemented if certain thresholds are exceeded. The thresholds are applied by comparing the investor's share for either its associates in aggregate or its joint ventures in aggregate or its individual associates or joint ventures, as appropriate, of the following:**

- **gross assets**
- **gross liabilities**
- **turnover**
- **operating results (on a three-year average)**

with the corresponding amounts for the investor group (excluding any amount included by the equity method for associates and the gross equity method for joint ventures). If any of the relevant amounts for the investor's share exceeds the specified proportion of the same amounts for the investor group, the threshold has been exceeded and the additional disclosures in paragraph 58 should be made.

The following are the additional disclosures that should be made. 58

(a) Where the aggregate of the investor's share in its associates exceeds a 15 per cent threshold with respect to the investor group, a note should give the aggregate of the investor's share in its associates of the following:
- **turnover (unless it is already included as a memorandum item)**
- **fixed assets**
- **current assets**
- **liabilities due within one year**
- **liabilities due after one year or more.**

(b) Where the aggregate of the investor's share in its joint ventures exceeds a 15 per cent threshold with respect to the investor group, a note should give the aggregate of the investor's share in its joint ventures of the following:
- **fixed assets**
- **current assets**
- **liabilities due within one year**
- **liabilities due after one year or more.**

(c) Where the investor's share in any individual associate or joint venture exceeds a 25 per cent threshold with respect to the investor group, a note should name that associate or joint venture and give its share of each of the following:
- **turnover**
- **profit before tax**
- **taxation**
- **profit after tax**
- **fixed assets**
- **current assets**
- **liabilities due within one year**
- **liabilities due after one year or more.**

If that individual associate or joint venture accounts for nearly all of the amounts included for that class of investment, only the aggregate, not the individual, information need be given, provided that this is explained and the associate or joint venture identified.

In addition to the disclosures in (a)–(c) above, further analysis should be given where this is necessary to understand the nature of the total amounts disclosed. In deciding into which balance sheet headings the amounts should be analysed, regard should be had to the nature of the businesses and, therefore, which are the most relevant and descriptive balance sheet amounts to disclose. It may be important to give an indication of the size and maturity profile of the liabilities held.

DATE FROM WHICH EFFECTIVE

The accounting practices set out in the FRS should be regarded as standard in respect of financial statements relating to accounting periods ending on or after 23 June 1998. Earlier adoption is encouraged but not required. 59

WITHDRAWAL OF SSAP 1 AND INTERIM STATEMENT AND AMENDMENT OF FRS 1 (REVISED 1996)

The FRS supersedes SSAP 1 'Accounting for associated companies' and withdraws the remaining paragraphs of the Interim Statement 'Consolidated Accounts'. 60

The FRS makes the following changes to FRS 1 (Revised 1996) 'Cash Flow Statements' in respect of the treatment of dividends received from associates and joint ventures. 61

[*Not reproduced as all changes have been reflected in the material reproduced in this volume.*]

Adoption of FRS 9 by the Board

Financial Reporting Standard 9 – 'Associates and Joint Ventures' was approved for issue by the ten members of the Accounting Standards Board.

Sir David Tweedie	(Chairman)
Allan Cook	(Technical Director)
David Allvey	
Ian Brindle	
Dr John Buchanan	
John Coombe	
Raymond Hinton	
Huw Jones	
Professor Geoffrey Whittington	
Ken Wild	

Appendix I
Note on legal requirements

The general legal background to the requirements of the FRS are considered in paragraphs 2–6. Paragraphs 7–11 set out the relevant legal provisions in Great Britain with the corresponding references for Northern Ireland in paragraph 12 and the Republic of Ireland in paragraph 13. 1

GREAT BRITAIN

*The Companies Act 1985 and the approach taken in the FRS**

An associate is defined in the FRS as an entity in which the investor holds a participating interest, and over which it exercises significant influence, with the result that an associate will also qualify as an associated undertaking as defined in the Companies Act 1985. The requirement for associates to be included in the investor's consolidated financial statements using the equity method of accounting is also consistent with the requirement for associated undertakings in the Act. 2

A joint venture is defined in the FRS as an entity in which each joint venturer has a long-term interest and has joint control. A joint venturer, therefore, fulfils the conditions for having a participating interest and exercising a significant influence, with the result that all joint ventures meeting the definition in the FRS will also qualify as associated undertakings as defined in the Act. The Act does not define a 'joint venture', although it refers to 'managing jointly' in its description of non-corporate joint ventures that are permitted to be included using proportional consolidation. 3

The FRS requires joint ventures to be included in the investor's consolidated financial statements using the gross equity method. This method provides information in addition to that given by the traditional equity method and its use is therefore consistent with the requirement of the Act for associated undertakings to be included by the equity method. 4

The FRS notes that a reporting entity sometimes carries out some of its operations through entities with the form of a joint venture but where there is limited commonality of interest between the venturers as each, in effect, operates its own business within the structure. Unless these arrangements constitute an undertaking (as defined in section 259 of the Act), the Act is silent on the treatment, and the 5

***Editor's note:** *The various statutory references change with the introduction of the Companies Act 2006, which affects accounting for periods beginning on or after 6 April 2008. The various statutory references have changed as follows:*

Companies Act 1985 reference	*Companies Act 2006 reference*
Section 259	*Section 1161*
Paragraph 20 of Schedule 4A	*Paragraph 19 of Schedule 6 to The Large and Medium-sized Companies and Groups (Accounts and Reports) Regulations 2008 (SI 2008/410)*
Section 260	*Paragraph 11 of Sch. 10 to SI 2008/410.*
Paragraph 22 of Schedule 4A	*Paragraph 21 of Sch. 6 to SI 2008/410.*
Paragraph 21 of Schedule 4A	*Paragraph 20 of Sch. 6 to SI 2008/410.*
Paragraph 19 of Schedule 4A	*Paragraph 18 of Sch. 6 to SI 2008/410.*

requirement of the FRS is that each of the participants should account for its share of the assets and liabilities directly as its own. Even in cases where the contractual arrangements are performed through the medium of an undertaking, if the nature of those arrangements means that the undertaking acts merely as an agent for the participants then, in such cases, they should follow the requirements of the FRS by accounting directly for their share of the assets and liabilities.

6 A similar analysis applies to the treatment of joint arrangements that are not entities. The FRS requires participants in such arrangements to account directly for their own assets, liabilities and cash flows. However, a joint arrangement may qualify as an undertaking under the Act even though it does not carry on its own trade or business (eg where the joint arrangement is a body corporate or a partnership). In such cases the nature of those arrangements means that the undertaking acts merely as an agent for the venturers and, therefore, they should account directly for their share of the assets and liabilities.

The provisions of the Companies Act 1985

7 The Act defines an "associated undertaking" in paragraph 20 of Schedule 4A.

"(1) An "associated undertaking" means an undertaking in which an undertaking included in the consolidation has a participating interest and over whose operating and financial policy it exercises a significant influence, and which is not–

(a) a subsidiary undertaking of the parent company, or
(b) a joint venture dealt with in accordance with paragraph 19 [of Schedule 4A].

(2) Where an undertaking holds 20 per cent or more of the voting rights in another undertaking, it shall be presumed to exercise such an influence over it unless the contrary is shown.
(3) The voting rights in an undertaking mean the rights conferred on shareholders in respect of their shares or, in the case of an undertaking not having a share capital, on members, to vote at general meetings of the undertaking on all, or substantially all, matters.
(4) The provisions of paragraphs 5 to 11 of Schedule 10A (rights to be taken into account and attribution of rights) apply in determining for the purposes of this paragraph whether an undertaking holds 20 per cent or more of the voting rights in another undertaking."

8 Section 260 of the Act defines a "participating interest" as follows:

"(1) ... an interest held by an undertaking in the shares of another undertaking which it holds on a long-term basis for the purpose of securing a contribution to its activities by the exercise of control or influence arising from or related to that interest.
(2) A holding of 20 per cent or more of the shares of an undertaking shall be presumed to be a participating interest unless the contrary is shown.
(3) The reference in subsection (1) to an interest in shares includes–

(a) an interest which is convertible into an interest in shares, and
(b) an option to acquire shares or any such interest;

and an interest or option falls within paragraph (a) or (b) notwithstanding that the shares to which it relates are, until the conversion or the exercise of the option, unissued.

(4) For the purposes of this section an interest held on behalf of an undertaking shall be treated as held by it."

Paragraph 22 of Schedule 4A requires that: **9**

"(1) The interest of an undertaking in an associated undertaking, and the amount of profit or loss attributable to such an interest, shall be shown by the equity method of accounting (including dealing with any goodwill arising in accordance with paragraphs 17 to 19 and 21 of Schedule 4).

(2) Where the associated undertaking is itself a parent undertaking, the net assets and profits or losses to be taken into account are those of the parent and its subsidiary undertakings (after making any consolidation adjustments)."

Paragraph 21 of Schedule 4A stipulates the position in the balance sheet and the profit and loss account formats of interests in associated undertakings and other participating interests and income from such interests. **10**

The Act does not define a joint venture. However, paragraph 19 of Schedule 4A provides that: **11**

"(1) Where an undertaking included in the consolidation manages another undertaking jointly with one or more undertakings not included in the consolidation, that other undertaking ("the joint venture") may, if it is not –

(a) a body corporate, or
(b) a subsidiary undertaking of the parent company,

be dealt with in the group accounts by the method of proportional consolidation.

(2) The provisions of this Part* relating to the preparation of consolidated accounts apply, with any necessary modifications, to proportional consolidation under this paragraph."

NORTHERN IRELAND

The legal requirements in Northern Ireland equivalent to those in Great Britain quoted in paragraphs 7–11 are set out in the following table. **12**

Great Britain: Companies Act 1985	*Northern Ireland: Companies (Northern Ireland) Order 1986*
paragraph 20 of Schedule 4A	paragraph 20 of Schedule 4A
section 260	Article 268
paragraph 22 of Schedule 4A	paragraph 22 of Schedule 4A
paragraph 21 of Schedule 4A	paragraph 21 of Schedule 4A
paragraph 19 of Schedule 4A	paragraph 19 of Schedule 4A

**The reference to 'Part' appears to mean Schedule 4A.*

REPUBLIC OF IRELAND

13 The legal requirements in the Republic of Ireland equivalent to those in Great Britain quoted in paragraphs 7–11 are set out in the following table.

Great Britain: Companies Act 1985	*Republic of Ireland: European Communities (Companies: Group Accounts) Regulations 1992*
paragraph 20 of Schedule 4A	Regulation 34
section 260	Regulation 35
paragraph 22 of Schedule 4A	Regulation 33
paragraph 21 of Schedule 4A	paragraph 10 of the Schedule
paragraph 19 of Schedule 4A	Regulation 32

Appendix II
Compliance with international accounting standards

The International Accounting Standards Committee (IASC) has one standard for associates – IAS 28 'Accounting for Investments in Associates' – and another for joint ventures and other joint arrangements – IAS 31 'Financial Reporting of Interests in Joint Ventures'.* 1

IAS 28 'Accounting for Investments in Associates'

For associates, the requirements of the FRS and IAS 28 are similar, both requiring the use of the equity method in the investor's consolidated financial statements. There are the following minor differences. 2

- IAS 28 defines an associate as an enterprise in which the investor has significant influence, whereas the FRS is consistent with companies legislation and defines an associate by the investor's holding of a participating interest and exercise of significant influence. Furthermore, the emphasis in the FRS is on the actual exercise of significant influence, whereas IAS 28 defines significant influence as "the power to participate in the financial and operating policy decisions of the investee". The IAS 28 definition would therefore apply to investors that had the ability to exercise significant influence but were not actually exercising it. This difference may have a limited effect in practice because the best evidence of an entity's ability to exercise significant influence is the fact that it is exercising such an influence.
- IAS 28 contains a rebuttable presumption of significant influence where an investor holds, directly or indirectly through subsidiaries, 20 per cent or more of the voting power of the investee. There is a similar presumption of the exercise of significant influence in companies legislation. However, the FRS moves away from using a 20 per cent threshold as the defining threshold, noting that a holding of 20 per cent or more of the voting rights in another entity suggests, but does not ensure, that the investor exercises significant influence over that entity. The presumption of the exercise of significant influence at the 20 per cent threshold is rebutted if the investor does not fulfil the criteria for the exercise of significant influence.
- IAS 28 excludes from equity accounting any associate that is acquired and held exclusively with a view to its subsequent disposal in the near future or which operates under severe long-term restrictions that significantly impair its ability to transfer funds to the investor. The FRS does not have any specific exclusions but the conditions relating to the exercise of significant influence are unlikely to be fulfilled by an investment operating under severe long-term restrictions and the definition of a participating interest specifies an interest that is held on a long-term basis, which excludes one held exclusively with a view to disposal.
- IAS 28 requires an associate to be included in its investor's individual financial statements using the equity method or at cost or revalued amount. The FRS

****Editor's note:*** *Both IAS 28 and IAS 31 were revised in 1998. They have now been revised further with new versions published in December 2003. Among the changes made to IAS 28 are that there is a specific exclusion for venture capital organisations and similar holding interests that would otherwise be associates, potential voting rights are to be taken into account in determining if an entity is an associate, there is some clarification on temporary influence and long-term restrictions, and there are revised rules on recognition of losses. Among the changes to IAS 31 are a similar exemption for venture capital organisations and similar, and similar rules on temporary joint control and long-term restrictions. From 2013, IFRS 11 replaces IAS 31, requiring the use of the equity method, while there are a number of further changes to IAS 28, including its scope.*

requires an associate to be carried at cost or valuation in its investor's individual financial statements.

- IAS 28 requires that the investor's consolidated income statement should reflect its share of the results of the operations of the investee. The FRS specifies that the investor's share of its associates' operating results should be brought into its consolidated profit and loss account immediately after the line showing group operating profit but after its share of the operating results of its joint ventures, if any.
- The FRS requires additional disclosures to the amounts shown under the equity method for associates that in aggregate exceed 15 per cent of gross assets, gross liabilities, turnover or, on a three-year average, operating result for the investing group and for each individual associate that exceeds 25 per cent of gross assets, gross liabilities, turnover or, on a three-year average, operating result for the investing group. These are not required by IAS 28.

IAS 31 'Financial Reporting of Interests in Joint Ventures'

3 Although both the FRS and IAS 31 take joint control as the defining relationship between an investor and its joint ventures, IAS 31 defines a joint venture in terms of a contractual arrangement while the FRS defines a joint venture in terms of an entity.* The effect of this difference in definition is that of the three types of joint venture identified in IAS 31 – jointly controlled operations, jointly controlled assets and jointly controlled entities – only the last qualifies as a joint venture as defined in the FRS. IAS 31 does not include an explicit definition of an entity or guidance on how to distinguish jointly controlled operations and jointly controlled assets from jointly controlled entities. The FRS provides guidance on whether an entity exists, which depends on whether the joint activities amount to the carrying on of a trade or business. In the FRS jointly controlled operations and jointly controlled assets are dealt with as joint arrangements that are not entities. However, the treatment required for jointly controlled operations and jointly controlled assets is the same in the FRS and IAS 31 – participants should recognise directly in their own financial statements, and consequently in their consolidated financial statements, their share of the assets and liabilities of jointly controlled operations and of any jointly controlled assets.

4 The FRS requires joint ventures to be included in their investor's consolidated financial statements using the gross equity method – which expands the traditional equity method with a note of the investor's share of the turnover, gross assets and liabilities of the joint ventures. In IAS 31, the equity method is an 'allowed alternative' for jointly controlled entities but the 'benchmark' treatment is proportional consolidation, with a choice of two reporting formats – including the investor's share of its joint ventures either line-by-line or as separate line items for assets, liabilities, profit and expenses.

5 IAS 31 requires interests in jointly controlled entities to be treated as ordinary investments if they:

(a) are acquired and held exclusively with a view to subsequent disposal in the near future; or
(b) operate under severe long-term restrictions that significantly impair their ability to transfer funds to the venturer.

**As noted in Appendix I, the definition in the FRS is in line with companies legislation, where only 'associated undertakings' qualify to use the equity method.*

The FRS has no need for such exclusions, because the conditions relating to the definition of a joint venture are unlikely to be fulfilled in these circumstances.

IAS 31 requires a venturer to disclose the aggregate amounts of each of current assets, long-term assets, current liabilities, long-term liabilities, income and expenses related to its interests in jointly controlled entities.* The FRS requires instead additional levels of disclosure where joint ventures in aggregate exceed a 15 per cent threshold or individual joint ventures exceed a 25 per cent threshold of certain key indicators (paragraphs 57 and 58). The FRS requires amounts included for joint ventures to be analysed into at least fixed assets, current assets, liabilities due within one year and liabilities due after one year or more. 6

**Unless the venturer uses the reporting format for proportional consolidation where separate line items are included for the venturer's share of the assets, liabilities, income and expenses of its joint venture.*

Appendix III
The development of the FRS

HISTORY

1 For a variety of legal, tax, economic and other reasons, business activities are often conducted through a network of connected entities, including subsidiaries, joint ventures and associates. Joint ventures are increasingly popular as a means of gaining access to new markets, new technologies or scarce resources and sometimes as a means of sharing risks.

2 In March 1996 the Board issued FRED 11 'Associates and Joint Ventures' containing proposals developed in the light of comments on its earlier Discussion Paper (July 1994) to revise the current standard, SSAP 1 'Accounting for associated companies'. SSAP 1 was originally issued in 1971 as a response to the growing practice of entities of conducting parts of their businesses through associates. The standard ensured that the investor's consolidated financial statements reflected the effect of a reporting entity's investments in associates by including such entities using the equity method. SSAP 1 was revised in 1982.

3 The Board decided to carry out a full review of SSAP 1 because that standard:

- did not cover the identification of, and accounting for, joint ventures.
- encouraged but did not require additional disclosures where significant interests were included by equity accounting. There was little evidence of additional disclosures being made.
- permitted in the Board's view an, at times, too literal interpretation of the definition of an associated company (associate), which was applied to the form of the reporting entity's interest in another entity rather than the substance.

4 The proposals in FRED 11 were generally well received and the FRS carries forward unchanged the proposals on the following topics:-

- the definitions of associates and joint ventures
- the inclusion of associates in the investor's consolidated financial statements using the equity method
- the measurement principles required by the equity method
- the commencement or cessation of an associate or joint venture relationship
- the treatment of losses and interests in the net liabilities where losses have accumulated.

5 On three topics some respondents, albeit a minority, did not support the proposals in FRED 11 and put forward some well argued objections. The Board has considered carefully the comments made and has consulted further on these issues. To meet some of the concerns expressed, the proposed treatments in FRED 11 have been modified.

- Joint ventures are now treated as a single class of investment rather than the two classes proposed by FRED 11 and the gross equity method is now required for all joint ventures. The result is to give a better impression of the scale of resources committed to joint ventures in relation to those of the reporting entity than is conveyed by the traditional equity method.
- The investor's share of the results of its equity accounted entities is now included immediately after group operating profit rather than in group operating profit, as proposed in FRED 11.

- The level of detail required for additional disclosures for associates or joint ventures at a 15 per cent threshold has been reduced from that proposed in FRED 11 – but further analysis is required where this is necessary to understand the nature of the amounts shown. The disclosures for individual associates or joint ventures that individually exceed a 25 per cent threshold in relation to the investor have been aligned with the disclosures in aggregate at the 15 per cent threshold.

THE BASIC PRINCIPLES

A key issue for the Board in considering associates and joint ventures has been the need to develop proposals for them that would form part of a coherent and consistent policy for the treatment of all of a reporting entity's interests in other entities and other joint arrangements that are not entities. The Board has therefore addressed how to distinguish joint ventures from associates on the one hand and subsidiaries on the other and how to distinguish associates from simple investments. In the FRS these distinctions are based on the nature of the investor's relationship with the investee – which is also what justifies the different accounting treatments proposed to reflect the different interests. 6

- If the investor controls its investee, the investee is its subsidiary and should be consolidated.
- If the reporting entity participates in a joint arrangement that is not an entity (ie it does not carry on a trade or business of its own), it should account directly for its share of the assets, liabilities and cash flows of the joint arrangement according to the terms of the agreement governing the arrangement.
- If the investor controls the investee not by itself but jointly with other entities, the investee is its joint venture. A special accounting treatment – the gross equity method – is proposed to reflect this relationship.
- If the investor neither controls nor jointly controls its investee but still has significant influence over the investee's operating and financial policies, the investee is its associate. The equity method is traditionally used to reflect this relationship.
- If the investor neither controls nor jointly controls its investee, nor has significant influence over the investee's operating and financial policies, the investee is merely an investment. There is no special relationship to account for and the investor should include the investment in both its individual and consolidated financial statements in the same way.

The principles set out above are very similar to those underlying the proposals in FRED 11, but the latter have been modified in two following respects. 7

(a) Joint arrangements that are not entities

FRED 11 defined joint ventures as entities in a similar way to the FRS, thus also departing from the IASC standard on joint ventures, IAS 31, which includes as joint ventures not only jointly controlled entities but also jointly controlled operations and jointly controlled assets. FRED 11 considered jointly controlled operations and jointly controlled assets only briefly in its 'Explanation' section. The FRS addresses joint arrangements that are not entities much more fully by including a definition with an explanation of how to determine whether a set of activities constitutes an entity. In the FRS the treatment for such joint arrangements is the same as that proposed in FRED 11.

(b) Joint ventures

FRED 11 proposed identifying two classes of joint ventures: those where the venturers shared in common the benefits and risks, which were to be included by the equity method, and those where each venturer had its own separate interest, which were to be included by proportional consolidation. The FRS now emphasises the special nature of joint control by identifying joint ventures as a single class of investments wholly separate from associates, to be included by a special method of accounting – the gross equity method. However, in practice the difference from the proposals in FRED 11 may be limited because the sort of arrangement that, under FRED 11, would have been most clearly identifiable as a joint venture to be proportionally consolidated will, under the FRS, be accounted for by each participant bringing in directly its share of any assets, liabilities and cash flows to reflect the substance of the arrangement as a structure within which each participant carries on its own business.

A JOINT ARRANGEMENT THAT IS NOT AN ENTITY

8 Paragraph 6 of the FRS identifies a joint arrangement that is not an entity as the way in which a reporting entity can further its economic activities through investments or joint arrangements that involves the reporting entity most directly. The FRS requires each participant in such a joint arrangement to account directly for its own share of the assets, liabilities and cash flows relating to the joint arrangement, its share being measured by reference to the terms of the joint arrangement. If a joint arrangement is not an entity, accounting treatments whose purpose is to reflect a reporting entity's interests in other entities in its consolidated financial statements – such as consolidation, proportional consolidation and equity accounting – are irrelevant in deciding how to treat that arrangement. The 'Explanation' section of FRED 11 dealt in a similar way with joint arrangements.

JOINT VENTURES

Definition

9 The FRS sets out three conditions to be fulfilled for a joint arrangement to meet the definition of a joint venture.

(a) The business activities undertaken under the joint arrangement must constitute an entity.
(b) The venturer must jointly control the entity.
(c) The investor's interest must be held for the long term.

In FRED 11 condition (c) was not stated explicitly.

10 The definition of an entity in the FRS is built on that of an undertaking in companies legislation as proposed in FRED 11 but, in response to the comments, the FRS gives more guidance on the application of the definition, elaborating on a key aspect – the carrying on of a trade or business. The distinction between joint arrangements that are entities and those that are not is important because the equity method can apply only to interests in entities. For a joint arrangement that does not amount to an entity, the only possible accounting procedure is that each party involved should recognise directly its own share of assets, liabilities and cash flows, measured by reference to the agreement governing the joint arrangement.

Treatment

The gross equity method required by the FRS for joint ventures amplifies the net amounts included under the equity method by showing in the consolidated profit and loss account and balance sheet the investor's share of its joint ventures' turnover, gross assets and gross liabilities. The manner in which these additional details are presented expands the information given by the traditional equity method without changing its nature – the investment in joint ventures is still shown as a net amount and joint ventures' turnover is excluded from that of the group. The effect of this is that the gross equity method, like the traditional equity method, is consistent with the use of control as the basis of asset recognition (in that the net investment represents the asset that is controlled by the venturer) while going some way to meet concerns expressed by a minority of respondents that the traditional equity method understated the scale of activity undertaken through joint ventures. 11

In addition to concerns about the adequacy of the equity method for joint ventures, some respondents who opposed the proposals in FRED 11 for joint ventures believed that either: 12

(a) all joint ventures should be included by proportional consolidation, particularly because that is the benchmark treatment for joint ventures in IAS 31; or

(b) the division of joint ventures into two classes proposed in FRED 11 was either not valid in principle or difficult to apply in practice. FRED 11 proposed distinguishing between:

  (i) the majority of joint ventures, where the venturers shared in common the benefits, risks and obligations of their joint venture as a separate business, which were to be included using the equity method; and

  (ii) other joint ventures, where each venturer had a separate interest in the benefits, risks and obligations of the venture, which were to be included by proportional consolidation.

The difference of opinion between those supporting an equity method for joint ventures and those supporting proportional consolidation is reflected in an international debate on the treatment of joint ventures. IAS 31 notes that, in a jointly controlled entity (a joint venture under the FRS), a venturer has control over its share of future economic benefits through its share of the assets and liabilities of the venture. IAS 31 does not recommend the use of the equity method, on the grounds that proportional consolidation better reflects the substance and economic reality of a venturer's interest in a jointly controlled entity, ie control over the venturer's share of the future economic benefits. The Board rejects proportional consolidation for joint ventures because it believes that it can be misleading to represent each venturer's joint control of a joint venture – which allows it to direct the operating and financial policies of the joint venture only with the consent of the other venturers – as being in substance equivalent to its having sole control of its share of each of that entity's assets, liabilities and cash flows. The key features of control are that the controlling party has the ability to direct or deploy what it controls without consultation and the ability to take the benefit from what it directs or deploys without question of entitlement. The problems with treating a venturer's joint control as equivalent to its sole control of its share are particularly clear for cash flow reporting where, under proportional consolidation, the venturer would include its share of the cash flows of its joint venture directly as its own cash flows. 13

Another argument on which IAS 31 supports proportional consolidation for jointly controlled entities is that it results in the joint arrangements of the investor being reflected in the same way in its consolidated financial statements, whether its joint activities are carried on through jointly controlled assets, jointly controlled 14 operations or jointly controlled entities. However, the Board believes there is an essential difference between activities carried on directly by the reporting entity itself through its jointly controlled assets or operations and activities carried out through an entity controlled jointly with other entities. In jointly controlled assets or operations, the benefits, risks and obligations for each entity relate only to the entity's share of the assets and liabilities involved in the joint activity. In contrast, in a jointly controlled entity the investors usually share in common the benefits, risks and obligations of the entity as a whole rather than those of the individual assets and liabilities of that entity.

15 The Board believes that some flexibility is important to reflect the diversity of joint ventures and to enable reporting entities to reflect the nature of their interests. In some cases, the reporting entity may want to give more information about its joint venture on the face of its financial statements. Provided that any additional information given for joint ventures is in a form that is consistent with the gross equity method, the Board encourages experimentation. Appendix IV sets out an optional columnar presentation that may be used where joint ventures represent a major part of the reporting entity's business. The columnar presentation keeps separate the amounts relating to joint ventures from the amounts for the group itself and remains consistent with the equity method because it is formatted to provide an additional analysis of the net amounts included under the equity method.

A STRUCTURE WITH THE FORM BUT NOT THE SUBSTANCE OF A JOINT VENTURE

16 The FRS requires that venturers should account directly for their own share of the assets, liabilities and cash flows of a structure with the appearance of a joint venture used only as a means for the each participant to carry on their own business. In spite of its appearance, such a structure is not a joint venture because of the extremely limited commonality of interest between the participants. The proposal in FRED 11 for proportional consolidation where a joint venture acts only as a framework for each venturer carrying on its own activities also recognised that the equity method was not appropriate in such cases.

ASSOCIATES

Identification

17 As proposed in FRED 11, to be consistent with companies legislation, the FRS defines an associate by reference to its investor having a participating interest and exercising significant influence over it. In the earlier Discussion Paper, both associates and joint ventures were identified as a single class of investments called 'strategic alliances' and the emphasis was on the investor acting as a partner in the business of its investee. Some commentators found this emphasis on a partnership between an investor and its associate unhelpful and contrary to their understanding of a partnership. As a result the Board decided to drop the approach that used 'strategic alliances', and has reverted to the approach underlying SSAP 1, which emphasises participation in the operating and financial policies of the investee.

18 All investees qualifying as associates under the FRS would have qualified as associates under SSAP 1, which defined an associate as an interest held for the long term where the investor is in a position to exercise significant influence. However, an entity may have qualified as an associate under SSAP 1 yet not qualify as such under the definitions in the FRS because a long-term interest is not always a participating interest, and being in a position to exercise significant influence does not always amount to the actual exercise of such an influence. In practice, these differences may have a limited effect because the best evidence that an entity is in a position to exercise significant influence is that it is actually exercising such influence. Applying the definition in this FRS should ensure that the substance of the relationship between the investor and investee is reflected thus correcting any instances of the too literal application of the SSAP 1 definition – for example, where the investor has a 20 per cent holding but in practice does not actually exercise significant influence.

Treatment

The requirement in the FRS for associates to be included in the investor's consolidated financial statements using the equity method of accounting represents no change to the requirements of SSAP 1 or the proposals in the Discussion Paper and FRED 11, the overwhelming majority of commentators agreeing with equity accounting for associates. Using the equity method for associates is in keeping with the principle that the assets and liabilities of a group are delineated by the extent of the parent's control because the equity method represents an investor's interest in an associate as a single asset – an investment – albeit one that is measured in terms of net assets and changes in net assets. An investor controls its interest in an associate but does not control its share of its associate's underlying assets and liabilities. For these reasons proportional consolidation is not appropriate for associates because it misrepresents the extent of the investor's influence over its associate's underlying assets and liabilities (and, in particular, its cash flows). 19

One possible alternative to the equity method would be to include associates at market value. However, providing information on that basis would not be consistent with the information provided by consolidated financial statements about a parent and its subsidiaries. Equity accounting for associates is consistent with consolidation for subsidiaries because it recognises the investor's share of its associates' results and changes in net assets, reflecting that associates are used as media through which the investor carries on its business, sometimes as substitutes for subsidiaries. 20

APPLYING THE EQUITY METHOD

Paragraph 33 of the FRS deals with cases where part of the investor's interest in its associate or joint venture arises from its holding of options, convertibles or non-equity shares. The basis of this paragraph is the requirement in FRS 5 (paragraph 14) that the substance of transactions should be reported. "In determining the substance of a transaction, all its aspects and implications should be identified and greater weight given to those more likely to have a commercial effect in practice." The investor should therefore account for the substance of its interest in its associates or joint ventures in cases where this is affected by its holdings of options, convertibles or non-equity shares. One example where an adjustment to the investor's interest may be necessary is where the price of exercising or converting options or convertibles is so low that there is commercially near-certainty that they will be exercised or converted. 21

Consistently with the exclusion of the results of associates or joint ventures from group operating profit, the FRS amends FRS 1 (Revised 1996) to include the cash flows relating to dividends received from associates and joint ventures as separate items between operating activities and returns on investment and servicing of finance in the investor's consolidated cash flow statement. FRED 11 proposed that the results of equity accounted entities should be included as part of group operating profit and therefore proposed that dividends received from such entities should be included as operating cash flows. The treatment in this FRS reflects the fact that dividends from 22 associates and joint ventures are not on a comparable basis to the cash flows arising from the group's operating activities and have a different significance from its returns on investments.

DISCLOSURES

23 One of the Board's objectives in reviewing SSAP 1 was to improve the information given about associates and joint ventures, particularly where they play a significant part in the reporting entity's operations. The equity method, by including only the net assets and results, had been criticised as failing to show the full amount of resources and obligations arising from the venturer's involvement. SSAP 1 required more detailed information to be given where, in the context of the financial statements of the investing group, the results of one or more associated companies were so material, or the interests in them were so material, that more detailed information about them would assist in giving a true and fair view. This requirement resulted in little extra disclosure in practice.

24 The FRS follows FRED 11 and the earlier Discussion Paper in requiring a layered approach to disclosures, with additional disclosures of aggregate amounts only when associates or joint ventures represent a significant part of the reporting entity's business at a 15 per cent threshold and with additional disclosures on an individual basis only in the rare cases when an individual associate or joint venture exceeds a 25 per cent threshold. However, there are two changes in the disclosure requirements from those proposed in FRED 11.

(a) The FRS requires the 15 per cent threshold for additional aggregate disclosures to be applied separately for associates and joint ventures as these are now classified as two different categories of investment.
(b) The FRS reduces the disclosures required both in aggregate at the 15 per cent threshold and for individual associates and joint ventures at the 25 per cent threshold.

These changes should reduce the concerns about the level of required disclosures that some respondents noted on FRED 11 – adverse comment was particularly marked in respect of the proposal for the disclosure of condensed financial information for any associate or joint venture that exceeded a 25 per cent threshold. The Board has successively attempted to meet concerns about the level of the disclosures by carefully targeting any disclosures to be required. FRED 11 itself reduced the number of disclosures proposed from those proposed in the Discussion Paper. The disclosures required at the 25 per cent threshold for individual associates and joint ventures are now consistent with those required in aggregate at the 15 per cent threshold, in particular the investor's share of the relevant amounts is to be disclosed rather than the amount relating to the whole associate or joint venture.

25 However, the FRS still includes a requirement for some additional individual disclosures for any highly significant associate or joint venture. The main objections to the proposal for individual disclosures in FRED 11 were that it would entail greater disclosure for some individual associates and joint ventures than for individual subsidiaries and might lead to the disclosure of commercially sensitive information. The Board has carefully considered these objections and, as a response, stresses the very high threshold level that is set to trigger the disclosures. An individual associate or joint venture rarely breaches this threshold – however, when it does, it plays such a significant role in a reporting entity while, unlike a subsidiary, outside the reporting entity's control, that the Board believes the proposed disclosures are necessary for the reporting entity to discharge its accountability and to give a true and fair view of its financial position and performance.

Appendix IV
Examples of alternative ways of giving information on joint ventures

The examples set out in this appendix are provided for general guidance only and do not form part of the FRS.

EXAMPLE 1 – the normal presentation using the equity method for associates and the gross equity method for joint ventures.

EXAMPLE 2 – an optional columnar presentation for joint ventures where they constitute a major part of the reporting entity's business.

Examples 1 and 2 use the same underlying information.

EXAMPLE 1 – THE NORMAL PRESENTATION

CONSOLIDATED PROFIT AND LOSS ACCOUNT

This format is illustrative only. The amounts shown for 'Associates' and 'Joint ventures' are subdivisions of the item for which the statutory prescribed heading is 'Income from interests in associated undertakings'. The subdivisions may be shown in a note rather than on the face of the profit and loss account.

	£m	£m
Turnover: group and share of joint ventures	*320*	
Less: share of joint ventures' turnover	*(120)*	
Group turnover		200
Cost of sales		(120)
Gross profit		80
Administrative expenses		(40)
Group operating profit		40
Share of operating profit in		
Joint ventures	30	
Associates	24	
		54
		94
Interest receivable (group)		6
Interest payable		
Group	(26)	
Joint ventures	(10)	
Associates	(12)	
		(48)
Profit on ordinary activities before tax		52
Tax on profit on ordinary activities*		(12)
Profit on ordinary activities after tax		40
Minority interests		(6)
Profit on ordinary activities after taxation and minority interest		34
Equity dividends		(10)
Retained profit for group and its share of associates and joint ventures		24

*Tax relates to the following:	Parent and subsidiaries	(5)
	Joint ventures	(5)
	Associates	(2)

CONSOLIDATED BALANCE SHEET

	£m	£m	£m
Fixed assets			
Tangible assets		480	
Investments			
Investments in joint ventures:			
Share of gross assets	130		
Share of gross liabilities	(80)		
		50	
Investments in associates		20	
			550
Current assets			
Stock		15	
Debtors		75	
Cash at bank and in hand		10	
		100	
Creditors (due within one year)		(50)	
Net current assets			50
Total assets less current liabilities			600
Creditors (due after more than one year)			(250)
Provisions for liabilities and charges			(10)
Equity minority interest			(40)
			300
Capital and reserves			
Called up share capital			50
Share premium account			150
Profit and loss account			100
Shareholders' funds (all equity)			300

NOTES

In the example, there is no individual associate or joint venture that accounts for more than 25 per cent of any of the following for the investor group (excluding any amount for associates and joint ventures):

- gross assets
- gross liabilities
- turnover
- operating results (on a three-year average).

Additional disclosures for joint ventures (which in aggregate exceed the 15 per cent threshold)

	£m	£m
Share of assets		
Share of fixed assets	100	
Share of current assets	30	
		130
Share of liabilities		
Liabilities due within one year or less	(10)	
Liabilities due after more than one year	(70)	
		(80)
Share of net assets		50

Additional disclosures for associates (which in aggregate exceed the 15 per cent threshold)

	£m	£m
Share of turnover of associates		90
Share of assets		
Share of fixed assets	4	
Share of current assets	28	
		32
Share of liabilities		
Liabilities due within one year or less	(3)	
Liabilities due after more than one year	(9)	
		(12)
Share of net assets		20

EXAMPLE 2 – AN OPTIONAL PRESENTATION

CONSOLIDATED PROFIT & LOSS ACCOUNT

This format is illustrative only. The amounts shown for 'Associates' and 'Joint ventures' are subdivisions of the item for which the statutory prescribed heading is 'Income from interests in associated undertakings'. The subdivisions may be shown in a note rather than on the face of the profit and loss account.

		£m ***Group***	£m ***Interests in joint ventures***	£m ***Total***
Turnover		200	120	*320*
Cost of sales		(120)	(85)	*(205)*
Gross profit		80	35	*115*
Administrative expenses		(40)	(5)	*(45)*
Operating profit		40	30	*70*
Share of operating profit in				
Joint ventures		30		
Associates		24		
Total operating profit: group and share of joint ventures and associates		94		
Interest receivable (group)		6		
Interest payable				
Group	(26)			
Joint ventures	(10)			
Associates	(12)			
		(48)		
Profit on ordinary activities before tax		52		
Tax on profit on ordinary activities*		(12)		
Profit on ordinary activities after tax *(carried forward)*		40		

* Tax relates to the following:	Parent and subsidiaries	(5)
	Joint ventures	(5)
	Associates	(2)

	£m
Profit on ordinary activities after tax *(brought forward)*	40
Minority interests	(6)
Profit on ordinary activities after taxation and minority interest	34
Equity dividends	(10)
Retained profit for group and its share of associates and joint ventures	24

CONSOLIDATED BALANCE SHEET

	£m *Group*	£m *Interests in joint ventures**	£m *Total*
Fixed assets			
Tangible assets	480	100	*580*
Investments			
Investments in joint ventures	50	*(50)*	
Investments in associates	20		*20*
	550		*600*
Current assets			
Stock	15	5	*20*
Debtors	75	23	*98*
Cash at bank and in hand	10	2	*12*
	100	30	*130*
Creditors (due within one year)	(50)	(10)	*(60)*
Net current assets	50	20	*70*
Total assets less current liabilities	600	120	*670*
Creditors (due after more than one year)	(250)	(70)	*(320)*
Provision for liabilities and charges	(10)		*(10)*
Net assets	340		340
Equity minority interest	(40)		
	300		
Capital and reserves			
Called up share capital	50		
Share premium account	150		
Profit and loss account	100		
Shareholders' funds (all equity)	300		

Additional disclosures

The same additional disclosures should be made as in Example 1.

** The boxed amounts, totalling 50 without the shaded amount, show the investor's share of the assets and liabilities of its joint ventures – the shaded (50) transfers this amount to the fixed assets of the group as 'investments in joint ventures'.*

Financial Reporting Standard 10 is set out in paragraphs 1–78.

The Statement of Standard Accounting Practice, which comprises the paragraphs set in bold type, should be read in the context of the Objective as stated in paragraph 1 and the definitions set out in paragraphs 2 and 3 and also of the Foreword to Accounting Standards and the Statement of Principles for Financial Reporting currently in issue.

The explanatory paragraphs contained in the FRS shall be regarded as part of the Statement of Standard Accounting Practice insofar as they assist in interpreting that statement.

Appendix III 'The development of the FRS' reviews considerations and arguments that were thought significant by members of the board in reaching the conclusions on the FRS. The views of the member who dissented are set out in Appendix IV.

[FRS 10] Goodwill and intangible assets*

(Issued December 1997)

Contents

Paragraphs

Summary

Financial Reporting Standard 10

Objective 1

Definitions 2–3

Scope 4–6

Initial recognition of positive goodwill and intangible assets 7–14
Goodwill 7–8
Intangible assets 9–14

Amortisation of positive goodwill and intangible assets 15–33
Requirement for amortisation 15–18
Determining useful economic lives 19–27
Residual value 28-29
Method of amortisation 30-32
Review of useful economic lives 33

Impairment of positive goodwill and intangible assets 34–42
Requirement for impairment reviews 34-38
Procedures for performing impairment reviews 39–42

Revaluation and restoration of past losses 43–47

Negative goodwill 48–51

Disclosures 52-64
Recognition and measurement 52-54
Amortisation of positive goodwill and intangible assets 55-60
Revaluation 61-62
Negative goodwill 63–64

Date from which effective 65

Transitional arrangements 66–76

Withdrawal of SSAP 22 and UITF Abstract 3 and amendment of FRS 2 77–78

****Editor's note**: The matters covered in FRS 10 are dealt with in Sections 19 of FRS 102 (in relation to goodwill) and 18 (in relation to other intangible assets).*

Appendices

I Note on legal requirements
II Compliance with International Accounting Standards
III The development of the FRS
IV Dissenting view
V Effect on realised profits of elimination of goodwill against reserves

Goodwill and intangible assets

Summary

GENERAL

Financial Reporting Standard 10 'Goodwill and Intangible Assets' sets out the principles of accounting for goodwill and intangible assets. Its objective is to ensure that purchased goodwill and intangible assets are charged in the profit and loss account in the periods in which they are depleted. **a**

THE NATURE OF GOODWILL AND INTANGIBLE ASSETS

The accounting requirements for goodwill reflect the view that goodwill arising on an acquisition is neither an asset like other assets nor an immediate loss in value. Rather, it forms the bridge between the cost of an investment shown as an asset in the acquirer's own financial statements and the values attributed to the acquired assets and liabilities in the consolidated financial statements. Although purchased goodwill is not in itself an asset, its inclusion amongst the assets of the reporting entity, rather than as a deduction from shareholders' equity, recognises that goodwill is part of a larger asset, the investment, for which management remains accountable. **b**

An intangible item may meet the definition of an asset when access to the future economic benefits that it represents is controlled by the reporting entity, either through custody or legal protection. However, intangible assets fall into a spectrum ranging from those that can readily be identified and measured separately from goodwill to those that are essentially very similar to goodwill. The basic principles set out for initial recognition, amortisation and impairment of intangible assets that are similar in nature to goodwill are therefore closely aligned with those set out for goodwill. **c**

INITIAL RECOGNITION

Purchased goodwill and intangible assets should be capitalised as assets. Internally generated goodwill should not be capitalised and internally developed intangible assets should be capitalised only where they have a readily ascertainable market value. **d**

AMORTISATION

The required approach seeks to charge goodwill to the profit and loss account only to the extent that the carrying value of the goodwill is not supported by the current value of the goodwill within the acquired business. Systematic amortisation is a practical means of recognising the reduction in value of goodwill that has a limited useful economic life. It is also a means of ensuring that where goodwill is not capable of continued measurement (so that impairment reviews cannot reasonably be performed each year), its depletion is recognised over a prudent, but not unrealistically short, period. **e**

Reflecting the view of goodwill as the bridge between the value of an acquired business in the entity's own financial statements and the values of its net identifiable assets shown in the consolidated financial statements, the useful economic life of purchased goodwill is defined as the period over which the value of an acquired business is expected to exceed the values of its identifiable assets and liabilities. **f**

g There is a rebuttable presumption that the useful economic lives of purchased goodwill and intangible assets are limited and do not exceed 20 years from the date of acquisition. However, there may be grounds for rebutting that presumption and regarding the useful economic life as greater than 20 years, or even indefinite. This may be done only if the goodwill or intangible asset is expected to be capable of continued measurement (so that annual impairment reviews can be performed).

h Where goodwill and intangible assets are regarded as having limited useful economic lives, they should be amortised over those lives. Where goodwill and intangible assets are regarded as having indefinite useful economic lives, they should not be amortised.

i Companies legislation requires goodwill to be amortised over a limited period. Hence, where the financial statements of a company include goodwill that is not amortised, they should explain that the departure from this specific requirement is necessary for the overriding purpose of providing a true and fair view, also detailing the reasons for and the effect of the departure.

IMPAIRMENT REVIEWS

j An asset is regarded as impaired if its recoverable amount (the higher of net realisable value and value in use) falls below its carrying value. Impairment reviews should be performed to ensure that goodwill and intangible assets are not carried at above their recoverable amounts. Where goodwill and intangible assets are amortised over a period that does not exceed 20 years, impairment reviews need be performed only at the end of the first full financial year following the initial recognition of the goodwill or intangible asset and, in other periods, if events or changes in circumstances indicate that its carrying value may not be recoverable in full. Where goodwill and intangible assets are not amortised, or are amortised over a period exceeding 20 years, impairment reviews should be performed each year.

REVALUATION AND RESTORATION OF PAST LOSSES

k Intangible assets with readily ascertainable market values may be revalued by reference to those market values.

l The reversal of a past impairment loss may be recognised only if it can clearly and demonstrably be attributed to the unforeseen reversal of the external event that caused the recognition of the original impairment loss. Past impairment losses may not be restored when the restoration in value is generated internally.

NEGATIVE GOODWILL

m Negative goodwill should be recognised and separately disclosed on the face of the balance sheet, immediately below the goodwill heading. It should be recognised in the profit and loss account in the periods in which the non-monetary assets acquired are depreciated or sold. Any negative goodwill in excess of the values of the non-monetary assets should be written back in the profit and loss account over the period expected to benefit from that negative goodwill.

DISCLOSURES

n There are few disclosure requirements other than those normally required for any type of fixed asset. Significant additional disclosure requirements include requirements to explain:

- the bases of valuation of intangible assets
- the grounds for believing a useful economic life to exceed 20 years or to be indefinite
- the treatment adopted for negative goodwill.

Financial Reporting Standard 10

Objective

1 The objective of this FRS is to ensure that:

(a) capitalised goodwill and intangible assets are charged in the profit and loss account in the periods in which they are depleted; and
(b) sufficient information is disclosed in the financial statements to enable users to determine the impact of goodwill and intangible assets on the financial position and performance of the reporting entity.

Definitions

2 The following definitions shall apply in the FRS and in particular in the Statement of Standard Accounting Practice set out **in bold type**.

Class of intangible assets:-
A category of intangible assets having a similar nature, function or use in the business of the entity.

Licences, quotas, patents, copyrights, franchises and trade marks are examples of categories that may be treated as separate classes of intangible assets. Further subdivision may be appropriate, for example where different types of licence have different functions within the business. Intangible assets that are used within different business segments may be treated as separate classes of intangible assets.

Identifiable assets and liabilities:-
The assets and liabilities of an entity that are capable of being disposed of or settled separately, without disposing of a business of the entity.

Impairment:-
A reduction in the recoverable amount of a fixed asset or goodwill below its carrying value.

Intangible assets:-
Non-financial fixed assets that do not have physical substance but are identifiable and are controlled by the entity through custody or legal rights.

An identifiable asset is defined by companies legislation as one that can be disposed of separately without disposing of a business of the entity. If an asset can be disposed of only as part of the revenue-earning activity to which it contributes, it is regarded as indistinguishable from the goodwill relating to that activity and is accounted for as such.

In the context of an intangible asset, control is normally secured by legal rights: a franchise or licence grants the entity access to the benefits for a fixed period; a patent or trade mark restricts the access of others. In the absence of legal rights, it is more difficult to demonstrate control. However, control may be obtained through custody. This could be the case where, for example, technical or intellectual knowledge arising from development activity is maintained secretly.

Where it is expected that future benefits will flow to the entity, but those benefits are not controlled through legal rights or custody, the entity does not have sufficient control over the benefits to recognise an intangible asset. For example, an entity may have a portfolio of clients or a team of skilled staff. There may be an expectation that the clients within the portfolio will continue to seek professional services from the entity, or that the team of staff will continue to make their expert skills available to the entity. However, in the absence of custody or legal rights to retain the clients or staff, the entity has insufficient control over the expected future benefits to recognise them as assets.

Software development costs that are directly attributable to bringing a computer system or other computer-operated machinery into working condition for its intended use within the business are treated as part of the cost of the related hardware rather than as a separate intangible asset.

The definition does not encompass assets, such as prepaid expenditure, that are not fixed assets.

Net realisable value:-
The amount at which an asset could be disposed of, less any direct selling costs.

Purchased goodwill:-
The difference between the cost of an acquired entity and the aggregate of the fair values of that entity's identifiable assets and liabilities. Positive goodwill arises when the acquisition cost exceeds the aggregate fair values of the identifiable assets and liabilities. Negative goodwill arises when the aggregate fair values of the identifiable assets and liabilities of the entity exceed the acquisition cost.

Readily ascertainable market value:-
The value of an intangible asset that is established by reference to a market where:

(a) the asset belongs to a homogeneous population of assets that are equivalent in all material respects; and
(b) an active market, evidenced by frequent transactions, exists for that population of assets.

Intangible assets that meet those conditions might include certain operating licences, franchises and quotas. Other intangible assets are by their nature unique: although there may be similar assets, they are not equivalent in all material respects and so do not have readily ascertainable market values. Examples of such assets include brands, publishing titles, patented drugs and engineering design patents.

Recoverable amount:-
The higher of net realisable value and value in use.

Residual value:-
The net realisable value of an asset at the end of its useful economic life. Residual values are based on prices prevailing at the date of acquisition (or revaluation) of the asset and do not take account of expected future price changes.

Useful economic life:-
The useful economic life of an intangible asset is the period over which the entity expects to derive economic benefit from that asset. The useful economic life of purchased goodwill is the period over which the value of the underlying business acquired is expected to exceed the values of its identifiable net assets.

If purchased goodwill includes intangible assets that have not been recognised separately because they cannot be measured reliably, the useful economic lives of those intangible assets will have a bearing on that of the goodwill as a whole.

Value in use:-
The present value of the future cash flows obtainable as a result of an asset's continued use, including those resulting from its ultimate disposal.

3 References to companies legislation mean:

(a) in Great Britain, the Companies Act 1985;*
(b) in Northern Ireland, the Companies (Northern Ireland) Order 1986; and
(c) in the Republic of Ireland, the Companies (Amendment) Act 1986 and the European Communities (Companies: Group Accounts) Regulations 1992.

SCOPE

4 **Subject to the provisions of paragraph 5, the FRS applies to all financial statements that are intended to give a true and fair view of a reporting entity's financial position and profit or loss (or income and expenditure) for a period. Although the requirements of the FRS that relate to business combinations are framed in terms of the acquisition of a subsidiary undertaking by a parent company that prepares consolidated accounts, they also apply whenever any reporting entity acquires a business or an investment accounted for using the equity method.**

5 **Reporting entities applying the Financial Reporting Standard for Smaller Entities (FRSSE) currently applicable are exempt from the FRS unless preparing consolidated financial statements, in which case they should apply the FRS to such statements as required by the FRSSE.**

6 **The requirements of the FRS apply to all intangible assets with the exception of:**

(a) oil and gas exploration and development costs;
(b) research and development costs; and
(c) any other intangible assets that are specifically addressed by another accounting standard.

Initial recognition of positive goodwill and intangible assets

Goodwill

7 **Positive purchased goodwill should be capitalised and classified as an asset on the balance sheet.**

8 **Internally generated goodwill should not be capitalised.**

Intangible assets

9 **An intangible asset purchased separately from a business should be capitalised at its cost.**

10 **An intangible asset acquired as part of the acquisition of a business should be capitalised separately from goodwill if its value can be measured reliably on initial recognition. It should initially be recorded at its fair value, subject to the constraint that, unless the asset has a readily ascertainable market value, the fair value should be**

**Editor's note:* *This should now be taken to refer to the Companies Act 2006 as well.*

limited to an amount that does not create or increase any negative goodwill arising on the acquisition.

FRS 7 'Fair Values in Acquisition Accounting' requires that where an intangible asset is recognised, its fair value should be based on its replacement cost. FRS 7 goes on to explain that the replacement cost will normally be the asset's estimated market value but that it may be estimated by other methods.* 11

It is not possible to determine a market value for unique intangible assets such as brands and publishing titles. Replacement cost may be equally difficult to determine directly. However, certain entities that are regularly involved in the purchase and sale of unique intangible assets have developed techniques for estimating their values indirectly and these may be used for initial recognition of such assets at the time of purchase. Techniques used can be based, for example, on 'indicators of value' – such as multiples of turnover – or on estimating the present value of the royalties that would be payable to license the asset from a third party. 12

If its value cannot be measured reliably, an intangible asset purchased as part of the acquisition of a business should be subsumed within the amount of the purchase price attributed to goodwill. 13

An internally developed intangible asset may be capitalised only if it has a readily ascertainable market value. 14

AMORTISATION OF POSITIVE GOODWILL AND INTANGIBLE ASSETS

Requirement for amortisation

Where goodwill and intangible assets are regarded as having limited useful economic lives, they should be amortised on a systematic basis over those lives. 15

The circumstances in which useful economic lives may be regarded as longer than 20 years are set out in paragraph 19. 16

Where goodwill and intangible assets are regarded as having indefinite useful economic lives, they should not be amortised. 17

Companies legislation requires goodwill that is treated as an asset to be amortised systematically over a finite period. Where a company's financial statements depart from this requirement, the departure must be justified as being required for the overriding purpose of providing a true and fair view. The circumstances in which useful economic lives may be regarded as indefinite are set out in paragraph 19. The necessary disclosure requirements are set out in paragraph 59. 18

Determining useful economic lives

There is a rebuttable presumption that the useful economic lives of purchased goodwill and intangible assets are limited to periods of 20 years or less. This presumption may be rebutted and a useful economic life regarded as a longer period or indefinite only if: 19

(a) the durability of the acquired business or intangible asset can be demonstrated and justifies estimating the useful economic life to exceed 20 years; and

**FRS 7 'Fair values in acquisition accounting', paragraph 10.*

(b) the goodwill or intangible asset is capable of continued measurement (so that annual impairment reviews will be feasible).

20 The transient nature of many business opportunities makes it appropriate for there to be a presumption that the 'premium' that an acquired business has over its net asset value cannot be maintained indefinitely. However, in some circumstances there may be grounds for regarding the premium as more durable and assigning it a longer or even indefinite economic life. Durability depends on a number of factors such as:

- the nature of the business
- the stability of the industry in which the acquired business operates
- typical lifespans of the products to which the goodwill attaches
- the extent to which the acquisition overcomes market entry barriers that will continue to exist
- the expected future impact of competition on the business.

21 The useful economic lives of goodwill and intangible assets will usually be uncertain. This uncertainty does not in itself form grounds for treating a useful economic life as indefinite or for adopting a 20-year period by default. Where, for example, the useful economic life of goodwill or an intangible asset is expected to be less than 20 years, the FRS requires an estimate of the useful economic life to be made.

22 Whilst uncertainty forms grounds for estimating the useful economic life on a prudent basis, it does not form grounds for choosing a life that is unrealistically short.

23 Goodwill and intangible assets will not be capable of continued measurement if the cost of such measurement is viewed as being unjustifiably high. This will be the case when, for example:

- acquired businesses are merged with existing businesses to such an extent that the goodwill associated with the acquired businesses cannot readily be tracked thereafter
- the management information systems used by the entity cannot identify and allocate cash flows at a detailed income-generating unit level
- the amounts involved are not sufficiently material to justify undertaking the detailed procedures of annual impairment reviews.

24 Where access to the economic benefits associated with an intangible asset is achieved through legal rights that have been granted for a finite period, the economic life of the asset may extend beyond that period only if, and to the extent that, the legal rights are renewable and renewal is assured. The amount of the asset that is treated as having the longer useful economic life should exclude those costs that will recur each time the legal right is renewed.

25 There may be both economic and legal factors influencing the useful economic life of an intangible asset: economic factors determine the period over which it is expected that future economic benefits will arise; legal factors may restrict the period over which the entity continues to control access to these benefits. The useful economic life of an asset is the shorter of the period over which it is expected that the future benefits will arise and that over which it is expected that the entity will control the benefits.

26 It follows that where a legal right securing access to an intangible asset has been granted for a finite period, as may be the case with a patent or licence, the useful economic life assigned to the asset cannot in general exceed that finite period. It would be appropriate to assign a longer useful economic life only if, and to the extent

that, the legal right is renewable and renewal is assured. Renewal may be regarded as being assured if:

(a) the value of the intangible asset does not reduce as the initial expiry date approaches, or reduces only by an amount reflecting the cost of renewal of the underlying legal right;
(b) there is evidence, possibly based on past experience, that the legal rights will be renewed; and
(c) where the entity is required to abide by any conditions under the terms of the legal right and breach of those conditions may prevent renewal, there is no evidence that any of those conditions have been or will be breached.

It follows that, where legal rights are essential to the benefits arising from the use of an intangible asset, the asset may be regarded as having an indefinite life only if such legal rights can remain in force indefinitely or are renewable indefinitely with each renewal process being assured. 27

Residual value

In amortising an intangible asset, a residual value may be assigned to that asset only if such residual value can be measured reliably. No residual value may be assigned to goodwill. 28

In practice, the residual value of an intangible asset is often insignificant. It is likely that the residual value of an intangible asset will be significant and capable of being measured reliably only when: 29

(a) there is a legal or contractual right to receive a certain sum at the end of the period of use of the intangible asset; or
(b) there is a readily ascertainable market value for the residual asset.

Method of amortisation

The method of amortisation should be chosen to reflect the expected pattern of depletion of the goodwill or intangible asset. A straight-line method should be chosen unless another method can be demonstrated to be more appropriate. 30

The pattern of depletion of intangible assets will normally be relatively uncertain and occur with the passing of time. A straight-line method of amortisation will normally be the most appropriate. However, there may be circumstances, for instance where a licence entitles the holder to produce a finite quantity of a product, where another method is more appropriate. It is unlikely that there will be circumstances in which there is justification and evidence to support a method of amortisation for goodwill that is less conservative than straight-line. 31

A method of amortisation that aims to produce a constant rate of return on the carrying value of an investment is not one that aims to reflect the pattern of depletion of goodwill. Hence, interest methods, such as the 'reverse sum of digits' method, are not appropriate methods of amortising goodwill. 32

Review of useful economic lives

The useful economic lives of goodwill and intangible assets should be reviewed at the end of each reporting period and revised if necessary. If a useful economic life is revised, the carrying value of the goodwill or intangible asset at the date of revision should be 33

amortised over the revised remaining useful economic life. If the effect of the revision is to increase the useful economic life to more than 20 years from the date of acquisition, the additional requirements of the FRS that apply to goodwill and intangible assets that are amortised over periods of more than 20 years or are not amortised become applicable.*

IMPAIRMENT OF POSITIVE GOODWILL AND INTANGIBLE ASSETS

Requirement for impairment reviews

34 **Goodwill and intangible assets that are amortised over a finite period not exceeding 20 years from the date of acquisition should be reviewed for impairment:**

(a) at the end of the first full financial year following the acquisition ('the first year review'); and

(b) in other periods if events or changes in circumstances indicate that the carrying values may not be recoverable.

35 If an impairment is identified at the time of the first year review, this impairment reflects:

(a) an overpayment;

(b) an event that occurred between the acquisition and the first year review; or

(c) depletion of the acquired goodwill or intangible asset between the acquisition and the first year review that exceeds the amount recognised through amortisation.

36 The requirements of the FRS are such that the recognition of an impairment loss must be justified in the same way as the absence of an impairment loss, ie by reference to expected future cash flows. In particular, a belief that the value of goodwill will not be capable of continued measurement in future does not justify writing off the whole balance at the time of the first year impairment review: it should be possible to perform the first year impairment review by updating investment appraisal calculations. The remaining carrying value would then be amortised over a period not exceeding 20 years.

37 **Goodwill and intangible assets that are amortised over a period exceeding 20 years from the date of acquisition or are not amortised should be reviewed for impairment at the end of each reporting period.**

38 After the first period the reviews need only be updated. If expectations of future cash flows and discount rates have not changed significantly, the updating procedure will be relatively quick to perform. If there have been no adverse changes in the key assumptions and variables, or if there was previously substantial leeway between the carrying value and estimated value in use, it may even be possible to ascertain immediately that an income-generating unit is not impaired.

Procedures for performing impairment reviews

39 **Except as permitted in paragraph 40, impairment reviews should be performed in accordance with the requirements of FRS 11 'Impairment of Fixed Assets and Goodwill.'**

****Editor's Note:*** *See also UITF Abstact 27 'Revisions to estimates of the useful economic life of goodwill and intangible assets'.*

The first year impairment review required by paragraph 34(a) may be performed in two stages: 40

(a) initially identifying any possible impairment by comparing post-acquisition performance in the first year with pre-acquisition forecasts used to support the purchase price; and

(b) performing a full impairment review in accordance with the requirements of FRS 11 only if the initial review indicates that the post-acquisition performance has failed to meet pre-acquisition expectations or if any other previously unforeseen events or changes in circumstances indicate that the carrying values may not be recoverable.

If an impairment loss is recognised, the revised carrying value, if being amortised, should be amortised over the current estimate of the remaining useful economic life. 41

If goodwill arising on consolidation is found to be impaired, the carrying amount of the investment held in the accounts of the parent undertaking should also be reviewed for impairment. 42

REVALUATION AND RESTORATION OF PAST LOSSES

Where an intangible asset has a readily ascertainable market value, the asset may be revalued to its market value. If one intangible asset is revalued, all other capitalised intangible assets of the same class should be revalued. Once an intangible asset has been revalued, further revaluations should be performed sufficiently often to ensure that the carrying value does not differ materially from the market value at the balance sheet date. 43

Where an external event caused the recognition of an impairment loss in previous periods, and subsequent external events clearly and demonstrably reverse the effects of that event in a way that was not foreseen in the original impairment calculations, any resulting reversal of the impairment loss that increases the recoverable amount of the goodwill or intangible asset above its current carrying value should be recognised in the current period. 44

Except as permitted or required by paragraphs 43 and 44, goodwill and intangible assets should not be revalued, either to increase the carrying value above original cost or to reverse prior period losses arising from impairment or amortisation. 45

An impairment review may identify that an impairment loss recognised in an earlier period has reversed in the current period. In general, such reversals will be the result of the internal generation of goodwill or intangible asset value. The FRS does not permit such restorations to be reflected in the financial statements. However, where the original impairment of goodwill or an intangible asset was caused by an external event and reverses because the external event reverses in a way that was not foreseen when the original impairment calculations were performed, the FRS requires the resulting restoration to be reflected in the financial statements. 46

The amortisation charge for revalued assets should be based on the revalued amounts and the remaining useful economic lives of the assets. Amortisation charged before the revaluation should not be written back in the profit and loss account. 47

NEGATIVE GOODWILL

If an acquisition appears to give rise to negative goodwill, the fair values of the acquired assets should be tested for impairment and the fair values of the acquired liabilities 48

checked carefully to ensure that none has been omitted or understated. Negative goodwill remaining after the fair values of the assets and liabilities have been checked should be recognised and separately disclosed on the face of the balance sheet, immediately below the goodwill heading and followed by a subtotal showing the net amount of the positive and negative goodwill.

49 **Negative goodwill up to the fair values of the non-monetary assets acquired should be recognised in the profit and loss account in the periods in which the non-monetary assets are recovered, whether through depreciation or sale.**

50 **Any negative goodwill in excess of the fair values of the non-monetary assets acquired should be recognised in the profit and loss account in the periods expected to be benefited.**

51 **Purchased goodwill (positive or negative) arising on a single transaction should not be divided into positive and negative components.**

DISCLOSURES

Recognition and measurement

52 **The financial statements should describe the method used to value intangible assets.**

53 **The following information should be disclosed separately for positive goodwill, negative goodwill and each class of intangible asset capitalised on the balance sheet:**

(a) the cost or revalued amount at the beginning of the financial period and at the balance sheet date;
(b) the cumulative amount of provisions for amortisation or impairment at the beginning of the financial period and at the balance sheet date;
(c) a reconciliation of the movements, separately disclosing additions, disposals, revaluations, transfers, amortisation, impairment losses, reversals of past impairment losses and amounts of negative goodwill written back in the financial period; and
(d) the net carrying amount at the balance sheet date.*

54 **The financial statements should disclose the profit or loss on each material disposal of a previously acquired business or business segment.**

Amortisation of positive goodwill and intangible assets

55 **The financial statements should disclose the methods and periods of amortisation of goodwill and intangible assets and the reasons for choosing those periods.†**

56 **Where an amortisation period is shortened or extended following a review of the remaining useful economic lives of goodwill and intangible assets, the reason and the effect, if material, should be disclosed in the year of change.**

57 **Where there has been a change in the amortisation method used, the reason and the effect, if material, should be disclosed in the year of change.**

**See paragraph 18 of Appendix 1 'Note on Legal Requirements'.*

†See paragraph 6 of Appendix 1 'Note on Legal Requirements'.

Where goodwill or an intangible asset is amortised over a period that exceeds 20 years from the date of acquisition or is not amortised, the grounds for rebutting the 20-year presumption should be given. This should be a reasoned explanation based on the specific factors contributing to the durability of the acquired business or intangible asset. 58

In addition, where goodwill in the financial statements of companies is not amortised, the financial statements should state that they depart from the specific requirement of companies legislation to amortise goodwill over a finite period* for the overriding purpose of giving a true and fair view. Particulars of the departure, the reasons for it and its effect should be given in sufficient detail to convey to the reader of the financial statements the circumstances justifying the use of the true and fair override† The reasons for the departure should incorporate the explanation of the specific factors contributing to the durability of the acquired business or intangible asset required by paragraph 58. 59

Companies legislation requires goodwill that is treated as an asset to be amortised systematically over a finite period. Where a company's financial statements depart from the specific requirements of companies legislation for the overriding purpose of providing a true and fair view, they are required to disclose particulars of the departure, the reasons for it and its effect. Paragraphs 62–65 of FRS 18 'Accounting policies' specify disclosures that should be made in order to provide the reader of the financial statements with a clear and unambiguous account of the reasons for the departure from the statutory requirement. The specific factors will be unique to the circumstances of each case. The requirements of FRS 18 encompass the disclosures necessary when it is not possible to quantify the effect of the departure, as will be the case when goodwill is not amortised. 60

Revaluation

Where a class of assets has been revalued, the financial statements should disclose: 61

(a) the year in which the assets were valued, the values and the bases of valuation; and
(b) the original cost (or original fair value) of the assets and the amount of any provision for amortisation that would have been recognised if the assets had been valued at their original cost or fair value.‡

Where any asset has been revalued during the year, the name and qualifications of the person who valued it should be disclosed.§ 62

Negative goodwill

The financial statements should disclose the period(s) in which negative goodwill is being written back in the profit and loss account. 63

Where negative goodwill exceeds the fair values of the non-monetary assets, the amount and source of the 'excess' negative goodwill and the period(s) in which it is being written back should be explained. 64

**See paragraph 6 of Appendix 1 'Note on Legal Requirements'.*

†*See paragraph 20 of Appendix 1 'Note on Legal Requirements'.*

‡*See paragraph 19 of Appendix 1 'Note on Legal Requirements'.*

§*See paragraph 19 of Appendix 1 'Note on Legal Requirements'.*

DATE FROM WHICH EFFECTIVE

65 **The accounting practices set out in the FRS should be regarded as standard in respect of financial statements relating to accounting periods ending on or after 23 December 1998. Earlier adoption is encouraged but not required.**

TRANSITIONAL ARRANGEMENTS

66 **Subject to the provisions of paragraphs 68 and 69, changes in accounting policy required to implement the requirements of the FRS should be applied retrospectively.**

67 The way in which prior period adjustments are made and disclosed is set out in FRS 3 'Reporting Financial Performance' and FRS 18 'Accounting policies'.

68 Ideally, all goodwill that had previously been eliminated against reserves but would not have been fully written down under the requirements of the FRS would be reinstated by means of prior year adjustment on implementation of the FRS. However, the Board recognises that this will not be practicable in all circumstances, and therefore does not require reinstatement.

69 **In those cases where all goodwill previously eliminated against reserves is not reinstated on implementation of the FRS, the goodwill remaining eliminated against reserves should comprise one of the following:**

(a) goodwill relating to acquisitions made before 23 December 1989 where the necessary information is unavailable or cannot be obtained without unreasonable expense or delay; or

(b) all goodwill eliminated before the implementation of FRS 7; or

(c) all goodwill previously eliminated.

70 **Where goodwill that was previously eliminated against reserves is reinstated on implementation of the FRS:**

(a) any impairment that is attributed to prior periods must be determined on the basis of impairment reviews performed in accordance with the FRS on impairment of fixed assets and goodwill;

(b) the notes to the financial statements should disclose the original cost of the goodwill and the amounts attributed to prior period amortisation and, separately, prior period impairment;

(c) it is not necessary to identify separately intangible assets that are subsumed within the goodwill.

71 **If goodwill remains eliminated against reserves:**

(a) the financial statements should state:

(i) the accounting policy followed in respect of that goodwill;

(ii) the cumulative amounts of positive goodwill eliminated against reserves and negative goodwill added to reserves, net of any goodwill attributable to businesses disposed of before the balance sheet date*; and

**In the UK, disclosure of amounts pertaining to an overseas business need not be given if it would be seriously prejudicial to the business and official agreement has been obtained. For acquisitions before 23 December 1989 (in Northern Ireland, 1 April 1990), disclosure need not be made if the information necessary to calculate the amount with material accuracy is unavailable or cannot be obtained without unreasonable expense or delay. The exclusion of such amounts and the grounds for the exclusion should be stated. See also paragraph 8 of Appendix 1 'Note on Legal Requirements'.*

(iii) the fact that this goodwill had been eliminated as a matter of accounting policy and would be charged or credited in the profit and loss account on subsequent disposal of the business to which it related.

(b) the eliminated goodwill should not be shown as a debit balance on a separate goodwill write-off reserve but should be offset against the profit and loss account or another appropriate reserve. The amount by which the reserve has been reduced by the elimination of goodwill (or increased by the addition of negative goodwill) should not be shown separately on the face of the balance sheet.

(c) in the reporting period in which the business with which the goodwill was acquired is disposed of or closed:

(i) the amount included in the profit or loss account in respect of the profit or loss on disposal or closure should include attributable goodwill to the extent that it has not previously been charged in the profit and loss account; and

(ii) the financial statements should disclose as a component of the profit or loss on disposal or closure the attributable amount of goodwill so included.

Where it is impractical or impossible to ascertain the goodwill attributable to a business that was acquired before 1 January 1989, this should be stated and the reasons given.

SSAP 22 provided guidance on the circumstances in which goodwill arising in the accounts of an individual company and eliminated against reserves should be regarded as a reduction in realised reserves. This guidance continues to apply to goodwill that remains eliminated against reserves under the transitional arrangements of the FRS. It is reproduced in Appendix V. **72**

[Withdrawn]. **73**

Any impairment loss relating to previously capitalised goodwill and intangible assets that is recognised on first implementing the FRS should be charged as an expense in the period. **74**

Companies legislation already requires a provision to be made for any permanent diminution in the value of a fixed asset. Therefore, any impairment loss relating to previously capitalised goodwill and intangible assets that is recognised on first implementing the FRS represents a change in an accounting estimate, which is charged as a loss in the period. **75**

Examples of the adjustments that will be required under the transitional arrangements are summarised as follows: **76**

Circumstances	Requirements	Method
(a) Goodwill previously eliminated against reserves	1 Leave eliminated against reserves until business disposed of.	If necessary, transfer from separate goodwill write-off reserve to another reserve. Deduct from profit on any future disposal.
	2 Capitalise at cost less amortisation or impairment attributed to previous periods. Amortise thereafter where appropriate.	Make prior year adjustment.
(b) Internally developed intangible assets that do not meet new recognition criteria	Write off.	Make prior year adjustment.
(c) Revalued purchased intangible assets	1 If asset has a readily ascertainable market value, update value.	Report value change as current year gain or loss.
	2 If asset does not have a readily ascertainable market value, restate at cost less amortisation or impairment attributed to previous periods.	Make prior year adjustment.

WITHDRAWAL OF SSAP 22 AND UITF ABSTRACT 3 AND AMENDMENT OF FRS 2

[*Not reproduced as it has been reflected in* FRS *2 reproduced in this volume.*]

Adoption of FRS 10 by the Board

Financial Reporting Standard 10 - 'Goodwill and Intangible Assets' was approved for issue by a vote of nine of the ten members of the Accounting Standards Board. Mr Hinton dissented. His dissenting view is set out in Appendix IV.

Members of the Accounting Standards Board

Sir David Tweedie (Chairman)
Allan Cook (Technical Director)
David Allvey
Ian Brindle
Dr John Buchanan
John Coombe
Raymond Hinton
Huw Jones
Professor Geoffrey Whittington
Ken Wild

Appendix I
Note on legal requirements

GREAT BRITAIN

1 In Great Britain, the statutory requirements relating to accounting for goodwill and intangible assets are set out in the Companies Act 1985. The main requirements that are directly relevant to goodwill and intangible assets and the requirements of FRS 10 are set out in Schedules 4 and 4A and are summarised below.*

2 Schedule 4 does not apply to banking and insurance companies and groups. Requirements equivalent to those of Schedule 4 are contained in Schedule 9 (for banking companies and groups) and in Schedule 9A (for insurance companies and groups).

Goodwill

3 The acquisition method of accounting and the calculation of goodwill are described by paragraph 9(4) and (5) of Schedule 4A. The interest of the parent company and its subsidiaries in the adjusted capital and reserves of an acquired subsidiary undertaking must be offset against the acquisition cost. The resulting amount if positive must be treated as goodwill, and if negative as a negative consolidation difference.

4 The balance sheet formats in Schedule 4 require purchased goodwill, to the extent that it has not been written off, to be included under the heading of intangible fixed assets, and shown separately from other intangible assets. Note (3) to the formats states that amounts representing goodwill should be included only to the extent that the goodwill was acquired for valuable consideration. Internally generated goodwill may not be capitalised.

5 Paragraph 5 of Schedule 4 states that amounts in respect of items representing assets may not be set off against amounts in respect of items representing liabilities. For

***Editor's note:** The various statutory references change with the introduction of the Companies Act 2006, which affects accounting for periods beginning on or after 6 April 2008. The various statutory references have changed as follows:*

Companies Act 1985 reference	***Companies Act 2006 reference***
Schedule 4	*Schedule 1 to the Large and Medium-sized Companies and Groups (Accounts and Reports) Regulations 2008 (SI 2008/410)*
Schedule 4A	*Schedule 6 to SI 2008/410*
Paragraph 9 of Schedule 4A	*Paragraph 9 of Schedule 6 to SI 2008/410*
Paragraph 5 of Schedule 4	*Paragraph 8 of Schedule 1 to SI 2008/410*
Paragraph 21 of Schedule 4	*Paragraph 22 of Schedule 1 to SI 2008/410*
Paragraph 31 (1) of Schedule 4	*Paragraph 32 of Schedule 1 to SI 2008/410*
Paragraph 14 of Schedule 4A	*Paragraph 9 of Schedule 6 to SI 2008/410*
Paragraph 16 of Schedule 4A	*Paragraph 16 of Schedule 6 to SI 2008/410*
Paragraph 18 of Schedule 4	*Paragraph 18 of Schedule 1 to SI 2008/410*
Paragraph 19 of Schedule 4	*Paragraph 19 of Schedule 1 to SI 2008/410*
Paragraph 36 of Schedule 4	*Paragraph 44 of Schedule 1 to SI 2008/410*
Paragraph 42 of Schedule 4	*Paragraph 51 of Schedule 1 to SI 2008/410*
Paragraph 33 of Schedule 4	*Paragraph 33 of Schedule 1 to SI 2008/410*
Paragraph 43 of Schedule 4	*Paragraph 52 of Schedule 1 to SI 2008/410*
Section 226	*Section 394*
Section 227	*Section 399*

this reason, the FRS requires negative goodwill to be shown separately from positive goodwill on the face of the balance sheet.

Paragraph 21 of Schedule 4 requires that, where goodwill is treated as an asset, it must be depreciated systematically over a period chosen by the directors. The period chosen must not exceed the useful economic life of the goodwill. The period chosen and the reason for choosing that period must be disclosed in a note. (No residual value is permitted for goodwill.) 6

Paragraph 31(1) of Schedule 4 prohibits the revaluation of goodwill. 7

Paragraph 14 of Schedule 4A requires the notes to the accounts to state the cumulative amount of goodwill resulting from acquisitions in that and earlier financial years that has been written off. That figure must be net of any goodwill attributable to subsidiary undertakings or businesses disposed of before the balance sheet date. Paragraph 16 of Schedule 4A states that disclosure of amounts pertaining to an overseas business need not be given if it would be seriously prejudicial to the group's business and agreement has been obtained from the Secretary of State. Further, for acquisitions before 23 December 1989, disclosure need not be made if the information necessary to calculate the amount with material accuracy is unavailable or cannot be obtained without unreasonable expense or delay (paragraph 9 of Schedule 2 to the Companies Act 1989 (Commencement No. 4 and Transitional and Saving Provisions) Order 1990). The exclusion of such amounts and the grounds for the exclusion must be stated. 8

Intangible assets

Paragraph 9(2) of Schedule 4A requires, under the acquisition method of accounting, the identifiable assets and liabilities of an acquired undertaking to be included in the consolidated balance sheet at their fair values as at the date of acquisition. It defines "identifiable" as capable of being disposed of or discharged separately, without disposing of a business of the undertaking. 9

The following headings for intangible assets are set out in the balance sheet formats in Schedule 4: 10

B Fixed assets
I Intangible assets
1. Development costs
2. Concessions, patents, licences, trade marks and similar rights and assets
3. Goodwill
4. Payments on account.

Note (2) on the balance sheet formats permits amounts in respect of assets to be included in a company's balance sheet under the heading of concessions, patents, licences, trade marks and similar rights and assets only if either (a) the assets were acquired for valuable consideration and are not required to be shown under goodwill; or (b) the assets in question were created by the company itself. 11

Paragraph 18 requires that, where a fixed asset has a limited useful economic life, the purchase price or production cost less any residual value is reduced by provisions for depreciation calculated to write off that amount systematically over the period of the asset's useful economic life. 12

Paragraph 31(1) permits intangible assets, other than goodwill, to be included at their current cost. Where an intangible asset is valued at its current cost, the depreciation rules are to be applied by substituting the most recently determined value for the purchase price or production cost (paragraph 32(1)). 13

Provisions for diminution in value

14 Paragraph 19(2) of Schedule 4 requires provisions for diminution in value to be made in respect of any fixed asset that has diminished in value if the reduction in its value is expected to be permanent. Any provisions that are not shown in the profit and loss account must be disclosed (either separately or in aggregate) in a note to the accounts.

15 Paragraph 19(3) of Schedule 4 requires that where the reasons for which a provision was made have ceased to apply to any extent, the provision must be written back to the extent that it is no longer necessary. Where any amounts written back are not shown in the profit and loss account, they must be disclosed (either separately or in aggregate) in a note to the accounts.

Amortisation and other amounts written off fixed assets

16 The formats set out in Schedule 4 prescribe the headings under which depreciation and other amounts written off tangible and intangible fixed assets are to be included in the profit and loss account. Under Formats 1 and 3, such amounts are to be included in cost of sales, distribution costs and administrative expenses. Under Formats 2 and 4, such amounts are to be shown as a separate heading.

Disclosure requirements

17 Disclosure of the accounting policies adopted by a company (including the policies regarding the depreciation and diminution in value of assets) is required by paragraph 36 of Schedule 4.

18 Paragraph 42 of Schedule 4 details the disclosures required of the movement on goodwill and intangible asset balances. The same level of detail is required as for other fixed assets.

19 Paragraphs 33 and 43 of Schedule 4 prescribe additional information to be given for any assets that have been revalued. This includes comparable amounts determined according to the historical cost accounting rules and details of the basis and date of the valuation and the qualifications of the valuer.

True and fair override

20 Sections 226(3) and 227(4) require the individual and group accounts of a company to comply with the provisions of Schedules 4 and 4A respectively. If, in exceptional circumstances, compliance with any of the provisions is inconsistent with the requirement to give a true and fair view, sections 226(5) and 227(6) require the directors to depart from those provisions to the extent necessary to give a true and fair view. Particulars of any such departure, the reasons for it and its effect are to be given in a note to the accounts.

NORTHERN IRELAND

21 The statutory requirements in Northern Ireland are set out in the Companies (Northern Ireland) Order 1986. They are similar to those in Great Britain. Most of the references cited above have parallel references in the Companies (Northern Ireland) Order 1986. The only exceptions are that:

(a) the requirements of sections 226 and 227 of the Companies Act 1985 are found in Articles 234 and 235 of the Companies (Northern Ireland) Order 1986; and
(b) the transitional arrangements permitted by paragraph 9 of Schedule 2 to the Companies Act 1989 (Commencement No. 4 and Transitional and Saving Provisions) Order 1990 are found in paragraph 9 of the Companies (1990 Order) (Commencement No. 1) Order (Northern Ireland) 1990. They apply to acquisitions made before 1 April 1990.

REPUBLIC OF IRELAND

The statutory requirements in the Republic of Ireland that correspond to those listed above for Great Britain are shown in the following table. **22**

Great Britain	*Republic of Ireland*
Section 226 of the Companies Act 1985	Section 3(1) of the Companies (Amendment) Act 1986
Section 227(4) and (6) of the Companies Act 1985	Regulations 15(1) and 14(4) of the European Communities (Companies: Group Accounts) Regulations 1992
Paragraph 5 of Schedule 4 to the Companies Act 1985	Section 4(11) of the Companies (Amendment) Act 1986
Schedule 4 to the Companies Act 1985:	The Schedule to the Companies (Amendment) Act 1986:
- notes (2) and (3) on the formats	- notes (1) and (2) on the formats
- paragraph 18	- paragraph 6
- paragraph 19(2) and (3)	- paragraph 7(1) and (2)
- paragraph 21	- paragraph 9
- paragraphs 31(1) and 32(1)	- paragraphs 19(1) and 20(1)
- paragraphs 33 and 36	- paragraphs 21 and 24
- paragraphs 42 and 43	- paragraphs 29 and 30
Schedule 4A to the Companies Act 1985:	European Communities (Companies: Group Accounts) Regulations 1992:
- paragraph 9(2), (4) and (5)	- Regulation 19(2), (4), (5) and (6)
- paragraphs 14 and 16	- no corresponding references

There are no transitional provisions in the Republic of Ireland that correspond to those given in paragraph 9 of Schedule 2 to the Companies Act 1989 (Commencement No. 4 and Transitional and Saving Provisions) Order 1990. **23**

Appendix II
Compliance with International Accounting Standards

1 At present, accounting for goodwill is addressed in International Accounting Standard (IAS) 22 'Business Combinations'. Other than IAS 9 'Research and Development Costs', there are at present no IASs addressing intangible assets.*

2 The objective of IAS 22 is to write off goodwill over the estimated useful economic life of the original purchased goodwill. The difference between this approach and the approach adopted in the FRS gives rise to a number of differences in the detailed requirements. IAS 22 states that:

(a) purchased goodwill should be amortised over its estimated useful economic life in all circumstances.
(b) the amortisation period should not exceed five years unless a longer period, not exceeding 20 years from the date of acquisition, can be justified.
(c) the unamortised balance of goodwill should be reviewed at each balance sheet date and, to the extent that it is not expected to be recoverable, it should be written down. The write-down may not subsequently be reversed.
(d) one of two treatments should be adopted for negative goodwill. The benchmark treatment requires the fair values of the non-monetary assets acquired to be reduced proportionately until the negative goodwill is eliminated. The permitted alternative treatment requires negative goodwill to be shown as deferred income in the balance sheet and released to the profit and loss account on a systematic basis over a period that does not exceed five years, unless a longer period not exceeding 20 years can be justified.

3 In August 1997, the International Accounting Standards Committee (IASC) published two Exposure Drafts, E60 'Intangible Assets' and E61 'Business Combinations'. The proposals in those Exposure Drafts would align the international requirements for goodwill with those for intangible assets and would reduce the extent of the differences between the FRS and IASs.

4 Like the FRS, E60 and E61 propose a rebuttable presumption that goodwill and intangible assets have useful economic lives of 20 years or less. They also propose that if the presumption can be rebutted, the goodwill or intangible asset may be amortised over a longer period providing that annual impairment reviews are also performed. The most significant difference between IASC's proposals and the requirements of the FRS is that, under the proposals in E60 and E61, goodwill and intangible assets cannot be regarded as having an indefinite life and must be amortised in all circumstances.

5 Other aspects of E60 and E61 that would give rise to differences between the FRS and international requirements include proposals that:

- internally developed intangible assets may be capitalised whenever their costs can be measured reliably, rather than only when they are of a type that is traded on an active market. E60 specifically states that the costs of generating brands, mastheads and other similar assets cannot be measured reliably. Given this, it is

***Editor's Note:** IAS 38 "Intangible Assets" was issued in October 1998. This has since been superseded by a revised version of the standard. IAS 22 has been withdrawn and replaced by IFRS 3. Goodwill is no longer amortized, but subject to an annual impairment review. Negative goodwill, although that term is not used, is first checked and then taken to income.*

expected that there will be few intangible assets which, in practice, can be capitalised under the proposals in E60 that could not be capitalised under the FRS.

- details of intangible assets whose individual values exceed 5 per cent of total assets should be disclosed.
- costs of research and development, software, advertising, pre-opening costs, and any other significant costs incurred on intangible items charged in the profit and loss account in the year should be disclosed.
- negative goodwill attributable to future costs or losses that were identified in the acquirer's purchase plan (and not provided for as identifiable liabilities) should be released as these costs or losses occur.
- other negative goodwill should be released on a systematic basis over the useful lives of the non-monetary assets acquired. Where such negative goodwill exceeds the value of the non-monetary assets, the excess should be released to the profit and loss account immediately.

E60 and E61 do not propose to require the values assigned to intangible assets to be capped at amounts that do not create or increase negative goodwill. Neither do they propose to require first year impairment reviews to be performed.

Appendix III
The development of the FRS

THE NEED FOR A REVIEW

1 The FRS, when implemented, replaces SSAP 22 'Accounting for goodwill'. The SSAP permitted a choice of two approaches to accounting for purchased goodwill. The preferred approach was immediate elimination against reserves. The permitted alternative approach was capitalisation as an asset, with subsequent write-off by systematic amortisation through the profit and loss account. SSAP 22 prohibited the recognition of internally generated goodwill.

2 In the late 1980s, the Accounting Standards Board's predecessor body, the Accounting Standards Committee, started a project to replace SSAP 22. On its inception, the Board decided to continue this project. The decision was taken for several reasons. First, the Board took the view that there was a need to restrict accounting for goodwill to a single method. Secondly, it believed that with the growing practice of separating intangible assets from goodwill, there was a need to codify best practice in accounting for intangible assets. The similarities between goodwill and certain types of intangible assets acquired with a business made it appropriate to review the two together. Finally, the Board recognised that SSAP 22's preferred method of accounting for goodwill, whereby it was eliminated immediately against reserves, attracted criticism and was becoming less accepted internationally. Following its revision in 1993, IAS 22, the International Accounting Standard on accounting for business combinations, prohibited SSAP 22's preferred approach.

DIFFERENT APPROACHES TO ACCOUNTING FOR GOODWILL

Elimination against reserves

3 The preferred method of accounting for purchased goodwill under SSAP 22 was immediate elimination against reserves. The principal rationale for this treatment was that it was consistent with the accepted practice of not including internally generated goodwill on the balance sheet. It can further be argued that goodwill is not an asset that should be recognised by a reporting entity since it is not a right to future economic benefits controlled by the entity.

4 However, the practice of eliminating goodwill against reserves has weaknesses:

- immediate elimination of goodwill gives the impression that the acquirer's net worth has been depleted or even eliminated.
- the problem of equity depletion has encouraged companies to reduce amounts attributed to purchased goodwill by separately valuing brands and similar intangible assets at the date of purchase. Given that such intangible assets are very similar in nature to goodwill and the allocation of value between the two can be subjective, it is widely thought to be inappropriate that the goodwill should be accounted for differently.
- management is not held accountable for the amount that it has invested in goodwill: it is not taken into account when measuring the assets on which a return must be earned, and there is no requirement to disclose a loss if the value of the goodwill is not maintained.
- although there is consistency in the balance sheet treatment of purchased and internally generated goodwill, there is no consistency in the profit and loss account treatment: the costs that can be attributed to building up internally

generated goodwill are offset against profits in the profit and loss account, whereas the costs of acquired goodwill are not charged against profits in this way unless the acquired business is sold.

- this inconsistency serves to make companies that grow by acquisition appear more profitable than those that grow organically.

Capitalisation and compulsory amortisation

An alternative approach to accounting for purchased goodwill, permitted by SSAP 22 and widely adopted internationally, is to capitalise it and amortise it on a systematic basis over a finite period. This approach is based on the rationale that purchased goodwill has a value at the time of recognition but that this value diminishes over time as the purchased goodwill is gradually replaced by internally generated goodwill. **5**

This approach is also open to criticism. In 1990, the Accounting Standards Committee issued Exposure Drafts ED 47 'Accounting for goodwill' and ED 52 'Accounting for intangible assets'. They proposed that purchased goodwill and intangible assets should be capitalised and amortised systematically over their estimated useful economic lives, which in general should not exceed 20 years and in no circumstance could exceed 40 years. Opposition to the proposals was strong: 93 per cent of corporate respondents and 73 per cent of all respondents opposed ED 47; 80 per cent of corporate respondents and 62 per cent of all respondents opposed ED 52. **6**

Those opposing the proposals argued primarily that, where large sums were spent on maintaining and developing the value of an acquired business, a requirement to amortise a significant part of the investment over an arbitrary period had no economic meaning. **7**

Capitalisation and annual impairment reviews

Many of the respondents opposed to amortisation of purchased goodwill agreed that it should be capitalised but thought that it should subsequently be written down only if and to the extent that the carrying value of the goodwill was not supported by the current value of goodwill in the acquired business. **8**

This approach is based on the premise that purchased goodwill is neither an identifiable asset like other assets nor an immediate loss in value. Rather, it represents the balance of the purchase consideration that remains after recognising all the identifiable assets and liabilities in the consolidated financial statements. Essentially, it forms a bridge between the cost of the investment shown as an asset in the acquirer's individual financial statements and the identifiable assets and liabilities recognised in the consolidated financial statements of the combined entities. Although purchased goodwill is not in itself an asset, its inclusion amongst the assets of the reporting entity, rather than as a deduction from shareholders' equity, recognises that goodwill is part of a larger asset, the investment, for which management remains accountable. **9**

This method ensures that the financial statements reflect management's success in maintaining the value of the goodwill and generating a return from its investment. It can be criticised for treating purchased goodwill differently from internally generated goodwill, although this is true for all methods of accounting for purchased goodwill. Other issues are that: **10**

- impairment reviews, which rely on forecasts of future cash flows, can be subjective.
- impairment reviews are onerous and may not be feasible on an annual basis. Where goodwill has a finite life, amortisation may provide a much simpler, yet adequate, method of reflecting the depletion in value of the goodwill.
- amortisation of goodwill is required by companies legislation.

THE FRS's APPROACH TO ACCOUNTING FOR GOODWILL

11 The Board recognised when it started its review that goodwill is something of an accounting anomaly. It arises from a distinct transaction that must be accounted for, yet – as illustrated above – each method of accounting for it results in inconsistencies with other aspects of financial reporting. No single method is universally accepted as being the correct one. Preferences for one method or another tend to be determined by the conceptual and practical issues deemed to be the most important in the light of each individual's particular experience.

12 To gather as many arguments as possible, the Board issued a Discussion Paper that explored a number of options.* Six possible methods were discussed:

1 Capitalisation and amortisation over a finite period.
2 Capitalisation and annual impairment reviews.
3 A combination of methods 1 and 2, with method 2 being used only in the special circumstances where goodwill had an indefinite life believed to exceed 20 years.
4 Immediate elimination against reserves.
5 Immediate elimination to a separate goodwill write-off reserve.
6 Transfer to a separate goodwill write-off reserve, with annual reviews of recoverability and any impairments being charged to the profit and loss account.

13 Methods 2, 3 and 6 represented a departure from traditional methods of accounting for goodwill. Their aim was to recognise the cost of goodwill as a loss only to the extent that the value of goodwill within the acquired business had reduced below the carrying value of the purchased goodwill.

14 No overall consensus emerged from the responses to the Discussion Paper. The method that individually achieved greatest support was method 5—immediate transfer to a separate write-off reserve. However, more respondents favoured capitalisation methods than favoured elimination methods.

15 Given the arguments made by respondents, and in the light of both the direction being taken internationally and the previous opposition to ED 47's proposals for compulsory amortisation, the Board decided to develop proposals based on method 3—capitalisation with a combination of amortisation for goodwill with a finite life and annual impairment reviews for goodwill with an indefinite life expected to exceed 20 years. In combining the amortisation and impairment options, the Board was seeking to overcome the practical and legal issues that would arise under method 2.

16 In favouring capitalisation rather than elimination against reserves, the Board was influenced in particular by the arguments that:

(a) a method requiring elimination against reserves would treat goodwill very differently from brands and similar intangible assets. Given that such assets are

**Discussion Paper 'Goodwill and intangible assets', December 1993.*

very similar in nature to goodwill and that the allocation of a purchase cost between the two can be subjective, it would be possible for a reporting entity's results to be shown in a more favourable light merely by classifying expenditure as an intangible asset rather than goodwill, or vice versa.

(b) immediate elimination of goodwill against reserves fails to demonstrate management's accountability for goodwill as part of the investment in an acquired business. The goodwill is not included in the assets on which a return must be earned, and under methods 4 and 5 no charge would be made in the profit and loss account if the value of the goodwill were not maintained.

The Board acknowledged that under method 6, whereby goodwill would be transferred to a separate goodwill write-off reserve and reviewed annually for impairment, there would be greater accountability. However, some companies told the Board that a requirement to perform detailed impairment reviews every year would be unacceptably onerous. An alternative could have been to require impairment reviews only when there was an indication that the goodwill had become impaired. But the Board took the view that, in the absence of amortisation, such a requirement would be insufficient to ensure that all impairment losses would be recognised on a timely basis. Losses could remain undetected until a major problem came to light. **17**

In developing its chosen approach, the Board conducted extensive consultations with preparers, users and auditors of financial statements, in particular addressing concerns that the procedures proposed for impairment reviews were too complicated. The simplified proposals were field-tested by seven large acquisitive groups and, after further refinement, formed the basis of the Working Paper* for subsequent debate at a public hearing. **18**

The proposals received broad support from the majority of those responding to the Working Paper. They formed the basis of the proposals for accounting for goodwill exposed in FRED 12 and the requirements subsequently included in the FRS. **19**

THE FRS's APPROACH TO ACCOUNTING FOR INTANGIBLE ASSETS

Intangible assets lie on a spectrum ranging from those that can readily be identified and measured separately from goodwill to those that are essentially very similar to goodwill. Companies legislation permits intangible assets to be recognised separately from goodwill only where they are capable of being disposed of separately from a business of the reporting entity.† **20**

In its Discussion Paper, the Board expressed a view that certain intangible assets such as brands and publishing titles could not be disposed of separately from a business and, further, that there was no generally accepted method of valuing such intangible assets. Given this, and given that the dividing line between goodwill and intangible assets can be unclear, the Board proposed in the Discussion Paper that intangible assets acquired as part of the acquisition of a business should be subsumed within the value attributed to goodwill. **21**

This proposal met with strong opposition. Corporate respondents stressed that intangible assets could be critical to their businesses and that it was important to account for them separately. **22**

**Working Paper 'Goodwill and intangible assets', June 1995.*

†*See paragraph 9 of Appendix 1 'Note on Legal Requirements'.*

23 The Board accepted these arguments and in its subsequent Working Paper proposed that intangible assets could be recognised separately from goodwill if they met the legal and conceptual requirements for identifiability and could be measured reliably on initial recognition. But to prevent the results of the reporting entity being shown in a more or less favourable light merely by classifying expenditure as an intangible asset rather than goodwill, or vice versa, the Board proposed that the accounting for intangible assets should be aligned with that for goodwill.

24 This proposal was accepted by most respondents to the Working Paper. It formed the basis of the accounting for intangible assets exposed in FRED 12 and subsequently required by the FRS.

THE DETAILED PROPOSALS FOR POSITIVE GOODWILL AND INTANGIBLE ASSETS

Capitalisation of internally generated intangible assets

25 In general, the FRS requires the costs of developing intangible assets internally to be charged as an expense as they are incurred. This requirement primarily reflects the Board's objective of aligning the treatment of intangible assets that are similar in nature to goodwill with the treatment of goodwill. The requirement also acknowledges that, at present, the measurement of the value of an intangible asset is often subjective. This is especially true in the absence of a transaction price, which establishes a ceiling on the value attributed to a purchased intangible asset.

26 The exception that permits capitalisation of intangible assets with readily ascertainable market values recognises that such assets are clearly distinguishable from goodwill and readily measurable. It is appropriate to treat those assets in the same way as tangible fixed assets, the costs of which can be capitalised whether they are purchased or self-constructed.

27 The Board acknowledges that there may be other intangible assets that would be more appropriately treated in the same way as tangible fixed assets, ie with the costs being capitalised even where the asset is developed internally. However, the Board believes that it would be very difficult to define the basis on which they could be distinguished from intangible assets that are similar in nature to goodwill. Hence, it would be difficult to ensure that only those assets that are genuinely different in nature from goodwill were treated as falling within this 'other' category. The approach that the Board has adopted is simpler and more objective.

Valuation of purchased intangible assets

28 There are two reasons for restricting the fair values that can be assigned to intangible assets to those that do not create or increase negative goodwill: first, the restriction aligns the treatment of purchased intangible assets with that of purchased goodwill and, secondly, it recognises that the values of intangible assets can be subject to a significant degree of uncertainty. Given this subjectivity, the Board regards it as appropriate to restrict the values to those that do not exceed the ceiling established by the purchase price.

Amortisation of goodwill

29 The required approach seeks to charge goodwill in the profit and loss account only to the extent that the carrying value of the goodwill is not supported by the current value of the goodwill within the acquired business. Systematic amortisation is a practical means of recognising the reduction in value of goodwill that has a limited useful economic life. It is also a means of ensuring that where goodwill is not capable of continued measurement (so that annual impairment reviews would not be feasible), its depletion is recognised over a prudent but not unrealistically short period.

The FRS defines the useful economic life of goodwill as the period over which the value of the underlying business is expected to exceed the values of the identifiable net assets. This reflects the link between the carrying value of the goodwill and the continuing value of the goodwill in the acquired investment. **30**

Useful economic lives in excess of 20 years

The economic benefits that goodwill and intangible assets represent are generally more nebulous than those of tangible assets. The useful economic lives of goodwill and intangible assets are correspondingly less certain than those of tangible assets and the Board believes that there should be a presumption that they do not exceed a specified maximum period, chosen to be 20 years. The Board recognises that there will be circumstances where there are valid grounds for rebutting the presumption. Such grounds will be based on the nature of the intangible asset or of the investment underlying a goodwill balance. **31**

Given the uncertainty in the useful economic life of goodwill or an intangible asset, the Board believes that it would be inappropriate to assume that it exceeds 20 years unless it will be possible to monitor the reasonableness of the resulting amortisation charge. For this reason, the ability to perform impairment reviews is one of the conditions that must be met in order to rebut the 20-year presumption. **32**

The choice of 20 years as the presumed maximum useful economic life of goodwill and intangible assets is based largely on judgement. This period was first proposed in the Working Paper. Most respondents to the Working Paper and FRED 12 regarded it as reasonable and accordingly the Board has not changed it in the FRS. Twenty years is not entirely consistent with IAS 22, the International Accounting Standard on goodwill: IAS 22 contains a presumption that the useful economic life of goodwill does not exceed five years and sets 20 years as the absolute maximum. Nevertheless, the alignment of the presumed maximum life in the FRS with the maximum life specified by IAS 22 avoids the unnecessary complexities created by introducing a third arbitrary period.* **33**

The inconsistency between IAS 22's presumed maximum life of five years and the FRS's presumed maximum life of 20 years reflects different underlying approaches. Whilst IAS 22 defines the useful economic life of goodwill as the period benefiting from the original purchased goodwill, the FRS defines it as the period over which the value of the underlying business continues to exceed the values of the identifiable net assets. The latter will normally be longer. **34**

Indefinite useful economic lives

There may be circumstances in which goodwill or an intangible asset can be regarded as having an indefinite life. In such circumstances, amortisation over an arbitrary period may not be an appropriate method of reflecting the depletion of the goodwill or intangible asset. This will be the case where the value of the goodwill or intangible **35**

At the date of publishing the FRS, IASC has published proposals that would remove the 20-year limit. For further details see Appendix II.* ***Editor's note:* *There is no longer a presumption of twenty year life under IAS 38, the relevant international standard.*

asset is expected to be capable of continued measurement in future. In such circumstances, the Board believes that a true and fair view will be given only if the goodwill or intangible asset is not amortised, but is instead subject to annual reviews for impairment.

36 The Board has been advised that non-amortisation of goodwill constitutes a departure from the specific requirement of companies legislation to depreciate the value attributed to goodwill over a limited period that does not exceed its useful economic life. However, departure from specific requirements such as this one is permitted by companies legislation in exceptional circumstances where it is necessary for the overriding purpose of providing a true and fair view.* Accordingly, the Board has limited the circumstances in which it proposes that goodwill is not amortised to those circumstances where systematic amortisation would not provide a true and fair view. It has also incorporated within the disclosure requirements the disclosures that are required by companies legislation where advantage has been taken of the true and fair override provisions.

Impairment reviews

37 It is accepted practice that an asset should not be carried at more than its recoverable amount, i.e. the higher of the amount for which it could be sold and the amount recoverable from its future use.

38 Systematic amortisation ensures that the carrying value of an asset is reduced to reflect any gradual reduction in the asset's recoverable amount over its useful economic life. An asset that is amortised in an appropriate manner is unlikely to become materially impaired unless it is impaired on initial recognition or subsequent events or changes in circumstances cause a sudden reduction in the estimate of the recoverable amount. Thus, where goodwill and intangible assets are amortised over a period not exceeding 20 years, a requirement for an impairment review to be performed each period would be unnecessary and unduly onerous. The Board believes that, in such circumstances, impairment reviews are necessary only at the end of the first full financial year following initial recognition and, thereafter, if subsequent events or changes in circumstances indicate that the carrying value may not be recoverable.

39 The requirement to perform an impairment review at the end of the first full financial year following the initial recognition of goodwill and intangible assets ensures that any impairment arising on acquisition (ie any overpayment) is recognised as a loss at that time, rather than being amortised over the life of the asset.

40 The longer the useful economic lives assigned to goodwill and intangible assets, the greater is the risk that the recoverable amounts will fall below the carrying values in future. Where an amortisation period exceeds 20 years, the Board believes that the risk is sufficiently high to require amortisation to be supplemented by annual reviews for impairment.

Revaluations and restoration of past losses

41 The FRS prohibits capitalisation of internally generated goodwill and permits internally developed intangible assets to be capitalised only if they have readily ascertainable market values. Revaluation of goodwill and intangible assets has the

**Editor's Note:* *Note the withdrawal of IAS 22 since the date of this statement and its replacement by IFRS 3. See paragraphs 6 and 20 of Appendix 1 'Note on Legal Requirements'.*

effect of recognising values that have been internally developed. Hence, the FRS permits revaluation only of intangible assets that have readily ascertainable market values.

Following the recognition of an impairment loss, the value of the impaired goodwill or intangible asset may return towards its previous carrying value. Such an increase will usually be attributable to the internal generation of goodwill or intangible asset value, and as such should not be recognised as a restoration of a past loss. **42**

Less frequently, the increase in value may be attributable to the unexpected reversal of an external event that caused the original impairment to be recognised. In these limited circumstances, the reversal of the impairment loss can be measured more reliably (by reference to the original impairment) and is required by companies legislation to be recognised in the financial statements.* Accordingly, the FRS permits restoration of past losses in such circumstances. **43**

NEGATIVE GOODWILL

Negative goodwill can be attributed to two causes: **44**

- a bargain purchase—the assets have been purchased for less than the aggregate of their individual fair values, perhaps because the vendor needs to achieve a quick sale
- future costs or losses—the purchase price has been reduced to take account of future costs, such as reorganisation costs, or losses that do not represent identifiable liabilities at the balance sheet date.

There are a number of methods of accounting for negative goodwill that can be regarded as consistent with the FRS's approach to positive goodwill. Those methods and the Board's reasons for choosing the method required by the FRS are discussed below. **45**

Goodwill attributable to a bargain purchase

Where negative goodwill is attributed to a bargain purchase, the acquirer can be viewed as having purchased the group of assets at a discount to their individual fair values. **46**

In these circumstances, the value of the business acquired is not less than the fair values of its net assets. It may therefore be argued that the negative goodwill should be recognised as an immediate gain, reflecting the advantageous transaction that the acquirer has undertaken. Since the gain is unrealised, it cannot be recognised in the profit and loss account. Instead, like other revaluation gains, it should be recognised in the statement of total recognised gains and losses. **47**

The Board believes that, in the same way as a revaluation reserve is treated as being realised as the asset is depreciated or sold, so negative goodwill becomes a realised gain as the asset purchased at a bargain price and valued at fair value is depreciated or sold. An alternative option is therefore to require negative goodwill to be recognised as a gain only when that asset is charged against realised profits, either through depreciation or cost of sales. At this point, the gain may be recognised in the profit and loss account. **48**

**See paragraph 15 of Appendix 1 'Note on Legal Requirements'.*

49 FRED 12 proposed that negative goodwill attributed to a bargain purchase should be released immediately in the statement of total recognised gains and losses. The Board took the view that this approach would be more consistent with the proposal that positive goodwill should be written down as soon as it became impaired. However, a majority of the respondents to FRED 12 opposed this proposal, arguing that a requirement to recognise a gain on non-monetary assets before the gain was realised was inconsistent with the requirements of other standards. The Board accepted this argument and the FRS requires negative goodwill to be released as the non-monetary assets acquired are used or sold.

50 The assets that are considered in determining the periods in which negative goodwill is released in the profit and loss account are the non-monetary assets only. This reflects the Board's view that, where a business with both monetary and non-monetary assets is purchased, it is unlikely that the monetary assets would be purchased at an artificially low price, since they can generally be disposed of individually at their fair values.

51 The Board considered a method of accounting for negative goodwill that would require negative goodwill to be eliminated against the fair values of the non-monetary assets acquired. Those supporting this method argue that it:

- is consistent with the principle that assets should initially be recognised at cost.
- helps to prevent unrealistically high fair values being assigned to assets whose values are very subjective. There is a view that true bargain purchases are not as common as optimistic purchasers tend to believe them to be and that cost may represent a realistic estimate of fair value.
- is objective and simple to apply.

52 However, the Board has taken the view that fair values can be different from cost and that a method that requires assets to be stated at amounts lower than their fair values is inconsistent with the requirements in FRS 7 'Fair Values in Acquisition Accounting'. The Board has also taken into consideration the fact that, if such a method were used, the impact of the negative goodwill on the financial statements would not be transparent.

53 The FRS instead requires negative goodwill to be shown separately. But just as positive goodwill is not viewed in the FRS as an asset, so negative goodwill is not viewed as a liability. The Board regards both as the bridge between the consolidated financial statements and the investment shown as an asset in the acquirer's own financial statements. Accordingly, negative goodwill is recognised next to positive goodwill.

Negative goodwill attributable to future reorganisation costs

54 Where negative goodwill is attributable to future costs and losses that do not represent identifiable liabilities at the acquisition date, the value of the acquired business is being viewed as being no higher than the price paid for it. The assets that have been acquired are encumbered in such a way that their combined value in use is less than their individual fair values, until the costs or losses materialise and eliminate the difference.

55 One method of accounting for the negative goodwill arising in these circumstances is to release it as the reorganisation costs or losses subsequently materialise. The rationale is that the negative goodwill is released to match the costs that gave rise to it. But this method raises a number of issues:

(a) the treatment of future reorganisation costs or losses varies depending on whether the acquisition gives rise to positive goodwill or to negative goodwill. Where the net goodwill is positive, the amount by which it has been reduced by an expectation of future costs or losses cannot be written back as the costs or losses are incurred.

(b) both the fair values of non-monetary assets and the allocation of negative goodwill between its two possible causes can be subjective. Stringent conditions would be necessary to ensure that fair values were not overstated thereby attributing too much negative goodwill to future costs and losses. Such conditions would add to the complexity of the requirements.

(c) views have been expressed that the gain in the value of the investment that arises when the future costs or losses have been incurred might not be a realised gain that can be recognised in the profit and loss account. However, respondents to FRED 12 strongly opposed the proposal that negative goodwill attributable to future reorganisation costs or losses should be released in the statement of total recognised gains and losses. They argued in particular that, if a loss of positive goodwill is charged in the profit and loss account, a reversal of negative goodwill should be credited in the same statement.

It can further be argued that a separate accounting treatment for negative goodwill arising in expectation of future costs or losses is unnecessary: such negative goodwill, like that arising from a bargain purchase, should be released as the non-monetary assets are recovered. The argument is that the value of the income-generating units acquired (which will be equal to the present value of the expected future cash flows) is less than the aggregate of the values attributed to the individual assets, so the non-monetary assets in their present state and condition can be viewed as being encumbered or impaired.* This impairment is recognised by deferring the release of the negative goodwill until the acquired assets are recovered through depreciation or sale. **56**

In requiring negative goodwill to be treated in the same manner, whatever its cause, the Board was influenced by the arguments set out above. It notes that the requirement to perform impairment reviews whenever negative goodwill appears to have arisen will eliminate much of the negative goodwill that would otherwise be attributed to future costs or losses. **57**

Negative goodwill in excess of the fair values of the non-monetary assets

As negative goodwill is expected to occur rarely, negative goodwill in excess of the fair values of the non-monetary assets acquired is expected to occur only extremely rarely and in unusual circumstances. Given this, the FRS does not prescribe the period over which 'excess' negative goodwill should be written back. **58**

The FRS does not permit purchased goodwill to be divided into positive and negative components. The Board believes that, since goodwill is viewed as a residual, it would be inappropriate to subdivide a net balance into positive and negative components. Thus, the amounts that can be attributed to any factors identified as causing negative goodwill are limited to the total negative goodwill arising on the acquisition. **59**

**The monetary assets are unlikely to be impaired, since it is likely that they will be capable of being realised individually at their fair values.*

TRANSITIONAL ARRANGEMENTS

60 Ideally, all goodwill that had previously been eliminated against reserves but would not have been fully written down under the requirements of the FRS would be reinstated by means of a prior year adjustment. However, the Board recognises that this will not be practicable in all circumstances and envisages that some or all of this goodwill will remain eliminated against reserves. In order to provide some degree of consistency to the various possibilities for reinstatement that might be chosen, the Board has limited them to those set out in paragraph 69 of the FRS. The 23 December 1989 cut-off point stems from the transitional provisions in companies legislation. The FRS 7 cut-off point recognises that goodwill calculated before then was measured on a different basis.

61 The Board considered including a requirement to reinstate goodwill acquired in the previous year. However, it concluded that, unless acquisitions made in the previous year were the only acquisitions for which goodwill remained at the balance sheet date, this limited requirement would not achieve proper comparability based on consistent application of the FRS's requirements. The profit and loss account would still reflect only part of the cost of the benefits conveyed by the goodwill of past acquisitions. Clearly, the further back any adjustments can be made, the greater the degree of comparability that will be achieved.

CHANGES MADE FOLLOWING EXPOSURE OF FRED 12

62 The majority of respondents to FRED 12 were broadly supportive of its overall approach. The minority who were opposed to the approach divided into those who would prefer compulsory amortisation and those who would prefer immediate elimination of goodwill against reserves. Only a small minority supported the alternative view put forward in Appendix IV of the FRED. The Board's reasons for rejecting compulsory amortisation and immediate elimination against reserves are set out above.

63 A number of changes to the detailed proposals were suggested by respondents and considered by the Board. The more significant changes that have been made in the light of the responses received are:

- the removal of the procedures to be used in performing impairment reviews. They are to be published as a separate FRS encompassing the impairment of all fixed assets and goodwill. FRED 15 'Impairment of Fixed Assets and Goodwill' sets out the procedures to be used for impairment reviews until that FRS is published. Changes that have been made to the impairment procedures as a result of responses to FRED 12 are explained in FRED 15.
- simplification of the procedures for performing 'first year' impairment reviews. The Board accepts the argument that a requirement to perform a full first year impairment review for every acquisition would be unduly onerous, particularly for smaller companies. The FRS permits the first year impairment review to be performed on a simpler basis, with a full review being required only if the simpler review indicates a potential impairment.
- a change in the requirements relating to negative goodwill. The changes are explained above.
- clarification of the transitional arrangements. A large majority of respondents to FRED 12 (including all who were users of financial statements) supported the Board's proposal to permit but not require reinstatement of goodwill that had previously been eliminated against reserves. However, many felt that it was unclear how goodwill would be reinstated and what, if any, constraints would be

placed on the extent and timing of reinstatement. The requirements have been clarified in the FRS.

- the addition of a new requirement for any 'old' goodwill that remains eliminated against reserves to be netted against another reserve and not shown separately on the face of the balance sheet. The Board agrees with respondents who suggested that it could be misleading and confusing to allow goodwill to appear in two places on the face of the balance sheet, with the two balances being subject to different impairment and amortisation requirements. The FRS now requires entities that wish to highlight goodwill as a separate balance to capitalise it as an asset and subject it to the new requirements for amortisation and/or impairment reviews.

A small minority of respondents to FRED 12 opposed the proposal that internally developed brands and mastheads could not be capitalised and the related proposal that purchased brands and mastheads could not be revalued. They argued that reliable valuation techniques exist and that, where brands and mastheads are fundamental to a business, their inclusion makes balance sheets more relevant and comparable and is important for accountability. **64**

The Board considered these arguments. However, it has concluded that the restrictions on capitalisation and revaluation of brands and mastheads stems more from the view that such assets are very similar in nature to goodwill and so should be treated in the same way as goodwill than from the view that their values cannot be measured reliably. The Board further notes that: **65**

- internationally, there are no moves to permit brands and similar assets to be carried at valuations
- reporting entities are not prevented from disclosing (and are indeed encouraged to disclose) estimated values for key intangible assets within the operating and financial review.

Appendix IV
Dissenting view

1 Mr Hinton dissents from the FRS because he does not agree that goodwill should be capitalised as an asset and amortised, or that revaluation of identifiable intangible assets should be prohibited. He advocates an alternative approach, which, he believes, places greater emphasis on the needs of users and the nature of goodwill, recognising that it is neither an asset nor an immediate loss in value. He concludes that goodwill should not be presented as an asset or in any way amortised but should be deducted from shareholders' equity. He notes that over 95 per cent of UK companies with goodwill at present deduct such goodwill from shareholders' equity by write-off to reserves or to a goodwill reserve.

NEEDS OF USERS

2 Users of financial statements in the UK have indicated that whilst they treat any amounts attributed to goodwill with considerable scepticism, they are concerned to hold management accountable for the amounts spent on goodwill. Immediate write-off with the amounts subsumed within reserves as practised by many companies reporting goodwill has clouded such accountability. The measure of such accountability is the relationship between the amounts spent and the likelihood and timing of improved earnings and cash flows. Mr Hinton believes that users are thus concerned with stewardship and whether goodwill has been impaired, but not with reporting goodwill as an asset with either indefinite retention or arbitrary amortisation to operating profit, both of which they have long ignored.

NATURE OF GOODWILL

3 Goodwill is not an asset as defined in the draft Statement of Principles for Financial Reporting and possesses unique characteristics that distinguish it from an asset. It may or may not have any relationship to the expenditures incurred to create it; there is no reliable or continuing relationship of value with any historical cost and such cost frequently and quickly loses any significance it may ever have possessed. Mr Hinton believes that, if goodwill is not an asset and is qualitatively different from assets as generally recognised, it is misleading to report it as such.

AMORTISATION

4 The FRS defines the useful economic life of purchased goodwill as the period over which the value of the underlying business acquired is expected to exceed the values of its identifiable net assets. Mr Hinton notes that this position is unique to the FRS in that traditional guidance on useful economic life emphasises the factors likely to impact the goodwill actually acquired. He regards the definition as inconsistent with the use of a rebuttable presumption that the useful life does not exceed 20 years. He notes that what is being reported is some measure of the current value of the acquired business compared with the current value of its identifiable assets and that this has little to do with the original purchased goodwill.

5 The original purchased goodwill cannot have an indefinite or long life. In reality, purchased goodwill is incapable of being separately measured in the years after purchase and inevitably wanes, only to be replaced in whole or in part by new goodwill arising from current expenditures and events. In effect, the FRS allows internally generated goodwill to be revalued (which is otherwise precluded by the FRS) and offset against declining purchased goodwill.

The approach taken in the FRS regards amortisation as necessary to recognise that goodwill has a limited useful life or as a surrogate for annual impairment reviews where such frequent reviews are not feasible. Mr Hinton does not accept this justification. He argues that: **6**

- FRED 17 'Measurement of Tangible Fixed Assets' defines depreciation as the measure of the cost of the economic benefits of tangible fixed assets that have been consumed during the period. Amortisation is the equivalent process for intangible fixed assets. Yet goodwill differs from other costs in that it is not consumed in any way in operations. Although it contributes to earnings, it arises primarily as a result of earnings or the expectation of them. Any decrease in the value of goodwill is not associated with the income of any period or allocable to any period on any rational or systematic basis.
- Where amortisation is viewed as a surrogate for annual impairment reviews, the FRS requires the goodwill (already acknowledged not to be an asset) to be reported in the balance sheet for up to 20 years irrespective of its value, providing that nothing has happened to indicate that the value might be less than that reported. Mr Hinton believes that this fails to hold management sufficiently accountable for the values assigned to the goodwill.
- In both cases, the FRS requires operating profit to be charged with a meaningless cost.

Mr Hinton takes the view that a proper matching of costs and revenue does not call for amortisation of every asset: it calls for amortisation of only those assets that can be related to operations on some realistic and systematic basis so that the charge reasonably reflects the cost of the economic benefits consumed during the period. Since goodwill is not consumed or depleted as a matter of course, amortisation is not relevant. Further, he believes that the life of purchased goodwill is indeterminable and not measurable and therefore that any period of amortisation is completely arbitrary. **7**

IDENTIFIABLE INTANGIBLE ASSETS

Mr Hinton notes that whilst the FRS recognises the growing importance attached to intangible assets and permits the inclusion at the date of purchase of intangible assets that are measurable on some recognised basis, it is inconsistent in precluding the subsequent revaluation of such intangibles. He takes the view that if an intangible asset is capable of measurement on some recognised basis at acquisition, it must be capable of subsequent measurement on such a basis and subsequent valuation should be permitted. He believes that this would encourage the development of methodology in this area to the ultimate benefit of users. **8**

AN ALTERNATIVE VIEW

Irrespective of whether the consideration is cash, shares or debt, purchased goodwill reduces shareholders' current equity for the prospect of enhanced profit in the future. Part of shareholders' funds (in terms of 'hard assets') has been disbursed: if cash is used, it has gone; if shares, the company could have received cash for the share issue as opposed to goodwill. In both cases, something tangible has been exchanged for something intangible. **9**

Mr Hinton believes that goodwill should be deducted from shareholders' equity to reflect the fact that shareholders' funds have been used. This treatment would **10** recognise that goodwill is neither an asset nor an immediate loss in value. In order to facilitate accountability and subsequent monitoring, the deduction should be by way of establishing a goodwill reserve within shareholders' equity. This presentation of goodwill as a separately identified balance (quasi-asset) would stress stewardship for the amounts spent but not in such a way as to suggest it is an asset, which it is not. It would also meet the requirements of the Companies Act as regards amortisation since such goodwill would be viewed as written off, thus avoiding arbitrary allocations to earnings.

11 While the business continued to be held, the goodwill would be kept under review for permanent impairment. This would be achieved by using high-level impairment indicators to identify possible impairment and using the full impairment reviews outlined in FRED 15 only for goodwill whose value was in doubt. Mr Hinton takes the view that the impairment reviews set forth in FRED 15 are highly subjective but that such subjectivity would be less sensitive where goodwill was not reported as an asset.

12 Intangible assets would be identified as set forth in the FRS. Only those intangible assets with a recognised market value or otherwise measurable on some recognised basis would be capitalised as assets at acquisition; the remainder would form part of goodwill. Only those intangible assets with a clear finite economic life and whose use could be related to earnings on a rational basis would be amortised. Intangible assets not amortised would be reviewed for impairment in the same manner as goodwill. Significantly, subsequent revaluation would be permitted.

Appendix V
Effect on realised profits of elimination of goodwill against reserves

This text reproduces guidance given in Appendix 2 of SSAP 22 'Accounting for goodwill'. The guidance has been reproduced in the FRS because it continues to apply to goodwill acquired before, and not reinstated on, implementation of the FRS. The text is largely unchanged from that contained in SSAP 22 to avoid losing any of the nuances that were considered carefully before SSAP 22 was published.

This appendix is for guidance only and does not form part of the Statement of Standard Accounting Practice.

"[The legal definition of realised profits] is relevant only in the case of an individual company. In the case of goodwill arising on consolidation, the distinction between realised and unrealised reserves is not relevant. Distributions are made from the profits of individual companies, not by groups, and hence the elimination of consolidation goodwill has no effect on the distributable profits of any company. **1**

Where it is the policy of an individual company to eliminate goodwill against reserves immediately on acquisition, the question arises whether such elimination constitutes a reduction of realised reserves. To the extent that the goodwill is considered to have suffered an actual diminution in value, the write-off should be charged against realised reserves. In other cases, where goodwill is written off on acquisition as a matter of accounting policy, rather than because of an actual diminution in value, realised reserves should not be reduced immediately. However, the standard is based on the concept in [UK companies legislation] that purchased goodwill has a limited useful life so that ultimately its elimination must constitute a realised loss. It may in some circumstances (e.g., where a company lacks sufficient distributable reserves to cover the purchase cost of the goodwill) be appropriate to charge the elimination of goodwill initially to a suitable unrealised reserve, thereby spreading the effect of the elimination of goodwill on realised reserves over its useful life rather than impairing realised reserves immediately. The Accounting Standards Committee is advised by the Department of Trade and Industry that the restriction regarding the use of the revaluation reserve set out in paragraph 34(3) of Schedule 4 has the effect that this reserve should not be charged with the write-off of goodwill.* A suitable unrealised reserve may exist as a result of the crediting to reserves of negative goodwill - see paragraph 3 below. To maintain parity of effect as regards distributable reserves with the amortisation method permitted by [ssap 22], the amount written off should then be transferred from unrealised reserves to realised reserves so as to reduce realised reserves on a systematic basis in the same way as if the goodwill had been amortised. In case of doubt on the points in this paragraph, legal advice should be sought. **2**

Where negative goodwill arises in the accounts of an individual company it should be credited initially to an unrealised reserve, from which it may be transferred to realised reserves in line with the depreciation or realisation of the assets acquired in the business combination which gave rise to the goodwill in question. On the introduction of this standard, amounts representing negative goodwill which arose on prior acquisitions may already have been credited to reserves. To the extent that **3**

Companies legislation has since been amended to clarify that the revaluation reserve may not be used for goodwill write-off. Paragraph 34(3B) of Schedule 4 to the Companies Act 1985 prohibits the reduction of the revaluation reserve in any circumstances other than those specified earlier in that paragraph. The specified circumstances do not include the write-off of goodwill.* ***Editor's note:* *For accounting periods beginning on or after 6 April 2008 this changes to Paragraph 35 of Schedule 1 to the Large and Medium-sized Companies and Groups (Accounts and Reports) Regulations 2008 (SI 2008/410).*

the assets acquired have, on the introduction of this standard, been depreciated or realised, the relevant amount or reserves may be regarded as realised."

Financial Reporting Standard 11 is set out in paragraphs 1–82.

The Statement of Standard Accounting Practice, which comprises the paragraphs set in bold type, should be read in the context of the Objective as stated in paragraph 1 and the definitions set out in paragraph 2 and also of the Foreword to Accounting Standards and the Statement of Principles for Financial Reporting currently in issue.

The explanatory paragraphs contained in the FRS shall be regarded as part of the Statement of Standard Accounting Practice insofar as they assist in interpreting that statement.

Appendix IV 'The development of the FRS' reviews considerations and arguments that were thought significant by members of the Board in reaching the conclusions of the FRS.

[FRS 11]
Impairment of fixed assets and goodwill*

(Issued July 1998)

Contents

Paragraphs

Summary

Financial Reporting Standard 11

Objective	1
Definitions	2
Scope	3–7
Indications of impairment	8–13
Recognition and measurement of impairment losses	14–21
Calculation of net realisable value	22–23
Calculation of value in use	24–46
Income-generating units	27–31
Central assets	32–35
Cash flows	36–40
Discount rate	41–46
Allocation of impairment losses	47–53
Allocation when acquired businesses are merged with existing operations	50–53
Subsequent monitoring of cash flows	54–55
Reversal of past impairments	56–62
Tangible fixed assets and investments in subsidiaries, associates and joint ventures	56–59
Goodwill and intangible assets	60–62
Revalued fixed assets	63–66
Presentation and disclosure	67–73
Date from which effective and transitional arrangements	74–76
Amendment of other accounting standards	77–82

****Editor's note****: The matters covered in FRS 11 are dealt with in Section 27 of FRS 102.*

Adoption of FRS 11 by the board

Appendices

- **I** Determining pre-tax discount rates
- **II** Note on legal requirements
- **III** Compliance with international accounting standards
- **IV** The development of the FRS

Impairment of fixed assets and goodwill

Summary

a Financial Reporting Standard 11 'Impairment of Fixed Assets and Goodwill' sets out the principles and methodology for accounting for impairments of fixed assets and goodwill. Investments covered by the Accounting Standards Board's project on derivatives and other financial instruments are excluded from the scope of the FRS. Also excluded are investment properties, which are being considered further in the light of other Board projects and the international project on investment properties.

b It would be unnecessarily onerous for all fixed assets and goodwill to be tested for impairment every year. In general, fixed assets and goodwill need be reviewed for impairment only if there is some indication that impairment has occurred. (Requirements for additional impairment reviews of goodwill and intangible assets in certain circumstances are included in FRS 10 'Goodwill and Intangible Assets'.)

c Where possible, individual fixed assets should be tested for impairment. However, impairment can often be tested only for groups of assets because the cash flows upon which the calculation is based do not arise from the use of a single asset. In these cases, impairment is measured for the smallest group of assets (the income-generating unit) that produces a largely independent income stream, subject to constraints of practicality and materiality.

d Impairment is measured by comparing the carrying value of the fixed asset or income-generating unit with its recoverable amount. The recoverable amount is the higher of the amounts that can be obtained from selling the fixed asset or income-generating unit (net realisable value) or using the fixed asset or income-generating unit (value in use).

e Net realisable value is the expected proceeds of selling the fixed asset or income-generating unit less any direct selling costs. Value in use is calculated by discounting the expected cash flows arising from the use of the fixed asset or assets in the income-generating unit at the rate of return that the market would expect from an equally risky investment.

f In some cases a detailed calculation of value in use will not be necessary. A simple estimate may be sufficient to demonstrate that either value in use is higher than carrying value, in which case there is no impairment, or value in use is lower than net realisable value, in which case impairment is measured by reference to net realisable value.

g If an acquisition that gives rise to goodwill is merged with an existing business, the requirements of the FRS necessitate the calculation of the amount of any internally generated goodwill in the existing business at the date of the merger because that amount will need to be used in the calculation of any subsequent impairment loss in the merged business.

h The reversal of past impairment losses is recognised when the recoverable amount of a tangible fixed asset or investment in a subsidiary, an associate or a joint venture has increased because of a change in economic conditions or in the expected use of the asset. Increases in the recoverable amount of goodwill and intangible assets are recognised only when an external event caused the recognition of the impairment loss in previous periods, and subsequent external events clearly and demonstrably reverse the effects of that event in a way that was not foreseen in the original impairment calculations.

Impairment losses are recognised in the profit and loss account, unless they arise on a previously revalued fixed asset. Impairment losses on revalued fixed assets are recognised in the statement of total recognised gains and losses until the carrying value of the asset falls below depreciated historical cost unless the impairment is clearly caused by a consumption of economic benefits, in which case the loss is recognised in the profit and loss account. Impairments below depreciated historical cost are recognised in the profit and loss account. i

Financial Reporting Standard 11

Objective

1 The objective of this FRS is to ensure that:

(a) fixed assets and goodwill are recorded in the financial statements at no more than their recoverable amount;

(b) any resulting impairment loss is measured and recognised on a consistent basis; and

(c) sufficient information is disclosed in the financial statements to enable users to understand the impact of the impairment on the financial position and performance of the reporting entity.

Definitions

2 The following definitions shall apply in the FRS and in particular in the Statement of Standard Accounting Practice set out **in bold type.**

Impairment:-

A reduction in the recoverable amount of a fixed asset or goodwill below its carrying amount.

Income-generating unit:-

A group of assets, liabilities and associated goodwill that generates income that is largely independent of the reporting entity's other income streams. The assets and liabilities include those directly involved in generating the income and an appropriate portion of those used to generate more than one income stream.

Intangible assets:-

Non-financial fixed assets that do not have physical substance but are identifiable and controlled by the entity through custody or legal rights.

Net realisable value:-

The amount at which an asset could be disposed of, less any direct selling costs.

Purchased goodwill:-

The difference between the cost of an acquired entity and the aggregate of the fair values of that entity's identifiable assets and liabilities.

Readily ascertainable market value:-

In relation to an intangible asset, the value that is established by reference to a market where:

(a) the asset belongs to a homogeneous population of assets that are equivalent in all material respects; and
(b) an active market, evidenced by frequent transactions, exists for that population of assets.

Recoverable amount:-

The higher of net realisable value and value in use.

Tangible fixed assets:-

Assets that have physical substance and are held for use in the production or supply of goods or services, for rental to others, or for administrative purposes on a continuing basis in the reporting entity's activities.

Value in use:-

The present value of the future cash flows obtainable as a result of an asset's continued use, including those resulting from its ultimate disposal.

SCOPE

The FRS applies to all financial statements that are intended to give a true and fair view of a reporting entity's financial position and profit or loss (or income and expenditure) for a period. 3

Reporting entities applying the Financial Reporting Standard for Smaller Entities (FRSSE) currently applicable are exempt from the FRS unless preparing consolidated financial statements, in which case they should apply the FRS to such statements as required by the FRSSE.* 4

The requirements of the FRS apply to purchased goodwill that is recognised in the balance sheet and all fixed assets, except: 5

(a) fixed assets within the scope of the FRS addressing disclosures of derivatives and other financial instruments†;
(b) investment properties as defined in SSAP 19 'Accounting for investment properties';
(c) an entity's own shares held by an ESOP and shown as a fixed asset in the entity's balance sheet under UITF Abstract 13 'Accounting for ESOP Trusts';‡
(d) costs capitalised pending determination (ie costs capitalised while a field is still being appraised) under the Oil Industry Accounting Committee's SORP 'Accounting for oil and gas exploration and development activities';§ and
(e) heritage assets to the extent specified in FRS 30 'Heritage assets'.¶¶

Reporting entities applying the* FRSSE *are generally exempt from applying this* FRS*. However, if they prepare consolidated financial statements, the* FRSSE *in force at the date of the publication of this* FRS *requires them to apply* SSAP *22 to purchased goodwill arising on consolidation. It is envisaged that a future revision of the* FRSSE *will required smaller entities adopting the* FRSSE *and preparing consolidated financial statements to replace that reference to* SSAP *22 with an equivalent reference to* FRS *10 and this* FRS*. (Editor's note:** The* FRSSE *(effective March 1999) did this.)*

†***Editor's note:** See FRS 25 and 29.*

‡***Editor's note**: The reference to UITF 13 should now be taken as a reference to UITF 38.*

§***Editor's note:** Superseded by updated SORP 'Accounting for oil and gas exploration, development, production and decommissioning activities' issued January 2000.*

¶¶***Editor's note**: Sub-paragraph added by FRS 30.*

6 Many investments are covered by the Accounting Standards Board's project on derivatives and other financial instruments and hence are excluded from this FRS. However, investments in subsidiary undertakings, associates and joint ventures are excluded from the scope of that project and are, therefore, included within the scope of this FRS

7 The FRS does not apply to purchased goodwill that was written off to reserves under SSAP 22 'Accounting for goodwill' and has not been recognised on the balance sheet under FRS 10 'Goodwill and Intangible Assets'.

INDICATIONS OF IMPAIRMENT

8 **A review for impairment of a fixed asset or goodwill should be carried out if events or changes in circumstances indicate that the carrying amount of the fixed asset or goodwill may not be recoverable.**

9 Impairment occurs because something has happened either to the fixed assets themselves or to the economic environment in which the fixed assets are operated. It is possible, therefore, to rely on the use of indicators of impairment to determine when a review for impairment is needed.

10 Examples of events and changes in circumstances that indicate an impairment may have occurred include:

- a current period operating loss in the business in which the fixed asset or goodwill is involved or net cash outflow from the operating activities of that business, combined with either past operating losses or net cash outflows from such operating activities or an expectation of continuing operating losses or net cash outflows from such operating activities
- a significant decline in a fixed asset's market value during the period
- evidence of obsolescence or physical damage to the fixed asset
- a significant adverse change in:
  - either the business or the market in which the fixed asset or goodwill is involved, such as the entrance of a major competitor
  - the statutory or other regulatory environment in which the business operates
  - any 'indicator of value' (for example turnover) used to measure the fair value of a fixed asset on acquisition
- a commitment by management to undertake a significant reorganisation
- a major loss of key employees
- a significant increase in market interest rates or other market rates of return that are likely to affect materially the fixed asset's recoverable amount.

11 The above indicators of impairment will trigger an impairment review only if they are relevant to the measurement of goodwill or fixed assets. For example, short-term market interest rates may increase without affecting the rate of return the market would require on long-term assets, with the result that there is no effect on the recoverable amount of such assets. Such increases in short-term rates would not trigger an impairment review.

12 If any such events or changes in circumstances are identified, a review of the useful economic lives and residual values of the fixed assets or goodwill affected is appropriate: even if the fixed assets or goodwill are not impaired, their remaining useful economic lives and residual values may have changed as a result of the events or changes in circumstances.

The requirements of this FRS are such that if no such events or changes in circumstances are identified, and there are no other indications that a tangible fixed asset or investment in a subsidiary, associate or joint venture has become impaired, there is no requirement for an impairment review. For tangible fixed assets, impairments will therefore be a relatively infrequent addition to depreciation. Additional requirements to perform impairment reviews for goodwill and intangible assets that are amortised over periods of more than 20 years or not at all are set out in FRS 10 'Goodwill and Intangible Assets'. 13

RECOGNITION AND MEASUREMENT OF IMPAIRMENT LOSSES

The impairment review should comprise a comparison of the carrying amount of the fixed asset or goodwill with its recoverable amount (the higher of net realisable value and value in use). To the extent that the carrying amount exceeds the recoverable amount, the fixed asset or goodwill is impaired and should be written down. The impairment loss should be recognised in the profit and loss account unless it arises on a previously revalued fixed asset, in which case it should be recognised as required by paragraph 63. 14

If either net realisable value or value in use is higher than the carrying amount of a fixed asset or goodwill, the fixed asset or goodwill is not impaired and there is no need to calculate the other amount. 15

If no reliable estimate of net realisable value can be made, the recoverable amount is determined by value in use alone. 16

If net realisable value is lower than the carrying amount of the fixed asset, before writing down the asset to net realisable value it is necessary to establish whether value in use is higher. If it is, the recoverable amount will be based on value in use, not net realisable value. 17

Requirements and guidance relating to the calculation of net realisable value and value in use are set out in paragraphs 22–46 below. In many cases, a detailed calculation of value in use will not be necessary because a simple estimate will be sufficient to demonstrate that value in use is either above carrying value, in which case there is no impairment, or is below net realisable value, in which case the recoverable amount will not be based on value in use. 18

In determining whether recoverable amount should be based on value in use or net realisable value, the deferred tax balances that would arise in each case need to be taken into account. For example, if net realisable value is £100 and would give rise to a deferred tax liability of £30 and value in use is £110 and would give rise to a deferred tax liability of £45, recoverable amount is based on net realisable value. 19

If a fixed asset is not held for the purpose of generating cash flows either by itself or in conjunction with other assets, for example certain fixed assets held for charitable purposes, it is not appropriate to measure the asset at an amount based on expected future cash flows. In such cases it may not be appropriate to write down the fixed asset to its recoverable amount – an alternative measure of its service potential may be more relevant. 20

When an impairment loss on a fixed asset or goodwill is recognised, the remaining useful economic life and residual value should be reviewed and revised if necessary. The revised carrying amount should be depreciated over the revised estimate of the remaining useful economic life. 21

CALCULATION OF NET REALISABLE VALUE

22 The net realisable value of an asset that is traded on an active market will be based on market value.

23 Net realisable value is defined as the amount at which an asset could be disposed of, less any direct selling costs. Examples of direct selling costs are legal costs and stamp duty. Any costs relating to the removal of a sitting tenant are also direct selling costs of a building. However, costs associated with reducing or reorganising the business rather than selling the fixed asset, such as redundancy costs incurred when a factory is sold, are not direct selling costs.

CALCULATION OF VALUE IN USE

24 **The value in use of a fixed asset should be estimated individually where reasonably practicable. Where it is not reasonably practicable to identify cash flows arising from an individual fixed asset, value in use should be calculated at the level of income-generating units. The carrying amount of each income-generating unit containing the fixed asset or goodwill under review should be compared with the higher of the value in use and the net realisable value (if it can be measured reliably) of the unit.**

25 The value in use of a fixed asset is the present value of the future cash flows obtainable as a result of the asset's continued use, including those resulting from its ultimate disposal. In practice, it is not normally possible to estimate the value in use of an individual fixed asset: it is the utilisation of groups of assets and liabilities, together with their associated goodwill, that generates cash flows. Hence value in use will usually have to be estimated in total for groups of assets and liabilities. These groups are referred to as income-generating units.

26 Because it is necessary to identify only material impairments, in some cases it may be acceptable to consider a group of income-generating units together rather than on an individual basis.

Income-generating units

27 **Income-generating units should be identified by dividing the total income of the entity into as many largely independent income streams as is reasonably practicable. Except as permitted by paragraph 32, each of the identifiable assets and liabilities of the entity, excluding deferred tax balances, interest-bearing debt, dividends payable and other items relating wholly to financing, should be attributed to (or apportioned between) one (or more) income-generating unit(s).**

28 To perform impairment reviews as accurately as possible:

- the groups of assets and liabilities that are considered together should be as small as is reasonably practicable, but
- the income stream underlying the future cash flows of one group should be largely independent of other income streams of the entity and should be capable of being monitored separately.

Income-generating units are therefore identified by dividing the total income of the business into as many largely independent income streams as is reasonably practicable in the light of the information available to management.

In general terms, the income streams identified are likely to follow the way in which management monitors and makes decisions about continuing or closing the different lines of business of the entity. Unique intangible assets, such as brands and mastheads, are generally seen to generate income independently of each other and are usually monitored separately. Hence they can often be used to identify income-generating units. Other income streams may be identified by reference to major products or services. **29**

Examples 1–4: Identification of income-generating units

Example 1

A transport company runs a network comprising trunk routes fed by a number of supporting routes. Decisions about continuing or closing the supporting routes are not based on the returns generated by the routes in isolation but on the contribution made to the returns generated by the trunk routes.

An income-generating unit comprises a trunk route plus the supporting routes associated with it because the cash inflows generated by the trunk routes are not independent of the supporting routes.

Example 2

A manufacturer can produce a product at a number of different sites. Not all the sites are used to full capacity and the manufacturer can choose how much to make at each site. However, there is not enough surplus capacity to enable any one site to be closed. The cash inflows generated by any one site therefore depend on the allocation of production across all sites.

The income-generating unit comprises all the sites at which the product can be made.

Example 3

A restaurant chain has a large number of restaurants across the country. The cash inflows of each restaurant can be individually monitored and sensible allocations of costs to each restaurant can be made.

Each restaurant is an income-generating unit by itself. However, any impairment of individual restaurants is unlikely to be material. A material impairment is likely to occur only when a number of restaurants are affected together by the same economic factors. It may therefore be acceptable to consider groupings of restaurants affected by the same economic factors rather than each individual restaurant.

Example 4

An entity comprises three stages of production, A (growing and felling trees), B (creating parts of wooden furniture) and C (assembling the parts from B into finished goods). The output of A is timber that is partly transferred to B and partly sold in an external market. If A did not exist, B could buy its timber from the market. The output of B has no external market and is transferred to C at an internal transfer price. C sells the finished product in an external market and the sales revenue achieved by C is not affected by the fact that the three stages of production are all performed by the entity (unlike example 1, where the sales revenue of the trunk routes is affected by the existence of supporting routes run by the same entity).

A forms an income-generating unit and its cash inflows should be based on the market price for its output. B and C together form one income-generating unit because there is no market available for the output of B. In calculating the cash outflows of the income-generating unit B+C, the timber received by B from A should be priced by reference to the market, not any internal transfer price.

30 Income-generating units are defined by allocating the assets and liabilities of the reporting entity, excluding deferred tax balances, interest-bearing debt, dividends payable and other items relating wholly to financing, to the identified income streams. Certain assets and liabilities that are directly involved in the production and distribution of individual products may be attributed directly to one unit. Central assets, such as group or regional head offices, and working capital may have to be apportioned across the units on a logical and systematic basis. The resulting income-generating units will be complete and non-overlapping, so that the sum of the carrying amounts of the units equals the carrying amount of the net assets (excluding tax and financing items) of the entity as a whole, as illustrated in example 5 below.

Example 5: Allocation of head office assets to income-generating units

An entity has three independent income streams, A, B and C, with net assets directly involved in the income streams with carrying amounts of £100 million, £150 million and £200 million respectively. In addition there are head office net assets with a carrying amount totalling £18 million. The relative proportion of the head office resources used by the income streams is 2:3:4. The income-generating units are defined as follows:

Income-generating unit	A	B	C	Total
Net assets directly attributable to income-generating unit (£ million)	100	150	200	450
Head office net assets (£ million)	4	6	8	18
Total (£ million)	104	156	208	468

If there were an indication that a fixed asset in income-generating unit B was impaired, the recoverable amount of B would be compared with £156 million, not £150 million. Similarly, the cash flows upon which the value in use of B is based would include the relevant portion of any cash outflows arising from central overheads.

31 The income stream of a fixed asset to be disposed of will be largely independent of the income stream of other assets. Such an asset therefore forms an income-generating unit of its own and does not belong to any other income-generating unit.

Central assets

32 **If it is not possible to apportion certain central assets meaningfully across the income-generating units to which they contribute, these assets may be excluded from the individual income-generating units. However, an additional impairment review should be performed on the excluded central assets. In this review, the income-generating units**

to which the central assets contribute should be combined and their combined carrying amount (including that of the central assets) should be compared with their combined value in use.

> **Example 6: Alternative approach to allocation of head office assets to income-generating units**
>
> With this approach, in example 5 above the recoverable amount of B would be compared with £150 million, not £156 million. Then a further impairment test would be required on the whole entity comparing its recoverable amount with the total carrying value of £468 million.

If there is any working capital in the balance sheet that will generate cash flows equal to its carrying amount, the carrying amount of the working capital may be excluded from the income-generating units and the cash flows arising from its realisation/settlement excluded from the value in use calculation. 33

Capitalised goodwill should be attributed to (or apportioned between) income-generating units or groups of similar units. If they were acquired as part of the same investment and are involved in similar parts of the business, individual units identified for the purpose of monitoring the recoverability of assets may be combined with other units to enable the recoverability of the related goodwill to be assessed. 34

Goodwill is allocated to income-generating units in the same way as are the assets and liabilities of the entity. However, where several similar income-generating units are acquired together in one investment, the units may be combined to assess the recoverability of the goodwill. The income-generating units are first reviewed individually for the purposes of assessing the recoverability of any capitalised intangible assets and tangible fixed assets and then, as illustrated in example 7 below, the combined unit is reviewed to assess the recoverability of the goodwill. 35

> **Example 7: Alternative approach to allocation of goodwill to income-generating units**
>
> An entity acquires a business comprising three income-generating units, A, B and C. After five years, the carrying amount of the net assets in the income-generating units and the purchased goodwill compares with the value in use as follows (there is no reliable estimate of net realisable value for any of the income-generating units or the business as a whole):

Income-generating unit	A	B	C	Goodwill	Total
Carrying amount (£ million)	80	120	140	50	390
Value in use (£ million)	100	140	120		360

> An impairment loss of £20 million is recognised in respect of income-generating unit C, reducing its carrying amount to £120 million and the total carrying amount to £370 million. A further impairment loss of £10 million is then recognised in respect of the goodwill.

Cash flows

The expected future cash flows of the income-generating unit, including any allocation of central overheads but excluding cash flows relating to financing and tax, should be 36

based on reasonable and supportable assumptions. The cash flows should be consistent with the most up-to-date budgets and plans that have been formally approved by management. Cash flows for the period beyond that covered by formal budgets and plans should assume a steady or declining growth rate. Only in exceptional circumstances should:

(a) the period before the steady or declining growth rate is assumed extend to more than five years; or

(b) the steady or declining growth rate exceed the long-term average growth rate for the country or countries in which the business operates.*

37 In exceptional circumstances, the use of a long-term growth rate that is higher than the average country growth rate may be justified. This may, for example, be the case where:

(a) the long-term growth rate for the relevant industry is expected to be significantly higher than the relevant country growth rate; and

(b) the business under review is expected to grow as rapidly as the industry as a whole, taking into account the likelihood of new competitors entering such an industry.

38 Subject to paragraph 39 below, future cash flows should be estimated for income-generating units or individual fixed assets in their current condition. They should not include:

(a) future cash outflows or related cost savings (for example reductions in staff costs) or benefits that are expected to arise from a future reorganisation for which provision has not yet been made; or

(b) future capital expenditure that will improve or enhance the income-generating units or assets in excess of their originally assessed standard of performance or the related future benefits of this future expenditure.

39 In the case of a newly acquired income-generating unit such as a subsidiary, the purchase price will reflect the synergies and other opportunities for making more effective use of the assets as a result of the acquisition. In some of these cases, in order to obtain the benefits from its investment, it may be necessary for the purchaser to undertake related capital expenditure and reorganisations. Consequently, in assessing the future cash flows of the investment, the costs and benefits of such reorganisations and capital expenditure anticipated at the time of performing impairment reviews up to the end of the first full year after acquisition and consistent with budgets and plans at that time may be taken into account in those and subsequent impairment reviews, to the extent that the investment or reorganisations are still to be incurred.

40 Failure to undertake capital investment or a reorganisation according to the planned schedule may call into question the validity of continuing to forecast that the investment or reorganisation will be undertaken in the future and may be an indication of impairment as discussed in paragraphs 8-13. The costs and benefits of the investment or reorganisation would then have to be omitted from forecasts performed for subsequent impairment reviews. Additionally, the monitoring of cash flows required by paragraph 54 may indicate that impairment has already occurred.

**The UK post-war average growth in gross domestic product, expressed in real terms, is 2.25 per cent (source: Financial Statement and Budget Report March 1998, HM Treasury).*

Discount rate

The present value of the income-generating unit under review should be calculated by discounting the expected future cash flows of the unit. The discount rate used should be an estimate of the rate that the market would expect on an equally risky investment. It should exclude the effects of any risk for which the cash flows have been adjusted and should be calculated on a pre-tax basis. 41

Estimates of this market rate may be made by a variety of means including reference to: 42

(a) the rate implicit in market transactions of similar assets;
(b) the current weighted average cost of capital (WACC) of a listed company whose cash flows have similar risk profiles to those of the income-generating unit; or
(c) the WACC for the entity *but only if* adjusted for the particular risks associated with the income-generating unit.

If method (c) is used the following matters are of note. 43

- Where the cash flow forecasts assume a real growth rate that exceeds the long-term average growth rate for more than five years, it is likely that the discount rate will be increased to reflect a higher level of risk.
- The discount rates applied to individual income-generating units will always be estimated such that, were they to be calculated for every unit, the weighted average discount rate would equal the entity's overall WACC.

The WACC will be a post-tax rate from the entity's point of view, whereas the required discount rate will be a pre-tax rate. Some of the issues that need to be considered in adjusting from a post-tax rate to a pre-tax rate are discussed in Appendix I. 44

Using a discount rate equal to the rate of return that the market would expect on an equally risky investment is a method of reflecting the risk associated with the cash flows in the value in use measurement. It is likely that this method will be the easiest method of reflecting risk. However, an acceptable alternative is to adjust the cash flows for risk and to discount them using a risk-free rate (eg a government bond rate). Whichever method of reflecting risk is adopted, care must be taken that the effect of risk is not double-counted by inclusion in both the cash flows and the discount rate. 45

If the cash flows to be discounted are expressed in current prices, a real discount rate will be used. If the cash flows are expressed in expected future prices, a nominal discount rate will be used. 46

ALLOCATION OF IMPAIRMENT LOSSES

The carrying amounts of the income-generating units under review should be calculated as the net of the carrying amounts of the assets, liabilities and goodwill allocated to the unit. 47

To the extent that the carrying amount of the income-generating unit exceeds its recoverable amount, the unit is impaired. In the absence of an obvious impairment of specific assets within the unit, the impairment should be allocated: 48

(a) first, to any goodwill in the unit;
(b) thereafter, to any capitalised intangible asset in the unit; and

(c) finally, to the tangible assets in the unit, on a pro rata or more appropriate basis.

49 In this allocation, which aims to write down the assets with the most subjective valuations first, no intangible asset with a readily ascertainable market value should be written down below its net realisable value. Similarly, no tangible asset with a net realisable value that can be measured reliably should be written down below its net realisable value.

Allocation when acquired businesses are merged with existing operations

50 Where an acquired business is merged with an existing business and results in an income-generating unit that contains both purchased and (unrecognised) internally generated goodwill:

(a) the value of the internally generated goodwill of the existing business at the date of merging the businesses should be estimated and added to the carrying amount of the income-generating unit for the purposes of performing impairment reviews;*

(b) any impairment arising on merging the businesses should be allocated solely to the purchased goodwill within the newly acquired business;

(c) subsequent impairments should be allocated pro rata between the goodwill of the acquired business and that of the existing business;

(d) the impairment allocated to the existing business should be allocated first to the (notional) internally generated goodwill; and

(e) only the impairments allocated to purchased goodwill (and, if necessary, to any recognised intangible or tangible assets) should be recognised in the financial statements.

51 An acquired business may be merged with an existing operation of the reporting entity in such a way that a single income-generating unit includes the assets and liabilities of both the acquired and the existing businesses. This combined income-generating unit contains both acquired and internally generated goodwill and any future impairment needs to be apportioned between the two. This can be done by notionally adjusting the carrying amount of the income-generating unit to recognise a notional carrying amount for the internally generated goodwill of the existing operation at the date of merging the two businesses.

52 The notional carrying amount of the internally generated goodwill is estimated by deducting the fair values of the net assets and purchased goodwill within the existing income-generating unit from its estimated value in use before combining the businesses. This calculation will need to be done whenever an acquisition that gives rise to goodwill is merged with an existing business. The notional balance is assumed to be subject to the same pattern of amortisation as is applied to the purchased goodwill.

53 Because the comparison with value in use will have resulted in the recognition of any impairment of the existing business at the time of merging it with the acquired business, any initial impairment in the combined income-generating unit will, by definition, relate to the acquired business. Any subsequent impairment cannot be attributed directly to either the acquired or the existing businesses and is therefore apportioned between the notional internally generated goodwill and the purchased goodwill pro rata to their current carrying values.

**The internally generated goodwill will not be recognised in the financial statements.*

Example 8: Allocation of impairment losses when an acquired business is merged with existing operations

Assumptions

An entity acquires for £60 million a business having net assets with a total fair value of £40 million, resulting in purchased goodwill of £20 million. The acquired business is merged with an existing operation that has net assets with a fair value of £100 million and a carrying amount of £70 million. The value in use of the existing operation at the time of the acquisition is £150 million, implying that the existing operation has internally generated goodwill of £50 million.

Five years later, the carrying amount of the net assets of the combined income-generating unit is £105 million and the carrying amount of the purchased goodwill is £10 million (goodwill is being amortised over 10 years). Value in use is £119 million and there is no reliable estimate of net realisable value.

Calculation of impairment loss	*£m*
Carrying amount of new assets	105
Carrying amount of goodwill	10
Notional carrying amount of the internally generated goodwill at the date of acquisition (assuming notional amortisation on same basis as for purchased goodwill)	25
Total	140
Value in use	119
Impairment	21

The impairment is allocated on a pro rata basis (2:5) to the purchased goodwill and internally generated goodwill, resulting in the recognition of an impairment loss of £6 million and purchased goodwill being written down to £4 million.

If value in use were £98 million, the resulting total impairment loss of £42 million would be allocated first to the goodwill (purchased and notional amount of internally generated) of £35 million, then to any intangible assets, then to the tangible fixed assets in the income-generating unit, resulting in the recognition of an impairment loss of £17 million (write-down of purchased goodwill £10 million, write-down of intangible and tangible assets £7 million).

SUBSEQUENT MONITORING OF CASH FLOWS

For the five years following each impairment review where the recoverable amount has been based on value in use, the cash flows achieved should be compared with those forecast. If the actual cash flows are so much less than those forecast that use of the actual cash flows could have required recognition of an impairment in previous periods, the original impairment calculations should be re-performed using the actual cash flows. Any impairment identified should be recognised in the current period unless the 54

impairment has reversed and the reversal of the loss is permitted to be recognised by paragraph 56 or 60 below.

55 In order to check whether an impairment would have arisen, the original calculation is re-performed using the cash flows that have actually occurred but without revising any other cash flows or assumptions (except those that change as a direct consequence of the occurrence of the actual cash flows, eg where a major cash inflow has been delayed for a year). If this recalculation identifies an impairment, the loss should be recognised in the current period. However, the entity may also recalculate value in use using revised assumptions in order to assess the current value in use. If this current value in use shows a reversal of the impairment that would have been recognised had the actual cash flows been used in the original calculation, and that reversal is permitted to be recognised under the FRS, recognition of an impairment loss is not required. Instead, the impairment that would have been recognised and its subsequent reversal are disclosed (paragraph 71).

REVERSAL OF PAST IMPAIRMENTS

Tangible fixed assets and investments in subsidiaries, associates and joint ventures

56 **If, after an impairment loss has been recognised, the recoverable amount of a tangible fixed asset or investment increases because of a change in economic conditions or in the expected use of the asset, the resulting reversal of the impairment loss should be recognised in the current period to the extent that it increases the carrying amount of the fixed asset up to the amount that it would have been had the original impairment not occurred. The reversal of the impairment loss should be recognised in the profit and loss account unless it arises on a previously revalued fixed asset, in which case it should be recognised as required by paragraph 66.**

57 Events and circumstances that are the reverse of those set out in paragraph 10 as triggers for an impairment review may indicate that the recoverable amount of a fixed asset has increased. The increase in the recoverable amount must arise from a change in economic conditions or in the expected use of the asset. This would include situations where the recoverable amount increases as a result of further capital investment or a reorganisation, the benefits of which had been excluded from the original measurement of value in use.

58 Increases in value in use may arise simply because of:

(a) the passage of time: as future cash inflows become closer, their discounted value increases. (Where value in use has been calculated using cash flows based on current prices and a real discount rate, value in use may also increase because of the effect of general inflation on current prices.)
(b) the occurrence of forecast cash outflows: once the cash outflows are past, they are no longer part of the value in use calculation and value in use therefore increases.

Such increases in value may not be recognised as reversals of an impairment loss.

59 The recognition of an increase in the recoverable amount of a tangible fixed asset above the amount that its carrying amount would have been had the original impairment not occurred is a revaluation, not a reversal of an impairment.

Goodwill and intangible assets

60 **The reversal of an impairment loss on intangible assets and goodwill should be recognised in the current period if, and only if:**

(a) an external event caused the recognition of the impairment loss in previous periods, and subsequent external events clearly and demonstrably reverse the effects of that event in a way that was not foreseen in the original impairment calculations; or

(b) the impairment loss arose on an intangible asset with a readily ascertainable market value and the net realisable value based on that market value has increased to above the intangible asset's impaired carrying amount.

The reversal of the impairment loss should be recognised to the extent that it increases the carrying amount of the goodwill or intangible asset up to the amount that it would have been had the original impairment not occurred. 61

The recognition of an increase in the recoverable amount of an intangible asset above the amount that its carrying amount would have been had the original impairment not occurred is a revaluation and is addressed by FRS 10 'Goodwill and Intangible Assets'. 62

Example 9: Allocation and reversal of impairment losses

Assumptions

An income-generating unit comprising a factory, plant and equipment etc and associated purchased goodwill becomes impaired because the product it makes is overtaken by a technologically more advanced model produced by a competitor. The recoverable amount of the income-generating unit falls to £60 million, resulting in an impairment loss of £80 million, allocated as follows:

	Carrying amounts before impairment £m	Carrying amounts after impairment £m
Goodwill	40	–
Patent (with no market value)	20	–
Tangible fixed assets	80	60
Total	140	60

After three years, the entity makes a technological breakthrough of its own, and the recoverable amount of the income-generating unit increases to £90 million. The carrying amount of the tangible fixed assets had the impairment not occurred would have been £70 million.

Calculation of reversal of the impairment loss

The reversal of the impairment loss is recognised to the extent that it increases the carrying amount of the tangible fixed assets to what it would have been had the impairment not taken place, ie a reversal of £10 million of the impairment loss is recognised and the tangible fixed assets written back to £70 million. Reversal of the impairment is not recognised in relation to the goodwill and a patent because the effect of the external event that caused the original impairment has not reversed – the original product is still overtaken by a more advanced model.

REVALUED FIXED ASSETS

63 **An impairment loss on a revalued fixed asset should be recognised in the profit and loss account if it is caused by a clear consumption of economic benefits. Other impairments of revalued fixed assets should be recognised in the statement of total recognised gains and losses until the carrying amount of the asset reaches its depreciated historical cost and thereafter in the profit and loss account.**

64 An impairment loss arises on a revalued fixed asset whenever the recoverable amount of the asset falls below its carrying amount. In particular, a downward revaluation may comprise, at least in part, an impairment loss. Some of these impairments are caused by a consumption of economic benefits, for example physical damage or a deterioration in the quality of the service provided by the asset, and are operating costs similar to depreciation.

65 Other impairments of revalued fixed assets may result from general changes in prices, for example a general slump in the property market, and are recognised in the statement of total recognised gains and losses as valuation adjustments until the carrying amount of the asset reaches its depreciated historical cost, and thereafter in the profit and loss account.

66 **A reversal of an impairment loss should be recognised in the profit and loss account to the extent that the original impairment loss (adjusted for subsequent depreciation) was recognised in the profit and loss account. Any remaining balance of the reversal of an impairment should be recognised in the statement of total recognised gains and losses.**

PRESENTATION AND DISCLOSURE

67 **Impairment losses recognised in the profit and loss account should be included within operating profit under the appropriate statutory heading, and disclosed as an exceptional item if appropriate. Impairment losses recognised in the statement of total recognised gains and losses should be disclosed separately on the face of that statement.**

68 **In the notes to the financial statements in accounting periods after the impairment, the impairment loss should be treated as follows:**

(a) for assets held on a historical cost basis, the impairment loss should be included within cumulative depreciation: the cost of the asset should not be reduced.

(b) for revalued assets held at a market value (eg existing use value or open market value), the impairment loss should be included within the revalued carrying amount.

(c) for revalued assets held at depreciated replacement cost, an impairment loss charged to the profit and loss account should be included within cumulative depreciation: the carrying amount of the asset should not be reduced; an impairment loss charged to the statement of total recognised gains and losses should be deducted from the carrying amount of the asset.

69 **If the impairment loss is measured by discounting cash flows in order to estimate the value in use or the net realisable value of a fixed asset or income-generating unit, the discount rate applied to the cash flows should be disclosed. If the risk-free discount rate is used, some indication of the risk adjustments made to the cash flows should be given. Management shall disclose, in addition to the discount rate applied to the cash flows, the following assumptions used in determining those estimated amounts:**

(i) the period over which management has projected the cash flows; and
(ii) the growth rate used to extrapolate cash flow projections.*

Where an impairment loss recognised in a previous period is reversed in the current period, the financial statements should disclose the reason for the reversal, including any changes in the assumptions upon which the calculation of recoverable amount is based. **70**

Where an impairment loss would have been recognised in a previous period had the forecasts of future cash flows been more accurate but the impairment has reversed and the reversal of the loss is permitted to be recognised, the impairment now identified and its subsequent reversal should be disclosed. **71**

Where, in the measurement of value in use, the period before a steady or declining long-term growth rate has been assumed extends to more than five years, the financial statements should disclose the length of the longer period and the circumstances justifying it. **72**

Where, in the measurement of value in use, the long-term growth rate used has exceeded the long-term average growth rate for the country or countries in which the business operates, the financial statements should disclose the growth rate assumed and the circumstances justifying it. **73**

Date from which effective and transitional arrangements

The accounting practices set out in the FRS should be regarded as standard in respect of financial statements relating to accounting periods ending on or after 23 December 1998. Earlier adoption is encouraged but not required. **74**

Impairment losses recognised when the standard is implemented for the first time are not the result of a change in accounting policy and should be recognised in accordance with the requirements of the FRS and not as prior period adjustments. **75**

Paragraph 69 was amended by 'Improvements to Financial Reporting Standards' issued in December 2009. The requirement set out in that paragraph should be applied in annual periods beginning on or after 1 January 2010. Earlier application is permitted.† **75A**

The requirement that fixed assets should not be held at more than recoverable amount is a well-established principle. Achieving this objective by applying the method prescribed in the FRS is not a change in accounting policy but is similar to a change in accounting estimate. **76**

AMENDMENT OF OTHER ACCOUNTING STANDARDS

[*Not reproduced as all changes have been reflected in the material reproduced in this volume.*] **77–82**

****Editor's note**: Paragraph amended with effect for accounting periods beginning on or after 1 January 2010.*

†***Editor's note**: This paragraph was itself added by the improvements project referred to within it.*

Adoption of FRS 11 by the board

Financial Reporting Standard 11 - 'Impairment of Fixed Assets and Goodwill' was approved for issue by the ten members of the Accounting Standards Board.

Sir David Tweedie	(Chairman)
Allan Cook	(Technical Director)
David Allvey	
Ian Brindle	
Dr John Buchanan	
John Coombe	
Raymond Hinton	
Huw Jones	
Professor Geoffrey Whittington	
Ken Wild	

Appendix I
Determining pre-tax discount rates

The discount rate reflects the rate of return required on the assets being reviewed, not the way in which they have been financed. Hence it is not affected by any tax relief available on the cost of financing the asset or by any tax paid by the provider of finance. 1

The required pre-tax rate of return is simply the rate of return that will, after tax has been deducted, give the required post-tax rate of return. Because the tax consequence of different cash flows may be different, the pre-tax rate of return is not always the post-tax rate of return grossed up by a standard rate of tax. 2

The effect of discounting pre-tax cash flows at a pre-tax discount rate should be similar to the effect of discounting post-tax cash flows at a post-tax discount rate. 3

Example

An asset is required to generate a post-tax return of 14 per cent. If the asset cost £100, and generated all of its cash flows in one year's time, the required post-tax cash flows would be £114.

If tax was charged at 30 per cent, pre-tax cash flows of £120 would be required to generate the required post-tax cash flows of £114:

	£	£
Pre-tax cash flows		120
Tax at 30% of £120	(36)	
Allowance for cost of asset at 30%	30	
		(6)
		114

Thus the required pre-tax cash flows would be £120, making the required pre-tax rate of return 20 per cent.

The value assigned to the asset would be £100, whether calculated by discounting pre-tax cash flows (£120) by the pre-tax required rate of return (20 per cent) or by discounting post-tax cash flows (£114) by the post-tax required rate of return (14 per cent).

However, when an asset becomes impaired, the relationship between pre-tax and post-tax required rates of return may change. This is because, although future pre-tax cash flows reduce, the amount of future tax relief may not. This is taken into account by providing for deferred tax on any timing differences created by the recognition of the impairment loss, not by making any adjustment to the pre-tax discount rate. 4

Example

Suppose that in the previous example, £100 had been paid for the asset in the expectation that it would generate pre-tax cash flows of at lease £120. However, circumstances then changed and the pre-tax cash flows were expected to halve to £60. The cash flows expected in one year's time would therefore be:

	£	£
Pre-tax cash flows		60
Tax at 30% of £60	(18)	
Allowance for cost of asset (£100 at 30%)	30	
		12
		72

Although the pre-tax cash flows have halved, the post-tax cash flows have not reduced so much. Thus discounting the pre-tax cash flows of £60 by 20 per cent (to give a value of £50) no longer produces the same value for the asset as would be achieved by discounting the post-tax cash flows of £72 by 14 per cent (to give a value of £63).

The difference is not eliminated by making any adjustment to the pre-tax rate of return to reflect the tax status of the asset under review. Rather it is eliminated by providing for deferred tax on the timing difference created by the recognition of the impairment loss:

	£
Impaired carrying value of asset (£60 discounted by 20%)	50
Deferred tax asset (impairment of £50 at 30%, discounted by 14%)	13*
Total amount recognised in respect of asset	63

Under SSAP 15, the deferred tax asset might not be recognised and would not be discounted. (Editor's note:** SSAP 15 has now been superseded by FRS 19 'Deferred tax'.)*

Appendix II
Note on Legal requirements

GREAT BRITAIN*

Impairment losses

Paragraph 19(1) of Schedule 4 to the Companies Act 1985 allows provisions for diminutions in value of fixed asset investments to be made and the amount to be included in respect of the fixed asset investment to be reduced accordingly. Any provisions that are not shown in the profit and loss account must be disclosed (either separately or in aggregate) in a note to the accounts. 1

Paragraph 19(2) of Schedule 4 requires provisions for diminution in value to be made in respect of any fixed asset that has diminished in value if the reduction in its value is expected to be permanent. The amount to be included in respect of the asset must be reduced accordingly. Any provisions that are not shown in the profit and loss account must be disclosed (either separately or in aggregate) in a note to the accounts. 2

Clearly it is a matter of judgement whether any diminution in value should be treated as permanent (although there must be reasonable grounds for making such a judgement), as indicated by the requirement, referred to again below, that any provision subsequently found not to be necessary has to be reversed. 3

In addition to references to diminutions in value in the paragraphs noted above, the Act allows for the revaluation downwards of fixed assets dealt with under the alternative accounting rules in paragraph 34 of Schedule 4. 4

The FRS concerns itself with impairment rather than permanent diminutions in value. Nevertheless, the distinction between permanent and temporary diminutions in value is inherently recognised in the FRS. A principle is established that impairments that are clearly due to consumption of economic benefits are charged to the profit and loss account. Any such loss is clearly a permanent loss. Other cases of impairment raise separate considerations. 5

Where a fixed asset is impaired, it will always be the case that both the value in use and the net realisable value will be below the carrying amount. Although this does not inevitably signify a loss that is permanent, it would be prudent in relation to fixed assets held at depreciated historical cost to regard such a loss as permanent and, despite any element of uncertainty, charge it to the profit and loss account. In the case of a revalued fixed asset, it would be reasonable to reflect the uncertainty of the permanence of any impairment by treating it as a reversal of any temporary increase in value previously recognised. Such an impairment would be dealt with through the statement of total recognised gains and losses (ie as a revaluation reserve movement). However, if the impairment results in a carrying value below depreciated historical cost, then, as in a 6

****Editor's note:** The various statutory references change with the introduction of the Companies Act 2006, which affects accounting for periods beginning on or after 6 April 2008. The various statutory references have changed as follows:*

Companies Act 1985 reference	***Companies Act 2006 reference***
Paragraph 19 of Schedule 4	*Paragraph 19 of Schedule 1 to the Large and Medium-sized Companies and Groups (Accounts and Reports) Regulations 2008 (SI 2008/410)*
Paragraph 34 of Schedule 4	*Paragraph 32 of Schedule 1 to SI 2008/410*

pure historical cost context, it would be prudent and reasonable to treat that part of the impairment as being permanent and charge it to the profit and loss account.

Reversals of impairment losses

7 Paragraph 19(3) of Schedule 4 requires that where the reasons for which a provision was made have ceased to apply to any extent, the provision shall be written back to the extent that it is no longer necessary. Where any amounts written back are not shown in the profit and loss account, they must be disclosed (either separately or in aggregate) in a note to the accounts.

8 The FRS requires that, for tangible fixed assets, a reversal of an impairment loss should be recognised when the recoverable amount of an asset increases because of a change in economic conditions – the reason for the impairment was that the asset was not expected to generate sufficient returns to cover its carrying amount. Once it is expected to do so, the reason for the impairment ceases to apply.

9 The FRS explains that the increase in recoverable amount must arise from a change in economic conditions that results in a revised calculation of the recoverable amount. Increases in value in use may arise simply because of:

(a) the passage of time: as future cash inflows become closer, their discounted value increases; or

(b) the occurrence of forecast cash outflows: once the cash outflows are past, they are no longer part of the value in use calculation and value in use therefore increases.

The Board believes that these increases should not give rise to a write-back of the impairment loss because the reason for which the provision was made has not ceased to apply – all that has happened is that time has passed and the expected cash flows have occurred.

10 The Board has received legal advice that a reversal of an impairment loss on goodwill should be recognised only where an external event caused the recognition of the impairment loss in previous periods and subsequent external events clearly and demonstrably reverse the effects of that event in a way that was not foreseen in the original impairment calculations. The Board believes that, for the reasons set out in Appendix IV 'The development of the FRS', the same criterion should apply to intangible assets (except those that have a readily ascertainable market value).

NORTHERN IRELAND AND THE REPUBLIC OF IRELAND

11 The references to the equivalent statutory requirements in Northern Ireland and the Republic of Ireland are as follows:

Great Britain	*Northern Ireland*	*Republic of Ireland*
Schedule 4 to the Companies Act 1985:	Schedule 4 to the Companies (Northern Ireland) Order 1986:	The Schedule to the Companies (Amendment) Act 1986:
paragraph 19(1)	paragraph 19(1)	paragraph 7(1)
paragraph 19(2)	paragraph 19(2)	paragraph 7(2)
paragraph 19(3)	paragraph 19(3)	paragraph 7(3)
paragraph 34	paragraph 34	paragraph 22

Appendix III
Compliance with International Accounting Standards

The International Accounting Standards Committee approved its accounting standard IAS 36 'Impairment of Assets' in April 1998.* The basic approach in the IAS is the same as that in the FRS: impairment is measured by comparing the carrying value of fixed assets and goodwill with the higher of net selling price (equivalent to net realisable value) and value in use. Value in use is calculated by discounting the cash flows expected to be generated from the assets. **1**

The detailed requirements of the IAS are also very similar to those of the FRS. They differ insofar as: **2**

(a) the FRS requires impairments of revalued assets that are clearly caused by the consumption of economic benefits to be recognised in the profit and loss account (paragraph 63). In contrast, the IAS requires such impairments to be recognised in the profit and loss account only to the extent that the loss exceeds the balance on the revaluation reserve relating to the assets in question.

(b) to be consistent with FRS 10 'Goodwill and Intangible Assets', the FRS aligns the treatment of intangible assets with that of goodwill, whereas the IAS treats intangibles as being more similar to tangible fixed assets. This has two consequences:

   (i) the FRS allocates impairment losses in an income-generating unit first to goodwill, secondly to intangible assets and then to tangible fixed assets (paragraph 48). The IAS allocates impairment losses first to goodwill and then pro rata to intangible and tangible assets; and

   (ii) the FRS restricts the recognition of reversals of impairment losses on intangible assets (except those with a readily ascertainable market value) to the same limited circumstances in which reversals of impairments of goodwill are recognised (paragraph 60). The IAS recognises reversals of impairments of intangible assets under the same conditions that apply to reversals of impairments of tangible fixed assets.

(c) the FRS has a general rule that in all but exceptional circumstances, longer-term cash flow projections should assume that within five years a steady or declining growth rate of no more than the relevant country average growth rate is achieved (paragraph 36). It requires disclosure if these assumptions are not made. The IAS has a similar general rule but:
- does not require disclosure if the assumptions are not made
- rather than restricting growth rates to those of the relevant country, restricts them to those of the relevant products, industry or country.

(d) if an acquired business has been merged with existing operations, the FRS requires any subsequent impairment to be allocated between the acquired goodwill and the goodwill in the existing operations at the time of merging the two businesses (paragraph 50). The IAS does not include this requirement.

(e) the FRS requires the accuracy of previous estimates of value in use to be monitored for five years following an impairment review (paragraph 54). Any impairment that should have been recognised at the time must be recognised in the current period unless it has since reversed, in which case its non-recognition in past years should be disclosed. The IAS does not include these requirements.

(f) The IAS requires the amounts recognised as impairment losses and reversals of impairment losses to be disclosed in more detail than does the FRS.

***Editor's note:** *A revised version of IAS 36 was issued in March 2004 as part of the IASB's business combinations project.*

3 The rationale for including in the FRS each of the requirements mentioned above is addressed in Appendix IV 'The development of the FRS'.

Appendix IV
The development of the FRS

THE NEED FOR A STANDARD

It is accepted practice that a fixed asset should not be carried in financial statements at more than its recoverable amount, ie the higher of the amount for which it could be sold and the amount recoverable from its future use. However, there is little guidance on how recoverable amount should be measured and when impairment losses should be recognised. As a result, practice is inconsistent and perhaps some impairments may not be recognised on a timely basis. 1

The need for a standard on impairment is increased by the requirement in FRS 10 'Goodwill and Intangible Assets' that, where goodwill and intangible assets have a useful life in excess of twenty years (including those exceptional cases where the life is indefinite), the recoverable amount of the goodwill and intangible assets should be reviewed every year. 2

This FRS sets out a method for measuring and recognising impairment. In developing the FRS the Board has considered comments on its initial proposals that were set out in the Discussion Paper 'Impairment of Tangible Fixed Assets', on the related proposals on impairment set out in FRED 12 'Goodwill and Intangible Assets' and in FRED 15 'Impairment of Fixed Assets and Goodwill'. 3

INDICATIONS OF IMPAIRMENT

Systematic depreciation ensures that the carrying amount of a fixed asset is reduced to reflect over its useful economic life any reduction in the asset's recoverable amount arising from consumption of economic benefits. A tangible fixed asset that is depreciated in an appropriate manner is unlikely to become materially impaired unless events or changes in circumstances cause a sudden reduction in the estimate of the recoverable amount. Thus, where tangible fixed assets are depreciated, a requirement for an impairment review to be performed each period would be unnecessary and unduly onerous. The Board believes that, in such circumstances, impairment reviews are necessary only if events or changes in circumstances indicate that the carrying amount may not be recoverable. The additional occasions when impairment reviews are required for intangible assets and goodwill are set out and explained in FRS 10. 4

MEASUREMENT OF IMPAIRMENT

Measurement by reference to recoverable amount

The FRS requires impairment to be measured by comparing the carrying amount of a fixed asset or income-generating unit with its recoverable amount. The recoverable amount is based on the cash flows that can be generated by the fixed asset or income-generating unit either by sale (net realisable value) or by continued use (value in use). When fixed assets or goodwill are written down to the higher of the amount that can be recovered through sale or continued use, they are recorded at their greatest value to the entity. If the entity chooses not to use or sell the fixed asset or income-generating unit so as to recover the greatest value possible, the loss from not doing so is properly recorded in the period in which the fixed asset or income-generating unit 5 is sold when more could be recovered through use, or in the period(s) in which it is used when more could be recovered through sale.

6 The Board believes that this presents a faithful representation of the economic decisions that are made when a fixed asset or income-generating unit becomes impaired.

7 An alternative approach would be to measure impairment by reference to fair value, being the amount at which an asset or liability could be exchanged in an arm's length transaction between informed and willing parties, other than in a forced or liquidation sale. This is the approach adopted by the US standard FAS 121 'Accounting for the Impairment of Long-Lived Assets and for Long-Lived Assets to Be Disposed Of'. For many assets with a deep active market, fair value, net realisable value and value in use will not be materially different. Where there is no such market or where the entity uses the asset for a specific purpose not generally open to other participants in the market, there may well be a difference between net realisable value and value in use, and the notion of fair value is less well defined. It might, for example, be assumed that fair value is equal to net realisable value (subject to transaction costs) even if value in use is higher, but such an assumption does not reflect the fact that a willing seller would not dispose of the asset for much less than its value in use. Exactly what is the 'fair value' of the asset is open to question.

8 The Board believes that defining recoverable amount as the higher of net realisable value and value in use gives a more precise and clearer indication of the amount to which the asset should be written down and therefore prefers this terminology to the use of the term 'fair value'.

Constraints on estimates of value in use – growth rates and subsequent monitoring

9 The forecasts of future cash flows used to measure the value in use of a business are inevitably subjective. The FRS contains two key controls designed to reduce the risk of over-optimistic forecasting. First, it requires the longer-term projections of cash flows to assume a growth rate that does not normally exceed the long-term average growth rate for the country in which the business operates (paragraph 36). It allows higher rates to be used in the shorter-term forecasts, but states that only in exceptional (and disclosed) circumstances should these shorter-term forecasts extend beyond five years.

10 The Board recognises that, even in the longer-term, growth rates in certain industries will exceed average growth rates for the country as a whole. However, it takes the view that this does not necessarily mean that individual businesses within such industries will grow as quickly: in the longer-term, high growth industries may attract new businesses, reducing the opportunities for high growth rates in existing businesses. Hence, where an entity believes that it could justify using an industry growth rate for more than five years, it must disclose what it has done.

11 The second constraint placed on estimates of future cash flows is the requirement to monitor the accuracy of cash flow forecasts for the five years following an impairment review: any impairment that should have been recognised at the time must be recognised in the current period unless it has since reversed, in which case its non-recognition in past years should be disclosed. The aim of the disclosure requirement is primarily to ensure that cash flows are reliable: a record of continually falling short of forecast cash flows will tend to cast doubt on the reliability of current estimates; and awareness that this would have to be disclosed will be an incentive to management to build its forecasts on realistic assumptions.

The Board views these two controls as important checks on the reliability of forecasts. They were proposed early on in the development of the FRS and included within the proposals in both the Discussion Paper and the subsequent FRED. They were accepted by most respondents. 12

Discounting

Discounting is a method of reflecting the time value of money and the effect of risk in the valuation of a stream of future cash flows. All rational economic decisions and, hence, all arm's length transactions reflect the time value of money and the effect of risk. Given that the Board's definition of recoverable amount is based on the economic decisions made when an impairment occurs, value in use must also reflect these factors. If not, value in use would not be measured on a consistent basis with net realisable value and cost (both of which are based on observable transactions and, hence, reflect the time value of money and the effect of risk). A comparison between carrying amount (based on cost), net realisable value and value in use would be meaningless. 13

The Board therefore believes that the cash flows on which value in use is based should either be discounted at a risk-adjusted rate, ie the rate of return that the market would expect on an equally risky investment, or should themselves be adjusted for risk before being discounted at a risk-free rate. 14

Tax

FRED 15 proposed that impairments should be measured on a post-tax basis and the tax element split out for presentation in the financial statements. An alternative approach, adopted by the FASB in FAS 121 and by IASC in IAS 36 'Impairment of Assets', is for value in use to be calculated by discounting the pre-tax cash flows at a pre-tax rate and any further tax consequences recognised by applying a tax standard. The reason behind the approach in FRED 15 was that it discounted the effect of any future capital allowances still to be received, whereas the present tax standard, SSAP 15, does not. 15

A slight majority of respondents to FRED 15 preferred the pre-tax approach, primarily because it was thought to be easier to apply. Given this view and the desirability of harmonisation with the USA and IASC, the Board has decided to change to a pre-tax approach. The question of discounting deferred tax assets and liabilities will be considered as part of the Board's project on deferred tax. 16

Measurement of impairment when acquired businesses are merged with existing operations

The FRS includes specific requirements regarding the measurement of an impairment arising after a purchased business has been merged with existing operations. It requires that any subsequent impairment of the combined business is allocated on a pro rata basis between the (unrecognised) goodwill in the existing operations and the acquired goodwill. Had this requirement not been included, the effect would be that any impairment of the acquired goodwill would not be recognised unless, and to the extent that, the impairment of the combined business exceeded the value of the unrecognised goodwill at the time of merging. 17

IAS 36 does not include this requirement. Although IASC acknowledged that the requirement would be necessary to measure impairment accurately, it took the view 18 that it would be a difficult requirement to apply in practice. The Board considered this argument, but retained the requirement in the FRS on the grounds that:

- without the requirement, impairment losses would be understated in the circumstances where the requirement applied.
- the absence of such a requirement would create an opportunity to avoid the recognition of impairment losses by treating an acquired business as having been merged with a large existing business.
- the requirement will not have to be applied universally: it will have to be applied only when performing an impairment review of purchased goodwill where the acquired business was merged with an existing business and the goodwill has become partly, but not wholly, impaired. Especially where goodwill is being amortised, these circumstances may not arise often.

IMPAIRMENT OF REVALUED FIXED ASSETS

19 The Board believes that, in principle, impairments of revalued fixed assets fall into two general groups – those that are clearly caused by a consumption of economic benefits and those caused by a general fall in prices. The first type is similar to depreciation and is treated as such, whereas the second type is more like a valuation adjustment that would fall to be recognised in the statement of total recognised gains and losses.

20 However, in many cases it is difficult to allocate an impairment to one or other group with certainty. In order to provide objectivity in the treatment of impairments of revalued fixed assets, the FRS requires that where there is doubt whether the impairment is caused by a reduction in the quantum of the service potential, the impairment loss should be recognised in the statement of total recognised gains and losses until the carrying amount of the asset reaches its depreciated historical cost. Any further impairment should be recognised in the profit and loss account.

21 Although this split between the statement of total recognised gains and losses and the profit and loss account where the type of impairment is unclear is necessarily arbitrary, it has the advantage of being consistent with IAS 16 (revised 1993) 'Property, Plant and Equipment' and IAS 36. It is also likely to be perceived as an equitable approach that does not penalise entities that revalue their fixed assets.

REVERSAL OF PAST IMPAIRMENT LOSSES

22 Companies legislation requires provisions for diminutions in value to be written back if the reasons for the provision have ceased to apply. The Board agrees with this principle but is aware that in some cases it will be difficult to distinguish between increases in the value of a fixed asset or income-generating unit that arise because the reasons for the impairment have ceased to apply and increases in value that arise for some other reason.

23 For tangible fixed assets and investments the Board believes it is acceptable for any increase in value that reverses a previous impairment to be recognised, as long as it results from changed economic conditions or the expected use of the asset and not simply the passage of time or the occurrence of forecast cash flows. After all, increases in value arising from changed economic conditions could be recognised by revaluing the assets.

24 In relation to intangible assets that cannot be revalued and goodwill, the Board does not wish to recognise increases in value attributable to the internal generation of intangible asset value or goodwill. Accordingly, the FRS allows recognition of reversals of past impairments of intangible assets and goodwill only where the increase in value can be clearly attributed to the unexpected reversal of an external event that caused the original impairment to be recognised.

CHANGES MADE TO FRED 15

In the light of comments made by those responding to FRED 15, a number of changes have been made to its proposals. The most significant changes are that: 25

- investment properties are exempted from the requirements of the FRS. The treatment of investment properties is being considered further in the light of other Board projects and the international project on investment properties. The Board believes that, until this work is complete, it is appropriate to maintain the status quo as set out in SSAP 19 'Accounting for investment properties'.
- an entity's own shares held in an ESOP and shown as a fixed asset in the balance sheet under UITF Abstract 13 'Accounting for ESOP Trusts' are also exempt from the requirements of the FRS. The Board believes that an entity's own shares should be treated in a manner consistent with other investments, rather than as fixed assets. They will, therefore, be considered as part of the financial instruments project.*
- the FRS requires a pre-tax rather than a post-tax approach to measuring impairment (see paragraphs 15 and 16 above).
- examples to clarify the principles underlying the identification of income-generating units have been added.
- an alternative to allocating central assets across income-generating units is allowed – the central assets may instead be tested for impairment by reviewing the combination of all the income-generating units to which they contribute.
- a requirement has been added (paragraph 38 of the FRS) that value in use should reflect the asset or income-generating unit as it exists at the balance sheet date and hence that in general the costs and benefits of future investment should not be included in the value in use calculation.
- explanation has been added regarding the circumstances in which the reversal of past impairment losses may be recognised.

****Editor's note****: *UITF 13 has been replaced by UITF 38. This treats own shares held in an ESOP as negative equity, rather than assets.*

Financial Reporting Standard 12 is set out in paragraphs 1–102.

The Statement of Standard Accounting Practice, which comprises the paragraphs set in bold type, should be read in the context of the Objective as stated in paragraph 1 and the definitions set out in paragraph 2 and also of the Foreword to Accounting Standards and the Statement of Principles for Financial Reporting currently in issue.

The explanatory paragraphs contained in the FRS shall be regarded as part of the Statement of Standard Accounting Practice insofar as they assist in interpreting that statement.

Appendix VII 'The development of the FRS' reviews considerations and arguments that were thought significant by members of the Board in reaching the conclusions on the FRS.

[FRS 12]
Provisions, contingent liabilities and contingent assets*†

(Issued September 1998)

Contents

	Paragraphs
Summary	
Financial Reporting Standard 12	
Objective	1
Definitions	2
Scope	3–10
Provisions and other liabilities	11
Relationship between provisions and contingent liabilities	12–13
Recognition	14–35
Provisions	14–26
Present obligation	15–16
Past event	17–22
Probable transfer of economic benefits	23–24
Reliable estimate of the obligation	25–26
Contingent liabilities	27–30
Contingent assets	31–35
Measurement	36–55
Best estimate	36–41
Risks and uncertainties	42–44
Present value	45–50
Future events	51–53
Expected disposal of assets	54–55
Reimbursements	56–61
Changes in provisions	62–63
Use of provisions	64–65
Recognising an asset when recognising a provision	66–67

****Editor's note:*** *FRS 12 was amended by FRS 17, FRS 21 and FRS 26.*

†***Editor's note:*** *The matters covered in FRS 12 are dealt with in Section 21 of FRS 102.*

Application of the recognition and measurement rules	68–88
Future operating losses	68–70
Onerous contracts	71–74
Restructuring	75–88
Disclosure	89–97
Date from which effective	98
Withdrawal of SSAP 18 and amendment of FRS 3	99–100
Application of the new requirements	101–102

Adoption of FRS 12 by the board

Appendices

I Tables – Main requirements of the FRS
II Decision tree
III Examples – Recognition
IV Examples – Disclosures
V Note on legal requirements
VI Compliance with International Accounting Standards
VII The Development of the FRS

Provisions, contingent liabilities and contingent assets

Summary

GENERAL

Financial Reporting Standard 12 'Provisions, Contingent Liabilities and Contingent Assets' sets out the principles of accounting for provisions, contingent liabilities and contingent assets. Its objective is to ensure that appropriate recognition criteria and measurement bases are applied to provisions, contingent liabilities and contingent assets and that sufficient information is disclosed in the notes to the financial statements to enable users to understand their nature, timing and amount. **a**

DEFINITIONS

In the FRS a *provision* is a liability that is of uncertain timing or amount, to be settled by the transfer of economic benefits. A *contingent liability* is either (i) a possible obligation arising from past events whose existence will be confirmed only by the occurrence of one or more uncertain future events not wholly within the entity's control; or (ii) a present obligation that arises from past events but is not recognised because it is not probable that a transfer of economic benefits will be required to settle the obligation or because the amount of the obligation cannot be measured with sufficient reliability. A *contingent asset* is a possible asset arising from past events whose existence will be confirmed only by the occurrence of one or more uncertain future events not wholly within the entity's control. **b**

SCOPE

The FRS applies to all financial statements that are intended to give a true and fair view in accounting for provisions, contingent liabilities and contingent assets except: **c**

- those resulting from financial instruments that are carried at fair value
- those resulting from executory contracts, except where the contract is onerous
- those arising in insurance entities from contracts with policy-holders
- those covered by more specific requirements in another FRS or a SSAP.

RECOGNITION

Provisions

A provision should be recognised when an entity has a present obligation (legal or constructive) as a result of a past event, it is probable that a transfer of economic benefits will be required to settle the obligation, and a reliable estimate can be made of the amount of the obligation. Unless these conditions are met, no provision should be recognised. **d**

Present obligation

Where it is not clear whether a present obligation exists, a past event is deemed to give rise to a present obligation if, taking account of all available evidence, it is more likely than not that a present obligation exists at the balance sheet date. **e**

Past event

f For an event to be an obligating event, it is necessary that the entity has no realistic alternative to settling the obligation created by the event. This will be the case only where the settlement of the obligation can be enforced by law or, in the case of a constructive obligation, the event (which may be an action of the entity) creates valid expectations in other parties that the entity will discharge the obligation. The only liabilities recognised in an entity's balance sheet are those that exist at the balance sheet date. Where an entity can avoid future expenditure by its future actions, for example by changing its method of operation, it has no present liability for that future expenditure and no provision is recognised.

g An event that does not immediately give rise to an obligation may do so at a later date, because of changes in the law or because an act (for example, a sufficiently specific public statement) by the entity gives rise to a constructive obligation. Where details of a proposed new law have yet to be finalised, an obligation arises only when the legislation is virtually certain to be enacted as drafted.

Probable transfer of economic benefits

h For a liability to qualify for recognition there must be not only a present obligation but also the probability of a transfer of economic benefits to settle that obligation. A transfer of economic benefits in settlement of an obligation is regarded as probable if the outflow is more likely than not to occur. Where there are a number of similar obligations (eg product warranties or similar contracts) the probability that a transfer will be required in settlement is determined by considering the class of obligations as a whole.

Reliable estimate of the obligation

i An entity will normally be able to determine a range of possible outcomes and can therefore make an estimate of the obligation that is sufficiently reliable to use in recognising a provision. In the extremely rare case where no reliable estimate can be made, a liability exists that cannot be recognised. That liability is therefore disclosed as a contingent liability.

Contingent liabilities

j An entity should not recognise a contingent liability.

Contingent assets

k An entity should not recognise a contingent asset.

MEASUREMENT

Best estimate

l The amount recognised as a provision should be the best estimate of the expenditure required to settle the present obligation at the balance sheet date. The provision is measured before tax, as the tax consequences of the provision, and changes in it, are dealt with under FRS 19 'Deferred tax'.

Risks and uncertainties

The risks and uncertainties that inevitably surround many events and circumstances should be taken into account in reaching the best estimate of the amount of the provision. Care is needed to avoid duplicating adjustments for risk and uncertainty with consequent overstatement of a provision. **m**

Present value

Where the effect of the time value of money is material, the amount of a provision should be the present value of the expenditures expected to be required to settle the obligation. The discount rate (or rates) should be a pre-tax rate (or rates) that reflect(s) current market assessments of the time value of money and the risks specific to the liability. The discount rate(s) should not reflect risks for which future cash flow estimates have been adjusted. **n**

Future events

Future events that may affect the amount required to settle the entity's obligation should be reflected in the amount of a provision where there is sufficient objective evidence that they will occur. The effect of possible new legislation is taken into consideration in measuring an existing obligation when sufficient objective evidence exists that the legislation is virtually certain to be enacted. **o**

Expected disposal of assets

Gains from the expected disposal of assets should not be taken into account in measuring a provision. Instead such gains are assessed for recognition under the principles of asset recognition, which include the requirements in FRS 11 'Impairment of Fixed Assets and Goodwill'. **p**

REIMBURSEMENTS

Where some or all of the expenditure required to settle a provision is expected to be reimbursed by another party, the reimbursement should be recognised only when it is virtually certain that reimbursement will be received if the entity settles the obligation. The reimbursement should be treated as a separate asset. The amount recognised for the reimbursement should not exceed that of the provision. In the profit and loss account, the expense relating to a provision may be presented net of the amount recognised for a reimbursement. **q**

CHANGES IN PROVISIONS

Provisions should be reviewed at each balance sheet date and adjusted to reflect the current best estimate. If it is no longer probable that a transfer of economic benefits will be required to settle the obligation, the provision should be reversed. **r**

Where discounting is used, the size of a provision will change in each period to reflect the passage of time. This change is recognised as interest expense and disclosed separately from other interest on the face of the profit and loss account. **s**

USE OF PROVISIONS

t A provision should be used only for expenditures for which the provision was originally recognised.

DISCLOSURE

u For each class of provision, an entity should disclose:

- the carrying amount at the beginning and end of the period
- additional provisions made in the period, including increases to existing provisions
- amounts used (ie incurred and charged against the provision)
- amounts reversed unused
- the change in the discounted amount arising from the passage of time and the effect of any change in the discount rate.

Comparative information need not be disclosed for these items. In addition the entity should give:

(i) a brief description of the nature of the obligation, and the expected timing of any resulting outflows of economic benefits;
(ii) an indication of the uncertainties about the amount or timing of those outflows; and
(iii) the amount of any reimbursement, and of any asset that has been recognised for that expected reimbursement.

v Unless the possibility of any transfer in settlement is remote, for each class of contingent liability at the balance sheet date a brief description of the nature of the contingent liability should be disclosed and, where practicable, an estimate of its financial effect and an indication of the uncertainties relating to the amount or timing of any outflow. The entity should also disclose the possibility of any reimbursement.

w Where an inflow of economic benefits is probable, the entity should give a brief description of the nature of the contingent assets at the balance sheet date and, where practicable, an estimate of their financial effect.

x In extremely rare cases, disclosure of some or all of the information required can be expected to prejudice seriously the position of the entity in a dispute with other parties on the subject matter of the provision, contingent liability or contingent asset. In such cases the information need not be disclosed; but the general nature of the dispute should be disclosed, together with the fact that, and reason why, the information has not been disclosed.

Financial Reporting Standard 12

Objective

The objective of this FRS is to ensure that appropriate recognition criteria and measurement bases are applied to provisions, contingent liabilities and contingent assets and that sufficient information is disclosed in the notes to the financial statements to enable users to understand their nature, timing and amount. 1

Definitions

The following definitions shall apply in the FRS and in particular in the Statement of Standard Accounting Practice set out **in bold type.** 2

Constructive obligation:-

An obligation that derives from an entity's actions where:

(a) by an established pattern of past practice, published policies or a sufficiently specific current statement, the entity has indicated to other parties that it will accept certain responsibilities; and
(b) as a result, the entity has created a valid expectation on the part of those other parties that it will discharge those responsibilities.

Contingent asset:-

A possible asset that arises from past events and whose existence will be confirmed only by the occurrence of one or more uncertain future events not wholly within the entity's control.

Contingent liability:-

(a) A possible obligation that arises from past events and whose existence will be confirmed only by the occurrence of one or more uncertain future events not wholly within the entity's control; or
(b) a present obligation that arises from past events but is not recognised because:
    (i) it is not probable that a transfer of economic benefits will be required to settle the obligation; or
    (ii) the amount of the obligation cannot be measured with sufficient reliability.

Legal obligation:-

An obligation that derives from:

(a) a contract (through its explicit or implicit terms);
(b) legislation; or
(c) other operation of law.

Liabilities:-

Obligations of an entity to transfer economic benefits as a result of past transactions or events.

Obligating event:-

An event that creates a legal or constructive obligation that results in an entity having no realistic alternative to settling that obligation.

Onerous contract:-

A contract in which the unavoidable costs of meeting the obligations under it exceed the economic benefits expected to be received under it.

Provision:-

A liability of uncertain timing or amount.

Restructuring:-

A programme that is planned and controlled by management, and materially changes either:

(a) the scope of a business undertaken by an entity; or
(b) the manner in which that business is conducted.

SCOPE

3 **The FRS applies to all financial statements that are intended to give a true and fair view in accounting for provisions, contingent liabilities and contingent assets, except:**

(a) those resulting from financial instruments that are carried at fair value;
(b) those resulting from executory contracts, except where the contract is onerous;
(c) those arising in insurance entities from contracts with policy-holders; or
(d) those covered by another Standard.*

4 **Reporting entities applying the Financial Reporting Standard for Smaller Entities currently applicable are exempt from the FRS.**

***Editor's note:** *The text of FRS 12 has been amended by FRS 26, but only for those companies which are applying the measurement provisions of FRS 26. Where a company is applying FRS 26 then paragraph 3 reads as follows:*

This standard shall be applied by all entities in accounting for provisions, contingent liabilities and contingent assets, except:

(a) those resulting from executory contracts, except where the contract is onerous;
(b) those arising in insurance entities from contracts with policyholders, and
(c) those covered by another FRS or a Statement of Standard Accounting Practice (SSAP).

The FRS applies to financial instruments (including guarantees) that are not carried at fair value.* **5**

Executory contracts are contracts under which neither party has performed any of its obligations or both parties have partially performed their obligations to an equal extent. The FRS does not apply to executory contracts unless they are onerous. **6**

The FRS applies to provisions, contingent liabilities and contingent assets of insurance entities other than those arising from contracts with policy-holders. **7**

Where another FRS or a SSAP deals with a more specific type of provision, contingent liability or contingent asset, an entity applies that standard instead of this FRS. For example, certain types of provisions are also addressed in standards on: **8**

- long-term contracts (see SSAP 9 'Stocks and long-term contracts').
- deferred tax (see FRS 19 'Deferred tax').
- leases (see SSAP 21 'Accounting for leases and hire purchase contracts'). However, as SSAP 21 contains no specific requirements to deal with operating leases that have become onerous, the FRS applies to such cases.
- pension costs (see FRS 17 'Retirement Benefits').

The FRS defines provisions as liabilities of uncertain timing or amount. The term 'provision' is also used sometimes in the context of items such as depreciation, impairment of assets and doubtful debts: these are adjustments to the carrying amounts of assets and are not addressed in the FRS. **9**

The FRS applies to provisions for restructuring (including discontinued operations). Where a restructuring meets the definition of a discontinued operation, additional disclosures may be required by FRS 3 'Reporting Financial Performance'. **10**

PROVISIONS AND OTHER LIABILITIES

Provisions can be distinguished from other liabilities such as trade creditors and accruals because there is uncertainty about the timing or amount of the future expenditure required in settlement. By contrast: **11**

(a) trade creditors are liabilities to pay for goods or services that have been received or supplied and have been invoiced or formally agreed with the supplier; and

(b) accruals are liabilities to pay for goods or services that have been received or supplied but have not been paid, invoiced or formally agreed with the supplier, including amounts due to employees (for example amounts relating to accrued holiday pay). Although it is sometimes necessary to estimate the amount or timing of accruals, the uncertainty is generally much less than for provisions.

Accruals are often reported as part of trade and other creditors, whereas provisions are reported separately.

*****Editor's note:*** *The text of FRS 12 has been amended by FRS 26, but only for those companies which are applying the measurement provisions of FRS 26. Where a company is applying FRS 26 then paragraph 5 reads as follows:*

This standard does not apply to financial instruments (including guarantees) that are within the scope of FRS 26 (IAS 39) *Financial Instruments: Measurement*. For financial guarantees excluded from the scope of FRS 26, this Standard applies as set out in paragraph 2(f) of FRS 26.

RELATIONSHIP BETWEEN PROVISIONS AND CONTINGENT LIABILITIES

12 In a general sense, all provisions are contingent because they are uncertain in timing or amount. However, in the FRS the term 'contingent' is used for liabilities and assets that are not recognised because their existence will be confirmed only by the occurrence of one or more uncertain future events not wholly within the entity's control. In addition, the term 'contingent liability' is used for liabilities that do not meet the recognition criteria.

13 The FRS distinguishes between:

(a) provisions – which are recognised as liabilities (assuming that a reliable estimate can be made) because they are present obligations where it is probable that a transfer of economic benefits will be required to settle the obligations; and

(b) contingent liabilities – which are not recognised as liabilities because they are either:

   (i) possible obligations, as it has yet to be confirmed whether the entity has an obligation that could lead to a transfer of economic benefits; or

   (ii) present obligations that do not meet the recognition criteria in the FRS because either it is not probable that a transfer of economic benefits will be required to settle the obligation, or a sufficiently reliable estimate of the amount of the obligation cannot be made.

RECOGNITION

Provisions

14 **A provision should be recognised when:**

(a) an entity has a present obligation (legal or constructive) as a result of a past event;

(b) it is probable that a transfer of economic benefits will be required to settle the obligation; and

(c) a reliable estimate can be made of the amount of the obligation.

If these conditions are not met, no provision should be recognised.

Present obligation

15 **In rare cases it is not clear whether there is a present obligation. In these cases, a past event is deemed to give rise to a present obligation if, taking account of all available evidence, it is more likely than not that a present obligation exists at the balance sheet date.**

16 In almost all cases it will be clear whether a past event has given rise to a present obligation. In rare cases, for example in a lawsuit, it may be disputed whether certain events have occurred or whether those events result in a present obligation. In such a case, an entity determines whether a present obligation exists at the balance sheet date by taking account of all available evidence, including, for example, the opinion of experts. The evidence considered includes any additional evidence provided by events occurring after the balance sheet date. On the basis of such evidence:

(a) where it is more likely than not that a present obligation exists at the balance sheet date, the entity recognises a provision (if the recognition criteria are met); and

(b) where it is more likely that no present obligation exists at the balance sheet date, the entity discloses a contingent liability, unless the possibility of a transfer of economic resources is remote (see paragraph 91).

Past event

A past event that leads to a present obligation is called an obligating event. For an event to be an obligating event, it is necessary that the entity has no realistic alternative to settling the obligation created by the event. This is the case only: **17**

(a) where the settlement of the obligation can be enforced by law; or
(b) in the case of a constructive obligation, where the event (which may be an action of the entity) creates valid expectations in other parties that the entity will discharge the obligation.

Financial statements deal with the financial position of an entity at the end of its reporting period and not its possible position in the future. Therefore no provision is recognised for costs that need to be incurred to operate in the future. The only liabilities recognised in an entity's balance sheet are those that exist at the balance sheet date. **18**

It is only those obligations arising from past events existing independently of an entity's future actions (ie the future conduct of its business) that are recognised as provisions. Examples of such obligations are penalties or clean-up costs for unlawful environmental damage, both of which would lead to a transfer of economic benefits in settlement regardless of the future actions of the entity. Similarly, an entity recognises a provision for the decommissioning costs of an oil installation or a nuclear power station to the extent that the entity is obliged to rectify damage already caused. In contrast, because of commercial pressures or legal requirements, an entity may intend or need to carry out expenditure to operate in a particular way in the future (for example, by fitting smoke filters in a certain type of factory). Because the entity can avoid the future expenditure by its future actions, for example by changing its method of operation, it has no present obligation for that future expenditure and no provision is recognised. **19**

An obligation always involves another party to whom the obligation is owed. It is not necessary, however, to know the identity of the party to whom the obligation is owed – indeed the obligation may be to the public at large. Because an obligation always involves a commitment to another party, it follows that a management or board decision does not give rise to a constructive obligation at the balance sheet date unless the decision has been communicated before the balance sheet date to those affected by it in a sufficiently specific manner to raise a valid expectation in them that the entity will discharge its responsibilities. **20**

An event that does not give rise to an obligation immediately may do so at a later date, because of changes in the law or because an act (for example, a sufficiently specific public statement) by the entity gives rise to a constructive obligation. For example, when environmental damage is caused there may be no obligation to remedy the consequences. However, the causing of the damage will become an obligating event when a new law requires the existing damage to be rectified or when the entity publicly accepts responsibility for rectification in a way that creates a constructive obligation. **21**

Where details of a proposed new law have yet to be finalised, an obligation arises only when the legislation is virtually certain to be enacted as drafted. For the purposes of the FRS, such an obligation is treated as a legal obligation. Differences in **22** circumstances surrounding enactment make it impossible to specify a single event that would make the enactment of a law virtually certain. In many cases it will be impossible to be virtually certain of the enactment of a law until it is enacted.

Probable transfer of economic benefits

23 For a liability to qualify for recognition there must be not only a present obligation but also the probability of a transfer of economic benefits to settle that obligation. For the purpose of the FRS, a transfer of economic benefits or other event is regarded as probable if the event is more likely than not to occur, ie the probability that the event will occur is greater than the probability that it will not. Where it is not probable that a present obligation exists, an entity discloses a contingent liability, unless the possibility of a transfer of economic resources is remote (see paragraph 91).

24 Where there are a number of similar obligations (eg product warranties or similar contracts) the probability that a transfer will be required in settlement is determined by considering the class of obligations as a whole. Although the likelihood of outflow for any one item may be small, it may well be probable that some transfer of economic benefits will be needed to settle the class of obligations as a whole. If that is the case, a provision is recognised (if the other recognition criteria are met).

Reliable estimate of the obligation

25 The use of estimates is an essential part of the preparation of financial statements and does not undermine their reliability. This is especially true in the case of provisions, which by their nature are more uncertain than most other balance sheet items. Except in extremely rare cases, an entity will be able to determine a range of possible outcomes and can therefore make an estimate of the obligation that is sufficiently reliable to use in recognising a provision.

26 In the extremely rare case where no reliable estimate can be made, a liability exists that cannot be recognised. That liability is disclosed as a contingent liability (see paragraph 91).

Contingent liabilities

27 **An entity should not recognise a contingent liability.**

28 A contingent liability is disclosed, as required by paragraph 91, unless the possibility of a transfer of economic benefits is remote.

29 Where an entity is jointly and severally liable for an obligation, the part of the obligation that is expected to be met by other parties is treated as a contingent liability. The entity recognises a provision for the part of the obligation for which a transfer of economic benefits is probable (except in the extremely rare circumstances where no reliable estimate can be made).

30 Contingent liabilities may develop in a way not initially expected. Therefore, they are assessed continually to determine whether a transfer of economic benefits has become probable. If it becomes probable that a transfer of future economic benefits will be required for an item previously dealt with as a contingent liability, a provision is recognised in the financial statements of the period in which the change in probability occurs (except in the extremely rare circumstances where no reliable estimate can be made).

Contingent assets

An entity should not recognise a contingent asset. 31

Contingent assets usually arise from unplanned or other unexpected events that give rise to the possibility of an inflow of economic benefits to the entity. An example is a claim that an entity is pursuing through legal processes, where the outcome is uncertain. 32

Contingent assets are not recognised in financial statements because it could result in the recognition of profit that may never be realised. However, when the realisation of the profit is virtually certain, then the related asset is not a contingent asset and its recognition is appropriate. 33

A contingent asset is disclosed, as required by paragraph 94, where an inflow of economic benefits is probable. 34

Contingent assets are assessed continually to ensure that developments are appropriately reflected in the financial statements. If it has become virtually certain that an inflow of economic benefits will arise, the asset and the related profit are recognised in the financial statements of the period in which the change occurs. If an inflow of economic benefits has become probable, an entity discloses the contingent asset (see paragraph 94). 35

MEASUREMENT

Best estimate

The amount recognised as a provision should be the best estimate of the expenditure required to settle the present obligation at the balance sheet date. 36

The best estimate of the expenditure required to settle the present obligation is the amount that an entity would rationally pay to settle the obligation at the balance sheet date or to transfer it to a third party at that time. It will often be impossible or prohibitively expensive to settle or transfer an obligation at the balance sheet date. However, the estimate of the amount that an entity would rationally pay to settle or transfer the obligation gives the best estimate of the expenditure required to settle the present obligation at the balance sheet date. 37

The estimates of outcome and financial effect are determined by the judgement of the entity's management, supplemented by experience of similar transactions and, in some cases, reports from independent experts. The evidence considered will include any additional evidence provided by events after the balance sheet date. 38

Uncertainties surrounding the amount to be recognised as a provision are dealt with by various means according to the circumstances. Where the provision being measured involves a large population of items, the obligation is estimated by weighting all possible outcomes by their associated probabilities. The name for this statistical method of estimation is 'expected value'. The provision will therefore be different depending on whether the probability of a loss of a given amount is, for example, 60 per cent or 90 per cent. Where there is a continuous range of possible outcomes, and each point in that range is as likely as any other, the mid-point of the range is used. 39

> **Example**
>
> An entity sells goods with a warranty under which customers are covered for the cost of repairs of any manufacturing defects that become apparent within the first six months after purchase. If minor defects were detected in all products sold, repair costs of £1 million would result. If major defects were detected in all products sold, repair costs of £4 million would result. The entity's past experience and future expectations indicate that, for the coming year, 75 per cent of the goods sold will have no defects, 20 per cent of the goods sold will have minor defects and 5 per cent of the goods sold will have major defects. In accordance with paragraph 24 an entity assesses the probability of a transfer for the warranty obligations as a whole.
>
> The expected value of the cost of repairs is:
> (75% of nil) + (20% of £1m) + (5% of £4m) = £400,000

40 Where a single obligation is being measured, the individual most likely outcome may be the best estimate of the liability. However, even in such a case, the entity considers other possible outcomes. Where other possible outcomes are either mostly higher or mostly lower than the most likely outcome, the best estimate will be a higher or lower amount. For example, if an entity has to rectify a serious fault in a major plant that it has constructed for a customer, the individual most likely outcome may be for the repair to succeed at the first attempt at a cost of £1 million but a provision for a larger amount is made if there is a significant chance that further attempts will be necessary.

41 The provision is measured before tax, as the tax consequences of the provision, and changes in it, are dealt with under FRS 19 'Deferred tax'.

Risks and uncertainties

42 **The risks and uncertainties that inevitably surround many events and circumstances should be taken into account in reaching the best estimate of a provision.**

43 Risk describes variability of outcome. A risk adjustment may increase the amount at which a liability is measured. Caution is needed in making judgements under conditions of uncertainty, so that profit or assets are not overstated and expenses or liabilities are not understated. However, uncertainty does not justify the creation of excessive provisions or a deliberate overstatement of liabilities. For example, if the projected costs of a particularly adverse outcome are estimated on a prudent basis, that outcome is not then deliberately treated as more probable than is realistically the case. Care is needed to avoid duplicating adjustments for risk and uncertainty with consequent overstatement of a provision.

44 Disclosure of the uncertainties surrounding the amount of the expenditure is made under paragraph 90(b).

Present value

45 **Where the effect of the time value of money is material, the amount of a provision should be the present value of the expenditures expected to be required to settle the obligation.**

Because of the time value of money, provisions relating to cash outflows that arise soon after the balance sheet date are more onerous than those where cash outflows of the same amount arise later. Provisions are therefore discounted, where the effect is material. 46

The discount rate (or rates) should be a pre-tax rate (or rates) that reflect(s) current market assessments of the time value of money and the risks specific to the liability. The discount rate(s) should not reflect risks for which future cash flow estimates have been adjusted. 47

The unwinding of the discount should be included as other finance costs adjacent to interest.* 48

Using a discount rate that reflects current market assessments of the time value of money and the risks specific to the liability is a method of reflecting the risk associated with the cash flows in the present value calculation. It is likely that this method will be the easiest method of reflecting risk. However, an acceptable alternative is to adjust the cash flows for risk and to discount them using a risk-free rate (eg a government bond rate). Whichever method of reflecting risk is adopted, care must be taken that the effect of risk is not double-counted by inclusion in both the cash flows and the discount rate. 49

If the cash flows to be discounted are expressed in current prices, a real discount rate will be used. If the cash flows are expressed in expected future prices, a nominal discount rate will be used. 50

Future events

Future events that may affect the amount required to settle an obligation should be reflected in the amount of a provision where there is sufficient objective evidence that they will occur. 51

Expected future events may be particularly important in measuring provisions. For example, an entity may believe that the cost of cleaning up a site at the end of its life will be reduced by future changes in technology. The amount recognised reflects a reasonable expectation of technically qualified, objective observers, taking account of all available evidence as to the technology that will be available at the time of the clean-up. Thus it is appropriate to include, for example, expected cost reductions associated with increased experience in applying existing technology or the expected cost of applying existing technology to a larger or more complex clean-up operation than has previously been carried out. However, an entity does not anticipate the development of a completely new technology for cleaning up unless it is supported by sufficient objective evidence. 52

The effect of possible new legislation is taken into consideration in measuring an existing obligation when sufficient objective evidence exists that the legislation is virtually certain to be enacted. The variety of circumstances that arise in practice makes it impossible to specify a single event that will provide sufficient, objective *evidence in every case. Evidence* is required both of what legislation will demand and of whether it is virtually certain to be enacted and implemented in due course. In many cases sufficient objective evidence will not exist until the new legislation is enacted. 53

****Editor's note:*** *Paragraph amended by FRS 17.*

Expected disposal of assets

54 **Gains from the expected disposal of assets should not be taken into account in measuring a provision.**

55 Gains on the expected disposal of assets are not taken into account in measuring a provision, even if the expected disposal is closely linked to the event giving rise to the provision. Instead, an entity assesses such gains for recognition under the principles of asset recognition, which include the requirements in FRS 11 'Impairment of Fixed Assets and Goodwill'.

Reimbursements

56 **Where some or all of the expenditure required to settle a provision is expected to be reimbursed by another party, the reimbursement should be recognised only when it is virtually certain that reimbursement will be received if the entity settles the obligation. The reimbursement should be treated as a separate asset. The amount recognised for the reimbursement should not exceed the amount of the provision.**

57 **In the profit and loss account, the expense relating to a provision may be presented net of the amount recognised for a reimbursement.**

58 Sometimes, an entity is able to look to another party to pay part or all of the expenditure required to settle a provision (for example, through insurance contracts, indemnity clauses or suppliers' warranties). The other party may either reimburse amounts paid by the entity or pay the amounts directly.

59 In most cases, the entity will remain liable for the whole of the amount in question so that the entity would have to settle the full amount if the third party failed to pay for any reason. In this situation, a provision is recognised for the full amount of the liability, and a separate asset for the expected reimbursement is recognised when it is virtually certain that reimbursement will be received if the entity settles the liability.

60 In some cases the entity will not be liable for the costs in question if the third party fails to pay. In such a case the entity has no liability for those costs and they are not included in the provision.

61 As noted in paragraph 29, an obligation for which an entity is jointly and severally liable is a contingent liability to the extent that it is expected that the obligation will be settled by the other parties.

CHANGES IN PROVISIONS

62 **Provisions should be reviewed at each balance sheet date and adjusted to reflect the current best estimate. If it is no longer probable that a transfer of economic benefits will be required to settle the obligation, the provision should be reversed.**

63 Where discounting is used, the carrying amount of a provision increases in each period to reflect the passage of time. As required in paragraph 48, this increase is recognised as an interest expense.

USE OF PROVISIONS

64 **A provision should be used only for expenditures for which the provision was originally recognised.**

Only expenditures that relate to the original provision are set against it. Setting expenditures against a provision that was originally recognised for another purpose would conceal the impact of two different events. 65

RECOGNISING AN ASSET WHEN RECOGNISING A PROVISION

When a provision or a change in a provision is recognised, an asset should also be recognised when, and only when, the incurring of the present obligation recognised as a provision gives access to future economic benefits; otherwise the setting up of the provision should be charged immediately to the profit and loss account. 66

Where a provision is recognised for a present obligation that has been incurred to gain rights or other access to future economic benefits that are to be enjoyed over more than one period, the part of the provision incurred that relates to such future benefits is capitalised. For example, an obligation for decommissioning costs is incurred by commissioning an oil rig but the commissioning also gives access to oil reserves over the years of the oil rig's operation – an asset representing future access to oil reserves is therefore recognised at the same time as the provision for decommissioning costs. 67

APPLICATION OF THE RECOGNITION AND MEASUREMENT RULES

Future operating losses

Provisions should not be recognised for future operating losses. 68

Future operating losses do not meet the definition of a liability in paragraph 2 and the general recognition criteria set out for provisions in paragraph 14. 69

An expectation of future operating losses is an indication that certain assets of the operation may be impaired. An entity tests these assets for impairment under FRS 11. 70

Onerous contracts

If an entity has a contract that is onerous, the present obligation under the contract should be recognised and measured as a provision. 71

Many contracts (for example, some routine purchase orders) can be cancelled without paying compensation to the other party, and therefore there is no obligation. Other contracts establish both rights and obligations for each of the contracting parties. Where events make such a contract onerous, the contract falls within the scope of the FRS and a liability exists which is recognised. Executory contracts that are not onerous fall outside the scope of the FRS. 72

The FRS defines an onerous contract as a contract in which the unavoidable costs of meeting the obligations under it exceed the economic benefits expected to be received under it. The unavoidable costs under a contract reflect the least net cost of exiting from the contract, ie the lower of the cost of fulfilling it and any compensation or penalties arising from failure to fulfil it. 73

Before a separate provision for an onerous contract is established, an entity recognises any impairment loss that has occurred on assets dedicated to that contract. 74

Restructuring

75 The following are examples of events that may fall under the definition of restructuring:

(a) sale or termination of a line of business;
(b) the closure of business locations in a country or region or the relocation of business activities from one country or region to another;
(c) changes in management structure, for example, eliminating a layer of management; and
(d) fundamental reorganisations that have a material effect on the nature and focus of the entity's operations.

76 A provision for restructuring costs is recognised only when the general recognition criteria for provisions set out in paragraph 14 are met. Paragraphs 77-88 set out how those criteria apply to restructurings.

77 **A constructive obligation to restructure arises only when an entity:**

(a) has a detailed formal plan for the restructuring identifying at least:

(i) the business or part of a business concerned;
(ii) the principal locations affected;
(iii) the location, function, and approximate number of employees who will be compensated for terminating their services;
(iv) the expenditures that will be undertaken; and
(v) when the plan will be implemented; and

(b) has raised a valid expectation in those affected that it will carry out the restructuring by starting to implement that plan or announcing its main features to those affected by it.

78 Evidence that an entity has started to implement a restructuring plan would be provided, for example, by dismantling plant or selling assets or by the public announcement of the main features of the plan. A public announcement of a detailed plan to restructure constitutes a constructive obligation to restructure only if it is made in such a way and in sufficient detail (ie setting out the main features of the plan) that it gives rise to valid expectations in other parties such as customers, suppliers and employees (or their representatives) that the entity will carry out the restructuring.

79 For a plan to be sufficient to give rise to a constructive obligation when communicated to those affected by it, its implementation needs to be planned to begin as soon as possible and to be completed in a timeframe that makes significant changes to the plan unlikely. If it is expected that there will be a long delay before the restructuring begins or that the restructuring will take an unreasonably long time, it is unlikely that the plan will raise a valid expectation on the part of others that the entity is at present committed to restructuring, because the timeframe allows opportunities for the entity to change its plans.

80 A management or board decision to restructure taken before the balance sheet date does not give rise to a constructive obligation at the balance sheet date unless the entity has, before the balance sheet date:

(a) started to implement the restructuring plan; or
(b) announced the main features of the restructuring plan to those affected by it in a sufficiently specific manner to raise a valid expectation in them that the entity will carry out the restructuring.

If an entity starts to implement the restructuring plan, or announces its main features to those affected, only after the balance sheet date, disclosure is required under FRS 21, *Events after the Balance Sheet Date*, if the restructuring is material and non-disclosure could influence the economic decisions of users taken on the basis of the financial statements.*

Although a constructive obligation is not created solely by a management decision, an obligation may result from other earlier events together with such a decision. For example, negotiations with employee representatives for termination payments, or with purchasers for the sale of an operation, may have been concluded subject only to board approval. Once that approval has been obtained and communicated to the other parties, the entity has a constructive obligation to restructure, if the conditions of paragraph 77 are met. **81**

In some countries the ultimate authority is vested in a board whose membership includes representatives of interests other than management (eg employees); alternatively, notification to such representatives may be necessary before the board decision is taken. Because a decision by the board in these circumstances involves communication to these representatives, it may result in a constructive obligation to restructure. **82**

No obligation arises for the sale of an operation until the entity is committed to the sale, ie there is a binding sale agreement. **83**

Even when an entity has taken a decision to sell an operation and announced that decision publicly, it cannot be committed to the sale until a purchaser has been identified and there is a binding sale agreement. Until there is such an agreement, the entity will be able to change its mind and indeed will have to take another course of action if a purchaser cannot be found on acceptable terms. When the sale of an operation is envisaged as part of a restructuring, the assets of the operation are reviewed for impairment, under FRS 11. When a sale is only part of a restructuring, a constructive obligation can arise for the other parts of the restructuring before a binding sale agreement exists. **84**

A restructuring provision should include only the direct expenditures arising from the restructuring, which are those that are both: **85**

(a) necessarily entailed by the restructuring and
(b) not associated with the ongoing activities of the entity.

A restructuring provision does not include such costs as: **86**
(a) retraining or relocating continuing staff;
(b) marketing; or
(c) investment in new systems and distribution networks.

These expenditures relate to the future conduct of the business and are not liabilities for restructuring at the balance sheet date. Such expenditures are recognised on the same basis as if they arose independently of a restructuring.

Identifiable future operating losses up to the date of a restructuring are not included in a provision, unless they relate to an onerous contract as defined in paragraph 2. **87**

****Editor's note:*** *Last section of paragraph amended by FRS 21.*

88 As required by paragraph 54, gains on the expected disposal of assets are not taken into account in measuring a restructuring provision, even if the sale of assets is envisaged as part of the restructuring.

DISCLOSURE

89 **For each class of provision, an entity should disclose:**

(a) the carrying amount at the beginning and end of the period;
(b) additional provisions made in the period, including increases to existing provisions;
(c) amounts used (ie incurred and charged against the provision) during the period;
(d) unused amounts reversed during the period; and
(e) the increase during the period in the discounted amount arising from the passage of time and the effect of any change in the discount rate.

Comparative information is not required.

90 **An entity should disclose the following for each class of provision:**

(a) a brief description of the nature of the obligation, and the expected timing of any resulting transfers of economic benefits;
(b) an indication of the uncertainties about the amount or timing of those transfers of economic benefits. Where necessary to provide adequate information, an entity should disclose the major assumptions made concerning future events, as addressed in paragraph 51; and
(c) the amount of any expected reimbursement, stating the amount of any asset that has been recognised for that expected reimbursement.

91 **Unless the possibility of any transfer in settlement is remote, an entity should disclose for each class of contingent liability at the balance sheet date a brief description of the nature of the contingent liability and, where practicable:**

(a) an estimate of its financial effect, measured in accordance with paragraphs 36-55;
(b) an indication of the uncertainties relating to the amount or timing of any outflow; and
(c) the possibility of any reimbursement.

92 In determining which provisions or contingent liabilities may be aggregated to form a class, it is necessary to consider whether the nature of the items is sufficiently similar for a single statement about them to fulfil the requirements of paragraph 90(a) and (b) or 91(a) and (b). Thus it may be appropriate to treat as a single class of provision amounts relating to warranties of different products, but it would not be appropriate to treat as a single class amounts relating to normal warranties and amounts that are subject to legal proceedings.

93 Where a provision and a contingent liability arise from the same set of circumstances, an entity makes the disclosures required by paragraphs 89–91 in a way that shows the link between the provision and the contingent liability.

94 **Where an inflow of economic benefits is probable, an entity should disclose a brief description of the nature of the contingent assets at the balance sheet date and, where practicable, an estimate of their financial effect, measured using the principles set out for provisions in paragraphs 36-55.**

95 It is important that disclosures for contingent assets avoid giving misleading indications of the likelihood of a profit arising.

Where any of the information required by paragraphs 91 and 94 is not disclosed because it is not practicable to do so, that fact should be stated. 96

In extremely rare cases, disclosure of some or all of the information required by paragraphs 89-94 can be expected to prejudice seriously the position of the entity in a dispute with other parties on the subject matter of the provision, contingent liability or contingent asset. In such cases an entity need not disclose the information, unless its disclosure is required by law; but should disclose the general nature of the dispute, together with the fact that, and reason why, the information has not been disclosed. 97

DATE FROM WHICH EFFECTIVE

The accounting practices set out in the FRS should be regarded as standard in respect of financial statements relating to accounting periods ending on or after 23 March 1999. Earlier adoption is encouraged but not required. 98

WITHDRAWAL OF SSAP 18 AND AMENDMENT OF FRS 3

The FRS supersedes SSAP 18 'Accounting for contingencies'. 99

In FRS 3 'Reporting Financial Performance' paragraph 18 is amended as follows: 100

[*Not reproduced as it has been reflected in FRS 3 reproduced in this volume.*]

APPLICATION OF THE NEW REQUIREMENTS

Changes in accounting policy arising from the initial application of the FRS should be dealt with as prior period adjustments in accordance with FRS 3 (paragraphs 7, 29 and 62). Corrections of accounting estimates should be dealt with in the profit and loss account of the period of initial application, and their effect stated where material (FRS 3, paragraph 60). 101

The initial application of the FRS will in some circumstances entail a change in accounting policy, and, in other cases, a correction of accounting estimate. For example, where no provision was previously recognised for decommissioning costs but the FRS requires that a provision is recognised, or where a provision was previously recognised that is not permitted by the FRS (for example, a provision for self-insurance), the application of the recognition principles set out in the FRS is a change in accounting policy. In contrast, where, for example, an entity already provides for its warranties but the initial application of the FRS causes the provision to be measured at a different amount, the change is a change in accounting estimate. 102

Adoption of FRS 12 by the Board

Financial Reporting Standard 12 – 'Provisions, Contingent Liabilities and Contingent Assets' was approved for issue by the ten members of the Accounting Standards Board.

Sir David Tweedie	(Chairman)
Allan Cook	(Technical Director)
David Allvey	
Ian Brindle	
Dr John Buchanan	
John Coombe	
Raymond Hinton	
Huw Jones	
Professor Geoffrey Whittington	
Ken Wild	

Appendix I
Tables: main requirements of the FRS

This appendix summarises the main requirements of the FRS. It does not form part of the FRS and should be read in the context of the full text.

Provisions and contingent liabilities

Where, as a result of past events, there may be a transfer of future economic benefits in settlement of (a) a present obligation or (b) a possible obligation whose existence will be confirmed by the occurrence of one or more uncertain future events not wholly within the entity's control, and		
there is a present obligation that probably requires a transfer of economic benefits in settlement,	**there is a possible obligation or a present obligation that may, but probably will not, require a transfer of economic benefits in settlement,**	**there is a possible obligation or a present obligation where the likelihood of a transfer of economic benefits in settlement is remote,**
a provision is recognised (paragraph 14); and disclosures are required for the provision (paragraphs 89 and 90).	no provision is recognised (paragraph 27); but disclosures are required for the contingent liability (paragraph 91).	no provision is recognised (paragraph 27); and no disclosure is required (paragraph 91).

A contingent liability also arises in the extremely rare case where there is a liability that cannot be recognised because it cannot be measured reliably (paragraph 2). Disclosures are required for the contingent liability (paragraph 91).

Contingent assets

Where, as a result of past events, there is a possible asset whose existence will be confirmed by the occurrence of one or more uncertain future events not wholly within the entity's control, and		
the inflow of economic benefits is virtually certain,	**the inflow of economic benefits is probably but not virtually certain,**	**the inflow is not probable,**
the asset is not contingent (paragraph 33).	no asset is recognised (paragraph 31); but disclosures are required (paragraph 94).	no asset is recognised (paragraph 31); and no disclosure is required (paragraph 94).

Reimbursements

Where some or all of the expenditure required to settle a provision is expected to be reimbursed by another party, and		
the entity has no obligation for the part of the expenditure to be reimbursed by the other party,	**the obligation for the amount expected to be reimbursed remains with the entity and it is virtually certain that reimbursement will be received if the entity settles the provision,**	**the obligation for the amount expected to be reimbursed remains with the entity and the reimbursement is not virtually certain if the entity settles the provision,**
the entity has no liability for the amount to be reimbursed (paragraph 60); and no disclosure is required.	the reimbursement is recognised as a separate asset in the balance sheet and may be offset against the charge in the profit and loss account. The amount recognised for the expected reimbursement does not exceed the liability (paragraphs 56 and 57); and the reimbursement is disclosed together with the amount recognised for the reimbursement (paragraph 90(c)).	the expected reimbursement is not recognised as an asset (paragraph 56); but the expected reimbursement is disclosed (paragraph 90(c)).

Appendix II
Decision Tree

This appendix summarises the main requirements of the FRS. It does not form part of the FRS and should be read in the context of the full text.

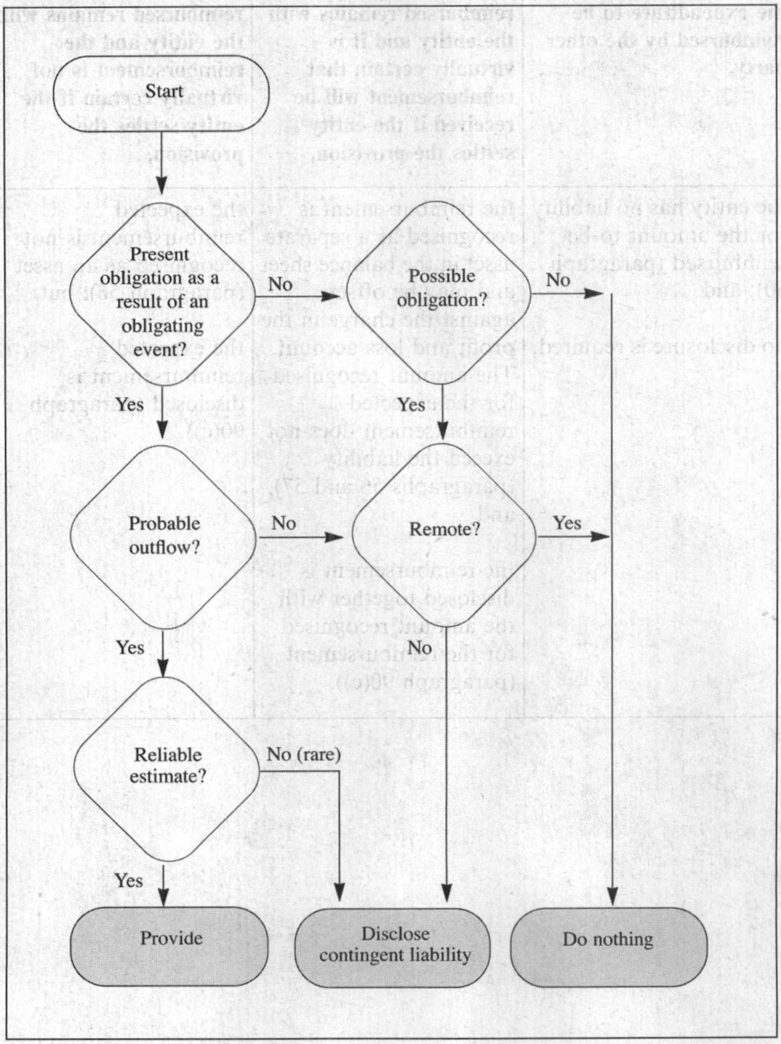

Note: in rare cases it is not clear whether there is a present obligation. In these cases, a past event is deemed to give rise to a present obligation if, taking account of all available evidence, it is more likely than not that a present obligation exists at the balance sheet date (see paragraph 15).

Appendix III
Examples: Recognition

This appendix illustrates the application of the FRS to assist in clarifying its meaning. It does not form part of the FRS.

All the entities in the examples have 31 December year-ends. In all cases it is assumed that a reliable estimate can be made of any outflows expected. In some examples the circumstances described may have resulted in impairment of the assets – this aspect is not dealt with in the examples.

The cross-references in the examples are to paragraphs of the FRS that are particularly relevant. The appendix should be read in the context of the full text of the FRS.

References to 'best estimate' are to the present value amount where the effect of the time value of money is material.

Example 1:

Warranties

A manufacturer gives warranties at the time of sale to purchasers of its product. Under the terms of the contract for sale the manufacturer undertakes to make good, by repair or replacement, manufacturing defects that become apparent within three years from the date of sale. On past experience, it is probable (ie more likely than not) that there will be some claims under the warranties.

Present obligation as a result of a past obligating event – The obligating event is the sale of the product with a warranty, which gives rise to a legal obligation.

Transfer of economic benefits in settlement – Probable for the warranties as a whole (see paragraph 24).

Conclusion – A provision is recognised for the best estimate of the costs of making good under the warranty products sold before the balance sheet date (see paragraphs 14 and 24).

Example 2A:

Contaminated land - legislation virtually certain to be enacted

An entity in the oil industry causes contamination but cleans up only when required to do so under the laws of the particular country in which it operates. One country in which it operates has had no legislation requiring cleaning up, and the entity has been contaminating land in that country for several years. At 31 December it is virtually certain that a draft law requiring a clean-up of land already contaminated will be enacted shortly after the year-end.

Present obligation as a result of a past obligating event – The obligating event is the contamination of the land because of the virtual certainty of legislation requiring cleaning up.

Transfer of economic benefits in settlement – Probable.

Conclusion – A provision is recognised for the best estimate of the costs of the clean-up (see paragraphs 14 and 22).

Example 2B:

Contaminated land and constructive obligation

An entity in the oil industry causes contamination and operates in a country where there is no environmental legislation. However, the entity has a widely published environmental policy in which it undertakes to clean up all contamination that it causes. The entity has a record of honouring this published policy.

Present obligation as a result of a past obligating event – The obligating event is the contamination of the land, which gives rise to a constructive obligation because the conduct of the entity has created a valid expectation on the part of those affected by it that the entity will clean up contamination.

Transfer of economic benefits in settlement – Probable.

Conclusion – A provision is recognised for the best estimate of the costs of clean-up (see paragraphs 2 (the definition of a constructive obligation), 14 and 17).

Example 3:

Offshore oilfield

An entity operates an offshore oilfield where its licensing agreement requires it to remove the oil rig at the end of production and restore the seabed. Ninety per cent of the eventual costs of undertaking this work relate to the removal of the oil rig and restoration of damage caused by building it, and ten per cent arise through the extraction of oil. At the balance sheet date, the rig has been constructed but no oil has been extracted.

Present obligation as a result of a past obligating event – The construction of the oil rig creates a legal obligation under the terms of the licence to remove the rig and restore the seabed and is thus an obligating event. At the balance sheet date, however, there is no obligation to rectify the damage that will be caused by extraction of the oil.

Transfer of economic benefits in settlement – Probable.

Conclusion – A provision is recognised for the best estimate of the ninety per cent of the eventual costs that relate to the removal of the oil rig and restoration of damage caused by building it (see paragraphs 17-19). These costs are included as part of the cost of the oil rig. The ten per cent of costs that arise through the extraction of oil are recognised as a liability when the oil is extracted.

Example 4:

Refunds policy

A retail store has a policy of refunding purchases by dissatisfied customers, even though it is under no legal obligation to do so. Its policy of making refunds is generally known.

Present obligation as a result of a past obligating event – The obligating event is the sale of the product, which gives rise to a constructive obligation because the conduct of the store has created a valid expectation on the part of its customers that the store will refund purchases.

Transfer of economic benefits in settlement – Probable, as a proportion of goods are returned for refund (see paragraph 24).

Conclusion – A provision is recognised for the best estimate of the costs of refunds (see paragraphs 2 (the definition of a constructive obligation), 14, 17 and 24).

Example 5A:

Closure of a division – no implementation before balance sheet date

On 12 December 2000 the board of an entity decided to close down a division. Before the balance sheet date (31 December 2000) the decision was not communicated to any of those affected and no other steps were taken to implement the decision.

Present obligation as a result of a past obligating event – There has been no obligating event and so there is no obligation.

Conclusion – No provision is recognised (see paragraphs 14 and 77).

Example 5B:

Closure of a division – communication/implementation before balance sheet date

On 12 December 2000 the board of an entity decided to close down a division making a particular product. On 20 December 2000 a detailed plan for closing down the division was agreed by the board; letters were sent to customers warning them to seek an alternative source of supply and redundancy notices were sent to the staff of the division.

Present obligation as a result of a past obligating event – The obligating event is the communication of the decision to the customers and employees, which gives rise to a constructive obligation from that date because it creates a valid expectation that the division will be closed.

Transfer of economic benefits in settlement – Probable.

Conclusion – A provision is recognised at 31 December 2000 for the best estimate of the costs of closing the division (see paragraphs 14 and 77).

Example 6:

Legal requirement to fit smoke filters

Under new legislation, an entity is required to fit smoke filters to its factories by 30 June 2000. The entity has not fitted the smoke filters.

(a) At the balance sheet date of 31 December 1999

Present obligation as a result of a past obligating event – There is no obligation because there is no obligating event either for the costs of fitting smoke filters or for fines under the legislation.

Conclusion – No provision is recognised for the cost of fitting the smoke filters (see paragraphs 14, 17 and 18).

(b) At the balance sheet date of 31 December 2000

Present obligation as a result of a past obligating event – There is still no obligation for the costs of fitting smoke filters because no obligating event (the fitting of the filters) has occurred. However, an obligation might arise to pay fines or penalties under the legislation because the obligating event has occurred (the non-compliant operation of the factory).

Transfer of economic benefits in settlement – Assessment of probability of incurring fines and penalties by non-compliant operation depends on the details of the legislation and the stringency of the enforcement regime.

Conclusion – No provision is recognised for the costs of fitting smoke filters. However, a provision is recognised for the best estimate of any fines and penalties that are more likely than not to be imposed (see paragraphs 14 and 17-19).

Example 7:

Staff retraining as a result of changes in the income tax system

The government introduces a number of changes to the income tax system. As a result of these changes an entity in the financial services sector will need to retrain a large proportion of its administrative and sales workforce in order to ensure continued compliance with financial services regulation. At the balance sheet date no retraining of staff has taken place.

Present obligation as a result of a past obligating event – There is no obligation because no obligating event (retraining) has taken place.

Conclusion – No provision is recognised (see paragraphs 14 and 17-19).

Example 8:

An onerous contract

An entity operates profitably from a factory that it has leased under an operating lease. During December 2000 the entity relocates its operations to a new factory. The lease on the old factory continues for the next four years, it cannot be cancelled and the factory cannot be re-let to another user.

Present obligation as a result of a past obligating event – The obligating event is the signing of the lease contract, which gives rise to a legal obligation.

Transfer of economic benefits in settlement – When the lease becomes onerous, a transfer of economic benefits is probable. (Until the lease becomes onerous, the entity accounts for the lease by applying SSAP 21 'Accounting for leases and hire purchase contracts'.)

Conclusion – A provision is recognised for the best estimate of the unavoidable lease payments (see paragraphs 14 and 71).

Example 9:

A single guarantee

During 1999 Entity A gives a guarantee of certain borrowings of Entity B, whose financial condition at that time is sound. During 2000, the financial condition of Entity B deteriorates and at 30 June 2000 Entity B files for protection from its creditors.

(a) At 31 December 1999

Present obligation as a result of a past obligating event – The obligating event is the giving of the guarantee, which gives rise to a legal obligation.

Transfer of economic benefits in settlement – No transfer of benefits is probable at 31 December 1999.

Conclusion – No provision is recognised (see paragraphs 14 and 23). The guarantee is disclosed as a contingent liability unless the probability of any transfer is regarded as remote (see paragraph 91).

(b) At 31 December 2000

Present obligation as a result of a past obligating event – The obligating event is the giving of the guarantee, which gives rise to a legal obligation.

Transfer of economic benefits in settlement – At 31 December 2000 it is probable that a transfer of economic benefits will be required to settle the obligation.

Conclusion – A provision is recognised for the best estimate of the obligation (see paragraphs 14 and 23).

*Note: This example deals with a single guarantee. If an entity has a portfolio of similar guarantees, it will assess that portfolio as a whole in determining whether a transfer of economic benefit is probable (see paragraph 24). Where an entity gives guarantees in exchange for a fee, revenue is recognised only when earned.**

Example 10:

A court case

After a wedding in 2000 ten people died, possibly as a result of food poisoning from products sold by the entity. Legal proceedings are started seeking damages from the entity but it disputes liability. Up to the date of approval of the financial statements for the year to 31 December 2000, the entity's lawyers advise that it is probable that the entity will not be found liable. However, when the entity prepares the financial statements for the year to 31 December 2001 its lawyers advise that, owing to developments in the case, it is probable that the entity will be found liable.

****Editor's note:*** *Example 9 has been amended by FRS 26, but only for those companies which are applying the measurement provisions of FRS 26. Where a company is applying FRS 26 then Example 9 reads as follows:*

A single guarantee

On 31 December 1999, Entity A gives a guarantee of certain borrowings of Entity B, whose financial condition at that time is sound. During 2000, the financial condition of Entity B deteriorates and at 30 June 2000 Entity B files for protection from its creditors.

(a) *At 31 December 1999*

Present obligation as a result of a past obligating event - The obligating event is the giving of the guarantee, which gives rise to a legal obligation.

An outflow of resources embodying economic benefits in settlement - No outflow of benefits is probable at 31 December 1999.

Conclusion - The guarantee is recognised at fair value.

(b) *At 31 December 2000*

Present obligation as a result of a past obligating event - The obligating event is the giving of the guarantee, which gives rise to a legal obligation.

An outflow of resources embodying economic benefits in settlement - At 31 December 2000, it is probable that an outflow of resources embodying economic benefits will be required to settle the obligation.

Conclusion - The guarantee is subsequently measured at the higher of (a) the best estimate of the obligation (see paragraphs 14 and 23) and (b) the amount initially recognised less, when appropriate, cumulative amortisation.

(a) At 31 December 2000

Present obligation as a result of a past obligating event – On the basis of the evidence available when the financial statements were approved, there is no obligation as a result of past events.

Conclusion – No provision is recognised (see paragraphs 14-16). The matter is disclosed as a contingent liability unless the probability of any transfer is regarded as remote.

(b) At 31 December 2001

Present obligation as a result of a past obligating event – On the basis of the evidence available, there is a present obligation.

Transfer of economic benefits in settlement – Probable.

Conclusion – A provision is recognised for the best estimate of the amount needed to settle the present obligation (paragraphs 14-16).

Example 11:

Repairs and maintenance

Some assets require, in addition to routine maintenance, substantial expenditure every few years for major refits or refurbishment and the replacement of major components.

Example 11A:

Refurbishment costs – no legislative requirement

A furnace has a lining that needs to be replaced every five years for technical reasons. At the balance sheet date, the lining has been in use for three years.

Present obligation as a result of a past obligating event – There is no present obligation.

Conclusion – No provision is recognised (see paragraphs 14 and 19).

The cost of replacing the lining is not recognised because, at the balance sheet date, no obligation to replace the lining exists independently of the entity's future actions – even the intention to incur the expenditure depends on the entity deciding to continue operating the furnace or to replace the lining. Instead of a provision being recognised, the depreciation of the lining takes account of its consumption, ie it is depreciated over five years. The re-lining costs then incurred are capitalised with the consumption of each new lining shown by depreciation over the subsequent five years.

Example 11B:

Refurbishment costs – legislative requirement

An airline is required by law to overhaul its aircraft once every three years.

Present obligation as a result of a past obligating event – There is no present obligation.

Conclusion – No provision is recognised (see paragraphs 14 and 19).

The costs of overhauling aircraft are not recognised as a provision for the same reasons as the cost of replacing the lining is not recognised as a provision in example 11A. Even a legal requirement to overhaul does not make the costs of overhaul a liability because no obligation exists to overhaul the aircraft independently of the entity's future actions – the entity could avoid the future expenditure by its future actions, for example by selling the aircraft. Instead of a provision being recognised, the depreciation of the aircraft takes account of the future incidence of maintenance costs, ie an amount equivalent to the expected maintenance costs is depreciated over three years.

Example 12:

Self-insurance

An entity that operates a chain of retail outlets decides not to insure itself in respect of the risk of minor accidents to its customers: instead it will 'self insure'. Based on its past experience, it expects to pay £100,000 a year in respect of these accidents. Should provision be made for the amount expected to arise in a normal year?

Present obligation as a result of a past obligating event – There is no present obligation.

Conclusion – No provision is recognised. There is no present obligation because there is no other party involved in insuring the risks (see paragraph 20).

Appendix IV
Examples: disclosures

These examples are illustrative only and do not form part of the FRS.

Examples 1 and 2 provide examples of the disclosures required by paragraph 90.

Example 1:

Warranties

A manufacturer gives warranties at the time of sale to purchasers of its three product lines. Under the terms of the warranty the manufacturer undertakes to repair or replace items that fail to perform satisfactorily for two years from the date of sale. At the balance sheet date a provision of £60,000 has been recognised. The provision has not been discounted as the effect of discounting is not material. The following information is disclosed:

'*A provision of £60,000 has been recognised for expected warranty claims on products sold during the last three financial years. It is expected that most of this expenditure will be incurred in the next financial year, and all will be incurred within two years of the balance sheet date.*'

Example 2:

Decommissioning costs

In 2000 an entity involved in nuclear activities recognises a provision for decommissioning costs of £300 million. The provision is estimated using the assumption that decommissioning will take place in 60–70 years' time. However, there is a possibility that it will not take place until 100–110 years' time, in which case the present value of the costs will be significantly reduced. The following information is disclosed:

'*A provision of £300 million has been recognised for decommissioning costs. These costs are expected to be incurred between 2060 and 2070. However, there is a possibility that decommissioning will not take place until 2100–2110. If the costs were measured based upon the expectation that they would not be incurred until 2100–2110 the provision would be reduced to £136 million. The provision has been estimated using existing technology, at current prices, and discounted using a real discount rate of 2 per cent.*'

Example 3 provides an example of the disclosures required by paragraph 97, where some of the information required is not given because it can be expected to prejudice seriously the position of the entity.

Example 3:

Disclosure exemption

An entity is involved in a dispute with a competitor, who is alleging that the entity has infringed patents and is seeking damages of £100 million. The entity recognises a provision for its best estimate of the obligation, but discloses none of the information required by paragraphs 89 and 90. The following information is disclosed:

'*Litigation is in process against the company relating to a dispute with a competitor which alleges that the company has infringed patents and which is seeking damages of £100 million. The information usually required by* FRS *12 is not disclosed on the grounds that it can be expected to prejudice seriously the outcome of the litigation. The directors are of the opinion that the claim can be successfully resisted by the company.*'

Appendix V
Note on Legal Requirements

GREAT BRITAIN*

The statutory requirements on accounting for provisions and contingencies are set out in the Companies Act 1985. The main requirements that are directly relevant are set out in Schedules 4 and 4A and are summarised below. 1

Schedule 4 to the Act does not apply to banking and insurance companies and groups. Banking companies and groups are dealt with in Schedule 9 and insurance companies and groups are dealt with in Schedule 9A. 2

Paragraph 12(b) of Schedule 4 states the general requirement that 'all liabilities and losses which have arisen or are likely to arise in respect of the financial year to which the accounts relate or a previous financial year shall be taken into account ...' 3

Provisions represent one aspect of the manner in which this general requirement is met. Provisions are defined in paragraph 89 of Schedule 4 in the following manner: 4

> 'References to provisions for liabilities or charges are to any amount retained as reasonably necessary for the purposes of providing for any liability or loss which is either likely to be incurred, or certain to be incurred but uncertain as to amount or as to the date on which it will arise.'†

The FRS defines a provision as:

> 'A liability of uncertain timing or amount.'

The requirements of the FRS are expressed in more specific terms than the requirements in Schedule 4. However, although the Act and the FRS define provisions in different terms, the Board believes that, when taken in their respective contexts, the FRS is consistent with the requirements of Schedule 4. 5

The legal definition refers to '... any amount retained as reasonably necessary for the purposes ...'. The reference to reasonableness recognises that the appropriate 6

***Editor's note:** The various statutory references change with the introduction of the Companies Act 2006, which affects accounting for periods beginning on or after 6 April 2008. The various statutory references have changed as follows:*

Companies Act 1985 reference	***Companies Act 2006 reference***
Schedule 4	*Schedule 1 to the Large and Medium-sized Companies and Groups (Accounts and Reports) Regulations 2008 (SI 2008/410)*
Schedule 4A	*Schedule 6 to SI 2008/410*
Schedules 9 and 9A	*Schedules 2 and 3 to SI 2008/410*
Paragraph 12 (b) of Schedule 4	Paragraph 13 (b) of Schedule 1 to SI 2008/410
Paragraph 89 of Schedule 4	*Paragraph 2 of Schedule 9 to SI 2008/410*
Paragraph 46 of Schedule 4	*Paragraph 59 of Schedule 1 to SI 2008/410*
Paragraph 50 of Schedule 4	*Paragraph 63 of Schedule 1 to SI 2008/410*

†***Editor's note:** References to 'provisions for liabilities and charges' in the legislation are now to 'provisions for liabilities'.*

amount to set aside as a provision for a specific matter will often be a matter of judgement. The FRS sets out the manner in which this judgement should be exercised in the context of giving a true and fair view.

7 In addition, the legal definition refers to '... any liability or loss ... [whether likely to be incurred or certain to be incurred]' and this needs to be considered in conjunction with the general requirement that 'liabilities or losses have arisen or are likely to arise in respect of the financial year to which the accounts relate [or a previous financial year]' (paragraph 12(b) of Schedule 4). These requirements are consistent with the Board's approach of requiring there to be a past transaction or event that gives rise to an obligation, before a provision can be recognised. Without a past transaction or event the liability or loss will not have arisen or be likely to arise in respect of the financial year or a previous financial year. Before a liability can be recognised, the draft Statement of Principles for Financial Reporting* requires sufficient evidence that a future transfer of benefits will occur.

8 In addition to covering liabilities that are certain to be incurred, the statutory definition also refers to liabilities as losses that are 'likely to be incurred'. This aspect of likelihood is covered in the FRS in two respects. The FRS requires provisions to be recognised arising from 'constructive obligations', which are liabilities that pass the test of sufficient certainty without constituting legal liabilities. The FRS also requires the recognition of provisions where a transfer of economic benefit is more likely than not to occur.

9 Where any amount is transferred to any provision for liabilities and charges or from any provision for liabilities and charges otherwise than for the purpose for which the provision was established, paragraph 46(1) and (2) of Schedule 4 requires the following information to be disclosed:

(a) the amount of the provisions as at the date of the beginning of the financial year and as at the balance sheet date respectively;
(b) any amounts transferred to or from provisions during that year; and
(c) the source and application respectively of any amounts so transferred.

10 Paragraph 46(3) of Schedule 4 requires particulars to be given of each material provision included in the item "other provisions" in the company's balance sheet.

11 Paragraph 50(2) of Schedule 4 requires the following information to be given in respect of any other contingent liability not provided for:

(a) the amount or estimated amount of that liability;
(b) its legal nature; and
(c) whether any valuable security has been provided by the company in connection with that liability and, if so, what.

NORTHERN IRELAND

12 The statutory requirements in Northern Ireland are set out in the Companies (Northern Ireland) Order 1986. They are identical to and parallel the references in the legislation for Great Britain cited above.

REPUBLIC OF IRELAND

13 The statutory requirements in the Republic of Ireland that correspond to those cited above for Great Britain are shown in the following table.

Exposure Draft, November 1995.* (*Editor's note:*** *also final Statement issued December 1999.*)

Great Britain	*Republic of Ireland*
Schedule 4 to the Companies Act 1985	The Schedule to the Companies (Amendment) Act 1986
Schedule 4A to the Companies Act 1985	Regulation 15(1) of the European Communities (Companies: Group Accounts) Regulations 1992
Schedule 9 to the Companies Act 1985	European Communities (Credit Institutions: Accounts) Regulations 1992
Schedule 9A to the Companies Act 1985	European Communities (Insurance Undertakings: Accounts) Regulations 1996
Paragraph 12(b) of Schedule 4 to the Companies Act 1985	Section 5(c)(ii) of the Companies (Amendment) Act 1986
Paragraph 89 of Schedule 4 to the Companies Act 1985	Paragraph 70 of the Schedule to the Companies (Amendment) Act 1986
Paragraph 46(1) and (2) of Schedule 4 to the Companies Act 1985	Paragraph 32(1) and (2) of the Schedule to the Companies (Amendment) Act 1986
Paragraph 46(3) of Schedule 4 to the Companies Act 1985	Paragraph 32(3) of the Schedule to the Companies (Amendment) Act 1986
Paragraph 50(2) of Schedule 4 to the Companies Act 1985	Paragraph 36(2) of the Schedule to the Companies (Amendment) Act 1986

Appendix VI
Compliance with International Accounting Standards

Because the FRS was developed jointly with the international standard on the same topic, IAS 37 'Provisions, Contingent Liabilities and Contingent Assets', all the requirements of the IAS are included in the FRS and there are no differences of substance between these common requirements. The FRS, additionally, deals with the circumstances under which an asset should be recognised when a provision is recognised and gives more guidance than the IAS on the discount rate to be used in the present value calculation.

Appendix VII
The development of the FRS

THE NEED FOR A STANDARD

Provisions often have a substantial effect on an entity's financial position and performance. They arise in a wide range of circumstances and businesses covering such matters as warranties, onerous contracts, restructuring costs, environmental liabilities and decommissioning costs. Published guidance on the subject, however, has tended to concentrate on particular forms of provision rather than the general principles underlying all provisions. 1

To portray the financial position of an entity, it is important that a provision should be recognised whenever a relevant liability exists; but it is equally important to recognise a provision only when such a liability exists. The basis of a liability is the existence of an obligation to one or more third parties. It follows that the *intention* to incur expenditure does not, of itself, result in a liability. This point needs to be made in an accounting standard because in some cases a mere intention to incur expenditure has been used to justify recognising a provision. 2

In the absence of an accounting standard on provisions the practice has grown up of aggregating liabilities with expected liabilities of future years, and sometimes even with expected expenditures related to ongoing operations, in one large provision, often reported as an exceptional item. The effect of such 'big bath' provisions has been not only to report excessive liabilities at the outset but also to boost profitability during the subsequent years, when the liabilities are in fact being incurred. 3

The FRS addresses these concerns, first by requiring that provisions should be recognised only where a liability exists at the period-end (based on the definition of a liability in FRS 5 'Reporting the Substance of Transactions' and in the Board's draft Statement of Principles for Financial Reporting*) and secondly by showing in examples how this principle should apply to a number of commonly occurring circumstances. The FRS deals with recognition, measurement and disclosure for provisions. Because contingent liabilities and contingent assets are closely linked to provisions, the FRS also covers their treatment. 4

The Board has taken the opportunity to develop a complete framework of disclosure requirements for provisions, contingent liabilities and contingent assets. The new disclosure requirements give information about the significance of a provision and any changes in it during the year and show how provisions have been used as expenditure occurs. 5

In developing the FRS, the Board has considered the comments on its proposals set out initially in the Discussion Paper 'Provisions' published in November 1995 and then in FRED 14 'Provisions and Contingencies' issued in June 1997. At both stages the majority of respondents have supported the issue of an FRS on provisions and the general principles proposed as its basis. 6

The FRS has been developed as part of a joint project with the International Accounting Standards Committee. The parallel development of the FRS and IAS 37 'Provisions, Contingent Liabilities and Contingent Assets' has meant that each standard has been able to benefit from the comments and discussion on the other 7

Exposure Draft, November 1995.* (*Editor's note:*** *also final Statement issued December 1999.)*

project. Apart from the two minor additions to the FRS noted in Appendix VI, the two standards are identical except for phraseology and structure necessary to conform to established practice in each constituency.

THE GENERAL PRINCIPLES

8 The central principle of the FRS is that a provision should be recognised only where at the period-end a liability exists that can be measured reliably. An entity may feel less well-off at the prospect of future cash flows entailed by its method of operation from the moment it becomes aware that they are likely to be necessary – it may wish to communicate such prospects by a note – but future expenditure, however necessary, does not justify the recognition of a provision unless a liability exists at the period-end. For a liability to exist the entity must have, as a result of past transactions or events, an obligation to transfer economic benefits in settlement. Future expenditure not relating to present obligations should be recognised in the period when the obligation to incur that expenditure arises.

9 FRED 14 distinguished between a legal and a constructive obligation. The responses indicated that it would be helpful to clarify the concept of a constructive obligation as a present obligation arising otherwise than by operation of law. The essence of an obligation is commitment to a third party: for a constructive obligation, that commitment arises through actions of the entity – its establishing a pattern of practice, publishing its policies or making a current statement setting out in detail its intended future actions – that raise in those dealing with it or affected by it a valid expectation that the entity will discharge its responsibilities. A constructive obligation is often the basis for recognising a provision for restructuring. The examples deal also with whether a constructive obligation exists for habitual refunds, cleaning up contamination and the closure of a division.

10 The proposals in FRED 14 defined 'contingency' and dealt with contingent losses and contingent gains rather than contingent liabilities and contingent assets. The draft Statement of Principles deals with the recognition of assets and liabilities and therefore the FRS now bases its analysis on contingent liabilities and contingent assets.

11 The FRS has clarified the relationship between provisions and contingent liabilities, which was the source of some concern to those commenting on the FRED 14 proposals. FRED 14 proposed that some contingent losses should be recognised while others should not. Under the FRS contingent liabilities as defined never qualify for recognition as liabilities – if circumstances change and a provision needs to be recognised there is no longer a contingent liability.

12 Similarly, the effect of the definition of a contingent asset in the FRS is that nothing that meets the criteria for recognition as an asset will count as a contingent asset. This distinction is clearer than the equivalent proposal in FRED 14 that some contingent gains should be recognised while others should not.

SCOPE

13 FRED 14 proposed that the FRS should apply to all financial statements that are intended to give a true and fair view of the reporting entity's financial position and profit or loss for a period. This proposal was widely supported by the respondents. However, because the accounting framework for financial instruments is under review, the Board has decided to exclude financial instruments carried at market value from the scope of the FRS. The special regulatory position of insurance

companies (for which provisions are particularly important) and the review of the accounting framework for insurance companies have led the Board to leave outside the scope of the FRS provisions arising in insurance entities from contracts with policy-holders. Because there are other accounting standards that specifically consider provisions in certain cases (eg pensions), the FRS does not apply to provisions covered by more specific requirements in other standards.

RECOGNITION

A present obligation

As explained above, the FRS follows the general principle proposed in the Discussion Paper and FRED 14 – and already embodied in FRS 3 'Reporting Financial Performance' and FRS 7 'Fair Values in Acquisition Accounting' – that a provision should be recognised only where a liability exists that can be reliably estimated. The recognition criteria in the FRS therefore require that: **14**

(a) an entity has a present obligation (legal or constructive) as a result of a past event;
(b) it is probable that a transfer of economic benefits will be required to settle the obligation; and
(c) a reliable estimate can be made of the amount of the obligation.

Conditions (a) and (b) must be fulfilled for a liability to exist. Condition (c) requires that it should be able to be measured with sufficient reliability. These conditions are therefore consistent with the recognition criteria set out in the draft Statement of Principles.

Past event

For there to be a present obligation the FRS requires that an obligating event has taken place. An obligating event creates a legal or constructive obligation that results in an entity having no realistic alternative to settling that obligation. In FRED 14 the proposals for recognition were also based on the existence of a present obligation, the key notion being that the entity had no realistic alternative to making a transfer of economic benefits. The Board decided that it would be helpful to include more guidance on the obligating event that gives rise to a present obligation. The FRS notes that it is only those obligations arising independently of the entity's future actions that are recognised as provisions. Where the entity can avoid future expenditure by its future actions, it has no present liability for that future expenditure and no provision is recognised. The examples in Appendix III illustrate the effect in practice of applying the FRS in assessing whether an obligating event has taken place – in particular examples 3 (offshore oilfield), 6 (smoke filters), 7 (staff retraining) and 11 (repairs and maintenance). **15**

By basing the recognition of a provision on the existence of a present obligation, the FRS rules out the recognition of any provision made simply to allocate results over more than one period or otherwise to smooth the results reported. For example, in a regulated industry the results achieved in the current period may cause the pricing structure in the next period to be adjusted, eg the higher the profits in this year the lower the prices permitted for next year. There is no justification under the FRS for a provision to be recognised in such circumstances. The purpose of such a provision would be to transfer some of the current year's profit to the following year, which would suffer from lower prices because of the current year's profits. However, there **16** is no present obligation that requires the transfer of economic benefits to settle it and nothing to justify recognition of a provision.

Probable outflow of economic resources

17 An essential part of the definition of a liability is the existence of an obligation to transfer economic benefits. This condition will be met where the transfer of economic benefits is probable, ie more likely than not to occur. Where there are a number of similar obligations the probability of a transfer is determined by considering the class of obligations as a whole.

Reliable estimate of the obligation

18 Some respondents to FRED 14 were concerned that the proposals would allow scope for abuse and the avoidance of proper provision because they permitted the non-recognition of a provision where a reliable estimate of the obligation could not be made. In response to these concerns the FRS notes that, except in extremely rare cases, an entity will be able to determine a range of possible outcomes and can therefore make an estimate that is sufficiently reliable to use in recognising a provision.

CONTINGENT LIABILITIES

19 The recognition of contingent losses on the basis of whether they were probable was supported by the respondents to FRED 14. As explained in paragraphs 10 and 11 above, the FRS bases its analysis on contingent liabilities rather than contingent losses and classifies as a provision, rather than a contingent liability, an obligation that is recognised because it will probably require the transfer of economic benefits in settlement. The effect of these requirements of the FRS on the recognition of losses is the same as proposed in FRED 14.

CONTINGENT ASSETS

20 The recognition of contingent gains on the basis of whether they were virtually certain was supported by the respondents to FRED 14. As explained in paragraphs 10 and 12 above, the FRS bases its analysis on contingent assets, rather than contingent gains, and requires that a contingent asset should not be recognised. When, however, the realisation of a profit becomes virtually certain, the related asset is not a contingent asset and recognition is appropriate. Accordingly, the effect of the requirements of the FRS on the recognition of gains is the same as proposed in FRED 14.

MEASUREMENT

21 The FRS requires a provision to be recognised at the best estimate of the expenditure required to settle the present obligation at the balance sheet date. The risks and uncertainties that surround events should be taken into account in calculating the amount of the provision. Whatever method of estimation is adopted full disclosure of the uncertainties surrounding the amount of the expenditure is required.

22 For a liability where there is a market, the best estimate of that liability at the balance sheet date would be its market value. The FRS recognises that it will often be impossible or prohibitively expensive to settle or transfer an obligation at the balance sheet date because of the uncertainty relating to provisions. By acknowledging this impossibility, the FRS reflects some of the points raised by the respondents to FRED 14.

However, a provision should, in principle, be recognised at the amount of the obligation that existed at the balance sheet date – ie the least cost amount to settle the existing present obligation. Even where it is not possible either to settle or transfer the obligation at the balance sheet date, the process of estimating the amounts at which such hypothetical transactions would take place provides a useful approach to calculating the least cost amount.

Assuming that it is possible to specify all the possible outcomes and their associated probabilities, the amount to be provided for an obligation could be estimated as: **23**

- *the most likely outcome* (ie the outcome with the highest probability). The problem with calculating the estimate using this method is that it ignores the other possible outcomes: for example, where the most likely outcome is nil it could also lead to the inference that an entity has no obligation.
- *the maximum amount* (ie the highest possible outcome). Use of this method to calculate the estimate could result in extremely large amounts being recognised even though the possibility of the outcome is remote.
- *at least the minimum amount in the range* (ie any amount from the lowest possible outcome to the highest possible outcome). This formula results in a wide range of possible estimates and would therefore be likely to impair comparability in financial reporting.
- *the expected value* (ie the amount that takes account of all possible outcomes using probabilities to weight the outcomes). Expected value as a method of estimation has a number of desirable features. The method provides an estimate that reflects the entire probability distribution, ie all the possible outcomes weighted by their probabilities. For a given assessed distribution, the method has the advantage of objectivity in that different measurers would calculate the same estimate. Furthermore, expected value is additive (ie the expected value of a number of items is the sum of the expected values of the individual items).

Where there is a large population of items, the expected value – adjusted as appropriate for risk – will provide the best estimate of a provision.

DISCOUNTING

Some provisions that are to be recognised require outflows of economic benefits in settlement far in the future. For some provisions, therefore, the effect of the time value of money – the greater value of a present sum than the certain payment of the same sum some time in the future – can be material and should be taken into account in estimating the amount to be recognised as a provision. Discounting was proposed for provisions in FRED 14 and received the support of the majority of the respondents. The background to the requirements on discounting is set out in the Working Paper 'Discounting in Financial Reporting' (published in April 1997). The proposals in the FRS are consistent with that Paper. **24**

The FRS requires the unwinding of the discount to be included in the profit and loss account as a financial item adjacent to but shown separately from interest. The respondents to FRED 14 were divided over whether the unwinding discount should be shown as interest or as an operating cost. Those who favoured showing it as an operating cost tended to argue that putting this amount in interest would be misleading and confusing to users of accounts and would distort or obscure the view given by the interest and funding disclosures. The Board has met these concerns by requiring that the unwinding discount should be shown clearly as a separate item from interest. The Board believes that the unwinding discount is a financial item – it relates to the time value of money, reflecting the effect of the passage of time on an amount specified in money terms. **25**

26 Provisions that are calculated at a discounted amount should take into account risk as well as the time value of money. Risk can be taken into account either by discounting at a risk-free rate cash flows that take risk into account or by discounting at a risk-adjusted rate cash flows that take no account of risk. The important point is that risk should be taken into account in the best way possible and that care should be taken not to double-count the effect of risk. Among the considerations to be borne in mind are whether it is feasible to derive an appropriate risk-adjusted rate of interest and whether the incidence of risk over the discount period may follow a different pattern from that of compound interest.

27 Where the amount recognised is discounted, the cash flows to be discounted are the pre-tax cash flows and the discount rate should be the rate of return that will, after tax has been deducted, give the required post-tax rate of return. Because the tax consequences of different cash flows may be different, the pre-tax rate of return is not always the post-tax rate of return grossed up by the standard rate of tax. The Board requires the effect of tax to be shown separately in financial statements rather than netting tax directly off the assets and liabilities. This is in line with the general requirement that tax effects shall be shown separately.

Expected disposal of assets

28 FRED 14 did not refer to the treatment of gains from the expected disposal of assets in measuring provisions. The FRS prohibits such gains from being taken into account in measuring a provision. The principle of the FRS is that provisions should be recognised and measured as liabilities independently of considerations affecting the recognition and measurement of assets held. As a practical matter, if in certain circumstances gains on expected disposals were netted off against the provision to be recognised, it would be difficult to limit the assets whose expected disposal could be set off. There would also need to be guidance on the treatment when the provision was both recognised and used before the gain was achieved.

REIMBURSEMENTS

29 The FRS requires that a provision and any expected reimbursement should be recognised separately as a liability and an asset – although shown net in the profit and loss account. This approach is consistent with the general principle contained in FRS 5 and is designed to reflect the fact that the entity often continues to be liable if the third party from which the reimbursement is due fails to pay. Reimbursement is recognised only when it is virtually certain to be received if the entity settles the liability.

APPLICATION OF THE RECOGNITION AND MEASUREMENT RULES

30 The FRS includes paragraphs applying its recognition and measurement rules to operating losses, onerous contracts and reorganisations. Although the text has changed from FRED 14, the FRS applies the same basic principles as the FRED and has the same effect.

Restructuring provisions

31 The most controversial aspect of the proposals in FRED 14 related to the date on which a provision for restructuring should be recognised – the FRED proposed that the date when the entity became demonstrably committed to a reorganisation should

be the date a provision was recognised. On this principle, no provision should be recognised if the only relevant event before the balance sheet date was a board decision. The majority of those disagreeing with this proposal argued that it was unrealistically strict and that a provision should be recognised where there was a formal board decision before the year-end and either implementation of that decision began before the signing of the financial statements or the decision was communicated in sufficient detail to those affected by it before that date.

The Board has discussed the issues raised by the respondents but has concluded that, for the consistent application of its principles, it must require a constructive obligation to restructure to exist at the balance sheet date for a provision for restructuring to be recognised. This is required also for consistency with the treatment of assets: the entity includes in its financial statements only those assets that it controls at the balance sheet date and does not include assets that come under its control only between the balance sheet date and the signing of the financial statements. 32

A constructive obligation to restructure arises only when the entity has a detailed formal plan for the reorganisation and, by beginning to implement that plan or communicating it to those affected, raises in them a valid expectation that it will carry out the restructuring as expected. Therefore a board decision alone (unless one of a supervisory board whose members include employees and possibly other affected interests (see paragraph 82 of the FRS)) does not amount to a constructive obligation to restructure. 33

DISCLOSURE

Respondents raised no major concerns with the disclosures proposed by FRED 14. 34

The reordering of the FRS to incorporate more fully contingent liabilities and contingent assets has led to the disclosure requirements for these to be set out alongside those for provisions, making clear the consistent basis for the requirements. As part of this rearrangement, the dispensation from providing disclosures that can be expected to prejudice seriously the position of the entity in its negotiations with other parties now applies to contingent liabilities and contingent assets as well as to provisions. The respondents to FRED 14 overwhelmingly supported a 'seriously prejudicial' exemption for disclosures on provisions. 35

DECOMMISSIONING COSTS AND REPAIRS AND MAINTENANCE PROVISIONS

The examples in Appendix III describe two cases where the effect of applying the requirements remains controversial, although the treatment in the examples received general support from the majority of respondents on FRED 14. These are example 3 on decommissioning costs and example 11 on repairs and maintenance. 36

Decommissioning costs

Before the introduction of the FRS, the treatment generally accorded to decommissioning costs was to account for them on the 'units of production' method. Under this method, the amount required for decommissioning is built up year by year, in line with production levels, to reach the amount of the expected decommissioning costs by the time production ceases. The FRS requires that, to the extent that decommissioning costs relate to damage already done or goods and services already received, that present obligation should be recognised as a provision. The following 37

points should be noted when considering the effects of the FRS's requirements on decommissioning costs.

- On installation of the oil rig, the effect of the time value of money is that the true measure of the extra cost of the rig represented by decommissioning costs is the discounted amount of the eventual cost.
- Decommissioning costs will be included in the cost of the oil rig only to the extent that they are incurred by the installation of the rig. If any damage is incurred by production, the costs of restoring that damage is a cost of production – the classic case of this in another industry is open-cast mining where the production process itself increases the damage caused and the consequent cost of restoration.
- The unwinding of the discount reflects the effect of the passage of time and that unwinding is matched in principle by interest or income earned as a result of having a liability that has not yet required the transfer of economic resources in settlement. Setting aside a sinking fund equal to the discounted amount of the liability at any time would provide sufficient cumulative interest income to settle the decommissioning liability directly without any additional transfer of resources.
- Some respondents have been concerned that the profile over time of the charge arising for decommissioning costs (lower at first but rising over time) could lead to payments of dividends early in the production process in excess of what the business could bear after taking into account its long-term liability for decommissioning costs. However, provided that the assets in the business earn a return in excess of the interest rate used to discount the decommissioning costs, there will be at least sufficient assets to settle the decommissioning costs liabilities when these need to be paid.

Repairs and maintenance

38 It is the present practice of some entities to recognise as a provision the future costs of repairing or maintaining part of their fixed assets. Example 11 illustrates the application of the FRS to repairs and maintenance for fixed assets. Because future repairs and maintenance are not present obligations of the entity resulting from past events, no provision should be made for them, even if they are required by legislation if the asset is to continue to be used. There are no grounds for recognising a provision for future repairs and maintenance expenditures because these relate to the future operation of the business, the restoration of service potential, and are therefore either to be capitalised as assets or written off as operating expenses when incurred. Where a part of the asset can be identified as declining in service potential because of the need for repairs or maintenance, it should be depreciated to show the declining service potential. Expenditure on repairs and maintenance should be capitalised to show the restoration of service potential.

39 In some operating leases the lessee is required to incur periodic charges for maintenance of the leased asset or to make good dilapidations or other damage occurring during the rental period. The principle illustrated in example 11 does not preclude the recognition of such liabilities once the event giving rise to the obligation under the lease has occurred.

Financial Reporting Standard 13 is set out in paragraphs 1–135.

The Statement of Standard Accounting Practice, which comprises the paragraphs set in bold type, should be read in the context of the Objective as stated in paragraph 1 and the definitions set out in paragraphs 2, 81 and 119 and also of the Foreword to Accounting Standards and the Statement of Principles for Financial Reporting currently in issue.

The explanatory paragraphs contained in the FRS shall be regarded as part of the Statement of Standard Accounting Practice insofar as they assist in interpreting that statement.

Appendix VII 'The development of the FRS' reviews considerations and arguments that were thought significant by members of the Board in reaching the conclusions on the FRS*.

**FRS 13 is withdrawn in virtually all cases with effect for accounting periods beginning on or after 1 January 2007, and is replaced by FRS 29. However, it continues to apply to a small number of companies.*

[FRS 13] Derivatives and other financial instruments: disclosures*

(Issued September 1998)

Contents

Paragraphs

Summary

Guide to the FRS

Financial Reporting Standard 13

Objective 1

Part A – Reporting entities other than financial institutions and financial institution groups

Definitions 2

Entities required to provide the disclosures set out in this part of the FRS 3–4

Instruments to be dealt with in the disclosures 5–10
Financial assets and financial liabilities to be dealt with in the disclosures 5
Short-term debtors and creditors 6–7
Non-equity shares issued by the reporting entity 8–9
Commodity contracts 10

Disclosure of objectives, policies and strategies 11–23

Numerical disclosures – general matters 24–25

Interest rate risk disclosures 26–33
Financial liabilities 26–31
Financial assets 32–33

Currency risk disclosures 34–37

Liquidity disclosures 38–43

Fair value disclosures 44–56
Disclosures about financial assets and financial liabilities held or issued for trading 57

Disclosures about hedges 58–63

****Editor's note***: *The matters covered in FRS 13 are dealt with in Sections 11 and 12 of FRS 102, but primarily in Section 34 in relation to the disclosures required by financial institutions.*

Disclosures about commodity contracts 64–65

Additional disclosures about market price risk 66–72

Disclosure of accounting policies 73–76

Amendment to FRS 4 77–78

Date from which effective 79–80

Part B – Banks and similar institutions and banking and similar groups

Definitions 81

Entities required to provide the disclosures set out in this part of the FRS 82

Instruments to be dealt with in the disclosures 83

Disclosure of objectives, policies and strategies 84

Numerical disclosures – general matters 85

Interest rate risk disclosures 86–89

Currency risk disclosures 90–97

Fair value disclosures 98–102

Disclosures about financial assets and financial liabilities held or issued for trading 103–111

Disclosures about hedges 112

Disclosures about commodity contracts 113–114

Additional disclosures about market price risk 115

Disclosure of accounting policies 116

Amendment to FRS 4 117

Date from which effective 118

Part C – Financial institutions and financial institution groups, other than banks and similar institutions and banking and similar groups

Definitions 119

Entities required to provide the disclosures set out in this part of the FRS 120

Instruments to be dealt with in the disclosures 121

Disclosure of objectives, policies and strategies 122

Numerical disclosures – general matters 123

Interest rate and currency risk disclosures 124

Liquidity disclosures 125–126

Fair value disclosures 127

Disclosures about financial assets and financial liabilities held or issued for trading 128

Disclosures about hedges 129

Disclosures about commodity contracts 130–131

Additional disclosures about market price risk 132

Disclosure of accounting policies 133

Amendment to FRS 4 134

Date from which effective 135

Adoption of FRS 13 by the board

Appendices

I Types of risk arising from financial instruments
II Examples applying the definition of a financial instrument
III Illustrations of the disclosures
IV Guidance on procedures for estimating fair values
V Note on legal requirements
VI Compliance with international accounting standards
VII The development of the FRS

Derivatives and other financial instruments: disclosures

Summary

GENERAL

Financial Reporting Standard 13 applies to all entities, other than insurance companies, that have one or more of their capital instruments listed or publicly traded on a stock exchange or market and to all banks and similar institutions. **a**

Such entities are required by the FRS to disclose in their financial statements certain information on their financial instruments. The objective of these disclosures is to provide information about the impact of financial instruments on the entity's risk profile, how the risks arising from financial instruments might affect the entity's performance and financial condition, and how these risks are being managed. **b**

THE APPROACH ADOPTED IN THE FRS

The FRS requires both narrative and numerical disclosures. The narrative disclosures describe the role that financial instruments have in creating or changing the risks that the entity faces, including its objectives and policies in using financial instruments to manage these risks. The numerical disclosures show how these objectives and policies were implemented in the period and provide supplementary information for evaluating significant or potentially significant exposures. Together these disclosures provide a broad overview of the entity's financial instruments and of the risk positions created by them, focusing on those risks and instruments that are of greatest significance. **c**

NARRATIVE DISCLOSURES

The FRS requires an explanation to be provided of the role that financial instruments play in creating or changing the risks that the entity faces in its activities. The entity should also explain the directors' approach to managing each of those risks, including a description of the objectives, policies and strategies for holding and issuing financial instruments. Where the directors decide, before the balance sheet date, to change these objectives, policies or strategies, that change should also be explained. **d**

The narrative disclosures are mandatory, although the FRS permits them to be given in a statement accompanying the financial statements (such as the operating and financial review or the directors' report) provided that they are incorporated into the financial statements by a suitable cross-reference. **e**

NUMERICAL DISCLOSURES

Although all entities within the scope of the FRS are required to provide the same type of narrative disclosures, the FRS requires different numerical disclosures for each of: **f**

- entities that are not financial institutions

- banks and similar institutions
- other types of financial institution.

These different disclosures reflect differences in the significance of the main risks that arise from financial instruments.

g The FRS requires specified numerical disclosures to be provided about:

- interest rate risk
- currency risk
- liquidity risk (except for banks and similar institutions, which are covered by existing requirements)
- fair values
- financial instruments used for trading (including, for banks and some other financial institutions, information on the market price risk of their trading book)
- financial instruments used for hedging
- certain commodity contracts.

h To avoid the numerical disclosures becoming so detailed that their message is obscured, the FRS encourages, and in some cases requires, a high degree of aggregation.

ILLUSTRATIONS

i Appendix III contains three illustrations of the required disclosures. The first shows the sort of information that the vast majority of companies to which the FRS applies will need to provide and the second the sort of information to be provided by companies that are more complex. The third illustration focuses on the disclosures that banks and certain other financial institutions will need to provide.

INSURANCE COMPANIES

j Insurance companies are at present excluded from the scope of the FRS. This is to allow the Accounting Standards Board to consider the disclosures to be provided by insurance companies in the context of developments in insurance company accounting generally.

Guide to the FRS

The disclosures required by this FRS depend on the type of reporting entity involved. The FRS distinguishes three types of reporting entity and, for ease of reference, the requirements (and related definitions) are set out in separate parts. The three types of reporting entity, and the part of the FRS that is relevant to each, are as follows:

- Reporting entities other than financial institutions and financial institution groups — Part A
- Banks and similar institutions and banking and similar groups — Part B
- Other financial institutions and financial institution groups. — Part C

Financial Reporting Standard 13

Objective

1 The objective of this FRS is to ensure that reporting entities within its scope provide in their financial statements disclosures that enable users to assess the entity's objectives, policies and strategies for holding or issuing financial instruments. In particular, such information should enable users to assess:

(a) the risk profile of the entity for each of the main financial risks that arise in connection with financial instruments and commodity contracts with similar characteristics; and

(b) the significance of such instruments and contracts to the entity's reported financial position, performance and cash flows, regardless of whether the instruments and contracts are on balance sheet (recognised) or off balance sheet (unrecognised).

Part A - Reporting entities other than financial institutions and financial institution groups

Definitions

2 The following definitions shall apply in Part A of the FRS and in particular in the Statement of Standard Accounting Practice set out **in bold type**.

Capital instruments:-

All instruments that are issued by reporting entities as a means of raising finance, including shares, debentures, loans and debt instruments, options and warrants that give the holder the right to subscribe for or obtain capital instruments. In the case of consolidated financial statements the term includes capital instruments issued by subsidiaries except those that are held by another member of the group included in the consolidation.

The definition set out above is taken from FRS 4 'Capital Instruments'.

Commodity contract and cash-settled commodity contract:-

A *commodity contract* is a contract that provides for settlement by receipt or delivery of a commodity.

A *cash-settled commodity contract* is a commodity contract (including a contract for the delivery of gold) which, though having contract terms that require settlement by physical delivery, is of a type that is normally extinguished other than by physical delivery in accordance with general market practice.

'Commodities' in this context means hard commodities (such as metals) and soft commodities (such as oils, grains, cocoa, coffee, cotton, soya beans and sugar).

It is not intended that cash or government securities should be treated as commodities for the purposes of the FRS.

Derivative financial instrument:-

A financial instrument that derives its value from the price or rate of some underlying item.

Underlying items include equities, bonds, commodities, interest rates, exchange rates and stock market and other indices.

Derivative financial instruments include futures, options, forward contracts, interest rate and currency swaps, interest rate caps, collars and floors, forward interest rate agreements, commitments to purchase shares or bonds, note issuance facilities and letters of credit.

Equity instrument:-

See 'Financial instrument, financial asset, financial liability and equity instrument'.

Equity shares:-

Shares other than non-equity shares.

Fair value:-

The amount at which an asset or liability could be exchanged in an arm's length transaction between informed and willing parties, other than in a forced or liquidation sale.

Financial institution and financial institution group:-

These terms are defined in paragraph 119 of Part C.

Financial instrument, financial asset, financial liability and equity instrument:-

A *financial instrument* is any contract that gives rise to both a financial asset of one entity and a financial liability or equity instrument of another entity.

Financial instruments include both primary financial instruments – such as bonds, debtors, creditors and shares – and derivative financial instruments. Types of financial instruments are discussed further in Appendix II.

A *financial asset* is any asset that is:

(a) cash;
(b) a contractual right to receive cash or another financial asset from another entity;
(c) a contractual right to exchange financial instruments with another entity under conditions that are potentially favourable; or

(d) an equity instrument of another entity.

A *financial liability* is any liability that is a contractual obligation:

(a) to deliver cash or another financial asset to another entity; or
(b) to exchange financial instruments with another entity under conditions that are potentially unfavourable.

An *equity instrument* is an instrument that evidences an ownership interest in an entity, ie a residual interest in the assets of the entity after deducting all of its liabilities.

> 'Equity instrument' has a wider meaning than equity shares because it includes some non-equity shares, as well as warrants and options to subscribe for or purchase equity shares in the issuing entity.

Floating rate financial assets and financial liabilities:-

Financial assets and financial liabilities that attract an interest charge and have their interest rate reset at least once a year.

> For the purposes of the FRS, financial assets and financial liabilities that have their interest rate reset less frequently than once a year are to be treated as fixed rate financial assets and financial liabilities.

Functional currency:-

The currency of the primary economic environment in which an entity operates and generates net cash flows.

> SSAP 20 'Foreign currency translation' uses the term 'local currency' rather than the term 'functional currency', although the definitions of the two terms are identical.

Insurance company or group:-

A company that carries on an insurance business and is regulated accordingly or an insurance group as defined in the relevant legislation.*

Non-equity shares:-

Shares possessing any of the following characteristics:

In the UK an insurance company is one to which Part II of the Insurance Companies Act 1982 applies. The equivalent reference in the Republic of Ireland is the Companies (Amendment) Act 1986 section 2(3). An insurance group is defined in Great Britain in section 255A of the Companies Act 1985 and in Northern Ireland in Article 263A of the Companies (Northern Ireland) Order 1986. In the Republic of Ireland an insurance company or group is one to which Regulation 3 of the European Community (Insurance Undertakings: Accounts) Regulation 1996 applies.* ***Editor's note**: Insurance companies are now defined in section 1165 of the Companies Act 2006.*

(a) any of the rights of the shares to receive payments (whether in respect of dividends, in respect of redemption or otherwise) are for a limited amount that is not calculated by reference to the company's assets or profits or the dividends on any class of equity share.
(b) any of their rights to participate in a surplus in a winding-up are limited to a specific amount that is not calculated by reference to the company's assets or profits and such limitation had a commercial effect in practice at the time the shares were issued or, if later, at the time the limitation was introduced.
(c) the shares are redeemable either according to their terms, or because the holder, or any party other than the issuer, can require their redemption.*

Short-term debtors and creditors:-

Financial assets and financial liabilities that meet all of the following criteria:

(a) they would be included under one of the following balance sheet headings if the entity was preparing its financial statements in accordance with Schedule 4 to the Companies Act 1985:†
   (i) debtors;
   (ii) prepayments and accrued income;
   (iii) creditors: amounts falling due within one year, other than items that would be included under the 'debenture loans' and 'bank loans and overdrafts' subheadings;
   (iv) provisions for liabilities and charges; or
   (v) accruals and deferred income;

(b) they mature or become payable within 12 months of the balance sheet date; and
(c) they are not a derivative financial instrument.

Trading in financial assets and financial liabilities:-

Buying, selling, issuing or holding financial assets and financial liabilities in order to take advantage of short-term changes in market prices or rates or, in the case of financial institutions and financial institution groups, in order to facilitate customer transactions.

Financial assets and financial liabilities bought, sold, issued or held in order to hedge the risks associated with another transaction or position are deemed to be trading in financial assets and financial liabilities only if that other transaction or position involves such trading.

****Editor's note:*** *This is no longer consistent with UK practice in other areas, since FRS 4 was largely replaced by FRS 25.*

†*in Great Britain. The equivalent legislation in Northern Ireland is Schedule 4 to the Companies (Northern Ireland) Order 1986 and in the Republic of Ireland the Schedule to the Companies (Amendment) Act 1986.* ***Editor's Note:*** *Schedule 4 is replaced by Schedule 1 to the Large and Medium-sized Companies and Groups (Accounts and Reports) Regulations 2008 (SI 2008/410) for accounting periods beginning on or after 6 April 2008.*

ENTITIES REQUIRED TO PROVIDE THE DISCLOSURES SET OUT IN THIS PART OF THE FRS

3 **Part A of the FRS applies to all financial statements that are intended to give a true and fair view of the reporting entity's financial position and profit or loss (or income and expenditure) for a period and are prepared by a reporting entity that has any of its capital instruments listed or publicly traded on a stock exchange or market, except that it does not apply:**

(a) if the entity is:

(i) a financial institution or financial institution group;
(ii) an entity that is applying the Financial Reporting Standard for Smaller Entities currently applicable; or
(iii) an insurance company or group.

(b) to a parent's own financial statements when those statements are presented together with the parent's consolidated financial statements.

4 The term 'stock exchange or market' includes domestic and foreign exchanges and markets and it also includes markets other than the main market. It therefore includes markets such as the London and Irish Stock Exchanges, EASDAQ, NASDAQ and the Alternative Investment Market.

INSTRUMENTS TO BE DEALT WITH IN THE DISCLOSURES

Financial assets and financial liabilities to be dealt with in the disclosures

5 **The FRS applies to all financial assets and financial liabilities, except that those listed below are to be excluded from the disclosures (other than the currency disclosures set out in paragraphs 34-37):**

(a) interests in subsidiary, quasi-subsidiary and associated undertakings, partnerships and joint ventures that fall within the relevant FRS concerned with such interests, other than an interest in such entities that is held exclusively with a view to subsequent resale;*
(b) employers' obligations to employees under employee share option and employee share schemes, and any shares held in order to fulfil such obligations;
(c) pension and other post-retirement benefit assets and liabilities that fall within the scope of FRS 17 'Retirement Benefits';
(d) rights and obligations arising under operating leases, as defined by SSAP 21 'Accounting for leases and hire purchase contracts';
(e) equity shares issued by the reporting entity and warrants and options on such shares issued by the reporting entity, other than those that are held exclusively with a view to subsequent resale;
(f) financial assets, financial liabilities and cash-settled commodity contracts of an insurance company or group.

**Subsidiary undertakings are dealt with in FRS 2 'Accounting for Subsidiary Undertakings', quasi-subsidiary undertakings are dealt with in FRS 5 'Reporting the Substance of Transactions', and associated undertakings, partnerships and joint ventures are dealt with in FRS 9 'Associates and Joint Ventures'. Equity minority interests in subsidiaries and quasi-subsidiaries are not financial instruments and therefore also do not need to be dealt with in the disclosures.*

Short-term debtors and creditors

An entity should exclude from all the disclosures (other than the currency disclosures set out in paragraphs 34-37) either all or none of its short-term debtors and creditors. An explanation of how such items have been dealt with should be provided. 6

The main focus of the FRS is on financial instruments that are complex or play a significant medium- to long-term role in the financial risk profile of the entity. Such financial instruments do not generally include short-term debtors and creditors. The FRS therefore does not require such items to be included in the disclosures. On the other hand, some entities may regard it as useful to include such items or may find it easier to do so. Paragraph 6 therefore permits entities either to include or to exclude such items. However, in order to achieve a degree of consistency and comparability, either all such items should be excluded from all the disclosures (other than the currency disclosures) or none of the items should be excluded from any of the disclosures. 7

Non-equity shares issued by the reporting entity

All non-equity shares issued by the reporting entity should be dealt with in the disclosures in the same way as its financial liabilities, except that they should be disclosed separately. 8

Although all non-equity shares issued by the reporting entity are financial instruments, only some of them are financial liabilities of that entity; the rest are equity instruments. However, rather than introduce complexity into the FRS by requiring entities to categorise non-equity shares into equity instruments and financial liabilities, paragraph 8 adopts a pragmatic approach. 9

Commodity contracts

Similarly, although commodity contracts requiring settlement by physical delivery are not financial instruments, paragraph 64 requires some such contracts to be included in certain of the disclosures as if they were. 10

DISCLOSURE OF OBJECTIVES, POLICIES AND STRATEGIES

The disclosures required by the FRS focus primarily on the risks that arise in connection with financial instruments (and certain similar contracts) and how they have been managed. These risks will typically include credit risk, liquidity risk, cash flow risk, interest rate risk, currency risk and other types of market price risk – all of which are discussed in greater detail in Appendix I – although the risks may be categorised in some other way. 11

It is envisaged, but not required, that the information provided about these risks – in other words, the disclosures required by the FRS – will usually be presented in the context of a discussion, in a statement such as the operating and financial review, of the entity's activities, structure and financing. This discussion will typically also consider the financial risk profile of the entity as a whole, before focusing specifically on financial instruments. Such an approach enables the disclosures required by the 12

FRS to be put into their proper context and it ensures that the disclosures required focus on the risks of greatest significance to the entity.

13 **An explanation should be provided of the role that financial instruments have had during the period in creating or changing the risks the entity faces in its activities. This should include an explanation of the objectives and policies for holding or issuing financial instruments and similar contracts, and the strategies for achieving those objectives – in both cases as agreed by the directors – that have been followed during the period.**

14 This disclosure would usually include a discussion of the nature of, and purposes for which, the main types of financial instruments and similar contracts are held or issued. Instruments used for financing, for risk management or hedging and for trading or speculation would all need to be covered, though separately from each other.

15 The disclosure would also typically include a description of the main financial risk management and treasury policies agreed by the directors, including the policies, quantified where appropriate, on:

(a) the fixed/floating split, maturity profile and currency profile of financial assets and liabilities;
(b) the extent to which foreign currency financial assets and financial liabilities are hedged to the functional currency of the business unit concerned;
(c) the extent to which foreign currency borrowings and other financial instruments are used to hedge foreign currency net investments; and
(d) any other hedging.

16 **If the disclosure described in paragraph 13 reflects a significant change from the explanations provided for the previous accounting period, this should be disclosed and the reasons for the change explained.**

17 This disclosure would include changes resulting from changes in the entity's main market price risks and from changes in the way that its exposures are managed.

18 **If the directors agreed, before the date of approval of the financial statements, to make a significant change to the role that financial instruments will have in creating or changing the risks of the entity, that change should be explained.**

19 The disclosures described in paragraphs 11-17 focus on the position during and at the end of the reporting period. However, to help users in making assessments about the entity, it is also important that details are provided of any changes the directors have agreed to make during the course of the next accounting period to the role that financial instruments will have. Paragraph 18 requires such information. This disclosure is supplemented by the requirements of SSAP 17 'Accounting for post balance sheet events' concerning the disclosure of certain events that occur after the balance sheet date.

20 **An explanation should be provided of how the period-end numerical disclosures shown in the financial statements reflect the objectives, policies and strategies disclosed under paragraph 13. If the period-end position is regarded as materially unrepresentative of the entity's position during the period or of its agreed objectives, policies and strategies, an explanation of the extent to which it is regarded as unrepresentative should be provided.**

If an entity uses financial instruments as hedges, it should describe: 21

(a) the transactions and risks that have been hedged, including the period of time until they are expected to occur; and
(b) the instruments used for hedging purposes, distinguishing between those that have been accounted for using hedge accounting and those that have not.

In this context a 'hedge' is an instrument that individually, or with other instruments, has a value or cash flow that is expected, wholly or partly, to move inversely with changes in the value or cash flows of the position being hedged. 22

The required disclosures described in paragraphs 11-22 should be given either in the financial statements or in some other statement, such as the operating and financial review, that is made available with the financial statements, provided that, if the disclosures are not included in the financial statements, they are incorporated therein by means of a cross-reference in the notes to the financial statements to the exact location of the disclosures. 23

NUMERICAL DISCLOSURES – GENERAL MATTERS

The disclosures required by the FRS are intended to be highly summarised, which is why the FRS prescribes in some detail the offsetting and aggregation to be used. It needs to be recognised, however, that the disclosures will involve a greater degree of aggregation and more offsetting than would be appropriate for recognition purposes. For example, the currency risk disclosures require various derivative financial instruments to be offset or aggregated with other financial assets and financial liabilities and the resulting, combined figure to be analysed. Whilst such a treatment is appropriate for the purposes of that particular disclosure, it does not follow that it would be appropriate for recognition purposes. 24

One effect of the high degree of aggregation and offsetting required, or encouraged, by the FRS is that it may not be possible to trace the components of the disclosures back to their respective balance sheet captions. Where this is the case, it will often be helpful to provide additional detail to enable the figures to be traced back unless that additional detail would unduly complicate the disclosure. 25

INTEREST RATE RISK DISCLOSURES

Financial liabilities

The aggregate carrying amount of financial liabilities should be analysed, by principal currency, to show separately those liabilities at fixed interest rates, those at floating interest rates and those on which no interest is paid. In preparing the analysis: 26

(a) interest rate swaps, currency swaps, forward contracts and other derivative financial instruments whose effect is to alter the interest or currency basis of the financial liabilities should, as far as possible, be taken into account;
(b) any financial liabilities and derivative financial instruments that cannot be adequately reflected in the analysis should be excluded and a summary of their main effects provided instead.

27 Finance lease obligations, and deep discounted bonds and similar liabilities whose finance costs are allocated in accordance with FRS 4, are not 'financial liabilities on which no interest is paid'. Financial assets accounted for in a similar way are similarly not 'financial assets on which no interest is earned'.

28 The requirement that derivative financial instruments should be taken into account in preparing the analysis means, for example, that, if the reporting entity has taken out a floating rate borrowing and has also entered into an interest rate swap that has the economic effect of replacing that floating rate borrowing with a fixed rate borrowing, the borrowing should be shown as a fixed rate borrowing in the disclosure.

29 The information to be provided about instruments excluded from the main analysis will need to be sufficient to enable the reader to understand their significance for the entity's interest rate risk profile, without providing excessive detail. Amongst other things, this might include disclosing, on a summarised basis:

(a) the notional amounts of principal involved;
(b) the rates of interest;
(c) the period for which the contracts are operative; and
(d) the terms of any options contained within the instrument.

30 **The following should also be disclosed by reference to principal currency:**

(a) the weighted average interest rate of the fixed rate financial liabilities;
(b) the weighted average period for which interest rates on the fixed rate financial liabilities are fixed;
(c) the weighted average period until maturity for financial liabilities on which no interest is paid; and
(d) the benchmark rate for determining interest payments for the floating rate financial liabilities.

31 Some entities manage the interest rate risk on their borrowings on a gross basis (in other words, without netting off cash, other liquid resources and perhaps similar items), while others manage it on a net basis. The FRS requires the interest rate risk disclosures to be prepared on a gross basis, although this does not prevent entities from showing the figures on a net basis if the difference is not material. If the difference is material but an entity still wishes to show the position on a net basis, additional information showing the net position may be included in the analysis so long as the gross position is also shown.

Financial assets

32 **If an entity has material holdings of financial assets, the same required information as is described by paragraphs 26-31 should be provided about them.**

33 An entity's holdings of financial assets may include investments in equity shares and in other instruments that neither pay interest nor have a maturity date. The disclosures to be provided under paragraph 32 for such instruments will typically be limited to information about any currency exposures involved.

CURRENCY RISK DISCLOSURES

An analysis should be provided of the net amount of monetary assets and liabilities* at the balance sheet date showing the amount denominated in each currency, analysed by reference to the functional currencies of the operations involved. In preparing this analysis: **34**

(a) to avoid excessive detail, the focus should be on the principal functional currencies and on the principal currencies in which the monetary items are denominated.

(b) monetary assets and liabilities denominated in the same currency as the functional currency of the operations involved should not be included in the analysis.

(c) if an entity has used foreign currency borrowings to finance, or provide a hedge against, foreign net investments† and the exchange gains or losses on those borrowings are included in the statement of total recognised gains and losses in accordance with SSAP 20, those borrowings should not be included in the analysis.

(d) account should as far as possible be taken of the effect of currency swaps, forward contracts and other derivative financial instruments that contribute to the matching of foreign currency exposures and a summary should be provided of the main effect of any such financial instruments that have not been taken into account.

The purpose of the disclosure required by paragraph 34 is to show an analysis of the currency exposures that give rise to the net currency gains and losses recognised in the profit and loss account. **35**

The analysis will therefore need to be constructed to reflect the entity's application of SSAP 20. SSAP 20 requires financial statements to reflect the financial results and relationships as measured in the functional currency of each operation's financial statements before translation. This means that: **36**

(a) assets and liabilities denominated in the same currency as the functional currency of the entity that utilises them will not need to be remeasured using the entity's functional currency, which is why paragraph 34(b) requires such assets and liabilities to be excluded from the analysis.

(b) assets and liabilities that are not denominated in the same currency as the functional currency of the entity that utilises them will need to be remeasured using the entity's functional currency and will therefore result in translation gains and losses. Under SSAP 20, all such gains and losses, other than those referred to in paragraph 37 below, will be included in the profit and loss account. The disclosure set out in paragraph 34 focuses on the currency exposures giving rise to these gains and losses.

(c) assets and liabilities, once expressed in the functional currency of the entity that utilises them, give rise to further differences on translation of the net investment in that currency to the reporting currency of the reporting entity. For the reasons explained in SSAP 20, this translation difference is required to be

As the currency disclosure required by the FRS is intended to reflect the reporting entity's application of SSAP 20, the terminology of SSAP 20 (ie 'monetary assets' and 'monetary liabilities') has been used instead of the FRS's usual references to financial assets and financial liabilities.* ***Editor's Note:* *For companies complying with FRS 26, FRS 23 is now the relevant standard. For such companies, all further references to SSAP 20 also need to be considered against FRS 23.*

†Although the FRS uses the term 'foreign net investment', SSAP 20 uses two different terms to describe the same item: 'foreign equity investments' and 'net investments'.

included in the statement of total recognised gains and losses, rather than the profit and loss account, and is therefore not dealt with in the analysis set out above.

37 Under SSAP 20, if a foreign currency borrowing qualifies as a hedge against a foreign net investment, the translation gains and losses on the foreign currency borrowing may be excluded from the profit and loss account and, instead, reported in the statement of total recognised gains and losses where they offset those on the foreign net investment. Paragraph 34(c) requires the currency exposures giving rise to such gains and losses to be excluded from the disclosure required by the FRS.

LIQUIDITY DISCLOSURES

38 **A maturity profile of the carrying amount of financial liabilities should be presented, showing amounts falling due:**

(a) in one year or less, or on demand;
(b) in more than one year but not more than two years;
(c) in more than two years but not more than five years; and
(d) in more than five years.

The maturity profile should be determined by reference to the earliest date on which payment can be required or on which the liability falls due.

39 In order to provide the disclosure required by paragraph 38, the maturity analyses of debt and finance lease obligations required by FRS 4 and SSAP 21 respectively could be brought together and extended. If this approach is adopted, the analyses of debt and finance lease obligations will need to be based on the carrying amounts and not, for example, on the amounts to be paid on maturity or, in the case of lease obligations, on the gross obligations before deduction of finance charges. In addition:

(a) an analysis of the carrying amount of financial liabilities other than debt and finance lease obligations would need to be provided; and
(b) those obligations under finance leases that are payable in the second to fifth years would need to be analysed into those that are payable in more than one year but not more than two years and those that are payable in more than two years but not more than five years.

40 **An analysis of the maturity of any material undrawn committed borrowing facilities of the entity should also be provided, showing those amounts expiring:**

(a) in one year or less;
(b) in more than one year but not more than two years; and
(c) in more than two years.

If conditions precedent are attached to a committed facility, it should be included in the analysis only if all the conditions were satisfied at the balance sheet date.

41 The maturity analysis of debt required by paragraphs 33-36 of FRS 4 takes into account certain committed borrowing facilities. To avoid double-counting, such facilities should not also be included in the disclosure set out in paragraph 40 above.

The adequacy of undrawn committed borrowing facilities will usually depend on a number of factors. In order to help the reader to assess the significance of the facilities, it will often be useful to provide details of the purpose and the period for which material facilities are committed and the extent to which the facilities are subject to annual review by the provider of the finance. 42

Although the FRS does not require a maturity analysis of financial assets, some entities may find it helpful to provide one in order to show the maturity analyses of financial liabilities and borrowing facilities in their proper context. 43

FAIR VALUE DISCLOSURES

An entity should group its financial assets and financial liabilities (whether recognised or unrecognised) into appropriate categories and for each category should disclose either: 44

(a) the aggregate fair value as at the balance sheet date together with the aggregate carrying amount; or

(b) the aggregate fair value of items with a positive fair value and, separately, the aggregate fair value of items with a negative fair value, in both cases as at the balance sheet date and in each case accompanied by the relevant aggregate carrying amount.

Entities can choose whether to disclose a single net figure for each category of financial asset and financial liability or to disclose two 'gross' figures. Entities developing systems to meet this requirement need to be aware, however, that, if a subsequent FRS requires most or all financial assets and financial liabilities to be carried on the balance sheet at fair value, gross figures would then be required. 45

Financial assets and financial liabilities are to be grouped into appropriate categories for the purpose of disclosing fair values. It will usually help users' understanding if those categories take into account the purpose for which each asset or liability is held or issued and the type of asset or liability involved. The categories will typically follow the same structure as – but be in more detail than – that used in discussing the objectives, policies and strategies for holding or issuing financial instruments. For example, interest rate derivatives would usually be shown separately from currency derivatives and interest rate derivatives would usually be split between interest rate swaps and instruments such as caps and collars. As it will generally be helpful to categorise like with like, financial assets would not usually be included in a category that also included financial liabilities. However, an exception to this might be that similar derivative financial instruments held or issued for the same purpose would be grouped together, regardless of whether their fair value was positive or negative. 46

Fair values are to be disclosed regardless of whether the financial asset or financial liability involved is held as a hedge. However, if the item is a hedge, it may be useful, in providing the fair value information, to indicate the link between the hedge and the hedged item and to explain whether the fair value of the hedged item is also disclosed. 47

If the estimated difference between the carrying amount of a financial asset or financial liability (or of a category of them) and its fair value is not material, the carrying amount may be used as the fair value. 48

For some financial assets and financial liabilities, the historical cost carrying amount will approximate to fair value. Examples of such assets and liabilities might include 49 debtors and creditors subject to normal trade credit terms,* other short-term financial assets and liabilities and other financial instruments (such as floating rate debt) where payments are reset to market rates at frequent intervals.

50 However, not all debtors and creditors will have a historical cost carrying amount that approximates to fair value. For example, the fair value of the reporting entity's own long-term fixed rate debt may be materially greater or lower than its carrying amount depending on changes in interest rates since the debt was issued. Another example may be a long-term debtor where the delay in settlement is not compensated for by interest at current market rates.

51 **The method(s) and any significant assumptions used in determining fair value should be disclosed.**

52 Guidance on procedures for estimating the fair value of financial assets and financial liabilities is set out in Appendix IV.

53 **No fair value need be disclosed if it is not practicable for the reporting entity to estimate with sufficient reliability the fair value of any financial asset or financial liability, or category of them, that is not traded on an organised market in a standard form. In such circumstances, the following should be provided instead:**

(a) a description of the financial asset or financial liability (or category of them) and its carrying amount.

(b) the reasons why it is not practicable for the reporting entity to estimate the fair value with sufficient reliability.

(c) information about the principal characteristics of the underlying financial asset or financial liability (or category of them) that is pertinent to estimating its fair value – for example the factors that determine or affect the instrument's cash flow – and the market for such instruments. Such information need not be provided if, at the level of aggregation and date at which the information would otherwise be disclosed, its disclosure is likely, in the opinion of the directors, to be seriously prejudicial to the entity's interests. The fact that such information has not been disclosed and the reasons for the omission should be stated.

54 Before this exemption can be invoked, the entity will need to have exhausted all viable methods of estimating and disclosing a sufficiently reliable fair value.

(a) If it is possible to estimate the range of amounts within which the fair value may lie, the requirement in paragraph 44 can be met by disclosing that range.

(b) If it is impracticable to estimate the fair value of individual instruments, it may be practicable to estimate the fair value of a portfolio of them. In those cases the FRS requires the fair value of the portfolio to be used.

(c) If it is practicable for an entity to estimate the fair value of some, but not all, of a class of financial instruments, the FRS requires the fair value of that subset to be disclosed and the disclosures described in paragraph 53 to be provided for the rest of that class.

55 Factors that would generally be present for the exemption described in paragraph 53 to apply include:

**Such items will usually be short-term debtors and creditors and therefore – depending on whether advantage is taken of paragraph 6 of the FRS – may not need to be dealt with in the disclosures.*

(a) the financial asset or financial liability is unique and no comparable instruments exist;
(b) the future cash flows of the financial asset or financial liability are difficult to predict reliably; and
(c) a reliable valuation model is not available from internal or external sources.

Whether the exemption will need to be applied will depend on the circumstances involved. These circumstances may vary over time and, as a result, what is not practicable in one year may be practicable in another. **56**

DISCLOSURES ABOUT FINANCIAL ASSETS AND FINANCIAL LIABILITIES HELD OR ISSUED FOR TRADING

If the reporting entity trades in financial assets and financial liabilities, the following information should be provided: **57**

(a) the net gain or loss from trading in financial assets and financial liabilities that has been included in the profit and loss account during the period, analysed by type of financial instrument, business activity, risk or in such other way as is consistent with the entity's management of this activity.
(b) if the analysis provided in accordance with subparagraph (a) is other than by type of financial instrument, a description, for each line of that analysis, of the types of financial instruments involved.
(c) the period-end fair value of financial assets and, separately, of financial liabilities, held or issued for trading.
(d) if the period-end position disclosed in accordance with subparagraph (c) is regarded as materially unrepresentative of the entity's typical position during the period, the average fair value over the period of financial assets and financial liabilities held or issued for trading. The average fair value should be calculated using daily figures or, if the figures are not calculated daily, using the most frequent interval that an entity's systems generate for management, regulatory or other reasons.

DISCLOSURES ABOUT HEDGES

Some entities use financial assets and financial liabilities as hedges to manage their risk profile. When instruments are used in this way, they are usually accounted for using hedge accounting. Under hedge accounting, changes in fair values of the hedge (referred to hereafter as 'the gain or loss on the hedge')* are usually not recognised in the profit and loss account immediately they arise. Instead, they either are not recognised at all or are recognised and carried forward in the balance sheet; then, when the hedged transaction occurs, the gain or loss on the hedge is usually either used to adjust the amount at which the hedged item is dealt with in the financial statements or recognised in the profit and loss account at the same time as the hedged item. **58**

**For ease of reference, all changes in the fair value or cash flows of financial assets and financial liabilities used as hedges are referred to in the FRS as 'gains' and 'losses'.*

59 The following information should be provided about gains and losses on financial assets and financial liabilities for which hedge accounting has been used:

(a) the cumulative aggregate gains and losses that are unrecognised at the balance sheet date. If the item's fair value is not disclosed under the FRS, any gain or loss on the item need not be dealt with in this disclosure.

(b) the cumulative aggregate gains and losses carried forward in the balance sheet at the balance sheet date, pending their recognition in the profit and loss account.

(c) the extent to which the gains and losses disclosed under (a) and (b) are expected to be recognised in the profit and loss account in the next accounting period.

(d) the amount of gains and losses included in the reporting period's profit and loss account that arose in previous years and were either unrecognised or carried forward in the balance sheet at the start of the reporting period.

60 The disclosures described in paragraph 59(b), (c) and (d) should not include gains or losses on hedges that have been accounted for by adjusting the carrying amount of a fixed asset recognised on the balance sheet.

61 Paragraph 60 is intended as a pragmatic response to the practical difficulties involved in trying to keep a record of the gains and losses on hedges that have been accounted for by adjusting the carrying amount of a fixed asset and are now being recognised in the profit and loss account through the depreciation charge. Although similar problems can arise on gains and losses accounted for by adjusting the carrying amount of other assets and liabilities, the paragraph deals only with fixed assets because that is where the difficulties are greatest.

62 If financial assets or financial liabilities previously accounted for as hedges are reclassified during the period and no longer accounted for as hedges and, as a result, gains and losses that arose in previous years have been recognised in the reporting period's profit and loss account, the amount of those gains and losses should be disclosed.

63 Although it will be rare for an entity to reclassify instruments previously accounted for (or designated) as hedges, it may happen. Such reclassifications are accounted for in a variety of ways and paragraph 62 requires disclosure only to the extent that gains and losses that arose in previous periods are recognised, on reclassification, in the profit and loss account.

DISCLOSURES ABOUT COMMODITY CONTRACTS

64 Subject to paragraph 65, entities within the scope of this part of the FRS should treat cash-settled commodity contracts as if they were financial assets or financial liabilities for the purposes of:

(a) the narrative disclosures described in paragraphs 11-23;

(b) the fair value disclosures described in paragraphs 44-56;

(c) the disclosures about financial assets and financial liabilities held or issued for trading described in paragraph 57; and

(d) the disclosures about hedges described in paragraphs 58-63.

65 Where an entity participates in an illiquid commodity market and it can demonstrate that:

(a) the market is dominated by very few participants; and

(b) **disclosure of some of the information required by paragraph 64(b), (c) or (d) at the time that its financial statements become publicly available is likely to move the market significantly and, in the directors' opinion, would be seriously prejudicial to the interests of the entity,**

that part of the disclosures need not be given. The fact that such information has not been disclosed and the reasons for the omission should be stated.

ADDITIONAL DISCLOSURES ABOUT MARKET PRICE RISK

Entities are encouraged, but not required, to provide numerical disclosures that show the magnitude of market price risk arising over the period for all financial instruments and cash-settled commodity contracts and, if significant, all other items carrying market price risk. This information should be provided using a technique or other basis that is consistent with the way the entity manages its risk exposures. Entities that use one approach to manage market price risk in one part of their business and a different approach in another part are encouraged to provide separate disclosures for each part. **66**

Entities are also encouraged to provide a discussion of their approach to market price risk so as to set the numerical information in context and to assist in its interpretation. **67**

It is important to choose a disclosure approach that gives meaningful information without oversimplifying the position or inundating the user with unmanageable amounts of data. Entities are encouraged to report in ways that reflect how the risk is managed. This could involve one of the methods described below, another method or a combination of approaches. **68**

(a) *More details about positions at the reporting date* and perhaps activity during the period. For example, an entity with a small number of swaps might disclose for each material swap the fixed rate, the benchmark used to determine the floating rate and the maturity. However, entities that use a large number of financial instruments may find such disclosures impractical.

(b) *Sensitivity analysis,* ie the hypothetical effects on net assets or profits of various possible changes in market prices. This might involve disclosing, for example, the effects of one percentage point and two percentage point increases and decreases in all interest rates; flattening or steepening of the yield curve; a 10 per cent increase or decrease in all or selected exchange rates; and 20 per cent changes in prices of securities held. (These amounts of change are illustrative only.) Entities providing this disclosure would usually show some of the changes in market prices that they actually use in managing or adjusting risk.

One of the limitations of sensitivity analysis is that it shows the effect of only the chosen changes in market prices; a very different effect could arise from greater or smaller changes, particularly if the instruments involve options. Another limitation is that a market price change rarely occurs in isolation. For example, a change in inflation expectations may cause changes in all of interest rates, exchange rates and equity prices, perhaps with a time delay, yet sensitivity analysis will typically show the effect of one of these changes while assuming that all other prices and rates remain unchanged. Another limitation is that sensitivity analysis takes no account of the fact that some market price changes are more likely than others.

(c) *'Gap' analysis* of interest rate repricing and/or maturity dates. This approach involves analysing assets and liabilities into time bands by reference to interest rate repricing dates or maturity dates. It should be noted that gap analysis reports on interest rate risk only, is not always able to capture the effect of all options and is less useful where instruments are not all denominated in the same currency (unless separate analyses are provided for each currency).

(d) *'Duration' of instruments*. This approach, which also deals only with interest rate risk, is a method of measuring sensitivity to interest rate changes. Duration is the length (in years) of a hypothetical zero coupon bond whose value would change by the same amount as that of the instrument(s) in response to a change in interest rates. A shorter duration indicates a lower level of interest rate sensitivity. This approach suffers from the same drawbacks as gap analysis.

(e) *Value at risk*. The value at risk of a group of assets and liabilities is the expected loss that will arise on those assets and liabilities from an adverse market movement with a specified probability over a specified period of time. For example, based on a simulation of a large number of possible scenarios, an entity might determine with 95 per cent probability that any adverse change in the fair value of its financial instruments over a ten-day holding period will not exceed £N, in which case £N will be the value at risk of that group of instruments.

69 If the disclosures described in paragraph 66 are provided, they should be supplemented by:

(a) an explanation of the method used and of the main parameters and assumptions underlying the data provided;

(b) an explanation of the objective of the method used and of the limitations that may result in the information not fully reflecting the market price risk of the assets and liabilities involved; and

(c) reasons for any material changes in the amount of reported market price risk when compared with that reported for the previous period.

70 Whilst many entities, particularly financial institutions, are very interested in value at risk as a way of monitoring and managing risk, there is, as yet, no consensus on the methodology or assumptions to be used. Different methodologies and assumptions produce very different value at risk numbers. This is also true of sensitivity analysis. Requiring the disclosure of the methodology and assumptions used will put the user on notice of this fact. In the case of value at risk, for example, the details to be disclosed will usually include the holding period and confidence limits, and might also include the historical observation period and weightings applied to observations within that period, an explanation of how options are dealt with in the calculations and which volatilities and correlations (or, alternatively, Monte Carlo probability distribution simulations) are used. The FRS also requires the limitations and objectives of the method used to be disclosed. This disclosure is intended to ensure that users understand that the information provided is a relative estimate of risk and not a precise and accurate number.

71 If material changes are made to the method, or key assumptions and parameters, used in providing the disclosure described in paragraph 66, the reasons for the change should be given and the previous period's information should be restated using the basis adopted in the current period.

72 The purpose of the requirement set out in paragraph 71 is to provide a degree of comparability between the information provided for the reporting period and the

previous period. The intention is that any material change in method, assumptions or parameters that has had a significant effect on the comparability of the information should be dealt with by restating the figures for the previous period; changes that do not have such an effect do not require restatement.

DISCLOSURE OF ACCOUNTING POLICIES

FRS 18 'Accounting policies' requires a description to be given of each of the accounting policies that is material in the context of an entity's financial statements. Disclosing the accounting policies used for financial instruments is of particular importance in view of the wide variety of accounting treatments that are adopted. **73**

In order to comply with FRS 18 'Accounting policies', the description of accounting policies will usually need to include (if the choice of policy applied has had a material effect) a description of: **74**

(a) the methods used to account for derivative financial instruments, the types of derivative financial instruments accounted for under each method and the criteria that determine the method used.
(b) the basis for recognising, measuring (both on initial recognition and subsequently), and ceasing to recognise financial assets and financial liabilities.
(c) how income and expenses (and other gains and losses) are recognised and measured.
(d) the treatment of financial assets and financial liabilities not recognised, including an explanation of how provisions for losses are recognised on financial assets and financial liabilities that have not been recognised.
(e) policies on offsetting.

Where financial instruments are carried on the historical cost basis, features covered by the description of accounting policies would typically include (where the choice of policy applied has had a material effect) the treatment of: **75**

(a) premiums and discounts on financial assets;
(b) changes in the estimated amount of determinable future cash flows associated with a financial instrument, such as a debenture indexed to a commodity price;
(c) a fall in the fair value of a financial asset to below the asset's carrying amount; and
(d) restructured financial liabilities.

Where financial instruments are used as hedges and accounted for using hedge accounting, the description of accounting policies will usually need to include (if the choice of policy has had a material effect) a description of: **76**

(a) the circumstances in which a financial instrument is accounted for as a hedge;
(b) the recognition and measurement treatment applied to an instrument used as a hedge;
(c) the method used to account for an instrument that ceases to be accounted for as a hedge;
(d) the method used to account for the hedge when the underlying item or position matures, is sold, extinguished, or terminated; and
(e) the method used to account for the hedge of a future transaction when that transaction is no longer likely to occur.

AMENDMENT TO FRS 4

77 **FRS 4 is amended by replacing paragraph 33 with the following paragraph:**

'An analysis of the maturity of debt should be provided showing amounts falling due:

(a) in one year or less, or on demand;
(b) in more than one year but not more than two years;
(c) in more than two years but not more than five years; and
(d) in more than five years.'

78 The effect of this amendment will be to change the band into which amounts that are due exactly five years after the balance sheet date will fall. Depending on the interpretation that has been used in the past, amounts that are due exactly two years after the balance sheet date may also now be dealt with in a different band.

DATE FROM WHICH EFFECTIVE

79 **The accounting practices set out in the FRS should be regarded as standard in respect of accounting periods ending on or after 23 March 1999. Earlier adoption is encouraged but not required.**

80 Corresponding amounts should be disclosed for each of the disclosures required by the FRS. However, this may not be practicable in all circumstances for the first accounting period in which the FRS comes into effect. Accordingly, such disclosure is not required for that period, although it is encouraged.

Part B - Banks and Similar Institutions and Banking and Similar Groups

Definitions

81 The following definitions, in addition to those set out in paragraph 2, shall apply in Part B of the FRS and in particular in the Statement of Standard Accounting Practice set out **in bold type** in Part B.

Bank or similar institution:-

An entity that:

(a) is authorised under the Banking Act 1987 (in the UK) or the Central Bank Acts 1942-1989 (in the Republic of Ireland); or
(b) whose business is to receive deposits or other repayable funds from the public and to grant credits for its own account.

The purpose of subparagraph (b), which repeats the definition of credit institution contained in the First Banking Coordination Directive (77/780/EEC), is to include within the term 'bank or similar institution' entities such as building societies and credit unions.

Banking or similar groups:-

Groups where:

(a) the parent company is a bank or similar institution; or
(b) the parent company:

  (i) does not itself carry on any material business apart from the acquisition, management and disposal of interests in subsidiary undertakings; and
  (ii) its principal subsidiary undertakings are wholly or mainly entities that are banks or similar institutions.

Trading book and non-trading book:-

The trading book comprises all the assets and liabilities held or issued as part of the entity's trading in financial assets and financial liabilities. The assets and liabilities that are not held in a trading book are non-trading book assets and liabilities.

The trading activities of banks and similar institutions, and many other financial institutions and groups, include:

- providing financial instruments to clients (other than through traditional lending and deposit-taking activities or by granting finance leases) – ie customer facilitation
- providing liquidity to the market – ie market-making
- acting as a connecting link between different markets – ie arbitrage
- taking proprietary positions
- related hedges.

The non-trading book comprises all the assets and liabilities that are not in the trading book, including structural and strategic positions. Non-trading activities include:

- traditional lending and deposit-taking
- granting of finance leases
- asset/liability and liquidity management
- investment activity, including activity of a strategic nature
- related hedges.

Although many financial institutions and groups are already required for capital adequacy purposes to categorise their assets and liabilities into trading book items and non-trading book items, the FRS does not require assets and liabilities to be categorised for its purposes in exactly the same way as for the purposes of the Capital Adequacy Directive (93/6/EEC).

ENTITIES REQUIRED TO PROVIDE THE DISCLOSURES SET OUT IN THIS PART OF THE FRS

Part B of the FRS applies to all financial statements that are intended to give a true and 82
fair view of the reporting entity's financial position and profit or loss (or income and expenditure) for a period and are prepared by a reporting entity that is a bank or similar institution or a banking or similar group, except that it does not apply to a parent's own financial statements when those statements are presented together with the parent's consolidated financial statements.

INSTRUMENTS TO BE DEALT WITH IN THE DISCLOSURES

83 The instruments to be dealt with in the disclosures set out in this part of the FRS are those referred to in paragraphs 5-10, except that:

(a) in paragraphs 5 and 6 the references to paragraphs 34-37 shall be taken to refer to paragraphs 90-97; and
(b) in paragraph 10 the reference to paragraph 64 shall be taken to refer to paragraphs 113 and 114; and
(c) financial assets and financial liabilities arising from traditional lending and deposit-taking activities shall not be treated as falling within the meaning of the term 'short-term debtors and creditors'.

DISCLOSURE OF OBJECTIVES, POLICIES AND STRATEGIES

84 Entities within the scope of this part of the FRS should provide the required disclosures, after taking into account the explanations, set out in paragraphs 11-23.

NUMERICAL DISCLOSURES – GENERAL MATTERS

85 Paragraphs 24 and 25 are also relevant in the context of the numerical disclosures required in this part of the FRS.

Interest rate risk disclosures

86 Interest rate risk may arise both on the trading book and on the non-trading book. The disclosures set out in paragraphs 87-89 focus on the interest rate exposures arising from the non-trading book; interest rate risk arising from the trading book is dealt with in the trading book disclosures described in paragraphs 104-111.

87 A table should be provided showing the aggregate carrying amounts of assets and liabilities in the non-trading book, analysed by category of asset and liability and, within those categories, into time bands. In this analysis:

(a) items should be allocated to time bands by reference to the earlier of the next interest rate repricing date and the maturity date.
(b) the time bands used should include at least the following:

(i) three months or less;
(ii) more than three months but not more than six months;
(iii) more than six months but not more than one year;
(iv) more than one year but not more than five years; and
(v) more than five years.

(c) the analysis should show the net position for each time band.
(d) account should as far as possible be taken of derivative financial instruments whose effect is to alter the interest basis of non-trading book assets and liabilities. Those that cannot be adequately reflected in the analysis should be excluded and a summary of their main effect provided instead.

88 A significant dimension of interest rate risk is the currency in which assets and liabilities are denominated. For example, a floating rate asset and a floating rate

liability denominated in different currencies will not appear, from the table required by paragraph 87, to create an interest rate sensitivity gap if their current sterling equivalent and repricing dates are the same. There may, however, be substantial interest rate risk exposure if one item is denominated in the currency of a country with high and fluctuating interest rates while the other is denominated in the currency of a country with low and stable interest rates. In such circumstances, entities are encouraged to incorporate details of the currency of denomination in the table.

The information provided on derivative financial instruments not taken into account in the table described in paragraph 87 will need to be sufficient to enable the reader to understand the significance of such instruments for the entity's non-trading book interest rate risk, without providing excessive detail. Amongst other things, this might include disclosing, on a summarised basis: **89**

(a) the notional amounts of principal involved;
(b) the period for which the instruments are operative;
(c) the main potential effect of the instruments on information provided in the analysis described in paragraph 87; and
(d) terms of any options contained within the instruments.

CURRENCY RISK DISCLOSURES

Viewed from the same perspective as that adopted in SSAP 20, the currency risk exposure of banks and similar institutions comprises three elements: **90**

(a) the structural currency exposures that arise from the entity's foreign equity investments as mitigated by the foreign currency borrowings taken out to finance or hedge such investments.
(b) the currency exposures arising on the monetary assets and monetary liabilities held in the non-trading book.
(c) the currency exposures that arise on the monetary assets and monetary liabilities held in the trading book.

The currency exposures that arise on the trading book are dealt with in the trading book disclosures set out in paragraphs 104-111. The other currency exposures are dealt with in the disclosures described in paragraphs 92-97, which will need to be constructed to reflect the entity's application of SSAP 20. **91**

The entity should provide an analysis of its foreign net investments:* **92**

(a) by reference to the principal functional currencies involved; and
(b) showing the extent to which such investments are financed or hedged by foreign currency borrowings that qualify under SSAP 20 as hedges of those investments.

This disclosure focuses on the entity's structural currency exposures. These exposures arise because the entity's operations involve functional currencies other than its reporting currency. As a result, the entity will need to translate the foreign currency denominated results and foreign currency net assets of subsidiaries, branches and associates into its reporting currency. This gives rise to translation gains and losses which, under SSAP 20, are recognised in the statement of total recognised gains and losses. **93**

**Although the FRS uses the term 'foreign net investment', SSAP 20 uses two different terms to describe the same item: 'foreign equity investments' and 'net investments'.*

94 To mitigate the effect of such exposures, the reporting entity may take out foreign currency borrowings to finance or hedge its foreign net investments. Under SSAP 20, if these borrowings meet certain criteria, the gains and losses on the borrowing can be offset against the translation gains and losses on the foreign net investments.

95 **An analysis should be provided of the net amount of monetary assets and liabilities* in the non-trading book at the balance sheet date showing the amount denominated in each principal currency, analysed by reference to the principal functional currencies of the operations involved. The analysis should not, however, include:**

(a) monetary assets and liabilities denominated in the same currency as the functional currency of the operations involved; and
(b) those foreign currency borrowings referred to in paragraph 92(b).

96 This disclosure focuses on the currency exposures on the monetary items in the entity's non-trading book. Many banks and similar institutions transfer all their currency risk arising from the commercial banking/lending activities to their trading book. If there are no remaining currency exposures in the non-trading book – or if the remaining exposures are immaterial – the disclosure set out in paragraph 95 will not need to be given. In such circumstances it will often be helpful to explain why no disclosures have been provided.

97 **In preparing the disclosures set out in paragraphs 92 and 95, account should as far as possible be taken of the effect of currency swaps, forward contracts and other derivative financial instruments that contribute to the matching of currency exposures and a summary should be provided of the main effect of any such instruments that have not been taken into account.**

FAIR VALUE DISCLOSURES

98 **The disclosures required by paragraphs 101 and 102 should be provided in respect of:**

(a) all financial assets and financial liabilities held in the trading book; and
(b) the following financial assets and financial liabilities held in the non-trading book:
(i) all derivative financial instruments;
(ii) all listed and/or publicly traded securities; and
(iii) any other financial asset or financial liability for which a liquid and active market exists, either for the asset or liability itself or for its component parts,

regardless of whether they are recognised or unrecognised.

99 For the purposes of paragraph 98(b)(iii), a market for a financial asset (or financial liability) is liquid and active if all of the following apply:

(a) assets (or liabilities) of the same type are regularly traded on the market.

**As the currency disclosure required by the* FRS *is intended to reflect the entity's application of* SSAP *20, the terminology of* SSAP *20 (ie 'monetary asset' and 'monetary liabilities') has been used instead of the* FRS*'s usual references to financial assets and financial liabilities.*

(b) the price determined from the market (by reference to, for example, quoted prices or last traded prices) is a reliable indicator of the price that would be obtained if some or all of the asset (or liability) was actually sold in the market in normal market conditions.

(c) there are willing buyers and sellers in the market at all times during normal business hours at the price referred to in subparagraph (b).

As markets are evolving rapidly, the fact that a liquid and active market does not exist for an item at present does not mean that such a market will not exist in the future. **100**

The financial assets and financial liabilities referred to in paragraph 98 should be grouped into appropriate categories of trading book and non-trading book items and, for each category, the reporting entity should disclose either: **101**

(a) the aggregate fair value as at the balance sheet date, together with the aggregate carrying amount; or

(b) the aggregate fair value of items with a positive fair value and, separately, the aggregate fair value of items with a negative fair value, in both cases as at the balance sheet date and in each case accompanied by the relevant aggregate carrying amount.

Entities within the scope of this part of the FRS should also provide the required disclosures, after taking into account the explanations, set out in paragraphs 45-52. **102**

DISCLOSURES ABOUT FINANCIAL ASSETS AND FINANCIAL LIABILITIES HELD OR ISSUED FOR TRADING

Entities within the scope of this part of the FRS should provide the disclosures required by paragraph 57. **103**

Subject to paragraph 111, the entity should disclose the highest, lowest and average exposure of its trading book to market price risk during the reporting period, together with the exposure at the balance sheet date, using at least one of the following methods: **104**

(a) The value at risk of the trading book as a whole.

(b) Sensitivity analysis showing the potential effect on earnings or net assets of selected hypothetical changes in market prices and rates. In this analysis:

(i) separate disclosures should be provided for each type of market price risk; and

(ii) the hypothetical changes used should be reasonably possible during the twelve months following the date on which the financial statements are approved by the directors. Furthermore, one of these hypothetical changes should be a fall of at least 10 per cent in the period-end market prices or rates unless such a fall can be shown not to be reasonably possible.

(c) Some other market price risk measure, but only if:

(i) the entity's management uses the model from which the measure has been derived for the purpose of managing the market price risk of the trading book; and

(ii) the entity's model has been approved by the entity's prudential regulator for the purpose of providing that regulator with capital adequacy returns on the entity.

105 Value at risk and sensitivity analysis are discussed further in paragraph 68. Although value at risk is generally regarded at present as the most sophisticated means available for measuring market price risk, in time to come risk management models may well be developed that are then regarded as more sophisticated than value at risk. The purpose of paragraph 104(c) is to allow for this possibility by permitting the use of unspecified models that have gained the approval of, inter alia, the prudential regulator.

106 Although a separate value at risk figure could be calculated for each type of market price risk to which the trading book is exposed, such a disclosure would not take account of the extent to which different market prices (such as interest rates and exchange rates) move together. The FRS therefore requires disclosure of a single value at risk figure that encapsulates the total market price risk of all kinds to which the entity's trading book is exposed. This is not practicable with sensitivity analysis, which is why paragraph 104(b)(i) requires separate disclosures for each type of market price risk.

107 **If one of the methods described in paragraph 104 is used to provide disclosures, those disclosures should be supplemented by the following:**

(a) **an explanation of the method used and of the main parameters and assumptions underlying the data provided.**

(b) **an explanation of the objective of the method used and of the limitations that may result in the information not fully reflecting the market price risk of the trading book.**

(c) **the frequency with which the figures were calculated when determining the highest, lowest and average figures for the period. This should, as a minimum, be the frequency at which the figures are calculated for risk management purposes. However, if those figures are calculated more frequently than daily, it will be sufficient to use daily figures for the purposes of the disclosure.**

(d) **reasons for any material changes in the amount of reported market price risk when compared with that reported for the previous period.**

108 **If material changes are made to the method, or the main assumptions and parameters, used in providing the disclosure required by paragraph 104, the reasons for the change should be given and the previous period's balance sheet date information should be restated using the basis adopted in the current period.**

109 The purpose of the requirement described in paragraph 108 is to provide a degree of comparability between the trading book information provided for the reporting period and for the previous period. The requirement refers to the restatement of balance sheet date information only, rather than also to the highest, lowest and average information required by paragraph 104, in order to avoid imposing a burden on those entities that might find such restatement particularly burdensome. However, entities are encouraged to restate all the information provided in respect of the previous period wherever possible.

110 The intention is that any material change in method, assumptions or parameters that has had a significant effect on the comparability of the information should be dealt with by restating the balance sheet date figures for the previous period; changes that do not have a significant effect on the comparability of the information do not require such restatement.

If none of the methods described in paragraph 104 is used by the entity to manage the market price risk of its trading book, the entity may provide, instead of the disclosures required by that paragraph, trading book disclosures in the format described for the non-trading book in paragraphs 87-89 and 95-97. Such disclosures should be provided separately from those for the non-trading book. 111

DISCLOSURES ABOUT HEDGES

Entities within the scope of this part of the FRS should provide the required disclosures, taking into account the explanations, set out in paragraphs 58-63. 112

DISCLOSURES ABOUT COMMODITY CONTRACTS

Subject to the exemption referred to in paragraph 114, entities within the scope of this part of the FRS should treat cash-settled commodity contracts and all other contracts for the delivery of gold as if they were financial assets or financial liabilities for the purposes of: 113

(a) the narrative disclosures required by paragraph 84;
(b) the required fair value disclosures described in paragraphs 98-102;
(c) the required disclosures, about financial assets and financial liabilities held or issued for trading, described in paragraphs 103-111; and
(d) the disclosures about hedges required by paragraph 112.

The exemption given by paragraph 65 applies also to entities required to provide the disclosures set out in this part of the FRS except that, in paragraph 65(b), the reference to paragraph 64(b), (c) and (d) shall be taken to refer to paragraph 113(b), (c) and (d). 114

ADDITIONAL DISCLOSURES ABOUT MARKET PRICE RISK

Entities within the scope of this part of the FRS are encouraged to disclose the information described in paragraphs 66-68. If they do so, they should also provide the required disclosures, after taking into account the explanations, set out in paragraphs 69-72. 115

DISCLOSURE OF ACCOUNTING POLICIES

Paragraphs 73-76 are of relevance also to entities required to provide the disclosures set out in this part of the FRS. 116

AMENDMENT TO FRS 4

The amendment to FRS 4 described in paragraphs 77 and 78 applies also in the context of entities within the scope of this part of the FRS. 117

DATE FROM WHICH EFFECTIVE

118 **Paragraphs 79 and 80, which set out the date from which the FRS is to take effect and refer to the need for corresponding amounts to be disclosed, apply also to entities within the scope of this part of the FRS.**

Part C - Financial institutions and financial institution groups, other than banks and similar institutions and banking and similar groups

Definitions

119 The following definitions, in addition to those set out in paragraphs 2 and 81, shall apply in Part C of the FRS and in particular in the Statement of Standard Accounting Practice set out **in bold type**.

Financial institution:-

An entity whose principal activity is to carry on one or more of the following activities:

(a) acceptance of deposits and other repayable funds from the public.
(b) lending.
(c) financial leasing.
(d) money transmission services.
(e) issuing and administering means of payment (eg credit cards, travellers' cheques and bankers' drafts).
(f) guarantees and commitments.
(g) trading for own account or for account of customers, or investing for own account, in:

    (i) money market instruments (cheques, bills, certificates of deposit, etc).
    (ii) foreign exchange.
    (iii) financial futures and options.
    (iv) exchange and interest rate instruments.
    (v) transferable securities.

(h) participation in share issues and the provision of services related to such issues.
(i) advice to undertakings on capital structure, industrial strategy, and related questions and advice and services relating to mergers and the purchase of undertakings.
(j) money broking.
(k) portfolio management and advice.
(l) safekeeping and administration of services.

The definition set out above is based on the definition of financial institution contained in the Second Banking Coordination Directive (89/646/EEC), although it has been extended slightly to include – primarily through the inclusion of subparagraph (a) – banks and similar institutions (as defined in the FRS) and – through the inclusion of the phrase 'investing for own account' in subparagraph (g) – investment vehicles such as investment trusts and unit trusts.

Financial institution group:-

A group where:

(a) the parent company is a financial institution; or
(b) the parent company:

  (i) does not itself carry on any material business apart from the acquisition, management and disposal of interests in subsidiary undertakings; and
  (ii) its principal subsidiary undertakings are wholly or mainly entities that are financial institutions.

ENTITIES REQUIRED TO PROVIDE THE DISCLOSURES SET OUT IN THIS PART OF THE FRS

Part C of the FRS applies to all financial statements that are intended to give a true and fair view of the reporting entity's financial position and profit or loss (or income and expenditure) for a period and are prepared by a reporting entity that is a financial institution or financial institution group and has any of its capital instruments listed or publicly traded on a stock exchange or market, except that it does not apply: 120

(a) if the entity is:

  (i) a bank or similar institution or a banking or similar group; or
  (ii) an entity that is applying the Financial Reporting Standard for Smaller Entities (FRSSE).

(b) to a parent's own financial statements when those statements are presented together with the parent's consolidated financial statements.

INSTRUMENTS TO BE DEALT WITH IN THE DISCLOSURES

The instruments to be dealt with in the disclosures set out in this part of the FRS are those referred to in paragraphs 5-10, except that: 121

(a) in paragraphs 5 and 6 the references to paragraphs 34-37 shall be taken to refer to paragraphs 34-37 or 90-97 (as applicable);
(b) in paragraph 10 the reference to paragraph 64 shall be taken to refer to paragraph 64 or 113 (as applicable); and
(c) financial assets and financial liabilities arising from traditional lending and deposit-taking activities shall not be treated as falling within the meaning of the term 'short-term debtors and creditors'.

DISCLOSURE OF OBJECTIVES, POLICIES AND STRATEGIES

Entities within the scope of this part of the FRS should provide the required disclosures, after taking into account the explanations, set out in paragraphs 11-23. 122

NUMERICAL DISCLOSURES – GENERAL MATTERS

Paragraphs 24 and 25 are relevant also in the context of the numerical disclosures required in this part of the FRS. 123

INTEREST RATE AND CURRENCY RISK DISCLOSURES

124 **Entities within the scope of this part of the FRS should:**

(a) provide all the required disclosures, after taking into account the explanations, set out in paragraphs 26-37; or
(b) provide all the required disclosures, after taking into account the explanations, set out in paragraphs 86-97.

LIQUIDITY DISCLOSURES

125 **Entities within the scope of this part of the FRS should provide the required disclosures, after taking into account the explanations, set out in paragraphs 38-43.**

126 Paragraph 43 will often be of particular relevance to entities providing the disclosures set out in this part of the FRS.

FAIR VALUE DISCLOSURES

127 **Entities within the scope of this part of the FRS should provide the required disclosures, after taking into account the explanations, set out in paragraphs 44-56.**

DISCLOSURES ABOUT FINANCIAL ASSETS AND FINANCIAL LIABILITIES HELD OR ISSUED FOR TRADING

128 **Entities within the scope of this part of the FRS should provide the disclosures required by paragraph 57. Furthermore, if they provide the disclosures required by paragraphs 86-97, they should also provide the required disclosures, after taking into account the explanations, set out in paragraphs 104-111.**

DISCLOSURES ABOUT HEDGES

129 **Entities within the scope of this part of the FRS should provide the required disclosures, after taking into account the explanations, set out in paragraphs 58-63.**

DISCLOSURES ABOUT COMMODITY CONTRACTS

130 **Subject to the exemption referred to in paragraph 131, entities within the scope of this part of the FRS should treat cash-settled commodity contracts and all other contracts for the delivery of gold as if they were financial assets or financial liabilities for the purposes of:**

(a) the narrative disclosures required by paragraph 122;
(b) the fair value disclosures required by paragraph 127;
(c) the disclosures, about financial assets and financial liabilities held or issued for trading, required by paragraph 128; and
(d) the disclosures about hedges required by paragraph 129.

The exemption given by paragraph 65 applies also to entities required to provide the disclosures set out in this part of the FRS except that, in paragraph 65(b), the reference to paragraph 64(b), (c) or (d) shall be taken to refer to paragraph 130(b), (c) or (d). 131

ADDITIONAL DISCLOSURES ABOUT MARKET PRICE RISK

Entities within the scope of this part of the FRS are encouraged to disclose the information described in paragraphs 66-68. If they do so, they should also provide the required disclosures, after taking into account the explanations, set out in paragraphs 69-72. 132

DISCLOSURE OF ACCOUNTING POLICIES

Paragraphs 73-76 are of relevance also to entities required to provide the disclosures set out in this part of the FRS. 133

AMENDMENT TO FRS 4

The amendment to FRS 4 described in paragraphs 77 and 78 applies also in the context of entities within the scope of this part of the FRS. 134

DATE FROM WHICH EFFECTIVE

Paragraphs 79 and 80, which set out the date from which the FRS is to take effect and refer to the need for corresponding amounts to be disclosed, apply also to entities within the scope of this part of the FRS. 135

Adoption of FRS 13 by the Board

Financial Reporting Standard 13 – 'Derivatives and other Financial Instruments: Disclosures' was approved for issue by the ten members of the Accounting Standards Board.

Sir David Tweedie	(Chairman)
Allan Cook	(Technical Director)
David Allvey	
Ian Brindle	
Dr John Buchanan	
John Coombe	
Raymond Hinton	
Huw Jones	
Professor Geoffrey Whittington	
Ken Wild	

Contents of Appendices

APPENDIX I
Types of risk arising from financial instruments

APPENDIX II
Examples applying the definition of a financial instrument
General principles
Contracts and contractual rights
Cash and bank deposits
Stocks, plant, equipment, patents and trade marks
Prepayments
Provisions
Lease obligations
Derivative financial instruments

APPENDIX III
Illustrations of the disclosures

APPENDIX IV
Guidance on procedures for estimating fair values
Fair value
Types of market price information available
Financial instruments with quoted market prices
Financial instruments with no quoted market prices

APPENDIX V
Note on legal requirements

APPENDIX VI
Compliance with International Accounting Standards

APPENDIX VII
The development of the FRS

Appendix I
Types of risk arising from financial instruments

1 The two most familiar risks arising from financial instruments are credit risk and liquidity risk. These risks can be defined as follows:

> **Credit risk** - *the possibility that a loss may occur from the failure of another party to perform according to the terms of a contract.*

> **Liquidity risk** *(also referred to as funding risk) - the risk that an entity will encounter difficulty in realising assets or otherwise raising funds to meet commitments associated with financial instruments.*

2 These risks are generally well understood and traditionally have been the main focus of what little disclosure on risk has appeared in financial statements. For example, some information about credit risk can be obtained from the nature of an entity's business and the numerical disclosures of debtors and provisions. Similarly, the disclosure of the terms and conditions of borrowings and broad indicators, such as the current ratio and quick assets ratio, provide some information about liquidity risk.

3 However, financial instruments also entail two other important types of risk – cash flow risk and market price risk. These can be defined as follows:

> **Cash flow risk** - *the risk that future cash flows generated by a monetary financial instrument will fluctuate in amount.*

> **Market price risk** - *the possibility that future changes in market prices may change the value, or the burden, of a financial instrument.*

The main components of market price risk likely to affect most entities are:

> **Interest rate risk** - *the risk that the value of a financial instrument will fluctuate because of changes in market interest rates.*

> **Currency risk** - *the risk that the value of a financial instrument will fluctuate because of changes in foreign exchange rates.*

> **Other market price risk** - *the risk that the value of a financial instrument will fluctuate as a result of changes in market prices caused by factors other than interest rates or currencies. This category includes risks stemming from commodity prices and share prices.*

4 Typically, information in financial statements on these risks has been scant and lacking a focus. For example, in the case of borrowings and interest-bearing assets, the fact that market price risk and cash flow risk are diametrically opposed is rarely mentioned, yet the relationship between the two has a significant impact on the risk profile. A fixed rate interest-earning asset exposes an entity to a change in the market value of the asset as a consequence of a change in market rates of interest ('market price risk') but, as the entity is not exposed to a change in future cash flow arising from interest rate changes, credit risk aside it has no cash flow risk. By contrast, a floating rate asset exposes an entity to a change in future cash flow if interest rates change ('cash flow risk' of reduced or increased cash receipts) but, aside from credit

risk, has no risk of a gain or loss due to a change in the market value of that asset ('market price risk').

Depending on management's attitude to these particular risks, transactions may be undertaken to reduce one of the risks at the expense of increasing the other. Consequently, the choice of which risk it seeks to reduce will have an important bearing on the entity's financial position, financial results and cash flows. **5**

Appendix II
Examples applying the definition of a financial instrument

The examples set out in this appendix are intended to clarify the meaning of the FRS but do not form part of it.

The FRS does not deal with the recognition or measurement of financial instruments. Therefore, although certain recognition and measurement practices have been assumed in this appendix in order to illustrate various points, the FRS does not require their use.

GENERAL PRINCIPLES

1 As defined in the FRS, a financial instrument is a contract that gives rise to both a financial asset of one entity and a financial liability or equity instrument of another entity.

(a) A financial asset is any asset that is cash, a contractual right of an entity to receive a financial asset from another entity, a contractual right of an entity to exchange financial instruments with another entity under conditions that are potentially favourable or an equity instrument of another entity.

(b) A financial liability is any liability that is a contractual obligation to deliver a financial asset to another entity or to exchange financial instruments with another entity under conditions that are potentially unfavourable.

2 Although the definitions of a financial asset and a financial liability include the terms 'financial asset' and 'financial instruments', the definitions are not circular. When there is a contractual right or obligation to exchange financial instruments, the instruments to be exchanged give rise to financial assets, financial liabilities, or equity instruments. A chain of contractual rights or obligations may be established but it ultimately leads to the receipt or payment of cash or to the acquisition or issue of an equity instrument.

3 As more fully explained in the paragraphs below, these definitions mean that the following are financial instruments:

(a) deposits, debtors, creditors, notes, loans, bonds, and debentures to be settled in cash.

(b) unconditional lease obligations.

(c) shares, including ordinary shares, preference shares and deferred shares.

(d) warrants or options to subscribe for shares of, or purchase shares from, the issuing entity.

(e) obligations of an entity to issue or deliver its own shares, such as a share option or warrant.

(f) derivative financial instruments such as forward contracts, futures, swaps and options that will be settled in cash or another financial instrument. An example of the latter is an option to purchase shares.

(g) contingent liabilities that arise from contracts and, if they crystallise, will be settled in cash – an example is a financial guarantee.

4 Similarly, the definitions mean, again as more fully explained in the paragraphs below, that the following are not financial instruments:

(a) physical assets, such as stock, property, plant and equipment.
(b) intangible assets, such as patents and trade marks.
(c) prepayments for goods or services, since these will not be settled in cash or another financial instrument.
(d) obligations to be settled by the delivery of goods or the rendering of services, such as most warranty obligations.
(e) income taxes (including deferred tax), since these are statutory rather than contractual obligations.
(f) forwards, swaps and options to be settled by the delivery of goods or the rendering of services.
(g) contingent items that do not arise from contracts, for example a contingent liability for a tort judgment.
(h) the minority interest that arises on consolidating a subsidiary that is not wholly-owned.

CONTRACTS AND CONTRACTUAL RIGHTS

The terms 'contract', 'contractual right' and 'contractual obligation' are fundamental to the definition of financial instrument, financial asset and financial liability. Paragraphs 6-10 below explain how these terms are to be applied in the context of the definitions in the FRS. **5**

The reference to a 'contract' is to an agreement between two or more parties that has clear economic consequences and which the parties have little, if any, discretion to avoid, usually because the agreement is enforceable at law. Contracts, and thus financial instruments, may take a variety of forms and need not be in writing. **6**

Contractual rights and contractual obligations are rights and obligations that arise out of a contract. Assets and liabilities that are not contractual in nature are not financial assets or financial liabilities. For this reason, tax liabilities, which arise not from a contract but from statutory requirements imposed by governments, are not financial liabilities. **7**

Most contracts give rise to a variety of rights and obligations, and the rights and obligations arising from a contract will often change or be added to as the contract is performed. Some of these rights and obligations may fall within the definition of a financial instrument and some may not. For example, an unperformed contract for the purchase or sale of a tangible asset usually gives rise to rights and obligations to exchange a physical asset for a financial asset (although it is possible that, if the contract is breached, the exchange will involve the payment of compensation). These rights and obligations do not represent a financial instrument. Under the same contract, once the physical asset has been delivered, a debtor or creditor will usually arise and this will be a financial instrument. A contract that, at some point in its performance, gives rise to rights and obligations that are financial assets and financial liabilities will, however, not be a financial instrument until those particular rights and obligations arise and it will cease to be a financial instrument when those rights and obligations no longer exist. **8**

'Contractual rights' and 'contractual obligations' encompass both rights and obligations that are contingent on the occurrence of a future event and those that are not. Examples of contingent rights and obligations are those arising under a financial guarantee. Such a guarantee meets the definition of a financial instrument since it **9** gives rise to both a liability for the guarantor (the contractual obligation to pay the lender if the borrower defaults) and an asset for the lender (the contractual right to receive cash from the guarantor if the borrower defaults).

10 Common examples of financial assets representing a contractual right to receive cash in the future and corresponding financial liabilities representing a contractual obligation to deliver cash in the future are:

(a) trade debtors and creditors;
(b) notes receivable and payable;
(c) bonds held or issued; and
(d) other debt instruments held or issued.

In each case, one party's contractual right to receive (or obligation to pay) cash is matched by the other party's corresponding obligation to pay (or right to receive), meaning that each case is an example of a financial instrument.

CASH AND BANK DEPOSITS

11 Cash, including foreign currency, is a financial asset because it represents the medium of exchange and is the basis on which all transactions are measured and reported in financial statements.

12 Cash deposited in banks and other institutions is a financial instrument of both the depositors and the deposit-takers. The depositors have a contractual right to receive currency, and the deposit-takers have a contractual obligation to deliver cash.

STOCKS, PLANT, EQUIPMENT, PATENTS AND TRADE MARKS

13 Although control of tangible assets, such as stocks, plant and equipment, and intangible assets, such as patents and trade marks, creates an opportunity to generate an inflow of cash or other assets, it does not give rise to a present contractual right to receive cash or other financial assets. Such assets are therefore not financial assets.

PREPAYMENTS

14 Assets, such as prepayments, for which the future economic benefit is the receipt of goods rather than a financial asset are not financial assets.

PROVISIONS

15 Some provisions are financial liabilities and some are not: it will depend on the nature of the obligation (ie whether it is contractual) and how that obligation is to be met (ie whether it will be met by the transfer of cash or other financial assets).

(a) Most warranty obligations are not financial liabilities because the outflow of economic benefits associated with them is the delivery of goods and services rather than cash or another financial asset. However, where a warranty involves a contractual obligation to pay compensation (for example, to cover the cost of a repair by an approved supplier), the provision will be a financial liability because the contractual obligation relates to the transfer of cash.

(b) Usually provisions for redundancy costs will not initially involve a contractual obligation to pay cash and, as such, will not be a financial liability. Similarly, many provisions to cover the cost of making good environmental damage will not initially involve contractual obligations.

LEASE OBLIGATIONS

Under SSAP 21 'Accounting for leases and hire purchase contracts', a finance lease contract is regarded as a contract for payments that are substantially the same as those under a loan agreement. In other words, the finance lease is accounted for as a sale with delayed payment terms. A finance lease is therefore a financial instrument. **16**

An operating lease, on the other hand, is regarded under SSAP 21 as primarily an uncompleted contract committing the lessor to provide the use of an asset in future periods in exchange for consideration similar to a fee for a service. The lessor therefore continues to account for the leased asset itself rather than any amount receivable in the future under the contract. Accordingly, the only operating lease assets and liabilities recognised in accordance with SSAP 21 that are financial instruments are the individual payments currently due and payable. However, some of the rights and obligations in respect of future payments that arise from certain types of operating lease are financial instruments even though they are not at present recognised in financial statements. To avoid unnecessary complexity, such financial instruments are excluded from the scope of the FRS. **17**

DERIVATIVE FINANCIAL INSTRUMENTS

A derivative is a contract that derives its value from the price or rate of an underlying item such as equities, bonds, commodities, interest rates, exchange rates and stock market and other indices. A derivative financial instrument is a derivative that is also a financial instrument. **18**

On inception, derivative financial instruments give one party a contractual right to exchange financial assets with another party under conditions that are potentially favourable, or a contractual obligation to exchange financial assets with another party under conditions that are potentially unfavourable. Some instruments embody both a right and an obligation to make an exchange. Since the terms of the exchange are determined on inception of the derivative financial instrument, those terms may become either favourable or unfavourable as prices in financial markets change. **19**

A put or call option to exchange financial instruments gives the holder a right to obtain potential future economic benefits associated with changes in the fair value of the financial instruments underlying the contract. Conversely, the writer of an option assumes an obligation to forgo potential future economic benefits or bear potential losses of economic benefits associated with changes in the fair value of the underlying financial instruments. The contractual right of the holder and the obligation of the writer meet the definition of a financial asset and a financial liability respectively. **20**

21 An example of a derivative that is not a financial instrument is an option to buy or sell an asset other than a financial asset (such as a commodity). Such an option does not give rise to a financial asset or financial liability because it does not fit the requirements of the definitions for the receipt or delivery of financial assets or exchange of financial instruments.

Appendix III
Illustrations of the disclosures

The following illustrations are provided for general guidance only and do not form part of the FRS.

The illustrations are intended to show the kind of information that could result from the application of the disclosures described in the Statement of Standard Accounting Practice contained in the FRS. They should not be taken as suggesting policies that companies should adopt.

The appendix contains three illustrations:

- ***Illustration 1 shows the sort of information that the majority of companies will need to provide to comply with the FRS.***
- ***Illustration 2 is for a more complex company.***
- ***Illustration 3 shows an example of some of the information that a bank or similar institution will need to provide to comply with the FRS.***

The paragraph numbers in the side-headings and footnotes refer to paragraphs in the FRS.

Illustration 1

A Simpler Company

Narrative disclosures (paragraphs 11-23)

For the purposes of this illustration, it has been assumed that the narrative disclosures are provided in the operating and financial review. As such, the notes to the financial statements will need to contain a cross-reference to the disclosures below. This cross-reference is not shown in this illustration.

It is envisaged that the discussion set out below will usually be preceded by a general discussion of, inter alia, the entity's activities, structure and financing. This discussion will typically consider the financial risk profile of the entity as a whole as a prelude to the narrative disclosures required by the FRS.

The Group's financial instruments, other than derivatives, comprise borrowings, some cash and liquid resources, and various items, such as trade debtors, trade creditors etc, that arise directly from its operations. The main purpose of these financial instruments is to raise finance for the Group's operations.

The Group also enters into derivatives transactions (principally interest rate swaps and forward foreign currency contracts). The purpose of such transactions is to manage the interest rate and currency risks arising from the Group's operations and its sources of finance.

It is, and has been throughout the period under review, the Group's policy that no trading in financial instruments shall be undertaken.

The main risks arising from the Group's financial instruments are interest rate risk, liquidity risk and foreign currency risk. The Board reviews and agrees policies for managing each of these risks and they are summarised below. These policies have remained unchanged since the beginning of 19X0.

INTEREST RATE RISK

The Group finances its operations through a mixture of retained profits and bank borrowings. The Group borrows in the desired currencies at both fixed and floating rates of interest and then uses interest rate swaps to generate the desired interest profile and to manage the Group's exposure to interest rate fluctuations. The Group's policy is to keep between 50 per cent and 65 per cent of its borrowings at fixed rates of interest. At the year-end, 62 per cent of the Group's borrowings were at fixed rates after taking account of interest rate swaps.

LIQUIDITY RISK

As regards liquidity, the Group's policy has throughout the year been that, to ensure continuity of funding, at least 50 per cent of its borrowings should mature in more than five years. At the year-end, 57 per cent of the Group's borrowings were due to mature in more than five years.

Short-term flexibility is achieved by overdraft facilities.

FOREIGN CURRENCY RISK

The Group has one significant overseas subsidiary – Foreign – which operates in the USA and whose revenues and expenses are denominated exclusively in US dollars. In order to protect the Group's sterling balance sheet from the movements in the US dollar/sterling exchange rate, the Group finances its net investment in this subsidiary by means of US dollar borrowings.

About one-third of the sales of the Group's UK businesses are to customers in continental Europe. These sales are priced in sterling but invoiced in the currencies of the customers involved. The Group's policy is to eliminate all currency exposures on sales at the time of sale through forward currency contracts. All the other sales of the UK businesses are denominated in sterling.

Numerical information (Notes to the accounts)

Although not shown in this illustration, an explanation of the material accounting policies adopted in accounting for financial instruments will need to be provided. The Group would also need to explain that it has taken advantage of the exemption available for short-term debtors and creditors.

The accounting period dealt with in this illustration is the 12 months to 31 December 19X1. Although corresponding amounts are not shown in the illustration, they will need to be provided except in respect of the first accounting period in which the FRS comes into effect.

INTEREST RATE RISK PROFILE OF FINANCIAL ASSETS AND FINANCIAL LIABILITIES (PARAGRAPHS 26-33)

Financial assets

The Group has no financial assets, other than short-term debtors and an immaterial amount of cash at bank.

Financial liabilities

After taking into account the various interest rate swaps and forward foreign currency contracts entered into by the Group, the interest rate profile of the Group's financial liabilities at 31 December 19X1 was:

Currency	Total	Floating rate financial liabilities	Fixed rate financial liabilities	Financial liabilities on which no interest is paid
	£ millions	£ millions	£ millions	£ millions
Sterling	415	150	250	15
US dollar	200	80	120	–
Total	615	230	370	15

	Fixed rate financial liabilities		Financial liabilities on which no interest is paid
Currency	Weighted average interest rate	Weighted average period for which rate is fixed	Weighted average period until maturity
	%	Years	Years
Sterling	10	5	1.4
US dollar	7	8	–
Total	–	6	1.4

The floating rate financial liabilities* comprise:

- sterling denominated bank borrowings and overdrafts that bear interest at rates based on the six-month LIBOR, and
- US dollar denominated bank borrowings that bear interest at rates based on the US Prime rate.

**It should be noted that other accounting standards or legislation may require additional information to be provided on these liabilities. For example, Schedule 4 to the Companies Act 1985 and to the Companies (Northern Ireland) Order 1986 both require disclosure of the rate of any interest payable on creditors, unless that would result in a statement of excessive length in which case it shall be sufficient to give a general indication of the rates of interest payable. As such, although not required by the FRS, the interest rate differential will often need to be stated as well as identification of the benchmark rate.*

CURRENCY EXPOSURES (paragraphs 34-37)

As at 31 December 19X1, after taking into account the effects of forward foreign exchange contracts the Group had no currency exposures.

MATURITY OF FINANCIAL LIABILITIES (paragraphs 38 and 39)

The maturity profile of the Group's financial liabilities at 31 December 19X1 was as follows:

	£m
In one year or less, or on demand	200
In more than one year but not more than two years	15
In more than two years but not more than five years	60
In more than five years	340
	615

BORROWING FACILITIES (paragraphs 40-42)

The Group has various undrawn committed borrowing facilities. The facilities available at 31 December 19X1 in respect of which all conditions precedent had been met were as follows:

	£m
Expiring in one year or less	40
Expiring in more than one year but not more than two years	7
Expiring in more than two years	3
	50

FAIR VALUES OF FINANCIAL ASSETS AND FINANCIAL LIABILITIES (paragraphs 44-56)

Set out below is a comparison by category of book values and fair values of the Group's financial assets and liabilities as at 31 December 19X1.

	Book value £ millions	Fair value £ millions
Primary financial instruments held or issued to finance the Group's operations:		
Short-term financial liabilities and current portion of long-term borrowings	(215)	(223)
Long-term borrowings	(400)	(370)
Financial assets	7	8
Derivative financial instruments held to manage the interest rate and currency profile:		
Interest rate swaps	–	15
Forward foreign currency contracts	–	(5)

The fair values of the interest rate swaps, forward foreign currency contracts and sterling denominated long-term fixed rate debt with a carrying amount of £250 million have been determined by reference to prices available from the markets on which the instruments involved are traded. All the other fair values shown above have been calculated by discounting cash flows at prevailing interest rates.

GAINS AND LOSSES ON HEDGES (paragraphs 58-63)

The Group enters into forward foreign currency contracts to eliminate the currency exposures that arise on sales denominated in foreign currencies immediately those sales are transacted. It also uses interest rate swaps to manage its interest rate profile. Changes in the fair value of instruments used as hedges are not recognised in the financial statements until the hedged position matures. An analysis of these unrecognised gains and losses is as follows:

	Gains	Losses	Total net gains/(losses)
	£ millions	**£ millions**	**£ millions**
Unrecognised gains and losses on hedges at 1.1.X1	**9**	**12**	**(3)**
Gains and losses arising in previous years that were recognised in 19X1	8	9	1
Gains and losses arising before 1.1.X1 that were not recognised in 19X1	**1**	**3**	**(2)**
Gains and losses arising in 19X1 that were not recognised in 19X1	18	6	12
Unrecognised gains and losses on hedges at 31.12.X1	**19**	**9**	**10**
Of which:			
Gains and losses expected to be recognised in 19X2	12	6	6
Gains and losses expected to be recognised in 19X3 or later	7	3	4

MARKET PRICE RISK (paragraphs 66-72)

The Group's exposure to market price risk comprises interest rate and currency risk exposures. It monitors these exposures primarily through a process known as sensitivity analysis. This involves estimating the effect on profit before tax over various periods of a range of possible changes in interest rates and exchange rates. The sensitivity analysis model used for this purpose makes no assumptions about any interrelationships between such rates or about the way in which such changes may affect the economies involved. As a consequence, figures derived from the Group's sensitivity analysis model should be used in conjunction with other information about the Group's risk profile.

The Group's policy towards currency risk is to eliminate all exposures that will impact on reported profit as soon as they arise. This is reflected in the sensitivity analysis, which estimates that five and ten percentage point increases in the value of sterling against all other currencies would have had minimal impact on profit before tax.

On the other hand, the Group's policy is to accept a degree of interest rate risk as long as the effects of various changes in rates remain within certain prescribed ranges. On the basis of the Group's analysis, it is estimated that a rise of one percentage point in all interest rates would have reduced 19X1 profit before tax by approximately 1.5 per cent and that a three percentage point increase would have reduced such profits by 4.2 per cent. This is well within the ranges that the Group regards as acceptable.

Illustration 2

A More complex company

Narrative disclosures (paragraphs 11-23)*

For the purposes of this illustration, it has been assumed that the narrative disclosures are provided in the operating and financial review. As such, the notes to the financial statements will need to contain a cross-reference to the disclosures below. This cross-reference is not shown in this illustration.

It is envisaged that the discussion set out below will usually be preceded by a general discussion of, inter alia, the entity's activities, structure and financing, including a brief description of the entity's group treasury arrangements. This discussion will typically consider the financial risk profile of the entity as a whole as a prelude to the narrative disclosures required by the FRS.

The Group holds or issues financial instruments for three main purposes:

- to finance its operations
- to manage the interest rate and currency risks arising from its operations and from its sources of finance
- for trading purposes.

In addition, various financial instruments – for example, trade debtors, trade creditors, accruals and prepayments – arise directly from the Group's operations.

The Group finances its operations by a mixture of retained profits, bank borrowings, long-term loans and commercial paper. The Group's long-term loans are raised centrally by Group finance companies and on-lent to operating subsidiaries on commercial terms. The Group borrows in the major global debt markets in a range of currencies at both fixed and floating rates of interest, using derivatives where appropriate to generate the desired effective currency profile and interest rate basis. The derivatives used for this purpose are principally interest rate swaps, interest rate caps and collars, currency swaps and forward foreign currency contracts.

The types of financial instrument used for trading purposes must be approved in advance by the Board, which also sets down limits, both in terms of capital invested and market price risk taken on, for this trading activity. During the period under review, the only instruments that have been traded are listed debt securities, FTSE futures and forward foreign currency contracts.

**If the narrative disclosures reflect a significant change from the explanations provided for the previous period, paragraph 16 requires this fact to be disclosed and reasons for the change to be given. In addition, if the directors have agreed to change the role that financial instruments have in creating or changing the risks of the reporting entity, paragraph 18 requires the change to be explained. Neither of these disclosures is illustrated here. Furthermore, as the period-end position is representative of the entity's agreed objectives, policies and strategies, the additional explanations required by paragraph 20 are not provided in this illustration.*

The main risks arising from the Group's financial instruments are interest rate risk, liquidity risk, foreign currency risk and market price risk. The Board reviews and agrees policies for managing each of these risks and they are summarised below. These policies have remained unchanged since the beginning of 19X0.

FINANCE AND INTEREST RATE RISK

The Group's exposure to interest rate fluctuations on its borrowings and deposits is managed by using interest rate swaps, interest rate options (caps and collars) and forward rate agreements. The Group's policy is to keep between 30 per cent and 70 per cent of net borrowings at fixed or capped rates of interest for a period of up to ten years. The minimum proportion fixed or capped is higher in the near term than in the longer term, with the aim of reducing the volatility of short-term interest costs whilst maintaining the opportunity to benefit from movements in longer-term rates. At the year-end and after taking account of interest rate swaps, the proportion of the Group's borrowings at fixed rates was 36 per cent, fixed for an average period of 4.1 years. In addition, 14 per cent of the Group's borrowings were floating rate but were covered by interest rate caps; the remaining 50 per cent were at floating rates of interest and were not capped.

LIQUIDITY RISK

The Group's objective is to maintain a balance between continuity of funding and flexibility through the use of borrowings with a range of maturities. The Group's policy is that not more than 30 per cent of borrowings should mature in any twelve-month period. In addition, to preserve continuity of funding, at least 50 per cent of borrowings should mature in more than two years and at least 30 per cent in more than five years. During the year the maturity profile of borrowings was extended, mainly by three new debt issues with an average maturity of nine years. As detailed in Note [x], only 17 per cent of the Group's total borrowings at the year-end will mature in the next twelve months, 69 per cent will mature in more than two years and over 50 per cent will mature in more than five years.

It is, in addition, the Group's policy to maintain undrawn committed borrowing facilities of at least 10 per cent of borrowings in order to provide flexibility in the management of the Group's liquidity and backing for the Group's commercial paper programme. At the year-end, the Group had multicurrency committed facilities of £400 million with three banks, none of which was drawn (commercial paper outstanding at the year-end was £200 million). The weighted average period until maturity of these facilities was 1.6 years.

CURRENCY RISK

Although the Group is based in the UK, it has a significant investment in overseas operations in Australia, Japan and the USA. As a result, the Group's sterling balance sheet can be significantly affected by movements in the Australian dollar/sterling, yen/sterling and US dollar/sterling exchange rates. The Group seeks to mitigate the effect of these structural currency exposures by borrowing in the same currencies as the operating (or 'functional') currencies of its main operating units and by using currency swaps to match the currency of some of its other borrowing to its various functional currencies. Generally speaking, between 30 per cent and 50 per cent of the Group's investment in non-sterling operations will be hedged back into sterling in this way, with the exact percentage varying depending on the Group's transactional currency exposures (which are described below). In managing its structural currency exposures, the Group's objectives are to maintain a low cost of borrowings and to retain some potential for currency-related appreciation while partially hedging against currency depreciation.

The Group also has transactional currency exposures. Such exposures arise from sales or purchases by an operating unit in currencies other than the unit's functional currency. The Group requires all its operating units to use forward currency contracts to eliminate the currency exposure on any balance that is not expected to mature within thirty days of its arising.

The Group also hedges foreign currency sales that are expected to occur in future periods. Over 70 per cent of the Group's sales are denominated in currencies other than the functional currency of the operating unit making the sale, whilst almost 95 per cent of costs are denominated in the unit's functional currency. The Group's policy is actively to manage the resulting currency risk, taking out more cover at times when rates are judged to be favourable, within overall limits. Expected future net cash flows are covered on a rolling basis at levels from 40 per cent to 90 per cent for sales expected in the next year and from 10 per cent to 60 per cent for sales expected in one to two years. Cover takes the form of currency swaps or forward contracts. At 31 December 19X1, the Group had hedged 85 per cent of the foreign currency sales expected in 19X2 and 50 per cent of those expected in 19X3.

Numerical information (Notes to the accounts)

Although not shown in this illustration, an explanation of the material accounting policies adopted in accounting for financial instruments will need to be provided. The Group would also need to explain that it has taken advantage of the exemption available for short-term debtors and creditors.

The accounting period dealt with in this illustration is the 12 months to 31 December 19X1. Although corresponding amounts are not shown in the illustration, they will need to be provided except in respect of the first accounting period in which the FRS comes into effect.

The FRS requires non-equity shares issued and certain commodity contracts to be included in – but shown separately from – the disclosures as if they were financial assets and financial liabilities. Such disclosures are not shown in this illustration.

INTEREST RATE RISK PROFILE OF FINANCIAL LIABILITIES (paragraphs 26-31)

The interest rate profile of the financial liabilities of the Group as at 31 December 19X1 was:

Currency	Total	Floating rate financial liabilities	Fixed rate financial liabilities	Financial liabilities on which no interest is paid
	£ millions	£ millions	£ millions	£ millions
Sterling	474	340	110	24
US dollar	325	200	120	5
Japanese yen	357	150	200	7
Australian dollar	149	100	40	9
Other	53	50	–	3
Total	1,358	840	470	48

	Fixed rate financial liabilities		Financial liabilities on which no interest is paid
Currency	Weighted average interest rate	Weighted average period for which rate is fixed	Weighted average period until maturity
	%	Years	Years
Sterling	12	4.2	0.8
US dollar	9	2.3	0.6
Japanese yen	6	5.4	1.2
Australian dollar	5	2.8	0.3
Other	–	–	0.5
Total	–	4.1	0.7

The floating rate financial liabilities comprise bank borrowings bearing interest at rates fixed in advance for periods ranging from three to six months by reference to the six-month LIBOR (in the case of the sterling and Australian dollar borrowings), the US Prime rate (in the case of US dollar borrowings) and the Japanese Government Bond rate (in the case of all other borrowings).*

The figures shown in the tables above take into account various interest rate and currency swaps used to manage the interest rate and currency profile of financial liabilities. Further protection from interest rate movements is provided by interest rate caps on £150 million at 10 per cent until June 19x4 and US$60 million at 6.5 per cent until August 19X5. The Group also has a A$120 million collar at 6.5 per cent floor/7.5 per cent cap commencing in June 19X2 for four years.

INTEREST RATE RISK OF FINANCIAL ASSETS (paragraphs 32 and 33)

The Group held the following financial assets as at 31 December 19X1:

	£m
Assets held as part of the financing arrangements of the Group:	
Sterling cash deposits	36
Assets held or issued for trading purposes:	
Investments in sterling denominated debt securities	32
Forward foreign currency contracts	6
	74

The sterling cash deposits comprise deposits placed on money markets at call, 7-day and monthly rates. All the investments in debt securities are in fixed rate securities; the weighted average interest rate on these securities is 4.3 per cent and the weighted average time for which the rate is fixed is 2.4 years. The weighted average period until maturity of the forward foreign currency contracts held for trading purposes is 4.7 months.

CURRENCY EXPOSURES (paragraphs 34-37)

As explained on page [x] of the operating and financial review, the Group's objectives in managing the currency exposures arising from its net investment overseas (in other words, its structural currency exposures) are to maintain a low cost of borrowings

**It should be noted that other accounting standards or legislation may require additional information to be provided on these liabilities. For example, Schedule 4 to the Companies Act 1985 and to the Companies (Northern Ireland) Order 1986 both require disclosure of the rate of any interest payable on creditors, unless that would result in a statement of excessive length in which case it shall be sufficient to give a general indication of the rates of interest payable. As such, although not required by the FRS, the interest rate differential will often need to be stated as well as identification of the benchmark rate.*

and to retain some potential for currency-related appreciation while partially hedging against currency depreciation. Gains and losses arising from these structural currency exposures are recognised in the statement of total recognised gains and losses.

The table below shows the Group's currency exposures; in other words, those transactional (or non-structural) exposures that give rise to the net currency gains and losses recognised in the profit and loss account. Such exposures comprise the monetary assets and monetary liabilities of the Group that are not denominated in the operating (or 'functional') currency of the operating unit involved, other than certain non-sterling borrowings treated as hedges of net investments in overseas operations. As at 31 December 19X1, these exposures were as follows:

	Net foreign currency monetary assets/(liabilities) in £ millions					
Functional currency of Group operation	Sterling	US Dollar	Yen	Australian dollar	Other	Total
Sterling	–	80	30	–	–	110
US dollar	45	–	–	–	–	45
Yen	(60)	80	–	(90)	–	(70)
Australian dollar	75	(120)	40	–	–	(5)
Other	(10)	(30)	–	40	10	10
Total	50	10	70	(50)	10	90

The amounts shown in the table above take into account the effect of any currency swaps, forward contracts and other derivatives entered into to manage these currency exposures.

As at 31 December 19X1, the Group also held open various currency swaps and forward contracts that the Group had taken out to hedge expected future foreign currency sales.

MATURITY OF FINANCIAL LIABILITIES (paragraphs 38 and 39)

The maturity profile of the Group's financial liabilities, other than short-term creditors such as trade creditors and accruals, at 31 December 19X1 was as follows:

	£m
In one year or less, or on demand	220
In more than one year but not more than two years	235
In more than two years but not more than five years	243
In more than five years	660
	1,358

BORROWING FACILITIES (paragraphs 40-42)

The Group has various borrowing facilities available to it. The undrawn committed facilities available at 31 December 19X1 in respect of which all conditions precedent had been met at that date were as follows:

	£m
Expiring in one year or less	150
Expiring in more than one year but not more than two years	220
Expiring in more than two years	30
	400

FAIR VALUES OF FINANCIAL ASSETS AND FINANCIAL LIABILITIES (paragraphs 44-56)

Set out below is a comparison by category of book values and fair values of all the Group's financial assets and financial liabilities as at 31 December 19X1.

	Book value £ millions	Fair value £ millions
Primary financial instruments held or issued to finance the Group's operations:		
Short-term borrowings and current portion of long-term borrowings	(220)	(234)
Long-term borrowings	(1,090)	(1,223)
Cash deposits	36	36
Other financial liabilities	(48)	(46)
Derivative financial instruments held to manage the interest rate and currency profile:		
Interest rate swaps and similar instruments	–	(35)
Interest rate caps and collars	–	15
Currency swaps	–	25
Forward foreign currency contracts	–	12
Derivative financial instruments held or issued to hedge the currency exposure on expected future sales:		
Currency swaps	–	15
Forward foreign currency contracts	–	17
Financial instruments held or issued for trading:		
Debt securities	32	32
Forward foreign currency contracts	6	6

All financial instruments held or issued for trading purposes are carried in the financial statements at fair value.

Market values have been used to determine the fair value of all swaps, forward foreign currency contracts and all listed debt issued and held. The fair values of the interest rate caps and collars have been calculated using option-pricing models. The fair values of all other items have been calculated by discounting expected future cash flows at prevailing interest rates.*

GAINS AND LOSSES ON FINANCIAL ASSETS AND FINANCIAL LIABILITIES HELD OR ISSUED FOR TRADING (paragraph 57)†

The net gain from trading in financial assets and financial liabilities shown in the profit and loss account for the period to 31 December 19X1 can be analysed as follows:

	£m
Investments in debt securities	2
FTSE futures	1
Forward foreign currency contracts	7
	10

HEDGES (paragraphs 58-63)‡

As explained in the operating and financial review on page [x], the Group's policy is to hedge the following exposures:

- interest rate risk – using interest swaps, caps and collars; currency swaps; and forward foreign currency contracts;
- structural and transactional currency exposures, and currency exposures on future expected sales – using currency swaps and forward foreign currency contracts.

Gains and losses on instruments used for hedging are not recognised until the exposure that is being hedged is itself recognised. Unrecognised gains and losses on instruments used for hedging, and the movements therein, are as follows:

**By virtue of paragraph 53, fair values of certain assets and liabilities do not need to be disclosed if they cannot be determined with sufficient reliability. In such circumstances, paragraph 53 requires other information to be provided. These disclosures are not shown in this illustration.*

†*Paragraph 57(c) requires the disclosure of the fair value of financial assets and of financial liabilities held or issued for trading. This information is given in this illustration in the disclosure provided to comply with paragraphs 44-56. If these fair values are materially unrepresentative of the entity's typical position during the period, paragraph 57(d) also requires the average fair value of financial assets and of financial liabilities held or issued for trading to be disclosed.*

‡*Paragraph 62 requires further disclosures if an instrument used as a hedge has been redesignated before the hedged position has matured. Such disclosures are not shown in this illustration.*

	Gains	Losses	Total net gains/(losses)
	£ millions	£ millions	£ millions
Unrecognised gains and losses on hedges at 1.1.X1	**53**	**28**	**25**
Gains and losses arising in previous years that were recognised in 19X1	22	21	1
Gains and losses arising before 1.1.X1 that were not recognised in 19X1	**31**	**7**	**24**
Gains and losses arising in 19X1 that were not recognised in 19X1	66	41	25
Unrecognised gains and losses on hedges at 31.12.X1	**97**	**48**	**49**
Of which:			
Gains and losses expected to be recognised in 19X2	71	40	31
Gains and losses expected to be recognised in 19X3 or later	26	8	18

Paragraph 59 also requires certain disclosures to be provided about deferred gains and losses on hedges. However, as there are no such gains or losses in this example, these disclosures are not illustrated.

MARKET PRICE RISK (paragraphs 66-72)*

The Group monitors its interest rate and currency risks and other market price risks to which it is exposed primarily through a process known as 'sensitivity analysis'. This involves estimating the effect on profit before tax over various periods of a range of possible changes in interest rates and exchange rates.

The model used for this purpose makes various assumptions about the inter-relationships between movements in interest rates and exchange rates and about the way in which such movements may impact on the economies involved. Although these assumptions are based on past experience, such experience may not be reflected in the future. Furthermore, the results of the analysis cannot be simply extrapolated to other price changes. For these reasons, the figures disclosed below need to be treated with a degree of caution.

**As already mentioned, corresponding amounts will usually need to be provided for all disclosures. If there are material changes in the amount of market price risk disclosed for the reporting period when compared with that disclosed for the previous period, paragraph 69(c) requires the reasons for the changes to be disclosed. Furthermore, if material changes have been made to the method, or main assumptions of parameters, used since the previous period, paragraph 71 requires the reasons for the changes to be given and the previous period's information to be restated.*

The Group accepts a degree of interest rate risk, currency risk and other market price risk as long as the effects of various changes in rates and prices, as calculated using its sensitivity analysis model, remain within certain prescribed ranges. The figures disclosed below are well within those ranges.

On the basis of the Group's analysis, it is estimated that the maximum effect of a rise of one percentage point in one of the principal interest rates to which the Group is exposed would, after taking into account the most likely consequential impact on other interest rates and on exchange rates, be a reduction in profit before tax for 19x1 of between 1.6 per cent and 2.4 per cent and the maximum effect of a rise of three percentage points would be a reduction in profit before tax for 19X1 of between 6.5 per cent and 9.8 per cent. Similarly, it is estimated that a strengthening of sterling by 10 per cent against all the currencies in which the Group does business would generate currency losses equal to about 3 per cent of profit before tax for 19X1, whereas a 30 per cent strengthening would have generated currency losses equal to about 8.4 per cent of 19X1 profit before tax. The Group's exposure to other market price risk is not material.

ILLUSTRATION 3

A BANK OR SIMILAR INSTITUTION

The examples set out below are intended to illustrate the disclosure requirements in the FRS that are in Part B of the FRS but not in Part A.

The accounting period dealt with in this illustration is the 12 months to 31 December 19X1. Although corresponding amounts are not shown in the illustration, they will need to be provided except in respect of the first accounting period in which the FRS comes into effect.

INTEREST RATE SENSITIVITY GAP ANALYSIS (paragraphs 86-89)

Part of the Bank's return on financial instruments is obtained from controlled mismatching of the dates on which interest receivable on assets and interest payable on liabilities are next reset to market rates or, if earlier, the dates on which the instruments mature. The table below summarises these repricing mismatches on the Bank's non-trading book as at 31 December 19X1. Items are allocated to time bands by reference to the earlier of the next contractual interest rate repricing date and the maturity date.

	Not more than three months	*More than three months but not more than six months*	*More than six months but not more than one year*	*More than one year but not more than five years*	*More than five years*	*Non-interest bearing*	*Total*
	£m	**£m**	**£m**	**£m**	**£m**	**£m**	**£m**
Assets:							
Treasury bills and other eligible bills	6,243	1,231	643	125	207	92	8,541
Loans & advances to banks	25,876	4,124	2,439	648	371	840	34,298
Loans & advances to customers	59,435	10,354	8,639	11,453	7,633	4,958	102,472
Debt securities & equity shares	5,657	4,321	6,125	7,345	9,620	7,401	40,469
Other assets	1,032	854	523	595	–	28,945	31,949
Total assets	98,243	20,884	18,369	20,166	17,831	42,236	217,729
Liabilities:							
Deposits by banks	23,921	5,168	1,641	261	96	217	31,304
Customer accounts	73,654	2,101	1,561	1,353	121	13,611	92,401
Debt securities in issue	21,961	3,142	3,189	789	376	52	29,509
Other liabilities	673	265	134	1,311	2,064	12,192	16,639
Loan capital & other subordinated liabilities	2,631	1,692	211	2,164	10,617	60	17,375
Minority interests & shareholders' funds	–	–	–	–	–	30,501	30,501
Total liabilities	122,840	12,368	6,736	5,878	13,274	56,633	217,729
Off balance sheet items	(3,931)	(2,962)	3,381	2,916	212	384	–
Interest rate sensitivity gap	(28,528)	5,554	15,014	17,204	4,769	(14,013)	
Cumulative gap	(28,528)	(22,974)	(7,960)	9,244	14,013		

This table does not take into account the effect of interest rate options used by the Bank to hedge its own positions. Details of these options are set out in note [x].

A negative interest rate sensitivity gap exists when more liabilities than assets reprice during a given period. Although a negative gap position tends to benefit net interest income in a declining interest rate environment, the actual effect will depend on a number of factors, including the extent to which repayments are made earlier or later than the contracted date and variations in interest rate sensitivity within repricing periods and among currencies.

CURRENCY RISK DISCLOSURES (paragraphs 90-97)

The Group's main overseas operations are in the European Union, the USA and Japan, although it also has operations elsewhere in Asia, and in Canada and Eastern Europe. The main operating (or 'functional') currencies of its operations are therefore sterling, the euro, US dollars, and the yen. As the currency in which the Group prepares its consolidated financial statements is sterling, it follows that the Group's consolidated balance sheet is affected by movements in the exchange rates between these functional currencies and sterling. These currency exposures are referred to as structural currency exposures. Translation gains and losses arising from these exposures are recognised in the statement of total recognised gains and losses.

The Group mitigates the effect of these exposures by financing a significant proportion of its net investment in its overseas operations with borrowings in the same currencies as the functional currencies involved. Currency swaps are also used to match the currency of some of its other borrowings to the functional currencies involved.

The Group's structural currency exposures as at 31 December 19X1 were as follows:

Functional currency of the operation involved	Net investments in overseas operations	Borrowings taken out in the functional currencies of the overseas operations in order to hedge the net investments in such operations	Remaining structural currency exposures
	£ millions	£ millions	£ millions
US dollar	10,123	8,867	1,256
Yen	8,891	8,831	150
Euro	5,621	5,146	475
Other non-sterling	648	593	55
Total	25,283	23,437	1,936

The entity would also need to produce numerical currency disclosures similar to those shown in the illustration for a complex company.

TRADING BOOK DISCLOSURES (paragraphs 104-111)

Although the Bank uses a range of techniques to manage the market price risk in its trading book, the main method involves the use of value at risk (VAR) limits. The VAR of a trading book is the expected loss that will arise on the trading book over a specified period of time (holding period) from an adverse market movement with a specified probability (confidence level). The Bank sets a range of VAR limits, using different confidence levels and holding periods, for the purposes of monitoring the level of various market price risks arising from its trading book and action is taken to keep the VAR within the ranges specified. Actual outcomes are monitored to test the validity of the assumptions made in the calculation of VAR.

Assuming a 95 per cent confidence level and a one-day holding period, the VAR for the Bank's trading book as at 31 December 19X1 was £3.6 million and the average, highest and lowest VARs for the trading book during 19X1 were £4.5 million, £8.3 million and £2.9 million respectively. This means, inter alia, that, on the basis of the risks in the trading book at 31 December 19X1, the Bank expected not to incur a loss on its trading book of more than £3.6 million in any one day more than 5 per cent of the time.*

Although the Bank is satisfied that the package of controls it uses to manage the market price risk in its trading book is an effective means of controlling that risk, it recognises that all measures of market price risk, when considered in isolation, have limitations. The VAR figures disclosed above, for example, have the following main limitations.

- The historical data on which the calculations have been based may not reflect all the factors that are relevant to the estimation of VAR, give the correct weight to these factors, or be the best estimate of risk factor changes that will occur in the future.
- Using a one-day time horizon does not fully capture the market price risk of positions that cannot be closed off within one day. Similarly, focusing on the maximum loss that is expected to be incurred 95 per cent of the time says little about the, admittedly smaller, losses that are expected to be incurred more frequently or the size of the losses in excess of the VAR that are expected to be incurred 5 per cent of the time.
- The highest, lowest and average figures disclosed are based on calculations performed at the end of each business day, and the balance sheet date figure is also an end-of-day figure. The VAR during the course of a single day may change substantially and there is no reason why the end-of-day figure should be representative of the figure at other times of the day.

**As already mentioned, corresponding amounts will usually need to be provided for all disclosures. If there are material changes in the amount of market price risk disclosed for the reporting period when compared with that disclosed for the previous period, paragraph 107(d) requires the reason for the changes to be disclosed. Furthermore, if material changes have been made to the method, or main assumptions or parameters, used since the previous period, paragraph 108 requires the reasons for the changes to be given and the previous period's balance sheet date information to be restated.*

Appendix IV
Guidance on procedures for estimating fair values

This appendix provides examples of procedures for estimating the fair value of financial assets and financial liabilities. The examples are illustrative and do not portray all possible ways of estimating fair value to comply with the provisions of the FRS.

FAIR VALUE

1 The fair value of a financial asset or financial liability is the amount at which it could be exchanged in an arm's length transaction between informed and willing parties, other than in a forced or liquidation sale.

2 Underlying the concept of fair value is therefore a presumption that the entity, being a going concern, has no intention or need to liquidate or otherwise wind up its operations or undertake a transaction on adverse terms. For example, if the entity is able to dispose of a large position in an orderly manner over a period of time and therefore does not have to accept a discount to the market price, the quoted market price will be the fair value.

3 On the other hand, an entity's current circumstances should be taken into account in determining the fair values of its financial assets and financial liabilities. For example, the fair value of an asset that an entity is committed to sell for cash in the immediate future is the amount that it expects to receive from such a sale.

TYPES OF MARKET PRICE INFORMATION AVAILABLE

4 Fair value information is frequently based on information obtained from market sources. In broad terms, there are four kinds of markets in which financial instruments can be bought, sold, or originated and the information available about prices varies from market to market.

(a) *Exchange market*. An exchange or 'auction' market provides high visibility and order to the trading of financial instruments. Typically, closing prices and volume levels are readily available in an exchange market.

(b) *Dealer market*. In a dealer market, dealers stand ready to trade – either buy or sell – for their own account, thereby providing liquidity to the market. Typically, current bid and offer prices are more readily available than information about closing prices and volume levels. 'Over-the-counter' markets are dealer markets.

(c) *Brokered market*. In a brokered market, brokers attempt to match buyers with sellers but do not stand ready to trade for their own account. The broker knows the prices bid and asked by the respective parties, but each party is typically unaware of another party's price requirements. In such a market, prices of completed transactions are sometimes available.

(d) *Principal-to-principal market*. Principal-to-principal transactions, both originations and resales, are negotiated independently with no intermediary and typically little, if any, information is released publicly.

FINANCIAL INSTRUMENTS WITH QUOTED MARKET PRICES

Quoted market prices, if available, usually provide the best evidence of fair value of financial instruments. Where more than one quoted price is available, the price in the most active market for transactions of the relevant size should normally be used. 5

When current bid and offer prices are unavailable, the price of the most recent transaction may provide evidence of the fair value provided that there has not been a significant change in economic circumstances between the transaction date and the reporting date. 6

FINANCIAL INSTRUMENTS WITH NO QUOTED MARKET PRICES

Quoted market prices may not be indicative of the fair value of the instrument if there is infrequent activity in the market, the market is not well established (as is the case, for example, for some 'over-the-counter' markets) or small volumes are traded relative to the number of units of a financial instrument to be valued. Where this is the case, as well as when a quoted market price is not available, estimation techniques will need to be used and are in most cases capable of determining fair value with sufficient reliability to satisfy the requirements of the FRS 7

Estimation techniques that are well established in financial markets include reference to the current market value of another instrument that is substantially the same, discounted cash flow analysis and option-pricing models. One method of applying discounted cash flow analysis is to discount the cash flows at a rate equal to the prevailing market rate of interest for financial instruments having substantially the same terms and characteristics, including the creditworthiness of the debtor, the remaining term over which the contractual interest rate is fixed, the remaining term to repayment of the principal and the currency in which payments are to be made. 8

When it is difficult to determine fair value of a financial asset or financial liability or of a class of financial assets or financial liabilities, it may be useful to disclose a range of amounts within which the fair value of the financial instrument or class is reasonably believed to lie. 9

Short-term financial instruments and loans that reprice frequently at market rates

For some short-term financial instruments, the carrying amount in the financial statements may approximate to fair value because of the relatively short period of time between the origination of the instruments and their expected realisation. This would also be true of loans that reprice frequently at market rates, provided there was no significant change in credit risk. 10

Custom-tailored financial instruments

Some financial instruments (for example, interest rate swaps and foreign currency contracts) may be 'custom-tailored' and, thus, may not have a quoted market price. 11

(a) In the case of some 'custom-tailored' financial instruments (for example, interest rate swaps and foreign currency contracts), it is often possible to base an estimate of fair value on the quoted market price of a similar financial instrument, adjusted as appropriate for the effects of the tailoring. Alternatively, the estimate might be based on the estimated current replacement cost of that instrument.

(b) In the case of 'custom-tailored' options, a variety of option-pricing models (such as the Black-Scholes model and binomial models) are available. The use of such pricing models to estimate fair value is appropriate under the requirements of the FRS.

Loans receivable

12 Quoted market prices may be more readily available for some categories of loans receivable than for others. If no quoted market price exists for a category of loans, an estimate of fair value may be based on:

(a) the market prices of traded loans with similar credit ratings, interest rates, and maturity dates;
(b) current prices (interest rates) offered for similar loans in the entity's own lending activities; or
(c) valuations obtained from loan-pricing services offered by various specialist firms or from other sources.

13 An estimate of the fair value of a loan or group of loans may be based on the discounted value of the future cash flows expected to be received from the loan or group of loans. The selection of an appropriate current discount rate reflecting the relative risks involved requires judgement, and several alternative rates and approaches are available to an entity.

(a) A single discount rate could be used to estimate the fair value of a homogeneous category of loans. For example, an entity might apply a single rate to each aggregated category of loans.
(b) An entity could use a discount rate commensurate with the credit, interest rate, and prepayment risks involved, which could be the rate at which the same loans would be made under current conditions.
(c) An entity could select a discount rate that reflects the effects of interest rate changes and then make adjustments to reflect the effects of changes in expected credit losses and in the variability of those losses. Those adjustments could include:

   (i) revising cash flow estimates;
   (ii) revising the discount rate; or
   (iii) some combination of (i) and (ii).

Financial liabilities

14 The fair value of financial liabilities for which quoted market prices are not available can generally be estimated using the same techniques used for estimating the value of financial assets. For example, a loan payable to a bank could be valued at the discounted amount of future cash flows using an entity's current incremental rate of borrowing for a similar liability. Alternatively, the discount rate could be the rate that an entity would have to pay to a creditworthy third party to assume its obligation, with the creditor's legal consent (sometimes referred to as the 'settlement rate') or the rate that an entity would have to pay to acquire essentially matching assets to extinguish the obligation.

Deposit liabilities with defined maturities

For deposit liabilities with defined maturities such as certificates of deposit, an estimate of fair value might be based on the discounted value of the future cash flows expected to be paid on the deposits. The discount rate could be the current rate offered for similar deposits with the same remaining maturities. 15

Appendix V
Note on legal requirements

1 This note sets out the main statutory requirements relating to the disclosures to be provided on financial instruments.

GREAT BRITAIN

2 The Companies Act 1985 requires a range of general disclosures about assets and liabilities that are, or will sometimes be, financial assets and financial liabilities. The Act also requires some disclosures about issues specifically addressed in the FRS, and paragraphs 3-11 below summarise these specific disclosure requirements*.

Interest rate risk disclosures

3 Paragraph 48(2) and (3) of Schedule 4 to the Act requires the disclosure of the interest terms on certain items of debt shown under 'creditors' in the balance sheet or, if in the opinion of the directors this would result in a statement of excessive length, a general indication of the rates of any interest repayable on such debt.

Liquidity disclosures

4 Paragraph 48(1) and (3) of Schedule 4 requires, for each item included in the balance sheet under 'creditors', the disclosure of:

(a) the aggregate of:

  (i) the amount that is payable or repayable otherwise than by instalments and is due for repayment in more than five years from the balance sheet date; and
  (ii) in respect of any amounts payable or repayable by instalments, the amount of any instalments falling due for payment in more than five years from the balance sheet date.

(b) the terms of payment or repayment of each item or, if this would in the opinion of the directors result in a statement of excessive length, a general indication of the terms of payment or repayment.

5 Note 5 to the Schedule 4 balance sheet formats requires the amount falling due after more than one year to be shown separately for each item included under debtors.

6 Paragraph 38(2) of Schedule 4 requires, in the case of any part of the alloted share capital that consists of redeemable shares, the disclosure of:

(a) the earliest and latest dates on which the company has the power to redeem those shares; and
(b) an explanation whether redemption is mandatory or is at the option of either the company or the shareholder.

****Editor's Note:*** *Schedule 4 is replaced by Schedule 1 to the Large and Medium-sized Companies and Groups (Accounts and Reports) Regulations 2008 (SI 2008/410) for accounting periods beginning on or after 6 April 2008. Paragraph 48 is now paragraph 61, paragraph 38 is paragraph 47, and paragraph 45 is paragraph 54.*

Fair value disclosures

Paragraph 45(2) of Schedule 4 requires: 7

(a) the disclosure of the aggregate market value of those listed investments held that are not carried in the balance sheet at market value; and
(b) the disclosure of both the market value and the stock exchange value of any listed investments held of which the former value is, for the purposes of the accounts, taken as higher than the latter.

Banking companies and groups (references are to Schedule 9)

Maturity disclosures

Paragraph 61 requires banking companies and groups to provide a maturity analysis of certain assets in the form of loans and advances and of certain liabilities in the form of deposits by banks, customer accounts and debt securities in issue. Paragraph 62 requires banking companies and groups to disclose the amount of debt securities and other fixed income securities that will become due within one year. Paragraph 63 requires, inter alia, disclosure of the maturity date of subordinated liabilities. **8**

Paragraph 51(2) contains an identical requirement for banking companies and groups to that referred to in paragraph 6 above. **9**

Fair value disclosures

Paragraph 68(2) contains an identical requirement for banking companies and groups to that described in paragraph 7(a) above. **10**

Disclosures about hedges

Paragraph 72(1) requires banking companies and groups to disclose the following information about unmatured forward transactions outstanding at the balance sheet date: **11**

(a) the categories of such transactions, by reference to an appropriate system of classification; and
(b) whether, in the case of each such category, they have been made, to any material extent, for the purpose of hedging the effects of fluctuations in interest rates, exchange rates and market prices or whether they have been made, to any material extent, for dealing purposes.

NORTHERN IRELAND

Schedules 4 and 9 to the Companies (Northern Ireland) Order 1986 require similar information about financial instruments to that required by Schedules 4 and 9 to the Companies Act 1985 and described in paragraphs 3-11 above. **12**

REPUBLIC OF IRELAND

The statutory requirements in the Republic of Ireland are similar to those in Great Britain. The following table shows the references to the legislation in the Republic of Ireland that correspond to the references in paragraphs 3-11 above. **13**

The following abbreviations have been used in the table:

1986 Act	Companies (Amendment) Act 1986
1992 Regulations	European Communities (Credit Institutions: Accounts) Regulations 1992

Paragraph above	*Great Britain*	*Republic of Ireland*
3	Schedule 4, paragraph 48(2)	No equivalent
3, 4	Schedule 4, paragraph 48(3)	No equivalent
4	Schedule 4, paragraph 48(1)	Paragraph 34(1) of the Schedule to 1986 Act
5	Note 5 to Schedule 4 balance sheet formats	Note 4 to the Schedule balance sheet formats 1986 Act
6	Schedule 4, paragraph 38(2)	Paragraph 26(2) of the Schedule to 1986 Act
7	Schedule 4, paragraph 45(2)	Paragraph 31(2) of the Schedule to 1986 Act
8	Schedule 9, paragraphs 61-63	Paragraphs 61-63 of Part I, the Schedule to 1992 Regulations
9	Schedule 9, paragraph 51(2)	Paragraph 51(2) of Part I, the Schedule to 1992 Regulations
10	Schedule 9, paragraph 68(2)	Paragraph 68(2) of Part I, the Schedule to 1992 Regulations
11	Schedule 9, paragraph 72(1)	Paragraph 72(1) of Part I, the Schedule to 1992 Regulations

Appendix VI
Compliance with international accounting standards

The International Accounting Standards Committee has issued IAS 32 'Financial Instruments: Disclosure and Presentation'. Features of IAS 32 are covered by FRS 4 'Capital Instruments', FRS 5 'Reporting the Substance of Transactions', this FRS and companies legislation. Compliance with those FRSS, this FRS and companies legislation will ensure compliance in all material respects with IAS 32 except in respect of the matters set out below. The Board's reasons for adopting certain disclosure requirements that are not consistent with the provisions of IAS 32 are set out in Appendix VII.* 1

SCOPE

IAS 32 applies to the financial statements of all entities. The FRS, on the other hand: 2

(a) applies only to entities that have a capital instrument listed or publicly traded and to banks, banking groups and similar institutions and groups; and
(b) does not apply to insurance companies or groups, to entities applying the Financial Reporting Standard for Smaller Entities (FRSSE) or to a parent's own financial statements where they are presented together with its consolidated financial statements.

IAS 32 applies to all financial instruments held or issued by entities, other than those instruments specifically excluded from its scope. The same approach is adopted in the FRS, although there are certain differences in the financial instruments excluded. 3

(a) Whilst IAS 32 exempts all interests in subsidiaries, associates and joint ventures, the FRS exempts only those not held exclusively with a view to subsequent resale.
(b) The FRS exempts certain equity shares issued by the reporting entity and certain warrants and options on such shares that are issued by the reporting entity. IAS 32 has no similar exemption.
(c) The FRS permits short-term debtors and creditors to be excluded from the disclosures. IAS 32 has no similar exemption.
(d) The FRS requires all the financial assets and financial liabilities of an insurance company or group to be excluded from the disclosures. IAS 32 exempts obligations arising under insurance contracts only.

In addition, the FRS requires certain contracts and instruments that are not financial assets and financial liabilities – in particular non-equity shares issued by the reporting entity that are equity instruments and certain types of commodity contracts – to be dealt with in the disclosures. IAS 32 has no similar requirement. 4

DISCLOSURE

Generally speaking, the FRS's disclosure requirements are more specific than the requirements in IAS 32. They are also more extensive in certain respects. For example, IAS 32 does not require the narrative disclosures required by the FRS. Compliance with IAS 32 will not therefore ensure compliance with the FRS. On the 5

* ***Editor's note:*** *The disclosure requirements of IAS 32 have been withdrawn. Disclosure requirements in relation to financial instruments are currently included in IFRS 7, with some changes in 2013 when IFRS 13 comes into force.*

other hand, compliance with the FRS will ensure compliance with the disclosure requirements of IAS 32 except as discussed in paragraphs 6-8 below.

6 IAS 32 requires, for each class of financial asset, financial liability and equity instrument, information to be provided on the extent and nature of the instruments, including specific terms and conditions that may affect the amount, timing and certainty of future cash flows. The FRS does not require the disclosure of significant terms and conditions, although it does require disclosures that show the effect of the instruments on the entity's interest rate and currency profiles, liquidity position and other market price risk exposures.

7 IAS 32 requires numerical disclosures to be provided about credit risk exposures. The FRS does not require numerical disclosures on these matters although, where an entity has significant exposure to credit risk, a discussion of the entity's policy for controlling and managing the risk is required.

8 IAS 32 requires that, when an entity carries one or more financial assets at an amount in excess of fair value, the entity should disclose the carrying amount and the fair value involved and the reasons for not reducing the carrying amount. The FRS does not require a similar disclosure.

PRESENTATION

9 IAS 32 requires preferred shares where the holder has the right to require redemption to be classified as liabilities. It also requires compound instruments that have equity and liability rights to be divided, with the liability element classified as liabilities and the equity element treated as part of shareholders' funds (so-called 'split accounting'). Neither the FRS nor FRS 4 adopts these requirements, for the reasons given in Appendix II to FRS 4.

10 There are also differences in the way in which offsetting is dealt with.

(a) Whilst IAS 32's offsetting provisions apply to all financial assets and financial liabilities, FRS 5's offsetting provisions apply only to some, and no other FRS deals with offsetting in the context of those financial assets and financial liabilities that are not covered in FRS 5.

(b) Whilst IAS 32 treats offsetting as a matter of presentation, FRS 5 treats it as a recognition issue. Therefore, whilst IAS 32 permits financial assets and financial liabilities to be offset in certain limited cases, under FRS 5 assets and liabilities should not be offset, although a debit and credit balance are required to be added together when they constitute a single asset or liability.

(c) IAS 32 requires a financial asset and a financial liability to be offset and the net amount reported in the balance sheet only when an entity has a legally enforceable right to set off the recognised amounts and it intends either to settle on a net basis, or to realise the asset and settle the liability simultaneously. This reference to an intention to settle either net or simultaneously is not included in FRS 5 (for the reasons given in Appendix III to FRS 5).

Appendix VII
The development of the FRS

BACKGROUND AND HISTORY

The dynamic nature of international financial markets has resulted in the widespread use by entities of both traditional primary financial instruments, such as bonds and shares, and various forms of derivative financial instruments, such as futures, options, forward contracts and swaps. This growth in the use of financial instruments has outstripped the development of guidance for their accounting. As a result, although many entities now use financial instruments in a way that can transform their financial position, financial performance and risk profile overnight, the accounting treatment of the instruments does not always portray effectively their impact and risks. 1

Accounting for financial instruments has been a topic of international concern for some time. For example, in 1993 a study by the Group of Thirty* stressed the need for improved disclosures in financial statements about transactions in derivatives and other financial instruments. The US financial reporting standard-setter, the Financial Accounting Standards Board, has been working on financial instruments for more than ten years and has issued a number of standards on the subject. Standards on financial instruments have also been issued in the last few years by the financial reporting standard-setters in Australia, Canada and New Zealand and the International Accounting Standards Committee (IASC). 2

The Accounting Standards Board's own concerns over the apparent inadequacy of accounting rules and guidance in this area caused it to issue a wide-ranging Discussion Paper 'Derivatives and other Financial Instruments' in July 1996. The Paper highlighted three main concerns – the measurement of financial instruments, the use of hedge accounting, and the disclosures provided about financial instruments (both generally and in the context of hedge accounting) – and tentatively reached the following main conclusions. 3

(a) It was not appropriate to continue to measure financial instruments on a historical cost basis. They should, instead, be measured at fair value (the term used in the Discussion Paper was 'current value'). The Paper recognised, however, that such a change would have far-reaching implications and therefore proposed that time should be allowed to explore the implications and debate the issues involved.

(b) Disclosures about financial instruments needed to be improved urgently. The Paper concluded that it was feasible to make these improvements relatively quickly and therefore proposed that priority should be given to this aspect of the subject.

Amongst those responding to the Discussion Paper there was general agreement with its conclusions on disclosure and with the specific disclosures proposed. The Board refined these disclosure proposals in the light of the comments received, and published them in April 1997 as FRED 13 'Derivatives and other Financial Instruments: Disclosures'. The Board also concluded that a separate set of disclosures was needed for banks, and these were issued in draft form in July 1997 as FRED 13 Supplement 4

**The Group of Thirty (or G30) is an international association of bankers and former government officials which provides a forum for discussion of economic issues of global significance. The study referred to is entitled 'Derivatives: Practices and Principles' and was published in July 1993.*

'Derivatives and other Financial Instruments: Disclosures by banks and similar institutions'.

5 These proposals were generally well received and consequently form the basis of this FRS. However, some changes have been made in the light of the comments received, and these are discussed in this appendix.

6 As already mentioned, the Discussion Paper also dealt with the measurement of financial instruments and the extent to which hedge accounting should be allowed. These topics stimulated much debate, although there was general support for an accounting standard on them. Work on measurement and hedge accounting is therefore continuing and the Board expects to publish proposals on these subjects in due course.

APPROACH ADOPTED IN THE FRS

7 The FRS is based on the premise that, in order to be able to make assessments about the financial performance and financial position of an entity, users of financial statements need information on the main aspects of the entity's risk profile and an understanding of how this risk profile is being managed. Since financial instruments contribute to this risk profile and are often used to manage it, they need to be dealt with fully in the disclosures provided. Although some disclosures are already required for financial instruments,* they do not represent a coherent set of requirements that cover all the main risks involved. The main purpose of the FRS is therefore to build a set of such requirements.

8 In developing the FRS, the Board has taken the view that the most meaningful form in which the information can be provided is through a structured mixture of narrative and numerical disclosures. The narrative disclosures will explain the entity's chosen risk profile, including its risk-management policies, and the numerical disclosures will show how these policies were implemented in the period and will provide information to enable significant or potentially significant exposures to be evaluated. Taken together, the disclosures are intended to give a broad overview of the risks arising on financial instruments, focusing on those instruments and risks that are of greatest significance. The approach, in particular, seeks to avoid requiring a mass of detail.

9 In framing the disclosure requirements, the Board has drawn on the work of other financial reporting standard-setters with the result that the FRS is broadly consistent with present international practice. However, the Board recognises that this is a developing area and it intends to review the FRS in the light of experience and in the context of its proposals on measurement and hedge accounting.

TO WHICH ENTITIES SHOULD THE FRS APPLY?

10 It is the Board's view that all entities should provide disclosures on their risk position and on how their financial instruments affect that position. Notwithstanding this, it also took the view in FRED 13 that it would be best, initially, to require the proposed

**For example, in Great Britain the Companies Act 1985 requires companies preparing their financial statements in accordance with Schedule 4 to the Act to disclose information about the maturity and interest rate terms of indebtedness; FRS 4 'Capital Instruments' and SSAP 21 'Accounting for leases and hire purchase contracts' also require certain maturity analyses; and the Board's Statement 'Operating and Financial Review' encourages disclosures on undrawn committed borrowing facilities. Similarly, in the case of banks and certain similar institutions, the Companies Act 1985 and the SORP 'Derivatives' issued by the British Bankers' Association and the Irish Bankers' Federation require the disclosure of some fair value information.*

disclosures only where the case for them was most compelling – the intention being that, in due course, the requirement would be extended to other entities – and that the case for disclosure was most compelling for entities whose capital instruments are listed or publicly traded on a stock exchange or market and for entities that are banks or insurance companies.

This proposal attracted much comment, with some respondents suggesting that the scope of the FRS should be narrower and some that it should be wider. Others agreed that it was necessary to limit the scope of the FRS, but disagreed on how it should be done. Although these comments have been considered at length, the Board remains of the view that the approach adopted in FRED 13 is the most realistic and pragmatic approach available at present. Therefore, with one exception (see 'Insurance companies' below), the scope of the FRS is the same as that proposed in the FRED. **11**

It nevertheless remains the Board's view that there is no reason in principle why all entities should not, in due course, be required to provide disclosures on the risks arising on their financial instruments. Accordingly, when the Board comes to review the FRS it intends to consider extending the scope to all entities. **12**

SPECIALISED INDUSTRIES

In developing the requirements set out in the FRS, the Board decided that a degree of prescription as to the form and content of the disclosures was necessary to help ensure that those provided are of a satisfactory standard and will achieve some consistency. In order to prescribe disclosures that are clear and reasonably precise as well as conforming to the objectives of the FRS, assumptions have had to be made about the way in which financial instruments are used and the main types of risk that arise from that use. Although the Board recognised that its assumptions would not be equally valid for all entities, at the time that it issued FRED 13 its view was that the assumptions it had made could be applied to all entities other than banks and certain similar institutions. It therefore developed and published one set of disclosure proposals for most types of entity (FRED 13) and a second set of disclosure proposals for banks and certain similar institutions (FRED 13 Supplement). **13**

Banks and similar institutions

Financial instruments play an integral part in the wealth-generating activities of banks, often being the primary source of a bank's net income. This net income arises from the management of the mismatches in the exposures arising from financial instruments and the margins earned on them. This is quite different from a typical non-financial institution, where the entity's financial instruments are primarily a result of the entity's financing arrangements or are a by-product of its operating activities. This difference makes it difficult for the traditional accounting model, supplemented by some general risk disclosures, to convey the true significance that the exposures arising from financial instruments have for a bank. For example, the interest rate risk disclosures in FRED 13 assumed that the main interest rate risk arises from borrowings that are used to finance operating activities. This assumption is not, however, appropriate for banks, where the main interest rate risk arises from mismatches between interest rate exposures on assets and on liabilities that form an integral part of the bank's operations. **14**

Another difference that has to be taken into account is that most banks operate a trading book that is distinct from their other assets and liabilities. The risks arising from the trading book tend to be a rapidly changing mix of different types of risk, whilst the risks arising from the non-trading book tend to be more stable and long- **15** term. The different nature of these risks can best be reflected by dealing with them separately in the disclosures.

Other financial institutions

16 When it published FRED 13 Supplement, the Board explained that, although it recognised that there are other types of entity whose business – like banks – is concerned with the handling of financial instruments, it had not been convinced that any of these entities had characteristics that meant that the disclosures proposed in FRED 13 would not be appropriate for them. This issue was by far and away the most controversial aspect of the Supplement, with very few of the respondents agreeing with the approach adopted.

17 In the light of the comments received, and after further discussions with some of the entities involved, the Board has accepted that some financial institutions other than banks would find the disclosures described in the Supplement (subject to certain amendments) better suited to their circumstances than those prescribed in FRED 13. On the other hand, it has also concluded that for some financial institutions the opposite will be true. Various ways of identifying which type of financial institution should provide which set of disclosures have been considered but, as none appears able to achieve a satisfactory fit between entities and disclosures, it has been decided to give financial institutions other than banks and certain similar institutions the choice of providing either the FRED 13 disclosures or (subject to certain amendments) the Supplement's disclosures. In this way different types of financial institution will be able to provide the disclosures in the form that best suits their circumstances.

Insurance companies

18 The Board believes that insurance companies should be required to provide disclosures on their financial instruments and the risks that arise from them. However, a number of those responding to FRED 13 argued that the disclosures described in FRED 13 were not well-suited to insurance companies, primarily because:

- the matching of the investment portfolio to the obligations of the insurer is crucial to an insurer's business, and financial risk disclosures that do not take this matching fully into account will be misleading; and
- financial risk disclosures that do not differentiate between risks borne by the shareholders and risks borne by the policy-holders will provide a misleading picture of the risk profile of the entity.

19 The Board has accepted that there is merit in these arguments and that, as a result, it would not be appropriate to require insurance companies to provide the disclosures set out in FRED 13 or its Supplement. Therefore, rather than delay publication until a suitable set of disclosures for insurance companies has been developed, it has chosen to exempt all insurance companies from the scope of the FRS. It is expected that the Board will shortly add to its work programme a project on certain aspects of insurance accounting. One of the issues that will be considered in this project is the disclosures that should be provided on derivatives and other financial instruments.

TO WHICH INSTRUMENTS SHOULD THE DISCLOSURES APPLY?

Exempt financial instruments

20 FRED 13 proposed that the FRS would not apply to certain specified financial instruments. These items are, generally speaking, already adequately dealt with in

other accounting standards (for example, interests in subsidiaries), or are the subject of other projects (for example, pension and operating lease obligations) or seem to fall outside the main focus of the disclosures being proposed and involve a number of potentially difficult issues (for example, take-or-pay or similar executory contracts that are financial instruments). In the light of the comments received, the list of exempted items in the FRED has been simplified and brought more into line with that contained in IAS 32 'Financial Instruments: Disclosure and Presentation'.

None of these exemptions apply in the case of the currency disclosures. That is because those disclosures are to be based on the way in which the entity has applied SSAP 20 'Foreign currency translation' and, as a result, need to take into account all the assets and liabilities relevant to that standard's application. 21

Short-term debtors and creditors

Many respondents expressed concern at the inclusion of trade debtors, trade creditors, prepayments, accruals and similar items (referred to in the FRS as short-term debtors and creditors) within the scope of the disclosures, arguing that the primary focus of the FRS should be complex financial instruments such as derivative financial instruments. The Board does not believe it appropriate to narrow the focus of the FRS so that it applies merely to complex financial instruments. On the other hand, although short-term debtors and creditors *are* financial instruments and *do* give rise to the sort of risks that the FRS is seeking to address, it is accepted that they are not the primary target of the disclosures. In recognition of this, the Board was minded to exempt such items from the FRS in order to simplify its implementation. It is understood, however, that some entities may find it easier, or regard it as preferable, to include such items in their disclosures. In the light of this, one option might have been to allow complete flexibility as to which short-term debtors and creditors are included in each disclosure. However, this would not have resulted in simple or consistent disclosure. The Board has therefore chosen to give entities the flexibility to decide whether all such items should be included in all the disclosures or whether they should all be excluded from all the disclosures (other than the currency disclosures). 22

Commodity contracts

Contracts that require settlement by the delivery of non-financial assets are not financial instruments. An example of such a contract is one that provides for settlement by receipt or delivery of a commodity (a commodity contract). Notwithstanding the settlement terms of commodity contracts, it is not uncommon for those that are standard in form to be traded on organised markets whose general practice is to permit the contracts to be 'closed out' through settlement in cash or with another financial instrument rather than by taking physical delivery of the underlying commodity. Where this is the case, such contracts are, in many ways, very similar to financial instruments and, as a result, are often used for the same purposes (for example, for hedging or speculative purposes), seen as interchangeable and managed in a similar manner to each other. The FRED therefore proposed that these types of commodity contract (referred to as cash-settled commodity contracts) should be included in the disclosures in the same way as financial instruments. There was general support for this proposal, and it has therefore been carried forward into the FRS. 23

Contracts for the delivery of gold are commodity contracts. Many of them are also cash-settled commodity contracts and will therefore be dealt with in the disclosures for the reasons set out in the previous paragraph. However, gold is used by many 24 entities as a reserve currency and so, even when settlement is achieved through physical delivery, gold contracts are often seen as interchangeable with certain financial instruments. It was for this reason that FRED 13 proposed that all other contracts for the delivery of gold should also be included in the disclosures. However, as a number of respondents pointed out, this would have the effect, in the case of gold producers and entities using gold in their production processes, of bringing stock-in-trade within the scope of the FRS, which was not the Board's intention. The requirement to include all gold contracts has therefore been amended so that it now applies only in the case of the type of entities most likely to be using gold as a reserve currency, ie financial institutions.

Non-equity shares issued by the reporting entity

25 The definitions of the terms 'financial instrument', 'financial asset' and 'financial liability' used in the FRS are taken from IAS 32. These definitions rely, in part, on the definition of 'equity instrument', a term that assumes that all shares are categorised as either evidence of an ownership interest in an entity (in other words, equity instruments) or liabilities. Such a categorisation is not adopted for accounting purposes in the UK. FRS 4, for example, does not permit shares to be treated as liabilities. FRED 13 attempted to reconcile these two different approaches by proposing that non-equity shares that behaved like debt should be treated as liabilities for the purpose of the disclosures. This proposal was not supported by respondents, who argued that it would, in view of FRS 4's requirements, cause confusion; would introduce unwelcome complexity to the disclosures; and, in any event, would still not achieve consistency with IAS 32. In the light of these comments, the Board has decided not to proceed with this approach. Instead, it has decided to require all non-equity shares issued by the reporting entity to be treated in the same way as the entity's financial liabilities, regardless of whether such shares are financial liabilities or equity instruments. This approach has been adopted for pragmatic reasons in order to address the most significant of the anomalies that would otherwise arise but is not intended to set a precedent for, or to indicate the future direction of, accounting for non-equity shares generally.

NARRATIVE DISCLOSURES

26 The detailed content of the narrative disclosures proposed in FRED 13 received general support, although some concerns were expressed that the requirements lacked clarity and precision. The requirements have therefore been extensively rewritten, although the objective of the disclosures remains unchanged: to explain the main risks that arise from financial instruments and to explain what the entity's response is to those risks. As such, the disclosures are intended to be a summary of the facts – drawing on documented policies and decisions and on transactions and exposures that have occurred – not subjective statements or a forecast of what will happen in the future.

27 The Board believes that the narrative disclosures are very important, not least because they set the numerical disclosures in their proper context. Indeed, without the narrative disclosures some of the numerical disclosures might be misunderstood. Because of this central role, the Board concluded during the development of FRED 13 that the narrative disclosures should be a necessary disclosure in financial statements intended to show a true and fair view. This means, amongst other things, that:

(a) such disclosures will need to be audited in the same way as other information that is included in the financial statements; and

(b) if the reporting entity chooses to locate the narrative disclosures outside of the financial statements – by, for example, including them in the operating and financial review – they will need to be incorporated into the financial statements by means of a cross-reference in the notes.

A number of respondents expressed concern at this, arguing that: **28**

(a) by making the disclosures mandatory the Board might inhibit the flexibility entities need to tailor the discussion to reflect their circumstances;
(b) making the narrative disclosures subject to audit might result in entities providing rather bland and unhelpful disclosures; and
(c) the disclosures, or at least parts of them, are not capable of being audited.

The Board does not accept the first two criticisms. Although the disclosures make it clear what information is required, they still leave plenty of scope for entities to tailor the discussion to reflect their circumstances. Furthermore, if required disclosures are provided in a way that is not meaningful it will be difficult for the financial statements to show a true and fair view. In the case of the third criticism, the Board believes that the disclosures as amended are capable of being audited. **29**

NUMERICAL DISCLOSURES TO BE PROVIDED BY NON-FINANCIAL INSTITUTIONS

The main purpose of the numerical disclosures is to illustrate the narrative disclosures by showing how the entity's objectives and policies for holding and issuing financial instruments were implemented during the period. To this end, detailed disclosures focusing on the risks that are likely to be the most significant in practice are prescribed. Furthermore, in order to avoid a mass of detail that obscures more than it enlightens, the FRS encourages, and in places requires, the disclosures to be provided in a highly aggregated form; the emphasis being on the effect of the instruments as a whole rather than on their individual terms and conditions. **30**

With the exception of the fair value and hedging disclosures and, to a lesser extent, the currency disclosures, the detailed numerical disclosures proposed in FRED 13 were generally well received and, as a result, have been carried forward to the FRS largely unchanged. The main amendments that have been made to the proposals were made to simplify and clarify the requirements, to make them easier to implement and to make the resulting disclosures easier to understand. The paragraphs below discuss the most significant changes made to the proposals as well as the most debated issues. **31**

Interest rate risk disclosures

FRED 13 proposed that entities other than banks (and certain similar institutions) should provide an analysis of the interest rate risk exposure arising from certain of their financial assets and financial liabilities. This proposal received a broad level of support and has therefore, with one exception, been retained largely unchanged. The exception relates to the instruments to be dealt with in the disclosure. FRED 13 proposed that the disclosures should focus on borrowings and on investments in interest-bearing assets and other debt instruments. However, some respondents criticised this proposal, arguing that the terms and definitions involved were imprecise; the disclosure would not include all the items that needed to be included; and, by including only some financial instruments in the disclosure, unnecessary complexity was being introduced. In order to address these concerns, the scope of the disclosures has been amended so that the focus is now on financial liabilities and financial assets. This change, taken together with the exemption available for short-term debtors and **32** creditors, will have the effect of extending the scope of the disclosure a little while simplifying implementation.

33 Some entities manage the interest rate risk on their assets separately from the interest rate risk on their liabilities. On the other hand, some deduct cash and liquid resources, and sometimes even other financial assets, from their borrowings and manage the interest rate risk on a 'net borrowings' basis. It has been argued that entities should be required, or at least allowed, to prepare the interest rate risk disclosures on a basis that reflects how they manage the risks. Although this argument was considered during the development of FRED 13, it was thought important, if there were material amounts of cash and liquid resources, that they be shown separately from borrowings. The FRED therefore proposed that a gross analysis should be provided unless the amount of cash and liquid resources was immaterial, in which case net or gross figures could be used. This approach was generally supported by those responding to the FRED, and has been retained in the FRS.

Liquidity disclosures

34 FRED 13 proposed that entities should provide a maturity analysis of borrowings and of undrawn committed borrowing facilities. The two main issues that arose in respect of these proposals were as follows:

(a) *The instruments to be dealt with* - For the reasons set out in paragraph 32 above, the FRED's proposal that only borrowings should be included in the first analysis has been amended; the disclosure now needs to be provided for financial liabilities rather than borrowings only.

(b) *The need for the analysis of undrawn committed borrowing facilities* - FRED 13's proposal that entities should provide an analysis of undrawn committed borrowing facilities met with a mixed response. Some respondents argued that the liquidity profile of an entity can be properly understood only if such an analysis is given. Some of these respondents pointed out that this disclosure is already required in the USA and by IAS 32 and is one of the disclosures suggested in the Board's own Statement 'Operating and Financial Review'. Others argued that the level and profile of undrawn committed borrowing facilities is of limited relevance and could, in fact, mislead users because it says nothing about the facilities that could be obtained should the entity need to obtain them. Having considered the arguments, the Board believes that, on balance, this information is useful to an understanding of the liquidity profile of the entity and should be disclosed. The FRS therefore continues to require a maturity analysis of undrawn committed borrowing facilities.

Currency disclosures

35 The currency risk disclosures proposed in FRED 13 were criticised by a number of respondents, who argued variously that the disclosures were misleading, meaningless, too complex, not practicable or very costly to prepare. Although the Board had thought that the disclosures were capable of being produced relatively easily and at little additional cost, it now understands that that will not always be the case. A particular difficulty for some entities that are not financial institutions stemmed from the fact that their application of SSAP 20 did not easily lend itself to providing the proposed structural disclosures. The currency risk disclosure requirements for such entities have therefore been simplified to focus on the underlying primary purpose of the disclosure, which is to show the currency exposures that give rise to the net currency gains and losses recognised in the profit and loss account. Such exposures

are the main currency exposures that arise from financial instruments in the case of most entities that are not financial institutions.

One consequence of this is that the FRS does not require such entities to provide any disclosures relating to their structural currency exposures (in other words, relating to the exposures that give rise to the translation gains and losses that are recognised in the statement of total recognised gains and losses under SSAP 20). Although these exposures are not the primary focus of the FRS, for many entities they are important. The Board will therefore be considering whether to propose that SSAP 20 should be amended to require disclosure of information about such exposures.* 36

Fair value disclosures

FRED 13 proposed that entities should be required to disclose the fair value of all financial instruments (other than those for which a reliable fair value could not be determined). These proposals were the subject of more comment from respondents than any other matter. Some, for example, argued that there should not be any requirement to disclose fair values. Others argued that fair values should not be required for certain financial assets and financial liabilities such as own debt, instruments that management intends to hold to maturity or instruments held for hedging purposes. Despite these comments, the Board remains convinced of the need to disclose the fair values of all financial assets and financial liabilities. It believes that fair value is a useful measure in the case of assets and liabilities that are not recognised because their cost on acquisition is nil. Even in the case of instruments that are recognised, fair value is a useful additional measure, enabling the instruments to be viewed from a different perspective from that used for recognition purposes. The requirement to disclose fair values has therefore been retained in the FRS. 37

As already mentioned FRED 13 recognised that there will be circumstances, albeit limited, in which it will not be practicable for non-financial institutions to determine with sufficient reliability the fair value of a non-traded financial instrument. In such circumstances, the FRED proposed that it should not be necessary to disclose fair value. This approach was generally supported and has been carried forward into the FRS. 38

However, in two important respects the fair value disclosure proposals have been modified. 39

(a) FRED 13 proposed that the FRS should require the fair value of financial instruments that are not traded on organised markets in a standard form to be shown separately from the fair values of other financial instruments. This proposal was criticised by respondents, who thought that its focus was inappropriate and that it was too detailed a disclosure. In the light of these comments, the requirement has not been included in the FRS.

(b) It had been proposed that financial assets and financial liabilities should be grouped into appropriate categories and that a single fair value should be given for each category. Whilst this approach was supported by the majority of respondents, a number thought that one aggregate figure should be given for instruments with a positive fair value and another for instruments with a negative fair value. The Board has reconsidered the matter and has decided that, as the arguments involved are evenly balanced and the issue is not central to the usefulness of the disclosure, the FRS should permit a choice.

****Editor's note:** An exposure draft of an amendment to SSAP 20 was published in February 1999, but withdrawn in May 1999.*

40 FRED 13 also contained an appendix setting out guidance on procedures for estimating fair values, and those responding to the FRED were asked to comment on whether this guidance was sufficient. Most respondents thought that it was sufficient, although a few suggested that the guidance should be much more specific on matters such as bid, offer or mid-market prices; large holdings; changes in creditworthiness of own debt; and portfolios. The Board believes, however, that it is not appropriate at this stage to be prescriptive on such matters. The guidance has therefore been carried forward into the FRS largely unchanged.

41 IAS 32 contains a requirement that, if a financial asset is carried in the balance sheet at an amount in excess of fair value, the reasons why the carrying amount has not been written down to the fair value should be disclosed, together with details of the carrying amount and fair value concerned. As IAS 32 goes on to say, "management exercises judgement in determining the amount it expects to recover from a financial asset and whether to write down the carrying amount of the asset when it is in excess of fair value. [This disclosure] provides users of financial statements with a basis for understanding management's exercise of judgement and assessing the possibility that circumstances may change and lead to a reduction in the asset's carrying amount in the future". When FRED 13 was published, it was explained that, although consideration had been given to including a similar requirement in the FRS, it had been decided that, whilst this disclosure was likely to be of relevance in the context of an FRS dealing with the measurement of financial instruments, it was unlikely to contribute to an understanding of the main risks arising from the entity's use of financial instruments. Those who responded to FRED 13 supported this conclusion. The FRS therefore adopts the same approach as the FRED.

Disclosures about financial assets and financial liabilities held or issued for trading

42 In response to comments received on FRED 13, the disclosures required for financial instruments held or issued for trading have been simplified in that the proposed requirement to analyse net gains and losses by type of financial instrument has not been retained.

Disclosures about hedges

43 As mentioned already, the Board's work on hedge accounting continues. One of the concerns about the use of hedge accounting is that, because practice varies widely and because it is management intention that determines what is a hedge, it is difficult to know how to interpret the financial statements of an entity that uses hedge accounting extensively. Therefore, although it is possible that the Board will in due course restrict or even prohibit the use of hedge accounting, there is a need now to improve the disclosures about its use. For this reason, proposals on disclosures for hedges of future transactions were put forward in FRED 13. The purpose of the disclosures proposed was to explain how the entity accounts for hedges of future transactions and, if it uses hedge accounting, to show the effect on the performance statements.

44 These proposals attracted much comment. Some respondents thought that few, if any, hedging disclosures should be required, some accepted the need for some disclosures but viewed the proposed disclosures as excessive, and some thought the disclosures would reveal commercially sensitive information and therefore should be subject to a commercial sensitivity exemption. Generally speaking, the Board has not been persuaded by such arguments and continues to believe that, in the absence of an accounting standard on the recognition and measurement aspects of hedge accounting, extensive disclosures are essential.

That said, the FRS makes two significant changes from the hedging disclosures proposed in FRED 13. 45

(a) The FRED proposed that the disclosures should apply only to hedges of future transactions. This left a gap in the information provided about hedges, and the disclosures in the FRS therefore extend to all hedges.
(b) The FRED proposed that the disclosures should be analysed to show information on hedges of firm contracts separately from information on other hedges. However, in response to the comments received, this requirement has not been included in the FRS.

Disclosures about commodity contracts treated as financial instruments

As already mentioned, FRED 13 proposed that certain types of commodity contract should be included in the disclosures as if they were financial instruments. The FRED also proposed that, if any of these disclosures were commercially sensitive, in certain circumstances that disclosure need not be given. Some respondents, however, thought that this exemption should also be available in other circumstances. The Board has considered at great length the comments made on this matter but, having taken into account: 46

- the degree of aggregation required or permitted by the FRS
- the flexibility given regarding the form that the disclosures should take
- the delay that will usually arise before the financial statements become publicly available

it has not been convinced that there is a need to extend the exemption.

Three changes have nevertheless been made to the exemption proposed by FRED 13. 47

(a) The FRED proposed that the exemption should be available in respect of all disclosures provided on commodity contracts. However, as the Board does not believe that the narrative disclosures could require the disclosure of commercially sensitive information, the FRS excludes such disclosures from the scope of the exemption.
(b) The FRS requires that to take advantage of the exemption, it is necessary that, inter alia, disclosure would be 'seriously prejudicial' to the interests of the entity; FRED 13 referred only to 'prejudicial'. This amendment brings the wording of the exemption in the FRS into line with the wording of the commercial sensitivity exemptions contained in other accounting standards.
(c) The FRS acknowledges that whether disclosure will be seriously prejudicial to the interests of the entity is essentially a matter of the directors' opinion.

Encouraged additional disclosures about market price risk

There is much concern about the absence of good quality disclosures about the market price risk that entities take on through financial instruments and similar contracts. On the other hand, the measurement of market price risk is evolving and a consensus has yet to emerge on the best method of providing adequate and meaningful information in a cost-effective manner. For these reasons, FRED 13 proposed to encourage, but not require, additional numerical disclosures concerning market risk. This approach was generally supported by respondents and has therefore been retained in the FRED. 48

Offsetting

49 FRED 13 proposed the extension, subject to minor amendments, of the offset provisions of FRS 5 'Reporting the Substance of Transactions' to all financial assets and financial liabilities. The proposal was criticised by respondents, who thought it inappropriate or confusing. Others argued that it was inappropriate for an FRS on disclosure to prescribe the rules to be applied when offsetting for recognition purposes. The Board accepts that, whilst it is necessary for the FRS to make it clear what level of aggregation and offsetting should be used in preparing the disclosures, it is not necessary for this FRS to address offsetting in the primary accounting statements themselves. The proposal has therefore been dropped.

NUMERICAL DISCLOSURES TO BE PROVIDED BY BANKS AND CERTAIN OTHER INSTITUTIONS

Main changes

50 Respondents generally supported the detailed disclosure requirements proposed in FRED 13 Supplement and, as a result, there have been only three significant changes to the disclosures.

(a) *Currency disclosures* - There was much debate about the currency disclosures proposed. This is discussed in paragraph 54 below.

(b) *Maturity analysis* - The Supplement proposed that the FRS should repeat the maturity analysis disclosure requirements for banks that are contained in other accounting standards and in legislation and it proposed that the FRS should require all these analyses to be provided together in a single note. Neither of these proposals has been carried forward to the FRS.

(c) *Trading book disclosures* - The Supplement proposed that the trading book disclosures should show the position at the balance sheet date (unless such information is not typical of the figures during the period). However, in the light of comments received, the Board concluded that providing information about the position at the balance sheet date only will not enable the user to understand the significance of the trading book to the reporting entity. The requirement in the FRS has therefore been extended to include disclosure of the highest, lowest and average positions during the period.

Currency disclosures

51 Although worded somewhat differently from the proposals set out in FRED 13, the Supplement's currency disclosure proposals were in essence very similar to the FRED's in that they proposed that banks and similar institutions should disclose details of their structural currency exposures and of the currency exposures in the non-trading book that give rise to the net currency gains and losses recognised in their profit and loss account. Although these proposals were criticised for some of the same reasons as the FRED's proposals, the Board has decided that the requirement to disclose the structural currency exposures should be retained for banks and certain similar institutions, albeit in a simplified form. There are two main reasons why this approach is not the same as the approach adopted for non-financial institutions.

(a) The structural currency exposures of most financial institutions arise primarily from financial instruments and therefore need to be dealt with in the FRS's disclosures if its objective is to be met.

(b) It would appear that the disclosures would not cause the same practical problems for banks and similar institutions as they would cause for non-financial institutions.

FAIR VALUE DISCLOSURES

In developing FRED 13 Supplement, the Board decided that the fair value disclosure requirements proposed in FRED 13 should be slightly modified for banks and similar institutions. For such entities, markets for some non-trading book items have generally not evolved to the point where fair values can be determined by reference to a readily available market price. Furthermore, although valuation techniques may exist that will enable entities with a few of those assets and liabilities to determine a reliable fair value reasonably easily, they have not yet developed to the point where fair values for large numbers of such assets and liabilities can be determined without incurring significant expense. The Board therefore concluded that the disclosure of fair values for these assets and liabilities should not, at present, be required. This approach was generally supported by those responding to the Supplement and has been reflected in the FRS. This is, however, a developing area and the Board intends to keep the matter under review, particularly in the light of developments in valuation techniques and as markets evolve. 52

As already mentioned, when the Board came to devise a disclosure regime for financial institutions other than banks, it concluded that, in the main, such entities should be able to choose to provide either the 'FRED 13 disclosures' or the 'Supplement's disclosures'. However, after careful consideration it concluded that it would be inappropriate to allow such flexibility for fair value disclosures. This conclusion was based on the Board's view that the circumstances described in paragraph 52 above do not hold true for the majority of financial institutions other than banks, and it is not practicable to try to differentiate between those institutions where it does hold true and those where it does not. Such entities will, of course, be able to avail themselves of the exemption referred to in paragraph 38 above. 53

Value at risk

Value at risk methods are widely viewed as the most sophisticated means available at present for measuring market price risk. For this reason, the Board was minded, in developing the proposals in the Supplement, to require all banks to disclose the value at risk of their trading books. However, this is not realistic at present; although there is a trend towards the use of value at risk for both internal risk management purposes and external prudential supervisory purposes, there are many banks that do not use the technique. The Board therefore concluded that it would be necessary to permit banks to use an alternative method to provide the disclosures. Similarly, although 'value at risk' is a generic term for a type of method it is not realistic at present to specify the precise method to be used by banks for external reporting purposes. These conclusions were reflected in the proposals set out in the Supplement and were supported by most respondents. The same approach has therefore been adopted in the FRS. 54

CREDIT RISK DISCLOSURES

Although IAS 32 requires numerical disclosures about an entity's exposure to maximum credit risk and concentrations of such risk, the FRS contains no similar requirements. When the Board was developing its Discussion Paper it took soundings to discover which information about financial instruments users thought was most relevant. This revealed that further disclosures relating to the credit risk of financial instruments in general, and derivative financial instruments in particular, were not normally of concern to users of financial statements, particularly for reporting entities that are not financial institutions. The Board therefore concluded that it should not require the disclosure of such information. This issue was 55 specifically highlighted in the preface to FRED 13 and the Board's conclusion was generally supported by respondents.

56 The Board accepts that, whilst this approach may be appropriate for non-financial institutions, it may progressively become less appropriate in the context of financial institutions, particularly in view of the use of credit derivatives and similar instruments. This matter will be kept under review in the light of developments in the markets and accounting techniques for such instruments.

AMENDMENT TO FRS 4

57 Paragraph 38 of the FRS requires certain entities to provide a liquidity analysis of financial liabilities. As mentioned in paragraph 39 of the FRS, maturity analyses of debt and obligations under finance leases are already required by paragraph 33 of FRS 4 and paragraph 52 of SSAP 21 respectively. The Board believes that many preparers and users would like to be able to meet those requirements and the requirements of paragraph 38 of this FRS through a single disclosure. However, paragraph 33 of FRS 4 requires very slightly different time bands to be used in its analysis from those that are required to be used by paragraph 52 of SSAP 21. The purpose of the amendment to FRS 4 is to eliminate these differences and thereby enable entities to meet all these requirements through a single disclosure.

Financial Reporting Standard 15 is set out in paragraphs 1–110.

The Statement of Standard Accounting Practice, which comprises the paragraphs set in bold type, should be read in the context of the Objective as stated in paragraph 1 and the definitions set out in paragraph 2 and also of the Foreword to Accounting Standards and the Statement of Principles for Financial Reporting currently in issue.

The explanatory paragraphs contained in the FRS shall be regarded as part of the Statement of Standard Accounting Practice insofar as they assist in interpreting that statement.

Appendix IV 'The development of the FRS' reviews considerations and arguments that were thought significant by members of the Board in reaching the conclusions on the FRS.

[FRS 15]
Tangible fixed assets*

(Issued February 1999)

Contents

	Paragraphs
Summary	
Financial Reporting Standard 15	
Objective	1
Definitions	2
Scope	3–5
Initial measurement	6–41
Cost	6–18
Finance costs	19–30
Disclosures – finance costs	31
Recoverable amount	32–33
Subsequent expenditure	34–41
Valuation	42–76
Frequency	43–52
Valuation basis	53–60
Class of assets	61–62
Reporting gains and losses on revaluation	63–71
Reporting gains and losses on disposal	72–73
Disclosures	74–76
Depreciation	77–102
Depreciable amount	77–92
Review of useful economic life and residual value	93–96
Renewals accounting	97–99
Disclosures	100–102
Date from which effective and transitional arrangements	103–108
Amendment to SSAP 19 and withdrawal of SSAP 12	109–110
Adoption of FRS 15 by the Board	

Appendices
- **I** RICS definitions
- **II** Note on legal requirements
- **III** Compliance with International accounting standards
- **IV** The development of the FRS

****Editor's note****: The matters covered in FRS 15 are dealt with in Section 17 of FRS 102.*

Summary

GENERAL

Financial Reporting Standard 15 'Tangible Fixed Assets' sets out the principles of accounting for the initial measurement, valuation and depreciation of tangible fixed assets, with the exception of investment properties. Investment properties continue to be accounted for in accordance with SSAP 19 'Accounting for investment properties', but are being considered further in the light of other Board projects and the international project on investment properties. **a**

The FRS codifies much of existing accounting practice. Its objective is to ensure that tangible fixed assets are accounted for on a consistent basis and, where a policy of revaluation is adopted, that revaluations are kept up-to-date. **b**

INITIAL MEASUREMENT

Whether acquired or self-constructed, a tangible fixed asset should initially be measured at its cost. Only costs that are directly attributable to bringing the asset into working condition for its intended use should be included. Such costs should be capitalised only for the period in which the activities that are necessary to get the asset ready for use are in progress. **c**

The capitalisation of finance costs, including interest, is optional. However, if an entity adopts such a policy then it should be applied consistently. All finance costs that are directly attributable to the construction of a tangible fixed asset should be capitalised as part of the cost of that asset, subject to the proviso that the total amount of finance costs capitalised during a period should not exceed the amount of finance costs incurred during the period. The FRS also sets limits on the period of capitalisation and specifies certain disclosure requirements. **d**

If the amount recognised when a tangible fixed asset is acquired or constructed exceeds its recoverable amount, it should be written down to recoverable amount. However, on initial recognition the asset needs to be reviewed for impairment only if there is an indication of impairment, in accordance with FRS 11 'Impairment of Fixed Assets and Goodwill'. **e**

Subsequent expenditure undertaken to ensure that the asset maintains its previously assessed standard of performance, for example routine repairs and maintenance expenditure, should be recognised in the profit and loss account as it is incurred. Without such expenditure the depreciation expense would be increased because the useful economic life or residual value of the asset would be reduced. However, subsequent expenditure should be capitalised in three circumstances, where the expenditure: **f**

(i) enhances the economic benefits of the asset in excess of its previously assessed standard of performance; or
(ii) replaces or restores a component of the asset that has been treated separately for depreciation purposes and depreciated over its individual useful economic life; or
(iii) relates to a major inspection or overhaul that restores the economic benefits of the asset that have been consumed by the entity and have already been reflected in depreciation.

VALUATION

g An entity has the option of revaluing its tangible fixed assets. However, where such a policy is adopted it should be applied consistently to all tangible fixed assets of the same class.

h Where a tangible fixed asset is revalued its carrying amount should be its current value at the balance sheet date. Generally this requirement is achieved by performing a full valuation at least every five years and an interim valuation in year 3, with an interim valuation in the intervening years where it is likely that there has been a material change in value. Alternatively, for a portfolio of non-specialised properties, a full valuation may be performed on a rolling basis over a five-year cycle, together with an interim valuation on the remaining portfolio where it is likely that there has been a material change in value. For tangible fixed assets other than properties where there is an active second-hand market or appropriate indices, such that the entity's directors can establish the asset's value with reasonable reliability, an annual revaluation by the directors may be sufficient, without necessarily using the services of a qualified valuer.

i Where tangible fixed assets are revalued the following valuation bases for unimpaired assets should be used:

- non-specialised properties – existing use value,* with the addition of notional directly attributable acquisition costs, where material
- specialised properties – depreciated replacement cost
- properties surplus to an entity's requirements – open market value,† after deducting expected directly attributable selling costs, where material
- tangible fixed assets other than properties – market value, or depreciated replacement cost where market value is not available.

j Revaluation gains are recognised in the statement of total recognised gains and losses except to the extent that they reverse revaluation losses on the same asset that were previously recognised in the profit and loss account, in which case they, too, should be recognised in the profit and loss account, after adjusting for subsequent depreciation.

k All revaluation losses that are caused by a clear consumption of economic benefits are recognised in the profit and loss account. Other revaluation losses are recognised in the statement of total recognised gains and losses until the carrying amount of the asset falls below depreciated historical cost. Revaluation losses below depreciated historical cost are recognised in the profit and loss account, except where it can be demonstrated that the recoverable amount of the asset is greater than its revalued amount, in which case the loss is recognised in the statement of total recognised gains and losses to the extent that the recoverable amount of the asset is greater than its revalued amount.

l Profits and losses on the disposal of tangible fixed assets are treated in accordance with FRS 3 'Reporting Financial Performance' – ie calculated as the difference between the net sale proceeds and the carrying amount and recorded in the profit and loss account in the period in which the disposal occurs.

**As defined by the Royal Institution of Chartered Surveyors (RICS). These definitions are reproduced in Appendix I.*

†As defined by the Royal Institution of Chartered Surveyors (RICS). These definitions are reproduced in Appendix I.

Where an entity revalues its tangible fixed assets the FRS requires specific disclosures about the valuation. m

DEPRECIATION

The fundamental objective of depreciation is to reflect in operating profit the cost of use of the tangible fixed assets (ie the amount of economic benefits consumed by the entity) in the period. Therefore, the depreciable amount (ie cost, or revalued amount, less residual value) of a tangible fixed asset should be recognised in the profit and loss account on a systematic basis that reflects as fairly as possible the pattern in which the asset's economic benefits are consumed by the entity, over its useful economic life. n

Where the tangible fixed asset comprises two or more major components with substantially different useful economic lives, each component should be accounted for separately for depreciation purposes and depreciated over its individual useful economic life. o

Subsequent expenditure on a tangible fixed asset that maintains or enhances the previously assessed standard of performance of the asset does not negate the need to charge depreciation, as, other than non-depreciable land, all tangible fixed assets have finite lives. However, where the remaining useful economic life of a tangible fixed asset is estimated to be greater than 50 years or where the depreciation charge is immaterial owing to a long useful economic life or high residual value, then, to ensure that the carrying amount can be supported, the tangible fixed asset should be subjected to impairment reviews at the end of each reporting period, performed in accordance with FRS 11. p

The useful economic life of a tangible fixed asset and its residual value (based on the price level that existed when the asset was purchased or last revalued) where material, should be reviewed at the end of each reporting period. If expectations are significantly different from previous estimates, the change should be accounted for prospectively over the tangible fixed asset's remaining useful economic life, except to the extent that the asset has been impaired at the balance sheet date. q

The FRS requires specific disclosures about the depreciation policies adopted by an entity and changes in those policies. r

Financial Reporting Standard 15

Objective

1 The objective of this FRS is to ensure that:

(a) consistent principles are applied to the initial measurement of tangible fixed assets.

(b) where an entity chooses to revalue tangible fixed assets the valuation is performed on a consistent basis and kept up-to-date and gains and losses on revaluation are recognised on a consistent basis.

(c) depreciation of tangible fixed assets is calculated in a consistent manner and recognised as the economic benefits are consumed over the assets' useful economic lives.

(d) sufficient information is disclosed in the financial statements to enable users to understand the impact of the entity's accounting policies regarding initial measurement, valuation and depreciation of tangible fixed assets on the financial position and performance of the entity.

Definitions

2 The following definitions shall apply in the FRS and in particular in the Statement of Standard Accounting Practice set out **in bold type**.

Class of tangible fixed assets:-

A category of tangible fixed assets having a similar nature, function or use in the business of the entity.

Current value:-

The current value of a tangible fixed asset to the business is the lower of replacement cost and recoverable amount.

Depreciable amount:-

The cost of a tangible fixed asset (or, where an asset is revalued, the revalued amount) less its residual value.

Depreciated replacement cost (of property):-

Has the same meaning as in the *Appraisal and Valuation Manual* published by the Royal Institution of Chartered Surveyors (RICS). The definition is reproduced in Appendix I.*

*****Editor's note**: There are various references to RICS guidance in FRS 15. The RICS guidance has altered since the date of publication of FRS 15, and some of the terms used in FRS 15 are no longer defined by RICS.*

Depreciated replacement cost (of tangible fixed assets other than property):-

The cost of replacing an existing tangible fixed asset with an identical or substantially similar new asset having a similar production or service capacity, from which appropriate deductions are made to reflect the value attributable to the remaining portion of the total useful economic life of the asset and the residual value at the end of the asset's useful economic life.

> Costs directly attributable to bringing the tangible fixed asset into working condition for its intended use, such as costs of transport, installation, commissioning, consultants' fees, non-recoverable taxes and duties, are included in depreciated replacement cost. The deductions from gross replacement cost should take into account the age and condition of the asset, economic and functional obsolescence, and environmental and other relevant factors.

Depreciation:-

The measure of the cost or revalued amount of the economic benefits of the tangible fixed asset that have been consumed during the period.

> Consumption includes the wearing out, using up or other reduction in the useful economic life of a tangible fixed asset whether arising from use, effluxion of time or obsolescence through either changes in technology or demand for the goods and services produced by the asset.

Existing use value:-

Has the same meaning as in the *Appraisal and Valuation Manual* published by the RICS. The definition is reproduced in Appendix I.

Finance costs:-

The difference between the net proceeds of an instrument and the total amount of payments (or other transfers of economic benefits) that the issuer may be required to make in respect of the instrument.*

Impairment:-

A reduction in the recoverable amount of a tangible fixed asset below its carrying amount.

> The definition set out above is taken from FRS 11 'Impairment of Fixed Assets and Goodwill'.

Non-specialised properties:-

Has the same meaning as in the *Appraisal and Valuation Manual* published by the RICS. The definition is reproduced in Appendix I.

Open market value:-

Has the same meaning as in the *Appraisal and Valuation Manual* published by the RICS. The definition is reproduced in Appendix I.

***Editor's note:** The explanatory paragraph on finance costs, which was based on FRS 4, has been deleted by FRS 25.*

Qualified (internal or external) valuer:-

A person conducting the valuation who holds a recognised and relevant professional qualification and having recent post-qualification experience, and sufficient knowledge of the state of the market, in the location and category of the tangible fixed asset being valued. An internal valuer is a director, officer or employee of the entity. An external valuer is not an internal valuer and does not have a significant financial interest in the entity.

Recoverable amount:-

The higher of net realisable value and value in use.*

Residual value:-

The net realisable value of an asset at the end of its useful economic life. Residual values are based on prices prevailing at the date of the acquisition (or revaluation) of the asset and do not take account of expected future price changes.

Specialised properties:-

Has the same meaning as in the *Appraisal and Valuation Manual* published by the RICS. The definition is reproduced in Appendix I.

Tangible fixed assets:-

Assets that have physical substance and are held for use in the production or supply of goods or services, for rental to others, or for administrative purposes on a continuing basis in the reporting entity's activities.

Useful economic life:-

The useful economic life of a tangible fixed asset is the period over which the entity expects to derive economic benefit from that asset.

SCOPE

3 **The FRS applies to all financial statements that are intended to give a true and fair view of a reporting entity's financial position and profit or loss (or income and expenditure) for a period.**

4 **The requirements of the FRS apply to all tangible fixed assets, with the exception of investment properties as defined in SSAP 19 'Accounting for investment properties'.**

4A **The recognition and measurement requirements in paragraphs 6 to 99 of this standard apply to heritage assets subject to the requirements set out in paragraphs 18 to 25 of FRS 30 'Heritage assets'. The disclosure requirements in paragraphs 100 to 108 of this standard do not apply to heritage assets.†**

5 **Reporting entities applying the Financial Reporting Standard for Smaller Entities (FRSSE) currently applicable are exempt from the FRS.**

**Refer to FRS 11 'Impairment of Fixed Assets and Goodwill' for a definition of value in use and details about its calculation.*

*†**Editor's note**: Paragraph added by FRS 30 with effect for accounting periods beginning on or after 1 April 2010.*

INITIAL MEASUREMENT

Cost

A tangible fixed asset should initially be measured at its cost. 6

Costs, but only those costs, that are directly attributable to bringing the asset into working condition for its intended use should be included in its measurement. 7

The cost of a tangible fixed asset (whether acquired or self-constructed) comprises its purchase price (after deducting any trade discounts and rebates) and any costs directly attributable to bringing it into working condition for its intended use. 8

Directly attributable costs are: 9

(a) the labour costs of own employees (eg site workers, in-house architects and surveyors) arising directly from the construction, or acquisition, of the specific tangible fixed asset; and

(b) the incremental costs to the entity that would have been avoided only if the tangible fixed asset had not been constructed or acquired.

It follows that administration and other general overhead costs would be excluded from the cost of a tangible fixed asset. Employee costs not related to the specific asset (such as site selection activities) are not directly attributable costs.

Examples of directly attributable costs include: 10

- acquisition costs (such as stamp duty, import duties and non-refundable purchase taxes)
- the cost of site preparation and clearance
- initial delivery and handling costs
- installation costs
- professional fees (such as legal, architects' and engineers' fees)
- the estimated cost of dismantling and removing the asset and restoring the site, to the extent that it is recognised as a provision under FRS 12 'Provisions, Contingent Liabilities and Contingent Assets'. The fact that the prospect of such expenditures emerges only some time after the original capitalisation of the asset (eg because of legislative changes) does not preclude their capitalisation.

Abnormal costs (such as those relating to design errors, industrial disputes, idle capacity, wasted materials, labour or other resources and production delays) and costs such as operating losses that occur because a revenue activity has been suspended during the construction of a tangible fixed asset are not directly attributable to bringing the asset into working condition for its intended use. 11

Capitalisation of directly attributable costs should cease when substantially all the activities that are necessary to get the tangible fixed asset ready for use are complete, even if the asset has not yet been brought into use. 12

A tangible fixed asset is ready for use when its physical construction is complete. 13

The costs associated with a start-up or commissioning period should be included in the cost of the tangible fixed asset only where the asset is available for use but incapable of operating at normal levels without such a start-up or commissioning period. 14

15 A distinction can be made between:

(a) the commissioning period for plant, in which it is impossible for it to operate at normal levels because of, for example, the need to run in machinery, to test equipment and generally to ensure the proper functioning of the plant; and
(b) an initial operating period in which, although the plant is available for use and capable of running at normal levels, it is operated at below normal levels because demand has not yet built up.

16 The costs of an essential commissioning period are included as part of the cost of bringing the asset up to its normal operating potential, and therefore as part of its cost. However, there is no justification for regarding costs relating to other start-up periods, where the asset is available for use but not yet operating at normal levels, for example because of a lack of demand, as part of the cost of the asset. An example is the start-up period of a new hotel or bookshop, which could operate at normal levels almost immediately, but for which experience teaches that demand will build up slowly and full utilisation or sales levels will be achieved only over a period of several months.

17 **The initial carrying amount of tangible fixed assets received as gifts and donations by charities should be the current value of the assets at the date they are received. Where these gifts and donations are heritage assets, entities should report these assets in accordance with FRS 30 'Heritage assets'.***

18 Donated assets are particularly common in the charity sector. Such organisations often receive tangible fixed assets that the entity cannot dispose of without external consent and other tangible fixed assets of particular historic, scientific or artistic importance. On occasion, such assets may present measurement difficulties where conventional valuation approaches lack sufficient reliability. In addition, even where valuation is practical, if significant costs are involved they may be onerous compared with the additional benefit derived by users of the accounts in assessing management's stewardship of the assets. Where it can be demonstrated that these factors are significant alternative approaches to the valuation of those tangible fixed assets may be appropriate, provided that adequate disclosure of the reason for the different treatment, and of the age, nature and scale of the assets is given in the notes to the accounts. A similar approach is acceptable on the first implementation of the FRS where, under previously permitted accounting policies, a charity holds tangible fixed assets that were not capitalised as required by the FRS and for which reliable estimates of cost or value are not available on a cost-benefit basis. Generally, these issues will be addressed in the relevant sector-specific guidance and Statements of Recommended Practice (SORPs). The requirements for heritage assets are addressed in FRS 30 'Heritage assets'.†

Finance costs

19 **Where an entity adopts a policy of capitalising finance costs, finance costs that are directly attributable to the construction of tangible fixed assets should be capitalised as part of the cost of those assets. The total amount of finance costs capitalised during a period should not exceed the total amount of finance costs incurred during that period.**

20 An entity need not capitalise finance costs. However, if an entity adopts a policy of capitalisation of finance costs, then it should be applied consistently to all tangible

Editor's note: *Final sentence added by FRS 30 with effect for accounting periods beginning on or after 1 April 2010.*

†***Editor's note:*** *Final sentence added by FRS 30 with effect for accounting periods beginning on or after 1 April 2010.*

fixed assets where finance costs fall to be capitalised in accordance with the above requirement.

Only finance costs that are directly attributable to the construction of a tangible fixed asset, or the financing of progress payments in respect of the construction of a tangible fixed asset by others for the entity, should be capitalised. Directly attributable finance costs are those that would have been avoided (for example by avoiding additional borrowings or by using the funds expended for the asset to repay existing borrowings) if there had been no expenditure on the asset. Finance costs are capitalised on a gross basis, ie before the deduction of any tax relief to which they give rise. **21**

Where the entity has borrowed funds specifically for the purpose of financing the construction of a tangible fixed asset, the amount of finance costs capitalised is limited to the actual costs incurred on the borrowings during the period in respect of expenditures to date on the tangible fixed asset. Finance costs in respect of leased tangible fixed assets should be accounted for in accordance with SSAP 21 'Accounting for leases and hire purchase contracts'. **22**

Where the funds used to finance the construction of a tangible fixed asset form part of the entity's general borrowings, the amount of finance costs capitalised is determined by applying a capitalisation rate to the expenditure on that asset. For this purpose the expenditure on the asset is the weighted average carrying amount of the asset during the period, including finance costs previously capitalised. The capitalisation rate used in an accounting period is based on the weighted average of rates applicable to the entity's general borrowings that are outstanding during the period. This excludes borrowings by the entity that are specifically for the purpose of constructing or acquiring other tangible fixed assets (eg obligations in respect of finance leases), or for other specific purposes, such as loans used to hedge foreign investments. **23**

In determining the borrowings to be included in the weighted average, the objective is a reasonable measure of the finance costs that are directly attributable to the construction of the asset. Accordingly, judgement will be required to make a selection of borrowings that best accomplishes the objective. In some circumstances, it is appropriate to include all borrowings by the parent and its subsidiaries when computing a weighted average of the finance costs; in other circumstances, it is appropriate for each subsidiary to use a weighted average of the finance costs applicable to its own borrowings. **24**

Where finance costs are capitalised, capitalisation should begin when: **25**

(a) finance costs are being incurred; and
(b) expenditures for the asset are being incurred; and
(c) activities that are necessary to get the asset ready for use are in progress.

The activities necessary to get the asset ready for use encompass more than its physical construction. They include technical and administrative work before construction begins, such as obtaining permits. However, such activities exclude the holding of an asset when no production or development that changes the asset's condition is taking place. For example, finance costs incurred while land is under development are capitalised during the period in which activities related to the development are being undertaken. However, finance costs incurred while land acquired for building purposes is held without any associated development activity do not qualify for capitalisation. **26**

27 **Capitalisation of finance costs should be suspended during extended periods in which active development is interrupted.**

28 Finance costs may be incurred during an extended period in which the activities necessary to get the asset ready for use are interrupted. Such costs are costs of holding partially completed assets and do not qualify for capitalisation.

29 **Capitalisation of finance costs should cease when substantially all the activities that are necessary to get the tangible fixed asset ready for use are complete. When construction of a tangible fixed asset is completed in parts and each part is capable of being used while construction continues on other parts, capitalisation of finance costs relating to a part should cease when substantially all the activities that are necessary to get that part ready for use are completed.**

30 A business park comprising several buildings, each of which can be used individually, is an example of an asset of which parts are usable while construction continues on other parts. An example of an asset that needs to be completed before any part can be used is an industrial plant involving several processes that are carried out in sequence at different parts of the plant within the same site, such as a steel mill.

Disclosures – finance costs

31 **Where a policy of capitalisation of finance costs is adopted, the financial statements should disclose:**

(a) the accounting policy adopted;
(b) the aggregate amount of finance costs included in the cost of tangible fixed assets;*
(c) the amount of finance costs capitalised during the period;
(d) the amount of finance costs recognised in the profit and loss account during the period; and
(e) the capitalisation rate used to determine the amount of finance costs capitalised during the period.

Recoverable amount

32 **If the amount recognised when a tangible fixed asset is acquired or constructed exceeds its recoverable amount, it should be written down to its recoverable amount.**

33 A tangible fixed asset needs to be reviewed for impairment on initial recognition only if there is some indication that impairment has occurred, as set out in FRS 11 'Impairment of Fixed Assets and Goodwill'. A tangible fixed asset that is impaired on initial recognition should be written down in accordance with FRS 11.

Subsequent expenditure

34 **Subsequent expenditure to ensure that the tangible fixed asset maintains its previously assessed standard of performance should be recognised in the profit and loss account as it is incurred.**

**This disclosure is required by companies legislation as follows:*
*in Great Britain, the Companies Act 1985, Schedule 4, paragraph 26(3). (**Editor's note:** For accounting periods beginning on or after 6 April 2008 this changes to Paragraph 27 of Schedule 1 to the Large and Medium-sized Companies and Groups (Accounts and Reports) Regulations 2008 (SI 2008/410).)*
in Northern Ireland, the Companies (Northern Ireland) Order 1986, Schedule 4, paragraph 26(3).
in the Republic of Ireland, the Companies (Amendment) Act 1986, Schedule, paragraph 14(3).

This type of expenditure is often referred to as 'repairs and maintenance' expenditure. An entity will assess the standard of performance of an asset (or a component of the asset) to determine its useful economic life and residual value. It will also assume that certain 'repairs and maintenance' expenditure will be carried out to maintain the standard of performance of the asset over its estimated useful economic life. Examples are the cost of servicing or the routine overhauling of plant and equipment and repainting a building structure. Without such expenditure the depreciation expense would be increased because the useful economic life or residual value of the asset would be reduced. 35

Subsequent expenditure should be capitalised in three circumstances: 36

(a) where the subsequent expenditure provides an enhancement of the economic benefits of the tangible fixed asset in excess of the previously assessed standard of performance.

(b) where a component of the tangible fixed asset that has been treated separately for depreciation purposes and depreciated over its individual useful economic life, is replaced or restored.

(c) where the subsequent expenditure relates to a major inspection or overhaul of a tangible fixed asset that restores the economic benefits of the asset that have been consumed by the entity and have already been reflected in depreciation.

Subsequent expenditure on a tangible fixed asset is recognised as an addition to the asset to the extent that the expenditure improves the condition of the asset beyond its previously assessed standard of performance. Examples of subsequent expenditure that results in an enhancement of economic benefits include: 37

- modification of an item of plant to extend its useful economic life or increase its capacity
- upgrading machine parts to achieve a substantial improvement in the quality of output.

Some tangible fixed assets require, in addition to routine repairs and maintenance (which is treated in accordance with paragraph 34), substantial expenditure every few years for major refits or refurbishment or the replacement or restoration of major components. For example, a furnace may require relining every five years. In accordance with paragraph 83, for depreciation purposes an entity accounts separately for major components (eg the furnace lining) that have substantially different useful economic lives from the rest of the asset. In such a case, each component is depreciated over its individual useful economic life, so that the depreciation profile of the whole asset more accurately reflects the actual consumption of the asset's economic benefits. Subsequent expenditure incurred in replacing or renewing the component is accounted for as an addition to the tangible fixed asset and the carrying amount of the replaced component is removed from the balance sheet in accordance with paragraphs 72 and 73. 38

The same approach may also be applied to major inspections and overhauls of tangible fixed assets. For example, an aircraft may be required by law to be overhauled once every three years. Unless the overhaul is undertaken the aircraft cannot continue to be flown. The entity reflects the need to undertake the overhaul or inspection by depreciating an amount of the asset that is equivalent to the expected inspection or overhaul costs over the period until the next inspection or overhaul. In such a case, the cost of the inspection or overhaul is capitalised when incurred because it restores the economic benefits of the tangible fixed asset and the carrying amount representing the cost of the benefits consumed is removed from the balance sheet in accordance with paragraphs 72 and 73. 39

40 The accounting treatment for subsequent expenditure should reflect the circumstances that were taken into account on the initial recognition of the asset and the depreciation profile adopted (or subsequent revisions thereof). Therefore, when the carrying amount of the asset already takes into account a consumption of economic benefits, eg by depreciating components of the asset at a faster rate than the asset as a whole (or by a previous impairment of the asset or component), the subsequent expenditure to restore those economic benefits is capitalised. The decision whether to identify separate components or future expenditures on overhauls or inspections for depreciation over a shorter useful economic life than the rest of the tangible fixed asset is likely to reflect:

- whether the useful economic lives of the components are, or the period until the next inspection or overhaul is, substantially different from the useful economic life of the remainder of the asset;
- the degree of irregularity in the level of expenditures required to restate the component or asset in different accounting periods; and
- their materiality in the context of the financial statements.

41 Where it has been determined not to account for each tangible fixed asset as several different asset components or to depreciate part of the asset over a different timescale from the rest of the asset, the cost of replacing, restoring, overhauling or inspecting the asset or components of the asset is not capitalised, but instead is recognised in the profit and loss account as incurred in accordance with paragraph 34.

Valuation

42 **Tangible fixed assets should be revalued only where the entity adopts a policy of revaluation. Where such a policy is adopted then it should be applied to individual classes of tangible fixed assets (in accordance with paragraph 61), but need not be applied to all classes of tangible fixed assets held by the entity.**

Frequency

43 **Where a tangible fixed asset is subject to a policy of revaluation* its carrying amount should be its current value as at the balance sheet date.**

44 The FRS does not insist on annual revaluations, although the objective of a revaluation policy is to reflect current values as at the balance sheet date. Paragraphs 45-52 outline the procedures to be adopted in order to satisfy the requirements of paragraph 43, although more frequent valuations may be undertaken where appropriate. However, for cost/benefit reasons, the details specified in paragraphs 45-52 may not be appropriate for charities and other not-for-profit and public sector organisations adopting a revaluation policy, in which case alternative approaches may be acceptable. Generally, these approaches will be addressed in the relevant sector-specific guidance and SORPs.

45 Where properties are revalued the requirements of paragraph 43 will be met by a full valuation at least every five years and an interim valuation in year 3. Interim valuations in years 1, 2 and 4 should be carried out where it is likely that there has been a material change in value.

**The term 'revaluation' does not encompass either the write-down of the carrying amount of a tangible fixed asset held at historical cost for an impairment in accordance with FRS 11, or determination of the cost of an asset acquired as a result of a business combination stated at its fair value at the date of acquisition, in accordance with FRS 7 'Fair Values in Acquisition Accounting', or, for charities, the initial measurement at current value of a donated tangible fixed asset in accordance with paragraph 17.*

Alternatively, for portfolios of non-specialised properties, a full valuation may be performed on a rolling basis designed to cover all the properties over a five-year cycle, together with an interim valuation on the remaining four-fifths of the portfolio where it is likely that there has been a material change in value. This approach is appropriate only where the property portfolio held by the entity either: **46**

(a) consists of a number of broadly similar properties whose characteristics are such that their values are likely to be affected by the same market factors; or
(b) can be divided on a continuing basis into five groups of a broadly similar spread.

A full valuation of a property normally involves, inter alia, the following: **47**

(a) detailed inspection of the interior and exterior of the property (on an initial valuation this will involve detailed measurement of floor space etc, but this would need to be reperformed in future full valuations only if there was evidence of a physical change to the buildings);
(b) inspection of the locality;
(c) enquiries of the local planning and similar authorities;
(d) enquiries of the entity or its solicitors; and
(e) research into market transactions in similar properties, identification of market trends, and the application of these to determine the value of the property under consideration.

A full valuation of a property is conducted by either: **48**

(a) a qualified external valuer; or
(b) a qualified internal valuer, provided that the valuation has been subject to review by a qualified external valuer. The review involves the valuation of a sample of the entity's properties by the external valuer and comparison with the internal valuer's figures leading to expression of opinion on the overall accuracy of the valuation, based upon analysis of this sample. The external valuer must be satisfied that the sample represents a genuine cross-section of the entity's portfolio.

An interim valuation of a property is conducted by a qualified (external or internal) valuer and consists of: **49**

(a) research into market transactions in similar properties, identification of market trends, and the application of these to determine the value of the property under consideration (as in paragraph 47(e));
(b) confirmation that there have been no changes of significance to the physical buildings, the legal rights, or local planning considerations; and
(c) an inspection of the property or the locality by the valuer to the extent that this is regarded as professionally necessary, having regard to all the circumstances of the case, including recent changes to the property or the locality and the date on which the valuer previously inspected the property.

For certain tangible fixed assets other than properties, for example company cars, there may be an active second-hand market for the asset, or appropriate indices may exist, such that the entity's directors can establish the asset's value with reasonable reliability. In such cases it may be unnecessary to use the services of a qualified valuer and the valuation should instead be updated annually by the directors. Otherwise, the valuation should be performed by a qualified valuer at least every five years, with an update in year 3, also performed by a qualified valuer. In addition, the valuation should be updated in the intervening years where it is likely that there has been a material change in value. If a qualified internal valuer is used for the five-yearly valuation, the valuation should be subject to review by a qualified external valuer. **50**

51 For an index to be appropriate for use by the directors in valuing a tangible fixed asset other than property, the index table will:

(a) be appropriate to the class of asset to which it is to be applied, as well as to the asset's location and condition, and take into account technological change; and
(b) have a proven record of regular publication and use and be expected to be available in the foreseeable future.

52 As explained in paragraphs 45, 46 and 50, valuations are to be updated where it is likely that there has been a material change in value. A material change in value is a change in value that would reasonably influence the decisions of a user of the accounts. In assessing whether a material change in value is likely, the combined impact of all relevant factors (eg physical deterioration in the property, general movements in market prices in the area etc) should be considered.

Valuation basis

53 **The following valuation bases should be used for revalued properties that are not impaired:**

(a) non-specialised properties should be valued on the basis of existing use value (EUV),* with the addition of notional directly attributable acquisition costs where material. Where the open market value (OMV) is materially different from EUV, the OMV and the reasons for the difference should be disclosed in the notes to the accounts.
(b) specialised properties should be valued on the basis of depreciated replacement cost.
(c) properties surplus to an entity's requirements should be valued on the basis of OMV, with expected directly attributable selling costs deducted where material.

54 Where there is an indication of impairment, an impairment review should be performed in accordance with FRS 11. The asset should be recorded at the lower of the revalued amount, determined in accordance with the above paragraph, and recoverable amount (which is the higher of net realisable value† and value in use).

55 Notional directly attributable acquisition costs includes normal dealing costs, such as professional fees, non-recoverable taxes and duties. It does not include expenditure incurred with the objective of enhancing the site value, such as site improvements, costs involved in obtaining planning consent, the cost of site preparation and clearance, or other costs that would already be reflected in EUV. For practical purposes, where notional acquisition costs (or expected selling costs for properties surplus to requirements) are not material they may be ignored.

56 Certain types of non-specialised properties are bought and sold, and therefore valued, as businesses. The EUV of a property valued as an operational entity is determined by having regard to trading potential, but excludes personal goodwill that has been created in the business by the present owner or management and is not expected to remain with the business in the event of the property being sold.

57 Some entities make structural changes to their properties or include special fittings within their properties in order to meet the particular needs of their individual businesses

**In the case of registered social landlords the valuation of non-specialised properties is based on Existing Use Value for Social Housing as defined in the RICS Appraisal and Valuation Manual.*

†*As the revalued amount of a tangible fixed asset is often close to its net realisable value, any further consideration of impairment is not generally necessary.*

(for example specialised shop fronts on a retail unit). These structural changes and specialised fittings are referred to as 'adaptation works' and have a low or nil market value owing to their specialised nature. In such cases, the adaptation works and shell of the property (ie the property in its state before adaptation) may be treated separately,* with only the shell of the property revalued using EUV. In such a case, the adaptation works are held at depreciated replacement cost or depreciated historical cost.

Specialised properties, where a market value is not available, are valued using depreciated replacement cost. The objective of depreciated replacement cost is to make a realistic estimate of the current cost of constructing an asset that has the same service potential as the existing asset. 58

Tangible fixed assets other than properties should be valued using market value, where possible. Where market value is not obtainable, assets should be valued on the basis of depreciated replacement cost.† 59

For tangible fixed assets other than property that are used in the business, notional directly attributable acquisition costs should be added to market value where material. For other tangible fixed assets that are surplus to requirements, expected selling costs should be deducted if material. Where market value is not obtainable, depreciated replacement cost, which provides a realistic estimate of the value attributable to the remaining service potential of the total useful economic life of the asset, should be used, with the assistance of a qualified valuer. 60

Class of assets

Where a tangible fixed asset is revalued all tangible fixed assets of the same class should be revalued. In those rare cases where it is impossible to obtain a reliable valuation of an asset held outside the UK or the Republic of Ireland the asset may be excluded from the class of assets for the purposes of this paragraph. However, the carrying amount of the tangible fixed asset and the fact that it has not been revalued must be stated. 61

The separate classes of tangible fixed assets that are shown in the formats in companies legislation are: 62

(a) land and buildings;
(b) plant and machinery; and
(c) fixtures, fittings, tools and equipment.‡

These are broad classes. For the purposes of valuation, entities may, within reason, adopt other, narrower classes that meet the definition of a class of tangible fixed assets and are appropriate to their business. For example, land and buildings may be split into specialised properties, non-specialised properties and short leasehold properties. The disclosures required by paragraphs 74 and 100 should be given for each class of asset adopted by an entity for revaluation purposes.

**In accordance with the RICS Appraisal and Valuation Manual, Practice Statement 12.4.*

†In accordance with guidance on the 'Value of Plant and Machinery to the Business' set out in Practice Statement 4 in the RICS Appraisal and Valuation Manual. The definition of Value of Plant and Machinery to the Business is reproduced in Appendix 1.

*‡In Great Britain, the Companies Act 1985, Schedule 4, Part I. (**Editor's note:** For accounting periods beginning on or after 6 April 2008 this changes to Schedule 1 to the Large and Medium-sized Companies and Groups (Accounts and Reports) Regulations 2008 (SI 2008/410).)*
In Northern Ireland, the Companies (Northern Ireland) Order 1986, Schedule 4, Part I.
In the Republic of Ireland, the Companies (Amendment) Act 1986, section 4 and Schedule, Part I.

Reporting gains and losses on revaluation

63 **Revaluation gains should be recognised in the profit and loss account only to the extent (after adjusting for subsequent depreciation) that they reverse revaluation losses on the same asset that were previously recognised in the profit and loss account. All other revaluation gains should be recognised in the statement of total recognised gains and losses.**

64 Where a revaluation gain reverses a revaluation loss that was previously recognised in the profit and loss account, the gain recognised in the profit and loss account is reduced by the amount of depreciation that would have been charged had the loss previously taken to the profit and loss account not been recognised in the first place. This is to achieve the same overall effect that would have been reached had the original downward revaluation reflected in the profit and loss account not occurred.

65 **All revaluation losses that are caused by a clear consumption of economic benefits should be recognised in the profit and loss account. Other revaluation losses should be recognised:**

(a) in the statement of total recognised gains and losses until the carrying amount reaches its depreciated historical cost; and

(b) thereafter, in the profit and loss account unless it can be demonstrated that the recoverable amount of the asset is greater than its revalued amount, in which case the loss should be recognised in the statement of total recognised gains and losses to the extent that the recoverable amount of the asset is greater than its revalued amount.

66 **For the purposes of paragraph 65(b), the recoverable amount of an asset should be calculated in accordance with the requirements of FRS 11.**

67 **In determining in which performance statement gains and losses on revaluation should be recognised, material gains and losses on individual assets in a class of asset should not be aggregated.**

68 A downward revaluation may comprise, at least in part, an impairment loss. When it is obvious that there has been a consumption of economic benefits (eg physical damage or a deterioration in the quality of the service provided by the asset), the asset is clearly impaired and the loss recognised in the profit and loss account, as an operating cost similar to depreciation.

69 Other revaluation losses may be due in part to a general fall in prices (eg a general slump in the property market) and in part to a consumption of economic benefits. Unless there is evidence to the contrary, it is assumed that the fall in value from the asset's previous carrying amount to depreciated historical cost is due to a general fall in prices (which is recognised in the statement of total recognised gains and losses, as a valuation adjustment) and the fall in value from depreciated historical cost to the revalued amount is due to a consumption of economic benefits (and therefore recognised in the profit and loss account).

70 However, where it can be demonstrated that recoverable amount is greater than the revalued amount, the difference between recoverable amount and the revalued amount is clearly not an impairment and should therefore be recognised in the statement of total recognised gains and losses as a valuation adjustment, rather than the profit and loss account.

Paragraphs 63-70 do not apply to assets held by insurance companies and insurance groups (including assets of the long-term business), as part of their insurance operations, where revaluation changes are included in the profit and loss account. 71

Example – Reporting revaluation gains and losses

Assumptions

A non-specialised property costs £1 million and has a useful life of 10 years and no residual value. It is depreciated on a straight-line basis and revalued annually. The entity has a policy of calculating depreciation based on the opening book amount. At the end of years 1 and 2 the asset has an EUV of £1,080,000 and £700,000 respectively. At the end of year 2, the recoverable amount of the asset is £760,000 and its depreciated historical cost is £800,000. There is no obvious consumption of economic benefits in year 2, other than that accounted for through the depreciation charge.

Accounting treatment under modified historical cost

	Year 1	Year 2
	£000	£000
Opening book amount	1,000	1,080
Depreciation	(100)	(120)*
Adjusted book amount	900	960
Revaluation gain (loss)	180	(220)
• recognised in the STRGL		
• recognised in the profit and loss account	–	(40)
Closing book amount	1,080	700

In year 1, after depreciation of £100,000, a revaluation gain of £180,000 is recognised in the statement of total recognised gains and losses, in accordance with paragraph 63.

In year 2, after a depreciation charge of £120,000, the revaluation loss on the property is £260,000. According to paragraph 65, where there is not a clear consumption of economic benefits, revaluation losses should be recognised in the statement of total recognised gains and losses until the carrying amount reaches its depreciated historical cost. Therefore, the fall in value from the adjusted book amount (£960,000) to depreciated historical cost (£800,000) of £160,000 is recognised in the statement of total recognised gains and losses.

The rest of the revaluation loss, £100,000 (ie the fall in value from depreciated historical cost (£800,000) to the revalued amount (£700,000)), should be recognised in the profit and loss account, unless it can be demonstrated that recoverable amount is greater than the revalued amount. In this case, recoverable amount of £760,000 is greater than the revalued amount of £700,000 by £60,000. Therefore £60,000 of the revaluation loss is recognised in the statement of total recognised gains and losses, rather than the profit and loss account – giving rise to a total revaluation loss of £220,000 (£60,000 + £160,000) that is recognised in the statement of total recognised gains and losses. The remaining loss (representing the fall in value from depreciated historical cost of £800,000 to recoverable amount of £760,000) of £40,000 is recognised in the profit and loss account.

** As the remaining useful economic life of the asset is nine years, the depreciation charge in year 2 is 1/9th of the opening book amount (£1,080,000/9 = £120,000).*

Reporting gains and losses on disposal

72 **The profit or loss on the disposal of a tangible fixed asset should be accounted for in the profit and loss account of the period in which the disposal occurs as the difference between the net sale proceeds and the carrying amount, whether carried at historical cost (less any provisions made) or at a valuation. Profits or losses on the disposal of fixed assets should be shown in accordance with FRS 3 'Reporting Financial Performance'.**

73 Where an asset (or a component of an asset) is replaced, its carrying amount is removed from the balance sheet (by eliminating its cost (or revalued amount) and related accumulated depreciation) and the resulting gain or loss on disposal is recorded in accordance with paragraph 72. For example, a new tangible fixed asset may be acquired from insurance proceeds when a previously held tangible fixed asset has been lost or destroyed. In such cases the lost or destroyed asset is removed from the balance sheet and the resulting gain or loss on disposal (being the difference between the carrying amount and the insurance proceeds) is recognised. The replacement asset is recorded at its cost.

Disclosures

74 **In addition to the disclosures required by paragraphs 53(a), 61 and 72, where any class of tangible fixed assets of an entity has been revalued the following information should be disclosed in each reporting period:**

(a) for each class of revalued assets:

(i) the name and qualifications of the valuer(s) or the valuer's organisation and a description of its nature;
(ii) the basis or bases of valuation (including whether notional directly attributable acquisition costs have been included or expected selling costs deducted);
(iii) the date and amounts of the valuations;
(iv) where historical cost records are available, the carrying amount that would have been included in the financial statements had the tangible fixed assets been carried at historical cost less depreciation;
(v) whether the person(s) carrying out the valuation is (are) internal or external to the entity;
(vi) where the directors are not aware of any material change in value and therefore the valuation(s) have not been updated, as described in paragraphs 45, 46 and 50, a statement to that effect; and
(vii) where the valuation has not been updated, or is not a full valuation, the date of the last full valuation.

(b) in addition, for revalued properties:

(i) where properties have been valued as fully-equipped operational entities having regard to their trading potential, a statement to that effect and the carrying amount of those properties; and
(ii) the total amount of notional directly attributable acquisition costs (or the total amount of expected selling costs deducted), included in the carrying amount, where material.

75 Other professional bodies may require disclosures in the financial statements in addition to the above disclosures. For example, the RICS requires confirmation in a published document containing a reference to a valuation report that the valuation has been made in accordance with the RICS *Appraisal and Valuation Manual* or a

(named) alternative pursuant to Practice Statement 1.2.2, or the extent of and reason(s) for departure therefrom.

In addition, companies legislation* requires disclosure, in the directors' report, of the difference, with such precision as is practicable, between the carrying amount and market value of interests in land,† where, in the opinion of the directors, it is of such significance that it needs to be drawn to the attention of the members of the entity. **76**

DEPRECIATION

Depreciable amount

The depreciable amount of a tangible fixed asset should be allocated on a systematic basis over its useful economic life. The depreciation method used should reflect as fairly as possible the pattern in which the asset's economic benefits are consumed by the entity. The depreciation charge for each period should be recognised as an expense in the profit and loss account unless it is permitted to be included in the carrying amount of another asset. **77**

The fundamental objective of depreciation is to reflect in operating profit the cost of use of the tangible fixed assets (ie amount of economic benefits consumed) in the period. This requires a charge to operating profit even if the asset has risen in value or been revalued. **78**

Where an asset has been revalued the current period's depreciation charge is based on the revalued amount and the remaining useful economic life. Ideally, the average value of the asset for the period should be used to calculate the depreciation charge. In practice, however, either the opening or closing balance may be used instead, provided that it is used consistently each period. **79**

The economic benefits embodied in a tangible fixed asset are consumed by the entity principally through the use of the asset. However, other factors often also result in the diminution of the economic benefits that might have been expected to be available from the asset. Consequently, all the following factors need to be considered in determining the useful economic life, residual value and depreciation method of an asset: **80**

- the expected usage of the asset by the entity, assessed by reference to the asset's expected capacity or physical output
- the expected physical deterioration of the asset through use or effluxion of time; this will depend upon the repair and maintenance programme of the entity both when the asset is in use and when it is idle

In Great Britain, the Companies Act 1985, Schedule 7, paragraph 1(2). (Editor's note:** For accounting periods beginning on or after 6 April 2008 this changes to Paragraph 2 of Schedule 7 to the Large and Medium-sized Companies and Groups (Accounts and Reports) Regulations 2008 (SI 2008/410).)*

In Northern Ireland, the Companies (Northern Ireland) Order 1986, Schedule 7, paragraph 1(2).

In the Republic of Ireland, the Companies Act 1963, section 158. (Note: this section includes a general requirement for the directors' report to deal with the state of affairs of the company; there is no specific requirement as in the UK references.)

†In Great Britain, Schedule 1 to the Interpretation Act 1987 states that '"Land" includes buildings and other structures, land covered with water, and any estate, interest, easement, servitude or right in or over land'.

In Northern Ireland, section 45 (i)(a) of the Interpretation Act (Northern Ireland) 1954 states that '(a) "Land" shall include- (i) messuages, tenements and hereditaments of any tenure; (ii) land covered by water; (iii) any estate in land or water; and (iv) houses or other buildings or structures whatsoever;'.

- economic or technological obsolescence, for example arising from changes or improvements in production, or a change in the market demand for the product or service output of that asset
- legal or similar limits on the use of the asset, such as the expiry dates of related leases.

81 A variety of methods can be used to allocate the depreciable amount of a tangible fixed asset on a systematic basis over its useful economic life. The method chosen should result in a depreciation charge throughout the asset's useful economic life and not just towards the end of its useful economic life or when the asset is falling in value. Two of the more common methods are:

(a) Straight-line – Here it is assumed that equal amounts of the asset's economic benefits are consumed in each year of the asset's estimated useful economic life. Therefore the asset is written off in equal instalments over its estimated useful economic life.

(b) Reducing balance – This method more closely reflects the pattern of consumption of the economic benefits of assets that clearly provide greater benefits when new than as they become older – perhaps as a result of general wear causing them to become more prone to breakdown, or less capable of producing a high-quality product, or because they will necessarily be less technologically advanced than the latest model.

Where the pattern of consumption of an asset's economic benefits is uncertain, a straight-line method of depreciation is usually adopted.

82 **A change from one method of providing depreciation to another is permissible only on the grounds that the new method will give a fairer presentation of the results and of the financial position. Such a change does not, however, constitute a change of accounting policy; the carrying amount of the tangible fixed asset is depreciated using the revised method over the remaining useful economic life, beginning in the period in which the change is made.**

83 **Where the tangible fixed asset comprises two or more major components with substantially different useful economic lives, each component should be accounted for separately for depreciation purposes and depreciated over its individual useful economic life.**

84 Land and buildings are separable components and are dealt with separately for accounting purposes, even when they are acquired together. With certain exceptions, such as sites used for extractive purposes or landfill, land has an unlimited life and therefore is not depreciated. Buildings have a limited life and therefore are depreciated. An increase in the existing use value of the land on which a building stands does not affect the determination of the useful economic life or residual value of the building. Another example of separable components that may have substantially different useful economic lives is the structure of a building and items within the structure such as general fittings.

85 It would not be appropriate, however, to treat the trading potential associated with a property that is valued as an operational entity, such as a public house or hotel, as a separate component, where the value and life of any such trading potential is inherently inseparable from that of the property.

86 **Subsequent expenditure on a tangible fixed asset that maintains or enhances the previously assessed standard of performance of the asset does not negate the need to charge depreciation.**

In calculating the useful economic life of an asset it is assumed that subsequent expenditure will be undertaken to maintain the previously assessed standard of performance of the asset (for example the cost of servicing or routine overhauling of plant and equipment). Without such expenditure the depreciation expense would be increased because the useful economic life or residual value of the asset would be reduced. This type of expenditure is recognised as an expense when incurred in accordance with paragraph 34. **87**

In addition, subsequent expenditure may be undertaken that results in an enhancement of the economic benefits of the asset in excess of the previously assessed standard of performance, or the restoration or replacement of a component of the asset that has been separately depreciated, or the restoration of the economic benefits of a tangible fixed asset where the cost of an overhaul or inspection of the tangible fixed asset has been reflected in previous depreciation. This type of expenditure may result in an extension of the useful economic life of the asset, but cannot extend the useful economic life of the asset indefinitely and does not negate the need to charge depreciation. In accordance with paragraph 36 the subsequent expenditure is capitalised as it is incurred and depreciated over the asset's or the component's useful economic life, or the period to the next major overhaul or inspection, as appropriate. **88**

Tangible fixed assets, other than non-depreciable land and heritage assets, should be reviewed for impairment, in accordance with FRS 11, at the end of each reporting period when either: **89**

(a) no depreciation charge is made on the grounds that it would be immaterial (either because of the length of the estimated remaining useful economic life or because the estimated residual value of the tangible fixed asset is not materially different from the carrying amount of the asset); or

(b) the estimated remaining useful economic life of the tangible fixed asset exceeds 50 years.*

For tangible fixed assets other than non-depreciable land and heritage assets, the only grounds for not charging depreciation are that the depreciation charge and accumulated depreciation are immaterial. The depreciation charge and accumulated depreciation are immaterial if they would not reasonably influence the decisions of a user of the accounts.† **90**

An entity must be able to justify that the uncharged depreciation is not material in aggregate as well as for each tangible fixed asset. Depreciation may be immaterial because of very long useful economic lives or high residual values (or both). A high residual value will reflect the remaining economic value of the asset at the end of its useful economic life to the entity. These conditions may occur when: **91**

(a) the entity has a policy and practice of regular maintenance and repair (charges for which are recognised in the profit and loss account) such that the asset is kept to its previously assessed standard of performance; and

(b) the asset is unlikely to suffer from economic or technological obsolescence (eg due to potential changes in demand in the market following changes in fashion); and

(c) where estimated residual values are material:

   (i) the entity has a policy and practice of disposing of similar assets well before the end of their economic lives; and

****Editor's note:*** *Reference to heritage assets added by FRS 30 with effect for accounting periods beginning on or after 1 April 2010.*

†***Editor's note:*** *Reference to heritage assets added by FRS 30 with effect for accounting periods beginning on or after 1 April 2010.*

(ii) the disposal proceeds of similar assets (after excluding the effect of price changes since the date of acquisition or last revaluation) have not been materially less than their carrying amounts.

92 Where it is not reasonably practicable to perform impairment reviews on an individual asset basis, they should be performed for groups of assets, as part of income-generating units, in accordance with FRS 11. After the first period the reviews need only be updated. If expectations of future cash flows and discount rates have not changed significantly, the updating procedure will be relatively quick to perform. If there have been no adverse changes in the key assumptions and variables, or if the estimated recoverable amount was previously substantially in excess of the carrying amount, it may even be possible to ascertain immediately that the asset or income-generating unit is not impaired.

Review of useful economic life and residual value

93 **The useful economic life of a tangible fixed asset should be reviewed at the end of each reporting period and revised if expectations are significantly different from previous estimates. If a useful economic life is revised, the carrying amount of the tangible fixed asset at the date of revision should be depreciated over the revised remaining useful economic life.**

94 If a tangible fixed asset is carried in the balance sheet at a revaluation (particularly if valued using depreciated replacement cost), a reassessment of useful economic life may necessitate a revaluation of the asset, in accordance with paragraphs 43, 45, 46 and 50. The revalued amount should be depreciated over the revised useful economic life.

95 **Where the residual value is material it should be reviewed at the end of each reporting period to take account of reasonably expected technological changes based on prices prevailing at the date of acquisition (or revaluation). A change in its estimated residual value should be accounted for prospectively over the asset's remaining useful economic life, except to the extent that the asset has been impaired at the balance sheet date.**

96 The reassessed residual value is, where practicable, restated in terms of the price level that existed when the asset was purchased (or revalued). Where such a restatement is not practicable, the residual value is restated in terms of current values only where the residual value at current prices is below the original estimate of residual value. Events or changes in circumstances that cause the residual value to fall may also be indicative of an impairment of the asset (ie when the asset's recoverable amount falls below its carrying amount), in which case an impairment review should be performed in accordance with FRS 11.

Renewals accounting

97 **Definable major assets or components within an infrastructure system or network with determinable finite lives should be treated separately and depreciated over their useful economic lives. For the remaining tangible fixed assets within the system or network ('the infrastructure asset'), renewals accounting (as outlined in paragraph 98) may be used as a method of estimating depreciation in the following circumstances:**

(a) the infrastructure asset is a system or network that as a whole is intended to be maintained at a specified level of service potential by the continuing replacement and refurbishment of its components; and

(b) the level of annual expenditure required to maintain the operating capacity (or service capability) of the infrastructure asset is calculated from an asset management plan that is certified by a person who is appropriately qualified and independent; and

(c) the system or network is in a mature or steady state.

Where renewals accounting is adopted, the level of annual expenditure required to maintain the operating capacity of the infrastructure asset is treated as the depreciation charged for the period and is deducted from the carrying amount of the asset (as part of accumulated depreciation). Actual expenditure is capitalised (as part of the cost of the asset) as incurred. 98

In the above circumstances, it is appropriate to treat the infrastructure asset as a single network of systems (ie one asset, except for definable major components with determinable finite lives), rather than as a number of individual assets. Evidence that a system or network is in a mature and steady state is provided when the annual cost of maintaining that system is relatively constant. In addition, attention should be given to removing the carrying amount of that part of the infrastructure asset that is replaced or restored by the subsequent expenditure. If the above treatment of accounting for infrastructure assets is not adopted, then expenditure to maintain the operating capacity of the infrastructure assets would be recognised in accordance with paragraphs 34 and 36, and depreciation calculated in the conventional manner, in accordance with paragraphs 77-96. 99

Disclosures

The following information should be disclosed separately in the financial statements for each class of tangible fixed assets: 100

- **(a) the depreciation methods used;**
- **(b) the useful economic lives or the depreciation rates used;**
- **(c) total depreciation charged for the period;**
- **(d) where material, the financial effect of a change during the period in either the estimate of useful economic lives (made in accordance with paragraph 93) or the estimate of residual values (made in accordance with paragraph 95);**
- **(e) the cost or revalued amount at the beginning of the financial period and at the balance sheet date;**
- **(f) the cumulative amount of provisions for depreciation or impairment at the beginning of the financial period and at the balance sheet date;**
- **(g) a reconciliation of the movements, separately disclosing additions, disposals, revaluations, transfers, depreciation, impairment losses, and reversals of past impairment losses written back in the financial period; and**
- **(h) the net carrying amount at the beginning of the financial period and at the balance sheet date.**

When a tangible fixed asset is revalued, the carrying amount of the asset is restated at its revalued amount. Usually any accumulated depreciation at the date of revaluation is eliminated and the cost or revalued amount of the asset is restated at its revalued amount. Alternatively, where the valuation is calculated on a depreciated replacement cost basis, both the cost or revalued amount and the accumulated depreciation at the date of revaluation may be restated, so that the carrying amount of the asset after revaluation equals its revalued amount. 101

Where there has been a change in the depreciation method used, the effect, if material, should be disclosed in the period of change. The reason for the change should also be disclosed. 102

DATE FROM WHICH EFFECTIVE AND TRANSITIONAL ARRANGEMENTS

The accounting practices set out in the FRS should be regarded as standard in respect of financial statements relating to accounting periods ending on or after 23 March 2000. Earlier adoption is encouraged. 103

104 **Where, on implementation of the FRS for the first time, an entity does not adopt a policy of revaluation, but the carrying amount of its tangible fixed assets reflects previous revaluations, it may:**

(a) retain the book amounts (subject to the requirement to test the assets for impairment in accordance with FRS 11 where there is an indication that an impairment may have occurred). In these circumstances the entity should disclose the fact that the transitional provisions of the FRS are being followed and that the valuation has not been updated and give the date of the last revaluation; or

(b) restate the carrying amount of the tangible fixed assets to historical cost (less restated accumulated depreciation), as a change in accounting policy.

105 The transitional arrangement set out in paragraph 104(a) is available only on the first application of the FRS.

106 **Except as provided for in paragraph 108, revisions to the useful economic lives and residual values of tangible fixed assets recognised on adoption of the FRS are not the result of a change in accounting policy and should be treated in accordance with paragraphs 93-96 and not as prior period adjustments.***

107 Revisions to the useful economic lives or residual values of tangible fixed assets may result in the depreciation of tangible fixed assets that were previously not depreciated by the entity on the grounds of immateriality. In such cases, the carrying amounts of the tangible fixed assets should be depreciated prospectively over the remaining useful economic lives of the assets.

108 **Where, on adoption of the FRS, entities separate tangible fixed assets into different components with significantly different useful economic lives for depreciation purposes, in accordance with paragraphs 36-41 and 83-85, the changes should be dealt with as prior period adjustments, as a change in accounting policy.†**

AMENDMENT TO SSAP 19 AND WITHDRAWAL OF SSAP 12

109 **Paragraph 9 of SSAP 19 'Accounting for investment properties' is deleted.**

110 **The FRS supersedes SSAP 12 'Accounting for depreciation'.**

Adoption of FRS 15 by the Board

Financial Reporting Standard 15 - 'Tangible Fixed Assets' was approved for issue by the ten members of the Accounting Standards Board.

Sir David Tweedie (Chairman)
Allan Cook (Technical Director)
David Allvey
Ian Brindle
Dr John Buchanan
John Coombe
Raymond Hinton
Huw Jones
Professor Geoffrey Whittington
Ken Wild

****Editor's note:*** *See also UITF Abstract 23 'Application of the transitional rules in FRS 15'.*

†*In accordance with FRS 3 and FRS 18.*

Appendix I
RICS definitions*

The following definitions have been extracted from the *Appraisal and Valuation Manual* published by RICS Books and are reproduced with the permission of the Royal Institution of Chartered Surveyors, which owns the copyright.

Specialised properties:-

"those which, due to their specialised nature, are rarely, if ever, sold on the open market for single occupation for a continuation of their existing use, except as part of a sale of the business in occupation. Their specialised nature may arise from the construction, arrangement, size or location of the property, or a combination of these factors, or may be due to the nature of the plant and machinery and items of equipment which the buildings are designed to house, or the function, or the purpose for which the buildings are provided. Examples of specialised properties, which are usually valued on the Depreciated Replacement Cost (DRC) basis, are:

(a) oil refineries and chemical works where, usually, the buildings are no more than housings or cladding for highly specialised plant;
(b) power stations and dock installations where the buildings and site engineering works are related directly to the business of the owner, it being highly unlikely that they would have a value to anyone other than a company acquiring the undertaking;
(c) properties of such construction, arrangement, size or specification that there would be no market (for a sale to a single owner occupier for the continuation of existing use) for those buildings;
(d) standard properties in particular geographical areas and remote from main business centres, located there for operational or business reasons, which are of such an abnormal size for that district, that there would be no market for such buildings there;
(e) schools, colleges, universities and research establishments where there is no competing market demand from other organisations using these types of property in the locality;
(f) hospitals, other specialised health care premises and leisure centres where there is no competing market demand from other organisations wishing to use these types of property in the locality; and
(g) museums, libraries, and other similar premises provided by the public sector."

Non-specialised properties:-

"all properties except those coming within the definition of specialised properties. Hence they are those for which there is a general demand, with or without adaptation, and which are commonly bought, sold or leased on the open market for their existing or similar uses, either with vacant possession for single occupation, or (whether tenanted or vacant) as investments or for development. Residential properties, shops, offices, standard industrial and warehouse buildings, public houses, petrol filling stations, and many others, are usually *non-specialised properties*."

***Editor's note**: These definitions are no longer current under RICS guidance.*

Open market value:-

"An opinion of the best price at which the sale of an interest in property would have been completed unconditionally for cash consideration on the date of valuation, assuming:

(a) a willing seller;
(b) that, prior to the date of valuation, there had been a reasonable period (having regard to the nature of the property and the state of the market) for the proper marketing of the interest, for the agreement of the price and terms and for the completion of the sale;
(c) that the state of the market, level of values and other circumstances were, on any earlier assumed date of exchange of contracts, the same as on the date of valuation;
(d) that no account is taken of any additional bid by a prospective purchaser with a special interest; and
(e) that both parties to the transaction had acted knowledgeably, prudently and without compulsion."

Existing use value:-

"An opinion of the best price at which the sale of an interest in property would have been completed unconditionally for cash consideration on the date of valuation, assuming:

(a) a willing seller;
(b) that, prior to the date of valuation, there had been a reasonable period (having regard to the nature of the property and the state of the market) for the proper marketing of the interest, for the agreement of the price and terms and for the completion of the sale;
(c) that the state of the market, level of values and other circumstances were, on any earlier assumed date of exchange of contracts, the same as on the date of valuation;
(d) that no account is taken of any additional bid by a prospective purchaser with a special interest;
(e) that both parties to the transaction had acted knowledgeably, prudently and without compulsion;
(f) that the property can be used for the foreseeable future only for the existing use; and
(g) that vacant possession is provided on completion of the sale of all parts of the property occupied by the business."

Depreciated replacement cost (of property):-

"The aggregate amount of the value of the land for the existing use or a notional replacement site in the same locality, and the gross replacement cost of the buildings and other site works, from which appropriate deductions may then be made to allow for the age, condition, economic or functional obsolescence, environmental and other relevant factors; all of these might result in the existing property being worth less to the undertaking in occupation than would a new replacement."

Value of plant and machinery to the business:-

"An opinion of the price at which an interest in the plant and machinery utilised in a business would have been transferred at the date of valuation assuming:

(a) that the plant and machinery will continue in its present uses in the business;
(b) adequate potential profitability of the business, or continuing viability of the undertaking, both having due regard to the value of the total assets employed and the nature of the operation; and
(c) that the transfer is part of an arm's length sale of the business wherein both parties acted knowledgeably, prudently and without compulsion."

Appendix II
Note on legal requirements

GREAT BRITAIN

1 In Great Britain, the statutory requirements relating to accounting for tangible fixed assets are set out in the Companies Act 1985. The main requirements that are directly relevant to tangible fixed assets and the requirements of FRS 15 are set out in Schedules 4 and 4A and are summarised below.*

2 Schedule 4 does not apply to banking and insurance companies or groups. Requirements equivalent to those of Schedule 4 are contained in Schedule 9 (for banking companies and groups) and in Schedule 9A (for insurance companies and groups).

Initial cost

3 Paragraph 17 of Schedule 4 requires the amount to be included in respect of any fixed asset to be its purchase price or production cost. The purchase price is to be determined by adding to the actual price any expenses incidental to its acquisition (paragraph 26(1) of Schedule 4). Paragraph 26(2) requires the cost of production of an asset to comprise the purchase price of raw materials and consumables used and the amount of costs incurred by the company that are directly attributable to the production of that asset. In addition, paragraph 26(3) allows the inclusion of:

(a) indirectly attributable costs incurred by the company relating to the period of production; and
(b) interest on capital borrowed to finance the production of the asset. (However, the amount of the interest capitalised is required to be disclosed in the notes to the accounts.)

4 Where there is no record of the purchase price or production cost of any asset of a company, paragraph 28 of Schedule 4 requires the asset value to be determined using

***Editor's note:** *The various statutory references change with the introduction of the Companies Act 2006, which affects accounting for periods beginning on or after 6 April 2008. The various statutory references have changed as follows:*

Companies Act 1985 reference	***Companies Act 2006 reference***
Schedule 4	*Schedule 1 to the Large and Medium-sized Companies and Groups (Accounts and Reports) Regulations 2008 (SI 2008/410)*
Schedule 4A	*Schedule 6 to SI 2008/410*
Schedules 9 and 9A	*Schedules 2 and 3 to SI 2008/410*
Paragraph 17 of Schedule 4	*Paragraph 17 of Schedule 1 to SI 2008/410*
Paragraph 26 of Schedule 4	*Paragraph 27 of Schedule 1 to SI 2008/410*
Paragraph 28 of Schedule 4	*Paragraph 29 of Schedule 1 to SI 2008/410*
Paragraph 31 of Schedule 4	*Paragraph 32 of Schedule 1 to SI 2008/410*
Paragraph 33 of Schedule 4	*Paragraph 34 of Schedule 1 to SI 2008/410*
Paragraph 43 of Schedule 4	*Paragraph 52 of Schedule 1 to SI 2008/410*
Paragraph 34 of Schedule 4	*Paragraph 35 of Schedule 1 to SI 2008/410*
Paragraph 19 of Schedule 4	*Paragraph 19 of Schedule 1 to SI 2008/410*
Paragraph 18 of Schedule 4	*Paragraph 18 of Schedule 1 to SI 2008/410*
Paragraph 32 of Schedule 4	*Paragraph 33 of Schedule 1 to SI 2008/410*
Paragraph 36 of Schedule 4	*Paragraph 44 of Schedule 1 to SI 2008/410*
Paragraph 42 of Schedule 4	*Paragraph 51 of Schedule 1 to SI 2008/410*
Paragraph 1 of Schedule 7	*Paragraph 2 of Schedule 7 to SI 2008/410*

the earliest available record of the value of the asset on or after its acquisition or production by the company. Such earliest available records may also be used where there are no relevant prices, expenses or costs against which the purchase price may be determined or where the record of such purchase price cannot be obtained without unreasonable expense or delay.

Valuation

The alternative accounting rules set out in paragraph 31(2) of Schedule 4 permit tangible fixed assets to be included at a market value determined as at the date of their last valuation or at their current cost. **5**

Where the alternative accounting rules set out in paragraph 31(2) of Schedule 4 are adopted by a company the following additional information is required to be included in the company's accounts: **6**

(a) the assets revalued and the basis of valuation (paragraph 33(2) of Schedule 4).
(b) either the comparable amounts determined according to the historical cost accounting rules or the differences between those amounts and the revalued amounts (paragraph 33(3) of Schedule 4).
(c) the year and amount of the valuation (paragraph 43(a) of Schedule 4).
(d) in the case of assets that have been valued during the financial year, the names of the persons who valued them or particulars of their qualifications for doing so and the bases of valuation used by them (paragraph 43(b) of Schedule 4).

Reporting revaluation gains and losses

A revaluation gain is required by the FRS to be recognised in the statement of total recognised gains and losses, unless it reverses a previous revaluation loss that has been recognised in the profit and loss account. This requirement is consistent with paragraph 34(1) of Schedule 4, which requires the "amount of any profit" (ie gain) "or loss" calculated under the alternative accounting rules to be "credited to a separate reserve (the revaluation reserve)". The requirement for a revaluation gain to be recognised in the profit and loss account to the extent that it reverses a revaluation loss previously recognised in the profit and loss account is consistent with paragraph 34(3) of Schedule 4, which explicitly authorises transfers to take place between the revaluation reserve and the profit and loss account provided that the relevant amount was previously charged to that account. **7**

The FRS requires all revaluation losses that are clearly due to the consumption of economic benefits to be recognised in the profit and loss account. This requirement is consistent with paragraph 19(2) of Schedule 4, which requires provisions for depreciation or permanent diminution in value to be recognised in the profit and loss account. **8**

For other revaluation losses where it *can* be demonstrated that the recoverable amount of the asset is greater than its revalued amount, the FRS requires the difference between recoverable amount and revalued amount to be recognised in the statement of total recognised gains and losses. In this situation there has been no diminution in value under paragraph 19(2) of Schedule 4 and therefore the loss can remain in the revaluation reserve in accordance with paragraph 34(1) of Schedule 4. **9**

For other revaluation losses where it *cannot* be demonstrated that the recoverable amount of the asset is greater than its revalued amount, an impairment loss arises. Where a fixed asset is impaired, it will always be the case that both the value in use **10** and the net realisable value will be below the carrying amount. In the case of a revalued fixed asset, it would be reasonable to reflect the uncertainty as to the permanence of any impairment by treating it as a reversal of any revaluation previously recognised. Such an impairment would be dealt with through the statement of total recognised gains and losses (ie as a revaluation reserve movement). However, if the impairment results in a carrying amount below depreciated historical cost, then, as in a pure historical cost context, it would be reasonable to treat that part of the impairment as being of a permanent nature and charge it to the profit and loss account.

Depreciation

11 Where a fixed asset has a limited useful economic life, paragraph 18 of Schedule 4 requires its purchase price or production cost less its estimated residual value to be written off systematically over the period of the asset's useful economic life.

12 Paragraph 32(1) of Schedule 4 requires the depreciation of revalued assets to be calculated on the basis of their latest valuations. Paragraph 32(3) allows a company to include under the relevant profit and loss account heading provisions for depreciation for the revalued assets based only on their historical cost, provided that the difference between that and the provision for depreciation calculated on the revalued amount is shown separately either in the profit and loss account or in the notes. It is unclear, however, whether the whole depreciation charge is required to be recognised in the profit and loss account (see discussion in Appendix IV 'The development of the FRS').

Disclosure requirements

13 In addition to the disclosures mentioned in paragraph 6 above in connection with the revaluation of tangible fixed assets, the following disclosures are required:

(a) Paragraph 36 of Schedule 4 requires the disclosure of the accounting policies adopted by a company (including the policies regarding the depreciation and diminution in value of assets).

(b) Paragraph 26(3) requires the disclosure of the amount of interest capitalised, where such a policy is adopted.

(c) Paragraph 42 details the disclosures required of the movement on tangible fixed asset balances for the items under each of the headings for tangible fixed assets set out in the balance sheet formats in Schedule 4, as follows:

1. Land and buildings
2. Plant and machinery
3. Fixtures, fittings, tools and equipment
4. Payments on account and assets in the course of construction.

(d) Paragraph 1(2) of Schedule 7 requires disclosure, in the directors' report, of the difference, with such precision as is practicable, between the carrying amount and market value of interests in land, where, in the opinion of the directors, it is of such significance that it needs to be drawn to the attention of the members of the entity.

NORTHERN IRELAND

14 The statutory requirements in Northern Ireland are set out in the Companies (Northern Ireland) Order 1986. They are identical to and parallel the references in the legislation for Great Britain cited above.

REPUBLIC OF IRELAND

The statutory requirements in the Republic of Ireland that correspond to those cited above for Great Britain are shown in the following table. 15

Great Britain	*Republic of Ireland*
Schedule 4 to the Companies Act 1985:	The Schedule to the Companies (Amendment) Act 1986:
paragraph 17	paragraph 5
paragraph 18	paragraph 6
paragraph 19(2)	paragraph 7(2)
paragraph 26(1), (2) and (3)	paragraph 14(1), (2) and (3)
paragraph 28	paragraph 16
paragraph 31(2)	paragraph 19(2)
paragraph 32(1) and (3)	paragraph 20(1) and (3)
paragraph 33(2) and (3)	paragraph 21(2) and (3)
paragraph 34(1) and (3)	paragraph 22(1) and (4)
paragraph 36	paragraph 24
paragraph 42	paragraph 29
paragraph 43(a) and (b)	paragraph 30(a) and (b)
Schedule 4A to the Companies Act 1985	European Communities (Companies: Group Accounts) Regulations 1992
Schedule 7 to the Companies Act 1985, paragraph 1(2)	The Companies Act 1963, section 158*
Schedule 9 to the Companies Act 1985	European Communities (Credit Institutions: Accounts) Regulations 1992
Schedule 9A to the Companies Act 1985	European Communities (Insurance Undertakings: Accounts) Regulations 1996

Note: this section includes a general requirement for the directors' report to deal with the state of affairs of the company; there is no specific requirement as in the UK references.

Appendix III
Compliance with international accounting standards

1 The main requirements for the recognition, measurement and depreciation of tangible fixed assets are included in International Accounting Standard (IAS) 16 (revised 1998) 'Property, Plant and Equipment'. In addition, some other relevant requirements are included in IAS 23 (revised 1993) 'Borrowing Costs'.*

2 The requirements in the FRS lead to compliance with IAS 16 and the relevant requirements of IAS 23 in all main respects, except as discussed below.

Fair/current value

3 Both the FRS and IAS 16 require that, where a policy of revaluation is adopted, the revalued tangible fixed assets should be carried at current values. IAS 16 uses the term 'fair value' and states that the fair value of land and buildings, plant and equipment is usually their market value, but where there is no evidence of market value depreciated replacement cost should be used instead.

4 As explained in Appendix IV 'The development of the FRS', the valuation requirements in the FRS are based on the value to the business model and therefore define current value as the lower of replacement cost and recoverable amount. The Board believes that this gives a more precise and clearer indication of the amount at which the asset should be revalued and therefore prefers this terminology to the use of the term 'fair value'.

5 Accordingly, the FRS requires non-specialised properties to be valued at existing use value, with the addition of notional directly attributable acquisition costs, if material, to reflect replacement cost. Similarly, specialised properties should be valued using depreciated replacement cost. However, properties surplus to requirements should be valued at net realisable value – ie open market value less expected selling costs, if material. Similar valuation bases are required for tangible fixed assets other than property. IAS 16 is silent in respect of whether valuations should be on an existing use basis and whether material direct acquisition or selling costs should be added/deducted.

Revaluation gains and losses

6 The requirements of IAS 16 differ from those in the FRS in two main respects:

- To be consistent with FRS 11 'Impairment of Fixed Assets and Goodwill', the FRS requires revaluation losses that are clearly caused by the consumption of economic benefits to be recognised in the profit and loss account (paragraph 65). The Board believes that such losses are operating costs similar to depreciation and should be treated as such by recognition in the profit and loss account. IAS 16 does not have a similar requirement.
- IAS 16 permits only those losses that reverse revaluation gains that were previously recognised in the statement of total recognised gains and losses to be recognised in that statement. The FRS requires other losses to be recognised in the

***Editor's note:** *IAS 16 has been revised, with a new version of the standard issued in December 2003. There are a number of detailed changes, but one major change is that the IAS no longer has separate principles for initial measurement of costs and subsequent expenditure. A revised version of IAS 23, effective for accounting periods beginning on or after 1 January 2009, requires the capitalisation of appropriate borrowing costs.*

statement of total recognised gains and losses to the extent that the asset's recoverable amount is greater than its revalued amount. The Board believes that such losses, which have been demonstrated not to be impairments, are in the nature of losses caused by a general fall in prices.

Depreciation

Both the FRS and IAS 16 state that subsequent expenditure does not negate the need for depreciation. However, the FRS takes this one step further by also requiring impairment reviews at the end of each reporting period where depreciation is not charged on the basis of immateriality or where the remaining useful economic life is estimated to be greater than 50 years. **7**

Disclosures

IAS 16 requires the following additional disclosures: **8**

(a) in general:
- property, plant and equipment pledged as security for liabilities,* and the existence and amounts of restrictions on title
- the amount of expenditures on account of property, plant and equipment in the course of construction
- the amount of commitments for the acquisition of property, plant and equipment.*

(b) in respect of each class of property, plant and equipment:
- the measurement bases used for determining the gross carrying amount

(c) in respect of each revalued class of property, plant and equipment:
- the nature of any indices used to determine replacement cost
- the revaluation surplus,† indicating the movement for the period and any restrictions on the distribution of the balance to shareholders.

**These disclosures are required by companies legislation, as follows:*
*in Great Britain, the Companies Act 1985, Schedule 4, paragraphs 48(4), 50(1), 50(3) and 50(5). (**Editor's note:** For accounting periods beginning on or after 6 April 2008 this changes to Paragraph 63 of Schedule 1 to the Large and Medium-sized Companies and Groups (Accounts and Reports) Regulations 2008 (SI 2008/410).)*
in Northern Ireland, the Companies (Northern Ireland) Order 1986, Schedule 4, paragraphs 48(4), 50(1), 50(3) and 50(5).
in the Republic of Ireland, the Companies (Amendment) Act 1986, Schedule, paragraphs 34(1), 36(1), 36(3) and 36(6).

†These disclosures are required by companies legislation, as follows:
*in Great Britain, the Companies Act 1985, Schedule 4, paragraphs 34(2), 42(1) and 46(1). (**Editor's note:** For accounting periods beginning on or after 6 April 2008 this changes to Paragraphs 35, 51 and 59 of Schedule 1 to the Large and Medium-sized Companies and Groups (Accounts and Reports) Regulations 2008 (SI 2008/410).)*
in Northern Ireland, the Companies (Northern Ireland) Order 1986, Schedule 4, paragraphs 34(2), 42(1) and 46(1).
in the Republic of Ireland, the Companies (Amendment) Act 1986, Schedule, paragraphs 22(3), 29(1) and 32(1).

Appendix IV
The development of the FRS

The need for a standard

1 Many of the principles for determining the cost of tangible fixed assets when they are initially recognised and measured are well known and accepted. However, as no previous accounting standard dealt with these issues, differences in practice have arisen.

2 Many entities adopted a policy of valuing specific tangible fixed assets as permitted by the alternative accounting rules in companies legislation.* Previous practices allowed valuations of assets to be made at an entity's discretion and there was no requirement for valuations to be updated in subsequent accounting periods. Replacing the historical cost of an asset with a valuation provides more relevant information to the user of the accounts. Nevertheless, the relevance of this information diminishes over time as it no longer reflects the current value of the tangible fixed asset. Finally, an entity could revalue some but not all of its tangible fixed assets, with little constraint imposed by the need to treat similar assets consistently. As a result, it was often difficult to understand the amounts attributable to the entity's assets and accordingly to make comparisons from year to year and between similar entities.

3 In respect of depreciation, SSAP 12 'Accounting for depreciation', which this FRS supersedes, was generally regarded as broadly satisfactory. However, it became apparent that some of the requirements of SSAP 12 required clarification. In particular, clarification was sought on the accounting treatment adopted by a number of entities that did not depreciate certain assets, most commonly properties, on the grounds that they were either increasing in value or being maintained or refurbished regularly.

4 The FRS addresses these concerns by specifying accounting rules for the initial recognition, valuation and depreciation of tangible fixed assets, other than investment properties. In developing the FRS, the Board has considered the comments on its initial proposals which were set out in the Discussion Paper 'Measurement of Tangible Fixed Assets' and on its subsequent proposals in FRED 17 'Measurement of Tangible Fixed Assets'.

Initial cost

Decommissioning costs

5 In accordance with FRS 12 'Provisions, Contingent Liabilities and Contingent Assets' a provision may be recognised for a present obligation in respect of decommissioning costs: such costs may include those relating to the dismantling and removal of a facility and the restoration of a site. Providing for these costs reflects the obligation of the entity that arises as a consequence of the construction or acquisition of the asset, and which cannot be avoided by the entity's future actions.

6 This FRS states that these costs, to the extent that they qualify for recognition as a provision under FRS 12, should be capitalised as a directly attributable cost of the

**For example 65 per cent of companies included in the Company Reporting database carried revalued tangible fixed assets in their accounts. However, Company Reporting noted that half of these companies did not have any valuations that were more recent than five years old. (Company Reporting No 80 February 1997).*

relevant asset (even though they may not be paid until the end of the asset's life). Treating these costs as part of the cost of the relevant asset acknowledges that the entity has undertaken the obligation to meet these costs in order to derive the benefits of the service potential provided by the asset. This has the consequence that these costs are charged to the profit and loss account as depreciation over the asset's life.

Donated tangible fixed assets

Charities often receive gifts and donations of assets. Donated tangible fixed assets do not have a cost to the charity, and therefore their initial measurement should be their current value at the date of donation. As this is a particular issue for charities, apart from the above key principle, the FRS leaves more detailed guidance to the relevant sector-specific guidance and Statements of Recommended Practice (SORPs). **7**

Inalienable, historic and similar assets

The Board believes that, in principle, inalienable,* historic and similar tangible fixed assets should be recognised in the balance sheet, to reflect that: **8**

(a) the assets give rise to future economic benefits (although not necessarily in terms of cash inflows),
(b) the entity has stewardship of the assets, and
(c) the entity has invested funds in the assets (through acquisition, maintenance, restoration etc).

However, the Board accepts that for some assets that were not capitalised in the past and for some donated inalienable, historic and similar assets, the cost of obtaining a valuation (if indeed a reliable valuation is available) may outweigh the benefit to users of the accounts. In such cases, appropriate disclosures should be made in the notes to the accounts instead. Further guidance is available in the relevant sector-specific guidance and SORPs. **9**

Capitalisation of finance costs

The FRS permits the optional capitalisation of finance costs, such as interest. The Board acknowledges that it would be preferable either to prohibit or to mandate the capitalisation of finance costs. Conceptually, directly attributable finance costs should be capitalised, for the following reasons: **10**

(a) finance costs are just as much a cost of constructing the tangible fixed asset as other directly attributable costs.
(b) capitalising finance costs results in a tangible fixed asset cost that more closely matches the market price of completed assets. Treating the finance costs as an expense distorts the choice between purchasing and constructing a tangible fixed asset.
(c) the accounts are more likely to reflect the true success or failure of the project.

However, the Board was influenced by the argument that if capitalisation is to become mandatory, in theory notional interest should also be capitalised. This is a contentious issue and until an internationally acceptable approach is agreed, the Board favours maintaining the optional capitalisation of finance costs, which is consistent with the approach in IAS 23 'Borrowing Costs'.† **11**

**Inalienable assets are tangible fixed assets that an entity cannot dispose of without external consent.*

†***Editor's note:*** *IAS 23 is revised with effect for accounting periods beginning on or after 1 January 2009 and will require the capitalisation of qualifying interest.*

Subsequent expenditure

12 The FRS codifies generally accepted accounting practice that subsequent expenditure on a tangible fixed asset undertaken to ensure that the asset maintains its previously assessed standard of performance (ie 'repairs and maintenance' expenditure) is recognised in the profit and loss account as it is incurred, whereas subsequent expenditure that enhances the previously assessed standard of performance of the tangible fixed asset is capitalised.

13 However, the FRS also recognises that it may be appropriate to capitalise certain subsequent expenditure that would have been written off to the profit and loss account in the past as repairs or maintenance expenditure, but to do so only where the depreciation of the asset already reflects the reduction of the service potential of the asset that has been restored by the expenditure. Where appropriate, tangible fixed assets may be divided into two or more major asset components, each component being treated separately for depreciation purposes and depreciated over its own individual useful economic life. Therefore, when a component is restored or replaced, that expenditure should be capitalised.

14 The decision to record a tangible fixed asset as several different components with different useful economic lives will depend upon the individual circumstances. In practice the Board expects a commonsense approach, so that only significant, major components with substantially different useful economic lives are identified and treated separately for depreciation purposes.

15 Before FRS 12 became applicable, some entities recognised as a provision significant costs of future repairs, maintenance, inspections or overhauls of their tangible fixed assets. Under FRS 12, such future costs are not present obligations of the entity resulting from past events, and therefore no provision should be made for them, even if they are required by legislation if the asset is to continue to be used. In these circumstances, an entity should charge such expenditure to the profit and loss account as it is incurred.

16 Alternatively, the entity may depreciate the relevant part of the asset that is declining in service potential to reflect the need for future repairs, maintenance, inspections or overhauls (ie to take account of the actual consumption of the asset's economic benefits) and to capitalise the subsequent expenditure because it results in the restoration of the asset or replacement of some of its components. This latter approach results in a charge being recognised in the profit and loss account that is similar to what would have been recognised under previous (pre-FRS 12) practices. However, the charge takes the form not of a provision for future expenditure but of depreciation, in recognition of the fact that economic benefits of the asset have been consumed at a different rate from that applicable to the remainder of the asset.

Valuation

Optional valuation

17 The FRS codifies present practice whereby the valuation of tangible fixed assets is optional. By not imposing a requirement either to revalue or not to revalue, the Board is, exceptionally, leaving to individual preparers of financial statements the task of weighing the costs and benefits of the alternative accounting treatments. However, where a revaluation policy is adopted, the FRS imposes conditions to prevent 'cherry-picking' which assets are revalued and when, by requiring up-to-date valuations of all assets in the same class.

Frequency of valuation

In determining the guidance in the FRS regarding the frequency of revaluations in 18
paragraphs 43-52, the Board had regard to the views of both the Royal Institution of Chartered Surveyors (RICS) and respondents to the earlier proposals in the Discussion Paper and FRED 17. It has balanced the benefits to users of the financial statements of up-to-date and reliable current values with the cost to preparers of obtaining regular, reliable valuations. This guidance was prepared primarily for commercial entities. Therefore, charities, public sector and other not-for-profit organisations, which have different cost/benefit considerations, may find that different approaches are more appropriate. Alternative guidance may be found in the relevant sector-specific guidance and SORPs.

Basis of valuation

As mentioned in the Board's draft Statement of Principles for Financial Reporting, 19
the current value of an asset is determined by reference to the value to the business model. The value of an asset to the business (ie its current value) is the value that is relevant to economic decision-making, ie the loss that the entity would suffer if it were deprived of the asset. This can be portrayed diagrammatically as follows:

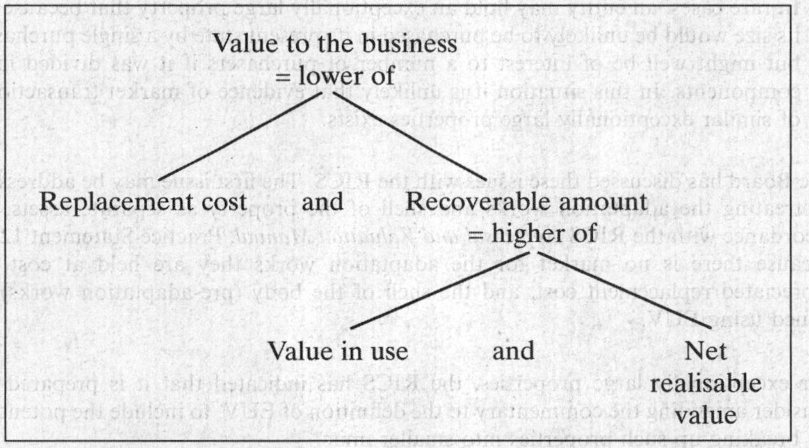

If the entity is to continue in its existing business at its current volume (or greater), 20
the value to the business of a tangible fixed asset that is used in the business will normally be its replacement cost. As long as the asset is not impaired (in which case recoverable amount would be less than replacement cost), the entity, if deprived of the asset, would replace it with another similar asset for the same use.

For non-specialised properties, existing use value (EUV), with the addition of 21
notional directly attributable acquisition costs (where material), is the basis that more closely approaches the concept of replacement cost (ie the least cost of purchasing the remaining service potential of the asset at the date of valuation). Notional directly attributable acquisition costs are included where material, as they form part of the cost to the entity of replacing the asset. EUV reflects the replacement of the service potential that is used by the owner rather than alternative possible uses.

Normally EUV will be no greater than open market value (OMV) as the latter 22
reflects the additional possible uses that are ignored in arriving at EUV (for example,

a factory located on the edge of an expanding town may have greater value as a potential residential property development than as an industrial site). In most cases, where a non-specialised property is fully developed for its most beneficial use, it is expected that the EUV will equal OMV with vacant possession. However, in some circumstances EUV may be higher than OMV. This may be the effect, for example, of restrictive alienation clauses in headleases, planning consents that are personal to the present occupier, or known contamination that does not affect the existing use of the non-specialised property. All of these would lower OMV, but would be disregarded in determining EUV as they do not affect the cost of replacement. Therefore, the FRS requires further information about OMV in the notes to the financial statements where OMV is materially different from EUV.

23 A concern was raised that in certain limited circumstances EUV may not provide an adequate measure of the replacement cost of a non-specialised property. This was due, in part, to the following two factors:

- When valuing a property with adaptation works (ie structural changes and specialised fittings made to the shell of a property to meet the particular needs of the individual business), both OMV and EUV are often lower than the original cost of the property. This is because the specialised nature of the adaptation works means that they are either not required by other entities or could not be used by them and therefore they are ascribed a low or nil market value.
- In rare cases, an entity may hold an exceptionally large property that because of its size would be unlikely to be purchased in its present state by a single purchaser but might well be of interest to a number of purchasers if it was divided into components. In this situation it is unlikely that evidence of market transactions of similar exceptionally large properties exists.

24 The Board has discussed these issues with the RICS. The first issue may be addressed by treating the adaptation works and shell of the property as separate assets, in accordance with the RICS *Appraisal and Valuation Manual*, Practice Statement 12.4. Because there is no market for the adaptation works they are held at cost or depreciated replacement cost, and the shell of the body (pre-adaptation works) is valued using EUV.

25 For exceptionally large properties, the RICS has indicated that it is prepared to consider amending the commentary to the definition of EUV, to include the potential for breaking up such properties into smaller units.

26 For certain properties no EUV or OMV can be determined, owing to their specialised nature and because they are rarely sold on the open market, except as part of a sale of the business in occupation. Such specialised properties are therefore valued on the basis of depreciated replacement cost.

27 If an entity were deprived of a tangible fixed asset that was surplus to requirements, then it would not replace that asset with another similar asset with the same service potential. In this situation, consistently with the value to the business model, the relevant valuation basis is not replacement cost or value in use, but rather net realisable value. Therefore, the FRS requires properties surplus to requirements to be valued using OMV less any material expected directly attributable selling costs. Selling costs are deducted to reflect the net realisable value of the asset to the entity.

28 Similar valuation bases are to be used for tangible fixed assets other than properties.

Reporting gains and losses on revaluation

The Board believes that, in principle, downward revaluations fall into two general groups – those that are clearly caused by a consumption of economic benefits (eg physical damage or a deterioration in the quality of the service provided by the asset) and those caused by a general fall in prices (eg a general slump in the property market). The first type is similar to depreciation and is treated as such, whereas the second type is more like a valuation adjustment that would fall to be recognised in the statement of total recognised gains and losses. **29**

When it is obvious that there has been a consumption of economic benefits, the asset is clearly impaired and the loss recognised in the profit and loss account, which is consistent with the treatment in FRS 11 'Impairment of Fixed Assets and Goodwill'. **30**

However, in most cases it is difficult to allocate a downward revaluation to one or other group with certainty. In order to provide objectivity in the treatment of revaluation losses, the FRS requires that where there is doubt whether the fall in value is caused by a reduction in the quantum of the service potential, the loss should be recognised in the statement of total recognised gains and losses until the carrying amount of the asset reaches its depreciated historical cost. Any further fall in value should be recognised in the profit and loss account, except to the extent that it can be demonstrated that the tangible fixed asset is not impaired – ie that the recoverable amount exceeds the revalued amount; such a fall is recognised in the statement of total recognised gains and losses instead. **31**

Where the type of fall in value is unclear, splitting the revaluation loss between the statement of total recognised gains and losses and the profit and loss account is necessarily arbitrary, because it depends upon whether the fall in value is above or below depreciated historical cost. However, this treatment has the advantage of being consistent with FRS 11, IAS 16 (revised 1998) 'Property, Plant and Equipment' and IAS 36 'Impairment of Assets' (although some other aspects of the treatment of revaluation gains and losses in the FRS are not consistent with IAS 16, as noted in Appendix III 'Compliance with International Accounting Standards'). **32**

The Board recognises that the treatment of revaluation losses in the FRS represents a pragmatic solution and, together with the other members of the G4 + 1,* is developing the above approach further in connection with its project on reporting financial performance. To this end, the Board, as part of the G4 + 1, intends to issue later in 1999 a Discussion Paper that will consider the development of a new framework for reporting gains and losses with different characteristics.† The Paper will explore the above concepts further and consider ways of refining the approach to revaluation losses. This process may, in due course, lead to revisions to the FRS in this area, in conjunction with future developments in the reporting of financial performance and revisions to FRS 3 'Reporting Financial Performance'. **33**

Revaluation gains are most likely to reflect a general rise in prices and therefore are recognised in the statement of total recognised gains and losses as valuation adjustments. Nevertheless, revaluation gains that reverse previous revaluation losses on the same tangible fixed asset are recognised in the same performance statement (after adjusting for subsequent depreciation) as the revaluation loss it reverses. **34**

**The G4 + 1 is a group of representatives from the standard-setting bodies of Australia, Canada, New Zealand, the UK and the USA, and from the International Accounting Standards Committee.*

*†**Editor's note:** The Discussion Paper 'Reporting financial performance: proposals for change' was published in June 1999 and is reproduced in Part Nine of this volume.*

Reporting gains and losses on disposal

35 FRS 3 requires gains and losses on disposal to be recognised in the profit and loss account in the period in which the disposal took place, calculated as the difference between carrying amount and the net sale proceeds. This treatment of gains and losses on disposals is inconsistent with the treatment of gains and losses on revaluation. For example, a revaluation gain would be recognised in the statement of total recognised gains and losses, whereas a subsequent gain on disposal would be recognised in the profit and loss account, even though both gains were due to the same factors (ie rising market prices).

36 FRED 17 therefore proposed amending the requirement in FRS 3, so that immediately before recording the disposal of a tangible fixed asset, the carrying amount of the asset would be adjusted to the disposal proceeds and any gain or loss resulting from such an adjustment would be recognised in accordance with the requirements for reporting revaluation gains and losses. Under these proposals those losses on disposal that would be recognised in the profit and loss account are regarded as a form of consumption similar to depreciation. This proposal was to apply to all tangible fixed assets, whether or not a policy of revaluation had been adopted.

37 The responses to FRED 17 made it clear that this proposal was not acceptable at present. Respondents argued that:

- the development of the role of the statement of total recognised gains and losses in FRED 17 was premature, particularly as the direction and outcome of the Board's intended project to review FRS 3 was unclear.
- the proposal raised anomalies for tangible fixed assets held at historical cost. Gains and losses on disposal reflect the accuracy of depreciation policies and estimated residual values, and therefore it was argued that they should be recognised in the same performance statement as depreciation.
- the proposal is inconsistent with the treatment of gains and losses on disposals of businesses, subsidiaries and investments.

38 The Board acknowledges that more work needs to be carried out in this area and intends to revisit this aspect in the course of its review of FRS 3. Accordingly the FRS retains the requirements of FRS 3 for the treatment of gains and losses on disposal.

Depreciation

The objective of depreciation

39 Depreciation is a measure of the cost (historical cost or revalued amount) of the economic benefits of the tangible fixed asset that have been consumed by the entity during the period.

40 It is sometimes argued that a valuation approach to depreciation should be adopted especially where an entity revalues its tangible fixed assets. The Board disagrees with this approach because it does not distinguish between depreciation (ie the amount consumed) and other sources of value changes and therefore results in a reduced or nil depreciation expense in a period of rising prices, even though there is a cost to the entity of using the asset to generate its revenues.

41 The Board does not accept that the increase in the value of a tangible fixed asset justifies non-depreciation. Wherever the asset has a finite expected life, part of the asset representing one year's economic benefits of the asset is consumed in the year. The revenues generated by the entity through using the tangible fixed asset in the

business justify a charge to the profit and loss account for using that asset. An increase in value, or an increase in residual value, whether arising from external factors or from refurbishment, should impact only on the parts of the asset representing future economic benefits.

Split depreciation

Some have argued that the depreciation charge on a revalued tangible fixed asset should be split, and only that part relating to the historical cost of the asset charged to the profit and loss account. The part of the depreciation charge that corresponds to the revaluation movement would be charged instead to the statement of total recognised gains and losses. Such split depreciation would remove a disincentive to revalue fixed assets and the depreciation charged to the profit and loss account would represent an allocation of the actual cash outlay. **42**

The issue of split depreciation raises legal considerations. In Great Britain, paragraph 32(3) of Schedule 4 to the Companies Act 1985* states that: **43**

> "Where sub-paragraph (1) applies in the case of any fixed asset the amount of the provision for depreciation in respect of that asset ... may be the *historical cost amount instead of the adjusted amount, provided that the amount of any difference between the two is shown separately in the profit and loss account or in a note to the accounts.*" (emphasis added)

It is unclear whether the above-mentioned paragraph permits split depreciation. The Board therefore obtained a legal opinion on this issue. That opinion noted that the practical effect of the paragraph as drafted makes it arguable that the entirety of a given charge need not pass through the profit and loss account. However, the opinion went on to note the implications of the *Marleasing*† decision. This case indicates that national courts of EU Member States are under a Community law obligation to interpret national law so that it conforms, so far as possible, with the underlying directive (in this case, the Fourth Directive). Articles 33.3 and 35.1 (c)(cc) of the Fourth Directive prohibit split depreciation. **44**

The Board also considered an alternative method of achieving split depreciation. With this method the full depreciation charge would be included in the profit and loss account along with a credit from the revaluation reserve equal to the depreciation on the revaluation surplus. In Great Britain, section 275(2) of the Companies Act 1985‡ permits depreciation on a revaluation surplus to be treated as a realised profit and paragraph 34(3) of Schedule 4† permits an amount to be transferred from the revaluation reserve to the profit and loss account if it represents a realised profit. However, total depreciation and the credit from the revaluation reserve would be **45**

**In Northern Ireland, the Companies (Northern Ireland) Order 1986, Schedule 4, paragraph 32(3).*
*In the Republic of Ireland, the Companies (Amendment) Act 1986, Schedule, paragraph 20(3). (**Editor's note:** For accounting periods beginning on or after 6 April 2008 this changes to Paragraph 33 of Schedule 1 to the Large and Medium-sized Companies and Groups (Accounts and Reports) Regulations 2008 (SI 2008/410).)*

†Marleasing S.A. vs La Commercial Internacional de Alimentation S.A. (C-106/89) [1992 CMLR 305].

‡In Northern Ireland, the Companies (Northern Ireland) Order 1986, article 283(2) and Schedule 4, paragraph 34(3).
*In the Republic of Ireland, the Companies (Amendment) Act 1983, section 45(6) and the Companies (Amendment) Act 1986, Schedule, paragraph 22(4). (**Editor's note:** For accounting periods beginning on or after 6 April 2008 this changes to Section 841 of the Companies Act 2006 and Paragraph 35 of Schedule 1 to the Large and Medium-sized Companies and Groups (Accounts and Reports) Regulations 2008 (SI 2008/410).)*

required to be separately disclosed in the profit and loss account (ie the credit from the revaluation reserve would not be permitted to be offset against the charge for depreciation).

46 The Board disagrees with the introduction of this alternative for three reasons:

(a) It would involve recycling amounts previously recognised in the statement of total recognised gains and losses – ie via a transfer from the revaluation reserve to the profit and loss account. The transfer from the revaluation reserve would result in a charge to the statement of total recognised gains and losses. Such a charge has no meaning.

(b) It is inconsistent with the Board's view of depreciation as a measure of the cost of the economic benefits consumed during the period.

(c) An approach that recognises depreciation on the historical amount of an asset in the profit and loss account and depreciation on the revalued amount in the statement of total recognised gains and losses implies that the purpose of the profit and loss account is invariably to report historical cost profits and losses. The Board rejected such an objective during its development of FRS 3. In addition, FRS 3 requires a note of historical cost profits and losses where there is a material difference between the results as disclosed in the profit and loss account and the result on an unmodified historical cost basis.

47 The Board believes that depreciation measured at current prices represents the best measure of the operating cost of using the asset in question. This is because the purpose of charging depreciation to the profit and loss account is to show the cost of the economic benefits consumed during the period, and depreciation based on current value reflects the cost that the entity could have avoided if it had not used the asset. In addition, it also provides a consistency between the profit and loss account and the balance sheet and is consistent with companies legislation. Hence, the FRS requires the depreciation charge in the profit and loss account to be based on the revalued amount of the asset, whenever the asset has been revalued.

Non-depreciation of tangible fixed assets

48 There has been a growing trend towards the non-depreciation of certain tangible fixed assets, particularly property. The main circumstances in which it is argued that no depreciation need be charged are where maintenance or refurbishment is carried out regularly, significantly extending the useful economic life of the asset or maintaining the residual value of the asset.

49 The Board believes that the estimate of a tangible fixed asset's useful economic life cannot be extended limitlessly through maintenance, refurbishment, overhaul or replacement of components of the asset. This is because the physical life of a tangible fixed asset, other than non-depreciable land, cannot be indefinite. At some point in time it will not be economic to continue to maintain and restore the asset and it will have scrap value only. Accordingly, the FRS states that subsequent expenditure on a tangible fixed asset that maintains or enhances the previously assessed standard of performance of the asset does not negate the need to charge depreciation.

50 The Board acknowledges that, with regular maintenance and restoration and where economic or technological obsolescence is unlikely, some tangible fixed assets (eg heritage buildings, fine art) may have very long useful economic lives before they need a major refit or restoration or are scrapped. In such cases the periodic depreciation charge may be immaterial.

The useful economic life of a tangible fixed asset is defined as the period in which the asset is expected to be used by the entity in its business. Therefore the useful economic life to the entity may be substantially shorter than the asset's total economic life, particularly where the asset management policy of the entity involves the disposal of assets after a specified time or after consumption of a limited portion of the economic benefits embodied in the asset. In addition, the asset may have an alternative use that has a longer economic life. In these circumstances, with regular maintenance and repairs, the residual value of the asset at the end of the useful economic life to the entity, which will reflect the remaining economic value of the asset, may not be insignificant or materially different from the carrying amount of the asset. 51

The Board believes that, apart from non-depreciable land, the only grounds for not charging depreciation on a tangible fixed asset are that the depreciation charge and related accumulated depreciation balance are not material, owing to a long estimated remaining useful economic life or high residual value. By not charging depreciation, however, there is greater risk that recoverable amount will fall below the carrying amount in the future. Where depreciation is not charged, therefore, the FRS requires impairment reviews to be undertaken at the end of each reporting period. 52

Similarly, the longer the useful economic lives assigned to tangible fixed assets, the greater is the risk that the recoverable amounts will fall below the carrying amounts in future. Where a depreciation period exceeds 50 years, the Board believes that the risk is sufficiently high to require depreciation to be supplemented by reviews for impairment at the end of each reporting period. 53

Review of useful economic life and residual value

Changes in the useful economic life or residual value of a tangible fixed asset generally arise from new information or developments and therefore do not relate to past periods. For that reason the FRS requires changes in the useful economic life and residual value of an asset to be accounted for prospectively over its remaining useful economic life. Estimates of residual value should be based on prices prevailing at the date of acquisition or latest revaluation. Unless the asset is being revalued, therefore, the estimate of residual value should not be altered simply because of changing prices. 54

Changes made following exposure of FRED 17

The majority of respondents to FRED 17 were broadly supportive of its proposals, with the exception of the proposals in respect of the treatment of gains and losses on disposal and the consequential amendment to FRS 3, which proved controversial. The Board has accepted the argument that the changes to recognition of gains and losses on disposal should not be introduced in isolation from a review of other aspects of FRS 3. It has, therefore, not incorporated these proposals in the requirements of the FRS, maintaining the treatment in FRS 3, as outlined above.* 55

In the light of other comments made by those responding to FRED 17, a number of changes have been made to its proposals. The most significant changes are: 56

- the exemption of investment properties from the requirements of the FRS. The treatment of investment properties is being considered further by the Board, in

**Editor's note:* 'FRED 22 Revision of FRS 3 "Reporting Financial Performance"' was issued by the ASB in December 2000.*

tandem with the international project on investment properties. The Board believes that, until this work is complete, it is appropriate to maintain the status quo as set out in SSAP 19 'Accounting for investment properties'.

- the inclusion of an explanatory paragraph explaining that, when valuing a non-specialised property, the adaptation works may be treated separately from the shell of the building.
- the amendment of the requirements for reporting gains and losses on revaluation that reverse previous losses or gains, to take into account subsequent depreciation. This ensures that the requirements are consistent with the equivalent requirements in FRS 11.
- the deletion of the proposed requirement in FRED 17 to disclose in the notes to the financial statements any significant differences between the current value and the carrying amount of properties that are not revalued. The Board agreed with respondents that the requirement in companies legislation to make a similar disclosure in the directors' report was sufficient.
- the addition of a new requirement for impairment reviews to be performed in each reporting period when either no depreciation charge on a tangible fixed asset is made on the grounds that it would be immaterial or the estimated remaining useful economic life of the asset exceeds 50 years. This replaces the proposal in FRED 17 that it should be assumed that the residual value of a tangible fixed asset was materially different from its carrying amount, unless the entity intends to dispose of the asset within about a year from its date of acquisition. The Board accepted respondents' comments that the assumption in FRED 17 did not reflect economic reality in certain circumstances. The new requirement is explained in paragraphs 48–53 above.
- the addition of a new requirement in respect of the use of renewals accounting as a method of estimating the depreciation of infrastructure assets.
- the addition of a requirement to disclose a reconciliation of the movements on the carrying amount for each class of tangible fixed assets. This is consistent with the equivalent requirement in companies legislation, but is repeated in the FRS for those entities that do not fall within the scope of companies legislation, and to ensure that the reconciliation is given for each class of assets adopted for revaluation purposes.
- the removal of the paragraph in SSAP 19 'Accounting for investment properties' that exempts charities with investment properties from following the requirements of SSAP 19, to be consistent with the SORP 'Accounting by Charities' issued by the Charity Commissioners for England and Wales.

Financial Reporting Standard 16 is set out in paragraphs 1–22.

The Statement of Standard Accounting Practice, which comprises the paragraphs set in bold type, should be read in the context of the Objective as stated in paragraph 1 and the definitions set out in paragraph 2 and also of the Foreword to Accounting Standards and the Statement of Principles for Financial Reporting currently in issue.

The explanatory paragraphs contained in the FRS shall be regarded as part of the Statement of Standard Accounting Practice insofar as they assist in interpreting that statement.

Appendix V 'The development of the FRS' reviews considerations and arguments that were thought significant by members of the Board in reaching the conclusions on the FRS.

[FRS 16]
Current tax*

(Issued December 1999)

Contents

	Paragraphs
Summary	
Financial Reporting Standard 16	
Objective	1
Definitions	2
Scope	3–4
Recognition	5–16
Disclosure	17
Date from which effective and transitional arrangements	18–21
Withdrawal of SSAP 8 and UITF Abstract 16	22
Adoption of FRS 16 by the board	
Appendices	
I Illustration of profit and loss account disclosure	
II Transitional arrangements for advance corporation tax (UK only)	
III Note on legal requirements	
IV Compliance with international accounting standards	
V The development of the FRS	

****Editor's note****: The matters covered in FRS 16 are dealt with in Section 29 of FRS 102.*

Current tax

Summary

Financial Reporting Standard 16 'Current Tax' specifies how current tax, in particular withholding tax and tax credits, should be reflected in financial statements. **a**

Current tax should be recognised in the profit and loss account for the period, except to the extent that it is attributable to a gain or loss that has been recognised directly in the statement of total recognised gains and losses. Where a gain or loss has been recognised directly in the statement of total recognised gains and losses, the tax relating to that gain or loss should also be recognised directly in that statement. **b**

Dividends, interest and other amounts payable or receivable should be recognised at an amount that: **c**

- includes withholding taxes payable to the tax authorities wholly on behalf of the recipient.
- excludes any other taxes, such as attributable tax credits, not payable wholly on behalf of the recipient.

Subject to the above, income and expenses should be included in the pre-tax results on the basis of the income or expenses actually receivable or payable, without any adjustment to reflect a notional amount of tax that would have been paid or relieved in respect of the transaction if it had been taxable, or allowable for tax purposes, on a different basis. **d**

Current tax should be measured using tax rates and laws that have been enacted or substantively enacted by the balance sheet date. **e**

[Financial Reporting Standard 16]

Objective

The objective of this FRS is to ensure that reporting entities recognise current taxes in a consistent and transparent manner. **1**

Definitions

The following definitions shall apply in the FRS and in particular in the Statement of Standard Accounting Practice set out **in bold type**. **2**

Current tax:-

The amount of tax estimated to be payable or recoverable in respect of the taxable profit or loss for a period, along with adjustments to estimates in respect of previous periods.

Tax credit:-

The tax credit given under UK tax legislation to the recipient of a dividend from a UK company.

The credit is given to acknowledge that the income out of which the dividend has been paid has already been charged to tax, rather than because any withholding tax has been deducted at source. The tax credit may discharge or reduce the recipient's liability to tax on the dividend. Non-taxpayers may or may not be able to recover the tax credit.

Taxable profit or loss:-

The profit or loss for the period, determined in accordance with the rules established by the tax authorities, upon which taxes are assessed.

Withholding tax:-

Tax on dividends or other income that is deducted by the payer of the income and paid to the tax authorities wholly on behalf of the recipient.

SCOPE

3 **The FRS applies to all financial statements that are intended to give a true and fair view of a reporting entity's financial position and profit or loss (or income and expenditure) for a period.**

4 **Reporting entities applying the Financial Reporting Standard for Smaller Entities currently applicable are exempt from the FRS.**

RECOGNITION

5 **Current tax should be recognised in the profit and loss account for the period, except to the extent that it is attributable to a gain or loss that is or has been recognised directly in the statement of total recognised gains and losses.**

6 **Where a gain or loss is or has been recognised directly in the statement of total recognised gains and losses, the tax attributable to that gain or loss should also be recognised directly in that statement.**

7 Accounting standards (or, in their absence, legislation) require or permit certain gains or losses to be credited or charged directly in the statement of total recognised gains and losses (ie not in the profit and loss account). The FRS requires any attributable tax to be treated in the same way. In exceptional circumstances it may be difficult to determine the amount of current tax that is attributable to gains or losses that have been recognised directly in the statement of total recognised gains and losses. In such circumstances, the attributable tax is based on a reasonable pro rata allocation, or another allocation that is more appropriate in the circumstances.

8 **Outgoing dividends paid and proposed (or declared and not yet payable), interest and other amounts payable should be recognised at an amount that:**

(a) includes any withholding taxes; but
(b) excludes any other taxes, such as attributable tax credits, not payable wholly on behalf of the recipient.

9 **Incoming dividends, interest or other income receivable should be recognised at an amount that:**

(a) includes any withholding taxes; but

(b) **excludes any other taxes, such as attributable tax credits, not payable wholly on behalf of the recipient.**

The effect of any withholding tax suffered should be taken into account as part of the tax charge.

The amount recognised therefore excludes attributable tax credits of the type defined in the FRS and underlying tax.* 10

Subject to paragraphs 8 and 9, income and expenses should be included in the pre-tax results on the basis of the income or expenses actually receivable or payable. No adjustment should be made to reflect a notional amount of tax that would have been paid or relieved in respect of the transaction if it had been taxable, or allowable for tax purposes, on a different basis. 11

The requirement in paragraph 11 applies, for example, to non-taxable income, non-deductible expenditure and income and expenditure subject to non-standard rates of tax. 12

The requirement applies only to notional tax, ie tax that is not actually paid or recovered. In some specialised industries, such as leasing and life insurance, profit from transactions is allocated to accounting periods on a post-tax basis and the tax charge and pre-tax profit relating to the accounting period is found by applying the effective rate of tax to the post-tax profit. Where, as is usually the case, such post-tax methods result in the actual pre-tax profit and the actual tax charge being recorded over the life of the transactions, their use is consistent with the requirements of the FRS. 13

Current tax should be measured at the amounts expected to be paid (or recovered) using the tax rates and laws that have been enacted or substantively enacted by the balance sheet date. 14

A UK tax rate can be regarded as having been substantively enacted if it is included in either: 15

(a) a Bill that has been passed by the House of Commons and is awaiting only passage through the House of Lords and Royal Assent; or
(b) a resolution having statutory effect that has been passed under the Provisional Collection of Taxes Act 1968.†

A Republic of Ireland tax rate can be regarded as having been substantively enacted if it is included in a Bill that has been passed by the Dail. 16

DISCLOSURE

The following major components of the current tax expense (or income) for the period in the profit and loss account and the statement of total recognised gains and losses should be disclosed separately: 17

**In certain circumstances, a UK company receiving dividends from an overseas company obtains relief for the tax (underlying tax) that the overseas company has paid on the profits from which the dividend has been paid. The UK company's taxable income is increased by the amount of underlying tax attributed to the dividend and relief is given against the resulting UK tax charge.*

†*Such a resolution could be used to collect taxes at a new rate before that rate has been enacted. In practice, corporation tax rates are now set a year ahead to avoid having to invoke the Provisional Collection of Taxes Act for the quarterly payment system.*

(a) UK or Republic of Ireland tax (depending on the companies legislation in accordance with which the entity is reporting); and
(b) foreign tax.

Both (a) and (b) should be analysed to distinguish tax estimated for the current period and any adjustments recognised in respect of prior periods. The domestic tax should be disclosed before and after double taxation relief.

DATE FROM WHICH EFFECTIVE AND TRANSITIONAL ARRANGEMENTS

18 **The accounting practices set out in the FRS should be regarded as standard in respect of accounting periods ending on or after 23 March 2000. Earlier adoption is encouraged.**

19 **Non-taxpaying entities that, at the date of implementation of the FRS, are entitled to transitional relief following the removal of their right to reclaim tax credits may continue to present that transitional relief as part of the income to which it relates. The nature and amount of the relief should be separately disclosed.**

20 **Any unrelieved advance corporation tax (ACT) that at the date of implementation of the FRS is carried forward for relief against future taxable profits should be recognised on the balance sheet only to the extent that it is regarded as recoverable. Any change in the amount of ACT regarded as recoverable should be recognised as part of the tax expense (or income) for the period in the profit and loss account and separately disclosed on the face of the profit and loss account or in a note.**

21 Guidance on the circumstances in which ACT can be regarded as recoverable is included in Appendix II.

WITHDRAWAL OF SSAP 8 AND UITF ABSTRACT 16

22 **The FRS supersedes SSAP 8 'The treatment of taxation under the imputation system in the accounts of companies' and UITF Abstract 16 'Income and expenses subject to non-standard rates of tax'.**

Adoption of FRS 16 by the board

Financial Reporting Standard 16 'Current Tax' was approved for issue by the ten members of the Accounting Standards Board.

Sir David Tweedie	(Chairman)
Allan Cook CBE	(Technical Director)
David Allvey	
Ian Brindle	
Dr John Buchanan	
John Coombe	
Raymond Hinton	
Huw Jones	
Professor Geoffrey Whittington	
Ken Wild	

Appendix I
Illustration of profit and loss account disclosure

This example illustrates one method of showing (by way of note) the tax items required to be disclosed under companies legislation* and the FRS.

This appendix is for general guidance and does not form part of the Statement of Standard Accounting Practice.

	£000	£000
UK† corporation tax		
Current tax on income for the period	a	
Adjustments in respect of prior periods	b	
	c	
Double taxation relief	(d)	
		e
Foreign tax		
Current tax on income for the period	f	
Adjustments in respect of prior periods	g	
		h
Tax on profit on ordinary activities		i

In Great Britain, the Companies Act 1985; in Northern Ireland, the Companies (Northern Ireland) Order 1986; and in the Republic of Ireland, the Companies (Amendment) Act 1986.* ***Editor's note:* *This should now be taken to refer to the Companies Act 2006 as well.*

†Companies reporting in accordance with companies legislation in the Republic of Ireland would instead show the Republic of Ireland tax.

Appendix II
Transitional arrangements for advance corporation tax (UK only)

The definition of recoverable advance corporation tax (ACT) and the treatments for ACT set out below are based on the requirements of SSAP *8. These continue to be relevant for the shadow ACT system, which is designed to ensure that ACT carried forward after April 1999 is recovered only if it could have been recovered had the ACT system still existed.*

Recoverable ACT:- 1

ACT is regarded as recoverable where the amount of the ACT previously paid on outgoing dividends can be:

(a) set off against a corporation tax liability on the profits of the period under review or of previous periods;

(b) properly set off against a credit balance on the deferred tax account; or

(c) expected to be recoverable taking into account expected profits and dividends—normally those of the next accounting period only.

Although ACT can be carried forward indefinitely if necessary, in each year there is an overriding restriction on the use of ACT for set-off imposed by the shadow ACT system. The shadow ACT system is designed to be no more generous than the old ACT system. Its effect is to ensure that ACT that was previously irrecoverable becomes recoverable only to the extent that it would have become recoverable under the old ACT system. 2

In deciding whether ACT should be carried forward as recoverable, regard should be had only to the immediate and foreseeable future. How long this future period should be will depend upon the circumstances of each case, but it is suggested that where there is no deferred tax account it should normally not extend beyond the next accounting period. 3

ACT should be offset against a credit balance on the deferred tax account only if, in the period in which the underlying timing differences are expected to reverse, the reversal will create sufficient taxable profits to enable ACT to be recovered under the shadow ACT system. 4

Subject to the preceding paragraph, if the ACT on dividends relating to previous periods is regarded as recoverable but has not yet been recovered, it should be deducted from the deferred tax account if such an account is available for this purpose. In the absence of a deferred tax account ACT recoverable should be shown as a deferred tax asset. 5

If ACT that was previously regarded as recoverable becomes irrecoverable, it is required to be charged in the profit and loss account as a separately disclosed component of the tax charge. 6

Where the recovery of the ACT was not regarded as reasonably certain and foreseeable, it will have been written off in the profit and loss account. Events may occur under the system applying from April 1999 (the shadow ACT system) causing ACT that has previously been written off as irrecoverable to be recovered. Such ACT is required to be credited in the profit and loss account as a separately disclosed component of the tax charge. 7

Appendix III
Note on legal requirements

GREAT BRITAIN

1 The main requirements that are directly relevant are set out in Schedule 4 to the Companies Act 1985 and are summarised below.*

2 Paragraph 3(7) of Schedule 4 requires every profit and loss account to show separately as additional items the aggregate amount of any dividends paid and proposed.

3 The formats in Schedule 4 set out where tax is to be shown in the balance sheet and the profit and loss account.

4 Paragraph 54(2) of Schedule 4 requires particulars to be given of any special circumstances that affect liability in respect of taxation of profits, income or capital gains for the financial year or liability in respect of taxation of profits, income or capital gains for succeeding financial years.

5 Paragraph 54(3) of Schedule 4 requires the following components of tax on profit or loss on ordinary activities to be stated:

(a) the amount of the charge for UK corporation tax;
(b) if the amount would have been greater but for relief from double taxation, the amount which it would have been but for such relief;
(c) the amount of the charge for UK income tax; and
(d) the amount of the charge for taxation imposed outside the UK of profits, income and (so far as charged to revenue) capital gains.

NORTHERN IRELAND

6 The statutory requirements in Northern Ireland are set out in the Companies (Northern Ireland) Order 1986. They are identical to and parallel the references for Great Britain in the Companies Act 1985.

REPUBLIC OF IRELAND

7 The main requirements that are directly relevant are set out in the Companies (Amendment) Act 1986 and are summarised below.

8 Section 4(15)(a) requires every profit and loss account to show separately the aggregate amount of the dividends paid and the aggregate amount of the dividends proposed to be paid.

****Editor's note:*** *The various statutory references change with the introduction of the Companies Act 2006, which affects accounting for periods beginning on or after 6 April 2008. The various statutory references have changed as follows:*

Companies Act 1985 reference	***Companies Act 2006 reference***
Schedule 4	*Schedule 1 to the Large and Medium-sized Companies and Groups (Accounts and Reports) Regulations 2008 (SI 2008/410)*
Paragraph 3 of Schedule 4	*Repealed*
Paragraph 54 of Schedule 4	*Paragraph 67 of Schedule 1 to SI 2008/410*

The formats in the Schedule set out where taxation is to be shown in the balance sheet and the profit and loss account. **9**

Paragraph 40(1) of the Schedule requires the basis on which the charge for corporation tax, income tax and other taxation on profits (whether payable in or outside the State) is computed to be stated. **10**

Paragraph 40(2) of the Schedule requires particulars to be given of any special circumstances which affect liability in respect of taxation on profits, income or capital gains for the financial year concerned or liability in respect of taxation of profits, income or capital gains for succeeding financial years. **11**

Paragraph 40(3) of the Schedule requires that the amount of the charge for corporation tax, income tax and other taxation on profits or capital gains, so far as charged to revenue, including taxation payable outside the State on profits (distinguishing where practicable between corporation tax and other taxation) shall be stated. **12**

Any amounts required to be stated under paragraph 40(1)-(3) shall be stated separately in respect of each of the amounts which is or would, but for section 4(6)(b) (items combined in the accounts) of the Act, be shown under the following items in the profit and loss account—'tax on profit or loss on ordinary activities' and 'tax on extraordinary profit or loss'. **13**

Paragraph 33 of the Schedule requires that the amount of any provision for taxation other than deferred taxation shall be stated. **14**

Paragraph 3 (note 7 on the balance sheet formats) of the Schedule requires the notes to the balance sheet to show separately the combined amounts included under the heading 'Other creditors including tax and social welfare' (format 1, items C8 and F8 and format 2, item C8) in respect of taxation and social welfare, specifying separately the amount due under the different categories of tax payable and the total amount of social welfare due. **15**

Appendix IV
Compliance with international accounting standards

1 The International Accounting Standard on current tax is IAS 12 (revised 1996) 'Income Taxes'.*

2 The main differences between the two standards are that:

- the IAS requires current tax to be presented separately on the face of the balance sheet; the FRS does not.
- the FRS specifies how a reporting entity should account for the tax consequences of outgoing or incoming dividends and other distributions; the IAS does not.
- the FRS requires all current tax income or expense for the period to be included in the statements of performance (ie profit and loss account or statement of total recognised gains and losses). The IAS requires current tax to be charged directly to equity if it relates to items that are also charged or credited directly to equity.
- the IAS requires disclosure of the tax expense relating to discontinued operations; the FRS does not.

****Editor's note:*** *IAS 12 was further revised in 2000.*

Appendix V
The development of the FRS

BACKGROUND

In the last few years there have been important changes in the tax systems of the UK and the Republic of Ireland. Amongst other changes, the reclaimability of tax credits became restricted in July 1997* and advance corporation tax (ACT) was abolished in April 1999. Further, in the Republic of Ireland, the previous imputation system was replaced by a system of withholding taxes. 1

The changes raised questions about the continuing relevance of SSAP 8 'The treatment of taxation under the imputation system in the accounts of companies'. SSAP 8 had been introduced in August 1974 for the UK, with Appendix 3 for the Republic of Ireland added in December 1977. It required incoming dividends to be recognised at the amount received plus the attributable tax credit and contained detailed requirements regarding the treatment of ACT. 2

In response to the earlier change in the UK that restricted the ability of non-tax-payers to reclaim tax credits attributed to dividends received, the Board published proposals for a limited amendment to SSAP 8.† The main proposal was that dividend income should not be grossed up to include tax credits. 3

This proposal received substantial support from commentators. However, in November 1997, the Chancellor of the Exchequer announced a far-reaching review of the UK tax system, part of which was a plan to abolish ACT. Similarly, in December 1997, the Minister for Finance in the Republic of Ireland announced changes to the Irish tax system that included abolition of ACT. 4

The Board therefore accepted a recommendation of its Urgent Issues Task Force that, rather than make a limited amendment to SSAP 8, the whole standard should be reviewed. At the time it was thought that it might be possible to incorporate revised requirements for current tax into the FRS being developed on deferred tax. However, this would have meant a delay in the introduction of the requirements for current tax. To avoid such a delay, the Board decided to issue two separate FRSS. 5

In June 1999, the Board published its proposals for revising SSAP 8 in an Exposure Draft, FRED 18 'Current Taxation'. The basic requirements proposed were widely supported and have remained largely unchanged in the FRS. 6

CHANGES TO THE REQUIREMENTS OF SSAP 8

The main changes introduced by the FRS are in the treatment of tax credits, with-holding taxes and similar methods of collecting tax at source: 7

(a) the FRS requires dividends to be recognised at an amount that does not include any attributable tax credit or underlying tax. SSAP 8 had required dividends to be recognised at an amount that included the attributable tax credit.

**In 1998 in the Republic of Ireland.*

†Exposure Draft: Amendment to SSAP 8 'The treatment of taxation under the imputation system in the accounts of companies', October 1997.

(b) the FRS addresses the treatment of withholding taxes, which SSAP 8 did not. It requires dividends to be recognised at an amount that includes any withholding taxes.

The reasons for these changes are discussed further in paragraphs 9-20 below.

8 Other changes introduced by the FRS are:

(a) *inclusion of requirements prescribing the circumstances in which current taxes should be recognised directly in the statement of total recognised gains and losses rather than in the profit and loss account.* The requirements reflect the principle underlying the consensus in UITF Abstract 19 'Tax on gains and losses on foreign currency borrowings that hedge an investment in a foreign enterprise' ie that tax should be charged in the same performance statement as the gains and losses on which it arises. The FRS does not fully supersede Abstract 19, which also covers other issues.

(b) *inclusion of the consensus from UITF Abstract 16, which is now withdrawn.* The FRS thus requires income and expenses to be included in the pre-tax results on the basis of the income or expenses actually receivable or payable. No adjustment is made to reflect a notional amount of tax that would have been paid or relieved had the transaction been taxable or allowable on a different basis.

(c) *removal of requirements relating to ACT.* With the abolition of ACT in both the UK and the Republic of Ireland, the requirements in SSAP 8 will not be relevant in future. Residual issues arising under the 'shadow' ACT system have been addressed as transitional arrangements in the FRS.

(d) *a requirement to use 'substantively enacted' tax rates and laws to measure current taxes.* This requirement is discussed further in paragraphs 21 and 22 below.

TAX CREDITS AND WITHHOLDING TAX

Proposals in FRED 18

9 FRED 18 proposed that incoming dividends should be recognised at the amount received or receivable without any attributable tax credit but including any withholding tax deducted at source.

10 The proposal arose from reconsidering the principles underlying the standard rather than as a result of the restriction in the reclaimability of tax credits or the abolition of ACT. The Board took the view that, whilst these changes affected those entities that are not taxpayers (through the restrictions on reclaimability*) and the timing of the tax payments (through ACT†), they did not fundamentally change the underlying tax system. The central feature of the tax credit system—dividends received with a tax credit fall outside the corporation tax computation altogether for companies and have no basic rate tax liability for individuals (and partnerships)—remained unchanged.

11 In developing its proposals, the Board considered the three possible amounts at which dividends could be recognised, ie:

(a) *including* withholding taxes but *excluding* tax credits;

* *Recipients of dividends that are taxpayers receive the benefit from the tax credit through no further tax being payable (except higher rate tax for some individuals). It is only for non-taxpayers that the extent to which the tax credit is recoverable is relevant.*

† *ACT, except where irrecoverable, affects only the timing and not the amount of tax due.*

(b) *including* both withholding taxes and tax credits; or
(c) *excluding* both withholding taxes and tax credits.

In support of (a), it was argued that there is a difference in nature between tax credits and withholding tax. It is not only that a withholding tax is tax that has actually been paid by (or at least on behalf of) the recipient of the dividend. The differences are more than merely technical matters of how the tax is collected, at what rates it is levied and whether the income to which the tax relates is included in a company's corporation tax computation. There are also differences of substance: **12**

- in many circumstances, no further tax is payable on dividends received with a tax credit: the dividend is treated as non-taxable income. In contrast, income on which withholding tax has been suffered is treated as taxable and subject to further tax, unless (unusually) the amount of the withholding tax is sufficient to discharge the full liability.
- the amount at which the dividend is measured if it is subject to further tax is different. When dividends are received subject to withholding tax, further tax is levied on the amount received plus the withholding tax. When reporting entities have further tax to pay on dividends received with tax credits (for example, when the investments are held by a bank as part of its trading portfolio), the further tax is levied on the amount received without the tax credit.

In support of option (b)—ie including both withholding taxes and tax credits—it was argued that any differences between a tax credit and a withholding tax are a matter of technical form rather than economic substance. Differences arise in the rate of the tax, the method of payment, the system for gaining credit for the tax suffered etc. But in both cases the recipient entity is liable for a reduced or nil amount of tax on the income received as a result of tax paid by the payer of the income. (The payer of the dividend has paid the tax either as corporation tax on the income out of which the dividend is paid or as withholding tax on behalf of the recipient.) Taking this view, it is further argued that the tax credit and the withholding tax have a real effect on the recipient of the dividend or other income and should therefore be reflected in the amount of income received. Grossing up is necessary to reflect the greater value of 100 received as dividend (no tax consequences) compared with 100 earned as trading profit (taxable). **13**

In favour of option (c)—ie excluding both withholding taxes and tax credits—it was argued that, given the diversity of tax systems and their implications for different types of recipient, it would be impossible to unravel and account for each system in accordance with its economic substance. Consistency would be achieved, and both the substance and form followed, if this approach were adopted because the financial statements could show that different sources of income had different tax consequences. These could be highlighted in the entity's tax charge. **14**

It was further argued that approach (c) can be regarded as consistent with UITF Abstract 16. This is because it applies a consistent rule that tax collections at source are not taken into account by grossing up. This approach also has the advantage of simplicity: it avoids the difficult issue of when such tax collections are 'real' (and should be taken into account) and when they are 'notional' (and should not be taken into account). **15**

The majority of the Board found the arguments in favour of option (a)—ie measuring dividends at an amount that included withholding tax but not tax credits—the most persuasive. They took the view that to show only the net amount of income received subject to withholding tax failed to reflect the full amount taxable in the hands of the recipient. And they noted that the distinction between notional and real **16** tax collections had already received general support in UITF Abstract 16. Hence, option (a) formed the basis of the proposals in the FRED.

Changes to the FRED proposals

17 The proposal to recognise dividends at an amount that includes withholding taxes but not attributable tax credits received widespread support from respondents to the FRED. Eighty-two per cent of respondents agreed with the proposal, and the preferences of the remaining 18 per cent were spread across a range of options.

18 However, a number of respondents noted that, by specifying requirements only for withholding taxes and tax credits of the type given to the recipients of dividends from UK companies, the FRS would fail to clarify how other forms of 'tax credit', some of which would have some of the characteristics of withholding taxes, should be treated. Examples included relief for 'underlying' tax and other credits given under double tax treaties.

19 Most of the respondents who raised this issue thought that underlying taxes and other forms of tax credit should be treated in the same way as UK tax credits. They argued that underlying tax is more like a tax credit than a withholding tax. It is more concerned with the taxes paid by the payer of a dividend rather than those paid by (or on behalf of) the recipient. To gross up a dividend received for the tax on the paying company's profits would fail to represent the substance of the dividend income. They noted that the grossed up amount would be difficult to interpret, being determined on the basis of accounts prepared using different accounting standards from those used in the UK and the Republic of Ireland. They further argued that whilst the measurement of withholding tax is relatively straightforward, underlying tax can be difficult to calculate and often takes time to agree with the Inland Revenue. The Board accepted these arguments, and reworded the requirements of the FRS to clarify that dividends should not be grossed up for any taxes other than withholding taxes.

20 The general proposal that dividends should not be grossed up for UK tax credits has not changed. Rather it has been extended to other taxes that were not addressed by the FRED.

TAX RATES

21 SSAP 8 required current tax to be measured at the latest known rate. The FRS instead requires current tax to be measured at the amount expected to be payable or recoverable based on tax rates and laws that have been enacted or substantively enacted by the balance sheet date. The change has been made to increase consistency and align the FRS with the requirements of the international accounting standard, IAS 12 (revised 1996) 'Income Taxes'.

22 The change was proposed in the FRED and widely supported by those commenting on it. A number of respondents suggested that the requirement should be to use rates that had been substantively enacted by the date of signing the accounts rather than the balance sheet date. The Board acknowledged that this could lead to more accurate measures of the tax that would actually be paid in respect of the period. But it took the view that:

- it was desirable that a universal effect, such as a tax rate, should be applied by all reporting entities from the same date. This would not happen if the cut-off point were the date of signing the accounts.

- practical problems could arise if a new tax rate or law was substantively enacted between the date on which a company announced its results and the date of signing the financial statements.

DISCLOSURES

The disclosures required by the FRS are very similar to those required by SSAP 8. A significant difference is the removal of the requirement to disclose certain special reliefs that have been available in the Republic of Ireland. These reliefs are now being phased out. 23

The FRED had proposed a more general requirement to disclose the impact of any special reliefs. However, the Board has removed this proposal, having accepted the views expressed by some respondents that: 24

- to quantify the effects of all special reliefs obtained would be an onerous requirement for entities with worldwide operations, and
- the effects of significant reliefs are already disclosed because of the general requirement to explain any significant factors affecting the tax charge.

TRANSITIONAL ARRANGEMENTS

Charities and other entities at present receive a tapering transitional relief following the changes in the tax system that removed their right to reclaim tax credits. As a concession to these entities, the FRS permits them to continue to show that particular transitional relief as part of the income to which it relates, rather than as a tax refund. 25

The FRS contains no other transitional concessions. The application of the FRS for the first time will therefore be treated as a change in accounting policy, effective from the start of the accounting period in which it was first implemented. The Board chose this approach because the changes required arise from a review of the fundamental principles underlying the standard and not as a result of the changes to the tax system. 26

Financial Reporting Standard 17 is set out in paragraphs 1–105.

The Statement of Standard Accounting Practice, which comprises the paragraphs set in bold type, should be read in the context of the Objective as stated in paragraph 1 and the definitions set out in paragraph 2 and also of the Foreword to Accounting Standards and the Statement of Principles for Financial Reporting currently in issue.

The explanatory paragraphs contained in the FRS shall be regarded as part of the Statement of Standard Accounting Practice insofar as they assist in interpreting that statement.

Appendix IV 'The development of the FRS' reviews considerations and arguments that were thought significant by members of the Board in reaching the conclusions on the FRS.

[FRS 17]
Retirement benefits*

(Issued November 2000)

Contents

	Paragraphs
Summary	
Financial Reporting Standard 17	
Objective	1
Definitions	2
Scope	3–6
Defined contribution schemes	7
Multi-employer schemes	8–12
Measurement of defined benefit schemes	13–36
Scheme assets	14–19
Scheme liabilities	20–34
Actuarial method and assumptions	20–31
The discount rate	32–34
Frequency of valuations	35–36
Recognition of defined benefit schemes	37–74
Recognition in the balance sheet	37–49
Recognition in the performance statements	50–74
Current service cost, interest cost and expected return on assets	51–56
Actuarial gains and losses	57–59
Past service costs	60–63
Settlements and curtailments	64–66
Impact of limit on balance sheet asset	67–70
Tax	71–72
Death-in-service and incapacity benefits	73–74
Disclosures	75–93
Defined contribution schemes	75
Defined benefit schemes	76–93
Date from which effective and transitional arrangements	94–97
Withdrawal of SSAP 24 and UITF Abstracts 6 and 18 and amendment of other accounting standards	98–105
Adoption of FRS 17 By The Board	
Appendices	
I Disclosure Example	
II Note on Legal Requirements	
III Compliance with International Accounting Standards	
IV The Development of the FRS	

***Editor's note**: The matters covered in FRS 17 are dealt with in Section 28 of FRS 102.*

Retirement benefits

Summary

a Financial Reporting Standard 17 sets out the requirements for accounting for retirement benefits.

Defined contribution schemes

b The cost of a defined contribution scheme is equal to the contributions payable to the scheme for the period.

Measurement of defined benefit scheme assets and liabilities

c Defined benefit scheme assets are measured at fair value.

d Defined benefit scheme liabilities are measured using the projected unit method.

e Defined benefit scheme liabilities are discounted at the current rate of return on a high quality corporate bond of equivalent term and currency to the liability.

f Full actuarial valuations should be obtained at intervals not exceeding three years and should be updated at each balance sheet date.

Recognition of defined benefit schemes

g An asset is recognised to the extent that an employer can recover a surplus in a defined benefit scheme through reduced contributions and refunds. A liability is recognised to the extent that the deficit reflects the employer's legal or constructive obligation.

h The resulting defined benefit asset or liability is presented separately on the face of the balance sheet after other net assets.

i The change in the defined benefit asset or liability (other than that arising from contributions to the scheme) is analysed into the following components:

(i) the current service cost
(ii) the interest cost
(iii) the expected return on assets
(iv) actuarial gains and losses
(v) past service costs (if any)
(vi) settlements and curtailments (if any).

j The current service cost and interest cost are based on the discount rate at the beginning of the period. The expected return on assets is based on the expected rate of return at the beginning of the period. The current service cost is shown within the appropriate statutory heading for pension costs in the profit and loss account. The interest cost and expected return on assets are shown as a net amount of other finance costs (or income) adjacent to interest.

k The expected return is calculated by applying the expected rate of return over the long term to the market value of scheme assets at the beginning of the year, adjusted for any contributions received and benefits paid during the year. Although the expected rate of return will vary according to market conditions it is expected that the amount of the return will normally be relatively stable.

Actuarial gains and losses are recognised immediately in the statement of total recognised gains and losses. They are not recycled into the profit and loss account in subsequent periods. **l**

Past service costs are recognised in the profit and loss account over the period until the benefits vest. If the benefits vest immediately, the past service cost is recognised immediately. **m**

Gains and losses arising on settlements and curtailments are recognised immediately in the profit and loss account. **n**

Disclosures for defined benefit schemes

The following disclosures are required: **o**

(i) the principal assumptions underlying the scheme;
(ii) a reconciliation of the opening and closing balances of the fair value of scheme assets and the opening and closing balances of scheme liabilities showing effects during the period which gave rise to the movement in the opening and closing balances;
(iii) for each major category of scheme assets the percentage or the amount that each major category constitutes of the fair value of the total scheme assets;
(iv) a narrative description of the basis used to determine the overall expected rate of return on assets; and
(v) the amounts for the current and previous four periods of the present value of the scheme liabilities, the fair value of the scheme assets and the surplus or deficit in the scheme.*

Financial Reporting Standard 17

OBJECTIVE

The objective of this FRS is to ensure that: **1**

(a) financial statements reflect at fair value the assets and liabilities arising from an employer's retirement benefit obligations and any related funding;
(b) the operating costs of providing retirement benefits to employees are recognised in the accounting period(s) in which the benefits are earned by the employees, and the related finance costs and any other changes in value of the assets and liabilities are recognised in the accounting periods in which they arise; and
(c) the financial statements contain adequate disclosure of the cost of providing retirement benefits and the related gains, losses, assets and liabilities.

***Editor's note:** Changed with effect for accounting periods beginning on or after 6 April 2007 as a result of the Amendment to FRS 17* Retirement Benefits *issued in December 2006.*

DEFINITIONS

2 The following definitions shall apply in the FRS and in particular in the Statement of Standard Accounting Practice set out **in bold type**.

Actuarial gains and losses:-

Changes in actuarial deficits or surpluses that arise because:

(a) events have not coincided with the actuarial assumptions made for the last valuation (experience gains and losses) or

(b) the actuarial assumptions have changed.

Current service cost:-

The increase in the present value of the scheme liabilities expected to arise from employee service in the current period.

Curtailment:-

An event that reduces the expected years of future service of present employees or reduces for a number of employees the accrual of defined benefits for some or all of their future service. Curtailments include:

(a) termination of employees' services earlier than expected, for example as a result of closing a factory or discontinuing a segment of a business, and

(b) termination of, or amendment to the terms of, a defined benefit scheme so that some or all future service by current employees will no longer qualify for benefits or will qualify only for reduced benefits.

Defined benefit scheme:-

A pension or other retirement benefit scheme other than a defined contribution scheme.

Usually, the scheme rules define the benefits independently of the contributions payable, and the benefits are not directly related to the investments of the scheme. The scheme may be funded or unfunded.

Defined contribution scheme:-

A pension or other retirement benefit scheme into which an employer pays regular contributions fixed as an amount or as a percentage of pay and will have no legal or constructive obligation to pay further contributions if the scheme does not have sufficient assets to pay all employee benefits relating to employee service in the current and prior periods.

An individual member's benefits are determined by reference to contributions paid into the scheme in respect of that member, usually increased by an amount based on the investment return on those contributions.

Defined contribution schemes may also provide death-in-service benefits. For the purposes of this definition, death-in-service benefits are not deemed to relate to employee service in the current and prior periods.

Expected rate of return on assets:-

The average rate of return, including both income and changes in fair value but net of scheme expenses, expected over the remaining life of the related obligation on the actual assets held by the scheme.

Interest cost:-

The expected increase during the period in the present value of the scheme liabilities because the benefits are one period closer to settlement.

Past service cost:-

The increase in the present value of the scheme liabilities related to employee service in prior periods arising in the current period as a result of the introduction of, or improvement to, retirement benefits.

Projected unit method:-

An accrued benefits valuation method in which the scheme liabilities make allowance for projected earnings. An accrued benefits valuation method is a valuation method in which the scheme liabilities at the valuation date relate to:

(a) the benefits for pensioners and deferred pensioners (ie individuals who have ceased to be active members but are entitled to benefits payable at a later date) and their dependants, allowing where appropriate for future increases, and
(b) the accrued benefits for members in service on the valuation date.

The accrued benefits are the benefits for service up to a given point in time, whether vested rights or not.

Guidance on the projected unit method is given in the Guidance Note GN26 issued by the Faculty and Institute of Actuaries.

Retirement benefits:-

All forms of consideration given by an employer in exchange for services rendered by employees that are payable after the completion of employment.

Retirement benefits do not include termination benefits payable as a result of either (i) an employer's decision to terminate an employee's employment before the normal retirement date or (ii) an employee's decision to accept voluntary redundancy in exchange for those benefits, because these are not given in exchange for services rendered by employees.

Scheme liabilities:-

The liabilities of a defined benefit scheme for outgoings due after the valuation date.

Scheme liabilities measured using the projected unit method reflect the benefits that the employer is committed to provide for service up to the valuation date.

Settlement:-

An irrevocable action that relieves the employer (or the defined benefit scheme) of the primary responsibility for a pension obligation and eliminates significant risks relating to the obligation and the assets used to effect the settlement. Settlements include:

(a) a lump-sum cash payment to scheme members in exchange for their rights to receive specified pension benefits;
(b) the purchase of an irrevocable annuity contract sufficient to cover vested benefits; and
(c) the transfer of scheme assets and liabilities relating to a group of employees leaving the scheme.

Vested rights:-

These are:

(a) for active members, benefits to which they would unconditionally be entitled on leaving the scheme;
(b) for deferred pensioners, their preserved benefits;
(c) for pensioners, pensions to which they are entitled.

Vested rights include where appropriate the related benefits for spouses or other dependants.

SCOPE

3 **The FRS applies to all financial statements that are intended to give a true and fair view of a reporting employer's financial position and profit or loss (or income and expenditure) for a period.**

4 The FRS covers all retirement benefits that an employer is committed to providing, whether the commitment is statutory, contractual or implicit in the employer's actions. It applies to retirement benefits arising overseas, as well as those arising in the UK and the Republic of Ireland. Retirement benefits include, for example, pensions and medical care during retirement.

5 The FRS covers funded and unfunded retirement benefits, including schemes that are operated on a pay-as-you-go basis, whereby benefits are paid by the employer in the period they fall due and no payments are made to fund benefits earned in the period. The FRS requires a liability to be recognised as the benefits are earned, not when they are due to be paid. The fact that the employer is funded by central government (or any other body) is not a reason for the employer not to recognise its own liabilities arising under the FRS.

6 **Reporting entities applying the Financial Reporting Standard for Smaller Entities currently applicable are exempt from the FRS.**

DEFINED CONTRIBUTION SCHEMES

7 **The cost of a defined contribution scheme is equal to the contributions payable to the scheme for the accounting period. The cost should be recognised within operating profit in the profit and loss account.**

MULTI-EMPLOYER SCHEMES

Where more than one employer participates in a defined contribution scheme, no special problems arise, since the employer's cost is limited to the contributions payable. 8

Where more than one employer participates in a defined benefit scheme the employer should account for the scheme as a defined benefit scheme unless: 9

(a) the employer's contributions are set in relation to the current service period only (ie are not affected by any surplus or deficit in the scheme relating to past service of its own employees or any other members of the scheme). If this is the case, the employer should account for the contributions to the scheme as if it were a defined contribution scheme.

(b) the employer's contributions are affected by a surplus or deficit in the scheme but the employer is unable to identify its share of the underlying assets and liabilities in the scheme on a consistent and reasonable basis. If this is the case, the employer should account for the contributions to the scheme as if it were a defined contribution scheme but, in addition, disclose:

(i) the fact that the scheme is a defined benefit scheme;
(ii) then reason why sufficient information is not available to enable the employer to account for the scheme as a defined benefit scheme;
(iii) any available information about that surplus or deficit;
(iv) the basis used to determine that surplus or deficit;
(v) the implications, if any, for the employer.*

Most multi-employer schemes will set contributions from employers so as to make good any deficit in the scheme and may reduce contributions to enable employers to benefit from a surplus. However, in some multi-employer schemes, an employer may have no obligation other than to pay a contribution that reflects only the benefits earned in the current period. In this case, from the point of view of the employer, the scheme is a defined contribution scheme and is accounted for as such. For this to be the case, there must be clear evidence that the employer cannot be required to pay additional contributions to the scheme relating to past service, including the existence of a third party that accepts that it has an obligation to fund the pension payments should the scheme have insufficient assets. 10

An employer may be required to make contributions set at a level to make good any deficit but may be unable to identify its share of the underlying assets and liabilities in the scheme on a consistent and reasonable basis. This may be the case if the scheme exposes the participating employers to actuarial risks associated with the current and former employees of other entities, for example when the contributions from employers are set at a common level rather than reflecting the characteristics of the workforces of individual employers. 11

Subsidiaries are not exempt from the FRS and, where possible, will account for defined benefit schemes in accordance with its requirements. However, many group schemes are run on a basis that does not enable individual companies within the group to identify their share of the underlying assets and liabilities. In these circumstances, the individual companies (including the parent company) within the group will account for the scheme as a defined contribution scheme and will give the additional disclosures required above. From the point of view of the group entity, a 12

**Editor's note: Changed with effect for accounting periods beginning on or after 6 April 2007 as a result of the Amendment to FRS 17* Retirement Benefits *issued in December 2006.*

group defined benefit scheme is not a multi-employer scheme and is treated as any other defined benefit scheme.

MEASUREMENT OF DEFINED BENEFIT SCHEMES

13 Paragraphs 14–36 of the FRS set out the requirements for measuring the assets and liabilities within a defined benefit scheme (the scheme assets and the scheme liabilities). The recognition of an asset or liability and the movements therein in the financial statements of the employer arising from the defined benefit scheme measured on this basis is covered in paragraphs 37–74.

Scheme assets

14 **Assets in a defined benefit scheme should be measured at their fair value at the balance sheet date.**

15 Scheme assets include current assets as well as investments. Any liabilities such as accrued expenses should be deducted.

16 For quoted securities, the current bid price is taken as the fair value. For unquoted securities, an estimate of fair value is used. The fair value of unitised securities is taken to be the current bid price.*

17 Property should be valued at open market value or on another appropriate basis of valuation determined in accordance with the Appraisal and Valuation Manual published by the Royal Institution of Chartered Surveyors and the Practice Statements contained therein.

18 Insurance policies that exactly match the amount and timing of some or all of the benefits payable under the scheme should be measured at the same amount as the related obligations. For other insurance policies there are a number of possible valuation methods. A method should be chosen which gives the best approximation to fair value given the circumstances of the scheme.

19 Notional funding of a pension scheme does not give rise to assets in a scheme for the purposes of the FRS.

Scheme liabilities

Actuarial method and assumptions

20 **Defined benefit scheme liabilities should be measured on an actuarial basis using the projected unit method. The scheme liabilities comprise:**

(a) any benefits promised under the formal terms of the scheme; and
(b) any constructive obligations for further benefits where a public statement or past practice by the employer has created a valid expectation in the employees that such benefits will be granted.

21 Where the scheme rules require a surplus arising in the scheme to be shared between the employer and members (perhaps in conjunction with a similar sharing of deficits), or where past practice has established a valid expectation that this will be done, the

__Editor's note__: Changed with effect for accounting periods beginning on or after 1 January 2009.

amount that will be passed to members should be treated as increasing the scheme liabilities.

The benefits should be attributed to periods of service according to the scheme's benefit formula, except where the benefit formula attributes a disproportionate share of the total benefits to later years of service. In such cases, the benefit should be attributed on a straight-line basis over the period during which it is earned. 22

The assumptions underlying the valuation should be mutually compatible and lead to the best estimate of the future cash flows that will arise under the scheme liabilities. The assumptions are ultimately the responsibility of the directors (or equivalent) but should be set upon advice given by an actuary. Any assumptions that are affected by economic conditions (financial assumptions) should reflect market expectations at the balance sheet date. 23

Because of the long-term nature of most defined benefit schemes and the inherent uncertainties affecting them, the liabilities of the scheme are measured on an actuarial basis. This involves estimating the future cash flows arising under the scheme liabilities based on a number of actuarial assumptions such as mortality rates, employee turnover rates and salary growth, then discounting the cash flows at an appropriate rate. 24

Some of these assumptions are affected by the same economic factors. Actuarial assumptions are mutually compatible if they reflect the underlying economic factors consistently. To be consistent with the measurement of the assets of the scheme at fair value, they must also reflect market expectations at the balance sheet date. 25

For example, the rate of increase in salaries and the discount rate must reflect the same rate of general inflation. In jurisdictions where there is a liquid market in long-dated inflation-linked bonds, the yields on such bonds relative to those on fixed interest bonds of similar credit standing will give an indication of the expected rate of general inflation. 26

The actuarial assumptions should reflect expected future events that will affect the cost of the benefits to which the employer is committed (either legally or through a constructive obligation) at the balance sheet date. 27

Expected future events that will affect the cost of the benefits include: 28

(a) any expected cost of living increases either provided for in the scheme rules, publicly announced or awarded under an established practice that creates among the employees a valid expectation of receiving them;
(b) in the case of pensions based on final salary, any expected salary increases; and
(c) expected early retirement where the employee has that right under the scheme rules.

These events affect the measurement of benefits to which the employer is committed at the balance sheet date.

Expected future redundancies are not reflected in the actuarial assumptions because the employer is not committed (either legally or constructively) to making such redundancies in advance. When the employer does become committed to making the redundancies, any impact on the defined benefit scheme is treated as a settlement and/or curtailment (see paragraph 64). 29

30 Expected future changes in the cost of retirement healthcare are particularly difficult to estimate—the cost often increases at a faster rate than either the retail price index or national earnings rate. Relevant considerations in determining the assumptions used to arrive at the retirement healthcare obligation include:

(a) advances in medical skills and technologies, often involving more expensive treatment;
(b) the rise in the expectations of prospective patients; and
(c) the effect of the above on companies, governments and insurance schemes in cutting back benefits, or making the patient pay a proportion.

31 It is not appropriate to assume a reduction in benefits below those currently promised on the grounds that the employer will curtail the scheme at some time in the future.

The discount rate

32 **Defined benefit scheme liabilities should be discounted at a rate that reflects the time value of money and the characteristics of the liability. Such a rate should be assumed to be the current rate of return on a high quality corporate bond of equivalent currency and term to the scheme liabilities.**

33 For this purpose, a high quality corporate bond means a bond that has been rated at the level of AA or equivalent status. The rate of return for such a bond reflects the time value of money and a small premium for risk. That premium is taken to reflect the options that the employer has to reduce the assumed scheme liabilities, including in extremis the option of closing down the scheme. If there is no liquid market in bonds of this type or duration, then a reasonable proxy should be used. This may be government bonds plus a margin for assumed credit risk spreads derived from global bond markets.

34 Many pension schemes provide benefits at least partly linked to inflation. One way to reflect that characteristic would be to consider the return on an index-linked corporate bond. However, given that there are few such bonds in existence, a more reliable alternative is to consider fixed interest corporate bonds and increase the cash flows to be discounted in line with inflation (ie project the liability to be discounted in nominal terms). Guidance on the inflation assumption is given in paragraph 26.

Frequency of valuations

35 **Full actuarial valuations by a professionally qualified actuary should be obtained for a defined benefit scheme at intervals not exceeding three years. The actuary should review the most recent actuarial valuation at the balance sheet date and update it to reflect current conditions.**

36 The actuarial valuations required for the FRS may use different assumptions and measurement methods from those used for a scheme's funding valuation. Full actuarial valuations under the FRS are not needed at every balance sheet date. Some aspects of the valuation will need to be updated at each balance sheet date, for example the fair value of the assets and financial assumptions such as the discount rate. Other assumptions, such as the expected leaving rate and mortality rate, may not need to be updated annually.

RECOGNITION OF DEFINED BENEFIT SCHEMES

Recognition in the balance sheet

The surplus/deficit in a defined benefit scheme is the excess/shortfall of the value of the assets in the scheme over/below the present value of the scheme liabilities. The employer should recognise an asset to the extent that it is able to recover a surplus either through reduced contributions in the future or through refunds from the scheme. The employer should recognise a liability to the extent that it reflects its legal or constructive obligation. **37**

A surplus in the scheme gives rise to an asset of the employer to the extent that: **38**

(a) the employer controls its use, ie has the ability to use the surplus to generate future economic benefits for itself, either in the form of a reduction in future contributions or a refund from the scheme; and

(b) that control is a result of past events (contributions paid by the employer and investment growth in excess of rights earned by the employees).

Usually the employer's obligation under the trust deed is to pay such contributions as the actuary believes to be necessary to keep the scheme fully funded but without building up a surplus. When a surplus arises, it is unlikely that the employer can be required to make contributions to maintain the surplus. In addition, the award of benefit improvements is also usually in the hands of the employer. Thus, in general, the employer controls the use of a surplus in the scheme.

Conversely, the employer has a liability if it has a legal or constructive obligation to make good a deficit in the defined benefit scheme. In general, the employer will either have a legal obligation under the terms of the scheme trust deed or will have by its past actions and statements created a constructive obligation as defined in FRS 12 'Provisions, Contingent Liabilities and Contingent Assets'. The legal or constructive obligation to fund the deficit should be assumed to apply to the deficit based on assumptions used under the FRS. **39**

In a scheme where employees as well as the employer make contributions, any deficit should be assumed to be borne by the employer unless the scheme rules require members' contributions to be increased to help fund a deficit. In this case, the present value of the required additional contributions should be treated as reducing the deficit to be recognised by the employer. **40**

In determining the asset to be recognised in accordance with paragraph 37, the amount that can be recovered through reduced contributions in the future is the present value of the liability expected to arise from future service by current and future scheme members less the present value of future employee contributions. No growth in the number of active scheme members should be assumed but a declining membership should be reflected if appropriate. The amount that can be recovered should be based on the assumptions used under the FRS, not the funding assumptions. The present value of the reduction in future contributions is determined using the discount rate applied to measure the defined benefit liability. **41**

The amount to be recovered from refunds from the scheme should reflect only refunds that have been agreed by the pension scheme trustees at the balance sheet date. **42**

The employer may not control or be able to benefit from the whole of a surplus—it may be so large that the employer cannot absorb it all through reduced contributions, and refunds from the scheme may be difficult to obtain. **43**

44 The amount recoverable through reduced contributions reflects the maximum possible to be recovered without assuming an increase in the number of employees covered by the scheme. There is no restriction on the period over which the reduction in contributions can be obtained, but the effect of discounting will increasingly reduce the impact of the reductions the further into the future they are, leading to an absolute limit on the amount that can be recognised equal to the service cost divided by the discount rate.

45 In practice, a surplus that potentially could be recovered will instead often be used in part to provide benefit improvements to members, thereby reducing the amount that the employer recovers through reduced contributions. The use of a potentially recoverable surplus in this way should be treated as a past service cost when it occurs (see paragraph 60) and not anticipated by reducing the amount recognised as an asset.

46 Paragraphs 67–70 specify how the limit on the amount that can be recognised as an asset should be recognised in the performance statements.

47 **Any unpaid contributions to the scheme should be presented in the balance sheet as a creditor due within one year. The defined benefit asset or liability should be presented separately on the face of the balance sheet:**

(a) in balance sheets of the type prescribed for companies in the United Kingdom by The Large and Medium-sized Companies and Groups (Accounts and Reports) Regulations 2008, Schedule 1, format 1: after item J Accruals and deferred income but before item K Capital and reserves; and

(b) in balance sheets of the type prescribed for companies in the United Kingdom by The Large and Medium-sized Companies and Groups (Accounts and Reports) Regulations 2008, Schedule 1, format 2: any asset after ASSETS item D Prepayments and accrued income and any liability after LIABILITIES item D Accruals and deferred income.*

Where an employer has more than one scheme, the total of any defined benefit assets and the total of any defined benefit liabilities should be shown separately on the face of the balance sheet.

48 [Withdrawn]†

49 **The deferred tax relating to the defined benefit asset or liability should be offset against the defined benefit asset or liability and not included with other deferred tax assets or liabilities.**

Recognition in the performance statements

50 **The change in the defined benefit asset or liability (other than that arising from contributions to the scheme) should be analysed into the following components:**

PERIODIC COSTS

(a) the current service cost;

(b) the interest cost;

(c) the expected return on assets;

(d) actuarial gains and losses;

****Editor's note:*** *Statutory reference amended by ASB Editorial Correction.*

†***Editor's note:*** *Withdrawn as a result of the Amendment to FRS 17* Retirement Benefits *issued in December 2006.*

NON-PERIODIC COSTS

(e) past service costs; and

(f) gains and losses on settlements and curtailments.

Current service cost, interest cost and expected return on assets

The current service cost should be based on the most recent actuarial valuation at the beginning of the period, with the financial assumptions updated to reflect conditions at that date. It should be included within operating profit in the profit and loss account (except insofar as the related employee remuneration is capitalised in accordance with another accounting standard). Any contributions from employees should be set off against the current service cost. 51

The current service cost will be based on the discount rate at the beginning of the period and will therefore reflect current long-term market interest rates at that time. 52

The interest cost should be based on the discount rate and the present value of the scheme liabilities at the beginning of the period. The interest cost should, in addition, reflect changes in the scheme liabilities during the period. 53

The expected return on assets is based on long-term expectations at the beginning of the period and is expected to be reasonably stable. For quoted corporate or government bonds, the expected return should be calculated by applying the current redemption yield at the beginning of the period to the market value of the bonds held by the scheme at the beginning of the period. For other assets (for example, equities), the expected return should be calculated by applying the rate of return expected over the long term at the beginning of the period (given the value of the assets at that date) to the fair value of the assets held by the scheme at the beginning of the period. The expected return on assets should, in addition, reflect changes in the assets in the scheme during the period as a result of contributions paid into and benefits paid out of the scheme. The expected rate of return should be set by the directors (or equivalent) having taken advice from an actuary. 54

For quoted fixed and index-linked securities, the expected return can be observed from the market. For other assets, the expected return has to be based on assumptions about the expected long-term rate of return. The rate of return expected over the long term will vary according to market conditions, but it is expected that the amount of the return will be reasonably stable. 55

The net of the interest cost and the expected return on assets should be included as other finance costs (or income) adjacent to interest. 56

Actuarial gains and losses

Actuarial gains and losses arising from any new valuation and from updating the latest actuarial valuation to reflect conditions at the balance sheet date should be recognised in the statement of total recognised gains and losses for the period. 57

Actuarial gains and losses may arise on both the defined benefit scheme liabilities and any scheme assets. They comprise: 58

(a) on the scheme assets, differences between the expected return and the actual return (for example, a sudden change in the value of the scheme assets);

(b) on the scheme liabilities, (i) differences between the actuarial assumptions underlying the scheme liabilities and actual experience during the period and (ii) the effect of changes in actuarial assumptions; and

(c) any adjustment necessary in accordance with paragraph 67 resulting from the limit on the amount that can be recognised as an asset in the balance sheet.

59 Once an actuarial gain or loss has been recognised in the statement of total recognised gains and losses it is not recognised again in the profit and loss account in subsequent periods.

Past service costs

60 **Past service costs should be recognised in the profit and loss account on a straight-line basis over the period in which the increases in benefit vest. To the extent that the benefits vest immediately, the past service cost should be recognised immediately. Any unrecognised past service costs should be deducted from the scheme liabilities and the balance sheet asset or liability adjusted accordingly.**

61 Past service costs arise when the employer makes a commitment to provide a higher level of benefit than previously promised, for example the creation of a pension benefit for a spouse where such a benefit did not previously exist or a grant of early retirement with added-on years of service.

62 Past service costs do not include increases in the expected cost of benefits that the employer is already statutorily, contractually or implicitly committed to, for example cost of living increases to pensions in payment and deferred pensions. Such increases are covered by the actuarial assumptions and any difference between actual experience and the assumptions or the effects of any changes in the assumptions are actuarial gains and losses.

63 Past service costs include benefit improvements awarded as a result of a surplus arising in the scheme. The fact that they are funded out of a surplus does not result in there being no cost to the employer if the surplus was potentially recoverable by the employer—the use of the surplus for benefit improvements means that the employer cannot then benefit from it in other ways.

Settlements and curtailments

64 **Losses arising on a settlement or curtailment not allowed for in the actuarial assumptions should be measured at the date on which the employer becomes demonstrably committed to the transaction and recognised in the profit and loss account covering that date. Gains arising on a settlement or curtailment not allowed for in the actuarial assumptions should be measured at the date on which all parties whose consent is required are irrevocably committed to the transaction and recognised in the profit and loss account covering that date.**

65 Where under the scheme rules the employees have the option to retire early or transfer out of the scheme, the resulting settlements and curtailments are allowed for in the normal demographic assumptions made by the actuary and any gains and losses arising are actuarial gains and losses.

66 In contrast, some settlements and curtailments arise from specific decisions made by an employer that are not covered by actuarial assumptions, for example major changes in the circumstances of the scheme instigated by the employer, such as the transfer of accrued benefits of some or all the members into a defined contribution

scheme or a reduction in employees because of the sale or termination of an operation. Gains and losses arising from such events are part of the employer's operating results for the period (unless they attach to one of the items shown immediately after operating profit).

Impact of limit on balance sheet asset

The limit set out in paragraph 41 on the amount that can be recognised as an asset may result in there being some part of a defined benefit scheme surplus that is not recognised. Where this is the case, the amounts recognised in the performance statements should be adjusted as follows. 67

(a) **First, if any refund is agreed and is covered by the unrecognised surplus, it should be recognised as other finance income adjacent to interest, with separate disclosure in the notes.**

Refunds from schemes where the whole surplus is regarded as recoverable do not give rise to gains. The cash received simply reduces the balance sheet asset (along with any related tax effect).

(b) **Next, the unrecognised surplus should be applied to extinguish past service costs or losses on settlements or curtailments that would otherwise be charged in the profit and loss account for the period, with disclosure in the notes of the items and amounts so extinguished.**

(c) **Next, the expected return on assets should be restricted so that it does not exceed the total of the current service cost, interest cost (and any past service costs and losses on settlements and curtailments not covered by the unrecognised surplus) and any increase in the recoverable surplus.**

(d) **Finally, any further adjustment necessary should be treated as an actuarial gain or loss.**

An increase in the recoverable amount of a surplus arising from an increase in the active membership of the scheme should be recognised as an operating gain. 68

An increase in the active membership can arise either from an increase in general recruitment or from the transfer of employees following an acquisition. The gain arising in the latter case is a post-acquisition operating gain, not an adjustment to the purchase price and goodwill. 69

A decrease in the recoverable amount of a surplus arising from a fall in the active membership should be treated as an actuarial loss unless it arises from an event not covered by the assumptions underlying the amount originally regarded as recoverable, for example a settlement or curtailment. If it does arise from such an event, it should be treated as part of the loss arising on that event. 70

Tax

When current tax relief arises on contributions made to a defined benefit scheme, it should be allocated to the profit and loss account or statement of total recognised gains and losses on the basis that the contribution covers first the items reported in the profit and loss account and then any actuarial losses reported in the statement of total recognised gains and losses, unless it is clear that some other allocation is more appropriate. To the extent that the contribution exceeds these items, the current tax relief attributable to the excess should be allocated to the profit and loss account, again unless it is clearly more appropriate to allocate it to the statement of total recognised gains and losses. 71

72 Current tax relief is usually available on contributions paid to the scheme and deferred tax usually arises on the balance of the charges/credits. The tax follows the relevant item, ie tax on the service cost, interest cost and expected return on assets will be recognised in the profit and loss account and tax on the actuarial gains and losses will be recognised in the statement of total recognised gains and losses. FRS 16 'Current Tax' requires disclosure of the current tax recognised in the profit and loss account and statement of total recognised gains and losses. The question arises of where the current tax relief arising on contributions should be deemed to belong. Sometimes it will be clear what the contribution relates to, for example when a special contribution is made to fund a deficit arising from an identifiable cause, say an actuarial loss, in which case the current tax relief should be allocated to the statement of total recognised gains and losses. In the absence of a clear link between the contribution and the items recognised in the performance statements, the allocation in paragraph 71 should be followed.

Death-in-service and incapacity benefits

73 **A charge should be made to operating profit to reflect the expected cost of providing any death-in-service or incapacity benefits for the period. Any difference between that expected cost and amounts actually incurred should be treated as an actuarial gain or loss.**

74 Where a scheme insures the death-in-service costs, the expected cost for the accounting period is simply the premium payable for the period. Where the costs are not insured, the expected cost reflects the probability of any employees dying in the period and the benefit that would then be paid out.

DISCLOSURES

Defined contribution schemes

75 **The following disclosures should be made in respect of a defined contribution scheme:**

(a) the nature of the scheme (ie defined contribution);
(b) the cost for the period; and
(c) any outstanding or prepaid contributions at the balance sheet date.

76 **An employer shall disclose information that enables users of financial statements to evaluate the nature of its defined benefit schemes and the financial effects of changes in those schemes during the period.**

77 **An employer shall disclose the following information about defined benefit schemes:**

(a) a general description of the type of scheme.
(b) a reconciliation of opening and closing balances of the present value of scheme liabilities showing separately, if applicable, the effects during the period attributable to each of the following:

(i) current service cost,
(ii) interest cost,
(iii) contributions by scheme participants,
(iv) actuarial gains and losses,
(v) foreign currency exchange rate changes on schemes measured in a currency different from the entity's presentation* currency,

**ASB Note: For entities that apply SSAP 20 'Foreign Currency Translation' the phrase 'entity's presentation currency' should be replaced with 'entity's local currency'.*

(vi) benefits paid,
(vii) past service cost,
(viii) business combinations,
(ix) curtailments, and
(x) settlements.

(c) an analysis of scheme liabilities into amounts arising from schemes that are wholly unfunded and amounts arising from schemes that are wholly or partly funded.

(d) a reconciliation of the opening and closing balances of the fair value of scheme assets showing separately, if applicable, the effects during the period attributable to each of the following:

(i) expected rate of return on scheme assets,
(ii) actuarial gains and losses,
(iii) foreign currency exchange rate changes on schemes measured in a currency different from the entity's presentation* currency,
(iv) contributions by the employer,
(v) contributions by scheme participants,
(vi) benefits paid,
(vii) business combinations and
(viii) settlements.

(e) a reconciliation of the present value of scheme liabilities in (b) and the fair value of the scheme assets in (d) to the assets and liabilities recognised in the balance sheet, showing at least:

(i) any past service cost not recognised in the balance sheet (see paragraph 60);
(ii) any amount not recognised as an asset, because of the limit in paragraph 41; and
(iii) any other amounts recognised in the balance sheet.

(f) the total expense recognised in profit or loss for each of the following, and the line item(s) in which they are included:

(i) current service cost;
(ii) interest cost;
(iii) expected return on scheme assets;
(iv) past service cost;
(v) the effect of any curtailment or settlement; and
(vi) the effect of the limit in paragraph 41.

(g) the total amounts recognised in the statement of total recognised gains and losses for each of the following:

(i) actuarial gains and losses; and
(ii) the effect of the limit in paragraph 41.

(h) the cumulative amount of actuarial gains and losses recognised in the statement of total recognised gains and losses.

(i) for each major category of scheme assets, which shall include, but is not limited to, equity instruments, debt instruments, property, and all other assets, the percentage or amount that each major category constitutes of the fair value of the total scheme assets.

(j) the amounts included in the fair value of scheme assets for:

(i) each category of the entity's own financial instruments; and
(ii) any property occupied by, or other assets used by, the entity.

**ASB Note: For entities that apply SSAP 20 'Foreign Currency Translation' the phrase 'entity's presentation currency' should be replaced with 'entity's local currency'.*

(k) a narrative description of the basis used to determine the overall expected rate of return on assets, including the effect of the major categories of scheme assets.

(l) the actual return on scheme assets.

(m) the principal actuarial assumptions used as at the balance sheet date, including, when applicable:

(i) the discount rates;

(ii) the expected rates of return on any assets of the scheme for the periods presented in the financial statements*;

(iii) the expected rates of salary increases (and of changes in an index or other variable specified in the formal or constructive terms of a scheme as the basis for future benefit increases);

(iv) retirement healthcare cost trend rates; and

(v) any other material actuarial assumptions used.

An employer shall disclose each actuarial assumption in absolute terms (for example, as an absolute percentage) and not just as a margin between different percentages or other variables.

(n) the effect of an increase of one percentage point and the effect of a decrease of one percentage point in the assumed retirement healthcare cost trend rates on:

(i) the aggregate of the current service cost and interest cost components of net periodic retirement healthcare costs; and

(ii) the accumulated retirement healthcare obligation for healthcare costs.

For the purposes of this disclosure, all other assumptions shall be held constant. For schemes operating in a high inflation environment, the disclosure shall be the effect of a percentage increase or decrease in the assumed healthcare cost trend rate of a significance similar to one percentage point in a low inflation environment.

(o) the amounts for the current accounting period and previous four accounting periods of:

(i) the present value of the scheme liabilities, the fair value of the scheme assets and the surplus or deficit in the scheme; and

(ii) the experience adjustments arising on:

(A) the scheme liabilities expressed either as (1) an amount or (2) a percentage of the scheme liabilities at the balance sheet date and

(B) the assets of the scheme expressed either as (1) an amount or (2) a percentage of the assets of the scheme at the balance sheet date.

(p) the employer's best estimate, as soon as it can reasonably be determined, of contributions expected to be paid to the scheme during the accounting period beginning after the balance sheet date.

78 Paragraph 77(a) requires a general description of the type of scheme. Such a description distinguishes, for example, flat salary pension schemes from final salary pension schemes and from retirement healthcare schemes. The description of the scheme shall include informal practices that give rise to constructive obligations included in the measurement of the scheme liabilities in accordance with paragraph 20(b). Further detail is not required.

79 When an employer has more than one defined benefit scheme, disclosures may be made in total, separately for each scheme, or in such groupings as are considered to be the most useful. It may be useful to distinguish groupings by criteria such as the following:

**ASB note: This requirement is for information as at the beginning of each period presented.*

(a) the geographical location of the schemes, for example, by distinguishing domestic schemes from foreign schemes; or
(b) whether schemes are subject to materially different risks, for example, by distinguishing flat salary pension schemes from final salary pension schemes and from retirement healthcare schemes.

When an employer provides disclosures in total for a grouping of schemes, such disclosures are provided in the form of weighted averages or of relatively narrow ranges.

Paragraph 9(b) requires additional disclosures about multi-employer defined benefit schemes that are treated as if they were defined contribution schemes. 80

Where required by FRS 8 'Related Party Disclosures' an employer discloses information about related party transactions with retirement benefit schemes. 81

Where required by FRS 12 'Provisions, Contingent Liabilities and Contingent Assets' an employer discloses information about contingent liabilities arising from retirement benefit obligations. 82

DATE FROM WHICH EFFECTIVE AND TRANSITIONAL ARRANGEMENTS

The following amounts, measured in accordance with the requirements of the FRS, should be disclosed in the notes to the financial statements: 94

(a) for financial statements relating to accounting periods ending on or after 22 June 2001: the disclosures required by paragraphs 76–81 and 88–93 of the FRS relating to the closing balance sheet (without comparatives for the previous period);
(b) in addition, for financial statements relating to accounting periods ending on or after 22 June 2002:
  (i) the disclosures required by paragraphs 76–81 and 88–93 of the FRS relating to the opening balance sheet (without comparatives for the previous period);
  (ii) the disclosures required by paragraphs 82–85 of the FRS relating to the performance statements (without comparatives for the previous period); and
  (iii) the disclosures required by paragraph 86 for the current period only.
(c) In addition, for financial statements relating to accounting periods ending on or after 22 June 2003, the disclosures required by paragraphs 82–85 for the comparative period and the disclosures required by paragraph 86 for periods ending on or after 22 June 2002.

None of these amounts need be recognised in the primary statements in these financial statements.

Subject to the requirements of paragraphs 95A to 95C below, all the requirements of the FRS should be regarded as standard for accounting periods beginning on or after 1 January 2005. Early adoption is encouraged.* 95

The requirements of this amendment (which has amended paragraphs 9b, 16 and paragraphs 76 to 82) become effective for financial statements covering periods beginning on or after 6 April 2007. In accordance with FRS 28 "Corresponding 95A

****Editor's note****: Changed with effect for accounting periods beginning on or after 6 April 2007 as a result of the Amendment to FRS 17*Retirement Benefits *issued in December 2006.*

Amounts" this amendment requires corresponding amounts. Early adoption is encouraged.

95B **Paragraph 77(h) of the FRS requires disclosure of the cumulative amount of actuarial gains and losses recognised in the statement of total recognised gains and losses. The amount to be disclosed should be the amount recognised in the statement of total recognised gains and losses for accounting periods ending on or after 22 June 2002 and subsequently included by prior year adjustment under paragraph 96 of the FRS.**

95C **Paragraph 77(o) of the FRS requires disclosure for the current accounting period and previous four accounting periods of the fair value of the scheme assets. This amendment changes paragraph 16 of the FRS and requires quoted securities to be valued at current bid-price. An entity is not required to restate corresponding amounts for the first two of the previous four accounting periods required by paragraph 77(o). Where an entity selects not to restate corresponding amounts it should disclose that corresponding amounts are not restated.**

95D Paragraph 16 was amended by 'Improvements to FRS' in December 2008. An entity shall apply that amendment for accounting periods beginning on or after 1 January 2009. If an entity applies the amendment for an earlier period, it shall disclose that fact. Consistent with paragraph 95C, an entity is not required to restate corresponding amounts for the first two of the previous four accounting periods required by paragraph 77(o).*

96 **Gains and losses arising on the initial recognition of items in the primary statements under the FRS should be dealt with as prior period adjustments in accordance with FRS 3. It is not required to create retrospectively the five-year history of amounts recognised in the statement of total recognised gains and losses beyond those figures already disclosed in financial statements under paragraph 94 above.**

97 FRS 7 requires the fair value of the deficit or surplus to be recognised as part of a business acquisition. This FRS applies the same policy in requiring the fair value of the defined benefit asset/liability to be recognised. The method of arriving at fair value under this FRS may be different from that previously used on acquisition, but any such difference should be treated as a change in assumptions (ie an actuarial gain or loss) arising since acquisition. Goodwill arising on the acquisition should not, therefore, be restated.

WITHDRAWAL OF SSAP 24 AND UITF ABSTRACTS 6 AND 18 AND AMENDMENT OF OTHER ACCOUNTING STANDARDS

98 **When applied in full, the FRS supersedes SSAP 24 'Accounting for pension costs', UITF Abstract 6 'Accounting for post-retirement benefits other than pensions' and UITF Abstract 18 'Pension costs following the 1997 tax changes in respect of dividend income'.**

99-105 [Not reproduced, as all changes that continue to be relevant have been made to the underlying standards or abstracts.]

* ***Editor's note***: Paragraph added in December 2008.

Adoption of FRS 17 by the board

Financial Reporting Standard 17 'Retirement Benefits' was approved for issue by the ten members of the Accounting Standards Board.

Sir David Tweedie	(Chairman)
Allan Cook CBE	(Technical Director)
David Allvey	
Ian Brindle	
Dr John Buchanan	
John Coombe	
Huw Jones	
Isobel Sharp	
Professor Geoffrey Whittington	
Ken Wild	

Appendix I*
Illustrative Disclosures

This appendix accompanies, but is not part of, FRS 17. Extracts from notes show how the required disclosures may be aggregated in the case of a large multi-national group that provides a variety of employee benefits. These extracts do not necessarily conform with all the disclosure and presentation requirements of FRS 17 and other Standards. In particular, they do not illustrate the disclosure of:

(a) a general description of the type of plan (paragraph 77(a)).
(b) a narrative description of the basis used to determine the overall expected rate of return on assets (paragraph 77(k)).

Employee benefit obligations

The amounts recognised in the balance sheet are as follows:

	Defined benefit pension plans†		Retirement healthcare benefits	
	20X2	*20X1*	*20X2*	*20X1*
Present value of funded obligations	20,300	17,400	–	–
Fair value of plan assets	(18,420)	(17,280)	–	–
	1,880	120	–	–
Present value of unfunded obligations	2,000	1,000	7,337	6,405
Unrecognised past service cost	(450)	(650)	–	–
Deficit	3,430	470	7,337	6,405
Related deferred tax asset‡:	(1,030)	(140)	(2,200)	(1,922)-
Net liability	2,400	330	5,137	4,483

**Editor's note*: *This is the replacement example effective for accounting periods beginning on or after 6 April 2007.*

†ASB Note: FRS 17 refers to 'defined benefit schemes' whereas IAS 19 uses the term 'defined benefit plans'.

‡ASB Note: Paragraph 49 of FRS 17 requires the deferred tax relating to the defined benefit asset or liability to be offset against the defined benefit asset or liability and not included with other deferred tax assets or liabilities. Differences between the asset or liability in the balance sheet and the surplus or deficit in the scheme will arise because of the related deferred tax balance.

Amounts in the balance sheet

Liabilities	2,400	420	5,137	4,483
Assets	–	(90)	–	–
Net liability	2,400	330	5,137	4,483

The pension plan assets include ordinary shares issued by [name of reporting entity] with a fair value of 317 (20X1: 281). Plan assets also include property occupied by [name of reporting entity] with a fair value of 200 (20X1: 185).

> *ASB Note: FRS 17 sets out where changes in the defined benefit asset or liability (other than that arising from contributions to the scheme) should be reported in the performance statements.*

The amounts recognised in profit or loss are as follows:

	Defined benefit pension plans		Retirement healthcare benefits	
	20X2	*20X1*	*20X2*	*20X1*
Current service cost	850	750	479	411
Interest on obligation	950	1,000	803	705
Expected return on plan assets	(900)	(650)		
Past service cost	200	200		
Losses (gains) on curtailments and settlements	175	(390)		
Total	1,275	910	1,282	1,116
Actual return on plan assets	600	2,250	–	–

Changes in the present value of the defined benefit obligation are as follows:

	Defined benefit pension plans		Retirement healthcare benefits	
	20X2	*20X1*	*20X2*	*20X1*
Opening defined benefit obligation	18,400	11,600	6,405	5,439
Service cost	850	750	479	411
Interest cost	950	1,000	803	705
Actuarial losses (gains)	2,350	950	250	400
Losses (gains) on curtailments	(500)	–		
Liabilities extinguished on settlements	–	(350)		
Liabilities assumed in a business combination	–	5,000		
Exchange differences on foreign plans	900	(150)		
Benefits paid	(650)	(400)	(600)	(550)
Closing defined benefit obligation	22,300	18,400	7,337	6,405

Changes in the fair value of plan assets are as follows:

	Defined benefit pension plans	
	20X2	*20X1*
Opening fair value of plan assets	17,280	9,200
Expected return	900	650
Actuarial gains and (losses)	(300)	1,600
Assets distributed on settlements	(400)	–
Contributions by employer	700	350
Assets acquired in a business combination	–	6,000
Exchange differences on foreign plans	890	(120)
Benefits paid	(650)	(400)
	18,420	17,280

The group expects to contribute 900 to its defined benefit pension plans in 20X3.

The major categories of plan assets as a percentage of total plan assets are as follows:

	20X2	*20X1*
European equities	30%	35%
North American equities	16%	15%
European bonds	31%	28%
North American bonds	18%	17%
Property	5%	5%

Principal actuarial assumptions at the balance sheet date (expressed as weighted averages):

	20X2	*20X1*
Discount rate at 31 December	5.0%	6.5%
Expected return on plan assets at 31 December	5.4%	7.0%
Future salary increases	5%	4%
Future pension increases	3%	2%
Proportion of employees opting for early retirement	30%	30%
Annual increase in healthcare costs	8%	8%
Future changes in maximum state healthcare benefits	3%	2%

Assumed healthcare cost trend rates have a significant effect on the amounts recognised in profit or loss. A one percentage point change in assumed healthcare cost trend rates would have the following effects:

	One percentage point increase	One percentage point decrease
Effect on the aggregate of the service cost and interest cost	190	(150)
Effect on defined benefit obligation	1,000	(900)

Amounts for the current and previous four periods are as follows:

Defined benefit pension plans

	20X2	*20X1*	*20X0*	*20W9*	*20W8*
Defined benefit obligation	(22,300)	(18,400)	(11,600)	(10,582)	(9,144)
Plan assets	18,420	17,280	9,200	8,502	10,000
Surplus/(deficit)	(3,880)	(1,120)	(2,400)	(2,080)	856
Experience adjustments on plan liabilities	(1,111)	(768)	(69)	543	(642)
Experience adjustments on plan assets	(300)	1,600	(1,078)	(2,890)	2,777

Retirement healthcare benefits

	20X2	*20X1*	*20X0*	*20W9*	*20W8*
Defined benefit obligation	7,337	6,405	5,439	4,923	4,221
Experience adjustments on plan liabilities	(232)	829	490	(174)	(103)

The group also participates in an industry-wide defined benefit plan that provides pensions linked to final salaries and is funded on a pay-as-you-go basis. It is not practicable to determine the present value of the group's obligation or the related current service cost as the plan computes its obligations on a basis that differs materially from the basis used in [name of reporting entity's] financial statements. [describe basis] On that basis, the plan's financial statements to 30 June 20X0 show an unfunded liability of 27,525. The unfunded liability will result in future payments by participating employers. The plan has approximately 75,000 members, of whom approximately 5,000 are current or former employees of [name of reporting entity] or their dependants. The expense recognised in the income statement, which is equal to contributions due for the year, and is not included in the above amounts, was 230 (20X1: 215). The group's future contributions may be increased substantially if other entities withdraw from the plan.

Appendix II
Note on legal requirements

Great Britain*

1 The statutory requirements relating to the presentation of pension costs in company accounts are set out in the Companies Act 1985. The relevant requirements are contained in Schedule 4 and are summarised below. Schedule 4 to the Act does not apply to banking and insurance companies and groups, nor to small companies to the extent that they choose instead to comply with the reduced requirements set out in Schedule 8. Requirements corresponding to those of Schedule 4 are set out for banking companies and groups in Schedule 9 and for insurance companies and groups in Schedule 9A.

2 The specific references in Schedule 4 include the following:

(a) the balance sheet formats include a heading:
'Provisions for liabilities and charges:†
1 Pensions and similar obligations'.

(b) the profit and loss formats 2 and 4 include a heading:
'Staff costs:
(a) wages and salaries
(b) social security costs
(c) other pension costs'.

(c) When profit and loss formats 1 and 3 are used, paragraph 56(4) requires the information in (b) to be disclosed.

3 Pension costs are defined in paragraph 94 of Schedule 4 as follows:

> '"Pension costs" includes any costs incurred by the company in respect of any pension scheme established for the purpose of providing pensions for persons currently or formerly employed by the company, any sums set aside for the future payment of pensions directly by the company to current or former employees and any pensions paid directly to such persons without having first been set aside.'

4 Paragraph 50(4) requires disclosure of particulars of any pension commitments under any provision shown in the company's balance sheet and any such commitments for which no provision has been made.

***Editor's note:** *The various statutory references change with the introduction of the Companies Act 2006, which affects accounting for periods beginning on or after 6 April 2008. The various statutory references have changed as follows:*

Companies Act 1985 reference	***Companies Act 2006 reference***
Schedule 4	*Schedule 1 to the Large and Medium-sized Companies and Groups (Accounts and Reports) Regulations 2008 (SI 2008/410)*
Schedule 8	*Schedule 1 to The Small Companies and Groups (Accounts and Directors' Report) Regulations 2008 (SI 2008/409)*
Schedules 9 and 9A	*Schedules 2 and 3 to SI 2008/410*
Paragraph 94 of Schedule 4	*Paragraph 14 of Schedule 10 to SI 2008/410*
Paragraph 50 of Schedule 4	*Paragraph 63 of Schedule 1 to SI 2008/410*

†***Editor's note:*** *Now 'provisions for liabilities'.*

5 The requirements in the FRS regarding the recognition of the amounts arising from a defined benefit scheme are that:

(a) the service cost should be presented within operating profit in the profit and loss account;
(b) the interest cost and expected return on assets should be presented as a net financial item in the profit and loss account;
(c) actuarial gains and losses should be recognised in the statement of total recognised gains and losses; and
(d) the net pension asset or liability should be presented separately on the face of the balance sheet following other net assets and before capital and reserves.

6 The Board has received legal advice that these requirements do not contravene the Companies Act 1985 but that the interest cost and expected return should be presented in a new format heading separate from 'interest and similar charges'. Accordingly the FRS requires these items to be included as other finance costs (or income) adjacent to interest.

Northern Ireland and the Republic of Ireland

7 The relevant references to companies legislation in Northern Ireland and the Republic of Ireland are as follows:

Great Britain	Northern Ireland	Republic of Ireland
Companies Act 1985: Schedule 4:	Companies (Northern Ireland) Order 1986: Schedule 4:	The Schedule to the Companies (Amendment) Act 1986:
paragraph 8	paragraph 8	paragraph 3
paragraph 50(4)	paragraph 50(4)	paragraph 36(4)
paragraph 56(4)	paragraph 56(4)	paragraph 42(2)
paragraph 94	paragraph 92	paragraph 74*
Schedule 8	Schedule 8	no equivalent
Schedule 9	Schedule 9	European Communities (Credit Institutions: Accounts) Regulations 1992
Schedule 9A	Schedule 9A	European Communities (Insurance Undertakings: Accounts) Regulations 1996

* *Note* The definition of pension costs in the Republic of Ireland legislation is slightly different from that in UK legislation (see paragraph 3) and is as follows:

> '... "pension costs" include any other contributions by a company for the purposes of any pension scheme established for the purpose of providing pensions for persons employed by the company, any sum set aside for that purpose and any amounts paid by the company in respect of pensions without first being so set aside'

Appendix III
Compliance with International Accounting Standards

The requirements for retirement benefit costs are included in International Accounting Standard (IAS) 19 (revised 1998) 'Employee Benefits'.* The requirements of the FRS are consistent with IAS 19 (revised) in most respects. 1

The FRS requires actuarial gains and losses to be recognised, immediately they occur, in the statement of total recognised gains and losses. IAS 19 (revised) requires an entity to either: 2

(i) recognise a specified portion of the net cumulative actuarial gains and losses in the profit and loss account to the extent that they exceed the greater of 10 per cent of the fair value of the scheme assets and 10 per cent of the present value of the defined benefit obligation (before deducting scheme assets). The portion of the actuarial gains and losses to be recognised for each defined benefit plan is the excess that fell outside the 10 per cent 'corridor' spread forward over the remaining working lives of employees participating in the scheme; or

(ii) recognise immediately all actuarial gains and losses in the period in which they occur outside the profit and loss account in a statement of recognised income and expense; or

(iii) use (as permitted by the Standard) systematic methods of faster recognition, provided that the same basis is applied to both gains and losses and the basis is applied consistently from period to period. Such permitted methods include immediate recognition of gains and losses in the profit and loss.

***Editor's note:** IAS 19 was further revised in 2000. It was then revised again in 2004. While not the only treatment possible, IAS 19 can now be applied in such a way as to result in a very similar treatment to that required by FRS 17.*

Appendix IV
The development of the FRS

BACKGROUND TO THE FRS

1 The FRS has been developed from the proposals set out in FRED 20 'Retirement Benefits', which was published in November 1999. FRED 20 was itself the result of many years' deliberations by the Board in which a number of factors were influential, in particular:

(a) concerns in the UK about the existing standard, SSAP 24 'Accounting for pension costs';
(b) the trend internationally towards the use of fair values for pension cost accounting; and
(c) the move within the UK actuarial profession away from traditional actuarial valuation methodologies to a greater use of market values.

2 The main concerns about SSAP 24 were:
(a) there were too many options available to the preparers of accounts, leading to inconsistency in accounting practice and allowing a great deal of flexibility to adjust results on a short-term basis; and
(b) the disclosure requirements did not necessarily ensure that the pension cost and related amounts in the balance sheet were adequately explained.

3 In response to these concerns, in June 1995 the Board published a Discussion Paper 'Pension Costs in the Employer's Financial Statements' which set out two contrasting approaches to accounting for pension costs:

(a) an actuarial approach, which relied on actuarial measurement of pension scheme assets but removed many of the options in SSAP 24 and enhanced the disclosure requirements; and
(b) a market value approach, which was based on measuring the pension scheme assets at market value.

4 The Discussion Paper noted that the Board's initial view was that the actuarial approach was preferable. The market value approach was included because the Board was aware that the International Accounting Standards Committee (IASC) was likely to propose such an approach and the Board wished to gauge UK reaction to it.

5 IASC published an exposure draft, E54, in October 1996 and a revised standard was issued in February 1998. As expected, IAS 19 (revised 1998) 'Employee Benefits' adopts a market value approach that is very similar to the US standard, FAS 87.

6 The Board set out its views on IAS 19 (revised) in a Discussion Paper 'Aspects of Accounting for Pension Costs', published in July 1998. It explained that the Board did not believe that there were sufficient reasons to stand out against the global trend to a market value approach as long as such an approach could be developed in a way that did not introduce undue volatility into the profit and loss account. It was clear that a pensions standard based on actuarial values for assets would be regarded internationally as weak and would not be an approach that other standard-setters would follow. Given this, and the increasing use of market values by the actuarial profession, it concluded that the UK and the Republic of Ireland should move into line with international practice and use market values rather than actuarial values for

scheme assets. This view was accepted by a majority of the respondents to the Discussion Paper.

The Discussion Paper then set out some options for how the Board might proceed in developing a standard based on market values. FRED 20 took forward some of those options, and they are now embodied in the FRS, as explained below. The resulting main changes from SSAP 24 are: 7

(a) measuring pension scheme assets: a move from using an actuarial basis to using market values (this is consistent with IAS 19 (revised) and FAS 87*).
(b) the discount rate for scheme liabilities: a move from using the expected rate of return on the scheme assets to a rate that reflects the characteristics of the liabilities (resulting in the use of a high quality corporate bond rate, again consistently with IAS 19 (revised) and FAS 87).
(c) recognition of actuarial gains and losses: a move from gradual recognition of such gains and losses in the profit and loss account to immediate recognition in the statement of total recognised gains and losses (an approach that IAS 19 (revised) indicated a willingness to revisit once further developments have taken place in the IASC project on reporting financial performance (see Appendix III) and which the G4 + 1 has also supported in general terms†).
(d) as a consequence of (c), the balance sheet shows a pension liability or asset equal to the deficit or recoverable surplus in the scheme.

The Board believes that these changes, as well as moving practice in the UK and the Republic of Ireland more into line with international practice, reflect the underlying economics of providing defined benefit promises. The detailed reasoning behind the changes is set out below. 8

In practical terms, the Board believes that the FRS will, when implemented, make the reported amounts for retirement benefits more transparent and easier to understand. The pension scheme assets and liabilities will be measured at fair value. The balance sheet will show the surplus/deficit in the scheme to the extent that the employer expects to benefit/suffer from it. The profit and loss account will show the ongoing service cost, interest cost and expected return on assets while the market fluctuations will be recorded in the statement of total recognised gains and losses. 9

MEASUREMENT OF SCHEME ASSETS AND SCHEME LIABILITIES

Scheme assets

As noted above, the Board did not believe that there were sufficient reasons for the UK to differ from the rest of the world by measuring scheme assets at an actuarial value that did not equal fair value. In addition, and perhaps more importantly, it was clear that substantial changes were taking place within the actuarial profession relating to the traditional actuarial methodologies for measuring assets in a pension scheme. Of the actuaries responding to the 1995 Discussion Paper, all but one supported the use of actuarial valuations. Of the actuaries responding to the 1998 Discussion Paper, all but one supported the use of market values. Given this, and the 10

**However, FAS 87 allows the market values to be averaged over a period up to five years, which the FRS and IAS 19 (revised) do not.*

†The G4 + 1 is a group of representatives of the national standard-setters of Australia, Canada, New Zealand, the UK and the USA, and of IASC. In the communiqué issued by the G4 + 1 after its meeting in April 2000, the Group expressed support for the direction of the conclusions in FRED 20.

advantages of market values in terms of objectivity and understandability, the Board believes there is no credible alternative to their use.

Scheme liabilities

11 Ideally, under a market value approach, the scheme liabilities would, like the scheme assets, be measured at market value. However, there is no active market for most defined benefit scheme liabilities. Their fair value has therefore to be estimated using actuarial techniques. There are two families of actuarial methods for valuing defined benefit liabilities: accrued benefits methods and prospective benefits methods. The difference between them lies in their treatment of the time value of money. Under an accrued benefits method each period is allocated its share of the eventual undiscounted cost, the liability arising from the costs to date is discounted and the discount unwinds in the normal manner over the employee's service life. This results in a higher cost at the end of an employee's service life than at the beginning because the effect of discounting the cost lessens as the employee approaches retirement. Under a prospective benefits method, the total cost including all the interest that will accrue is spread evenly over the employee's service life. This does not represent the economic reality that, because of the time value of money, the cost of providing a defined benefit increases nearer retirement and such valuation methods do not, therefore, approximate the fair value of the liability. For this reason, the FRS requires the use of an accrued benefits method.

12 The FRS requires the defined benefit liability to be the best estimate of the present value of the amount that will actually be paid out. For this to be the case, all expected changes in factors affecting the payments should be taken into account. For final salary liabilities, the liability will therefore be based on the expected final salary, not the current salary. Some argue that this is not consistent with FRS 12 'Provisions, Contingent Liabilities and Contingent Assets' because the employer has some control over the future increases in salary and hence does not have a present obligation relating to those increases. However, there is a difference between a present commitment to pay a pension based on present salary and a present commitment to pay a pension based on final salary, which the Board believes should be reflected in the measurement of the liabilities. The use of expected final salaries is also consistent with IAS 19 (revised) and FAS 87. For retirement healthcare liabilities, calculating the best estimate of the payments to be made in the future means taking into account expected changes in the cost of medical care.

The discount rate

13 In the UK, actuaries have traditionally discounted the liabilities in a defined benefit scheme at the expected rate of return on the assets in the scheme (prudently estimated). IAS 19 (revised) and FAS 87 require the use of a high quality corporate bond rate.

14 The Board believes that the discount rate should reflect the time value of money and the risk associated with the liability. The view put forward in the Discussion Paper published in 1998 was that such a rate could be determined by looking at the rate of return on matching assets. (If the assets exactly matched the liability they must have the same fair value and hence the discount rate appropriate for the liability must be the same as the rate of return on the asset.) Matching assets were expected to be:

(a) for pensions fixed in monetary terms, fixed rate government bonds;
(b) for index-linked pensions in payment and deferred pensions, index-linked government bonds;

(c) for final salary liabilities, a portfolio containing some element of equity investments.

However, later research conducted by the Faculty and Institute of Actuaries demonstrated from past data that the correlation between equities and salaries had not been close and that the best match for final salary liabilities was probably index-linked bonds. 15

Some argue that even if there is no close correlation between equity and salary growth, it is appropriate to use the expected return on equities as the discount rate if the scheme is invested therein because, over the long term, that return is relatively secure. However, the higher return expected on equities is a reward for the risk involved in equity investment. Unless the risk matches that associated with the liabilities, discounting the liabilities at the higher return anticipates the expected benefit of equity investment without recognising the risks involved. The higher return should instead be recognised as it is earned over the period the equities are held. 16

On the other hand, although index-linked bonds seem to have been a better match for final salary liabilities, they are not a perfect match and an index-linked bond discount rate would ignore some important aspects of a final salary pension liability, for example the uncertainty of the amounts ultimately to be paid out. The Board has therefore decided not to try to find matching assets but to build up the discount rate from its components. As noted above, it believes that, if possible, the discount rate should reflect: 17

(a) the time value of money (given by the rate of return on an investment regarded as being risk-free); and
(b) the risks associated with the liability because of the uncertainty surrounding the ultimate cash payments due.

The FRS requires the assumptions to reflect the best estimate of the ultimate cash flows. The resulting liability is clearly subject to uncertainty – the ultimate cash flows are not contractually fixed and will depend on final salaries, length of retirement etc. The uncertainty of the future cash outflows might be expected to make the liability more onerous – most entities are risk-averse and would prefer to avoid the possibility that the cash flows might be more than expected. 18

However, in many defined benefit schemes, the employer has the option of preventing the cash flows being greater than expected and even of reducing the cash flows if necessary (eg if investment performance has been consistently poor for a long period). These options exist because the best estimate of the cash flows will include expected benefit increases likely to be granted by the employer such as (i) increases in pensions in payment and deferred pensions at above the minimum required by statute or the scheme rules and (ii) increases in benefits arising from salary increases for active members over and above the rate applicable if they left service (it is assumed that an employer would, over any substantial period, have to increase salaries by at least the indexing rate applied to deferred pensions). Although the employer expects to give these increases, they are not guaranteed. If necessary the employer could, in many cases, give lower than expected increases in benefits and give lower than expected salary increases. In extremis, the employer could even close the scheme down. 19

These options are a crucial factor in the operation of UK defined benefit schemes and the level of benefits that is given. Employers' willingness to provide the expected benefits is often based, at least partly, on the assumption that the liability can be funded in equities. The expectation is that a higher return on equities compared with 20 that on less risky investments will make such promises affordable. The employer can bear the risk associated with the higher return because, if equities were to underperform for a long period, the options described above allow the employer to take action to mitigate the financial impact.

21 These options make the liability less onerous and can be reflected by using a discount rate higher than a risk-free rate. In principle, the premium over the risk-free rate should vary from scheme to scheme (and within schemes), reflecting the differing levels of discretion that exist for different scheme liabilities. However, assessing the appropriate premium is difficult and subjective. In the interests of objectivity and international harmonisation, the Board has therefore decided to adopt a standard discount rate: the rate of return on a high quality corporate bond, ie one rated at the level of AA or equivalent status. This includes a small premium above the risk-free rate, which can be regarded as reflecting the options open to the employer to limit the pension scheme liabilities.

22 Reflecting these options in the discount rate is not inconsistent with the proposal in paragraph 31 of the FRS that it is not appropriate to assume a reduction in benefits below those currently promised. It is not appropriate to assume that a curtailment of the scheme will take place in the future but it is appropriate to reflect the value of the *option* to make that curtailment.

Frequency of valuations

23 The FRS requires the actuarial valuation to be updated at each balance sheet date to reflect current conditions. The Board does not believe that this imposes an excessively onerous or impracticable burden on preparers of accounts for two reasons.

(a) The figures in the profit and loss account are based on assumptions at the beginning of the period, and will therefore be known before the balance sheet date. It is only the figures in the statement of total recognised gains and losses and the balance sheet that depend on the valuation updated at the balance sheet date.

(b) Unless there have been major changes to the scheme, only the financial assumptions and the fair value of the assets need to be updated at the balance sheet date. The actuarial profession is preparing guidance on what the annual update should involve.

Recognition in the balance sheet

24 Pension schemes will not usually be subsidiary (or quasi-subsidiary) undertakings of the employer because defined benefit schemes are controlled by the trustees, not the employer. It is not, therefore, appropriate to consolidate the scheme into the employer's financial statements. A pension scheme can give rise to assets and liabilities of the employer but these are not the gross amounts of the pension scheme assets and liabilities – the employer does not control the assets nor is it directly liable for the pension payments. Instead, the employer has a pension asset or liability to the extent that it is entitled to benefit from any surplus or has a legal or constructive obligation to make good any deficit.

25 Pension schemes differ in this respect from employee share ownership plans (ESOPs). The key difference lies in the control that the employer has over the trust. ESOP trusts are such that the actions that the trustees can take are very limited – the ESOP exists only to hold the sponsoring company's own shares for future distribution to employees. ESOP trusts are designed to ensure that there is minimal risk in practice that the trustees would act other than in accordance with the sponsoring company's wishes. The sponsoring company has, in effect, de facto control. In contrast, for a pension scheme, the trustees' rights and duties are much wider. The employer cannot in practice ensure that the trustees will act as it would wish in many significant areas and, hence, does not control the assets and liabilities in the scheme.

Many respondents to FRED 20 questioned whether a surplus in the pension scheme should give rise to any asset in the balance sheet of the employer. Their view was that the employer did not own or control the surplus in the scheme and, hence, it was not appropriate to recognise an asset. The Board's view is that the employer has an asset if it has the right to reduce its contributions in the future. It is unlikely that an employer could be required to make contributions to a scheme in order to maintain a surplus. Accordingly, in general, a surplus will give rise to an asset for the employer. **26**

The amount recognised as an asset cannot, of course, exceed the amount that the employer can recover and such a limit is included in the FRS. The limit reflects the maximum that can be recovered through reduced contributions together with any refunds that have been agreed at the balance sheet date. Some argue that the reductions in contributions must be assessed in relation to the funding assumptions rather than the accounting assumptions because it is in relation to funding assumptions alone that the trustees of the scheme will agree to any such reductions. It is true that the trustees will set the contributions based on the funding assumptions, but over the life of the scheme the accounting and funding assumptions must come together. The delay in accessing the surplus does not affect its measurement because, in the period where the company is still making contributions based on funding assumptions, the accounting surplus will be growing because of the return earned by the excess assets in the scheme with the result that the surplus that the employer will eventually recover through reduced contributions in future will be larger. In present value terms (which is how the surplus is measured), the amount by which the employer can benefit is the same. **27**

Furthermore, the assumptions required by the FRS are a best estimate. Funding assumptions may well build in an element of prudence. It is not appropriate to reflect an arbitrary element of prudence in the measurement of the pension asset for financial reporting purposes. **28**

RECOGNITION IN THE PERFORMANCE STATEMENTS

Analysis of pension cost

The FRS requires the ongoing defined benefit cost to be analysed into (i) the service cost (ii) the interest cost and (iii) the expected return on assets, with (ii) and (iii) presented as finance costs (or income). The Board believes that including the interest cost and the expected return on assets with the service cost within operating activities distorts the operating cost that is shown. For example, the pension cost recorded for an unfunded scheme would be higher than that recorded for a funded scheme with exactly the same pension obligations. This does not properly reflect the fact that the *pension* in both cases costs the same, it is only the funding policy that is different. The interest cost and expected return are matters relating to the financing of the pension promise. The Board believes that the three components of the pension cost and their underlying economic nature are well accepted and understood and, hence, should be reflected in their presentation in the profit and loss account. **29**

Expected return on assets

30 Although the Board wishes to move to market values for retirement benefit accounting, it does not believe that it would be appropriate for the short-term volatility associated with equity returns to be reflected in the profit and loss account. Rather, the profit and loss account should reflect the long-term return that equities are expected to produce with any fluctuations around that return shown in the statement of total recognised gains and losses. The rationale for this view is explained further below (see paragraph 37).

31 In practice, it is difficult to judge the long-term rate of return on equities at any particular date, given that it needs to reflect the current state of the market. The FRS, therefore, requires the disclosure of an analysis of the assets in the scheme and the expected rates of return assumed so that users may assess the assumptions and calculate the effects of making different assumptions. It is to be expected that those using rates at the extremes of the range at any particular date will come under close scrutiny and possible challenge.

32 The higher long-term return expected on equities compensates for the uncertainty over the return. FRED 20 noted that some believe, therefore, that it is not appropriate to recognise the expected higher long-term return in the profit and loss account every year with the fluctuations around the return going to the statement of total recognised gains and losses. Doing so separates the reward for risk (the expected higher return) from the results of taking the risk (the variability in the actual return). It was suggested that an alternative approach would be to record in the profit and loss account a risk-free return on assets (removing the effects of risk to the statement of total recognised gains and losses completely).

33 There was almost no support for this alternative approach in the responses to FRED 20 and it has therefore not been taken forward in the FRS.

Recognition of actuarial gains and losses

34 SSAP 24 required actuarial gains and losses (variations from regular cost) to be recognised gradually over the service lives of the employees. In the 1995 Discussion Paper, under the alternative market value approach, a different treatment was proposed. The profit and loss account would be charged with the cost of pensions earned in the period. Actuarial gains and losses would be recorded in the statement of total recognised gains and losses.

35 This approach was explored in more detail in the 1998 Discussion Paper and in FRED 20. It is based on the view that items of financial performance should be grouped together according to their characteristics. The Board's approach was set out in detail in its Discussion Paper "Reporting Financial Performance: proposals for change' (June 1999). That Paper explained that, where gains and losses arise predominantly from price changes and relate to assets and liabilities that are held not with a view to benefiting directly from changes in their value but because they are needed for the employer's operating activities (eg a head office), it would be misleading to include those gains and losses within operating profit. Instead, they should be reported as "other' gains and losses, ie at present within the statement of total recognised gains and losses rather than the profit and loss account.

36 The Board expects to publish shortly a FRED on reporting financial performance. The proposals in the FRED on the reporting of holding gains and losses will be consistent with those in the Discussion Paper noted above.

The Board regards actuarial gains and losses as similar in nature to revaluation gains and losses on fixed assets. In relation to the assets in the pension scheme, they are held with a view to producing a relatively secure long-term return that will assist in financing the pension cost. The length of the term, coupled with the options available to the employer to restrict the liability in extreme circumstances, mean that much of the fluctuations in market values does not affect the relatively stable cash flows between the employer and its pension scheme. Market fluctuations are incidental to the main purpose of the pension scheme just as the revaluation gains and losses on a fixed asset are incidental to its main operating role. They are therefore best reported within the statement of total recognised gains and losses. **37**

On the scheme liabilities side, the effect of both experience gains and losses and changes in actuarial assumptions is to update the liabilities to reflect current conditions consistent with the current market value used to measure the assets. As with fixed assets, where the profit and loss account reflects the current depreciation charge, so for scheme liabilities the profit and loss account reflects the service cost and interest cost of providing the pension promise. Subsequent changes in the value of the liabilities are generally related to financial assumptions and are caused by general changes in economic conditions. These fluctuations of the liabilities to reflect current market conditions are, like the market value fluctuations of the assets, incidental to the main operating business of the employer. **38**

In the periods after their recognition in the statement of total recognised gains and losses, actuarial gains and losses do not change in nature to become operating costs. They should not, therefore, be "recycled" by recognition in the profit and loss account in later years. (An additional, pragmatic, reason for not recycling the gains and losses is that doing so would introduce volatility into the profit and loss account. Actuarial gains and losses arising under a market value approach are such that, even when spread over the remaining service lives of the employees, they would cause significant fluctuations in the total amount charged to the profit and loss account. Further, there would be problems in knowing how to allocate the recycled amount between operating and financial costs.) **39**

In addition to the fact that this approach is consistent with its views on reporting financial performance, the Board prefers immediate recognition in the statement of total recognised gains and losses to the spreading approach required under SSAP 24 for the following reasons. **40**

(a) The balance sheet reflects the surplus (to the extent that the employer can benefit from it) or deficit (to the extent that the employer is obliged to fund it) in the scheme based on the latest actuarial valuation. These amounts meet the Board's definitions of assets and liabilities of the employer. In contrast, under SSAP 24, some actuarial gains and losses were not recognised at the balance sheet date. In a market value model, there is no conceptual reason to defer the recognition of these gains and losses. Deferral means that the asset/liability in the balance sheet does not equal the recoverable surplus or the deficit in the scheme. In fact, it was not uncommon under SSAP 24 for a deficit in the scheme to give rise to a supposed asset in the balance sheet which built up as the deficit was funded faster than it was recognised. Such figures do not meet the Board's definition of assets.

(b) The figures in the balance sheet and performance statements are transparent and easy to understand.

(c) The complex and arbitrary rules needed to govern spreading gains and losses forward are not required.

41 The main concerns expressed about this approach in the responses to the FRED were the following.

(a) The figures in the statement of total recognised gains and losses and balance sheet can be large and volatile. They will distort the financial statements of the employer and will not be understood by users of the accounts.

(b) Some gains and losses are never recorded in the profit and loss account. This concern had two aspects:

(i) Some believed that all gains and losses (in particular, all losses) should be recorded in the profit and loss account at some point. Doing so is necessary for the profit and loss account to show the true margins achieved by the employer.

(ii) Others accepted the distinction in principle between actuarial gains and losses and operating costs but were concerned at the possibility of understating the costs that should be reflected in the profit and loss account. Over-optimistic actuarial assumptions could lead to lower service and interest costs in the profit and loss account, while the difference between the assumptions and actual experience would be reflected as a loss in the statement of total recognised gains and losses.

42 In relation to the point (a), the Board believes that users of accounts are sufficiently sophisticated to view the figures in their proper context. It is important to remember that the amounts reported in the statement of total recognised gains and losses *in any one period* have relatively little significance and should not necessarily cause concern. What matters is *the pattern that emerges over a number of years*. For example, if a substantial actuarial loss arises in one year, but then reverses over the next few years, there may well be no impact on future cash flows. If, on the other hand, the loss does not reverse and perhaps even is repeated, then it is more likely that additional contributions to the pension scheme will be required. Repeated gains or losses may also imply that pension costs in the future will be lower or higher as experience causes the actuary to change his assumptions. These trends will be highlighted by the disclosure of a five-year history of actuarial gains and losses.

43 The different context in which the figures in the statement of total recognised gains and losses and balance sheet need to be viewed is also highlighted by their position in the accounts: the actuarial gains and losses are reported in the statement of total recognised gains and losses, not the profit and loss account (or earnings per share), and the pension asset/liability is presented at the foot of the balance sheet separately from and after all other net assets.

44 It is of note that all the users responding to FRED 20 supported the approach in the FRED.

45 The Board's view on the fact that the approach in the FRS does not report actuarial gains and losses in the profit and loss account at any time (paragraph 41(b)(i)) is that this is entirely in line with the approach to reporting financial performance set out in the Board's Discussion Paper on the subject – some gains and losses have different characteristics from those that arise from the employer's mainstream operating activities and it is therefore appropriate for them to be reported separately. This does not imply that they are unimportant or can be disregarded in assessing the employer's performance. It is simply a reflection of the fact that they are different in nature from operating gains and losses.

46 The Board accepts that the concern about understating the costs in the profit and loss account is valid (paragraph 41(b)(ii)), although as, with experience, more attention than hitherto is paid to gains and losses reported in the statement of total

recognised gains and losses, such manipulation will become less effective. In the meantime, the five-year history of actuarial gains and losses will separately highlight experience gains and losses so that users of the accounts are aware when actuarial assumptions are consistently not being met. It would be expected that, although the assumptions would probably not be met in each and every year, the experience gains and losses would over time compensate for each other. A consistent trend of experience losses (or gains) should cause the preparers of accounts and the auditors to re-examine the assumptions.

It is worth noting that an approach that spreads the actuarial gains and losses forward in the profit and loss account is equally open to abuse. Although the losses arising from over-optimistic assumptions are recognised in the profit and loss account, only a small proportion is recognised in any one year. The beneficial effects of the over-optimistic assumptions outweigh that small proportion until the effect has built up over many (typically twelve to fifteen) years. Such a delay in the bad news hitting the accounts is likely to be more of an incentive to manipulate the assumptions than immediate recognition of the losses in the statement of total recognised gains and losses. **47**

Recognition of past service costs

Under SSAP 24 past service costs for current employees were spread forward in the profit and loss account and past service costs for former employees were recognised immediately in the profit and loss account to the extent that they were not covered by a surplus in the scheme. **48**

The decision to improve benefits or award new benefits in relation to past service increases the scheme liabilities immediately. If an employee left the day after the increased benefits vested (usually at the time of the award), the transfer value would reflect those increased benefits – no further service from the employee would be required to earn them. The Board does not, therefore, believe that there is any reason to defer recognition of the increased liability beyond the date the benefits vest. **49**

This leaves the question of how the cost should be recognised in the performance statements. Many of the respondents to the FRED believed that the cost of the improved benefits should be offset against any surplus in the scheme, with only the excess cost being recognised in the profit and loss account. They argued that this properly reflects the fact that such benefit improvements may have been awarded only because there was a surplus in the scheme and therefore no cash cost to the employer. **50**

The Board's view is that although there may be no direct cash cost, by using a surplus in this way the employer loses some of the advantages that it could otherwise obtain, for example reduced contributions. Further, by awarding such benefit improvements, it may be able to reduce other aspects of its staff costs. From this perspective, it seems appropriate that the cost of the benefit improvements should be recognised as an employment cost. The manner in which the cost is funded, whether through cash or the use of a surplus that could otherwise have been used to reduce contributions, does not affect that classification. However, sometimes the benefit improvements are funded out of a surplus that the employer could not otherwise benefit from, ie a surplus so large that the employer could not absorb it fully through reduced contributions (or agreed refunds). In these cases, the surplus will not have been recognised in full previously and to the extent that it has been used to fund the past service costs the unrecognised amount should now be offset against the past service cost in the profit and loss account. **51**

52 This treatment of past service costs (including the use of any irrecoverable surplus) is consistent with IAS 19 (revised).

Impact of limit on balance sheet asset

53 The limit on the amount that can be recognised as an asset in the balance sheet may mean that some part of a surplus is not recognised. The effect of the balance sheet limit might be allocated to the various pension components in the performance statements in a number of ways. The allocation required by the FRS is one that preserves the structure of the ongoing items (ie the current service cost, interest cost and expected return on assets) as far as possible but allows one-off costs (eg past service costs) to be offset against the unrecognised surplus.

DISCLOSURES

54 FRED 20 proposed sufficient disclosures for a reader to understand the various elements that constitute the pension cost and the relationship between the actuarial valuation and the amounts recorded in the balance sheet. These disclosures were largely supported by the respondents to the FRED, with the exception of:

(a) a comment on the difference between the expected rate of return on equities and the AA corporate bond rate; and
(b) the five-year history of amounts recognised in the statement of total recognised gains and losses.

55 The first of these disclosures has been dropped, because the two rates are required to be disclosed anyway and any comment was likely to be couched in terms that added little extra information.

56 The second disclosure has been retained because the Board believes that it helps place in context the actuarial gains or losses in any one year and hence plays an important role in the FRS.

AMENDMENT TO FRS 17 (2006)*

56A In 2006 the Accounting Standards Board issued a Financial Reporting Exposure Draft (FRED) that proposed to replace the disclosure requirements of FRS 17 with those of International Accounting Standard 19 (IAS 19) 'Employee Benefits'. In making its proposal the ASB took into consideration the fact that, in December 2004, the International Accounting Standards Board (IASB) amended the disclosure requirements of IAS 19 following a review of national standards on accounting for post-employment benefits.

56B In replacing the disclosure requirements of FRS 17 with those of IAS 19 the ASB made changes only where the accounting treatment of items differed between the two accounting standards or where necessary to make the terminology consistent.

56C Respondents to the FRED were generally in agreement with the proposal to replace the disclosure requirements of FRS 17 with those of IAS 19 and so increase convergence between the two standards.

56D Some respondents did, however, raise a concern regarding disclosures that were required by the current FRS 17 but would no longer be required by the amended

***Editor's note**: Inserted by Amendment to FRS 17 issued December 2006.*

FRS 17. The ASB considered this view but decided it did not wish to extend the disclosure requirements for entities applying UK Financial Reporting Standards beyond the disclosure requirements of entities applying International Financial Reporting Standards. The ASB therefore decided not to amend the disclosure requirements set out in the amended FRS 17 beyond those of IAS 19. The ASB did, however, note that where an entity considers the information provided by a disclosure that is no longer required by the amended FRS would enhance the understanding of the financial statements to users, the disclosure could be provided on a voluntary basis.

A few respondents to the FRED considered that the amendment should address some of the other differences that exist between FRS 17 and IAS 19. The ASB gave due consideration to the views of these respondents. However, it decided that in view of the longer term research project that it was undertaking into pension accounting it should not extend the scope of this short-term project. The ASB did, however, decide to include in this amendment its proposal set out in Financial Reporting Exposure Draft 39 'Proposed amendment to FRS 12 Provisions, Contingent Liabilities and Contingent Assets and Amendment to FRS 17 Retirement Benefits' to amendment paragraph 16 of FRS 17. The amendment replaces the term in paragraph 16 'mid-market price' with 'current bid price'. **56E**

TRANSITIONAL ARRANGEMENTS

The FRS allows for a long implementation period, with disclosures building up in the notes to the accounts. The reasons for this are: **57**

(a) to avoid companies having to revisit previous actuarial valuations;
(b) to give the Board a chance to persuade IASC to follow the UK approach on the immediate recognition of actuarial gains and losses; and
(c) to give preparers and users of accounts the opportunity to become accustomed to the figures arising under the FRS before they are recognised in the primary statements.

In 2006 the Accounting Standards Board, following convergence of the disclosure requirements with those of IAS 19, required the new disclosure requirements to be effective for accounting periods beginning on or after 6 April 2007.* **57A**

IMPACT ON DISTRIBUTABLE PROFITS

Appendix III to FRED 20 set out a possible approach to mitigate the impact on distributable profits of a pension deficit measured and recognised in accordance with the FRED. Some respondents to FRED 20 thought this approach was unsatisfactory in a number of respects. In the light of these responses and because a distribution problem is unlikely to arise often,† the Board has decided not to proceed with this approach. It believes that it is better for those few companies that are affected to find appropriate solutions with the help of their legal advisers. **58**

****Editor's note****: *Added by the Amendment to FRS 17* Retirement Benefits *issued in December 2006.*

†*A distribution problem will arise only when individual company accounts show a defined benefit liability so large that it reduces distributable reserves to below that needed to cover any intended distribution. In this context, it should be noted that the FRS allows an exemption in some circumstances from the recognition of a defined benefit liability in the accounts of individual companies that are members of a group defined benefit scheme.*

ALTERNATIVE CASH-BASED APPROACH TO PENSION COST ACCOUNTING

59 Throughout the development of the FRS, a number of respondents to the various consultation documents raised the possibility of a return to a cash-based method of accounting for pension costs. It was suggested that in the UK the Pensions Act 1995, together with the existing tax regime, would impose such constraints on the contributions that an employer made to an approved UK pension scheme that, for such schemes, the contributions made in each period could be regarded as an appropriate measure for the pension cost for that period. The argument was that, because the scheme could be neither substantially overfunded (the tax limit) nor underfunded (the minimum funding requirement (MFR) of the Pensions Act), the contributions each year must be equivalent to the increase in the pension obligation that had arisen that year, ie the pension cost. The cost of implementing an accruals-based system, therefore, exceeded the benefits.

60 This argument does not apply to unfunded or overseas schemes, for which an accruals-based method would still need to be prescribed. Also, pension regulation still allows substantial scope for employers and trustees to agree on different and varying contribution schedules.

61 For example, for a typical UK pension scheme, it would not be unusual for a scheme to be regarded as 100 per cent funded when measured using the test for the upper tax limit on funding, but 150 per cent funded using the MFR test. The profile of some schemes may lead to even larger discrepancies than this. A pension scheme funded between the 100 per cent level on the MFR basis and 100 per cent level on the maximum funding basis may be able to justify paying contributions at any level between zero (ie a temporary contribution holiday) and the full regular cost calculated on a conservative basis. With typical regular cost levels being between 10 per cent and 15 per cent of pensionable salaries, the difference between full regular cost and no contributions whatsoever is likely to be material.

62 The Board does not, therefore, believe that a return to a cash-based method would ensure that the proper cost of a pension is measured and recognised as it arises over the service lives of the employees.

ALTERNATIVE ACCOUNTING STANDARDS

63 Some respondents to the consultation papers have suggested that if overseas pension schemes have been accounted for under a "recognised' standard (for example, FAS 87), those figures could be included in UK financial statements without restatement. The same suggestion was made for retirement benefits other than pensions that have been accounted for under FAS 106. The Board does not accept this suggestion. While it may sometimes be possible, using options in standards, to achieve a high degree of convergence between the effect of each, where there are differences the Board's standards must be followed.

Financial Reporting Standard 18 is set out in paragraphs 1–69.

The Statement of Standard Accounting Practice, which comprises the paragraphs set in bold type, should be read in the context of the Objective as stated in paragraph 1 and the definitions set out in paragraph 2 and also of the Foreword to Accounting Standards and the Statement of Principles for Financial Reporting currently in issue.

The explanatory paragraphs contained in the FRS shall be regarded as part of the Statement of Standard Accounting Practice insofar as they assist in interpreting that statement.

Appendix IV 'The development of the FRS' reviews considerations and arguments that were thought significant by members of the Board in reaching the conclusions on the FRS.

FRS 18
Accounting policies*†

(Issued December 2000)

Contents

	Paragraphs
Summary	
Financial Reporting Standard 18	
Objective	**1**
Scope	**2–3**
Definitions	
Applying the definitions in practice	**6–13**
Distinguishing accounting policies from estimation techniques	6–8
Recognition	9
Measurement bases for fungible assets	10–11
Changes to presentation	12–13
Accounting policies	**14–49**
Accounting policies and financial statements	14–29
Objectives and constraints in selecting accounting policies	30–44
Reviewing and changing accounting policies	45–49
Estimation techniques	**50–54**
Disclosures	**55–65**
Date from which effective	**66–67**
Withdrawal of SSAP 2 and UITF Abstracts 7 and 14 and amendment of other accounting standards and UITF Abstracts	**68–69**
Adoption of FRS 18 by the Board	

Appendices
- **I** Examples of changes to accounting policies and to estimation techniques
- **II** note on legal requirements
- **III** compliance with international accounting standards
- **IV** the development of the FRS

****Editor's note:*** *FRS 18 has been amended by FRS 21 with effect for accounting periods beginning on or after 1 January 2005.*

†***Editor's note:*** *The matters covered in FRS 18 are dealt with in Section 10 of FRS 102.*

Accounting policies

Summary

Financial Reporting Standard 18 sets out the principles to be followed in selecting accounting policies and the disclosures needed to help users to understand the accounting policies adopted and how they have been applied. **a**

The FRS defines accounting policies, and estimation techniques used in implementing those policies. Accounting policies should be consistent with accounting standards, Urgent Issues Task Force (UITF) Abstracts and companies legislation. Where this requirement allows a choice, the FRS requires an entity to select those accounting policies judged to be most appropriate to its particular circumstances for the purpose of giving a true and fair view. **b**

An entity should judge the appropriateness of accounting policies to its particular circumstances against the objectives of relevance, reliability, comparability and understandability. The constraints that an entity should take into account are the need to balance the different objectives, and the need to balance the cost of providing information with the likely benefit of such information to users of the entity's financial statements. **c**

An entity's accounting policies should be reviewed regularly to ensure that they remain the most appropriate to its particular circumstances. An entity should implement a new accounting policy if it is judged more appropriate to the entity's particular circumstances than the present accounting policy. **d**

The FRS requires specific disclosures about the accounting policies followed and changes to those policies. It also requires, in some circumstances, disclosures about the estimation techniques used in applying those policies. **e**

Financial Reporting Standard 18

OBJECTIVE

The objective of this FRS is to ensure that for all material items: 1

(a) an entity adopts the accounting policies most appropriate to its particular circumstances for the purpose of giving a true and fair view;

(b) the accounting policies adopted are reviewed regularly to ensure that they remain appropriate, and are changed when a new policy becomes more appropriate to the entity's particular circumstances; and

(c) sufficient information is disclosed in the financial statements to enable users to understand the accounting policies adopted and how they have been implemented.

SCOPE

The FRS applies to all financial statements that are intended to give a true and fair view of a reporting entity's financial position and profit or loss (or income and expenditure) for a period. 2

3 **Reporting entities applying the Financial Reporting Standard for Smaller Entities currently applicable are exempt from the FRS.**

DEFINITIONS

4 The following definitions shall apply in the FRS and in particular in the Statement of Standard Accounting Practice set out **in bold type**.

Accounting policies:-

Those principles, bases, conventions, rules and practices applied by an entity that specify how the effects of transactions and other events are to be reflected in its financial statements through

(i) recognising,
(ii) selecting measurement bases for, and
(iii) presenting

assets, liabilities, gains, losses and changes to shareholders' funds. Accounting policies do not include estimation techniques.

Accounting policies define the process whereby transactions and other events are reflected in financial statements. For example, an accounting policy for a particular type of expenditure may specify whether an asset or a loss is to be recognised; the basis on which it is to be measured; and where in the profit and loss account or balance sheet it is to be presented.

Estimation techniques:-

The methods adopted by an entity to arrive at estimated monetary amounts, corresponding to the measurement bases selected, for assets, liabilities, gains, losses and changes to shareholders' funds.

Estimation techniques implement the measurement aspects of accounting policies. An accounting policy will specify the basis on which an item is to be measured; where there is uncertainty over the monetary amount corresponding to that basis, the amount will be arrived at by using an estimation technique.

Estimation techniques include, for example:

(a) methods of depreciation, such as straight-line and reducing balance, applied in the context of a particular measurement basis, used to estimate the proportion of the economic benefits of a tangible fixed asset consumed in a period;
(b) different methods used to estimate the proportion of trade debts that will not be recovered, particularly where such methods consider a population as a whole rather than individual balances.

Measurement bases:-

Those monetary attributes of the elements of financial statements – assets, liabilities, gains, losses and changes to shareholders' funds – that are reflected in financial statements.

Where a business holds an asset that was purchased, the asset will have a number of qualities that may be expressed in terms of 'values'. As well as the amount for which it was acquired, it will have a current net realisable value and, if it is capable of being replaced, it will have a current replacement cost. These are examples of monetary attributes of the asset. Other examples arise when different monetary attributes are combined in a formula. For example, in a historical cost system, stocks are stated at the lower of historical cost and net realisable value. Similarly, in a current value measurement system, the current value of an asset, using the value to the business rule, is the lower of replacement cost and recoverable amount.*

Monetary attributes fall into two broad categories – those that reflect current values and those that reflect historical values. Some monetary attributes will be suitable for use in financial statements only in conjunction with others.† A monetary attribute, or combination of attributes, that may be reflected in financial statements is called a measurement basis.

SORP:-

An extant Statement of Recommended Practice (SORP) either developed in accordance with the Board's policy on SORPs, and including a statement by the Board‡, or 'franked' by the former Accounting Standards Committee.

SORPs recommend accounting practices for specialised industries or sectors. They supplement accounting standards and other legal and regulatory requirements in the light of the special factors prevailing or transactions undertaken in a particular industry or sector.

References to companies legislation mean, for a company: 5

(a) in Great Britain, the Companies Act 1985§;
(b) in Northern Ireland, the Companies (Northern Ireland) Order 1986; and
(c) in the Republic of Ireland, the Companies Acts 1963–90 and the European Communities (Companies: Group Accounts) Regulations 1992;

and for an entity other than a company, any equivalent legislation.

APPLYING THE DEFINITIONS IN PRACTICE

Distinguishing accounting policies from estimation techniques

Often, accounting standards or companies legislation will prescribe the measurement bases to be used in respect of particular assets and liabilities. Whether prescribed or selected, measurement bases are a matter of accounting policy. Accordingly, if an entity has previously reported certain assets on a historical cost basis, but now reports them on a current value basis, that is a change of accounting policy. 6

**Recoverable amount is itself the higher of value in use and net realisable value.*

†*For example, value in use is unlikely to be appropriate for use in financial statements unless the competing claims of alternative monetary attributes are also considered, as in the value to the business rule.*

‡*The Statement 'SORPs: Policy and Code of Practice' sets out the Board's policy on SORPs and the basis on which a SORP will include a statement by the Board.*

§***Editor's note:** This should now be read as a reference to the Companies Act 2006.*

7 By contrast, the choice of method used to arrive at a monetary amount corresponding to a measurement basis is not a matter of accounting policy. For example, an entity may wish to measure the current disposal value of an asset. It might estimate this by reference to its own recent disposals of similar assets, or by reference to prices quoted in advertisements. Both methods are intended to arrive at the same unknown figure, and therefore a change from one method to another is a change of estimate, not of accounting policy. These methods are referred to in the FRS as estimation techniques.

8 Financial statements present information about their elements – assets, liabilities, gains, losses and changes to shareholders' funds – but not all the information that is available can be presented in an entity's primary financial statements. For example, although information may be available about two different monetary attributes of a particular asset – its historical cost and its current value under the value to the business rule – it will not be possible to reflect both in the entity's balance sheet. Therefore, accounting policies are used to determine which information is to be presented – ie which attribute of the asset is to be measured – and also how it is to be presented. By contrast, where it is either impossible or impractical to measure directly the amount corresponding to that attribute, estimation techniques are used to arrive at a suitable approximation. In simple terms, accounting policies determine which facts about a business are to be presented in financial statements, and how those facts are to be presented; estimation techniques are used to establish what those facts are. Some examples of changes to accounting policies and to estimation techniques are set out in Appendix I.

Recognition

9 For certain transactions, accounting standards allow a choice of what is to be recognised. Examples arise in FRS 15 'Tangible Fixed Assets', which allows directly attributable interest to be treated either as part of an asset or as an expense, and in SSAP 13 'Accounting for research and development', which allows expenditure satisfying asset recognition criteria to be treated either as an asset or as an expense. Where accounting standards allow a choice over what is to be recognised, that choice is a matter of accounting policy.

Measurement bases for fungible assets

10 Fungible assets are assets that are substantially indistinguishable one from another, in that there is no basis on which to distinguish between them in economic terms. Companies legislation, accounting standards and Urgent Issues Task Force (UITF) Abstracts may specify accounting policies for particular types of fungible asset. Subject to any such constraints, where fungible assets are recorded at historical cost, an entity's accounting policy may be to determine cost on an asset-by-asset basis, or the entity may select an accounting policy that considers those assets in aggregate, rather than individually. Accounting policies that consider fungible assets in aggregate will use measurement bases such as weighted average historical cost and historical cost measured on a 'first in, first out' (FIFO) basis.

11 However, an accounting policy that determines cost for fungible assets on an asset-by-asset basis may not enhance the comparability of financial statements. This is because the results reported under such a policy will be affected by the order in which fungible assets are disposed of or consumed, even though there is no basis on which to distinguish between those assets in economic terms. Accordingly, an accounting policy that considers fungible assets in aggregate will be more consistent with the objective of comparability set out in paragraph 30.

Changes to presentation

When an entity changes the way it presents a particular item in the balance sheet or in the profit and loss account, that is a change of accounting policy. However, it is not a change of accounting policy merely to provide additional information. Accordingly, where a more detailed analysis of a particular item in the balance sheet or in the profit and loss account is presented, or where information is disclosed for the first time, that is not of itself a change of accounting policy. Nevertheless, it will still be necessary to disclose corresponding amounts in similar detail. **12**

Care is needed when an accounting change involves both a change of presentation and a change of estimation technique. The former will be treated as a change of accounting policy but the latter will not.* **13**

ACCOUNTING POLICIES

Accounting policies and financial statements

An entity should adopt accounting policies that enable its financial statements to give a true and fair view. Those accounting policies should be consistent with the requirements of accounting standards, Urgent Issues Task Force (UITF) Abstracts and companies legislation. **14**

If in exceptional circumstances compliance with the requirements of an accounting standard or UITF Abstract is inconsistent with the requirement to give a true and fair view, the requirements of the accounting standard or UITF Abstract should be departed from to the extent necessary to give a true and fair view. In such circumstances, the disclosures set out in paragraph 62 should be provided. **15**

An entity will not depart from the requirements of an accounting standard or UITF Abstract where a true and fair view can be achieved by additional disclosure. In such circumstances, the requirements of the accounting standard or UITF Abstract are not inconsistent with the requirement to give a true and fair view. **16**

Where it is necessary to choose between accounting policies that satisfy the conditions in paragraph 14, an entity should select whichever of those accounting policies is judged by the entity to be most appropriate to its particular circumstances for the purpose of giving a true and fair view. **17**

The provision of additional disclosures will not justify or remedy the adoption of an accounting policy other than that which is judged by the entity to be most appropriate to its particular circumstances for the purpose of giving a true and fair view. The appropriateness of accounting policies to an entity's particular circumstances is judged by reference to the objectives and constraints set out in paragraphs 30 and 31. **18**

Financial statements need to reflect, in an appropriate manner and as far as is practicable, the effects of transactions and other events on an entity's financial performance and financial position. Accounting policies assist in this process by providing a framework within which elements of financial statements, such as assets and liabilities, are recognised, measured and presented. They enhance the comparability of financial statements by helping to ensure that similar transactions are reflected in a similar way. **19**

**This is illustrated in Example 4b in Appendix I.*

20 Two concepts – the going concern assumption and accruals – play a pervasive role in financial statements, and hence in the selection of accounting policies.

Going concern

21 **An entity should prepare its financial statements on a going concern basis, unless**

(a) the entity is being liquidated or has ceased trading, or
(b) the directors either intend to liquidate the entity or to cease trading, or have no realistic alternative but to do so,

in which circumstances the entity should prepare its financial statements on a basis other than that of a going concern.*

22 The information provided by financial statements is usually most relevant if prepared on the hypothesis that the entity is to continue in operational existence for the foreseeable future. This hypothesis is commonly referred to as the going concern assumption. Financial statements are usually prepared on the basis that the reporting entity is a going concern because measures based on break-up values tend not to be relevant to users seeking to assess the entity's cash-generation ability and financial adaptability.

23 **When preparing financial statements, directors should assess whether there are significant doubts about an entity's ability to continue as a going concern.**

24 If the directors, when making the assessment required by paragraph 23, are aware of material uncertainties related to events or conditions that may cast significant doubt upon the entity's ability to continue as a going concern, paragraph 61 requires them to disclose those uncertainties. In making their assessment, the directors take into account all available information about the foreseeable future.

25 The degree of consideration necessary to make the assessment required by paragraph 23 depends on the facts in each case. When an entity has a history of profitable operations, which are expected to continue, and ready access to financial resources, detailed analysis may not be necessary. In other cases, the directors may, in making their assessment, need to consider a wide range of factors surrounding current and expected profitability, debt repayment schedules and potential sources of replacement financing. Such considerations also govern the length of time in respect of which the assessment should be made.

Accruals

26 **An entity should prepare its financial statements, except for cash flow information, on the accrual basis of accounting.**

27 The accrual basis of accounting requires the non-cash effects of transactions and other events to be reflected, as far as is possible†, in the financial statements for the accounting period in which they occur, and not, for example, in the period in which any cash involved is received or paid. The accruals concept lies at the heart of the definitions of assets and liabilities, which are set out in FRS 5 'Reporting the

***Editor's note:** *Paragraph amended by FRS 21.*

†*In rare cases, it may not be possible to reflect the non-cash effects of transactions and other events in the financial statements for the accounting period in which they occur because they are not yet capable of reliable measurement. In such circumstances, recognition will be deferred until reliable measurement is possible.*

Substance of Transactions'. Accordingly, the use of those definitions to determine items to be recognised in an entity's balance sheet is consistent with the accruals concept.

Realisation

In preparing financial statements, an entity will have regard to requirements in companies legislation that only profits realised at the balance sheet date should be included in the profit and loss account. Companies legislation requires realised profits to be determined in accordance with principles generally accepted at the time that financial statements are prepared. It is generally accepted that profits shall be treated as realised,* for these purposes, only when realised in the form either of cash or of other assets the ultimate cash realisation of which can be assessed with reasonable certainty. 28

The requirements in paragraph 28 relating to realised profits and the profit and loss account apply unless there are special reasons for departing from them. However, such reasons will not exist unless, as a minimum, it is possible to be reasonably certain that, although a gain is unrealised, it nevertheless exists, and to measure it with sufficient reliability.† 29

Objectives and constraints in selecting accounting policies

The objectives against which an entity should judge the appropriateness of accounting policies to its particular circumstances are: 30

(a) relevance;
(b) reliability;
(c) comparability; and
(d) understandability.

The constraints that an entity should take into account in judging the appropriateness of accounting policies to its particular circumstances are: 31

(a) the need to balance the different objectives set out in paragraph 30; and
(b) the need to balance the cost of providing information with the likely benefit of such information to users of the entity's financial statements.

Although these objectives and constraints are discussed individually below, they are considered together in judging the appropriateness of accounting policies to an entity's particular circumstances. 32

Relevance

The objective of financial statements is to provide information about an entity's financial performance and financial position that is useful for assessing the stewardship of management and for making economic decisions. Financial information is relevant if it has the ability to influence the economic decisions of users and is 33

**In this context, 'realised' may also encompass profits relating to assets that are readily realisable.*

†In addition, where there are special reasons for departing from the requirements described in paragraph 28, directors will also consider whether a departure would result in the use of valuation bases or other accounting treatments not permitted by companies legislation, which would be available only if use of the true and fair override was justified.

provided in time to influence those decisions. Relevant information possesses either predictive or confirmatory value or both.

34 Appropriate accounting policies will result in financial information being presented that is relevant. Where more than one accounting policy would achieve this result, an entity will consider which of those policies presents the most relevant financial information in the context of the financial statements as a whole. In identifying that accounting policy, an entity will consider which measurement basis is most relevant and how to present information in the most relevant way.

Reliability

35 Financial information is reliable if:

(a) it can be depended upon by users to represent faithfully what it either purports to represent or could reasonably be expected to represent, and therefore reflects the substance of the transactions and other events that have taken place;
(b) it is free from deliberate or systematic bias (ie it is neutral);
(c) it is free from material error;
(d) it is complete within the bounds of materiality; and
(e) under conditions of uncertainty, it has been prudently prepared (ie a degree of caution has been applied in exercising judgement and making the necessary estimates).

36 Appropriate accounting policies will result in financial information being presented that is reliable. They will present transactions and other events in a way that reflects their substance. A transaction or other event is faithfully represented in financial statements if the way in which it is recognised, measured and presented in those statements corresponds closely to the effect of that transaction or event.

37 Often there is uncertainty, either about the existence of assets, liabilities, gains, losses and changes to shareholders' funds, or about the amount at which they should be measured. Prudence requires that accounting policies take account of such uncertainty in recognising and measuring those assets, liabilities, gains, losses and changes to shareholders' funds. In conditions of uncertainty, appropriate accounting policies will require more confirmatory evidence about the existence of an asset or gain than about the existence of a liability or loss, and a greater reliability of measurement for assets and gains than for liabilities and losses.

38 However, it is not necessary to exercise prudence where there is no uncertainty. Nor is it appropriate to use prudence as a reason for, for example, creating hidden reserves or excessive provisions, deliberately understating assets or gains, or deliberately overstating liabilities or losses, because that would mean that the financial statements are not neutral and therefore not reliable.

Comparability

39 Information in an entity's financial statements gains greatly in usefulness if it can be compared with similar information about the entity for some other period or point in time, and with similar information about other entities. Such comparability can usually be achieved through a combination of consistency and disclosure. The disclosures required in respect of an entity's accounting policies, and any changes to those policies, are set out in paragraph 55.

Appropriate accounting policies will result in financial information being presented in a way that enables users to discern and evaluate similarities in, and differences between, the nature and effects of transactions and other events taking place over time. In selecting accounting policies, an entity will assess whether accepted industry practices are appropriate to its particular circumstances. Such practices will be particularly persuasive if set out in a SORP that has been generally accepted by an industry or sector. **40**

Understandability

Information provided by financial statements needs to be capable of being understood by users having a reasonable knowledge of business and economic activities and accounting and a willingness to study with reasonable diligence the information provided. Appropriate accounting policies will result in financial information being presented in a way that enables its significance to be perceived by such users. **41**

Balancing the different objectives

There can be tensions between the different objectives set out in paragraph 30. In particular, sometimes the accounting policy that is most relevant to a particular entity's circumstances is not the most reliable, and vice versa. In such circumstances, the most appropriate accounting policy will usually be that which is the most relevant of those that are reliable. **42**

There can also be tension between two aspects of reliability – neutrality and prudence. Whilst neutrality involves freedom from deliberate or systematic bias, prudence is a potentially biased concept that seeks to ensure that, under conditions of uncertainty, gains and assets are not overstated and losses and liabilities are not understated. This tension exists only where there is uncertainty, because it is only then that prudence needs to be exercised. In the selection of accounting policies, the competing demands of neutrality and prudence are reconciled by finding a balance that ensures that the deliberate and systematic understatement of assets and gains and overstatement of liabilities and losses do not occur. **43**

Cost and benefit considerations

Paragraph 14 emphasises that accounting policies should be consistent with the requirements of accounting standards, UITF Abstracts and companies legislation. Accordingly, cost and benefit considerations will not justify the adoption of an accounting policy that is inconsistent with those requirements. **44**

Reviewing and changing accounting policies

An entity's accounting policies should be reviewed regularly to ensure that they remain the most appropriate to its particular circumstances for the purpose of giving a true and fair view. However, in judging whether a new policy is more appropriate than the existing policy, an entity will give due weight to the impact on comparability, as explained in paragraph 49. **45**

An entity may take account of recently issued FRSS – ie those for which the effective date falls in a later accounting period – in judging whether its present accounting policies are still the most appropriate to its particular circumstances. Paragraph 45 does not require early adoption of a new FRS, because the effective date of a new FRS allows an appropriate period for entities to consider and address any issues **46** surrounding its implementation. However, where it is necessary either to implement a new accounting policy or to change an existing accounting policy, an entity will ensure wherever possible that the new accounting policy is in accordance with recently issued FRSS.

47 An entity may take account of Financial Reporting Exposure Drafts (FREDS) in judging which accounting policies are most appropriate to its particular circumstances. However, in accordance with paragraph 14, an entity will not be free to adopt an accounting policy based on a FRED unless that policy is consistent with the requirements of existing accounting standards and UITF Abstracts. Moreover, there may be changes between a FRED and the ensuing FRS. Accordingly, where an entity believes that an accounting policy based on a FRED may be more appropriate than its existing policy, the entity will, in reaching a judgement, consider the factors discussed in paragraph 49.

48 Unless other accounting standards, UITF Abstracts or companies legislation require otherwise, a material adjustment applicable to prior periods arising from a change to an accounting policy is accounted for as a prior period adjustment, in accordance with the requirements of FRS 3 'Reporting Financial Performance'.

49 Frequent changes to accounting policies will not enhance comparability over the longer term, because they make it more difficult for users to compare an entity's financial statements with those of earlier periods. Consequently, the impact of past and expected future changes is considered when determining whether a potential change is desirable, and accounting policies are not changed unless the benefit to users outweighs the corresponding disadvantages. Nevertheless, consistency is not an end in itself and therefore does not impede the introduction of improved accounting practices that result in an overall benefit to users.

ESTIMATION TECHNIQUES

50 **Where estimation techniques are required to enable the accounting policies adopted to be applied, an entity should select estimation techniques that enable its financial statements to give a true and fair view and are consistent with the requirements of accounting standards, UITF Abstracts and companies legislation.**

51 **Where it is necessary to choose between estimation techniques that satisfy the conditions in paragraph 50, an entity should select whichever of those estimation techniques is judged by the entity to be most appropriate to its particular circumstances for the purpose of giving a true and fair view.**

52 The purpose of an estimation technique is to arrive at a monetary amount corresponding to a particular measurement basis. Accordingly, it is important for estimation techniques to be reliable and, all other things being equal, an entity will ideally select whichever estimation technique best approximates that monetary amount. However, it may not be possible to identify that estimation technique with certainty, at least at the time that financial statements are prepared, because estimation techniques are used only in circumstances where an amount is unknown. Moreover, materiality and cost and benefit considerations will usually play a part; greater accuracy of estimation often comes at an incremental cost, which may not be justified once improvements in accuracy cease to be material.

53 In addition, other factors will sometimes be relevant. In certain circumstances, paragraph 55(b) requires a description of the estimation technique selected to be given, so that users may consider the impact that different judgements might have had on the entity's financial statements and to enable comparisons to be made with the financial statements of other entities. When choosing between estimation techniques in circumstances where disclosures are likely to be required, an entity will also consider the extent to which each technique may be understood by users, and the extent to which each will facilitate comparisons with other entities.

A change to an estimation technique should not be accounted for as a prior period adjustment, unless 54

(a) it represents the correction of a fundamental error, or
(b) another accounting standard, a UITF Abstract or companies legislation requires the change to be accounted for as a prior period adjustment.

DISCLOSURES

The following information should be disclosed in the financial statements: 55

(a) a description of each of the accounting policies that is material in the context of the entity's financial statements.
(b) a description of those estimation techniques adopted that are significant, as explained in paragraph 57.
(c) details of any changes to the accounting policies that were followed in preparing financial statements for the preceding period, including:

(i) a brief explanation of why each new accounting policy is thought more appropriate;
(ii) where practicable, the effect of a prior period adjustment on the results for the preceding period, in accordance with FRS 3 'Reporting Financial Performance'; and
(iii) where practicable, an indication of the effect of a change in accounting policy on the results for the current period.
Where it is not practicable to make the disclosures described in (ii) or (iii) above, that fact, together with the reasons, should be stated.

(d) where the effect of a change to an estimation technique is material, a description of the change and, where practicable, the effect on the results for the current period.

The objective of the disclosures required by paragraph 55(a) is to enable the accounting policies adopted by an entity to be understood by users having a reasonable knowledge of business and economic activities and accounting and a willingness to study with reasonable diligence the information provided. Where an accounting policy is prescribed by, and fully described in, an accounting standard, a UITF Abstract or companies legislation, a succinct description of the policy will satisfy the requirements of paragraph 55(a). Where an accounting policy is not prescribed by an accounting standard, a UITF Abstract or companies legislation, or the entity uses an option permitted therein, a fuller description will be provided. 56

Estimation techniques are used where there is uncertainty over the monetary amount at which an item is to be measured. The amount that is determined will depend both on the estimation technique selected and on any assumptions (such as interest rates and useful lives) used in applying that technique. Although many estimation techniques are used in preparing financial statements, most do not require disclosure because, in most instances, the monetary amounts that might reasonably be ascribed to an item will fall within a relatively narrow range. An estimation technique is significant for the purposes of paragraph 55(b) only if the range of reasonable monetary amounts is so large that the use of a different amount from within that 57 range could materially affect the view shown by the entity's financial statements. To judge whether disclosures are required in respect of a particular estimation technique, an entity will consider the impact of varying the assumptions underlying that technique. The description of a significant estimation technique will include details of those underlying assumptions to which the monetary amount is particularly sensitive.

SORPs

58 **Where an entity's financial statements fall within the scope of a SORP, the entity should state the title of the SORP and whether its financial statements have been prepared in accordance with those of the SORP's provisions currently in effect.* In the event of a departure, the entity should give a brief description of how the financial statements depart from the recommended practice set out in the SORP, which should include:**

(a) for any treatment that is not in accordance with the SORP, the reasons why the treatment adopted is judged more appropriate to the entity's particular circumstances, and

(b) details of any disclosures recommended by the SORP that have not been provided, and the reasons why they have not been provided.

59 SORPs recommend particular accounting treatments with the aim of narrowing areas of difference and variety between comparable entities. Compliance with a SORP that has been generally accepted by an industry or sector leads to enhanced comparability between the financial statements of entities in that industry or sector. Comparability is further enhanced if users are made aware of the extent to which an entity complies with a SORP, and the reasons for any departures. The effect of a departure from a SORP need not be quantified, except in those rare cases where such quantification is necessary for the entity's financial statements to give a true and fair view.

60 Entities whose financial statements do not fall within the scope of a SORP may nevertheless choose to comply with the SORP's recommendations when preparing financial statements. Where this is the case, entities are encouraged to disclose that fact.

Going concern

61 **The following information should be disclosed in the financial statements in relation to the going concern assessment required by paragraph 23:**

(a) any material uncertainties, of which the directors are aware in making their assessment, related to events or conditions that may cast significant doubt upon the entity's ability to continue as a going concern.

(b) where the foreseeable future considered by the directors has been limited to a period of less than one year from the date of approval of the financial statements, that fact.

(c) when the financial statements are not prepared on a going concern basis, that fact, together with the basis on which the financial statements are prepared and the reason why the entity is not regarded as a going concern.

**The provisions of a SORP will cease to have effect, for example, to the extent that they conflict with a more recent accounting standard or UITF Abstract.*

True and fair view override

For any material departure from the requirements of an accounting standard, a UITF Abstract or companies legislation, particulars of the departure, the reasons for it and its effect should be disclosed. The information disclosed should include: 62

(a) a clear and unambiguous statement that there has been a departure from the requirements of an accounting standard, a UITF Abstract or companies legislation, as the case may be, and that the departure is necessary to give a true and fair view.
(b) a statement of the treatment that the accounting standard, UITF Abstract or companies legislation would normally require in the circumstances and a description of the treatment actually adopted.
(c) a statement of why the treatment prescribed would not give a true and fair view.
(d) a description of how the position shown in the financial statements is different as a result of the departure, normally with quantification, except where
(i) quantification is already evident in the financial statements themselves;* or
(ii) the effect cannot reasonably be quantified, in which case the directors should explain the circumstances.

Where a departure continues in subsequent financial statements, the disclosures should be made in all such subsequent statements, and should include corresponding amounts for the previous year. Where a departure affects only the corresponding amounts, the disclosures should be given for those corresponding amounts. 63

Where companies legislation requires an entity to make a statement of whether its financial statements have been prepared in accordance with applicable accounting standards†, that statement should either include or cross-reference any disclosures required by paragraph 62. 64

Where companies legislation requires disclosure of particulars of a departure from a specific statutory requirement, the reasons for it and its effect, disclosures equivalent to those set out in paragraph 62 should be provided.‡ 65

DATE FROM WHICH EFFECTIVE

Subject to paragraph 67, the accounting practices set out in the FRS should be regarded as standard in respect of accounting periods ending on or after 22 June 2001. Earlier adoption is encouraged. 66

**An example might be a matter of presentation rather than measurement.*

†*This disclosure is required by companies legislation as follows:*
*in Great Britain, the Companies Act 1985, Schedule 4, paragraph 36A (**Editor's note:** For accounting periods beginning on or after 6 April 2008 this changes to Paragraph 45 of Schedule 1 to the Large and Medium-sized Companies and Groups (Accounts and Reports) Regulations 2008 (SI 2008/410).); and*
in Northern Ireland, the Companies (Northern Ireland) Order 1986, Schedule 4, paragraph 36A. There is no equivalent requirement in the Republic of Ireland.

‡*In Great Britain, such disclosures in connection with a departure are required by the Companies Act 1985, sections 226(5) and 227(6), Schedule 4 paragraph 15, Schedule 4A paragraph 3(2), Schedule 8 paragraph 15, Schedule 9 paragraph 22 and Schedule 9A paragraph 19. The equivalent requirements in Northern Ireland and in the Republic of Ireland are set out in Appendix II. **Editor's note:** For accounting periods beginning on or after 6 April 2008 this changes to Sections 396 and 404 of the Companies Act 2006 and Paragraph 10 of Schedule 1 to the Large and Medium-sized Companies and Groups (Accounts and Reports) Regulations 2008 (SI 2008/410) with equivalent requirements for small companies, banks and insurance companies.*

67 Paragraphs 58–60 and the last sentence of paragraph 40 need not be applied in respect of accounting periods beginning on or before 23 December 2001, but earlier application is encouraged.

WITHDRAWAL OF SSAP 2 AND UITF ABSTRACTS 7 AND 14 AND AMENDMENT OF OTHER ACCOUNTING STANDARDS AND UITF ABSTRACTS

68 The FRS supersedes SSAP 2 'Disclosure of accounting policies', UITF Abstract 7 'True and fair view override disclosures' and UITF Abstract 14 'Disclosure of changes in accounting policy'.

69 The FRS makes the following changes to other accounting standards and UITF Abstracts:

[Not reproduced as all changes have been reflected in the material reproduced in this volume.]

Adoption of FRS 18 by the Board

Financial Reporting Standard 18 'Accounting Policies' was approved for issue by the ten members of the Accounting Standards Board.

Sir David Tweedie	(Chairman)
Allan Cook CBE	(Technical Director)
David Allvey	
Ian Brindle	
Dr John Buchanan	
John Coombe	
Huw Jones	
Isobel Sharp	
Professor Geoffrey Whittington	
Ken Wild	

Appendix I
Examples of changes to accounting policies and to estimation techniques

This appendix illustrates the application of the FRS to assist in clarifying its meaning. It does not form part of the FRS.

Example 1:
Capitalised finance costs

An entity has previously charged to the profit and loss account interest incurred in connection with the construction of tangible fixed assets. It now proposes to capitalise such interest, as permitted by FRS 15 'Tangible Fixed Assets', since it believes this better reflects the cost of constructing those assets.

Does this involve a change to:	
Recognition?	✓
Presentation?	✓
Measurement basis?	×

Explanation – The transaction whose effects are being reflected is the incurring of directly attributable finance costs. That transaction is still being measured in the same way, but there is a change to recognition, in that it is now being recognised as (part of) an asset rather than as an expense.* There is also, consequently, a change to the presentation of the transaction in the balance sheet and the profit and loss account.

Conclusion – This is a change of accounting policy.

Example 2:
Indirect overheads recorded in the value of stock

A manufacturing entity has three indirect cost centres (A, B and C). It has previously assessed that the indirect costs attributable to production are 30 per cent of A and 40 per cent of B. Having reassessed the nature of those cost centres' activities, it now assesses that the indirect costs attributable to production are 25 per cent of A, 40 per cent of B and 10 per cent of C.

Does this involve a change to:	
Recognition?	×
Presentation?	×
Measurement basis?	×

Explanation – This example has similarities with Example 1; cost centre C may be contrasted with interest in that example. The key difference is that, in Example 1, FRS 15 allows the entity a choice of how to treat directly attributable interest – as an asset

**Paragraph 9 of the FRS notes that where accounting standards allow a choice over what is to be recognised, that choice is a matter of accounting policy.*

or as an expense. There is no such choice here; directly attributable costs, once estimated, must be treated as part of an asset. Accordingly there is no change to recognition. In addition, both stocks and overheads continue to be presented in the same way and measured on the same basis (stocks are measured at the amount of directly attributable historical costs).

Conclusion – This is a change of estimation technique.

Example 3:
Classification of overheads

An entity has previously shown certain overheads within cost of sales. It now proposes to show those overheads within administrative expenses.

Does this involve a change to:	
Recognition?	×
Presentation?	✓
Measurement basis?	×

Explanation – Although there is no change to the recognition and measurement of costs, they are being presented differently.

Conclusion – This is a change of accounting policy.

Example 4a:
Depreciation of vehicles

An entity has previously depreciated vehicles using the reducing balance method at 40 per cent per year. It now proposes to depreciate vehicles using the straight-line method over five years, since it believes this better reflects the pattern of consumption of economic benefits.

Does this involve a change to:	
Recognition?	×
Presentation?	×
Measurement basis?	×

Explanation – Vehicles are being recognised and presented in the same way as before, and using the same, historical cost measurement basis. The only change is to the estimation technique used to measure the unexpired portion of each vehicle's economic benefits.

Conclusion – This is not a change of accounting policy.*

Example 4b:
Depreciation of vehicles

As in Example 4a, an entity has previously depreciated vehicles using the reducing balance method at 40 per cent per year and now proposes to depreciate vehicles using the straight-line method over five years. In addition, it has previously recorded the

**Paragraph 82 of FRS 15 also states that a change from one method of providing depreciation to another does not constitute a change of accounting policy.*

depreciation charge within cost of sales, but now proposes to include it within administrative expenses.

Does this involve a change to:	
Recognition?	×
Presentation?	✓
Measurement basis?	×

Explanation – This accounting change involves both a change to presentation, as in Example 3 above, and a change of estimation technique, as in Example 4a above. For the reasons set out in those examples, the former is a change of accounting policy but the latter is not.

Conclusion – The two changes are accounted for separately. No change is made to the amount of depreciation charged in earlier periods, but the profit and loss account for the preceding period is restated to move the depreciation charge from cost of sales to administrative expenses.

Example 5:
Accounting for fungible stocks

An entity has fungible stocks and its accounting policy has previously been to consider those stocks in aggregate, measuring them at weighted average historical cost. However, it determines that the normal accounting policy in its industry is to measure such stocks at historical cost on a FIFO basis. It concludes, for reasons of comparability, that it should adopt the normal industry policy.

Does this involve a change to:	
Recognition?	×
Presentation?	×
Measurement basis?	✓

Explanation – There is explicitly a change of measurement basis.*

Conclusion – This is a change of accounting policy, and it should be disclosed. However, a prior period adjustment will be required only if the difference between weighted average and FIFO is material.

Example 6a:
Discounting

An entity has previously reported deferred tax on an undiscounted basis. However, the norm in its industry is to report deferred tax on a discounted basis. It concludes, for reasons of comparability, that it should adopt the normal industry approach.

**As explained in paragraph 10 of the FRS, an entity with fungible assets will make clear, when disclosing its accounting policy, whether it is to consider those assets individually or, if in aggregate, which measurement basis is reflected (FIFO, weighted average etc.). For many entities, however, the difference between measurement bases in value terms may not be material.*

Does this involve a change to:	
Recognition?	×
Presentation?	×
Measurement basis?	✓

Explanation – FRS 19 allows entities to report deferred tax on either a discounted or an undiscounted basis. These are two different measurement bases, and it is a matter of accounting policy which an entity chooses to adopt.

Conclusion – This is a change of accounting policy.

Example 6b:
Discounting

An entity has previously measured a particular provision on an undiscounted basis, in accordance with FRS 12 'Provisions, Contingent Liabilities and Contingent Assets', as the effect of discounting was not material. However, this year it has revised upwards its estimates of future cash flows associated with the provision and, as a result, the effect of discounting is now material. FRS 12 therefore requires it to report the provision at the discounted amount.

Does this involve a change to:	
Recognition?	×
Presentation?	×
Measurement basis?	×

Explanation – FRS 12 requires entities to report provisions at the best estimate of the expenditure required to settle the present obligation at the balance sheet date. Where that estimate is based on future cash flows, it is permissible to use undiscounted amounts only where the effect of the time value of money is not material. In such circumstances, the use of undiscounted future cash flows is, in effect, an estimation technique for arriving at the present value.

Conclusion – This is not a change of accounting policy.

Example 7:
Translating the financial statements of a foreign subsidiary

A group has previously translated the profit and loss account of its foreign subsidiary using the closing rate. However, it now proposes to use the average rate for the accounting period, on the basis that this reflects more fairly the group's profits and losses as they arise throughout the accounting period.

Does this involve a change to:	
Recognition?	×
Presentation?	×
Measurement basis?	✓

Explanation – SSAP 20 'Foreign currency translation' allows a group translating the profit and loss account of a foreign subsidiary under the closing rate/net investment method to use either the closing rate or the average rate for the accounting period. These are two different measurement bases for the profit and loss account, and it is a matter of accounting policy which an entity chooses to adopt.

Conclusion – This is a change of accounting policy.

Appendix II
Note on legal requirements

Great Britain*

The statutory requirements relating to accounting policies are set out in the Companies Act 1985. The main requirements that are directly relevant are set out in Schedules 4 and 4A and are summarised below. 1

Schedules 4 and 4A to the Act do not apply to banking and insurance companies and groups. Corresponding requirements are set out in Schedule 9 for banking companies and groups and in Schedule 9A for insurance companies and groups. Schedule 4 to the Act does not apply to small companies to the extent that they choose instead to comply with the reduced requirements set out in Schedule 8. 2

Accounting principles

Paragraph 9 of Schedule 4 requires the amounts to be included in a company's accounts to be determined in accordance with the following principles set out in paragraphs 10–14 of Schedule 4, unless there are special reasons for departing from any of those principles: 3

(a) the company shall be presumed to be carrying on business as a going concern;
(b) accounting policies shall be applied consistently within the same accounts and from one financial year to the next;
(c) the amount of any item shall be determined on a prudent basis, and in particular–
   (i) only profits realised at the balance sheet date shall be included in the profit and loss account; and
   (ii) all liabilities and losses which have arisen or are likely to arise in respect of the financial year to which the accounts relate or a previous financial year shall be taken into account, including those which only become apparent between the balance sheet date and the date on which it is signed on behalf of the board of directors;

****Editor's note:** The various statutory references change with the introduction of the Companies Act 2006, which affects accounting for periods beginning on or after 6 April 2008. The various statutory references have changed as follows:*

Companies Act 1985 reference	***Companies Act 2006 reference***
Schedule 4	*Schedule 1 to the Large and Medium-sized Companies and Groups (Accounts and Reports) Regulations 2008 (SI 2008/410)*
Schedule 8	*Schedule 1 to The Small Companies and Groups (Accounts and Directors' Report) Regulations 2008 (SI 2008/409)*
Schedules 9 and 9A	*Schedules 2 and 3 to SI 2008/410*
Paragraphs 9 to 14 of Schedule 4	*Paragraph 10 to 15 of Schedule 1 to SI 2008/410*
Paragraph 15 of Schedule 4	*Paragraph 10 of Schedule 1 to SI 2008/410*
Paragraph 36 of Schedule 4	*Paragraph 44 of Schedule 1 to SI 2008/410*
Paragraphs 17 to 28 of Schedule 4	*Paragraphs 16 to 29 of Schedule 1 to SI 2008/410*
Paragraphs 29 to 34 of Schedule 4	*Paragraphs 30 to 35 of Schedule 1 to SI 2008/410*
Paragraph 45 of Schedule 4	*Paragraph 54 of Schedule 1 to SI 2008/410*
Paragraph 58 of Schedule 4	*Paragraph 70 of Schedule 1 to SI 2008/410*
Paragraph 4 (2) of Schedule 4	*Repealed*
Paragraphs 3 and 4 of Schedule 4A	*Paragraphs 3 and 4 of Schedule 6 to SI 2008/410*
Sections 226 and 227	*Sections 396 and 404*
Section 262 (3)	*Section 853*

(d) all income and charges relating to the financial year to which the accounts relate shall be taken into account, without regard to the date of receipt or payment; and
(e) in determining the aggregate amount of any item the amount of each individual asset or liability that falls to be taken into account shall be determined separately.

4 Paragraph 15 of Schedule 4 permits the directors of a company to depart from any of the principles stated above in preparing the company's accounts in respect of any financial year if it appears to them that there are special reasons for such a departure. Particulars of the departure, the reasons for it and its effect are required to be given in a note to the accounts.

5 Although 'prudence' is not defined in the Act, the Act describes the requirement that the amount of any item shall be determined on a prudent basis in a way that differs from the FRS. Nevertheless, the Board believes that the requirements of the FRS are not inconsistent with those of the Act.*

Disclosure of accounting policies

6 Paragraph 36 of Schedule 4 requires disclosure of the accounting policies adopted by a company (including the policies regarding the depreciation and diminution in value of assets).†

Measurement bases

7 Except to the extent that a company chooses to adopt the alternative accounting rules, the amounts to be included in a company's accounts are to be determined in accordance with the historical cost accounting rules set out in paragraphs 17–28 of Schedule 4. The alternative accounting rules are set out in paragraphs 29–34 of Schedule 4.

8 The following paragraphs of Schedule 4 require disclosures in respect of measurement bases:

(a) where stocks or other fungible assets are measured using 'first in, first out' (FIFO), 'last in, first out' (LIFO),‡ weighted average price or a similar method, paragraph 27(3) requires the difference between the amount measured using that method and on the basis of replacement cost at the balance sheet date, or of most recent actual cost, to be disclosed if material.

**This matter is discussed in greater detail in paragraphs 3–8 of Appendix V to FRS 12 'Provisions, Contingent Liabilities and Contingent Assets'.*

†According to legal advice received by the Financial Reporting Review Panel, a statement that accounts have been prepared in accordance with applicable accounting standards, as required by paragraph 36A, does not satisfy the requirement in paragraph 36. To satisfy that requirement, there must be a brief statement of each relevant accounting policy, either in the accounts themselves or in the notes to the accounts. However, paragraph 36 does not require disclosure of accounting policies that are immaterial in the context of the accounts in question.

‡SSAP 9 'Stocks and long-term contracts' notes that 'the use of the LIFO method can result in the reporting of current assets at amounts that bear little relationship to recent costs. This may result in not only a significant misstatement of balance sheet amounts but also a potential distortion of current and future results. This places a special responsibility on the directors to be assured that the circumstances of the company require the adoption of such a valuation method in order for the accounts to give a true and fair view.'

(b) where the alternative accounting rules set out in paragraph 31 are adopted as the measurement bases for certain assets, paragraph 33(2) requires disclosure of each item affected and the basis of valuation, and paragraph 33(3) requires disclosure for each item affected (except stocks) either of the amount that would have been determined under the historical cost accounting rules, or of the difference between the amount measured under the historical cost accounting rules and under the alternative accounting rule adopted.

(c) paragraph 45(2) requires disclosure of the aggregate market value of listed investments where this differs from the amount included in a company's accounts, and of both the market value and the stock exchange value of any investments of which the former value is, for the purposes of a company's accounts, taken as being higher than the latter.

(d) paragraph 58(1) requires disclosure of the basis on which any amounts originally denominated in foreign currencies have been translated into sterling for inclusion in the balance sheet or profit and loss account.

Comparability

Paragraph 4(2) of Schedule 4 requires the corresponding amount for any item in a company's balance sheet or profit and loss account to be adjusted if it is not comparable with the amount for the current financial year. Particulars of the adjustment and the reasons for it are to be disclosed. Paragraph 58(2) of Schedule 4 extends this requirement to corresponding amounts stated in notes to the accounts, with the exception of the items listed in paragraph 58(3) of Schedule 4. **9**

Group accounts

Where assets and liabilities to be included in group accounts have been valued or otherwise determined according to accounting rules differing from those used for the group accounts, paragraph 3 of Schedule 4A requires the values or amounts to be adjusted so as to accord with the rules used for the group accounts, unless it appears to the directors of the parent company that there are special reasons for departing from this rule. Particulars of any such departure, the reasons for it and its effect shall be given in a note to the accounts. **10**

Paragraph 4 of Schedule 4A requires any differences of accounting rules as between a parent company's individual accounts for a financial year and its group accounts to be disclosed in a note to the group accounts and the reasons for the difference to be given. **11**

The true and fair view override

In special circumstances, compliance with a provision of the Act on the matters to be included in a company's accounts (or notes thereto) may be inconsistent with the requirement to give a true and fair view of the state of affairs and profit or loss. Sections 226(5) and 227(6) of the Act provide, for individual company accounts and for group accounts, that in such circumstances the directors shall depart from that provision to the extent necessary to give a true and fair view* Where this true and fair view override is used, the Act requires particulars of the departure, the reasons for it and its effect to be given in a note to the accounts. **12**

**However, if a true and fair view can be achieved by the provision of additional information, there is no inconsistency. No departure is allowed in such circumstances.*

Realisation

13 Part VIII of the Act sets limits on a company's ability to make distributions to its members. Different rules apply to public companies, private companies, investment companies and insurance companies, but those rules are in part concerned with whether gains and losses have been realised. Realised profits and realised losses are defined in section 262(3) of the Act:

> 'References in this Part to "realised profits" and "realised losses", in relation to a company's accounts, are to such profits or losses of the company as fall to be treated as realised in accordance with principles generally accepted, at the time when the accounts are prepared, with respect to the determination for accounting purposes of realised profits or losses.
>
> This is without prejudice to –
>
> (a) the construction of any other expression (where appropriate) by reference to accepted accounting principles or practice, or
> (b) any specific provision for the treatment of profits or losses of any description as realised.'

14 The concept of realisation is discussed further in paragraphs 15–20 of Appendix IV.

Northern Ireland

15 The statutory requirements in Northern Ireland are set out in the Companies (Northern Ireland) Order 1986. Those requirements are identical to the legislation for Great Britain cited above.

Republic of Ireland

16 The statutory requirements in the Republic of Ireland that correspond to those cited above for Great Britain are shown in the following table.

Great Britain	*Republic of Ireland*
section 226(5) of the Companies Act 1985	section 3(1) of the Companies (Amendment) Act 1986
section 227(6) of the Companies Act 1985	Regulation 14(3) and (4) of the European Communities (Companies: Group Accounts) Regulations 1992
section 262(3) of the Companies Act 1985	paragraph 72 of the Schedule to the Companies (Amendment) Act 1986
Part VIII of the Companies Act 1985	Part IV of the Companies (Amendment) Act 1983
Schedule 4 to the Companies Act 1985:	The Companies (Amendment) Act 1986:
paragraph 4(2)	section 4(8)
paragraph 9	section 5
paragraph 10	section 5(a)
paragraph 11	section 5(b)
paragraph 12	section 5(c)

paragraph 13	section 5(d)
paragraph 14	section 5(e)
paragraph 15	section 6
Schedule 4 to the Companies Act 1985:	The Schedule to the Companies (Amendment) Act 1986:
paragraphs 17—28	paragraphs 5—16*
paragraph 27(3)	paragraph 15(3)
paragraphs 29—34	paragraphs 17—22†
paragraph 33(2)	paragraph 21(2)
paragraph 33(3)	paragraph 21(3)
paragraph 36	paragraph 24
paragraph 36A	no equivalent
paragraph 45(2)	paragraph 31(2)
paragraph 58(1)	paragraph 44(1)
paragraph 58(2)	paragraph 44(2)
paragraph 58(3)(a)–(c)	no equivalent
paragraph 58(3)(d)	paragraph 44(3)
Schedule 4A to the Companies Act 1985:	European Communities(Companies: Group Accounts) Regulations 1992:
paragraph 3	Regulation 30
paragraph 4	Regulation 29
Schedule 8 to the Companies Act 1985	no equivalent
Schedule 9 to the Companies Act 1985	European Communities (Credit Institutions: Accounts) Regulations 1992
Schedule 9A to the Companies Act 1985	European Communities (Insurance Undertakings: Accounts) Regulations 1996

**Note: there is no requirement corresponding to paragraph 27(2)(b) of Schedule 4.*

†*Note: there is no requirement corresponding to paragraph 34(3A) of Schedule 4.*

Appendix III
Compliance with International Accounting Standards

1 The International Accounting Standards Committee deals with accounting policies in its standards IAS 1 (revised 1997) 'Presentation of Financial Statements' and IAS 8 (revised 1993) 'Net Profit or Loss for the Period, Fundamental Errors and Changes in Accounting Policies'. The general requirements for accounting policies in the FRS are consistent with those standards, except as discussed below.*

2 IAS 8 (revised 1993) defines accounting policies as the specific principles, bases, conventions, rules and practices adopted by an enterprise in preparing and presenting financial statements. The definition in the FRS also refers to principles, bases, conventions, rules and practices, but it is more specific about the role that accounting policies play in the preparation and presentation of financial statements. Specifically, accounting policies are applied by an entity in order to reflect the effects of transactions and other events through recognising, selecting measurement bases for, and presenting assets, liabilities, gains, losses and changes to shareholders' funds.

3 The FRS defines estimation techniques and distinguishes them from accounting policies. IAS 8 (revised 1993) distinguishes between a change of accounting policy and a change of accounting estimate, but does not include an equivalent definition.

4 IAS 1 (revised 1997) requires management to develop accounting policies that provide information that is relevant and reliable, and that provide the most useful information to users, but only in the absence both of a specific IAS and of an interpretation of the Standing Interpretations Committee.† Accordingly, where specific IASs or interpretations of the Standing Interpretations Committee allow different treatments, an entity is permitted a free choice; it is not required in such circumstances to choose whichever policy will provide the most useful information to users. By contrast, the FRS requires that, where more than one treatment is allowed, an entity should use the criteria of relevance, reliability, comparability and understandability to select the policy that is the most appropriate of those allowed.

5 IAS 1 (revised 1997) requires management to make an assessment of an enterprise's ability to continue as a going concern, taking into account all available information for the foreseeable future, which should be at least, but is not limited to, twelve months from the balance sheet date. The FRS includes a similar requirement but, like the UK Auditing Standard SAS 130 'The going concern basis in financial statements', it does not specify a minimum length for the foreseeable future. Instead, it requires disclosure where the directors have considered a period of less than twelve months from the date of approval of the financial statements.‡

6 IAS 1 (revised 1997) requires financial statements to be prepared on a going concern basis unless management either intends to liquidate the enterprise or to cease trading, or has no realistic alternative but to do so. The FRS includes a requirement that is similar except that management intent is not sufficient to justify a departure from the going concern basis. Accordingly, the FRS requires an entity's financial statements to be prepared on a going concern basis unless the entity is being liquidated or has ceased trading, or the directors have no realistic alternative but to liquidate the entity or to cease trading.

***Editor's note:** *IAS 1 and IAS 8 have both been revised. IAS 8 now contains all guidance on accounting policies.*

†**Editor's note:** *The Standard Interpretations Committee has now been replaced by the International Financial Reporting Interpretations Committee.*

‡**Editor's note:** *SAS 130 is no longer applicable, and has now been replaced by ISA (UK and Ireland) 570,* Going Concern.

Appendix IV
The development of the FRS

History

The FRS sets out the principles to be followed in selecting accounting policies and the disclosures needed to help users to understand the accounting policies adopted and how they have been implemented. It supersedes SSAP 2 'Disclosure of accounting policies', which was issued in November 1971. 1

The objective of SSAP 2 was to ensure disclosure in an entity's financial statements of clear explanations of the accounting policies followed insofar as they were significant for the purpose of giving a true and fair view. At the time it was issued, no statement of principles existed in the UK and the Republic of Ireland to provide a framework within which 'accounting policies' might be defined. Accordingly, SSAP 2 introduced and defined 'fundamental accounting concepts', singling out four – going concern, accruals, consistency and prudence – which have since been reflected in the EC Accounting Directives and in companies legislation in the UK and the Republic of Ireland.* 2

SSAP 2 made clear that this approach was expedient rather than theoretical. The fundamental accounting concepts were to be regarded as working assumptions having general acceptance at the time of issue of the standard – practical rules rather than theoretical ideals. It was envisaged that, as accounting thought and practice developed, the concepts would be capable of variation and evolution. 3

In December 1999, the Board issued its Statement of Principles for Financial Reporting, which reflected, among other things, how accounting developments in the 28 years since SSAP 2 was issued had affected the fundamental accounting concepts identified in that standard. Although the Statement of Principles discussed each of the concepts individually, they were no longer referred to as 'fundamental accounting concepts' and their respective roles had changed, as explained further below. 4

A number of respondents to the Revised Exposure Draft of the Statement of Principles commented that SSAP 2 should be amended in the light of that document. The Board agreed and in December 1999 it published FRED 21 'Accounting Policies', which set out proposals to update the concepts underpinning SSAP 2. In other respects, the Board regarded SSAP 2 as broadly satisfactory, retaining many of its requirements in FRED 21, but it took the opportunity to clarify and to expand on certain matters. Accordingly, the FRED: 5

- sought to make the distinction between a change of accounting policy and a change of estimate more robust, by including a more specific definition of accounting policies and a new definition of estimation techniques
- set out clearly a requirement, implied but not explicit in SSAP 2, that an entity should adopt those accounting policies that are most appropriate to its particular circumstances for the purpose of giving a true and fair view
- set out the objectives and constraints to be considered when selecting and changing accounting policies
- set out circumstances in which an entity should also disclose details of the estimation techniques used in implementing its accounting policies

**See paragraphs 3 and 4 of Appendix II 'Note on legal requirements' (and paragraph 16 for the Republic of Ireland).*

6 The Board has considered the comments of respondents to FRED 21 in developing the FRS. The most significant comments, and the resulting changes made to the proposals in FRED 21, are discussed in the following sections.

The fundamental accounting concepts in SSAP 2

7 As SSAP 2 envisaged, the meanings attaching to the fundamental accounting concepts, and their individual importance relative to one another, have developed and evolved over time. Accordingly, they are treated somewhat differently in the FRS from the way in which they were treated in SSAP 2.

Going concern and accruals

8 Two of the concepts – going concern and accruals – have a particularly prominent role in the FRS. That is because they are part of the bedrock of accounting, and hence critical to the selection of accounting policies. The going concern assumption determines the perspective from which the objectives and constraints set out in the FRS should be viewed, particularly with regard to measurement. The accruals concept lies at the heart of the definitions of assets, liabilities, gains, losses and changes to shareholders' funds, and both notions play an important role in the recognition of those items.

9 In discussing the accruals concept, SSAP 2 explained that revenues and costs should be matched with one another so far as their relationship can be established or justifiably assumed, and dealt with in the profit and loss account of the period to which they relate. The FRS takes a slightly different approach to the accruals concept. Rather than focusing on when a relationship can be established or justifiably assumed, it emphasises instead that the non-cash effects of transactions and other events should be reflected, as far as is possible, in the financial statements for the accounting period in which they occur, and not, for example, in the period in which any cash involved is received or paid.* Together with the definitions of assets and liabilities, set out in FRS 5 'Reporting the Substance of Transactions', this provides a discipline within which the matching process can operate, while still resulting in the simultaneous recognition of revenues and costs that result from the same transactions or events.

10 SSAP 2 did not require financial statements to be prepared in accordance with the going concern and accruals concepts; rather, where this was not the case, it required the facts to be disclosed and explained. This approach was also taken in FRED 21, but several respondents suggested that the role of these concepts should be strengthened. Respondents also suggested that disclosure should be required of any material uncertainties that might cast doubt on an entity's ability to continue as a going concern, as is the case under the International Accounting Standard IAS 1 (revised 1997) 'Presentation of Financial Statements'.

11 The Board has accepted these proposals. Accordingly the FRS requires financial statements to be prepared on a going concern basis† and on the accruals basis. The FRS also requires directors to assess whether there are significant doubts about the entity's ability to continue as a going concern and to disclose any material

**This approach is consistent with that taken in the Statement of Principles.*

†*Except where an entity is being liquidated or has ceased trading, or the directors have no realistic alternative but to liquidate the entity or to cease trading.*

uncertainties, of which they are aware, related to events or conditions that may raise such doubts.*

FRS 21 'Events after the Balance Sheet Date' was issued in May 2004. It was based on IAS 10 'Events after the Balance Sheet Date' and is effective for accounting periods beginning on or after 1 January 2005. To conform with FRS 21 and international accounting standards a consequential amendment was made to paragraph 21. **11A**

21 An entity should prepare its financial statements on a going concern basis, unless

(a) the entity is being liquidated or has ceased trading, or
(b) the directors either intend to liquidate the entity or to cease trading, or have no realistic alternative but to do so,

in which circumstances the entity should prepare its financial statements on a basis other than that of a going concern.†

Consistency and prudence

The other two concepts from SSAP 2 – consistency and prudence – are rather different in that they are desirable qualities of financial information rather than part of the bedrock of accounting. The FRS therefore discusses them in the context of the objectives against which an entity should judge the appropriateness of accounting policies to its particular circumstances. **12**

Like the Statement of Principles, the FRS regards comparability as a more fundamental objective than consistency. Information in financial statements should be prepared and presented in a way that enables users to discern and evaluate similarities in, and differences between, the nature and effects of transactions and other events taking place over time and across different reporting entities. Although comparability is usually achieved through consistency, the latter is not an end in itself and there will be circumstances in which it needs to be sacrificed. In particular, whilst consistency is important, it should not be allowed to prevent improvements in accounting. Where the introduction of a new accounting policy would result in an overall benefit to users, an entity should not use consistency to justify retaining an existing policy that is no longer the most appropriate to its particular circumstances. **13**

The FRS also reflects how the prudence concept has evolved from the way in which it was described in SSAP 2. Since SSAP 2 was issued, the smoothing of reported profits has become as great a concern as their overstatement and, as a result, the deliberate understatement of assets and gains and the deliberate overstatement of liabilities are no longer seen as a virtue. Accordingly, like the Statement of Principles, the FRS treats prudence as one aspect of the overall objective of reliability. In conditions of uncertainty, prudence requires more confirmatory evidence about the existence of an asset or gain than about the existence of a liability or loss, and a greater reliability of measurement for assets and gains than for liabilities and losses. **14**

**Differences between the requirements of the FRS and of IAS 1 (revised 1997) are discussed in Appendix III.*

†***Editor's note:** Paragraph inserted by FRS 21.*

Realisation

15 One aspect of prudence as described in SSAP 2 was that revenue and profits should be included in the profit and loss account only when realised in the form either of cash or of other assets the ultimate cash realisation of which could be assessed with reasonable certainty. However, the FRS does not refer to the notion of realisation in discussing prudence.

16 The realisation notion was originally concerned with the conversion into cash of non-cash resources and rights, and was intended to ensure that sufficient cash was available to distribute profits without an entity becoming insolvent. By the time SSAP 2 was issued, the notion had evolved so that it was also concerned with claims to cash, and was used to ensure that only gains that were reasonably certain, and unlikely to reverse, were included in the profit and loss account.

17 By the time that FRED 21 was being developed, however, the linking of prudence to realisation in SSAP 2 had itself become out of date. Markets have developed so that it is often possible to be reasonably certain that a gain exists, and to measure it with sufficient reliability, even if no disposal has occurred. One approach to this problem might have been to try to update the notion of realisation. However, the Board believes that it is preferable to focus on the underlying objective. In the Board's view, this is that a gain should be recognised only if there is reasonable certainty that it exists and if it can be measured reliably. Accordingly, the FRED and the FRS both discuss the concept of prudence in these terms, rather than in terms of realisation.

18 This approach provoked much comment from respondents to the FRED, with some supportive but many expressing concern. Two themes emerged strongly from the responses:

- although the Board does not believe that it is useful to link prudence and realisation, requirements based on the notion of realisation are nevertheless part of companies legislation. Respondents were concerned that the Board appeared, in effect, to be encouraging entities to ignore or flout those requirements.
- rather than fixing the interpretation of the notion of realisation, companies legislation requires it to be determined in accordance with principles generally accepted at the time when financial statements are prepared. The description of realisation in SSAP 2 provided a strong underpinning to those principles, and respondents were concerned that its omission from the FRED would lead to that underpinning being removed.

19 As regards the first concern, it was never the Board's intention to encourage entities to ignore or flout requirements of companies legislation. Certain paragraphs from the FRED have been redrafted to reduce any risk of ambiguity in that regard. In particular, paragraph 14 of the FRS makes clear that entities should adopt accounting policies that are consistent with the requirements of other accounting standards and of companies legislation, which will include any requirements relating to realisation. Paragraph 29 and its footnote have also been redrafted to avoid wrongly giving the impression that the Board is encouraging entities to depart from such requirements.

20 The words from SSAP 2 describing the notion of realisation have been included in paragraph 28 of the FRS in order to address the second concern. Although the FRS does not maintain the link between prudence and realisation from SSAP 2, the Board had not intended to create uncertainty in respect of existing realisation requirements, and the inclusion of these words is intended to preserve the status quo.

Definitions

Accounting bases

SSAP 2 defined both accounting bases and accounting policies. It explained that accounting bases are the methods developed for applying fundamental accounting concepts to financial transactions and items, while accounting policies are the specific accounting bases adopted by an entity. In developing the FRS, the Board considered whether the concept of accounting bases was useful in defining accounting policies. 21

The Board noted that definitions of accounting policies adopted by other standard-setters do not refer to accounting bases in this way. In addition, it noted that there are no other UK accounting standards in which the phrase 'accounting bases' is used, and that a distinction between accounting bases and accounting policies does not appear to have any practical consequences for recognition, measurement or disclosure in financial statements. Finally, it noted that references in SSAP 2 to accounting bases had led in some instances to confusion, for example about whether a choice of depreciation method was an accounting basis. 22

For these reasons, the Board concluded that it is not necessary, and might be confusing, to continue to define accounting policies as the specific accounting bases adopted by an entity. Instead, the FRS makes clear by its context whether the phrase 'accounting policies' refers to such policies in general or to the specific policies adopted by an entity. 23

Accounting policies and estimation techniques

Having recognised that it is not always easy to distinguish between a change of accounting policy and a change of estimate, the Board also looked again at the definition of an accounting policy. SSAP 2 referred to 'the methods developed for applying fundamental accounting concepts to financial transactions and items', but it is clear that some methods adopted by an entity are merely estimates rather than accounting policies. 24

Accordingly, the FRS introduces a more specific definition of an accounting policy. As defined in the FRS, accounting policies are concerned with the recognition and presentation of assets, liabilities, gains, losses and changes to shareholders' funds, and with the selection of measurement bases for those items. However, methods used to arrive at a monetary amount corresponding to the measurement basis selected are in the nature of estimates rather than accounting policies. Accordingly, the FRS defines such methods as 'estimation techniques' and makes clear that they are not accounting policies. 25

The Board believes that this approach will make it easier to distinguish between a change of accounting policy and a change of accounting estimate. Where an accounting change leads to an asset, liability or other item being measured in a different way, an important question is whether this involves a change of measurement basis – ie whether a different attribute of the item is being measured. If so, it will be a change of accounting policy. Otherwise, it will be merely a change of estimation technique. 26

FRS 3 'Reporting Financial Performance'

Some respondents suggested that material relating to prior period adjustments included in FRS 3 'Reporting Financial Performance' might more appropriately be 27 included in an FRS developed from FRED 21. However, in June 1999 the Board published a Discussion Paper entitled 'Reporting Financial Performance: proposals for change', which included a proposal that might affect the circumstances in which errors in earlier financial statements would lead to prior period adjustments. Accordingly, while the Board agrees that, in the longer term, it may be appropriate for material relating to prior period adjustments to be included with the material in this FRS, it does not believe it is appropriate to move material from FRS 3 at present.

Adopting and changing accounting policies

Requiring adoption of the most appropriate accounting policies

28 The standard accounting practice required by SSAP 2 was concerned, explicitly, only with disclosure. Nevertheless, the explanatory note to SSAP 2 described accounting policies as being those 'judged by business enterprises to be most appropriate to their circumstances', while the definition of an enterprise's accounting policies referred to them being 'best suited to present fairly its results and financial position'. The FRS makes explicit that an entity should adopt those accounting policies judged to be the most appropriate to its particular circumstances for the purpose of giving a true and fair view.

29 A minority of respondents suggested that an FRS developed from FRED 21 should require only that accounting policies be appropriate, rather than most appropriate. The Board rejected this as being a step backwards from the position under SSAP 2. Other respondents suggested that the approach set out in the FRED would be more onerous than SSAP 2; however, although the FRS uses the phrase 'most appropriate' whereas the SSAP sometimes used the phrase 'best suited', the Board believes both phrases reflect the same underlying objective.

30 In addition, some respondents expressed concern that the approach taken in the FRED might create difficulties for directors and auditors, particularly if similar entities adopt different accounting policies or if an entity's choice of accounting policies is subsequently challenged. The Board does not believe that such difficulties should arise. The FRS makes clear that the most appropriate accounting policies are to be judged in the context of an entity's particular circumstances; different policies may be most appropriate in different circumstances. Further, the choice of accounting policies is only one of many judgements involved in the preparation of financial statements. For any such judgement it may become clear, with the benefit of hindsight, that a different judgement would have been more appropriate, but that does not invalidate an earlier judgement arrived at in good faith. In particular, where an entity changes accounting policies it does not follow that its former accounting policies were in some sense wrong, or that financial statements prepared under those former policies did not give a true and fair view.

31 Finally, a small number of respondents thought the FRED was proposing that an entity should disregard or overrule the requirements of other accounting standards and legislation in determining the most appropriate accounting policies. As explained below, this was not the case; however, the FRS has been amended to avoid any confusion in this respect.

Identifying the most appropriate accounting policies

32 In identifying the accounting policies to be followed, directors need to ensure that an entity complies with the provisions of other accounting standards and specific statutory requirements. This will often mean that the policies available to an entity are restricted, and on occasions there may be only one acceptable accounting policy to be followed. However, where more than one policy is acceptable the FRS requires the entity to adopt whichever of those policies is judged to be the most appropriate.

The Board acknowledges that the judgement of which accounting policy is most appropriate for the purpose of giving a true and fair view will to an extent be subjective, since it must take into account an entity's particular circumstances. Nevertheless, it is important that different entities have the same goal in sight when selecting policies, which is that they should reflect, as far as is practicable, the effects of transactions and other events on the entity's financial performance and financial position in an appropriate manner. Accordingly, the FRS specifies objectives and constraints that an entity should take into account in judging which accounting policies are most appropriate. **33**

The FRS does not prescribe measurement bases, but some examples of changes to accounting policies and to estimation techniques are set out in Appendix I. However, some respondents suggested that the proposals in FRED 21 implied that the Board was seeking to require entities to make greater use of current values and to restrict legitimate options to report assets at historical cost. This was not the Board's intention, nor does it believe that this will be the effect of the FRS. Where it is permissible to report an asset on either a historical cost or a current value basis, as under FRS 15 'Tangible Fixed Assets' for example, an entity will judge which of those policies is most appropriate to its particular circumstances. Factors to be taken into account will include, among others, the relevance of the information to users, comparability with other entities and also the relative costs and benefits of the different policies. Moreover, different judgements may be likely depending on the nature both of the asset and of the reporting entity. **34**

Changing accounting policies

The FRS requires accounting policies to be reviewed regularly to ensure that they remain the most appropriate to an entity's particular circumstances, and a new accounting policy to be implemented if judged more appropriate. Although the objectives and constraints to be considered by an entity will not change, the relative merits of a particular accounting policy, and of the associated measurement basis, may change over time. **35**

Many respondents expressed the view that it is unhelpful to users for an entity to change accounting policy too frequently, and that the FRED had placed insufficient emphasis on this longer-term aspect of comparability. The Board agrees that there is a balance to be achieved in this regard. Accordingly, paragraph 49 of the FRS makes clear that, in judging whether a change of accounting policy is appropriate, an entity will assess whether the benefit to users arising from the new policy outweighs the corresponding disadvantages. **36**

Disclosures: estimation techniques

In developing the FRED, the Board considered whether disclosures should be required in respect of estimation techniques. Very often, such disclosures will not be necessary because it is sufficient for users to understand the measurement basis that is being reflected. This is particularly the case where an amount may be estimated with reasonable certainty, ie whichever estimation technique is used the amount estimated will fall within a relatively narrow range. Accordingly, the FRED did not propose to require disclosures in respect of an estimation technique merely because it produces an amount that is material. **37**

38 Instead, the FRED proposed that a description of an estimation technique should be provided where the use of that technique is material. It explained that this would be the case where another estimation technique, other than that adopted, is also relevant and reliable and, had that other estimation technique instead been adopted, the figures presented in the financial statements would have been materially different. Where a range of methods and estimates would be acceptable, the entity would need to consider the range of amounts resulting from using those different estimates and methods.

39 Many respondents disliked this approach, objecting that it was too complex and that it was onerous to expect entities to assess amounts using many different estimation techniques. Some respondents suggested that disclosures should be required in respect of all estimation techniques used for material items. However, the Board believes that this alternative approach would also be onerous, in that many estimation techniques are used in the preparation of financial statements, and that it would result in users being swamped with irrelevant information.

40 Estimation techniques are used where there is uncertainty over the monetary amount to be associated with the measurement basis chosen for a particular item. The Board believes that information about estimation techniques should be provided where that uncertainty is significant in the context of the accounts as a whole. Nevertheless, it accepts the criticisms of the FRED's proposals, and has reconsidered how this objective should be encapsulated. Accordingly, the FRS instead focuses on the degree to which judgement is needed in applying whichever estimation technique has been chosen, and the sensitivity of the resulting amounts to such judgement.

FRED 21 Supplement 'Accounting Policies: Compliance with Statements of Recommended Practice'

41 In March 2000, the Board published a Supplement to FRED 21, which proposed additional disclosures where a significant part of an entity's activities falls within the scope of a Statement of Recommended Practice (SORP). The Supplement's proposals were well received by most respondents, and they have been reflected in the FRS. However, respondents raised a number of practical issues, particularly relating to the scope of SORPs and to possible conflicts between SORPs. In response to these, the FRS:

- requires disclosures where an entity's financial statements fall within the scope of a SORP, rather than where a significant part of its activities falls within the scope of a SORP
- makes clear that where an entity fails to provide disclosures recommended by a SORP, it should describe those disclosures and explain why they have been omitted
- emphasises that quantification of a departure from a SORP is not required except in those rare cases where such quantification is necessary for the entity's financial statements to give a true and fair view.

42 In July 2000 the Board issued a Statement 'SORPs: Policy and Code of Practice'. The Code of Practice requires, amongst other things, that a SORP should state its scope by indicating the types of entity to whose financial statements the SORP is intended to apply. However, the Board recognises that some SORPs may need to be updated in order to comply with this requirement. Until that updating has taken place, it may not be possible for an entity to determine whether it falls within the scope of a SORP and, hence, is required to make disclosures under the FRS. Accordingly, those paragraphs of the FRS that relate directly to the Supplement's proposals need not be applied in respect of accounting periods beginning on or before 23 December 2001, though earlier application is encouraged.

Financial Reporting Standard 19 'Deferred Tax' is issued by the Accounting Standards Board in respect of its application in the United Kingdom and by the Institute of Chartered Accountants in Ireland in respect of its application in the Republic of Ireland.

Financial Reporting Standard 19 is set out in paragraphs 1–72.

The Statement of Standard Accounting Practice, which comprises the paragraphs set in bold type, should be read in the context of the Objective as stated in paragraph 1 and the definitions set out in paragraph 2 and also of the Foreword to Accounting Standards and the Statement of Principles for Financial Reporting currently in issue.

The explanatory paragraphs contained in the FRS shall be regarded as part of the Statement of Standard Accounting Practice insofar as they assist in interpreting that statement.

Appendix V 'The development of the FRS' reviews considerations and arguments that were thought significant by members of the Board in reaching the conclusions on the FRS.

[FRS 19]
Deferred tax*

(Issued December 2000)

Contents

Paragraphs

Summary

Financial Reporting Standard 19

Objective	1
Definitions	2
Scope	3–6
Recognition of deferred tax assets and liabilities	7–33
General requirements	7–8
Allowances for fixed asset expenditure	9–11
Non-monetary assets – revaluations and gains on disposal	12–20
Assets continuously revalued to fair value with changes in fair value recognised in the profit and loss account	12–13
Other non-monetary assets	14–20
Unremitted earnings of subsidiaries, associates and joint ventures	21–22
Deferred tax assets	23–33
General requirements	23
Suitable taxable profits	24–25
Deferred tax assets that can be recovered against deferred tax liabilities	26
Deferred tax assets that cannot be recovered against deferred tax liabilities	27–32
Reassessment of recoverability	33
Recognition in the statements of performance	34–36
Measurement	37–54
Tax rates	37–41
Discounting	42–54
Criteria for discounting	42–46
Scheduling the cash flows to be discounted	47–51
Discount rates	52–54
Presentation	55–59
Presentation in the balance sheet	55–58
Presentation in the statements of performance	59
Disclosures	60–65
Deferred tax included in the statements of performance	60
Deferred tax included in the balance sheet	61–63
Circumstances affecting current and future tax charges	64–65

***Editor's note**: The matters covered in FRS 19 are dealt with in Section 29 of FRS 102.*

Date from which effective 66

Withdrawal of SSAP 15 and amendment of other accounting standards 67–72

Adoption of FRS 19 by the board

Appendices

I Discounting example
II Disclosure illustrations
III Note on legal requirements
IV Compliance with international accounting standards
V the development of the FRS

Summary

a Financial Reporting Standard 19 'Deferred Tax' requires full provision to be made for deferred tax assets and liabilities arising from timing differences between the recognition of gains and losses in the financial statements and their recognition in a tax computation.

b The general principle underlying the requirements is that deferred tax should be recognised as a liability or asset if the transactions or events that give the entity an obligation to pay more tax in future or a right to pay less tax in future have occurred by the balance sheet date. The FRS:

(a) requires deferred tax to be recognised on most types of timing difference, including those attributable to:

- accelerated capital allowances
- accruals for pension costs and other post-retirement benefits that will be deductible for tax purposes only when paid
- elimination of unrealised intragroup profits on consolidation unrelieved tax losses
- other sources of short-term timing differences.

(b) prohibits the recognition of deferred tax on timing differences arising when:

- a fixed asset is revalued without there being any commitment to sell the asset
- the gain on sale of an asset is rolled over into replacement assets
- the remittance of a subsidiary, associate or joint venture's earnings would cause tax to be payable, but no commitment has been made to the remittance of the earnings.

(c) requires deferred tax assets to be recognised to the extent that it is regarded as more likely than not that they will be recovered.

c As an exception to the general requirement not to recognise deferred tax on revaluation gains and losses, the FRS requires deferred tax to be recognised when assets are continuously revalued to fair value, with changes in fair value being recognised in the profit and loss account.

d The FRS permits but does not require entities to adopt a policy of discounting deferred tax assets and liabilities.

e The FRS includes other requirements regarding the measurement and presentation of deferred tax assets and liabilities. These include requirements for the deferred tax to be:

- measured using tax rates that have been enacted or substantively enacted
- presented separately on the face of the balance sheet if the amounts are so material that, in the absence of such disclosure, readers may misinterpret the financial statements.

f The FRS requires information to be disclosed about factors affecting current and future tax charges. A key element of this is a requirement to disclose a reconciliation of the current tax charge for the period to the charge that would arise if the profits reported in the financial statements were charged at a standard rate of tax.

g The FRS amends FRS 7 'Fair Values in Acquisition Accounting'. The amendment requires deferred tax recognised in a fair value exercise to be measured in accordance with the requirements of the FRS. Thus, deferred tax would not be recognised on an adjustment to recognise a non-monetary asset acquired with the business at its fair value on acquisition.

Financial Reporting Standard 19

OBJECTIVE

The objective of this FRS is to ensure that: 1

(a) future tax consequences of past transactions and events are recognised as liabilities or assets in n the financial statements; and

(b) the financial statements disclose any other special circumstances that may have an effect on future tax charges.

DEFINITIONS

The following definitions shall apply in the FRS and in particular in the Statement of Standard Accounting Practice set out **in bold type**. 2

Current tax:

The amount of tax estimated to be payable or recoverable in respect of the taxable profit or loss for a period, along with adjustments to estimates in respect of previous periods.

Deferred tax:

Estimated future tax consequences of transactions and events recognised in the financial statements of the current and previous periods.

Permanent differences:

Differences between an entity's taxable profits and its results as stated in the financial statements that arise because certain types of income and expenditure are non-taxable or disallowable, or because certain tax charges or allowances have no corresponding amount in the financial statements.

Timing differences:

Differences between an entity's taxable profits and its results as stated in the financial statements that arise from the inclusion of gains and losses in tax assessments in periods different from those in which they are recognised in financial statements. Timing differences originate in one period and are capable of reversal in one or more subsequent periods.

Timing differences arise when, for example:

- tax deductions for the cost of a fixed asset* are accelerated or decelerated, ie received before or after the cost of the fixed asset is recognised in the profit and loss account
- pension liabilities are accrued in the financial statements but are allowed for tax purposes only when paid or contributed at a later date
- interest charges or development costs are capitalised on the balance sheet but are treated as revenue expenditure and allowed as incurred for tax purposes
- intragroup profits in stock, unrealised at group level, are reversed on consolidation
- an asset is revalued in the financial statements but the revaluation gain becomes taxable only if and when the asset is sold
- a tax loss is not relieved against past or present taxable profits but can be carried forward to reduce future taxable profits
- the unremitted earnings of subsidiary and associated undertakings and joint ventures are recognised in the group results but will be subject to further taxation only if and when remitted to the parent undertaking.

SCOPE

3 **The FRS applies to all financial statements that are intended to give a true and fair view of a reporting entity's financial position and profit or loss (or income and expenditure) for a period.**

4 **The FRS applies to taxes calculated on the basis of taxable profits, including withholding taxes paid on behalf of the reporting entity.**

5 In the UK and the Republic of Ireland, the taxes that are calculated on the basis of taxable profits are primarily corporation tax and income tax. Other taxes, such as value added tax and petroleum revenue tax, that are not assessed directly on profits for an accounting period are not within the scope of the FRS.

6 **Reporting entities applying the Financial Reporting Standard for Smaller Entities (FRSSE) currently applicable are exempt from the FRS.**

RECOGNITION OF DEFERRED TAX ASSETS AND LIABILITIES

General requirements

7 **Except as set out in paragraphs 9–33, deferred tax:**

(a) should be recognised in respect of all timing differences that have originated but not reversed by the balance sheet date;

(b) should not be recognised on permanent differences.

8 The requirements of paragraph 7 are not intended to prevent lessors preparing financial statements in accordance with SSAP 21 'Accounting for leases and hire purchase contracts' from allocating profit from transactions over the term of the lease on a post-tax basis and measuring the tax charge and pre-tax profit relating to the accounting period by applying the effective rate of tax to the post-tax profit. The way in which finance lessors should determine the amount of deferred tax to be provided for is illustrated in Part II of the Guidance Notes on SSAP 21.

**Including deductions for expenditure on infrastructure assets capitalised and depreciated using renewals accounting.*

Allowances for fixed asset expenditure

Deferred tax should be recognised when the allowances for the cost of a fixed asset are received before or after the cost of the fixed asset is recognised in the profit and loss account. However, if and when all conditions for retaining the allowances have been met, the deferred tax should be reversed. 9

If an asset is not being depreciated (and has not otherwise been written down to a carrying value less than cost), the timing difference is the amount of capital allowances received. 10

Most capital allowances are received on a conditional basis, ie they are repayable (for example, via a balancing charge) if the assets to which they relate are sold for more than their tax written-down value. However, some, such as industrial buildings allowances, are repayable only if the assets to which they relate are sold within a specified period. Once that period has expired, all conditions for retaining the allowance have been met. At that point, deferred tax that has been recognised (ie on the excess of the allowance over any depreciation) is reversed. 11

Non-monetary assets – revaluations and gains on disposal

Assets continuously revalued to fair value with changes in fair value recognised in the profit and loss account

Deferred tax should be recognised on timing differences arising when an asset is continuously revalued to fair value with changes in fair value being recognised in the profit and loss account. 12

The assets to which paragraph 12 applies are typically investments and current assets that are 'marked to market' with fluctuations being recognised in the profit and loss account. In many circumstances, the gains and losses are subject to current tax when they are recognised, and no timing difference (and hence no deferred tax) arises. Paragraph 12 is relevant only if the gains and losses are not taxed until realised at a later date. 13

Other non-monetary assets

Deferred tax should not be recognised on timing differences arising when other non-monetary assets are revalued, unless, by the balance sheet date, the reporting entity has: 14

(a) entered into a binding agreement to sell the revalued assets; and
(b) recognised the gains and losses expected to arise on sale.

Deferred tax should not be recognised on timing differences arising when non-monetary assets (other than those referred to in paragraph 12) are revalued or sold if, on the basis of all available evidence, it is more likely than not that the taxable gain will be rolled over, being charged to tax only if and when the assets into which the gain has been rolled over are sold.* 15

Where an entity has entered into a binding agreement to sell a fixed asset, such as land and buildings, and has revalued the fixed asset at the net sale proceeds, it will have recognised the expected gain or loss on sale. To the extent that rollover relief is 16

**or are deemed to have been sold for tax purposes.*

not expected to be obtained and a timing difference has arisen – ie the gain will not be chargeable to current tax – the FRS requires deferred tax to be recognised.

17 An asset may have been purchased with a view to resale. Stock, for example, may be purchased for the sole purpose of resale. But this does not in itself mean that the entity has entered into a binding agreement to sell the asset.

18 Stock may be adjusted to its fair value on the acquisition of a business. However, even where such stock has been manufactured under the terms of a binding contract, that contract will generally be treated as an executory contract. The rights and obligations under that contract (and hence the gain on sale) will not have been recognised. In adjusting the value of the stock, the entity is merely recognising a movement in the replacement cost of the stock. In such circumstances, the FRS does not allow provision to be made for deferred tax on the adjustment.

19 The requirement not to provide for deferred tax if it is more likely than not that a taxable gain will be rolled over into replacement assets applies only if the terms of the relief are such that the gain will not be taxed unless and until the replacement assets are themselves sold (rollover relief). It does not apply if the terms of the relief are such that taxation of the gain is merely postponed (held over) for a finite period (holdover relief).* Sometimes, holdover relief can be converted into rollover relief if qualifying replacement assets are purchased before the held-over gain crystallises. Where this is the case, the requirements regarding rollover relief apply. However, it may be more difficult to arrive at the conclusion that it is more likely than not that the gain will be rolled over and, in consequence, that no provision is required.

20 The need to make a judgement regarding the availability of rollover relief will arise when the entity has not yet reinvested the proceeds of sale in qualifying replacement assets but may still do so within the period allowed by the tax authorities.† All available evidence, including that provided by events occurring after the balance sheet date, is considered when judging whether it is more likely than not that the gain will be rolled over. The available evidence will change with time and will therefore be reassessed continually until the entity either claims rollover relief or loses its right to do so. Any adjustment to recognise a previously unrecognised deferred tax provision (or to release a provision previously recognised) is a change in estimate, which, in accordance with the requirements of FRS 3 'Reporting Financial Performance', is charged or credited as part of the tax charge for the period in the profit and loss account or statement of total recognised gains and losses.

Unremitted earnings of subsidiaries, associates and joint ventures

21 **Tax that could be payable (taking account of any double taxation relief) on any future remittance of the past earnings of a subsidiary, associate or joint venture should be provided for only to the extent that, at the balance sheet date:**

(a) dividends have been accrued as receivable; or
(b) a binding agreement to distribute the past earnings in future has been entered into by the subsidiary, associate or joint venture.

22 It is unlikely that there will be a binding agreement for the future distribution of the past earnings of a subsidiary, associate or joint venture. In most circumstances,

**At present (December 2000), holdover relief can postpone the payment of tax for up to ten years from acquisition of the replacement asset.*

†At present (December 2000), within three years of the sale of the original asset.

therefore, the deferred tax provision comprises only tax that will become payable (taking account of double taxation relief) on receipt of dividends accrued at the balance sheet date.

Deferred tax assets

General requirements

Deferred tax assets should be recognised to the extent that they are regarded as recoverable. They should be regarded as recoverable to the extent that, on the basis of all available evidence, it can be regarded as more likely than not that there will be suitable taxable profits from which the future reversal of the underlying timing differences can be deducted. **23**

Suitable taxable profits

Suitable taxable profits from which the future reversal of timing differences could be deducted are those that are: **24**

(a) generated in the same taxable entity (or in an entity whose profits would be available via group relief) and assessed by the same taxation authority as the income or expenditure giving rise to the deferred tax asset;
(b) generated in the same period as that in which the deferred tax asset is expected to reverse, or in a period to which a tax loss arising from the reversal of the deferred tax asset may be carried back or forward; and
(c) of a type (such as capital or trading) from which the taxation authority allows the reversal of the timing difference to be deducted.

Account may be taken of tax planning opportunities, ie actions that the entity would take if necessary to create suitable taxable profits. Such actions could include: **25**

(a) accelerating taxable amounts or deferring claims for writing down allowances to recover losses being carried forward (perhaps before they expire);
(b) changing the character of taxable or deductible amounts from trading gains or losses to capital gains or losses or vice versa; or
(c) switching from tax-free to taxable investments.

Deferred tax assets that can be recovered against deferred tax liabilities

It can be assumed that the future reversal of any deferred tax liabilities recognised at the balance sheet date will give rise to taxable profits. To the extent that those profits will be suitable for the deduction of the reversing deferred tax asset, the asset can always be regarded as recoverable. **26**

Deferred tax assets that cannot be recovered against deferred tax liabilities

To the extent that the deferred tax asset cannot be recovered against the reversal of deferred tax liabilities, it is necessary to consider the likelihood of there being other suitable taxable profits. **27**

All available evidence is considered. Historical information about the entity's financial performance and position may provide the most objective evidence. Other evidence may be important if historical information is either not available or of limited relevance because of recent or forthcoming changes in circumstances. **28**

29 The existence of unrelieved tax losses of a certain character (for example, trading or capital) at the balance sheet date is strong evidence that there will not be suitable taxable profits of that character in future against which the losses (and other deferred tax assets) can be recovered. In such circumstances, the unrelieved losses (and other deferred tax assets affected) are recognised only if there is other persuasive and reliable evidence suggesting that suitable taxable profits will be generated in future.

30 In the case of unrelieved trading losses, such evidence may exist if the loss resulted from an identifiable and non-recurring cause and the reporting entity has otherwise been consistently profitable over a long period, with any past losses being more than offset by income in later periods.

31 If an unrelieved capital loss can be relieved only against future capital gains, there is likely to be persuasive and reliable evidence that there will be suitable taxable gains against which the loss can be relieved only to the extent that:

(a) a potential chargeable gain not expected to be covered by rollover relief is present in assets but has not been recognised as a deferred tax liability;
(b) plans are in place for the sale of these assets; and
(c) the carried-forward loss will be offset against the resulting chargeable gain for tax purposes.

32 If it is expected that it will take some time for tax losses to be relieved, the recoverability of the resulting deferred tax asset is likely to be relatively uncertain. In such circumstances, it may not be appropriate to recognise the deferred tax asset at all.

Reassessment of recoverability

33 Changes in circumstances from one balance sheet date to the next might affect the extent to which a deferred tax asset is regarded as recoverable and therefore require an adjustment to the amount recognised. For example, an improvement in trading conditions or the acquisition of a new subsidiary might make it more likely that a previously unrecognised tax loss in the acquiring entity will be recovered. As changes in estimates, the resulting movements in the deferred tax balance are required by FRS 3 'Reporting Financial Performance' to be reflected in the results for the period.

RECOGNITION IN THE STATEMENTS OF PERFORMANCE

34 Deferred tax should be recognised in the profit and loss account for the period, except to the extent that it is attributable to a gain or loss that is or has been recognised directly in the statement of total recognised gains and losses.

35 Where a gain or loss is or has been recognised directly in the statement of total recognised gains and losses, deferred tax attributable to that gain or loss should also be recognised directly in that statement.

36 Accounting standards (or, in their absence, legislation) require or permit certain gains or losses to be credited or charged directly in the statement of total recognised gains and losses (ie not in the profit and loss account). The FRS requires any attributable deferred tax to be treated in the same way. In exceptional circumstances it may be difficult to determine the amount of deferred tax that is attributable to gains or losses that have been recognised directly in the statement of total recognised gains and losses. In such circumstances, the attributable deferred tax is based on a reasonable pro rata allocation, or another allocation that is more appropriate in the circumstances.

MEASUREMENT

Tax rates

Deferred tax should be measured at the average tax rates that are expected to apply in the periods in which the timing differences are expected to reverse, based on tax rates and laws that have been enacted or substantively enacted by the balance sheet date. 37

It will normally be necessary to calculate an average tax rate only if the enacted or substantively enacted tax rates are graduated, ie if different rates apply to different levels of taxable income. To calculate the average tax rate it is necessary to estimate the levels of profits expected in the periods in which the timing differences reverse. 38

The requirement to calculate an average tax rate is not intended to lead to averaging of different rates expected to apply to different types of taxable profit or in different tax jurisdictions. If different rates of tax apply to different types of taxable profits (for example, trading profits and capital gains), the rate used will reflect the nature of the timing difference. The rates used for measuring deferred tax arising in a specific tax jurisdiction will be the rates expected to apply in that jurisdiction. 39

A UK tax rate can be regarded as having been substantively enacted if it is included in either: 40

(a) a Bill that has been passed by the House of Commons and is awaiting only passage through the House of Lords and Royal Assent; or
(b) a resolution having statutory effect that has been passed under the Provisional Collection of Taxes Act 1968.*

A Republic of Ireland tax rate can be regarded as having been substantively enacted if it is included in a Bill that has been passed by the Dail. 41

Discounting

Criteria for discounting

Reporting entities are permitted but not required to discount deferred tax assets and liabilities to reflect the time value of money. 42

Requirements and guidance on selecting and changing accounting policies are set out in FRS 18 'Accounting Policies'. Factors that are likely to be especially relevant to selecting a policy of either discounting or not discounting deferred tax include: 43

(a) how material the impact of discounting would tend to be to the overall results and position reported in the entity's financial statements;
(b) whether the benefits of discounting to users would outweigh the costs of collating the necessary information and performing discounting calculations; and
(c) whether there is an established industry practice, adherence to which would enhance comparability.

**Such a resolution could be used to collect taxes at a new rate before that rate has been enacted. In practice, corporation tax rates are now set a year ahead to avoid having to invoke the Provisional Collection of Taxes Act for the quarterly payment system.*

44 If a reporting entity adopts a policy of discounting, all deferred tax (and recoverable advance corporation tax*) balances that have been measured by reference to undiscounted cash flows and for which the impact of discounting is material should be discounted.

45 Certain timing differences, such as those arising on:

- provisions for pension costs and other long-term liabilities
- a lessor's investment in finance leases,

are measured by reference to cash flows that have already been discounted. The deferred tax provisions to which they give rise already incorporate discounting. They are not eligible for further discounting and are not subject to any of the detailed requirements for discounting, or disclosures of amounts arising from discounting, in the FRS. They are disclosed as if they were undiscounted amounts.

46 Timing differences that are eligible for discounting include those arising from accelerated capital allowances, revaluation gains and losses and carried- forward tax losses. (However, as noted in paragraph 32, if it is expected that it will take some time for tax losses to be relieved, it may not be appropriate to recognise the losses as an asset at all.)

Scheduling the cash flows to be discounted

47 **If deferred tax balances are discounted, the discount period(s) should be the number of years between the balance sheet date and the date(s) on which it is estimated that the underlying timing differences will reverse. Assumptions made when estimating the date(s) of reversal should be consistent with those made elsewhere in the financial statements. The scheduling of the reversal(s) should take into account the remaining tax effects of transactions that have already been reflected in the financial statements. However, no account should be taken either of other timing differences expected to arise on future transactions or of future tax losses.**

48 Where, for example, assets are depreciated over their useful economic lives but receive capital allowances early in their lives, the timing of the reversal of accelerated capital allowances is determined:

(a) by scheduling all expected future movements (increases as well as decreases) in the accelerated capital allowances on assets that are held at the balance sheet date, taking account of both future depreciation patterns and the expected timing of remaining capital allowances to be received on these assets; but
(b) without taking into consideration timing differences that might arise on fixed assets to be purchased in future.

The assumptions about future depreciation charges and residual value should be consistent with those used to account for the related fixed assets. It may be possible to use approximations or averages to simplify the calculations without introducing material errors. Illustrative examples are given below and in Appendix I.

49 A timing difference might be expected to reverse in a period in which it is also expected that the entity will make tax losses. In this situation, the reversal of the timing difference may not have an incremental effect on a tax payment until an even

**Advance corporation tax (ACT) was abolished in 1999. ACT that had been paid but not relieved by that date may still be recoverable under the shadow ACT system. FRS 16 'Current Tax' sets out requirements and guidance regarding the recognition of recoverable ACT.*

later period, when the future losses are relieved. However, the FRS requires deferred tax to be discounted without taking into consideration the possibility of future losses.

Simple example illustrating the scheduling of the reversal of accelerated capital allowances on a single asset

An entity purchases an asset for £100,000 at the start of 20X0. It is estimated that the asset will have a useful economic life of ten years and no residual value. Capital allowances can be claimed at a rate of 25 per cent of cost in each of the first four years.

At the end of 20X0, there is a timing difference of £15,000, which is the difference between the allowances of £25,000 received and the depreciation of £10,000. The timing difference is treated as reversing according to the following schedule (even if the entity expects to make losses at some point during the life of the asset):

Years from now:	**1**	**2**	**3**	**4**	**5**	**6**	**7**	**8**	**9**	**Total**
Depreciation (£000)	10	10	10	10	10	10	10	10	10	90
Allowances (£000)	25	25	25	–	–	–	–	–	–	75
(Increase)/Reversal	(15)	(15)	(15)	10	10	10	10	10	10	15

Where deferred tax is recognised on changes in the carrying amount of an asset that is revalued to fair value (ie as required by paragraph 12), the objective is to provide for the incremental tax that the entity will pay or recover on selling the asset, above the amount that it would have paid if it had purchased the asset at its carrying amount at the balance sheet date. The timing difference is therefore discounted from the future date on which it is estimated that the tax will become payable, taking account of any available reliefs. 50

The amount of tax that will be payable and the time at which it is likely to be paid may be uncertain and, hence, may have to be estimated on the basis of available evidence. Where the entity holds a portfolio of assets for investment or trading purposes, evidence can be obtained from historical data regarding average turnover periods, average amounts of tax paid as a percentage of the book gain and other variables. But evidence of how these variables are likely to change in future also has to be considered. 51

Discount rates

If deferred tax balances are discounted, the discount rates used should be the post-tax yields to maturity that could be obtained at the balance sheet date on government bonds with maturity dates and in currencies similar to those of the deferred tax assets or liabilities. 52

The yields to maturity on government bonds can be obtained from published sources. The post-tax yield is estimated by deducting tax at the rate at which it would be paid by an entity holding the bond, based on enacted or substantively enacted tax rates and laws. 53

The need to match the discount rate with the maturity date and currency of the deferred tax asset or liability in theory requires a different discount rate to be applied to each year in which a timing difference is forecast to reverse and for each different tax jurisdiction. It may, however, be possible to use approximations and averages to simplify the calculations without introducing material errors. This is illustrated in the example in Appendix I. 54

PRESENTATION

Presentation in the balance sheet

55 With the exception of deferred tax relating to a defined benefit asset or liability recognised in accordance with FRS 17 'Retirement Benefits'*:

(a) net deferred tax liabilities should be classified as provisions for liabilities and charges.

(b) net deferred tax assets should be classified as debtors, as a separate subheading of debtors where material.

56 Deferred tax debit and credit balances should be offset within the above headings to the extent, and only to the extent, that they:

(a) relate to taxes levied by the same tax authority; and

(b) arise in the same taxable entity or in a group of taxable entities where the tax losses of one entity can reduce the taxable profits of another.

57 Typically, each company in the UK is a single taxable entity and can offset current corporation tax payable to the Inland Revenue against current corporation tax due from the Inland Revenue. Where this is the case, deferred tax balances relating to the corporation tax of a single company are offset on the balance sheet. It may be appropriate to offset the deferred tax assets and liabilities of different entities within the same tax jurisdiction. This will be the case if and to the extent that the entities are treated as a group for tax purposes, being able to use the tax losses of one entity to reduce the amount of tax paid by another. The deferred tax assets and liabilities of different entities cannot be offset when they relate to taxes levied in different jurisdictions.

58 Deferred tax liabilities and assets should be disclosed separately on the face of the balance sheet if the amounts are so material in the context of the total net current assets or net assets that, in the absence of such disclosure, readers may misinterpret the financial statements.

Presentation in the statements of performance

59 All deferred tax recognised in the profit and loss account should be included within the heading 'tax on profit or loss on ordinary activities'.

DISCLOSURES

Deferred tax included in the statements of performance

60 The notes to the financial statements should disclose the amount of deferred tax charged or credited within:

(a) tax on ordinary activities in the profit and loss account, separately disclosing material components, including those attributable to:

(i) changes in deferred tax balances (before discounting, where applicable) arising from:

- **the origination and reversal of timing differences;**
- **changes in tax rates and laws; and**

**FRS 17 requires such deferred tax to be offset against the defined benefit asset or liability to which it relates.*

- **adjustments to the estimated recoverable amount of deferred tax assets arising in previous periods.**

(ii) where applicable, changes in the amounts of discount deducted in arriving at the deferred tax balance.

(b) tax charged or credited directly in the statement of total recognised gains and losses for the period, separately disclosing material components, including those listed in (a) above.

Deferred tax included in the balance sheet

The financial statements should disclose: 61

(a) the total deferred tax balance (before discounting, where applicable), showing the amount recognised for each significant type of timing difference separately;

(b) the impact of discounting on, and the discounted amount of, the deferred tax balance; and

(c) the movement between the opening and closing net deferred tax balance, analysing separately:

(i) the amount charged or credited in the profit and loss account for the period;

(ii) the amount charged or credited directly in the statement of total recognised gains and losses for the period; and

(iii) movements arising from the acquisition or disposal of businesses.

The financial statements should disclose the amount of a deferred tax asset and the nature of the evidence supporting its recognition if: 62

(a) the recoverability of the deferred tax asset is dependent on future taxable profits in excess of those arising from the reversal of deferred tax liabilities; and

(b) the reporting entity has suffered a loss in either the current or preceding period in the tax jurisdiction to which the deferred tax asset relates.

The evidence supporting the recognition of the deferred tax asset is the specific circumstances that make it reasonable to forecast that there will be future profits against which the deferred tax assets can be recovered. Such circumstances are discussed in paragraphs 28–31. 63

Circumstances affecting current and future tax charges

The notes to the financial statements should highlight circumstances that affect the current and total tax charges or credits for the current period or may affect the current and total tax charges or credits in future periods. This disclosure (illustrated in Appendix II) **should include:** 64

(a) a reconciliation of the current tax charge or credit on ordinary activities for the period reported in the profit and loss account to the current tax charge that would result from applying a relevant standard rate of tax to the profit on ordinary activities before tax. Either the monetary amounts or the rates (as a percentage of profits on ordinary activities before tax) may be reconciled. Where material, positive amounts should not be offset against negative amounts or vice versa: they should be shown as separate reconciling items. The basis on which the standard rate of tax has been determined should be disclosed.

(b) – if assets have been revalued in the financial statements without deferred tax having been recognised on the revaluation gain or loss, or if the market values of assets that have not been revalued have been disclosed in a note – an estimate of tax that could be payable or recoverable if the assets were sold at the values

shown, the circumstances in which the tax would be payable or recoverable and an indication of the amount that may become payable or recoverable in the foreseeable future.

(c) – if the reporting entity has sold (or entered into a binding agreement to sell) an asset but has not recognised deferred tax on a taxable gain because the gain has been or is expected to be rolled over into replacement assets – the conditions that will have to be met to obtain the rollover relief and an estimate of the tax that would become payable if those conditions were not met.

(d) – if a deferred tax asset has not been recognised on the grounds that there is insufficient evidence that the asset will be recoverable – the amount that has not been recognised and the circumstances in which the asset would be recovered.

(e) – if any other deferred tax has not been recognised – the nature of the amounts not recognised, the circumstances in which the tax would become payable or recoverable and an indication of the amount that may become payable or recoverable in the foreseeable future.

65 Relevant 'standard' tax rates vary from entity to entity. A relevant rate for a group whose profits are earned primarily in the UK is the standard rate of corporation tax in the UK, even if some of the group's operations are conducted in other countries. The impact of different rates of tax applied to profits earned in other countries would be shown as a reconciling item. The standard rate of tax in the UK might be regarded as being of limited relevance for a group that operates primarily outside the UK. For such a group, it may be more appropriate to use the average rate of tax (weighted in proportion to accounting profits) applicable across the group. Such a reconciliation could be performed by preparing and aggregating separate reconciliations for each country using the local rate of tax as the standard tax rate for each reconciliation.

DATE FROM WHICH EFFECTIVE

66 The accounting practices set out in the FRS should be regarded as standard for financial statements relating to accounting periods ending on or after 23 January 2002. Earlier adoption is encouraged.

WITHDRAWAL OF SSAP 15 AND AMENDMENT OF OTHER ACCOUNTING STANDARDS

67 The FRS supersedes SSAP 15 'Accounting for deferred tax'.

68–71 [*Not reproduced as all changes have been reflected in the material reproduced in this volume.*]

72 The Guidance Notes to SSAP 21 'Accounting for leases and hire purchase contracts' were issued by the former Accounting Standards Committee of the CCAB and were not adopted by the Board. Nonetheless, it would be consistent with the FRS if paragraphs 170 and 173–175 of the Notes, and the references to them in paragraphs 47, 101 and 110, were deemed to be deleted.

Adoption of FRS 19 by the board

Financial Reporting Standard 19 'Deferred Tax' was approved for issue by a vote of nine of the ten members of the Accounting Standards Board. Ms Sharp, recognising that she had not participated in the Board's key earlier debates in the development of this standard and its important role in promoting international convergence, abstained from voting in accordance with the Board's agreed procedure for newly appointed members.

Sir David Tweedie	(Chairman)
Allan Cook CBE	(Technical Director)
David Allvey	
Ian Brindle	
Dr John Buchanan	
John Coombe	
Huw Jones	
Professor Geoffrey Whittington	
Ken Wild	

Appendix I
Discounting example

1 This appendix illustrates how deferred tax arising from accelerated capital allowances on a plant and machinery pool is discounted.

Assumptions

2 A company that operates solely in the UK depreciates its plant and machinery on a straight-line basis over 10 years. Residual value is estimated to be $1/11^{th}$ of cost. The company receives capital allowances at a rate of 25 per cent per year on a reducing balance basis. It is taxed on its profits at 30 per cent.

3 The company has three groups of assets costing £1,100 each, purchased six years, three years and one year ago (in each case at the end of the financial year). The net book value of plant and machinery at the balance sheet date (year 0) is:

	£
Original cost	3,300
Cumulative depreciation	(1,000)
Net book value	2,300

4 The tax written-down values of the plant and machinery pool, and the consequential timing difference, at the balance sheet date are:

	£
Net book value	2,300
Tax written-down value	(1,114)
Timing difference at end of year 0	1,114

Scheduling the reversal of the deferred tax liability

5 The future reversals of the liability are scheduled in Table 1 below. The future depreciation of the existing pool of fixed assets (column b) is compared with the future writing-down allowances available on the pool (column c) to determine the years of reversal of the capital allowances (column d). When forecasting capital allowances for future periods, it is assumed that allowances will be claimed as early as possible and that the residual values of the assets will equal those forecast for depreciation purposes.

TABLE 1

Years from now	Depreciation £	Capital allowances £	Reversal of timing difference £	Deferred tax liability (undiscounted) £
a	b	c	d = b−c	**e** = d × 30%
1	300	278	22	7
2	300	209	91	27
3	300	157	143	43
4	300	93	207	62
5	200	69	131	39
6	200	52	148	44
7	200	14	186	56
8	100	11	89	27
9	100	(17)*	117	35
10+	–	(52)	52	16
Total	2,000†	814	1,186	356

Discount rates

The prices of and yields on UK Treasury gilts are published in the Financial Times. An appropriate post-tax rate is obtained by deducting the rate of tax that the entity pays on investment income (30 per cent) from these returns. **6**

TABLE 2

Years to maturity	Coupon rate %	Bid Price	Bid Yield %	Post-tax return (Bid yield less tax of 30%)
	Published information			
1	6	99.37	6.67	4.7
3	7	102.82	6.01	4.2
5	6.5	104.27	5.55	3.9
9	7.2	114.16	5.29	3.7
30	6	114.00	5.09	3.6

Appropriate rates of return for other maturity dates are estimated by interpolation. See column f of Table 3 below.

**It is assumed that the plant and machinery pool on which the writing-down allowances are claimed will continue beyond year 9 and hence that the incremental effect of the sale of the third asset in year 9 will be to reduce the writing-down allowances obtained in that and following years.*

†The future depreciation and capital allowances are £300 less than the net book value and tax written-down value respectively owing to the assumption that assets will be sold for £100 in each of years 4, 7 and 9.

Discounting the liability

7 Table 3 below illustrates how the discounted liability of £290 is calculated. The guidance in the FRS notes that it may be possible to use simplifying assumptions without introducing material errors into the measurement of the discounted liability. In this example, all timing differences reversing in years 10 onwards are treated as reversing in year 10.

TABLE 3

Years from now	Deferred tax liability (undiscounted) £	Discount rate %		Deferred tax liability (discounted) £
a	**e** (from Table 1)	**f** (from Table 2)		**g** = e/[(1+f)^a]
1	7	4.7		7
2	27	4.4	i	25
3	43	4.2		38
4	62	4.0	i	53
5	39	3.9		33
6	44	3.8	i	35
7	56	3.8	i	43
8	27	3.7	i	20
9	35	3.7		25
10+	16	3.7	i	11
Total	356			290

i = estimate based on interpolation of rates known for years 1, 3, 5, 9 and 30*

8 The discount reduces the deferred tax liability at year 0 by £66, ie from £356 to £290.

**In practice, it might be possible to limit the number of rates used without introducing material differences. For example, in the above illustration, the rates could be simplified to:*
4.5 per cent for short-term reversals (years 1–4)
3.8 per cent for medium-term reversals (years 5–9)
3.7 per cent for long-term reversals (years 10+).

Appendix II
Disclosure illustrations

The following illustrates how the disclosures required by paragraphs 60-65 of the FRS could be presented in the notes to the accounts. (Not illustrated is the disclosure that would be required of any deferred tax that had been charged or credited in the statement of total recognised gains and losses for the period.)

In this illustration, the analysis of the deferred tax charge for the period required by paragraph 60 (a) of the FRS has been combined with the analysis of the current tax charge for the period required by paragraph 17 of FRS 16 'Current Tax'.

The reconciliation of the tax charge, illustrated as a reconciliation of monetary amounts in note 1 (b) below, could alternatively be given as a reconciliation of the standard rate of tax to the effective rate.

1 TAX ON PROFIT ON ORDINARY ACTIVITIES

(a) Analysis of charge in period	**200Y**		200X	
	£m	**£m**	£m	£m
Current tax:				
UK corporation tax on profits of the period	**40**		26	
Adjustments in respect of previous periods	**4**		(6)	
		44		20
Foreign tax		**12**		16
Total current tax (note 1(b))		**56**		36
Deferred tax:				
Origination and reversal of timing differences	**67**		60	
Effect of increased tax rate on opening liability	**12**		–	
Increase in discount	**(14)**		(33)	
Total deferred tax (note 2)		**65**		27
Tax on profit on ordinary activities		**121**		63

(b) Factors affecting tax charge for period

The tax assessed for the period is lower than the standard rate of corporation tax in the UK (31 per cent). The differences are explained below:

	200Y £m	200X £m
Profit on ordinary activities before tax	**361**	327
Profit on ordinary activities multiplied by standard rate of corporation tax in the UK of 31% (200X: 30%)	**112**	98
Effects of:		
Expenses not deductible for tax purposes (primarily goodwill amortisation)	**22**	10
Capital allowances for period in excess of depreciation	**(58)**	(54)
Utilisation of tax losses	**(17)**	(18)
Rollover relief on profit on disposal of property	**(10)**	–
Higher tax rates on overseas earnings	**3**	6
Adjustments to tax charge in respect of previous periods	**4**	(6)
Current tax charge for period (note 1(a))	**56**	36

(c) Factors that may affect future tax charges

Based on current capital investment plans, the group expects to continue to be able to claim capital allowances in excess of depreciation in future years but at a slightly lower level than in the current year.

The group has now used all brought-forward tax losses, which have significantly reduced tax payments in recent years.

No provision has been made for deferred tax on gains recognised on revaluing property to its market value or on the sale of properties where potentially taxable gains have been rolled over into replacement assets. Such tax would become payable only if the property were sold without it being possible to claim rollover relief. The total amount unprovided for is £21 million. At present, it is not envisaged that any tax will become payable in the foreseeable future.

The group's overseas tax rates are higher than those in the UK primarily because the profits earned in country X are taxed at a rate of 45 per cent. The group expects a reduction in future tax rates following a recent announcement that the rate of tax in that country is to reduce to 40 per cent.

No deferred tax is recognised on the unremitted earnings of overseas subsidiaries, associates and joint ventures. As the earnings are continually reinvested by the group, no tax is expected to be payable on them in the foreseeable future.

2 PROVISION FOR DEFERRED TAX

	31.12.200Y	31.12.200X
	£m	£m
Accelerated capital allowances	**426**	356
Tax losses carried forward	–	(9)
Undiscounted provision for deferred tax	**426**	347
Discount	**(80)**	(66)
Discounted provision for deferred tax	**346**	281
Provision at start of period	**281**	
Deferred tax charge in profit and loss account for period (note 1)	**65**	
Provision at end of period	**346**	

Appendix III
Note on legal requirements

Great Britain*

1 The Companies Act 1985 sets out requirements for companies on accounting for provisions and current assets in general and deferred tax in particular. The main requirements that are directly relevant are set out in Schedule 4 and are summarised below.

2 Schedule 4 does not apply to banking and insurance companies and groups, nor to small companies to the extent that they choose instead to comply with the reduced requirements set out in Schedule 8. Requirements corresponding to those of Schedule 4 are set out for banking companies and groups in Schedule 9 and for insurance companies and groups in Schedule 9A.

****Editor's note:*** *The various statutory references change with the introduction of the Companies Act 2006, which affects accounting for periods beginning on or after 6 April 2008. The various statutory references have changed as follows:*

Companies Act 1985 reference	***Companies Act 2006 reference***
Schedule 4	*Schedule 1 to The Large and Medium-sized Companies and Groups (Accounts and Reports) Regulations 2008 (SI 2008/410)*
Schedule 8	*Schedule 1 to The Small Companies and Groups (Accounts and Directors' Report) Regulations 2008 (SI 2008/409)*
Schedules 9 and 9A	*Schedules 2 and 3 to SI 2008/410*
Paragraph 12 (b) of Schedule 4	*Paragraph 13 (b) of Schedule 1 to SI 2008/410*
Paragraph 89 of Schedule 4	*Paragraph 2 of Schedule 9 to SI 2008/410*
Paragraph 34 of Schedule 4	*Paragraph 32 of Schedule 1 to SI 2008/410*
Paragraph 3 (6) of Schedule 4	*Paragraph 6 of Schedule 1 to SI 2008/410*
Paragraph 47 of Schedule 4	*Paragraph 60 of Schedule 1 to SI 2008/410*
Paragraph 46 of Schedule 4	*Paragraph 59 of Schedule 1 to SI 2008/410*
Paragraph 5 of Schedule 4	*Paragraph 8 of Schedule 1 to SI 2008/410*
Paragraph 50 (2) of Schedule 4	*Paragraph 63 (2) of Schedule 1 to SI 2008/410*
Paragraph 54 (2) of Schedule 4	*Paragraph 67 (1) of Schedule 1 to SI 2008/410*
Section 275	*S. 841*

Recognition and measurement

Paragraph 12(b) of Schedule 4 states the general requirement to provide for all liabilities that have arisen in respect of the financial year to which the accounts relate or a previous financial year. Under the full provision method of accounting for deferred tax a timing difference is viewed as creating a liability because, as a result of that timing difference, a future tax assessment will be higher than it would otherwise have been (whether or not the timing difference will be replaced). 3

Paragraph 89 of Schedule 4 defines provisions as: 4

> 'any amount retained as reasonably necessary for the purposes of providing for any liability or loss which is either likely to be incurred, or certain to be incurred but uncertain as to amount or as to the date on which it will arise.'

The deferred tax liabilities provided for in accordance with the FRS, which are typically uncertain in terms of both timing and amount, are categorised as provisions in the balance sheet formats prescribed by Schedule 4.

The reference to 'liability or loss' in the definition of provisions needs to be considered in conjunction with the general requirement that the liabilities have arisen or are likely to arise *in respect of the financial year to which the accounts relate [or a previous financial year]*. Thus deferred tax can be regarded as giving rise to a liability that is required to be provided for only if the events causing the future reversal of a timing difference (such as a commitment to sell a revalued asset or to remit overseas earnings) have occurred before the end of the financial year. Without that past event the future 'liability' does not relate to the financial year or a previous financial year. 5

In addition to covering liabilities that are certain to be incurred the statutory definition also refers to liabilities as losses that are likely to be incurred. Typically, if the events causing the future reversal of a timing difference have occurred, the deferred tax liability, although not certain, is likely to be incurred. An exception is the deferred tax that might be payable following the sale of a fixed asset, if it is not yet certain whether rollover relief will be obtained. The FRS requires such deferred tax to be provided for only if it is likely that rollover relief will not be obtained. The amount unprovided for is regarded as a contingent liability. 6

Paragraph 34(3)(b) of Schedule 4 allows taxation to be transferred to or from the revaluation reserve if it relates to any profit or loss credited or debited to that reserve. Paragraph 34(4) requires the treatment for taxation purposes of amounts credited or debited to the revaluation reserve to be disclosed. The FRS requires the deferred tax to be included either in the profit and loss account or directly in the statement of total recognised gains and losses and requires the amounts to be disclosed. 7

Presentation and disclosure

Paragraph 3(6) of Schedule 4 requires the profit and loss accounts of companies to show the profit or loss on ordinary activities before taxation. 8

The balance sheet formats set out in Schedule 4 require provisions for taxation, including deferred taxation, to be included within the total for provisions for liabilities and charges. Provisions for taxation need not be shown separately on the face of the balance sheet (paragraph 3(4)), providing that material amounts are disclosed in a note to the accounts. Paragraph 47 requires the provision for deferred 9 taxation to be shown separately from any other tax provision. Paragraph 46 requires the movements on provisions for taxation to be disclosed in a note to the accounts.

10 Paragraph 5 of Schedule 4 states that assets and income should not be offset against liabilities and expenditure in the balance sheet and profit and loss account. Deferred tax debit and credit balances that arise with the same taxation authority and that the entity would have a right to settle on a net basis are not separate assets and liabilities and should therefore be shown on a net basis in the financial statements. Net debit balances, however, must be shown as assets rather than as negative amounts within provisions. The formats set out in Schedule 4 do not specify a heading for net deferred tax assets but paragraph 3(2) permits assets not covered by the prescribed headings to be included in the balance sheet. The FRS requires material deferred tax assets to be included as a separate subheading within debtors. Note (5) on the balance sheet formats requires the amount falling due after more than one year to be shown separately for each item included under debtors.

11 Paragraph 50(2) of Schedule 4 requires the following information to be given in respect of any contingent liability not provided for:

(a) the amount or estimated amount of that liability;
(b) its legal nature; and
(c) whether any valuable security has been provided by the company in connection with that liability, and if so, what.

Any deferred tax not provided for because it is expected that rollover relief will be obtained is a contingent liability. The FRS requires the estimated amount and the circumstances in which it will become payable to be disclosed.

12 Paragraph 54(2) of Schedule 4 requires any special circumstances affecting the liability to tax on profits, income or capital gains for the current or future years to be disclosed. The FRS details specific circumstances that should be disclosed.

Impact on distributable profits

13 As discussed in paragraphs 3 and 4 above, the deferred tax provisions that are required to be recognised by the FRS are, in general, regarded as liabilities that arise from past events and, hence, as 'provisions for liabilities and charges' of the type given in paragraph 89 of Schedule 4. Section 275(1) requires provisions of the type mentioned in paragraph 89 of Schedule 4 to be treated as realised losses for the purposes of determining a company's profits available for distribution.

14 The FRS additionally requires deferred tax to be provided for when assets are revalued to their fair values with changes being recorded in the profit and loss account. In such circumstances, the purpose of the deferred tax is to recognise the tax attributable to the gain resulting from the change in fair value. As such a gain on which deferred tax is provided for is regarded as unrealised, the deferred tax on that gain should be treated as a reduction in that unrealised gain rather than a realised loss. The fact that the deferred tax is presented with other tax provisions within the heading 'provisions for liabilities and charges' does not alter that position.

Northern Ireland

15 The statutory requirements in Northern Ireland are set out in Schedule 4 to the Companies (Northern Ireland) Order 1986. They are identical to and have the same paragraph references as those cited above for Great Britain.

Republic of Ireland

The statutory requirements in the Republic of Ireland that correspond to those listed above for Great Britain are shown in the following table. **16**

Great Britain	*Republic of Ireland*
Section 275(1) of the Companies Act 1985	section 45(4) of the Companies (Amendment) Act 1983 and paragraphs 69 and 70 of the Schedule to the Companies (Amendment) Act 1986.
Schedule 4 to the Companies Act 1985:	Companies (Amendment) Act 1986:
paragraph 3(2), 3(4) and 3(6)	section 4(12), 4(6) and 4(16)
paragraph 5	section 4(11)
paragraph 12(b)	section 5(c)(ii)
Schedule 4 to the Companies Act 1985:	The Schedule to the Companies (Amendment) Act 1986:
note (5) on the formats	note 4 on the formats
paragraph 34(4)	paragraph 22(5)
paragraph 46	paragraph 32
paragraph 47	paragraph 33
paragraph 50(2)	paragraph 36(2)
paragraph 54(2)	paragraph 40(2)
paragraph 89	paragraph 70
Schedule 8 to the Companies Act 1985	no equivalent
Schedule 9 to the Companies Act 1985	European Communities (Credit Institutions: Accounts) Regulations 1992
Schedule 9A to the Companies Act 1985	European Communities (Insurance Undertakings: Accounts) Regulations 1996

There is no equivalent to paragraph 34(3)(b) of Schedule 4 to The Companies Act 1985. **17**

Appendix IV
Compliance with International Accounting Standards

1 The International Accounting Standard (IAS) that addresses deferred tax is IAS 12 (revised 1996) 'Income Taxes'.* Like the FRS, IAS 12 (revised) requires deferred tax to be recognised on a full provision basis. But it requires deferred tax to be recognised on the basis of 'temporary differences' rather than on the basis of obligations arising from timing differences. The conceptual differences between temporary differences and timing differences are explained in Appendix V 'The development of the FRS'. This appendix sets out the resulting differences in the requirements of the two standards.

2 The circumstances in which deferred tax is provided for are wider under IAS 12 (revised) than under the FRS. This is for two reasons: temporary differences can arise from both timing and permanent differences; and IAS 12 (revised) requires provisions to be made even when the critical events causing the deferred tax to become payable in future have not occurred by the balance sheet date. The main areas where compliance with IAS 12 (revised) could require additional provisions to be recognised by UK and Irish companies are set out in the following table.

Differences between the recognition requirements of IAS 12 (revised 1996) and those of the FRS

Circumstances giving rise to deferred tax	Deferred tax required to be recognised: by FRS 19	by IAS 12 (revised 1996)
1 Revaluation of non-monetary assets	Provision is required only if either: (a) the asset is revalued to fair value each period with changes in fair value being recognised in the profit and loss account; or (b) the entity has entered into a binding agreement to sell the revalued asset, has revalued the asset to its selling price and does not expect to obtain rollover relief.	Provision is required whether or not it is intended that the asset will be sold and whether or not rollover relief could be claimed.
2 Sale of assets, where gain has been or might be rolled over into replacement assets.	Provision is required only if rollover relief has not been obtained and is not expected to be obtained.	Provision is required. The deferred tax is measured on the difference between the replacement asset's cost and its tax base (ie cost less taxable gain rolled over).

****Editor's note:*** *IAS 12 was further revised in 2000.*

Circumstances giving rise to deferred tax	Deferred tax required to be recognised: by FRS 19	by IAS 12 (revised 1996)
3 Adjustments to recognise assets and liabilities at their fair values on the acquisition of a business.	The amendment to FRS 7 'Fair Values in Acquisition Accounting' introduced by FRS 19 requires deferred tax to be provided for as if the adjustments had been gains or losses recognised before the acquisition. Deferred tax would not normally be recognised on adjusting non-monetary assets to market values. No provision is recognised in respect of acquired goodwill.	Provision is made for all differences between the fair values recognised for assets and liabilities and their tax bases. The only exception is that no provision is required in respect of the temporary difference arising on the recognition of non-deductible goodwill.
4 Unremitted earnings of subsidiaries, associates and joint ventures.	Provision is required only to the extent that dividends payable by a subsidiary, associate or joint venture have been accrued at the balance sheet date or a binding agreement to distribute the past earnings in future has been made.	Provision is required on the unremitted earnings of associates in all circumstances. Provision is required on the unremitted profits of subsidiaries, branches and joint ventures if either the parent/investor is unable to control the timing of the remittance of the earnings or it is probable that remittance will take place in the foreseeable future.
5 Exchange differences arising on consolidation of non-monetary assets of an entity accounted for under the temporal method.	No provision is required because there is no timing difference.	Provision is required on the temporary difference between the carrying amount (at historical exchange rates) and the tax base (at balance sheet date exchange rates).

Circumstances giving rise to deferred tax	Deferred tax required to be recognised: by FRS 19	by IAS 12 (revised 1996)
6 Unrealised intragroup profits (for example, in stock) are eliminated on consolidation.	Provision is required on the timing difference, ie the profit that has been taxed but not recognised in the consolidated financial statements. It is therefore measured using the supplying company's rate of tax.	Provision is required on the temporary difference. IAS 12 (revised) states that this is the difference between the (reduced) carrying amount of the stock in the balance sheet and its higher tax base (the amount paid by the receiving company). The provision is measured using the receiving company's rate of tax.

3 The requirements in the FRS regarding the rates of tax used to measure deferred tax assets and liabilities are very similar to those in IAS 12 (revised). However, IAS 12 (revised) does not permit deferred tax balances to be discounted.

4 The FRS requires deferred tax to be shown separately on the face of the balance sheet if the amounts are so material that failure to do so could cause readers to misinterpret the financial statements. IAS 12 (revised) requires all (material) deferred tax balances to be shown separately on the face of the balance sheet.

5 The amendment to FRS 7 'Fair Values in Acquisition Accounting' introduced by FRS 19 refers to previously unrecognised deferred tax assets (typically carried forward losses) that meet the criteria for recognition as a result of the acquisition. The amendment requires the benefit of the assets to be recognised as part of the fair value exercise only if the assets have arisen in the acquired entity: if the assets have arisen in the acquiring entity, the benefit is required to be recognised as part of post-acquisition performance. IAS 22 'Business Combinations' requires the benefit to be recognised as part of the fair value exercise whether the assets have arisen in the acquired or the acquiring entities.

6 The disclosures required by the FRS are similar overall to those required by IAS 12 (revised). The main differences comprise:

(a) *disclosures required by IAS 12 (revised) but not by FRS 19:*

– the aggregate amount of temporary differences associated with investments in subsidiaries, branches, associates and joint ventures for which deferred tax liabilities have not been recognised
– the tax expense relating to discontinued operations;

(b) *disclosures required by FRS 19 but not by IAS 12 (revised):*

– disclosures of the effects of discounting
– a general explanation of circumstances that have affected the current and total tax charges for the current period or that may affect the charges in future periods
– the circumstances in which deferred tax relating to revaluation and rolled over gains (and other deferred tax unprovided for) would become payable and an indication of the amounts that are expected to become payable in the foreseeable future;

(*c*) *other differences:*

IAS 12 (revised) requires disclosure of a reconciliation of the entity's actual tax charge (current and deferred) for the period to the tax that would be payable using a standard rate of tax. The FRS requires a different reconciliation to be disclosed: a reconciliation of the *current* tax assessed for the period to a standard rate of tax. (It is of note, however, that although the two reconciliations are different, the IAS 12 (revised) reconciliation can be constructed from information required to be disclosed by the FRS.)

Appendix V
The development of the FRS

Contents

	Paragraphs
Requirement for full provision	1–22
The source of deferred tax	1–3
Three methods of accounting for tax	4–11
Reasons for rejecting the partial provision method	12–19
Reasons for rejecting flow-through accounting	20–22
Recognition criteria – incremental liability approach	23–75
Overview	23–27
Reasons for rejecting the temporary difference approach	28–37
Reasons for adopting the incremental liability approach	38–52
Detailed aspects of the recognition requirements	53–75
Recoverability of deferred tax assets	76–79
Measurement – tax rates	80–83
Measurement – discounting	84–123
Overview	84
Arguments for and against discounting	85–99
Reasons for making discounting optional	100–105
Detailed requirements for discounting	106–123
Presentation of deferred tax balances	124–130
Disclosures	131–138
Amendment to FRS 7	139–146
Changes to requirements proposed in FRED 19	

The development of the FRS

REQUIREMENT FOR FULL PROVISION

The source of deferred tax

In most tax jurisdictions, including the UK and the Republic of Ireland, the starting point for computing corporation tax is the accounting profit as reported in the financial statements. However, adjustments are made to the accounting profit to arrive at taxable profits. These differences can be analysed into two types: 'permanent' and 'timing'. 1

Permanent differences arise because certain gains or losses that are recognised in the financial statements are not taxable or tax-deductible at all. An example is a non-taxable government grant. Timing differences arise when gains or losses are recognised in accounting profits in periods different from those in which they are recognised in taxable profits. An example is a capital allowance that is obtained before the depreciation of the asset to which it relates is recognised in the financial statements. 2

Because timing differences reverse, tax charged in later periods may be increased or reduced as a result of transactions or events that have taken place before the balance sheet date. The issue in accounting for deferred tax is the extent to which provision should be made for the future tax consequences of past transactions and events. Three different methods – flow-through accounting, full provision and partial provision – exist. 3

Three methods of accounting for tax

Flow-through accounting

Flow-through accounting makes no provision at all for deferred tax. Rather, tax is accounted for as it is assessed. 4

The rationale for this method of accounting is that tax is assessed annually on profits as determined for tax purposes, not on accounting profits. The tax authorities impose a single tax assessment on the entity and that is its only liability to tax for that period. Any tax assessed in future years will depend on future events and hence is not a present liability as defined in the Board's Statement of Principles for Financial Reporting. 5

Supporters of flow-through accounting also argue that it is the most transparent and intuitively sensible way of communicating an entity's tax position. The financial statements show the actual tax charge for the year in the clearest possible manner, and the associated notes (which would disclose such matters as accumulated timing differences and the items reconciling the actual tax charge to a standard rate) would be no more detailed and possibly more intelligible than those resulting from other possible accounting methods. 6

Some supporters of flow-through accounting further argue that even if, in principle, timing differences did give rise to tax liabilities,* in practice such liabilities could not always be measured reliably. The future tax consequences of current transactions depend upon a complex interaction of future events, such as the profitability, investment and financing transactions of the entity, and changes in tax rates and laws. Only those that could be measured reliably – typically very short-term discrete 7

**To avoid making the text unduly cumbersome, this discussion focuses on deferred tax liabilities (which tend to be more significant and frequent than deferred tax assets). The same principles extend to deferred tax assets, although the precise arguments may be slightly different.*

timing differences – should be provided for. Thus they advocate a modified flow-through approach.

Full provision method

8 The full provision method is based on the view that every transaction has a tax consequence and it is possible to make a reasonable estimate of the future tax consequences of transactions that have occurred by the balance sheet date. Such future tax consequences cannot be avoided: whatever happens in future, the entity will pay less or more tax as a result of the reversal of a timing difference that exists at the balance sheet date than it would have done in the absence of that timing difference. Deferred tax should therefore be provided for in full on timing differences.

Partial provision method

9 The partial provision method also starts from the premise that the future reversal of timing differences gives rise to a tax asset or liability. However, rather than focusing on the individual components of the tax computation, the partial provision method emphasises the interaction of those components in a single net assessment. To the extent that timing differences are expected to continue in future (ie the existing timing differences being replaced by future timing differences as they reverse), the tax is viewed as being deferred permanently.

10 Where, for example, fixed asset expenditure attracts tax deductions before the fixed assets are depreciated, timing differences arise. The timing differences increase with time under conditions of inflation or expansion, with the result that new timing differences more than replace those that reverse. In consequence, effective tax rates are reduced. The partial provision method allows the lower effective tax rates to be reflected in the profit and loss account, to the extent that the reduction is not expected to reverse in future years.

11 The attraction of the partial provision method is that it reflects an entity's ongoing effective tax rate. It results in tax charges that reflect the amount of tax that it is expected will actually be paid and excludes amounts that are expected to be deferred 'permanently'.

Reasons for rejecting the partial provision method

12 The FRS supersedes SSAP 15 'Accounting for deferred tax'. SSAP 15 required deferred tax to be accounted for using the partial provision method.

13 SSAP 15 and the partial provision method were first implemented in the UK and the Republic of Ireland in 1978, when they were viewed as a pragmatic response to the corporation tax system of the time. A key feature of that system was very generous capital and stock allowances: companies could deduct for tax purposes 100 per cent of the cost of plant and equipment in the year of purchase and inflationary increases in the value of stock. The effect of these deductions was that companies could indefinitely postpone payment of some or all of their deferred tax and paid tax at well below the enacted rate of 52 per cent.

14 The partial provision method allowed companies to avoid creating provisions for tax that they argued they were unlikely to pay. However, by the early 1990s, concerns were being expressed about the method and the way in which it was being applied. It was noted in particular that:

- the recognition rules and anticipation of future events were subjective and inconsistent with the principles underlying other aspects of accounting.
- the partial provision method had not been regarded as appropriate for dealing with the long-term deferred tax assets associated with provisions for post-retirement benefits. As a result, SSAP 15 had been amended in 1992 to permit such assets to be accounted for on a full provision basis. The amendment introduced inconsistencies into SSAP 15.
- there were variations in the way in which SSAP 15 was applied in practice. Different entities within the same industry and with similar prospects seemed to take quite different views on the levels of provisions necessary. There was evidence that some companies provided for deferred tax in full for simplicity's sake rather than because their circumstances required it. The different approaches being taken reduced the comparability of financial statements.
- because of its recognition rules and anticipation of future events, the partial provision method was increasingly being rejected by standard-setters in other countries. The US Financial Accounting Standards Board (FASB) had issued a standard FAS 109 'Accounting for Income Taxes' requiring full provision. The International Accounting Standards Committee (IASC) had published proposals for similar requirements and other standard-setters had started to move in the same direction.

When rejecting the partial provision method, the FASB and IASC argued in particular that: **15**

(a) every tax timing difference represented a real liability, since every one would reverse and, whatever else happened, an entity would pay more tax in future as a result of the reversal than it would have done in the absence of the timing difference.
(b) it was only the impact of new timing differences arising in future that prevented the total liability from reducing. It was inappropriate (and inconsistent with other areas of accounting) to take account of future transactions when measuring an existing liability.
(c) the assessment of the liability using the partial provision method relied on management intentions regarding future events. Standard-setters were uncomfortable with this, having already embodied in a number of other standards the principle that liabilities should be determined on the basis of obligations rather than management decisions or intentions.

In view of the criticisms of the partial provision method, the Board decided to review SSAP 15. In 1995 it published a Discussion Paper 'Accounting for Tax'. The Discussion Paper proposed that SSAP 15 should be replaced with an FRS requiring full provision for deferred tax. **16**

Most respondents to the Discussion Paper opposed the move to full provision at that stage, preferring instead to retain the partial provision method. In the meantime, however, IASC had approved its standard, IAS 12 (revised 1996) 'Income Taxes', which required use of the full provision method. The Board reconsidered the arguments and arrived at the view that: **17**

- whilst it did not agree with all of the criticisms of the partial provision method expressed internationally and could see the logic for all three methods of accounting for tax, it shared some of the concerns regarding the subjectivity of the partial provision method and its reliance on future events; and
- as more companies adopted international accounting standards, the partial provision method would become less well understood and accepted, particularly as it was regarded as less prudent than the internationally accepted method.

Hence, the retention of the partial provision method in the UK could damage the credibility of UK financial reporting.

18 For these reasons, the Board took the view that deferred tax was not an area where a good case could be made for departing from principles that had been widely accepted internationally. Following informal consultations, it developed a draft FRS, FRED 19 'Deferred Tax', which proposed requirements based more closely on a full provision method. The FRED was published for consultation in August 1999.

19 The responses to FRED 19 indicated that, whilst many amongst the financial community remained disappointed that there had not been international acceptance of the partial provision method, most accepted the arguments for greater harmonisation with international practice and supported the proposed move to a full provision method.

Reasons for rejecting flow-through accounting

20 For the reasons outlined in paragraphs 5–7 above, a number of Board members believe that the clearest and most transparent method of communicating an entity's tax position is by flow-through accounting combined with detailed disclosures. The possibility of moving to flow-through accounting was therefore suggested in the Board's Discussion Paper.

21 However, flow-through accounting would not have moved UK accounting more into line with international practice and received little support from those responding to the Board's Discussion Paper. Most respondents agreed with the view that taxable profit was, in both form and substance, an adjusted accounting profit and that it was possible to attribute tax effects to individual transactions. Further, they regarded tax systems as sufficiently stable to allow reasonable estimates to be made of the deferred tax consequences of events reported up to the balance sheet date. They added their concerns that flow-through accounting would make their results more volatile, could sometimes understate an entity's liability to tax and that any modification to it would require arbitrary cut-off points that could be difficult to rationalise.

22 In view of the lack of support from respondents and the Board's commitment to international harmonisation, Board members who would have preferred flow-through accounting accepted that the FRS should instead require full provision for deferred tax.

RECOGNITION CRITERIA – INCREMENTAL LIABILITY APPROACH

Overview

23 Traditionally, deferred tax has been identified and recognised on the basis of timing differences. And, even under full provision methods, not all types of timing difference have necessarily been provided for. Varying approaches have been taken, depending on views regarding the nature and purpose of deferred tax.

24 A completely different approach, which requires deferred tax to be recognised on 'temporary' rather than timing differences, was developed for FAS 109 and adopted in IAS 12 (revised).

25 Given that the move to full provision accounting in the UK was driven primarily by international harmonisation, it would have been ideal if the requirements of the FRS could have mirrored those of IAS 12 (revised). However, the Board did not accept

some of the assumptions underlying the temporary difference approach and opposed some of the practical consequences of the approach. The Board therefore considered alternative approaches that did not rely on the same assumptions and were designed to be consistent with its Statement of Principles for Financial Reporting.

The Board developed two approaches. The first required deferred tax to be recognised only when it could be regarded as meeting the definition of an asset or a liability in its own right (the 'incremental liability' approach). The second required deferred tax to be recognised as a necessary adjustment to the values at which other assets and liabilities were recognised (the 'valuation adjustment' approach). **26**

Most Board members preferred the incremental liability approach and based the requirements of FRED 19 on this approach. A majority of respondents who expressed a preference supported the proposed approach, with the rest supporting either a valuation adjustment approach or full harmonisation with IAS 12 (revised). The incremental liability approach therefore remains the approach on which the requirements in the FRS have been based. **27**

Reasons for rejecting the temporary difference approach

The meaning of 'temporary difference'

A temporary difference is defined as any difference between the amount at which an asset or liability is recognised in financial statements and its tax base. The tax base is the amount that will be deductible or taxable in respect of the asset or liability in the future. **28**

Most temporary differences are created by timing differences. For example, the tax base of a fixed asset that attracts capital allowances is its cost less allowances received. A temporary difference arises if the tax base is less than the net book value recognised in the financial statements. The temporary difference equals the timing difference created if the allowances received have exceeded depreciation. **29**

But temporary differences can also be created by permanent differences between accounting profits and taxable profits. If a government grant is non-taxable, any portion that is deferred as a liability has a tax base of zero. Similarly, a non-deductible cost capitalised as an asset has a tax base of zero. In some tax jurisdictions, certain fixed asset expenditure is 'super- deductible' and qualifies for tax allowances for, say, 150 per cent of cost. The tax base will initially be greater than cost. In each of these cases, a temporary difference arises as soon as the asset or liability is recognised. **30**

Rationale for the temporary difference approach

The rationale for recognising deferred tax on temporary differences is that the entity should provide for the unavoidable tax consequences of recovering the carrying values of assets or settling liabilities at the amounts shown in the accounts. It is argued that it is inherent in the carrying value of an asset that the asset will generate pre-tax cash flows at least equal to that carrying value. Any tax payable on generating such cash flows is therefore inherently a liability of the entity. The temporary difference measures the amount on which tax will be payable. **31**

Reasons for rejecting the temporary difference approach

The Board did not accept one of the fundamental assumptions underlying the temporary difference approach, ie that the carrying value of an asset represented the **32** minimum pre-tax cash flows that the asset would generate. It identified circumstances in which tax cash flows might also be reflected in the carrying value. For example, if an entity had bought a non-deductible asset for 100 and carried it at its historical cost of 100, this would not be because it had expected to generate pre-tax cash flows of 100, on which it would pay tax of 33. Rather it would have expected to generate pre-tax cash flows of at least 150, on which it would pay tax of 50. The carrying value of 100 would therefore have already taken account of future tax cash flows.

33 The circumstances in which future tax cash flows are not reflected in the carrying value of an asset (and hence should potentially be provided for) are those in which there has been a timing difference. This could arise when one of the future tax cash flows inherent in the original cost of an asset had been received without the asset having been depreciated (as would be the case on receipt of an accelerated capital allowance). Or it could arise when an asset had been revalued to a market value that assumed the whole cost was deductible.

34 Thus the Board concluded that deferred tax should be provided for on timing but not permanent differences.

35 IASC board members also had concerns about the need to provide for deferred tax on permanent differences. They decided that, as an exception to the general rule that deferred tax should be provided for on all temporary differences, IAS 12 (revised) should not require recognition of deferred tax arising on initial recognition of an asset or liability (ie permanent differences).

36 In the Board's view, a standard based on timing differences would be preferable to IAS 12 (revised), which is based on temporary differences but permits exceptions for temporary differences that are not timing differences. In the Board's view, a timing difference approach would not only be easier to justify conceptually, it would also be simpler to understand and apply. Timing differences are relatively easily identified from tax computations. Temporary differences can be more difficult to identify and measure. A substantial amount of guidance was required in IAS 12 (revised).

37 A substantial majority of respondents to FRED 19 supported the Board's decision not to adopt the temporary difference approach.

Reasons for adopting the incremental liability approach

Overview

38 There are two different views on how an approach based on timing differences should be implemented. The first view is that deferred tax should be recognised only when it meets the strict criteria for recognition as a liability (or asset) in its own right – the incremental liability approach. The alternative view is that deferred tax should be recognised even if it does not itself meet the strict recognition criteria if it can be regarded as a necessary adjustment to the values at which other assets and liabilities are recognised – the valuation adjustment approach. The requirements of the FRS are based on an incremental liability approach.

Incremental liability approach

39 The Board's Statement of Principles for Financial Reporting defines liabilities as 'obligations of an entity to transfer economic benefits as a result of past transactions or events'.* The assessment of whether deferred tax is a liability requires conclusions to be reached about whether the transactions and events giving rise to an obligation to pay tax in future (the obligating events) are past events, ie have occurred at the balance sheet date.

Typically, a series of events must take place before an entity becomes required to pay tax: the entity must undertake a potentially taxable transaction, generate taxable profits and be required by tax laws to pay tax on these profits. The Statement of Principles provides guidance: **40**

> 'Sometimes a series of events must take place before the entity will have an obligation to transfer economic benefits. In such circumstances, whether the obligation exists depends on whether any of the events that have still to take place are under the entity's control. If they are, the entity retains discretion to avoid the transfer, so no obligation exists.'†

Thus the obligating event is the one that leaves the entity with no realistic alternative to paying tax, or in other words the event that will trigger the reversal of a timing difference in future.

For most types of timing difference, the events that trigger the reversal of the timing difference can be regarded as having taken place by the year-end. Suppose, for example, that the entity has accrued interest on cash deposits, but will pay tax on that interest only when it is received. Having placed the funds on deposit, it has a right to the interest they will generate. And by recognising the right to the interest, it also has to recognise the obligation to pay tax on that interest. The entity no longer has the discretion to avoid paying the tax. And as the future events that will confirm the existence of the liability (ie the inclusion of the interest received in a future tax computation and a request for the payment of tax based on that computation) are relatively certain, they do not affect its recognition. **41**

However, this is not the case with timing differences arising when assets are revalued. In the UK, the revaluation of a fixed asset to its replacement cost is not a taxable event. The taxable event is the sale of the revalued asset. Therefore, as long as the management of the entity has the discretion not to sell the fixed asset, the entity does not have an obligation to pay any tax as a result of the increase in value. An obligation can arise only when the reporting entity enters into a binding sale agreement. **42**

Similarly, a parent company can incur a tax liability when the earnings of overseas subsidiaries, associates and joint ventures are remitted to it, for example by the payment of a dividend. Therefore, the existence of unremitted earnings can be regarded as giving rise to a tax timing difference. However, their existence does not give rise to an obligation to pay tax, as long as the entity has the discretion to avoid remitting the earnings. The obligating event is the distribution of earnings. Hence, the liability arises, and, under an incremental liability approach, should be recognised, only when a dividend is accrued as receivable or a binding agreement has been made for the sale of the investment. **43**

Following the incremental liability approach, therefore, leads to a conclusion that deferred tax should not be provided for on timing differences arising from revaluation of assets or non-remittance of earnings to the parent entity. The obligating **44**

**Paragraph 4.23, Statement of Principles for Financial Reporting.*

†*Paragraph 4.32, Statement of Principles for Financial Reporting.*

event has not occurred and the entity does not have a liability at the balance sheet date.

Valuation adjustment approach

45 An alternative view is that, even where timing differences do not give rise to obligations in their own right, recognition of deferred tax could still be argued to be consistent with the Board's Statement of Principles. The argument would be that the deferred tax might need to be provided for in order to ensure that other assets were not valued at more than their economic (ie post-tax) values to the business.

46 Suppose, for example, that a company revalued an asset such as a building to its market value of 100. A timing difference would arise because the revaluation gain would be taxable only if and when the asset was sold. This timing difference would not in itself give rise to an obligation to pay more tax in future. But the valuation adjustment argument would be that deferred tax should be provided for to reflect the fact that the economic value to the business was not the market value of 100. Rather, in principle, it was the market value of 100 less the present value of the tax that would be payable on selling the asset for 100.

47 The valuation adjustment argument would apply even when the purpose of revaluing the asset to market value was to recognise its replacement cost rather than its net realisable value. It would be argued that the market values were established in the expectation that the full market value would be tax-deductible on sale (or earlier, if capital allowances were available). Unadjusted market value would not reflect that there would be more tax payable on the sale of the existing asset than there would be on the sale of an asset purchased at the market value. The true economic replacement cost of the existing asset would be measured by valuing the asset at the market value of an 'equivalent' asset and then adjusting it by providing for deferred tax.

48 The present value of the additional tax paid on the sale of a revalued asset would depend on when that tax was paid. Hence, deferred tax provided for on revaluation gains would in theory be discounted. Where an asset was not eligible for capital allowances and there was an assumption that it would be retained in the business (or replaced only when rollover relief could be claimed), the difference in the future tax deductions would materialise only very far into the future or perhaps not at all. In such cases it could be argued that the present value of the tax on the revaluation gain was negligible. A valuation adjustment approach could be simplified to require deferred tax to be provided for on revaluation gains only if it were expected that the timing difference would reverse without rollover relief being obtained.

49 In theory, deferred tax provided for as a valuation adjustment rather than as a liability might most appropriately be reflected by netting the tax provision against the value of the asset. However, it is generally accepted, both in the UK and internationally, that an entity's results and position are more clearly communicated if tax effects are shown separately from the items or transactions to which they relate.

Reasons for adopting the incremental liability approach

50 A minority of Board members favoured the valuation adjustment approach. They regarded it as important that assets recognised at their fair values – and in particular financial assets and assets adjusted to their fair values on acquisition – should be recognised at their true economic fair values, taking into consideration all future cash flows, including tax. Unless a valuation adjustment approach was adopted, assets could be valued at more than their economic (ie post-tax) recoverable

amounts. The Board members also noted that an FRS based on a valuation adjustment approach would more closely align UK accounting requirements with those of IAS 12 (revised).

However, most Board members favoured the incremental liability approach. They took the view that: 51

- the incremental liability approach was more clearly consistent with FRS 12 'Provisions, Contingent Liabilities and Contingent Assets' than one that recognised deferred tax liabilities that were not obligations.
- the valuation adjustment approach relied on theoretical models of the way in which asset values were determined. The fact that these models did not always hold in practice, combined with the difficulty in estimating the amount and timing of tax that was likely to be paid on the possible future sale of an asset, meant that the deferred tax provisions could be somewhat artificial. The tax position would be communicated much more clearly to users by recognising the amounts payable only when the entity became obliged to pay them.
- the effect of the creation and reversal of provisions under a valuation adjustment approach could be simply to standardise the tax charge rather than reflect the accrual and eventual payment of tax. For example, if a revalued asset was recovered through use in the business (ie depreciation) rather than sale, any deferred tax provision recognised on revaluing the asset would simply be reversed over the life of the asset, without any tax having become payable.

Accepting the views of the majority, the Board chose to base the FRS's requirements on the incremental liability approach. The way in which the detailed requirements fit into that approach is explained below. 52

Detailed aspects of the recognition requirements

Accelerated capital allowances

Capital allowances in excess of depreciation (accelerated capital allowances) give rise to timing differences, the reversals of which occur automatically in future and cannot be avoided by the reporting entity. 53

It was suggested to the Board that the receipt of an accelerated capital allowance for the purchase of an asset did not give rise to a deferred tax obligation since it would not in itself increase a future tax assessment. The entity had no more than a contingent liability to repay the allowance – it would be repayable only if the fixed asset was sold. Any future sale was a future event that should not be taken into account at the balance sheet date. 54

However, the Board took the view that, in commercial and economic terms, capital allowances were given for the loss arising from the consumption of the service potential of an asset – not simply for the purchase of the asset. An entity that had received capital allowances in excess of depreciation had received allowances in advance, ie on service potential that would be consumed in future. As with any consideration received in advance of performance, the entity had an obligation either to perform or to repay the consideration. This obligation remained until, as a result of future events, the service potential was consumed. 55

Hence, the Board concluded that under an incremental liability approach, deferred tax should be provided for on accelerated capital allowances. 56

Industrial buildings allowances

57 In general, allowances for capital expenditure are repayable to the tax authorities if the assets purchased are sold for more than their tax written-down value. However, this is not always the case. Industrial buildings allowances (IBAs),* for example, are repayable only if the building is sold within a certain time – 25 years of purchase.

58 FRED 19 did not specify whether and for how long deferred tax should be provided for on accelerated IBAs (or similar non-repayable allowances). Several respondents asked for clarification.

59 Some argued that, from the outset, the deferred tax was not a liability (or at least was no more than a contingent liability) because, like the deferred tax on a revaluation gain, it would be repayable only upon an uncertain future event within management's control, ie sale within 25 years. It should therefore be provided for only if and when there was an intention or commitment to sell.

60 However, the Board noted that in this respect an IBA was no different from other capital allowances – all were repayable only if the asset was sold rather than being consumed within the business. The argument (in paragraph 55 above) for requiring accelerated capital allowances to be recognised as liabilities was that, until the conditions for retaining the allowances had been met (ie through consumption of the asset), they remained unearned – a liability had not been discharged – and hence should be provided for. The deferred tax on an accelerated capital allowance was different from that on a revaluation gain because it arose from a past event. Applying the same argument to accelerated IBAs led the Board to conclude that the deferred tax thereon should be provided for until the condition for retaining the IBAs (ie the expiry of 25 years) had been met. Thus, the FRS clarifies that accelerated capital allowances of all types should be recognised as liabilities until the conditions for retaining them (ie the expiry of 25 years) have been met.

61 One respondent further noted that if industrial buildings were not being depreciated (for example, if they were investment properties), and there was no intention of selling them within 25 years, the allowances could be regarded as giving rise to permanent differences. FRED 19 had proposed that deferred tax should not be provided for on permanent differences. The Board considered this suggestion but concluded that the obligation to repay an IBA remained until all conditions for retaining it had been met, irrespective of whether the asset was being depreciated. The requirement to provide for accelerated IBAs until the conditions for retaining them have been met therefore applies to depreciating and non-depreciating assets.

Infrastructure assets

62 The FRS requires deferred tax to be provided for on all accelerated capital allowances, including those arising on infrastructure assets that, in accordance with the requirements of FRS 15 'Tangible Fixed Assets', are accounted for using renewals accounting. As clarified in the definitions section of the FRS, capital allowances obtained for such assets can give rise to timing differences in the same way as capital allowances obtained for any other assets.

**IBAs are given for expenditure on some buildings – factories, warehouses and hotels, and any commercial buildings in enterprise zones. Buildings in enterprise zones can qualify for 100 per cent first year allowances. Other industrial buildings receive IBAs at a rate of 4 per cent per year.*

Assets continuously revalued to fair value with changes recognised in profit and loss account

In line with the incremental liability approach on which it was based, FRED 19 proposed that deferred tax should not be recognised on revaluation gains. The rationale was that the rise in value of an asset was not an event that in itself obliged an entity to pay more tax in future. **63**

A significant number of respondents, whilst accepting this approach for most types of revalued asset, regarded it as inappropriate where assets were 'marked to market', ie continuously revalued to fair value with changes being recognised in the profit and loss account. Such assets could include the investments of financial institutions and some commodities. **64**

The respondents took the view that when assets were marked to market in this way, the gains and losses were recognised in the profit and loss account because, although not necessarily realised, they were readily realisable. To give a true and fair view of the entity's performance, any tax that would be payable on realising the gains should also be recognised. The respondents suggested that the arguments that deferred tax provisions on revaluation gains were somewhat artificial (paragraph 51 above) did not hold in these circumstances. **65**

The Board accepted this view and amended the FRS to require deferred tax to be provided for if it arose when assets were marked to market with gains and losses being recognised in the profit and loss account. **66**

Current assets (other than those that are marked to market)

It is rare for current assets (other than those, such as commodities, that are marked to market with gains and losses being recognised in the profit and loss account) to be held at fair value. But they are more frequently adjusted to their fair values on the acquisition of a business. **67**

The FRS permits deferred tax to be recognised on the adjustment only if there is a binding agreement for the sale of the asset at the acquisition date and the gains and losses on selling the asset have also been recognised in the fair value exercise. **68**

It was suggested to the Board that an entity always had a constructive or commercial commitment to sell stock, since that was the whole purpose of purchasing it in the first place. But the Board took the view that, whilst there could be an expectation that stock would be sold, the expectation alone did not give rise to a binding commitment. **69**

It acknowledged that a binding agreement to sell stock could exist if goods were being manufactured under the terms of a binding contract. In such circumstances, one of the obligations associated with the contract was the obligation to pay tax on the profits made. But if the contract was being accounted for as an executory contract (ie if neither the rights nor the obligations had yet been recognised because both parties had yet to perform), it would be inappropriate to recognise the tax obligation alone. **70**

Rollover relief

As an extension of the requirement not to provide for deferred tax on revaluation gains and losses, the FRS does not require deferred tax to be provided for on taxable gains that have been deferred via 'rollover relief'. **71**

72 Rollover relief can be claimed in a number of tax jurisdictions when the proceeds of sale of 'qualifying' assets (such as land and buildings) are reinvested in other qualifying assets within a specified period. The taxable gain is not charged to tax immediately but is instead rolled over into the replacement assets, becoming chargeable only if and when the replacement assets are sold.

73 The Board took the view that, where such rollover relief had been obtained, the entity retained the discretion to avoid paying tax on the chargeable gain. That tax would be paid only if and when the replacement assets were sold. Hence, where an entity had sold or agreed to sell an asset and had recognised the gain on sale, it still did not have a liability for any tax if it had already met the conditions for rolling the gain over into a replacement asset. (This would not be the case if the terms of the relief were different and merely postponed the payment of tax for a specified period.)

74 It was suggested that the justification for not providing for rolled-over gains (ie that the tax was not a liability because it would be deferred by the purchase of new assets) should also justify providing on a partial basis for accelerated capital allowances. However, the arguments are different. When a gain is rolled over into a replacement asset, it does not enter a tax computation and will not do so unless and until a decision is made to sell the replacement asset. It might not make future tax charges higher than they would otherwise have been. The tax authorities are in effect recognising successive assets as if they were a single asset. So, even using full provision arguments, the deferred tax should not be provided for. In contrast, an accelerated capital allowance will reverse automatically over the life of the asset, entering into a future tax computation and making a future tax assessment higher than it would otherwise have been, whether or not more assets are purchased. The purchase of another asset does not prevent the original accelerated capital allowance from reversing, it merely originates a new one that offsets it.

75 Tax legislation may allow rollover relief to be claimed even if the proceeds of sale are not reinvested immediately, but are reinvested within a specified period. In such circumstances, an entity could have sold or entered into a binding agreement to sell one asset by the balance sheet date without being certain that it would be able to roll the gain over into a replacement asset. The Board took the view that in such circumstances the deferred tax represented a contingent liability as defined in FRS 12 'Provisions, Contingent Liabilities and Contingent Assets'. Consistently with the recognition requirements in FRS 12, the FRS requires that for as long as it appears more likely than not that the entity will be able to roll over the gain, the deferred tax on that gain should not be provided for.

RECOVERABILITY OF DEFERRED TAX ASSETS

General recognition requirement – transfer of economic benefits

76 Assets or liabilities are recognised only if there is sufficient evidence that the rights or obligations that give rise to them will result in the transfer of economic benefits in future.* In respect of deferred tax assets and liabilities, there would be such a transfer of economic benefits only if the future reversal of the timing difference had an incremental effect on a future tax payment or receipt. This would be the case only if the reporting entity generated taxable profits in future (or tax losses that could be relieved against past taxable profits). If, instead, it were to generate unrelieved tax losses, the reversal of the timing differences would not result in any cash flows: it would simply alter the amount of losses for which no relief had been received. Deferred tax assets and liabilities should therefore be recognised only when there is

**Chapter 4, Statement of Principles for Financial Reporting.*

evidence that the entity will make sufficient taxable profits in future for the reversal of the timing difference to affect the amount of tax actually paid.

Deferred tax liabilities

In theory, therefore, there could be circumstances in which entities need not recognise deferred tax liabilities. However, the FRS requires all deferred tax liabilities to be recognised, without referring at all to future tax losses. The Board's rationale for this proposal was that: 77

- it was very unlikely that there would be persuasive evidence on which to base a prudent and reliable prediction that an entity that was a going concern was more likely than not to make tax losses in future that would remain unrelieved; and
- a requirement to make a judgement on this matter would make the FRS more difficult to understand and apply.

Deferred tax assets

With deferred tax assets, the situation is slightly different. To recover a deferred tax asset, an entity would have to do more than simply *not make losses* in future: it would have to *make sufficient profits* that would be charged to tax if it were not for the reversal of the timing difference. Further, the need for prudence would suggest that more evidence of the likelihood of future profits was needed for recognition of a deferred tax asset than for recognition of a deferred tax liability. For these reasons, the FRS permits deferred tax assets to be recognised only when, on the basis of available evidence, it is more likely than not that there will be taxable profits in future against which the deferred tax asset can be offset. The requirements are the same as those of both FAS 109 and IAS 12 (revised). 78

SSAP 15 permitted deferred tax assets arising from tax losses to be recognised only if the availability of future taxable profits against which the losses could be offset was 'assured beyond reasonable doubt'. The Board agreed that the recognition of tax losses as assets should be restricted, since the very existence of losses provided strong evidence that they would not be recovered. However, in the Board's view, it was more appropriate to restrict the recognition of the losses by emphasising that the 'more likely than not' threshold must be met rather than by setting a recognition threshold that was higher than that set for other deferred tax assets (such as those arising on accruals for retirement benefits). 79

MEASUREMENT – TAX RATES

The FRS follows IAS 12 (revised) in requiring deferred tax to be measured using tax rates that have been enacted or substantively enacted by the balance sheet date. 80

Although it could be argued that the rates used should instead be the best estimates of the future rates that would apply, the Board concluded that: 81

- given that future tax rates are influenced by political and economic considerations that are very difficult to predict, the best estimates of future tax rates would normally be the most recently enacted or substantively enacted rates
- where there was evidence of possible future changes (for example, when proposals had been announced for consultation), it was generally difficult for individuals to assess the likelihood that the changes would be enacted. Different views could be taken and different rates used by different entities. Given that these entities would actually be paying tax at the same rate, such inconsistencies would be unhelpful.

82 Guidance has been given on the meaning of 'substantively enacted' in the UK and the Republic of Ireland to help ensure that the requirement is interpreted consistently. In developing this guidance the Board considered, but rejected, suggestions that a Budget announcement should be viewed as substantive enactment in the UK providing that the changes were very likely to be enacted. The Board took the view that 'substantive enactment' meant that the process of enactment was substantively complete. Whilst in some circumstances it could be very likely that a change proposed at the first reading of a Finance Bill would be enacted, the process of enactment was not at that stage substantively complete. In particular, the Bill still had to pass through committee and two further readings in the House of Commons. Similarly, in the Republic of Ireland, the process of enactment would not be substantively complete until the Bill had been passed by the Dail.

83 The FRS requires that, where tax rates are graduated – ie where different tax rates apply to different bands of taxable profit – entities should use the *average* rate expected to be paid in the year in which the timing difference reverses. IAS 12 (revised) has the same requirement. The Board was aware that arguments could be made for using instead the rate that applied to the bottom, or the top, band of taxable profits. However, it believed that there were insufficient grounds for departing from international practice in this respect, in particular because most UK companies were unaffected by graduated tax rates.

MEASUREMENT – DISCOUNTING

Overview

84 FRED 19 tentatively proposed that deferred tax balances should be discounted where the effect of discounting was material and asked for respondents' views on the proposal. In the light of the responses received, the Board decided that the FRS should neither prohibit nor require discounting but should allow entities a choice of accounting policy.

Arguments for and against discounting

Conceptual validity

85 A key feature of the UK tax system is that there can be a significant delay between the recognition of certain items in the accounts and their recognition in a tax computation and vice versa. The delay suggests that there would be a case for discounting deferred tax assets and liabilities where the effect was material. However, views differ on whether there is a conceptual justification for discounting certain deferred tax balances, such as those arising from accelerated capital allowances.

86 The purpose of discounting is to measure future cash flows at their present value. It is therefore valid to discount deferred tax balances only if they can be viewed as representing future cash flows that are not already measured at their present value.

87 There are some types of timing differences that clearly represent future tax cash flows. Where, for example, an accrual is made for expenses that are to be paid far into the future and tax relief will be received only when the expenses are paid, the tax relief represents a future tax cash flow that should be discounted to its present value. In practice, however, it is rarely necessary to perform separate discounting calculations for this type of deferred tax, since long-term accruals, such as those for retirement benefits, are usually themselves measured on a discounted basis. Thus the

timing differences already incorporate discounting and it is not appropriate to discount the resulting deferred tax as well.

Separate discounting would, however, be required if the timing difference giving rise to a future tax cash flow were not discounted. An example of such a timing difference is that provided for (in the limited circumstances set out in paragraph 12 of the FRS) on revaluation gains. Discounting of deferred tax on revaluation gains is discussed in paragraphs 47 and 48 above. **88**

More controversial is the issue of whether it is valid to discount deferred tax when tax cash flows have already occurred. This situation arises most commonly when capital allowances have been received before an asset has been depreciated. **89**

Undoubtedly, an entity that receives a capital allowance as soon as it purchases an asset is better off than one that receives the same allowance as it depreciates the asset. *Without discounting*, this benefit materialises in the form of higher interest income over the period in which the asset is being depreciated. *With discounting*, the benefit of the additional interest income is pulled forward and recognised immediately. **90**

The question is whether the benefit should be recognised immediately by discounting. One view – typically held by those who regard deferred tax as an adjustment to the values at which other assets are recognised rather than as a liability in its own right – is that it should not. Those holding this view argue that: **91**

- the deferred tax provision represents a cash inflow that has already been received. It is therefore already stated at its present value. There are no future tax cash flows to occur.
- the carrying value of an asset reflects the present value of the future economic benefits that it will generate. At the outset, one of these future benefits is the present value of the capital allowance that will be received (including the value of receiving it early in the life of the asset). Once the capital allowance has been received, the remaining future benefits are reduced by that amount. The reduction in the value of the asset is recognised by providing for deferred tax. If the amount provided for is discounted, the entity is recognising a 'gain' that has not necessarily been earned.
- the cash outflow arising from the purchase of a fixed asset is recognised as depreciation evenly over the life of the asset. If the cash inflow arising from a capital allowance is seen as an adjustment to the value of the asset, it too should be recognised evenly over the life of the asset.

However, a different view can be taken under the incremental liability approach required by the FRS. Under this approach, an accelerated capital allowance is viewed as a liability that will be repaid in the form of higher tax assessments in the future. Although one tax cash flow has already occurred, creating the timing difference, it can be argued that there will be a second tax cash flow when, on reversal of the timing difference, a future tax payment is higher than it would otherwise have been. And, where the higher future tax payment will occur some distance into the future, it is valid to discount it to reflect the fact that, at the balance sheet date, it represents a lower obligation than a liability that is payable immediately. **92**

Another way of viewing the accelerated capital allowance is as an interest-free loan from the tax authorities. And just as it can be argued that an interest-free loan is a smaller obligation than a loan paying a commercial rate of interest, so it can be argued that a deferred tax liability should be discounted. **93**

The different conclusions on discounting that are reached depending on whether deferred tax is rationalised as a liability or a valuation adjustment can be reconciled. When a capital allowance is received, the cash-generating capability of the fixed asset (and hence its value in *absolute* terms) is reduced by the amount of that past tax cash **94** flow. A valuation adjustment approach seeks to recognise that absolute reduction in future cash flows. However, if deferred tax is rationalised as a liability, all that is being provided for is the additional tax cash flows that the entity will pay *relative* to the tax that it would have paid had it not received capital allowances until they were earned. The liability is being measured without reference to changes in the values of fixed assets.

Cost/benefit considerations

95 One of the messages that emerged strongly from the responses to FRED 19 was that for most industries the benefits of discounting were not perceived to outweigh the costs.

96 Significant time and effort may be required to collate the information required to discount accelerated capital allowances and perform the discounting calculations, especially for large organisations with operations spread across a wide range of tax jurisdictions. Some respondents argued that they would have to collate substantial amounts of information even if only to establish that the impact of discounting was not material in that period.

97 There were also reservations expressed about the benefit of discounting to users of financial statements. Users who responded to the FRED were divided in their opinions. And preparers were concerned that the impact on the profit and loss account would be difficult to understand: movements caused, for example, by changes in discount rate from one period to the next could be difficult to explain to users.

98 Support for discounting was strong only from companies for which the effect of discounting would be fundamental.

International practice

99 Both IAS 12 (revised) and the US accounting standard FAS 109 prohibit discounting of deferred tax balances. IASC took the view that the scheduling of the reversal of timing differences was often impracticable or highly complex and hence that it should not be made mandatory. It rejected the possibility of permitting discounting without requiring it, because the option would make the results of different entities less comparable. It is, however, now reconsidering, as part of a general project on discounting, whether deferred tax should be discounted. *Reasons for making discounting optional*

100 One Board member opposed discounting, primarily on the grounds that it impeded international harmonisation. The Board member also took the view (explained in paragraphs 89-91 above) that discounting was conceptually wrong for timing differences – such as accelerated capital allowances – where tax cash flows had already occurred.

101 The rest of the Board supported discounting in principle, regarding it as consistent with the incremental liability approach on which the FRS requirements were based and as a means of providing more relevant information to users. However, taking into consideration the practical arguments made by respondents, the Board concluded that:

(a) in many circumstances, the costs were widely perceived to outweigh the benefits. Discounting should not be required in those circumstances.

(b) this was especially the case given that discounting was not yet well established in the context of deferred tax (either in theory or in practice). A methodology was being introduced in the UK before an international consensus had been reached.

(c) providing that discounting was applied consistently from one period to the next, and the impact of discounting on the financial statements was highlighted clearly, there would not be a serious loss of comparability if not all entities discounted deferred tax.

The Board considered first whether it could achieve its aims by emphasising that discounting was required only where the effect was genuinely material to the overall results and performance portrayed in the financial statements. It considered whether 'indicators of materiality' could be prescribed to make it easier for companies to determine that the effect would not be material. **102**

However, it took the view that such indicators would be difficult to define other than in vague (and hence not very useful) terms. Further, basing decisions on discounting purely on materiality would not entirely eliminate the practical problems. First, there would remain some companies for which the effect of discounting deferred tax would border on being material. Such companies would certainly have to perform discounting calculations and would probably take the view that they should report discounted amounts, even though they would probably regard the costs as exceeding the benefits. **103**

The second problem would be that by concentrating only on materiality, it would be difficult to emphasise the importance of consistency. For some companies, the effect of discounting could be material in some periods but not others. In such circumstances, it could be argued that it was more important that the company reported consistently from one period to the next (either discounting or not) than that it discounted only when the effect was material. **104**

For these reasons, the Board concluded that the FRS should not require all entities to discount deferred tax. Instead, it should allow them a choice of accounting policy that they would then apply consistently. In taking this approach, the FRS has followed a precedent set in FRS 15 'Tangible Fixed Assets', which allows entities a choice of policies with regard to capitalisation of finance costs attributable to the construction of a fixed asset. The factors set out in paragraph 101 above are very similar to those that led the Board to permit a choice of policies in FRS 15. **105**

Detailed requirements for discounting

The 'full reversal' approach to scheduling reversals

To discount a deferred tax liability or asset, it is necessary to forecast the timing of the future cash flows that the deferred tax represents. Two alternative approaches were considered by the Board: **106**

- *the full reversal basis*, whereby the future cash flows are treated as occurring when the timing differences constituting the deferred tax balance at the year-end are expected to reverse
- *the net reversal basis*, whereby the future cash flows are treated as occurring when the timing differences as a whole (ie after taking account of new timing differences to replace those that reverse) are expected to reduce.

The rationale for the full reversal basis is the same as that for full provision accounting: every individual timing difference reverses and, when it does so, has an **107** incremental or decremental effect on future cash flows. Similarly, the rationale for the net reversal basis is the same as that for the partial provision method: the deferred tax is viewed as a homogeneous whole and is regarded as giving rise to a future cash flow only to the extent that reversing timing differences will not be replaced by new originating timing differences.

108 The Board took the view that the net reversal basis for discounting could be justified only within a partial provision framework. Within a full provision framework, it would be inconsistent not to treat the cash flows as occurring when the individual timing differences reversed. The FRS therefore requires that where deferred tax is discounted, it is to be discounted on a full reversal basis.

109 The FRS does, however, require the scheduling of reversals to take account of the remaining capital allowances to be received on the existing assets on which the timing differences have arisen. It was suggested that the remaining capital allowances should be ignored on the grounds that they were future events that created further timing differences (rather than delaying the reversal of the existing timing differences). The existing timing differences would be viewed as reversing as soon as further depreciation occurred. However, the Board did not view the remaining capital allowances as arising from future events. Rather it regarded the allowances, like depreciation, as one of the expected consequences of a past event (the purchase of an asset) that had to be taken into account in measuring the tax liability arising from that event.

Future losses

110 Future tax losses could affect the time at which deferred tax liabilities and assets were paid or recovered. Suppose, for example, that an accelerated capital allowance was expected to reverse over the next five years but that the entity expected to generate in that period tax losses that would themselves be relieved only in later periods. The deferred tax liability would not have an incremental effect on the amount of tax actually paid until the future losses were relieved. It could therefore be argued that the liability should be discounted further to reflect the expected delay.

111 However, in addition to possible conceptual reasons, the Board concluded that there were practical reasons why possible future losses should not be taken into account when assessing the period over which deferred tax assets and liabilities were discounted:

(a) whilst little judgement was required to schedule the reversal of timing differences, far more judgement would be required if predictions regarding future tax losses had to be made. It would be difficult to forecast patterns of future losses reliably, especially those expected to arise in later years (ie those for which discounting would be most relevant). The discounting calculations could be more difficult to perform and the discounted amount could be significantly less reliable.

(b) whilst there was a theoretical risk that deferred tax assets would be overstated if future losses were not taken into consideration when estimating the timing of the recovery of the assets, this risk was unlikely to give rise to problems in practice. The overstatement would arise only if future losses were expected to delay significantly the recovery of a deferred tax asset. In such circumstances, it is unlikely that there would be sufficient evidence to support the recognition of the deferred tax asset at all. Guidance to this effect is included in the FRS.

For these reasons, the Board concluded that future losses should not be taken into consideration when determining the period over which deferred tax assets and liabilities should be discounted. 112

Discount rate

General conclusions on discounting were set out in the Board's Working Paper 'Discounting in Financial Reporting', published in April 1997. The requirements of the FRS are consistent with the conclusions reached in that Paper. 113

Chapter 4 of the Working Paper concluded that the discount rate for a liability should reflect only the characteristics of the liability. Hence the discount rate used to measure a liability should not be based on the entity's cost of capital. Rather it should aim to measure the least cost of settling the liability, which would be either: 114

(a) the amount that a third party would have to be paid to take over the liability; or
(b) the amount that would have to be invested in assets that would grow to match the amount due and settle the liability at the due date.

In practice, it is unlikely that there would be a third party willing to take over a deferred tax liability. Hence it is necessary to determine the amount that the entity would have to invest at the balance sheet date in assets that would grow to match the liability. 115

When deferred tax liabilities are discounted on a full reversal basis, the future cash flows that they represent are relatively certain. In most circumstances, they are fixed at the amount of the timing difference multiplied by the rate of tax paid by the entity. The most appropriate 'matching assets' are therefore those that provide a fixed income that is taxable at the same rate. This is most likely to be government bonds of a maturity date and in a currency similar to those of the deferred tax liability. 116

The Working Paper suggested that the rate at which assets should be discounted was the rate that the market would expect on an equally risky investment. The rate would be reduced to the extent that any of the risk had been taken into account by lowering the estimates of future cash flows. The FRS requires uncertainty about the recoverability of a deferred tax asset to be taken into account in determining the extent to which the undiscounted asset is recognised. This uncertainty should not therefore be reflected in the discount rate. In other respects, the future cash flows associated with a deferred tax asset are relatively certain. For this reason the return that would be expected by the market is approximately equal to the effective return on a government bond. 117

The FRS therefore requires both deferred tax assets and liabilities to be discounted at the effective rates of return on government bonds of maturity dates and in currencies similar to those of the deferred tax. These rates are not only consistent with the conclusions reached in the Working Paper on discounting, they also have the advantage of being simpler to determine and less subjective than other possible rates. 118

The FRS requires the government bond rates used to discount deferred tax to be measured on a post-tax basis, ie after taking account of the tax that the reporting entity would pay on income generated by the bonds. This is because the cost of the reversing timing differences is not tax-deductible. The whole reversing timing difference would therefore have to be funded from the post-tax yield on the government bond. 119

Presentation of movement in discount

120 When deferred tax is discounted, there is a charge or credit to the profit and loss account each period that represents the movement on the discount. The net movement has three components:

(a) changes in the underlying timing differences and tax rates;
(b) an 'unwinding' of the discount on timing differences that had existed at the start of the period (because these differences are now one year closer to reversal); and
(c) changes in the rates at which the opening deferred tax balance is discounted.

121 The Board takes the view that, in principle, an expense should be measured in the profit and loss account at the present value (when the expense is recognised) of the amount to be paid. Thus, an operating expense that was not payable immediately would be recognised in the profit and loss account at a discounted amount. The additional charge attributable to the unwinding of the discount as the payment date approached would not be presented as an additional operating expense. Rather, because it arose as a consequence of not settling the liability immediately, it would be presented as a financing item, ie next to interest payable and receivable. An argument in support of such an approach is that it avoids the amounts reported as operating profit being distorted by funding decisions: an operating expense that was not payable immediately would be recorded at the same amount whether or not it had been funded. The Board believes that such an approach, which it regards as correct in principle, should be required when it is practicable and results in a presentation that corresponds to the reader's understanding of the underlying economic nature of the transaction.

122 However, even though the unwinding of the discount on a deferred tax liability (or asset) can be regarded in principle as a financing item, the FRS does not require it to be shown as part of the financing section in the profit and loss account. The reason is that profit and loss account formats require all of the tax consequences of pre-tax profits to be shown separately, below the subtotal 'profits on ordinary activities before taxation'. The unwinding of a discount on a deferred tax balance, whether viewed conceptually as part of the tax expense or as a finance item, is not part of profits before tax. Hence, it is shown after the subtotal of profits before tax.

123 For similar reasons the FRS also requires the movement in the discount attributable to a change in the rate at which the opening deferred tax liability or asset has been discounted to be shown as part of the tax charge.

PRESENTATION OF DEFERRED TAX BALANCES

Offset of deferred tax assets and liabilities

124 The Board's Statement of Principles* states that:

> 'If a right to receive future economic benefits and an obligation to transfer future economic benefits exist and the reporting entity has the ability – which is assured – to insist on net settlement of the balances, the right and obligation together form a single net asset or liability regardless of how the parties intend to settle the balances.'

**Paragraph 4.34, Statement of Principles for Financial Reporting.*

If this principle is applied, deferred tax debit and credit balances might be regarded as being capable of being offset and presented as a single net asset or liability only if: 125

(a) they relate to the same tax authority;
(b) they arise within the same taxable entities or within different taxable entities that are entitled to settle their tax liabilities on a net basis; and
(c) the timing differences giving rise to a deferred tax asset reverse before or at the same time as those giving rise to a deferred tax liability. (If those giving rise to the liability reverse first, there will be a requirement to pay tax before any entitlement to recover tax.)

However, the requirements in the FRS do not restrict the offsetting of deferred tax debit and credit balances to circumstances where the above criteria are met. The Board took the view that: 126

(a) it could be argued that all deferred tax balances of a single taxable entity* with a single tax authority were adjustments to future liabilities of that entity (rather than assets or liabilities in their own right) and so should be shown as a single balance;
(b) the costs of scheduling the timings of reversals to measure the extent to which the balances should be offset would greatly exceed any benefit to users. Indeed, the needs of many users would probably best be served by presenting the deferred tax in as uncomplicated a manner as possible.

The view that a requirement to take account of the timing of reversals would be impracticable has also been taken in IAS 12 (revised). The offset requirements required by the FRS are therefore very similar to those of IAS 12 (revised). A significant difference is that IAS 12 (revised) adds a criterion based on whether or not it is intended that current tax balances will be settled on a net basis. The difference reflects differences between the Board's and IASC's general principles regarding offset. 127

Presentation on the face of the balance sheet

The requirements for separate presentation of deferred tax (at least in the notes to the accounts) reflect the Board's view that deferred tax is different from most other debtors and provisions. In general it does not have a direct relationship with future cash receipts or payments. Rather than being a payment or receipt in its own right, it affects other (possibly very distant) future payments, which will also be affected by a number of other factors. 128

To identify the deferred tax assets and provisions that should be presented separately on the face of the balance sheet, the Board followed the consensus reached in UITF Abstract 4 in respect of any long- term debtor included within current assets: 129

> 'In most cases, it will be satisfactory to disclose the size ... in the notes to the accounts. There will be some instances, however, where the amount is so material in the context of the total net current assets that in the absence of disclosure ... on the face of the balance sheet readers may misinterpret the accounts.'

The FRS does not go as far as IAS 12 (revised), which requires all (material) deferred tax balances to be presented separately from other debtors and provisions on the face of the balance sheet. In the Board's view, such a requirement would add unnecessary 130

**or of entities within a single tax group, where the losses of one entity could be used to reduce the taxable profits of another.*

detail when deferred tax assets and liabilities did not have a fundamental impact on the company's net asset or net current asset position.

DISCLOSURES

Unrecognised deferred tax

131 The FRS requires disclosure of the amounts of deferred tax not provided for on the unremitted earnings of subsidiaries, associates and joint ventures only to the extent that the earnings are expected to be remitted in the foreseeable future. Unlike IAS 12 (revised), it does not require any quantification of the total timing differences arising from unremitted earnings because the Board was not persuaded that such a disclosure would provide relevant information to users of financial statements. (In most circumstances, the possibility of all of the earnings being remitted is remote, and the tax that would become payable would be subject to a number of uncertainties.)

Other factors affecting future tax charges

132 Companies legislation requires information to be given about special circumstances that have affected the tax charge for the current period and might affect the tax charges of future periods. Users of financial statements frequently told the Board that they particularly valued information that helped them to make more accurate predictions about future tax payments. The FRED therefore specifies the information that an entity should include.

133 The Board decided that the requirement to disclose a reconciliation of the entity's current tax charge for the period to an 'expected' charge – ie the charge that would result if accounting profits were taxed at a standard rate – was especially important. The reconciliation would provide users of financial statements with a complete picture of the factors that had influenced the current tax charge for the period. They could then use other information about the company (for example, the nature of its deferred tax liabilities and its capital investment plans) to arrive at a judgement about the extent to which the reconciling items would recur. The requirement received strong support from those responding to the FRED on behalf of institutional investors.

134 IAS 12 (revised) and FAS 109 also require reconciliations to be disclosed. However, both of those standards require a reconciliation of the total tax charge for the period (ie the total of current and deferred tax) to a standard tax charge. The Board chose to focus the reconciliation on the current tax charge instead because it believed that that was the element of the total tax charge that was of most importance to users. A reconciliation based on the current tax charge was the clearest and most direct way of providing information on the factors that might affect future current tax charges.

135 FAS 109 requires the reconciliation to be given only by listed companies. Other entities need disclose only the nature of significant reconciling items. The Board considered whether it should propose a similar distinction in FRED 19. It concluded that a full reconciliation would be of use to the users of the financial statements of all entities. And, since the information would normally be readily available from tax computations, it ought not to be an onerous requirement.

Other disclosures required by IAS 12 (revised)

IAS 12 (revised) requires entities that have recently made losses to explain (where relevant) why they have recognised deferred tax assets. 136

It could be argued that this disclosure is not necessary: the recognition of the asset in itself shows that the directors and auditors have satisfied themselves that it is more likely than not that the asset will be recovered. 137

However, the Board took the view that additional information about the assumptions underlying the recognition of a deferred tax asset alerted users to the uncertainties surrounding the asset's recoverability and helped them to assess the financial position of the entity. The FRS therefore includes a disclosure requirement identical to that included in IAS 12 (revised). 138

AMENDMENT TO FRS 7

General changes

FRS 7 'Fair Values in Acquisition Accounting' aims to recognise in a fair value exercise only the identifiable assets and liabilities of the acquired entity that existed at the date of acquisition. It aims to measure them based on their condition at that date, independent of the intentions of the acquirer. However, its requirements regarding deferred tax (ie to measure the extent to which the liabilities would crystallise considering the enlarged group as a whole) were slightly inconsistent with this general aim, since they had to be consistent with the partial provision method of accounting for deferred tax required by SSAP 15. 139

With the replacement of SSAP 15 it is no longer necessary to consider the enlarged group when measuring deferred tax liabilities. The amendment to FRS 7 implemented by the FRS clarifies that this is the case. And it ensures that deferred tax recognised in a fair value exercise is recognised on the same basis as it is recognised in the group financial statements thereafter. 140

Previously unrecognised deferred tax assets

The amendment to FRS 7 adds guidance on how to treat deferred tax assets – typically, unrelieved tax losses – that were not regarded as recoverable before the acquisition but, as a result of the acquisition, become sufficiently recoverable within the enlarged group to be recognised as assets after the acquisition. FRS 7 previously gave no guidance on whether such assets should be recognised in the fair value exercise or as a credit in the post-acquisition profit and loss account. The Board received anecdotal evidence that practice varied. 141

The Board concluded that, if the losses had arisen in the acquiring group, it would be inconsistent with the principles of FRS 7 to require them to be recognised as part of the fair value exercise. They could not be regarded as assets of the acquired entity. Rather, as a result of the acquisition, the acquiring group was expected to be more profitable in future. The FRS 7 therefore requires the benefit to be recognised as a credit in the post-acquisition profit and loss account. 142

It was less clear how any previously unrecognised losses in the acquired entity should be recognised. One view was that the recoverability of the acquired entity's deferred tax asset stemmed from the future actions of the acquiring group. In its condition before acquisition, the asset had not been recoverable. Hence it was argued that it 143 would be inconsistent with the principles underlying FRS 7 to recognise an asset as part of the fair value exercise. This was the view taken in FRED 19, which proposed that the losses should not be recognised as assets in the fair value exercise.

144 However, another view was that deferred tax losses (unlike, say, provisions for future reorganisations) were identifiable contingent assets of the acquired entity that had existed before the acquisition. Especially if a large proportion of the purchase price related to the losses, a requirement not to reflect them as an asset (but to recognise a larger goodwill balance instead) seemed not to reflect the economics of the purchase.

145 Those taking this view noted that paragraph 37 of FRS 7 specifically addressed such contingent assets:

> 'Certain contingent assets and liabilities that crystallise as a result of the acquisition would also be recognised, provided that the underlying contingency was in existence before the acquisition. An example is where the acquired entity has previously entered into a contract that contains a clause under which the obligations are triggered in the event of a change of ownership.'

146 After consideration of the arguments, the Board decided that it would be consistent with the treatment of other contingent assets to recognise the recoverable tax losses of an acquired entity in the fair value exercise. The requirements proposed in FRED 19 have therefore been amended in the FRS.

CHANGES TO REQUIREMENTS PROPOSED IN FRED 19

Change	Paragraph reference: FRS (Requirement)	Paragraph reference: This Appendix (Explanation)
1 New requirement clarifying that deferred tax should be provided for on capital allowances until all conditions for retaining them have been met. Applies in practice to industrial buildings allowances.	9	57–61
2 New exception to general requirement that deferred tax should not be recognised on revaluation gains and losses. Exception requires deferred tax to be recognised on timing differences arising when an asset or liability is continuously revalued to its fair value with revaluation gains and losses being recognised in the profit and loss account.	12	63–66
3 Discounting made optional (rather than mandatory as had been proposed).	42	100–105
4 Removal of requirement to present as finance costs the movement in deferred tax balances in the year resulting from unwinding of discounts and changes in discount rates. These are now required to be shown as part of the deferred tax charge.	59	120–123
5 Amendment of proposal regarding recognition of deferred tax assets on the acquisition of a business. The FRS requires deferred tax assets of the acquired entity to be included in the fair value exercise, even if they had not been recognised before the acquisition. The FRED had proposed that they should be recognised as credits to post-acquisition profits.	71	141–146

Financial Reporting Standard 20 embodies IFRS 2 'Share-based Payment' and some amendments to that standard adopted for entities subject to UK accounting standards.

The Statement of Standard Accounting Practice in FRS 20 is set out in paragraphs 1-64 and Appendices A-C. All the paragraphs have equal authority. Paragraphs in bold type state the main principles. Terms defined in Appendix A are in italics the first time they appear.*

Accompanying the Statement of Standard Accounting Practice is the basis for the conclusions reached in the Statement and some implementation guidance, neither of which forms part of the Statement.

The Statement of Standard Accounting Practice should be read in the context of its objective as stated in paragraph 1, the Basis for Conclusions set out in paragraphs BC1-BC333, and the Accounting Standards Board's 'Foreword to Accounting Standards' and 'Statement of Principles for Financial Reporting'.

***Editor's note**: *Paragraph amended in August 2009.*

FRS 20
(IFRS 2) Share-based payment*

(Issued April 2004)

Contents

	paragraphs
Introduction	**IN1-IN8**
Reasons for issuing the IFRS	**IN1-IN2**
Main features of the IFRS	**IN3-IN8**
Financial Reporting Standard 20 (IFRS 2)	
Share-based Payment	
Objective	**1**
Scope	**1A-6**
Recognition	**7-9**
Equity-settled share-based payment transactions	**10-29**
Overview	**10-13**
Transactions in which services are received	**14-15**
Transactions measured by reference to the fair value of the equity instruments granted	**16-25**
Determining the fair value of equity instruments granted	16-18
Treatment of vesting conditions	19-21A
Treatment of a reload feature	22
After vesting date	23
If the fair value of the equity instruments cannot be estimated reliably	24-25
Modifications to the terms and conditions on which equity instruments were granted, including cancellations and settlements	**26-29**
Cash-settled share-based payment transactions	**30-33**
Share-based payment transactions with cash alternatives	**34-43**
Share-based payment transactions in which the terms of the arrangement provide the counterparty with a choice of settlement	**35-40**
Share-based payment transactions in which the terms of the arrangement provide the entity with a choice of settlement	**41-43**
Disclosures	**44-52**
Transitional provisions	**53-59**

****Editor's note****: *The matters covered in FRS 20 are dealt with in Section 26 of FRS 102.*

Effective date 60

Appendices

A Defined terms
B Application guidance
C Amendments to other standards and UITF Abstracts

Preface by the Accounting Standards Board

This Financial Reporting Standard (FRS) has the effect of implementing the International Accounting Standards Board's (IASB's) International Financial Reporting Standard (IFRS) 2 *Share-based Payment* in the UK and the Republic of Ireland for entities not preparing their financial statements in accordance with international accounting standards adopted pursuant to the Regulation of the European Parliament and of the Council on the Application of International Accounting Standards. a

IFRS 2 sets out requirements on the accounting treatment of share-based payment transactions. It applies to all entities and to all share-based payment transactions, and it comes into effect for accounting periods beginning on or after 1 January 2005. The requirements, scope and effective date of FRS 20 are identical to IFRS 2 with two exceptions: b

- entities applying the FRSSE will be exempt from the FRS, and
- for unlisted entities that are not applying the FRSSE, the FRS will come into effect for accounting periods beginning on or after 1 January 2006, rather than 2005.

For this purpose an unlisted entity is an entity that has neither shares nor debt admitted to trading on a regulated market in the EU.

The text of IFRS 2 contains various references to other IFRSs. In FRS 20 those references have been amended where necessary to enable the Standard to be applied in a UK context. The Accounting Standards Board believes that those amendments do not change the requirements of IFRS 2 in any way. c

Appendix C of IFRS 2 contains amendments that the IASB has made to existing IFRS in the light of the main requirements in IFRS 2. In FRS 20 this material has been amended and added to so that the FRS can be applied in a UK context. In particular, from the relevant date of the Standard paragraphs C9 and C10 withdraw UITF Abstract 17 *Employee share schemes* and UITF Abstract 30 *Date of award to employees of shares or rights to shares* and amend UITF Abstract 38 *Accounting for ESOP trusts*. d

In all other respects the FRS is identical to IFRS 2. e

In January 2008 the Board amended FRS 20 to incorporate changes made by the IASB to IFRS 2 *Share-based Payments 'Vesting Conditions and Cancellations.'* h

In August 2009 the Board amended FRS 20 to incorporate changes made by the IASB to IFRS 2 – *Share-based payments 'Group Cash-settled Share-based Payment Transactions'*.* i

****Editor's note**: Paragraph added in August 2009.*

Introduction

REASONS FOR ISSUING THE IFRS*

IN1 Entities often grant shares or share options to employees or other parties. Share plans and share option plans are a common feature of employee remuneration, for directors, senior executives and many other employees. Some entities issue shares or share options to pay suppliers, such as suppliers of professional services.

IN2 Until this IFRS was issued, there was no IFRS covering the recognition and measurement of these transactions. Concerns were raised about this gap in IFRSs, given the increasing prevalence of share-based payment transactions in many countries.

REASONS FOR AMENDING IFRS 2 IN JUNE 2009

IN2A In June 2009 the International Accounting Standards Board amended IFRS 2 to clarify its scope and the accounting for group cash-settled share-based payment transactions in the separate or individual financial statements of the entity receiving the goods or services when that entity has no obligation to settle the share-based payment transaction. The amendments also incorporate the guidance contained in the following Interpretations:

- IFRIC 8 Scope of IFRS 2
- IFRIC 11 IFRS 2—Group and Treasury Share Transactions.

As a result, the Board withdrew IFRIC 8 and IFRIC 11.†

MAIN FEATURES OF THE IFRS

IN3 The IFRS requires an entity to recognise share-based payment transactions in its financial statements, including transactions with employees or other parties to be settled in cash, other assets, or equity instruments of the entity. There are no exceptions to the IFRS, other than for transactions to which other Standards apply.

IN4 The IFRS sets out measurement principles and specific requirements for three types of share-based payment transactions:

(a) equity-settled share-based payment transactions, in which the entity receives goods or services as consideration for equity instruments of the entity (including shares or share options);
(b) cash-settled share-based payment transactions, in which the entity acquires goods or services by incurring liabilities to the supplier of those goods or services for amounts that are based on the price (or value) of the entity's shares or other equity instruments of the entity; and
(c) transactions in which the entity receives or acquires goods or services and the terms of the arrangement provide either the entity or the supplier of those goods or services with a choice of whether the entity settles the transaction in cash or by issuing equity instruments.

* ***ASB footnote:*** *Although references to specific IFRSs have been amended so that the standard can be applied in a UK context, the standard's references to itself as an 'IFRS' and its references to other extant accounting standards as 'other IFRS' have been left unchanged. They should though be taken to be references to this FRS and to extant standards issued in the UK and the Republic of Ireland respectively.*

†***Editor's note****: Paragraph added in August 2009.*

For equity-settled share-based payment transactions, the IFRS requires an entity to measure the goods or services received, and the corresponding increase in equity, directly, at the fair value of the goods or services received, unless that fair value cannot be estimated reliably. If the entity cannot estimate reliably the fair value of the goods or services received, the entity is required to measure their value, and the corresponding increase in equity, indirectly, by reference to the fair value of the equity instruments granted. Furthermore: **IN5**

(a) for transactions with employees and others providing similar services, the entity is required to measure the fair value of the equity instruments granted, because it is typically not possible to estimate reliably the fair value of employee services received. The fair value of the equity instruments granted is measured at grant date.

(b) for transactions with parties other than employees (and those providing similar services), there is a rebuttable presumption that the fair value of the goods or services received can be estimated reliably. That fair value is measured at the date the entity obtains the goods or the counterparty renders service. In rare cases, if the presumption is rebutted, the transaction is measured by reference to the fair value of the equity instruments granted, measured at the date the entity obtains the goods or the counterparty renders service.

(c) for goods or services measured by reference to the fair value of the equity instruments granted, the FRS specifies that all non-vesting conditions are taken into account in the estimate of the fair value of the equity instruments. However, vesting conditions that are not market conditions are not taken into account when estimating the fair value of the shares or options at the relevant measurement date (as specified above). Instead, vesting conditions are taken into account by adjusting the number of equity instruments included in the measurement of the transaction amount so that, ultimately, the amount recognised for goods or services received as consideration for the equity instruments granted is based on the number of equity instruments that eventually vest. Hence, on a cumulative basis, no amount is recognised for goods or services received if the equity instruments granted do not vest because of failure to satisfy a vesting condition (other than a market condition).*

(d) the IFRS requires the fair value of equity instruments granted to be based on market prices, if available, and to take into account the terms and conditions upon which those equity instruments were granted. In the absence of market prices, fair value is estimated, using a valuation technique to estimate what the price of those equity instruments would have been on the measurement date in an arm's length transaction between knowledgeable, willing parties.

(e) the IFRS also sets out requirements if the terms and conditions of an option or share grant are modified (eg an option is repriced) or if a grant is cancelled, repurchased or replaced with another grant of equity instruments. For example, irrespective of any modification, cancellation or settlement of a grant of equity instruments to employees, the IFRS generally requires the entity to recognise, as a minimum, the services received measured at the grant date fair value of the equity instruments granted.

For cash-settled share-based payment transactions, the IFRS requires an entity to measure the goods or services acquired and the liability incurred at the fair value of the liability. Until the liability is settled, the entity is required to remeasure the fair value of the liability at each reporting date and at the date of settlement, with any changes in value recognised in profit or loss for the period. **IN6**

****Editor's note:*** *Amended for accounting periods beginning on or after 1 January 2009.*

IN7 For share-based payment transactions in which the terms of the arrangement provide either the entity or the supplier of goods or services with a choice of whether the entity settles the transaction in cash or by issuing equity instruments, the entity is required to account for that transaction, or the components of that transaction, as a cash-settled share-based payment transaction if, and to the extent that, the entity has incurred a liability to settle in cash (or other assets), or as an equity-settled share-based payment transaction if, and to the extent that, no such liability has been incurred.

IN8 The IFRS prescribes various disclosure requirements to enable users of financial statements to understand:

(a) the nature and extent of share-based payment arrangements that existed during the period;
(b) how the fair value of the goods or services received, or the fair value of the equity instruments granted, during the period was determined; and
(c) the effect of share-based payment transactions on the entity's profit or loss for the period and on its financial position.

Financial Reporting Standard 20 (IFRS 2)

'Share-based Payment'

OBJECTIVE

1 The objective of this IFRS is to specify the financial reporting by an entity when it undertakes a *share-based payment transaction*. In particular, it requires an entity to reflect in its profit or loss and financial position the effects of share-based payment transactions, including expenses associated with transactions in which *share options* are granted to employees.

SCOPE

1A This IFRS applies to all financial statements that are intended to give a true and fair view of a reporting entity's financial position and profit or loss (or income or expenditure), except that reporting entities applying the Financial Reporting Standard for Smaller Entities (FRSSE) currently applicable are exempt from the IFRS.

2 An entity shall apply this IFRS in accounting for all share-based payment transactions, whether or not the entity can identify specifically some or all of the goods or services received, including:

(a) *equity-settled share-based payment transactions,*
(b) *cash-settled share-based payment transactions,* and
(c) transactions in which the entity receives or acquires goods or services and the terms of the arrangement provide either the entity or the supplier of those goods or services with a choice of whether the entity settles the transaction in cash (or other assets) or by issuing equity instruments, except as noted in paragraphs 3A–6. In the absence of specifically identifiable goods or services, other circumstances may indicate that goods or services have been (or will be) received, in which case this FRS applies.*

****Editor's note**: Paragraph 2 amended, paragraph 3 deleted and paragraph 3A added with effect for accounting periods beginning on or after 1 January 2010.*

[Deleted] 3

A share-based payment transaction may be settled by another group entity (or a shareholder of any group entity) on behalf of the entity receiving or acquiring the goods or services. Paragraph 2 also applies to an entity that 3A

(a) receives goods or services when another entity in the same group (or a shareholder of any group entity) has the obligation to settle the share-based payment transaction, or
(b) has an obligation to settle a share-based payment transaction when another entity in the same group receives the goods or services unless the transaction is clearly for a purpose other than payment for goods or services supplied to the entity receiving them.

For the purposes of this IFRS, a transaction with an employee (or other party) in his/her capacity as a holder of equity instruments of the entity is not a share-based payment transaction. For example, if an entity grants all holders of a particular class of its equity instruments the right to acquire additional equity instruments of the entity at a price that is less than the fair value of those equity instruments, and an employee receives such a right because he/she is a holder of equity instruments of that particular class, the granting or exercise of that right is not subject to the requirements of this IFRS. 4

As noted in paragraph 2, this FRS applies to share-based payment transactions in which an entity acquires or receives goods or services. Goods includes inventories, consumables, property, plant and equipment, intangible assets and other non-financial assets. However, an entity shall not apply this FRS to transactions in which the entity acquires goods as part of the net assets acquired in a business combination as defined by FRS 6 *Acquisitions and Mergers* applies. Hence, equity instruments issued in a business combination in exchange for control of the acquiree are not within the scope of this IFRS. However, equity instruments granted to employees of the acquiree in their capacity as employees (eg in return for continued service) are within the scope of this IFRS. Similarly, the cancellation, replacement or other modification of *share-based payment arrangements* because of a business combination or other equity restructuring shall be accounted for in accordance with this FRS.* 5

This IFRS does not apply to share-based payment transactions in which the entity receives or acquires goods or services under a contract to buy or sell a non-financial item that can be settled net in cash or another financial instrument, or by exchanging financial instruments, as if the contracts were financial instruments, except that it does apply to contracts that were entered into and continue to be held for the purpose of the receipt or delivery of a non-financial item in accordance with the entity's expected purchase, sale or usage requirements. 6

RECOGNITION

An entity shall recognise the goods or services received or acquired in a share-based payment transaction when it obtains the goods or as the services are received. The entity shall recognise a corresponding increase in equity if the goods or services were received in an equity-settled share-based payment transaction, or a liability if the goods or services were acquired in a cash-settled share-based payment transaction. 7

****Editor's note:*** *Paragraph amended in December 2008 and April 2009.*

8 **When the goods or services received or acquired in a share-based payment transaction do not qualify for recognition as assets, they shall be recognised as expenses.**

9 Typically, an expense arises from the consumption of goods or services. For example, services are typically consumed immediately, in which case an expense is recognised as the counterparty renders service. Goods might be consumed over a period of time or, in the case of inventories, sold at a later date, in which case an expense is recognised when the goods are consumed or sold. However, sometimes it is necessary to recognise an expense before the goods or services are consumed or sold, because they do not qualify for recognition as assets. For example, an entity might acquire goods as part of the research phase of a project to develop a new product. Although those goods have not been consumed, they might not qualify for recognition as assets under the applicable IFRS.

EQUITY-SETTLED SHARE-BASED PAYMENT TRANSACTIONS

Overview

10 **For equity-settled share-based payment transactions, the entity shall measure the goods or services received, and the corresponding increase in equity, directly, at the *fair value* of the goods or services received, unless that fair value cannot be estimated reliably. If the entity cannot estimate reliably the fair value of the goods or services received, the entity shall measure their value, and the corresponding increase in equity, indirectly, by reference to* the fair value of the *equity instruments granted*.**

11 To apply the requirements of paragraph 10 to transactions with *employees and others providing similar services*,† the entity shall measure the fair value of the services received by reference to the fair value of the equity instruments granted, because typically it is not possible to estimate reliably the fair value of the services received, as explained in paragraph 12. The fair value of those equity instruments shall be measured at *grant date*.

12 Typically, shares, share options or other equity instruments are granted to employees as part of their remuneration package, in addition to a cash salary and other employment benefits. Usually, it is not possible to measure directly the services received for particular components of the employee's remuneration package. It might also not be possible to measure the fair value of the total remuneration package independently, without measuring directly the fair value of the equity instruments granted. Furthermore, shares or share options are sometimes granted as part of a bonus arrangement, rather than as a part of basic remuneration, eg as an incentive to the employees to remain in the entity's employ or to reward them for their efforts in improving the entity's performance. By granting shares or share options, in addition to other remuneration, the entity is paying additional remuneration to obtain additional benefits. Estimating the fair value of those additional benefits is likely to be difficult. Because of the difficulty of measuring directly the fair value of the services received, the entity shall measure the fair value of the employee services received by reference to the fair value of the equity instruments granted.

13 To apply the requirements of paragraph 10 to transactions with parties other than employees, there shall be a rebuttable presumption that the fair value of the goods or

**This IFRS uses the phrase 'by reference to' rather than 'at', because the transaction is ultimately measured by multiplying the fair value of the equity instruments granted, measured at the date specified in paragraph 11 or 13 (whichever is applicable), by the number of equity instruments that vest, as explained in paragraph 19.*

†*In the remainder of this IFRS, all references to employees also includes others providing similar services.*

services received can be estimated reliably. That fair value shall be measured at the date the entity obtains the goods or the counterparty renders service. In rare cases, if the entity rebuts this presumption because it cannot estimate reliably the fair value of the goods or services received, the entity shall measure the goods or services received, and the corresponding increase in equity, indirectly, by reference to the fair value of the equity instruments granted, measured at the date the entity obtains the goods or the counterparty renders service.

In particular, if the identifiable consideration received (if any) by the entity appears to be less than the fair value of the equity instruments granted or liability incurred, typically this situation indicates that other consideration (ie unidentifiable goods or services) has been (or will be) received by the entity. The entity shall measure the identifiable goods or services received in accordance with this FRS. The entity shall measure the unidentifiable goods or services received (or to be received) as the difference between the fair value of the share-based payment and the fair value of any identifiable goods or services received (or to be received). The entity shall measure the unidentifiable goods or services received at the grant date. However, for cash-settled transactions, the liability shall be remeasured at the end of each reporting period until it is settled in accordance with paragraphs 30–33.* **13A**

Transactions in which services are received

If the equity instruments granted *vest* immediately, the counterparty is not required to complete a specified period of service before becoming unconditionally entitled to those equity instruments. In the absence of evidence to the contrary, the entity shall presume that services rendered by the counterparty as consideration for the equity instruments have been received. In this case, on grant date the entity shall recognise the services received in full, with a corresponding increase in equity. **14**

If the equity instruments granted do not vest until the counterparty completes a specified period of service, the entity shall presume that the services to be rendered by the counterparty as consideration for those equity instruments will be received in the future, during the *vesting period*. The entity shall account for those services as they are rendered by the counterparty during the vesting period, with a corresponding increase in equity. For example: **15**

(a) if an employee is granted share options conditional upon completing three years' service, then the entity shall presume that the services to be rendered by the employee as consideration for the share options will be received in the future, over that three-year vesting period.

(b) if an employee is granted share options conditional upon the achievement of a performance condition and remaining in the entity's employ until that performance condition is satisfied, and the length of the vesting period varies depending on when that performance condition is satisfied, the entity shall presume that the services to be rendered by the employee as consideration for the share options will be received in the future, over the expected vesting period. The entity shall estimate the length of the expected vesting period at grant date, based on the most likely outcome of the performance condition. If the performance condition is a *market condition*, the estimate of the length of the expected vesting period shall be consistent with the assumptions used in estimating the fair value of the options granted, and shall not be subsequently revised. If the performance condition is not a market condition, the entity shall revise its estimate of the length of the vesting period, if necessary, if subsequent

****Editor's note:** *Paragraph added in August 2009. This paragraph is applicable only for accounting periods beginning on or after 1 January 2010.*

information indicates that the length of the vesting period differs from previous estimates.

Transactions measured by reference to the fair value of the equity instruments granted

Determining the fair value of equity instruments granted

16 For transactions measured by reference to the fair value of the equity instruments granted, an entity shall measure the fair value of equity instruments granted at the *measurement date*, based on market prices if available, taking into account the terms and conditions upon which those equity instruments were granted (subject to the requirements of paragraphs 19–22).

17 If market prices are not available, the entity shall estimate the fair value of the equity instruments granted using a valuation technique to estimate what the price of those equity instruments would have been on the measurement date in an arm's length transaction between knowledgeable, willing parties. The valuation technique shall be consistent with generally accepted valuation methodologies for pricing financial instruments, and shall incorporate all factors and assumptions that knowledgeable, willing market participants would consider in setting the price (subject to the requirements of paragraphs 19–22).

18 Appendix B contains further guidance on the measurement of the fair value of shares and share options, focusing on the specific terms and conditions that are common features of a grant of shares or share options to employees.

Treatment of vesting conditions

19 A grant of equity instruments might be conditional upon satisfying specified *vesting conditions*. For example, a grant of shares or share options to an employee is typically conditional on the employee remaining in the entity's employ for a specified period of time. There might be performance conditions that must be satisfied, such as the entity achieving a specified growth in profit or a specified increase in the entity's share price. Vesting conditions, other than market conditions, shall not be taken into account when estimating the fair value of the shares or share options at the measurement date. Instead, vesting conditions shall be taken into account by adjusting the number of equity instruments included in the measurement of the transaction amount so that, ultimately, the amount recognised for goods or services received as consideration for the equity instruments granted shall be based on the number of equity instruments that eventually vest. Hence, on a cumulative basis, no amount is recognised for goods or services received if the equity instruments granted do not vest because of failure to satisfy a vesting condition, eg the counterparty fails to complete a specified service period, or a performance condition is not satisfied, subject to the requirements of paragraph 21.

20 To apply the requirements of paragraph 19, the entity shall recognise an amount for the goods or services received during the vesting period based on the best available estimate of the number of equity instruments expected to vest and shall revise that estimate, if necessary, if subsequent information indicates that the number of equity instruments expected to vest differs from previous estimates. On vesting date, the entity shall revise the estimate to equal the number of equity instruments that ultimately vested, subject to the requirements of paragraph 21.

Market conditions, such as a target share price upon which vesting (or exercisability) is conditioned, shall be taken into account when estimating the fair value of the equity instruments granted. Therefore, for grants of equity instruments with market conditions, the entity shall recognise the goods or services received from a counterparty who satisfies all other vesting conditions (eg services received from an employee who remains in service for the specified period of service), irrespective of whether that market condition is satisfied. **21**

Treatment of non-vesting conditions

Similarly, an entity shall take into account all non-vesting conditions when estimating the fair value of the equity instruments granted. Therefore, for grants of equity instruments with non-vesting conditions, the entity shall recognise the goods or services received from a counterparty that satisfies all vesting conditions that are not market conditions (eg services received from an employee who remains in service for the specified period of service), irrespective of whether those non-vesting conditions are satisfied.* **21A**

Treatment of a reload feature

For options with a *reload feature*, the reload feature shall not be taken into account when estimating the fair value of options granted at the measurement date. Instead, a *reload option* shall be accounted for as a new option grant, if and when a reload option is subsequently granted. **22**

After vesting date

Having recognised the goods or services received in accordance with paragraphs 10–22, and a corresponding increase in equity, the entity shall make no subsequent adjustment to total equity after vesting date. For example, the entity shall not subsequently reverse the amount recognised for services received from an employee if the vested equity instruments are later forfeited or, in the case of share options, the options are not exercised. However, this requirement does not preclude the entity from recognising a transfer within equity, ie a transfer from one component of equity to another. **23**

If the fair value of the equity instruments cannot be estimated reliably

The requirements in paragraphs 16–23 apply when the entity is required to measure a share-based payment transaction by reference to the fair value of the equity instruments granted. In rare cases, the entity may be unable to estimate reliably the fair value of the equity instruments granted at the measurement date, in accordance with the requirements in paragraphs 16–22. In these rare cases only, the entity shall instead: **24**

(a) measure the equity instruments at their *intrinsic value*, initially at the date the entity obtains the goods or the counterparty renders service and subsequently at each reporting date and at the date of final settlement, with any change in intrinsic value recognised in profit or loss. For a grant of share options, the share-based payment arrangement is finally settled when the options are exercised, are forfeited (eg upon cessation of employment) or lapse (eg at the end of the option's life).

****Editor's note:*** *Heading and paragraph added with effect for accounting periods beginning on or after 1 January 2009.*

(b) recognise the goods or services received based on the number of equity instruments that ultimately vest or (where applicable) are ultimately exercised. To apply this requirement to share options, for example, the entity shall recognise the goods or services received during the vesting period, if any, in accordance with paragraphs 14 and 15, except that the requirements in paragraph 15(b) concerning a market condition do not apply. The amount recognised for goods or services received during the vesting period shall be based on the number of share options expected to vest. The entity shall revise that estimate, if necessary, if subsequent information indicates that the number of share options expected to vest differs from previous estimates. On vesting date, the entity shall revise the estimate to equal the number of equity instruments that ultimately vested. After vesting date, the entity shall reverse the amount recognised for goods or services received if the share options are later forfeited, or lapse at the end of the share option's life.

25 If an entity applies paragraph 24, it is not necessary to apply paragraphs 26-29, because any modifications to the terms and conditions on which the equity instruments were granted will be taken into account when applying the intrinsic value method set out in paragraph 24. However, if an entity settles a grant of equity instruments to which paragraph 24 has been applied:

(a) if the settlement occurs during the vesting period, the entity shall account for the settlement as an acceleration of vesting, and shall therefore recognise immediately the amount that would otherwise have been recognised for services received over the remainder of the vesting period.

(b) any payment made on settlement shall be accounted for as the repurchase of equity instruments, ie as a deduction from equity, except to the extent that the payment exceeds the intrinsic value of the equity instruments, measured at the repurchase date. Any such excess shall be recognised as an expense.

Modifications to the terms and conditions on which equity instruments were granted, including cancellations and settlements

26 An entity might modify the terms and conditions on which the equity instruments were granted. For example, it might reduce the exercise price of options granted to employees (ie reprice the options), which increases the fair value of those options. The requirements in paragraphs 27–29 to account for the effects of modifications are expressed in the context of share-based payment transactions with employees. However, the requirements shall also be applied to share-based payment transactions with parties other than employees that are measured by reference to the fair value of the equity instruments granted. In the latter case, any references in paragraphs 27–29 to grant date shall instead refer to the date the entity obtains the goods or the counterparty renders service.

27 The entity shall recognise, as a minimum, the services received measured at the grant date fair value of the equity instruments granted, unless those equity instruments do not vest because of failure to satisfy a vesting condition (other than a market condition) that was specified at grant date. This applies irrespective of any modifications to the terms and conditions on which the equity instruments were granted, or a cancellation or settlement of that grant of equity instruments. In addition, the entity shall recognise the effects of modifications that increase the total fair value of the share-based payment arrangement or are otherwise beneficial to the employee. Guidance on applying this requirement is given in Appendix B.

If a grant of equity instruments is cancelled or settled during the vesting period (other than a grant cancelled by forfeiture when the vesting conditions are not satisfied):* 28

(a) the entity shall account for the cancellation or settlement as an acceleration of vesting, and shall therefore recognise immediately the amount that otherwise would have been recognised for services received over the remainder of the vesting period.
(b) any payment made to the employee on the cancellation or settlement of the grant shall be accounted for as the repurchase of an equity interest, ie as a deduction from equity, except to the extent that the payment exceeds the fair value of the equity instruments granted, measured at the repurchase date. Any such excess shall be recognised as an expense. However, if the share-based payment arrangement included liability components, the entity shall remeasure the fair value of the liability at the date of cancellation or settlement. Any payment made to settle the liability component shall be accounted for as an extinguishment of the liability.†
(c) if new equity instruments are granted to the employee and, on the date when those new equity instruments are granted, the entity identifies the new equity instruments granted as replacement equity instruments for the cancelled equity instruments, the entity shall account for the granting of replacement equity instruments in the same way as a modification of the original grant of equity instruments, in accordance with paragraph 27 and the guidance in Appendix B. The incremental fair value granted is the difference between the fair value of the replacement equity instruments and the net fair value of the cancelled equity instruments, at the date the replacement equity instruments are granted. The net fair value of the cancelled equity instruments is their fair value, immediately before the cancellation, less the amount of any payment made to the employee on cancellation of the equity instruments that is accounted for as a deduction from equity in accordance with (b) above. If the entity does not identify new equity instruments granted as replacement equity instruments for the cancelled equity instruments, the entity shall account for those new equity instruments as a new grant of equity instruments.

If an entity or counterparty can choose whether to meet a non-vesting condition, the entity shall treat the entity's or counterparty's failure to meet that non-vesting condition during the vesting period as a cancellation.‡ 28A

If an entity repurchases vested equity instruments, the payment made to the employee shall be accounted for as a deduction from equity, except to the extent that the payment exceeds the fair value of the equity instruments repurchased, measured at the repurchase date. Any such excess shall be recognised as an expense. 29

CASH-SETTLED SHARE-BASED PAYMENT TRANSACTIONS

For cash-settled share-based payment transactions, the entity shall measure the goods or services acquired and the liability incurred at the fair value of the liability. Until the liability is settled, the entity shall remeasure the fair value of the liability at each reporting date and at the date of settlement, with any changes in fair value recognised in profit or loss for the period. 30

****Editor's note:*** *Paragraph amended with effect for accounting periods beginning on or after 1 January 2009.*

†***Editor's note:*** *Sub-paragraph amended with effect for accounting periods beginning on or after 1 January 2009.*

‡***Editor's note:*** *Paragraph added with effect for accounting periods beginning on or after 1 January 2009.*

31 For example, an entity might grant share appreciation rights to employees as part of their remuneration package, whereby the employees will become entitled to a future cash payment (rather than an equity instrument), based on the increase in the entity's share price from a specified level over a specified period of time. Or an entity might grant to its employees a right to receive a future cash payment by granting to them a right to shares (including shares to be issued upon the exercise of share options) that are redeemable, either mandatorily (eg upon cessation of employment) or at the employee's option.

32 The entity shall recognise the services received, and a liability to pay for those services, as the employees render service. For example, some share appreciation rights vest immediately, and the employees are therefore not required to complete a specified period of service to become entitled to the cash payment. In the absence of evidence to the contrary, the entity shall presume that the services rendered by the employees in exchange for the share appreciation rights have been received. Thus, the entity shall recognise immediately the services received and a liability to pay for them. If the share appreciation rights do not vest until the employees have completed a specified period of service, the entity shall recognise the services received, and a liability to pay for them, as the employees render service during that period.

33 The liability shall be measured, initially and at each reporting date until settled, at the fair value of the share appreciation rights, by applying an option pricing model, taking into account the terms and conditions on which the share appreciation rights were granted, and the extent to which the employees have rendered service to date.

SHARE-BASED PAYMENT TRANSACTIONS WITH CASH ALTERNATIVES

34 **For share-based payment transactions in which the terms of the arrangement provide either the entity or the counterparty with the choice of whether the entity settles the transaction in cash (or other assets) or by issuing equity instruments, the entity shall account for that transaction, or the components of that transaction, as a cash-settled share-based payment transaction if, and to the extent that, the entity has incurred a liability to settle in cash or other assets, or as an equity-settled share-based payment transaction if, and to the extent that, no such liability has been incurred.**

Share-based payment transactions in which the terms of the arrangement provide the counterparty with a choice of settlement

35 If an entity has granted the counterparty the right to choose whether a share-based payment transaction is settled in cash* or by issuing equity instruments, the entity has granted a compound financial instrument, which includes a debt component (ie the counterparty's right to demand payment in cash) and an equity component (ie the counterparty's right to demand settlement in equity instruments rather than in cash). For transactions with parties other than employees, in which the fair value of the goods or services received is measured directly, the entity shall measure the equity component of the compound financial instrument as the difference between the fair value of the goods or services received and the fair value of the debt component, at the date when the goods or services are received.

36 For other transactions, including transactions with employees, the entity shall measure the fair value of the compound financial instrument at the measurement

**In paragraphs 35-43, all references to cash also include other assets of the entity.*

date, taking into account the terms and conditions on which the rights to cash or equity instruments were granted.

To apply paragraph 36, the entity shall first measure the fair value of the debt component, and then measure the fair value of the equity component – taking into account that the counterparty must forfeit the right to receive cash in order to receive the equity instrument. The fair value of the compound financial instrument is the sum of the fair values of the two components. However, share-based payment transactions in which the counterparty has the choice of settlement are often structured so that the fair value of one settlement alternative is the same as the other. For example, the counterparty might have the choice of receiving share options or cash-settled share appreciation rights. In such cases, the fair value of the equity component is zero, and hence the fair value of the compound financial instrument is the same as the fair value of the debt component. Conversely, if the fair values of the settlement alternatives differ, the fair value of the equity component usually will be greater than zero, in which case the fair value of the compound financial instrument will be greater than the fair value of the debt component. 37

The entity shall account separately for the goods or services received or acquired in respect of each component of the compound financial instrument. For the debt component, the entity shall recognise the goods or services acquired, and a liability to pay for those goods or services, as the counterparty supplies goods or renders service, in accordance with the requirements applying to cash-settled share-based payment transactions (paragraphs 30–33). For the equity component (if any), the entity shall recognise the goods or services received, and an increase in equity, as the counterparty supplies goods or renders service, in accordance with the requirements applying to equity-settled share-based payment transactions (paragraphs 10–29). 38

At the date of settlement, the entity shall remeasure the liability to its fair value. If the entity issues equity instruments on settlement rather than paying cash, the liability shall be transferred direct to equity, as the consideration for the equity instruments issued. 39

If the entity pays in cash on settlement rather than issuing equity instruments, that payment shall be applied to settle the liability in full. Any equity component previously recognised shall remain within equity. By electing to receive cash on settlement, the counterparty forfeited the right to receive equity instruments. However, this requirement does not preclude the entity from recognising a transfer within equity, ie a transfer from one component of equity to another. 40

Share-based payment transactions in which the terms of the arrangement provide the entity with a choice of settlement

For a share-based payment transaction in which the terms of the arrangement provide an entity with the choice of whether to settle in cash or by issuing equity instruments, the entity shall determine whether it has a present obligation to settle in cash and account for the share-based payment transaction accordingly. The entity has a present obligation to settle in cash if the choice of settlement in equity instruments has no commercial substance (eg because the entity is legally prohibited from issuing shares), or the entity has a past practice or a stated policy of settling in cash, or generally settles in cash whenever the counterparty asks for cash settlement. 41

If the entity has a present obligation to settle in cash, it shall account for the transaction in accordance with the requirements applying to cash-settled share-based payment transactions, in paragraphs 30–33. 42

43 If no such obligation exists, the entity shall account for the transaction in accordance with the requirements applying to equity-settled share-based payment transactions, in paragraphs 10–29. Upon settlement:

(a) if the entity elects to settle in cash, the cash payment shall be accounted for as the repurchase of an equity interest, ie as a deduction from equity, except as noted in (c) below.
(b) if the entity elects to settle by issuing equity instruments, no further accounting is required (other than a transfer from one component of equity to another, if necessary), except as noted in (c) below.
(c) if the entity elects the settlement alternative with the higher fair value, as at the date of settlement, the entity shall recognise an additional expense for the excess value given, ie the difference between the cash paid and the fair value of the equity instruments that would otherwise have been issued, or the difference between the fair value of the equity instruments issued and the amount of cash that would otherwise have been paid, whichever is applicable.

Share-based payment transactions among group entities (2009 amendments)*

43A For share-based payment transactions among group entities, in its separate or individual financial statements, the entity receiving the goods or services shall measure the goods or services received as either an equity-settled or a cash-settled share-based payment transaction by assessing:

(a) the nature of the awards granted, and
(b) its own rights and obligations.

The amount recognised by the entity receiving the goods or services may differ from the amount recognised by the consolidated group or by another group entity settling the share-based payment transaction.

43B The entity receiving the goods or services shall measure the goods or services received as an equity-settled share-based payment transaction when:

(a) the awards granted are its own equity instruments, or
(b) the entity has no obligation to settle the share-based payment transaction.

The entity shall subsequently remeasure such an equity-settled share-based payment transaction only for changes in non-market vesting conditions in accordance with paragraphs 19–21. In all other circumstances, the entity receiving the goods or services shall measure the goods or services received as a cash-settled share-based payment transaction.

43C The entity settling a share-based payment transaction when another entity in the group receives the goods or services shall recognise the transaction as an equity-settled share-based payment transaction only if it is settled in the entity's own equity instruments. Otherwise, the transaction shall be recognised as a cash-settled share-based payment transaction.

43D Some group transactions involve repayment arrangements that require one group entity to pay another group entity for the provision of the share-based payments to the suppliers of goods or services. In such cases, the entity that receives the goods or services shall account for the share-based payment transaction in accordance with paragraph 43B regardless of intragroup repayment arrangements.

****Editor's note**: Heading and paragraphs 43A to 43D added in August 2009. These paragraphs are applicable only for accounting periods beginning on or after 1 January 2010.*

DISCLOSURES

An entity shall disclose information that enables users of the financial statements to understand the nature and extent of share-based payment arrangements that existed during the period. 44

To give effect to the principle in paragraph 44, the entity shall disclose at least the following: 45

(a) a description of each type of share-based payment arrangement that existed at any time during the period, including the general terms and conditions of each arrangement, such as vesting requirements, the maximum term of options granted, and the method of settlement (eg whether in cash or equity). An entity with substantially similar types of share-based payment arrangements may aggregate this information, unless separate disclosure of each arrangement is necessary to satisfy the principle in paragraph 44.

(b) the number and weighted average exercise prices of share options for each of the following groups of options:

 (i) outstanding at the beginning of the period;
 (ii) granted during the period;
 (iii) forfeited during the period;
 (iv) exercised during the period;
 (v) expired during the period;
 (vi) outstanding at the end of the period; and
 (vii) exercisable at the end of the period.

(c) for share options exercised during the period, the weighted average share price at the date of exercise. If options were exercised on a regular basis throughout the period, the entity may instead disclose the weighted average share price during the period.

(d) for share options outstanding at the end of the period, the range of exercise prices and weighted average remaining contractual life. If the range of exercise prices is wide, the outstanding options shall be divided into ranges that are meaningful for assessing the number and timing of additional shares that may be issued and the cash that may be received upon exercise of those options.

An entity shall disclose information that enables users of the financial statements to understand how the fair value of the goods or services received, or the fair value of the equity instruments granted, during the period was determined. 46

If the entity has measured the fair value of goods or services received as consideration for equity instruments of the entity indirectly, by reference to the fair value of the equity instruments granted, to give effect to the principle in paragraph 46, the entity shall disclose at least the following: 47

(a) for share options granted during the period, the weighted average fair value of those options at the measurement date and information on how that fair value was measured, including:

 (i) the option pricing model used and the inputs to that model, including the weighted average share price, exercise price, expected volatility, option life, expected dividends, the risk-free interest rate and any other inputs to the model, including the method used and the assumptions made to incorporate the effects of expected early exercise;
 (ii) how expected volatility was determined, including an explanation of the extent to which expected volatility was based on historical volatility; and

(iii) whether and how any other features of the option grant were incorporated into the measurement of fair value, such as a market condition.

(b) for other equity instruments granted during the period (ie other than share options), the number and weighted average fair value of those equity instruments at the measurement date, and information on how that fair value was measured, including:

(i) if fair value was not measured on the basis of an observable market price, how it was determined;
(ii) whether and how expected dividends were incorporated into the measurement of fair value; and
(iii) whether and how any other features of the equity instruments granted were incorporated into the measurement of fair value.

(c) for share-based payment arrangements that were modified during the period:

(i) an explanation of those modifications;
(ii) the incremental fair value granted (as a result of those modifications); and
(iii) information on how the incremental fair value granted was measured, consistently with the requirements set out in (a) and (b) above, where applicable.

48 If the entity has measured directly the fair value of goods or services received during the period, the entity shall disclose how that fair value was determined, eg whether fair value was measured at a market price for those goods or services.

49 If the entity has rebutted the presumption in paragraph 13, it shall disclose that fact, and give an explanation of why the presumption was rebutted.

50 **An entity shall disclose information that enables users of the financial statements to understand the effect of share-based payment transactions on the entity's profit or loss for the period and on its financial position.**

51 To give effect to the principle in paragraph 50, the entity shall disclose at least the following:

(a) the total expense recognised for the period arising from share-based payment transactions in which the goods or services received did not qualify for recognition as assets and hence were recognised immediately as an expense, including separate disclosure of that portion of the total expense that arises from transactions accounted for as equity-settled share-based payment transactions;
(b) for liabilities arising from share-based payment transactions:

(i) the total carrying amount at the end of the period; and
(ii) the total intrinsic value at the end of the period of liabilities for which the counterparty's right to cash or other assets had vested by the end of the period (eg vested share appreciation rights).

52 If the information required to be disclosed by this IFRS does not satisfy the principles in paragraphs 44, 46 and 50, the entity shall disclose such additional information as is necessary to satisfy them.

TRANSITIONAL PROVISIONS

For equity-settled share-based payment transactions, the entity shall apply this IFRS to grants of shares, share options or other equity instruments that were granted after 7 November 2002 and had not yet vested at the relevant effective date of this IFRS. 53

The entity is encouraged, but not required, to apply this IFRS to other grants of equity instruments if the entity has disclosed publicly the fair value of those equity instruments, determined at the measurement date. 54

For all grants of equity instruments to which this IFRS is applied, the entity shall restate comparative information and, where applicable, adjust the opening balance of retained earnings for the earliest period presented. 55

For all grants of equity instruments to which this IFRS has not been applied (eg equity instruments granted on or before 7 November 2002), the entity shall nevertheless disclose the information required by paragraphs 44 and 45. 56

If, after the IFRS becomes effective, an entity modifies the terms or conditions of a grant of equity instruments to which this IFRS has not been applied, the entity shall nevertheless apply paragraphs 26–29 to account for any such modifications. 57

For liabilities arising from share-based payment transactions existing at the effective date of this IFRS, the entity shall apply the IFRS retrospectively. For these liabilities, the entity shall restate comparative information, including adjusting the opening balance of retained earnings in the earliest period presented for which comparative information has been restated, except that the entity is not required to restate comparative information to the extent that the information relates to a period or date that is earlier than 7 November 2002. 58

The entity is encouraged, but not required, to apply retrospectively the IFRS to other liabilities arising from share-based payment transactions, for example, to liabilities that were settled during a period for which comparative information is presented. 59

EFFECTIVE DATE

A *listed entity* shall apply this IFRS for accounting periods beginning on or after 1 January 2005; and an *unlisted entity* shall apply it for accounting periods beginning on or after 1 January 2006. In both cases earlier application is encouraged. If an entity applies the IFRS before the relevant effective date, it shall disclose that fact. 60

[Not used]. 61

An entity shall apply the following amendments retrospectively in annual periods beginning on or after 1 January 2009: 62

(a) the requirements in paragraph 21A in respect of the treatment of non-vesting conditions;
(b) the revised definitions of 'vest' and 'vesting conditions' in Appendix A;
(c) the amendments in paragraphs 28 and 28A in respect of cancellations.

Earlier application is permitted. If an entity applies these amendments for a period beginning before 1 January 2009, it shall disclose that fact.

An entity shall apply the following amendments made by Group Cash-settled Share-based Payment Transactions issued in August 2009 retrospectively, subject to the 63 transitional provisions in paragraphs 53–59, in accordance with FRS 3 Reporting financial performance for annual periods beginning on or after 1 January 2010:

(a) the amendment of paragraph 2, the deletion of paragraph 3 and the addition of paragraphs 3A and 43A–43D and of paragraphs B45, B47, B50, B54, B56–B58 and B60 in Appendix B in respect of the accounting for transactions among group entities.

(b) the revised definitions in Appendix A of the following terms:
- cash-settled share-based payment transaction,
- equity-settled share-based payment transaction,
- share-based payment arrangement, and
- share-based payment transaction.

If the information necessary for retrospective application is not available, an entity shall reflect in its separate or individual financial statements the amounts previously recognised in the group's consolidated financial statements. Earlier application is permitted. If an entity applies the amendments for a period beginning before 1 January 2010, it shall disclose that fact.

Withdrawal of Abstracts

64 *Group Cash-settled Share-based Payment Transactions* issued in August 2009 supersedes UITF 41 *Scope of FRS 20* and UITF 44 *FRS 20 — Group and Treasury Share Transactions*. The amendments made by that document incorporated the previous requirements set out in UITF 41 and UITF 44 as follows:

(a) amended paragraph 2 and added paragraph 13A in respect of the accounting for transactions in which the entity cannot identify specifically some or all of the goods or services received. Those requirements were effective for annual periods beginning on or after 1 May 2006.

(b) added paragraphs B46, B48, B49, B51–B53, B55, B59 and B61 in Appendix B in respect of the accounting for transactions among group entities. Those requirements were effective for annual periods beginning on or after 1 March 2007.

Those requirements were applied retrospectively in accordance with the requirements of FRS 18, subject to the transitional provisions of FRS 20.

Appendix A
Defined terms

This appendix is an integral part of the IFRS.

cash-settled share-based payment transaction A **share-based payment transaction** in which the entity acquires goods or services by incurring a liability to transfer cash or other assets to the supplier of those goods or services for amounts that are based on the price (or value) of **equity instruments** (including shares or **share options**) of the entity or another group entity.*

employees and others providing similar services Individuals who render personal services to the entity and either (a) the individuals are regarded as employees for legal or tax purposes, (b) the individuals work for the entity under its direction in the same way as individuals who are regarded as employees for legal or tax purposes, or (c) the services rendered are similar to those rendered by employees. For example, the term encompasses all management personnel, ie those persons having authority and responsibility for planning, directing and controlling the activities of the entity, including non-executive directors.

equity instrument A contract that evidences a residual interest in the assets of an entity after deducting all of its liabilities.†

equity instrument granted The right (conditional or unconditional) to an **equity instrument** of the entity conferred by the entity on another party, under a **share-based payment arrangement**.

equity-settled share-based payment transaction A **share-based payment transaction** in which the entity

(a) receives goods or services as consideration for its own **equity instruments** (including shares or **share options**), or

(b) receives goods or services but has no obligation to settle the transaction with the supplier.‡

fair value The amount for which an asset could be exchanged, a liability settled, or an **equity instrument granted** could be exchanged, between knowledgeable, willing parties in an arm's length transaction.

****Editor's note**: Definition amended in August 2009 with effect for accounting periods beginning on or after 1 January 2010.*

†The Framework defines a liability as a present obligation of the entity arising from past events, the settlement of which is expected to result in an outflow from the entity of resources embodying economic benefits (ie an outflow of cash or other assets of the entity).

*‡**Editor's note**: Definition amended in August 2009 with effect for accounting periods beginning on or after 1 January 2010.*

grant date — The date at which the entity and another party (including an employee) agree to a **share-based payment arrangement**, being when the entity and the counterparty have a shared understanding of the terms and conditions of the arrangement. At grant date the entity confers on the counterparty the right to cash, other assets, or **equity instruments** of the entity, provided the specified **vesting conditions**, if any, are met. If that agreement is subject to an approval process (for example, by shareholders), grant date is the date when that approval is obtained.

intrinsic value — The difference between the **fair value** of the shares to which the counterparty has the (conditional or unconditional) right to subscribe or which it has the right to receive, and the price (if any) the counterparty is (or will be) required to pay for those shares. For example, a **share option** with an exercise price of CU15,* on a share with a **fair value** of CU20, has an intrinsic value of CU5.

listed entity — An entity that has in issue one or more securities that are admitted to trading on a regulated market of any Member State within the meaning of Article 1(13) of Council Directive 93/22/EEC of 10 May 1993 on investment services in the securities field.

market condition — A condition upon which the exercise price, vesting or exercisability of an **equity instrument** depends that is related to the market price of the entity's **equity instruments**, such as attaining a specified share price or a specified amount of **intrinsic value** of a **share option**, or achieving a specified target that is based on the market price of the entity's **equity instruments** relative to an index of market prices of **equity instruments** of other entities.

measurement date — The date at which the **fair value** of the **equity instruments granted** is measured for the purposes of this IFRS. For transactions with **employees and others providing similar services**, the measurement date is **grant date**. For transactions with parties other than employees (and those providing similar services), the measurement date is the date the entity obtains the goods or the counterparty renders service.

reload feature — A feature that provides for an automatic grant of additional **share options** whenever the option holder exercises previously granted options using the entity's shares, rather than cash, to satisfy the exercise price.

reload option — **A new share option** granted when a share is used to satisfy the exercise price of a previous **share option**.

**In this appendix, monetary amounts are denominated in 'currency units' (CU).*

share-based payment arrangement An agreement between the entity (or another group* entity or any shareholder of any group entity) and another party (including an employee) that entitles the other party to receive

(a) cash or other assets of the entity for amounts that are based on the price (or value) of **equity instruments** (including shares or **share options**) of the entity or another group entity, or
(b) **equity instruments** (including shares or **share options**) of the entity or another group entity,

provided the specified **vesting conditions**, are met.†

share-based payment transaction A transaction in which the entity

(a) receives goods or services from the supplier of those goods or services (including an employee) in a **share-based payment arrangement**, or
(b) incurs an obligation to settle the transaction with the supplier in a **share-based payment arrangement** when another group entity receives those goods or services.‡

share option A contract that gives the holder the right, but not the obligation, to subscribe to the entity's shares at a fixed or determinable price for a specified period of time.

unlisted entity An entity that is not a **listed entity**.

vest To become an entitlement. Under a **share-based payment arrangement**, a counterparty's right to receive cash, other assets, or **equity instruments** of the entity vests when the counterparty's entitlement is no longer conditional on the satisfaction of any **vesting conditions**.§

vesting conditions The conditions that determine whether the conditions entity receives the services that entitle the counterparty to receive cash, other assets or **equity instruments** of the entity, under a **share-based payment arrangement**. Vesting conditions are either service conditions or performance conditions. Service conditions require the counterparty to complete a specified period of service. Performance conditions require the counterparty to complete a specified period of service and specified performance targets to be met (such as a specified increase in the entity's profit over a specified period of time). A performance condition might include a **market condition**.

**A 'group' is defined in paragraph 9 of FRS 2 Subsidiary undertakings as 'a parent undertaking and its subsidiary undertakings' from the perspective of the reporting entity's ultimate parent.*

†***Editor's note**: Definition amended in August 2009 with effect for accounting periods beginning on or after 1 January 2010.*

‡***Editor's note**: Definition amended in August 2009 with effect for accounting periods beginning on or after 1 January 2010.*

§***Editor's note:** Definition, amended with effect for accounting periods beginning on or after 1 January 2009.*

vesting period	The period during which all the specified **vesting conditions** of a **share-based payment arrangement** are to be satisfied.

Appendix B
Application Guidance

This appendix is an integral part of the IFRS.

ESTIMATING THE FAIR VALUE OF EQUITY INSTRUMENTS GRANTED

Paragraphs B2–B41 of this appendix discuss measurement of the fair value of shares and share options granted, focusing on the specific terms and conditions that are common features of a grant of shares or share options to employees. Therefore, it is not exhaustive. Furthermore, because the valuation issues discussed below focus on shares and share options granted to employees, it is assumed that the fair value of the shares or share options is measured at grant date. However, many of the valuation issues discussed below (eg determining expected volatility) also apply in the context of estimating the fair value of shares or share options granted to parties other than employees at the date the entity obtains the goods or the counterparty renders service. **B1**

Shares

For shares granted to employees, the fair value of the shares shall be measured at the market price of the entity's shares (or an estimated market price, if the entity's shares are not publicly traded), adjusted to take into account the terms and conditions upon which the shares were granted (except for vesting conditions that are excluded from the measurement of fair value in accordance with paragraphs 19–21). **B2**

For example, if the employee is not entitled to receive dividends during the vesting period, this factor shall be taken into account when estimating the fair value of the shares granted. Similarly, if the shares are subject to restrictions on transfer after vesting date, that factor shall be taken into account, but only to the extent that the post-vesting restrictions affect the price that a knowledgeable, willing market participant would pay for that share. For example, if the shares are actively traded in a deep and liquid market, post-vesting transfer restrictions may have little, if any, effect on the price that a knowledgeable, willing market participant would pay for those shares. Restrictions on transfer or other restrictions that exist during the vesting period shall not be taken into account when estimating the grant date fair value of the shares granted, because those restrictions stem from the existence of vesting conditions, which are accounted for in accordance with paragraphs 19–21. **B3**

Share options

For share options granted to employees, in many cases market prices are not available, because the options granted are subject to terms and conditions that do not apply to traded options. If traded options with similar terms and conditions do not exist, the fair value of the options granted shall be estimated by applying an option pricing model. **B4**

The entity shall consider factors that knowledgeable, willing market participants would consider in selecting the option pricing model to apply. For example, many employee options have long lives, are usually exercisable during the period between vesting date and the end of the options' life, and are often exercised early. These factors should be considered when estimating the grant date fair value of the options. **B5**

For many entities, this might preclude the use of the Black-Scholes-Merton formula, which does not allow for the possibility of exercise before the end of the option's life and may not adequately reflect the effects of expected early exercise. It also does not allow for the possibility that expected volatility and other model inputs might vary over the option's life. However, for share options with relatively short contractual lives, or that must be exercised within a short period of time after vesting date, the factors identified above may not apply. In these instances, the Black-Scholes-Merton formula may produce a value that is substantially the same as a more flexible option pricing model.

B6 All option pricing models take into account, as a minimum, the following factors:

(a) the exercise price of the option;
(b) the life of the option;
(c) the current price of the underlying shares;
(d) the expected volatility of the share price;
(e) the dividends expected on the shares (if appropriate); and
(f) the risk-free interest rate for the life of the option.

B7 Other factors that knowledgeable, willing market participants would consider in setting the price shall also be taken into account (except for vesting conditions and reload features that are excluded from the measurement of fair value in accordance with paragraphs 19–22).

B8 For example, a share option granted to an employee typically cannot be exercised during specified periods (eg during the vesting period or during periods specified by securities regulators). This factor shall be taken into account if the option pricing model applied would otherwise assume that the option could be exercised at any time during its life. However, if an entity uses an option pricing model that values options that can be exercised only at the end of the options' life, no adjustment is required for the inability to exercise them during the vesting period (or other periods during the options' life), because the model assumes that the options cannot be exercised during those periods.

B9 Similarly, another factor common to employee share options is the possibility of early exercise of the option, for example, because the option is not freely transferable, or because the employee must exercise all vested options upon cessation of employment. The effects of expected early exercise shall be taken into account, as discussed in paragraphs B16-B21.

B10 Factors that a knowledgeable, willing market participant would not consider in setting the price of a share option (or other equity instrument) shall not be taken into account when estimating the fair value of share options (or other equity instruments) granted. For example, for share options granted to employees, factors that affect the value of the option from the individual employee's perspective only are not relevant to estimating the price that would be set by a knowledgeable, willing market participant.

Inputs to option pricing models

B11 In estimating the expected volatility of and dividends on the underlying shares, the objective is to approximate the expectations that would be reflected in a current market or negotiated exchange price for the option. Similarly, when estimating the effects of early exercise of employee share options, the objective is to approximate the expectations that an outside party with access to detailed information about employees' exercise behaviour would develop based on information available at the grant date.

Often, there is likely to be a range of reasonable expectations about future volatility, dividends and exercise behaviour. If so, an expected value should be calculated, by weighting each amount within the range by its associated probability of occurrence. **B12**

Expectations about the future are generally based on experience, modified if the future is reasonably expected to differ from the past. In some circumstances, identifiable factors may indicate that unadjusted historical experience is a relatively poor predictor of future experience. For example, if an entity with two distinctly different lines of business disposes of the one that was significantly less risky than the other, historical volatility may not be the best information on which to base reasonable expectations for the future. **B13**

In other circumstances, historical information may not be available. For example, a newly listed entity will have little, if any, historical data on the volatility of its share price. Unlisted and newly listed entities are discussed further below. **B14**

In summary, an entity should not simply base estimates of volatility, exercise behaviour and dividends on historical information without considering the extent to which the past experience is expected to be reasonably predictive of future experience. **B15**

Expected early exercise

Employees often exercise share options early, for a variety of reasons. For example, employee share options are typically non-transferable. This often causes employees to exercise their share options early, because that is the only way for the employees to liquidate their position. Also, employees who cease employment are usually required to exercise any vested options within a short period of time, otherwise the share options are forfeited. This factor also causes the early exercise of employee share options. Other factors causing early exercise are risk aversion and lack of wealth diversification. **B16**

The means by which the effects of expected early exercise are taken into account depends upon the type of option pricing model applied. For example, expected early exercise could be taken into account by using an estimate of the option's expected life (which, for an employee share option, is the period of time from grant date to the date on which the option is expected to be exercised) as an input into an option pricing model (eg the Black-Scholes-Merton formula). Alternatively, expected early exercise could be modelled in a binomial or similar option pricing model that uses contractual life as an input. **B17**

Factors to consider in estimating early exercise include: **B18**

(a) the length of the vesting period, because the share option typically cannot be exercised until the end of the vesting period. Hence, determining the valuation implications of expected early exercise is based on the assumption that the options will vest. The implications of vesting conditions are discussed in paragraphs 19–21.
(b) the average length of time similar options have remained outstanding in the past.
(c) the price of the underlying shares. Experience may indicate that the employees tend to exercise options when the share price reaches a specified level above the exercise price.

(d) the employee's level within the organisation. For example, experience might indicate that higher-level employees tend to exercise options later than lower-level employees (discussed further in paragraph B21).
(e) expected volatility of the underlying shares. On average, employees might tend to exercise options on highly volatile shares earlier than on shares with low volatility.

B19 As noted in paragraph B17, the effects of early exercise could be taken into account by using an estimate of the option's expected life as an input into an option pricing model. When estimating the expected life of share options granted to a group of employees, the entity could base that estimate on an appropriately weighted average expected life for the entire employee group or on appropriately weighted average lives for subgroups of employees within the group, based on more detailed data about employees' exercise behaviour (discussed further below).

B20 Separating an option grant into groups for employees with relatively homogeneous exercise behaviour is likely to be important. Option value is not a linear function of option term; value increases at a decreasing rate as the term lengthens. For example, if all other assumptions are equal, although a two-year option is worth more than a one-year option, it is not worth twice as much. That means that calculating estimated option value on the basis of a single weighted average life that includes widely differing individual lives would overstate the total fair value of the share options granted. Separating options granted into several groups, each of which has a relatively narrow range of lives included in its weighted average life, reduces that overstatement.

B21 Similar considerations apply when using a binomial or similar model. For example, the experience of an entity that grants options broadly to all levels of employees might indicate that top-level executives tend to hold their options longer than middle-management employees hold theirs and that lower-level employees tend to exercise their options earlier than any other group. In addition, employees who are encouraged or required to hold a minimum amount of their employer's equity instruments, including options, might on average exercise options later than employees not subject to that provision. In those situations, separating options by groups of recipients with relatively homogeneous exercise behaviour will result in a more accurate estimate of the total fair value of the share options granted.

Expected volatility

B22 Expected volatility is a measure of the amount by which a price is expected to fluctuate during a period. The measure of volatility used in option pricing models is the annualised standard deviation of the continuously compounded rates of return on the share over a period of time. Volatility is typically expressed in annualised terms that are comparable regardless of the time period used in the calculation, for example, daily, weekly or monthly price observations.

B23 The rate of return (which may be positive or negative) on a share for a period measures how much a shareholder has benefited from dividends and appreciation (or depreciation) of the share price.

B24 The expected annualised volatility of a share is the range within which the continuously compounded annual rate of return is expected to fall approximately two-thirds of the time. For example, to say that a share with an expected continuously compounded rate of return of 12 per cent has a volatility of 30 per cent means that the probability that the rate of return on the share for one year will be between –18 per cent (12% – 30%) and 42 per cent (12% + 30%) is approximately two-thirds. If the share price is CU100 at the beginning of the year and no dividends are paid, the year-end share price would be expected to be between CU83.53 (CU100 × $e^{-0.18}$) and CU152.20 (CU100 × $e^{0.42}$) approximately two-thirds of the time.

Factors to consider in estimating expected volatility include: **B25**

(a) implied volatility from traded share options on the entity's shares, or other traded instruments of the entity that include option features (such as convertible debt), if any.
(b) the historical volatility of the share price over the most recent period that is generally commensurate with the expected term of the option (taking into account the remaining contractual life of the option and the effects of expected early exercise).
(c) the length of time an entity's shares have been publicly traded. A newly listed entity might have a high historical volatility, compared with similar entities that have been listed longer. Further guidance for newly listed entities is given below.
(d) the tendency of volatility to revert to its mean, ie its long-term average level, and other factors indicating that expected future volatility might differ from past volatility. For example, if an entity's share price was extraordinarily volatile for some identifiable period of time because of a failed takeover bid or a major restructuring, that period could be disregarded in computing historical average annual volatility.
(e) appropriate and regular intervals for price observations. The price observations should be consistent from period to period. For example, an entity might use the closing price for each week or the highest price for the week, but it should not use the closing price for some weeks and the highest price for other weeks. Also, the price observations should be expressed in the same currency as the exercise price.

Newly listed entities

As noted in paragraph B25, an entity should consider historical volatility of the share price over the most recent period that is generally commensurate with the expected option term. If a newly listed entity does not have sufficient information on historical volatility, it should nevertheless compute historical volatility for the longest period for which trading activity is available. It could also consider the historical volatility of similar entities following a comparable period in their lives. For example, an entity that has been listed for only one year and grants options with an average expected life of five years might consider the pattern and level of historical volatility of entities in the same industry for the first six years in which the shares of those entities were publicly traded. **B26**

Unlisted entities

An unlisted entity will not have historical information to consider when estimating expected volatility. Some factors to consider instead are set out below. **B27**

In some cases, an unlisted entity that regularly issues options or shares to employees (or other parties) might have set up an internal market for its shares. The volatility of those share prices could be considered when estimating expected volatility. **B28**

Alternatively, the entity could consider the historical or implied volatility of similar listed entities, for which share price or option price information is available, to use **B29** when estimating expected volatility. This would be appropriate if the entity has based the value of its shares on the share prices of similar listed entities.

B30 If the entity has not based its estimate of the value of its shares on the share prices of similar listed entities, and has instead used another valuation methodology to value its shares, the entity could derive an estimate of expected volatility consistent with that valuation methodology. For example, the entity might value its shares on a net asset or earnings basis. It could consider the expected volatility of those net asset values or earnings.

Expected dividends

B31 Whether expected dividends should be taken into account when measuring the fair value of shares or options granted depends on whether the counterparty is entitled to dividends or dividend equivalents.

B32 For example, if employees were granted options and are entitled to dividends on the underlying shares or dividend equivalents (which might be paid in cash or applied to reduce the exercise price) between grant date and exercise date, the options granted should be valued as if no dividends will be paid on the underlying shares, ie the input for expected dividends should be zero.

B33 Similarly, when the grant date fair value of shares granted to employees is estimated, no adjustment is required for expected dividends if the employee is entitled to receive dividends paid during the vesting period.

B34 Conversely, if the employees are not entitled to dividends or dividend equivalents during the vesting period (or before exercise, in the case of an option), the grant date valuation of the rights to shares or options should take expected dividends into account. That is to say, when the fair value of an option grant is estimated, expected dividends should be included in the application of an option pricing model. When the fair value of a share grant is estimated, that valuation should be reduced by the present value of dividends expected to be paid during the vesting period.

B35 Option pricing models generally call for expected dividend yield. However, the models may be modified to use an expected dividend amount rather than a yield. An entity may use either its expected yield or its expected payments. If the entity uses the latter, it should consider its historical pattern of increases in dividends. For example, if an entity's policy has generally been to increase dividends by approximately 3 per cent per year, its estimated option value should not assume a fixed dividend amount throughout the option's life unless there is evidence that supports that assumption.

B36 Generally, the assumption about expected dividends should be based on publicly available information. An entity that does not pay dividends and has no plans to do so should assume an expected dividend yield of zero. However, an emerging entity with no history of paying dividends might expect to begin paying dividends during the expected lives of its employee share options. Those entities could use an average of their past dividend yield (zero) and the mean dividend yield of an appropriately comparable peer group.

Risk-free interest rate

B37 Typically, the risk-free interest rate is the implied yield currently available on zero-coupon government issues of the country in whose currency the exercise price is expressed, with a remaining term equal to the expected term of the option being valued (based on the option's remaining contractual life and taking into account the effects of expected early exercise). It may be necessary to use an appropriate substitute, if no such government issues exist or circumstances indicate that the implied yield on zero-coupon government issues is not representative of the risk-free interest rate (for example, in high inflation economies). Also, an appropriate substitute should be used if market participants would typically determine the risk-free interest rate by using that substitute, rather than the implied yield of zero-coupon government issues, when estimating the fair value of an option with a life equal to the expected term of the option being valued.

Capital structure effects

Typically, third parties, not the entity, write traded share options. When these share options are exercised, the writer delivers shares to the option holder. Those shares are acquired from existing shareholders. Hence the exercise of traded share options has no dilutive effect. **B38**

In contrast, if share options are written by the entity, new shares are issued when those share options are exercised (either actually issued or issued in substance, if shares previously repurchased and held in treasury are used). Given that the shares will be issued at the exercise price rather than the current market price at the date of exercise, this actual or potential dilution might reduce the share price, so that the option holder does not make as large a gain on exercise as on exercising an otherwise similar traded option that does not dilute the share price. **B39**

Whether this has a significant effect on the value of the share options granted depends on various factors, such as the number of new shares that will be issued on exercise of the options compared with the number of shares already issued. Also, if the market already expects that the option grant will take place, the market may have already factored the potential dilution into the share price at the date of grant. **B40**

However, the entity should consider whether the possible dilutive effect of the future exercise of the share options granted might have an impact on their estimated fair value at grant date. Option pricing models can be adapted to take into account this potential dilutive effect. **B41**

Modifications to equity-settled share-based payment arrangements

Paragraph 27 requires that, irrespective of any modifications to the terms and conditions on which the equity instruments were granted, or a cancellation or settlement of that grant of equity instruments, the entity should recognise, as a minimum, the services received measured at the grant date fair value of the equity instruments granted, unless those equity instruments do not vest because of failure to satisfy a vesting condition (other than a market condition) that was specified at grant date. In addition, the entity should recognise the effects of modifications that increase the total fair value of the share-based payment arrangement or are otherwise beneficial to the employee. **B42**

To apply the requirements of paragraph 27: **B43**

(a) if the modification increases the fair value of the equity instruments granted (eg by reducing the exercise price), measured immediately before and after the modification, the entity shall include the incremental fair value granted in the measurement of the amount recognised for services received as consideration for the equity instruments granted. The incremental fair value granted is the difference between the fair value of the modified equity instrument and that of the original equity instrument, both estimated as at the date of the modification. If the modification occurs during the vesting period, the incremental fair value granted is included in the measurement of the amount recognised for services received over the period from the modification date until the date when the modified equity instruments vest, in addition to the amount based on the grant date fair value of the original equity instruments, which is recognised over the remainder of the original vesting period. If the modification occurs after vesting date, the incremental fair value granted is recognised immediately, or over the vesting period if the employee is required to complete an additional period of service before becoming unconditionally entitled to those modified equity instruments.

(b) similarly, if the modification increases the number of equity instruments granted, the entity shall include the fair value of the additional equity instruments granted, measured at the date of the modification, in the measurement of the amount recognised for services received as consideration for the equity instruments granted, consistently with the requirements in (a) above. For example, if the modification occurs during the vesting period, the fair value of the additional equity instruments granted is included in the measurement of the amount recognised for services received over the period from the modification date until the date when the additional equity instruments vest, in addition to the amount based on the grant date fair value of the equity instruments originally granted, which is recognised over the remainder of the original vesting period.

(c) if the entity modifies the vesting conditions in a manner that is beneficial to the employee, for example, by reducing the vesting period or by modifying or eliminating a performance condition (other than a market condition, changes to which are accounted for in accordance with (a) above), the entity shall take the modified vesting conditions into account when applying the requirements of paragraphs 19–21.

B44 Furthermore, if the entity modifies the terms or conditions of the equity instruments granted in a manner that reduces the total fair value of the share-based payment arrangement, or is not otherwise beneficial to the employee, the entity shall nevertheless continue to account for the services received as consideration for the equity instruments granted as if that modification had not occurred (other than a cancellation of some or all the equity instruments granted, which shall be accounted for in accordance with paragraph 28). For example:

(a) if the modification reduces the fair value of the equity instruments granted, measured immediately before and after the modification, the entity shall not take into account that decrease in fair value and shall continue to measure the amount recognised for services received as consideration for the equity instruments based on the grant date fair value of the equity instruments granted.

(b) if the modification reduces the number of equity instruments granted to an employee, that reduction shall be accounted for as a cancellation of that portion of the grant, in accordance with the requirements of paragraph 28.

(c) if the entity modifies the vesting conditions in a manner that is not beneficial to the employee, for example, by increasing the vesting period or by modifying or adding a performance condition (other than a market condition, changes to which are accounted for in accordance with (a) above), the entity shall not take the modified vesting conditions into account when applying the requirements of paragraphs 19–21.

Share-based payment transactions among group entities (2009 amendments)

Paragraphs 43A–43C address the accounting for share-based payment transactions among group entities in each entity's separate or individual financial statements. Paragraphs B46–B61 discuss how to apply the requirements in paragraphs 43A–43C. As noted in paragraph 43D, share-based payment transactions among group entities may take place for a variety of reasons depending on facts and circumstances. Therefore, this discussion is not exhaustive and assumes that when the entity receiving the goods or services has no obligation to settle the transaction, the transaction is a parent's equity contribution to the subsidiary, regardless of any intragroup repayment arrangements. **B45**

Although the discussion below focuses on transactions with employees, it also applies to similar share-based payment transactions with suppliers of goods or services other than employees. An arrangement between a parent and its subsidiary may require the subsidiary to pay the parent for the provision of the equity instruments to the employees. The discussion below does not address how to account for such an intragroup payment arrangement. **B46**

Four issues are commonly encountered in share-based payment transactions among group entities. For convenience, the examples below discuss the issues in terms of a parent and its subsidiary. **B47**

Share-based payment arrangements involving an entity's own equity instruments

The first issue is whether the following transactions involving an entity's own equity instruments should be accounted for as equity-settled or as cash-settled in accordance with the requirements of this IFRS: **B48**

(a) an entity grants to its employees rights to equity instruments of the entity (eg share options), and either chooses or is required to buy equity instruments (ie treasury shares) from another party, to satisfy its obligations to its employees; and

(b) an entity's employees are granted rights to equity instruments of the entity (eg share options), either by the entity itself or by its shareholders, and the shareholders of the entity provide the equity instruments needed.

The entity shall account for share-based payment transactions in which it receives services as consideration for its own equity instruments as equity-settled. This applies regardless of whether the entity chooses or is required to buy those equity instruments from another party to satisfy its obligations to its employees under the share-based payment arrangement. It also applies regardless of whether: **B49**

(a) the employee's rights to the entity's equity instruments were granted by the entity itself or by its shareholder(s); or

(b) the share-based payment arrangement was settled by the entity itself or by its shareholder(s).

If the shareholder has an obligation to settle the transaction with its investee's employees, it provides equity instruments of its investee rather than its own. Therefore, if its investee is in the same group as the shareholder, in accordance with paragraph 43C, the shareholder shall measure its obligation in accordance with the requirements applicable to cash-settled share-based payment transactions in the shareholder's separate financial statements and those applicable to equity-settled share-based payment transactions in the shareholder's consolidated financial statements. **B50**

Share-based payment arrangements involving equity instruments of the parent

B51 The second issue concerns share-based payment transactions between two or more entities within the same group involving an equity instrument of another group entity. For example, employees of a subsidiary are granted rights to equity instruments of its parent as consideration for the services provided to the subsidiary.

B52 Therefore, the second issue concerns the following share-based payment arrangements:

(a) a parent grants rights to its equity instruments directly to the employees of its subsidiary: the parent (not the subsidiary) has the obligation to provide the employees of the subsidiary with the equity instruments; and
(b) a subsidiary grants rights to equity instruments of its parent to its employees: the subsidiary has the obligation to provide its employees with the equity instruments.

A parent grants rights to its equity instruments to the employees of its subsidiary (paragraph B52(a))

B53 The subsidiary does not have an obligation to provide its parent's equity instruments to the subsidiary's employees. Therefore, in accordance with paragraph 43B, the subsidiary shall measure the services received from its employees in accordance with the requirements applicable to equity-settled share-based payment transactions, and recognise a corresponding increase in equity as a contribution from the parent.

B54 The parent has an obligation to settle the transaction with the subsidiary's employees by providing the parent's own equity instruments. Therefore, in accordance with paragraph 43C, the parent shall measure its obligation in accordance with the requirements applicable to equity-settled share-based payment transactions.

A subsidiary grants rights to equity instruments of its parent to its employees (paragraph B52(b))

B55 Because the subsidiary does not meet either of the conditions in paragraph 43B, it shall account for the transaction with its employees as cash-settled. This requirement applies irrespective of how the subsidiary obtains the equity instruments to satisfy its obligations to its employees.

Share-based payment arrangements involving cash-settled payments to employees

B56 The third issue is how an entity that receives goods or services from its suppliers (including employees) should account for share-based arrangements that are cash-settled when the entity itself does not have any obligation to make the required payments to its suppliers. For example, consider the following arrangements in which the parent (not the entity itself) has an obligation to make the required cash payments to the employees of the entity:

(a) the employees of the entity will receive cash payments that are linked to the price of its equity instruments.
(b) the employees of the entity will receive cash payments that are linked to the price of its parent's equity instruments.

B57 The subsidiary does not have an obligation to settle the transaction with its employees. Therefore, the subsidiary shall account for the transaction with its employees as equity-settled, and recognise a corresponding increase in equity as a contribution from its parent. The subsidiary shall remeasure the cost of the transaction subsequently for any changes resulting from non-market vesting conditions not being met in accordance with paragraphs 19–21. This differs from the measurement of the transaction as cash-settled in the consolidated financial statements of the group.

Because the parent has an obligation to settle the transaction with the employees, and the consideration is cash, the parent (and the consolidated group) shall measure its obligation in accordance with the requirements applicable to cash-settled share-based payment transactions in paragraph 43C. **B58**

Transfer of employees between group entities

The fourth issue relates to group share-based payment arrangements that involve employees of more than one group entity. For example, a parent might grant rights to its equity instruments to the employees of its subsidiaries, conditional upon the completion of continuing service with the group for a specified period. An employee of one subsidiary might transfer employment to another subsidiary during the specified vesting period without the employee's rights to equity instruments of the parent under the original share-based payment arrangement being affected. If the subsidiaries have no obligation to settle the share-based payment transaction with their employees, they account for it as an equity-settled transaction. Each subsidiary shall measure the services received from the employee by reference to the fair value of the equity instruments at the date the rights to those equity instruments were originally granted by the parent as defined in Appendix A, and the proportion of the vesting period the employee served with each subsidiary. **B59**

If the subsidiary has an obligation to settle the transaction with its employees in its parent's equity instruments, it accounts for the transaction as cash-settled. Each subsidiary shall measure the services received on the basis of grant date fair value of the equity instruments for the proportion of the vesting period the employee served with each subsidiary. In addition, each subsidiary shall recognise any change in the fair value of the equity instruments during the employee's service period with each subsidiary. **B60**

Such an employee, after transferring between group entities, may fail to satisfy a vesting condition other than a market condition as defined in Appendix A, eg the employee leaves the group before completing the service period. In this case, because the vesting condition is service to the group, each subsidiary shall adjust the amount previously recognised in respect of the services received from the employee in accordance with the principles in paragraph 19. Hence, if the rights to the equity instruments granted by the parent do not vest because of an employee's failure to meet a vesting condition other than a market condition, no amount is recognised on a cumulative basis for the services received from that employee in the financial statements of any group entity. **B61**

Appendix C
Amendments to other standards and UITF Abstracts

[Not reproduced, as all changes have been made to the underlying standards and abstracts]

Adoption of the standard
Approval of IFRS 2 by the International Accounting Standards Board

International Financial Reporting Standard 2 Share-based Payment was approved for issue by the fourteen members of the International Accounting Standards Board.

Sir David Tweedie	Chairman
Thomas E Jones	Vice-Chairman
Mary E Barth	
Hans-Georg Bruns	
Anthony T Cope	
Robert P Garnett	
Gilbert Gélard	
James J Leisenring	
Warren J McGregor	
Patricia L O'Malley	
Harry K Schmid	
John T Smith	
Geoffrey Whittington	
Tatsumi Yamada	

Adoption of FRS 20 by the Accounting Standards Board

Financial Reporting Standard 20 (IFRS 2) Share-based Payment was approved for issue by the nine members of the Accounting Standards Board.

Mary Keegan	Chairman
Andrew Lennard	Technical Director
Michael Ashley	
Douglas Flint	
Huw Jones	
Roger Marshall	
Isobel Sharp	
John Smith	
Jonathan Symonds	

Approval by the IASB of Group Cash-settled Share-based Payment Transactions (Amendments to IFRS 2) issued in June 2009

Group Cash-settled Share-based Payment Transactions (Amendments to IFRS 2) was approved for issue by thirteen of the fourteen members of the International Accounting Standards Board. Mr Kalavacherla abstained in view of his recent appointment to the Board.

Sir David Tweedie	Chairman
Thomas E Jones	Vice-Chairman
Mary E Barth	
Stephen Cooper	
Philippe Danjou	
Jan Engström	
Robert P Garnett	
Gilbert Gélard	
Prabhakar Kalavacherla	
James J Leisenring	
Warren J McGregor	
John T Smith	
Tatsumi Yamada	
Wei-Guo Zhang	

Adoption of Amendment to FRS 20 by the Accounting Standards Board

Amendment to Financial Reporting Standard 20 (IFRS 2) 'Share-based payment' – Group Cash-settled Share-based Payment Transactions was approved for issue by the eleven members of the Accounting Standards Board.

Ian Mackintosh	Chairman
David Loweth	Technical Director
Nick Anderson	
Michael Ashley	
Edward Beale	
Marisa Cassoni	
Peter Elwin	
Ken Lever	
Robert Overend	
Andy Simmonds	
Professor Geoffrey Whittington CBE	

Notes on the standard's application in the UK and the Republic of Ireland

THE NEED FOR AN FRS ON SHARE-BASED PAYMENTS

In November 2002, the IASB published a draft International Financial Reporting Standard (IFRS) on share-based payments. It indicated that it expected the final IFRS to come into effect for accounting periods beginning on or after 1 January 2004. The ASB (the Board) proposed in FRED 31 that a Financial Reporting Standard (FRS) based on the draft IFRS should be implemented in the UK and the Republic of Ireland* from that same date. **N1**

The Board had for many years been concerned about the accounting treatment of share-based payment transactions. In its view, such transactions give rise to an expense and that expense should be measured at fair value and recognised in full in the profit and loss account (or included as part of the cost of an asset recognised on the balance sheet). Unless and until that is done, the financial statements will not fully reflect the substance of the transactions the reporting entity has entered into. A standard like the draft IFRS that requires all entities to recognise an expense, measured at fair value, in relation to all their share-based payments was therefore needed urgently to improve the UK financial reporting framework. **N2**

Some respondents to FRED 31 thought it wrong to require recognition of a fair value expense, either because the entity was not thought to incur an expense or because fair value was not believed to be the appropriate measure. The Board was not persuaded by these arguments for the same reasons the IASB was not persuaded (see paragraphs BC34-BC60). **N3**

Some respondents argued that there was no need for the Board to issue an FRS because listed entities preparing consolidated financial statements would be required by the EU Regulation on International Accounting Standards† to apply EU adopted IFRS rather than the UK financial reporting framework from 2005. Notwithstanding the EU Regulation, the Board's responsibility continues to be to establish and improve the UK financial reporting framework for the benefit of users, preparers, and auditors of financial information. Therefore, if it believes that a material aspect of accounting practice in the UK is deficient and is capable of improvement – as it does with share-based payments – its responsibility is to achieve the necessary improvement. **N4**

Some respondents disagreed with the timetable proposed in the FRED. **N5**

(a) Some thought the FRS should be implemented in 2005 to coincide with the substantial changes that many UK entities would be making to their financial reporting to comply with the EU Regulation.

**For simplicity, the remainder of this section uses 'UK' to mean 'UK and the Republic of Ireland' unless the context indicates otherwise.*

†*Regulation (EC) No 1606/2002 of the European Parliament and of the Council of 19 July 2002 on the application of international accounting standards.*

(b) Others thought it inappropriate for the UK to implement the IFRS in advance of an equivalent standard being implemented in the USA because to do so would put UK entities at a competitive disadvantage.* The Board does not accept this argument, not least because it implies that no improvement – however worthy and necessary – should be made to the UK's accounting requirements unless those same improvements are being made at the same time, or have already been made, in the USA. The Board also believes that users are generally sufficiently sophisticated to take superior accounting practices into account in evaluating an entity's financial statements, even if those superior accounting practices result in the recognition of additional expenses.

N6 In February 2004, the IASB issued its standard as IFRS 2 *Share-based Payment*. Having considered the responses received to FRED 31, the Board decided it should implement an FRS based on that IFRS as soon as possible. It took the view that, for listed entities, that means implementation for accounting periods beginning on or after 1 January 2005.

SCOPE EXEMPTIONS FROM FRS 20

N7 The Board has followed its usual practice by exempting from the FRS all entities falling within the scope of the Financial Reporting Standard for Smaller Entities (FRSSE).

N7A In April 2009, as part of its annual 'Improvements to IFRS' the IASB amended paragraph 5 of the IFRS to clarify that an entity shall not apply the IFRS to transactions in which an entity acquires goods or services as part of the net assets acquired in a combination of entities or businesses under common control as described in paragraphs B1 to B4 of IFRS 3 'Business Combinations' (as revised in 2008), or the contributions of a business on the formation of a joint venture as defined by IAS 31 'Interests in Joint Ventures'. The ASB amended the text of paragraph 5 of the FRS to retain consistency between the text of IFRS 2 and FRS 20. It was not, however, necessary to amend further the wording in FRS 20 as the definition of a business combination set out in FRS 6 'Acquisition and Mergers' includes within its scope combination of entities or businesses under common control and the contributions of a business on the formation of a joint venture.

All-employee schemes

N8 A number of respondents argued for some sort of exemption for broadly-based employee schemes such as Save-As-You-Earn (SAYE) schemes. In their view:

(a) even though other share-based payment arrangements involve the sponsoring entity incurring an expense, broadly-based employee schemes do not;

(b) requiring entities to recognise a fair value expense for such schemes would involve them taking on a burden that was not commensurate with the benefits derived from such an accounting treatment; and

**At the moment, the USA has a non-mandatory standard that adopts a fair value approach to share-based payment expense recognition. It also has an active project that involves working with the IASB on a single, high-quality global accounting standard on share-based payments. A US exposure draft on equity-settled share-based payments is expected soon, with a final standard scheduled by the end of the year. The draft standard is expected to be similar to IFRS 2 in many important respects, although there will be some differences. The intention is that a convergence project will be undertaken as soon as is reasonably possible to bring the IFRS and the eventual US standard fully into line.*

(c) the Board should take into account that, if entities were required to recognise a fair value expense for broadly-based employee schemes, many would discontinue the schemes which would not be a good thing.

As the IASB makes clear in its Basis for Conclusions, it does not find such arguments persuasive. In its view, broadly-based schemes such as all-employee schemes *do* involve an expense and the benefits of recognising that expense in the financial statements justify the costs involved. Furthermore, the role of accounting is to report transactions and events in a neutral manner, not to permit or require favourable treatments of particular transactions so as to encourage entities to engage in those transactions. The Board shares those views. **N9**

Unlisted entities

Some respondents suggested that unlisted entities also needed some sort of exemption. Some stated that the public's interest in such entities was not as great as for listed entities, so the benefits of recognising a fair value expense would not be as great. Furthermore, unlisted entities would often have difficulty fair valuing their share-based payments. Therefore, unlisted entities should be exempt from the Standard or permitted to use some sort of simplified methodology. Other respondents thought unlisted entities needed more time to prepare for the FRS. **N10**

The IASB received similar comments in response to its draft IFRS and responded by amending its proposals to permit a simplified methodology to be used in circumstances in which an entity is unable to estimate reliably the measurement date fair value of the equity instruments granted (see paragraphs 24 and 25 of FRS 20). No specific exemption for unlisted entities was granted. **N11**

The Board agrees that there is no conceptual or practical reason for excluding unlisted entities from the scope of the FRS. However, anecdotal evidence suggests that many of the unlisted entities that make share-based payments will not be ready to implement the Standard in 2005; they need more time to gather the necessary information and develop the necessary systems and valuation techniques. The Board has decided therefore to delay implementation of FRS 20 for unlisted entities by one year until accounting periods beginning on or after 1 January 2006. **N12**

This decision meant it was necessary to include definitions of 'listed entity' and 'unlisted entity' in the FRS. Existing FRSs and FREDs suggested some possible definitions: FRS 13 *Derivatives and other Financial Instruments: Disclosures* refers to instruments that are "listed or publicly traded on a stock exchange or market" and FRS 22 (IAS 33) *Earnings per share* refers also to entities that are in the process of issuing instruments in public securities markets. However, the Board thought it would be best, and also least confusing, if it adopted the definition of a listed entity set out in the EU Regulation. **N13**

Parents' and subsidiaries' single entity financial statements

The other exemption that the Board considered concerns the single entity financial statements of parent and subsidiary entities whose financial information is also included in consolidated financial statements. **N14**

IFRS 2 does not differentiate between individual entity financial statements and consolidated financial statements, nor between subsidiaries or parents; the Standard applies to all entities and to all their financial statements. **N15**

N16 The Board recognises that there is generally less interest from users in an entity's single entity financial statements if its financial information is also included in consolidated financial statements. However, it does not believe that is sufficient reason to justify exempting single entity financial statements from the scope of the Standard. The expense that arises on a share-based payment is no different from any other expense an entity incurs and should be treated in exactly the same way regardless of the type of financial statements being prepared.

IAS 32

N17 One of the issues that the Board will need to consider whenever it is implementing an FRS based on an IFRS is whether that IFRS relies on other IFRSs that have not yet been implemented in the UK.

N18 In the case of IFRS 2 it would appear that the only IFRS it assumes is already in place is IAS 32 *Financial Instruments: Disclosure and Presentation*; in particular the material in that standard on the equity/liability classification (the so-called 'presentation requirements'). The Board has recently announced* that it intends to implement those presentation requirements in the UK for all entities for accounting periods beginning on or after 1 January 2005.†

CONSEQUENTIAL AMENDMENTS TO EXISTING STANDARDS AND UITF ABSTRACTS

N19-N26 [Not reproduced, as all changes have been made to the underlying standards and abstracts]

THE FRS' IMPLICATIONS FOR DISTRIBUTABLE PROFITS

N27 A number of those responding to FRED 31 raised questions about the effect that the proposals would have on distributable profits. The Board's general policy is not to comment on distribution matters of this kind because, if they are material to the amount that an entity may wish to distribute, the entity will need to take its own legal advice.

N28 As explained above, FRS 20 supersedes UITF 17. When developing the original version of that Abstract, the UITF took legal advice on the implications of the required accounting treatment for the share premium account. A summary of the advice received was included in the Abstract. Some respondents have suggested that, although the Abstract itself is to be withdrawn, that legal advice will still have relevance in the context of FRS 20 and should therefore be repeated in the FRS. UITF 17's summary of the legal advice the UITF received is set out below, although it needs to be borne in mind that the accounting treatment required by FRS 20 is very different from that required by UITF 17, as is the rationale that underpins the respective requirements.

> "The UITF has received legal advice on the implications for share premium account when the accounting treatment required by this Abstract is followed. It has been advised that where new shares are issued in connection with an employee share scheme the share premium account will normally have to reflect

**In its UK Accounting Standards: A Strategy for Convergence with IFRS Discussion Paper, which was issued in March 2004.*

†***Editor's note:*** *Now FRS 25.*

only the cash subscribed for the shares (eg by the employee or by an ESOP). In such cases, any difference between the cash subscribed for the shares (which must be at least as much as the nominal value, as shares cannot be issued at a discount) and the fair value at the date of grant of rights should be credited to reserves other than the share premium account. This is on the basis that the services of the employee do not, as a matter of law, form part of the consideration received for the shares issued, and the UITF has been advised that this would be the usual legal interpretation of such transactions. Exceptionally, however, the terms of a transaction might be such as to lead to the opposite interpretation, and companies may need to take legal advice on this point. In such a case, the operation of section 99(2) of the Companies Act 1985 [prohibition of public company accepting undertaking to perform services in payment up of its shares] and section 103 [non-cash consideration to be valued before allotment of shares] would also have to be considered."

In March 2006 the ASB issued an exposure draft inviting comments on the proposed IASB's amendments to IFRS 2, which addressed vesting conditions and cancellations. The ASB acknowledge that while many people shared its concerns in relation to the accounting treatment of cancellations by parties other than the entity they were not considered sufficient to justify FRS 20 diverging from IFRS 2. The consultation process had not identified a fundamental reason to diverge. **N29**

In January 2008 the Board issued an amendment to FRS 20 to incorporate changes made by the IASB to IFRS 2 *Share-based Payments 'Vesting Conditions and Cancellations'*. **N30**

In January 2008 the ASB issued a Financial Reporting Exposure Draft (FRED) inviting comments on the proposed IASB's amendments for group cash-settled share-based payment transactions. Respondents replied that they were not aware of any issues that would affect UK entities in implementing the proposals set out in the FRED and consider that the benefits of the proposal would outweigh any additional costs involved. The consultation process had found no fundamental reason to diverge from IFRS 2. **N31**

In August 2009 the Board amended FRS 20 (IFRS 2) to incorporate changes made by the IASB to IFRS 2 *Share-based Payment 'Group Cash-settled Share-based Payments Transactions'*. **N32**

Basis for conclusions

Contents

paragraphs

Introduction **BC1-BC6**

Scope **BC7-BC28**

Broad-based employee share plans, including employee share purchase plans **BC8-BC18**

Transfers of equity instruments to employees **BC19-BC22**

Transactions within the scope of IAS 22 *Business Combinations* **BC23-BC24**

Transactions within the scope of IAS 32 *Financial Instruments: Disclosure and Presentation* and IAS 39 *Financial Instruments: Recognition and Measurement* **BC25-BC28**

Recognition of equity-settled share-based payment transactions **BC29-BC60**

'The entity is not a party to the transaction' **BC34-BC35**

'The employees do not provide services' **BC36-BC39**

'There is no cost to the entity, therefore there is no expense' **BC40-BC44**

'Expense recognition is inconsistent with the definition of an expense' **BC45-BC53**

'Earnings per share is "hit twice"' **BC54-BC57**

'Adverse economic consequences' **BC58-BC60**

Measurement of equity-settled share-based payment transactions **BC61-BC128**

Measurement basis **BC69-BC87**

Historical cost BC70-BC74

Intrinsic value BC75-BC79

Minimum value BC80-BC83

Fair value BC84-BC87

Measurement date **BC88-BC128**

The debit side of the transaction BC91-BC96

The credit side of the transaction BC97-BC105

Exercise date BC98

Vesting date, service date and grant date BC99-BC105

Other issues BC106-BC118

IAS 32 Financial Instruments: Disclosure and Presentation BC106-BC110

Suggestions to change the definitions of liabilities and equity BC111-BC118

Share-based payment transactions with parties other than employees BC119-BC128

Fair value of employee share options **BC129-BC199**

Application of option pricing models to unlisted and newly listed entities **BC137-BC144**

Application of option pricing models to employee options **BC145-BC199**
Inability to exercise during the vesting period BC146-BC152
Non-transferability BC153-BC169
Vesting conditions BC170-BC184
Option term BC185-BC187
Other features of employee share options BC188-BC199

Recognition and measurement of services received in an equity-settled share-based payment transaction **BC200-BC221**

During the vesting period **BC200-BC217**

Share options that are forfeited or lapse after the end of the vesting period **BC218-BC221**

Modifications to the terms and conditions of share-based payment arrangements **BC222-BC237B**

Share appreciation rights settled in cash **BC238-BC255**

Is there a liability before vesting date? **BC243-BC245**

How should the liability be measured? **BC246-BC251**

How should the associated expense be presented in the income statement? **BC252-BC255**

Share-based payment transactions with cash alternatives **BC256-BC268**

The terms of the arrangement provide the employee with a choice of settlement **BC258-BC264**

The terms of the arrangement provide the entity with a choice of settlement **BC265-BC268**

Overall conclusions on accounting for employee share options **BC269-BC312**

Convergence with US GAAP **BC270-BC286**
APB 25 BC272-BC275
SFAS 123 BC276-BC286

Recognition versus disclosure **BC287-BC293**

Reliability of measurement **BC294-BC310**

Consequential amendments to other standards **BC311-BC333**

Tax effects of share-based payment transactions **BC311-BC329**

Accounting for own shares held **BC330-BC333**

Basis for conclusions

This Basis for Conclusions accompanies, but is not part of, IFRS 2.

> *ASB note:* The IASB's Basis for Conclusions, which accompanies IFRS 2, is set out below in full. It should be noted though that some of the discussion it contains concerns IASB requirements that have no equivalent in the UK or Republic of Ireland. Footnotes have been used to highlight those parts of the discussion.
>
> All references in this section to 'the Board' and 'Board members' are references to the IASB Board and IASB Board members.

INTRODUCTION

BC1 This Basis for Conclusions summarises the International Accounting Standards Board's considerations in reaching the conclusions in IFRS 2 *Share-based Payment*. Individual Board members gave greater weight to some factors than to others.

BC2 Entities often issue* shares or share options to pay employees or other parties. Share plans and share option plans are a common feature of employee remuneration, not only for directors and senior executives, but also for many other employees. Some entities issue shares or share options to pay suppliers, such as suppliers of professional services.

BC3 Until the issue of IFRS 2, there has been no International Financial Reporting Standard (IFRS) covering the recognition and measurement of these transactions. Concerns have been raised about this gap in international standards. For example, the International Organization of Securities Commissions (IOSCO), in its 2000 report on international standards, stated that IASC (the IASB's predecessor body) should consider the accounting treatment of share-based payment.

BC4 Few countries have standards on the topic. This is a concern in many countries, because the use of share-based payment has increased in recent years and continues to spread. Various standard-setting bodies have been working on this issue. At the time the IASB added a project on share-based payment to its agenda in July 2001, some standard-setters had recently published proposals. For example, the German Accounting Standards Committee published a draft accounting standard *Accounting for Share Option Plans and Similar Compensation Arrangements* in June 2001. The UK Accounting Standards Board led the development of the Discussion Paper *Accounting for Share-based Payment*, published in July 2000 by IASC, the ASB and other bodies represented in the G4 + 1.† The Danish Institute of State Authorised Public Accountants issued a Discussion Paper *The Accounting Treatment of Share-Based Payment* in April 2000. More recently, in December 2002, the Accounting Standards Board of Japan published a Summary Issues Paper on share-based payment. In March 2003, the US Financial Accounting Standards Board (FASB) added

**The word 'issue' is used in a broad sense. For example, a transfer of shares held in treasury (own shares held) to another party is regarded as an 'issue' of equity instruments. Some argue that if options or shares are granted with vesting conditions, they are not 'issued' until those vesting conditions have been satisfied. However, even if this argument is accepted, it does not change the Board's conclusions on the requirements of the IFRS, and therefore the word 'issue' is used broadly, to include situations in which equity instruments are conditionally transferred to the counterparty, subject to the satisfaction of specified vesting conditions.*

†The G4 + 1 comprised members of the national accounting standard-setting bodies of Australia, Canada, New Zealand, the UK and the US, and IASC.

to its agenda a project to review US accounting requirements on share-based payment. Also, the Canadian Accounting Standards Board (AcSB) recently completed its project on share-based payment. The AcSB standard requires recognition of all share-based payment transactions, including transactions in which share options are granted to employees (discussed further in paragraphs BC281 and BC282).

Users of financial statements and other commentators are calling for improvements in the accounting treatment of share-based payment. For example, the proposal in the IASC/G4 + 1 Discussion Paper and ED 2 *Share-based Payment*, that share-based payment transactions should be recognised in the financial statements, resulting in an expense when the goods or services are consumed, received strong support from investors and other users of financial statements. Recent economic events have emphasised the importance of high quality financial statements that provide neutral, transparent and comparable information to help users make economic decisions. In particular, the omission of expenses arising from share-based payment transactions with employees has been highlighted by investors, other users of financial statements and other commentators as causing economic distortions and corporate governance concerns. **BC5**

As noted above, the Board began a project to develop an IFRS on share-based payment in July 2001. In September 2001, the Board invited additional comment on the IASC/G4 + 1 Discussion Paper, with a comment deadline of 15 December 2001. The Board received over 270 letters. During the development of ED 2, the Board was also assisted by an Advisory Group, consisting of individuals from various countries and with a range of backgrounds, including persons from the investment, corporate, audit, academic, compensation consultancy, valuation and regulatory communities. The Board received further assistance from other experts at a panel discussion held in New York in July 2002. In November 2002, the Board published an Exposure Draft, ED 2 *Share-based Payment*, with a comment deadline of 7 March 2003. The Board received over 240 letters. The Board also worked with the FASB after that body added to its agenda a project to review US accounting requirements on share-based payment. This included participating in meetings of the FASB's Option Valuation Group and meeting the FASB to discuss convergence issues. **BC6**

In 2007 the Board added to its agenda a project to clarify the scope and accounting for group cash-settled share-based payment transactions in the separate or individual financial statements of the entity receiving the goods or services when that entity has no obligation to settle the share-based payment. In December 2007 the Board published *Group Cash-settled Share-based Payment Transactions* (proposed amendments to IFRS 2). The resulting amendments issued in June 2009 also incorporate the requirements of two Interpretations—IFRIC 8 *Scope of IFRS 2* and IFRIC 11 *IFRS 2—Group and Treasury Share Transactions*. As a consequence, the Board withdrew both Interpretations.* **BC6A**

SCOPE

Much of the controversy and complexity surrounding the accounting for share-based payment relates to employee share options. However, the scope of IFRS 2 is broader than that. It applies to transactions in which shares or other equity instruments are granted to employees. It also applies to transactions with parties other than employees, in which goods or services are received as consideration for the issue of shares, share options or other equity instruments. The term 'goods' includes inventories, consumables, property, plant and equipment, intangible assets and other non- **BC7**

****Editor's note**: Paragraph added in August 2009.*

financial assets. Lastly, the IFRS applies to payments in cash (or other assets) that are 'share-based' because the amount of the payment is based on the price of the entity's shares or other equity instruments, eg cash share appreciation rights.

Broad-based employee share plans, including employee share purchase plans

BC8 Some employee share plans are described as 'broad-based' or 'allemployee' plans, in which all (or virtually all) employees have the opportunity to participate, whereas other plans are more selective, covering individual or specific groups of employees (eg senior executives). Employee share purchase plans are often broad-based plans. Typically, employee share purchase plans provide employees with an opportunity to buy a specific number of shares at a discounted price, ie at an amount that is less than the fair value of the shares. The employee's entitlement to discounted shares is usually conditional upon specific conditions being satisfied, such as remaining in the service of the entity for a specified period.

BC9 The issues that arise with respect to employee share purchase plans are:

(a) are these plans somehow so different from other employee share plans that a different accounting treatment is appropriate?
(b) even if the answer to the above question is 'no', are there circumstances, such as when the discount is very small, when it is appropriate to exempt employee share purchase plans from an accounting standard on share-based payment?

BC10 Some respondents to ED 2 argued that broad-based employee share plans should be exempt from an accounting standard on share-based payment. The reason usually given was that these plans are different from other types of employee share plans and, in particular, are not a part of remuneration for employee services. Some argued that requiring the recognition of an expense in respect of these types of plans was perceived to be contrary to government policy to encourage employee share ownership. In contrast, other respondents saw no difference between employee share purchase plans and other employee share plans, and argued that the same accounting requirements should therefore apply. However, some suggested that there should be an exemption if the discount is small.

BC11 The Board concluded that, in principle, there is no reason to treat broad-based employee share plans, including broad-based employee share purchase plans, differently from other employee share plans (the issue of 'small' discounts is considered later). The Board noted that the fact that these schemes are available only to employees is in itself sufficient to conclude that the benefits provided represent employee remuneration. Moreover, the term 'remuneration' is not limited to remuneration provided as part of an individual employee's contract: it encompasses all benefits provided to employees. Similarly, the term services encompasses all benefits provided by the employees in return, including increased productivity, commitment or other enhancements in employee work performance as a result of the incentives provided by the share plan.

BC12 Moreover, distinguishing regular employee services from the additional benefits received from broad-based employee share plans would not change the conclusion that it is necessary to account for such plans. No matter what label is placed on the benefits provided by employees – or the benefits provided by the entity – the transaction should be recognised in the financial statements.

BC13 Furthermore, that governments in some countries have a policy of encouraging employee share ownership is not a valid reason for according these types of plans a different accounting treatment, because it is not the role of financial reporting to give favourable accounting treatment to particular transactions to encourage entities to enter into them. For example, governments might wish to encourage entities to provide pensions to their employees, to lessen the future burden on the state, but that does not mean that pension costs should be excluded from the financial statements. To do so would impair the quality of financial reporting. The purpose of financial reporting is to provide information to users of financial statements, to assist them in making economic decisions. The omission of expenses from the financial statements does not change the fact that those expenses have been incurred. The omission of expenses causes reported profits to be overstated and hence the financial statements are not neutral, are less transparent and comparable, and are potentially misleading to users.

There remains the question whether there should be an exemption for some plans, when the discount is small. For example, FASB Statement of Financial Accounting Standards No. 123 *Accounting for Stock-Based Compensation* contains an exemption for employee share purchase plans that meet specified criteria, of which one is that the discount is small. **BC14**

On the one hand, it seems reasonable to exempt an employee share purchase plan if it has substantially no option features and the discount is small. In such situations, the rights given to the employees under the plan probably do not have a significant value, from the entity's perspective. **BC15**

On the other hand, even if one accepts that an exemption is appropriate, specifying its scope is problematic, eg deciding what constitutes a small discount. Some argue that a 5 per cent discount from the market price (as specified in SFAS 123) is too high, noting that a block of shares can be sold on the market at a price close to the current share price. Furthermore, it could be argued that it is unnecessary to exempt these plans from the standard. If the rights given to the employees do not have a significant value, this suggests that the amounts involved are immaterial. Because it is not necessary to include immaterial information in the financial statements, there is no need for a specific exclusion in an accounting standard. **BC16**

For the reasons given in the preceding paragraph, the Board concluded that broad-based employee share plans, including broad-based employee share purchase plans, should not be exempted from the IFRS. **BC17**

However, the Board noted that there might be instances when an entity engages in a transaction with an employee in his/her capacity as a holder of equity instruments, rather than in his/her capacity as an employee. For example, an entity might grant all holders of a particular class of its equity instruments the right to acquire additional equity instruments of the entity at a price that is less than the fair value of those equity instruments. If an employee receives such a right because he/she is a holder of that particular class of equity instruments, the Board concluded that the granting or exercise of that right should not be subject to the requirements of the IFRS, because the employee has received that right in his/her capacity as a shareholder, rather than as an employee. **BC18**

Transactions in which an entity cannot identify some or all of the goods or services received (paragraph 2)*

BC18A The Board incorporated into IFRS 2 the consensus of IFRIC 8 in *Group Cash-settled Share-based Payment Transactions* issued in June 2009. This section summarises the IFRIC's considerations in reaching that consensus, as approved by the Board.

BC18B IFRS 2 applies to share-based payment transactions in which the entity receives or acquires goods or services. However, in some situations it might be difficult to demonstrate that the entity has received goods or services. This raises the question of whether IFRS 2 applies to such transactions. In addition, if the entity has made a share-based payment and the identifiable consideration received (if any) appears to be less than the fair value of the share-based payment, does this situation indicate that goods or services have been received, even though those goods or services are not specifically identified, and therefore that IFRS 2 applies?

BC18C When the Board developed IFRS 2, it concluded that the directors of an entity would expect to receive some goods or services in return for equity instruments issued (paragraph BC37). This implies that it is not necessary to identify the specific goods or services received in return for the equity instruments granted to conclude that goods or services have been (or will be) received. Furthermore, paragraph 8 of the IFRS establishes that it is not necessary for the goods or services received to qualify for recognition as an asset in order for the share-based payment to be within the scope of IFRS 2. In this case, the IFRS requires the cost of the goods or services received or receivable to be recognised as expenses.

BC18D Accordingly, the Board concluded that the scope of IFRS 2 includes transactions in which the entity cannot identify some or all of the specific goods or services received. If the value of the identifiable consideration received appears to be less than the fair value of the equity instruments granted or liability incurred, typically,† this circumstance indicates that other consideration (ie unidentifiable goods or services) has been (or will be) received.

Transfers of equity instruments to employees (paragraphs 3 and 3A)

BC19 In some situations, an entity might not issue shares or share options to employees (or other parties) direct. Instead, a shareholder (or shareholders) might transfer equity instruments to the employees (or other parties).

BC20 Under this arrangement, the entity has received services (or goods) that were paid for by its shareholders. The arrangement could be viewed as being, in substance, two transactions – one transaction in which the entity has reacquired equity instruments for nil consideration, and a second transaction in which the entity has received services (or goods) as consideration for equity instruments issued to the employees (or other parties).

BC21 The second transaction is a share-based payment transaction. Therefore, the Board concluded that the entity should account for transfers of equity instruments by

**Paragraphs BC18A–BC18D are added as a consequence of* Group Cash-settled Share-based Payment Transactions *(Amendments to IFRS 2) issued in June 2009.*

†*In some cases, the reason for the transfer would explain why no goods or services have been or will be received. For example, a principal shareholder, as part of estate planning, transfers some of his shares to a family member. In the absence of factors that indicate that the family member has provided, or is expected to provide, any goods or services to the entity in return for the shares, such a transaction would be outside the scope of IFRS 2.*

shareholders to employees or other parties in the same way as other share-based payment transactions. The Board reached the same conclusion with respect to transfers of equity instruments of the entity's parent, or of another entity within the same group as the entity, to the entity's employees or other suppliers.

However, such a transfer is not a share-based payment transaction if the transfer of equity instruments to an employee or other party is clearly for a purpose other than payment for goods or services supplied to the entity. This would be the case, for example, if the transfer is to settle a shareholder's personal obligation to an employee that is unrelated to employment by the entity, or if the shareholder and employee are related and the transfer is a personal gift because of that relationship. **BC22**

In December 2007 the Board published an exposure draft *Group Cash-settled Share-based Payment Transactions* proposing amendments to IFRS 2 and IFRIC 11 to clarify the accounting for such transactions in the separate or individual financial statements of the entity receiving goods or services. The Board proposed to include specified types of such transactions within the scope of IFRS 2 (not IAS 19 *Employee Benefits*), regardless of whether the group share-based payment transaction is cash-settled or equity-settled. **BC22A**

Nearly all of the respondents to the exposure draft agreed that the group cash-settled transactions between a parent and a subsidiary described in the exposure draft should be within the scope of IFRS 2. Respondents generally believed that including these transactions is consistent with IFRS 2's main principle that the entity should recognise the goods or services that it receives in a share-based transaction. However, respondents also expressed concerns that the proposed scope: **BC22B**

(a) adopted a case-by-case approach and was inconsistent with the definitions of share-based payment transactions in IFRS 2.
(b) was unclear and increased the inconsistency in the scope requirements among the applicable IFRSs, including IFRIC 11.

Many respondents expressed concerns that similar transactions would continue to be treated differently. Because no amendments to the definitions of share-based payment transactions were proposed, some transactions might not be included within the scope of IFRS 2 because they did not meet those definitions. The Board agreed with respondents that the proposals did not achieve the objective of including all share-based payment transactions within the scope of IFRS 2 as intended. **BC22C**

When finalising the amendments issued in June 2009, the Board reaffirmed the view it had intended to convey in the proposed amendments, namely that the entity receiving the goods or services should account for group share-based payment transactions in accordance with IFRS 2. Consequently, IFRS 2 applies even when the entity receiving the goods or services has no obligation to settle the transaction and regardless of whether the payments to the suppliers are equity-settled or cash-settled. To avoid the need for further guidance on the scope of IFRS 2 for group transactions, the Board decided to amend some of the defined terms and to supersede paragraph 3 by a new paragraph 3A to state clearly the principles applicable to those transactions. **BC22D**

During its redeliberations of the proposed amendments, the Board agreed with respondents' comments that, as proposed, the scope of IFRS 2 remained unclear and inconsistent between the standard and related Interpretations. For example, the terms 'shareholder' and 'parent' have different meanings: a shareholder is not necessarily a parent, and a parent does not have to be a shareholder. The Board noted that share-based payment transactions among group entities are often directed **BC22E** by the parent, indicating a level of control. Therefore, the Board clarified the boundaries of a 'group' by adopting the same definition as in paragraph 4 of IAS 27 *Consolidated and Separate Financial Statements*, which includes only a parent and its subsidiaries.

BC22F Some respondents to the exposure draft questioned whether the proposals should apply to joint ventures. Before the Board's amendments, the guidance in paragraph 3 (now superseded by paragraph 3A) stated that when a shareholder transferred equity instruments of the entity (or another group entity), the transaction would be within the scope of IFRS 2 for the entity receiving the goods or services. However, that guidance did not specify the accounting by a shareholder transferor. The Board noted that the defined terms in Appendix A, as amended, would clearly state that any entity (including a joint venture) that receives goods or services in a share-based payment transaction should account for the transaction in accordance with the IFRS, regardless of whether that entity also settles the transaction.

BC22G Furthermore, the Board noted that the exposure draft and related discussions focused on clarifying guidance for transactions involving group entities in the separate or individual financial statements of the entity receiving the goods or services. Addressing transactions involving related parties outside a group structure in their separate or individual financial statements would significantly expand the scope of the project and change the scope of IFRS 2. Therefore, the Board decided not to address transactions between entities not in the same group that are similar to share-based payment transactions but outside the definitions as amended. This carries forward the existing guidance of IFRS 2 for entities not in the same group and the Board does not intend to change that guidance.

Transactions within the scope of IAS 22 *Business Combinations**

BC23 An entity might acquire goods (or other non-financial assets) as part of the net assets acquired in a business combination for which the consideration paid included shares or other equity instruments issued by the entity. Because IAS 22 applies to the acquisition of assets and issue of shares in connection with a business combination, that is the more specific standard that should be applied to that transaction.

BC24 Therefore, equity instruments issued in a business combination in exchange for control of the acquiree are not within the scope of IFRS 2. However, equity instruments granted to employees of the acquiree in their capacity as employees, eg in return for continued service, are within the scope of IFRS 2. Also, the cancellation, replacement, or other modifications to share-based payment arrangements because of a business combination or other equity restructuring should be accounted for in accordance with IFRS 2.

Transactions within the scope of IFRS 3 *Business Combinations*

BC24A IFRS 3 (as revised in 2008) changed the definition of a business combination. The previous definition of a business combination was 'the bringing together of separate entities or businesses into one reporting entity'. The revised definition of a business combination is 'a transaction or other event in which an acquirer obtains control of one or more businesses'.

ASB footnote: *The equivalent standard in the UK and Republic of Ireland to IAS 22 is FRS 6 Acquisitions and Mergers. The reference in paragraph 5 of IFRS 2 to IAS 22 has therefore been replaced in FRS 20 with a reference to FRS 6.*

The Board was advised that the changes to that definition caused the accounting for the contribution of a business in exchange for shares issued on formation of a joint venture by the venturers to be within the scope of IFRS 2. The Board noted that common control transactions may also be within the scope of IFRS 2 depending on which level of the group reporting entity is assessing the combination. **BC24B**

The Board noted that during the development of revised IFRS 3 it did not discuss whether it intended IFRS 2 to apply to these types of transactions. The Board also noted that the reason for excluding common control transactions and the accounting by a joint venture upon its formation from the scope of revised IFRS 3 was to give the Board more time to consider the relevant accounting issues. When the Board revised IFRS 3, it did not intend to change existing practice by bringing such transactions within the scope of IFRS 2, which does not specifically address them. **BC24C**

Accordingly, in *Improvements to IFRSs* issued in April 2009, the Board amended paragraph 5 of IFRS 2 to confirm that the contribution of a business on the formation of a joint venture and common control transactions are not within the scope of IFRS 2. **BC24D**

Transactions within the scope of IAS 32 *Financial Instruments: Disclosure and Presentation* and IAS 39 *Financial Instruments: Recognition and Measurement**

The IFRS includes consequential amendments to IAS 32 and IAS 39 to exclude from their scope transactions within the scope of IFRS 2. **BC25**

For example, suppose the entity enters into a contract to purchase cloth for use in its clothing manufacturing business, whereby it is required to pay cash to the counterparty in an amount equal to the value of 1,000 of the entity's shares at the date of delivery of the cloth. The entity will acquire goods and pay cash at an amount based on its share price. This meets the definition of a share-based payment transaction. Moreover, because the contract is to purchase cloth, which is a non-financial item, and the contract was entered into for the purpose of taking delivery of the cloth for use in the entity's manufacturing business, the contract is not within the scope of IAS 32 and IAS 39. **BC26**

The scope of IAS 32 and IAS 39 includes contracts to buy non-financial items that can be settled net in cash or another financial instrument, or by exchanging financial instruments, with the exception of contracts that were entered into and continue to be held for the purpose of the receipt or delivery of a non-financial item in accordance with the entity's expected purchase, sale or usage requirements. A contract that can be settled net in cash or another financial instrument or by exchanging financial instruments includes (a) when the terms of the contract permit either party to settle it net in cash or another financial instrument or by exchanging financial instruments; (b) when the ability to settle net in cash or another financial instrument, or by exchanging financial instruments, is not explicit in the terms of the contract, but the entity has a practice of settling similar contracts net in cash or another financial instrument, or by exchanging financial instruments (whether with the counterparty, by entering into offsetting contracts, or by selling the contract before its exercise or lapse); (c) when, for similar contracts, the entity has a practice of taking delivery of the underlying and selling it within a short period after delivery for **BC27**

**ASB footnote:* *There is no equivalent standard in the UK and Republic of Ireland to IAS 39. The equivalent standards to IAS 32 are FRS 4 Capital Instruments and FRS 13 Derivatives and other Financial Instruments: Disclosures. The implications of FRS 20 for those standards is explained in 'Notes on the standard's application in the UK and the Republic of Ireland' section.*

the purpose of generating a profit from short-term fluctuations in price or dealer's margin; and (d) when the non-financial item that is the subject of the contract is readily convertible to cash (IAS 32, paragraphs 8-10 and IAS 39, paragraphs 5-7).

BC28 The Board concluded that the contracts discussed in paragraph BC27 should remain within the scope of IAS 32 and IAS 39 and they are therefore excluded from the scope of IFRS 2.

RECOGNITION OF EQUITY-SETTLED SHARE-BASED PAYMENT TRANSACTIONS

BC29 When it developed ED 2, the Board first considered conceptual arguments relating to the recognition of an expense arising from equity-settled share-based payment transactions, including arguments advanced by respondents to the Discussion Paper and other commentators. Some respondents who disagreed with the recognition of an expense arising from particular share-based payment transactions (ie those involving employee share options) did so for practical, rather than conceptual, reasons. The Board considered those practical issues later (see paragraphs BC294-BC310).

BC30 The Board focused its discussions on employee share options, because that is where most of the complexity and controversy lies, but the question of whether expense recognition is appropriate is broader than that it covers all transactions involving the issue of shares, share options or other equity instruments to employees or suppliers of goods and services. For example, the Board noted that arguments made by respondents and other commentators against expense recognition are directed solely at employee share options. However, if conceptual arguments made against recognition of an expense in relation to employee share options are valid (eg that there is no cost to the entity), those arguments ought to apply equally to transactions involving other equity instruments (eg shares) and to equity instruments issued to other parties (eg suppliers of professional services).

BC31 The rationale for recognising all types of share-based payment transactions – irrespective of whether the equity instrument is a share or a share option, and irrespective of whether the equity instrument is granted to an employee or to some other party – is that the entity has engaged in a transaction that is in essence the same as any other issue of equity instruments. In other words, the entity has received resources (goods or services) as consideration for the issue of shares, share options or other equity instruments. It should therefore account for the inflow of resources (goods or services) and the increase in equity. Subsequently, either at the time of receipt of the goods or services or at some later date, the entity should also account for the expense arising from the consumption of those resources.

BC32 Many respondents to ED 2 agreed with this conclusion. Of those who disagreed, some disagreed in principle, some disagreed for practical reasons, and some disagreed for both reasons. The arguments against expense recognition in principle were considered by the Board when it developed ED 2, as were the arguments against expense recognition for practical reasons, as explained below and in paragraphs BC294-BC310.

BC33 Arguments commonly made against expense recognition include:

(a) the transaction is between the shareholders and the employees, not the entity and the employees.
(b) the employees do not provide services for the options.

(c) there is no cost to the entity, because no cash or other assets are given up; the shareholders bear the cost, in the form of dilution of their ownership interests, not the entity.

(d) the recognition of an expense is inconsistent with the definition of an expense in the conceptual frameworks used by accounting standard-setters, including the IASB's *Framework for the Preparation and Presentation of Financial Statements*.*

(e) the cost borne by the shareholders is recognised in the dilution of earnings per share (EPS); if the transaction is recognised in the entity's accounts, the resulting charge to the income statement would mean that EPS is 'hit twice'.

(f) requiring the recognition of a charge would have adverse economic consequences, because it would discourage entities from introducing or continuing employee share plans.

'The entity is not a party to the transaction'

Some argue that the effect of employee share plans is that the existing shareholders transfer some of their ownership interests to the employees and that the entity is not a party to this transaction. **BC34**

The Board did not accept this argument. Entities, not shareholders, set up employee share plans and entities, not shareholders, issue share options to their employees. Even if that were not the case, eg if shareholders transferred shares or share options direct to the employees, this would not mean that the entity is not a party to the transaction. The equity instruments are issued in return for services rendered by the employees and the entity, not the shareholders, receives those services. Therefore, the Board concluded that the entity should account for the services received in return for the equity instruments issued. The Board noted that this is no different from other situations in which equity instruments are issued. For example, if an entity issues warrants for cash, the entity recognises the cash received in return for the warrants issued. Although the effect of an issue, and subsequent exercise, of warrants might be described as a transfer of ownership interests from the existing shareholders to the warrant holders, the entity nevertheless is a party to the transaction because it receives resources (cash) for the issue of warrants and further resources (cash) for the issue of shares upon exercise of the warrants. Similarly, with employee share options, the entity receives resources (employee services) for the issue of the options and further resources (cash) for the issue of shares on the exercise of options. **BC35**

'The employees do not provide services'

Some who argue that the entity is not a party to the transaction counter the points made above with the argument that employees do not provide services for the options, because the employees are paid in cash (or other assets) for their services. **BC36**

Again, the Board was not convinced by this argument. If it were true that employees do not provide services for their share options, this would mean that entities are issuing valuable share options and getting nothing in return. Employees do not pay cash for the share options they receive. Hence, if they do not provide services for the options, the employees are providing nothing in return. If this were true, by issuing such options the entity's directors would be in breach of their fiduciary duties to their shareholders. **BC37**

****ASB footnote:*** The equivalent document in the UK and Republic of Ireland to the IASB's Framework is the ASB's Statement of Principles for Financial Reporting. Although the Statement of Principles is very similar to the Framework, it is not identical.

BC38 Typically, shares or share options granted to employees form one part of their remuneration package. For example, an employee might have a remuneration package consisting of a basic cash salary, company car, pension, healthcare benefits, and other benefits including shares and share options. It is usually not possible to identify the services received in respect of individual components of that remuneration package, eg the services received in respect of healthcare benefits. But that does not mean that the employee does not provide services for those healthcare benefits. Rather, the employee provides services for the entire remuneration package.

BC39 In summary, shares, share options or other equity instruments are granted to employees because they are employees. The equity instruments granted form a part of their total remuneration package, regardless of whether that represents a large part or a small part.

'There is no cost to the entity, therefore there is no expense'

BC40 Some argue that because share-based payments do not require the entity to sacrifice any cash or other assets, there is no cost to the entity, and therefore no expense should be recognised.

BC41 The Board regards this argument as unsound, because it overlooks that:

(a) every time an entity receives resources as consideration for the issue of equity instruments, there is no outflow of cash or other assets, and on every other occasion the resources received as consideration for the issue of equity instruments are recognised in the financial statements; and

(b) the expense arises from the consumption of those resources, not from an outflow of assets.

BC42 In other words, irrespective of whether one accepts that there is a cost to the entity, an accounting entry is required to recognise the resources received as consideration for the issue of equity instruments, just as it is on other occasions when equity instruments are issued. For example, when shares are issued for cash, an entry is required to recognise the cash received. If a non-monetary asset, such as plant and machinery, is received for those shares instead of cash, an entry is required to recognise the asset received. If the entity acquires another business or entity by issuing shares in a business combination, the entity recognises the net assets acquired.

BC43 The recognition of an expense arising out of such a transaction represents the consumption of resources received, ie the 'using up' of the resources received for the shares or share options. In the case of the plant and machinery mentioned above, the asset would be depreciated over its expected life, resulting in the recognition of an expense each year. Eventually, the entire amount recognised for the resources received when the shares were issued would be recognised as an expense (including any residual value, which would form part of the measurement of the gain or loss on disposal of the asset). Similarly, if another business or entity is acquired by an issue of shares, an expense is recognised when the assets acquired are consumed. For example, inventories acquired will be recognised as an expense when sold, even though no cash or other assets were disbursed to acquire those inventories.

BC44 The only difference in the case of employee services (or other services) received as consideration for the issue of shares or share options is that usually the resources received are consumed immediately upon receipt. This means that an expense for the consumption of resources is recognised immediately, rather than over a period of time. The Board concluded that the timing of consumption does not change the principle; the financial statements should recognise the receipt and consumption of resources, even when consumption occurs at the same time as, or soon after, receipt. This point is discussed further in paragraphs BC45-BC53.

'Expense recognition is inconsistent with the definition of an expense'

Some have questioned whether recognition of an expense arising from particular share-based payment transactions is consistent with accounting standard-setters' conceptual frameworks, in particular, the *Framework*, which states: **BC45**

> Expenses are decreases in economic benefits during the accounting period in the form of outflows or *depletions of assets* or incurrences of liabilities that result in decreases in equity, other than those relating to distributions to equity participants. (paragraph 70, emphasis added)

Some argue that if services are received in a share-based payment transaction, there is no transaction or event that meets the definition of an expense. They contend that there is no outflow of assets and that no liability is incurred. Furthermore, because services usually do not meet the criteria for recognition as an asset, it is argued that the consumption of those services does not represent a depletion of assets. **BC46**

The *Framework* defines an asset and explains that the term 'asset' is not limited to resources that can be recognised as assets in the balance sheet (*Framework*, paragraphs 49 and 50). Although services to be received in the future might not meet the definition of an asset,* services are assets when received. These assets are usually consumed immediately. This is explained in FASB Statement of Financial Accounting Concepts No. 6 *Elements of Financial Statements*: **BC47**

> Services provided by other entities, including personal services, cannot be stored and are received and used simultaneously. They can be assets of an entity only momentarily as the entity receives and uses them although their use may create or add value to other assets of the entity... (paragraph 31)

This applies to all types of services, eg employee services, legal services and telephone services. It also applies irrespective of the form of payment. For example, if an entity purchases services for cash, the accounting entry is: **BC48**

Dr Services received

Cr Cash paid

Sometimes, those services are consumed in the creation of a recognisable asset, such as inventories, in which case the debit for services received is capitalised as part of a recognised asset. But often the services do not create or form part of a recognisable asset, in which case the debit for services received is charged immediately to the income statement as an expense. The debit entry above (and the resulting expense) does not represent the cash outflow that is what the credit entry was for. Nor does it represent some sort of balancing item, to make the accounts balance. The debit entry above represents the resources received, and the resulting expense represents the consumption of those resources. **BC49**

The same analysis applies if the services are acquired with payment made in shares or share options. The resulting expense represents the consumption of services, ie a depletion of assets. **BC50**

**For example, the entity might not have control over future services.*

BC51 To illustrate this point, suppose that an entity has two buildings, both with gas heating, and the entity issues shares to the gas supplier instead of paying cash. Suppose that, for one building, the gas is supplied through a pipeline, and so is consumed immediately upon receipt. Suppose that, for the other building, the gas is supplied in bottles, and is consumed over a period of time. In both cases, the entity has received assets as consideration for the issue of equity instruments, and should therefore recognise the assets received, and a corresponding contribution to equity. If the assets are consumed immediately (the gas received through the pipeline), an expense is recognised immediately; if the assets are consumed later (the gas received in bottles), an expense is recognised later when the assets are consumed.

BC52 Therefore, the Board concluded that the recognition of an expense arising from share-based payment transactions is consistent with the definition of an expense in the *Framework*.

BC53 The FASB considered the same issue and reached the same conclusion in SFAS 123:

> Some respondents pointed out that the definition of expenses in FASB Concepts Statement No. 6, *Elements of Financial Statements*, says that expenses result from outflows or using up of assets or incurring of liabilities (or both). They asserted that because the issuance of stock options does not result in the incurrence of a liability, no expense should be recognised. The Board agrees that employee stock options are not a liability – like stock purchase warrants, employee stock options are equity instruments of the issuer. However, equity instruments, including employee stock options, are valuable financial instruments and thus are issued for valuable consideration, which...for employee stock options is employee services. Using in the entity's operations the benefits embodied in the asset received results in an expense... (Concepts Statement 6, paragraph 81, footnote 43, notes that, in concept most expenses decrease assets. However, if receipt of an asset, such as services, and its use occur virtually simultaneously, the asset often is not recorded.) [paragraph 88]

'Earnings per share is "hit twice"'

BC54 Some argue that any cost arising from share-based payment transactions is already recognised in the dilution of earnings per share (EPS). If an expense were recognised in the income statement, EPS would be 'hit twice'.

BC55 However, the Board noted that this result is appropriate. For example, if the entity paid the employees in cash for their services and the cash was then returned to the entity, as consideration for the issue of share options, the effect on EPS would be the same as issuing those options direct to the employees.

BC56 The dual effect on EPS simply reflects the two economic events that have occurred: the entity has issued shares or share options, thereby increasing the number of shares included in the EPS calculation – although, in the case of options, only to the extent that the options are regarded as dilutive – and it has also consumed the resources it received for those options, thereby decreasing earnings. This is illustrated by the plant and machinery example mentioned in paragraphs BC42 and BC43. Issuing shares affects the number of shares in the EPS calculation, and the consumption (depreciation) of the asset affects earnings.

BC57 In summary, the Board concluded that the dual effect on diluted EPS is not doublecounting the effects of a share or share option grant – the same effect is not counted twice. Rather, two different effects are each counted once.

'Adverse economic consequences'

Some argue that to require recognition (or greater recognition) of employee share-based payment would have adverse economic consequences, in that it might discourage entities from introducing or continuing employee share plans. **BC58**

Others argue that if the introduction of accounting changes did lead to a reduction in the use of employee share plans, it might be because the requirement for entities to account properly for employee share plans had revealed the economic consequences of such plans. They argue that this would correct the present economic distortion, whereby entities obtain and consume resources by issuing valuable shares or share options without accounting for those transactions. **BC59**

In any event, the Board noted that the role of accounting is to report transactions and events in a neutral manner, not to give 'favourable' treatment to particular transactions to encourage entities to engage in those transactions. To do so would impair the quality of financial reporting. The omission of expenses from the financial statements does not change the fact that those expenses have been incurred. Hence, if expenses are omitted from the income statement, reported profits are overstated. The financial statements are not neutral, are less transparent and are potentially misleading to users. Comparability is impaired, given that expenses arising from employee share-based payment transactions vary from entity to entity, from sector to sector, and from year to year. More fundamentally, accountability is impaired, because the entities are not accounting for transactions they have entered into and the consequences of those transactions. **BC60**

MEASUREMENT OF EQUITY-SETTLED SHARE-BASED PAYMENT TRANSACTIONS

To recognise equity-settled share-based payment transactions, it is necessary to decide how the transactions should be measured. The Board began by considering how to measure share-based payment transactions in principle. Later, it considered practical issues arising from the application of its preferred measurement approach. In terms of accounting principles, there are two basic questions: **BC61**

(a) which measurement basis should be applied?
(b) when should that measurement basis be applied?

To answer these questions, the Board considered the accounting principles applying to equity transactions. The *Framework* states: **BC62**

> Equity is the residual interest in the assets of the enterprise after deducting all of its liabilities...The amount at which equity is shown in the balance sheet is dependent upon the measurement of assets and liabilities. Normally, the aggregate amount of equity only by coincidence corresponds with the aggregate market value of the shares of the enterprise... (paragraphs 49 and 67).

The accounting equation that corresponds to this definition of equity is: **BC63**

> assets minus liabilities equals equity

Equity is a residual interest, dependent on the measurement of assets and liabilities. Therefore, accounting focuses on recording changes in the left side of the equation (assets minus liabilities, or net assets), rather than the right side. Changes in equity arise from changes in net assets. For example, if an entity issues shares for cash, it recognises the cash received and a corresponding increase in equity. Subsequent **BC64** changes in the market price of the shares do not affect the entity's net assets and therefore those changes in value are not recognised.

BC65 Hence, the Board concluded that, when accounting for an equity-settled share-based payment transaction, the primary accounting objective is to account for the goods or services received as consideration for the issue of equity instruments. Therefore, equity-settled share-based payment transactions should be accounted for in the same way as other issues of equity instruments, by recognising the consideration received (the change in net assets), and a corresponding increase in equity.

BC66 Given this objective, the Board concluded that, in principle, the goods or services received should be measured at their fair value at the date when the entity obtains those goods or as the services are received. In other words, because a change in net assets occurs when the entity obtains the goods or as the services are received, the fair value of those goods or services at that date provides an appropriate measure of the change in net assets.

BC67 However, for share-based payment transactions with employees, it is usually difficult to measure directly the fair value of the services received. As noted earlier, typically shares or share options are granted to employees as one component of their remuneration package. It is usually not possible to identify the services rendered in respect of individual components of that package. It might also not be possible to measure independently the fair value of the total package, without measuring directly the fair value of the equity instruments granted. Furthermore, options or shares are sometimes granted as part of a bonus arrangement, rather than as a part of basic remuneration, eg as an incentive to the employees to remain in the entity's employ, or to reward them for their efforts in improving the entity's performance. By granting share options, in addition to other remuneration, the entity is paying additional remuneration to obtain additional benefits. Estimating the fair value of those additional benefits is likely to be difficult.

BC68 Given these practical difficulties in measuring directly the fair value of the employee services received, the Board concluded that it is necessary to measure the other side of the transaction, ie the fair value of the equity instruments granted, as a surrogate measure of the fair value of the services received. In this context, the Board considered the same basic questions, as mentioned above:

(a) which measurement basis should be applied?
(b) when should that measurement basis be applied?

Measurement basis

BC69 The Board discussed the following measurement bases, to decide which should be applied in principle:

(a) historical cost
(b) intrinsic value
(c) minimum value
(d) fair value.

Historical cost

BC70 In jurisdictions where legislation permits, entities commonly repurchase their own shares, either directly or through a vehicle such as a trust, which are used to fulfil promised grants of shares to employees or the exercise of employee share options. A possible basis for measuring a grant of options or shares would be the historical cost (purchase price) of its own shares that an entity holds (own shares held), even if they were acquired before the award was made.

For share options, this would entail comparing the historical cost of own shares held with the exercise price of options granted to employees. Any shortfall would be recognised as an expense. Also, presumably, if the exercise price exceeded the historical cost of own shares held, the excess would be recognised as a gain. **BC71**

At first sight, if one simply focuses on the cash flows involved, the historical cost basis appears reasonable: there is a cash outflow to acquire the shares, followed by a cash inflow when those shares are transferred to the employees (the exercise price), with any shortfall representing a cost to the entity. If the cash flows related to anything other than the entity's own shares, this approach would be appropriate. For example, suppose ABC Ltd bought shares in another entity, XYZ Ltd, for a total cost of CU500,000,* and later sold the shares to employees for a total of CU400,000. The entity would recognise an expense for the CU100,000 shortfall. **BC72**

But when this analysis is applied to the entity's own shares, the logic breaks down. The entity's own shares are not an asset of the entity.† Rather, the shares are an interest in the entity's assets. Hence, the distribution of cash to buy back shares is a return of capital to shareholders, and should therefore be recognised as a decrease in equity. Similarly, when the shares are subsequently reissued or transferred, the inflow of cash is an increase in shareholders' capital, and should therefore be recognised as an increase in equity. It follows that no revenue or expense should be recognised. Just as the issue of shares does not represent revenue to the entity, the repurchase of those shares does not represent an expense. **BC73**

Therefore, the Board concluded that historical cost is not an appropriate basis upon which to measure equity-settled share-based payment transactions. **BC74**

Intrinsic value

An equity instrument could be measured at its intrinsic value. The intrinsic value of a share option at any point in time is the difference between the market price of the underlying shares and the exercise price of the option. **BC75**

Often, employee share options have zero intrinsic value at the date of grant – commonly the exercise price is at the market value of the shares at grant date. Therefore, in many cases, valuing share options at their intrinsic value at grant date is equivalent to attributing no value to the options. **BC76**

**All monetary amounts in this Basis for Conclusions are denominated in 'currency units' (CU).*

†*The Discussion Paper discusses this point:*

> *Accounting practice in some jurisdictions may present own shares acquired as an asset, but they lack the essential feature of an asset – the ability to provide future economic benefits. The future economic benefits usually provided by an interest in shares are the right to receive dividends and the right to gain from an increase in value of the shares. When a company has an interest in its own shares, it will receive dividends on those shares only if it elects to pay them, and such dividends do not represent a gain to the company, as there is no change in net assets: the flow of funds is simply circular. Whilst it is true that a company that holds its own shares in treasury may sell them and receive a higher amount if their value has increased, a company is generally able to issue shares to third parties at (or near) the current market price. Although there may be legal, regulatory or administrative reasons why it is easier to sell shares that are held as treasury shares than it would be to issue new shares, such considerations do not seem to amount to a fundamental contrast between the two cases. (Footnote to paragraph 4.7)*

BC77 However, the intrinsic value of an option does not fully reflect its value. Options sell in the market for more than their intrinsic value. This is because the holder of an option need not exercise it immediately and benefits from any increase in the value of the underlying shares. In other words, although the ultimate benefit realised by the option holder is the option's intrinsic value at the date of exercise, the option holder is able to realise that future intrinsic value because of having held the option. Thus, the option holder benefits from the right to participate in future gains from increases in the share price. In addition, the option holder benefits from the right to defer payment of the exercise price until the end of the option term. These benefits are commonly referred to as the option's 'time value'.

BC78 For many options, time value represents a substantial part of their value. As noted earlier, many employee share options have zero intrinsic value at grant date, and hence the option's value consists entirely of time value. In such cases, ignoring time value by applying the intrinsic value method at grant date understates the value of the option by 100 per cent.

BC79 The Board concluded that, in general, the intrinsic value measurement basis is not appropriate for measuring share-based payment transactions, because omitting the option's time value ignores a potentially substantial part of an option's total value. Measuring share-based payment transactions at such an understated value would fail to represent those transactions faithfully in the financial statements.

Minimum value

BC80 A share option could be measured at its minimum value. Minimum value is based on the premise that someone who wants to buy a call option on a share would be willing to pay at least (and the option writer would demand at least) the value of the right to defer payment of the exercise price until the end of the option's term. Therefore, minimum value can be calculated using a present value technique. For a dividend-paying share, the calculation is:

(a) the current price of the share, minus
(b) the present value of expected dividends on that share during the option term (if the option holder does not receive dividends), minus
(c) the present value of the exercise price.

BC81 Minimum value can also be calculated using an option pricing model with an expected volatility of effectively zero (not exactly zero, because some option pricing models use volatility as a divisor, and zero cannot be a divisor).

BC82 The minimum value measurement basis captures part of the time value of options, being the value of the right to defer payment of the exercise price until the end of the option's term. It does not capture the effects of volatility. Option holders benefit from volatility because they have the right to participate in gains from increases in the share price during the option term without having to bear the full risk of loss from decreases in the share price. By ignoring volatility, the minimum value method produces a value that is lower, and often much lower, than values produced by methods designed to estimate the fair value of an option.

BC83 The Board concluded that minimum value is not an appropriate measurement basis, because ignoring the effects of volatility ignores a potentially large part of an option's value. As with intrinsic value, measuring share-based payment transactions at the option's minimum value would fail to represent those transactions faithfully in the financial statements.

Fair value

Fair value is already used in other areas of accounting, including other transactions in which non-cash resources are acquired through the issue of equity instruments. For example, consideration transferred in a business combination* is measured at fair value, including the fair value of any equity instruments issued by the entity. **BC84**

Fair value, which is the amount at which an equity instrument granted could be exchanged between knowledgeable, willing parties in an arm's length transaction, captures both intrinsic value and time value and therefore provides a measure of the share option's total value (unlike intrinsic value or minimum value). It is the value that reflects the bargain between the entity and its employees, whereby the entity has agreed to grant share options to employees for their services to the entity. Hence, measuring share-based payment transactions at fair value ensures that those transactions are represented faithfully in the financial statements, and consistently with other transactions in which the entity receives resources as consideration for the issue of equity instruments. **BC85**

Therefore, the Board concluded that shares, share options or other equity instruments granted should be measured at their fair value. **BC86**

Of the respondents to ED 2 who addressed this issue, many agreed with the proposal to measure the equity instruments granted at their fair value. Some respondents who disagreed with the proposal, or who agreed with reservations, expressed concerns about measurement reliability, particularly in the case of smaller or unlisted entities. The issues of measurement reliability and unlisted entities are discussed in paragraphs BC294-BC310 and BC137-BC144, respectively. **BC87**

Measurement date

The Board first considered at which date the fair value of equity instruments should be determined for the purpose of measuring share-based payment transactions with employees (and others providing similar services).† The possible measurement dates discussed were grant date, service date, vesting date and exercise date. Much of this discussion was in the context of share options rather than shares or other equity instruments, because only options have an exercise date. **BC88**

In the context of an employee share option, grant date is when the entity and the employee enter into an agreement, whereby the employee is granted rights to the share option, provided that specified conditions are met, such as the employee's **BC89**

ASB footnote*: *FRS 6 'Acquisition and Mergers' permits the use of merger accounting. Where merger accounting is applied, the carrying values of the assets and liabilities of the parties to the combination are not required to be adjusted to fair value on consolidation.* ***Editor's note**: Paragraph BC84 amended in December 2008.*

†*When the Board developed the proposals in ED 2, it focused on the measurement of equity-settled transactions with employees and with parties other than employees. ED 2 did not propose a definition of the term 'employees'. When the Board reconsidered the proposals in ED 2 in the light of comments received, it discussed whether the term might be interpreted too narrowly. This could result in a different accounting treatment of services received from individuals who are regarded as employees (eg for legal or tax purposes) and substantially similar services received from other individuals. The Board therefore concluded that the requirements of the IFRS for transactions with employees should also apply to transactions with other parties providing similar services. This includes services received from (1) individuals who work for the entity under its direction in the same way as individuals who are regarded as employees for legal or tax purposes and (2) individuals who are not employees but who render personal services to the entity similar to those rendered by employees. All references to employees therefore include other parties providing similar services.*

remaining in the entity's employ for a specified period. Service date is the date when the employee renders the services necessary to become entitled to the share option.* Vesting date is the date when the employee has satisfied all the conditions necessary to become entitled to the share option. For example, if the employee is required to remain in the entity's employ for three years, vesting date is at the end of that threeyear period. Exercise date is when the share option is exercised.

BC90 To help determine the appropriate measurement date, the Board applied the accounting concepts in the *Framework* to each side of the transaction. For transactions with employees, the Board concluded that grant date is the appropriate measurement date, as explained in paragraphs BC91-BC105. The Board also considered some other issues, as explained in paragraphs BC106-BC118. For transactions with parties other than employees, the Board concluded that delivery date is the appropriate measurement date (ie the date the goods or services are received, referred to as service date in the context of transactions with employees), as explained in paragraphs BC119-BC128.

The debit side of the transaction

BC91 Focusing on the debit side of the transaction means focusing on measuring the fair value of the resources received. This measurement objective is consistent with the primary objective of accounting for the goods or services received as consideration for the issue of equity instruments (see paragraphs BC64-BC66). The Board therefore concluded that, in principle, the goods or services received should be measured at their fair value at the date when the entity obtains those goods or as the services are received.

BC92 However, if the fair value of the services received is not readily determinable, then a surrogate measure must be used, such as the fair value of the share options or shares granted. This is the case for employee services.

BC93 If the fair value of the equity instruments granted is used as a surrogate measure of the fair value of the services received, both vesting date and exercise date measurement are inappropriate because the fair value of the services received during a particular accounting period is not affected by subsequent changes in the fair value of the equity instrument. For example, suppose that services are received during years 13 as the consideration for share options that are exercised at the end of year 5. For services received in year 1, subsequent changes in the value of the share option in years 25 are unrelated to, and have no effect on, the fair value of those services when received.

BC94 Service date measurement measures the fair value of the equity instrument at the same time as the services are received. This means that changes in the fair value of the equity instrument during the vesting period affect the amount attributed to the services received. Some argue that this is appropriate, because, in their view, there is a correlation between changes in the fair value of the equity instrument and the fair value of the services received. For example, they argue that if the fair value of a share option falls, so does its incentive effects, which causes employees to reduce the level of services provided for that option, or demand extra remuneration. Some argue that when the fair value of a share option falls because of a general decline in share prices,

**Service date measurement theoretically requires the entity to measure the fair value of the share option at each date when services are received. For pragmatic reasons, an approximation would probably be used, such as the fair value of the share option at the end of each accounting period, or the value of the share option measured at regular intervals during each accounting period.*

remuneration levels also fall, and therefore service date measurement reflects this decline in remuneration levels.

The Board concluded, however, that there is unlikely to be a high correlation between changes in the fair value of an equity instrument and the fair value of the services received. For example, if the fair value of a share option doubles, it is unlikely that the employees work twice as hard, or accept a reduction in the rest of their remuneration package. Similarly, even if a general rise in share prices is accompanied by a rise in remuneration levels, it is unlikely that there is a high correlation between the two. Furthermore, it is likely that any link between share prices and remuneration levels is not universally applicable to all industry sectors. **BC95**

The Board concluded that, at grant date, it is reasonable to presume that the fair value of both sides of the contract are substantially the same, ie the fair value of the services expected to be received is substantially the same as the fair value of the equity instruments granted. This conclusion, together with the Board's conclusion that there is unlikely to be a high correlation between the fair value of the services received and the fair value of the equity instruments granted at later measurement dates, led the Board to conclude that grant date is the most appropriate measurement date for the purposes of providing a surrogate measure of the fair value of the services received. **BC96**

The credit side of the transaction

Although focusing on the debit side of the transaction is consistent with the primary accounting objective, some approach the measurement date question from the perspective of the credit side of the transaction, ie the issue of an equity instrument. The Board therefore considered the matter from this perspective too. **BC97**

Exercise date

Under exercise date measurement, the entity recognises the resources received (eg employee services) for the issue of share options, and also recognises changes in the fair value of the option until it is exercised or lapses. Thus, if the option is exercised, the transaction amount is ultimately 'trued up' to equal the gain made by the option holder on exercise of the option. However, if the option lapses at the end of the exercise period, any amounts previously recognised are effectively reversed, hence the transaction amount is ultimately trued up to equal zero. The Board rejected exercise date measurement because it requires share options to be treated as liabilities, which is inconsistent with the definition of liabilities in the *Framework*. Exercise date measurement requires share options to be treated as liabilities because it requires the remeasurement of share options after initial recognition, which is inappropriate if the share options are equity instruments. A share option does not meet the definition of a liability, because it does not contain an obligation to transfer cash or other assets. **BC98**

Vesting date, service date and grant date

The Board noted that the IASC/G4+1 Discussion Paper supported vesting date measurement, and rejected grant date and service date measurement, because it concluded that the share option is not issued until vesting date. It noted that the employees must perform their side of the arrangement by providing the necessary services and meeting any other performance criteria before the entity is obliged to perform its side of the arrangement. The provision of services by the employees is not merely a condition of the arrangement, it is the consideration they use to 'pay' for the **BC99** share option. Therefore, the Discussion Paper concluded, in economic terms the share option is not issued until vesting date. Because the entity performs its side of the arrangement on vesting date, that is the appropriate measurement date.

BC100 The Discussion Paper also proposed recognising an accrual in equity during the vesting period to ensure that the services are recognised when they are received. It proposed that this accrual should be revised on vesting date to equal the fair value of the share option at that date. This means that amounts credited to equity during the vesting period will be subsequently remeasured to reflect changes in the value of that equity interest before vesting date. That is inconsistent with the *Framework* because equity interests are not subsequently remeasured, ie any changes in their value are not recognised. The Discussion Paper justified this remeasurement by arguing that because the share option is not issued until vesting date, the option is not being remeasured. The credit to equity during the vesting period is merely an interim measure that is used to recognise the partially completed transaction.

BC101 However, the Board noted that even if one accepts that the share option is not issued until vesting date, this does not mean that there is no equity interest until then. If an equity interest exists before vesting date, that interest should not be remeasured. Moreover, the conversion of one type of equity interest into another should not, in itself, cause a change in total equity, because no change in net assets has occurred.

BC102 Some supporters of vesting date suggest that the accrual during the performance period meets the definition of a liability. However, the basis for this conclusion is unclear. The entity is not required to transfer cash or other assets to the employees. Its only commitment is to issue equity instruments.

BC103 The Board concluded that vesting date measurement is inconsistent with the *Framework*, because it requires the remeasurement of equity.

BC104 Service date measurement does not require remeasurement of equity interests after initial recognition. However, as explained earlier, the Board concluded that incorporating changes in the fair value of the share option into the transaction amount is unlikely to produce an amount that fairly reflects the fair value of the services received, which is the primary objective.

BC105 The Board therefore concluded that, no matter which side of the transaction one focuses upon (ie the receipt of resources or the issue of an equity instrument), grant date is the appropriate measurement date under the *Framework*, because it does not require remeasurement of equity interests and it provides a reasonable surrogate measure of the fair value of the services received from employees.

Other issues

IAS 32 Financial Instruments: Disclosure and Presentation*

BC106 As discussed above, under the definitions of liabilities and equity in the *Framework*, both shares and share options are equity instruments, because neither instrument requires the entity to transfer cash or other assets. Similarly, all contracts or arrangements that will be settled by the entity issuing shares or share options are classified as equity. However, this differs from the distinction between liabilities and equity applied in IAS 32. Although IAS 32 also considers, in its debt/equity

***Editor's note**: *IAS 32 now deals only with the presentation of financial instruments. Disclosure is now covered by IFRS 7.*

distinction, whether an instrument contains an obligation to transfer cash or other assets, this is supplemented by a second criterion, which considers whether the number of shares to be issued (and cash to be received) on settlement is fixed or variable. IAS 32 classifies a contract that will or may be settled in the entity's own equity instruments as a liability if the contract is a non-derivative for which the entity is or may be obliged to deliver a variable number of the entity's own equity instruments; or a derivative that will or may be settled other than by the exchange of a fixed amount of cash or another financial asset for a fixed number of the entity's own equity instruments.

In some cases, the number of share options to which employees are entitled varies. For example, the number of share options to which the employees will be entitled on vesting date might vary depending on whether, and to the extent that, a particular performance target is exceeded. Another example is share appreciation rights settled in shares. In this situation, a variable number of shares will be issued, equal in value to the appreciation of the entity's share price over a period of time. **BC107**

Therefore, if the requirements of IAS 32 were applied to equity-settled share-based payment transactions, in some situations an obligation to issue equity instruments would be classified as a liability. In such cases, final measurement of the transaction would be at a measurement date later than grant date. **BC108**

The Board concluded that different considerations applied in developing IFRS 2. For example, drawing a distinction between fixed and variable option plans and requiring a later measurement date for variable option plans has undesirable consequences, as discussed in paragraphs BC272-BC275. **BC109**

The Board concluded that the requirements in IAS 32, whereby some obligations to issue equity instruments are classified as liabilities, should not be applied in the IFRS on share-based payment. The Board recognises that this creates a difference between IFRS 2 and IAS 32. Before deciding whether and how that difference should be eliminated, the Board concluded that it is necessary to address this issue in a broader context, as part of a fundamental review of the definitions of liabilities and equity in the *Framework*, particularly because this is not the only debt/ equity classification issue that has arisen in the share-based payment project, as explained below. **BC110**

Suggestions to change the definitions of liabilities and equity

In concluding that, for transactions with employees, grant date is the appropriate measurement date under the *Framework*, the Board noted that some respondents to ED 2 and the Discussion Paper support other measurement dates because they believe that the definitions of liabilities and equity in the *Framework* should be revised. **BC111**

For example, some supporters of vesting date argue that receipt of employee services between grant date and vesting date creates an obligation for the entity to pay for those services, and that the method of settlement should not matter. In other words, it should not matter whether that obligation is settled in cash or in equity instruments – both ought to be treated as liabilities. Therefore, the definition of a liability should be modified so that all types of obligations, however settled, are included in liabilities. But it is not clear that this approach would necessarily result in vesting date measurement. A share option contains an obligation to issue shares. Hence, if all types of obligations are classified as liabilities, then a share option would be a liability, which would result in exercise date measurement. **BC112**

BC113 Some support exercise date measurement on the grounds that it produces the same accounting result as 'economically similar' cash-settled share-based payments. For example, it is argued that share appreciation rights (SARs) settled in cash are substantially similar to SARs settled in shares, because in both cases the employee receives consideration to the same value. Also, if the SARs are settled in shares and the shares are immediately sold, the employee ends up in exactly the same position as under a cash-settled SAR, ie with cash equal to the appreciation in the entity's share price over the specified period. Similarly, some argue that share options and cash-settled SARs are economically similar. This is particularly true when the employee realises the gain on the exercise of share options by selling the shares immediately after exercise, as commonly occurs. Either way, the employee ends up with an amount of cash that is based on the appreciation of the share price over a period of time. If cash-settled transactions and equity-settled transactions are economically similar, the accounting treatment should be the same.

BC114 However, it is not clear that changing the distinction between liabilities and equity to be consistent with exercise date measurement is the only way to achieve the same accounting treatment. For example, the distinction could be changed so that cash-settled employee share plans are measured at grant date, with the subsequent cash payment debited directly to equity, as a distribution to equity participants.

BC115 Others who support exercise date measurement do not regard share option holders as part of the ownership group, and therefore believe that options should not be classified as equity. Option holders, some argue, are only potential owners of the entity. But it is not clear whether this view is held generally, ie applied to all types of options. For example, some who support exercise date measurement for employee share options do not necessarily advocate the same approach for share options or warrants issued for cash in the market. However, any revision to the definitions of liabilities and equity in the *Framework* would affect the classification of all options and warrants issued by the entity.

BC116 Given that there is more than one suggestion to change the definitions of liabilities and equity, and these suggestions have not been fully explored, it is not clear exactly what changes to the definitions are being proposed.

BC117 Moreover, the Board concluded that these suggestions should not be considered in isolation, because changing the distinction between liabilities and equity affects all sorts of financial interests, not just those relating to employee share plans. All of the implications of any suggested changes should be explored in a broader project to review the definitions of liabilities and equity in the *Framework*. If such a review resulted in changes to the definitions, the Board would then consider whether the IFRS on share-based payment should be revised.

BC118 Therefore, after considering the issues discussed above, the Board confirmed its conclusion that grant date is the appropriate date at which to measure the fair value of the equity instruments granted for the purposes of providing a surrogate measure of the fair value of services received from employees.

Share-based payment transactions with parties other than employees

BC119 In many share-based payment transactions with parties other than employees, it should be possible to measure reliably the fair value of the goods or services received. The Board therefore concluded that the IFRS should require an entity to presume that the fair value of the goods or services received can be measured reliably.* However, in rare cases in which the presumption is rebutted, it is necessary to measure the transaction at the fair value of the equity instruments granted.

Some measurement issues that arise in respect of share-based payment transactions with employees also arise in transactions with other parties. For example, there might be performance (ie vesting) conditions that must be met before the other party is entitled to the shares or share options. Therefore, any conclusions reached on how to treat vesting conditions in the context of share-based payment transactions with employees also apply to transactions with other parties. **BC120**

Similarly, performance by the other party might take place over a period of time, rather than on one specific date, which again raises the question of the appropriate measurement date. **BC121**

SFAS 123 does not specify a measurement date for share-based payment transactions with parties other than employees, on the grounds that this is usually a minor issue in such transactions. However, the date at which to estimate the fair value of equity instruments issued to parties other than employees is specified in the US interpretation EITF 9618 *Accounting for Equity Instruments That Are Issued to Other Than Employees for Acquiring, or in Conjunction with Selling, Goods or Services*: **BC122**

> [The measurement date is] the earlier of the following:
>
> 1. The date at which a commitment for performance by the counterparty to earn the equity instruments is reached (a "performance commitment"), or
>
> 2. The date at which the counterparty's performance is complete. (extract from Issue 1, footnotes excluded)

The second of these two dates corresponds to vesting date, because vesting date is when the other party has satisfied all the conditions necessary to become unconditionally entitled to the share options or shares. The first of the two dates does not necessarily correspond to grant date. For example, under an employee share plan, the employees are (usually) not committed to providing the necessary services, because they are usually able to leave at any time. Indeed, EITF 9618 makes it clear that the fact that the equity instrument will be forfeited if the counterparty fails to perform is not sufficient evidence of a performance commitment (Issue 1, footnote 3). Therefore, in the context of share-based payment transactions with parties other than employees, if the other party is not committed to perform, there would be no performance commitment date, in which case the measurement date would be vesting date. **BC123**

**ED 2 proposed that equity-settled share-based payment transactions should be measured at the fair value of the goods or services received, or by reference to the fair value of the equity instruments granted, whichever fair value is more readily determinable. For transactions with parties other than employees, ED 2 proposed that there should be a rebuttable presumption that the fair value of the goods or services received is the more readily determinable fair value. The Board reconsidered these proposed requirements when finalising the IFRS. It concluded that it would be more consistent with the primary accounting objective (explained in paragraphs BC64-BC66) to require equity-settled share-based payment transactions to be measured at the fair value of the goods or services received, unless that fair value cannot be estimated reliably (eg in transactions with employees). For transactions with parties other than employees, the Board concluded that, in many cases, it should be possible to measure reliably the fair value of the goods or services received, as noted above. Hence, the Board concluded that the IFRS should require an entity to presume that the fair value of the goods or services received can be measured reliably.*

BC124 Accordingly, under SFAS 123 and EITF 9618, the measurement date for share-based payment transactions with employees is grant date, but for transactions with other parties the measurement date could be vesting date, or some other date between grant date and vesting date.

BC125 In developing the proposals in ED 2, the Board concluded that for transactions with parties other than employees that are measured by reference to the fair value of the equity instruments granted, the equity instruments should be measured at grant date, the same as for transactions with employees.

BC126 However, the Board reconsidered this conclusion during its redeliberations of the proposals in ED 2. The Board considered whether the delivery (service) date fair value of the equity instruments granted provided a better surrogate measure of the fair value of the goods or services received from parties other than employees than the grant date fair value of those instruments. For example, some argue that if the counterparty is not firmly committed to delivering the goods or services, the counterparty would consider whether the fair value of the equity instruments at the delivery date is sufficient payment for the goods or services when deciding whether to deliver the goods or services. This suggests that there is a high correlation between the fair value of the equity instruments at the date the goods or services are received and the fair value of those goods or services. The Board noted that it had considered and rejected a similar argument in the context of transactions with employees (see paragraphs BC94 and BC95). However, the Board found the argument more compelling in the case of transactions with parties other than employees, particularly for transactions in which the counterparty delivers the goods or services on a single date (or over a short period of time) that is substantially later than grant date, compared with transactions with employees in which the services are received over a continuous period that typically begins on grant date.

BC127 The Board was also concerned that permitting entities to measure transactions with parties other than employees on the basis of the fair value of the equity instruments at grant date would provide opportunities for entities to structure transactions to achieve a particular accounting result, causing the carrying amount of the goods or services received, and the resulting expense for the consumption of those goods or services, to be understated.

BC128 The Board therefore concluded that for transactions with parties other than employees in which the entity cannot measure reliably the fair value of the goods or services received at the date of receipt, the fair value of those goods or services should be measured indirectly, based on the fair value of the equity instruments granted, measured at the date the goods or services are received.

Transactions in which the entity cannot identify specifically some or all of the goods or services received (paragraph 13A)*

BC128A The Board incorporated into IFRS 2 the consensus of IFRIC 8 in *Group Cash-settled Share-based Payment Transactions* issued in June 2009. This section summarises the IFRIC's considerations in reaching that consensus, as approved by the Board.

BC128B IFRS 2 presumes that the consideration received for share-based payments is consistent with the fair value of those share-based payments. For example, if the entity cannot estimate reliably the fair value of the goods or services received, paragraph 10

**Paragraphs BC128A–BC128H are added as a consequence of amendments to IFRS 2* Group Cash-settled Share-based Payment Transactions *issued in June 2009.*

of the IFRS requires the entity to measure the fair value of the goods or services received by reference to the fair value of the share-based payment made to acquire those goods or services.

The Board noted that it is neither necessary nor appropriate to measure the fair value of goods or services as well as the fair value of the share-based payment for every transaction in which the entity receives goods or non-employee services. However, when the value of the identifiable consideration received appears to be less than the fair value of the share-based payment, measurement of both the goods or the services received and the share-based payment may be necessary in order to measure the value of the unidentifiable goods or services received. **BC128C**

Paragraph 13 of the IFRS stipulates a rebuttable presumption that the value of identifiable goods or services received can be reliably measured. The Board noted that goods or services that are unidentifiable cannot be reliably measured and that this rebuttable presumption is relevant only for identifiable goods or services. **BC128D**

The Board noted that when the goods or services received are identifiable, the measurement principles in the IFRS should be applied. When the goods or services received are unidentifiable, the Board concluded that the grant date is the most appropriate date for the purposes of providing a surrogate measure of the value of the unidentifiable goods or services received (or to be received). **BC128E**

The Board noted that some transactions include identifiable and unidentifiable goods or services. In this case, it would be necessary to measure at the grant date the fair value of the unidentifiable goods or services received and to measure the value of the identifiable goods or services in accordance with the IFRS. **BC128F**

For cash-settled transactions in which unidentifiable goods or services are received, it is necessary to remeasure the liability at each subsequent reporting date in order to be consistent with the IFRS. **BC128G**

The Board noted that the IFRS's requirements in respect of the recognition of the expense arising from share-based payments would apply to identifiable and unidentifiable goods or services. Therefore, the Board decided not to issue additional guidance on this point. **BC128H**

FAIR VALUE OF EMPLOYEE SHARE OPTIONS

The Board spent much time discussing how to measure the fair value of employee share options, including how to take into account common features of employee share options, such as vesting conditions and non-transferability. These discussions focused on measuring fair value at grant date, not only because the Board regarded grant date as the appropriate measurement date for transactions with employees, but also because more measurement issues arise at grant date than at later measurement dates. In reaching its conclusions in ED 2, the Board received assistance from the project's Advisory Group and from a panel of experts. During its redeliberations of the proposals in ED 2, the Board considered comments by respondents and advice received from valuation experts on the FASB's Option Valuation Group. **BC129**

Market prices provide the best evidence of the fair value of share options. However, share options with terms and conditions similar to employee share options are seldom traded in the markets. The Board therefore concluded that, if market prices are not available, it will be necessary to apply an option pricing model to estimate the fair value of share options. **BC130**

BC131 The Board decided that it is not necessary or appropriate to prescribe the precise formula or model to be used for option valuation. There is no particular option pricing model that is regarded as theoretically superior to the others, and there is the risk that any model specified might be superseded by improved methodologies in the future. Entities should select whichever model is most appropriate in the circumstances. For example, many employee share options have long lives, are usually exercisable during the period between vesting date and the end of the option's life, and are often exercised early. These factors should be considered when estimating the grant date fair value of share options. For many entities, this might preclude the use of the Black-Scholes-Merton formula, which does not take into account the possibility of exercise before the end of the share option's life and may not adequately reflect the effects of expected early exercise. This is discussed further below (paragraphs BC160-BC162).

BC132 All option pricing models take into account the following option features:

- the exercise price of the option
- the current market price of the share
- the expected volatility of the share price
- the dividends expected to be paid on the shares
- the rate of interest available in the market
- the term of the option.

BC133 The first two items define the intrinsic value of a share option; the remaining four are relevant to the share option's time value. Expected volatility, dividends and interest rate are all based on expectations over the option term. Therefore, the option term is an important part of calculating time value, because it affects the other inputs.

BC134 One aspect of time value is the value of the right to participate in future gains, if any. The valuation does not attempt to predict what the future gain will be, only the amount that a buyer would pay at the valuation date to obtain the right to participate in any future gains. In other words, option pricing models estimate the value of the share option at the measurement date, not the value of the underlying share at some future date.

BC135 The Board noted that some argue that any estimate of the fair value of a share option is inherently uncertain, because it is not known what the ultimate outcome will be, eg whether the share option will expire worthless or whether the employee (or other party) will make a large gain on exercise. However, the valuation objective is to measure the fair value of the rights granted, not to predict the outcome of having granted those rights. Hence, irrespective of whether the option expires worthless or the employee makes a large gain on exercise, that outcome does not mean that the grant date estimate of the fair value of the option was unreliable or wrong.

BC136 A similar analysis applies to the argument that share options do not have any value until they are in the money, ie the share price is greater than the exercise price. This argument refers to the share option's intrinsic value only. Share options also have a time value, which is why they are traded in the markets at prices greater than their intrinsic value. The option holder has a valuable right to participate in any future increases in the share price. So even share options that are at the money have a value when granted. The subsequent outcome of that option grant, even if it expires worthless, does not change the fact that the share option had a value at grant date.

Application of option pricing models to unlisted and newly listed entities

As explained above, two of the inputs to an option pricing model are the entity's share price and the expected volatility of its share price. For an unlisted entity, there is no published share price information. The entity would therefore need to estimate the fair value of its shares (eg based on the share price of similar entities that are listed, or on a net assets or earnings basis). It would also need to estimate the expected volatility of that value. **BC137**

The Board considered whether unlisted entities should be permitted to use the minimum value method instead of a fair value measurement method. The minimum value method is explained earlier, in paragraphs BC80-BC83. Because it excludes the effects of expected volatility, the minimum value method produces a value that is lower, often much lower, than that produced by methods designed to estimate the fair value of an option. Therefore, the Board discussed how an unlisted entity could estimate expected volatility. **BC138**

An unlisted entity that regularly issues share options or shares to employees (or other parties) might have an internal market for its shares. The volatility of the internal market share prices provides a basis for estimating expected volatility. Alternatively, an entity could use the historical or implied volatility of similar entities that are listed, and for which share price or option price information is available, as the basis for an estimate of expected volatility. This would be appropriate if the entity has estimated the value of its shares by reference to the share prices of these similar listed entities. If the entity has instead used another methodology to value its shares, the entity could derive an estimate of expected volatility consistent with that methodology. For example, the entity might value its shares on the basis of net asset values or earnings, in which case it could use the expected volatility of those net asset values or earnings as a basis for estimating expected share price volatility. **BC139**

The Board acknowledged that these approaches for estimating the expected volatility of an unlisted entity's shares are somewhat subjective. However, the Board thought it likely that, in practice, the application of these approaches would result in underestimates of expected volatility, rather than overestimates, because entities were likely to exercise caution in making such estimates, to ensure that the resulting option values are not overstated. Therefore, estimating expected volatility is likely to produce a more reliable measure of the fair value of share options granted by unlisted entities than an alternative valuation method, such as the minimum value method. **BC140**

Newly listed entities would not need to estimate their share price. However, like unlisted entities, newly listed entities could have difficulties in estimating expected volatility when valuing share options, because they might not have sufficient historical share price information upon which to base an estimate of expected volatility. **BC141**

SFAS 123 requires such entities to consider the historical volatility of similar entities during a comparable period in their lives: **BC142**

> For example, an entity that has been publicly traded for only one year that grants options with an average expected life of five years might consider the pattern and level of historical volatility of more mature entities in the same industry for the first six years the stock of those entities were publicly traded. (paragraph 285b)

The Board concluded that, in general, unlisted and newly listed entities should not be exempt from a requirement to apply fair value measurement and that the IFRS **BC143** should include implementation guidance on estimating expected volatility for the purposes of applying an option pricing model to share options granted by unlisted and newly listed entities.

BC144 However, the Board acknowledged that there might be some instances in which an entity – such as (but not limited to) an unlisted or newly listed entity – cannot estimate reliably the grant date fair value of share options granted. In this situation, the Board concluded that the entity should measure the share option at its intrinsic value, initially at the date the entity obtains the goods or the counterparty renders service and subsequently at each reporting date until the final settlement of the share-based payment arrangement, with the effects of the remeasurement recognised in profit or loss. For a grant of share options, the share-based payment arrangement is finally settled when the options are exercised, forfeited (eg upon cessation of employment) or lapse (eg at the end of the option's life). For a grant of shares, the share-based payment arrangement is finally settled when the shares vest or are forfeited.

Application of option pricing models to employee share options

BC145 Option pricing models are widely used in, and accepted by, the financial markets. However, there are differences between employee share options and traded share options. The Board considered the valuation implications of these differences, with assistance from its Advisory Group and other experts, including experts in the FASB's Option Valuation Group, and comments made by respondents to ED 2. Employee share options usually differ from traded options in the following ways, which are discussed further below:

(a) there is a vesting period, during which time the share options are not exercisable;

(b) the options are non-transferable;

(c) there are conditions attached to vesting which, if not satisfied, cause the options to be forfeited; and

(d) the option term is significantly longer.

Inability to exercise during the vesting period

BC146 Typically, employee share options have a vesting period, during which the options cannot be exercised. For example, a share option might be granted with a tenyear life and a vesting period of three years, so the option is not exercisable for the first three years and can then be exercised at any time during the remaining seven years. Employee share options cannot be exercised during the vesting period because the employees must first 'pay' for the options, by providing the necessary services. Furthermore, there might be other specified periods during which an employee share option cannot be exercised (eg during a closed period).

BC147 In the finance literature, employee share options are sometimes called Bermudian options, being partly European and partly American. An American share option can be exercised at any time during the option's life, whereas a European share option can be exercised only at the end of the option's life. An American share option is more valuable than a European share option, although the difference in value is not usually significant.

BC148 Therefore, other things being equal, an employee share option would have a higher value than a European share option and a lower value than an American share option, but the difference between the three values is unlikely to be significant.

If the entity uses the Black-Scholes-Merton formula, or another option pricing model that values European share options, there is no need to adjust the model for the inability to exercise an option in the vesting period (or any other period), because the model already assumes that the option cannot be exercised during that period. **BC149**

If the entity uses an option pricing model that values American share options, such as the binomial model, the inability to exercise an option during the vesting period can be taken into account in applying such a model. **BC150**

Although the inability to exercise the share option during the vesting period does not, in itself, have a significant effect on the value of the option, there is still the question whether this restriction has an effect when combined with non-transferability. This is discussed in the following section. **BC151**

The Board therefore concluded that: **BC152**

(a) if the entity uses an option pricing model that values European share options, such as the Black-Scholes-Merton formula, no adjustment is required for the inability to exercise the options during the vesting period, because the model already assumes that they cannot be exercised during that period.
(b) if the entity uses an option pricing model that values American share options, such as a binomial model, the application of the model should take account of the inability to exercise the options during the vesting period.

Non-transferability

From the option holder's perspective, the inability to transfer a share option limits the opportunities available when the option has some time yet to run and the holder wishes either to terminate the exposure to future price changes or to liquidate the position. For example, the holder might believe that over the remaining term of the share option the share price is more likely to decrease than to increase. Also, employee share option plans typically require employees to exercise vested options within a fixed period of time after the employee leaves the entity, or to forfeit the options. **BC153**

In the case of a conventional share option, the holder would sell the option rather than exercise it and then sell the shares. Selling the share option enables the holder to receive the option's fair value, including both its intrinsic value and remaining time value, whereas exercising the option enables the holder to receive intrinsic value only. **BC154**

However, the option holder is not able to sell a non-transferable share option. Usually, the only possibility open to the option holder is to exercise it, which entails forgoing the remaining time value. (This is not always true. The use of other derivatives, in effect, to sell or gain protection from future changes in the value of the option is discussed later.) **BC155**

At first sight, the inability to transfer a share option could seem irrelevant from the entity's perspective, because the entity must issue shares at the exercise price upon exercise of the option, no matter who holds it. In other words, from the entity's perspective, its commitments under the contract are unaffected by whether the shares are issued to the original option holder or to someone else. Therefore, in valuing the entity's side of the contract, from the entity's perspective, non-transferability seems irrelevant. **BC156**

However, the lack of transferability often results in early exercise of the share option, because that is the only way for the employees to liquidate their position. Therefore, **BC157** by imposing the restriction on transferability, the entity has caused the option holder to exercise the option early, thereby resulting in the loss of time value. For example, one aspect of time value is the value of the right to defer payment of the exercise price until the end of the option term. If the option is exercised early because of non-transferability, the entity receives the exercise price much earlier than it would otherwise have done.

BC158 Non-transferability is not the only reason why employees might exercise share options early. Other reasons include risk aversion, lack of wealth diversification, and termination of employment (typically, employees must exercise vested options soon after termination of employment; otherwise the options are forfeited).

BC159 Recent accounting standards and proposed standards (including ED 2) address the issue of early exercise by requiring the expected life of a non-transferable share option to be used in valuing it, rather than the contractual option term. Expected life can be estimated either for the entire share option plan or for subgroups of employees participating in the plan. The estimate takes into account factors such as the length of the vesting period, the average length of time similar options have remained outstanding in the past and the expected volatility of the underlying shares.

BC160 However, comments from respondents to ED 2 and advice received from valuation experts during the Board's redeliberations led the Board to conclude that using a single expected life as an input into an option pricing model (eg the Black-Scholes-Merton formula) was not the best solution for reflecting in the share option valuation the effects of early exercise. For example, such an approach does not take into account the correlation between the share price and early exercise. It would also mean that the share option valuation does not take into account the possibility that the option might be exercised at a date that is later than the end of its expected life. Therefore, in many instances, a more flexible model, such as a binomial model, that uses the share option's contractual life as an input and takes into account the possibility of early exercise on a range of different dates in the option's life, allowing for factors such as the correlation between the share price and early exercise and expected employee turnover, is likely to produce a more accurate estimate of the option's fair value.

BC161 Binomial lattice and similar option pricing models also have the advantage of permitting the inputs to the model to vary over the share option's life. For example, instead of using a single expected volatility, a binomial lattice or similar option pricing model can allow for the possibility that volatility might change over the share option's life. This would be particularly appropriate when valuing share options granted by entities experiencing higher than usual volatility, because volatility tends to revert to its mean over time.

BC162 For these reasons, the Board considered whether it should require the use of a more flexible model, rather than the more commonly used Black-Scholes-Merton formula. However, the Board concluded that it was not necessary to prohibit the use of the Black-Scholes-Merton formula, because there might be instances in which the formula produces a sufficiently reliable estimate of the fair value of the share options granted. For example, if the entity has not granted many share options, the effects of applying a more flexible model might not have a material impact on the entity's financial statements. Also, for share options with relatively short contractual lives, or share options that must be exercised within a short period of time after vesting date, the issues discussed in paragraph BC160 may not be relevant, and hence the Black-Scholes-Merton formula may produce a value that is substantially the same as that produced by a more flexible option pricing model. Therefore, rather than prohibit the use of the Black-Scholes-Merton formula, the Board concluded that the IFRS should include guidance on selecting the most appropriate model to apply. This includes the requirement that the entity should consider factors that knowledgeable, willing market participants would consider in selecting the option pricing model to apply.

Although non-transferability often results in the early exercise of employee share options, some employees can mitigate the effects of non-transferability, because they are able, in effect, to sell the options or protect themselves from future changes in the value of the options by selling or buying other derivatives. For example, the employee might be able, in effect, to sell an employee share option by entering into an arrangement with an investment bank whereby the employee sells a similar call option to the bank, ie an option with the same exercise price and term. A zerocost collar is one means of obtaining protection from changes in the value of an employee share option, by selling a call option and buying a put option. **BC163**

However, it appears that such arrangements are not always available. For example, the amounts involved have to be sufficiently large to make it worthwhile for the investment bank, which would probably exclude many employees (unless a collective arrangement was made). Also, it appears that investment banks are unlikely to enter into such an arrangement unless the entity is a top listed company, with shares traded in a deep and active market, to enable the investment bank to hedge its own position. **BC164**

It would not be feasible to stipulate in an accounting standard that an adjustment to take account of non-transferability is necessary only if the employees cannot mitigate the effects of non-transferability through the use of other derivatives. However, using expected life as an input into an option pricing model, or modelling early exercise in a binomial or similar model, copes with both situations. If employees were able to mitigate the effects of non-transferability by using derivatives, this would often result in the employee share options being exercised later than they would otherwise have been. By taking this factor into account, the estimated fair value of the share option would be higher, which makes sense, given that non-transferability is not a constraint in this case. If the employees cannot mitigate the effects of non-transferability through the use of derivatives, they are likely to exercise the share options much earlier than is optimal. In this case, allowing for the effects of early exercise would significantly reduce the estimated value of the share option. **BC165**

This still leaves the question whether there is a need for further adjustment for the combined effect of being unable to exercise or transfer the share option during the vesting period. In other words, the inability to exercise a share option does not, in itself, appear to have a significant effect on its value. But if the share option cannot be transferred and cannot be exercised, and assuming that other derivatives are not available, the holder is unable to extract value from the share option or protect its value during the vesting period. **BC166**

However, it should be noted why these restrictions are in place: the employee has not yet 'paid' for the share option by providing the required services (and fulfilling any other performance conditions). The employee cannot exercise or transfer a share option to which he/she is not yet entitled. The share option will either vest or fail to vest, depending on whether the vesting conditions are satisfied. The possibility of forfeiture resulting from failure to fulfil the vesting conditions is taken into account through the application of the modified grant date method (discussed in paragraphs BC170-BC184). **BC167**

Moreover, for accounting purposes, the objective is to estimate the fair value of the share option, not the value from the employee's perspective. The fair value of any item depends on the expected amounts, timing, and uncertainty of the future cash **BC168** flows relating to the item. The share option grant gives the employee the right to subscribe to the entity's shares at the exercise price, provided that the vesting conditions are satisfied and the exercise price is paid during the specified period. The effect of the vesting conditions is considered below. The effect of the share option being nonexercisable during the vesting period has already been considered above, as has the effect of non-transferability. There does not seem to be any additional effect on the expected amounts, timing or uncertainty of the future cash flows arising from the combination of nonexercisability and non-transferability during the vesting period.

BC169 After considering all of the above points, the Board concluded that the effects of early exercise, because of non-transferability and other factors, should be taken into account when estimating the fair value of the share option, either by modelling early exercise in a binomial or similar model, or using expected life rather than contracted life as an input into an option pricing model, such as the Black-Scholes-Merton formula.

Vesting conditions

BC170 Employee share options usually have vesting conditions. The most common condition is that the employee must remain in the entity's employ for a specified period, say three years. If the employee leaves during that period, the options are forfeited. There might also be other performance conditions, eg that the entity achieves a specified growth in share price or earnings.

BC171 Vesting conditions ensure that the employees provide the services required to 'pay' for their share options. For example, the usual reason for imposing service conditions is to retain staff; the usual reason for imposing other performance conditions is to provide an incentive for the employees to work towards specified performance targets.

BC171A In 2005 the Board decided to take on a project to clarify the definition of vesting conditions and the accounting treatment of cancellations. In particular, the Board noted that it is important to distinguish between non-vesting conditions, which need to be satisfied for the counterparty to become entitled to the equity instrument, and vesting conditions such as performance conditions. In February 2006 the Board published an exposure draft Vesting Conditions and Cancellations, which proposed to restrict vesting conditions to service conditions and performance conditions. Those are the only conditions that determine whether the entity receives the services that entitle the counterparty to the share-based payment, and therefore whether the share-based payment vests. In particular, a share-based payment may vest even if some non-vesting conditions have not been met. The feature that distinguishes a performance condition from a non-vesting condition is that the former has an explicit or implicit service requirement and the latter does not.

BC171B In general, respondents to the exposure draft agreed with the Board's proposals but asked for clarification of whether particular restrictive conditions, such as 'non-compete provisions', are vesting conditions. The Board noted that a share-based payment vests when the counterparty's entitlement to it is no longer conditional on future service or performance conditions. Therefore, conditions such as non-compete provisions and transfer restrictions, which apply after the counterparty has become entitled to the share-based payment, are not vesting conditions. The Board revised the definition of 'vest' accordingly.

Some argue that the existence of vesting conditions does not necessarily imply that the value of employee share options is significantly less than the value of traded share options. The employees have to satisfy the vesting conditions to fulfil their side of the arrangement. In other words, the employees' performance of their side of the arrangement is what they do to pay for their share options. Employees do not pay for the options with cash, as do the holders of traded share options; they pay with their services. Having to pay for the share options does not make them less valuable. On the contrary, it proves that the share options are valuable. **BC172**

Others argue that the possibility of forfeiture without compensation for part-performance suggests that the share options are less valuable. The employees might partly perform their side of the arrangement, eg by working for part of the period, then have to leave for some reason, and forfeit the share options without compensation for that part performance. If there are other performance conditions, such as achieving a specified growth in the share price or earnings, the employees might work for the entire vesting period, but fail to meet the vesting conditions and therefore forfeit the share options. **BC173**

Similarly, some argue that the entity would take into account the possibility of forfeiture when entering into the agreement at grant date. In other words, in deciding how many share options to grant in total, the entity would allow for expected forfeitures. Hence, if the objective is to estimate at grant date the fair value of the entity's commitments under the share option agreement, that valuation should take into account that the entity's commitment to fulfil its side of the option agreement is conditional upon the vesting conditions being satisfied. **BC174**

In developing the proposals in ED 2, the Board concluded that the valuation of rights to share options or shares granted to employees (or other parties) should take into account all types of vesting conditions, including both service conditions and performance conditions. In other words, the grant date valuation should be reduced to allow for the possibility of forfeiture due to failure to satisfy the vesting conditions. **BC175**

Such a reduction might be achieved by adapting an option pricing model to incorporate vesting conditions. Alternatively, a more simplistic approach might be applied. One such approach is to estimate the possibility of forfeiture at grant date, and reduce the value produced by an option pricing model accordingly. For example, if the valuation calculated using an option pricing model was CU15, and the entity estimated that 20 per cent of the share options would be forfeited because of failure to satisfy the vesting conditions, allowing for the possibility of forfeiture would reduce the grant date value of each option granted from CU15 to CU12. **BC176**

The Board decided against proposing detailed guidance on how the grant date value should be adjusted to allow for the possibility of forfeiture. This is consistent with the Board's objective of setting principles-based standards. The measurement objective is to estimate fair value. That objective might not be achieved if detailed, prescriptive rules were specified, which would probably become outdated by future developments in valuation methodologies. **BC177**

However, respondents to ED 2 raised a variety of concerns about the inclusion of vesting conditions in the grant date valuation. Some respondents were concerned about the practicality and subjectivity of including non-market performance conditions in the share option valuation. Some were also concerned about the practicality of including service conditions in the grant date valuation, particularly in conjunction with the units of service method proposed in ED 2 (discussed further in paragraphs BC203-BC217). **BC178**

BC179 Some respondents suggested the alternative approach applied in SFAS 123, referred to as the modified grant date method. Under this method, service conditions and non-market performance conditions are excluded from the grant date valuation (ie the possibility of forfeiture is not taken into account when estimating the grant date fair value of the share options or other equity instruments, thereby producing a higher grant date fair value), but are instead taken into account by requiring the transaction amount to be based on the number of equity instruments that eventually vest. Under this method, on a cumulative basis, no amount is recognised for goods or services received if the equity instruments granted do not vest because of failure to satisfy a vesting condition (other than a market condition), eg the counterparty fails to complete a specified service period, or a performance condition (other than a market condition) is not satisfied.

BC180 After considering respondents' comments and obtaining further advice from valuation experts, the Board decided to adopt the modified grant date method applied in SFAS 123. However, the Board decided that it should not permit the choice available in SFAS 123 to account for the effects of expected or actual forfeitures of share options or other equity instruments because of failure to satisfy a service condition. For a grant of equity instruments with a service condition, SFAS 123 permits an entity to choose at grant date to recognise the services received based on an estimate of the number of share options or other equity instruments expected to vest, and to revise that estimate, if necessary, if subsequent information indicates that actual forfeitures are likely to differ from previous estimates. Alternatively, an entity may begin recognising the services received as if all the equity instruments granted that are subject to a service requirement are expected to vest. The effects of forfeitures are then recognised when those forfeitures occur, by reversing any amounts previously recognised for services received as consideration for equity instruments that are forfeited.

BC181 The Board decided that the latter method should not be permitted. Given that the transaction amount is ultimately based on the number of equity instruments that vest, it is appropriate to estimate the number of expected forfeitures when recognising the services received during the vesting period. Furthermore, by ignoring expected forfeitures until those forfeitures occur, the effects of reversing any amounts previously recognised might result in a distortion of remuneration expense recognised during the vesting period. For example, an entity that experiences a high level of forfeitures might recognise a large amount of remuneration expense in one period, which is then reversed in a later period.

BC182 Therefore, the Board decided that the IFRS should require an entity to estimate the number of equity instruments expected to vest and to revise that estimate, if necessary, if subsequent information indicates that actual forfeitures are likely to differ from previous estimates.

BC183 Under SFAS 123, market conditions (eg a condition involving a target share price, or specified amount of intrinsic value on which vesting or exercisability is conditioned) are included in the grant date valuation, without subsequent reversal. That is to say, when estimating the fair value of the equity instruments at grant date, the entity takes into account the possibility that the market condition may not be satisfied. Having allowed for that possibility in the grant date valuation of the equity instruments, no adjustment is made to the number of equity instruments included in the calculation of the transaction amount, irrespective of the outcome of the market condition. In other words, the entity recognises the goods or services received from a counterparty that satisfies all other vesting conditions (eg services received from an employee who remains in service for the specified service period), irrespective of whether that market condition is satisfied. The treatment of market conditions therefore contrasts with the treatment of other types of vesting conditions. As explained in paragraph BC179, under the modified grant date method, vesting conditions are not taken into account when estimating the fair value of the equity instruments at grant date, but are instead taken into account by requiring the transaction amount to be based on the number of equity instruments that eventually vest.

The Board considered whether it should apply the same approach to market conditions as is applied in SFAS 123. It might be argued that it is not appropriate to distinguish between market conditions and other types of performance conditions, because to do so could create opportunities for arbitrage, or cause an economic distortion by encouraging entities to favour one type of performance condition over another. However, the Board noted that it is not clear what the result would be. On the one hand, some entities might prefer the 'truing up' aspect of the modified grant date method, because it permits a reversal of remuneration expense if the condition is not met. On the other hand, if the performance condition is met, and it has not been incorporated into the grant date valuation (as is the case when the modified grant date method is used), the expense will be higher than it would otherwise have been (ie if the performance condition had been incorporated into the grant date valuation). Furthermore, some entities might prefer to avoid the potential volatility caused by the truing up mechanism. Therefore, it is not clear whether having a different treatment for market and non-market performance conditions will necessarily cause entities to favour market conditions over non-market performance conditions, or vice versa. Furthermore, the practical difficulties that led the Board to conclude that non-market performance conditions should be dealt with via the modified grant date method rather than being included in the grant date valuation do not apply to market conditions, because market conditions can be incorporated into option pricing models. Moreover, it is difficult to distinguish between market conditions, such as a target share price, and the market condition that is inherent in the option itself, ie that the option will be exercised only if the share price on the date of exercise exceeds the exercise price. For these reasons, the Board concluded that the IFRS should apply the same approach as is applied in SFAS 123. **BC184**

Option term

Employee share options often have a long contractual life, eg ten years. Traded options typically have short lives, often only a few months. Estimating the inputs required by an option pricing model, such as expected volatility, over long periods can be difficult, giving rise to the possibility of significant estimation error. This is not usually a problem with traded share options, given their much shorter lives. **BC185**

However, some share options traded over the counter have long lives, such as ten or fifteen years. Option pricing models are used to value them. Therefore, contrary to the argument sometimes advanced, option pricing models can be (and are being) applied to long-lived share options. **BC186**

Moreover, the potential for estimation error is mitigated by using a binomial or similar model that allows for changes in model inputs over the share option's life, such as expected volatility, and interest and dividend rates, that could occur and the probability of those changes occurring during the term of the share option. The potential for estimation error is further mitigated by taking into account the possibility of early exercise, either by using expected life rather than contracted life as an input into an option pricing model or by modelling exercise behaviour in a binomial or similar model, because this reduces the expected term of the share option. Because **BC187** employees often exercise their share options relatively early in the share option's life, the expected term is usually much shorter than contracted life.

Other features of employee share option plans

BC188 Whilst the features discussed above are common to most employee share options, some might include other features. For example, some share options have a reload feature. This entitles the employee to automatic grants of additional share options whenever he/she exercises previously granted share options and pays the exercise price in the entity's shares rather than in cash. Typically, the employee is granted a new share option, called a reload option, for each share surrendered when exercising the previous share option. The exercise price of the reload option is usually set at the market price of the shares on the date the reload option is granted.

BC189 When SFAS 123 was developed, the FASB concluded that, ideally, the value of the reload feature should be included in the valuation of the original share option at grant date. However, at that time the FASB believed that it was not possible to do so. Accordingly, SFAS 123 does not require the reload feature to be included in the grant date valuation of the original share option. Instead, reload options granted upon exercise of the original share options are accounted for as a new share option grant.

BC190 However, recent academic research indicates that it is possible to value the reload feature at grant date, eg Saly, Jagannathan and Huddart (1999).* However, if significant uncertainties exist, such as the number and timing of expected grants of reload options, it might not be practicable to include the reload feature in the grant date valuation.

BC191 When it developed ED 2, the Board concluded that the reload feature should be taken into account, where practicable, when measuring the fair value of the share options granted. However, if the reload feature was not taken into account, then when the reload option is granted, it should be accounted for as a new share option grant.

BC192 Many respondents to ED 2 agreed with the proposals in ED 2. However, some disagreed. For example, some disagreed with there being a choice of treatments. Some respondents supported always treating reload options granted as new grants whereas others supported always including the reload feature in the grant date valuation. Some expressed concerns about the practicality of including the reload feature in the grant date valuation. After reconsidering this issue, the Board concluded that the reload feature should not be included in the grant date valuation and therefore all reload options granted should be accounted for as new share option grants.

BC193 There may be other features of employee (and other) share options that the Board has not yet considered. But even if the Board were to consider every conceivable feature of employee (and other) share options that exist at present, new features might be developed in the future.

BC194 The Board therefore concluded that the IFRS should focus on setting out clear principles to be applied to share-based payment transactions, and provide guidance

**P J Saly, R Jagannathan and S J Huddart. 1999. Valuing the Reload Features of Executive Stock Options. Accounting Horizons 13 (3): 219240.*

on the more common features of employee share options, but should not prescribe extensive application guidance, which would be likely to become outdated.

Nevertheless, the Board considered whether there are share options with such unusual or complex features that it is too difficult to make a reliable estimate of their fair value and, if so, what the accounting treatment should be. **BC195**

SFAS 123 states that "it should be possible to reasonably estimate the fair value of most stock options and other equity instruments at the date they are granted" (paragraph 21). However, it states that, "in unusual circumstances, the terms of the stock option or other equity instrument may make it virtually impossible to reasonably estimate the instrument's fair value at the date it is granted". The standard requires that, in such situations, measurement should be delayed until it is possible to estimate reasonably the instrument's fair value. It notes that this is likely to be the date at which the number of shares to which the employee is entitled and the exercise price are determinable. This could be vesting date. The standard requires that estimates of compensation expense for earlier periods (ie until it is possible to estimate fair value) should be based on current intrinsic value. **BC196**

The Board thought it unlikely that entities could not reasonably determine the fair value of share options at grant date, particularly after excluding vesting conditions* and reload features from the grant date valuation. The share options form part of the employee's remuneration package, and it seems reasonable to presume that an entity's management would consider the value of the share options to satisfy itself that the employee's remuneration package is fair and reasonable. **BC197**

When it developed ED 2, the Board concluded that there should be no exceptions to the requirement to apply a fair value measurement basis, and therefore it was not necessary to include in the proposed IFRS specific accounting requirements for share options that are difficult to value. **BC198**

However, after considering respondents' comments, particularly with regard to unlisted entities, the Board reconsidered this issue. The Board concluded that, in rare cases only, in which the entity could not estimate reliably the grant date fair value of the equity instruments granted, the entity should measure the equity instruments at intrinsic value, initially at grant date and subsequently at each reporting date until the final settlement of the share-based payment arrangement, with the effects of the remeasurement recognised in profit or loss. For a grant of share options, the share-based payment arrangement is finally settled when the share options are exercised, are forfeited (eg upon cessation of employment) or lapse (eg at the end of the option's life). For a grant of shares, the share-based payment arrangement is finally settled when the shares vest or are forfeited. This requirement would apply to all entities, including listed and unlisted entities. **BC199**

RECOGNITION AND MEASUREMENT OF SERVICES RECEIVED IN AN EQUITY-SETTLED SHARE-BASED PAYMENT TRANSACTION

During the vesting period

In an equity-settled share-based payment transaction, the accounting objective is to recognise the goods or services received as consideration for the entity's equity instruments, measured at the fair value of those goods or services when received. For **BC200**

**ie vesting conditions other than market conditions.*

transactions in which the entity receives employee services, it is often difficult to measure directly the fair value of the services received. In this case, the Board concluded that the fair value of the equity instruments granted should be used as a surrogate measure of the fair value of the services received. This raises the question how to use that surrogate measure to derive an amount to attribute to the services received. Another related question is how the entity should determine when the services are received.

BC201 Starting with the latter question, some argue that shares or share options are often granted to employees for past services rather than future services, or mostly for past services, irrespective of whether the employees are required to continue working for the entity for a specified future period before their rights to those shares or share options vest. Conversely, some argue that shares or share options granted provide a future incentive to the employees and those incentive effects continue after vesting date, which implies that the entity receives services from employees during a period that extends beyond vesting date. For share options in particular, some argue that employees render services beyond vesting date, because employees are able to benefit from an option's time value between vesting date and exercise date only if they continue to work for the entity (since usually a departing employee must exercise the share options within a short period, otherwise they are forfeited).

BC202 However, the Board concluded that if the employees are required to complete a specified service period to become entitled to the shares or share options, this requirement provides the best evidence of when the employees render services in return for the shares or share options. Consequently, the Board concluded that the entity should presume that the services are received during the vesting period. If the shares or share options vest immediately, it should be presumed that the entity has already received the services, in the absence of evidence to the contrary. An example of when immediately vested shares or share options are not for past services is when the employee concerned has only recently begun working for the entity, and the shares or share options are granted as a signing bonus. But in this situation, it might nevertheless be necessary to recognise an expense immediately, if the future employee services do not meet the definition of an asset.

BC203 Returning to the first question in paragraph BC200, when the Board developed ED 2 it developed an approach whereby the fair value of the shares or share options granted, measured at grant date and allowing for all vesting conditions, is divided by the number of units of service expected to be received to determine the deemed fair value of each unit of service subsequently received.

BC204 For example, suppose that the fair value of share options granted, before taking into account the possibility of forfeiture, is CU750,000. Suppose that the entity estimates the possibility of forfeiture because of failure of the employees to complete the required threeyear period of service is 20 per cent (based on a weighted average probability), and hence it estimates the fair value of the options granted at CU600,000 (CU750,000 × 80%). The entity expects to receive 1,350 units of service over the three year vesting period.

BC205 Under the units of service method proposed in ED 2, the deemed fair value per unit of service subsequently received is CU444.44 (CU600,000/ 1,350). If everything turns out as expected, the amount recognised for services received is CU600,000 (CU444.44 × 1,350).

BC206 This approach is based on the presumption that there is a fairly bargained contract at grant date. Thus the entity has granted share options valued at CU600,000 and expects to receive services valued at CU600,000 in return. It does not expect all share options granted to vest because it does not expect all employees to complete three years' service. Expectations of forfeiture because of employee departures are taken into account when estimating the fair value of the share options granted, and when determining the fair value of the services to be received in return.

Under the units of service method, the amount recognised for services received during the vesting period might exceed CU600,000, if the entity receives more services than expected. This is because the objective is to account for the services subsequently received, not the fair value of the share options granted. In other words, the objective is not to estimate the fair value of the share options granted and then spread that amount over the vesting period. Rather, the objective is to account for the services subsequently received, because it is the receipt of those services that causes a change in net assets and hence a change in equity. Because of the practical difficulty of valuing those services directly, the fair value of the share options granted is used as a surrogate measure to determine the fair value of each unit of service subsequently received, and therefore the transaction amount is dependent upon the number of units of service actually received. If more are received than expected, the transaction amount will be greater than CU600,000. If fewer services are received, the transaction amount will be less than CU600,000. **BC207**

Hence, a grant date measurement method is used as a practical expedient to achieve the accounting objective, which is to account for the services actually received in the vesting period. The Board noted that many who support grant date measurement do so for reasons that focus on the entity's commitments under the contract, not the services received. They take the view that the entity has conveyed to its employees valuable equity instruments at grant date and that the accounting objective should be to account for the equity instruments conveyed. Similarly, supporters of vesting date measurement argue that the entity does not convey valuable equity instruments to the employees until vesting date, and that the accounting objective should be to account for the equity instruments conveyed at vesting date. Supporters of exercise date measurement argue that, ultimately, the valuable equity instruments conveyed by the entity to the employees are the shares issued on exercise date and the objective should be to account for the value given up by the entity by issuing equity instruments at less than their fair value. **BC208**

Hence all of these arguments for various measurement dates are focused entirely on what the entity (or its shareholders) has given up under the share-based payment arrangement, and accounting for that sacrifice. Therefore, if 'grant date measurement' were applied as a matter of principle, the primary objective would be to account for the value of the rights granted. Depending on whether the services have already been received and whether a prepayment for services to be received in the future meets the definition of an asset, the other side of the transaction would either be recognised as an expense at grant date, or capitalised as a prepayment and amortised over some period of time, such as over the vesting period or over the expected life of the share option. Under this view of grant date measurement, there would be no subsequent adjustment for actual outcomes. No matter how many share options vest or how many share options are exercised, that does not change the value of the rights given to the employees at grant date. **BC209**

Therefore, the reason why some support grant date measurement differs from the reason why the Board concluded that the fair value of the equity instruments granted should be measured at grant date. This means that some will have different views about the consequences of applying grant date measurement. Because the units of service method is based on using the fair value of the equity instruments granted, measured at grant date, as a surrogate measure of the fair value of the services **BC210** received, the total transaction amount is dependent upon the number of units of service received.

BC211 Some respondents to ED 2 disagreed with the units of service method in principle, because they did not accept that the fair value of the services received should be the accounting focus. Rather, the respondents focused on accounting for the 'cost' of the equity instruments issued (ie the credit side of the transaction rather than the debit side), and took the view that if the share options or shares are forfeited, no cost was incurred, and thus any amounts recognised previously should be reversed, as would happen with a cash-settled transaction.

BC212 Some respondents also disagreed with the treatment of performance conditions under the units of service method, because if the employee completes the required service period but the equity instruments do not vest because of the performance condition not being satisfied, there is no reversal of amounts recognised during the vesting period. Some argue that this result is unreasonable because, if the performance condition is not satisfied, then the employee did not perform as required, hence it is inappropriate to recognise an expense for services received or consumed, because the entity did not receive the specified services.

BC213 The Board considered and rejected the above arguments made against the units of service method in principle. For example, the Board noted that the objective of accounting for the services received, rather than the cost of the equity instruments issued, is consistent with the accounting treatment of other issues of equity instruments, and with the IASB *Framework*. With regard to performance conditions, the Board noted that the strength of the argument in paragraph BC212 depends on the extent to which the employee has control or influence over the achievement of the performance target. One cannot necessarily conclude that the nonattainment of the performance target is a good indication that the employee has failed to perform his/her side of the arrangement (ie failed to provide services).

BC214 Therefore, the Board was not persuaded by those respondents who disagreed with the units of service method in principle. However, the Board also noted that some respondents raised practical concerns about the method. Some respondents regarded the units of service method as too complex and burdensome to apply in practice. For example, if an entity granted share options to a group of employees but did not grant the same number of share options to each employee (eg the number might vary according to their salary or position in the entity), it would be necessary to calculate a different deemed fair value per unit of service for each individual employee (or for each subgroup of employees, if there are groups of employees who each received the same number of options). Then the entity would have to track each employee, to calculate the amount to recognise for each employee. Furthermore, in some circumstances, an employee share or share option scheme might not require the employee to forfeit the shares or share options if the employee leaves during the vesting period in specified circumstances. Under the terms of some schemes, employees can retain their share options or shares if they are classified as a 'good leaver', eg a departure resulting from circumstances not within the employee's control, such as compulsory retirement, ill health or redundancy. Therefore, in estimating the possibility of forfeiture, it is not simply a matter of estimating the possibility of employee departure during the vesting period. It is also necessary to estimate whether those departures will be 'good leavers' or 'bad leavers'. And because the share options or shares will vest upon departure of 'good leavers', the expected number of units to be received and the expected length of the vesting period will be shorter for this group of employees. These factors would need to be incorporated into the application of the units of service method.

Some respondents also raised practical concerns about applying the units of service method to grants with performance conditions. These concerns include the difficulty of incorporating non-market and complex performance conditions into the grant date valuation, the additional subjectivity that this introduces, and that it was unclear how to apply the method when the length of the vesting period is not fixed, because it depends on when a performance condition is satisfied. **BC215**

The Board considered the practical concerns raised by respondents, and obtained further advice from valuation experts concerning the difficulties highlighted by respondents of including non-market performance conditions in the grant date valuation. Because of these practical considerations, the Board concluded that the units of service method should not be retained in the IFRS. Instead, the Board decided to adopt the modified grant date method applied in SFAS 123. Under this method, service conditions and non-market performance conditions are excluded from the grant date valuation (ie the possibility of forfeiture is not taken into account when estimating the grant date fair value of the share options or other equity instruments, thereby producing a higher grant date fair value), but are instead taken into account by requiring that the transaction amount be based on the number of equity instruments that eventually vest.* Under this method, on a cumulative basis, no amount is recognised for goods or services received if the equity instruments granted do not vest because of failure to satisfy a vesting condition (other than a market condition), eg the counterparty fails to complete a specified service period, or a performance condition (other than a market condition) is not satisfied. **BC216**

However, as discussed earlier (paragraphs BC180-BC182), the Board decided that it should not permit the choice available in SFAS 123 to account for the effects of expected or actual forfeitures of share options or other equity instruments because of failure to satisfy a service condition. The Board decided that the IFRS should require an entity to estimate the number of equity instruments expected to vest and to revise that estimate, if necessary, if subsequent information indicates that actual forfeitures are likely to differ from previous estimates. **BC217**

Share options that are forfeited or lapse after the end of the vesting period

Some share options might not be exercised. For example, a share option holder is unlikely to exercise a share option if the share price is below the exercise price throughout the exercise period. Once the last date for exercise is passed, the share option will lapse. **BC218**

The lapse of a share option at the end of the exercise period does not change the fact that the original transaction occurred, ie goods or services were received as consideration for the issue of an equity instrument (the share option). The lapsing of the share option does not represent a gain to the entity, because there is no change to the entity's net assets. In other words, although some might see such an event as being a benefit to the remaining shareholders, it has no effect on the entity's financial position. In effect, one type of equity interest (the share option holders' interest) becomes part of another type of equity interest (the shareholders' interest). The Board therefore concluded that the only accounting entry that might be required is a movement within equity, to reflect that the share options are no longer outstanding (ie as a transfer from one type of equity interest to another). **BC219**

**The treatment of market conditions is discussed in paragraphs BC183 and BC184. As noted in paragraph BC184, the practical difficulties that led the Board to conclude that non-market conditions should be dealt with via the modified grant date method rather than being included in the grant date valuation do not apply to market conditions, because market conditions can be incorporated into option pricing models.*

BC220 This is consistent with the treatment of other equity instruments, such as warrants issued for cash. When warrants subsequently lapse unexercised, this is not treated as a gain; instead the amount previously recognised when the warrants were issued remains within equity.*

BC221 The same analysis applies to equity instruments that are forfeited after the end of the vesting period. For example, an employee with vested share options typically must exercise those options within a short period after cessation of employment, otherwise the options are forfeited. If the share options are not in the money, the employee is unlikely to exercise the options and hence they will be forfeited. For the same reasons as are given in paragraph BC219, no adjustment is made to the amounts previously recognised for services received as consideration for the share options. The only accounting entry that might be required is a movement within equity, to reflect that the share options are no longer outstanding.

MODIFICATIONS TO THE TERMS AND CONDITIONS OF SHARE-BASED PAYMENT ARRANGEMENTS

BC222 An entity might modify the terms of or conditions under which the equity instruments were granted. For example, the entity might reduce the exercise price of share options granted to employees (ie reprice the options), which increases the fair value of those options. During the development of ED 2, the Board focused mainly on the repricing of share options.

BC223 The Board noted that the IASC/G4+1 Discussion Paper argued that if the entity reprices its share options it has, in effect, replaced the original share option with a more valuable share option. The entity presumably believes that it will receive an equivalent amount of benefit from doing so, because otherwise the directors would not be acting in the best interests of the entity or its shareholders. This suggests that the entity expects to receive additional or enhanced employee services equivalent in value to the incremental value of the repriced share options. The Discussion Paper therefore proposed that the incremental value given (ie the difference between the value of the original share option and the value of the repriced share option, as at the date of repricing) should be recognised as additional remuneration expense. Although the Discussion Paper discussed repricing in the context of vesting date measurement, SFAS 123, which applies a grant date measurement basis for employee share-based payment, contains reasoning similar to that in the Discussion Paper.

BC224 This reasoning seems appropriate if grant date measurement is applied on the grounds that the entity made a payment to the employees on grant date by granting them valuable rights to equity instruments of the entity. If the entity is prepared to replace that payment with a more valuable payment, it must believe it will receive an equivalent amount of benefit from doing so.

BC225 The same conclusion is drawn if grant date measurement is applied on the grounds that some type of equity interest is created at grant date, and thereafter changes in the value of that equity interest accrue to the option holders as equity participants, not as employees. Repricing is inconsistent with the view that share option holders bear changes in value as equity participants. Hence it follows that the incremental value has been granted to the share option holders in their capacity as employees (rather than equity participants), as part of their remuneration for services to the

**However, an alternative approach is followed in some jurisdictions (eg Japan and the UK), where the entity recognises a gain when warrants lapse. But under the Framework, recognising a gain on the lapse of warrants would be appropriate only if warrants were liabilities, which they are not.*

entity. Therefore additional remuneration expense arises in respect of the incremental value given.

It could be argued that if (a) grant date measurement is used as a surrogate measure of the fair value of the services received and (b) the repricing occurs between grant date and vesting date and (c) the repricing merely restores the share option's original value at grant date, then the entity may not receive additional services. Rather, the repricing might simply be a means of ensuring that the entity receives the services it originally expected to receive when the share options were granted. Under this view, it is not appropriate to recognise additional remuneration expense to the extent that the repricing restores the share option's original value at grant date. **BC226**

Some argue that the effect of a repricing is to create a new deal between the entity and its employees, and therefore the entity should estimate the fair value of the repriced share options at the date of repricing to calculate a new measure of the fair value of the services received subsequent to repricing. Under this view, the entity would cease using the grant date fair value of the share options when measuring services received after the repricing date, but without reversal of amounts recognised previously. The entity would then measure the services received between the date of repricing and the end of the vesting period by reference to the fair value of the modified share options, measured at the date of repricing. If the repricing occurs after the end of the vesting period, the same process applies. That is to say, there is no adjustment to previously recognised amounts, and the entity recognises – either immediately or over the vesting period, depending on whether the employees are required to complete an additional period of service to become entitled to the repriced share options – an amount equal to the fair value of the modified share options, measured at the date of repricing. **BC227**

In the context of measuring the fair value of the equity instruments as a surrogate measure of the fair value of the services received, after considering the above points, the Board concluded when it developed ED 2 that the incremental value granted on repricing should be taken into account when measuring the services received, because: **BC228**

(a) there is an underlying presumption that the fair value of the equity instruments, at grant date, provides a surrogate measure of the fair value of the services received. That fair value is based on the share option's original terms and conditions. Therefore, if those terms or conditions are modified, the modification should be taken into account when measuring the services received.

(b) a share option that will be repriced if the share price falls is more valuable than one that will not be repriced. Therefore, by presuming at grant date that the share option will not be repriced, the entity underestimated the fair value of that option. The Board concluded that, because it is impractical to include the possibility of repricing in the estimate of fair value at grant date, the incremental value granted on repricing should be taken into account as and when the repricing occurs.

Many of the respondents to ED 2 who addressed the issue of repricing agreed with the proposed requirements. After considering respondents' comments, the Board decided to retain the approach to repricing as proposed in ED 2, ie recognise the incremental value granted on repricing, in addition to continuing to recognise amounts based on the fair value of the original grant. **BC229**

The Board also discussed situations in which repricing might be effected by cancelling share options and issuing replacement share options. For example, suppose an entity grants atthemoney share options with an estimated fair value of CU20 **BC230** each. Suppose the share price falls, so that the share options become significantly out of the money, and are now worth CU2 each. Suppose the entity is considering repricing, so that the share options are again at the money, which would result in them being worth, say, CU10 each. (Note that the share options are still worth less than at grant date, because the share price is now lower. Other things being equal, an atthemoney option on a low priced share is worth less than an atthemoney option on a high priced share.)

BC231 Under ED 2's proposed treatment of repricing, the incremental value given on repricing (CU10 – CU2 = CU8 increment in fair value per share option) would be accounted for when measuring the services rendered, resulting in the recognition of additional expense, ie additional to any amounts recognised in the future in respect of the original share option grant (valued at CU20). If the entity instead cancelled the existing share options and then issued what were, in effect, replacement share options, but treated the replacement share options as a new share option grant, this could reduce the expense recognised. Although the new grant would be valued at CU10 rather than incremental value of CU8, the entity would not recognise any further expense in respect of the original share option grant, valued at CU20. Although some regard such a result as appropriate (and consistent with their views on repricing, as explained in paragraph BC227), it is inconsistent with the Board's treatment of repricing.

BC232 By this means, the entity could, in effect, reduce its remuneration expense if the share price falls, without having to increase the expense if the share price rises (because no repricing would be necessary in this case). In other words, the entity could structure a repricing so as to achieve a form of service date measurement if the share price falls and grant date measurement if the share price rises, ie an asymmetrical treatment of share price changes.

BC233 When it developed ED 2, the Board concluded that if an entity cancels a share or share option grant during the vesting period (other than cancellations because of employees' failing to satisfy the vesting conditions), it should nevertheless continue to account for services received, as if that share or share option grant had not been cancelled. In the Board's view, it is very unlikely that a share or share option grant would be cancelled without some compensation to the counterparty, either in the form of cash or replacement share options. Moreover, the Board saw no difference between a repricing of share options and a cancellation of share options followed by the granting of replacement share options at a lower exercise price, and therefore concluded that the accounting treatment should be the same. If cash is paid on the cancellation of the share or share option grant, the Board concluded that the payment should be accounted for as the repurchase of an equity interest, ie as a deduction from equity.

BC234 The Board noted that its proposed treatment means that an entity would continue to recognise services received during the remainder of the original vesting period, even though the entity might have paid cash compensation to the counterparty upon cancellation of the share or share option grant. The Board discussed an alternative approach applied in SFAS 123: if an entity settles unvested shares or share options in cash, those shares or share options are treated as having immediately vested. The entity is required to recognise immediately an expense for the amount of compensation expense that would otherwise have been recognised during the remainder of the original vesting period. Although the Board would have preferred to adopt this approach, it would have been difficult to apply in the context of the proposed accounting method in ED 2, given that there is not a specific amount of unrecognised compensation expense – the amount recognised in the future would have depended on the number of units of service received in the future.

Many respondents who commented on the treatment of cancellations disagreed with the proposals in ED 2. They commented that it was inappropriate to continue recognising an expense after a grant has been cancelled. Some suggested other approaches, including the approach applied in SFAS 123. After considering these comments, and given that the Board had decided to replace the units of service method with the modified grant date method in SFAS 123, the Board concluded that it should adopt the same approach as applied in SFAS 123 to cancellations and settlements. Under SFAS 123, a settlement (including a cancellation) is regarded as resulting in the immediate vesting of the equity instruments. The amount of remuneration expense measured at grant date but not yet recognised is recognised immediately at the date of settlement or cancellation. **BC235**

In addition to the above issues, during its redeliberation of the proposals in ED 2 the Board also considered more detailed issues relating to modifications and cancellations. Specifically, the Board considered: **BC236**

(a) a modification that results in a decrease in fair value (ie the fair value of the modified instrument is less than the fair value of the original instrument, measured at the date of the modification).
(b) a change in the number of equity instruments granted (increase and decrease).
(c) a change in services conditions, thereby changing the length of the vesting period (increase and decrease).
(d) a change in performance conditions, thereby changing the probability of vesting (increase and decrease).
(e) a change in the classification of the grant, from equity to liabilities.

The Board concluded that having adopted a grant date measurement method, the requirements for modifications and cancellations should ensure that the entity cannot, by modifying or cancelling the grant of shares or share options, avoid recognising remuneration expense based on the grant date fair values. Therefore, the Board concluded that, for arrangements that are classified as equity-settled arrangements (at least initially), the entity must recognise the grant date fair value of the equity instruments over the vesting period, unless the employee fails to vest in those equity instruments under the terms of the original vesting conditions. **BC237**

During the deliberations of its proposals in the exposure draft *Vesting Conditions and Cancellations* published in February 2006, the Board considered how failure to meet a non-vesting condition should be treated. The Board concluded that in order to be consistent with the grant date measurement method, failure to meet a non-vesting condition should have no accounting effect when neither the entity nor the counterparty can choose whether that condition is met. The entity should continue to recognise the expense, based on the grant date fair value, over the vesting period unless the employee fails to meet a vesting condition. **BC237A**

However, the Board concluded that the entity's failure to meet a non-vesting condition is a cancellation if the entity can choose whether that non-vesting condition is met. Furthermore, the Board noted that no non-arbitrary or unambiguous criteria exist to distinguish between a decision by the counterparty not to meet a non-vesting condition and a cancellation by the entity. The Board considered establishing a rebuttable presumption that a counterparty's failure to meet a non-vesting condition is (or is not) a cancellation, unless it can be demonstrated that the entity had no (or had some) influence over the counterparty's decision. The Board did not believe that the information about the entity's decision-making processes that is publicly available would be sufficient to determine whether the presumption has been rebutted. Therefore, the Board concluded that a failure to meet a non-vesting condition should **BC237B** be treated as a cancellation when either the entity or the counterparty can choose whether that non-vesting condition is met.

SHARE APPRECIATION RIGHTS SETTLED IN CASH

BC238 Some transactions are 'share-based', even though they do not involve the issue of shares, share options or any other form of equity instrument. Share appreciation rights (SARs) settled in cash are transactions in which the amount of cash paid to the employee (or another party) is based upon the increase in the share price over a specified period, usually subject to vesting conditions, such as the employee's remaining with the entity during the specified period. (Note that the following discussion focuses on SARs granted to employees, but also applies to SARs granted to other parties.)

BC239 In terms of accounting concepts, share-based payment transactions involving an outflow of cash (or other assets) are different from transactions in which goods or services are received as consideration for the issue of equity instruments.

BC240 In an equity-settled transaction, only one side of the transaction causes a change in assets, ie an asset (services) is received but no assets are disbursed. The other side of the transaction increases equity; it does not cause a change in assets. Accordingly, not only is it not necessary to remeasure the transaction amount upon settlement, it is not appropriate, because equity interests are not remeasured.

BC241 In contrast, in a cash-settled transaction, both sides of the transaction cause a change in assets, ie an asset (services) is received and an asset (cash) is ultimately disbursed. Therefore, no matter what value is attributed to the first asset (services received), eventually it will be necessary to recognise the change in assets when the second asset (cash) is disbursed. Thus, no matter how the transaction is accounted for between the receipt of services and the settlement in cash, it will be 'trued up' to equal the amount of cash paid out, to account for both changes in assets.

BC242 Because cash-settled SARs involve an outflow of cash (rather than the issue of equity instruments) cash SARs should be accounted for in accordance with the usual accounting for similar liabilities. That sounds straightforward, but there are some questions to consider:

(a) should a liability be recognised before vesting date, ie before the employees have fulfilled the conditions to become unconditionally entitled to the cash payment?
(b) if so, how should that liability be measured?
(c) how should the expense be presented in the income statement?

Is there a liability before vesting date?

BC243 It could be argued that the entity does not have a liability until vesting date, because the entity does not have a present obligation to pay cash to the employees until the employees fulfil the conditions to become unconditionally entitled to the cash; between grant date and vesting date there is only a contingent liability.

BC244 The Board noted that this argument applies to all sorts of employee benefits settled in cash, not just SARs. For example, it could be argued that an entity has no liability for pension payments to employees until the employees have met the specified vesting conditions. This argument was considered by IASC in IAS 19 *Employee Benefits*. The Basis for Conclusions states:

> Paragraph 54 of the new IAS 19 summarises the recognition and measurement of liabilities arising from defined benefit plans...Paragraph 54 of the new IAS 19 is based on the definition of, and recognition criteria for, a liability in IASC's Framework...The Board believes that an enterprise has an obligation under a defined benefit plan when an employee has rendered service in return for the benefits promised under the plan...The Board believes that an obligation exists even if a benefit is not vested, in other words if the employee's right to receive the benefit is conditional upon future employment. For example, consider an enterprise that provides a benefit of 100 to employees who remain in service for two years. At the end of the first year, the employee and the enterprise are not in the same position as at the beginning of the first year, because the employee will only need to work for one year, instead of two, before becoming entitled to the benefit. Although there is a possibility that the benefit may not vest, that difference is an obligation and, in the Board's view, should result in the recognition of a liability at the end of the first year. The measurement of that obligation at its present value reflects the enterprise's best estimate of the probability that the benefit may not vest. (IAS 19, Basis for Conclusions, paragraphs 11-14)

Therefore, the Board concluded that, to be consistent with IAS 19, which covers other cash-settled employee benefits, a liability should be recognised in respect of cash-settled SARs during the vesting period, as services are rendered by the employees. Thus, no matter how the liability is measured, the Board concluded that it should be accrued over the vesting period, to the extent that the employees have performed their side of the arrangement. For example, if the terms of the arrangement require the employees to perform services over a threeyear period, the liability would be accrued over that threeyear period, consistently with the treatment of other cash-settled employee benefits. **BC245**

How should the liability be measured?

A simple approach would be to base the accrual on the entity's share price at the end of each reporting period. If the entity's share price increased over the vesting period, expenses would be larger in later reporting periods compared with earlier reporting periods. This is because each reporting period will include the effects of (a) an increase in the liability in respect of the employee services received during that reporting period and (b) an increase in the liability attributable to the increase in the entity's share price during the reporting period, which increases the amount payable in respect of past employee services received. **BC246**

This approach is consistent with SFAS 123 (paragraph 25) and FASB Interpretation No. 28 *Accounting for Stock Appreciation Rights and Other Variable Stock Option or Award Plans*. **BC247**

However, this is not a fair value approach. Like share options, the fair value of SARs includes both their intrinsic value (the increase in the share price to date) and their time value (the value of the right to participate in future increases in the share price, if any, that may occur between the valuation date and the settlement date). An option pricing model can be used to estimate the fair value of SARs. **BC248**

Ultimately, however, no matter how the liability is measured during the vesting period, the liability – and therefore the expense – will be remeasured, when the SARs are settled, to equal the amount of the cash paid out. The amount of cash paid will be based on the SARs' intrinsic value at the settlement date. Some support measuring the SAR liability at intrinsic value for this reason, and because intrinsic value is easier to measure. **BC249**

BC250 The Board concluded that measuring SARs at intrinsic value would be inconsistent with the fair value measurement basis applied, in most cases, in the rest of the IFRS. Furthermore, although a fair value measurement basis is more complex to apply, it was likely that many entities would be measuring the fair value of similar instruments regularly, eg new SAR or share option grants, which would provide much of the information required to remeasure the fair value of the SAR at each reporting date. Moreover, because the intrinsic value measurement basis does not include time value, it is not an adequate measure of either the SAR liability or the cost of services consumed.

BC251 The question of how to measure the liability is linked with the question how to present the associated expense in the income statement, as explained below.

How should the associated expense be presented in the income statement?

BC252 SARs are economically similar to share options. Hence some argue that the accounting treatment of SARs should be the same as the treatment of share options, as discussed earlier (paragraph BC113). However, as noted in paragraphs BC240 and BC241, in an equity-settled transaction there is one change in net assets (the goods or services received) whereas in a cash-settled transaction there are two changes in net assets (the goods or services received and the cash or other assets paid out). To differentiate between the effects of each change in net assets in a cash-settled transaction, the expense could be separated into two components:

- an amount based on the fair value of the SARs at grant date, recognised over the vesting period, in a manner similar to accounting for equity-settled share-based payment transactions, and
- changes in estimate between grant date and settlement date, ie all changes required to remeasure the transaction amount to equal the amount paid out on settlement date.

BC253 In developing ED 2, the Board concluded that information about these two components would be helpful to users of financial statements. For example, users of financial statements regard the effects of remeasuring the liability as having little predictive value. Therefore, the Board concluded that there should be separate disclosure, either on the face of the income statement or in the notes, of that portion of the expense recognised during each accounting period that is attributable to changes in the estimated fair value of the liability between grant date and settlement date.

BC254 However, some respondents to ED 2 disagreed with the proposed disclosure, arguing that it was burdensome and inappropriate to require the entity to account for the transaction as a cash-settled transaction and also calculate, for the purposes of the disclosure, what the transaction amount would have been if the arrangement was an equity-settled transaction.

BC255 The Board considered these comments and also noted that its decision to adopt the SFAS 123 modified grant date method will make it more complex for entities to determine the amount to disclose, because it will be necessary to distinguish between the effects of forfeitures and the effects of fair value changes when calculating the amount to disclose. The Board therefore concluded that the disclosure should not be retained as a mandatory requirement, but instead should be given as an example of an additional disclosure that entities should consider providing. For example, entities with a significant amount of cash-settled arrangements that experience significant share price volatility will probably find that the disclosure is helpful to users of their financial statements.

SHARE-BASED PAYMENT TRANSACTIONS WITH CASH ALTERNATIVES

Under some employee share-based payment arrangements the employees can choose to receive cash instead of shares or share options, or instead of exercising share options. There are many possible variations of share-based payment arrangements under which a cash alternative may be paid. For example, the employees may have more than one opportunity to elect to receive the cash alternative, eg the employees may be able to elect to receive cash instead of shares or share options on vesting date, or elect to receive cash instead of exercising the share options. The terms of the arrangement may provide the entity with a choice of settlement, ie whether to pay the cash alternative instead of issuing shares or share options on vesting date or instead of issuing shares upon the exercise of the share options. The amount of the cash alternative may be fixed or variable and, if variable, may be determinable in a manner that is related, or unrelated, to the price of the entity's shares. **BC256**

The IFRS contains different accounting methods for cash-settled and equity-settled share-based payment transactions. Hence, if the entity or the employee has the choice of settlement, it is necessary to determine which accounting method should be applied. The Board considered situations when the terms of the arrangement provide (a) the employee with a choice of settlement and (b) the entity with a choice of settlement. **BC257**

The terms of the arrangement provide the employee with a choice of settlement

Share-based payment transactions without cash alternatives do not give rise to liabilities under the *Framework*, because the entity is not required to transfer cash or other assets to the other party. However, this is not so if the contract between the entity and the employee gives the employee the contractual right to demand the cash alternative. In this situation, the entity has an obligation to transfer cash to the employee and hence a liability exists. Furthermore, because the employee has the right to demand settlement in equity instead of cash, the employee also has a conditional right to equity instruments. Hence, on grant date the employee was granted rights to a compound financial instrument, ie a financial instrument that includes both debt and equity components. **BC258**

It is common for the alternatives to be structured so that the fair value of the cash alternative is always the same as the fair value of the equity alternative, eg where the employee has a choice between share options and SARs. However, if this is not so, then the fair value of the compound financial instrument will usually exceed both the individual fair value of the cash alternative (because of the possibility that the shares or share options may be more valuable than the cash alternative) and that of the shares or options (because of the possibility that the cash alternative may be more valuable than the shares or options). **BC259**

Under IAS 32, a financial instrument that is accounted for as a compound instrument is separated into its debt and equity components, by allocating the proceeds received for the issue of a compound instrument to its debt and equity components. This entails determining the fair value of the liability component and then assigning the remainder of the proceeds received to the equity component. This is possible if those proceeds are cash or noncash consideration whose fair value can be reliably measured. If that is not the case, it will be necessary to estimate the fair value of the compound instrument itself. **BC260**

BC261 The Board concluded that the compound instrument should be measured by first valuing the liability component (the cash alternative) and then valuing the equity component (the equity instrument) – with that valuation taking into account that the employee must forfeit the cash alternative to receive the equity instrument – and adding the two component values together. This is consistent with the approach adopted in IAS 32, whereby the liability component is measured first and the residual is allocated to equity. If the fair value of each settlement alternative is always the same, then the fair value of the equity component of the compound instrument will be zero and hence the fair value of the compound instrument will be the same as the fair value of the liability component.

BC262 The Board concluded that the entity should separately account for the services rendered in respect of each component of the compound financial instrument, to ensure consistency with the IFRS's requirements for equity-settled and cash-settled share-based payment transactions. Hence, for the debt component, the entity should recognise the services received, and a liability to pay for those services, as the employees render services, in the same manner as other cash-settled share-based payment transactions (eg SARs). For the equity component (if any), the entity should recognise the services received, and an increase in equity, as the employees render services, in the same way as other equity-settled share-based payment transactions.

BC263 The Board concluded that the liability should be remeasured to its fair value as at the date of settlement, before accounting for the settlement of the liability. This ensures that, if the entity settles the liability by issuing equity instruments, the resulting increase in equity is measured at the fair value of the consideration received for the equity instruments issued, being the fair value of the liability settled.

BC264 The Board also concluded that, if the entity pays cash rather than issuing equity instruments on settlement, any contributions to equity previously recognised in respect of the equity component should remain in equity. By electing to receive cash rather than equity instruments, the employee has surrendered his/her rights to receive equity instruments. That event does not cause a change in net assets and hence there is no change in total equity. This is consistent with the Board's conclusions on other lapses of equity instruments (see paragraphs BC218-BC221).

The terms of the arrangement provide the entity with a choice of settlement

BC265 For share-based payment transactions in which the terms of the arrangement provide the entity with a choice of whether to settle in cash or by issuing equity instruments, the entity would need first to determine whether it has an obligation to settle in cash and therefore does not, in effect, have a choice of settlement. Although the contract might specify that the entity can choose whether to settle in cash or by issuing equity instruments, the Board concluded that the entity will have an obligation to settle in cash if the choice of settlement in equity has no commercial substance (eg because the entity is legally prohibited from issuing shares), or if the entity has a past practice or a stated policy of settling in cash, or generally settles in cash whenever the counterparty asks for cash settlement. The entity will also have an obligation to settle in cash if the shares issued (including shares issued upon the exercise of share options) are redeemable, either mandatorily (eg upon cessation of employment) or at the counterparty's option.

BC266 During its redeliberations of the proposals in ED 2, the Board noted that the classification as liabilities or equity of arrangements in which the entity appears to have the choice of settlement differs from the classification under IAS 32, which requires such an arrangement to be classified either wholly as a liability (if the contract is a derivative contract) or as a compound instrument (if the contract is a non-derivative contract). However, consistently with its conclusions on the other differences between IFRS 2 and IAS 32 (see paragraphs BC106-BC110), the Board decided to retain this difference, pending the outcome of its longer-term Concepts project, which includes reviewing the definitions of liabilities and equity.

Even if the entity is not obliged to settle in cash until it chooses to do so, at the time it makes that election a liability will arise for the amount of the cash payment. This raises the question how to account for the debit side of the entry. It could be argued that any difference between (a) the amount of the cash payment and (b) the total expense recognised for services received and consumed up to the date of settlement (which would be based on the grant date value of the equity settlement alternative) should be recognised as an adjustment to the employee remuneration expense. However, given that the cash payment is to settle an equity interest, the Board concluded that it is consistent with the *Framework* to treat the cash payment as the repurchase of an equity interest, ie as a deduction from equity. In this case, no adjustment to remuneration expense is required on settlement. **BC267**

However, the Board concluded that an additional expense should be recognised if the entity chooses the settlement alternative with the higher fair value because, given that the entity has voluntarily paid more than it needed to, presumably it expects to receive (or has already received) additional services from the employees in return for the additional value given. **BC268**

SHARE-BASED PAYMENT TRANSACTIONS AMONG GROUP ENTITIES (2009 AMENDMENTS)*

This section summarises the Board's considerations when finalising its proposals contained in the exposure draft *Group Cash-settled Share-based Payment Transactions* published in December 2007. Until the Board amended IFRS 2 in 2009, IFRIC 11 provided guidance on how an entity that received the goods or services from its suppliers should account for some specific group equity-settled share-based payment transactions in its separate or individual financial statements. Therefore, the amendments issued in June 2009 incorporated substantially the same consensus contained in IFRIC 11. The relevant matters the IFRIC considered when reaching the consensus contained in IFRIC 11, as approved by the Board, are also carried forward in this section. **BC268A**

The exposure draft published in December 2007 addressed two arrangements in which the parent (not the entity itself) has an obligation to make the required cash payments to the suppliers of the entity: **BC268B**

(a) Arrangement 1 – the supplier of the entity will receive cash payments that are linked to the price of the equity instruments of the entity.
(b) Arrangement 2 – the supplier of the entity will receive cash payments that are linked to the price of the equity instruments of the parent of the entity.

The Board noted that, like those group equity-settled share-based payment transactions originally addressed in IFRIC 11, the two arrangements described in paragraph BC268B did not meet the definition of either an equity-settled or a cash-settled share-based payment transaction. The Board considered whether a different conclusion should be reached for such arrangements merely because they are cash- **BC268C**

**Paragraphs BC268A–BC268O are added as a consequence of amendments to IFRS 2* Group Cash-settled Share-based Payment Transactions *issued in June 2009.*

settled rather than equity-settled. Paragraphs BC22A–BC22F explain the Board's considerations in finalising the amendments to clarify the scope of IFRS 2. The section below summarises the Board's considerations in finalising the amendments relating to the measurement of such transactions.

BC268D The Board noted that the arrangements described in paragraph BC268B are

(a) for the purpose of providing benefits to the employees of the subsidiary in return for employee services, and
(b) share-based and cash-settled.

In addition, the Board noted that the guidance in paragraph 3 (now superseded by paragraph 3A) already stated that when a shareholder transferred equity instruments of the entity (or another group entity), the transaction would be within the scope of IFRS 2 for the entity receiving the goods or services.

BC268E For these reasons, in the exposure draft published in December 2007 the Board proposed to amend IFRS 2 and IFRIC 11 to require that, in the separate or individual financial statements of the entity receiving the goods or services, the entity should measure the employee services in accordance with the requirements applicable to cash-settled share-based payment transactions on the basis of the fair value of the corresponding liability incurred by the parent. Specifically, until the liability incurred by the parent is settled, the entity should recognise any changes in the fair value of the liability in profit or loss and changes in the entity's equity as adjustments to contributions from the parent.

BC268F Because group cash-settled share-based payment transactions did not meet the definition of either an equity-settled or a cash-settled share-based payment transaction, some respondents did not object to measuring them as cash-settled on the basis that the accounting reflects the form of the payment received by the entity's suppliers. However, many respondents questioned the basis for the conclusions reached, citing reasons that included:

(a) the lack of a 'push-down' accounting concept in current IFRSs that would require the parent's costs incurred on behalf of the subsidiary to be attributed to the subsidiary,
(b) conflicts with the *Framework* and with other IFRSs that prohibit remeasurement of equity, and
(c) conflicts with the rationale in the Basis for Conclusions on IFRS 2 related to the remeasurement of cash-settled share-based payment transactions when the entity itself has no obligation to its suppliers.

BC268G The Board agreed with respondents that the entity receiving goods or services has no obligation to distribute assets and that the parent's settlement is an equity contribution to the entity. The Board noted that regardless of how such group transactions are structured or accounted for in the separate or individual financial statements of the group entities, the accounting measurement in the consolidated financial statements of the group will be the same. The Board also noted that the share-based payment expense measured on grant date results in the same fair value for both the entity receiving goods or services and the entity settling the transaction, regardless of whether it is measured as equity-settled or as cash-settled.

BC268H To address the comments received from respondents, the Board reviewed two issues to determine the appropriate subsequent measurement in the separate or individual financial statements of the entity receiving the goods or services. The first issue was whether the entity should recognise in its separate or individual financial statements:

(a) Approach 1 – an expense of the same amount as in the consolidated financial statements, or

(b) Approach 2 – an expense measured by classifying the transaction as equity-settled or cash-settled evaluated from its own perspective, which may not always be the same as the amount recognised by the consolidated group.

The Board noted that IFRSs have no broad-based guidance to address 'push-down' accounting or the accounting in separate or individual financial statements for the allocation of costs among group entities. When addressing defined benefit plans that share risks between entities under common control, IAS 19 requires an expense to be recognised by the subsidiary on the basis of the cash amount charged by the group plan. When there are no repayment arrangements, in the separate or individual financial statements, the subsidiary should recognise a cost equal to its contribution payable for the period. This is consistent with Approach 2 described in paragraph BC268H. **BC268I**

The Board therefore decided to adopt Approach 2. However, the approach adopted in IFRS 2 is different from that in IAS 19 in that the entity receiving goods or services in a share-based payment transaction recognises an expense even when it has no obligation to pay cash or other assets. The Board concluded that this approach is consistent with the expense attribution principles underlying IFRS 2. **BC268J**

The Board noted that Approach 2 is consistent with the rationale that the information provided by general purpose financial reporting should 'reflect the perspective of the entity rather than the perspective of the entity's equity investors ....' because the reporting entity is deemed to have substance of its own, separate from that of its owners. Approach 1 reflects the perspective of the entity's owners (the group) rather than the rights and obligations of the entity itself. **BC268K**

The Board also noted that the consensus reached in IFRIC 11 reflected Approach 1 described in paragraph BC268H for some scenarios and Approach 2 for others. The Board concluded that this was undesirable and decided that there should be a single approach to measurement that would apply in all situations. **BC268L**

The second issue the Board considered was identifying the criteria for classifying group share-based payment transactions as equity-settled or cash-settled. How a transaction is classified determines the subsequent measurement in the separate or individual financial statements of both the entity receiving the goods or services and the entity settling the transaction, if different. The Board reviewed the two classification criteria set out in the consensus in IFRIC 11 for group equity-settled transactions: **BC268M**

(a) based on the nature of the award given to the employees—therefore, classified as *equity-settled* if the entity's own equity instruments are given, regardless of which entity grants or settles it; otherwise classified as *cash-settled* even when the entity receiving the goods or services has no obligation.

(b) based on the entity's own rights and obligations—therefore, classified as *cash-settled* if the entity has an obligation to settle, regardless of the nature of the consideration; otherwise classified as *equity-settled*.

The Board noted that, on its own, either of the two criteria described above would not consistently reflect the entity's perspective when assessing the appropriate classification for transactions described in paragraph BC268B. The Board concluded that the entity should consider both criteria in IFRIC 11, ie *equity-settled* when suppliers are given the entity's own equity instruments or when the entity receiving the goods or services has no obligation to settle; and *cash-settled* in all other **BC268N** circumstances. The Board also noted that when the entity receiving goods or services has no obligation to deliver cash or other assets to its suppliers, accounting for the transaction as cash-settled in its separate or individual financial statements is not appropriate. The equity-settled basis is more consistent with the principles and rationales in both IFRS 2 and IFRIC 11. Therefore, the Board decided that the entity receiving the goods or services should classify both of the group cash-settled share-based payment transactions described in paragraph BC268B as *equity-settled* in its separate or individual financial statements.

BC268O This conclusion is the main change to the proposals in the exposure draft. The Board concluded that the broader principles it developed during its redeliberations addressed the three main concerns expressed by respondents described in paragraph BC268F. Those principles apply to all group share-based payment transactions, whether they are cash-settled or equity-settled. The Board's conclusions do not result in any changes to the guidance in IFRIC 11 that addressed similar group equity-settled share-based payment transactions. Other than the change described above, the Board reaffirmed the proposals in the exposure draft. Therefore, the Board concluded that it was not necessary to re-expose the amendments before finalising them.

Transfers of employees between group entities (paragraphs B58–B61)

BC268P When it developed the consensus in IFRIC 11, the IFRIC noted that some share-based payment arrangements involve a parent granting rights to the employees of more than one subsidiary with a vesting condition that requires the employees to work for the group for a particular period. Sometimes, an employee of one subsidiary transfers employment to another subsidiary during the vesting period, without the employee's rights under the original share-based payment arrangements being affected.

BC268Q The IFRIC noted that the terms of the original share-based payment arrangement require the employees to work for the group, rather than for a particular group entity. Thus, the IFRIC concluded that the change of employment should not result in a new grant of equity instruments in the financial statements of the subsidiary to which the employees transferred employment. The subsidiary to which the employee transfers employment should measure the fair value of the services received from the employee by reference to the fair value of the equity instruments at the date those equity instruments were originally granted to the employee by the parent. For the same reason, the IFRIC concluded that the transfer itself should not be treated as an employee's failure to satisfy a vesting condition. Thus, the transfer should not trigger any reversal of the charge previously recognised in respect of the services received from the employee in the separate or individual financial statements of the subsidiary from which the employee transfers employment.

BC268R The IFRIC noted that paragraph 19 of the IFRS requires the cumulative amount recognised for goods or services as consideration for the equity instruments granted to be based on the number of equity instruments that eventually vest. Accordingly, on a cumulative basis, no amount is recognised for goods or services if the equity instruments do not vest because of failure to satisfy a vesting condition other than a market condition as defined in Appendix A. Applying the principles in paragraph 19, the IFRIC concluded that when the employee fails to satisfy a vesting condition other than a market condition, the services from that employee recognised in the financial statements of each group entity during the vesting period should be reversed.

When finalising the 2009 amendments to IFRS 2 for group share-based payment transactions, the Board concluded that the guidance in IFRIC 11 should apply to all group share-based payment transactions classified as equity-settled in the entity's separate or individual financial statements in accordance with paragraphs 43A–43C. **BC268S**

OVERALL CONCLUSIONS ON ACCOUNTING FOR EMPLOYEE SHARE OPTIONS

The Board first considered all major issues relating to the recognition and measurement of share-based payment transactions, and reached conclusions on those issues. It then drew some overall conclusions, particularly on the treatment of employee share options, which is one of the most controversial aspects of the project. In arriving at those conclusions, the Board considered the following issues: **BC269**

- convergence with US GAAP
- recognition versus disclosure of expenses arising from employee share-based payment transactions
- reliability of measurement of the fair value of employee share options.

Convergence with US GAAP

Some respondents to the Discussion Paper and ED 2 urged the Board to develop an IFRS that was based on existing requirements under US generally accepted accounting principles (US GAAP). **BC270**

More specifically, respondents urged the Board to develop a standard based on SFAS 123. However, given that convergence of accounting standards was commonly given as a reason for this suggestion, the Board considered US GAAP overall, not just one aspect of it. The main pronouncements of US GAAP on share-based payment are Accounting Principles Board Opinion No. 25 *Accounting for Stock Issued to Employees*, and SFAS 123. **BC271**

APB 25

APB 25 was issued in 1972. It deals with employee share plans only, and draws a distinction between nonperformance-related (fixed) plans and performance-related and other variable plans. **BC272**

For fixed plans, an expense is measured at intrinsic value (ie the difference between the share price and the exercise price), if any, at grant date. Typically, this results in no expense being recognised for fixed plans, because most share options granted under fixed plans are granted at the money. For performance-related and other variable plans, an expense is measured at intrinsic value at the measurement date. The measurement date is when both the number of shares or share options that the employee is entitled to receive and the exercise price are fixed. Because this measurement date is likely to be much later than grant date, any expense is subject to uncertainty and, if the share price is increasing, the expense for performance-related plans would be larger than for fixed plans. **BC273**

In SFAS 123, the FASB noted that APB 25 is criticised for producing anomalous results and for lacking any underlying conceptual rationale. For example, the requirements of APB 25 typically result in the recognition of an expense for performance-related share options but usually no expense is recognised for fixed share options. This result is anomalous because fixed share options are usually more valuable at grant date than performance-related share options. Moreover, the **BC274** omission of an expense for fixed share options impairs the quality of financial statements:

> The resulting financial statements are less credible than they could be, and the financial statements of entities that use fixed employee share options extensively are not comparable to those of entities that do not make significant use of fixed options. (SFAS 123, paragraph 56)

BC275 The Discussion Paper, in its discussion of US GAAP, noted that the different accounting treatments for fixed and performance-related plans also had the perverse effect of discouraging entities from setting up performance-related employee share plans.

SFAS 123

BC276 SFAS 123 was issued in 1995. It requires recognition of share-based payment transactions with parties other than employees, based on the fair value of the shares or share options issued or the fair value of the goods or services received, whichever is more reliably measurable. Entities are also encouraged, but not required, to apply the fair value accounting method in SFAS 123 to share-based payment transactions with employees. Generally speaking, SFAS 123 draws no distinction between fixed and performance-related plans.

BC277 If an entity applies the accounting method in APB 25 rather than that in SFAS 123, SFAS 123 requires disclosures of pro forma net income and earnings per share in the annual financial statements, as if the standard had been applied. Recently, a significant number of major US companies have voluntarily adopted the fair value accounting method in SFAS 123 for transactions with employees.

BC278 The FASB regards SFAS 123 as superior to APB 25, and would have preferred recognition based on the fair value of employee options to be mandatory, not optional. SFAS 123 makes it clear that the FASB decided to permit the disclosurebased alternative for political reasons, not because it thought that it was the best accounting solution:

> ...the Board...continues to believe that disclosure is not an adequate substitute for recognition of assets, liabilities, equity, revenues and expenses in financial statements...The Board chose a disclosurebased solution for stockbased employee compensation to bring closure to the divisive debate on this issuenot because it believes that solution is the best way to improve financial accounting and reporting. (SFAS 123, paragraphs 61 and 62)

BC279 Under US GAAP, the accounting treatment of share-based payment transactions differs, depending on whether the other party to the transaction is an employee or non-employee, and whether the entity chooses to apply SFAS 123 or APB 25 to transactions with employees. Having a choice of accounting methods is generally regarded as undesirable. Indeed, the Board recently devoted much time and effort to developing improvements to existing international standards, one of the objectives of which is to eliminate choices of accounting methods.

BC280 Research in the US demonstrates that choosing one accounting method over the other has a significant impact on the reported earnings of US entities. For example, research by Bear Stearns and Credit Suisse First Boston on the S&P 500 shows that, had the fair value measurement method in SFAS 123 been applied for the purposes of recognising an expense for employee stockbased compensation, the earnings of the

S&P 500 companies would have been significantly lower, and that the effect is growing. The effect on reported earnings is substantial in some sectors, where companies make heavy use of share options.

The Canadian Accounting Standards Board (AcSB) recently completed its project on share-based payment. In accordance with the AcSB's policy of harmonising Canadian standards with those in the US, the AcSB initially proposed a standard that was based on US GAAP, including APB 25. After considering respondents' comments, the AcSB decided to delete the guidance drawn from APB 25. The AcSB reached this decision for various reasons, including that, in its view, the intrinsic value method is flawed. Also, incorporating the requirements of APB 25 into an accounting standard would result in preparers of financial statements incurring substantial costs for which users of financial statements would derive no benefit – entities would spend a great deal of time and effort on understanding the rules and then redesigning option plans, usually by deleting existing performance conditions, to avoid recognising an expense in respect of such plans, thereby producing no improvement in the accounting for share option plans. **BC281**

The Canadian standard was initially consistent with SFAS 123. That included permitting a choice between fair valuebased accounting for employee stockbased compensation expense in the income statement and disclosure of pro forma amounts in the notes to both interim and annual financial statements. However, the AcSB recently amended its standard to remove the choice between recognition and disclosure, and therefore expense recognition is mandatory for financial periods beginning on or after 1 January 2004. **BC282**

Because APB 25 contains serious flaws, the Board concluded that basing an IFRS on it is unlikely to represent much, if any, improvement in financial reporting. Moreover, the perverse effects of APB 25, particularly in discouraging performance-related share option plans, may cause economic distortions. Accounting standards are intended to be neutral, not to give favourable or unfavourable accounting treatments to particular transactions to encourage or discourage entities from entering into those transactions. APB 25 fails to achieve that objective. Performance-related employee share plans are common in Europe (performance conditions are often required by law) and in other parts of the world outside the US, and investors are calling for greater use of performance conditions. Therefore, the Board concluded that introducing an accounting standard based on APB 25 would be inconsistent with its objective of developing high quality accounting standards. **BC283**

That leaves SFAS 123. Comments from the FASB, in the SFAS 123 Basis for Conclusions, and from the Canadian AcSB when it developed a standard based on SFAS 123, indicate that both standard-setters regard it as inadequate, because it permits a choice between recognition and disclosure. (This issue is discussed further below.) The FASB added to its agenda in March 2003 a project to review US accounting requirements on share-based payment, including removing the disclosure alternative in SFAS 123, so that expense recognition is mandatory. The Chairman of the FASB commented: **BC284**

> Recent events have served as a reminder to all of us that clear, credible and comparable financial information is essential to the health and vitality of our capital market system. In the wake of the market meltdown and corporate reporting scandals, the FASB has received numerous requests from individual and institutional investors, financial analysts and many others urging the Board to mandate the expensing of the compensation cost relating to employee stock options...While a number of major companies have voluntarily opted to reflect these costs as an expense in reporting their earnings, other companies continue

> to show these costs in the footnotes to their financial statements. In addition, a move to require an expense treatment would be consistent with the FASB's commitment to work toward convergence between U.S. and international accounting standards. In taking all of these factors into consideration, the Board concluded that it was critical that it now revisit this important subject. (FASB News Release, 12 March 2003)

BC285 During the Board's redeliberations of the proposals in ED 2, the Board worked with the FASB to achieve convergence of international and US standards, to the extent possible, bearing in mind that the FASB was at an earlier stage in its project – the FASB was developing an Exposure Draft to revise SFAS 123 whereas the IASB was finalising its IFRS. The Board concluded that, although convergence is an important objective, it would not be appropriate to delay the issue of the IFRS, because of the pressing need for a standard on share-based payment, as explained in paragraphs BC2BC5. In any event, at the time the IASB concluded its deliberations, a substantial amount of convergence had been achieved. For example, the FASB agreed with the IASB that all share-based payment transactions should be recognised in the financial statements, measured on a fair value measurement basis, including transactions in which share options are granted to employees. Hence, the FASB agreed that the disclosure alternative in SFAS 123 should be eliminated.

BC286 The IASB and FASB also agreed that, once both boards have issued final standards on share-based payment, the two boards will consider undertaking a convergence project, with the objective of eliminating any remaining areas of divergence between international and US standards on this topic.

Recognition versus disclosure

BC287 A basic accounting concept is that disclosure of financial information is not an adequate substitute for recognition in the financial statements. For example, the *Framework* states:

> Items that meet the recognition criteria should be recognised in the balance sheet or income statement. The failure to recognise such items is not rectified by disclosure of the accounting policies used nor by notes or explanatory material. (paragraph 82)

BC288 A key aspect of the recognition criteria is that the item can be measured with reliability. This issue is discussed further below. Therefore, this discussion focuses on the 'recognition versus disclosure' issue in principle, not on measurement reliability. Once it has been determined that an item meets the criteria for recognition in the financial statements, failing to recognise it is inconsistent with the basic concept that disclosure is not an adequate substitute for recognition.

BC289 Some disagree with this concept, arguing that it makes no difference whether information is recognised in the financial statements or disclosed in the notes. Either way, users of financial statements have the information they require to make economic decisions. Hence, they believe that note disclosure of expenses arising from particular employee share-based payment transactions (ie those involving awards of share options to employees), rather than recognition in the income statement, is acceptable.

BC290 The Board did not accept this argument. The Board noted that if note disclosure is acceptable, because it makes no difference whether the expense is recognised or disclosed, then recognition in the financial statements must also be acceptable for the same reason. If recognition is acceptable, and recognition rather than mere disclosure accords with the accounting principles applied to all other expense items, it is not acceptable to leave one particular expense item out of the income statement.

The Board also noted that there is significant evidence that there is a difference between recognition and disclosure. First, academic research indicates that whether information is recognised or merely disclosed affects market prices (eg Barth, Clinch and Shibano, 2003).* If information is disclosed only in the notes, users of financial statements have to expend time and effort to become sufficiently expert in accounting to know (a) that there are items that are not recognised in the financial statements, (b) that there is information about those items in the notes, and (c) how to assess the note disclosures. Because gaining that expertise comes at a cost, and not all users of financial statements will become accounting experts, information that is merely disclosed may not be fully reflected in share prices. **BC291**

Second, both preparers and users of financial statements appear to agree that there is an important difference between recognition and disclosure. Users of financial statements have strongly expressed the view that all forms of share-based payment, including employee share options, should be recognised in the financial statements, resulting in the recognition of an expense when the goods or services received are consumed, and that note disclosure alone is inadequate. Their views have been expressed by various means, including: **BC292**

(a) users' responses to the Discussion Paper and ED 2.
(b) the 2001 survey by the Association for Investment Management and Research of analysts and fund managers – 83 per cent of survey respondents said the accounting method for all share-based payment transactions should require recognition of an expense in the income statement.
(c) public comments by users of financial statements, such as those reported in the press or made at recent US Senate hearings.

Preparers of financial statements also see a major difference between recognition and disclosure. For example, some preparers who responded to the Discussion Paper and ED 2 were concerned that unless expense recognition is required in all countries, entities that are required to recognise an expense would be at a competitive disadvantage compared with entities that are permitted a choice between recognition and disclosure. Comments such as these indicate that preparers of financial statements regard expense recognition as having consequences that are different from those of disclosure. **BC293**

Reliability of measurement

One reason commonly given by those who oppose the recognition of an expense arising from transactions involving grants of share options to employees is that it is not possible to measure those transactions reliably. **BC294**

The Board discussed these concerns about reliability, after first putting the issue into context. For example, the Board noted that when estimating the fair value of share options, the objective is to measure that fair value at the measurement date, not the value of the underlying share at some future date. Some regard the fair value estimate as inherently uncertain because it is not known, at the measurement date, what the final outcome will be, ie how much the gain on exercise (if any) will be. However, the valuation does not attempt to estimate the future gain, only the amount that the other party would pay to obtain the right to participate in any future gains. **BC295**

**M E Barth, G Clinch and T Shibano. 2003. Market Effects of Recognition and Disclosure. Journal of Accounting Research 41(4): 581609.*

Therefore, even if the share option expires worthless or the employee makes a large gain on exercise, this does not mean that the grant date estimate of the fair value of that option was unreliable or wrong.

BC296 The Board also noted that accounting often involves making estimates, and therefore reporting an estimated fair value is not objectionable merely because that amount represents an estimate rather than a precise measure. Examples of other estimates made in accounting, which may have a material effect on the income statement and the balance sheet, include estimates of the collectability of doubtful debts, estimates of the useful life of fixed assets and the pattern of their consumption, and estimates of employee pension liabilities.

BC297 However, some argue that including in the financial statements an estimate of the fair value of employee share options is different from including other estimates, because there is no subsequent correction of the estimate. Other estimates, such as employee pension costs, will ultimately be revised to equal the amount of the cash paid out. In contrast, because equity is not remeasured, if the estimated fair value of employee share options is recognised, there is no remeasurement of the fair value estimate – unless exercise date measurement is used – so any estimation error is permanently embedded in the financial statements.

BC298 The FASB considered and rejected this argument in developing SFAS 123. For example, for employee pension costs, the total cost is never completely trued up unless the scheme is terminated, the amount attributed to any particular year is never trued up, and it can take decades before the amounts relating to particular employees are trued up. In the meantime, users of financial statements have made economic decisions based on the estimated costs.

BC299 Moreover, the Board noted that if no expense (or an expense based on intrinsic value only, which is typically zero) is recognised in respect of employee share options, that also means that there is an error that is permanently embedded in the financial statements. Reporting zero (or an amount based on intrinsic value, if any) is never trued up.

BC300 The Board also considered the meaning of reliability. Arguments about whether estimates of the fair value of employee share options are sufficiently reliable focus on one aspect of reliability only – whether the estimate is free from material error. The *Framework*, in common with the conceptual frameworks of other accounting standard-setters, makes it clear that another important aspect of reliability is whether the information can be depended upon by users of financial statements to represent faithfully what it purports to represent. Therefore, in assessing whether a particular accounting method produces reliable financial information, it is necessary to consider whether that information is representationally faithful. This is one way in which reliability is linked to another important qualitative characteristic of financial information, relevance.

BC301 For example, in the context of share-based payment, some commentators advocate measuring employee share options at intrinsic value rather than fair value, because intrinsic value is regarded as a much more reliable measure. Whether intrinsic value is a more reliable measure is doubtful – it is certainly less subject to estimation error, but is unlikely to be a representationally faithful measure of remuneration. Nor is intrinsic value a relevant measure, especially when measured at grant date. Many employee share options are issued at the money, so have no intrinsic value at grant date. A share option with no intrinsic value consists entirely of time value. If a share option is measured at intrinsic value at grant date, zero value is attributed to the share option. Therefore, by ignoring time value, the amount attributed to the share option is 100 per cent understated.

Another qualitative characteristic is comparability. Some argue that, given the uncertainties relating to estimating the fair value of employee share options, it is better for all entities to report zero, because this will make financial statements more comparable. They argue that if, for example, for two entities the 'true' amount of expense relating to employee share options is CU500,000, and estimation uncertainties cause one entity to report CU450,000 and the other to report CU550,000, the two entities' financial statements would be more comparable if both reported zero, rather than these divergent figures. **BC302**

However, it is unlikely that any two entities will have the same amount of employee share-based remuneration expense. Research (eg by Bear Stearns and Credit Suisse First Boston) indicates that the expense varies widely from industry to industry, from entity to entity, and from year to year. Reporting zero rather than an estimated amount is likely to make the financial statements much less comparable, not more comparable. For example, if the estimated employee share-based remuneration expense of Company A, Company B and Company C is CU10,000, CU100,000 and CU1,000,000 respectively, reporting zero for all three companies will not make their financial statements comparable. **BC303**

In the context of the foregoing discussion of reliability, the Board addressed the question whether transactions involving share options granted to employees can be measured with sufficient reliability for the purpose of recognition in the financial statements. The Board noted that many respondents to the Discussion Paper asserted that this is not possible. They argue that option pricing models cannot be applied to employee share options, because of the differences between employee options and traded options. **BC304**

The Board considered these differences, with the assistance of the project's Advisory Group and other experts, and has reached conclusions on how to take account of these differences when estimating the fair value of employee share options, as explained in paragraphs BC145-BC199. In doing so, the Board noted that the objective is to measure the fair value of the share options, ie an estimate of what the price of those equity instruments would have been on grant date in an arm's length transaction between knowledgeable, willing parties. The valuation methodology applied should therefore be consistent with valuation methodologies that market participants would use for pricing similar financial instruments, and should incorporate all factors and assumptions that knowledgeable, willing market participants would consider in setting the price. **BC305**

Hence, factors that a knowledgeable, willing market participant would not consider in setting the price of an option are not relevant when estimating the fair value of shares, share options or other equity instruments granted. For example, for share options granted to employees, factors that affect the value of the option from the individual employee's perspective only are not relevant to estimating the price that would be set by a knowledgeable, willing market participant. Many respondents' comments about measurement reliability, and the differences between employee share options and traded options, often focused on the value of the option from the employee's perspective. Therefore, the Board concluded that the IFRS should emphasise that the objective is to estimate the fair value of the share option, not an employee specific value. **BC306**

The Board noted that there is evidence to support a conclusion that it is possible to make a reliable estimate of the fair value of employee share options. First, there is **BC307** academic research to support this conclusion (eg Carpenter 1998, Maller, Tan and Van De Vyver 2002).* Second, users of financial statements regard the estimated fair values as sufficiently reliable for recognition in the financial statements. Evidence of this can be found in a variety of sources, such as the comment letters received from users of financial statements who responded to the Discussion Paper and ED 2. Users' views are important, because the objective of financial statements is to provide high quality, transparent and comparable information to help users make economic decisions. In other words, financial statements are intended to meet the needs of users, rather than preparers or other interest groups. The purpose of setting accounting standards is to ensure that, wherever possible, the information provided in the financial statements meets users' needs. Therefore, if the people who use the financial statements in making economic decisions regard the fair value estimates as sufficiently reliable for recognition in the financial statements, this provides strong evidence of measurement reliability.

BC308 The Board also noted that, although the FASB decided to permit a choice between recognition and disclosure of expenses arising from employee share-based payment transactions, it did so for nontechnical reasons, not because it agreed with the view that reliable measurement was not possible:

> The Board continues to believe that use of optionpricing models, as modified in this statement, will produce estimates of the fair value of stock options that are sufficiently reliable to justify recognition in financial statements. Imprecision in those estimates does not justify failure to recognize compensation cost stemming from employee stock options. That belief underlies the Board's encouragement to entities to adopt the fair value based method of recognizing stockbased employee compensation cost in their financial statements. (SFAS 123, Basis for Conclusions, paragraph 117)

BC309 In summary, if expenses arising from grants of share options to employees are omitted from the financial statements, or recognised using the intrinsic value method (which typically results in zero expense) or the minimum value method, there will be a permanent error embedded in the financial statements. So the question is, which accounting method is more likely to produce the smallest amount of error and the most relevant, comparable information – a fair value estimate, which might result in some understatement or overstatement of the associated expense, or another measurement basis, such as intrinsic value (especially if measured at grant date), that will definitely result in substantial understatement of the associated expense?

BC310 Taking all of the above into consideration, the Board concluded that, in virtually all cases, the estimated fair value of employee share options at grant date can be measured with sufficient reliability for the purposes of recognising employee share-based payment transactions in the financial statements. The Board therefore concluded that, in general, the IFRS on share-based payment should require a fair value measurement method to be applied to all types of share-based payment transactions, including all types of employee share-based payment. Hence, the Board concluded that the IFRS should not allow a choice between a fair value measurement method and an intrinsic value measurement method, and should not permit a choice between recognition and disclosure of expenses arising from employee share-based payment transactions.

**J N Carpenter. 1998. The exercise and valuation of executive stock options. Journal of Financial Economics 48: 127158.*

R A Maller, R Tan and M Van De Vyver. 2002. How Might Companies Value ESOs? Australian Accounting Review 12 (1): 1124.

TRANSITIONAL PROVISIONS

Share-based payment transactions among group entities

The Board noted a potential difficulty when an entity retrospectively applies the amendments made by *Group Cash-settled Share-based Payment Transactions* issued in June 2009. An entity might not have accounted for some group share-based payment transactions in accordance with IFRS 2 in its separate or individual financial statements. In a few cases, an entity that settles a group share-based payment transaction may have to apply hindsight to measure the fair value of awards now required to be accounted for as cash-settled. However, the Board noted that such transactions would have been accounted for in accordance with IFRS 2 in the group's consolidated financial statements. For these reasons and those outlined in paragraph BC268G, if the information necessary for retrospective application is not available, the Board decided to require an entity to use amounts previously recognised in the group's consolidated financial statements when applying the new requirements retrospectively in the entity's separate or individual financial statements. **BC310A**

CONSEQUENTIAL AMENDMENTS TO OTHER STANDARDS*

Tax effects of share-based payment transactions

Whether expenses arising from share-based payment transactions are deductible, and if so, whether the amount of the tax deduction is the same as the reported expense and whether the tax deduction arises in the same accounting period, varies from country to country. **BC311**

If the amount of the tax deduction is the same as the reported expense, but the tax deduction arises in a later accounting period, this will result in a deductible temporary difference under IAS 12 *Income Taxes*. Temporary differences usually arise from differences between the carrying amount of assets and liabilities and the amount attributed to those assets and liabilities for tax purposes. However, IAS 12 also deals with items that have a tax base but are not recognised as assets and liabilities in the balance sheet. It gives an example of research costs that are recognised as an expense in the financial statements in the period in which the costs are incurred, but are deductible for tax purposes in a later accounting period. The Standard states that the difference between the tax base of the research costs, being the amount that will be deductible in a future accounting period, and the carrying amount of nil is a deductible temporary difference that results in a deferred tax asset (IAS 12, paragraph 9). **BC312**

Applying this guidance indicates that if an expense arising from a share-based payment transaction is recognised in the financial statements in one accounting period and is taxdeductible in a later accounting period, this should be accounted for as a deductible temporary difference under IAS 12. Under that Standard, a deferred tax asset is recognised for all deductible temporary differences to the extent that it is probable that taxable profit will be available against which the deductible temporary difference can be used (IAS 12, paragraph 24). **BC313**

****ASB footnote:** The section of IFRS 2 dealing with the consequential amendments to other standards needed to be amended very significantly before being included in FRS 20 so that it can be applied in a UK context. In the context of the discussion in paragraphs BC311-BC333, it should be noted that the ASB has decided not to make amendments to its tax standards (FRS 16 Current Tax and FRS 19 Deferred Tax) equivalent to those made in IFRS 2 to IAS 12 Income Taxes. The ASB's rationale is explained in the 'Notes on the standard's application in the UK and the Republic of Ireland' section.*

BC314 Whilst IAS 12 does not discuss reverse situations, the same logic applies. For example, suppose the entity is able to claim a tax deduction for the total transaction amount at the date of grant but the entity recognises an expense arising from that transaction over the vesting period. Applying the guidance in IAS 12 suggests that this should be accounted for as a taxable temporary difference, and hence a deferred tax liability should be recognised.

BC315 However, the amount of the tax deduction might differ from the amount of the expense recognised in the financial statements. For example, the measurement basis applied for accounting purposes might not be the same as that used for tax purposes, eg intrinsic value might be used for tax purposes and fair value for accounting purposes. Similarly, the measurement date might differ. For example, US entities receive a tax deduction based on intrinsic value at the date of exercise in respect of some share options, whereas for accounting purposes an entity applying SFAS 123 would recognise an expense based on the option's fair value, measured at the date of grant. There could also be other differences in the measurement method applied for accounting and tax purposes, eg differences in the treatment of forfeitures or different valuation methodologies applied.

BC316 SFAS 123 requires that, if the amount of the tax deduction exceeds the total expense recognised in the financial statements, the tax benefit for the excess deduction should be recognised as additional paidin capital, ie as a direct credit to equity. Conversely, if the tax deduction is less than the total expense recognised for accounting purposes, the write-off of the related deferred tax asset in excess of the benefits of the tax deduction is recognised in the income statement, except to the extent that there is remaining additional paidin capital from excess tax deductions from previous share-based payment transactions (SFAS 123, paragraph 44).

BC317 At first sight, it may seem questionable to credit or debit directly to equity amounts that relate to differences between the amount of the tax deduction and the total recognised expense. The tax effects of any such differences would ordinarily flow through the income statement. However, some argue that the approach in SFAS 123 is appropriate if the reason for the difference between the amount of the tax deduction and the recognised expense is that a different measurement date is applied.

BC318 For example, suppose grant date measurement is used for accounting purposes and exercise date measurement is used for tax purposes. Under grant date measurement, any changes in the value of the equity instrument after grant date accrue to the employee (or other party) in their capacity as equity participants. Therefore, some argue that any tax effects arising from those valuation changes should be credited to equity (or debited to equity, if the value of the equity instrument declines).

BC319 Similarly, some argue that the tax deduction arises from an equity transaction (the exercise of options), and hence the tax effects should be reported in equity. It can also be argued that this treatment is consistent with the requirement in IAS 12 to account for the tax effects of transactions or events in the same way as the entity accounts for those transactions or events themselves. If the tax deduction relates to both an income statement item and an equity item, the associated tax effects should be allocated between the income statement and equity.

BC320 Others disagree, arguing that the tax deduction relates to employee remuneration expense, ie an income statement item only, and therefore all of the tax effects of the deduction should be recognised in the income statement. The fact that the taxing authority applies a different method in measuring the amount of the tax deduction does not change this conclusion. A further argument is that this treatment is consistent with the *Framework*, because reporting amounts directly in equity would be inappropriate, given that the government is not an owner of the entity.

The Board noted that, if one accepts that it might be appropriate to debit/ credit to equity the tax effect of the difference between the amount of the tax deduction and the total recognised expense where that difference relates to changes in the value of equity interests, there could be other reasons why the amount of the tax deduction differs from the total recognised expense. For example, grant date measurement may be used for both tax and accounting purposes, but the valuation methodology used for tax purposes might produce a higher value than the methodology used for accounting purposes (eg the effects of early exercise might be ignored when valuing an option for tax purposes). The Board saw no reason why, in this situation, the excess tax benefits should be credited to equity. **BC321**

In developing ED 2, the Board concluded that the tax effects of share-based payment transactions should be recognised in the income statement by being taken into account in the determination of tax expense. It agreed that this should be explained in the form of a worked example in a consequential amendment to IAS 12. **BC322**

During the Board's redeliberation of the proposals in ED 2, the Board reconsidered the points above, and concluded that the tax effects of an equity-settled share-based payment transaction should be allocated between the income statement and equity. The Board then considered how this allocation should be made and related issues, such as the measurement of the deferred tax asset. **BC323**

Under IAS 12, the deferred tax asset for a deductible temporary difference is based on the amount the taxation authorities will permit as a deduction in future periods. Therefore, the Board concluded that the measurement of the deferred tax asset should be based on an estimate of the future tax deduction. If changes in the share price affect that future tax deduction, the estimate of the expected future tax deduction should be based on the current share price. **BC324**

These conclusions are consistent with the proposals in ED 2 concerning the measurement of the deferred tax asset. However, this approach differs from SFAS 123, which measures the deferred tax asset on the basis of the cumulative recognised expense. The Board rejected the SFAS 123 method of measuring the deferred tax asset because it is inconsistent with IAS 12. As noted above, under IAS 12, the deferred tax asset for a deductible temporary difference is based on the amount the taxation authorities will permit as a deduction in future periods. If a later measurement date is applied for tax purposes, it is very unlikely that the tax deduction will ever equal the cumulative expense, except by coincidence. For example, if share options are granted to employees, and the entity receives a tax deduction measured as the difference between the share price and the exercise price at the date of exercise, it is extremely unlikely that the tax deduction will ever equal the cumulative expense. By basing the measurement of the deferred tax asset on the cumulative expense, the SFAS 123 method is likely to result in the understatement or overstatement of the deferred tax asset. In some situations, such as when share options are significantly out of the money, SFAS 123 requires the entity to continue to recognise a deferred tax asset even when the possibility of the entity recovering that asset is remote. Continuing to recognise a deferred tax asset in this situation is not only inconsistent with IAS 12, it is inconsistent with the definition of an asset in the *Framework*, and the requirements of other IFRSs for the recognition and measurement of assets, including requirements to assess impairment. **BC325**

The Board also concluded that: **BC326**

(a) if the tax deduction received (or expected to be received, measured as described in paragraph BC324) is less than or equal to the cumulative expense, the associated tax benefits received (or expected to be received) should be recognised as tax income and included in profit or loss for the period.
(b) if the tax deduction received (or expected to be received, measured as described in paragraph BC324) exceeds the cumulative expense, the excess associated tax benefits received (or expected to be received) should be recognised directly in equity.

BC327 The above allocation method is similar to that applied in SFAS 123, with some exceptions. First, the above allocation method ensures that the total tax benefits recognised in the income statement in respect of a particular share-based payment transaction do not exceed the tax benefits ultimately received. The Board disagreed with the approach in SFAS 123, which sometimes results in the total tax benefits recognised in the income statement exceeding the tax benefits ultimately received because, in some situations, SFAS 123 permits the unrecovered portion of the deferred tax asset to be written off to equity.

BC328 Second, the Board concluded that the above allocation method should be applied irrespective of why the tax deduction received (or expected to be received) differs from the cumulative expense. The SFAS 123 method is based on US tax legislation, under which the excess tax benefits credited to equity (if any) arise from the use of a later measurement date for tax purposes. The Board agreed with respondents who commented that the accounting treatment must be capable of being applied in various tax jurisdictions. The Board was concerned that requiring entities to examine the reasons why there is a difference between the tax deduction and the cumulative expense, and then account for the tax effects accordingly, would be too complex to be applied consistently across a wide range of different tax jurisdictions.

BC329 The Board noted that it might need to reconsider its conclusions on accounting for the tax effects of share-based payment transactions in the future, for example, if the Board reviews IAS 12 more broadly.

Accounting for own shares held

BC330 IAS 32 requires the acquisition of treasury shares to be deducted from equity, and no gain or loss is to be recognised on the sale, issue or cancellation of treasury shares. Consideration received on the subsequent sale or issue of treasury shares is credited to equity.

BC331 This is consistent with the *Framework*. The repurchase of shares and their subsequent reissue or transfer to other parties are transactions with equity participants that should be recognised as changes in equity. In accounting terms, there is no difference between shares that are repurchased and cancelled, and shares that are repurchased and held by the entity. In both cases, the repurchase involves an outflow of resources to shareholders (ie a distribution), thereby reducing shareholders' investment in the entity. Similarly, there is no difference between a new issue of shares and an issue of shares previously repurchased and held in treasury. In both cases, there is an inflow of resources from shareholders, thereby increasing shareholders' investment in the entity. Although accounting practice in some jurisdictions treats own shares held as assets, this is not consistent with the definition of assets in the *Framework* and the conceptual frameworks of other standard-setters, as explained in the Discussion Paper (footnote to paragraph 4.7 of the Discussion Paper, reproduced earlier in the footnote to paragraph BC73).

Given that treasury shares are treated as an asset in some jurisdictions, it will be necessary to change that accounting treatment when this IFRS is applied, because otherwise an entity would be faced with two expense items – an expense arising from the share-based payment transaction (for the consumption of goods and services received as consideration for the issue of an equity instrument) and another expense arising from the write-down of the 'asset' for treasury shares issued or transferred to employees at an exercise price that is less than their purchase price. **BC332**

Hence, the Board concluded that the requirements in the relevant paragraphs of IAS 32 regarding treasury shares should also be applied to treasury shares purchased, sold, issued or cancelled in connection with employee share plans or other share-based payment arrangements. **BC333**

Implementation guidance

Contents

paragraphs

Definition of grant date **IG1-IG4A**

Measurement date for transactions with parties other than employees **IG5-IG7**

Transitional arrangements **IG8**

Illustrative examples **IG9-IG22**

Equity-settled share-based payment transactions IG9-IG17

Cash-settled share-based payment transactions IG18-IG19

Share-based payment arrangements with cash alternatives IG20-IG22

Illustrative disclosures **IG23**

Summary of conditions for a counterparty to receive an equity instrument granted and of accounting treatments **IG24**

Implementation Guidance

This guidance accompanies, but is not part of, IFRS 2.

ASB note: This Implementation Guidance was prepared by the IASB.

Definition of grant date

IFRS 2 defines grant date as the date at which the entity and the employee (or other party providing similar services) agree to a share-based payment arrangement, being when the entity and the counterparty have a shared understanding of the terms and conditions of the arrangement. At grant date the entity confers on the counterparty the right to cash, other assets, or equity instruments of the entity, provided the specified vesting conditions, if any, are met. If that agreement is subject to an approval process (for example, by shareholders), grant date is the date when that approval is obtained. **IG1**

As noted above, grant date is when both parties agree to a share-based payment arrangement. The word 'agree' is used in its usual sense, which means that there must be both an offer and acceptance of that offer. Hence, the date at which one party makes an offer to another party is not grant date. The date of grant is when that other party accepts the offer. In some instances, the counterparty explicitly agrees to the arrangement, eg by signing a contract. In other instances, agreement might be implicit, eg for many share-based payment arrangements with employees, the employees' agreement is evidenced by their commencing to render services. **IG2**

Furthermore, for both parties to have agreed to the share-based payment arrangement, both parties must have a shared understanding of the terms and conditions of the arrangement. Therefore, if some of the terms and conditions of the arrangement are agreed on one date, with the remainder of the terms and conditions agreed on a later date, then grant date is on that later date, when all of the terms and conditions have been agreed. For example, if an entity agrees to issue share options to an employee, but the exercise price of the options will be set by a compensation committee that meets in three months' time, grant date is when the exercise price is set by the compensation committee. **IG3**

In some cases, grant date might occur after the employees to whom the equity instruments were granted have begun rendering services. For example, if a grant of equity instruments is subject to shareholder approval, grant date might occur some months after the employees have begun rendering services in respect of that grant. The IFRS requires the entity to recognise the services when received. In this situation, the entity should estimate the grant date fair value of the equity instruments (eg by estimating the fair value of the equity instruments at the end of the reporting period), for the purposes of recognising the services received during the period between service commencement date and grant date. Once the date of grant has been established, the entity should revise the earlier estimate so that the amounts recognised for services received in respect of the grant are ultimately based on the grant date fair value of the equity instruments. **IG4**

IFRS 2 defines vesting conditions as the conditions that determine whether the entity receives the services that entitle the counterparty to receive cash, other assets or equity instruments of the entity under a share-based payment arrangement. The following flowchart illustrates the evaluation of whether a condition is a service or performance condition or a non-vesting condition. **IG4A**

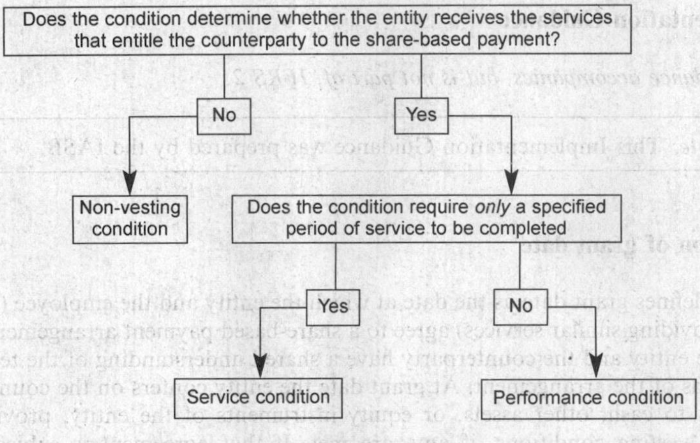

Transactions with parties other than employees

IG5 For transactions with parties other than employees (and others providing similar services) that are measured by reference to the fair value of the equity instruments granted, paragraph 13 of IFRS 2 includes a rebuttable presumption that the fair value of the goods or services received can be estimated reliably. In these situations, paragraph 13 of IFRS 2 requires the entity to measure that fair value at the date the entity obtains the goods or the counterparty renders service.

Transaction in which the entity cannot identify specifically some or all of the goods or services received

IG5A In some cases, however, it might be difficult to demonstrate that goods or services have been (or will be) received. For example, an entity may grant shares to a charitable organisation for nil consideration. It is usually not possible to identify the specific goods or services received in return for such a transaction. A similar situation might arise in transactions with other parties.

IG5B Paragraph 11 of IFRS 2 requires transactions in which share-based payments are made to employees to be measured by reference to the fair value of the share-based payments at grant date.* Hence, the entity is not required to measure directly the fair value of the employee services received.

IG5C It should be noted that the phrase 'the fair value of the share-based payment' refers to the fair value of the particular share-based payment concerned. For example, an entity might be required by government legislation to issue some portion of its shares to nationals of a particular country that may be transferred only to other nationals of that country. Such a transfer restriction may affect the fair value of the shares concerned, and therefore those shares may have a fair value that is less than the fair value of otherwise identical shares that do not carry such restrictions. In this situation, the phrase 'the fair value of the share-based payment' would refer to the fair value of the restricted shares, not the fair value of other, unrestricted shares.

IG5D Paragraph 13A of IFRS 2 specifies how such transactions should be measured. The following example illustrates how the entity should apply the requirements of the IFRS to a transaction in which the entity cannot identify specifically some or all of the goods or services received.

**In IFRS 2, all references to employees include others providing similar services.*

IG Example 1

Share-based payment transaction in which the entity cannot identify specifically some or all of the goods or services received

BACKGROUND

An entity granted shares with a total fair value of CU100,000[(a)] to parties other than employees who are from a particular section of the community (historically disadvantaged individuals), as a means of enhancing its image as a good corporate citizen. The economic benefits derived from enhancing its corporate image could take a variety of forms, such as increasing its customer base, attracting or retaining employees, or improving or maintaining its ability to tender successfully for business contracts.

The entity cannot identify the specific consideration received. For example, no cash was received and no service conditions were imposed. Therefore, the identifiable consideration (nil) is less than the fair value of the equity instruments granted (CU100,000).

APPLICATION OF REQUIREMENTS

Although the entity cannot identify the specific goods or services received, the circumstances indicate that goods or services have been (or will be) received, and therefore IFRS 2 applies.

In this situation, because the entity cannot identify the specific goods or services received, the rebuttable presumption in paragraph 13 of IFRS 2, that the fair value of the goods or services received can be estimated reliably, does not apply. The entity should instead measure the goods or services received by reference to the fair value of the equity instruments granted.

(a) In this example, and in all other examples in this guidance, monetary amounts are denominated in 'currency units (CU)'.

If the goods or services are received on more than one date, the entity should measure the fair value of the equity instruments granted on each date when goods or services are received. The entity should apply that fair value when measuring the goods or services received on that date. **IG6**

However, an approximation could be used in some cases. For example, if an entity received services continuously during a three-month period, and its share price did not change significantly during that period, the entity could use the average share price during the three-month period when estimating the fair value of the equity instruments granted. **IG7**

Transitional arrangements

In paragraph 54 of IFRS 2, the entity is encouraged, but not required, to apply the requirements of the IFRS to other grants of equity instruments (ie grants other than those specified in paragraph 53 of the IFRS), if the entity has disclosed publicly the fair value of those equity instruments, measured at the measurement date. For example, such equity instruments include equity instruments for which the entity has disclosed in the notes to its financial statements the information required in the US by SFAS 123 *Accounting for Stock-Based Compensation*. **IG8**

Equity-settled share-based payment transactions

IG9 For equity-settled transactions measured by reference to the fair value of the equity instruments granted, paragraph 19 of IFRS 2 states that vesting conditions, other than market conditions,* are not taken into account when estimating the fair value of the shares or share options at the measurement date (ie grant date, for transactions with employees and others providing similar services). Instead, vesting conditions are taken into account by adjusting the number of equity instruments included in the measurement of the transaction amount so that, ultimately, the amount recognised for goods or services received as consideration for the equity instruments granted is based on the number of equity instruments that eventually vest. Hence, on a cumulative basis, no amount is recognised for goods or services received if the equity instruments granted do not vest because of failure to satisfy a vesting condition, eg the counterparty fails to complete a specified service period, or a performance condition is not satisfied. This accounting method is known as the modified grant date method, because the number of equity instruments included in the determination of the transaction amount is adjusted to reflect the outcome of the vesting conditions, but no adjustment is made to the fair value of those equity instruments. That fair value is estimated at grant date (for transactions with employees and others providing similar services) and not subsequently revised. Hence, neither increases nor decreases in the fair value of the equity instruments after grant date are taken into account when determining the transaction amount (other than in the context of measuring the incremental fair value transferred if a grant of equity instruments is subsequently modified).

IG10 To apply these requirements, paragraph 20 of IFRS 2 requires the entity to recognise the goods or services received during the vesting period based on the best available estimate of the number of equity instruments expected to vest and to revise that estimate, if necessary, if subsequent information indicates that the number of equity instruments expected to vest differs from previous estimates. On vesting date, the entity revises the estimate to equal the number of equity instruments that ultimately vested (subject to the requirements of paragraph 21 concerning market conditions).

IG11 In the examples below, the share options granted all vest at the same time, at the end of a specified period. In some situations, share options or other equity instruments granted might vest in instalments over the vesting period. For example, suppose an employee is granted 100 share options, which will vest in instalments of 25 share options at the end of each year over the next four years. To apply the requirements of the IFRS, the entity should treat each instalment as a separate share option grant, because each instalment has a different vesting period, and hence the fair value of each instalment will differ (because the length of the vesting period affects, for example, the likely timing of cash flows arising from the exercise of the options).

**In the remainder of this paragraph, the discussion of vesting conditions excludes market conditions, which are subject to the requirements of paragraph 21 of IFRS 2.*

IG Example 1

BACKGROUND

An entity grants 100 share options to each of its 500 employees. Each grant is conditional upon the employee working for the entity over the next three years. The entity estimates that the fair value of each share option is CU15.*

On the basis of a weighted average probability, the entity estimates that 20 per - cent of employees will leave during the three-year period and therefore forfeit their rights to the share options.

APPLICATION OF REQUIREMENTS

Scenario 1

If everything turns out exactly as expected, the entity recognises the following amounts during the vesting period, for services received as consideration for the share options.

Year	Calculation	Remuneration expense for period CU	Cumulative remuneration expense CU
1	50,000 options × 80% × CU15 × 1/3 years	200,000	200,000
2	(50,000 options × 80% × CU15 × 2/3 years) – CU200,000	200,000	400,000
3	(50,000 options × 80% × CU15 × 3/3 years) – CU400,000	200,000	600,000

Scenario 2

During year 1, 20 employees leave. The entity revises its estimate of total employee departures over the three-year period from 20 per cent (100employees) to 15 per cent (75 employees). During year 2, a further 22employees leave. The entity revises its estimate of total employee departures over the three-year period from 15 per cent to 12 per cent (60 employees). During year 3, a further 15 employees leave. Hence, a total of 57 employees forfeited their rights to the share options during the three-year period, and a total of 44,300 share options (443 employees × 100 options per employee) vested at the end of year 3.

Year	Calculation	Remuneration expense for period CU	Cumulative remuneration expense CU
1	50,000 options × 85% × CU15 × 1/3 years	212,500	212,500
2	(50,000 options × 88% × CU15 × 2/3 years) CU212,500	227,500	440,000
3	(44,300 options × CU15) CU440,000	224,500	664,500

In Example 1, the share options were granted conditionally upon the employees' completing a specified service period. In some cases, a share option or share grant IG12

**In this example, and in all other examples in this guidance, monetary amounts are denominated in 'currency units' (CU).*

might also be conditional upon the achievement of a specified performance target. Examples 2, 3 and 4 illustrate the application of the IFRS to share option or share grants with performance conditions (other than market conditions, which are discussed in paragraph IG5 and illustrated in Examples 5 and 6). In Example 2, the length of the vesting period varies, depending on when the performance condition is satisfied. Paragraph 15 of the IFRS requires the entity to estimate the length of the expected vesting period, based on the most likely outcome of the performance condition, and to revise that estimate, if necessary, if subsequent information indicates that the length of the vesting period is likely to differ from previous estimates.

IG Example 2

Grant with a performance condition, in which the length of the vesting period varies

BACKGROUND

At the beginning of year 1, the entity grants 100 shares each to 500 employees, conditional upon the employees' remaining in the entity's employ during the vesting period. The shares will vest at the end of year 1 if the entity's earnings increase by more than 18 per cent; at the end of year 2 if the entity's earnings increase by more than an average of 13 per cent per year over the two-year period; and at the end of year 3 if the entity's earnings increase by more than an average of 10 per cent per year over the three-year period. The shares have a fair value of CU30 per share at the start of year 1, which equals the share price at grant date. No dividends are expected to be paid over the three-year period.

By the end of year 1, the entity's earnings have increased by 14 per cent, and 30 employees have left. The entity expects that earnings will continue to increase at a similar rate in year 2, and therefore expects that the shares will vest at the end of year 2. The entity expects, on the basis of a weighted average probability, that a further 30 employees will leave during year 2, and therefore expects that 440 employees will vest in 100 shares each at the end of year 2.

By the end of year 2, the entity's earnings have increased by only 10 per cent and therefore the shares do not vest at the end of year 2. 28 employees have left during the year. The entity expects that a further 25 employees will leave during year 3, and that the entity's earnings will increase by at least 6 per cent, thereby achieving the average of 10 per cent per year.

By the end of year 3, 23 employees have left and the entity's earnings had increased by 8 per cent, resulting in an average increase of 10.67 per cent per year. Therefore, 419 employees received 100 shares at the end of year 3.

APPLICATION OF REQUIREMENTS

Year	Calculation	Remuneration expense for period CU	Cumulative remuneration expense CU
1	440 employees × 100 shares × CU30 × 1/2	660,000	660,000
2	(417 employees × 100 shares × CU30 × 2/3) – CU660,000	174,000	834,000
3	(419 employees × 100 shares × CU30 × 3/3) – CU834,000	423,000	1,257,000

IG Example 3

Grant with a performance condition, in which the number of equity instruments varies

BACKGROUND

At the beginning of year 1, Entity A grants share options to each of its 100 employees working in the sales department. The share options will vest at the end of year 3, provided that the employees remain in the entity's employ, and provided that the volume of sales of a particular product increases by at least an average of 5 per cent per year. If the volume of sales of the product increases by an average of between 5 per cent and 10 per cent per year, each employee will receive 100 share options. If the volume of sales increases by an average of between 10 per cent and 15 per cent each year, each employee will receive 200 share options. If the volume of sales increases by an average of 15 per cent or more, each employee will receive 300 share options.

On grant date, Entity A estimates that the share options have a fair value of CU20 per option. Entity A also estimates that the volume of sales of the product will increase by an average of between 10 per cent and 15 per cent per year, and therefore expects that, for each employee who remains in service until the end of year 3, 200 share options will vest. The entity also estimates, on the basis of a weighted average probability, that 20 per cent of employees will leave before the end of year 3.

By the end of year 1, seven employees have left and the entity still expects that a total of 20 employees will leave by the end of year 3. Hence, the entity expects that 80 employees will remain in service for the three-year period. Product sales have increased by 12 per cent and the entity expects this rate of increase to continue over the next 2 years.

By the end of year 2, a further five employees have left, bringing the total to 12 to date. The entity now expects only three more employees will leave during year 3, and therefore expects a total of 15 employees will have left during the three-year period, and hence 85 employees are expected to remain. Product sales have increased by 18 per cent, resulting in an average of 15 per cent over the two years to date. The entity now expects that sales will average 15 per cent or more over the three-year period, and hence expects each sales employee to receive 300 share options at the end of year 3.

By the end of year 3, a further two employees have left. Hence, 14 employees have left during the three-year period, and 86 employees remain. The entity's sales have increased by an average of 16 per cent over the three years. Therefore, each of the 86 employees receives 300 share options.

APPLICATION OF REQUIREMENTS

Year	Calculation	Remuneration expense for period CU	Cumulative remuneration expense CU
1	80 employees × 200 options × CU20 × 1/3	106,667	106,667
2	(85 employees × 300 options × CU20 × 2/3) – CU106,667	233,333	340,000
3	(86 employees × 300 options × CU20 × 3/3) – CU340,000	176,000	516,000

IG Example 4

Grant with a performance condition, in which the exercise price varies

BACKGROUND

At the beginning of year 1, an entity grants to a senior executive 10,000 share options, conditional upon the executive's remaining in the entity's employ until the end of year 3. The exercise price is CU40. However, the exercise price drops to CU30 if the entity's earnings increase by at least an average of 10 per cent per year over the three-year period.

On grant date, the entity estimates that the fair value of the share options, with an exercise price of CU30, is CU16 per option. If the exercise price is CU40, the entity estimates that the share options have a fair value of CU12 per option.

During year 1, the entity's earnings increased by 12 per cent, and the entity expects that earnings will continue to increase at this rate over the next two years. The entity therefore expects that the earnings target will be achieved, and hence the share options will have an exercise price of CU30.

During year 2, the entity's earnings increased by 13 per cent, and the entity continues to expect that the earnings target will be achieved.

During year 3, the entity's earnings increased by only 3 per cent, and therefore the earnings target was not achieved. The executive completes three years' service, and therefore satisfies the service condition. Because the earnings target was not achieved, the 10,000 vested share options have an exercise price of CU40.

APPLICATION OF REQUIREMENTS

Because the exercise price varies depending on the outcome of a performance condition that is not a market condition, the effect of that performance condition (ie the possibility that the exercise price might be CU40 and the possibility that the exercise price might be CU30) is not taken into account when estimating the fair value of the share options at grant date. Instead, the entity estimates the fair value of the share options at grant date under each scenario (ie exercise price of CU40 and exercise price of CU30) and ultimately revises the transaction amount to reflect the outcome of that performance condition, as illustrated below.

Year	Calculation	Remuneration expense for period CU	Cumulative remuneration expense CU
1	10,000 options × CU16 × 1/3	53,333	53,333
2	(10,000 options × CU16 × 2/3) – CU53,333	53,334	106,667
3	(10,000 options × CU12 × 3/3) – CU106,667	13,333	120,000

IG13 Paragraph 21 of the IFRS requires market conditions, such as a target share price upon which vesting (or exercisability) is conditional, to be taken into account when estimating the fair value of the equity instruments granted. Therefore, for grants of equity instruments with market conditions, the entity recognises the goods or services received from a counterparty who satisfies all other vesting conditions (eg services received from an employee who remains in service for the specified period of service), irrespective of whether that market condition is satisfied. Example 5 illustrates these requirements.

IG Example 5

Grant with a market condition

BACKGROUND

At the beginning of year 1, an entity grants to a senior executive 10,000 share options, conditional upon the executive remaining in the entity's employ until the end of year 3. However, the share options cannot be exercised unless the share price has increased from CU50 at the beginning of year 1 to above CU65 at the end of year 3. If the share price is above CU65 at the end of year 3, the share options can be exercised at any time during the next seven years, ie by the end of year 10.

The entity applies a binomial option pricing model, which takes into account the possibility that the share price will exceed CU65 at the end of year 3 (and hence the share options become exercisable) and the possibility that the share price will not exceed CU65 at the end of year 3 (and hence the options will be forfeited). It estimates the fair value of the share options with this market condition to be CU24 per option.

APPLICATION OF REQUIREMENTS

Because paragraph 21 of the IFRS requires the entity to recognise the services received from a counterparty who satisfies all other vesting conditions (eg services received from an employee who remains in service for the specified service period), irrespective of whether that market condition is satisfied, it makes no difference whether the share price target is achieved. The possibility that the share price target might not be achieved has already been taken into account when estimating the fair value of the share options at grant date. Therefore, if the entity expects the executive to complete the three-year service period, and the executive does so, the entity recognises the following amounts in years 1, 2 and 3:

Year	Calculation	Remuneration expense for period CU	Cumulative remuneration expense CU
1	10,000 options × CU24 × 1/3	80,000	80,000
2	(10,000 options × CU24 × 2/3) – CU80,000	80,000	160,000
3	(10,000 options × CU24) – CU160,000	80,000	240,000

As noted above, these amounts are recognised irrespective of the outcome of the market condition. However, if the executive left during year 2 (or year 3), the amount recognised during year 1 (and year 2) would be reversed in year 2 (or year 3). This is because the service condition, in contrast to the market condition, was not taken into account when estimating the fair value of the share options at grant date. Instead, the service condition is taken into account by adjusting the transaction amount to be based on the number of equity instruments that ultimately vest, in accordance with paragraphs 19 and 20 of the IFRS.

In Example 5, the outcome of the market condition did not change the length of the vesting period. However, if the length of the vesting period varies depending on when a performance condition is satisfied, paragraph 15 of the IFRS requires the entity to presume that the services to be rendered by the employees as consideration for the equity instruments granted will be received in the future, over the expected vesting period. The entity is required to estimate the length of the expected vesting period at **IG14** grant date, based on the most likely outcome of the performance condition. If the performance condition is a market condition, the estimate of the length of the expected vesting period must be consistent with the assumptions used in estimating the fair value of the share options granted, and is not subsequently revised. Example 6 illustrates these requirements.

IG Example 6

Grant with a market condition, in which the length of the vesting period varies

BACKGROUND

At the beginning of year 1, an entity grants 10,000 share options with a ten-year life to each of ten senior executives. The share options will vest and become exercisable immediately if and when the entity's share price increases from CU50 to CU70, provided that the executive remains in service until the share price target is achieved.

The entity applies a binomial option pricing model, which takes into account the possibility that the share price target will be achieved during the ten-year life of the options, and the possibility that the target will not be achieved. The entity estimates that the fair value of the share options at grant date is CU25 per option. From the option pricing model, the entity determines that the mode of the distribution of possible vesting dates is five years. In other words, of all the possible outcomes, the most likely outcome of the market condition is that the share price target will be achieved at the end of year 5. Therefore, the entity estimates that the expected vesting period is five years. The entity also estimates that two executives will have left by the end of year 5, and therefore expects that 80,000 share options (10,000 share options x 8 executives) will vest at the end of year 5.

Throughout years 1–4, the entity continues to estimate that a total of two executives will leave by the end of year 5. However, in total three executives leave, one in each of years 3, 4 and 5. The share price target is achieved at the end of year 6. Another executive leaves during year 6, before the share price target is achieved.

Application of requirements

Paragraph 15 of the IFRS requires the entity to recognise the services received over the expected vesting period, as estimated at grant date, and also requires the entity not to revise that estimate. Therefore, the entity recognises the services received from the executives over years 1–5. Hence, the transaction amount is ultimately based on 70,000 share options (10,000 share options × 7 executives who remain in service at the end of year 5). Although another executive left during year 6, no adjustment is made, because the executive had already completed the expected vesting period of five years. Therefore, the entity recognises the following amounts in years 1–5:

Year	Calculation	Remuneration expense for period CU	Cumulative remuneration expense CU
1	80,000 options × CU25 × 1/5	400,000	400,000
2	(80,000 options × CU25 × 2/5) – CU400,000	400,000	800,000
3	(80,000 options × CU25 × 3/5) – CU800,000	400,000	1,200,000
4	(80,000 options × CU25 × 4/5) – CU1,200,000	400,000	1,600,000
5	(70,000 options × CU25) – CU1,600,000	150,000	1,750,000

Paragraphs 26–29 and B42–B44 of the IFRS set out requirements that apply if a share option is repriced (or the entity otherwise modifies the terms or conditions of a share-based payment arrangement). Examples 7–9 illustrate some of these requirements. **IG15**

IG Example 7

Grant of share options that are subsequently repriced

BACKGROUND

At the beginning of year 1, an entity grants 100 share options to each of its 500 employees. Each grant is conditional upon the employee remaining in service over the next three years. The entity estimates that the fair value of each option is CU15. On the basis of a weighted average probability, the entity estimates that 100 employees will leave during the three-year period and therefore forfeit their rights to the share options.

Suppose that 40 employees leave during year 1. Also suppose that by the end of year 1, the entity's share price has dropped, and the entity reprices its share options, and that the repriced share options vest at the end of year 3. The entity estimates that a further 70 employees will leave during years 2 and 3, and hence the total expected employee departures over the three-year vesting period is 110 employees. During year 2, a further 35 employees leave, and the entity estimates that a further 30 employees will leave during year 3, to bring the total expected employee departures over the three-year vesting period to 105 employees. During year 3, a total of 28 employees leave, and hence a total of 103 employees ceased employment during the vesting period. For the remaining 397 employees, the share options vested at the end of year 3.

The entity estimates that, at the date of repricing, the fair value of each of the original share options granted (ie before taking into account the repricing) is CU5 and that the fair value of each repriced share option is CU8.

APPLICATION OF REQUIREMENTS

Paragraph 27 of the IFRS requires the entity to recognise the effects of modifications that increase the total fair value of the share-based payment arrangement or are otherwise beneficial to the employee. If the modification increases the fair value of the equity instruments granted (eg by reducing the exercise price), measured immediately before and after the modification, paragraph B43(a) of Appendix B requires the entity to include the incremental fair value granted (ie the difference between the fair value of the modified equity instrument and that of the original equity instrument, both estimated as at the date of the modification) in the measurement of the amount recognised for services received as consideration for the equity instruments granted. If the modification occurs during the vesting period, the incremental fair value granted is included in the measurement of the amount recognised for services received over the period from the modification date until the date when the modified equity instruments vest, in addition to the amount based on the grant date fair value of the original equity instruments, which is recognised over the remainder of the original vesting period.

The incremental value is CU3 per share option (CU8 – CU5). This amount is recognised over the remaining two years of the vesting period, along with remuneration expense based on the original option value of CU15.

The amounts recognised in years 1–3 are as follows:

Year	Calculation	Remuneration expense for period CU	Cumulative remuneration expense CU
1	(500 – 110) employees × 100 options × CU15 × 1/3	195,000	195,000
2	(500 – 105) employees × 100 options × (CU15 × 2/3 + CU3 × 1/2) – CU195,000	259,250	454,250
3	(500 – 103) employees × 100 options × (CU15 + CU3) – CU454,250	260,350	714,600

IG Example 8

Grant of share options with a vesting condition that is subsequently modified

BACKGROUND

At the beginning of year 1, the entity grants 1,000 share options to each member of its sales team, conditional upon the employee's remaining in the entity's employ for three years, and the team selling more than 50,000 units of a particular product over the three-year period. The fair value of the share options is CU15 per option at the date of grant.

During year 2, the entity increases the sales target to 100,000 units. By the end of year 3, the entity has sold 55,000 units, and the share options are forfeited. Twelve members of the sales team have remained in service for the three-year period.

APPLICATION OF REQUIREMENTS

Paragraph 20 of the IFRS requires, for a performance condition that is not a market condition, the entity to recognise the services received during the vesting period based on the best available estimate of the number of equity instruments expected to vest and to revise that estimate, if necessary, if subsequent information indicates that the number of equity instruments expected to vest differs from previous estimates. On vesting date, the entity revises the estimate to equal the number of equity instruments that ultimately vested. However, paragraph 27 of the IFRS requires, irrespective of any modifications to the terms and conditions on which the equity instruments were granted, or a cancellation or settlement of that grant of equity instruments, the entity to recognise, as a minimum, the services received, measured at the grant date fair value of the equity instruments granted, unless those equity instruments do not vest because of failure to satisfy a vesting condition (other than a market condition) that was specified at grant date. Furthermore, paragraph B44(c) of Appendix B specifies that, if the entity modifies the vesting conditions in a manner that is not beneficial to the employee, the entity does not take the modified vesting conditions into account when applying the requirements of paragraphs 19–21 of the IFRS.

Therefore, because the modification to the performance condition made it less likely that the share options will vest, which was not beneficial to the employee, the entity takes no account of the modified performance condition when recognising the services received. Instead, it continues to recognise the services received over the three-year period based on the original vesting conditions. Hence, the entity ultimately recognises cumulative remuneration expense of CU180,000 over the three-year period (12 employees × 1,000 options × CU15).

The same result would have occurred if, instead of modifying the performance target, the entity had increased the number of years of service required for the share options to vest from three years to ten years. Because such a modification would make it less likely that the options will vest, which would not be beneficial to the employees, the entity would take no account of the modified service condition when recognising the services received. Instead, it would recognise the services received from the twelve employees who remained in service over the original three-year vesting period.

IG Example 9

Grant of shares, with a cash alternative subsequently added

BACKGROUND

At the beginning of year 1, the entity grants 10,000 shares with a fair value of CU33 per share to a senior executive, conditional upon the completion of three years' service. By the end of year 2, the share price has dropped to CU25 per share. At that date, the entity adds a cash alternative to the grant, whereby the executive can choose whether to receive 10,000 shares or cash equal to the value of 10,000 shares on vesting date. The share price is CU22 on vesting date.

APPLICATION OF REQUIREMENTS

Paragraph 27 of the IFRS requires, irrespective of any modifications to the terms and conditions on which the equity instruments were granted, or a cancellation or settlement of that grant of equity instruments, the entity to recognise, as a minimum, the services received measured at the grant date fair value of the equity instruments granted, unless those equity instruments do not vest because of failure to satisfy a vesting condition (other than a market condition) that was specified at grant date. Therefore, the entity recognises the services received over the three-year period, based on the grant date fair value of the shares.

Furthermore, the addition of the cash alternative at the end of year 2 creates an obligation to settle in cash. In accordance with the requirements for cash-settled share-based payment transactions (paragraphs 30–33 of the IFRS), the entity recognises the liability to settle in cash at the modification date, based on the fair value of the shares at the modification date and the extent to which the specified services have been received. Furthermore, the entity remeasures the fair value of the liability at each reporting date and at the date of settlement, with any changes in fair value recognised in profit or loss for the period. Therefore, the entity recognises the following amounts:

Year	Calculation	Expense CU	Equity CU	Liability CU
1	Remuneration expense for year: 10,000 shares × CU33 × 1/3	110,000	110,000	
2	Remuneration expense for year: (10,000 shares × CU33 × 2/3) – CU110,000	110,000	110,000	
	Reclassify equity to liabilities: 10,000 shares × CU25 × 2/3		(166,667)	166,667
3	Remuneration expense for year: (10,000 shares × CU33 × 3/3) – CU220,000	110,000	26,667*	83,333*
	Adjust liability to closing fair value: (CU166,667 + CU83,333) – (CU22 × 10,000 shares)	(30,000)		(30,000)
	Total	300,000	80,000	220,000

IG15A If a share-based payment has a non-vesting condition that the counterparty can choose not to meet and the counterparty does not meet that non-vesting condition during the vesting period, paragraph 28A of the IFRS requires that event to be treated as a cancellation. Example 9A illustrates the accounting for this type of event.

IG Example 9A

Share-based payment with vesting and non-vesting conditions when the counterparty can choose whether the non-vesting condition is met

BACKGROUND

An entity grants an employee the opportunity to participate in a plan in which the employee obtains share options if he agrees to save 25 per cent of his monthly salary of CU400 for a three-year period. The monthly payments are made by deduction from the employee's salary. The employee may use the accumulated savings to exercise his options at the end of three years, or take a refund of his contributions at any point during the three-year period. The estimated annual expense for the share-based payment arrangement is CU120.

After 18 months, the employee stops paying contributions to the plan and takes a refund of contributions paid to date of CU1,800.

APPLICATION OF REQUIREMENTS

There are three components to this plan: paid salary, salary deduction paid to the savings plan and share-based payment. The entity recognises an expense in respect of each component and a corresponding increase in liability or equity as appropriate. The requirement to pay contributions to the plan is a non-vesting condition, which the employee chooses not to meet in the second year. Therefore, in accordance with paragraphs 28(b) and 28A of the IFRS, the repayment of contributions is treated as an extinguishment of the liability and the cessation of contributions in year 2 is treated as a cancellation.

* *Allocated between liabilities and equity, to bring in the final third of the liability based on the fair value of the shares as at the date of the modification.*

YEAR 1	Expense CU	Cash CU	Liability CU	Equity CU
Paid salary	3,600 (75% x 400 x 12)	(3,600)		
Salary deduction paid to the savings plan	1,200 (25% x 400 x 12)		(1,200)	
Share-based payment	120			(120)
Total	4,920	(3,600)	(1,200)	(120)
YEAR 2				
Paid salary	4,200 (75% x 400 x 6 + 100% x 400 x 6)	(4,200)		
Salary deduction paid to the savings plan	600 (25% x 400 x 6)		(600)	
Refund of contributions to the employee	(1,800)		1,800	
Share-based payment (acceleration of remaining expense)	240 (120 x 3 – 120)			(240)
Total	5,040	(6,000)	1,200	(240)

Paragraph 24 of the IFRS requires that, in rare cases only, in which the IFRS requires the entity to measure an equity-settled share-based payment transaction by reference to the fair value of the equity instruments granted, but the entity is unable to estimate reliably that fair value at the specified measurement date (eg grant date, for transactions with employees), the entity shall instead measure the transaction using an intrinsic value measurement method. Paragraph 24 also contains requirements on how to apply this method. The following example illustrates these requirements. **IG16**

IG Example 10

Grant of share options that is accounted for by applying the intrinsic value method

BACKGROUND

At the beginning of year 1, an entity grants 1,000 share options to 50 employees. The share options will vest at the end of year 3, provided the employees remain in service until then. The share options have a life of 10 years. The exercise price is CU60 and the entity's share price is also CU60 at the date of grant.

At the date of grant, the entity concludes that it cannot estimate reliably the fair value of the share options granted.

At the end of year 1, three employees have ceased employment and the entity estimates that a further seven employees will leave during years 2 and 3. Hence, the entity estimates that 80 per cent of the share options will vest.

Two employees leave during year 2, and the entity revises its estimate of the number of share options that it expects will vest to 86 per cent.

Two employees leave during year 3. Hence, 43,000 share options vested at the end of year 3.

The entity's share price during years 1-10, and the number of share options exercised during years 4-10, are set out below. Share options that were exercised during a particular year were all exercised at the end of that year.

Year	Share price at year-end	Number of share options exercised at year-end
1	63	0
2	65	0
3	75	0
4	88	6,000
5	100	8,000
6	90	5,000
7	96	9,000
8	105	8,000
9	108	5,000
10	115	2,000

APPLICATION OF REQUIREMENTS

In accordance with paragraph 24 of the IFRS, the entity recognises the following amounts in years 1-10.

Year	Calculation	Expense for period CU	Cumulative expense CU
1	50,000 options × 80% × (CU63 – CU60) × 1/3 years	40,000	40,000
2	50,000 options × 86% × (CU65 – CU60) × 2/3 years – CU40,000	103,333	143,333
3	43,000 options × (CU75 – CU60) – CU143,333	501,667	645,000
4	37,000 outstanding options × (CU88 – CU75) + 6,000 exercised options × (CU88 – CU75)	559,000	1,204,000
5	29,000 outstanding options × (CU100 – CU88) + 8,000 exercised options × (CU100 – CU88)	444,000	1,648,000
6	24,000 outstanding options × (CU90 – CU100) + 5,000 exercised options × (CU90 – CU100)	(290,000)	1,358,000
7	15,000 outstanding options × (CU96 – CU90) + 9,000 exercised options × (CU96 – CU90)	144,000	1,502,000
8	7,000 outstanding options × (CU105 – CU96) + 8,000 exercised options × (CU105 – CU96)	135,000	1,637,000
9	2,000 outstanding options × (CU108 – CU105) + 5,000 exercised options × (CU108 – CU105)	21,000	1,658,000
10	2,000 exercised options × (CU115 – CU108)	14,000	1,672,000

There are many different types of employee share and share option plans. The following example illustrates the application of IFRS 2 to one particular type of plan – an employee share purchase plan. Typically, an employee share purchase plan provides employees with the opportunity to purchase the entity's shares at a discounted price. The terms and conditions under which employee share purchase plans operate differ from country to country. That is to say, not only are there many different types of employee share and share options plans, there are also many different types of employee share purchase plans. Therefore, the following example illustrates the application of IFRS 2 to one specific employee share purchase plan. **IG17**

IG Example 11

Employee share purchase plan

BACKGROUND

An entity offers all its 1,000 employees the opportunity to participate in an employee share purchase plan. The employees have two weeks to decide whether to accept the offer. Under the terms of the plan, the employees are entitled to purchase a maximum of 100 shares each. The purchase price will be 20 per cent less than the market price of the entity's shares at the date the offer is accepted, and the purchase price must be paid immediately upon acceptance of the offer. All shares purchased must be held in trust for the employees, and cannot be sold for five years. The employee is not permitted to withdraw from the plan during that period. For example, if the employee ceases employment during the five-year period, the shares must nevertheless remain in the plan until the end of the five-year period. Any dividends paid during the five-year period will be held in trust for the employees until the end of the five-year period.

In total, 800 employees accept the offer and each employee purchases, on average, 80 shares, ie the employees purchase a total of 64,000 shares. The weighted-average market price of the shares at the purchase date is CU30 per share, and the weighted-average purchase price is CU24 per share.

APPLICATION OF REQUIREMENTS

For transactions with employees, IFRS 2 requires the transaction amount to be measured by reference to the fair value of the equity instruments granted (IFRS 2, paragraph 11). To apply this requirement, it is necessary first to determine the type of equity instrument granted to the employees. Although the plan is described as an employee share purchase plan (ESPP), some ESPPs include option features and are therefore, in effect, share option plans. For example, an ESPP might include a 'lookback feature', whereby the employee is able to purchase shares at a discount, and choose whether the discount is applied to the entity's share price at the date of grant or its share price at the date of purchase. Or an ESPP might specify the purchase price, and then allow the employees a significant period of time to decide whether to participate in the plan. Another example of an option feature is an ESPP that permits the participating employees to cancel their participation before or at the end of a specified period and obtain a refund of amounts previously paid into the plan.

However, in this example, the plan includes no option features. The discount is applied to the share price at the purchase date, and the employees are not permitted to withdraw from the plan.

Another factor to consider is the effect of post-vesting transfer restrictions, if any. Paragraph B3 of IFRS 2 states that, if shares are subject to restrictions on transfer after vesting date, that factor should be taken into account when estimating the fair value of those shares, but only to the extent that the postvesting restrictions affect the price that a knowledgeable, willing market participant would pay for that share. For example, if the shares are actively traded in a deep and liquid market, post-vesting transfer restrictions may have little, if any, effect on the price that a knowledgeable, willing market participant would pay for those shares.

In this example, the shares are vested when purchased, but cannot be sold for five years after the date of purchase. Therefore, the entity should consider the valuation effect of the five-year post-vesting transfer restriction. This entails using a valuation technique to estimate what the price of the restricted share would have been on the purchase date in an arm's length transaction between knowledgeable, willing parties. Suppose that, in this example, the entity estimates that the fair value of each restricted share is CU28. In this case, the fair value of the equity instruments granted is CU4 per share (being the fair value of the restricted share of CU28 less the purchase price of CU24). Because 64,000 shares were purchased, the total fair value of the equity instruments granted is CU256,000.

In this example, there is no vesting period. Therefore, in accordance with paragraph 14 of IFRS 2, the entity should recognise an expense of CU256,000 immediately.

However, in some cases, the expense relating to an ESPP might not be material. IAS 8 *Accounting Policies, Changes in Accounting Policies and Errors* states that the accounting policies in IFRSs need not be applied when the effect of applying them is immaterial (IAS 8, paragraph 8). IAS 8 also states that an omission or misstatement of an item is material if it could, individually or collectively, influence the economic decisions of users taken on the basis of the financial statements. Materiality depends on the size and nature of the omission or misstatement judged in the surrounding circumstances. The size or nature of the item, or a combination of both, could be the determining factor (IAS 8, paragraph 5). Therefore, in this example, the entity should consider whether the expense of CU256,000 is material.

Cash-settled share-based payment transactions

IG18 Paragraphs 30–33 of the IFRS set out requirements for transactions in which an entity acquires goods or services by incurring liabilities to the supplier of those goods or services in amounts based on the price of the entity's shares or other equity instruments. The entity is required to recognise initially the goods or services acquired, and a liability to pay for those goods or services, when the entity obtains the goods or as the services are rendered, measured at the fair value of the liability. Thereafter, until the liability is settled, the entity is required to recognise changes in the fair value of the liability.

IG19 For example, an entity might grant share appreciation rights to employees as part of their remuneration package, whereby the employees will become entitled to a future cash payment (rather than an equity instrument), based on the increase in the entity's share price from a specified level over a specified period of time. If the share appreciation rights do not vest until the employees have completed a specified period of service, the entity recognises the services received, and a liability to pay for them, as the employees render service during that period. The liability is measured, initially and at each reporting date until settled, at the fair value of the share appreciation rights, by applying an option pricing model, and the extent to which the employees have rendered service to date. Changes in fair value are recognised in profit or loss. Therefore, if the amount recognised for the services received was included in the carrying amount of an asset recognised in the entity's balance sheet (eg inventory), the carrying amount of that asset is not adjusted for the effects of the liability remeasurement. Example 12 illustrates these requirements.

IG Example 12

BACKGROUND

An entity grants 100 cash share appreciation rights (SARs) to each of its 500 employees, on condition that the employees remain in its employ for the next three years.

During year 1, 35 employees leave. The entity estimates that a further 60 will leave during years 2 and 3. During year 2, 40 employees leave and the entity estimates that a further 25 will leave during year 3. During year 3, 22 employees leave. At the end of year 3, 150 employees exercise their SARs, another 140 employees exercise their SARs at the end of year 4 and the remaining 113 employees exercise their SARs at the end of year 5.

The entity estimates the fair value of the SARs at the end of each year in which a liability exists as shown below. At the end of year 3, all SARs held by the remaining employees vest. The intrinsic values of the SARs at the date of exercise (which equal the cash paid out) at the end of years 3, 4 and 5 are also shown below.

Year	Fair value	Intrinsic value
1	CU14.40	
2	CU15.50	
3	CU18.20	CU15.00
4	CU21.40	CU20.00
5		CU25.00

APPLICATION OF REQUIREMENTS

Year	Calculation		Expense CU	Liability CU
1	(500 – 95) employees × 100 SARs × CU14.40 × 1/3		194,400	194,400
2	(500 – 100) employees × 100 SARs × CU15.50 × 2/3 – CU194,400		218,933	413,333
3	(500 – 97 – 150) employees × 100 SARs × CU18.20 – CU413,333	47,127		460,460
	+ 150 employees × 100 SARs × CU15.00	225,000		
	Total		272,127	
4	(253 – 140) employees × 100 SARs × CU21.40 – CU460,460	(218,640)		241,820
	+ 140 employees × 100 SARs × CU20.00	280,000		
	Total		61,360	
5	CU0 – CU241,820	(241,820)		0
	+ 113 employees × 100 SARs × CU25.00	282,500		
	Total		40,680	
	Total		787,500	

Share-based payment arrangements with cash alternatives

IG20 Some employee share-based payment arrangements permit the employee to choose whether to receive cash or equity instruments. In this situation, a compound financial instrument has been granted, ie a financial instrument with debt and equity components. Paragraph 37 of the IFRS requires the entity to estimate the fair value of the compound financial instrument at grant date, by first measuring the fair value of the debt component, and then measuring the fair value of the equity component – taking into account that the employee must forfeit the right to receive cash to receive the equity instrument.

IG21 Typically, share-based payment arrangements with cash alternatives are structured so that the fair value of one settlement alternative is the same as the other. For example, the employee might have the choice of receiving share options or cash share appreciation rights. In such cases, the fair value of the equity component will be zero, and hence the fair value of the compound financial instrument will be the same as the fair value of the debt component. However, if the fair values of the settlement alternatives differ, usually the fair value of the equity component will be greater than zero, in which case the fair value of the compound financial instrument will be greater than the fair value of the debt component.

IG22 Paragraph 38 of the IFRS requires the entity to account separately for the services received in respect of each component of the compound financial instrument. For the debt component, the entity recognises the services received, and a liability to pay for those services, as the counterparty renders service, in accordance with the requirements applying to cash-settled share-based payment transactions. For the equity component (if any), the entity recognises the services received, and an increase in equity, as the counterparty renders service, in accordance with the requirements applying to equity-settled share-based payment transactions. Example 13 illustrates these requirements.

IG Example 13

BACKGROUND

An entity grants to an employee the right to choose either 1,000 phantom shares, ie a right to a cash payment equal to the value of 1,000 shares, or 1,200 shares. The grant is conditional upon the completion of three years' service. If the employee chooses the share alternative, the shares must be held for three years after vesting date.

At grant date, the entity's share price is CU50 per share. At the end of years 1, 2 and 3, the share price is CU52, CU55 and CU60 respectively. The entity does not expect to pay dividends in the next three years. After taking into account the effects of the post-vesting transfer restrictions, the entity estimates that the grant date fair value of the share alternative is CU48 per share.

At the end of year 3, the employee chooses:

<u>Scenario 1</u>: The cash alternative

<u>Scenario 2</u>: The equity alternative

APPLICATION OF REQUIREMENTS

The fair value of the equity alternative is CU57,600 (1,200 shares × CU48). The fair value of the cash alternative is CU50,000 (1,000 phantom shares × CU50). Therefore, the fair value of the equity component of the compound instrument is CU7,600 (CU57,600 – CU50,000).

The entity recognises the following amounts:

Year		Expense CU	Equity CU	Liability CU
1	Liability component: (1,000 × CU52 × 1/3)	17,333		17,333
	Equity component: (CU7,600 × 1/3)	2,533	2,533	
2	Liability component: (1,000 × CU55 × 2/3) – CU17,333	19,333		19,333
	Equity component: (CU7,600 × 1/3)	2,533	2,533	
3	Liability component: (1,000 × CU60) – CU36,666	23,334		23,334
	Equity component: (CU7,600 × 1/3)	2,534	2,534	
End Year 3	Scenario 1: cash of CU60,000 paid			(60,000)
	Scenario 1 totals	67,600	7,600	0
	Scenario 2: 1,200 shares issued		60,000	(60,000)
	Scenario 2 totals	67,600	67,600	0

Share-based payment transactions among group entities

Paragraphs 43A and 43B of IFRS 2 specify the accounting requirements for share-based payment transactions among group entities in the separate or individual financial statements of the entity receiving the goods or services. Example 14 illustrates the journal entries in the separate or individual financial statements for a group transaction in which a parent grants rights to its equity instruments to the employees of its subsidiary. **IG22A**

IG Example 14

Share-based payment transactions in which a parent grants rights to its equity instruments to the employees of its subsidiary

BACKGROUND

A parent grants 200 share options to each of 100 employees of its subsidiary, conditional upon the completion of two years' service with the subsidiary. The fair value of the share options on grant date is CU30 each. At grant date, the subsidiary estimates that 80 per cent of the employees will complete the two-year service period. This estimate does not change during the vesting period. At the end of the vesting period, 81 employees complete the required two years of service. The parent does not require the subsidiary to pay for the shares needed to settle the grant of share options.

APPLICATION OF REQUIREMENTS

As required by paragraph B53 of the IFRS, over the two-year vesting period, the subsidiary measures the services received from the employees in accordance with the requirements applicable to equity-settled share-based payment transactions. Thus, the subsidiary measures the services received from the employees on the basis of the fair value of the share options at grant date. An increase in equity is recognised as a contribution from the parent in the separate or individual financial statements of the subsidiary.

The journal entries recorded by the subsidiary for each of the two years are as follows:

Year 1

Dr Remuneration expense (200 × 100 × CU30 × 0.8/2)	CU240,000	
Cr Equity (Contribution from the parent)		CU240,000

Year 2

Dr Remuneration expense (200 × 100 × CU30 × 0.81 – 240,000)	CU246,000	
Cr Equity (Contribution from the parent)		CU246,000

ILLUSTRATIVE DISCLOSURES

IG23 The following example illustrates the disclosure requirements in paragraphs 44-52 of the IFRS.*

Extract from the Notes to the Financial Statements of Company Z for the year ended 31 December 20X5.

Share-based Payment

During the period ended 31 December 20X5, the Company had four share-based payment arrangements, which are described below.

Type of arrangement	Senior management share option plan	General employee share option plan	Executive share plan	Senior management share appreciation cash plan
Date of grant	1 January 20X4	1 January 20X5	1 January 20X5	1 July 20X5
Number granted	50,000	75,000	50,000	25,000
Contractual life	10 years	10 years	N/A	10 years
Vesting conditions	1.5 years' service and achievement of a share price target, which was achieved.	Three years' service.	Three years' service and achievement of a target growth in earnings per share.	Three years' service and achievement of a target increase in market share.

**Note that the illustrative example is not intended to be a template or model and is therefore not exhaustive. For example, it does not illustrate the disclosure requirements in paragraphs 47(c), 48 and 49 of the IFRS.*

The estimated fair value of each share option granted in the general employee share option plan is CU23.60. This was calculated by applying a binomial option pricing model. The model inputs were the share price at grant date of CU50, exercise price of CU50, expected volatility of 30 per cent, no expected dividends, contractual life of ten years, and a risk-free interest rate of 5 per cent. To allow for the effects of early exercise, it was assumed that the employees would exercise the options after vesting date when the share price was twice the exercise price. Historical volatility was 40 per cent, which includes the early years of the Company's life; the Company expects the volatility of its share price to reduce as it matures.

The estimated fair value of each share granted in the executive share plan is CU50.00, which is equal to the share price at the date of grant.

Further details of the two share option plans are as follows:

	20X4		20X5	
	Number of options	Weighted average exercise price	Number of options	Weighted average exercise price
Outstanding at start of year	0	–	45,000	CU40
Granted	50,000	CU40	75,000	CU50
Forfeited	(5,000)	CU40	(8,000)	CU46
Exercised	0	–	(4,000)	CU40
Outstanding at end of year	45,000	CU40	108,000	CU46
Exercisable at end of year	0	CU40	38,000	CU40

The weighted average share price at the date of exercise for share options exercised during the period was CU52. The options outstanding at 31 December 20X5 had an exercise price of CU40 or CU50, and a weighted average remaining contractual life of 8.64 years.

	20X4 CU	20X5 CU
Expense arising from share-based payment transactions	495,000	1,105,867
Expense arising from share and share option plans	495,000	1,007,000
Closing balance of liability for cash share appreciation plan	-	98,867
Expense arising from increase in fair value of liability for cash share appreciation plan	-	9,200

SUMMARY OF CONDITIONS FOR A COUNTERPARTY TO RECEIVE AN EQUITY INSTRUMENT GRANTED AND OF ACCOUNTING TREATMENTS

IG24 The table below categorises, with examples, the various conditions that determine whether a counterparty receives an equity instrument granted and the accounting treatment of share-based payments with those conditions.

	Summary of conditions that determine whether a counterparty receives an equity instrument granted					
	VESTING CONDITIONS			NON-VESTING CONDITIONS		
	Service conditions	**Performance conditions**				
		Performance conditions that are market conditions	**Other performance conditions**	**Neither the entity nor the counterparty can choose whether the condition is met**	**Counterparty can choose whether to meet the condition**	**Entity can choose whether to meet the condition**
Example conditions	Requirement to remain in service for three years	Target based on the market price of the entity's equity instruments	Target based on a successful initial public offering with a specified service requirement	Target based on a commodity index	Paying contributions towards the exercise price of a share based payment	Continuation of the plan by the entity
Include in grant-date fair value?	No	Yes	No	Yes	Yes	Yes[a]
Accounting treatment if the condition is not met after the grant date and during the vesting period	Forfeiture. The entity revises the expense to reflect the best available estimate of the number of equity instruments expected to vest. (paragraph 19)	No change to accounting. The entity continues to recognise the expense over the remainder of the vesting period. (paragraph 21)	Forfeiture. The entity revises the expense to reflect the best available estimate of the number of equity instruments expected to vest. (paragraph 19)	No change to accounting. The entity continues to recognise the expense over the remainder of the vesting period. (paragraph 21A)	Cancellation. The entity recognises immediately the amount of the expense that would otherwise have been recognised over the remainder of the vesting period. (paragraph 28A)	Cancellation. The entity recognises immediately the amount of the expense that would otherwise have been recognised over the remainder of the vesting period. (paragraph 28A)

a In the calculation of the fair value of the share-based payment, the probability of continuation of the plan by the entity is assumed to be 100 per cent.

Financial Reporting Standard 21 embodies IAS 10 (revised 2003) 'Events after the Balance Sheet Date' and some amendments to that standard adopted for entities subject to UK accounting standards.

The Statement of Standard Accounting Practice in FRS 21 is set out in paragraphs 1-23 and the Appendix. All the paragraphs have equal authority. Paragraphs in bold type state the main principles.

Accompanying the Statement of Standard Accounting Practice is the basis for the conclusions reached in the Statement which does not form part of the Statement.

The Statement of Standard Accounting Practice should be read in the context of its objective as stated in paragraph 1, the Basis for Conclusions set out in paragraphs BC1-BC4, and the Accounting Standards Board's 'Foreword to Accounting Standards' and 'Statement of Principles for Financial Reporting'.

FRS 21
(IAS 10) Events after the balance sheet date*

(Issued May 2004)

Contents

paragraphs

Introduction	**IN1-IN4**
Financial Reporting Standard 21 (IAS 10)	
Events after the Balance Sheet Date	
Objective	**1**
Scope	**1a-2**
Definitions	**3-7**
Recognition and Measurement	**8-13**
Adjusting Events after the Balance Sheet Date	**8-9**
Non-adjusting Events after the Balance Sheet Date	**10-11**
Dividends	**12-13**
Going Concern	**14-16**
Disclosure	**17-22**
Date of Authorisation for Issue	**17-18**
Updating Disclosure about Conditions at the Balance Sheet Date	**19-20**
Non-adjusting Events after the Balance Sheet Date	**21-22**
Effective Date	**23**

Appendix
Amendments to other Standards

***Editor's note**: The matters covered in FRS 21 are dealt with in Section 32 of FRS 102.*

Preface by the Accounting Standards Board

This Financial Reporting Standard (FRS) has the effect of implementing the International Accounting Standards Board's (IASB's) International Accounting Standard (IAS) 10 (revised 2003) *Events after the Balance Sheet Date* in the UK and the Republic of Ireland for entities not preparing their financial statements in accordance with international accounting standards adopted pursuant to the Regulation of the European Parliament and of the Council on the Application of International Accounting Standards. It replaces SSAP 17 *Accounting for post balance sheet events,* and reflects the proposals of FRED 27 which was published in May 2002. **a**

In March 2004 the Department of Trade and Industry (DTI) issued a consultation document 'Modernisation of Accounting Directives/IAS Infrastructure'. These proposals include draft Regulations amending the Companies Act 1985 which will apply in respect of companies' financial years which begin on or after 1 January 2005*. The proposals remove the requirement to report proposed dividends in the profit and loss account. This is in accordance with the now generally accepted view that dividends declared after the balance sheet date should not be reported as liabilities. This is reflected in this FRS and is the principal difference between this FRS and SSAP 17.† **b**

The accounting practice set out in this FRS should be applied for accounting periods beginning on or after 1 January 2005 which is consistent with the proposed legislative changes. **c**

The requirements, scope and effective date of FRS 21 are identical to IAS 10 except that: **d**

- entities applying the FRSSE will be exempt from the FRS, and
- early adoption is not permitted because proposed changes to the legal requirements for recognising dividend payments come into effect for accounting periods beginning on or after 1 January 2005 and compliance with the FRS before then will not be compatible with the law.

The text of IAS 10 contains various references to other IASs and IFRSs. In FRS 21 those references have been amended where necessary to enable the Standard to be applied in the UK context. Deleted text has been struck through and inserted text is underlined. The Accounting Standards Board believes that those amendments do not change the requirements of IAS 10 in any way. **e**

The Appendix of IAS 10 contains amendments that the IASB has made to existing IASs in the light of the main requirements in IAS 10. In FRS 21 this material has been amended and added to so that the FRS can be applied in a UK context. In particular, from the relevant effective date of the Standard, paragraphs A5 to A8 withdraw SSAP 17 *Accounting for post balance sheet events* and amend FRS 12 *Provisions, Contingent Liabilities and Contingent Assets* and FRS 18 *Accounting Policies.* **f**

In all other respects the FRS is identical to IAS 10. **g**

**Similar amendments are proposed to the statutory requirements in Northern Ireland and the Republic of Ireland.*

*†**Editor's note:** The law was changed as a result of the proposals referred to. The changes have been carried over into the Companies Act 2006.*

Introduction

IN1 International Accounting Standard 10 *Events after the Balance Sheet Date* (IAS 10) replaces IAS 10 *Events after the Balance Sheet Date* (revised in 1999)* and should be applied for accounting periods beginning on or after 1 January 2005.

REASONS FOR REVISING IAS 10

IN2 The International Accounting Standards Board developed this revised IAS 10 as part of its project on Improvements to International Accounting Standards. The project was undertaken in the light of queries and criticisms raised in relation to the Standards by securities regulators, professional accountants and other interested parties. The objectives of the project were to reduce or eliminate alternatives, redundancies and conflicts within the Standards, to deal with some convergence issues and to make other improvements.

IN3 For IAS 10 the Board's main objective was a limited clarification of the accounting for dividends declared after the balance sheet date. The Board did not reconsider the fundamental approach to the accounting for events after the balance sheet date contained in IAS 10.

THE MAIN CHANGES

IN4 The main change from the previous version of IAS 10 was a limited clarification of paragraphs 12 and 13 (paragraphs 11 and 12 of the previous version of IAS 10). As revised, those paragraphs state that if an entity declares dividends after the balance sheet date, the entity shall not recognise those dividends as a liability at the balance sheet date.

'In September 2007 the IASB amended the title of IAS 10 from 'Events after the Balance Sheet Date' to 'Events after the Reporting Period' as a consequence of the revision of IAS 1 Presentation of Financial Statements in 2007†.

† ***ASB footnote:*** *The ASB decided not to amend UK FRSs for terminology changes and, consequently, has not amended the title of FRS 21. The ASB issued FRS 21 in December 2004'.*

Financial Reporting Standard 21 (IAS 10)

'Events after the Balance Sheet Date'

OBJECTIVE

The objective of this Standard is to prescribe: 1

(a) when an entity should adjust its financial statements for events after the balance sheet date; and
(b) the disclosures that an entity should give about the date when the financial statements were authorised for issue and about events after the balance sheet date.

The Standard also requires that an entity should not prepare its financial statements on a going concern basis if events after the balance sheet date indicate that the going concern assumption is not appropriate.

SCOPE

This Standard applies to all financial statements that are intended to give a true and fair view of a reporting entity's financial position and profit or loss (or income and expenditure), except that reporting entities applying the Financial Reporting Standard for Smaller Entities (FRSSE) currently applicable are exempt. 1A

This Standard shall be applied in the accounting for, and disclosure of, events after the balance sheet date. 2

DEFINITIONS

The following terms are used in this Standard with the meanings specified: 3

Events after the balance sheet date are those events, favourable and unfavourable, that occur between the balance sheet date and the date when the financial statements are authorised for issue. Two types of events can be identified:

(a) those that provide evidence of conditions that existed at the balance sheet date (adjusting events after the balance sheet date); and
(b) those that are indicative of conditions that arose after the balance sheet date (non-adjusting events after the balance sheet date).

The process involved in authorising the financial statements for issue will vary depending upon the management structure, statutory requirements and procedures followed in preparing and finalising the financial statements. 4

In some cases, an entity is required to submit its financial statements to its shareholders for approval after the financial statements have been issued. In such cases, the financial statements are authorised for issue on the date of issue, not the date when shareholders approve the financial statements. 5

Example

The management of an entity completes draft financial statements for the year to 31 December 20X1 on 28 February 20X2. On 18 March 20X2, the board of directors reviews the financial statements and authorises them for issue. The entity announces its profit and selected other financial information on 19 March 20X2. The financial statements are made available to shareholders and others on 1 April 20X2. The shareholders approve the financial statements at their annual meeting on 15 May 20X2 and the approved financial statements are then filed with a regulatory body on 17 May 20X2.

The financial statements are authorised for issue on 18 March 20X2 (date of board authorisation for issue).

6 In some cases, the management of an entity is required to issue its financial statements to a supervisory board (made up solely of non-executives) for approval. In such cases, the financial statements are authorised for issue when the management authorises them for issue to the supervisory board.

Example

On 18 March 20X2, the management of an entity authorises financial statements for issue to its supervisory board. The supervisory board is made up solely of non-executives and may include representatives of employees and other outside interests. The supervisory board approves the financial statements on 26 March 20X2. The financial statements are made available to shareholders and others on 1 April 20X2. The shareholders approve the financial statements at their annual meeting on 15 May 20X2 and the financial statements are then filed with a regulatory body on 17 May 20X2.

The financial statements are authorised for issue on 18 March 20X2 (date of management authorisation for issue to the supervisory board).

7 Events after the balance sheet date include all events up to the date when the financial statements are authorised for issue, even if those events occur after the public announcement of profit or of other selected financial information.

RECOGNITION AND MEASUREMENT

Adjusting Events after the Balance Sheet Date

8 **An entity shall adjust the amounts recognised in its financial statements to reflect adjusting events after the balance sheet date.**

9 The following are examples of adjusting events after the balance sheet date that require an entity to adjust the amounts recognised in its financial statements, or to recognise items that were not previously recognised:

(a) the settlement after the balance sheet date of a court case that confirms that the entity had a present obligation at the balance sheet date. The entity adjusts any previously recognised provision related to this court case in accordance with

FRS 12 *Provisions, Contingent Liabilities and Contingent Assets* or recognises a new provision. The entity does not merely disclose a contingent liability because the settlement provides additional evidence that would be considered in accordance with paragraph 16 of FRS 12.

(b) the receipt of information after the balance sheet date indicating that an asset was impaired at the balance sheet date, or that the amount of a previously recognised impairment loss for that asset needs to be adjusted. For example:

   (i) the bankruptcy of a customer that occurs after the balance sheet date usually confirms that a loss existed at the balance sheet date on a trade receivable and that the entity needs to adjust the carrying amount of the trade receivable; and

   (ii) the sale of inventories after the balance sheet date may give evidence about their net realisable value at the balance sheet date.

(c) the determination after the balance sheet date of the cost of assets purchased, or the proceeds from assets sold, before the balance sheet date.

(d) the determination after the balance sheet date of the amount of profit-sharing or bonus payments, if the entity had a present legal or constructive obligation at the balance sheet date to make such payments as a result of events before that date.

(e) the discovery of fraud or errors that show that the financial statements are incorrect.

Non-adjusting Events after the Balance Sheet Date

An entity shall not adjust the amounts recognised in its financial statements to reflect non-adjusting events after the balance sheet date. 10

An example of a non-adjusting event after the balance sheet date is a decline in market value of investments between the balance sheet date and the date when the financial statements are authorised for issue. The decline in market value does not normally relate to the condition of the investments at the balance sheet date, but reflects circumstances that have arisen subsequently. Therefore, an entity does not adjust the amounts recognised in its financial statements for the investments. Similarly, the entity does not update the amounts disclosed for the investments as at the balance sheet date, although it may need to give additional disclosure under paragraph 21. 11

Dividends

If an entity declares dividends to holders of equity instruments (as defined in FRS 25 *(IAS 32) Financial Instruments: Presentation) after the balance sheet date, the entity shall not recognise those dividends as a liability at the balance sheet date.** 12

If dividends are declared (ie the dividends are appropriately authorised and no longer at the discretion of the entity) after the balance sheet date but before the financial statements are authorised for issue, the dividends are not recognised as a liability at the balance sheet date because no obligation exists at that time. Such dividends are disclosed in the notes to the financial statements.† 13

***Editor's note**: Paragraph amended in December 2008.*

*†**Editor's note**: Paragraph amended with effect for accounting periods beginning on or after 1 January 2009.*

GOING CONCERN

14 **An entity shall not prepare its financial statements on a going concern basis if management determines after the balance sheet date either that it intends to liquidate the entity or to cease trading, or that it has no realistic alternative but to do so.**

15 Deterioration in operating results and financial position after the balance sheet date may indicate a need to consider whether the going concern assumption is still appropriate. If the going concern assumption is no longer appropriate, the effect is so pervasive that this Standard requires a fundamental change in the basis of accounting, rather than an adjustment to the amounts recognised within the original basis of accounting.

16 FRS 18 *Accounting Policies* specifies required disclosures in relation to the assessment of going concern:

(a) any material uncertainties, of which the directors are aware in making their assessment, related to events or conditions that may cast significant doubt upon the entity's ability to continue as a going concern;
(b) where the foreseeable future considered by the directors has been limited to a period of less than one year from the date of approval of the financial statements, that fact;
(c) when the financial statements are not prepared on a going concern basis, that fact, together with the basis on which the financial statements are prepared and the reason why the entity is not regarded as a going concern.

DISCLOSURE

Date of Authorisation for Issue

17 **An entity shall disclose the date when the financial statements were authorised for issue and who gave that authorisation. If the entity's owners or others have the power to amend the financial statements after issue, the entity shall disclose that fact.**

18 It is important for users to know when the financial statements were authorised for issue, because the financial statements do not reflect events after this date.

Updating Disclosure about Conditions at the Balance Sheet Date

19 **If an entity receives information after the balance sheet date about conditions that existed at the balance sheet date, it shall update disclosures that relate to those conditions, in the light of the new information.**

20 In some cases, an entity needs to update the disclosures in its financial statements to reflect information received after the balance sheet date, even when the information does not affect the amounts that it recognises in its financial statements. One example of the need to update disclosures is when evidence becomes available after the balance sheet date about a contingent liability that existed at the balance sheet date. In addition to considering whether it should recognise or change a provision under FRS 12 *Provisions, Contingent Liabilities and Contingent Assets*, an entity updates its disclosures about the contingent liability in the light of that evidence.

Non-adjusting Events after the Balance Sheet Date

If non-adjusting events after the balance sheet date are material, non-disclosure could influence the economic decisions that users make on the basis of the financial statements. Accordingly, an entity shall disclose the following for each material category of non-adjusting events after the balance sheet date: 21

- **(a) the nature of the event; and**
- **(b) an estimate of its financial effect, or a statement that such an estimate cannot be made.***

The following are examples of non-adjusting events after the balance sheet date that would generally result in disclosure: 22

- (a) a major business combination after the balance sheet date or disposing of a major subsidiary;
- (b) announcing a plan to discontinue an operation;
- (c) major purchases of assets, and disposals of assets, or expropriation of major assets by government;
- (d) the destruction of a major production plant by a fire after the balance sheet date;
- (e) announcing, or commencing the implementation of, a major restructuring (see FRS 12);
- (f) major ordinary share transactions and potential ordinary share transactions after the balance sheet date (FRS 22 (IAS 33) *Earnings per Share* requires an entity to disclose a description of such transactions, other than when such transactions involve capitalisation or bonus issues, share splits or reverse share splits all of which are required to be adjusted under FRS 22);
- (g) abnormally large changes after the balance sheet date in asset prices or foreign exchange rates;
- (h) changes in tax rates or tax laws enacted or announced after the balance sheet date that have a significant effect on current and deferred tax assets and liabilities;
- (i) entering into significant commitments or contingent liabilities, for example, by issuing significant guarantees; and
- (j) commencing major litigation arising solely out of events that occurred after the balance sheet date.†

EFFECTIVE DATE

An entity shall apply this Standard for accounting periods beginning on or after 1 January 2005. 23

****Editor's note**: Paragraph amended in December 2008.*

*†**Editor's note**: Paragraph amended in December 2008.*

Appendix
Amendments to other Standards

[Not reproduced, as all changes have been made to the underlying standards]

Adoption of the standard
Approval of IAS 10 by the International Accounting Standards Board

International Accounting Standard 10 *Events after the Balance Sheet Date* was approved for issue by the fourteen members of the International Accounting Standards Board.

Sir David Tweedie	Chairman
Thomas E Jones	Vice-Chairman
Mary E Barth	
Hans-Georg Bruns	
Anthony T Cope	
Robert P Garnett	
Gilbert Gélard	
James J Leisenring	
Warren J McGregor	
Patricia L O'Malley	
Harry K Schmid	
John T Smith	
Geoffrey Whittington	
Tatsumi Yamada	

Adoption of FRS 21 by the Accounting Standards Board

Financial Reporting Standard 21 (IAS 10) *Events after the Balance Sheet Date* was approved for issue by the nine members of the Accounting Standards Board.

Mary Keegan	Chairman
Andrew Lennard	Technical Director
Michael Ashley	
Douglas Flint	
Huw Jones	
Roger Marshall	
Isobel Sharp	
John Smith	
Jonathan Symonds	

Notes on the standard's application in the UK and the Republic of Ireland

NOTE ON LEGAL REQUIREMENTS

Great Britain*

Paid and proposed dividends

N1 The statutory requirements relating to paid and proposed dividends are set out in Schedule 4 paragraph 3(7) to the Companies Act 1985. Schedule 4 does not apply to banking and insurance groups. Corresponding requirements are set out in Schedule 9 paragraph 8 for banking companies and groups and in Schedule 9A paragraph 5 for insurance companies and groups.

N2 The UK Government has recently published its proposals† to amend the Companies Act 1985 through a draft Statutory Instrument – *The Companies Act 1985 (International Accounting Standards and Other Accounting Amendments) Regulations 2004*. The draft Regulations will apply in respect of companies' financial years which begin on or after 1 January 2005.‡

N3 The draft Regulations amend paragraph 3(7) of Schedule 4 to the 1985 Act, by replacing the requirement for companies to show the aggregate amount of any dividends paid and proposed in the profit and loss account, with a requirement to show dividends which are paid or liable to be paid at the balance sheet date. The draft Regulations introduce a new requirement, as paragraph 3(7A), to disclose in the notes to the accounts the aggregate amount of dividends proposed before the date of approval of the accounts, which have not been shown in the profit and loss account in accordance with the requirement in paragraph 3(7).

N4 The draft Regulations make corresponding amendments to Schedules 9 and 9A to the 1985 Act.

N5 The accounting practice set out in paragraphs 12 and 13 of the FRS is consistent with the proposed changes to the 1985 Act and will take effect from the same date.

****Editor's note:** The various statutory references change with the introduction of the Companies Act 2006, which affects accounting for periods beginning on or after 6 April 2008. The various statutory references, not already noted as removed, have changed as follows:*

Companies Act 1985 reference	***Companies Act 2006 reference***
Schedule 4	*Schedule 1 to the Large and Medium-sized Companies and Groups (Accounts and Reports) Regulations 2008 (SI 2008/410)*
Schedules 9 and 9A	*Schedules 2 and 3 to SI 2008/410*
Paragraph 10 of Schedule 4	*Paragraph 11 of Schedule 1 to SI 2008/410*
Paragraph 15 of Schedule 4	*Paragraph 10 of Schedule 1 to SI 2008/410*

†DTI/HM Treasury – Modernisation of accounting directives/IAS infrastructure – a consultation document. March 2004.

‡***Editor's note**: This statutory instrument was issued as SI 2004 No. 2947.*

Going Concern

Paragraph 10 of Schedule 4 to the Companies Act 1985 requires that the company shall be presumed to be carrying on business as a going concern. Paragraph 15 of Schedule 4 permits the directors of a company to depart from this principle in preparing the company's accounts in respect of any financial year if it appears to them that there are special reasons for such a departure. Particulars of the departure, the reasons for it and its effect are required to be given in a note to the accounts. Schedule 4 does not apply to banking and insurance groups. Corresponding requirements are set out in Schedule 9 paragraphs 17 and 22 for banking companies and groups and in Schedule 9A paragraphs 14 and 19 for insurance companies and groups. **N6**

Northern Ireland

The statutory requirements in Northern Ireland are set out in the Companies (Northern Ireland) Order 1986. These requirements are identical to the legislation for Great Britain cited above. Under the Northern Ireland Act 1998 company law is a transferred matter. Northern Ireland will therefore make Statutory Regulations, with provisions similar to those in the Statutory Instrument being prepared in Great Britain to amend the Companies (Northern Ireland) Order 1986. It is intended that these should be effective from 1 January 2005. **N7**

Republic of Ireland

The statutory requirements in the Republic of Ireland that correspond to those cited above for Great Britain are shown in the following table: **N8**

Great Britain	*Republic of Ireland*
Schedule 4 to the Companies Act 1985:	The Companies (Amendment) Act 1986:
paragraph 3(7)	Section 4(15)(a)
paragraph 10	Section 5(a)
paragraph 15	Section 6
Schedule 9 to the Companies Act 1985	European Communities (Credit Institutions: Accounts) Regulations 1992
Schedule 9A to the Companies Act 1985	European Communities (Insurance Undertakings: Accounts) Regulations 1996

The Republic of Ireland has under consideration similar amendments to those proposed for Great Britain.

DEVELOPMENT OF THE FRS

This FRS is based on IAS 10 (revised 2003) *Events after the Balance Sheet Date* and it supersedes SSAP 17 *Accounting for post balance sheet events*, which was issued in August 1980. The draft standard was published as FRED 27 in May 2002. Respondents were concerned that the proposed reference to FRS 4 in paragraph 12 was unhelpful. In light of the ASB's decision to introduce a standard based on IAS 32 *Financial Instruments: Disclosure and Presentation* effective from 1 January 2005 the reference has been amended to refer to this standard. Respondents also raised practical issues regarding the proposed removal of references to Going Concern and possible deficiencies in FRS 18 *Accounting Policies*; and if the references to **N9**

Going Concern were retained, possible conflicts with FRS 18. In response to this the FRS retains references to Going Concern in paragraphs 1, 14 and 15 to minimise divergence from IAS 10. As a consequence an amendment has been made to FRS 18 paragraph 21 to bring the assessment of going concern into line with that used in paragraph 14 of IAS 10. Paragraph 16 of the FRS is amended to refer to the disclosure requirements of FRS 18.

Basis for Conclusions on IAS 10 '*Events after the Reporting Period*'*†

This Basis for Conclusions accompanies, but is not part of IAS 10.

ASB note: All references in this section to 'the Board' and 'Board members' are references to the IASB Board and IASB Board members.

INTRODUCTION

This Basis for Conclusions summarises the International Accounting Standards Board's considerations in reaching its conclusions on revising IAS 10 *Events After the Balance Sheet Date* in 2003. Individual Board members gave greater weight to some factors than to others. **BC1**

In July 2001 the Board announced that, as part of its initial agenda of technical projects, it would undertake a project to improve a number of Standards, including IAS 10. The project was undertaken in the light of queries and criticisms raised in relation to the Standards by securities regulators, professional accountants and other interested parties. The objectives of the Improvements project were to reduce or eliminate alternatives, redundancies and conflicts within Standards, to deal with some convergence issues and to make other improvements. In May 2002 the Board published its proposals in an Exposure Draft of *Improvements to International Accounting Standards*, with a comment deadline of 16 September 2002. The Board received over 160 comment letters on the Exposure Draft. **BC2**

Because the Board's intention was not to reconsider the fundamental approach to the accounting for events after the balance sheet date established by IAS 10, this Basis for Conclusions does not discuss requirements in IAS 10 that the Board has not reconsidered. **BC3**

LIMITED CLARIFICATION

For this limited clarification of IAS 10 the main change made is in paragraphs 12 and 13 (paragraphs 11 and 12 of the previous version of IAS 10). As revised, those paragraphs state that if dividends are declared after the balance sheet date,‡ an entity shall not recognise those dividends as a liability at the balance sheet date. This is because undeclared dividends do not meet the criteria of a present obligation in IAS **BC4**

In September 2007 the IASB amended the title of IAS 10 from* Events after the Balance Sheet Date *to* Events after the Reporting Period *as a consequence of the amendments in IAS 1 Presentation of Financial Statements (as revised in 2007).

**The ASB decided not to make the terminology changes to UK FRS that arose from IAS 1 and, consequently, did not amend the title of FRS 21.*

†***Editor's note**: The title of this section was changed in December 2008, and all of the footnotes added.*

‡*IAS 1* Presentation of Financial Statements *(as revised in 2007) replaced the term 'balance sheet date' with 'end of the reporting period'.*

In 2007, the Board was advised that paragraph 13, taken in isolation, could be read to imply that a liability should be recognised in some circumstances on the basis that a constructive obligation exists, such as when there is an established pattern of paying a dividend. Therefore, the Board amended paragraph 13 by Improvements to IFRSs *issued in May 2008 to state that no such obligation exists.*

37 *Provisions, Contingent Liabilities and Contingent Assets*. The Board discussed whether or not an entity's past practice of paying dividends could be considered a constructive obligation. The Board concluded that such practices do not give rise to a liability to pay dividends.

Financial Reporting Standard 22 embodies IAS 33 (revised 2003) 'Earnings per Share' and some amendments to that standard adopted for entities subject to UK accounting standards.

The Statement of Standard Accounting Practice in FRS 22 is set out in paragraphs 1-75 and Appendices A-C. All the paragraphs have equal authority. Paragraphs in bold type state the main principles.

Accompanying the Statement of Standard Accounting Practice is the basis for the conclusions reached in the Statement and some illustrative examples, which do not form part of the Statement.

The Statement of Standard Accounting Practice should be read in the context of its objective as stated in paragraph 1, the Basis for Conclusions set out in paragraphs BC1-BC15, and the Accounting Standards Board's 'Foreword to Accounting Standards' and 'Statement of Principles for Financial Reporting'.

FRS 22
(IAS 33) Earnings per share*

(Issued December 2004)

Contents

	paragraphs
Introduction	**IN1-IN3**
Financial Reporting Standard 22 (IAS 33) Earnings per Share	
Objective	**1**
Scope	**2-4**
Definitions	**5-8**
Measurement	**9-63**
Basic Earnings per Share	**9-29**
Earnings	12-18
Shares	19-29
Diluted Earnings per Share	**30-63**
Earnings	33-35
Shares	36-40
Dilutive Potential Ordinary Shares	41-63
Options, warrants and their equivalents	*45-48*
Convertible instruments	*49-51*
Contingently issuable shares	*52-57*
Contracts that may be settled in ordinary shares or cash	*58-61*
Purchased options	*62*
Written put options	*63*
Retrospective Adjustments	**64-65**
Presentation	**66-69**
Disclosure	**70-73**
Effective date	**74**
Withdrawal of Other Pronouncements	**75**

Appendices:

A. Application Guidance
B. Amendments to Other Standards and UITF Abstracts
C. Application to Merger Accounting
D. Non-mandatory Application Guidance

****Editor's note****: FRS 102 does not directly deal with earnings per share. Entities within the scope of FRS 102, but which have ordinary shares or potential ordinary shares that are publicly traded, file or are in the process of filing financial statements with a securities commission or other regulatory organisation for the purpose of issuing ordinary shares in a public market, or which choose to disclose earnings per share will be required to comply with IAS 33* Earnings Per Share *(as adopted in the EU).*

Preface by the Accounting Standards Board

This Financial Reporting Standard (FRS) prescribes the basis for calculating and presenting earnings per share in the financial statements of entities whose shares are, or will be, publicly traded and other entities that choose to disclose earnings per share. It has the effect of implementing the International Accounting Standards Board's (IASB's) International Accounting Standard (IAS) 33 (revised 2003) *Earnings per Share* in the UK and the Republic of Ireland for such entities not preparing their financial statements in accordance with international accounting standards adopted pursuant to the Regulation of the European Parliament and of the Council on the Application of International Accounting Standards. It replaces FRS 14 *Earnings per Share*. **a**

An exposure draft of the proposed standard, FRED 26 *Earnings per Share*, was published in May 2002. FRED 26 was based on the IASB's exposure draft of a proposed revision of IAS 33 but under the assumption that the UK and Republic of Ireland equivalent standards of IAS 32 *Financial Instruments: Disclosure and Presentation* and IAS 39 *Financial Instruments: Recognition and Measurement* would not be effective and that the requirements of FRS 4 *Capital Instruments* would therefore remain. The UK and Republic of Ireland equivalent standards of IAS 32 and IAS 39 have now been issued and therefore this standard no longer contains the differences from IAS 33 that it was necessary to propose in FRED 26. The IASB made a number of changes to the exposure draft of IAS 33 when it issued IAS 33 (revised 2003) in addressing comments received from respondents. This standard contains only limited differences from IAS 33 (revised 2003). **b**

The accounting practice set out in this FRS should be applied for accounting periods beginning on or after 1 January 2005. **c**

MAIN CHANGES TO EXISTING UK REQUIREMENTS

This standard requires that basic and diluted earnings per share should be disclosed on the face of the profit and loss account both for net profit or loss for the period and also for profit or loss from continuing operations. Basic and diluted earnings per share for discontinued operations (if reported) should be reported either on the face of the profit and loss account or in a note to the accounts. Entities will be permitted to present additional per share amounts in the notes to the accounts. Under FRS 14, basic and diluted earnings per share for net profit or loss were required on the face of the profit and loss account. Companies were encouraged to provide additional per share amounts which they could disclose where they wished, providing they were no more prominent than the per share amounts required by FRS 14. **d**

Where additional earnings per share amounts were presented, FRS 14 required a reconciliation to the amounts required by FRS 14, listing the items for which an adjustment was being made and their individual effect on the calculation. The reason for the additional per share amount was also required to be given. This standard requires less disclosure than FRS 14 where additional per share amounts are presented – if the component of the income statement used for the additional earnings per share amount is not reported as a line item in the income statement, a reconciliation should be provided between the component and a line item. **e**

This standard gives more guidance than FRS 14 did on the adjustments required in calculating basic earnings per share for transactions involving preference shares. **f**

g FRS 14 and this standard both use profit or loss from continuing operations as the control number that is used to establish whether potential ordinary shares are dilutive or anti-dilutive. However, as FRS 3 *Reporting Financial Performance* requires an analysis of continuing operations, acquisitions and discontinued operations only to the level of profit before interest, FRS 14 gave additional guidance on how to allocate interest and tax in order to achieve a reasonable estimate of profit or loss from continuing operations. This standard does not provide any guidance on how to estimate this number, which is also required for basic earnings per share disclosure purposes. The guidance in FRS 14, which entities applying FRS 3 may find a useful reference, is reproduced in Appendix D, as non-mandatory application guidance.

h For contracts that may be settled in ordinary shares or cash, the treatment under FRS 14 depended on the facts available each period. Unless past experience or a stated policy provided a basis for concluding how the contract would be satisfied, it was presumed that the contract would be settled by the more dilutive method. This standard distinguishes between those contracts where settlement is to be determined by the entity and those by the holder. For those contracts that may be settled at the holder's option, the more dilutive of cash or share settlement should be used. For those contracts that may be settled in cash or shares at the entity's option, it should be presumed for the purpose of calculating diluted earnings per share that the contract will be settled in shares, and this presumption is not rebuttable.

i This standard provides a specific requirement in respect of written put options (contracts that require the entity to repurchase its own shares). These are included in the calculation of diluted earnings per share if the effect is dilutive (ie the contracts are 'in the money' during the period). Although not specified in FRS 14, the guidance is consistent with its principles.

j The standard requires disclosure of securities that could potentially dilute basic earnings per share in the future but which were not included in the calculation because they were anti-dilutive for the periods presented.

k FRS 14 included additional guidance in respect of the presentation of financial statistics in historical summaries. There is no equivalent guidance in this standard.

MAIN DIFFERENCES BETWEEN UK REQUIREMENTS AND IAS 33

l The requirements, scope and effective date of FRS 22 are identical to IAS 33 except that:

- early adoption is not permitted consistent with FRS 25 (IAS 32) *Financial Instruments: Disclosure and Presentation.*
- The guidance on earnings per share for business combinations accounted for as mergers under FRS 6 *Acquisitions and Mergers* that was exposed in FRED 26 has been retained in Appendix C.
- The text of IAS 33 contains various references to other IASs and IFRSs. In FRS 22 those references have been amended where necessary to enable the Standard to be applied in the UK context. Deleted text has been struck through and inserted text is underlined. The Accounting Standards Board believes that those amendments do not change the requirements of IAS 33 in any way.

AMENDMENTS TO OTHER UK STANDARDS AND UITF ABSTRACTS

Implementation of this standard requires, from the relevant effective date of the standard, amendment to FRS 3 *Reporting Financial Performance* and amendment of references to FRS 14 in FRS 20 *Share-Based Payment*, FRS 21 *Events after the Balance Sheet Date*, the Financial Reporting Standard for Smaller Entities (FRSSE), UITF 37 *Purchases and Sales of Own Shares* and UITF 38 *Accounting for ESOP Trusts*. **m**

Introduction

IN1 [Not reproduced].

REASONS FOR REVISING IAS 33

IN2 The International Accounting Standards Board has developed this revised IAS 33 as part of its project on Improvements to International Accounting Standards. The project was undertaken in the light of queries and criticisms raised in relation to the Standards by securities regulators, professional accountants and other interested parties. The objectives of the project were to reduce or eliminate alternatives, redundancies and conflicts within the Standards, to deal with some convergence issues and to make other improvements.

IN3 For IAS 33 the Board's main objective was a limited revision to provide additional guidance and illustrative examples on selected complex matters, such as the effects of contingently issuable shares; potential ordinary shares of subsidiaries, joint ventures or associates; participating equity instruments; written put options; purchased put and call options; and mandatorily convertible instruments. The Board did not reconsider the fundamental approach to the determination and presentation of earnings per share contained in IAS 33.

Financial Reporting Standard 22 (IAS 33)

'Earnings per Share'

OBJECTIVE

The objective of this Standard is to prescribe principles for the determination and presentation of earnings per share, so as to improve performance comparisons between different entities in the same reporting period and between different reporting periods for the same entity. Even though earnings per share data have limitations because of the different accounting policies that may be used for determining 'earnings', a consistently determined denominator enhances financial reporting. The focus of this Standard is on the denominator of the earnings per share calculation. 1

SCOPE

This Standard shall apply to: 2

(a) the separate or individual financial statements of an entity:

(i) whose ordinary shares or potential ordinary shares are traded in a public market (a domestic or foreign stock exchange or an over-the-counter market, including local and regional markets) or

(ii) that files, or is in the process of filing, its financial statements with a securities commission or other regulatory organisation for the purpose of issuing ordinary shares in a public market; and

(b) the consolidated financial statements of a group with a parent:

(i) whose ordinary shares or potential ordinary shares are traded in a public market (a domestic or foreign stock exchange or an over-the-counter market, including local and regional markets) or

(ii) that files, or is in the process of filing, its financial statements with a securities commission or other regulatory organisation for the purpose of issuing ordinary shares in a public market.*

Reporting entities applying the Financial Reporting Standard for Smaller Entities currently applicable are exempt from the FRS. 2A

An entity that discloses earnings per share shall calculate and disclose earnings per share in accordance with this Standard. 3

Entities that use merger accounting as required or permitted by FRS 6 'Acquisitions and Mergers' should follow the requirements in Appendix C 'Application to Merger Accounting'. 3A

When an entity presents both consolidated financial statements and separate financial statements, the disclosures required by this Standard need be presented only on the basis of the consolidated information. An entity that chooses to disclose earnings per share based on its separate financial statements shall present such earnings per share information only on the face of its separate income statement. An entity shall not present such earnings per share information in the consolidated financial statements. 4

**Editor's note*: *Paragraph amended with effect for accounting periods beginning on or after 1 January 2009.*

DEFINITIONS

5 ***The following terms are used in this Standard with the meanings specified:***

Antidilution is an increase in earnings per share or a reduction in loss per share resulting from the assumption that convertible instruments are converted, that options or warrants are exercised, or that ordinary shares are issued upon the satisfaction of specified conditions.

A contingent share agreement is an agreement to issue shares that is dependent on the satisfaction of specified conditions.

Contingently issuable ordinary shares are ordinary shares issuable for little or no cash or other consideration upon the satisfaction of specified conditions in a contingent share agreement.

Dilution is a reduction in earnings per share or an increase in loss per share resulting from the assumption that convertible instruments are converted, that options or warrants are exercised, or that ordinary shares are issued upon the satisfaction of specified conditions.

Options, warrants and their equivalents are financial instruments that give the holder the right to purchase ordinary shares.

An ordinary share is an equity instrument that is subordinate to all other classes of equity instruments.

A potential ordinary share is a financial instrument or other contract that may entitle its holder to ordinary shares.

Put options on ordinary shares are contracts that give the holder the right to sell ordinary shares at a specified price for a given period.

6 Ordinary shares participate in profit for the period only after other types of shares such as preference shares have participated. An entity may have more than one class of ordinary shares. Ordinary shares of the same class have the same rights to receive dividends.

7 Examples of potential ordinary shares are:

(a) financial liabilities or equity instruments, including preference shares, that are convertible into ordinary shares;
(b) options and warrants;
(c) shares that would be issued upon the satisfaction of conditions resulting from contractual arrangements, such as the purchase of a business or other assets.

8 Terms defined in FRS 25 (IAS 32) *Financial Instruments: Disclosure and Presentation** are used in this Standard with the meanings specified in paragraph 11 of FRS 25 (IAS 32), unless otherwise noted. FRS 25 (IAS 32) defines financial instrument, financial asset, financial liability, equity instrument and fair value, and provides guidance on applying those definitions.

****Editor's note:*** *The title of FRS 25 no longer makes reference to disclosure.*

MEASUREMENT

Basic Earnings per Share

An entity shall calculate basic earnings per share amounts for profit or loss attributable to ordinary equity holders of the parent entity and, if presented, profit or loss from continuing operations attributable to those equity holders. 9

Basic earnings per share shall be calculated by dividing profit or loss attributable to ordinary equity holders of the parent entity (the numerator) by the weighted average number of ordinary shares outstanding (the denominator) during the period. 10

The objective of basic earnings per share information is to provide a measure of the interests of each ordinary share of a parent entity in the performance of the entity over the reporting period. 11

Earnings

For the purpose of calculating basic earnings per share, the amounts attributable to ordinary equity holders of the parent entity in respect of: 12

(a) profit or loss from continuing operations attributable to the parent entity; and
(b) profit or loss attributable to the parent entity

shall be the amounts in (a) and (b) adjusted for the after-tax amounts of preference dividends, differences arising on the settlement of preference shares, and other similar effects of preference shares classified as equity.

All items of income and expense attributable to ordinary equity holders of the parent entity that are recognised in a period, including tax expense and dividends on preference shares classified as liabilities are included in the determination of profit or loss for the period attributable to ordinary equity holders of the parent entity. 13

The after-tax amount of preference dividends that is deducted from profit or loss is: 14

(a) the after-tax amount of any preference dividends on noncumulative preference shares declared in respect of the period; and
(b) the after-tax amount of the preference dividends for cumulative preference shares required for the period, whether or not the dividends have been declared. The amount of preference dividends for the period does not include the amount of any preference dividends for cumulative preference shares paid or declared during the current period in respect of previous periods.

Preference shares that provide for a low initial dividend to compensate an entity for selling the preference shares at a discount, or an above market dividend in later periods to compensate investors for purchasing preference shares at a premium, are sometimes referred to as increasing rate preference shares. Any original issue discount or premium on increasing rate preference shares is amortised to retained earnings using the effective interest method and treated as a preference dividend for the purposes of calculating earnings per share. 15

Preference shares may be repurchased under an entity's tender offer to the holders. The excess of the fair value of the consideration paid to the preference shareholders over the carrying amount of the preference shares represents a return to the holders of the preference shares and a charge to retained earnings for the entity. This amount 16 is deducted in calculating profit or loss attributable to ordinary equity holders of the parent entity.

17 Early conversion of convertible preference shares may be induced by an entity through favourable changes to the original conversion terms or the payment of additional consideration. The excess of the fair value of the ordinary shares or other consideration paid over the fair value of the ordinary shares issuable under the original conversion terms is a return to the preference shareholders, and is deducted in calculating profit or loss attributable to ordinary equity holders of the parent entity.

18 Any excess of the carrying amount of preference shares over the fair value of the consideration paid to settle them is added in calculating profit or loss attributable to ordinary equity holders of the parent entity.

Shares

19 ***For the purpose of calculating basic earnings per share, the number of ordinary shares shall be the weighted average number of ordinary shares outstanding during the period.***

20 Using the weighted average number of ordinary shares outstanding during the period reflects the possibility that the amount of shareholders' capital varied during the period as a result of a larger or smaller number of shares being outstanding at any time. The weighted average number of ordinary shares outstanding during the period is the number of ordinary shares outstanding at the beginning of the period, adjusted by the number of ordinary shares bought back or issued during the period multiplied by a time-weighting factor. The timeweighting factor is the number of days that the shares are outstanding as a proportion of the total number of days in the period; a reasonable approximation of the weighted average is adequate in many circumstances.

21 Shares are usually included in the weighted average number of shares from the date consideration is receivable (which is generally the date of their issue), for example:

(a) ordinary shares issued in exchange for cash are included when cash is receivable;
(b) ordinary shares issued on the voluntary reinvestment of dividends on ordinary or preference shares are included when dividends are reinvested;
(c) ordinary shares issued as a result of the conversion of a debt instrument to ordinary shares are included from the date that interest ceases to accrue;
(d) ordinary shares issued in place of interest or principal on other financial instruments are included from the date that interest ceases to accrue;
(e) ordinary shares issued in exchange for the settlement of a liability of the entity are included from the settlement date;
(f) ordinary shares issued as consideration for the acquisition of an asset other than cash are included as of the date on which the acquisition is recognised; and
(g) ordinary shares issued for the rendering of services to the entity are included as the services are rendered.

The timing of the inclusion of ordinary shares is determined by the terms and conditions attaching to their issue. Due consideration is given to the substance of any contract associated with the issue.

22 Ordinary shares issued as part of the cost of a business combination are included in the weighted average number of shares from the acquisition date. This is because the

acquirer incorporates into its profit and loss account the acquiree's profits and losses from that date.*

Ordinary shares that will be issued upon the conversion of a mandatorily convertible instrument are included in the calculation of basic earnings per share from the date the contract is entered into. 23

Contingently issuable shares are treated as outstanding and are included in the calculation of basic earnings per share only from the date when all necessary conditions are satisfied (ie the events have occurred). Shares that are issuable solely after the passage of time are not contingently issuable shares, because the passage of time is a certainty. 24

Outstanding ordinary shares that are contingently returnable (ie subject to recall) are not treated as outstanding and are excluded from the calculation of basic earnings per share until the date the shares are no longer subject to recall. 25

The weighted average number of ordinary shares outstanding during the period and for all periods presented shall be adjusted for events, other than the conversion of potential ordinary shares, that have changed the number of ordinary shares outstanding without a corresponding change in resources. 26

Ordinary shares may be issued, or the number of ordinary shares outstanding may be reduced, without a corresponding change in resources. Examples include: 27

(a) a capitalisation or bonus issue (sometimes referred to as a stock dividend);
(b) a bonus element in any other issue, for example a bonus element in a rights issue to existing shareholders;
(c) a share split; and
(d) a reverse share split (consolidation of shares).

In a capitalisation or bonus issue or a share split, ordinary shares are issued to existing shareholders for no additional consideration. Therefore, the number of ordinary shares outstanding is increased without an increase in resources. The number of ordinary shares outstanding before the event is adjusted for the proportionate change in the number of ordinary shares outstanding as if the event had occurred at the beginning of the earliest period presented. For example, on a two for-one bonus issue, the number of ordinary shares outstanding before the issue is multiplied by three to obtain the new total number of ordinary shares, or by two to obtain the number of additional ordinary shares. 28

A consolidation of ordinary shares generally reduces the number of ordinary shares outstanding without a corresponding reduction in resources. However, when the overall effect is a share repurchase at fair value, the reduction in the number of ordinary shares outstanding is the result of a corresponding reduction in resources. An example is a share consolidation combined with a special dividend. The weighted average number of ordinary shares outstanding for the period in which the combined transaction takes place is adjusted for the reduction in the number of ordinary shares from the date the special dividend is recognised. 29

****Editor's note****: *Paragraph amended in December 2008.*

Diluted Earnings per Share

30 ***An entity shall calculate diluted earnings per share amounts for profit or loss attributable to ordinary equity holders of the parent entity and, if presented, profit or loss from continuing operations attributable to those equity holders.***

31 ***For the purpose of calculating diluted earnings per share, an entity shall adjust profit or loss attributable to ordinary equity holders of the parent entity, and the weighted average number of shares outstanding, for the effects of all dilutive potential ordinary shares.***

32 The objective of diluted earnings per share is consistent with that of basic earnings per share—to provide a measure of the interest of each ordinary share in the performance of an entity—while giving effect to all dilutive potential ordinary shares outstanding during the period. As a result:

(a) profit or loss attributable to ordinary equity holders of the parent entity is increased by the after-tax amount of dividends and interest recognised in the period in respect of the dilutive potential ordinary shares and is adjusted for any other changes in income or expense that would result from the conversion of the dilutive potential ordinary shares; and

(b) the weighted average number of ordinary shares outstanding is increased by the weighted average number of additional ordinary shares that would have been outstanding assuming the conversion of all dilutive potential ordinary shares.

Earnings

33 ***For the purpose of calculating diluted earnings per share, an entity shall adjust profit or loss attributable to ordinary equity holders of the parent entity, as calculated in accordance with paragraph 12, by the after-tax effect of:***

(a) any dividends or other items related to dilutive potential ordinary shares deducted in arriving at profit or loss attributable to ordinary equity holders of the parent entity as calculated in accordance with paragraph 12;

(b) any interest recognised in the period related to dilutive potential ordinary shares; and

(c) any other changes in income or expense that would result from the conversion of the dilutive potential ordinary shares.

34 After the potential ordinary shares are converted into ordinary shares, the items identified in paragraph 33(a)-(c) no longer arise. Instead, the new ordinary shares are entitled to participate in profit or loss attributable to ordinary equity holders of the parent entity. Therefore, profit or loss attributable to ordinary equity holders of the parent entity calculated in accordance with paragraph 12 is adjusted for the items identified in paragraph 33(a)-(c) and any related taxes. The expenses associated with potential ordinary shares include transaction costs and discounts accounted for in accordance with the effective interest method (see paragraph 9 of FRS 26 (Part of IAS 39) *Financial Instruments: Measurement*).

35 The conversion of potential ordinary shares may lead to consequential changes in income or expenses. For example, the reduction of interest expense related to potential ordinary shares and the resulting increase in profit or reduction in loss may lead to an increase in the expense related to a nondiscretionary employee profit sharing plan. For the purpose of calculating diluted earnings per share, profit or loss attributable to ordinary equity holders of the parent entity is adjusted for any such consequential changes in income or expense.

Shares

For the purpose of calculating diluted earnings per share, the number of ordinary shares shall be the weighted average number of ordinary shares calculated in accordance with paragraphs 19 and 26, plus the weighted average number of ordinary shares that would be issued on the conversion of all the dilutive potential ordinary shares into ordinary shares. Dilutive potential ordinary shares shall be deemed to have been converted into ordinary shares at the beginning of the period or, if later, the date of the issue of the potential ordinary shares. 36

Dilutive potential ordinary shares shall be determined independently for each period presented. The number of dilutive potential ordinary shares included in the year-to-date period is not a weighted average of the dilutive potential ordinary shares included in each interim computation. 37

Potential ordinary shares are weighted for the period they are outstanding. Potential ordinary shares that are cancelled or allowed to lapse during the period are included in the calculation of diluted earnings per share only for the portion of the period during which they are outstanding. Potential ordinary shares that are converted into ordinary shares during the period are included in the calculation of diluted earnings per share from the beginning of the period to the date of conversion; from the date of conversion, the resulting ordinary shares are included in both basic and diluted earnings per share. 38

The number of ordinary shares that would be issued on conversion of dilutive potential ordinary shares is determined from the terms of the potential ordinary shares. When more than one basis of conversion exists, the calculation assumes the most advantageous conversion rate or exercise price from the standpoint of the holder of the potential ordinary shares. 39

A subsidiary, joint venture or associate may issue to parties other than the parent, venturer or investor potential ordinary shares that are convertible into either ordinary shares of the subsidiary, joint venture or associate, or ordinary shares of the parent, venturer or investor (the reporting entity). If these potential ordinary shares of the subsidiary, joint venture or associate have a dilutive effect on the basic earnings per share of the reporting entity, they are included in the calculation of diluted earnings per share. 40

Dilutive Potential Ordinary Shares

Potential ordinary shares shall be treated as dilutive when, and only when, their conversion to ordinary shares would decrease earnings per share or increase loss per share from continuing operations. 41

An entity uses profit or loss from continuing operations attributable to the parent entity as the control number to establish whether potential ordinary shares are dilutive or antidilutive. Profit or loss from continuing operations attributable to the parent entity is adjusted in accordance with paragraph 12 and excludes items relating to discontinued operations* 42

Potential ordinary shares are antidilutive when their conversion to ordinary shares would increase earnings per share or decrease loss per share from continuing operations. The calculation of diluted earnings per share does not assume 43

****ASB footnote:* *Discontinued operations are defined in FRS 3* Reporting Financial Performance.

conversion, exercise, or other issue of potential ordinary shares that would have an antidilutive effect on earnings per share.

44 In determining whether potential ordinary shares are dilutive or antidilutive, each issue or series of potential ordinary shares is considered separately rather than in aggregate. The sequence in which potential ordinary shares are considered may affect whether they are dilutive. Therefore, to maximise the dilution of basic earnings per share, each issue or series of potential ordinary shares is considered in sequence from the most dilutive to the least dilutive, ie dilutive potential ordinary shares with the lowest 'earnings per incremental share' are included in the diluted earnings per share calculation before those with a higher earnings per incremental share. Options and warrants are generally included first because they do not affect the numerator of the calculation.

Options, warrants and their equivalents

45 ***For the purpose of calculating diluted earnings per share, an entity shall assume the exercise of dilutive options and warrants of the entity. The assumed proceeds from these instruments shall be regarded as having been received from the issue of ordinary shares at the average market price of ordinary shares during the period. The difference between the number of ordinary shares issued and the number of ordinary shares that would have been issued at the average market price of ordinary shares during the period shall be treated as an issue of ordinary shares for no consideration.***

46 Options and warrants are dilutive when they would result in the issue of ordinary shares for less than the average market price of ordinary shares during the period. The amount of the dilution is the average market price of ordinary shares during the period minus the issue price. Therefore, to calculate diluted earnings per share, potential ordinary shares are treated as consisting of both the following:

(a) a contract to issue a certain number of the ordinary shares at their average market price during the period. Such ordinary shares are assumed to be fairly priced and to be neither dilutive nor antidilutive. They are ignored in the calculation of diluted earnings per share.
(b) a contract to issue the remaining ordinary shares for no consideration. Such ordinary shares generate no proceeds and have no effect on profit or loss attributable to ordinary shares outstanding. Therefore, such shares are dilutive and are added to the number of ordinary shares outstanding in the calculation of diluted earnings per share.

47 Options and warrants have a dilutive effect only when the average market price of ordinary shares during the period exceeds the exercise price of the options or warrants (ie they are 'in the money'). Previously reported earnings per share are not retroactively adjusted to reflect changes in prices of ordinary shares.

47A For share options and other share-based payment arrangement to which FRS 20 (IFRS 2) *Share-based Payment* applies, the issue price referred to in paragraph 46 and the exercise price referred to in paragraph 47 shall include the fair value of any goods or services to be supplied to the entity in the future under the share option or other share-based payment arrangement.

48 Employee share options with fixed or determinable terms and nonvested ordinary shares are treated as options in the calculation of diluted earnings per share, even though they may be contingent on vesting. They are treated as outstanding on the grant date. Performance-based employee share options are treated as contingently

issuable shares because their issue is contingent upon satisfying specified conditions in addition to the passage of time.

Convertible instruments

49 The dilutive effect of convertible instruments shall be reflected in diluted earnings per share in accordance with paragraphs 33 and 36.

50 Convertible preference shares are antidilutive whenever the amount of the dividend on such shares declared in or accumulated for the current period per ordinary share obtainable on conversion exceeds basic earnings per share. Similarly, convertible debt is antidilutive whenever its interest (net of tax and other changes in income or expense) per ordinary share obtainable on conversion exceeds basic earnings per share.

51 The redemption or induced conversion of convertible preference shares may affect only a portion of the previously outstanding convertible preference shares. In such cases, any excess consideration referred to in paragraph 17 is attributed to those shares that are redeemed or converted for the purpose of determining whether the remaining outstanding preference shares are dilutive. The shares redeemed or converted are considered separately from those shares that are not redeemed or converted.

Contingently issuable shares

52 As in the calculation of basic earnings per share, contingently issuable ordinary shares are treated as outstanding and included in the calculation of diluted earnings per share if the conditions are satisfied (ie the events have occurred). Contingently issuable shares are included from the beginning of the period (or from the date of the contingent share agreement, if later). If the conditions are not satisfied, the number of contingently issuable shares included in the diluted earnings per share calculation is based on the number of shares that would be issuable if the end of the period were the end of the contingency period. Restatement is not permitted if the conditions are not met when the contingency period expires.

53 If attainment or maintenance of a specified amount of earnings for a period is the condition for contingent issue and if that amount has been attained at the end of the reporting period but must be maintained beyond the end of the reporting period for an additional period, then the additional ordinary shares are treated as outstanding, if the effect is dilutive, when calculating diluted earnings per share. In that case, the calculation of diluted earnings per share is based on the number of ordinary shares that would be issued if the amount of earnings at the end of the reporting period were the amount of earnings at the end of the contingency period. Because earnings may change in a future period, the calculation of basic earnings per share does not include such contingently issuable ordinary shares until the end of the contingency period because not all necessary conditions have been satisfied.

54 The number of ordinary shares contingently issuable may depend on the future market price of the ordinary shares. In that case, if the effect is dilutive, the calculation of diluted earnings per share is based on the number of ordinary shares that would be issued if the market price at the end of the reporting period were the market price at the end of the contingency period. If the condition is based on an average of market prices over a period of time that extends beyond the end of the reporting period, the average for the period of time that has lapsed is used. Because the market price may change in a future period, the calculation of basic earnings per share does

not include such contingently issuable ordinary shares until the end of the contingency period because not all necessary conditions have been satisfied.

55 The number of ordinary shares contingently issuable may depend on future earnings and future prices of the ordinary shares. In such cases, the number of ordinary shares included in the diluted earnings per share calculation is based on both conditions (ie earnings to date and the current market price at the end of the reporting period). Contingently issuable ordinary shares are not included in the diluted earnings per share calculation unless both conditions are met.

56 In other cases, the number of ordinary shares contingently issuable depends on a condition other than earnings or market price (for example, the opening of a specific number of retail stores). In such cases, assuming that the present status of the condition remains unchanged until the end of the contingency period, the contingently issuable ordinary shares are included in the calculation of diluted earnings per share according to the status at the end of the reporting period.

57 Contingently issuable potential ordinary shares (other than those covered by a contingent share agreement, such as contingently issuable convertible instruments) are included in the diluted earnings per share calculation as follows:

(a) an entity determines whether the potential ordinary shares may be assumed to be issuable on the basis of the conditions specified for their issue in accordance with the contingent ordinary share provisions in paragraphs 52-56; and

(b) if those potential ordinary shares should be reflected in diluted earnings per share, an entity determines their impact on the calculation of diluted earnings per share by following the provisions for options and warrants in paragraphs 45-48, the provisions for convertible instruments in paragraphs 49-51, the provisions for contracts that may be settled in ordinary shares or cash in paragraphs 58-61, or other provisions, as appropriate.

However, exercise or conversion is not assumed for the purpose of calculating diluted earnings per share unless exercise or conversion of similar outstanding potential ordinary shares that are not contingently issuable is assumed.

Contracts that may be settled in ordinary shares or cash

58 ***When an entity has issued a contract that may be settled in ordinary shares or cash at the entity's option, the entity shall presume that the contract will be settled in ordinary shares, and the resulting potential ordinary shares shall be included in diluted earnings per share if the effect is dilutive.***

59 When such a contract is presented for accounting purposes as an asset or a liability, or has an equity component and a liability component, the entity shall adjust the numerator for any changes in profit or loss that would have resulted during the period if the contract had been classified wholly as an equity instrument. That adjustment is similar to the adjustments required in paragraph 33.

60 ***For contracts that may be settled in ordinary shares or cash at the holder's option, the more dilutive of cash settlement and share settlement shall be used in calculating diluted earnings per share.***

61 An example of a contract that may be settled in ordinary shares or cash is a debt instrument that, on maturity, gives the entity the unrestricted right to settle the principal amount in cash or in its own ordinary shares. Another example is a written put option that gives the holder a choice of settling in ordinary shares or cash.

Purchased options

Contracts such as purchased put options and purchased call options (ie options held by the entity on its own ordinary shares) are not included in the calculation of diluted earnings per share because including them would be antidilutive. The put option would be exercised only if the exercise price were higher than the market price and the call option would be exercised only if the exercise price were lower than the market price. 62

Written put options

Contracts that require the entity to repurchase its own shares, such as written put options and forward purchase contracts, are reflected in the calculation of diluted earnings per share if the effect is dilutive. If these contracts are 'in the money' during the period (ie the exercise or settlement price is above the average market price for that period), the potential dilutive effect on earnings per share shall be calculated as follows: 63

(a) it shall be assumed that at the beginning of the period sufficient ordinary shares will be issued (at the average market price during the period) to raise proceeds to satisfy the contract;
(b) it shall be assumed that the proceeds from the issue are used to satisfy the contract (ie to buy back ordinary shares); and
(c) the incremental ordinary shares (the difference between the number of ordinary shares assumed issued and the number of ordinary shares received from satisfying the contract) shall be included in the calculation of diluted earnings per share.

RETROSPECTIVE ADJUSTMENTS

If the number of ordinary or potential ordinary shares outstanding increases as a result of a capitalisation, bonus issue or share split, or decreases as a result of a reverse share split, the calculation of basic and diluted earnings per share for all periods presented shall be adjusted retrospectively. If these changes occur after the balance sheet date but before the financial statements are authorised for issue, the per share calculations for those and any prior period financial statements presented shall be based on the new number of shares. The fact that per share calculations reflect such changes in the number of shares shall be disclosed. In addition, basic and diluted earnings per share of all periods presented shall be adjusted for the effects of errors and adjustments resulting from changes in accounting policies accounted for retrospectively. 64

An entity does not restate diluted earnings per share of any prior period presented for changes in the assumptions used in earnings per share calculations or for the conversion of potential ordinary shares into ordinary shares. 65

PRESENTATION

An entity shall present on the face of the income statement basic and diluted earnings per share for profit or loss from continuing operations attributable to the ordinary equity holders of the parent entity and for profit or loss attributable to the ordinary equity holders of the parent entity for the period for each class of ordinary shares that has a different right to share in profit for the period. An entity shall present basic and diluted earnings per share with equal prominence for all periods presented. 66

Earnings per share is presented for every period for which an income statement is presented. If diluted earnings per share is reported for at least one period, it shall be reported for all periods presented, even if it equals basic earnings per share. If basic 67 and diluted earnings per share are equal, dual presentation can be accomplished in one line on the income statement.

68 ***An entity that reports a discontinued operation shall disclose the basic and diluted amounts per share for the discontinued operation either on the face of the income statement or in the notes to the financial statements.***

69 ***An entity shall present basic and diluted earnings per share, even if the amounts are negative (ie a loss per share).***

DISCLOSURE

70 ***An entity shall disclose the following:***

(a) the amounts used as the numerators in calculating basic and diluted earnings per share, and a reconciliation of those amounts to profit or loss attributable to the parent entity for the period. The reconciliation shall include the individual effect of each class of instruments that affects earnings per share.
(b) the weighted average number of ordinary shares used as the denominator in calculating basic and diluted earnings per share, and a reconciliation of these denominators to each other. The reconciliation shall include the individual effect of each class of instruments that affects earnings per share.
(c) instruments (including contingently issuable shares) that could potentially dilute basic earnings per share in the future, but were not included in the calculation of diluted earnings per share because they are antidilutive for the period(s) presented.
(d) a description of ordinary share transactions or potential ordinary share transactions, other than those accounted for in accordance with paragraph 64, that occur after the balance sheet date and that would have changed significantly the number of ordinary shares or potential ordinary shares outstanding at the end of the period if those transactions had occurred before the end of the reporting period.

71 Examples of transactions in paragraph 70(d) include:

(a) an issue of shares for cash;
(b) an issue of shares when the proceeds are used to repay debt or preference shares outstanding at the balance sheet date;
(c) the redemption of ordinary shares outstanding;
(d) the conversion or exercise of potential ordinary shares outstanding at the balance sheet date into ordinary shares;
(e) an issue of options, warrants, or convertible instruments; and
(f) the achievement of conditions that would result in the issue of contingently issuable shares.

Earnings per share amounts are not adjusted for such transactions occurring after the balance sheet date because such transactions do not affect the amount of capital used to produce profit or loss for the period.

72 Financial instruments and other contracts generating potential ordinary shares may incorporate terms and conditions that affect the measurement of basic and diluted earnings per share. These terms and conditions may determine whether any potential ordinary shares are dilutive and, if so, the effect on the weighted average number of shares outstanding and any consequent adjustments to profit or loss attributable to ordinary equity holders. The disclosure of the terms and conditions of such financial

instruments and other contracts is encouraged, if not otherwise required (see FRS 29 (IFRS 7) Financial Instruments: Disclosures).*

If an entity discloses, in addition to basic and diluted earnings per share, amounts per share using a reported component of the income statement other than one required by this Standard, such amounts shall be calculated using the weighted average number of ordinary shares determined in accordance with this Standard. Basic and diluted amounts per share relating to such a component shall be disclosed with equal prominence and presented in the notes to the financial statements. An entity shall indicate the basis on which the numerator(s) is (are) determined, including whether amounts per share are before tax or after tax. If a component of the income statement is used that is not reported as a line item in the income statement, a reconciliation shall be provided between the component used and a line item that is reported in the income statement. 73

EFFECTIVE DATE

An entity shall apply this Standard for accounting periods beginning on or after 1 January 2005. 74

WITHDRAWAL OF OTHER PRONOUNCEMENTS

This Standard supersedes FRS 14 *Earnings per Share.* 75

***Editor's note:** *Amended by FRS 29.*

Appendix A
Application Guidance

This appendix is an integral part of the Standard.

Profit or Loss Attributable to the Parent Entity

A1 For the purpose of calculating earnings per share based on the consolidated financial statements, profit or loss attributable to the parent entity refers to profit or loss of the consolidated entity after adjusting for minority interests.

Rights Issues

A2 The issue of ordinary shares at the time of exercise or conversion of potential ordinary shares does not usually give rise to a bonus element. This is because the potential ordinary shares are usually issued for full value, resulting in a proportionate change in the resources available to the entity. In a rights issue, however, the exercise price is often less than the fair value of the shares. Therefore, as noted in paragraph 27(b), such a rights issue includes a bonus element. If a rights issue is offered to all existing shareholders, the number of ordinary shares to be used in calculating basic and diluted earnings per share for all periods before the rights issue is the number of ordinary shares outstanding before the issue, multiplied by the following factor:

$$\frac{\text{Fair value per share immediately before the exercise of rights}}{\text{Theoretical ex-rights fair value per share}}$$

The theoretical ex-rights fair value per share is calculated by adding the aggregate market value of the shares immediately before the exercise of the rights to the proceeds from the exercise of the rights, and dividing by the number of shares outstanding after the exercise of the rights. Where the rights are to be publicly traded separately from the shares before the exercise date, fair value for the purposes of this calculation is established at the close of the last day on which the shares are traded together with the rights.

Control Number

A3 To illustrate the application of the control number notion described in paragraphs 42 and 43, assume that an entity has profit from continuing operations attributable to the parent entity of CU4,800,* a loss from discontinued operations attributable to the parent entity of (CU7,200), a loss attributable to the parent entity of (CU2,400), and 2,000 ordinary shares and 400 potential ordinary shares outstanding. The entity's basic earnings per share is CU2.40 for continuing operations, (CU3.60) for discontinued operations and (CU1.20) for the loss. The 400 potential ordinary shares are included in the diluted earnings per share calculation because the resulting CU2.00 earnings per share for continuing operations is dilutive, assuming no profit or loss impact of those 400 potential ordinary shares. Because profit from continuing operations attributable to the parent entity is the control number, the entity also includes those 400 potential ordinary shares in the calculation of the other earnings per share amounts, even though the resulting earnings per share amounts are anti-dilutive to their comparable basic earnings per share amounts, ie the loss per share is

**In this guidance, monetary amounts are denominated in 'currency units' (CU).*

less [(CU3.00) per share for the loss from discontinued operations and (CU1.00) per share for the loss].

Average Market Price of Ordinary Shares

For the purpose of calculating diluted earnings per share, the average market price of ordinary shares assumed to be issued is calculated on the basis of the average market price of the ordinary shares during the period. Theoretically, every market transaction for an entity's ordinary shares could be included in the determination of the average market price. As a practical matter, however, a simple average of weekly or monthly prices is usually adequate. **A4**

Generally, closing market prices are adequate for calculating the average market price. When prices fluctuate widely, however, an average of the high and low prices usually produces a more representative price. The method used to calculate the average market price is used consistently unless it is no longer representative because of changed conditions. For example, an entity that uses closing market prices to calculate the average market price for several years of relatively stable prices might change to an average of high and low prices if prices start fluctuating greatly and the closing market prices no longer produce a representative average price. **A5**

Options, Warrants and Their Equivalents

Options or warrants to purchase convertible instruments are assumed to be exercised to purchase the convertible instrument whenever the average prices of both the convertible instrument and the ordinary shares obtainable upon conversion are above the exercise price of the options or warrants. However, exercise is not assumed unless conversion of similar outstanding convertible instruments, if any, is also assumed. **A6**

Options or warrants may permit or require the tendering of debt or other instruments of the entity (or its parent or a subsidiary) in payment of all or a portion of the exercise price. In the calculation of diluted earnings per share, those options or warrants have a dilutive effect if (a) the average market price of the related ordinary shares for the period exceeds the exercise price or (b) the selling price of the instrument to be tendered is below that at which the instrument may be tendered under the option or warrant agreement and the resulting discount establishes an effective exercise price below the market price of the ordinary shares obtainable upon exercise. In the calculation of diluted earnings per share, those options or warrants are assumed to be exercised and the debt or other instruments are assumed to be tendered. If tendering cash is more advantageous to the option or warrant holder and the contract permits tendering cash, tendering of cash is assumed. Interest (net of tax) on any debt assumed to be tendered is added back as an adjustment to the numerator. **A7**

Similar treatment is given to preference shares that have similar provisions or to other instruments that have conversion options that permit the investor to pay cash for a more favourable conversion rate. **A8**

The underlying terms of certain options or warrants may require the proceeds received from the exercise of those instruments to be applied to redeem debt or other instruments of the entity (or its parent or a subsidiary). In the calculation of diluted earnings per share, those options or warrants are assumed to be exercised and the proceeds applied to purchase the debt at its average market price rather than to purchase ordinary shares. However, the excess proceeds received from the assumed **A9** exercise over the amount used for the assumed purchase of debt are considered (ie assumed to be used to buy back ordinary shares) in the diluted earnings per share calculation. Interest (net of tax) on any debt assumed to be purchased is added back as an adjustment to the numerator.

Written Put Options

A10 To illustrate the application of paragraph 63, assume that an entity has outstanding 120 written put options on its ordinary shares with an exercise price of CU35. The average market price of its ordinary shares for the period is CU28. In calculating diluted earnings per share, the entity assumes that it issued 150 shares at CU28 per share at the beginning of the period to satisfy its put obligation of CU4,200. The difference between the 150 ordinary shares issued and the 120 ordinary shares received from satisfying the put option (30 incremental ordinary shares) is added to the denominator in calculating diluted earnings per share.

Instruments of Subsidiaries, Joint Ventures or Associates

A11 Potential ordinary shares of a subsidiary, joint venture or associate convertible into either ordinary shares of the subsidiary, joint venture or associate, or ordinary shares of the parent, venturer or investor (the reporting entity) are included in the calculation of diluted earnings per share as follows:

(a) instruments issued by a subsidiary, joint venture or associate that enable their holders to obtain ordinary shares of the subsidiary, joint venture or associate are included in calculating the diluted earnings per share data of the subsidiary, joint venture or associate. Those earnings per share are then included in the reporting entity's earnings per share calculations based on the reporting entity's holding of the instruments of the subsidiary, joint venture or associate.

(b) instruments of a subsidiary, joint venture or associate that are convertible into the reporting entity's ordinary shares are considered among the potential ordinary shares of the reporting entity for the purpose of calculating diluted earnings per share. Likewise, options or warrants issued by a subsidiary, joint venture or associate to purchase ordinary shares of the reporting entity are considered among the potential ordinary shares of the reporting entity in the calculation of consolidated diluted earnings per share.

A12 For the purpose of determining the earnings per share effect of instruments issued by a reporting entity that are convertible into ordinary shares of a subsidiary, joint venture or associate, the instruments are assumed to be converted and the numerator (profit or loss attributable to ordinary equity holders of the parent entity) adjusted as necessary in accordance with paragraph 33. In addition to those adjustments, the numerator is adjusted for any change in the profit or loss recorded by the reporting entity (such as dividend income or equity method income) that is attributable to the increase in the number of ordinary shares of the subsidiary, joint venture or associate outstanding as a result of the assumed conversion. The denominator of the diluted earnings per share calculation is not affected because the number of ordinary shares of the reporting entity outstanding would not change upon assumed conversion.

Participating Equity Instruments and Two-Class Ordinary Shares

A13 The equity of some entities includes:

(a) instruments that participate in dividends with ordinary shares according to a predetermined formula (for example, two for one) with, at times, an upper limit on the extent of participation (for example, up to, but not beyond, a specified amount per share).

(b) a class of ordinary shares with a different dividend rate from that of another class of ordinary shares but without prior or senior rights.

For the purpose of calculating diluted earnings per share, conversion is assumed for those instruments described in paragraph A13 that are convertible into ordinary shares if the effect is dilutive. For those instruments that are not convertible into a class of ordinary shares, profit or loss for the period is allocated to the different classes of shares and participating equity instruments in accordance with their dividend rights or other rights to participate in undistributed earnings. To calculate basic and diluted earnings per share: **A14**

(a) profit or loss attributable to ordinary equity holders of the parent entity is adjusted (a profit reduced and a loss increased) by the amount of dividends declared in the period for each class of shares and by the contractual amount of dividends (or interest on participating bonds) that must be paid for the period (for example, unpaid cumulative dividends).
(b) the remaining profit or loss is allocated to ordinary shares and participating equity instruments to the extent that each instrument shares in earnings as if all of the profit or loss for the period had been distributed. The total profit or loss allocated to each class of equity instrument is determined by adding together the amount allocated for dividends and the amount allocated for a participation feature.
(c) the total amount of profit or loss allocated to each class of equity instrument is divided by the number of outstanding instruments to which the earnings are allocated to determine the earnings per share for the instrument.

For the calculation of diluted earnings per share, all potential ordinary shares assumed to have been issued are included in outstanding ordinary shares.

Partly Paid Shares

Where ordinary shares are issued but not fully paid, they are treated in the calculation of basic earnings per share as a fraction of an ordinary share to the extent that they were entitled to participate in dividends during the period relative to a fully paid ordinary share. **A15**

To the extent that partly paid shares are not entitled to participate in dividends during the period they are treated as the equivalent of warrants or options in the calculation of diluted earnings per share. The unpaid balance is assumed to represent proceeds used to purchase ordinary shares. The number of shares included in diluted earnings per share is the difference between the number of shares subscribed and the number of shares assumed to be purchased. **A16**

Appendix B
Amendments to other Standards and UITF Abstracts

[Not reproduced, as all changes have been made to the underlying standards and abstracts].

Appendix C

ASB note: This Appendix has been prepared by the ASB

APPLICATION TO MERGER ACCOUNTING

Entities that use merger accounting as required by FRS 6* Acquisitions and Mergers *should apply FRS 22 in full with the following amendments:

Paragraph 22 of FRS 22 should not be applied. Instead: **C1**

Ordinary shares issued as part of a business combination that is merger accounted under FRS 6 *Acquisitions and Mergers* are included in the calculation of the weighted average number of shares for all periods presented because the financial statements of the combined entity are prepared as if the combined entity had always existed. Therefore, the number of ordinary shares used for the calculation of basic earnings per share in a business combination that is merger accounted under FRS 6 is the aggregate of the weighted average number of shares of the combined entities, adjusted to equivalent shares of the entity whose shares are outstanding after the combination.

Basic and diluted earnings per share of all periods presented shall be adjusted for the effects of a business combination that is merger accounted under FRS 6. **C2**

Appendix D

ASB note: This Appendix has been prepared by the ASB

NON-MANDATORY APPLICATION GUIDANCE

This appendix does not form part of the standard

Net profit from continuing operations

This Appendix reproduces the text of paragraphs 59 and 60 of FRS 14 *Earnings per Share*. Entities applying FRS 3 *Reporting Financial Performance* may find this guidance to be a useful reference.

D1 FRS 3 'Reporting Financial Performance' requires an analysis of continuing operations, acquisitions (as a component of continuing operations) and discontinued operations only to the level of profit before interest, because interest payable often reflects an entity's overall financing policy rather than an aggregation of the particular types of finance allocated to its operations. Although FRS 3 does not encourage further allocation without disclosure of the method and underlying assumptions adopted, many entities will have the data necessary to allocate interest and tax between continuing and discontinued operations. In particular, it will often be possible to allocate a specific amount of tax and interest to exceptional items that are reported after operating profit under paragraph 20 of FRS 3. Where practicable, such an allocation is adopted for determination of the 'control number'.

D2 In the absence of a practical, more reliable method of allocation, however, net profit from continuing operations will need to be estimated. In these restricted circumstances, and following any specific allocation of tax and interest that may be possible in respect of exceptional items shown after operating profit, it is permitted to allocate interest and taxation in the proportion of profits from continuing operations to total profit at the operating profit level. In practice a profit-based allocation method may be more suitable for taxation, which is levied on profits, than for interest, which finances capital.

Adoption of the Standard

APPROVAL OF IAS 33 BY THE INTERNATIONAL ACCOUNTING STANDARDS BOARD

International Accounting Standard 33 *Earnings per Share* was approved for issue by the fourteen members of the International Accounting Standards Board.

Sir David Tweedie	Chairman
Thomas E Jones	Vice-Chairman
Mary E Barth	
Hans-Georg Bruns	
Anthony T Cope	
Robert P Garnett	
Gilbert Gélard	
James J Leisenring	
Warren J McGregor	
Patricia L O'Malley	
Harry K Schmid	
John T Smith	
Geoffrey Whittington	
Tatsumi Yamada	

ADOPTION OF FRS 22 BY THE ACCOUNTING STANDARDS BOARD

Financial Reporting Standard 22 (IAS33) *Earnings per Share* was approved for issue by the ten members of the Accounting Standards Board.

Ian Mackintosh	Chairman
Andrew Lennard	Technical Director
Michael Ashley	
Douglas Flint	
Anthony Good	
Roger Marshall	
Isobel Sharp	
John Smith	
Jonathan Symonds	
Peter Westlake	

DEVELOPMENT OF THE FRS

1 This FRS is based on IAS 33 (revised 2003) *Earnings per Share* and supersedes FRS 14 *Earnings per Share*, which was issued in October 1998. The draft standard was published as FRED 26 in May 2002. Respondents expressed a number of concerns over the proposed standard, and many also expressed their concerns directly with the IASB, but the majority stated that they did not want the ASB to make any additional amendments to the IASB's final standard over and above those necessary for cross-referencing and consequential amendments to align the standard to UK GAAP and legal requirements. The IASB addressed many of the concerns raised when it issued IAS 33 (revised 2003) as explained in their basis for conclusions which accompanies this FRS.

2 Many UK respondents objected to IAS 33 (revised 2003) paragraphs 66 and 73 which require an entity to present additional per share amounts in the notes to the financial statements, but the respondents also stated that they did not want the ASB to make changes to IAS 33 (revised 2003) because this would hinder convergence. The ASB has not therefore amended the requirements in IAS 33 (revised 2003).

3 The accounting practices set out in this FRS require an entity to have adopted FRS 25 (IAS 32) and, therefore, this FRS takes effect from the same date, being accounting periods beginning on or after 1 January 2005, and earlier application is not permitted.

Basis for Conclusions

This Basis for Conclusions accompanies, but is not part of, IAS 33.

ASB note: The IASB's Basis for Conclusions, which accompanies IAS 33, is set out below in full. All references in this section to 'the Board' and 'Board members' are references to the IASB Board and IASB Board members.

INTRODUCTION

This Basis for Conclusions summarises the International Accounting Standards Board's considerations in reaching its conclusions on revising IAS 33 *Earnings Per Share* in 2003. Individual Board members gave greater weight to some factors than to others. BC1

In July 2001 the Board announced that, as part of its initial agenda of technical projects, it would undertake a project to improve a number of Standards, including IAS 33. The project was undertaken in the light of queries and criticisms raised in relation to the Standards by securities regulators, professional accountants and other interested parties. The objectives of the Improvements project were to reduce or eliminate alternatives, redundancies and conflicts within Standards, to deal with some convergence issues and to make other improvements. In May 2002 the Board published its proposals in an Exposure Draft of *Improvements to International Accounting Standards*, with a comment deadline of 16 September 2002. The Board received over 160 comment letters on the Exposure Draft. BC2

Because the Board's intention was not to reconsider the fundamental approach to the determination and presentation of earnings per share established by IAS 33, this Basis for Conclusions does not discuss requirements in IAS 33 that the Board has not reconsidered. BC3

PRESENTATION OF PARENT'S SEPARATE EARNINGS PER SHARE

The Exposure Draft published in May 2002 proposed deleting paragraphs 2 and 3 of the previous version of IAS 33, which stated that when the parent's separate financial statements and consolidated financial statements are presented, earnings per share need be presented only on the basis of consolidated information. BC4

Some respondents expressed concern that the presentation of two earnings per share figures (one for the parent's separate financial statements and one for the consolidated financial statements) might be misleading. BC5

The Board noted that disclosing the parent's separate earnings per share amount is useful in limited situations, and therefore decided to retain the option. However, the Board decided that the Standard should prohibit presentation of the parent's separate earnings per share amounts in the consolidated financial statements (either on the face of the financial statements or in the notes). BC6

CONTRACTS THAT MAY BE SETTLED IN ORDINARY SHARES OR CASH

BC7 The Exposure Draft proposed that an entity should include in the calculation of the number of potential ordinary shares in the diluted earnings per share calculation contracts that may be settled in ordinary shares or cash, at the issuer's option, based on a rebuttable presumption that the contracts will be settled in shares. This proposed presumption could be rebutted if the issuer had acted through an established pattern of past practice, published policies, or by having made a sufficiently specific current statement indicating to other parties the manner in which it expected to settle, and, as a result, the issuer had created a valid expectation on the part of those other parties that it would settle in a manner other than by issuing shares.

BC8 The majority of the respondents on the Exposure Draft agreed with the proposed treatment of contracts that may be settled in ordinary shares or cash at the issuer's option. However, the Board decided to withdraw the notion of a rebuttable presumption and to incorporate into the Standard the requirements of SIC-24 *Earnings Per Share—Financial Instruments and Other Contracts that May Be Settled in Shares.* SIC24 requires financial instruments or other contracts that may result in the issue of ordinary shares of the entity to be considered potential ordinary shares of the entity.

BC9 Although the proposed treatment would have converged with that required by several liaison standard-setters, for example, in US SFAS 128 *Earnings per Share*, the Board concluded that the notion of a rebuttable presumption is inconsistent with the stated objective of diluted earnings per share. The US Financial Accounting Standards Board has agreed to consider this difference as part of the joint shortterm convergence project with the IASB.

CALCULATION OF YEAR-TO-DATE DILUTED EARNINGS PER SHARE

BC10 The Exposure Draft proposed the following approach to the yeartodate calculation of diluted earnings per share:

(a) The number of potential ordinary shares is a year-to-date weighted average of the number of potential ordinary shares included in each interim diluted earnings per share calculation, rather than a year-to-date weighted average of the number of potential ordinary shares weighted for the period they were outstanding (ie without regard for the diluted earnings per share information reported during the interim periods).

(b) The number of potential ordinary shares is computed using the average market price during the interim periods, rather than using the average market price during the year-to-date period.

(c) Contingently issuable shares are weighted for the interim periods in which they were included in the computation of diluted earnings per share, rather than being included in the computation of diluted earnings per share (if the conditions are satisfied) from the beginning of the year-to-date reporting period (or from the date of the contingent share agreement, if later).

BC11 The majority of the respondents on the Exposure Draft disagreed with the proposed approach to the year-to-date calculation of diluted earnings per share. The most significant argument against the proposed approach was that the proposed calculation of diluted earnings per share could result in an amount for year-to-date diluted earnings per share that was different for entities that report more frequently, for example, on a quarterly or half-yearly basis, and for entities that report only annually. It was also noted that this problem would be exacerbated for entities with seasonal businesses.

The Board considered whether to accept that differences in the frequency of interim reporting would result in different earnings per share amounts being reported. However, IAS 34 *Interim Financial Reporting* states "the frequency of an entity's reporting (annual, halfyearly, or quarterly) should not affect the measurement of its annual results. To achieve that objective, measurements for interim reporting purposes should be made on a year-to-date basis." **BC12**

The Board also considered whether it could mandate the frequency of interim reporting to ensure consistency between all entities preparing financial statements in accordance with IFRSs, ie those that are brought within the scope of IAS 33 by virtue of issuing publicly traded instruments or because they elect to present earnings per share. However, IAS 34 states that, "This Standard does not mandate which entities should be required to publish interim financial reports, how frequently, or how soon after the end of an interim period." The frequency of interim reporting is mandated by securities regulators, stock exchanges, governments, and accountancy bodies, and varies by jurisdiction. **BC13**

Although the proposed approach for the calculation of year-to-date diluted earnings per share would have converged with US SFAS 128, the Board concluded that the approach was inconsistent with IAS 34 and that it could not mandate the frequency of interim reporting. The US Financial Accounting Standards Board has agreed to consider this difference as part of the joint shortterm convergence project with the IASB as well as the issue noted in paragraph BC9. **BC14**

OTHER CHANGES

Implementation questions have arisen since the previous version of IAS 33 was issued, typically concerning the application of the Standard to complex capital structures and arrangements. In response, the Board decided to provide additional application guidance in the Appendix as well as illustrative examples on more complex matters that were not addressed in the previous version of IAS 33. These matters include the effects of contingently issuable shares, potential ordinary shares of subsidiaries, joint ventures or associates, participating equity instruments, written put options, and purchased put and call options. **BC15**

Illustrative Examples

These examples accompany, but are not part of, IAS 33.

ASB note: These Illustrative Examples have been prepared by the IASB

Contents

Example 1	Increasing Rate Preference Shares
Example 2	Weighted Average Number of Ordinary Shares
Example 3	Bonus Issue
Example 4	Rights Issue
Example 5	Effects of Share Options on Diluted Earnings per Share
Example 5A	Determining the Exercise Price of Employee Share Options
Example 6	Convertible Bonds
Example 7	Contingently Issuable Shares
Example 8	Convertible Bonds Settled in Shares or Cash at the Issuer's Option
Example 9	Calculation of Weighted Average Number of Shares: Determining the Order in Which to Include Dilutive Instruments
Example 10	Instruments of a Subsidiary: Calculation of Basic and Diluted Earnings per Share
Example 11	Participating Equity Instruments and Two-Class Ordinary Shares
Example 12	Calculation of Basic and Diluted Earnings per Share and Income Statement Presentation (Comprehensive Example)

Example 1 - Increasing Rate Preference Shares

Reference: FRS 22 (IAS 33), paragraphs 12 and 15

Entity D issued non-convertible, non-redeemable class A cumulative preference shares of CU100 par value on 1 January 20X1. The class A preference shares are entitled to a cumulative annual dividend of CU7 per share starting in 20X4.

At the time of issue, the market rate dividend yield on the class A preference shares was 7 per cent a year. Thus, Entity D could have expected to receive proceeds of approximately CU100 per class A preference share if the dividend rate of CU7 per share had been in effect at the date of issue.

In consideration of the dividend payment terms, however, the class A preference shares were issued at CU81.63 per share, ie at a discount of CU18.37 per share. The issue price can be calculated by taking the present value of CU100, discounted at 7 per cent over a three-year period.

Because the shares are classified as equity, the original issue discount is amortised to retained earnings using the effective interest method and treated as a preference dividend for earnings per share purposes. To calculate basic earnings per share, the following imputed dividend per class A preference share is deducted to determine the profit or loss attributable to ordinary equity holders of the parent entity:

Year	*Carrying amount of class A preference shares 1 January*	*Imputed dividend*[1]	*Carrying amount of class A preference shares 31 December*[2]	*Dividend paid*
	CU	CU	CU	CU
20X1	81.63	5.71	87.34	-
20X2	87.34	6.12	93.46	-
20X3	93.46	6.54	100.00	-
Thereafter:	100.00	7.00	107.00	(7.00)

[1] at 7%
[2] This is before dividend payment.

Example 2 - Weighted Average Number of Ordinary Shares

Reference: FRS 22 (IAS 33), paragraphs 19-21

		Shares issued	*Treasury shares*[3]	*Shares outstanding*
1 January 20X1	Balance at beginning of year	2,000	300	1,700
31 May 20X1	Issue of new shares for cash	800	–	2,500
1 December 20X1	Purchase of treasury shares for cash	–	250	2,250
31 December 20X1	Balance at yearend	2,800	550	2,250

Calculation of weighted average:

(1,700 × 5/12) + (2,500 × 6/12) + (2,250 × 1/12) = 2,146 shares *or*
(1,700 × 12/12) + (800 × 7/12) – (250 × 1/12) = 2,146 shares

[3] Treasury shares are equity instruments reacquired and held by the issuing entity itself or by its subsidiaries.

Example 3 - Bonus Issue

Reference: FRS 22 (IAS 33), paragraphs 26, 27(a) and 28

Profit attributable to ordinary equity holders of the parent entity 20X0	CU180
Profit attributable to ordinary equity holders of the parent entity 20X1	CU600
Ordinary shares outstanding until 30 September 20X1	200
Bonus issue 1 October 20X1	2 ordinary shares for each ordinary share outstanding at 30 September 20X1 $200 \times 2 = 400$
Basic earnings per share 20X1	$\frac{CU600}{(200+400)} = CU1.00$
Basic earnings per share 20X0	$\frac{CU600}{(200+400)} = CU0.30$

Because the bonus issue was without consideration, it is treated as if it had occurred before the beginning of 20X0, the earliest period presented.

Example 4 - Rights Issue

Reference: FRS 22 (IAS 33), paragraphs 26, 27(b) and A2

	20X0	20X1	20X2
Profit attributable to ordinary equity holders of the parent entity	CU1,100	CU1,500	CU1,800
Shares outstanding before rights issue	500 shares		
Rights issue	One new share for each five outstanding shares (100 new shares total) Exercise price: CU5.00 Date of rights issue: 1 January 20X1 Last date to exercise rights: 1 March 20X1		
Market price of one ordinary share immediately before exercise on 1 March 20X1:	CU11.00		
Reporting date	31 December		

Calculation of theoretical ex-rights value per share

$$\frac{\text{Fair value of all outstanding shares before the exercise of rights + total amount received from exercise of rights}}{\text{Number of shares outstanding before exercise + number of shares issued in the exercise}}$$

$$\frac{(\text{CU}11.00 \times 500 \text{ shares}) + (\text{CU}5.00 \times 100 \text{ shares})}{500 \text{ shares} + 100 \text{ shares}}$$

Theoretical ex-rights value per share = CU10.00

Calculation of adjustment factor

$$\frac{\text{Fair value per share before exercise of rights}}{\text{Theoretical ex-rights value per share}} \qquad \frac{\text{CU}11.00}{\text{CU}10.00} = 1.10$$

continued...

Calculation of basic earnings per share

		20X0	20X1	20X2
20X0 basic EPS as originally reported:	CU 1,100 ÷ 500 shares	CU2.20		
20X0 basic EPS restated for rights issue:	$\frac{\text{CU1,100}}{(500 \text{ shares} \times 1.1)}$	CU2.00		
20X1 basic EPS including effects of rights issue:			CU2.54	
20X2 basic EPS:	CU1,800 ÷ 600 shares			CU3.00

Example 5 - Effects of Share Options on Diluted Earnings per Share

Reference: FRS 22 (IAS 33), paragraphs 45-47

Profit attributable to ordinary equity holders of the parent entity for year 20X1	CU1,200,000
Weighted average number of ordinary shares outstanding during year 20X1	500,000 shares
Average market price of one ordinary share during year 20X1	CU20.00
Weighted average number of shares under option during year 20X1	100,000 shares
Exercise price for shares under option during year 20X1	CU15.00

Calculation of earnings per share

	Earnings	*Shares*	*Per share*
Profit attributable to ordinary equity holders of the parent entity for year 20X1	CU1,200,000		
Weighted average shares outstanding during year 20X1		500,000	
Basic earnings per share			CU2.40
Weighted average number of shares under option		100,000	
Weighted average number of shares that would have been issued at average market price: (100,000 × CU15.00) ÷ CU20.00		*(75,000)	
Diluted earnings per share	CU1,200,000	525,000	CU2.29

* Earnings have not increased because the total number of shares has increased only by the number of shares (25,000) deemed to have been issued for no consideration (see paragraph 46(b) of the Standard).

Example 5A - Determining the Exercise Price of Employee Share Options

Weighted average number of unvested share options per employee	1,000
Weighted average amount per employee to be recognised over the remainder of the vesting period for employee services to be rendered as consideration for the share options, determined in accordance with FRS 20 (IFRS 2) *Share-based Payment*	CU1,200
Cash exercise price of unvested share options	CU15

Calculation of adjusted exercise price

Fair value of services yet to be rendered per employee:	CU1,200
Fair value of services yet to be rendered per option: (CU1,200/ 1,000)	CU1.20
Total exercise price of share options: (CU 15.00 + CU1.20)	CU16.20

Example 6 - Convertible Bonds[4]

Reference: FRS 22 (IAS 33), paragraphs 33, 34, 36 and 49

Profit attributable to ordinary equity holders of the parent entity	CU1,004
Ordinary shares outstanding	1,000
Basic earnings per share	CU1.00
Convertible bonds	100
Each block of 10 bonds is convertible into three ordinary shares	
Interest expense for the current year relating to the liability component of the convertible bonds	CU10
Current and deferred tax relating to that interest expense	CU4

Note: the interest expense includes amortisation of the discount arising on initial recognition of the liability component (see FRS 25 (IAS 32) Financial Instruments: Disclosure and Presentation*).*

Adjusted profit attributable to ordinary equity holders of the parent entity	CU1,004 + CU10 – CU4 = CU1,010
Number of ordinary shares resulting from conversion of bonds	30
Number of ordinary shares used to calculate diluted earnings per share	1,000 + 30 = 1,030
Diluted earnings per share	$\frac{CU1,010}{1,030} = CU0.98$

[4] This example does not illustrate the classification of the components of convertible financial instruments as liabilities and equity or the classification of related interest and dividends as expenses and equity as required by *FRS 25* (IAS 32).

Example 7 - Contingently Issuable Shares

Reference: FRS 22 (IAS 33), paragraphs 19, 24, 36, 37, 41-43 and 52

Ordinary shares outstanding during 20X1	1,000,000 (there were no options, warrants or convertible instruments outstanding during the period)

An agreement related to a recent business combination provides for the issue of additional ordinary shares based on the following conditions:

	5,000 additional ordinary shares for each new retail site opened during 20X1
	1,000 additional ordinary shares for each CU1,000 of consolidated profit in excess of CU2,000,000 for the year ended 31 December 20X1
Retail sites opened during the year:	one on 1 May 20X1
	one on 1 September 20X1
Consolidated year-to-date profit attributable to ordinary equity holders of the parent entity:	CU1,100,000 as of 31 March 20X1
	CU2,300,000 as of 30 June 20X1
	CU1,900,000 as of 30 September 20X1 (including a CU450,000 loss from a discontinued operation)
	CU2,900,000 as of 31 December 20X1

continued...

Basic earnings per share

	First quarter	*Second quarter*	*Third quarter*	*Fourth quarter*	*Full year*
Numerator (CU)	1,100,000	1,200,000	(400,000)	1,000,000	2,900,000
Denominator:					
Ordinary shares outstanding	1,000,000	1,000,000	1,000,000	1,000,000	1,000,000
Retail site contingency	–	3,333[(a)]	6,667[(b)]	10,000	5,000[(c)]
Earnings contingency [(d)]	–	–	–	–	–
Total shares	1,000,000	1,003,333	1,006,667	1,010,000	1,005,000
Basic earnings per share (CU)	1.10	1.20	(0.40)	0.99	2.89

(a) 5,000 shares × 2/3

(b) 5,000 shares + (5,000 shares × 1/3)

(c) (5,000 shares × 8/12) + (5,000 shares × 4/12)

(d) The earnings contingency has no effect on basic earnings per share because it is not certain that the condition is satisfied until the end of the contingency period. The effect is negligible for the fourth-quarter and full-year calculations because it is not certain that the condition is met until the last day of the period.

Diluted earnings per share

	First quarter	*Second quarter*	*Third quarter*	*Fourth quarter*	*Full year*
Numerator (CU)	1,100,000	1,200,000	(400,000)	1,000,000	2,900,000
Denominator:					
Ordinary shares outstanding	1,000,000	1,000,000	1,000,000	1,000,000	1,000,000
Retail site contingency	–	5,000	10,000	10,000	10,000
Earnings contingency	–[(e)]	300,000[(f)]	–[(g)]	900,000[(h)]	900,000[(h)]
Total shares	1,000,000	1,305,000	1,010,000	1,910,000	1,910,000
Diluted earnings per share (CU)	1.10	0.92	(0.40)[(i)]	0.52	1.52

[(e)] Company A does not have year-to-date profit exceeding CU2,000,000 at 31 March 20X1. The Standard does not permit projecting future earnings levels and including the related contingent shares.

[(f)] [(CU2,300,000 – CU2,000,000) ÷ 1,000] × 1,000 shares = 300,000 shares.

[(g)] Year-to-date profit is less than CU2,000,000.

[(h)] [(CU2,900,000 – CU2,000,000) ÷ 1,000] × 1,000 shares = 900,000 shares.

[(i)] Because the loss during the third quarter is attributable to a loss from a discontinued operation, the antidilution rules do not apply. The control number (ie profit or loss from continuing operations attributable to the equity holders of the parent entity) is positive. Accordingly, the effect of potential ordinary shares is included in the calculation of diluted earnings per share.

Example 8 – Convertible Bonds Settled in Shares or Cash at the Issuer's Option

Reference: FRS 22 (IAS 33), paragraphs 31-33, 36, 58 and 59

An entity issues 2,000 convertible bonds at the beginning of Year 1. The bonds have a three year term, and are issued at par with a face value of CU1,000 per bond, giving total proceeds of CU2,000,000. Interest is payable annually in arrears at a nominal annual interest rate of 6 per cent. Each bond is convertible at any time up to maturity into 250 common shares. The entity has an option to settle the principal amount of the convertible bonds in ordinary shares or in cash.

When the bonds are issued, the prevailing market interest rate for similar debt without a conversion option is 9 per cent. At the issue date, the market price of one common share is CU3. Income tax is ignored.

Profit attributable to ordinary equity holders of the	CU1,000,000
parent entity Year 1	1,000,000
Ordinary shares outstanding	1,200,000
Convertible bonds outstanding	2,000

Allocation of proceeds of the bond issue:

Liability component	CU1,848,122[5]
Equity component	CU151,878
	CU2,000,000

The liability and equity components would be determined in accordance with FRS 25 (IAS 32) *Financial Instruments: Disclosure and Presentation*. These amounts are recognised as the initial carrying amounts of the liability and equity components. The amount assigned to the issuer conversion option equity element is an addition to equity and is not adjusted.

continued...

[5] This represents the present value of the principal and interest discounted at 9% – CU2,000,000 payable at the end of three years; CU120,000 payable annually in arrears for three years.

Basic earnings per share Year 1:

$$\frac{CU1,000,000}{1,200,000} = CU0.83 \text{ per ordinary share}$$

Diluted earnings per share Year 1:

It is presumed that the issuer will settle the contract by the issue of ordinary shares. The dilutive effect is therefore calculated in accordance with paragraph 59 of the Standard.

$$\frac{CU1,000,000 + CU166,331^{(a)}}{1,200,000 + 500,000^{(b)}} = CU0.69 \text{ per ordinary share}$$

(a) Profit is adjusted for the accretion of CU166,331 (CU1,848,122 × 9%) of the liability because of the passage of time.

(b) 500,000 ordinary shares = 250 ordinary shares × 2,000 convertible bonds

Example 9 – Calculation of Weighted Average Number of Shares: Determining the Order in Which to Include Dilutive Instruments[6]

Primary reference: FRS 22 (IAS 33), paragraph 44

Secondary reference: FRS 22 (IAS 33), paragraphs 10, 12, 19, 31-33, 36, 41-47, 49 and 50

Earnings	CU
Profit from continuing operations attributable to the parent entity	16,400,000
Less dividends on preference shares	(6,400,000)
Profit from continuing operations attributable to ordinary equity holders of the parent entity	10,000,000
Loss from discontinued operations attributable to the parent entity	(4,000,000)
Profit attributable to ordinary equity holders of the parent entity	6,000,000
Ordinary shares outstanding	2,000,000
Average market price of one ordinary share during year	CU75.00

Potential Ordinary Shares

Options	100,000 with exercise price of CU60
Convertible preference shares	800,000 shares with a par value of CU100 entitled to a cumulative dividend of CU8 per share. Each preference share is convertible to two ordinary shares.
5% convertible bonds	Nominal amount CU100,000,000. Each CU1,000 bond is convertible to 20 ordinary shares. There is no amortisation of premium or discount affecting the determination of interest expense.
Tax rate	40%

continued...

6 This example does not illustrate the classification of the components of convertible financial instruments as liabilities and equity or the classification of related interest and dividends as expenses and equity as required by FRS 25 (IAS 32).

Increase in Earnings Attributable to Ordinary Equity Holders on Conversion of Potential Ordinary Shares

		Increase in earnings	*Increase in number of ordinary shares*	*Earnings per incremental share*
		CU		CU
Options				
Increase in earnings		Nil		
Incremental shares issued for no consideration	100,000 ×(CU75 − CU60) ÷ CU75		20,000	Nil
Convertible preference shares				
Increase in profit	CU800,000 × 100 × 0.08	6,400,000		
Incremental shares	2 × 800,000		1,600,000	4.00
5% convertible bonds				
Increase in profit	CU100,000,000 × 0.05 × (1 − 0.40)	3,000,000		
Incremental shares	100,000 × 20		2,000,000	1.50

The order in which to include the dilutive instruments is therefore:

(1) Options
(2) 5% convertible bonds
(3) Convertible preference shares

continued...

Calculation of Diluted Earnings per Share

	Profit from continuing operations attributable to ordinary equity holders of the parent entity (control number)	*Ordinary shares*	*Per share*	
	CU		CU	
As reported	10,000,000	2,000,000	5.00	
Options	-	20,000		
	10,000,000	2,020,000	4.95	Dilutive
5% convertible bonds	3,000,000	2,000,000		
	13,000,000	4,020,000	3.23	Dilutive
Convertible preference shares	6,400,000	1,600,000		
	19,400,000	5,620,000	3.45	Antidilutive

Because diluted earnings per share is increased when taking the convertible preference shares into account (from CU3.23 to CU3.45), the convertible preference shares are antidilutive and are ignored in the calculation of diluted earnings per share. Therefore, diluted earnings per share for profit from continuing operations is CU3.23:

	Basic EPS	*Diluted EPS*
	CU	CU
Profit from continuing operations attributable to ordinary equity holders of the parent entity	5.00	3.23
Loss from discontinued operations attributable to ordinary equity holders of the parent entity	(2.00)[(a)]	(0.99)[(b)]
Profit attributable to ordinary equity holders of the parent entity	3.00[(c)]	2.24[(d)]

(a) (CU4,000,000) ÷ 2,000,000 = (CU2.00)
(b) (CU4,000,000) ÷ 4,020,000 = (CU0.99)
(c) CU6,000,000 ÷ 2,000,000 = CU3.00
(d) (CU6,000,000 + CU3,000,000) ÷ 4,020,000 = CU2.24

Example 10 - Instruments of a Subsidiary: Calculation of Basic and Diluted Earnings per Share[7]

Reference: FRS 22 (IAS 33), paragraphs 40, A11 and A12

Parent:

Profit attributable to ordinary equity holders of the parent entity	CU12,000 (excluding any earnings of, or dividends paid by, the subsidiary)
Ordinary shares outstanding	10,000
Instruments of subsidiary owned by the parent	800 ordinary shares 30 warrants exercisable to purchase ordinary shares of subsidiary 300 convertible preference shares

Subsidiary:

Profit	CU5,400
Ordinary shares outstanding	1,000
Warrants	150, exercisable to purchase ordinary shares of the subsidiary
Exercise price	CU10
Average market price of one ordinary share	CU20
Convertible preference shares	400, each convertible into one ordinary share
Dividends on preference shares	CU1 per share

No inter-company eliminations or adjustments were necessary except for dividends.

For the purposes of this illustration, income taxes have been ignored.

continued...

[7] This example does not illustrate the classification of the components of convertible financial instruments as liabilities and equity or the classification of related interest and dividends as expenses and equity as required by FRS 25 (IAS 32).

Subsidiary's earnings per share

Basic EPS CU5.00 calculated: $\frac{CU5,400^{(a)} - CU400^{(b)}}{1,000^{(c)}}$

Diluted EPS CU3.66 calculated: $\frac{CU5,400^{(d)}}{(1,000 + 75^{(e)} + 400^{(f)})}$

(a) Subsidiary's profit attributable to ordinary equity holders.
(b) Dividends paid by subsidiary on convertible preference shares.
(c) Subsidiary's ordinary shares outstanding.
(d) Subsidiary's profit attributable to ordinary equity holders (CU5,000) increased by CU400 preference dividends for the purpose of calculating diluted earnings per share.
(e) Incremental shares from warrants, calculated: [(CU20 − CU10) ÷ CU20] × 150.
(f) Subsidiary's ordinary shares assumed outstanding from conversion of convertible preference shares, calculated: 400 convertible preference shares × conversion factor of 1.

Consolidated earnings per share

Basic EPS CU1.63 calculated: $\frac{CU12,000^{(g)} + CU4,300^{(h)}}{10,000^{(i)}}$

Diluted EPS CU1.61 calculated:

$$\frac{CU12,000 + CU2,928^{(j)} + CU55^{(k)} + CU1,098^{(l)}}{10,000}$$

(g) Parent's profit attributable to ordinary equity holders of the parent entity.
(h) Portion of subsidiary's profit to be included in consolidated basic earnings per share, calculated: (800 × CU5.00) + (300 × CU1.00).
(i) Parent's ordinary shares outstanding.
(j) Parent's proportionate interest in subsidiary's earnings attributable to ordinary shares, calculated: (800 ÷ 1,000) × (1,000 shares × CU3.66 per share).
(k) Parent's proportionate interest in subsidiary's earnings attributable to warrants, calculated: (30 ÷ 150) × (75 incremental shares × CU3.66 per share).
(l) Parent's proportionate interest in subsidiary's earnings attributable to convertible preference shares, calculated: (300 ÷ 400) × (400 shares from conversion × CU3.66 per share).

Example 11 - Participating Equity Instruments and Two-class Ordinary Shares[8]

Reference: FRS 22 (IAS 33), paragraphs A13 and A14

Profit attributable to equity holders of the parent entity	CU100,000
Ordinary shares outstanding	10,000
Non-convertible preference shares	6,000
Non-cumulative annual dividend on preference shares (before any dividend is paid on ordinary shares)	CU5.50 per share

After ordinary shares have been paid a dividend of CU2.10 per share, the preference shares participate in any additional dividends on a 20:80 ratio with ordinary shares (ie after preference and ordinary shares have been paid dividends of CU5.50 and CU2.10 per share, respectively, preference shares participate in any additional dividends at a rate of one-fourth of the amount paid to ordinary shares on a per-share basis).

Dividends on preference shares paid	CU33,000	(CU5.50 per share)
Dividends on ordinary shares paid	CU21,000	(CU2.10 per share)

continued...

[8] This example does not illustrate the classification of the components of convertible financial instruments as liabilities and equity or the classification of related interest and dividends as expenses and equity as required by *FRS 25* (IAS 32).

Basic earnings per share is calculated as follows:

	CU	CU
Profit attributable to equity holders of the parent entity		100,000
Less dividends paid:		
Preference	33,000	
Ordinary	21,000	
		(54,000)
Undistributed earnings		46,000

Allocation of undistributed earnings:

Allocation per ordinary share = A
Allocation per preference share = B; B = 1/4 A

$$(A \times 10{,}000) + (1/4 \times A \times 6{,}000) = CU46{,}000$$
$$A = CU46{,}000 \div (10{,}000 + 1{,}500)$$
$$A = CU4.00$$
$$B = 1/4\ A$$
$$B = CU1.00$$

Basic per share amounts:

	Preference shares	*Ordinary shares*
Distributed earnings	CU5.50	CU2.10
Undistributed earnings	CU1.00	CU4.00
Totals	CU6.50	CU6.10

Example 12 - Calculation and Presentation of Basic and Diluted Earnings per Share (Comprehensive Example)[9]

This example illustrates the quarterly and annual calculations of basic and diluted earnings per share in the year 20X1 for Company A, which has a complex capital structure. The control number is profit or loss from continuing operations attributable to the parent entity. Other facts assumed are as follows:

Average market price of ordinary shares: The average market prices of ordinary shares for the calendar year 20X1 were as follows:

First quarter	CU49
Second quarter	CU60
Third quarter	CU67
Fourth quarter	CU67

The average market price of ordinary shares from 1 July to 1 September 20X1 was CU65.

Ordinary shares: The number of ordinary shares outstanding at the beginning of 20X1 was 5,000,000. On 1 March 20X1, 200,000 ordinary shares were issued for cash.

Convertible bonds: In the last quarter of 20X0, 5 per cent convertible bonds with a principal amount of CU12,000,000 due in 20 years were sold for cash at CU1,000 (par). Interest is payable twice a year, on 1 November and 1 May. Each CU1,000 bond is convertible into 40 ordinary shares. No bonds were converted in 20X0. The entire issue was converted on 1 April 20X1 because the issue was called by Company A.

Convertible preference shares: In the second quarter of 20X0, 800,000 convertible preference shares were issued for assets in a purchase transaction. The quarterly dividend on each convertible preference share is CU0.05, payable at the end of the quarter for shares outstanding at that date. Each share is convertible into one ordinary share. Holders of 600,000 convertible preference shares converted their preference shares into ordinary shares on 1 June 20X1.

continued...

9 This example does not illustrate the classification of the components of convertible financial instruments as liabilities and equity or the classification of related interest and dividends as expenses and equity as required by *FRS 25* (IAS 32).

Warrants: Warrants to buy 600,000 ordinary shares at CU55 per share for a period of five years were issued on 1 January 20X1. All outstanding warrants were exercised on 1 September 20X1.

Options: Options to buy 1,500,000 ordinary shares at CU75 per share for a period of 10 years were issued on 1 July 20X1. No options were exercised during 20X1 because the exercise price of the options exceeded the market price of the ordinary shares.

Tax rate: The tax rate was 40 per cent for 20X1.

20X1	*Profit (loss) from continuing operations attributable to the parent entity*[(a)]	*Profit (loss) attributable to the parent entity*
	CU	CU
First quarter	5,000,000	5,000,000
Second quarter	6,500,000	6,500,000
Third quarter	1,000,000	(1,000,000)[(b)]
Fourth quarter	(700,000)	(700,000)
Full year	11,800,000	9,800,000

First Quarter 20X1	
Basic EPS calculation	CU
Profit from continuing operations attributable to the parent entity	5,000,000
Less: preference shares dividends	(40,000)[(c)]
Profit attributable to ordinary equity holders of the parent entity	4,960,000

continued...

(a) This is the control number (before adjusting for preference dividends).

(b) Company A had a CU2,000,000 loss (net of tax) from discontinued operations in the third quarter.

(c) 800,000 shares × CU0.05

Dates	*Shares Outstanding*	*Fraction of period*	*Weighted-average shares*
1 January–28 February	5,000,000	2/3	3,333,333
Issue of ordinary shares on 1 March	200,000		
1 March–31 March	5,200,000	1/3	1,733,333
Weighted-average shares			5,066,666
Basic EPS			***CU0.98***

Diluted EPS calculation

Profit attributable to ordinary equity holders of the parent entity		CU4,960,000
Plus: profit impact of assumed conversions		
Preference share dividends	CU40,000[(d)]	
Interest on 5% convertible bonds	CU90,000[(e)]	
Effect of assumed conversions		CU130,000
Profit attributable to ordinary equity holders of the parent entity including assumed conversions		CU5,090,000
Weighted-average shares		5,066,666
Plus: incremental shares from assumed conversions		
Warrants	0[(f)]	

continued...

[(d)] 800,000 shares × CU0.05

[(e)] (CU12,000,000 × 5%) ÷ 4; less taxes at 40%

[(f)] The warrants were not assumed to be exercised because they were antidilutive in the period (CU55 [exercise price] > CU49 [average price]).

Convertible preference shares	800,000	
5% convertible bonds	480,000	
Dilutive potential ordinary shares		1,280,000
Adjusted weighted-average shares		6,346,666
Diluted EPS		***CU0.80***

Second Quarter 20X1

Basic EPS calculation	CU
Profit from continuing operations attributable to the parent entity	6,500,000
Less: preference shares dividends	(10,000)[(g)]
Profit attributable to ordinary equity holders of the parent entity	6,490,000

Dates	*Shares outstanding*	*Fraction of period*	*Weighted-average shares*
1 April	5,200,000		
Conversion of 5% bonds on 1 April	480,000		
1 April–31 May	5,680,000	2/3	3,786,666
Conversion of preference shares on 1 June	600,000		
1 June–30 June	6,280,000	1/3	2,093,333
Weighted-average shares			5,880,000
Basic EPS			***CU1.10***

(g) 200,000 shares × CU0.05

continued...

Diluted EPS calculation

Profit attributable to ordinary equity holders of the parent entity		CU6,490,000
Plus: profit impact of assumed conversions		
Preference share dividends	CU10,000[h]	
Effect of assumed conversions		CU10,000
Profit attributable to ordinary equity holders of the parent entity including assumed conversions		CU6,500,000
Weighted-average shares		5,880,000
Plus: incremental shares from assumed conversions		
Warrants	50,000[i]	
Convertible preference shares	600,000[j]	
Dilutive potential ordinary shares		650,000
Adjusted weighted-average shares		6,530,000
Diluted EPS		***CU1.00***

(h) 200,000 shares × CU0.05

(i) CU55 × 600,000 = CU33,000,000; CU33,000,000 ÷ CU60 = 550,000;
600,000 – 550,000 = 50,000 shares OR [(CU60 – CU55) ÷ CU60] × 600,000 shares = 50,000 shares

(j) (800,000 shares × 2/3) + (200,000 shares × 1/3)

continued...

Third Quarter 20X1

Basic EPS calculation	CU
Profit from continuing operations attributable to the parent entity	1,000,000
Less: preference shares dividends	(10,000)
Profit from continuing operations attributable to ordinary equity holders of the parent entity	990,000
Loss from discontinued operations attributable to the parent entity	(2,000,000)
Loss attributable to ordinary equity holders of the parent entity	(1,010,000)

Dates	*Shares outstanding*	*Fraction of period*	*Weighted-average shares*
1 July–31 August	6,280,000	2/3	4,186,666
Exercise of warrants on 1 September	600,000		
1 September-30 September	6,880,000	1/3	2,293,333
Weighted-average shares			6,480,000

Basic EPS	
Profit from continuing operations	***CU0.15***
Loss from discontinued operations	***(CU0.31)***
Loss	***(CU0.16)***

continued...

Diluted EPS calculation

Profit from continuing operations attributable to ordinary equity holders of the parent entity		CU990,000
Plus: profit impact of assumed conversions		
Preference shares dividends	CU10,000	
Effect of assumed conversions		CU10,000
Profit from continuing operations attributable to ordinary equity holders of the parent entity including assumed conversions		CU1,000,000
Loss from discontinued operations attributable to the parent entity		(CU2,000,000)
Loss attributable to ordinary equity holders of the parent entity including assumed conversions		(CU1,000,000)
Weighted-average shares		6,480,000
Plus: incremental shares from assumed conversions		
Warrants	61,538[(k)]	
Convertible preference shares	200,000	
Dilutive potential ordinary shares		261,538
Adjusted weighted-average shares		6,741,538
Diluted EPS		
Profit from continuing operations		***CU0.15***
Loss from discontinued operations		***(CU0.30)***
Loss		***(CU0.15)***

(k) [(CU65 − CU55) ÷ CU65] × 600,000 = 92,308 shares; 92,308 × 2/3 = 61,538 shares

Note: The incremental shares from assumed conversions are included in calculating the diluted per-share amounts for the loss from discontinued operations and loss even though they are antidilutive. This is because the control number (profit from continuing operations attributable to ordinary equity holders of the parent entity, adjusted for preference dividends) was positive (ie profit, rather than loss).

continued...

Fourth Quarter 20X1

Basic and diluted EPS calculation	CU
Loss from continuing operations attributable to the parent entity	(700,000)
Add: preference shares dividends	(10,000)
Loss attributable to ordinary equity holders of the parent entity	(710,000)

Dates	*Shares outstanding*	*Fraction of period*	*Weighted-average shares*
1 October–31 December	6,880,000	3/3	6,880,000
Weighted-average shares			6,880,000
Basic and diluted EPS			
Loss attributable to ordinary equity holders of the parent entity			***(CU0.10)***

Note: The incremental shares from assumed conversions are not included in calculating the diluted per-share amounts because the control number (loss from continuing operations attributable to ordinary equity holders of the parent entity adjusted for preference dividends) was negative (ie a loss, rather than profit).

continued...

Full Year 20X1

Basic EPS calculation	CU
Profit from continuing operations attributable to the parent entity	11,800,000
Less: preference shares dividends	(70,000)
Profit from continuing operations attributable to ordinary equity holders of the parent entity	11,730,000
Loss from discontinued operations attributable to the parent entity	(2,000,000)
Profit attributable to ordinary equity holders of the parent entity	9,730,000

Dates	*Shares Outstanding*	*Fraction of period*	*Weighted-average shares*
1 January-28 February	5,000,000	2/12	833,333
Issue of ordinary shares on 1 March	200,000		
1 March-31 March	5,200,000	1/12	433,333
Conversion of 5% bonds on 1 April	480,000		
1 April-31 May	5,680,000	2/12	946,667
Conversion of preference shares on 1 June	600,000		
1 June-31 August	6,280,000	3/12	1,570,000
Exercise of warrants on 1 September	600,000		
1 September-31 December	6,880,000	4/12	2,293,333
Weighted-average shares			6,076,667

Basic EPS	
Profit from continuing operations	***CU1.93***
Loss from discontinued operations	***(CU0.33)***
Profit	***CU 1.60***

continued...

Diluted EPS calculation

Profit from continuing operations attributable to ordinary equity holders of the parent entity		CU11,730,000
Plus: profit impact of assumed conversions		
Preference share dividends	CU70,000	
Interest on 5% convertible bonds	CU90,000[(l)]	
Effect of assumed conversions		CU160,000
Profit from continuing operations attributable to ordinary equity holders of the parent entity including assumed conversions		CU11,890,000
Loss from discontinued operations attributable to the parent entity		(CU2,000,000)
Profit attributable to ordinary equity holders of the parent entity including assumed conversions		CU9,890,000
Weighted-average shares		6,076,667
Plus: incremental shares from assumed conversions		
Warrants	14,880[(m)]	
Convertible preference shares	450,000[(n)]	
5% convertible bonds	120,000[(o)]	
Dilutive potential ordinary shares		584,880
Adjusted weighted-average shares		6,661,547
Diluted EPS		
Profit from continuing operations		***CU1.78***
Loss from discontinued operations		***(CU0.30)***
Profit		***CU1.48***

(l) (CU12,000,000 × 5%) ÷ 4; less taxes at 40%

(m) [(CU57.125* – CU55) ÷ CU57.125] × 600,000 = 22,320 shares; 22,320 × 8/12 = 14,880 shares

* The average market price from 1 January 20X1 to 1 September 20X1

(n) (800,000 shares × 5/12) + (200,000 shares × 7/12)

(o) 480,000 shares × 3/12

continued...

The following illustrates how Company A might present its earnings per share data on its income statement. Note that the amounts per share for the loss from discontinued operations are not required to be presented on the face of the income statement.

	For the year ended 20X1
	CU
Earnings per ordinary share	
Profit from continuing operations	1.93
Loss from discontinued operations	(0.33)
Profit	1.60
Diluted earnings per ordinary share	
Profit from continuing operations	1.78
Loss from discontinued operations	(0.30)
Profit	1.48

The following table includes the quarterly and annual earnings per share data for Company A. The purpose of this table is to illustrate that the sum of the four quarters' earnings per share data will not necessarily equal the annual earnings per share data. The Standard does not require disclosure of this information.

	First quarter	*Second quarter*	*Third quarter*	*Fourth quarter*	*Full year*
	CU	CU	CU	CU	CU
Basic EPS					
Profit (loss) from continuing operations	0.98	1.10	0.15	(0.10)	1.93
Loss from discontinued operations	–	–	(0.31)	–	(0.33)
Profit (loss)	0.98	1.10	(0.16)	(0.10)	1.60
Diluted EPS					
Profit (loss) from continuing operations	0.80	1.00	0.15	(0.10)	1.78
Loss from discontinued operations	–	–	(0.30)	–	(0.30)
Profit (loss)	0.80	1.00	(0.15)	(0.10)	1.48

Financial Reporting Standard 23 embodies IAS 21 'The Effects of Changes in Foreign Exchange Rates' and some amendments to that standard adopted for entities subject to UK accounting standards.

The Statement of Standard Accounting Practice in FRS 23 is set out in paragraphs 1-62 and the appendix. All the paragraphs have equal authority. Paragraphs in bold type state the main principles.

Accompanying the Statement of Standard Accounting Practice is the basis for the conclusions reached in the Statement. This does not form part of the Statement.

The Statement of Standard Accounting Practice should be read in the context of its objective as stated in paragraphs 1-2, the Basis for Conclusions set out in paragraphs BC1-BC32, and the Accounting Standards Board's 'Foreword to Accounting Standards' and 'Statement of Principles for Financial Reporting'.

FRS 23
(IAS 21) The effects of changes in foreign exchange rates*

(Issued December 2004)

Contents

	paragraphs
Introduction	**IN1-IN17**
Financial Reporting Standard 23 (IAS 21) The Effects of Changes in Foreign Exchange Rates	
Objective	**1-2**
Scope	**2a-7**
Definitions	**8-16**
Elaboration on the Definitions	**9-16**
Functional Currency	9-14
Net Investment in a Foreign Operation	15
Monetary Items	16
Summary of the approach required by this standard	**17-19**
Reporting foreign currency transactions in the functional currency	**20-37**
Initial Recognition	**20-22**
Reporting at Subsequent Balance Sheet Dates	**23-26**
Recognition of Exchange Differences	**27-34**
Change in Functional Currency	**35-37**
Use of a presentation currency other than the functional currency	**38-49**
Translation to the Presentation Currency	**38-43**
Translation of a Foreign Operation	**44-47**
Disposal of a Foreign Operation	**48-49**
Tax effects of all exchange differences	**50**
Disclosure	**51-57**
Effective date and transition	**58-60**
Withdrawal of other pronouncements	**61-62**
Appendix Amendments to Other Pronouncements	

****Editor's note**: The matters covered in FRS 23 are dealt with in Section 30 of FRS 102.*

Preface by the Accounting Standards Board

This Financial Reporting Standard (FRS) has the effect, for those entities that are applying it, of: **a**

- implementing in the UK and the Republic of Ireland the International Accounting Standards Board's (IASB's) International Accounting Standard (IAS) 21 *The Effects of Changes in Foreign Exchange Rates*;
- withdrawing an existing UK standard, SSAP 20 *Foreign currency translation*; and
- making consequential amendments to certain other UK standards and UITF Abstracts.

SSAP 20 remains in place unamended—and the various other UK standards and UITF Abstracts amended by this FRS remain in place unamended—for entities not applying this FRS.

This FRS is, in effect, part of a package of UK standards comprising: **b**

- this FRS,
- FRS 24 (IAS 29) *Financial Reporting in Hyperinflationary Economies*,
- the disclosure requirements of FRS 25 (IAS 32) *Financial Instruments: Disclosure and Presentation*,*; and
- FRS 26 (IAS 39) *Financial Instruments: Measurement*.

The application of the package of standards is determined by reference to FRS 26's application. **c**

- For accounting periods beginning on or after 1 January 2005, FRS 26—and therefore the entire package of standards listed above, including this FRS—applies to all listed entities preparing their financial statements in accordance with UK requirements—including listed parent undertakings preparing individual financial statements in accordance with those requirements.† Other entities are permitted to apply the entire package of standards from that date, although entities are not permitted to apply some of the standards in the package but not others—except that FRS 25 exempts certain entities from applying the disclosure requirements and also permits entities to apply those disclosure requirements in advance of the other standards in the package if they wish.
- For accounting periods beginning on or after 1 January 2006, unlisted entities using accounting policies that are consistent with the fair value measurement rules incorporated into the Companies Act 1985 (or equivalent legislation) to implement the Fair Value Directive will also be required to comply with FRS 26—and therefore the entire package of standards including this one.

The Accounting Standards Board (the Board) will in due course be issuing proposals for the application of the standards to other unlisted entities. **d**

The text of IAS 21 contains various references to other International Financial Reporting Standards (IFRSs). In the FRS those references have been amended where necessary to enable the Standard to be applied in a UK context. The Board **e**

**The other requirements of FRS 25 apply to all entities—regardless of whether they are listed or unlisted— for accounting periods beginning on or after 1 January 2005.*

†For this purpose a listed entity is an entity that has shares or debt admitted to trading on a regulated market in the EU.

believes that those amendments do not change the requirements of IAS 21 in any way.

d The appendix of IAS 21 contains amendments that the IASB has made to existing IFRSs in the light of the main requirements in IAS 21. In the FRS that material has been amended and added to so that the FRS can be applied in a UK context.

e IFRS 1 *First-time Adoption of International Financial Reporting Standards* sets out additional transitional provisions for the application of IAS 21 by a first-time adopter of IFRSs. Those transitional provisions have been incorporated into the FRS as paragraph 59A.

f In all other respects the FRS is identical to IAS 21.

g In December 2005 the Board amended FRS 23 to incorporate changes made to IAS 21 by the IASB in the Amendments to IAS 21 *The Effect of Changes In Foreign Exchange Rates* – Net Investment in a Foreign Operation, also issued in December 2005.*

Editor's note: *Made by 'Amendment to FRS 23 (IAS 21) The Effects of Changes In Foreign Exchange Rates – Net Investment in a Foreign Operation.'*

Introduction*

ASB note: The IASB's Introduction to IAS 21 is set out in full below. It should be noted that the discussion focuses on the changes that the IASB made in December 2003 to the previous version of IAS 21. Neither that previous version of IAS 21 nor the various SIC Interpretations that were incorporated in the December 2003 revision of IAS 21 had been implemented as UK standards.

Footnotes have been used to provide some UK context to the discussion.

International Accounting Standard 21 *The Effects of Changes in Foreign Exchange Rates* (IAS 21) replaces IAS 21 *The Effects of Changes in Foreign Exchange Rates* (revised in 1993), and should be applied for annual periods beginning on or after 1 January 2005. Earlier application is encouraged. The Standard also replaces the following Interpretations:† **IN1**

- SIC-11 *Foreign Exchange—Capitalisation of Losses Resulting from Severe Currency Devaluations*
- SIC-19 *Reporting Currency—Measurement and Presentation of Financial Statements under IAS 21 and IAS 29*
- SIC-30 *Reporting Currency—Translation from Measurement Currency to Presentation Currency.*

REASONS FOR REVISING IAS 21

The International Accounting Standards Board developed this revised IAS 21 as part of its project on Improvements to International Accounting Standards. The project was undertaken in the light of queries and criticisms raised in relation to the Standards by securities regulators, professional accountants and other interested parties. The objectives of the project were to reduce or eliminate alternatives, redundancies and conflicts within the Standards, to deal with some convergence issues and to make other improvements. **IN2**

For IAS 21 the Board's main objective was to provide additional guidance on the translation method and on determining the functional and presentation currencies. The Board did not reconsider the fundamental approach to accounting for the effects of changes in foreign exchange rates contained in IAS 21. **IN3**

THE MAIN CHANGES

The main changes from the previous version of IAS 21 are described below. **IN4**

**ASB Footnote:* *Throughout this standard, although references to specific IFRSs have been amended so that the standard can be applied in a UK context, the standard's references to itself as an 'IFRS' and its references to other extant accounting standards as 'other IFRS' have been left unchanged. They should though be taken to be references to this FRS and to extant standards issued in the UK and the Republic of Ireland respectively.*

†***ASB footnote:*** *None of these SIC Interpretations had a UK equivalent.*

Scope

IN5 The Standard excludes from its scope foreign currency derivatives that are within the scope of IAS 39 *Financial Instruments: Recognition and Measurement*.* Similarly, the material on hedge accounting has been moved to IAS 39.

Definitions

IN6 The notion of 'reporting currency' has been replaced with two notions:

- functional currency, ie the currency of the primary economic environment in which the entity operates. The term 'functional currency' is used in place of 'measurement currency' (the term used in SIC-19) because it is the more commonly used term, but with essentially the same meaning.
- presentation currency, ie the currency in which financial statements are presented.

Definitions—Functional Currency

IN7 When a reporting entity prepares financial statements, the Standard requires each individual entity included in the reporting entity—whether it is a stand-alone entity, an entity with foreign operations (such as a parent) or a foreign operation (such as a subsidiary or branch)—to determine its functional currency and measure its results and financial position in that currency. The new material on functional currency incorporates some of the guidance previously included in SIC-19 on how to determine a measurement currency. However, the Standard gives greater emphasis than SIC-19 gave to the currency of the economy that determines the pricing of transactions, as opposed to the currency in which transactions are denominated.

IN8 As a result of these changes and the incorporation of guidance previously in SIC19:

- an entity (whether a stand-alone entity or a foreign operation) does not have a free choice of functional currency.
- an entity cannot avoid restatement in accordance with IAS 29 *Financial Reporting in Hyperinflationary Economies* by, for example, adopting a stable currency (such as the functional currency of its parent) as its functional currency.†

IN9 The Standard revises the requirements in the previous version of IAS 21 for distinguishing between foreign operations that are integral to the operations of the reporting entity (referred to below as 'integral foreign operations') and foreign entities. The requirements are now among the indicators of an entity's functional currency. As a result:

- there is no distinction between integral foreign operations and foreign entities. Rather, an entity that was previously classified as an integral foreign operation will have the same functional currency as the reporting entity.
- only one translation method is used for foreign operations—namely that described in the previous version of IAS 21 as applying to foreign entities (see paragraph IN13).

**ASB footnote:* *The measurement and hedge accounting requirements of IAS 39 (but not its requirements on recognition and derecognition) have been implemented in the UK and the Republic of Ireland as FRS 26 (IAS 39)* Financial Instruments: Measurement.

†*IAS 29 has been implemented in the UK and the Republic of Ireland as FRS 24 (IAS 29)* Financial Reporting in Hyperinflationary Economies.

- the paragraphs dealing with the distinction between an integral foreign operation and a foreign entity and the paragraph specifying the translation method to be used for the former have been deleted.

Reporting Foreign Currency Transactions in the Functional Currency—Recognition of Exchange Differences

The Standard removes the limited option in the previous version of IAS 21 to capitalise exchange differences resulting from a severe devaluation or depreciation of a currency against which there is no means of hedging. Under the Standard, such exchange differences are now recognised in profit or loss. Consequently, SIC-11, which outlined restricted circumstances in which such exchange differences may be capitalised, has been superseded since capitalisation of such exchange differences is no longer permitted in any circumstances. **IN10**

Reporting Foreign Currency Transactions in the Functional Currency—Change in Functional Currency

The Standard replaces the previous requirement for accounting for a change in the classification of a foreign operation (which is now redundant) with a requirement that a change in functional currency is accounted for prospectively. **IN11**

Use of a Presentation Currency other than the Functional Currency—Translation to the Presentation Currency

The Standard permits an entity to present its financial statements in any currency (or currencies). For this purpose, an entity could be a standalone entity, a parent preparing consolidated financial statements or a parent, an investor or a venturer preparing separate financial statements in accordance with IAS 27 *Consolidated and Separate Financial Statements*. **IN12**

An entity is required to translate its results and financial position from its functional currency into a presentation currency (or currencies) using the method required for translating a foreign operation for inclusion in the reporting entity's financial statements. Under this method, assets and liabilities are translated at the closing rate, and income and expenses are translated at the exchange rates at the dates of the transactions (or at the average rate for the period when this is a reasonable approximation). **IN13**

The Standard requires comparative amounts to be translated as follows: **IN14**

(a) for an entity whose functional currency is not the currency of a hyperinflationary economy:

    (i) assets and liabilities in each balance sheet presented are translated at the closing rate at the date of that statement of financial position (ie last year's comparatives are translated at last year's closing rate).

    (ii) income and expenses in each statement of comprehensive income or separate income statement presented are translated at exchange rates at the dates of the transactions (ie last year's comparatives are translated at last year's actual or average rate).

(b) for an entity whose functional currency is the currency of a hyperinflationary economy, and for which the comparative amounts are translated into the currency of a different hyperinflationary economy, all amounts (eg amounts in a statement of financial position and statement of comprehensive income) are translated at the closing rate of the most recent balance sheet presented (ie last year's comparatives, as adjusted for subsequent changes in the price level, are translated at this year's closing rate).

(c) for an entity whose functional currency is the currency of a hyperinflationary economy, and for which the comparative amounts are translated into the currency of a nonhyperinflationary economy, all amounts are those presented in the prior year financial statements (ie not adjusted for subsequent changes in the price level or subsequent changes in exchange rates).

This translation method, like that described in paragraph IN13, applies when translating the financial statements of a foreign operation for inclusion in the financial statements of the reporting entity, and when translating the financial statements of an entity into a different presentation currency.*

Use of a Presentation Currency other than the Functional Currency—Translation of a Foreign Operation

IN15 The Standard requires goodwill and fair value adjustments to assets and liabilities that arise on the acquisition of a foreign entity to be treated as part of the assets and liabilities of the acquired entity and translated at the closing rate.

Disclosure

IN16 The Standard includes most of the disclosure requirements of SIC-30. These apply when a translation method different from that described in paragraphs IN13 and IN14 is used or other supplementary information (such as an extract from the full financial statements) is displayed in a currency other than the functional currency or the presentation currency.

IN17 In addition, entities must disclose when there has been a change in functional currency, and the reasons for the change.

***Editor's note**: *Paragraph amended in December 2008.*

Financial Reporting Standard 23 (IAS 21)

The Effects of Changes in Foreign Exchange Rates

OBJECTIVE

An entity may carry on foreign activities in two ways. It may have transactions in foreign currencies or it may have foreign operations. In addition, an entity may present its financial statements in a foreign currency. The objective of this Standard is to prescribe how to include foreign currency transactions and foreign operations in the financial statements of an entity and how to translate financial statements into a presentation currency. **1**

The principal issues are which exchange rate(s) to use and how to report the effects of changes in exchange rates in the financial statements. **2**

SCOPE

This Standard applies to all financial statements that are intended to give a true and fair view of a reporting entity's financial position and profit or loss (or income or expenditure), except that: **2A**

(a) it should not be applied to any financial statements to which FRS 26 (IAS 39) **Financial Instruments: Recognition and Measurement** ***has not also been applied; and***

(b) entities applying the **Financial Reporting Standard for Smaller Entities** ***(FRSSE) currently applicable are exempt from the Standard.****

For accounting periods beginning on or after 1 January 2005, FRS 26—and therefore this Standard—will apply to listed entities. Other entities have the option of applying the Standard, though only if they also apply FRS 26 (and certain other Standards). From 2006 unlisted entities using accounting policies that are consistent with the fair value measurement rules incorporated into the Companies Act or equivalent legislation will also be required to apply FRS 26, and therefore this Standard. **2B**

This Standard shall be applied:† **3**

(a) in accounting for transactions and balances in foreign currencies, except for those derivative transactions and balances that are within the scope of FRS 26;

(b) in translating the results and financial position of foreign operations that are included in the financial statements of the entity by consolidation, proportionate consolidation or the equity method;‡ and

(c) in translating an entity's results and financial position into a presentation currency.

FRS 26 applies to many foreign currency derivatives and, accordingly, these are excluded from the scope of this Standard. However, those foreign currency **4**

****Editor's note:*** *Reference to FRS 26 altered by amendments to FRS 26, to reflect the change in its title.*

†*See also UITF Abstract 21* Accounting issues arising from the proposed introduction of the euro.

‡***ASB footnote****: Although IFRSs permit proportional consolidation in certain circumstances, existing FRSs do not so the reference here and elsewhere in the standard to proportional consolidation can be disregarded. Also, for the avoidance of doubt the reference here and elsewhere in the standard to 'the equity method' should be taken to include the gross equity method.*

derivatives that are not within the scope of FRS 26 (eg some foreign currency derivatives that are embedded in other contracts) are within the scope of this Standard. In addition, this Standard applies when an entity translates amounts relating to derivatives from its functional currency to its presentation currency.

5 This Standard does not apply to hedge accounting for foreign currency items, including the hedging of a net investment in a foreign operation. FRS 26 applies to hedge accounting.

6 This Standard applies to the presentation of an entity's financial statements in a foreign currency and sets out requirements for the resulting financial statements to be described as complying with Financial Reporting Standards (FRS). For translations of financial information into a foreign currency that do not meet these requirements, this Standard specifies information to be disclosed.

7 This Standard does not apply to the presentation in a cash flow statement of cash flows arising from transactions in a foreign currency, or to the translation of cash flows of a foreign operation (see FRS 1 *Cash Flow Statements*).

DEFINITIONS

8 ***The following terms are used in this Standard with the meanings specified:***

Closing rate is the spot exchange rate at the balance sheet date.

Exchange difference is the difference resulting from translating a given number of units of one currency into another currency at different exchange rates.

Exchange rate is the ratio of exchange for two currencies.

Fair value is the amount for which an asset could be exchanged, or a liability settled, between knowledgeable, willing parties in an arm's length transaction.

Foreign currency is a currency other than the functional currency of the entity.

Foreign operation is an entity that is a subsidiary, associate, joint venture or branch of a reporting entity, the activities of which are based or conducted in a country or currency other than those of the reporting entity.

Functional currency is the currency of the primary economic environment in which the entity operates.

A group is a parent and all its subsidiaries.

Monetary items are units of currency held and assets and liabilities to be received or paid in a fixed or determinable number of units of currency.

Net investment in a foreign operation is the amount of the reporting entity's interest in the net assets of that operation.

Presentation currency is the currency in which the financial statements are presented.

Spot exchange rate is the exchange rate for immediate delivery.

Elaboration on the Definitions

Functional Currency

The primary economic environment in which an entity operates is normally the one in which it primarily generates and expends cash. An entity considers the following factors in determining its functional currency: 9

(a) the currency:

(i) that mainly influences sales prices for goods and services (this will often be the currency in which sales prices for its goods and services are denominated and settled); and
(ii) of the country whose competitive forces and regulations mainly determine the sales prices of its goods and services.

(b) the currency that mainly influences labour, material and other costs of providing goods or services (this will often be the currency in which such costs are denominated and settled).

The following factors may also provide evidence of an entity's functional currency: 10

(a) the currency in which funds from financing activities (ie issuing debt and equity instruments) are generated.
(b) the currency in which receipts from operating activities are usually retained.

The following additional factors are considered in determining the functional currency of a foreign operation, and whether its functional currency is the same as that of the reporting entity (the reporting entity, in this context, being the entity that has the foreign operation as its subsidiary, branch, associate or joint venture): 11

(a) whether the activities of the foreign operation are carried out as an extension of the reporting entity, rather than being carried out with a significant degree of autonomy. An example of the former is when the foreign operation only sells goods imported from the reporting entity and remits the proceeds to it. An example of the latter is when the operation accumulates cash and other monetary items, incurs expenses, generates income and arranges borrowings, all substantially in its local currency.
(b) whether transactions with the reporting entity are a high or a low proportion of the foreign operation's activities.
(c) whether cash flows from the activities of the foreign operation directly affect the cash flows of the reporting entity and are readily available for remittance to it.
(d) whether cash flows from the activities of the foreign operation are sufficient to service existing and normally expected debt obligations without funds being made available by the reporting entity.

When the above indicators are mixed and the functional currency is not obvious, management uses its judgement to determine the functional currency that most faithfully represents the economic effects of the underlying transactions, events and conditions. As part of this approach, management gives priority to the primary indicators in paragraph 9 before considering the indicators in paragraphs 10 and 11, which are designed to provide additional supporting evidence to determine an entity's functional currency. 12

An entity's functional currency reflects the underlying transactions, events and conditions that are relevant to it. Accordingly, once determined, the functional currency is not changed unless there is a change in those underlying transactions, events and conditions. 13

14 If the functional currency is the currency of a hyperinflationary economy, the entity's financial statements are restated in accordance with FRS 24 (IAS 29) *Financial Reporting in Hyperinflationary Economies*. An entity cannot avoid restatement in accordance with FRS 24 by, for example, adopting as its functional currency a currency other than the functional currency determined in accordance with this Standard (such as the functional currency of its parent).

Net Investment in a Foreign Operation

15 An entity may have a monetary item that is receivable from or payable to a foreign operation. An item for which settlement is neither planned nor likely to occur in the foreseeable future is, in substance, a part of the entity's net investment in that foreign operation, and is accounted for in accordance with paragraphs 32 and 33. Such monetary items may include long-term receivables or loans. They do not include trade receivables or trade payables.

15A The entity that has a monetary item receivable from or payable to a foreign operation described in paragraph 15 may be any subsidiary of the group. For example, an entity has two subsidiaries, A and B. Subsidiary B is a foreign operation. Subsidiary A grants a loan to Subsidiary B. Subsidiary A's loan receivable from Subsidiary B would be part of the entity's net investment in Subsidiary B if settlement of the loan is neither planned nor likely to occur in the foreseeable future. This would also be true if Subsidiary A were itself a foreign operation.*

Monetary Items

16 The essential feature of a monetary item is a right to receive (or an obligation to deliver) a fixed or determinable number of units of currency. Examples include: pensions and other employee benefits to be paid in cash; provisions that are to be settled in cash; and cash dividends that are recognised as a liability. Similarly, a contract to receive (or deliver) a variable number of the entity's own equity instruments or a variable amount of assets in which the fair value to be received (or delivered) equals a fixed or determinable number of units of currency is a monetary item. Conversely, the essential feature of a non-monetary item is the absence of a right to receive (or an obligation to deliver) a fixed or determinable number of units of currency. Examples include: amounts prepaid for goods and services (eg prepaid rent); goodwill; intangible assets; inventories; property, plant and equipment; and provisions that are to be settled by the delivery of a non-monetary asset.

SUMMARY OF THE APPROACH REQUIRED BY THIS STANDARD

17 In preparing financial statements, each entity—whether a stand-alone entity, an entity with foreign operations (such as a parent) or a foreign operation (such as a subsidiary or branch)—determines its functional currency in accordance with paragraphs 9-14. The entity translates foreign currency items into its functional currency and reports the effects of such translation in accordance with paragraphs 20-37 and 50.

18 Many reporting entities comprise a number of individual entities (eg a group is made up of a parent and one or more subsidiaries). Various types of entities, whether members of a group or otherwise, may have investments in associates or joint ventures. They may also have branches. It is necessary for the results and financial

****Editor's note:*** *Paragraph 15A added by 'Amendment to FRS 23 (IAS 21)* The Effects of Changes In Foreign Exchange Rates – Net Investment in a Foreign Operation*' with effect for accounting periods beginning on or after 1 January 2006, although early adoption is encouraged.*

position of each individual entity included in the reporting entity to be translated into the currency in which the reporting entity presents its financial statements. This Standard permits the presentation currency of a reporting entity to be any currency (or currencies). The results and financial position of any individual entity within the reporting entity whose functional currency differs from the presentation currency are translated in accordance with paragraphs 38-50.

This Standard also permits a stand-alone entity preparing financial statements or an entity that has an investment in a subsidiary, a jointly-controlled entity or an associate and is preparing separate financial statements to present its financial statements in any currency (or currencies). If the entity's presentation currency differs from its functional currency, its results and financial position are also translated into the presentation currency in accordance with paragraphs 38-50. **19**

REPORTING FOREIGN CURRENCY TRANSACTIONS IN THE FUNCTIONAL CURRENCY

Initial Recognition

A foreign currency transaction is a transaction that is denominated or requires settlement in a foreign currency, including transactions arising when an entity: **20**

(a) buys or sells goods or services whose price is denominated in a foreign currency;
(b) borrows or lends funds when the amounts payable or receivable are denominated in a foreign currency; or
(c) otherwise acquires or disposes of assets, or incurs or settles liabilities, denominated in a foreign currency.

A foreign currency transaction shall be recorded, on initial recognition in the functional currency, by applying to the foreign currency amount the spot exchange rate between the functional currency and the foreign currency at the date of the transaction. **21**

The date of a transaction is the date on which the transaction first qualifies for recognition in accordance with FRS. For practical reasons, a rate that approximates the actual rate at the date of the transaction is often used, for example, an average rate for a week or a month might be used for all transactions in each foreign currency occurring during that period. However, if exchange rates fluctuate significantly, the use of the average rate for a period is inappropriate. **22**

Reporting at Subsequent Balance Sheet Dates

At each balance sheet date: **23**

(a) foreign currency monetary items shall be translated using the closing rate;
(b) non-monetary items that are measured in terms of historical cost in a foreign currency shall be translated using the exchange rate at the date of the transaction; and
(c) non-monetary items that are measured at fair value in a foreign currency shall be translated using the exchange rates at the date when the fair value was determined.

The carrying amount of an item is determined in conjunction with other relevant Standards. For example, property, plant and equipment may be measured in terms of current value or historical cost in accordance with FRS 15 *Tangible fixed assets*. Whether the carrying amount is determined on the basis of historical cost or on the **24** basis of current value, if the amount is determined in a foreign currency it is then translated into the functional currency in accordance with this Standard.

25 The carrying amount of some items is determined by comparing two or more amounts. For example, the carrying amount of inventories is the lower of cost and net realisable value in accordance with SSAP 9 *Stocks and long-term contracts.* Similarly, in accordance with FRS 11 *Impairment of fixed assets and goodwill,* the carrying amount of an asset for which there is an indication of impairment is the lower of its carrying amount before considering possible impairment losses and its recoverable amount. When such an asset is nonmonetary and is measured in a foreign currency, the carrying amount is determined by comparing:

(a) the cost or carrying amount, as appropriate, translated at the exchange rate at the date when that amount was determined (ie the rate at the date of the transaction for an item measured in terms of historical cost); and
(b) the net realisable value or recoverable amount, as appropriate, translated at the exchange rate at the date when that value was determined (eg the closing rate at the balance sheet date).

The effect of this comparison may be that an impairment loss is recognised in the functional currency but would not be recognised in the foreign currency, or vice versa.

26 When several exchange rates are available, the rate used is that at which the future cash flows represented by the transaction or balance could have been settled if those cash flows had occurred at the measurement date. If exchangeability between two currencies is temporarily lacking, the rate used is the first subsequent rate at which exchanges could be made.

Recognition of Exchange Differences

27 As noted in paragraph 3, FRS 26 applies to hedge accounting for foreign currency items. The application of hedge accounting requires an entity to account for some exchange differences differently from the treatment of exchange differences required by this Standard. For example, FRS 26 requires that exchange differences on monetary items that qualify as hedging instruments in a cash flow hedge are recognised initially through the statement of total recognised gains and losses to the extent that the hedge is effective.*

28 ***Exchange differences arising on the settlement of monetary items or on translating monetary items at rates different from those at which they were translated on initial recognition during the period or in previous financial statements shall be recognised in profit or loss in the period in which they arise, except as described in paragraph 32.***

29 When monetary items arise from a foreign currency transaction and there is a change in the exchange rate between the transaction date and the date of settlement, an exchange difference results. When the transaction is settled within the same accounting period as that in which it occurred, all the exchange difference is recognised in that period. However, when the transaction is settled in a subsequent accounting period, the exchange difference recognised in each period up to the date of settlement is determined by the change in exchange rates during each period.

****ASB footnote:*** *There are a number of references in this standard to certain exchange differences being "reported initially in equity", "recognised directly in equity" or being "recognised initially in a separate component of equity". Under UK standards such exchange differences are recognised in the statement of total recognised gains and losses.*

When a gain or loss on a non-monetary item is recognised through the statement of total recognised gains and losses, any exchange component of that gain or loss shall be recognised through the statement of total recognised gains and losses. Conversely, when a gain or loss on a non-monetary item is recognised in profit or loss, any exchange component of that gain or loss shall be recognised in profit or loss. **30**

Other FRS require some gains and losses to be recognised through the statement of total recognised gains and losses. For example, FRS 15 requires some gains and losses arising on a revaluation of property, plant and equipment to be recognised through the statement of total recognised gains and losses. When such an asset is measured in a foreign currency, paragraph 23(c) of this Standard requires the revalued amount to be translated using the rate at the date the value is determined, resulting in an exchange difference that is also recognised through the statement of total recognised gains and losses. **31**

Exchange differences arising on a monetary item that forms part of a reporting entity's net investment in a foreign operation (see paragraph 15) shall be recognised in profit or loss in the separate financial statements of the reporting entity or the individual financial statements of the foreign operation, as appropriate. In the financial statements that include the foreign operation and the reporting entity (eg consolidated financial statements when the foreign operation is a subsidiary), such exchange differences shall be recognised initially through the statement of total recognised gains and losses and recognised in profit or loss on disposal of the net investment in accordance with paragraph 48. **32**

When a monetary item forms part of a reporting entity's net investment in a foreign operation and is denominated in the functional currency of the reporting entity, an exchange difference arises in the foreign operation's individual financial statements in accordance with paragraph 28. If such an item is denominated in the functional currency of the foreign operation, an exchange difference arises in the reporting entity's separate financial statements in accordance with paragraph 28. If such an item is denominated in a currency other the functional currency of either the reporting entity or the foreign operation, an exchange difference arises in the reporting entity's separate financial statements and in the foreign operation's individual financial statements in accordance with paragraph 28. Such exchange differences are recognised through the statement of total recognised gains and losses in the financial statements that include the foreign operation and the reporting entity (ie financial statements in which the foreign operation is consolidated, proportionately consolidated or accounted for using the equity method).* **33**

When an entity keeps its books and records in a currency other than its functional currency, at the time the entity prepares its financial statements all amounts are translated into the functional currency in accordance with paragraphs 20-26. This produces the same amounts in the functional currency as would have occurred had the items been recorded initially in the functional currency. For example, monetary items are translated into the functional currency using the closing rate, and nonmonetary items that are measured on a historical cost basis are translated using the exchange rate at the date of the transaction that resulted in their recognition. **34**

Editor's note: *Paragraph 33 amended by 'Amendment to FRS 23 (IAS 21)* The Effects of Changes In Foreign Exchange Rates – Net Investment in a Foreign Operation*' with effect for accounting periods beginning on or after 1 January 2006, although early adoption is encouraged.*

Change in Functional Currency

35 ***When there is a change in an entity's functional currency, the entity shall apply the translation procedures applicable to the new functional currency prospectively from the date of the change.***

36 As noted in paragraph 13, the functional currency of an entity reflects the underlying transactions, events and conditions that are relevant to the entity. Accordingly, once the functional currency is determined, it can be changed only if there is a change to those underlying transactions, events and conditions. For example, a change in the currency that mainly influences the sales prices of goods and services may lead to a change in an entity's functional currency.

37 The effect of a change in functional currency is accounted for prospectively. In other words, an entity translates all items into the new functional currency using the exchange rate at the date of the change. The resulting translated amounts for non-monetary items are treated as their historical cost. Exchange differences arising from the translation of a foreign operation previously recognised through the statement of total recognised gains and losses in accordance with paragraphs 32 and 39(c) are not reclassified from reserves to profit or loss until the disposal of the operation.*

USE OF A PRESENTATION CURRENCY OTHER THAN THE FUNCTIONAL CURRENCY

Translation to the Presentation Currency

38 An entity may present its financial statements in any currency (or currencies). If the presentation currency differs from the entity's functional currency, it translates its results and financial position into the presentation currency. For example, when a group contains individual entities with different functional currencies, the results and financial position of each entity are expressed in a common currency so that consolidated financial statements may be presented.

39 ***The results and financial position of an entity whose functional currency is not the currency of a hyperinflationary economy shall be translated into a different presentation currency using the following procedures:***

(a) assets and liabilities for each balance sheet presented (ie including comparatives) shall be translated at the closing rate at the date of that balance sheet;

(b) income and expenses for each income statement (ie including comparatives) shall be translated at exchange rates at the dates of the transactions; and

(c) all resulting exchange differences shall be recognised through the statement of total recognised gains and losses.

40 For practical reasons, a rate that approximates the exchange rates at the dates of the transactions, for example an average rate for the period, is often used to translate income and expense items. However, if exchange rates fluctuate significantly, the use of the average rate for a period is inappropriate.

41 The exchange differences referred to in paragraph 39(c) result from:

(a) translating income and expenses at the exchange rates at the dates of the transactions and assets and liabilities at the closing rate.

***Editor's note**: Paragraph amended in December 2008.*

(b) translating the opening net assets at a closing rate that differs from the previous closing rate.

These exchange differences are not recognised in profit or loss because the changes in exchange rates have little or no direct effect on the present and future cash flows from operations. The cumulative amount of the exchange differences is presented separately in reserves until disposal of the foreign operation. When the exchange differences relate to a foreign operation that is consolidated but not wholly owned, accumulated exchange differences arising from translation and attributable to minority interests are allocated to, and recognised as part of, minority interest in the consolidated balance sheet.*

The results and financial position of an entity whose functional currency is the currency of a hyperinflationary economy shall be translated into a different presentation currency using the following procedures: 42

(a) all amounts (ie assets, liabilities, amounts recognised through the statement of total recognised gains and losses, income and expenses, including comparatives) shall be translated at the closing rate at the date of the most recent balance sheet, except that

(b) when amounts are translated into the currency of a nonhyperinflationary economy, comparative amounts shall be those that were presented as current year amounts in the relevant prior year financial statements (ie not adjusted for subsequent changes in the price level or subsequent changes in exchange rates).

When an entity's functional currency is the currency of a hyperinflationary economy, the entity shall restate its financial statements in accordance with FRS 24 before applying the translation method set out in paragraph 42, except for comparative amounts that are translated into a currency of a non-hyperinflationary economy (see paragraph 42(b)). When the economy ceases to be hyperinflationary and the entity no longer restates its financial statements in accordance with FRS 24, it shall use as the historical costs for translation into the presentation currency the amounts restated to the price level at the date the entity ceased restating its financial statements. 43

Translation of a Foreign Operation

Paragraphs 45-47, in addition to paragraphs 38-43, apply when the results and financial position of a foreign operation are translated into a presentation currency so that the foreign operation can be included in the financial statements of the reporting entity by consolidation, proportionate consolidation or the equity method. 44

The incorporation of the results and financial position of a foreign operation with those of the reporting entity follows normal consolidation procedures, such as the elimination of intragroup balances and intragroup transactions of a subsidiary (see FRS 2 *Accounting for subsidiary undertakings*). However, an intragroup monetary asset (or liability), whether short-term or long-term, cannot be eliminated against the corresponding intragroup liability (or asset) without showing the results of currency fluctuations in the consolidated financial statements. This is because the monetary item represents a commitment to convert one currency into another and exposes the reporting entity to a gain or loss through currency fluctuations. Accordingly, in the consolidated financial statements of the reporting entity, such an exchange difference is recognised in profit or loss or, if it arises from the circumstances described in paragraph 32, it is recognised through the statement of total recognised gains and 45

****Editor's note****: Paragraph amended in December 2008.*

losses and accumulated in a separate component of reserves until the disposal of the foreign operation.*

46 When the financial statements of a foreign operation are as of a date different from that of the reporting entity, the foreign operation often prepares additional statements as of the same date as the reporting entity's financial statements. When this is not done, FRS 2 allows the use of a different reporting date provided that the difference is no greater than three months before the relevant period-end of the parent of the group and adjustments are made for the effects of any significant transactions or other events that occur between the different dates. In such a case, the assets and liabilities of the foreign operation are translated at the exchange rate at the balance sheet date of the foreign operation. Adjustments are made for significant changes in exchange rates up to the balance sheet date of the reporting entity in accordance with FRS 2. The same approach is used in applying the equity method to associates and joint ventures and in applying proportionate consolidation to joint ventures in accordance with FRS 9 *Associates and joint ventures*, except that if using these statements would release restricted, price-sensitive information, financial statements prepared for a period that ended not more than six months before the investor's period-end may be used.

47 ***Any goodwill arising on the acquisition of a foreign operation and any fair value adjustments to the carrying amounts of assets and liabilities arising on the acquisition of that foreign operation shall be treated as assets and liabilities of the foreign operation. Thus they shall be expressed in the functional currency of the foreign operation and shall be translated at the closing rate in accordance with paragraphs 39 and 42.***

Disposal of a Foreign Operation

48 On the disposal of a foreign operation, the cumulative amount of the exchange differences relating to that foreign operation, recognised through the statement of total recognised gains and losses and accumulated in a separate component of reserves, shall be reclassified from reserves to the profit or loss when the gain or loss on disposal is recognised.†

49 An entity may dispose or partially dispose of its interest in a foreign operation through sale, liquidation, repayment of share capital or abandonment of all, or part of, that entity. A write-down of the carrying amount of a foreign operation, either because of its own losses or because of an impairment recognised by the investor, does not constitute a partial disposal. Accordingly, no part of the foreign exchange gain or loss recognised though the statement of total recognised gains and losses is reclassified to profit or loss at the time of a write-down.‡

TAX EFFECTS OF ALL EXCHANGE DIFFERENCES

50 Gains and losses on foreign currency transactions and exchange differences arising on translating the results and financial position of an entity (including a foreign operation) into a different currency may have tax effects. FRS 16 *Current tax* and FRS 19 *Deferred tax* apply to these tax effects.

***Editor's note**: Paragraph amended in December 2008.*

*†**Editor's note**: Paragraph amended in December 2008. Strictly, new paragraphs 48A to 48D were also added at this time, but have been omitted since they all derive from IAS 21 and have been struck through by the ASB for FRS 23.*

*‡**Editor's note**: Paragraph amended in December 2008.*

DISCLOSURE

In paragraphs 53 and 55-57 references to 'functional currency' apply, in the case of a group, to the functional currency of the parent. 51

An entity shall disclose: 52

(a) the amount of exchange differences recognised in profit or loss except for those arising on financial instruments measured at fair value through profit or loss in accordance with FRS 26; and

(b) net exchange differences recognised through the statement of total recognised gains and losses, and accumulated in a separate reserve, and a reconciliation of the amount of such exchange differences at the beginning and end of the period.*

When the presentation currency is different from the functional currency, that fact shall be stated, together with disclosure of the functional currency and the reason for using a different presentation currency. 53

When there is a change in the functional currency of either the reporting entity or a significant foreign operation, that fact and the reason for the change in functional currency shall be disclosed. 54

When an entity presents its financial statements in a currency that is different from its functional currency, it shall describe the financial statements as complying with FRS only if they comply with all the requirements of FRS including the translation method set out in paragraphs 39 and 42. 55

An entity sometimes presents its financial statements or other financial information in a currency that is not its functional currency without meeting the requirements of paragraph 55. For example, an entity may convert into another currency only selected items from its financial statements. Or, an entity whose functional currency is not the currency of a hyperinflationary economy may convert the financial statements into another currency by translating all items at the most recent closing rate. Such conversions are not in accordance with FRS and the disclosures set out in paragraph 57 are required. 56

When an entity displays its financial statements or other financial information in a currency that is different from either its functional currency or its presentation currency and the requirements of paragraph 55 are not met, it shall: 57

(a) clearly identify the information as supplementary information to distinguish it from the information that complies with FRS;

(b) disclose the currency in which the supplementary information is displayed; and

(c) disclose the entity's functional currency and the method of translation used to determine the supplementary information.

EFFECTIVE DATE AND TRANSITION

An entity shall apply this Standard for accounting periods in which they also apply FRS 26 but not in any other accounting period. 58

Net Investment in a Foreign Operation *(Amendment to FRS 23), issued in December 2005, added paragraph 15A and amended paragraph 33. An entity shall apply those* 58A

**Editor's note: Paragraph amendид in December 2008.*

amendments for accounting periods beginning on or after 1 January 2006. Earlier application is encouraged.*

58B Unless and until an entity applies FRS 26 it is not permitted to adopt this Standard; and if it applies FRS 26 it must also apply this Standard. Listed entities are required to apply FRS 26 for accounting periods beginning on or after 1 January 2005 (and other entities are permitted to apply it from that same date). As explained in paragraph 2B, certain unlisted entities are required to apply FRS 26 for accounting periods beginning on or after 1 January 2006.

59 ***An entity shall apply paragraph 47 prospectively to all acquisitions occurring after the beginning of the financial reporting period in which this Standard is first applied. Retrospective application of paragraph 47 to earlier acquisitions is permitted. For an acquisition of a foreign operation treated prospectively but which occurred before the date on which this Standard is first applied, the entity shall not restate prior years and accordingly may, when appropriate, treat goodwill and fair value adjustments arising on that acquisition as assets and liabilities of the entity rather than as assets and liabilities of the foreign operation. Therefore, those goodwill and fair value adjustments either are already expressed in the entity's functional currency or are non-monetary foreign currency items, which are reported using the exchange rate at the date of the acquisition.***

59A† ***Paragraphs 48 and 49 require an entity to recognise some translation differences through the statement of total recognised gains and losses as a separate component of equity and, on disposal of a foreign operation, to transfer the cumulative translation difference for that foreign operation (including, if applicable, gains and losses on related hedges) to the income statement as part of the gain or loss on disposal. However, on first applying this standard an entity need not comply with these requirements for cumulative translation differences that existed at the effective date. If an entity uses this exemption:***

(a) the cumulative translation differences for all foreign operations are deemed to be zero at the effective date; and

(b) the gain or loss on a subsequent disposal of any foreign operation shall exclude translation differences that arose before the effective date and shall include later translation differences.

60 ***All other changes resulting from the application of this Standard shall be accounted for in accordance with the requirements of FRS 18* Accounting policies.**

60A The ASB amended paragraphs 37, 41, 45, 48 and 52 as part of its 'Improvements to Financial Reporting Standards' issued in December 2008.‡

****Editor's note:** *Added by the amendment to which reference is made. The current paragraph 58B was previously paragraph 58A.*

† ***ASB footnote:*** *This ASB amendment inserts into the FRS paragraphs 21 and 22 of IFRS 1* First-time Adoption of International Financial Reporting Standards. *Those paragraphs have been amended to refer to recognising translation differences 'through the statement of total recognised gains and losses' rather than 'as a separate component of equity'.*

‡***Editor's note:*** *Paragraph added in December 2008.*

WITHDRAWAL OF OTHER PRONOUNCEMENTS

For entities applying this Standard, it supersedes SSAP 20 *Foreign currency translation*. **61**

[*ASB note:* Deleted] **62**

Appendix
Amendments to other pronouncements

[Not reproduced, as all changes have been made to the underlying standards and abstracts].

Adoption of the standard

APPROVAL OF IAS 21 BY THE INTERNATIONAL ACCOUNTING STANDARDS BOARD

International Accounting Standard 21 *The Effects of Changes in Foreign Exchange Rates* was approved for issue by the fourteen members of the International Accounting Standards Board.

Sir David Tweedie	Chairman
Thomas E Jones	Vice-Chairman
Mary E Barth	
Hans-Georg Bruns	
Anthony T Cope	
Robert P Garnett	
Gilbert Gélard	
James J Leisenring	
Warren J McGregor	
Patricia L O'Malley	
Harry K Schmid	
John T Smith	
Geoffrey Whittington	
Tatsumi Yamada	

ADOPTION OF FRS 23 BY THE ACCOUNTING STANDARDS BOARD

Financial Reporting Standard 23 (IAS 21) *The Effects of Changes in Foreign Exchange Rates* was approved for issue by the ten members of the Accounting Standards Board.

Ian Mackintosh	Chairman
Andrew Lennard	Technical Director
Michael Ashley	
Douglas Flint	
Anthony Good	
Roger Marshall	
Isobel Sharp	
John Smith	
Jonathan Symonds	
Peter Westlake	

Notes on the standard's application in the UK and the Republic of Ireland

N1 SSAP 20 *Foreign currency translation* was issued in April 1983. It was developed at the same time as the original version of IAS 21 and the US Financial Accounting Standard (FAS) 52 *Foreign Currency Translation* as part of an international convergence project on accounting for foreign currency. As a result, the main requirements of the three standards were similar, although they differed somewhat in the terminology used and the matters of emphasis.

THE IASB'S IMPROVEMENTS PROJECT

N2 In 2001 the IASB announced that it would be reviewing a number of existing standards, including IAS 21. The revised IAS 21 was issued in December 2003.

N3 The main changes made are summarised in the IASB's Introduction to the standard; and the rationale behind the changes made is set out in the Basis for Conclusions material that the IASB prepared to accompany the standard.

FRED 24

N4 In recent years, the Accounting Standards Board (the Board) has been placing increasing emphasis on the convergence aspects of its standard-setting role: listed entities in the UK and the Republic of Ireland preparing consolidated financial statements will from 2005 be required to prepare those statements in accordance with EU-adopted international accounting standards (International Financial Reporting Standards or IFRSs) and, although entities can continue to prepare other financial statements in accordance with the requirements of the UK and the Republic of Ireland, the Board's view is that there can be no case for the use of two sets of wholly different standards in the medium term.

N5 As part of this convergence strategy, the Board issued FRED 24 *The Effects of Changes in Foreign Exchange Rates & Financial Reporting in Hyperinflationary Economies*. FRED 24 set out for comment two proposed UK standards, based on the IASB's proposals for a revised IAS 21 and the IASB's existing IAS 29. The FRED proposed that, with certain amendments, both IFRSs should be implemented as standards in the UK and the Republic of Ireland and should apply to all UK and Republic of Ireland entities. At the same time the FRED proposed withdrawing the existing UK requirements in this area, which are mainly in SSAP 20 *Foreign currency translation*.

N6 Those responding to FRED 24 were broadly supportive of the Board's strategy to converge its standards in this area with those of the IASB. However, concerns were raised about recycling, hedge accounting and some detailed aspects of the UK implementation plan proposed.

Recycling

N7 'Recycling' is the term commonly used to describe the practice of reversing out of the statement of total recognised gains and losses (STRGL) gains and losses that have been recognised in prior periods and recognising them instead in the profit and loss account (P&L).

IAS 21 requires exchange differences on a monetary item that is part of a net investment in a foreign operation to be recognised initially in the STRGL, then recycled to the P&L on disposal of the foreign operation. Existing UK standards, on the other hand, do not permit such gains and losses to be recycled; indeed, they do not permit any gains and losses to be recycled. **N8**

FRED 24 proposed to retain the prohibition on recycling, primarily because the IASB was reviewing its use of recycling as part of its comprehensive income project and it was understood at the time that the result of that review was likely to be that the IASB would converge on UK practice and prohibit recycling. **N9**

Respondents were split on how the Board should deal with recycling in implementing IAS 21. Some agreed with the approach taken in the FRED; others thought that if the Board decides to implement an IFRS in the UK it should not amend that IFRS. The issue was discussed again in the Board's recent Discussion Paper *UK Accounting Standards: A Strategy for Convergence with IFRS* and this time the clear majority of respondents favoured making no amendment to IAS 21. **N10**

The Board continues to have concerns about recycling, primarily because it is not consistent with the *Statement of Principles*. That is because it involves (depending precisely on how one looks at it) either the recognition in the performance statements of items that are not gains and losses or the recognition in the performance statements of the same gains and losses twice. **N11**

The IASB is actively considering the future of recycling in its comprehensive income project, and the Board intends to continue to argue strongly for the practice's prohibition. Nevertheless, the Board has concluded that it would be inconsistent with its stated policy of convergence were it to amend IAS 21's recycling provisions simply because it does not like them and thinks the UK has a better solution. It is therefore implementing IAS 21 unamended. **N12**

Hedge accounting

SSAP 20 sets out the UK requirements on the accounting treatment of hedges of net investments in foreign operations. IAS 21 contains no equivalent requirements, because hedge accounting is dealt with in another standard (IAS 39). Therefore, when developing the proposals in FRED 24 the Board had a choice. **N13**

(a) It could include in the UK version of IAS 21 (or issue as some form of standalone standard) some hedge accounting requirements. Those requirements could be those set out in SSAP 20, those set out in IAS 39, or some other hedge accounting requirements.
(b) It could allow entities to adopt the UK version of IAS 21 (rather than SSAP 20) only if they are apply the UK version of IAS 39.
(c) It could implement IAS 21 without any hedge accounting requirements, take a separate independent decision on UK implementation of IAS 39, and accept that some entities may—for an interim period—no longer be subject to any requirements concerning the accounting treatment of hedges of net investments in foreign operations.

The Board decided to adopt option (a) in FRED 24. Furthermore, rather than import either SSAP 20's requirements or IAS 39's requirements, it proposed (in FRED 23 *Financial instruments: Hedge accounting*) issuing a standalone hedge accounting standard, albeit one based on the principles set out in IAS 39. This proposal was not supported by respondents who thought that the development of a UK standard on hedge accounting was not consistent with the convergence **N14** objective. Others thought the proposal introduced additional complexity in the financial reporting framework at a time when what was needed most of all was simplicity. As a result, the Board announced in its Convergence Strategy Discussion Paper that, although it has not withdrawn FRED 23, it has no present intention to develop it into a standard.

N15 The Board has now decided to address the issue described in paragraph N13 by adopting option (b)—in other words, implementing IAS 21 (as FRS 23) and the hedge accounting requirements of IAS 39 (as FRS 26) in the UK and the Republic of Ireland at the same time and for the same entities.

Application of the FRS

N16 Having reached this conclusion, the Board then decided that it was sensible to implement the UK standard based on IAS 29 *Financial Reporting in Hyperinflationary Economies* at the same time as this standard, and that it was sensible to implement the disclosure aspects of the UK standard based on IAS 32 *Financial Instruments: Disclosures and Presentation* at the same time as the measurement aspects of the UK standard based on IAS 39. This approach has the advantage of simplicity—entities are either applying the financial instruments and foreign currency standards or they are not—and simplicity is a desirable attribute at this time. The Board recognises that the approach does mean though that there will be some entities that wanted to start applying FRS 23 in 2005 but will not now do so because they are not ready to implement the whole package of standards.

Timetable

N17 FRED 24 proposed that IAS 21 should be implemented as a standard in the UK and the Republic of Ireland as soon as the IASB had finalised its revisions to IAS 21—which the IASB expected at the time to be in early 2003. In fact, the revised standard was not issued until December 2003. In any event, many respondents to FRED 24—and to the other convergence proposals the Board issued at the time in FREDs 25-30—argued that it would be more appropriate to implement the proposed new standards from 2005.

N18 As just explained, the Board has decided to implement IAS 21 and IAS 39 in the UK together and for the same entities. The Board furthermore decided that the implementation timetable for both standards should be determined by reference to the UK version of IAS 39 (FRS 26). FRS 26 will apply to all listed entities for accounting periods starting on or after 1 January 2005 and to all unlisted [fair value volunteers] for accounting periods beginning on or after 1 January 2006. It follows that FRS 23 will apply to the same entities from the same dates. Earlier adoption is permitted, as long as both standards (together with the other standards that the Board has decided should be implemented at the same time*) are implemented at the same time.

N19 The Board intends to issue proposals on the implementation of the standards for other entities in due course.

N20 Another issue raised by respondents concerned the transitional provisions. Some respondents suggested that the transitional arrangements proposed in the IASB's exposure draft of a revised IAS 21 (and therefore in FRED 24) were not practicable and that additional transitional relief needed to be given in respect of the treatment

****FRSs 23-26, excluding the presentation requirements of FRS 25. Entities are permitted to apply the disclosure requirements of FRS 25 ahead of the other FRSs.***

of purchased goodwill (paragraph 47 of the FRS) and the treatment of disposals of foreign operations (paragraphs 48 and 49). In finalising the standard the IASB included in its standard additional relief on the first point; it also included transitional relief on the second point in IFRS 1 *First-time Adoption of International Financial Reporting Standards* and the Board has incorporated that relief into FRS 23.

CHANGES TO EXISTING UK REQUIREMENTS

As already mentioned, SSAP 20 and IAS 21 were developed together and, as a result, their main requirements are similar. In its improvement project, the IASB did not reconsider the fundamental approach adopted in IAS 21—the main objective was to provide additional guidance on the translation method and on determining the functional and presentation currencies—so the main requirements of the revised version of IAS 21 (and therefore of this standard) are also similar to SSAP 20's requirements. The main differences between FRS 23 and SSAP 20 are described in the following paragraphs. **N21**

Preparing the individual entity financial statements

Presentation currency

SSAP 20 and FRS 23 both require each entity to determine its functional currency and measure its results in that currency (although SSAP 20 refers to the 'functional currency' as the 'local currency'). FRS 23, but not SSAP 20, also deals explicitly with the currency in which financial statements are then presented (the presentation currency). **N22**

(a) The implication in SSAP 20 is that the presentation currency will be the entity's local currency (or, in the case of consolidated financial statements, the parent entity's local currency).

(b) FRS 23, on the other hand, states that an entity may present its financial statements in any currency or currencies. The standard also specifies the method to be used to translate the results and financial position into that presentation currency when the functional currency and presentation currency are different.

Use of contracted rates of exchange

The terms on which some foreign currency transactions are carried out specify the rate of exchange that is to be used for settlement purposes and SSAP 20 permits such transactions and any resulting assets and liabilities to be translated into the functional currency at that contracted rate. FRS 23, on the other hand, requires the transaction to be measured on initial recognition at the then spot rate; subsequently, if a monetary item is involved it should be retranslated each balance sheet date at the relevant closing rate. **N23**

Monetary items forming part of a net investment in a foreign operation

SSAP 20 permits exchange differences arising on an entity's net investment in a foreign operation to be recognised in the STRGL of the individual financial statements of that investing entity. FRS 23, however, requires some of these exchange differences—in particular those that arise on monetary items that are part of the investing entity's net investment—to be recognised in the P&L of the investee's individual financial statements. **N24**

Exchange gains on long-term monetary items

N25 SSAP 20 generally requires exchange gains and losses on monetary items to be recognised immediately in the profit and loss account. However, when long-term monetary items are involved, SSAP 20 permits the recognition of some or all of such gains (but not losses) to be deferred if there are doubts as to the convertibility or marketability of the currency in question. Deferring the recognition of such gains is not permitted under FRS 23.

Preparing the consolidated financial statements

Net investment method or temporal method?

N26 If an entity is preparing consolidated financial statements for a group that includes one or more foreign operations, SSAP 20 generally requires the net investment method to be used to incorporate the results and financial position of a foreign operation. (SSAP 20 called this method the 'closing rate/net investment method'.) However, if the foreign operation is deemed to be an integral part of the investing company (ie the affairs of a foreign entity are so closely interlinked with those of the investing company that its results are regarded as being more dependent on the economic environment of the investing company's currency than on that of its own currency), the temporal method should be used.* FRS 23 permits only one method to be used: the net investment method.

N27 This difference in the requirements ought not, however, to result in a difference in accounting practice. As explained in paragraph BC6 of the Basis for Conclusions, if a foreign operation is integral to the investing company, the functional currency of the foreign operation will be the same as the investing company's, so the overall effect will be the same in the consolidated financial statements as under SSAP 20 when the temporal method was applied.

Exchange rate to be used for P&L items under the net investment method

N28 Under SSAP 20's version of the net investment method, the profit and loss account (the P&L) of the foreign operation is translated at either the closing rate or an appropriate average rate. FRS 23, on the other hand, requires the rate of exchange at the transaction date to be used, although it accepts that an average rate will often be a good approximation of that rate.

Translation of goodwill and fair value adjustments

N29 SSAP 20 does not specifically address the treatment of goodwill and fair value adjustments to the carrying amounts of assets and liabilities on the acquisition of a foreign operation. FRS 23 requires such items to be treated as assets and liabilities of the foreign operation and translated at the closing rate.

**Put another way, the net investment method is used under SSAP 20 when a foreign operation is largely self-contained and is not dependent upon the economic environment of the investing company's functional currency. In such circumstances, the foreign currency exposure that the investing company has relates to its net investment in the foreign operation, rather than in the individual assets and liabilities of the foreign operation. The net investment method reflects this by translating the net investment at the closing rate of exchange. The temporal method treats the foreign operation's transactions as if they had been entered into by the investing company itself in its own currency.*

Disposal of a foreign operation

SSAP 20 does not explicitly deal with the disposal of a foreign operation. However, the implication of the standard (when taken together with other UK standards) is that, when a foreign operation is sold, no adjustment should be made to the cumulative amount of the exchange differences previously recognised in the STRGL in respect of that foreign operation—other than perhaps moving the amounts from one reserve to another. FRS 23 requires the cumulative amount of those exchange differences to be reversed out of the STRGL and recognised in full in the P&L (in other words, they should be recycled to the P&L). **N30**

Hedge accounting

SSAP 20 sets out the requirements to be followed in accounting for hedges of net investments in foreign operations. As already explained, FRS 23 does not contain equivalent requirements; instead, they are set out in FRS 26. FRS 26's requirements are also different from SSAP 20's. The main differences are **N31**

(a) Although the net investment hedging provisions of SSAP 20 apply both to individual financial statements and consolidated financial statements, under FRS 26 they apply only to consolidated financial statements. To be able to use hedge accounting in the individual financial statements to account for a hedge of a net investment in a foreign operation, the hedge will need to qualify as a fair value hedge of the foreign exchange risk involved. Under FRS 26, gains and losses arising on the hedging instrument and hedged item in a net investment hedge are recognised in the STRGL; and gains and losses arising on the hedging instrument and hedged item in a fair value hedge are recognised in the P&L.

(b) FRS 26 is more restrictive than SSAP 20 on what will qualify for hedge accounting,

(b) Unlike SSAP 20, FRS 26 requires entities to recognise gains and losses on any ineffective element of a hedge in the P&L immediately.

(c) Although both standards require gains and losses on a net investment hedge to be recognised in the consolidated financial statements in the STRGL, FRS 26 requires those gains and losses to be recycled to the P&L on disposal of the foreign operation. SSAP 20 does not.

Disclosure requirements

The disclosure requirements of the two standards are also somewhat different. **N32**

Basis for Conclusions

ASB note: The IASB's Basis for Conclusions, which accompanies IAS 21, is set out below in full. It should be noted though that some of the discussion it contains concerns IASB requirements that have no equivalent in the UK or Republic of Ireland. Footnotes have been used to highlight those parts of the discussion.

All references in this section to 'the Board' and 'Board members' are references to the IASB Board and IASB Board members.

This Basis for Conclusions accompanies, but is not part of, IAS 21.

Paragraph BC1 was amended and paragraphs BC25A–BC25F were added in relation to the amendment to IAS 21 issued in December 2005.

*In this Basis for Conclusions the terminology has not been amended to reflect the changes made by IAS 1 Presentation of Financial Statements (as revised in 2007).**

INTRODUCTION

BC1 This Basis for Conclusions summarises the International Accounting Standards Board's considerations in reaching its conclusions on revising IAS 21 *The Effects of Changes in Foreign Exchange Rates* in 2003, and on the amendment to IAS 21 *Net Investment in a Foreign Operation* in December 2005. Individual Board members gave greater weight to some factors than to others.†

BC2 In July 2001 the Board announced that, as part of its initial agenda of technical projects, it would undertake a project to improve a number of Standards, including IAS 21. The project was undertaken in the light of queries and criticisms raised in relation to the Standards by securities regulators, professional accountants and other interested parties. The objectives of the Improvements project were to reduce or eliminate alternatives, redundancies and conflicts within Standards, to deal with some convergence issues and to make other improvements. In May 2002 the Board published its proposals in an Exposure Draft of *Improvements to International Accounting Standards*, with a comment deadline of 16 September 2002. The Board received over 160 comment letters on the Exposure Draft.

BC3 Because the Board's intention was not to reconsider the fundamental approach to accounting for the effects of changes in foreign exchange rates established by IAS 21, this Basis for Conclusions does not discuss requirements in IAS 21 that the Board has not reconsidered.

FUNCTIONAL CURRENCY

BC4 The term 'reporting currency' was previously defined as "the currency used in presenting the financial statements". This definition comprises two separate notions (which were identified in SIC-19 *Reporting Currency—Measurement and Presentation of Financial Statements under IAS 21 and IAS 29*):

****Editor's note:*** *Paragraphs amended in December 2008.*

*†**Editor's note:** Amended by 'Amendment to FRS 23 (IAS 21) The Effects of Changes In Foreign Exchange Rates – Net Investment in a Foreign Operation'.*

- the measurement currency (the currency in which the entity measures the items in the financial statements); and
- the presentation currency (the currency in which the entity presents its financial statements).

The Board decided to revise the previous version of IAS 21 to incorporate the SIC19 approach of separating these two notions. The Board also noted that the term 'functional currency' is more commonly used than 'measurement currency' and decided to adopt the more common term.

The Board noted a concern that the guidance in SIC-19 on determining a measurement currency could permit entities to choose one of several currencies, or to select an inappropriate currency. In particular, some believed that SIC-19 placed too much emphasis on the currency in which transactions are denominated and too little emphasis on the underlying economy that determines the pricing of those transactions. To meet these concerns, the Board defined functional currency as "the currency of the primary economic environment in which the entity operates". The Board also provided guidance on how to determine the functional currency (see paragraphs 9-14 of the Standard). This guidance draws heavily on SIC-19 and equivalent guidance in US and other national standards, but also reflects the Board's decision that some factors merit greater emphasis than others. **BC5**

The Board also discussed whether a foreign operation that is integral to the reporting entity (as described in the previous version of IAS 21) could have a functional currency that is different from that of its 'parent'.* The Board decided that the functional currencies will always be the same, because it would be contradictory for an integral foreign operation that "carries on business as if it were an extension of the reporting enterprise's operations"† to operate in a primary economic environment different from its parent. **BC6**

It follows that it is not necessary to translate the results and financial position of an integral foreign operation when incorporating them into the financial statements of the parent—they will already be measured in the parent's functional currency. Furthermore, it is not necessary to distinguish between an integral foreign operation and a foreign entity. When a foreign operation's functional currency is different from that of its parent, it is a foreign entity, and the translation method in paragraphs 38-49 of the Standard applies. **BC7**

The Board also decided that the principles in the previous version of IAS 21 for distinguishing an integral foreign operation from a foreign entity are relevant in determining an operation's functional currency. Hence it incorporated these principles into the Standard in that context. **BC8**

The Board agreed that the indicators in paragraph 9 are the primary indicators for determining the functional currency and that paragraphs 10 and 11 are secondary. This is because the indicators in paragraphs 10 and 11 are not linked to the primary economic environment in which the entity operates but provide additional supporting evidence to determine an entity's functional currency. **BC9**

**The term 'parent' is used broadly in this context to mean an entity that has a branch, associate or joint venture, as well as one with a subsidiary.*

†IAS 21 (revised 1993), paragraph 24

PRESENTATION CURRENCY

BC10 A further issue is whether an entity should be permitted to present its financial statements in a currency (or currencies) other than its functional currency. Some believe it should not. They believe that the functional currency, being the currency of the primary economic environment in which the entity operates, most usefully portrays the economic effect of transactions and events on the entity. For a group that comprises operations with a number of functional currencies, they believe that the consolidated financial statements should be presented in the functional currency that management uses when controlling and monitoring the performance and financial position of the group. They also believe that allowing an entity to present its financial statements in more than one currency may confuse, rather than help, users of those financial statements. Supporters of this view believe that any presentation in a currency other than that described above should be regarded as a 'convenience translation' that is outside the scope of IFRSs.

BC11 Others believe that the choice of presentation currency should be limited, for example, to the functional currency of one of the substantive entities within a group. However, such a restriction might be easily overcome—an entity that wished to present its financial statements in a different currency might establish a substantive, but relatively small operation with that functional currency.

BC12 Still others believe that, given the rising trend towards globalisation, entities should be permitted to present their financial statements in any currency. They note that most large groups do not have a single functional currency, but rather comprise operations with a number of functional currencies. For such entities, they believe it is not clear which currency should be the presentation currency, or why one currency is preferable to another. They also point out that management may not use a single currency when controlling and monitoring the performance and financial position of such a group. In addition, they note that in some jurisdictions, entities are required to present their financial statements in the local currency, even when this is not the functional currency.* Hence, if IFRSs required the financial statements to be presented in the functional currency, some entities would have to present two sets of financial statements: financial statements that comply with IFRSs presented in the functional currency and financial statements that comply with local regulations presented in a different currency.

BC13 The Board was persuaded by the arguments in the previous paragraph. Accordingly, it decided that entities should be permitted to present their financial statements in any currency (or currencies).

BC14 The Board also clarified that the Standard does not prohibit the entity from providing, as supplementary information, a 'convenience translation'. Such a 'convenience translation' may display financial statements (or selected portions of financial statements) in a currency other than the presentation currency, as a convenience to some users. The 'convenience translation' may be prepared using a translation method other than that required by the Standard. These types of 'convenience translations' should be clearly identified as supplementary information to distinguish them from information required by IFRSs and translated in accordance with the Standard.

**This includes entities operating in another country and, for example, publishing financial statements to comply with a listing requirement of that country.*

TRANSLATION METHOD

The Board debated which method should be used to translate financial statements from an entity's functional currency into a different presentation currency. **BC15**

The Board agreed that the translation method should not have the effect of substituting another currency for the functional currency. Put another way, presenting the financial statements in a different currency should not change the way in which the underlying items are measured. Rather, the translation method should merely express the underlying amounts, as measured in the functional currency, in a different currency. **BC16**

Given this, the Board considered two possible translation methods. The first is to translate all amounts (including comparatives) at the most recent closing rate. This method has several advantages: it is simple to apply; it does not generate any new gains and losses; and it does not change ratios such as return on assets. This method is supported by those who believe that the process of merely expressing amounts in a different currency should preserve the relationships among amounts as measured in the functional currency and, as such, should not lead to any new gains or losses. **BC17**

The second method considered by the Board is the one that the previous version of IAS 21 required for translating the financial statements of a foreign operation.* This method results in the same amounts in the presentation currency regardless of whether the financial statements of a foreign operation are: **BC18**

(a) first translated into the functional currency of another group entity (eg th-e parent) and then into the presentation currency, or

(b) translated directly into the presentation currency.

This method avoids the need to decide the currency in which to express the financial statements of a multinational group before they are translated into the presentation currency. As noted above, many large groups do not have a single functional currency, but comprise operations with a number of functional currencies. For such entities it is not clear which functional currency should be chosen in which to express amounts before they are translated into the presentation currency, or why one currency is preferable to another. In addition, this method produces the same amounts in the presentation currency for a standalone entity as for an identical subsidiary of a parent whose functional currency is the presentation currency. **BC19**

The Board decided to require the second method, ie that the financial statements of any entity (whether a stand-alone entity, a parent or an operation within a group) whose functional currency differs from the presentation currency used by the reporting entity are translated using the method set out in paragraphs 3849 of the Standard. **BC20**

With respect to translation of comparative amounts, the Board adopted the approach required by SIC-30 for: **BC21**

(a) an entity whose functional currency is not the currency of the hyperinflationary economy (assets and liabilities in the comparative balance sheet are translated at the closing rate at the date of that balance sheet and income and expenses in the comparative income statement are translated at exchange rates at the dates of the transactions); and

**This is to translate balance sheet items at the closing rate and income and expense items at actual (or average) rates, except for an entity whose functional currency is that of a hyperinflationary economy.*

(b) an entity whose functional currency is the currency of a hyperinflationary economy, and for which the comparative amounts are being translated into the currency of a hyperinflationary economy (both balance sheet and income statement items are translated at the closing rate of the most recent balance sheet presented).

BC22 However, the Board decided not to adopt the SIC-30 approach for the translation of comparatives for an entity whose functional currency is the currency of a hyperinflationary economy, and for which the comparative amounts are being translated into a presentation currency of a nonhyperinflationary economy. The Board noted that in such a case, the SIC30 approach requires restating the comparative amounts from those shown in last year's financial statements for both the effects of inflation and for changes in exchange rates. If exchange rates fully reflect differing price levels between the two economies to which they relate, the SIC-30 approach will result in the same amounts for the comparatives as were reported as current year amounts in the prior year financial statements. Furthermore, the Board noted that in the prior year, the relevant amounts had been already expressed in the non-hyperinflationary presentation currency, and there was no reason to change them. For these reasons the Board decided to require that all comparative amounts are those presented in the prior year financial statements (ie there is no adjustment for either subsequent changes in the price level or subsequent changes in exchange rates).

BC23 The Board decided to incorporate into the Standard most of the disclosure requirements of SIC-30 *Reporting Currency—Translation from Measurement Currency to Presentation Currency* that apply when a different translation method is used or other supplementary information, such as an extract from the full financial statements, is displayed in a currency other than the functional currency (see paragraph 57 of the Standard). These disclosures enable users to distinguish information prepared in accordance with IFRSs from information that may be useful to users but is not the subject of IFRSs, and also tell users how the latter information has been prepared.

CAPITALISATION OF EXCHANGE DIFFERENCES

BC24 The previous version of IAS 21 allowed a limited choice of accounting for exchange differences that arise "from a severe devaluation or depreciation of a currency against which there is no practical means of hedging and that affects liabilities which cannot be settled and which arise directly on the recent acquisition of an asset".* The benchmark treatment was to recognise such exchange differences in profit or loss. The allowed alternative was to recognise them as an asset.

BC25 The Board noted that the allowed alternative (of recognition as an asset) was not in accordance with the *Framework for the Preparation and Presentation of Financial Statements* because exchange losses do not meet the definition of an asset.† Moreover, recognition of exchange losses as an asset is neither allowed nor required by any liaison standard-setter, so its deletion would improve convergence. Finally, in many cases when the conditions for recognition as an asset are met, the asset would

**IAS 21 (revised 1993), paragraph 21*

†***ASB footnote:*** *The equivalent document in the UK and the Republic of Ireland to the IASB's* Framework for the Preparation and Presentation of Financial Statements *is the* Statement of Principles for Financial Reporting. *Exchange losses do not meet the* Statement of Principles' *asset definition either.*

be restated in accordance with IAS 29 *Financial Reporting in Hyperinflationary Economies*.* Thus, to the extent that an exchange loss reflects hyperinflation, this effect is taken into account by IAS 29. For all of these reasons, the Board removed the allowed alternative treatment and the related SIC Interpretation is superseded.

Net investment in a foreign operation

The principle in paragraph 32 is that exchange differences arising on a monetary item that is, in substance, part of the reporting entity's net investment in a foreign operation are initially recognised in a separate component of equity† in the consolidated financial statements of the reporting entity. Among the revisions to IAS 21 made in 2003 was the provision of guidance on this principle that required the monetary item to be denominated in the functional currency of either the reporting entity or the foreign operation. The previous version of IAS 21 did not include such guidance. **BC25A**

The requirements can be illustrated by the following example. Parent P owns 100 per cent of Subsidiary S. Parent P has a functional currency of UK sterling. Subsidiary S has a functional currency of Mexican pesos. Parent P grants a loan of 100 US dollars to Subsidiary S, for which settlement is neither planned nor likely to occur in the foreseeable future. IAS 21 (as revised in 2003) requires the exchange differences arising on the loan to be recognised in profit or loss in the consolidated financial statements of Parent P, whereas those differences would be recognised initially in equity‡ in the consolidated financial statements of Parent P, if the loan were to be denominated in sterling or Mexican pesos. **BC25B**

After the revised IAS 21 was issued in 2003, constituents raised the following concerns: **BC25C**

(a) It is common practice for a monetary item that forms part of an entity's investment in a foreign operation to be denominated in a currency that is not the functional currency of either the reporting entity or the foreign operation. An example is a monetary item denominated in a currency that is more readily convertible than the local domestic currency of the foreign operation.
(b) An investment in a foreign operation denominated in a currency that is not the functional currency of the reporting entity or the foreign operation does not expose the group to a greater foreign currency exchange difference than arises when the investment is denominated in the functional currency of the reporting entity or the foreign operation. It simply results in exchange differences arising in the foreign operation's individual financial statements and the reporting entity's separate financial statements.
(c) It is not clear whether the term 'reporting entity' in paragraph 32 should be interpreted as the single entity or the group comprising a parent and all its subsidiaries. As a result, constituents questioned whether the monetary item must be transacted between the foreign operation and the reporting entity, or whether it could be transacted between the foreign operation and any member of the consolidated group, ie the reporting entity or any of its subsidiaries.

ASB footnote: *IAS 29 is being implemented in the UK and the Republic of Ireland at the same time as this standard as FRS 24 (IAS 29)* Financial Reporting in Hyperinflationary Economies.

†*As a consequence of the revision of IAS 1* Presentation of Financial Statements *in 2007 such differences are recognised in other comprehensive income.*

‡*As a consequence of the revision of IAS 1* Presentation of Financial Statements *in 2007 such differences are recognised in other comprehensive income.*

BC25D The Board noted that the nature of the monetary item referred to in paragraph 15 is similar to an equity investment in a foreign operation, ie settlement of the monetary item is neither planned nor likely to occur in the foreseeable future. Therefore, the principle in paragraph 32 to recognise exchange differences arising on a monetary item initially in a separate component of equity* effectively results in the monetary item being accounted for in the same way as an equity investment in the foreign operation when consolidated financial statements are prepared. The Board concluded that the accounting treatment in the consolidated financial statements should not be dependent on the currency in which the monetary item is denominated, nor on which entity within the group conducts the transaction with the foreign operation.

BC25E Accordingly, in 2005 the Board decided to amend IAS 21. The amendment requires exchange differences arising on a monetary item that forms part of a reporting entity's net investment in a foreign operation to be recognised initially in a separate component of equity† in the consolidated financial statements. This requirement applies irrespective of the currency of the monetary item and of whether the monetary item results from a transaction with the reporting entity or any of its subsidiaries.

BC25F The Board also proposed amending IAS 21 to clarify that an investment in a foreign operation made by an associate of the reporting entity is not part of the reporting entity's net investment in that foreign operation. Respondents to the exposure draft disagreed with this proposal. Many respondents said that the proposed amendment added a detailed rule that was not required because the principle in paragraph 15 was clear. In redeliberations, the Board agreed with those comments and decided not to proceed with that proposed amendment.‡

GOODWILL AND FAIR VALUE ADJUSTMENTS

BC26 The previous version of IAS 21 allowed a choice of translating goodwill and fair value adjustments to assets and liabilities that arise on the acquisition of a foreign entity at (a) the closing rate or (b) the historical transaction rate.

BC27 The Board agreed that, conceptually, the correct treatment depends on whether goodwill and fair value adjustments are part of:

(a) the assets and liabilities of the acquired entity (which would imply translating them at the closing rate); or

(b) the assets and liabilities of the parent (which would imply translating them at the historical rate).

BC28 The Board agreed that fair value adjustments clearly relate to the identifiable assets and liabilities of the acquired entity and should therefore be translated at the closing rate.

BC29 Goodwill is more complex, partly because it is measured as a residual. In addition, the Board noted that difficult issues can arise when the acquired entity comprises businesses that have different functional currencies (eg if the acquired entity is a

**As a consequence of the revision of IAS 1* Presentation of Financial Statements *in 2007 such differences are recognised in other comprehensive income.*

†As a consequence of the revision of IAS 1 Presentation of Financial Statements *in 2007 such differences are recognised in other comprehensive income.*

*‡**Editor's note:** Paragraphs BC25A to BC25F added by 'Amendment to FRS 23 (IAS 21) The Effects of Changes in Foreign Exchange Rates – Net Investment in a Foreign Operation'.*

multinational group). The Board discussed how to assess any resulting goodwill for impairment and, in particular, whether the goodwill would need to be 'pushed down' to the level of each different functional currency or could be accounted for and assessed at a higher level.

One view is that when the parent acquires a multinational operation comprising businesses with many different functional currencies, any goodwill may be treated as an asset of the parent/acquirer and tested for impairment at a consolidated level. Those who support this view believe that, in economic terms, the goodwill is an asset of the parent because it is part of the acquisition price paid by the parent. Thus, they believe, it would be incorrect to allocate the goodwill to the many acquired businesses and translate it into their various functional currencies. Rather, the goodwill, being treated as an asset of the parent, is not exposed to foreign currency risks, and translation differences associated with it should not be recognised. In addition, they believe that such goodwill should be tested for impairment at a consolidated level. Under this view, allocating or 'pushing down' the goodwill to a lower level, such as each different functional currency within the acquired foreign operation, would not serve any purpose. **BC30**

Others take a different view. They believe that the goodwill is part of the parent's net investment in the acquired entity. In their view, goodwill should be treated no differently from other assets of the acquired entity, in particular intangible assets, because a significant part of the goodwill is likely to comprise intangible assets that do not qualify for separate recognition. They also note that goodwill arises only because of the investment in the foreign entity and has no existence apart from that entity. Lastly, they point out that when the acquired entity comprises a number of businesses with different functional currencies, the cash flows that support the continued recognition of goodwill are generated in those different functional currencies. **BC31**

The Board was persuaded by the reasons set out in the preceding paragraph and decided that goodwill is treated as an asset of the foreign operation and translated at the closing rate. Consequently, goodwill should be allocated to the level of each functional currency of the acquired foreign operation. This means that the level to which goodwill is allocated for foreign currency translation purposes may be different from the level at which the goodwill is tested for impairment. Entities follow the requirements in IAS 36 *Impairment of Assets* to determine the level at which goodwill is tested for impairment.* **BC32**

Disposal and partial disposal of a foreign operation†

In the second phase of the business combinations project, the Board decided that the loss of control, significant influence or joint control of an entity is accounted for as a disposal for the purposes of IAS 21. Accordingly, a former parent accounts for the loss of control over a subsidiary as a disposal of the subsidiary, even if the former subsidiary becomes an associate or jointly controlled entity of the former parent. Similarly, an investor accounts for the loss of significant influence over an associate or the loss of joint control over a jointly controlled entity as a disposal. The Board **BC33**

****ASB footnote****: The equivalent standard in the UK and the Republic of Ireland to IAS 36 is FRS 11* Impairment of fixed assets and goodwill.

†*These paragraphs were added to the Basis for Conclusions as a consequence of amendments to IAS 27* Consolidated and Separate Financial Statements *made as part of the second phase of the business combinations project in 2008.*

decided that the change in the nature of the investment is a significant economic event.

BC34 The Board also decided in the second phase of the business combinations project that:

(a) changes in the parent's ownership interest in a subsidiary that do not result in a loss of control are accounted for as equity transactions (ie transactions with owners in their capacity as owners);
(b) if a parent loses control of a subsidiary, the parent reclassifies from equity to profit or loss (as a reclassification adjustment) the parent's share of the exchange differences recognised in other comprehensive income relating to a foreign operation in that subsidiary; and
(c) if an investor loses significant influence over an associate or loses joint control over a jointly controlled entity, the investor reclassifies from equity to profit or loss (as a reclassification adjustment) the exchange differences recognised in other comprehensive income relating to a foreign operation in that associate or jointly controlled entity.

The amendments in paragraphs 48A–49 of the Standard reflect those decisions for the disposal or partial disposal of a foreign operation.

Financial Reporting Standard 24 embodies IAS 29 'Financial Reporting in Hyperinflationary Economies' and some amendments to that standard adopted for entities subject to UK accounting standards.

The Statement of Standard Accounting Practice in FRS 24 is set out in paragraphs 1-42. All the paragraphs have equal authority. Paragraphs in bold type state the main principles.

The Statement of Standard Accounting Practice should be read in the context of the Accounting Standards Board's 'Foreword to Accounting Standards' and 'Statement of Principles for Financial Reporting'.

FRS 24
(IAS 29) Financial reporting in hyperinflationary economies*

(Issued December 2004)

Contents

	paragraphs
Financial Reporting Standard 24 (IAS 29) Financial Reporting in Hyperinflationary Economies	
Scope	**1-4**
The restatement of financial statements	**5-10**
Historical Cost Financial Statements	**11-28**
Balance Sheet	11-25
Income Statement	26
Gain or Loss on Net Monetary Position	27-28
Taxes	**32**
Cash Flow Statement	**33**
Corresponding Figures	**34**
Consolidated Financial Statements	**35-36**
Selection and Use of the General Price Index	**37**
Economies ceasing to be hyperinflationary	**38**
Disclosures	**39-40**
Effective date	**41-41a**
Withdrawal of other pronouncements	**42**

****Editor's note****: *The matters covered in FRS 24 are dealt with in Section 31 of FRS 102.*

Preface by the Accounting Standards Board

This Financial Reporting Standard (FRS) has the effect, for those entities that are applying it, of: **a**

- implementing in the UK and the Republic of Ireland the International Accounting Standards Board's (IASB's) International Accounting Standard (IAS) 29 *Financial Reporting in Hyperinflationary Economies*; and
- withdrawing the existing UK requirements on the subject, which are contained in UITF Abstract 9 *Accounting for operations in hyper-inflationary economies.*

UITF Abstract 9 remains in place unamended for entities not applying this FRS.

This FRS is, in effect, part of a package of UK standards comprising: **b**

- this FRS,
- FRS 23 (IAS 21) *The Effects of Changes in Foreign Exchange Rates*,
- the disclosure requirements of FRS 25 (IAS 32) *Financial Instruments: Disclosure and Presentation*,* and
- FRS 26 (IAS 39) *Financial Instruments: Measurement*.

The applicability of the package of standards is determined by reference to FRS 26's application. **c**

- For accounting periods beginning on or after 1 January 2005, FRS 26—and therefore the entire package of standards listed above, including this FRS—applies to all listed entities preparing their financial statements in accordance with UK requirements—including listed parent undertakings preparing individual financial statements in accordance with those requirements.† Other entities are permitted to apply the entire package of standards from that date, although entities are not permitted to apply some of the standards in the package but not others—except that FRS 25 exempts certain entities from applying its disclosure requirements and also permits entities to apply those disclosure requirements in advance of the other standards in the package if they wish.
- For accounting periods beginning on or after 1 January 2006, unlisted entities using accounting policies that are consistent with the fair value measurement rules incorporated into the Companies Act 1985 (or equivalent legislation) to implement the Fair Value Directive will also be required to comply with FRS 26—and therefore the entire package of standards including this one.

The Accounting Standards Board (the Board) will in due course be issuing proposals for the application of the standards to other unlisted entities. **d**

The text of IAS 29 contains various references to other International Financial Reporting Standards (IFRSs). In the FRS those references have been amended where necessary to enable the Standard to be applied in a UK context. The text has also been amended to remove the material relating to current cost financial statements, because that material is not relevant in the UK. The Board believes that those amendments do not change the basic requirements of IAS 29 in any way. **e**

In all other respects the FRS is identical to IAS 29. **f**

**The other requirements of FRS 25 apply to all entities—regardless of whether they are listed or unlisted— for accounting periods beginning on or after 1 January 2005.*

†For this purpose a listed entity is an entity that has shares or debt admitted to trading on a regulated market in the EU.

International Accounting Standard 29 (IAS 29)*

Financial Reporting in Hyperinflationary Economies

SCOPE

1 ***This Standard applies to all financial statements that are intended to give a true and fair view of a reporting entity's financial position and profit or loss (or income or expenditure) and which are the financial statements of a reporting entity whose functional currency is the currency of a hyperinflationary economy, except that:***

(a) it should not be applied to any financial statements to which FRS 26 (IAS 39) **Financial Instruments: Recognition and Measurement** ***has not also been applied; and***

(b) entities applying the **Financial Reporting Standard for Smaller Entities** ***(FRSSE) currently applicable are exempt from the Standard.***†

1A For accounting periods beginning on or after 1 January 2005, FRS 26—and therefore this Standard—will apply to listed entities; other entities have the option of applying the Standard, though only if they also apply FRS 26 (and certain other Standards). From 2006, unlisted entities using accounting policies that are consistent with the fair value measurement rules incorporated into the Companies Act or equivalent legislation will also be required to apply FRS 26 and, therefore, this Standard.

2 In a hyperinflationary economy, reporting of operating results and financial position in the local currency without restatement is not useful. Money loses purchasing power at such a rate that comparison of amounts from transactions and other events that have occurred at different times, even within the same accounting period, is misleading.

3 This Standard does not establish an absolute rate at which hyperinflation is deemed to arise. It is a matter of judgement when restatement of financial statements in accordance with this Standard becomes necessary. Hyperinflation is indicated by characteristics of the economic environment of a country which include, but are not limited to, the following:

(a) the general population prefers to keep its wealth in non-monetary assets or in a relatively stable foreign currency. Amounts of local currency held are immediately invested to maintain purchasing power;

(b) the general population regards monetary amounts not in terms of the local currency but in terms of a relatively stable foreign currency. Prices may be quoted in that currency;

(c) sales and purchases on credit take place at prices that compensate for the expected loss of purchasing power during the credit period, even if the period is short;

(d) interest rates, wages and prices are linked to a price index; and

(e) the cumulative inflation rate over three years is approaching, or exceeds, 100%.

**As part of Improvements to IFRSs issued in May 2008, the Board changed terms used in IAS 29 to be consistent with other IFRSs as follows: (a) 'market value' was amended to 'fair value', and (b) 'results of operations' and 'net income' were amended to 'profit or loss'. In this footnote 'the Board' refers to the IASB. The ASB made the same amendment to FRS 24 as part of its 'Improvements to FRS' issued in December 2008.*

†***Editor's note:*** *Reference to FRS 26 altered by amendments to FRS 26, to reflect the change in its title.*

It is preferable that all entities that report in the currency of the same hyperinflationary economy apply this Standard from the same date. Nevertheless, this Standard applies to the financial statements of any entity from the beginning of the reporting period in which it identifies the existence of hyperinflation in the country in whose currency it reports. 4

THE RESTATEMENT OF FINANCIAL STATEMENTS

Prices change over time as the result of various specific or general political, economic and social forces. Specific forces such as changes in supply and demand and technological changes may cause individual prices to increase or decrease significantly and independently of each other. In addition, general forces may result in changes in the general level of prices and therefore in the general purchasing power of money. 5

Entities that prepare financial statements on the historical cost basis of accounting do so without regard either to changes in the general level of prices or to increases in specific prices of recognised assets or liabilities. The exceptions to this are those assets and liabilities that the entity is required, or chooses where applicable in accordance with the relevant accounting Standard, to measure at current value. Some entities, however, present financial statements that are based on a current cost approach that reflects the effects of changes in the specific prices of assets held.* 6

In a hyperinflationary economy, financial statements, whether they are based on a historical cost approach or a current cost approach, are useful only if they are expressed in terms of the measuring unit current at the balance sheet date. As a result, this Standard applies to the financial statements of entities reporting in the currency of a hyperinflationary economy. Presentation of the information required by this Standard as a supplement to unrestated financial statements is not permitted. Furthermore, separate presentation of the financial statements before restatement is discouraged. 7

The financial statements of an entity whose functional currency is the currency of a hyperinflationary economy shall be stated in terms of the measuring unit current at the balance sheet date. The corresponding amounts for the previous period required by FRS 28 'Corresponding Amounts' and any information in respect of earlier periods shall also be stated in terms of the measuring unit current at the balance sheet date. For the purpose of presenting corresponding amounts in a different presentation currency, paragraphs 42(b) and 43 of FRS 23 (IAS 21) *The Effects of Changes in Foreign Exchange Rates* apply.† 8

The gain or loss on the net monetary position shall be included in profit or loss and separately disclosed. 9

The restatement of financial statements in accordance with this Standard requires the application of certain procedures as well as judgement. The consistent application of these procedures and judgements from period to period is more important than the precise accuracy of the resulting amounts included in the restated financial statements. 10

***Editor's note:** *Paragraph amended in December 2008.*

†***Editor's note:*** *Paragraph amended in December 2008.*

Historical Cost Financial Statements

Balance Sheet

11 Balance sheet amounts not already expressed in terms of the measuring unit current at the balance sheet date are restated by applying a general price index.

12 Monetary items are not restated because they are already expressed in terms of the monetary unit current at the balance sheet date. Monetary items are money held and items to be received or paid in money.

13 Assets and liabilities linked by agreement to changes in prices, such as index linked bonds and loans, are adjusted in accordance with the agreement in order to ascertain the amount outstanding at the balance sheet date. These items are carried at this adjusted amount in the restated balance sheet.

14 All other assets and liabilities are non-monetary. Some non-monetary items are carried at amounts current at the balance sheet date, such as net realisable value and fair value, so they are not restated. All other non-monetary assets and liabilities are restated.*

15 Most non-monetary items are carried at cost or cost less depreciation; hence they are expressed at amounts current at their date of acquisition. The restated cost, or cost less depreciation, of each item is determined by applying to its historical cost and accumulated depreciation the change in a general price index from the date of acquisition to the balance sheet date. For example, property, plant and equipment, inventories of raw materials and merchandise, goodwill, patents, trademarks and similar assets are restated from the dates of their purchase. Inventories of partly-finished and finished goods are restated from the dates on which the costs of purchase and of conversion were incurred.†

16 Detailed records of the acquisition dates of items of property, plant and equipment may not be available or capable of estimation. In these rare circumstances, it may be necessary, in the first period of application of this Standard, to use an independent professional assessment of the value of the items as the basis for their restatement.

17 A general price index may not be available for the periods for which the restatement of property, plant and equipment is required by this Standard. In these circumstances, it may be necessary to use an estimate based, for example, on the movements in the exchange rate between the functional currency and a relatively stable foreign currency.

18 Some non-monetary items are carried at amounts current at dates other than that of acquisition or that of the balance sheet, for example property, plant and equipment that has been revalued at some earlier date. In these cases, the carrying amounts are restated from the date of the revaluation.

19 The restated amount of a non-monetary item is reduced, in accordance with appropriate Standards, when it exceeds its recoverable amount. For example, restated amounts of property, plant and equipment, goodwill, patents and

****Editor's note**: Paragraph amended in December 2008.*

†***Editor's note**: Paragraph amended in December 2008.*

trademarks are reduced to recoverable amount and restated amounts of inventories are reduced to net realisable value.*

An investee that is accounted for under the equity method may report in the currency of a hyperinflationary economy. The balance sheet and profit and loss account of such an investee are restated in accordance with this Standard in order to calculate the investor's share of its net assets and profit or loss. When the restated financial statements of the investee are expressed in a foreign currency they are translated at closing rates.† **20**

The impact of inflation is usually recognised in borrowing costs. It is not appropriate both to restate the capital expenditure financed by borrowing and to capitalise that part of the borrowing costs that compensates for the inflation during the same period. This part of the borrowing costs is recognised as an expense in the period in which the costs are incurred. **21**

An entity may acquire assets under an arrangement that permits it to defer payment without incurring an explicit interest charge. Where it is impracticable to impute the amount of interest, such assets are restated from the payment date and not the date of purchase. **22**

[Deleted] **23**

At the beginning of the first period of application of this Standard, the components of owners' equity, except retained earnings and any revaluation surplus, are restated by applying a general price index from the dates the components were contributed or otherwise arose. Any revaluation surplus that arose in previous periods is eliminated. Restated retained earnings are derived from all the other amounts in the restated balance sheet. **24**

At the end of the first period and in subsequent periods, all components of owners' equity are restated by applying a general price index from the beginning of the period or the date of contribution, if later. The movements for the period in owners' equity are disclosed in accordance with FRS 3 *Reporting Financial Performance*. **25**

Income Statement

This Standard requires that all items in the income statement are expressed in terms of the measuring unit current at the balance sheet date. Therefore all amounts need to be restated by applying the change in the general price index from the dates when the items of income and expenses were initially recorded in the financial statements. **26**

Gain or Loss on Net Monetary Position

In a period of inflation, an entity holding an excess of monetary assets over monetary liabilities loses purchasing power and an entity with an excess of monetary liabilities over monetary assets gains purchasing power to the extent the assets and liabilities are not linked to a price level. This gain or loss on the net monetary position may be derived as the difference resulting from the restatement of non-monetary assets, owners' equity and income statement items and the adjustment of index linked assets and liabilities. The gain or loss may be estimated by applying the change in a general **27**

* ***Editor's note**: Paragraph amended in December 2008.*

† ***Editor's note**: Paragraph amended in December 2008.*

price index to the weighted average for the period of the difference between monetary assets and monetary liabilities.

28 The gain or loss on the net monetary position is included in the profit and loss account. The adjustment to those assets and liabilities linked by agreement to changes in prices made in accordance with paragraph 13 is offset against the gain or loss on net monetary position. Other profit and loss items, such as interest income and expense, and foreign exchange differences related to invested or borrowed funds are also associated with the net monetary position. Although such items are separately disclosed, it may be helpful if they are presented together with the gain or loss on net monetary position in the profit and loss account.*

29-31 [*ASB note:* Deleted]

Taxes

32 The restatement of financial statements in accordance with this Standard may give rise to differences between the carrying amount of individual assets and liabilities in the balance sheet and their tax bases. Consequential timing differences are accounted for in accordance with FRS 19 *Deferred Tax*.

Cash Flow Statement

33 This Standard requires that all items in the cash flow statement are expressed in terms of the measuring unit current at the balance sheet date.

Corresponding Amounts

34 Corresponding amounts for the previous reporting period, whether they were based on a historical cost approach or a current cost approach, are restated by applying a general price index so that the corresponding financial statements are presented in terms of the measuring unit current at the balance sheet date. Information that is disclosed in respect of earlier periods is also expressed in terms of the measuring unit current at the balance sheet date. For the purpose of presenting corresponding amounts in a different presentation currency, paragraphs 42(b) and 43 of FRS 23 apply.†

Consolidated Financial Statements

35 A parent that reports in the currency of a hyperinflationary economy may have subsidiaries that also report in the currencies of hyperinflationary economies. The financial statements of any such subsidiary need to be restated by applying a general price index of the country in whose currency it reports before they are included in the consolidated financial statements issued by its parent. Where such a subsidiary is a foreign subsidiary, its restated financial statements are translated at closing rates. The financial statements of subsidiaries that do not report in the currencies of hyperinflationary economies are dealt with in accordance with FRS 23.

36 If financial statements with different reporting dates are consolidated, all items, whether non-monetary or monetary, need to be restated into the measuring unit current at the date of the consolidated financial statements.

* ***Editor's note****: Paragraph amended in December 2008.*

† ***Editor's note****: Paragraph amended in December 2008.*

Selection and Use of the General Price Index

The restatement of financial statements in accordance with this Standard requires the use of a general price index that reflects changes in general purchasing power. It is preferable that all entities that report in the currency of the same economy use the same index. **37**

ECONOMIES CEASING TO BE HYPERINFLATIONARY

When an economy ceases to be hyperinflationary and an entity discontinues the preparation and presentation of financial statements prepared in accordance with this Standard, it shall treat the amounts expressed in the measuring unit current at the end of the previous reporting period as the basis for the carrying amounts in its subsequent financial statements. **38**

DISCLOSURES

The following disclosures shall be made: **39**

(a) the fact that the financial statements and the corresponding figures for previous periods have been restated for the changes in the general purchasing power of the functional currency and, as a result, are stated in terms of the measuring unit current at the balance sheet date;
(b) whether the financial statements are based on a historical cost approach or a current cost approach; and
(c) the identity and level of the price index at the balance sheet date and the movement in the index during the current and the previous reporting period.

The disclosures required by this Standard are needed to make clear the basis of dealing with the effects of inflation in the financial statements. They are also intended to provide other information necessary to understand that basis and the resulting amounts. **40**

EFFECTIVE DATE

An entity shall apply this Standard for accounting periods in which they also apply FRS 26 but not in any other accounting period. **41**

Unless and until an entity applies FRS 26 it is not permitted to adopt this Standard; and if it applies FRS 26 it must also apply this Standard. Listed entities are required to apply FRS 26 for accounting periods beginning on or after 1 January 2005 (and other entities are permitted to apply it from that date). As explained in paragraph 1A, certain unlisted entities are required to apply FRS 26 for accounting periods beginning on or after 1 January 2006. **41A**

WITHDRAWAL OF OTHER PRONOUNCEMENTS

***For entities applying this Standard, it supersedes UITF Abstract 9* Accounting for operations in hyper-inflationary economies.** **42**

Adoption of the standard

APPROVAL OF IAS 21 BY THE INTERNATIONAL ACCOUNTING STANDARDS BOARD

[*ASB note:* IAS 29 was originally approved by the International Accounting Standards Committee, the IASB's predecessor body, in 1989. It was subsequently reformatted and, in 2001, was adopted by the IASB.]

ADOPTION OF FRS 24 BY THE ACCOUNTING STANDARDS BOARD

Financial Reporting Standard 24 (IAS 29) *Financial Reporting in Hyperinflationary Economies* was approved for issue by the ten members of the Accounting Standards Board.

Ian Mackintosh	Chairman
Andrew Lennard	Technical Director
Michael Ashley	
Douglas Flint	
Anthony Good	
Roger Marshall	
Isobel Sharp	
John Smith	
Jonathan Symonds	
Peter Westlake	

Notes on the standard's application in the UK and the Republic of Ireland

FRED 24

In recent years, the Accounting Standards Board (the Board) has been placing increasing emphasis on the convergence aspects of its standard-setting role: listed entities in the UK and the Republic of Ireland preparing consolidated financial statements will from 2005 be required to prepare those statements in accordance with EU-adopted international accounting standards (International Financial Reporting Standards or IFRSs) and, although entities can continue to prepare other financial statements in accordance with the requirements of the UK and the Republic of Ireland, the Board's view is that there can be no case for the use of two sets of wholly different standards in the medium term. **N1**

As part of this convergence strategy, the Board issued in May 2002 FRED 24 *The Effects of Changes in Foreign Exchange Rates & Financial Reporting in Hyperinflationary Economies*. FRED 24 proposed replacing the existing UK material on accounting for foreign currency (set out in SSAP 20 *Foreign currency translation)* and accounting in inflationary economies (set out in UITF Abstract 9 *Accounting for operations in hyper-inflationary economies*) with two new UK standards based on IAS 21 *The Effects of Changes in Foreign Exchange Rates* and IAS 29 *Financial Reporting in Hyperinflationary Economies*. **N2**

Those responding to FRED 24 were broadly supportive of the Board's strategy to converge its standards in this area with those of the IASB, and there was in particular relatively little negative comment on the proposal to implement IAS 29 in the UK and the Republic of Ireland. The issue raised by most of those who did comment on the proposal concerned the main proposed change: **N3**

(a) UITF 9 specifies two methods of eliminating the distortions caused by hyperinflation—the current price level approach and the stable currency approach*—but also permits entities to adopt an alternative approach if neither of those methods is considered appropriate.
(b) IAS 29, on the other hand, is much more prescriptive in that it requires use of the current price level approach.

Some respondents thought that the proposed new standard should be amended to incorporate the stable currency approach. Some argued that this should be done because the stable currency approach was better than (or as good as) the current price level approach, and some argued that some flexibility was needed because it would not always be practicable to apply IAS 29's current price level approach. **N4**

The Board noted that IAS 29 has been in place for fifteen years and has apparently proved workable. It was therefore unconvinced that an amendment was needed for practicability reasons. It also noted that, having decided to adopt a convergence objective, it is difficult to justify an amendment to an international accounting standard on the grounds that some other approach is better. It therefore decided not to amend the IAS 29 requirements in the way suggested. **N5**

**The current price level approach involves adjusting the functional currency financial statements to reflect current price levels before the translation process is undertaken. The stable currency approach involves using a relatively stable currency as the functional currency of the relevant foreign operation.*

N6 FRED 24 proposed that a UK standard based on IAS 29 should be implemented for all entities in 2004. That proposal was however based on the assumption that a UK standard based on the revised version of IAS 21 that the IASB was then developing would also be implemented in 2004 for all entities. It also assumed that the UK standard based on IAS 21 would be supplemented in some way by a hedge accounting standard based on the principles underlying the hedge accounting requirements in the revised version of IAS 39 that the IASB was developing. However, the revised versions of IASs 21 and 39 were not issued until December 2003, making their application in the UK for 2004 impracticable. In any event, as explained more fully in the UK version of IAS 21 which has now been issued (FRS 23), the Board decided to change its approach to the implementation of IAS 21 in the light of the comments received in response to FRED 24. IAS 21 will now be implemented in the UK in tandem with IAS 39—in other words, all entities applying the UK version of IAS 39 (ie FRS 26) must also apply FRS 23 and an entity that is not applying FRS 26 is not permitted to apply FRS 23.

N7 The Board has also decided that IAS 29 should be implemented in the UK in tandem with FRS 23.

N8 The Board further decided that it should be the implementation of FRS 26 that should determine when the other standards are implemented. In other words, because all listed entities are required to apply FRS 26 for all accounting periods beginning on or after 1 January 2005, all listed entities will be required to apply FRS 23 and this standard from that date as well. Similarly, certain unlisted entities will be required to apply FRS 26 for all accounting periods beginning on or after 1 January 2006, so they will also be required to apply FRS 23 and this standard from that date.

Changes to existing UK requirements

N9 As mentioned already, the existing UK requirements on accounting for operations in hyperinflationary economies are set out in UITF Abstract 9. The main differences between that Abstract and FRS 24 are as follows:

(a) The scope of FRS 24 is wider than UITF 9. UITF 9 applies only to "group financial statements". FRS 24, on the other hand, also deals with the accounting to be adopted in individual financial statements when the entity has a functional currency that is the currency of a hyperinflationary economy.

(b) As explained in paragraph N3 above, UITF 9 is considerably less prescriptive than IAS 29 as to the method to be used to eliminate the distortions caused by hyperinflation.

(c) FRS 24 is in other ways also more detailed and more prescriptive than UITF 9. FRS 24's disclosure requirements are also a little more extensive.

Basis for Conclusions on FRS 24 (IAS 29) 'Financial Reporting in Hyperinflationary Economies'*

ASB note: The IASB's Basis for Conclusions, which accompanies IAS 29, is set out below in full. All references in this section to 'the Board' and 'Board members' are references to the IASB Board and IASB Board members.

This Basis for Conclusions accompanies, but is not part of, IAS 29.

This Basis for Conclusions summarises the International Accounting Standards Board's considerations in reaching its conclusions on amending IAS 29 Financial Reporting in Hyperinflationary Economies in 2008. Individual Board members gave greater weight to some factors than to others. **BC1**

Paragraph 6 of the previous version of the Standard did not reflect the fact that a number of assets and liabilities may or must be measured on the basis of a current value rather than a historical value. Therefore, the Board included examples rather than a definitive list of such items by Improvements to IFRSs issued in May 2008. **BC2**

****Editor's note****: This section added in December 2008.*

Financial Reporting Standard 25 embodies IAS 32 'Financial Instruments: Disclosure and Presentation' and some amendments to that standard adopted for entities subject to UK accounting standards.

The Statement of Standard Accounting Practice in FRS 25 is set out in paragraphs 1 to 100D and the application guidance set out in the appendix. All the paragraphs have equal authority. Paragraphs in bold type state the main principles.

Accompanying the Statement of Standard Accounting Practice is the basis for the conclusions reached in the Statement and illustrative examples. These do not form part of the Statement.

The Statement of Standard Accounting Practice should be read in the context of its objective as stated in paragraphs 1-3, the Basis for Conclusions set out in paragraphs BC1-BC49, and the Accounting Standards Board's 'Foreword to Accounting Standards' and 'Statement of Principles for Financial Reporting'.

FRS 25
(IAS 32) Financial instruments: Presentation*†

(Issued December 2004)

Contents

	paragraphs
Introduction	**IN1-IN21**
Reasons for Revising IAS 32	**IN1-IN3**
The Main Changes	**IN4-IN19**
Withdrawal of Other Pronouncements	**IN20**
International Accounting Standard 32 Financial Instruments: Disclosure and Presentation	
Objective	**1-3**
Scope	**3A-10**
Definitions	**11-14**
Presentation	**15-50E**
Liabilities and Equity	**15-27**
No Contractual Obligation to Deliver Cash or Another Financial Asset	17-20
Settlement in the Entity's Own Equity Instruments	21-24
Contingent Settlement Provisions	25
Settlement Options	26-27
Compound Financial Instruments	**28-32**
Treasury Shares	**33-34**
Interest, Dividends, Losses and Gains	**35-41**
Offsetting a Financial Asset and a Financial Liability	**42-50**
Disclosure	**51-59**
Format, Location and Classes of Financial Instruments	**53-55**
Risk Management Policies and Hedging Activities	**56-59**
Terms, Conditions and Accounting Policies	**60-66**
Interest Rate Risk	**67-75**

****Editor's note:*** *The disclosure requirements of FRS 25 are replaced by FRS 29 with effect for accounting periods beginning on or after 1 January 2007.*

†***Editor's note****: The matters covered in FRS 25 are dealt with in Sections 11, 12 and 25 of FRS 102.*

Credit Risk	**76-85**
Fair Value	**86-93**
Other Disclosures	**94-95**
Effective date	**96-97**
Withdrawal of other pronouncements	**98-100**
Appendix: application guidance	
Definitions	**AG3-AG24**
Financial Assets and Financial Liabilities	AG3-AG12
Equity Instruments	AG13-AG14
Derivative Financial Instruments	AG15-AG19
Contracts to Buy or Sell Non-Financial Items	AG20-AG24
Presentation	**AG25-AG39**
Liabilities and Equity	AG25-AG29
No Contractual Obligation to Deliver Cash or Another Financial Asset	*AG25-AG26*
Settlement in the Entity's Own Equity Instruments	*AG27*
Contingent Settlement Provisions	*AG28*
Treatment in Consolidated Financial Statements	*AG29*
Compound Financial Instruments	AG30-AG35
Treasury Shares	AG36
Interest, Dividends, Losses and Gains	AG37
Offsetting a Financial Asset and a Financial Liability	AG38-AG39
Disclosure	**AG40**
Financial Assets and Financial Liabilities at Fair Value Through Profit or Loss	AG40

Preface by the Accounting Standards Board

This Financial Reporting Standard (FRS) has the effect of implementing the International Accounting Standards Board's (IASB's) International Accounting Standard (IAS) 32 'Financial Instruments: Disclosure and Presentation' in the UK and the Republic of Ireland for entities not preparing their financial statements in accordance with international accounting standards adopted pursuant to the Regulation of the European Parliament and of the Council on the Application of International Accounting Standards. a

IAS 32 sets out requirements for the presentation of, and disclosures relating to, financial instruments. FRS 25 is based on the text of IAS 32 as at 31 March 2004, incorporating the revised version of IAS 32 issued by the IASB in December 2003 and includes amendments made by IFRS 4 'Insurance Contracts'. b

The presentation requirements of FRS 25 are applicable to all entities other than entities applying the FRSSE, and apply for accounting periods beginning on or after 1 January 2005, corresponding to the effective date of amendments to the Companies Act 1985 implementing the EU Modernisation Directive*; early adoption is not permitted for this part of the standard. c

The disclosure requirements of the FRS are, in effect, part of a package of UK standards comprising d

- the disclosure requirements of this FRS,
- FRS 23 (IAS 21) *The Effects of Changes in Foreign Exchange Rates*, and
- FRS 24 (IAS 29) *Financial Reporting in Hyperinflationary Economies*,
- FRS 26 (IAS 39) *Financial Instruments: Measurement*.

Listed entities preparing their financial statements in accordance with UK and Republic of Ireland requirements—including listed parent undertakings preparing individual financial statements in accordance with those requirements—are required to comply with the entire package of standards for accounting periods beginning on or after 1 January 2005.† Other entities are permitted to apply the entire package of standards from that date, although entities are not permitted to apply some of the standards in the package but not others—except that FRS 25 exempts certain entities from applying its disclosure requirements and also permits entities to apply those disclosure requirements in advance of the other standards in the package if they wish. e

For accounting periods beginning on or after 1 January 2006, unlisted entities using accounting policies that are consistent with the fair value measurement rules incorporated into the Companies Act to implement the EU Fair Value Directive‡ will also be required to comply with the entire package of standards. f

**Directive 2003/51/EC was originally implemented in the Companies Act 1985 by the Companies Act 1985 (International Accounting Standards and other Accounting Amendments) Regulations 2004 and re-enacted in Part 15 of the Companies Act 2006 and the regulations made under it. These extend to Northern Ireland.*

†For this purpose a listed entity is an entity that has shares or debt admitted to trading on a regulated market in the EU.

‡Section D of Schedule 4, and equivalents in other schedules, inserted by the Companies Act 1985 (International Accounting Standards and Other Accounting Amendments) Regulations 2004, and equivalent Northern Ireland and Republic of Ireland legislation. Section D Part 2 of Schedule 1 of The Large and Medium-sized Companies and Groups (Accounts and Reports) Regulations 2008 and the provisions in equivalent Schedules replaces Section D of Schedule 4 to the Companies Act 1985 and equivalent Schedules.

g The Accounting Standards Board (the Board) will in due course be issuing proposals for the application of the standards to other unlisted entities.

h The Board expects in due course to issue revised disclosure requirements, as proposed in FRED 33 and the IASB's ED 7 'Financial Instruments: Disclosures', amending those set out in FRS 25. It is envisaged that these revised disclosures would be required from 2007, but entities would have the option to adopt them early in place of the requirements of FRS 25.

i The requirements of FRS 25 are identical to the revised IAS 32 with the following exceptions in addition to the differences in scope and implementation date set out above:

- disclosures are not required for certain subsidiaries where at least 90 per cent of the voting rights are held within the group, and parent companies in their single-entity financial statements;
- the Board has added certain requirements for those entities not applying the requirements of FRS 26 (IAS 39) 'Financial Instruments: Measurement' but who wish to comply with the disclosure requirements of this standard voluntarily;
- *
- material relating to the classification of liabilities as current or non-current has been incorporated from IAS 1 'Presentation of Financial Statements';
- the Board has added transitional provisions from IFRS 1 'First-time Adoption of International Financial Reporting Standards' allowing entities not to separate elements of equity for compound instruments no longer in outstanding; the ASB has not included transitional provisions permitting non-restatement of comparatives in relation to the presentation requirements of the FRS; and
- the Board has also added transitional provisions from IFRS 1 permitting entities that apply this standard for accounting periods commencing before 1 January 2007 not to restate comparatives to comply with this standard.

j The text of IAS 32 contains various references to other International Financial Reporting Standards (IFRSs). In FRS 25 those references have been amended where necessary to enable the standard to be applied in a UK context. The ASB believes that those amendments do not change the requirements of IAS 32 in any way.

k The FRS withdraws parts of FRS 4 'Capital Instruments'. For convenience, the text of FRS 4 following these amendments is set out in the appendix to the FRS.

l The FRS also has the effect of withdrawing FRS 13 for those entities complying with the disclosure requirements of the FRS. It also supersedes UITF Abstract 33 'Obligations in capital instruments' and Abstract 37 'Purchases and sales of own shares'. Consequential amendments to other UK standards are also made.

m IAS 32 sets out amendments to other IFRSs. These amendments are not relevant in a UK context and have not been included in FRS 25.

n In October 2005 the Board amended FRS 25 to incorporate consequential amendments made to IAS 32 by the IASB in amendments to IAS 39:

- The Fair Value Option (June 2005)
- Financial Guarantee Contracts and Credit Insurance (August 2005).

****Editor's note:** Bullet point deleted by amendments to FRS 26 for those entities applying the revised version of FRS 26 which also deals with derecognition requirements.*

The Board did not include certain disclosure requirements relating to the designation of financial assets and financial liabilities as at fair value through profit and loss account as it does not consider them to be necessary.* **o**

In April 2006 the Board amended FRS 26 to include the IAS 39 material on recognition and derecognition into the Standard. Accordingly, on implementation of this amendment the corresponding disclosure requirements of IAS 32 are implemented in FRS 25. Those new disclosure requirements replace disclosures required for financial assets and liabilities by FRS 5 'Reporting the Substance of Transactions'. These amendments are effective for accounting periods on or after 1 January 2007, with earlier adoption permitted.† **p**

In August 2008 the Board amended FRS 25 to incorporate amendments made to IAS 32 by the IASB in relation to the classification as equity of certain puttable financial instruments and instruments that impose an obligation on the entity to deliver a pro rata share of the net assets of the entity on liquidation to another entity. The Board also took this opportunity to incorporate into FRS 25 certain consequential amendments by the IASB to the disclosure requirements of IAS 1 in its amendment to IAS 32.‡ **q**

These amendments are applicable for accounting periods commencing on or after 1 January 2010. Entities wishing to adopt the requirements of this amendment earlier than this date will be able to do so from periods commencing on or after 1 January 2009. **r**

In January 2010 the Board amended FRS 25 to incorporate changes made by the IASB to IAS 32 Financial Instruments: Presentation '*Classification of Rights Issues*'. The amendment is applicable for accounting periods beginning on or after 1 February 2010 with earlier application permitted.'§ **s**

**Editor's note:* *Paragraph n and o added in October 2005.*

†***Editor's note:*** *Paragraph p added in April 2006.*

‡***Editor's note:*** *Paragraphs q and r added in December 2008.*

§***Editor's note:*** *Paragraph added in January 2010.*

Introduction*

Reasons for revising IAS 32 in December 2003

IN1 International Accounting Standard 32 *Financial Instruments: Disclosure and Presentation* (IAS 32)† replaces IAS 32 *Financial Instruments: Disclosure and Presentation* (revised in 2000), and should be applied for annual periods beginning on or after 1 January 2005. Earlier application is permitted. The Standard also replaces the following Interpretations and draft Interpretation:

- SIC-5 *Classification of Financial Instruments—Contingent Settlement Provisions*;
- SIC-16 *Share Capital—Reacquired Own Equity Instruments (Treasury Shares)*;
- SIC-17 *Equity—Costs of an Equity Transaction*; and
- draft SIC-D34 *Financial Instruments—Instruments or Rights Redeemable by the Holder*.

IN2 The International Accounting Standards Board developed this revised IAS 32 as part of its project to improve IAS 32 and IAS 39 *Financial Instruments: Recognition and Measurement*. The objective of the project was to reduce complexity by clarifying and adding guidance, eliminating internal inconsistencies and incorporating into the Standards elements of Standing Interpretations Committee (SIC) Interpretations and IAS 39 implementation guidance published by the Implementation Guidance Committee (IGC).

IN3 For IAS 32, the Board's main objective was a limited revision to provide additional guidance on selected matters—such as the measurement of the components of a compound financial instrument on initial recognition, and the classification of derivatives based on an entity's own shares—and to locate all disclosures relating to financial instruments in one Standard.‡ The Board did not reconsider the fundamental approach to the presentation and disclosure of financial instruments contained in IAS 32.

The Main Changes

IN4 The main changes from the previous version of IAS 32 are described below.

Scope

IN5 The scope of IAS 32 has, where appropriate, been conformed to the scope of IAS 39.

This Introduction refers to IAS 32 as revised in December 2003. In August 2005 the IASB amended IAS 32 by relocating all disclosures relating to financial instruments to IFRS 7* Financial Instruments: Disclosures. *In February 2008 the IASB amended IAS 32 by requiring some puttable financial instruments and some financial instruments that impose on the entity an obligation to deliver to another party a pro rata share of the net assets of the entity only on liquidation to be classified as equity.* ***Editor's note**: This footnote was added in August 2008.*

†***ASB Footnote****: Although references to specific IFRSs have been amended in the main section of the standard, references in the amendment to the Introduction, which describe the revision of IAS 32 and other IFRSs, have been left unchanged.* ***Editor's note****: Heading and IN1 amended in August 2008.*

‡*In August 2005 the IASB relocated all disclosures relating to financial instruments to IFRS 7* Financial Instruments: Disclosures. ***Editor's note:*** *This footnote was added by FRS 29.*

Principle

In summary, when an issuer determines whether a financial instrument is a financial liability or an equity instrument, the instrument is an equity instrument if, and only if, both conditions (a) and (b) are met. **IN6**

(a) The instrument includes no contractual obligation:

 (i) to deliver cash or another financial asset to another entity; or
 (ii) to exchange financial assets or financial liabilities with another entity under conditions that are potentially unfavourable to the issuer.

(b) If the instrument will or may be settled in the issuer's own equity instruments, it is:

 (i) a non-derivative that includes no contractual obligation for the issuer to deliver a variable number of its own equity instruments; or
 (ii) a derivative that will be settled by the issuer exchanging a fixed amount of cash or another financial asset for a fixed number of its own equity instruments. For this purpose, the issuer's own equity instruments do not include instruments that are themselves contracts for the future receipt or delivery of the issuer's own equity instruments.

In addition, when an issuer has an obligation to purchase its own shares for cash or another financial asset, there is a liability for the amount that the issuer is obliged to pay. **IN7**

The definitions of a financial asset and a financial liability, and the description of an equity instrument, are amended consistently with this principle. **IN8**

Classification of Contracts Settled in an Entity's Own Equity Instruments

The classification of derivative and non-derivative contracts indexed to, or settled in, an entity's own equity instruments has been clarified consistently with the principle in paragraph IN6 above. In particular, when an entity uses its own equity instruments 'as currency' in a contract to receive or deliver a variable number of shares whose value equals a fixed amount or an amount based on changes in an underlying variable (eg a commodity price), the contract is not an equity instrument, but is a financial asset or a financial liability. **IN9**

Puttable Instruments

IAS 32 incorporates the guidance previously proposed in draft SIC Interpretation 34 *Financial Instruments—Instruments or Rights Redeemable by the Holder*. Consequently, a financial instrument that gives the holder the right to put the instrument back to the issuer for cash or another financial asset (a 'puttable instrument') is a financial liability of the issuer. In response to comments received on the Exposure Draft, the Standard provides additional guidance and illustrative examples for entities that, because of this requirement, have no equity or whose share capital is not equity as defined in IAS 32. **IN10**

Contingent Settlement Provisions

IAS 32 incorporates the conclusion previously in SIC-5 *Classification of Financial Instruments—Contingent Settlement Provisions* that a financial instrument is a financial liability when the manner of settlement depends on the occurrence or **IN11** nonoccurrence of uncertain future events or on the outcome of uncertain circumstances that are beyond the control of both the issuer and the holder. Contingent settlement provisions are ignored when they apply only in the event of liquidation of the issuer or are not genuine.

Settlement Options

IN12 Under IAS 32, a derivative financial instrument is a financial asset or a financial liability when it gives one of the parties to it a choice of how it is settled unless all of the settlement alternatives would result in it being an equity instrument.

Measurement of the Components of a Compound Financial Instrument on Initial Recognition

IN13 The revisions eliminate the option previously in IAS 32 to measure the liability component of a compound financial instrument on initial recognition either as a residual amount after separating the equity component, or by using a relative fair-value method. Thus, any asset and liability components are separated first and the residual is the amount of any equity component. These requirements for separating the liability and equity components of a compound financial instrument are conformed to both the definition of an equity instrument as a residual and the measurement requirements in IAS 39.

Treasury Shares

IN14 IAS 32 incorporates the conclusion previously in SIC-16 *Share Capital—Reacquired Own Equity Instruments (Treasury Shares)* that the acquisition or subsequent resale by an entity of its own equity instruments does not result in a gain or loss for the entity. Rather it represents a transfer between those holders of equity instruments who have given up their equity interest and those who continue to hold an equity instrument.

Interest, Dividends, Losses and Gains

IN15 IAS 32 incorporates the guidance previously in SIC-17 *Equity—Costs of an Equity Transaction*. Transaction costs incurred as a necessary part of completing an equity transaction are accounted for as part of that transaction and are deducted from equity.

Disclosure*

IN16–19 [Withdrawn]

IN19A In August 2005 the Board revised disclosures about financial instruments and relocated them to IFRS 7 *Financial Instruments: Disclosures.*

Withdrawal of Other Pronouncements

IN20 As a consequence of the revisions to this Standard, the Board withdrew the three Interpretations and one draft Interpretation of the former Standing Interpretations Committee noted in paragraph IN1.

****Editor's note:** *Paragraphs IN16 to IN19 deleted by FRS 29, with effect for accounting periods beginning on or after 1 January 2007, and replaced with IN19A.*

Potential Impact of Proposals in Exposure Drafts

[Deleted] **IN21**

Reasons for Amending IAS 32 in February 2008*

In February 2008 the IASB amended IAS 32 by requiring some financial instruments that meet the definition of a financial liability to be classified as equity. Entities should apply the amendments for annual periods beginning on or after 1 January 2009. Earlier application is permitted. **IN22**

The amendment addresses the classification of some: **IN23**

(a) puttable financial instruments, and
(b) instruments, or components of instruments, that impose on the entity an obligation to deliver to another party a pro rata share of the net assets of the entity only on liquidation.

The objective was a short-term, limited scope amendment to improve the financial reporting of particular types of financial instruments that meet the definition of a financial liability but represent the residual interest in the net assets of the entity. **IN24**

***Editor's note**: *Heading and paragraphs IN22 to IN24 added in August 2008.*

Financial Instruments: Disclosure and Presentation

Objective

1* [Withdrawn]

2† The objective of this Standard is to establish principles for presenting financial instruments as liabilities or equity and for offsetting financial assets and financial liabilities. It applies to the classification of financial instruments, from the perspective of the issuer, into financial assets, financial liabilities and equity instruments; the classification of related interest, dividends, losses and gains; and the circumstances in which financial assets and financial liabilities should be offset.

3‡ The principles in this Standard complement the principles for measuring financial assets and financial liabilities in FRS 26 (IAS 39) *Financial Instruments: Measurement*, and for disclosing information about them in FRS 29 (IFRS 7) *Financial Instruments: Disclosures*.§

SCOPE

3A ***This Standard applies to all financial statements that are intended to give a true and fair view of a reporting entity's financial position and profit or loss (or income and expenditure). Reporting entities applying the Financial Reporting Standard for Smaller Entities (FRSSE) are exempt from this Standard.***

3B§§

4 **This Standard shall be applied to all types of financial instruments except:**

(a) those interests in subsidiary, quasi-subsidiary and associated undertakings, partnerships and joint ventures, including those which are accounted for under FRS 5 'Reporting the Substance of Transactions'; and FRS 9 'Associates and Joint Ventures'. However, entities shall apply this Standard to all derivatives linked to interests in subsidiaries, quasi-subsidiary or associated undertakings, partnerships or joint ventures.||

(b) employers' rights and obligations under employee benefit plans, to which FRS 17 **Retirement Benefits*, applies.***

(c) contracts for contingent consideration in a business combination (see paragraph 27 of FRS 7 **Fair Values in Acquisition Accounting*). This exemption applies only to the acquirer.***

****Editor's note:** Paragraph 1 deleted by FRS 29 with effect for accounting periods beginning on or after 1 January 2007.*

*†**Editor's note:** Paragraph 2 amended by FRS 29 with effect for accounting periods beginning on or after 1 January 2007.*

*‡**Editor's note:** Paragraph 3 amended by FRS 29 with effect for accounting periods beginning on or after 1 January 2007.*

*§**Editor's note:** Reference to FRS 26 altered by amendments to FRS 26, to reflect the change in its title.*

*§§**Editor's note:** Paragraphs 3B to 3D deleted by FRS 29 with effect for accounting periods beginning on or after 1 January 2007.*

*||**Editor's note:** Paragraph amended with effect for accounting periods beginning on or after 1 January 2010.*

(*d*) ***insurance contracts as defined in* Appendix C to FRS 26. However, this Standard applies to derivatives that are embedded in insurance contracts if FRS 26 requires the entity to account for them separately. Moreover, an issuer shall apply this Standard to financial guarantee contracts if the issuer applies FRS 26 in measuring the contracts.***

(*e*) ***financial instruments that an entity issues with a discretionary participation feature as defined in Appendix C to FRS 26). The issuer of these instruments is exempt from applying to these features paragraphs 15-32 and AG25-AG35 of this Standard regarding the distinction between financial liabilities and equity instruments. However, these instruments are subject to all other requirements of this Standard. Furthermore, this Standard applies to derivatives that are embedded in these instruments (see FRS 26).***

(*f*) ***financial instruments, contracts and obligations under share-based payment transactions to which FRS 20* Share-based Payment *applies, except for***

(*i*) ***contracts within the scope of paragraphs 8-10 of this Standard, to which this Standard applies,***

(*ii*) ***paragraphs 33 and 34 of this Standard, which shall be applied to treasury shares purchased, sold, issued or cancelled in connection with employee share option plans, employee share purchase plans, and all other share-based payment arrangements.***

[Withdrawn] 5†

[Deleted] 6

[Withdrawn] 7

This Standard shall be applied to those contracts to buy or sell a nonfinancial item that can be settled net in cash or another financial instrument, or by exchanging financial instruments, as if the contracts were financial instruments, with the exception of contracts that were entered into and continue to be held for the purpose of the receipt or delivery of a non-financial item in accordance with the entity's expected purchase, sale or usage requirements. 8

There are various ways in which a contract to buy or sell a non-financial item can be settled net in cash or another financial instrument or by exchanging financial instruments. These include: 9

(a) when the terms of the contract permit either party to settle it net in cash or another financial instrument or by exchanging financial instruments;

(b) when the ability to settle net in cash or another financial instrument, or by exchanging financial instruments, is not explicit in the terms of the contract, but the entity has a practice of settling similar contracts net in cash or another financial instrument, or by exchanging financial instruments (whether with the counterparty, by entering into offsetting contracts or by selling the contract before its exercise or lapse);

(c) when, for similar contracts, the entity has a practice of taking delivery of the underlying and selling it within a short period after delivery for the purpose of generating a profit from short-term fluctuations in price or dealer's margin; and

(*d*) *when the non-financial* item that is the subject of the contract is readily convertible to cash.

****Editor's note:*** *Amended with effect from 1 January 2005.*

†***Editor's note:*** *Paragraphs 5 and 7 deleted by FRS 29 with effect for accounting periods beginning on or after 1 January 2007.*

A contract to which (b) or (c) applies is not entered into for the purpose of the receipt or delivery of the non-financial item in accordance with the entity's expected purchase, sale or usage requirements, and, accordingly, is within the scope of this Standard. Other contracts to which paragraph 8 applies are evaluated to determine whether they were entered into and continue to be held for the purpose of the receipt or delivery of the non-financial item in accordance with the entity's expected purchase, sale or usage requirement, and accordingly, whether they are within the scope of this Standard.

10 A written option to buy or sell a non-financial item that can be settled net in cash or another financial instrument, or by exchanging financial instruments, in accordance with paragraph 9(a) or (d) is within the scope of this Standard. Such a contract cannot be entered into for the purpose of the receipt or delivery of the non-financial item in accordance with the entity's expected purchase, sale or usage requirements.

DEFINITIONS (see also paragraphs AG3-AG23)*

11 ***The following terms are used in this Standard with the meanings specified:***

A financial instrument is any contract that gives rise to a financial asset of one entity and a financial liability or equity instrument of another entity.

A financial asset is any asset that is:

(a) cash;
(b) an equity instrument of another entity;
(c) a contractual right:

(i) to receive cash or another financial asset from another entity; or
(ii) to exchange financial assets or financial liabilities with another entity under conditions that are potentially favourable to the entity; or

(d) a contract that will or may be settled in the entity's own equity instruments and is:

(i) a non-derivative for which the entity is or may be obliged to receive a variable number of the entity's own equity instruments; or
(ii) a derivative that will or may be settled other than by the exchange of a fixed amount of cash or another financial asset for a fixed number of the entity's own equity instruments. For this purpose the entity's own equity instruments do not include puttable financial instruments classified as equity instruments in accordance with paragraphs 16A and 16B, instruments that impose on the entity an obligation to deliver to another party a pro rata share of the net assets of the entity only on liquidation and are classified as equity instruments in accordance with paragraphs 16C and 16D, or instruments that are contracts for the future receipt or delivery of the entity's own equity instruments.†

A financial liability is any liability that is:

(a) a contractual obligation:

(i) to deliver cash or another financial asset to another entity; or
(ii) to exchange financial assets or financial liabilities with another entity under conditions that are potentially unfavourable to the entity; or

***Editor's note**: *Amended in December 2008.*

†**Editor's note**: *Paragraph amended with effect for accounting periods beginning on or after 1 January 2010.*

(b) a contract that will or may be settled in the entity's own equity instruments and is:

(i) a non-derivative for which the entity may be obliged to deliver a variable number of the entity's own equity instruments; or

(ii) a derivative that will or may be settled other than by the exchange of a fixed amount of cash or another financial asset for a fixed number of the entity's own equity instruments. For this purpose, rights, options or warrants to acquire a fixed number of the entity's own equity instruments for a fixed amount of any currency are equity instruments if the entity offers the rights, options or warrants pro rata to all of its existing owners of the same class of its own non-derivative equity instruments. Also, for these purposes the entity's own equity instruments do not include instruments that are themselves contracts for the future receipt or delivery of the entity's own instruments.

(iii) a derivative that will or may be settled other than by the exchange of a fixed amount of cash or another financial asset for a fixed number of the entity's own equity instruments. For this purpose the entity's own equity instruments do not include puttable financial instruments that are classified as equity instruments in accordance with paragraphs 16A and 16B, instruments that impose on the entity an obligation to deliver to another party a pro rata share of the net assets of the entity only on liquidation and are classified as equity instruments in accordance with paragraphs 16C and 16D, or instruments that are contracts for the future receipt or delivery of the entity's own equity instruments

As an exception, an instrument that meets the definition of a financial liability is classified as an equity instrument if it has all the features and meets the conditions in paragraphs 16A and 16B or paragraphs 16C and 16D.*

An equity instrument is any contract that evidences a residual interest in the assets of an entity after deducting all of its liabilities.

Fair value is the amount for which an asset could be exchanged, or a liability settled, between knowledgeable, willing parties in an arm's length transaction.

A* **puttable instrument** *is a financial instrument that gives the holder the right to put the instrument back to the issuer for cash or another financial asset or is automatically put back to the issuer on the occurrence of an uncertain future event or the death or retirement of the instrument holder.†

The following terms are defined in paragraph 9 of FRS 26 and are used in this Standard with the meaning specified in FRS 26. **12**

- amortised cost of a financial asset or financial liability
- available-for-sale financial assets
- derecognition
- derivative
- effective interest method
- financial asset or financial liability at fair value through profit or loss
- financial guarantee contract‡
- firm commitment
- forecast transaction

****Editor's note**: *Paragraph amended with effect for accounting periods beginning on or after 1 January 2010.*

†***Editor's note**: Paragraph added with effect for accounting periods beginning on or after 1 January 2010.*

‡***Editor's note:** Added with effect from 1 January 2006.*

- hedge effectiveness
- hedged item
- hedging instrument
- held-to-maturity investments
- loans and receivables
- regular way purchase or sale
- transaction costs.

13 In this Standard, 'contract' and 'contractual' refer to an agreement between two or more parties that has clear economic consequences that the parties have little, if any, discretion to avoid, usually because the agreement is enforceable by law. Contracts, and thus financial instruments, may take a variety of forms and need not be in writing.

14 In this Standard, 'entity' includes individuals, partnerships, incorporated bodies, trusts and government agencies.

PRESENTATION

Liabilities and Equity (see also paragraphs AG13-AG145 and AG25-AG29)

15 ***The issuer of a financial instrument shall classify the instrument, or its component parts, on initial recognition as a financial liability, a financial asset or an equity instrument in accordance with the substance of the contractual arrangement and the definitions of a financial liability, a financial asset and an equity instrument.***

16 When an issuer applies the definitions in paragraph 11 to determine whether a financial instrument is an equity instrument rather than a financial liability, the instrument is an equity instrument if, and only if, both conditions (a) and (b) below are met.

(a) The instrument includes no contractual obligation:

(i) to deliver cash or another financial asset to another entity; or
(ii) to exchange financial assets or financial liabilities with another entity under conditions that are potentially unfavourable to the issuer.

(b) If the instrument will or may be settled in the issuer's own equity instruments, it is:

(i) a non-derivative that includes no contractual obligation for the issuer to deliver a variable number of its own equity instruments; or
(ii) a derivative that will be settled only by the issuer exchanging a fixed amount of cash or another financial asset for a fixed number of its own equity instruments. For this purpose the issuer's own equity instruments do not include instruments that have all the features and meet the conditions described in paragraphs 16A and 16B or paragraphs 16C and 16D, or instruments that are contracts for the future receipt or delivery of the issuer's own equity instruments.

A contractual obligation, including one arising from a derivative financial instrument, that will or may result in the future receipt or delivery of the issuer's own equity instruments, but does not meet conditions (a) and (b) above, is not an equity instrument. As an exception, an instrument that meets the definition of a financial liability is classified as an equity instrument if it has all the features and meets the conditions in paragraphs 16A and 16B or paragraphs 16C and 16D.*

Puttable instruments

A puttable financial instrument includes a contractual obligation for the issuer to repurchase or redeem that instrument for cash or another financial asset on exercise of the put. As an exception to the definition of a financial liability, an instrument that includes such an obligation is classified as an equity instrument if it has all the following features: **16A**

(a) It entitles the holder to a pro rata share of the entity's net assets in the event of the entity's liquidation. The entity's net assets are those assets that remain after deducting all other claims on its assets. A pro rata share is determined by:

   (i) dividing the entity's net assets on liquidation into units of equal amount; and

   (ii) multiplying that amount by the number of the units held by the financial instrument holder.

(b) The instrument is in the class of instruments that is subordinate to all other classes of instruments. To be in such a class the instrument:

   (i) has no priority over other claims to the assets of the entity on liquidation, and

   (ii) does not need to be converted into another instrument before it is in the class of instruments that is subordinate to all other classes of instruments.

(c) All financial instruments in the class of instruments that is subordinate to all other classes of instruments have identical features. For example, they must all be puttable, and the formula or other method used to calculate the repurchase or redemption price is the same for all instruments in that class.

(d) Apart from the contractual obligation for the issuer to repurchase or redeem the instrument for cash or another financial asset, the instrument does not include any contractual obligation to deliver cash or another financial asset to another entity, or to exchange financial assets or financial liabilities with another entity under conditions that are potentially unfavourable to the entity, and it is not a contract that will or may be settled in the entity's own equity instruments as set out in subparagraph (b) of the definition of a financial liability.

(e) The total expected cash flows attributable to the instrument over the life of the instrument are based substantially on the profit or loss, the change in the recognised net assets or the change in the fair value of the recognised and unrecognised net assets of the entity over the life of the instrument (excluding any effects of the instrument).

For an instrument to be classified as an equity instrument, in addition to the instrument having all the above features, the issuer must have no other financial instrument or contract that has: **16B**

(a) total cash flows based substantially on the profit or loss, the change in the recognised net assets or the change in the fair value of the recognised and unrecognised net assets of the entity (excluding any effects of such instrument or contract) and

***Editor's note**: Paragraph amended with effect for accounting periods beginning on or after 1 January 2010, and paragraphs 16A to 16F added.*

(b) the effect of substantially restricting or fixing the residual return to the puttable instrument holders.

For the purposes of applying this condition, the entity shall not consider non-financial contracts with a holder of an instrument described in paragraph 16A that have contractual terms and conditions that are similar to the contractual terms and conditions of an equivalent contract that might occur between a non-instrument holder and the issuing entity. If the entity cannot determine that this condition is met, it shall not classify the puttable instrument as an equity instrument.

Instruments, or components of instruments, that impose on the entity an obligation to deliver to another party a pro rata share of the net assets of the entity only on liquidation

16C Some financial instruments include a contractual obligation for the issuing entity to deliver to another entity a pro rata share of its net assets only on liquidation. The obligation arises because liquidation either is certain to occur and outside the control of the entity (for example, a limited life entity) or is uncertain to occur but is at the option of the instrument holder. As an exception to the definition of a financial liability, an instrument that includes such an obligation is classified as an equity instrument if it has all the following features:

(a) It entitles the holder to a pro rata share of the entity's net assets in the event of the entity's liquidation. The entity's net assets are those assets that remain after deducting all other claims on its assets. A pro rata share is determined by:

  (i) dividing the net assets of the entity on liquidation into units of equal amount; and
  (ii) multiplying that amount by the number of the units held by the financial instrument holder.

(b) The instrument is in the class of instruments that is subordinate to all other classes of instruments. To be in such a class the instrument:

  (i) has no priority over other claims to the assets of the entity on liquidation, and
  (ii) does not need to be converted into another instrument before it is in the class of instruments that is subordinate to all other classes of instruments.

(c) All financial instruments in the class of instruments that is subordinate to all other classes of instruments must have an identical contractual obligation for the issuing entity to deliver a pro rata share of its net assets on liquidation.

16D For an instrument to be classified as an equity instrument, in addition to the instrument having all the above features, the issuer must have no other financial instrument or contract that has:

(a) total cash flows based substantially on the profit or loss, the change in the recognised net assets or the change in the fair value of the recognised and unrecognised net assets of the entity (excluding any effects of such instrument or contract) and
(b) the effect of substantially restricting or fixing the residual return to the instrument holders.

For the purposes of applying this condition, the entity shall not consider non-financial contracts with a holder of an instrument described in paragraph 16C that have contractual terms and conditions that are similar to the contractual terms and conditions of an equivalent contract that might occur between a non-instrument holder and the issuing entity. If the entity cannot determine that this condition is met, it shall not classify the instrument as an equity instrument.

Reclassification of puttable instruments and instruments that impose on the entity an obligation to deliver to another party a pro rata share of the net assets of the entity only on liquidation

An entity shall classify a financial instrument as an equity instrument in accordance with paragraphs 16A and 16B or paragraphs 16C and 16D from the date when the instrument has all the features and meets the conditions set out in those paragraphs. An entity shall reclassify a financial instrument from the date when the instrument ceases to have all the features or meet all the conditions set out in those paragraphs. For example, if an entity redeems all its issued non-puttable instruments and any puttable instruments that remain outstanding have all the features and meet all the conditions in paragraphs 16A and 16B, the entity shall reclassify the puttable instruments as equity instruments from the date when it redeems the non-puttable instruments. **16E**

An entity shall account as follows for the reclassification of an instrument in accordance with paragraph 16E: **16F**

(a) It shall reclassify an equity instrument as a financial liability from the date when the instrument ceases to have all the features or meet the conditions in paragraphs 16A and 16B or paragraphs 16C and 16D. The financial liability shall be measured at the instrument's fair value at the date of reclassification. The entity shall recognise in equity any difference between the carrying value of the equity instrument and the fair value of the financial liability at the date of reclassification.

(b) It shall reclassify a financial liability as equity from the date when the instrument has all the features and meets the conditions set out in paragraphs 16A and 16B or paragraphs 16C and 16D. An equity instrument shall be measured at the carrying value of the financial liability at the date of reclassification.

No Contractual Obligation to Deliver Cash or Another Financial Asset (paragraph 16(a))

With the exception of the circumstances described in paragraphs 16A and 16B or paragraphs 16C and 16D, a critical feature in differentiating a financial liability from an equity instrument is the existence of a contractual obligation of one party to the financial instrument (the issuer) either to deliver cash or another financial asset to the other party (the holder) or to exchange financial assets or financial liabilities with the holder under conditions that are potentially unfavourable to the issuer. Although the holder of an equity instrument may be entitled to receive a pro rata share of any dividends or other distributions of equity, the issuer does not have a contractual obligation to make such distributions because it cannot be required to deliver cash or another financial asset to another party.* **17**

The substance of a financial instrument, rather than its legal form, governs its classification in the entity's statement of financial position. Substance and legal form are commonly consistent, but not always. Some financial instruments take the legal form of equity but are liabilities in substance and others may combine features associated with equity instruments and features associated with financial liabilities. For example: **18**

* ***Editor's note**: Paragraph amended with effect for accounting periods beginning on or after 1 January 2010.*

(a) a preference share that provides for mandatory redemption by the issuer for a fixed or determinable amount at a fixed or determinable future date, or gives the holder the right to require the issuer to redeem the instrument at or after a particular date for a fixed or determinable amount, is a financial liability.

(b) a financial instrument that gives the holder the right to put it back to the issuer for cash or another financial asset (a 'puttable instrument') is a financial liability, except for those instruments classified as equity instruments in accordance with paragraphs 16A and 16B or paragraphs 16C and 16D. The financial instrument is a financial liability even when the amount of cash or other financial assets is determined on the basis of an index or other item that has the potential to increase or decrease. The existence of an option for the holder to put the instrument back to the issuer for cash or another financial asset means that the puttable instrument meets the definition of a financial liability, except for those instruments classified as equity instruments in accordance with paragraphs 16A and 16B or paragraphs 16C and 16D. For example, open-ended mutual funds, unit trusts, partnerships and some co-operative entities may provide their unitholders or members with a right to redeem their interests in the issuer at any time for cash, which results in the unitholders' or members' interests being classified as financial liabilities, except for those instruments classified as equity instruments in accordance with paragraphs 16A and 16B or paragraphs 16C and 16D. However, classification as a financial liability does not preclude the use of descriptors such as 'net asset value attributable to unitholders' and 'change in net asset value attributable to unitholders' in the financial statements of an entity that has no contributed equity (such as some mutual funds and unit trusts, see Illustrative Example 7) or the use of additional disclosure to show that total members' interests comprise items such as reserves that meet the definition of equity and puttable instruments that do not (see Illustrative Example 8).*

19 If an entity does not have an unconditional right to avoid delivering cash or another financial asset to settle a contractual obligation, the obligation meets the definition of a financial liability, except for those instruments classified as equity instruments in accordance with paragraphs 16A and 16B or paragraphs 16C and 16D. For example:†

(a) a restriction on the ability of an entity to satisfy a contractual obligation, such as lack of access to foreign currency or the need to obtain approval for payment from a regulatory authority, does not negate the entity's contractual obligation or the holder's contractual right under the instrument.

(b) a contractual obligation that is conditional on a counterparty exercising its right to redeem is a financial liability because the entity does not have the unconditional right to avoid delivering cash or another financial asset.

20 A financial instrument that does not explicitly establish a contractual obligation to deliver cash or another financial asset may establish an obligation indirectly through its terms and conditions. For example:

(a) a financial instrument may contain a non-financial obligation that must be settled if, and only if, the entity fails to make distributions or to redeem the instrument. If the entity can avoid a transfer of cash or another financial asset only by settling the non-financial obligation, the financial instrument is a financial liability.

****Editor's note**: Paragraph amended with effect for accounting periods beginning on or after 1 January 2010.*

†***Editor's note**: Paragraph amended with effect for accounting periods beginning on or after 1 January 2010.*

(b) a financial instrument is a financial liability if it provides that on settlement the entity will deliver either:

   (i) cash or another financial asset; or
   (ii) its own shares whose value is determined to exceed substantially the value of the cash or other financial asset.

   Although the entity does not have an explicit contractual obligation to deliver cash or another financial asset, the value of the share settlement alternative is such that the entity will settle in cash. In any event, the holder has in substance been guaranteed receipt of an amount that is at least equal to the cash settlement option (see paragraph 21).

Settlement in the Entity's Own Equity Instruments (paragraph 16(b))

A contract is not an equity instrument solely because it may result in the receipt or delivery of the entity's own equity instruments. An entity may have a contractual right or obligation to receive or deliver a number of its own shares or other equity instruments that varies so that the fair value of the entity's own equity instruments to be received or delivered equals the amount of the contractual right or obligation. Such a contractual right or obligation may be for a fixed amount or an amount that fluctuates in part or in full in response to changes in a variable other than the market price of the entity's own equity instruments (eg an interest rate, a commodity price or a financial instrument price). Two examples are (a) a contract to deliver as many of the entity's own equity instruments as are equal in value to CU100,* and (b) a contract to deliver as many of the entity's own equity instruments as are equal in value to the value of 100 ounces of gold. Such a contract is a financial liability of the entity even though the entity must or can settle it by delivering its own equity instruments. It is not an equity instrument because the entity uses a variable number of its own equity instruments as a means to settle the contract. Accordingly, the contract does not evidence a residual interest in the entity's assets after deducting all of its liabilities. **21**

Except as stated in paragraph 22A, a contract that will be settled by the entity (receiving or) delivering a fixed number of its own equity instruments in exchange for a fixed amount of cash or another financial asset is an equity instrument. For example, an issued share option that gives the counterparty a right to buy a fixed number of the entity's shares for a fixed price or for a fixed stated principal amount of a bond is an equity instrument. Changes in the fair value of a contract arising from variations in market interest rates that do not affect the amount of cash or other financial assets to be paid or received, or the number of equity instruments to be received or delivered, on settlement of the contract do not preclude the contract from being an equity instrument. Any consideration received (such as the premium received for a written option or warrant on the entity's own shares) is added directly to equity. Any consideration paid (such as the premium paid for a purchased option) is deducted directly from equity. Changes in the fair value of an equity instrument are not recognised in the financial statements. **22**

If the entity's own equity instruments to be received, or delivered, by the entity upon settlement of a contract are puttable financial instruments with all the features and meeting the conditions described in paragraphs 16A and 16B, or instruments that impose on the entity an obligation to deliver to another party a pro rata share of the net assets of the entity only on liquidation with all the features and meeting the conditions described in paragraphs 16C and 16D, the contract is a financial asset or a **22A**

**In this Standard, monetary amounts are denominated in 'currency units' (CU).*

financial liability. This includes a contract that will be settled by the entity receiving or delivering a fixed number of such instruments in exchange for a fixed amount of cash or another financial asset.

23 With the exception of the circumstances described in paragraphs 16A and 16B or paragraphs 16C and 16D, a contract that contains an obligation for an entity to purchase its own equity instruments for cash or another financial asset gives rise to a financial liability for the present value of the redemption amount (for example, for the present value of the forward repurchase price, option exercise price or other redemption amount). This is the case even if the contract itself is an equity instrument. One example is an entity's obligation under a forward contract to purchase its own equity instruments for cash. When the financial liability is recognised initially under IAS 39, its fair value (the present value of the redemption amount) is reclassified from equity. Subsequently, the financial liability is measured in accordance with IAS 39. If the contract expires without delivery, the carrying amount of the financial liability is reclassified to equity. An entity's contractual obligation to purchase its own equity instruments gives rise to a financial liability for the present value of the redemption amount even if the obligation to purchase is conditional on the counterparty exercising a right to redeem (eg a written put option that gives the counterparty the right to sell an entity's own equity instruments to the entity for a fixed price).*

24 A contract that will be settled by the entity delivering or receiving a fixed number of its own equity instruments in exchange for a variable amount of cash or another financial asset is a financial asset or financial liability. An example is a contract for the entity to deliver 100 of its own equity instruments in return for an amount of cash calculated to equal the value of 100 ounces of gold.

Contingent Settlement Provisions

25 A financial instrument may require the entity to deliver cash or another financial asset, or otherwise to settle it in such a way that it would be a financial liability, in the event of the occurrence or non-occurrence of uncertain future events (or on the outcome of uncertain circumstances) that are beyond the control of both the issuer and the holder of the instrument, such as a change in a stock market index, consumer price index, interest rate or taxation requirements, or the issuer's future revenues, net income or debt-to-equity ratio. The issuer of such an instrument does not have the unconditional right to avoid delivering cash or another financial asset (or otherwise to settle it in such a way that it would be a financial liability). Therefore, it is a financial liability of the issuer unless:

(a) the part of the contingent settlement provision that could require settlement in cash or another financial asset (or otherwise in such a way that it would be a financial liability) is not genuine; or
(b) the issuer can be required to settle the obligation in cash or another financial asset (or otherwise to settle it in such a way that it would be a financial liability) only in the event of liquidation of the issuer; or
(c) the instrument has all the features and meets the conditions in paragraphs 16A and 16B.†

****Editor's note:*** *Paragraphs 22 and 23 amended, and paragraph 22A added, with effect for accounting periods beginning on or after 1 January 2010.*

†***Editor's note:*** *Sub-paragraph (c) added with effect for accounting periods beginning on or after 1 January 2010.*

Settlement Options

When a derivative financial instrument gives one party a choice over how it is settled (eg the issuer or the holder can choose settlement net in cash or by exchanging shares for cash), it is a financial asset or a financial liability unless all of the settlement alternatives would result in it being an equity instrument. 26

An example of a derivative financial instrument with a settlement option that is a financial liability is a share option that the issuer can decide to settle net in cash or by exchanging its own shares for cash. Similarly, some contracts to buy or sell a non-financial item in exchange for the entity's own equity instruments are within the scope of this Standard because they can be settled either by delivery of the non-financial item or net in cash or another financial instrument (see paragraphs 8-10). Such contracts are financial assets or financial liabilities and not equity instruments. 27

Compound Financial Instruments (see also paragraphs AG30-AG35 and Illustrative Examples 9-12)

The issuer of a non-derivative financial instrument shall evaluate the terms of the financial instrument to determine whether it contains both a liability and an equity component. Such components shall be classified separately as financial liabilities, financial assets or equity instruments in accordance with paragraph 15. 28

An entity recognises separately the components of a financial instrument that (a) creates a financial liability of the entity and (b) grants an option to the holder of the instrument to convert it into an equity instrument of the entity. For example, a bond or similar instrument convertible by the holder into a fixed number of ordinary shares of the entity is a compound financial instrument. From the perspective of the entity, such an instrument comprises two components: a financial liability (a contractual arrangement to deliver cash or another financial asset) and an equity instrument (a call option granting the holder the right, for a specified period of time, to convert it into a fixed number of ordinary shares of the entity). The economic effect of issuing such an instrument is substantially the same as issuing simultaneously a debt instrument with an early settlement provision and warrants to purchase ordinary shares, or issuing a debt instrument with detachable share purchase warrants. Accordingly, in all cases, the entity presents the liability and equity components separately on its balance sheet. 29

Classification of the liability and equity components of a convertible instrument is not revised as a result of a change in the likelihood that a conversion option will be exercised, even when exercise of the option may appear to have become economically advantageous to some holders. Holders may not always act in the way that might be expected because, for example, the tax consequences resulting from conversion may differ among holders. Furthermore, the likelihood of conversion will change from time to time. The entity's contractual obligation to make future payments remains outstanding until it is extinguished through conversion, maturity of the instrument or some other transaction. 30

IAS 39 deals with the measurement of financial assets and financial liabilities. Equity instruments are instruments that evidence a residual interest in the assets of an entity after deducting all of its liabilities. Therefore, when the initial carrying amount of a compound financial instrument is allocated to its equity and liability components, the equity component is assigned the residual amount after deducting from the fair value of the instrument as a whole the amount separately determined for the liability component. The value of any derivative features (such as a call option) embedded in the compound financial instrument other than the equity component (such as an 31 equity conversion option) is included in the liability component. The sum of the carrying amounts assigned to the liability and equity components on initial recognition is always equal to the fair value that would be ascribed to the instrument as a whole. No gain or loss arises from initially recognising the components of the instrument separately.*

32 Under the approach described in paragraph 31, the issuer of a bond convertible into ordinary shares first determines the carrying amount of the liability component by measuring the fair value of a similar liability (including any embedded non-equity derivative features) that does not have an associated equity component. The carrying amount of the equity instrument represented by the option to convert the instrument into ordinary shares is then determined by deducting the fair value of the financial liability from the fair value of the compound financial instrument as a whole.

Treasury Shares (see also paragraph AG36)

33 ***If an entity reacquires its own equity instruments, those instruments ('treasury shares') shall be deducted from equity. No gain or loss shall be recognised in profit or loss on the purchase, sale, issue or cancellation of an entity's own equity instruments. Such treasury shares may be acquired and held by the entity or by other members of the consolidated group. Consideration paid or received shall be recognised directly in equity.***

34 The amount of treasury shares held is disclosed separately either on the face of the balance sheet or in the notes. An entity provides disclosure in accordance with FRS 8 *Related Party Disclosures* if the entity reacquires its own equity instruments from related parties.

Interest, Dividends, Losses and Gains (see also paragraph AG37)

35 ***Interest, dividends, losses and gains relating to a financial instrument or a component that is a financial liability shall be recognised as income or expense in profit or loss. Distributions to holders of an equity instrument shall be debited by the entity directly to equity, net of any related income tax benefit. Transaction costs of an equity transaction, other than costs of issuing an equity instrument that are directly attributable to the acquisition of a business (which shall be accounted for under FRS 6*** **Acquisitions and Mergers*****), shall be accounted for as a deduction from equity, net of any related income tax benefit.***

36 The classification of a financial instrument as a financial liability or an equity instrument determines whether interest, dividends, losses and gains relating to that instrument are recognised as income or expense in profit or loss. Thus, dividend payments on shares wholly recognised as liabilities are recognised as expenses in the same way as interest on a bond. Similarly, gains and losses associated with redemptions or refinancings of financial liabilities are recognised in profit or loss, whereas redemptions or refinancings of equity instruments are recognised as changes in equity. Changes in the fair value of an equity instrument are not recognised in the financial statements.

37 An entity typically incurs various costs in issuing or acquiring its own equity instruments. Those costs might include registration and other regulatory fees, amounts paid to legal, accounting and other professional advisers, printing costs and stamp duties. The transaction costs of an equity transaction are accounted for as a

***Editor's note:** *Amended by amendments to FRS 26. Reference to IAS 39 should be read as reference to FRS 26.*

deduction from equity (net of any related income tax benefit) to the extent they are incremental costs directly attributable to the equity transaction that otherwise would have been avoided. The costs of an equity transaction that is abandoned are recognised as an expense.

Transaction costs that relate to the issue of a compound financial instrument are allocated to the liability and equity components of the instrument in proportion to the allocation of proceeds. Transaction costs that relate jointly to more than one transaction (for example, costs of a concurrent offering of some shares and a stock exchange listing of other shares) are allocated to those transactions using a basis of allocation that is rational and consistent with similar transactions. **38**

The amount of transaction costs accounted for as a deduction from equity in the period shall be disclosed separately. **39**

Dividends classified as an expense may be presented in the income statement either with interests on other liabilities or as a separate item. In addition to the requirements of this Standard, disclosure of interests and dividends is subject to the requirements of FRS 29. In some circumstances, because of the differences between interest and dividends with respect to matters such as tax deductibility, it is desirable to disclose them separately in the income statement.* **40**

Gains and losses related to changes in the carrying amount of a financial liability are recognised as income or expense in profit or loss even when they relate to an instrument that includes a right to the residual interest in the assets of the entity in exchange for cash or another financial asset (see paragraph 18(b)). **41**

Offsetting a Financial Asset and a Financial Liability (see also paragraphs AG38 and AG39)

A financial asset and a financial liability shall be offset and the net amount presented in the balance sheet when, and only when, an entity: **42**

(a) currently has a legally enforceable right to set off the recognised amounts; and
(b) intends either to settle on a net basis, or to realise the asset and settle the liability simultaneously.

In accounting for a transfer of a financial asset that does not qualify for derecognition, the entity shall not offset the transferred asset and the associated liability (see IAS 39, paragraph 36).†

This Standard requires the presentation of financial assets and financial liabilities on a net basis when doing so reflects an entity's expected future cash flows from settling two or more separate financial instruments. When an entity has the right to receive or pay a single net amount and intends to do so, it has, in effect, only a single financial asset or financial liability. In other circumstances, financial assets and financial liabilities are presented separately from each other consistently with their characteristics as resources or obligations of the entity. **43**

Offsetting a recognised financial asset and a recognised financial liability and presenting the net amount differs from the derecognition of a financial asset or a **44**

****Editor's note:*** *Amended by FRS 29 with effect for accounting periods beginning on or after 1 January 2007.*

†***Editor's note:*** *Last sentence added by amendments to FRS 26. Reference to IAS 39 should be read as reference to FRS 26.*

financial liability. Although offsetting does not give rise to recognition of a gain or loss, the derecognition of a financial instrument not only results in the removal of the previously recognised item from the balance sheet but also may result in recognition of a gain or loss.

45 A right of set-off is a debtor's legal right, by contract or otherwise, to settle or otherwise eliminate all or a portion of an amount due to a creditor by applying against that amount an amount due from the creditor. In unusual circumstances, a debtor may have a legal right to apply an amount due from a third party against the amount due to a creditor provided that there is an agreement between the three parties that clearly establishes the debtor's right of set-off. Because the right of setoff is a legal right, the conditions supporting the right may vary from one legal jurisdiction to another and the laws applicable to the relationships between the parties need to be considered.

46 The existence of an enforceable right to set off a financial asset and a financial liability affects the rights and obligations associated with a financial asset and a financial liability and may affect an entity's exposure to credit and liquidity risk. However, the existence of the right, by itself, is not a sufficient basis for offsetting. In the absence of an intention to exercise the right or to settle simultaneously, the amount and timing of an entity's future cash flows are not affected. When an entity intends to exercise the right or to settle simultaneously, presentation of the asset and liability on a net basis reflects more appropriately the amounts and timing of the expected future cash flows, as well as the risks to which those cash flows are exposed. An intention by one or both parties to settle on a net basis without the legal right to do so is not sufficient to justify offsetting because the rights and obligations associated with the individual financial asset and financial liability remain unaltered.

47 An entity's intentions with respect to settlement of particular assets and liabilities may be influenced by its normal business practices, the requirements of the financial markets and other circumstances that may limit the ability to settle net or to settle simultaneously. When an entity has a right of set-off, but does not intend to settle net or to realise the assets and settle the liability simultaneously, the effect of the right on the credit risk exposure is disclosed in accordance with paragraph 36 of FRS 29.*

48 Simultaneous settlement of two financial instruments may occur through, for example, the operation of a clearing house in an organised financial market or a face-to-face exchange. In these circumstances the cash flows are, in effect, equivalent to a single net amount and there is no exposure to credit or liquidity risk. In other circumstances, an entity may settle two instruments by receiving and paying separate amounts, becoming exposed to credit risk for the full amount of the asset or liquidity risk for the full amount of the liability. Such risk exposures may be significant even though relatively brief. Accordingly, realisation of a financial asset and settlement of a financial liability are treated as simultaneous only when the transactions occur at the same moment.

49 The conditions set out in paragraph 42 are generally not satisfied and offsetting is usually inappropriate when:

(a) several different financial instruments are used to emulate the features of a single financial instrument (a 'synthetic instrument');
(b) financial assets and financial liabilities arise from financial instruments having the same primary risk exposure (for example, assets and liabilities within a

***Editor's note:** *Amended by FRS 29 with effect for accounting periods beginning on or after 1 January 2007.*

portfolio of forward contracts or other derivative instruments) but involve different counterparties;
(c) financial or other assets are pledged as collateral for non-recourse financial liabilities;
(d) financial assets are set aside in trust by a debtor for the purpose of discharging an obligation without those assets having been accepted by the creditor in settlement of the obligation (for example, a sinking fund arrangement); or
(e) obligations incurred as a result of events giving rise to losses are expected to be recovered from a third party by virtue of a claim made under an insurance contract.

An entity that undertakes a number of financial instrument transactions with a single counterparty may enter into a 'master netting arrangement' with that counterparty. Such an agreement provides for a single net settlement of all financial instruments covered by the agreement in the event of default on, or termination of, any one contract. These arrangements are commonly used by financial institutions to provide protection against loss in the event of bankruptcy or other circumstances that result in a counterparty being unable to meet its obligations. A master netting arrangement commonly creates a right of set-off that becomes enforceable and affects the realisation or settlement of individual financial assets and financial liabilities only following a specified event of default or in other circumstances not expected to arise in the normal course of business. A master netting arrangement does not provide a basis for offsetting unless both of the criteria in paragraph 42 are satisfied. When financial assets and financial liabilities subject to a master netting arrangement are not offset, the effect of the arrangement on an entity's exposure to credit risk is disclosed in accordance with paragraph 36 of FRS 29.* **50**

***Current liabilities*†**

An entity classifies its financial liabilities as current when they are due to be settled within twelve months after the balance sheet date, even if: **50A**

(a) the original term was for a period longer than twelve months, and
(b) an agreement to refinance, or to reschedule payments, on a long-term basis is completed after the balance sheet date and before the financial statements are authorised for issue.

If an entity expects, and has the discretion, to refinance or roll over an obligation for at least twelve months after the balance sheet date under an existing loan facility, it classifies the obligation as non-current, even if it would otherwise be due within a shorter period. However, when refinancing or rolling over the obligation is not at the discretion of the entity (for example, there is no arrangement for refinancing), the entity does not consider the potential to refinance the obligation as current. **50B**

When an entity breaches a provision of a long-term loan arrangement on or before the balance sheet date, with the effect that the liability becomes payable on demand, it classifies the liability as current, even if the lender agreed, after the balance sheet date and before the authorisation of the financial statements for issue, not to demand payment as a consequence of the breach. An entity classifies the liability as current because, at the balance sheet date, it does not have an unconditional right to defer its settlement for at least twelve months after that date. **50C**

****Editor's note:** *Amended by FRS 29 with effect for accounting periods beginning on or after 1 January 2007.*

†***Editor's note:*** *Paragraphs 50A to 50E amended with effect for accounting periods beginning on or after 1 January 2009.*

50D However, an entity classifies the liability as non-current if the lender agreed by the balance sheet date to provide a period of grace ending at least twelve months after the balance sheet date, within which the entity can rectify the breach and during which the lender cannot demand immediate repayment.

50E In respect of loans classified as current liabilities, if the following events occur between the balance sheet date and the date the financial statements are authorised for issue, those events are disclosed as non-adjusting events in accordance with FRS 21 (IAS 10) *Events after the Balance Sheet Date*:

(a) refinancing on a long-term basis;
(b) rectification of a breach of a long-term loan arrangement; and
(c) the granting by the lender of a period of grace to rectify a breach of a long-term loan arrangement ending at least twelve months after the balance sheet date.

DISCLOSURE REQUIREMENTS FOR PUTTABLE FINANCIAL INSTRUMENTS AND OBLIGATIONS ARISING ON LIQUIDATION CLASSIFIED AS EQUITY*

Information to be presented either in the statement of financial position or in the notes

50F If an entity has reclassified

(a) a puttable financial instrument classified as an equity instrument, or
(b) an instrument that imposes on the entity an obligation to deliver to another party a pro rata share of the net assets of the entity only on liquidation and is classified as an equity instrument

between financial liabilities and equity, it shall disclose the amount reclassified into and out of each category (financial liabilities or equity), and the timing and reason for that reclassification.

Puttable financial instruments classified as equity

50G For puttable financial instruments classified as equity instruments, an entity shall disclose (to the extent not disclosed elsewhere):

(a) summary quantitative data about the amount classified as equity;
(b) its objectives, policies and processes for managing its obligation to repurchase or redeem the instruments when required to do so by the instrument holders, including any changes from the previous period;
(c) the expected cash outflow on redemption or repurchase of that class of financial instruments; and
(d) information about how the expected cash outflow on redemption or repurchase was determined.

Other disclosures

50H An entity shall disclose the following, if not disclosed elsewhere in information published with the financial statements:

***Editor's note:** *Paragraphs 50F to 50H added with effect for accounting periods beginning on or after 1 January 2010.*

(a) the domicile and legal form of the entity, its country of incorporation and the address of its registered office (or principal place of business, if different from the registered office);
(b) a description of the nature of the entity's operations and its principal activities;
(c) the name of the parent and the ultimate parent of the group; and
(d) if it is a limited life entity, information regarding the length of its life.

EFFECTIVE DATE AND TRANSITION

An entity shall apply paragraphs 15 to 50 of this Standard for accounting periods beginning on or after 1 January 2005. Earlier application of these paragraphs of the Standard is not permitted. An entity shall apply paragraphs 51 to 95 of the Standard no later than the accounting period the entity is applying FRS 26. Where, in an accounting period commencing before 1 January 2007, an entity applies the measurement provisions of FRS 26 but not the derecognition provisions of that Standard, it is not required to make the disclosures required by paragraph 94(a).* **96**

Puttable Financial Instruments and Obligations Arising on Liquidation (Amendments to FRS 25), issued in August 2008, required financial instruments that contain all the features and meet the conditions in paragraphs 16A and 16B or paragraphs 16C and 16D to be classified as an equity instrument, amended paragraphs 11, 16, 17–19, 22, 23, 25, AG13, AG14 and AG27, and inserted paragraphs 16A–16F, 22A, 96B, 96C, 97C, AG14A–AG14J and AG29A. An entity shall apply those amendments for annual periods beginning on or after 1 January 2010. Earlier application is permitted only for annual periods beginning on or after 1 January 2009. If an entity applies the changes for an earlier period, it shall disclose that fact and apply the related amendments to FRS 26, FRS 29 and UITF 39 at the same time. **96A**

Puttable Financial Instruments and Obligations Arising on Liquidation introduced a limited scope exception; therefore, an entity shall not apply the exception by analogy. **96B**

The classification of instruments under this exception shall be restricted to the accounting for such an instrument under FRS 25, FRS 36 and FRS 29. The instrument shall not be considered an equity instrument under other guidance, for example FRS 20 (IFRS 2) Share-based Payment.† **96C**

This Standard shall be applied retrospectively, subject to paragraphs 97A and 97B. **97**

This Standard requires an entity to split a compound financial instrument at inception into separate liability and equity components. If the liability component is no longer outstanding, retrospective application of this Standard involves separating two portions of equity. The first portion is in retained earnings and represents the cumulative interest accreted on the liability component. The other portion represents the original equity component. On first applying this Standard, an entity need not separate these two portions if the liability component is no longer outstanding at the date of transition to this Standard. The date of transition to this standard is the beginning of the earliest period for which an entity presents comparative information in compliance with this standard. **97A**

An entity that first adopts the presentation requirements in paragraphs 15 to 50 of this Standard for an accounting period that commences before 1 January 2006, or that adopts the disclosure requirements in paragraphs 51 to 95 of this Standard for **97B**

****Editor's note:*** *Last sentence added by amendments to FRS 26.*

†***Editor's note****: Heading changed and paragraphs 96A to 96C added in August 2008.*

an accounting period that commences before 1 January 2007, need not restate comparative information to comply with those requirements An entity that chooses to present comparative information that does not comply with those requirements in their first year of adoption shall:

(a) apply its existing accounting policies to financial instruments within the scope of this standard and FRS 26 in the comparative information;
(b) disclose this fact together with the basis used to prepare this information; and
(c) disclose the nature of the main adjustments that would make the information comply with this Standard. The entity need not quantify those adjustments. However, the entity shall treat any adjustment between the balance sheet at the comparative period's reporting date (ie the balance sheet that includes comparative information under previous accounting policies) and the balance sheet at the start of the first reporting period that includes information that complies with this Standard and FRS 25 as arising from a change in accounting policy and give the disclosures required by FRS 18 *Accounting Policies*.

97C When applying the amendments described in paragraph 96A, an entity is required to split a compound financial instrument with an obligation to deliver to another party a pro rata share of the net assets of the entity only on liquidation into separate liability and equity components. If the liability component is no longer outstanding, a retrospective application of those amendments to IAS 32 would involve separating two components of equity. The first component would be in retained earnings and represent the cumulative interest accreted on the liability component. The other component would represent the original equity component. Therefore, an entity need not separate these two components if the liability component is no longer outstanding at the date of application of the amendments.*

97D Paragraph 4 was amended by 'Improvements to Financial Reporting Standards' issued in December 2008. An entity shall apply this amendment for annual periods beginning on or after 1 January 2009. Earlier application is permitted. If an entity applies the amendment for an earlier period, it shall disclose that fact and apply the amendments to paragraph 2 of FRS 26 and paragraph 3 of FRS 29. An entity is permitted to apply these amendments prospectively.†

97E Paragraphs 11 and 16 were amended by Classification of Rights Issues issued in October 2009 January 2010. An entity shall apply that amendment for annual periods beginning on or after 1 February 2010. Earlier application is permitted. If an entity applies the amendment for an earlier period, it shall disclose that fact.‡

98A In December 2005 the ASB relocated all disclosures relating to financial instruments to FRS 29 (IFRS 7) *Financial Instruments: Disclosures*.§

****Editor's note**: Paragraph 97C added in August 2008.*

*†**Editor's note**: Paragraph 97D added in December 2008.*

*‡**Editor's note**: Paragraph added in January 2010.*

*§**Editor's note:** This paragraph is added by FRS 29 with effect for accounting periods beginning on or after 1 January 2007.*

Withdrawal of, and amendments to, existing UK Standards and UITF Abstracts

[Not reproduced, as all changes have been made to the underlying standards and abstracts].

Appendix
Application Guidance
FRS 25 Financial Instruments: Disclosure and Presentation

This appendix is an integral part of the Standard.

AG1 This Application Guidance explains the application of particular aspects of the Standard.

AG2 The Standard does not deal with the recognition or measurement of financial instruments. Requirements about the recognition and measurement of financial assets and financial liabilities are set out in FRS 26 (IAS 39) *Financial Instruments: Recognition and Measurement*.*

Definitions (paragraphs 11-14)

Financial Assets and Financial Liabilities

AG3 Currency (cash) is a financial asset because it represents the medium of exchange and is therefore the basis on which all transactions are measured and recognised in financial statements. A deposit of cash with a bank or similar financial institution is a financial asset because it represents the contractual right of the depositor to obtain cash from the institution or to draw a cheque or similar instrument against the balance in favour of a creditor in payment of a financial liability.

AG4 Common examples of financial assets representing a contractual right to receive cash in the future and corresponding financial liabilities representing a contractual obligation to deliver cash in the future are:

(a) trade accounts receivable and payable;
(b) notes receivable and payable;
(c) loans receivable and payable; and
(d) bonds receivable and payable.

In each case, one party's contractual right to receive (or obligation to pay) cash is matched by the other party's corresponding obligation to pay (or right to receive).

AG5 Another type of financial instrument is one for which the economic benefit to be received or given up is a financial asset other than cash. For example, a note payable in government bonds gives the holder the contractual right to receive and the issuer the contractual obligation to deliver government bonds, not cash. The bonds are financial assets because they represent obligations of the issuing government to pay cash. The note is, therefore, a financial asset of the note holder and a financial liability of the note issuer.

AG6 'Perpetual' debt instruments (such as 'perpetual' bonds, debentures and capital notes) normally provide the holder with the contractual right to receive payments on account of interest at fixed dates extending into the indefinite future, either with no right to receive a return of principal or a right to a return of principal under terms that make it very unlikely or very far in the future. For example, an entity may issue

Editor's note: *Reference to FRS 26 altered by amendments to FRS 26 to reflect the change in its title.*

a financial instrument requiring it to make annual payments in perpetuity equal to a stated interest rate of 8 per cent applied to a stated par or principal amount of CU1,000.* Assuming 8 per cent to be the market rate of interest for the instrument when issued, the issuer assumes a contractual obligation to make a stream of future interest payments having a fair value (present value) of CU1,000 on initial recognition. The holder and issuer of the instrument have a financial asset and a financial liability, respectively.

A contractual right or contractual obligation to receive, deliver or exchange financial instruments is itself a financial instrument. A chain of contractual rights or contractual obligations meets the definition of a financial instrument if it will ultimately lead to the receipt or payment of cash or to the acquisition or issue of an equity instrument. **AG7**

The ability to exercise a contractual right or the requirement to satisfy a contractual obligation may be absolute, or it may be contingent on the occurrence of a future event. For example, a financial guarantee is a contractual right of the lender to receive cash from the guarantor, and a corresponding contractual obligation of the guarantor to pay the lender, if the borrower defaults. The contractual right and obligation exist because of a past transaction or event (assumption of the guarantee), even though the lender's ability to exercise its right and the requirement for the guarantor to perform under its obligation are both contingent on a future act of default by the borrower. A contingent right and obligation meet the definition of a financial asset and a financial liability, even though such assets and liabilities are not always recognised in the financial statements. Some of their contingent rights and obligations may be insurance contracts as defined in Appendix C to FRS 26. **AG8**

Under SSAP 21 *Accounting for leases and hire purchase contracts* a finance lease is regarded as primarily an entitlement of the lessor to receive, and an obligation of the lessee to pay, a stream of payments that are substantially the same as blended payments of principal and interest under a loan agreement. The lessor accounts for its investment in the amount receivable under the lease contract rather than the leased asset itself. An operating lease, on the other hand, is regarded as primarily an uncompleted contract committing the lessor to provide the use of an asset in future periods in exchange for consideration similar to a fee for a service. The lessor continues to account for the leased asset itself rather than any amount receivable in the future under the contract. Accordingly, a finance lease is regarded as a financial instrument and an operating lease is not regarded as a financial instrument (except as regards individual payments currently due and payable). **AG9**

Physical assets (such as inventories, property, plant and equipment), leased assets and intangible assets (such as patents and trademarks) are not financial assets. Control of such physical and intangible assets creates an opportunity to generate an inflow of cash or another financial asset, but it does not give rise to a present right to receive cash or another financial asset. **AG10**

Assets (such as prepaid expenses) for which the future economic benefit is the receipt of goods or services, rather than the right to receive cash or another financial asset, are not financial assets. Similarly, items such as deferred revenue and most warranty obligations are not financial liabilities because the outflow of economic benefits associated with them is the delivery of goods and services rather than a contractual obligation to pay cash or another financial asset. **AG11**

**In this guidance, monetary amounts are denominated in 'currency units' (CU).*

AG12 Liabilities or assets that are not contractual (such as income taxes that are created as a result of statutory requirements imposed by governments) are not financial liabilities or financial assets. Accounting for income taxes is dealt with in FRS 16 *Current Tax* and FRS 19 *Deferred Tax*. Similarly, constructive obligations, as defined in FRS 12 *Provisions, Contingent Liabilities and Contingent Assets*, do not arise from contracts and are not financial liabilities.

Equity Instruments

AG13 Examples of equity instruments include non-puttable ordinary shares, some puttable instruments (see paragraphs 16A and 16B), some instruments that impose on the entity an obligation to deliver to another party a pro rata share of the net assets of the entity only on liquidation (see paragraphs 16C and 16D), some types of preference shares (see paragraphs AG25 and AG26), and warrants or written call options that allow the holder to subscribe for or purchase a fixed number of non-puttable ordinary shares in the issuing entity in exchange for a fixed amount of cash or another financial asset. An entity's obligation to issue or purchase a fixed number of its own equity instruments in exchange for a fixed amount of cash or another financial asset is an equity instrument of the entity (except as stated in paragraph 22A). However, if such a contract contains an obligation for the entity to pay cash or another financial asset (other than a contract classified as equity in accordance with paragraphs 16A and 16B or paragraphs 16C and 16D), it also gives rise to a liability for the present value of the redemption amount (see paragraph AG27(a)). An issuer of non-puttable ordinary shares assumes a liability when it formally acts to make a distribution and becomes legally obliged to the shareholders to do so. This may be the case following the declaration of a dividend or when the entity is being wound up and any assets remaining after the satisfaction of liabilities become distributable to shareholders.*

AG14 A purchased call option or other similar contract acquired by an entity that gives it the right to reacquire a fixed number of its own equity instruments in exchange for delivering a fixed amount of cash or another financial asset is not a financial asset of the entity (except as stated in paragraph 22A). Instead, any consideration paid for such a contract is deducted from equity.

The class of instruments that is subordinate to all other classes (paragraphs 16A(b) and 16C(b))

AG14A One of the features of paragraphs 16A and 16C is that the financial instrument is in the class of instruments that is subordinate to all other classes.

AG14B When determining whether an instrument is in the subordinate class, an entity evaluates the instrument's claim on liquidation as if it were to liquidate on the date when it classifies the instrument. An entity shall reassess the classification if there is a change in relevant circumstances. For example, if the entity issues or redeems another financial instrument, this may affect whether the instrument in question is in the class of instruments that is subordinate to all other classes.

AG14C An instrument that has a preferential right on liquidation of the entity is not an instrument with an entitlement to a pro rata share of the net assets of the entity. For example, an instrument has a preferential right on liquidation if it entitles the holder to a fixed dividend on liquidation, in addition to a share of the entity's net assets,

***Editor's note:** *Paragraphs AG13 and AG14 were replaced and paragraphs AG41A to AG14J added in August 2008.*

when other instruments in the subordinate class with a right to a pro rata share of the net assets of the entity do not have the same right on liquidation.

If an entity has only one class of financial instruments, that class shall be treated as if it were subordinate to all other classes. **AG14D**

Total expected cash flows attributable to the instrument over the life of the instrument (paragraph 16A(e))

The total expected cash flows of the instrument over the life of the instrument must be substantially based on the profit or loss, change in the recognised net assets or fair value of the recognised and unrecognised net assets of the entity over the life of the instrument. Profit or loss and the change in the recognised net assets shall be measured in accordance with the relevant standards. **AG14E**

Transactions entered into by an instrument holder other than as owner of the entity (paragraphs 16A and 16C)

The holder of a puttable financial instrument or an instrument that imposes on the entity an obligation to deliver to another party a pro rata share of the net assets of the entity only on liquidation may enter into transactions with the entity in a role other than that of an owner. For example, an instrument holder may also be an employee of the entity. Only the cash flows and the contractual terms and conditions of the instrument that relate to the instrument holder as an owner of the entity shall be considered when assessing whether the instrument should be classified as equity under paragraph 16A or paragraph 16C. **AG14F**

An example is a limited partnership that has limited and general partners. Some general partners may provide a guarantee to the entity and may be remunerated for providing that guarantee. In such situations, the guarantee and the associated cash flows relate to the instrument holders in their role as guarantors and not in their roles as owners of the entity. Therefore, such a guarantee and the associated cash flows would not result in the general partners being considered subordinate to the limited partners, and would be disregarded when assessing whether the contractual terms of the limited partnership instruments and the general partnership instruments are identical. **AG14G**

Another example is a profit or loss sharing arrangement that allocates profit or loss to the instrument holders on the basis of services rendered or business generated during the current and previous years. Such arrangements are transactions with instrument holders in their role as non-owners and should not be considered when assessing the features listed in paragraph 16A or paragraph 16C. However, profit or loss sharing arrangements that allocate profit or loss to instrument holders based on the nominal amount of their instruments relative to others in the class represent transactions with the instrument holders in their roles as owners and should be considered when assessing the features listed in paragraph 16A or paragraph 16C. **AG14H**

The cash flows and contractual terms and conditions of a transaction between the instrument holder (in the role as a non-owner) and the issuing entity must be similar to an equivalent transaction that might occur between a non-instrument holder and the issuing entity. **AG14I**

No other financial instrument or contract with total cash flows that substantially fixes or restricts the residual return to the instrument holder (paragraphs 16B and 16D)

AG14J A condition for classifying as equity a financial instrument that otherwise meets the criteria in paragraph 16A or paragraph 16C is that the entity has no other financial instrument or contract that has (a) total cash flows based substantially on the profit or loss, the change in the recognised net assets or the change in the fair value of the recognised and unrecognised net assets of the entity and (b) the effect of substantially restricting or fixing the residual return. The following instruments, when entered into on normal commercial terms with unrelated parties, are unlikely to prevent instruments that otherwise meet the criteria in paragraph 16A or paragraph 16C from being classified as equity:

(a) instruments with total cash flows substantially based on specific assets of the entity.
(b) instruments with total cash flows based on a percentage of revenue.
(c) contracts designed to reward individual employees for services rendered to the entity.
(d) contracts requiring the payment of an insignificant percentage of profit for services rendered or goods provided.

Derivative Financial Instruments

AG15 Financial instruments include primary instruments (such as receivables, payables and equity instruments) and derivative financial instruments (such as financial options, futures and forwards, interest rate swaps and currency swaps). Derivative financial instruments meet the definition of a financial instrument and, accordingly, are within the scope of this Standard.

AG16 Derivative financial instruments create rights and obligations that have the effect of transferring between the parties to the instrument one or more of the financial risks inherent in an underlying primary financial instrument. On inception, derivative financial instruments give one party a contractual right to exchange financial assets or financial liabilities with another party under conditions that are potentially favourable, or a contractual obligation to exchange financial assets or financial liabilities with another party under conditions that are potentially unfavourable. However, they generally* do not result in a transfer of the underlying primary financial instrument on inception of the contract, nor does such a transfer necessarily take place on maturity of the contract. Some instruments embody both a right and an obligation to make an exchange. Because the terms of the exchange are determined on inception of the derivative instrument, as prices in financial markets change those terms may become either favourable or unfavourable.

AG17 A put or call option to exchange financial assets or financial liabilities (ie financial instruments other than an entity's own equity instruments) gives the holder a right to obtain potential future economic benefits associated with changes in the fair value of the financial instrument underlying the contract. Conversely, the writer of an option assumes an obligation to forgo potential future economic benefits or bear potential losses of economic benefits associated with changes in the fair value of the underlying financial instrument. The contractual right of the holder and obligation of the writer meet the definition of a financial asset and a financial liability, respectively. The financial instrument underlying an option contract may be any financial asset, including shares in other entities and interestbearing instruments. An option may

**This is true of most, but not all derivatives, eg in some cross-currency interest rate swaps principal is exchanged on inception (and re-exchanged on maturity).*

require the writer to issue a debt instrument, rather than transfer a financial asset, but the instrument underlying the option would constitute a financial asset of the holder if the option were exercised. The option-holder's right to exchange the financial asset under potentially favourable conditions and the writer's obligation to exchange the financial asset under potentially unfavourable conditions are distinct from the underlying financial asset to be exchanged upon exercise of the option. The nature of the holder's right and of the writer's obligation are not affected by the likelihood that the option will be exercised.

Another example of a derivative financial instrument is a forward contract to be settled in six months' time in which one party (the purchaser) promises to deliver CU1,000,000 cash in exchange for CU1,000,000 face amount of fixed rate government bonds, and the other party (the seller) promises to deliver CU1,000,000 face amount of fixed rate government bonds in exchange for CU1,000,000 cash. During the six months, both parties have a contractual right and a contractual obligation to exchange financial instruments. If the market price of the government bonds rises above CU1,000,000, the conditions will be favourable to the purchaser and unfavourable to the seller; if the market price falls below CU1,000,000, the effect will be the opposite. The purchaser has a contractual right (a financial asset) similar to the right under a call option held and a contractual obligation (a financial liability) similar to the obligation under a put option written; the seller has a contractual right (a financial asset) similar to the right under a put option held and a contractual obligation (a financial liability) similar to the obligation under a call option written. As with options, these contractual rights and obligations constitute financial assets and financial liabilities separate and distinct from the underlying financial instruments (the bonds and cash to be exchanged). Both parties to a forward contract have an obligation to perform at the agreed time, whereas performance under an option contract occurs only if and when the holder of the option chooses to exercise it. **AG18**

Many other types of derivative instruments embody a right or obligation to make a future exchange, including interest rate and currency swaps, interest rate caps, collars and floors, loan commitments, note issuance facilities and letters of credit. An interest rate swap contract may be viewed as a variation of a forward contract in which the parties agree to make a series of future exchanges of cash amounts, one amount calculated with reference to a floating interest rate and the other with reference to a fixed interest rate. Futures contracts are another variation of forward contracts, differing primarily in that the contracts are standardised and traded on an exchange. **AG19**

Contracts to Buy or Sell Non-Financial Items (paragraphs 8-10)

Contracts to buy or sell non-financial items do not meet the definition of a financial instrument because the contractual right of one party to receive a nonfinancial asset or service and the corresponding obligation of the other party do not establish a present right or obligation of either party to receive, deliver or exchange a financial asset. For example, contracts that provide for settlement only by the receipt or delivery of a non-financial item (eg an option, futures or forward contract on silver) are not financial instruments. Many commodity contracts are of this type. Some are standardised in form and traded on organised markets in much the same fashion as some derivative financial instruments. For example, a commodity futures contract may be bought and sold readily for cash because it is listed for trading on an exchange and may change hands many times. However, the parties buying and selling the contract are, in effect, trading the underlying commodity. The ability to buy or sell a commodity contract for cash, the ease with which it may be bought or sold and the possibility of negotiating a cash settlement of the obligation to receive or **AG20** deliver the commodity do not alter the fundamental character of the contract in a way that creates a financial instrument. Nevertheless, some contracts to buy or sell non-financial items that can be settled net or by exchanging financial instruments, or in which the non-financial item is readily convertible to cash, are within the scope of the Standard as if they were financial instruments (see paragraph 8).

AG21 A contract that involves the receipt or delivery of physical assets does not give rise to a financial asset of one party and a financial liability of the other party unless any corresponding payment is deferred past the date on which the physical assets are transferred. Such is the case with the purchase or sale of goods on trade credit.

AG22 Some contracts are commodity-linked, but do not involve settlement through the physical receipt or delivery of a commodity. They specify settlement through cash payments that are determined according to a formula in the contract, rather than through payment of fixed amounts. For example, the principal amount of a bond may be calculated by applying the market price of oil prevailing at the maturity of the bond to a fixed quantity of oil. The principal is indexed by reference to a commodity price, but is settled only in cash. Such a contract constitutes a financial instrument.

AG23 The definition of a financial instrument also encompasses a contract that gives rise to a non-financial asset or non-financial liability in addition to a financial asset or financial liability. Such financial instruments often give one party an option to exchange a financial asset for a non-financial asset. For example, an oil-linked bond may give the holder the right to receive a stream of fixed periodic interest payments and a fixed amount of cash on maturity, with the option to exchange the principal amount for a fixed quantity of oil. The desirability of exercising this option will vary from time to time depending on the fair value of oil relative to the exchange ratio of cash for oil (the exchange price) inherent in the bond. The intentions of the bondholder concerning the exercise of the option do not affect the substance of the component assets. The financial asset of the holder and the financial liability of the issuer make the bond a financial instrument, regardless of the other types of assets and liabilities also created.

AG24 [Withdrawn]*

PRESENTATION

Liabilities and Equity (paragraphs 15-27)

No Contractual Obligation to Deliver Cash or Another Financial Asset (paragraphs 17-20)

AG25 Preference shares may be issued with various rights. In determining whether a preference share is a financial liability or an equity instrument, an issuer assesses the particular rights attaching to the share to determine whether it exhibits the fundamental characteristic of a financial liability. For example, a preference share that provides for redemption on a specific date or at the option of the holder contains a financial liability because the issuer has an obligation to transfer financial assets to the holder of the share. The potential inability of an issuer to satisfy an obligation to redeem a preference share when contractually required to do so, whether because of a lack of funds, a statutory restriction or insufficient profits or reserves, does not negate the obligation. An option of the issuer to redeem the shares for cash does not

***Editor's note:** *AG24 deleted by FRS 29 with effect for accounting periods beginning on or after 1 January 2007.*

satisfy the definition of a financial liability because the issuer does not have a present obligation to transfer financial assets to the shareholders. In this case, redemption of the shares is solely at the discretion of the issuer. An obligation may arise, however, when the issuer of the shares exercises its option, usually by formally notifying the shareholders of an intention to redeem the shares.

When preference shares are non-redeemable, the appropriate classification is determined by the other rights that attach to them. Classification is based on an assessment of the substance of the contractual arrangements and the definitions of a financial liability and an equity instrument. When distributions to holders of the preference shares, whether cumulative or non-cumulative, are at the discretion of the issuer, the shares are equity instruments. The classification of a preference share as an equity instrument or a financial liability is not affected by, for example: **AG26**

(a) a history of making distributions;
(b) an intention to make distributions in the future;
(c) a possible negative impact on the price of ordinary shares of the issuer if distributions are not made (because of restrictions on paying dividends on the ordinary shares if dividends are not paid on the preference shares);
(d) the amount of the issuer's reserves;
(e) an issuer's expectation of a profit or loss for a period; or
(f) an ability or inability of the issuer to influence the amount of its profit or loss for the period.

Settlement in the Entity's Own Equity Instruments (paragraphs 21-24)

The following examples illustrate how to classify different types of contracts on an entity's own equity instruments: **AG27**

(a) A contract that will be settled by the entity receiving or delivering a fixed number of its own shares for no future consideration, or exchanging a fixed number of its own shares for a fixed amount of cash or another financial asset, is an equity instrument (except as stated in paragraph 22A). Accordingly, any consideration received or paid for such a contract is added directly to or deducted directly from equity. One example is an issued share option that gives the counterparty a right to buy a fixed number of the entity's shares for a fixed amount of cash. However, if the contract requires the entity to purchase (redeem) its own shares for cash or another financial asset at a fixed or determinable date or on demand, the entity also recognises a financial liability for the present value of the redemption amount (with the exception of instruments that have all the features and meet the conditions in paragraphs 16A and 16B or paragraphs 16C and 16D). One example is an entity's obligation under a forward contract to repurchase a fixed number of its own shares for a fixed amount of cash.
(b) An entity's obligation to purchase its own shares for cash gives rise to a financial liability for the present value of the redemption amount even if the number of shares that the entity is obliged to repurchase is not fixed or if the obligation is conditional on the counterparty exercising a right to redeem (except as stated in paragraphs 16A and 16B or paragraphs 16C and 16D). One example of a conditional obligation is an issued option that requires the entity to repurchase its own shares for cash if the counterparty exercises the option.
(c) A contract that will be settled in cash or another financial asset is a financial asset or financial liability even if the amount of cash or another financial asset that will be received or delivered is based on changes in the market price of the entity's own equity (except as stated in paragraphs 16A and 16B or paragraphs 16C and 16D). One example is a net cash-settled share option.

(d) A contract that will be settled in a variable number of the entity's own shares whose value equals a fixed amount or an amount based on changes in an underlying variable (eg a commodity price) is a financial asset or a financial liability. An example is a written option to buy gold that, if exercised, is settled net in the entity's own instruments by the entity delivering as many of those instruments as are equal to the value of the option contract. Such a contract is a financial asset or financial liability even if the underlying variable is the entity's own share price rather than gold. Similarly, a contract that will be settled in a fixed number of the entity's own shares, but the rights attaching to those shares will be varied so that the settlement value equals a fixed amount or an amount based on changes in an underlying variable, is a financial asset or a financial liability.*

Contingent Settlement Provisions (paragraph 25)

AG28 Paragraph 25 requires that if a part of a contingent settlement provision that could require settlement in cash or another financial asset (or in another way that would result in the instrument being a financial liability) is not genuine, the settlement provision does not affect the classification of a financial instrument. Thus, a contract that requires settlement in cash or a variable number of the entity's own shares only on the occurrence of an event that is extremely rare, highly abnormal and very unlikely to occur is an equity instrument. Similarly, settlement in a fixed number of an entity's own shares may be contractually precluded in circumstances that are outside the control of the entity, but if these circumstances have no genuine possibility of occurring, classification as an equity instrument is appropriate.

Treatment in Consolidated Financial Statements

AG29 In consolidated financial statements, an entity presents minority interests—ie the interests of other parties in the equity and income of its subsidiaries—in accordance with FRS 2 *Subsidiary Undertakings*. When classifying a financial instrument (or a component of it) in consolidated financial statements, an entity considers all terms and conditions agreed between members of the group and the holders of the instrument in determining whether the group as a whole has an obligation to deliver cash or another financial asset in respect of the instrument or to settle it in a manner that results in liability classification. When a subsidiary in a group issues a financial instrument and a parent or other group entity agrees additional terms directly with the holders of the instrument (eg a guarantee), the group may not have discretion over distributions or redemption. Although the subsidiary may appropriately classify the instrument without regard to these additional terms in its individual financial statements, the effect of other agreements between members of the group and the holders of the instrument is considered in order to ensure that consolidated financial statements reflect the contracts and transactions entered into by the group as a whole. To the extent that there is such an obligation or settlement provision, the instrument (or the component of it that is subject to the obligation) is classified as a financial liability in consolidated financial statements.

AG29A Some types of instruments that impose a contractual obligation on the entity are classified as equity instruments in accordance with paragraphs 16A and 16B or paragraphs 16C and 16D. Classification in accordance with those paragraphs is an exception to the principles otherwise applied in this Standard to the classification of an instrument. This exception is not extended to the classification of non-controlling interests in the consolidated financial statements. Therefore, instruments classified as

****Editor's note*: *Paragraph AG27 amended in August 2008.**

equity instruments in accordance with either paragraphs 16A and 16B or paragraphs 16C and 16D in the separate or individual financial statements that are non-controlling interests are classified as liabilities in the consolidated financial statements of the group.*

Compound Financial Instruments (paragraphs 28-32)

Paragraph 28 applies only to issuers of non-derivative compound financial instruments. Paragraph 28 does not deal with compound financial instruments from the perspective of holders. FRS 26 deals with the separation of embedded derivatives from the perspective of holders of compound financial instruments that contain debt and equity features. **AG30**

A common form of compound financial instrument is a debt instrument with an embedded conversion option, such as a bond convertible into ordinary shares of the issuer, and without any other embedded derivative features. Paragraph 28 requires the issuer of such a financial instrument to present the liability component and the equity component separately on the balance sheet, as follows: **AG31**

(a) The issuer's obligation to make scheduled payments of interest and principal is a financial liability that exists as long as the instrument is not converted. On initial recognition, the fair value of the liability component is the present value of the contractually determined stream of future cash flows discounted at the rate of interest applied at that time by the market to instruments of comparable credit status and providing substantially the same cash flows, on the same terms, but without the conversion option.
(b) The equity instrument is an embedded option to convert the liability into equity of the issuer. The fair value of the option comprises its time value and its intrinsic value, if any. This option has value on initial recognition even when it is out of the money.

On conversion of a convertible instrument at maturity, the entity derecognises the liability component and recognises it as equity. The original equity component remains as equity (although it may be transferred from one line item within equity to another). There is no gain or loss on conversion at maturity. **AG32**

When an entity extinguishes a convertible instrument before maturity through an early redemption or repurchase in which the original conversion privileges are unchanged, the entity allocates the consideration paid and any transaction costs for the repurchase or redemption to the liability and equity components of the instrument at the date of the transaction. The method used in allocating the consideration paid and transaction costs to the separate components is consistent with that used in the original allocation to the separate components of the proceeds received by the entity when the convertible instrument was issued, in accordance with paragraphs 28-32. **AG33**

Once the allocation of the consideration is made, any resulting gain or loss is treated in accordance with accounting principles applicable to the related component, as follows: **AG34**

(a) the amount of gain or loss relating to the liability component is recognised in profit or loss; and
(b) the amount of consideration relating to the equity component is recognised in equity.

***Editor's note**: Paragraph AG29A added in August 2008.*

AG35 An entity may amend the terms of a convertible instrument to induce early conversion, for example by offering a more favourable conversion ratio or paying other additional consideration in the event of conversion before a specified date. The difference, at the date the terms are amended, between the fair value of the consideration the holder receives on conversion of the instrument under the revised terms and the fair value of the consideration the holder would have received under the original terms is recognised as a loss in profit or loss.

Treasury Shares (paragraphs 33 and 34)

AG36 An entity's own equity instruments are not recognised as a financial asset regardless of the reason for which they are reacquired. Paragraph 33 requires an entity that reacquires its own equity instruments to deduct those equity instruments from equity. However, when an entity holds its own equity on behalf of others, eg a financial institution holding its own equity on behalf of a client, there is an agency relationship and as a result those holdings are not included in the entity's balance sheet.

Interest, Dividends, Losses and Gains (paragraphs 35-41)

AG37 The following example illustrates the application of paragraph 35 to a compound financial instrument. Assume that a non-cumulative preference share is mandatorily redeemable for cash in five years, but that dividends are payable at the discretion of the entity before the redemption date. Such an instrument is a compound financial instrument, with the liability component being the present value of the redemption amount. The unwinding of the discount on this component is recognised in profit or loss and classified as interest expense. Any dividends paid relate to the equity component and, accordingly, are recognised as a distribution of profit or loss. A similar treatment would apply if the redemption was not mandatory but at the option of the holder, or if the share was mandatorily convertible into a variable number of ordinary shares calculated to equal a fixed amount or an amount based on changes in an underlying variable (eg commodity). However, if any unpaid dividends are added to the redemption amount, the entire instrument is a liability. In such a case, any dividends are classified as interest expense.

Offsetting a Financial Asset and a Financial Liability (paragraphs 42-50)

AG38 To offset a financial asset and a financial liability, an entity must have a currently enforceable legal right to set off the recognised amounts. An entity may have a conditional right to set off recognised amounts, such as in a master netting agreement or in some forms of nonrecourse debt, but such rights are enforceable only on the occurrence of some future event, usually a default of the counterparty. Thus, such an arrangement does not meet the conditions for offset.

AG39 The Standard does not provide special treatment for so-called 'synthetic instruments', which are groups of separate financial instruments acquired and held to emulate the characteristics of another instrument. For example, a floating rate long-term debt combined with an interest rate swap that involves receiving floating payments and making fixed payments synthesises a fixed rate long-term debt. Each of the individual financial instruments that together constitute a 'synthetic instrument' represents a contractual right or obligation with its own terms and conditions and each may be transferred or settled separately. Each financial instrument is exposed to risks that may differ from the risks to which other financial instruments are exposed. Accordingly, when one financial instrument in a 'synthetic instrument' is an asset and another is a liability, they are not offset and presented on an entity's balance sheet on a net basis unless they meet the criteria for offsetting in paragraph 42. Disclosures are provided about the significant terms and conditions of each financial instrument, although an entity may indicate in addition the nature of the relationship between the individual instruments (see paragraph 65).*

DISCLOSURE

Financial Assets and Financial Liabilities at Fair Value Through Profit or Loss (paragraph 94(f))

[Withdrawn]† **AG40**

* ***Editor's note:*** *The last sentence of this paragraph is deleted by FRS 29 with effect for accounting periods beginning on or after 1 January 2007, or where FRS 29 is adopted early.*

†***Editor's note:*** *Paragraph deleted by FRS 29.*

APPROVAL OF IAS 32 BY THE BOARD

International Accounting Standard 32 *Financial Instruments: Disclosure and Presentation* was approved for issue by thirteen of the fourteen members of the International Accounting Standards Board. Mr Leisenring dissented. His dissenting opinion is set out after the Basis for Conclusions.

Sir David Tweedie	Chairman
Thomas E Jones	Vice-Chairman
Mary E Barth	
Hans-Georg Bruns	
Anthony T Cope	
Robert P Garnett	
Gilbert Gélard	
James J Leisenring	
Warren J McGregor	
Patricia L O'Malley	
Harry K Schmid	
John T Smith	
Geoffrey Whittington	
Tatsumi Yamada	

ADOPTION OF FRS 25 BY THE ACCOUNTING STANDARDS BOARD

Financial Reporting Standard 25 (IAS 32) *Financial Instruments: Disclosure and Presentation* was approved for issue by the ten members of the Accounting Standards Board.

Ian Mackintosh	Chairman
Andrew Lennard	Technical Director
Michael Ashley	
Douglas Flint	
Anthony Good	
Roger Marshall	
Isobel Sharp	
John Smith	
Jonathan Symonds	
Peter Westlake	

Notes on the standard's application in the UK and the Republic of Ireland

The need for an FRS on financial instruments disclosure and presentation

In June 2002 the Accounting Standards Board (the Board) issued FRED 30 'Financial Instruments: Disclosure and Presentation & Recognition and Measurement'. In August 2003, April 2004 and July 2004 it issued three supplements to that FRED. Together, the four documents proposed that: **N1**

(a) a standard for use in the UK and Republic or Ireland based on IAS 32 'Financial Instruments: Disclosure and Presentation' should be implemented for all entities, other than those that apply the FRSSE, for accounting periods beginning on or after 1 January 2005; and

(b) a standard for use in the UK and the Republic of Ireland based on the measurement and hedge accounting requirements of IAS 39 'Financial Instruments: Recognition and Measurement' (but not its recognition and derecognition requirements) should be implemented from the same date for all listed entities and for any unlisted entity that chooses to apply fair value accounting in its financial statements.

The Board has now decided to issue FRS 25 which, together with FRS 26 (IAS 39) 'Financial Instruments: Measurement', implements these proposals.

The issue of these two standards forms part of the Board's programme to bring about convergence between its accounting standards and International Accounting Standards (IFRSs). Under this programme, the Board is seeking to bring its standards into line with IFRS over the medium term, dealing first with areas where implementation of an international standard would enhance existing UK and Republic of Ireland financial reporting requirements and keep them in step with changes in the law. **N2**

The Board is strongly of the view that a standard on disclosures relating to financial instruments including derivatives is important beyond the limited scope of the existing UK standard on these disclosures, FRS 13 'Derivatives and Other Financial Instruments'. **N3**

Furthermore, the Board considers it necessary to implement the presentation requirements of the IASB's standard on financial instruments in place of the requirements of FRS 4 'Capital Instruments' to correspond with the amendments to the Companies Act 1985 resulting from the Modernisation Directive*. These amendments will require the classification of items on the balance sheet to have regard to their substance, and as a result preference shares that contain obligations to transfer economic benefits will be classified as liabilities rather than shareholders' funds. The Board therefore believes that it is necessary to issue a standard providing guidance on the application of these new requirements in the Companies Act, to be effective from the same date as the amendments to the Act. **N4**

**Directive 2003/51/EC; similar amendments are to be made to the equivalent Northern Ireland and Republic of Ireland legislation. The implementation of the Modernisation Directive is continued in Part 15 of the Companies Act 2006 and regulations made under it, which extend to Northern Ireland.*

Effective date

N5 The presentation requirements of the FRS are effective for accounting periods beginning on or after 1 January 2005, to correspond to the effective date of the regulations amending the Companies Act to implement the Modernisation Directive, and accordingly early implementation is not permitted. The disclosure requirements apply for accounting periods beginning on or after 1 January 2007; earlier compliance is required for entities that are required, or choose, to comply with FRS 26, as explained in the notes on application of that standard.

Exemptions from FRS 25

N6 The Board has followed its usual practice of exempting from the FRS all entities falling within the scope of the Financial Reporting Standard for Smaller Entities (FRSSE).

N7 The Board did not consider any other exemptions from the presentation requirements of the standard were necessary. The Board did, however, decide that some exemptions were appropriate from the disclosure requirements.

Disclosure exemptions

N8 The Board first developed disclosure requirements for financial instruments in FRS 13, which applied only to banks and listed entities. Since the issue of that standard, experience in disclosing information relating to financial instruments has developed, and in FRED 30 Third Supplement the Board expressed its view that it was time for disclosures on financial instruments to be required from a wider range of entities.

N9 However, many respondents pointed out the considerable burden these disclosures would place on entities, particularly smaller ones. They also pointed out the major changes to the disclosure requirements proposed by the IASB in its exposure draft ED 7 'Financial Instruments: Disclosures' (issued by the Board as FRED 33). The Board has decided to require the IAS 32 disclosures from 2005 only for those entities that applied the measurement rules set out in FRS 26 (IAS 39) 'Financial Instruments: Measurement'. Other entities are required to adopt the amended requirements of FRS 25 from 2007, although early adoption is encouraged. Furthermore, if the IASB and ASB issue a standard based on ED 7 and FRED 33 during 2005, as is expected, it is envisaged that entities will be permitted to implement the requirements of this new standard in place of the FRS 25 disclosure requirements.

N10 The Board also noted that the amendments to the Companies Act that are being introduced to implement the Fair Value Directive include additional disclosure requirements for all companies on financial instruments. Most of these requirements are similar to those set out in FRS 25. The Board would encourage those entities outside the scope of the disclosure requirements of FRS 25 to have regard to the standard to guide them in applying the new requirements of the Companies Act.

N11 In FRED 30 the Board proposed additional disclosure requirements for those entities applying the disclosure provisions of IAS 32 but not the measurement provisions of IAS 39. These additional requirements called for additional detail of accounting policies for financial instruments to be given. Although the disclosures are no longer required for those entities not adopting FRS 26, the Board has retained these additional requirements, in paragraphs 66A and 66B, for those entities voluntarily making FRS 25 disclosures, to emphasise the importance of full disclosure of accounting policies. The Board has also, in paragraph 3C, included clarification that entities not applying the measurement requirements set out in FRS

26 but voluntarily giving the FRS 25 disclosures should adapt these disclosure requirements in line with the entity's accounting policies for the relevant transactions. In particular, an entity would disclose the interest rate used for accruing interest under its accounting policies, rather than the effective interest rate calculated in accordance with IAS 39; would classify contracts as insurance contracts for disclosure purposes in line with their accounting treatment rather than in accordance with the definition in IFRS 4; and would make disclosures relating to hedge accounting that correspond to its accounting policies for hedging transactions.

Parents and subsidiaries

IAS 39 does not differentiate between individual entity financial statements and consolidated financial statements, nor between subsidiaries and parents; it applies to all entities and to all their financial statements. **N12**

Several respondents expressed the view that applying the disclosure requirements to the single-entity financial statements of parent companies and wholly-owned subsidiaries may result in lengthy disclosures for little benefit, particularly where the financial risks of the entity were managed as part of the risks of the group. The Board agreed that there was a balance to be struck between the value of this information and the additional burden of requiring it to be published, and in many such cases this information is likely to be of less importance. It also noted that the legislative amendments implementing the Fair Value Directive would require disclosure of some, though not all, of the information. It therefore agreed that the benefits of applying the full disclosure requirements to all such entities were outweighed by the likely costs of so doing, and has included an exemption in the FRS. This exemption applies to parent companies in their own single-entity financial statements, and to subsidiaries where at least 90 per cent of the voting rights are controlled within the group. In each case it is dependent on the entity being included in consolidated financial statements that are publicly available and which include the disclosures on a group basis. **N13**

However, the arguments for full disclosure were stronger in the case of certain entities where there is a substantial public interest – banks and insurance companies – and the Board has therefore not included these in the above exemption. **N14**

Derecognition

[Deleted]* **N15**

Material on current liabilities

In FRED 30 the Board also proposed that the requirements in IAS 1 'Presentation of Financial Statements' on the classification of financial liabilities as current or non-current should be implemented in the UK and Republic of Ireland to support the disclosures in IAS 32, and these have been included in the standard, with minor drafting amendments. **N16**

Transitional provisions

The Board considered whether to allow entities adopting this FRS to be able to take advantage of the same transitional provisions as entities adopting the corresponding **N17**

Editor's note: *Paragraph deleted by amendments to FRS 26.*

international standard as part of their transition to IFRS, which are set out in IFRS 1 'First-time Adoption of International Financial Reporting Standards'. Under IFRS 1, entities first adopting IFRS for an accounting period commencing before 1 January 2006 are not required to restate comparatives to comply with IAS 32 and IAS 39, subject to additional disclosure requirements. The Board agreed to include this exemption for those entities adopting both this FRS and FRS 26 for that accounting period. The relevant paragraphs from IFRS 1 have therefore been incorporated in FRS 26 and referred to in this FRS. The FRS does not prohibit restatement and entities are encouraged to restate comparatives for the presentation changes where practicable.

N18 The Board intends that entities adopting this FRS should be able to take advantage of the same transitional provisions as entities adopting the corresponding international standards as part of their transition to IFRS, which are set out in IFRS 1 'First-time Adoption of International Financial Reporting Standards', and consistently with its reasons for deferring the effective date for some entities to 2006, has extended the period for which these transitional provisions apply. Restatement of comparatives is therefore not required for an entity adopting the presentation requirements of this standard for an accounting period commencing before 1 January 2006, or adopting the disclosure requirements of the standard together with the requirements of FRS 26 for an accounting period commencing before 1 January 2007.

N19 The Board has, in adopting the transition requirements in IFRS 1, followed the practice adopted in several previous UK standards that applied prospectively and therefore not required corresponding amounts on a comparable basis. Some commentators have recently raised concerns that this might not be in compliance with the requirements of the Companies Act. The Board does not believe that it was ever the intention that prospective application of a new standard should be prevented. However, in view of these concerns, it has noted that a minor change to the Act could clarify the issue by explicitly permitting entities not to restate comparatives in certain circumstances; the DTI has agreed to consider such an amendment if this would remove Uncertainty over the application of the transitional provisions of the FRS.

N20 Where an entity has previously issued a convertible instrument that the FRS requires to be split into its equity and liability components, and the instrument is not longer outstanding, retrospective application of the FRS would require separating two portions of equity. The Board has included the transitional provision in IFRS 1 that permits entities not to make this allocation if the liability component is no longer outstanding at the beginning of the earliest period for which comparative information is given.

ASB consequential amendments

N21 Amendments to existing UK standards and UITF Abstracts are set out in paragraphs 100A to 100D.

N22 The existing UK standard on financial instrument disclosures, FRS 13, applies only to listed entities and to banks and similar institutions. Most of these entities will be required to adopt the measurement rules of FRS 26 and accordingly fall within the scope of FRS 25's disclosure requirements. For such entities, FRS 13 is withdrawn. However, it remains in force for any banking or similar institution that does not fall within the scope of FRS 26 and does not voluntarily adopt that standard.

The FRS also has the effect of withdrawing FRS 4, except for material on measurement of debt and gains and loses on repurchase of debt. This material is withdrawn for those entities applying the measurement requirements set out in FRS 26, but remains applicable for other entities. In addition, a UITF Abstract interpreting the requirements of FRS 4 is withdrawn: Abstract 33 'Obligations in capital instruments'. Abstract 11 'Capital instruments: issue call options' relates to the measurement requirements of FRS 4 and continues in force for those entities not applying the requirements of FRS 26. **N23**

A further UITF Abstract, Abstract 37 'Purchase and sales of own shares' is also withdrawn as these requirements are incorporated in the FRS. **N24**

The offset rules in FRS 5 'Reporting the Substance of Transactions' are withdrawn, as these are replaced by requirements in the FRS. **N25**

Minor consequential amendments to other UK standards are set out in paragraph 100D. **N26**

Other consequential amendments set out in IAS 32 do not affect UK standards and are not included in FRS 25. **N27**

In October 2005 the Board amended FRS 25 to incorporate consequential amendments made to IAS 32 by the IASB in amendments to IAS 39: **N28**

- The Fair Value Option (June 2005)
- Financial Guarantee Contracts and Credit Insurance (August 2005)

Fair Value Option

In June 2005 the IASB amended IAS 39 to restrict the circumstances in which a financial asset or financial liability could be designated as at fair value through profit and loss, and incorporated additional disclosure requirements in IAS 32 for information on the circumstances in which an entity designated items at fair value through profit and loss, and on the items so designated. **N29**

The ASB has amended FRS 25 to include certain of these additional disclosure requirements. The ASB does, however, have considerable reservations over the value of some of the disclosures introduced by the IASB's amendment which in its view are intended to provide information that is relevant to regulatory returns rather than general purpose financial statements. The ASB has not, therefore, implemented all the disclosure requirements inserted in IAS 32.* **N30**

Implementation of derecognition material

In April 2006 the Board amended FRS 26 to include the IAS 39 material on recognition and derecognition into the Standard. Accordingly, on implementation of this amendment the corresponding disclosure requirements of IAS 32 are implemented in FRS 25. These new disclosure requirements replace disclosures required for financial assets and liabilities by FRS 5 'Reporting the Substance of Transactions'. These amendments are effective for accounting periods on or after 1 January 2007, with earlier adoption permitted.† **N31**

****Editor's note:*** *Paragraphs N28 to N30 added in October 2005.*

†***Editor's note:*** *Paragraph N31 added in April 2006.*

Classification of Rights Issues

N32 An amendment to FRS 25 was issued by the Board in January 2010 following the IASB's amendment to IAS 32 Financial Instruments: Presentation '*Classification of Rights Issues*' issued in October 2009. The objective of issuing this amendment to UK GAAP is to ensure that FRS 25 remains converged with IAS 32.

Basis for Conclusions

Definitions **BC4**

Financial Asset, Financial Liability and Equity Instrument **BC4**

Presentation **BC5-BC33**

Liabilities and Equity **BC5-BC6**
No Contractual Obligation to Deliver Cash or Another Financial Asset **BC7-BC21**
Puttable Instruments BC7-BC8
Implicit Obligations BC9
Settlement in the Entity's Own Equity Instruments BC10-BC15
Contingent Settlement Provisions BC16-BC19
Settlement Options BC20
Alternative Approaches Considered BC21
Compound Financial Instruments **BC22-BC31**
Treasury Shares **BC32**
Interest, Dividends, Losses and Gains **BC33**

Disclosure **BC34-BC48**

Interest Rate Risk and Credit Risk **BC34**
Fair Value **BC35-BC36**
Financial Assets Carried at an Amount in Excess of Fair Value **BC37**
Other Disclosures **BC39-BC48**
Multiple Embedded Derivative Features BC39-BC42
Financial Assets and Financial Liabilities at Fair Value Through Profit or Loss BC43-BC47
Defaults and Breaches BC48

Summary of changes from the exposure draft **BC49**

Dissenting Opinion **DO1-DO3**

Basis for Conclusions

This Basis for Conclusions accompanies, but is not part of, IAS 32.

> *ASB note:* The IASB's Basis for Conclusions, which accompanies IAS 32, is set out below in full. It should be noted though that some of the discussion it contains concerns IASB requirements that have no equivalent in the UK or Republic of Ireland. Footnotes have been used to indicate corresponding requirements in the UK and Republic of Ireland where applicable.

All references in this section to 'the Board' and 'Board members' are references to the IASB Board and IASB Board members.

BC1 This Basis for Conclusions summarises the International Accounting Standards Board's considerations in reaching its conclusions on revising IAS 32 *Financial Instruments: Disclosure and Presentation* in 2003*. Individual Board members gave greater weight to some factors than to others.

BC2 In July 2001 the Board announced that, as part of its initial agenda of technical projects, it would undertake a project to improve a number of Standards, including IAS 32 and IAS 39 *Financial Instruments: Recognition and Measurement*. The objectives of the Improvements project were to reduce the complexity in the Standards by clarifying and adding guidance, eliminating internal inconsistencies, and incorporating into the Standards elements of Standing Interpretations Committee (SIC) Interpretations and IAS 39 implementation guidance. In June 2002 the Board published its proposals in an Exposure Draft of proposed amendments to IAS 32 *Financial Instruments: Disclosure and Presentation* and IAS 39 *Financial Instruments: Recognition and Measurement*, with a comment deadline of 14 October 2002. The Board received over 170 comment letters on the Exposure Draft.

BC3 Because the Board did not reconsider the fundamental approach to the accounting for financial instruments established by IAS 32 and IAS 39, this Basis for Conclusions does not discuss requirements in IAS 32 that the Board has not reconsidered.

BC3A In July 2006 the Board published an exposure draft of proposed amendments to IAS 32 relating to the classification of puttable instruments and instruments with obligations arising on liquidation. The Board subsequently confirmed the proposals and in 2008 issued an amendment that now forms part of IAS 32. A summary of the Board's considerations and reasons for its conclusions is in paragraphs BC50–BC74.†

DEFINITIONS (PARAGRAPHS 11-14 AND AG3AG24)

Financial Asset, Financial Liability and Equity Instrument (paragraphs 11 and AG3 – AG 14)

BC4 The revised IAS 32 addresses the classification as financial assets, financial liabilities or equity instruments of financial instruments that are indexed to, or settled in, an

**ASB footnote: In August 2005, the IASB relocated all disclosures relating to financial instruments to IFRS 7. The paragraphs relating to disclosures that were originally published in this Basis for Conclusions were relocated, if still relevant, to the Basis for Conclusions to IFRS 7. The ASB issued FRS 29 in December 2005. All disclosures relating to financial instrument, and so all relevant paragraphs from this Basis for Conclusions were similarly relocated.*

*†**Editor's note**: Paragraph added August 2008.*

entity's own equity instruments. As discussed further in paragraphs BC6–BC15, the Board decided to preclude equity classification for such contracts when they (a) involve an obligation to deliver cash or another financial asset or to exchange financial assets or financial liabilities under conditions that are potentially unfavourable to the entity, (b) in the case of a nonderivative, are not for the receipt or delivery of a fixed number of shares or (c) in the case of a derivative, are not for the exchange of a fixed number of shares for a fixed amount of cash or another financial asset. The Board also decided to preclude equity classification for contracts that are derivatives on derivatives on an entity's own equity. Consistently with this decision, the Board also decided to amend the definitions of financial asset, financial liability and equity instrument in IAS 32 to make them consistent with the guidance about contracts on an entity's own equity instruments. The Board did not reconsider other aspects of the definitions as part of this project to revise IAS 32, for example the other changes to the definitions proposed by the Joint Working Group in its Draft Standard *Financial Instruments and Similar Items* published by the Board's predecessor body, IASC, in 2000*.

Foreign currency denominated pro rata rights issues

In 2005 the International Financial Reporting Interpretations Committee (IFRIC) was asked whether the equity conversion option embedded in a convertible bond denominated in a foreign currency met IAS 32's requirements to be classified as an equity instrument. IAS 32 states that a derivative instrument relating to the purchase or issue of an entity's own equity instruments is classified as equity only if it results in the exchange of a fixed number of equity instruments for a fixed amount of cash or other assets. At that time, the IFRIC concluded that if the conversion option was denominated in a currency other than the issuing entity's functional currency, the amount of cash to be received in the functional currency would be variable. Consequently, the instrument was a derivative liability that should be measured at its fair value with changes in fair value included in profit or loss. **BC4A**

However, the IFRIC also concluded that this outcome was not consistent with the Board's approach when it introduced the 'fixed for fixed' notion in IAS 32. Therefore, the IFRIC decided to recommend that the Board amend IAS 32 to permit a conversion or stand-alone option to be classified as equity if the exercise price was fixed in any currency. In September 2005 the Board decided not to proceed with the proposed amendment. **BC4B**

In 2009 the Board was asked by the IFRIC to consider a similar issue. This issue was whether a right entitling the holder to receive a fixed number of the issuing entity's own equity instruments for a fixed amount of a currency other than the issuing entity's functional currency (foreign currency) should be accounted for as a derivative liability. **BC4C**

These rights are commonly described as 'rights issues' and include rights, options and warrants. Laws or regulations in many jurisdictions throughout the world require the use of rights issues when raising capital. The entity issues one or more rights to acquire a fixed number of additional shares pro rata to all existing shareholders of a class of non-derivative equity instruments. The exercise price is normally below the current market price of the shares. Consequently, a shareholder must exercise its rights if it does not wish its proportionate interest in the entity to be diluted. Issues with those characteristics are discussed in IFRS 2 *Share-based Payment* and IAS 33 *Earnings per Share*. **BC4D**

****ASB footnote:** *This document was also published by the ASB.*

BC4E The Board was advised that rights with the characteristics discussed above were being issued frequently in the current economic environment. The Board was also advised that many issuing entities fixed the exercise price of the rights in currencies other than their functional currency because the entities were listed in more than one jurisdiction and might be required to do so by law or regulation. Therefore, the accounting conclusions affected a significant number of entities in many jurisdictions. In addition, because these are usually relatively large transactions, they can have a substantial effect on entities' financial statement amounts.

BC4F The Board agreed with the IFRIC's 2005 conclusion that a contract with an exercise price denominated in a foreign currency would not result in the entity receiving a fixed amount of cash. However, the Board also agreed with the IFRIC that classifying rights as derivative liabilities was not consistent with the substance of the transaction. Rights issues are issued only to existing shareholders on the basis of the number of shares they already own. In this respect they partially resemble dividends paid in shares.

BC4G The Board decided that a financial instrument that gives the holder the right to acquire a fixed number of the entity's own equity instruments for a fixed amount of any currency is an equity instrument if, and only if, the entity offers the financial instrument pro rata to all of its existing owners of the same class of its own non-derivative equity instruments.

BC4H In excluding grants of rights with these features from the scope of IFRS 2, the Board explicitly recognised that the holder of the right receives it as a holder of equity instruments, ie as an owner. The Board noted that IAS 1 *Presentation of Financial Statements* requires transactions with owners in their capacity as owners to be recognised in the statement of changes in equity rather than in the statement of comprehensive income.

BC4I Consistently with its conclusion in IFRS 2, the Board decided that a pro rata issue of rights to all existing shareholders to acquire additional shares is a transaction with an entity's owners in their capacity as owners. Consequently, those transactions should be recognised in equity, not comprehensive income. Because the Board concluded that the rights were equity instruments, it decided to amend the definition of a financial liability to exclude them.

BC4J Some respondents to the exposure draft expressed concerns that the wording of the amendment was too open-ended and could lead to structuring risks. The Board rejected this argument because of the extremely narrow amendment that requires the entity to treat all of its existing owners of the same class of its own non-derivative equity instruments equally. The Board also noted that a change in the capital structure of an entity to create a new class of non-derivative equity instruments would be transparent because of the presentation and disclosure requirements in IFRSs.

BC4K The Board decided not to extend this conclusion to other instruments that grant the holder the right to purchase the entity's own equity instruments such as the conversion feature in convertible bonds. The Board also noted that long-dated foreign currency rights issues are not primarily transactions with owners in their capacity as owners. The equal treatment of all owners of the same class of equity instruments was also the basis on which, in IFRIC 17 *Distributions of Non-cash Assets to Owners*, the IFRIC distinguished non-reciprocal distributions to owners from exchange transactions. The fact that the rights are distributed pro rata to existing shareholders is critical to the Board's conclusion to provide an exception to the 'fixed for fixed' concept in IAS 32 as this is a narrow targeted transaction with owners in their capacity as owners.

PRESENTATION (PARAGRAPHS 15-50 AND AG25AG39)

Liabilities and Equity (paragraphs 15-27 and AG25-AG29)

The revised IAS 32 addresses whether derivative and non-derivative contracts indexed to, or settled in, an entity's own equity instruments are financial assets, financial liabilities or equity instruments. The original IAS 32 dealt with aspects of this issue piecemeal and it was not clear how various transactions (eg net share settled contracts and contracts with settlement options) should be treated under the Standard. The Board concluded that it needed to clarify the accounting treatment for such transactions. **BC5**

The approach agreed by the Board can be summarised as follows: **BC6**

A contract on an entity's own equity is an equity instrument if, and only if:

(a) it contains no contractual obligation to transfer cash or another financial asset, or to exchange financial assets or financial liabilities with another entity under conditions that are potentially unfavourable to the entity; and

(b) if the instrument will or may be settled in the entity's own equity instruments, it is either (i) a non-derivative that includes no contractual obligation for the entity to deliver a variable number of its own equity instruments, or (ii) a derivative that will be settled by the entity exchanging a fixed amount of cash or another financial asset for a fixed number of its own equity instruments.

No Contractual Obligation to Deliver Cash or Another Financial Asset (paragraphs 17-20 and AG25 and AG26)*

Puttable Instruments (paragraph 18(b))

The Board decided that a financial instrument that gives the holder the right to put the instrument back to the entity for cash or another financial asset is a financial liability of the entity. Such financial instruments are commonly issued by mutual funds, unit trusts, co-operative and similar entities, often with the redemption amount being equal to a proportionate share in the net assets of the entity. Although the legal form of such financial instruments often includes a right to the residual interest in the assets of an entity available to holders of such instruments, the inclusion of an option for the holder to put the instrument back to the entity for cash or another financial asset means that the instrument meets the definition of a financial liability. The classification as a financial liability is independent of considerations such as when the right is exercisable, how the amount payable or receivable upon exercise of the right is determined, and whether the puttable instrument has a fixed maturity. **BC7**

The Board reconsidered its conclusions with regards to some puttable instruments and amended IAS 32 in February 2008 (see paragraphs BC50–BC74).† **BC7A**

The Board noted that the classification of a puttable instrument as a financial liability does not preclude the use of descriptors such as 'net assets attributable to **BC8**

***Editor's note:** *Amended in December 2008.*

†***Editor's note:** *Paragraph added August 2008.*

unitholders' and 'change in net assets attributable to unitholders' on the face of the financial statements of an entity that has no equity (such as some mutual funds and unit trusts) or whose share capital is a financial liability under IAS 32 (such as some cooperatives). The Board also agreed that it should provide examples of how such entities might present their income statement* and balance sheet† (see Illustrative Examples 7 and 8).

Implicit Obligations (paragraph 20)

BC9 The Board did not debate whether an obligation can be established implicitly rather than explicitly because this is not within the scope of an improvements project. This question will be considered by the Board in its project on revenue, liabilities and equity. Consequently, the Board retained the existing notion that an instrument may establish an obligation indirectly through its terms and conditions (see paragraph 20). However, it decided that the example of a preference share with a contractually accelerating dividend which, within the foreseeable future, is scheduled to yield a dividend so high that the entity will be economically compelled to redeem the instrument, was insufficiently clear. The example was therefore removed and replaced with others that are clearer and deal with situations that have proved problematic in practice.

Settlement in the Entity's Own Equity Instruments (paragraphs 21-24 and AG27)

BC10 The approach taken in the revised IAS 32 includes two main conclusions:

(a) When an entity has an obligation to purchase its own shares for cash (such as under a forward contract to purchase its own shares), there is a financial liability for the amount of cash that the entity has an obligation to pay.

(b) When an entity uses its own equity instruments 'as currency' in a contract to receive or deliver a variable number of shares whose value equals a fixed amount or an amount based on changes in an underlying variable (eg a commodity price), the contract is not an equity instrument, but is a financial asset or a financial liability. In other words, when a contract is settled in a variable number of the entity's own equity instruments, or by the entity exchanging a fixed number of its own equity instruments for a variable amount of cash or another financial asset, the contract is not an equity instrument but is a financial asset or a financial liability.

When an entity has an obligation to purchase its own shares for cash, there is a financial liability for the amount of cash that the entity has an obligation to pay.

BC11 An entity's obligation to purchase its own shares establishes a maturity date for the shares that are subject to the contract. Therefore, to the extent of the obligation, those shares cease to be equity instruments when the entity assumes the obligation. This treatment under IAS 32 is consistent with the treatment of shares that provide for mandatory redemption by the entity. Without a requirement to recognise a financial liability for the present value of the share redemption amount, entities with identical obligations to deliver cash in exchange for their own equity instruments could report different information in their financial statements depending on whether

IAS 1 Presentation of Financial Statements (as revised in 2007) requires an entity to present all income and expense items in one statement of comprehensive income or in two statements (a separate income statement and a statement of comprehensive income). **Editor's note: Footnote added in December 2008.*

*†IAS 1 (revised 2007) replaced the term 'balance sheet' with 'statement of financial position'. **Editor's note:** Footnote added in December 2008.*

the redemption clause is embedded in the equity instrument or is a free-standing derivative contract.

Some respondents to the Exposure Draft suggested that when an entity writes an option that, if exercised, will result in the entity paying cash in return for receiving its own shares, it is incorrect to treat the full amount of the exercise price as a financial liability because the obligation is conditional upon the option being exercised. The Board rejected this argument because the entity has an obligation to pay the full redemption amount and cannot avoid settlement in cash or another financial asset for the full redemption amount unless the counterparty decides not to exercise its redemption right or specified future events or circumstances beyond the control of the entity occur or do not occur. The Board also noted that a change would require a reconsideration of other provisions in IAS 32 that require liability treatment for obligations that are conditional on events or choices that are beyond the entity's control. These include, for example, (a) the treatment of financial instruments with contingent settlement provisions as financial liabilities for the full amount of the conditional obligation, (b) the treatment of preference shares that are redeemable at the option of the holder as financial liabilities for the full amount of the conditional obligation, and (c) the treatment of financial instruments (puttable instruments) that give the holder the right to put the instrument back to the issuer for cash or another financial asset, the amount of which is determined by reference to an index, and which therefore has the potential to increase and decrease, as financial liabilities for the full amount of the conditional obligation. **BC12**

When an entity uses its own equity instruments as currency in a contract to receive or deliver a variable number of shares, the contract is not an equity instrument, but is a financial asset or a financial liability.

The Board agreed that it would be inappropriate to account for a contract as an equity instrument when an entity's own equity instruments are used as currency in a contract to receive or deliver a variable number of shares whose value equals a fixed amount or an amount based on changes in an underlying variable (eg a net share-settled derivative contract on gold or an obligation to deliver as many shares as are equal in value to CU10,000). Such a contract represents a right or obligation of a specified amount rather than a specified equity interest. A contract to pay or receive a specified amount (rather than a specified equity interest) is not an equity instrument. For such a contract, the entity does not know, before the transaction is settled, how many of its own shares (or how much cash) it will receive or deliver and the entity may not even know whether it will receive or deliver its own shares. **BC13**

In addition, the Board noted that precluding equity treatment for such a contract limits incentives for structuring potentially favourable or unfavourable transactions to obtain equity treatment. For example, the Board believes that an entity should not be able to obtain equity treatment for a transaction simply by including a share settlement clause when the contract is for a specified value, rather than a specified equity interest. **BC14**

The Board rejected the argument that a contract that is settled in the entity's own shares must be an equity instrument because no change in assets or liabilities, and thus no gain or loss, arises on settlement of the contract. The Board noted that any gain or loss arises before settlement of the transaction, not when it is settled. **BC15**

Contingent Settlement Provisions (paragraphs 25 and AG28)

BC16 The revised Standard incorporates the conclusion previously in SIC-5 *Classification of Financial Instruments—Contingent Settlement Provisions** that a financial instrument for which the manner of settlement depends on the occurrence or non-occurrence of uncertain future events, or on the outcome of uncertain circumstances that are beyond the control of both the issuer and the holder (ie a 'contingent settlement provision'), is a financial liability.

BC17 The amendments do not include the exception previously provided in paragraph 6 of SIC5 for circumstances in which the possibility of the entity being required to settle in cash or another financial asset is remote at the time the financial instrument is issued. The Board concluded that it is not consistent with the definitions of financial liabilities and equity instruments to classify an obligation to deliver cash or another financial asset as a financial liability only when settlement in cash is probable. There is a contractual obligation to transfer economic benefits as a result of past events because the entity is unable to avoid a settlement in cash or another financial asset unless an event occurs or does not occur in the future.

BC18 However, the Board also concluded that contingent settlement provisions that would apply only in the event of liquidation of an entity should not influence the classification of the instrument because to do so would be inconsistent with a going concern assumption. A contingent settlement provision that provides for payment in cash or another financial asset only on the liquidation of the entity is similar to an equity instrument that has priority in liquidation and therefore should be ignored in classifying the instrument.

BC19 Additionally, the Board decided that if the part of a contingent settlement provision that could require settlement in cash or a variable number of own shares is not genuine, it should be ignored for the purposes of classifying the instrument. The Board also agreed to provide guidance on the meaning of 'genuine' in this context (see paragraph AG28).

Settlement Options (paragraphs 26 and 27)

BC20 The revised Standard requires that if one of the parties to a contract has one or more options as to how it is settled (eg net in cash or by exchanging shares for cash), the contract is a financial asset or a financial liability unless all of the settlement alternatives would result in equity classification. The Board concluded that entities should not be able to circumvent the accounting requirements for financial assets and financial liabilities simply by including an option to settle a contract through the exchange of a fixed number of shares for a fixed amount. The Board had proposed in the Exposure Draft that past practice and management intentions should be considered in determining the classification of such instruments. However, respondents to the Exposure Draft noted that such requirements can be difficult to apply because some entities do not have any history of similar transactions and the assessment of whether an established practice exists and of what is management's intention can be subjective. The Board agreed with these comments and accordingly concluded that past practice and management intentions should not be determining factors.

****ASB footnote****: no equivalent requirement in the UK and Republic of Ireland.*

Alternative Approaches Considered

BC21 In finalising the revisions to IAS 32 the Board considered, but rejected, a number of alternative approaches:

(a) To classify as an equity instrument any contract that will be settled in the entity's own shares. The Board rejected this approach because it does not deal adequately with transactions in which an entity is using its own shares as currency, eg when an entity has an obligation to pay a fixed or determinable amount that is settled in a variable number of its own shares.

(b) To classify a contract as an equity instrument only if (i) the contract will be settled in the entity's own shares, and (ii) the changes in the fair value of the contract move in the same direction as the changes in the fair value of the shares from the perspective of the counterparty. Under this approach, contracts that will be settled in the entity's own shares would be financial assets or financial liabilities if, from the perspective of the counterparty, their value moves inversely with the price of the entity's own shares. An example is an entity's obligation to buy back its own shares. The Board rejected this approach because its adoption would represent a fundamental shift in the concept of equity. The Board also noted that it would result in a change to the classification of some transactions, compared with the existing *Framework** and IAS 32, that had not been exposed for comment.

(c) To classify as an equity instrument a contract that will be settled in the entity's own shares unless its value changes in response to something other than the price of the entity's own shares. The Board rejected this approach to avoid an exception to the principle that non-derivative contracts that are settled in a variable number of an entity's own shares should be treated as financial assets or financial liabilities.

(d) To limit classification as equity instruments to outstanding ordinary shares, and classify as financial assets or financial liabilities all contracts that involve future receipt or delivery of the entity's own shares. The Board rejected this approach because its adoption would represent a fundamental shift in the concept of equity. The Board also noted that it would result in a change to the classification of some transactions compared with the existing IAS 32 that had not been exposed for comment.

Compound Financial Instruments (paragraphs 28-32 and AG30-AG35)

BC22 The Standard requires the separate presentation on an entity's balance sheet† of liability and equity components of a single financial instrument. It is more a matter of form than a matter of substance that both liabilities and equity interests are created by a single financial instrument rather than two or more separate instruments. The Board believes that an entity's financial position is more faithfully represented by separate presentation of liability and equity components contained in a single instrument.

Allocation of the initial carrying amount to the liability and equity components (paragraphs 31, 32, AG36-AG38 and Illustrative Examples 9-12)

****ASB footnote****: The equivalent document in the UK and Republic of Ireland to the IASB's* Framework *is the ASB's* Statement of Principles for Financial Reporting. *Although the Statement of Principles is very similar to the Framework, it is not identical.*

†*IAS 1 (as revised in 2007) replaced the term 'balance sheet' with 'statement of financial position'.* ***Editor's note****: Footnote added in December 2008.*

BC23 The previous version of IAS 32 did not prescribe a particular method for assigning the initial carrying amount of a compound financial instrument to its separated liability and equity components. Rather, it suggested approaches that might be considered, such as:

(a) assigning to the less easily measurable component (often the equity component) the residual amount after deducting from the instrument as a whole the amount separately determined for the component that is more easily determinable (a 'withandwithout' method); and
(b) measuring the liability and equity components separately and, to the extent necessary, adjusting these amounts pro rata so that the sum of the components equals the amount of the instrument as a whole (a 'relative fair value' method).

BC24 This choice was originally justified on the grounds that IAS 32 did not deal with the measurement of financial assets, financial liabilities and equity instruments.

BC25 However, since the issue of IAS 39*, IFRSs contain requirements for the measurement of financial assets and financial liabilities. Therefore, the view that IAS 32 should not prescribe a particular method for separating compound financial instruments because of the absence of measurement requirements for financial instruments is no longer valid. IAS 39, paragraph 43, requires a financial liability to be measured on initial recognition at its fair value. Therefore, a relative fair value method could result in an initial measurement of the liability component that is not in compliance with IAS 39.

BC26 After initial recognition, a financial liability that is classified as at fair value through profit or loss is measured at fair value under IAS 39, and other financial liabilities are measured at amortised cost. If the liability component of a compound financial instrument is classified as at fair value through profit or loss, an entity could recognise an immediate gain or loss after initial recognition if it applies a relative fair value method. This is contrary to IAS 32, paragraph 31, which states that no gain or loss arises from recognising the components of the instrument separately.

BC27 Under the *Framework*, and IASs 32 and 39, an equity instrument is defined as any contract that evidences a residual interest in the assets of an entity after deducting all of its liabilities. Paragraph 67 of the *Framework* further states that the amount at which equity is recognised in the balance sheet is dependent on the measurement of assets and liabilities.

BC28 The Board concluded that the alternatives in IAS 32 to measure on initial recognition the liability component of a compound financial instrument as a residual amount after separating the equity component or on the basis of a relative fair value method should be eliminated. Instead the liability component should be measured first (including the value of any embedded non-equity derivative features, such as an embedded call feature), and the residual amount assigned to the equity component.

BC29 The objective of this amendment is to make the requirements about the entity's separation of the liability and equity components of a single compound financial instrument consistent with the requirements about the initial measurement of a financial liability in IAS 39 and the definitions in IAS 32 and the *Framework* of an equity instrument as a residual interest.

BC30 This approach removes the need to estimate inputs to, and apply, complex option pricing models to measure the equity component of some compound financial

**ASB footnote: now being implemented in the UK as FRS 26.*

instruments. The Board also noted that the absence of a prescribed approach led to a lack of comparability among entities applying IAS 32 and that it therefore was desirable to specify a single approach.

The Board noted that a requirement to use the with-and-without method, under which the liability component is determined first, is consistent with the proposals of the Joint Working Group of Standard Setters in its Draft Standard and Basis for Conclusions in *Financial Instruments and Similar Items,* published by IASC in December 2000 (see Draft Standard, paragraphs 74 and 75 and Application Supplement, paragraph 318). BC31

Treasury Shares (paragraphs 33, 34 and AG36)

The revised Standard incorporates the guidance in SIC-16 *Share Capital—Reacquired Own Equity Instruments (Treasury Shares)**. The acquisition and subsequent resale by an entity of its own equity instruments represents a transfer between those holders of equity instruments who have given up their equity interest and those who continue to hold an equity instrument, rather than a gain or loss to the entity. BC32

Interest, Dividends, Losses and Gains (paragraphs 35-41 and AG37)

Costs of an equity transaction (paragraphs 35 and 37-39)

The revised Standard incorporates the guidance in SIC-17 *Equity—Costs of an Equity Transaction*†. *Transaction costs incurred as a necessary part of completing an equity transaction are accounted for as part of the transaction to which they relate. Linking the equity transaction and costs of the transaction reflects in equity the total cost of the transaction.* BC33

DISCLOSURE (PARAGRAPHS 51-95)‡

SUMMARY OF CHANGES FROM THE EXPOSURE DRAFT

The main changes from the Exposure Draft's proposals are as follows: BC49

(a) The Exposure Draft proposed to define a financial liability as a contractual obligation to deliver cash or another financial asset to another entity or to exchange financial instruments with another entity under conditions that are potentially unfavourable. The definition in the Standard has been expanded to include some contracts that will or may be settled in the entity's own equity instruments. The Standard's definition of a financial asset has been similarly expanded.

(b) The Exposure Draft proposed that a financial instrument that gives the holder the right to put it back to the entity for cash or another financial asset is a financial liability. The Standard retains this conclusion, but provides additional guidance and illustrative examples to assist entities that, as a result of this requirement, either have no equity as defined in IAS 32 or whose share capital is not equity as defined in IAS 32.

****ASB footnote****: similar provisions were included in UITF Abstract 37* Purchases and sales of own shares.

†***ASB footnote****: similar provisions were included in FRS 4* Capital Instruments.

‡***Editor's note****: BC34 to BC48 withdrawn by FRS 29.*

(c) The Standard retains and clarifies the proposal in the Exposure Draft that terms and conditions of a financial instrument may indirectly create an obligation.

(d) The Exposure Draft proposed to incorporate in IAS 32 the conclusion previously in SIC-5 *Classification of Financial Instruments—Contingent Settlement Provisions.* This is that a financial instrument for which the manner of settlement depends on the occurrence or non-occurrence of uncertain future events or on the outcome of uncertain circumstances that are beyond the control of both the issuer and the holder is a financial liability. The Standard clarifies this conclusion by requiring contingent settlement provisions that apply only in the event of liquidation of an entity or are not genuine to be ignored.

(e) The Exposure Draft proposed that a derivative contract that contains an option as to how it is settled meets the definition of an equity instrument if the entity had all of the following: (i) an unconditional right and ability to settle the contract gross; (ii) an established practice of such settlement; and (iii) the intention to settle the contract gross. These conditions have not been carried forward into the Standard. Rather, a derivative with settlement options is classified as a financial asset or a financial liability unless all the settlement alternatives would result in equity classification.

(f) The Standard provides explicit guidance on accounting for the repurchase of a convertible instrument.

(g) The Standard provides explicit guidance on accounting for the amendment of the terms of a convertible instrument to induce early conversion.

(h) The Exposure Draft proposed that a financial instrument that is an equity instrument of a subsidiary should be eliminated on consolidation when held by the parent, or presented in the consolidated balance sheet within equity when not held by the parent (as a minority interest* separate from the equity of the parent). The Standard requires all terms and conditions agreed between members of the group and the holders of the instrument to be considered when determining if the group as a whole has an obligation that would give rise to a financial liability. To the extent there is such an obligation, the instrument (or component of the instrument that is subject to the obligation) is a financial liability in consolidated financial statements.

(i) [Withdrawn]

(j) [Withdrawn]

(k) In August 2005, the IASB issued IFRS 7 Financial Instruments: Disclosures. As a result, disclosures relating to financial instruments, if still relevant, were relocated to IFRS 7.†

Amendment for puttable instruments

BC50 As discussed in paragraphs BC7 and BC8, puttable instruments meet the definition of a financial liability and the Board concluded that all such instruments should be classified as liabilities. However, constituents raised the following concerns about classifying such instruments as financial liabilities if they represent the residual claim to the net assets of the entity:

In January 2008 the IASB issued an amended IAS 27* Consolidated and Separate Financial Statements, *which amended 'minority interest' to 'non-controlling interests*'.* ***ASB Footnote:* *The ASB has retained the term 'minority interest.'* ***Editor's note:*** *Footnote added in December 2008.*

†***ASB footnote:*** *The ASB issued FRS 29 in December 2005. All disclosures relating to financial instruments were similarly relocated.*

(a) On an ongoing basis, the liability is recognised at not less than the amount payable on demand. This can result in the entire market capitalisation of the entity being recognised as a liability depending on the basis for which the redemption value of the financial instrument is calculated.
(b) Changes in the carrying value of the liability are recognised in profit or loss. This results in counter-intuitive accounting (if the redemption value is linked to the performance of the entity) because:

  (i) when an entity performs well, the present value of the settlement amount of the liabilities increases, and a loss is recognised.
  (ii) when the entity performs poorly, the present value of the settlement amount of the liability decreases, and a gain is recognised.

(c) It is possible, again depending on the basis for which the redemption value is calculated, that the entity will report negative net assets because of unrecognised intangible assets and goodwill, and because the measurement of recognised assets and liabilities may not be at fair value.
(d) The issuing entity's statement of financial position portrays the entity as wholly, or mostly, debt funded.
(e) Distributions of profits to shareholders are recognised as expenses. Hence, it may appear that profit or loss is a function of the distribution policy, not performance.

Furthermore, constituents contended that additional disclosures and adapting the format of the statement of comprehensive income and statement of financial position did not resolve these concerns.

The Board agreed with constituents that many puttable instruments, despite meeting the definition of a financial liability, represent a residual interest in the net assets of the entity. The Board also agreed with constituents that additional disclosures and adapting the format of the entity's financial statements did not resolve the problem of the lack of relevance and understandability of that current accounting treatment. Therefore, the Board decided to amend IAS 32 to improve the financial reporting of these instruments. **BC51**

The Board considered the following ways to improve the financial reporting of instruments that represent a residual interest in the net assets of the entity: **BC52**

(a) to continue to classify these instruments as financial liabilities, but amend their measurement so that changes in their fair value would not be recognised;
(b) to amend IAS 32 to require separation of all puttable instruments into a put option and a host instrument; or
(c) to amend IAS 32 to provide a limited scope exception so that financial instruments puttable at fair value would be classified as equity, if specified conditions were met.

Amend the measurement of some puttable financial instruments so that changes in their fair value would not be recognised

The Board decided against this approach because: **BC53**

(a) it is inconsistent with the principle in IAS 32 and IAS 39 that only equity instruments are not remeasured after their initial recognition;
(b) it retains the disadvantage that entities whose instruments are all puttable would have no equity instruments; and
(c) it introduces a new category of financial liabilities to IAS 39, and thus increases complexity.

Separate all puttable instruments into a put option and a host instrument

BC54 The Board concluded that conducting further research into an approach that splits a puttable share into an equity component and a written put option component (financial liability) would duplicate efforts of the Board's longer-term project on liabilities and equity. Consequently, the Board decided not to proceed with a project at this stage to determine whether a puttable share should be split into an equity component and a written put option component.

Classify as equity instruments puttable instruments that represent a residual interest in the entity

BC55 The Board decided to proceed with proposals to amend IAS 32 to require puttable financial instruments that represent a residual interest in the net assets of the entity to be classified as equity provided that specified conditions are met. The proposals represented a limited scope exception to the definition of a financial liability and a short-term solution, pending the outcome of the longer-term project on liabilities and equity. In June 2006 the Board published an exposure draft proposing that financial instruments puttable at fair value that meet specific criteria should be classified as equity.

BC56 In response to comments received from respondents to that exposure draft, the Board amended the criteria for identifying puttable instruments that represent a residual interest in the entity, to those included in paragraphs 16A and 16B. The Board decided on those conditions for the following reasons:

(a) to ensure that the puttable instruments, as a class, represent the residual interest in the net assets of the entity;
(b) to ensure that the proposed amendments are consistent with a limited scope exception to the definition of a financial liability; and
(c) to reduce structuring opportunities that might arise as a result of the amendments.

BC57 The Board decided that the instrument must entitle the holder to a pro rata share of the net assets on liquidation because the net assets on liquidation represent the ultimate residual interest of the entity.

BC58 The Board decided that the instrument must be in the class of instruments that is subordinate to all other classes of instruments on liquidation in order to represent the residual interest in the entity.

BC59 The Board decided that all instruments in the class that is subordinate to all other classes of instruments must have identical contractual terms and conditions. In order to ensure that the class of instruments as a whole is the residual class, the Board decided that no instrument holder in that class can have preferential terms or conditions in its position as an owner of the entity.

BC60 The Board decided that the puttable instruments should contain no contractual obligation to deliver a financial asset to another entity other than the put. That is because the amendments represent a limited scope exception to the definition of a financial liability and extending that exception to instruments that also contain other contractual obligations is not appropriate. Moreover, the Board concluded that if the puttable instrument contains another contractual obligation, that instrument may not represent the residual interest because the holder of the puttable instrument may have a claim to some of the net assets of the entity in preference to other instruments.

As well as requiring a direct link between the puttable instrument and the performance of the entity, the Board also decided that there should be no financial instrument or contract with a return that is more residual. The Board decided to require that there must be no other financial instrument or contract that has total cash flows based substantially on the performance of the entity and has the effect of significantly restricting or fixing the return to the puttable instrument holders. This criterion was included to ensure that the holders of the puttable instruments represent the residual interest in the net assets of the entity. **BC61**

An instrument holder may enter into transactions with the issuing entity in a role other than that of an owner. The Board concluded that it is inappropriate to consider cash flows and contractual features related to the instrument holder in a non-owner role when evaluating whether a financial instrument has the features set out in paragraph 16A or paragraph 16C. That is because those cash flows and contractual features are separate and distinct from the cash flows and contractual features of the puttable financial instrument. **BC62**

The Board also decided that contracts (such as warrants and other derivatives) to be settled by the issue of puttable financial instruments should be precluded from equity classification. That is because the Board noted that the amendments represent a limited scope exception to the definition of a financial liability and extending that exception to such contracts is not appropriate. **BC63**

Amendment for obligations to deliver to another party a pro rata share of the net assets of the entity only on liquidation

Issues similar to those raised by constituents relating to classification of puttable financial instruments apply to some financial instruments that create an obligation only on liquidation of the entity. **BC64**

In the exposure draft published in June 2006, the Board proposed to exclude from the definition of a financial liability a contractual obligation that entitles the holder to a pro rata share of the net assets of the entity only on liquidation of the entity. The liquidation of the entity may be: **BC65**

(a) certain to occur and outside the control of the entity (limited life entities); or
(b) uncertain to occur but at the option of the holder (for example, some partnership interests).

Respondents to that exposure draft were generally supportive of the proposed amendment. **BC66**

The Board decided that an exception to the definition of a financial liability should be made for instruments that entitle the holder to a pro rata share of the net assets of an entity only on liquidation if particular requirements are met. Many of those requirements, and the reasons for them, are similar to those for puttable financial instruments. The differences between the requirements are as follows: **BC67**

(a) there is no requirement that there be no other contractual obligations;
(b) there is no requirement to consider the expected total cash flows throughout the life of the instrument;
(c) the only feature that must be identical among the instruments in the class is the obligation for the issuing entity to deliver to the holder a pro rata share of its net assets on liquidation.

The reason for the differences is the timing of settlement of the obligation. The life of the financial instrument is the same as the life of the issuing entity; the extinguishment of the obligation can occur only at liquidation. Therefore, the Board concluded that it was appropriate to focus only on the obligations that exist at liquidation. The instrument must be subordinate to all other classes of instruments and represent the residual interests only at that point in time. However, if the instrument contains other contractual obligations, those obligations may need to be accounted for separately in accordance with the requirements of IAS 32.

Non-controlling interests

BC68 The Board decided that puttable financial instruments or instruments that impose on the entity an obligation to deliver to another party a pro rata share of the net assets of the entity only on liquidation should be classified as equity in the separate financial statements of the issuer if they represent the residual class of instruments (and all the relevant requirements are met). The Board decided that such instruments were not the residual interest in the consolidated financial statements and therefore that non-controlling interests that contain an obligation to transfer a financial asset to another entity should be classified as a financial liability in the consolidated financial statements.

Analysis of costs and benefits

BC69 The Board acknowledged that the amendments made in February 2008 are not consistent with the definition of a liability in the *Framework*, or with the underlying principle of IAS 32, which is based on that definition. Consequently, those amendments added complexity to IAS 32 and introduced the need for detailed rules. However, the Board also noted that IAS 32 contains other exceptions to its principle (and the definition of a liability in the Framework) that require instruments to be classified as liabilities that otherwise would be treated as equity. Those exceptions highlight the need for a comprehensive reconsideration of the distinctions between liabilities and equity, which the Board is undertaking in its long-term project.

BC70 In the interim, the Board concluded that classifying as equity the instruments that have all the features and meet the conditions in paragraphs 16A and 16B or paragraphs 16C and 16D would improve the comparability of information provided to the users of financial statements. That is because financial instruments that are largely equivalent to ordinary shares would be consistently classified across different entity structures (eg some partnerships, limited life entities and co-operatives). The specified instruments differ from ordinary shares in one respect; that difference is the obligation to deliver cash (or another financial asset). However, the Board concluded that the other characteristics of the specified instruments are sufficiently similar to ordinary shares for the instruments to be classified as equity. Consequently, the Board concluded that the amendments will result in financial reporting that is more understandable and relevant to the users of financial statements.

BC71 Furthermore, in developing the amendments, the Board considered the costs to entities of obtaining information necessary to determine the required classification. The Board believes that the costs of obtaining any new information would be slight because all of the necessary information should be readily available.

BC72 The Board also acknowledged that one of the costs and risks of introducing exceptions to the definition of a financial liability is the structuring opportunities that may result. The Board concluded that financial structuring opportunities are minimised by the detailed criteria required for equity classification and the related disclosures.

Consequently, the Board believed that the benefits of the amendments outweigh the costs. **BC73**

The Board took the view that, in most cases, entities should be able to apply the amendments retrospectively. The Board noted that IAS 8 *Accounting Policies, Changes in Accounting Estimates and Errors* provides relief when it is impracticable to apply a change in accounting policy retrospectively as a result of a new requirement. Furthermore, the Board took the view that the costs outweighed the benefits of separating a compound financial instrument with an obligation to deliver a pro rata share of the net assets of the entity only on liquidation when the liability component is no longer outstanding on the date of initial application. Hence, there is no requirement on transition to separate such compound instruments. **BC74**

DISSENTING OPINION

Dissent of James J Leisenring

Mr Leisenring dissents from IAS 32 because, in his view, the conclusions about the accounting for forward purchase contracts and written put options on an issuer's equity instruments that require physical settlement in exchange for cash are inappropriate. IAS 32 requires a forward purchase contract to be recognised as though the future transaction had already occurred. Similarly it requires a written put option to be accounted for as though the option had already been exercised. Both of these contracts result in combining the separate forward contract and the written put option with outstanding shares to create a synthetic liability. **DO1**

Recording a liability for the present value of the fixed forward price as a result of a forward contract is inconsistent with the accounting for other forward contracts. Recording a liability for the present value of the strike price of an option results in recording a liability that is inconsistent with the *Framework* as there is no present obligation for the strike price. In both instances the shares considered to be subject to the contracts are outstanding, have the same rights as any other shares and should be accounted for as outstanding. The forward and option contracts meet the definition of a derivative and should be accounted for as derivatives rather than create an exception to the accounting required by IAS 39. Similarly, if the redemption feature is embedded in the equity instrument (for example, a redeemable preference share) rather than being a free-standing derivative contract, the redemption feature should be accounted for as a derivative. **DO2**

Mr Leisenring also objects to the conclusion that a purchased put or call option on a fixed number of an issuer's equity instruments is not an asset. The rights created by these contracts meet the definition of an asset and should be accounted for as assets and not as a reduction in equity. These contracts also meet the definition of derivatives that should be accounted for as such consistently with IAS 39. **DO3**

Dissent of Mary E Barth and Robert P Garnett from the issue of Puttable Financial Instruments and Obligations Arising on Liquidation (Amendments to IAS 32 and IAS 1) in February 2008

Professor Barth and Mr Garnett voted against the publication of *Puttable Financial Instruments and Obligations Arising on Liquidation* (Amendments to IAS 32 and IAS **DO1**

1 *Presentation of Financial Statements*). The reasons for their dissent are set out below.

DO2 These Board members believe that the decision to permit entities to classify as equity some puttable financial instruments and some financial instruments that entitle the holder to a pro rata share of the net assets of the entity only on liquidation is inconsistent with the *Framework*. The contractual provisions attached to those instruments give the holders the right to put the instruments to the entity and demand cash. The *Framework*'s definition of a liability is that it is a present obligation of the entity arising from a past event, the settlement of which is expected to result in an outflow of resources of the entity. Thus, financial instruments within the scope of the amendments clearly meet the definition of a liability in the *Framework*.

DO3 These Board members do not agree with the Board that an exception to the *Framework* is justified in this situation. First, the Board has an active project on the *Framework*, which will revisit the definition of a liability. Although these Board members agree that standards projects can precede decisions in the *Framework* project, the discussions to date in the *Framework* project do not make it clear that the Board will modify the existing elements definitions in such a way that these instruments would be equity. Second, the amendments would require disclosure of the expected cash outflow on redemption or repurchase of puttable instruments classified as equity. These disclosures are similar to those for financial liabilities; existing standards do not require similar disclosure for equity instruments. The Board's decision to require these disclosures reveals its implicit view these instruments are, in fact, liabilities. Yet, the *Framework* is clear that disclosure is not a substitute for recognition. Third, these Board members see no cost-benefit or practical reasons for making this exception. The amendments require the same or similar information to be obtained and disclosed as would be the case if these obligations were classified as liabilities. Existing standards offer presentation alternatives for entities that have no equity under the Framework's definitions.

DO4 These Board members also do not agree with the Board that there are benefits to issuing these amendments. First, paragraph BC70 in the Basis for Conclusions states that the amendments will result in more relevant and understandable financial reporting. However, as noted above, these Board members do not believe that presenting as equity items that meet the *Framework's* definition of a liability results in relevant information. Also as noted above, existing standards offer presentation alternatives that result in understandable financial reporting.

DO5 Second, paragraph BC70 states that the amendments would increase comparability by requiring more consistent classification of financial instruments that are largely equivalent to ordinary shares. These Board members believe that the amendments decrease comparability. These instruments are not comparable to ordinary shares because these instruments oblige the entity to transfer its economic resources; ordinary shares do not. Also, puttable instruments and instruments that entitle the holder to a pro rata share of the net assets of the entity only on liquidation will be classified as equity by some entities and as liabilities by other entities, depending on whether the other criteria specified in the amendments are met. Thus, these amendments account similarly for economically different instruments, which decreases comparability.

DO6 Finally, these Board members do not believe that the amendments are based on a clear principle. Rather, they comprise several paragraphs of detailed rules crafted to achieve a desired accounting result. Although the Board attempted to craft these rules to minimise structuring opportunities, the lack of a clear principle leaves open the possibility that economically similar situations will be accounted for differently and economically different situations will be accounted for similarly. Both of these outcomes also result in lack of comparability.

Dissent of James J Leisenring and John T Smith from the issue of *Classification of Rights Issues*

Messrs Leisenring and Smith dissent from the amendment *Classification of Rights Issues* for the reasons set out below. DO1

Mr Smith agrees with the concept of accounting for a rights issue as equity in specified circumstances and supports both the IFRIC recommendation and staff recommendation in July 2009 that the Board make 'an extremely narrow amendment' to IAS 32 to deal with this issue. However, he dissents because he believes the change is not extremely narrow and will provide a means for an entity to use its equity instruments as a way to engage in speculative foreign currency transactions and structure them as equity transactions, a concern identified by the Board in the Basis for Conclusions on IAS 32. DO2

In their comment letters on the exposure draft, some respondents expressed concerns that the wording of the amendment was too open-ended and could lead to structuring risks. Mr Smith believes that these concerns are well-founded because there is no limitation on what qualifies as a class of equity. Without some limitation, an entity could, for example, establish a foreign currency trading subsidiary, issue shares to a non-controlling interest and deem the shares to be a class of equity in the consolidated group. DO3

The staff acknowledged the concerns expressed in comment letters that a new class of equity could be created for the purpose of obtaining a desired accounting treatment. However, the Board decided not to attempt to limit such structuring opportunities. The Board was concerned that a requirement that a pro rata offer of rights must be made to all existing owners (rather than only all existing owners of a particular class) of equity instruments would mean that the amendment would not be applicable to most of the transactions to which the Board intended the amendment to apply. DO4

Instead of trying to narrow the amendment, the Board simply acknowledged that under the amendment, 'You could set up a new class of shares today and one minute later issue shares to that class and ... speculate in foreign currency without it going through the income statement'. Mr Smith believes the Board should have explored other alternatives. Mr Smith believes that the Board should have sought solutions that could in fact provide a means of narrowing the amendment to limit structuring while accommodating appropriate transactions. DO5

Mr Smith believes that structuring opportunities could be curtailed significantly if some limitations were placed on the type of class of equity instruments that qualify for the exemption. There are a number of factors or indicators that could have been incorporated into the amendment that would limit the exception. For example, the amendment could have specified that non-controlling interests do not constitute a class. The amendment could have further required that qualification for the exemption is limited to those classes of equity instruments in which (a) ownership in the class is diverse or (b) the class is registered on an exchange and shares are exchanged in the marketplace or (c) shares in that class when issued were offered to the public at large and sold in more than one jurisdiction and there was no agreement to subsequently offer rights to shares of the entity; and the amount of capital provided by the class is substantial relative to the other classes of equity. Clearly, some combination of these and other alternatives could have been used to limit structuring DO6 opportunities. Mr Smith believes that a better solution could have been found and without introducing some limits around the type of class of equity instruments that qualify, the Board did not produce an extremely narrow amendment.

DO7 Mr Leisenring agrees that when an entity issues rights to acquire its own equity instruments those rights should be classified as equity. However, he does not accept that the issue must be pro rata to all existing shareholders of a class of non-derivative equity instruments. He does not accept that whether or not the offer is pro rata is relevant to determining if the transaction meets the definition of a liability.

DO8 Paragraph BC4J suggests that the Board limited its conclusion to those transactions issued on a pro rata basis because of concerns about structuring risks. If that is of concern the suggestions contained in Mr Smith's dissent would be much more effective and desirable than introducing a precedent that transactions such as this rights offering must simply be pro rata to be considered a transaction with owners as owners.

DO9 Mr Leisenring would have preferred to conclude that a right granted for a fixed amount of a currency was a 'fixed for fixed' exchange rather than create additional conditions to the determination of a liability.

Illustrative Examples

Accounting for contracts on equity instruments of an entity	**IE1-IE31**
Example 1: Forward to buy shares	IE2-IE6
Example 2: Forward to sell shares	IE7-IE11
Example 3: Purchased call option on shares	IE12-IE16
Example 4: Written call option on shares	IE17-IE21
Example 5: Purchased put option on shares	IE22-IE26
Example 6: Written put option on shares	IE27-IE31
Entities such as mutual funds and cooperatives whose share capital is not equity as defined in IAS 32	**IE32-IE33**
Example 7: Entities with no equity	IE32
Example 8: Entities with some equity	IE33
Accounting for compound financial instruments	**IE34-IE50**
Example 9: Separation of a compound financial instrument on initial recognition	IE34-IE36
Example 10: Separation of a compound financial instrument with multiple embedded derivative features	IE37-IE38
Example 11: Repurchase of a convertible instrument	IE39-IE46
Example 12: Amendment of the terms of a convertible instrument to induce early conversion	IE47-IE50

Illustrative Examples

These examples accompany, but are not part of, FRS 25.

Accounting for Contracts on Equity Instruments of an Entity

IE1 The following examples* illustrate the application of paragraphs 15-27 and FRS 26 to the accounting for contracts on an entity's own equity instruments (other than the financial instruments specified in paragraphs 16A and 16B or paragraphs 16C and 16D).†

Example 1: Forward to buy shares

IE2 This example illustrates the journal entries for forward purchase contracts on an entity's own shares that will be settled (a) net in cash, (b) net in shares or (c) by delivering cash in exchange for shares. It also discusses the effect of settlement options (see (d) below). To simplify the illustration, it is assumed that no dividends are paid on the underlying shares (ie the 'carry return' is zero) so that the present value of the forward price equals the spot price when the fair value of the forward contract is zero. The fair value of the forward has been computed as the difference between the market share price and the present value of the fixed forward price.

Assumptions:

Contract date	1 February 2002
Maturity date	31 January 2003
Market price per share on 1 February 2002	CU100
Market price per share on 31 December 2002	CU110
Market price per share on 31 January 2003	CU106
Fixed forward price to be paid on 31 January 2003	CU104
Present value of forward price on 1 February 2002	CU100
Number of shares under forward contract	1,000
Fair value of forward on 1 February 2002	CU0
Fair value of forward on 31 December 2002	CU6,300
Fair value of forward on 31 January 2003	CU2,000

(a) Cash for cash ('net cash settlement')

IE3 In this subsection, the forward purchase contract on the entity's own shares will be settled net in cash, ie there is no receipt or delivery of the entity's own shares upon settlement of the forward contract.

On 1 February 2002, Entity A enters into a contract with Entity B to receive the fair value of 1,000 of Entity A's own outstanding ordinary shares as of 31 January 2003 in exchange for a payment of CU104,000 in cash (ie CU104 per share) on 31 January 2003. The contract will be settled net in cash. Entity A records the following journal entries.

**In these examples, monetary amounts are denominated in 'currency units' (CU).*

† ***Editor's note**: Paragraph amended in August 2008.*

1 February 2002

The price per share when the contract is agreed on 1 February 2002 is CU100. The initial fair value of the forward contract on 1 February 2002 is zero.

No entry is required because the fair value of the derivative is zero and no cash is paid or received.

31 December 2002

On 31 December 2002, the market price per share has increased to CU110 and, as a result, the fair value of the forward contract has increased to CU6,300.

Dr	Forward asset	CU6,300	
Cr	Gain		CU6,300

To record the increase in the fair value of the forward contract.

31 January 2003

On 31 January 2003, the market price per share has decreased to CU106. The fair value of the forward contract is CU2,000
([CU106 x 1,000] – CU104,000).

On the same day, the contract is settled net in cash. Entity A has an obligation to deliver CU104,000 to Entity B and Entity B has an obligation to deliver CU106,000 (CU106 x 1,000) to Entity A, so Entity B pays the net amount of CU2,000 to Entity A.

Dr	Loss	CU4,300	
Cr	Forward asset		CU4,300

To record the decrease in the fair value of the forward contract (ie CU4,300 = CU6,300 – CU2,000).

Dr	Cash	CU2,000	
Cr	Forward asset		CU2,000

To record the settlement of the forward contract.

(b) Shares for shares ('net share settlement')

Assume the same facts as in (a) except that settlement will be made net in shares instead of net in cash. Entity A's journal entries are the same as those shown in (a) above, except for recording the settlement of the forward contract, as follows: **IE4**

31 January 2003

The contract is settled net in shares. Entity A has an obligation to deliver CU104,000 (CU104 x 1,000) worth of its shares to Entity B and Entity B has an obligation to deliver CU106,000 (CU106 x 1,000) worth of shares to Entity A. Thus, Entity B delivers a net amount of CU2,000 (CU106,000 – CU104,000) worth of shares to Entity A, ie 18.9 shares (CU2,000 / CU106).

Dr	Equity	CU2,000	
Cr	Forward asset		CU2,000

To record the settlement of the forward contract.

(c) Cash for shares ('gross physical settlement')

IE5 Assume the same facts as in (a) except that settlement will be made by delivering a fixed amount of cash and receiving a fixed number of Entity A's shares. Similarly to (a) and (b) above, the price per share that Entity A will pay in one year is fixed at CU104. Accordingly, Entity A has an obligation to pay CU104,000 in cash to Entity B (CU104 x 1,000) and Entity B has an obligation to deliver 1,000 of Entity A's outstanding shares to Entity A in one year. Entity A records the following journal entries.

1 February 2002

Dr	Equity	CU100,000	
Cr	Liability		CU100,000

To record the obligation to deliver CU104,000 in one year at its present value of CU100,000 discounted using an appropriate interest rate (see IAS 39, paragraph AG64).

31 December 2002

Dr	Interest expense	CU3,660	
Cr	Liability		CU3,660

To accrue interest in accordance with the effective interest method on the liability for the share redemption amount.

31 January 2003

Dr	Interest expense	CU340	
Cr	Liability		CU340

To accrue interest in accordance with the effective interest method on the liability for the share redemption amount.

Entity A delivers CU104,000 in cash to Entity B and Entity B delivers 1,000 of Entity A's shares to Entity A.

Dr	Liability	CU104,000	
Cr	Cash		CU104,000

To record the settlement of the obligation to redeem Entity A's own shares for cash.

(d) Settlement options

IE6 The existence of settlement options (such as net in cash, net in shares or by an exchange of cash and shares) has the result that the forward repurchase contract is a financial asset or a financial liability. If one of the settlement alternatives is to exchange cash for shares ((c) above), Entity A recognises a liability for the obligation to deliver cash, as illustrated in (c) above. Otherwise, Entity A accounts for the forward contract as a derivative.

Example 2: Forward to sell shares

This example illustrates the journal entries for forward sale contracts on an entity's own shares that will be settled (a) net in cash, (b) net in shares or (c) by receiving cash in exchange for shares. It also discusses the effect of settlement options (see (d) below). To simplify the illustration, it is assumed that no dividends are paid on the underlying shares (ie the 'carry return' is zero) so that the present value of the forward price equals the spot price when the fair value of the forward contract is zero. The fair value of the forward has been computed as the difference between the market share price and the present value of the fixed forward price. IE7

Assumptions:

Contract date	1 February 2002
Maturity date	31 January 2003
Market price per share on 1 February 2002	CU100
Market price per share on 31 December 2002	CU110
Market price per share on 31 January 2003	CU106
Fixed forward price to be received on 31 January 2003	CU104
Present value of forward price on 1 February 2002	CU100
Number of shares under forward contract	1,000
Fair value of forward on 1 February 2002	CU0
Fair value of forward on 31 December 2002	CU(6,300)
Fair value of forward on 31 January 2003	CU(2,000)

(a) Cash for cash ('net cash settlement')

On 1 February 2002, Entity A enters into a contract with Entity B to pay the fair value of 1,000 of Entity A's own outstanding ordinary shares as of 31 January 2003 in exchange for CU104,000 in cash (ie CU104 per share) on 31 January 2003. The contract will be settled net in cash. Entity A records the following journal entries. IE8

1 February 2002

No entry is required because the fair value of the derivative is zero and no cash is paid or received.

31 December 2002

Dr	Loss	CU6,300	
Cr	Forward liability		CU6,300

To record the decrease in the fair value of the forward contract.

31 January 2003

Dr	Forward liability	CU4,300	
Cr	Gain		CU4,300

To record the increase in the fair value of the forward contract (ie CU4,300 = CU6,300 – CU2,000).

The contract is settled net in cash. Entity B has an obligation to deliver CU104,000 to Entity A, and Entity A has an obligation to deliver CU106,000 (CU106 x 1,000) to Entity B. Thus, Entity A pays the net amount of CU2,000 to Entity B.

Dr	Forward liability	CU2,000	
Cr	Cash		CU2,000

To record the settlement of the forward contract.

(b) Shares for shares ('net share settlement')

IE9 Assume the same facts as in (a) except that settlement will be made net in shares instead of net in cash. Entity A's journal entries are the same as those shown in (a), except:

31 January 2003

The contract is settled net in shares. Entity A has a right to receive CU104,000 (CU104 x 1,000) worth of its shares and an obligation to deliver CU106,000 (CU106 x 1,000) worth of its shares to Entity A. Thus, Entity A delivers a net amount of CU2,000 (CU106,000 – CU104,000) worth of its shares to Entity B, ie 18.9 shares (CU2,000 / CU106).

Dr	Forward liability	CU2,000	
Cr	Equity		CU2,000

To record the settlement of the forward contract. The issue of the entity's own shares is treated as an equity transaction.

(c) Shares for cash ('gross physical settlement')

IE10 Assume the same facts as in (a), except that settlement will be made by receiving a fixed amount of cash and delivering a fixed number of the entity's own shares. Similarly to (a) and (b) above, the price per share that Entity A will receive in one year is fixed at CU104. Accordingly, Entity A has a right to receive CU104,000 in cash (CU104 x 1,000) and an obligation to deliver 1,000 of its own shares in one year. Entity A records the following journal entries.

1 February 2002

No entry is made on 1 February. No cash is paid or received because the forward has an initial fair value of zero. A forward contract to deliver a fixed number of Entity A's own shares in exchange for a fixed amount of cash or another financial asset meets the definition of an equity instrument because it cannot be settled otherwise than through the delivery of shares in exchange for cash.

31 December 2002

No entry is made on 31 December because no cash is paid or received and a contract to deliver a fixed number of Entity A's own shares in exchange for a fixed amount of cash meets the definition of an equity instrument of the entity.

31 January 2003

On 31 January 2003, Entity A receives CU104,000 in cash and delivers 1,000 shares.

Dr	Cash	CU104,000	
Cr	Equity		CU104,000

To record the settlement of the forward contract.

(d) Settlement options

The existence of settlement options (such as net in cash, net in shares or by an exchange of cash and shares) has the result that the forward contract is a financial asset or a financial liability. It does not meet the definition of an equity instrument because it can be settled otherwise than by Entity A repurchasing a fixed number of its own shares in exchange for paying a fixed amount of cash or another financial asset. Entity A recognises a derivative asset or liability, as illustrated in (a) and (b) above. The accounting entry to be made on settlement depends on how the contract is actually settled. **IE11**

Example 3: Purchased call option on shares

This example illustrates the journal entries for a purchased call option right on the entity's own shares that will be settled (a) net in cash, (b) net in shares or (c) by delivering cash in exchange for the entity's own shares. It also discusses the effect of settlement options (see (d) below): **IE12**

Assumptions:

Contract date	1 February 2002
Exercise date	31 January 2003 (European terms, ie it can be exercised only at maturity)
Exercise right holder	Reporting entity (Entity A)
Market price per share on 1 February 2002	CU100
Market price per share on 31 December 2002	CU104
Market price per share on 31 January 2003	CU104
Fixed exercise price to be paid on 31 January 2003	CU102
Number of shares under option contract	1,000
Fair value of option on 1 February 2002	CU5,000
Fair value of option on 31 December 2002	CU3,000
Fair value of option on 31 January 2003	CU2,000

(a) Cash for cash ('net cash settlement')

On 1 February 2002, Entity A enters into a contract with Entity B that gives Entity B the obligation to deliver, and Entity A the right to receive the fair value of 1,000 of Entity A's own ordinary shares as of 31 January 2003 in exchange for CU102,000 in **IE13** cash (ie CU102 per share) on 31 January 2003, if Entity A exercises that right. The contract will be settled net in cash. If Entity A does not exercise its right, no payment will be made. Entity A records the following journal entries.

1 February 2002

The price per share when the contract is agreed on 1 February 2002 is CU100. The initial fair value of the option contract on 1 February 2002 is CU5,000, which Entity A pays to Entity B in cash on that date. On that date, the option has no intrinsic value, only time value, because the exercise price of CU102 exceeds the market price per share of CU100 and it would therefore not be economic for Entity A to exercise the option. In other words, the call option is out of the money.

Dr	Call option asset	CU5,000	
Cr	Cash		CU5,000

To recognise the purchased call option.

31 December 2002

On 31 December 2002, the market price per share has increased to CU104. The fair value of the call option has decreased to CU3,000, of which CU2,000 is intrinsic value ([CU104 – CU102] x 1,000), and CU1,000 is the remaining time value.

Dr	Loss	CU2,000	
Cr	Call option asset		CU2,000

To record the decrease in the fair value of the call option.

31 January 2003

On 31 January 2003, the market price per share is still CU104. The fair value of the call option has decreased to CU2,000, which is all intrinsic value ([CU104 – CU102] x 1,000) because no time value remains.

Dr	Loss	CU1,000	
Cr	Call option asset		CU1,000

To record the decrease in the fair value of the call option.

On the same day, Entity A exercises the call option and the contract is settled net in cash. Entity B has an obligation to deliver CU104,000 (CU104 x 1,000) to Entity A in exchange for CU102,000 (CU102 x 1,000) from Entity A, so Entity A receives a net amount of CU2,000.

Dr	Cash	CU2,000	
Cr	Call option asset		CU2,000

To record the settlement of the option contract.

(b) Shares for shares ('net share settlement')

IE14 Assume the same facts as in (a) except that settlement will be made net in shares instead of net in cash. Entity A's journal entries are the same as those shown in (a) except for recording the settlement of the option contract as follows:

31 January 2003

Entity A exercises the call option and the contract is settled net in shares. Entity B has an obligation to deliver CU104,000 (CU104 x 1,000) worth of Entity A's shares to Entity A in exchange for CU102,000 (CU102 x 1,000) worth of Entity A's shares. Thus, Entity B delivers the net amount of CU2,000 worth of shares to Entity A, ie 19.2 shares (CU2,000 / CU104).

Dr	Equity	CU2,000	
Cr	Call option asset		CU2,000

To record the settlement of the option contract. The settlement is accounted for as a treasury share transaction (ie no gain or loss).

(c) Cash for shares ('gross physical settlement')

Assume the same facts as in (a) except that settlement will be made by receiving a fixed number of shares and paying a fixed amount of cash, if Entity A exercises the option. Similarly to (a) and (b) above, the exercise price per share is fixed at CU102. Accordingly, Entity A has a right to receive 1,000 of Entity A's own outstanding shares in exchange for CU102,000 (CU102 x 1,000) in cash, if Entity A exercises its option. Entity A records the following journal entries. **IE15**

1 February 2002

Dr	Equity	CU5,000	
Cr	Cash		CU5,000

To record the cash paid in exchange for the right to receive Entity A's own shares in one year for a fixed price. The premium paid is recognised in equity.

31 December 2002

No entry is made on 31 December because no cash is paid or received and a contract that gives a right to receive a fixed number of Entity A's own shares in exchange for a fixed amount of cash meets the definition of an equity instrument of the entity.

31 January 2003

Entity A exercises the call option and the contract is settled gross. Entity B has an obligation to deliver 1,000 of Entity A's shares in exchange for CU102,000 in cash.

Dr	Equity	CU102,000	
Cr	Cash		CU102,000

To record the settlement of the option contract.

(d) Settlement options

The existence of settlement options (such as net in cash, net in shares or by an exchange of cash and shares) has the result that the call option is a financial asset. It does not meet the definition of an equity instrument because it can be settled otherwise than by Entity A repurchasing a fixed number of its own shares in exchange for paying a fixed amount of cash or another financial asset. Entity A recognises a derivative asset, as illustrated in (a) and (b) above. The accounting entry to be made on settlement depends on how the contract is actually settled. **IE16**

Example 4: Written call option on shares

IE17 This example illustrates the journal entries for a written call option obligation on the entity's own shares that will be settled (a) net in cash, (b) net in shares or (c) by delivering cash in exchange for shares. It also discusses the effect of settlement options (see (d) below).

Assumptions:

Contract date	1 February 2002
Exercise date	31 January 2003 (European terms, ie it can be exercised only at maturity)
Exercise right holder	Counterparty (Entity B)
Market price per share on 1 February 2002	CU100
Market price per share on 31 December 2002	CU104
Market price per share on 31 January 2003	CU104
Fixed exercise price to be received on 31 January 2003	CU102
Number of shares under option contract	1,000
Fair value of option on 1 February 2002	CU5,000
Fair value of option on 31 December 2002	CU3,000
Fair value of option on 31 January 2003	CU2,000

(a) Cash for cash ('net cash settlement')

IE18 Assume the same facts as in Example 3(a) above except that Entity A has written a call option on its own shares instead of having purchased a call option on them. Accordingly, on 1 February 2002 Entity A enters into a contract with Entity B that gives Entity B the right to receive and Entity A the obligation to pay the fair value of 1,000 of Entity A's own ordinary shares as of 31 January 2003 in exchange for CU102,000 in cash (ie CU102 per share) on 31 January 2003, if Entity B exercises that right. The contract will be settled net in cash. If Entity B does not exercise its right, no payment will be made. Entity A records the following journal entries.

1 February 2002

Dr	Cash	CU5,000	
Cr	Call option obligation		CU5,000

To recognise the written call option.

31 December 2002

Dr	Call option obligation	CU2,000	
Cr	Gain		CU2,000

To record the decrease in the fair value of the call option.

31 January 2003

Dr	Call option obligation	CU1,000	
Cr	Gain		CU1,000

To record the decrease in the fair value of the option.

On the same day, Entity B exercises the call option and the contract is settled net in cash. Entity A has an obligation to deliver CU104,000 (CU104 x 1,000) to Entity B in exchange for CU102,000 (CU102 x 1,000) from Entity B, so Entity A pays a net amount of CU2,000.

Dr	Call option obligation	CU2,000	
Cr	Cash		CU2,000

To record the settlement of the option contract.

(b) Shares for shares ('net share settlement')

Assume the same facts as in (a) except that settlement will be made net in shares instead of net in cash. Entity A's journal entries are the same as those shown in (a), except for recording the settlement of the option contract, as follows: **IE19**

31 January 2003

Entity B exercises the call option and the contract is settled net in shares. Entity A has an obligation to deliver CU104,000 (CU104 x 1,000) worth of Entity A's shares to Entity B in exchange for CU102,000 (CU102 x 1,000) worth of Entity A's shares. Thus, Entity A delivers the net amount of CU2,000 worth of shares to Entity B, ie 19.2 shares (CU2,000 / CU104).

Dr	Call option obligation	CU2,000	
Cr	Equity		CU2,000

To record the settlement of the option contract. The settlement is accounted for as an equity transaction.

(c) Cash for shares ('gross physical settlement')

Assume the same facts as in (a) except that settlement will be made by delivering a fixed number of shares and receiving a fixed amount of cash, if Entity B exercises the option. Similarly to (a) and (b) above, the exercise price per share is fixed at CU102. Accordingly, Entity B has a right to receive 1,000 of Entity A's own outstanding shares in exchange for CU102,000 (CU102 x 1,000) in cash, if Entity B exercises its option. Entity A records the following journal entries. **IE20**

1 February 2002

Dr	Cash	CU5,000	
Cr	Equity		CU5,000

To record the cash received in exchange for the obligation to deliver a fixed number of Entity A's own shares in one year for a fixed price. The premium received is recognised in equity. Upon exercise, the call would result in the issue of a fixed number of shares in exchange for a fixed amount of cash.

31 December 2002

No entry is made on 31 December because no cash is paid or received and a contract to deliver a fixed number of Entity A's own shares in exchange for a fixed amount of cash meets the definition of an equity instrument of the entity.

31 January 2003

Entity B exercises the call option and the contract is settled gross. Entity A has an obligation to deliver 1,000 shares in exchange for CU102,000 in cash.

Dr	Cash	CU102,000	
Cr	Equity		CU102,000

To record the settlement of the option contract.

(d) Settlement options

IE21 The existence of settlement options (such as net in cash, net in shares or by an exchange of cash and shares) has the result that the call option is a financial liability. It does not meet the definition of an equity instrument because it can be settled otherwise than by Entity A issuing a fixed number of its own shares in exchange for receiving a fixed amount of cash or another financial asset. Entity A recognises a derivative liability, as illustrated in (a) and (b) above. The accounting entry to be made on settlement depends on how the contract is actually settled.

Example 5: Purchased put option on shares

IE22 This example illustrates the journal entries for a purchased put option on the entity's own shares that will be settled (a) net in cash, (b) net in shares or (c) by delivering cash in exchange for shares. It also discusses the effect of settlement options (see (d) below).

Assumptions:

Contract date	1 February 2002
Exercise date	31 January 2003 (European terms, ie it can be exercised only at maturity)
Exercise right holder	Reporting entity (Entity A)
Market price per share on 1 February 2002	CU100
Market price per share on 31 December 2002	CU95
Market price per share on 31 January 2003	CU95
Fixed exercise price to be received on 31 January 2003	CU98
Number of shares under option contract	1,000
Fair value of option on 1 February 2002	CU5,000
Fair value of option on 31 December 2002	CU4,000
Fair value of option on 31 January 2003	CU3,000

(a) Cash for cash ('net cash settlement')

On 1 February 2002, Entity A enters into a contract with Entity B that gives Entity A the right to sell, and Entity B the obligation to buy the fair value of 1,000 of Entity A's own outstanding ordinary shares as of 31 January 2003 at a strike price of CU98,000 (ie CU98 per share) on 31 January 2003, if Entity A exercises that right. The contract will be settled net in cash. If Entity A does not exercise its right, no payment will be made. Entity A records the following journal entries. **IE23**

1 February 2002

The price per share when the contract is agreed on 1 February 2002 is CU100. The initial fair value of the option contract on 1 February 2002 is CU5,000, which Entity A pays to Entity B in cash on that date. On that date, the option has no intrinsic value, only time value, because the exercise price of CU98 is less than the market price per share of CU100. Therefore it would not be economic for Entity A to exercise the option. In other words, the put option is out of the money.

Dr	Put option asset	CU5,000	
Cr	Cash		CU5,000

To recognise the purchased put option.

31 December 2002

On 31 December 2002 the market price per share has decreased to CU95. The fair value of the put option has decreased to CU4,000, of which CU3,000 is intrinsic value ([CU98 – CU95] x 1,000) and CU1,000 is the remaining time value.

Dr	Loss	CU1,000	
Cr	Put option asset		CU1,000

To record the decrease in the fair value of the put option.

31 January 2003

On 31 January 2003 the market price per share is still CU95. The fair value of the put option has decreased to CU3,000, which is all intrinsic value ([CU98 – CU95] x 1,000) because no time value remains.

Dr	Loss	CU1,000	
Cr	Put option asset		CU1,000

To record the decrease in the fair value of the option.

On the same day, Entity A exercises the put option and the contract is settled net in cash. Entity B has an obligation to deliver CU98,000 to Entity A and Entity A has an obligation to deliver CU95,000 (CU95 x 1,000) to Entity B, so Entity B pays the net amount of CU3,000 to Entity A.

Dr	Cash	CU3,000	
Cr	Put option asset		CU3,000

To record the settlement of the option contract.

(b) Shares for shares ('net share settlement')

IE24 Assume the same facts as in (a) except that settlement will be made net in shares instead of net in cash. Entity A's journal entries are the same as shown in (a), except:

31 January 2003

Entity A exercises the put option and the contract is settled net in shares. In effect, Entity B has an obligation to deliver CU98,000 worth of Entity A's shares to Entity A, and Entity A has an obligation to deliver CU95,000 worth of Entity A's shares (CU95 x 1,000) to Entity B, so Entity B delivers the net amount of CU3,000 worth of shares to Entity A, ie 31.6 shares (CU3,000 / CU95).

Dr	Equity	CU3,000	
Cr	Put option asset		CU3,000

To record the settlement of the option contract.

(c) Cash for shares ('gross physical settlement')

IE25 Assume the same facts as in (a) except that settlement will be made by receiving a fixed amount of cash and delivering a fixed number of Entity A's shares, if Entity A exercises the option. Similarly to (a) and (b) above, the exercise price per share is fixed at CU98. Accordingly, Entity B has an obligation to pay CU98,000 in cash to Entity A (CU98 x 1,000) in exchange for 1,000 of Entity A's outstanding shares, if Entity A exercises its option. Entity A records the following journal entries.

1 February 2002

Dr	Equity	CU5,000	
Cr	Cash		CU5,000

To record the cash received in exchange for the right to deliver Entity A's own shares in one year for a fixed price. The premium paid is recognised directly in equity. Upon exercise, it results in the issue of a fixed number of shares in exchange for a fixed price.

31 December 2002

No entry is made on 31 December because no cash is paid or received and a contract to deliver a fixed number of Entity A's own shares in exchange for a fixed amount of cash meets the definition of an equity instrument of Entity A.

31 January 2003

Entity A exercises the put option and the contract is settled gross. Entity B has an obligation to deliver CU98,000 in cash to Entity A in exchange for 1,000 shares.

Dr	Cash	CU98,000	
Cr	Equity		CU98,000

To record the settlement of the option contract.

(d) Settlement options

The existence of settlement options (such as net in cash, net in shares or by an exchange of cash and shares) has the result that the put option is a financial asset. It does not meet the definition of an equity instrument because it can be settled otherwise than by Entity A issuing a fixed number of its own shares in exchange for receiving a fixed amount of cash or another financial asset. Entity A recognises a derivative asset, as illustrated in (a) and (b) above. The accounting entry to be made on settlement depends on how the contract is actually settled. **IE26**

Example 6: Written put option on shares

This example illustrates the journal entries for a written put option on the entity's own shares that will be settled (a) net in cash, (b) net in shares or (c) by delivering cash in exchange for shares. It also discusses the effect of settlement options (see (d) below). **IE27**

Assumptions:

Contract date	1 February 2002
Exercise date	31 January 2003 (European terms, ie it can be exercised only at maturity)
Exercise right holder	Counterparty (Entity B)
Market price per share on 1 February 2002	CU100
Market price per share on 31 December 2002	CU95
Market price per share on 31 January 2003	CU95
Fixed exercise price to be paid on 31 January 2003	CU98
Present value of exercise price on 1 February 2002	CU95
Number of shares under option contract	1,000
Fair value of option on 1 February 2002	CU5,000
Fair value of option on 31 December 2002	CU4,000
Fair value of option on 31 January 2003	CU3,000

(a) Cash for cash ('net cash settlement')

IE28 Assume the same facts as in Example 5(a) above, except that Entity A has written a put option on its own shares instead of having purchased a put option on its own shares. Accordingly, on 1 February 2002, Entity A enters into a contract with Entity B that gives Entity B the right to receive and Entity A the obligation to pay the fair value of 1,000 of Entity A's outstanding ordinary shares as of 31 January 2003 in exchange for CU98,000 in cash (ie CU98 per share) on 31 January 2003, if Entity B exercises that right. The contract will be settled net in cash. If Entity B does not exercise its right, no payment will be made. Entity A records the following journal entries.

1 February 2002

Dr	Cash	CU5,000	
Cr	Put option liability		CU5,000

To recognise the written put option.

31 December 2002

Dr	Put option liability	CU1,000	
Cr	Gain		CU1,000

To record the decrease in the fair value of the put option.

31 January 2003

Dr	Put option liability	CU1,000	
Cr	Gain		CU1,000

To record the decrease in the fair value of the put option.

On the same day, Entity B exercises the put option and the contract is settled net in cash. Entity A has an obligation to deliver CU98,000 to Entity B, and Entity B has an obligation to deliver CU95,000 (CU95 x 1,000) to Entity A. Thus, Entity A pays the net amount of CU3,000 to Entity B.

Dr	Put option liability	CU3,000	
Cr	Cash		CU3,000

To record the settlement of the option contract.

(b) Shares for shares ('net share settlement')

IE29 Assume the same facts as in (a) except that settlement will be made net in shares instead of net in cash. Entity A's journal entries are the same as those in (a), except for the following:

31 January 2003

Entity B exercises the put option and the contract is settled net in shares. In effect, Entity A has an obligation to deliver CU98,000 worth of shares to Entity B, and Entity B has an obligation to deliver CU95,000 worth of Entity A's shares (CU95 x 1,000) to Entity A. Thus, Entity A delivers the net amount of CU3,000 worth of Entity A's shares to Entity B, ie 31.6 shares (3,000 / 95).

Dr	Put option liability	CU3,000	
Cr	Equity		CU3,000

To record the settlement of the option contract. The issue of Entity A's own shares is accounted for as an equity transaction.

(c) Cash for shares ('gross physical settlement')

Assume the same facts as in (a) except that settlement will be made by delivering a fixed amount of cash and receiving a fixed number of shares, if Entity B exercises the option. Similarly to (a) and (b) above, the exercise price per share is fixed at CU98. Accordingly, Entity A has an obligation to pay CU98,000 in cash to Entity B (CU98 x 1,000) in exchange for 1,000 of Entity A's outstanding shares, if Entity B exercises its option. Entity A records the following journal entries. **IE30**

1 February 2002

Dr	Cash	CU5,000	
Cr	Equity		CU5,000

To recognise the option premium received of CU5,000 in equity.

Dr	Equity	CU95,000	
Cr	Liability		CU95,000

To recognise the present value of the obligation to deliver CU98,000 in one year, ie CU95,000, as a liability.

31 December 2002

Dr	Interest expense	CU2,750	
Cr	Liability		CU2,750

To accrue interest in accordance with the effective interest method on the liability for the share redemption amount.

31 January 2003

Dr	Interest expense	CU250	
Cr	Liability		CU250

To accrue interest in accordance with the effective interest method on the liability for the share redemption amount.

On the same day, Entity B exercises the put option and the contract is settled gross. Entity A has an obligation to deliver CU98,000 in cash to Entity B in exchange for CU95,000 worth of shares (CU95 x 1,000).

Dr	Liability	CU98,000	
Cr	Cash		CU98,000

To record the settlement of the option contract.

(d) Settlement options

IE31 The existence of settlement options (such as net in cash, net in shares or by an exchange of cash and shares) has the result that the written put option is a financial liability. If one of the settlement alternatives is to exchange cash for shares ((c) above), Entity A recognises a liability for the obligation to deliver cash, as illustrated in (c) above. Otherwise, Entity A accounts for the put option as a derivative liability.

Entities such as Mutual Funds and Co-operatives whose Share Capital is not Equity as Defined in IAS 32

Example 7: Entities with no equity

The following example illustrates an income statement and balance sheet format that may be used by entities such as mutual funds that do not have equity as defined in FRS 25. Other formats are possible. **IE32**

Income statement for the year ended 31 December 20x1

	20x1	*20x0*
	CU	CU
Revenue	2,956	1,718
Expenses (classified by nature or function)	(644)	(614)
Profit from operating activities	2,312	1,104
Finance costs – other finance costs	(47)	(47)
– distributions to unitholders	(50)	(50)
Change in net assets attributable to unitholders	2,215	1,007

Balance sheet at 31 December 20x1

		20x1		*20x0*
	CU	CU	CU	CU
ASSETS				
Non-current assets (classified in accordance with IAS 1)	91,374		78,484	
Total non-current assets		91,374		78,484
Current assets (classified in accordance with IAS 1)	1,422		1,769	
Total current assets		1,422		1,769
Total assets		92,796		80,253
LIABILITIES				
Current liabilities (classified in accordance with IAS 1)	647		66	
Total current liabilities		(647)		(66)
Non-current liabilities excluding net assets attributable to unitholders (classified in accordance with IAS 1)	280		136	
		(280)		(136)
Net assets attributable to unitholders		91,869		80,051

Example 8: Entities with some equity

The following example illustrates a format of a statement of comprehensive income and statement of financial position that may be used by entities whose share capital is not equity as defined in FRS 25 because the entity has an obligation to repay the share capital on demand but does not have all the features or meet the conditions in paragraphs 16A and 16B or paragraphs 16C and 16D. Other formats are possible.* **IE33**

Income statement for the year ended 31 December 20x1

	20x1	***20x0***
	CU	CU
Revenue	472	498
Expenses (classified by nature or function)	(367)	(396)
Profit from operating activities	105	102
Finance costs – other finance costs	(4)	(4)
– distributions to members	(50)	(50)
Change in net assets attributable to members	51	48

* ***Editor's note**: Paragraph amended in August 2008.*

Balance sheet at 31 December 20x1

	20x1			***20x0***
	CU	CU	CU	CU
ASSETS				
Non-current assets (classified in accordance with IAS 1)	908		830	
Total non-current assets		908		830
Current assets (classified in accordance with IAS 1)	383			350
Total current assets		383		350
Total assets		1,291		1,180
LIABILITIES				
Current liabilities (classified in accordance with IAS 1)	372			338
Share capital repayable on demand	202			161
Total current liabilities		(574)		(499)
Total assets less current liabilities		717		681
Non-current liabilities (classified in accordance with IAS 1)	187		196	
		187		196
RESERVES*				
Reserves eg revaluation reserve, retained earnings etc	530		485	
		530		485
		717		681

**In this example, the entity has no obligation to deliver a share of its reserves to its members.*

MEMORANDUM NOTE – Total Members' Interests

Share capital repayable on demand	202	161
Reserves	530	485
	732	646

Accounting for Compound Financial Instruments

Example 9: Separation of a compound financial instrument on initial recognition

Paragraph 28 describes how the components of a compound financial instrument are separated by the entity on initial recognition. The following example illustrates how such a separation is made. **IE34**

An entity issues 2,000 convertible bonds at the start of year 1. The bonds have a three-year term, and are issued at par with a face value of CU1,000 per bond, giving total proceeds of CU2,000,000. Interest is payable annually in arrears at a nominal annual interest rate of 6 per cent. Each bond is convertible at any time up to maturity into 250 ordinary shares. When the bonds are issued, the prevailing market interest rate for similar debt without conversion options is 9 per cent. **IE35**

The liability component is measured first, and the difference between the proceeds of the bond issue and the fair value of the liability is assigned to the equity component. The present value of the liability component is calculated using a discount rate of 9 per cent, the market interest rate for similar bonds having no conversion rights, as shown below. **IE36**

	CU
Present value of the principal – CU2,000,000 payable at the end of three years	1,544,367
Present value of the interest – CU120,000 payable annually in arrears for three years	303,755
Total liability component	1,848,122
Equity component (by deduction)	151,878
Proceeds of the bond issue	2,000,000

Example 10: Separation of a compound financial instrument with multiple embedded derivative features

IE37 The following example illustrates the application of paragraph 31 to the separation of the liability and equity components of a compound financial instrument with multiple embedded derivative features.

IE38 Assume that the proceeds received on the issue of a callable convertible bond are CU60. The value of a similar bond without a call or equity conversion option is CU57. Based on an option pricing model, it is determined that the value to the entity of the embedded call feature in a similar bond without an equity conversion option is CU2. In this case, the value allocated to the liability component under paragraph 31 is CU55 (CU57 – CU2) and the value allocated to the equity component is CU5 (CU60 – CU55).

Example 11: Repurchase of a convertible instrument

IE39 The following example illustrates how an entity accounts for a repurchase of a convertible instrument. For simplicity, at inception, the face amount of the instrument is assumed to be equal to the aggregate carrying amount of its liability and equity components in the financial statements, ie no original issue premium or discount exists. Also, for simplicity, tax considerations have been omitted from the example.

IE40 On 1 January 1999, Entity A issued a 10 per cent convertible debenture with a face value of CU1,000 maturing on 31 December 2008. The debenture is convertible into ordinary shares of Entity A at a conversion price of CU25 per share. Interest is payable half-yearly in cash. At the date of issue, Entity A could have issued non-convertible debt with a ten-year term bearing a coupon interest rate of 11 per cent.

IE41 In the financial statements of Entity A the carrying amount of the debenture was allocated on issue as follows:

	CU
Liability component	
Present value of 20 half-yearly interest payments of CU50, discounted at 11%	597
Present value of CU1,000 due in 10 years, discounted at 11%, compounded half-yearly	343
	940
Equity component	
(difference between CU1,000 total proceeds and CU940 allocated above)	60
Total proceeds	1,000

IE42 On 1 January 2004, the convertible debenture has a fair value of CU1,700.

IE43 Entity A makes a tender offer to the holder of the debenture to repurchase the debenture for CU1,700, which the holder accepts. At the date of repurchase, Entity A could have issued non-convertible debt with a five-year term bearing a coupon interest rate of 8 per cent.

IE44 The repurchase price is allocated as follows:

	Carrying Value	Fair Value	Difference
Liability component:	CU	CU	CU
Present value of 10 remaining halfyearly interest payments of CU50, discounted at 11% and 8%, respectively	377	405	
Present value of CU1,000 due in 5 years, discounted at 11% and 8%, compounded half-yearly, respectively	585	676	
	962	1,081	(119)
Equity component	60	619*	(559)
Total	1,022	1,700	(678)

Entity A recognises the repurchase of the debenture as follows: IE45

Dr	Liability component	CU962	
Dr	Debt settlement expense (income statement)	CU119	
Cr	Cash		CU1,081

To recognise the repurchase of the liability component.

Dr	Equity	CU619	
Cr	Cash		CU619

To recognise the cash paid for the equity component.

The equity component remains as equity, but may be transferred from one line item within equity to another. IE46

Example 12: Amendment of the terms of a convertible instrument to induce early conversion

The following example illustrates how an entity accounts for the additional consideration paid when the terms of a convertible instrument are amended to induce early conversion. IE47

On 1 January 1999, Entity A issued a 10 per cent convertible debenture with a face value of CU1,000 with the same terms as described in Example 11. On 1 January 2000, to induce the holder to convert the convertible debenture promptly, Entity A reduces the conversion price to CU20 if the debenture is converted before 1 March 2000 (ie within 60 days). IE48

Assume the market price of Entity A's ordinary shares on the date the terms are amended is CU40 per share. The fair value of the incremental consideration paid by Entity A is calculated as follows: IE49

Number of ordinary shares to be issued to debenture holders under ***amended*** *conversion terms:*

**This amount represents the difference between the fair value amount allocated to the liability component and the repurchase price of CU1,700.*

Face amount	CU1,000	
New conversion price	/CU20	per share
Number of ordinary shares to be issued on conversion	50	shares

Number of ordinary shares to be issued to debenture holders under ***original*** *conversion terms:*

Face amount	CU1,000	
Original conversion price	/CU25	per share
Number of ordinary shares issued upon conversion	40	shares
Number of ***incremental*** *ordinary shares issued upon conversion*	10	shares

Value of incremental ordinary shares issued upon conversion

CU40 per share x 10 incremental shares	CU400

IE50 The incremental consideration of CU400 is recognised as a loss in profit or loss.

Financial Reporting Standard 26 embodies part of IAS 39 'Financial Instruments: Recognition and Measurement' and some amendments to that standard adopted for entities subject to UK accounting standards.

The Statement of Standard Accounting Practice in FRS 26 is set out in paragraphs 1-110A and the appendices. All the paragraphs have equal authority. Paragraphs in bold type state the main principles.

Accompanying the Statement of Standard Accounting Practice is the basis for the conclusions reached in the Statement. This does not form part of the Statement.

The Statement of Standard Accounting Practice should be read in the context of its objective as stated in paragraph 1, the Basis for Conclusions set out in paragraphs BC1-BC222, and the Accounting Standards Board's 'Foreword to Accounting Standards' and 'Statement of Principles for Financial Reporting'.

FRS 26
(IAS 39) Financial instruments: recognition and measurement*†

(Issued December 2004)

Contents

	paragraphs
Introduction	**IN1-IN26**
International Accounting Standard 39 **Financial Instruments: Recognition and Measurement**	
Objective	**1**
Scope	**2-7**
Definitions	**8-9**
Embedded derivatives	**10-13**
Measurement	**43-70**
Initial Measurement of Financial Assets and Financial Liabilities	**43-44**
Subsequent Measurement of Financial Assets	**45-46**
Subsequent Measurement of Financial Liabilities	**47**
Fair Value Measurement Considerations	**48-49**
Reclassifications	**50-54**
Gains and Losses	**55-57**
Impairment and Uncollectibility of Financial Assets	**58-70**
Financial Assets Carried at Amortised Cost	63-65
Financial Assets Carried at Cost	66
Available-for-Sale Financial Assets	67-70
Hedging	**71-102**
Hedging Instruments	**72-77**
Qualifying Instruments	72-73
Designation of Hedging Instruments	74-77
Hedged Items	**78-84**
Qualifying Items	78-80
Designation of Financial Items as Hedged Items	81-81A

****Editor's note:*** *Title changed in April 2006.*

†***Editor's note****: The matters covered in FRS 26 are dealt with in Sections 11 and 12 of FRS 102. Entities adopting FRS 102 also have the choice of applying IAS 39* Financial Instruments: Recognition and Measurement, *the standard on which FRS 26 is based.*

Designation of Non-Financial Items as Hedged Items 82
Designation of Groups of Items as Hedged Items 83-84

Hedge Accounting **85-102**
Fair Value Hedges 89-94
Cash Flow Hedges 95-101
Hedges of a Net Investment 102

Effective date and transition **103-108**

Withdrawal of other pronouncements **109-110**

Appendix A: Application guidance **AG1-AG111**

Scope **AG1-AG4**

Definitions **AG5-AG26**
Effective Interest Rate AG5-AG8
Derivatives AG9-AG12A
Transaction Costs AG13
Financial Assets and Financial Liabilities Held for Trading AG14-AG15
Held-to-Maturity Investments AG16-AG25
Loans and Receivables AG26

Embedded Derivatives **AG27-AG33**

Recognition and Derecognition **AG34-AG63**
Initial Recognition AG34-AG35
Derecognition of a Financial Asset AG36-AG52
Transfers that Qualify for Derecognition *AG45-AG46*
Transfers that Do Not Qualify for Derecognition *AG47*
Continuing Involvement in Transferred Assets *AG48*
All Transfers *AG49-AG50*
Examples *AG51-AG52*
Regular Way Purchase or Sale of a Financial Asset AG53-AG56
Derecognition of a Financial Liability AG57-AG63

Measurement **AG64-AG92**
Initial Measurement of Financial Assets and Financial Liabilities AG64-AG65
Subsequent Measurement of Financial Assets AG66-AG68
Fair Value Measurement Considerations AG69-AG82
Active Market: Quoted Price *AG71-AG73*
No Active Market: Valuation Technique *AG74-AG79*
No Active Market: Equity Instruments *AG80-AG81*
Inputs to Valuation Techniques *AG82*
Gains and Losses AG83
Impairment and Uncollectibility of Financial Assets AG84-AG93
Financial Assets Carried at Amortised Cost *AG84-AG92*
Interest Income After Impairment Recognition *AG93*

Hedging **AG94-AG113**
Hedging Instruments AG94-AG97
Qualifying Instruments *AG94-AG97*
Hedged Items AG98-AG101
Qualifying Items *AG98-AG99*
Designation of Financial Items as Hedged Items AG99A-AG99B
Designation of Non-Financial Items as Hedged Items *AG100*
Designation of Groups of Items as Hedged Items *AG101*

Hedge Accounting	AG102-AG132
Assessing Hedge Effectiveness	*AG105-AG113*
Fair Value Hedge Accounting for a Portfolio Hedge of Interest Rate Risk	*AG114-AG132*

Appendix B: Amendments to other pronouncements

Appendix C: Insurance Contracts

Preface by the Accounting Standards Board

This Financial Reporting Standard (FRS) has the effect, for those entities applying it, of implementing the International Accounting Standards Board's (IASB's) International Accounting Standard (IAS) 39 'Financial Instruments: Recognition and Measurement' in the UK and the Republic of Ireland. **a**

IAS 39 sets out requirements for the measurement, recognition and derecognition of financial instruments. FRS 26 is based on the text of IAS 39 as at 31 March 2004, incorporating the revised version of IAS 39 issued by the IASB in December 2003 together with the amendments to IAS 39 on 'Fair Value Hedge Accounting for a Portfolio Hedge of Interest Rate Risk' and those made by IFRS 4 'Insurance Contracts', both issued in March 2004. **b**

The FRS is, in effect, part of a package of UK standards comprising: **c**

- this FRS,
- FRS 23 (IAS 21) *The Effects of Changes in Foreign Exchange Rates*,
- FRS 24 (IAS 29) *Financial Reporting in Hyperinflationary Economies*, and
- the disclosure requirements of FRS 25 (IAS 32) *Financial Instruments: Disclosure and Presentation*.*

Listed entities preparing their financial statements in accordance with UK requirements—including listed parent undertakings preparing individual financial statements in accordance with those requirements—are required to comply with the entire package of standards for accounting periods beginning on or after 1 January 2005.† Other entities are permitted to apply the entire package of standards from that date, although entities are not permitted to apply some of the standards in the package but not others—except that FRS 25 exempts certain entities from applying its disclosure requirements and also permits entities to apply those disclosure requirements in advance of the other standards in the package if they wish. **d**

For accounting periods beginning on or after 1 January 2006, unlisted entities using accounting policies that are consistent with the fair value measurement rules incorporated into the Companies Act‡ to implement the EU Fair Value Directive§ will also be required to comply with the entire package of standards. **e**

The Board will in due course be issuing proposals for the application of the entire package of standards to other unlisted entities. **f**

The requirements, scope and effective date of FRS 26 are identical to the revised IAS 39 with the following exceptions: **g**

**The other requirements of FRS 25 apply to all entities—regardless of whether they are listed or unlisted— for accounting periods beginning on or after 1 January 2005.*

†For this purpose a listed entity is an entity that has shares or debt admitted to trading on a regulated market in the EU.

‡Section D of Schedule 4, and equivalents in other schedules, inserted by The Companies Act 1985 (International Accounting Standards and Other Accounting Amendments) Regulations 2004; and equivalent Northern Ireland and Republic of Ireland legislation. Now re-enacted for the whole of the UK in Schedule 1 of The Large and Medium-sized Companies and Groups (Accounts and Reports) Regulations 2008 and equivalents in other Schedules to those Regulations.

§Directive 2001/65/EC.

- entities applying the FRSSE are exempt from the FRS;
- only those entities that are listed entities or whose financial statements are prepared in accordance with the fair value accounting rules set out in the The Large and Medium-sized Companies and Groups (Accounts and Reports) Regulations 2008 or The Large and Medium-sized Limited Liability Partnerships (Accounts) Regulations 2008* are required to adopt the standard;
- changes in fair value that are recognised directly in equity under IAS 39 are required by FRS 26 to be recognised in the statement of total recognised gains and losses;
- commencement of the FRS for listed entities corresponds to the effective date of amendments to the Companies Act implementing the Fair Value Directive†, and earlier adoption is not permitted; other entities required to apply the FRS are permitted to defer its application for one year from this date;
- the Board has added transitional provisions from IFRS 1 'First-time Adoption of International Financial Reporting Standards' to enable prospective application of the requirements of the FRS without the need for full restatement of comparatives; and
- the scope of IAS 39 includes a reference to the definition of an insurance contract, as set out in IFRS 4; the ASB has included, in an appendix forming an integral part of FRS 26, this definition and supporting material from IFRS 4.

h The text of IAS 39 and the material included from IFRS 4 contain various references to other International Financial Reporting Standards (IFRSs). In FRS 26 those references have been amended where necessary to enable the standard to be applied in a UK context. The ASB believes that those amendments do not change the requirements of IAS 39 or the definition of insurance contract in IFRS 4 in any way.

i IAS 39 sets out amendments to other IFRSs. The Board has made amendments to FRS 12 'Provisions, Contingent Liabilities and Contingent Assets' corresponding to those made by IAS 39 to IAS 37 'Provisions, Contingent Liabilities and Contingent Assets'. The amendments clarify the interaction between FRS 12 and FRS 26, and apply only to those entities applying FRS 26. Other amendments set out in IAS 39 are not relevant in a UK context and have not been included in FRS 26.

j This FRS supersedes, for those entities applying the standard, UITF Abstract 11 'Capital instruments: issuer call options'.

k The illustrative example and implementation guidance issued by the IASB, which accompanies but does not form part of IAS 39, has also been issued by the ASB. Implementation guidance from IFRS 1 that relates to IAS 39 has also been included.

l In October 2005 the Board amended FRS 26 to incorporate five amendments made to IAS 39 by the IASB:

- Transition and Initial Recognition of Financial Assets and Financial Liabilities (December 2004)
- Cash Flow Hedge Accounting of Forecast Intragroup Transactions (April 2005)
- The Fair Value Option (June 2005)
- Financial Guarantee Contracts and Credit Insurance (August 2005)
- IFRIC Interpretation 5 'Rights to Interests arising from Decommissioning, Restoration and Environmental Rehabilitation Funds' (December 2004).

**and equivalent Northern Ireland and Republic of Ireland legislation.*

†Similar amendments are to be made to Northern Ireland and Republic of Ireland legislation.

The requirements of these amendments to FRS 26 are identical to the amendments to IAS 39 except that for the Fair Value Option the Board has: **m**

- added transitional provisions that IASB has inserted in IFRS 1 'First-time Adoption of International Financial Reporting Standards'
- amended the date by which transitional designations must be made from 1 September 2005 to 1 December 2005. This applies only to those entities adopting the amended fair value option for accounting periods commencing before 1 January 2006.

The Board has agreed, in response to a request from the Irish Government, to permit a limited deferral of the effective date of the standard for certain securitisation entities in the Republic of Ireland with listed debt securities but no listed equity.* **n**

In the exposure drafts preceding FRS 26 the Board had decided not to implement in the UK the sections of IAS 39 relating to recognition and derecognition of financial instruments. The Board had taken this approach as it doubted the validity of the method of derecognition that the IASB had been considering at the time and had exposed to its constituents in June 2002. The IASB did not proceed with that approach to derecognition and issued a clarified version of its existing derecognition model in 2003. This Board has therefore decided to bring FRS 26 fully into line with IAS 39 by implementing the IAS 39 recognition and derecognition material into the Standard. **o**

In April 2006 the Board amended FRS 26 to include the IAS 39 material on recognition and derecognition into the Standard. Upon implementation of the amendment the requirements and scope of FRS 26 will be identical to that of IAS 39 except as described in paragraphs g and m above. **p**

Upon implementation of this amendment entities within the scope of FRS 26 will apply the derecognition requirements in FRS 26 to financial assets and liabilities and the derecognition principles of FRS 5 to non-financial assets and liabilities. **q**

For entities within the scope of FRS 26 the recognition and derecognition material is applicable to accounting periods commencing on or after 1 January 2007; earlier adoption is permitted. **r**

The Board took into consideration that on initial application of the new requirements, it may not be practicable to obtain the necessary information to restate all past transactions and that to require such restatement would also be inconsistent with international standards. It has, therefore, permitted transitional provisions similar to those set out in international standards, allowing an entity to choose to apply the requirements either: **s**

(a) only to transactions entered into after the beginning of the comparative period for the accounting period the entity first applied the derecognition requirements of the standard; or

(b) only to transactions entered into after an earlier date of the entity's choosing, provided information sufficient to apply the standard was obtained at the time of initial accounting for each transaction.

The Board has allowed the application of the derecognition provisions from a date related to the entity's first application of the standard rather than a fixed date; but notes that entities wishing to adopt IFRS in due course may wish to choose an **t**

****Editor's note:*** *Paragraphs l to n added in October 2005.*

earlier date for this purpose, for example 1 January 2004, the equivalent transition provisions of IFRS 1, for this purpose.

u At the same time the Board made consequential amendments to FRS 25 which incorporate into that Standard the corresponding disclosure requirements relating to the recognition and derecognition material from IAS 32; to FRS 29 'Financial Instruments: Disclosures' to reinstate the disclosure requirements relating to recognition and derecognition; and to FRS 5 to exclude from its scope those transactions falling within FRS 26.

v In the FRED the Board had proposed to extend the scope of FRS 26 to all entities, excluding those applying the FRSSE, in the UK. The Board has decided to defer a decision on the extension of scope until it has decided on the wider issue of convergence of UK standards with IFRS.*

w In October 2008 the Board issued an amendment to FRS 26 to incorporate changes made by the IASB to IAS 39 *Financial Instruments: Recognition and Measurement 'Reclassification of Financial Assets'*. The amendment permits entities to reclassify certain financial assets, including: non-derivative held-for-trading financial assets (other than those designated at Fair Value Through Profit or Loss by the entity upon initial recognition) out of the Fair Value Through Profit or Loss category in rare circumstances; and certain financial assets to the loans and receivables category (if the financial asset had not been designated as available for sale) if the entity has the intention and ability to hold that financial asset for the foreseeable future.†

x At the same time the Board made consequential amendments to FRS 29 which incorporate into that Standard the consequential disclosure requirements implemented into IFRS 7 by the IASB.

y The October 2008 amendments to FRS 26 and FRS 29 are applicable from 1 July 2008.

z In November 2008 the Board issued an amendment to FRS 26 to incorporate changes made by the IASB to IAS 39 *Financial Instruments: recognition and Measurement 'Eligible Hedged Items'*.‡

a1 In September 2009 the Board amended FRS 26 to incorporate changes made by the IASB to IAS 39 'Financial Instruments: Recognition and Measurement' '*Embedded Derivatives*'. The amendments are applicable for accounting periods ending on or after 31 December 2009.

* ***Editor's note:*** *Paragraphs o to v added in April 2006.*

† ***Editor's note:*** *Paragraphs w to y added in October 2008.*

‡ ***Editor's note:*** *Paragraph z added in November 2008.*

Introduction

Reasons for Revising IAS 39*

International Accounting Standard 39 *Financial Instruments: Recognition and Measurement* (IAS 39) replaces IAS 39 *Financial Instruments: Recognition and Measurement* (revised in 2000) and should be applied for annual periods beginning on or after 1 January 2005. Earlier application is permitted. Implementation Guidance accompanying this revised IAS 39 replaces the Questions and Answers published by the former Implementation Guidance Committee (IGC). **IN1**

The International Accounting Standards Board has developed this revised IAS 39 as part of its project to improve IAS 32 *Financial Instruments: Disclosure and Presentation* and IAS 39. The objective of this project was to reduce complexity by clarifying and adding guidance, eliminating internal inconsistencies and incorporating into the Standard elements of Standing Interpretations Committee (SIC) Interpretations and Questions and Answers published by the IGC. **IN2**

For IAS 39, the Board's main objective was a limited revision to provide additional guidance on selected matters such as derecognition, when financial assets and financial liabilities may be measured at fair value, how to assess impairment, how to determine fair value and some aspects of hedge accounting. The Board did not reconsider the fundamental approach to the accounting for financial instruments contained in IAS 39. **IN3**

The Main Changes

The main changes from the previous version of IAS 39 are described below. **IN4**

Scope

A scope exclusion has been made for loan commitments that are not designated as at fair value through profit or loss, cannot be settled net, and do not involve loan at a below-market interest rate. A commitment to provide a loan at a below-market interest rate is initially recognised at fair value, and subsequently measured at the higher of (a) the amount that would be recognised in accordance with IAS 37 *Provisions, Contingent Liabilities and Contingent Assets* and (b) the amount initially recognised less, when appropriate, cumulative amortisation recognised in accordance with IAS 18 *Revenue*. **IN5**

The scope of the Standard includes financial guarantee contracts issued. However, if an issuer of financial guarantee contracts has previously asserted explicitly that it regards such contracts as insurance contracts and has used accounting applicable to insurance contracts, the issuer may elect to apply either this Standard or IFRS 4 to such financial guarantee contracts. Under this Standard, a financial guarantee contract is initially recognised at fair value and is subsequently measured at the higher of (a) the amount determined in accordance with IAS 37 and (b) the amount initially recognised less, when appropriate, cumulative amortisation recognised in accordance with IAS 18. Different requirements apply for the subsequent measurement of financial guarantee contracts that prevent derecognition of financial assets or result in continuing involvement. Financial guarantee contracts held are not within the **IN6**

****ASB footnote:* Although references to specific IFRSs have been amended in the main section of the Standard, references in the Introduction, which describes the revision of IAS 39, have been left unchanged.***

scope of the Standard because they are insurance contracts and are therefore outside the scope of the Standard because of the general scope exclusion for such contracts.*

IN7 The Standard continues to require that a contract to buy or sell a nonfinancial item is within the scope of IAS 39 if it can be settled net in cash or another financial instrument, unless it is entered into and continues to be held for the purpose of receipt or delivery of a non- financial item in accordance with the entity's expected purchase, sale or usage requirements. However, the Standard clarifies that there are various ways in which a contract to buy or sell a nonfinancial asset can be settled net. These include: when the entity has a practice of settling similar contracts net in cash or another financial instrument, or by exchanging financial instruments; when the entity has a practice of taking delivery of the underlying and selling it within a short period after delivery for the purpose of generating a profit from shortterm fluctuations in price or dealer's margin; and when the non-financial item that is the subject of the contract is readily convertible to cash. The Standard also clarifies that a written option that can be settled net in cash or another financial instrument, or by exchanging financial instruments, is within the scope of the Standard.

Definitions

IN8 The Standard amends the definition of 'originated loans and receivables' to become 'loans and receivables'. Under the revised definition, an entity is permitted to classify as loans and receivables purchased loans that are not quoted in an active market.

Reclassifications

IN8A An amendment to the Standard, issued in October 2008, permits an entity to reclassify non-derivative financial assets (other than those designated at fair value through profit or loss by the entity upon initial recognition) out of the fair value through profit or loss category in particular circumstances. The amendment also permits an entity to transfer from the available-for-sale category to the loans and receivables category a financial asset that would have met the definition of loans and receivables (if the financial asset had not been designated as available for sale), if the entity has the intention and ability to hold that financial asset for the foreseeable future.†

Derecognition of a Financial Asset

IN9 Under the original IAS 39, several concepts governed when a financial asset should be derecognised. Although the revised Standard retains the two main concepts of *risks and rewards* and *control*, it clarifies that the evaluation of the transfer of risks and rewards of ownership precedes the evaluation of the transfer of control for all derecognition transactions.

IN10 Under the Standard, an entity determines what asset is to be considered for derecognition. The Standard requires a part of a larger financial asset to be considered for derecognition if, and only if, the part is one of:

(a) specifically identified cash flows from a financial asset; or
(b) a fully proportionate (pro rata) share of the cash flows from a financial asset; or

****Editor's Note:** Paragraphs IN5 and IN6 amended with effect from 1 January 2006. IN6 further amended in December 2008.*

*†**Editor's note:** Paragraph added in October 2008.*

(c) a fully proportionate (pro rata) share of specifically identified cash flows from a financial asset.

In all other cases, the Standard requires the financial asset to be considered for derecognition in its entirety.

The Standard introduces the notion of a 'transfer' of a financial asset. A financial asset is derecognised when (a) an entity has transferred a financial asset and (b) the transfer qualifies for derecognition. **IN11**

The Standard states that an entity has transferred a financial asset if, and only if, it either: **IN12**

(a) retains the contractual rights to receive the cash flows of the financial asset, but assumes a contractual obligation to pay those cash flows to one or more recipients in an arrangement that meets three specified conditions; or
(b) transfers the contractual rights to receive the cash flows of a financial asset.

Under the Standard, if an entity has transferred a financial asset, it assesses whether it has transferred substantially all the risks and rewards of ownership of the transferred asset. If an entity has retained substantially all such risks and rewards, it continues to recognise the transferred asset. If it has transferred substantially all such risks and rewards, it derecognises the transferred asset. **IN13**

The Standard specifies that if an entity has neither transferred nor retained substantially all the risks and rewards of ownership of the transferred asset, it assesses whether it has retained control over the transferred asset. If it has retained control, the entity continues to recognise the transferred asset to the extent of its continuing involvement in the transferred asset. If it has not retained control, the entity derecognises the transferred asset. **IN14**

The Standard provides guidance on how to apply the concepts of risks and rewards and of control.* **IN15**

Measurement: Fair Value Option

The Standard permits an entity to designate any financial asset or financial liability on initial recognition as one to be measured at fair value, with changes in fair value recognised in profit or loss. To impose discipline on this categorisation, an entity is precluded from reclassifying financial instruments into or out of this category. **IN16**

The option previously contained in IAS 39 to recognise in profit or loss gains and losses on available-for-sale financial assets has been eliminated. Such an option is no longer necessary because under the amendments to IAS 39 an entity is now permitted by designation to measure any financial asset or financial liability at fair value with gains and losses recognised in profit or loss. **IN17**

How to Determine Fair Value

The Standard provides the following additional guidance about how to determine fair values using valuation techniques. **IN18**

**Editor's note:* *Paragraphs IN9 to IN15 added in April 2006.*

- The objective is to establish what the transaction price would have been on the measurement date in an arm's length exchange motivated by normal business considerations.
- A valuation technique (a) incorporates all factors that market participants would consider in setting a price and (b) is consistent with accepted economic methodologies for pricing financial instruments.
- In applying valuation techniques, an entity uses estimates and assumptions that are consistent with available information about the estimates and assumptions that market participants would use in setting a price for the financial instrument.
- The best estimate of fair value at initial recognition of a financial instrument that is not quoted in an active market is the transaction price unless the fair value of the instrument is evidenced by other observable market transactions or is based on a valuation technique whose variables include only data from observable markets.

IN19 The Standard also clarifies that the fair value of a liability with a demand feature, eg a demand deposit, is not less than the amount payable on demand, discounted from the first date that the amount could be required to be paid.

Impairment of Financial Assets

IN20 The Standard clarifies that an impairment loss is recognised only when it has been incurred. It also provides additional guidance on what events provide objective evidence of impairment for investments in equity instruments.

IN21 The Standard provides additional guidance about how to evaluate impairment that is inherent in a group of loans, receivables or held to maturity investments, but cannot yet be identified with any individual financial asset in the group, as follows:

- An asset that is individually assessed for impairment and found to be impaired should not be included in a group of assets that are collectively assessed for impairment.
- An asset that has been individually assessed for impairment and found *not* to be individually impaired should be included in a collective assessment of impairment. The occurrence of an event or a combination of events should not be a precondition for including an asset in a group of assets that are collectively evaluated for impairment.
- When performing a collective assessment of impairment, an entity groups assets by similar credit risk characteristics that are indicative of the debtors' ability to pay all amounts due according to the contractual terms.
- Contractual cash flows and historical loss experience provide the basis for estimating expected cash flows. Historical loss rates are adjusted on the basis of relevant observable data that reflect current economic conditions.
- The methodology for measuring impairment should ensure that an impairment loss is not recognised on the initial recognition of an asset.

IN22 The Standard requires that impairment losses on available-for-sale equity instruments cannot be reversed through profit or loss, ie any subsequent increase in fair value is recognised in equity.

Hedge Accounting

IN23 Hedges of firm commitments are now treated as fair value hedges rather than cash flow hedges. However, the Standard clarifies that a hedge of the foreign currency risk of a firm commitment can be treated as either a cash flow hedge or a fair value hedge.

The Standard requires that when a hedged forecast transaction occurs and results in the recognition of a *financial* asset or a *financial* liability, the gain or loss recognised in other comprehensive income does not adjust the initial carrying amount of the asset or liability (ie basis adjustment is prohibited), but remains in equity and is reclassified from equity to profit or loss consistently with the recognition of gains and losses on the asset or liability as a reclassification adjustment. For hedges of forecast transactions that result in the recognition of a *non-financial asset* or a *non-financial liability*, the entity has a choice of whether to apply basis adjustment or retain the hedging gain or loss in equity and reclassify it from equity to profit or loss when the asset or liability affects profit or loss as a reclassification adjustment.* **IN24**

This Standard permits fair value hedge accounting to be used more readily for a portfolio hedge of interest rate risk than previous versions of IAS 39. In particular, for such a hedge, it allows: **IN24A**

(a) the hedged item to be designated as an amount of a currency (eg an amount of dollars, euro, pounds or rand) rather than as individual assets (or liabilities).

(b) the gain or loss attributable to the hedged item to be presented either:

  (i) in a single separate line item within assets, for those repricing time periods for which the hedged item is an asset; or

  (ii) in a single separate line item within liabilities, for those repricing time periods for which the hedged item is a liability.

(c) prepayment risk to be incorporated by scheduling prepayable items into repricing time periods based on expected, rather than contractual, repricing dates. However, when the portion hedged is based on expected repricing dates, the effect that changes in the hedged interest rate have on those expected repricing dates are included when determining the change in the fair value of the hedged item. Consequently, if a portfolio that contains prepayable items is hedged with a non-prepayable derivative, ineffectiveness arises if the dates on which items in the hedged portfolio are expected to prepay are revised, or actual prepayment dates differ from those expected.

In July 2008† the Board amended the Standard, by Eligible Hedged Items, to clarify how the principles that determine whether a hedged risk or portion of cash flows is eligible for designation should be applied in particular situations. **IN24B**

Disclosure

The disclosure requirements previously in IAS 39 have been moved to IAS 32.‡ **IN25**

Amendments to and Withdrawal of Other Pronouncements

As a consequence of the revisions to this Standard, the Implementation Guidance developed by IASC's IAS 39 Implementation Guidance Committee is superseded by this Standard and its accompanying Implementation Guidance. **IN26**

****Editor's note****: Paragraph amended in December 2008.*

†***ASB Footnote****: In November 2008 the ASB approved the amendment.*

‡*In August 2005 the IASB relocated all disclosures relating to financial instruments to IFRS 7* Financial Instruments: Disclosures. ***Editor's note:*** *Footnote added by FRS 29.*

Potential Impact of Proposals in Exposure Drafts

IN27 [Deleted]

Financial Instruments: Recognition and Measurement

OBJECTIVE

The objective of this Standard is to establish principles for recognising and measuring financial assets, financial liabilities and some contracts to buy or sell non-financial items. Requirements for presenting information about financial instruments are in FRS 25 (IAS 32) *Financial Instruments: Presentation.* Requirements for disclosing information about financial instruments are in FRS 29 (IFRS 7) *Financial Instruments: Disclosures.** 1

SCOPE

This Standard applies to all financial statements that are intended to give a true and fair view of a reporting entity's financial position and profit or loss (or income and expenditure) and are: 1A

(a) for an entity that is a listed entity, or

(b) prepared in accordance with the fair value accounting rules set out in The Large and Medium-sized Companies and Groups (Accounts and Reports) Regulations 2008 or The Large and Medium-sized Limited Liability Partnerships (Accounts) Regulations 2008 ('Accounting Regulations')

except that reporting entities applying the Financial Reporting Standard for Smaller Entities currently applicable are exempt.

The fair value accounting rules are those set out in the following schedules to the Accounting Regulations. Entities that apply the fair value accounting rules for financial instruments fall within the scope of FRS 26 1B

	Old reference Companies Act 1985†	New reference Accounting Regulations
SI 2008/410 Companies		
Companies which are not banking or insurance companies	Schedule 4 paragraphs 34A and 34C	Schedule 1 Part 2 paragraphs 36 and 38
Banking companies	Schedule 9 paragraphs 44A and 44C	Schedule 2 Part 2 paragraphs 44 and 46
Insurance companies	Schedule 9A paragraphs 29A and 29C	Schedule 3 Part 2 paragraphs 30 and 32
SI 2008/1913 Limited Liability Partnerships		
LLP	Schedule 4 paragraphs 34A and 34C	Schedule 1 Part 2 paragraphs 36 and 38

This Standard shall be applied to all types of financial instruments except: 2

(a) interests in subsidiaries, quasi-subsidiaries and associated undertakings, partnerships and joint ventures, including those which are accounted for under FRS 5

****Editor's note:*** *Amended by FRS 29 with effect for accounting periods beginning on or after 1 January 2007.*

†*In this paragraph, all references to schedules of the Companies Act 1985 should be read as including equivalent Northern Ireland and Republic of Ireland legislation. The Companies Act 2006 and regulations under it extend to Northern Ireland.*

Reporting the Substance of Transactions; *and FRS 9 Associates and Joint Ventures. However, entities shall also apply this Standard to derivatives on an interest in a subsidiary, quasi-subsidiary or associated undertaking, partnership or joint venture unless the derivative meets the definition of an equity instrument of the entity in FRS 25.**

(b) *rights and obligations under leases to which SSAP 21* **Accounting for leases and hire purchase contracts** *applies. However:*

(i) *lease receivables recognised by a lessor are subject to the derecognition and impairment provisions of this Standard (see paragraphs 15-37, 58, 59, 63-65 and Appendix A paragraphs AG36-AG52 and AG84-AG93); and*

(ii) *finance lease payables recognised by a lessee are subject to the derecognition provisions of this Standard (see paragraphs 39-42 and Appendix A paragraphs AG57-AG63); and†*

(iii) *derivatives that are embedded in leases are subject to the embedded derivatives provisions of this Standard (see paragraphs 10-13 and Appendix A paragraphs AG27-AG33).*

(c) *employers' rights and obligations under employee benefit plans, to which FRS 17* **Retirement Benefits** *applies.*

(d) *financial instruments issued by the entity that meet the definition of an equity instrument in FRS 25 (including options and warrants) or that are required to be classified as an equity instrument in accordance with paragraphs 16A and 16B or paragraphs 16C and 16D of FRS 25. However, the holder of such equity instruments shall apply this Standard to those instruments, unless they meet the exception in (a) above.‡*

(e) *rights and obligations arising under (i) an insurance contract as defined in Appendix C to FRS 26, other than an issuer's rights and obligations arising under an insurance contract that meets the definition of a financial guarantee contract in paragraph 9, or (ii) a contract that contains a discretionary participation feature as defined in that Appendix. However, this Standard applies to a derivative that is embedded in such a contract if the derivative is not itself an insurance contract (see paragraphs 10–13 and Appendix A paragraphs AG27–AG33). Moreover, if an issuer of financial guarantee contracts has previously asserted explicitly that it regards such contracts as insurance contracts and has used accounting applicable to insurance contracts, the issuer may elect to apply either this Standard or continue to use accounting applicable to insurance contracts to such financial guarantee contracts (see paragraphs AG4 and AG4A). The issuer may make that election contract by contract, but the election for each contract is irrevocable.*

(f) *contracts for contingent consideration in a business combination (see paragraph 27 of FRS 7* **Fair Values in Acquisition Accounting***). This exemption applies only to the acquirer.*

(g) *any forward contracts between an acquirer and a selling shareholder to buy or sell an acquiree that will result in a business combination at a future acquisition date. The term of the forward contract should not exceed a reasonable period normally necessary to obtain any required approvals and to complete the transaction.§*

* **Editor's note**: *Sub-paragraph is amended with effect for accounting periods beginning on or after 1 January 2009.*

†**Editor's note:** *(i) amended and (ii) added in April 2006.*

‡**Editor's note**: *Sub-paragraph amended with effect for accounting periods beginning on or after 1 January 2010.*

§**Editor's note**: *Sub-paragraph amended with effect for accounting periods beginning on or after 1 January 2010.*

(h) ***loan commitments other than those loan commitments described in paragraph 4. An issuer of loan commitments shall apply FRS 12 to loan commitments that are not within the scope of this Standard.****

(i) ***financial instruments, contracts and obligations under share- based payment transactions to which FRS 20*** **Share-based Payment** ***applies, except for contracts within the scope of paragraphs 5-7 of this Standard, to which this Standard applies.***

(j) ***rights to payments to reimburse the entity for expenditure it is required to make to settle a liability it recognises as a provision in accordance with FRS 12 or for which, in an earlier period, it recognised a provision in accordance with FRS 12.†***

[‡] 3

The following loan commitments are within the scope of this Standard: 4

(a) **loan commitments that the entity designates as financial liabilities at fair value through profit or loss. An entity that has a past practice of selling the assets resulting from its loan commitments shortly after origination shall apply this Standard to all its loan commitments in the same class.**

(b) **loan commitments that can be settled net in cash or by delivering or issuing another financial instrument. These loan commitments are derivatives. A loan commitment is not regarded as settled net merely because the loan is paid out in instalments (for example, a mortgage construction loan that is paid out in instalments in line with the progress of construction).**

(c) **commitments to provide a loan at a below-market interest rate. Paragraph 47(d) specifies the subsequent measurement of liabilities arising from these loan commitments.**

This Standard shall be applied to those contracts to buy or sell a nonfinancial item that can be settled net in cash or another financial instrument, or by exchanging financial instruments, as if the contracts were financial instruments, with the exception of contracts that were entered into and continue to be held for the purpose of the receipt or delivery of a non-financial item in accordance with the entity's expected purchase, sale or usage requirements. 5

There are various ways in which a contract to buy or sell a non-financial item can be settled net in cash or another financial instrument or by exchanging financial instruments. These include: 6

(a) when the terms of the contract permit either party to settle it net in cash or another financial instrument or by exchanging financial instruments;

(b) when the ability to settle net in cash or another financial instrument, or by exchanging financial instruments, is not explicit in the terms of the contract, but the entity has a practice of settling similar contracts net in cash or another financial instrument or by exchanging financial instruments (whether with the counterparty, by entering into offsetting contracts or by selling the contract before its exercise or lapse);

(c) when, for similar contracts, the entity has a practice of taking delivery of the underlying and selling it within a short period after delivery for the purpose of generating a profit from shortterm fluctuations in price or dealer's margin; and

****Editor's note:** *(e) and (h) amended with effect from 1 January 2006.*

†***Editor's note:*** *Added with effect from 1 January 2006.*

‡***Editor's note:*** *Paragraph 3 deleted with effect from 1 January 2006.*

(d) when the non-financial item that is the subject of the contract is readily convertible to cash.

A contract to which (b) or (c) applies is not entered into for the purpose of the receipt or delivery of the non-financial item in accordance with the entity's expected purchase, sale or usage requirements and, accordingly, is within the scope of this Standard. Other contracts to which paragraph 5 applies are evaluated to determine whether they were entered into and continue to be held for the purpose of the receipt or delivery of the non-financial item in accordance with the entity's expected purchase, sale or usage requirements and, accordingly, whether they are within the scope of this Standard.

7 A written option to buy or sell a non-financial item that can be settled net in cash or another financial instrument, or by exchanging financial instruments, in accordance with paragraph 6(a) or (d) is within the scope of this Standard. Such a contract cannot be entered into for the purpose of the receipt or delivery of the non-financial item in accordance with the entity's expected purchase, sale or usage requirements.

DEFINITIONS

8 The terms defined in FRS 25 are used in this Standard with the meanings specified in paragraph 11 of FRS 25. FRS 25 defines the following terms:

- financial instrument
- financial asset
- financial liability
- equity instrument

and provides guidance on applying those definitions.

9 ***The following terms are used in this Standard with the meanings specified:***

Definition of a Derivative

A <u>derivative</u> is a financial instrument or other contract within the scope of this Standard (see paragraphs 2-7) with all three of the following characteristics:

(a) its value changes in response to the change in a specified interest rate, financial instrument price, commodity price, foreign exchange rate, index of prices or rates, credit rating or credit index, or other variable, provided in the case of a non-financial variable that the variable is not specific to a party to the contract (sometimes called the 'underlying');
(b) it requires no initial net investment or an initial net investment that is smaller than would be required for other types of contracts that would be expected to have a similar response to changes in market factors; and
(c) it is settled at a future date.

Definitions of Four Categories of Financial Instruments

A <u>financial asset or financial liability at fair value through profit or loss</u> is a financial asset or financial liability that meets either of the following conditions.

(a) It is classified as held for trading. A financial asset or financial liability is classified as held for trading if:

(i) it is acquired or incurred principally for the purpose of selling or repurchasing it in the near term;

(ii) ***on initial recognition it is part of a portfolio of identified financial instruments that are managed together and for which there is evidence of a recent actual pattern of short-term profit-taking; or***

(iii) ***it is a derivative (except for a derivative that is a financial guarantee contract or a designated and effective hedging instrument).****

(b) ***Upon initial recognition it is designated by the entity as at fair value through profit or loss. An entity may use this designation only when permitted by paragraph 11A, or when doing so results in more relevant information, because either***

(i) ***it eliminates or significantly reduces a measurement or recognition inconsistency (sometimes referred to as 'an accounting mismatch') that would otherwise arise from measuring assets or liabilities or recognising the gains and losses on them on different bases; or***

(ii) ***a group of financial assets, financial liabilities or both is managed and its performance is evaluated on a fair value basis, in accordance with a documented risk management or investment strategy, and information about the group is provided internally on that basis to the entity's key management personnel. For the purposes of this standard, key management personnel are those persons having authority and responsibility for planning, directing and controlling the activities of the entity, directly or indirectly, including any director (whether executive or otherwise) of that entity. For example the entity's board of directors and chief executive officer.†***

In FRS 29, paragraphs 9–11 and B4 require the entity to provide disclosures about financial assets and financial liabilities it has designated as at fair value through profit or loss, including how it has satisfied these conditions. For instruments qualifying in accordance with (ii) above, that disclosure includes a narrative description of how designation as at fair value through profit or loss is consistent with the entity's documented risk management or investment strategy.

Investments in equity instruments that do not have a quoted market price in an active market, and whose fair value cannot be reliably measured (see paragraph 46(c) and Appendix A paragraphs AG80 and AG81), shall not be designated as at fair value through profit or loss.

It should be noted that paragraphs 48, 48A, 49 and Appendix A paragraphs AG69-AG82, which set out requirements for determining a reliable measure of the fair value of a financial asset or financial liability, apply equally to all items that are measured at fair value, whether by designation or otherwise, or whose fair value is disclosed.‡

Held-to-maturity investments are non-derivative financial assets with fixed or determinable payments and fixed maturity that an entity has the positive intention and ability to hold to maturity (see Appendix A paragraphs AG16-AG25) other than:

(a) ***those that the entity upon initial recognition designates as at fair value through profit or loss;***

(b) ***those that the entity designates as available for sale; and***

(c) ***those that meet the definition of loans and receivables.***

****Editor's note:** *Sub-paragraph amended with effect for accounting periods beginning on or after 1 January 2009.*

†***ASB Footnote:*** *The IASB's definition of key management personnel is contained in IAS 24* Related Party Disclosures. *In the UK key management is defined in FRS 8* Related Party Disclosures. *For the purposes of this standard the ASB Board considered it appropriate to use the IASB's definition.*

‡***Editor's note:*** *Definition amended October 2005, with effect from 1 January 2006.*

An entity shall not classify any financial assets as held to maturity if the entity has, during the current financial year or during the two preceding financial years, sold or reclassified more than an insignificant amount of held-to-maturity investments before maturity (more than insignificant in relation to the total amount of heldtomaturity investments) other than sales or reclassifications that:

(i) are so close to maturity or the financial asset's call date (for example, less than three months before maturity) that changes in the market rate of interest would not have a significant effect on the financial asset's fair value;
(ii) occur after the entity has collected substantially all of the financial asset's original principal through scheduled payments or prepayments; or
(iii) are attributable to an isolated event that is beyond the entity's control, is non-recurring and could not have been reasonably anticipated by the entity.

Loans and receivables are non-derivative financial assets with fixed or determinable payments that are not quoted in an active market, other than:
(a) those that the entity intends to sell immediately or in the near term, which shall be classified as held for trading, and those that the entity upon initial recognition designates as at fair value through profit or loss;
(b) those that the entity upon initial recognition designates as available for sale; or
(c) those for which the holder may not recover substantially all of its initial investment, other than because of credit deterioration, which shall be classified as available for sale.

An interest acquired in a pool of assets that are not loans or receivables (for example, an interest in a mutual fund or a similar fund) is not a loan or receivable.

Available-for-sale financial assets are those non-derivative financial assets that are designated as available for sale or are not classified as (a) loans and receivables, (b) held-to-maturity investments or (c) financial assets at fair value through profit or loss.

Definition of a financial guarantee contract

A *financial guarantee contract* is a contract that requires the issuer to make specified payments to reimburse the holder for a loss it incurs because a specified debtor fails to make payment when due in accordance with the original or modified terms of a debt instrument.*

Definitions Relating to Recognition and Measurement

For the purposes of paragraph 19, cash comprises cash on hand and demand deposits, and cash equivalents are short-term, highly liquid investments that are readily convertible to known amounts of cash and which are subject to insignificant risk of changes in value.†

The amortised cost of a financial asset or financial liability is the amount at which the financial asset or financial liability is measured at initial recognition minus principal repayments, plus or minus the cumulative amortisation using the effective interest method of any difference between that initial amount and the maturity amount, and minus any reduction (directly or through the use of an allowance account) for impairment or uncollectibility.

****Editor's note:** Definition added with effect from 1 January 2006.*

*†**Editor's note:** Definition added in April 2006.*

The effective interest method is a method of calculating the amortised cost of a financial asset or a financial liability (or group of financial assets or financial liabilities) and of allocating the interest income or interest expense over the relevant period. The effective interest rate is the rate that exactly discounts estimated future cash payments or receipts through the expected life of the financial instrument or, when appropriate, a shorter period to the net carrying amount of the financial asset or financial liability. When calculating the effective interest rate, an entity shall estimate cash flows considering all contractual terms of the financial instrument (for example, prepayment, call and similar options) but shall not consider future credit losses. The calculation includes all fees and points paid or received between parties to the contract that are an integral part of the effective interest rate (see IAS 18), transaction costs, and all other premiums or discounts. There is a presumption that the cash flows and the expected life of a group of similar financial instruments can be estimated reliably. However, in those rare cases when it is not possible to estimate reliably the cash flows or the expected life of a financial instrument (or group of financial instruments), the entity shall use the contractual cash flows over the full contractual term of the financial instrument (or group of financial instruments).

Derecognition is the removal of a previously recognised financial asset or financial liability from an entity's balance sheet.*

Fair value is the amount for which an asset could be exchanged, or a liability settled, between knowledgeable, willing parties in an arm's length transaction.†

A regular way purchase or sale is a purchase or sale of a financial asset under a contract whose terms require delivery of the asset within the time frame established generally by regulation or convention in the marketplace concerned.

Transaction costs are incremental costs that are directly attributable to the acquisition, issue or disposal of a financial asset or financial liability (see Appendix A paragraph AG13). An incremental cost is one that would not have been incurred if the entity had not acquired, issued or disposed of the financial instrument.

Definitions Relating to Hedge Accounting

A firm commitment is a binding agreement for the exchange of a specified quantity of resources at a specified price on a specified future date or dates.

A forecast transaction is an uncommitted but anticipated future transaction.

A hedging instrument is a designated derivative or (for a hedge of the risk of changes in foreign currency exchange rates only) a designated nonderivative financial asset or nonderivative financial liability whose fair value or cash flows are expected to offset changes in the fair value or cash flows of a designated hedged item (paragraphs 72-77 and Appendix A paragraphs AG94-AG97 elaborate on the definition of a hedging instrument).

A hedged item is an asset, liability, firm commitment, highly probable forecast transaction or net investment in a foreign operation that (a) exposes the entity to risk of changes in fair value or future cash flows and (b) is designated as being hedged

**Editor's note:* *Definition added in April 2006.*

†*Paragraphs 48, 49 and AG69-AG82 of Appendix A contain requirements for determining the fair value of a financial asset or financial liability.*

(paragraphs 78-84 and Appendix A paragraphs AG98-AG101 elaborate on the definition of hedged items).

Hedge effectiveness is the degree to which changes in the fair value or cash flows of the hedged item that are attributable to a hedged risk are offset by changes in the fair value or cash flows of the hedging instrument (see Appendix A paragraphs AG105-AG113).

9A ***A listed entity is an entity that has in issue one or more securities that are admitted to trading on a regulated market of any Member State by Council Directive 2004/39/EC.***

9B ***The date of transition to this standard is the beginning of the earliest period for which an entity presents comparative information in compliance with this standard. In the case of an entity that chooses to apply the option in paragraph 108D not to restate comparative information, the date of transition is the beginning of the accounting period in which the standard is first applied.***

EMBEDDED DERIVATIVES

10 An embedded derivative is a component of a hybrid (combined) instrument that also includes a non-derivative host contract—with the effect that some of the cash flows of the combined instrument vary in a way similar to a stand-alone derivative. An embedded derivative causes some or all of the cash flows that otherwise would be required by the contract to be modified according to a specified interest rate, financial instrument price, commodity price, foreign exchange rate, index of prices or rates, credit rating or credit index, or other variable, provided in the case of a non-financial variable that the variable is not specific to a party to the contract. A derivative that is attached to a financial instrument but is contractually transferable independently of that instrument, or has a different counterparty from that instrument, is not an embedded derivative, but a separate financial instrument.

11 ***An embedded derivative shall be separated from the host contract and accounted for as a derivative under this Standard if, and only if:***

(a) the economic characteristics and risks of the embedded derivative are not closely related to the economic characteristics and risks of the host contract (see Appendix A paragraphs AG30 and AG33);
(b) a separate instrument with the same terms as the embedded derivative would meet the definition of a derivative; and
(c) the hybrid (combined) instrument is not measured at fair value with changes in fair value recognised in profit or loss (ie a derivative that is embedded in a financial asset or financial liability at fair value through profit or loss is not separated).

If an embedded derivative is separated, the host contract shall be accounted for under this Standard if it is a financial instrument, and in accordance with other appropriate Standards if it is not a financial instrument. This Standard does not address whether an embedded derivative shall be presented separately on the face of the financial statements.

11A ***Notwithstanding paragraph 11, if a contract contains one or more embedded derivatives, an entity may designate the entire hybrid (combined) contract as a financial asset or financial liability at fair value through profit or loss unless:***

(a) the embedded derivative(s) does not significantly modify the cash flows that otherwise would be required by the contract; or

(b) ***it is clear with little or no analysis when a similar hybrid (combined) instrument is first considered that separation of the embedded derivative(s) is prohibited, such as a prepayment option embedded in a loan that permits the holder to prepay the loan for approximately its amortised cost.***

If an entity is required by this Standard to separate an embedded derivative from its host contract, but is unable to measure the embedded derivative separately either at acquisition or at the end of a subsequent financial reporting period, it shall designate the entire hybrid (combined) contract as at fair value through profit or loss. Similarly, if an entity is unable to measure separately the embedded derivative that would have to be separated on reclassification of a hybrid (combined) contract out of the fair value through profit or loss category, that reclassification is prohibited. In such circumstances the hybrid (combined) contract remains classified as at fair value through profit or loss in its entirety.* **12**

If an entity is unable to determine reliably the fair value of an embedded derivative on the basis of its terms and conditions (for example, because the embedded derivative is based on an unquoted equity instrument), the fair value of the embedded derivative is the difference between the fair value of the hybrid (combined) instrument and the fair value of the host contract, if those can be determined under this Standard. If the entity is unable to determine the fair value of the embedded derivative using this method, paragraph 12 applies and the hybrid (combined) instrument is designated as at fair value through profit or loss.† **13**

Recognition and Derecognition

Initial Recognition

An entity shall recognise a financial asset or a financial liability on its balance sheet when, and only when, the entity becomes a party to the contractual provisions of the instrument. (See paragraph 38 with respect to regular way purchases of financial assets.) **14**

Derecognition of a Financial Asset

In consolidated financial statements, paragraphs 16–23 and Appendix A paragraphs AG34–AG52 are applied at a consolidated level. Hence, an entity first consolidates all subsidiaries in accordance with FRS 2 and quasi-subsidiaries in accordance with FRS 5‡ and then applies paragraphs 16–23 and Appendix A paragraphs AG34–AG52 to the resulting group. **15**

Before evaluating whether, and to what extent, derecognition is appropriate under paragraphs 17–23, an entity determines whether those paragraphs should be applied to a part of a financial asset (or a part of a group of similar financial assets) or a financial asset (or a group of similar financial assets) in its entirety, as follows. **16**

***Editor's note:** *Paragraph amended in September 2009 with effect for accounting periods ending on or after 31 December 2009.*

†**Editor's note:** *Paragraph 11A added, and 12 and 13 amended, with effect from 1 January 2006.*

‡**ASB footnote**: *Where an entity has a quasi-subsidiary but no subsidiary undertakings and therefore does not prepare group financial statements, it should provide in its financial statements consolidated financial statements of itself and its quasi-subsidiary in accordance with paragraph 35 of FRS 5.*

***(a)* Paragraphs 17–23 are applied to a part of a financial asset (or a part of a group of similar financial assets) if, and only if, the part being considered for derecognition meets one of the following three conditions.**

***(i)* The part comprises only specifically identified cash flows from a financial asset (or a group of similar financial assets). For example, when an entity enters into an interest rate strip whereby the counterparty obtains the right to the interest cash flows, but not the principal cash flows from a debt instrument, paragraphs 17–23 are applied to the interest cash flows.**

***(ii)* The part comprises only a fully proportionate (pro rata) share of the cash flows from a financial asset (or a group of similar financial assets). For example, when an entity enters into an arrangement whereby the counterparty obtains the rights to a 90 per cent share of all cash flows of a debt instrument, paragraphs 17–23 are applied to 90 per cent of those cash flows. If there is more than one counterparty, each counterparty is not required to have a proportionate share of the cash flows provided that the transferring entity has a fully proportionate share.**

***(iii)* The part comprises only a fully proportionate (pro rata) share of specifically identified cash flows from a financial asset (or a group of similar financial assets). For example, when an entity enters into an arrangement whereby the counterparty obtains the rights to a 90 per cent share of interest cash flows from a financial asset, paragraphs 17–23 are applied to 90 per cent of those interest cash flows. If there is more than one counterparty, each counterparty is not required to have a proportionate share of the specifically identified cash flows provided that the transferring entity has a fully proportionate share.**

***(b)* In all other cases, paragraphs 17–23 are applied to the financial asset in its entirety (or to the group of similar financial assets in their entirety). For example, when an entity transfers (i) the rights to the first or the last 90 per cent of cash collections from a financial asset (or a group of financial assets), or (ii) the rights to 90 per cent of the cash flows from a group of receivables, but provides a guarantee to compensate the buyer for any credit losses up to 8 per cent of the principal amount of the receivables, paragraphs 17–23 are applied to the financial asset (or a group of similar financial assets) in its entirety.**

In paragraphs 17–26, the term 'financial asset' refers to either a part of a financial asset (or a part of a group of similar financial assets) as identified in (a) above or, otherwise, a financial asset (or a group of similar financial assets) in its entirety.

17 ***An entity shall derecognise a financial asset when, and only when:***

***(a)* the contractual rights to the cash flows from the financial asset expire; or**

***(b)* it transfers the financial asset as set out in paragraphs 18 and 19 and the transfer qualifies for derecognition in accordance with paragraph 20.**

(See paragraph 38 for regular way sales of financial assets.)

18 ***An entity transfers a financial asset if, and only if, it either:***

***(a)* transfers the contractual rights to receive the cash flows of the financial asset; or**

***(b)* retains the contractual rights to receive the cash flows of the financial asset, but assumes a contractual obligation to pay the cash flows to one or more recipients in an arrangement that meets the conditions in paragraph 19.**

19 ***When an entity retains the contractual rights to receive the cash flows of a financial asset (the 'original asset'), but assumes a contractual obligation to pay those cash flows***

to one or more entities (the 'eventual recipients'), the entity treats the transaction as a transfer of a financial asset if, and only if, all of the following three conditions are met.

(a) The entity has no obligation to pay amounts to the eventual recipients unless it collects equivalent amounts from the original asset. Short-term advances by the entity with the right of full recovery of the amount lent plus accrued interest at market rates do not violate this condition.

(b) The entity is prohibited by the terms of the transfer contract from selling or pledging the original asset other than as security to the eventual recipients for the obligation to pay them cash flows.

(c) The entity has an obligation to remit any cash flows it collects on behalf of the eventual recipients without material delay. In addition, the entity is not entitled to reinvest such cash flows, except for investments in cash or cash equivalents (as defined in paragraph 9) during the short settlement period from the collection date to the date of required remittance to the eventual recipients, and interest earned on such investments is passed to the eventual recipients.

When an entity transfers a financial asset (see paragraph 18), it shall evaluate the extent to which it retains the risks and rewards of ownership of the financial asset. In this case: 20

(a) if the entity transfers substantially all the risks and rewards of ownership of the financial asset, the entity shall derecognise the financial asset and recognise separately as assets or liabilities any rights and obligations created or retained in the transfer.

(b) if the entity retains substantially all the risks and rewards of ownership of the financial asset, the entity shall continue to recognise the financial asset.

(c) if the entity neither transfers nor retains substantially all the risks and rewards of ownership of the financial asset, the entity shall determine whether it has retained control of the financial asset. In this case:

(i) if the entity has not retained control, it shall derecognise the financial asset and recognise separately as assets or liabilities any rights and obligations created or retained in the transfer.

(ii) if the entity has retained control, it shall continue to recognise the financial asset to the extent of its continuing involvement in the financial asset (see paragraph 30).

The transfer of risks and rewards (see paragraph 20) is evaluated by comparing the entity's exposure, before and after the transfer, with the variability in the amounts and timing of the net cash flows of the transferred asset. An entity has retained substantially all the risks and rewards of ownership of a financial asset if its exposure to the variability in the present value of the future net cash flows from the financial asset does not change significantly as a result of the transfer (eg because the entity has sold a financial asset subject to an agreement to buy it back at a fixed price or the sale price plus a lender's return). An entity has transferred substantially all the risks and rewards of ownership of a financial asset if its exposure to such variability is no longer significant in relation to the total variability in the present value of the future net cash flows associated with the financial asset (eg because the entity has sold a financial asset subject only to an option to buy it back at its fair value at the time of repurchase or has transferred a fully proportionate share of the cash flows from a larger financial asset in an arrangement, such as a loan sub-participation, that meets the conditions in paragraph 19). 21

Often it will be obvious whether the entity has transferred or retained substantially all risks and rewards of ownership and there will be no need to perform any computations. In other cases, it will be necessary to compute and compare the entity's 22 exposure to the variability in the present value of the future net cash flows before and after the transfer. The computation and comparison is made using as the discount rate an appropriate current market interest rate. All reasonably possible variability in net cash flows is considered, with greater weight being given to those outcomes that are more likely to occur.

23 Whether the entity has retained control (see paragraph 20(c)) of the transferred asset depends on the transferee's ability to sell the asset. If the transferee has the practical ability to sell the asset in its entirety to an unrelated third party and is able to exercise that ability unilaterally and without needing to impose additional restrictions on the transfer, the entity has not retained control. In all other cases, the entity has retained control.

Transfers that Qualify for Derecognition (see paragraph 20(a) and (c)(i))

24 ***If an entity transfers a financial asset in a transfer that qualifies for derecognition in its entirety and retains the right to service the financial asset for a fee, it shall recognise either a servicing asset or a servicing liability for that servicing contract. If the fee to be received is not expected to compensate the entity adequately for performing the servicing, a servicing liability for the servicing obligation shall be recognised at its fair value. If the fee to be received is expected to be more than adequate compensation for the servicing, a servicing asset shall be recognised for the servicing right at an amount determined on the basis of an allocation of the carrying amount of the larger financial asset in accordance with paragraph 27.***

25 ***If, as a result of a transfer, a financial asset is derecognised in its entirety but the transfer results in the entity obtaining a new financial asset or assuming a new financial liability, or a servicing liability, the entity shall recognise the new financial asset, financial liability or servicing liability at fair value.***

26 ***On derecognition of a financial asset in its entirety, the difference between:***

(a) the carrying amount and
(b) the sum of (i) the consideration received (including any new asset obtained less any new liability assumed) and (ii) any cumulative gain or loss that had been recognised directly in equity (see paragraph 55(b))

shall be recognised in profit or loss.

27 ***If the transferred asset is part of a larger financial asset (eg when an entity transfers interest cash flows that are part of a debt instrument, see paragraph 16(a)) and the part transferred qualifies for derecognition in its entirety, the previous carrying amount of the larger financial asset shall be allocated between the part that continues to be recognised and the part that is derecognised, based on the relative fair values of those parts on the date of the transfer. For this purpose, a retained servicing asset shall be treated as a part that continues to be recognised. The difference between:***

(a) the carrying amount allocated to the part derecognised and
(b) the sum of (i) the consideration received for the part derecognised (including any new asset obtained less any new liability assumed) and (ii) any cumulative gain or loss allocated to it that had been recognised directly in equity (see paragraph 55(b))

shall be recognised in profit or loss. A cumulative gain or loss that had been recognised in equity is allocated between the part that continues to be recognised and the part that is derecognised, based on the relative fair values of those parts.

When an entity allocates the previous carrying amount of a larger financial asset between the part that continues to be recognised and the part that is derecognised, the fair value of the part that continues to be recognised needs to be determined. When the entity has a history of selling parts similar to the part that continues to be recognised or other market transactions exist for such parts, recent prices of actual transactions provide the best estimate of its fair value. When there are no price quotes or recent market transactions to support the fair value of the part that continues to be recognised, the best estimate of the fair value is the difference between the fair value of the larger financial asset as a whole and the consideration received from the transferee for the part that is derecognised. 28

Transfers that Do Not Qualify for Derecognition (see paragraph 20(b))

If a transfer does not result in derecognition because the entity has retained substantially all the risks and rewards of ownership of the transferred asset, the entity shall continue to recognise the transferred asset in its entirety and shall recognise a financial liability for the consideration received. In subsequent periods, the entity shall recognise any income on the transferred asset and any expense incurred on the financial liability. 29

Continuing Involvement in Transferred Assets *(see paragraph 20(c)(ii))*

If an entity neither transfers nor retains substantially all the risks and rewards of ownership of a transferred asset, and retains control of the transferred asset, the entity continues to recognise the transferred asset to the extent of its continuing involvement. The extent of the entity's continuing involvement in the transferred asset is the extent to which it is exposed to changes in the value of the transferred asset. For example: 30

(a) when the entity's continuing involvement takes the form of guaranteeing the transferred asset, the extent of the entity's continuing involvement is the lower of (i) the amount of the asset and (ii) the maximum amount of the consideration received that the entity could be required to repay ('the guarantee amount').

(b) when the entity's continuing involvement takes the form of a written or purchased option (or both) on the transferred asset, the extent of the entity's continuing involvement is the amount of the transferred asset that the entity may repurchase. However, in case of a written put option on an asset that is measured at fair value, the extent of the entity's continuing involvement is limited to the lower of the fair value of the transferred asset and the option exercise price (see paragraph AG48).

(c) when the entity's continuing involvement takes the form of a cash-settled option or similar provision on the transferred asset, the extent of the entity's continuing involvement is measured in the same way as that which results from non-cash settled options as set out in (b) above.

When an entity continues to recognise an asset to the extent of its continuing involvement, the entity also recognises an associated liability. Despite the other measurement requirements in this Standard, the transferred asset and the associated liability are measured on a basis that reflects the rights and obligations that the entity has retained. The associated liability is measured in such a way that the net carrying amount of the transferred asset and the associated liability is: 31

(a) the amortised cost of the rights and obligations retained by the entity, if the transferred asset is measured at amortised cost; or

(b) equal to the fair value of the rights and obligations retained by the entity when measured on a stand-alone basis, if the transferred asset is measured at fair value.

32 ***The entity shall continue to recognise any income arising on the transferred asset to the extent of its continuing involvement and shall recognise any expense incurred on the associated liability.***

33 ***For the purpose of subsequent measurement, recognised changes in the fair value of the transferred asset and the associated liability are accounted for consistently with each other in accordance with paragraph 55, and shall not be offset.***

34 ***If an entity's continuing involvement is in only a part of a financial asset (eg when an entity retains an option to repurchase part of a transferred asset, or retains a residual interest that does not result in the retention of substantially all the risks and rewards of ownership and the entity retains control), the entity allocates the previous carrying amount of the financial asset between the part it continues to recognise under continuing involvement, and the part it no longer recognises on the basis of the relative fair values of those parts on the date of the transfer. For this purpose, the requirements of paragraph 28 apply. The difference between:***

(a) the carrying amount allocated to the part that is no longer recognised; and
(b) the sum of (i) the consideration received for the part no longer recognised and (ii) any cumulative gain or loss allocated to it that had been recognised directly in equity (see paragraph 55(b))

shall be recognised in profit or loss. A cumulative gain or loss that had been recognised in equity is allocated between the part that continues to be recognised and the part that is no longer recognised on the basis of the relative fair values of those parts.

35 If the transferred asset is measured at amortised cost, the option in this Standard to designate a financial liability as at fair value through profit or loss is not applicable to the associated liability.

All Transfers

36 ***If a transferred asset continues to be recognised, the asset and the associated liability shall not be offset. Similarly, the entity shall not offset any income arising from the transferred asset with any expense incurred on the associated liability (see FRS 25 paragraph 42).***

37 ***If a transferor provides non-cash collateral (such as debt or equity instruments) to the transferee, the accounting for the collateral by the transferor and the transferee depends on whether the transferee has the right to sell or repledge the collateral and on whether the transferor has defaulted. The transferor and transferee shall account for the collateral as follows:***

(a) If the transferee has the right by contract or custom to sell or repledge the collateral, then the transferor shall reclassify that asset in its balance sheet (eg as a loaned asset, pledged equity instruments or repurchase receivable) separately from other assets.
(b) If the transferee sells collateral pledged to it, it shall recognise the proceeds from the sale and a liability measured at fair value for its obligation to return the collateral.
(c) If the transferor defaults under the terms of the contract and is no longer entitled to redeem the collateral, it shall derecognise the collateral, and the transferee shall recognise the collateral as its asset initially measured at fair value or, if it has already sold the collateral, derecognise its obligation to return the collateral.
(d) Except as provided in (c), the transferor shall continue to carry the collateral as its asset, and the transferee shall not recognise the collateral as an asset.

Regular Way Purchase or Sale of a Financial Asset

A regular way purchase or sale of financial assets shall be recognised and derecognised, as applicable, using trade date accounting or settlement date accounting (see Appendix A paragraphs AG53–AG56). 38

Derecognition of a Financial Liability

An entity shall remove a financial liability (or a part of a financial liability) from its balance sheet when, and only when, it is extinguished—ie when the obligation specified in the contract is discharged or cancelled or expires. 39

An exchange between an existing borrower and lender of debt instruments with substantially different terms shall be accounted for as an extinguishment of the original financial liability and the recognition of a new financial liability. Similarly, a substantial modification of the terms of an existing financial liability or a part of it (whether or not attributable to the financial difficulty of the debtor) shall be accounted for as an extinguishment of the original financial liability and the recognition of a new financial liability. 40

The difference between the carrying amount of a financial liability (or part of a financial liability) extinguished or transferred to another party and the consideration paid, including any non-cash assets transferred or liabilities assumed, shall be recognised in profit or loss. 41

If an entity repurchases a part of a financial liability, the entity shall allocate the previous carrying amount of the financial liability between the part that continues to be recognised and the part that is derecognised based on the relative fair values of those parts on the date of the repurchase. The difference between (a) the carrying amount allocated to the part derecognised and (b) the consideration paid, including any non-cash assets transferred or liabilities assumed, for the part derecognised shall be recognised in profit or loss. 42

MEASUREMENT

Initial Measurement of Financial Assets and Financial Liabilities

When a financial asset or financial liability is recognised initially, an entity shall measure it at its fair value plus, in the case of a financial asset or financial liability not at fair value through profit or loss, transaction costs that are directly attributable to the acquisition or issue of the financial asset or financial liability. 43

When an entity uses settlement date accounting for an asset that is subsequently measured at cost or amortised cost, the asset is recognised initially at its fair value on the trade date (see Appendix A paragraphs AG53-AG56). 44

Subsequent Measurement of Financial Assets

For the purpose of measuring a financial asset after initial recognition, this Standard classifies financial assets into the following four categories defined in paragraph 9: 45

(a) financial assets at fair value through profit or loss;
(b) held-to-maturity investments;
(c) loans and receivables; and
(d) available-for-sale financial assets.

These categories apply to measurement and profit or loss recognition under this Standard. The entity may use other descriptors for these categories or other categorisations when presenting information on the face of the financial statements. The entity shall disclose in the notes the information required by FRS 29.*

46 ***After initial recognition, an entity shall measure financial assets, including derivatives that are assets, at their fair values, without any deduction for transaction costs it may incur on sale or other disposal, except for the following financial assets:***

(a) loans and receivables as defined in paragraph 9, which shall be measured at amortised cost using the effective interest method;
(b) held-to-maturity investments as defined in paragraph 9, which shall be measured at amortised cost using the effective interest method; and
(c) investments in equity instruments that do not have a quoted market price in an active market and whose fair value cannot be reliably measured and derivatives that are linked to and must be settled by delivery of such unquoted equity instruments, which shall be measured at cost (see Appendix A paragraphs AG80 and AG81).

Financial assets that are designated as hedged items are subject to measurement under the hedge accounting requirements in paragraphs 89-102. All financial assets except those measured at fair value through profit or loss are subject to review for impairment in accordance with paragraphs 58-70 and Appendix A paragraphs AG84-AG93.

Subsequent Measurement of Financial Liabilities

47 **After initial recognition, an entity shall measure all financial liabilities at amortised cost using the effective interest method, except for:**

(a) financial liabilities at fair value through profit or loss. Such liabilities, including derivatives that are liabilities, shall be measured at fair value except for a derivative liability that is linked to and must be settled by delivery of an unquoted equity instrument whose fair value cannot be reliably measured which shall be measured at cost.
(b) financial liabilities that arise when a transfer of a financial asset does not qualify for derecognition.
(c) financial liabilities that arise when a transfer of a non-financial asset does not qualify for derecognition.†
(c) financial guarantee contracts as defined in paragraph 9. After initial recognition, an issuer of such a contract shall (unless paragraph 47(a) or (b) applies) measure it at the higher of:

(i) the amount determined in accordance with FRS 12; and
(ii) the amount initially recognised (see paragraph 43) less, when appropriate, cumulative amortisation.

(d) commitments to provide a loan at a below-market interest rate. After initial recognition, an issuer of such a commitment shall (unless paragraph 47(a) applies) measure it at the higher of:

(i) the amount determined in accordance with FRS 12; and

****Editor's note:*** *Reference to FRS 25 replaced with a reference to FRS 29 with effect for accounting periods beginning on or after 1 January 2007.*

†***Editor's note:*** *Added in April 2006. There would now appear to be two sub-paragraphs (c).*

(ii) the amount initially recognised (see paragraph 43) less, when appropriate, cumulative amortisation.*

Fair Value Measurement Considerations

In determining the fair value of a financial asset or a financial liability for the purpose of applying this Standard, FRS 25 or FRS 29, an entity shall apply paragraphs AG69-AG82 of Appendix A.† **48**

The best evidence of fair value is quoted prices in an active market. If the market for a financial instrument is not active, an entity establishes fair value by using a valuation technique. The objective of using a valuation technique is to establish what the transaction price would have been on the measurement date in an arm's length exchange motivated by normal business considerations. Valuation techniques include using recent arm's length market transactions between knowledgeable, willing parties, if available, reference to the current fair value of another instrument that is substantially the same, discounted cash flow analysis and option pricing models. If there is a valuation technique commonly used by market participants to price the instrument and that technique has been demonstrated to provide reliable estimates of prices obtained in actual market transactions, the entity uses that technique. The chosen valuation technique makes maximum use of market inputs and relies as little as possible on entity-specific inputs. It incorporates all factors that market participants would consider in setting a price and is consistent with accepted economic methodologies for pricing financial instruments. Periodically, an entity calibrates the valuation technique and tests it for validity using prices from any observable current market transactions in the same instrument (ie without modification or repackaging) or based on any available observable market data.‡ **48A**

The fair value of a financial liability with a demand feature (eg a demand deposit) is not less than the amount payable on demand, discounted from the first date that the amount could be required to be paid. **49**

Reclassifications

An entity: **50**

(a) shall not reclassify a derivative out of the fair value through profit or loss category while it is held or issued;

(b) shall not reclassify any financial instrument out of the fair value through profit or loss category if upon initial recognition it was designated by the entity as at fair value through profit or loss; and

(c) may, if a financial asset is no longer held for the purpose of selling or repurchasing it in the near term (notwithstanding that the financial asset may have been acquired or incurred principally for the purpose of selling or repurchasing it in the near term), reclassify that financial asset out of the fair value through profit or loss category if the requirements in paragraph 50B or 50D are met.

****Editor's note:*** *Paragraph amended with effect from 1 January 2006.*

†***Editor's note:*** *This paragraph replaced by FRS 29 with effect for accounting periods beginning on or after 1 January 2007, or where FRS 29 is adopted early.*

‡***Editor's note:*** *Paragraph 48A added with effect from 1 January 2006.*

An entity shall not reclassify any financial instrument into the fair value through profit or loss category after initial recognition.*

50A The following changes in circumstances are not reclassifications for the purposes of paragraph 50:

(a) a derivative that was previously a designated and effective hedging instrument in a cash flow hedge or net investment hedge no longer qualifies as such;
(b) a derivative becomes a designated and effective hedging instrument in a cash flow hedge or net investment hedge;
(c) financial assets are reclassified when an insurance company changes its accounting policies in accordance with FRS 18 Accounting Policies.

50B A financial asset to which paragraph 50(c) applies (except a financial asset of the type described in paragraph 50D) may be reclassified out of the fair value through profit or loss category only in rare circumstances.

50C If an entity reclassifies a financial asset out of the fair value through profit or loss category in accordance with paragraph 50B, the financial asset shall be reclassified at its fair value on the date of reclassification. Any gain or loss already recognised in profit or loss shall not be reversed. The fair value of the financial asset on the date of reclassification becomes its new cost or amortised cost, as applicable.

50D A financial asset to which paragraph 50(c) applies that would have met the definition of loans and receivables (if the financial asset had not been required to be classified as held for trading at initial recognition) may be reclassified out of the fair value through profit or loss category if the entity has the intention and ability to hold the financial asset for the foreseeable future or until maturity.

50E A financial asset classified as available for sale that would have met the definition of loans and receivables (if it had not been designated as available for sale) may be reclassified out of the available-for-sale category to the loans and receivables category if the entity has the intention and ability to hold the financial asset for the foreseeable future or until maturity.

50F If an entity reclassifies a financial asset out of the fair value through profit or loss category in accordance with paragraph 50D or out of the available-for-sale category in accordance with paragraph 50E, it shall reclassify the financial asset at its fair value on the date of reclassification. For a financial asset reclassified in accordance with paragraph 50D, any gain or loss already recognised in profit or loss shall not be reversed. The fair value of the financial asset on the date of reclassification becomes its new cost or amortised cost, as applicable. For a financial asset reclassified out of the available-for-sale category in accordance with paragraph 50E, any previous gain or loss on that asset that has been recognised in other comprehensive income in accordance with paragraph 55(b) shall be accounted for in accordance with paragraph 54.

51 ***If, as a result of a change in intention or ability, it is no longer appropriate to classify an investment as held to maturity, it shall be reclassified as available for sale and remeasured at fair value, and the difference between its carrying amount and fair value shall be accounted for in accordance with paragraph 55(b).***

****Editor's note:** *Paragraph 50 amended and paragraphs 50B to 50F added in October 2008. In addition, paragraph 50A was added with effect for accounting periods beginning on or after from 1 January 2009.*

Whenever sales or reclassification of more than an insignificant amount of heldto-maturity investments do not meet any of the conditions in paragraph 9, any remaining held-to-maturity investments shall be reclassified as available for sale. On such reclassification, the difference between their carrying amount and fair value shall be accounted for in accordance with paragraph 55(b). 52

If a reliable measure becomes available for a financial asset or financial liability for which such a measure was previously not available, and the asset or liability is required to be measured at fair value if a reliable measure is available (see paragraphs 46(c) and 47), the asset or liability shall be remeasured at fair value, and the difference between its carrying amount and fair value shall be accounted for in accordance with paragraph 55. 53

If, as a result of a change in intention or ability or in the rare circumstance that a reliable measure of fair value is no longer available (see paragraphs 46(c) and 47) or because the 'two preceding financial years' referred to in paragraph 9 have passed, it becomes appropriate to carry a financial asset or financial liability at cost or amortised cost rather than at fair value, the fair value carrying amount of the financial asset or the financial liability on that date becomes its new cost or amortised cost, as applicable. Any previous gain or loss on that asset that has been recognised through the statement of total recognised gains and losses in accordance with paragraph 55(b) shall be accounted for as follows: 54

(a) In the case of a financial asset with a fixed maturity, the gain or loss shall be amortised to profit or loss over the remaining life of the held-to-maturity investment using the effective interest method. Any difference between the new amortised cost and maturity amount shall also be amortised over the remaining life of the financial asset using the effective interest method, similar to the amortisation of a premium and a discount. If the financial asset is subsequently impaired, any gain or loss that has been recognised through the statement of total recognised gains and losses is reclassified from reserve(s) to profit or loss in accordance with paragraph 67.

(b) In the case of a financial asset that does not have a fixed maturity, the gain or loss shall be recognised in profit or loss when the financial asset is sold or otherwise disposed of. If the financial asset is subsequently impaired any previous gain or loss that has been recognised through the statement of total recognised gains and losses is reclassified from reserve(s) to profit or loss in accordance with paragraph 67.*

Gains and Losses

A gain or loss arising from a change in the fair value of a financial asset or financial liability that is not part of a hedging relationship (see paragraphs 89-102), shall be recognised, as follows. 55

(a) A gain or loss on a financial asset or financial liability classified as at fair value through profit or loss shall be recognised in profit or loss.

(b) A gain or loss on an available-for-sale financial asset shall be recognised through the statement of total recognised gains and losses, except for impairment losses (see paragraphs 67–70) and foreign exchange gains and losses (see Appendix A paragraph AG83), until the financial asset is derecognised. At that time, the cumulative gain or loss previously recognised through the statement of total recognised gains and losses shall be reclassified from reserves to profit or loss.

**Editor's note*: *With effect for accounting periods beginning on or after 1 January 2009, paragraphs 54 and 55 are amended.*

However, interest calculated using the effective interest method (see paragraph 9) is recognised in profit or loss. Dividends on an available-for-sale equity instrument are recognised in profit or loss when the entity's right to receive payment is established.

56 ***For financial assets and financial liabilities carried at amortised cost (see paragraphs 46 and 47), a gain or loss is recognised in profit or loss when the financial asset or financial liability is derecognised or impaired, and through the amortisation process. However, for financial assets or financial liabilities that are hedged items (see paragraphs 78-84 and Appendix A paragraphs AG98-AG101) the accounting for the gain or loss shall follow paragraphs 89-102.***

57 ***If an entity recognises financial assets using settlement date accounting (see paragraph 38 and Appendix A paragraphs AG53 and AG56), any change in the fair value of the asset to be received during the period between the trade date and the settlement date is not recognised for assets carried at cost or amortised cost (other than impairment losses). For assets carried at fair value, however, the change in fair value shall be recognised in profit or loss or through the statement of total recognised gains and losses, as appropriate under paragraph 55.***

Impairment and Uncollectibility of Financial Assets

58 ***An entity shall assess at each balance sheet date whether there is any objective evidence that a financial asset or group of financial assets is impaired. If any such evidence exists, the entity shall apply paragraph 63 (for financial assets carried at amortised cost), paragraph 66 (for financial assets carried at cost) or paragraph 67 (for available-for-sale financial assets) to determine the amount of any impairment loss.***

59 A financial asset or a group of financial assets is impaired and impairment losses are incurred if, and only if, there is objective evidence of impairment as a result of one or more events that occurred after the initial recognition of the asset (a 'loss event') and that loss event (or events) has an impact on the estimated future cash flows of the financial asset or group of financial assets that can be reliably estimated. It may not be possible to identify a single, discrete event that caused the impairment. Rather the combined effect of several events may have caused the impairment. Losses expected as a result of future events, no matter how likely, are not recognised. Objective evidence that a financial asset or group of assets is impaired includes observable data that comes to the attention of the holder of the asset about the following loss events:

(a) significant financial difficulty of the issuer or obligor;
(b) a breach of contract, such as a default or delinquency in interest or principal payments;
(c) the lender, for economic or legal reasons relating to the borrower's financial difficulty, granting to the borrower a concession that the lender would not otherwise consider;
(d) it becoming probable that the borrower will enter bankruptcy or other financial reorganisation;
(e) the disappearance of an active market for that financial asset because of financial difficulties; or
(f) observable data indicating that there is a measurable decrease in the estimated future cash flows from a group of financial assets since the initial recognition of those assets, although the decrease cannot yet be identified with the individual financial assets in the group, including:

    (i) adverse changes in the payment status of borrowers in the group (eg an increased number of delayed payments or an increased number of credit card borrowers who have reached their credit limit and are paying the minimum monthly amount); or

(ii) national or local economic conditions that correlate with defaults on the assets in the group (eg an increase in the unemployment rate in the geographical area of the borrowers, a decrease in property prices for mortgages in the relevant area, a decrease in oil prices for loan assets to oil producers, or adverse changes in industry conditions that affect the borrowers in the group).

The disappearance of an active market because an entity's financial instruments are no longer publicly traded is not evidence of impairment. A downgrade of an entity's credit rating is not, of itself, evidence of impairment, although it may be evidence of impairment when considered with other available information. A decline in the fair value of a financial asset below its cost or amortised cost is not necessarily evidence of impairment (for example, a decline in the fair value of an investment in a debt instrument that results from an increase in the risk-free interest rate). **60**

In addition to the types of events in paragraph 59, objective evidence of impairment for an investment in an equity instrument includes information about significant changes with an adverse effect that have taken place in the technological, market, economic or legal environment in which the issuer operates, and indicates that the cost of the investment in the equity instrument may not be recovered. A significant or prolonged decline in the fair value of an investment in an equity instrument below its cost is also objective evidence of impairment. **61**

In some cases the observable data required to estimate the amount of an impairment loss on a financial asset may be limited or no longer fully relevant to current circumstances. For example, this may be the case when a borrower is in financial difficulties and there are few available historical data relating to similar borrowers. In such cases, an entity uses its experienced judgement to estimate the amount of any impairment loss. Similarly an entity uses its experienced judgement to adjust observable data for a group of financial assets to reflect current circumstances (see paragraph AG89). The use of reasonable estimates is an essential part of the preparation of financial statements and does not undermine their reliability. **62**

Financial Assets Carried at Amortised Cost

If there is objective evidence that an impairment loss on loans and receivables or held-to-maturity investments carried at amortised cost has been incurred, the amount of the loss is measured as the difference between the asset's carrying amount and the present value of estimated future cash flows (excluding future credit losses that have not been incurred) discounted at the financial asset's original effective interest rate (ie the effective interest rate computed at initial recognition). The carrying amount of the asset shall be reduced either directly or through use of an allowance account. The amount of the loss shall be recognised in profit or loss. **63**

An entity first assesses whether objective evidence of impairment exists individually for financial assets that are individually significant, and individually or collectively for financial assets that are not individually significant (see paragraph 59). If an entity determines that no objective evidence of impairment exists for an individually assessed financial asset, whether significant or not, it includes the asset in a group of financial assets with similar credit risk characteristics and collectively assesses them for impairment. Assets that are individually assessed for impairment and for which an impairment loss is or continues to be recognised are not included in a collective assessment of impairment. **64**

65 ***If, in a subsequent period, the amount of the impairment loss decreases and the decrease can be related objectively to an event occurring after the impairment was recognised (such as an improvement in the debtor's credit rating), the previously recognised impairment loss shall be reversed either directly or by adjusting an allowance account. The reversal shall not result in a carrying amount of the financial asset that exceeds what the amortised cost would have been had the impairment not been recognised at the date the impairment is reversed. The amount of the reversal shall be recognised in profit or loss.***

Financial Assets Carried at Cost

66 ***If there is objective evidence that an impairment loss has been incurred on an unquoted equity instrument that is not carried at fair value because its fair value cannot be reliably measured, or on a derivative asset that is linked to and must be settled by delivery of such an unquoted equity instrument, the amount of the impairment loss is measured as the difference between the carrying amount of the financial asset and the present value of estimated future cash flows discounted at the current market rate of return for a similar financial asset (see paragraph 46(c) and Appendix A paragraphs AG80 and AG81). Such impairment losses shall not be reversed.***

Available-for-Sale Financial Assets

67 ***When a decline in the fair value of an available-for-sale financial asset has been recognised through the statement of total recognised gains and losses and there is objective evidence that the asset is impaired (see paragraph 59), the cumulative loss that had been recognised through the statement of total recognised gains and losses shall be removed from reserves and recognised in profit or loss even though the financial asset has not been derecognised.***

68 ***The amount of the cumulative loss that is reclassified from reserves and recognised in profit or loss under paragraph 67 shall be the difference between the acquisition cost (net of any principal repayment and amortisation) and current fair value, less any impairment loss on that financial asset previously recognised in profit of loss.****

69 ***Impairment losses recognised in profit or loss for an investment in an equity instrument classified as available for sale shall not be reversed through profit or loss.***

70 ***If, in a subsequent period, the fair value of a debt instrument classified as available for sale increases and the increase can be objectively related to an event occurring after the impairment loss was recognised in profit or loss, the impairment loss shall be reversed, with the amount of the reversal recognised in profit or loss.***

HEDGING

71 ***If there is a designated hedging relationship between a hedging instrument and a hedged item as described in paragraphs 85-88 and Appendix A paragraphs AG102-AG104, accounting for the gain or loss on the hedging instrument and the hedged item shall follow paragraphs 89-102.***

**Editor's note*: *With effect for accounting periods beginning on or after 1 January 2009, this paragraph was amended.*

Hedging Instruments

Qualifying Instruments

This Standard does not restrict the circumstances in which a derivative may be designated as a hedging instrument provided the conditions in paragraph 88 are met, except for some written options (see Appendix A paragraph AG94). However, a non-derivative financial asset or non-derivative financial liability may be designated as a hedging instrument only for a hedge of a foreign currency risk. **72**

For hedge accounting purposes, only instruments that involve a party external to the reporting entity (ie external to the group or individual entity that is being reported on) can be designated as hedging instruments. Although individual entities within a consolidated group or divisions within an entity may enter into hedging transactions with other entities within the group or divisions within the entity, any such intragroup transactions are eliminated on consolidation. Therefore, such hedging transactions do not qualify for hedge accounting in the consolidated financial statements of the group. However, they may qualify for hedge accounting in the individual or separate financial statements of individual entities within the group, provided that they are external to the individual entity that is being reported on.* **73**

Designation of Hedging Instruments

There is normally a single fair value measure for a hedging instrument in its entirety, and the factors that cause changes in fair value are codependent. Thus, a hedging relationship is designated by an entity for a hedging instrument in its entirety. The only exceptions permitted are: **74**

(a) separating the intrinsic value and time value of an option contract and designating as the hedging instrument only the change in intrinsic value of an option and excluding change in its time value; and
(b) separating the interest element and the spot price of a forward contract.

These exceptions are permitted because the intrinsic value of the option and the premium on the forward can generally be measured separately. A dynamic hedging strategy that assesses both the intrinsic value and time value of an option contract can qualify for hedge accounting.

A proportion of the entire hedging instrument, such as 50 per cent of the notional amount, may be designated as the hedging instrument in a hedging relationship. However, a hedging relationship may not be designated for only a portion of the time period during which a hedging instrument remains outstanding. **75**

A single hedging instrument may be designated as a hedge of more than one type of risk provided that (a) the risks hedged can be identified clearly; (b) the effectiveness of the hedge can be demonstrated; and (c) it is possible to ensure that there is specific designation of the hedging instrument and different risk positions. **76**

Two or more derivatives, or proportions of them (or, in the case of a hedge of currency risk, two or more non-derivatives or proportions of them, or a combination of derivatives and non-derivatives or proportions of them), may be viewed in combination and jointly designated as the hedging instrument, including when the risk(s) arising from some derivatives offset(s) those arising from others. However, an interest rate collar or other derivative instrument that combines a written option and **77**

***Editor's note**: *Paragraph amended with effect for accounting periods beginning on or after 1 January 2009.*

a purchased option does not qualify as a hedging instrument if it is, in effect, a net written option (for which a net premium is received). Similarly, two or more instruments (or proportions of them) may be designated as the hedging instrument only if none of them is a written option or a net written option.

Hedged Items

Qualifying Items

78 A hedged item can be a recognised asset or liability, an unrecognised firm commitment, a highly probable forecast transaction or a net investment in a foreign operation. The hedged item can be (a) a single asset, liability, firm commitment, highly probable forecast transaction or net investment in a foreign operation, (b) a group of assets, liabilities, firm commitments, highly probable forecast transactions or net investments in foreign operations with similar risk characteristics or (c) in a portfolio hedge of interest rate risk only, a portion of the portfolio of financial assets or financial liabilities that share the risk being hedged.

79 Unlike loans and receivables, a held-to-maturity investment cannot be a hedged item with respect to interest-rate risk or prepayment risk because designation of an investment as held to maturity requires an intention to hold the investment until maturity without regard to changes in the fair value or cash flows of such an investment attributable to changes in interest rates. However, a held-to-maturity investment can be a hedged item with respect to risks from changes in foreign currency exchange rates and credit risk.

80 For hedge accounting purposes, only assets, liabilities, firm commitments or highly probable forecast transactions that involve a party external to the entity can be designated as hedged items. It follows that hedge accounting can be applied to transactions between entities in the same group only in the individual or separate financial statements of those entities and not in the consolidated financial statements of the group. As an exception, the foreign currency risk of an intragroup monetary item (eg a payable/receivable between two subsidiaries) may qualify as a hedged item in the consolidated financial statements if it results in an exposure to foreign exchange rate gains or losses that are not fully eliminated on consolidation in accordance with FRS 23 (IAS 21) The Effects of Changes in Foreign Exchange Rates. In accordance with FRS 23 (IAS 21), foreign exchange rate gains and losses on intragroup monetary items are not fully eliminated on consolidation when the intragroup monetary item is transacted between two group entities that have different functional currencies. In addition, the foreign currency risk of a highly probable forecast intragroup transaction may qualify as a hedged item in consolidated financial statements provided that the transaction is denominated in a currency other than the functional currency of the entity entering into that transaction and the foreign currency risk will affect consolidated profit or loss.*

Designation of Financial Items as Hedged Items

81 If the hedged item is a financial asset or financial liability, it may be a hedged item with respect to the risks associated with only a portion of its cash flows or fair value (such as one or more selected contractual cash flows or portions of them or a percentage of the fair value) provided that effectiveness can be measured. For example, an identifiable and separately measurable portion of the interest rate exposure of an interest-bearing asset or interest-bearing liability may be designated

**Editor's note:* *Paragraph amended with effect for accounting periods beginning on or after 1 January 2010.*

as the hedged risk (such as a risk-free interest rate or benchmark interest rate component of the total interest rate exposure of a hedged financial instrument).

In a fair value hedge of the interest rate exposure of a portfolio of financial assets or financial liabilities (and only in such a hedge), the portion hedged may be designated in terms of an amount of a currency (eg an amount of dollars, euro, pounds or rand) rather than as individual assets (or liabilities). Although the portfolio may, for risk management purposes, include assets and liabilities, the amount designated is an amount of assets or an amount of liabilities. Designation of a net amount including assets and liabilities is not permitted. The entity may hedge a portion of the interest rate risk associated with this designated amount. For example, in the case of a hedge of a portfolio containing prepayable assets, the entity may hedge the change in fair value that is attributable to a change in the hedged interest rate on the basis of expected, rather than contractual, repricing dates. When the portion hedged is based on expected repricing dates, the effect that changes in the hedged interest rate have on those expected repricing dates shall be included when determining the change in the fair value of the hedged item. Consequently, if a portfolio that contains prepayable items is hedged with a non-prepayable derivative, ineffectiveness arises if the dates on which items in the hedged portfolio are expected to prepay are revised, or actual prepayment dates differ from those expected. **81A**

Designation of Non-Financial Items as Hedged Items

If the hedged item is a non-financial asset or non-financial liability, it shall be designated as a hedged item (a) for foreign currency risks, or (b) in its entirety for all risks, because of the difficulty of isolating and measuring the appropriate portion of the cash flows or fair value changes attributable to specific risks other than foreign currency risks. **82**

Designation of Groups of Items as Hedged Items

Similar assets or similar liabilities shall be aggregated and hedged as a group only if the individual assets or individual liabilities in the group share the risk exposure that is designated as being hedged. Furthermore, the change in fair value attributable to the hedged risk for each individual item in the group shall be expected to be approximately proportional to the overall change in fair value attributable to the hedged risk of the group of items. **83**

Because an entity assesses hedge effectiveness by comparing the change in the fair value or cash flow of a hedging instrument (or group of similar hedging instruments) and a hedged item (or group of similar hedged items), comparing a hedging instrument with an overall net position (eg the net of all fixed rate assets and fixed rate liabilities with similar maturities), rather than with a specific hedged item, does not qualify for hedge accounting. **84**

Hedge Accounting

Hedge accounting recognises the offsetting effects on profit or loss of changes in the fair values of the hedging instrument and the hedged item. **85**

Hedging relationships are of three types: **86**

(a) fair value hedge: a hedge of the exposure to changes in fair value of a recognised asset or liability or an unrecognised firm commitment, or an identified portion of

such an asset, liability or firm commitment, that is attributable to a particular risk and could affect profit or loss.

(b) cash flow hedge: a hedge of the exposure to variability in cash flows that (i) is attributable to a particular risk associated with a recognised asset or liability (such as all or some future interest payments on variable rate debt) or a highly probable forecast transaction and (ii) could affect profit or loss.

(c) hedge of a net investment in a foreign operation as defined in FRS 23.

87 A hedge of the foreign currency risk of a firm commitment may be accounted for as a fair value hedge or as a cash flow hedge.

88 ***A hedging relationship qualifies for hedge accounting under paragraphs 89-102 if, and only if, all of the following conditions are met.***

(a) At the inception of the hedge there is formal designation and documentation of the hedging relationship and the entity's risk management objective and strategy for undertaking the hedge. That documentation shall include identification of the hedging instrument, the hedged item or transaction, the nature of the risk being hedged and how the entity will assess the hedging instrument's effectiveness in offsetting the exposure to changes in the hedged item's fair value or cash flows attributable to the hedged risk.

(b) The hedge is expected to be highly effective (see Appendix A paragraphs AG105-AG113) in achieving offsetting changes in fair value or cash flows attributable to the hedged risk, consistently with the originally documented risk management strategy for that particular hedging relationship.

(c) For cash flow hedges, a forecast transaction that is the subject of the hedge must be highly probable and must present an exposure to variations in cash flows that could ultimately affect profit or loss.

(d) The effectiveness of the hedge can be reliably measured, ie the fair value or cash flows of the hedged item that are attributable to the hedged risk and the fair value of the hedging instrument can be reliably measured (see paragraphs 46 and 47 and Appendix A paragraphs AG80 and AG81 for guidance on determining fair value).

(e) The hedge is assessed on an ongoing basis and determined actually to have been highly effective throughout the financial reporting periods for which the hedge was designated.

Fair Value Hedges

89 ***If a fair value hedge meets the conditions in paragraph 88 during the period, it shall be accounted for as follows:***

(a) the gain or loss from remeasuring the hedging instrument at fair value (for a derivative hedging instrument) or the foreign currency component of its carrying amount measured in accordance with FRS 23 (for a non-derivative hedging instrument) shall be recognised in profit or loss; and

(b) the gain or loss on the hedged item attributable to the hedged risk shall adjust the carrying amount of the hedged item and be recognised in profit or loss. This applies if the hedged item is otherwise measured at cost. Recognition of the gain or loss attributable to the hedged risk in profit or loss applies if the hedged item is an available-for-sale financial asset.

89A For a fair value hedge of the interest rate exposure of a portion of a portfolio of financial assets or financial liabilities (and only in such a hedge), the requirement in paragraph 89(b) may be met by presenting the gain or loss attributable to the hedged item either:

(a) in a single separate line item within assets, for those repricing time periods for which the hedged item is an asset; or
(b) in a single separate line item within liabilities, for those repricing time periods for which the hedged item is a liability.

The separate line items referred to in (a) and (b) above shall be presented next to financial assets or financial liabilities. Amounts included in these line items shall be removed from the balance sheet when the assets or liabilities to which they relate are derecognised.

If only particular risks attributable to a hedged item are hedged, recognised changes in the fair value of the hedged item unrelated to the hedged risk are recognised as set out in paragraph 55. **90**

An entity shall discontinue prospectively the hedge accounting specified in paragraph 89 if: **91**

(a) the hedging instrument expires or is sold, terminated or exercised (for this purpose, the replacement or rollover of a hedging instrument into another hedging instrument is not an expiration or termination if such replacement or rollover is part of the entity's documented hedging strategy);
(b) the hedge no longer meets the criteria for hedge accounting in paragraph 88; or
(c) the entity revokes the designation.

Any adjustment arising from paragraph 89(b) to the carrying amount of a hedged financial instrument for which the effective interest method is used (or, in the case of a portfolio hedge of interest rate risk, to the separate balance sheet line item described in paragraph 89A) shall be amortised to profit or loss. Amortisation may begin as soon as an adjustment exists and shall begin no later than when the hedged item ceases to be adjusted for changes in its fair value attributable to the risk being hedged. The adjustment is based on a recalculated effective interest rate at the date amortisation begins. However, if, in the case of a fair value hedge of the interest rate exposure of a portfolio of financial assets or financial liabilities (and only in such a hedge), amortising using a recalculated effective interest rate is not practicable, the adjustment shall be amortised using a straightline method. The adjustment shall be amortised fully by maturity of the financial instrument or, in the case of a portfolio hedge of interest rate risk, by expiry of the relevant repricing time period. **92**

When an unrecognised firm commitment is designated as a hedged item, the subsequent cumulative change in the fair value of the firm commitment attributable to the hedged risk is recognised as an asset or liability with a corresponding gain or loss recognised in profit or loss (see paragraph 89(b)). The changes in the fair value of the hedging instrument are also recognised in profit or loss. **93**

When an entity enters into a firm commitment to acquire an asset or assume a liability that is a hedged item in a fair value hedge, the initial carrying amount of the asset or liability that results from the entity meeting the firm commitment is adjusted to include the cumulative change in the fair value of the firm commitment attributable to the hedged risk that was recognised in the balance sheet. **94**

Cash Flow Hedges

If a cash flow hedge meets the conditions in paragraph 88 during the period, it shall be accounted for as follows: **95**

(a) ***the portion of the gain or loss on the hedging instrument that is determined to be an effective hedge (see paragraph 88) shall be recognised through the statement of total recognised gains and losses; and***

(b) ***the ineffective portion of the gain or loss on the hedging instrument shall be recognised in profit or loss.***

96 More specifically, a cash flow hedge is accounted for as follows:

(a) the separate amount recognised through the statement of total recognised gains and losses associated with the hedged item is adjusted to the lesser of the following (in absolute amounts):

  (i) the cumulative gain or loss on the hedging instrument from inception of the hedge; and

  (ii) the cumulative change in fair value (present value) of the expected future cash flows on the hedged item from inception of the hedge;

(b) any remaining gain or loss on the hedging instrument or designated component of it (that is not an effective hedge) is recognised in profit or loss; and

(c) if an entity's documented risk management strategy for a particular hedging relationship excludes from the assessment of hedge effectiveness a specific component of the gain or loss or related cash flows on the hedging instrument (see paragraphs 74, 75 and 88(a)), that excluded component of gain or loss is recognised in accordance with paragraph 55.

97 ***If a hedge of a forecast transaction subsequently results in the recognition of a financial asset or a financial liability, the associated gains or losses that were recognised through the statement of total recognised gains and losses in accordance with paragraph 95 shall be reclassified into profit or loss in the same period or periods during which the hedged forecast cash flows affect profit or loss (such as in the periods that interest income or interest expense is recognised). However, if an entity expects that all or a portion of a loss recognised through the statement of total recognised gains and losses will not be recovered in one or more future periods, it shall recognise into profit or loss the amount that is not expected to be recovered.****

98 ***If a hedge of a forecast transaction subsequently results in the recognition of a non-financial asset or a non-financial liability, or a forecast transaction for a non-financial asset or non-financial liability becomes a firm commitment for which fair value hedge accounting is applied, then the entity shall adopt (a) or (b) below:***

(a) ***It reclassifies the associated gains and losses that were recognised through the statement of total recognised gains and losses in accordance with paragraph 95 to profit or loss in the same period or periods during which the asset acquired or liability assumed affects profit or loss (such as in the periods that depreciation expense or cost of sales is recognised). However, if an entity expects that all or a portion of a loss recognised through the statement of total recognised gains and losses will not be recovered in one or more future periods, it shall reclassify from reserves to profit or loss the amount that is not expected to be recovered.***

(b) ***It removes the associated gains and losses that were recognised through the statement of total recognised gains and losses in accordance with paragraph 95.†***

99 ***An entity shall adopt either (a) or (b) in paragraph 98 as its accounting policy and shall apply it consistently to all hedges to which paragraph 98 relates.***

****Editor's note:*** *Paragraph amended with effect for accounting periods beginning on or after 1 January 2010.*

†***Editor's note:*** *With effect for accounting periods beginning on or after 1 January 2009, this paragraph is amended.*

For cash flow hedges other than those covered by paragraphs 97 and 98, amounts that had been recognised in reserves shall be recognised in profit or loss in the same period or periods during which the hedged forecast cash flows affects profit or loss (for example, when a forecast sale occurs).* 100

In any of the following circumstances an entity shall discontinue prospectively the hedge accounting specified in paragraphs 95-100: 101

(a) The hedging instrument expires or is sold, terminated or exercised (for this purpose, the replacement or rollover of a hedging instrument into another hedging instrument is not an expiration or termination if such replacement or rollover is part of the entity's documented hedging strategy). In this case, the cumulative gain or loss on the hedging instrument that has been recognised through the statement of total recognised gains and losses from the period when the hedge was effective (see paragraph 95(a)) shall remain separately in reserves until the forecast transaction occurs. When the transaction occurs, paragraph 97, 98 or 100 applies.

(b) The hedge no longer meets the criteria for hedge accounting in paragraph 88. In this case, the cumulative gain or loss on the hedging instrument that has been recognised through the statement of total recognised gains and losses from the period when the hedge was effective (see paragraph 95(a)) shall remain separately in reserves until the forecast transaction occurs. When the transaction occurs, paragraph 97, 98 or 100 applies.

(c) The forecast transaction is no longer expected to occur, in which case any related cumulative gain or loss on the hedging instrument that remains recognised directly in reserves from the period when the hedge was effective (see paragraph 95(a)) shall be recognised in profit or loss. A forecast transaction that is no longer highly probable (see paragraph 88(c)) may still be expected to occur.

(d) The entity revokes the designation. For hedges of a forecast transaction, the cumulative gain or loss on the hedging instrument that remains recognised directly in reserves from the period when the hedge was effective (see paragraph 95(a)) shall remain separately in reserves until the forecast transaction occurs or is no longer expected to occur. When the transaction occurs, paragraph 97, 98 or 100 applies. If the transaction is no longer expected to occur, the cumulative gain or loss that had been recognised directly in the reserves shall be recognised in profit or loss.

Hedges of a Net Investment

Hedges of a net investment in a foreign operation, including a hedge of a monetary item that is accounted for as part of the net investment (see FRS 23), shall be accounted for similarly to cash flow hedges: 102

(a) the portion of the gain or loss on the hedging instrument that is determined to be an effective hedge (see paragraph 88) shall be recognised through the statement of total recognised gains and losses; and

(b) the ineffective portion shall be recognised in profit or loss.

The gain or loss on the hedging instrument relating to the effective portion of the hedge that has been recognised through the statement of total recognised gains and losses shall be recognised in profit or loss in accordance with paragraphs 48-49 of FRS 23 on disposal or partial disposal of the foreign operation.†

****Editor's note**: Paragraph amended with effect for accounting periods beginning on or after 1 January 2010.*

*†**Editor's note**: Paragraph amended with effect for accounting periods beginning on or after 1 January 2009.*

EFFECTIVE DATE AND TRANSITION

103 ***A listed entity shall apply this Standard for accounting periods beginning on or after 1 January 2005. Other entities falling within the scope of this Standard shall apply it for accounting periods beginning on or after 1 January 2006, and may voluntarily apply it for accounting periods beginning on or after 1 January 2005. Earlier application is not permitted.***

103A **An entity shall apply the amendment in paragraph 2(j) for annual periods beginning on or after 1 January 2006.**

103B **This amendment to FRS 26 amended paragraphs 2(e) and (h), 4, 47 and AG4, added paragraph AG4A, added a new definition of financial guarantee contracts in paragraph 9, and deleted paragraph 3. An entity shall apply those amendments for annual periods beginning on or after 1 January 2006. Earlier application is encouraged. If an entity applies these changes for an earlier period, it shall disclose that fact and apply the related amendments to FRS 25 at the same time.**

103C **For accounting periods commencing before 1 January 2006, the definition of listed entity in paragraph 9A shall not be treated as including entities in the Republic of Ireland that (i) have debt securities but not equity securities admitted to trading on a regulated market as referred to in that paragraph and (ii) are qualifying companies within the meaning of Section 110 of the Taxes Consolidation Act 1997 of the Republic of Ireland.**

103D The amendments to the standard made in March 2006, including the insertion of paragraphs 14 to 42 and AG34 to AG63, are effective for accounting periods commencing on or after 1 January 2007. Earlier implementation of this amendment is permitted.

103E The ASB amended the terminology in paragraphs 98 and 100-102 as part of its 'Improvements to Financial Reporting Standards' issued in December 2008. An entity shall apply those amendments for annual periods beginning on or after 1 January 2009.

103F An entity shall apply the amendment in paragraph 2 for annual periods beginning on or after 1 January 2010. If an entity applies Puttable Financial Instruments and Obligations Arising on Liquidation (Amendments to FRS 25), issued in August 2008, for an earlier period, the amendment in paragraph 2 shall be applied for that earlier period.

103G Reclassification of Financial Assets (Amendments to FRS 26 and FRS 29), issued in October 2008, amended paragraphs 50 and AG8, and added paragraphs 50B–50F. An entity shall apply those amendments from 1 July 2008. An entity shall not reclassify a financial asset in accordance with paragraph 50B, 50D or 50E before 1 July 2008. Any reclassification of a financial asset made in periods beginning on or after 1 November 2008 shall take effect only from the date when the reclassification is made. Any reclassification of a financial asset in accordance with paragraph 50B, 50D or 50E shall not be applied retrospectively to reporting periods ended before the effective date set out in this paragraph.

103H An entity shall apply paragraphs AG99BA, AG99E, AG99F, AG110A and AG110B retrospectively for annual periods beginning on or after 1 July 2009, in accordance with FRS 18 *Accounting Policies*. Earlier application is permitted. If an entity applies

Eligible Hedged Items (Amendment to FRS 26) for periods beginning before 1 July 2009, it shall disclose that fact.*

An entity shall apply paragraph 12, as amended by *Embedded Derivatives* (Amendments to UITF Abstract 42 and FRS 26), issued in September 2009, for annual periods ending on or after 31 December 2009. Earlier application is permitted. **103J**

'Improvements to Financial Reporting Standards' issued in December 2009 amended paragraphs 2(g), 97, 100 and AG30(g). An entity shall apply the amendments to paragraphs 2(g), 97 and 100 prospectively to all unexpired contracts for annual periods beginning on or after 1 January 2010. An entity shall apply the amendment to paragraph AG30(g) for annual periods beginning on or after 1 January 2010. Earlier application is permitted. If an entity applies the amendment for an earlier period it shall disclose that fact. **103K**

This Standard shall be applied retrospectively except as specified in paragraphs 105-108D. The opening balance of retained earnings for the earliest prior period presented and all other comparative amounts shall be adjusted as if this Standard had always been in use unless restating the information would be impracticable. If restatement is impracticable, the entity shall disclose that fact and indicate the extent to which the information was restated. **104**

When this Standard is first applied, an entity is permitted to designate a previously recognised financial asset as available for sale. For any such financial asset, the entity shall recognise all cumulative changes in fair value in a separate component of equity reserves until subsequent derecognition or impairment, when the entity shall reclassify that cumulative gain or loss from reserves to profit or loss. The entity shall also: **105**

(a) restate the financial asset using the new designation in the comparative financial statements; and
***(b) disclose the fair value of the financial assets at the date of designation and their classification and carrying amount in the previous financial statements.*†**

An entity shall apply paragraphs 11A, 48A, AG4B-AG4K, AG33A and AG33B and the 2005 amendments in paragraphs 9, 12 and 13 for accounting periods beginning on or after 1 January 2006. Earlier application is encouraged. **105A**

An entity that is not adopting the standard for the first time that first applies paragraphs 11A, 48A, AG4B-AG4K, AG33A and AG33B and the 2005 amendments in paragraphs 9, 12 and 13 in its accounting period beginning on or after 1 January 2006: **105C**

(a) shall de-designate any financial asset or financial liability previously designated as at fair value through profit or loss only if it does not qualify for such designation in accordance with those new and amended paragraphs. When a financial asset or financial liability will be measured at amortised cost after de-designation, the date of de-designation is deemed to be its date of initial recognition.
(b) shall not designate as at fair value through profit or loss any previously recognised financial assets or financial liabilities.
(c) shall disclose the fair value of any financial assets or financial liabilities de-designated in accordance with subparagraph (a) at the date of de-designation and their new classifications.

***Editor's note:** *The references have been changed to those under UK accounting standards.*

†**Editor's note:** *Paragraph amended with effect for accounting periods beginning on or after 1 January 2009.*

105D *An entity falling within paragraph 105C shall restate its comparative financial statements using the new designations in that paragraph provided that, in the case of a financial asset, financial liability, or group of financial assets, financial liabilities or both, designated as at fair value through profit or loss, those items or groups would have met the criteria in paragraph 9(b)(i), 9(b)(ii) or 11A at the beginning of the comparative period or, if acquired after the beginning of the comparative period, would have met the criteria in paragraph 9(b)(i), 9(b)(ii) or 11A at the date of initial recognition.*

105E ***An entity that first adopts this Standard for an accounting period beginning on or after 1 January 2006*—such an entity is permitted to designate, at the date of transition to this standard, any financial asset or financial liability as at fair value through profit or loss provided the asset or liability meets the criteria in paragraph 9(b)(i), 9(b)(ii) or 11A of FRS 26 at that date.**

105F **When the date of transition to this standard is before 1 December 2005, such designations need not be completed until 1 December 2005 and may also include financial assets and financial liabilities recognised between the date of transition to this standard and 1 December 2005.**

105G ***An entity that first adopts this Standard for an accounting period beginning before 1 January 2006 and applies paragraphs 11A, 48A, AG4B-AG4K, AG33A and AG33B and the 2005 amendments in paragraphs 9, 12 and 13 of FRS 26*—such an entity is permitted at the start of the first period in which it adopts the standard to designate as at fair value through profit or loss any financial asset or financial liability that qualifies for such designation in accordance with these new and amended paragraphs at that date. When the entity's period of first adopting the Standard begins before 1 December 2005, such designations need not be completed until 1 December 2005 and may also include financial assets and financial liabilities recognised between the beginning of that period and 1 December 2005. If the entity restates comparative information for FRS 26 it shall restate that information for the financial assets, financial liabilities, or group of financial assets, financial liabilities or both, designated at the start of the period in which the Standard is adopted. Such restatement of comparative information shall be made only if the designated items or groups would have met the criteria for such designation in paragraph 9(b)(i), 9(b)(ii) or 11A of FRS 26 at the date of transition to this standard or, if acquired after the date of transition to this standard, would have met the criteria in paragraph 9(b)(i), 9(b)(ii) or 11A at the date of initial recognition.**

105H **Where any financial assets and financial liabilities are designated as at fair value through profit or loss in accordance with subparagraph 105F or 105G above and were previously designated as the hedged item in fair value hedge accounting relationships, they shall be de-designated from those hedging relationships at the same time they are designated as at fair value through profit or loss, notwithstanding the requirements of paragraph 91 of FRS 26.**

107A Notwithstanding paragraph 104, an entity may apply the requirements in the last sentence of paragraph AG76, and paragraph AG76A, in either of the following ways:

(a) prospectively to transactions entered into after 25 October 2002; or
(b) prospectively to transactions entered into after 1 January 2004.*

108 *An entity shall not adjust the carrying amount of non-financial assets and non-financial liabilities to exclude gains and losses related to cash flow hedges that were included in the carrying amount before the beginning of the financial year in which this Standard is*

****Editor's note:** Paragraph added October 2005.*

first applied. At the beginning of the financial period in which this Standard is first applied, any amount recognised outside profit or loss (through the statement of total recognised gains and losses or directly in reserves) for a hedge of a firm commitment that under this Standard is accounted for as a fair value hedge shall be reclassified as an asset or liability, except for a hedge of foreign currency risk that continues to be treated as a cash flow hedge.*

At the date of transition to this Standard, an entity shall: **108A**

(a) measure all derivatives at fair value; and
(b) eliminate all deferred losses and gains arising on derivatives that were reported under its previous accounting policies as if they were assets or liabilities.

An entity shall not reflect in its opening balance sheet at the date of transition to this standard a hedging relationship of a type that does not qualify for hedge accounting under this Standard (for example, many hedging relationships where the hedging instrument is a cash instrument or written option; where the hedged item is a net position; or where the hedge covers interest risk in a held-to-maturity investment). However, if an entity designated a net position as a hedged item under its previous accounting policies, it may designate an individual item within that net position as a hedged item under this Standard, provided that it does so no later than the date of transition to this Standard. **108B**

If, before the date of transition to this Standard, an entity had designated a transaction as a hedge but the hedge does not meet the conditions for hedge accounting in this Standard the entity shall apply paragraphs 91 and 101 to discontinue hedge accounting. Transactions entered into before the date of transition to this Standard shall not be retrospectively designated as hedges. **108C**

An entity that first adopts this Standard for an accounting period that commences before 1 January 2007 need not restate comparative information to comply with this Standard and FRS 25. An entity that chooses to present comparative information that does not comply with this Standard and FRS 25 in its first year of adoption shall: **108D**

(a) apply its existing accounting policies to financial instruments within the scope of this standard and FRS 25 in the comparative information;
(b) disclose this fact together with the basis used to prepare this information; and
(c) disclose the nature of the main adjustments that would make the information comply with this Standard and FRS 25. The entity need not quantify those adjustments. However, the entity shall treat any adjustment between the balance sheet at the comparative period's reporting date (ie the balance sheet that includes comparative information under previous accounting policies) and the balance sheet at the start of the first reporting period that includes information that complies with this Standard and FRS 25 as arising from a change in accounting policy and give the disclosures required by FRS 18 *Accounting Policies*.

Except as permitted by paragraph 108F, an entity adopting paragraphs 15-37 and AG36-AG52 for the first time shall apply these requirements prospectively for **108E**

****Editor's note***: *Paragraph amended with effect for accounting periods beginning on or after 1 January 2009.*

transactions occurring on or after the beginning of the comparative period for the accounting period in which the entity first applies these paragraphs. In other words, if the entity derecognised non-derivative financial assets or non-derivative financial liabilities under its previous accounting policies as a result of a transaction that occurred before that date, if shall not recognise those assets and liabilities (unless they qualify for recognition as a result of a later transaction or event). When an entity has previously shown a transaction using the linked presentation of FRS 5, it shall not treat this as derecognition for the purposes of this paragraph.

...

108F Notwithstanding paragraph 108H, an entity may apply the derecognition requirements in paragraphs 15-37 and AG36-52 retrospectively from a date of the entity's choosing, provided that the information needed to apply these paragraphs to financial assets and financial liabilities derecognised as a result of past transactions was obtained at the time of initially accounting for those transactions.

108G An entity shall apply the last sentence of paragraph 80, and paragraphs AG99A and AG99B, for accounting periods beginning on or after 1 January 2006. Earlier application is encouraged. If an entity has designated as the hedged item an external forecast transaction that

(a) is denominated in the functional currency of the entity entering into the transaction,
(b) gives rise to an exposure that will have an effect on consolidated profit or loss (ie is denominated in a currency other than the group's presentation currency), and
(c) would have qualified for hedge accounting had it not been denominated in the functional currency of the entity entering into it,

it may apply hedge accounting in the consolidated financial statements in the period(s) before the date of application of the last sentence of paragraph 80, and paragraphs AG99A and AG99B.

108H An entity need not apply paragraph AG99B to comparative information relating to periods before the date of application of the last sentence of paragraph 80 and paragraph AG99A.

108I Paragraph 2(a) was amended by Improvements to Financial Reporting Standards issued in December 2008. An entity shall apply this amendment for annual periods beginning on or after 1 January 2009. Earlier application is permitted. If an entity applies the amendment for an earlier period, it shall disclose that fact and apply the amendments to paragraph 4 of FRS 25 and paragraph 3 of FRS 29. An entity is permitted to apply these amendments prospectively.

108J Paragraphs 9, 73 and AG8 are amended and paragraph 50A is added by *Improvements to FRSs* issued December 2008. Paragraph 80 was amended by 'Improvements to Financial Reporting Standards' issued in December 2009. An entity shall apply those amendments for annual periods beginning on or after 1 January 2009. An entity shall apply the amendments in paragraphs 9 and 50A as of the date and in the manner it applied the 2005 amendments described in paragraph 105A. Earlier application of all these amendments is permitted. If an entity applies the amendments for an earlier period, it shall disclose that fact.

WITHDRAWAL OF OTHER PRONOUNCEMENTS

This Standard supersedes UITF Abstract 11* Capital instruments: issuer call options *for those entities applying this Standard. **110A**

Appendix A
Application Guidance

This appendix is an integral part of the Standard.

SCOPE (PARAGRAPHS 2-7)

AG1 Some contracts require a payment based on climatic, geological or other physical variables. (Those based on climatic variables are sometimes referred to as 'weather derivatives'.) If those contracts are not insurance contracts as defined in Appendix C to FRS 26, they are within the scope of this Standard.

AG2 This Standard does not change the requirements relating to employee benefit plans that comply with FRS 17 *Retirement Benefits* and royalty agreements based on the volume of sales or service revenues.

AG3 Sometimes, an entity makes what it views as a 'strategic investment' in equity instruments issued by another entity, with the intention of establishing or maintaining a long-term operating relationship with the entity in which the investment is made. The investor entity uses FRS 9 *Associates and Joint Ventures* to determine whether the equity method of accounting, gross equity method, or treatment as a joint arrangement that is not an entity is appropriate for such an investment. If none of these is appropriate, the entity applies this Standard to that strategic investment.

AG3A This Standard applies to the financial assets and financial liabilities of insurers, other than rights and obligations that paragraph 2(e) excludes because they arise under contracts that are insurance contracts as defined in Appendix C to FRS 26.

AG4 Financial guarantee contracts may have various legal forms, such as a guarantee, some types of letter of credit, a credit default contract or an insurance contract. Their accounting treatment does not depend on their legal form. The following are examples of the appropriate treatment (see paragraph 2(e)):

(a) Although a financial guarantee contract meets the definition of an insurance contract in Appendix C to FRS 26 if the risk transferred is significant, the issuer applies this Standard. Nevertheless, if the issuer has previously asserted explicitly that it regards such contracts as insurance contracts and has used accounting applicable to insurance contracts, the issuer may elect to apply this Standard to such financial guarantee contracts. If this Standard applies, paragraph 43 requires the issuer to recognise a financial guarantee contract initially at fair value. If the financial guarantee contract was issued to an unrelated party in a stand-alone arm's length transaction, its fair value at inception is likely to equal the premium received, unless there is evidence to the contrary. Subsequently, unless the financial guarantee contract was designated at inception as at fair value through profit or loss, the issuer measures it at the higher of:

   (i) the amount determined in accordance with FRS 12; and
   (ii) the amount initially recognised less, when appropriate, cumulative amortisation (see paragraph 47(c)).

(b) Some credit-related guarantees do not, as a precondition for payment, require that the holder is exposed to, and has incurred a loss on, the failure of the debtor to make payments on the guaranteed asset when due. An example of such a guarantee is one that requires payments in response to changes in a specified credit rating or credit index. Such guarantees are not financial guarantee contracts, as defined in this Standard, and are not insurance contracts, as defined in Appendix C to FRS 26. Such guarantees are derivatives and the issuer applies this Standard to them.

(c) If a financial guarantee contract was issued in connection with the sale of goods, the issuer applies Application Note G to FRS 5 *Reporting the Substance of Transactions* in determining when it recognises the revenue from the sale of goods.

Assertions that an issuer regards contracts as insurance contracts are typically found throughout the issuer's communications with customers and regulators, contracts, business documentation and financial statements. Furthermore, insurance contracts are often subject to accounting requirements that are distinct from the requirements for other types of transaction, such as contracts issued by banks or commercial companies. In such cases, an issuer's financial statements typically include a statement that the issuer has used those accounting requirements.* **AG4A**

Paragraph 9 of this Standard allows an entity to designate a financial asset, a financial liability, or a group of financial instruments (financial assets, financial liabilities or both) as at fair value through profit or loss provided that doing so results in more relevant information. **AG4B**

The decision of an entity to designate a financial asset or financial liability as at fair value through profit or loss is similar to an accounting policy choice (although, unlike an accounting policy choice, it is not required to be applied consistently to all similar transactions). Paragraph 30 of FRS 18 *Accounting Policies* states that the objectives against which an entity should judge the appropriateness of accounting policies include relevance and reliability. In the case of designation as at fair value through profit or loss paragraph 9 sets out the two circumstances in which more relevant information will be provided. Accordingly, to choose such designation in accordance with paragraph 9, the entity needs to demonstrate that it falls within one (or both) of these two circumstances. **AG4C**

Paragraph 9(b)(i): Designation eliminates or significantly reduces a measurement or recognition inconsistency that would otherwise arise

Under FRS 26, measurement of a financial asset or financial liability and classification of recognised changes in its value are determined by the item's classification and whether the item is part of a designated hedging relationship. Those requirements can create a measurement or recognition inconsistency (sometimes referred to as an 'accounting mismatch') when, for example, in the absence of designation as at fair value through profit or loss, a financial asset would be classified as available for sale (with most changes in fair value recognised directly in equity) and a liability the entity considers related would be measured at amortised cost (with changes in fair value not recognised). In such circumstances, an entity may conclude that its financial statements would provide more relevant information if both the asset and the liability were classified as at fair value through profit or loss. **AG4D**

The following examples show when this condition could be met. In all cases, an entity may use this condition to designate financial assets or financial liabilities as at fair value through profit or loss only if it meets the principle in paragraph 9(b)(i). **AG4E**

(a) An entity has liabilities whose cash flows are contractually based on the performance of assets that would otherwise be classified as available for sale. For

* ***Editor's note:*** *AG4 amended and AG4A added with effect from 1 January 2006.*

example, an insurer may have liabilities containing a discretionary participation feature that pay benefits based on realised and/or unrealised investment returns of a specified pool of the insurer's assets. If the measurement of those liabilities reflects current market prices, classifying the assets as at fair value through profit or loss means that changes in the fair value of the financial assets are recognised in profit or loss in the same period as related changes in the value of the liabilities.

(b) An entity has liabilities under insurance contracts whose measurement incorporates current information and financial assets it considers related that would otherwise be classified as available for sale or measured at amortised cost.

(c) An entity has financial assets, financial liabilities or both that share a risk, such as interest rate risk, that gives rise to opposite changes in fair value that tend to offset each other. However, only some of the instruments would be measured at fair value through profit or loss (ie are derivatives, or are classified as held for trading). It may also be the case that the requirements for hedge accounting are not met, for example because the requirements for effectiveness in paragraph 88 are not met.

(d) An entity has financial assets, financial liabilities or both that share a risk, such as interest rate risk, that gives rise to opposite changes in fair value that tend to offset each other and the entity does not qualify for hedge accounting because none of the instruments is a derivative. Furthermore, in the absence of hedge accounting there is a significant inconsistency in the recognition of gains and losses. For example:

    (i) the entity has financed a portfolio of fixed rate assets that would otherwise be classified as available for sale with fixed rate debentures whose changes in fair value tend to offset each other. Reporting both the assets and the debentures at fair value through profit or loss corrects the inconsistency that would otherwise arise from measuring the assets at fair value with changes reported in equity and the debentures at amortised cost.

    (ii) the entity has financed a specified group of loans by issuing traded bonds whose changes in fair value tend to offset each other. If, in addition, the entity regularly buys and sells the bonds but rarely, if ever, buys and sells the loans, reporting both the loans and the bonds at fair value through profit or loss eliminates the inconsistency in the timing of recognition of gains and losses that would otherwise result from measuring them both at amortised cost and recognising a gain or loss each time a bond is repurchased.

AG4F In cases such as those described in the preceding paragraph, to designate, at initial recognition, the financial assets and financial liabilities not otherwise so measured as at fair value through profit or loss may eliminate or significantly reduce the measurement or recognition inconsistency and produce more relevant information. For practical purposes, the entity need not enter into all of the assets and liabilities giving rise to the measurement or recognition inconsistency at exactly the same time. A reasonable delay is permitted provided that each transaction is designated as at fair value through profit or loss at its initial recognition and, at that time, any remaining transactions are expected to occur.

AG4G It would not be acceptable to designate only some of the financial assets and financial liabilities giving rise to the inconsistency as at fair value through profit or loss if to do so would not eliminate or significantly reduce the inconsistency and would therefore not result in more relevant information. However, it would be acceptable to designate only some of a number of similar financial assets or similar financial liabilities if doing so achieves a significant reduction (and possibly a greater reduction than other allowable designations) in the inconsistency. For example, assume an entity has a number of similar financial liabilities that sum to CU100* and a number of similar financial assets that sum to CU50 but are measured on a different basis. The entity may significantly reduce the measurement inconsistency by designating at initial recognition all of the assets but only some of the liabilities (for example, individual liabilities with a combined total of CU45) as at fair value through profit or loss. However, because designation as at fair value through profit or loss can be applied only to the whole of a financial instrument, the entity in this example must designate one or more liabilities in their entirety. It could not designate either a component of a liability (eg changes in value attributable to only one risk, such as changes in a benchmark interest rate) or a proportion (ie percentage) of a liability.

Paragraph 9(b)(ii): A group of financial assets, financial liabilities or both is managed and its performance is evaluated on a fair value basis, in accordance with a documented risk management or investment strategy

An entity may manage and evaluate the performance of a group of financial assets, financial liabilities or both in such a way that measuring that group at fair value through profit or loss results in more relevant information. The focus in this instance is on the way the entity manages and evaluates performance, rather than on the nature of its financial instruments. **AG4H**

The following examples show when this condition could be met. In all cases, an entity may use this condition to designate financial assets or financial liabilities as at fair value through profit or loss only if it meets the principle in paragraph 9(b)(ii). **AG4I**

(a) The entity is a venture capital organisation, mutual fund, unit trust or similar entity whose business is investing in financial assets with a view to profiting from their total return in the form of interest or dividends and changes in fair value.†

(b) The entity has financial assets and financial liabilities that share one or more risks and those risks are managed and evaluated on a fair value basis in accordance with a documented policy of asset and liability management. An example could be an entity that has issued 'structured products' containing multiple embedded derivatives and manages the resulting risks on a fair value basis using a mix of derivative and non-derivative financial instruments. A similar example could be an entity that originates fixed interest rate loans and manages the resulting benchmark interest rate risk using a mix of derivative and non-derivative financial instruments.

(c) The entity is an insurer that holds a portfolio of financial assets, manages that portfolio so as to maximise its total return (ie interest or dividends and changes in fair value), and evaluates its performance on that basis. The portfolio may be held to back specific liabilities, equity or both. If the portfolio is held to back specific liabilities, the condition in paragraph 9(b)(ii) may be met for the assets regardless of whether the insurer also manages and evaluates the liabilities on a fair value basis. The condition in paragraph 9(b)(ii) may be met when the insurer's objective is to maximise total return on the assets over the longer term even if amounts paid to holders of participating contracts depend on other factors such as the amount of gains realised in a shorter period (eg a year) or are subject to the insurer's discretion.

**In this Standard, monetary amounts are denominated in 'currency units' (CU)*

†ASB Footnote: *Under FRS 9* Associates and Joint Ventures*, investment funds account for their investments at cost or market value. Unlike IFRS, where a market value approach is taken it is not a requirement for the period movement in market value to be recorded in the profit and loss account. Accordingly the second sentence of paragraph AG 41(a) has been deleted for the purposes of FRS 26.*

AG4J As noted above, this condition relies on the way the entity manages and evaluates performance of the group of financial instruments under consideration. Accordingly, (subject to the requirement of designation at initial recognition) an entity that designates financial instruments as at fair value through profit or loss on the basis of this condition shall so designate all eligible financial instruments that are managed and evaluated together.

AG4K Documentation of the entity's strategy need not be extensive but should be sufficient to demonstrate compliance with paragraph 9(b)(ii). Such documentation is not required for each individual item, but may be on a portfolio basis. For example, if the performance management system for a department—as approved by the entity's key management personnel (as defined in paragraph 9(b)(ii))—clearly demonstrates that its performance is evaluated on a total return basis, no further documentation is required to demonstrate compliance with paragraph 9(b)(ii).*

DEFINITIONS (PARAGRAPHS 8 AND 9)

Effective Interest Rate

AG5 In some cases, financial assets are acquired at a deep discount that reflects incurred credit losses. Entities include such incurred credit losses in the estimated cash flows when computing the effective interest rate.

AG6 When applying the effective interest method, an entity generally amortises any fees, points paid or received, transaction costs and other premiums or discounts included in the calculation of the effective interest rate over the expected life of the instrument. However, a shorter period is used if this is the period to which the fees, points paid or received, transaction costs, premiums or discounts relate. This will be the case when the variable to which the fees, points paid or received, transaction costs, premiums or discounts relate is repriced to market rates before the expected maturity of the instrument. In such a case, the appropriate amortisation period is the period to the next such repricing date. For example, if a premium or discount on a floating rate instrument reflects interest that has accrued on the instrument since interest was last paid, or changes in market rates since the floating interest rate was reset to market rates, it will be amortised to the next date when the floating interest is reset to market rates. This is because the premium or discount relates to the period to the next interest reset date because, at that date, the variable to which the premium or discount relates (ie interest rates) is reset to market rates. If, however, the premium or discount results from a change in the credit spread over the floating rate specified in the instrument, or other variables that are not reset to market rates, it is amortised over the expected life of the instrument.

AG7 For floating rate financial assets and floating rate financial liabilities, periodic reestimation of cash flows to reflect movements in market rates of interest alters the effective interest rate. If a floating rate financial asset or floating rate financial liability is recognised initially at an amount equal to the principal receivable or payable on maturity, re-estimating the future interest payments normally has no significant effect on the carrying amount of the asset or liability.

AG8 If an entity revises its estimates of payments or receipts, the entity shall adjust the carrying amount of the financial asset or financial liability (or group of financial instruments) to reflect actual and revised estimated cash flows. The entity recalculates the carrying amount by computing the present value of estimated future cash flows at

***Editor's note:** *AG4B to AG4K added with effect from 1 January 2006.*

the financial instrument's original effective interest rate or, when applicable, the revised effective interest rate calculated in accordance with paragraph 92. The adjustment is recognised in profit or loss as income or expense. If a financial asset is reclassified in accordance with paragraph 50B, 50D or 50E, and the entity subsequently increases its estimates of future cash receipts as a result of increased recoverability of those cash receipts, the effect of that increase shall be recognised as an adjustment to the effective interest rate from the date of the change in estimate rather than as an adjustment to the carrying amount of the asset at the date of the change in estimate.*

Derivatives

Typical examples of derivatives are futures and forward, swap and option contracts. A derivative usually has a notional amount, which is an amount of currency, a number of shares, a number of units of weight or volume or other units specified in the contract. However, a derivative instrument does not require the holder or writer to invest or receive the notional amount at the inception of the contract. Alternatively, a derivative could require a fixed payment or payment of an amount that can change (but not proportionally with a change in the underlying) as a result of some future event that is unrelated to a notional amount. For example, a contract may require a fixed payment of CU1,000† if sixmonth LIBOR increases by 100 basis points. Such a contract is a derivative even though a notional amount is not specified. **AG9**

The definition of a derivative in this Standard includes contracts that are settled gross by delivery of the underlying item (eg a forward contract to purchase a fixed rate debt instrument). An entity may have a contract to buy or sell a nonfinancial item that can be settled net in cash or another financial instrument or by exchanging financial instruments (eg a contract to buy or sell a commodity at a fixed price at a future date). Such a contract is within the scope of this Standard unless it was entered into and continues to be held for the purpose of delivery of a non-financial item in accordance with the entity's expected purchase, sale or usage requirements (see paragraphs 5-7). **AG10**

One of the defining characteristics of a derivative is that it has an initial net investment that is smaller than would be required for other types of contracts that would be expected to have a similar response to changes in market factors. An option contract meets that definition because the premium is less than the investment that would be required to obtain the underlying financial instrument to which the option is linked. A currency swap that requires an initial exchange of different currencies of equal fair values meets the definition because it has a zero initial net investment. **AG11**

A regular way purchase or sale gives rise to a fixed price commitment between trade date and settlement date that meets the definition of a derivative. However, because of the short duration of the commitment it is not recognised as a derivative financial instrument. Rather, this Standard provides for special accounting for such regular way contracts (see paragraphs 38 and AG53-AG56). **AG12**

The definition of a derivative refers to non-financial variables that are not specific to a party to the contract. These include an index of earthquake losses in a particular **AG12A**

**Editor's note*: *Paragraph amended in October 2008. Strictly, there is a prima facie change in December 2008. However, the October changes are based on IASB changes which were made later than the December changes. It has therefore been assumed that it is the October changes which continue to apply.*

†*In this Standard, monetary amounts are denominated in 'currency units' (CU).*

region and an index of temperatures in a particular city. Nonfinancial variables specific to a party to the contract include the occurrence or nonoccurrence of a fire that damages or destroys an asset of a party to the contract. A change in the fair value of a nonfinancial asset is specific to the owner if the fair value reflects not only changes in market prices for such assets (a financial variable) but also the condition of the specific nonfinancial asset held (a nonfinancial variable). For example, if a guarantee of the residual value of a specific car exposes the guarantor to the risk of changes in the car's physical condition, the change in that residual value is specific to the owner of the car.

Transaction Costs

AG13 Transaction costs include fees and commissions paid to agents (including employees acting as selling agents), advisers, brokers and dealers, levies by regulatory agencies and securities exchanges, and transfer taxes and duties. Transaction costs do not include debt premiums or discounts, financing costs or internal administrative or holding costs.

Financial Assets and Financial Liabilities Held for Trading

AG14 Trading generally reflects active and frequent buying and selling, and financial instruments held for trading generally are used with the objective of generating a profit from short-term fluctuations in price or dealer's margin.

AG15 Financial liabilities held for trading include:

(a) derivative liabilities that are not accounted for as hedging instruments;
(b) obligations to deliver financial assets borrowed by a short seller (ie an entity that sells financial assets it has borrowed and does not yet own);
(c) financial liabilities that are incurred with an intention to repurchase them in the near term (eg a quoted debt instrument that the issuer may buy back in the near term depending on changes in its fair value); and
(d) financial liabilities that are part of a portfolio of identified financial instruments that are managed together and for which there is evidence of a recent pattern of short-term profit-taking.

The fact that a liability is used to fund trading activities does not in itself make that liability one that is held for trading.

Held-to-Maturity Investments

AG16 An entity does not have a positive intention to hold to maturity an investment in a financial asset with a fixed maturity if:

(a) the entity intends to hold the financial asset for an undefined period;
(b) the entity stands ready to sell the financial asset (other than if a situation arises that is non-recurring and could not have been reasonably anticipated by the entity) in response to changes in market interest rates or risks, liquidity needs, changes in the availability of and the yield on alternative investments, changes in financing sources and terms or changes in foreign currency risk; or
(c) the issuer has a right to settle the financial asset at an amount significantly below its amortised cost.

AG17 A debt instrument with a variable interest rate can satisfy the criteria for a heldto-maturity investment. Equity instruments cannot be heldtomaturity investments either because they have an indefinite life (such as ordinary shares) or because the amounts the holder may receive can vary in a manner that is not predetermined (such as for share options, warrants and similar rights). With respect to the definition of heldtomaturity investments, fixed or determinable payments and fixed maturity mean that a contractual arrangement defines the amounts and dates of payments to the holder, such as interest and principal payments. A significant risk of non-payment does not preclude classification of a financial asset as held to maturity as long as its contractual payments are fixed or determinable and the other criteria for that classification are met. If the terms of a perpetual debt instrument provide for interest payments for an indefinite period, the instrument cannot be classified as held to maturity because there is no maturity date.

The criteria for classification as a held-to-maturity investment are met for a financial asset that is callable by the issuer if the holder intends and is able to hold it until it is called or until maturity and the holder would recover substantially all of its carrying amount. The call option of the issuer, if exercised, simply accelerates the asset's maturity. However, if the financial asset is callable on a basis that would result in the holder not recovering substantially all of its carrying amount, the financial asset cannot be classified as a held-to-maturity investment. The entity considers any premium paid and capitalised transaction costs in determining whether the carrying amount would be substantially recovered. **AG18**

A financial asset that is puttable (ie the holder has the right to require that the issuer repay or redeem the financial asset before maturity) cannot be classified as a held-to-maturity investment because paying for a put feature in a financial asset is inconsistent with expressing an intention to hold the financial asset until maturity. **AG19**

For most financial assets, fair value is a more appropriate measure than amortised cost. The held-to-maturity classification is an exception, but only if the entity has a positive intention and the ability to hold the investment to maturity. When an entity's actions cast doubt on its intention and ability to hold such investments to maturity, paragraph 9 precludes the use of the exception for a reasonable period of time. **AG20**

A disaster scenario that is only remotely possible, such as a run on a bank or a similar situation affecting an insurer, is not something that is assessed by an entity in deciding whether it has the positive intention and ability to hold an investment to maturity. **AG21**

Sales before maturity could satisfy the condition in paragraph 9—and therefore not raise a question about the entity's intention to hold other investments to maturity—if they are attributable to any of the following: **AG22**

(a) a significant deterioration in the issuer's creditworthiness. For example, a sale following a downgrade in a credit rating by an external rating agency would not necessarily raise a question about the entity's intention to hold other investments to maturity if the downgrade provides evidence of a significant deterioration in the issuer's creditworthiness judged by reference to the credit rating at initial recognition. Similarly, if an entity uses internal ratings for assessing exposures, changes in those internal ratings may help to identify issuers for which there has been a significant deterioration in creditworthiness, provided the entity's approach to assigning internal ratings and changes in those ratings give a consistent, reliable and objective measure of the credit quality of the issuers. If there is evidence that a financial asset is impaired (see paragraphs 58 and 59), the deterioration in creditworthiness is often regarded as significant.

(b) a change in tax law that eliminates or significantly reduces the tax-exempt status of interest on the held-to-maturity investment (but not a change in tax law that revises the marginal tax rates applicable to interest income).
(c) a major business combination or major disposition (such as a sale of a segment) that necessitates the sale or transfer of heldto-maturity investments to maintain the entity's existing interest rate risk position or credit risk policy (although the business combination is an event within the entity's control, the changes to its investment portfolio to maintain an interest rate risk position or credit risk policy may be consequential rather than anticipated).
(d) a change in statutory or regulatory requirements significantly modifying either what constitutes a permissible investment or the maximum level of particular types of investments, thereby causing an entity to dispose of a heldto-maturity investment.
(e) a significant increase in the industry's regulatory capital requirements that causes the entity to downsize by selling heldto-maturity investments.
(f) a significant increase in the risk weights of held-to-maturity investments used for regulatory risk-based capital purposes.

AG23 An entity does not have a demonstrated ability to hold to maturity an investment in a financial asset with a fixed maturity if:

(a) it does not have the financial resources available to continue to finance the investment until maturity; or
(b) it is subject to an existing legal or other constraint that could frustrate its intention to hold the financial asset to maturity. (However, an issuer's call option does not necessarily frustrate an entity's intention to hold a financial asset to maturity—see paragraph AG18.)

AG24 Circumstances other than those described in paragraphs AG16-AG23 can indicate that an entity does not have a positive intention or the ability to hold an investment to maturity.

AG25 An entity assesses its intention and ability to hold its held-to-maturity investments to maturity not only when those financial assets are initially recognised, but also at each subsequent balance sheet date.

Loans and Receivables

AG26 Any non-derivative financial asset with fixed or determinable payments (including loan assets, trade receivables, investments in debt instruments and deposits held in banks) could potentially meet the definition of loans and receivables. However, a financial asset that is quoted in an active market (such as a quoted debt instrument, see paragraph AG71) does not qualify for classification as a loan or receivable. Financial assets that do not meet the definition of loans and receivables may be classified as held-to-maturity investments if they meet the conditions for that classification (see paragraphs 9 and AG16-AG25). On initial recognition of a financial asset that would otherwise be classified as a loan or receivable, an entity may designate it as a financial asset at fair value through profit or loss, or available for sale.

EMBEDDED DERIVATIVES (PARAGRAPHS 10-13)

AG27 If a host contract has no stated or predetermined maturity and represents a residual interest in the net assets of an entity, then its economic characteristics and risks are those of an equity instrument, and an embedded derivative would need to possess equity characteristics related to the same entity to be regarded as closely related. If the host contract is not an equity instrument and meets the definition of a financial instrument, then its economic characteristics and risks are those of a debt instrument.

An embedded non-option derivative (such as an embedded forward or swap) is separated from its host contract on the basis of its stated or implied substantive terms, so as to result in it having a fair value of zero at initial recognition. An embedded option-based derivative (such as an embedded put, call, cap, floor or swaption) is separated from its host contract on the basis of the stated terms of the option feature. The initial carrying amount of the host instrument is the residual amount after separating the embedded derivative. **AG28**

Generally, multiple embedded derivatives in a single instrument are treated as a single compound embedded derivative. However, embedded derivatives that are classified as equity (see FRS 25) are accounted for separately from those classified as assets or liabilities. In addition, if an instrument has more than one embedded derivative and those derivatives relate to different risk exposures and are readily separable and independent of each other, they are accounted for separately from each other. **AG29**

The economic characteristics and risks of an embedded derivative are not closely related to the host contract (paragraph 11(a)) in the following examples. In these examples, assuming the conditions in paragraph 11(b) and (c) are met, an entity accounts for the embedded derivative separately from the host contract. **AG30**

(a) A put option embedded in an instrument that enables the holder to require the issuer to reacquire the instrument for an amount of cash or other assets that varies on the basis of the change in an equity or commodity price or index is not closely related to a host debt instrument.

(b) A call option embedded in an equity instrument that enables the issuer to reacquire that equity instrument at a specified price is not closely related to the host equity instrument from the perspective of the holder (from the issuer's perspective, the call option is an equity instrument provided it meets the conditions for that classification under FRS 25, in which case it is excluded from the scope of this Standard).

(c) An option or automatic provision to extend the remaining term to maturity of a debt instrument is not closely related to the host debt instrument unless there is a concurrent adjustment to the approximate current market rate of interest at the time of the extension. If an entity issues a debt instrument and the holder of that debt instrument writes a call option on the debt instrument to a third party, the issuer regards the call option as extending the term to maturity of the debt instrument provided the issuer can be required to participate in or facilitate the remarketing of the debt instrument as a result of the call option being exercised.

(d) Equity-indexed interest or principal payments embedded in a host debt instrument or insurance contract—by which the amount of interest or principal is indexed to the value of equity instruments—are not closely related to the host instrument because the risks inherent in the host and the embedded derivative are dissimilar.

(e) Commodity-indexed interest or principal payments embedded in a host debt instrument or insurance contract—by which the amount of interest or principal is indexed to the price of a commodity (such as gold)—are not closely related to the host instrument because the risks inherent in the host and the embedded derivative are dissimilar.

(f) An equity conversion feature embedded in a convertible debt instrument is not closely related to the host debt instrument from the perspective of the holder of the instrument (from the issuer's perspective, the equity conversion option is an equity instrument and excluded from the scope of this Standard provided it meets the conditions for that classification under FRS 25).

(g) A call, put, or prepayment option embedded in a host debt contract or host insurance contract is not closely related to the host contract unless:

 (i) the option's exercise price is approximately equal on each exercise date to the amortised cost of the host debt instrument or the carrying amount of the host insurance contract; or

 (ii) the exercise price of a prepayment option reimburses the lender for an amount up to the approximate present value of lost interest for the remaining term of the host contract. Lost interest is the product of the principal amount prepaid multiplied by the interest rate differential. The interest rate differential is the excess of the effective interest rate of the host contract over the effective interest rate the entity would receive at the prepayment date if it reinvested the principal amount prepaid in a similar contract for the remaining term of the host contract.

The assessment of whether the call or put option is closely related to the host debt contract is made before separating the equity element of a convertible debt instrument in accordance with FRS 25.

(h) Credit derivatives that are embedded in a host debt instrument and allow one party (the 'beneficiary') to transfer the credit risk of a particular reference asset, which it may not own, to another party (the 'guarantor') are not closely related to the host debt instrument. Such credit derivatives allow the guarantor to assume the credit risk associated with the reference asset without directly owning it.

AG31 An example of a hybrid instrument is a financial instrument that gives the holder a right to put the financial instrument back to the issuer in exchange for an amount of cash or other financial assets that varies on the basis of the change in an equity or commodity index that may increase or decrease (a 'puttable instrument'). Unless the issuer on initial recognition designates the puttable instrument as a financial liability at fair value through profit or loss, it is required to separate an embedded derivative (ie the indexed principal payment) under paragraph 11 because the host contract is a debt instrument under paragraph AG27 and the indexed principal payment is not closely related to a host debt instrument under paragraph AG30(a). Because the principal payment can increase and decrease, the embedded derivative is a non-option derivative whose value is indexed to the underlying variable.

AG32 In the case of a puttable instrument that can be put back at any time for cash equal to a proportionate share of the net asset value of an entity (such as units of an openended mutual fund or some unitlinked investment products), the effect of separating an embedded derivative and accounting for each component is to measure the combined instrument at the redemption amount that is payable at the balance sheet date if the holder exercised its right to put the instrument back to the issuer.

AG33 The economic characteristics and risks of an embedded derivative are closely related to the economic characteristics and risks of the host contract in the following examples. In these examples, an entity does not account for the embedded derivative separately from the host contract.

(a) An embedded derivative in which the underlying is an interest rate or interest rate index that can change the amount of interest that would otherwise be paid or received on an interest-bearing host debt contract or insurance contract is closely related to the host contract unless the combined instrument can be settled in such a way that the holder would not recover substantially all of its recognised investment or the embedded derivative could at least double the holder's initial rate of return on the host contract and could result in a rate of return that is at least twice what the market return would be for a contract with the same terms as the host contract.

(b) An embedded floor or cap on the interest rate on a debt contract or insurance contract is closely related to the host contract, provided the cap is at or above the market rate of interest and the floor is at or below the market rate of interest when the contract is issued, and the cap or floor is not leveraged in relation to the host contract. Similarly, provisions included in a contract to purchase or sell an asset (eg a commodity) that establish a cap and a floor on the price to be paid or received for the asset are closely related to the host contract if both the cap and floor were out of the money at inception and are not leveraged.

(c) An embedded foreign currency derivative that provides a stream of principal or interest payments that are denominated in a foreign currency and is embedded in a host debt instrument (eg a dual currency bond) is closely related to the host debt instrument. Such a derivative is not separated from the host instrument because FRS 23 requires foreign currency gains and losses on monetary items to be recognised in profit or loss.

(d) An embedded foreign currency derivative in a host contract that is an insurance contract or not a financial instrument (such as a contract for the purchase or sale of a non-financial item where the price is denominated in a foreign currency) is closely related to the host contract provided it is not leveraged, does not contain an option feature, and requires payments denominated in one of the following currencies:

   (i) the functional currency of any substantial party to that contract;

   (ii) the currency in which the price of the related good or service that is acquired or delivered is routinely denominated in commercial transactions around the world (such as the US dollar for crude oil transactions); or

   (iii) a currency that is commonly used in contracts to purchase or sell non-financial items in the economic environment in which the transaction takes place (eg a relatively stable and liquid currency that is commonly used in local business transactions or external trade).

(e) An embedded prepayment option in an interest-only or principal-only strip is closely related to the host contract provided the host contract (i) initially resulted from separating the right to receive contractual cash flows of a financial instrument that, in and of itself, did not contain an embedded derivative, and (ii) does not contain any terms not present in the original host debt contract.

(f) An embedded derivative in a host lease contract is closely related to the host contract if the embedded derivative is (i) an inflation-related index such as an index of lease payments to a consumer price index (provided that the lease is not leveraged and the index relates to inflation in the entity's own economic environment), (ii) contingent rentals based on related sales or (iii) contingent rentals based on variable interest rates.

(g) A unit-linking feature embedded in a host financial instrument or host insurance contract is closely related to the host instrument or host contract if the unit-denominated payments are measured at current unit values that reflect the fair values of the assets of the fund. A unit-linking feature is a contractual term that requires payments denominated in units of an internal or external investment fund.

(h) A derivative embedded in an insurance contract is closely related to the host insurance contract if the embedded derivative and host insurance contract are so interdependent that an entity cannot measure the embedded derivative separately (ie without considering the host contract).

AG33A When an entity becomes a party to a hybrid (combined) instrument that contains one or more embedded derivatives, paragraph 11 requires the entity to identify any such embedded derivative, assess whether it is required to be separated from the host contract and, for those that are required to be separated, measure the derivatives at fair value at initial recognition and subsequently. These requirements can be more complex, or result in less reliable measures, than measuring the entire instrument at fair value through profit or loss. For that reason this Standard permits the entire instrument to be designated as at fair value through profit or loss.

AG33B Such designation may be used whether paragraph 11 requires the embedded derivatives to be separated from the host contract or prohibits such separation. However, paragraph 11A would not justify designating the hybrid (combined) instrument as at fair value through profit or loss in the cases set out in paragraph 11A(a) and (b) because doing so would not reduce complexity or increase reliability.*

RECOGNITION AND DERECOGNITION (PARAGRAPHS 14–42)

Initial Recognition (paragraph 14)

AG34 As a consequence of the principle in paragraph 14, an entity recognises all of its contractual rights and obligations under derivatives in its balance sheet as assets and liabilities, respectively, except for derivatives that prevent a transfer of financial assets from being accounted for as a sale (see paragraph AG49). If a transfer of a financial asset does not qualify for derecognition, the transferee does not recognise the transferred asset as its asset (see paragraph AG50).

AG35 The following are examples of applying the principle in paragraph 14:

(a) unconditional receivables and payables are recognised as assets or liabilities when the entity becomes a party to the contract and, as a consequence, has a legal right to receive or a legal obligation to pay cash.
(b) assets to be acquired and liabilities to be incurred as a result of a firm commitment to purchase or sell goods or services are generally not recognised until at least one of the parties has performed under the agreement. For example, an entity that receives a firm order does not generally recognise an asset (and the entity that places the order does not recognise a liability) at the time of the commitment but, rather, delays recognition until the ordered goods or services have been shipped, delivered or rendered. If a firm commitment to buy or sell non-financial items is within the scope of this Standard under paragraphs 5–7, its net fair value is recognised as an asset or liability on the commitment date (see (c) below). In addition, if a previously unrecognised firm commitment is designated as a hedged item in a fair value hedge, any change in the net fair value attributable to the hedged risk is recognised as an asset or liability after the inception of the hedge (see paragraphs 93 and 94).
(c) a forward contract that is within the scope of this Standard (see paragraph 27) is recognised as an asset or a liability on the commitment date, rather than on the date on which settlement takes place. When an entity becomes a party to a forward contract, the fair values of the right and obligation are often equal, so that the net fair value of the forward is zero. If the net fair value of the right and obligation is not zero, the contract is recognised as an asset or liability.
(d) option contracts that are within the scope of this Standard (see paragraph 27) are recognised as assets or liabilities when the holder or writer becomes a party to the contract.

**Editor's note:* *AG33A and AG33B added with effect from 1 January 2006.*

(e) planned future transactions, no matter how likely, are not assets and liabilities because the entity has not become a party to a contract.

Derecognition of a Financial Asset (paragraphs 15–37)

The following flow chart illustrates the evaluation of whether and to what extent a financial asset is derecognised. **AG36**

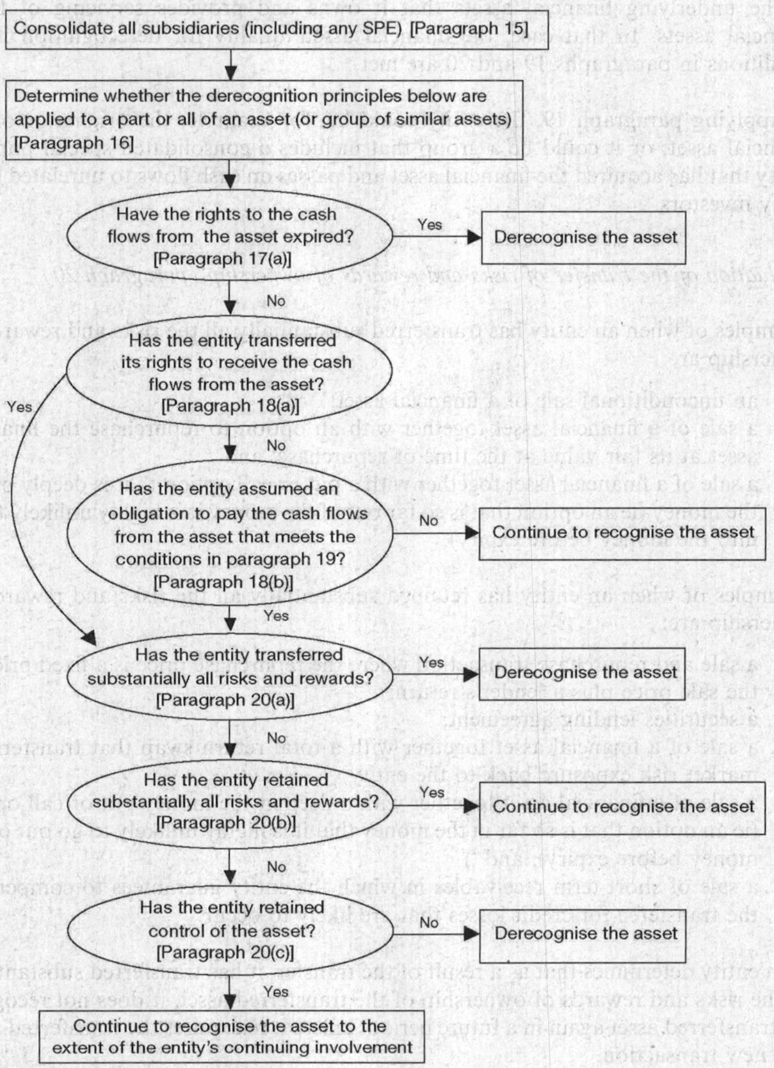

Arrangements under which an entity retains the contractual rights to receive the cash flows of a financial asset, but assumes a contractual obligation to pay the cash flows to one or more recipients (paragraph 18(b))

AG37 The situation described in paragraph 18(b) (when an entity retains the contractual rights to receive the cash flows of the financial asset, but assumes a contractual obligation to pay the cash flows to one or more recipients) occurs, for example, if the entity is a special purpose entity* or trust, and issues to investors beneficial interests in the underlying financial assets that it owns and provides servicing of those financial assets. In that case, the financial assets qualify for derecognition if the conditions in paragraphs 19 and 20 are met.

AG38 In applying paragraph 19, the entity could be, for example, the originator of the financial asset, or it could be a group that includes a consolidated special purpose entity that has acquired the financial asset and passes on cash flows to unrelated third party investors.

Evaluation of the transfer of risks and rewards of ownership (paragraph 20)

AG39 Examples of when an entity has transferred substantially all the risks and rewards of ownership are:

(a) an unconditional sale of a financial asset;
(b) a sale of a financial asset together with an option to repurchase the financial asset at its fair value at the time of repurchase; and
(c) a sale of a financial asset together with a put or call option that is deeply out of the money (ie an option that is so far out of the money it is highly unlikely to go into the money before expiry).

AG40 Examples of when an entity has retained substantially all the risks and rewards of ownership are:

(a) a sale and repurchase transaction where the repurchase price is a fixed price or the sale price plus a lender's return;
(b) a securities lending agreement;
(c) a sale of a financial asset together with a total return swap that transfers the market risk exposure back to the entity;
(d) a sale of a financial asset together with a deep in-the-money put or call option (ie an option that is so far in the money that it is highly unlikely to go out of the money before expiry); and
(e) a sale of short-term receivables in which the entity guarantees to compensate the transferee for credit losses that are likely to occur.

AG41 If an entity determines that as a result of the transfer, it has transferred substantially all the risks and rewards of ownership of the transferred asset, it does not recognise the transferred asset again in a future period, unless it reacquires the transferred asset in a new transaction.

Evaluation of the transfer of control

AG42 An entity has not retained control of a transferred asset if the transferee has the practical ability to sell the transferred asset. An entity has retained control of a transferred asset if the transferee does not have the practical ability to sell the

***ASB footnote**: *a special purpose entity is consolidated if it meets the definition of subsidiary undertaking in FRS 2 or quasi-subsidiary in FRS 5.*

transferred asset. A transferee has the practical ability to sell the transferred asset if it is traded in an active market because the transferee could repurchase the transferred asset in the market if it needs to return the asset to the entity. For example, a transferee may have the practical ability to sell a transferred asset if the transferred asset is subject to an option that allows the entity to repurchase it, but the transferee can readily obtain the transferred asset in the market if the option is exercised. A transferee does not have the practical ability to sell the transferred asset if the entity retains such an option and the transferee cannot readily obtain the transferred asset in the market if the entity exercises its option.

The transferee has the practical ability to sell the transferred asset only if the transferee can sell the transferred asset in its entirety to an unrelated third party and is able to exercise that ability unilaterally and without imposing additional restrictions on the transfer. The critical question is what the transferee is able to do in practice, not what contractual rights the transferee has concerning what it can do with the transferred asset or what contractual prohibitions exist. In particular: **AG43**

(a) a contractual right to dispose of the transferred asset has little practical effect if there is no market for the transferred asset; and
(b) an ability to dispose of the transferred asset has little practical effect if it cannot be exercised freely. For that reason:
    (i) the transferee's ability to dispose of the transferred asset must be independent of the actions of others (ie it must be a unilateral ability); and
    (ii) the transferee must be able to dispose of the transferred asset without needing to attach restrictive conditions or 'strings' to the transfer (eg conditions about how a loan asset is serviced or an option giving the transferee the right to repurchase the asset).

That the transferee is unlikely to sell the transferred asset does not, of itself, mean that the transferor has retained control of the transferred asset. However, if a put option or guarantee constrains the transferee from selling the transferred asset, then the transferor has retained control of the transferred asset. For example, if a put option or guarantee is sufficiently valuable it constrains the transferee from selling the transferred asset because the transferee would, in practice, not sell the transferred asset to a third party without attaching a similar option or other restrictive conditions. Instead, the transferee would hold the transferred asset so as to obtain payments under the guarantee or put option. Under these circumstances the transferor has retained control of the transferred asset. **AG44**

Transfers that Qualify for Derecognition

An entity may retain the right to a part of the interest payments on transferred assets as compensation for servicing those assets. The part of the interest payments that the entity would give up upon termination or transfer of the servicing contract is allocated to the servicing asset or servicing liability. The part of the interest payments that the entity would not give up is an interest-only strip receivable. For example, if the entity would not give up any interest upon termination or transfer of the servicing contract, the entire interest spread is an interest-only strip receivable. For the purposes of applying paragraph 27, the fair values of the servicing asset and interest-only strip receivable are used to allocate the carrying amount of the receivable between the part of the asset that is derecognised and the part that continues to be recognised. If there is no servicing fee specified or the fee to be received is not expected to compensate the entity adequately for performing the servicing, a liability for the servicing obligation is recognised at fair value. **AG45**

AG46 In estimating the fair values of the part that continues to be recognised and the part that is derecognised for the purposes of applying paragraph 27, an entity applies the fair value measurement requirements in paragraphs 48-49 and AG69–AG82 in addition to paragraph 28.

Transfers that Do Not Qualify for Derecognition

AG47 The following is an application of the principle outlined in paragraph 29. If a guarantee provided by the entity for default losses on the transferred asset prevents a transferred asset from being derecognised because the entity has retained substantially all the risks and rewards of ownership of the transferred asset, the transferred asset continues to be recognised in its entirety and the consideration received is recognised as a liability.

Continuing Involvement in Transferred Assets

AG48 The following are examples of how an entity measures a transferred asset and the associated liability under paragraph 30.

All assets

(a) If a guarantee provided by an entity to pay for default losses on a transferred asset prevents the transferred asset from being derecognised to the extent of the continuing involvement, the transferred asset at the date of the transfer is measured at the lower of (i) the carrying amount of the asset and (ii) the maximum amount of the consideration received in the transfer that the entity could be required to repay ('the guarantee amount'). The associated liability is initially measured at the guarantee amount plus the fair value of the guarantee (which is normally the consideration received for the guarantee). Subsequently, the initial fair value of the guarantee is recognised in profit or loss on a time proportion basis (see IAS 18) and the carrying value of the asset is reduced by any impairment losses.

Assets measured at amortised cost

(b) If a put option obligation written by an entity or call option right held by an entity prevents a transferred asset from being derecognised and the entity measures the transferred asset at amortised cost, the associated liability is measured at its cost (ie the consideration received) adjusted for the amortisation of any difference between that cost and the amortised cost of the transferred asset at the expiration date of the option. For example, assume that the amortised cost and carrying amount of the asset on the date of the transfer is CU98 and that the consideration received is CU95. The amortised cost of the asset on the option exercise date will be CU100. The initial carrying amount of the associated liability is CU95 and the difference between CU95 and CU100 is recognised in profit or loss using the effective interest method. If the option is exercised, any difference between the carrying amount of the associated liability and the exercise price is recognised in profit or loss.

Assets measured at fair value

(c) If a call option right retained by an entity prevents a transferred asset from being derecognised and the entity measures the transferred asset at fair value, the asset continues to be measured at its fair value. The associated liability is measured at (i) the option exercise price less the time value of the option if the option is in or at the money, or (ii) the fair value of the transferred asset less the time value of the option if the option is out of the money. The adjustment to the measurement of the associated liability ensures that the net carrying amount of the asset and the associated liability is the fair value of the call option right. For example, if the fair value of the underlying asset is CU80, the option exercise price is CU95 and the time value of the option is CU5, the carrying amount of the associated liability is CU75 (CU80 – CU5) and the carrying amount of the transferred asset is CU80 (ie its fair value).

(d) If a put option written by an entity prevents a transferred asset from being derecognised and the entity measures the transferred asset at fair value, the associated liability is measured at the option exercise price plus the time value of the option. The measurement of the asset at fair value is limited to the lower of the fair value and the option exercise price because the entity has no right to increases in the fair value of the transferred asset above the exercise price of the option. This ensures that the net carrying amount of the asset and the associated liability is the fair value of the put option obligation. For example, if the fair value of the underlying asset is CU120, the option exercise price is CU100 and the time value of the option is CU5, the carrying amount of the associated liability is CU105 (CU100 + CU5) and the carrying amount of the asset is CU100 (in this case the option exercise price).

(e) If a collar, in the form of a purchased call and written put, prevents a transferred asset from being derecognised and the entity measures the asset at fair value, it continues to measure the asset at fair value. The associated liability is measured at (i) the sum of the call exercise price and fair value of the put option less the time value of the call option, if the call option is in or at the money, or (ii) the sum of the fair value of the asset and the fair value of the put option less the time value of the call option if the call option is out of the money. The adjustment to the associated liability ensures that the net carrying amount of the asset and the associated liability is the fair value of the options held and written by the entity. For example, assume an entity transfers a financial asset that is measured at fair value while simultaneously purchasing a call with an exercise price of CU120 and writing a put with an exercise price of CU80. Assume also that the fair value of the asset is CU100 at the date of the transfer. The time value of the put and call are CU1 and CU5 respectively. In this case, the entity recognises an asset of CU100 (the fair value of the asset) and a liability of CU96 [(CU100 + CU1) – CU5]. This gives a net asset value of CU4, which is the fair value of the options held and written by the entity.

All Transfers

To the extent that a transfer of a financial asset does not qualify for derecognition, the transferor's contractual rights or obligations related to the transfer are not accounted for separately as derivatives if recognising both the derivative and either the transferred asset or the liability arising from the transfer would result in recognising the same rights or obligations twice. For example, a call option retained by the transferor may prevent a transfer of financial assets from being accounted for as a sale. In that case, the call option is not separately recognised as a derivative asset. **AG49**

To the extent that a transfer of a financial asset does not qualify for derecognition, the transferee does not recognise the transferred asset as its asset. The transferee derecognises the cash or other consideration paid and recognises a receivable from the transferor. If the transferor has both a right and an obligation to reacquire control of the entire transferred asset for a fixed amount (such as under a repurchase agreement), the transferee may account for its receivable as a loan or receivable. **AG50**

Examples

AG51 The following examples illustrate the application of the derecognition principles of this Standard.

(a) *Repurchase agreements and securities lending*. If a financial asset is sold under an agreement to repurchase it at a fixed price or at the sale price plus a lender's return or if it is loaned under an agreement to return it to the transferor, it is not derecognised because the transferor retains substantially all the risks and rewards of ownership. If the transferee obtains the right to sell or pledge the asset, the transferor reclassifies the asset on its balance sheet, for example, as a loaned asset or repurchase receivable.

(b) *Repurchase agreements and securities lending—assets that are substantially the same*. If a financial asset is sold under an agreement to repurchase the same or substantially the same asset at a fixed price or at the sale price plus a lender's return or if a financial asset is borrowed or loaned under an agreement to return the same or substantially the same asset to the transferor, it is not derecognised because the transferor retains substantially all the risks and rewards of ownership.

(c) *Repurchase agreements and securities lending—right of substitution*. If a repurchase agreement at a fixed repurchase price or a price equal to the sale price plus a lender's return, or a similar securities lending transaction, provides the transferee with a right to substitute assets that are similar and of equal fair value to the transferred asset at the repurchase date, the asset sold or lent under a repurchase or securities lending transaction is not derecognised because the transferor retains substantially all the risks and rewards of ownership.

(d) *Repurchase right of first refusal at fair value*. If an entity sells a financial asset and retains only a right of first refusal to repurchase the transferred asset at fair value if the transferee subsequently sells it, the entity derecognises the asset because it has transferred substantially all the risks and rewards of ownership.

(e) *Wash sale transaction*. The repurchase of a financial asset shortly after it has been sold is sometimes referred to as a wash sale. Such a repurchase does not preclude derecognition provided that the original transaction met the derecognition requirements. However, if an agreement to sell a financial asset is entered into concurrently with an agreement to repurchase the same asset at a fixed price or the sale price plus a lender's return, then the asset is not derecognised.

(f) *Put options and call options that are deeply in the money*. If a transferred financial asset can be called back by the transferor and the call option is deeply in the money, the transfer does not qualify for derecognition because the transferor has retained substantially all the risks and rewards of ownership. Similarly, if the financial asset can be put back by the transferee and the put option is deeply in the money, the transfer does not qualify for derecognition because the transferor has retained substantially all the risks and rewards of ownership.

(g) *Put options and call options that are deeply out of the money*. A financial asset that is transferred subject only to a deep out-of-the-money put option held by the transferee or a deep out-of-the-money call option held by the transferor is derecognised. This is because the transferor has transferred substantially all the risks and rewards of ownership.

(h) *Readily obtainable assets subject to a call option that is neither deeply in the money nor deeply out of the money*. If an entity holds a call option on an asset that is readily obtainable in the market and the option is neither deeply in the money nor deeply out of the money, the asset is derecognised. This is because the entity (i) has neither retained nor transferred substantially all the risks and rewards of ownership, and (ii) has not retained control. However, if the asset is not readily obtainable in the market, derecognition is precluded to the extent of the amount of the asset that is subject to the call option because the entity has retained control of the asset.

(i) *A not readily obtainable asset subject to a put option written by an entity that is neither deeply in the money nor deeply out of the money*. If an entity transfers a financial asset that is not readily obtainable in the market, and writes a put option that is not deeply out of the money, the entity neither retains nor transfers substantially all the risks and rewards of ownership because of the written put option. The entity retains control of the asset if the put option is sufficiently valuable to prevent the transferee from selling the asset, in which case the asset continues to be recognised to the extent of the transferor's continuing involvement (see paragraph AG44). The entity transfers control of the asset if the put option is not sufficiently valuable to prevent the transferee from selling the asset, in which case the asset is derecognised.

(j) *Assets subject to a fair value put or call option or a forward repurchase agreement*. A transfer of a financial asset that is subject only to a put or call option or a forward repurchase agreement that has an exercise or repurchase price equal to the fair value of the financial asset at the time of repurchase results in derecognition because of the transfer of substantially all the risks and rewards of ownership.

(k) *Cash settled call or put options*. An entity evaluates the transfer of a financial asset that is subject to a put or call option or a forward repurchase agreement that will be settled net in cash to determine whether it has retained or transferred substantially all the risks and rewards of ownership. If the entity has not retained substantially all the risks and rewards of ownership of the transferred asset, it determines whether it has retained control of the transferred asset. That the put or the call or the forward repurchase agreement is settled net in cash does not automatically mean that the entity has transferred control (see paragraphs AG44 and (g), (h) and (i) above).

(l) *Removal of accounts provision*. A removal of accounts provision is an unconditional repurchase (call) option that gives an entity the right to reclaim assets transferred subject to some restrictions. Provided that such an option results in the entity neither retaining nor transferring substantially all the risks and rewards of ownership, it precludes derecognition only to the extent of the amount subject to repurchase (assuming that the transferee cannot sell the assets). For example, if the carrying amount and proceeds from the transfer of loan assets are CU100,000 and any individual loan could be called back but the aggregate amount of loans that could be repurchased could not exceed CU10,000, CU90,000 of the loans would qualify for derecognition.

(m) *Clean-up calls*. An entity, which may be a transferor, that services transferred assets may hold a clean-up call to purchase remaining transferred assets when the amount of outstanding assets falls to a specified level at which the cost of servicing those assets becomes burdensome in relation to the benefits of servicing. Provided that such a clean-up call results in the entity neither retaining nor transferring substantially all the risks and rewards of ownership and the transferee cannot sell the assets, it precludes derecognition only to the extent of the amount of the assets that is subject to the call option.

(n) *Subordinated retained interests and credit guarantees*. An entity may provide the transferee with credit enhancement by subordinating some or all of its interest retained in the transferred asset. Alternatively, an entity may provide the transferee with credit enhancement in the form of a credit guarantee that could be unlimited or limited to a specified amount. If the entity retains substantially all the risks and rewards of ownership of the transferred asset, the asset continues to be recognised in its entirety. If the entity retains some, but not substantially all, of the risks and rewards of ownership and has retained control, derecognition is precluded to the extent of the amount of cash or other assets that the entity could be required to pay.

(o) *Total return swaps.* An entity may sell a financial asset to a transferee and enter into a total return swap with the transferee, whereby all of the interest payment cash flows from the underlying asset are remitted to the entity in exchange for a fixed payment or variable rate payment and any increases or declines in the fair value of the underlying asset are absorbed by the entity. In such a case, derecognition of all of the asset is prohibited.

(p) *Interest rate swaps.* An entity may transfer to a transferee a fixed rate financial asset and enter into an interest rate swap with the transferee to receive a fixed interest rate and pay a variable interest rate based on a notional amount that is equal to the principal amount of the transferred financial asset. The interest rate swap does not preclude derecognition of the transferred asset provided the payments on the swap are not conditional on payments being made on the transferred asset.

(q) *Amortising interest rate swaps.* An entity may transfer to a transferee a fixed rate financial asset that is paid off over time, and enter into an amortising interest rate swap with the transferee to receive a fixed interest rate and pay a variable interest rate based on a notional amount. If the notional amount of the swap amortises so that it equals the principal amount of the transferred financial asset outstanding at any point in time, the swap would generally result in the entity retaining substantial prepayment risk, in which case the entity either continues to recognise all of the transferred asset or continues to recognise the transferred asset to the extent of its continuing involvement. Conversely, if the amortisation of the notional amount of the swap is not linked to the principal amount outstanding of the transferred asset, such a swap would not result in the entity retaining prepayment risk on the asset. Hence, it would not preclude derecognition of the transferred asset provided the payments on the swap are not conditional on interest payments being made on the transferred asset and the swap does not result in the entity retaining any other significant risks and rewards of ownership on the transferred asset.

AG52 This paragraph illustrates the application of the continuing involvement approach when the entity's continuing involvement is in a part of a financial asset.

Assume an entity has a portfolio of prepayable loans whose coupon and effective interest rate is 10 per cent and whose principal amount and amortised cost is CU10,000. It enters into a transaction in which, in return for a payment of CU9,115, the transferee obtains the right to CU9,000 of any collections of principal plus interest thereon at 9.5 per cent. The entity retains rights to CU1,000 of any collections of principal plus interest thereon at 10 per cent, plus the excess spread of 0.5 per cent on the remaining CU9,000 of principal. Collections from prepayments are allocated between the entity and the transferee proportionately in the ratio of 1:9, but any defaults are deducted from the entity's interest of CU1,000 until that interest is exhausted. The fair value of the loans at the date of the transaction is CU10,100 and the estimated fair value of the excess spread of 0.5 per cent is CU40.

The entity determines that it has transferred some significant risks and rewards of ownership (for example, significant prepayment risk) but has also retained some significant risks and rewards of ownership (because of its subordinated retained interest) and has retained control. It therefore applies the continuing involvement approach.

To apply this Standard, the entity analyses the transaction as (a) a retention of a fully proportionate retained interest of CU1,000, plus (b) the subordination of that retained interest to provide credit enhancement to the transferee for credit losses.

The entity calculates that CU9,090 (90 per cent × CU10,100) of the consideration received of CU9,115 represents the consideration for a fully proportionate 90 per cent share. The remainder of the consideration received (CU25) represents consideration received for subordinating its retained interest to provide credit enhancement to the transferee for credit losses. In addition, the excess spread of 0.5 per cent represents consideration received for the credit enhancement. Accordingly, the total consideration received for the credit enhancement is CU65 (CU25 + CU40).

The entity calculates the gain or loss on the sale of the 90 per cent share of cash flows. Assuming that separate fair values of the 10 per cent part transferred and the 90 per cent part retained are not available at the date of the transfer, the entity allocates the carrying amount of the asset in accordance with paragraph 28 as follows:

	Estimated Fair Value	*Percentage*	*Allocated Carrying Amount*
Portion transferred	9,090	90%	9,000
Portion retained	1,010	10%	1,000
Total	**10,100**		**10,000**

The entity computes its gain or loss on the sale of the 90 per cent share of the cash flows by deducting the allocated carrying amount of the portion transferred from the consideration received, ie CU90 (CU9,090 – CU9,000). The carrying amount of the portion retained by the entity is CU1,000.

In addition, the entity recognises the continuing involvement that results from the subordination of its retained interest for credit losses. Accordingly, it recognises an asset of CU1,000 (the maximum amount of the cash flows it would not receive under the subordination), and an associated liability of CU1,065 (which is the maximum amount of the cash flows it would not receive under the subordination, ie CU1,000 plus the fair value of the subordination of CU65).

The entity uses all of the above information to account for the transaction as follows:

	Debit	*Credit*
Original asset	-	9,000
Asset recognised for subordination or the residual interest	1,000	-
Asset for the consideration received in the form of excess spread	40	-
Profit or loss (gain on transfer)	-	90
Liability	-	1,065
Cash received	9,115	-
Total	**10,155**	**10,155**

Immediately following the transaction, the carrying amount of the asset is CU2,040 comprising CU1,000, representing the allocated cost of the portion retained, and CU1,040, representing the entity's additional continuing involvement from the subordination of its retained interest for credit losses (which includes the excess spread of CU40).

In subsequent periods, the entity recognises the consideration received for the credit enhancement (CU65) on a time proportion basis, accrues interest on the recognised asset using the effective interest method and recognises any credit impairment on the recognised assets. As an example of the latter, assume that in the following year there is a credit impairment loss on the underlying loans of CU300. The entity reduces its recognised asset by CU600 (CU300 relating to its retained interest and CU300 relating to the additional continuing involvement that arises from the subordination of its retained interest for credit losses), and reduces its recognised liability by CU300. The net result is a charge to profit or loss for credit impairment of CU300.

Regular Way Purchase or Sale of a Financial Asset (paragraph 38)

AG53 A regular way purchase or sale of financial assets is recognised using either trade date accounting or settlement date accounting as described in paragraphs AG55 and AG56. The method used is applied consistently for all purchases and sales of financial assets that belong to the same category of financial assets defined in paragraph 9. For this purpose assets that are held for trading form a separate category from assets designated at fair value through profit and loss.

AG54 A contract that requires or permits net settlement of the change in the value of the contract is not a regular way contract. Instead, such a contract is accounted for as a derivative in the period between the trade date and the settlement date.

AG55 The trade date is the date that an entity commits itself to purchase or sell an asset. Trade date accounting refers to (a) the recognition of an asset to be received and the liability to pay for it on the trade date, and (b) derecognition of an asset that is sold, recognition of any gain or loss on disposal and the recognition of a receivable from the buyer for payment on the trade date. Generally, interest does not start to accrue on the asset and corresponding liability until the settlement date when title passes.

AG56 The settlement date is the date that an asset is delivered to or by an entity. Settlement date accounting refers to (a) the recognition of an asset on the day it is received by the entity, and (b) the derecognition of an asset and recognition of any gain or loss on disposal on the day that it is delivered by the entity. When settlement date accounting is applied an entity accounts for any change in the fair value of the asset to be received during the period between the trade date and the settlement date in the same way as it accounts for the acquired asset. In other words, the change in value is not recognised for assets carried at cost or amortised cost; it is recognised in profit or loss for assets classified as financial assets at fair value through profit or loss; and it is recognised in equity for assets classified as available for sale.

Derecognition of a Financial Liability (paragraphs 39–42)

AG57 A financial liability (or part of it) is extinguished when the debtor either:

(a) discharges the liability (or part of it) by paying the creditor, normally with cash, other financial assets, goods or services; or

(b) is legally released from primary responsibility for the liability (or part of it) either by process of law or by the creditor. (If the debtor has given a guarantee this condition may still be met.)

If an issuer of a debt instrument repurchases that instrument, the debt is extinguished even if the issuer is a market maker in that instrument or intends to resell it in the near term. **AG58**

Payment to a third party, including a trust (sometimes called 'insubstance defeasance'), does not, by itself, relieve the debtor of its primary obligation to the creditor, in the absence of legal release. **AG59**

If a debtor pays a third party to assume an obligation and notifies its creditor that the third party has assumed its debt obligation, the debtor does not derecognise the debt obligation unless the condition in paragraph AG57(b) is met. If the debtor pays a third party to assume an obligation and obtains a legal release from its creditor, the debtor has extinguished the debt. However, if the debtor agrees to make payments on the debt to the third party or direct to its original creditor, the debtor recognises a new debt obligation to the third party. **AG60**

Although legal release, whether judicially or by the creditor, results in derecognition of a liability, the entity may recognise a new liability if the derecognition criteria in paragraphs 15–37 are not met for the financial assets transferred. If those criteria are not met, the transferred assets are not derecognised, and the entity recognises a new liability relating to the transferred assets. **AG61**

For the purpose of paragraph 40, the terms are substantially different if the discounted present value of the cash flows under the new terms, including any fees paid net of any fees received and discounted using the original effective interest rate, is at least 10 per cent different from the discounted present value of the remaining cash flows of the original financial liability. If an exchange of debt instruments or modification of terms is accounted for as an extinguishment, any costs or fees incurred are recognised as part of the gain or loss on the extinguishment. If the exchange or modification is not accounted for as an extinguishment, any costs or fees incurred adjust the carrying amount of the liability and are amortised over the remaining term of the modified liability. **AG62**

In some cases, a creditor releases a debtor from its present obligation to make payments, but the debtor assumes a guarantee obligation to pay if the party assuming primary responsibility defaults. In this circumstance the debtor: **AG63**

(a) recognises a new financial liability based on the fair value of its obligation for the guarantee; and
(b) recognises a gain or loss based on the difference between (i) any proceeds paid and (ii) the carrying amount of the original financial liability less the fair value of the new financial liability.

MEASUREMENT (PARAGRAPHS 43-70)

Initial Measurement of Financial Assets and Financial Liabilities (paragraph 43)

The fair value of a financial instrument on initial recognition is normally the transaction price (ie the fair value of the consideration given or received, see also paragraph AG76). However, if part of the consideration given or received is for something other than the financial instrument, the fair value of the financial **AG64** instrument is estimated, using a valuation technique (see paragraphs AG74-AG79). For example, the fair value of a long-term loan or receivable that carries no interest can be estimated as the present value of all future cash receipts discounted using the prevailing market rate(s) of interest for a similar instrument (similar as to currency, term, type of interest rate and other factors) with a similar credit rating. Any additional amount lent is an expense or a reduction of income unless it qualifies for recognition as some other type of asset.

AG65 If an entity originates a loan that bears an off-market interest rate (eg 5 per cent when the market rate for similar loans is 8 per cent), and receives an up-front fee as compensation, the entity recognises the loan at its fair value, ie net of the fee it receives. The entity accretes the discount to profit or loss using the effective interest rate method.

Subsequent Measurement of Financial Assets (paragraphs 45 and 46)

AG66 If a financial instrument that was previously recognised as a financial asset is measured at fair value and its fair value falls below zero, it is a financial liability in accordance with paragraph 47.

AG67 The following example illustrates the accounting for transaction costs on the initial and subsequent measurement of an available-for-sale financial asset. An asset is acquired for CU100 plus a purchase commission of CU2. Initially, the asset is recognised at CU102. The next financial reporting date occurs one day later, when the quoted market price of the asset is CU100. If the asset were sold, a commission of CU3 would be paid. On that date, the asset is measured at CU100 (without regard to the possible commission on sale) and a loss of CU2 is recognised in equity. If the availableforsale financial asset has fixed or determinable payments, the transaction costs are amortised to profit or loss using the effective interest method. If the available-for-sale financial asset does not have fixed or determinable payments, the transaction costs are recognised in profit or loss when the asset is derecognised or becomes impaired.

AG68 Instruments that are classified as loans and receivables are measured at amortised cost without regard to the entity's intention to hold them to maturity.

Fair Value Measurement Considerations (paragraphs 48-49)

AG69 Underlying the definition of fair value is a presumption that an entity is a going concern without any intention or need to liquidate, to curtail materially the scale of its operations or to undertake a transaction on adverse terms. Fair value is not, therefore, the amount that an entity would receive or pay in a forced transaction, involuntary liquidation or distress sale. However, fair value reflects the credit quality of the instrument.

AG70 This Standard uses the terms 'bid price' and 'asking price' (sometimes referred to as 'current offer price') in the context of quoted market prices, and the term 'the bid-ask spread' to include only transaction costs. Other adjustments to arrive at fair value (eg for counterparty credit risk) are not included in the term 'bid-ask spread'.

Active Market: Quoted Price

AG71 A financial instrument is regarded as quoted in an active market if quoted prices are readily and regularly available from an exchange, dealer, broker, industry group, pricing service or regulatory agency, and those prices represent actual and regularly occurring market transactions on an arm's length basis. Fair value is defined in terms of a price agreed by a willing buyer and a willing seller in an arm's length transaction. The objective of determining fair value for a financial instrument that is traded in an active market is to arrive at the price at which a transaction would occur at the balance sheet date in that instrument (ie without modifying or repackaging the instrument) in the most advantageous active market to which the entity has immediate access. However, the entity adjusts the price in the more advantageous market to reflect any differences in counterparty credit risk between instruments traded in that market and the one being valued. The existence of published price quotations in an active market is the best evidence of fair value and when they exist they are used to measure the financial asset or financial liability.

The appropriate quoted market price for an asset held or liability to be issued is usually the current bid price and, for an asset to be acquired or liability held, the asking price. When an entity has assets and liabilities with offsetting market risks, it may use mid-market prices as a basis for establishing fair values for the offsetting risk positions and apply the bid or asking price to the net open position as appropriate. When current bid and asking prices are unavailable, the price of the most recent transaction provides evidence of the current fair value as long as there has not been a significant change in economic circumstances since the time of the transaction. If conditions have changed since the time of the transaction (eg a change in the risk-free interest rate following the most recent price quote for a corporate bond), the fair value reflects the change in conditions by reference to current prices or rates for similar financial instruments, as appropriate. Similarly, if the entity can demonstrate that the last transaction price is not fair value (eg because it reflected the amount that an entity would receive or pay in a forced transaction, involuntary liquidation or distress sale), that price is adjusted. The fair value of a portfolio of financial instruments is the product of the number of units of the instrument and its quoted market price. If a published price quotation in an active market does not exist for a financial instrument in its entirety, but active markets exist for its component parts, fair value is determined on the basis of the relevant market prices for the component parts. **AG72**

If a rate (rather than a price) is quoted in an active market, the entity uses that market-quoted rate as an input into a valuation technique to determine fair value. If the market-quoted rate does not include credit risk or other factors that market participants would include in valuing the instrument, the entity adjusts for those factors. **AG73**

No Active Market: Valuation Technique

If the market for a financial instrument is not active, an entity establishes fair value by using a valuation technique. Valuation techniques include using recent arm's length market transactions between knowledgeable, willing parties, if available, reference to the current fair value of another instrument that is substantially the same, discounted cash flow analysis and option pricing models. If there is a valuation technique commonly used by market participants to price the instrument and that technique has been demonstrated to provide reliable estimates of prices obtained in actual market transactions, the entity uses that technique. **AG74**

The objective of using a valuation technique is to establish what the transaction price would have been on the measurement date in an arm's length exchange motivated by normal business considerations. Fair value is estimated on the basis of the results of a valuation technique that makes maximum use of market inputs, and relies as little as possible on entity-specific inputs. A valuation technique would be expected to arrive at a realistic estimate of the fair value if (a) it reasonably reflects how the market **AG75** could be expected to price the instrument and (b) the inputs to the valuation technique reasonably represent market expectations and measures of the risk-return factors inherent in the financial instrument.

AG76 Therefore, a valuation technique (a) incorporates all factors that market participants would consider in setting a price and (b) is consistent with accepted economic methodologies for pricing financial instruments. Periodically, an entity calibrates the valuation technique and tests it for validity using prices from any observable current market transactions in the same instrument (ie without modification or repackaging) or based on any available observable market data. An entity obtains market data consistently in the same market where the instrument was originated or purchased. The best evidence of the fair value of a financial instrument at initial recognition is the transaction price (ie the fair value of the consideration given or received) unless the fair value of that instrument is evidenced by comparison with other observable current market transactions in the same instrument (ie without modification or repackaging) or based on a valuation technique whose variables include only data from observable markets.

AG76A The subsequent measurement of the financial asset or financial liability and the subsequent recognition of gains and losses shall be consistent with the requirements of this Standard. The application of paragraph AG76 may result in no gain or loss being recognised on the initial recognition of a financial asset or financial liability. In such a case, FRS 26 requires that a gain or loss shall be recognised after initial recognition only to the extent that it arises from a change in a factor (including time) that market participants would consider in setting a price.*

AG77 The initial acquisition or origination of a financial asset or incurrence of a financial liability is a market transaction that provides a foundation for estimating the fair value of the financial instrument. In particular, if the financial instrument is a debt instrument (such as a loan), its fair value can be determined by reference to the market conditions that existed at its acquisition or origination date and current market conditions or interest rates currently charged by the entity or by others for similar debt instruments (ie similar remaining maturity, cash flow pattern, currency, credit risk, collateral and interest basis). Alternatively, provided there is no change in the credit risk of the debtor and applicable credit spreads after the origination of the debt instrument, an estimate of the current market interest rate may be derived by using a benchmark interest rate reflecting a better credit quality than the underlying debt instrument, holding the credit spread constant, and adjusting for the change in the benchmark interest rate from the origination date. If conditions have changed since the most recent market transaction, the corresponding change in the fair value of the financial instrument being valued is determined by reference to current prices or rates for similar financial instruments, adjusted as appropriate, for any differences from the instrument being valued.

AG78 The same information may not be available at each measurement date. For example, at the date that an entity makes a loan or acquires a debt instrument that is not actively traded, the entity has a transaction price that is also a market price. However, no new transaction information may be available at the next measurement date and, although the entity can determine the general level of market interest rates, it may not know what level of credit or other risk market participants would consider in pricing the instrument on that date. An entity may not have information from recent transactions to determine the appropriate credit spread over the basic interest rate to use in determining a discount rate for a present value computation. It would be reasonable to assume, in the absence of evidence to the contrary, that no changes

Editor's note: Paragraph added in October 2005.

have taken place in the spread that existed at the date the loan was made. However, the entity would be expected to make reasonable efforts to determine whether there is evidence that there has been a change in such factors. When evidence of a change exists, the entity would consider the effects of the change in determining the fair value of the financial instrument.

In applying discounted cash flow analysis, an entity uses one or more discount rates equal to the prevailing rates of return for financial instruments having substantially the same terms and characteristics, including the credit quality of the instrument, the remaining term over which the contractual interest rate is fixed, the remaining term to repayment of the principal and the currency in which payments are to be made. Short-term receivables and payables with no stated interest rate may be measured at the original invoice amount if the effect of discounting is immaterial. **AG79**

No Active Market: Equity Instruments

The fair value of investments in equity instruments that do not have a quoted market price in an active market and derivatives that are linked to and must be settled by delivery of such an unquoted equity instrument (see paragraphs 46(c) and 47) is reliably measurable if (a) the variability in the range of reasonable fair value estimates is not significant for that instrument or (b) the probabilities of the various estimates within the range can be reasonably assessed and used in estimating fair value. **AG80**

There are many situations in which the variability in the range of reasonable fair value estimates of investments in equity instruments that do not have a quoted market price and derivatives that are linked to and must be settled by delivery of such an unquoted equity instrument (see paragraphs 46(c) and 47) is likely not to be significant. Normally it is possible to estimate the fair value of a financial asset that an entity has acquired from an outside party. However, if the range of reasonable fair value estimates is significant and the probabilities of the various estimates cannot be reasonably assessed, an entity is precluded from measuring the instrument at fair value. **AG81**

Inputs to Valuation Techniques

An appropriate technique for estimating the fair value of a particular financial instrument would incorporate observable market data about the market conditions and other factors that are likely to affect the instrument's fair value. The fair value of a financial instrument will be based on one or more of the following factors (and perhaps others). **AG82**

(a) *The time value of money (ie interest at the basic or risk-free rate)*. Basic interest rates can usually be derived from observable government bond prices and are often quoted in financial publications. These rates typically vary with the expected dates of the projected cash flows along a yield curve of interest rates for different time horizons. For practical reasons, an entity may use a well-accepted and readily observable general rate, such as LIBOR or a swap rate, as the benchmark rate. (Because a rate such as LIBOR is not the riskfree interest rate, the credit risk adjustment appropriate to the particular financial instrument is determined on the basis of its credit risk in relation to the credit risk in this benchmark rate.) In some countries, the central government's bonds may carry a significant credit risk and may not provide a stable benchmark basic interest rate for instruments denominated in that currency. Some entities in these countries may have a better credit standing and a lower borrowing rate than the central government. In such a case, basic interest rates may be more appropriately determined by reference to interest rates for the highest rated corporate bonds issued in the currency of that jurisdiction.

(b) *Credit risk*. The effect on fair value of credit risk (ie the premium over the basic interest rate for credit risk) may be derived from observable market prices for traded instruments of different credit quality or from observable interest rates charged by lenders for loans of various credit ratings.

(c) *Foreign currency exchange prices*. Active currency exchange markets exist for most major currencies, and prices are quoted daily in financial publications.

(d) *Commodity prices*. There are observable market prices for many commodities.

(e) *Equity prices*. Prices (and indexes of prices) of traded equity instruments are readily observable in some markets. Present value based techniques may be used to estimate the current market price of equity instruments for which there are no observable prices.

(f) *Volatility (ie magnitude of future changes in price of the financial instrument or other item)*. Measures of the volatility of actively traded items can normally be reasonably estimated on the basis of historical market data or by using volatilities implied in current market prices.

(g) *Prepayment risk and surrender risk*. Expected prepayment patterns for financial assets and expected surrender patterns for financial liabilities can be estimated on the basis of historical data. (The fair value of a financial liability that can be surrendered by the counterparty cannot be less than the present value of the surrender amount—see paragraph 49.)

(h) *Servicing costs for a financial asset or a financial liability*. Costs of servicing can be estimated using comparisons with current fees charged by other market participants. If the costs of servicing a financial asset or financial liability are significant and other market participants would face comparable costs, the issuer would consider them in determining the fair value of that financial asset or financial liability. It is likely that the fair value at inception of a contractual right to future fees equals the origination costs paid for them, unless future fees and related costs are out of line with market comparables.

Gains and Losses (paragraphs 55-57)

AG83 An entity applies FRS 23 to financial assets and financial liabilities that are monetary items in accordance with FRS 23 and denominated in a foreign currency. Under FRS 23, any foreign exchange gains and losses on monetary assets and monetary liabilities are recognised in profit or loss. An exception is a monetary item that is designated as a hedging instrument in either a cash flow hedge (see paragraphs 95-101) or a hedge of a net investment (see paragraph 102). For the purpose of recognising foreign exchange gains and losses under FRS 23, a monetary available-for-sale financial asset is treated as if it were carried at amortised cost in the foreign currency. Accordingly, for such a financial asset, exchange differences resulting from changes in amortised cost are recognised in profit or loss and other changes in carrying amount are recognised in accordance with paragraph 55(b). For available-for-sale financial assets that are not monetary items under FRS 23 (for example, equity instruments), the gain or loss that is recognised through the statement of total recognised gains and losses under paragraph 55(b) includes any related foreign exchange component. If there is a hedging relationship between a non-derivative monetary asset and a non-derivative monetary liability, changes in the foreign currency component of those financial instruments are recognised in profit or loss.

Impairment and Uncollectibility of Financial Assets (paragraphs 58-70)

Financial Assets Carried at Amortised Cost (paragraphs 63-65)

Impairment of a financial asset carried at amortised cost is measured using the financial instrument's original effective interest rate because discounting at the current market rate of interest would, in effect, impose fair value measurement on financial assets that are otherwise measured at amortised cost. If the terms of a loan, receivable or held-to-maturity investment are renegotiated or otherwise modified because of financial difficulties of the borrower or issuer, impairment is measured using the original effective interest rate before the modification of terms. Cash flows relating to short-term receivables are not discounted if the effect of discounting is immaterial. If a loan, receivable or held-to-maturity investment has a variable interest rate, the discount rate for measuring any impairment loss under paragraph 63 is the current effective interest rate(s) determined under the contract. As a practical expedient, a creditor may measure impairment of a financial asset carried at amortised cost on the basis of an instrument's fair value using an observable market price. The calculation of the present value of the estimated future cash flows of a collateralised financial asset reflects the cash flows that may result from foreclosure less costs for obtaining and selling the collateral, whether or not foreclosure is probable. **AG84**

The process for estimating impairment considers all credit exposures, not only those of low credit quality. For example, if an entity uses an internal credit grading system it considers all credit grades, not only those reflecting a severe credit deterioration. **AG85**

The process for estimating the amount of an impairment loss may result either in a single amount or in a range of possible amounts. In the latter case, the entity recognises an impairment loss equal to the best estimate within the range* taking into account all relevant information available before the financial statements are issued about conditions existing at the balance sheet date. **AG86**

For the purpose of a collective evaluation of impairment, financial assets are grouped on the basis of similar credit risk characteristics that are indicative of the debtors' ability to pay all amounts due according to the contractual terms (for example, on the basis of a credit risk evaluation or grading process that considers asset type, industry, geographical location, collateral type, past-due status and other relevant factors). The characteristics chosen are relevant to the estimation of future cash flows for groups of such assets by being indicative of the debtors' ability to pay all amounts due according to the contractual terms of the assets being evaluated. However, loss probabilities and other loss statistics differ at a group level between (a) assets that have been individually evaluated for impairment and found not to be impaired and (b) assets that have not been individually evaluated for impairment, with the result that a different amount of impairment may be required. If an entity does not have a group of assets with similar risk characteristics, it does not make the additional assessment. **AG87**

Impairment losses recognised on a group basis represent an interim step pending the identification of impairment losses on individual assets in the group of financial assets that are collectively assessed for impairment. As soon as information is available that specifically identifies losses on individually impaired assets in a group, those assets are removed from the group. **AG88**

**IAS 37, paragraph 39 contains guidance on how to determine the best estimate in a range of possible outcomes.*

AG89 Future cash flows in a group of financial assets that are collectively evaluated for impairment are estimated on the basis of historical loss experience for assets with credit risk characteristics similar to those in the group. Entities that have no entity-specific loss experience or insufficient experience, use peer group experience for comparable groups of financial assets. Historical loss experience is adjusted on the basis of current observable data to reflect the effects of current conditions that did not affect the period on which the historical loss experience is based and to remove the effects of conditions in the historical period that do not exist currently. Estimates of changes in future cash flows reflect and are directionally consistent with changes in related observable data from period to period (such as changes in unemployment rates, property prices, commodity prices, payment status or other factors that are indicative of incurred losses in the group and their magnitude). The methodology and assumptions used for estimating future cash flows are reviewed regularly to reduce any differences between loss estimates and actual loss experience.

AG90 As an example of applying paragraph AG89, an entity may determine, on the basis of historical experience, that one of the main causes of default on credit card loans is the death of the borrower. The entity may observe that the death rate is unchanged from one year to the next. Nevertheless, some of the borrowers in the entity's group of credit card loans may have died in that year, indicating that an impairment loss has occurred on those loans, even if, at the year-end, the entity is not yet aware which specific borrowers have died. It would be appropriate for an impairment loss to be recognised for these 'incurred but not reported' losses. However, it would not be appropriate to recognise an impairment loss for deaths that are expected to occur in a future period, because the necessary loss event (the death of the borrower) has not yet occurred.

AG91 When using historical loss rates in estimating future cash flows, it is important that information about historical loss rates is applied to groups that are defined in a manner consistent with the groups for which the historical loss rates were observed. Therefore, the method used should enable each group to be associated with information about past loss experience in groups of assets with similar credit risk characteristics and relevant observable data that reflect current conditions.

AG92 Formula-based approaches or statistical methods may be used to determine impairment losses in a group of financial assets (eg for smaller balance loans) as long as they are consistent with the requirements in paragraphs 63-65 and AG87-AG91. Any model used would incorporate the effect of the time value of money, consider the cash flows for all of the remaining life of an asset (not only the next year), consider the age of the loans within the portfolio and not give rise to an impairment loss on initial recognition of a financial asset.

Interest Income After Impairment Recognition

AG93 Once a financial asset or a group of similar financial assets has been written down as a result of an impairment loss, interest income is thereafter recognised using the rate of interest used to discount the future cash flows for the purpose of measuring the impairment loss.

HEDGING (PARAGRAPHS 71-102)

Hedging Instruments (paragraphs 72-77)

Qualifying Instruments (paragraphs 72 and 73)

The potential loss on an option that an entity writes could be significantly greater than the potential gain in value of a related hedged item. In other words, a written option is not effective in reducing the profit or loss exposure of a hedged item. Therefore, a written option does not qualify as a hedging instrument unless it is designated as an offset to a purchased option, including one that is embedded in another financial instrument (for example, a written call option used to hedge a callable liability). In contrast, a purchased option has potential gains equal to or greater than losses and therefore has the potential to reduce profit or loss exposure from changes in fair values or cash flows. Accordingly, it can qualify as a hedging instrument. **AG94**

A held-to-maturity investment carried at amortised cost may be designated as a hedging instrument in a hedge of foreign currency risk. **AG95**

An investment in an unquoted equity instrument that is not carried at fair value because its fair value cannot be reliably measured or a derivative that is linked to and must be settled by delivery of such an unquoted equity instrument (see paragraphs 46(c) and 47) cannot be designated as a hedging instrument. **AG96**

An entity's own equity instruments are not financial assets or financial liabilities of the entity and therefore cannot be designated as hedging instruments. **AG97**

Hedged Items (paragraphs 78-84)

Qualifying Items (paragraphs 78-80)

A firm commitment to acquire a business in a business combination cannot be a hedged item, except for foreign exchange risk, because the other risks being hedged cannot be specifically identified and measured. These other risks are general business risks. **AG98**

An equity method investment cannot be a hedged item in a fair value hedge because the equity method recognises in profit or loss the investor's share of the associate's profit or loss, rather than changes in the investment's fair value. For a similar reason, an investment in a consolidated subsidiary cannot be a hedged item in a fair value hedge because consolidation recognises in profit or loss the subsidiary's profit or loss, rather than changes in the investment's fair value. A hedge of a net investment in a foreign operation is different because it is a hedge of the foreign currency exposure, not a fair value hedge of the change in the value of the investment. **AG99**

An entity can designate all changes in the cash flows or fair value of a hedged item in a hedging relationship. An entity can also designate only changes in the cash flows or fair value of a hedged item above or below a specified price or other variable (a one-sided risk). The intrinsic value of a purchased option hedging instrument (assuming that it has the same principal terms as the designated risk), but not its time value, reflects a one-sided risk in a hedged item. For example, an entity can designate the variability of future cash flow outcomes resulting from a price increase of a forecast commodity purchase. In such a situation, only cash flow losses that result from an increase in the price above the specified level are designated. The hedged risk does **AG99BA** not include the time value of a purchased option because the time value is not a component of the forecast transaction that affects profit or loss (paragraph 86(b)).*

Designation of Financial Items as Hedged Items (paragraphs 81 and 81A)

AG99A Paragraph 80 states that in consolidated financial statements the foreign currency risk of a highly probable forecast intragroup transaction may qualify as a hedged item in a cash flow hedge, provided the transaction is denominated in a currency other than the functional currency of the entity entering into that transaction and the foreign currency risk will affect consolidated profit or loss. For this purpose an entity can be a parent, subsidiary, associate, joint venture or branch. If the foreign currency risk of a forecast intragroup transaction does not affect consolidated profit or loss, the intragroup transaction cannot qualify as a hedged item. This is usually the case for royalty payments, interest payments or management charges between members of the same group unless there is a related external transaction. However, when the foreign currency risk of a forecast intragroup transaction will affect consolidated profit or loss, the intragroup transaction can qualify as a hedged item. An example is forecast sales or purchases of inventories between members of the same group if there is an onward sale of the inventory to a party external to the group. Similarly, a forecast intragroup sale of plant and equipment from the group entity that manufactured it to a group entity that will use the plant and equipment in its operations may affect consolidated profit or loss. This could occur, for example, because the plant and equipment will be depreciated by the purchasing entity and the amount initially recognised for the plant and equipment may change if the forecast intragroup transaction is denominated in a currency other than the functional currency of the purchasing entity.

AG99B If a hedge of a forecast intragroup transaction qualifies for hedge accounting, any gain or loss that is recognised through the statement of total recognised gains and losses in accordance with paragraph 95(a) shall be reclassified from reserves to profit or loss in the same period or periods during which the foreign currency risk of the hedged transaction affects consolidated profit or loss.†

AG99C If a portion of the cash flows of a financial asset or financial liability is designated as the hedged item, that designated portion must be less than the total cash flows of the asset or liability. For example, in the case of a liability whose effective interest rate is below LIBOR, an entity cannot designate (a) a portion of the liability equal to the principal amount plus interest at LIBOR and (b) a negative residual portion. However, the entity may designate all of the cash flows of the entire financial asset or financial liability as the hedged item and hedge them for only one particular risk (eg only for changes that are attributable to changes in LIBOR). For example, in the case of a financial liability whose effective interest rate is 100 basis points below LIBOR, an entity can designate as the hedged item the entire liability (ie principal plus interest at LIBOR minus 100 basis points) and hedge the change in the fair value or cash flows of that entire liability that is attributable to changes in LIBOR. The entity may also choose a hedge ratio of other than one to one in order to improve the effectiveness of the hedge as described in paragraph AG100.

AG99D In addition, if a fixed rate financial instrument is hedged some time after its origination and interest rates have changed in the meantime, the entity can designate a portion equal to a benchmark rate that is higher than the contractual rate paid on the

****Editor's note****: Paragraph added in November 2008.*

†***Editor's note****: Paragraph amended with effect for accounting periods beginning on or after 1 January 2009.*

item. The entity can do so provided that the benchmark rate is less than the effective interest rate calculated on the assumption that the entity had purchased the instrument on the day it first designates the hedged item. For example, assume an entity originates a fixed rate financial asset of CU100 that has an effective interest rate of 6 per cent at a time when LIBOR is 4 per cent. It begins to hedge that asset some time later when LIBOR has increased to 8 per cent and the fair value of the asset has decreased to CU90. The entity calculates that if it had purchased the asset on the date it first designates it as the hedged item for its then fair value of CU90, the effective yield would have been 9.5 per cent. Because LIBOR is less than this effective yield, the entity can designate a LIBOR portion of 8 per cent that consists partly of the contractual interest cash flows and partly of the difference between the current fair value (ie CU90) and the amount repayable on maturity (ie CU100).

Paragraph 81 permits an entity to designate something other than the entire fair value change or cash flow variability of a financial instrument. For example: **AG99E**

(a) all of the cash flows of a financial instrument may be designated for cash flow or fair value changes attributable to some (but not all) risks; or
(b) some (but not all) of the cash flows of a financial instrument may be designated for cash flow or fair value changes attributable to all or only some risks (ie a 'portion' of the cash flows of the financial instrument may be designated for changes attributable to all or only some risks).*

To be eligible for hedge accounting, the designated risks and portions must be separately identifiable components of the financial instrument, and changes in the cash flows or fair value of the entire financial instrument arising from changes in the designated risks and portions must be reliably measurable. For example: **AG99F**

(a) for a fixed rate financial instrument hedged for changes in fair value attributable to changes in a risk-free or benchmark interest rate, the risk-free or benchmark rate is normally regarded as both a separately identifiable component of the financial instrument and reliably measurable.
(b) inflation is not separately identifiable and reliably measurable and cannot be designated as a risk or a portion of a financial instrument unless the requirements in (c) are met.
(c) a contractually specified inflation portion of the cash flows of a recognised inflation-linked bond (assuming there is no requirement to account for an embedded derivative separately) is separately identifiable and reliably measurable as long as other cash flows of the instrument are not affected by the inflation portion.

Designation of Non-Financial Items as Hedged Items (paragraph 82)

Changes in the price of an ingredient or component of a non-financial asset or non-financial liability generally do not have a predictable, separately measurable effect on the price of the item that is comparable to the effect of, say, a change in market interest rates on the price of a bond. Thus, a non-financial asset or nonfinancial liability is a hedged item only in its entirety or for foreign exchange risk. If there is a difference between the terms of the hedging instrument and the hedged item (such as for a hedge of the forecast purchase of Brazilian coffee using a forward contract to purchase Colombian coffee on otherwise similar terms), the hedging relationship nonetheless can qualify as a hedge relationship provided all the conditions in paragraph 88 are met, including that the hedge is expected to be highly effective. For this purpose, the amount of the hedging instrument may be greater or less than that **AG100**

**Editor's note*: *Paragraphs AG99E and AG99F were added in November 2008.*

of the hedged item if this improves the effectiveness of the hedging relationship. For example, a regression analysis could be performed to establish a statistical relationship between the hedged item (eg a transaction in Brazilian coffee) and the hedging instrument (eg a transaction in Colombian coffee). If there is a valid statistical relationship between the two variables (ie between the unit prices of Brazilian coffee and Colombian coffee), the slope of the regression line can be used to establish the hedge ratio that will maximise expected effectiveness. For example, if the slope of the regression line is 1.02, a hedge ratio based on 0.98 quantities of hedged items to 1.00 quantities of the hedging instrument maximises expected effectiveness. However, the hedging relationship may result in ineffectiveness that is recognised in profit or loss during the term of the hedging relationship.

Designation of Groups of Items as Hedged Items (paragraphs 83 and 84)

AG101 A hedge of an overall net position (eg the net of all fixed rate assets and fixed rate liabilities with similar maturities), rather than of a specific hedged item, does not qualify for hedge accounting. However, almost the same effect on profit or loss of hedge accounting for this type of hedging relationship can be achieved by designating as the hedged item part of the underlying items. For example, if a bank has CU100 of assets and CU90 of liabilities with risks and terms of a similar nature and hedges the net CU10 exposure, it can designate as the hedged item CU10 of those assets. This designation can be used if such assets and liabilities are fixed rate instruments, in which case it is a fair value hedge, or if they are variable rate instruments, in which case it is a cash flow hedge. Similarly, if an entity has a firm commitment to make a purchase in a foreign currency of CU100 and a firm commitment to make a sale in the foreign currency of CU90, it can hedge the net amount of CU10 by acquiring a derivative and designating it as a hedging instrument associated with CU10 of the firm purchase commitment of CU100.

Hedge Accounting (paragraphs 85-102)

AG102 An example of a fair value hedge is a hedge of exposure to changes in the fair value of a fixed rate debt instrument as a result of changes in interest rates. Such a hedge could be entered into by the issuer or by the holder.

AG103 An example of a cash flow hedge is the use of a swap to change floating rate debt to fixed rate debt (ie a hedge of a future transaction where the future cash flows being hedged are the future interest payments).

AG104 A hedge of a firm commitment (eg a hedge of the change in fuel price relating to an unrecognised contractual commitment by an electric utility to purchase fuel at a fixed price) is a hedge of an exposure to a change in fair value. Accordingly, such a hedge is a fair value hedge. However, under paragraph 87 a hedge of the foreign currency risk of a firm commitment could alternatively be accounted for as a cash flow hedge.

Assessing Hedge Effectiveness

AG105 A hedge is regarded as highly effective only if both of the following conditions are met:

(a) At the inception of the hedge and in subsequent periods, the hedge is expected to be highly effective in achieving offsetting changes in fair value or cash flows attributable to the hedged risk during the period for which the hedge is designated. Such an expectation can be demonstrated in various ways, including a comparison of past changes in the fair value or cash flows of the hedged item that are attributable to the hedged risk with past changes in the fair value or cash flows of the hedging instrument, or by demonstrating a high statistical correlation between the fair value or cash flows of the hedged item and those of the hedging instrument. The entity may choose a hedge ratio of other than one to one in order to improve the effectiveness of the hedge as described in paragraph AG100.

(b) The actual results of the hedge are within a range of 80-125 per cent. For example, if actual results are such that the loss on the hedging instrument is CU120 and the gain on the cash instrument is CU100, offset can be measured by 120 / 100, which is 120 per cent, or by 100 / 120, which is 83 per cent. In this example, assuming the hedge meets the condition in (a), the entity would conclude that the hedge has been highly effective.

Effectiveness is assessed, at a minimum, at the time an entity prepares its annual or interim financial statements. **AG106**

This Standard does not specify a single method for assessing hedge effectiveness. The method an entity adopts for assessing hedge effectiveness depends on its risk management strategy. For example, if the entity's risk management strategy is to adjust the amount of the hedging instrument periodically to reflect changes in the hedged position, the entity needs to demonstrate that the hedge is expected to be highly effective only for the period until the amount of the hedging instrument is next adjusted. In some cases, an entity adopts different methods for different types of hedges. An entity's documentation of its hedging strategy includes its procedures for assessing effectiveness. Those procedures state whether the assessment includes all of the gain or loss on a hedging instrument or whether the instrument's time value is excluded. **AG107**

If an entity hedges less than 100 per cent of the exposure on an item, such as 85 per cent, it shall designate the hedged item as being 85 per cent of the exposure and shall measure ineffectiveness based on the change in that designated 85 per cent exposure. However, when hedging the designated 85 per cent exposure, the entity may use a hedge ratio of other than one to one if that improves the expected effectiveness of the hedge, as explained in paragraph AG100. **AG107A**

If the principal terms of the hedging instrument and of the hedged asset, liability, firm commitment or highly probable forecast transaction are the same, the changes in fair value and cash flows attributable to the risk being hedged may be likely to offset each other fully, both when the hedge is entered into and afterwards. For example, an interest rate swap is likely to be an effective hedge if the notional and principal amounts, term, repricing dates, dates of interest and principal receipts and payments, and basis for measuring interest rates are the same for the hedging instrument and the hedged item. In addition, a hedge of a highly probable forecast purchase of a commodity with a forward contract is likely to be highly effective if: **AG108**

(a) the forward contract is for the purchase of the same quantity of the same commodity at the same time and location as the hedged forecast purchase;
(b) the fair value of the forward contract at inception is zero; and
(c) either the change in the discount or premium on the forward contract is excluded from the assessment of effectiveness and recognised in profit or loss or the change in expected cash flows on the highly probable forecast transaction is based on the forward price for the commodity.

Sometimes the hedging instrument offsets only part of the hedged risk. For example, a hedge would not be fully effective if the hedging instrument and hedged item are denominated in different currencies that do not move in tandem. Also, a hedge of **AG109** interest rate risk using a derivative would not be fully effective if part of the change in the fair value of the derivative is attributable to the counterparty's credit risk.

AG110 To qualify for hedge accounting, the hedge must relate to a specific identified and designated risk, and not merely to the entity's general business risks, and must ultimately affect the entity's profit or loss. A hedge of the risk of obsolescence of a physical asset or the risk of expropriation of property by a government is not eligible for hedge accounting; effectiveness cannot be measured because those risks are not measurable reliably.

AG110A Paragraph 74(a) permits an entity to separate the intrinsic value and time value of an option contract and designate as the hedging instrument only the change in the intrinsic value of the option contract. Such a designation may result in a hedging relationship that is perfectly effective in achieving offsetting changes in cash flows attributable to a hedged one-sided risk of a forecast transaction, if the principal terms of the forecast transaction and hedging instrument are the same.*

AG110B If an entity designates a purchased option in its entirety as the hedging instrument of a one-sided risk arising from a forecast transaction, the hedging relationship will not be perfectly effective. This is because the premium paid for the option includes time value and, as stated in paragraph AG99BA, a designated one-sided risk does not include the time value of an option. Therefore, in this situation, there will be no offset between the cash flows relating to the time value of the option premium paid and the designated hedged risk.

AG111 In the case of interest rate risk, hedge effectiveness may be assessed by preparing a maturity schedule for financial assets and financial liabilities that shows the net interest rate exposure for each time period, provided that the net exposure is associated with a specific asset or liability (or a specific group of assets or liabilities or a specific portion of them) giving rise to the net exposure, and hedge effectiveness is assessed against that asset or liability.

AG112 In assessing the effectiveness of a hedge, an entity generally considers the time value of money. The fixed interest rate on a hedged item need not exactly match the fixed interest rate on a swap designated as a fair value hedge. Nor does the variable interest rate on an interest-bearing asset or liability need to be the same as the variable interest rate on a swap designated as a cash flow hedge. A swap's fair value derives from its net settlements. The fixed and variable rates on a swap can be changed without affecting the net settlement if both are changed by the same amount.

AG113 If an entity does not meet hedge effectiveness criteria, the entity discontinues hedge accounting from the last date on which compliance with hedge effectiveness was demonstrated. However, if the entity identifies the event or change in circumstances that caused the hedging relationship to fail the effectiveness criteria, and demonstrates that the hedge was effective before the event or change in circumstances occurred, the entity discontinues hedge accounting from the date of the event or change in circumstances.

Fair Value Hedge Accounting for a Portfolio Hedge of Interest Rate Risk

AG114 For a fair value hedge of interest rate risk associated with a portfolio of financial assets or financial liabilities, an entity would meet the requirements of this Standard

Editor's note: *Paragraphs AG110A and AG110B added in November 2008.*

if it complies with the procedures set out in (a)-(i) and paragraphs AG115-AG132 below.

(a) As part of its risk management process the entity identifies a portfolio of items whose interest rate risk it wishes to hedge. The portfolio may comprise only assets, only liabilities or both assets and liabilities. The entity may identify two or more portfolios (eg the entity may group its available-for-sale assets into a separate portfolio), in which case it applies the guidance below to each portfolio separately.

(b) The entity analyses the portfolio into repricing time periods based on expected, rather than contractual, repricing dates. The analysis into repricing time periods may be performed in various ways including scheduling cash flows into the periods in which they are expected to occur, or scheduling notional principal amounts into all periods until repricing is expected to occur.

(c) On the basis of this analysis, the entity decides the amount it wishes to hedge. The entity designates as the hedged item an amount of assets or liabilities (but not a net amount) from the identified portfolio equal to the amount it wishes to designate as being hedged. This amount also determines the percentage measure that is used for testing effectiveness in accordance with paragraph AG126(b).

(d) The entity designates the interest rate risk it is hedging. This risk could be a portion of the interest rate risk in each of the items in the hedged position, such as a benchmark interest rate (eg LIBOR).

(e) The entity designates one or more hedging instruments for each repricing time period.

(f) Using the designations made in (c)-(e) above, the entity assesses at inception and in subsequent periods, whether the hedge is expected to be highly effective during the period for which the hedge is designated.

(g) Periodically, the entity measures the change in the fair value of the hedged item (as designated in (c)) that is attributable to the hedged risk (as designated in (d)), on the basis of the expected repricing dates determined in (b). Provided that the hedge is determined actually to have been highly effective when assessed using the entity's documented method of assessing effectiveness, the entity recognises the change in fair value of the hedged item as a gain or loss in profit or loss and in one of two line items in the balance sheet as described in paragraph 89A. The change in fair value need not be allocated to individual assets or liabilities.

(h) The entity measures the change in fair value of the hedging instrument(s) (as designated in (e)) and recognises it as a gain or loss in profit or loss. The fair value of the hedging instrument(s) is recognised as an asset or liability in the balance sheet.

(i) Any ineffectiveness* will be recognised in profit or loss as the difference between the change in fair value referred to in (g) and that referred to in (h).

This approach is described in more detail below. The approach shall be applied only to a fair value hedge of the interest rate risk associated with a portfolio of financial assets or financial liabilities. **AG115**

The portfolio identified in paragraph AG114(a) could contain assets and liabilities. Alternatively, it could be a portfolio containing only assets, or only liabilities. The portfolio is used to determine the amount of the assets or liabilities the entity wishes to hedge. However, the portfolio is not itself designated as the hedged item. **AG116**

**The same materiality considerations apply in this context as apply throughout IFRSs.*

AG117 In applying paragraph AG114(b), the entity determines the expected repricing date of an item as the earlier of the dates when that item is expected to mature or to reprice to market rates. The expected repricing dates are estimated at the inception of the hedge and throughout the term of the hedge, based on historical experience and other available information, including information and expectations regarding prepayment rates, interest rates and the interaction between them. Entities that have no entity-specific experience or insufficient experience use peer group experience for comparable financial instruments. These estimates are reviewed periodically and updated in the light of experience. In the case of a fixed rate item that is prepayable, the expected repricing date is the date on which the item is expected to prepay unless it reprices to market rates on an earlier date. For a group of similar items, the analysis into time periods based on expected repricing dates may take the form of allocating a percentage of the group, rather than individual items, to each time period. An entity may apply other methodologies for such allocation purposes. For example, it may use a prepayment rate multiplier for allocating amortising loans to time periods based on expected repricing dates. However, the methodology for such an allocation shall be in accordance with the entity's risk management procedures and objectives.

AG118 As an example of the designation set out in paragraph AG114(c), if in a particular repricing time period an entity estimates that it has fixed rate assets of CU100 and fixed rate liabilities of CU80 and decides to hedge all of the net position of CU20, it designates as the hedged item assets in the amount of CU20 (a portion of the assets).* The designation is expressed as an 'amount of a currency' (eg an amount of dollars, euro, pounds or rand) rather than as individual assets. It follows that all of the assets (or liabilities) from which the hedged amount is drawn—ie all of the CU100 of assets in the above example—must be:

(a) items whose fair value changes in response to changes in the interest rate being hedged; and
(b) items that could have qualified for fair value hedge accounting if they had been designated as hedged individually. In particular, because the Standard† specifies that the fair value of a financial liability with a demand feature (such as demand deposits and some types of time deposits) is not less than the amount payable on demand, discounted from the first date that the amount could be required to be paid, such an item cannot qualify for fair value hedge accounting for any time period beyond the shortest period in which the holder can demand payment. In the above example, the hedged position is an amount of assets. Hence, such liabilities are not a part of the designated hedged item, but are used by the entity to determine the amount of the asset that is designated as being hedged. If the position the entity wished to hedge was an amount of liabilities, the amount representing the designated hedged item must be drawn from fixed rate liabilities other than liabilities that the entity can be required to repay in an earlier time period, and the percentage measure used for assessing hedge effectiveness in accordance with paragraph AG126(b) would be calculated as a percentage of these other liabilities. For example, assume that an entity estimates that in a particular repricing time period it has fixed rate liabilities of CU100, comprising CU40 of demand deposits and CU60 of liabilities with no demand feature, and CU70 of fixed rate assets. If the entity decides to hedge all

**The Standard permits an entity to designate any amount of the available qualifying assets or liabilities, ie in this example any amount of assets between CU0 and CU100.*

†see paragraph 49

of the net position of CU30, it designates as the hedged item liabilities of CU30 or 50 per cent* of the liabilities with no demand feature.

The entity also complies with the other designation and documentation requirements set out in paragraph 88(a). For a portfolio hedge of interest rate risk, this designation and documentation specifies the entity's policy for all of the variables that are used to identify the amount that is hedged and how effectiveness is measured, including the following: **AG119**

(a) which assets and liabilities are to be included in the portfolio hedge and the basis to be used for removing them from the portfolio.
(b) how the entity estimates repricing dates, including what interest rate assumptions underlie estimates of prepayment rates and the basis for changing those estimates. The same method is used for both the initial estimates made at the time an asset or liability is included in the hedged portfolio and for any later revisions to those estimates.
(c) the number and duration of repricing time periods.
(d) how often the entity will test effectiveness and which of the two methods in paragraph AG126 it will use.
(e) the methodology used by the entity to determine the amount of assets or liabilities that are designated as the hedged item and, accordingly, the percentage measure used when the entity tests effectiveness using the method described in paragraph AG126(b).
(f) when the entity tests effectiveness using the method described in paragraph AG126(b), whether the entity will test effectiveness for each repricing time period individually, for all time periods in aggregate, or by using some combination of the two.

The policies specified in designating and documenting the hedging relationship shall be in accordance with the entity's risk management procedures and objectives. Changes in policies shall not be made arbitrarily. They shall be justified on the basis of changes in market conditions and other factors and be founded on and consistent with the entity's risk management procedures and objectives.

The hedging instrument referred to in paragraph AG114(e) may be a single derivative or a portfolio of derivatives all of which contain exposure to the hedged interest rate risk designated in paragraph AG114(d) (eg a portfolio of interest rate swaps all of which contain exposure to LIBOR). Such a portfolio of derivatives may contain offsetting risk positions. However, it may not include written options or net written options, because the Standard† does not permit such options to be designated as hedging instruments (except when a written option is designated as an offset to a purchased option). If the hedging instrument hedges the amount designated in paragraph AG114(c) for more than one repricing time period, it is allocated to all of the time periods that it hedges. However, the whole of the hedging instrument must be allocated to those repricing time periods because the Standard‡ does not permit a hedging relationship to be designated for only a portion of the time period during which a hedging instrument remains outstanding. **AG120**

When the entity measures the change in the fair value of a prepayable item in accordance with paragraph AG114(g), a change in interest rates affects the fair value of the prepayable item in two ways: it affects the fair value of the contractual cash **AG121**

**CU30 ÷ (CU100 – CU40) = 50 per cent*

†see paragraphs 77 and AG94

‡see paragraph 75

flows and the fair value of the prepayment option that is contained in a prepayable item. Paragraph 81 of the Standard permits an entity to designate a portion of a financial asset or financial liability, sharing a common risk exposure, as the hedged item, provided effectiveness can be measured. For prepayable items, paragraph 81A permits this to be achieved by designating the hedged item in terms of the change in the fair value that is attributable to changes in the designated interest rate on the basis of *expected*, rather than *contractual*, repricing dates. However, the effect that changes in the hedged interest rate have on those expected repricing dates shall be included when determining the change in the fair value of the hedged item. Consequently, if the expected repricing dates are revised (eg to reflect a change in expected prepayments), or if actual repricing dates differ from those expected, ineffectiveness will arise as described in paragraph AG126. Conversely, changes in expected repricing dates that (a) clearly arise from factors other than changes in the hedged interest rate, (b) are uncorrelated with changes in the hedged interest rate and (c) can be reliably separated from changes that are attributable to the hedged interest rate (eg changes in prepayment rates clearly arising from a change in demographic factors or tax regulations rather than changes in interest rate) are excluded when determining the change in the fair value of the hedged item, because they are not attributable to the hedged risk. If there is uncertainty about the factor that gave rise to the change in expected repricing dates or the entity is not able to separate reliably the changes that arise from the hedged interest rate from those that arise from other factors, the change is assumed to arise from changes in the hedged interest rate.

AG122 The Standard does not specify the techniques used to determine the amount referred to in paragraph AG114(g), namely the change in the fair value of the hedged item that is attributable to the hedged risk. If statistical or other estimation techniques are used for such measurement, management must expect the result to approximate closely that which would have been obtained from measurement of all the individual assets or liabilities that constitute the hedged item. It is not appropriate to assume that changes in the fair value of the hedged item equal changes in the value of the hedging instrument.

AG123 Paragraph 89A requires that if the hedged item for a particular repricing time period is an asset, the change in its value is presented in a separate line item within assets. Conversely, if the hedged item for a particular repricing time period is a liability, the change in its value is presented in a separate line item within liabilities. These are the separate line items referred to in paragraph AG114(g). Specific allocation to individual assets (or liabilities) is not required.

AG124 Paragraph AG114(i) notes that ineffectiveness arises to the extent that the change in the fair value of the hedged item that is attributable to the hedged risk differs from the change in the fair value of the hedging derivative. Such a difference may arise for a number of reasons, including:

(a) actual repricing dates being different from those expected, or expected repricing dates being revised;

(b) items in the hedged portfolio becoming impaired or being derecognised;

(c) the payment dates of the hedging instrument and the hedged item being different; and

(d) other causes (eg when a few of the hedged items bear interest at a rate below the benchmark rate for which they are designated as being hedged, and the resulting ineffectiveness is not so great that the portfolio as a whole fails to qualify for hedge accounting).

Such ineffectiveness* shall be identified and recognised in profit or loss.

Generally, the effectiveness of the hedge will be improved: **AG125**

(a) if the entity schedules items with different prepayment characteristics in a way that takes account of the differences in prepayment behaviour.
(b) when the number of items in the portfolio is larger. When only a few items are contained in the portfolio, relatively high ineffectiveness is likely if one of the items prepays earlier or later than expected. Conversely, when the portfolio contains many items, the prepayment behaviour can be predicted more accurately.
(c) when the repricing time periods used are narrower (eg 1-month as opposed to 3-month repricing time periods). Narrower repricing time periods reduces the effect of any mismatch between the repricing and payment dates (within the repricing time period) of the hedged item and those of the hedging instrument.
(d) the greater the frequency with which the amount of the hedging instrument is adjusted to reflect changes in the hedged item (eg because of changes in prepayment expectations).

An entity tests effectiveness periodically. If estimates of repricing dates change between one date on which an entity assesses effectiveness and the next, it shall calculate the amount of effectiveness either: **AG126**

(a) as the difference between the change in the fair value of the hedging instrument (see paragraph AG114(h)) and the change in the value of the entire hedged item that is attributable to changes in the hedged interest rate (including the effect that changes in the hedged interest rate have on the fair value of any embedded prepayment option); or
(b) using the following approximation. The entity:
    (i) calculates the percentage of the assets (or liabilities) in each repricing time period that was hedged, on the basis of the estimated repricing dates at the last date it tested effectiveness.
    (ii) applies this percentage to its revised estimate of the amount in that repricing time period to calculate the amount of the hedged item based on its revised estimate.
    (iii) calculates the change in the fair value of its revised estimate of the hedged item that is attributable to the hedged risk and presents it as set out in paragraph AG114(g).
    (iv) recognises ineffectiveness equal to the difference between the amount determined in (iii) and the change in the fair value of the hedging instrument (see paragraph AG114(h)).

When measuring effectiveness, the entity distinguishes revisions to the estimated repricing dates of existing assets (or liabilities) from the origination of new assets (or liabilities), with only the former giving rise to ineffectiveness. All revisions to estimated repricing dates (other than those excluded in accordance with paragraph AG121), including any reallocation of existing items between time periods, are included when revising the estimated amount in a time period in accordance with paragraph AG126(b)(ii) and hence when measuring effectiveness. Once ineffectiveness has been recognised as set out above, the entity establishes a new estimate of the total assets (or liabilities) in each repricing time period, including new assets (or liabilities) that have been originated since it last tested effectiveness, and designates a new amount as the hedged item and a new percentage as the hedged percentage. The **AG127**

**The same materiality considerations apply in this context as apply throughout IFRSs.*

procedures set out in paragraph AG126(b) are then repeated at the next date it tests effectiveness.

AG128 Items that were originally scheduled into a repricing time period may be derecognised because of earlier than expected prepayment or writeoffs caused by impairment or sale. When this occurs, the amount of change in fair value included in the separate line item referred to in paragraph AG114(g) that relates to the derecognised item shall be removed from the balance sheet, and included in the gain or loss that arises on derecognition of the item. For this purpose, it is necessary to know the repricing time period(s) into which the derecognised item was scheduled, because this determines the repricing time period(s) from which to remove it and hence the amount to remove from the separate line item referred to in paragraph AG114(g). When an item is derecognised, if it can be determined in which time period it was included, it is removed from that time period. If not, it is removed from the earliest time period if the derecognition resulted from higher than expected prepayments, or allocated to all time periods containing the derecognised item on a systematic and rational basis if the item was sold or became impaired.

AG129 In addition, any amount relating to a particular time period that has not been derecognised when the time period expires is recognised in profit or loss at that time (see paragraph 89A). For example, assume an entity schedules items into three repricing time periods. At the previous redesignation, the change in fair value reported in the single line item on the balance sheet was an asset of CU25. That amount represents amounts attributable to periods 1, 2 and 3 of CU7, CU8 and CU10, respectively. At the next redesignation, the assets attributable to period 1 have been either realised or rescheduled into other periods. Therefore, CU7 is derecognised from the balance sheet and recognised in profit or loss. CU8 and CU10 are now attributable to periods 1 and 2, respectively. These remaining periods are then adjusted, as necessary, for changes in fair value as described in paragraph AG114(g).

AG130 As an illustration of the requirements of the previous two paragraphs, assume that an entity scheduled assets by allocating a percentage of the portfolio into each repricing time period. Assume also that it scheduled CU100 into each of the first two time periods. When the first repricing time period expires, CU110 of assets are derecognised because of expected and unexpected repayments. In this case, all of the amount contained in the separate line item referred to in paragraph AG114(g) that relates to the first time period is removed from the balance sheet, plus 10 per cent of the amount that relates to the second time period.

AG131 If the hedged amount for a repricing time period is reduced without the related assets (or liabilities) being derecognised, the amount included in the separate line item referred to in paragraph AG114(g) that relates to the reduction shall be amortised in accordance with paragraph 92.

AG132 An entity may wish to apply the approach set out in paragraphs AG114-AG131 to a portfolio hedge that had previously been accounted for as a cash flow hedge in accordance with IAS 39. Such an entity would revoke the previous designation of a cash flow hedge in accordance with paragraph 101(d), and apply the requirements set out in that paragraph. It would also redesignate the hedge as a fair value hedge and apply the approach set out in paragraphs AG114-AG131 prospectively to subsequent accounting periods.

AG133 An entity may have designated a forecast intragroup transaction as a hedged item at the start of an annual period beginning on or after 1 January 2005 (or, for the purpose of restating comparative information, the start of an earlier comparative period) in a hedge that would qualify for hedge accounting in accordance with this

Standard (as amended by the last sentence of paragraph 80). Such an entity may use that designation to apply hedge accounting in consolidated financial statements from the start of the annual period beginning on or after 1 January 2005 (or the start of the earlier comparative period). Such an entity shall also apply paragraphs AG99A and AG99B from the start of the annual period beginning on or after 1 January 2005. However, in accordance with paragraph 108F, it need not apply paragraph AG99B to comparative information for earlier periods.*

****Editor's note:*** *Paragraph added October 2005.*

Appendix B
Amendments to Other Pronouncements

[Not reproduced, as all changes have been made to the underlying standards and abstracts].

Appendix C

This appendix is an integral part of the Standard.

Insurance Contracts – extracts from IFRS 4

Paragraphs C2 to C4 are taken from the Standard section of IFRS 4, paragraphs 7 to 9. **C1**

Embedded derivatives

IAS 39 requires an entity to separate some embedded derivatives from their host contract, measure them at *fair value* and include changes in their fair value in profit or loss. IAS 39 applies to derivatives embedded in an insurance contract unless the embedded derivative is itself an insurance contract. **C2**

As an exception to the requirement in IAS 39, an insurer need not separate, and measure at fair value, a policyholder's option to surrender an insurance contract for a fixed amount (or for an amount based on a fixed amount and an interest rate), even if the exercise price differs from the carrying amount of the host *insurance liability*. However, the requirement in IAS 39 does apply to a put option or cash surrender option embedded in an insurance contract if the surrender value varies in response to the change in a financial variable (such as an equity or commodity price or index), or a non-financial variable that is not specific to a party to the contract. Furthermore, that requirement also applies if the holder's ability to exercise a put option or cash surrender option is triggered by a change in such a variable (for example, a put option that can be exercised if a stock market index reaches a specified level). **C3**

Paragraph 8 applies equally to options to surrender a financial instrument containing a discretionary participation feature. **C4**

The following definitions are taken from Appendix A of IFRS 4 'Defined Terms'. This appendix is an integral part of IFRS 4. **C5**

Discretionary participation feature — A contractual right to receive, as a supplement to guaranteed benefits, additional benefits:

(a) that are likely to be a significant portion of the total contractual benefits;

(b) whose amount or timing is contractually at the discretion of the issuer; and

(c) that are contractually based on:

  (i) the performance of a specified pool of contracts or a specified type of contract;

  (ii) realised and/or unrealised investment returns on a specified pool of assets held by the issuer; or

  (iii) the profit or loss of the company, fund or other entity that issues the contract.

Financial risk — The risk of a possible future change in one or more of a specified interest rate, financial instrument price, commodity price, foreign exchange rate, index of prices or rates, credit rating or credit index or other

	variable, provided in the case of a non-financial variable that the variable is not specific to a party to the contract.
Guaranteed benefits	Payments or other benefits to which a particular policyholder or investor has an unconditional right that is not subject to the contractual discretion of the issuer.
Insurance contract	A contract under which one party (the insurer) accepts significant insurance risk from another party (the policyholder) by agreeing to compensate the policyholder if a specified uncertain future event (the insured event) adversely affects the policyholder. (See Appendix B for guidance on this definition.)
Insurance liability	An insurer's net contractual obligations under an insurance contract.
Insurance risk	Risk, other than financial risk, transferred from the holder of a contract to the issuer.
Insured event	An uncertain future event that is covered by an insurance contract and creates insurance risk.
Insurer	The party that has an obligation under an insurance contract to compensate a policyholder if an insured event occurs.
Policyholder	A party that has a right to compensation under an insurance contract if an insured event occurs.

C6 Paragraphs C7 to C36 are taken from Appendix B of IFRS 4 'Definition of an insurance contract', paragraphs B1 to B30; this appendix is an integral part of IFRS 4.

C7 Paragraphs C8 to C36 give guidance on the definition of an insurance contract in paragraph C5. They addresses the following issues:

(a) the term 'uncertain future event' (paragraphs C8-C10);
(b) payments in kind (paragraphs C11-C13);
(c) insurance risk and other risks (paragraphs C14-C23);
(d) examples of insurance contracts (paragraphs C24-C27);
(e) significant insurance risk (paragraphs C28-C34); and
(f) changes in the level of insurance risk (paragraphs C35 and C36).

Uncertain future event

C8 Uncertainty (or risk) is the essence of an insurance contract. Accordingly, at least one of the following is uncertain at the inception of an insurance contract:

(a) whether an *insured event* will occur;
(b) when it will occur; or
(c) how much the insurer will need to pay if it occurs.

C9 In some insurance contracts, the insured event is the discovery of a loss during the term of the contract, even if the loss arises from an event that occurred before the inception of the contract. In other insurance contracts, the insured event is an event that occurs during the term of the contract, even if the resulting loss is discovered after the end of the contract term.

Some insurance contracts cover events that have already occurred, but whose financial effect is still uncertain. An example is a reinsurance contract that covers the direct insurer against adverse development of claims already reported by policyholders. In such contracts, the insured event is the discovery of the ultimate cost of those claims. **C10**

Payments in kind

Some insurance contracts require or permit payments to be made in kind. An example is when the insurer replaces a stolen article directly, instead of reimbursing the policyholder. Another example is when an insurer uses its own hospitals and medical staff to provide medical services covered by the contracts. **C11**

Some fixed-fee service contracts in which the level of service depends on an uncertain event meet the definition of an insurance contract in this Appendix but are not regulated as insurance contracts in some countries. One example is a maintenance contract in which the service provider agrees to repair specified equipment after a malfunction. The fixed service fee is based on the expected number of malfunctions, but it is uncertain whether a particular machine will break down. The malfunction of the equipment adversely affects its owner and the contract compensates the owner (in kind, rather than cash). Another example is a contract for car breakdown services in which the provider agrees, for a fixed annual fee, to provide roadside assistance or tow the car to a nearby garage. The latter contract could meet the definition of an insurance contract even if the provider does not agree to carry out repairs or replace parts. **C12**

Distinction between insurance risk and other risks

The definition of an insurance contract refers to insurance risk, which this Appendix defines as risk, other than *financial risk*, transferred from the holder of a contract to the issuer. A contract that exposes the issuer to financial risk without significant insurance risk is not an insurance contract. **C14**

The definition of financial risk in paragraph C5 includes a list of financial and non-financial variables. That list includes non-financial variables that are not specific to a party to the contract, such as an index of earthquake losses in a particular region or an index of temperatures in a particular city. It excludes non-financial variables that are specific to a party to the contract, such as the occurrence or nonoccurrence of a fire that damages or destroys an asset of that party. Furthermore, the risk of changes in the fair value of a non-financial asset is not a financial risk if the fair value reflects not only changes in market prices for such assets (a financial variable) but also the condition of a specific non-financial asset held by a party to a contract (a non-financial variable). For example, if a guarantee of the residual value of a specific car exposes the guarantor to the risk of changes in the car's physical condition, that risk is insurance risk, not financial risk. **C15**

Some contracts expose the issuer to financial risk, in addition to significant insurance risk. For example, many life insurance contracts both guarantee a minimum rate of return to policyholders (creating financial risk) and promise death benefits that at some times significantly exceed the policyholder's account balance (creating insurance risk in the form of mortality risk). Such contracts are insurance contracts. **C16**

Under some contracts, an insured event triggers the payment of an amount linked to a price index. Such contracts are insurance contracts, provided the payment that is contingent on the insured event can be significant. For example, a life-contingent **C17** annuity linked to a cost-of-living index transfers insurance risk because payment is triggered by an uncertain event—the survival of the annuitant. The link to the price index is an embedded derivative, but it also transfers insurance risk. If the resulting transfer of insurance risk is significant, the embedded derivative meets the definition of an insurance contract, in which case it need not be separated and measured at fair value (see paragraph C2 of this Appendix).

C18 The definition of insurance risk refers to risk that the insurer accepts from the policyholder. In other words, insurance risk is a pre-existing risk transferred from the policyholder to the insurer. Thus, a new risk created by the contract is not insurance risk.

C19 The definition of an insurance contract refers to an adverse effect on the policyholder. The definition does not limit the payment by the insurer to an amount equal to the financial impact of the adverse event. For example, the definition does not exclude 'new-for-old' coverage that pays the policyholder sufficient to permit replacement of a damaged old asset by a new asset. Similarly, the definition does not limit payment under a term life insurance contract to the financial loss suffered by the deceased's dependants, nor does it preclude the payment of predetermined amounts to quantify the loss caused by death or an accident.

C20 Some contracts require a payment if a specified uncertain event occurs, but do not require an adverse effect on the policyholder as a precondition for payment. Such a contract is not an insurance contract even if the holder uses the contract to mitigate an underlying risk exposure. For example, if the holder uses a derivative to hedge an underlying non-financial variable that is correlated with cash flows from an asset of the entity, the derivative is not an insurance contract because payment is not conditional on whether the holder is adversely affected by a reduction in the cash flows from the asset. Conversely, the definition of an insurance contract refers to an uncertain event for which an adverse effect on the policyholder is a contractual precondition for payment. This contractual precondition does not require the insurer to investigate whether the event actually caused an adverse effect, but permits the insurer to deny payment if it is not satisfied that the event caused an adverse effect.

C21 Lapse or persistency risk (ie the risk that the counterparty will cancel the contract earlier or later than the issuer had expected in pricing the contract) is not insurance risk because the payment to the counterparty is not contingent on an uncertain future event that adversely affects the counterparty. Similarly, expense risk (ie the risk of unexpected increases in the administrative costs associated with the servicing of a contract, rather than in costs associated with insured events) is not insurance risk because an unexpected increase in expenses does not adversely affect the counterparty.

C22 Therefore, a contract that exposes the issuer to lapse risk, persistency risk or expense risk is not an insurance contract unless it also exposes the issuer to insurance risk. However, if the issuer of that contract mitigates that risk by using a second contract to transfer part of that risk to another party, the second contract exposes that other party to insurance risk.

C23 An insurer can accept significant insurance risk from the policyholder only if the insurer is an entity separate from the policyholder. In the case of a mutual insurer, the mutual accepts risk from each policyholder and pools that risk. Although policyholders bear that pooled risk collectively in their capacity as owners, the mutual has still accepted the risk that is the essence of an insurance contract.

Examples of insurance contracts

The following are examples of contracts that are insurance contracts, if the transfer of insurance risk is significant: C24

(a) insurance against theft or damage to property.
(b) insurance against product liability, professional liability, civil liability or legal expenses.
(c) life insurance and prepaid funeral plans (although death is certain, it is uncertain when death will occur or, for some types of life insurance, whether death will occur within the period covered by the insurance).
(d) life-contingent annuities and pensions (ie contracts that provide compensation for the uncertain future event—the survival of the annuitant or pensioner—to assist the annuitant or pensioner in maintaining a given standard of living, which would otherwise be adversely affected by his or her survival).
(e) disability and medical cover.
(f) surety bonds, fidelity bonds, performance bonds and bid bonds (ie contracts that provide compensation if another party fails to perform a contractual obligation, for example an obligation to construct a building).
(g) credit insurance that provides for specified payments to be made to reimburse the holder for a loss it incurs because a specified debtor fails to make payment when due under the original or modified terms of a debt instrument. These contracts could have various legal forms, such as that of a guarantee, some types of letter of credit, a credit derivative default contract or an insurance contract. However, although these contracts meet the definition of an insurance contract, they also meet the definition of a financial guarantee contract in FRS 26 and are within the scope of FRS 25 and FRS 26. Nevertheless, if an issuer of financial guarantee contracts has previously asserted explicitly that it regards such contracts as insurance contracts and has used accounting applicable to insurance contracts, the issuer may elect to apply FRS 26 and FRS 25 to such financial guarantee contracts.*
(h) product warranties. Product warranties issued by another party for goods sold by a manufacturer, dealer or retailer are within the scope of this IFRS. However, product warranties issued directly by a manufacturer, dealer or retailer are outside its scope, because they are within the scope of FRS 12 *Provisions, Contingent Liabilities and Contingent Assets*.
(i) title insurance (ie insurance against the discovery of defects in title to land that were not apparent when the insurance contract was written). In this case, the insured event is the discovery of a defect in the title, not the defect itself.
(j) travel assistance (ie compensation in cash or in kind to policyholders for losses suffered while they are travelling). Paragraphs C11 and C12 discuss some contracts of this kind.
(k) catastrophe bonds that provide for reduced payments of principal, interest or both if a specified event adversely affects the issuer of the bond (unless the specified event does not create significant insurance risk, for example if the event is a change in an interest rate or foreign exchange rate).
(l) insurance swaps and other contracts that require a payment based on changes in climatic, geological or other physical variables that are specific to a party to the contract.
(m) reinsurance contracts.

The following are examples of items that are not insurance contracts: C25

(a) investment contracts that have the legal form of an insurance contract but do not expose the insurer to significant insurance risk, for example life insurance

****Editor's note:*** *Amended with effect from 1 January 2006.*

contracts in which the insurer bears no significant mortality risk (such contracts are noninsurance financial instruments or service contracts, see paragraphC26).

(b) contracts that have the legal form of insurance, but pass all significant insurance risk back to the policyholder through non-cancellable and enforceable mechanisms that adjust future payments by the policyholder as a direct result of insured losses, for example some financial reinsurance contracts or some group contracts (such contracts are normally non-insurance financial instruments or service contracts, see paragraph C26).

(c) self-insurance, in other words retaining a risk that could have been covered by insurance (there is no insurance contract because there is no agreement with another party).

(d) contracts (such as gambling contracts) that require a payment if a specified uncertain future event occurs, but do not require, as a contractual precondition for payment, that the event adversely affects the policyholder. However, this does not preclude the specification of a predetermined payout to quantify the loss caused by a specified event such as death or an accident (see also paragraph C19).

(e) derivatives that expose one party to financial risk but not insurance risk, because they require that party to make payment based solely on changes in one or more of a specified interest rate, financial instrument price, commodity price, foreign exchange rate, index of prices or rates, credit rating or credit index or other variable, provided in the case of a non-financial variable that the variable is not specific to a party to the contract (see FRS 26).

(f) a credit-related guarantee (or letter of credit, credit derivative default contract or credit insurance contract) that requires payments even if the holder has not incurred a loss on the failure of the debtor to make payments when due.*

(g) contracts that require a payment based on a climatic, geological or other physical variable that is not specific to a party to the contract (commonly described as weather derivatives).

(h) catastrophe bonds that provide for reduced payments of principal, interest or both, based on a climatic, geological or other physical variable that is not specific to a party to the contract.

C26 If the contracts described in paragraph C25 create financial assets or financial liabilities, they are within the scope of FRS 26. Among other things, this means that the parties to the contract use what is sometimes called deposit accounting, which involves the following:

(a) one party recognises the consideration received as a financial liability, rather than as revenue.

(b) the other party recognises the consideration paid as a financial asset, rather than as an expense.

Significant insurance risk

C28 A contract is an insurance contract only if it transfers significant insurance risk. Paragraphs C13-C26 discuss insurance risk. The following paragraphs discuss the assessment of whether insurance risk is significant.

C29 Insurance risk is significant if, and only if, an insured event could cause an insurer to pay significant additional benefits in any scenario, excluding scenarios that lack commercial substance (ie have no discernible effect on the economics of the transaction). If significant additional benefits would be payable in scenarios that have commercial substance, the condition in the previous sentence may be met even if the

****Editor's note:*** *Amended with effect from 1 January 2006.*

insured event is extremely unlikely or even if the expected (ie probability-weighted) present value of contingent cash flows is a small proportion of the expected present value of all the remaining contractual cash flows.

The additional benefits described in paragraph C29 refer to amounts that exceed those that would be payable if no insured event occurred (excluding scenarios that lack commercial substance). Those additional amounts include claims handling and claims assessment costs, but exclude: **C30**

(a) the loss of the ability to charge the policyholder for future services. For example, in an investment-linked life insurance contract, the death of the policyholder means that the insurer can no longer perform investment management services and collect a fee for doing so. However, this economic loss for the insurer does not reflect insurance risk, just as a mutual fund manager does not take on insurance risk in relation to the possible death of the client. Therefore, the potential loss of future investment management fees is not relevant in assessing how much insurance risk is transferred by a contract.

(b) waiver on death of charges that would be made on cancellation or surrender. Because the contract brought those charges into existence, the waiver of these charges does not compensate the policyholder for a pre-existing risk. Hence, they are not relevant in assessing how much insurance risk is transferred by a contract.

(c) a payment conditional on an event that does not cause a significant loss to the holder of the contract. For example, consider a contract that requires the issuer to pay one million currency units if an asset suffers physical damage causing an insignificant economic loss of one currency unit to the holder. In this contract, the holder transfers to the insurer the insignificant risk of losing one currency unit. At the same time, the contract creates non-insurance risk that the issuer will need to pay 999,999 currency units if the specified event occurs. Because the issuer does not accept significant insurance risk from the holder, this contract is not an insurance contract.

(d) possible reinsurance recoveries. The insurer accounts for these separately.

An insurer shall assess the significance of insurance risk contract by contract, rather than by reference to materiality to the financial statements.* Thus, insurance risk may be significant even if there is a minimal probability of material losses for a whole book of contracts. This contract-by-contract assessment makes it easier to classify a contract as an insurance contract. However, if a relatively homogeneous book of small contracts is known to consist of contracts that all transfer insurance risk, an insurer need not examine each contract within that book to identify a few non-derivative contracts that transfer insignificant insurance risk. **C31**

It follows from paragraphs C29-C31 that if a contract pays a death benefit exceeding the amount payable on survival, the contract is an insurance contract unless the additional death benefit is insignificant (judged by reference to the contract rather than to an entire book of contracts). As noted in paragraph B24(b), the waiver on death of cancellation or surrender charges is not included in this assessment if this waiver does not compensate the policyholder for a pre-existing risk. Similarly, an annuity contract that pays out regular sums for the rest of a policyholder's life is an insurance contract, unless the aggregate lifecontingent payments are insignificant. **C32**

Paragraph C29 refers to additional benefits. These additional benefits could include a requirement to pay benefits earlier if the insured event occurs earlier and the payment **C33**

**For this purpose, contracts entered into simultaneously with a single counterparty (or contracts that are otherwise interdependent) form a single contract.*

is not adjusted for the time value of money. An example is whole life insurance for a fixed amount (in other words, insurance that provides a fixed death benefit whenever the policyholder dies, with no expiry date for the cover). It is certain that the policyholder will die, but the date of death is uncertain. The insurer will suffer a loss on those individual contracts for which policyholders die early, even if there is no overall loss on the whole book of contracts.

C34 If an insurance contract is unbundled into a deposit component and an insurance component, the significance of insurance risk transfer is assessed by reference to the insurance component. The significance of insurance risk transferred by an embedded derivative is assessed by reference to the embedded derivative.

Changes in the level of insurance risk

C35 Some contracts do not transfer any insurance risk to the issuer at inception, although they do transfer insurance risk at a later time. For example, consider a contract that provides a specified investment return and includes an option for the policyholder to use the proceeds of the investment on maturity to buy a life-contingent annuity at the current annuity rates charged by the insurer to other new annuitants when the policyholder exercises the option. The contract transfers no insurance risk to the issuer until the option is exercised, because the insurer remains free to price the annuity on a basis that reflects the insurance risk transferred to the insurer at that time. However, if the contract specifies the annuity rates (or a basis for setting the annuity rates), the contract transfers insurance risk to the issuer at inception.

C36 A contract that qualifies as an insurance contract remains an insurance contract until all rights and obligations are extinguished or expire.

APPROVAL OF IAS 39 BY THE BOARD

International Accounting Standard 39 *Financial Instruments: Recognition and Measurement* was approved for issue by eleven of the fourteen members of the International Accounting Standards Board. Messrs Cope, Leisenring and McGregor dissented. Their dissenting opinions are set out after the Basis for Conclusions.

The amendments made in March 2004 in International Accounting Standard 39 Financial Instruments: Recognition and Measurement *Fair Value Hedge Accounting for a Portfolio Hedge of Interest Rate Risk* were approved for issue by thirteen of the fourteen members of the International Accounting Standards Board. Mr Smith dissented. His dissenting opinion is set out after the Basis for Conclusions.

Sir David Tweedie	Chairman
Thomas E Jones	Vice-Chairman
Mary E Barth	
Hans-Georg Bruns	
Anthony T Cope	
Robert P Garnett	
Gilbert Gélard	
James J Leisenring	
Warren J McGregor	
Patricia L O'Malley	
Harry K Schmid	
John T Smith	
Geoffrey Whittington	
Tatsumi Yamada	

ADOPTION OF FRS 26 BY THE ACCOUNTING STANDARDS BOARD

Financial Reporting Standard 26 (IAS 39) *Financial Instruments: Measurement* was approved for issue by the ten members of the Accounting Standards Board.

Ian Mackintosh	Chairman
Andrew Lennard	Technical Director
Michael Ashley	
Douglas Flint	
Anthony Good	
Roger Marshall	
Isobel Sharp	
John Smith	
Jonathan Symonds	
Peter Westlake	

Notes on the standard's application in the UK and the Republic of Ireland

The need for an FRS on measurement of financial instruments

N1 In June 2002 the Accounting Standards Board (the Board) issued FRED 30 'Financial Instruments: Disclosure and Presentation & Recognition and Measurement'. In August 2003, April 2004 and July 2004 it issued three supplements to that FRED. Together, the four documents proposed that:

(a) a standard for use in the UK and Republic of Ireland based on IAS 32 'Financial Instruments: Disclosure and Presentation' should be implemented for all entities, other than those that apply the FRSSE, for accounting periods beginning on or after 1 January 2005; and

(b) a standard for use in the UK and Republic of Ireland based on the measurement and hedge accounting requirements of IAS 39 'Financial Instruments: Recognition and Measurement' (but not its recognition and derecognition requirements) should be implemented from the same date for all listed entities and for any unlisted entity that chooses to apply fair value accounting in its financial statements (so-called 'fair value volunteers').

The Board has now decided to issue FRS 26 which, together with FRS 25 (IAS 32) 'Financial Instruments: Disclosure and Presentation', implements these proposals.

N2 The issue of these two standards forms part of the Accounting Standards Board's programme to bring about convergence between UK accounting standards and International Accounting Standards (IFRSs). Under this programme, the Board is seeking to bring UK standards into line with IFRS over the medium term, dealing first with areas where implementation of an international standard would enhance existing UK financial reporting requirements and keep them in step with changes in the law.

N3 The Board is strongly of the view that a standard on measurement of derivatives and other financial instruments is important, and that the initial implementation of this standard in the UK and Republic of Ireland should not be delayed.

N4 Furthermore, amendments that have been made to the Companies Act 1985 (the Act) to implement the Fair Value Directive* will enable companies to adopt fair value accounting for some types of asset and liability. In the Board's view the application of the fair value rules set out in the Act should be governed by an accounting standard.

Application of FRS 26

N5 The Board's phased approach to implementation of IAS 39 envisages that in due course all the sections of IAS 39 will be applied generally in the UK and Republic of Ireland. However, the initial application of IAS 39, as implemented by FRS 26, is limited in two major respects; in relation to its scope, and in relation to the exclusion of the part of the standard dealing with recognition and derecognition.

**Similar amendments are to be made to Northern Ireland and Republic of Ireland legislation. The fair value rules previously included in the Companies Act 1985 and equivalent Northern Ireland legislation can be found in The Large and Medium-sized Companies and Groups (Accounts and Reports) Regulations 2008.*

Scope

The Board considers that because of the complexity of the measurement requirements of IAS 39, and the delays in IASB issuing a final version of this standard, these requirements should be implemented on a phased basis in the UK and Republic of Ireland. The Board has restricted the scope of FRS 26 to apply as follows: **N6**

(a) for accounting periods beginning on or after 1 January 2005, to all listed entities (other than those implementing IFRS under the IAS Regulation), and
(b) for accounting periods beginning on or after 1 January 2006, to other entities only if they adopt an accounting policy that complies with the fair value accounting rules in the Act.*

The Board has explained the definition of the scope of (b) to make it clear that this is to be interpreted widely, to include all entities whose accounting policies for financial instruments are consistent with the fair value rules of the Act. This includes any entity that accounts for financal instruments at fair value through profit and loss account, except where this practice is specifically permitted under rules other than the fair value accounting rules in the Act.* **N7**

For those entities reporting under Schedule 4† of the Act, no provision is made in the historical cost or alternative accounting rules for fair value accounting with the gains and losses recognised in the profit and loss account for financial instruments of any kind. An accounting policy to measure any financial instruments (for example, trading book securities) at fair value and recognise the resulting gains and losses in the profit and loss account (for example, marking to market trading positions in securities, derivatives or other financial instruments) falls within the fair value rules in the Schedule. Accordingly, an entity using such an accounting policy will be required to adopt FRS 26. **N8**

For banking entities reporting under Schedule 9‡, the historical cost accounting rules§ permit fair value accounting through the profit and loss account for some classes of financial instrument. Where such an entity applies fair value accounting only to those financial instruments which those rules specifically permit to be fair valued through the profit and loss account, it does not fall within the scope of FRS 26. However, if an entity reporting under these Schedules uses fair value accounting through the profit and loss account for financial instruments that are not specifically covered by the historical cost rules but are within the scope of the fair value rules – such as derivatives or loans and advances – the entity will be required to adopt FRS 26. The standard will therefore apply inter alia to banks and similar entities that use mark to market or fair value accounting through profit and loss account for derivatives, for example those held for trading. **N9**

**Replaced by The Large and Medium-sized Companies and Groups (Accounts and Reports) Regulations 2008.*

†Replaced by paragraphs 16 to 35 of Part 2 of Schedule 1 of The Large and Medium-sized Companies and Groups (Accounts and Reports) Regulations 2008.

‡Replaced by paragraphs 22 to 37 of Part 2 of Schedule 2 of The Large and Medium-sized Companies and Groups (Accounts and Reports) Regulations 2008

§Paragraphs 23 to 38 of Schedule 9 and equivalent requirements in Northern Ireland and Republic of Ireland legislation.

N10 Similarly, for insurance entities under Schedule 9A*, the current value rules† permit or require fair value accounting through the profit and loss account for investments and certain other assets. Where an insurance entity applies fair value accounting only to those financial instruments for which it is specifically permitted under these rules, it does not fall within the scope of FRS 26. However, the standard will apply to insurance entities that use fair value accounting through profit and loss account for any derivatives, or for any other financial instruments that are not specifically covered by the current value rules in Schedule 9A.

N11 The Board decided that, in the light of uncertainties expressed by some respondents over the interpretation of the scope set out in the exposure draft, that the effective date of entities falling within paragraph (b) above should be deferred for one year, to 2006. However, it confirmed the proposed effective date of 2005 for listed entities falling under paragraph (a) above.

N12 The Board intends bringing forward proposals extending the scope of application of the FRS to other entities after 2006, and intends to issue an exposure draft shortly.

Recycling

N15 IAS 39 requires gains and losses on remeasurement of available for sale assets to be recognised in equity and subsequently included in profit and loss on derecognition of the assets (e.g. on sale). Similarly gains and losses arising on a hedging instrument under cash flow hedging are recognised in equity and subsequently reclassified to profit and loss in accordance with the cash flow hedge accounting requirements. Existing UK standards, however, do not permit such gains and losses to be recycled.

N16 In FRED 30 the Board proposed amending the IAS 39 requirements to prohibit recycling, as the IASB was at that time reviewing its use of recycling as part of its comprehensive income project. Respondents were concerned that this would result in a UK standard that was not consistent with the equivalent international standard, and in the amended version of the draft FRS set out in FRED 30 Second Supplement the Board amended its approach to retain the IAS 39 requirements for recycling, although gains and losses recognised directly in equity under IAS 39 would be reflected in the statement of total recognised gains and losses under UK standards.

N17 The Board continues to have concerns over recycling, primarily because it is not consistent with the *Statement of Principles*. The IASB is actively considering the future of recycling in its comprehensive income project, and the Board intends to continue to argue strongly for the practice's prohibition. Nevertheless, the Board has concluded that it would be inconsistent with its stated policy of convergence were it to amend IAS 39's recycling provisions, and it is therefore implementing this aspect of IAS 39 unamended.

Relationship of the UK standard to the Fair Value Directive

N18 The Fair Value Directive, adopted in 2001, was drafted to correspond to the version of IAS 39 issued in 2000. Since then, IAS 39 has been revised, but these revisions have not been reflected in the directive, nor in the amendments to the Companies Act implementing the directive. In particular, IAS 39 now allows a reporting entity to

**Replaced by paragraphs 22 to 29 of Part 2 of Schedule 3 of The Large and Medium-sized Companies and Groups (Accounts and Reports) Regulations 2008.*

†Paragraphs 20 to 29 of Schedule 9A and equivalent requirements in Northern Ireland and Republic of Ireland legislation.

designate *any* financial asset or financial liability to be measured at fair value through profit or loss. This unrestricted 'fair value option' is not available under the amendments to the Act implementing the directive, which limit the use of fair values to specified categories of asset and liability. In FRS 26 the Board has implemented the current version of IAS 39 rather than the 2000 version; since the inconsistencies with the Act relate to an optional designation rather than a requirement, entities may comply with both the FRS and the Act by not choosing to use this option.

There may be circumstances in which an entity's financial statements will not present a true and fair view if certain financial liabilities are not accounted for at fair value. In such circumstances the entity should use the true and fair override and adopt an accounting policy that measures these liabilities at fair value in accordance with the FRS. It is difficult for the Board to provide guidance as to the circumstances that might merit the use of such an override because the use of the override must be justified by the particular circumstances of the entity in question. The Board would envisage that: **N19**

(a) if the override is to be applied there would need to be potential for substantial artificial volatility to arise otherwise. 'Artificial volatility' in this context means that the financial statements show volatility that would not be present were the financial liabilities concerned measured at fair value through profit or loss like the financial assets they are managed with. The Board believes that the *potential* for volatility, rather than the existence of actual volatility, is important in order to ensure that consistency in accounting practice from year to year is to be achieved.

(b) it would not generally be appropriate to apply the override if the result would be the recognition in the profit and loss account of a substantial gain arising from a fall in the fair value of financial liabilities caused by a deterioration in the entity's own credit standing.

The IASB issued an exposure draft proposing an amendment to IAS 39 to restrict the circumstances in which the fair value option may be adopted, and this exposure draft was issued by the Board as part of FRED 30 Third Supplement. If implemented, this proposal would reduce the significance of the difference between IAS 39 and the Fair Value Directive referred to in the previous paragraph. The Board will issue any IASB amendment to IAS 39 as an amendment to this FRS. **N20**

Transitional provisions

The Board intends that entities adopting this FRS should be able to take advantage of the same transitional provisions as entities adopting the corresponding international standards as part of their transition to IFRS, which are set out in IFRS 1 'First-time Adoption of International Financial Reporting Standards', and consistently with its reasons for deferring the effective date for some entities to 2006, has extended the period for which these transitional provisions apply. An entity that first applies the requirements of the FRS for accounting periods commencing before 1 January 2007 need not restate comparatives to comply with the requirements of the FRS or those of FRS 25. **N21**

The relevant paragraphs from IFRS 1 have been incorporated in the FRS, including the implementation guidance in IFRS 1 that relates to IAS 39 which is included at the end of the implementation guidance section of this FRS. **N22**

The Board has, in adopting the transition requirements in IFRS 1, followed the practice adopted in several previous UK standards that applied prospectively and therefore not required corresponding amounts on a comparable basis. Some **N23** commentators have recently raised concerns that this might not be in compliance with the requirements of the Companies Act. The Board does not believe that it was ever the intention that prospective application of a new standard should be prevented. However, in view of these concerns, it has noted that a minor change to the Act could clarify the issue by explicitly permitting entities not to restate comparatives in certain circumstances; the DTI has agreed to consider such an amendment if this would remove uncertainty over the application of the transitional provisions of the FRS.

Consequential amendments

N24 Measurement of financial instruments is addressed in FRS 4 'Capital Instruments'. Most of the requirements of FRS are superseded by FRS 25; the remaining paragraphs of FRS 4, relating to measurement of debt instruments, are superseded by this FRS. UITF Abstract 11 'Capital instruments: issuer call options' is also superseded by this FRS. No other amendments of substance are required to these on issue of FRS 26.

N25 IAS 39 made minor changes to IAS 37 'Provisions, Contingent Liabilities and Contingent Assets' clarifying the interaction between the two standards. IAS 37 is substantially the same as FRS 12 37 'Provisions, Contingent Liabilities and Contingent Assets', and the Board has implemented the same changes to FRS 12, applicable only to those entities applying FRS 26.

N26 Other amendments set out in IAS 39 do not affect UK standards and are not included in FRS 26.

N27 In July 2004 the ASB issued an exposure draft FRED 30 Third Supplement 'Further Amendments to the Proposed Standards on Financial Instruments'. This set out, inter alia, four exposure drafts issued by the IASB of proposed amendments to IAS 39.

N28 Subsequent to those exposure drafts, the IASB has made five amendments to IAS 39:

- Transition and Initial Recognition of Financial Assets and Financial Liabilities (December 2004)
- Cash Flow Hedge Accounting of Forecast Intragroup Transactions (April 2005)
- The Fair Value Option (June 2005)
- Financial Guarantee Contracts and Credit Insurance (August 2005)
- IFRIC Interpretation 5 'Rights to Interests arising from Decommissioning, Restoration and Environmental Rehabilitation Funds' (December 2004).

N29 The ASB has considered those amendments and decided to make corresponding changes to FRS 26.

Transition and initial recognition of financial assets and financial liabilities

N30 FRS 26 requires that the fair value of a financial instrument on its initial recognition should be the transaction price unless a different fair value can be evidenced by observable market data – thus limiting the circumstances in which a 'day one' profit or loss is recognised. On initial application of FRS 26 prior to the amendment, all financial instruments held by the entity would need to be assessed to determine any profit or loss recognised on initial recognition, even if this occurred in previous accounting periods. The amendment permits entities to restrict this reassessment to transactions that occurred after 1 January 2004, or to those that occurred after 25 October 2002 (the effective date for equivalent US GAAP requirements).

The ASB agreed that the IASB's amendment was an appropriate simplification and should be incorporated into FRS 26. **N31**

In line with the amendment to IAS 39, the amendment is effective for accounting periods commencing on or after 1 January 2005. The transitional provisions of FRS 26 are consistent with the provisions for first-time adopters under IFRS 1 *First-time Adoption of International Reporting Standards*. **N32**

Cash flow hedge accounting of forecast intragroup transactions

Prior to the amendment, FRS 26 did not permit hedge accounting to be used where the hedged risk arises on a forecast intragroup transaction; hedge accounting is only permitted for risks arising from transactions with parties external to the group. However, in some circumstances forecast intragroup transactions denominated in a currency other than the functional currency of one or both of the parties to the transaction can give rise to a foreign currency risk that affects consolidated profit and loss. The IASB have amended IAS 39 to permit cash flow hedge accounting of forecast intragroup transactions in these circumstances. **N33**

The ASB agreed that it was appropriate to amend FRS 26 in line with the amendment to IAS 39. **N34**

In line with the amendment to IAS 39, the amendment is effective for accounting periods commencing on or after 1 January 2006. Earlier adoption is encouraged. **N35**

The Fair Value Option

Prior to the amendment, IAS 39 permitted entities to designate any financial asset or financial liability as at fair value through profit and loss. The amendment restricted this to circumstances where fair value accounting provided more relevant information, either by eliminating or reducing a measurement inconsistency or where a group of financial items is managed, and its performance evaluated, on a fair value basis in accordance with documented risk management or investment strategy. Fair value measurement is also permitted for certain contracts that contain embedded derivatives. **N36**

The ASB stated, when it issued FRED 30 Third Supplement, that it had considerable reservations about the proposed restriction on the use of the fair value option. However, it now agrees that, although the restricted amendment results in greater complexity in implementation, there are unlikely to be cases where the use of fair value accounting would be appropriate but not permitted by the amended standard, and that the disadvantages of implementing these restrictions are outweighed by the benefits of keeping UK standards in line with IFRS. It has therefore agreed to implement the changes by amending FRS 26. **N37**

Under the amendment to IAS 39, an entity must take into account criteria set out in IAS 8 'Accounting Policies' when deciding whether to designate items as at fair value through profit and loss. As there is no UK standard equivalent to IAS 8, the ASB has amended the guidance in AG4C and subsequent paragraphs to refer to the need to consider objectives against which an entity should judge the appropriateness of accounting policies as set out in FRS 18 'Accounting Policies'. **N38**

Paragraph 9(b)(ii) of the amended standard refers to information provided internally to the entity's key management personnel, as defined in IAS 24 'Related Party Disclosures'. This definition is not identical to the definition of key management in **N39**

FRS 8 'Related Party Disclosures' and has therefore been included in the amended standard.

N40 In line with the amendment to IAS 39, the amendment is effective for accounting periods commencing on or after 1 January 2006. Earlier adoption is permitted. The ASB has also amended the transitional provisions of FRS 26 to remain consistent with the provisions for first-time adopters under IFRS 1.

N41 The ASB has also amended FRS 25 to include certain additional disclosure requirements. The ASB does, however, have considerable reservations over the value of some of the disclosures introduced by the IASB's amendment. These include disclosures introduced as paragraph 94 (g) relating to the credit risk of loans and receivables designated as at fair value through profit and loss which in the ASB's view are intended to provide information that is relevant to regulatory returns rather than general purpose financial statements. The ASB has not, therefore, implemented all the disclosure requirements inserted in IAS 32.

N42 The ASB has, however, amended the date by which transitional designations must be made from 1 September 2005 to 1 December 2005. This applies only to those entities adopting the amended fair value option for accounting periods commencing before 1 January 2006.

Credit insurance and financial guarantees

N43 Before the amendment, IAS 39 excluded credit insurance and financial guarantee contracts from its scope where these met the definition of an insurance contract. The IASB considered that although there may be differences in the way insurance entities and banks currently account for these contracts, there was no fundamental difference between credit insurance and financial guarantees, although those entered into by insurance companies were often longer term and more complex arrangements. The IASB considered that financial guarantees are similar in nature to financial instruments, and should be within the scope of IAS 39. However, some aspects of the more complex types of contract issued by insurance companies were not dealt with in IAS 39; furthermore, applying IAS 39 to these contracts would cause insurance companies to change their systems in advance of the completion of the IASB's insurance project. The IASB agreed that all such contracts should be included in the scope of IAS 39 except where these have been regarded by the issuer as an insurance contract and previously accounted for as such.

N44 The ASB has considered the amendment and agreed that it was appropriate to make a corresponding amendment to FRS 26.

N45 In line with the amendment to IAS 39, the amendment is effective for accounting periods commencing on or after 1 January 2006. Earlier adoption is encouraged.

N46 The IASB amended example 9 in Appendix C to IAS 37 *Provisions, Contingent Liabilities and Contingent Assets* so that it refers to accounting in accordance with IAS 39. The equivalent example is contained in FRS 12 and the ASB has made a corresponding amendment. However, as the amendment is only applicable to entities adopting FRS 26 the change is noted in Appendix B to the Standard.

IFRIC Interpretation 5

N47 In IFRIC Interpretation 5 'Rights to Interests arising from Decommissioning, Restoration and Environmental Rehabilitation Funds' (December 2004) the IASB amended the scope of IAS 39 to exclude rights to payments to reimburse the entity for expenditure required to settle a liability that it recognises as a provision in accordance with IAS 37 *Provisions, Contingent Liabilities and Contingent Assets*. The ASB has made a corresponding amendment to FRS 26.

In line with the amendment to IAS 39, the amendment is effective for accounting periods commencing on or after 1 January 2006. Earlier adoption is encouraged. **N48**

Securitisation entities in the Republic of Ireland

The Board notes that the implementation of the IAS Regulation in the Republic of Ireland took advantage of the member state option to defer the effective date of the Regulation to accounting periods commencing on or after 1 January 2007 for entities with listed debt but no listed equity. The Board considered a request from the Irish Government for an equivalent exemption from the Standard on the ground of practicalities. It agreed to permit a deferral for one year for Irish securitisation entities, as defined in Irish tax legislation, that have listed debt but no listed equities.* **N49**

Recognition and derecognition of financial assets and liabilities

In April 2006 the Board amended FRS 26 to include the IAS 39 material on recognition and derecognition into the Standard. Upon implementation of this amendment entities within the scope of FRS 26 will apply the derecognition requirements in FRS 26 to financial assets and liabilities and the derecognition principles of FRS 5 to non-financial assets and liabilities. **N50**

Consolidation requirements – subsidiaries and quasi-subsidiaries

The first step in considering derecognition for a particular transaction is to ensure that all subsidiaries and quasi-subsidiaries are consolidated. Some respondents to the Exposure Draft noted that the consolidation requirements relating to subsidiaries and quasi-subsidiaries in FRS 2 and FRS 5 are not completely equivalent to those in IAS 27 and SIC 12, leading to differences in accounting for subsidiaries under IFRS and UK GAAP. The Board considered whether it would be appropriate to amend the requirements in the UK to make them compliant with IFRS. It decided to postpone this due to the following considerations: a number of the FRS 2 requirements are derived from company law (until this is amended entities applying UK standards would also need to consider the Companies Act definition of a subsidiary); and the IASB is currently considering the long term future of SIC 12 which may lead to an amendment of IAS 27 to clarify the situation of SPEs. **N51**

Transactions that result in assets being transferred but not derecognised

The amendment also sets out a clarification of the treatment of liabilities that are recognised when a transaction is entered into that transfers an asset but does not result in derecognition; for example, where the entity retains a call option over the asset. Application of the subsequent measurement provisions of FRS 26 to such liabilities may not be appropriate, as there may not be any contracted cash outflows. Paragraph 47 of FRS 26 currently exempts such liabilities from the continuing measurement provisions of the standard where they arise from a transaction in *financial* assets. The amendment would extend this exception to financial liabilities that arise as a result of not derecognising a *non-financial* asset, under FRS 5. **N52**

**Editor's note:* *Paragraph N27 to N49 added in October 2005.*

Overlap between the requirements of FRS 26 and FRS 5

N53 Some respondents to the FRED were concerned about the interaction between FRS 5 and FRS 26. For example Application Note F of FRS 5 can sometimes lead to a financial asset being recognised, which the Application Note requires should be recorded at fair value. Some constituents noted that this financial asset may need to be recognised under the 'available for sale' category of FRS 26, thus leading to confusion as to the accounting for such assets. The Board considered paragraph 13 of FRS 5 and in its view the accounting is clear in that an entity would comply with FRS 5 in determining what assets and liabilities should be recognised. If, as a result of applying FRS 5, a financial asset or liability arises this should be accounted for in accordance with FRS 26.

N54 The Board also noted that where a transaction in a non-financial asset incorporates options, these might also be within the scope of FRS 26 and it might be unclear which standard applies. The Board's view is that such options will often fall outside the definition of derivative, as the option will be based on a non-financial variable that is specific to a party to the contract. However, where a transaction includes an option that falls within the scope of FRS 26, it should be accounted for under that standard as well as taken into account in determining the substance of the transaction in the non-financial asset.

Treatment of transactions previously accounted for under linked presentation

N55 In its deliberations over the transitional arrangements the Board considered the issue of transactions previously accounted for under linked presentation. As a result, the Board decided that if a transaction that occurred before the transition date resulted in linked presentation under FRS 5, the derecognition of the gross asset and liability must be re-examined under the new derecognition requirements of FRS 26.

Explanatory material describing non-financial assets in FRS 5

N56 As a consequence of excluding derecognition of financial assets and liabilities from the scope of FRS 5, some material in the explanation section and application notes which addresses transactions involving financial assets is no longer relevant. The consequential amendment has the effect of deleting this material, including the illustrations of the linked presentation, and application notes dealing with factoring of debt, securitised assets (which is discussed only in terms of securitisation of financial assets) and loan transfers.

N57 Some respondents to the Exposure Draft requested that the deleted material be replaced with explanatory material describing transactions in non-financial assets. The Board did not incorporate such material in this amendment. In doing so it took the following into consideration: it believes that the principles in FRS 5 are now widely understood so the examples are less necessary; and until the scope of FRS 26 is extended to all entities in the UK the examples will not completely disappear from UK standards. It also noted that additional material in FRS 5 would need to be exposed to the UK constituents which would mean a further delay in issuing this amendment.

Effective date and transitional provisions

For entities within the scope of FRS 26 the recognition and derecognition material would be applicable to accounting periods commencing on or after 1 January 2007; earlier adoption is permitted. **N58**

The Board took into consideration that on initial application of the new requirements, it may not be practicable to obtain the necessary information to restate all past transactions and that to require such restatement would also be inconsistent with international standards. It has, therefore, included transitional provisions equivalent to those set out in IFRS 1 – First–time Adoption of International Financial Reporting Standards, allowing an entity to choose to apply the requirements either: **N59**

(a) only to transactions entered into after the beginning of the comparative period for the accounting period the entity first applied the derecognition requirements of the standard; or

(b) only to transactions entered into after an earlier date of the entity's choosing, provided information sufficient to apply the standard was obtained at the time of initial accounting for each transaction.

The Board has allowed the application of the derecognition provisions from a date related to the entity's first application of the standard rather than a fixed date; but notes that entities wishing to adopt IFRS in due course may wish to choose 1 January 2004 (or an earlier date), the equivalent transition provisions of IFRS 1, for this purpose.* **N60**

In October 2008 the International Accounting Standards Board (IASB) published amendments to IAS 39 'Financial Instruments: Recognition and Measurement' and IFRS 7 'Financial Instruments: Disclosures'. The amendments permit the reclassification of certain financial assets, including: non-derivative held-for-trading financial assets out of the Fair Value Through Profit or Loss (FVTPL) category in rare circumstances; and certain financial assets to the loans and receivables category in a selection of cases. The amendments do not permit reclassification if an entity has applied an option to fair value financial instruments on initial recognition. **N61**

In moving to issue the amendments, the ASB – like the IASB – did not follow its normal due process, given the need to take urgent action to address the rare circumstances of the current credit crisis. The ASB wants to ensure that entities applying FRS 26 and FRS 29 have the same ability to be able to make reclassifications as those applying IFRS.† **N62**

In October 2007 the ASB issued its exposure draft inviting comments on the proposed IASB's amendments. The ASB welcomed the IASB initiative of clarifying the Board's original intentions regarding what could be designated as a hedged risk and when an entity may designate a portion of the cash flows of a financial instrument as a hedged tem. The ASB recognised that the approach proposed was rules based rather than principle based and was concerned that this approach may lead to unintended consequences and prevent hedging opportunities for items that should, in principle, be hedged.‡ **N63**

****Editor's note:** Paragraphs N50 to N60 added in April 2006.*

*†**Editor's note**: N61 and N62 added in October 2008.*

*‡**Editor's note**: N63 to N66 added in November 2008.*

N64 Many respondents to the IASB raised concerns about the rules based approach proposed in the Exposure Draft. Their response indicated that there was little diversity in practice regarding the designation of hedged items. However, the responses demonstrated that diversity in practice existed, or was likely to occur, in the two situations set out in paragraph BC 172C namely:

(a) the designation of a one-sided risk in a hedged item; and
(b) the designation of inflation as a hedged risk or portion in particular situations.

N65 After considering the responses the IASB decided top focus on these two situations. Rather than specifying eligible risks and portions, as proposed in the Exposure Draft, the IASB decided to address those situations by adding additional application guidance to illustrate how the principles underlying hedge accounting should be applied.

N66 In November 2008 the Board issued an amendments to FRS 26 to incorporate the changes made by the IASB to IAS 39 *Financial Instruments: Recognition and Measurement 'Eligible Hedged Items'*.

N67 An amendment to FRS 26 was issued by the Board in September 2009 following the IASB's amendments to IFRIC 9 'Reassessment of Embedded Derivatives' and IAS 39 Financial Instruments: Recognition and Measurement '*Embedded Derivatives*'. The amendments clarify the treatment of embedded derivatives when an entity reclassifies a financial asset out of the fair value through profit or loss category. The effective date for the amendment is for annual periods ending on or after 31 December 2009. Earlier application is permitted to enable entities to align the accounting under UK GAAP with the equivalent IFRS amendment which has an effective date for annual periods ending on or after 30 June 2009.

Basis for Conclusions

Background **BC4-BC14**

Scope **BC15-BC24**
Loan Commitments BC15-BC20
Financial Guarantee Contracts BC21-BC23
Contracts to Buy or Sell a Non-Financial Item BC24

Definitions **BC25-BC36**
Loans and Receivables BC25-BC29
Effective Interest Rate BC30-BC35
Accounting for a Change in Estimates BC36

Embedded derivatives **BC37-BC40**
Embedded Foreign Currency Derivatives BC37-BC40

Recognition and Derecognition **BC41-BC70**
Derecognition of a Financial Asset **BC41-BC53**
The Original IAS 39 BC41-BC43
Exposure Draft BC44-BC45
Comments Received BC46-BC47
Revisions to IAS 39 BC48-BC53
Arrangements Under Which an Entity Retains the Contractual Rights to Receive the Cash Flows of a Financial Asset but Assumes a Contractual Obligation to Pay the Cash Flows to One or More Recipients **BC54-BC64**
Transfers that Do Not Qualify for Derecognition **BC65-BC66**
Continuing Involvement in a Transferred Asset **BC67-BC70**

Measurement **BC71-BC174**
Fair Value Measurement Option **BC71-BC94**
Application of the Fair Value Measurement Option to a Portion (Rather than the Entirety) of a Financial Asset or a Financial Liability BC85-BC86
Own Credit Risk BC87-BC92
Measurement of Financial Liabilities with a Demand Feature BC93-BC94
Fair Value Measurement Guidance **BC95-BC104**
Use of Quoted Prices in Active Markets BC96-BC101
No Active Market BC102-BC104
Impairment and Uncollectibility of Financial Assets **BC105-BC130**
Impairment of Investments in Equity Instruments BC105-BC130

Hedging **BC131-BC220**
Consideration of the Shortcut Method in SFAS 133 BC132-BC135
Hedging of Portions of Financial Assets and Financial Liabilities BC135A
Expected Effectiveness BC136-BC136B

Hedges of Portions of Non-Financial Assets and Non-Financial Liabilities for Risk Other Than Foreign Currency Risk BC137-BC139
Loan Servicing Rights BC140-BC143
Whether to Permit Hedge Accounting Using Cash Instruments BC144-BC145
Whether to Treat Hedges of Forecast Transactions as Fair Value Hedges BC146-BC148
Hedges of Firm Commitments BC149-BC154
Basis Adjustments BC155-BC164
Hedging Using Internal Contracts BC165-BC172
Fair Value Accounting for a Portfolio Hedge of Interest Rate Risk BC173-BC220
Background BC173-BC174
Scope BC175
The issue: why fair value hedge accounting was difficult to achieve in accordance with previous versions of IAS 39 BC176-BC177
Prepayment Risk BC178-BC181
Designation of the hedged item and liabilities with a demand feature BC182-BC192
What portion of assets should be designated and the impact on ineffectiveness BC193-BC206
The carrying amount of the hedged item BC207-BC209
Derecognition of amounts included in the separate line items BC210-BC212
The hedging instrument BC213-BC215
Hedge effectiveness for a portfolio hedge of interest rate risk BC216-BC218
Transition to fair value hedge accounting for portfolios of interest rate risk BC219-BC220

Elimination of selected differences from US GAAP BC221

Summary of changes from the Exposure Draft BC222

Dissenting opinions

Dissent of Anthony T Cope, James J Leisenring and Warren J McGregor from the issue of IAS 39 in December 2003 **DO1-DO15**

Dissent of John T Smith from the issue in March 2004 of amendments to International Accounting Standard IAS 39 on Fair Value Hedge Accounting for a Portfolio Hedge of Interest Rate Risk **DO1-DO2**

Basis for Conclusions

This Basis for Conclusions accompanies, but is not part of, IAS 39.

In this Basis for Conclusions the terminology has not been amended to reflect the changes made by IAS 1 Presentation of Financial Statements (as revised in 2007).

ASB note: The IASB's Basis for Conclusions, which accompanies IAS 39, is set out below in full. It should be noted though that some of the discussion it contains concerns IASB requirements that have no equivalent in the UK or Republic of Ireland. Footnotes have been used to indicate corresponding requirements in the UK and Republic of Ireland where applicable.

All references in this section to 'the Board' and 'Board members' are references to the IASB Board and IASB Board members.

This Basis for Conclusions summarises the International Accounting Standards Board's considerations in reaching the conclusions on revising IAS 39 *Financial Instruments: Recognition and Measurement* in 2003. Individual Board members gave greater weight to some factors than to others. **BC1**

In July 2001 the Board announced that, as part of its initial agenda of technical projects, it would undertake a project to improve a number of Standards, including IAS 32 *Financial Instruments: Disclosure and Presentation* and IAS 39 *Financial Instruments: Recognition and Measurement*. The objectives of the Improvements project were to reduce the complexity in the Standards by clarifying and adding guidance, eliminating internal inconsistencies and incorporating into the Standards elements of Standing Interpretations Committee (SIC) Interpretations and IAS 39 implementation guidance. In June 2002 the Board published its proposals in an Exposure Draft of Proposed Amendments to IAS 32 *Financial Instruments: Disclosure and Presentation* and IAS 39 *Financial Instruments: Recognition and Measurement*, with a comment deadline of 14 October 2002. In August 2003 the Board published a further Exposure Draft of Proposed Amendments to IAS 39 on *Fair Value Hedge Accounting for a Portfolio Hedge of Interest Rate Risk*, with a comment deadline of 14 November 2003. **BC2**

Because the Board's intention was not to reconsider the fundamental approach to the accounting for financial instruments established by IAS 32 and IAS 39, this Basis for Conclusions does not discuss requirements in IAS 39 that the Board has not reconsidered. **BC3**

BACKGROUND

The original version of IAS 39 became effective for financial statements covering financial years beginning on or after 1 January 2001. It reflected a mixed measurement model in which some financial assets and financial liabilities are measured at fair value and others at cost or amortised cost, depending in part on an entity's intention in holding an instrument. **BC4**

The Board recognises that accounting for financial instruments is a difficult and controversial subject. The Board's predecessor body, the International Accounting Standards Committee (IASC) began its work on the issue some 15 years ago, in 1988. During the next eight years it published two Exposure Drafts, culminating in the issue of IAS 32 on disclosure and presentation in 1995. IASC decided that its **BC5** initial proposals on recognition and measurement should not be progressed to a Standard, in view of:

- the critical response they had attracted;
- evolving practices in financial instruments; and
- the developing thinking by national standard-setters.

BC6 Accordingly, in 1997 IASC published, jointly with the Canadian Accounting Standards Board, a discussion paper that proposed a different approach, namely that all financial assets and financial liabilities should be measured at fair value. The responses to that paper indicated both widespread unease with some of its proposals and that more work needed to be done before a standard requiring a full fair value approach could be contemplated.

BC7 In the meantime, IASC concluded that a standard on the recognition and measurement of financial instruments was needed urgently. It noted that although financial instruments were widely held and used throughout the world, few countries apart from the United States had any recognition and measurement standards for them. In addition, IASC had agreed with the International Organization of Securities Commissions (IOSCO) that it would develop a set of 'core' International Accounting Standards that could be endorsed by IOSCO for the purpose of cross-border capital raising and listing in all global markets. Those core standards included one on the recognition and measurement of financial instruments. Accordingly, IASC developed the version of IAS 39 that was issued in 2000.

BC8 In December 2000 a Financial Instruments Joint Working Group of Standard Setters (JWG), comprising representatives or members of accounting standardsetters and professional organisations from a range of countries, published a Draft Standard and Basis for Conclusions entitled *Financial Instruments and Similar Items*. That Draft Standard proposed far-reaching changes to accounting for financial instruments and similar items, including the measurement of virtually all financial instruments at fair value. In the light of feedback on the JWG's proposals, it is evident that much more work is needed before a comprehensive fair value accounting model could be introduced.

BC9 In July 2001 the Board announced that it would undertake a project to improve the existing requirements on the accounting for financial instruments in IAS 32 and IAS 39. The improvements deal with practice issues identified by audit firms, national standard-setters, regulators and others, and issues identified in the IAS 39 implementation guidance process or by IASB staff.

BC10 In June 2002 the Board published an Exposure Draft of proposed amendments to IAS 32 and IAS 39 for a 116-day comment period. More than 170 comment letters were received.

BC11 Subsequently, the Board took steps to enable constituents to inform it better about the main issues arising out of the comment process, and to enable the Board to explain its views of the issues and its tentative conclusions. These consultations included:

(a) discussions with the Standards Advisory Council on the main issues raised in the comment process.

(b) nine roundtable discussions with constituents during March 2003 conducted in Brussels and London. Over 100 organisations and individuals took part in those discussions.

(c) discussions with the Board's liaison standard-setters of the issues raised in the roundtable discussions.

(d) meetings between members of the Board and its staff and various groups of constituents to explore further issues raised in comment letters and at the roundtable discussions.

Some of the comment letters on the June 2002 Exposure Draft and participants in the roundtables raised a significant issue for which the June 2003 Exposure Draft had not proposed any changes. This was hedge accounting for a portfolio hedge of interest rate risk (sometimes referred to as 'macro hedging') and the related question of the treatment in hedge accounting of deposits with a demand feature (sometimes referred to as 'demand deposits' or 'demandable liabilities'). In particular, some were concerned that it was very difficult to achieve fair value hedge accounting for a macro hedge in accordance with previous versions of IAS 39. **BC11A**

In the light of these concerns, the Board decided to explore whether and how IAS 39 might be amended to enable fair value hedge accounting to be used more readily for a portfolio hedge of interest rate risk. This resulted in a further Exposure Draft of Proposed Amendments to IAS 39 that was published in August 2003 and on which more than 120 comment letters were received. The amendments proposed in the Exposure Draft were finalised in March 2004. **BC11B**

After those amendments were issued in March 2004 the Board received further comments from constituents calling for further amendments to the Standard. In particular, as a result of continuing discussions with constituents, the Board became aware that some, including prudential supervisors of banks, securities companies and insurers, were concerned that the fair value option might be used inappropriately. These constituents were concerned that: **BC11C**

(a) entities might apply the fair value option to financial assets or financial liabilities whose fair value is not verifiable. If so, because the valuation of these financial assets and financial liabilities is subjective, entities might determine their fair value in a way that inappropriately affects profit or loss.

(b) the use of the option might increase, rather than decrease, volatility in profit or loss, for example if an entity applied the option to only one part of a matched position.

(c) if an entity applied the fair value option to financial liabilities, it might result in an entity recognising gains or losses in profit or loss associated with changes in its own creditworthiness.

In response to those concerns, the Board published in April 2004 an Exposure Draft of proposed restrictions to the fair value option*. In March 2005 the Board held a series of round-table meetings to discuss proposals with invited constituents. As a result of this process, the Board issued an amendment to IAS 39 in June 2005 relating to the fair value option.†

In September 2007, following a request from the International Financial Reporting Interpretations Committee (IFRIC), the Board published Exposures Qualifying for Hedge Accounting, an exposure draft of proposed amendments to IAS 39. The Board's objective was to clarify its requirements on exposures qualifying for hedge accounting and to provide additional guidance by specifying eligible risks and portions of cash flows. The Board received 75 responses to the exposure draft. Many respondents raised concerns about the rule-based approach proposed in the exposure **BC11D**

*ASB Footnote: *equivalent proposals were published in the UK by the ASB as part of FRED 30 Third Supplement.*

†***Editor's note:*** *BC11C added with effect from 1 January 2006.*

draft. Their responses indicated that there was little diversity in practice regarding the designation of hedged items. However, the responses demonstrated that diversity in practice existed, or was likely to occur, in the two situations set out in paragraph BC172C. After considering the responses, the Board decided to focus on those two situations. Rather than specifying eligible risks and portions as proposed in the exposure draft, the Board decided to address those situations by adding application guidance to illustrate how the principles underlying hedge accounting should be applied. The Board subsequently issued Eligible Hedged Items (Amendment to IAS 39) in July 2008. The rationale for the amendment is set out in paragraphs BC172B–BC172J.*

BC11E In October 2008 the Board received requests to address differences between the reclassification requirements of IAS 39 and US GAAP (Statements of Financial Accounting Standards No. 115 *Accounting for Certain Investments in Debt and Equity Securities* (SFAS 115) and No. 65 *Accounting for Certain Mortgage Banking Activities* (SFAS 65) issued by the US Financial Accounting Standards Board). In response the Board issued *Reclassification of Financial Assets* (Amendments to IAS 39 and IFRS 7) in October 2008. The amendments to IAS 39 permit non-derivative financial assets held for trading and available-for-sale financial assets to be reclassified in particular situations. The rationale for the amendments is set out in paragraphs BC104A–BC104E.†

BC11F Following the issue of *Reclassification of Financial Assets* (Amendments to IAS 39 and IFRS 7) in October 2008 constituents told the Board that there was uncertainty about the interaction between those amendments and IFRIC 9 regarding the assessment of embedded derivatives. In response the Board issued *Embedded Derivatives* (Amendments to IFRIC 9 and IAS 39) in March 2009. The amendment to IAS 39 clarifies the consequences if the fair value of the embedded derivative that would have to be separated cannot be measured separately.

BC12 The Board did not reconsider the fundamental approach to accounting for financial instruments contained in IAS 39. Some of the complexity in existing requirements is inevitable in a mixed measurement model based in part on management's intentions for holding financial instruments and given the complexity of finance concepts and fair value estimation issues. The amendments reduce some of the complexity by clarifying the Standard, eliminating internal inconsistencies and incorporating additional guidance into the Standard.

BC13 The amendments also eliminate or mitigate some differences between IAS 39 and US GAAP related to the measurement of financial instruments. Already, the measurement requirements in IAS 39 are, to a large extent, similar to equivalent requirements in US GAAP, in particular, those in FASB SFAS 114 *Accounting by Creditors for Impairment of a Loan*, SFAS 115 *Accounting for Certain Investments in Debt and Equity Securities* and SFAS 133 *Accounting for Derivative Instruments and Hedging Activities*.

BC14 The Board will continue its consideration of issues related to the accounting for financial instruments. However, it expects that the basic principles in the improved IAS 39 will be in place for a considerable period.

****Editor's note****: Paragraph added in November 2008.*

†***Editor's note****: Paragraph added in October 2008.*

SCOPE

Loan Commitments (paragraphs 2(i) and 4)

Loan commitments are firm commitments to provide credit under prespecified terms and conditions. In the IAS 39 implementation guidance process, the question was raised whether a bank's loan commitments are derivatives accounted for at fair value under IAS 39. This question arises because a commitment to make a loan at a specified rate of interest during a fixed period of time meets the definition of a derivative. In effect, it is a written option for the potential borrower to obtain a loan at a specified rate. **BC15**

To simplify the accounting for holders and issuers of loan commitments, the Board decided to exclude particular loan commitments from the scope of IAS 39. The effect of the exclusion is that an entity will not recognise and measure changes in fair value of these loan commitments that result from changes in market interest rates or credit spreads. This is consistent with the measurement of the loan that results if the holder of the loan commitment exercises its right to obtain financing, because changes in market interest rates do not affect the measurement of an asset measured at amortised cost (assuming it is not designated in a category other than loans and receivables). **BC16**

However, the Board decided that an entity should be permitted to measure a loan commitment at fair value with changes in fair value recognised in profit or loss on the basis of designation at inception of the loan commitment as a financial liability through profit or loss. This may be appropriate, for example, if the entity manages risk exposures related to loan commitments on a fair value basis. **BC17**

The Board further decided that a loan commitment should be excluded from the scope of IAS 39 only if it cannot be settled net. If the value of a loan commitment can be settled net in cash or another financial instrument, including when the entity has a past practice of selling the resulting loan assets shortly after origination, it is difficult to justify its exclusion from the requirement in IAS 39 to measure at fair value similar instruments that meet the definition of a derivative. **BC18**

Some comments received on the Exposure Draft disagreed with the Board's proposal that an entity that has a past practice of selling the assets resulting from its loan commitments shortly after origination should apply IAS 39 to all of its loan commitments. The Board considered this concern and agreed that the words in the Exposure Draft did not reflect the Board's intention. Thus, the Board clarified that if an entity has a past practice of selling the assets resulting from its loan commitments shortly after origination, it applies IAS 39 only to its loan commitments in the same class. **BC19**

Finally, the Board decided that commitments to provide a loan at a below-market interest rate should be initially measured at fair value, and subsequently measured at the higher of (a) the amount that would be recognised under IAS 37* and (b) the amount initially recognised less, where appropriate, cumulative amortisation recognised in accordance with IAS 18 *Revenue*†. It noted that without such a **BC20**

****ASB footnote****: the equivalent standard in the UK and the Republic of Ireland is FRS 12* Provisions, Contingent Liabilities and Contingent Assets.

†***ASB footnote****: the requirements of IAS 18 are more specific than those of the equivalent in the UK and Republic of Ireland, Application Note G* Revenue Recognition *to FRS 5* Reporting the Substance of Transactions.

requirement, liabilities that result from such commitments might not be recognised in the balance sheet, because in many cases no cash consideration is received.

BC20A As discussed in paragraphs BC21–BC23E, the Board amended IAS 39 in 2005 to address financial guarantee contracts. In making those amendments, the Board moved the material on loan commitments from the scope section of the Standard to the section on subsequent measurement (paragraph 47(d)). The purpose of this change was to rationalise the presentation of this material without making substantive changes.

Financial guarantee contracts (paragraphs 2(e), 9, 47(c), AG4 and AG4A)

BC21 In finalising IFRS 4 *Insurance Contracts** in early 2004, the Board reached the following conclusions:

(a) Financial guarantee contracts can have various legal forms, such as that of a guarantee, some types of letter of credit, a credit default contract or an insurance contract. However, although this difference in legal form may in some cases reflect differences in substance, the accounting for these instruments should not depend on their legal form.

(b) If a financial guarantee contract is not an insurance contract, as defined in IFRS 4, it should be within the scope of IAS 39. This was the case before the Board finalised IFRS 4.

(c) As required before the Board finalised IFRS 4, if a financial guarantee contract was entered into or retained on transferring to another party financial assets or financial liabilities within the scope of IAS 39, the issuer should apply IAS 39 to that contract even if it is an insurance contract, as defined in IFRS 4.

(d) Unless (c) applies, the following treatment is appropriate for a financial guarantee contract that meets the definition of an insurance contract:

(i) At inception, the issuer of a financial guarantee contract has a recognisable liability and should measure it at fair value. If a financial guarantee contract was issued in a stand-alone arm's length transaction to an unrelated party, its fair value at inception is likely to equal the premium received, unless there is evidence to the contrary.

(ii) Subsequently, the issuer should measure the contract at the higher of the amount determined in accordance with IAS 37 *Provisions, Contingent Liabilities and Contingent Assets*† and the amount initially recognised less, when appropriate, cumulative amortisation recognised in accordance with IAS 18 *Revenue*.‡

BC22 Mindful of the need to develop a 'stable platform' of Standards for 2005, the Board finalised IFRS 4 in early 2004 without specifying the accounting for these contracts and then published an Exposure Draft *Financial Guarantee Contracts and Credit Insurance* in July 2004 to expose for public comment the conclusion set out in paragraph BC21(d). The Board set a comment deadline of 8 October 2004 and

*ASB footnote: *There is no UK standard equivalent to IFRS 4; the IFRS 4 definition of insurance contract is set out in Appendix C to FRS 26.*

†ASB footnote: *The equivalent standard in the UK and the Republic of Ireland is FRS 12* Provisions, Contingent Liabilities and Contingent Assets.

‡ASB footnote: *The requirements of IAS 18 are more specific than those of the equivalent in the UK and Republic of Ireland, Application Note G* Revenue recognition *to FRS 5* Reporting the Substance of transactions.

received more than 60 comment letters. Before reviewing the comment letters, the Board held a public education session at which it received briefings from representatives of the International Credit Insurance & Surety Association and of the Association of Financial Guaranty Insurers.

Some respondents to the Exposure Draft of July 2004 argued that there were important economic differences between credit insurance contracts and other forms of contract that met the proposed definition of a financial guarantee contract. However, both in developing the Exposure Draft and in subsequently discussing the comments received, the Board was unable to identify differences that would justify differences in accounting treatment. **BC23**

Some respondents to the Exposure Draft of July 2004 noted that some credit insurance contracts contain features, such as cancellation and renewal rights and profit-sharing features, that the Board will not address until phase II of its project on insurance contracts. They argued that the Exposure Draft did not give enough guidance to enable them to account for these features. The Board concluded it could not address such features in the short term. The Board noted that when credit insurers issue credit insurance contracts, they typically recognise a liability measured as either the premium received or an estimate of the expected losses. However, the Board was concerned that some other issuers of financial guarantee contracts might argue that no recognisable liability existed at inception. To provide a temporary solution that balances these competing concerns, the Board decided the following: **BC23A**

(a) If the issuer of financial guarantee contracts has previously asserted explicitly that it regards such contracts as insurance contracts and has used accounting applicable to insurance contracts, the issuer may elect to apply either IAS 39 or IFRS 4 to such financial guarantee contracts.
(b) In all other cases, the issuer of a financial guarantee contract should apply IAS 39.

The Board does not regard criteria such as those described in paragraph BC23A(a) as suitable for the long term, because they can lead to different accounting for contracts that have similar economic effects. However, the Board could not find a more compelling approach to resolve its concerns for the short term. Moreover, although the criteria described in paragraph BC23A(a) may appear imprecise, the Board believes that the criteria would provide a clear answer in the vast majority of cases. Paragraph AG4A gives guidance on the application of those criteria. **BC23B**

The Board considered convergence with US GAAP. In US GAAP, the requirements for financial guarantee contracts (other than those covered by US standards specific to the insurance sector) are in FASB Interpretation 45 *Guarantor's Accounting and Disclosure Requirements for Guarantees, Including Indirect Guarantees of Indebtedness of Others* (FIN 45). The recognition and measurement requirements of FIN 45 do not apply to guarantees issued between parents and their subsidiaries, between entities under common control, or by a parent or subsidiary on behalf of a subsidiary or the parent. Some respondents to the Exposure Draft of July 2004 asked the Board to provide a similar exemption. They argued that the requirement to recognise these financial guarantee contracts in separate or individual financial statements would cause costs disproportionate to the likely benefits, given that intragroup transactions are eliminated on consolidation. However, to avoid the omission of material liabilities from separate or individual financial statements, the Board did not create such an exemption. **BC23C**

The Board issued the amendments for financial guarantee contracts in August 2005. After those amendments, the recognition and measurement requirements for **BC23D** financial guarantee contracts within the scope of IAS 39 are consistent with FIN 45 in some areas, but differ in others:

(a) Like FIN 45, IAS 39 requires initial recognition at fair value.
(b) IAS 39 requires systematic amortisation, in accordance with IAS 18, of the liability recognised initially. This is compatible with FIN 45, though FIN 45 contains less prescriptive requirements on subsequent measurement. Both IAS 39 and FIN 45 include a liability adequacy (or loss recognition) test, although the tests differ because of underlying differences in the Standards to which those tests refer (IAS 37 and SFAS 5).
(c) Like FIN 45, IAS 39 permits a different treatment for financial guarantee contracts issued by insurers.
(d) Unlike FIN 45, IAS 39 does not contain exemptions for parents, subsidiaries or other entities under common control. However, any differences are reflected only in the separate or individual financial statements of the parent, subsidiaries or common control entities.

BC23E Some respondents to the Exposure Draft of July 2004 asked for guidance on the treatment of financial guarantee contracts by the holder. However, this was beyond the limited scope of the project.*

Contracts to Buy or Sell a Non-Financial Item (paragraphs 5-7 and AG10)

BC24 Before the amendments, IAS 39 and IAS 32 were not consistent with respect to the circumstances in which a commodity-based contract meets the definition of a financial instrument and is accounted for as a derivative. The Board concluded that the amendments should make them consistent on the basis of the notion that a contract to buy or sell a non-financial item should be accounted for as a derivative when it (i) can be settled net or by exchanging financial instruments and (ii) is not held for the purpose of receipt or delivery of the non-financial item in accordance with the entity's expected purchase, sale or usage requirements (a 'normal' purchase or sale). In addition, the Board concluded that the notion of when a contract can be settled net should include contracts:

(a) where the entity has a practice of settling similar contracts net in cash or another financial instrument or by exchanging financial instruments;
(b) for which the entity has a practice of taking delivery of the underlying and selling it within a short period after delivery for the purpose of generating a profit from short-term fluctuations in price or dealer's margin; and
(c) in which the non-financial item that is the subject of the contract is readily convertible to cash.

Because practices of settling net or taking delivery of the underlying and selling it within a short period after delivery also indicate that the contracts are not 'normal' purchases or sales, such contracts are within the scope of IAS 39 and are accounted for as derivatives. The Board also decided to clarify that a written option that can be settled net in cash or another financial instrument, or by exchanging financial instruments, is within the scope of the Standard and cannot qualify as a 'normal' purchase or sale.

Business combination forward contracts

BC24A The Board was advised that there was diversity in practice regarding the application of the exemption in paragraph 2(g) of IAS 39. Paragraph 2(g) applies to particular

****Editor's note:*** *BC20A to BC23E added with effect from 1 January 2006.*

contracts associated with a business combination and results in those contracts not being accounted for as derivatives while, for example, necessary regulatory and legal processes are being completed.

As part of the *Improvements to IFRSs* issued in April 2009, the Board concluded that paragraph 2(g) should be restricted to forward contracts between an acquirer and a selling shareholder to buy or sell an acquiree in a business combination at a future acquisition date and should not apply to option contracts, whether or not currently exercisable, that on exercise will result in control of an entity. **BC24B**

The Board concluded that the purpose of paragraph 2(g) is to exempt from the provisions of IAS 39 contracts for business combinations that are firmly committed to be completed. Once the business combination is consummated, the entity follows the requirements of IFRS 3. Paragraph 2(g) applies only when completion of the business combination is not dependent on further actions of either party (and only the passage of a normal period of time is required). Option contracts allow one party to control the occurrence or non-occurrence of future events depending on whether the option is exercised. **BC24C**

Several respondents to the exposure draft expressed the view that the proposed amendment should also apply to contracts to acquire investments in associates, referring to paragraph 20 of IAS 28. However, the acquisition of an interest in an associate represents the acquisition of a financial instrument. The acquisition of an interest in an associate does not represent an acquisition of a business with subsequent consolidation of the constituent net assets. The Board noted that paragraph 20 of IAS 28 explains only the methodology used to account for investments in associates. This should not be taken to imply that the principles for business combinations and consolidations can be applied by analogy to accounting for investments in associates and joint ventures. The Board concluded that paragraph 2(g) should not be applied by analogy to contracts to acquire investments in associates and similar transactions. This conclusion is consistent with the conclusion the Board reached regarding impairment losses on investments in associates as noted in the *Improvements to IFRSs* issued in May 2008 and stated in paragraph BC27 of the Basis for Conclusions on IAS 28. **BC24D**

Some respondents to the exposure draft raised concerns about the proposed transition requirement. The Board noted that determining the fair value of a currently outstanding contract when its inception was before the effective date of this amendment would require the use of hindsight and might not achieve comparability. Accordingly, the Board decided not to require retrospective application. The Board also rejected applying the amendment prospectively only to new contracts entered into after the effective date because that would create a lack of comparability between contracts outstanding as of the effective date and contracts entered into after the effective date. Therefore, the Board concluded that the amendment to paragraph 2(g) should be applied prospectively to all unexpired contracts for annual periods beginning on or after 1 January 2010. **BC24E**

DEFINITIONS

Loans and Receivables (paragraphs 9, 46(a) and AG26)

The principal difference between loans and receivables and other financial assets is that loans and receivables are not subject to the tainting provisions that apply to held-to-maturity investments. Loans and receivables that are not held for trading **BC25** may be measured at amortised cost even if an entity does not have the positive intention and ability to hold the loan asset until maturity.

BC26 The Board decided that the ability to measure a financial asset at amortised cost without consideration of the entity's intention and ability to hold the asset until maturity is most appropriate when there is no liquid market for the asset. It is less appropriate to extend the category to debt instruments traded in liquid markets. The distinction for measurement purposes between liquid debt instruments that are acquired upon issue and liquid debt instruments that are acquired shortly afterwards is difficult to justify on conceptual grounds. Why should a liquid debt instrument that is purchased on the day of issue be treated differently from a liquid debt instrument that is purchased one week after issue? Why should it not be possible to classify a liquid debt instrument that is acquired directly from the issuer as available for sale, with fair value gains and losses recognised in equity? Why should a liquid debt instrument that is bought shortly after it is issued be subject to tainting provisions, if a liquid debt instrument that is bought at the time of issue is not subject to tainting provisions?

BC27 The Board therefore decided to add a condition to the definition of a loan or receivable. More specifically, an entity should not be permitted to classify as a loan or receivable an investment in a debt instrument that is quoted in an active market. For such an investment, an entity should be required to demonstrate its positive intention and ability to hold the investment until maturity to be permitted to measure the investment at amortised cost by classifying it as held to maturity.

BC28 The Board considered comments received on the proposal in the Exposure Draft (which was unchanged from the requirement in the original IAS 39) that 'loans and receivables' must be originated (rather than purchased) to meet that classification. Such comments suggested that purchased loans should be eligible for classification as loans and receivables, for example, if an entity buys a loan portfolio, and the purchased loans meet the definition other than the fact that they were purchased. Such comments also noted that (a) some entities typically manage purchased and originated loans together, and (b) there are systems problems of segregating purchased loans from originated loans given that a distinction between them is likely to be made only for accounting purposes. In the light of these concerns, the Board decided to remove the requirement that loans or receivables must be originated by the entity to meet the definition of 'loans and receivables'.

BC29 However, the Board was concerned that removing this requirement might result in some instruments that should be measured at fair value meeting the definition of loans and receivables and thus being measured at amortised cost. In particular, the Board was concerned that this would be the case for a debt instrument in which the purchaser may not recover its investment, for example a fixed rate interest-only strip created in a securitisation and subject to prepayment risk. The Board therefore decided to exclude from the definition of loans and receivables instruments for which the holder may not recover substantially all of its initial investment, other than because of credit deterioration. Such assets are accounted for as available for sale or at fair value through profit or loss.

Effective Interest Rate (paragraphs 9 and AG5-AG8)

BC30 The Board considered whether the effective interest rate for all financial instruments should be calculated on the basis of estimated cash flows (consistently with the original IAS 39) or whether the use of estimated cash flows should be restricted to groups of financial instruments with contractual cash flows being used for individual financial instruments. The Board agreed to reconfirm the position in the original IAS 39 because it achieves consistent application of the effective interest method throughout the Standard.

The Board noted that future cash flows and the expected life can be reliably estimated for most financial assets and financial liabilities, in particular for a group of similar financial assets or similar financial liabilities. However, the Board acknowledged that in some rare cases it might not be possible to estimate the timing or amount of future cash flows reliably. It therefore decided to require that if it is not possible to estimate reliably the future cash flows or the expected life of a financial instrument, the entity should use contractual cash flows over the full contractual term of the financial instrument. **BC31**

The Board also decided to clarify that expected future defaults should not be included in estimates of cash flows because this would be a departure from the incurred loss model for impairment recognition. At the same time, the Board noted that in some cases, for example, when a financial asset is acquired at a deep discount, credit losses have occurred and are reflected in the price. If an entity does not take into account such credit losses in the calculation of the effective interest rate, the entity would recognise a higher interest income than that inherent in the price paid. The Board therefore decided to clarify that such credit losses are included in the estimated cash flows when computing the effective interest rate. **BC32**

The revised IAS 39 refers to all fees "that are an integral part of the effective interest rate". The Board included this reference to clarify that IAS 39 relates only to those fees that are determined to be an integral part of the effective interest rate in accordance with IAS 18. **BC33**

Some commentators noted that it was not always clear how to interpret the requirement in the original IAS 39 that the effective interest rate must be based on discounting cash flows through maturity or the next market-based repricing date. In particular, it was not always clear whether fees, transaction costs and other premiums or discounts included in the calculation of the effective interest rate should be amortised over the period until maturity or the period to the next market-based repricing date. **BC34**

For consistency with the estimated cash flows approach, the Board decided to clarify that the effective interest rate is calculated over the expected life of the instrument or, when applicable, a shorter period. A shorter period is used when the variable (eg interest rates) to which the fee, transaction costs, discount or premium relates is repriced to market rates before the expected maturity of the instrument. In such a case, the appropriate amortisation period is the period to the next such repricing date. **BC35**

The Board identified an apparent inconsistency in the guidance in the revised IAS 39. It related to whether the revised or the original effective interest rate of a debt instrument should be applied when remeasuring the instrument's carrying amount on the cessation of fair value hedge accounting. A revised effective interest rate is calculated when fair value hedge accounting ceases. The Board removed this inconsistency as part of *Improvements to IFRSs* issued in May 2008 by clarifying that the remeasurement of an instrument in accordance with paragraph AG8 is based on the revised effective interest rate calculated in accordance with paragraph 92, when applicable, rather than the original effective interest rate.* **BC35A**

***Editor's note:** *Paragraph added in December 2008.*

Accounting for a Change in Estimates

BC36 The Board considered the accounting for a change in the estimates used in calculating the effective interest rate. The Board agreed that if an entity revises its estimates of payments or receipts, it should adjust the carrying amount of the financial instrument to reflect actual and revised estimated cash flows. The adjustment is recognised as income or expense in profit or loss. The entity recalculates the carrying amount by computing the present value of remaining cash flows at the original effective interest rate of the financial instrument. The Board noted that this approach has the practical advantage that it does not require recalculation of the effective interest rate, ie the entity simply recognises the remaining cash flows at the original rate. As a result, this approach avoids a possible conflict with the requirement when assessing impairment to discount estimated cash flows using the original effective interest rate.

EMBEDDED DERIVATIVES

Embedded Foreign Currency Derivatives (paragraphs 10 and AG33(d))

BC37 A rationale for the embedded derivatives requirements is that an entity should not be able to circumvent the recognition and measurement requirements for derivatives merely by embedding a derivative in a non-derivative financial instrument or other contract, for example, a commodity forward in a debt instrument. To achieve consistency in accounting for such embedded derivatives, all derivatives embedded in financial instruments that are not measured at fair value with gains and losses recognised in profit or loss ought to be accounted for separately as derivatives. However, as a practical expedient IAS 39 provides that an embedded derivative need not be separated if it is regarded as closely related to its host contract. When the embedded derivative bears a close economic relationship to the host contract, such as a cap or a floor on the interest rate on a loan, it is less likely that the derivative was embedded to achieve a desired accounting result.

BC38 The original IAS 39 specified that a foreign currency derivative embedded in a non-financial host contract (such as a supply contract denominated in a foreign currency) was not separated if it required payments denominated in the currency of the primary economic environment in which any substantial party to the contract operates (their functional currencies) or the currency in which the price of the related good or service that is acquired or delivered is routinely denominated in international commerce (such as the US dollar for crude oil transactions). Such foreign currency derivatives are regarded as bearing such a close economic relationship to their host contracts that they do not have to be separated.

BC39 The requirement to separate embedded foreign currency derivatives may be burdensome for entities that operate in economies in which business contracts denominated in a foreign currency are common. For example, entities domiciled in small countries may find it convenient to denominate business contracts with entities from other small countries in an internationally liquid currency (such as the US dollar, euro or yen) rather than the local currency of any of the parties to the transaction. In addition, an entity operating in a hyperinflationary economy may use a price list in a hard currency to protect against inflation, for example, an entity that has a foreign operation in a hyperinflationary economy that denominates local contracts in the functional currency of the parent.

BC40 In revising IAS 39, the Board concluded that an embedded foreign currency derivative may be integral to the contractual arrangements in the cases mentioned in the previous paragraph. It decided that a foreign currency derivative in a contract should not be required to be separated if it is denominated in a currency that is commonly used in business transactions (that are not financial instruments) in the environment in which the transaction takes place. A foreign currency derivative would be viewed as closely related to the host contract if the currency is commonly used in local business transactions, for example, when monetary amounts are viewed by the general population not in terms of the local currency but in terms of a relatively stable foreign currency, and prices may be quoted in that foreign currency (see IAS 29 *Financial Reporting in Hyperinflationary Economies**).

Inability to measure an embedded derivative separately (paragraph 12)

As described in paragraph BC11F, the Board also considered another issue related to a reclassification of a hybrid (combined) financial asset out of the fair value through profit or loss category. If the fair value of the embedded derivative that would have to be separated cannot be measured separately, the Board decided to clarify that the hybrid (combined) financial asset in its entirety should remain in the fair value through profit or loss category. The Board noted that the clarification to paragraph 12 would prevent reclassification of a hybrid (combined) financial asset out of that category between financial reporting dates, and hence avoid a requirement to reclassify the hybrid (combined) financial asset back into the fair value through profit or loss category at the end of the financial reporting period. The amendments were issued in March 2009. **BC40A**

Embedded prepayment penalties (paragraph AG30(g))

The Board identified an apparent inconsistency in the guidance in IAS 39. The inconsistency related to embedded prepayment options in which the exercise price represented a penalty for early repayment (ie prepayment) of the loan. The inconsistency related to whether these are considered closely related to the loan. **BC40B**

The Board decided to remove this inconsistency by amending paragraph AG30(g). The amendment makes an exception to the examples in paragraph AG30(g) of embedded derivatives that are not closely related to the underlying. This exception is in respect of prepayment options, the exercise prices of which compensate the lender for the loss of interest income because the loan was prepaid. This exception is conditional on the exercise price compensating the lender for loss of interest by reducing the economic loss from reinvestment risk. **BC40C**

RECOGNITION AND DERECOGNITION

Derecognition of a Financial Asset (paragraphs 15–37)

The Original IAS 39

Under the original IAS 39, several concepts governed when a financial asset should be derecognised. It was not always clear when and in what order to apply these concepts. As a result, the derecognition requirements in the original IAS 39 were not applied consistently in practice. **BC41**

****ASB footnote:*** *the ASB is implementing IAS 29 as FRS 24 (IAS 29)* Financial Reporting in Hyperinflationary Economies.

BC42 As an example, the original IAS 39 was unclear about the extent to which risks and rewards of a transferred asset should be considered for the purpose of determining whether derecognition is appropriate and how risks and rewards should be assessed. In some cases (eg transfers with total returns swaps or unconditional written put options), the Standard specifically indicated whether derecognition was appropriate, whereas in others (eg credit guarantees) it was unclear. Also, some questioned whether the assessment should focus on risks and rewards or only risks and how different risks and rewards should be aggregated and weighed.

BC43 To illustrate, assume an entity sells a portfolio of short-term receivables of CU100* and provides a guarantee to the buyer for credit losses up to a specified amount (say CU20) that is less than the total amount of the receivables, but higher than the amount of expected losses (say CU5). In this case, should (a) the entire portfolio continue to be recognised, (b) the portion that is guaranteed continue to be recognised or (c) the portfolio be derecognised in full and a guarantee be recognised as a financial liability? The original IAS 39 did not give a clear answer and the IAS 39 Implementation Guidance Committee—a group set up by the Board's predecessor body to resolve interpretive issues raised in practice—was unable to reach an agreement on how IAS 39 should be applied in this case. In developing proposals for improvements to IAS 39, the Board concluded that it was important that IAS 39 should provide clear and consistent guidance on how to account for such a transaction.

Exposure Draft

BC44 To resolve the problems, the Exposure Draft proposed an approach to derecognition under which a transferor of a financial asset continues to recognise that asset to the extent the transferor has a continuing involvement in it. Continuing involvement could be established in two ways: (a) a reacquisition provision (such as a call option, put option or repurchase agreement) and (b) a provision to pay or receive compensation based on changes in value of the transferred asset (such as a credit guarantee or net cash settled option).

BC45 The purpose of the approach proposed in the Exposure Draft was to facilitate consistent implementation and application of IAS 39 by eliminating conflicting concepts and establishing an unambiguous, more internally consistent and workable approach to derecognition. The main benefits of the proposed approach were that it would greatly clarify IAS 39 and provide transparency on the face of the balance sheet about any continuing involvement in a transferred asset.

Comments Received

BC46 Many respondents agreed that there were inconsistencies in the existing derecognition requirements in IAS 39. However, there was limited support for the continuing involvement approach proposed in the Exposure Draft. Respondents expressed conceptual and practical concerns, including:

(a) any benefits of the proposed changes did not outweigh the burden of adopting a different approach that had its own set of (as yet unidentified and unsolved) problems;

(b) the proposed approach was a fundamental change from that in the original IAS 39;

(c) the proposal did not achieve convergence with US GAAP;

(d) the proposal was untested; and

**In this Basis for Conclusions, monetary amounts are denominated in 'currency units' (CU).*

(e) the proposal was not consistent with the *Framework**

Many respondents expressed the view that the basic approach in the original IAS 39 should be retained in the revised Standard and the inconsistencies removed. The reasons included: (a) the existing IAS 39 was proven to be reasonable in concept and operational in practice and (b) the approach should not be changed until the Board developed an alternative comprehensive approach. **BC47**

Revisions to IAS 39

In response to the comments received, the Board decided to revert to the derecognition concepts in the original IAS 39 and to clarify how and in what order the concepts should be applied. In particular, the Board decided that an evaluation of the transfer of risks and rewards should precede an evaluation of the transfer of control for all types of transactions. **BC48**

Although the structure and wording of the derecognition requirements have been substantially amended, the Board concluded that the requirements in the revised IAS 39 are not substantially different from those in the original IAS 39. In support of this conclusion, it noted that the application of the requirements in the revised IAS 39 generally results in answers that could have been obtained under the original IAS 39. In addition, although there will be a need to apply judgement to evaluate whether substantially all risks and rewards have been retained, this type of judgement is not new compared with the original IAS 39. However, the revised requirements clarify the application of the concepts in circumstances in which it was previously unclear how IAS 39 should be applied. The Board concluded that it would be inappropriate to revert to the original IAS 39 without such clarifications. **BC49**

The Board also decided to include guidance in the Standard that clarifies how to evaluate the concepts of risks and rewards and of control. The Board regards such guidance as important to provide a framework for applying the concepts in IAS 39. Although judgement is still necessary to apply the concepts in practice, the guidance should increase consistency in how the concepts are applied. **BC50**

More specifically, the Board decided that the transfer of risks and rewards should be evaluated by comparing the entity's exposure before and after the transfer to the variability in the amounts and timing of the net cash flows of the transferred asset. If the entity's exposure, on a present value basis, has not changed significantly, the entity would conclude that it has retained substantially all risks and rewards. In this case, the Board concluded that the asset should continue to be recognised. This accounting treatment is consistent with the treatment of repurchase transactions and some assets subject to deep in-the-money options under the original IAS 39. It is also consistent with how some interpreted the original IAS 39 when an entity sells a portfolio of short-term receivables but retains all substantive risks through the issue of a guarantee to compensate for all expected credit losses (see the example in paragraph BC43). **BC51**

The Board decided that control should be evaluated by looking to whether the transferee has the practical ability to sell the asset. If the transferee can sell the asset (eg because the asset is readily obtainable in the market and the transferee can obtain a replacement asset should it need to return the asset to the transferor), the transferor has not retained control because the transferor does not control the transferee's use **BC52**

ASB footnote: The equivalent document in the UK and Republic of Ireland to the IASB's* Framework *is the ASB's* Statement of Principles for Financial Reporting. *Although the Statement of Principles is very similar to the Framework, it is not identical.*

of the asset. If the transferee cannot sell the asset (eg because the transferor has a call option and the asset is not readily obtainable in the market, so that the transferee cannot obtain a replacement asset), the transferor has retained control because the transferee is not free to use the asset as its own.

BC53 The original IAS 39 also did not contain guidance on when a part of a financial asset could be considered for derecognition. The Board decided to include such guidance in the Standard to clarify the issue. It decided that an entity should apply the derecognition principles to a part of a financial asset only if that part contains no risks and rewards relating to the part not being considered for derecognition. Accordingly, a part of a financial asset is considered for derecognition only if it comprises:

(a) only specifically identified cash flows from a financial asset (or a group of similar financial assets);
(b) only a fully proportionate (pro rata) share of the cash flows from a financial asset (or a group of similar financial assets); or
(c) only a fully proportionate (pro rata) share of specifically identified cash flows from a financial asset (or a group of similar financial assets).

In all other cases the derecognition principles are applied to the financial asset in its entirety.

Arrangements Under Which an Entity Retains the Contractual Rights to Receive the Cash Flows of a Financial Asset but Assumes a Contractual Obligation to Pay the Cash Flows to One or More Recipients (paragraph 19)

BC54 The original IAS 39 did not provide explicit guidance about the extent to which derecognition is appropriate for contractual arrangements in which an entity retains its contractual right to receive the cash flows from an asset, but assumes a contractual obligation to pay those cash flows to another entity (a 'pass-through arrangement'). Questions were raised in practice about the appropriate accounting treatment and divergent interpretations evolved for more complex structures.

BC55 To illustrate the issue using a simple example, assume the following. Entity A makes a five-year interest-bearing loan (the 'original asset') of CU100 to Entity B. Entity A then enters into an agreement with Entity C in which, in exchange for a cash payment of CU90, Entity A agrees to pass to Entity C 90 per cent of all principal and interest payments collected from Entity B (as, when and if collected). Entity A accepts no obligation to make any payments to Entity C other than 90 per cent of exactly what has been received from Entity B. Entity A provides no guarantee to Entity C about the performance of the loan and has no rights to retain 90 per cent of the cash collected from Entity B nor any obligation to pay cash to Entity C if cash has not been received from Entity B. In the example above, does Entity A have a loan asset of CU100 and a liability of CU90 or does it have an asset of CU10? To make the example more complex, what if Entity A first transfers the loan to a consolidated special purpose entity (SPE), which in turn passes through to investors the cash flows from the asset? Does the accounting treatment change because Entity A first sold the asset to an SPE?

BC56 To address these issues, the Exposure Draft of proposed amendments to IAS 39 included guidance to clarify under which conditions pass-through arrangements can be treated as a transfer of the underlying financial asset. The Board concluded that an entity does not have an asset and a liability, as defined in the *Framework*, when it enters into an arrangement to pass through cash flows from an asset and that arrangement meets specified conditions. In these cases, the entity acts more as an agent of the eventual recipients of the cash flows than as an owner of the asset. Accordingly, to the extent that those conditions are met the arrangement is treated as a transfer and considered for derecognition even though the entity may continue to collect cash flows from the asset. Conversely, to the extent the conditions are not met, the entity acts more as an owner of the asset with the result that the asset should continue to be recognised.

Respondents to the Exposure Draft were generally supportive of the proposed changes. Some respondents asked for further clarification of the requirements and the interaction with the requirements for consolidation of special purpose entities (in SIC-12)*. Respondents in the securitisation industry noted that under the proposed guidance many securitisation structures would not qualify for derecognition. **BC57**

Considering these and other comments, the Board decided to proceed with its proposals to issue guidance on pass-through arrangements and to clarify that guidance in finalising the revised IAS 39. **BC58**

The Board concluded that the following three conditions must be met for treating a contractual arrangement to pass through cash flows from a financial asset as a transfer of that asset: **BC59**

(a) The entity has no obligation to pay amounts to the eventual recipients unless it collects equivalent amounts from the original asset. However, the entity is allowed to make short-term advances to the eventual recipient so long as it has the right of full recovery of the amount lent plus accrued interest.
(b) The entity is prohibited by the terms of the transfer contract from selling or pledging the original asset other than as security to the eventual recipients for the obligation to pay them cash flows.
(c) The entity has an obligation to remit any cash flows it collects on behalf of the eventual recipients without material delay. In addition, during the short settlement period, the entity is not entitled to reinvest such cash flows except for investments in cash or cash equivalents and where any interest earned from such investments is remitted to the eventual recipients.

These conditions follow from the definitions of assets and liabilities in the *Framework*. Condition (a) indicates that the transferor has no liability (because there is no present obligation to pay cash), and conditions (b) and (c) indicate that the transferor has no asset (because the transferor does not control the future economic benefits associated with the transferred asset). **BC60**

The Board decided that the derecognition tests that apply to other transfers of financial assets (ie the tests of transferring substantially all the risks and rewards and control) should also apply to arrangements to pass through cash flows that meet the three conditions but do not involve a fully proportional share of all or specifically identified cash flows. Thus, if the three conditions are met and the entity passes on a fully proportional share, either of all cash flows (as in the example in paragraph BC55) or of specifically identified cash flows (eg 10 per cent of all interest cash flows), the proportion sold is derecognised, provided the entity has transferred substantially all the risks and rewards of ownership. Thus, in the example in paragraph BC55, Entity A would report a loan asset of CU10 and derecognise CU90. Similarly, if an entity enters into an arrangement that meets the three conditions above, but the arrangement is not on a fully proportionate basis, the contractual arrangement **BC61**

* ***ASB footnote**: under FRS 26, special purpose entities are consolidated if they meet the definition of subsidiary undertaking in FRS 2 'Accounting for Subsidiary Undertakings' or quasi-subsidiary in FRS 5 'Reporting the Substance of Transactions'.*

would have to meet the general derecognition conditions to qualify for derecognition. This ensures consistency in the application of the derecognition model, whether a transaction is structured as a transfer of the contractual right to receive the cash flows of a financial asset or as an arrangement to pass through cash flows.

BC62 To illustrate a disproportionate arrangement using a simple example, assume the following. Entity A originates a portfolio of five-year interest-bearing loans of CU10,000. Entity A then enters into an agreement with Entity C in which, in exchange for a cash payment of CU9,000, Entity A agrees to pay to Entity C the first CU9,000 (plus interest) of cash collected from the loan portfolio. Entity A retains rights to the last CU1,000 (plus interest), ie it retains a subordinated residual interest. If Entity A collects, say, only CU8,000 of its loans of CU10,000 because some debtors default, Entity A would pass on to Entity C all of the CU8,000 collected and Entity A keeps nothing of the CU8,000 collected. If Entity A collects CU9,500, it passes CU9,000 to Entity C and retains CU500. In this case, if Entity A retains substantially all the risks and rewards of ownership because the subordinated retained interest absorbs all of the likely variability in net cash flows, the loans continue to be recognised in their entirety even if the three pass-through conditions are met.

BC63 The Board recognises that many securitisations may fail to qualify for derecognition either because one or more of the three conditions in paragraph 19 are not met or because the entity has retained substantially all the risks and rewards of ownership.

BC64 Whether a transfer of a financial asset qualifies for derecognition does not differ depending on whether the transfer is direct to investors or through a consolidated SPE or trust that obtains the financial assets and, in turn, transfers a portion of those financial assets to third party investors.

Transfers that Do Not Qualify for Derecognition (paragraph 29)

BC65 The original IAS 39 did not provide guidance about how to account for a transfer of a financial asset that does not qualify for derecognition. The amendments include such guidance. To ensure that the accounting reflects the rights and obligations that the transferor has in relation to the transferred asset, there is a need to consider the accounting for the asset as well as the accounting for the associated liability.

BC66 When an entity retains substantially all the risks and rewards of the asset (eg in a repurchase transaction), there are generally no special accounting considerations because the entity retains upside and downside exposure to gains and losses resulting from the transferred asset. Therefore, the asset continues to be recognised in its entirety and the proceeds received are recognised as a liability. Similarly, the entity continues to recognise any income from the asset along with any expense incurred on the associated liability.

Continuing Involvement in a Transferred Asset (paragraphs 30–35)

BC67 The Board decided that if the entity determines that it has neither retained nor transferred substantially all of the risks and rewards of an asset and that it has retained control, the entity should continue to recognise the asset to the extent of its continuing involvement. This is to reflect the transferor's continuing exposure to the risks and rewards of the asset and that this exposure is not related to the entire asset, but is limited in amount. The Board noted that precluding derecognition to the extent of the continuing involvement is useful to users of financial statements in such cases, because it reflects the entity's retained exposure to the risks and rewards of the financial asset better than full derecognition.

When the entity transfers some significant risks and rewards and retains others and derecognition is precluded because the entity retains control of the transferred asset, the entity no longer retains all the upside and downside exposure to gains and losses resulting from the transferred asset. Therefore, the revised IAS 39 requires the asset and the associated liability to be measured in a way that ensures that any changes in value of the transferred asset that are not attributed to the entity are not recognised by the entity. **BC68**

For example, special measurement and income recognition issues arise if derecognition is precluded because the transferor has retained a call option or written a put option and the asset is measured at fair value. In those situations, in the absence of additional guidance, application of the general measurement and income recognition requirements for financial assets and financial liabilities in IAS 39 may result in accounting that does not represent the transferor's rights and obligations related to the transfer. **BC69**

As another example, if the transferor retains a call option on a transferred available-for-sale financial asset and the fair value of the asset decreases below the exercise price, the transferor does not suffer a loss because it has no obligation to exercise the call option. In that case, the Board decided that it is appropriate to adjust the measurement of the liability to reflect that the transferor has no exposure to decreases in the fair value of the asset below the option exercise price. Similarly, if a transferor writes a put option and the fair value of the asset exceeds the exercise price, the transferee need not exercise the put. Because the transferor has no right to increases in the fair value of the asset above the option exercise price, it is appropriate to measure the asset at the lower of (a) the option exercise price and (b) the fair value of the asset. **BC70**

MEASUREMENT

Definitions (paragraph 9)

The definition of a financial asset or financial liability at fair value through profit or loss excludes derivatives that are designated and effective hedging instruments. Paragraph 50 of IAS 39 prohibits the reclassification of financial instruments into or out of the fair value through profit or loss category after initial recognition. The Board noted that the prohibition on reclassification in paragraph 50 might be read by some as preventing a derivative financial instrument that becomes a designated and effective hedging instrument from being excluded from the fair value through profit or loss category in accordance with the definition. Similarly, it might be read as preventing a derivative that ceases to be a designated and effective hedging instrument from being accounted for at fair value through profit or loss.* **BC70A**

The Board decided that the prohibition on reclassification in paragraph 50 should not prevent a derivative from being accounted for at fair value through profit or loss when it does not qualify for hedge accounting and vice versa. Therefore, in *Improvements to IFRSs* issued in May 2008, the Board amended the definitions in paragraph 9(a) and added paragraph 50A to address this point. **BC70B**

* ***Editor's note****: Paragraphs BC70A and BC70B added in December 2008.*

Fair Value Option (paragraph 9)*

BC71 The Board concluded that it could simplify the application of IAS 39 (as revised in 2000) for some entities by permitting the use of fair value measurement for any financial instrument. With one exception (see paragraph 9), this greater use of fair value is optional. The fair value option does not require entities to measure more financial instruments at fair value.

BC72 IAS 39 (as revised in 2000) did not permit an entity to measure particular categories of financial instruments at fair value with changes in fair value recognised in profit or loss. Examples included:

(a) originated loans and receivables, including a debt instrument acquired directly from the issuer, unless they met the conditions for classification as held for trading in paragraph 9.
(b) financial assets classified as available for sale, unless as an accounting policy choice gains and losses on all available-for-sale financial assets were recognised in profit or loss or they met the conditions for classification as held for trading in paragraph 9.
(c) non-derivative financial liabilities, even if the entity had a policy and practice of actively repurchasing such liabilities or they formed part of an arbitrage/customer facilitation strategy or fund trading activities.

BC73 The Board decided in IAS 39 (as revised in 2003) to permit entities to designate irrevocably on initial recognition any financial instruments as ones to be measured at fair value with gains and losses recognised in profit or loss ('fair value through profit or loss'). To impose discipline on this approach, the Board decided that financial instruments should not be reclassified into or out of the category of fair value through profit or loss. In particular, some comments received on the Exposure Draft of proposed amendments to IAS 39 published in June 2002 suggested that entities could use the fair value option to recognise selectively changes in fair value in profit or loss. The Board noted that the requirement to designate irrevocably on initial recognition the financial instruments for which the fair value option is to be applied results in an entity being unable to 'cherry pick' in this way. This is because it will not be known at initial recognition whether the fair value of the instrument will increase or decrease.

BC73A Following the issue of IAS 39 (as revised in 2003), as a result of continuing discussions with constituents on the fair value option, the Board became aware that some, including prudential supervisors of banks, securities companies and insurers, were concerned that the fair value option might be used inappropriately (as discussed in paragraph BC11C). In response to those concerns, the Board published in April 2004 an Exposure Draft of proposed restrictions to the fair value option contained in IAS 39 (as revised in 2003). After discussing comments received from constituents and a series of public roundtable meetings, the Board issued an amendment to IAS 39 in June 2005 permitting entities to designate irrevocably on initial recognition financial instruments that meet one of three conditions (see paragraphs 9(b)(i), 9(b)(ii) and 11A) as ones to be measured at fair value through profit or loss.

BC74 In the amendment to the fair value option, the Board identified three situations in which permitting designation at fair value through profit or loss either results in more relevant information (cases (a) and (b) below) or is justified on the grounds of

****Editor's note:*** *whole section amended with effect from 1 January 2006.*

reducing complexity or increasing measurement reliability (case (c) below). These are:

(a) when such designation eliminates or significantly reduces a measurement or recognition inconsistency (sometimes referred to as an 'accounting mismatch') that would otherwise arise (paragraphs BC75-BC75B);
(b) when a group of financial assets, financial liabilities or both is managed and its performance is evaluated on a fair value basis, in accordance with a documented risk management or investment strategy (paragraphs BC76-BC76B); and
(c) when an instrument contains an embedded derivative that meets particular conditions (paragraphs BC77-BC78).

The ability for entities to use the fair value option simplifies the application of IAS 39 by mitigating some anomalies that result from the different measurement attributes in the Standard. In particular, for financial instruments designated in this way: **BC74A**

(a) it eliminates the need for hedge accounting for hedges of fair value exposures when there are natural offsets, and thereby eliminates the related burden of designating, tracking and analysing hedge effectiveness.
(b) it eliminates the burden of separating embedded derivatives.
(c) it eliminates problems arising from a mixed measurement model when financial assets are measured at fair value and related financial liabilities are measured at amortised cost. In particular, it eliminates volatility in profit or loss and equity that results when matched positions of financial assets and financial liabilities are not measured consistently.
(d) the option to recognise unrealised gains and losses on available for-sale financial assets in profit or loss is no longer necessary.
(e) it de-emphasises interpretative issues around what constitutes trading.

Designation as at fair value through profit or loss eliminates or significantly reduces a measurement or recognition inconsistency (paragraph 9(b)(i))

IAS 39, like comparable standards in some national jurisdictions, imposes a mixed-attribute measurement model. It requires some financial assets and liabilities to be measured at fair value, and others to be measured at amortised cost. It requires some gains and losses to be recognised in profit or loss, and others to be recognised initially as a component of equity.* This combination of measurement and recognition requirements can result in inconsistencies, which some refer to as 'accounting mismatches', between the accounting for an asset (or group of assets) and a liability (or group of liabilities). The notion of an accounting mismatch necessarily involves two propositions. First, an entity has particular assets and liabilities that are measured, or on which gains and losses are recognised, inconsistently; second, there is a perceived economic relationship between those assets and liabilities. For example, a liability may be considered to be related to an asset when they share a risk that gives rise to opposite changes in fair value that tend to offset, or when the entity considers that the liability funds the asset. **BC75**

Some entities can overcome measurement or recognition inconsistencies by using hedge accounting or, in the case of insurers, shadow accounting. However, the Board recognises that those techniques are complex and do not address all situations. In developing the amendment to the fair value option, the Board considered whether **BC75A**

**As a consequence of the revision of IAS 1* Presentation of Financial Statements *in 2007 these other gains and losses are recognised in other comprehensive income.*

it should impose conditions to limit the situations in which an entity could use the option to eliminate an accounting mismatch. For example, it considered whether entities should be required to demonstrate that particular assets and liabilities are managed together, or that a management strategy is effective in reducing risk (as is required for hedge accounting to be used), or that hedge accounting or other ways of overcoming the inconsistency are not available.

BC75B The Board concluded that accounting mismatches arise in a wide variety of circumstances. In the Board's view, financial reporting is best served by providing entities with the opportunity to eliminate perceived accounting mismatches whenever that results in more relevant information. Furthermore, the Board concluded that the fair value option may validly be used in place of hedge accounting for hedges of fair value exposures, thereby eliminating the related burden of designating, tracking and analysing hedge effectiveness. Hence, the Board decided not to develop detailed prescriptive guidance about when the fair value option could be applied (such as requiring effectiveness tests similar to those required for hedge accounting) in the amendment on the fair value option. Rather, the Board decided to require disclosures in IAS 32* about:

- the criteria an entity uses for designating financial assets and financial liabilities as at fair value through profit or loss
- how the entity satisfies the conditions in this Standard for such designation
- the nature of the assets and liabilities so designated
- the effect on the financial statement of using this designation, namely the carrying amounts and net gains and losses on assets and liabilities so designated, information about the effect of changes in a financial liability's credit quality on changes in its fair value, and information about the credit risk of loans or receivables and any related credit derivatives or similar instruments.

A group of financial assets, financial liabilities or both is managed and its performance is evaluated on a fair value basis, in accordance with a documented risk management or investment strategy (paragraph 9(b)(ii))

BC76 The Standard requires financial instruments to be measured at fair value through profit or loss in only two situations, namely when an instrument is held for trading or when it contains an embedded derivative that the entity is unable to measure separately. However, the Board recognised that some entities manage and evaluate the performance of financial instruments on a fair value basis in other situations. Furthermore, for instruments managed and evaluated in this way, users of financial statements may regard fair value measurement as providing more relevant information. Finally, it is established practice in some industries in some jurisdictions to recognise all financial assets at fair value through profit or loss. (This practice was permitted for many assets in IAS 39 (as revised in 2000) as an accounting policy choice in accordance with which gains and losses on all available-for-sale financial assets were reported in profit or loss.)

BC76A In the amendment to IAS 39 relating to the fair value option issued in June 2005, the Board decided to permit financial instruments managed and evaluated on a fair value basis to be measured at fair value through profit or loss. The Board also decided to introduce two requirements to make this category operational. These requirements are that the financial instruments are managed and evaluated on a fair value basis in accordance with a documented risk management or investment strategy, and that

*ASB Footnote: *In the UK IAS 32 is implemented as FRS 25* Financial Instruments: Disclosure and Presentation.

information about the financial instruments is provided internally on that basis to the entity's key management personnel.

In looking to an entity's documented risk management or investment strategy, the Board makes no judgement on what an entity's strategy should be. However, the Board noted that users, in making economic decisions, would find useful both a description of the chosen strategy and how designation at fair value through profit or loss is consistent with it. Accordingly, IAS 32 requires such disclosures. The Board also noted that the required documentation of the entity's strategy need not be on an item-by-item basis, nor need it be in the level of detail required for hedge accounting. However, it should be sufficient to demonstrate that using the fair value option is consistent with the entity's risk management or investment strategy. In many cases, the entity's existing documentation, as approved by its key management personnel, should be sufficient for this purpose. **BC76B**

The instrument contains an embedded derivative that meets particular conditions (paragraph 11A)

The Standard requires virtually all derivative financial instruments to be measured at fair value. This requirement extends to derivatives that are *embedded* in an instrument that also includes a non-derivative host contract if the embedded derivative meets the conditions in paragraph 11. Conversely, if the embedded derivative does not meet those conditions, separate accounting with measurement of the embedded derivative at fair value is prohibited. Therefore, to satisfy these requirements, the entity must: **BC77**

(a) identify whether the instrument contains one or more embedded derivatives,
(b) determine whether each embedded derivative is one that must be separated from the host instrument or one for which separation is prohibited, and
(c) if the embedded derivative is one that must be separated, determine its fair value at initial recognition and subsequently.

For some embedded derivatives, like the prepayment option in an ordinary residential mortgage, this process is fairly simple. However, entities with more complex instruments have reported that the search for and analysis of embedded derivatives (steps (a) and (b) in paragraph BC77) significantly increase the cost of complying with the Standard. They report that this cost could be eliminated if they had the option to fair value the combined contract. **BC77A**

Other entities report that one of the most common uses of the fair value option is likely to be for structured products that contain several embedded derivatives. Those structured products will typically be hedged with derivatives that offset all (or nearly all) of the risks they contain, whether or not the embedded derivatives that give rise to those risks are separated for accounting purposes. Hence, the simplest way to account for such products is to apply the fair value option so that the combined contract (as well as the derivatives that hedge it) is measured at fair value through profit or loss. Furthermore, for these more complex instruments, the fair value of the combined contract may be significantly easier to measure and hence be more reliable than the fair value of only those embedded derivatives that IAS 39 requires to be separated. **BC77B**

The Board sought to strike a balance between reducing the costs of complying with the embedded derivatives provisions of this Standard and the need to respond to the concerns expressed regarding possible inappropriate use of the fair value option. The Board determined that allowing the fair value option to be used for *any* instrument with an embedded derivative would make other restrictions on the use of the option **BC78** ineffective, because many financial instruments include an embedded derivative. In contrast, limiting the use of the fair value option to situations in which the embedded derivative must otherwise be separated would not significantly reduce the costs of compliance and could result in less reliable measures being included in the financial statements. Therefore, the Board decided to specify situations in which an entity cannot justify using the fair value option in place of assessing embedded derivatives—when the embedded derivative does not significantly modify the cash flows that would otherwise be required by the contract or is one for which it is clear with little or no analysis when a similar hybrid instrument is first considered that separation is prohibited.

The role of prudential supervisors

BC78A The Board considered the circumstances of regulated financial institutions such as banks and insurers in determining the extent to which conditions should be placed on the use of the fair value option. The Board recognised that regulated financial institutions are extensive holders and issuers of financial instruments and so are likely to be among the largest potential users of the fair value option. However, the Board noted that some of the prudential supervisors that oversee these entities expressed concern that the fair value option might be used inappropriately.

BC79 The Board noted that the primary objective of prudential supervisors is to maintain the financial soundness of individual financial institutions and the stability of the financial system as a whole. Prudential supervisors achieve this objective partly by assessing the risk profile of each regulated institution and imposing a risk-based capital requirement.

BC79A The Board noted that these objectives of prudential supervision differ from the objectives of general purpose financial reporting. The latter is intended to provide information about the financial position, performance and changes in financial position of an entity that is useful to a wide range of users in making economic decisions. However, the Board acknowledged that for the purposes of determining what level of capital an institution should maintain, prudential supervisors may wish to understand the circumstances in which a regulated financial institution has chosen to apply the fair value option and evaluate the rigour of the institution's fair value measurement practices and the robustness of its underlying risk management strategies, policies and practices. Furthermore, the Board agreed that certain disclosures would assist both prudential supervisors in their evaluation of capital requirements and investors in making economic decisions. In particular, the Board decided to require an entity to disclose how it has satisfied the conditions in paragraphs 9(b), 11A and 12 for using the fair value option, including, for instruments within paragraph 9(b)(ii), a narrative description of how designation at fair value through profit or loss is consistent with the entity's documented risk management or investment strategy.

Other matters

BC80 IAS 39 (as revised in 2000) contained an accounting policy choice for the recognition of gains and losses on available-for-sale financial assets—such gains and losses could be recognised either in equity or in profit or loss. The Board concluded that the fair value option removed the need for such an accounting policy choice. An entity can achieve recognition of gains and losses on such assets in profit or loss in appropriate cases by using the fair value option. Accordingly, the Board decided that the choice that was in IAS 39 (as revised in 2000) should be removed and that gains and losses on available-for-sale financial assets should be recognised in equity when IAS 39 was revised in 2003.

The fair value option permits (but does not require) entities to measure financial instruments at fair value with changes in fair value recognised in profit or loss. Accordingly, it does not restrict an entity's ability to use other accounting methods (such as amortised cost). Some respondents to the Exposure Draft of proposed amendments to IAS 39 published in June 2002 would have preferred more pervasive changes to expand the use of fair values and limit the choices available to entities, such as the elimination of the held-to-maturity category or the cash flow hedge accounting approach. Although such changes have the potential to make the principles in IAS 39 more coherent and less complex, the Board did not consider such changes as part of the project to improve IAS 39. **BC80A**

Comments received on the Exposure Draft of proposed amendments to IAS 39 published in June 2002 also questioned the proposal that all items measured at fair value through profit or loss should have the descriptor 'held for trading'. Some comments noted that 'held for trading' is commonly used with a narrower meaning, and it may be confusing for users if instruments designated at fair value through profit or loss are also called 'held for trading'. Therefore, the Board considered using a fifth category of financial instruments—'fair value through profit or loss'—to distinguish those instruments to which the fair value option was applied from those classified as held for trading. The Board rejected this possibility because it believed that adding a fifth category of financial instruments would unnecessarily complicate the Standard. Rather, the Board concluded that 'fair value through profit or loss' should be used to describe a category that encompasses financial instruments classified as held for trading and those to which the fair value option is applied. **BC81**

The Board also decided to include in IAS 39 (as revised in 2003) the ability for entities to designate a loan or receivable as available for sale (see paragraph 9). The Board decided that, in the context of the existing mixed measurement model, there are no reasons to limit to any particular type of asset the ability to designate an asset as available for sale. **BC84**

Application of the Fair Value Option to a Component or a Proportion (Rather than the Entirety) of a Financial Asset or a Financial Liability

Some comments received on the Exposure Draft of proposed amendments to IAS 39 published in June 2002 argued that the fair value option should be extended so that it could also be applied to a component of a financial asset or a financial liability (eg changes in fair value attributable to one risk such as changes in a benchmark interest rate). The arguments included (a) concerns regarding inclusion of own credit risk in the measurement of financial liabilities and (b) the prohibition on using non-derivatives as hedging instruments (cash instrument hedging). **BC85**

The Board concluded that IAS 39 should not extend the fair value option to components of financial assets or financial liabilities. It was concerned (a) about difficulties in measuring the change in value of the component because of ordering issues and joint effects (ie if the component is affected by more than one risk, it may be difficult to isolate accurately and measure the component); (b) that the amounts recognised in the balance sheet would be neither fair value nor cost; and (c) that a fair value adjustment for a component may move the carrying amount of an instrument away from its fair value. In finalising the 2003 amendments to IAS 39, the Board separately considered the issue of cash instrument hedging (see paragraphs BC144 and BC145). **BC86**

BC86A Other comments received on the April 2004 Exposure Draft of proposed restrictions to the fair value option contained in IAS 39 (as revised in 2003) suggested that the fair value option should be extended so that it could be applied to a proportion (ie a percentage) of a financial asset or financial liability. The Board was concerned that such an extension would require prescriptive guidance on how to determine a proportion. For example if an entity were to issue a bond totalling CU100 million in the form of 100 certificates each of CU1 million, would a proportion of 10 per cent be identified as 10 per cent of each certificate, CU10 million specified certificates, the first (or last) CU10 million certificates to be redeemed, or on some other basis? The Board was also concerned that the remaining proportion, not being subject to the fair value option, could give rise to incentives for an entity to 'cherry pick' (ie to realise financial assets or financial liabilities selectively so as to achieve a desired accounting result). For these reasons, the Board decided not to allow the fair value option to be applied to a proportion of a single financial asset or financial liability. However, if an entity simultaneously issues two or more identical financial instruments, it is not precluded from designating only some of those instruments as being subject to the fair value option (for example, if doing so achieves a significant reduction in a recognition or measurement inconsistency, as explained in paragraph AG4G). Thus, in the above example, the entity could designate CU10 million specified certificates if to do so would meet one of the three criteria in paragraph BC74.

Credit Risk of Liabilities

BC87 The Board discussed the issue of including changes in the credit risk of a financial liability in its fair value measurement. It considered responses to the Exposure Draft of proposed amendments to IAS 39 published in June 2002 that expressed concern about the effect of including this component in the fair value measurement and that suggested the fair value option should be restricted to exclude all or some financial liabilities. However, the Board concluded that the fair value option could be applied to any financial liability, and decided not to restrict the option in the Standard (as revised in 2003) because to do so would negate some of the benefits of the fair value option set out in paragraph BC74A.

BC88 The Board considered comments on the same Exposure Draft that disagreed with the view that, in applying the fair value option to financial liabilities, an entity should recognise income as a result of deteriorating credit quality (and a loan expense as a result of improving credit quality). Commentators noted that it is not useful to report lower liabilities when an entity is in financial difficulty precisely because its debt levels are too high, and that it would be difficult to explain to users of financial statements the reasons why income would be recognised when a liability's creditworthiness deteriorates. These comments suggested that fair value should exclude the effects of changes in the instrument's credit risk.

BC89 However, the Board noted that because financial statements are prepared on a going concern basis, credit risk affects the value at which liabilities could be repurchased or settled. Accordingly, the fair value of a financial liability reflects the credit risk relating to that liability. Therefore, it decided to include credit risk relating to a financial liability in the fair value measurement of that liability for the following reasons:

(a) entities realise changes in fair value, including fair value attributable to the liability's credit risk, for example, by renegotiating or repurchasing liabilities or by using derivatives;

(b) changes in credit risk affect the observed market price of a financial liability and hence its fair value;

(c) it is difficult from a practical standpoint to exclude changes in credit risk from an observed market price; and
(d) the fair value of a financial liability (ie the price of that liability in an exchange between a knowledgeable, willing buyer and a knowledgeable, willing seller) on initial recognition reflects its credit risk. The Board believes that it is inappropriate to include credit risk in the initial fair value measurement of financial liabilities, but not subsequently.

The Board also considered whether the component of the fair value of a financial liability attributable to changes in credit quality should be specifically disclosed, separately presented in the income statement, or separately presented in equity. The Board decided that whilst separately presenting or disclosing such changes might be difficult in practice, disclosure of such information would be useful to users of financial statements and would help alleviate the concerns expressed. Therefore, it decided to include in IAS 32* a disclosure to help identify the changes in the fair value of a financial liability that arise from changes in the liability's credit risk. The Board believes this is a reasonable proxy for the change in fair value that is attributable to changes in the liability's credit risk, in particular when such changes are large, and will provide users with information with which to understand the profit or loss effect of such a change in credit risk. **BC90**

The Board decided to clarify that this issue relates to the credit risk of the financial liability, rather than the creditworthiness of the entity. The Board noted that this more appropriately describes the objective of what is included in the fair value measurement of financial liabilities. **BC91**

The Board also noted that the fair value of liabilities secured by valuable collateral, guaranteed by third parties or ranking ahead of virtually all other liabilities is generally unaffected by changes in the entity's creditworthiness. **BC92**

Measurement of Financial Liabilities with a Demand Feature

Some comments received on the Exposure Draft requested clarification of how to determine fair value for financial liabilities with a demand feature (eg demand deposits), when the fair value measurement option is applied or the liability is otherwise measured at fair value. In other words, could the fair value be less than the amount payable on demand, discounted from the first date that an amount could be required to be paid (the 'demand amount'), such as the amount of the deposit discounted for the period that the entity expects the deposit to be outstanding? Some commentators believe that the fair value of financial liabilities with a demand feature is less than the demand amount, for reasons that include the consistency of such measurement with how those financial liabilities are treated for risk management purposes. **BC93**

The Board agreed that this issue should be clarified in IAS 39. It confirmed that the fair value of a financial liability with a demand feature is not less than the amount payable on demand discounted from the first date that the amount could be required to be paid. This conclusion is the same as in the original IAS 32. The Board noted that in many cases, the market price observed for such financial liabilities is the price at which they are originated between the customer and the deposit-taker—ie the demand amount. It also noted that recognising a financial liability with a demand **BC94**

In August 2005, the IASB relocated all disclosures relating to financial instruments to IFRS 7* Financial Instruments: Disclosures. ***ASB footnote**: In December 2005, the ASB similarly relocated all disclosures relating to financial instruments to FRS 29.*

feature at less than the demand amount would give rise to an immediate gain on the origination of such a deposit, which the Board believes is inappropriate.

Fair Value Measurement Guidance (paragraphs AG69-AG82)

BC95 The Board decided to include in the revised IAS 39 expanded guidance about how to determine fair values, in particular for financial instruments for which no quoted market price is available (Appendix A paragraphs AG74-AG82). The Board decided that it is desirable to provide clear and reasonably detailed guidance about the objective and use of valuation techniques to achieve reliable and comparable fair value estimates when financial instruments are measured at fair value.

Use of Quoted Prices in Active Markets (paragraphs AG71-AG73)

BC96 The Board considered comments received that disagreed with the proposal in the Exposure Draft that a quoted price is the appropriate measure of fair value for an instrument quoted in an active market. Some respondents argued that (a) valuation techniques are more appropriate for measuring fair value than a quoted price in an active market (eg for derivatives) and (b) valuation models are consistent with industry best practice, and are justified because of their acceptance for regulatory capital purposes.

BC97 However, the Board confirmed that a quoted price is the appropriate measure of fair value for an instrument quoted in an active market, notably because (a) in an active market, the quoted price is the best evidence of fair value, given that fair value is defined in terms of a price agreed by a knowledgeable, willing buyer and a knowledgeable, willing seller; (b) it results in consistent measurement across entities; and (c) fair value as defined in the Standard does not depend on entityspecific factors. The Board further clarified that a quoted price includes market-quoted rates as well as prices.

Entities that have access to more than one active market (paragraph AG71)

BC98 The Board considered situations in which entities operate in different markets. An example is a trader that originates a derivative with a corporate in an active corporate retail market and offsets the derivative by taking out a derivative with a dealer in an active dealers' wholesale market. The Board decided to clarify that the objective of fair value measurement is to arrive at the price at which a transaction would occur at the balance sheet date in the same instrument (ie without modification or repackaging) in the most advantageous active market to which an entity has immediate access. Thus, if a dealer enters into a derivative instrument with the corporate, but has immediate access to a more advantageously priced dealers' market, the entity recognises a profit on initial recognition of the derivative instrument. However, the entity adjusts the price observed in the dealer market for any differences in counterparty credit risk between the derivative instrument with the corporate and that with the dealers' market.

Bid-ask spreads in active markets (paragraph AG72)

BC99 The Board confirmed the proposal in the Exposure Draft that the appropriate quoted market price for an asset held or liability to be issued is usually the current bid price and, for an asset to be acquired or liability held, the asking price. It concluded that applying midmarket prices to an individual instrument is not appropriate because it would result in entities recognising up-front gains or losses for the difference between the bid-ask price and the mid-market price.

The Board discussed whether the bid-ask spread should be applied to the net open position of a portfolio containing offsetting market risk positions, or to each instrument in the portfolio. It noted the concerns raised by constituents that applying the bid-ask spread to the net open position better reflects the fair value of the risk retained in the portfolio. The Board concluded that for offsetting risk positions, entities could use mid-market prices to determine fair value, and hence may apply the bid or asking price to the net open position as appropriate. The Board believes that when an entity has offsetting risk positions, using the mid-market price is appropriate because the entity (a) has locked in its cash flows from the asset and liability and (b) potentially could sell the matched position without incurring the bid-ask spread. **BC100**

Comments received on the Exposure Draft revealed that some interpret the term 'bid-ask spread' differently from others and from the Board. Thus, IAS 39 clarifies that the spread represents only transaction costs. **BC101**

No Active Market (paragraphs AG74-AG82)

The Exposure Draft proposed a three-tier fair value measurement hierarchy as follows: **BC102**

(a) For instruments traded in active markets, use a quoted price.
(b) For instruments for which there is not an active market, use a recent market transaction.
(c) For instruments for which there is neither an active market nor a recent market transaction, use a valuation technique.

The Board decided to simplify the proposed fair value measurement hierarchy by requiring the fair value of financial instruments for which there is not an active market to be determined on the basis of valuation techniques, including the use of recent market transactions between knowledgeable, willing parties in an arm's length transaction. **BC103**

The Board also considered constituents' comments regarding whether an instrument should always be recognised on initial recognition at the transaction price or whether gains or losses may be recognised on initial recognition when an entity uses a valuation technique to estimate fair value. The Board concluded that an entity may recognise a gain or loss at inception only if fair value is evidenced by comparison with other observable current market transactions in the same instrument (ie without modification or repackaging) or is based on a valuation technique incorporating only observable market data. The Board concluded that those conditions were necessary and sufficient to provide reasonable assurance that fair value was other than the transaction price for the purpose of recognising up-front gains or losses. The Board decided that in other cases, the transaction price gave the best evidence of fair value. The Board also noted that its decision achieved convergence with US GAAP. **BC104**

Reclassification of financial instruments (paragraphs 50–54)

As described in paragraph BC11E, in October 2008 the Board received requests to address differences between the reclassification requirements of IAS 39 and US GAAP. SFAS 115 permits a security to be reclassified out of the trading category in rare situations. SFAS 65 permits a loan to be reclassified out of the Held for Sale category if the entity has the intention and ability to hold the loan for the foreseeable future or until maturity. IAS 39 permitted no reclassifications for financial assets classified as held for trading. The Board was asked to consider allowing entities **BC104A** applying IFRSs the same ability to reclassify a financial asset out of the held-for-trading category as is permitted by SFAS 115 and SFAS 65.*

BC104B The Board noted that allowing reclassification, even in limited circumstances, could allow an entity to manage its reported profit or loss by avoiding future fair value gains or losses on the reclassified assets.

BC104C The Board was also informed that, in practice under US GAAP, reclassification out of the trading category of SFAS 115 is extremely rare. However, the Board noted that the possibility of reclassification of securities and loans under US GAAP is available and that entities applying IFRSs do not have that possibility.

BC104D The Board therefore decided to permit non-derivative financial assets to be reclassified out of the held-for-trading category in the same circumstances as are permitted in SFAS 115 and SFAS 65. The Board also noted that rare circumstances arise from a single event that is unusual and highly unlikely to recur in the near term. In addition, the Board decided that a financial asset that would have met the definition of loans and receivables (if it had not been designated as available for sale) should be permitted to be transferred from the available-for-sale category to loans and receivables, if the entity intends to hold the loan or receivable for the foreseeable future or until maturity. The Board decided that this substantially aligns the accounting for reclassifications of loans and receivables with that permitted under US GAAP.

BC104E The Board normally publishes an exposure draft of any proposed amendments to standards to invite comments from interested parties. However, given the requests to address this issue urgently in the light of market conditions, and after consultation with the Trustees of the IASC Foundation, the Board decided to proceed directly to issuing the amendments. In taking this exceptional step the Board noted that the amendments to IAS 39 relaxed the existing requirements to provide short-term relief for some entities. The Board also noted that the amendments were a short-term response to the requests and therefore the Board decided to restrict the scope of the amendments.

Impairment and Uncollectibility of Financial Assets

Impairment of Investments in Equity Instruments (paragraph 61)

BC105 Under IAS 39, investments in equity instruments that are classified as available for sale and investments in unquoted equity instruments whose fair value cannot be reliably measured are subject to an impairment assessment. The original IAS 39 did not include guidance about impairment indicators that are specific to investments in equity instruments. Questions were raised about when in practice such investments become impaired.

BC106 The Board agreed that for marketable investments in equity instruments any impairment trigger other than a decline in fair value below cost is likely to be arbitrary to some extent. If markets are reasonably efficient, today's market price is the best estimate of the discounted value of the future market price. However, the Board also concluded that it is important to provide guidance to address the questions raised in practice.

BC107 The revised IAS 39 includes impairment triggers that the Board concluded were reasonable in the case of investments in equity instruments (paragraph 61). They

***Editor's note**: Paragraphs BC104A to BC104E added in October 2008.*

apply in addition to those specified in paragraph 59, which focus on the assessment of impairment in debt instruments.

Incurred versus expected losses

Some respondents to the Exposure Draft were confused about whether the Exposure **BC108** Draft reflected an 'incurred loss' model or an 'expected loss' model. Others expressed concern about the extent to which 'future losses' could be recognised as impairment losses. They suggested that losses should be recognised only when they are incurred (ie a deterioration in the credit quality of an asset or a group of assets after their initial recognition). Other respondents favoured the use of an expected loss approach. They suggested that expected future losses should be considered in the determination of the impairment loss for a group of assets even if the credit quality of a group of assets has not deteriorated from original expectations.

In considering these comments, the Board decided that impairment losses should be **BC109** recognised only if they have been incurred. The Board reasoned that it was inconsistent with an amortised cost model to recognise impairment on the basis of expected future transactions and events. The Board also decided that guidance should be provided about what 'incurred' means when assessing whether impairment exists in a group of financial assets. The Board was concerned that, in the absence of such guidance, there could be a range of interpretations about when a loss is incurred or what events cause a loss to be incurred in a group of assets.

Therefore, the Board included guidance in IAS 39 that specifies that for a loss to be **BC110** incurred, an event that provides objective evidence of impairment must have occurred after the initial recognition of the financial asset, and IAS 39 now identifies types of such events. Possible or expected future trends that may lead to a loss in the future (eg an expectation that unemployment will rise or a recession will occur) do not provide objective evidence of impairment. In addition, the loss event must have a reliably measurable effect on the present value of estimated future cash flows and be supported by current observable data.

Assets assessed individually and found not to be impaired (paragraphs 59(f) and 64)

It was not clear in the original IAS 39 whether loans and receivables and some other **BC111** financial assets, when reviewed for impairment and determined not to be impaired, could or should subsequently be included in the assessment of impairment for a group of financial assets with similar characteristics.

The Exposure Draft proposed that a loan asset or other financial asset that is **BC112** measured at amortised cost and has been individually assessed for impairment and found not to be impaired should be included in a collective assessment of impairment. The Exposure Draft also included proposed guidance about how to evaluate impairment inherent in a group of financial assets.

The comment letters received on the Exposure Draft indicated considerable support **BC113** for the proposal to include in a collective evaluation of impairment an individually assessed financial asset that is found not to be impaired.

The Board noted the following arguments in favour of an additional portfolio **BC114** assessment for individually assessed assets that are found not to be impaired.

(a) Impairment that cannot be identified with an individual loan may be identifiable on a portfolio basis. The *Framework** states that for a large population of receivables, some degree of nonpayment is normally regarded as probable. In that case, an expense representing the expected reduction in economic benefits is recognised (*Framework*, paragraph 85). For example, a lender may have some concerns about identified loans with similar characteristics, but not have sufficient evidence to conclude that an impairment loss has occurred on any of those loans on the basis of an individual assessment. Experience may indicate that some of those loans are impaired even though an individual assessment may not reveal this. The amount of loss in a large population of items can be estimated on the basis of experience and other factors by weighing all possible outcomes by their associated probabilities.

(b) Some time may elapse between an event that affects the ability of a borrower to repay a loan and actual default of the borrower. For example, if the market forward price for wheat decreases by 10 per cent, experience may indicate that the estimated payments from borrowers that are wheat farmers will decrease by 1 per cent over a one-year period. When the forward price decreases, there may be no objective evidence that any individual wheat farmer will default on an individually significant loan. On a portfolio basis, however, the decrease in the forward price may provide objective evidence that the estimated future cash flows on loans to wheat farmers have decreased by 1 per cent over a one-year period.

(c) Under IAS 39, impairment of loans is measured on the basis of the present value of estimated future cash flows. Estimations of future cash flows may change because of economic factors affecting a group of loans, such as country and industry factors, even if there is no objective evidence of impairment of an individual loan. For example, if unemployment increases by 10 per cent in a quarter in a particular region, the estimated future cash flows from loans to borrowers in that region for the next quarters may have decreased even though no objective evidence of impairment exists that is based on an individual assessment of loans to borrowers in that region. In that case, objective evidence of impairment exists for the group of financial assets, even though it does not exist for an individual asset. A requirement for objective evidence to exist to recognise and measure impairment in individually significant loans might result in delayed recognition of loan impairment that has already occurred.

(d) Accepted accounting practice in some countries is to establish a provision to cover impairment losses that, although not specifically identified to individual assets, are known from experience to exist in a loan portfolio as of the balance sheet date.

(e) If assets that are individually not significant are collectively assessed for impairment and assets that are individually significant are not, assets will not be measured on a consistent basis because impairment losses are more difficult to identify asset by asset.

(f) What is an individually significant loan that is assessed on its own will differ from one entity to another. Thus, identical exposures will be evaluated on different bases (individually or collectively), depending on their significance to the entity holding them. If a collective evaluation were not to be required, an entity that wishes to minimise its recognised impairment losses could elect to assess all loans individually. Requiring a collective assessment of impairment for all exposures judged not to be impaired individually enhances consistency between entities rather than reduces it.

****ASB footnote**: The equivalent document in the UK and Republic of Ireland to the IASB's* Framework *is the ASB's* Statement of Principles for Financial Reporting. *Although the Statement of Principles is very similar to the Framework, it is not identical.*

Arguments against an additional portfolio assessment for individually assessed loans that are found not to be impaired are as follows. **BC115**

(a) It appears illogical to make an impairment provision on a group of loans that have been assessed for impairment on an individual basis and have been found not to be impaired.
(b) The measurement of impairment should not depend on whether a lender has only one loan or a group of similar loans. If the measurement of impairment is affected by whether the lender has groups of similar loans, identical loans may be measured differently by different lenders. To ensure consistent measurement of identical loans, impairment in individually significant financial assets should be recognised and measured asset by asset.
(c) The *Framework* specifies that financial statements are prepared on the accrual basis of accounting, according to which the effects of transactions and events are recognised when they occur and are recognised in the financial statements in the periods to which they relate. Financial statements should reflect the outcome of events that took place before the balance sheet date and should not reflect events that have not yet occurred. If an impairment loss cannot be attributed to a specifically identified financial asset or a group of financial assets that are not individually significant, it is questionable whether an event has occurred that justifies the recognition of impairment. Even though the risk of loss may have increased, a loss has not yet materialised.
(d) The *Framework*, paragraph 94, requires an expense to be recognised only if it can be measured reliably. The process of estimating impairment in a group of loans that have been individually assessed for impairment but found not to be impaired may involve a significant degree of subjectivity. There may be a wide range of reasonable estimates of impairment. In practice, the establishment of general loan loss provisions is sometimes viewed as more of an art than a science. This portfolio approach should be applied only if it is necessary on practical grounds and not to override an assessment made on an individual loan, which must provide a better determination of whether an allowance is necessary.
(e) IAS 39 requires impairment to be measured on a present value basis using the original effective interest rate. Mechanically, it may not be obvious how to do this for a group of loans with similar characteristics that have different effective interest rates. In addition, measurement of impairment in a group of loans based on the present value of estimated cash flows discounted using the original effective interest rate may result in doublecounting of losses that were expected on a portfolio basis when the loans were originated because the lender included compensation for those losses in the contractual interest rate charged. As a result, a portfolio assessment of impairment may result in the recognition of a loss almost as soon as a loan is issued. (This question arises also in measuring impairment on a portfolio basis for loans that are not individually assessed for impairment under IAS 39.)

The Board was persuaded by the arguments in favour of a portfolio assessment for individually assessed assets that are found not to be impaired and decided to confirm that a loan or other financial asset measured at amortised cost that is individually assessed for impairment and found not to be impaired should be included in a group of similar financial assets that are assessed for impairment on a portfolio basis. This is to reflect that, in the light of the law of large numbers, impairment may be evident in a group of assets, but not yet meet the threshold for recognition when any individual asset in that group is assessed. The Board also confirmed that it is important to provide guidance about how to assess impairment on a portfolio basis to introduce discipline into a portfolio assessment. Such guidance promotes consistency in practice and comparability of information across entities. It should also mitigate **BC116** concerns that collective assessments of impairment should not be used to conceal changes in asset values or as a cushion for potential future losses.

BC117 Some respondents expressed concerns about some of the detailed guidance proposed in the Exposure Draft, such as the guidance about adjusting the discount rate for expected losses. Many entities indicated that they do not have the data and systems necessary to implement the proposed approach. The Board decided to eliminate some of the detailed application guidance (eg whether to make an adjustment of the discount rate for originally expected losses and an illustration of the application of the guidance).

Assets that are assessed individually and found to be impaired (paragraph 64)

BC118 In making a portfolio assessment of impairment, one issue that arises is whether the collective assessment should include assets that have been individually evaluated and identified as impaired.

BC119 One view is that methods used to estimate impairment losses on a portfolio basis are equally valid whether or not an asset has been specifically identified as impaired. Those who support this view note that the law of large numbers applies equally whether or not an asset has been individually identified as impaired and that a portfolio assessment may enable a more accurate prediction to be made of estimated future cash flows.

BC120 Another view is that there should be no need to complement an individual assessment of impairment for an asset that is specifically identified as impaired by an additional portfolio assessment, because objective evidence of impairment exists on an individual basis and expectations of losses can be incorporated in the measurement of impairment for the individual assets. Double-counting of losses in terms of estimated future cash flows should not be permitted. Moreover, recognition of impairment losses for groups of assets should not be a substitute for the recognition of impairment losses on individual assets.

BC121 The Board decided that assets that are individually assessed for impairment and identified as impaired should be excluded from a portfolio assessment of impairment. Excluding assets that are individually identified as impaired from a portfolio assessment of impairment is consistent with the view that collective evaluation of impairment is an interim step pending the identification of impairment losses on individual assets. A collective evaluation identifies losses that have been incurred on a group basis as of the balance sheet date, but cannot yet be identified with individual assets. As soon as information is available to identify losses on individually impaired assets, those assets are removed from the group that is collectively assessed for impairment.

Grouping of assets that are collectively evaluated for impairment(paragraphs 64 and AG87)

BC122 The Board considered how assets that are collectively assessed for impairment should be grouped for the purpose of assessing impairment on a portfolio basis. In practice, different methods are conceivable for grouping assets for the purposes of assessing impairment and computing historical and expected loss rates. For example, assets may be grouped on the basis of one or more of the following characteristics: (a) estimated default probabilities or credit risk grades; (b) type (for example, mortgage loans or credit card loans); (c) geographical location; (d) collateral type; (e) counterparty type (for example, consumer, commercial or sovereign); (f) past-due status; and (g) maturity. More sophisticated credit risk models or methodologies for estimating expected future cash flows may combine several factors, for example, a credit risk evaluation or grading process that considers asset type, industry, geographical location, collateral type, past-due status, and other relevant characteristics of the assets being evaluated and associated loss data.

The Board decided that for the purpose of assessing impairment on a portfolio basis, the method employed for grouping assets should, as a minimum, ensure that individual assets are allocated to groups of assets that share similar credit risk characteristics. It also decided to clarify that when assets that are assessed individually and found not to be impaired are grouped with assets with similar credit risk characteristics that are assessed only on a collective basis, the loss probabilities and other loss statistics differ between the two types of asset with the result that a different amount of impairment may be required. **BC123**

Estimates of future cash flows in groups (paragraphs AG89-AG92)

The Board decided that to promote consistency in the estimation of impairment on groups of financial assets that are collectively evaluated for impairment, guidance should be provided about the process for estimating future cash flows in such groups. It identified the following elements as critical to an adequate process: **BC124**

(a) Historical loss experience should provide the basis for estimating future cash flows in a group of financial assets that are collectively assessed for impairment.
(b) Entities that have no loss experience of their own or insufficient experience should use peer group experience for comparable groups of financial assets.
(c) Historical loss experience should be adjusted, on the basis of observable data, to reflect the effects of current conditions that did not affect the period on which the historical loss experience is based and to remove the effects of conditions in the historical period that do not exist currently.
(d) Changes in estimates of future cash flows should be directionally consistent with changes in underlying observable data.
(e) Estimation methods should be adjusted to reduce differences between estimates of future cash flows and actual cash flows.

Impairment of investments in available-for-sale financial assets (paragraphs 67-70)

In the Exposure Draft, the Board proposed that impairment losses on debt and equity instruments classified as available for sale should not be reversed through profit or loss if conditions changed after the recognition of the impairment loss. The Board arrived at this decision because of the difficulties in determining objectively when impairment losses on debt and equity instruments classified as available-for-sale have been recovered and hence of distinguishing a reversal of an impairment (recognised in profit or loss) from other increases in value (recognised in equity). Accordingly, the Board proposed that any increase in the fair value of an available-for-sale financial asset would be recognised directly in equity even though the entity had previously recognised an impairment loss on that asset. The Board noted that this was consistent with the recognition of changes in the fair value of available-for-sale financial assets directly in equity* (see paragraph 55(b)). **BC125**

The Board considered the comments received on its proposal to preclude reversals of impairment on available-for-sale financial assets. It concluded that available-for-sale debt instruments and available-for-sale equity instruments should be treated differently. **BC126**

**As a consequence of the revision of IAS 1* Presentation of Financial Statements *in 2007 such changes are recognised in other comprehensive income.*

Reversals of impairment on available-for-sale debt instruments (paragraph 70)

BC127 For available-for-sale debt instruments, the Board decided that impairment should be reversed through profit or loss when fair value increases and the increase can be objectively related to an event occurring after the loss was recognised.

BC128 The Board noted that (a) other Standards require the reversal of impairment losses if circumstances change (eg IAS 2 *Inventories*, IAS 16 *Property, Plant and Equipment* and IAS 38 *Intangible Assets**); (b) the decision provides consistency with the requirement to reverse impairment losses on loans and receivables, and on assets classified as held to maturity; and (c) reversals of impairment in debt instruments (ie determining an increase in fair value attributable to an improvement in credit standing) are more objectively determinable than those in equity instruments.

Reversals of impairment on available-for-sale equity instruments (paragraph 69)

BC129 For available-for-sale equity instruments, the Board concluded that if impairment is recognised, and the fair value subsequently increases, the increase in value should be recognised in equity (and not as a reversal of the impairment loss through profit or loss).

BC130 The Board could not find an acceptable way to distinguish reversals of impairment losses from other increases in fair value. Therefore, it decided that precluding reversals of impairment on available-for-sale equity instruments was the only appropriate solution. In its deliberations, the Board considered:

(a) limiting reversals to those cases in which specific facts that caused the original impairment reverse. However, the Board questioned the operationality of applying this approach (ie how to decide whether the same event that caused the impairment caused the reversal).

(b) recognising all changes in fair value below cost as impairments and reversals of impairment through profit or loss, ie all changes in fair value below cost would be recognised in profit or loss, and all changes above cost would be recognised in equity. Although this approach achieves consistency with IAS 16 and IAS 38, and eliminates any subjectivity involved in determining what constitutes impairment or reversal of impairment, the Board noted that it would significantly change the notion of 'available for sale' in practice. The Board believed that introducing such a change to the available-for-sale category was not appropriate at this time.

HEDGING

BC131 The Exposure Draft proposed few changes to the hedge accounting guidance in the original IAS 39. The comments on the Exposure Draft raised several issues in the area of hedge accounting suggesting that the Board should consider these issues in the revised IAS 39. The Board's decisions with regard to these issues are presented in the following paragraphs.

Consideration of the Shortcut Method in SFAS 133

BC132 SFAS 133 *Accounting for Derivative Instruments and Hedging Activities* issued by the FASB allows an entity to assume no ineffectiveness in a hedge of interest rate risk

****ASB footnote**: the corresponding requirements in the UK and the Republic of Ireland are in SSAP 9* Stocks and long-term contracts *and FRS 11* Impairment of Fixed Assets and Goodwill.

using an interest rate swap as the hedging instrument, provided specified criteria are met (the 'shortcut method').

The original IAS 39 and the Exposure Draft precluded the use of the shortcut method. Many comments received on the Exposure Draft argued that IAS 39 should permit use of the shortcut method. The Board considered the issue in developing the Exposure Draft, and discussed it in the roundtable discussions that were held in the process of finalising IAS 39. **BC133**

The Board noted that, if the shortcut method were permitted, an exception would have to be made to the principle in IAS 39 that ineffectiveness in a hedging relationship is measured and recognised in profit or loss. The Board agreed that no exception to this principle should be made, and therefore concluded that IAS 39 should not permit the shortcut method. **BC134**

Additionally, IAS 39 permits the hedging of portions of financial assets and financial liabilities in cases when US GAAP does not. The Board noted that under IAS 39 an entity may hedge a portion of a financial instrument (eg interest rate risk or credit risk), and that if the critical terms of the hedging instrument and the hedged item are the same, the entity would, in many cases, recognise no ineffectiveness. **BC135**

Hedges of Portions of Financial Assets and Financial Liabilities (paragraphs 81, 81A, AG99A and AG99B)

IAS 39 permits a hedged item to be designated as a portion of the cash flows or fair value of a financial asset or financial liability. In finalising the Exposure Draft *Fair Value Hedge Accounting for a Portfolio Hedge of Interest Rate Risk*, the Board received comments that demonstrated that the meaning of a 'portion' was unclear in this context. Accordingly, the Board decided to amend IAS 39 to provide further guidance on what may be designated as a hedged portion, including confirmation that it is not possible to designate a portion that is greater than the total cash flows of the asset or liability. **BC135A**

Expected Effectiveness (paragraphs AG105–AG113)

Qualification for hedge accounting is based on expectations of future effectiveness (prospective) and evaluation of actual effectiveness (retrospective). In the original IAS 39, the prospective test was expressed as "almost fully offset", whereas the retrospective test was "within a range of 80-125 per cent". The Board considered whether to amend IAS 39 to permit the prospective effectiveness to be within the range of 80-125 per cent rather than "almost fully offset". The Board noted that an undesirable consequence of such an amendment could be that entities would deliberately underhedge a hedged item in a cash flow hedge so as to reduce recognised ineffectiveness. Therefore, the Board initially decided to retain the guidance in the original IAS 39. **BC136**

However, when subsequently finalising the requirements for portfolio hedges of interest rate risk, the Board received representations from constituents that some hedges would fail the "almost fully offset" test in IAS 39, including some hedges that would qualify for the short-cut method in US GAAP and thus be assumed to be 100 per cent effective. The Board was persuaded that the concern described in the previous paragraph that an entity might deliberately underhedge would be met by an explicit statement that an entity could not deliberately hedge less than 100 per cent of the exposure on an item and designate the hedge as a hedge of 100 per cent of the exposure. Therefore, the Board decided to amend IAS 39: **BC136A**

(a) to remove the words "almost fully offset" from the prospective effectiveness test, and replace them by a requirement that the hedge is expected to be "highly effective". (This amendment is consistent with the wording in US GAAP.)

(b) to include a statement in the Application Guidance in IAS 39 that if an entity hedges less than 100 per cent of the exposure on an item, such as 85 per cent, it shall designate the hedged item as being 85 per cent of the exposure and shall measure ineffectiveness on the basis of the change in the whole of that designated 85 per cent exposure.

BC136B Additionally, comments made in response to the Exposure Draft *Fair Value Hedge Accounting for a Portfolio Hedge of Interest Rate Risk* demonstrated that it was unclear how the prospective effectiveness test was to be applied. The Board noted that the objective of the test was to ensure there was firm evidence to support an expectation of high effectiveness. Therefore, the Board decided to amend the Standard to clarify that an expectation of high effectiveness may be demonstrated in various ways, including a comparison of past changes in the fair value or cash flows of the hedged item that are attributable to the hedged risk with past changes in the fair value or cash flows of the hedging instrument, or by demonstrating a high statistical correlation between the fair value of cash flows of the hedged item and those of the hedging instrument. The Board noted that the entity may choose a hedge ratio of other than one to one in order to improve the effectiveness of the hedge as described in paragraph AG100.

Hedges of Portions of Non-Financial Assets and Non-Financial Liabilities for Risk Other Than Foreign Currency Risk (paragraph 82)

BC137 The Board considered comments on the Exposure Draft that suggested that IAS 39 should permit designating as the hedged risk a risk portion of a non-financial item other than foreign currency risk.

BC138 The Board concluded that IAS 39 should not be amended to permit such designation. It noted that in many cases, changes in the cash flows or fair value of a portion of a non-financial hedged item are difficult to isolate and measure. Moreover, the Board noted that permitting portions of non-financial assets and non-financial liabilities to be designated as the hedged item for risk other than foreign currency risk would compromise the principles of identification of the hedged item and effectiveness testing that the Board has confirmed because the portion could be designated so that no ineffectiveness would ever arise.

BC139 The Board confirmed that non-financial items may be hedged in their entirety when the item the entity is hedging is not the standard item underlying contracts traded in the market. In this context, the Board decided to clarify that a hedge ratio of other than one-to-one may maximise expected effectiveness, and to include guidance on how the hedge ratio that maximises expected effectiveness can be determined.

Loan Servicing Rights

BC140 The Board also considered whether IAS 39 should permit the interest rate risk portion of loan servicing rights to be designated as the hedged item.

BC141 The Board considered the argument that interest rate risk can be separately identified and measured in loan servicing rights, and that changes in market interest rates have a predictable and separately measurable effect on the value of loan servicing rights. The Board also considered the possibility of treating loan servicing rights as financial assets (rather than non-financial assets).

However, the Board concluded that no exceptions should be permitted for this matter. The Board noted that (a) the interest rate risk and prepayment risk in loan servicing rights are interdependent, and thus inseparable, (b) the fair values of loan servicing rights do not change in a linear fashion as interest rates increase or decrease, and (c) concerns exist about how to isolate and measure the interest rate risk portion of a loan servicing right. Moreover, the Board expressed concern that in jurisdictions in which loan servicing right markets are not developed, the interest rate risk portion may not be measurable. **BC142**

The Board also considered whether IAS 39 should be amended to allow, on an elective basis, the inclusion of loan servicing rights in its scope provided that they are measured at fair value with changes in fair value recognised immediately in profit or loss. The Board noted that this would create two exceptions to the general principles in IAS 39. First, it would create a scope exception because IAS 39 applies only to financial assets and financial liabilities; loan servicing rights are non-financial assets. Second, *requiring* an entity to measure loan servicing rights at fair value through profit or loss would create a further exception, because this treatment is optional (except for items that are held for trading). The Board therefore decided not to amend the scope of IAS 39 for loan servicing rights. **BC143**

Whether to Permit Hedge Accounting Using Cash Instruments

In finalising the amendments to IAS 39, the Board discussed whether an entity should be permitted to designate a financial asset or financial liability other than a derivative (ie a 'cash instrument') as a hedging instrument in hedges of risks other than foreign currency risk. The original IAS 39 precluded such designation because of the different bases for measuring derivatives and cash instruments. The Exposure Draft did not propose a change to this limitation. However, some commentators suggested a change, noting that entities do not distinguish between derivative and non-derivative financial instruments in their hedging and other risk management activities and that entities may have to use a non-derivative financial instrument to hedge risk if no suitable derivative financial instrument exists. **BC144**

The Board acknowledged that some entities use non-derivatives to manage risk. However, it decided to retain the restriction against designating non-derivatives as hedging instruments in hedges of risks other than foreign currency risk. It noted the following arguments in support of this conclusion: **BC145**

(a) The need for hedge accounting arises in part because derivatives are measured at fair value, whereas the items they hedge may be measured at cost or not recognised at all. Without hedge accounting, an entity might recognise volatility in profit or loss for matched positions. For non-derivative items that are not measured at fair value or for which changes in fair value are not recognised in profit or loss, there is generally no need to adjust the accounting of the hedging instrument or the hedged item to achieve matched recognition of gains and losses in profit or loss.
(b) To allow designation of cash instruments as hedging instruments would diverge from US GAAP: SFAS 133 precludes the designation of non-derivative instruments as hedging instruments except for some foreign currency hedges.
(c) To allow designation of cash instruments as hedging instruments would add complexity to the Standard. More financial instruments would be measured at an amount that represents neither amortised cost nor fair value. Hedge accounting is, and should be, an exception to the normal measurement requirements.
(d) If cash instruments were permitted to be designated as hedging instruments, there would be much less discipline in the accounting model because, in the

absence of hedge accounting, a non-derivative may not be selectively measured at fair value. If the entity subsequently decides that it would rather not apply fair value measurement to a cash instrument that had been designated as a hedging instrument, it can breach one of the hedge accounting requirements, conclude that the non-derivative no longer qualifies as a hedging instrument and selectively avoid recognising the changes in fair value of the non-derivative instrument in equity (for a cash flow hedge) or profit or loss (for a fair value hedge).

(e) The most significant use of cash instruments as hedging instruments is to hedge foreign currency exposures, which is permitted under IAS 39.

Whether to Treat Hedges of Forecast Transactions as Fair Value Hedges

BC146 The Board considered a suggestion made in some of the comment letters received on the Exposure Draft that a hedge of a forecast transaction should be treated as a fair value hedge, rather than as a cash flow hedge. Some argued that the hedge accounting provisions should be simplified by having only one type of hedge accounting. Some also raised concern about an entity's ability, in some cases, to choose between two hedge accounting methods for the same hedging strategy (ie the choice between designating a forward contract to sell an existing asset as a fair value hedge of the asset or a cash flow hedge of a forecast sale of the asset).

BC147 The Board acknowledged that the hedge accounting provisions would be simplified, and their application more consistent in some situations, if the Standard permitted only one type of hedge accounting. However, the Board concluded that IAS 39 should continue to distinguish between fair value hedge accounting and cash flow hedge accounting. It noted that removing either type of hedge accounting would narrow the range of hedging strategies that could qualify for hedge accounting.

BC148 The Board also noted that treating a hedge of a forecast transaction as a fair value hedge is not appropriate for the following reasons: (a) it would result in the recognition of an asset or liability before the entity has become a party to the contract; (b) amounts would be recognised in the balance sheet that do not meet the definitions of assets and liabilities in the *Framework*; and (c) transactions in which there is no fair value exposure would be treated as if there were a fair value exposure.

Hedges of Firm Commitments (paragraphs 93 and 94)

BC149 The previous version of IAS 39 required a hedge of a firm commitment to be accounted for as a cash flow hedge. In other words, hedging gains and losses, to the extent that the hedge is effective, were initially recognised in equity and were subsequently 'recycled' to profit or loss in the same period(s) that the hedged firm commitment affected profit or loss (although, when basis adjustment was used, they adjusted the initial carrying amount of an asset or liability recognised in the meantime). Some believe this is appropriate because cash flow hedge accounting for hedges of firm commitments avoids partial recognition of the firm commitment that would otherwise not be recognised. Moreover, some believe it is conceptually incorrect to recognise the hedged fair value exposure of a firm commitment as an asset or liability merely because it has been hedged.

BC150 The Board considered whether hedges of firm commitments should be treated as cash flow hedges or fair value hedges. The Board concluded that hedges of firm commitments should be accounted for as fair value hedges.

The Board noted that, in concept, a hedge of a firm commitment is a fair value hedge. This is because the fair value of the item being hedged (the firm commitment) changes with changes in the hedged risk. **BC151**

The Board was not persuaded by the argument that it is conceptually incorrect to recognise an asset or liability for a firm commitment merely because it has been hedged. It noted that for all fair value hedges, applying hedge accounting has the effect that amounts are recognised as assets or liabilities that would otherwise not be recognised. For example, assume an entity hedges a fixed rate loan asset with a payfixed, receive-variable interest rate swap. If there is a loss on the swap, applying fair value hedge accounting requires the offsetting gain on the loan to be recognised, ie the carrying amount of the loan is increased. Thus, applying hedge accounting has the effect of recognising a part of an asset (the increase in the loan's value attributable to interest rate movements) that would otherwise not have been recognised. The only difference in the case of a firm commitment is that, without hedge accounting, none of the commitment is recognised, ie the carrying amount is zero. However, this difference merely reflects that the historical cost of a firm commitment is usually zero. It is not a fundamental difference in concept. **BC152**

Furthermore, the Board's decision converges with SFAS 133, and thus eliminates practical problems and eases implementation for entities that report under both standards. **BC153**

However, the Board clarified that a hedge of the foreign currency risk of a firm commitment may be treated as either a fair value hedge or a cash flow hedge because foreign currency risk affects both the cash flows and the fair value of the hedged item. Accordingly a foreign currency cash flow hedge of a forecast transaction need not be re-designated as a fair value hedge when the forecast transaction becomes a firm commitment. **BC154**

Basis Adjustments (paragraphs 97-99)

The question of basis adjustment arises when an entity hedges the future purchase of an asset or the future issue of a liability. One example is that of a US entity that expects to make a future purchase of a German machine that it will pay for in euro. The entity enters into a derivative to hedge against possible future changes in the US dollar / euro exchange rate. Such a hedge is classified as a cash flow hedge under IAS 39, with the effect that gains and losses on the hedging instrument (to the extent that the hedge is effective) are initially recognised in equity.* The question the Board considered is what the accounting should be once the future transaction takes place. In its deliberations on this issue, the Board discussed the following approaches: **BC155**

(a) to remove the hedging gain or loss from equity and recognise it as part of the initial carrying amount of the asset or liability (in the example above, the machine). In future periods, the hedging gain or loss is automatically recognised in profit or loss by being included in amounts such as depreciation expense (for a fixed asset), interest income or expense (for a financial asset or financial liability), or cost of sales (for inventories). This treatment is commonly referred to as 'basis adjustment'.

(b) to leave the hedging gain or loss in equity. In future periods, the gain or loss on the hedging instrument is 'recycled' to profit or loss in the same period(s) as the acquired asset or liability affects profit or loss. This recycling requires a separate adjustment and is not automatic.

**As a consequence of the revision of IAS 1* Presentation of Financial Statements *in 2007 such gains and losses are recognised in other comprehensive income.*

BC156 It should be noted that both approaches have the same effect on profit or loss and net assets for all periods affected, so long as the hedge is accounted for as a cash flow hedge. The difference relates to balance sheet presentation and, possibly, the line item in the income statement.

BC157 In the Exposure Draft, the Board proposed that the 'basis adjustment' approach for forecast transactions (approach (a)) should be eliminated and replaced by approach (b) above. It further noted that eliminating the basis adjustment approach would enable IAS 39 to converge with SFAS 133.

BC158 Many of the comments received from constituents disagreed with the proposal in the Exposure Draft. Those responses argued that it would unnecessarily complicate the accounting to leave the hedging gain or loss in equity when the hedged forecast transaction occurs. They particularly noted that tracking the effects of cash flow hedges after the asset or liability is acquired would be complicated and would require systems changes. They also pointed out that treating hedges of firm commitments as fair value hedges has the same effect as a basis adjustment when the firm commitment results in the recognition of an asset or liability. For example, for a perfectly effective hedge of the foreign currency risk of a firm commitment to buy a machine, the effect is to recognise the machine initially at its foreign currency price translated at the forward rate in effect at the inception of the hedge rather than the spot rate. Therefore, they questioned whether it is consistent to treat a hedge of a firm commitment as a fair value hedge while precluding basis adjustments for hedges of forecast transactions.

BC159 Others believe that a basis adjustment is difficult to justify in principle for forecast transactions, and also argue that such basis adjustments impair comparability of financial information. In other words, two identical assets that are purchased at the same time and in the same way, except for the fact that one was hedged, should not be recognised at different amounts.

BC160 The Board concluded that IAS 39 should distinguish between hedges of forecast transactions that will result in the recognition of a *financial* asset or a *financial* liability and those that will result in the recognition of a *non-financial* asset or a *non-financial* liability.

Basis adjustments for hedges of forecast transactions that will result in the recognition of a financial asset or a financial liability

BC161 For hedges of forecast transactions that will result in the recognition of a financial asset or a financial liability, the Board concluded that basis adjustments are not appropriate. Its reason was that basis adjustments cause the initial carrying amount of acquired assets (or assumed liabilities) arising from forecast transactions to move away from fair value and hence would override the requirement in IAS 39 to measure a financial instrument initially at its fair value.

BC161A If a hedged forecast transaction results in the recognition of a financial asset or a financial liability, paragraph 97 of IAS 39 required the associated gains or losses on hedging instruments to be reclassified from equity to profit or loss as a reclassification adjustment in the same period or periods during which the hedged item affects profit or loss (such as in the periods that interest income or interest expense is recognised).

BC161B The Board was informed that there was uncertainty about how paragraph 97 should be applied when the designated cash flow exposure being hedged differs from the financial instrument arising from the hedged forecast cash flows.

The example below illustrates the issue: BC161C

> An entity applies the guidance in the answer to Question F.6.2 of the guidance on implementing IAS 39. On 1 January 20X0 the entity designates forecast cash flows for the risk of variability arising from changes in interest rates. Those forecast cash flows arise from the repricing of existing financial instruments and are scheduled for 1 April 20X0. The entity is exposed to variability in cash flows for the three-month period beginning on 1 April 20X0 attributable to changes in interest rate risk that occur from 1 January 20X0 to 31 March 20X0.
>
> The occurrence of the forecast cash flows is deemed to be highly probable and all the other relevant hedge accounting criteria are met.
>
> The financial instrument that results from the hedged forecast cash flows is a five-year interest-bearing instrument.

Paragraph 97 required the gains or losses on the hedging instrument to be reclassified from equity to profit or loss as a reclassification adjustment in the same period or periods during which the asset acquired or liability assumed affected profit or loss. The financial instrument that was recognised is a five-year instrument that will affect profit or loss for five years. The wording in paragraph 97 suggested that the gains or losses should be reclassified over five years, even though the cash flows designated as the hedged item were hedged for the effects of interest rate changes over only a three-month period. BC161D

The Board believes that the wording of paragraph 97 did not reflect the underlying rationale in hedge accounting, ie that the gains or losses on the hedging instrument should offset the gains or losses on the hedged item, and the offset should be reflected in profit or loss by way of reclassification adjustments. BC161E

The Board believes that in the example set out above the gains or losses should be reclassified over a period of three months beginning on 1 April 20X0, and not over a period of five years beginning on 1 April 20X0. BC161F

Consequently, in *Improvements to IFRSs* issued in April 2009, the Board amended paragraph 97 of IAS 39 to clarify that the gains or losses on the hedged instrument should be reclassified from equity to profit or loss during the period that the hedged forecast cash flows affect profit or loss. The Board also decided that to avoid similar confusion paragraph 100 of IAS 39 should be amended to be consistent with paragraph 97. BC161G

Basis adjustments for hedges of forecast transactions that will result in the recognition of a non-financial asset or a non-financial liability

For hedges of forecast transactions that will result in the recognition of a non-financial asset or a non-financial liability, the Board decided to permit entities a choice of whether to apply basis adjustment. BC162

The Board considered the argument that changes in the fair value of the hedging instrument are appropriately included in the initial carrying amount of the recognised asset or liability because such changes represent a part of the "cost" of that asset or liability. Although the Board has not yet considered the broader issue of what costs may be capitalised at initial recognition, the Board believes that its decision to provide an option for basis adjustments in the case of non-financial items will not pre-empt that future discussion. The Board also recognised that financial BC163 items and non-financial items are not necessarily measured at the same amount on initial recognition, because financial items are measured at fair value and non-financial items are measured at cost.

BC164 The Board concluded that, on balance, providing entities with a choice in this case was appropriate. The Board took the view that allowing basis adjustments addresses the concern that precluding basis adjustments complicates the accounting for hedges of forecast transactions. In addition, the number of balance sheet line items that could be affected is quite small, generally being only property, plant and equipment, inventory and the cash flow hedge line item in equity. The Board also noted that US GAAP precludes basis adjustments and that applying a basis adjustment is inconsistent with the accounting for hedges of forecast transactions that will result in the recognition of a financial asset or a financial liability. The Board acknowledged the merits of these arguments, and recognised that by permitting a choice in IAS 39, entities could apply the accounting treatment required by US GAAP.

Hedging Using Internal Contracts

BC165 IAS 39 does not preclude entities from using internal contracts as a risk management tool, or as a tracking device in applying hedge accounting for external contracts that hedge external positions. Furthermore, IAS 39 permits hedge accounting to be applied to transactions between entities in the same group in the *separate reporting* of those entities. However, IAS 39 does not permit hedge accounting for transactions between entities in the same group in consolidated financial statements. The reason is the fundamental requirement of consolidation that the accounting effects of internal contracts should be eliminated in consolidated financial statements, including any internally generated gains or losses. Designating internal contracts as hedging instruments could result in non-elimination of internal gains and losses and have other accounting effects. The Exposure Draft did not propose any change in this area.

BC166 To illustrate, assume the banking book division of Bank A enters into an internal interest rate swap with the trading book division of the same bank. The purpose is to hedge the net interest rate risk exposure in the banking book of a group of similar fixed rate loan assets funded by floating rate liabilities. Under the swap, the banking book pays fixed interest payments to the trading book and receives variable interest rate payments in return. The bank wants to designate the internal interest rate swap in the banking book as a hedging instrument in its consolidated financial statements.

BC167 If the internal swap in the banking book is designated as a hedging instrument in a cash flow hedge of the liabilities, and the internal swap in the trading book is classified as held for trading, internal gains and losses on that internal swap would not be eliminated. This is because the gains and losses on the internal swap in the banking book would be recognised in equity* to the extent the hedge is effective and the gains and losses on the internal swap in the trading book would be recognised in profit or loss.

BC168 If the internal swap in the banking book is designated as a hedging instrument in a fair value hedge of the loan assets and the internal swap in the trading book is classified as held for trading, the changes in the fair value of the internal swap would offset both in total net assets in the balance sheet and profit or loss. However, without elimination of the internal swap, there would be an adjustment to the

* *As a consequence of the revision of IAS 1* Presentation of Financial Statements *in 2007 such gains and losses are recognised in other comprehensive income.*

carrying amount of the hedged loan asset in the banking book to reflect the change in the fair value attributable to the risk hedged by the internal contract. Moreover, to reflect the effect of the internal swap the bank would in effect recognise the fixed rate loan at a floating interest rate and recognise an offsetting trading gain or loss in the income statement. Hence the internal swap would have accounting effects.

Some respondents to the Exposure Draft and some participants in the roundtables objected to not being able to obtain hedge accounting in the consolidated financial statements for internal contracts between subsidiaries or between a subsidiary and the parent (as illustrated above). Among other things, they emphasised that the use of internal contracts is a key risk management tool and that the accounting should reflect the way in which risk is managed. Some suggested that IAS 39 should be changed to make it consistent with US GAAP, which allows the designation of internal derivative contracts as hedging instruments in cash flow hedges of forecast foreign currency transactions in specified, limited circumstances. **BC169**

In considering these comments, the Board noted that the following principles apply to consolidated financial statements: **BC170**

(a) financial statements provide financial information about an entity or group as a whole (as that of a single entity). Financial statements do not provide financial information about an entity as if it were two separate entities.

(b) a fundamental principle of consolidation is that intragroup balances and intragroup transactions are eliminated in full. Permitting the designation of internal contracts as hedging instruments would require a change to the consolidation principles.

(c) it is conceptually wrong to permit an entity to recognise internally generated gains and losses or make other accounting adjustments because of internal transactions. No external event has occurred.

(d) an ability to recognise internally generated gains and losses could result in abuse in the absence of requirements about how entities should manage and control the associated risks. It is not the purpose of accounting standards to prescribe how entities should manage and control risks.

(e) permitting the designation of internal contracts as hedging instruments violates the following requirements in IAS 39:

  (i) the prohibition against designating as a hedging instrument a non-derivative financial asset or non-derivative financial liability for other than foreign currency risk. To illustrate, if an entity has two offsetting internal contracts and one is the designated hedging instrument in a fair value hedge of a non-derivative asset and the other is the designated hedging instrument in a fair value hedge of a non-derivative liability, from the entity's perspective the effect is to designate a hedging relationship between the asset and the liability (ie a non-derivative asset or non-derivative liability is used as the hedging instrument).

  (ii) the prohibition on designating a net position of assets and liabilities as the hedged item. To illustrate, an entity has two internal contracts. One is designated in a fair value hedge of an asset and the other in a fair value hedge of a liability. The two internal contracts do not fully offset, so the entity lays off the net risk exposure by entering into a net external derivative. In that case, the effect from the entity's perspective is to designate a hedging relationship between the net external derivative and a net position of an asset and a liability.

  (iii) the option to fair value assets and liabilities does not extend to portions of assets and liabilities.

(f) the Board is considering separately whether to make an amendment to IAS 39 to facilitate fair value hedge accounting for portfolio hedges of interest rate risk. The Board believes that that is a better way to address the concerns raised about symmetry with risk management systems than permitting the designation of internal contracts as hedging instruments.

(g) the Board decided to permit an option to measure any financial asset or financial liability at fair value with changes in fair value recognised in profit or loss. This enables an entity to measure matching asset/liability positions at fair value without a need for hedge accounting.

BC171 The Board reaffirmed that it is a fundamental principle of consolidation that any accounting effect of internal contracts is eliminated on consolidation. The Board decided that no exception to this principle should be made in IAS 39. Consistently with this decision, the Board also decided not to explore an amendment to permit internal derivative contracts to be designated as hedging instruments in hedges of some forecast foreign currency transactions, as is permitted by SFAS 138 *Accounting for Certain Derivative Instruments and Certain Hedging Activities*.

BC172 The Board also decided to clarify that IAS 39 does not preclude hedge accounting for transactions between entities in the same group in individual or separate financial statements of those entities because they are not internal to the entity (ie the individual entity).

BC172A Previously, paragraph 73 and 80 referred to the need for hedging instruments to involve a party external to the reporting entity. In doing so, they used a segment as an example of a reporting entity. However, IFRS 8 *Operating Segments* requires disclosure of information that is reported to the chief operating decision maker even if this is on a non-IFRS basis. Therefore, the two IFRSs appeared to conflict. In *Improvements to IFRSs* issued in May 2008 and April 2009, the Board removed from paragraphs 73 and 80 references to the designation of hedging instruments at the segment level.*

Eligible hedged items in particular situations (paragraphs AG99BA, AG99E, AG99F, AG110A and AG110B)

BC172B The Board amended IAS 39 in July 2008 to clarify the application of the principles that determine whether a hedged risk or portion of cash flows is eligible for designation in particular situations. This followed a request by the IFRIC for guidance.†

BC172C The responses to the exposure draft Exposures Qualifying for Hedge Accounting demonstrated that diversity in practice existed, or was likely to occur, in two situations:

(a) the designation of a one-sided risk in a hedged item;

(b) the designation of inflation as a hedged risk or portion in particular situations.

Designation of a one-sided risk in a hedged item

BC172D The IFRIC received requests for guidance on whether an entity can designate a purchased option in its entirety as the hedging instrument in a cash flow hedge of a highly probable forecast transaction in such a way that all changes in the fair value of

****Editor's note**: Paragraphs BC172A added in December 2008.*

†***Editor's note**: Paragraphs BC172B to BC172J added in November 2008.*

the purchased option, including changes in the time value, are regarded as effective and would be recognised in other comprehensive income. The exposure draft proposed to amend IAS 39 to clarify that such a designation was not allowed.

After considering the responses to the exposure draft, the Board confirmed that the designation set out in paragraph BC172D is not permitted. **BC172E**

The Board reached that decision by considering the variability of future cash flow outcomes resulting from a price increase of a forecast commodity purchase (a one-sided risk). The Board noted that the forecast transaction contained no separately identifiable risk that affects profit or loss that is equivalent to the time value of a purchased option hedging instrument (with the same principal terms as the designated risk). The Board concluded that the intrinsic value of a purchased option, but not its time value, reflects a one-sided risk in a hedged item. The Board then considered a purchased option designated in its entirety as the hedging instrument. The Board noted that hedge accounting is based on a principle of offsetting changes in fair value or cash flows between the hedging instrument and the hedged item. Because a designated one-sided risk does not contain the time value of a purchased option hedging instrument, the Board noted that there will be no offset between the cash flows relating to the time value of the option premium paid and the designated hedged risk. Therefore, the Board concluded that a purchased option designated in its entirety as the hedging instrument of a one-sided risk will not be perfectly effective. **BC172F**

Designation of inflation in particular situations

The IFRIC received a request for guidance on whether, for a hedge of a fixed rate financial instrument, an entity can designate inflation as the hedged item. The exposure draft proposed to amend IAS 39 to clarify that such a designation was not allowed. **BC172G**

After considering the responses to the exposure draft, the Board acknowledged that expectations of future inflation rates can be viewed as an economic component of nominal interest. However, the Board also noted that hedge accounting is an exception to normal accounting principles for the hedged item (fair value hedges) or hedging instrument (cash flow hedges). To ensure a disciplined use of hedge accounting the Board noted that restrictions regarding eligible hedged items are necessary, especially if something other than the entire fair value or cash flow variability of a hedged item is designated. **BC172H**

The Board noted that paragraph 81 permits an entity to designate as the hedged item something other than the entire fair value change or cash flow variability of a financial instrument. For example, an entity may designate some (but not all) risks of a financial instrument, or some (but not all) cash flows of a financial instrument (a 'portion'). **BC172I**

The Board noted that, to be eligible for hedge accounting, the designated risks and portions must be separately identifiable components of the financial instrument, and changes in the fair value or cash flows of the entire financial instrument arising from changes in the designated risks and portions must be reliably measurable. The Board noted that these principles were important in order for the effectiveness requirements set out in paragraph 88 to be applied in a meaningful way. The Board also noted that deciding whether designated risks and portions are separately identifiable and reliably measurable requires judgement. However, the Board confirmed that unless the inflation portion is a contractually specified portion of cash flows and other cash **BC172J** flows of the financial instrument are not affected by the inflation portion, inflation is not separately identifiable and reliably measurable and is not eligible for designation as a hedged risk or portion of a financial instrument.

Fair Value Hedge Accounting for a Portfolio Hedge of Interest Rate Risk

Background

BC173 The Exposure Draft of proposed improvements to IAS 39 published in June 2002 did not propose any substantial changes to the requirements for hedge accounting as they applied to a portfolio hedge of interest rate risk. However, some of the comment letters on the Exposure Draft and participants in the roundtable discussions raised this issue. In particular, some were concerned that portfolio hedging strategies they regarded as effective hedges would not have qualified for fair value hedge accounting in accordance with previous versions of IAS 39. Rather, they would have either:

(a) not qualified for hedge accounting at all, with the result that reported profit or loss would be volatile; or

(b) qualified only for cash flow hedge accounting, with the result that reported equity would be volatile.

BC174 In the light of these concerns, the Board decided to explore whether and how IAS 39 could be amended to enable fair value hedge accounting to be used more readily for portfolio hedges of interest rate risk. As a result, in August 2003 the Board published a second Exposure Draft, *Fair Value Hedge Accounting for a Portfolio Hedge of Interest Rate Risk*, with a comment deadline of 14 November 2003. More than 120 comment letters were received. The amendments proposed in this second Exposure Draft were finalised in March 2004. Paragraphs BC135A-BC136B and BC175-BC220 summarise the Board's considerations in reaching conclusions on the issues raised.

Scope

BC175 The Board decided to limit any amendments to IAS 39 to applying fair value hedge accounting to a hedge of interest rate risk on a portfolio of items. In making this decision it noted that:

(a) implementation guidance on IAS 39* explains how to apply cash flow hedge accounting to a hedge of the interest rate risk on a portfolio of items.

(b) the issues that arise for a portfolio hedge of interest rate risk are different from those that arise for hedges of individual items and for hedges of other risks. In particular, the three issues discussed in paragraph BC176 do not arise in combination for such other hedging arrangements.

The issue: why fair value hedge accounting was difficult to achieve in accordance with previous versions of IAS 39

BC176 The Board identified the following three main reasons why a portfolio hedge of interest rate risk might not have qualified for fair value hedge accounting in accordance with previous versions of IAS 39.

(a) Typically, many of the assets that are included in a portfolio hedge are prepayable, ie the counterparty has a right to repay the item before its contractual repricing date. Such assets contain a prepayment option whose fair value

see Q&A F.6.1 and F.6.2

changes as interest rates change. However, the derivative that is used as the hedging instrument typically is not prepayable, ie it does not contain a prepayment option. When interest rates change, the resulting change in the fair value of the hedged item (which is prepayable) differs from the change in fair value of the hedging derivative (which is not prepayable), with the result that the hedge may not meet IAS 39's effectiveness tests.* Furthermore, prepayment risk may have the effect that the items included in a portfolio hedge fail the requirement† that a group of hedged assets or liabilities must be "similar" and the related requirement‡ that "the change in fair value attributable to the hedged risk for each individual item in the group shall be expected to be approximately proportional to the overall change in fair value attributable to the hedged risk of the group of items".

(b) IAS 39§ prohibits the designation of an overall net position (eg the net of fixed rate assets and fixed rate liabilities) as the hedged item. Rather, it requires individual assets (or liabilities), or groups of similar assets (or similar liabilities), that share the risk exposure equal in amount to the net position to be designated as the hedged item. For example, if an entity has a portfolio of CU100 of assets and CU80 of liabilities, IAS 39 requires that individual assets or a group of similar assets of CU20 are designated as the hedged item. However, for risk management purposes, entities often seek to hedge the net position. This net position changes each period as items are repriced or derecognised and as new items are originated. Hence, the individual items designated as the hedged item also need to be changed each period. This requires de- and redesignation of the individual items that constitute the hedged item, which gives rise to significant systems needs.

(c) Fair value hedge accounting requires the carrying amount of the hedged item to be adjusted for the effect of changes in the hedged risk.¶¶ Applied to a portfolio hedge, this could involve changing the carrying amounts of many thousands of individual items. Also, for any items subsequently de-designated from being hedged, the revised carrying amount must be amortised over the item's remaining life.|| This, too, gives rise to significant systems needs.

The Board decided that any change to IAS 39 must be consistent with the principles that underlie IAS 39's requirements on derivatives and hedge accounting. The three principles that are most relevant to a portfolio hedge of interest rate risk are: **BC177**

(a) derivatives should be measured at fair value;

(b) hedge ineffectiveness should be identified and recognised in profit or loss;** and

(c) only items that are assets and liabilities should be recognised as such in the balance sheet. Deferred losses are not assets and deferred gains are not liabilities. However, if an asset or liability is hedged, any change in its fair value that is attributable to the hedged risk should be recognised in the balance sheet.

**see IAS 39, paragraph AG105*

†*see IAS 39, paragraph 78*

‡*see IAS 39, paragraph 83*

§*see IAS 39, paragraph AG101*

¶¶*see IAS 39, paragraph 89 (b)*

||*see IAS 39, paragraph 92*

***Subject to the same materiality considerations that apply in this context as throughout IFRSs.*

Prepayment risk

BC178 In considering the issue described in paragraph BC176(a), the Board noted that a prepayable item can be viewed as a combination of a non-prepayable item and a prepayment option. It follows that the fair value of a fixed rate prepayable item changes for two reasons when interest rates move:

(a) the fair value of the contracted cash flows to the contractual repricing date changes (because the rate used to discount them changes); and
(b) the fair value of the prepayment option changes (reflecting, among other things, that the likelihood of prepayment is affected by interest rates).

BC179 The Board also noted that, for risk management purposes, many entities do not consider these two effects separately. Instead they incorporate the effect of prepayments by grouping the hedged portfolio into repricing time periods based on *expected* repayment dates (rather than contractual repayment dates). For example, an entity with a portfolio of 25-year mortgages of CU100 may expect 5 per cent of that portfolio to repay in one year's time, in which case it schedules an amount of CU5 into a 12-month time period. The entity schedules all other items contained in its portfolio in a similar way (ie on the basis of expected repayment dates) and hedges all or part of the resulting overall net position in each repricing time period.

BC180 The Board decided to permit the scheduling that is used for risk management purposes, ie on the basis of expected repayment dates, to be used as a basis for the designation necessary for hedge accounting. As a result, an entity would not be required to compute the effect that a change in interest rates has on the fair value of the prepayment option embedded in a prepayable item. Instead, it could incorporate the effect of a change in interest rates on prepayments by grouping the hedged portfolio into repricing time periods based on expected repayment dates. The Board noted that this approach has significant practical advantages for preparers of financial statements, because it allows them to use the data they use for risk management. The Board also noted that the approach is consistent with paragraph 81 of IAS 34, which permits hedge accounting for a portion of a financial asset or financial liability. However, as discussed further in paragraphs BC193-BC206, the Board also concluded that if the entity changes its estimates of the time periods in which items are expected to repay (eg in the light of recent prepayment experience), ineffectiveness will arise, regardless of whether the revision in estimates results in more or less being scheduled in a particular time period.

BC181 The Board also noted that if the items in the hedged portfolio are subject to different amounts of prepayment risk, they may fail the test in paragraph 78 of being similar and the related requirement in paragraph 83 that the change in fair value attributable to the hedged risk for each individual item in the group is expected to be approximately proportional to the overall change in fair value attributable to the hedged risk of the group of items. The Board decided that, in the context of a portfolio hedge of interest rate risk, these requirements could be inconsistent with the Board's decision, set out in the previous paragraph, on how to incorporate the effects of prepayment risk. Accordingly, the Board decided that they should not apply. Instead, the financial assets or financial liabilities included in a portfolio hedge of interest rate risk need only share the risk being hedged.

Designation of the hedged item and liabilities with a demand feature

BC182 The Board considered two main ways to overcome the issue noted in paragraph BC176(b). These were:

(a) to designate the hedged item as the overall net position that results from a portfolio containing assets and liabilities. For example, if a repricing time period contains CU100 of fixed rate assets and CU90 of fixed rate liabilities, the net position of CU10 would be designated as the hedged item.
(b) to designate the hedged item as a portion of the assets (ie assets of CU10 in the above example), but not to require individual assets to be designated.

Some of those who commented on the Exposure Draft favoured designation of the overall net position in a portfolio that contains assets and liabilities. In their view, existing asset-liability management (ALM) systems treat the identified assets and liabilities as a natural hedge. Management's decisions about additional hedging focus on the entity's remaining net exposure. They observe that designation based on a portion of either the assets or the liabilities is not consistent with existing ALM systems and would entail additional systems costs. **BC183**

In considering questions of designation, the Board was also concerned about questions of measurement. In particular, the Board observed that fair value hedge accounting requires measurement of the change in fair value of the hedged item attributable to the risk being hedged. Designation based on the net position would require the assets and the liabilities in a portfolio each to be measured at fair value (for the risk being hedged) in order to compute the fair value of the net position. Although statistical and other techniques can be used to estimate these fair values, the Board concluded that it is not appropriate to assume that the change in fair value of the hedging instrument is equal to the change in fair value of the net position. **BC184**

The Board noted that under the first approach in paragraph BC182 (designating an overall net position), an issue arises if the entity has liabilities that are repayable on demand or after a notice period (referred to below as 'demandable liabilities'). This includes items such as demand deposits and some types of time deposits. The Board was informed that, when managing interest rate risk, many entities that have demandable liabilities include them in a portfolio hedge by scheduling them to the date when they *expect* the total amount of demandable liabilities in the portfolio to be due because of net withdrawals from the accounts in the portfolio. This expected repayment date is typically a period covering several years into the future (eg 0-10 years hence). The Board was also informed that some entities wish to apply fair value hedge accounting based on this scheduling, ie they wish to include demandable liabilities in a fair value portfolio hedge by scheduling them on the basis of their expected repayment dates. The arguments for this view are: **BC185**

(a) it is consistent with how demandable liabilities are scheduled for risk management purposes. Interest rate risk management involves hedging the interest rate margin resulting from assets and liabilities and not the fair value of all or part of the assets and liabilities included in the hedged portfolio. The interest rate margin of a specific period is subject to variability as soon as the amount of fixed rate assets in that period differs from the amount of fixed rate liabilities in that period.
(b) it is consistent with the treatment of prepayable assets to include demandable liabilities in a portfolio hedge based on expected repayment dates.
(c) as with prepayable assets, expected maturities for demandable liabilities are based on the historical behaviour of customers.
(d) applying the fair value hedge accounting framework to a portfolio that includes demandable liabilities would not entail an immediate gain on origination of such liabilities because all assets and liabilities enter the hedged portfolio at their carrying amounts. Furthermore, IAS 39* requires the carrying amount of

**see IAS 39, paragraph AG76*

a financial liability on its initial recognition to be its fair value, which normally equates to the transaction price (ie the amount deposited).

(e) historical analysis shows that a base level of a portfolio of demandable liabilities, such as chequing accounts, is very stable. Whilst a portion of the demandable liabilities varies with interest rates, the remaining portion—the base level—does not. Hence, entities regard this base level as a long-term fixed rate item and include it as such in the scheduling that is used for risk management purposes.

(f) the distinction between 'old' and 'new' money makes little sense at a portfolio level. The portfolio behaves like a long-term item even if individual liabilities do not.

BC186 The Board noted that this issue is related to that of how to measure the fair value of a demandable liability. In particular, it interrelates with the requirement in IAS 39* that the fair value of a liability with a demand feature is not less than the amount payable on demand, discounted from the first date that the amount could be required to be paid. This requirement applies to all liabilities with a demand feature, not only to those included in a portfolio hedge.

BC187 The Board also noted that:

(a) although entities, when managing risk, may schedule demandable liabilities based on the expected repayment date of the total balance of a portfolio of accounts, the deposit liabilities included in that balance are unlikely to be outstanding for an extended period (eg several years). Rather, these deposits are usually expected to be withdrawn within a short time (eg a few months or less), although they may be replaced by new deposits. Put another way, the balance of the portfolio is relatively stable only because withdrawals on some accounts (which usually occur relatively quickly) are offset by new deposits into others. Thus, the liability being hedged is actually the forecast replacement of existing deposits by the receipt of new deposits. IAS 39 does not permit a hedge of such a forecast transaction to qualify for fair value hedge accounting. Rather, fair value hedge accounting can be applied only to the liability (or asset) or firm commitment that exists today.

(b) a portfolio of demandable liabilities is similar to a portfolio of trade payables. Both comprise individual balances that usually are expected to be paid within a short time (eg a few months or less) and replaced by new balances. Also, for both, there is an amount—the base level—that is expected to be stable and present indefinitely. Hence, if the Board were to permit demandable liabilities to be included in a fair value hedge on the basis of a stable base level created by expected replacements, it should similarly allow a hedge of a portfolio of trade payables to qualify for fair value hedge accounting on this basis.

(c) a portfolio of similar core deposits is not different from an individual deposit, other than that, in the light of the 'law of large numbers', the behaviour of the portfolio is more predictable. There are no diversification effects from aggregating many similar items.

(d) it would be inconsistent with the requirement in IAS 39 that the fair value of a liability with a demand feature is not less than the amount payable on demand, discounted from the first date that the amount could be required to be paid, to schedule such liabilities for hedging purposes using a different date. For example, consider a deposit of CU100 that can be withdrawn on demand without penalty. IAS 39 states that the fair value of such a deposit is CU100. That fair value is unaffected by interest rates and does not change when interest

see IAS 39, paragraph 49

rates move. Accordingly, the demand deposit cannot be included in a fair value hedge of interest rate risk—there is no fair value exposure to hedge.

For these reasons, the Board concluded that demandable liabilities should not be included in a portfolio hedge on the basis of the expected repayment date of the *total balance of a portfolio* of demandable liabilities, ie including expected rollovers or replacements of existing deposits by new ones. However, as part of its consideration of comments received on the Exposure Draft, the Board also considered whether a demandable liability, such as a demand deposit, could be included in a portfolio hedge based on the expected repayment date of the *existing balance of individual deposits*, ie ignoring any rollovers or replacements of existing deposits by new deposits. The Board noted the following. **BC188**

(a) For many demandable liabilities, this approach would imply a much earlier expected repayment date than is generally assumed for risk management purposes. In particular, for chequing accounts it would probably imply an expected maturity of a few months or less. However, for other demandable liabilities, such as fixed term deposits that can be withdrawn only by the depositor incurring a significant penalty, it might imply an expected repayment date that is closer to that assumed for risk management.

(b) This approach implies that the *fair value* of the demandable liability should also reflect the expected repayment date of the existing balance, ie that the fair value of a demandable deposit liability is the present value of the amount of the deposit discounted from the expected repayment date. The Board noted that it would be inconsistent to permit fair value hedge accounting to be based on the expected repayment date, but to measure the fair value of the liability on initial recognition on a different basis. The Board also noted that this approach would give rise to a difference on initial recognition between the amount deposited and the fair value recognised in the balance sheet. This, in turn, gives rise to the issue of what the difference represents. Possibilities the Board considered include (i) the value of the depositor's option to withdraw its money before the expected maturity, (ii) prepaid servicing costs or (iii) a gain. The Board did not reach a conclusion on what the difference represents, but agreed that if it were to require such differences to be recognised, this would apply to all demandable liabilities, not only to those included in a portfolio hedge. Such a requirement would represent a significant change from present practice.

(c) If the fair value of a demandable deposit liability at the date of initial recognition is deemed to equal the amount deposited, a fair value portfolio hedge based on an expected repayment date is unlikely to be effective. This is because such deposits typically pay interest at a rate that is significantly lower than that being hedged (eg the deposits may pay interest at zero or at very low rates, whereas the interest rate being hedged may be LIBOR or a similar benchmark rate). Hence, the fair value of the deposit will be significantly less sensitive to interest rate changes than that of the hedging instrument.

(d) The question of how to fair value a demandable liability is closely related to issues being debated by the Board in other projects, including Insurance (phase II), Revenue Recognition, Leases and Measurement. The Board's discussions in these other projects are continuing and it would be premature to reach a conclusion in the context of portfolio hedging without considering the implications for these other projects.

As a result, the Board decided: **BC189**

(a) to confirm the requirement in IAS 39* that "the fair value of a financial liability with a demand feature (eg a demand deposit) is not less than the amount

**see paragraph 49*

payable on demand, discounted from the first date that the amount could be required to be paid", and

(b) consequently, that a demandable liability cannot qualify for fair value hedge accounting for any time period beyond the shortest period in which the counterparty can demand payment.

The Board noted that, depending on the outcome of its discussions in other projects (principally Insurance (phase II), Revenue Recognition, Leases and Measurement), it might reconsider these decisions at some time in the future.

BC190 The Board also noted that what is designated as the hedged item in a portfolio hedge affects the relevance of this issue, at least to some extent. In particular, if the hedged item is designated as a portion *of the assets* in a portfolio, this issue is irrelevant. To illustrate, assume that in a particular repricing time period an entity has CU100 of fixed rate assets and CU80 of what it regards as fixed rate liabilities and the entity wishes to hedge its net exposure of CU20. Also assume that all of the liabilities are demandable liabilities and the time period is later than that containing the earliest date on which the items can be repaid. If the hedged item is designated as CU20 of *assets*, then the demandable *liabilities* are not included in the hedged item, but rather are used only to determine how much of the assets the entity wishes to designate as being hedged. In such a case, whether the demandable liabilities can be designated as a hedged item in a fair value hedge is irrelevant. However, if the overall net position were to be designated as the hedged item, because the net position comprises CU100 of assets and CU80 of demandable liabilities, whether the demandable liabilities can be designated as a hedged item in a fair value hedge becomes critical.

BC191 Given the above points, the Board decided that a portion of assets or liabilities (rather than an overall net position) may be designated as the hedged item, to overcome part of the demandable liabilities issue. It also noted that this approach is consistent with IAS 39*, whereas designating an overall net position is not. IAS 39† prohibits an overall net position from being designated as the hedged item, but permits a similar effect to be achieved by designating an amount of assets (or liabilities) equal to the net position.

BC192 However, the Board also recognised that this method of designation would not fully resolve the demandable liabilities issue. In particular, the issue is still relevant if, in a particular repricing time period, the entity has so many demandable liabilities whose earliest repayment date is before that time period that (a) they comprise nearly all of what the entity regards as its fixed rate liabilities and (b) its fixed rate liabilities (including the demandable liabilities) exceed its fixed rate assets in this repricing time period. In this case, the entity is in a net liability position. Thus, it needs to designate an amount of the *liabilities* as the hedged item. But unless it has sufficient fixed rate liabilities other than those that can be demanded before that time period, this implies designating the demandable liabilities as the hedged item. Consistently with the Board's decision discussed above, such a hedge does not qualify for fair value hedge accounting. (If the liabilities are non-interest bearing, they cannot be designated as the hedged item in a cash flow hedge because their cash flows do not vary with changes in interest rates, ie there is no cash flow exposure to interest rates.‡ However, the hedging relationship may qualify for cash flow hedge accounting if designated as a hedge of associated assets.)

**see IAS 39, paragraph 84*

†see IAS 39, paragraph AG101

‡see Guidance on Implementing IAS 39, Question and Answer F.6.3.

What portion of assets should be designated and the impact on ineffectiveness

Having decided that a portion of assets (or liabilities) could be designated as the hedged item, the Board considered how to overcome the systems problems noted in paragraph BC176(b) and (c). The Board noted that these problems arise from designating individual assets (or liabilities) as the hedged item. Accordingly, the Board decided that the hedged item could be expressed as an *amount* (of assets or liabilities) rather than as individual assets or liabilities. **BC193**

The Board noted that this decision—that the hedged item may be designated as an amount of assets or liabilities rather than as specified items—gives rise to the issue of how the amount designated should be specified. The Board considered comments received on the Exposure Draft that it should not specify any method for designating the hedged item and hence measuring effectiveness. However, the Board concluded that if it provided no guidance, entities might designate in different ways, resulting in little comparability between them. The Board also noted that its objective, when permitting an amount to be designated, was to overcome the systems problems associated with designating individual items whilst achieving a very similar accounting result. Accordingly, it concluded that it should require a method of designation that closely approximates the accounting result that would be achieved by designating individual items. **BC194**

Additionally, the Board noted that designation determines how much, if any, ineffectiveness arises if actual repricing dates in a particular repricing time period vary from those estimated or if the estimated repricing dates are revised. Taking the above example of a repricing time period in which there are CU100 of fixed rate assets and the entity designates as the hedged item an amount of CU20 of assets, the Board considered two approaches (a layer approach and a percentage approach) that are summarised below. **BC195**

Layer approach

The first of these approaches, illustrated in figure 1, designates the hedged item as a 'layer' (eg (a) the bottom layer, (b) the top layer or (c) a portion of the top layer) of the assets (or liabilities) in a repricing time period. In this approach, the portfolio of CU100 in the above example is considered to comprise a hedged layer of CU20 and an unhedged layer of CU80. **BC196**

Figure 1: Illustrating the designation of an amount of assets as a layer

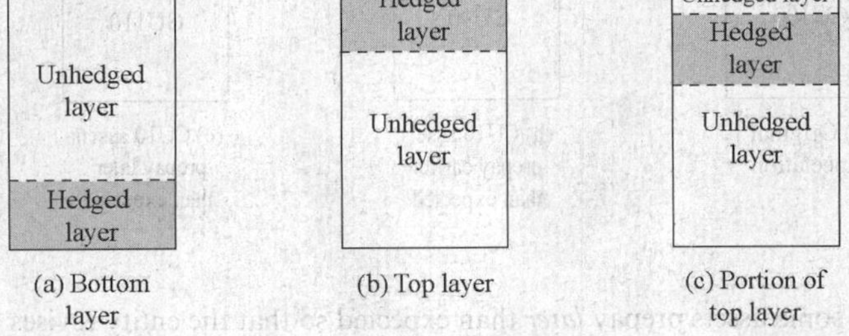

The Board noted that the layer approach does not result in the recognition of ineffectiveness in all cases when the estimated amount of assets (or liabilities) **BC197**

changes. For example, in a bottom layer approach (see figure 2), if some assets prepay earlier than expected so that the entity revises downward its estimate of the amount of assets in the repricing time period (eg from CU100 to CU90), these reductions are assumed to come first from the unhedged top layer (figure 2(b)). Whether any ineffectiveness arises depends on whether the downward revision reaches the hedged layer of CU20. Thus, if the bottom layer is designated as the hedged item, it is unlikely that the hedged (bottom) layer will be reached and that any ineffectiveness will arise. Conversely, if the top layer is designated (see figure 3), any downward revision to the estimated amount in a repricing time period will reduce the hedged (top) layer and ineffectiveness will arise (figure 3(b)).

Figure 2: Illustrating the effect on changes in prepayments in a bottom layer approach

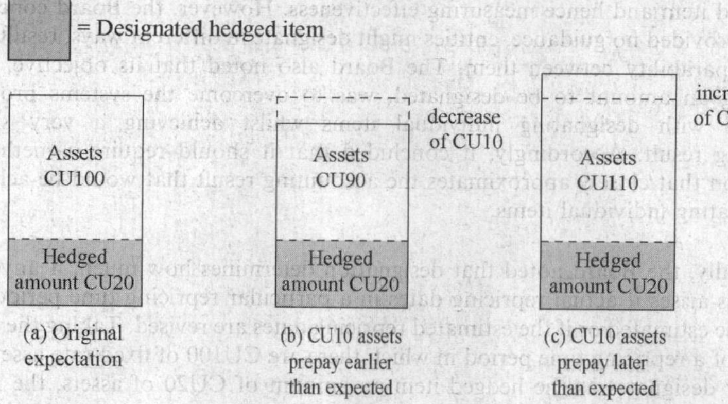

Figure 3: Illustrating the effect on changes in prepayments in a top layer approach

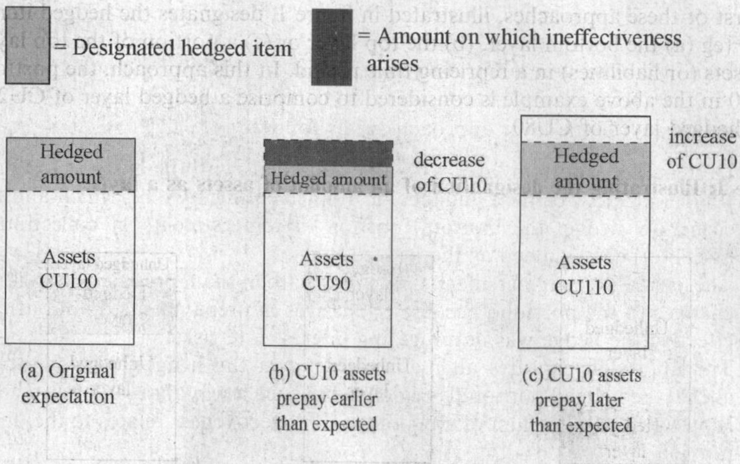

BC198 Finally, if some assets prepay *later* than expected so that the entity revises *upward* its estimate of the amount of assets in this repricing time period (eg from CU100 to CU110, see figures 2(c) and 3(c)), no ineffectiveness arises no matter how the layer is designated, on the grounds that the hedged layer of CU20 is still there and that was all that was being hedged.

Percentage approach

The percentage approach, illustrated in figure 4, designates the hedged item as a percentage of the assets (or liabilities) in a repricing time period. In this approach, in the portfolio in the above example, 20 per cent of the assets of CU100 in this repricing time period is designated as the hedged item (figure 4(a)). As a result, if some assets prepay *earlier* than expected so that the entity revises *downwards* its estimate of the amount of assets in this repricing time period (eg from CU100 to CU90, figure 4(b)), ineffectiveness arises on 20 per cent of the decrease (in this case ineffectiveness arises on CU2). Similarly, if some assets prepay *later* than expected so that the entity revises *upwards* its estimate of the amount of assets in this repricing time period (eg from CU100 to CU110, figure 4(c)), ineffectiveness arises on 20 per cent of the increase (in this case ineffectiveness arises on CU2). **BC199**

Illustrating the designation of an amount of assets as a percentage

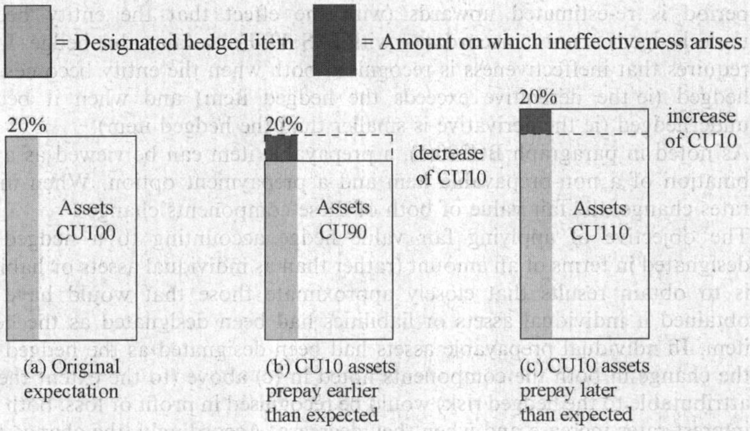

Arguments for and against the layer approach

The arguments for the layer approach are as follows: **BC200**

(a) Designating a bottom layer would be consistent with the answers to Questions F.6.1 and F.6.2 of the Guidance on Implementing IAS 39, which allow, for a cash flow hedge, the 'bottom' portion of reinvestments of collections from assets to be designated as the hedged item.

(b) The entity is hedging interest rate risk rather than prepayment risk. Any - changes to the portfolio because of changes in prepayments do not affect how effective the hedge was in mitigating interest rate risk.

(c) The approach captures all ineffectiveness on the hedged portion. It merely allows the hedged portion to be defined in such a way that, at least in a bottom layer approach, the first of any potential ineffectiveness relates to the unhedged portion.

(d) It is correct that no ineffectiveness arises if changes in prepayment estimates cause more assets to be scheduled into that repricing time period. So long as assets equal to the hedged layer remain, there is no ineffectiveness and upward revisions of the amount in a repricing time period do not affect the hedged layer.

(e) A prepayable item can be viewed as a combination of a non-prepayable item and a prepayment option. The designation of a bottom layer can be viewed as hedging a part of the life of the non-prepayable item, but none of the prepayment option. For example, a 25-year prepayable mortgage can be viewed as a combination of (i) a non-prepayable, fixed term, 25-year mortgage and (ii) a written prepayment option that allows the borrower to repay the mortgage early. If the entity hedges this asset with a 5year derivative, this is equivalent to hedging the first five years of component (i). If the position is viewed in this way, no ineffectiveness arises when interest rate changes cause the value of the prepayment option to change (unless the option is exercised and the asset prepaid) because the prepayment option was not hedged.

BC201 The arguments against the layer approach are as follows:

(a) The considerations that apply to a fair value hedge are different from those that apply to a cash flow hedge. In a cash flow hedge, it is the cash flows associated with the reinvestment of probable future collections that are hedged. In a fair value hedge it is the fair value of the assets that currently exist.

(b) The fact that no ineffectiveness is recognised if the amount in a repricing time period is re-estimated upwards (with the effect that the entity becomes underhedged) is not in accordance with IAS 39. For a fair value hedge, IAS 39 requires that ineffectiveness is recognised both when the entity becomes overhedged (ie the derivative exceeds the hedged item) and when it becomes underhedged (ie the derivative is smaller than the hedged item).

(c) As noted in paragraph BC200(e), a prepayable item can be viewed as a combination of a non-prepayable item and a prepayment option. When interest rates change, the fair value of both of these components changes.

(d) The objective of applying fair value hedge accounting to a hedged item designated in terms of an amount (rather than as individual assets or liabilities) is to obtain results that closely approximate those that would have been obtained if individual assets or liabilities had been designated as the hedged item. Ifi ndividual prepayable assets had been designated as the hedged item, the change in both the components noted in (c) above (to the extent they are attributable to the hedged risk) would be recognised in profit or loss, both when interest rates increase and when they decrease. Accordingly, the change in the fair value of the hedged asset would differ from the change in the fair value of the hedging derivative (unless that derivative includes an equivalent prepayment option) and ineffectiveness would be recognised for the difference. It follows that in the simplified approach of designating the hedged item as an amount, ineffectiveness should similarly arise.

(e) *All* prepayable assets in a repricing time period, and not just a layer of them, contain a prepayment option whose fair value changes with changes in interest rates. Accordingly, when interest rates change, the fair value of the hedged assets (which include a prepayment option whose fair value has changed) will change by an amount different from that of the hedging derivative (which typically does not contain a prepayment option), and ineffectiveness will arise. This effect occurs regardless of whether interest rates increase or decrease—ie regardless of whether re-estimates of prepayments result in the amount in a time period being more or less.

(f) Interest rate risk and prepayment risk are so closely interrelated that it is not appropriate to separate the two components referred to in paragraph BC200(e) and designate only one of them (or a part of one of them) as the hedged item. Often the biggest single cause of changes in prepayment rates is changes in interest rates. This close relationship is the reason why IAS 39* prohibits a held-to-maturity asset from being a hedged item with respect to either interest rate risk or prepayment risk. Furthermore, most entities do not separate the

**see IAS 39, paragraph 79*

two components for risk management purposes. Rather, they incorporate the prepayment option by scheduling amounts based on expected maturities. When entities choose to use risk management practices—based on not separating prepayment and interest rate risk—as the basis for designation for hedge accounting purposes, it is not appropriate to separate the two components referred to in paragraph BC200(e) and designate only one of them (or a part of one of them) as the hedged item.

(g) If interest rates change, the effect on the fair value of a portfolio of prepayable items will be different from the effect on the fair value of a portfolio of otherwise identical but non-prepayable items. However, using a layer approach, this difference would not be recognised—if both portfolios were hedged to the same extent, both would be recognised in the balance sheet at the same amount.

The Board was persuaded by the arguments in paragraph BC201 and rejected layer approaches. In particular, the Board concluded that the hedged item should be designated in such a way that if the entity changes its estimates of the repricing time periods in which items are expected to repay or mature (eg in the light of recent prepayment experience), ineffectiveness arises. It also concluded that ineffectiveness should arise both when estimated prepayments decrease, resulting in more assets in a particular repricing time period, and when they increase, resulting in fewer. **BC202**

Arguments for a third approach—measuring directly the change in fair value of the entire hedged item

The Board also considered comments on the Exposure Draft that: **BC203**

(a) some entities hedge prepayment risk and interest rate risk separately, by hedging to the expected prepayment date using interest rate swaps, and hedging possible variations in these expected prepayment dates using swaptions.

(b) the embedded derivatives provisions of IAS 39 require some prepayable assets to be separated into a prepayment option and a non-prepayable host contract* (unless the entity is unable to measure separately the prepayment option, in which case it treats the entire asset as held for trading†). This seems to conflict with the view in the Exposure Draft that the two risks are too difficult to separate for the purposes of a portfolio hedge.

In considering these arguments, the Board noted that the percentage approach described in paragraph AG126(b) is a proxy for measuring the change in the fair value of the *entire* asset (or liability)—including any embedded prepayment option—that is attributable to changes in interest rates. The Board had developed this proxy in the Exposure Draft because it had been informed that most entities (a) do not separate interest rate risk and prepayment risk for risk management purposes and hence (b) were unable to value the change in the value of the entire asset (including any embedded prepayment option) that is attributable to changes in the hedged interest rates. However, the comments described in BC203 indicated that in some cases, entities may be able to measure this change in value directly. The Board noted that such a direct method of measurement is conceptually preferable to the proxy described in paragraph AG126(b) and, accordingly, decided to recognise it explicitly. Thus, for example, if an entity that hedges prepayable assets using a combination of interest rate swaps and swaptions is able to measure directly the change in fair value of the entire asset, it could measure effectiveness by comparing **BC204**

**see IAS 39, paragraphs 11 and AG30(g)*

†see IAS 39, paragraph 12

the change in the value of the swaps and swaptions with the change in the fair value of the entire asset (including the change in the value of the prepayment option embedded in them) that is attributable to changes in the hedged interest rate. However, the Board also decided to permit the proxy proposed in the Exposure Draft for those entities that are unable to measure directly the change in the fair value of the entire asset.

Consideration of systems requirements

BC205 Finally, the Board was informed that, to be practicable in terms of systems needs, any approach should not require tracking of the amount in a repricing time period for multiple periods. Therefore it decided that ineffectiveness should be calculated by determining the change in the estimated amount in a repricing time period between one date on which effectiveness is measured and the next, as described more fully in paragraphs AG126 and AG127. This requires the entity to track how much of the change in each repricing time period between these two dates is attributable to revisions in estimates and how much is attributable to the origination of new assets (or liabilities). However, once ineffectiveness has been determined as set out above, the entity in essence starts again, ie it establishes the new amount in each repricing time period (including new items that have been originated since it last tested effectiveness), designates a new hedged item, and repeats the procedures to determine ineffectiveness at the next date it tests effectiveness. Thus the tracking is limited to movements between one date when effectiveness is measured and the next. It is not necessary to track for multiple periods. However, the entity will need to keep records relating to each repricing time period (a) to reconcile the amounts for each repricing time period with the total amounts in the two separate line items in the balance sheet (see paragraph AG114(f)), and (b) to ensure that amounts in the two separate line items are derecognised no later than when the repricing time period to which they relate expires.

BC206 The Board also noted that the amount of tracking required by the percentage approach is no more than what would be required by any of the layer approaches. Thus, the Board concluded that none of the approaches was clearly preferable from the standpoint of systems needs.

The carrying amount of the hedged item

BC207 The last issue noted in paragraph BC176 is how to present in the balance sheet the change in fair value of the hedged item. The Board noted the concern of respondents that the hedged item may contain many—even thousands of—individual assets (or liabilities) and that to change the carrying amounts of each of these individual items would be impracticable. The Board considered dealing with this concern by permitting the change in value to be presented in a single line item in the balance sheet. However, the Board noted that this could result in a decrease in the fair value of a financial asset (financial liability) being recognised as a financial liability (financial asset). Furthermore, for some repricing time periods the hedged item may be an asset, whereas for others it may be a liability. The Board concluded that it would be incorrect to present together the changes in fair value for such repricing time periods, because to do so would combine changes in the fair value of assets with changes in the fair value of liabilities.

BC208 Accordingly, the Board decided that two line items should be presented, as follows:

(a) for those repricing time periods for which the hedged item is an asset, the change in its fair value is presented in a single separate line item within assets; and

(b) for those repricing time periods for which the hedged item is a liability, the change in its fair value is presented in a single separate line item within liabilities.

The Board noted that these line items represent changes in the fair value of the hedged item. For this reason, the Board decided that they should be presented next to financial assets or financial liabilities. **BC209**

Derecognition of amounts included in the separate line items

Derecognition of an asset (or liability) in the hedged portfolio

The Board discussed how and when amounts recognised in the separate balance sheet line items should be removed from the balance sheet. The Board noted that the objective is to remove such amounts from the balance sheet in the same periods as they would have been removed had individual assets or liabilities (rather than an amount) been designated as the hedged item. **BC210**

The Board noted that this objective could be fully met only if the entity schedules individual assets or liabilities into repricing time periods and tracks both for how long the scheduled individual items have been hedged and how much of each item was hedged in each time period. In the absence of such scheduling and tracking, some assumptions would need to be made about these matters and, hence, about how much should be removed from the separate balance sheet line items when an asset (or liability) in the hedged portfolio is derecognised. In addition, some safeguards would be needed to ensure that amounts included in the separate balance sheet line items are removed from the balance sheet over a reasonable period and do not remain in the balance sheet indefinitely. With these points in mind, the Board decided to require that: **BC211**

(a) whenever an asset (or liability) in the hedged portfolio is derecognised—whether through earlier than expected prepayment, sale or write-off from impairment—any amount included in the separate balance sheet line item relating to that derecognised asset (or liability) should be removed from the balance sheet and included in the gain or loss on derecognition.

(b) if an entity cannot determine into which time period(s) a derecognised asset (or liability) was scheduled:

  (i) it should assume that higher than expected prepayments occur on assets scheduled into the first available time period; and

  (ii) it should allocate sales and impairments to assets scheduled into all time periods containing the derecognised item on a systematic and rational basis.

(c) the entity should track how much of the total amount included in the separate line items relates to each repricing time period, and should remove the amount that relates to a particular time period from the balance sheet no later than when that time period expires.

Amortisation

The Board also noted that if the designated hedged amount for a repricing time period is reduced, IAS 39* requires that the separate balance sheet line item described in paragraph 89A relating to that reduction is amortised on the basis of a recalculated effective interest rate. The Board noted that for a portfolio hedge of **BC212**

**see paragraph 92*

interest rate risk, amortisation based on a recalculated effective interest rate could be complex to determine and could demand significant additional systems requirements. Consequently, the Board decided that in the case of a portfolio hedge of interest rate risk (and only in such a hedge), the line item balance may be amortised using a straight-line method when a method based on a recalculated effective interest rate is not practicable.

The hedging instrument

BC213 The Board was asked by commentators to clarify whether the hedging instrument may be a portfolio of derivatives containing offsetting risk positions. Commentators noted that previous versions of IAS 39 were unclear on this point.

BC214 The issue arises because the assets and liabilities in each repricing time period change over time as prepayment expectations change, as items are derecognised and as new items are originated. Thus the net position, and the amount the entity wishes to designate as the hedged item, also changes over time. If the hedged item decreases, the hedging instrument needs to be reduced. However, entities do not normally reduce the hedging instrument by disposing of some of the derivatives contained in it. Instead, entities adjust the hedging instrument by entering into new derivatives with an offsetting risk profile.

BC215 The Board decided to permit the hedging instrument to be a portfolio of derivatives containing offsetting risk positions for both individual and portfolio hedges. It noted that all of the derivatives concerned are measured at fair value. It also noted that the two ways of adjusting the hedging instrument described in the previous paragraph can achieve substantially the same effect. Therefore the Board clarified paragraph 77 to this effect.

Hedge effectiveness for a portfolio hedge of interest rate risk

BC216 Some respondents to the Exposure Draft questioned whether IAS 39's effectiveness tests* should apply to a portfolio hedge of interest rate risk. The Board noted that its objective in amending IAS 39 for a portfolio hedge of interest rate risk is to permit fair value hedge accounting to be used more easily, whilst continuing to meet the principles of hedge accounting. One of these principles is that the hedge is highly effective. Thus, the Board concluded that the effectiveness requirements in IAS 39 apply equally to a portfolio hedge of interest rate risk.

BC217 Some respondents to the Exposure Draft sought guidance on how the effectiveness tests are to be applied to a portfolio hedge. In particular, they asked how the prospective effectiveness test is to be applied when an entity periodically 'rebalances' a hedge (ie adjusts the amount of the hedging instrument to reflect changes in the hedged item). The Board decided that if the entity's risk management strategy is to change the amount of the hedging instrument periodically to reflect changes in the hedged position, that strategy affects the determination of the term of the hedge. Thus, the entity needs to demonstrate that the hedge is expected to be highly effective only for the period until the amount of the hedging instrument is next adjusted. The Board noted that this decision does not conflict with the requirement in paragraph 75 that "a hedging relationship may not be designated for only a portion of the time period during which a hedging instrument remains outstanding". This is because the entire hedging instrument is designated (and not only some of its cash flows, for example, those to the time when the hedge is next adjusted). However, expected

**see paragraph AG105*

effectiveness is assessed by considering the change in the fair value of the entire hedging instrument only for the period until it is next adjusted.

A third issue raised in the comment letters was whether, for a portfolio hedge, the retrospective effectiveness test should be assessed for all time buckets in aggregate or individually for each time bucket. The Board decided that entities could use any method to assess retrospective effectiveness, but noted that the chosen method would form part of the documentation of the hedging relationship made at the inception of the hedge in accordance with paragraph 88(a) and hence could not be decided at the time the retrospective effectiveness test is performed. **BC218**

Transition to fair value hedge accounting for portfolios of interest rate risk

In finalising the amendments to IAS 39, the Board considered whether to provide additional guidance for entities wishing to apply fair value hedge accounting to a portfolio hedge that had previously been accounted for using cash flow hedge accounting. The Board noted that such entities could apply paragraph 101(d) to revoke the designation of a cash flow hedge and re-designate a new fair value hedge using the same hedged item and hedging instrument, and decided to clarify this in the Application Guidance. Additionally, the Board concluded that clarification was not required for first-time adopters because IFRS 1 already contained sufficient guidance. **BC219**

The Board also considered whether to permit retrospective designation of a portfolio hedge. The Board noted that this would conflict with the principle in paragraph 88(a) that "at the inception of the hedge there is formal designation and documentation of the hedging relationship" and accordingly, decided not to permit retrospective designation. **BC220**

ELIMINATION OF SELECTED DIFFERENCES FROM US GAAP

The Board considered opportunities to eliminate differences between IAS 39 and US GAAP. The guidance on measurement and hedge accounting under revised IAS 39 is generally similar to that under US GAAP. The amendments will further reduce or eliminate differences between IAS 39 and US GAAP in the areas listed below. In some other areas, a difference will remain. For example, US GAAP in many, but not all, areas is more detailed, which may result in a difference in accounting when an entity applies an accounting approach under IAS 39 that would not be permitted under US GAAP. **BC221**

Contracts to buy or sell a non-financial item

(a) The Board decided that a contract to buy or sell a non-financial item is a derivative within the scope of IAS 39 if the non-financial item that is the subject of the contract is readily convertible to cash and the contract is not a 'normal' purchase or sale. This requirement is comparable to the definition of a derivative in SFAS 133, which also includes contracts for which the underlying is readily convertible to cash, and to the scope exclusion in SFAS 133 for 'normal' purchases and sales.

Scope: loan commitments

(b) The Board decided to add a paragraph to IAS 39 to exclude particular loan commitments that are not settled net. Such loan commitments were within the scope of the original IAS 39. The amendment moves IAS 39 closer to US GAAP.

Unrealised gains and losses on available-for-sale financial assets

(c) The Board decided to eliminate the option to recognise in profit or loss gains and losses on available-for-sale financial assets (IAS 39, paragraph 55(b)), and thus require such gains and losses to be recognised in equity.* The change is consistent with SFAS 115, which does not provide the option in the original IAS 39 to recognise gains and losses on available-for-sale financial assets in profit or loss. SFAS 115 requires those unrealised gains and losses to be recognised in other comprehensive income (not profit or loss).

Fair value in active markets

(d) The Board decided to amend the wording in IAS 39, paragraph AG71, to state that, instead of a quoted market price *normally* being the best evidence of fair value, a quoted market price *is* the best evidence of fair value. This is similar to SFAS 107 *Disclosures about Fair Value of Financial Instruments*.

Fair value in inactive markets

(e) The Board decided to include in IAS 39 a requirement that the best evidence of the fair value of an instrument that is not traded in an active market is the transaction price, unless the fair value is evidenced by comparison with other observable current market transactions in the same instrument (ie without modification or repackaging) or based on a valuation technique incorporating only observable market data. This is similar to the requirements of EITF 0-23 *Issues Involved in Accounting for Derivative Contracts Held for Trading Purposes and Contracts Involved in Energy Trading and Risk Management Activities*.

Impaired fixed rate loans: observable market price

(f) The Board decided to permit an impaired fixed interest rate loan to be measured using an observable market price. SFAS 114 allows impairment to be measured on the basis of a loan's observable market price.

Reversal of impairment losses on investments in equity instruments

(g) The Board decided that if an entity recognises an impairment loss on an available-for-sale equity investment and the fair value of the investment subsequently increases, the increase in fair value should be recognised in equity. This is comparable to US GAAP under which reversals of impairment losses are not permitted.

Hedges of firm commitments

(h) The Board decided to require hedges of firm commitments to be treated as fair value hedges instead of cash flow hedges as was required under the original IAS 39 (except foreign currency risk when the hedge may be designated as

* *As a consequence of the revision of IAS 1* Presentation of Financial Statements *in 2007 such gains and losses are recognised in other comprehensive income.*

either a cash flow hedge or a fair value hedge). This change brings IAS 39 closer to SFAS 133.

Basis adjustments to financial assets or financial liabilities resulting from hedges of forecast transactions

(i) Basis adjustments to financial assets or financial liabilities resulting from hedges of forecast transactions are not permitted under SFAS 133. The revised IAS 39 also precludes such basis adjustments.

Basis adjustments to non-financial assets or non-financial liabilities resulting from hedges of forecast transactions

(j) The Board decided to permit entities to apply basis adjustments to non-financial assets or non-financial liabilities that result from hedges of forecast transactions. Although US GAAP precludes basis adjustments, permitting a choice in IAS 39 allows entities to meet the US GAAP requirements.

SUMMARY OF CHANGES FROM THE EXPOSURE DRAFT

The main changes from the Exposure Draft's proposals are as follows: **BC222**

Scope

(a) The Standard adopts the proposal in the Exposure Draft that loan commitments that cannot be settled net and are not classified at fair value through profit or loss are excluded from the scope of the Standard. The Standard requires, however, that a commitment to extend a loan at a below-market interest rate is initially recognised at fair value, and subsequently measured at the higher of (i) the amount determined under IAS 37 and (ii) the amount initially recognised, less where appropriate, cumulative amortisation recognised in accordance with IAS 18.

(b) The Standard adopts the proposal in the Exposure Draft that financial guarantees are initially recognised at fair value, but clarifies that subsequently they are measured at the higher of (a) the amount determined under IAS 37 and (b) the amount initially recognised, less, where appropriate, cumulative amortisation recognised in accordance with IAS 18.

Definitions

(c) The Standard amends the definition of 'originated loans and receivables' to 'loans and receivables'. Under the revised definition, an entity is permitted to classify as loans and receivables purchased loans that are not quoted in an active market.

(d) The Standard amends the definition of transaction costs in the Exposure Draft to include internal costs, provided they are incremental and directly attributable to the acquisition, issue or disposal of a financial asset or financial liability.

(e) The Standard amends the definition of the effective interest rate proposed in the Exposure Draft so that the effective interest rate is calculated using estimated cash flows for all instruments. An exception is made for those rare cases in which it is not possible to estimate cash flows reliably, when the Standard requires the use of contractual cash flows over the contractual life of the instrument. The Standard further stipulates that when accounting for a change in estimates, entities adjust the carrying amount of the instrument in the period of change with a corresponding gain or loss recognised in profit or loss. To calculate the new carrying amount, entities discount revised estimated cash flows at the original effective rate.

Derecognition of a financial asset

(f) The Exposure Draft proposed that an entity would continue to recognise a financial asset to the extent of its continuing involvement in that asset. Hence, an entity would derecognise a financial asset only if it did not have any continuing involvement in that asset. The Standard uses the concepts of control and of risks and rewards of ownership to determine whether, and to what extent, a financial asset is derecognised. The continuing involvement approach applies only if an entity retains some, but not substantially all, the risks and rewards of ownership and also retains control (see also (i) below).

(g) Unlike the Exposure Draft, the Standard clarifies when a part of a larger financial asset should be considered for derecognition. The Standard requires a part of a larger financial asset to be considered for derecognition if, and only if, the part is one of:
- only specifically identified cash flows from a financial asset;
- only a fully proportionate (pro rata) share of the cash flows from a financial asset; or
- only a fully proportionate (pro rata) share of specifically identified cash flows from a financial asset.

In all other cases, the Standard requires the financial asset to be considered for derecognition in its entirety.

(h) The Standard retains the conditions proposed in the Exposure Draft for 'pass-through arrangements' in which an entity retains the contractual rights to receive cash flows of a financial asset, but assumes a contractual obligation to pay those cash flows to one or more entities. However, because of confusion over the meaning of the term 'pass-through arrangements', the Standard does not use this term.

(i) The Standard requires that an entity first assesses whether it has transferred substantially all the risks and rewards of ownership. If an entity has retained substantially all such risks and rewards, it continues to recognise the transferred asset. If it has transferred substantially all such risks and rewards, it derecognises the transferred asset. If an entity has neither transferred nor retained substantially all the risks and rewards of ownership of the transferred asset, it assesses whether it has retained control over the transferred asset. Ifi t has retained control, the Standard requires the entity to continue recognising the transferred asset to the extent of its continuing involvement in the transferred asset. If it has not retained control, the entity derecognises the transferred asset.

(j) The Standard provides guidance on how to evaluate the concepts of risks and rewards and of control for derecognition purposes.

Measurement

(k) The Standard adopts the option proposed in the Exposure Draft to permit designation of any financial asset or financial liability on initial recognition as one to be measured at fair value, with changes in fair value recognised in profit or loss. However, the Standard clarifies that the fair value of liabilities with a demand feature, for example, demand deposits, is not less than the amount payable on demand discounted from the first date that the amount could be required to be paid.

(l) The Standard adopts the proposal in the Exposure Draft that quoted prices in active markets should be used to determine fair value in preference to other valuation techniques. The Standard adds guidance that if a rate (rather than a price) is quoted, these quoted rates are used as inputs into valuation techniques to determine the fair value. The Standard further clarifies that if an entity operates in more than one active market, the entity uses the price at which a transaction would occur at the balance sheet date in the same instrument (ie without modification or repackaging) in the most advantageous active market to which the entity has immediate access.

(m) The Standard simplifies the fair value measurement hierarchy in an inactive market so that recent market transactions do not take precedence over a valuation technique. Rather, when there is not a price in an active market, a valuation technique is used. Such valuation techniques include using recent arm's length market transactions.

(n) The Standard also clarifies that the best estimate of fair value at initial recognition of a financial instrument that is not quoted in an active market is the transaction price, unless the fair value of the instrument is evidenced by other observable market transactions or is based on a valuation technique whose variables include only data from observable markets.

Impairment of financial assets

(o) The Standard clarifies that an impairment loss is recognised only when it has been incurred. The Standard eliminates some of the detailed guidance in the Exposure Draft, in particular, the example of how to calculate the discount rate for the purpose of measuring impairment in a group of financial assets.

(p) The Exposure Draft proposed that impairment losses recognised on investments in debt or equity instruments that are classified as available for sale cannot be reversed through profit or loss. The Standard requires that for available-for-sale debt instruments, an impairment loss is reversed through profit or loss when fair value increases and the increase can be objectively related to an event occurring after the loss was recognised. Impairment losses recognised on available-for-sale equity instruments cannot be reversed through profit or loss, ie any subsequent increase in fair value is recognised in equity.*

Hedge accounting

(q) The Standard requires that when a hedged forecast transaction actually occurs and results in the recognition of a financial asset or a financial liability, the gain or loss deferred in equity does not adjust the initial carrying amount of the asset or liability (ie 'basis adjustment' is prohibited), but remains in equity and is recognised in profit or loss consistently with the recognition of gains and losses on the asset or liability. For hedges of forecast transactions that will result in the recognition of a non-financial asset or a non-financial liability, the entity has a choice of whether to apply basis adjustment or retain the hedging gain or loss in equity and recognise it in profit or loss when the asset or liability affects profit or loss.

(r) The Exposure Draft proposed to treat hedges of firm commitments as fair value hedges (rather than as cash flow hedges). The Standard adopts this requirement

**As a consequence of the revision of IAS 1* Presentation of Financial Statements *in 2007 such gains and losses are recognised in other comprehensive income.*

but clarifies that a hedge of the foreign currency risk of a firm commitment may be accounted for as either a fair value hedge or a cash flow hedge.

Transition

(s) The Exposure Draft maintained the prior guidance that a forecast intragroup transaction may be designated as the hedged item in a foreign currency cash flow hedge provided the transaction is highly probable, meets all other hedge accounting criteria, and will result in the recognition of an intragroup monetary item. The Standard (as revised in 2003) did not include this guidance in the light of comments received from some constituents questioning its conceptual basis. After the revised Standard was issued, constituents raised concerns that it was common practice for entities to designate a forecast intragroup transaction as the hedged item and that the revised IAS 39 created a difference from US GAAP. In response to these concerns, the Board published an Exposure Draft in July 2004*. That Exposure Draft proposed to allow an entity to apply hedge accounting in the consolidated financial statements to a highly probable forecast external transaction denominated in the functional currency of the entity entering into the transaction, provided the transaction gave rise to an exposure that would have an effect on the consolidated profit or loss (ie was denominated in a currency other than the group's presentation currency). After discussing the comment letters received on that Exposure Draft, the Board decided to permit the foreign currency risk of a forecast intragroup transaction to be the hedged item in a cash flow hedge in consolidated financial statements provided the transaction is denominated in a currency other than the functional currency of the entity entering into that transaction and the foreign currency risk will affect consolidated profit or loss. In issuing this amendment the Board concluded that:

(i) allowing a forecast intragroup transaction to be designated as the hedged item in consolidated financial statements is consistent with the functional currency framework in IAS 21 *The Effects of Changes in Foreign Exchange Rates*†, which recognises a functional currency exposure whenever a transaction (including a forecast transaction) is denominated in a currency different from the functional currency of the entity entering into the transaction.

(ii) allowing a forecast transaction (intragroup or external) to be designated as the hedged item in consolidated financial statements would not be consistent with the functional currency framework in IAS 21 if the transaction is denominated in the functional currency of the entity entering into it. Accordingly, such transactions should not be permitted to be designated as hedged items in a foreign currency cash flow hedge.

(iii) it is consistent with paragraphs 97 and 98 that any gain or loss that is recognised directly in equity‡ in a cash flow hedge of a forecast intragroup transaction should be reclassified into consolidated profit or loss in the same period or periods during which the foreign currency risk of the hedged transaction affects consolidated profit or loss.§

*ASB footnote: *In the UK equivalent proposed amendments were contained in FRED 30 Third Supplement published in July 2004.*

†ASB footnote: *The corresponding requirements in the UK and the Republic of Ireland are in FRS 23 (IAS 21)* The Effects of Changes in Foreign Exchange Rates.

‡*As a consequence of the revision of IAS 1* Presentation of Financial Statements *in 2007 such gains and losses are recognised in other comprehensive income.*

§***Editor's note:*** *section (s) added October 2005, with consequential re-referencing.*

(t) The revised Standard adopts the proposal in the Exposure Draft that, on transition, an entity is permitted to designate a previously recognised financial asset or financial liability as a financial asset or a financial liability at fair value through profit or loss or available for sale. However, a disclosure requirement has been added to IAS 32* to provide information about the fair value of the financial assets or financial liabilities designated into each category and the classification and carrying amount in the previous financial statements.

(u) The Exposure Draft proposed retrospective application of the derecognition provisions of the revised IAS 39 to financial assets derecognised under the original IAS 39. The Standard requires prospective application, namely that entities do not recognise those assets that were derecognised under the original Standard, but permits retrospective application from a date of the entity's choosing, provided that the information needed to apply IAS 39 to assets and liabilities derecognised as a result of past transactions was obtained at the time of initially accounting for those transactions.

(v) The Exposure Draft proposed, and the revised Standard originally required, retrospective application of the 'day 1' gain or loss recognition requirements in paragraph AG76. After the revised Standard was issued, constituents raised concerns that retrospective application would diverge from the requirements of US GAAP, would be difficult and expensive to implement, and might require subjective assumptions about what was observable and what was not. In response to these concerns, the Board decided:

(i) to permit entities to apply the requirements in the last sentence of paragraph AG76 in any one of the following ways:

- retrospectively, as previously required by IAS 39
- prospectively to transactions entered into after 25 October 2002, the effective date of equivalent US GAAP requirements
- prospectively to transactions entered into after 1 January 2004, the date of transition to IFRSs for many entities.

(ii) to clarify that a gain or loss should be recognised after initial recognition only to the extent that it arises from a change in a factor (including time) that market participants would consider in setting a price. Some constituents asked the Board to clarify that straight-line amortisation is an appropriate method of recognising the difference between a transaction price (used as fair value in accordance with paragraph AG76) and a valuation made at the time of the transaction that was not based solely on data from observable markets. The Board decided not to do this. It concluded that although straight-line amortisation may be an appropriate method in some cases, it will not be appropriate in others.†

DISSENTING OPINIONS

Dissent of Anthony T Cope, James J Leisenring and Warren J McGregor from the issue of IAS 39 in December 2003

Messrs Cope, Leisenring and McGregor dissent from the issue of this Standard. **DO1**

Mr Leisenring dissents because he disagrees with the conclusions concerning derecognition, impairment of certain assets and the adoption of basis adjustment hedge accounting in certain circumstances. **DO2**

**In August 2005, the IASB relocated all disclosures relating to financial instruments to IFRS 7* Financial Instruments: Disclosures. ***ASB footnote*: In December 2005, the ASB similarly relocated all disclosures relating to financial instruments to FRS 29.*

†*Editor's note: Section V added in October 2005.*

DO3 The Standard requires in paragraphs 30 and 31 that to the extent of an entity's continuing involvement in an asset, a liability should be recognised for the consideration received. Mr Leisenring believes that the result of that accounting is to recognise assets that fail to meet the definition of assets and to record liabilities that fail to meet the definition of liabilities. Furthermore, the Standard fails to recognise forward contracts, puts or call options and guarantees that are created, but instead records a fictitious 'borrowing' as a result of rights and obligations created by those contracts. There are other consequences of the continuing involvement approach that has been adopted. For transferors, it results in very different accounting by two entities when they have identical contractual rights and obligations only because one entity once owned the transferred financial asset. Furthermore, the 'borrowing' that is recognised is not accounted for like other loans, so no interest expense may be recorded. Indeed, implementing the proposed approach requires the specific override of measurement and presentation standards applicable to other similar financial instruments that do not arise from derecognition transactions. For example, derivatives created by derecognition transactions are not accounted for at fair value. For transferees, the approach also requires the override of the recognition and measurement requirements applicable to other similar financial instruments. If an instrument is acquired in a transfer transaction that fails the derecognition criteria, the transferee recognises and measures it differently from an instrument that is acquired from the same counterparty separately.

DO4 Mr Leisenring also disagrees with the requirement in paragraph 64 to include an asset that has been individually judged not to be impaired in a portfolio of similar assets for an additional portfolio assessment of impairment. Once an asset is judged not to be impaired, it is irrelevant whether the entity owns one or more similar assets as those assets have no implications for whether the asset that was individually considered for impairment is or is not impaired. The result of this accounting is that two entities could each own 50 per cent of a single loan. Both entities could conclude the loan is not impaired. However, if one of the two entities happens to have other loans that are similar, it would be allowed to recognise an impairment with respect to the loan where the other entity is not. Accounting for identical exposures differently is unacceptable. Mr Leisenring believes that the arguments in paragraph BC115 are compelling.

DO5 Mr Leisenring also dissents from paragraph 98 which allows but does not require basis adjustment for hedges of forecast transactions that result in the recognition of non-financial assets or liabilities. This accounting results in always adjusting the recorded asset or liability at the date of initial recognition away from its fair value. It also records an asset, if the basis adjustment alternative is selected, at an amount other than its cost as defined in IAS 16 *Property, Plant and Equipment* and further described in paragraph 16 of that Standard. If a derivative were to be considered a part of the cost of acquiring an asset, hedge accounting in these circumstances should not be elective to be consistent with IAS 16. Mr Leisenring also objects to creating this alternative as a result of an improvement project that ostensibly had as an objective the reduction of alternatives. The noncomparability that results from this alternative is both undesirable and unnecessary.

DO6 Mr Leisenring also dissents from the application guidance in paragraph AG71 and in particular the conclusion contained in paragraph BC98. He does not believe that an entity that originates a contract in one market should measure the fair value of the contract by reference to a different market in which the transaction did not take place. If prices change in the transacting market, that price change should be recognised when subsequently measuring the fair value of the contract. However, there are many implications of switching between markets when measuring fair value that the Board has not yet addressed. Mr Leisenring believes a gain or loss should not be recognised based on the fact a transaction could occur in a different market.

Mr Cope dissents from paragraph 64 and agrees with Mr Leisenring's analysis and conclusions on loan impairment as set out above in paragraph DO4. He finds it counter-intuitive that a loan that has been determined not to be impaired following careful analysis should be subsequently accounted for as if it were impaired when included in a portfolio. **DO7**

Mr Cope also dissents from paragraph 98, and, in particular, the Board's decision to allow a free choice over whether basis adjustment is used when accounting for hedges of forecast transactions that result in the recognition of non-financial assets or non-financial liabilities. In his view, of the three courses of action open to the Board—retaining IAS 39's requirement to use basis adjustment, prohibiting basis adjustment as proposed in the June 2002 Exposure Draft, or providing a choice—the Board has selected the worst course. Mr Cope believes that the best approach would have been to prohibit basis adjustment, as proposed in the Exposure Draft, because, in his opinion, basis adjustments result in the recognition of assets and liabilities at inappropriate amounts. **DO8**

Mr Cope believes that increasing the number of choices in international standards is bad policy. The Board's decision potentially creates major differences between entities choosing one option and those choosing the other. This lack of comparability will adversely affect users' ability to make sound economic decisions. **DO9**

In addition, Mr Cope notes that entities that are US registrants may choose not to adopt basis adjustment in order to avoid a large reconciling difference to US GAAP. Mr Cope believes that increasing differences between IFRS-compliant entities that are US registrants and those that are not is undesirable. **DO10**

Mr McGregor dissents from paragraph 98 and agrees with Mr Cope's and Mr Leisenring's analyses and conclusions as set out above in paragraphs DO5 and DO8-DO10. **DO11**

Mr McGregor also dissents from this Standard because he disagrees with the conclusions about impairment of certain assets. **DO12**

Mr McGregor disagrees with paragraphs 67 and 69, which deal with the impairment of equity investments classified as available for sale. These paragraphs require impairment losses on such assets to be recognised in profit or loss when there is objective evidence that the asset is impaired. Previously recognised impairment losses are not to be reversed through profit and loss when the assets' fair value increases. Mr McGregor notes that the Board's reasoning for prohibiting reversals through profit or loss of previously impaired available-for-sale equity investments, set out in paragraph BC130 of the Basis for Conclusions, is that it "..could not find an acceptable way to distinguish reversals of impairment losses from other increases in fair value". He agrees with this reasoning but believes that it applies equally to the recognition of impairment losses in the first place. Mr McGregor believes that the significant subjectivity involved in assessing whether a reduction in fair value represents an impairment (and thus should be recognised in profit or loss) or another decrease in value (and should be recognised directly in equity) will at best lead to a lack of comparability within an entity over time and between entities, and at worst provide an opportunity for entities to manage reported profit or loss. **DO13**

Mr McGregor believes that all changes in the fair value of assets classified as available for sale should be recognised in profit or loss. However, such a major change to the Standard would need to be subject to the Board's full due process. At **DO14** this time, to overcome the concerns expressed in paragraph DO13, he believes that for equity investments classified as available for sale, the Standard should require all changes in fair value below cost to be recognised in profit or loss as impairments and reversals of impairments and all changes in value above cost to be recognised in equity. This approach treats all changes in value the same way, no matter what their cause. The problem of how to distinguish an impairment loss from another decline in value (and of deciding whether there is an impairment in the first place) is eliminated because there is no longer any subjectivity involved. In addition, the approach is consistent with IAS 16 *Property, Plant and Equipment* and IAS 38 *Intangible Assets*.

DO15 Mr McGregor disagrees with paragraph 106 of the Standard and with the consequential amendments to paragraph 27 of IFRS 1 *First-time Adoption of International Financial Reporting Standards*. Paragraph 106 requires entities to apply the derecognition provisions prospectively to financial assets. Paragraph 27 of IFRS 1 requires first-time adopters to apply the derecognition provisions of IAS 39 (as revised in 2003) prospectively to non-derivative financial assets and financial liabilities. Mr McGregor believes that existing IAS 39 appliers should apply the derecognition provisions retrospectively to financial assets, and that first-time adopters should apply the derecognition provisions of IAS 39 retrospectively to all financial assets and financial liabilities. He is concerned that financial assets may have been derecognised under the original IAS 39 by entities that were subject to it, which might not have been derecognised under the revised IAS 39. He is also concerned that non-derivative financial assets and financial liabilities may have been derecognised by first-time adopters under previous GAAP that would not have been derecognised under the revised IAS 39. These amounts may be significant in many cases. Not requiring recognition of such amounts will result in the loss of relevant information and will impair the ability of users of financial statements to make sound economic decisions.

Dissent of John T Smith from the issue in March 2004 of amendments to International Accounting Standard IAS 39 on Fair Value Hedge Accounting for a Portfolio Hedge of Interest Rate Risk

DO1 Mr Smith dissents from these Amendments to IAS 39 Financial Instruments: Recognition and Measurement *Fair Value Hedge Accounting for a Portfolio Hedge of Interest Rate Risk*. He agrees with the objective of finding a macro hedging solution that would reduce systems demands without undermining the fundamental accounting principles related to derivative instruments and hedging activities. However, Mr Smith believes that some respondents' support for these Amendments and their willingness to accept IAS 39 is based more on the extent to which the Amendments reduce recognition of ineffectiveness, volatility of profit or loss, and volatility of equity than on whether the Amendments reduce systems demands without undermining the fundamental accounting principles.

DO2 Mr Smith believes some decisions made during the Board's deliberations result in an approach to hedge accounting for a portfolio hedge that does not capture what was originally intended, namely a result that is substantially equivalent to designating an individual asset or liability as the hedged item. He understands some respondents will not accept IAS 39 unless the Board provides still another alternative that will further reduce reported volatility. Mr Smith believes that the Amendments already go beyond their intended objective. In particular, he believes that features of these Amendments can be applied to smooth out ineffectiveness and achieve results substantially equivalent to the other methods of measuring ineffectiveness that the Board considered when developing the Exposure Draft. The Board rejected those methods because they did not require the immediate recognition of all ineffectiveness. He also believes those features could be used to manage earnings.

FRS 26 'Financial Instruments: Measurement'

ILLUSTRATIVE EXAMPLE

This example accompanies, but is not part of, FRS 26.

Facts

On 1 January 20x1, Entity A identifies a portfolio comprising assets and liabilities whose interest rate risk it wishes to hedge. The liabilities include demandable deposit liabilities that the depositor may withdraw at any time without notice. For risk management purposes, the entity views all of the items in the portfolio as fixed rate items. **IE1**

For risk management purposes, Entity A analyses the assets and liabilities in the portfolio into repricing time periods based on expected repricing dates. The entity uses monthly time periods and schedules items for the next five years (ie it has 60 separate monthly time periods).* The assets in the portfolio are prepayable assets that Entity A allocates into time periods based on the expected prepayment dates, by allocating a percentage of all of the assets, rather than individual items, into each time period. The portfolio also includes demandable liabilities that the entity expects, on a portfolio basis, to repay between one month and five years and, for risk management purposes, are scheduled into time periods on this basis. On the basis of this analysis, Entity A decides what amount it wishes to hedge in each time period. **IE2**

This example deals only with the repricing time period expiring in three months' time, ie the time period maturing on 31 March 20x1 (a similar procedure would be applied for each of the other 59 time periods). Entity A has scheduled assets of CU100 million and liabilities of CU80 million into this time period. All of the liabilities are repayable on demand. **IE3**

Entity A decides, for risk management purposes, to hedge the net position of CU20 million and accordingly enters into an interest rate swap† on 1 January 20x1 to pay a fixed rate and receive LIBOR, with a notional principal amount of CU20 million and a fixed life of three months. **IE4**

This Example makes the following simplifying assumptions: **IE5**

(a) the coupon on the fixed leg of the swap is equal to the fixed coupon on the asset;
(b) the coupon on the fixed leg of the swap becomes payable on the same dates as the interest payments on the asset; and
(c) the interest on the variable leg of the swap is the overnight LIBOR rate. As a result, the entire fair value change of the swap arises from the fixed leg only, because the variable leg is not exposed to changes in fair value due to changes in interest rates.

**In this Example principal cash flows have been scheduled into time periods but the related interest cash flows have been included when calculating the change in the fair value of the hedged item. Other methods of scheduling assets and liabilities are also possible. Also, in this Example, monthly repricing time periods have been used. An entity may choose narrower or wider time periods.*

†The Example uses a swap as the hedging instrument. An entity may use forward rate agreements or other derivatives as hedging instruments.

In cases when these simplifying assumptions do not hold, greater ineffectiveness will arise.

The ineffectiveness arising from (a) could be eliminated by designating as the hedged item a portion of the cash flows on the asset that are equivalent to the fixed leg of the swap.)

IE6 It is also assumed that Entity A tests effectiveness on a monthly basis.

IE7 The fair value of an equivalent non-prepayable asset of CU20 million, ignoring changes in value that are not attributable to interest rate movements, at various times during the period of the hedge is as follows:

	1 Jan 20x1	31 Jan 20x1	1 Feb 20x1	28 Feb 20x1	31 Mar 20x1
Fair value (asset) (CU)	20,000,000	20,047,408	20,047,408	20,023,795	Nil

IE8 The fair value of the swap at various times during the period of the hedge is as follows.

	1 Jan 20x1	31 Jan 20x1	1 Feb 20x1	28 Feb 20x1	31 Mar 20x1
Fair value (liability) (CU)	Nil	(47,408)	(47,408)	(23,795)	Nil

Accounting Treatment

IE9 On 1 January 20x1, Entity A designates as the hedged item an amount of CU20 million of assets in the three-month time period. It designates as the hedged risk the change in the value of the hedged item (ie the CU20 million of assets) that is attributable to changes in LIBOR. It also complies with the other designation requirements set out in paragraphs 88(d) and AG119 of the Standard.

IE10 Entity A designates as the hedging instrument the interest rate swap described in paragraph IE4.

End of month 1 (31 January 20x1)

IE11 On 31 January 20x1 (at the end of month 1) when Entity A tests effectiveness, LIBOR has decreased. Based on historical prepayment experience, Entity A estimates that, as a consequence, prepayments will occur faster than previously estimated. As a result it re-estimates the amount of assets scheduled into this time period (excluding new assets originated during the month) as CU96 million.

IE12 The fair value of the designated interest rate swap with a notional principal of CU20 million is (CU47,408)* (the swap is a liability).

IE13 Entity A computes the change in the fair value of the hedged item, taking into account the change in estimated prepayments, as follows.

(a) First, it calculates the percentage of the initial estimate of the assets in the time period that was hedged. This is 20 per cent (CU20 million ÷ CU100 million).

(b) Second, it applies this percentage (20 per cent) to its revised estimate of the amount in that time period (CU96 million) to calculate the amount that is the hedged item based on its revised estimate. This is CU19.2 million.

*see paragraph IE8.

(c) Third, it calculates the change in the fair value of this revised estimate of the hedged item (CU19.2 million) that is attributable to changes in LIBOR. This is CU45,511 (CU47,408* × (CU19.2 million ÷ CU20 million)).

Entity A makes the following accounting entries relating to this time period: † **IE14**

Dr	Cash	CU172,097	
Cr	Profit or loss (interest income)[§]		CU172,097

To recognise the interest received on the hedged amount

Dr	Profit or loss (interest expense)	CU179,268	
Cr	Profit or loss (interest income)		CU179,268
Cr	Cash		Nil

To recognise the interest received and paid on the swap designated as the hedging instrument.

Dr	Profit or loss (loss)		CU47,408
Cr	Derivative liability		CU47,408

To recognise the change in the fair value of the swap.

Dr	Separate line item in the statement of financial position		CU45,511
Cr	Profit or loss (gain)		CU45,511

To recognise the change in the fair value of the hedged amount.

The net result on profit or loss (excluding interest income and interest expense) is to recognise a loss of (CU1,897). This represents ineffectiveness in the hedging relationship that arises from the change in estimated prepayment dates. **IE15**

Beginning of month 2

On 1 February 20x1 Entity A sells a proportion of the assets in the various time periods. Entity A calculates that it has sold $8^1/_3$ per cent of the entire portfolio of assets. Because the assets were allocated into time periods by allocating a percentage of the assets (rather than individual assets) into each time period, Entity A determines that it cannot ascertain into which specific time periods the sold assets were scheduled. Hence it uses a systematic and rational basis of allocation. Based on the fact that it sold a representative selection of the assets in the portfolio, Entity A allocates the sale proportionately over all time periods. **IE16**

On this basis, Entity A computes that it has sold $8^1/_3$ per cent of the assets allocated to the three-month time period, ie CU8 million ($8^1/_3$ per cent of CU96 million). The proceeds received are CU8,018,400, equal to the fair value of the assets.‡ On derecognition of the assets, Entity A also removes from the separate line item in the statement of financial position an amount that represents the change in the fair value of the hedged assets that it has now sold. This is $8^1/_3$ per cent of the total line item balance of CU45,511, ie CU3,793. **IE17**

**ie CU20,047,408 – CU20,000,000. See paragraph IE7.*

†This Example does not show how amounts of interest income and interest expense are calculated.

‡The amount realised on sale of the asset is the fair value of a prepayable asset, which is less than the fair value of the equivalent non-prepayable asset shown in paragraph IE7.

IE18 Entity A makes the following accounting entries to recognise the sale of the asset and the removal of part of the balance in the separate balance sheet line item.

Dr	Cash	CU8,018,400	
Cr	Asset		CU8,000,000
Cr	Separate line item in the statement of financial position		CU3,793
Cr	Profit or loss (gain)		CU14,607

To recognise the sale of the asset at fair value and to recognise a gain on sale.

Because the change in the amount of the assets is not attributable to a change in the hedged interest rate no ineffectiveness arises.

IE19 Entity A now has CU88 million of assets and CU80 million of liabilities in this time period. Hence the net amount Entity A wants to hedge is now CU8 million and, accordingly, it designates CU8 million as the hedged amount.

IE20 Entity A decides to adjust the hedging instrument by designating only a proportion of the original swap as the hedging instrument. Accordingly, it designates as the hedging instrument CU8 million or 40 per cent of the notional amount of the original swap with a remaining life of two months and a fair value of CU18,963.* It also complies with the other designation requirements in paragraphs 88(a) and AG119 of the Standard. The CU12 million of the notional amount of the swap that is no longer designated as the hedging instrument is either classified as held for trading with changes in fair value recognised in profit or loss, or is designated as the hedging instrument in a different hedge. †

IE21 As at 1 February 20x1 and after accounting for the sale of assets, the separate line item in the statement of financial position is CU41,718 (CU45,511 – CU3,793), which represents the cumulative change in fair value of CU17.6‡ million of assets. However, as at 1 February 20x1, Entity A is hedging only CU8 million of assets that have a cumulative change in fair value of CU18,963.§ The remaining separate line item in the statement of financial position of CU22,755¶¶ relates to an amount of assets that Entity A still holds but is no longer hedging. Accordingly Entity A amortises this amount over the remaining life of the time period, ie it amortises CU22,755 over two months.

IE22 Entity A determines that it is not practicable to use a method of amortisation based on a recalculated effective yield and hence uses a straight-line method.

End of month 2 (28 February 20x1)

IE23 On 28 February 20x1 when Entity A next tests effectiveness, LIBOR is unchanged. Entity A does not revise its prepayment expectations. The fair value of the designated

**CU47,408* ∞ 40 per cent

†*The entity could instead enter into an offsetting swap with a notional principal of CU12 million to adjust its position and designate as the hedging instrument all CU20 million of the existing swap and all CU12 million of the new offsetting swap.*

‡*CU19.2 million-($8^1/_3$% ∞ CU19.2 million)*

§*CU41,718 ∞ (CU8 million ≥ CU17.6 million)*

¶¶*CU41,718 – CU18,963*

interest rate swap with a notional principal of CU8 million is (CU9,518)* (the swap is a liability). Also, Entity A calculates the fair value of the CU8 million of the hedged assets as at 28 February 20x1 as CU8,009,518†.

Entity A makes the following accounting entries relating to the hedge in this time period: **IE24**

Dr	Cash	CU71,707	
Cr	Profit or loss (interest income)		CU71,707

To recognise the interest received on the hedged amount (CU8 million).

Dr	Profit or loss (interest expense)	CU71,707	
Cr	Profit or loss (interest income)		CU62,115
Cr	Cash		CU9,592

To recognise the interest received and paid on the portion of the swap designated as the hedging instrument (CU8 million).

Dr	Derivative liability	CU9,445	
Cr	Profit or loss (gain)		CU9,445

To recognise the change in the fair value of the portion of the swap designated as the hedging instrument (CU8 million) (CU9,518 – CU18,963).

Dr	Profit or loss (loss)	CU9,445	
Cr	Separate line item in the statement of financial position		CU9,445

To recognise the change in the fair value of the hedged amount (CU8,009,518 – CU8,018,963).

The net effect on profit or loss (excluding interest income and interest expense) is nil reflecting that the hedge is fully effective. **IE25**

Entity A makes the following accounting entry to amortise the line item balance for this time period: ‡ **IE26**

Dr	Profit or loss (loss)	CU11,378	
Cr	Separate item in the statement of financial position		CU11,378*

To recognise the amortisation charge for the period.

End of month 3

During the third month there is no further change in the amount of assets or liabilities in the three-month time period. On 31 March 20x1 the assets and the swap mature and all balances are recognised in profit or loss. **IE27**

Entity A makes the following accounting entries relating to this time period: **IE28**

Dr	Cash	CU8,071,707	
Cr	Asset (balance sheet)		CU8,000,000
Cr	Profit or loss (interest income)		CU71,707

**CU23,795 [see paragraph IE8] ∞ (CU8 million ≥ CU20 million)*

†CU20,023,795 [see paragraph IE7] ∞ (CU8 million ≥ CU20 million)

‡CU22,755 ≥ 2

To recognise the interest and cash received on maturity of the hedged amount (CU8 million).

Dr	Profit or loss (interest expense)	CU71,707	
Cr	Profit or loss (interest income)		CU62,115
Cr	Cash		CU9,592

To recognise the interest received and paid on the portion of the swap designated as the hedging instrument (CU8 million).

Dr	Derivative liability	CU9,518	
Cr	Profit or loss (gain)		CU9,518

To recognise the expiry of the portion of the swap designated as the hedging instrument (CU8 million).

Dr	Profit or loss (loss)	CU9,518	
Cr	Separate line item in the statement of financial position		CU9,518

To remove the remaining line item balance on expiry of the time period.

IE29 The net effect on profit or loss (excluding interest income and interest expense) is nil reflecting that the hedge is fully effective.

IE30 Entity A makes the following accounting entry to amortise the line item balance for this time period: *

Dr	Profit or loss (loss)	CU11,377	
Cr	Separate line item in the statement of financial position		CU11,377*

To recognise the amortisation charge for the period.

Summary

IE31 The tables below summarise:

(a) changes in the separate line item in the statement of financial position;
(b) the fair value of the derivative;
(c) the profit or loss effect of the hedge for the entire three-month period of the hedge; and
(d) interest income and interest expense relating to the amount designated as hedged.

**CU22,755 ≥ 2*

Description	**1 Jan 20x1 CU**	**31 Jan 20x1 CU**	**1 Feb 20x1 CU**	**28 Feb 20x1 CU**	**31 Mar 20x1 CU**
Amount of asset hedged	**20,000,000**	**19,200,000**	**8,000,000**	**8,000,000**	**8,000,000**

(a) Changes in the separate line item in the statement of financial position

Brought forward:					
Balance to be amortised	Nil	Nil	Nil	22,755	11,377
Remaining balance	Nil	Nil	45,511	18,963	9,518
Less: Adjustment on sale of asset	Nil	Nil	(3,793)	Nil	Nil
Adjustment for change in fair value of the hedged asset	Nil	45,511	Nil	(9,445)	(9,518)
Amortisation	Nil	Nil	Nil	(11,378)	(11,377)
Carried forward:					
Balance to be amortised	**Nil**	**Nil**	**22,755**	**11,377**	**Nil**
Remaining balance	**Nil**	**45,511**	**18,963**	**9,518**	**Nil**

(b) The fair value of the derivative

	1 Jan 20x1	**31 Jan 20x1**	**1 Feb 20x1**	**28 Feb 20x1**	**31 Mar 20x1**
CU20,000,000	Nil	47,408	-	-	-
CU12,000,000	Nil	-	28,445	No longer designated as the hedging instrument.	
CU8,000,000	Nil	-	18,963	9,518	Nil
Total	**Nil**	**47,408**	**47,408**	**9,518**	**Nil**

(c) Profit or loss effect of the hedge

	1 Jan 20x1	**31 Jan 20x1**	**1 Feb 20x1**	**28 Feb 20x1**	**31 Mar 20x1**
Change in line item: asset	Nil	45,511	N/A	(9,445)	(9,518)
Change in derivative fair value	Nil	(47,408)	N/A	9,445	9,518
Net effect	**Nil**	**(1,897)**	**N/A**	**Nil**	**Nil**
Amortisation	**Nil**	**Nil**	**N/A**	**(11,378)**	**(11,377)**

In addition, there is a gain on sale of assets of CU14,607 at 1 February 20x1.

(d) Interest income and interest expense relating to the amount designated as hedged

Profit or loss recognised for the amount hedged	**1 Jan20x1**	**31 Jan20x1**	**1 Feb20x1**	**28 Feb 20x1**	**31 Mar20x1**
Interest income					
- on the asset	Nil	172,097	N/A	71,707	71,707
- on the swap	Nil	179,268	N/A	62,115	62,115
Interest expense					
- on the swap	Nil	(179,268)	N/A	(71,707)	(71,707)

Guidance on Implementing International Accounting Standard 39

Financial Instruments: Recognition and Measurement

Contents

Guidance on Implementing IAS 39
Financial Instruments: Recognition and Measurement

SECTION A: SCOPE
A.1 Practice of settling net: forward contract to purchase a commodity
A.2 Option to put a non-financial asset

SECTION B: DEFINITIONS
B.1 Definition of a financial instrument: gold bullion
B.2 Definition of a derivative: examples of derivatives and underlyings
B.3 Definition of a derivative: settlement at a future date, interest rate swap with net or gross settlement
B.4 Definition of a derivative: prepaid interest rate swap (fixed rate payment obligation prepaid at inception or subsequently)
B.5 Definition of a derivative: prepaid pay-variable, receive-fixed interest rate swap
B.6 Definition of a derivative: offsetting loans
B.7 Definition of a derivative: option not expected to be exercised
B.8 Definition of a derivative: foreign currency contract based on sales volume
B.9 Definition of a derivative: prepaid forward
B.10 Definition of a derivative: initial net investment
B.11 Definition of held for trading: portfolio with a recent actual pattern of short-term profit taking
B.12 Definition of held for trading: balancing a portfolio
B.13 Definition of held-to-maturity financial assets: index-linked principal
B.14 Definition of held-to-maturity financial assets: index-linked interest
B.15 Definition of held-to-maturity financial assets: sale following rating downgrade
B.16 Definition of held-to-maturity financial assets: permitted sales
B.17 Definition of held-to-maturity investments: sales in response to entity-specific capital requirements
B.18 Definition of held-to-maturity financial assets: pledged collateral, repurchase agreements (repos) and securities lending agreements
B.19 Definition of held-to-maturity financial assets: 'tainting'
B.20 Definition of held-to-maturity investments: subcategorisation for the purpose of applying the 'tainting' rule
B.21 Definition of held-to-maturity investments: application of the 'tainting' rule on consolidation
B.22 Definition of loans and receivables: equity instrument
B.23 Definition of loans and receivables: banks' deposits in other banks
B.24 Definition of amortised cost: perpetual debt instruments with fixed or market-based variable rate

B.25 Definition of amortised cost: perpetual debt instruments with decreasing interest rate
B.26 Example of calculating amortised cost: financial asset
B.27 Example of calculating amortised cost: debt instruments with stepped interest payments
B.28 Regular way contracts: no established market
B.29 Regular way contracts: forward contract
B.30 Regular way contracts: which customary settlement provisions apply?
B.31 Regular way contracts: share purchase by call option
B.32 Recognition and derecognition of financial liabilities using trade date or settlement date accounting

SECTION C: EMBEDDED DERIVATIVES
C.1 Embedded derivatives: separation of host debt instrument
C.2 Embedded derivatives: separation of embedded option
C.3 Embedded derivatives: accounting for a convertible bond
C.4 Embedded derivatives: equity kicker
C.5 Embedded derivatives: debt or equity host contract
C.6 Embedded derivatives: synthetic instruments
C.7 Embedded derivatives: purchases and sales contracts in foreign currency instruments
C.8 Embedded foreign currency derivatives: unrelated foreign currency provision
C.9 Embedded foreign currency derivatives: currency of international commerce
C.10 Embedded derivatives: holder permitted, but not required, to settle without recovering substantially all of its recognised investment
C.11 Embedded derivatives: reliable determination of fair value

SECTION D: RECOGNITION AND DERECOGNITION
D.1 Initial Recognition
D.1.1 Recognition: cash collateral
D.2 Regular Way Purchase or Sale of a Financial Asset
D.2.1 Trade date vs settlement date: amounts to be recorded for a purchase
D.2.2 Trade date vs settlement date: amounts to be recorded for a sale
D.2.3 Settlement date accounting: exchange of non-cash financial assets

SECTION E: MEASUREMENT
E.1 Initial Measurement of Financial Assets and Financial Liabilities
E.1.1 Initial measurement: transaction costs
E.2 Fair Value Measurement Considerations
E.2.1 Fair value measurement considerations for investment funds
E.2.2 Fair value measurement: large holding
E.3 Gains and Losses
E.3.1 Available-for-sale financial assets: exchange of shares
E.3.2 IAS 39 and IAS 21 – Available-for-sale financial assets: separation of currency component
E.3.3 IAS 39 and IAS 21 – Exchange differences arising on translation of foreign entities: equity or income?
E.3.4 IAS 39 and IAS 21 – Interaction between IAS 39 and IAS 21
E.4 Impairment and Uncollectibility of Financial Assets
E.4.1 Objective evidence of impairment
E.4.2 Impairment: future losses
E.4.3 Assessment of impairment: principal and interest
E.4.4 Assessment of impairment: fair value hedge
E.4.5 Impairment: provision matrix
E.4.6 Impairment: excess losses
E.4.7 Recognition of impairment on a portfolio basis

E.4.8 Impairment: recognition of collateral
E.4.9 Impairment of non-monetary available-for-sale financial asset
E.4.10 Impairment: whether the available-for-sale reserve in equity can be negative

SECTION F: HEDGING

F.1 Hedging Instruments

F.1.1 Hedging the fair value exposure of a bond denominated in a foreign currency
F.1.2 Hedging with a non-derivative financial asset or liability
F.1.3 Hedge accounting: use of written options in combined hedging instruments
F.1.4 Internal hedges
F.1.5 Offsetting internal derivative contracts used to manage interest rate risk
F.1.6 Offsetting internal derivative contracts used to manage foreign currency risk
F.1.7 Internal derivatives: examples of applying Question F.1.6
F.1.8 Combination of written and purchased options
F.1.9 Delta-neutral hedging strategy
F.1.10 Hedging instrument: out of the money put option
F.1.11 Hedging instrument: proportion of the cash flows of a cash instrument
F.1.12 Hedges of more than one type of risk
F.1.13 Hedging instrument: dual foreign currency forward exchange contract
F.1.14 Concurrent offsetting swaps and use of one as a hedging instrument

F.2 Hedged Items

F.2.1 Whether a derivative can be designated as a hedged item
F.2.2 Cash flow hedge: anticipated issue of fixed rate debt
F.2.3 Hedge accounting: unrecognised assets
F.2.4 Hedge accounting: hedging of future foreign currency revenue streams
F.2.5 Cash flow hedges: 'all in one' hedge
F.2.6 Hedge relationships: entity-wide risk
F.2.7 Cash flow hedge: forecast transaction related to an entity's equity
F.2.8 Hedge accounting: risk of a transaction not occurring
F.2.9 Held-to-maturity investments: hedging variable interest rate payments
F.2.10 Hedged items: purchase of held-to-maturity investment
F.2.11 Cash flow hedges: reinvestment of funds obtained from held-to-maturity investments
F.2.12 Hedge accounting: prepayable financial asset
F.2.13 Fair value hedge: risk that could affect profit or loss
F.2.14 Intragroup and intra-entity hedging transactions
F.2.15 Internal contracts: single offsetting external derivative
F.2.16 Internal contracts: external derivative contracts that are settled net
F.2.17 Partial term hedging
F.2.18 Hedging instrument: cross-currency interest rate swap
F.2.19 Hedged items: hedge of foreign currency risk of publicly traded shares
F.2.20 Hedge accounting: stock index
F.2.21 Hedge accounting: netting of assets and liabilities

F.3 Hedge Accounting

F.3.1 Cash flow hedge: fixed interest rate cash flows
F.3.2 Cash flow hedge: reinvestment of fixed interest rate cash flows
F.3.3 Foreign currency hedge
F.3.4 Foreign currency cash flow hedge
F.3.5 Fair value hedge: variable rate debt instrument
F.3.6 Fair value hedge: inventory
F.3.7 Hedge accounting: forecast transaction

F.3.8 Retrospective designation of hedges
F.3.9 Hedge accounting: designation at the inception of the hedge
F.3.10 Hedge accounting: identification of hedged forecast transaction
F.3.11 Cash flow hedge: documentation of timing of forecast transaction

F.4 Hedge Effectiveness

F.4.1 Hedging on an after-tax basis
F.4.2 Hedge effectiveness: assessment on cumulative basis
F.4.3 Hedge effectiveness: counterparty credit risk
F.4.4 Hedge effectiveness: effectiveness tests
F.4.5 Hedge effectiveness: less than 100 per cent offset
F.4.6 [Deleted]
F.4.7 Assuming perfect hedge effectiveness

F.5 Cash Flow Hedges

F.5.1 Hedge accounting: non-derivative monetary asset or non-derivative monetary liability used as a hedging instrument
F.5.2 Cash flow hedges: performance of hedging instrument (1)
F.5.3 Cash flow hedges: performance of hedging instrument (2)
F.5.4 Cash flow hedges: forecast transaction occurs before the specified period
F.5.5 Cash flow hedges: measuring effectiveness for a hedge of a forecast transaction in a debt instrument
F.5.6 Cash flow hedges: firm commitment to purchase inventory in a foreign currency

F.6 Hedging: Other Issues

F.6.1 Hedge accounting: management of interest rate risk in financial institutions
F.6.2 Hedge accounting considerations when interest rate risk is managed on a net basis
F.6.3 Illustrative example of applying the approach in Question F.6.2
F.6.4 Hedge accounting: premium or discount on forward exchange contract
F.6.5 IAS 39 and IAS 21 – Fair value hedge of asset measured at cost

SECTION G: OTHER

G.1 Disclosure of changes in fair value
G.2 IAS 39 and IAS 7 – Hedge accounting: cash flow statements

Implementation guidance relating to IAS 39 extracted from IFRS 1 *First-time Application of International Financial Reporting Standards*

IAS 39 *Financial Instruments: Recognition and Measurement*	IG52–IG60
Recognition	IG53–IG54
Embedded derivatives	IG55
Measurement	IG56–IG58
Transition adjustments	IG58A-IG59
Hedge accounting	IG60-IG60B

Guidance on Implementing

IAS 39 *Financial Instruments: Recognition and Measurement*

This guidance accompanies, but is not part of, IAS 39.

SECTION A: SCOPE

A.1 Practice of settling net: forward contract to purchase a commodity

Entity XYZ enters into a fixed price forward contract to purchase one million kilograms of copper in accordance with its expected usage requirements. The contract permits XYZ to take physical delivery of the copper at the end of twelve months or to pay or receive a net settlement in cash, based on the change in fair value of copper. Is the contract accounted for as a derivative?

While such a contract meets the definition of a derivative, it is not necessarily accounted for as a derivative. The contract is a derivative instrument because there is no initial net investment, the contract is based on the price of copper, and it is to be settled at a future date. However, if XYZ intends to settle the contract by taking delivery and has no history for similar contracts of settling net in cash or of taking delivery of the copper and selling it within a short period after delivery for the purpose of generating a profit from short-term fluctuations in price or dealer's margin, the contract is not accounted for as a derivative under IAS 39. Instead, it is accounted for as an executory contract.

A.2 Option to put a non-financial asset

Entity XYZ owns an office building. XYZ enters into a put option with an investor that permits XYZ to put the building to the investor for CU150 million. The current value of the building is CU175* million. The option expires in five years. The option, if exercised, may be settled through physical delivery or net cash, at XYZ's option. How do both XYZ and the investor account for the option?

XYZ's accounting depends on XYZ's intention and past practice for settlement. Although the contract meets the definition of a derivative, XYZ does not account for it as a derivative if XYZ intends to settle the contract by delivering the building if XYZ exercises its option and there is no past practice of settling net (IAS 39.5 and IAS 39.AG10).

The investor, however, cannot conclude that the option was entered into to meet the investor's expected purchase, sale or usage requirements because the investor does not have the ability to require delivery (IAS 39.7). In addition, the option may be settled net in cash. Therefore, the investor has to account for the contract as a derivative. Regardless of past practices, the investor's intention does not affect whether settlement is by delivery or in cash. The investor has written an option, and a written option in which the holder has a choice of physical settlement or net cash settlement can never satisfy the normal delivery requirement for the exemption from IAS 39 because the option writer does not have the ability to require delivery.

However, if the contract were a forward contract rather than an option, and if the contract required physical delivery and the reporting entity had no past practice of settling net in cash or of taking delivery of the building and selling it within a short period after delivery for the purpose of generating a profit from short-term fluctuations in price or dealer's margin, the contract would not be accounted for as a derivative.

**In this Guidance, monetary amounts are denominated in 'currency units' (CU).*

SECTION B: DEFINITIONS

B.1 Definition of a financial instrument: gold bullion

Is gold bullion a financial instrument (like cash) or is it a commodity?

It is a commodity. Although bullion is highly liquid, there is no contractual right to receive cash or another financial asset inherent in bullion.

B.2 Definition of a derivative: examples of derivatives and underlyings

What are examples of common derivative contracts and the identified underlying?

IAS 39 defines a derivative as follows:

"A derivative is a financial instrument or other contract within the scope of this Standard with all three of the following characteristics:

(a) its value changes in response to the change in a specified interest rate, financial instrument price, commodity price, foreign exchange rate, index of prices or rates, credit rating or credit index, or other variable, provided in the case of a non-financial variable that the variable is not specific to a party to the contract (sometimes called the 'underlying');
(b) it requires no initial net investment or an initial net investment that is smaller than would be required for other types of contracts that would be expected to have a similar response to changes in market factors; and
(c) it is settled at a future date."

Type of Contract	*Main Pricing-Settlement Variable (Underlying Variable)*
Interest Rate Swap	Interest rates
Currency Swap (Foreign Exchange Swap)	Currency rates
Commodity Swap	Commodity prices
Equity Swap	Equity prices (equity of another entity)
Credit Swap	Credit rating, credit index or credit price
Total Return Swap	Total fair value of the reference asset and interest rates
Purchased or Written Treasury Bond Option (call or put)	Interest rates
Purchased or Written Currency Option (call or put)	Currency rates
Purchased or Written Commodity Option (call or put)	Commodity prices
Purchased or Written Stock Option (call or put)	Equity prices (equity of another entity)
Interest Rate Futures Linked to Government Debt (Treasury Futures)	Interest rates
Currency Futures	Currency rates
Commodity Futures	Commodity prices
Interest Rate Forward Linked to Government Debt (Treasury Forward)	Interest rates
Currency Forward	Currency rates

Commodity Forward	Commodity prices
Equity Forward	Equity prices (equity of another entity)

The above list provides examples of contracts that normally qualify as derivatives under IAS 39. The list is not exhaustive. Any contract that has an underlying may be a derivative. Moreover, even if an instrument meets the definition of a derivative contract, special provisions of IAS 39 may apply, for example, if it is a weather derivative (see IAS 39.AG1), a contract to buy or sell a non-financial item such as commodity (see IAS 39.5 and IAS 39.AG10) or a contract settled in an entity's own shares (see IAS 32.21-IAS 32.24). Therefore, an entity must evaluate the contract to determine whether the other characteristics of a derivative are present and whether special provisions apply.

B.3 Definition of a derivative: settlement at a future date, interest rate swap with net or gross settlement

For the purpose of determining whether an interest rate swap is a derivative financial instrument under IAS 39, does it make a difference whether the parties pay the interest payments to each other (gross settlement) or settle on a net basis?

No. The definition of a derivative does not depend on gross or net settlement.

To illustrate: Entity ABC enters into an interest rate swap with a counterparty (XYZ) that requires ABC to pay a fixed rate of 8 per cent and receive a variable amount based on threemonth LIBOR, reset on a quarterly basis. The fixed and variable amounts are determined based on a CU100 million notional amount. ABC and XYZ do not exchange the notional amount. ABC pays or receives a net cash amount each quarter based on the difference between 8 per cent and three-month LIBOR. Alternatively, settlement may be on a gross basis.

The contract meets the definition of a derivative regardless of whether there is net or gross settlement because its value changes in response to changes in an underlying variable (LIBOR), there is no initial net investment, and settlements occur at future dates.

B.4 Definition of a derivative: prepaid interest rate swap (fixed rate payment obligation prepaid at inception or subsequently)

If a party prepays its obligation under a pay-fixed, receive-variable interest rate swap at inception, is the swap a derivative financial instrument?

Yes.

To illustrate: Entity S enters into a CU100 million notional amount five-year pay-fixed, receive-variable interest rate swap with Counterparty C. The interest rate of the variable part of the swap is reset on a quarterly basis to threemonth LIBOR. The interest rate of the fixed part of the swap is 10 per cent per year. Entity S prepays its fixed obligation under the swap of CU50 million (CU100 million · 10 per cent · 5 years) at inception, discounted using market interest rates, while retaining the right to receive interest payments on the CU100 million reset quarterly based on three-month LIBOR over the life of the swap.

The initial net investment in the interest rate swap is significantly less than the notional amount on which the variable payments under the variable leg will be calculated. The contract requires an initial net investment that is smaller than would be required for other types of contracts that would be expected to have a similar response to changes in market factors, such as a variable rate bond. Therefore, the contract fulfils the "no initial net investment or an initial net investment that is smaller than would be required for other types of contracts that would be expected to have a similar response to changes in market factors" provision of IAS 39. Even though Entity S has no future performance obligation, the ultimate settlement of the contract is at a future date and the value of the contract changes in response to changes in the LIBOR index. Accordingly, the contract is regarded as a derivative contract.

Would the answer change if the fixed rate payment obligation is prepaid subsequent to initial recognition?

If the fixed leg is prepaid during the term, that would be regarded as a termination of the old swap and an origination of a new instrument that is evaluated under IAS 39.

B.5 Definition of a derivative: prepaid pay-variable, receive-fixed interest rate swap

If a party prepays its obligation under a pay-variable, receive-fixed interest rate swap at inception of the contract or subsequently, is the swap a derivative financial instrument?

No. A prepaid pay-variable, receive-fixed interest rate swap is not a derivative if it is prepaid at inception and it is no longer a derivative if it is prepaid after inception because it provides a return on the prepaid (invested) amount comparable to the return on a debt instrument with fixed cash flows. The prepaid amount fails the "no initial net investment or an initial net investment that is smaller than would be required for other types of contracts that would be expected to have a similar response to changes in market factors" criterion of a derivative.

To illustrate: Entity S enters into a CU100 million notional amount five-year pay-variable, receive-fixed interest rate swap with Counterparty C. The variable leg of the swap is reset on a quarterly basis to three-month LIBOR. The fixed interest payments under the swap are calculated as 10 per cent times the swap's notional amount, ie CU10 million per year. Entity S prepays its obligation under the variable leg of the swap at inception at current market rates, while retaining the right to receive fixed interest payments of 10 per cent on CU100 million per year.

The cash inflows under the contract are equivalent to those of a financial instrument with a fixed annuity stream since Entity S knows it will receive CU10 million per year over the life of the swap. Therefore, all else being equal, the initial investment in the contract should equal that of other financial instruments that consist of fixed annuities. Thus, the initial net investment in the pay-variable, receive-fixed interest rate swap is equal to the investment required in a non-derivative contract that has a similar response to changes in market conditions. For this reason, the instrument fails the "no initial net investment or an initial net investment that is smaller than would be required for other types of contracts that would be expected to have a similar response to changes in market factors" criterion of IAS 39. Therefore, the contract is not accounted for as a derivative under IAS 39. By discharging the obligation to pay variable interest rate payments, Entity S in effect provides a loan to Counterparty C.

B.6 Definition of a derivative: offsetting loans

Entity A makes a five-year fixed rate loan to Entity B, while B at the same time makes a five-year variable rate loan for the same amount to A. There are no transfers of principal at inception of the two loans, since A and B have a netting agreement. Is this a derivative under IAS 39?

Yes. This meets the definition of a derivative (that is to say, there is an underlying variable, no initial net investment or an initial net investment that is smaller than would be required for other types of contracts that would be expected to have a similar response to changes in market factors, and future settlement). The contractual effect of the loans is the equivalent of an interest rate swap arrangement with no initial net investment. Non-derivative transactions are aggregated and treated as a derivative when the transactions result, in substance, in a derivative. Indicators of this would include:

- they are entered into at the same time and in contemplation of one another
- they have the same counterparty
- they relate to the same risk
- there is no apparent economic need or substantive business purpose for structuring the transactions separately that could not also have been accomplished in a single transaction.

The same answer would apply if Entity A and Entity B did not have a netting agreement, because the definition of a derivative instrument in IAS 39.9 does not require net settlement.

B.7 Definition of a derivative: option not expected to be exercised

The definition of a derivative in IAS 39.9 requires that the instrument "is settled at a future date". Is this criterion met even if an option is expected not to be exercised, for example, because it is out of the money?

Yes. An option is settled upon exercise or at its maturity. Expiry at maturity is a form of settlement even though there is no additional exchange of consideration.

B.8 Definition of a derivative: foreign currency contract based on sales volume

Entity XYZ, whose functional currency is the US dollar, sells products in France denominated in euro. XYZ enters into a contract with an investment bank to convert euro to US dollars at a fixed exchange rate. The contract requires XYZ to remit euro based on its sales volume in France in exchange for US dollars at a fixed exchange rate of 6.00. Is that contract a derivative?

Yes. The contract has two underlying variables (the foreign exchange rate and the volume of sales), no initial net investment or an initial net investment that is smaller than would be required for other types of contracts that would be expected to have a similar response to changes in market factors, and a payment provision. IAS 39 does not exclude from its scope derivatives that are based on sales volume.

B.9 Definition of a derivative: prepaid forward

An entity enters into a forward contract to purchase shares of stock in one year at the forward price. It prepays at inception based on the current price of the shares. Is the forward contract a derivative?

No. The forward contract fails the "no initial net investment or an initial net investment that is smaller than would be required for other types of contracts that would be expected to have a similar response to changes in market factors" test for a derivative.

To illustrate: Entity XYZ enters into a forward contract to purchase one million T ordinary shares in one year. The current market price of T is CU50 per share; the one-year forward price of T is CU55 per share. XYZ is required to prepay the forward contract at inception with a CU50 million payment. The initial investment in the forward contract of CU50 million is less than the notional amount applied to the underlying, one million shares at the forward price of CU55 per share, ie CU55 million. However, the initial net investment approximates the investment that would be required for other types of contracts that would be expected to have a similar response to changes in market factors because T's shares could be purchased at inception for the same price of CU50. Accordingly, the prepaid forward contract does not meet the initial net investment criterion of a derivative instrument.

B.10 Definition of a derivative: initial net investment

Many derivative instruments, such as futures contracts and exchange traded written options, require margin accounts. Is the margin account part of the initial net investment?

No. The margin account is not part of the initial net investment in a derivative instrument. Margin accounts are a form of collateral for the counterparty or clearing house and may take the form of cash, securities or other specified assets, typically liquid assets. Margin accounts are separate assets that are accounted for separately.

B.11 Definition of held for trading: portfolio with a recent actual pattern of short-term profit taking

The definition of a financial asset or financial liability held for trading states that "a financial asset or financial liability is classified as held for trading if it is ... part of a portfolio of identified financial instruments that are managed together and for which there is evidence of a recent actual pattern of short-term profit taking". What is a 'portfolio' for the purposes of applying this definition?

Although the term 'portfolio' is not explicitly defined in IAS 39, the context in which it is used suggests that a portfolio is a group of financial assets or financial liabilities that are managed as part of that group (IAS 39.9). If there is evidence of a recent actual pattern of short-term profit taking on financial instruments included in such a portfolio, those financial instruments qualify as held for trading even though an individual financial instrument may in fact be held for a longer period of time.

B.12 Definition of held for trading: balancing a portfolio

Entity A has an investment portfolio of debt and equity instruments. The documented portfolio management guidelines specify that the equity exposure of the portfolio should be limited to between 30 and 50 per cent of total portfolio value. The investment manager of the portfolio is authorised to balance the portfolio within the designated guidelines by buying and selling equity and debt instruments. Is Entity A permitted to classify the instruments as available for sale?

It depends on Entity A's intentions and past practice. If the portfolio manager is authorised to buy and sell instruments to balance the risks in a portfolio, but there is no intention to trade and there is no past practice of trading for short-term profit, the instruments can be classified as available for sale. If the portfolio manager actively buys and sells instruments to generate short-term profits, the financial instruments in the portfolio are classified as held for trading.

B.13 Definition of held-to-maturity financial assets: index-linked principal

Entity A purchases a five-year equity-index-linked note with an original issue price of CU10 at a market price of CU12 at the time of purchase. The note requires no interest payments before maturity. At maturity, the note requires payment of the original issue price of CU10 plus a supplemental redemption amount that depends on whether a specified share price index exceeds a predetermined level at the maturity date. If the share index does not exceed or is equal to the predetermined level, no supplemental redemption amount is paid. If the share index exceeds the predetermined level, the supplemental redemption amount equals the product of 1.15 and the difference between the level of the share index at maturity and the level of the share index when the note was issued divided by the level of the share index at the time of issue. Entity A has the positive intention and ability to hold the note to maturity. Can Entity A classify the note as a held-to-maturity investment?

Yes. The note can be classified as a held-to-maturity investment because it has a fixed payment of CU10 and fixed maturity and Entity A has the positive intention and ability to hold it to maturity (IAS 39.9). However, the equity index feature is a call option not closely related to the debt host, which must be separated as an embedded derivative under IAS 39.11. The purchase price of CU12 is allocated between the host debt instrument and the embedded derivative. For example, if the fair value of the embedded option at acquisition is CU4, the host debt instrument is measured at CU8 on initial recognition. In this case, the discount of CU2 that is implicit in the host bond (principal of CU10 minus the original carrying amount of CU8) is amortised to profit or loss over the term to maturity of the note using the effective interest method.

B.14 Definition of held-to-maturity financial assets: index-linked interest

Can a bond with a fixed payment at maturity and a fixed maturity date be classified as a held-to-maturity investment if the bond's interest payments are indexed to the price of a commodity or equity, and the entity has the positive intention and ability to hold the bond to maturity?

Yes. However, the commodity-indexed or equity-indexed interest payments result in an embedded derivative that is separated and accounted for as a derivative at fair value (IAS 39.11). IAS 39.12 is not applicable since it should be straightforward to separate the host debt investment (the fixed payment at maturity) from the embedded derivative (the index-linked interest payments).

B.15 Definition of held-to-maturity financial assets: sale following rating downgrade

Would a sale of a held-to-maturity investment following a downgrade of the issuer's credit rating by a rating agency raise a question about the entity's intention to hold other investments to maturity?

Not necessarily. A downgrade is likely to indicate a decline in the issuer's creditworthiness. IAS 39 specifies that a sale due to a significant deterioration in the issuer's creditworthiness could satisfy the condition in IAS 39 and therefore not raise a question about the entity's intention to hold other investments to maturity. However, the deterioration in creditworthiness must be significant judged by reference to the credit rating at initial recognition. Also, the rating downgrade must not have been reasonably anticipated when the entity classified the investment as held to maturity in order to meet the condition in IAS 39. A credit downgrade of a notch within a class or from one rating class to the immediately lower rating class could often be regarded as reasonably anticipated. If the rating downgrade in combination with other information provides evidence of impairment, the deterioration in creditworthiness often would be regarded as significant.

B.16 Definition of held-to-maturity financial assets: permitted sales

Would sales of held-to-maturity financial assets due to a change in management compromise the classification of other financial assets as held to maturity?

Yes. A change in management is not identified under IAS 39.AG22 as an instance where sales or transfers from held-to-maturity do not compromise the classification as held to maturity. Sales in response to such a change in management would, therefore, call into question the entity's intention to hold investments to maturity.

To illustrate: Entity X has a portfolio of financial assets that is classified as held to maturity. In the current period, at the direction of the board of directors, the senior management team has been replaced. The new management wishes to sell a portion of the held-to-maturity financial assets in order to carry out an expansion strategy designated and approved by the board. Although the previous management team had been in place since the entity's inception and Entity X had never before undergone a major restructuring, the sale nevertheless calls into question Entity X's intention to hold remaining held-to- maturity financial assets to maturity.

B.17 Definition of held-to-maturity investments: sales in response to entity-specific capital requirements

In some countries, regulators of banks or other industries may set *entityspecific* capital requirements that are based on an assessment of the risk in that particular entity. IAS 39.AG22(e) indicates that an entity that sells held-to-maturity investments in response to an unanticipated significant increase by the regulator in the *industry's* capital requirements may do so under IAS 39 without necessarily raising a question about its intention to hold other investments to maturity. Would sales of held-to-maturity investments that are due to a significant increase in *entityspecific* capital requirements imposed by regulators (ie capital requirements applicable to a particular entity, but not to the industry) raise such doubt?

Yes, such sales 'taint' the entity's intention to hold other financial assets as held to maturity unless it can be demonstrated that the sales fulfil the condition in IAS 39.9 in that they result from an increase in capital requirements, which is an isolated event that is beyond the entity's control, is nonrecurring and could not have been reasonably anticipated by the entity.

B.18 Definition of held-to-maturity financial assets: pledged collateral, repurchase agreements (repos) and securities lending agreements

An entity cannot have a demonstrated ability to hold to maturity an investment if it is subject to a constraint that could frustrate its intention to hold the financial asset to maturity. Does this mean that a debt instrument that has been pledged as collateral, or transferred to another party under a repo or securities lending transaction, and continues to be recognised cannot be classified as a held-to-maturity investment?

No. An entity's intention and ability to hold debt instruments to maturity is not necessarily constrained if those instruments have been pledged as collateral or are subject to a repurchase agreement or securities lending agreement. However, an entity does not have the positive intention and ability to hold the debt instruments until maturity if it does not expect to be able to maintain or recover access to the instruments.

B.19 Definition of held-to-maturity financial assets: 'tainting'

In response to unsolicited tender offers, Entity A sells a significant amount of financial assets classified as held to maturity on economically favourable terms. Entity A does not classify any financial assets acquired after the date of the sale as held to maturity. However, it does not reclassify the remaining held-to-maturity investments since it maintains that it still intends to hold them to maturity. Is Entity A in compliance with IAS 39?

No. Whenever a sale or transfer of more than an insignificant amount of financial assets classified as held to maturity (HTM) results in the conditions in IAS 39.9 and IAS 39.AG22 not being satisfied, no instruments should be classified in that category. Accordingly, any remaining HTM assets are reclassified as available-for-sale financial assets. The reclassification is recorded in the reporting period in which the sales or transfers occurred and is accounted for as a change in classification under IAS 39.51. IAS 39.9 makes it clear that at least two full financial years must pass before an entity can again classify financial assets as HTM.

B.20 Definition of held-to-maturity investments: sub-categorisation for the purpose of applying the 'tainting' rule

Can an entity apply the conditions for held-to-maturity classification in IAS 39.9 separately to different categories of held-to-maturity financial assets, such as debt instruments denominated in US dollars and debt instruments denominated in euro?

No. The 'tainting rule' in IAS 39.9 is clear. If an entity has sold or reclassified more than an insignificant amount of held-to-maturity investments, it cannot classify any financial assets as held-to-maturity financial assets.

B.21 Definition of held-to-maturity investments: application of the 'tainting' rule on consolidation

Can an entity apply the conditions in IAS 39.9 separately to held-to-maturity financial assets held by different entities in a consolidated group, for example, if those group entities are in different countries with different legal or economic environments?

No. If an entity has sold or reclassified more than an insignificant amount of investments classified as held-to-maturity in the consolidated financial statements, it cannot classify any financial assets as held-to-maturity financial assets in the consolidated financial statements unless the conditions in IAS 39.9 are met.

B.22 Definition of loans and receivables: equity instrument

Can an equity instrument, such as a preference share, with fixed or determinable payments be classified within loans and receivables by the holder?

Yes. If a non-derivative equity instrument would be recorded as a liability by the issuer, and it has fixed or determinable payments and is not quoted in an active market, it can be classified within loans and receivables by the holder, provided the definition is otherwise met. IAS 32.15-IAS 32.22 provide guidance about the classification of a financial instrument as a liability or as equity from the perspective of the issuer of a financial instrument. If an instrument meets the definition of an equity instrument under IAS 32, it cannot be classified within loans and receivables by the holder.

B.23 Definition of loans and receivables: banks' deposits in other banks

Banks make term deposits with a central bank or other banks. Sometimes, the proof of deposit is negotiable, sometimes not. Even if negotiable, the depositor bank may or may not intend to sell it. Would such a deposit fall within loans and receivables under IAS 39.9?

Such a deposit meets the definition of loans and receivables, whether or not the proof of deposit is negotiable, unless the depositor bank intends to sell the instrument immediately or in the near term, in which case the deposit is classified as a financial asset held for trading.

B.24 Definition of amortised cost: perpetual debt instruments with fixed or market-based variable rate

Sometimes entities purchase or issue debt instruments that are required to be measured at amortised cost and in respect of which the issuer has no obligation to repay the principal amount. Interest may be paid either at a fixed rate or at a variable rate. Would the difference between the initial amount paid or received and zero ('the maturity amount') be amortised immediately on initial recognition for the purpose of determining amortised cost if the rate of interest is fixed or specified as a market-based variable rate?

No. Since there are no repayments of principal, there is no amortisation of the difference between the initial amount and the maturity amount if the rate of interest is fixed or specified as a market-based variable rate. Because interest payments are fixed or market-based and will be paid in perpetuity, the amortised cost (the present value of the stream of future cash payments discounted at the effective interest rate) equals the principal amount in each period (IAS 39.9).

B.25 Definition of amortised cost: perpetual debt instruments with decreasing interest rate

If the stated rate of interest on a perpetual debt instrument decreases over time, would amortised cost equal the principal amount in each period?

No. From an economic perspective, some or all of the interest payments are repayments of the principal amount. For example, the interest rate may be stated as 16 per cent for the first ten years and as zero per cent in subsequent periods. In that case, the initial amount is amortised to zero over the first ten years using the effective interest method, since a portion of the interest payments represents repayments of the principal amount. The amortised cost is zero after year 10 because the present value of the stream of future cash payments in subsequent periods is zero (there are no further cash payments of either principal or interest in subsequent periods).

B.26 Example of calculating amortised cost: financial asset

Financial assets that are excluded from fair valuation and have a fixed maturity should be measured at amortised cost. How is amortised cost calculated?

Under IAS 39, amortised cost is calculated using the effective interest method. The effective interest rate inherent in a financial instrument is the rate that exactly discounts the estimated cash flows associated with the financial instrument through the expected life of the instrument or, where appropriate, a shorter period to the net carrying amount at initial recognition. The computation includes all fees and points paid or received that are an integral part of the effective interest rate, directly attributable transaction costs and all other premiums or discounts.

The following example illustrates how amortised cost is calculated using the effective interest method. Entity A purchases a debt instrument with five years remaining to maturity for its fair value of CU1,000 (including transaction costs). The instrument has a principal amount of CU1,250 and carries fixed interest of 4.7 per cent that is paid annually (CU1,250 · 4.7 per cent = CU59 per year). The contract also specifies that the borrower has an option to prepay the instrument and that no penalty will be charged for prepayment. At inception, the entity expects the borrower not to prepay.

It can be shown that in order to allocate interest receipts and the initial discount over the term of the debt instrument at a constant rate on the carrying amount, they must be accrued at the rate of 10 per cent annually. The table below provides information about the amortised cost, interest income and cash flows of the debt instrument in each reporting period.

Year	*(a) Amortised cost at the beginning of the year*	*(b = a 10%) Interest income*	*(c) Cash flows*	*(d = a + b - c) Amortised cost at the end of the year*
20x0	1,000	100	59	1,041
20x1	1,041	104	59	1,086
20x2	1,086	109	59	1,136
20x3	1,136	113	59	1,190
20x4	1,190	119	1,250 + 59	-

On the first day of 20x2 the entity revises its estimate of cash flows. It now expects that 50 per cent of the principal will be prepaid at the end of 20x2 and the remaining 50 per cent at the end of 20x4. In accordance with IAS 39.AG8, the opening balance of the debt instrument in 20x2 is adjusted. The adjusted amount is calculated by discounting the amount the entity expects to receive in 20x2 and subsequent years using the original effective interest rate (10 per cent). This results in the new opening balance in 20x2 of CU1,138. The adjustment of CU52 (CU1,138 – CU1,086) is recorded in profit or loss in 20x2. The table below provides information about the amortised cost, interest income and cash flows as they would be adjusted taking into account the change in estimate.

Year	*(a) Amortised cost at the beginning of the year*	*(b = a × 10%) Interest income*	*(c) Cash flows*	*(d = a + b - c) Amortised cost at the end of the year*
20x0	1,000	100	59	1,041
20x1	1,041	104	59	1,086
20x2	1,086 + 52	114	625 + 59	568
20x3	568	57	30	595
20x4	595	60	625 + 30	-

If the debt instrument becomes impaired, say, at the end of 20x3, the impairment loss is calculated as the difference between the carrying amount (CU595) and the present value of estimated future cash flows discounted at the original effective interest rate (10 per cent).

B.27 Example of calculating amortised cost: debt instruments with stepped interest payments

Sometimes entities purchase or issue debt instruments with a predetermined rate of interest that increases or decreases progressively ('stepped interest') over the term of the debt instrument. If a debt instrument with stepped interest and no embedded derivative is issued at CU1,250 and has a maturity amount of CU1,250, would the amortised cost equal CU1,250 in each reporting period over the term of the debt instrument?

No. Although there is no difference between the initial amount and maturity amount, an entity uses the effective interest method to allocate interest payments over the term of the debt instrument to achieve a constant rate on the carrying amount (IAS 39.9).

The following example illustrates how amortised cost is calculated using the effective interest method for an instrument with a predetermined rate of interest that increases or decreases over the term of the debt instrument ('stepped interest').

On 1 January 2000, Entity A issues a debt instrument for a price of CU1,250. The principal amount is CU1,250 and the debt instrument is repayable on 31 December 2004. The rate of interest is specified in the debt agreement as a percentage of the principal amount as follows: 6.0 per cent in 2000 (CU75), 8.0 per cent in 2001 (CU100), 10.0 per cent in 2002 (CU125), 12.0 per cent in 2003 (CU150), and 16.4 per cent in 2004 (CU205). In this case, the interest rate that exactly discounts the stream of future cash payments through maturity is 10 per cent. Therefore, cash interest payments are reallocated over the term of the debt instrument for the purposes of determining amortised cost in each period. In each period, the amortised cost at the beginning of the period is multiplied by the effective interest rate of 10 per cent and added to the amortised cost. Any cash payments in the period are deducted from the resulting number. Accordingly, the amortised cost in each period is as follows:

Year	*(a)* *Amortised cost at the beginning of the year*	*(b= a 10%)* *Reported interest*	*(c)* *Cash flows*	*(d = a+b-c)* *Amortised cost at the end of the year*
2000	1,250	125	75	1,300
2001	1,300	130	100	1,330
2002	1,330	133	125	1,338
2003	1,338	134	150	1,322
2004	1,322	133	1,250+205	-

B.28 Regular way contracts: no established market

Can a contract to purchase a financial asset be a regular way contract if there is no established market for trading such a contract?

Yes. IAS 39.9 refers to terms that require delivery of the asset within the time frame established generally by regulation or convention in the marketplace concerned. Marketplace, as that term is used in IAS 39.9, is not limited to a formal stock exchange or organised over-the-counter market. Rather, it means the environment in which the financial asset is customarily exchanged. An acceptable time frame would be the period reasonably and customarily required for the parties to complete the transaction and prepare and execute closing documents.

For example, a market for private issue financial instruments can be a marketplace.

B.29 Regular way contracts: forward contract

Entity ABC enters into a forward contract to purchase one million of M's ordinary shares in two months for CU10 per share. The contract is with an individual and is not an exchange-traded contract. The contract requires ABC to take physical delivery of the shares and pay the counterparty CU10 million in cash. M's shares trade in an active public market at an average of 100,000 shares a day. Regular way delivery is three days. Is the forward contract regarded as a regular way contract?

No. The contract must be accounted for as a derivative because it is not settled in the way established by regulation or convention in the marketplace concerned.

B.30 Regular way contracts: which customary settlement provisions apply?

If an entity's financial instruments trade in more than one active market, and the settlement provisions differ in the various active markets, which provisions apply in assessing whether a contract to purchase those financial instruments is a regular way contract?

The provisions that apply are those in the market in which the purchase actually takes place.

To illustrate: Entity XYZ purchases one million shares of Entity ABC on a US stock exchange, for example, through a broker. The settlement date of the contract is six business days later. Trades for equity shares on US exchanges customarily settle in three business days. Because the trade settles in six business days, it does not meet the exemption as a regular way trade.

However, if XYZ did the same transaction on a foreign exchange that has a customary settlement period of six business days, the contract would meet the exemption for a regular way trade.

B.31 Regular way contracts: share purchase by call option

Entity A purchases a call option in a public market permitting it to purchase 100 shares of Entity XYZ at any time over the next three months at a price of CU100 per share. If Entity A exercises its option, it has 14 days to settle the transaction according to regulation or convention in the options market. XYZ shares are traded in an active public market that requires three-day settlement. Is the purchase of shares by exercising the option a regular way purchase of shares?

Yes. The settlement of an option is governed by regulation or convention in the marketplace for options and, therefore, upon exercise of the option it is no longer accounted for as a derivative because settlement by delivery of the shares within 14 days is a regular way transaction.

B.32 Recognition and derecognition of financial liabilities using trade date or settlement date accounting

IAS 39 has special rules about recognition and derecognition of financial assets using trade date or settlement date accounting. Do these rules apply to transactions in financial instruments that are classified as financial liabilities, such as transactions in deposit liabilities and trading liabilities?

No. IAS 39 does not contain any specific requirements about trade date accounting and settlement date accounting in the case of transactions in financial instruments that are classified as financial liabilities. Therefore, the general recognition and derecognition requirements in IAS 39.14 and IAS 39.39 apply. IAS 39.14 states that financial liabilities are recognised on the date the entity "becomes a party to the contractual provisions of the instrument". Such contracts generally are not recognised unless one of the parties has performed or the contract is a derivative contract not exempted from the scope of IAS 39. IAS 39.39 specifies that financial liabilities are derecognised only when they are extinguished, ie when the obligation specified in the contract is discharged or cancelled or expires.

SECTION C: EMBEDDED DERIVATIVES

C.1 Embedded derivatives: separation of host debt instrument

If an embedded non-option derivative is required to be separated from a host debt instrument, how are the terms of the host debt instrument and the embedded derivative identified? For example, would the host debt instrument be a fixed rate instrument, a variable rate instrument or a zero coupon instrument?

The terms of the host debt instrument reflect the stated or implied substantive terms of the hybrid instrument. In the absence of implied or stated terms, the entity makes its own judgement of the terms. However, an entity may not identify a component that is not specified or may not establish terms of the host debt instrument in a manner that would result in the separation of an embedded derivative that is not already clearly present in the hybrid instrument, that is to say, it cannot create a cash flow that does not exist. For example, if a five-year debt instrument has fixed interest payments of CU40,000 annually and a principal payment at maturity of CU1,000,000 multiplied by the change in an equity price index, it would be inappropriate to identify a floating rate host contract and an embedded equity swap that has an offsetting floating rate leg in lieu of identifying a fixed rate host. In that example, the host contract is a fixed rate debt instrument that pays CU40,000 annually because there are no floating interest rate cash flows in the hybrid instrument.

In addition, the terms of an embedded non-option derivative, such as a forward or swap, must be determined so as to result in the embedded derivative having a fair value of zero at the inception of the hybrid instrument. If it were permitted to separate embedded non-option derivatives on other terms, a single hybrid instrument could be decomposed into an infinite variety of combinations of host debt instruments and embedded derivatives, for example, by separating embedded derivatives with terms that create leverage, asymmetry or some other risk exposure not already present in the hybrid instrument. Therefore, it is inappropriate to separate an embedded non-option derivative on terms that result in a fair value other than zero at the inception of the hybrid instrument. The determination of the terms of the embedded derivative is based on the conditions existing when the financial instrument was issued.

C.2 Embedded derivatives: separation of embedded option

The response to Question C.1 states that the terms of an embedded nonoption derivative should be determined so as to result in the embedded derivative having a fair value of zero at the initial recognition of the hybrid instrument. When an embedded option-based derivative is separated, must the terms of the embedded option be determined so as to result in the embedded derivative having either a fair value of zero or an intrinsic value of zero (that is to say, be at the money) at the inception of the hybrid instrument?

No. The economic behaviour of a hybrid instrument with an option-based embedded derivative depends critically on the strike price (or strike rate) specified for the option feature in the hybrid instrument, as discussed below. Therefore, the separation of an option-based embedded derivative (including any embedded put, call, cap, floor, caption, floortion or swaption feature in a hybrid instrument) should be based on the stated terms of the option feature documented in the hybrid instrument. As a result, the embedded derivative would not necessarily have a fair value or intrinsic value equal to zero at the initial recognition of the hybrid instrument.

If an entity were required to identify the terms of an embedded option-based derivative so as to achieve a fair value of the embedded derivative of zero, the strike price (or strike rate) generally would have to be determined so as to result in the option being infinitely out of the money. This would imply a zero probability of the option feature being exercised. However, since the probability of the option feature in a hybrid instrument being exercised generally is not zero, it would be inconsistent with the likely economic behaviour of the hybrid instrument to assume an initial fair value of zero. Similarly, if an entity were required to identify the terms of an embedded option-based derivative so as to achieve an intrinsic value of zero for the embedded derivative, the strike price (or strike rate) would have to be assumed to equal the price (or rate) of the underlying variable at the initial recognition of the hybrid instrument. In this case, the fair value of the option would consist only of time value. However, such an assumption would not be consistent with the likely economic behaviour of the hybrid instrument, including the probability of the option feature being exercised, unless the agreed strike price was indeed equal to the price (or rate) of the underlying variable at the initial recognition of the hybrid instrument.

The economic nature of an option-based embedded derivative is fundamentally different from a forward-based embedded derivative (including forwards and swaps), because the terms of a forward are such that a payment based on the difference between the price of the underlying and the forward price will occur at a specified date, while the terms of an option are such that a payment based on the difference between the price of the underlying and the strike price of the option may or may not occur depending on the relationship between the agreed strike price and the price of the underlying at a specified date or dates in the future. Adjusting the strike price of an option-based embedded derivative, therefore, alters the nature of the hybrid instrument. On the other hand, if the terms of a non-option embedded derivative in a host debt instrument were determined so as to result in a fair value of any amount other than zero at the inception of the hybrid instrument, that amount would essentially represent a borrowing or lending. Accordingly, as discussed in the answer to Question C.1, it is not appropriate to separate a non-option embedded derivative in a host debt instrument on terms that result in a fair value other than zero at the initial recognition of the hybrid instrument.

C.3 Embedded derivatives: accounting for a convertible bond

What is the accounting treatment of an investment in a bond (financial asset) that is convertible into shares of the issuing entity or another entity before maturity?

An investment in a convertible bond that is convertible before maturity generally cannot be classified as a held-to-maturity investment because that would be inconsistent with paying for the conversion feature—the right to convert into equity shares before maturity.

An investment in a convertible bond can be classified as an available-for-sale financial asset provided it is not purchased for trading purposes. The equity conversion option is an embedded derivative.

If the bond is classified as available for sale (ie fair value changes recognised in other comprehensive income until the bond is sold), the equity conversion option (the embedded derivative) is separated. The amount paid for the bond is split between the debt instrument without the conversion option and the equity conversion option. Changes in the fair value of the equity conversion option are recognised in profit or loss unless the option is part of a cash flow hedging relationship.

If the convertible bond is measured at fair value with changes in fair value recognised in profit or loss, separating the embedded derivative from the host bond is not permitted.

C.4 Embedded derivatives: equity kicker

In some instances, venture capital entities providing subordinated loans agree that if and when the borrower lists its shares on a stock exchange, the venture capital entity is entitled to receive shares of the borrowing entity free of charge or at a very low price (an 'equity kicker') in addition to interest and repayment of principal. As a result of the equity kicker feature, the interest on the subordinated loan is lower than it would otherwise be. Assuming that the subordinated loan is not measured at fair value with changes in fair value recognised in profit or loss (IAS 39.11(c)), does the equity kicker feature meet the definition of an embedded derivative even though it is contingent upon the future listing of the borrower?

Yes. The economic characteristics and risks of an equity return are not closely related to the economic characteristics and risks of a host debt instrument (IAS 39.11(a)). The equity kicker meets the definition of a derivative because it has a value that changes in response to the change in the price of the shares of the borrower, it requires no initial net investment or an initial net investment that is smaller than would be required for other types of contracts that would be expected to have a similar response to changes in market factors, and it is settled at a future date (IAS 39.11(b) and IAS 39.9(a)). The equity kicker feature meets the definition of a derivative even though the right to receive shares is contingent upon the future listing of the borrower. IAS 39.AG9 states that a derivative could require a payment as a result of some future event that is unrelated to a notional amount. An equity kicker feature is similar to such a derivative except that it does not give a right to a fixed payment, but an option right, if the future event occurs.

C.5 Embedded derivatives: debt or equity host contract

Entity A purchases a five-year 'debt' instrument issued by Entity B with a principal amount of CU1 million that is indexed to the share price of Entity C. At maturity, Entity A will receive from Entity B the principal amount plus or minus the change in the fair value of 10,000 shares of Entity C. The current share price is CU110. No separate interest payments are made by Entity B. The purchase price is CU1 million. Entity A classifies the debt instrument as available for sale. Entity A concludes that the instrument is a hybrid instrument with an embedded derivative because of the equity-indexed principal. For the purposes of separating an embedded derivative, is the host contract an equity instrument or a debt instrument?

The host contract is a debt instrument because the hybrid instrument has a stated maturity, ie it does not meet the definition of an equity instrument (IAS 32.11 and IAS 32.16). It is accounted for as a zero coupon debt instrument. Thus, in accounting for the host instrument, Entity A imputes interest on CU1 million over five years using the applicable market interest rate at initial recognition. The embedded non-option derivative is separated so as to have an initial fair value of zero (see Question C.1).

C.6 Embedded derivatives: synthetic instruments

Entity A acquires a five-year floating rate debt instrument issued by Entity B. At the same time, it enters into a five-year pay-variable, receive-fixed interest rate swap with Entity C. Entity A regards the combination of the debt instrument and swap as a synthetic fixed rate instrument and classifies the instrument as a held-to-maturity investment, since it has the positive intention and ability to hold it to maturity. Entity A contends that separate accounting for the swap is inappropriate since IAS 39.AG33(a) requires an embedded derivative to be classified together with its host instrument if the derivative is linked to an interest rate that can change the amount of interest that would otherwise be paid or received on the host debt contract. Is the entity's analysis correct?

No. Embedded derivative instruments are terms and conditions that are included in non-derivative host contracts. It is generally inappropriate to treat two or more separate financial instruments as a single combined instrument ('synthetic instrument' accounting) for the purpose of applying IAS 39. Each of the financial instruments has its own terms and conditions and each may be transferred or settled separately. Therefore, the debt instrument and the swap are classified separately. The transactions described here differ from the transactions discussed in Question B.6, which had no substance apart from the resulting interest rate swap.

C.7 Embedded derivatives: purchases and sales contracts in foreign currency instruments

A supply contract provides for payment in a currency other than (a) the functional currency of either party to the contract, (b) the currency in which the product is routinely denominated in commercial transactions around the world and (c) the currency that is commonly used in contracts to purchase or sell non-financial items in the economic environment in which the transaction takes place. Is there an embedded derivative that should be separated under IAS 39?

Yes. To illustrate: a Norwegian entity agrees to sell oil to an entity in France. The oil contract is denominated in Swiss francs, although oil contracts are routinely denominated in US dollars in commercial transactions around the world, and Norwegian krone are commonly used in contracts to purchase or sell non-financial items in Norway. Neither entity carries out any significant activities in Swiss francs. In this case, the Norwegian entity regards the supply contract as a host contract with an embedded foreign currency forward to purchase Swiss francs. The French entity regards the supply contact as a host contract with an embedded foreign currency forward to sell Swiss francs. Each entity includes fair value changes on the currency forward in profit or loss unless the reporting entity designates it as a cash flow hedging instrument, if appropriate.

C.8 Embedded foreign currency derivatives: unrelated foreign currency provision

Entity A, which measures items in its financial statements on the basis of the euro (its functional currency), enters into a contract with Entity B, which has the Norwegian krone as its functional currency, to purchase oil in six months for 1,000 US dollars. The host oil contract is not within the scope of IAS 39 because it was entered into and continues to be for the purpose of delivery of a non-financial item in accordance with the entity's expected purchase, sale or usage requirements (IAS 39.5 and IAS 39.AG10). The oil contract includes a leveraged foreign exchange provision that states that the parties, in addition to the provision of, and payment for, oil will exchange an amount equal to the fluctuation in the exchange rate of the US dollar and Norwegian krone applied to a notional amount of 100,000 US dollars. Under IAS 39.11, is that embedded derivative (the leveraged foreign exchange provision) regarded as closely related to the host oil contract?

No, that leveraged foreign exchange provision is separated from the host oil contract because it is not closely related to the host oil contract (IAS 39.33(d)).

The payment provision under the host oil contract of 1,000 US dollars can be viewed as a foreign currency derivative because the US dollar is neither Entity A's nor Entity B's functional currency. This foreign currency derivative would not be separated because it follows from IAS 39.AG33(d) that a crude oil contract that requires payment in US dollars is not regarded as a host contract with a foreign currency derivative.

The leveraged foreign exchange provision that states that the parties will exchange an amount equal to the fluctuation in the exchange rate of the US dollar and Norwegian krone applied to a notional amount of 100,000 US dollars is in addition to the required payment for the oil transaction. It is unrelated to the host oil contract and therefore separated from the host oil contract and accounted for as an embedded derivative under IAS 39.11.

C.9 Embedded foreign currency derivatives: currency of international commerce

IAS 39.AG33(d) refers to the currency in which the price of the related goods or services is routinely denominated in commercial transactions around the world. Could it be a currency that is used for a certain product or service in commercial transactions within the local area of one of the substantial parties to the contract?

No. The currency in which the price of the related goods or services is routinely denominated in commercial transactions around the world is only a currency that is used for similar transactions all around the world, not just in one local area. For example, if crossborder transactions in natural gas in North America are routinely denominated in US dollars and such transactions are routinely denominated in euro in Europe, neither the US dollar nor the euro is a currency in which the goods or services is routinely denominated in commercial transactions around the world.

C.10 Embedded derivatives: holder permitted, but not required, to settle without recovering substantially all of its recognised investment

If the terms of a combined instrument permit, but do not require, the holder to settle the combined instrument in a manner that causes it not to recover substantially all of its recognised investment and the issuer does not have such a right (for example, a puttable debt instrument), does the contract satisfy the condition in IAS 39.AG33(a) that the holder would not recover substantially all of its recognised investment?

No. The condition that "the holder would not recover substantially all of its recognised investment" is not satisfied if the terms of the combined instrument permit, but do not require, the investor to settle the combined instrument in a manner that causes it not to recover substantially all of its recognised investment and the issuer has no such right. Accordingly, an interest-bearing host contract with an embedded interest rate derivative with such terms is regarded as closely related to the host contract. The condition that "the holder would not recover substantially all of its recognised investment" applies to situations in which the holder can be forced to accept settlement at an amount that causes the holder not to recover substantially all of its recognised investment.

C.11 Embedded derivatives: reliable determination of fair value

If an embedded derivative that is required to be separated cannot be reliably measured because it will be settled by an unquoted equity instrument whose fair value cannot be reliably measured, is the embedded derivative measured at cost?

No. In this case, the entire combined contract is treated as a financial instrument held for trading (IAS 39.12). If the fair value of the combined instrument can be reliably measured, the combined contract is measured at fair value. The entity might conclude, however, that the equity component of the combined instrument may be sufficiently significant to preclude it from obtaining a reliable estimate of the entire instrument. In that case, the combined instrument is measured at cost less impairment.

SECTION D: RECOGNITION AND DERECOGNITION

D.1 Initial Recognition

D.1.1 Recognition: cash collateral

Entity B transfers cash to Entity A as collateral for another transaction with Entity A (for example, a securities borrowing transaction). The cash is not legally segregated from Entity A's assets. Should Entity A recognise the cash collateral it has received as an asset?

Yes. The ultimate realisation of a financial asset is its conversion into cash and, therefore, no further transformation is required before the economic benefits of the cash transferred by Entity B can be realised by Entity A. Therefore, Entity A recognises the cash as an asset and a payable to Entity B while Entity B derecognises the cash and recognises a receivable from Entity A.

D.2 Regular Way Purchase or Sale of a Financial Asset

D.2.1 Trade date vs settlement date: amounts to be recorded for a purchase

How are the trade date and settlement date accounting principles in the Standard applied to a purchase of a financial asset?

The following example illustrates the application of the trade date and settlement date accounting principles in the Standard for a purchase of a financial asset. On 29 December 20x1, an entity commits itself to purchase a financial asset for CU1,000, which is its fair value on commitment (trade) date. Transaction costs are immaterial. On 31 December 20x1 (financial year-end) and on 4 January 20x2 (settlement date) the fair value of the asset is CU1,002 and CU1,003, respectively. The amounts to be recorded for the asset will depend on how it is classified and whether trade date or settlement date accounting is used, as shown in the two tables below.

SETTLEMENT DATE ACCOUNTING			
Balances	**Held-to-Maturity Investments Carried at Amortised Cost**	**Available-for-Sale Assets Remeasured to Fair Value with Changes in other comprehensive income**	**Assets at Fair Value through Profit or Loss Remeasured to Fair Value with Changes in Profit or Loss**
29 December 20x1			
Financial asset	-	-	
Financial liability	-	-	
31 December 20x1	-		
Receivable	-	2	2
Financial asset	-	-	-
Financial liability	-	-	-
Equity (fair value adjustment)	-	(2)	-
Retained earnings (through profit or loss)	-	-	(2)
4 January 20x2			
Receivable	-	-	-
Financial asset	1,000	1,003	1,003
Financial liability	-	-	-
Equity (fair value adjustment)	-	(3)	-
Retained earnings (through profit or loss)	-	-	(3)

TRADE DATE ACCOUNTING			
Balances	**Held-to-Maturity Investments Carried at Amortised Cost**	**Available-for-Sale Assets Remeasured to Fair Value with Changes in other comprehensive income**	**Assets at Fair Value through Profit or Loss Remeasured to Fair Value with Changes in Profit or Loss**
29 December 20x1			
Financial asset	1,000	1,000	1,000
Financial liability	(1,000)	(1,000)	(1,000)
31 December 20x1			
Receivable	-	-	-
Financial asset	1,000	1,002	1,002
Financial liability	(1,000)	(1,000)	(1,000)
Equity (fair value adjustment)	-	(2)	-
Retained earnings (through profit or loss)	-	-	(2)
4 January 20x2			
Receivable	-	-	-
Financial asset	1,000	1,003	1,003
Financial liability	-	-	-
Equity (fair value adjustment)	-	(3)	-
Retained earnings (through profit or loss)	-	-	(3)

D.2.2 Trade date vs settlement date: amounts to be recorded for a sale

How are the trade date and settlement date accounting principles in the Standard applied to a sale of a financial asset?

The following example illustrates the application of the trade date and settlement date accounting principles in the Standard for a sale of a financial asset. On 29 December 20x2 (trade date) an entity enters into a contract to sell a financial asset for its current fair value of CU1,010. The asset was acquired one year earlier for CU1,000 and its amortised cost is CU1,000. On 31 December 20x2 (financial year-end), the fair value of the asset is CU1,012. On 4 January 20x3 (settlement date), the fair value is CU1,013. The amounts to be recorded will depend on how the asset is classified and whether trade date or settlement date accounting is used as shown in the two tables below (any interest that might have accrued on the asset is disregarded).

A change in the fair value of a financial asset that is sold on a regular way basis is not recorded in the financial statements between trade date and settlement date even if the entity applies settlement date accounting because the seller's right to changes in the fair value ceases on the trade date.

SETTLEMENT DATE ACCOUNTING			
Balances	**Held-to-Maturity Investments Carried at Amortised Cost**	**Available-for-Sale Assets Remeasured to Fair Value with Changes in other comprehensive income**	**Assets at Fair Value through Profit or Loss Remeasured to Fair Value with Changes in Profit or Loss**
29 December 20x2			
Receivable	-	-	-
Financial asset	1,000	1,010	1,010
Equity (fair value adjustment)	-	10	-
Retained earnings (through profit or loss)	-	-	10
31 December 20x2			
Receivable	-	-	-
Financial asset	1,000	1,010	1,010
Equity (fair value adjustment)	-	10	-
Retained earnings (through profit or loss)	-	-	10
4 January 20x3	-	-	
Equity (fair value adjustment)	-	-	-
Retained earnings (through profit or loss)	10	10	10

TRADE DATE ACCOUNTING			
Balances	**Held-to-Maturity Investments Carried at Amortised Cost**	**Available-for-Sale Assets Remeasured to Fair Value with Changes in other comprehensive income**	**Assets at Fair Value through Profit or Loss Remeasured to Fair Value with Changes in Profit or Loss**
29 December 20x2			
Receivable			
Financial asset	1,010	1,010	1,010
Equity (fair value adjustment)	-	-	-
Retained earnings (through profit or loss)	10	10	10
31 December 20x2			
Receivable	1,010	1,010	1,010
Financial asset	-	-	-
Equity (fair value adjustment)	-	-	-
Retained earnings (through profit or loss)	10	10	10
4 January 20x3			
Equity (fair value adjustment)	-	-	-
Retained earnings (through profit or loss)	10	10	10

D.2.3 Settlement date accounting: exchange of non-cash financial assets

If an entity recognises sales of financial assets using settlement date accounting, would a change in the fair value of a financial asset to be received in exchange for the noncash financial asset that is sold be recognised in accordance with IAS 39.57?

It depends. Any change in the fair value of the financial asset to be received would be accounted for under IAS 39.57 if the entity applies settlement date accounting for that category of financial assets. However, if the entity classifies the financial asset to be received in a category for which it applies trade date accounting, the asset to be received is recognised on the trade date as described in IAS 39.AG55. In that case, the entity recognises a liability of an amount equal to the carrying amount of the financial asset to be delivered on settlement date.

To illustrate: on 29 December 20x2 (trade date) Entity A enters into a contract to sell Note Receivable A, which is carried at amortised cost, in exchange for Bond B, which will be classified as held for trading and measured at fair value. Both assets have a fair value of CU1,010 on 29 December, while the amortised cost of Note Receivable A is CU1,000. Entity A uses settlement date accounting for loans and receivables and trade date accounting for assets held for trading. On 31 December 20x2 (financial year-end), the fair value of Note Receivable A is CU1,012 and the fair value of Bond B is CU1,009. On 4 January 20x3, the fair value of Note Receivable A is CU1,013 and the fair value of Bond B is CU1,007. The following entries are made:

29 December 20x2		
Dr Bond B	CU1,010	
Cr Payable		CU1,010
31 December 20x2		
Dr Trading loss	CU1	
Cr Bond B		CU1
4 January 20x3		
Dr Payable	CU1,010	
Dr Trading loss	CU2	
Cr Note Receivable A		CU1,000
Cr Bond B		CU2
Cr Realisation gain		CU10

SECTION E: MEASUREMENT

E.1 Initial Measurement of Financial Assets and Financial Liabilities

E.1.1 Initial measurement: transaction costs

Transaction costs should be included in the initial measurement of financial assets and financial liabilities other than those at fair value through profit or loss. How should this requirement be applied in practice?

For financial assets, incremental costs that are directly attributable to the acquisition of the asset, for example fees and commissions, are added to the amount originally recognised. For financial liabilities, directly related costs of issuing debt are deducted from the amount of debt originally recognised. For financial instruments that are measured at fair value through profit or loss, transaction costs are not added to the fair value measurement at initial recognition.

For financial instruments that are carried at amortised cost, such as held-to-maturity investments, loans and receivables, and financial liabilities that are not at fair value through profit or loss, transaction costs are included in the calculation of amortised cost using the effective interest method and, in effect, amortised through profit or loss over the life of the instrument.

For available-for-sale financial assets, transaction costs are recognised in other comprehensive income as part of a change in fair value at the next remeasurement. If an available-for-sale financial asset has fixed or determinable payments and does not have an indefinite life, the transaction costs are amortised to profit or loss using the effective interest method. If an available-for-sale financial asset does not have fixed or determinable payments and has an indefinite life, the transaction costs are recognised in profit or loss when the asset is derecognised or becomes impaired.

Transaction costs expected to be incurred on transfer or disposal of a financial instrument are not included in the measurement of the financial instrument.

E.2 Fair Value Measurement Considerations

E.2.1 Fair value measurement considerations for investment funds

IAS 39.AG72 states that the current bid price is usually the appropriate price to be used in measuring the fair value of an asset held. The rules applicable to some investment funds require net asset values to be reported to investors on the basis of mid-market prices. In these circumstances, would it be appropriate for an investment fund to measure its assets on the basis of mid-market prices?

No. The existence of regulations that require a different measurement for specific purposes does not justify a departure from the general requirement in IAS 39.AG72 to use the current bid price in the absence of a matching liability position. In its financial statements, an investment fund measures its assets at current bid prices. In reporting its net asset value to investors, an investment fund may wish to provide a reconciliation between the fair values recognised in its statement of financial position and the prices used for the net asset value calculation.

E.2.2 Fair value measurement: large holding

Entity A holds 15 per cent of the share capital in Entity B. The shares are publicly traded in an active market. The currently quoted price is CU100. Daily trading volume is 0.1 per cent of outstanding shares. Because Entity A believes that the fair value of the Entity B shares it owns, if sold as a block, is greater than the quoted market price, Entity A obtains several independent estimates of the price it would obtain if it sells its holding. These estimates indicate that Entity A would be able to obtain a price of CU105, ie a 5 per cent premium above the quoted price. Which figure should Entity A use for measuring its holding at fair value?

Under IAS 39.AG71, a published price quotation in an active market is the best estimate of fair value. Therefore, Entity A uses the published price quotation (CU100). Entity A cannot depart from the quoted market price solely because independent estimates indicate that Entity A would obtain a higher (or lower) price by selling the holding as a block.

E.3 Gains and Losses

E.3.1 Available-for-sale financial assets: exchange of shares

Entity A holds a small number of shares in Entity B. The shares are classified as available for sale. On 20 December 20X0, the fair value of the shares is CU120 and the cumulative gain recognised in other comprehensive income is CU20. On the same day, Entity B is acquired by Entity C, a large public entity. As a result, Entity A receives shares in Entity C in exchange for those it had in Entity B of equal fair value. Under IAS 39.55(b), should Entity A reclassify the cumulative gain of CU20 recognised in other comprehensive income from equity to profit or loss as a reclassification adjustment?

Yes. The transaction qualifies for derecognition under IAS 39. IAS 39.55(b) requires that the cumulative gain or loss on an available-for-sale financial asset that has been recognised in other comprehensive income be reclassified from equity to profit or loss when the asset is derecognised. In the exchange of shares, Entity A disposes of the shares it had in Entity B and receives shares in Entity C.

E.3.2 IAS 39 and IAS 21 – Available-for-sale financial assets: separation of currency component

For an available-for-sale monetary financial asset, the entity reports changes in the carrying amount relating to changes in foreign exchange rates in profit or loss in accordance with IAS 21.23(a) and IAS 21.28 and other changes in the carrying amount in other comprehensive income in accordance with IAS 39. How is the cumulative gain or loss that is recognised in other comprehensive income determined?

It is the difference between the amortised cost (adjusted for impairment, if any) and fair value of the available-for-sale monetary financial asset in the functional currency of the reporting entity. For the purpose of applying IAS 21.28 the asset is treated as an asset measured at amortised cost in the foreign currency.

To illustrate: on 31 December 20X1 Entity A acquires a bond denominated in a foreign currency (FC) for its fair value of FC1,000. The bond has five years remaining to maturity and a principal amount of FC1,250, carries fixed interest of 4.7 per cent that is paid annually (FC1,250 · 4.7 per cent = FC59 per year), and has an effective interest rate of 10 per cent. Entity A classifies the bond as available for sale, and thus recognises gains and losses in other comprehensive income. The entity's functional currency is its local currency (LC). The exchange rate is FC1 to LC1.5 and the carrying amount of the bond is LC1,500 (= FC1,000 · 1.5).

Dr	Bond	LC1,500	
	Cr Cash		LC1,500

On 31 December 20X2, the foreign currency has appreciated and the exchange rate is FC1 to LC2. The fair value of the bond is FC1,060 and thus the carrying amount is LC2,120 (= FC1,060 · 2). The amortised cost is FC1,041 (= LC2,082). In this case, the cumulative gain or loss to be recognised in other comprehensive income and accumulated in equity is the difference between the fair value and the amortised cost on 31 December 20X2, ie LC38 (= LC2,120 – LC2,082).

Interest received on the bond on 31 December 20X2 is FC59 (= LC118). Interest income determined in accordance with the effective interest method is FC100 (=1,000□· 10 per cent). The average exchange rate during the year is FC1 to LC1.75. For the purpose of this question, it is assumed that the use of the average exchange rate provides a reliable approximation of the spot rates applicable to the accrual of interest income during the year (IAS 21.22). Thus, reported interest income is LC175 (= FC100 · 1.75) including accretion of the initial discount of LC72 (= [FC100 – FC59] · 1.75). Accordingly, the exchange difference on the bond that is recognised in profit or loss is LC510 (= LC2,082 – LC1,500 – LC72). Also, there is an exchange gain on the interest receivable for the year of LC15 (= FC59 × [2.00 – 1.75]).

Dr	Bond	LC620	
Dr	Cash	LC118	
	Cr Interest income		LC175
	Cr Exchange gain		LC525
	Cr Fair value change in other comprehensive income		LC38

On 31 December 20X3, the foreign currency has appreciated further and the exchange rate is FC1 to LC2.50. The fair value of the bond is FC1,070 and thus the

carrying amount is LC2,675 (= FC1,070 · 2.50). The amortised cost is FC1,086 (= LC2,715). The cumulative gain or loss to be accumulated in other comprehensive income is the difference between the fair value and the amortised cost on 31 December 20X3, ie negative LC40 (= LC2,675 – LC2,715). Thus, the amount recognised in other comprehensive income equals the change in the difference during 20X3 of LC78 (= LC40 + LC38).

Interest received on the bond on 31 December 20X3 is FC59 (= LC148). Interest income determined in accordance with the effective interest method is FC104 (= FC1,041· 10 per cent). The average exchange rate during the year is FC1 to LC2.25. For the purpose of this question, it is assumed that the use of the average exchange rate provides a reliable approximation of the spot rates applicable to the accrual of interest income during the year (IAS 21.22). Thus, recognised interest income is LC234 (= FC104 · 2.25) including accretion of the initial discount of LC101 (= [FC104 – FC59] · 2.25). Accordingly, the exchange difference on the bond that is recognised in profit or loss is LC532 (= LC2,715 – LC2,082 – LC101). Also, there is an exchange gain on the interest receivable for the year of LC15 (= FC59 · [2.50 – 2.25]).

Dr	Bond	LC555	
Dr	Cash	LC148	
Dr	Fair value change in other comprehensive income	LC78	
	Cr Interest income		LC234
	Cr Exchange gain		LC547

E.3.3 IAS 39 and IAS 21 – Exchange differences arising on translation of foreign entities: other comprehensive income or profit or loss?

IAS 21.32 and IAS 21.48 states that all exchange differences resulting from translating the financial statements of a foreign operation should be recognised in other comprehensive income until disposal of the net investment. This would include exchange differences arising from financial instruments carried at fair value, which would include both financial assets classified as at fair value through profit or loss and financial assets that are available for sale.

IAS 39.55 requires that changes in fair value of financial assets classified as at fair value through profit or loss should be recognised in profit or loss and changes in fair value of available-for-sale investments should be recognised in other comprehensive income.

If the foreign operation is a subsidiary whose financial statements are consolidated with those of its parent, in the consolidated financial statements how are IAS 39.55 and IAS 21.39 applied?

IAS 39 applies in the accounting for financial instruments in the financial statements of a foreign operation and IAS 21 applies in translating the financial statements of a foreign operation for incorporation in the financial statements of the reporting entity.

To illustrate: Entity A is domiciled in Country X and its functional currency and presentation currency are the local currency of Country X (LCX). A has a foreign subsidiary (Entity B) in Country Y whose functional currency is the local currency of Country Y (LCY). B is the owner of a debt instrument, which is held for trading and therefore carried at fair value under IAS 39.

In B's financial statements for year 20x0, the fair value and carrying amount of the debt instrument is LCY100 in the local currency of Country Y. In A's consolidated financial statements, the asset is translated into the local currency of Country X at the spot exchange rate applicable at the balance sheet date (2.00). Thus, the carrying amount is LCX200 (= LCY100 · 2.00) in the consolidated financial statements.

At the end of year 20x1, the fair value of the debt instrument has increased to LCY110 in the local currency of Country Y. B recognises the trading asset at LCY110 in its balance sheet and recognises a fair value gain of LCY10 in its profit or loss. During the year, the spot exchange rate has increased from 2.00 to 3.00 resulting in an increase in the fair value of the instrument from LCX200 to LCX330 (= LCY110 · 3.00) in the currency of Country X. Therefore, Entity A recognises the trading asset at LCX330 in its consolidated financial statements.

Entity A translates the income statement of B "at the exchange rates at the dates of the transactions" (IAS 21.39(b)). Since the fair value gain has accrued through the year, A uses the average rate as a practical approximation ([3.00 + 2.00] / 2 = 2.50, in accordance with IAS 21.22). Therefore, while the fair value of the trading asset has increased by LCX130 (= LCX330 - LCX200), Entity A recognises only LCX25 (= LCY10 · 2.5) of this increase in consolidated profit or loss to comply with IAS 21.39(b). The resulting exchange difference, ie the remaining increase in the fair value of the debt instrument (LCX130 – LCX25 = LCX105), is accumulated in equity until the disposal of the net investment in the foreign operation in accordance with IAS 21.48.

E.3.4 IAS 39 and IAS 21 – Interaction between IAS 39 and IAS 21

IAS 39 includes requirements about the measurement of financial assets and financial liabilities and the recognition of gains and losses on remeasurement in profit or loss. IAS 21 includes rules about the reporting of foreign currency items and the recognition of exchange differences in profit or loss. In what order are IAS 21 and IAS 39 applied?

Balance sheet

Generally, the measurement of a financial asset or financial liability at fair value, cost or amortised cost is first determined in the foreign currency in which the item is denominated in accordance with IAS 39. Then, the foreign currency amount is translated into the functional currency using the closing rate or a historical rate in accordance with IAS 21 (IAS 39.AG83). For example, if a monetary financial asset (such as a debt instrument) is carried at amortised cost under IAS 39, amortised cost is calculated in the currency of denomination of that financial asset. Then, the foreign currency amount is recognised using the closing rate in the entity's financial statements (IAS 21.23). That applies regardless of whether a monetary item is measured at cost, amortised cost or fair value in the foreign currency (IAS 21.24). A non-monetary financial asset (such as an investment in an equity instrument) is translated using the closing rate if it is carried at fair value in the foreign currency (IAS 21.23(c)) and at a historical rate if it is not carried at fair value under IAS 39 because its fair value cannot be reliably measured (IAS 21.23(b) and IAS 39.46(c)).

As an exception, if the financial asset or financial liability is designated as a hedged item in a fair value hedge of the exposure to changes in foreign currency rates under IAS 39, the hedged item is remeasured for changes in foreign currency rates even if it would otherwise have been recognised using a historical rate under IAS 21 (IAS 39.89), ie the foreign currency amount is recognised using the closing rate. This exception applies to non-monetary items that are carried in terms of historical cost in the foreign currency and are hedged against exposure to foreign currency rates (IAS 21.23(b)).

Profit or loss

The recognition of a change in the carrying amount of a financial asset or financial liability in profit or loss depends on a number of factors, including whether it is an exchange difference or other change in carrying amount, whether it arises on a monetary item (for example, most debt instruments) or non-monetary item (such as most equity investments), whether the associated asset or liability is designated as a cash flow hedge of an exposure to changes in foreign currency rates, and whether it results from translating the financial statements of a foreign operation. The issue of recognising changes in the carrying amount of a financial asset or financial liability held by a foreign operation is addressed in a separate question (see Question E.3.3).

Any exchange difference arising on recognising a *monetary item* at a rate different from that at which it was initially recognised during the period, or recognised in previous financial statements, is recognised in profit or loss or in equity in accordance with IAS 21 (IAS 39.AG83, IAS 21.28 and IAS 21.32), unless the monetary item is designated as a cash flow hedge of a highly probable forecast transaction in foreign currency, in which case the requirements for recognition of gains and losses on cash flow hedges in IAS 39 apply (IAS 39.95). Differences arising from recognising a monetary item at a foreign currency amount different from that at which it was previously recognised are accounted for in a similar manner, since all changes in the carrying amount relating to foreign currency movements should be treated consistently. All other changes in the balance sheet measurement of a monetary item are recognised in profit or loss or in other comprehensive income in accordance with IAS 39. For example, although an entity recognises gains and losses on available-for-sale monetary financial assets in other comprehensive income (IAS 39.55(b)), the entity nevertheless recognises the changes in the carrying amount relating to changes in foreign exchange rates in profit or loss (IAS 21.23(a)).

Any changes in the carrying amount of a *non-monetary item* are recognised in profit or loss or in equity in accordance with IAS 39 (IAS 39.AG83). For example, for available-for-sale financial assets the entire change in the carrying amount, including the effect of changes in foreign currency rates, is recognised in other comprehensive income. If the non-monetary item is designated as a cash flow hedge of an unrecognised firm commitment or a highly probable forecast transaction in foreign currency, the requirements for recognition of gains and losses on cash flow hedges in IAS 39 apply (IAS 39.95).

When some portion of the change in carrying amount is recognised in other comprehensive income and some portion is recognised in profit or loss, for example, if the amortised cost of a foreign currency bond classified as available for sale has increased in foreign currency (resulting in a gain in profit or loss) but its fair value has decreased in the functional currency (resulting in a loss recognised in other comprehensive income), an entity cannot offset those two components for the purposes of determining gains or losses that should be recognised in profit or loss or in equity.

E.4 Impairment and Uncollectibility of Financial Assets

E.4.1 Objective evidence of impairment

Does IAS 39 require that an entity be able to identify a single, distinct past causative event to conclude that it is probable that an impairment loss on a financial asset has been incurred?

No. IAS 39.59 states "It may not be possible to identify a single, discrete event that caused the impairment. Rather the combined effect of several events may have caused the impairment." Also, IAS 39.60 states that "a downgrade of an entity's credit rating is not, of itself, evidence of impairment, although it may be evidence of impairment when considered with other available information". Other factors that an entity considers in determining whether it has objective evidence that an impairment loss has been incurred include information about the debtors' or issuers' liquidity, solvency and business and financial risk exposures, levels of and trends in delinquencies for similar financial assets, national and local economic trends and conditions, and the fair value of collateral and guarantees. These and other factors may, either individually or taken together, provide sufficient objective evidence that an impairment loss has been incurred in a financial asset or group of financial assets.

E.4.2 Impairment: future losses

Does IAS 39 permit the recognition of an impairment loss through the establishment of an allowance for future losses when a loan is given? For example, if Entity A lends CU1,000 to Customer B, can it recognise an immediate impairment loss of CU10 if Entity A, based on historical experience, expects that 1 per cent of the principal amount of loans given will not be collected?

No. IAS 39.14 requires a financial asset to be initially measured at fair value. For a loan asset, the fair value is the amount of cash lent adjusted for any fees and costs (unless a portion of the amount lent is compensation for other stated or implied rights or privileges). In addition, IAS 39.58 requires that an impairment loss is recognised only if there is objective evidence of impairment as a result of a past event that occurred after initial recognition. Accordingly, it is inconsistent with IAS 39.14 and IAS 39.58 to reduce the carrying amount of a loan asset on initial recognition through the recognition of an immediate impairment loss.

E.4.3 Assessment of impairment: principal and interest

Because of Customer B's financial difficulties, Entity A is concerned that Customer B will not be able to make all principal and interest payments due on a loan in a timely manner. It negotiates a restructuring of the loan. Entity A expects that Customer B will be able to meet its obligations under the restructured terms. Would Entity A recognise an impairment loss if the restructured terms are as reflected in any of the following cases?

(a) Customer B will pay the full principal amount of the original loan five years after the original due date, but none of the interest due under the original terms.
(b) Customer B will pay the full principal amount of the original loan on the original due date, but none of the interest due under the original terms.
(c) Customer B will pay the full principal amount of the original loan on the original due date with interest only at a lower interest rate than the interest rate inherent in the original loan.
(d) Customer B will pay the full principal amount of the original loan five years after the original due date and all interest accrued during the original loan term, but no interest for the extended term.
(e) Customer B will pay the full principal amount of the original loan five years after the original due date and all interest, including interest for both the original term of the loan and the extended term.

IAS 39.58 indicates that an impairment loss has been incurred if there is objective evidence of impairment. The amount of the impairment loss for a loan measured at amortised cost is the difference between the carrying amount of the loan and the present value of future principal and interest payments discounted at the loan's original effective interest rate. In cases (a)-(d) above, the present value of the future principal and interest payments discounted at the loan's original effective interest rate will be lower than the carrying amount of the loan. Therefore, an impairment loss is recognised in those cases.

In case (e), even though the timing of payments has changed, the lender will receive interest on interest, and the present value of the future principal and interest payments discounted at the loan's original effective interest rate will equal the carrying amount of the loan. Therefore, there is no impairment loss. However, this fact pattern is unlikely given Customer B's financial difficulties.

E.4.4 Assessment of impairment: fair value hedge

A loan with fixed interest rate payments is hedged against the exposure to interest rate risk by a receive-variable, pay-fixed interest rate swap. The hedge relationship qualifies for fair value hedge accounting and is reported as a fair value hedge. Thus, the carrying amount of the loan includes an adjustment for fair value changes attributable to movements in interest rates. Should an assessment of impairment in the loan take into account the fair value adjustment for interest rate risk?

Yes. The loan's original effective interest rate before the hedge becomes irrelevant once the carrying amount of the loan is adjusted for any changes in its fair value attributable to interest rate movements. Therefore, the original effective interest rate and amortised cost of the loan are adjusted to take into account recognised fair value changes. The adjusted effective interest rate is calculated using the adjusted carrying amount of the loan.

An impairment loss on the hedged loan is calculated as the difference between its carrying amount after adjustment for fair value changes attributable to the risk being hedged and the estimated future cash flows of the loan discounted at the adjusted effective interest rate. When a loan is included in a portfolio hedge of interest rate risk, the entity should allocate the change in the fair value of the hedged portfolio to the loans (or groups of similar loans) being assessed for impairment on a systematic and rational basis.

E.4.5 Impairment: provision matrix

A financial institution calculates impairment in the unsecured portion of loans and receivables on the basis of a provision matrix that specifies fixed provision rates for the number of days a loan has been classified as nonperforming (zero per cent if less than 90 days, 20 per cent if 90-180 days, 50 per cent if 181-365 days and 100 per cent if more than 365 days). Can the results be considered to be appropriate for the purpose of calculating the impairment loss on loans and receivables under IAS 39.63?

Not necessarily. IAS 39.63 requires impairment or bad debt losses to be calculated as the difference between the asset's carrying amount and the present value of estimated future cash flows discounted at the financial instrument's original effective interest rate.

E.4.6 Impairment: excess losses

Does IAS 39 permit an entity to recognise impairment or bad debt losses in excess of impairment losses that are determined on the basis of objective evidence about impairment in identified individual financial assets or identified groups of similar financial assets?

No. IAS 39 does not permit an entity to recognise impairment or bad debt losses in addition to those that can be attributed to individually identified financial assets or identified groups of financial assets with similar credit risk characteristics (IAS 39.64) on the basis of objective evidence about the existence of impairment in those assets (IAS 39.58). Amounts that an entity might want to set aside for additional possible impairment in financial assets, such as reserves that cannot be supported by objective evidence about impairment, are not recognised as impairment or bad debt losses under IAS 39. However, if an entity determines that no objective evidence of impairment exists for an individually assessed financial asset, whether significant or not, it includes the asset in a group of financial assets with similar credit risk characteristics (IAS 39.64).

E.4.7 Recognition of impairment on a portfolio basis

IAS 39.63 requires that impairment be recognised for financial assets carried at amortised cost. IAS 39.64 states that impairment may be measured and recognised individually or on a portfolio basis for a group of similar financial assets. If one asset in the group is impaired but the fair value of another asset in the group is above its amortised cost, does IAS 39 allow non-recognition of the impairment of the first asset?

No. If an entity knows that an individual financial asset carried at amortised cost is impaired, IAS 39.63 requires that the impairment of that asset should be recognised. It states: "the amount of the loss is measured as the difference between *the asset's* carrying amount and the present value of estimated future cash flows (excluding future credit losses that have not been incurred) discounted at the financial asset's original effective interest rate" (emphasis added). Measurement of impairment on a portfolio basis under IAS 39.64 may be applied to groups of small balance items and to financial assets that are individually assessed and found not to be impaired when there is indication of impairment in a group of similar assets and impairment cannot be identified with an individual asset in that group.

E.4.8 Impairment: recognition of collateral

If an impaired financial asset is secured by collateral and foreclosure is probable, is the collateral recognised as an asset separate from the impaired financial asset?

No. The measurement of the impaired financial asset reflects the fair value of the collateral. The collateral would generally not meet the recognition criteria until it is transferred to the lender. Accordingly, the collateral is not recognised as an asset separate from the impaired financial asset before foreclosure.

E.4.9 Impairment of non-monetary available-for-sale financial asset

If a non-monetary financial asset, such as an equity instrument, measured at fair value with gains and losses recognised in other comprehensive income becomes impaired, should the cumulative net loss recognised in equity, including any portion attributable to foreign currency changes, be reclassified from equity to profit as a reclassification adjustment?

Yes. IAS 39.67 states that when a decline in the fair value of an available-for-sale financial asset has been recognised in other comprehensive income and there is objective evidence that the asset is impaired, the cumulative net loss that had been recognised in other comprehensive income should be reclassified from equity to profit or loss even though the asset has not been derecognised. Any portion of the cumulative net loss that is attributable to foreign currency changes on that asset that had been recognised in other comprehensive income is also recognised in profit or loss. Any subsequent losses, including any portion attributable to foreign currency changes, are also reclassified from equity to profit or loss until the asset is derecognised.

E.4.10 Impairment: whether the available-for-sale reserve in equity can be negative

IAS 39 requires that gains and losses arising from changes in fair value on available-for-sale financial assets are recognised in other comprehensive income. If the aggregate fair value of such assets is less than their carrying amount, should the aggregate net loss that has been recognised in other comprehensive income be removed from equity and recognised in profit or loss?

Not necessarily. The relevant criterion is not whether the aggregate fair value is less than the carrying amount, but whether there is objective evidence that a financial asset or group of assets is impaired. An entity assesses at each balance sheet date whether there is any objective evidence that a financial asset or group of assets may be impaired, in accordance with IAS 39.59-61. IAS 39.60 states that a downgrade of an entity's credit rating is not, of itself, evidence of impairment, although it may be evidence of impairment when considered with other available information. Additionally, a decline in the fair value of a financial asset below its cost or amortised cost is not necessarily evidence of impairment (for example, a decline in the fair value of an investment in a debt instrument that results from an increase in the basic, riskfree interest rate).

SECTION F HEDGING

F.1 Hedging Instruments

F.1.1 Hedging the fair value exposure of a bond denominated in a foreign currency

Entity J, whose functional currency is the Japanese yen, has issued 5 million five-year US dollar fixed rate debt. Also, it owns a 5 million fiveyear fixed rate US dollar bond which it has classified as available for sale. Can Entity J designate its US dollar liability as a hedging instrument in a fair value hedge of the entire fair value exposure of its US dollar bond?

No. IAS 39.72 permits a non-derivative to be used as a hedging instrument only for a hedge of a foreign currency risk. Entity J's bond has a fair value exposure to foreign currency and interest rate changes and credit risk.

Alternatively, can the US dollar liability be designated as a fair value hedge or cash flow hedge of the foreign currency component of the bond?

Yes. However, hedge accounting is unnecessary because the amortised cost of the hedging instrument and the hedged item are both remeasured using closing rates. Regardless of whether Entity J designates the relationship as a cash flow hedge or a fair value hedge, the effect on profit or loss is the same. Any gain or loss on the non-derivative hedging instrument designated as a cash flow hedge is immediately recognised in profit or loss to correspond with the recognition of the change in spot rate on the hedged item in profit or loss as required by IAS 21.

F.1.2 Hedging with a non-derivative financial asset or liability

Entity J's functional currency is the Japanese yen. It has issued a fixed rate debt instrument with semi-annual interest payments that matures in two years with principal due at maturity of 5 million US dollars. It has also entered into a fixed price sales commitment for 5 million US dollars that matures in two years and is not accounted for as a derivative because it meets the exemption for normal sales in paragraph 5. Can Entity J designate its US dollar liability as a fair value hedge of the entire fair value exposure of its fixed price sales commitment and qualify for hedge accounting?

No. IAS 39.72 permits a non-derivative asset or liability to be used as a hedging instrument only for a hedge of a foreign currency risk.

Alternatively, can Entity J designate its US dollar liability as a cash flow hedge of the foreign currency exposure associated with the future receipt of US dollars on the fixed price sales commitment?

Yes. IAS 39 permits the designation of a non-derivative asset or liability as a hedging instrument in either a cash flow hedge or a fair value hedge of the exposure to changes in foreign exchange rates of a firm commitment (IAS 39.87). Any gain or loss on the non-derivative hedging instrument that is recognised in other comprehensive income during the period preceding the future sale is reclassified from equity to profit or loss as a reclassification adjustment when the sale takes place (IAS 39.95).

Alternatively, can Entity J designate the sales commitment as the hedging instrument instead of the hedged item?

No. Only a derivative instrument or a non-derivative financial asset or liability can be designated as a hedging instrument in a hedge of a foreign currency risk. A firm commitment cannot be designated as a hedging instrument. However, if the foreign currency component of the sales commitment is required to be separated as an embedded derivative under IAS 39.11 and IAS 39.AG33(d), it could be designated as a hedging instrument in a hedge of the exposure to changes in the fair value of the maturity amount of the debt attributable to foreign currency risk.

F.1.3 Hedge accounting: use of written options in combined hedging instruments

Issue (a) - Does IAS 39.AG94 preclude the use of an interest rate collar or other derivative instrument that combines a written option component and a purchased option component as a hedging instrument?

It depends. An interest rate collar or other derivative instrument that includes a written option cannot be designated as a hedging instrument if it is a net written option, because IAS 39.AG94 precludes the use of a written option as a hedging instrument unless it is designated as an offset to a purchased option. An interest rate collar or other derivative instrument that includes a written option may be designated as a hedging instrument, however, if the combination is a net purchased option or zero cost collar.

Issue (b) - What factors indicate that an interest rate collar or other derivative instrument that combines a written option component and a purchased option component is not a net written option?

The following factors taken together suggest that an interest rate collar or other derivative instrument that includes a written option is not a net written option.

(a) No net premium is received either at inception or over the life of the combination of options. The distinguishing feature of a written option is the receipt of a premium to compensate the writer for the risk incurred.

(b) Except for the strike prices, the critical terms and conditions of the written option component and the purchased option component are the same (including underlying variable or variables, currency denomination and maturity date). Also, the notional amount of the written option component is not greater than the notional amount of the purchased option component.

F.1.4 Internal hedges

Some entities use internal derivative contracts (internal hedges) to transfer risk exposures between different companies within a group or divisions within a single legal entity. Does IAS 39.73 prohibit hedge accounting in such cases?

Yes, if the derivative contracts are internal to the entity being reported on. IAS 39 does not specify how an entity should manage its risk. However, it states that internal hedging transactions do not qualify for hedge accounting. This applies both (a) in consolidated financial statements for intragroup hedging transactions, and (b) in the individual or separate financial statements of a legal entity for hedging transactions between divisions in the entity. The principles of preparing consolidated financial statements in IAS 27.24 require that "intragroup balances, transactions, income and expenses shall be eliminated in full".

On the other hand, an intragroup hedging transaction may be designated as a hedge in the individual or separate financial statements of a group entity, if the intragroup transaction is an external transaction from the perspective of the group entity. In addition, if the internal contract is offset with an external party the external contract may be regarded as the hedging instrument and the hedging relationship may qualify for hedge accounting.

The following summarises the application of IAS 39 to internal hedging transactions.

- IAS 39 does not preclude an entity from using internal derivative contracts for risk management purposes and it does not preclude internal derivatives from being accumulated at the treasury level or some other central location so that risk can be managed on an entitywide basis or at some higher level than the separate legal entity or division.
- Internal derivative contracts between two separate entities within a consolidated group can qualify for hedge accounting by those entities in their individual or separate financial statements, even though the internal contracts are not offset by derivative contracts with a party external to the consolidated group.
- Internal derivative contracts between two separate divisions within the same legal entity can qualify for hedge accounting in the individual or separate financial statements of that legal entity only if those contracts are offset by derivative contracts with a party external to the legal entity.
- Internal derivative contracts between separate divisions within the same legal entity and between separate entities within the consolidated group can qualify for hedge accounting in the consolidated financial statements only if the internal contracts are offset by derivative contracts with a party external to the consolidated group.
- If the internal derivative contracts are not offset by derivative contracts with external parties, the use of hedge accounting by group entities and divisions using internal contracts must be reversed on consolidation.

To illustrate: the banking division of Entity A enters into an internal interest rate swap with the trading division of the same entity. The purpose is to hedge the interest rate risk exposure of a loan (or group of similar loans) in the loan portfolio. Under the swap, the banking division pays fixed interest payments to the trading division and receives variable interest rate payments in return.

If a hedging instrument is not acquired from an external party, IAS 39 does not allow hedge accounting treatment for the hedging transaction undertaken by the banking and trading divisions. IAS 39.73 indicates that only derivatives that involve a party external to the entity can be designated as hedging instruments and, further, that any gains or losses on intragroup or intra-entity transactions should be eliminated on consolidation. Therefore, transactions between different divisions within Entity A do not qualify for hedge accounting treatment in the financial statements of Entity A. Similarly, transactions between different entities within a group do not qualify for hedge accounting treatment in consolidated financial statements.

However, if in addition to the internal swap in the above example the trading division enters into an interest rate swap or other contract with an external party that offsets the exposure hedged in the internal swap, hedge accounting is permitted under IAS 39. For the purposes of IAS 39, the hedged item is the loan (or group of similar loans) in the banking division and the hedging instrument is the external interest rate swap or other contract.

The trading division may aggregate several internal swaps or portions of them that are not offsetting each other and enter into a single third party derivative contract that offsets the aggregate exposure. Under IAS 39, such external hedging transactions may qualify for hedge accounting treatment provided that the hedged items in the banking division are identified and the other conditions for hedge accounting are met. It should be noted, however, that IAS 39.79 does not permit hedge accounting treatment for held-to-maturity investments if the hedged risk is the exposure to interest rate changes.

F.1.5 Offsetting internal derivative contracts used to manage interest rate risk

If a central treasury function enters into internal derivative contracts with subsidiaries and various divisions within the consolidated group to manage interest rate risk on a centralised basis, can those contracts qualify for hedge accounting in the consolidated financial statements if, before laying off the risk, the internal contracts are first netted against each other and only the net exposure is offset in the marketplace with external derivative contracts?

No. An internal contract designated at the subsidiary level or by a division as a hedge results in the recognition of changes in the fair value of the item being hedged in profit or loss (a fair value hedge) or in the recognition of the changes in the fair value of the internal derivative in other comprehensive income (a cash flow hedge). There is no basis for changing the measurement attribute of the item being hedged in a fair value hedge unless the exposure is offset with an external derivative. There is also no basis for recognising the gain or loss on the internal derivative in other comprehensive income for one entity and recognising it in profit or loss by the other entity unless it is offset with an external derivative. In cases where two or more internal derivatives are used to manage interest rate risk on assets or liabilities at the subsidiary or division level and those internal derivatives are offset at the treasury level, the effect of designating the internal derivatives as hedging instruments is that the hedged non-derivative exposures at the subsidiary or division levels would be used to offset each other on consolidation. Accordingly, since IAS 39.72 does not permit designating non-derivatives as hedging instruments, except for foreign currency exposures, the results of hedge accounting from the use of internal derivatives at the subsidiary or division level that are not laid off with external parties must be reversed on consolidation.

It should be noted, however, that there will be no effect on profit or loss and other comprehensive income of reversing the effect of hedge accounting in consolidation for internal derivatives that offset each other at the consolidation level if they are used in the same type of hedging relationship at the subsidiary or division level and, in the case of cash flow hedges, where the hedged items affect profit or loss in the same period. Just as the internal derivatives offset at the treasury level, their use as fair value hedges by two separate entities or divisions within the consolidated group will also result in the offset of the fair value amounts recognised in profit or loss, and their use as cash flow hedges by two separate entities or divisions within the consolidated group will also result in the fair value amounts being offset against each other in other comprehensive income. However, there may be an effect on individual line items in both the consolidated statement of comprehensive income and the consolidated statement of financial position, for example when internal derivatives that hedge assets (or liabilities) in a fair value hedge are offset by internal derivatives that are used as a fair value hedge of other assets (or liabilities) that are recognised in a different line item in the statement of financial position or statement of comprehensive income. In addition, to the extent that one of the internal contracts is used as a cash flow hedge and the other is used in a fair value hedge, gains and losses recognised would not offset since the gain (or loss) on the internal derivative used as a fair value hedge would be recognised in profit or loss and the corresponding loss (or gain) on the internal derivative used as a cash flow hedge would be recognised in other comprehensive income.

Question F.1.4 describes the application of IAS 39 to internal hedging transactions.

F.1.6 Offsetting internal derivative contracts used to manage foreign currency risk

If a central treasury function enters into internal derivative contracts with subsidiaries and various divisions within the consolidated group to manage foreign currency risk on a centralised basis, can those contracts be used as a basis for identifying external transactions that qualify for hedge accounting in the consolidated financial statements if, before laying off the risk, the internal contracts are first netted against each other and only the net exposure is offset by entering into a derivative contract with an external party?

It depends. IAS 27 *Consolidated and Separate Financial Statements* requires all internal transactions to be eliminated in consolidated financial statements. As stated in IAS 39.73, internal hedging transactions do not qualify for hedge accounting in the consolidated financial statements of the group. Therefore, if an entity wishes to achieve hedge accounting in the consolidated financial statements, it must designate a hedging relationship between a qualifying external hedging instrument and a qualifying hedged item.

As discussed in Question F.1.5, the accounting effect of two or more internal derivatives that are used to manage interest rate risk at the subsidiary or division level and are offset at the treasury level is that the hedged non-derivative exposures at those levels would be used to offset each other on consolidation. There is no effect on profit or loss or other comprehensive income if (a) the internal derivatives are used in the same type of hedge relationship (ie fair value or cash flow hedges) and (b), in the case of cash flow hedges, any derivative gains and losses that are initially recognised in other comprehensive income are reclassified from equity to profit or loss in the same period(s). When these two conditions are met, the gains and losses on the internal derivatives that are recognised in profit or loss or in equity will offset on consolidation resulting in the same profit or loss and other comprehensive income as if the derivatives had been eliminated. However, there may be an effect on individual line items, in both the consolidated income statement and the consolidated balance sheet, that would need to be eliminated. In addition, there is an effect on profit or loss and equity if some of the offsetting internal derivatives are used in cash flow hedges, while others are used in fair value hedges. There is also an effect on profit or loss and equity for offsetting internal derivatives that are used in cash flow hedges if the derivative gains and losses that are initially recognised in other comprehensive income are recognised in profit or loss in different periods (because the hedged items affect profit or loss in different periods).

As regards foreign currency risk, provided that the internal derivatives represent the transfer of foreign currency risk on underlying non-derivative financial assets or liabilities, hedge accounting can be applied because IAS 39.72 permits a non-derivative financial asset or liability to be designated as a hedging instrument for hedge accounting purposes for a hedge of a foreign currency risk. Accordingly, in this case the internal derivative contracts can be used as a basis for identifying external transactions that qualify for hedge accounting in the consolidated financial statements even if they are offset against each other. However, for consolidated financial statements, it is necessary to designate the hedging relationship so that it involves only external transactions.

Furthermore, the entity cannot apply hedge accounting to the extent that two or more offsetting internal derivatives represent the transfer of foreign currency risk on underlying forecast transactions or unrecognised firm commitments. This is because an unrecognised firm commitment or forecast transaction does not qualify as a hedging instrument under IAS 39. Accordingly, in this case the internal derivatives cannot be used as a basis for identifying external transactions that qualify for hedge accounting in the consolidated financial statements. As a result, any cumulative net gain or loss on an internal derivative that has been included in the initial carrying amount of an asset or liability (basis adjustment) or recognised in other comprehensive income would have to be reversed on consolidation if it cannot be demonstrated that the offsetting internal derivative represented the transfer of a foreign currency risk on a financial asset or liability to an external hedging instrument.

F.1.7 Internal derivatives: examples of applying Question F.1.6

In each case, FC = foreign currency, LC = local currency (which is the entity's functional currency), and TC = treasury centre.

Case 1: Offset of fair value hedges

Subsidiary A has trade receivables of FC100, due in 60 days, which it hedges using a forward contract with TC. Subsidiary B has payables of FC50, also due in 60 days, which it hedges using a forward contact with TC.

TC nets the two internal derivatives and enters into a net external forward contract to pay FC50 and receive LC in 60 days.

At the end of month 1, FC weakens against LC. A incurs a foreign exchange loss of LC10 on its receivables, offset by a gain of LC10 on its forward contract with TC. B makes a foreign exchange gain of LC5 on its payables offset by a loss of LC5 on its forward contract with TC. TC makes a loss of LC10 on its internal forward contract with A, a gain of LC5 on its internal forward contract with B, and a gain of LC5 on its external forward contract.

At the end of month 1, the following entries are made in the individual or separate financial statements of A, B and TC. Entries reflecting intragroup transactions or events are shown in italics.

A's entries

Dr	Foreign exchange loss	LC10	
	Cr Receivables		LC10
Dr	*Internal contract TC*	*LC10*	
	Cr Internal gain TC		*LC10*

B's entries

Dr	Payables	LC5	
	Cr Foreign exchange gain		LC5
Dr	*Internal loss TC*	*LC5*	
	Cr Internal contract TC		*LC5*

TC's entries

Dr	*Internal loss A*	*LC10*	
	Cr Internal contract A		*LC10*
Dr	*Internal contract B*	*LC5*	
	Cr Internal gain B		*LC5*
Dr	External forward contract	LC5	
	Cr Foreign exchange gain		LC5

Both A and B could apply hedge accounting in their individual financial statements provided all conditions in IAS 39 are met. However, in this case, no hedge accounting is required because gains and losses on the internal derivatives and the offsetting losses and gains on the hedged receivables and payables are recognised immediately in the profit or loss of A and B without hedge accounting.

In the consolidated financial statements, the internal derivative transactions are eliminated. In economic terms, the payable in B hedges FC50 of the receivables in A. The external forward contract in TC hedges the remaining FC50 of the receivable in A. Hedge accounting is not necessary in the consolidated financial statements because monetary items are measured at spot foreign exchange rates under IAS 21 irrespective of whether hedge accounting is applied.

The net balances before and after elimination of the accounting entries relating to the internal derivatives are the same, as set out below. Accordingly, there is no need to make any further accounting entries to meet the requirements of IAS 39.

	Debit	*Credit*
Receivables	-	LC10
Payables	LC5	-
External forward contract	LC5	-
Gains and losses	-	-
Internal contracts	-	-

Case 2: Offset of cash flow hedges

To extend the example, A also has highly probable future revenues of FC200 on which it expects to receive cash in 90 days. B has highly probable future expenses of FC500 (advertising cost), also to be paid for in 90 days. A and B enter into separate forward contracts with TC to hedge these exposures and TC enters into an external forward contract to receive FC300 in 90 days.

As before, FC weakens at the end of month 1. A incurs a 'loss' of LC20 on its anticipated revenues because the LC value of these revenues decreases. This is offset by a 'gain' of LC20 on its forward contract with TC.

B incurs a 'gain' of LC50 on its anticipated advertising cost because the LC value of the expense decreases. This is offset by a 'loss' of LC50 on its transaction with TC.

TC incurs a 'gain' of LC50 on its internal transaction with B, a 'loss' of LC20 on its internal transaction with A and a loss of LC30 on its external forward contract.

A and B complete the necessary documentation, the hedges are effective, and both A and B qualify for hedge accounting in their individual financial statements. A recognises the gain of LC20 on its internal derivative transaction in other comprehensive income and B recognises the loss of LC50 in other comprehensive income. TC does not claim hedge accounting, but measures both its internal and external derivative positions at fair value, which net to zero.

At the end of month 1, the following entries are made in the individual or separate financial statements of A, B and TC. Entries reflecting intragroup transactions or events are shown in italics.

A's entries

Dr	*Internal contract TC*	*LC20*	
	Cr Other comprehensive income		*LC20*

B's entries

Dr	*Other comprehensive income*	*LC50*	
	Cr Internal contract TC		*LC50*

TC's entries

Dr	*Internal loss A*	*LC20*	
	Cr Internal contract A		*LC20*
Dr	*Internal contract B*	*LC50*	
	Cr Internal gain B		*LC50*
Dr	Foreign exchange loss	LC30	
	Cr External forward contract		LC30

For the consolidated financial statements, TC's external forward contract on FC300 is designated, at the beginning of month 1, as a hedging instrument of the first FC300 of B's highly probable future expenses. IAS 39 requires that in the consolidated financial statements at the end of month 1, the accounting effects of the internal derivative transactions must be eliminated.

However, the net balances before and after elimination of the accounting entries relating to the internal derivatives are the same, as set out below. Accordingly, there is no need to make any further accounting entries in order for the requirements of IAS 39 to be met.

	Debit	*Credit*
External forward contract	-	LC30
Other comprehensive income	LC30	-
Gains and losses	-	-
Internal contracts	-	-

Case 3: Offset of fair value and cash flow hedges

Assume that the exposures and the internal derivative transactions are the same as in cases 1 and 2. However, instead of entering into two external derivatives to hedge separately the fair value and cash flow exposures, TC enters into a single net external derivative to receive FC250 in exchange for LC in 90 days.

TC has four internal derivatives, two maturing in 60 days and two maturing in 90 days. These are offset by a net external derivative maturing in 90 days. The interest rate differential between FC and LC is minimal, and therefore the ineffectiveness resulting from the mismatch in maturities is expected to have a minimal effect on profit or loss in TC.

As in cases 1 and 2, A and B apply hedge accounting for their cash flow hedges and TC measures its derivatives at fair value. A recognises a gain of LC20 on its internal derivative transaction in other comprehensive income and B defers a loss of LC50 on its internal derivative transaction in other comprehensive income.

At the end of month 1, the following entries are made in the individual or separate financial statements of A, B and TC. Entries reflecting intragroup transactions or events are shown in italics.

A's entries

Dr	Foreign exchange loss	LC10	
	Cr Receivables		LC10
Dr	*Internal contract TC*	*LC10*	
	Cr Internal gain TC		*LC10*
Dr	*Internal contract TC*	*LC20*	
	Cr Other comprehensive income		*LC20*

B's entries

Dr	Payables	LC5	
	Cr Foreign exchange gain		LC5
Dr	*Internal loss TC*	*LC5*	
	Cr Internal contract TC		*LC5*
Dr	*Other comprehensive income*	*LC50*	
	Cr Internal contract TC		*LC50*

TC's entries

Dr	*Internal loss A*	*LC10*	
	Cr Internal contract A		*LC10*
Dr	*Internal loss A*	*LC20*	
	Cr Internal contract A		*LC20*
Dr	*Internal contract B*	*LC5*	
	Cr Internal gain B		*LC5*
Dr	*Internal contract B*	*LC50*	
	Cr Internal gain B		*LC50*
Dr	Foreign exchange loss	LC25	
	Cr External forward contract		LC25

TOTAL (for the internal derivatives)	*A* *LC*	*B* *LC*	*Total* *LC*
Profit or loss (fair value hedges)	10	(5)	5
Other comprehensive income (cash flow hedges)	20	(50)	(30)
Total	30	(55)	(25)

Combining these amounts with the external transactions (ie those not marked in italics above) produces the total net balances before elimination of the internal derivatives as follows:

	Debit	*Credit*
Receivables	-	LC10
Payables	LC5	-
Forward contract	-	LC25
Other comprehensive income	LC30	-
Gains and losses	-	-
Internal contracts	-	-

For the consolidated financial statements, the following designations are made at the beginning of month 1:

- the payable of FC50 in B is designated as a hedge of the first FC50 of the highly probable future revenues in A. Therefore, at the end of month 1, the following entries are made in the consolidated financial statements: Dr Payable LC5; Cr Equity LC5;
- the receivable of FC100 in A is designated as a hedge of the first FC100 of the highly probable future expenses in B. Therefore, at the end of month 1, the following entries are made in the consolidated financial statements: Dr Equity LC10, Cr Receivable LC10; and
- the external forward contract on FC250 in TC is designated as a hedge of the next FC250 of highly probable future expenses in B. Therefore, at the end of month 1, the following entries are made in the consolidated financial statements: Dr Equity LC25; Cr External forward contract LC25.

In the consolidated financial statements at the end of month 1, IAS 39 requires the accounting effects of the internal derivative transactions to be eliminated.

However, the total net balances before and after elimination of the accounting entries relating to the internal derivatives are the same, as set out below. Accordingly, there is no need to make any further accounting entries to meet the requirements of IAS 39.

	Debit	*Credit*
Receivables	-	LC10
Payables	LC5	-
Forward contract	-	LC25
Equity	LC30	
Gains and losses	-	-
Internal contracts	-	-

Case 4: Offset of fair value and cash flow hedges with adjustment to carrying amount of inventory

Assume similar transactions as in case 3, except that the anticipated cash outflow of FC500 in B relates to the purchase of inventory that is delivered after 60 days. Assume also that the entity has a policy of basis-adjusting hedged forecast non-financial items. At the end of month 2, there are no further changes in exchange rates or fair values. At that date, the inventory is delivered and the loss of LC50 on B's internal derivative, recognised in other comprehensive income in month 1, is adjusted against the carrying amount of inventory in B. The gain of LC20 on A's internal derivative is deferred in equity as before.

In the consolidated financial statements, there is now a mismatch compared with the result that would have been achieved by unwinding and redesignating the hedges. The external derivative (FC250) and a proportion of the receivable (FC50) offset FC300 of the anticipated inventory purchase. There is a natural hedge between the remaining FC200 of anticipated cash outflow in B and the anticipated cash inflow of FC200 in A. This relationship does not qualify for hedge accounting under IAS 39 and this time there is only a partial offset between gains and losses on the internal derivatives that hedge these amounts.

At the end of months 1 and 2, the following entries are made in the individual or separate financial statements of A, B and TC. Entries reflecting intragroup transactions or events are shown in italics.

A's entries (all at the end of month 1)

Dr	Foreign exchange loss	LC10	
	Cr Receivables		LC10
Dr	*Internal contract TC*	*LC10*	
	Cr Internal gain TC		*LC10*
Dr	*Internal contract TC*	*LC20*	
	Cr Other comprehensive income		*LC20*

B's entries

At the end of month 1:

Dr	Payables	LC5	
	Cr Foreign exchange gain		LC5
Dr	*Internal loss TC*	*LC5*	
	Cr Internal contract TC		*LC5*
Dr	*Other comprehensive income*	*LC50*	
	Cr Internal contract TC		*LC50*

At the end of month 2:

Dr	Inventory	LC50	
	Cr Other comprehensive income		LC50

TC's entries (all at the end of month 1)

Dr	*Internal loss A*	*LC10*	
	Cr Internal contract A		*LC10*
Dr	*Internal loss A*	*LC20*	
	Cr Internal contract A		*LC20*
Dr	*Internal contract B*	*LC5*	
	Cr Internal gain B		*LC5*
Dr	*Internal contract B*	*LC50*	
	Cr Internal gain B		*LC50*
Dr	Foreign exchange loss	LC25	
	Cr Forward		LC25

TOTAL (for the internal derivatives)	*A* *LC*	*B* *LC*	*Total* *LC*
Income (fair value hedges)	10	(5)	5
Equity (cash flow hedges)	20	-	20
Basis adjustment (inventory)	-	(50)	(50)
Total	30	(55)	(25)

Combining these amounts with the external transactions (ie those not marked in italics above) produces the total net balances before elimination of the internal derivatives as follows:

	Debit	*Credit*
Receivables	-	LC10
Payables	LC5	-
Forward contract	-	LC25
Other comprehensive income	-	LC20
Basis adjustment (inventory)	LC50	-
Gains and losses	-	-
Internal contracts	-	-

For the consolidated financial statements, the following designations are made at the beginning of month 1:

- the payable of FC50 in B is designated as a hedge of the first FC50 of the highly probable future revenues in A. Therefore, at the end of month 1, the following entry is made in the consolidated financial statements: Dr Payables LC5; Cr Equity LC5.
- the receivable of FC100 in A is designated as a hedge of the first FC100 of the highly probable future expenses in B. Therefore, at the end of month 1, the following entries are made in the consolidated financial statements: Dr Equity LC10; Cr Receivable LC10; and at the end of month 2, Dr Inventory LC10; Cr Equity LC10.
- the external forward contract on FC250 in TC is designated as a hedge of the next FC250 of highly probable future expenses in B. Therefore, at the end of month 1, the following entry is made in the consolidated financial statements: Dr Equity LC25; Cr External forward contract LC25; and at the end of month 2, Dr Inventory LC25; Cr Equity LC25.

The total net balances after elimination of the accounting entries relating to the internal derivatives are as follows:

	Debit	*Credit*
Receivables	-	LC10
Payables	LC5	-
Forward contract	-	LC25
Other comprehensive income	-	LC5
Basis adjustment (inventory)	LC35	-
Gains and losses	-	-
Internal contracts	-	-

These total net balances are different from those that would be recognised if the internal derivatives were not eliminated, and it is these net balances that IAS 39 requires to be included in the consolidated financial statements. The accounting entries required to adjust the total net balances before elimination of the internal derivatives are as follows:

(a) to reclassify LC15 of the loss on B's internal derivative that is included in inventory to reflect that FC150 of the forecast purchase of inventory is not hedged by an external instrument (neither the external forward contract of FC250 in TC nor the external payable of FC100 in A); and
(b) to reclassify the gain of LC15 on A's internal derivative to reflect that the forecast revenues of FC150 to which it relates is not hedged by an external instrument.

The net effect of these two adjustments is as follows:

Dr	Other comprehensive income	LC15	
	Cr Inventory		LC15

F.1.8 Combination of written and purchased options

In most cases, IAS 39.AG94 prohibits the use of written options as hedging instruments. If a combination of a written option and purchased option (such as an interest rate collar) is transacted as a single instrument with one counterparty, can an entity split the derivative instrument into its written option component and purchased option component and designate the purchased option component as a hedging instrument?

No. IAS 39.74 specifies that a hedging relationship is designated by an entity for a hedging instrument in its entirety. The only exceptions permitted are splitting the time value and intrinsic value of an option and splitting the interest element and spot price on a forward. Question F.1.3 addresses the issue of whether and when a combination of ptions is considered as a written option.

F.1.9 Delta-neutral hedging strategy

Does IAS 39 permit an entity to apply hedge accounting for a 'deltaneutral' hedging strategy and other dynamic hedging strategies under which the quantity of the hedging instrument is constantly adjusted in order to maintain a desired hedge ratio, for example, to achieve a deltaneutral position insensitive to changes in the fair value of the hedged item?

Yes. IAS 39.74 states that "a dynamic hedging strategy that assesses both the intrinsic value and time value of an option contract can qualify for hedge accounting". For example, a portfolio insurance strategy that seeks to ensure that the fair value of the hedged item does not drop below a certain level, while allowing the fair value to increase, may qualify for hedge accounting.

To qualify for hedge accounting, the entity must document how it will monitor and update the hedge and measure hedge effectiveness, be able to track properly all terminations and redesignations of the hedging instrument, and demonstrate that all other criteria for hedge accounting in IAS 39.88 are met. Also, it must be able to demonstrate an expectation that the hedge will be highly effective for a specified short period of time during which the hedge is not expected to be adjusted.

F.1.10 Hedging instrument: out of the money put option

Entity A has an investment in one share of Entity B, which it has classified as available for sale. To give itself partial protection against decreases in the share price of Entity B, Entity A acquires a put option on one share of Entity B and designates the change in the intrinsic value of the put as a hedging instrument in a fair value hedge of changes in the fair value of its share in Entity B. The put gives Entity A the right to sell one share of Entity B at a strike price of CU90. At the inception of the hedging relationship, the share has a quoted price of CU100. Since the put option gives Entity A the right to dispose of the share at a price of CU90, the put should normally be fully effective in offsetting price declines below CU90 on an intrinsic value basis. Price changes above CU90 are not hedged. In this case, are changes in the fair value of the share of Entity B for prices above CU90 regarded as hedge ineffectiveness under IAS 39.88 and recognised in profit or loss under IAS 39.89?

No. IAS 39.74 permits Entity A to designate changes in the intrinsic value of the option as the hedging instrument. The changes in the intrinsic value of the option provide protection against the risk of variability in the fair value of one share of Entity B below or equal to the strike price of the put of CU90. For prices above CU90, the option is out of the money and has no intrinsic value. Accordingly, gains and losses on one share of Entity B for prices above CU90 are not attributable to the hedged risk for the purposes of assessing hedge effectiveness and recognising gains and losses on the hedged item.

Therefore, Entity A recognises changes in the fair value of the share in other comprehensive income if it is associated with variation in its price above CU90 (IAS 39.55 and IAS 39.90). Changes in the fair value of the share associated with price declines below CU90 form part of the designated fair value hedge and are recognised in profit or loss under IAS 39.89(b). Assuming the hedge is effective, those changes are offset by changes in the intrinsic value of the put, which are also recognised in profit or loss (IAS 39.89(a)). Changes in the time value of the put are excluded from the designated hedging relationship and recognised in profit or loss under IAS 39.55(a).

F.1.11 Hedging instrument: proportion of the cash flows of a cash instrument

In the case of foreign exchange risk, a non-derivative financial asset or non-derivative financial liability can potentially qualify as a hedging instrument. Can an entity treat the cash flows for specified periods during which a financial asset or financial liability that is designated as a hedging instrument remains outstanding as a proportion of the hedging instrument under IAS 39.75, and exclude the other cash flows from the designated hedging relationship?

No. IAS 39.75 indicates that a hedging relationship may not be designated for only a portion of the time period in which the hedging instrument is outstanding. For example, the cash flows during the first three years of a tenyear borrowing denominated in a foreign currency cannot qualify as a hedging instrument in a cash flow hedge of the first three years of revenue in the same foreign currency. On the other hand, a non-derivative financial asset or financial liability denominated in a foreign currency may potentially qualify as a hedging instrument in a hedge of the foreign currency risk associated with a hedged item that has a remaining time period until maturity that is equal to or longer than the remaining maturity of the hedging instrument (see Question F.2.17).

F.1.12 Hedges of more than one type of risk

Issue (a) - Normally a hedging relationship is designated between an entire hedging instrument and a hedged item so that there is a single measure of fair value for the hedging instrument. Does this preclude designating a single financial instrument simultaneously as a hedging instrument in both a cash flow hedge and a fair value hedge?

No. For example, entities commonly use a combined interest rate and currency swap to convert a variable rate position in a foreign currency to a fixed rate position in the functional currency. IAS 39.76 allows the swap to be designated separately as a fair value hedge of the currency risk and a cash flow hedge of the interest rate risk provided the conditions in IAS 39.76 are met.

Issue (b) - If a single financial instrument is a hedging instrument in two different hedges, is special disclosure required?

IAS 32.58 requires disclosures separately for designated fair value hedges, cash flow hedges and hedges of a net investment in a foreign operation. The instrument in question would be reported in the IAS 32.58 disclosures separately for each type of hedge.

F.1.13 Hedging instrument: dual foreign currency forward exchange contract

Entity A's functional currency is the Japanese yen. Entity A has a fiveyear floating rate US dollar liability and a ten-year fixed rate pound sterling-denominated note receivable. The principal amounts of the asset and liability when converted into the Japanese yen are the same. Entity A enters into a single foreign currency forward contract to hedge its foreign currency exposure on both instruments under which it receives US dollars and pays pounds sterling at the end of five years. If Entity A designates the forward exchange contract as a hedging instrument in a cash flow hedge against the foreign currency exposure on the principal repayments of both instruments, can it qualify for hedge accounting?

Yes. IAS 39.76 permits designating a single hedging instrument as a hedge of multiple types of risk if three conditions are met. In this example, the derivative hedging instrument satisfies all of these conditions, as follows.

(a) The risks hedged can be identified clearly. The risks are the exposures to changes in the exchange rates between US dollars and yen, and yen and pounds, respectively.

(b) The effectiveness of the hedge can be demonstrated. For the pound sterling loan, the effectiveness is measured as the degree of offset between the fair value of the principal repayment in pounds sterling and the fair value of the pound sterling payment on the forward exchange contract. For the US dollar liability, the effectiveness is measured as the degree of offset between the fair value of the principal repayment in US dollars and the US dollar receipt on the forward exchange contract. Even though the receivable has a ten-year life and the forward protects it for only the first five years, hedge accounting is permitted for only a portion of the exposure as described in Question F.2.17.

(c) It is possible to ensure that there is specific designation of the hedging instrument and different risk positions. The hedged exposures are identified as the principal amounts of the liability and the note receivable in their respective currency of denomination.

F.1.14 Concurrent offsetting swaps and use of one as a hedging instrument

Entity A enters into an interest rate swap and designates it as a hedge of the fair value exposure associated with fixed rate debt. The fair value hedge meets the hedge accounting criteria of IAS 39. Entity A simultaneously enters into a second interest rate swap with the same swap counterparty that has terms that fully offset the first interest rate swap. Is Entity A required to view the two swaps as one unit and therefore precluded from applying fair value hedge accounting to the first swap?

It depends. IAS 39 is transaction-based. If the second swap was not entered into in contemplation of the first swap or there is a substantive business purpose for structuring the transactions separately, then the swaps are not viewed as one unit.

For example, some entities have a policy that requires a centralised dealer or treasury subsidiary to enter into third-party derivative contracts on behalf of other subsidiaries within the organisation to hedge the subsidiaries' interest rate risk exposures. The dealer or treasury subsidiary also enters into internal derivative transactions with those subsidiaries in order to track those hedges operationally within the organisation. Because the dealer or treasury subsidiary also enters into derivative contracts as part of its trading operations, or because it may wish to rebalance the risk of its overall portfolio, it may enter into a derivative contract with the same third party during the same business day that has substantially the same terms as a contract entered into as a hedging instrument on behalf of another subsidiary. In this case, there is a valid business purpose for entering into each contract.

Judgement is applied to determine whether there is a substantive business purpose for structuring the transactions separately. For example, if the sole purpose is to obtain fair value accounting treatment for the debt, there is no substantive business purpose.

F.2 Hedged Items

F.2.1 Whether a derivative can be designated as a hedged item

Does IAS 39 permit designating a derivative instrument (whether a standalone or separately recognised embedded derivative) as a hedged item either individually or as part of a hedged group in a fair value or cash flow hedge, for example, by designating a pay-variable, receive-fixed Forward Rate Agreement (FRA) as a cash flow hedge of a pay-fixed, receive-variable FRA?

No. Derivative instruments are always deemed held for trading and measured at fair value with gains and losses recognised in profit or loss unless they are designated and effective hedging instruments (IAS 39.9). As an exception, IAS 39.AG94 permits the designation of a purchased option as the hedged item in a fair value hedge.

F.2.2 Cash flow hedge: anticipated issue of fixed rate debt

Is hedge accounting allowed for a hedge of an anticipated issue of fixed rate debt?

Yes. This would be a cash flow hedge of a highly probable forecast transaction that will affect profit or loss (IAS 39.86) provided that the conditions in IAS 39.88 are met.

To illustrate: Entity R periodically issues new bonds to refinance maturing bonds, provide working capital and for various other purposes. When Entity R decides it will be issuing bonds, it may hedge the risk of changes in the long-term interest rate from the date it decides to issue the bonds to the date the bonds are issued. If long-term interest rates go up, the bond will be issued either at a higher rate or with a higher discount or smaller premium than was originally expected. The higher rate being paid or decrease in proceeds is normally offset by the gain on the hedge. If long-term interest rates go down, the bond will be issued either at a lower rate or with a higher premium or a smaller discount than was originally expected. The lower rate being paid or increase in proceeds is normally offset by the loss on the hedge.

For example, in August 2000 Entity R decided it would issue CU200 million seven-year bonds in January 2001. Entity R performed historical correlation studies and determined that a seven-year treasury bond adequately correlates to the bonds Entity R expected to issue, assuming a hedge ratio of 0.93 futures contracts to one debt unit. Therefore, Entity R hedged the anticipated issue of the bonds by selling (shorting) CU186 million worth of futures on seven-year treasury bonds. From August 2000 to January 2001 interest rates increased. The short futures positions were closed in January 2001, the date the bonds were issued, and resulted in a CU1.2 million gain that will offset the increased interest payments on the bonds and, therefore, will affect profit or loss over the life of the bonds. The hedge qualifies as a cash flow hedge of the interest rate risk on the forecast issue of debt.

F.2.3 Hedge accounting: core deposit intangibles

Is hedge accounting treatment permitted for a hedge of the fair value exposure of core deposit intangibles?

It depends on whether the core deposit intangible is generated internally or acquired (eg as part of a business combination).

Internally generated core deposit intangibles are not recognised as intangible assets under IAS 38. Because they are not recognised, they cannot be designated as a hedged item.

If a core deposit intangible is acquired together with a related portfolio of deposits, the core deposit intangible is required to be recognised separately as an intangible asset (or as part of the related acquired portfolio of deposits) if it meets the recognition criteria in paragraph 21 of IAS 38 *Intangible Assets*. A recognised core deposit intangible asset could be designated as a hedged item, but only if it meets the conditions in paragraph 88, including the requirement in paragraph 88(b) that the effectiveness of the hedge can be measured reliably. Because it is often difficult to measure reliably the fair value of a core.

F.2.4 Hedge accounting: hedging of future foreign currency revenue streams

Is hedge accounting permitted for a currency borrowing that hedges an expected but not contractual revenue stream in foreign currency?

Yes, if the revenues are highly probable. Under IAS 39.86(b) a hedge of an anticipated sale may qualify as a cash flow hedge. For example, an airline entity may use sophisticated models based on experience and economic data to project its revenues in various currencies. If it can demonstrate that forecast revenues for a period of time into the future in a particular currency are "highly probable", as required by IAS 39.88, it may designate a currency borrowing as a cash flow hedge of the future revenue stream. The portion of the gain or loss on the borrowing that is determined to be an effective hedge is recognised in other comprehensive income until the revenues occur.

It is unlikely that an entity can reliably predict 100 per cent of revenues for a future year. On the other hand, it is possible that a portion of predicted revenues, normally those expected in the short term, will meet the "highly probable" criterion.

F.2.5 Cash flow hedges: 'all in one' hedge

If a derivative instrument is expected to be settled gross by delivery of the underlying asset in exchange for the payment of a fixed price, can the derivative instrument be designated as the hedging instrument in a cash flow hedge of that gross settlement assuming the other cash flow hedge accounting criteria are met?

Yes. A derivative instrument that will be settled gross can be designated as the hedging instrument in a cash flow hedge of the variability of the consideration to be paid or received in the future transaction that will occur on gross settlement of the derivative contract itself because there would be an exposure to variability in the purchase or sale price without the derivative. This applies to all fixed price contracts that are accounted for as derivatives under IAS 39.

For example, if an entity enters into a fixed price contract to sell a commodity and that contract is accounted for as a derivative under IAS 39 (for example, because the entity has a practice of settling such contracts net in cash or of taking delivery of the underlying and selling it within a short period after delivery for the purpose of generating a profit from short-term fluctuations in price or dealer's margin), the entity may designate the fixed price contract as a cash flow hedge of the variability of the consideration to be received on the sale of the asset (a future transaction) even though the fixed price contract is the contract under which the asset will be sold. Also, if an entity enters into a forward contract to purchase a debt instrument that will be settled by delivery, but the forward contract is a derivative because its term exceeds the regular way delivery period in the marketplace, the entity may designate the forward as a cash flow hedge of the variability of the consideration to be paid to acquire the debt instrument (a future transaction), even though the derivative is the contract under which the debt instrument will be acquired.

F.2.6 Hedge relationships: entity-wide risk

An entity has a fixed rate asset and a fixed rate liability, each having the same principal amount. Under the terms of the instruments, interest payments on the asset and liability occur in the same period and the net cash flow is always positive because the interest rate on the asset exceeds the interest rate on the liability. The entity enters into an interest rate swap to receive a floating interest rate and pay a fixed interest rate on a notional amount equal to the principal of the asset and designates the interest rate swap as a fair value hedge of the fixed rate asset. Does the hedging relationship qualify for hedge accounting even though the effect of the interest rate swap on an entity-wide basis is to create an exposure to interest rate changes that did not previously exist?

Yes. IAS 39 does not require risk reduction on an entity-wide basis as a condition for hedge accounting. Exposure is assessed on a transaction basis and, in this instance, the asset being hedged has a fair value exposure to interest rate increases that is offset by the interest rate swap.

F.2.7 Cash flow hedge: forecast transaction related to an entity's equity

Can a forecast transaction in the entity's own equity instruments or forecast dividend payments to shareholders be designated as a hedged item in a cash flow hedge?

No. To qualify as a hedged item, the forecast transaction must expose the entity to a particular risk that can affect profit or loss (IAS 39.86). The classification of financial instruments as liabilities or equity generally provides the basis for determining whether transactions or other payments relating to such instruments are recognised in profit or loss (IAS 32). For example, distributions to holders of an equity instrument are debited by the issuer directly to equity (IAS 32.35). Therefore, such distributions cannot be designated as a hedged item. However, a declared dividend that has not yet been paid and is recognised as a financial liability may qualify as a hedged item, for example, for foreign currency risk if it is denominated in a foreign currency.

F.2.8 Hedge accounting: risk of a transaction not occurring

Does IAS 39 permit an entity to apply hedge accounting to a hedge of the risk that a transaction will not occur, for example, if that would result in less revenue to the entity than expected?

No. The risk that a transaction will not occur is an overall business risk that is not eligible as a hedged item. Hedge accounting is permitted only for risks associated with recognised assets and liabilities, firm commitments, highly probable forecast transactions and net investments in foreign operations (IAS 39.86).

F.2.9 Held-to-maturity investments: hedging variable interest rate payments

Can an entity designate a pay-variable, receive-fixed interest rate swap as a cash flow hedge of a variable rate, held-to-maturity investment?

No. It is inconsistent with the designation of a debt investment as being held to maturity to designate a swap as a cash flow hedge of the debt investment's variable interest rate payments. IAS 39.79 states that a held-tomaturity investment cannot be a hedged item with respect to interest rate risk or prepayment risk "because designation of an investment as held to maturity requires an intention to hold the investment until maturity without regard to changes in the fair value or cash flows of such an investment attributable to changes in interest rates".

F.2.10 Hedged items: purchase of held-to-maturity investment

An entity forecasts the purchase of a financial asset that it intends to classify as held to maturity when the forecast transaction occurs. It enters into a derivative contract with the intent to lock in the current interest rate and designates the derivative as a hedge of the forecast purchase of the financial asset. Can the hedging relationship qualify for cash flow hedge accounting even though the asset will be classified as a held-to-maturity investment?

Yes. With respect to interest rate risk, IAS 39 prohibits hedge accounting for financial assets that are classified as held-to-maturity (IAS 39.79). However, even though the entity intends to classify the asset as held to maturity, the instrument is not classified as such until the transaction occurs.

F.2.11 Cash flow hedges: reinvestment of funds obtained from held-to-maturity investments

An entity owns a variable rate asset that it has classified as held to maturity. It enters into a derivative contract with the intention to lock in the current interest rate on the reinvestment of variable rate cash flows, and designates the derivative as a cash flow hedge of the forecast future interest receipts on debt instruments resulting from the reinvestment of interest receipts on the held-to-maturity asset. Assuming that the other hedge accounting criteria are met, can the hedging relationship qualify for cash flow hedge accounting even though the interest payments that are being reinvested come from an asset that is classified as held to maturity?

Yes. IAS 39.79 states that a held-to-maturity investment cannot be a hedged item with respect to interest rate risk. Question F.2.9 specifies that this applies not only to fair value hedges, ie hedges of the exposure to fair value interest rate risk associated with held-to-maturity investments that pay fixed interest, but also to cash flow hedges, ie hedges of the exposure to cash flow interest rate risk associated with held-to-maturity investments that pay variable interest at current market rates. However, in this instance, the derivative is designated as an offset of the exposure to cash flow risk associated with forecast future interest receipts on debt instruments resulting from the forecast reinvestment of variable rate cash flows on the held-to-maturity investment. The source of the funds forecast to be reinvested is not relevant in determining whether the reinvestment risk can be hedged. Accordingly, designation of the derivative as a cash flow hedge is permitted. This answer applies also to a hedge of the exposure to cash flow risk associated with the forecast future interest receipts on debt instruments resulting from the reinvestment of interest receipts on a fixed rate asset classified as held to maturity.

F.2.12 Hedge accounting: prepayable financial asset

If the issuer has the right to prepay a financial asset, can the investor designate the cash flows after the prepayment date as part of the hedged item?

Cash flows after the prepayment date may be designated as the hedged item to the extent it can be demonstrated that they are "highly probable" (IAS 39.88). For example, cash flows after the prepayment date may qualify as highly probable if they result from a group or pool of similar assets (for example, mortgage loans) for which prepayments can be estimated with a high degree of accuracy or if the prepayment option is significantly out of the money. In addition, the cash flows after the prepayment date may be designated as the hedged item if a comparable option exists in the hedging instrument.

F.2.13 Fair value hedge: risk that could affect profit or loss

Is fair value hedge accounting permitted for exposure to interest rate risk in fixed rate loans that are classified as loans and receivables?

Yes. Under IAS 39, loans and receivables are carried at amortised cost. Banking institutions in many countries hold the bulk of their loans and receivables until maturity. Thus, changes in the fair value of such loans and receivables that are due to changes in market interest rates will not affect profit or loss. IAS 39.86 specifies that a fair value hedge is a hedge of the exposure to changes in fair value that is attributable to a particular risk and that can affect profit or loss. Therefore, IAS 39.86 may appear to preclude fair value hedge accounting for loans and receivables. However, it follows from IAS 39.79 that loans and receivables can be hedged items with respect to interest rate risk since they are not designated as held-to-maturity investments. The entity could sell them and the change in fair values would affect profit or loss. Thus, fair value hedge accounting is permitted for loans and receivables.

F.2.14 Intragroup and intra-entity hedging transactions

An Australian entity, whose functional currency is the Australian dollar, has forecast purchases in Japanese yen that are highly probable. The Australian entity is wholly owned by a Swiss entity, which prepares consolidated financial statements (which include the Australian subsidiary) in Swiss francs. The Swiss parent entity enters into a forward contract to hedge the change in yen relative to the Australian dollar. Can that hedge qualify for hedge accounting in the consolidated financial statements, or must the Australian subsidiary that has the foreign currency exposure be a party to the hedging transaction?

Yes. The hedge can qualify for hedge accounting provided the other hedge accounting criteria in IAS 39 are met. Since the Australian entity did not hedge the foreign currency exchange risk associated with the forecast purchases in yen, the effects of exchange rate changes between the Australian dollar and the yen will affect the Australian entity's profit or loss and, therefore, would also affect consolidated profit or loss. IAS 39 does not require that the operating unit that is exposed to the risk being hedged be a party to the hedging instrument.

F.2.15 Internal contracts: single offsetting external derivative

An entity uses what it describes as internal derivative contracts to document the transfer of responsibility for interest rate risk exposures from individual divisions to a central treasury function. The central treasury function aggregates the internal derivative contracts and enters into a single external derivative contract that offsets the internal derivative contracts on a net basis. For example, if the central treasury function has entered into three internal receive-fixed, pay-variable interest rate swaps that lay off the exposure to variable interest cash flows on variable rate liabilities in other divisions and one internal receive-variable, pay-fixed interest rate swap that lays off the exposure to variable interest cash flows on variable rate assets in another division, it would enter into an interest rate swap with an external counterparty that exactly offsets the four internal swaps. Assuming that the hedge accounting criteria are met, in the entity's financial statements would the single offsetting external derivative qualify as a hedging instrument in a hedge of a part of the underlying items on a gross basis?

Yes, but only to the extent the external derivative is designated as an offset of cash inflows or cash outflows on a gross basis. IAS 39.84 indicates that a hedge of an overall net position does not qualify for hedge accounting. However, it does permit designating a part of the underlying items as the hedged position on a gross basis. Therefore, even though the purpose of entering into the external derivative was to offset internal derivative contracts on a net basis, hedge accounting is permitted if the hedging relationship is defined and documented as a hedge of a part of the underlying cash inflows or cash outflows on a gross basis. An entity follows the approach outlined in IAS 39.84 and IAS 39.AG101 to designate part of the underlying cash flows as the hedged position.

F.2.16 Internal contracts: external derivative contracts that are settled net

Issue (a) - An entity uses internal derivative contracts to transfer interest rate risk exposures from individual divisions to a central treasury function. For each internal derivative contract, the central treasury function enters into a derivative contract with a single external counterparty that offsets the internal derivative contract. For example, if the central treasury function has entered into a receive-5 per cent-fixed, pay-LIBOR interest rate swap with another division that has entered into the internal contract with central treasury to hedge the exposure to variability in interest cash flows on a pay-LIBOR borrowing, central treasury would enter into a pay-5 per cent-fixed, receive-LIBOR interest rate swap on the same principal terms with the external counterparty. Although each of the external derivative contracts is formally documented as a separate contract, only the net of the payments on all of the external derivative contracts is settled since there is a netting agreement with the external counterparty. Assuming that the other hedge accounting criteria are met, can the individual external derivative contracts, such as the pay-5 per cent-fixed, receive-LIBOR interest rate swap above, be designated as hedging instruments of underlying gross exposures, such as the exposure to changes in variable interest payments on the pay-LIBOR borrowing above, even though the external derivatives are settled on a net basis?

Generally, yes. External derivative contracts that are legally separate contracts and serve a valid business purpose, such as laying off risk exposures on a gross basis, qualify as hedging instruments even if those external contracts are settled on a net basis with the same external counterparty, provided the hedge accounting criteria in IAS 39 are met. See also Question F.1.14.

Issue (b) - Treasury observes that by entering into the external offsetting contracts and including them in the centralised portfolio, it is no longer able to evaluate the exposures on a net basis. Treasury wishes to manage the portfolio of offsetting external derivatives separately from other exposures of the entity. Therefore, it enters into an additional, single derivative to offset the risk of the portfolio. Can the individual external derivative contracts in the portfolio still be designated as hedging instruments of underlying gross exposures even though a single external derivative is used to offset fully the market exposure created by entering into the external contracts?

Generally, yes. The purpose of structuring the external derivative contracts in this manner is consistent with the entity's risk management objectives and strategies. As indicated above, external derivative contracts that are legally separate contracts and serve a valid business purpose qualify as hedging instruments. Moreover, the answer to Question F.1.14 specifies that hedge accounting is not precluded simply because the entity has entered into a swap that mirrors exactly the terms of another swap with the same counterparty if there is a substantive business purpose for structuring the transactions separately.

F.2.17 Partial term hedging

IAS 39.75 indicates that a hedging relationship may not be designated for only a portion of the time period during which a hedging instrument remains outstanding. Is it permitted to designate a derivative as hedging only a portion of the time period to maturity of a hedged item?

Yes. A financial instrument may be a hedged item for only a portion of its cash flows or fair value, if effectiveness can be measured and the other hedge accounting criteria are met.

To illustrate: Entity A acquires a 10 per cent fixed rate government bond with a remaining term to maturity of ten years. Entity A classifies the bond as available for sale. To hedge itself against fair value exposure on the bond associated with the present value of the interest rate payments until year 5, Entity A acquires a five-year pay-fixed, receive-floating swap. The swap may be designated as hedging the fair value exposure of the interest rate payments on the government bond until year 5 and the change in value of the principal payment due at maturity to the extent affected by changes in the yield curve relating to the five years of the swap.

F.2.18 Hedging instrument: cross-currency interest rate swap

Entity A's functional currency is the Japanese yen. Entity A has a fiveyear floating rate US dollar liability and a 10-year fixed rate pound sterling-denominated note receivable. Entity A wishes to hedge the foreign currency exposure on its asset and liability and the fair value interest rate exposure on the receivable and enters into a matching cross-currency interest rate swap to receive floating rate US dollars and pay fixed rate pounds sterling and to exchange the dollars for the pounds at the end of five years. Can Entity A designate the swap as a hedging instrument in a fair value hedge against both foreign currency risk and interest rate risk, although both the pound sterling and US dollar are foreign currencies to Entity A?

Yes. IAS 39.81 permits hedge accounting for components of risk, if effectiveness can be measured. Also, IAS 39.76 permits designating a single hedging instrument as a hedge of more than one type of risk if the risks can be identified clearly, effectiveness can be demonstrated, and specific designation of the hedging instrument and different risk positions can be ensured. Therefore, the swap may be designated as a hedging instrument in a fair value hedge of the pound sterling receivable against exposure to changes in its fair value associated with changes in UK interest rates for the initial partial term of five years and the exchange rate between pounds and US dollars. The swap is measured at fair value with changes in fair value recognised in profit or loss. The carrying amount of the receivable is adjusted for changes in its fair value caused by changes in UK interest rates for the first fiveyear portion of the yield curve. The receivable and payable are remeasured using spot exchange rates under IAS 21 and the changes to their carrying amounts recognised in profit or loss.

F.2.19 Hedged items: hedge of foreign currency risk of publicly traded shares

Entity A acquires shares in Entity B on a foreign stock exchange for their fair value of 1,000 in foreign currency (FC). It classifies the shares as available for sale. To protect itself from the exposure to changes in the foreign exchange rate associated with the shares, it enters into a forward contract to sell FC750. Entity A intends to roll over the forward exchange contract for as long as it retains the shares. Assuming that the other hedge accounting criteria are met, could the forward exchange contract qualify as a hedge of the foreign exchange risk associated with the shares?

Yes, but only if there is a clear and identifiable exposure to changes in foreign exchange rates. Therefore, hedge accounting is permitted if (a) the equity instrument is not traded on an exchange (or in another established marketplace) where trades are denominated in the same currency as the functional currency of Entity A and (b) dividends to Entity A are not denominated in that currency. Thus, if a share is traded in multiple currencies and one of those currencies is the functional currency of the reporting entity, hedge accounting for the foreign currency component of the share price is not permitted.

If so, could the forward exchange contract be designated as a hedging instrument in a hedge of the foreign exchange risk associated with the portion of the fair value of the shares up to FC750 in foreign currency?

Yes. IAS 39 permits designating a portion of the cash flow or fair value of a financial asset as the hedged item if effectiveness can be measured (IAS 39.81). Therefore, Entity A may designate the forward exchange contract as a hedge of the foreign exchange risk associated with only a portion of the fair value of the shares in foreign currency. It could either be designated as a fair value hedge of the foreign exchange exposure of FC750 associated with the shares or as a cash flow hedge of a forecast sale of the shares, provided the timing of the sale is identified. Any variability in the fair value of the shares in foreign currency would not affect the assessment of hedge effectiveness unless the fair value of the shares in foreign currency was to fall below FC750.

F.2.20 Hedge accounting: stock index

An entity may acquire a portfolio of shares to replicate a stock index and a put option on the index to protect itself from fair value losses. Does IAS 39 permit designating the put on the stock index as a hedging instrument in a hedge of the portfolio of shares?

No. If similar financial instruments are aggregated and hedged as a group, IAS 39.83 states that the change in fair value attributable to the hedged risk for each individual item in the group is expected to be approximately proportional to the overall change in fair value attributable to the hedged risk of the group. In the scenario above, the change in the fair value attributable to the hedged risk for each individual item in the group (individual share prices) is not expected to be approximately proportional to the overall change in fair value attributable to the hedged risk of the group.

F.2.21 Hedge accounting: netting of assets and liabilities

May an entity group financial assets together with financial liabilities for the purpose of determining the net cash flow exposure to be hedged for hedge accounting purposes?

An entity's hedging strategy and risk management practices may assess cash flow risk on a net basis but IAS 39.84 does not permit designating a net cash flow exposure as a hedged item for hedge accounting purposes. IAS 39.AG101 provides an example of how a bank might assess its risk on a net basis (with similar assets and liabilities grouped together) and then qualify for hedge accounting by hedging on a gross basis.

F.3 Hedge Accounting

F.3.1 Cash flow hedge: fixed interest rate cash flows

An entity issues a fixed rate debt instrument and enters into a receive-fixed, pay-variable interest rate swap to offset the exposure to interest rate risk associated with the debt instrument. Can the entity designate the swap as a cash flow hedge of the future interest cash outflows associated with the debt instrument?

No. IAS 39.86(b) states that a cash flow hedge is "a hedge of the exposure to variability in cash flows". In this case, the issued debt instrument does not give rise to any exposure to variability in cash flows since the interest payments are fixed. The entity may designate the swap as a fair value hedge of the debt instrument, but it cannot designate the swap as a cash flow hedge of the future cash outflows of the debt instrument.

F.3.2 Cash flow hedge: reinvestment of fixed interest rate cash flows

An entity manages interest rate risk on a net basis. On 1 January 2001, it forecasts aggregate cash inflows of CU100 on fixed rate assets and aggregate cash outflows of CU90 on fixed rate liabilities in the first quarter of 2002. For risk management purposes it uses a receive-variable, pay-fixed Forward Rate Agreement (FRA) to hedge the forecast net cash inflow of CU10. The entity designates as the hedged item the first CU10 of cash inflows on fixed rate assets in the first quarter of 2002. Can it designate the receive-variable, pay-fixed FRA as a cash flow hedge of the exposure to variability to cash flows in the first quarter of 2002 associated with the fixed rate assets?

No. The FRA does not qualify as a cash flow hedge of the cash flow relating to the fixed rate assets because they do not have a cash flow exposure. The entity could, however, designate the FRA as a hedge of the fair value exposure that exists before the cash flows are remitted.

In some cases, the entity could also hedge the interest rate exposure associated with the forecast reinvestment of the interest and principal it receives on fixed rate assets (see Question F.6.2). However, in this example, the FRA does not qualify for cash flow hedge accounting because it increases rather than reduces the variability of interest cash flows resulting from the reinvestment of interest cash flows (for example, if market rates increase, there will be a cash inflow on the FRA and an increase in the expected interest cash inflows resulting from the reinvestment of interest cash inflows on fixed rate assets). However, potentially it could qualify as a cash flow hedge of a portion of the refinancing of cash outflows on a gross basis.

F.3.3 Foreign currency hedge

Entity A has a foreign currency liability payable in six months' time and it wishes to hedge the amount payable on settlement against foreign currency fluctuations. To that end, it takes out a forward contract to buy the foreign currency in six months' time. Should the hedge be treated as:

(a) a fair value hedge of the foreign currency liability with gains and losses on revaluing the liability and the forward contract at the year-end both recognised in profit or loss; or

(b) a cash flow hedge of the amount to be settled in the future with gains and losses on revaluing the forward contract recognised in other comprehensive income?

IAS 39 does not preclude either of these two methods. If the hedge is treated as a fair value hedge, the gain or loss on the fair value remeasurement of the hedging instrument and the gain or loss on the fair value remeasurement of the hedged item for the hedged risk are recognised immediately in profit or loss. If the hedge is treated as a cash flow hedge with the gain or loss on remeasuring the forward contract recognised in other comprehensive income, that amount is recognised in profit or loss in the same period or periods during which the hedged item (the liability) affects profit or loss, ie when the liability is remeasured for changes in foreign exchange rates. Therefore, if the hedge is effective, the gain or loss on the derivative is released to profit or loss in the same periods during which the liability is remeasured, not when the payment occurs. See Question F.3.4.

F.3.4 Foreign currency cash flow hedge

An entity exports a product at a price denominated in a foreign currency. At the date of the sale, the entity obtains a receivable for the sale price payable in 90 days and takes out a 90-day forward exchange contract in the same currency as the receivable to hedge its foreign currency exposure.

Under IAS 21, the sale is recorded at the spot rate at the date of sale, and the receivable is restated during the 90-day period for changes in exchange rates with the difference being taken to profit or loss (IAS 21.23 and IAS 21.28).

If the foreign exchange contract is designated as a hedging instrument, does the entity have a choice whether to designate the foreign exchange contract as a fair value hedge of the foreign currency exposure of the receivable or as a cash flow hedge of the collection of the receivable?

Yes. If the entity designates the foreign exchange contract as a fair value hedge, the gain or loss from remeasuring the forward exchange contract at fair value is recognised immediately in profit or loss and the gain or loss on remeasuring the receivable is also recognised in profit or loss.

If the entity designates the foreign exchange contract as a cash flow hedge of the foreign currency risk associated with the collection of the receivable, the portion of the gain or loss that is determined to be an effective hedge is recognised in other comprehensive income, and the ineffective portion in profit or loss (IAS 39.95). The amount recognised in other comprehensive income is reclassified for equity to profit or loss as a reclassified adjustment in the same period or periods during which changes in the measurement of the receivable affect profit or loss (IAS 39.100).

F.3.5 Fair value hedge: variable rate debt instrument

Does IAS 39 permit an entity to designate a portion of the risk exposure of a variable rate debt instrument as a hedged item in a fair value hedge?

Yes. A variable rate debt instrument may have an exposure to changes in its fair value due to credit risk. It may also have an exposure to changes in its fair value relating to movements in the market interest rate in the periods between which the variable interest rate on the debt instrument is reset. For example, if the debt instrument provides for annual interest payments reset to the market rate each year, a portion of the debt instrument has an exposure to changes in fair value during the year.

F.3.6 Fair value hedge: inventory

IAS 39.86(a) states that a fair value hedge is "a hedge of the exposure to changes in fair value of a recognised asset or liability ... that is attributable to a particular risk and could affect profit or loss". Can an entity designate inventories, such as copper inventory, as the hedged item in a fair value hedge of the exposure to changes in the price of the inventories, such as the copper price, although inventories are measured at the lower of cost and net realisable value under IAS 2 *Inventories*?

Yes. The inventories may be hedged for changes in fair value due to changes in the copper price because the change in fair value of inventories will affect profit or loss when the inventories are sold or their carrying amount is written down. The adjusted carrying amount becomes the cost basis for the purpose of applying the lower of cost and net realisable value test under IAS 2. The hedging instrument used in a fair value hedge of inventories may alternatively qualify as a cash flow hedge of the future sale of the inventory.

F.3.7 Hedge accounting: forecast transaction

For cash flow hedges, a forecast transaction that is subject to a hedge must be "highly probable". How should the term "highly probable" be interpreted?

The term "highly probable" indicates a much greater likelihood of happening than the term "more likely than not". An assessment of the likelihood that a forecast transaction will take place is not based solely on management's intentions because intentions are not verifiable. A transaction's probability should be supported by observable facts and the attendant circumstances.

In assessing the likelihood that a transaction will occur, an entity should consider the following circumstances:

(a) the frequency of similar past transactions;
(b) the financial and operational ability of the entity to carry out the transaction;
(c) substantial commitments of resources to a particular activity (for example, a manufacturing facility that can be used in the short run only to process a particular type of commodity);
(d) the extent of loss or disruption of operations that could result if the transaction does not occur;
(e) the likelihood that transactions with substantially different characteristics might be used to achieve the same business purpose (for example, an entity that intends to raise cash may have several ways of doing so, ranging from a short-term bank loan to an offering of ordinary shares); and
(f) the entity's business plan.

The length of time until a forecast transaction is projected to occur is also a factor in determining probability. Other factors being equal, the more distant a forecast transaction is, the less likely it is that the transaction would be regarded as highly probable and the stronger the evidence that would be needed to support an assertion that it is highly probable.

For example, a transaction forecast to occur in five years may be less likely to occur than a transaction forecast to occur in one year. However, forecast interest payments for the next 20 years on variable rate debt would typically be highly probable if supported by an existing contractual obligation.

In addition, other factors being equal, the greater the physical quantity or future value of a forecast transaction in proportion to the entity's transactions of the same nature, the less likely it is that the transaction would be regarded as highly probable and the stronger the evidence that would be required to support an assertion that it is highly probable. For example, less evidence generally would be needed to support forecast sales of 100,000 units in the next month than 950,000 units in that month when recent sales have averaged 950,000 units per month for the past three months.

A history of having designated hedges of forecast transactions and then determining that the forecast transactions are no longer expected to occur would call into question both an entity's ability to predict forecast transactions accurately and the propriety of using hedge accounting in the future for similar forecast transactions.

F.3.8 Retrospective designation of hedges

Does IAS 39 permit an entity to designate hedge relationships retrospectively?

No. Designation of hedge relationships takes effect prospectively from the date all hedge accounting criteria in IAS 39.88 are met. In particular, hedge accounting can be applied only from the date the entity has completed the necessary documentation of the hedge relationship, including identification of the hedging instrument, the related hedged item or transaction, the nature of the risk being hedged, and how the entity will assess hedge effectiveness.

F.3.9 Hedge accounting: designation at the inception of the hedge

Does IAS 39 permit an entity to designate and formally document a derivative contract as a hedging instrument after entering into the derivative contract?

Yes, prospectively. For hedge accounting purposes, IAS 39 requires a hedging instrument to be designated and formally documented as such from the inception of the hedge relationship (IAS 39.88); in other words, a hedge relationship cannot be designated retrospectively. Also, it precludes designating a hedging relationship for only a portion of the time period during which the hedging instrument remains outstanding (IAS 39.75). However, it does not require the hedging instrument to be acquired at the inception of the hedge relationship.

F.3.10 Hedge accounting: identification of hedged forecast transaction

Can a forecast transaction be identified as the purchase or sale of the last 15,000 units of a product in a specified period or as a percentage of purchases or sales during a specified period?

No. The hedged forecast transaction must be identified and documented with sufficient specificity so that when the transaction occurs, it is clear whether the transaction is or is not the hedged transaction. Therefore, a forecast transaction may be identified as the sale of the first 15,000 units of a specific product during a specified three-month period, but it could not be identified as the last 15,000 units of that product sold during a three-month period because the last 15,000 units cannot be identified when they are sold. For the same reason, a forecast transaction cannot be specified solely as a percentage of sales or purchases during a period.

F.3.11 Cash flow hedge: documentation of timing of forecast transaction

For a hedge of a forecast transaction, should the documentation of the hedge relationship that is established at inception of the hedge identify the date on, or time period in which, the forecast transaction is expected to occur?

Yes. To qualify for hedge accounting, the hedge must relate to a specific identified and designated risk (IAS 39.AG110) and it must be possible to measure its effectiveness reliably (IAS 39.88(d)). Also, the hedged forecast transaction must be highly probable (IAS 39.88(c)). To meet these criteria, an entity is not required to predict and document the exact date a forecast transaction is expected to occur. However, it is required to identify and document the time period during which the forecast transaction is expected to occur within a reasonably specific and generally narrow range of time from a most probable date, as a basis for assessing hedge effectiveness. To determine that the hedge will be highly effective in accordance with IAS 39.88(d), it is necessary to ensure that changes in the fair value of the expected cash flows are offset by changes in the fair value of the hedging instrument and this test may be met only if the timing of the cash flows occur within close proximity to each other. If the forecast transaction is no longer expected to occur, hedge accounting is discontinued in accordance with IAS 39.101(c).

F.4 Hedge Effectiveness

F.4.1 Hedging on an after-tax basis

Hedging is often done on an after-tax basis. Is hedge effectiveness assessed after taxes?

IAS 39 permits, but does not require, assessment of hedge effectiveness on an after-tax basis. If the hedge is undertaken on an after-tax basis, it is so designated at inception as part of the formal documentation of the hedging relationship and strategy.

F.4.2 Hedge effectiveness: assessment on cumulative basis

IAS 39.88(b) requires that the hedge is expected to be highly effective. Should expected hedge effectiveness be assessed separately for each period or cumulatively over the life of the hedging relationship?

Expected hedge effectiveness may be assessed on a cumulative basis if the hedge is so designated, and that condition is incorporated into the appropriate hedging documentation. Therefore, even if a hedge is not expected to be highly effective in a particular period, hedge accounting is not precluded if effectiveness is expected to remain sufficiently high over the life of the hedging relationship. However, any ineffectiveness is required to be recognised in profit or loss as it occurs.

To illustrate: an entity designates a LIBOR-based interest rate swap as a hedge of a borrowing whose interest rate is a UK base rate plus a margin. The UK base rate changes, perhaps, once each quarter or less, in increments of 25-50 basis points, while LIBOR changes daily. Over a period of 1-2 years, the hedge is expected to be almost perfect. However, there will be quarters when the UK base rate does not change at all, while LIBOR has changed significantly. This would not necessarily preclude hedge accounting.

F.4.3 Hedge effectiveness: counterparty credit risk

Must an entity consider the likelihood of default by the counterparty to the hedging instrument in assessing hedge effectiveness?

Yes. An entity cannot ignore whether it will be able to collect all amounts due under the contractual provisions of the hedging instrument. When assessing hedge effectiveness, both at the inception of the hedge and on an ongoing basis, the entity considers the risk that the counterparty to the hedging instrument will default by failing to make any contractual payments to the entity. For a cash flow hedge, if it becomes probable that a counterparty will default, an entity would be unable to conclude that the hedging relationship is expected to be highly effective in achieving offsetting cash flows. As a result, hedge accounting would be discontinued. For a fair value hedge, if there is a change in the counterparty's creditworthiness, the fair value of the hedging instrument will change, which affects the assessment of whether the hedge relationship is effective and whether it qualifies for continued hedge accounting.

F.4.4 Hedge effectiveness: effectiveness tests

How should hedge effectiveness be measured for the purposes of initially qualifying for hedge accounting and for continued qualification?

IAS 39 does not provide specific guidance about how effectiveness tests are performed. IAS 39.AG105 specifies that a hedge is normally regarded as highly effective only if at inception and in subsequent periods, the hedge is expected to be highly effective in achieving offsetting changes in fair value or cash flows attributable to the hedged risk during the period for which the hedge is designated, and (b) the actual results are within a range of 80125 per cent. IAS 39.AG105 also states that the expectation in (a) can be demonstrated in various ways.

The appropriateness of a given method of assessing hedge effectiveness will depend on the nature of the risk being hedged and the type of hedging instrument used. The method of assessing effectiveness must be reasonable and consistent with other similar hedges unless different methods are explicitly justified. An entity is required to document at the inception of the hedge how effectiveness will be assessed and then to apply that effectiveness test on a consistent basis for the duration of the hedge.

Several mathematical techniques can be used to measure hedge effectiveness, including ratio analysis, ie a comparison of hedging gains and losses with the corresponding gains and losses on the hedged item at a point in time, and statistical measurement techniques such as regression analysis. If regression analysis is used, the entity's documented policies for assessing effectiveness must specify how the results of the regression will be assessed.

F.4.5 Hedge effectiveness: less than 100 per cent offset

If a cash flow hedge is regarded as highly effective because the actual risk offset is within the allowed 80-125 per cent range of deviation from full offset, is the gain or loss on the ineffective portion of the hedge recognised in other comprehensive income?

No. IAS 39.95(a) indicates that only the effective portion is recognised in other comprehensive income. IAS 39.95(b) requires the ineffective portion to be recognised in profit or loss.

F.4.7 Assuming perfect hedge effectiveness

If the principal terms of the hedging instrument and of the entire hedged asset or liability or hedged forecast transaction are the same, can an entity assume perfect hedge effectiveness without further effectiveness testing?

No. IAS 39.88(e) requires an entity to assess hedges on an ongoing basis for hedge effectiveness. It cannot assume hedge effectiveness even if the principal terms of the hedging instrument and the hedged item are the same, since hedge ineffectiveness may arise because of other attributes such as the liquidity of the instruments or their credit risk (IAS 39.AG109). It may, however, designate only certain risks in an overall exposure as being hedged and thereby improve the effectiveness of the hedging relationship. For example, for a fair value hedge of a debt instrument, if the derivative hedging instrument has a credit risk that is equivalent to the AA-rate, it may designate only the risk related to AA-rated interest rate movements as being hedged, in which case changes in credit spreads generally will not affect the effectiveness of the hedge.

F.5 Cash Flow Hedges

F.5.1 Hedge accounting: non-derivative monetary asset or non-derivative monetary liability used as a hedging instrument

If an entity designates a non-derivative monetary asset as a foreign currency cash flow hedge of the repayment of the principal of a non-derivative monetary liability, would the exchange differences on the hedged item be recognised in profit or loss (IAS 21.28) and the exchange differences on the hedging instrument be recognised in other comprehensive income until the repayment of the liability (IAS 39.95)?

No. Exchange differences on the monetary asset and the monetary liability are both recognised in profit or loss in the period in which they arise (IAS 21.28). IAS 39.AG83 specifies that if there is a hedge relationship between a non-derivative monetary asset and a non-derivative monetary liability, changes in fair values of those financial instruments are recognised in profit or loss.

F.5.2 Cash flow hedges: performance of hedging instrument (1)

Entity A has a floating rate liability of CU1,000 with five years remaining to maturity. It enters into a five-year pay-fixed, receive-floating interest rate swap in the same currency and with the same principal terms as the liability to hedge the exposure to variable cash flow payments on the floating rate liability attributable to interest rate risk. At inception, the fair value of the swap is zero. Subsequently, there is an increase of CU49 in the fair value of the swap. This increase consists of a change of CU50 resulting from an increase in market interest rates and a change of minus CU1 resulting from an increase in the credit risk of the swap counterparty. There is no change in the fair value of the floating rate liability, but the fair value (present value) of the future cash flows needed to offset the exposure to variable interest cash flows on the liability increases by CU50. Assuming that Entity A determines that the hedge is still highly effective, is there ineffectiveness that should be recognised in profit or loss?

No. A hedge of interest rate risk is not fully effective if part of the change in the fair value of the derivative is attributable to the counterparty's credit risk (IAS 39.AG109). However, because Entity A determines that the hedge relationship is still highly effective, it recognises the effective portion of the change in fair value of the swap, ie the net change in fair value of CU49 in other comprehensive income. There is no debit to profit or loss for the change in fair value of the swap attributable to the deterioration in the credit quality of the swap counterparty, because the cumulative change in the present value of the future cash flows needed to offset the exposure to variable interest cash flows on the hedged item, ie CU50, exceeds the cumulative change in value of the hedging instrument, ie CU49.

Dr	Swap	CU49	
	Cr Other comprehensive income		CU49

If Entity A concludes that the hedge is no longer highly effective, it discontinues hedge accounting prospectively as from the date the hedge ceased to be highly effective in accordance with IAS 39.101.

Would the answer change if the fair value of the swap instead increases to CU51 of which CU50 results from the increase in market interest rates and CU1 from a decrease in the credit risk of the swap counterparty?

Yes. In this case, there is a credit to profit or loss of CU1 for the change in fair value of the swap attributable to the improvement in the credit quality of the swap counterparty. This is because the cumulative change in the value of the hedging instrument, ie CU51, exceeds the cumulative change in the present value of the future cash flows needed to offset the exposure to variable interest cash flows on the hedged item, ie CU50. The difference of CU1 represents the excess ineffectiveness attributable to the derivative hedging instrument, the swap, and is recognised in profit or loss.

Dr	Swap	CU51	
	Cr Other comprehensive income		CU50
	Cr Profit or loss		CU1

F.5.3 Cash flow hedges: performance of hedging instrument (2)

On 30 September 20X1, Entity A hedges the anticipated sale of 24 tonnes of pulp on 1 March 20X2 by entering into a short forward contract on 24 tonnes of pulp. The contract requires net settlement in cash determined as the difference between the future spot price of pulp on a specified commodity exchange and CU1,000. Entity A expects to sell the pulp in a different, local market. Entity A determines that the forward contract is an effective hedge of the anticipated sale and that the other conditions for hedge accounting are met. It assesses hedge effectiveness by comparing the entire change in the fair value of the forward contract with the change in the fair value of the expected cash inflows. On 31 December, the spot price of pulp has increased both in the local market and on the exchange. The increase in the local market exceeds the increase on the exchange. As a result, the present value of the expected cash inflow from the sale on the local market is CU1,100. The fair value of Entity A's forward contract is negative CU80. Assuming that Entity A determines that the hedge is still highly effective, is there ineffectiveness that should be recognised in profit or loss?

No. In a cash flow hedge, ineffectiveness is not recognised in the financial statements when the cumulative change in the fair value of the hedged cash flows exceeds the cumulative change in the value of the hedging instrument. In this case, the cumulative change in the fair value of the forward contract is CU80, while the fair value of the cumulative change in expected future cash flows on the hedged item is CU100. Since the fair value of the cumulative change in expected future cash flows on the hedged item from the inception of the hedge exceeds the cumulative change in fair value of the hedging instrument (in absolute amounts), no portion of the gain or loss on the hedging instrument is recognised in profit or loss (IAS 39.95(a)). Because Entity A determines that the hedge relationship is still highly effective, it recognises the entire change in fair value of the forward contract (CU80) in other comprehensive income.

Dr	Other comprehensive income	CU80	
	Cr Forward		CU80

If Entity A concludes that the hedge is no longer highly effective, it discontinues hedge accounting prospectively as from the date the hedge ceases to be highly effective in accordance with IAS 39.101.

F.5.4 Cash flow hedges: forecast transaction occurs before the specified period

An entity designates a derivative as a hedging instrument in a cash flow hedge of a forecast transaction, such as a forecast sale of a commodity. The hedging relationship meets all the hedge accounting conditions, including the requirement to identify and document the period in which the transaction is expected to occur within a reasonably specific and narrow range of time (see Question F.1.17). If, in a subsequent period, the forecast transaction is expected to occur in an earlier period than originally anticipated, can the entity conclude that this transaction is the same as the one that was designated as being hedged?

Yes. The change in timing of the forecast transaction does not affect the validity of the designation. However, it may affect the assessment of the effectiveness of the hedging relationship. Also, the hedging instrument would need to be designated as a hedging instrument for the whole remaining period of its existence in order for it to continue to qualify as a hedging instrument (see IAS 39.75 and Question F.2.17).

F.5.5 Cash flow hedges: measuring effectiveness for a hedge of a forecast transaction in a debt instrument

A forecast investment in an interest-earning asset or forecast issue of an interest-bearing liability creates a cash flow exposure to interest rate changes because the related interest payments will be based on the market rate that exists when the forecast transaction occurs. The objective of a cash flow hedge of the exposure to interest rate changes is to offset the effects of future changes in interest rates so as to obtain a single fixed rate, usually the rate that existed at the inception of the hedge that corresponds with the term and timing of the forecast transaction. During the period of the hedge, it is not possible to determine what the market interest rate for the forecast transaction will be at the time the hedge is terminated or when the forecast transaction occurs. In this case, how is the effectiveness of the hedge assessed and measured?

During this period, effectiveness can be measured on the basis of changes in interest rates between the designation date and the interim effectiveness measurement date. The interest rates used to make this measurement are the interest rates that correspond with the term and occurrence of the forecast transaction that existed at the inception of the hedge and that exist at the measurement date as evidenced by the term structure of interest rates.

Generally it will not be sufficient simply to compare cash flows of the hedged item with cash flows generated by the derivative hedging instrument as they are paid or received, since such an approach ignores the entity's expectations of whether the cash flows will offset in subsequent periods and whether there will be any resulting ineffectiveness.

The discussion that follows illustrates the mechanics of establishing a cash flow hedge and measuring its effectiveness. For the purpose of the illustrations, assume that an entity expects to issue a CU100,000 one-year debt instrument in three months. The instrument will pay interest quarterly with principal due at maturity. The entity is exposed to interest rate increases and establishes a hedge of the interest cash flows of the debt by entering into a forward starting interest rate swap. The swap has a term of one year and will start in three months to correspond with the terms of the forecast debt issue. The entity will pay a fixed rate and receive a variable rate, and the entity designates the risk being hedged as the LIBOR-based interest component in the forecast issue of the debt.

Yield curve

The yield curve provides the foundation for computing future cash flows and the fair value of such cash flows both at the inception of, and during, the hedging relationship. It is based on current market yields on applicable reference bonds that are traded in the marketplace. Market yields are converted to spot interest rates ('spot rates' or 'zero coupon rates') by eliminating the effect of coupon payments on the market yield. Spot rates are used to discount future cash flows, such as principal and interest rate payments, to arrive at their fair value. Spot rates also are used to compute forward interest rates that are used to compute variable and estimated future cash flows. The relationship between spot rates and one-period forward rates is shown by the following formula:

Spot–forward relationship

$$F = \frac{(1 + \mathrm{SR})}{(1 + \mathrm{SR})} - 1$$

where F = forward rate (%)
SR = spot rate (%)
t = period in time (eg 1, 2, 3, 4, 5)

Also, for the purpose of this illustration, assume that the following quarterlyperiod term structure of interest rates using quarterly compounding exists at the inception of the hedge.

Yield curve at inception – (beginning of period 1)

Forward periods	*1*	*2*	*3*	*4*	*5*
Spot rates	3.75%	4.50%	5.50%	6.00%	6.25%
Forward rates	3.75%	5.25%	7.51%	7.50%	7.25%

The one-period forward rates are computed on the basis of spot rates for the applicable maturities. For example, the current forward rate for Period 2 calculated using the formula above is equal to $[1.0450^2 / 1.0375] - 1 = 5.25$ per cent. The current one-period forward rate for Period 2 is different from the current spot rate for Period 2, since the spot rate is an interest rate from the beginning of Period 1 (spot) to the end of Period 2, while the forward rate is an interest rate from the beginning of Period 2 to the end of Period 2.

Hedged item

In this example, the entity expects to issue a CU100,000 one-year debt instrument in three months with quarterly interest payments. The entity is exposed to interest rate increases and would like to eliminate the effect on cash flows of interest rate changes that may happen before the forecast transaction takes place. If that risk is eliminated, the entity would obtain an interest rate on its debt issue that is equal to the one-year forward coupon rate currently available in the marketplace in three months. That forward coupon rate, which is different from the forward (spot) rate, is 6.86 per cent, computed from the term structure of interest rates shown above. It is the market rate of interest that exists at the inception of the hedge, given the terms of the forecast debt instrument. It results in the fair value of the debt being equal to par at its issue.

At the inception of the hedging relationship, the expected cash flows of the debt instrument can be calculated on the basis of the existing term structure of interest rates. For this purpose, it is assumed that interest rates do not change and that the debt would be issued at 6.86 per cent at the beginning of Period 2. In this case, the cash flows and fair value of the debt instrument would be as follows at the beginning of Period 2.

Issue of fixed rate debt

Beginning of period 2 - No rate changes (Spot based on forward rates)

	Total					
Original forward periods		*1*	*2*	*3*	*4*	*5*
Remaining periods			*1*	*2*	*3*	*4*
Spot rates			5.25%	6.38%	6.75%	6.88%
Forward rates			5.25%	7.51%	7.50%	7.25%
	CU		*CU*	*CU*	*CU*	*CU*
Cash flows:						
Fixed interest @ 6.86%			1,716	1,716	1,716	1,716
Principal						100,000
Fair value:						
Interest	6,592		1,694	1,663	1,632	1,603
Principal	93,408					93,408*
Total						100,000

* CU100,000 / (1 + [0.0688 / 4])^4

Since it is assumed that interest rates do not change, the fair value of the interest and principal amounts equals the par amount of the forecast transaction. The fair value amounts are computed on the basis of the spot rates that exist at the inception of the hedge for the applicable periods in which the cash flows would occur had the debt been issued at the date of the forecast transaction. They reflect the effect of discounting those cash flows on the basis of the periods that will remain after the debt instrument is issued. For example, the spot rate of 6.38 per cent is used to discount the interest cash flow that is expected to be paid in Period 3, but it is discounted for only two periods because it will occur two periods after the forecast transaction.

The forward interest rates are the same as shown previously, since it is assumed that interest rates do not change. The spot rates are different but they have not actually changed. They represent the spot rates one period forward and are based on the applicable forward rates.

Hedging instrument

The objective of the hedge is to obtain an overall interest rate on the forecast transaction and the hedging instrument that is equal to 6.86 per cent, which is the market rate at the inception of the hedge for the period from Period 2 to Period 5. This objective is accomplished by entering into a forward starting interest rate swap that has a fixed rate of 6.86 per cent. Based on the term structure of interest rates that exist at the inception of the hedge, the interest rate swap will have such a rate. At the inception of the hedge, the fair value of the fixed rate payments on the interest rate swap will equal the fair value of the variable rate payments, resulting in the interest rate swap having a fair value of zero. The expected cash flows of the interest rate swap and the related fair value amounts are shown as follows.

Interest rate swap

	Total					
Original forward periods		*1*	*2*	*3*	*4*	*5*
Remaining periods			*1*	*2*	*3*	*4*
	CU		*CU*	*CU*	*CU*	*CU*
Cash flows: Fixed interest @ 6.86%			1,716	1,716	1,716	1,716
Forecast variable interest			1,313	1,877	1,876	1,813
Forecast based on forward rate			*5.25%*	*7.51%*	*7.50%*	*7.25%*
Net interest			(403)	161	160	97
Fair value: *Discount rate (spot)*			*5.25%*	*6.38%*	*6.75%*	*6.88%*
Fixed interest	6,592		1,694	1,663	1,632	1,603
Forecast variable interest	6,592		1,296	1,819	1,784	1,693
Fair value of interest rate swap	0		(398)	156	152	90

At the inception of the hedge, the fixed rate on the forward swap is equal to the fixed rate the entity would receive if it could issue the debt in three months under terms that exist today.

Measuring hedge effectiveness

If interest rates change during the period the hedge is outstanding, the effectiveness of the hedge can be measured in various ways.

Assume that interest rates change as follows immediately before the debt is issued at the beginning of Period 2.

Yield curve - Rates increase 200 basis points

Forward periods	*1*	*2*	*3*	*4*	*5*
Remaining periods		*1*	*2*	*3*	*4*
Spot rates		5.75%	6.50%	7.50%	8.00%
Forward rates		5.75%	7.25%	9.51%	9.50%

Under the new interest rate environment, the fair value of the pay-fixed at 6.86 per cent, receive-variable interest rate swap that was designated as the hedging instrument would be as follows.

Fair value of interest rate swap

	Total					
Original forward periods		*1*	*2*	*3*	*4*	*5*
Remaining periods			*1*	*2*	*3*	*4*
	CU	*CU*	*CU*	*CU*	*CU*	*CU*
Cash flows:						
Fixed interest @ 6.86%			1,716	1,716	1,716	1,716
Forecast variable interest			1,438	1,813	2,377	2,376
Forecast based on new forward rate			*5.75%*	*7.25%*	*9.51%*	*9.50%*
Net interest			(279)	97	661	660
Fair value:						
New discount rate (spot)			*5.75%*	*6.50%*	*7.50%*	*8.00%*
Fixed interest	6,562		1,692	1,662	1,623	1,585
Forecast variable interest	7,615		1,417	1,755	2,248	2,195
Fair value of net interest	1,053		(275)	93	625	610

In order to compute the effectiveness of the hedge, it is necessary to measure the change in the present value of the cash flows or the value of the hedged forecast transaction. There are at least two methods of accomplishing this measurement.

Method A – Compute change in fair value of debt

	Total				
Original forward periods		*1*	*2*	*3*	*4*	*5*
Remaining periods			*1*	*2*	*3*	*4*
	CU		*CU*	*CU*	*CU*	*CU*
Cash flows:						
Fixed interest @ 6.86%			1,716	1,716	1,716	1,716
Principal				100,000		
Fair value:						
New discount rate (spot)			5.75%	6.50%	7.50%	8.00%
Interest	6,562		1,692	1,662	1,623	1,585
Principal	92,385					92,385*
Total	98,947					
Fair value at inception	100,000					
Fair value difference	(1,053)					

* = CU100,000 / (1 + [0.08 / 4])^4

Under Method A, a computation is made of the fair value in the new interest rate environment of debt that carries interest that is equal to the coupon interest rate that existed at the inception of the hedging relationship (6.86 per cent). This fair value is compared with the expected fair value as of the beginning of Period 2 that was calculated on the basis of the term structure of interest rates that existed at the inception of the hedging relationship, as illustrated above, to determine the change in the fair value. Note that the difference between the change in the fair value of the swap and the change in the expected fair value of the debt exactly offset in this example, since the terms of the swap and the forecast transaction match each other.

Method B - Compute change in fair value of cash flows

	Total				
Original forward periods		*1*	*2*	*3*	*4*	*5*
Remaining periods			*1*	*2*	*3*	*4*
Market rate at inception			6.86%	6.86%	6.86%	6.86%
Current forward rate			5.75%	7.25%	9.51%	9.50%
Rate difference			1.11%	(0.39%)	(2.64%)	(2.64%)
Cash flow difference (principal rate)			CU279	(CU97)	(CU661)	(CU660)
Discount rate (spot)			5.75%	6.50%	7.50%	8.00%
Fair value of difference	(CU1,053)		CU 275	(CU93)	(CU625)	(CU610)

Under Method B, the present value of the change in cash flows is computed on the basis of the difference between the forward interest rates for the applicable periods at the effectiveness measurement date and the interest rate that would have been obtained if the debt had been issued at the market rate that existed at the inception of the hedge. The market rate that existed at the inception of the hedge is the one-year forward coupon rate in three months. The present value of the change in cash flows is computed on the basis of the current spot rates that exist at the effectiveness measurement date for the applicable periods in which the cash flows are expected to occur. This method also could be referred to as the 'theoretical swap' method (or 'hypothetical derivative' method) because the comparison is between the hedged fixed rate on the debt and the current variable rate, which is the same as comparing cash flows on the fixed and variable rate legs of an interest rate swap.

As before, the difference between the change in the fair value of the swap and the change in the present value of the cash flows exactly offset in this example, since the terms match.

Other considerations

There is an additional computation that should be performed to compute ineffectiveness before the expected date of the forecast transaction that has not been considered for the purpose of this illustration. The fair value difference has been determined in each of the illustrations as of the expected date of the forecast transaction immediately before the forecast transaction, ie at the beginning of Period 2. If the assessment of hedge effectiveness is done before the forecast transaction occurs, the difference should be discounted to the current date to arrive at the actual amount of ineffectiveness. For example, if the measurement date were one month after the hedging relationship was established and the forecast transaction is now expected to occur in two months, the amount would have to be discounted for the remaining two months before the forecast transaction is expected to occur to arrive at the actual fair value. This step would not be necessary in the examples provided above because there was no ineffectiveness. Therefore, additional discounting of the amounts, which net to zero, would not have changed the result.

Under Method B, ineffectiveness is computed on the basis of the difference between the forward coupon interest rates for the applicable periods at the effectiveness measurement date and the interest rate that would have been obtained if the debt had been issued at the market rate that existed at the inception of the hedge. Computing the change in cash flows based on the difference between the forward interest rates that existed at the inception of the hedge and the forward rates that exist at the effectiveness measurement date is inappropriate if the objective of the hedge is to establish a single fixed rate for a series of forecast interest payments. This objective is met by hedging the exposures with an interest rate swap as illustrated in the above example. The fixed interest rate on the swap is a blended interest rate composed of the forward rates over the life of the swap. Unless the yield curve is flat, the comparison between the forward interest rate exposures over the life of the swap and the fixed rate on the swap will produce different cash flows whose fair values are equal only at the inception of the hedging relationship. This difference is shown in the table below.

	Total					
Original forward periods		*1*	*2*	*3*	*4*	*5*
Remaining periods			*1*	*2*	*3*	*4*
Forward rate at inception			5.25%	7.51%	7.50%	7.25%
Current forward rate			5.75%	7.25%	9.51%	9.50%
Rate difference			(0.50%)	0.26%	(2.00%)	(2.25%)
Cash flow difference (principal rate)			(CU125)	CU 64	(CU501)	(CU563)
Discount rate (spot)			5.75%	6.50%	7.50%	8.00%
Fair value of difference	(CU1,055)		(CU123)	CU 62	(CU474)	(CU520)
Fair value of interest rate swap	CU 1,053					
Ineffectiveness	(CU2)					

If the objective of the hedge is to obtain the forward rates that existed at the inception of the hedge, the interest rate swap is ineffective because the swap has a single blended fixed coupon rate that does not offset a series of different forward interest rates. However, if the objective of the hedge is to obtain the forward coupon rate that existed at the inception of the hedge, the swap is effective, and the comparison based on differences in forward interest rates suggests ineffectiveness when none may exist. Computing ineffectiveness based on the difference between the forward interest rates that existed at the inception of the hedge and the forward rates that exist at the effectiveness measurement date would be an appropriate measurement of ineffectiveness if the hedging objective is to lock in those forward interest rates. In that case, the appropriate hedging instrument would be a series of forward contracts each of which matures on a repricing date that corresponds with the date of the forecast transactions.

It also should be noted that it would be inappropriate to compare only the variable cash flows on the interest rate swap with the interest cash flows in the debt that would be generated by the forward interest rates. That methodology has the effect of measuring ineffectiveness only on a portion of the derivative, and IAS 39 does not permit the bifurcation of a derivative for the purposes of assessing effectiveness in this situation (IAS 39.74). It is recognised, however, that if the fixed interest rate on the interest rate swap is equal to the fixed rate that would have been obtained on the debt at inception, there will be no ineffectiveness assuming that there are no differences in terms and no change in credit risk or it is not designated in the hedging relationship.

F.5.6 Cash flow hedges: firm commitment to purchase inventory in a foreign currency

Entity A has the Local Currency (LC) as its functional currency and presentation currency. On 30 June 20X1, it enters into a forward exchange contract to receive Foreign Currency (FC) 100,000 and deliver LC109,600 on 30 June 20X2 at an initial cost and fair value of zero. It designates the forward exchange contract as a hedging instrument in a cash flow hedge of a firm commitment to purchase a certain quantity of paper on 31 March 20X2 and the resulting payable of FC100,000, which is to be paid on 30 June 20X2. All hedge accounting conditions in IAS 39 are met.

As indicated in the table below, on 30 June 20X1, the spot exchange rate is LC1.072 to FC1, while the twelve-month forward exchange rate is LC1.096 to FC1. On 31 December 20X1, the spot exchange rate is LC1.080 to FC1, while the six-month forward exchange rate is LC1.092 to FC1. On 31 March 20X2, the spot exchange rate is LC1.074 to FC1, while the three-month forward rate is LC1.076 to FC1. On 30 June 20X2, the spot exchange rate is LC1.072 to FC1. The applicable yield curve in the local currency is flat at 6 per cent per year throughout the period. The fair value of the forward exchange contract is negative LC388 on 31 December 20X1 $\{([1.092 \cdot 100{,}000] - 109{,}600) / 1.06^{(6/12)}\}$, negative LC1,971 on 31 March 20X2 $\{([1.076 \cdot 100{,}000] - 109{,}600) / 1.06^{(3/12)}\}$, and negative LC2,400 on 30 June 20X2 $\{1.072 \cdot 100{,}000 - 109{,}600\}$.

Date	*Spot rate*	*Forward rate to 30 June 20X2*	*Fair value offorward contract*
30 June 20X1	1.072	1.096	-
31 December 20X1	1.080	1.092	(388)
31 March 20X2	1.074	1.076	(1,971)
30 June 20X2	1.072	-	(2,400)

Issue (a) - What is the accounting for these transactions if the hedging relationship is designated as being for changes in the fair value of the forward exchange contract and the entity's accounting policy is to apply basis adjustment to non-financial assets that result from hedged forecast transactions?

The accounting entries are as follows.

30 June 20X1

Dr	Forward	LC0	
	Cr Cash		LC0

To record the forward exchange contract at its initial amount of zero (IAS 39.43). The hedge is expected to be fully effective because the critical terms of the forward exchange contract and the purchase contract and the assessment of hedge effectiveness are based on the forward price (IAS 39.AG108).

31 December 20X1

Dr	Other comprehensive income	LC388	
	Cr Forward liability		LC388

To record the change in the fair value of the forward exchange contract between 30 June 20X1 and 31 December 20X1, ie LC388 – 0 = LC388, directly in other comprehensive income (IAS 39.95). The hedge is fully effective because the loss on the forward exchange contract (LC388) exactly offsets the change in cash flows associated with the purchase contract based on the forward price [(LC388) = {([1.092 · 100,000] – 109,600)/1.06$^{(6/12)}$} – {([1.096 · 100,000] – 109,600) / 1.06}].

31 March 20X2

Dr	Other comprehensive income	LC1,583	
	Cr Forward liability		LC1,583

To record the change in the fair value of the forward exchange contract between 1 January 20X2 and 31 March 20X2 (ie LC1,971 – LC388 = LC1,583), directly in other comprehensive income (IAS 39.94). The hedge is fully effective because the loss on the forward exchange contract (LC1,583) exactly offsets the change in cash flows associated with the purchase contract based on the forward price [(LC1,583) = {([1.076 · 100,000] – 109,600)/1.06$^{(3/12)}$} – {([1.092 · 100,000] – 109,600) /1.06$^{(6/12)}$}].

Dr	Paper (purchase price)	LC107,400	
Dr	Paper (hedging loss)	LC1,971	
	Cr Other comprehensive income		LC1,971
	Cr Payable		LC107,400

To recognise the purchase of the paper at the spot rate (1.074 · FC100,000) and remove the cumulative loss on the forward exchange contract that has been recognised directly in other comprehensive income (LC1,971) and include it in the initial measurement of the purchased paper. Accordingly, the initial measurement of the purchased paper is LC109,371 consisting of a purchase consideration of LC107,400 and a hedging loss of LC1,971.

30 June 20X2

Dr	Payable	LC107,400	
	Cr Cash		LC107,200
	Cr Profit or loss		LC200

To record the settlement of the payable at the spot rate (FC100,000 · 1.072 = 107,200) and the associated exchange gain of LC200 (LC107,400- LC107,200).

Dr	Profit or loss	LC429	
	Cr Forward liability		LC429

To record the loss on the forward exchange contract between 1 April 20X2 and 30 June 20X2 (ie LC2,400 – LC1,971 = LC429) in profit or loss. The hedge is regarded as fully effective because the loss on the forward exchange contract (LC429) exactly offsets the change in the fair value of the payable based on the forward price (LC429 = ([1.072· 100,000] – 109,600 – {([1.076 · 100,000] – 109,600)/1.06$^{(3/12)}$}).

Dr	Forward liability	LC2,400	
	Cr Cash		LC2,400

To record the net settlement of the forward exchange contract.

Issue (b) - What is the accounting for these transactions if the hedging relationship instead is designated as being for changes in the spot element of the forward exchange contract and the interest element is excluded from the designated hedging relationship (IAS 39.74)?

The accounting entries are as follows.

30 June 20X1

Dr Forward	LC0	
Cr Cash		LC0

To record the forward exchange contract at its initial amount of zero (IAS 39.43). The hedge is expected to be fully effective because the critical terms of the forward exchange contract and the purchase contract are the same and the change in the premium or discount on the forward contract is excluded from the assessment of effectiveness (IAS 39.AG108).

31 December 20X1

Dr Profit or loss (interest element)	LC1,165	
Cr Other comprehensive income (spot element)		LC777
Cr Forward liability		LC388

To record the change in the fair value of the forward exchange contract between 30 June 20X1 and 31 December 20X1, ie LC388 – 0 = LC388. The change in the present value of spot settlement of the forward exchange contract is a gain of LC777 ({([1.080 · 100,000] – 107,200)/1.06$^{(6/12)}$} – {([1.072 · 100,000] – 107,200)/1.06}), which is recognised directly in other comprehensive income (IAS 39.95(a)). The change in the interest element of the forward exchange contract (the residual change in fair value) is a loss of LC1,165 (388 + 777), which is recognised in profit or loss (IAS 39.74 and IAS 39.55(a)). The hedge is fully effective because the gain in the spot element of the forward contract (LC777) exactly offsets the change in the purchase price at spot rates (LC777 = {([1.080 · 100,000] – 107,200)/1.06$^{(6/12)}$} – {([1.072 · 100,000] – 107,200)/ 1.06}).

31 March 20X2

Dr Other comprehensive income (spot element)	LC580	
Dr Profit or loss (interest element)	LC1,003	
Cr Forward liability		LC1,583

To record the change in the fair value of the forward exchange contract between 1 January 20X2 and 31 March 20X2, ie LC1,971 – LC388 = LC1,583. The change in the present value of the spot settlement of the forward exchange contract is a loss of LC580 ({([1.074 · 100,000] – 107,200)/1.06$^{(3/12)}$} – {([1.080 · 100,000] – 107,200) / 1.06$^{(6/12)}$}), which is recognised directly in other comprehensive income (IAS 39.95(a)). The change in the interest element of the forward exchange contract (the residual change in fair value) is a loss of LC1,003 (LC1,583 – LC580), which is recognised in profit or loss (IAS 39.74 and IAS 39.55(a)). The hedge is fully effective because the loss in the spot element of the forward contract (LC580) exactly offsets the change in the purchase price at spot rates [(580) = {([1.074 · 100,000] – 107,200)/ 1.06$^{(3/12)}$} – {([1.080 · 100,000] – 107,200) /1.06$^{(6/12)}$}].

Dr	Paper (purchase price)	LC107,400	
Dr	Other comprehensive income	LC197	
	Cr Paper (hedging gain)		LC197
	Cr Payable		LC107,400

To recognise the purchase of the paper at the spot rate (= 1.074 · FC100,000) and remove the cumulative gain on the spot element of the forward exchange contract that has been recognised directly in other comprehensive income (LC777 – LC580 = LC197) and include it in the initial measurement of the purchased paper. Accordingly, the initial measurement of the purchased paper is LC107,203, consisting of a purchase consideration of LC107,400 and a hedging gain of LC197.

30 June 20X2

Dr	Payable	LC107,400	
	Cr Cash		LC107,200
	Cr Profit or loss		LC200

To record the settlement of the payable at the spot rate (FC100,000 · 1.072 = LC107,200) and the associated exchange gain of LC200 (– [1.072 – 1.074] · FC100,000).

Dr	Profit or loss (spot element)	LC197	
Dr	Profit or loss (interest element)	LC232	
	Cr Forward liability		LC429

To record the change in the fair value of the forward exchange contract between 1 April 20X2 and 30 June 20X2 (ie LC2,400 – LC1,971 = LC429). The change in the present value of the spot settlement of the forward exchange contract is a loss of LC197 ([1.072 · 100,000] – 107,200 – {([1.074 · 100,000] – 107,200)/$1.06^{(3/12)}$}), which is recognised in profit or loss. The change in the interest element of the forward exchange contract (the residual change in fair value) is a loss of LC232 (LC429 – LC197), which is recognised in profit or loss. The hedge is fully effective because the loss in the spot element of the forward contract (LC197) exactly offsets the change in the present value of the spot settlement of the payable [(LC197) = {[1.072 · 100,000] – 107,200 – {([1.074 · 100,000] – 107,200)/$1.06^{(3/12)}$}].

Dr	Forward liability	LC2,400	
	Cr Cash		LC2,400

To record the net settlement of the forward exchange contract.

The following table provides an overview of the components of the change in fair value of the hedging instrument over the term of the hedging relationship. It illustrates that the way in which a hedging relationship is designated affects the *subsequent accounting for that* hedging relationship, including the assessment of hedge effectiveness and the recognition of gains and losses.

Period ending	*Change in spot settlement* LC	*Fair value of change in spot settlement* LC	*Change in forward settlement* LC	*Fair value of change in forward settlement* LC	*Fair value of change in interest element* LC
June 20X1	-	-	-	-	-
December 20X1	800	777	(400)	(388)	(1,165)
March 20X2	(600)	(580)	(1,600)	(1,583)	(1,003)
June 20X2	(200)	(197)	(400)	(429)	(232)
Total	-	-	(2,400)	(2,400)	(2,400)

F.6 Hedges: Other issues

F.6.1 Hedge accounting: management of interest rate risk in financial institutions

Banks and other financial institutions often manage their exposure to interest rate risk on a net basis for all or parts of their activities. They have systems to accumulate critical information throughout the entity about their financial assets, financial liabilities and forward commitments, including loan commitments. This information is used to estimate and aggregate cash flows and to schedule such estimated cash flows into the applicable future periods in which they are expected to be paid or received. The systems generate estimates of cash flows based on the contractual terms of the instruments and other factors, including estimates of prepayments and defaults. For risk management purposes, many financial institutions use derivative contracts to offset some or all exposure to interest rate risk on a net basis.

If a financial institution manages interest rate risk on a net basis, can its activities potentially qualify for hedge accounting under IAS 39?

Yes. However, to qualify for hedge accounting the derivative hedging instrument that hedges the net position for risk management purposes must be designated for accounting purposes as a hedge of a gross position related to assets, liabilities, forecast cash inflows or forecast cash outflows giving rise to the net exposure (IAS 39.84, IAS 39.AG101 and IAS 39.AG111). It is not possible to designate a net position as a hedged item under IAS 39 because of the inability to associate hedging gains and losses with a specific item being hedged and, correspondingly, to determine objectively the period in which such gains and losses should be recognised in profit or loss.

Hedging a net exposure to interest rate risk can often be defined and documented to meet the qualifying criteria for hedge accounting in IAS 39.88 if the objective of the activity is to offset a specific, identified and designated risk exposure that ultimately affects the entity's profit or loss (IAS 39.AG110) and the entity designates and documents its interest rate risk exposure on a gross basis. Also, to qualify for hedge accounting the information systems must capture sufficient information about the amount and timing of cash flows and the effectiveness of the risk management activities in accomplishing their objective.

The factors an entity must consider for hedge accounting purposes if it manages interest rate risk on a net basis are discussed in Question F.6.2.

F.6.2 Hedge accounting considerations when interest rate risk is managed on a net basis

If an entity manages its exposure to interest rate risk on a net basis, what are the issues the entity should consider in defining and documenting its interest rate risk management activities to qualify for hedge accounting and in establishing and accounting for the hedge relationship?

Issues (a)-(l) below deal with the main issues. First, Issues (a) and (b) discuss the designation of derivatives used in interest rate risk management activities as fair value hedges or cash flow hedges. As noted there, hedge accounting criteria and accounting consequences differ between fair value hedges and cash flow hedges. Since it may be easier to achieve hedge accounting treatment if derivatives used in interest rate risk management activities are designated as cash flow hedging instruments, Issues (c)-(l) expand on various aspects of the accounting for cash flow hedges. Issues (c)-(f) consider the application of the hedge accounting criteria for cash flow hedges in IAS 39, and Issues (g) and (h) discuss the required accounting treatment. Finally, Issues (i)-(l) elaborate on other specific issues relating to the accounting for cash flow hedges.

Issue (a) – Can a derivative that is used to manage interest rate risk on a net basis be designated under IAS 39 as a hedging instrument in a fair value hedge or a cash flow hedge of a gross exposure?

Both types of designation are possible under IAS 39. An entity may designate the derivative used in interest rate risk management activities either as a fair value hedge of assets, liabilities and firm commitments or as a cash flow hedge of forecast transactions, such as the anticipated reinvestment of cash inflows, the anticipated refinancing or rollover of a financial liability, and the cash flow consequences of the resetting of interest rates for an asset or a liability.

In economic terms, it does not matter whether the derivative instrument is regarded as a fair value hedge or as a cash flow hedge. Under either perspective of the exposure, the derivative has the same economic effect of reducing the net exposure. For example, a receive-fixed, pay-variable interest rate swap can be considered to be a cash flow hedge of a variable rate asset or a fair value hedge of a fixed rate liability. Under either perspective, the fair value or cash flows of the interest rate swap offset the exposure to interest rate changes. However, accounting consequences differ depending on whether the derivative is designated as a fair value hedge or a cash flow hedge, as discussed in Issue (b).

To illustrate: a bank has the following assets and liabilities with a maturity of two years.

	Variable interest	*Fixed interest*
	CU	*CU*
Assets	60	100
Liabilities	(100)	(60)
Net	(40)	40

The bank takes out a two-year swap with a notional principal of CU40 to receive a variable interest rate and pay a fixed interest rate to hedge the net exposure. As discussed above, this may be regarded and designated either as a fair value hedge of CU40 of the fixed rate assets or as a cash flow hedge of CU40 of the variable rate liabilities.

Issue (b) – What are the critical considerations in deciding whether a derivative that is used to manage interest rate risk on a net basis should be designated as a hedging instrument in a fair value hedge or a cash flow hedge of a gross exposure?

Critical considerations include the assessment of hedge effectiveness in the presence of prepayment risk and the ability of the information systems to attribute fair value or cash flow changes of hedging instruments to fair value or cash flow changes, respectively, of hedged items, as discussed below.

For accounting purposes, the designation of a derivative as hedging a fair value exposure or a cash flow exposure is important because both the qualification requirements for hedge accounting and the recognition of hedging gains and losses for these categories are different. It is often easier to demonstrate high effectiveness for a cash flow hedge than for a fair value hedge.

Effects of prepayments

Prepayment risk inherent in many financial instruments affects the fair value of an instrument and the timing of its cash flows and impacts on the effectiveness test for fair value hedges and the highly probable test for cash flow hedges, respectively.

Effectiveness is often more difficult to achieve for fair value hedges than for cash flow hedges when the instrument being hedged is subject to prepayment risk. For a fair value hedge to qualify for hedge accounting, the changes in the fair value of the derivative hedging instrument must be expected to be highly effective in offsetting the changes in the fair value of the hedged item (IAS 39.88(b)). This test may be difficult to meet if, for example, the derivative hedging instrument is a forward contract having a fixed term and the financial assets being hedged are subject to prepayment by the borrower. Also, it may be difficult to conclude that, for a portfolio of fixed rate assets that are subject to prepayment, the changes in the fair value for each individual item in the group will be expected to be approximately proportional to the overall changes in fair value attributable to the hedged risk of the group. Even if the risk being hedged is a benchmark interest rate, to be able to conclude that fair value changes will be proportional for each item in the portfolio, it may be necessary to disaggregate the asset portfolio into categories based on term, coupon, credit, type of loan and other characteristics.

In economic terms, a forward derivative instrument could be used to hedge assets that are subject to prepayment but it would be effective only for small movements in interest rates. A reasonable estimate of prepayments can be made for a given interest rate environment and the derivative position can be adjusted as the interest rate environment changes. If an entity's risk management strategy is to adjust the amount of the hedging instrument periodically to reflect changes in the hedged position, the entity needs to demonstrate that the hedge is expected to be highly effective only for the period until the amount of the hedging instrument is next adjusted. However, for that period, the expectation of effectiveness has to be based on existing fair value exposures and the potential for interest rate movements without consideration of future adjustments to those positions. Furthermore, the fair value exposure attributable to prepayment risk can generally be hedged with options.

For a cash flow hedge to qualify for hedge accounting, the forecast cash flows, including the reinvestment of cash inflows or the refinancing of cash outflows, must be highly probable (IAS 39.88(c)) and the hedge expected to be highly effective in achieving offsetting changes in the cash flows of the hedged item and hedging instrument (IAS 39.88(b)). Prepayments affect the timing of cash flows and, therefore, the probability of occurrence of the forecast transaction. If the hedge is established for risk management purposes on a net basis, an entity may have sufficient levels of highly probable cash flows on a gross basis to support the designation for accounting purposes of forecast transactions associated with a portion of the gross cash flows as the hedged item. In this case, the portion of the gross cash flows designated as being hedged may be chosen to be equal to the amount of net cash flows being hedged for risk management purposes.

Systems considerations

The accounting for fair value hedges differs from that for cash flow hedges. It is usually easier to use existing information systems to manage and track cash flow hedges than it is for fair value hedges.

Under fair value hedge accounting, the assets or liabilities that are designated as being hedged are remeasured for those changes in fair values during the hedge period that are attributable to the risk being hedged. Such changes adjust the carrying amount of the hedged items and, for interest sensitive assets and liabilities, may result in an adjustment of the effective interest rate of the hedged item (IAS 39.89). As a consequence of fair value hedging activities, the changes in fair value have to be allocated to the assets or liabilities being hedged in order for the entity to be able to recompute their effective interest rate, determine the subsequent amortisation of the fair value adjustment to profit or loss, and determine the amount that should be recognised in profit or loss when assets are sold or liabilities extinguished (IAS 39.89 and IAS 39.92). To comply with the requirements for fair value hedge accounting, it will generally be necessary to establish a system to track the changes in the fair value attributable to the hedged risk, associate those changes with individual hedged items, recompute the effective interest rate of the hedged items, and amortise the changes to profit or loss over the life of the respective hedged item.

Under cash flow hedge accounting, the cash flows relating to the forecast transactions that are designated as being hedged reflect changes in interest rates. The adjustment for changes in the fair value of a hedging derivative instrument is initially recognised in other comprehensive income (IAS 39.95). To comply with the requirements for cash flow hedge accounting, it is necessary to determine when the cumulative gains and losses recognised in other comprehensive income from changes in the fair value of a hedging instrument should be reclassified to profit or loss (IAS 39.100 and IAS 39.101). For cash flow hedges, it is not necessary to create a separate system to make this determination. The system used to determine the extent of the net exposure provides the basis for scheduling the changes in the cash flows of the derivative and the recognition of such changes in profit or loss.

The timing of the recognition in profit or loss can be predetermined when the hedge is associated with the exposure to changes in cash flows. The forecast transactions that are being hedged can be associated with a specific principal amount in specific future periods composed of variable rate assets and cash inflows being reinvested or variable rate liabilities and cash outflows being refinanced, each of which creates a cash flow exposure to changes in interest rates. The specific principal amounts in specific future periods are equal to the notional amount of the derivative hedging instruments and are hedged only for the period that corresponds to the repricing or maturity of the derivative hedging instruments so that the cash flow changes resulting from changes in interest rates are matched with the derivative hedging instrument. IAS 39.100 specifies that the amounts recognised in other comprehensive income should be reclassified from equity to profit or loss in the same period or periods during which the hedged item affects profit or loss.

Issue (c) – If a hedging relationship is designated as a cash flow hedge relating to changes in cash flows resulting from interest rate changes, what would be included in the documentation required by IAS 39.88(a)?

The following would be included in the documentation.

The hedging relationship - The maturity schedule of cash flows used for risk management purposes to determine exposures to cash flow mismatches on a net basis would provide part of the documentation of the hedging relationship.

The entity's risk management objective and strategy for undertaking the hedge - The entity's overall risk management objective and strategy for hedging exposures to interest rate risk would provide part of the documentation of the hedging objective and strategy.

The type of hedge - The hedge is documented as a cash flow hedge.

The hedged item - The hedged item is documented as a group of forecast transactions (interest cash flows) that are expected to occur with a high degree of probability in specified future periods, for example, scheduled on a monthly basis. The hedged item may include interest cash flows resulting from the reinvestment of cash inflows, including the resetting of interest rates on assets, or from the refinancing of cash outflows, including the resetting of interest rates on liabilities and rollovers of financial liabilities. As discussed in Issue (e), the forecast transactions meet the probability test if there are sufficient levels of highly probable cash flows in the specified future periods to encompass the amounts designated as being hedged on a gross basis.

The hedged risk - The risk designated as being hedged is documented as a portion of the overall exposure to changes in a specified market interest rate, often the risk-free interest rate or an interbank offered rate, common to all items in the group. To help ensure that the hedge effectiveness test is met at inception of the hedge and subsequently, the designated hedged portion of the interest rate risk could be documented as being based on the same yield curve as the derivative hedging instrument.

The hedging instrument - Each derivative hedging instrument is documented as a hedge of specified amounts in specified future time periods corresponding with the forecast transactions occurring in the specified future time periods designated as being hedged.

The method of assessing effectiveness - The effectiveness test is documented as being measured by comparing the changes in the cash flows of the derivatives allocated to the applicable periods in which they are designated as a hedge to the changes in the cash flows of the forecast transactions being hedged. Measurement of the cash flow changes is based on the applicable yield curves of the derivatives and hedged items.

Issue (d) – If the hedging relationship is designated as a cash flow hedge, how does an entity satisfy the requirement for an expectation of high effectiveness in achieving offsetting changes in IAS 39.88(b)?

An entity may demonstrate an expectation of high effectiveness by preparing an analysis demonstrating high historical and expected future correlation between the interest rate risk designated as being hedged and the interest rate risk of the hedging instrument. Existing documentation of the hedge ratio used in establishing the derivative contracts may also serve to demonstrate an expectation of effectiveness.

Issue (e) – If the hedging relationship is designated as a cash flow hedge, how does an entity demonstrate a high probability of the forecast transactions occurring as required by IAS 39.88(c)?

An entity may do this by preparing a cash flow maturity schedule showing that there exist sufficient aggregate gross levels of expected cash flows, including the effects of the resetting of interest rates for assets or liabilities, to establish that the forecast transactions that are designated as being hedged are highly probable to occur. Such a schedule should be supported by management's stated intentions and past practice of reinvesting cash inflows and refinancing cash outflows.

For example, an entity may forecast aggregate gross cash inflows of CU100 and aggregate gross cash outflows of CU90 in a particular time period in the near future. In this case, it may wish to designate the forecast reinvestment of gross cash inflows of CU10 as the hedged item in the future time period. If more than CU10 of the forecast cash inflows are contractually specified and have low credit risk, the entity has strong evidence to support an assertion that gross cash inflows of CU10 are highly probable to occur and to support the designation of the forecast reinvestment of those cash flows as being hedged for a particular portion of the reinvestment period. A high probability of the forecast transactions occurring may also be demonstrated under other circumstances.

Issue (f) – If the hedging relationship is designated as a cash flow hedge, how does an entity assess and measure effectiveness under IAS 39.88(d) and IAS 39.88(e)?

Effectiveness is required to be measured at a minimum at the time an entity prepares its annual or interim financial reports. However, an entity may wish to measure it more frequently on a specified periodic basis, at the end of each month or other applicable reporting period. It is also measured whenever derivative positions designated as hedging instruments are changed or hedges are terminated to ensure that the recognition in profit or loss of the changes in the fair value amounts on assets and liabilities and the recognition of changes in the fair value of derivative instruments designated as cash flow hedges are appropriate.

Changes in the cash flows of the derivative are computed and allocated to the applicable periods in which the derivative is designated as a hedge and are compared with computations of changes in the cash flows of the forecast transactions. Computations are based on yield curves applicable to the hedged items and the derivative hedging instruments and applicable interest rates for the specified periods being hedged.

The schedule used to determine effectiveness could be maintained and used as the basis for determining the period in which the hedging gains and losses recognised initially in other comprehensive income are reclassified from equity to profit or loss.

Issue (g) – If the hedging relationship is designated as a cash flow hedge, how does an entity account for the hedge?

The hedge is accounted for as a cash flow hedge in accordance with the provisions in IAS 39.95-IAS 39.100, as follows:

(i) the portion of gains and losses on hedging derivatives determined to result from effective hedges is recognised in other comprehensive income whenever effectiveness is measured; and
(ii) the ineffective portion of gains and losses resulting from hedging derivatives is recognised in profit or loss.

IAS 39.100 specifies that the amounts recognised in other comprehensive income should be reclassified from equity to profit or loss in the same period or periods during which the hedged item affects profit or loss. Accordingly, when the forecast transactions occur, the amounts previously recognised in other comprehensive income are reclassified from equity to profit or loss. For example, if an interest rate swap is designated as a hedging instrument of a series of forecast cash flows, the changes in the cash flows of the swap are recognised in profit or loss in the periods when the forecast cash flows and the cash flows of the swap offset each other.

Issue (h) – If the hedging relationship is designated as a cash flow hedge, what is the treatment of any net cumulative gains and losses recognised in other comprehensive income if the hedging instrument is terminated prematurely, the hedge accounting criteria are no longer met, or the hedged forecast transactions are no longer expected to take place?

If the hedging instrument is terminated prematurely or the hedge no longer meets the criteria for qualification for hedge accounting, for example, the forecast transactions are no longer highly probable, the net cumulative gain or loss recognised in other comprehensive income remains in equity until the forecast transaction occurs (IAS 39.101(a) and IAS 39.101(b)). If the hedged forecast transactions are no longer expected to occur, the net cumulative gain or loss is reclassified from equity to profit or loss (IAS 39.101(c)).

Issue (i) – IAS 39.75 states that a hedging relationship may not be designated for only a portion of the time period in which a hedging instrument is outstanding. If the hedging relationship is designated as a cash flow hedge, and the hedge subsequently fails the test for being highly effective, does IAS 39.75 preclude redesignating the hedging instrument?

No. IAS 39.75 indicates that a derivative instrument may not be designated as a hedging instrument for only a portion of its remaining period to maturity. IAS 39.75 does not refer to the derivative instrument's original period to maturity. If there is a hedge effectiveness failure, the ineffective portion of the gain or loss on the derivative instrument is recognised immediately in profit or loss (IAS 39.95(b)) and hedge accounting based on the previous designation of the hedge relationship cannot be continued (IAS 39.101). In this case, the derivative instrument may be redesignated prospectively as a hedging instrument in a new hedging relationship provided this hedging relationship satisfies the necessary conditions. The derivative instrument must be redesignated as a hedge for the entire time period it remains outstanding.

Issue (j) – For cash flow hedges, if a derivative is used to manage a net exposure to interest rate risk and the derivative is designated as a cash flow hedge of forecast interest cash flows or portions of them on a gross basis, does the occurrence of the hedged forecast transaction give rise to an asset or liability that will result in a portion of the hedging gains and losses that were recognised in other comprehensive income remaining in equity?

No. In the hedging relationship described in Issue (c) above, the hedged item is a group of forecast transactions consisting of interest cash flows in specified future periods. The hedged forecast transactions do not result in the recognition of assets or liabilities and the effect of interest rate changes that are designated as being hedged is recognised in profit or loss in the period in which the forecast transactions occur. Although this is not relevant for the types of hedges described here, if instead the derivative is designated as a hedge of a forecast purchase of a financial asset or issue of a financial liability, the associated gains or losses that were recognised in other comprehensive income are reclassified from equity to profit or loss in the same period or periods during which the hedged forecast cash flows affects profit or loss (such as in the periods that interest expenses are recognised). However, if an entity expects at any time that all or a portion of a loss recognised in other comprehensive income will not be recovered in one or more future periods, it shall reclassify immediately from equity to profit or loss the amount that is not expected to be recovered.

Issue (k) – In the answer to Issue (c) above it was indicated that the designated hedged item is a portion of a cash flow exposure. Does IAS 39 permit a portion of a cash flow exposure to be designated as a hedged item?

Yes. IAS 39 does not specifically address a hedge of a portion of a cash flow exposure for a forecast transaction. However, IAS 39.81 specifies that a financial asset or liability may be a hedged item with respect to the risks associated with only a portion of its cash flows or fair value, if effectiveness can be measured. The ability to hedge a portion of a cash flow exposure resulting from the resetting of interest rates for assets and liabilities suggests that a portion of a cash flow exposure resulting from the forecast reinvestment of cash inflows or the refinancing or rollover of financial liabilities can also be hedged. The basis for qualification as a hedged item of a portion of an exposure is the ability to measure effectiveness. This is further supported by IAS 39.82, which specifies that a non-financial asset or liability can be hedged only in its entirety or for foreign currency risk but not for a portion of other risks because of the difficulty of isolating and measuring the appropriate portion of the cash flows or fair value changes attributable to a specific risk. Accordingly, assuming effectiveness can be measured, a portion of a cash flow exposure of forecast transactions associated with, for example, the resetting of interest rates for a variable rate asset or liability can be designated as a hedged item.

Issue (l) – In the answer to Issue (c) above it was indicated that the hedged item is documented as a group of forecast transactions. Since these transactions will have different terms when they occur, including credit exposures, maturities and option features, how can an entity satisfy the tests in IAS 39.78 and IAS 39.83 requiring the hedged group to have similar risk characteristics?

IAS 39.78 provides for hedging a group of assets, liabilities, firm commitments or forecast transactions with similar risk characteristics. IAS 39.83 provides additional guidance and specifies that portfolio hedging is permitted if two conditions are met, namely: the individual items in the portfolio share the same risk for which they are designated, and the change in the fair value attributable to the hedged risk for each individual item in the group will be expected to be approximately proportional to the overall change in fair value.

When an entity associates a derivative hedging instrument with a gross exposure, the hedged item typically is a group of forecast transactions. For hedges of cash flow exposures relating to a group of forecast transactions, the overall exposure of the forecast transactions and the assets or liabilities that are repriced may have very different risks. The exposure from forecast transactions may differ depending on the terms that are expected as they relate to credit exposures, maturities, options and other features. Although the overall risk exposures may be different for the individual items in the group, a specific risk inherent in each of the items in the group can be designated as being hedged.

The items in the portfolio do not necessarily have to have the same overall exposure to risk, provided they share the same risk for which they are designated as being hedged. A common risk typically shared by a portfolio of financial instruments is exposure to changes in the risk-free or benchmark interest rate or to changes in a specified rate that has a credit exposure equal to the highest credit-rated instrument in the portfolio (ie the instrument with the lowest credit risk). If the instruments that are grouped into a portfolio have different credit exposures, they may be hedged as a group for a portion of the exposure. The risk they have in common that is designated as being hedged is the exposure to interest rate changes from the highest credit rated instrument in the portfolio. This ensures that the change in fair value attributable to the hedged risk for each individual item in the group is expected to be approximately proportional to the overall change in fair value attributable to the hedged risk of the group. It is likely there will be some ineffectiveness if the hedging instrument has a credit quality that is inferior to the credit quality of the highest credit-rated instrument being hedged, since a hedging relationship is designated for a hedging instrument in its entirety (IAS 39.74). For example, if a portfolio of assets consists of assets rated A, BB and B, and the current market interest rates for these assets are LIBOR + 20 basis points, LIBOR + 40 basis points and LIBOR + 60 basis points, respectively, an entity may use a swap that pays fixed interest rate and for which variable interest payments based on LIBOR are made to hedge the exposure to variable interest rates. If LIBOR is designated as the risk being hedged, credit spreads above LIBOR on the hedged items are excluded from the designated hedge relationship and the assessment of hedge effectiveness.

F.6.3 Illustrative example of applying the approach in Question F.6.2

The purpose of this example is to illustrate the process of establishing, monitoring and adjusting hedge positions and of qualifying for cash flow hedge accounting in applying the approach to hedge accounting described in Question F.6.2 when a financial institution manages its interest rate risk on an entity-wide basis. To this end, this example identifies a methodology that allows for the use of hedge accounting and takes advantage of existing risk management systems so as to avoid unnecessary changes to it and to avoid unnecessary bookkeeping and tracking.

The approach illustrated here reflects only one of a number of risk management processes that could be employed and could qualify for hedge accounting. Its use is not intended to suggest that other alternatives could not or should not be used. The approach being illustrated could also be applied in other circumstances (such as for cash flow hedges of commercial entities), for example, hedging the rollover of commercial paper financing.

Identifying, assessing and reducing cash flow exposures

The discussion and illustrations that follow focus on the risk management activities of a financial institution that manages its interest rate risk by analysing expected cash flows in a particular currency on an entity-wide basis. The cash flow analysis forms the basis for identifying the interest rate risk of the entity, entering into hedging transactions to manage the risk, assessing the effectiveness of risk management activities, and qualifying for and applying cash flow hedge accounting.

The illustrations that follow assume that an entity, a financial institution, had the following expected future net cash flows and hedging positions outstanding in a specific currency, consisting of interest rate swaps, at the beginning of Period X0. The cash flows shown are expected to occur at the end of the period and, therefore, create a cash flow interest exposure in the following period as a result of the reinvestment or repricing of the cash inflows or the refinancing or repricing of the cash outflows.

The illustrations assume that the entity has an ongoing interest rate risk management programme. Schedule I shows the expected cash flows and hedging positions that existed at the beginning of Period X0. It is included here to provide a starting point in the analysis. It provides a basis for considering existing hedges in connection with the evaluation that occurs at the beginning of Period X1.

Schedule I – End of period – Expected cash flows and hedging positions

Quarterly period (units)	*X0 CU*	*X1 CU*	*X2 CU*	*X3 CU*	*X4 CU*	*X5 CU*	*...n CU*
Expected net cash flows		1,100	1,500	1,200	1,400	1,500	x,xxx
Outstanding interest rate swaps:							
Receive-fixed, pay-variable (notional amounts)	2,000	2,000	2,000	1,200	1,200	1,200	x,xxx
Pay-fixed, receive-variable (notional amounts)	(1,000)	(1,000)	(1,000)	(500)	(500)	(500)	x,xxx
Net exposure after outstanding swaps		100	500	500	700	800	x,xxx

The schedule depicts five quarterly periods. The actual analysis would extend over a period of many years, represented by the notation '...n'. A financial institution that manages its interest rate risk on an entity-wide basis re-evaluates its cash flow exposures periodically. The frequency of the evaluation depends on the entity's risk management policy.

For the purposes of this illustration, the entity is re-evaluating its cash flow exposures at the end of Period X0. The first step in the process is the generation of forecast net cash flow exposures from existing interest-earning assets and interest-bearing liabilities, including the rollover of short-term assets and short-term liabilities. Schedule II below illustrates the forecast of net cash flow exposures. A common technique for assessing exposure to interest rates for risk management purposes is an interest rate sensitivity gap analysis showing the gap between interest rate-sensitive assets and interest rate-sensitive liabilities over different time intervals. Such an analysis could be used as a starting point for identifying cash flow exposures to interest rate risk for hedge accounting purposes.

Schedule II – Forecast net cash flow and repricing exposures

Quarterly period (units)	*Notes*	*X1 CU*	*X2 CU*	*X3 CU*	*X4 CU*	*X5 CU*	*...n CU*
CASH INFLOW AND REPRICING EXPOSURES - from assets							
Principal and interest payments:							
Long-term fixed rate	(1)	2,400	3,000	3,000	1,000	1,200	x,xxx
Short-term (roll over)	(1)(2)	1,575	1,579	1,582	1,586	1,591	x,xxx
Variable rate - principal payments	(1)	2,000	1,000	-	500	500	x,xxx
Variable rate - estimated interest	(2)	125	110	105	114	118	x,xxx
Total expected cash inflows		*6,100*	*5,689*	*4,687*	*3,200*	*3,409*	*x,xxx*
Variable rate asset balances	(3)	8,000	7,000	7,000	6,500	6,000	x,xxx
Cash inflows and repricings	***(4)***	***14,100***	***12,689***	***11,687***	***9,700***	***9,409***	***x,xxx***
CASH OUTFLOW AND REPRICING EXPOSURES - from liabilities							
Principal and interest payments:							
Long-term fixed rate	(1)	2,100	400	500	500	301	x,xxx
Short-term (roll over)	(1)(2)	735	737	738	740	742	x,xxx
Variable rate - principal payments	(1)	-	-	2,000	-	1,000	x,xxx
Variable rate - estimated interest	(2)	100	110	120	98	109	x,xxx
Total expected cash outflows		*2,935*	*1,247*	*3,358*	*1,338*	*2,152*	*x,xxx*
Variable rate liability balances	(3)	8,000	8,000	6,000	6,000	5,000	x,xxx
Cash outflows and repricings	***(4)***	***10,935***	***9,247***	***9,358***	***7,338***	***7,152***	***x,xxx***
NET EXPOSURES	*(5)*	*3,165*	*3,442*	*2,329*	*2,362*	*2,257*	*x,xxx*

(1) The cash flows are estimated using contractual terms and assumptions based on management's intentions and market factors. It is assumed that short-term assets and liabilities will continue to be rolled over in succeeding periods. Assumptions about prepayments and defaults and the withdrawal of deposits are based on market and historical data. It is assumed that principal and interest inflows and outflows will be reinvested and refinanced, respectively, at the end of each period at the then current market interest rates and share the benchmark interest rate risk to which they are exposed.

(2) Forward interest rates obtained from Schedule VI are used to forecast interest payments on variable rate financial instruments and expected rollovers of short-term assets and liabilities. All forecast cash flows are associated with the specific time periods (3 months, 6 months, 9 months and 12 months) in which

they are expected to occur. For completeness, the interest cash flows resulting from reinvestments, refinancings and repricings are included in the schedule and shown gross even though only the net margin may actually be reinvested. Some entities may choose to disregard the forecast interest cash flows for risk management purposes because they may be used to absorb operating costs and any remaining amounts would not be significant enough to affect risk management decisions.

(3) The cash flow forecast is adjusted to include the variable rate asset and liability balances in each period in which such variable rate asset and liability balances are repriced. The principal amounts of these assets and liabilities are not actually being paid and, therefore, do not generate a cash flow. However, since interest is computed on the principal amounts each period based on the then current market interest rate, such principal amounts expose the entity to the same interest rate risk as if they were cash flows being reinvested or refinanced.

(4) The forecast cash flow and repricing exposures that are identified in each period represent the principal amounts of cash inflows that will be reinvested or repriced and cash outflows that will be refinanced or repriced at the market interest rates that are in effect when those forecast transactions occur.

(5) The net cash flow and repricing exposure is the difference between the cash inflow and repricing exposures from assets and the cash outflow and repricing exposures from liabilities. In the illustration, the entity is exposed to interest rate declines because the exposure from assets exceeds the exposure from liabilities and the excess (ie the net amount) will be reinvested or repriced at the current market rate and there is no offsetting refinancing or repricing of outflows.

Note that some banks regard some portion of their non-interest bearing demand deposits as economically equivalent to long-term debt. However, these deposits do not create a cash flow exposure to interest rates and would therefore be excluded from this analysis for accounting purposes.

Schedule II *Forecast net cash flow and repricing exposures* provides no more than a starting point for assessing cash flow exposure to interest rates and for adjusting hedging positions. The complete analysis includes outstanding hedging positions and is shown in Schedule III *Analysis of expected net exposures and hedging positions*. It compares the forecast net cash flow exposures for each period (developed in Schedule II) with existing hedging positions (obtained from Schedule I), and provides a basis for considering whether adjustment of the hedging relationship should be made.

Schedule III – Analysis of expected net exposures and hedging positions

Quarterly period (units)	*X1 CU*	*X2 CU*	*X3 CU*	*X4 CU*	*X5 CU*	*...n CU*
Net cash flow and repricing exposures (Schedule II)	3,165	3,442	2,329	2,362	2,257	x,xxx
Pre-existing swaps outstanding:						
Receive-fixed, pay-variable (notional amounts)	2,000	2,000	1,200	1,200	1,200	x,xxx
Pay-fixed, receive-variable (notional amounts)	(1,000)	(1,000)	(500)	(500)	(500)	x,xxx
Net exposure after pre-existing swaps	*2,165*	*2,442*	*1,629*	*1,662*	*1,557*	*x,xxx*
Transactions to adjust outstanding hedging positions:						
Receive-fixed, pay variable swap 1 (notional amount, 10-years)	2,000	2,000	2,000	2,000	2,000	x,xxx
Pay-fixed, receive-variable swap 2 (notional amount, 3-years)			(1,000)	(1,000)	(1,000)	x,xxx
Swaps ...X						x,xxx
Unhedged cash flow and repricing exposure	*165*	*442*	*629*	*662*	*557*	*x,xxx*

The notional amounts of the interest rate swaps that are outstanding at the analysis date are included in each of the periods in which the interest rate swaps are outstanding to illustrate the impact of the outstanding interest rate swaps on the identified cash flow exposures. The notional amounts of the outstanding interest rate swaps are included in each period because interest is computed on the notional amounts each period, and the variable rate components of the outstanding swaps are repriced to the current market rate quarterly. The notional amounts create an exposure to interest rates that in part is similar to the principal balances of variable rate assets and variable rate liabilities.

The exposure that remains after considering the existing positions is then evaluated to determine the extent to which adjustments of existing hedging positions are necessary. The bottom portion of Schedule III shows the beginning of Period X1 using interest rate swap transactions to reduce the net exposures further to within the tolerance levels established under the entity's risk management policy.

Note that in the illustration, the cash flow exposure is not entirely eliminated. Many financial institutions do not fully eliminate risk but rather reduce it to within some tolerable limit.

Various types of derivative instruments could be used to manage the cash flow exposure to interest rate risk identified in the schedule of forecast net cash flows (Schedule II). However, for the purpose of the illustration, it is assumed that interest rate swaps are used for all hedging activities. It is also assumed that in periods in which interest rate swaps should be reduced, rather than terminating some of the outstanding interest rate swap positions, a new swap with the opposite return characteristics is added to the portfolio.

In the illustration in Schedule III above, swap 1, a receive-fixed, pay-variable swap, is used to reduce the net exposure in Periods X1 and X2. Since it is a 10year swap, it also reduces exposures identified in other future periods not shown. However, it has the effect of creating an over-hedged position in Periods X3-X5. Swap 2, a forward starting pay-fixed, receive-variable interest rate swap, is used to reduce the notional amount of the outstanding receive-fixed, pay-variable interest rate swaps in Periods X3-X5 and thereby reduce the over-hedged positions.

It also is noted that in many situations, no adjustment or only a single adjustment of the outstanding hedging position is necessary to bring the exposure to within an acceptable limit. However, when the entity's risk management policy specifies a very low tolerance of risk a greater number of adjustments to the hedging positions over the forecast period would be needed to further reduce any remaining risk.

To the extent that some of the interest rate swaps fully offset other interest rate swaps that have been entered into for hedging purposes, it is not necessary to include them in a designated hedging relationship for hedge accounting purposes. These offsetting positions can be combined, de-designated as hedging instruments, if necessary, and reclassified for accounting purposes from the hedging portfolio to the trading portfolio. This procedure limits the extent to which the gross swaps must continue to be designated and tracked in a hedging relationship for accounting purposes. For the purposes of this illustration it is assumed that CU500 of the pay-fixed, receive-variable interest rate swaps fully offset CU500 of the receive-fixed, pay-variable interest rate swaps at the beginning of Period X1 and for Periods X1-X5, and are dedesignated as hedging instruments and reclassified to the trading account.

After reflecting these offsetting positions, the remaining gross interest rate swap positions from Schedule III are shown in Schedule IV as follows.

Schedule IV – Interest rate swaps designated as hedges

Quarterly period (units)	*X1* CU	*X2* CU	*X3* CU	*X4* CU	*X5* CU	*...n* CU
Receive-fixed, pay-variable (notional amounts)	3,500	3,500	2,700	2,700	2,700	x,xxx
Pay-fixed, receive-variable (notional amounts)	(500)	(500)	(1,000)	(1,000)	(1,000)	x,xxx
Net outstanding swaps positions	*3,000*	*3,000*	*1,700*	*1,700*	*1,700*	*x,xxx*

For the purposes of the illustrations, it is assumed that Swap 2, entered into at the beginning of Period X1, only partially offsets another swap being accounted for as a hedge and therefore continues to be designated as a hedging instrument.

Hedge accounting considerations

Illustrating the designation of the hedging relationship

The discussion and illustrations thus far have focused primarily on economic and risk management considerations relating to the identification of risk in future periods and the adjustment of that risk using interest rate swaps. These activities form the basis for designating a hedging relationship for accounting purposes.

The examples in IAS 39 focus primarily on hedging relationships involving a single hedged item and a single hedging instrument, but there is little discussion and guidance on portfolio hedging relationships for cash flow hedges when risk is being managed centrally. In this illustration, the general principles are applied to hedging relationships involving a component of risk in a portfolio having multiple risks from multiple transactions or positions.

Although designation is necessary to achieve hedge accounting, the way in which the designation is described also affects the extent to which the hedging relationship is judged to be effective for accounting purposes and the extent to which the entity's existing system for managing risk will be required to be modified to track hedging activities for accounting purposes. Accordingly, an entity may wish to designate the hedging relationship in a manner that avoids unnecessary systems changes by taking advantage of the information already generated by the risk management system and avoids unnecessary bookkeeping and tracking. In designating hedging relationships, the entity may also consider the extent to which ineffectiveness is expected to be recognised for accounting purposes under alternative designations.

The designation of the hedging relationship needs to specify various matters. These are illustrated and discussed here from the perspective of the hedge of the interest rate risk associated with the cash inflows, but the guidance can also be applied to the hedge of the risk associated with the cash outflows. It is fairly obvious that only a portion of the gross exposures relating to the cash inflows is being hedged by the interest rate swaps. Schedule V *The general hedging relationship* illustrates the designation of the portion of the gross reinvestment risk exposures identified in Schedule II as being hedged by the interest rate swaps.

Schedule V – The general hedging relationship

Quarterly period (units)	*X1 CU*	*X2 CU*	*X3 CU*	*X4 CU*	*X5 CU*	*...n CU*
Cash inflow repricing exposure (Schedule II)	14,100	12,689	11,687	9,700	9,409	x,xxx
Receive-fixed, pay-variable swaps (Schedule IV)	3,500	3,500	2,700	2,700	2,700	x,xxx
Hedged exposure percentage	*24.8%*	*27.6%*	*23.1%*	*27.8%*	*28.7%*	*xx.x%*

The hedged exposure percentage is computed as the ratio of the notional amount of the receive-fixed, pay-variable swaps that are outstanding divided by the gross exposure. Note that in Schedule V there are sufficient levels of forecast reinvestments in each period to offset more than the notional amount of the receive-fixed, pay-variable swaps and satisfy the accounting requirement that the forecast transaction is highly probable.

It is not as obvious, however, how the interest rate swaps are specifically related to the cash flow interest risks designated as being hedged and how the interest rate swaps are effective in reducing that risk. The more specific designation is illustrated in Schedule VI *The specific hedging relationship* below. It provides a meaningful way of depicting the more complicated narrative designation of the hedge by focusing on the hedging objective to eliminate the cash flow variability associated with future changes in interest rates and to obtain an interest rate equal to the fixed rate inherent in the term structure of interest rates that exists at the commencement of the hedge.

The expected interest from the reinvestment of the cash inflows and repricings of the assets is computed by multiplying the gross amounts exposed by the forward rate for the period. For example, the gross exposure for Period X2 of CU14,100 is multiplied by the forward rate for Periods X2-X5 of 5.50 per cent, 6.00 per cent, 6.50 per cent and 7.25 per cent, respectively, to compute the expected interest for those quarterly periods based on the current term structure of interest rates. The hedged expected interest is computed by multiplying the expected interest for the applicable three-month period by the hedged exposure percentage.

Schedule VI – The specific hedging relationship

			Term structure of interest rates					
Quarterly period			*X1*	*X2*	*X3*	*X4*	*X5*	*...n*
Spot rates			5.00%	5.25%	5.50%	5.75%	6.05%	x.xx%
Forward rates*			5.00%	5.50%	6.00%	6.50%	7.25%	x.xx%
Cash flow exposures and expected interest amounts								
Repricing period	Time to forecast transaction	Gross amounts exposed	Expected interest					
			CU	CU	CU	CU	CU	CU
2	3 months	14,100	→	194	212	229	256	
3	6 months	12,689			190	206	230	xxx
4	9 months	11,687				190	212	xxx
5	12 months	9,700					176	xxx
6	15 months	9,409						xxx
Hedged percentage (Schedule V) in the previous period				24.8%	27.6%	23.1%	27.8%	xx.x%
Hedged expected interest				48	52	44	49	xx

* The forward interest rates are computed from the spot interest rates and rounded for the purposes of the presentation. Computations that are based on the forward interest rates are made based on the actual computed forward rate and then rounded for the purposes of the presentation.

It does not matter whether the gross amount exposed is reinvested in long-term fixed rate debt or variable rate debt, or in short-term debt that is rolled over in each subsequent period. The exposure to changes in the forward interest rate is the same. For example, if the CU14,100 is reinvested at a fixed rate at the beginning of Period X2 for six months, it will be reinvested at 5.75 per cent. The expected interest is based on the forward interest rates for Period X2 of 5.50 per cent and for Period X3 of 6.00 per cent, equal to a blended rate of 5.75 per cent $(1.055 \cdot 1.060)^{0.5}$, which is the Period X2 spot rate for the next six months.

However, only the expected interest from the reinvestment of the cash inflows or repricing of the gross amount for the first three-month period after the forecast transaction occurs is designated as being hedged. The expected interest being hedged is represented by the shaded cells. The exposure for the subsequent periods is not hedged. In the example, the portion of the interest rate exposure being hedged is the forward rate of 5.50 per cent for Period X2. In order to assess hedge effectiveness and compute actual hedge ineffectiveness on an ongoing basis, the entity may use the information on hedged interest cash inflows in Schedule VI and compare it with updated estimates of expected interest cash inflows (for example, in a table that looks like Schedule II). As long as expected interest cash inflows exceed hedged interest cash inflows, the entity may compare the cumulative change in the fair value of the hedged cash inflows with the cumulative change in the fair value of the hedging instrument to compute actual hedge effectiveness. If there are insufficient expected interest cash inflows, there will be ineffectiveness. It is measured by comparing the cumulative change in the fair value of the expected interest cash flows to the extent they are less than the hedged cash flows with the cumulative change in the fair value of the hedging instrument.

Describing the designation of the hedging relationship

As mentioned previously, there are various matters that should be specified in the designation of the hedging relationship that complicate the description of the designation but are necessary to limit ineffectiveness to be recognised for accounting purposes and to avoid unnecessary systems changes and bookkeeping. The example that follows describes the designation more fully and identifies additional aspects of the designation not apparent from the previous illustrations.

Example designation

Hedging objective

The hedging objective is to eliminate the risk of interest rate fluctuations over the hedging period, which is the life of the interest rate swap, and in effect obtain a fixed interest rate during this period that is equal to the fixed interest rate on the interest rate swap.

Type of hedge

Cash flow hedge.

Hedging instrument

The receive-fixed, pay-variable swaps are designated as the hedging instrument. They hedge the cash flow exposure to interest rate risk.
Each repricing of the swap hedges a three-month portion of the interest cash inflows that results from:

- the forecast reinvestment or repricing of the principal amounts shown in Schedule V.
- unrelated investments or repricings that occur after the repricing dates on the swap over its life and involve different borrowers or lenders.

The hedged item - General

The hedged item is a portion of the gross interest cash inflows that will result from the reinvestment or repricing of the cash flows identified in Schedule V and are expected to occur within the periods shown on such schedule. The portion of the interest cash inflow that is being hedged has three components:

- the principal component giving rise to the interest cash inflow and the period in which it occurs,
- the interest rate component, and
- the time component or period covered by the hedge.

The hedged item The principal component

The portion of the interest cash inflows being hedged is the amount that results from the first portion of the principal amounts being invested or repriced in each period:

- that is equal to the sum of the notional amounts of the received-fixed, pay-*variable interest rate* swaps that are designated as hedging instruments and outstanding in the period of the reinvestment or repricing, and
- that corresponds to the first principal amounts of cash flow exposures that are invested or repriced at or after the repricing dates of the interest rate swaps.

The hedged item The interest rate component

The portion of the interest rate change that is being hedged is the change in both of the following:

- the credit component of the interest rate being paid on the principal amount invested or repriced that is equal to the credit risk inherent in the interest rate swap. It is that portion of the interest rate on the investment that is equal to the interest index of the interest rate swap, such as LIBOR, and
- the yield curve component of the interest rate that is equal to the repricing period on the interest rate swap designated as the hedging instrument.

The hedged item The hedged period

The period of the exposure to interest rate changes on the portion of the cash flow exposures being hedged is:

- the period from the designation date to the repricing date of the interest rate swap that occurs within the quarterly period in which, but not before, the forecast transactions occur, and
- its effects for the period after the forecast transactions occur equal to the repricing interval of the interest rate swap.

It is important to recognise that the swaps are not hedging the cash flow risk for a single investment over its entire life. The swaps are designated as hedging the cash flow risk from different principal investments and repricings that are made in each repricing period of the swaps over their entire term. The swaps hedge only the interest accruals that occur in the first period following the reinvestment. They are hedging the cash flow impact resulting from a change in interest rates that occurs up to the repricing of the swap. The exposure to changes in rates for the period from the repricing of the swap to the date of the hedged reinvestment of cash inflows or repricing of variable rate assets is not hedged. When the swap is repriced, the interest rate on the swap is fixed until the next repricing date and the accrual of the net swap settlements is determined. Any changes in interest rates after that date that affect the amount of the interest cash inflow are no longer hedged for accounting purposes.

Designation objectives

Systems considerations

Many of the tracking and bookkeeping requirements are eliminated by designating each repricing of an interest rate swap as hedging the cash flow risk from forecast reinvestments of cash inflows and repricings of variable rate assets for only a portion of the lives of the related assets. Much tracking and bookkeeping would be necessary if the swaps were instead designated as hedging the cash flow risk from forecast principal investments and repricings of variable rate assets over the entire lives of these assets.

This type of designation avoids keeping track of deferred derivative gains and losses recognised in other comprehensive income after the forecast transactions occur (IAS 39.97 and IAS 39.98) because the portion of the cash flow risk being hedged is that portion that will be reclassified from equity to profit or loss in the period immediately following the forecast transactions that corresponds with the periodic net cash settlements on the swap. If the hedge were to cover the entire life of the assets being acquired, it would be necessary to associate a specific interest rate swap with the asset being acquired. If a forecast transaction is the acquisition of a fixed rate instrument, the fair value of the swap that hedged that transaction would be reclassified from equity to profit or loss to adjust the interest income on the asset when the interest income is recognised. The swap would then have to be terminated or redesignated in another hedging relationship. If a forecast transaction is the acquisition of a variable rate asset, the swap would continue in the hedging relationship but it would have to be tracked back to the asset acquired so that any fair value amounts on the swap recognised in equity could be reclassified from equity to profit or loss upon the subsequent sale of the asset.

It also avoids the necessity of associating with variable rate assets any portion of the fair value of the swaps that is recognised in equity. Accordingly, there is no portion of the fair value of the swap that is recognised in other comprehensive income that should be reclassified from equity to profit or loss when a forecast transaction occurs or upon the sale of a variable rate asset.

This type of designation also permits flexibility in deciding how to reinvest cash flows when they occur. Since the hedged risk relates only to a single period that corresponds with the repricing period of the interest rate swap designated as the hedging instrument, it is not necessary to determine at the designation date whether the cash flows will be reinvested in fixed rate or variable rate assets or to specify at the date of designation the life of the asset to be acquired.

Effectiveness considerations

Ineffectiveness is greatly reduced by designating a specific portion of the cash flow exposure as being hedged.

- Ineffectiveness due to credit differences between the interest rate swap and hedged forecast cash flow is eliminated by designating the cash flow risk being hedged as the risk attributable to changes in the interest rates that correspond with the rates inherent in the swap, such as the AA rate curve. This type of designation prevents changes resulting from changes in credit spreads from being considered as ineffectiveness.
- Ineffectiveness due to duration differences between the interest rate swap and hedged forecast cash flow is eliminated by designating the interest rate risk being hedged as the risk relating to changes in the portion of the yield curve that corresponds with the period in which the variable rate leg of the interest rate swap is repriced.
- Ineffectiveness due to interest rate changes that occur between the repricing date of the interest rate swap and the date of the forecast transactions is eliminated by simply not hedging that period of time. The period from the repricing of the swap and the occurrence of the forecast transactions in the period immediately following the repricing of the swap is left unhedged. Therefore, the difference in dates does not result in ineffectiveness.

Accounting considerations

The ability to qualify for hedge accounting using the methodology described here is founded on provisions in IAS 39 and on interpretations of its requirements. Some of those are described in the answer to Question F.6.2 *Hedge accounting considerations when interest rate risk is managed on a net basis*. Some additional and supporting provisions and interpretations are identified below.

Hedging a portion of the risk exposure

The ability to identify and hedge only a portion of the cash flow risk exposure resulting from the reinvestment of cash flows or repricing of variable rate instruments is found in IAS 39.81 as interpreted in the answers to Questions F.6.2 Issue (k) and F.2.17 *Partial term hedging*.

Hedging multiple risks with a single instrument

The ability to designate a single interest rate swap as a hedge of the cash flow exposure to interest rates resulting from various reinvestments of cash inflows or repricings of variable rate assets that occur over the life of the swap is founded on IAS 39.76 as interpreted in the answer to Question F.1.12 *Hedges of more than one type of risk*.

Hedging similar risks in a portfolio

The ability to specify the forecast transaction being hedged as a portion of the cash flow exposure to interest rates for a portion of the duration of the investment that gives rise to the interest payment without specifying at the designation date the expected life of the instrument and whether it pays a fixed or variable rate is founded on the answer to Question F.6.2 Issue (l), which specifies that the items in the portfolio do not necessarily have to have the same overall exposure to risk, providing they share the same risk for which they are designated as being hedged.

Hedge terminations

The ability to de-designate the forecast transaction (the cash flow exposure on an investment or repricing that will occur after the repricing date of the swap) as being hedged is provided for in IAS 39.101 dealing with hedge terminations. While a portion of the forecast transaction is no longer being hedged, the interest rate swap is not de-designated, and it continues to be a hedging instrument for the remaining transactions in the series that have not occurred. For example, assume that an interest rate swap having a remaining life of one year has been designated as hedging a series of three quarterly reinvestments of cash flows. The next forecast cash flow reinvestment occurs in three months. When the interest rate swap is repriced in three months at the then current variable rate, the fixed rate and the variable rate on the interest rate swap become known and no longer provide hedge protection for the next three months. If the next forecast transaction does not occur until three months and ten days, the ten-day period that remains after the repricing of the interest rate swap is not hedged.

F.6.4 Hedge accounting: premium or discount on forward exchange contract

A forward exchange contract is designated as a hedging instrument, for example, in a hedge of a net investment in a foreign operation. Is it permitted to amortise the discount or premium on the forward exchange contract to profit or loss over the term of the contract?

No. The premium or discount on a forward exchange contract may not be amortised to profit or loss under IAS 39. Derivatives are always measured at fair value in the balance sheet. The gain or loss resulting from a change in the fair value of the forward exchange contract is always recognised in profit or loss unless the forward exchange contract is designated and effective as a hedging instrument in a cash flow hedge or in a hedge of a net investment in a foreign operation, in which case the effective portion of the gain or loss is recognised in other comprehensive income. In that case, the amounts recognised in other comprehensive income are reclassified from equity to profit or loss when the hedged future cash flows occur or on the disposal of the net investment, as appropriate. Under IAS 39.74(b), the interest element (time value) of the fair value of a forward may be excluded from the designated hedge relationship. In that case, changes in the interest element portion of the fair value of the forward exchange contract are recognised in profit or loss.

F.6.5 IAS 39 and IAS 21 – Fair value hedge of asset measured at cost

If the future sale of a ship carried at historical cost is hedged against the exposure to currency risk by foreign currency borrowing, does IAS 39 require the ship to be remeasured for changes in the exchange rate even though the basis of measurement for the asset is historical cost?

No. In a fair value hedge, the hedged item is remeasured. However, a foreign currency borrowing cannot be classified as a fair value hedge of a ship since a ship does not contain any separately measurable foreign currency risk. If the hedge accounting conditions in IAS 39.88 are met, the foreign currency borrowing may be classified as a cash flow hedge of an anticipated sale in that foreign currency. In a cash flow hedge, the hedged item is not remeasured.

To illustrate: a shipping entity in Denmark has a US subsidiary that has the same functional currency (the Danish krone). The shipping entity measures its ships at historical cost less depreciation in the consolidated financial statements. In accordance with IAS 21.23(b), the ships are recognised in Danish krone using the historical exchange rate. To hedge, fully or partly, the potential currency risk on the ships at disposal in US dollars, the shipping entity normally finances its purchases of ships with loans denominated in US dollars.

In this case, a US dollar borrowing (or a portion of it) may be designated as a cash flow hedge of the anticipated sale of the ship financed by the borrowing provided the sale is highly probable, for example, because it is expected to occur in the immediate future, and the amount of the sales proceeds designated as being hedged is equal to the amount of the foreign currency borrowing designated as the hedging instrument. The gains and losses on the currency borrowing that are determined to constitute an effective hedge of the anticipated sale are recognised in other comprehensive income in accordance with IAS 39.95(a).

SECTION G: OTHER

G.1 Disclosure of changes in fair value

IAS 39 requires financial assets classified as available for sale (AFS) and financial assets and financial liabilities at fair value through profit or loss to be remeasured to fair value. Unless a financial asset or a financial liability is designated as a cash flow hedging instrument, fair value changes for financial assets and financial liabilities at fair value through profit or loss are recognised in profit or loss, and fair value changes for AFS assets are recognised in other comprehensive income. What disclosures are required regarding the amounts of the fair value changes during a reporting period?

IAS 32.94(h) requires material items of income, expense and gains and losses to be disclosed whether included in profit or loss or in other comprehensive income. This disclosure requirement encompasses material items of income, expense and gains and losses that arise on remeasurement to fair value. Therefore, an entity provides disclosures of material fair value changes, distinguishing between changes that are recognised in profit or loss and changes that are recognised in other comprehensive income. Further breakdown is provided of changes that relate to:

(a) AFS assets;

(b) financial assets and financial liabilities at fair value through profit or loss; and

(c) hedging instruments.

IAS 32 neither requires nor prohibits disclosure of components of the change in fair value by the way items are classified for internal purposes. For example, an entity may choose to disclose separately the change in fair value of those derivatives that IAS 39 classifies as held for trading but the entity classifies as part of risk management activities outside the trading portfolio.

In addition, IAS 32.94(e) requires disclosure of the carrying amounts of financial assets and financial liabilities that: (i) are classified as held for trading and (ii) were, upon initial recognition, designated by the entity as financial assets and financial liabilities at fair value through profit or loss (ie those not financial instruments classified as held for trading).

Implementation guidance relating to IAS 39 extracted from IFRS 1 *First-time Application of International Financial Reporting Standards*

IG52 An entity recognises and measures all financial assets and financial liabilities in its opening IFRS balance sheet in accordance with IAS 39, except as specified in paragraphs 27-30 of the IFRS, which address derecognition and hedge accounting, and paragraph 36A, which permits an exemption from restating comparative information.

Recognition

IG53 An entity recognises all financial assets and financial liabilities (including all derivatives) that qualify for recognition under IAS 39 and have not yet qualified for derecognition under IAS 39, except non-derivative financial assets and nonderivative financial liabilities derecognised under previous GAAP before 1 January 2004, to which the entity does not choose to apply paragraph 27A (see paragraphs 27 and 27A of the IFRS). For example, an entity that does not apply paragraph 27A does not recognise assets transferred in a securitisation, transfer or other derecognition transaction that occurred before 1 January 2004 if those transactions qualified for derecognition under previous GAAP. However, if the entity uses the same securitisation arrangement or other derecognition arrangement for further transfers after 1 January 2004, those further transfers qualify for derecognition only if they meet the derecognition criteria of IAS 39.

IG54 An entity does not recognise financial assets and financial liabilities that do not qualify for recognition under IAS 39, or have already qualified for derecognition under IAS 39.

Embedded derivatives

IG55 When IAS 39 requires an entity to separate an embedded derivative from a host contract, the initial carrying amounts of the components at the date when the instrument first satisfies the recognition criteria in IAS 39 reflect circumstances at that date (IAS 39, paragraph 11). If the entity cannot determine the initial carrying amounts of the embedded derivative and host contract reliably, it treats the entire combined contract as a financial instrument held for trading (IAS 39, paragraph 12). This results in fair value measurement (except when the entity cannot determine a reliable fair value, see IAS 39, paragraph 46(c)), with changes in fair value recognised in profit or loss.

Measurement

IG56 In preparing its opening IFRS balance sheet, an entity applies the criteria in IAS 39 to identify those financial assets and financial liabilities that are measured at fair value and those that are measured at amortised cost. In particular:

(a) to comply with IAS 39, paragraph 51, classification of financial assets as heldto-maturity investments relies on a designation made by the entity in applying IAS 39 reflecting the entity's intention and ability at the date of transition to IFRSs. It follows that sales or transfers of held-to-maturity investments before the date of transition to IFRSs do not trigger the 'tainting' rules in IAS 39, paragraph 9.

(b) to comply with IAS 39, paragraph 9, the category of 'loans and receivables' refers to the circumstances when the financial asset first satisfied the recognition criteria in IAS 39.

(c) under IAS 39, paragraph 9, derivative financial assets and derivative financial liabilities are always deemed held for trading (except for a derivative that is a designated and effective hedging instrument). The result is that an entity measures all derivative financial assets and derivative financial liabilities at fair value.

(d) to comply with IAS 39, paragraph 50, an entity classifies a nonderivative financial asset or non-derivative financial liability in its opening IFRS balance sheet as at fair value through profit or loss if, and only if, the asset or liability was:

(i) acquired or incurred principally for the purpose of selling or repurchasing it in the near term;
(ii) at the date of transition to IFRSs, part of a portfolio of identified financial instruments that were managed together and for which there was evidence of a recent actual pattern of shortterm profit-taking; or
(iii) designated as at fair value through profit or loss at the date of transition to IFRS, for an entity that presents its first IFRS financial statements for an annual period beginning on or after 1 January 2006.
(iv) designated as at fair value through profit or loss at the start of its first IFRS reporting period, for an entity that presents its first IFRS financial statements for an annual period beginning before 1 January 2006 and applies paragraphs 11A, 48A, AG4B-AG4K, AG33A and AG33B and the 2005 amendments in paragraphs 9, 12 and 13 of IAS 39. If the entity restates comparative information for IAS 39 it shall restate the comparative information only if the financial assets or financial liabilities designated at the start of its first IFRS reporting period would have met the criteria for such designation in paragraph 9(b)(i), 9(b)(ii) or 11A of IAS 39 at the date of transition to IFRS or, if acquired after the date of transition to IFRSs, would have met the criteria in paragraph 9(b)(i), 9(b)(ii) or 11A at the date of initial recognition. For groups of financial assets, financial liabilities or both that are designated in accordance with paragraph 9(b)(ii) of IAS 39 at the start of the first IFRS reporting period, the comparative financial statements should be restated for all the financial assets and financial liabilities within the groups at the date of transition to IFRSs even if individual financial assets or liabilities within a group were derecognised during the comparative period.*

(e) to comply with IAS 39, paragraph 9, available-for-sale financial assets are those non-derivative financial assets that are designated as available for sale and those non-derivative financial assets that are not in any of the previous categories.

For those financial assets and financial liabilities measured at amortised cost in the opening IFRS balance sheet, an entity determines their cost on the basis of circumstances existing when the assets and liabilities first satisfied the recognition criteria in IAS 39. However, if the entity acquired those financial assets and financial liabilities in a past business combination, their carrying amount under previous GAAP immediately following the business combination is their deemed cost under IFRSs at that date (paragraph B2(e) of the IFRS). **IG57**

Editor's note: *Paragraph amended with effect from 1 January 2006.*

IG58 An entity's estimates of loan impairments at the date of transition to IFRSs are consistent with estimates made for the same date under previous GAAP (after adjustments to reflect any difference in accounting policies), unless there is objective evidence that those assumptions were in error (paragraph 31 of the IFRS). The entity treats the impact of any later revisions to those estimates as impairment losses (or, if the criteria in IAS 39 are met, reversals of impairment losses) of the period in which it makes the revisions.

Transition adjustments

IG58A An entity shall treat an adjustment to the carrying amount of a financial asset or financial liability as a transition adjustment to be recognised in the opening balance of retained earnings at the date of transition to IFRSs only to the extent that it results from adopting IAS 39. Because all derivatives, other than those that are designated and effective hedging instruments, are classified as held for trading, the differences between the previous carrying amount (which may have been zero) and the fair value of the derivatives are recognised as an adjustment of the balance of retained earnings at the beginning of the financial year in which IAS 39 is initially applied (other than for a derivative that is a designated and effective hedging instrument).

IG58B IAS 8 (as revised in 2003) applies to adjustments resulting from changes in estimates. If an entity is unable to determine whether a particular portion of the adjustment is a transition adjustment or a change in estimate, it treats that portion as a change in accounting estimate under IAS 8, with appropriate disclosures (IAS 8, paragraphs 32-40).

IG59 An entity may, under its previous GAAP, have measured investments at fair value and recognised the revaluation gain directly in equity. If an investment is classified as at fair value through profit or loss, the preIAS 39 revaluation gain that had been recognised in other comprehensive income is reclassified into retained earnings on initial application of IAS 39. If, on initial application of IAS 39, an investment is classified as available for sale, then the preIAS 39 revaluation gain is recognised in a separate component of equity. Subsequently, the entity recognises gains and losses on the availableforsale financial asset in that separate component of equity until the investment is impaired, sold, collected or otherwise disposed of. On subsequent derecognition or impairment of the available-for-sale financial asset, the entity transfers to profit or loss the cumulative gain or loss remaining in equity (IAS 39, paragraph 55(b)).

Hedge accounting

IG60 Paragraphs 28-30 of the IFRS deal with hedge accounting. The designation and documentation of a hedge relationship must be completed on or before the date of transition to IFRSs if the hedge relationship is to qualify for hedge accounting from that date. Hedge accounting can be applied prospectively only from the date that the hedge relationship is fully designated and documented.

IG60A An entity may, under its previous GAAP, have deferred or not recognised gains and losses on a fair value hedge of a hedged item that is not measured at fair value. For such a fair value hedge, an entity adjusts the carrying amount of the hedged item at the date of transition to IFRSs. The adjustment is the lower of:

(a) that portion of the cumulative change in the fair value of the hedged item that reflects the designated hedged risk and was not recognised under previous GAAP; and
(b) that portion of the cumulative change in the fair value of the hedging instrument that reflects the designated hedged risk and, under previous GAAP, was either (i) not recognised or (ii) deferred in the balance sheet as an asset or liability.

An entity may, under its previous GAAP, have deferred gains and losses on a cash flow hedge of a forecast transaction. If, at the date of transition to IFRSs, the hedged forecast transaction is not highly probable, but is expected to occur, the entire deferred gain or loss is recognised in other comprehensive income. Any net cumulative gain or loss that has been reclassified to equity on initial application of IAS 39 remains in equity until (a) the forecast transaction subsequently results in the recognition of a nonfinancial asset or non-financial liability, (b) the forecast transaction affects profit or loss or (c) subsequently circumstances change and the forecast transaction is no longer expected to occur, in which case any related net cumulative gain or loss that had been recognised in other comprehensive income is recognised in profit or loss. If the hedging instrument is still held, but the hedge does not qualify as a cash flow hedge under IAS 39, hedge accounting is no longer appropriate starting from the date of transition to IFRSs. **IG60B**

Financial Reporting Standard 27 'Life Assurance' is set out in paragraphs 1-67.

The Statement of Standard Accounting Practice, which comprises the paragraphs set in bold type, should be read in the context of the Objective as stated in paragraph 1 and the definitions set out in paragraph 2 and also of the Foreword to Accounting Standards and the Statement of Principles for Financial Reporting currently in issue.

The explanatory paragraphs contained in the FRS shall be regarded as part of the Statement of Standard Accounting Practice insofar as they assist in interpreting that statement.

Appendix IV 'The development of the FRS' reviews considerations and arguments that were thought significant by members of the Board in reaching the conclusions on the FRS.

FRS 27
Life assurance*

(Issued December 2004)

Contents

Paragraph

Summary

Financial Reporting Standard

Objective	**1**
Definitions	**2**
Scope	**3**
Life assurance liabilities and assets	**4-29**
Measurement of with-profits liabilities and related assets	4-21
Disclosure and presentation relating to with-profits business	22-25
Value of in-force life assurance business	26-29
Capital and liabilities	**30-60**
Capital statement	32-44
Disclosures relating to liabilities and capital	45-52
Disclosure of analysis of liabilities	53-54
Movements in capital	55-60
Date from which effective and transitional arrangements	**61-67**

Adoption of FRS 27 by the Board

Appendices

I Illustration of the Capital Statement

II Note on Legal Requirements

III Compliance with International Accounting Standards

IV The Development of the FRS

****Editor's note**: The matters covered in FRS 27 are not dealt with in FRS 102. They are expected to be dealt with in FRS 103.*

Summary

a Financial Reporting Standard 27 applies to all entities that have a life assurance business, including a life reinsurance business.

b For large UK with-profits life assurance businesses falling within the scope of the FSA's realistic capital regime, liabilities to policyholders are required by the FRS to be measured on the basis determined in accordance with that regime, subject to adjustments specified in the FRS. Further adjustments are made to related assets and deferred tax for consistency with the measurement of the realistic liabilities, and the resulting effect on profit and loss account is offset by a corresponding transfer to the fund for future appropriations or, in the case of a mutual, to retained surplus.

c For all entities within the scope of the FRS, the fund for future appropriations must be separately presented on the balance sheet and an explanation given of a negative FFA balance.

d The FRS restricts the recognition of the value of in-force business, but permits entities that currently recognise such value to continue to do so, subject to limitations on the way this value may be determined.

e A capital statement is required setting out the total available capital for sections of the life assurance business of the entity.

f The capital statement is required to be supported by information on regulatory capital requirements or management's capital targets, the basis of determining regulatory capital, the sensitivity of liabilities and capital to changes in market variables and key assumptions, and the entity's capital management policies.

g Information is also required to be disclosed on the assumptions used in the measurement of liabilities, and the terms and conditions of options and guarantees relating to life assurance contracts. For those liabilities to policyholders resulting from options and guarantees that are not measured at fair value or on a statistical basis that takes into account all possible outcomes of the option or guarantee, entities must provide additional information on the nature and extent of the options and guarantees and the possible liabilities that may arise.

h A movements table is also required to show the changes in capital from one reporting date to the next.

Financial Reporting Standard

OBJECTIVE

The objective of this FRS is to require appropriate measurement of, and disclosures relating to, liabilities and assets of life assurance business; and disclosures relating to the financial strength of entities carrying on life assurance business. 1

DEFINITIONS

The following definitions shall apply in the FRS and in particular in the Statement of Standard Accounting Practice set out in **bold type**. 2

The **Financial Services Authority (FSA) realistic capital regime** is that set out in section 7.4 of its integrated prudential sourcebook.*

The **realistic value of liabilities** is that element of the amount defined by rule 7.4.40 in the FSA's integrated prudential sourcebook, excluding current liabilities falling within the definition in rule 7.4.190 that are recognised separately on the entity's balance sheet.

An entity's **existing accounting policies** are the accounting policies adopted in its last annual financial statements before adoption of this FRS.

The **modified statutory solvency basis (MSSB)** for determining insurance liabilities is the statutory solvency basis adjusted, in accordance with the Statement of Recommended Practice of the Association of British Insurers (the ABI SORP), for the following items:

(a) to defer new business acquisition costs incurred where the benefit of such costs will be obtained in subsequent accounting periods; and

(b) to treat investment, resilience and similar reserves, or reserves held in respect of general contingencies or the specific contingency that the fund will be closed to new business, where such items are held within the long term business fund, as reserves rather than provisions. These are included, as appropriate, within shareholders' capital and reserves or the Fund for Future Appropriations.

The **statutory solvency basis** is the basis of determination of insurance liabilities in accordance with rule 7.4.27 of the FSA's integrated prudential sourcebook.

The **Principles and Practices of Financial Management (PPFM)** is the statement that the FSA requires each with-profits life fund to make available to its policyholders containing, inter alia, a description of the fund's investment management and bonus distribution policies.

The **Fund for Future Appropriations (FFA)** is the balance sheet item required by Schedule 9A to the Companies Act 1985 to comprise all funds the allocation of

References to the FSA's integrated prudential sourcebook for insurers, and to individual rules therein, are to the rules made on 18 November 2004 by the Integrated Prudential Sourcebook (Insurers and Other Amendments) Instrument 2004.* ***Editor's note:* *All references to the FSA should now be taken as references to the Financial Conduct Authority or Prudential Regulation Authority.*

which, either to policyholders or to shareholders, has not been determined by the end of the accounting period.*

Directive friendly societies and **non-directive friendly societies** are as defined in section 7 of the FSA Interim Prudential Sourcebook for Friendly Societies.

SCOPE

3 **The FRS applies to all financial statements that are intended to give a true and fair view of a reporting entity's financial position and profit and loss (or income and expenditure) for a period, where the reporting entity includes a business that is a life assurance business (including reinsurance business).**

LIFE ASSURANCE LIABILITIES AND ASSETS

Measurement of with-profits liabilities and related assets

4 **For with-profits life funds falling within the scope of the FSA realistic capital regime:**

(a) liabilities to policyholders arising from with-profits life assurance business shall be stated at the amount of the realistic value of liabilities adjusted to exclude the shareholders' share of projected future bonuses;

(b) acquisition costs shall not be deferred;

(c) reinsurance recoveries that are recognised shall be measured on a basis that is consistent with the value of the policyholder liabilities to which the reinsurance applies;

(d) an amount may be recognised for the present value of future profits on non-participating business written in a with-profits fund if:

(i) the non-participating business is measured on this basis for the purposes of the regulatory returns made under the FSA realistic capital regime;

(ii) the value is determined in accordance with the FSA regulations†; and

(iii) the determination of the realistic value of liabilities in that with-profits fund takes account, directly or indirectly, of this value;

(e) where a with-profits life fund has an interest in a subsidiary or associated entity that is valued for FSA regulatory purposes at an amount in excess of the net amounts included in the entity's consolidated accounts, an amount may be recognised representing this excess if the determination of the realistic value of liabilities to with-profits policyholders takes account of this value; and

(f) adjustments to reflect the consequential tax effects of (a) to (e) above shall be made.

Adjustments from the modified statutory solvency basis necessary to meet the above requirements, including the recognition of an amount in accordance with paragraph 4(d) or 4(e), shall be included in the profit and loss account. An amount equal and opposite to the net amount of these adjustments shall be transferred to or from the FFA (or, in the case of a mutual, its retained surplus) and also included in the profit and loss account.

5 **Amounts recognised under paragraph 4(d) or 4(e) shall be presented in one of the following ways:**

****Editor's note:*** *Schedule 9A to the Companies Act 1985 is to be replaced, for accounting periods beginning on or after 6 April 2008, with Schedule 3 to the Large and Medium-sized Companies and Groups (Accounts and Reports) Regulations 2008 (SI 2008/410).*

†*FSA rule PRU 7.4.37.*

(a) Where it is possible to apportion the amount recognised under paragraph 4(d) or 4(e) between an amount relating to liabilities to policyholders and an amount relating to the FFA, these portions shall be presented in the balance sheet as a deduction in arriving at the amount of liabilities to policyholders and the FFA respectively.

(b) Where it is not possible to make a reasonably approximate apportionment of the amount recognised under paragraph 4(d) or 4(e), the amount shall be presented on the balance sheet as a separate item deducted from a sub-total of liabilities to policyholders and the FFA.

(c) Where the presentation under 5(a) or 5(b) does not comply with statutory requirements for balance sheet presentation applying to the entity, the amount recognised under paragraph 4(d) or 4(e) shall be recognised as an asset.

The established accounting treatment for UK life assurance business is to measure liabilities for policyholder benefits on the modified statutory solvency basis (MSSB). The FRS does not require any change to the accounting for those funds not within the scope of the FSA realistic capital regime, but requires those UK with-profits funds that fall under that regime to use the realistic value of liabilities as the basis for the estimated value of the liabilities to be included in the financial statements. Where the entity's returns to the FSA have not been completed at the time of completion of the financial statements, an estimate of the amount may be used provided it is in accordance with the FSA regulations. **6**

An entity may, but is not required to, adopt the requirements of paragraph 4 for UK* with-profits funds that do not fall within the scope of the FSA realistic capital regime or for which the FSA has granted a full waiver from compliance with this regime. **7**

Overseas insurance businesses that do not fall within the FSA's regulatory remit may determine insurance liabilities in accordance with local regulatory and accounting requirements. Adjustments on consolidation may be made to take account of the different bases of reporting, although insurance entities are exempt from the requirement in the Companies Act 1985† applicable to other businesses to adjust amounts recognised in the financial statements of subsidiary undertakings onto a consistent basis for the purposes of consolidated financial statements. The FRS does not require any change to the accounting treatment of the liabilities of overseas businesses, but voluntary adoption of the requirements of paragraph 4 is permitted. **8**

Liabilities determined in accordance with the FSA realistic capital regime include, in addition to amounts attributable to declared bonuses, amounts in respect of future bonuses, estimated in accordance with the entity's published Principles and Practices of Financial Management and representing a constructive obligation to policyholders. A liability is also included for policyholders' options and guarantees, measured at fair value or estimated using a stochastic model that has been calibrated to give market-consistent estimates of option and guarantee values. **9**

An adjustment is made to the realistic value of liabilities to exclude the portion attributed to shareholders, which represents the shareholders' share of future bonuses. Similar adjustments should be made if other amounts due to shareholders would otherwise be included in the realistic value of liabilities. **10**

**and Republic of Ireland with-profits funds*

†*and equivalent Republic of Ireland and Northern Ireland legislation*

11 Acquisition costs are deferred under MSSB to offset the effects of 'new business strain', being the requirement to establish liabilities on a statutory solvency basis on inception of a policy in excess of the premiums received. When liabilities are restated in accordance with the FSA realistic capital regime, there is no longer any justification for treating such costs as an asset. The FRS does not alter the treatment of deferred acquisition costs relating to business outside the scope of the FSA realistic capital regime (other than adjustments that may be made to deferred acquisition costs relating to business for which the value of in-force business is recognised under paragraph 4(d) or (e)).

12 Amounts recoverable under reinsurance contracts relating to life assurance shall be measured on a basis consistent with the measurement of the related liability, so that the net amount reflects the exposure of the entity. Changing the measurement of the liability may therefore give rise to a change in the related reinsurance asset. The amount of the change in the asset will depend on the terms of the reinsurance contract.

13 Under the FSA realistic capital regime, a with-profits life fund includes within assets the value of future profits expected to arise from non-participating business (ie life assurance policies that do not have a with-profits feature, such as term assurance, annuities and unit-linked policies) that form part of the with-profits fund—sometimes referred to as the value of in-force business. In the FSA realistic capital regime, this value is also taken into account in determining the returns earned by the fund and its financial strength, and thus gives rise to an increase in the estimated value of future bonuses included in the realistic value of liabilities, although there is not necessarily a direct link between the value of in-force business and the additional amount included in liabilities. To exclude from the balance sheet the value of in-force business whilst recognising the realistic value of liabilities in full, and valuing non-participating liabilities on a statutory basis, would give rise to an inconsistency in the fund's net assets. An entity is therefore permitted to recognise the value of in-force business if that business has been taken into account in measuring the liability, in the circumstances of paragraph 4(d), even though there is not a direct link between the value of the asset and the amount of the liabilities. Where there is not a direct link between the value of the business and the amount of realistic liabilities, but the value is taken into account in determining those liabilities, it is appropriate to recognise the total value of the business. Although not separately identifiable, any excess value over that included in realistic liabilities will be taken to the FFA. Paragraph 4(d) applies only to non-participating business written in a with-profits fund and not to such business outside a with-profits fund.

14 The amount recognised under paragraph 4(d) or 4(e) may be regarded either as an additional asset, representing the value of future cash flows from the related insurance business; or as an adjustment to the measurement of liabilities and the FFA, being the deduction from these items of the obligation to transfer an unrecognised asset or other source of value. The FRS requires entities to adopt the latter interpretation, unless this would not be in compliance with the statutory requirements that apply to the entity, in which case it permits the amount to be recognised as an asset. Where the amount is treated as an adjustment to a liability, the FRS requires an entity to apportion, if practicable, the amount between the amounts that have been taken into account in the measurement of liabilities and other amounts that should be shown as an adjustment to the FFA. Where this is not practicable, the amount recognised should be shown as an adjustment to a sub-total of the FFA and liabilities to policyholders.

15 The value of in-force non-participating business recognised within assets for regulatory purposes as described in paragraph 13 is determined as the discounted value of future profits expected to arise from the policies, taking into account liabilities

relating to the policies measured on a statutory solvency basis. When adjustments are made onto an MSSB basis for the purposes of the financial statements (for example, to adjust liabilities to exclude certain additional reserves included in the liabilities for regulatory purposes, or where future income included in the value of in-force business covers deferred acquisition costs included in the MSSB balance sheet), a corresponding adjustment to the value of in-force policies will need to be made in order to ensure a consistent valuation.

A similar situation may arise where an entity chooses to value an interest in a subsidiary that is held directly in the with-profits fund at a value that includes the value of in-force business within the subsidiary in addition to its net asset value, as permitted by the FSA regulations. In such a case, the value taken into account in determining the realistic value of liabilities is greater than the net assets included in the consolidated accounts. To exclude from the balance sheet the additional value of the investment in the subsidiary whilst recognising the realistic value of liabilities in full would result in an inconsistency in the fund's net assets. An entity is therefore permitted to recognise the excess of the market value of the subsidiary over the net amounts included in the consolidated financial statements as a deduction from the sub-total of the FFA and liabilities to policyholders in the same way as the value of in-force business described in paragraph 13. **16**

Where the amounts on a 'realistic' basis determined in accordance with paragraph 4 above are different from the amounts on a modified statutory solvency basis, a corresponding amount is transferred to or from the FFA, so that there is no effect on shareholders' funds. However, individual lines in the revenue (technical) account, including the line item for transfers to or from the FFA, will be affected. The potential shareholders' share corresponding to additional bonuses to policyholders that have been included in the policyholders' liability should be accounted for in the FFA. As a result, there will generally be no change in the profit for the financial year and, in the case of an entity that is not a mutual, generally no change to shareholders' funds. However, this will not be the case where the adjustments result in a negative balance on the FFA and the entity determines that this negative balance should result in a deduction from shareholders' funds through the profit and loss account. **17**

In the case of a mutual, which has no shareholders, an FFA or retained surplus account is maintained that represents amounts that have not yet been allocated to specific policyholders. For such entities, the adjustments required by paragraph 4 will be offset within the profit and loss account by a transfer directly to or from this FFA or retained surplus account, with the result that overall profit or loss for the year will be unchanged. **18**

Policyholders' options and guarantees

Entities with with-profits funds within the scope of the FSA's realistic capital regime are required to measure the liability of those funds in respect of options and guarantees relating to policyholders either at fair value or at an amount estimated using a market-consistent stochastic model in accordance with FSA regulations. **19**

For all life assurance businesses, the best basis for measuring policyholders' options and guarantees is one that includes their time value*. Any deterministic approach to **20**

**The value of an option or guarantee comprises two elements, the intrinsic value and the time value. The intrinsic value is the amount that would be payable if the option or guarantee were exercised immediately – that is, the amount it is currently 'in the money', or nil if it is 'out of the money'. The time value is the additional value that reflects the possibility of the intrinsic value increasing in future, before the expiry date of the option or guarantee.*

valuation of a policy with a guarantee or optionality feature will generally fail to deal appropriately with the time value of the option. In order to capture this time value it is necessary to use stochastic modelling techniques to evaluate the range of potential outcomes unless a market value for the option is available. The FSA realistic capital regime includes a requirement to value options and guarantees on this basis. For the liabilities of businesses not falling within the scope of the FSA realistic capital regime, entities are encouraged, but not required, to adopt these valuation techniques. Where options are not valued on this basis, additional disclosures are required; these are set out in paragraph 48(c).

21 Under the FSA realistic capital regime, a market-consistent stochastic method for estimating the value of guarantees and options involves:

(a) determining the market variables whose value will affect the additional amount payable under the guarantee or option, and the period in which they have such effect;
(b) determining the likely distribution of each of those variables within that time period, using assumptions calibrated to market observations;
(c) constructing a large number of possible scenarios combining different changes in each variable over the time period, reflecting the expected distribution of values determined in accordance with (b);
(d) evaluating the additional amounts payable under the option or guarantee under each scenario; and
(e) combining these, weighted according to the probability of each scenario occurring, to determine the expected value of the liability.

In determining the amount payable under each scenario, the entity will take into account management actions it anticipates would be taken in response to variations in market variables (such as changing the balance of the investment portfolio between debt instruments and equity, varying the amount charged to policyholders, or varying its bonus policy) that will affect the amount payable under the guarantee or option. Such actions must be realistically capable of being implemented within the time-scale assumed in the scenario analysis, and be consistent with the entity's published Principles and Practice of Financial Management.

Disclosure and presentation relating to with-profits business

22 **Entities shall present the FFA on the balance sheet separately from technical provisions and other liabilities.**

23 **Where the balance on the FFA of a with-profits life fund is negative, as a result of the transfer made in accordance with paragraph 4 or otherwise, the entity shall include in the notes to the financial statements an explanation of the nature of the negative balance and the circumstances in which it arose, and why no action to eliminate it has been considered necessary.**

24 The FFA should be disclosed separately on the balance sheet, and not combined with technical provisions. Entities that consolidate interests in a life assurance entity on a basis that combines the FFA and technical provisions into a single amount of liabilities to policyholders are required to show these elements separately.

25 A negative balance on the FFA may arise, either under MSSB or as a result of adjustments made under paragraph 4. Sometimes this will result in the entity taking action that results in the elimination of the negative balance. Where no such action has been considered necessary, details of the negative balance are required by paragraph 23, including an explanation of why the entity considers it appropriate not

to take action to eliminate this balance. Where an entity has more than one with-profits fund, a negative balance on the FFA in one fund should not be offset against a positive balance in another.

Value of in-force life assurance business

Where, other than under paragraph 4(d) or 4(e) above, an entity's existing accounting policies include the recognition of the value of in-force life assurance business as an asset (or as a deduction from a liability), it may continue to recognise such an item as an asset, but shall exclude from the value of that asset any value of in-force policies that reflects future investment margins. 26

Banking and other non-insurance entities with insurance subsidiaries* sometimes account for the insurance business in their consolidated financial statements on an embedded value or similar basis under which, in addition to the value of the retained surplus in the insurance subsidiary, an asset is recognised for the discounted value of the future profit to shareholders expected to arise from existing insurance business. The FRS permits the continuation of such a practice only if the existing policy is amended, if necessary, to exclude from the measurement of the value of the in-force business any value attributable to future investment margins. Investment margins are the amounts by which assumed investment returns exceed the risk-free return on assets. As a consequence of excluding these margins, the embedded value will not vary with the choice of assets in which the fund is invested (ignoring different tax treatments of various types of asset). An example of an accounting policy that reflects those margins, and is not permitted under the FRS, is projecting the returns on the insurer's assets at an estimated rate of return in excess of the risk-free rate, discounting those projected returns at a lower rate and including the result as part of the measurement of the value of in-force business. 27

No value shall be attributed to in-force life assurance business other than: 28

(a) in accordance with paragraphs 4(d), 4(e) or 26 above; or

(b) amounts recognised as an intangible asset as part of the allocation of fair values under acquisition accounting in accordance with FRS 7 'Fair Values in Acquisition Accounting', which are subject to the measurement requirements of that standard and not paragraph 26 above.

Where the value attributable to in-force life assurance business recognised under paragraph 26 or paragraph 28(b) includes an amount in relation to non-participating business for which the entity also recognises an amount under paragraph 4(d) or 4(e), the amount recognised under paragraph 4(d) or 4(e) shall be reduced to exclude the amount that is included in relation to that business under paragraph 26 or paragraph 28(b). 29

CAPITAL AND LIABILITIES

An entity shall present quantitative and narrative disclosures of its regulatory capital position, as set out below. 30

An entity is not required to include the disclosures required by paragraphs 32 to 47 and 53 to 60 if it is: 31

(a) a subsidiary undertaking where 90 per cent or more of the voting rights are controlled within the group; or

and insurance entities and groups in the Republic of Ireland.

(b) a parent entity, in relation to its individual financial statements

provided the entity is included in publicly available group financial statements which provide information on a group basis complying with the FRS.

Capital statement

32 **An entity shall present a statement setting out its total capital resources relating to life assurance business. The statement shall show, for each section of that business as defined in paragraph 34:**

(a) shareholders' funds (or in the case of a mutual, the equivalent, often described as disclosed surplus);
(b) adjustments to restate these amounts in accordance with regulatory requirements;
(c) each additional component of capital included for regulatory purposes, including capital retained within a life fund whether attributable to shareholders, policyholders or not yet allocated between shareholders and policyholders; and
(d) the total capital available to meet regulatory capital requirements.

33 Available capital will comprise a number of distinct elements, each of which will be separately disclosed, including:

(a) shareholders' funds as included in the published balance sheet, represented by surplus held within a life fund or by assets held separately from those of the fund itself;
(b) amounts that are wholly attributable to shareholders, but held within a life fund and where the distribution out of the fund is restricted by regulatory or other considerations;
(c) surplus held in life funds that has yet to be attributed or allocated between shareholders and policyholders (in the case of a mutual all such surplus is attributable to policyholders but is not treated as a liability); and
(d) qualifying debt capital, whether issued by the life entity itself or by another entity within the group.

34 **The capital statement shall show as separate sections:**

(a) each UK* with-profits life fund that is material to the group; and
(b) the entity's other life assurance business, showing the extent to which the various components of capital are subject to constraints such that they are available to meet requirements in only part of the entity's business, or are available to meet risks and regulatory capital requirements in all parts of the business.

35 The purpose of the capital statement is to set out the financial strength of the entity and to provide an analysis of the disposition and constraints over the availability of the capital to meet risks and regulatory requirements. It is particularly important to show the various sources of capital separately and the extent to which the capital in each section is subject to constraint as to its ability to meet requirements in other parts of the entity. Such constraints can arise for any of the following reasons:

(a) ownership—the capital may be subject to specific ownership considerations (for example, the FFA of a UK with-profits fund, for which the allocation between policyholders and shareholders has not been determined);
(b) regulatory—local regulatory limitations may require the maintenance of solvency margins in particular funds or countries; or

**or, for an entity in the Republic of Ireland, each with-profits fund in the Republic of Ireland.*

(c) financial—the availability of capital in certain cases can be restricted due to the imposition of taxes or other financial penalty in the event of the capital being required to be redeployed across the group.

An entity must consider how best to present information to meet the requirements of paragraph 34(b) in the particular circumstances of its own business. For example, those requirements might be met by sub-analysis of the part of the entity's life assurance business, other than the UK with-profit life funds, into two sections in the statement, one including amounts of capital that are constrained and the other amounts that are freely available to meet risks and regulatory capital requirements in all parts of the business. Alternatively, this information could be presented by means of a sub-analysis by the nature of the capital constraints applying to each business unit: one section in the capital statement would include those business units where there were no constraints on transferring surplus capital to other parts of the group, and another section in the statement would include those business units where surplus capital was constrained. Under either approach, the information would need to be supplemented by narrative explaining the nature and effect of the constraints. Where the capital constraints are more complex, it may be necessary to add additional sections in the capital statement providing further analysis of the different types of constraint that apply. Another way of meeting this requirement would be to provide aggregated information supplemented by fuller narrative disclosure of the constraints and their effect. **36**

The aggregate amount of regulatory capital resources included in the capital statement shall be reconciled to the shareholders' funds, FFA and other amounts shown in the entity's balance sheet, showing separately for each component of capital the amount relating to the entity's business other than life assurance. Where such other business is significant, an explanation shall be given of the extent to which this capital can be used to meet the requirements of the life assurance business. **37**

Although the detailed requirements apply to life assurance business, entities will need to incorporate information on other parts of the business, together with consolidation adjustments, in order to demonstrate how the aggregated capital attributed to the life assurance business reconciles to the total shown in the consolidated balance sheet, and the extent to which capital outside the life assurance business may be made available to meet the capital requirements of the life assurance business. This reconciliation applies to each different type of capital shown in the capital statement. **38**

Where the reporting entity is a subsidiary undertaking, narrative supporting the capital statement shall explain the extent to which the capital of the entity is able to be transferred to the parent or fellow subsidiaries, or the extent to which it is required to be retained within the reporting entity. **39**

For life funds within the scope of the FSA realistic capital regime, in determining available capital, liabilities will be taken into account at their 'realistic' amount (unless the capital requirement is higher on the regulatory basis). Further adjustments are necessary to adjust the capital shown in the balance sheet to the amount for regulatory purposes. The most significant differences are: **40**

(a) the inclusion in capital of the fund for future appropriations;
(b) the exclusion from capital of the shareholders' share of accrued bonus;
(c) the exclusion of goodwill and other intangible assets, such as an amount attributed to the acquired value of in-force business; and
(d) changes to the valuation of assets and the exclusion of certain non-admissible assets for regulatory purposes, for example any regulatory adjustment to a pension fund deficit that is recognised as a liability.

Disclosure of these adjustments should be sufficient to give a clear picture of the capital position from a regulatory perspective and its relationship to the shareholders' funds shown in the consolidated balance sheet.

41 **Where the amount of a capital instrument that qualifies for inclusion as regulatory capital is restricted (for example, where a limited percentage of total regulatory capital may be in the form of debt) the full amount of the instrument shall be included, with a separate deduction for the amount in excess of the restriction.**

42 **Disclosure shall be made of any formal intra-group arrangements to provide capital to particular funds or business units, including intra-group loans and contingent arrangements. Where the reporting entity is a subsidiary undertaking, disclosure shall also be made of similar arrangements between the entity and its parent or fellow subsidiary undertakings.**

43 Regulatory capital can include both shareholders' funds and surplus within the fund. Such surplus may be wholly attributable to shareholders, or form part of the fund that has not yet been appropriated and allocated between shareholders and policyholders. In a mutual fund, all surplus is attributable to policyholders. Debt instruments qualifying as capital may also be issued from the fund itself, or may form part of the shareholders' net assets outside the life fund; and a debt instrument issued by the fund to the shareholders may effectively transfer capital from the shareholders to the fund. Separate disclosure of each class of capital is important to an understanding of the funding of the business and the way any future losses would be absorbed or new business financed.

44 Intra-group arrangements should be included in the regulatory capital of a section only where they are subject to formal arrangements. Where capital in other parts of a group is available to meet the requirements of a particular section of the business, but no formal arrangement has been entered into to do so, no allocation of this capital to the section of the business should be shown in the capital position statement.

Disclosures relating to liabilities and capital

45 **The capital statement shall be supported by the following disclosures:**

(a) narrative or quantified information on the regulatory capital requirements applying to each section of the business shown in the capital statement, or on the capital targets set by management for that section;

(b) narrative disclosure of the basis of determining regulatory capital and the corresponding regulatory capital requirements and any major inconsistencies in this basis between the different sections of the business;

(c) narrative disclosure addressing the sensitivity of liabilities and the components of total capital to changes in market conditions, key assumptions and other variables, and assumptions about future management actions in response to changes in market conditions; and

(d) narrative disclosure of the entity's capital management policies and objectives, and its approach to managing the risks that would affect the capital position.

46 Although the capital statement itself deals only with capital available to meet regulatory requirements, the narrative discussion should address both this and the related regulatory requirements. Narrative explanation of the capital position, setting out its capital management objectives and risk management policies and the sensitivity to changes in assumptions, is important to the user's ability to understand the management of capital by the entity, its financial adaptability in changing circumstances, and the resources available to each group of policyholders.

Narrative discussion of sensitivity to changes in market conditions, assumptions and other variables is required to address both liabilities, including options and guarantees given to policyholders, and the components of total capital. Measurement of liabilities, including options and guarantees, may be determined using stochastic methods that take into account actions that are assumed would be taken by management in response to changes in market conditions. Incorporating management actions in this way can substantially alter the value of liabilities and disclosure of the effect of changes in such assumptions is required. In relation to UK life funds, management actions that are taken into account should be consistent with those disclosed in the life fund's Principles and Practices of Financial Management available to policyholders. **47**

In relation to life assurance liabilities, the entity shall include the following additional information: **48**

(a) the process used to determine the assumptions that have the greatest effect on the measurement of liabilities including options and guarantees and, where practicable, quantified disclosure of those assumptions;

(b) those terms and conditions of options and guarantees relating to life assurance contracts that could in aggregate have a material effect on the amount, timing and uncertainty of the entity's future cash flows; and

(c) information about exposures to interest rate risk or market risk under options and guarantees if the entity does not measure these at fair value or at an amount estimated using a market-consistent stochastic model.

It may be relatively easy to quantify some assumptions that are used in the measurement of liabilities – for example, discount rates or general inflation, where the rate used should be disclosed. For other assumptions, such as mortality tables, it may not be practicable to disclose quantified assumptions because there are too many, or they cannot be expressed as single values, in which case it is more important to describe the process used to generate the assumptions. The description of the process would include the objective – whether a best-estimate or a given level of assurance is intended; the sources of data; whether assumptions are consistent with observable market data or other published information; how past experience, current conditions and future trends are taken into account; correlations between different assumptions; management's policy for future bonuses; and the nature and extent of uncertainties affecting the assumptions. **49**

Options and guarantees are features of life assurance contracts that confer potentially valuable guarantees underlying the level or nature of policyholder benefits, or options to change these benefits exercisable at the discretion of the policyholder. For the purposes of this FRS, the term is used to refer only to those options and guarantees whose potential value is affected by the behaviour of financial variables, and not to those features of life assurance contracts where the potential changes in policyholder benefits arise solely from insurance risk (including mortality and morbidity), or from changes in the entity's creditworthiness. It includes a financial guarantee or option that applies if a policy lapses, but does not include the option to surrender or allow a policy to lapse. **50**

The requirements of 48(c) will require, for options and guarantees that are not measured at fair value or at an amount estimated using a market-consistent stochastic model, the following disclosures: **51**

(a) a description of the nature and extent of the options and guarantees;

(b) the basis of measurement for the amount at which these options and guarantees are stated, and the extent to which an amount is included for the additional payment that may arise under the option or guarantee in excess of the amounts

expected to be paid under the relevant policies if they did not include the option or guarantee feature;

(c) the main variables that determine the amount payable under the option or guarantee; and

(d) information on the potential effects of adverse changes in those market conditions that affect the entity's obligations under options and guarantees.

52 The requirement of 51(d) may be met by disclosing:

(a) for options and guarantees that would result in additional payments to policyholders if current asset values and market rates continued unchanged (ie those that are 'in the money'), an indication of the change in these amounts if the variables moved adversely by a stated amount;

(b) for options and guarantees that would result in additional payments to policyholders only if there was an adverse change in current asset values and market rates (ie those that are 'out of the money'):

(i) an indication of the change in these variables, from current levels, which would cause material amounts to become payable under the options and guarantees; and

(ii) an indication of the amount that would result from a specified adverse change in these variables from the levels at which amounts first become payable under the options and guarantees.

The above disclosures may be made in aggregate for classes of options and guarantees that do not differ materially, or which are not individually material.

Disclosure of analysis of liabilities

53 The capital statement shall show the amount of policyholder liabilities attributed to each section of the business shown in the statement, analysed between:

(a) with-profits business;

(b) unit-linked business;

(c) other life assurance business; and

(d) insurance business accounted for as financial instruments in accordance with the requirements of FRS 26 (IAS 39) 'Financial Instruments: Measurement'.

The total of these policyholder liabilities shall be the amounts shown in the entity's balance sheet.

54 The relationship between capital requirements and policyholder liabilities for each fund or business unit provides additional information on the interrelationship between the capital position and the extent of liabilities.

Movements in capital

55 An entity shall include an explanation of the movements in the total amount of available capital for life assurance business shown in the capital statement with the corresponding amounts at the end of the previous accounting period. This disclosure shall cover individually each UK life fund* that is separately shown in the capital statement required under paragraph 32, and other life assurance business in aggregate.

56 This disclosure shall set out in tabular form the effect of changes resulting from:

**or, for an entity in the Republic of Ireland, each life fund in the Republic of Ireland.*

(a) changes in assumptions used to measure life assurance liabilities, showing separately the effect of each change in an assumption that has had a material effect on the group;
(b) changes in management policy;
(c) changes in regulatory requirements and similar external developments; and
(d) new business and other factors, describing any material items.

An understanding of the underlying causes of changes in the capital position is valuable, giving an insight into the development of the entity's life assurance business. It is important to separate movements relating to changes in assumptions and management policy from other movements arising from the business. Those other movements might arise from changing market prices affecting assets and liabilities and movements resulting from surrenders, lapses and maturities of existing policies and new business written, and would be identified, where material, in accordance with paragraph 56(d). **57**

The movements analysis distinguishes between assumption changes, changes in management policy, and other factors. Changes in management policy relate to significant changes in the management of the fund such as changes in investment policy or changes in the use of the estate. Where management actions are clearly directly related to changes in assumptions or other factors, it will be appropriate to show the net impact but the narrative should discuss the constituent factors. An example might be the combined effect of a reduced level of bonuses assumed as a result of a reduction in the assumed level of future investment return and a reduction in investment returns earned in the period. **58**

Although it is important to explain all movements in liabilities and capital during the period that are material to the group, this does not imply that the impact of each assumption change needs to be shown separately. Where there is a common cause for the change of assumption the impact can be grouped together. As an example, the impact of changes in investment return attributable to changing market circumstances does not need to be broken down between the various classes of investment. **59**

Determination of the effect of assumption changes involves considerable recalculation of valuations using both old and new assumptions and, particularly in the case of option and guarantee models, this may result in impracticable demands on computer systems. This is especially so in the first year of applying the FRS, when the FSA realistic valuation methodology is relatively new and untried, and estimation and approximation methods for analysing and explaining movements for management purposes are in the early stages of development. Accordingly, less detailed analysis of changes, and less quantification of movements, may be expected in the first year of applying the FRS as a result of these practical difficulties; paragraph 66 permits entities to present this information in non-tabular form for an accounting period ending before 23 December 2006. **60**

DATE FROM WHICH EFFECTIVE AND TRANSITIONAL ARRANGEMENTS

Subject to paragraphs 62 and 63, the accounting practices set out in the FRS shall be regarded as standard for financial statements relating to accounting periods ending on or after 23 December 2005. Earlier adoption of all or part of the FRS is permitted. **61**

Entities that are directive friendly societies and are not within the scope of the FSA realistic capital regime are not required to apply the FRS for accounting periods ending before 23 December 2006. **62**

63 **Entities that are non-directive friendly societies are not required to apply the FRS for accounting periods ending before 23 December 2007.**

64 **Changes in accounting policy resulting from the adoption of the FRS shall be accounted for by restating prior periods in accordance with FRS 3 'Reporting Financial Performance', except that comparatives in the profit and loss account need not be restated for changes arising from the adoption of a new accounting policy in accordance with paragraph 4 where this is not practicable.**

65 For those entities that adopt the measurement requirements of paragraph 4, including adoption of the realistic value of liabilities as the basis of measurement, or adoption of stochastic methods for the measurement of options and guarantees, it may not be practicable to restate profit and loss account comparatives for the first year of adoption. Accordingly, the FRS permits such comparatives not to be restated. FRS 18 'Accounting Policies' sets out requirements for disclosures relating to changes in accounting policies.

66 **For accounting periods ending before 23 December 2006, an entity is not required to set out the analysis of movements in tabular form as required by paragraph 56, but should include quantified disclosure of changes where practicable. The narrative disclosure required by paragraph 55 should address the movements as categorised in paragraph 56. For the first accounting period for which a table of movements is presented, comparatives for the previous period are not required.**

67 Comparatives should be disclosed for the capital position statement, for the table of movements in the capital position and for the related disclosures. However, this may not be practicable in the case of the movements table for the first accounting period in which the FRS comes into effect. Accordingly, such disclosure is not required for that period, although it is encouraged if information is available.

Adoption of FRS 27 by the Board

Financial Reporting Standard 27 *Life Assurance* was approved for issue by the nine members of the Accounting Standards Board.

Ian Mackintosh	Chairman
Andrew Lennard	Technical Director
Michael Ashley	
Douglas Flint	
Anthony Good	
Roger Marshall	
Isobel Sharp	
Jonathan Symonds	
Peter Westlake	

Appendix I
Illustration of the Capital Statement

The following illustration of a capital statement and its supporting narrative is provided for general guidance only and does not form part of the FRS. It is intended to show a possible format for the capital statement, but is not intended to imply that this is the only form such a statement could take. Entities will need to consider the format for the statement that best meets their individual circumstances.

Available capital resources	A UK (with-profits)	B UK (with-profits)	UK non-participating	Overseas	Life Business Shareholders' Funds	TOTAL LIFE BUSINESS	Other Activities	Consol. adjusts.	GROUP TOTAL
Shareholders' funds outside fund					850	850	200	(50)	1,000
Shareholders' funds held in fund			350			350			350
Total shareholders' funds			**350**		**850**	**1,200**	**200**	**(50)**	**1,350**
Adjustments onto regulatory basis:									
FFA	350	150				500			500
Adjustment to assets	(25)	(20)				(45)			(45)
Shareholders' share in realistic liabilities	(25)	(30)				(55)			(55)
Other adjustments									
	300	100	350		850	1,600	200	(50)	1,750
Other qualifying capital:									
Loan capital							750		750
Internal loans		150			(150)				
Allocation of group capital		300		300	(600)				
Total available capital resources	**300**	**550**	**350**	**300**	**100**	**1,600**	**950**	**(50)**	**2,500**

With-profits liabilities on realistic basis:						
Options and guarantees	200	100				300
Other policyholder obligations	1,800	4,000		1,900		7,700
Total with-profits liabilities	**2,000**	**4,100**		**1,900**		**8,000**
Unit-linked	1,000	100	500	800		2,300
Non-participating life assurance	800	400	1,400	500		3,100
Technical provisions in balance sheet	**3,800**	**4,500**	**1,900**	**3,200**		**13,400**

The following paragraphs illustrate the explanation of the regulatory capital requirements required by paragraph 45(a) and (b), together with the analysis of liabilities required by paragraph 53. Further details of the determination of the regulatory capital position, including discussion of the sensitivity to changes in assumptions and management's policies and objectives, would need to be included to meet the requirements of paragraph 45(c) and (d) of the FRS.

The Group has two UK with-profit funds, A and B, shown separately in the capital position statement. The Group's UK non-participating business is shown in aggregate. The Group's overseas life businesses are also aggregated for the purposes of the statement.

For the Group's two UK with-profit funds the available capital is determined in accordance with the 'realistic balance sheet' regime prescribed by the FSA's regulations, under which liabilities to policyholders include both declared bonuses and the constructive obligation for future bonuses not yet declared. The available capital resources include an estimate of the value of their respective estates, included as part of the FFA. The estate represents the surplus in the fund that is in excess of any constructive obligation to policyholders. The allocation of the estate between policyholders and shareholders has not been determined. It represents capital resources of the individual with-profits fund to which it relates and is available to meet regulatory and other solvency requirements of the fund and, in certain circumstances, additional liabilities that may arise.

For these with-profit funds, the liabilities included in the balance sheet include only amounts relating to policyholders and do not include the amount representing the shareholders' share of future bonuses. However, the shareholders' share is treated as a deduction from capital that is available to meet regulatory requirements and is therefore shown as a separate adjustment in the capital statement.

Shareholders' funds held outside the life funds and overseas businesses are shown separately in the capital statement. In the case of Fund B and certain overseas funds the capital requirements are met in part from centrally-held Group capital, by means of internal loans, contingent loans and share capital. To the extent that this support is made under a formal arrangement, it is shown as an allocation of Group capital between the sections of the statement.

The total available capital resources for each section of the statement shows the capital on a regulatory basis that is available to meet the regulatory capital requirements of that part of the business, and the targets for the surplus capital management regards as appropriate protection against future adverse changes in circumstances. Such capital is generally subject to restrictions as to its availability to meet requirements that arise elsewhere in the Group. The principal restrictions are:

(a) *UK with-profits funds A and B* – the available surplus held in the fund can only be applied to meet the requirements of the fund itself or be distributed to policyholders and shareholders. Shareholders are entitled to an amount not exceeding one ninth of the amount distributed to policyholders in the form of bonuses, and the shareholders' share of distributions would also be subject to a tax charge.

(b) *UK non-participating funds* – the available surplus held in the fund is attributable to shareholders and, subject to meeting the regulatory requirements of these businesses, this capital is available to meet requirements elsewhere in the Group. Any transfer of the surplus would give rise to a tax charge.

(c) *Overseas businesses* – these include several smaller participating and non-participating businesses. In all cases the available capital resources are subject to local regulatory restrictions which restrict management's ability to redeploy these amounts in other parts of the Group and in most cases such transfers would also give rise to a tax charge. Because of the complex nature of these restrictions, the Group's management does not regard this capital as available to meet requirements in other parts of the Group.

For the UK life funds the group is required to hold sufficient capital to meet the FSA capital requirements, based on the 'risk capital margin' (RCM) determined in accordance with the FSA's regulatory rules under its realistic capital regime, together with the Individual Capital Assessment (ICA) which takes into account certain business risks not reflected in the RCM. The determination of the RCM depends on various actuarial and other assumptions about potential changes in market prices, and the actions management would take in the event of particular adverse changes in market conditions.

Management intends to maintain surplus capital in excess of the RCM and ICA to meet the FSA's total requirements, and to maintain an appropriate additional margin over this to absorb changes in both capital and capital requirements. For life fund A, the capital was 171% of the RCM of £175 million and for life fund B the capital was 140% of the RCM of £390 million, in line with management's target of maintaining a margin of at least 35% of the RCM.

For UK non-participating business, the relevant capital requirement is the minimum solvency requirement determined in accordance with FSA regulations. For this business, a lower capital surplus is targeted by management, since the capital requirement is less subject to fluctuation and the capital amount is after deducting liabilities that include additional prudential margins. At 31 December the available capital was 130% of the capital requirement of £270 million, in excess of management's target minimum of 120%.

For overseas businesses the amount shown is the minimum requirement under the locally applicable regulatory regimes. These are determined on various bases, and in practice the local regulators expect a significant margin over these minima to be maintained. Management also carries out its own assessment of the level of capital resources it regards as appropriate, in excess of these regulatory minima. Overall, overseas businesses held capital substantially in excess of management's target minimum capital level of £250 million. No individual overseas business held less that 150% of its regulatory capital requirement.

Additional narrative disclosures will cover:

- *sensitivity of liabilities (including options and guarantees) and components of capital (paragraph 45(c));*
- *capital management policies and the approach to managing risks (paragraph 45(d));*
- *information on liabilities, including information on assumptions, terms and conditions relating to options and guarantees, and exposure to risk in relation to options and guarantees not measured at fair value or by using a stochastic modelling method (paragraphs 48 and 51);*
- *information on movements in capital, including a movements table (paragraphs 55 and 56); and*
- *an explanation of the reasons for a negative balance on an FFA of any with-profits fund of the entity, and why no action to eliminate it has been considered necessary (paragraph 23).*

Appendix II
Note on Legal Requirements

GREAT BRITAIN

Insurance companies and insurance groups

For accounting periods beginning prior to 1 January 2005, all insurance companies and insurance groups (as defined by the Companies Act 1985) are required to prepare their financial statements in accordance with Schedule 9A to the Companies Act 1985 (the Schedule). For accounting periods beginning on or after 1 January 2005, the financial statements of some insurance companies and insurance groups will continue to be prepared in accordance with the Schedule. However, other financial statements of insurance companies and insurance groups will be prepared in accordance with EU-adopted IFRS and will, as a result, not be subject to any detailed legal requirements as to their form and content.* 1

The requirements of the Schedule that are relevant to the FRS are set out in paragraphs 3-10 below. It is the requirement in the FRS for some entities to recognise 'realistic' liabilities for certain policyholder liabilities that is most relevant to the Schedule's requirements, and the implications of that are analysed in paragraphs 4.47-4.65 of Appendix IV 'The Development of the FRS'. That analysis is not relevant to entities not required to recognise 'realistic' liabilities, nor is it relevant to entities that *are* required to recognise 'realistic' liabilities but, because they prepare their financial statements in accordance with EU-adopted IFRS, are not subject to the requirements of the Schedule. 2

The FFA

The Schedule requires disclosure, as a separate item on the face of the balance sheet immediately below 'Subordinated liabilities' and immediately above 'Technical provisions', of an item called 'Fund for future appropriations'. Note 19 on the balance sheet format in the Schedule states that the item shall comprise "all funds the allocation of which either to policy holders or shareholders has not been determined by the end of the financial year." 3

Technical provisions

The Schedule requires disclosure, as a separate item on the face of the balance sheet, of an item entitled 'Technical provisions'. That item is to be analysed between the provision for unearned premiums, long-term business provisions, claims outstanding, the provision for bonuses and rebates, the equalisation provision, and other technical provisions. 4

Note 21 on the balance sheet format in the Schedule requires that the long-term business provision shall comprise the actuarially estimated value of the company's liabilities (excluding technical provisions included under 'Technical provisions for linked liabilities'), including bonuses already declared and after deducting the actuarial value of future premiums. 5

***Editor's note:** *For accounting periods beginning on or after 6 April 2008 references to Schedule 9A to the Companies Act 1985 change to references to Schedule 3 to the Large and Medium-sized Companies and Groups (Accounts and Reports) Regulations 2008 (SI 2008/410)*

(a) A technical provision should be included under 'Technical provisions for linked liabilities' if it is constituted to cover liabilities relating to investment in the context of long-term policies under which the benefits payable to policyholders are wholly or partly to be determined by reference to the value of, or the income from, property of any description or by reference to fluctuations in, or in an index of, the value of property of any description. Any additional technical provisions constituted to cover death risks, operating expenses or other risks (such as benefits payable at the maturity date or guaranteed surrender values) shall be included under 'Technical provisions—Long-term business provision'.

(b) Note 20 permits the provision for unearned premiums to be included within the long-term business provision rather than the provision for unearned premiums.

6 Paragraph 43 of the Schedule requires that the amount of technical provisions must at all times be sufficient to cover any liabilities arising out of insurance contracts as far as can reasonably be foreseen.

7 Paragraph 46 of the Schedule goes on to require that:

"(1) The long term business provision shall in principle be computed separately for each long term contract, save that statistical or mathematical methods may be used where they may be expected to give approximately the same results as individual calculations.

(2) A summary of the principal assumptions in making the provision under sub-paragraph (1) shall be given in the notes to the accounts.

(3) The computation shall be made annually by a Fellow of the Institute or Faculty of Actuaries on the basis of recognised actuarial methods, with due regard to the actuarial principles laid down in Council Directive 92/96/EEC."

8 The reference in paragraph 46(3) to Council Directive 92/96/EEC is, in effect, a reference to Directive 2002/83/EC of the European Parliament and of the Council.* That Directive is concerned with prudential regulation, and many parts of the Directive have no relevance to the true and fair financial statements. However, the following parts of Article 20 appear to have indirect relevance to the financial statements by virtue of the cross reference in paragraph 46(3):

"Establishment of technical provisions

1. The home Member State shall require every assurance undertaking to establish sufficient technical provisions, including mathematical provisions, in respect of its entire business.

   The amount of such technical provisions shall be determined according to the following principles.

   A. (i) the amount of the technical life-assurance provisions shall be calculated by a sufficiently prudent prospective actuarial valuation, taking account of all future liabilities as determined by the policy conditions for each existing contract, including:
   - all guaranteed benefits, including guaranteed surrender values,
   - bonuses to which policy holders are already either collectively or individually entitled, however those bonuses are described - vested, declared or allotted,
   - all options available to the policy holder under the terms of the contract,

**Directive 2002/83/EC has replaced Council Directive 92/96/EEC, which has been repealed. The cross-reference in paragraph 46(3) has not yet been updated, but it is understood that it will be shortly.*

- expenses, including commissions, taking credit for future premiums due;

(ii) the use of a retrospective method is allowed, if it can be shown that the resulting technical provisions are not lower than would be required under a sufficiently prudent prospective calculation or if a prospective method cannot be used for the type of contract involved;

(iii) a prudent valuation is not a 'best estimate' valuation, but shall include an appropriate margin for adverse deviation of the relevant factors;

(iv) the method of valuation for the technical provisions must not only be prudent in itself, but must also be so having regard to the method of valuation for the assets covering those provisions;

(v) technical provisions shall be calculated separately for each contract. The use of appropriate approximations or generalisations is allowed, however, where they are likely to give approximately the same result as individual calculations. The principle of separate calculation shall in no way prevent the establishment of additional provisions for general risks which are not individualised;

(vi) where the surrender value of a contract is guaranteed, the amount of the mathematical provisions for the contract at any time shall be at least as great as the value guaranteed at that time;

B. the rate of interest used shall be chosen prudently. It shall be determined in accordance with the rules of the competent authority in the home Member State, applying the following principles:

(a) for all contracts, the competent authority of the assurance undertaking's home Member State shall fix one or more maximum rates of interest, in particular in accordance with the following rules:

(i) when contracts contain an interest rate guarantee, the competent authority in the home Member State shall set a single maximum rate of interest. It may differ according to the currency in which the contract is denominated, provided that it is not more than 60% of the rate on bond issues by the State in whose currency the contract is denominated.

If a Member State decides, pursuant to the second sentence of the first subparagraph, to set a maximum rate of interest for contracts denominated in another Member State's currency, it shall first consult the competent authority of the Member State in whose currency the contract is denominated;

(ii) however, when the assets of the assurance undertaking are not valued at their purchase price, a Member State may stipulate that one or more maximum rates may be calculated taking into account the yield on the corresponding assets currently held, minus a prudential margin and, in particular for contracts with periodic premiums, furthermore taking into account the anticipated yield on future assets. The prudential margin and the maximum rate or rates of interest applied to the anticipated yield on future assets shall be fixed by the competent authority of the home Member State;

(b) the establishment of a maximum rate of interest shall not imply that the assurance undertaking is bound to use a rate as high as that;

(c) the home Member State may decide not to apply paragraph (a) to the following categories of contracts:

- unit-linked contracts,
- single-premium contracts for a period of up to eight years,

- without-profits contracts, and annuity contracts with no surrender value.

In the cases referred to in the second and third indents of the first subparagraph, in choosing a prudent rate of interest, account may be taken of the currency in which the contract is denominated and corresponding assets currently held and where the undertaking's assets are valued at their current value, the anticipated yield on future assets.

Under no circumstances may the rate of interest used be higher than the yield on assets as calculated in accordance with the accounting rules in the home Member State, less an appropriate deduction;

(d) the Member State shall require an assurance undertaking to set aside in its accounts a provision to meet interest-rate commitments vis-à-vis policy holders if the present or foreseeable yield on the undertaking's assets is insufficient to cover those commitments;

(e) the Commission and the competent authorities of the Member States which so request shall be notified of the maximum rates of interest set under (a);

C. the statistical elements of the valuation and the allowance for expenses used shall be chosen prudently, having regard to the State of the commitment, the type of policy and the administrative costs and commissions expected to be incurred;

D. in the case of participating contracts, the method of calculation for technical provisions may take into account, either implicitly or explicitly, future bonuses of all kinds, in a manner consistent with the other assumptions on future experience and with the current method of distribution of bonuses;

E. allowance for future expenses may be made implicitly, for instance by the use of future premiums net of management charges. However, the overall allowance, implicit or explicit, shall be not less than a prudent estimate of the relevant future expenses;

F. the method of calculation of technical provisions shall not be subject to discontinuities from year to year arising from arbitrary changes to the method or the bases of calculation and shall be such as to recognise the distribution of profits in an appropriate way over the duration of each policy."

Deferred acquisition costs

9 The Schedule includes an item entitled 'deferred acquisition costs' to be shown separately on the balance sheet under the heading 'Prepayments and accrued income'. Note 17 on the balance sheet format requires that the item shall comprise the costs of acquiring insurance policies which are incurred during a financial year but relate to a subsequent financial year, except in so far as:

(a) allowance has been made in the computation of the long-term business provision made under paragraph 46 of the Schedule and shown under 'Technical provisions—Long-term business provisions' or 'Technical provisions for linked liabilities' in the balance sheet, for:

(i) the explicit recognition of such costs,

(ii) the implicit recognition of such costs by virtue of the anticipation of future income from which such costs may prudently be expected to be recovered, or

(b) allowance has been made for such costs in respect of general business policies by a deduction from the provision for unearned premiums made under paragraph 44 of the Schedule and shown under 'Technical provisions—Provision for unearned premiums' in the balance sheet.

Note 17 also requires that: 10

(a) deferred acquisition costs arising in general business shall be distinguished from those arising in long-term business;
(b) there shall be disclosed in the notes how the deferral of acquisition costs has been treated (unless otherwise expressly stated in the accounts);
(c) where such costs are included as a deduction from 'Technical provisions—Provision for unearned premiums', the amount of such deduction; and
(d) where the actuarial method used in the calculation of the 'Technical provisions—Long-term business provisions' or 'Technical provisions for linked liabilities' has made allowance for the explicit recognition of such costs, the amount of the costs so recognised.

Other entities

Paragraphs 1–10 above describe the accounting requirements in the legislation that apply to insurance companies or insurance groups as defined in the Companies Act 1985. The FRS also applies to: 11

(a) groups reporting under the Companies Act 1985 that are not insurance groups, including bancassurers and retail groups with life assurance subsidiaries. Bancassurers are required to prepare their financial statements in accordance with Schedule 9 of the Act; retail groups in accordance with Schedule 4 of the Act. Neither Schedule contains specific requirements on how to account for life assurance activities.
(b) friendly societies. Friendly societies are required to prepare their financial statements in accordance with The Friendly Societies (Accounts and Related Provisions) Regulations 1994.
    (i) The financial statements of directive friendly societies are required to prepare in accordance with Schedules 1 - 6 of the Regulations. The requirements on the form and content of the balance sheet are set out in Schedule 2 and are almost identical to the Companies Act requirements summarised above.
    (ii) The financial statements of non-directive friendly societies are required to prepare in accordance with Schedule 7 of the Regulations. Although Schedule 7 requires a prescribed analysis of liabilities to be provided, that prescribed analysis is, compared to the analysis required by Schedule 9A of the Companies Act, highly abbreviated.
(c) various other entities that prepare their financial statements in accordance with The Insurance Accounts Directive (Miscellaneous Insurance Undertakings) Regulations 1993. Those Regulations require the entities to which they apply to comply with the requirements of Schedule 9A of the Companies Act in preparing their financial statements.

NORTHERN IRELAND

The statutory requirements in Northern Ireland that apply to insurance companies and insurance groups are set out in Schedule 9A to the Companies (Northern Ireland) Order 1986. Those requirements are identical to the legislation for Great Britain cited above. 12

REPUBLIC OF IRELAND

13 The statutory requirements in the Republic of Ireland that correspond to those cited above for Great Britain are shown in the following table.

Great Britain	*Republic of Ireland*
Schedule 9A to the Companies Act 1985 (the Schedule)	European Communities (Insurance Undertakings: Accounts) Regulations, 1996
Note 17 on the balance sheet format in the Schedule	Schedule, Part I, Chapter 2, Section A, Note 17
Note 19 on the balance sheet format in the Schedule	Schedule, Part I, Chapter 2, Section A, Note 21
Note 20 on the balance sheet format in the Schedule	Schedule, Part I, Chapter 2, Section A, Note 23
Note 21 on the balance sheet format in the Schedule	Schedule, Part I, Chapter 2, Section A, Note 25
Paragraph 43 of the Schedule	Schedule, Part II, Chapter 3 – Paragraph 23
Paragraph 44 of the Schedule	Schedule, Part II, Chapter 3 – Paragraph 24
Paragraph 46 of the Schedule	Schedule, Part II, Chapter 3 – Paragraph 26
Paragraph 46(3) of the Schedule	Schedule, Part II, Chapter 3 – Paragraph 26(4)

Appendix III
Compliance with International Accounting Standards

Some of the entities applying the FRS will do so in financial statements prepared in accordance with EU-adopted IFRS; others will be applying it in financial statements prepared in accordance with UK standards and legal requirements. 1

(a) Paragraphs 10.1-10.4 of Appendix IV 'The Development of the FRS' discuss the implications of the FRS for the former entities.

(b) This appendix is addressed to the entities preparing their financial statements in accordance with UK standards and legal requirements. The appendix explains the extent to which compliance with the FRS will ensure compliance with the international accounting standard on insurance, IFRS 4 'Insurance Contracts'.

IFRS 4 contains definitions of 'insurance contracts' and various other insurance-related terms. Although those definitions are not included in the FRS, those that define the scope of IFRS 4, IAS 32 and IAS 39—including the definition of 'insurance contracts'—are included in FRS 26 and will therefore apply to entities complying with that standard. 2

Paragraph 10 of IFRS 4 notes that some insurance contracts contain both an insurance contract and a deposit component. Paragraphs 10-12 require those components in certain specified circumstances to be accounted for as if they were separate contracts (in other words, unbundled); permits, but does not require, them to be unbundled in certain other specified circumstances; and prohibits them from being unbundled in certain other specified circumstances. There is nothing in this FRS or any other UK standard requiring, permitting or prohibiting the unbundling of insurance contracts, save the general principle in FRS 5 'Reporting the Substance of Transactions' that transactions should be accounted for in accordance with their substance. 3

All accounting policies adopted by an insurer are required to meet the criteria set out in paragraph 14 of IFRS 4. Neither this FRS nor any other extant UK standard contains similar criteria. The accounting policies that the FRS requires to be adopted all meet the criteria, but some of the entity's other accounting policies might not. 4

Paragraphs 21-23 of IFRS 4 prohibit an insurer from changing its accounting policies for insurance contracts unless two criteria are met. 5

(a) The first criterion is that the new accounting policy shall make the financial statements more relevant to the economic decision-making needs of users and no less reliable, or more reliable and no less relevant to those needs. Although there is no similar requirement in the FRS, compliance with FRS 18 'Accounting Policies' would ensure compliance with this criterion.

(b) The second criterion is that the change shall be consistent with the requirements set out in paragraphs 24-30 of IFRS 4, which relate to changes of certain specific accounting policies. Compliance with the FRS would ensure compliance with the requirements in paragraphs 27 and 28 of IFRS 4 concerning the inclusion of future investment margins in the measurement of insurance contracts. However, compliance with the FRS and extant UK standards would not necessarily ensure compliance in all respects with the other requirements in paragraphs 24-30 of IFRS 4.

Paragraph 34(d) of IFRS 4 requires that, if an insurance contract contains a discretionary feature, a guaranteed element and an embedded derivative that is within 6 the scope of IAS 39 'Financial Instruments: Recognition and Measurement', that embedded derivative shall be accounted for in accordance with IAS 39. For accounting periods beginning on or after 1 January 2005, some entities are required—and all entities may choose—to apply FRS 26 (IAS 39) 'Financial Instruments: Measurement'.

(a) Compliance with FRS 26 would ensure compliance with paragraph 34(d) of IFRS 4.

(b) For entities not complying with FRS 26, neither this FRS nor any other extant UK standard currently requires embedded derivatives to be separated from their host contract.

7 Paragraphs 36-39 of IFRS 4 contain disclosure requirements. The disclosure requirements in paragraphs 37(c), 39(b), 39(e) and 37(d) are virtually identical to requirements in the FRS (paragraphs 48(a), (b) and (c) and paragraph 56(a) respectively), although the scope of the FRS' disclosures is more limited.

Appendix IV
The Development of the FRS

BACKGROUND

Life assurance accounting today

In Great Britain, financial reporting by most types of insurance entity is governed by the legislation implementing the EU Insurance Accounts Directive.*† These requirements are derived in the main from regulatory solvency requirements. The requirements are relatively prescriptive, leaving only a limited amount of scope for accounting developments, although a number of modifications to the underlying solvency principles have been made for the purposes of accounting for life assurance by the Statement of Recommended Practice of the Association of British Insurers (the ABI SORP)—resulting in the financial statements of life assurers being prepared on the so-called Modified Statutory Solvency Basis (MSSB). **1.1**

The MSSB basis of accounting has a number of distinctive features. They include: **1.2**

(a) *A non-standard liability model*—The liability model differs from the model that applies to other entities in at least three important respects:

  (i) Liabilities are recognised for legal obligations but not constructive obligations (such as constructive obligations in respect of terminal bonuses in with-profits funds). FRS 12 'Provisions, Contingent Liabilities and Contingent Assets' requires liabilities to be recognised both for legal obligations and constructive obligations.

  (ii) Recognised liabilities are measured on a particularly prudent basis. FRS 12 requires a best estimate measurement to be used.

  (iii) The Fund for Future Appropriations (FFA) is classified as a liability even though parts of it do not meet the definition of a liability set out in accounting standards.‡

(b) *Deferred acquisition costs*—In part to compensate for this liability model, life assurance policy selling costs are recognised as assets (deferred acquisition costs).

(c) *Profit recognition model*—The MSSB profit recognition model involves the use of statutory transfers from the with-profits fund and profit smoothing techniques such as the amortisation of deferred acquisition costs in line with margin earned. This is a very different profit recognition from the asset/liability framework that is now informing most developments in financial reporting.

**For example, Schedule 9A of the Companies Act 1985 implements the Directive for insurance companies and insurance groups. Schedules 1-6 of The Friendly Societies (Accounts and Related Provisions) Regulations 1994 implement the Directive for certain friendly societies.*

†*The legal framework in Great Britain is, as explained more fully in Appendix II, broadly similar to the framework that exists in Northern Ireland and the Republic of Ireland. However, for simplicity this appendix refers only to British legislation. Similarly, although the intention is that the FRS should apply in Great Britain, Northern Ireland and the Republic of Ireland, the text tends for simplicity to refer to 'UK entities', 'UK standards' etc rather than 'entities in the UK and the Republic of Ireland' and 'standards that apply in the UK and the Republic of Ireland'. However, the system of prudential regulation that applies in the UK differs from that that applies in the Republic of Ireland. so in that context 'UK' is not used to include 'the Republic of Ireland'.*

‡*The FFA represents the balance of surplus of a with-profits fund that has neither been declared as a bonus to policyholders nor distributed as profit to shareholders. The eventual allocation of the FFA between shareholders and policyholders will depend on future appropriations of bonus and profit, hence the name.*

1.3 This reporting framework also does not reflect well the distinctive features of with-profits life assurance: the participatory nature of the entity's relationship with its policyholders; policyholders' expectations about future bonus declarations; the nature of the options granted and guarantees given; and the ownership and nature of any estate* and of the capital more generally.

1.4 The resulting financial statements do not report on life assurance activities in as meaningful a way as they might.

The Penrose Report

1.5 In March 2004 the Accounting Standards Board (the Board or the ASB) received a request from the Financial Secretary to the Treasury to initiate an urgent study into accounting for with-profits business by life insurers. That request was part of the Financial Secretary's response to the Report of the Equitable Life Inquiry, prepared by the Right Honourable Lord Penrose (the Penrose Report).

1.6 The Penrose Report criticised a number of aspects of existing with-profits accounting:

(a) *The treatment of future bonuses*. The report found that the current practice of recognising (as part of the technical provision) a liability for bonuses declared, but not recognising a specific liability for accrued terminal bonuses was unsatisfactory. The conclusion was that the financial statements would not show a realistic position of the life office unless a liability was recognised for the constructive obligation in respect of terminal bonuses.

(b) *Reserves available to cover bonuses*. Insufficient information was provided about the amount of reserves available to meet expected future bonuses. The conclusion was that financial statements should include a disclosure that compares the value of the liability for such bonuses with the reserves available to cover them.

(c) *Changes during the period*. It was unsatisfactory that, under existing practice, life assurers could make important changes affecting policyholders without those changes being apparent from the financial statements. In particular, the report highlighted in this context changes in actuarial assumptions and reductions made to guaranteed benefits as a result of:

   (i) altering the mix of bonus between declared and final elements progressively towards terminal bonus; and
   (ii) changing policy conditions to reduce the scope of contractual benefits and increase the scope for allotting terminal bonus.

   It was suggested that the financial statements should provide an analysis of the movements over the year in the amount of realistic liabilities.

(d) *Complexity*. Addressing the complexity of life assurers' regulatory returns and financial statements and the inter-relationship between them, the report suggested that policyholders and other users should be provided with simplified summary versions of both reports. Furthermore, the objective in the longer-term should be to move to a single accounting basis for both reports.

(e) *The information needs of policyholders*. There was a danger in focusing exclusively on the information needs of investors when preparing financial statements covering life assurance products. Policyholders' interests needed to be taken into account; they were investors in the entity's products and their

**The estate of a with-profits fund is the excess of a fund's assets over its obligations—legal and constructive—to policyholders.*

interests, in financial terms in with-profits funds, usually exceeded those of shareholders by a factor of about 9:1.

The Financial Secretary's letter to the Board requested that the Board's study into accounting for with-profits business should be made against the background of the developments in the Financial Services Authority's (FSA's) regulatory regime and the requirement for listed companies to use EU-adopted International Financial Reporting Standards (IFRS) in their consolidated financial statements from 1 January 2005. **1.7**

The FSA's regulatory regime

Until recently, the system of prudential regulation for UK with-profits funds has been the basis that underlies Schedule 9A—the Statutory Solvency Basis (SSB). The FSA has, however, introduced a new system of prudential regulation for UK with-profits funds, which applies from 31 December 2004 to the UK with-profits funds of entities with UK with-profits liabilities of £500m or more. This new methodology is known as the Realistic Balance Sheet (RBS) approach.*,† **1.8**

The FSA has designed the RBS approach to be based on notions that are much closer than existing regulatory practice to the liability model in general financial reporting standards. For example, the policyholder liabilities are required to take into account both legal and constructive obligations, and they are required to be measured on a basis that is much closer than the current MSSB liability to FRS 12's best estimate approach. **1.9**

The development of the RBS approach has implications for the way in which the existing legal requirements are interpreted and, as a result, means the Board has been able to contemplate making changes to life assurance accounting that would not have been possible hitherto. (This is explained more fully in paragraphs 4.47-4.65.) **1.10**

The RBS approach therefore appears to provide both an opportunity and a means for the Board to improve life assurance accounting. **1.11**

The move to IFRS

From 1 January 2005, listed UK entities will be required‡ to prepare their consolidated financial statements in accordance with EU-adopted IFRS, rather than UK standards and legal requirements. In addition, from that date most unlisted entities will be permitted to use EU-adopted IFRS, rather than UK standards and legal requirements, in their financial statements. **1.12**

Entities reporting under EU-adopted IFRS are, by definition, not reporting under the existing UK legal requirements and, as such, are free of the constraints imposed on their accounting policies by the Companies Act 1985 (the Act). Thus, the move to **1.13**

**'Realistic' is the FSA's term for the methodology it has developed. In using the term in the FRS, the Board is not intending to imply anything other than that the items involved have been calculated by applying the FSA's RBS methodology. There is, for example, no suggestion that entities should be required to use the term in their true and fair financial statements.*

†The RBS approach has been implemented alongside the existing SSB) as part of a 'twin peaks' approach under which the higher of the RBS approach's 'realistic peak' and the SSB's 'regulatory peak' will be the regulatory requirement.

‡By EU Regulation 1606/2002.

EU-adopted IFRS provides a further opportunity for improvements in insurance accounting to be made. However, during the initial stages of this project the Board took the view that from 2005 those improvements would have to be made by the industry or by the International Accounting Standards Board (IASB) because the Board's standards would not apply to entities following EU-adopted IFRS. For that reason, the Board's focus initially was on the changes it could make in 2004 that would remain in place after 2005.

1.14 For UK reporting entities with life assurance activities, one of the key standards in 2005 for those following EU-adopted IFRS will be IFRS 4 'Insurance Contracts', which was issued in March 2004. Under IFRS 4, issuers of insurance contracts are permitted in the main to continue to use their pre-2005 accounting policies in preparing their financial statements from 2005 even if those policies do not meet the requirements of other IASB standards ('the grandfathering provisions'). However, if the entity wishes to change an accounting policy, it can do provided that the new accounting policy will make the financial statements more relevant to the economic decision-making needs of users and no less reliable, or more reliable and no less relevant to those needs.

1.15 The Board viewed these grandfathering provisions as highly relevant to its project because they provided a means by which the Board could make changes to life assurance accounting policies that would remain in place for some time after 2005. In other words, although IFRS 4 itself makes few improvements to insurance accounting, the timing of its introduction provided a one-year window of opportunity for a national standard-setter to do so.

1.16 IFRS 4 fulfils another important role. By setting out the criteria that need to be met if a new accounting policy is to be adopted, it provides an indication of the direction in which the IASB expects insurance accounting to develop. This enabled the UK Board to make changes to life assurance accounting and be reasonably confident that those changes would not be reversed by the IASB in the near future.

APPROACH ADOPTED BY THE BOARD

A two-part project

2.1 Bearing in mind the opportunity offered by the development of the RBS approach to prudential regulation of with-profits insurance business and the timing constraint imposed by the move to EU-adopted IFRS in 2005, the Board concluded that its project should comprise two parts:

(a) *To consider what improvements could be made to life assurance accounting in time for the 2004 accounts and to develop a standard requiring those improvements.* Within this timescale, it would not be realistic to make wholesale change to the existing insurance accounting framework nor would it be appropriate to do so ahead of phase 2 of the IASB's insurance project. However, it would be realistic to make limited improvements which could be implemented for 2004 reporting and would point in the direction of the further improvements the IASB has indicated it would like to see.

(b) *To develop views on the direction in which insurance accounting more generally should develop over the next few years and on the key issues that will need to be addressed in securing the changes necessary.* Although the Board may have less direct influence on the shape of insurance accounting from 2005, it intends to continue to play an active and influential role in phase 2 of the IASB's project and will therefore continue to develop its thinking on the issues that need to be addressed. Where the Board identifies potential improvements that it cannot introduce across the industry as a whole, it will recommend them to the IASB for consideration. In some cases, it might also incorporate them into UK standards.

In considering which issues it should attempt to address in the first part of the project, the Board recognised that, although the issues raised by Lord Penrose would represent an important part of its work, it would need to consider addressing other issues and concerns as well. The broad issues and concerns that the Board considered initially are summarised briefly in paragraphs 2.3-2.17 and those dealt with in this Financial Reporting Standard (the FRS) are explored more fully in sections 3-8 of this appendix. **2.2**

Financial strength

As mentioned in paragraph 1.3, the existing reporting framework struggles to reflect in the financial statements a number of the distinctive features of with-profits life assurance. One of those features is the rather unusual nature of the capital resources involved. Although some of the capital is fungible, much of it is subject to a variety of restrictions as to its availability and use. Some of the capital is shareholders' capital but the ownership of some other capital—and for with-profits funds this capital can be very significant—is uncertain and is perhaps best viewed as being jointly owned by policyholders and shareholders. Unless the nature, fungibility and extent of the capital available to a life assurer is properly explained in the financial statements, users of those financial statements will struggle to understand the insurer's prospective ability to continue to treat customers fairly whilst meeting all other obligations to third parties and providing an appropriate and secure return to shareholders. In other words, they will struggle to understand the insurer's financial strength. **2.3**

The Penrose Report also raised some concerns in this area, emphasising the importance of disclosing the amount of the reserves the insurer is holding against actual and contingent liabilities. **2.4**

The Board therefore concluded that one of the issues it should seek to address through its limited improvements project was the provision of information about the financial strength of UK with-profits funds. **2.5**

Liability accounting

The Board decided that another priority was to consider ways of improving the existing liability recognition, measurement and presentation model. This is one of the areas in which existing life assurance accounting is most out-of-step with general accounting principles. It is an issue that the Board highlighted in the statement it attached to the November 2003 revision of the ABI SORP; it is mentioned in the Penrose Report as a significant concern; and it is the aspect of with-profits life assurance accounting for which the FSA's new RBS approach has the most implications. **2.6**

Another of the issues raised by the Board in its statement attached to the November 2003 revision of the ABI SORP concerned the balance sheet classification of the FFA. The Board decided to consider this issue in its limited improvements project (although it eventually decided not to address the matter in the FRS). **2.7**

Options and guarantees

2.8 Many life funds over the last few years have experienced major reductions in their capital position as a consequence of the need to fund options and guarantees provided to policyholders. These options and guarantees can take a variety of forms, and some expose the entity to insurance variables such as mortality and morbidity, while others expose the entity to financial variables such as market prices.

2.9 Historically, UK entities with life assurance activities have tended to recognise a liability for an option or guarantee that exposes it to financial variables only if it is 'in the money'. The financial statements have, as a result, reported the impact on the estate and net assets of such options and guarantees as being more sudden and severe than might have been the case had the liability measurement basis taken appropriate account of the potential for future changes (for example, through stochastic modelling of possible outcomes or some form of fair valuing).*

2.10 The RBS approach requires the options and guarantees liabilities of large UK with-profits funds to be measured at fair value or at a stochastically modelled value. This makes it reasonable to consider whether the liability should be measured on the same basis in the true and fair financial statements, and also whether the treatment in the financial statements of other options and guarantees (for example, those granted on overseas life assurance contracts) could be improved. As the Board has previously made clear the importance it attaches to treating options and guarantees properly, it decided to consider these issues further in its limited improvements project.

Profit recognition and performance reporting

2.11 The Board recognised that the existing profit recognition, measurement and presentation model used by insurers is in need of improvement. It was also conscious though that, in looking predominately at with-profits reporting, any improvements it made to the model would inevitably be only a partial solution to a wider problem. It therefore decided that, to the extent that changes to the balance sheet were to be proposed, it would address the consequential profit recognition and performance reporting issues but, that apart, profit recognition and performance reporting issues would not be considered in the first part of the project.

Complexity and lack of transparency

2.12 The financial statements of an insurance company or group are complex and difficult for anyone who is not an expert to use. This complexity only partly derives from the nature of the business. The terminology used is not always helpful and the presentation of information calculated on different bases—without proper disclosure of how these different sets of information relate to each other—can be very confusing.

2.13 The complexity and lack of transparency of insurance financial statements was highlighted in the Penrose Report, which criticised both the regulatory returns and the financial statements for not being readily understandable.

2.14 This is an important issue. The purpose of financial statements is to communicate information. Financial statements that cannot be understood by a user with general financial knowledge, applying reasonable diligence, do not fulfil their purpose. However, the Board decided that it should not carry out a study of how the existing

**A stochastic modelling approach involves valuing the item by reference to the weighted average value under a large number of possible future market price scenarios.*

formats and terminology might be improved during the first part of its work because the formats and terminology used were largely determined by legislation and legislative change was not feasible in 2004.

The Penrose Report concluded that another source of complexity was the existence of multiple statements—regulatory returns, true and fair financial statements, and embedded value supplementary information—prepared on different bases with no means for the user to navigate their way between the statements. This is a matter which the Board considered in its limited improvements project. **2.15**

The use of embedded value in the primary financial statements

Generally speaking, entities with life assurance activities respond to the perceived inadequacies of MSSB financial statements by trying to focus users' attention on the value of in-force business. Some do this by supplementing the MSSB financial statements with information prepared on an embedded value basis. Some others recognise assets based on those embedded values in their primary financial statements and use them to drive the profit recognition model. This means that the same transactions are accounted for in the financial statements of different entities in fundamentally different ways. **2.16**

Such inconsistencies are unsatisfactory, so the Board decided to consider the use of embedded value—even though the matter is a more general concern and is not specifically linked to with-profits reporting—in its limited improvements project in order to determine whether it was appropriate and possible to achieve greater consistency.. **2.17**

Summary

In summary, the Board decided to focus on the following issues in the first part—the limited improvements project part—of its work: **2.18**

(a) the provision of information that helps users to assess the financial strength of UK with-profits funds (section 3);
(b) the liability model for with-profits policyholder liabilities (section 4);
(c) the balance sheet classification of the FFA (section 5);
(d) the treatment of options and guarantees not taken appropriately into account in measuring policyholder liabilities (section 6);
(e) recognising the value of in-force life assurance business (ie embedded value) in the primary financial statements (section 7); and
(f) the complexity caused by multiple statements prepared on different bases (section 8).

In July 2004 the Board issued Financial Reporting Exposure Draft (FRED) 34 'Life Assurance'. Sections 3 to 8 explain the issues the Board considered in developing the proposals in the FRED, as well as how the Board has addressed the main comments made on those issues by those responding to the FRED. **2.19**

The other sections of this appendix discuss: **2.20**

(a) other issues arising from the FRED 34 consultations (section 9);
(b) the memorandum of understanding and the application of the FRS by entities applying EU-adopted IFRS (section 10);
(c) future developments (section 11); and
(d) the ASB's advisory panel on life assurance (section 12).

FINANCIAL STRENGTH

3.1 Generally speaking, it is possible for users of financial statements to develop a good understanding of the financial strength of most entities from their balance sheet and supporting disclosures. This is possible because the capital of such entities is largely fungible. However, one of the unique features of with-profits life assurers is that their capital often comprises elements that exhibit widely different characteristics. These characteristics—which relate to the ownership, certainty of valuation and availability of use—mean that some analysis of the components of capital is needed to enable the entity's financial strength to be understood by both policyholders and shareholders. This is not information that the financial statements currently provide.

3.2 At first, the Board considered the possibility of changing the presentation of the balance sheet to provide this information. For example, the entity's capital could be shown as a series of layers each subject to a different set of restrictions. However, the Board concluded that such a presentation would not be able to do justice to the capital structures that currently exist. What was needed was a disclosure that focused on the amount and nature of capital held by, or available to, the life assurer, and that showed where the capital is held and the extent to which it is available to other parts of the business. (The FRS refers to this disclosure as a 'capital statement'.)

3.3 The remainder of section 3 discusses the main issues that the Board considered in developing its requirements on the capital statement.

ED 7

3.4 The Board issued the FRED that preceded this FRS in the same month that the IASB issued ED 7 'Financial Instruments: Disclosures'. ED 7 proposed, inter alia, that entities should be required to disclose certain information about the amount of their capital resources, their target capital levels and the way they manage their capital. The proposal was that the final standard would be published early in 2005 and would be mandatory from 2007, although entities could adopt it from 2005 if they wished. The Board issued ED 7 as a UK exposure draft (FRED 33 'Financial Instruments: Disclosures') and proposed that it should be implemented as a UK standard when it is implemented internationally.

3.5 A number of respondents to FRED 34 argued that, in view of the proposals in ED 7, the capital statement proposals in FRED 34 were superfluous. Some argued that the two sets of proposals merely set out alternative ways of achieving the same objective and, in the interests of convergence, FRED 34's proposals should be withdrawn in favour of ED 7's. However, the Board does not consider the proposals to be interchangeable; although the disclosures described in FRED 34 would meet most of the proposed capital disclosure requirements set out in ED 7, the opposite would not be the case because an entity could comply with proposed requirements in ED 7 without providing any information about the fungibility of its capital. During the development of the FRED the Board saw the two sets of proposals as complementary because, while ED 7 proposed some important, extremely useful general disclosures, FRED 34 proposed extending those disclosures to highlight some specific factors of particular importance in the life assurance industry. In finalising the FRS, the Board has emphasised the complementary nature of the two sets of disclosures.

Entity level or group level?

3.6 The Board took the view in developing the proposals in the FRED that, if a good understanding is to be obtained of a UK with-profits fund's overall financial strength, its capital position needs to be put in the context of the consolidated group of which it is a part. In the Board's view, such a presentation ensures that due account is taken of the extent to which shareholder or other finance exists in other parts of the Group and might be available to the UK with-profits funds. The FRED proposed therefore that, if the reporting entity has general insurance and other activities, these should be included in the disclosure—grouped together but shown separately from the life funds—with an indication of the availability or otherwise of this capital. In doing so, the Board recognised that the complex structure of many of the largest insurance and bancassurer groups, with intra-group and inter-fund lending and investing arrangements, made it likely that the consolidation of the various individual capital positions would be complicated and consolidation adjustments could be significant. It believed however that this was itself relevant to an understanding of the different aspects of the entity's capital position. The contrast between the simplicity of the capital position of the large, single fund of a traditional UK mutual and the complex capital structure of a diversified global group was important and was of relevance to users.

Some of those responding to the FRED disagreed with this focus on group-wide information, particularly as the FRED also exempted some single entities that are part of groups from the need to include the capital disclosures in their individual financial statements. Those respondents argued that what policyholders needed was information about financial strength at the level of their individual fund and, because of materiality and the inevitable need to aggregate, the information provided at the entity level was the nearest policyholders would get to that. Some respondents also argued a group-wide presentation could be misleading if the funds are ring-fenced. **3.7**

The Board has not been persuaded by these arguments for the following reasons: **3.8**

(a) Although prima facie a policyholders' interest lies at the individual fund level, it does not follow that policyholders are not interested in the financial strength of the group as a whole. Many groups seek to market on the basis of their group level financial strength and it is therefore reasonable to provide policyholders with an analysis that relates the position of the individual funds to the overall group capital position. Even if a group manages its individual funds on a strictly ring-fenced basis, it is of value to the policyholder to see the overall financial strength of the group and how 'their' fund fits in, thereby gaining some understanding of the likely financial imperatives that are going to govern the fund's management. Indeed, it is important for policyholders to know whether the group manages their fund on the basis of strict ring-fencing or on the basis of group-level financial strength (taking advantage of the benefit of financial diversification, for example). During discussions with major life assurers, the Board had both these diametrically opposing positions explained to it as the basis on which the capital position of that particular group was managed. Setting out which approach applies would be a key part of the narrative disclosures that should accompany the capital statement.

(b) Most insurers manage their capital both at the individual fund level and at the group level. For example, an entity with most of its available capital resources tied up in funds that it cannot easily access (for example a UK with-profits fund) might need a capital injection to raise capital for other purposes even if the capital resources within particular funds are substantial. Users need information that helps them understand the interrelationship between the financial position of individual funds and the group's capital position. The great variety of intra-group financial arrangements (such as reinsurance, contingent loans, guarantees etc) that can apply means there will often need to be careful explanation of the consolidation adjustments that are made in producing the group level information.

3.9 Some respondents recognised the objective behind the capital statement but argued that the objective would not be achievable unless the statement reflected the benefits of diversification. However, the fact that diversification benefits *are* particularly important for some groups—though not for those that manage their funds on a strictly ring-fenced basis—is one of the main reasons why it is essential for the aggregate of the individual entities' capital positions to be clearly reconciled to the group position as shown in the balance sheet. Without this reconciliation, there is a significant risk of the capital statement being unable to be related to other aspects of the group financial position.

3.10 As mentioned earlier, the FRED not only proposed that the capital statement should be prepared at a group level, it also proposed that some single entities should be exempt from the requirement to provide the statement. The proposal was that the exemption would apply to:

(a) an entity that is a wholly-owned subsidiary undertaking, if its ultimate or intermediate parent entity includes a capital statement complying with the FRS in its consolidated financial statements; and

(b) in a parent entity's own financial statements when presented together with the parent's consolidated financial statements.

3.11 In the light of the comments received in response to the FRED, the Board reconsidered the appropriateness of this exemption. The Board noted that, without the exemptions, much of the information provided by the subsidiary or parent company would be available to policyholders in the consolidated financial statements and, as such, there would be some duplication if the exemptions were deleted. On the other hand, it recognised that the information would often be provided at a higher level of aggregation in the consolidated financial statements than in, say, the subsidiary's financial statements and that some smaller funds would be 'visible' only at a subsidiary level.

3.12 In the Board's view, neither of the options available to it was ideal. It nevertheless decided, for pragmatic reasons, to retain the exemptions; entities would not be forced to provide disclosures at a subsidiary level but also would not be prevented from doing so if they considered the benefit of doing so justified the cost.

3.13 For consistency with other standards, the Board decided to amend the exemption for subsidiaries so that it applies to 90%-owned subsidiaries, rather than just wholly-owned subsidiaries.

Level of aggregation

3.14 As the focus of the capital statement should be on the different types of capital the entity has, the statement needed to show a disaggregated view of capital. On the other hand, showing each segment of capital and each restriction separately would, in some cases, make the disclosure so voluminous that it would be of little value. A balance needed to be found.

3.15 The Board took the view in the FRED that the primary focus should be on the individual UK with-profits funds (or, for an entity in the Republic of Ireland, on the individual with-profits funds in the Republic of Ireland) because it is in that context that the need for detailed information about financial strength is greatest. Respondents largely agreed with this view. Paragraph 34(a) of the FRS therefore requires information about each UK with-profits fund to be shown separately if the fund is material.

The FRED proposed that the information about the entity's other life assurance business should be provided separately for each material section of that business. It went on to propose that, for this purpose, a fund or business unit would be a separate section if the capital attributable to that business was subject to material restriction or limitation as to its availability to other parts of the business. **3.16**

A number of respondents criticised this proposal. Some argued that the level and manner of aggregation it implied was not appropriate for their business; some argued that, bearing in mind that the capital in most business sections would be subject to some constraints, the aggregation principle proposed was not particularly useful. Some respondents were concerned about how the information on the separate sections would be interpreted, with some arguing that the aggregation of fungible capital should be permitted to avoid confusion and others arguing that aggregating capital that is subject to different restrictions implies it is fungible when it is not. Concerns were also raised about whether showing funds that had interdependencies separately would be helpful. It was also clear that there was some confusion as to how the restrictions over the use of capital would be portrayed. **3.17**

The Board reconsidered its proposals in the light of the comments received, and decided that the FRS should be more flexible as to how the information about life assurance activities other than UK with-profits funds is presented. Paragraphs 34(b), 35 and 36 of the FRS now require that the disclosures show the extent to which the various components of capital are subject to constraints or are available to other parts of the business—how that is done is up to each entity. The result is that entities will be able to adopt a presentation that best suits their particular circumstances. **3.18**

Should the capital statement focus on capital resources, or also show capital requirements or targets?

The FRED proposed that the capital statement should show not only an analysis of the entity's capital resources but also the regulatory capital requirements relevant to each section of that capital. Disclosing the regulatory capital requirements provided context for the information about capital resources. Furthermore, as the regulatory capital requirements impose restrictions on the use of capital in other parts of the business, including them in the disclosure helped focus attention on available capital *after meeting regulatory capital requirements.* **3.19**

The proposal to require disclosure of the regulatory capital requirements in the capital statement was criticised by a significant number of respondents. **3.20**

(a) Some commentators argued that the target capital levels set by management, rather than the regulatory capital requirements, should be disclosed because what matters most is the basis on which the business is being managed and that would be by reference to target capital. These commentators also pointed out that ED 7 proposed the disclosure of information about internally-set capital target levels.

(b) Some commentators argued, in a similar vein, that disclosing a single regulatory capital requirement for each section would be misleading in jurisdictions where there was more than one regulatory requirement or where the requirements comprise a series of action levels or trigger points. In such jurisdictions, it is not immediately clear which regulatory requirement would be the most useful to use in the capital statement. The FRED's suggestion—that in such circumstances the disclosure should focus on the minimum requirement—was thought by many to be inappropriate.

(c) Under the proposals in the FRED, the regulatory requirements shown would be calculated on different bases. This, some respondents argued, meant they were inconsistent and, as a result, not additive.

(d) Some commentators suggested that the Board should not adopt a regulatory approach because it would not be practicable to prepare the relevant numbers to the required quality until after the end of the annual statutory reporting process.

3.21 The Board has not accepted all these arguments. For example, although those arguing that the requirements are not calculated on a consistent basis and are therefore not additive are right in pointing out that the insurance industry is not as fortunate as the banks in having a common approach, the numbers nevertheless *are* the regulatory capital requirements and hence *are* relevant. Similarly, although there may be some practical difficulties in preparing the relevant numbers to the required quality at short notice, this is an argument for deferring the disclosure, not for abandoning it.

3.22 The Board nevertheless concluded that the role of the regulatory capital requirements in the capital statement should be downgraded because a surplus of capital over the regulatory minimum is not a true surplus, and could even represent a shortfall below the target capital level; as a result, complex and lengthy notes would need to be provided to enable users to understand the true position. The regulatory capital requirements are just one of the constraints placed on the free use of capital. Therefore, rather than insist on the amount of the requirement to be disclosed for each business section disclosed separately in the capital statement, paragraph 45(a) of the FRS requires the capital statement to be supported by "narrative or quantified information on the regulatory capital requirements applying to each section of the business shown in the capital statement, or on the capital targets set by management for that section."

Clarity

3.23 In developing its proposals on the capital statement, the Board was very aware of the comments in the Penrose Report about different pieces of information in the financial statements being prepared on different bases with no explanation of those differences. For that reason the Board considered it important to ensure that the information in the capital statement could be reconciled to the balance sheet. This matter is discussed in more detail in section 8.

Practicalities of obtaining information

3.24 The proposal in the FRED was that the capital statement should be provided for the first time in the 2004 year-end financial statements. Some commentators expressed the view that, due in particular to the sequential process that is adopted by companies in the preparation of their year-end financial information—with the preliminary announcement and published financial statements preceding the regulatory returns—it would not be possible to include in their 2004 year-end financial statements information that, currently, is only required to be disclosed in the regulatory returns. This would be an issue in 2004 for information calculated on the FSA's RBS basis and for overseas regulatory information (which is often not produced until much later in the year).

3.25 Although the decision to downgrade the role of the regulatory capital requirements in the capital statement (see paragraph 3.22 above) changed the significance of this issue, it did not mean it was no longer a concern because:

(a) the Board still envisaged that the available capital amounts shown in the capital statement would be calculated on a regulatory basis; and
(b) some disclosures about the regulatory capital requirements would still be required.

The Board decided to defer the implementation of its capital statement disclosure requirement by one year to accounting periods ending on or after 23 December 2005. **3.26**

(a) As explained more fully in paragraphs 4.67–4.72 and section 10 of this appendix, the Board decided to defer for a year the changes it is making to the UK with-profits liability model. Having taken that decision, there were strong arguments for deferring the capital statement requirement as well.
(b) Allowing entities a year in which to prepare for this disclosure would, the Board believed, give them time to experiment with different forms of presentation and find a presentation that best fits their circumstances.
(c) The current expectation is that a standard based on ED 7 will be issued in 2005 and will be available for early adoption in accounting periods beginning on or after 1 January 2005. Deferring the capital statement requirements a year enables entities to implement the capital statement requirements at the same time as their ED 7 capital disclosures should they wish to do so.

Commercial sensitivity

Another concern that respondents raised was the commercial sensitivity of the information. The financial strength of an insurer is a key aspect of its customer proposition and is often used in marketing products. It is also of interest to shareholders. Requiring UK entities to disclose detailed information about the fungibility of their available capital when non-UK competitors in a similar position can remain silent or can point to an inappropriate indicator (such as the value of funds under management) would put UK entities at a disadvantage. Financial strength matters to current and prospective investors and policyholders, so putting an insurer at a competitive disadvantage could impact both on new business levels and on perception amongst the investor community. **3.27**

The Board did not find these arguments persuasive. Given the importance of financial strength to the commercial success of an insurer, it is inevitable that the requirement for a capital statement will be viewed as sensitive by companies (and very relevant and important by users). It is true that different standards of financial reporting requirements have been and continue to be a problem. It does not follow, however, that entities that are more forthcoming in their disclosures are at a disadvantage compared to those that remain wrapped in a cloak of silence and ambiguity. The principal reason for the movement in Europe to the use of improved and international accounting standards is that markets have rewarded companies that have been open about their financial position and performance and discussed frankly the strategy options facing them. Regulators, too, have moved from believing that secrecy was an essential means of maintaining public confidence in the financial system to acknowledging that early identification and public discussion of problems is a surer way of avoiding potential crises. Experience also shows that better disclosures and management discussion by leading entities serve to educate users and create pressures on their competitors to emulate their example. **3.28**

Communication to policyholders

The Penrose Report urged that policyholders, as well as shareholders, should be kept better informed on the financial strength of an insurer. It is outside the Board's remit to require this directly. However, the capital statement required by the FRS has been **3.29** designed with the idea that it could be extracted from the financial statements and sent to policyholders on an annual basis—or included as an annual annex to the Principles and Practices of Financial Management (PPFM)*—together with an appropriate introduction as to its purpose and explanation as to its form.

Movements analysis

3.30 One of the concerns expressed in the Penrose Report was that financial statements contain insufficient information on the changes over the accounting period in key numbers (such as liabilities) and the causes of those changes. As a result, changes that an insurer has made to assumptions and in policy might not be apparent to users of those financial statements.

3.31 The Board shares those concerns and, as a result, it proposed in the FRED that a movements analysis should be provided in support of the proposed capital statement. That analysis should show how the capital position had developed in the period in the light of changes in assumptions and policies; the impact of new business, surrenders and maturities; and changes in asset mix. It should also be show a separate analysis for each category of capital or fund set out in the capital statement.

3.32 A number of respondents expressed concerns about the practicality of what the FRED proposed. There were three common concerns. Two related to how the FRED proposed the movement during the year should be analysed.

(a) Respondents thought the difference between a change in assumption and a change in a management policy needed to be clarified and that guidance was needed on how to distinguish between the effect of an assumption change and the effect of a management policy caused by an assumption change. Additional guidance has now been provided in the FRS.

(b) Respondents also argued that the complexities of the stochastic models involved made it difficult to isolate the effect of new business on available capital and liability levels and that this would not be information they would need for management purposes. The FRS now does not require the effects of new business to be shown separately.

3.33 The third concern related to the difficulty of isolating the effect of any specific change when the numbers involved are calculated on a stochastic basis. For example, the Board has been told by some entities that it will take them nearly a month to run the stochastic models necessary to estimate their 'realistic' liabilities. Their intention had been to run these models just at the end of each accounting period. However, in order to produce the FRED's proposed movements analysis it would be necessary to run the models after every change. That would involve a substantial amount of additional work.

(a) The Board considered this to be a short-term difficulty caused by an understandable reluctance on the part of preparers to use short-cut methods to estimate the effects of changes until the stochastic models used are better understood.

(b) In the Board's view, even if some relief needs to be given for a year or so until preparers are comfortable using short-cut methods, the longer-term objective should still be to require entities to provide a full, quantitative analysis of the reasons for the movements in available capital.

**The PPFM is a new document that the FSA requires UK with-profits life funds to make available to their policyholders. It contains a description of the fund's investment management and bonus distribution policies.*

The FRS therefore retains the disclosure proposed in the FRED (subject to the amendment described in paragraph 3.32(b) above). However, for the first year (ie for 2005 year-ends), significant flexibility is given as to the form the disclosure should take. The Board believed that this additional flexibility would ease significantly the practical difficulties that would otherwise arise in the first year of implementation. **3.34**

LIABILITY ACCOUNTING

Existing accounting practice

As explained in Appendix II 'Note on legal requirements', most UK entities with life assurance activities are required to follow either the accounting requirements set out in Schedule 9A of the Companies Act 1985 (Schedule 9A) or requirements that are almost identical to those in Schedule 9A (for example, The Friendly Societies (Accounts and Related Provisions) Regulations 1994) in presenting their balance sheet information. The items in the prescribed format that relate in whole or in part to with-profits activities are: **4.1**

Debit balances

(a) *Investments*. Included within this item will be the aggregate fair value of the investments held within the with-profits fund.

(b) *Prepayments and accrued income: Deferred acquisition costs (DACs)*. Selling a with-profits policy typically involves the insurer incurring significant up-front costs (acquisition costs). Under existing accounting practice, those costs are usually not charged immediately to the profit and loss account; instead, they are carried forward on the balance sheet and amortised over the period in which they are expected to be recoverable out of margins earned by the insurer from the policy at a rate commensurate with the pattern of such margins. The unamortised costs are shown on the balance sheet as 'deferred acquisition costs'.

(c) *Reinsurers' share of technical provisions*. If the exposure on a with-profits policy has been reinsured, an asset may be recognised under this heading. The amount of any such asset will be determined by reference to the amount recognised as a liability for that reinsured risk and the nature of the reinsurance.

Credit balances

(d) *Technical provision for long-term business*. Currently this item represents an extremely prudent provision for bonuses already declared and claims incurred but not yet reported. It is calculated in accordance with regulatory guidance (the MSSB basis).

(e) *The FFA*. The FFA comprises all funds the allocation of which either to policyholders or shareholders has not been determined by the end of the financial year.

In its work on insurance liability accounting, the Board focused on: **4.2**

(a) *Recognition*—The technical provision for long-term business currently recognised takes into account the insurer's legal obligations to policyholders (for example, to pay declared bonuses), but not its constructive obligations (for example, in respect of future bonuses).

(b) *Measurement*—The liability to policyholders that is recognised (under technical provisions for long-term business) is measured using extremely prudent (and therefore biased) estimates; under general accounting principles a best estimate measurement basis is usually used.

(c) *Presentation*—The FFA is presented in the balance sheet amongst liabilities, even though significant elements of the FFA appear not to meet the definition of a liability.

4.3 Reporting entities that have insurance business but are not subject to Schedule 9A requirements or the equivalent—for example, bancassurers and some retail groups—tend to include the assets arising from their insurance business on one line of the balance sheet and the liabilities arising from their insurance business on another. Those recognising the value of in-force life assurance business in their primary financial statements also recognise, on a separate line in the balance sheet, an asset that represents the value of in-force business.* The analysis included in the notes of liabilities tends to follow Schedule 9A conventions, so a technical provision for long-term business and an FFA are shown. As such, the recognition, measurement and presentation liability issues that arise in Schedule 9A financial statements also arise in the context of these statements.

4.4 The remainder of this section focuses on the recognition and measurement issues; the presentation issue is addressed in section 5.

FRS 12

4.5 The liability recognition and measurement principles that apply to most entities are those set out in FRS 12. Liabilities are required to be recognised when:

(a) an entity has a present obligation (legal or constructive) as a result of a past event;

(b) it is probable that a transfer of economic benefits will be required to settle the obligation; and

(c) a best estimate of the expenditure required to settle the present obligation at the balance sheet date can be determined reliably.

4.6 However, FRS 12 does not apply to provisions, contingent liabilities and contingent assets that arise in insurance entities from contracts with policyholders. There were two main reasons for this exemption: the constraints imposed by Schedule 9A and the uncertainty as to how to apply the notion of a constructive obligation to with-profits business because of the ill-defined nature of the obligations owed to with-profits policyholders.

4.7 Although there may have been difficulties in applying FRS 12 to with-profits obligations, the Board has never doubted that the principles in the standard are just as applicable to those obligations as to any other obligation. In its view, policyholder liabilities should be recognised for constructive obligations, not just legal obligations, and those liabilities should be measured on a best estimate basis, rather than on an overly prudent basis.

4.8 The objective of the Board's work on insurance liability accounting has been to identify improvements that point in the direction in which insurance accounting is likely to develop and are capable of being implemented quickly. In the Board's view it is clear that the direction in which insurance liability accounting will develop will be to converge on the principles in FRS 12. However, the Board did not believe that it was possible to remove the FRS 12 scope exemption for insurance contracts without developing a substantial amount of additional guidance and without

**Embedded value is discussed further in section 7 of this appendix.*

addressing certain key issues—neither of which the Board would have been able to do in the time available for this project.

The RBS approach

Having concluded that it was not practicable in the short-term to remove the FRS 12 exemption for with-profits business, the Board considered what other options were available to it. In its view, any approach adopted needed to meet the following criteria: **4.9**

(a) If improvements are to be made in the near-future, time constraints suggest that they would have to be based either on a method that already exists and is widely used or on a new method for which preparations for implementation are already well underway.

(b) If the direction in which insurance liability accounting should develop is towards the principles in FRS 12, it seems reasonable to suppose that any change in the liability model that is in the direction of those principles will be an improvement, as long as it does not bring with it offsetting disadvantages. Any change being considered therefore needs to be closer to FRS 12 than the existing basis.

(c) Any proposed new liability model would need to be consistent with the relevant legal requirements and capable of being implemented in true and fair financial statements in the timescales envisaged by the project.

The Board saw the FSA's RBS approach as the only approach that might meet all these criteria. **4.10**

Is the 'realistic' liability closer to the FRS 12 basis than the existing basis?

The Board therefore examined the RBS method in detail to determine whether it was, in theory at least, an improvement on the existing basis. **4.11**

The RBS method involves restating the assets and liabilities of a with-profits fund onto a 'realistic' basis. The FSA's rules envisage that the 'realistic' liability* will comprise the 'with-profits benefits reserve' and 'future policy-related liabilities'. **4.12**

(a) The most significant element is the with-profits benefits reserve, which can be calculated in one of two ways: the retrospective method (ie asset share) or the prospective benefit method (ie the bonus reserve approach).

(b) Where not already taken into account in the with-profits benefits reserve, the future policy-related liabilities, among other things, add to the benefits reserve provisions for:

   (i) future costs of options and guarantees, of smoothing, and of non-contractual commitments and other amounts needed to ensure that customers are treated fairly;

   (ii) any past miscellaneous surplus or deficit that the entity intends to attribute to the benefits reserve and any future planned enhancements to the benefits reserve; and

   (iii) other long-term insurance liabilities.

The objective of the calculation is to estimate the discounted value of future payments on policies in force. **4.13**

**This appendix uses the term "'realistic' liability" as short-hand for the 'realistic value of liabilities', which is the term used in the FRS.*

4.14 Thus, the liability is not restricted to legal obligations—constructive obligations are taken into account as well—and the liability is not measured on an extremely prudent basis. This is similar to FRS 12's approach. However:

(a) there are a number of detailed differences in approach that the Board explored before concluding that the 'realistic' liability is an improvement, for accounting purposes, on the existing basis. These are considered in paragraphs 4.15-4.19;

(b) the estimate of future payments to be made on in-force policies used in the 'realistic' liabilities calculation takes into account the fair value of the investments held in the with-profits fund (because the future payments will, by-and-large, in normal circumstances be a distribution of the part of the fund that does not represent the estate). If some assets are taken into account in calculating the 'realistic' liability but are not recognised in the financial statements—or are not measured on the same basis—it could be argued that there will be a mismatch between the asset and liability sides of the balance sheet. The Board's approach to this issue is set out in paragraphs 4.20-4.31; and

(c) the FSA is requiring initially only some with-profits funds—those UK with-profits funds of entities with UK with-profits liabilities that are at least £500m in size—to implement the RBS method. RBS information is likely therefore to be available initially for only those funds. The implications of this are considered in paragraphs 4.32-4.35.

Differences between a 'realistic' liability and an FRS 12 liability

4.15 With most UK with-profits policies, when a bonus is declared an allocation is made both to policyholders and to shareholders. (For example, assume that policyholders and shareholders share fund profits on a 90:10 basis: if a bonus to policyholders of £90 is declared, an allocation of £10 will be made to shareholders.) When calculating the provision to be made for constructive obligations in respect of additional undeclared bonuses, the RBS approach requires both the constructive obligation to policyholders and the related shareholder allocation (the shareholders' share of undeclared bonus) to be included in the 'realistic' liability. Under FRS 12, the shareholders' share of undeclared bonus would not be treated as a liability. If the shareholders' share of undeclared bonus was to be left in the amount recognised for policyholder liabilities, that liability would always be overstated and in many cases that overstatement would be significant. However, as it appears to be a relatively straightforward matter to eliminate the shareholders' share of the undeclared bonus from the 'realistic' liability, this appears not to create any difficulties for the possible use of 'realistic' liabilities in true and fair financial statements.

4.16 The FSA's rules make it clear that, in estimating future payments to be made on in-force policies in order to estimate the 'realistic' liability, account should be taken of any intention of management to enhance (or reduce) permanently allocations to policyholders. Under FRS 12 such an intention would create a constructive obligation only where:

(a) an established pattern of past practice, published policies or a sufficiently specific current statement has meant that the entity has indicated to other parties that it will accept certain responsibilities; and

(b) as a result, the entity has created a valid expectation on the part of those other parties that it will discharge those responsibilities.

Thus a management intention to enhance (or reduce) allocations to policyholders might be reflected in the 'realistic' liability even though it does not give rise to a constructive obligation as defined by FRS 12.

There are also potential differences in the way that options and guarantees are measured. Under existing generally applicable accounting principles, options and guarantees giving rise to liabilities would usually be measured either on a best estimate basis or at fair value; under the RBS method they can be measured at either fair value or at a stochastically modelled value. Although the stochastically modelled value will often be the closest approximation to fair value that is available, it is not the same thing.* 4.17

Another apparent difference between the 'realistic' liability and the FRS 12 liability is the treatment of future premiums and future investment gains. Under the RBS method, if the 'realistic' liability is being determined by estimating the future payments to be made on in-force business, the entity will project the eventual outcome (using, inter alia, the expected rate of future investment gains) and deduct from that the expected future premiums. Although this is the technically most accurate way of estimating the future payments to be made on in-force business, it does involve the anticipation of future events. 4.18

The Board's understanding is that there is no easy way to adjust for the potential differences described in paragraphs 4.16-4.18 because the differences go to the core of the methodology used. Therefore, if the RBS method is to be used as a basis for insurance liability accounting, it has to be used with the 'potential differences' unresolved. The Board's judgement in developing the FRED was that, despite the potential differences, the 'realistic' liability would still be closer than the existing liability to FRS 12 and is therefore to be preferred. Few of those responding to the FRED disagreed with this view. 4.19

Potential balance sheet mismatches

In order to estimate the 'realistic' liability, it is necessary to estimate the future payments to be made on in-force policies. That estimate will need to take into account the fair value of all the investments in the with-profits fund since it is the overall financial strength of the fund that will be taken into account when determining bonuses. If non-participating business has been written in the with-profits fund, that business will be one of the with-profits fund's investments, and the fair value of that investment will be one of the fair values to be taken into account in estimating the amount of the 'realistic' liability. It seems to follow from this that, if 'realistic' liabilities are to be recognised, the fair value of non-participating business written in the with-profits fund—referred to in this appendix as the value of in-force, non-participating business (or the VIF of non-participating business)—needs to be recognised as well. 4.20

The VIF of non-participating business is, in effect, an embedded value. The Board has been asked to consider the merits of embedded value methodologies several times in the past and on each occasion has concluded that it could not support their use in true and fair financial statements. For that reason, when faced with the VIF of non-participating business issue, the Board's response was to consider whether recognition of the VIF could be avoided. 4.21

It could be argued that the basis on which the assets were being recognised and measured ought not to matter. FRS 12 takes no account of the basis of asset recognition and measurement; it focuses exclusively on the present obligations the entity has as a result of a past event to transfer economic benefits. On that analysis, the notion of a mismatch between assets and liabilities would not exist and there 4.22

**The measurement of options and guarantees is discussed further in section 6.*

would be no reason why the VIF of non-participating business would need to be recognised just because the 'realistic' liability is recognised.

4.23 Another way to look at the issue is to ask how one should account for an obligation to transfer to another party some or all of the valuable benefit to be derived from an item that is not recognised on the balance sheet—because, unless either the item was recognised on the asset side of the balance sheet or that element of the obligation is measured at nil, there would be a mismatch. For example, assume that an entity enters into an arrangement that involves it agreeing to pay a specified percentage of the next five years' profits to a third party. As future profits are not usually considered to be assets, they would not be recognised on the balance sheet; nor therefore is the liability under generally accepted practice.

4.24 The simplest treatment to adopt would be to show the VIF of non-participating business as an asset and to recognise as a liability the full amount of the 'realistic' liabilities. Under this approach the 'realistic' liabilities would be clearly shown, and the fair value of the investments being held against that liability would be shown on the asset side of the balance sheet. This was the approach proposed in the FRED.

4.25 Some respondents argued however that the VIF asset does not meet the definition of an asset and therefore should not be recognised on the balance sheet. Others argued that an insurance contract might meet the definition of an asset; the key question for them was whether measuring that asset by reference to the VIF of non-participating business would be appropriate bearing in mind that the value was an embedded value and the Board had not previously permitted the use of embedded values in the financial statements. As will be explained later in this section of the appendix, the Board has decided to defer implementation of the FRS until 2005, which has meant that the implications for the FRS of EU-adopted IFRS need also to be taken into account.

(a) The Board's view is that it may be difficult to recognise the VIF asset in full—and perhaps even at all—in financial statements prepared in accordance with EU-adopted IFRS if that VIF asset is recognised for the first time in 2005 financial statements.

  (i) IFRS 4 does not permit the introduction of new accounting policies in 2005 that involve including a value for future investment risk margins (and for investment management fees in excess of fair value) in an embedded value. It is possible that the amount at which the VIF asset has been measured for regulatory purposes would include some amounts for such items.

  (ii) The effect of paragraph 11 of IAS 8 'Accounting Policies, Changes in Accounting Estimates and Errors' is that entities are required to refer to and consider the applicability of "the definitions, recognition criteria and measurement concepts for assets" set out in the IASB's 'Framework for the Preparation and Presentation of Financial Statements' (the IASB's Framework). The VIF asset probably would not qualify for recognition on the balance sheet as an asset under the IASB's Framework, although some might argue that the reference to the need to "consider the applicability of" the IASB's Framework, coupled with IFRS 4's acceptance of the recognition of embedded value assets makes the position much less clear cut than that.

(b) In theory similar difficulties would arise for an entity preparing its financial statements in accordance with UK standards and legal requirements as the FRS would contain IFRS 4's embedded value restrictions and the Board's Framework (the 'Statement of Principles for Financial Reporting') is similar to the IASB's. However, the Board's Framework does not form part of the hierarchy of authoritative accounting literature that preparers are required to take into account.

An alternative approach more in keeping with the discussion in paragraph 4.23 would be to deduct the VIF of non-participating business from liabilities. Such an approach could be justified on the grounds that the liabilities would be calculated by taking into account the value of the fund's investments (including the VIF of non-participating business); if it is not appropriate to recognise the VIF of non-participating business as an asset, its effect on the liabilities should be removed. As one element of the VIF of non-participating business is often an amount to compensate for the excessive prudence included in the measurement of the non-participating business liabilities, deducting the VIF of non-participating business from liabilities would have the effect of netting off that compensation for over-prudence against the over-prudent liability, which seems reasonable. **4.26**

(a) In an ideal world, when applying this approach one would deduct that part of the VIF of non-participating business included in the policyholder liabilities from the 'realistic' liability number, that part of the VIF of non-participating business included in the FFA from the FFA, and that part of the VIF of non-participating business relating to the excessive prudence included in the non-participating liabilities from those liabilities. However, the Board's understanding is that it will seldom be practicable to allocate the VIF of non-participating business in this way.

(b) Another approach might be to deduct the whole of the VIF of non-participating business from policyholder liabilities, or alternatively to deduct the whole of the VIF from the FFA. The Board rejected both these alternatives, believing that neither method represented faithfully the actual underlying position (unless by coincidence). As such, the resulting information could be misleading.

(c) The Board then considered the possibility of deducting the VIF of non-participating business from the aggregate of policyholder liabilities and the FFA, while still displaying separately on the face of the balance sheet all three items. The Board concluded that such a presentation—showing the three elements separately—was superior to showing a single (net) number of the balance sheet (supported by a breakdown of the net number in the notes) because the three elements are so different in nature.

Such an approach appears consistent with the requirements of EU-adopted IFRS, especially as those standards contain flexibility as to the liability model to be adopted in accounting for insurance. However, it is not clear that such an approach could be reconciled with the requirements set out in Schedule 9A , which appear not to contemplate that amounts not calculated in accordance with the legal requirements could be shown as deductions from balance sheet items that have been calculated in accordance with those requirements (ie policyholder liabilities and the FFA). **4.27**

On the basis of the above analysis, it would appear that the 'asset presentation' approach described in paragraphs 4.24 and 4.25 might be the only option available for financial statements prepared in accordance with UK standards and legal requirements, while the 'liability presentation' approach described in paragraphs 4.26 and 4.27 might be the appropriate option for entities prepared in accordance with EU-adopted IFRS. Faced with the prospect of having to permit a choice on the issue, the Board considered whether it might be preferable to abandon the proposal to include 'realistic' liabilities on the balance sheet. **4.28**

4.29 The Board has always understood that the improvement it is seeking to make to insurance accounting through the recognition of 'realistic' liabilities on the balance sheet is just one step on what will be a long journey for insurance accounting. The improvement tackles a number of issues (such as the recognition of liabilities based on legal obligations only and not constructive obligations, the use of overly prudent measures and the recognition as assets of deferred acquisition costs), but leaves some other issues to be addressed another day. The objective throughout has been to ensure that the benefits (ie the advantages gained by tackling the various issues) continue to outweigh the disadvantages (ie the unresolved issues). The Board believes that this continues to be the case regardless of whether the asset or liability presentation approach is adopted.

4.30 The other issue that arose from FRED 34 concerned the extent to which the VIF of non-participating business has actually been taken into account in determining the amount of the 'realistic' liabilities. The FRED stated that the VIF of non-participating business could be recognised "to the extent that...the determination of the realistic value of liabilities ...takes account of this value". The objective of this statement was to prevent entities from recognising the VIF of non-participating business if it was not taken into account in determining 'realistic' liabilities. However, a number of respondents pointed out that there would generally be no direct link between the value of the VIF of non-participating business and the value of 'realistic' liabilities; in other words, if the former increased by a certain amount, it would not follow that the latter would increase by the same amount. The relationship between the two would be rather more indirect. Respondents were concerned that the FRED expected a direct link between the two to be present before it permitted the VIF of non-participating business to be recognised. The FRS has been amended to make it clear that a direct link of this kind is not expected and that the amount of the VIF to be recognised is not restricted to the value taken into account in determining the amount at which to measure the liabilities.

4.31 A similar potential mismatch situation to the VIF issue discussed above arises where the with-profits fund has an investment in a subsidiary undertaking. In some cases that subsidiary will be valued for the purposes of estimating the 'realistic' liability at a market value or other value in excess of the net amount at which the subsidiary is included in the consolidated balance sheet. For similar reasons to those outlined above, the Board concluded that in such circumstances a mismatch could be avoided only by allowing the recognition as part of the with-profits fund of the excess of the amount at which it is valued for regulatory purposes over the amount at which it would normally be included in the consolidated balance sheet.

Implications of the FSA limiting the application of its RBS method

4.32 Initially, only entities with UK with-profits life liabilities of at least £500m will be required by the FSA to implement the RBS method, and then only for their UK with-profits funds; the method will not have to be adopted for smaller firms or for other UK life funds or any overseas life funds. It is understood that this means initially between thirty and forty large UK funds will be applying the RBS method. They will together represent approximately 95% in value of UK with-profits funds, but probably less than 50% in value of all UK life office funds.

4.33 When the Board was developing FRED 34, it considered the possibility of including within the scope of its 'realistic' liability requirement some or all of the funds that are not within the scope of the FSA's RBS regime. However, at that time the proposal was that the Board's requirement would be implemented for 2004 year-ends and the Board took the view that the FSA was in the best position to judge how practicable it is to expect a fund to apply the RBS method in 2004 and had the FSA thought it possible to apply the RBS method more widely in 2004, it would have done so.

Later, when it became apparent that the FRS would not be implemented until 2005 year-ends, the Board considered the possibility again. However, the FSA had no immediate plans at that time to extend the scope of its RBS requirements or of the other FSA requirements that make it possible to apply the notion of a constructive obligation to with-profits business. That would have meant that the Board would have had to develop substantial additional guidance of its own. While that was feasible given time, it was not feasible given that the Board had decided that the FRS had to be finalised before the end of 2004. **4.34**

That meant that, if the Board were to require 'realistic' liabilities to be used in the true and fair financial statements, it would have to accept that 'realistic' liabilities would be used only for the funds required by the FSA to prepare RBS information. The Board considered whether a 'partial' implementation of this kind of accounting was appropriate. If the amount currently recognised for policyholder liabilities had been calculated on a consistent basis, that might have represented a powerful argument for not adopting a partial implementation approach. However, Schedule 9A does not require uniform accounting policies to be adopted, and local regulatory constraints mean that full advantage of this relief is often taken. As such, requiring the UK with-profits liabilities of some entities to be calculated using the RBS method would therefore not introduce inconsistency or additional diversity in those entities' accounting. It would, however, mean that an important element of the amount of the total liability would be calculated on a basis closer to that of FRS 12. **4.35**

Summary

The Board examined the RBS method to determine whether it was, in theory at least, an improvement on the existing basis. It concluded that: **4.36**

(a) there were differences between the 'realistic' liability basis (as amended to exclude the shareholders' share of undeclared bonus) and FRS 12;

(b) in order to state the with-profits assets and liabilities on the same basis, if a 'realistic' liability is to be recognised on the balance sheet it will be necessary also to recognise the value of in-force business written in the with-profits fund if that business has been taken into account in determining the 'realistic' liability. A similar adjustment would also be made if the amount of the 'realistic' liability takes into account, for an investment that the with-profits fund has in a subsidiary undertaking, a value that is in excess of the amount at which that investment is shown in the consolidated balance sheet; and

(c) it is not practicable initially to require the whole of the policyholder liability to be calculated on an RBS basis.

In the Board's view it would nevertheless still be an improvement for 'realistic' liability amounts to be used wherever they were available. **4.37**

Implications of recognising 'realistic' liabilities in the balance sheet for other balance sheet and profit and loss items

Recognising 'realistic' liabilities in the balance sheet has implications for a number of other balance sheet items and, potentially, the profit and loss account. **4.38**

Reinsurers' share of technical provisions

4.39 If the exposure on a with-profits policy has been reinsured, an asset called "Reinsurers' share of technical provisions" will be recognised. That asset will be measured at an amount that reflects the amount recognised as a liability for that reinsured risk. Therefore, if the basis used to determine the amount of the liability is to change, so must the basis used for the reinsurance asset.

Deferred acquisition costs

4.40 Under MSSB accounting, where liabilities are measured on an excessively prudent basis, acquisition costs are deferred in order to reduce the distortion to reported financial performance that results from overly prudent provisioning. Under the RBS approach, the need to recover acquisition costs incurred is taken into account in the estimate of future bonus levels used to calculate the amount of the 'realistic' liability, so it would be inappropriate to continue to defer such costs.

Tax effects of the proposed changes

4.41 It would also be necessary to account fully for the tax effects of the changes described above.

Implications for the FFA and for the profit and loss account

4.42 The implications of the changes suggested for the FFA and the profit and loss account also needed to be considered. (To summarise, those suggestions involve, for the balance sheet items relating to a UK with-profits fund falling within the scope of the FSA's RBS method:

(a) adjusting the liability onto a 'realistic' basis and making consequential adjustments to any reinsurance assets;
(b) removing the related deferred acquisition costs from the balance sheet;
(c) recognising the value of non-participating in-force business written in the with-profits fund;
(d) recognising the amount by which the value of an interest in a subsidiary undertaking held in the with-profits fund as estimated for the purposes of the 'realistic' liability calculation exceeds the net amount that would otherwise have been included in the consolidated balance sheet; and
(e) adjustments to reflect the consequential tax effects of the above adjustments.)

4.43 The Board took the view in developing the FRED that, in the case of an entity with shareholders, all these adjustments should be made to the profit and loss account with an offsetting transfer to the FFA. That would mean that, for such an entity, the proposals would have no direct net effect on the profit and loss account or shareholders' funds. Mutuals have no shareholders, and all the surplus is attributable to policyholders (though not yet allocated to specific policyholders). In some cases that retained surplus account is called 'the FFA'. The FRED therefore proposed for mutuals that the adjustment to liabilities should be offset by a direct transfer to or from this retained surplus account. Few of those responding to the FRED disagreed.

Shareholders' interest in the liability for undeclared bonuses

4.44 The RBS method requires a liability to be set up for a life assurer's constructive obligation in respect of additional bonuses. For the FSA's purposes, that liability is required to include the shareholders' share of the undeclared additional bonus but, as explained in 4.15, the FRS requires this shareholders' share to be excluded from the liability recognised in the financial statements. The effect of this is that for financial reporting the shareholders' share would remain in the FFA.

Some commentators argue that the shareholders' share should be treated as part of shareholders' funds. They reason that: **4.45**

(a) if the FFA is supposed to contain only funds the allocation of which has not been determined, and
(b) the undeclared additional bonuses to which the constructive obligation relates is deemed to have had its allocation,

the shareholders' interest in those undeclared bonuses should also be deemed to have been allocated—which means it should be excluded from the FFA.

However, in most cases the amount that would be allocated to shareholders is not fixed until the bonus is declared. The terms of the policy often state that the entitlement of shareholders is up to 10% but there are examples of shareholders taking less than 10% and in some cases not taking anything at all. In addition, as explained in more detail in section 5, providing for the 'realistic' liability does not mean that the balance of the FFA represents equity. After meeting policyholders' reasonable expectations the FFA will still include material elements of surplus the ownership of which remains uncertain. For that reason the Board believes it appropriate to leave the shareholders' share in the FFA. **4.46**

The legal position

The form and content of insurance financial statements are the subject of detailed legal requirements.* A number of those requirements have in the past been cited as constraining the ability of insurance entities to improve their liability model. Therefore, when the Board was developing the FRED it considered the implications of those requirements for the balance sheet changes it was contemplating making. In particular it considered the following issues: **4.47**

(a) If 'realistic' liabilities are to be recognised in the balance sheet for some UK with-profits funds, for some funds the technical provision would comprise just liabilities arising out of legal obligations and in other cases it would also include liabilities arising out of constructive obligations. Does the law permit the inclusion of liabilities arising out of constructive obligations in the technical provision and, if so, does it also permit the inclusion of such liabilities for some funds but not others?
(b) Another implication of recognising 'realistic' liabilities in the balance sheet for some UK with-profits funds is that some liabilities included in the technical provision would be measured using an extremely prudent basis and some would not. Does the law permit liabilities to be included in the technical provision on a less prudent basis than at present and, if so, does it also permit some liabilities to be measured on that less prudent basis while some others are measured on the existing extremely prudent basis?
(c) If a 'realistic' liability is being recognised for a particular fund, the intention is that the recognition of an asset for deferred acquisition costs arising on that fund would be prohibited. Is that consistent with the legal requirements?

**As explained more fully in Appendix II the detailed requirements that apply to British insurance entities are either contained in or almost identical to those contained in Schedule 9A of the Companies Act 1985. Similar requirements apply to insurance entities in Northern Ireland and the Republic of Ireland.*

(d) Are there any legal difficulties in recognising the value of in-force non-participating business written in the with-profits fund or the value of an interest in a subsidiary undertaking in excess of the net amount that would otherwise have been included in the consolidated balance sheet?

4.48 The Board's view at the time that it was developing the FRED was that there were no legal difficulties arising from any of those issues. The Board has since received legal advice that confirms that view. It has also considered the views expressed by respondents as to the meaning of some of Schedule 9A's requirements but has not changed its view that the changes it is making to the insurance liability model (and the consequential changes that are being made to other balance sheet items) are consistent with Schedule 9A's requirements.

4.49 The Board's detailed analysis of the issues highlighted above is set out in the paragraphs that follow.

Including constructive obligations in the technical provision

4.50 Currently, the liability to policyholders recognised in the technical provision for long-term business relates only to legal obligations owed to policyholders; it does not include constructive obligations in respect of additional bonuses. Some commentators argue that the law prohibits the inclusion in the technical provision of liabilities for bonuses not yet declared. That may well have been the case in the past, but the Board believes that the development of the RBS method and, with it, a means of applying FRS 12's constructive obligations notion to UK with-profits business has had the effect of making possible a wider range of interpretations of the legal restrictions than hitherto. One consequence of this is that it is now reasonable to interpret the law as permitting the inclusion of liabilities for additional bonuses in the technical provision. The analysis leading to this conclusion is set out in the following paragraphs.

4.51 Paragraph 16 of Schedule 9A requires "all liabilities and losses which have arisen or are likely to arise in respect of the financial year" to be taken into account in determining the amount at which to show items in the financial statements. This makes it clear that a liability should not be ignored; the Board believes it also means that all liabilities that have been identified should be recognised on the balance sheet. This interpretation seems to be supported by note 21 of the balance sheet format in Schedule 9A, which states that the long-term business provision shall comprise "the actuarially estimated value of the company's liabilities (excluding technical provisions [included under 'Technical provisions for linked liabilities']), including bonuses already declared and after deducting the actuarial value of future premiums."

(a) The reference to "bonuses already declared" appears not to be restrictive because it is preceded by the word 'including', which implies that the list is not exhaustive.

(b) The reference to the provision comprising "the company's liabilities" suggests that, if a liability is identified, note 21 expects it to be included in the long-term business provision. Under the MSSB basis the only liabilities identified were for bonuses already declared; under the RBS method liabilities are also identified in respect of additional bonuses not yet declared.

4.52 Paragraph 46(3) of Schedule 9A states that the computation of the long-term business provision "shall be made annually by a Fellow of the Institute or Faculty of Actuaries on the basis of recognised actuarial methods, with due regard to the actuarial principles laid down in Council Directive 92/96/EEC." This reference to

Council Directive 92/96/EEC is in effect a reference to Directive 2002/83/EC.* Article 20 of that Directive states, inter alia, that the amount of such technical provisions "shall be calculated by a sufficiently prudent prospective actuarial valuation, taking account of all future liabilities as determined by the policy conditions for each existing contract, including: all guaranteed benefits, including guaranteed surrender values; bonuses to which policy holders are already either collectively or individually entitled, however those bonuses are described—vested, declared or allotted; all options available to the policy holder under the terms of the contract; expenses, including commissions, taking credit for future premiums due..."

(a) Again, the use of the word 'including' means that the list at the end of this quote is not restrictive and, therefore, not significant. The technical provision must include bonuses to which policyholders are already entitled, but could also include other amounts relating to future bonuses. This is reinforced by the explanation in the Article (paragraph 1D) that "in the case of participating contracts, the method of calculation for technical provisions may take into account, either implicitly or explicitly, future bonuses of all kinds, in a manner consistent with the other assumptions on future experience and with the current method of distribution of bonuses."
(b) The reference to "taking account of all future liabilities" is significant in that it makes it clear that no liability should be ignored. 'Taking account of' is however a rather imprecise term open to interpretation in different ways. One interpretation which the Board believes is reasonable—though not necessarily the *only* interpretation that is reasonable—is that the paragraph requires all liabilities to be recognised in the balance sheet.

Paragraphs 4.50-4.52 analyse the legal requirements dealing with the items to be included in the long-term business provision. The legal requirements as to the content of the FFA are also relevant because, if an item is required to be included in the FFA, it cannot also be included in the long-term business provision. Note 19 of the balance sheet format in Schedule 9A states that the FFA should comprise "all funds the allocation of which either to policyholders or shareholders has not been determined by the end of the financial year." This means that amounts for which the allocation has not been determined should not be recognised in the long-term business provision. Some commentators have suggested that an allocation is determined only when a bonus is declared. Such a view would mean that amounts relating to constructive obligations for additional bonuses would be required to be included in the FFA rather than the technical provision. However, although the reference to 'allocations being determined' could be interpreted in that way, it could also be interpreted in other ways—for example, it could be that an allocation can be determined through the identification of a constructive obligation—and there is no reason to believe that the first interpretation is more appropriate than the second.† **4.53**

So, to summarise, a reasonable interpretation of: **4.54**

(a) paragraph 16 of Schedule 9A is that all liabilities that have been identified should be recognised on the balance sheet;
(b) note 21 of Schedule 9A's balance sheet formats is that the long-term business provision is required to show the company's liabilities; and
(c) paragraph 46(3) of Schedule 9A requires all future liabilities to be recognised in the long-term business provision.

**Directive 2002/83/EC has replaced Council Directive 92/96/EEC, which has been repealed. The cross-reference in paragraph 46(3) has not yet been updated, but it is understood that it will be shortly.*

†*The discussion, in paragraphs 4.44-4.46, on the balance sheet treatment of the shareholders' interest in the liability for undeclared bonuses is also relevant here.*

None of these paragraphs—nor indeed any other legal requirements—suggest that 'liabilities' can comprise only liabilities for bonuses already declared. Furthermore, it is reasonable to interpret the description of the contents of the FFA in note 19 of Schedule 9A's balance sheet formats as not prohibiting liabilities for additional bonuses not yet declared from being included in the long-term business provision.

4.55 As a result, there appears no legal restriction on including liabilities for additional bonuses in the long-term business provision. Indeed:

(a) in the case of funds for which 'realistic' liabilities are determined, constructive obligations (for additional bonuses not yet declared) that give rise to liabilities have been identified, so those liabilities should be recognised in the technical provision.

(b) for other funds, the only liabilities that have been identified are those based on legal obligations. As such, it seems reasonable to recognise only those amounts in the technical provision.

4.56 As explained more fully later in this appendix, the FRS requires entities to start recognising 'realistic' liabilities in their financial statements from December 2005 year-ends. This raises a further issue: is there an inconsistency between the conclusion (in subparagraph (a) above) that all liabilities that have been identified should be recognised in the financial statements and the Board's decision not to require recognition of 'realistic' liabilities for 2004 year-ends even though the FSA requires the RBS method to be used in prudential returns from December 2004? The Board does not believe so. In its view, there are issues surrounding the recognition of 'realistic' liabilities in financial statements that mean, for many entities, that it is not yet practicable for them to be recognised in financial statements for 2004 year-ends—and there seems no reason to suppose that Schedule 9A would require their use in such circumstances. However, if they are not recognised, as explained more fully under the next heading it will be necessary to take that into account in determining the amount of prudence to include in the measurement of the liabilities that are recognised.

Less prudent measurement bases

4.57 Currently those liabilities recognised in the technical provision are measured on an extremely prudent basis. 'Realistic' liabilities are measured on a less prudent basis and it has been suggested that the existing legal requirements prevent these 'less prudent' measures from being used in the financial statements. The Board does not agree. Its analysis is set out below.

4.58 The legal requirements are that the long-term business provision is measured at "the actuarially estimated value" (note 21 of the balance sheet format in Schedule 9A), the computation of the technical provision to be made "on the basis of recognised actuarial methods" (paragraph 46(3) of Schedule 9A), the amount of the technical life-assurance provisions shall be calculated "by a sufficiently prudent prospective actuarial valuation" (Directive 2002/83/EC). Legislation also makes clear that "a prudent valuation is not a 'best estimate' valuation, but shall include an appropriate margin for adverse deviation of the relevant factors". There is therefore no requirement that an extremely prudent measurement basis should be used.

(a) Both an MSSB measure and a RBS measure would meet the requirement that the liability be measured at the "actuarially estimated value" and on the basis of "recognised actuarial methods". Similarly, both would meet the requirement that a prudent measurement basis should be used rather than a best estimate measurement basis. (Although the RBS measure is closer than the MSSB measure to a best estimate, it still includes certain margins for adverse deviations.)

(b) Although the law requires that the measurement basis should be "sufficiently prudent" and that the measure should include "an appropriate margin" for adverse deviation, it provides no further guidance and, in particular, does not make clear the purpose for which the measure should be sufficiently prudent or for which the margin needs to be appropriate. For example, it has been argued that more prudence has been needed to date in arriving at a measure that is to be used for prudential regulatory purposes than in arriving at a measure for true and fair financial statements. It seems reasonable to argue therefore that what is sufficient and appropriate should be judged in the context in which the measurement is to be used.

In an accounting framework in which liabilities are not recognised for constructive obligations in respect of additional bonuses, substantial margins are necessary to take account of those obligations. However, in an accounting system in which liabilities are recognised for those constructive obligations, a less (possibly much less) prudent measurement basis can be used because the prudence 'margin' does not need to take account of those obligations.

Paragraph 43 of Schedule 9A states that "the amount of technical provisions must at all times be sufficient to cover any liabilities arising out of insurance contracts as far as can reasonably be foreseen." The meaning of this paragraph is open to different interpretations. **4.59**

(a) For example, some commentators suggest that it requires the maximum liability that might arise from an uncertain event to be recognised. This, they suggest, means that using a measurement basis in the financial statements that is as close to a best estimate basis as the RBS method would not be consistent with the law. Others point out that, if this interpretation were correct, options and guarantees would be measured by reference to the worst case scenario, assuming a catastrophe. Such a measurement approach is impractical and potentially misleading. It is also not how options and guarantees are measured currently.

(b) In the absence of any other indications as to its meaning, it seems reasonable to assume that the requirement has the same objective in mind as the requirements discussed in paragraph 4.53-4.54–a liability amount should be determined on a basis that is sufficiently prudent for the purpose to which the number is to be used, bearing in mind the context in which it is to be placed and taking appropriate account of the various risks and uncertainties in arriving at the measure.

Deferred acquisition costs

Note 17 of the balance sheet format in Schedule 9A states that the deferred acquisition costs line of the balance sheet shall comprise "the costs of acquiring insurance policies which are incurred during a financial year but relate to a subsequent financial year" (except for certain allowances not relevant to this discussion). Some commentators have suggested that this means that any accounting standard that prohibits deferral of acquisition costs (as the FRS does) is not consistent with the law. **4.60**

When costs are incurred is largely a matter of fact and nothing in the FRS seeks to change the existing view on when acquisition costs are incurred. However, which period such costs relate to is a matter of accounting convention and is therefore something that standards help determine. In effect, the FRS requires that, for funds required by the FSA to prepare RBS information, the acquisition costs should be **4.61** treated as relating to the period in which they were incurred. For other funds, the FRS does not prevent acquisition costs from being treated as relating to future periods.

Recognising the value of in-force non-participating business and the excess value of any investment that the with-profits fund has in a subsidiary

4.62 As explained above, the FRS permits entities to recognise the value of in-force (VIF of) non-participating business written in the with-profits fund as an asset or as a deduction from liabilities, although in both cases only if it has been taken into account in determining a 'realistic' liability that is recognised on the balance sheet. Some commentators have questioned whether the recognition of this amount is permitted by Schedule 9A.

4.63 Considering first the 'asset presentation' approach, Schedule 9A sets out in some detail the items that should be disclosed on the balance sheet and where they should be disclosed. An implication of this is that, if an entity intends to recognise a particular type of asset that has a line item allocated to it by Schedule 9A—for example, deferred acquisition costs—the only place that asset can be recognised on the balance sheet is on the deferred acquisition costs line. Some have suggested that the value of in-force non-participating business includes items that should more properly be disclosed under Schedule 9A's prescribed line items; and as such recognising the value separately is not consistent with the law. The Board does not share these concerns. Although the VIF of non-participating business may well be derived, inter alia, from the use of assets and liabilities shown on other lines in Schedule 9A's format that is not the same as saying the value comprises those other assets and liabilities and should therefore be shown on the lines allocated for those assets and liabilities by Schedule 9A.

4.64 The Board believes that a similar argument applies to the recognition of the excess value of any investment that the with-profits fund has in a subsidiary.

4.65 The FRS describes two different approaches to 'liability presentation'.

(a) The first approach will usually not be feasible but should be adopted if it is. It requires that part of the VIF of non-participating business included in the policyholder liabilities to be deducted from the 'realistic' liability number, and that part of the VIF of non-participating business included in the FFA to be deducted from the FFA. The Board believes that this approach would be consistent with Schedule 9A's requirements analysed above in that it is still a prudent measure derived from an actuarial valuation—it is just that no value has been attributed to an obligation to transfer an item that is not recognised as an asset.

(b) On the other hand, the Board believes that the 'liability presentation' approach that is usually feasible—deducting the VIF of non-participating business from the aggregate of policyholder liabilities and the FFA, although showing each of the three items separately on the face of the balance sheet—might not meet Schedule 9A's requirements. That is because Schedule 9A requires policyholder liabilities and the FFA to be shown separately, and that seems to require the VIF of non-participating business to be allocated between them rather than deducted from the sum of them.

Practicality

4.66 To summarise the discussion in section 4 so far:

(a) Although there were certain conceptual difficulties with 'realistic' liabilities, the Board still considers their use where available preferable to the continued use of the existing MSSB basis.
(b) If 'realistic' liabilities were to be used, it would be necessary to make certain consequential changes to other balance sheet items. However, those changes would not be problematical.
(c) It was possible to use 'realistic' liabilities where available and make the consequential balance sheet amendments deemed necessary and still comply with the requirements of Schedule 9A (and equivalent requirements).

Deferral until 2005

During the development of the FRED, the Board heard from a number of commentators who suggested that, regardless of the technical merits of recognising 'realistic' liabilities, there are practical considerations that mean that such a change should either not be made at all or should not be made for 2004 year-ends. **4.67**

(a) Some commentators questioned whether the FSA's rules on the RBS method will be sufficiently robust to bear the burden that the Board is proposing to put on them. These commentators characterised the RBS method as involving a negotiation with the FSA and this, they argued, was not a good basis for an accounting standard. It would also mean that the reporting timetable would become crucially dependent on the FSA's ability to provide timely input into the estimation process. They also argued that the estimation of the 'realistic' liability amount was a highly subjective exercise; too subjective for the information to be included in financial statements intended to show a true and fair view.
(b) Some had fewer doubts about the long-term practicality of the proposals, but questioned the wisdom of implementing the proposals for 2004 reporting. They argued that, as with any major change in practice, the RBS method would take time to 'bed down' and would be very approximate until it does. They also suggested it would take longer to implement in the first year than in subsequent years. In their view it would be better to defer implementation for a year rather than jeopardise the timeliness of the financial statements and significantly increase the risk of those statements containing errors or misstatements.
(c) Some argued that, even though auditors would be required to give an opinion on the FSA's 2004 regulatory returns which would include RBS information, the FRED's proposals would raise important audit issues that were not capable of resolution in time for 2004.

At the time the Board was developing the FRED, it did not find these arguments persuasive. In its view, 'realistic' liability numbers would be no less subjective than other numbers—such as loan loss provisions, provisions for decommissioning costs, perhaps even pension liabilities. Furthermore, although the Board recognised that the proposed FRS would set preparers and auditors a challenge—particularly in the first year of implementation—it was not convinced that this would be any more difficult to overcome than the difficulties that some other entities have had to overcome in preparing their financial statements. In its view it would not be credible for entities to publish financial statements including liabilities measured on the existing basis whilst, at the same time, measuring liabilities in publicly available regulatory returns on a basis that is generally perceived to be better. The Board therefore proposed in the FRED that the changes to the liability model should be implemented for 2004 year-ends. **4.68**

Implementation in 2004 also had the advantage of ensuring that the FRS would apply to the whole industry in 2004 and would, in the main, continue to be applied **4.69** by the whole industry in subsequent periods—including, because of the grandfathering provisions in IFRS 4, entities preparing their financial statements in accordance with EU-adopted IFRS. On the other hand, if the FRS was not implemented until 2005, entities preparing their financial statements in accordance with EU-adopted IFRS would not fall within its scope. The Board considered it important that the FRS should be applied across the industry.

4.70 Most of those responding to FRED 34 criticised the proposal that the FRS should be implemented for 2004 year-ends. Some simply stated that the timetable was impracticable; others suggested a one year deferral.

4.71 The Board noted that a number of entities due to be preparing their financial statements in accordance with EU-adopted IFRS from 2005 had offered, either in their formal responses to FRED 34 or in their discussions with the Board's staff, to implement the FRS from 2005 if the Board decided not to require its adoption in 2004. It therefore had discussions with the Association of British Insurers, the British Banking Association and some of those bodies' members about that possibility. As explained more fully in section 10 of this appendix, those discussions were positive, thus enabling the Board to consider the proposed implementation timetable in isolation from its desire to issue a standard that would be adopted across the industry as a whole.

4.72 The Board then reconsidered its proposal to implement this part of the FRS in 2004 and concluded that implementation should be deferred by a year. The advantage to be gained by implementing this part of the FRS in 2004 rather than 2005 were marginal and there was a risk that, if more time for implementation was not allowed, the information provided could prove misleading.

Implications of IFRS 4 for a delay in implementation of the proposed standard

4.73 IFRS 4 imposes restrictions on the accounting policies that can be used from 2005 in financial statements prepared in accordance with EU-adopted IFRS. Those restrictions differ depending on whether the accounting policy is an existing policy (ie was also used in 2004) or a new policy (ie is being implemented for the first time in 2005). When the Board was developing the proposals in FRED 34, it kept its eye firmly fixed on the former restrictions but ignored the latter restrictions. The decision to delay implementation of the proposed FRS until 2005 meant that the latter restrictions were now relevant.

4.74 The Board believed there were three restrictions to consider. The first is set out in paragraph 22 of IFRS 4. That paragraph requires that, subject to certain exceptions (none of which are relevant here), an accounting policy can be changed only if it represents an improvement; in other words, if the change makes the financial statements more relevant and no less reliable, or more reliable and no less relevant. Does a change of accounting policy to one that involves the recognition of 'realistic' liabilities represent an improvement under IFRS 4? The Board believes that it does and its reasons for reaching that conclusion are as follows:

(a) The Board believes that it is beyond dispute that 'realistic' liabilities are a more relevant measure of the obligation to policyholders than the existing MSSB basis. The question is therefore whether they are less reliable.

(b) IFRS 4 requires reliability to be judged by the criteria in IAS 8. Paragraph 10(b) of IAS 8 makes it clear that reliability should be judged by considering whether an accounting policy results in financial statements that:

(i) represent faithfully the financial position, financial performance and cash flows of the entity;
(ii) reflect the economic substance of transactions, other events and conditions, and not merely the legal form;
(iii) are neutral; in other words, free from bias;
(iv) are prudent; and
(v) are complete in all material respects.

There is no doubt that 'realistic' liabilities are generally 'softer' numbers than MSSB liabilities (because they are significantly affected by assumptions and non-market inputs). However, as IAS 8 makes clear, the reliability test is not about the softness (or otherwise) of the numbers per se. Rather it is about attributes such as faithful representation (the MSSB number is not a faithful representation of policyholder liabilities because it omits a major element of the obligation to the policyholders—the constructive obligation for future bonuses); neutrality (the 'realistic' liability is a more neutral number than the MSSB liability because the latter is prepared on a very prudent basis), and prudence (both bases are prudent, it is just that the MSSB basis is overly prudent). On that analysis, 'realistic' liabilities are also more reliable than MSSB liabilities.

The second restriction relates to paragraph 25(c) of IFRS 4, which stipulates that, except as permitted by paragraph 24 of the IFRS, an accounting policy change cannot be made if it would involve the use of non-uniform accounting policies for the insurance liabilities of subsidiaries. The question here is, is a requirement to change the basis of recognising and measuring the policyholder liabilities of some entities' UK with-profits liabilities—and at the same time making changes to the treatment of the deferred acquisition costs and reinsurance assets arising from such funds—without changing the basis for all with-profits liabilities permitted by IFRS 4? The Board believes that it does; its reasoning is as follows: **4.75**

(a) Most groups with UK life assurance activities currently adopt a wide diversity of accounting policies in determining their policyholder liabilities, especially in respect of various overseas subsidiaries. For them, the change from the MSSB basis to the 'realistic' basis can be described as changing one basis that is used for UK with-profits policyholder liabilities but no other policyholder liabilities to another basis that is used for UK with-profits policyholder liabilities but no other policyholder liabilities.
(b) An alternative way of viewing the change to 'realistic' liabilities is a move from applying a partial recognition basis to the recognition of with-profits liabilities (because it takes account only of declared bonuses) to a basis that attempts to recognise constructive obligations for future bonuses as well. Viewed in this way the change can be seen as improving the uniformity of accounting policies used in the group, because the recognition bases used in other parts of the group—including non-participating business and general insurance business—will also be close to a full recognition basis.
(c) The exemption in paragraph 24 of the IFRS also appears relevant and clearly demonstrates that partial changes are not prohibited by the standard:
"An insurer is permitted, but not required to change its accounting policies so that it remeasures designated insurance liabilities to reflect current market interest rates and recognises changes in those liabilities in profit or loss. At that time, it may also introduce accounting policies that require other current estimates and assumptions for the designated liabilities. The election in this paragraph permits an insurer to change its accounting policies for designated liabilities, without applying those policies to all similar liabilities as IAS 8 would otherwise require."

The adoption of realistic liabilities would represent the introduction of an accounting policy that requires the use of current estimates and assumptions and as such is envisaged by the IFRS.

4.76 The third restriction relates to the recognition of the VIF of non-participating business written in a with-profits fund. The FRS permits the whole of the amount to be recognised if the non-participating business is measured on that basis for the purpose of the regulatory returns, the value is determined in accordance with the FSA's requirements, and the 'realistic' liabilities amount took account of the value. However, most UK entities recognising this VIF amount in their balance sheet will be doing so for the first time in their 2005 financial statements, which means that entities preparing their financial statements in accordance with EU-adopted IFRS will need to be able to implement the changes the FRS requires under EU-adopted IFRS. The Board believes that they can. That is because paragraph 5 of the FRS gives entities a choice of ways in which to incorporate the VIF amount on the balance sheet and although recognising the VIF as an asset will not be possible under IFRS 4 unless that amount includes neither future investment risk margins or excess investment management fees—and may not be possible under the IASB's Framework—the other two approaches allowed by the FRS envisage the VIF amount being taken into account in determining liabilities and IFRS 4's embedded value restrictions will have no implications for such a treatment.

4.77 The Board's view is therefore that it is possible to implement the requirements of the FRS in full in 2005 in a set of financial statements that comply fully with EU-adopted IFRS.

BALANCE SHEET CLASSIFICATION OF THE FFA

What is the FFA?

5.1 As already explained, under existing UK requirements entities with with-profits funds recognise an item called the Fund for Future Appropriations (or FFA) amongst their liabilities. The FFA is the cumulative amount that is available for allocation to policyholders (current and future) and, where applicable, shareholders but remains unallocated at the balance sheet date. Therefore, for an entity with shareholders one of the issues concerning the FFA is its ownership. For all entities there will also be the inter-generational issue: how much of the FFA belongs to which generation of policyholders?

5.2 Currently the FFA includes amounts relating to obligations (for example, amounts relating to the constructive obligations that exist in respect of additional bonuses) . However, in many cases it also includes an 'estate'. The ownership and future application of the estate is uncertain; although the expectation might be that 90% or so of it will be allocated to policyholders, there is no current obligation to allocate or pay any of the estate to anyone—it can be held indefinitely or used for any or all of the following purposes:

(a) meeting the expenses incurred in writing new business;
(b) meeting investment or other losses arising on the assets backing the estate;
(c) meeting losses arising from non-participating business written by the with-profit fund;
(d) meeting liabilities to the with-profit policyholders arising from non-participating features of the policies (such as options or guarantees);

(e) distribution to current and or future policyholders through the declaration of bonuses in excess of their measured obligations. (This could, for example, be as a consequence of a marketing initiative or a tontine effect*); or

(f) distribution to shareholders in accordance with their rights of participation in bonus declaration or by way of a scheme of arrangement agreed with policyholders.†

The FRS requires changes to the existing liability model that would have the effect, inter alia, of removing from the FFA, for those funds required by the FSA to prepare RBS information, amounts relating to the fund's constructive obligations in respect of additional bonuses and amounts relating to options and guarantees. As a result, it seems reasonable to consider whether for those funds the FFA should continue to be classified, as it is currently in the UK, amongst liabilities. (Many entities will also have funds not required to prepare RBS information and the FFA for those funds will continue to have an element that is related to constructive obligations in respect of additional bonuses.) **5.3**

IFRS 4, which applies from 2005 to those entities preparing their financial statements in accordance with EU-adopted IFRS, requires the FFA to be classified as either equity or liability or in part as equity and in part as a liability. The standard allows almost total flexibility as to how the classification (and any split) is done and does not, for example, appear to require it to be based on the existing equity and liability definitions. However, it does require that all guaranteed elements are classified as liabilities and that, if the guaranteed element is not distinguished from other parts of the with-profits contract, all the amounts relating to the contract should be classified as a liability. **5.4**

Under most US GAAP approaches and under embedded value principles the FFA is classified on the assumption that it is to be shared between policyholders and shareholders, generally in a 90:10 ratio. In other words, 90% of the FFA is treated as a liability and the balance is classified as equity. **5.5**

Should the FRS address the classification of the FFA?

Against this background, the Board considered whether the FRS should address the classification of the FFA. Bearing in mind that the FFA appears to comprise both equity and liability elements, it seemed unlikely that accounting would be improved by requiring the entire FFA to be treated as a liability or to be classified as equity.‡ The options the Board considered were: **5.6**

(a) to require the FFA to be classified as equity to the extent that no liability is involved (in other words, classify the estate as equity) and as a liability to the extent that the liability definition is met; or

**If a closed fund has a surplus but those leaving the fund are paid an amount that is equal to the constructive obligation, the value of the fund per remaining policyholder will increase as policyholders leave until there is only one remaining policyholder, who would be entitled to the entire surplus. (The principle of the tontine is that the last remaining policyholder is entitled to the surplus.) To avoid the tontine effect, funds over-distribute when they foresee a tontine arising.*

†Normally in a life company that has shareholders, when a surplus is declared as a bonus, 10% of the surplus involved is attributed to shareholders and 90% to policyholders. A scheme of arrangement may allow a higher amount to be attributed to shareholders. This is generally as part of an agreement to share the surplus with current policyholders.

‡The Board's Framework envisages that credit balances will be classified as liabilities if they meet the definition of a liability and as part of the ownership interest (which might be called by a number of different names, including 'equity') otherwise. The FRS uses the term 'equity'.

(b) to adopt a similar approach to that set out in IFRS 4.

5.7 In order to apply the change described in option (a) to entities preparing their financial statements in accordance with UK standards and legal requirements, a change would be required to the law and the Board understands there is little prospect of such a change in the near-future. However, rather than dismissing this option out of hand because of the legal difficulties, the Board considered whether it would want to make the change, legal requirements permitting.

(a) The case for classifying the estate as equity is simply stated: the estate (if correctly calculated) is not a liability as defined and any credit balance that is not a liability is equity under the Board's Framework. Arguments that the estate does not have the characteristics that one would normally associate with something that is equity miss the point: the only characteristic that equity has is that it is a residual and the estate possesses that characteristic. However, as the Board's Framework itself admits, definitions of items like liabilities are developed with current and past accounting problems in mind and, although they will often help in tackling new accounting problems, those new problems will sometimes point up shortcomings that need to be addressed. Indeed, recent work by a number of standard-setters has revealed the need for the principles that underlie the equity/liability classification to be reviewed. The US standard-setter, FASB, is carrying out a review for the IASB and that project is likely to inform the IASB's work in phase 2 of its insurance project.

(b) In order to classify as equity all of the FFA other than the portion identified as a liability, the Board would want to be confident that its definitions of 'liabilities' and of 'equity' were appropriate in the context of with-profits activities. It would also want to be confident that all the liabilities had been recognised and appropriately measured because it would not be appropriate to classify as equity a balance that might contain some element of liabilities. Although the development of the FSA's RBS approach has made it possible to get much closer to identifying the liability element (as defined by FRS 12) for the funds to which the methodology relates, 'realistic' liabilities are not the same as 'liabilities calculated on an FRS 12 basis'. There also remains considerable difficulty in attempting to identify the liability element for other funds.

(c) A consequence of classifying some or all of the FFA as equity would be a fundamental change to the profit recognition model. The Board would not want to make changes of this kind without a more detailed consideration of the profit recognition model than has been possible in this project.

The Board therefore decided not to propose the reclassification of some or all of the FFA as equity.

5.8 The other change the Board could have made was to adopt a similar approach to that set out in IFRS 4. However, such a change would have no effect on entities preparing their financial statements under UK standards and legal requirements unless there was a change of law—and there is no prospect of that in the near-future. Adopting the IFRS 4 approach in the UK would also have created the possibility of a diversity of practice where currently there is uniformity. The Board therefore decided not to pursue this option.

5.9 The FRS therefore remains silent on the classification of the FFA. This means that:

(a) in financial statements prepared in accordance with UK standards and legal requirements, the FFA will be classified as a liability; and

(b) in financial statements prepared in accordance with EU-adopted IFRS, there will be almost complete flexibility as to how the FFA is classified, subject only to the caveats explained in paragraph 5.4 above and pending completion of phase 2 of the IASB's insurance project.

Showing the technical provision and the FFA separately on the balance sheet

Currently Schedule 9A requires that the FFA and the technical provision are shown on separate lines of the balance sheet. However, for entities applying EU-adopted IFRS are not subject to that legal requirement. Furthermore, IFRS 4 permits, but does not require, entities to combine the technical provision and FFA on a single line of the balance sheet. **5.10**

Combining the technical provision and the FFA on a single line of the balance sheet would lose the improvements that the FRS is requiring because, rather than a technical provision that is prepared on a basis that is closer than the existing basis to FRS 12 and an FFA, there would just be an aggregated liability that would bear no resemblance whatsoever to the FRS 12 liability. The Penrose Report's desire to see the financial statements show a realistic position of the life office would also have been frustrated. **5.11**

Furthermore, although the Board decided that it should not for the time being propose reclassification of any of the FFA, it did not consider the FFA to be like any other liability and believed it would be inappropriate for the FFA and the technical provision to be combined together on a single line of the balance sheet. **5.12**

The Board therefore took steps to preserve the improvement the FRS makes to insurance liability accounting and to preserve the distinction between the FFA and other liabilities by including in the FRS a requirement that the technical provision and FFA should always be shown separately on the face of the balance sheet. **5.13**

The Board recognised that this would involve a change in balance sheet presentation for those non-insurance entities with insurance activities that show the FFA and the technical provision, together with all other insurance liabilities, on a single line of the consolidated balance sheet. However, it believed the change to be justified for the reasons explained above. **5.14**

OPTIONS AND GUARANTEES

Many life assurance policies include option or guarantee features, such as guaranteed surrender values or guaranteed annuity options on vesting of a pension accumulation product. Such options and guarantees are, furthermore, not unique to UK with-profits funds. They can also arise, for example, in non-participating funds and overseas funds. **6.1**

Some of these options and guarantees expose the entity to insurance variables (for example, mortality or morbidity); some to financial variables (for example, market prices). The latter are similar to financial options in that the amount payable will depend on the level of a variable, relative to a predetermined value, on a specified maturity date (or in a specified time period). **6.2**

(a) If at the specified time the variable is lower than the predetermined value, an amount is payable—the exact amount depending on the amount of the variable—and, if the variable is higher than the predetermined value, no amount is payable.

(b) An option contract is 'in the money' if the current level of the variable is below the predetermined value such that, were the current value to remain unchanged, an amount would be payable under the option. It is 'out of the money' if, were the current value to remain unchanged, no amount would be payable on maturity. Of course, a contract that is in the money prior to maturity may be out of the money when it matures, and vice versa.

(c) The fair value of such a contract at any time prior to its maturity will reflect both the amount (if any) by which the option is in the money at that time (its 'intrinsic value') and the risk that the intrinsic value will change in the period to maturity (its 'time value'). A contract that is out of the money will still have value, unless there is no possibility that it could be in the money when it matures. Therefore, an accounting practice that considers merely the extent to which the contract is in the money at the valuation date (or on a single forecast of the position at maturity date)—and thus ignores the time value of the contract—does not reflect the fair value of the contract.

6.3 The Board has long held the view that in principle all financial derivatives should be measured in the primary financial statements at an amount that takes into account both intrinsic value and time value (ie typically fair value),* and it sees no reason why options and guarantees exposing the life assurer to financial variables life assurers should be any different.

6.4 The Board noted in this context that, in calculating the 'realistic' liability arising from options and guarantees on UK with-profits policies within the scope of its RBS approach, the FSA requires the options and guarantees to be measured at an amount that takes into account both intrinsic value and time value. Currently, there are two ways of doing this:

(a) *Fair value derived from a market value comparison.* Contracts traded on financial markets are traded at their fair value so, if an option or guarantee feature of a with-profits policy is similar to a traded contract (or is similar to a combination of traded contracts), its fair value can be estimated by reference to that (those) observable market value(s).

(b) *A probabilistic or stochastic valuation method.* For many option and guarantee features incorporated in with-profits policies, equivalent traded instruments do not exist. In such circumstances, in order to capture the time value involved a probabilistic or stochastic modelling approach has to be adopted. Under such an approach, all possible outcomes are considered and weighted according to the probability of that outcome occurring, and the weighted average of the outcomes calculated.

6.5 Stochastic models need careful calibration, with the probabilities used in the model being adjusted to ensure that the values produced are consistent with observable market values for similar traded instruments. The models are further complicated by the need to reflect future management actions that may be taken in response to changes in conditions. For example, it may be that, were equity market prices to fall by 10% from current levels, the intention would be to change the mix of the fund's investment portfolio so that a greater proportion of bonds is held. It may alternatively be that management would respond by varying bonus rates or charges to policyholders. Both these courses of action could reduce the cost of the options. Stochastically modelled values need to take account of such management actions to the extent that such actions are realistically possible in the timescale envisaged and are consistent with the PPFM.

6.6 Although the Board believed that options and guarantees written by life assurers should in principle be included in the balance sheet at amounts that take into account both intrinsic value and time value, it accepted that major difficulties would arise in

**See 'Derivatives and other Financial Instruments' Discussion Paper, which was issued in July 1996.*

the short-term were it to require that time value should be taken into account for options and guarantees which do not have to be measured on that basis currently.* Accordingly, it decided that it should not at this stage *require* all options and guarantees to be measured on that basis.

Instead the proposal in the FRED was that detailed disclosure should be provided about all the options and guarantees written by a life assurer that are not measured at amounts that include time value, including options and guarantees written in non-participating funds and overseas funds. Disclosure is a poor substitute for proper accounting, but it helps ensure that users of accounts are aware of such options and guarantees. **6.7**

One option open to the Board was to implement in the UK some or all of IFRS 4's disclosure requirements. Such an approach would achieve convergence with international standards. The Board took the view that, although the IFRS 4 requirements set out the high-level disclosure principle involved, they were not detailed enough to ensure that the disclosure would be focused on the aspects of the options and guarantees on which the Board thought the disclosure should focus. It therefore developed its own disclosure proposals. **6.8**

Mixed views were expressed about the FRED's proposals, with some respondents expressing the view that their scope should be extended to include options and guarantees that were shown in the balance sheet at fair value or at market-consistent stochastic values, and others arguing that the disclosure should be narrowly scoped. A number of respondents also thought the proposed disclosures would be onerous to produce and should be simplified. **6.9**

On the question of scope: **6.10**

(a) the Board reconsidered whether it was appropriate to restrict the scope of the disclosures just to those options and guarantees not shown on the balance sheet at fair value or at a market-consistent stochastic value. It noted that, for those entities preparing their financial statements in accordance with EU-adopted IFRS, the IFRS 4 disclosure requirements would apply to all options and guarantees. The Board thought there was a need for some general disclosures (similar to some of those required by IFRS 4) for all options and guarantees, and that those disclosures should be supplemented with some more targeted disclosures (similar to those in FRED 34) for options and guarantees not shown on the balance sheet at fair value or at a market-consistent stochastic value. Therefore, in the FRS the general disclosure principle (in paragraph 48) is based on requirements in IFRS 4, and the disclosure requirement for options and guarantees not shown on the balance sheet at fair value or at a market-consistent stochastic value (in paragraph 51) is based on FRED 34; and

(b) the Board recognised that the FRED had not been clear as to what exactly was meant by 'options and guarantees' and, as a result, it was possible to interpret the phrase much more widely than the Board intended. The intention had been for the disclosures to focus on the financial risk aspects of the options and guarantees granted, rather than the insurance risk. Paragraph 50 of the FRS now makes this clear.

As already mentioned, some respondents thought the disclosures would be extremely burdensome. This was thought to be a particular problem if the information provided had to be audited at the 2004 year-end, because there was little time to put in place the systems needed to gather the necessary information. **6.11**

*ie non-participatory funds, the smaller UK with-profits funds and some overseas with-profits funds. It is understood that some overseas regulators already require the use of a measurement basis that takes into account both intrinsic value and time value.

(a) In the light of these comments, the Board reconsidered its disclosure proposals but concluded that it was essential that there should be disclosures that enable users to understand the main variables that determine the amount payable under options and guarantees granted and the potential effects of adverse changes in those variables. However, it accepted that there are different ways of presenting that information and that the most appropriate presentation would often depend on the circumstances involved. The FRS is therefore more flexible than the FRED on the detailed nature of the disclosures to be provided.

(b) Furthermore, to give preparers more time to put in place the necessary systems (and in line with the decisions taken on other aspects of the FRS), the Board decided to defer implementation of the options and guarantee disclosure requirements until 2005 year-ends. At the same time, a number of the biggest entities with life assurance activities have volunteered to provide the FRS's disclosures on options and guarantees in their OFR (or equivalent statements) for 2004 year-ends (see section 10 of this appendix).

RECOGNISING THE VALUE OF IN-FORCE LIFE ASSURANCE IN FINANCIAL STATEMENTS

Background

7.1 One aspect of the embedded value debate—the recognition of an asset that represents the VIF of non-participating business written in a with-profits fund—has already been discussed in this appendix (see paragraphs 4.20-4.30 and 4.62-4.65). A different but related issue was also considered in this project: the recognition in the primary financial statements as an asset of the value of in-force life assurance business (the VIF of life assurance business). In other words, the recognition on the balance sheet by some entities of an asset that represents the value to shareholders of in-force life assurance business and (usually) the recognition in the profit and loss account of changes in the value of this asset (after adjustment for any capital transfers into or out of the fund in the period).*

7.2 The objective of embedded value techniques is to reflect the estimated economic value of the existing in-force life business and of any existing surplus in the life fund from the shareholders' perspective. For example, for a with-profit life fund, VIF comprises two elements:

(a) *The shareholders' share of any surplus of the assets of the fund over the 'realistic' liabilities to current policyholders.* This surplus represents the estate of the fund and is usually held to meet solvency requirements and as working capital.

(b) *The net present value of the shareholders' share of the future bonuses expected to be declared in respect of in-force policies.* This represents the capitalised future returns on existing business and, as such, is derived from expected future profits and, in some cases, assumptions about the distribution of the estate.

7.3 There is not one single, precisely designed embedded value methodology; there are a number of similar, but different techniques.†

**This use of embedded values in the primary financial statements is most commonly—though not exclusively—seen in consolidated financial statements when a non-insurance group is consolidating an insurance subsidiary.*

†A number of different terms are also used, some of which describe different techniques and some of which do not. These include: embedded value, European embedded value, market-consistent embedded value, certainty equivalent embedded value, achieved profits, and value of in-force business. The discussion that follows uses the term 'embedded value' in its widest sense.

The issue

Existing insurance accounting focuses more on the needs of prudential regulation than on the information needs of investors. As a result, the true and fair financial statements are not very good at providing shareholders with useful information about the value of their interest in the business. Many entities have sought to address this by including in the annual report information prepared on an embedded value basis. Some entities provide this embedded value information as supplementary information. Others include embedded values in the primary financial statements. **7.4**

When the ABI was carrying out its latest revision of its SORP, it discussed with the Board the then practice of several insurance groups of recognising the VIF of life assurance business in the primary financial statements. The Board's view was that an asset for the internally-generated VIF of life assurance business should not be recognised in a balance sheet prepared on an MSSB basis, and that was the view that prevailed in the 2003 revision of the SORP. As a result, entities within the scope of the SORP—British insurance companies and insurance groups—no longer recognise the internally-generated VIF of life assurance business in their primary statements. Instead, they usually provide supplementary embedded value information. **7.5**

However, there are entities that have insurance activities but do not fall within the scope of the SORP (for example, bancassurers, Irish insurance entities and some retail groups), and a number of them still recognise the VIF of life assurance business in their primary financial statements. Thus, the same transactions are accounted for in fundamentally different ways depending on the type of entity involved. Although the effect on the profit and loss account is only a timing difference, the impact can be significant and the periods involved can be very long. **7.6**

The Board believes that there is no reason in principle why all entities should not account for life assurance in the same way. It has therefore been considering how it should respond to this inconsistency. **7.7**

Courses of action open to the Board

One possible option was to reverse the position the Board took during its discussions with the ABI and allow entities falling within the scope of the SORP to recognise the VIF of life assurance business in their primary financial statements without restriction. The Board rejected this approach. It has long-standing concerns about aspects of the embedded value approach and was not prepared to put aside those concerns—at least not without undertaking a comprehensive analysis of embedded value methodologies.* **7.8**

Another possible option was to prohibit all entities from recognising the VIF of life assurance business in their financial statements. Such an approach would achieve consistency between different types of entity, and appears to be consistent with the position the Board took in its discussions with the ABI in 2003. It would however mean forcing entities that currently recognise the VIF of life assurance business back on to a basis of accounting that the Board has acknowledged is very unsatisfactory—the MSSB basis (albeit modified by the FRS). A standard that achieves convergence by requiring some entities to move from a useful basis of accounting to a less useful basis is not a good accounting standard. **7.9**

**The Board intends to carry out a more thorough analysis of embedded value methods in the second half of this project. That work will include a review of the European CFO Forum paper 'European Embedded Value Principles' (issued May 2004).*

7.10 The Board concluded therefore that its approach should lie somewhere between these two extremes.

7.11 The aspect of embedded value that has caused the Board greatest concern in the past is the inclusion of future investment risk margins in the VIF of life assurance business.* Under 'traditional' embedded value methodologies, the expected future bonuses element of the VIF of life assurance business is determined after estimating the projected investment returns on each of the asset classes held in the funds, then discounting those returns using a single discount rate. Thus, the projected differential investment risk premium from asset classes is included in the embedded value; in other words, as the investment mix of the fund's portfolio changes, so will the amount of the VIF. This, the Board believes, is not appropriate.

7.12 For that reason, the Board was interested to see that a recent development of an embedded value methodology (known as market-consistent embedded value or MCEV) under which the expected future investment return on each asset class is discounted using a discount rate that is equal to that assumed return—thus ensuring that the future investment risk margins for the different asset classes are not anticipated in the VIF of life assurance business recognised as an asset. The Board might view more favourably embedded values that exclude those margins.

7.13 Before the Board would be able to form a view on embedded value methods that exclude future investment risk margins, it would need to study carefully a number of other aspects of the methodology. Those aspects include:

(a) *Future bonus assumptions*—Embedded value approaches for with-profits business generally make a number of simplifying assumptions in respect of future bonuses. For example, it is generally assumed that the whole of the estate will be distributed to existing policyholders, and that this distribution will be achieved by a proportionate uplift in the projected level of bonuses. The effect of this assumption is to spread the distribution of the estate over the run off period of the existing policies. It could be argued that this is not appropriate because it in effect assumes artificially that the fund is going to go into run off with no new policies being written and therefore no need to maintain an estate to meet future solvency or other requirements.

(b) *'Lock in'*—Embedded value calculations generally reduce the value of the shareholders' interest in the life business if that capital is considered to be 'locked in' the fund by the requirement to maintain regulatory solvency margins and prudential margins. For example, some—though not all—life assurers assume under that basis that the amounts are available for shareholders only as the solvency margins decline and therefore apply a discount. It could be argued that this reduction in value is inconsistent with usual accounting practice, which generally does not impose measurement limitations when there are restrictions as to distributability.

(c) *'Burn through' of the estate*—Generally embedded value calculations do not at present stochastically model all possible outcomes for the fund, and in particular do not take full account of the asymmetry of the shareholders' interest. For example, although embedded value methodologies generally assume that the shareholders' interest is 10% (with the policyholders taking 90%), they do not necessarily take account of extreme adverse circumstances in which the estate is exhausted (burnt through) and the shareholders' exposure might increase. (The shareholders' exposure can become 100% of the increase in the

**IFRS 4 uses the term 'future investment margins'. The FRS does as well because it is implementing IFRS 4 requirements. This appendix uses 'future investment risk margin' because that is a more precise description of what is being discussed.*

liability, although the exact exposure will depend on the contract terms and the PPFM of the fund concerned.) Taking these extreme circumstances into account in the stochastic model will reduce the embedded value.

(d) *Movements analysis*—Currently there are a number of differing conventions as to how the movement in the VIF of life assurance business in a period—particularly the impact of changing assumptions—is presented. This movements analysis is an important part of the embedded value information set.

The suggestion at the end of paragraph 7.12—that embedded value with future investment risk margins excluded might be the way forward—seems to be echoed in IFRS 4. Although IFRS 4 does not require an entity already recognising an embedded value that includes future investment risk margins to change that accounting policy, it makes it difficult for an entity not recognising future investment risk margins to start recognising them. (It adopts a similar approach to excess investment management fees—see paragraph 7.19 below.) 7.14

The Board decided that it should propose a prohibition on including, as part of an asset of the VIF of life assurance business, any value attributed to future investment risk margins. Such a proposal had three advantages: 7.15

(a) It addressed the aspect of embedded value that most concerns the Board.
(b) It appeared to be in line with the direction IFRS 4 indicates the IASB is taking.
(c) If applied to all entities prior to them preparing their financial statements under EU-adopted IFRS, it would ensure that under EU-adopted IFRS they were all subject to the same restriction on the use of future investment risk margins (rather than different restrictions depending on whether the entity is already recognising such margins).

When the FRED was being developed, the intention was to implement the above proposal for 2004 year-ends. Against this background some commentators suggested that, in the interests of achieving immediate convergence on future investment risk margins, the Board should allow the ABI to amend its SORP to permit the recognition by insurance entities of assets representing the VIF of life assurance business. That amendment, plus the proposal in the FRED, would mean that all entities—whether or not they were within the scope of the SORP and whether reporting under UK standards or EU-adopted IFRS—would be subject to the same restrictions in 2004. However, the Board decided instead that the FRED should propose that: 7.16

(a) those entities currently recognising an asset that represents the VIF of life assurance business could continue to recognise such an asset as long as, from 2004, that VIF did not include future investment risk margins; and
(b) there should be no change in the Board's position towards entities preparing their financial statements in accordance with UK standards and not currently recognising the VIF of life assurance business unless and until the Board had studied embedded value methodologies that do not include future investment risk margins and concluded that they were acceptable for use in financial statements.

These proposals allowed an inconsistency in existing practice to persist for 2004 but, because of IFRS 4's grandfathering provisions, would mean that all entities preparing their financial statements in accordance with EU-adopted IFRS would be subject to the same restrictions from 2005. 7.17

The proposal to prohibit a value being attributed to future investment risk margins received a mixed response. 7.18

(a) Some respondents claimed that embedded value was outside the scope of the life assurance project, because the Financial Secretary to the Treasury had made no reference to the subject in her letter to the Board. However, it is the Board that decides the scope of its project work and it decided in this case that, as the objective was to improve life assurance accounting, the scope of its work should not be limited to the concerns raised in the Penrose Report—the use of embedded value in the primary financial statements should also be considered.

(b) Some respondents argued that the restriction should be omitted because it would have no effect on the amount at which the VIF asset was recognised. On the other hand, others argued that, even if it had no effect on the amount recognised, the restriction would ensure that a more disciplined approach would be taken to the valuation of the VIF asset.

(c) Some respondents argued that the Board was misdirecting itself by seeking to achieve convergence on the restrictions that apply to the recognition of the VIF asset; it would not result in practice converging because recognising the VIF asset was optional. The Board was aware that convergence would not be achieved in the short-term, but did not believe that invalidated the proposal.

(d) Some respondents criticised the proposal that the restriction should be implemented for 2004 year-ends, arguing that it was too late in the year to require entities already recognising the VIF of life assurance business to make a potentially major change to their basis of profit recognition. They also pointed out that they would have to make changes to the VIF of life assurance business in 2005 when they implemented IAS 39 'Financial Investments: Recognition and Measurement' and it would be preferable if they could make all the changes at the same time. One reason the Board was seeking to implement the change in 2004 was because it would not be able to mandate the change in 2005 for entities preparing their financial statements in accordance with EU-adopted IFRS. The Board therefore had discussions with the largest entities currently recognising a VIF asset in their financial statements about the possibility of deferring the implementation of the restriction in exchange for a commitment to implement the restriction in 2005. Those discussions proved positive and the Board decided that the FRS should apply for accounting periods ending on or after 23 December 2005.

7.19 As mentioned in paragraph 7.14, IFRS 4 also prohibits entities from changing their accounting policies to start recognising in their VIF for life assurance business a value attributed to future investment management fees that exceeds the fair value of those future fees. In line with the Board's objective of trying to ensure that all types of entity would be subject from 2005 to the same restrictions on the use of embedded value, the Board proposed in the FRED that the FRS should include a similar restriction. However, it was clear from the comments received that the restriction was not being interpreted consistently and that the differences in interpretation could have a significant effect on the amount at which the VIF asset was recognised. As the source of the ambiguity seemed to be the wording taken from IFRS 4 and the Board was reluctant to include a clarification of that wording in the FRS (because that would involve interpreting an IFRS), it was eventually decided that the restriction should be omitted from the FRS.

MULTIPLE STATEMENTS PREPARED ON DIFFERENT BASES

8.1 The financial statements of life assurers are not easy to follow. Partly that is because life assurance is a complex business that has to date proved difficult to represent faithfully and simply in financial statements—the uncertainty of ownership of the estate is, for example, difficult to portray simply, as is the measurement uncertainty that is involved in any insurance entity. This is not a matter that is easily fixed. Partly the complexity stems from the unfamiliar technical jargon and formats used. However, for entities preparing their financial statements in accordance with UK standards and legal requirements, that terminology and those formats are largely dictated by law and the Board understands that there is no prospect of the law being changed in the near future. Entities preparing their financial statements in accordance with EU-adopted IFRS are not constrained in the same way, but the Board has no ability to mandate change for such entities.

For these reasons, the Board believes that there is little it can do about the unfamiliar technical jargon and formats used in the short-term. **8.2**

Another source of complexity is the publication of multiple statements: the true and fair financial statements, the supplementary embedded value statements, and the regulatory returns—each of which is prepared on a different basis, designed to serve a distinct (but often unexplained) purpose, and all of which are typically presented with little or no means for the users to navigate their way from one statement to another. The complexity this creates was a particular concern noted in the Penrose Report. It is also an issue that the Board believes it can do something about. **8.3**

The Penrose Report makes the case for convergence of true and fair financial statements with regulatory returns. However, the statements and returns serve different purposes—regulatory returns are primarily focused on solvency whereas true and fair financial statements have a broader remit—and statements that have different purposes will in their optimal form often involve different structures and bases. Therefore, although alignment of regulatory and financial reporting is desirable, this is best achieved through convergence around the structure and basis that are 'right' for the true and fair financial statements. The Board has been able to base so much of the FRS on the FSA's methodology because that methodology is to some extent an attempt by the FSA to converge aspects of regulatory returns with the approach applied generally in financial statements. **8.4**

Where differences between the statements remain, the Board's preference is to seek to improve the clarity of the information provided by requiring reconciliations between the statements. **8.5**

If two statements have been prepared on bases that have nothing in common, a reconciliation between them is not very useful because it tends to involve simply the substitution of one set of numbers with a second set. Therefore, reconciliations between statements should be required only if they would be meaningful. **8.6**

The Board believes that, although the various statements currently prepared are each serving a different purpose, there is an underlying convergence of approach which means that it is reasonable to expect reconciliations between the true and fair financial statements and the prudential returns to be meaningful. For example: **8.7**

(a) apart from a few isolated exceptions, the same asset recognition and measurement model is used in all the statements;
(b) as a result of the changes in the liability model required by the FRS, the same basic liability model will underlie the big UK with-profits funds' policyholder liability numbers in the true and fair financial statements, the regulatory returns, and in many cases (depending on the exact methodology used) the embedded value information; and
(c) embedded value methodology seems to be developing in the direction of valuing options and guarantees written in policies in a manner consistent with that required for 'realistic' balance sheets (ie on a fair value or stochastic basis).

8.8 These developments mean that reconciliations can provide a useful service in highlighting the remaining issues of difference between the various statements. On implementing the FRS, the main areas of difference would be:

(a) any adjustments to asset valuation required by solvency regulation; and
(b) the treatment as a liability for RBS regulatory returns of the shareholders' share of future bonus.

8.9 The Board believes that the proposed capital statement lends itself well to a reconciliation requirement, which is why paragraph 37 of the FRS requires the aggregate amount of the capital resources included in the capital statement to be reconciled to the shareholders' funds, FFA and other amounts shown in the entity's balance sheet. The effect is that the capital statement provides a reconciliation between regulatory and financial reporting at the available capital level.

8.10 The Board has not included in the FRS any requirement to provide a reconciliation between the supplementary embedded value information and the other statements. That is primarily it seems likely that such a reconciliation would have to be included in the supplementary information rather than the financial statements (because otherwise at least some of the embedded value information would be brought within the scope of the true and fair view requirement and the implications of that have not yet been fully explored). The Board has no means of insisting on a reconciliation if it is not to be included in the financial statements.

OTHER ISSUES ARISING FROM THE FRED 34 CONSULTATIONS

Scope

9.1 FRED 34 proposed that the FRS should apply to all entities that include a life assurance business, regardless of how they are constituted, whether life assurance is their main business and their size.

9.2 A number of respondents thought the proposals were inappropriate for some friendly societies or for smaller entities. Some suggested exemptions; others suggested deferred implementation.

9.3 Friendly societies are either 'directive friendly societies' or 'non-directive friendly societies'.

(a) Directive friendly societies are those whose premium income exceeds 5 million euro. They are required to prepare true and fair financial statements and, in doing so, to comply with detailed legal requirements that are almost identical to those set out in Schedule 9A.
(b) Non-directive friendly societies are also subject to a true and fair requirement, although the requirements as to the form and content of their financial statements are much less onerous and less prescriptive than those applying to directive friendly societies.

9.4 Another way of categorising friendly societies is as either 'incorporated friendly societies' or 'registered friendly societies'.

(a) An incorporated friendly society is a friendly society constituted under the Friendly Societies Act 1992. That Act accords a friendly society a separate legal identity.
(b) A registered friendly society is a friendly society constituted under the Friendly Societies Act 1974. Such friendly societies have no separate legal identity and,

as a result, they carry out their transactions in the name of the appointed trustees.

The main implications of the FRS for friendly societies and for smaller entities can be summarised as follows. **9.5**

(a) The recognition of 'realistic' liabilities—Only a few of the biggest friendly societies are required by the FSA to adopt the RBS method in their prudential returns and will therefore be required by the FRS to recognise 'realistic' liabilities in their balance sheets. Unless and until the FSA extends the scope of its regulations to entities that have UK with-profits liabilities of less than £500m, this aspect of the FRS will not apply to other friendly societies or to the other smaller entities with life assurance activities.

(b) Capital statement—Policyholders have the same level of interest in financial strength, and fungibility of capital, in the case of a friendly society as for any other life assurer. The same is true regardless of the entity's size. As such, there seems to be no reason why the capital statement and its supporting disclosures would not be relevant for a friendly society or for a smaller entity.

(c) Options and guarantees—The objective of these disclosures is to highlight the existence of any options and guarantees, to provide information that helps users to understand the extent to which the options and guarantees granted expose the entity to risk, and to explain what that exposure is. This objective is valid regardless of the size or type of entity involved.

There seems therefore to be no technical reason why the requirements of the FRS are any less applicable to friendly societies than to any other type of entity with a life assurance business. Nor does there seem to be any technical reason why the requirements should not be applied to smaller entities. **9.6**

However, directive friendly societies do not have to submit prudential returns to the FSA until six months after their year-end. (From 2006 this will be reduced to four months, and from 2007 to three months.) As a result, their current practice tends to be to publish their true and fair financial statements and hold their AGMs long before the completion and submission of their prudential returns. **9.7**

If an FRS were to require the inclusion in the 2005 financial statements of regulatory information, it will be necessary either to delay the financial statements (perhaps until six months after the year-end) or to accelerate the computation of regulatory numbers. , which could be difficult for some friendly societies. The Board weighed this against the advantages to be gained by applying the FRS as soon as possible. It also noted that, by issuing the FRS in December 2004 for application to December 2005 year-ends, it was giving entities more time to prepare for the standard's implementation than the FRED had proposed. The Board decided: **9.8**

(a) to require friendly societies applying the RBS approach for the FSA's regulatory returns to implement the FRS from the same date that all other life assurers applying the RBS approach were implementing it; and

(b) for purely pragmatic grounds, to defer the FRS's application to all other directive friendly societies for a further year (ie until 2006 year-ends).

The smallest friendly societies—non-directive friendly societies—are subject to a less rigorous prudential reporting regime than directive friendly societies. For example, a full actuarial valuation for the prudential return is computed only triennially and, although interim valuations are made for the purposes of the financial statements, they are often no more than 'no material change' confirmations. Although the Board can see no reason why policyholders and other users of the financial statements of such friendly societies should not be as well-informed as any other policyholders **9.9** about the financial position of their life assurer, it accepts that the application of the FRS will cause considerable practical difficulties for these friendly societies and they will struggle to overcome those difficulties quickly. For that reason, the Board decided to give such friendly societies a further year to prepare for the FRS; in other words, it will not apply to non-directive friendly societies until 2007 year-ends.

Terminology

9.10 The FRS uses the term "'realistic' liabilities" to describe the basis of liability recognition and measurement that it requires to be adopted for certain with-profits funds. That term has been used because it is the term that the FSA also uses (and it *was* the FSA that developed the basis).Although there is little doubt that the new basis is "more realistic" than the existing (MSSB) basis, some of those responding to the FRED thought it was an exaggeration—and therefore potentially misleading—to call it the 'realistic' basis. They suggested that the Board use a different term.

9.11 One of the things that makes insurance accounting difficult for many users to understand is the terminology used. The Board does not wish to add to that difficulty. However, the FSA's new methodology *is* universally known as the 'realistic' basis, and the Board believed it would be unhelpful to use any other term in the FRS. However, entities are not required by the FRS to use the term in their financial statements.

Changes to the FSA's 'realistic' capital regime

9.12 The FRS requires what is, in effect, a slightly amended regulatory number (the 'realistic' liabilities number) to be recognised in the financial statements. When this was proposed in the FRED, several respondents sought clarification as to the implications of a change in the regulations from which the number is derived.

9.13 There are two possible types of regulatory change that could be made:

(a) The scope of the regulations could change, so that they apply to funds or entities not currently within their scope. The FRED was worded so that, if the FSA extends the scope of its regulations to include other with-profits funds, entities would automatically be required by the FRS to show 'realistic' liabilities for those funds in their financial statements. However, if the scope was extended to include non-with-profits funds, that change would be treated in the same way as the changes described in (b). This approach has also been adopted in the FRS.

(b) The basis of the calculation could be changed. Although the Board believes the current 'realistic' capital regime is a satisfactory basis to use in the financial statements, it recognises that—because prudential regulation and true and fair financial statements serve different purposes—a future version of the 'realistic' capital regime may not be a satisfactory basis for the financial statements. For that reason, the FRS makes it clear (through the footnote to the definition of the 'Financial Services Authority realistic capital regime') that the FRS is based on the original version of the regime (ie the 18 November 2004 version) and will continue to be based on that version if the 'realistic' capital regime is amended unless and until the FRS is amended. Similarly, if the scope of the 'realistic' capital regime is extended by the FSA to include non-with-profits funds, the scope of the FRS would not extend to such funds unless and until the FRS is amended.

Negative FFAs

Some funds currently have a negative FFA—in other words, the aggregate of the fund-related debits recognised on the balance sheet is lower than the aggregate of the fund-related credits (other than the FFA) recognised. As a result of the changes the FRS requires to be made to the liability model, it is likely that more negative FFAs will arise in the future. **9.14**

There are a number of reasons why a negative FFA might arise, and only some of those reasons would result in the entity taking action to eliminate the negative FFA. For example, if the negative FFA was caused by the measurement of a liability at an amount that takes into account unrecognised assets or by the excessive prudence that will continue to be incorporated in many policyholder liabilities, it may be that corrective action would be deemed unnecessary. However, in other cases corrective action might be expected. Some types of corrective action would address the cause of the negative FFA but would not be accounted for in a way that would result in the negative FFA as shown in the balance sheet being eliminated, some would not. **9.15**

A number of respondents noted that FRED 34 was silent on the accounting treatment of negative FFAs and suggested that the FRS should make clear the treatment to be adopted. Some suggested that a negative FFA should always be eliminated as soon as it arises by making a charge to the profit or loss account. **9.16**

The Board considered these comments, but concluded that the FRS should remain silent on the accounting treatment. To adopt a blanket requirement that a negative FFA should always be written off to profit and loss account would not be appropriate in all cases. On the other hand, it would be difficult to identify all the circumstances in which it *would* be appropriate. **9.17**

The FRS requires entities with a negative FFA to explain how the negative balance arose and why it is that corrective action is not considered necessary. **9.18**

ABI SORP

Because of the FRS, the ABI's SORP will, for accounting periods ending on or after 23 December 2005, no longer be consistent in all respects with UK standards. The Board intends to discuss with the ABI how best to amend the SORP to eliminate the inconsistencies. **9.19**

Corresponding amounts

The FRED's proposals on the restatement of the corresponding amounts were based on the FRS being implemented for 2004 year-ends, and are therefore not relevant to the final FRS, which is to be implemented for 2005 year-ends. **9.20**

Currently the Act requires corresponding amounts to be presented for all the amounts included in the primary financial statements and for those corresponding amounts to be calculated on the same basis as the amounts for the current period. However, paragraph 64 of the FRS states that, when the FRS is first adopted, it will not be necessary to restate certain corresponding amounts in the profit and loss account. That is because, if all the corresponding amounts in the profit and loss account are to be restated, it will be necessary to produce a restated opening balance sheet for 2004. The Board accepts that this will often not be practicable. **9.21**

9.22 EU-adopted IFRS permit entities not to restate corresponding amounts if it is impracticable to do so. Although there is no equivalent provision in UK standards or legislation, the Board has asked the Department of Trade and Industry to consider amending the legal requirements to achieve the same effect.

THE MEMORANDUM OF UNDERSTANDING AND EU-ADOPTED IFRS

10.1 As has already been mentioned, the proposal in FRED 34 was that the FRS would be implemented for accounting periods beginning on or after 23 December 2004. There were two main reasons for this:

(a) The Board believed that improvements to life assurance accounting were needed urgently and that the improvements it was proposing were capable of being implemented for 2004 year-ends.

(b) The Board wished the improvements to be adopted by all UK entities with life assurance activities. If it did not implement the FRS until 2005 year-ends, its standard would not apply to entities preparing their financial statements in accordance with EU-adopted IFRS. On the other hand, if it implemented the FRS in 2004, the grandfathering provisions of IFRS 4 meant that entities preparing their financial statements in accordance with EU-adopted IFRS were likely to be required to continue to adopt the accounting policy changes required in the FRS in 2005 and thereafter.

10.2 Almost all respondents questioned whether implementation of the proposals for 2004 year-ends was as practicable as the FRED suggested. In the light of those comments, the Board decided to discuss with the largest entities with life assurance activities a suggestion that they had made to the Board on several occasions: the possibility of the Board deferring its FRS until 2005 and entities preparing EU-adopted IFRS financial statements still complying with the FRS as if it applied directly to them.

10.3 The Board has entered into a memorandum of understanding with a number of large entities and with the ABI along exactly those lines. The preparers signing the memorandum have also volunteered to provide most of the information that the FRS requires to be provided in the financial statements from 2005 in the OFR (or equivalent document) in 2004. A copy of the memorandum of understanding, together with details of the entities that have signed it, can be downloaded from the Board's website (www.frc.org.uk/asb).

10.4 When the FRED was being developed, the Board considered how the standard would work in the context of existing UK standards and what the implications of IFRS 4 would be for those entities applying the FRS in 2004, then moving onto EU-adopted IFRS in 2005. The implications of IFRS 4 differ depending on whether an accounting policy is being changed in 2004 (and is therefore an existing accounting policy in 2005) or 2005. This meant that, before it could consider deferring the FRS, the Board had to consider the implications of EU-adopted IFRS for a 2005 implementation of the FRS.

(a) One issue that the Board considered was whether the changes that the FRS requires to be made to accounting policies could be made in 2005, bearing in mind IFRS 4's restrictions on changing accounting policies. As explained in paragraphs 4.73-4.77, the Board concluded that they could.

(b) Another issue concerned the implications for the FRS of IAS 39's requirement that contracts that have in the past been viewed as insurance but actually meet the definition of a financial instrument (savings business) should be accounted for in accordance with IAS 39 rather than IFRS 4. The question the Board asked itself was would the changes required by IAS 39 have any effect on the accounting and disclosures required by the FRS and, if they would, was that effect troublesome?

(i) The FRS's 'realistic' liability requirements apply only to certain UK with-profits funds and, under IFRS 4, all UK with-profits activities would be 'insurance contracts that contain discretionary participation features' and would be accounted for in accordance with IFRS 4 rather than IAS 39. As mentioned in subparagraph (a), there is nothing in IFRS 4 that prevents the FRS's 'realistic' liabilities requirements from being complied with. Therefore, IAS 39 has no significant effect on the FRS's 'realistic' liability requirements.

(ii) IAS 39 appears to have no significant impact on the capital statement disclosures.

(iii) The FRS requires certain disclosures to be provided in respect of those options and guarantees described in paragraph 50 of the FRS that are not measured at fair value or on the basis of a market-consistent stochastic model. Some of the options and guarantees described in paragraph 50 (and not merely those not measured at fair value or on the basis of a market-consistent stochastic model) will fall within the scope of IAS 39 and will therefore be covered by the disclosure requirements in IAS 32 'Financial Instruments: Disclosure and Presentation' as well.

(iv) Entities already recognising the value of in-force life assurance business that are reporting under EU-adopted IFRS in 2005 but wishing to comply with this FRS at the same time will find they may have to make three changes to the VIF asset in 2005: in order to comply with IAS 39 they will need to exclude any embedded value that arises on the contracts that IFRS treats as savings business rather than insurance business; in order to comply with IFRS 4 they will need to comply with that standard's restriction on excess investment management fees and, in order to comply with this FRS they will need to exclude any amounts attributed to future investment risk margins.

None of this seemed to suggest that implementing the FRS would be particularly troublesome.

FUTURE DEVELOPMENTS

The Board recognises that the FRS will not be the final word on insurance accounting. Further improvements are still necessary, but the Board has taken the view that it is not reasonable for it to require further substantial changes in accounting policy at this time. **11.1**

The Board has, over the last seven years, taken a close interest in the international project on insurance accounting which was started by the International Accounting Standards Committee (IASC) and was taken up by the IASC's successor body, the IASB. The Board continues to see this international project as the best chance of achieving a fundamental and long-lasting improvement in insurance accounting. It intends to do all that it can, working with the IASB, the FSA and others, to secure that improvement. **11.2**

In this context, the FRS can be seen as outlining the direction in which the Board believes insurance accounting should develop over the next few years—away from the excessively prudent, deferral, matching and smoothing model of today towards a model consistent with the reporting framework that applies more generally, supplemented in ways that ensure that the distinctive features of insurance activities can **11.3** properly be reflected in financial statements. The Board hopes that the industry, freed as most of the biggest UK entities with life assurance activities are from the constraints of Schedules 9 and 9A, will make further improvements in their accounting in this direction.

11.4 The FRS is the first output from the Board's insurance project. The Board will also be making a formal response to the Financial Secretary on some issues not addressed in the FRS. It intends also to develop its thinking on a range of insurance-related issues and to use that thinking to help the IASB in its work.

THE ASB'S ADVISORY PANEL ON LIFE ASSURANCE

12.1 To assist the Board in the development of the FRS and in its ongoing consideration of improvements needed to insurance accounting, the Board set up an Advisory Panel, chaired by Mr Julian Hance. Although the Board reached its own conclusions and those conclusions were not necessarily the same as those of individual Panel members, it reached those conclusions only after taking fully into account the advice of Panel members. The Board found the Panel's advice and expertise invaluable during the development of the FRS, and it wishes to place on record its gratitude to Panel members for their work over the last eight months.

Financial Reporting Standard 28 'Corresponding Amounts' is set out in paragraphs 1-18.

The Statement of Standard Accounting Practice, which comprises the paragraphs set in bold type, should be read in the context of the Objective as stated in paragraph 1 and also of the Foreword to Accounting Standards and the Statement of Principles for Financial Reporting currently in issue.

The explanatory paragraphs contained in the FRS shall be regarded as part of the Statement of Standard Accounting Practice insofar as they assist in interpreting that statement.

Appendix III 'The development of the FRS' reviews considerations and arguments that were thought significant by members of the Board in reaching the conslusions on the FRS.

FRS 28
Corresponding amounts*

Summary

a Financial Reporting Standard 28 sets out the requirements for the disclosure of corresponding amounts† for items shown in an entity's primary financial statements and notes to the financial statements.

b The requirements of the FRS apply to financial statements that are intended to give a true and fair view except where an accounting standard or Urgent Issues Task Force Abstract requires or permits an alternative treatment.

c Corresponding amounts should be shown for items in the primary financial statements and the notes to the financial statements.

d Where the corresponding amounts are not directly comparable with the amount to be shown in respect of the current financial year, they should be adjusted and the basis for adjustment disclosed in a note to the financial statements.

e The FRS permits a reporting entity not to show corresponding amounts for certain items in the notes to the financial statements that were previously exempted under company law. It also does not require corresponding amounts for the earliest period presented where financial statements for two or more consecutive periods are presented together.

***Editor's note**: The matters covered in FRS 28 are dealt with, to the extent they are dealt with at all, in Section 3 of FRS 102.*

†*Also described as 'comparative figures' or 'comparative information' in other accounting standards.*

Financial Reporting Standard

OBJECTIVE

The objective of this FRS is to require appropriate disclosures of corresponding amounts for items shown in an entity's primary financial statements and notes to the financial statements. 1

SCOPE

The FRS applies to all financial statements that are intended to give a true and fair view of a reporting entity's financial position and profit and loss (or income and expenditure) for a period. 2

The requirements of the FRS apply except where an accounting standard or an Urgent Issues Task Force Abstract requires or permits an alternative treatment. 3

Where financial statements intended to give a true and fair view for two or more consecutive periods are presented together this FRS does not require corresponding amounts for the earliest period presented. 4

Reporting entities applying the Financial Reporting Standard for Smaller Entities currently applicable are exempt from the FRS. 5

DISCLOSURE REQUIREMENTS

Primary financial statements

In respect of every item shown in an entity's primary financial statements the corresponding amount for the accounting period immediately preceding that to which the primary financial statements relate shall also be shown. 6

Primary financial statements generally comprise statements of financial performance (for example, profit and loss account and statement of total recognised gains and losses); a statement of financial position (for example, balance sheet) and a cash flow statement. FRS 3 'Reporting financial performance' notes that the reconciliation of movements in shareholders' funds may be presented as a primary statement. Other terminology may be used to describe these primary financial statements in some industries and sectors. 7

Where there is no amount to be shown for an item in respect of the accounting period to which the primary financial statements relate but a corresponding amount can be shown for the item in question for the accounting period immediately preceding that to which the primary financial statements relate, the corresponding amount shall be shown. 8

Where a corresponding amount given in accordance with paragraph 6 or 8 of this FRS is not comparable with the amount to be shown for the item in question in respect of the accounting period to which the primary financial statements relate, the former amount shall be adjusted and particulars of the adjustment and the reasons for it shall be disclosed in a note to the financial statements. 9

Notes to the financial statements

10 **In respect of every item stated in a note to the financial statements:**

(a) the corresponding amount for the accounting period immediately preceding that to which the financial statements relate shall also be stated, unless not required by paragraph 11 of this FRS; and

(b) where a corresponding amount is not comparable, it shall be adjusted and particulars of the adjustment and the reasons for it shall be given.

11 **A reporting entity is not required to apply paragraph 10(a) in relation to any amounts stated for the items listed below which correspond to the requirements of the Large and Medium-sized Companies and Groups (Accounts and Reports) Regulations 2008 identified in the marginal notes.***

(a) details of additions, disposals, revaluations, transfers and cumulative depreciation of fixed assets; *[From Sch1 Part 3, 51†]*

(b) transfers to or from reserves and provisions and the source and application of any transfers; *[From Sch1 Part 3, 59‡]*

(c) accounting treatment of acquisitions; *[From Sch6 Part 1, 13]*

(d) details of shareholdings in subsidiary undertakings held by a company or, where group accounts are prepared, held by the parent company and by the group; *[From Sch4 Part 2, 11 and Part 3, 17]*

(e) significant holdings in undertakings other than subsidiary undertakings where group accounts are not prepared, details of the identity of each class of share in the undertaking held by the company, and the proportion of the nominal value of the shares of that class represented by those shares; *[From Sch4 Part 1, 5 (3)]*

(f) the proportion of the capital of the joint venture held by undertakings included in the consolidation; *[From Sch4 Part 3, 18(1)(d)]*

(g) details of shareholdings of associated undertakings held by the parent company and group; and *[From Sch4 Part 3, 19(4) and 19(5)]*

(h) details of other significant shareholdings of the parent company or the group. *[From Sch4 Part 3, 20(1) and Part 1, 5(3)]*

**The corresponding requirements for small companies are set out in The Small Companies and Groups (Accounts and Directors' Report) Regulations 2008.*

†The corresponding requirement is set out in Schedule 2 paragraph 62 for banking companies and Schedule 3 paragraph 69 for insurance companies.

‡The corresponding requirement is set out in Schedule 2 paragraph 70 for banking companies and Schedule 3 paragraph 77 for insurance companies.

DATE FROM WHICH EFFECTIVE

The accounting practices set out in the FRS should be regarded as standard for financial statements relating to accounting periods which begin on or after 1 January 2005 and which end on or after 1 October 2005. 12

In 2009 the FRS was amended to update the legal references following the introduction of the Companies Act 2006 and The Large and Medium-sized Companies and Groups (Accounts and Reports) Regulations 2008 (SI 2008 No. 410). The amendments take effect for accounting periods beginning on or after 6 April 2008, or when the provisions of the Act and/or the Regulations are applied to other entities (eg limited liability partnerships), if later. 12A

AMENDMENTS TO THE FINANCIAL REPORTING STANDARD FOR SMALLER ENTITIES (EFFECTIVE JANUARY 2005)

[Not reproduced, as all changes have been made to the FRSSE]

Adoption of FRS 28 by the Board

Financial Reporting Standard 28 *Corresponding Amounts* was approved for issue by the ten members of the Accounting Standards Board.

Ian Mackintosh	Chairman
Andrew Lennard	Technical Director
Michael Ashley	
Marisa Cassoni	
Anthony Good	
Roger Marshall	
Isobel Sharp	
Jonathan Symonds	
Helen Weir	
Peter Westlake	

Appendix I
Note on Legal Requirements

UNITED KINGDOM

The statutory requirements relating to the disclosure of corresponding amounts for items presented in the balance sheet or profit and loss account are set out in paragraphs 5 and 7 of Schedule 1 to the Large and Medium-sized Companies and Groups (Accounts and Reports) Regulations 2008. Corresponding requirements are set out in paragraphs 6 and 7 of Schedule 2 of the 2008 Regulations for banking companies and groups, and in paragraphs 4 and 5 of Schedule 3 of the 2008 Regulations for insurance companies. 1

The equivalent statutory requirements for small companies are set out in The Small Companies and Groups (Accounts and Directors' Report) Regulations 2008. The equivalent provisions of those set out in paragraph 11 of the Financial Reporting Standard are: 2

Large and medium sized companies	**Small companies**
Schedule 1 Part 3 paragraph 51	Schedule 1 Part 3 paragraph 48
Schedule 1 Part 3 paragraph 59	Schedule 1 Part 3 paragraph 54
Schedule 6 Part 1 paragraph 13	Schedule 6 Part 1 paragraph 13
Schedule 4 Part 2 paragraph 11	Schedule 2 Part 1 paragraph 2
Schedule 4 Part 3 paragraph 17	Schedule 6 Part 2 paragraph 23
Schedule 4 Part 1 paragraph 5(3)	Schedule 2 Part 1 paragraph 6(3)
Schedule 4 Part 3 paragraph 18(1)(d)	Schedule 6 Part 2 paragraph 26(1)(d)
Schedule 4 Part 3 paragraph 19(4) and (5)	Schedule 6 Part 2 paragraph 27(4) and (5)
Schedule 4 Part 3 paragraph 20(1)	Schedule 6 Part 2 paragraph 28(1)
Schedule 4 Part 1 paragraph 5(3)	Schedule 2 part 1 paragraph 6(3)

REPUBLIC OF IRELAND

The following table shows the provisions in the Companies Acts 1963-2006 and various Regulations implementing EC Accounting Directives, corresponding to the provisions of the UK Companies Act 2006 ('the 2006 Act') and the Schedules to the Large and Medium-sized Companies and Groups (Accounts and Reports) Regulations 2008 ('the 2008 Regulations') referred to in the Standard. The principal pieces of Irish legislation referred to in the table below are: 6

- The Companies (Amendment) Act 1986 ('1986 Act');
- The European Communities (Companies: Group Accounts) Regulations 1992 – SI 201 of 1992 ('Group Accounts Regulations 1992' or 'GAR 1992');
- The European Communities (Credit Institutions: Accounts) Regulations 1992 – SI 294 of 1992 – ('Credit Institutions Regulations 1992' or 'CIR 1992');
- The European Communities (Insurance Undertakings: Accounts) Regulations 1996, SI 23 of 1996 – ('Insurance Undertakings Regulations 1996' or 'IUR 1996').

This section is intended as a reference guide to the corresponding provisions in Irish company law and does not purport to be comprehensive. Readers are advised to refer to the Irish legislation for an understanding of relevant legal points.

UK References	ROI References				
2006 Act and the 2008 Regulations	**1986 Act**	**GAR 1992**	**CIR 1992**	**IUR 1996**	**Comments**
Schedule 1 Part 1 Paragraphs 5 and 7 of the Regulations	Sections 4(8) to 4(10)	Regulation 15(1)			
Schedule 2 Part 1 Paragraphs 6 and 7 of the Regulations			Paragraphs 3(4) and 4 of Part I of the Schedule		
Schedule 3 Part 1 Paragraphs 4 and 5 of the Regulations				Regulations 6(6) to 6(8)	
Schedule 1 Part 3 Paragraph 51 of the Regulations	Paragraph 29 of the Schedule	Regulation 15(1)			
Schedule 1 Part 3 Paragraph 59 of the Regulations	Paragraph 32 of the Schedule	Regulation 15(1)			
Schedule 6 Part 1 Paragraph 13 of the Regulations		Regulation 27	Paragraph 16 of Part II of the Schedule	Paragraph 6 of Part IV of the Schedule	Irish company law requires that where the composition of the undertakings dealt with in the group accounts has changed significantly, information must be provided to make the comparison of successive

UK References	ROI References				
2006 Act and the 2008 Regulations	1986 Act	GAR 1992	CIR 1992	IUR 1996	Comments
					sets of group accounts meaningful.
Schedule 4 Part 2 Paragraph 11 of the Regulations	Section 16(1)		Paragraph 2 of Part III of the Schedule	Paragraph 19 of Part III of the Schedule	
Schedule 4 Part 3 Paragraph 17 of the Regulations	Section 16(1)	Paragraph 18 of the Schedule	Paragraph 12 of Part III of the Schedule	Paragraph 32 of Part IV of the Schedule	The provisions noted set out the requirements of Irish company law. Other than under paragraph 12 of Part III of the Schedule to the Credit Institutions Regulations 1992 (CIR 1992), Irish company law does not require the separate disclosure of the identity of each class of shares held, and the proportion of the nominal value of the shares of that class represented by those shares, distinguishing between shares held by the parent company and shares held by other group undertakings. However,

UK References	ROI References				
2006 Act and the 2008 Regulations	**1986 Act**	**GAR 1992**	**CIR 1992**	**IUR 1996**	**Comments**
					paragraph 18 of the Schedule to the Group Accounts Regulations 1992 (GAR 1992), paragraph 11 of Part III of the Schedule to the Credit Institutions Regulations (CIR 1992) and paragraph 32 of Part IV of the Schedule to the Insurance Undertakings Regulations (IUR 1996) require disclosure of the basis for consolidating a subsidiary undertaking which is controlled by a group undertaking other than the parent company.
Schedule 4 Part 1 Paragraph 5(3) of the Regulations	Section 16(1)	Paragraph 22 of the Schedule	Paragraphs 7, 8 and 19 of Part III of the Schedule	Paragraph 36 of Part IV of the Schedule	
Schedule 4 Part 3 Paragraph 18(1)(d) of the Regulations	Section 16(1)	Paragraph 21 of the Schedule	Paragraph 17 of Part III of the Schedule	Paragraph 35 of Part IV of the Schedule	

UK References	ROI References				
2006 Act and the 2008 Regulations	**1986 Act**	**GAR 1992**	**CIR 1992**	**IUR 1996**	**Comments**
Schedule 4 Part 3 Paragraphs 19(4) and 19(5) of the Regulations	Section 16(1)	Paragraph 20 of the Schedule	Paragraph 18 of Part III of the Schedule	Paragraph 34 of Part IV of the Schedule	
Schedule 4 Part 3 Paragraph 20(1) and Part 1 Paragraph 5(3)	Section 16(1)	Paragraph 22 of the Schedule ('undertaking of substantial interest')	Paragraph 19 of Part III of the Schedule	Paragraph 36 of Part IV of the Schedule ('undertaking of substantial interest')	
Schedule 2 Paragraph 62 of the Regulations			Paragraph 55 of Part I of the Schedule		
Schedule 3 Paragraph 69 of the Regulations				Paragraphs 10(1)(a) and 10(3) of Part III of the Schedule	
Schedule 2 Paragraph 70 of the Regulations			Paragraph 59 of Part I of the Schedule		
Schedule 3 Paragraph 77 of the Regulations				Paragraph 14 of Part III of the Schedule	

Appendix II
Compliance with International Accounting Standards

The International Accounting Standards Board deals with corresponding amounts in its standards IAS 1 'Presentation of Financial Statements', IAS 8 'Accounting Policies, Changes in Accounting Estimates and Errors' and IFRS 1 'First-time Adoption of International Financial Reporting Standards'. 1

IAS 1 'Presentation of Financial Statements' paragraphs 36 to 41 set out requirements for comparative information. IFRS 1 'First-time adoption of IFRS' paragraph 36A provides exemption from the requirement to restate comparative information for IAS 32, IAS 39 and IFRS 4 for entities adopting IFRSs before 1 January 2006. IAS 8 'Accounting Policies, Changes in Accounting Estimates and Errors' deals in general with adjustments to comparative information required when an entity changes an accounting policy or corrects an error. It also discusses the impracticability of retrospective restatement. 2

The requirements of the FRS are consistent with international accounting standards in most cases except that: 3

(a) the FRS does not explicitly require comparative information for narrative and descriptive information required under paragraph 36 of IAS 1;
(b) the FRS does not permit non-restatement of comparative amounts on first time adoption of certain accounting standards or require disclosures of this as set out in paragraph 36A of IFRS 1;
(c) IAS 1 paragraph 38 does not require reclassification of comparative amounts where reclassification is impractical. This FRS does not contain a similar exemption; and
(d) paragraph 11 of the FRS provides specific exemptions from the requirement to disclose corresponding amounts for certain items disclosed in a note to the financial statements, not all of which have equivalent exemptions in IFRS.

Appendix III
The development of the FRS

BACKGROUND

1 In March 2005 the Department of Trade and Industry (DTI) issued a Consultation Document 'A consultation on extending use of summary financial statements and other minor changes'. In parallel the ASB issued Financial Reporting Exposure Draft 35 'Corresponding Amounts'. FRED 35 related to one aspect of the Consultation Document: the proposals in respect of corresponding amounts.

2 Following the consultation period the Companies Act 1985 was amended by a statutory instrument SI 2005 No. 2280 'Companies Act 1985 (Investment Companies and Accounting and Audit Amendments) Regulations 2005'.

3 The amendments made by the statutory instrument removed from the law the requirement to restate corresponding amounts where they are not comparable – although it remains a legal requirement to provide corresponding amounts in respect of the balance sheet and the profit and loss account, and the law permits them to be restated where they are not comparable. The amendments also removed from the law the requirement to provide corresponding amounts for items disclosed in the notes to the financial statements.

4 As a consequence of the amendments to the Companies Act 1985 it falls to accounting standards to prescribe whether corresponding amounts should be restated and whether corresponding amounts should be provided for amounts disclosed in the notes to the financial statements. FRED 35 set out the Board's proposal for a new FRS to require disclosure of corresponding amounts, generally adjusted onto a comparable basis, in an entity's primary financial statements and items disclosed in the notes to the financial statements.

APPROACH ADOPTED BY THE BOARD

5 The Board considers that the disclosure of corresponding amounts, generally adjusted onto a comparable basis, is an important part of accepted accounting practice. This Financial Reporting Standard is intended to secure this. In the main, the FRS replicates the legal requirements on corresponding amounts that existed prior to amendments made by the statutory instrument.

6 The Board intends that entities using UK IFRS-based accounting standards should be able to take advantage of the same exemptions as entities adopting IFRS. To enable the Board to incorporate these exemptions in UK IFRS-based standards the requirements of this FRS do not apply where a UK accounting standard or Urgent Issues Task Force Abstract requires or permits an alternative accounting treatment. This will allow the Board to consider exemptions for IFRS-based UK standards as the individual standards are developed.

CONVERGENCE WITH INTERNATIONAL FINANCIAL REPORTING STANDARDS

7 The Board considered adopting the requirements of International Financial Reporting Standards for corresponding amounts. These are set out in IAS 1 'Presentation of Financial Statements', IFRS 1 'First-time Adoption of International

Financial Reporting Standards' and IAS 8 'Accounting Policies, Changes in Accounting Estimates and Errors'. However, the Board concluded it was undesirable to introduce on a piecemeal basis elements of individual international accounting standards. This might introduce unintended consequences for other UK standards, whilst not achieving a substantive step towards convergence.

The Board also considered whether to introduce a general exemption from restating corresponding amounts on a comparable basis on grounds of practicality. The Board noted there is no such exemption under present or past requirements and considered that practicality is better addressed as each new accounting standard is developed. **8**

In considering the comments made by respondents to FRED 35 the Board noted that most respondents supported the Board's approach in respect of these matters and the proposals have been retained in the FRS. **9**

SCOPE OF THE FRS

The requirements of the FRS to disclose corresponding amounts apply to all entities and not just entities reporting under the Companies Act 1985. In its Statement of Principles* the Board notes that information in an entity's financial statements gains greatly in usefulness if it can be compared with similar information about the entity for some other period or point in time in order to identify trends in financial performance and financial position. It has become widely accepted practice to provide corresponding amounts in the financial statements of all entities. The FRS requires that where corresponding amounts are not comparable they should be restated unless an accounting standard or Urgent Issues Task Force Abstract permits or requires an alternative treatment. **10**

During its redeliberations of FRED 35 the Board became aware that the requirements proposed in FRED 35 could, in certain circumstances, be considered to extend regulatory requirements. One possible example was where a regulator requires a three year financial record and that the information given for each of the three years is required to give a true and fair view. The impact of FRED 35 would be to require a further year of corresponding amounts (ie corresponding amounts for the earliest year presented and thereby a further year presented). The Board decided it would be appropriate to amend the scope of the FRS such that where financial statements intended to give a true and fair view for two or more consecutive periods are presented together the FRS does not require corresponding amounts for the earliest period presented. This would avoid the potential extension of reporting requirements, as set out in the example above, but preserve the requirement to present corresponding amounts for at least one period. **11**

EXEMPTIONS

As noted FRED 35 was issued in parallel with the DTI's Consultation Document; 'A consultation on extending use of summary financial statements and other minor changes'. The Consultation Document did not propose to amend the legal requirements relating to corresponding amounts required for the notes to the financial statements. The DTI sought views on whether the requirements for disclosure in the notes should be retained in the Companies Act 1985, or should be removed and any future requirements be a matter for the ASB. **12**

**Statement of Principles for Financial Reporting; December 1999.*

13 Previously the Companies Act 1985 (paragraph 58 of Schedule 4) required corresponding amounts for every item stated in a note to the accounts for the financial year immediately preceding that to which the accounts relate. It also provided a number of specific exemptions from this requirement. The amendments made by the statutory instrument deleted the requirement to provide corresponding amounts for every item stated in a note to the accounts and thereby the exemptions from this requirement.

14 FRED 35 replicated the legal requirements and exemptions to these requirements previously set out in paragraph 58 of Schedule 4 to the Companies Act 1985 and corresponding schedules for banking and insurance and companies, except that it did not include an exemption from the requirement to provide corresponding amounts for loans and other dealings in favour of directors and others*. This was on the basis that the corresponding amounts for these items can often be easily provided and inclusion would enhance the usefulness of the financial statements. It is also difficult to justify these specific exemptions as there is no general exemption for related party transactions. Respondents to FRED 35 were generally in favour of the Board's proposals and these have been retained.

DATE FROM WHICH EFFECTIVE

15 The Regulations are effective in respect of financial years which begin on or after 1 January 2005 and which end on or after 1 October 2005. The FRS is effective from the same date.

**Part II and III of Schedule 6 (loans and other dealings in favour of directors and others) to the Companies Act 1985.*

Financial Reporting Standard 29 embodies IFRS 7 'Financial Instruments: Disclosures' and some amendments to that standard adopted for entities subject to UK accounting standards.

The Statement of Standard Accounting Practice in FRS 29 is set out in paragraphs 1-45A and the appendices. All paragraphs have equal authority. Paragraphs in bold type state the main principles.

Accompanying the Statement of Standard Accounting Practice is the basis for the conclusions reached in the Statement and some implementation guidance, neither of which forms part of the Statement.

The Statement of Standard Accounting Practice should be read in the context of its objectives as stated in paragraph 1, the Basis for Conclusions set out in paragraphs BC1-EBC16, and the Accounting Standard Board's 'Foreword to Accounting Standards' and 'Statement of Principles for Financial Reporting'.

Preface by the Accounting Standards Board

a This Financial Reporting Standard (FRS) has the effect of implementing the International Accounting Standards Board's (IASB's) International Financial Reporting Standard (IFRS) 7 'Financial Instruments: Disclosures' in the UK and Republic of Ireland for entities not preparing their financial statements in accordance with international financial reporting standards pursuant to the Regulation of the European Parliament and of the Council on the Application of International Accounting Standards.

b This Standard sets out requirements for disclosures relating to financial instruments and capital. Unlike IFRS 7, it only applies to entities within the scope of FRS 26 'Financial Instruments: Measurement' and comes into effect for accounting periods beginning on or after 1 January 2007. This Standard replaces the disclosure requirements of FRS 25 'Financial Instruments: Disclosure and Presentation'.

c Entities not applying FRS 26 are not required to comply with this Standard, although voluntary compliance is permitted.*

d The Board has issued FRS 29 to enable entities within the current scope of FRS 26 to adopt this standard in 2005 or 2006 if they so wish, with identical scope exemptions for subsidiaries and parent companies to those for the disclosure requirements of FRS 25. However, the FRS may be amended at a later date to remove some or all scope exemptions.

e In addition to the differences in scope set out above, the following differences exist between the requirements, scope and effective date of FRS 29 and IFRS 7:

- entities applying the FRSSE will be exempt from the FRS;
- disclosures are not required for certain subsidiary undertakings where at least 90 percent of the voting rights are held within the group, and parent companies in their single-entity financial statements provided the entity is included in publicly available consolidated financial statements which include disclosures that comply with this Standard;
- the FRS contains certain additional requirements for those entities not applying the requirements of FRS 26 (IAS 39) 'Financial Instruments: Measurement' but who wish to comply with the disclosure requirements of this standard voluntarily;
- certain disclosure requirements relating to the designation of financial assets and financial liabilities as at fair value through profit and loss account were not included as they were not considered necessary;
- disclosure requirements relating to capital that the IASB made as an amendment to IAS 1 'Presentation of Financial Statements' have been included in Appendix E to FRS 29; and
- certain transitional provisions from IFRS 1 'First-time Adoption of International Financial Reporting Standards' permitting entities applying the requirements of the FRS before 1 January 2007 not to restate comparatives to comply with this standard have been added.

The Board is currently considering proposals to extend the scope of FRS 26, as set out in the exposure draft 'Amendment to FRS 26: Extension of Scope and Recognition and Derecognition' (April 2005), and may decide to: extend the scope of FRS 26 and thus the effective scope of FRS 29; require some or all of the disclosures of FRS 29 to be made by entities not within the scope of FRS 26; and amend the scope exemption for subsidiary undertakings and parent companies. The Board may also implement the derecognition parts of IAS 39, in which case it will also implement the related disclosures in IFRS 7 (and paragraph 13 in particular).* ***Editor's note:* *These changes have now been made.*

The text of IFRS 7 contains various references to other IFRSs. In FRS 29 those references have been amended where necessary to enable the Standard to be applied in a UK context. The Accounting Standards Board believes that those amendments do not change the requirements of IFRS 7 in any way. **f**

IFRS 7 sets out amendments to other IFRSs. The Board has made amendments to FRS 26 corresponding to those made by IFRS 7 to IAS 39 'Financial Instruments: Recognition and Measurement'. Other amendments set out in IFRS 7 are not relevant in a UK context and have not been included in FRS 29. **g**

For entities applying this Standard, it supersedes the disclosure requirements of FRS 25 and FRS 13 'Derivatives and Other Financial Instruments: Disclosures'. **h**

In April 2006 the Board amended FRS 26 to include the IAS 39 material on recognition and derecognition in the Standard. Accordingly, on implementation of this amendment the corresponding disclosure requirements of IAS 32 are implemented in FRS 25. These new disclosure requirements replace disclosures required for financial assets and liabilities by FRS 5 'Reporting the Substance of Transactions'. These amendments are effective for accounting periods on or after 1 January 2007, with earlier adoption permitted. **i**

In May 2009 the Board amended FRS 29 to incorporate changes made to IFRS 7 by the IASB to require enhanced disclosures about fair value measurements and liquidity risk. The Board also took this opportunity to incorporate the credit risk disclosures for loans and receivables. **j**

These amendments are applicable for accounting periods commencing on or after 1 January 2009. Earlier application is permitted. **k**

In June 2011 the Board amended FRS 29 to incorporate changes made to IFRS 7 by the IASB to require enhanced disclosures about transfers of financial assets. These amendments are applicable for accounting periods commencing on or after 1 July 2011. **l**

FRS 29
(IFRS 7) Financial instruments: disclosures*

(Issued December 2005)

Contents

	paragraphs
Introduction	**IN1–IN8**
Financial Reporting Standard 29 (IFRS 7) Financial instruments: disclosures	
Objective	**1–2**
Scope	**3–5**
Classes of financial instruments and level of disclosure	**6**
Significance of financial instruments for financial position and performance	**7–30**
Balance sheet	**8–19**
Categories of financial assets and financial liabilities	8
Financial assets or financial liabilities at fair value through profit or loss	9–11
Reclassification	12
Derecognition	13
Collateral	14–15
Allowance account for credit losses	16
Compound financial instruments with multiple embedded derivatives	17
Defaults and breaches	18–19
Income statement and equity	**20**
Items of income, expense, gains or losses	20
Other disclosures	**21–26**
Accounting policies	21
Hedge accounting	22–24
Fair value	25–30
Nature and extent of risks arising from financial instruments	**31–42**
Qualitative disclosures	**33**
Quantitative disclosures	**34–42**
Credit risk	36–38
Liquidity risk	39
Market risk	40–42
Capital disclosures	**42A**
Effective date and transition	**43–44**
Withdrawal of FRS 13	**45A**

****Editor's note***: *The matters covered in FRS 29 are dealt with in Sections 11 and 12 of FRS 102, but also in Section 34 in relation to the disclosures required by financial institutions.*

Introduction*

Reasons for issuing the IFRS

In recent years, the techniques used by entities for measuring and managing exposure to risks arising from financial instruments have evolved and new risk management concepts and approaches have gained acceptance. In addition, many public and private sector initiatives have proposed improvements to the disclosure framework for risks arising from financial instruments. IN1

The International Accounting Standards Board believes that users of financial statements need information about an entity's exposure to risks and how those risks are managed. Such information can influence a user's assessment of the financial position and financial performance of an entity or of the amount, timing and uncertainty of its future cash flows. Greater transparency regarding those risks allows users to make more informed judgements about risk and return. IN2

Consequently, the Board concluded that there was a need to revise and enhance the disclosures in IAS 30 *Disclosures in the Financial Statements of Banks and Similar Financial Institutions*† and IAS 32 *Financial Instruments: Disclosure and Presentation*‡. As part of this revision, the Board removed duplicative disclosures and simplified the disclosures about concentrations of risk, credit risk, liquidity risk and market risk in IAS 32. IN3

Main features of the IFRS

IFRS 7 applies to all risks arising from all financial instruments, except those instruments listed in paragraph 3. The IFRS applies to all entities, including entities that have few financial instruments (eg a manufacturer whose only financial instruments are accounts receivable and accounts payable) and those that have many financial instruments (eg a financial institution most of whose assets and liabilities are financial instruments). However, the extent of disclosure required depends on the extent of the entity's use of financial instruments and of its exposure to risk. IN4

The IFRS requires disclosure of: IN5

(a) the significance of financial instruments for an entity's financial position and performance. These disclosures incorporate many of the requirements previously in IAS 32.

(b) qualitative and quantitative information about exposure to risks arising from financial instruments, including specified minimum disclosures about credit risk, liquidity risk and market risk. The qualitative disclosures describe management's objectives, policies and processes for managing those risks. The quantitative disclosures provide information about the extent to which the entity is exposed to risk, based on information provided internally to the entity's key management personnel. Together, these disclosures provide an

*ASB Footnote: *Although references to specific IFRSs have been amended in the main section of the Standard, references in the Introduction, which describes the issue of IFRS 7, have been left unchanged.*

†ASB Footnote: *IAS 30 has no equivalent in the UK and Republic of Ireland.*

‡ASB Footnote: *The equivalent standard in the UK and Republic of Ireland is FRS 25 (IAS 32) Financial Instruments: Disclsoure and Presentation.*

overview of the entity's use of financial instruments and the exposures to risks they create.

IN5A Amendments to the IFRS, issued in March 2009, require enhanced disclosures about fair value measurements and liquidity risk. These have been made to address application issues and provide useful information to users.

IN5B *Disclosures – Transfers of Financial Assets* (Amendments to IFRS 7), issued in October 2010, amended the required disclosures to help users of financial statements evaluate the risk exposures relating to transfers of financial assets and the effect of those risks on an entity's financial position.

IN6 The IFRS includes in Appendix B mandatory application guidance that explains how to apply the requirements in the IFRS. The IFRS is accompanied by non-mandatory Implementation Guidance that describes how an entity might provide the disclosures required by the IFRS.

IN7 The IFRS supersedes IAS 30 and the disclosure requirements of IAS 32. The presentation requirements of IAS 32 remain unchanged.

IN8 The IFRS is effective for annual periods beginning on or after 1 January 2007. Earlier application is encouraged.

Financial Instruments: Disclosures

OBJECTIVE

The objective of this Standard is to require entities to provide disclosures in their financial statements that enable users to evaluate: 1

(a) the significance of financial instruments for the entity's financial position and performance; and

(b) the nature and extent of risks arising from financial instruments to which the entity is exposed during the period and at the reporting date, and how the entity manages those risks.

The principles in this Standard complement the principles for recognising, measuring and presenting financial assets and financial liabilities in FRS 25 (IAS 32) *Financial Instruments: Presentation* and FRS 26 (IAS 39) *Financial Instruments: Recognition and Measurement*. 2

SCOPE

This Standard applies to all financial statements that are intended to give a true and fair view of a reporting entity's financial position and profit or loss (or income and expenditure), subject to the exemptions in 2B to 2E below. 2A

Reporting entities applying the Financial Reporting Standard for Smaller Entities (FRSSE) currently applicable are exempt from this Standard. 2B

Entities that are not applying FRS 26 are exempt from this Standard. 2C

The following entities are exempted from this Standard: 2D

(a) subsidiary undertakings, other than banks or insurance companies, 90 percent or more of whose voting rights are controlled within the group; and

(b) parent companies in respect of their single-entity financial statements

provided the entity is included in publicly available consolidated financial statements which include disclosures that comply with this Standard.

Although not mandatory, entities that are not applying FRS 26 are encouraged to comply with the disclosure requirements of this Standard, adapting these in line with the entity's accounting policies for the relevant transactions, and describing those accounting policies as required by paragraphs 21, 21A and 21B. In particular: 2E

(a) interest rate disclosures should be based on the rates at which interest is accounted for under the entity's accounting policies if this is different from the effective interest rate defined in FRS 26;

(b) disclosures on hedge accounting set out in paragraphs 22 to 24 should be applied to the entity's own hedge accounting policies; and

(c) instruments should be treated as insurance contracts for the purposes of disclosure if they are accounted for as such under the entity's accounting policies, even if they meet the definition of a financial instrument in FRS 26.

This Standard shall be applied by all entities to all types of financial instruments, except: 3

(a) those interests in subsidiaries, quasi-subsidiaries and associated undertakings, partnerships and joint ventures, including those which are accounted for under FRS 5 *Reporting the Substance of Transactions*; and FRS 9 *Associates and Joint Ventures*. However, entities shall also apply this Standard to all derivatives linked to interests in subsidiaries, quasi-subsidiaries or associated undertakings, partnerships or joint ventures unless the derivative meets the definition of an equity instrument in FRS 25.*

(b) employers' rights and obligations arising from employee benefit plans, to which FRS 17 *Retirement Benefits* applies.

(c) contracts for contingent consideration in a business combination (see paragraph 27 of FRS 7 *Fair Values in Acquisition Accounting*). This exemption applies only to the acquirer.

(d) insurance contracts as defined in Appendix C to FRS 26. However, this Standard applies to derivatives that are embedded in insurance contracts if FRS 26 requires the entity to account for them separately. Moreover, an issuer shall apply this Standard to *financial guarantee contracts* if the issuer applies FRS 26 in measuring the contracts.

(e) financial instruments, contracts and obligations under share-based payment transactions to which FRS 20 (IFRS 2) *Share-based Payment* applies, except that this Standard applies to contracts within the scope of paragraphs 5–7 of FRS 26.

(f) instruments that are required to be classified as equity instruments in accordance with paragraphs 16A and 16B or paragraphs 16C and 16D of FRS 25. The disclosure requirements for these instruments required to be classified as equity have instead been included in paragraphs E4-E8 of Appendix E to this standard.†

4 This Standard applies to recognised and unrecognised financial instruments. Recognised financial instruments include financial assets and financial liabilities that are within the scope of FRS 26. Unrecognised financial instruments include some financial instruments that, although outside the scope of FRS 26, are within the scope of this Standard (such as some loan commitments).

5 This Standard applies to contracts to buy or sell a non-financial item that are within the scope of FRS 26 (see paragraphs 5–7 of FRS 26).

CLASSES OF FINANCIAL INSTRUMENTS AND LEVEL OF DISCLOSURE

6 When this Standard requires disclosures by class of financial instrument, an entity shall group financial instruments into classes that are appropriate to the nature of the information disclosed and that take into account the characteristics of those financial instruments. An entity shall provide sufficient information to permit reconciliation to the line items presented in the balance sheet.

SIGNIFICANCE OF FINANCIAL INSTRUMENTS FOR FINANCIAL POSITION AND PERFORMANCE

7 An entity shall disclose information that enables users of its financial statements to evaluate the significance of financial instruments for its financial position and performance.

****Editor's note**: Sub-paragraph amended with effect for accounting periods beginning on or after 1 January 2009.*

*†**Editor's note**: Sub-paragraph added with effect for accounting periods beginning on or after 1 January 2010.*

Balance sheet

Categories of financial assets and financial liabilities

The carrying amounts of each of the following categories, as defined in FRS 26, shall be disclosed either on the face of the balance sheet or in the notes: **8**

(a) financial assets at fair value through profit or loss, showing separately (i) those designated as such upon initial recognition and (ii) those classified as held for trading in accordance with FRS 26;
(b) held-to-maturity investments;
(c) loans and receivables;
(d) available-for-sale financial assets;
(e) financial liabilities at fair value through profit or loss, showing separately (i) those designated as such upon initial recognition and (ii) those classified as held for trading in accordance with FRS 26; and
(f) financial liabilities measured at amortised cost.

If the entity has designated a loan or receivable (or group of loans or receivables) as at fair value through profit or loss, it shall disclose: **9**

(a) the maximum exposure to *credit risk* (see paragraph 36(a)) of the loan or receivable (or group of loans or receivables) at the end of the reporting period.
(b) the amount by which any related credit derivatives or similar instruments mitigate that maximum exposure to credit risk.
(c) the amount of change, during the period and cumulatively, in the fair value of the loan or receivable (or group of loans or receivables) that is attributable to changes in the credit risk of the financial asset determined either:
   (i) as the amount of change in its fair value that is not attributable to changes in market conditions that give rise to *market risk*; or
   (ii) using an alternative method the entity believes more faithfully represents the amount of change in its fair value that is attributable to changes in the credit risk of the asset.

   Changes in market conditions that give rise to market risk include changes in an observed (benchmark) interest rate, commodity price, foreign exchange rate or index of prices or rates.
(d) the amount of the change in the fair value of any related credit derivatives or similar instruments that has occurred during the period and cumulatively since the loan or receivable was designated.*

Financial assets or financial liabilities at fair value through profit or loss

If the entity has designated a financial liability as at fair value through profit or loss in accordance with paragraph 9 of FRS 26, it shall disclose: **10**

(a) the amount of change, during the period and cumulatively, in the fair value of the financial liability that is attributable to changes in the credit risk of that liability determined either:
   (i) as the amount of change in its fair value that is not attributable to changes in market conditions that give rise to market risk (see Appendix B, paragraph B4); or

****Editor's note:*** *Paragraph added in May 2009.*

(ii) using an alternative method the entity believes more faithfully represents the amount of change in its fair value that is attributable to changes in the credit risk of the liability.

Changes in market conditions that give rise to market risk include changes in a benchmark interest rate, the price of another entity's financial instrument, a commodity price, a foreign exchange rate or an index of prices or rates. For contracts that include a unit-linking feature, changes in market conditions include changes in the performance of the related internal or external investment fund.

(b) the difference between the financial liability's carrying amount and the amount the entity would be contractually required to pay at maturity to the holder of the obligation.

11 The entity shall disclose:

(a) the methods used to comply with the requirements in paragraph 10(a).
(b) if the entity believes that the disclosure it has given to comply with the requirements in paragraph 10(a) does not faithfully represent the change in the fair value of the financial asset or financial liability attributable to changes in its credit risk, the reasons for reaching this conclusion and the factors it believes are relevant.

Reclassification

12 If the entity has reclassified a financial asset (in accordance with paragraphs 51-54 of FRS 26) as one measured:

(a) at cost or amortised cost, rather than fair value; or
(b) at fair value, rather than at cost or amortised cost,

it shall disclose the amount reclassified into and out of each category and the reason for that reclassification.*

12A If the entity has reclassified a financial asset out of the fair value through profit or loss category in accordance with paragraph 50B or 50D of FRS 26 or out of the available-for-sale category in accordance with paragraph 50E of FRS 26, it shall disclose:

(a) the amount reclassified into and out of each category;
(b) for each reporting period until derecognition, the carrying amounts and fair values of all financial assets that have been reclassified in the current and previous reporting periods;
(c) if a financial asset was reclassified in accordance with paragraph 50B, the rare situation, and the facts and circumstances indicating that the situation was rare;
(d) for the reporting period when the financial asset was reclassified, the fair value gain or loss on the financial asset recognised in profit or loss or the statement of total recognised gains and losses in that reporting period and in the previous reporting period;
(e) for each reporting period following the reclassification (including the reporting period in which the financial asset was reclassified) until derecognition of the financial asset, the fair value gain or loss that would have been recognised in profit or loss or the statement of total recognised gains and losses if the financial asset had not been reclassified, and the gain, loss, income and expense recognised in profit or loss; and

****Editor's note****: Paragraph 12 amended and paragraph 12A added in October 2008.*

(f) the effective interest rate and estimated amounts of cash flows the entity expects to recover, as at the date of reclassification of the financial asset.

Derecognition

An entity may have transferred financial assets in such a way that part or all of the financial assets do not qualify for derecognition (see paragraphs 15–37 of IAS 39). The entity shall disclose for each class of such financial assets: **13**

(a) the nature of the assets;
(b) the nature of the risks and rewards of ownership to which the entity remains exposed;
(c) when the entity continues to recognise all of the assets, the carrying amounts of the assets and of the associated liabilities; and
(d) when the entity continues to recognise the assets to the extent of its continuing involvement, the total carrying amount of the original assets, the amount of the assets that the entity continues to recognise, and the carrying amount of the associated liabilities.*

Collateral

An entity shall disclose: **14**

(a) the carrying amount of financial assets it has pledged as collateral for liabilities or contingent liabilities; and
(b) the terms and conditions relating to its pledge.

When an entity holds collateral (of financial or non-financial assets) and is permitted to sell or repledge the collateral in the absence of default by the owner of the collateral, it shall disclose: **15**

(a) the fair value of the collateral held;
(b) the fair value of any such collateral sold or repledged, and whether the entity has an obligation to return it; and
(c) the terms and conditions associated with its use of the collateral.

Allowance account for credit losses

When financial assets are impaired by credit losses and the entity records the impairment in a separate account (eg an allowance account used to record individual impairments or a similar account used to record a collective impairment of assets) rather than directly reducing the carrying amount of the asset, it shall disclose a reconciliation of changes in that account during the period for each class of financial assets. **16**

Compound financial instruments with multiple embedded derivatives

If an entity has issued an instrument that contains both a liability and an equity component (see paragraph 28 of FRS 25) and the instrument has multiple embedded derivatives whose values are interdependent (such as a callable convertible debt instrument), it shall disclose the existence of those features. **17**

****Editor's note:*** *This paragraph, and the preceding heading, is deleted with effect for accounting periods beginning on or after 1 July 2011.*

Defaults and breaches

18 For *loans payable* recognised at the reporting date, an entity shall disclose:

(a) details of any defaults during the period of principal, interest, sinking fund, or redemption terms of those loans payable;
(b) the carrying amount of the loans payable in default at the reporting date; and
(c) whether the default was remedied, or the terms of the loans payable were renegotiated, before the financial statements were authorised for issue.

19 If, during the period, there were breaches of loan agreement terms other than those described in paragraph 18, an entity shall disclose the same information as required by paragraph 18 if those breaches permitted the lender to demand accelerated repayment (unless the breaches were remedied, or the terms of the loan were renegotiated, on or before the reporting date).

Income statement and equity

Profit and loss account and statement of total recognised gains and losses

20 An entity shall disclose the following items of income, expense, gains or losses either in the profit and loss account, statement of total recognised gains and losses or in the notes:

(a) net gains or net losses on:

(i) financial assets or financial liabilities at fair value through profit or loss, showing separately those on financial assets or financial liabilities designated as such upon initial recognition, and those on financial assets or financial liabilities that are classified as held for trading in accordance with FRS 26;
(ii) available-for-sale financial assets, showing separately the amount of gain or loss recognised through the statement of recognised gains and losses during the period and the amount reclassified from reserves to the profit or loss for the period;
(iii) held-to-maturity investments;
(iv) loans and receivables; and
(v) financial liabilities measured at amortised cost;

(b) total interest income and total interest expense (calculated using the effective interest method) for financial assets or financial liabilities that are not at fair value through profit or loss;
(c) fee income and expense (other than amounts included in determining the effective interest rate) arising from:

(i) financial assets or financial liabilities that are not at fair value through profit or loss; and
(ii) trust and other fiduciary activities that result in the holding or investing of assets on behalf of individuals, trusts, retirement benefit plans, and other institutions;

(d) interest income on impaired financial assets accrued in accordance with paragraph AG93 of FRS 26; and
(e) the amount of any impairment loss for each class of financial asset.*

**Editor's note: with effect for accounting periods beginning on or after 1 January 2009, paragraph 20, and the preceding heading, is amended.*

An issuer applying paragraph 20(b) of this Standard to contracts with a discretionary participation feature shall disclose the total interest expense recognised in profit or loss, but need not calculate such interest expense using the effective interest method.* 20A

Accounting policies

In accordance with paragraph 55 of FRS 18 *Accounting Policies*, an entity discloses the accounting policies that are material in the context of the entity's financial statements. 21

†For entities that choose to apply this Standard but do not apply FRS 26, it will be particularly important to provide adequate information for users of financial statements to understand the basis on which financial assets and financial liabilities have been measured. Therefore, disclosures of accounting policies indicate not only whether cost, fair value or some other basis of measurement has been applied to a specific class of asset or liability but also the method of applying that basis. For example, for financial instruments carried on the cost basis, an entity may be required to disclose how it accounts for: 21A

(a) costs of acquisition or issuance;
(b) premiums and discounts on monetary financial assets and financial liabilities;
(c) changes in the estimated amount of determinable future cash flows associated with a monetary financial instrument such as a bond indexed to a commodity price;
(d) changes in circumstances that result in significant uncertainty about the timely collection of all contractual amounts due from monetary financial assets;
(e) declines in the fair value of financial assets below their carrying amount; and
(f) restructured financial liabilities.

For financial assets and financial liabilities carried at fair value, an entity indicates whether carrying amounts are determined from quoted market prices, independent appraisals, discounted cash flow analysis or another appropriate method, and discloses any significant assumptions made in applying those methods.

An entity discloses the basis for reporting in the income statement realised and unrealised gains and losses, interest and other items of income and expense associated with financial assets and financial liabilities. The disclosure includes information about the basis on which income and expense arising from financial instruments held for hedging purposes are recognised. When an entity presents income and expense items on a net basis even though the corresponding financial asset and financial liabilities on the balance sheet have not been offset, the reason for that presentation is disclosed if the effect is significant. 21B

*ASB Footnote: *The IASB have incorporated this exemption from the effective interest rate method for issuers of financial instruments with discretionary participation features in IFRS 4* Insurance Contracts. *The ASB have replicated the text here to afford UK GAAP preparers the same exemption.*

†ASB footnote: *This paragraph is identical (apart from a necessary but cosmetic change to the introductory text) to paragraph 54 of the 1998 version of IAS 32, which the IASB has subsequently deleted. The ASB has reinstated it because compliance with FRS 26 is not mandatory for all companies initially. Similarly, paragraph 21B is identical to paragraph 55 of the 1998 version of IAS 32, which the IASB has subsequently deleted but the ASB has reinstated.*

Hedge accounting

22 An entity shall disclose the following separately for each type of hedge described in FRS 26 (ie fair value hedges, cash flow hedges, and hedges of net investments in foreign operations):

(a) a description of each type of hedge;
(b) a description of the financial instruments designated as hedging instruments and their fair values at the reporting date; and
(c) the nature of the risks being hedged.

23 For cash flow hedges, an entity shall disclose:

(a) the periods when the cash flows are expected to occur and when they are expected to affect profit or loss;
(b) a description of any forecast transaction for which hedge accounting had previously been used, but which is no longer expected to occur;
(c) the amount that was recognised through the statement of total recognised gains and losses during the period;
(d) the amount that was reclassified from reserves to the profit or loss for the period, showing the amount included in each line item in the profit and loss account;
(e) the amount that was removed from equity during the period and included in the initial cost or other carrying amount of a non-financial asset or non-financial liability whose acquisition or incurrence was a hedged highly probable forecast transaction.*

24 An entity shall disclose separately:

(a) in fair value hedges, gains or losses:
   (i) on the hedging instrument; and
   (ii) on the hedged item attributable to the hedged risk.
(b) the ineffectiveness recognised in profit or loss that arises from cash flow hedges; and
(c) the ineffectiveness recognised in profit or loss that arises from hedges of net investments in foreign operations.

Fair value

25 Except as set out in paragraph 29, for each class of financial assets and financial liabilities (see paragraph 6), an entity shall disclose the fair value of that class of assets and liabilities in a way that permits it to be compared with its carrying amount.

26 In disclosing fair values, an entity shall group financial assets and financial liabilities into classes, but shall offset them only to the extent that their carrying amounts are offset in the balance sheet.

27 An entity shall disclose for each class of financial instruments the methods and, when a valuation technique is used, the assumptions applied in determining fair values of each class of financial assets or financial liabilities. For example, if applicable, an entity discloses information about the assumptions relating to prepayment rates, rates of estimated credit losses, and interest rates or discount rates. If there has been

****Editor's note*: *With effect for accounting periods beginning on or after 1 January 2009, paragraph 23 is amended.***

a change in valuation technique, the entity shall disclose that change and the reasons for making it.

To make the disclosures required by paragraph 27B an entity shall classify fair value measurements using a fair value hierarchy that reflects the significance of the inputs used in making the measurements. The fair value hierarchy shall have the following levels: **27A**

(a) quoted prices (unadjusted) in active markets for identical assets or liabilities (Level 1);
(b) inputs other than quoted prices included within Level 1 that are observable for the asset or liability, either directly (ie as prices) or indirectly (ie derived from prices) (Level 2); and
(c) inputs for the asset or liability that are not based on observable market data (unobservable inputs) (Level 3).

The level in the fair value hierarchy within which the fair value measurement is categorised in its entirety shall be determined on the basis of the lowest level input that is significant to the fair value measurement in its entirety. For this purpose, the significance of an input is assessed against the fair value measurement in its entirety. If a fair value measurement uses observable inputs that require significant adjustment based on unobservable inputs, that measurement is a Level 3 measurement. Assessing the significance of a particular input to the fair value measurement in its entirety requires judgement, considering factors specific to the asset or liability.

For fair value measurements recognised in the balance sheet, an entity shall disclose for each class of financial instruments: **27B**

(a) the level in the fair value hierarchy into which the fair value measurements are categorised in their entirety, segregating fair value measurements in accordance with the levels defined in paragraph 27A.
(b) any significant transfers between Level 1 and Level 2 of the fair value hierarchy and the reasons for those transfers. Transfers into each level shall be disclosed and discussed separately from transfers out of each level. For this purpose, significance shall be judged with respect to profit or loss, and total assets or total liabilities.
(c) for fair value measurements in Level 3 of the fair value hierarchy, a reconciliation from the beginning balances to the ending balances, disclosing separately changes during the period attributable to the following:
    (i) total gains or losses for the period recognised in profit or loss, and a description of where they are presented in the profit and loss account;
    (ii) total gains or losses recognised through the statement of total recognised gains and losses;
    (iii) purchases, sales, issues and settlements (each type of movement disclosed separately); and
    (iv) transfers into or out of Level 3 (eg transfers attributable to changes in the observability of market data) and the reasons for those transfers. For significant transfers, transfers into Level 3 shall be disclosed and discussed separately from transfers out of Level 3.
(d) the amount of total gains or losses for the period in (c)(i) above included in profit or loss that are attributable to gains or losses relating to those assets and liabilities held at the end of the reporting period and a description of where those gains or losses are presented in the profit and loss account.
(e) for fair value measurements in Level 3, if changing one or more of the inputs to reasonably possible alternative assumptions would change fair value significantly, the entity shall state that fact and disclose the effect of those changes.

The entity shall disclose how the effect of a change to a reasonably possible alternative assumption was calculated. For this purpose, significance shall be judged with respect to profit or loss, and total assets or total liabilities, or, when changes in fair value are recognised through the statement of total recognised gains and losses, total equity.

An entity shall present the quantitative disclosures required by this paragraph in tabular format unless another format is more appropriate.

28 If the market for a financial instrument is not active, an entity establishes its fair value using a valuation technique (see paragraphs AG74–AG79 of FRS 26). Nevertheless, the best evidence of fair value at initial recognition is the transaction price (ie the fair value of the consideration given or received), unless conditions described in paragraph AG76 of FRS 26 are met. It follows that there could be a difference between the fair value at initial recognition and the amount that would be determined at that date using the valuation technique. If such a difference exists, an entity shall disclose, by class of financial instrument:

(a) its accounting policy for recognising that difference in profit or loss to reflect a change in factors (including time) that market participants would consider in setting a price (see paragraph AG76A of FRS 26); and
(b) the aggregate difference yet to be recognised in profit or loss at the beginning and end of the period and a reconciliation of changes in the balance of this difference.

29 Disclosures of fair value are not required:

(a) when the carrying amount is a reasonable approximation of fair value, for example, for financial instruments such as short-term trade receivables and payables;
(b) for an investment in equity instruments that do not have a quoted market price in an active market, or derivatives linked to such equity instruments, that is measured at cost in accordance with FRS 26 because its fair value cannot be measured reliably; or
(c) for a contract containing a discretionary participation feature (as described in Appendix C to FRS 26) if the fair value of that feature cannot be measured reliably.

30 In the cases described in paragraph 29(b) and (c), an entity shall disclose information to help users of the financial statements make their own judgements about the extent of possible differences between the carrying amount of those financial assets or financial liabilities and their fair value, including:

(a) the fact that fair value information has not been disclosed for these instruments because their fair value cannot be measured reliably;
(b) a description of the financial instruments, their carrying amount, and an explanation of why fair value cannot be measured reliably;
(c) information about the market for the instruments;
(d) information about whether and how the entity intends to dispose of the financial instruments; and
(e) if financial instruments whose fair value previously could not be reliably measured are derecognised, that fact, their carrying amount at the time of derecognition, and the amount of gain or loss recognised.

Nature and extent of risks arising from financial instruments

An entity shall disclose information that enables users of its financial statements to evaluate the nature and extent of risks arising from financial instruments to which the entity is exposed at the reporting date. **31**

The disclosures required by paragraphs 33–42 focus on the risks that arise from financial instruments and how they have been managed. These risks typically include, but are not limited to, credit risk, *liquidity risk* and market risk. **32**

Providing qualitative disclosures in the context of quantitative disclosures enables users to link related disclosures and hence form an overall picture of the nature and extent of risks arising from financial instruments. The interaction between qualitative and quantitative disclosures contributes to disclosure of information in a way that better enables users to evaluate an entity's exposure to risks.* **32A**

QUALITATIVE DISCLOSURES

For each type of risk arising from financial instruments, an entity shall disclose: **33**

(a) the exposures to risk and how they arise;
(b) its objectives, policies and processes for managing the risk and the methods used to measure the risk; and
(c) any changes in (a) or (b) from the previous period.

QUANTITATIVE DISCLOSURES

For each type of risk arising from financial instruments, an entity shall disclose: **34**

(a) summary quantitative data about its exposure to that risk at the end of the reporting period. This disclosure shall be based on the information provided internally to key management personnel of the entity (as defined in FRS 8, 'Related party disclosures'), for example the entity's board of directors or chief executive officer.
(b) the disclosures required by paragraphs 36–42, to the extent not provided in accordance with (a).
(c) concentrations of risk if not apparent from the disclosures made in accordance with (a) and (b).†

If the quantitative data disclosed as at the reporting date are unrepresentative of an entity's exposure to risk during the period, an entity shall provide further information that is representative. **35**

Credit risk

An entity shall disclose by class of financial instrument: **36**

(a) the amount that best represents its maximum exposure to credit risk at the end of the reporting period without taking account of any collateral held or other credit enhancements (e.g. netting agreements that do not qualify for offset in accordance with FRS 25); this disclosure is not required for financial

****Editor's note:*** *Paragraph added with effect for accounting periods beginning on or after 1 January 2011.*

†***Editor's note:*** *Paragraph amended with effect for accounting periods beginning on or after 1 January 2011.*

instruments whose carrying amount best represents the maximum exposure to credit risk.

(b) a description of collateral held as security and of other credit enhancements, and their financial effect (e.g. a quantification of the extent to which collateral and other credit enhancements mitigate credit risk) in respect of the amount that best represents the maximum exposure to credit risk (whether disclosed in accordance with (a) or represented by the carrying amount of a financial instrument).

(c) information about the credit quality of financial assets that are neither *past due* nor impaired.

Financial assets that are either past due or impaired

37 An entity shall disclose by class of financial asset:

(a) an analysis of the age of financial assets that are past due as at the end of the reporting period but not impaired; and

(b) an analysis of financial assets that are individually determined to be impaired as at the end of the reporting period, including the factors the entity considered in determining that they are impaired.

Collateral and other credit enhancements obtained

38 When an entity obtains financial or non-financial assets during the period by taking possession of collateral it holds as security or calling on other credit enhancements (e.g. guarantees), and such assets meet the recognition criteria in other FRS, an entity shall disclose for such assets held at the reporting date:

(a) the nature and carrying amount of the assets; and

(b) when the assets are not readily convertible into cash, its policies for disposing of such assets or for using them in its operations.*

Liquidity risk

39 An entity shall disclose:

(a) a maturity analysis for non-derivative financial liabilities (including issued financial guarantee contracts) that shows the remaining contractual maturities.

(b) a maturity analysis for derivative financial liabilities. The maturity analysis shall include the remaining contractual maturities for those derivative financial liabilities for which contractual maturities are essential for an understanding of the timing of the cash flows (see paragraph B11B).

(c) a description of how it manages the liquidity risk inherent in (a) and (b).†

Market risk

Sensitivity analysis

40 Unless an entity complies with paragraph 41, it shall disclose:

(a) a sensitivity analysis for each type of market risk to which the entity is exposed at the reporting date, showing how profit or loss and equity would have been

****Editor's note:*** *Paragraphs 36 to 38 amended with effect for accounting periods beginning on or after 1 January 2011.*

†***Editor's note:*** *Paragraph amended in May 2009.*

affected by changes in the relevant risk variable that were reasonably possible at that date;

(b) the methods and assumptions used in preparing the sensitivity analysis; and

(c) changes from the previous period in the methods and assumptions used, and the reasons for such changes.

If an entity prepares a sensitivity analysis, such as value-at-risk, that reflects inter-dependencies between risk variables (eg interest rates and exchange rates) and uses it to manage financial risks, it may use that sensitivity analysis in place of the analysis specified in paragraph 40. The entity shall also disclose: **41**

(a) an explanation of the method used in preparing such a sensitivity analysis, and of the main parameters and assumptions underlying the data provided; and

(b) an explanation of the objective of the method used and of limitations that may result in the information not fully reflecting the fair value of the assets and liabilities involved.

Other market risk disclosures

When the sensitivity analyses disclosed in accordance with paragraph 40 or 41 are unrepresentative of a risk inherent in a financial instrument (for example because the year-end exposure does not reflect the exposure during the year), the entity shall disclose that fact and the reason it believes the sensitivity analyses are unrepresentative. **42**

The disclosure requirements in paragraphs 42B–42H relating to transfers of financial assets supplement the other disclosure requirements of this FRS. An entity shall present the disclosures required by paragraphs 42B–42H in a single note in its financial statements. An entity shall provide the required disclosures for all transferred financial assets that are not derecognised and for any continuing involvement in a transferred asset, existing at the reporting date, irrespective of when the related transfer transaction occurred. For the purposes of applying the disclosure requirements in those paragraphs, an entity transfers all or a part of a financial asset (the transferred financial asset), if, and only if, it either: **42A**

(a) transfers the contractual rights to receive the cash flows of that financial asset; or

(b) retains the contractual rights to receive the cash flows of that financial asset, but assumes a contractual obligation to pay the cash flows to one or more recipients in an arrangement.*

An entity shall disclose information that enables users of its financial statements: **42B**

(a) to understand the relationship between transferred financial assets that are not derecognised in their entirety and the associated liabilities; and

(b) to evaluate the nature of, and risks associated with, the entity's continuing involvement in derecognised financial assets.

For the purposes of applying the disclosure requirements in paragraphs 42E–42H, an entity has continuing involvement in a transferred financial asset if, as part of the transfer, the entity retains any of the contractual rights or obligations inherent in the transferred financial asset or obtains any new contractual rights or obligations relating to the transferred financial asset. For the purposes of applying the disclosure **42C**

**Editor's note: Paragraphs 42A to 42H added with effect for accounting periods beginning on or after 1 July 2011.*

requirements in paragraphs 42E–42H, the following do not constitute continuing involvement:

(a) normal representations and warranties relating to fraudulent transfer and concepts of reasonableness, good faith and fair dealings that could invalidate a transfer as a result of legal action;
(b) forward, option and other contracts to reacquire the transferred financial asset for which the contract price (or exercise price) is the fair value of the transferred financial asset; or
(c) an arrangement whereby an entity retains the contractual rights to receive the cash flows of a financial asset but assumes a contractual obligation to pay the cash flows to one or more entities and the conditions in paragraph 19(a)–(c) of FRS 26 are met.

Transferred financial assets that are not derecognised in their entirety

42D An entity may have transferred financial assets in such a way that part or all of the transferred financial assets do not qualify for derecognition. To meet the objectives set out in paragraph 42B(a), the entity shall disclose at each reporting date for each class of transferred financial assets that are not derecognised in their entirety:

(a) the nature of the transferred assets.
(b) the nature of the risks and rewards of ownership to which the entity is exposed.
(c) a description of the nature of the relationship between the transferred assets and the associated liabilities, including restrictions arising from the transfer on the reporting entity's use of the transferred assets.
(d) when the counterparty (counterparties) to the associated liabilities has (have) recourse only to the transferred assets, a schedule that sets out the fair value of the transferred assets, the fair value of the associated liabilities and the net position (the difference between the fair value of the transferred assets and the associated liabilities).
(e) when the entity continues to recognise all of the transferred assets, the carrying amounts of the transferred assets and the associated liabilities.
(f) when the entity continues to recognise the assets to the extent of its continuing involvement (see paragraphs 20(c)(ii) and 30 of FRS 26), the total carrying amount of the original assets before the transfer, the carrying amount of the assets that the entity continues to recognise, and the carrying amount of the associated liabilities.

Transferred financial assets that are derecognised in their entirety

42E To meet the objectives set out in paragraph 42B(b), when an entity derecognises transferred financial assets in their entirety (see paragraph 20(a) and (c)(i) of FRS 26) but has continuing involvement in them, the entity shall disclose, as a minimum, for each type of continuing involvement at each reporting date:

(a) the carrying amount of the assets and liabilities that are recognised in the entity's balance sheet and represent the entity's continuing involvement in the derecognised financial assets, and the line items in which the carrying amount of those assets and liabilities are recognised.
(b) the fair value of the assets and liabilities that represent the entity's continuing involvement in the derecognised financial assets.
(c) the amount that best represents the entity's maximum exposure to loss from its continuing involvement in the derecognised financial assets, and information showing how the maximum exposure to loss is determined.
(d) the undiscounted cash outflows that would or may be required to repurchase derecognised financial assets (eg the strike price in an option agreement) or

other amounts payable to the transferee in respect of the transferred assets. If the cash outflow is variable then the amount disclosed should be based on the conditions that exist at each reporting date.

(e) a maturity analysis of the undiscounted cash outflows that would or may be required to repurchase the derecognised financial assets or other amounts payable to the transferee in respect of the transferred assets, showing the remaining contractual maturities of the entity's continuing involvement.

(f) qualitative information that explains and supports the quantitative disclosures required in (a)–(e).

An entity may aggregate the information required by paragraph 42E in respect of a particular asset if the entity has more than one type of continuing involvement in that derecognised financial asset, and report it under one type of continuing involvement. 42F

In addition, an entity shall disclose for each type of continuing involvement: 42G

(a) the gain or loss recognised at the date of transfer of the assets.

(b) income and expenses recognised, both in the reporting period and cumulatively, from the entity's continuing involvement in the derecognised financial assets (eg fair value changes in derivative instruments).

(c) if the total amount of proceeds from transfer activity (that qualifies for derecognition) in a reporting period is not evenly distributed throughout the reporting period (eg if a substantial proportion of the total amount of transfer activity takes place in the closing days of a reporting period):

  (i) when the greatest transfer activity took place within that reporting period (eg the last five days before the end of the reporting period),

  (ii) the amount (eg related gains or losses) recognised from transfer activity in that part of the reporting period, and

  (iii) the total amount of proceeds from transfer activity in that part of the reporting period.

An entity shall provide this information for each period for which a profit and loss account is presented.

Supplementary information

An entity shall disclose any additional information that it considers necessary to meet the disclosure objectives in paragraph 42B. 42H

Capital disclosures

An entity shall make disclosures about its capital as required by Appendix E, which is an integral part of this Standard.* 42A

Effective date and transition

An entity shall apply this Standard for accounting periods beginning on or after 1 January 2007. Earlier application is encouraged. If an entity applies this Standard for an earlier period, it shall disclose that fact. 43

Editor's note: *With effect for accounting periods beginning on or after 1 July 2011, this paragraph is renumbered 42I.*

44A An entity that chooses to adopt this Standard for accounting periods beginning before 1 January 2007 may elect to:

(i) adopt the requirements of Appendix E only;
(ii) adopt the Standard with the exception of Appendix E; or
(iii) adopt the whole Standard.*

44B If an entity that has not previously adopted the disclosure requirements of FRS 25 applies this Standard for an accounting period beginning before 1 January 2007 it need not present the comparative disclosures required by this Standard in its first financial statements prepared in accordance with this Standard. This exemption from the requirement to present comparative information does not extend to the requirements of Appendix E.†

44C An entity shall apply the amendment in paragraph 3 for annual periods beginning on or after 1 January 2010. If an entity applies Puttable Financial Instruments and Obligations Arising on Liquidation *(Amendments to FRS 25)* issued in August 2008, for an earlier period, the amendment in paragraph 3 shall be applied for that earlier period.‡

44D Paragraph 3(a) was amended by 'Improvements to Financial Reporting Standards' issued in December 2008. An entity shall apply this amendment for annual periods beginning on or after 1 January 2009. Earlier application is permitted. If an entity applies the amendment for an earlier period, it shall disclose that fact and apply the amended paragraph 2 of FRS 26 and paragraph 4 of FRS 25 issued in May 2008 for that earlier period. An entity is permitted to apply the amendment prospectively.§

44E Reclassification of Financial Assets (FRS 26 and FRS 29), issued in October 2008, amended paragraph 12 and added paragraph 12A. An entity shall apply those amendments from 1 July 2008.¶¶

44F The ASB amended paragraphs 20, 21, 23 (c) and (d) as part of its 'Improvements to Financial Reporting Standards' issued in December 2008. An entity shall apply those amendments for annual periods beginning on or after 1 January 2009.||

44G 'Amendments to FRS 29 – Improving Disclosures about Financial Instruments', issued in May 2009, amended paragraphs 27, 39 and B11 and added paragraphs 9, 27A, 27B, B10A and B11A–B11F. An entity shall apply those amendments for annual periods beginning on or after 1 January 2009. In the first year of application,

*ASB Footnote: *A consequence of putting the Capital Disclosures in IAS 1 is the ability of IFRS preparers to adopt IFRS 7 and the amendments to IAS 1 separately. Paragraph 44B of FRS 29 enables UK GAAP preparers to likewise adopt the Capital Disclosures separately from the other disclosures of the Standard.*

†ASB Footnote: *This paragraph implements transitional provisions of IFRS 1 for entities that voluntarily adopt the requirements of this Standard prior to its effective date. As a result, the exemption in paragraph 44 is not applicable and has been deleted. Appendix E contains the* Capital Disclosures *requirements developed by the IASB as part of the IFRS 7 project but introduced as an amendment to IAS 1 rather than in IFRS 7. IFRS 1 has been amended to provide certain reliefs from the need to restate comparative information for the requirements of IFRS 7 but not IAS 1. This approach has been replicated by the ASB.*

‡***Editor's note****: Paragraph 44C added in August 2008.*

§***Editor's note****: Paragraph 44D added in December 2008.*

¶¶***Editor's note****: Paragraph 44E added in October 2008.*

||***Editor's note****: Paragraph added in December 2008.*

an entity need not provide comparative information for the disclosures required by the amendments. Earlier application is permitted. If an entity applies the amendments for an earlier period, it shall disclose that fact.

'Improvements to Financial Reporting Standards 2010' issued in November 2010 added paragraph 32A and amended paragraphs 34 and 36–38. An entity shall apply those amendments for annual periods beginning on or after 1 January 2011. Earlier application is permitted. If an entity applies the amendments for an earlier period it shall disclose that fact. **44L**

Disclosures – Transfers of Financial Assets (Amendments to FRS 29), issued in July 2011, deleted paragraph 13 and added paragraphs 42A–42H and B29–B39. An entity shall apply those amendments for annual periods beginning on or after 1 July 2011. Earlier application is permitted. If an entity applies the amendments from an earlier date, it shall disclose that fact. An entity need not provide the disclosures required by those amendments for any period presented that begins before the date of initial application of the amendments. **44M**

WITHDRAWAL OF FRS 13

For entities applying this Standard, it supersedes FRS 13 *Derivatives and other financial instruments: disclosures.* **45A**

Appendix A
Defined terms

This appendix is an integral part of the Standard.

credit risk	The risk that one party to a financial instrument will cause a financial loss for the other party by failing to discharge an obligation.
currency risk	The risk that the fair value or future cash flows of a financial instrument will fluctuate because of changes in foreign exchange rates.
interest rate risk	The risk that the fair value or future cash flows of a financial instrument will fluctuate because of changes in market interest rates.
liquidity risk	The risk that an entity will encounter difficulty in meeting obligations associated with financial liabilities that are settled by delivering cash or another financial asset.*
loans payable	Loans payable are financial liabilities, other than short-term trade payables on normal credit terms.
market risk	The risk that the fair value or future cash flows of a financial instrument will fluctuate because of changes in market prices. Market risk comprises three types of risk: **currency risk**, **interest rate risk** and **other price risk**.
other price risk	The risk that the fair value or future cash flows of a financial instrument will fluctuate because of changes in market prices (other than those arising from **interest rate risk** or **currency risk**), whether those changes are caused by factors specific to the individual financial instrument or its issuer, or factors affecting all similar financial instruments traded in the market.
past due	A financial asset is past due when a counterparty has failed to make a payment when contractually due.

The following terms are defined in paragraph 11 of FRS 25 or paragraph 9 of FRS 26 and are used in the Standard with the meaning specified in FRS 25 and FRS 26

- amortised cost of a financial asset or financial liability
- available-for-sale financial assets
- derivative
- effective interest method
- equity instrument
- fair value
- financial asset
- financial instrument
- financial liability

**Editor's note*: *Amended in May 2009.*

- financial asset or financial liability at fair value through profit or loss
- financial asset or financial liability held for trading
- financial guarantee contract
- forecast transaction
- hedging instrument
- held-to-maturity investments
- loans and receivables
- regular way purchase or sale

Appendix B
Application guidance

This appendix is an integral part of the Standard.

CLASSES OF FINANCIAL INSTRUMENTS AND LEVEL OF DISCLOSURE (PARAGRAPH 6)

B1 Paragraph 6 requires an entity to group financial instruments into classes that are appropriate to the nature of the information disclosed and that take into account the characteristics of those financial instruments. The classes described in paragraph 6 are determined by the entity and are, thus, distinct from the categories of financial instruments specified in FRS 26 (which determine how financial instruments are measured and where changes in fair value are recognised).

B2 In determining classes of financial instrument, an entity shall, at a minimum:

(a) distinguish instruments measured at amortised cost from those measured at fair value

(b) treat as a separate class or classes those financial instruments outside the scope of this Standard.

B3 An entity decides, in the light of its circumstances, how much detail it provides to satisfy the requirements of this Standard, how much emphasis it places on different aspects of the requirements and how it aggregates information to display the overall picture without combining information with different characteristics. It is necessary to strike a balance between overburdening financial statements with excessive detail that may not assist users of financial statements and obscuring important information as a result of too much aggregation. For example, an entity shall not obscure important information by including it among a large amount of insignificant detail. Similarly, an entity shall not disclose information that is so aggregated that it obscures important differences between individual transactions or associated risks.

SIGNIFICANCE OF FINANCIAL INSTRUMENTS FOR FINANCIAL POSITION AND PERFORMANCE

Financial liabilities at fair value through profit or loss (paragraphs 10 and 11)

B4 If an entity designates a financial liability as at fair value through profit or loss, paragraph 10(a) requires it to disclose the amount of change in the fair value of the financial liability that is attributable to changes in the liability's credit risk. Paragraph 10(a)(i) permits an entity to determine this amount as the amount of change in the liability's fair value that is not attributable to changes in market conditions that give rise to market risk. If the only relevant changes in market conditions for a liability are changes in an observed (benchmark) interest rate, this amount can be estimated as follows:

(a) First, the entity computes the liability's internal rate of return at the start of the period using the observed market price of the liability and the liability's contractual cash flows at the start of the period. It deducts from this rate of return the observed (benchmark) interest rate at the start of the period, to arrive at an instrument-specific component of the internal rate of return.

(b) Next, the entity calculates the present value of the cash flows associated with the liability using the liability's contractual cash flows at the end of the period and a discount rate equal to the sum of (i) the observed (benchmark) interest rate at the end of the period and (ii) the instrument-specific component of the internal rate of return as determined in (a).

(c) The difference between the observed market price of the liability at the end of the period and the amount determined in (b) is the change in fair value that is not attributable to changes in the observed (benchmark) interest rate. This is the amount to be disclosed.

This example assumes that changes in fair value arising from factors other than changes in the instrument's credit risk or changes in interest rates are not significant. If the instrument in the example contains an embedded derivative, the change in fair value of the embedded derivative is excluded in determining the amount to be disclosed in accordance with paragraph 10(a).

OTHER DISCLOSURE – ACCOUNTING POLICIES (PARAGRAPH 21)

Paragraph 21 requires disclosure of the measurement basis (or bases) used in preparing the financial statements and the other accounting policies used that are relevant to an understanding of the financial statements. For financial instruments, such disclosure may include: **B5**

(a) for financial assets or financial liabilities designated as at fair value through profit or loss:

  (i) the nature of the financial assets or financial liabilities the entity has designated as at fair value through profit or loss;
  (ii) the criteria for so designating such financial assets or financial liabilities on initial recognition; and
  (iii) how the entity has satisfied the conditions in paragraph 9, 11A or 12 of FRS 26 for such designation. For instruments designated in accordance with paragraph (b)(i) of the definition of a financial asset or financial liability at fair value through profit or loss in FRS 26, that disclosure includes a narrative description of the circumstances underlying the measurement or recognition inconsistency that would otherwise arise. For instruments designated in accordance with paragraph (b)(ii) of the definition of a financial asset or financial liability at fair value through profit or loss in FRS 26, that disclosure includes a narrative description of how designation at fair value through profit or loss is consistent with the entity's documented risk management or investment strategy.

(b) the criteria for designating financial assets as available for sale.
(c) whether regular way purchases and sales of financial assets are accounted for at trade date or at settlement date (see paragraph 38 of IAS 39).
(d) when an allowance account is used to reduce the carrying amount of financial assets impaired by credit losses:

  (i) the criteria for determining when the carrying amount of impaired financial assets is reduced directly (or, in the case of a reversal of a write-down, increased directly) and when the allowance account is used; and
  (ii) the criteria for writing off amounts charged to the allowance account against the carrying amount of impaired financial assets (see paragraph 16).

(e) how net gains or net losses on each category of financial instrument are determined (see paragraph 20(a)), for example, whether the net gains or net losses on items at fair value through profit or loss include interest or dividend income.

(f) the criteria the entity uses to determine that there is objective evidence that an impairment loss has occurred (see paragraph 20(e)).
(g) when the terms of financial assets that would otherwise be past due or impaired have been renegotiated, the accounting policy for financial assets that are the subject of renegotiated terms (see paragraph 36(d)).

NATURE AND EXTENT OF RISKS ARISING FROM FINANCIAL INSTRUMENTS (PARAGRAPHS 31–42)

B6 The disclosures required by paragraphs 31–42 shall be either given in the financial statements or incorporated by cross-reference from the financial statements to some other statement, such as a management commentary or risk report, that is available to users of the financial statements on the same terms as the financial statements and at the same time. Without the information incorporated by cross-reference, the financial statements are incomplete.

Quantitative disclosures (paragraph 34)

B7 Paragraph 34(a) requires disclosures of summary quantitative data about an entity's exposure to risks based on the information provided internally to key management personnel of the entity. When an entity uses several methods to manage a risk exposure, the entity shall disclose information using the method or methods that provide the most relevant and reliable information. FRS 18 *Accounting Policies* discusses relevance and reliability.

B8 Paragraph 34(c) requires disclosures about concentrations of risk. Concentrations of risk arise from financial instruments that have similar characteristics and are affected similarly by changes in economic or other conditions. The identification of concentrations of risk requires judgement taking into account the circumstances of the entity. Disclosure of concentrations of risk shall include:

(a) a description of how management determines concentrations;
(b) a description of the shared characteristic that identifies each concentration (eg counterparty, geographical area, currency or market); and
(c) the amount of the risk exposure associated with all financial instruments sharing that characteristic.

Maximum credit risk exposure (paragraph 36(a))

B9 Paragraph 36(a) requires disclosure of the amount that best represents the entity's maximum exposure to credit risk. For a financial asset, this is typically the gross carrying amount, net of:

(a) any amounts offset in accordance with FRS 25; and
(b) any impairment losses recognised in accordance with FRS 26.

B10 Activities that give rise to credit risk and the associated maximum exposure to credit risk include, but are not limited to:

(a) granting loans and receivables to customers and placing deposits with other entities. In these cases, the maximum exposure to credit risk is the carrying amount of the related financial assets.
(b) entering into derivative contracts, eg foreign exchange contracts, interest rate swaps and credit derivatives. When the resulting asset is measured at fair value, the maximum exposure to credit risk at the reporting date will equal the carrying amount.

(c) granting financial guarantees. In this case, the maximum exposure to credit risk is the maximum amount the entity could have to pay if the guarantee is called on, which may be significantly greater than the amount recognised as a liability.
(d) making a loan commitment that is irrevocable over the life of the facility or is revocable only in response to a material adverse change. If the issuer cannot settle the loan commitment net in cash or another financial instrument, the maximum credit exposure is the full amount of the commitment. This is because it is uncertain whether the amount of any undrawn portion may be drawn upon in the future. This may be significantly greater than the amount recognised as a liability.

Quantitative liquidity risk disclosures (paragraphs 34(a) and 39(a) and (b))

In accordance with paragraph 34(a) an entity discloses summary quantitative data about its exposure to liquidity risk on the basis of the information provided internally to key management personnel. An entity shall explain how those data are determined. If the outflows of cash (or another financial asset) included in those data could either: **B10A**

(a) occur significantly earlier than indicated in the data, or
(b) be for significantly different amounts from those indicated in the data (eg for a derivative that is included in the data on a net settlement basis but for which the counterparty has the option to require gross settlement),

the entity shall state that fact and provide quantitative information that enables users of its financial statements to evaluate the extent of this risk unless that information is included in the contractual maturity analyses required by paragraph 39(a) or (b).

In preparing the maturity analyses required by paragraph 39(a) and (b) an entity uses its judgement to determine an appropriate number of time bands. For example, an entity might determine that the following time bands are appropriate: **B11**

(a) not later than one month;
(b) later than one month and not later than three months;
(c) later than three months and not later than one year; and
(d) later than one year and not later than five years.

In complying with paragraph 39(a) and (b), an entity shall not separate an embedded derivative from a hybrid (combined) financial instrument. For such an instrument, an entity shall apply paragraph 39(a). **B11A**

Paragraph 39(b) requires an entity to disclose a quantitative maturity analysis for derivative financial liabilities that shows remaining contractual maturities if the contractual maturities are essential for an understanding of the timing of the cash flows. For example, this would be the case for: **B11B**

(a) an interest rate swap with a remaining maturity of five years in a cash flow hedge of a variable rate financial asset or liability.
(b) all loan commitments.

Paragraph 39(a) and (b) requires an entity to disclose maturity analyses for financial liabilities that show the remaining contractual maturities for some financial liabilities. In this disclosure: **B11C**

(a) when a counterparty has a choice of when an amount is paid, the liability is allocated to the earliest period in which the entity can be required to pay. For example, financial liabilities that an entity can be required to repay on demand (eg demand deposits) are included in the earliest time band. [includes text from deleted paragraph B12]

(b) when an entity is committed to make amounts available in instalments, each instalment is allocated to the earliest period in which the entity can be required to pay. For example, an undrawn loan commitment is included in the time band containing the earliest date it can be drawn down. [text from deleted paragraph B13]

(c) for issued financial guarantee contracts the maximum amount of the guarantee is allocated to the earliest period in which the guarantee could be called.

B11D The contractual amounts disclosed in the maturity analyses as required by paragraph 39(a) and (b) are the contractual undiscounted cash flows, for example:

(a) gross finance lease obligations (before deducting finance charges);
(b) prices specified in forward agreements to purchase financial assets for cash;
(c) net amounts for pay-floating/receive-fixed interest rate swaps for which net cash flows are exchanged;
(d) contractual amounts to be exchanged in a derivative financial instrument (eg a currency swap) for which gross cash flows are exchanged; and
(e) gross loan commitments.

Such undiscounted cash flows differ from the amount included in the balance sheet because the amount in that statement is based on discounted cash flows. When the amount payable is not fixed, the amount disclosed is determined by reference to the conditions existing at the end of the reporting period. For example, when the amount payable varies with changes in an index, the amount disclosed may be based on the level of the index at the end of the period. [includes text from deleted paragraphs B14 and B16]

B11E Paragraph 39(c) requires an entity to describe how it manages the liquidity risk inherent in the items disclosed in the quantitative disclosures required in paragraph 39(a) and (b). An entity shall disclose a maturity analysis of financial assets it holds for managing liquidity risk (eg financial assets that are readily saleable or expected to generate cash inflows to meet cash outflows on financial liabilities), if that information is necessary to enable users of its financial statements to evaluate the nature and extent of liquidity risk.

B11F Other factors that an entity might consider in providing the disclosure required in paragraph 39(c) include, but are not limited to, whether the entity:

(a) has committed borrowing facilities (eg commercial paper facilities) or other lines of credit (eg stand-by credit facilities) that it can access to meet liquidity needs;
(b) holds deposits at central banks to meet liquidity needs;
(c) has very diverse funding sources;
(d) has significant concentrations of liquidity risk in either its assets or its funding sources;
(e) has internal control processes and contingency plans for managing liquidity risk;
(f) has instruments that include accelerated repayment terms (eg on the downgrade of the entity's credit rating);
(g) has instruments that could require the posting of collateral (eg margin calls for derivatives);
(h) has instruments that allows the entity to choose whether it settles its financial liabilities by delivering cash (or another financial asset) or by delivering its own shares; or

(i) has instruments that are subject to master netting agreements. [includes text from deleted paragraph IG31]

Market risk – sensitivity analysis (paragraphs 40 and 41)

Paragraph 40(a) requires a sensitivity analysis for each type of market risk to which the entity is exposed. In accordance with paragraph B3, an entity decides how it aggregates information to display the overall picture without combining information with different characteristics about exposures to risks from significantly different economic environments. For example: **B17**

(a) an entity that trades financial instruments might disclose this information separately for financial instruments held for trading and those not held for trading.

(b) an entity would not aggregate its exposure to market risks from areas of hyperinflation with its exposure to the same market risks from areas of very low inflation.

If an entity has exposure to only one type of market risk in only one economic environment, it would not show disaggregated information.

Paragraph 40(a) requires the sensitivity analysis to show the effect on profit or loss and equity of reasonably possible changes in the relevant risk variable (eg prevailing market interest rates, currency rates, equity prices or commodity prices). For this purpose: **B18**

(a) entities are not required to determine what the profit or loss for the period would have been if relevant risk variables had been different. Instead, entities disclose the effect on profit or loss and equity at the balance sheet date assuming that a reasonably possible change in the relevant risk variable had occurred at the balance sheet date and had been applied to the risk exposures in existence at that date. For example, if an entity has a floating rate liability at the end of the year, the entity would disclose the effect on profit or loss (ie interest expense) for the current year if interest rates had varied by reasonably possible amounts.

(b) entities are not required to disclose the effect on profit or loss and equity for each change within a range of reasonably possible changes of the relevant risk variable. Disclosure of the effects of the changes at the limits of the reasonably possible range would be sufficient.

In determining what a reasonably possible change in the relevant risk variable is, an entity should consider: **B19**

(a) the economic environments in which it operates. A reasonably possible change should not include remote or 'worst case' scenarios or 'stress tests'. Moreover, if the rate of change in the underlying risk variable is stable, the entity need not alter the chosen reasonably possible change in the risk variable. For example, assume that interest rates are 5 per cent and an entity determines that a fluctuation in interest rates of ± 50 basis points is reasonably possible. It would disclose the effect on profit or loss and equity if interest rates were to change to 4.5 per cent or 5.5 per cent. In the next period, interest rates have increased to 5.5 per cent. The entity continues to believe that interest rates may fluctuate by ± 50 basis points (ie that the rate of change in interest rates is stable). The entity would disclose the effect on profit or loss and equity if interest rates were to change to 5 per cent or 6 per cent. The entity would not be required to revise its assessment that interest rates might reasonably fluctuate by ± 50 basis points, unless there is evidence that interest rates have become significantly more volatile.

(b) the time frame over which it is making the assessment. The sensitivity analysis shall show the effects of changes that are considered to be reasonably possible over the period until the entity will next present these disclosures, which is usually its next annual reporting period.

B20 Paragraph 41 permits an entity to use a sensitivity analysis that reflects interdependencies between risk variables, such as a value-at-risk methodology, if it uses this analysis to manage its exposure to financial risks. This applies even if such a methodology measures only the potential for loss and does not measure the potential for gain. Such an entity might comply with paragraph 41(a) by disclosing the type of value-at-risk model used (eg whether the model relies on Monte Carlo simulations), an explanation about how the model works and the main assumptions (eg the holding period and confidence level). Entities might also disclose the historical observation period and weightings applied to observations within that period, an explanation of how options are dealt with in the calculations, and which volatilities and correlations (or, alternatively, Monte Carlo probability distribution simulations) are used.

B21 An entity shall provide sensitivity analyses for the whole of its business, but may provide different types of sensitivity analysis for different classes of financial instruments.

Interest rate risk

B22 *Interest rate risk* arises on interest-bearing financial instruments recognised in the balance sheet (eg loans and receivables and debt instruments issued) and on some financial instruments not recognised in the balance sheet (eg some loan commitments).

Currency risk

B23 *Currency risk* (or foreign exchange risk) arises on financial instruments that are denominated in a foreign currency, ie in a currency other than the functional currency in which they are measured. For the purpose of this Standard, currency risk does not arise from financial instruments that are non-monetary items or from financial instruments denominated in the functional currency.

B24 A sensitivity analysis is disclosed for each currency to which an entity has significant exposure.

Other price risk

B25 *Other price risk* arises on financial instruments because of changes in, for example, commodity prices or equity prices. To comply with paragraph 40, an entity might disclose the effect of a decrease in a specified stock market index, commodity price, or other risk variable. For example, if an entity gives residual value guarantees that are financial instruments, the entity discloses an increase or decrease in the value of the assets to which the guarantee applies.

B26 Two examples of financial instruments that give rise to equity price risk are (a) a holding of equities in another entity and (b) an investment in a trust that in turn holds investments in equity instruments. Other examples include forward contracts and options to buy or sell specified quantities of an equity instrument and swaps that are indexed to equity prices. The fair values of such financial instruments are affected by changes in the market price of the underlying equity instruments.*

In accordance with paragraph 40(a), the sensitivity of profit or loss (that arises, for example, from instruments classified as at fair value through profit or loss and impairments of available-for-sale financial assets) is disclosed separately from the sensitivity of equity (that arises, for example, from instruments classified as available for sale). **B27**

Financial instruments that an entity classifies as equity instruments are not remeasured. Neither profit or loss nor equity will be affected by the equity price risk of those instruments. Accordingly, no sensitivity analysis is required. **B28**

DERECOGNITION (PARAGRAPHS 42C–42H)

Continuing involvement (paragraph 42C)

The assessment of continuing involvement in a transferred financial asset for the purposes of the disclosure requirements in paragraphs 42E–42H is made at the level of the reporting entity. For example, if a subsidiary transfers to an unrelated third party a financial asset in which the parent of the subsidiary has continuing involvement, the subsidiary does not include the parent's involvement in the assessment of whether it has continuing involvement in the transferred asset in its stand-alone financial statements (ie when the subsidiary is the reporting entity). However, a parent would include its continuing involvement (or that of another member of the group) in a financial asset transferred by its subsidiary in determining whether it has continuing involvement in the transferred asset in its consolidated financial statements (ie when the reporting entity is the group). **B29**

An entity does not have a continuing involvement in a transferred financial asset if, as part of the transfer, it neither retains any of the contractual rights or obligations inherent in the transferred financial asset nor acquires any new contractual rights or obligations relating to the transferred financial asset. An entity does not have continuing involvement in a transferred financial asset if it has neither an interest in the future performance of the transferred financial asset nor a responsibility under any circumstances to make payments in respect of the transferred financial asset in the future. **B30**

Continuing involvement in a transferred financial asset may result from contractual provisions in the transfer agreement or in a separate agreement with the transferee or a third party entered into in connection with the transfer. **B31**

Transferred financial assets that are not derecognised in their entirety

Paragraph 42D requires disclosures when part or all of the transferred financial assets do not qualify for derecognition. Those disclosures are required at each reporting date at which the entity continues to recognise the transferred financial assets, regardless of when the transfers occurred. **B32**

Types of continuing involvement (paragraphs 42E–42H)

Paragraphs 42E–42H require qualitative and quantitative disclosures for each type of continuing involvement in derecognised financial assets. An entity shall aggregate its **B33**

**Editor's note*: *Paragraph amended in December 2008.*

continuing involvement into types that are representative of the entity's exposure to risks. For example, an entity may aggregate its continuing involvement by type of financial instrument (eg guarantees or call options) or by type of transfer (eg factoring of receivables, securitisations and securities lending).

Maturity analysis for undiscounted cash outflows to repurchase transferred assets (paragraph 42E(e))

B34 Paragraph 42E(e) requires an entity to disclose a maturity analysis of the undiscounted cash outflows to repurchase derecognised financial assets or other amounts payable to the transferee in respect of the derecognised financial assets, showing the remaining contractual maturities of the entity's continuing involvement. This analysis distinguishes cash flows that are required to be paid (eg forward contracts), cash flows that the entity may be required to pay (eg written put options) and cash flows that the entity might choose to pay (eg purchased call options).

B35 An entity shall use its judgement to determine an appropriate number of time bands in preparing the maturity analysis required by paragraph 42E(e). For example, an entity might determine that the following maturity time bands are appropriate:

(a) not later than one month;
(b) later than one month and not later than three months;
(c) later than three months and not later than six months;
(d) later than six months and not later than one year;
(e) later than one year and not later than three years;
(f) later than three years and not later than five years; and
(g) more than five years.

B36 If there is a range of possible maturities, the cash flows are included on the basis of the earliest date on which the entity can be required or is permitted to pay.

Qualitative information (paragraph 42E(f))

B37 The qualitative information required by paragraph 42E(f) includes a description of the derecognised financial assets and the nature and purpose of the continuing involvement retained after transferring those assets. It also includes a description of the risks to which an entity is exposed, including:

(a) a description of how the entity manages the risk inherent in its continuing involvement in the derecognised financial assets.
(b) whether the entity is required to bear losses before other parties, and the ranking and amounts of losses borne by parties whose interests rank lower than the entity's interest in the asset (ie its continuing involvement in the asset).
(c) a description of any triggers associated with obligations to provide financial support or to repurchase a transferred financial asset.

Gain or loss on derecognition (paragraph 42G(a))

B38 Paragraph 42G(a) requires an entity to disclose the gain or loss on derecognition relating to financial assets in which the entity has continuing involvement. The entity shall disclose if a gain or loss on derecognition arose because the fair values of the components of the previously recognised asset (ie the interest in the asset derecognised and the interest retained by the entity) were different from the fair value of the previously recognised asset as a whole. In that situation, the entity also shall disclose whether the fair value measurements included significant inputs that were not based on observable market data, as described in paragraph 27A.

Supplementary information (paragraph 42H)

The disclosures required in paragraphs 42D–42G may not be sufficient to meet the disclosure objectives in paragraph 42B. If this is the case, the entity shall disclose whatever additional information is necessary to meet the disclosure objectives. The entity shall decide, in the light of its circumstances, how much additional information it needs to provide to satisfy the information needs of users and how much emphasis it places on different aspects of the additional information. It is necessary to strike a balance between burdening financial statements with excessive detail that may not assist users of financial statements and obscuring information as a result of too much aggregation.* **B39**

****Editor's note:*** *Paragraphs B29 to B39 added in July 2011.*

Appendix C
Amendments to other Standards

[*Not reproduced, as all changes have been made to the underlying standards*]

Appendix D
Amendments to FRS 29 if the Amendments to FRS 26 (IAS 39) Financial Instruments: Measurement—*The Fair Value Option* have not been applied

In October 2005, the ASB issued Amendments to FRS 26 (IAS 39): Financial Instruments: Measurement Part III – The Fair Value Option, *to be applied for accounting periods beginning on or after 1 January 2006. If an entity applies FRS 29 for accounting periods beginning before 1 January 2006 and it does not apply these amendments to FRS 26, it shall amend FRS 29 for that period, as follows.*

The heading above paragraph 9 and paragraph 11 are amended to read as follows. **D1**

Financial liabilities at fair value through profit or loss

11 The entity shall disclose:

(a) the methods used to comply with the requirements in paragraph 10(a).
(b) if the entity believes that the disclosure it has given to comply with the requirement in paragraph 10(a) does not faithfully represent the change in the fair value of the financial liability attributable to changes in its credit risk, the reasons for reaching this conclusion and the factors it believes to be relevant.

Paragraph B5(a) is amended as follows:

(a) the criteria for designating, on initial recognition, financial assets or financial liabilities as at fair value through profit or loss.

Appendix E
Capital disclosures

ASB Note: This appendix reproduces the IASB's Capital Disclosures requirements developed by the IASB as part of the IFRS 7 project and issued as amendments to IAS 1. The IASB's Basis for Conclusions that relate to the Capital Disclosures have been reproduced in the Basis for Conclusions at paragraphs EBC 1 to EBC 16. The IASB's Implementation Guidance has been reproduced in the Implementation Guidance at paragraphs EIG 1–EIG 2.

Paragraphs E1 to E3 are an integral part of the Standard. Subject to the transitional provisions contained in paragraphs 43 to 46 the requirements of this Appendix should be applied for accounting periods beginning on or after 1 January 2007.

Capital Disclosures

Capital

E1 **An entity shall disclose information that enables users of its financial statements to evaluate the entity's objectives, policies and processes for managing capital.**

E2 To comply with paragraph E1, the entity discloses the following:

(a) qualitative information about its objectives, policies and processes for managing capital, including (but not limited to):

- (i) a description of what it manages as capital;
- (ii) when an entity is subject to externally imposed capital requirements, the nature of those requirements and how those requirements are incorporated into the management of capital; and
- (iii) how it is meeting its objectives for managing capital.

(b) summary quantitative data about what it manages as capital. Some entities regard some financial liabilities (eg some forms of subordinated debt) as part of capital. Other entities regard capital as excluding some components of equity (eg components arising from cash flow hedges).

(c) any changes in (a) and (b) from the previous period.

(d) whether during the period it complied with any externally imposed capital requirements to which it is subject.

(e) when the entity has not complied with such externally imposed capital requirements, the consequences of such noncompliance.

These disclosures shall be based on the information provided internally to the entity's key management personnel.

E3 An entity may manage capital in a number of ways and be subject to a number of different capital requirements. For example, a conglomerate may include entities that undertake insurance activities and banking activities, and those entities may also operate in several jurisdictions. When an aggregate disclosure of capital requirements and how capital is managed would not provide useful information or distorts a financial statement user's understanding of an entity's capital resources, the entity shall disclose separate information for each capital requirement to which the entity is subject.

The following terms are described in FRS 25 *Financial Instruments: Presentation* and are used in this Standard with the meaning specified in FRS 25: **E4**

(a) puttable financial instrument classified as an equity instruments (described in paragraphs 16A and 16B of FRS 25).
(b) an instrument that imposes on the entity an obligation to deliver to another party a pro rata share of the net assets of the entity only on liquidation and is classified as an equity instrument (described in paragraphs 16C and 16D of FRS 25).*

DISCLOSURE REQUIREMENTS FOR PUTTABLE FINANCIAL INSTRUMENTS AND OBLIGATIONS ARISING ON LIQUIDATION CLASSIFIED AS EQUITY

Information to be presented either in the statement of financial position or in the notes

If an entity has reclassified: **E5**

(a) a puttable financial instrument classified as an equity instrument, or
(b) an instrument that imposes on the entity an obligation to deliver to another party a pro rata share of the net assets of the entity only on liquidation and is classified as an equity instrument

between financial liabilities and equity, it shall disclose the amount reclassified into and out of each category (financial liabilities or equity), and the timing and reason for that reclassification.

Puttable financial instruments classified as equity

For puttable financial instruments classified as equity instruments, an entity shall disclose (to the extent not disclosed elsewhere): **E6**

(a) summary quantitative data about the amount classified as equity;
(b) its objectives, policies and processes for managing its obligation to repurchase or redeem the instruments when required to do so by the instrument holders, including any changes from the previous period;
(c) the expected cash outflow on redemption or repurchase of that class of financial instruments; and
(d) information about how the expected cash outflow on redemption or repurchase was determined.

Other disclosures

An entity shall disclose the following, if not disclosed elsewhere in information published with the financial statements: **E7**

(a) the domicile and legal form of the entity, its country of incorporation and the address of its registered office (or principal place of business, if different from the registered office);
(b) a description of the nature of the entity's operations and its principal activities;
(c) the name of the parent and the ultimate parent of the group; and
(d) if it is a limited life entity, information regarding the length of its life.

****Editor's note****: Paragraphs E4 to E8 were added in August 2008. The application date and transitional provisions are set out in paragraph E8.*

E8 *Puttable Financial Instruments and Obligations Arising on Liquidation* (Amendments to FRS 25), issued in August 2008, inserted paragraphs E4 to E7. An entity shall apply those amendments for annual periods beginning on or after 1 January 2010. Earlier application is permitted only for annual periods beginning on or after 1 January 2009. If an entity applies the changes for an earlier period, it shall disclose that fact and apply the related amendments to FRS 25, FRS 26, FRS 29 and UITF 39 (IFRIC 2) *Members' Shares in Co-Operative Entities and Similar Instruments* at the same time.

Adoption of the standard

Approval of IFRS 7 by the Board

International Financial Reporting Standard 7 *Financial Instruments: Disclosures* was approved for issue by the fourteen members of the International Accounting Standards Board.

Sir David Tweedie	Chairman
Thomas E Jones	Vice-Chairman
Mary E Barth	
Hans-Georg Bruns	
Anthony T Cope	
Jan Engström	
Robert P Garnett	
Gilbert Gélard	
James J Leisenring	
Warren J McGregor	
Patricia L O'Malley	
John T Smith	
Geoffrey Whittington	
Tatsumi Yamada	

Approval of Amendments to IAS 1 by the Board

These Amendments to International Accounting Standard 1 *Presentation of Financial Statements: Capital Disclosures** were approved for issue by thirteen of the fourteen members of the International Accounting Standards Board. Mr Leisenring dissented. His dissenting opinion is set out on page 116.

Sir David Tweedie	Chairman
Thomas E Jones	Vice-Chairman
Mary E Barth	
Hans-Georg Bruns	
Anthony T Cope	
Jan Engström	
Robert P Garnett	
Gilbert Gélard	
James J Leisenring	
Warren J McGregor	
Patricia L O'Malley	
John T Smith	
Geoffrey Whittington	
Tatsumi Yamada	

*ASB Footnote: *The equivalent requirements have been reproduced in Appendix E of this Standard.*

Adoption of FRS 29 by the Accounting Standards Board

Financial Reporting Standard 29 (IFRS 7) 'Financial Instruments: Disclosures' was approved for issue by the ten members of the Accounting Standards Board.

Ian Mackintosh	Chairman
Andrew Lennard	Technical Director
Michael Ashley	
Marisa Cassoni	
Anthony Good	
Roger Marshall	
Isobel Sharp	
Jonathan Symonds	
Helen Weir	
Peter Westlake	

Approval by the IASB of *Disclosures – Transfers of Financial Assets* (Amendments to IFRS 7) Issued in October 2010

Disclosures – Transfers of Financial Assets (Amendments to IFRS 7) was approved for issue by the fourteen members of the International Accounting Standards Board.

Sir David Tweedie	Chairman
Stephen Cooper	
Philippe Danjou	
Jan Engström	
Patrick Finnegan	
Amaro Luiz de Oliveira Gomes	
Prabhakar Kalavacherla	
Elke König	
Patricia McConnell	
Warren J McGregor	
Paul Pacter	
John T Smith	
Tatsumi Yamada	
Wei-Guo Zhang	

Approval by the Accounting Standards Board of *Disclosures – Transfers of Financial Assets* (Amendments to FRS 29)

Amendments to Financial Reporting Standard 29 (IFRS 7) Financial Instruments: Disclosures was approved for issue by the eight members of the Accounting Standards Board.

Roger Marshall	Chairman
David Loweth	Technical Director
Nick Anderson	
Peter Elwin	
Ken Lever	
Robert Overend	
Andy Simmonds	
Pauline Wallace	

Notes on the Standard's Application in the UK and the Republic of Ireland

In July 2004, the IASB published exposure draft ED7 'Financial Instruments: Disclosures', setting out proposals for a new IFRS that would: **N1**

- contain some new disclosure requirements as well as disclosures already required by IAS 32, and
- require additional capital disclosure requirements in the new IFRS.

The ASB issued these proposals as FRED 33 'Financial Instruments: Disclosures' at the same time as the IASB. **N2**

As part of its convergence programme, the ASB then issued FRS 25 (IAS 32) 'Financial Instruments: Disclosure and Presentation' in December 2004. **N3**

Respondents to the FRED generally supported the implementation of the IFRS in the UK, although some expressed concern over the details of the proposals, and in particular aspects of the capital disclosures. Similar concerns were expressed to IASB, who agreed some changes in their redeliberation of the proposed standard. **N4**

In August 2005, the IASB issued its standard as IFRS 7 *Financial Instruments: Disclosures*, and the ASB then agreed to issue a UK standard based on that IFRS. **N5**

GENERAL

The requirements of Schedule 1* of The Large and Medium-sized Companies and Groups (Accounts and Reports) Regulations 2008 relating to the form and content of company and group financial statements set out formats for the balance sheet and profit and loss account which allow some flexibility in certain circumstances in the manner in which the information is presented. The provisions of the FRS supplement those legal requirements, while remaining within their bounds. **N6**

SCOPE

The ASB has followed its usual practice of exempting from the FRS all entities applying the Financial Reporting Standard for Smaller Entities (FRSSE). **N7**

Entities not applying FRS 26 measurement requirements

As with FRS 25, the Board has exempted entities not applying FRS 26 measurement requirements from the disclosure requirements of this FRS. The Board is currently discussing the possibility of extending the scope of FRS 26 which may lead to an extension in the scope of this Standard. However, the Board is also aware that some entities falling within the scope of FRS 26 may wish to adopt the disclosure requirements of this Standard, rather than those contained in FRS 25, in 2005 or 2006 thus avoiding the need to make two changes in quick succession. It has, **N8**

**The requirements relating to banking and insurance companies are set out in Schedules 2 and 3 respectively. The Regulations extend to Northern Ireland. The equivalent Republic of Ireland requirements are set out in the Sixth Schedule of the Companies Act 1963, and Section 3 and the Schedule of the Companies (Amendment) Act 1986, the European Communities (Companies: Group Accounts) Regulations 1992, the European Communities (Credit Institutions: Accounts) Regulations 1992 and the European Communities (Insurance Undertakings: Accounts) Regulations 1992.*

therefore, decided to issue this Standard in advance of a decision on the scope of FRS 26 with the provision that it may amend the scope of the Standard at a later date.

Parents and subsidiaries

N9 As for FRS 25, the Board has granted certain exemptions for parent companies and wholly-owned subsidiaries from complying with the disclosure requirements of this Standard. The exemption applies to parent companies in their own single-entity financial statements and to subsidiaries where at least 90 percent of the voting rights are controlled within the group. In each case it is dependent on the entity being included in consolidated financial statements that are publicly available and which include the disclosures on a group basis. The Board takes the view that applying the disclosure requirements to the single entity financial statements of parent companies and wholly-owned subsidiaries may result in lengthy disclosures for little benefit. Entities falling within the scope of this exemption may still be subject to the disclosure requirements of the Companies Act referred to in paragraph N13 below.

EFFECTIVE DATE

N10 The new standard is effective from the same date as the IFRS, for accounting periods commencing on or after 1 January 2007. Early adoption is permitted; in particular, entities required to adopt FRS 25 for periods commencing in 2005 or 2006 are permitted instead to adopt the requirements of the new FRS, thereby avoiding two changes in disclosure requirements in quick succession.

DISCLOSURES RELATING TO CAPITAL

N11 The standard proposed in ED 7 and FRED 33 included a requirement for certain disclosures relating to capital. The IASB has not included these in IFRS 7, but has amended IAS 1 to incorporate these disclosure requirements on the basis that they are not directly related to financial instruments. As the UK does not have a standard that corresponds to IAS 1, these requirements have been added as a separate appendix to FRS 29, with the same scope and scope exemptions as the main standard.

DISCLOSURES RELATING TO THE FAIR VALUE OPTION

N12 FRS 29 was first introduced in December 2005. At that time, the ASB noted its reservations about the value of disclosures of the credit risk of loans and receivables designated at fair value through the profit and loss. The ASB's view was that these disclosures were unnecessarily burdensome on some preparers, given the general credit risk disclosures required by paragraph 36. For this reason, the ASB decided not to adopt paragraph 9 of IFRS 7. Given developments in financial reporting standards on financial instruments, in November 2008, the ASB issued Financial Reporting Exposure Draft (FRED) 'Improvements to Financial Instrument Disclosures' which proposed, amongst other amendments, to adopt the credit risk disclosure requirements set out in paragraph 9 of IFRS 7. In responding to the FRED, constituents supported the adoption of those requirements and highlighted the importance of ensuring that FRS 29 is fully converged with IFRS 7. Accordingly, the ASB decided to adopt these disclosures in FRS 29.

FAIR VALUE DIRECTIVE

The Companies Act includes certain disclosure requirements relating to financial instruments, in particular those inserted in Schedules 4, 9 and 9A*, as a result of implementing the Fair Value Directive. These requirements apply to all entities within the scope of the Act, whether or not they are within the scope of the FRS; they are generally similar, but not identical, to certain requirements of the FRS. Entities within the scope of both the Act and the FRS will need to ensure that they comply with the requirements of both. **N13**

The table below provides an overview of the disclosure requirements contained in the Companies Act and their relationship to those in the Standard. **N14**

**Replaced by Schedule 1 of The Large and Medium-sized Companies and Groups (Accounts and Reports) Regulations 2008.*

Financial Statements

The Large and Medium-sized Companies and Groups (Accounts and Reports) Regulations 2008*	Republic of Ireland Companies Legislation	FRS 29
Sch 1 Part 3 Paragraph 55 (2) (a) (2) There must be stated- (a) the significant assumptions underlying the valuation models and techniques used where the fair value of the instruments has been determined in accordance with paragraph 37(4)	Para 31A (2)(a), Schedule, Companies (Amendment) Act, 1986 Regulation 16A(2)(a), European Communities (Companies: Group Accounts) Regulations 1992	Paragraph 27(a) An entity shall disclose: (a) the methods and, when a valuation technique is used, the assumptions applied in determining fair values of each class of financial assets or financial liabilities. For example, if applicable, an entity discloses information about the assumptions relating to prepayment rates, rates of estimated credit losses, and interest rates or discount rates.

* ASB Footnote: *The numbering provided here follows that contained in the amendments to Schdules 4 and 7 of the Companies Act 1985 as described in Statutory Instrument 2004 No. 2947 and the Companies (Northern Ireland) Order 1986 as described in S. R. 2004 No. 496. The requirements relating to banking and insurance companies are set out in Schedules 9 and 9A respectively.*

The Large and Medium-sized Companies and Groups (Accounts and Reports) Regulations 2008	Republic of Ireland Companies Legislation	FRS 29
Sch 1 Part 3 Paragraph 55 (2) (b) (2) There must be stated- (b) for each category of financial instrument, the fair value of the instruments in that category and the changes in value – (i) included in the profit and loss account, or (ii) credited to or (as the case my be) debited from the fair value reserve, in respect of those instruments.	Para 31A (2)(b), Schedule, Companies (Amendment) Act, 1986 Regulation 16A(2)(b), European Communities (Companies: Group Accounts) Regulations 1992	Paragraphs 20 and 25 **Paragraph 20**: An entity shall disclose the following items of income, expense, gains or losses either on the face of the financial statements or in the notes: (a) net gains or net losses on: (i) financial assets or financial liabilities at fair value through profit or loss, showing separately those on financial assets or financial liabilities designated as such upon initial recognition, and those on financial assets or financial liabilities that are classified as held for trading in accordance with FRS 26; (ii) available-for-sale financial assets, showing separately the amount of gain or loss recognised directly in equity during the period and the amount removed from equity and recognised in profit or loss for the period; (iii) held-to-maturity investments; (iv) loans and receivables; and

The Large and Medium-sized Companies and Groups (Accounts and Reports) Regulations 2008	Republic of Ireland Companies Legislation	FRS 29
		(v) financial liabilities measured at amortised cost; (b) total interest income and total interest expense (calculated using the effective interest method) for financial assets or financial liabilities that are not at fair value through profit or loss; (c) fee income and expense (other than amounts included in determining the effective interest rate) arising from: (i) financial assets or financial liabilities that are not at fair value through profit or loss; and (ii) trust and other fiduciary activities that result in the holding or investing of assets on behalf of individuals, trusts, retirement benefit plans, and other institutions; (d) interest income on impaired financial assets accrued in accordance with paragraph AG93 of IAS 39; and (e) the amount of any impairment loss for each class of financial asset.

The Large and Medium-sized Companies and Groups (Accounts and Reports) Regulations 2008	Republic of Ireland Companies Legislation	FRS 29
		Paragraph 25: Except as set out in paragraph 29, for each class of financial assets and financial liabilities (see paragraph 6), an entity shall disclose the fair value of that class of assets and liabilities in a way that permits it to be compared with its carrying amount.
Sch 1 Part 3 Paragraph 55 (2) (c) (2) There must be stated- (c) for each class of derivatives, the extent and nature of the instruments, including significant terms and conditions that may affect the amount, timing and certainty of future cash flows.	Para 31 A (2) (a), Schedule, Companies (Amendment) Act, 1986 Regulations 16A(2)(c), European Communities (Companies: Group Accounts) Regulations 1992	[the Standard does not specifically require these disclosures]
Sch 1 Part 3 Paragraph 55 (3) (3) Where any amount is transferred to or from the fair value reserve during the financial year, there must be stated in tabular form: (a) the amount of the reserve as at the date of the beginning of the financial year and as at the balance sheet date respectively;	–	[the Standard does not specifically require these disclosures]

The Large and Medium-sized Companies and Groups (Accounts and Reports) Regulations 2008	**Republic of Ireland Companies Legislation**	**FRS 29**
(b) the amount transferred to or from the reserve during that year; and (c) the source and application respectively of the amounts so transferred.		
Sch 1 Part 3 Paragraph 56 Where the company has derivatives that it has not included at fair value, there must be stated for each class of such derivative - (a) the fair value of the derivatives in that class, if such a value can be determined in accordance with paragraph 37, and (b) the extent and nature of the derivatives.	Para 31B, Schedule, Companies (Amendment) Act, 1986 Regulation 16B, European Communities (Companies: Group Accounts) Regulations 1992	Paragraph 25 Except as set out in paragraph 29, for each class of financial assets and financial liabilities (see paragraph 6), an entity shall disclose the fair value of that class of assets and liabilities in a way that permits it to be compared with its carrying amount.
Sch 1 Part 3 Paragraph 57 (1) This paragraph applies if – (a) the company has financial fixed assets which could be included at fair value by virtue of paragraph 36, (b) the amount at which those items are included under any item in the company's accounts is in excess of their fair value, and	Para 31C, Schedule, Companies (Amendment) Act, 1986 Regulation 16C, European Communities (Companies: Group Accounts) Regulations 1992	[the Standard does not specifically require these disclosures]

The Large and Medium-sized Companies and Groups (Accounts and Reports) Regulations 2008	Republic of Ireland Companies Legislation	FRS 29
(c) the company has not made provision for diminution in value of those assets in accordance with paragraph 19(1) of this Schedule. (2) There must be stated- (a) the amount at which either the individual assets or appropriate groupings of those individual assets are included in the company's accounts, (b) the fair value of those assets or groupings, and (c) the reasons for not making a provision for diminution in value of those assets, including the nature of the evidence that provides the basis for the belief that the amount at which they are stated in the accounts will be recovered.		

Directors' Report

The Large and Medium-sized Companies and Groups (Accounts and Reports) Regulations 2008	**Republic of Ireland Companies Legislation**	**FRS 29**
Sch 7 Paragraph 6 (1) (1) In relation to the use of financial instruments by a company, the directors' report must contain an indication of - (a) the financial risk management objectives and policies of the company, including the policy for hedging each major type of forecasted transaction for which hedge accounting is used, and (b) the exposure of the company to price risk, credit risk, liquidity risk and cashflow risk, unless such information is not material for the assessment of the assets, liabilities, financial position and profit or loss of the company and its subsidiary undertakings included in the consolidation.	Section 13(f), Companies (Amendment) Act 1986 Regulation 37 (1)(f), European Communities (Companies: Group Accounts) Regulations 1992	See paragraphs 31, 33 and 34-42 for disclosures in the financial statement relating to the nature and extent of risks arising from financial instruments

Implementation of derecognition material

In April 2006 the Board amended FRS 26 to include the IAS 39 material on recognition and derecognition into the Standard. Accordingly, on implementation of this amendment the corresponding disclosure requirements of IAS 32 are implemented in FRS 25. These new disclosure requirements replace disclosures required for financial assets and liabilities by FRS 5 'Reporting the Substance of Transactions'. These amendments are effective for accounting periods on or after 1 January 2007, with earlier adoption permitted. **N15**

Basis for Conclusions

paragraphs

Introduction **BC1–BC5**

Scope **BC6–BC11**

The entities to which the IFRS applies **BC6–BC8**

Exemptions considered by the Board **BC9–BC11**

Insurers BC9
Small and medium-sized entities BC10
Subsidiaries BC11

Disclosures about the significance of financial instruments for financial position and performance **BC12–BC39**

The principle **BC13**

Balance sheet disclosures **BC14–BC32**

Categories of financial assets and financial liabilities BC14–BC15
Financial assets or financial liabilities at fair value through profit or loss BC16–BC22
Reclassification BC23
Derecognition BC24
Collateral BC25
Allowance account for credit losses BC26–BC27
Compound financial instruments with multiple embedded derivatives BC28–BC31
Defaults and breaches BC32

Income statement and equity **BC33–BC35**

Items of income, expenses, gains or losses BC33–BC34
Fee income and expense BC35

Other disclosures—fair value **BC36–BC39**

Disclosures about the nature and extent of risks arising from financial instruments **BC40–BC65**

Location of disclosures of risks arising from financial instruments **BC43–BC46**

Quantitative disclosures **BC47–BC48**

Information based on how the entity manages risk BC47
Information on averages BC48

Credit risk **BC49–BC56**

Maximum exposure to credit risk BC49–BC50
Collateral held as security and other credit enhancements BC51–BC53
Credit quality of financial assets that are neither past due nor impaired BC54
Financial assets that are either past due or impaired BC55
Collateral and other credit enhancements obtained BC56

Liquidity risk **BC57–BC58**

Market risk **BC59–BC64**

Operational risk **BC65**

Effective date and transition **BC66–BC72**

Summary of main changes from the exposure draft **BC73**

Disclosures about capital **EBC1–EBC19**

Dissenting opinion **ED01**

Appendix

Amendments to Basis for Conclusions on other IFRSs

Basis for Conclusions

This Basis for Conclusions accompanies, but is not part of, IFRS 7.

*In this Basis for Conclusions the terminology has not been amended to reflect the changes made by IAS 1 Presentation of Financial Statements (as revised in 2007).**

> ASB Note: The IASB's Basis for Conclusion, which accompanies IFRS 7, is set out below in full. It should be noted though that some of the discussion it contains concerns IASB requirements that have no equivalent in the UK or Republic of Ireland. Footnotes have been used to indicate corresponding requirements in the UK and Republic of Ireland where applicable.
>
> All references to 'the Board' and 'Board members' are references to the IASB Board and IASB Board members.

INTRODUCTION

BC1 This Basis for Conclusions summarises the International Accounting Standards Board's considerations in reaching the conclusions in IFRS 7 *Financial Instruments: Disclosures*. Individual Board members gave greater weight to some factors than to others.

BC2 During the late 1990s, the need for a comprehensive review of IAS 30 *Disclosures in the Financial Statements of Banks and Similar Financial Institutions*† became apparent. The Board's predecessor, the International Accounting Standards Committee (IASC), issued a number of Standards that addressed, more comprehensively, some of the topics previously addressed only for banks in IAS 30. Also, fundamental changes were taking place in the financial services industry and in the way in which financial institutions manage their activities and risk exposures. This made it increasingly difficult for users of banks' financial statements to assess and compare their financial position and performance, their associated risk exposures, and their processes for measuring and managing those risks.

BC3 In 1999 IASC added a project to its agenda to revise IAS 30 and in 2000 it appointed a steering committee.

BC4 In 2001 the Board added this project to its agenda. To assist and advise it, the Board retained the IAS 30 steering committee, renamed the Financial Activities Advisory Committee (FAAC), as an expert advisory group. FAAC members had experience and expertise in banks, finance companies and insurance companies and included auditors, financial analysts, preparers and regulators. The FAAC's role was:

(a) to provide input from the perspective of preparers and auditors of financial statements of entities that have significant exposures to financial instruments; and
(b) to assist the Board in developing a standard and implementation guidance for risk disclosures arising from financial instruments and for other related disclosures.

* ***Editor's note***: *Rubric amended in December 2008.*

†ASB Footnote: *The Basis for Conclusions discusses the IAS 30 revision project. IAS 30 was not implemented in the UK.*

The Board published its proposals in July 2004 as ED 7 *Financial Instruments: Disclosures**. The deadline for comments was 27 October 2004. The Board received 105 comment letters. After reviewing the responses, the Board issued IFRS 7 in August 2005. **BC5**

In October 2008 the Board published an exposure draft *Improving Disclosures about Financial Instruments* (proposed amendments to IFRS 7). The aim of the proposed amendments was to enhance disclosures about fair value and liquidity risk. The Board received 89 comment letters. After reviewing the responses, the Board issued amendments to IFRS 7 in March 2009. The Board decided to require application of the amendments for periods beginning on or after 1 January 2009. The Board noted that, although the effective date of IFRSs and amendments to IFRSs is usually 6–18 months after issue, the urgent need for enhanced disclosures about financial instruments demanded earlier application. **BC5A**

SCOPE (PARAGRAPHS 3–5)

The entities to which the IFRS applies

Although IFRS 7 arose from a project to revise IAS 30 (a Standard that applied only to banks and similar financial institutions), it applies to all entities that have financial instruments. The Board observed that the reduction in regulatory barriers in many countries and increasing competition between banks, non-bank financial services firms, and financial conglomerates have resulted in many entities providing financial services that were traditionally provided only by entities regulated and supervised as banks. The Board concluded that this development would make it inappropriate to limit this project to banks and similar financial institutions. **BC6**

The Board considered whether entities that undertake specified activities commonly undertaken by banks and other financial institutions, namely deposit-taking, lending and securities activities, face unique risks that would require a standard specific to them. However, the Board decided that the scope of this project should include disclosures about risks arising from financial instruments in all entities for the following reasons: **BC7**

(a) disclosures about risks associated with financial instruments are useful to users of the financial statements of all entities.

(b) the Board found it could not satisfactorily define deposit-taking, lending, and securities activities. In particular, it could not satisfactorily differentiate an entity with securities activities from an entity holding a portfolio of financial assets for investment and liquidity management purposes.

(c) responses to the Exposure Draft of Improvements to IAS 32 *Financial Instruments: Disclosure and Presentation*†, published in June 2002, indicated that IAS 32's risk disclosure requirements, applicable to all entities, could be improved.

(d) the exclusion of some financial instruments would increase the danger that risk disclosures could be incomplete and possibly misleading. For example, a debt instrument issued by an entity could significantly affect its exposures to liquidity risk, interest rate risk and currency risk even if that instrument is not held as part of deposit-taking, lending and securities activities.

(e) users of financial statements need to be able to compare similar activities, transactions and events of different entities on a consistent basis. Hence, the

*ASB Footnote: *FRED 33 was based on ED 7 and was issued by the ASB in July 2004.*

†ASB Footnote: *FRS 25 implemented the IAS 32 requirements in the UK.*

disclosure principles that apply to regulated entities should not differ from those that apply to non-regulated, but otherwise similar, entities.

BC8 The Board decided that the scope of the IFRS should be the same as that of IAS 32 with one exception. The Board concluded that the IFRS should not apply to derivatives based on interests in subsidiaries, associates or joint ventures if the derivatives meet the definition of an equity instrument in IAS 32. This is because equity instruments are not remeasured and hence:

(a) they do not expose the issuer to balance sheet and income statement risk; and
(b) the disclosures about the significance of financial instruments for financial position and performance are not relevant to equity instruments.

Although these instruments are excluded from the scope of IFRS 7, they are within the scope of IAS 32 for the purpose of determining whether they meet the definition of equity instruments.

Exemptions considered by the Board

Insurers

BC9 The Board considered whether the IFRS should apply to entities that both have financial instruments and issue insurance contracts. The Board did not exempt these entities because financial instruments expose all entities to risks regardless of what other assets and liabilities they have. Accordingly, an entity that both issues insurance contracts and has financial instruments applies IFRS 4 *Insurance Contracts** to its insurance contracts and IFRS 7 to its financial assets and financial liabilities. However, many of the disclosure requirements in IFRS 4 were applications of, or relatively straightforward analogies with, existing requirements in IAS 32. Therefore, the Board also updated the disclosures required by IFRS 4 to make them consistent with IFRS 7, with modifications that reflect the interim nature of IFRS 4.

Small and medium-sized entities

BC10 The Board considered whether it should exempt small and medium-sized entities from the scope of the IFRS†. The Board noted that the extent of disclosures required by the IFRS will depend on the extent to which the entity uses financial instruments and the extent to which it has assumed associated risks. The IFRS requires entities with few financial instruments and few risks to give few disclosures. Also, many of the requirements in the IFRS are based on information provided internally to the entity's key management personnel. This helps to avoid unduly onerous requirements that would not be appropriate for smaller entities. Accordingly, the Board decided not to exempt such entities from the scope of IFRS 7. However, it will keep this decision under review in its project on financial reporting for small and medium-sized entities.

*ASB Footnote: *IFRS 4 has not been implemented in the UK but its definition of insurance contract was implemented as Appendix C to FRS 26. As a result the disclosure requirements for insurance contracts remain as those in FRS 27* Life Assurance *and in Schedule 9A of Companies Act 1985, supplemented by guidance in the SORP on Insurance Business issued by the Association of British Insurers.*

†ASB Footnote: *Reporting entities in the UK applying the Financial Reporting Standard for Smaller Entities (FRSSE) currently applicable are exempt from this Standard.*

Subsidiaries

Some respondents to ED 7 stated that there is little public interest in the financial statements of some entities, such as a wholly-owned subsidiary whose parent issues publicly available financial statements. These respondents stated that such subsidiaries should be exempt from some of the requirements of IFRS 7 in their individual financial statements. However, deciding whether such an entity should prepare general purpose financial statements is a matter for the entity and local legislators and regulators. If such an entity prepares financial statements in accordance with IFRSs, users of those statements should receive information of the same quality as users of any general purpose financial statements prepared in accordance with IFRSs. The Board confirmed its view that no exemptions from the general requirements of any Standard should be given for the financial statements of subsidiaries. **BC11**

DISCLOSURES ABOUT THE SIGNIFICANCE OF FINANCIAL INSTRUMENTS FOR FINANCIAL POSITION AND PERFORMANCE (PARAGRAPHS 7–30, B4 AND B5)

The Board relocated disclosures from IAS 32 to IFRS 7, so that all disclosure requirements for financial instruments are in one Standard. Many of the disclosure requirements about the significance of financial instruments for an entity's financial position and performance were previously in IAS 32. For these disclosures, the relevant paragraphs from the Basis for Conclusions on IAS 32 have been incorporated into this Basis for Conclusions. This Basis for Conclusions does not discuss requirements that the Board did not reconsider either in revising IAS 32 in 2003 or in developing IFRS 7. **BC12**

The principle (paragraph 7)

The Board decided that the disclosure requirements of IFRS 7 should result from the explicit disclosure principle in paragraph 7. The Board also decided to specify disclosures to satisfy this principle. In the Board's view, entities could not satisfy the principle in paragraph 7 unless they disclose the information required by paragraphs 8–30. **BC13**

Balance sheet disclosures (paragraphs 8–19 and B4)

Categories of financial assets and financial liabilities (paragraph 8)

Paragraph 8 requires entities to disclose financial assets and financial liabilities by the measurement categories in IAS 39 *Financial Instruments: Recognition and Measurement**. The Board concluded that the disclosure for each measurement category would assist users in understanding the extent to which accounting policies affect the amounts at which financial assets and financial liabilities are recognised. **BC14**

The Board also concluded that separate disclosure of the carrying amounts of financial assets and financial liabilities that are classified as held for trading and those designated upon initial recognition as financial assets and financial liabilities at fair value through profit or loss is useful because such designation is at the discretion of the entity. **BC15**

*ASB Footnote: *FRS 26 implemented the equivalent measurement categories in the UK.*

Financial assets or financial liabilities at fair value through profit or loss (paragraphs 9–11, B4 and B5)

BC16 IAS 39 permits entities to designate a non-derivative financial liability as at fair value through profit or loss, if specified conditions are met. If entities do so, they are required to provide the disclosures in paragraphs 10 and 11. The Board's reasons for these disclosures are set out in the Basis for Conclusions on IAS 39, paragraphs BC87–BC92.

BC17 The requirements in paragraphs 9, 11 and B5(a) are related to the Amendments to IAS 39 Financial Instruments: Recognition and Measurement—*The Fair Value Option**, issued in June 2005. The reasons for those requirements are discussed in the Basis for Conclusions on those Amendments.

BC18 Paragraph 10(a) requires disclosure of the change in fair value of a financial liability designated as at fair value through profit or loss that is attributable to changes in the liability's credit risk. The Board previously considered this disclosure in its deliberations on the fair value measurement of financial liabilities in IAS 39.

BC19 Although quantifying such changes might be difficult in practice, the Board concluded that disclosure of such information would be useful to users of financial statements and would help alleviate concerns that users may misinterpret the profit or loss effects of changes in credit risk, especially in the absence of disclosures. Therefore, in finalising the revisions to IAS 32 in 2003, it decided to require disclosure of the change in fair value of the financial liability that is not attributable to changes in a benchmark interest rate. The Board believed that this is often a reasonable proxy for the change in fair value that is attributable to changes in the liability's credit risk, in particular when such changes are large, and would provide users with information with which to understand the profit or loss effect of such a change in credit risk.

BC20 However, some respondents to ED 7 stated that they did not agree that the IAS 32 disclosure provided a reasonable proxy, except for straightforward debt instruments. In particular, there could be other factors involved in the change in an instrument's fair value unrelated to the benchmark interest rate, such as the effect of an embedded derivative. Respondents also cited difficulties for unit-linked insurance contracts, for which the amount of the liability reflects the performance of a defined pool of assets. The Board noted that the proxy that was developed in IAS 32 assumed that it is not practicable for entities to determine directly the change in fair value arising from changes in credit risk. However, the Board acknowledged and shared these concerns.

BC21 As a result, the Board amended this requirement to focus directly on the objective of providing information about the effects of changes in credit risk:

(a) by permitting entities to provide a more faithful representation of the amount of change in fair value that is attributable to changes in credit risk if they could do so. However, such entities are also required to disclose the methods used and provide their justification for concluding that those methods give a more faithful representation than the proxy in paragraph 10(a)(i).

(b) by amending the proxy disclosure to be the amount of change in fair value that is not attributable to changes in market conditions that give rise to market risk. For example, some entities may be able to identify part of the change in the fair value of the liability as attributable to a change in an index. In these cases, the

*ASB Footnote: *The Fair Value Option amendment was issued in the UK as part of the amendments to FRS 26 issued in October 2005.*

proxy disclosure would exclude the amount of change attributable to a change in an index. Similarly, excluding the amount attributable to a change in an internal or external investment fund makes the proxy more suitable for unit-linked insurance contracts.

The Board decided that when an entity has designated a financial liability as at fair value through profit or loss, it should disclose the difference between the carrying amount and the amount the entity would contractually be required to pay at maturity to the holders of the liability (see paragraph 10(b)). The fair value may differ significantly from the settlement amount, in particular for financial liabilities with a long duration when an entity has experienced a significant deterioration in creditworthiness since their issue. The Board concluded that knowledge of this difference would be useful to users of financial statements. Also, the settlement amount is important to some financial statement users, particularly creditors. **BC22**

Reclassification (paragraphs 12 and 12A)

IAS 32 required disclosure of the reason for reclassification of financial assets at cost or amortised cost rather than at fair value. The Board extended this requirement to include disclosure of the reason for reclassifications and of the amount reclassified into and out of each category. As noted in paragraph BC14, the Board regards such information as useful because the categorisation of financial instruments has a significant effect on their measurement. **BC23**

In October 2008 the Board amended IAS 39 to permit reclassification of particular financial assets in some circumstances. The Board decided to require additional disclosures about the situations in which any such reclassification is made, and the effects on the financial statements. The Board regards such information as useful because the reclassification of a financial asset can have a significant effect on the financial statements.* **BC23A**

[Paragraph deleted]. **BC24**

Collateral (paragraphs 14 and 15)

Paragraph 15 requires disclosures about collateral that the entity holds if it is permitted to sell or repledge the collateral in the absence of default by the owner. Some respondents to ED 7 argued for an exemption from this disclosure if it is impracticable to obtain the fair value of the collateral held. However, the Board concluded that it is reasonable to expect an entity to know the fair value of collateral that it holds and can sell even if there is no default. **BC25**

Allowance account for credit losses (paragraph 16)

When a separate account is used to record impairment losses (such as an allowance account or similar account used to record a collective impairment of assets), paragraph 16 requires a reconciliation of that account to be disclosed. The Board was informed that analysts and other users find this information useful in assessing the adequacy of the allowance for impairment losses for such entities and when comparing one entity with another. However, the Board decided not to specify the components of the reconciliation. This allows entities flexibility in determining the most appropriate format for their needs. **BC26**

***Editor's note**: *Paragraph added in October 2008.*

BC27 Respondents to ED 7 asked the Board to require entities to provide equivalent information if they do not use an allowance account. The Board decided not to add this disclosure in finalising the IFRS. It concluded that, for virtually all entities, IAS 39's requirement to consider impairment on a group basis would necessitate the use of an allowance or similar account. The accounting policy disclosures required by paragraph B5(d) also include information about the use of direct adjustments to carrying amounts of financial assets.

Compound financial instruments with multiple embedded derivatives (paragraph 17)

BC28 IAS 32 requires the separation of the liability and equity components of a compound financial instrument. The Board notes that this is more complicated for compound financial instruments with multiple embedded derivative features whose values are interdependent (for example, a convertible debt instrument that gives the issuer a right to call the instrument back from the holder, or the holder a right to put the instrument back to the issuer) than for those without such features. If the embedded equity and non-equity derivative features are interdependent, the sum of the separately determined values of the liability and equity components will not equal the value of the compound financial instrument as a whole.

BC29 For example, the values of an embedded call option feature and an equity conversion option feature in a callable convertible debt instrument depend in part on each other if the holder's equity conversion option is extinguished when the entity exercises the call option or vice versa. The following diagram illustrates the joint value arising from the interaction between a call option and an equity conversion option in a callable convertible bond. Circle L represents the value of the liability component, ie the value of the straight debt and the embedded call option on the straight debt, and Circle E represents the value of the equity component, ie the equity conversion option on the straight debt. The total area of the two circles represents the value of the callable convertible bond. The difference between the value of the callable convertible bond as a whole and the sum of the separately determined values for the liability and equity components is the joint value attributable to the interdependence between the call option feature and the equity conversion feature. It is represented by the intersection between the two circles.

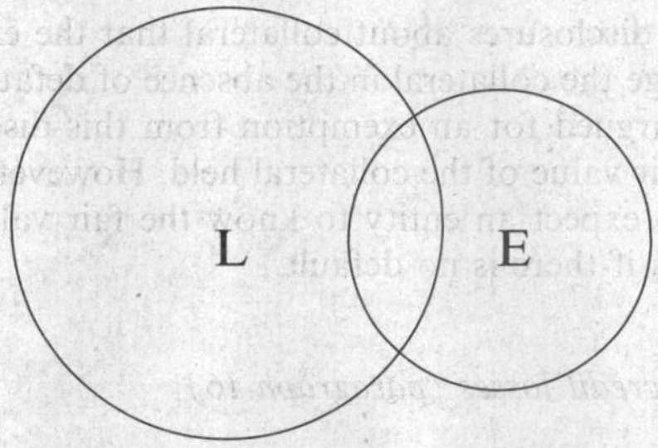

BC30 Under the approach in IAS 32, the joint value attributable to the interdependence between multiple embedded derivative features is included in the liability component. A numerical example is set out as Illustrative Example 10 accompanying IAS 32.

BC31 Even though this approach is consistent with the definition of equity as a residual interest, the Board recognises that the allocation of the joint value to either the liability component or the equity component is arbitrary because it is, by its nature, joint. Therefore, the Board concluded that it is important to disclose the existence of issued compound financial instruments with multiple embedded derivative features that have interdependent values. Such disclosure highlights the effect of multiple embedded derivative features on the amounts recognised as liabilities and equity.

Defaults and breaches (paragraphs 18 and 19)

Paragraphs 18 and 19 require disclosures about defaults and breaches of loans payable and other loan agreements. The Board concluded that such disclosures provide relevant information about the entity's creditworthiness and its prospects of obtaining future loans. **BC32**

Income statement and equity (paragraph 20)

Items of income, expenses, gains or losses (paragraph 20(a))

Paragraph 20(a) requires disclosure of income statement gains and losses by the measurement categories in IAS 39 (which complement the balance sheet disclosure requirement described in paragraph BC14). The Board concluded that the disclosure is needed for users to understand the financial performance of an entity's financial instruments, given the different measurement bases in IAS 39. **BC33**

Some entities include interest and dividend income in gains and losses on financial assets and financial liabilities held for trading and others do not. To assist users in comparing income arising from financial instruments across different entities, the Board decided that an entity should disclose how the income statement amounts are determined. For example, an entity should disclose whether net gains and losses on financial assets or financial liabilities held for trading include interest and dividend income (see Appendix B, paragraph B5(e)). **BC34**

Fee income and expense (paragraph 20(c))

Paragraph 20(c) requires disclosure of fee income and expense (other than amounts included in determining the effective interest rate) arising from financial assets or financial liabilities and from trust and other fiduciary activities that result in the entity holding or placing assets on behalf of individuals, trusts, retirement benefit plans, and other institutions. This information indicates the level of such activities and helps users to estimate possible future income of the entity. **BC35**

Other disclosures—fair value (paragraphs 25–30)

Many entities use fair value information internally in determining their overall financial position and in making decisions about individual financial instruments. It is also relevant to many decisions made by users of financial statements because, in many circumstances, it reflects the judgement of the financial markets about the present value of expected future cash flows relating to an instrument. Fair value information permits comparisons of financial instruments having substantially the same economic characteristics, regardless of why they are held and when and by whom they were issued or acquired. Fair values provide a neutral basis for assessing management's stewardship by indicating the effects of its decisions to buy, sell or hold financial assets and to incur, maintain or discharge financial liabilities. The - Board decided that when an entity does not measure a financial asset or financial liability in its balance sheet at fair value, it should provide fair value information through supplementary disclosures to assist users to compare entities on a consistent basis. **BC36**

BC37 Disclosure of fair value is not required for investments in unquoted equity instruments and derivatives linked to such equity instruments if their fair value cannot be measured reliably. Similarly, IFRS 4 does not specify the accounting required for contracts containing a discretionary participation feature pending phase II of the Board's project on insurance contracts. Accordingly, disclosure of fair value is not required for contracts containing a discretionary participation feature, if the fair value of that feature cannot be measured reliably. For all other financial assets and financial liabilities, it is reasonable to expect that fair value can be determined with sufficient reliability within constraints of timeliness and cost. Therefore, the Board concluded that there should be no other exception from the requirement to disclose fair value information for financial assets or financial liabilities.

BC38 To provide users of financial statements with a sense of the potential variability of fair value estimates, the Board decided that information about the use of valuation techniques should be disclosed, in particular the sensitivities of fair value estimates to the main valuation assumptions. In forming this conclusion, the Board considered the view that disclosure of sensitivities could be difficult, particularly when there are many assumptions to which the disclosure would apply and these assumptions are interdependent. However, the Board noted that a detailed quantitative disclosure of sensitivity to all assumptions is not required (only those that could result in a significantly different estimate of fair value are required) and that the disclosure does not require the entity to reflect interdependencies between assumptions when making the disclosure. Additionally, the Board considered whether this disclosure might imply that a fair value established by a valuation technique is less reliable than one established by other means. However, the Board noted that fair values estimated by valuation techniques are more subjective than those established from an observable market price, and concluded that users need information to help them assess the extent of this subjectivity.

BC39 Paragraph 28 requires disclosure about the difference that arises if the transaction price differs from the fair value of a financial instrument that is determined in accordance with paragraph AG76 of IAS 39. Those disclosures relate to matters addressed in the December 2004 amendment to IAS 39 *Transition and Initial Recognition of Financial Assets and Financial Liabilities**. That amendment does not specify how entities should account for those initial differences in subsequent periods. The disclosures required by paragraph 28 inform users about the amount of gain or loss that will be recognised in profit or loss in future periods. The Board noted that the information required to provide these disclosures would be readily available to the entities affected.

BC39A Statement of Financial Accounting Standards No. 157 *Fair Value Measurements* (SFAS 157) issued by the US Financial Accounting Standards Board requires disclosures that are based on a three-level fair value hierarchy for the inputs used in valuation techniques to measure fair value. The Board was asked by some users of financial statements to include similar disclosure requirements in IFRS 7 to provide more information about the relative reliability of the inputs to fair value measurements. The Board concluded that such a hierarchy would improve comparability between entities about the effects of fair value measurements as well as increase the convergence of IFRSs and US generally accepted accounting principles (GAAP). Therefore, the Board decided to require disclosures for financial instruments on the basis of a fair value hierarchy.

*ASB Footnote: *This amendment was issued in the UK as part of the amendments to FRS 26 issued in October 2005.*

Because its own fair value measurement project was not yet completed, the Board decided not to propose a fair value hierarchy for measurement, but only for disclosures. The fair value hierarchy for disclosures is the same as that in SFAS 157 but uses IFRS language pending completion of the fair value measurement project. Although the implicit fair value hierarchy for measurement in IAS 39 is different from the fair value hierarchy in SFAS 157, the Board recognised the importance of using a three-level hierarchy for disclosures that is the same as that in SFAS 157. **BC39B**

The Board noted the following three-level measurement hierarchy implicit in IAS 39: **BC39C**

(a) financial instruments quoted in an active market;
(b) financial instruments whose fair value is evidenced by comparison with other observable current market transactions in the same instrument (ie without modification or repackaging) or based on a valuation technique whose variables include only data from observable markets; and
(c) financial instruments whose fair value is determined in whole or in part using a valuation technique based on assumptions that are not supported by prices from observable current market transactions in the same instrument (ie without modification or repackaging) and not based on available observable market data.

For example, the Board acknowledged that some financial instruments that for measurement purposes are considered to have an active market in accordance with paragraphs AG71–AG73 of IAS 39 might be in Level 2 for disclosure purposes. Also, the application of paragraph AG76A of IAS 39 might result in no gain or loss being recognised on the initial recognition of a financial instrument that is in Level 2 for disclosure purposes. **BC39D**

The introduction of the fair value disclosure hierarchy does not affect any measurement or recognition requirements of other standards. In particular, the Board noted that the recognition of gains or losses at inception of a financial instrument (as required by paragraph AG76 of IAS 39) would not change as a result of the fair value disclosure hierarchy. **BC39E**

The Board decided to require additional disclosures for instruments with fair value measurements that are in Level 3 of the fair value hierarchy. These disclosures inform users of financial statements about the effects of those fair value measurements that use the most subjective inputs. **BC39F**

After reviewing comments received on the exposure draft, the Board decided not to require disclosure by level of the fair value hierarchy for financial instruments that are not measured at fair value in the statement of financial position. The Board noted that paragraphs 25 and 27 of IFRS 7, which require the disclosure of the fair value of each class of assets and liabilities in a way that permits it to be compared with its carrying amount, and the methods and assumptions applied in determining fair values, were retained. **BC39G**

DISCLOSURES ABOUT THE NATURE AND EXTENT OF RISKS ARISING FROM FINANCIAL INSTRUMENTS (PARAGRAPHS 31–42 AND B6–B28)

The Board was informed that users of financial statements value information about the risks arising from financial instruments, such as credit risk, liquidity risk and market risk, to which entities are exposed, and the techniques used to identify, measure, monitor and control those risks. Therefore, the Board decided to require disclosure of this information. The Board also decided to balance two objectives: **BC40**

(a) consistent requirements should apply to all entities so that users receive comparable information about the risks to which entities are exposed.

(b) the disclosures provided should depend on the extent of an entity's use of financial instruments and the extent to which it assumes associated risks. Entities with many financial instruments and related risks should provide more disclosure to communicate those risks to users of financial statements. Conversely, entities with few financial instruments and related risks may provide less extensive disclosure.

BC41 The Board decided to balance these two objectives by developing an IFRS that sets out principles and minimum requirements applicable to all entities, supported by guidance on implementing the IFRS. The requirements in paragraphs 33–42 combine qualitative disclosures of the entity's exposure to risks arising from financial instruments, and the way in which management views and manages these risks, with quantitative disclosures about material risks arising from financial instruments. The extent of disclosure depends on the extent of the entity's exposure to risks arising from financial instruments. The guidance on implementing the IFRS illustrates how an entity might apply the IFRS. This guidance is consistent with the disclosure requirements for banks developed by the Basel Committee (known as Pillar 3), so that banks can prepare, and users receive, a single co-ordinated set of disclosures about financial risk.

BC42 The Board noted that because entities view and manage risk in different ways, disclosures based on how an entity manages risk are unlikely to be comparable between entities. In addition, for an entity that undertakes limited management of risks arising from financial instruments, such disclosures would convey little or no information about the risks the entity has assumed. To overcome these limitations, the Board decided to specify disclosures about risk exposures applicable to all entities. These disclosures provide a common benchmark for financial statement users when comparing risk exposures across different entities and are expected to be relatively easy for entities to prepare. Entities with more developed risk management systems would provide more detailed information.

Interaction between qualitative and quantitative disclosures (paragraph 32A)

BC42A In Improvements to IFRSs issued in May 2010, the Board addressed a perceived lack of clarity in the intended interaction between the qualitative and quantitative disclosures of the nature and extent of risks arising from financial instruments. The Board emphasised the interaction between qualitative and quantitative disclosures about the nature and extent of risks arising from financial instruments. This enables users to link related disclosures and hence form an overall picture of the nature and extent of risks arising from financial instruments. The Board concluded that an explicit emphasis on the interaction between qualitative and quantitative disclosures will contribute to disclosure of information in a way that better enables users to evaluate an entity's exposure.*

Location of disclosures of risks arising from financial instruments (paragraph B6)

BC43 Many respondents to ED 7 argued that disclosures about risks in paragraphs 31–42 should not be part of the financial statements for the following reasons:

(a) the information would be difficult and costly to audit.

* ***Editor's note**: Paragraph, and preceding heading, added in November 2010.*

(b) the information is different from information generally included in financial statements because it is subjective, forward-looking and based on management's judgement. Thus, the information does not meet the criteria of comparability, faithful representation and completeness.
(c) inclusion of such information in a management commentary section outside the financial statements would be consistent with practice in other jurisdictions, including the US. Having this information in the financial statements would put IFRS preparers at a disadvantage relative to their US peers.

Respondents raised concerns that the disclosure of sensitivity analysis in particular should not be part of the financial statements. Respondents stated that sensitivity analysis cannot be prepared with the degree of reliability expected of information in the financial statements, and that the subjectivity in the sensitivity analysis and the hypothetical alternative values could undermine the credibility of the fair values recognised in the financial statements. **BC44**

The Board considered whether the disclosures should be part of the information provided by management outside the financial statements. The Board noted that respondents generally regarded the disclosures proposed in ED 7 as useful, even if they did not agree that they should be located in the financial statements. The Board's view is that financial statements would be incomplete and potentially misleading without disclosures about risks arising from financial instruments. Hence, it concluded that such disclosures should be part of the financial statements. The Board rejected the argument that increased transparency puts an entity at a disadvantage; greater certainty on the part of investors can provide a significant advantage by lowering the entity's cost of capital. **BC45**

The Board also noted that some entities might prefer to present the information required by the IFRS together with material such as a management commentary or risk report that is not part of the financial statements. Some entities might be required by regulatory authorities to provide in a separate report information similar to that required by the IFRS. Accordingly, the Board decided these disclosures should be given in the financial statements or incorporated by cross-reference from the financial statements to some other statement that is available to users of the financial statements on the same terms as the financial statements and at the same time. **BC46**

Quantitative disclosures (paragraphs 34–42 and B7–B28)

Information based on how the entity manages risk (paragraphs 34 and B7)

The Board concluded that disclosures about an entity's exposure to risks arising from financial instruments should be required, and should be based on how the entity views and manages its risks, ie using the information provided to key management personnel (for example, its board of directors or chief executive officer). This approach: **BC47**

(a) provides a useful insight into how the entity views and manages risk;
(b) results in information that has more predictive value than information based on assumptions and methods that management does not use, for instance, in considering the entity's ability to react to adverse situations;
(c) is more effective in adapting to changes in risk measurement and management techniques and developments in the external environment;

(d) has practical advantages for preparers of financial statements, because it allows them to use the data they use in managing risk; and
(e) is consistent with the approach used in IAS 14 *Segment Reporting**.

BC47A In Improvements to IFRSs issued in May 2010, the Board removed the reference to materiality from paragraph 34(b) of IFRS 7. The Board noted that the reference could imply that disclosures in IFRS 7 are required even if those disclosures are not material, which was not the Board's intention.†

Information on averages

BC48 The Board considered whether it should require quantitative information about average risk exposures during the period. It noted that information about averages is more informative if the risk exposure at the reporting date is not typical of the exposure during the period. However, information about averages is also more onerous to prepare. On balance, the Board decided to require disclosure of the exposures at the reporting date in all cases and to require additional information only if the information provided at the reporting date is unrepresentative of the entity's exposure to risk during the period.

Credit risk (paragraphs 36–38, B9 and B10)

Maximum exposure to credit risk (paragraphs 36(a), B9 and B10)

BC49 Paragraph 36(a) requires disclosure of an entity's maximum exposure to credit risk at the reporting date. Some respondents to ED 7 stated that these disclosures would not provide useful information when there are no identified problems in a loan portfolio, and it is not likely that collateral would be called on. However, the Board disagreed because it believes that such information:

(a) provides users of financial statements with a consistent measure of an entity's exposure to credit risk; and
(b) takes into account the possibility that the maximum exposure to loss may differ from the amount recognised in the balance sheet.

BC49A In Improvements to IFRSs issued in May 2010, the Board enhanced consistency within IFRS 7 by clarifying that the disclosure requirement in paragraph 36(a) applies only to financial assets whose carrying amounts do not show the reporting entity's maximum exposure to credit risk. Such an approach is consistent with the approach taken in paragraph 29(a), which states that disclosure of fair value is not required when the carrying amount is a reasonable approximation of fair value. Moreover, the Board concluded that the requirement might be duplicative for assets that are presented in the statement of financial position because the carrying amount of these assets often represents the maximum exposure to credit risk. In the Board's view, the disclosure requirement should focus on the entity's exposure to credit risk that is not already reflected in the statement of financial position.‡

BC50 Some respondents to ED 7 questioned whether the maximum exposure to credit risk for a derivative contract is its carrying amount because fair value does not always

*ASB Footnote: *IAS 14 has not been implemented in the UK. SSAP 25* Segmental Reporting *addresses issues that are addressed in some parts of IAS 14.*

†***Editor's note****: Paragraph added in November 2010.*

‡***Editor's note****: Paragraph added in November 2010.*

reflect potential future exposure to credit risk (see paragraph B10(b)). However, the Board noted that paragraph 36(a) requires disclosure of the amount that best represents the maximum exposure to credit risk *at the reporting date*, which is the carrying amount.

Collateral held as security and other credit enhancements (paragraphs 36(b) and 37(c))

ED 7 proposed that, unless impracticable, the entity should disclose the fair value of collateral held as security and other credit enhancements, to provide information about the loss the entity might incur in the event of default. However, many respondents to ED 7 disagreed with this proposal on cost/benefit grounds. Respondents indicated that fair value information might not be available for: **BC51**

(a) small entities and entities other than banks, which may find it onerous to acquire information about collateral;
(b) banks that collect precise information on the value of collateral only on origination, for loans whose payments are made on time and in full (for example a mortgage portfolio secured by properties, for which valuations are not kept up to date on an asset-by-asset basis);
(c) particular types of collateral, such as a floating charge on all the assets of an entity; and
(d) insurers that hold collateral for which fair value information is not readily available.

The Board also noted respondents' concerns that an aggregate disclosure of the fair value of collateral held would be misleading when some loans in a portfolio are over-collateralised, and other loans have insufficient collateral. In these circumstances, netting the fair value of the two types of collateral would under-report the amount of credit risk. The Board agreed with respondents that the information useful to users is not the total amount of credit exposure less the total amount of collateral, but rather is the amount of credit exposure that is left after available collateral is taken into account. **BC52**

Therefore, the Board decided not to require disclosure of the fair value of collateral held, but to require disclosure of only a description of collateral held as security and other credit enhancements. The Board noted that such disclosure does not require an entity to establish fair values for all its collateral (in particular when the entity has determined that the fair value of some collateral exceeds the carrying amount of the loan) and, thus, would be less onerous for entities to provide than fair values. **BC53**

Credit quality of financial assets that are neither past due nor impaired (paragraph 36(c))

The Board noted that information about credit quality gives a greater insight into the credit risk of assets and helps users assess whether such assets are more or less likely to become impaired in the future. Because this information will vary between entities, the Board decided not to specify a particular method for giving this information, but rather to allow each entity to devise a method that is appropriate to its circumstances. **BC54**

Financial assets with renegotiated terms (paragraph 36(d))

In Improvements to IFRSs issued in May 2010, the Board addressed a practical concern relating to the disclosure requirements for renegotiated financial assets. The **BC54A**

Board deleted the requirement in paragraph 36(d) to disclose the carrying amount of financial assets that would otherwise be past due or impaired whose terms have been renegotiated. The Board considered the difficulty in identifying financial assets whose terms have been renegotiated to avoid becoming past due or impaired (rather than for other commercial reasons). The Board noted that the original requirement was unclear about whether the requirement applies only to financial assets that were renegotiated in the current reporting period or whether past negotiations of those assets should be considered. Moreover, the Board was informed that commercial terms of loans are often renegotiated regularly for reasons that are not related to impairment. In practice it is difficult, especially for a large portfolio of loans, to ascertain which loans were renegotiated to avoid becoming past due or impaired.*

Financial assets that are either past due or impaired (paragraph 37)

BC55 The Board decided to require separate disclosure of financial assets that are past due or impaired to provide users with information about financial assets with the greatest credit risk (paragraph 37). This includes:

(a) an analysis of the age of financial assets, including trade receivables, that are past due at the reporting date, but not impaired (paragraph 37(a)). This information provides users with information about those financial assets that are more likely to become impaired and helps users to estimate the level of future impairment losses.

(b) an analysis of financial assets that are individually determined to be impaired at the reporting date, including the factors the entity considered in determining that the financial assets are impaired (paragraph 37(b)). The Board concluded that an analysis of impaired financial assets by factors other than age (eg nature of the counterparty, or geographical analysis of impaired assets) would be useful because it helps users to understand why the impairment occurred.

BC55A In Improvements to IFRSs issued in May 2010, the Board addressed a concern that the disclosure of the fair value of collateral was potentially misleading. Within a class of assets some might be over-collateralised while others might be under-collateralised. Hence, aggregate disclosure of the fair value might be misleading. Therefore, the Board removed from paragraph 37(c) the requirement to disclose the fair value of collateral and other credit enhancements. However, the Board believes that information on the financial effect of such assets is useful to users. Hence, the Board included in paragraph 36(b) a requirement to disclose a description of collateral held as security and of other credit enhancements and to disclose their financial effect.†

Collateral and other credit enhancements obtained (paragraph 38)

BC56 Paragraph 38 requires the entity to disclose the nature and carrying amount of assets obtained by taking possession of collateral held as security or calling on other credit enhancements and its policy for disposing of such assets. The Board concluded that this information is useful because it provides information about the frequency of such activities and the entity's ability to obtain and realise the value of the collateral. ED 7 had proposed that the entity should disclose the fair value of the assets obtained less the cost of selling them, rather than the carrying amount. The Board noted that this amount might be more relevant in the case of collateral obtained that is expected to be sold. However, it also noted that such an amount would be included

* ***Editor's note**: Paragraph, and preceding heading, added in November 2010.*

† ***Editor's note**: Paragraph added in November 2010.*

in the impairment calculation that is reflected in the amount recognised in the balance sheet and the purpose of the disclosure is to indicate the amount recognised in the balance sheet for such assets.

In Improvements to IFRSs issued in May 2010, the Board enhanced consistency within IFRS 7 by clarifying that paragraph 38 requires entities to disclose the amount of foreclosed collateral held at the reporting date. This is consistent with the objective in IFRS 7 to disclose information that enables users to evaluate the nature and extent of risks arising from financial instruments to which the entity is exposed at the end of the reporting period.* **BC56A**

Liquidity risk (paragraphs 34(a), 39, B10A and B11A–B11F)

The Board decided to require disclosure of a maturity analysis for financial liabilities showing the remaining earliest contractual maturities (paragraph 39(a) and paragraphs B11–B16 of Appendix B). Liquidity risk, ie the risk that the entity will encounter difficulty in meeting commitments associated with financial liabilities, arises because of the possibility (which may often be remote) that the entity could be required to pay its liabilities earlier than expected. The Board decided to require disclosure based on the earliest contractual maturity date because this disclosure shows a worst case scenario. **BC57**

Some respondents expressed concerns that such a contractual maturity analysis does not reveal the expected maturity of liabilities, which, for some entities—eg banks with many demand deposits—may be very different. They suggested that a contractual maturity analysis alone does not provide information about the conditions expected in normal circumstances or how the entity manages deviations from expected maturity. Therefore, the Board decided to require a description of how the entity manages the liquidity risk portrayed by the contractual maturity analysis. **BC58**

In March 2009 the Board amended the disclosure requirements on the nature and extent of liquidity risk by: **BC58A**

(a) amending the definition of liquidity risk to clarify that paragraph 39 applies only to financial liabilities that will result in the outflow of cash or another financial asset. This clarifies that the disclosure requirements would not apply to financial liabilities that will be settled in the entity's own equity instruments and to liabilities within the scope of IFRS 7 that are settled with non-financial assets.
(b) emphasising that an entity must provide summary quantitative data about its exposure to liquidity risk based on information provided internally to key management personnel of the entity as required by paragraph 34(a). This reinforces the principles of IFRS 7.
(c) amending the requirement in paragraph 39 to disclose a contractual maturity analysis.

The requirements in paragraph 39(a) and (b) relate to minimum benchmark disclosures as set out in paragraph 34(b) and are expected to be relatively easy to apply. However, the Board noted that the requirement to provide disclosures based on the remaining contractual maturities was difficult to apply for some derivative financial liabilities and did not always result in information that reflects how many entities manage liquidity risk for such instruments. Hence, for some circumstances the Board eliminated the previous requirement to disclose contractual maturity information for derivative financial liabilities. However, the Board retained minimum contractual **BC58B**

****Editor's note**: Paragraph added in November 2010.*

maturity disclosures for non-derivative financial liabilities (including issued financial guarantee contracts within the scope of the IFRS) and for some derivative financial liabilities.

BC58C The Board noted that for non-derivative financial liabilities (including issued financial guarantee contracts within the scope of the IFRS) and some derivative financial liabilities, contractual maturities are essential for an understanding of the timing of cash flows associated with the liabilities. Therefore, this information is useful to users of financial statements. The Board concluded that disclosures based on the remaining contractual maturities of these financial liabilities should continue to be required.

BC58D The Board also emphasised the existing requirement to disclose a maturity analysis for financial assets held for managing liquidity risk, if that information is required to enable users of its financial statements to evaluate the nature and extent of liquidity risk. The Board also emphasised that an entity must explain the relationship between qualitative and quantitative disclosures about liquidity risk so that users of financial statements can evaluate the nature and extent of liquidity risk.

Market risk (paragraphs 40–42 and B17–B28)

BC59 The Board decided to require disclosure of a sensitivity analysis for each type of market risk (paragraph 40) because:

(a) users have consistently emphasised the fundamental importance of sensitivity analysis;
(b) a sensitivity analysis can be disclosed for all types of market risk and by all entities, and is relatively easy to understand and calculate; and
(c) it is suitable for all entities—including non-financial entities—that have financial instruments. It is supported by disclosures of how the entity manages the risk. Thus, it is a simpler and more suitable disclosure than other approaches, including the disclosures of terms and conditions and the gap analysis of interest rate risk previously required by IAS 32.

The Board noted that information provided by a simple sensitivity analysis would not be comparable across entities. This is because the methodologies used to prepare the sensitivity analysis and the resulting disclosures would vary according to the nature of the entity and the complexity of its risk management systems.

BC60 The Board acknowledged that a simple sensitivity analysis that shows a change in only one variable has limitations. For example, the analysis may not reveal non-linearities in sensitivities or the effects of interdependencies between variables. The Board decided to meet the first concern by requiring additional disclosure when the sensitivity analysis is unrepresentative of a risk inherent in a financial instrument (paragraph 42). The Board noted that it could meet the second concern by requiring a more complex sensitivity analysis that takes into account the interdependencies between risks. Although more informative, such an analysis is also more complex and costly to prepare. Accordingly, the Board decided not to require such an analysis, but to permit its disclosure as an alternative to the minimum requirement when it is used by management to manage risk.

BC61 Respondents to ED 7 noted that a value-at-risk amount would not show the effect on profit or loss or equity. However, entities that manage on the basis of value at risk would not want to prepare a separate sensitivity analysis solely for the purpose of this disclosure. The Board's objective was to require disclosures about sensitivity, not to mandate a particular form of sensitivity disclosure. Therefore, the Board decided not to require disclosure of the effects on profit or loss and equity if an alternative disclosure of sensitivity is made.

Respondents to ED 7 requested the Board to provide more guidance and clarification about the sensitivity analysis, in particular: **BC62**

(a) what is a reasonably possible change in the relevant risk variable?
(b) what is the appropriate level of aggregation in the disclosures?
(c) what methodology should be used in preparing the sensitivity analysis?

The Board concluded that it would not be possible to provide comprehensive guidance on the methodology to be used in preparing the sensitivity analysis. The Board noted that more comparable information would be obtained if it imposed specific requirements about the inputs, process and methodology of the analysis, for example disclosure of the effects of a parallel shift of the yield curve by 100 basis points. However, the Board decided against such a specific requirement because a reasonably possible change in a relevant risk variable (such as interest rates) in one economic environment may not be reasonably possible in another (such as an economy with higher inflation). Moreover, the effect of a reasonably possible change will vary depending on the entity's risk exposures. As a result, entities are required to judge what those reasonably possible changes are. **BC63**

However, the Board decided that it would provide high level application guidance about how the entity should assess what is a reasonably possible change and on the appropriate level of aggregation in the disclosures. In response to comments received on ED 7, the Board also decided to clarify that: **BC64**

(a) an entity should not aggregate information about material exposures to risk from significantly different economic environments. However, if it has exposure to only one type of market risk in only one economic environment, it might not show disaggregated information.
(b) the sensitivity analysis does not require entities to determine what the profit or loss for the period would have been had the relevant risk variable been different. The sensitivity analysis shows the effect on current period profit or loss and equity if a reasonably possible change in the relevant risk variable had been applied to the risk exposures in existence at the balance sheet date.
(c) a reasonably possible change is judged relative to the economic environments in which the entity operates, and does not include remote or 'worst case' scenarios or 'stress tests'.
(d) entities are required to disclose only the effects of the changes at the limits of the reasonably possible range of the relevant risk variable, rather than all reasonably possible changes.
(e) the time frame for which entities should make an assessment about what is reasonably possible is the period until the entity next presents these disclosures, usually its next annual reporting period.

The Board also decided to add a simple example of what a sensitivity analysis might look like.

Operational risk

The Board discussed whether it should require disclosure of information about operational risk. However, the Board noted that the definition and measurement of operational risk are in their infancy and are not necessarily related to financial instruments. It also decided that such disclosures would be more appropriately **BC65** located outside the financial statements. Therefore, the Board decided to defer this issue to its research project on management commentary.

DISCLOSURES RELATING TO TRANSFERS OF FINANCIAL ASSETS

Background

BC65A In March 2009, in conjunction with the Memorandum of Understanding between the IASB and the US Financial Accounting Standards Board (FASB) to improve and achieve convergence of IFRS and US standards for derecognition, the IASB published an exposure draft to replace the derecognition requirements of IAS 39 and to improve the disclosure requirements in IFRS 7 relating to the transfer of financial assets and liabilities. In response to feedback received on the exposure draft the IASB developed more fully the alternative model described in the exposure draft and the boards discussed the alternative model.

BC65B In May 2010 the boards reconsidered their strategies and plans for the derecognition project in the light of:

(a) their joint discussions of the alternative derecognition model described in the exposure draft;
(b) the June 2009 amendments to the US GAAP derecognition guidance by the FASB, which reduced the differences between IFRSs and US GAAP by improving requirements relating to derecognition of financial assets and liabilities; and
(c) the feedback the IASB received from national standard-setters on the largely favourable effects of the IFRS derecognition requirements during the financial crisis.

BC65C As a result, in June 2010 the IASB and the FASB agreed that their near term priority was on increasing the transparency and comparability of their standards by improving and aligning the disclosure requirements in IFRSs and US GAAP for financial assets transferred to another entity. The boards also decided to conduct additional research and analysis, including a post-implementation review of some of the FASB's recently amended requirements, as a basis for assessing the nature and direction of any further efforts to improve or align IFRSs and US GAAP.

BC65D As a result, the Board decided to finalise the derecognition disclosures and related objectives, proposed in the exposure draft. Accordingly, in October 2010 the Board issued *Disclosures – Transfers of Financial Assets* (Amendments to IFRS 7), requiring disclosures to help users of financial statements:

(a) to understand the relationship between transferred financial assets that are not derecognised in their entirety and the associated liabilities; and
(b) to evaluate the nature of and risks associated with the entity's continuing involvement in derecognised financial assets.

Transferred financial assets that are not derecognised in their entirety

BC65E When financial assets are transferred but not derecognised, there has been an exchange transaction that is not reflected as such in the financial statements as a result of the accounting requirements. The Board concluded that in those situations, users of financial statements need to understand the relationship between those transferred financial assets and the associated liabilities that an entity recognises.

Understanding that relationship helps users of financial statements in assessing an entity's cash flow needs and the cash flows available to the entity from its assets.

The Board observed that IFRS 7 required disclosures about transferred financial assets that are not derecognised in their entirety. The Board decided to continue requiring those disclosures because they provide information that is useful in understanding the relationship between transferred financial assets that are not derecognised and associated liabilities. **BC65F**

However, the Board also decided that the following additional disclosures were necessary: **BC65G**

(a) a qualitative description of the nature of the relationship between transferred assets and associated liabilities, including restrictions arising from the transfer on the reporting entity's use of the transferred assets; and
(b) a schedule that sets out the fair value of the transferred financial assets, the associated liabilities and the net position when the counterparty to the associated liabilities has recourse only to the transferred assets.

The Board concluded that these disclosures would provide information that is useful in assessing the extent to which the economic benefits generated by assets of an entity cannot be used in an unrestricted manner, as is implied when assets are recognised in an entity's statement of financial position. In addition, the disclosures would provide information about liabilities that will be settled entirely from the proceeds received from the transferred assets, and thus identify liabilities for which the counterparties do not have claims on the assets of the entity in general. For those assets for which the underlying cash flows are committed to be used to satisfy related liabilities, the Board noted that a schedule that sets out the fair value of the transferred financial assets, the associated liabilities and the net position (in addition to showing the cash flow relationship between those assets and liabilities) also provides a means of understanding the net exposure of an entity following a transfer transaction that fails derecognition. **BC65H**

Transferred financial assets that are derecognised

The Board was asked by users of financial statements, regulators and others to review the disclosure requirements for what are often described as 'off balance sheet' activities. Transfers of financial assets, particularly securitisation of financial assets, were identified as forming part of such activities. **BC65I**

The Board concluded that when an entity retains continuing involvement in financial assets that it has derecognised, users of financial statements would benefit from information about the risks to which the entity remains exposed. Such information is relevant in assessing the amount, timing and uncertainty of the entity's future cash flows. **BC65J**

The Board observed that IFRS 7 already requires certain disclosures by class of financial instrument or by type of risk. However, the IFRS requires the information at an aggregated level, so information specific to derecognition transactions is often not available. In response to requests from users and others the Board concluded that disclosures specific to derecognition transactions were necessary. **BC65K**

The Board concluded that the disclosures should focus on the risk exposure of an entity, and should provide information about the timing of the return and the cash outflow that would or may be required to repurchase the derecognised financial assets in the future. The Board reasoned that a combination of disclosures about the **BC65L** strike price or repurchase price to repurchase assets, the fair value of its continuing involvement, the maximum exposure to loss and qualitative information about an entity's obligations to provide financial support are relevant in understanding an entity's exposure to risks.

BC65M In addition, the Board concluded that information about an entity's gain or loss on derecognition and the timing of recognition of that gain or loss provides information about the proportion of an entity's profit or loss that arises from transferring financial assets in which the entity also retains continuing involvement. Such information is useful in assessing the extent to which an entity generates profits from transferring financial assets while retaining some form of continuing involvement and thus exposure to risk.

BC65N The Board observed that the total amount of proceeds from transfer activity (that qualifies for derecognition) in a reporting period may not be evenly distributed throughout the reporting period (eg if a substantial proportion of the total amount of transfer activity takes place in the closing days of a reporting period). The Board decided that, if transfer activity is concentrated around the end of reporting periods, disclosure of this fact provides an indication of whether transfer transactions are undertaken for the purpose of altering the appearance of the statement of financial position rather than for an ongoing commercial or financing purpose. In such cases, the amendments require disclosure of when the greatest transfer activity took place within that reporting period, the amount recognised from the transfer activity in that part of the reporting period, and the total amount of proceeds from transfer activity in that part of the reporting period.*

EFFECTIVE DATE AND TRANSITION (PARAGRAPHS 43 AND 44)

BC66 The Board is committed to maintaining a 'stable platform' of substantially unchanged Standards for annual periods beginning on or before 1 January 2005, when many entities will adopt IFRSs for the first time. In addition, some preparers will need time to make the system changes necessary to comply with the IFRS. Therefore, the Board decided that the effective date of IFRS 7 should be annual periods beginning on or after 1 January 2007, with earlier application encouraged.

BC67 The Board noted that entities that apply IFRS 7 only when it becomes mandatory will have sufficient time to prepare comparative information. This conclusion does not apply to entities that apply IFRS 7 early. In particular, the time would be extremely short for those entities that would like to apply IFRS 7 when they first adopt IFRSs in 2005, to avoid changing from local GAAP to IAS 32 and IAS 30 when they adopt IFRSs and then changing again to IFRS 7 only one or two years later. Therefore, the Board gave an exemption from providing comparative disclosure in the first year of application of IFRS 7 to any entity that both (a) is a first-time adopter of IFRSs and (b) applies IFRS 7 before 1 January 2006. The Board noted that such an exemption for first-time adopters exists in IAS 32 and IFRS 4 and that the reasons for providing the exemption apply equally to IFRS 7.

BC68 The Board also considered whether it should provide an exemption from presenting all or some of the comparative information to encourage early adoption of IFRS 7 by entities that already apply IFRSs.

BC69 The Board noted that IFRS 7 contains two types of disclosures: accounting disclosures (in paragraphs 7–30) that are based on requirements previously in IAS 32

****Editor's note:** *Paragraphs BC65A to BC65N added in July 2011.*

and new risk disclosures (in paragraphs 31–42). The Board concluded that existing users of IFRSs already will have complied with the requirements of IAS 32 and will not encounter difficulty in providing comparative information for the accounting disclosures.

The Board noted that most of the risk disclosures, in particular those about market risk, are based on information collected at the end of the reporting period. The Board concluded that although IFRS 7 was published in August 2005, it will still be possible for entities to collect the information that they require to comply with IFRS 7 for accounting periods beginning in 2005. However, it would not always be possible to collect the information needed to provide comparative information about accounting periods that began in 2004. As a result, the Board decided that entities that apply IFRS 7 for accounting periods beginning in 2005 (ie before 1 January 2006) need not present comparative information about the risk disclosures. **BC70**

The Board also noted that comparative disclosures about risk are less relevant because these disclosures are intended to have predictive value. As a result information about risk loses relevance more quickly than other types of disclosure, and any disclosures required by previous GAAP are unlikely to be comparable with those required by IFRS 7. Accordingly, the Board decided that an entity that is not a first-time adopter and applies IFRS 7 for annual periods beginning before 1 January 2006 need not present comparative disclosures about the nature and extent of risks arising from financial instruments. In reaching this conclusion, the Board noted that the advantages of encouraging more entities to apply IFRS 7 early outweighed the disadvantage of the reduced information provided. **BC71**

The Board considered and rejected arguments that it should extend the exemption: **BC72**

(a) from providing comparative information to first-time adopters that applied IFRS 7 before 1 January 2007 (rather than only those that applied IFRS 7 before 1 January 2006). The Board concluded that an entity that intends to adopt IFRSs for the first time on or after 1 January 2006 will have sufficient time to collect information for its accounting period beginning on or after 1 January 2005 and, thus, should not have difficulty in providing the comparative disclosures for accounting periods beginning on or after 1 January 2006.

(b) from providing comparative disclosures about the significance of financial instruments to all entities adopting the IFRS for annual periods beginning before 1 January 2006 (rather than only to first-time adopters). The Board concluded that only first-time adopters warranted special relief so that they would be able to adopt IFRS 7 early without first having to adopt IAS 32 and IAS 30 for only one period. Entities that are not first-time adopters already apply IAS 32 and IAS 30 and have no particular need to adopt IFRS 7 before 1 January 2007.

(c) from providing comparative disclosures about risk to periods beginning before 1 January 2007 (rather than 2006). The Board noted that entities adopting IFRS 7 after 1 January 2006 would have a full calendar year to prepare after the publication of the IFRS.

Summary of main changes from the Exposure Draft

BC73 The main changes to the proposals in ED 7 are:

(a) ED 7 proposed disclosure of the amount of change in the fair value of a financial liability designated as at fair value through profit or loss that is not attributable to changes in a benchmark interest rate as a proxy for the amount of change in fair value attributable to changes in the instrument's credit risk. The IFRS permits entities to determine the amount of change in fair value attributable to changes in the instrument's credit risk using an alternative method if the entity believes that its alternative method gives more faithful representation. The proxy disclosure has been amended to be the amount of change in fair value that is not attributable to changes in market conditions that give rise to market risk. As a result, entities may exclude factors other than a change in a benchmark interest rate when calculating the proxy.

(b) a requirement has been added for disclosures about the difference between the transaction price at initial recognition (used as fair value in accordance with paragraph AG76 of IAS 39) and the results of a valuation technique that will be used for subsequent measurement.

(c) no disclosure is required of the fair value of collateral pledged as security and other credit enhancements as was proposed in ED 7.

(d) the sensitivity analysis requirements have been clarified.

(e) the exemption from presenting comparatives has been widened.

(f) the capital disclosures are a stand-alone amendment to IAS 1, rather than part of the IFRS. No disclosure is required of whether the entity has complied with capital targets set by management and of the consequences of any non-compliance with those targets.

(g) the amendments to IFRS 4 related to IFRS 7 have been modified to reduce systems changes for insurers.

Disclosures about capital

> ASB Note: The following is a reproduction of the IASB's Basis for Conclusions and related Dissenting Opinion in relation to the Capital Disclosures that were developed as part of the IFRS 7 project but implemented as amendments to IAS 1. The ASB has implemented the amendments to IAS 1 as Appendix E to FRS 29.

EBC1 In July 2004, the Board published an Exposure Draft—ED 7 *Financial Instruments: Disclosures*. As part of that project, the Board considered whether it should require disclosures about capital.

EBC2 The level of an entity's capital and how it manages capital are important factors for users to consider in assessing the risk profile of an entity and its ability to withstand unexpected adverse events. The level of capital might also affect the entity's ability to pay dividends. Consequently, ED 7 proposed disclosures about capital.

EBC3 In ED 7, the Board decided that it should not limit its requirements for disclosures about capital to entities that are subject to external capital requirements (eg regulatory capital requirements established by legislation or other regulation). The Board believes that information about capital is useful for all entities, as is evidenced by the fact that some entities set internal capital requirements and norms have been established for some industries. The Board noted that the capital disclosures are not intended to replace disclosures required by regulators. The Board also noted that the financial statements should not be regarded as a substitute for disclosures to regulators (which may not be available to all users) because the function of disclosures made to regulators may differ from those to other users. Therefore, the Board decided that information about capital should be required of all entities because it is useful to users of general purpose financial statements. Accordingly, the Board did not distinguish between the requirements for regulated and nonregulated entities.

Some respondents to ED 7 questioned the relevance of the capital disclosures in a Standard dealing with disclosures relating to financial instruments. The Board noted that an entity's capital does not relate solely to financial instruments and, thus, capital disclosures have more general relevance. Accordingly, the Board included these disclosures in IAS 1, rather than IFRS 7. **EBC4**

The Board also decided that an entity's decision to adopt the amendments to IAS 1 should be independent of the entity's decision to adopt IFRS 7. The Board noted that issuing a separate amendment facilitates separate adoption decisions. **EBC5**

Objectives, policies and processes for managing capital

The Board decided that disclosure about capital should be placed in the context of a discussion of the entity's objectives, policies and processes for managing capital. This is because the Board believes that such a discussion both communicates important information about the entity's capital strategy and provides the context for other disclosures. **EBC6**

The Board considered whether an entity can have a view of capital that differs from what IFRSs define as equity. The Board noted that, although for the purposes of this disclosure capital would often equate with equity as defined in IFRSs, it might also include or exclude some components. The Board also noted that this disclosure is intended to give entities the opportunity to describe how they view the components of capital they manage, if this is different from what IFRSs define as equity. **EBC7**

Externally imposed capital requirements

The Board considered whether it should require disclosure of any externally imposed capital requirements. Such a capital requirement could be: **EBC8**

(a) an industrywide requirement with which all entities in the industry must comply; or
(b) an entityspecific requirement imposed on a particular entity by its prudential supervisor or other regulator.

The Board noted that some industries and countries have industrywide capital requirements, and others do not. Thus, the Board concluded that it should not require disclosure of industrywide requirements, or compliance with such requirements, because such disclosure would not lead to comparability between different entities or between similar entities in different countries. **EBC9**

The Board concluded that disclosure of the existence and level of entityspecific capital requirements is important information for users, because it informs them about the risk assessment of the regulator. Such disclosure improves transparency and market discipline. **EBC10**

However, the Board noted the following arguments against requiring disclosure of externally imposed entityspecific capital requirements. **EBC11**

(a) Users of financial statements might rely primarily on the regulator's assessment of solvency risk without making their own risk assessment.
(b) The focus of a regulator's risk assessment is for those whose interests the regulations are intended to protect (eg depositors or policyholders). This emphasis is different from that of a shareholder. Thus, it could be misleading to suggest that the regulator's risk assessment could, or should, be a substitute for independent analysis by investors.
(c) The disclosure of entityspecific capital requirements imposed by a regulator might undermine that regulator's ability to impose such requirements. For example, the information could cause depositors to withdraw funds. Hence, this might discourage regulators from imposing requirements. Furthermore, an entity's regulatory dialogue would become public, which might not be appropriate in all circumstances.
(d) Because different regulators have different tools available, for example formal requirements and moral suasion, a requirement to disclose entityspecific capital requirements could not be framed in a way that would lead to the provision of information that is comparable across entities.
(e) Disclosure of capital requirements (and hence, regulatory judgements) could hamper clear communication to the entity of the regulator's assessment by creating incentives to use moral suasion and other informal mechanisms.
(f) Disclosure requirements should not focus on entityspecific capital requirements in isolation, but should focus on how entityspecific capital requirements affect how an entity manages and determines the adequacy of its capital resources.
(g) A requirement to disclose entityspecific capital requirements imposed by a regulator is not part of Pillar 3 of the Basel II Framework developed by the Basel Committee on Banking Supervision.

EBC12 Taking into account all of the above arguments, the Board decided not to require quantitative disclosure of externally imposed capital requirements. Rather, it decided to require disclosures about whether the entity complied with any externally imposed capital requirements during the period and, if not, the consequences of non-compliance. This retains confidentiality between regulators and the entity, but alerts users to breaches of capital requirements and their consequences.

EBC13 Some respondents to ED 7 did not agree that breaches of externally imposed capital requirements should be disclosed. They argued that disclosure about breaches of externally imposed capital requirements and the associated regulatory measures subsequently imposed could be disproportionately damaging to entities. The Board was not persuaded by these arguments because it believes that such concerns indicate that information about breaches of externally imposed capital requirements may often be material by its nature. The *Framework* states that 'Information is material if its omission or misstatement could influence the economic decisions of users taken on the basis of the financial statements.' Similarly, the Board decided not to provide an exemption for temporary noncompliance with regulatory requirements during the year. Information that an entity is sufficiently close to its limits to breach them, even on a temporary basis, is useful for users.

Internal capital targets

EBC14 The Board proposed in ED 7 that the requirement to disclose information about breaches of capital requirements should apply equally to breaches of internally imposed requirements, because it believed the information is also useful to a user of the financial statements.

However, this proposal was criticised by respondents to ED 7 for the following reasons: **EBC15**

(a) the information is subjective and, thus, not comparable between entities. In particular, different entities will set internal targets for different reasons, so a breach of a requirement might signify different things for different entities. In contrast, a breach of an external requirement has similar implications for all entities required to comply with similar requirements.
(b) capital targets are not more important than other internally set financial targets, and to require disclosure only of capital targets would provide users with incomplete and, perhaps, misleading information.
(c) internal targets are estimates that are subject to change by the entity. It is not appropriate to require the entity's performance against this benchmark to be disclosed.
(d) an internally set capital target can be manipulated by management. The disclosure requirement could cause management to set the target so that it would always be achieved, providing little useful information to users and potentially reducing the effectiveness of the entity's capital management.

As a result, the Board decided not to require disclosure of the capital targets set by management, whether the entity has complied with those targets, or the consequences of any noncompliance. However, the Board confirmed its view that when an entity has policies and processes for managing capital, qualitative disclosures about these policies and processes are useful. The Board also concluded that these disclosures, together with disclosure of the components of equity and their changes during the year (required by paragraphs 96–101)*, would give sufficient information about entities that are not regulated or subject to externally imposed capital requirements. **EBC16**

Amendments to IAS 32 and IAS 1 – Puttable Financial Instruments and Obligations Arising on Liquidation *(2008)*†

In July 2006 the Board published an exposure draft of proposed amendments to IAS 32 and IAS 1 relating to the classification of puttable instruments and instruments with obligations arising only on liquidation. The Board subsequently confirmed the proposals and in February 2008 issued an amendments that now forms part of IAS 1. **EBC17**

Puttable financial instruments and obligations arising on liquidation

The Board decided to require disclosure of information about puttable instruments and instruments that impose on the entity an obligation to deliver to another party a pro rata share of the net assets of the entity only on liquidation that are reclassified in accordance with paragraphs 16E and 16F of IAS 32. This is because the Board concluded that this disclosure allows users of financial statements to understand the effects of any reclassifications. **EBC18**

The Board also concluded that entities with puttable financial instruments classified as equity should be required to disclose additional information to allow users to assess any effect on the entity's liquidity arising from the ability of the holder to put the instruments to the issuer. Financial instruments classified as equity usually do not **EBC19**

*ASB Footnote: *IAS 1 has no equivalent in the UK.*

†***ASB Footnote****: These additions relate to changes made to IAS 1 by the IASB in February 2008. As IAS 1 has no equivalent in the UK or Republic of Ireland, the ASB incorporated additional equivalent paragraphs in Appendix E of FRS 29 as paragraphs E4 to E8.*

include any obligation for the entity to deliver a financial asset to another party. Therefore, the Board concluded that additional disclosures are needed in these circumstances. In particular, the Board concluded that entities should disclose the expected cash outflow on redemption or repurchase of those financial instruments that are classified as equity and information about how that amount was determined. That information allows liquidity risk associated with the put obligation and future cash flows to be evaluated.

DISSENTING OPINION

Dissent of James J Leisenring

EDO1 Mr Leisenring dissents from the amendments to IAS 1 Presentation of Financial Statements—*Capital Disclosures*. He disagrees with the assertion in paragraph BC43 that the information required by this amendment is useful for all entities. He notes that nothing would prohibit an entity making these disclosures if specific circumstances suggested the disclosures were particularly useful. Therefore he would not impose the disclosure requirements of paragraphs 124A–124C on entities that are not subject to external capital requirements.*

*ASB Footnote: *The ASB has included these amendments to IAS 1 in this Standard and these are contained within Appendix E. Paragraph BC43 in IAS 1 has been incorporated at EBC3 in this Standard and the IAS 1 disclosure requirements in paragraphs 124A – 124C have been incorporated at E1 – E3 in Appendix C.*

Appendix
Amendments to Basis for Conclusions on other IFRSs

This appendix contains amendments to the Basis for Conclusions on other Standards that are necessary in order to ensure consistency with FRS 29. In the amended paragraphs, new text is underlined and deleted text is struck through.

The Basis for Conclusions on FRS 25 *Financial Instruments: Disclosure and Presentation* is amended as described below. **BCA1**

The reference to FRS 25 in paragraph BC1 is footnoted as follows:

> In August 2005, the IASB relocated all disclosures relating to financial instruments to IFRS 7. The paragraphs relating to disclosures that were originally published in this Basis for Conclusions were relocated, if still relevant, to the Basis for Conclusions on IFRS 7.

An ASB footnote is also added as follows:

> The ASB issued FRS 29 in December 2005. All disclosures relating to financial instruments, and so all relevant paragraphs from this Basis for Conclusions were similarly relocated.

The headings above paragraph BC34 and paragraphs BC34–BC48 are deleted.

In paragraph BC49, subparagraphs (i) and (j) are deleted and new subparagraph (k) is added as follows:

(k) In August 2005, the IASB issued IFRS 7 *Financial Instruments: Disclosures*. As a result, disclosures relating to financial instruments, if still relevant, were relocated to IFRS 7.

The new subparagraph (k) is footnoted as follows:

> The ASB issued FRS 29 in December 2005. All disclosures relating to financial instruments were similarly relocated.

In the Basis for Conclusions on FRS 26 (IAS 39) *Financial Instruments: Measurement*, the references to FRS 25 in paragraphs BC90 and BC222(s) are footnoted as follows: **BCA2**

> In August 2005, the IASB relocated all disclosures relating to financial instruments to IFRS 7 *Financial Instruments: Disclosures*.

An ASB footnote is also added as follows:

> In December 2005, the ASB similarly relocated all disclosures relating to financial instruments to FRS 29.

Deleted by ASB (IAS 41) **BCA3**

Deleted by ASB (IFRS 4) **BCA4**

Guidance on implementing FRS 29 (IFRS 7) Financial instruments: disclosures

	paragraphs
Introduction	**IG1–IG4**
Materiality	**IG3–IG4**
Classes of financial instruments and level of disclosure	**IG5–IG6**
Significance of financial instruments for financial position and performance	**IG7–IG14**
Financial liabilities at fair value through profit or loss	**IG7–IG11**
Defaults and breaches	**IG12**
Total interest income and total interest expense	**IG13**
Fair value	**IG14**
Nature and extent of risks arising from financial instruments	**IG15–IG40**
Qualitative disclosures	**IG15–IG17**
Quantitative disclosures	**IG18–IG40**
Credit risk	IG21–IG29
Collateral and other credit enhancements pledged	*IG22*
Credit quality	IG23–IG25
Financial assets that are either past due or impaired	IG26–IG29
Liquidity risk	IG30–IG31
Liquidity management	IG30–IG31
Market risk	IG32–IG40
Other market risk disclosures	IG37–IG40
Transition	**IG41**
Appendix	
Amendments to guidance on other IFRSs	

Guidance on Implementing FRS 29 (IFRS 7) Financial Instruments: Disclosures

This guidance accompanies, but is not part of, FRS 29.

INTRODUCTION

This guidance suggests possible ways to apply some of the disclosure requirements in *FRS 29*. The guidance does not create additional requirements. IG1

For convenience, each disclosure requirement in the FRS is discussed separately. In practice, disclosures would normally be presented as an integrated package and individual disclosures might satisfy more than one requirement. For example, information about concentrations of risk might also convey information about exposure to credit or other risk. IG2

[Deleted]* IG3

CLASSES OF FINANCIAL INSTRUMENTS AND LEVEL OF DISCLOSURE (PARAGRAPHS 6 AND B1–B3)

Paragraph B3 states that 'an entity decides in the light of its circumstances how much detail it provides to satisfy the requirements of this FRS, how much emphasis it places on different aspects of the requirements and how it aggregates information to display the overall picture without combining information with different characteristics.' To satisfy the requirements, an entity may not need to disclose all the information suggested in this guidance. IG5

SIGNIFICANCE OF FINANCIAL INSTRUMENTS FOR FINANCIAL POSITION AND PERFORMANCE (PARAGRAPHS 7–30, B4 AND B5)

Financial liabilities at fair value through profit or loss (paragraphs 10(a)(i) and B4)

The following example illustrates the calculation that an entity might perform in accordance with paragraph B4 of Appendix B of the FRS. IG7

On 1 January 20X1, an entity issues a 10-year bond with a par value of CU150,000 and an annual fixed coupon rate of 8 per cent, which is consistent with market rates for bonds with similar characteristics. IG8

The entity uses LIBOR as its observable (benchmark) interest rate. At the date of inception of the bond, LIBOR is 5 per cent. At the end of the first year: IG9

(a) LIBOR has decreased to 4.75 per cent.

**Editor's note*: Paragraph deleted in November 2010.*

(b) the fair value for the bond is CU153,811, consistent with an interest rate of 7.6 per cent.*

IG10 The entity assumes a flat yield curve, all changes in interest rates result from a parallel shift in the yield curve, and the changes in LIBOR are the only relevant changes in market conditions.

IG11 The entity estimates the amount of change in the fair value of the bond that is not attributable to changes in market conditions that give rise to market risk as follows:

[paragraph B4(a)] First, the entity computes the liability's internal rate of return at the start of the period using the observed market price of the liability and the liability's contractual cash flows at the start of the period. It deducts from this rate of return the observed (benchmark) interest rate at the start of the period, to arrive at an instrument-specific component of the internal rate of return.	At the start of the period of a 10-year bond with a coupon of 8 per cent, the bond's internal rate of return is 8 per cent. Because the observed (benchmark) interest rate (LIBOR) is 5 per cent, the instrument-specific component of the internal rate of return is 3 per cent.
[paragraph B4(b)] Next, the entity calculates the present value of the cash flows associated with the liability using the liability's contractual cash flows at the end of the period and a discount rate equal to the sum of (i) the observed (benchmark) interest rate at the end of the period and (ii) the instrument-specific component of the internal rate of return as determined in accordance with paragraph B4(a).	The contractual cash flows of the instrument at the end of the period are: • interest: CU12,000[(a)] per year for each of years 2–10. • principal: CU150,000 in year 10. The discount rate to be used to calculate the present value of the bond is thus 7.75 per cent, which is 4.75 per cent end of period LIBOR rate, plus the 3 per cent instrument-specific component. This gives a present value of CU152,367.[(b)]
[paragraph B4(c)] The difference between the observed market price of the liability at the end of the period and the amount determined in accordance with paragraph B4(b) is the change in fair value that is not attributable to changes in the observed (benchmark) interest rate. This is the amount to be disclosed.	The market price of the liability at the end of the period is CU153,811.[(c)] Thus, the entity discloses CU1,444, which is CU153,811–CU152,367, as the increase in fair value of the bond that is not attributable to changes in market conditions that give rise to market risk.

**This reflects a shift in LIBOR from 5 per cent to 4.75 per cent and a movement of 0.15 per cent which, in the absence of other relevant changes in market conditions, is assumed to reflect changes in credit risk of the instrument.*

(a) CU150,000 × 8% = CU12,000
(b) PV = $[CU12{,}000 \times (1-(1+0.0775)^{-9})/0.0775] + CU150{,}000 \times (1+0.0775)^{-9}$
(c) market price = $[CU12{,}000 \times (1-(1+0.076)^{-9})/0.076] + CU150{,}000 \times (1+0.076)^{-9}$

Defaults and breaches (paragraphs 18 and 19)

Paragraphs 18 and 19 require disclosures when there are any defaults or breaches of loans payable. Any defaults or breaches may affect the classification of the liability as current or non-current in accordance with paragraphs 50A to 50E of FRS 25. **IG12**

Total interest expense (paragraph 20(b))*

Total interest expense disclosed in accordance with paragraph 20(b) is a component of the line item for finance costs which may also include amounts associated with non-financial liabilities. **IG13**

Fair value (paragraphs 27-28)

FRS 29 requires disclosures about the level in the fair value hierarchy in which fair value measurements are categorised for assets and liabilities measured in the balance sheet. A tabular format is required unless another format is more appropriate. An entity might disclose the following for assets to comply with paragraph 27B(a). (Disclosure of comparative information is also required, but is not included in the following example.) **IG13A**

Assets measured at fair value

		Fair value measurement at the balance sheet date using:		
Description	**31 Dec 20X2**	**Level 1 CU million**	**Level 2 CU million**	**Level 3 CU million**
Financial assets at fair value through profit or loss				
Trading securities	100	40	55	5
Trading derivatives	39	17	20	2
Available-for-sale financial assets				
Equity investments	75	30	40	5
Total	214	87	115	12

(Note: For liabilities, a similar table might be presented.)

FRS 29 requires a reconciliation from beginning to ending balances for those assets and liabilities that are measured in the balance sheet at fair value based on a valuation technique for which any significant input is not based on observable market data (Level 3). A tabular format is required unless another format is more **IG13B**

In* Improvements to IFRSs *issued in May 2008, the Board amended paragraph IG13 and removed 'total interest income' as a component of finance costs. This amendment removed an inconsistency with paragraph 32 of IAS 1 Presentation of Financial Statements, which precludes the offsetting of income and expenses (except when required or permitted by an IFRS). The ASB notes that UK FRS and the requirements of the Companies Act do not prohibit the netting of finance costs with finance income on the face of the profit and loss account, providing the gross amounts are disclosed in the notes to the financial statements.* ***Editor's note**: Paragraph amended and footnote added December 2008.*

appropriate. An entity might disclose the following for assets to comply with paragraph 27B(c). (Disclosure of comparative information is also required, but is not included in the following example.)

Assets measured at fair value based on Level 3

	Fair value measurement at the balance sheet date			
	Financial assets at fair value through profit or loss		**Available-for-sale financial assets**	**Total**
	Trading securities	Trading derivatives	Equity investments	
	CU million	CU million	CU million	CU million
Opening balance	6	5	4	15
Total gains or losses				
in profit or loss	(2)	(2)	–	(4)
in the statement of total recognised gains and losses	–	–	(1)	(1)
Purchases	1	2	2	5
Issues	–	–	–	
Settlements	–	(1)	–	(1)
Transfers out of Level 3	–	(2)	–	(2)
Closing balance	5	2	5	12
Total gains or losses for the period included in profit or loss for assets held at the balance sheet date	(1)	(1)	–	(2)

(Note: For liabilities, a similar table might be presented.)

Gains or losses included in profit or loss for the period (above) are presented in trading income and in other income as follows:

	Trading income
Total gains or losses included in profit or loss for the period	(4)
Total gains or losses for the period included in profit or loss for assets held at the balance sheet date	(2)

(Note: For liabilities, a similar table might be presented.)

IG14 The fair value at initial recognition of financial instruments that are not traded in active markets is determined in accordance with paragraph AG76 of FRS26. However, when, after initial recognition, an entity will use a valuation technique that incorporates data not obtained from observable markets, there may be a difference between the transaction price at initial recognition and the amount determined at initial recognition using that valuation technique. In these circumstances, the difference will be recognised in profit or loss in subsequent periods in accordance with FRS26 and the entity's accounting policy. Such recognition reflects changes in factors (including time) that market participants would consider in setting a price (see paragraph AG76A of FRS26). Paragraph 28 requires disclosures in these circumstances. An entity might disclose the following to comply with paragraph 28:

Background

On 1 January 20X1 an entity purchases for CU15 million financial assets that are not traded in an active market. The entity has only one class of such financial assets.

The transaction price of CU15 million is the fair value at initial recognition.

After initial recognition, the entity will apply a valuation technique to establish the financial assets' fair value. This valuation technique includes variables other than data from observable markets.

At initial recognition, the same valuation technique would have resulted in an amount of CU14 million, which differs from fair value by CU1 million.

The entity has existing differences of CU5 million at 1 January 20X1.

Application of requirements

The entity's 20X2 disclosure would include the following:

Accounting policies

The entity uses the following valuation technique to determine the fair value of financial instruments that are not traded in an active market: [description of technique, not included in this example]. Differences may arise between the fair value at initial recognition (which, in accordance with FRS26, is generally the transaction price) and the amount determined at initial recognition using the valuation technique. Any such differences are [description of the entity's accounting policy].

In the notes to the financial statements

As discussed in note X, the entity uses [name of valuation technique] to measure the fair value of the following financial instruments that are not traded in an active market. However, in accordance with FRS26, the fair value of an instrument at inception is generally the transaction price. If the transaction price differs from the amount determined at inception using the valuation technique, that difference is [description of the entity's accounting policy]. The differences yet to be recognised in profit or loss are as follows:

	31 Dec X2 CU million	31 Dec X1 CU million
Balance at beginning of year	5.3	5.0
New transactions	–	1.0
Amounts recognised in profit or loss during the year	(0.7)	(0.8)
Other increases	–	0.2
Other decreases	(0.1)	(0.1)
Balance at end of year	4.5	5.3

NATURE AND EXTENT OF RISKS ARISING FROM FINANCIAL INSTRUMENTS (PARAGRAPHS 31–42 AND B6–B28)

Qualitative disclosures (paragraph 33)

IG15 The type of qualitative information an entity might disclose to meet the requirements in paragraph 33 includes, but is not limited to, a narrative description of:

(a) the entity's exposures to risk and how they arose. Information about risk exposures might describe exposures both gross and net of risk transfer and other risk-mitigating transactions.

(b) the entity's policies and processes for accepting, measuring, monitoring and controlling risk, which might include:

- (i) the structure and organisation of the entity's risk management function(s), including a discussion of independence and accountability;
- (ii) the scope and nature of the entity's risk reporting or measurement systems;
- (iii) the entity's policies for hedging or mitigating risk, including its policies and procedures for taking collateral; and
- (iv) the entity's processes for monitoring the continuing effectiveness of such hedges or mitigating devices.

(c) the entity's policies and procedures for avoiding excessive concentrations of risk.

IG16 Information about the nature and extent of risks arising from financial instruments is more useful if it highlights any relationship between financial instruments that can affect the amount, timing or uncertainty of an entity's future cash flows. The extent to which a risk exposure is altered by such relationships might be apparent to users from the disclosures required by this Standard, but in some cases further disclosures might be useful.

IG17 In accordance with paragraph 33(c), entities disclose any change in the qualitative information from the previous period and explain the reasons for the change. Such changes may result from changes in exposure to risk or from changes in the way those exposures are managed.

Quantitative disclosures (paragraphs 34–42 and B7–B28)

IG18 Paragraph 34 requires disclosure of quantitative data about concentrations of risk. For example, concentrations of credit risk may arise from:

(a) industry sectors. Thus, if an entity's counterparties are concentrated in one or more industry sectors (such as retail or wholesale), it would disclose separately exposure to risks arising from each concentration of counterparties.
(b) credit rating or other measure of credit quality. Thus, if an entity's counterparties are concentrated in one or more credit qualities (such as secured loans or unsecured loans) or in one or more credit ratings (such as investment grade or speculative grade), it would disclose separately exposure to risks arising from each concentration of counterparties.
(c) geographical distribution. Thus, if an entity's counterparties are concentrated in one or more geographical markets (such as Asia or Europe), it would disclose separately exposure to risks arising from each concentration of counterparties.
(d) a limited number of individual counterparties or groups of closely related counterparties.

Similar principles apply to identifying concentrations of other risks, including liquidity risk and market risk. For example, concentrations of liquidity risk may arise from the repayment terms of financial liabilities, sources of borrowing facilities or reliance on a particular market in which to realise liquid assets. Concentrations of foreign exchange risk may arise if an entity has a significant net open position in a single foreign currency, or aggregate net open positions in several currencies that tend to move together.

In accordance with paragraph B8, disclosure of concentrations of risk includes a description of the shared characteristic that identifies each concentration. For example, the shared characteristic may refer to geographical distribution of counterparties by groups of countries, individual countries or regions within countries. **IG19**

When quantitative information at the reporting date is unrepresentative of the entity's exposure to risk during the period, paragraph 35 requires further disclosure. To meet this requirement, an entity might disclose the highest, lowest and average amount of risk to which it was exposed during the period. For example, if an entity typically has a large exposure to a particular currency, but at year-end unwinds the position, the entity might disclose a graph that shows the exposure at various times during the period, or disclose the highest, lowest and average exposures. **IG20**

Credit risk (paragraphs 36–38, B9 and B10)

Paragraph 36 requires an entity to disclose information about its exposure to credit risk by class of financial instrument. Financial instruments in the same class share economic characteristics with respect to the risk being disclosed (in this case, credit risk). For example, an entity might determine that residential mortgages, unsecured consumer loans, and commercial loans each have different economic characteristics. **IG21**

Collateral and other credit enhancements pledged (paragraph 36(b))

Paragraph 36(b) requires an entity to describe collateral available as security for assets it holds and other credit enhancements obtained. An entity might meet this requirement by disclosing: **IG22**

(a) the policies and processes for valuing and managing collateral and other credit enhancements obtained;
(b) a description of the main types of collateral and other credit enhancements (examples of the latter being guarantees, credit derivatives, and netting agreements that do not qualify for offset in accordance with FRS 25);

(c) the main types of counterparties to collateral and other credit enhancements and their creditworthiness; and
(d) information about risk concentrations within the collateral or other credit enhancements.

Credit quality (paragraph 36(c))

IG23 Paragraph 36(c) requires an entity to disclose information about the credit quality of financial assets with credit risk that are neither past due nor impaired. In doing so, an entity might disclose the following information:

(a) an analysis of credit exposures using an external or internal credit grading system;
(b) the nature of the counterparty;
(c) historical information about counterparty default rates; and
(d) any other information used to assess credit quality.

IG24 When the entity considers external ratings when managing and monitoring credit quality, the entity might disclose information about:

(a) the amounts of credit exposures for each external credit grade;
(b) the rating agencies used;
(c) the amount of an entity's rated and unrated credit exposures; and
(d) the relationship between internal and external ratings.

IG25 When the entity considers internal credit ratings when managing and monitoring credit quality, the entity might disclose information about:

(a) the internal credit ratings process;
(b) the amounts of credit exposures for each internal credit grade; and
(c) the relationship between internal and external ratings.

Financial assets that are either past due or impaired (paragraph 37)

IG26 A financial asset is past due when the counterparty has failed to make a payment when contractually due. As an example, an entity enters into a lending agreement that requires interest to be paid every month. On the first day of the next month, if interest has not been paid, the loan is past due. Past due does not mean that a counterparty will never pay, but it can trigger various actions such as renegotiation, enforcement of covenants, or legal proceedings.

IG27 When the terms and conditions of financial assets that have been classified as past due are renegotiated, the terms and conditions of the new contractual arrangement apply in determining whether the financial asset remains past due.

IG28 Paragraph 37(a) requires an analysis by class of the age of financial assets that are past due but not impaired. An entity uses its judgement to determine an appropriate number of time bands. For example, an entity might determine that the following time bands are appropriate:

(a) not more than three months;
(b) more than three months and not more than six months;
(c) more than six months and not more than one year; and
(d) more than one year.

IG29 Paragraph 37(b) requires an analysis of impaired financial assets by class. This analysis might include:

(a) the carrying amount, before deducting any impairment loss;
(b) the amount of any related impairment loss; and
(c) the nature and fair value of collateral available and other credit enhancements obtained.

[IG30–IG31 Deleted]

Market risk (paragraphs 40–42 and B17–B28)

Paragraph 40(a) requires a sensitivity analysis for each type of market risk to which the entity is exposed. There are three types of market risk: interest rate risk, currency risk and other price risk. Other price risk may include risks such as equity price risk, commodity price risk, prepayment risk (ie the risk that one party to a financial asset will incur a financial loss because the other party repays earlier or later than expected), and residual value risk (eg a lessor of motor cars that writes residual value guarantees is exposed to residual value risk). Risk variables that are relevant to disclosing market risk include, but are not limited to: **IG32**

(a) the yield curve of market interest rates. It may be necessary to consider both parallel and non-parallel shifts in the yield curve.
(b) foreign exchange rates.
(c) prices of equity instruments.
(d) market prices of commodities.

Paragraph 40(a) requires the sensitivity analysis to show the effect on profit or loss and equity of reasonably possible changes in the relevant risk variable. For example, relevant risk variables might include: **IG33**

(a) prevailing market interest rates, for interest-sensitive financial instruments such as a variable-rate loan; or
(b) currency rates and interest rates, for foreign currency financial instruments such as foreign currency bonds.

For interest rate risk, the sensitivity analysis might show separately the effect of a change in market interest rates on: **IG34**

(a) interest income and expense;
(b) other line items of profit or loss (such as trading gains and losses); and
(c) when applicable, equity.

An entity might disclose a sensitivity analysis for interest rate risk for each currency in which the entity has material exposures to interest rate risk.

Because the factors affecting market risk vary depending on the specific circumstances of each entity, the appropriate range to be considered in providing a sensitivity analysis of market risk varies for each entity and for each type of market risk. **IG35**

The following example illustrates the application of the disclosure requirement in paragraph 40(a): **IG36**

Interest rate risk

At 31 December 20X2, if interest rates at that date had been 10 basis points lower with all other variables held constant, post-tax profit for the year would have been CU1.7 million (20X1—CU2.4 million) higher, arising mainly as a result of lower interest expense on variable borrowings, and other components of equity would have been CU2.8 million (20X1—CU3.2 million) higher, arising mainly as a result of an increase in the fair value of fixed rate financial assets classified as available for sale. If interest rates had been 10 basis points higher, with all other variables held constant, post-tax profit would have been CU1.5 million (20X1—CU2.1 million) lower, arising mainly as a result of higher interest expense on variable borrowings, and other components of equity would have been CU3.0 million (20X1—CU3.4 million) lower, arising mainly as a result of a decrease in the fair value of fixed rate financial assets classified as available for sale. Profit is more sensitive to interest rate decreases than increases because of borrowings with capped interest rates. The sensitivity is lower in 20X2 than in 20X1 because of a reduction in outstanding borrowings that has occurred as the entity's debt has matured (see note X).[a]

Foreign currency exchange rate risk

At 31 December 20X2, if the CU had weakened 10 per cent against the US dollar with all other variables held constant, post-tax profit for the year would have been CU2.8 million (20X1—CU6.4 million) lower, and other components of equity would have been CU1.2 million (20X1—CU1.1 million) higher. Conversely, if the CU had strengthened 10 per cent against the US dollar with all other variables held constant, post-tax profit would have been CU2.8 million (20X1—CU6.4 million) higher, and other components of equity would have been CU1.2 million (20X1—CU1.1 million) lower. The lower foreign currency exchange rate sensitivity in profit in 20X2 compared with 20X1 is attributable to a reduction in foreign currency denominated debt. Equity is more sensitive in 20X2 than in 20X1 because of the increased use of hedges of foreign currency purchases, offset by the reduction in foreign currency debt.

(a) Paragraph 39(a) requires disclosure of a maturity analysis of liabilities.

Other market risk disclosures (paragraph 42)

IG37 Paragraph 42 requires the disclosure of additional information when the sensitivity analysis disclosed is unrepresentative of a risk inherent in a financial instrument. For example, this can occur when:

(a) a financial instrument contains terms and conditions whose effects are not apparent from the sensitivity analysis, eg options that remain out of (or in) the money for the chosen change in the risk variable;
(b) financial assets are illiquid, eg when there is a low volume of transactions in similar assets and an entity finds it difficult to find a counterparty; or
(c) an entity has a large holding of a financial asset that, if sold in its entirety, would be sold at a discount or premium to the quoted market price for a smaller holding.

IG38 In the situation in paragraph IG37(a), additional disclosure might include:

(a) the terms and conditions of the financial instrument (eg the options);
(b) the effect on profit or loss if the term or condition were met (ie if the options were exercised); and

(c) a description of how the risk is hedged.

For example, an entity may acquire a zero-cost interest rate collar that includes an out-of-the-money leveraged written option (eg the entity pays ten times the amount of the difference between a specified interest rate floor and the current market interest rate). The entity may regard the collar as an inexpensive economic hedge against a reasonably possible increase in interest rates. However, an unexpectedly large decrease in interest rates might trigger payments under the written option that, because of the leverage, might be significantly larger than the benefit of lower interest rates. Neither the fair value of the collar nor a sensitivity analysis based on reasonably possible changes in market variables would indicate this exposure. In this case, the entity might provide the additional information described above.

In the situation described in paragraph IG37(b), additional disclosure might include the reasons for the lack of liquidity and how the entity hedges the risk. **IG39**

In the situation described in paragraph IG37(c), additional disclosure might include: **IG40**

(a) the nature of the security (eg entity name);
(b) the extent of holding (eg 15 per cent of the issued shares);
(c) the effect on profit or loss; and
(d) how the entity hedges the risk.

The following examples illustrate how an entity might meet the quantitative disclosure requirements in paragraphs 42D and 42E.* **IG40C**

Transferred financial assets that are not derecognised in their entirety

Illustrating the application of paragraph 42D(d) and (e)

	Financial assets at fair value through profit or loss		**Loans and receivables**		**Available-for-sale financial assets**
	CU million		CU million		CU million
	Trading securities	Derivatives	Mortgages	Consumer loans	Equity investments
Carrying amount of assets	x	x	x	x	x
Carrying amount of associated liabilities	(x)	(x)	(x)	(x)	(x)
For those liabilities that have recourse only to the transferred assets:					
Fair value of assets	x	x	x	x	x
Fair value of associated liabilities	(x)	(x)	(x)	(x)	(x)
Net position	x	x	x	x	x

****Editor's note:*** *Paragraph IG40C added July 2011. (IG40A and IG40B are not used in FRS 29, as they relate to the application of IFRS 7 to those entities which have adopted IFRS 9. There is no UK equivalent to IFRS 9.*

Transferred financial assets that are derecognised in their entirety

Illustrating the application of paragraph 42E(a) to (d)

	Cash outflows to repurchase transferred (derecognised) assets	Carrying amount of continuing involvement in statement of financial position			Fair value of continuing involvement		Maximum exposure to loss
	CU million	CU million			CU million		CU million
Type of continuing involvement		**Held for trading**	**Available-for-sale financial assets**	**Financial liabilities at fair value through profit or loss**	**Assets**	**Liabilities**	
Written put options	(x)			(x)		(x)	x
Purchased call options	(x)	x			x		x
Securities lending	(x)		x	(x)	x	(x)	x
Total		x	x	(x)	x	(x)	x

Illustrating the application of paragraph 42E(e)

Undiscounted cash flow to repurchase transferred assets								
	Maturity of continuing involvement CU million							
Type of continuing involvement	Total	less than 1 month	1–3 months	3–6 months	6 months–1 year	1–3 years	3–5 years	more than 5 years
Written put options	x		x	x	x	x		
Purchased call options	x			x	x	x		x
Securities lending	x	x	x					

TRANSITION (PARAGRAPH 44)

IG41 The following table* summarises the effect of the exemption from presenting comparative accounting and risk disclosures for accounting periods beginning before 1 January 2006, before 1 January 2007, and on or after 1 January 2007. In this table:

(a) a **first-time adopter** is an entity that is adopting FRS 26 for the first time in preparing its financial statements.

(b) an **existing user** is an entity that applies this standard when preparing its second or subsequent financial statements in accordance with FRS 26.

*ASB Footnote: *The ASB has removed an IASB table, providing the effect of exemption from presenting comparatives for accounting and risk disclosures for entities producing IFRS financial statements, and replaced it with the table on the following page which summarises the various transition options availble to UK entities applying this standard.*

	Accounting and Risk disclosures	**Capital Disclosures**
Accounting periods beginning before 1 January 2006		
First-time adopter not applying FRS 29 early	Applies FRS 25 but exempt from providing FRS 25 comparative information.	May choose to provide capital disclosures contained within Appendix E. Must provide comparative information if Appendix E adopted.
First-time adopter applying FRS 29 early	Exempt from presenting FRS 29 comparative information[(a)].	May choose to provide capital disclosures contained within Appendix E. Must provide comparative information if Appendix E adopted.
Accounting periods beginning on or after 1 January 2006 and before 1 January 2007		
First-time adopter not applying FRS 29 early	Applies FRS 25 but exempt from providing FRS 25 comparative information.	May choose to provide capital disclosures contained within Appendix E. Must provide comparative information if Appendix E adopted.
First-time adopter applying FRS 29 early	Exempt from presenting FRS 29 comparative information.	Has the option to provide capital disclosures contained within Appendix E but is not required to do so.
Existing user not applying FRS 29 early	Applies FRS 25. Provides full FRS 25 comparative information.	Has the option to provide capital disclosures contained within Appendix E.
Existing user applying FRS 29 early	Provides full FRS 29 comparative information.	Has the option to provide capital disclosures contained within Appendix E but is not required to do so.
Accounting periods beginning on or after 1 January 2007 (mandatory application of FRS 29)		
First-time adopter	Provides full FRS 29 comparative information.	Provides full FRS 29 capital disclosures.
Existing user	Provides full FRS 29 comparative information.	Provides full FRS 29 capital disclosures.
(a) See paragraph 44B of FRS 29.		

Disclosures about capital

> ASB Note: the following is a reproduction of the IASB's guidance on implementing disclosures on capital that were developed as part of the IFRS 7 project but implemented an amendment to IAS 1. The ASB has implemented the amendments to IAS 1 as Appendix E to FRS 29.

ILLUSTRATIVE EXAMPLES OF CAPITAL DISCLOSURES (PARAGRAPHS E1–E3)

This implementation guidance accompanies but is not part of the standard

An entity that is not a regulated financial institution

EIG1 The following example illustrates the application of paragraphs E1 and E3 for an entity that is not a financial institution and is not subject to an externally imposed capital requirement. In this example, the entity monitors capital using a debt-to-adjusted capital ratio. Other entities may use different methods to monitor capital. The example is also relatively simple. An entity decides, in the light of its circumstances, how much detail it provides to satisfy the requirements of paragraphs E1 and E3.

Facts

Group A manufactures and sells cars. Group A includes a finance subsidiary that provides finance to customers, primarily in the form of leases. Group A is not subject to any externally imposed capital requirements.

Example disclosure

The Group's objectives when managing capital are:

- to safeguard the entity's ability to continue as a going concern, so that it can continue to provide returns for shareholders and benefits for other stakeholders, and
- to provide an adequate return to shareholders by pricing products and services commensurately with the level of risk.

The Group sets the amount of capital in proportion to risk. The Group manages the capital structure and make adjustments to it in the light of changes in economic conditions and the risk characteristics of the underlying assets. In order to maintain or adjust the capital structure, the Group may adjust the amount of dividends paid to shareholders, return capital to shareholders, issue new shares, or sell assets to reduce debt.

Consistently with others in the industry, the Group monitors capital on the basis of the debt-to-adjusted capital ratio. This ratio is calculated as net debt ÷ adjusted capital. Net debt is calculated as total debt (as shown in the balance sheet) less cash and cash equivalents. Adjusted capital comprises all components of equity (ie share capital, share premium, minority interest, retained earnings, and revaluation reserve) other than amounts recognised in equity relating to cash flow hedges, and includes some forms of subordinated debt.

During 20X4, the Group's strategy, which was unchanged from 20X3, was to maintain the debt-to-adjusted capital ratio at the lower end of the range 6:1 to 7:1, in order to secure access to finance at a reasonable cost by maintaining a BB credit rating. The debt-to-adjusted capital ratios at 31 December 20X4 and at 31 December 20X3 were as follows:

	31 Dec X4 CU million	**31 Dec X3 CU million**
Total debt	1,000	1,100
Less: cash and cash equivalents	(90)	(150)
Net debt	910	950
Total equity	110	105
Add: subordinated debt instruments	38	38
Less: amounts recognised in equity relating to cash flow hedges	(10)	(5)
Adjusted capital	138	138
Debt-to-adjusted capital ratio	6.6	6.9

The decrease in the debt-to-adjusted capital ratio during 20X4 resulted primarily from the reduction in net debt that occurred on the sale of subsidiary Z. As a result of this reduction in net debt, improved profitability and lower levels of managed receivables, the dividend payment was increased to CU2.8 million for 20X4 (from CU2.5 million for 20X3).

An entity that has not complied with externally imposed capital requirements

The following example illustrates the application of paragraph E2(e) when an entity has not complied with externally imposed capital requirements during the period. Other disclosures would be provided to comply with the other requirements of paragraphs E1 and E2. EIG2

Facts
Entity A provides financial services to its customers and is subject to capital requirements imposed by Regulator B. During the year ended 31 December 20X7, Entity A did not comply with the capital requirements imposed by Regulator B. In its financial statements for the year ended 31 December 20X7, Entity A provides the following disclosure relating to its noncompliance.

Example disclosure
Entity A filed its quarterly regulatory capital return for 30 September 20X7 on 20 October 20X7. At that date, Entity A's regulatory capital was below the capital requirement imposed by Regulator B by CU1 million. As a result, Entity A was required to submit a plan to the regulator indicating how it would increase its regulatory capital to the amount required. Entity A submitted a plan that entailed selling part of its unquoted equities portfolio with a carrying amount of CU11.5 million in the fourth quarter of 20X7. In the fourth quarter of 20X7, Entity A sold its fixed interest investment portfolio for CU12.6 million and met its regulatory capital requirement.

Appendix
Amendments to guidance on other IFRSs

This appendix contains amendments to guidance on other Standards that are necessary in order to ensure consistency with FRS 29. *In the amended paragraphs, new text is underlined and deleted text is struck through.*

IGA1 The Guidance on Implementing FRS 26 (IAS 39) *Financial Instruments: Recognition and Measurement* is amended to read below.

Q&A E.4.8 is amended as follows:

If an impaired financial asset is secured by collateral that does not meet the recognition criteria for assets in other Standards, is the collateral recognised as an asset separate from the impaired financial asset?

No. The measurement of the impaired financial asset reflects the fair value of the collateral. The collateral is not recognised as an asset separate from the impaired financial asset unless it meets the recognition criteria for an asset in another Standard.

In Q&A F.1.12 issue (b), both references to 'IAS 32.58' are replaced by 'IFRS 7.22'.

In Q&A G.1, the answer is amended as follows:

IFRS 7.20 requires items of income, expense and gains and losses to be disclosed. This disclosure requirement encompasses items of income, expense and gains and losses that arise on remeasurement to fair value. Therefore, an entity provides disclosures of fair value changes, distinguishing between changes that are recognised in profit or loss and changes that are recognised in equity. Further breakdown is provided of changes that relate to:

(a) AFS assets, showing separately the amount of gain or loss recognised directly in equity during the period and the amount that was removed from equity and recognised in profit or loss for the period;
(b) financial assets or financial liabilities at fair value through profit or loss, showing separately those fair value changes on financial assets or financial liabilities (i) designated as such upon initial recognition and (ii) classified as held for trading in accordance with IAS 39; and
(c) hedging instruments.

IFRS 7 neither requires nor prohibits disclosure of components of the change in fair value by the way items are classified for internal purposes. For example, an entity may choose to disclose separately the change in fair value of those derivatives that in accordance with IAS 39 it categorises as held for trading, but the entity classifies as part of risk management activities outside the trading portfolio.

In addition, IFRS 7.8 requires disclosure of the carrying amounts of financial assets or financial liabilities at fair value through profit or loss, showing separately : (i) those designated as such upon initial recognition and (ii) those held for trading in accordance with IAS 39.

Financial Reporting Standard 30 'Heritage assets' is set out in paragraphs 1 to 32.

The Statement of Standard Accounting Practice, which comprises the paragraphs set in bold type, should be read in the context of the Objective, as stated in paragraph 1 and the Definition set out in paragraph 2 and also the Foreword to Accounting Standards, the Statement of Principles for Financial Reporting currently in issue and the Interpretation of the Statement of Principles for Public Benefit Entities. The explanatory paragraphs contained in the FRS shall be regarded as part of the Statement of Standard Accounting Practice insofar as they assist in interpreting that Statement.

Appendix I 'The Development of the FRS' reviews the considerations and arguments that were thought significant by members of the Board in reaching their conclusions on the FRS.

FRS 30
Heritage assets*

(Issued June 2009)

Contents

Pages

Summary

Financial Reporting Standard 30

Objective

Definition

Scope

Disclosures

Recognition and measurement

Date from which effective and transitional arrangements

Amendment to FRS 11 'Impairment of fixed assets and goodwill'

Amendments to FRS 15 'Tangible fixed assets'

Adoption of FRS 30 by the Board

Appendices

I The Development of the FRS
II Illustrative examples of disclosures

***Editor's note**: The matters covered in FRS 30 are dealt with within Section 34 of FRS 102.*

Summary

Financial Reporting Standard (FRS) 30 '*Heritage assets*' applies to all heritage assets that are held and maintained by an entity principally for their contribution to knowledge and culture. Heritage assets can have historical, artistic, scientific, geophysical or environmental qualities. 1

Assets that are used by an entity in its operations should be accounted for as operational assets in accordance with FRS 15 '*Tangible fixed assets*', notwithstanding historical or other heritage qualities. 2

The FRS sets out new disclosure requirements for the reporting of heritage assets, which apply whether or not they are reported in the balance sheet. Where heritage assets fall within the scope of FRS 30, the disclosure requirements of FRS 15 do not apply. 3

The FRS retains the recognition and measurement requirements in FRS 15 which require heritage assets to be reported as tangible fixed assets in the balance sheet where information is available on cost or valuation. There are however some relaxations to the measurement requirements of FRS 15 to encourage the reporting of heritage assets in the balance sheet at valuation. 4

The main features of this standard are as follows. 5

(i) the disclosures should apply to all entities that hold heritage assets, regardless of whether these assets are reported in the balance sheet. These disclosures will provide information about an entity's total holding of heritage assets and the entity's stewardship of these assets.

(ii) The disclosures should make clear the accounting policies adopted for an entity's holding of heritage assets and the extent to which these assets are recognised in the balance sheet. The disclosures should provide readers with an understanding of the asset values being reported as well as the entity's policies for managing its total holding of heritage assets.

(iii) The accounting in respect of the recognition and measurement of heritage assets should follow the requirements of FRS 15, as supplemented by the requirements of this standard.

(iv) To encourage a valuation approach, the FRS allows entities to use internal valuations without the need for a full valuation every five years.

Illustrative examples of disclosures are set out at Appendix II. 6

Financial Reporting Standard 30 'Heritage Assets'

OBJECTIVE

1 The objective of this **FRS** is to ensure that:

(i) enhanced disclosures apply to all heritage assets, regardless of whether they are reported in the balance sheet; and
(ii) where information is available on cost or value, heritage assets are reported in the balance sheet.

DEFINITION

2 The following definition shall apply in this FRS

HERITAGE ASSET

A tangible asset with historical, artistic, scientific, technological, geophysical or environmental qualities that is held and maintained principally for its contribution to knowledge and culture.

SCOPE

3 **All heritage assets should be accounted for in accordance with the requirements of this standard.**

4 **The FRS applies to all financial statements that are intended to give a true and fair view of a reporting entity's financial position and profit or loss (or income and expenditure) for a period, except that reporting entities applying the Financial Reporting Standard for Smaller Entities (FRSSE) currently applicable are exempt.**

DISCLOSURES

5 **The disclosures required by paragraphs 6 to 15 are required, except where noted otherwise, for all heritage assets regardless of whether they are reported in the balance sheet.**

6 **An entity's financial statements should contain an indication of the nature and scale of heritage assets held by the entity.**

7 **The financial statements should set out the entity's policy for the acquisition, preservation, management and disposal of heritage assets. This should include a description of the records maintained by the entity of its collection of heritage assets and information on the extent to which access to the assets is permitted. The information required by this paragraph may alternatively be provided in a document that is cross-referenced from the financial statements.**

8 **The accounting policies adopted for an entity's holding of heritage assets should be stated, including details of the measurement bases used.**

9 **For heritage assets that are not reported in the balance sheet, the reasons why should be explained and the notes to the financial statements should explain the significance and nature of those assets that are not reported in the balance sheet.**

The disclosures relating to assets that are not reported in the balance sheet should aim to ensure that, when read in the context of information about capitalised assets, the financial statements provide useful and relevant information about the entity's overall holding of heritage assets. 10

Where heritage assets are reported in the balance sheet, the following should be disclosed: 11

(i) the carrying amount of heritage assets at the beginning of the financial period and at the balance sheet date, including an analysis between those classes or groups of heritage assets that are reported at cost and those that are reported at valuation; and

(ii) where assets are reported at valuation, sufficient information to assist in an understanding of the valuations being reported and their significance. This should include:

(a) the date of the valuation;
(b) the methods used to produce the valuation;
(c) whether the valuation was carried out by external valuers and, where this is the case, the valuer's name and professional qualification, if any; and
(d) any significant limitations on the valuation.

An example of a limitation to be disclosed under paragraph 11 (ii) (d) would be where an asset has a particular provenance, the effect of which is not fully captured by valuation. 12

Information that is available to the entity and is helpful in assessing the value of those heritage assets that are not reported in the entity's balance sheet should be disclosed. 13

The financial statements should contain a summary of transactions relating to heritage assets disclosing, for the accounting period and each of the previous four accounting periods: 14

(a) the cost of acquisitions of heritage assets;
(b) the value of heritage assets acquired by donation;
(c) the carrying amount of heritage assets disposed of in the period and the proceeds received; and
(d) any impairment recognised in the period.

This summary should show separately transactions in assets that are reported in the balance sheet and those that are not.

Where, exceptionally, it is not practicable to obtain a valuation of heritage assets acquired by donation, the reasons why should be stated. Disclosures should also be provided on the nature and extent of significant donations of heritage assets. 15

The information required by paragraph 14 may be supplemented by disclosure of other information, for example the sources of funding for acquisition of heritage assets, or expenditure on major restoration costs, but this is not required by this standard. 16

The disclosures required by paragraphs 6 to 15 may be presented in aggregate for groups or classes of heritage assets provided this aggregation does not obscure significant information. Separate disclosures should be provided for those assets reported at cost and those reported at valuation. Amounts in respect of assets that are not reported in the balance sheet should not be aggregated with amounts for assets that are recognised at cost or valuation. 17

RECOGNITION AND MEASUREMENT

18 **An entity should report heritage assets as tangible fixed assets and recognise and measure these assets in accordance with FRS 15 'Tangible fixed assets', subject to the requirements set out in paragraphs 19 to 25 below.**

19 **Where information is available on the cost or value of heritage assets:**

(i) they should be presented in the balance sheet separately from other tangible fixed assets;
(ii) the balance sheet or the notes to the accounts should identify separately those classes of heritage assets being reported at cost and those at valuation; and
(ii) changes in the valuation should be recognised in the statement of total recognised gains and losses, except for impairment losses that should be recognised in accordance with paragraph 24.

20 **Where assets have previously been capitalised or are recently purchased, information on their cost or value will be available. Where this information is not available, and cannot be obtained at a cost which is commensurate with the benefits to users of the financial statements, the assets will not be recognised in the balance sheet and the disclosures required by this standard should be made.**

21 **Valuations may be made by any method that is appropriate and relevant.**

22 There is no requirement for valuations to be carried out or verified by external valuers, nor is there any prescribed minimum period between valuations. However, where heritage assets are reported at valuation, the carrying amount should be reviewed with sufficient frequency to ensure the valuations remain current.

Depreciation and Impairment

23 **Depreciation need not be provided on heritage assets which have indefinite lives.**

24 **The carrying amount of an asset should be reviewed where there is evidence of impairment, for example where it has suffered physical deterioration or breakage or new doubts arise as to its authenticity. Any impairment recognised should be dealt with in accordance with the recognition and measurement requirements of FRS 11 '*Impairment of fixed assets and goodwill*'.**

Donations

25 **The receipt of donations of heritage assets should be reported in the profit and loss account at valuation. Where, exceptionally, it is not practicable to obtain a valuation for a donated heritage asset, the disclosures required by paragraph 15 apply.**

DATE FROM WHICH EFFECTIVE AND TRANSITIONAL ARRANGEMENTS

26 **This standard should be applied in respect of accounting periods beginning on or after 1 April 2010. Earlier application is encouraged.**

27 **The information required by paragraph 14 need not be given for any accounting period earlier than the period immediately before the period in which this standard is first applied where it is not practicable to do so and a statement to the effect that it is not practicable is made.**

AMENDMENT TO FRS 11 'IMPAIRMENT OF FIXED ASSETS AND GOODWILL'

Paragraph 5 of FRS 11 is amended by adding the following sub-paragraph: **28**

(e) heritage assets to the extent specified in FRS 30 'Heritage assets'

AMENDMENTS TO FRS 15 'TANGIBLE FIXED ASSETS'

The scope section of FRS 15 is amended by inserting the following additional paragraph: **29**

4A The recognition and measurement requirements in paragraphs 6 to 99 of this standard apply to heritage assets subject to the requirements set out in paragraphs 18 to 25 of FRS 30 'Heritage assets'. The disclosure requirements in paragraphs 100 to 108 of this standard do not apply to heritage assets.

Paragraph 17 of FRS 15 is amended by inserting the following additional text: **30**

17 Where these gifts and donations are heritage assets, entities should report these assets in accordance with FRS 30 'Heritage assets'.

Paragraph 18 of FRS 15 is amended by inserting the following additional text: **31**

18 The requirements for heritage assets are addressed in FRS 30 'Heritage assets'.

Paragraphs 89 and 90 of FRS 15 are amended by inserting '**and heritage assets**' after 'non-depreciable land'. **32**

Adoption of FRS 30 by the Accounting Standards Board

Financial Reporting Standard (FRS) 30 'Heritage assets' was approved for issue by the eleven members of the Accounting Standards Board.

MEMBERS OF THE ACCOUNTING STANDARDS BOARD

Ian Mackintosh	Chairman
David Loweth	Technical Director
Nick Anderson	
Michael Ashley	
Edward Beale	
Marisa Cassoni	
Peter Elwin	
Ken Lever	
Robert Overend	
Andy Simmonds	
Professor Geoffrey Whittington CBE	

Appendix I
The Development of the FRS

INTRODUCTION

This Appendix reviews the considerations and arguments that were thought significant by the Board in reaching its conclusions on heritage assets. It explains the different approaches considered by the Board and why it has issued a new Financial Reporting Standard (FRS) that requires enhanced disclosures for heritage assets. 1

In developing the FRS, the Board has considered the comments on its initial proposals which were set out in the Discussion Paper '*Heritage assets – Can accounting do better?*' (January 2006) and on its subsequent proposals in FRED 40 '*Accounting for heritage assets*' (December 2006) and FRED 42 '*Heritage assets*' (June 2008). 2

THE NEED FOR A NEW STANDARD

The Board's project on heritage assets was undertaken to address criticisms of the current financial reporting requirements. Although a few museums and galleries account for their heritage assets at valuation, most adopt an approach under which assets purchased in 2001 and later years are reflected in the balance sheet at cost but previously acquired assets are not. 3

In many cases, this results in an amount in the balance sheet that appears significant but bears little or no relationship to the total value of an entity's collection of heritage assets. Some entities aim to compensate for this by providing supplementary disclosures, although the quality of these is uneven, with significant differences in the information provided by different entities, which impairs its usefulness. 4

The current accounting is based upon the requirements of FRS 15 '*Tangible fixed assets*' and the Statement of Recommended Practice (SORP) for Charities. The Financial Reporting Advisory Board (FRAB)* has in the past reported to Parliament its concerns over the existing accounting treatment applied by charities and public sector bodies, including the national museums and galleries, citing the problems noted above. 5

The ASB therefore agreed to carry out a review of the current accounting and reporting requirements for heritage assets in the UK, to determine whether a change to these requirements was desirable and, if so, to develop alternative proposals. 6

THE BOARD'S CONCLUSIONS

Any debate on accounting for heritage assets will inevitably generate a wide range of views. The Board has listened carefully to these views over the course of its project and acknowledges that the financial reporting of heritage assets presents some very difficult and challenging issues. Yet, after considering a number of alternative approaches, the Board is not persuaded that there is a better accounting solution for heritage assets than the current approach which is based on FRS 15 and results in entities capitalising those heritage assets that have been acquired since 2001. 7

**The FRAB is an independent statutory body which advises the Treasury and devolved administrations in the UK on financial reporting principles and standards applicable to government departments, executive agencies, executive non-departmental public bodies, trading funds, health bodies and, from accounting periods beginning 1 April 2010, local government.*

8 The Board has therefore concluded that the main improvement in the financial reporting of heritage assets will be secured by issuing a new FRS that requires enhanced disclosures for all heritage assets, regardless of whether they are reported in the balance sheet. In reaching this conclusion the Board has considered responses to its three consultation papers. It has also met with key stakeholders to discuss their views.

9 The new FRS will result in the continued reporting of at least some of an entity's heritage assets in the balance sheet. In the Board's view, this is preferable to not reporting any assets in the balance sheet, even where, as under the current approach, it results in the reporting of recently acquired assets at cost. The improved disclosures prescribed by the new FRS will make clear the extent to which heritage assets are reported in the balance sheet and mitigate the disadvantages of an entity reporting only part of their total holding of heritage assets in the balance sheet.

10 Some respondents to the consultation papers questioned whether there was any purpose in reporting the value of heritage assets. Although many museums and galleries do not see their principal objectives in financial terms, they nonetheless use and command economic resources and it is the purpose of the financial statements to provide an account of these resources and how they have changed. In the Board's view, reporting the cost or value of heritage assets provides an important context in which other elements of financial performance may be assessed.

Heritage assets are assets

11 Throughout the project, the Board has retained the view that, conceptually, heritage assets are assets. They are central to the purpose of an entity such as a museum or gallery: without them the entity could not function. An artefact held by a museum might be realisable for cash, it might generate income indirectly through admission charges or the exploitation of reproduction rights. However, and in most cases much more importantly, the museum needs the artefact to function as a museum. The artefact has utility: it can be displayed to provide an educational or cultural experience to the public or it can be preserved for future display or for academic or scientific research. The future economic benefits associated with the artefact are primarily in the form of its service potential rather than cash flows. In the Board's view, by virtue of the service potential they provide, heritage assets meet the definition of an asset; that is, they provide 'rights or other access to future economic benefits controlled by an entity as a result of past transactions or events'*.

Inalienability

12 Heritage assets are often described as 'inalienable', ie the entity cannot dispose of them without external consent. Such a restriction may, for example, be imposed by trust law, arise from a charity's governing documents or, in some cases, by statute. The key feature of inalienability is that it prevents an asset being readily realisable. Some argue that assets held in trust are not assets of the entity, equating the inability to sell such items with foregoing the economic benefit inherent in them. But assets that are inalienable may well have utility to the entity and therefore, as noted in paragraph 11 above, meet the definition of an asset.

13 Inalienability is not a robust concept – it is possible that a donor's wishes may be revoked and even statutory restrictions are not immutable from amendment or revocation by Parliament. Some assets are so central to the purpose of an entity that

**Paragraph 4.6 of the Board's Statement of Principles for Financial Reporting (December 1999).*

it is inconceivable they would ever be sold; so, in substance, they are inalienable. Because it is imprecise, the concept of 'inalienability' does not therefore provide a suitable criterion for framing accounting requirements.

The best accounting

If heritage assets are not capitalised, the balance sheet will provide an incomplete picture of an entity's financial position. For this reason, it is better to report heritage assets in the balance sheet where information is available on cost or value rather than leave these assets out of the balance sheet. **14**

The Board considers the best financial reporting is achieved when heritage assets are reported as tangible fixed assets at values that provide useful and relevant information at the balance sheet date. It is therefore likely that a current valuation will be more useful than historical cost, although it is acknowledged there can be difficulties in obtaining valuations for heritage assets. **15**

ALTERNATIVE APPROACHES

The Board considered a number of alternative approaches during the course of its work, ranging from capitalising no heritage assets through to a requirement to capitalise all heritage assets. The non-capitalisation approach, although straightforward to apply, has little conceptual merit and will result in heritage assets not being capitalised where information is available on their cost or value. It also raises issues regarding the reporting of acquisitions and disposals of heritage assets. In particular, it would be wrong to report the purchase of a heritage asset as an expense. **16**

On the other hand, a full capitalisation approach is unlikely to be applied consistently, given the unique nature of many heritage assets and the many practical difficulties associated with identifying cost or determining a current value. **17**

Discussion Paper

Neither of these approaches provides an appropriate basis for a standard; hence the Board developed an approach that it considered conceptually sound as well as being pragmatic. This approach was exposed in the Discussion Paper and required the valuation of heritage assets where *it is* ***practicable*** *to obtain valuations, which, when supplemented with appropriate disclosures, provide useful and relevant information sufficient to assist in an assessment of the value of heritage assets held by the entity at the balance sheet date.* **18**

The Discussion Paper required the valuation, where practicable, of an entity's total holding of heritage assets, where it could obtain, at reasonable cost, reliable current values for the majority, by value, of these assets. Where an entity was able to demonstrate a valuation approach was not practicable, a non-recognition approach was to be adopted. **19**

FRED 40

Despite considerable support from respondents, the Board was concerned that preparers might use the assessment of practicability to keep their heritage assets off the balance sheet. The Board therefore exposed in FRED 40 an approach that retained the principle of practicability but, rather than carrying out this assessment **20** for an entity's total holding of heritage assets, required it to be carried out at the level of an individual collection.

21 The responses to FRED 40 highlighted two main problems. Firstly, respondents noted problems with the definition of a collection and that dividing up an entity's overall collection would provide scope for manipulation and confusion. Some large museums also suggested their heritage assets comprised a single collection – something that was not the Board's intention in publishing FRED 40.

22 Respondents to FRED 40 also noted that the judgements made by an entity in making its assessment of practicability could raise difficulties for auditors, particularly where a valuation approach is adopted and where valuations have been generated internally. Some auditors suggested this may result in a need for the audit opinion to include a limitation of scope.

23 The Board acknowledged that an approach that requires valuation, where practicable, raises issues for auditors, but it was keen to introduce a high level, principle-based standard and felt the issues raised should not be that dissimilar from other balance sheet issues, for example surrounding the reporting of intangibles.

FRED 42

24 Following its review of the responses to FRED 40, the Board re-considered its approach. It decided not to proceed with 'practicability', as envisaged in the Discussion Paper and FRED 40 but, instead, revert to an approach that would require heritage assets to be reported in the balance sheet where information on cost or value is available. This is the approach that was in FRED 42 and is the approach required by this standard.

25 The Board notes the importance of disclosures and the strong support that its proposals for enhanced disclosures have received from respondents throughout its consultations. The majority of respondents who commented said that the proposed disclosures are both appropriate and necessary for the proper discharge of an entity's accountability for its heritage assets.

26 In the Board's view, the enhanced disclosures remain the most important benefit of this project in terms of the improved financial reporting of heritage assets. The proposed disclosures, which have been developed from the Discussion Paper, and are similar to those included in FRED 40 and FRED 42, are therefore retained in this FRS. An important aim of the disclosures is to provide relevant and useful information on an entity's overall holding of heritage assets and not just those that are reported as assets in the balance sheet.

SPECIFIC ISSUES

Scope and definition

27 Works of art and similar objects are sometimes held by commercial entities but fall outside the scope of the new FRS because they are not maintained principally for their contribution to knowledge and culture. Respondents to the Discussion Paper said this issue should not be dealt with in a standard on heritage assets. These assets should therefore be accounted for in accordance with FRS 15 '*Tangible fixed assets*'.

28 Historic assets used by the entity itself, for example historical buildings used for teaching by education establishments, should also be accounted for under the

existing requirements for fixed assets. This is based on the view that an operational perspective is likely to be most relevant for most users of financial statements. However, entities that use historical buildings and similar assets may wish to consider whether it might be appropriate to apply the disclosures required by this FRS.

Valuation

To encourage entities to report heritage assets in their balance sheets, the new FRS includes the option available in FRS 15 to report assets at either cost or valuation. The Board would encourage entities to adopt a valuation approach where at all possible as it should provide more relevant and useful information. **29**

The Board acknowledges that it may not always be possible to obtain current valuations but, to encourage entities to adopt a valuation approach, paragraphs 21 and 22 of the new FRS relax some of the valuation requirements of FRS 15. For example, the standard allows valuations to be made by any method that is appropriate and relevant. **30**

Disclosures

Whilst some respondents raised concerns about the need for a five year summary of transactions relating to heritage assets, the majority supported this proposal and it has been retained. To avoid undue burdens in implementation, the standard permits the summary to be built-up going forward: only two years' information is required in the year in which the standard is first applied, provided it is stated that it is not practicable to provide information for earlier periods. This is consistent with the proposals in FRED 40 and FRED 42. **31**

Paragraph 7 of the FRS requires an entity to disclose its policy for the acquisition, preservation, management and disposal of heritage assets. The FRS allows this disclosure to be made in the financial statements; in the information accompanying the financial statements; or in another document that is made publicly available by the entity. Where this information is not provided in the financial statements, the financial statements should contain a cross-reference to the document that sets out this information. **32**

To clarify the Board's intentions in framing the disclosure requirements, illustrative examples are provided in Appendix II. **33**

Depreciation and impairment

The Discussion Paper and FRED 40 both proposed that heritage assets should be reported at valuation. Depreciation and impairment therefore were unnecessary refinements because any changes in value should be reflected in the regular revaluation of heritage assets. This FRS requires some assets to be reported at cost and therefore addresses depreciation and impairment. The requirements are consistent with those exposed in FRED 42. **34**

Respondents to FRED 42 agreed with the proposal that entities should not be expected to charge depreciation on heritage assets that have indefinite lives. Respondents also agreed that for other assets depreciation will be required in accordance with FRS 15 '*Tangible fixed assets*' and that the requirement in FRS 15 for annual impairment reviews for long-lived assets should not apply to heritage assets within the scope of this FRS. **35**

36 FRED 42 reflected the view that not all of the indications of impairment identified in FRS 11 '*Impairment of fixed assets and goodwill*' are relevant to heritage assets, for example, a fall in market prices is not relevant to the main purpose for which the asset is being held and maintained, i.e. for its contribution to knowledge and culture. For this reason, it proposed that impairment reviews should be required only where an asset has suffered physical deterioration or breakage.

37 Some respondents suggested that impairment reviews should be required in other cases, including some of those included in FRS 11 '*Impairment of fixed assets and goodwill*'. The Board considered that it would be unduly burdensome to require impairment reviews when any of the indicators in FRS 11 is present. For this reason, the FRS simply requires an impairment review where there is evidence of impairment and specifically requires such a review only in the case of physical deterioration or breakage or where new doubts arise as to authenticity. It does not specify or restrict other circumstances in which an impairment review is required. This is a matter for professional judgement.

Donations

38 The proposals for donations of heritage assets are the same as set out in FRED 42. These require that heritage assets should be recognised in the profit and loss account, or equivalent statement, at the current value of the assets at the date they are received. This approach is also the same as that of FRS 15 '*Tangible fixed assets*' which recognises that heritage assets may present measurement difficulties. In the Board's view, it should only be impracticable to obtain a current value in exceptional cases and, where this is the case, paragraph 15 of the FRS requires disclosure in the notes to the accounts of why a valuation cannot be obtained.

39 Some respondents to FRED 42 questioned whether it was appropriate to report donations of heritage assets in the profit and loss account when the asset is not depreciated and cannot be sold. In addition to introducing volatility into the financial performance being reported, it was argued the accounting would generate substantial reserves that would give a misleading impression as to the true extent of an entity's expendable reserves. The Board's view remains that, where no conditions are attached to the receipt of a donation, a gain equivalent to the value of the asset should be reported in the profit and loss account. The notes to the accounts and the accompanying information provide an opportunity for the entity to explain the impact of donations on its financial performance and expendable reserves.

40 Some respondents to FRED 42 noted that the proposals in respect of donated assets might be difficult to reconcile with the accounting principle in the Companies Act that only profits realised at the balance sheet date should be included in the profit and loss account. However, the Act provides that its accounting principles may be departed from if there are special reasons*. The Board concluded that the receipt of a donation, and the need to ensure comparability with other entities that are subject to this FRS, would constitute such special reasons.

**Paragraph 15, Schedule 4 of the 1985 Companies Act and, from 6 April 2008, paragraph 10 of Schedule 1 of The Large and Medium-sized Companies and Groups (Accounts and Reports) Regulations 2008: Statutory Instrument 2008/410, require that particulars of the departure, the reasons for it and its effect must be given in a note to the accounts. The equivalent reference in the Republic of Ireland is Section 6 of the Companies (Amendment) Act 1986 and paragraph 28 of the Group Accounts Regulations 1992.*

Reporting acquisitions and disposals of heritage assets

The proposals in the Discussion Paper and FRED 40 prohibited the reporting of acquisitions and disposals in the profit and loss account, or an equivalent statement. This was considered necessary to avoid acquisitions of heritage assets, where a non-recognition approach was being adopted, being reported as an expense. The proposals were also intended to avoid any distortion of the profit and loss account by prohibiting the reporting of disposal proceeds as gains. **41**

The Board does not consider this FRS should require the separate reporting of acquisitions and disposals in the primary statements. This is because, other than donations where a current value cannot be obtained (something that should only happen in exceptional cases), acquisitions are required to be reported as assets. **42**

There remains an issue for disposals of heritage assets that are not reported in the balance sheet, although this is not expected to be a significant issue for most entities on the grounds that few heritage assets are disposed of. There is also a requirement in paragraph 14 of the FRS for the financial statements to contain a summary of transactions in heritage assets, including information on proceeds and gains from disposals. **43**

REGULATORY IMPACT

The Board has carried out an extensive consultation exercise as part of this project and, in doing so, sought views about the benefits and costs of applying its proposals for heritage assets. It noted the concerns expressed by a number of respondents that, where a valuation approach was adopted, the costs could be significant. The Board does, however, continue to believe there are significant benefits in reporting heritage assets in the balance sheet. **44**

The costs of introducing the new requirements will largely fall on preparers, although it is not envisaged that, in the majority of cases, this will be burdensome. This is because the requirements will permit the current practice of reporting recent acquisitions at cost (or, in the case of donations, at current value). **45**

Where an entity decides to report some or all of its heritage assets at a current value, it will do so having considered the benefits and costs of obtaining valuations. For this reason, there will not be disproportionate cost for those entities that choose to report heritage assets at valuation. **46**

In addition, this standard includes new disclosure requirements, and there will be some cost in complying with them. However, the information should be readily available; hence any new cost will be confined to presenting and publishing the information. **47**

In light of the above, it appears to the ASB that the cost of the new requirements will not be disproportionate to their benefits. **48**

FUTURE DEVELOPMENTS

The ASB will continue to monitor how entities are accounting for heritage assets and may revise the requirements in the light of developments in reporting practice and the outcome of work being taken forward internationally, in particular the International Public Sector Accounting Standards Board's project on heritage assets. **49**

Appendix II
Illustrative examples of disclosures

The following examples illustrate disclosures that might be made to comply with the requirements set out in paragraphs 6 to 15 of the FRS. To keep the illustrations simple, comparative information is not given, although this would normally be required.

EXAMPLE 1 — THE VINTAGE CAR MUSEUM

The Museum holds a collection of vintage cars and a collection of motoring ephemera for the purpose of fostering and promoting a public interest in the history of vintage cars.

The vintage car collection is capitalised at market value and was acquired through donations and purchases.

The collection of motoring ephemera has been assembled over many years and includes manuals, brochures and advertising material. The collection does not include items whose value is significant to the financial position of the Museum and is not capitalised because valuations could only be obtained at disproportionate cost.

Note 1 Accounting policies

Tangible fixed assets and depreciation

Heritage assets

The museum's collection of vintage and classic cars is reported in the Balance Sheet at market value. Valuations are made by professional valuers (Parker, Glass and Co). Approximately one-third of the collection is valued each year on a rolling basis. Gains and losses on revaluation are recognised in the Statement of Total Recognised Gains and Losses.

It is the Museum's policy to maintain its collection of cars in full working order and maintenance costs are charged to the Income and Expenditure Account when incurred. The cars are deemed to have indeterminate lives and the Trustees do not therefore consider it appropriate to charge depreciation.

Subject to the approval of the Trustees, the Museum may dispose of items from the collection, although this will only happen in exceptional circumstances, for example when the item cannot be properly displayed or the disposal proceeds can be used to purchase a better example.

In addition, the Museum holds a collection of motoring ephemera which is not recognised in the Balance Sheet as cost information is not readily available and the Trustees believe the benefits of obtaining valuations for these items would not justify the cost. Nearly all items in the collection are thought to have a financial value of less than £50 and, as far as the Trustees are aware, no individual item is worth more than £1,000. The vast majority of the items in the collection were acquired over twenty years ago.

The Museum's management policy in respect of its heritage assets is summarised in Note 8. Further information is available from the March 2006 publication

"*Bringing Vintage Cars to Life*" which is available from the Museum's website. The Museum also makes available on its website a full listing of its collection of vintage and classic cars. This includes information on the history, provenance and date of acquisition of each vehicle and contains a commentary on their historical significance.

Note 7(a) Tangible fixed assets – heritage assets

	Vintage cars £000
Cost or valuation	
1 April 2007	6,700
Additions	200
Disposals	(50)
Revaluation	335
31 March 2008	**7,185**

The above represents valuations made in the following financial years:

2007-08	3,000
2006-07	2,185
2005-06	2,000
	7,185

The vintage car collection includes the S4 Bentley Sport driven to victory by John Duff and Frank Clement in the 1924 Le Mans race. This vehicle has been included in the accounts at a valuation made in 2006-07 of £150,000 reflecting cars of a similar model and vintage. However, the Museum's professional valuers have advised that the car would probably realise significantly more than this if it were to be sold on the open market.

Additions in 2007-08 comprise:

£200,000 purchase of a private collection of 1950s Jaguar sports cars.

Disposals in 2007-08 comprise:

£50,000 sale of Lotus Elite and Triumph TR2.

Note 7(b) Five year financial summary of heritage asset transactions:

	2007-08 £000	2006-07 £000	2005-06 £000	2004-05 £000	2003-04 £000
Additions:					
Purchases	200	130	100	160	50
Donations	–	25	20	–	–
Total additions	200	155	120	160	50
Disposals					
Carrying value	50	–	30	50	–
Sale proceeds	50	–	25	55	–

The above information relates only to transactions in cars.

There were very few transactions in ephemera during the periods and these were acquisitions by donation. In the Trustees' view, the value of these donations is not material and obtaining a current valuation would involve disproportionate cost. The Museum wishes to acknowledge in particular the donation of 85 workshop manuals in 2007-08 from the estate of the late Toad of Toad Hall.

Note 8 Heritage assets management policy

The Museum maintains a collection of 250 vintage and classic cars which reflect the history of the British sports car from 1900-1960. Approximately 240 of these are on display to the public, while the remainder are held in the Museum's maintenance depot undergoing or awaiting repair.

Acquisitions are made by purchase or donation. The Museum occasionally disposes of objects from the collection in order to fund new acquisitions where the Trustees determine this does not detract from the integrity of the collection.

The Museum also holds a collection of motoring ephemera associated with the history of the British sports car. The collection comprises some 2,000 objects including manuals, brochures and advertising material. This collection of ephemera was originally purchased in the early 1970s, although a few items have been acquired since mostly through direct donation and occasionally by purchase. The Museum draws upon this collection for displays in the public rooms and arranges for private inspection by prior arrangement.

EXAMPLE 2 — THE BARSETSHIRE MUSEUM

The Museum's collections relate to the natural and man-made history of Barsetshire. There are three distinct collections: artefacts, fossils and paintings of local interest. The vast majority of the objects held were acquired in the late 19th century.

In the opinion of the Trustees, reliable information on cost or valuation is not available for the Museum's collections of fossils and artefacts. This is owing to the lack of information on purchase cost; the lack of comparable market values; the diverse nature of the objects; and the volume of items held. These collections are therefore not reported as assets in the balance sheet, other than recent purchases which are reported at cost.

The Trustees have obtained valuations for the collection of local paintings which is regularly being updated through acquisitions either by purchase or donation. The Trustees have also approved the sale of certain paintings.

The following disclosures would be provided in the notes to the financial statements.

Note 1 Accounting policies

Tangible fixed assets and depreciation

Heritage assets

The Museum has three collections of heritage assets which are held in support of the Museum's primary objective of increasing knowledge, understanding and appreciation of the Barsetshire landscape. The collections are accounted for as follows:

Paintings

The collection of paintings, which also includes sketches and photographs, is reported in the Balance Sheet at market value. Individual items in the collection are periodically revalued by an external valuer with any surplus or deficit on revaluation being reported in the Statement of Total Recognised Gains and Losses. The paintings are deemed to have indeterminate lives and a high residual value; hence the Trustees do not consider it appropriate to charge depreciation.

Acquisitions are made by purchase or donation. Purchases are initially recorded at cost and donations are recorded at current value ascertained by the Museum's curators with reference, where possible, to commercial markets using recent transaction information from auctions.

Artefacts and fossils

The Trustees do not consider that reliable cost or valuation information can be obtained for the vast majority of items held in the collections of artefacts and fossils. This is because of the diverse nature of the assets held, the number of assets held and the lack of comparable market values. The Museum does not therefore recognise these assets on its Balance Sheet, other than recent acquisitions which are reported at cost, where the object is purchased, or at the Museum curator's best estimate of current value where the object is donated.

Preservation costs

Expenditure which, in the Trustees' view, is required to preserve or clearly prevent further deterioration of individual collection items is recognised in the Income and Expenditure account when it is incurred.

Further information on the collections is given in Notes 7, 8 and 9 to the accounts.

Note 7 Tangible fixed assets – heritage assets

	Paintings £000	Artefacts and fossils £000	Total assets £000
Cost or valuation			
1 April 2007	28,900	1,250	30,150
Additions	400	150	550
Disposals	(80)	-	(80)
Revaluation	2,600	-	2,600
31 March 2008	**30,820**	**1,400**	**32,220**

The Museum's external valuer (Turner, Constable and Co) carried out a full valuation of the collection of paintings as at 31 March 2008. The valuations were based on commercial markets, including recent transaction information from auctions where similar types of paintings are regularly being purchased. During the year, a painting that was valued in last year's accounts at £175,000 suffered major damage and was revalued at £25,000 at 31 March 2008. The write-down of £150,000 was charged to the Income and Expenditure account.

A particularly significant exhibit within the collection is the portrait of the Lady Elinor May, Countess of Barset by William Maclean ca 1750. The portrait is unusual as Maclean is more widely known for his landscapes of the Scottish Highlands. The painting has been valued by an external valuer at £2.5 million. Expert opinion is divided as to the artistic merit of the portrait. A Maclean landscape was recently sold at auction for £3 million.

The values reported for the collections of artefacts and fossils are transaction costs for recent purchases or the Museum curator's best estimate of a current valuation for recent donations.

Additions in 2007-08 comprise:

- £200,000 purchase of a collection of 20 watercolours of Barsetshire landscapes by a local artist.
- £150,000 purchase at auction of a private collection of oil paintings from the estate of a local family.
- £50,000 donation of various paintings of local interest whose public display will, in the opinion of the Trustees, support the Museum's objective.
- £150,000 donation of fossils and artefacts received from the Dorsetshire Museum. The Trustees of the Dorsetshire Museum approved the donation because the objects were unlikely to be displayed at their Museum and it was becoming increasingly difficult to maintain them in good condition.

Disposals in 2007-08 comprise:

- The disposal relates to a piece of contemporary art that was donated to the Museum by a local artist in 2006-07. The disposal, which is to a private gallery that specialises in contemporary art, was approved by both the artist and the Trustees. The proceeds of £120,000 were used to fund additions to the collection of paintings in 2007-08.

Note 8 Five year financial summary of heritage asset transactions:

	2007-08 £000	2006-07 £000	2005-06 £000	2004-05 £000	2003-04 £000
Purchases					
Paintings	350	70	100	160	50
Artefacts and Fossils	150	5	65	10	20
Donations					
Paintings	50	20	20	–	–
Total additions	550	95	185	170	70
Disposal of Paintings					
Carrying value	80	20	–	–	10
Sale proceeds	120	25	–	–	12

Note 9 Further information on the Museum's collections of heritage assets

Paintings

The collection consists of 3,000 paintings, sketches and photographs from the last 150 years illustrating the changing landscape and local populace. The collection has been significantly enhanced in 2007-08 by the acquisition of a collection of watercolours from a local artist and a collection of oil paintings from the estate of a local family. The watercolours comprise modern Barsetshire landscapes with the oil paintings depicting more traditional Barsetshire landscapes from the late 19th and early 20th centuries.

The Museum occasionally makes available on loan items from the collection to other regional museums and also accepts paintings and other items on loan. At any time, approximately 50 per cent of the collections are on display. The remaining items are held in storage but access is permitted to scholars and others for research purposes.

Artefacts and fossils

The Museum's collections of artefacts and fossils have been developed over 120 years and are used for reference, research and education. The Museum occasionally makes available on loan objects to other regional museums and also accepts objects on loan. The Trustees are indebted to the Dorsetshire Museum for the permanent transfer to the Museum of a collection of fossils and artefacts.

At any time approximately 20 per cent of the items in the collections are on display. The remaining items are held in storage but access is permitted to scholars for research purposes.

Artefacts

The collection consists of 5,000 miscellaneous, man-made objects including flints, pottery and coins from the period 3000 BC to 1900 AD and reflects the activity of man in the local area over this period. The collection has been developed over many years from digs and field surveys undertaken by the county archaeologists.

Fossils

The collection consists of 2,000 specimens from the Cretaceous to the Pleistocene period (145 million to 2 million years ago) and includes fossil fish remains such as shark and ray teeth, marine molluscs and sponges and disarticulated remains of fossil dinosaurs and mammals. It records the development of fauna from the local area. The collection was principally created from a bequest from Octavius Bayley, Victorian philanthropist and fossil enthusiast.

Heritage assets of particular importance

As explained in note 7, the Museum holds one painting which, in the opinion of the Trustees, is of particular significance and has been valued by an external valuer at £2.5 million. The overall value of the collection, as reported in note 7, at 31 March 2008 is £30.8 million.

The Museum also holds certain items which the Trustees regard as particularly important to the collections of artefacts and fossils and are likely to have a significant monetary value in comparison with other items in these collections. Of particular importance are artefacts from the tomb of Baron Percy de Barsette ca 1100-1160 comprising chain mail armour, a long shield and a sword. These objects are in poor condition but are of great rarity. They were acquired by the Museum in the late 19th century and, in the Trustees' opinion, it is not possible to provide a reliable estimate of their value.

Preservation and management

The Museum has a rolling programme of major restoration developed from a comprehensive review of the condition of the Museum's collections that was carried out in 2002-03. The review was commissioned by the Trustees following a major flood in the basement areas where items not on public display are stored.

The total cost of the restoration programme is £250,000 which is being partly funded by a £100,000 grant from the Heritage Preservation Fund. At the end of 2007-08, the programme is around 80 per cent complete and the Trustees expect the programme to be completed in 2008-09. The costs of the programme have been charged to the Income and Expenditure Account.

Each of the collections is managed by a Curator who reports to the Director of Collections. The Curators manage the collections in accordance with policies that are approved by the Trustees. Further information is provided in the Museum's separate publication "*The Management and Preservation of the Barsetshire Museum's Collections*", which is available on the Museum's website. As is explained in that publication, assets in the collection are only disposed of where, in the opinion of the Trustees, an item does not contribute to the interest and diversity of the Museum's collection.

The Museum maintains a register for its collections of heritage assets which records the nature, provenance and current location of each asset. Due to the large volume of items received in the period, the register is not currently complete. It is expected that it will be fully comprehensive by the end of March 2009.

EXAMPLE 3 — THE ANCIENT MONUMENT MUSEUM

The Museum maintains four Neolithic burial mounds and, although it periodically undertakes restoration work, none has been undertaken recently. In the Trustees' opinion, conventional valuation approaches lack sufficient reliability and any valuation is likely to involve costs that are likely to be onerous. For this reason the burial mounds, which were gifted to the Museum at nil cost, are not recognised as assets in the Museum's Balance Sheet. Other than routine maintenance works, there have been no transactions in heritage assets for many years.

The following disclosures are provided in the financial statements.

Note 1 Accounting policies

Tangible fixed assets and depreciation

Heritage assets

The Museum maintains four Neolithic burial mounds in support of the Museum's objective to protect these historic monuments for the benefit of future generations. The Trustees consider that owing to the incomparable nature of the burial mounds, conventional valuation approaches lack sufficient reliability and that, even if valuations could be obtained, the costs would be onerous compared with the additional benefits derived by the Museum and users of the accounts. As a result, no value is reported for these assets in the Museum's Balance Sheet.

Expenditure on major restoration

The cost of associated major repairs is reported in the Income and Expenditure Account in the year it is incurred.

Further information is given in Note 8 to the accounts.

Note 8 Heritage Assets not recognised in the balance sheet

The Museum maintains four Neolithic burial mounds which were acquired during the 19th century as a gift from the former landowner at no cost to the Museum. No related artefacts are held.

There have been no acquisitions or disposals of heritage assets during the last five years.

The Museum aims to maintain the condition of the earthworks in a steady state of repair. Detailed surveys are undertaken at least every five years. The last survey was carried out during 2003-04 following a landslip. As a result, some underpinning work was undertaken. The cost of these works was not capitalised in the Balance Sheet. No major restoration costs were incurred during 2007-08.

Public access to the burial mounds is permitted at weekends and public holidays between March and October and, by prior arrangement, at other times.

EXAMPLE 4 — THE STONEWORKS MUSEUM OF INDUSTRIAL HERITAGE

The Museum charts the impact of the Industrial Revolution on the county of Slateshire which became famous for stonecutting and the manufacture of tiles. The Museum has two main parts; the Stoneworks Site, which includes the old quarry and stonecutting factory; and Stoneworth House, which was the country residence of the family which founded the Stoneworks Site. The majority of exhibits were acquired in the late 19th and early 20th centuries.

In the opinion of the Trustees, most of the items of machinery and equipment that are exhibited in the quarry and factory on the Stoneworks Site cannot be valued because conventional valuation approaches lack sufficient reliability. The Trustees are also of the opinion that the costs of obtaining valuations for these items would be disproportionate in terms of the benefits derived by the Museum and users of the accounts. Valuations are, however, provided for the majority of items exhibited in Stoneworth House, including the House itself.

The following disclosures would be provided in the notes to the financial statements.

Note 1 Accounting policies

Tangible fixed assets and depreciation

Heritage assets

The Museum holds heritage assets relating to the Stoneworks Site, founded by the Stoneworth family that has made the Slateshire area famous for stonecutting and the manufacture of tiles. The Museum also includes Stoneworth House, the country estate of the Stoneworth family, which includes collections of paintings, furniture and other household and business items. In addition to donations from the Stoneworth estate, the Museum also houses exhibits donated by other local families and businesses, as well as exhibits that have been acquired from other museums or purchased at auction.

These items are held in support of the Museum's primary objective of increasing knowledge, understanding and appreciation of the industrial heritage of the Slateshire area. The Museum's exhibits are accounted for as follows:

Stoneworks Site

A valuation is provided for the land that is used for the factory and for other parts of the Site that do not form part of the quarry. This is because, subject to appropriate planning consents, the land may have an alternative commercial use. The valuation was updated in March 2008 by a local firm of estate agents with the increase in valuation charged to the Statement of Total Recognised Gains and Losses. The estate agents that valued the land also confirmed that sufficiently reliable valuations could not be obtained either for the factory building, which is now largely derelict, or for the quarry which is a heritage site and has no existing or alternative use.

The Trustees consider that obtaining valuations for the vast majority of the machinery and equipment that is exhibited in the quarry and factory would involve disproportionate cost. This is because of the diverse nature of the assets held and the lack of comparable market values. Other than a few items that have been acquired recently, for example purchased at auction or bequeathed, or where there may be an active market, the Museum does not recognise these assets on its Balance Sheet.

Valuations are, however, available for a small number of exhibits, including the two most significant items on display, a steam-driven stonecutter at the quarry site and a steam locomotive that ran between the quarry and the Stoneworks factory and the county town of Tilemouth. The Museum has also been able to value some recent donations that are reported at values indicative of prices for similar items achieved at auction. There are also some donations from the estate of the late Lord Gravelstone, who also owned a quarry and stonecutting company in the late 19th century, that are reported at values provided by executors administering the estate.

The Trustees will occasionally approve the disposal of items of machinery and equipment, for example when an item is of doubtful provenance or is unsuitable for public display. Where items that are not recognised as fixed assets are disposed of, the proceeds are reported in the Income and Expenditure Account. Disposal proceeds are also disclosed separately in the notes to the accounts.

Recent purchases are recorded at cost with the Museum's curators making a best estimate of current value for reporting donations.

Stoneworth House

Stoneworth House was built in 1846 and remained the home of the Stoneworth family until 1910. It is a Grade II listed building and forms an integral part of the Museum. It is reported in the Balance Sheet as a tangible fixed asset.

The House and all of the paintings and furniture within it are stated at valuation with subsequent restoration work on the House stated at cost. Certain other household items, such as tapestries, statues and children's toys, are also included at valuation but, for the majority of household items, valuations could not be obtained at reasonable cost. This is because of the size and diversity of the collection.

The assets that are not valued include a collection of around 25,000 documents representing the business records of the Stoneworth company.

Where valuations are reported, Stoneworth House and items from the collections of paintings and furniture are periodically revalued by an external valuer. Other items that can be valued, for example the late Lord Stoneworth's 1910 Model T Ford motor car, are valued by the Museum's curator. Any surplus or deficit on revaluation is charged to the Statement of Total Recognised Gains and Losses.

Acquisitions are normally made by purchase or donation. Purchases are initially recorded at cost and donations are recorded at a current valuation ascertained by the Museum's curator with reference, where possible, to commercial markets using recent transaction information from auctions.

The Trustees have approved the sale of certain paintings and items of furniture to fund the restoration and maintenance work that is considered necessary to preserve the Stoneworks Site, maintain exhibits on display and keep the Museum open for the public.

The disposal proceeds from items that are not classified as fixed assets, are included in the Income and Expenditure Account and are separately disclosed in the notes to the accounts.

Preservation costs

Expenditure which, in the Trustees' view, is required to preserve or prevent further deterioration of individual items, including preservation work on Stoneworth House, is recognised in the Income and Expenditure Account when it is incurred.

Further information on the exhibits held by the Museum is given in Notes 7, 8 and 9 to the accounts.

Note 7 Tangible fixed assets – heritage assets

	Stoneworth House	Stoneworth House Exhibits	Stoneworks Land	Site Exhibits	**Total**
	£000	£000	£000	£000	**£000**
Cost or valuation					
1 April 2007	6,386	2,448	750	421	**10,005**
Additions	120	–	–	95	**215**
Disposals	-	(500)	–	–	**(500)**
Revaluation	–	1,120	50	–	**1,170**
31 March 2008	**6,506**	**3,068**	**800**	**516**	**10,890**
Valuation	**6,366**	**3,068**	**800**	**471**	**10,705**
Cost	**140**	**–**	**–**	**45**	**185**
Total	**6,506**	**3,068**	**800**	**516**	**10,890**

The Museum's external valuer (Granite, Marble and Co) carried out a full valuation of Stoneworth House at 31 March 2006. In the Trustees' opinion, the only material change in the valuation since this date results from the subsequent restoration work that has been carried out on the outhouses and paddocks. This expenditure, which allows these premises to display more of the Museum's exhibits, has been capitalised. The next full external valuation of Stoneworth House is scheduled for 31 March 2009.

Granite, Marble and Co also carried out valuations of paintings and furniture in Stoneworth House, as at 31 March 2008 and of other exhibits relevant to the House where valuation is practicable. The valuations were based on commercial markets, including recent transaction information from auctions where comparable items are regularly being traded.

The land valuation for the Stoneworks Site is provided by a local estate agent and was updated at 31 March 2008.

There are only a few items on display in the quarry and factory where valuations can be obtained. These items, including the steam-driven stonecutter at the quarry and the steam locomotive, have been valued by the Museum's curator.

The collection of paintings includes six works by the local artist Alexander Pebble (1836–1902). These paintings are valued at significantly higher amounts than other paintings held by the Museum, reflecting the popularity of paintings depicting the Industrial Revolution, including those by Pebble. The revaluation of the six Pebble paintings exhibited at Stoneworth House results in an increase of £1,120,000 which has been taken to the Statement of Total Recognised Gains and Losses.

Additions in 2007-08 comprise:

- £120,000 restoration of outhouses and paddocks at Stoneworth House.
- £45,000 purchase at auction of a steam-driven stonecutter similar to the one that would have been used at the Stoneworks Quarry in the mid 19th century.
- £50,000 donation of various items of machinery and equipment from the estate of the late Lord Gravelstone. The public display of these items will, in the opinion of the Trustees, support the Museum's objective.

Disposals in 2007-08 comprise:

The disposal relates to the sale of Pebble's highly acclaimed 1873 landscape of the Stoneworks Site. The painting's carrying amount in the balance sheet was £500,000 and the £360,000 surplus is separately reported in the Income and Expenditure Account. The disposal, which is to a gallery that specialises in local art, was approved by the Trustees. The proceeds of £860,000 are being used to fund further restoration work on Stoneworth House.

Note 8 Five year financial summary of heritage asset transactions

	2007-08 £000	2006-07 £000	2005-06 £000	2004-05 £000	2003-04 £000
Purchases:					
Stoneworth House	120	20	-	40	30
Other Exhibits	45	25	65	10	20
Donations	50	30	20	10	15
Total additions	215	75	85	60	65
Disposals					
Carrying amount	500	25	15	5	20
Sale proceeds	860	28	20	6	24

Note 9 Further information on the Museum's heritage assets

The Museum's heritage

The Museum provides an excellent example of how the Industrial Revolution transformed a small, family-run business into a successful large company employing hundreds of people locally and selling its products throughout the United Kingdom. The story of the Stonehouse family and the Stoneworks Site forms an important part of the industrial heritage of the Slateshire area.

A full inventory is maintained of all items held, including valuations where these can be obtained and provide a meaningful insight into the value of the asset.

Stoneworks Site

The factory and quarry are classified as heritage sites and retain many features from when the Stoneworks Site was operational during the period 1830 to 1910. The machinery and equipment on display cover the early years, when the stone was quarried by hand with horses used for transport, through to the late 19th century when a steam-driven stonecutter was used to cut stone from the quarry which was then transported by a steam locomotive to the factory for shaping and polishing. The equipment used to process and polish the quarried stone, including that used to manufacture the world renowned Stoneworks tiles, is also on display in the factory.

All of the Museum's machinery and equipment relevant to the Stoneworks Site is on public display.

Stoneworth House

The Stoneworth family built their family residence in 1876 following a particularly successful period for their Stoneworks company. The House is an excellent example of a mid Victorian family residence with furnishings and other items exhibited throughout the house that demonstrate the increasingly extravagant lifestyle of the Stonehouse family, their pursuit of leisure and the need to employ a large number of domestic staff.

At any one time, around 70 per cent of exhibits are on display in Stoneworth House. The remaining exhibits are not displayed, either because of preservation work or because of the Museum's policy of rotating some of the items on display. When not on display, items are stored in rooms that are not open to the public, although access is permitted to historians and others for research purposes.

Paintings

The collection, which was assembled by the Stoneworth family in the period 1850 to 1895, consists of 215 paintings by a number of artists, including Alexander Pebble. All of these paintings are recognised as fixed assets at a total value of £2.3 million as at 31 March 2008.

Furniture and other exhibits

The collection of furniture consists of around 1,200 items, including chairs, tables, beds and cabinets. Valuations are available for around 800 of these items which are reported in the Balance Sheet at a total value of £600,000. Whilst valuations are available for the majority of the items of furniture, very few valuations are available for the other exhibits displayed in the House. There are around 2,600 other exhibits, such as clothes, kitchen and gardening equipment, children's toys and chandeliers. The items that are valued, including a model T Ford motor car, are reported at a total value of £168,000 as at 31 March 2008.

Heritage assets of particular importance

As explained in note 7, the Museum holds a number of paintings by the well known local artist, Alexander Pebble. In the opinion of the external valuer, the six remaining Pebble paintings held by the Museum have a total value of £1.65 million, and have given rise to a £1.12 million revaluation gain that is reported in these financial statements. No other individual painting or item of furniture has a value in excess of £25,000.

Although the majority of other exhibits on display at the Museum are of low financial value, there are three items which, in the opinion of the Trustees, are of particular importance and have a significant market value which is reported in the Museum's Balance Sheet. These items are:

- A steam-driven stonecutter which was purchased in 1881 for 68 guineas and has an estimated current market value of £95,000.
- A steam locomotive which was purchased in 1884 for 145 guineas and has an estimated current market value of £180,000.
- A Ford motor car which was purchased in 1910 for $750 and has an estimated current market value of £65,000.

Preservation and management

The Museum has a rolling programme of major restoration developed from a comprehensive review of the condition of the Stoneworks Site, Stoneworth House and all the Museum's exhibits that was carried out in 2004-05. The review was commissioned by the Trustees following major storm damage to the factory which in turn resulted in some damage to exhibits on display.

The total cost of the restoration programme is £950,000 which is being partly funded by a £100,000 grant from Slateshire County Council and proceeds from the sale of exhibits. The sale of the Alexander Pebble painting means that the restoration programme is now fully funded and is scheduled to start in 2008-09.

The Museum's exhibits are managed by a Curator who reports to the Museum Director. The Curator manages the exhibits in accordance with policies that are approved by the Trustees.

Further information is provided in the Museum's separate publication "*The Management and Preservation of the Stoneworks Museum of Industrial Heritage*", which is available on the Museum's website. As explained in that publication, assets are only disposed of where, in the opinion of the Trustees, an item does not contribute to the interest and diversity of the Museum's collection or, in exceptional circumstances, where the disposal will provide the Museum with funding that, in the opinion of the Trustees, is considered essential to the Museum being able to fulfil its charitable objects in the future.

The Museum maintains a full catalogue of its collection of heritage assets and this can be consulted by appointment with the Curator. Information provided by the catalogue includes the nature and provenance of each item.

Financial Reporting Standard for Smaller Entities (effective April 2008) is set out in parts A–D.

The Statement of Standard Accounting Practice set out in sections 1–20 of Part B should be read in the context of the Objective as stated in Part A, the Definitions set out in Part C and the Foreword to Accounting Standards. In addition, recommended Voluntary Disclosures, which do not form part of the Statement of Standard Accounting Practice, are set out in Part D.

As stated in the Foreword to Accounting Standards, accounting standards, which include the FRSSE, need not be applied to immaterial items.

Appendix IV 'The development of the FRSSE' reviews considerations and arguments that were thought significant by members of the Board in reaching the conclusions on the document.

The Financial Reporting Standard for Smaller Entities (effective April 2008) updates and supersedes the FRSSE (effective January 2007). It should be regarded as standard for financial statements relating to accounting periods beginning on or after 6 April 2008. The revised and new paragraphs in Parts B–D are highlighted by the use of sidelines. The FRSSE (effective January 2007) remains in force for financial statements relating to accounting periods beginning on or after 1 January 2007 and on or before 5 April 2008.

The FRSSE (effective April 2008) introduces no changes to the accounting requirements. The only differences between the FRSSE (effective April 2008) and the FRSSE (effective January 2007) are in respect of the legal requirements which have been updated to reflect the Companies Act 2006. Earlier adoption is not permitted.

Financial Reporting Standard for Smaller Entities (effective April 2008)*

(Issued April 2008)

Contents

Status of the FRSSE

Financial Reporting Standard for Smaller Entities (effective April 2008)

A – Objective

B – Statement of Standard Accounting Practice

1 **Scope**

2 **General**
Requirement to prepare financial statements
True and fair view
Accounting principles and policies
Going concern
Prudence
Accruals
Prior period adjustments
Formats – general rules
Balance sheet format
Profit and loss account formats
Approval and signing of accounts
Delivery to the registrar
Exemptions from audit
Liability limitation agreement

3 **Profit and loss account**
General
Exceptional items
Profit or loss on disposal
Disclosure of auditor remuneration

4 **Revenue recognition**
Basic principles
Turnover
Contracts for services

5 **Statement of total recognised gains and losses**

6 **Fixed assets and goodwill**
Disclosure
Research and development
Other intangible assets and goodwill

***Editor's note**: The FRSSE is amended with effect for periods beginning on or after 1 January 2015, and retitled accordingly. The changes have been included within footnotes.*

Tangible fixed assets
Investments
Revaluation reserve
Depreciation
Write-downs to recoverable amount
Investment properties
Government grants

7 Leases
Hire purchase and leasing
Accounting by lessees
Accounting by lessors
Manufacturer/dealer lessor
Sale and leaseback transactions – accounting by the seller/lessee
Sale and leaseback transactions – accounting by the buyer/lessor
Disclosure by lessees

8 Current assets
Stocks and long-term contracts
Consignment stock
Debt factoring
Current asset investments
Start-up costs and pre-contract costs

9 Taxation
General
Deferred tax
Tax on dividends
Value added tax (VAT)

10 Pensions

11 Provisions, contingent liabilities and contingent assets
Provisions
Contingent liabilities and contingent assets

12 Financial instruments, share capital and share-based payments
General
The company's share capital
Share-based payments

13 Foreign currency translation
Transactions in foreign currencies
Incorporating accounts of foreign entities

14 Post balance sheet events

15 Related party disclosures
Parent undertaking drawing up accounts for larger group
Directors' benefits: advances, credit and guarantees
Subsidiary undertakings
Holdings in subsidiary undertakings
Financial information about subsidiary undertakings
Membership of certain undertakings

16 Consolidated financial statements
Form and content of small group accounts

17 Directors' remuneration

18 The directors' report
Introduction
The principal activities of the company
Details of the company's directors
Disclosure of qualifying third party indemnity provisions
Political donations and expenditure and charitable donations
Acquisition of own shares
Employment, etc of disabled persons
Statement as to disclosure of information to auditors
Approval and signing of the directors' report

19 Date from which effective and transitional arrangements
Transitional arrangements – goodwill
Transitional arrangements – tangible fixed assets

20 Withdrawal of the FRSSE (effective January 2007)

C – Definitions

D – Voluntary disclosures

Cash flow information

E – Adoption of the FRSSE (Effective April 2008) by the Board

Appendices
I Note on legal requirements for companies
II Accounting for retirement benefits: defined benefit schemes
III Illustrative examples and practical considerations
Statement of total recognised gains and losses
Disclosure – defined contribution pension scheme
Disclosure – defined benefit pension scheme
Stocks and long-term contracts
Consignment stock
Debt factoring
Bill and hold arrangements
Sales with rights of return
Presentation of turnover as principal or as agent
Classification of preference shares
Cash flow statement
Discounting when making a provision
IV The development of the FRSSE
V Amendment to the FRSSE (Effective January 2007)

Status of the FRSSE

GENERAL

1 The Financial Reporting Standard for Smaller Entities (effective April 2008) – the FRSSE – prescribes the basis, for those entities within its scope that have chosen to adopt it, for preparing and presenting their financial statements. The definitions and accounting treatments are consistent with the requirements of companies legislation and, for the generality of small entities, are the same as those required by other accounting standards or a simplified version of those requirements. The disclosure requirements exclude a number of those stipulated in other accounting standards.*

2 Reporting entities that apply the FRSSE are exempt from complying with other accounting standards (Statements of Standard Accounting Practice and Financial Reporting Standards) and Urgent Issues Task Force (UITF) Abstracts, unless preparing consolidated financial statements, in which case certain other accounting standards apply, as set out in paragraph 16.1.†

3 For the convenience of companies using the FRSSE, the requirements of company law in the United Kingdom on full financial statements have been reflected in this standard. THESE ARE SHOWN IN SMALL CAPITALS TO DISTINGUISH THEM FROM THE REQUIREMENTS OF THE FRSSE‡. The legal requirements set out in the FRSSE are intended to reflect company law, including the Companies Act 2006 and amendments and Regulations issued thereunder which are effective from 6 April 2008. This does not affect directors' responsibilities regarding compliance with company law and in all matters regarding interpretation of the legal requirements reference should be to the relevant legislation.

4 The only differences between this version of the FRSSE (effective April 2008) and the FRSSE (effective January 2007) are in respect of the legislative requirements which have been updated to reflect the Companies Act 2006. The main change relates to increases in the thresholds for companies to qualify as small. The other changes, such as an increase in the threshold for reporting political and charitable donations and removal of the requirement to maintain a register of directors' interests, are set out at

***Editor's note**: With effect for accounting periods beginning on or after 1 January 2015 this is replaced with:*

The Financial Reporting Standard for Smaller Entities (effective January 2015) – the FRSSE – prescribes the basis, for those entities within its scope that have chosen to adopt it, for preparing and presenting their financial statements. The definitions and accounting treatments are consistent with the requirements of companies legislation.

†***Editor's note**: With effect for accounting periods beginning on or after 1 January 2015 this is replaced with:*

Reporting entities that apply the FRSSE, together with FRS 100 *Application of Financial Reporting Requirements*, are exempt from complying with other Financial Reporting Standards (FRSs).

‡*The detail of the requirements in company law in the Republic of Ireland in many cases differs from the UK requirements reflected in the FRSSE. Tables showing the source of legislative requirements in British law and the equivalent sources in Northern Ireland and the Republic of Ireland are available on the ASB website (www.frc.org.uk/asb) In addition, there are a number of Republic of Ireland legal requirements that are not reflected in the FRSSE. There is no equivalent to SI 2008/409 The Small Companies and Groups (Accounts and Directors' Report) Regulations 2008 providing certain exemptions for small companies when preparing annual accounts for shareholders. Exemptions from company law requirements for small companies in the Republic of Ireland are therefore limited and relate primarily to information that must be filed with the Companies Registration Office. This does not affect directors' responsibilities regarding compliance with company law and in all matters regarding interpretation of the legal requirements in the Republic of Ireland reference should be to the relevant legislation.*

Appendix V. These do not impact upon the accounting requirements but do alter some of the disclosures. A derivation table, available on the ASB website, provides a full cross-reference between the legal requirements set out in the FRSSE (effective April 2008) and the Companies Act 2006.*

Financial statements will generally be prepared using accepted practice and, accordingly, for transactions or events not dealt with in the FRSSE, smaller entities should have regard to other accounting standards and UITF Abstracts, not as mandatory documents, but as a means of establishing current practice.† 5

CRITERIA

When considering the application of accounting standards and UITF Abstracts to smaller entities, the Accounting Standards Board has had, and will continue to have, regard to the following criteria:‡§ 6

(a) The standard or requirement is likely to be regarded as having general application and as an essential element of generally accepted accounting practice for all entities.
(b) The standard or requirement is likely to lead to a transaction being treated in a way that would be readily recognised by the proprietor or manager of the business as corresponding to his or her understanding of the transaction.
(c) The standard or requirement is likely to meet the information needs and legitimate expectations of a user of a small entity's accounts.
(d) The standard or requirement results in disclosures that are likely to be meaningful and comprehensive to such a user. Where disclosures are aimed at a particular group of users, that group would be likely to receive the information, given that they may have access only to abbreviated accounts.

*****Editor's note**: With effect for accounting periods beginning on or after 1 January 2015 this is replaced with:*

The significant differences between this version of the FRSSE (effective January 2015) and the FRSSE (effective April 2008) are in respect of the revised reporting framework introduced into the UK effective January 2015. As part of the revised reporting framework, the FRC has withdrawn extant Financial Reporting Standards and Urgent Issues Task Force (UITF) Abstracts. It has made consequential amendments to the FRSSE where it previously referred to standards or Abstracts that are now withdrawn.

*†**Editor's note**: With effect for accounting periods beginning on or after 1 January 2015 this is replaced with:*

Financial statements will generally be prepared using accepted practice and, accordingly, for transactions or events not dealt with in the FRSSE, smaller entities should first have regard to their own existing accounting policies. Where an entity applying the FRSSE undertakes a new transaction not dealt with in the FRSSE for which it has no existing policy, in developing a new policy it should have regard to FRS 102 *The Financial Reporting Standard applicable in the UK and Republic ofIreland*, not as a mandatory document, but as a means of establishing current practice.

and the following paragraph is added:

5A Public benefit entities (PBEs), only, shall have regard to the requirements in FRS 102 that are specific to PBEs not as mandatory requirements, but as a means of establishing current practice.

‡Legal advice has been obtained that in accounting standards smaller entities may properly be allowed exemptions or differing treatments provided that there are rational grounds for doing so: see Appendix I.

*§**Editor's note**: With effect for accounting periods beginning on or after 1 January 2015 this part of this paragraph is replaced with:*

When considering the application of accounting standards, including FRS 102 *The Financial Reporting Standard applicable in the UK and Republic of Ireland*, to smaller entities, the FRC has had, and will continue to have, regard to the following criteria.

(e) The requirements of the standard significantly augment the treatment prescribed by legislation.
(f) The treatment prescribed by the standard or requirement is compatible with that already used, or expected to be used, by the Inland Revenue in computing taxable profits.
(g) The standard or requirement provides the least cumbersome method of achieving the desired accounting treatment and/or disclosure for an entity that is not complex.
(h) The standard provides guidance that is expected to be widely relevant to the transactions of small entities and is written in terms that can be understood by such businesses.
(i) The measurement methods prescribed in the standard are likely to be reasonably practical for small entities.

7 The satisfaction of a majority of the above criteria would suggest that the standard or requirement under consideration may also be appropriate for application to smaller entities, whereas failure to satisfy a majority of the above criteria would suggest that exemption, or differing treatment, from the standard, or a specific requirement within that standard, may be more appropriate.

SCOPE

8 The FRSSE may be applied to all financial statements intended to give a true and fair view of the financial position and profit or loss (or income and expenditure) of all entities* that are:

(a) small companies or small groups as defined in companies legislation† preparing Companies Act individual or group accounts; or
(b) entities that would also qualify under (a) if they had been incorporated under companies legislation, with the exception of building societies.

9 Accordingly, the FRSSE does not apply to:

(a) large or medium-sized companies, groups and other entities;
(b) public companies;
(c) companies preparing individual or group accounts in accordance with international accounting standards;
(d) companies preparing individual or group accounts in accordance with the fair value accounting rules for certain assets and liabilities set out in Section D of Schedule 1 of Regulation 2008/409 to the 2006 Companies Act;‡
(e) a company that is an authorised insurance company, a banking company, an e-money issuer, a MifId investment firm§ or a UCITS management company or a company that carries on insurance market activity;

**Some older accounting standards are drafted in terms of application to companies. References to companies and associated terms, such as board of directors and shareholders, in the FRSSE should therefore be taken to apply also to unincorporated entities.*

†*The legal definitions of small companies and small groups in the UK are set out in Appendix I. In the Republic of Ireland the FRSSE can be applied to those companies meeting the criteria as set out in companies legislation that allow them to be treated as 'small' for the purposes of filing information with the Companies Registration Office.*

‡*Companies accounting for fixed assets and investments at valuation are not precluded from using the FRSSE*

§*The Markets in Financial Instruments Directive (Consequential Amendments) Regulations 2007 (SI 2007/2932) substituted the term "MifId iinvestment firm" for "ISD investment firm"*

(f) a person (other than a small company) who has permission under Part 4 of the Financial Services and Markets Act 2000 (in the UK) to carry on a regulated activity or, notwithstanding the definition of a small company in the legislation, companies authorised under the Investment Intermediaries Act 1995 (in the Republic of Ireland); or

(g) members of an ineligible group. A group is ineligible if any of its members is:

  (i) a public company;
  (ii) a body corporate (other than a company) whose shares are admitted to trading on a regulated market in an EEA State;
  (iii) a person (other than a small company) who has permission under Part 4 of the Financial Services and Markets Act 2000 to carry on a regulated activity;
  (iv) a small company that is an authorised insurance company, a banking company, an e-money issuer, a MifId investment firm or a UCITS management company; or
  (v) a person who carries on insurance market activity.

Reporting entities that are entitled to adopt the FRSSE, but choose not to do so, should apply Statements of Standard Accounting Practice (SSAPs), other Financial Reporting Standards (FRSs) and UITF Abstracts when preparing financial statements intended to give a true and fair view of the financial position and profit or loss of the entity.* **10**

Statements of Recommended Practice

Statements of Recommended Practice (SORPs) and other equivalent guidance developed or revised after the FRSSE was first issued (in November 1997) may specify the circumstances, if any, in which entities in the industry or sector addressed in the SORP or equivalent guidance may adopt the current version of the FRSSE. Financial statements that purport to comply with existing SORPs that are drafted on the basis that the financial statements comply with the requirements of SSAPs, FRSs (other than the FRSSE) and UITF Abstracts, should also observe those requirements, rather than adopt the FRSSE.† **11**

****Editor's note****: With effect for accounting periods beginning on or after 1 January 2015 this is replaced with the following paragraph and footnote:*

Reporting entities that are entitled to adopt the FRSSE, but choose not to do so, are required to apply EU-adopted IFRS, FRS 101 *Reduced Disclosure Framework* (in the individual financial statements of qualifying entities) or FRS 102 *The Financial Reporting Standard applicable in the UK and Republic of Ireland*, in accordance with the requirements of FRS 100 *Application of Financial Reporting Requirements*, when preparing financial statements intended to give a true and fair view of the assets, liabilities, financial position and profit or loss of the entity.[8]

[8] Under company law in the Republic of Ireland, certain companies are permitted to prepare Companies Act accounts using a financial reporting framework based on accounting standards other than those issued by the FRC.

†***Editor's note****: With effect for accounting periods beginning on or after 1 January 2015 this is replaced with the following two paragraphs:*

Statements of Recommended Practice (SORPs) and other equivalent guidance may specify the circumstances, if any, in which entities in the industry or sector addressed in the SORP or equivalent guidance may adopt the current version of the FRSSE.

Where SORPs are drafted on the basis of the requirements of FRS 102 *The Financial Reporting Standard applicable in the UK and Republic of Ireland*, financial statements cannot be said to comply with those SORPs if they are prepared in accordance with the FRSSE.

Financial Reporting Standard for Smaller Entities (effective April 2008)

A – Objective

1 The objective of the FRSSE is to ensure that reporting entities falling within its scope provide in their financial statements information about the financial position, performance and financial adaptability of the entity that is useful to users in assessing the stewardship of management and for making economic decisions, recognising that the balance between users' needs in respect of stewardship and economic decision-making for smaller entities is different from that for other reporting entities.

B – Statement of Standard Accounting Practice

1 SCOPE

The FRSSE may be applied to all financial statements intended to give a true and fair view of the financial position and profit or loss (or income and expenditure) of all entities that are: 1.1

(a) companies incorporated under **companies legislation*** and entitled to the exemptions available in the legislation for small companies when filing accounts with the Registrar of Companies;† or

(b) entities that would have come into category (a) above had they been companies incorporated under **companies legislation,** excluding building societies. While not bound by the requirements of **companies legislation** reflected in the FRSSE (set out in SMALL CAPITALS), such entities shall have regard to the **accounting principles,** presentation and disclosure requirements in **companies legislation** (or other equivalent legislation) that, taking into account the FRSSE, are necessary to present a true and fair view.

2 GENERAL

Requirement to prepare financial statements

THE **DIRECTORS** MUST PREPARE FOR EACH **FINANCIAL YEAR** OF THE COMPANY‡ – 2.1

(A) A BALANCE SHEET AS AT THE LAST DAY OF THE **FINANCIAL YEAR**, AND

(B) A PROFIT AND LOSS ACCOUNT.

True and fair view

THE BALANCE SHEET MUST GIVE A TRUE AND FAIR VIEW OF THE STATE OF AFFAIRS OF THE COMPANY AS AT THE END OF THE **FINANCIAL YEAR**; AND THE PROFIT AND LOSS ACCOUNT MUST GIVE A TRUE AND FAIR VIEW OF THE PROFIT OR LOSS OF THE COMPANY FOR THE **FINANCIAL YEAR**. THE DIRECTORS OF A COMPANY MUST, IN DETERMINING HOW AMOUNTS ARE PRESENTED WITHIN ITEMS IN THE PROFIT AND LOSS ACCOUNT AND BALANCE SHEET, HAVE REGARD TO THE SUBSTANCE OF THE REPORTED TRANSACTION OR ARRANGEMENT, IN ACCORDANCE WITH GENERALLY ACCEPTED ACCOUNTING PRINCIPLES OR PRACTICE. To determine the substance of a transaction it is necessary to identify whether the transaction has given rise to new **assets** or **liabilities** for the reporting entity and whether it has changed the entity's existing **assets** or **liabilities**. 2.2

IF IN SPECIAL CIRCUMSTANCES COMPLIANCE WITH ANY OF THE PROVISIONS OF THE FRSSE OR COMPANIES ACT IS INCONSISTENT WITH THE REQUIREMENT TO GIVE A TRUE AND FAIR VIEW, THE **DIRECTORS** MUST DEPART FROM THAT PROVISION TO THE EXTENT NECESSARY TO GIVE A TRUE AND FAIR VIEW. PARTICULARS OF THE DEPARTURE, THE REASONS FOR IT AND ITS EFFECT MUST BE GIVEN IN A NOTE TO THE ACCOUNTS as follows: 2.3

Terms appearing in* **bold *in the text are explained in the Definitions set out in Part C.*

†*The legal definitions of small companies and small groups in the UK are set out in Appendix I. In the Republic of Ireland the FRSSE can be applied to those companies meeting the criteria as set out in companies legislation that allow them to be treated as 'small' for the purposes of filing information with the Companies Registration Office.*

‡*Text appearing in SMALL CAPITALS refers to UK company legislation requirements.*

(a) a statement that there has been a departure from the requirements of the FRSSE or Companies Act and that the departure is necessary to give a true and fair view;
(b) a statement of the treatment that the FRSSE or Companies Act would normally require and a description of the treatment adopted;
(c) a statement of the reasons why the treatment prescribed would not give a true and fair view; and
(d) a description of how the position shown in the financial statements is different as a result of the departure, normally with quantification, except where:
    (i) quantification is already evident in the financial statements themselves; or
    (ii) the effect cannot be reasonably quantified, in which case the **directors** shall explain the circumstances.

2.4 Where a departure continues in subsequent financial statements, the disclosures shall be made in all subsequent statements and shall include comparative amounts for the previous period. Where a departure affects only the comparative amounts, the disclosures shall be given for those comparative amounts.

2.5 Where there is doubt whether applying provisions of the FRSSE would be sufficient to give a true and fair view, adequate explanation shall be given in the notes to the accounts of the transaction or arrangement concerned and the treatment adopted.

Accounting principles and policies

2.6 The financial statements shall state that they have been prepared in accordance with the Financial Reporting Standard for Smaller Entities (effective April 2008)*†.

2.7 Financial statements shall include:

(a) a description of each material **accounting policy** followed;
(b) details of any changes to the **accounting policies** followed in the preceding period including, in addition to the disclosures necessary for **prior period adjustments**, a brief explanation of why each new **accounting policy** is thought

**This statement may be included with the note of accounting policies or, for those entities taking advantage of the exemptions for small companies in companies legislation, in the statement required by companies legislation to be given on the balance sheet. For example, in the United Kingdom the combined statement could read as follows "These accounts have been prepared in accordance with the special provisions relating to small companies within Part 15 of the Companies Act 2006 and with the Financial Reporting Standard for Smaller Entities (effective April 2008)." If abbreviated accounts are also to be prepared, the statement referring to the Financial Reporting Standard for Smaller Entities (effective April 2008) shall be included with the note of accounting policies so that it is reproduced in the abbreviated accounts.*

†***Editor's note**: With effect for accounting periods beginning on or after 1 January 2015 this paragraph, and its footnote, are replaced with:*

The financial statements shall state that they have been prepared in accordance with the Financial Reporting Standard for Smaller Entities (effective January 2015). *

* This statement may be included with the note of accounting policies or, for those entities taking advantage of the exemptions for small companies in companies legislation, in the statement required by companies legislation to be given on the balance sheet. For example, in the United Kingdom the combined statement could read as follows "These accounts have been prepared in accordance with the provisions applicable to small companies within Part 15 of the Companies Act 2006 and with the Financial Reporting Standard for Smaller Entities (effective January 2015)." If abbreviated accounts are also to be prepared, the statement referring to the Financial Reporting Standard for Smaller Entities (effective January 2015) shall be included with the note of accounting policies so that it is reproduced in the abbreviated accounts.

more appropriate and, where practicable, an indication of the effect of the change on the results for the current period; and

(c) where the effect of a change to an **estimation technique** is material, a description of the change and, where practicable, the effect on the results for the current period.

THE **ACCOUNTING POLICIES** ADOPTED BY THE COMPANY IN DETERMINING THE AMOUNTS TO BE INCLUDED IN RESPECT OF ITEMS SHOWN IN THE BALANCE SHEET AND IN DETERMINING THE PROFIT OR LOSS OF THE COMPANY MUST BE STATED (INCLUDING SUCH POLICIES WITH RESPECT TO THE **DEPRECIATION** AND DIMINUTION IN VALUE OF ASSETS). **2.8**

Accounting policies and **estimation techniques** shall be consistent with the requirements of the FRSSE and of **companies legislation** (or other equivalent legislation). Where this permits a choice, an entity shall select the policies and techniques most appropriate to its particular circumstances for the purpose of giving a true and fair view, taking account of the objectives of relevance, **reliability**, comparability and understandability. **2.9**

Accounting policies MUST BE APPLIED CONSISTENTLY WITHIN THE SAME ACCOUNTS AND FROM ONE **FINANCIAL YEAR** TO THE NEXT. They shall be reviewed regularly to ensure that they remain the most appropriate to the entity's particular circumstances for the purpose of giving a true and fair view. However, in judging whether a new policy is more appropriate than the existing policy, due weight shall be given to the impact on consistency and comparability. Following a change in **accounting policy**, the amounts for the current and corresponding periods shall be restated on the basis of the new policies. **2.10**

IN DETERMINING THE AGGREGATE AMOUNT OF ANY ITEM, THE AMOUNT OF EACH INDIVIDUAL ASSET OR LIABILITY THAT FALLS TO BE TAKEN INTO ACCOUNT MUST BE DETERMINED SEPARATELY. AMOUNTS IN RESPECT OF ASSETS OR INCOME MAY NOT BE SET OFF AGAINST AMOUNTS IN RESPECT OF LIABILITIES OR EXPENDITURE (AS THE CASE MAY BE), OR VICE VERSA. **2.11**

Going concern

THE COMPANY IS PRESUMED TO BE CARRYING ON BUSINESS AS A GOING CONCERN. When preparing financial statements, **directors** shall assess whether there are significant doubts about the entity's ability to continue as a going concern. Any material uncertainties, of which the **directors** are aware in making their assessment, shall be disclosed. Where the period considered by the **directors** in making this assessment has been limited to a period of less than one year from the date of approval of the financial statements, that fact shall be stated. The financial statements shall not be prepared on a going concern basis if the **directors** determine after the balance sheet date either that they intend to liquidate the entity or to cease trading, or that they have no realistic alternative but to do so. **2.12**

Prudence

THE *AMOUNT OF* ANY *ITEM* MUST BE DETERMINED ON A PRUDENT BASIS. Prudence is the inclusion of a degree of caution in the exercise of the judgements needed in making the estimates required under conditions of uncertainty, such that gains and assets are not overstated and liabilities are not understated. However it is not necessary to exercise prudence where there is no uncertainty. Nor is it appropriate to use prudence as a reason to understate deliberately assets or gains or overstate liabilities or losses. **2.13**

Accruals

2.14 The financial statements, with the exception of cash flow information, shall be prepared on the accruals basis of accounting. HENCE, ALL INCOME AND CHARGES RELATING TO THE **FINANCIAL YEAR** TO WHICH THE ACCOUNTS RELATE MUST BE TAKEN INTO ACCOUNT, WITHOUT REGARD TO THE DATE OF PAYMENT OR RECEIPT.

Prior period adjustments

2.15 **Prior period adjustments** shall be accounted for by restating the comparative figures for the preceding period in the primary statements and notes and adjusting the opening balance of reserves for the cumulative effect. The cumulative effect of the adjustments shall also be noted at the foot of the statement of **total recognised gains and losses** of the current period. The effect of **prior period adjustments** on the results for the preceding period shall be disclosed where practicable.

Formats – general rules

2.16 THE FORMATS FOR THE BALANCE SHEET AND PROFIT AND LOSS ACCOUNT ARE SET OUT BELOW. A COMPANY'S INDIVIDUAL ACCOUNTS MUST COMPLY WITH THE PROVISIONS SET OUT BELOW AS TO THE FORM AND CONTENT OF THE BALANCE SHEET AND PROFIT AND LOSS ACCOUNT AND ADDITIONAL INFORMATION TO BE PROVIDED BY WAY OF NOTES TO THE ACCOUNTS.

2.17 THE **DIRECTORS** OF THE COMPANY MUST ADOPT THE SAME FORMAT IN PREPARING THE ACCOUNTS FOR SUBSEQUENT **FINANCIAL YEARS** OF THE COMPANY UNLESS IN THEIR OPINION THERE ARE SPECIAL REASONS FOR A CHANGE. PARTICULARS OF ANY CHANGE IN THE FORMAT ADOPTED IN A COMPANY'S PROFIT AND LOSS ACCOUNT OR BALANCE SHEET MUST BE DISCLOSED, AND THE REASONS FOR THE CHANGE MUST BE EXPLAINED IN A NOTE TO THE ACCOUNTS IN WHICH THE NEW FORMAT IS FIRST ADOPTED.

2.18 WHERE COMPLIANCE WITH THE PROVISIONS OF COMPANIES LEGISLATION AS TO THE MATTERS TO BE INCLUDED IN A COMPANY'S INDIVIDUAL ACCOUNTS OR IN NOTES TO THOSE ACCOUNTS WOULD NOT BE SUFFICIENT TO GIVE A TRUE AND FAIR VIEW, THE NECESSARY ADDITIONAL INFORMATION MUST BE GIVEN IN THE ACCOUNTS OR IN A NOTE TO THEM.

2.19 ANY ITEM REQUIRED TO BE SHOWN IN THE ACCOUNTS MAY BE SHOWN IN GREATER DETAIL THAN REQUIRED BY THE FORMAT ADOPTED. THE ACCOUNTS MAY INCLUDE AN ITEM REPRESENTING OR COVERING THE AMOUNT OF ANY ASSET OR LIABILITY, INCOME OR EXPENDITURE NOT OTHERWISE COVERED BY ANY OF THE ITEMS LISTED IN THE FORMAT ADOPTED*.

2.20 ITEMS LISTED IN THE FORMATS MUST NOT BE INCLUDED IF THERE IS NO AMOUNT TO BE SHOWN FOR THAT ITEM IN RESPECT OF THE **FINANCIAL YEAR** TO WHICH THE ACCOUNTS RELATE AND FOR THE IMMEDIATELY PRECEDING **FINANCIAL YEAR**.

2.21 IN PREPARING THE BALANCE SHEET OR PROFIT AND LOSS ACCOUNT, THE **DIRECTORS** MUST ADAPT THE ARRANGEMENT, HEADINGS AND SUBHEADINGS OF ITEMS TO WHICH AN ARABIC NUMBER IS ASSIGNED IN THE FORMATS, WHERE THE SPECIAL NATURE OF THE COMPANY'S BUSINESS REQUIRES SUCH ADAPTATION.

**PRELIMINARY EXPENSES, EXPENSES OF AND COMMISSION ON ANY ISSUE OF SHARES OR DEBENTURES AND COSTS OF RESEARCH SHALL NOT BE TREATED AS ASSETS.*

ITEMS TO WHICH ARABIC NUMBERS ARE ASSIGNED IN ANY OF THE FORMATS MAY BE COMBINED FOR ANY **FINANCIAL YEAR** IF: 2.22

(A) THEIR INDIVIDUAL AMOUNTS ARE NOT MATERIAL TO ASSESSING THE STATE OF AFFAIRS OR PROFIT AND LOSS OF THE COMPANY FOR THAT YEAR; OR
(B) THEIR COMBINATION FACILITATES THAT ASSESSMENT OF THE BALANCE SHEET OR PROFIT AND LOSS ACCOUNT. WHERE THIS APPLIES, THE INDIVIDUAL AMOUNTS OF ANY ITEMS WHICH HAVE BEEN COMBINED MUST BE DISCLOSED IN A NOTE TO THE ACCOUNTS.

Corresponding amounts for the previous accounting period shall be shown for every item disclosed in the balance sheet, profit and loss account and notes to the financial statements. Where there is no amount to be shown for an item in the balance sheet or profit and loss account for the current accounting period but a corresponding amount can be shown for the previous accounting period, the corresponding amount shall be shown. Where a corresponding amount is not comparable with that for the current accounting period, it shall be adjusted and particulars of the adjustment and the reasons for it shall be disclosed in a note to the financial statements. Corresponding amounts are not required in relation to any amounts stated in the notes to the financial statements for the items listed below: 2.23

(a) details of additions, disposals, revaluations, transfers and cumulative depreciation of fixed assets;
(b) transfers to or from reserves and provisions and the source and application of any transfers;
(c) details of a company's shareholdings in subsidiary undertakings and;
(d) details of a company's significant holdings in undertakings other than subsidiary undertakings.

IF NOT GIVEN IN THE COMPANY'S ACCOUNTS THERE MUST BE STATED BY WAY OF A NOTE TO THOSE ACCOUNTS ANY AMOUNT SET ASIDE OR PROPOSED TO BE SET ASIDE, OR WITHDRAWN OR PROPOSED TO BE WITHDRAWN FROM RESERVES. FOR EACH RESERVE DISCLOSED SEPARATELY IN THE ACCOUNTS, THE FOLLOWING INFORMATION MUST BE PROVIDED: 2.24

(A) THE AMOUNT OF THE RESERVE AT THE BEGINNING AND THE END OF THE **FINANCIAL YEAR**;
(B) ANY AMOUNTS TRANSFERRED TO OR FROM THE RESERVES DURING THE YEAR; AND
(C) THE SOURCE AND APPLICATION OF THE AMOUNTS TRANSFERRED.

FOR THE AGGREGATE OF ALL ITEMS SHOWN AS CREDITORS IN THE BALANCE SHEET, THE AGGREGATE OF THE AMOUNTS WHICH FALL DUE FOR PAYMENT MORE THAN FIVE YEARS AFTER THE END OF THE CURRENT PERIOD MUST BE DISCLOSED. AMOUNTS PAYABLE OR REPAYABLE BY INSTALMENTS AND THOSE PAYABLE OR REPAYABLE OTHERWISE THAN BY INSTALMENTS MUST BE SEPARATELY DISCLOSED. 2.25

FOR EACH ITEM SHOWN UNDER CREDITORS, THE AGGREGATE AMOUNT OF ANY DEBTS INCLUDED WHERE ANY SECURITY HAS BEEN GIVEN BY THE COMPANY MUST BE DISCLOSED. 2.26

Balance sheet format*

2.27 THE BALANCE SHEET MUST SHOW THE ITEMS LISTED IN THE ORDER, AND UNDER THE HEADINGS AND SUB-HEADINGS, SHOWN IN THE FORMAT BELOW†.

BALANCE SHEET FORMAT‡

A. CALLED UP SHARE CAPITAL NOT PAID

B. FIXED ASSETS
- I. INTANGIBLE ASSETS
  1. GOODWILL
  2. OTHER INTANGIBLE ASSETS
- II. TANGIBLE ASSETS
  1. LAND AND BUILDINGS
  2. PLANT AND MACHINERY ETC
- III. INVESTMENTS
  1. SHARES IN GROUP UNDERTAKINGS AND PARTICIPATING INTERESTS
  2. LOANS TO GROUP UNDERTAKINGS AND UNDERTAKINGS IN WHICH THE COMPANY HAS A PARTICIPATING INTEREST
  3. OTHER INVESTMENTS OTHER THAN LOANS
  4. OTHER INVESTMENTS

C. CURRENT ASSETS
- I. STOCKS
  1. STOCKS
  2. PAYMENTS ON ACCOUNT
- II. DEBTORS§
  1. TRADE DEBTORS
  2. AMOUNTS OWED BY GROUP UNDERTAKINGS AND UNDERTAKINGS IN WHICH THE COMPANY HAS A PARTICIPATING INTEREST
  3. OTHER DEBTORS
- III. INVESTMENTS
  1. SHARES IN GROUP UNDERTAKINGS
  2. OTHER INVESTMENTS
- IV. CASH AT BANK AND IN HAND

D. PREPAYMENTS AND ACCRUED INCOME¶¶

E. CREDITORS: AMOUNTS FALLING DUE WITHIN ONE YEAR
  1. BANK LOANS AND OVERDRAFTS
  2. TRADE CREDITORS

**An alternative format is available under companies legislation and may be adopted.*

†*Note: this does not mean that the items, headings and sub-headings need be identified by the letters and numbers assigned to them in the format.*

‡*There are certain differences in the format requirements for the balance sheet under companies legislation in the Republic of Ireland. The format requirements are contained in Part 1 of the Schedule to the Companies (Amendment) Act 1986 with references available in the derivation tables on the ASB website.*

§*THE AMOUNT FALLING DUE AFTER MORE THAN ONE YEAR MUST BE SHOWN SEPARATELY FOR EACH ITEM INCLUDED UNDER DEBTORS UNLESS THE AGGREGATE AMOUNT OF DEBTORS FALLING DUE AFTER MORE THAN ONE YEAR IS DISCLOSED IN THE NOTES TO THE ACCOUNTS.*

¶¶*THIS ITEM MAY ALTERNATIVELY BE INCLUDED UNDER ITEM C.II.3.*

3. AMOUNTS OWED TO GROUP UNDERTAKINGS AND UNDERTAKINGS IN WHICH THE COMPANY HAS A PARTICIPATING INTEREST
4. OTHER CREDITORS*

F. NET CURRENT ASSETS/LIABILITIES†

G. TOTAL ASSETS LESS CURRENT LIABILITIES

H. CREDITORS: AMOUNTS FALLING DUE AFTER MORE THAN ONE YEAR
1. BANK LOANS AND OVERDRAFTS
2. TRADE CREDITORS
3. AMOUNTS OWED TO GROUP UNDERTAKINGS AND UNDERTAKINGS IN WHICH THE COMPANY HAS A PARTICIPATING INTEREST
4. OTHER CREDITORS

I. PROVISIONS FOR LIABILITIES

J. ACCRUALS AND DEFERRED INCOME ‡

K. CAPITAL AND RESERVES
I. CALLED UP SHARE CAPITAL
II. SHARE PREMIUM ACCOUNT
III. REVALUATION RESERVE
IV. OTHER RESERVES
V. PROFIT AND LOSS ACCOUNT

Profit and loss account formats§

THE FORMAT OF THE PROFIT AND LOSS ACCOUNT MUST COMPLY WITH ONE OF THE FORMATS SET OUT BELOW. 2.28

THE ACCOUNT MUST SHOW THE ITEMS LISTED IN THE ORDER, AND UNDER THE HEADINGS AND SUB-HEADINGS, SHOWN IN THE FORMATS SET OUT BELOW¶¶. 2.29

PROFIT AND LOSS ACCOUNT FORMAT 1||

1. TURNOVER
2. COST OF SALES**
3. GROSS PROFIT OR LOSS
4. DISTRIBUTION COSTS
5. ADMINISTRATIVE EXPENSES
6. OTHER OPERATING INCOME

**ITEMS E4, H4 AND J: THERE MUST BE SHOWN SEPARATELY THE AMOUNT OF ANY CONVERTIBLE LOANS AND THE AMOUNT OF CREDITORS IN RESPECT OF TAXATION AND SOCIAL SECURITY.*

†IN DETERMINING THE AMOUNT TO BE SHOWN UNDER THIS ITEM ANY PREPAYMENTS AND ACCRUED INCOME MUST BE TAKEN INTO ACCOUNT.

‡THIS ITEM MAY ALTERNATIVELY BE INCLUDED UNDER ITEM E4 OR H4 OR BOTH (AS THE CASE MAY REQUIRE)

§Alternative formats are available under companies legislation and may be adopted.

¶¶Note, this does not mean that the items, headings and sub-headings need be identified by the letters and numbers assigned to them in the formats.

||There are certain differences in the format requirements for the profit and loss account under companies legislation in the Republic of Ireland. The format requirements are contained in Part 1 of the Schedule to the Companies (Amendment) Act 1986. References are available in the derivation tables on the ASB website.

***COST OF SALES, DISTRIBUTION COSTS AND ADMINISTRATIVE EXPENSES SHALL INCLUDE THE PROVISIONS FOR DEPRECIATION AND DIMINUTIONS IN VALUE OF ASSETS. THESE AMOUNTS SHALL ALSO BE SEPARATELY DISCLOSED IN A NOTE TO THE ACCOUNTS.*

7. Income from shares in group undertakings
8. Income from participating interests
9. Income from other fixed asset investments
10. Other interest receivable and similar income
11. Amounts written off investments
12. Interest payable and similar charges
12A. Profit or loss on ordinary activities before taxation
13. Tax on profit or loss on ordinary activities
14. Profit or loss on ordinary activities after taxation*
19. Other taxes not shown under the above items
20. Profit or loss for the financial year

PROFIT AND LOSS ACCOUNT FORMAT 2

1. Turnover
2. Change in stocks of finished goods and in work in progress
3. Own work capitalised
4. Other operating income
5. a. Raw materials and consumables
   b. Other external charges
6. Staff costs:
   a. wages and salaries
   b. social security costs
   c. other pension costs
7. a. Depreciation and other amounts written off tangible and intangible fixed assets
   b. Exceptional amounts written off current assets
8. Other operating charges
9. Income from shares in group undertakings
10. Income from participating interests
11. Income from other fixed asset investments
12. Other interest receivable and similar income
13. Amounts written off investments
14. Interest payable and similar charges
14A. Profit or loss on ordinary activities before taxation
15. Tax on profit or loss on ordinary activities
16. Profit or loss on ordinary activities after taxation†
21. Other taxes not shown under the above items
22. Profit or loss for the financial year

Approval and signing of accounts

2.30 A company's annual accounts must be approved by the board of **directors** and signed on behalf of the board by a director of the company. The signature must be on the company's balance sheet. The date on which the financial statements are approved by the board of **directors** shall be disclosed in the financial statements. The balance sheet must contain, in a prominent position above the signature, a

**Extraordinary items, which are extremely rare, shall be shown separately after the profit or loss on ordinary activities after taxation.*

†*Extraordinary items, which are extremely rare, shall be shown separately after the profit or loss on ordinary activities after taxation.*

STATEMENT THAT THE ACCOUNTS HAVE BEEN PREPARED IN ACCORDANCE WITH THE SPECIAL PROVISIONS IN PART 15 OF THE COMPANIES ACT 2006 RELATING TO SMALL COMPANIES.

EVERY COPY OF THE BALANCE SHEET WHICH IS PUBLISHED BY OR ON BEHALF OF THE BOARD MUST STATE THE NAME OF THE PERSON WHO SIGNED THE BALANCE SHEET ON BEHALF OF THE BOARD. **2.31**

THE COPY OF THE COMPANY'S BALANCE SHEET WHICH IS DELIVERED TO THE REGISTRAR MUST STATE THE NAME OF THE PERSON WHO SIGNED IT ON BEHALF OF THE BOARD. **2.32**

IF ANNUAL ACCOUNTS ARE APPROVED WHICH DO NOT COMPLY WITH THE REQUIREMENTS OF THE COMPANIES ACT, EVERY DIRECTOR OF THE COMPANY WHO KNOWS THAT THEY DO NOT COMPLY OR IS RECKLESS AS TO WHETHER THEY COMPLY COMMITS AN OFFENCE AND IS LIABLE TO A FINE. FOR THIS PURPOSE EVERY DIRECTOR OF THE COMPANY AT THE TIME THE ACCOUNTS ARE APPROVED SHALL BE TAKEN TO BE A PARTY TO THEIR APPROVAL UNLESS HE SHOWS THAT HE TOOK ALL REASONABLE STEPS TO SECURE COMPLIANCE WITH THOSE REQUIREMENTS OR, AS THE CASE MAY BE, PREVENT THEIR BEING APPROVED. **2.33**

IF A COPY OF THE BALANCE SHEET – **2.34**

(A) IS LAID BEFORE THE COMPANY, OR OTHERWISE CIRCULATED, PUBLISHED OR ISSUED, WITHOUT THE BALANCE SHEET HAVING BEEN SIGNED OR WITHOUT THE REQUIRED STATEMENT OF THE SIGNATORY'S NAME BEING INCLUDED, OR

(B) IS DELIVERED TO THE REGISTRAR WITHOUT BEING SIGNED,

EVERY PERSON WHO WAS A DIRECTOR OF THE COMPANY COMMITS AN OFFENCE AND IS LIABLE TO A FINE.

Delivery to the registrar

THE COPY OF THE FINANCIAL STATEMENTS DELIVERED TO THE REGISTRAR MUST STATE IN A PROMINENT POSITION THE REGISTERED NUMBER OF THE COMPANY, BE SIGNED BY, AND STATE THE NAME OF, THE **DIRECTORS** WHO SIGNED ON BEHALF OF THE BOARD AND REGISTERED AUDITORS AS APPROPRIATE. **2.35**

THE FINANCIAL STATEMENTS MUST ALSO CONTAIN A STATEMENT IN A PROMINENT POSITION ON THE BALANCE SHEET THAT THEY HAVE BEEN PREPARED IN ACCORDANCE WITH THE SPECIAL PROVISIONS IN PART 15 OF THE COMPANIES ACT 2006 RELATING TO SMALL COMPANIES. **2.36**

Exemptions from audit

WHERE A COMPANY MEETS THE CONDITIONS FOR EXEMPTION FROM AUDIT, AND HAS TAKEN ADVANTAGE OF THAT EXEMPTION, THE BALANCE SHEET MUST CONTAIN A STATEMENT BY THE **DIRECTORS** THAT: **2.37**

(A) FOR THE YEAR IN QUESTION, THE COMPANY WAS ENTITLED TO EXEMPTION (UNDER SECTIONS 475 AND 477 OF THE COMPANIES ACT 2006);

(B) NO MEMBER OR MEMBERS ELIGIBLE TO DO SO HAVE DEPOSITED A NOTICE REQUESTING AN AUDIT WITHIN THE SPECIFIED TIME PERIOD; AND

(C) THE **DIRECTORS** ACKNOWLEDGE THEIR RESPONSIBILITIES FOR COMPLYING WITH THE REQUIREMENTS OF THE 2006 COMPANIES ACT WITH RESPECT TO ACCOUNTING RECORDS AND FOR PREPARING ACCOUNTS WHICH GIVE A TRUE AND FAIR VIEW OF THE STATE OF AFFAIRS OF THE COMPANY AS AT THE END OF THE **FINANCIAL YEAR** AND OF ITS PROFIT OR LOSS FOR THE **FINANCIAL YEAR** IN ACCORDANCE WITH THE REQUIREMENTS OF SECTIONS 394 AND 395 (DUTY TO PREPARE INDIVIDUAL COMPANY

ACCOUNTS AND APPLICABLE ACCOUNTING FRAMEWORK), AND WHICH OTHERWISE COMPLY WITH THE REQUIREMENTS OF THE COMPANIES ACT 2006 RELATING TO ACCOUNTS, SO FAR AS APPLICABLE TO THE COMPANY.

2.38 WHERE THE **DIRECTORS** HAVE TAKEN ADVANTAGE OF THE EXEMPTION FROM AUDIT DUE TO THE FACT THAT THE COMPANY IS DORMANT, AND THE COMPANY HAS DURING THE **FINANCIAL YEAR** IN QUESTION ACTED AS AN AGENT FOR ANY PERSON, THE FACT THAT IT HAS SO ACTED MUST BE STATED.

Liability Limitation Agreement

2.39 WHERE EXEMPTION FROM AUDIT IS NOT AVAILABLE, OR THE DIRECTORS HAVE NOT TAKEN ADVANTAGE OF THE EXEMPTION FROM AUDIT AND THE COMPANY HAS ENTERED INTO A LIABILITY LIMITATION AGREEMENT WITH ITS AUDITORS, THE NOTES TO THE ACCOUNTS MUST DISCLOSE THE PRINCIPAL TERMS OF THE AGREEMENT AND EITHER THE DATE OF THE RESOLUTION APPROVING THE AGREEMENT OR THE AGREEMENT'S PRINCIPAL TERMS OR THE DATE OF THE RESOLUTION WAIVING THE NEED FOR SUCH APPROVAL.

3 PROFIT AND LOSS ACCOUNT

General

3.1 All gains and losses **recognised** in the financial statements for the period shall be included in the profit and loss account or the statement of **total recognised gains and losses**. ONLY PROFITS THAT ARE REALISED AT THE BALANCE SHEET DATE MUST BE INCLUDED IN THE PROFIT AND LOSS ACCOUNT. ALL LIABILITIES WHICH HAVE ARISEN IN RESPECT OF THE PERIOD OR IN RESPECT OF A PREVIOUS FINANCIAL YEAR, MUST BE TAKEN INTO ACCOUNT, INCLUDING THOSE WHICH ONLY BECOME APPARENT BETWEEN THE BALANCE SHEET DATE AND THE DATE ON WHICH IT IS SIGNED.

3.2 Gains and losses may be excluded from the profit and loss account only if they are specifically permitted or required to be taken direct to reserves by this standard or by **companies legislation** or equivalent legislation.

3.3 WHERE AN AMOUNT RELATING TO ANY PRECEDING **FINANCIAL YEAR** IS INCLUDED IN THE PROFIT AND LOSS ACCOUNT, THE EFFECT OF ITS INCLUSION MUST BE STATED.

3.4 IF THE COMPANY HAS SUPPLIED GEOGRAPHICAL MARKETS OUTSIDE THE UNITED KINGDOM DURING THE **FINANCIAL YEAR**, THE PERCENTAGE OF TURNOVER THAT IS ATTRIBUTABLE TO THOSE MARKETS MUST BE SEPARATELY DISCLOSED. IN ANALYSING THE SOURCE OF TURNOVER, REGARD MUST BE PAID TO THE MANNER IN WHICH THE COMPANY'S ACTIVITIES ARE ORGANISED.

Exceptional items

3.5 All **exceptional items**, other than those included in the items listed in the next paragraph, shall be credited or charged in arriving at the profit or loss on **ordinary activities** by inclusion under the statutory format headings to which they relate. The amount of each **exceptional item**, either individually or as an aggregate of items of a similar type, shall be disclosed separately by way of a note, or on the face of the profit and loss account if that degree of prominence is necessary in order to give a true and fair view. An adequate description of each **exceptional item** shall be given to enable its nature to be understood. THE EFFECT MUST BE STATED OF ANY TRANSACTIONS

THAT ARE EXCEPTIONAL BY VIRTUE OF SIZE OR INCIDENCE THOUGH THEY FALL WITHIN THE ORDINARY ACTIVITIES OF THE COMPANY.

The following items, including provisions in respect of such items, shall be shown separately on the face of the profit and loss account after operating profit (which is normally profit before income from shares in group undertakings) and before interest: **3.6**

(a) profits or losses on the sale or termination of an operation;
(b) costs of a fundamental reorganisation or restructuring having a material effect on the nature and focus of the reporting entity's operations; and
(c) profits or losses on the disposal of fixed assets.

Profit or loss on disposal

The profit or loss on the disposal of an asset shall be accounted for in the profit and loss account of the period in which the disposal occurs as the difference between the net sale proceeds and the net carrying amount, whether carried at historical cost (less any provisions made) or at a valuation. Profit or loss on disposal of a previously acquired business shall include the attributable amount of **purchased goodwill** that has previously been eliminated against reserves as a matter of **accounting policy** and has not previously been charged in the profit and loss account. **3.7**

Disclosure of auditor remuneration

WHERE A SMALL COMPANY CHOOSES NOT TO TAKE ADVANTAGE OF THE EXEMPTION IN THE 2006 COMPANIES ACT RELATING TO THE AUDIT OF ACCOUNTS, THE REMUNERATION OF THE COMPANY'S AUDITOR, INCLUDING SUMS PAID IN RESPECT OF EXPENSES, MUST BE DISCLOSED IN A NOTE TO THE ACCOUNTS, INCLUDING THE NATURE AND ESTIMATED MONETARY VALUE OF ANY BENEFITS IN KIND. WHERE MORE THAN ONE PERSON HAS BEEN APPOINTED AS A COMPANY'S AUDITOR IN RESPECT OF THE PERIOD TO WHICH THE ACCOUNTS RELATE, SEPARATE DISCLOSURE IS REQUIRED IN RESPECT OF THE REMUNERATION OF EACH SUCH PERSON. **3.8**

4 REVENUE RECOGNITION

Basic principles*

A seller recognises revenue under an **exchange transaction** with a customer, when, and to the extent that, it obtains the **right to consideration** in exchange for its **performance**. At the same time, it typically recognises a new asset, usually a debtor. **4.1**

When a seller receives payment from a customer in advance of **performance**, it recognises a liability equal to the amount received, representing its **obligation** under the contract. When the seller obtains the **right to consideration** through its **performance**, that liability is reduced and the amount of the reduction in the liability is simultaneously reported as revenue. **4.2**

A seller may obtain a **right to consideration** when some, but not all, of its contractual **obligations** have been fulfilled. Where a seller has partially performed its contractual **obligations**, it recognises revenue to the extent that it has obtained the **right to consideration** through its **performance**. **4.3**

**Guidance on the practical considerations for recognising revenue in respect of service contracts, bill and hold arrangements, presentation of turnover as principal or as agent and sales with rights of return is given in Appendix III.*

4.4 Revenue shall be measured at the **fair value** of the **right to consideration**. Subject to paragraphs 4.5-4.6 or other evidence to the contrary, this will normally be the price specified in the contractual arrangement, net of discounts, value added tax and similar sales taxes.

4.5 Where the effect of the time value of money is material to reported revenue, the amount of revenue **recognised** shall be the present value of the cash inflows expected to be received from the customer in settlement. The unwinding of the discount shall be credited to finance income as this represents a gain from a financing transaction.

4.6 Where at the time revenue is **recognised** on a transaction there is a significant risk that there will be default on the amount of consideration due and the effect is material to reported revenue, an adjustment to the price specified in the contractual arrangement will be necessary to arrive at the amount of revenue to be **recognised**.

4.7 Subsequent adjustments to a debtor as a result of changes in the time value of money and credit risk shall not be included within revenue.

Turnover

4.8 Turnover (which may be described as 'sales' in a seller's financial statements) is the revenue resulting from **exchange transactions** under which a seller supplies to customers the goods or services that it is in business to provide.*

4.9 A seller may enter into other **exchange transactions** such as the sale of fixed assets. Such transactions do not normally give rise to turnover, as they do not normally fall within the class of transactions set out in paragraph 4.8.

Contracts for services

4.10 Where there are distinguishable phases of a single contract it may be appropriate to account for the contract as two or more separate transactions, provided the value of each phase can be reliably estimated.

4.11 Contracts for services should not be accounted for as long-term contracts unless they involve the provision of a single service, or a number of services that constitute a single project.

4.12 A contract for services should be accounted for as a long-term contract where contract activity falls into different accounting periods and it is concluded that the effect is material. In determining whether contracts should be accounted for as long-term contracts, the aggregate effect of all such contracts on the financial statements as a whole should be considered.

4.13 Where the substance of a contract is that the seller's contractual obligations are performed gradually over time, revenue should be recognised as contract activity progresses to reflect the seller's partial performance of its contractual obligations. The amount of revenue should reflect the accrual of the right to consideration as contract activity progresses by reference to value of the work performed.

4.14 Where the substance of a contract is that a right to consideration does not arise until the occurrence of a critical event, revenue is not recognised until that event occurs. This only applies where the right to consideration is conditional or contingent on a

**These transactions are often referred to as being part of the seller's operating activities.*

specified future event or outcome, the occurrence of which is outside the control of the seller.

The amount of revenue recognised on any contract for services should reflect any uncertainties as to the amount that the customer will accept and pay. 4.15

5 STATEMENT OF TOTAL RECOGNISED GAINS AND LOSSES

A primary statement shall be presented, with the same prominence as the profit and loss account, showing the **total of recognised gains and losses** and its components. The components shall be the gains and losses that are **recognised** in the period insofar as they are attributable to shareholders, excluding transactions with shareholders.* Where the only **recognised** gains and losses are the results included in the profit and loss account no separate statement to this effect need be made. 5.1

6 FIXED ASSETS AND GOODWILL

Disclosure

THE FOLLOWING INFORMATION MUST BE PROVIDED FOR ALL FIXED ASSETS AND GOODWILL: 6.1

(A) THE COST OR VALUATION AT THE BEGINNING AND THE END OF THE YEAR; AND
(B) THE EFFECT OF ANY:

- (I) REVALUATION MADE DURING THE YEAR;
- (II) ACQUISITIONS DURING THE YEAR;
- (III) DISPOSALS DURING THE YEAR; AND
- (IV) TRANSFERS DURING THE YEAR.

THE FOLLOWING INFORMATION MUST BE PROVIDED IN RESPECT OF PROVISIONS FOR DEPRECIATION OR DIMINUTION IN VALUE: 6.2

(A) THE CUMULATIVE AMOUNT OF SUCH PROVISIONS AS AT THE BEGINNING AND END OF THE YEAR;
(B) THE AMOUNT OF ANY SUCH PROVISIONS MADE DURING THE YEAR;
(C) THE AMOUNT OF ANY ADJUSTMENTS MADE ON DISPOSAL DURING THE YEAR; AND
(D) THE AMOUNT OF ANY OTHER ADJUSTMENTS MADE DURING THE YEAR.

Research and development

The cost of fixed assets acquired or constructed in order to provide facilities for **research and development** activities over a number of accounting periods shall be capitalised and written off over their useful lives through the profit and loss account. 6.3

Expenditure on **pure** and **applied research** shall be written off in the period of expenditure through the profit and loss account. 6.4

Development expenditure shall be written off in the period of expenditure except in the following circumstances when it may be deferred to future periods: 6.5

(a) there is a clearly defined project; and
(b) the related expenditure is separately identifiable; and
(c) the outcome of such a project has been assessed with reasonable certainty as to:

- (i) its technical feasibility; and

**An illustration of a statement of total recognised gains and losses is given in Appendix III.*

(ii) its ultimate commercial viability considered in the light of factors such as likely market conditions (including competing products), public opinion, consumer and environmental legislation; and

(d) the aggregate of the deferred **development** costs, any further **development** costs, and related production, selling and administration costs is reasonably expected to be exceeded by related future sales or other revenues; and

(e) adequate resources exist, or are reasonably expected to be available, to enable the project to be completed and to provide any consequential increases in working capital.

6.6 In the foregoing circumstances **development** expenditure may be deferred to the extent that its recovery can be reasonably regarded as assured.

6.7 If an **accounting policy** of deferral of **development** expenditure is adopted, it shall be applied to all **development** projects that meet the criteria in paragraph 6.5.

6.8 If **development** costs are deferred to future periods, they shall be amortised. The amortisation shall commence with the commercial production or application of the product, service, process or system and shall be allocated on a systematic basis to each accounting period, by reference to either the sale or use of the product, service, process or system or the period over which these are expected to be sold or used.

6.9 Deferred **development** expenditure for each product shall be reviewed at the end of each accounting period and where the circumstances that justified the deferral of expenditure no longer apply, or are considered doubtful, the expenditure, to the extent to which it is considered to be irrecoverable, shall be written off immediately project by project.

6.10 The amount of deferred **development** expenditure carried forward at the beginning and end of the period shall be disclosed under **intangible assets** in the balance sheet or in the notes to the balance sheet. THE REASON FOR CAPITALISING THESE COSTS AND THE PERIOD OVER WHICH THEY ARE BEING DEPRECIATED MUST BE DISCLOSED IN A NOTE TO THE ACCOUNTS. IF **DEVELOPMENT** COSTS ARE NOT TREATED AS A REALISED LOSS, THIS MUST BE STATED TOGETHER WITH AN EXPLANATION OF THE CIRCUMSTANCES RELIED UPON BY THE **DIRECTORS** TO JUSTIFY THEIR DECISION.

Other intangible assets and goodwill

6.11 Positive **purchased goodwill** and purchased **intangible assets** shall be capitalised. Internally generated goodwill and intangible assets shall not be capitalised.

6.12 An **intangible asset** purchased with a business shall be **recognised** separately from the **purchased goodwill** if its value can be measured reliably.

6.13 Capitalised goodwill and **intangible assets** shall be **depreciated** on a straight-line (or more appropriate) basis over their **useful economic lives**, which shall not exceed 20 years. THE PERIOD CHOSEN FOR DEPRECIATING GOODWILL AND THE REASONS FOR CHOOSING THAT PERIOD MUST BE DISCLOSED IN A NOTE TO THE ACCOUNTS.*

****Editor's note**: With effect for accounting periods beginning on or after 1 January 2015 this is replaced with:*

Capitalised goodwill and intangible assets shall be considered to have a finite useful life, and shall be depreciated on a straight-line (or more appropriate) basis over their useful economic lives. If an entity is unable to make a reliable estimate of the useful life of goodwill or intangible assets, the life shall be presumed not to exceed five years. THE PERIOD CHOSEN FOR DEPRECIATING GOODWILL AND THE REASONS FOR CHOOSING THAT PERIOD MUST BE DISCLOSED IN A NOTE TO THE ACCOUNTS.

The **residual value** assigned to goodwill shall be zero. A higher **residual value** may be assigned to an **intangible asset** only when this value can be established reliably, for example when it has been agreed contractually. **6.14**

Useful economic lives shall be reviewed at the end of each reporting period and revised if necessary, subject to the constraint that the revised life shall not exceed 20 years from the date of acquisition. The carrying amount at the date of revision shall be **depreciated** over the revised estimate of remaining **useful economic life**. **6.15**

Goodwill and **intangible assets** shall not be revalued. **6.16**

If an acquisition appears to give rise to negative goodwill, **fair values** shall be checked to ensure that those of the acquired **assets** have not been overstated and those of the acquired **liabilities** have not been understated. Once this has been done, remaining negative goodwill up to the **fair values** of the non-monetary **assets** acquired shall be released in the profit and loss account over the lives of those assets. Any additional negative goodwill shall be **recognised** in the profit and loss account over the period expected to benefit from it. The amount of negative goodwill on the balance sheet and the period(s) in which it is being written back shall be disclosed. **6.17**

Tangible fixed assets

Paragraphs 6.19-6.26 apply to all **tangible fixed assets** other than **investment properties**. **6.18**

A **tangible fixed asset** shall initially be measured at its cost, then written down to its **recoverable amount** if necessary. The initial carrying amount of a **tangible fixed asset** received as a gift or donation by a charity shall be its current value, i.e. the lower of replacement cost and **recoverable amount**, at the date it is received.* WHERE THERE IS NO RECORD OF THE PURCHASE PRICE OR PRODUCTION COST OF AN ASSET, OR ANY SUCH RECORD CANNOT BE OBTAINED WITHOUT UNREASONABLE EXPENSE OR DELAY, THE VALUE ASCRIBED MUST BE THE EARLIEST AVAILABLE RECORD OF ITS VALUE. PARTICULARS MUST BE GIVEN OF ANY CASE WHERE THE PURCHASE PRICE OR PRODUCTION COST OF ANY ASSET IS FOR THE FIRST TIME DETERMINED IN THIS WAY. **6.19**

Costs that are directly attributable to bringing the **tangible fixed asset** into working condition for its intended use shall be included in its measurement. Other costs shall not be included. An entity may adopt an **accounting policy** of capitalising **finance costs** (such as interest). Where such a policy is adopted, **finance costs** that are directly attributable to the construction of **tangible fixed assets** shall be capitalised as part of the cost of those assets. The total amount of **finance costs** capitalised during a period shall not exceed the total amount of **finance costs** incurred during that period. WHERE APPLICABLE, THE NOTES TO THE ACCOUNTS MUST DISCLOSE THAT FINANCE COSTS ARE INCLUDED IN DETERMINING THE COST OF THE ASSET AND THE AMOUNT OF FINANCE COSTS SO INCLUDED. **6.20**

Capitalisation of directly attributable costs, including **finance costs**, shall be suspended during extended periods in which active **development** is interrupted. Capitalisation shall cease when substantially all the activities that are necessary to get the **tangible fixed asset** ready for use are complete, even if the asset has not yet been brought into use. **6.21**

**Generally, where issues of practicality or of cost-benefit arise, these will be addressed in the relevant sector-specific guidance and Statements of Recommended Practice (SORPs).*

6.22 Subsequent expenditure shall be capitalised only if:

(a) it enhances the economic benefits of a **tangible fixed asset** in excess of the previously assessed standard of performance (i.e. if it is an 'improvement'); or

(b) it replaces or restores a component that has been separately depreciated over its **useful economic life**.

Otherwise it shall be **recognised** in the profit and loss account as it is incurred.

6.23 Where an entity adopts an **accounting policy** of revaluation in respect of a **tangible fixed asset**, its carrying amount shall be its market value (or the best estimate thereof) as at the balance sheet date. Where the **directors** believe that market value is not an appropriate basis, current value (i.e. the lower of replacement cost and **recoverable amount**) may be used instead. Where a **tangible fixed asset** is revalued, all **tangible fixed assets** of the same class (i.e. having a similar nature, function or use in the business) shall be revalued, but a policy of revaluation need not be applied to all classes of **tangible fixed assets**.

6.24 It may be possible to establish with reasonable **reliability** the values of certain **tangible fixed assets**, other than properties, by reference to active second-hand markets or appropriate publicly available indices. For other **tangible fixed assets**, including properties, a valuation shall be performed by an experienced valuer (i.e. one who has recognised and relevant recent professional experience, and sufficient knowledge of the state of the market, in the location and category of the **tangible fixed asset** being valued) at least every five years. It shall be updated by an experienced valuer in the intervening years where it is likely that there has been a material change in value.*

6.25 Revaluation losses caused only by changing market prices shall be **recognised** in the statement of **total recognised gains and losses** until the carrying amount of the asset reaches its depreciated historical cost. Other revaluation losses shall be **recognised** in the profit and loss account.

6.26 Revaluation gains shall be **recognised** in the statement of **total recognised gains and losses**, except to the extent (after adjusting for subsequent **depreciation**) that they reverse revaluation losses on the same asset that were previously **recognised** in the profit and loss account. To that extent they shall be **recognised** in the profit and loss account. The adjustment for subsequent **depreciation** is to achieve the same overall effect that would have been reached had the original downward revaluation reflected in the profit and loss account not occurred.

6.27 WHERE TANGIBLE FIXED ASSETS HAVE BEEN REVALUED EITHER – THE COMPARABLE AMOUNTS DETERMINED UNDER THE HISTORICAL COST ACCOUNTING RULES (i.e. the aggregate historical cost amount that would have been included had the **assets** not been revalued, reflecting any write-downs to **recoverable amount** that would have been necessary); OR THE DIFFERENCES BETWEEN THOSE AMOUNTS AND THE CORRESPONDING AMOUNTS ACTUALLY SHOWN IN THE BALANCE SHEET MUST BE SHOWN SEPARATELY IN THE BALANCE SHEET OR IN A NOTE TO THE ACCOUNTS.

6.28 WHERE TANGIBLE FIXED ASSETS ARE CONSTANTLY BEING REPLACED AND THEIR VALUE IS NOT MATERIAL TO ASSESSING THE COMPANY'S STATE OF AFFAIRS AND THEIR QUANTITY, VALUE AND COMPOSITION ARE NOT SUBJECT TO MATERIAL VARIATION, THEY MAY BE INCLUDED AT A FIXED QUANTITY AND VALUE.

**Where, for cost/benefit reasons, alternative approaches are set out in relevant sector-specific guidance and SORPs, these may be adopted instead of the approach in paragraph 6.24.*

WHERE TANGIBLE FIXED ASSETS HAVE BEEN REVALUED, THE YEAR IN WHICH THEY WERE VALUED MUST BE DISCLOSED. IN THE CASE OF ASSETS THAT HAVE BEEN REVALUED DURING THE CURRENT **FINANCIAL YEAR**, THE NAMES OF THE PERSONS WHO VALUED THEM OR PARTICULARS OF THEIR QUALIFICATIONS FOR DOING SO AND THE BASES OF THE VALUATION MUST BE DISCLOSED. **6.29**

Investments

FIXED ASSET INVESTMENTS MUST INITIALLY BE MEASURED AT COST. ALTERNATIVELY, THEY MAY BE MEASURED AT A MARKET VALUE DETERMINED AS AT THE DATE OF THEIR LAST VALUATION OR ON ANY OTHER VALUE DETERMINED ON A BASIS WHICH APPEARS TO THE **DIRECTORS** TO BE APPROPRIATE IN THE CIRCUMSTANCES OF THE COMPANY (IN THE LATTER CASE, THE METHOD OF VALUATION ADOPTED AND OF THE REASONS FOR ADOPTING IT MUST BE DISCLOSED IN A NOTE TO THE ACCOUNTS). Gains and losses shall be **recognised** (in the profit and loss account or statement of **total recognised gains and losses**) using the same basis applied to **tangible fixed assets** in paragraphs 6.25 and 6.26 above. **6.30**

WHERE FIXED ASSET INVESTMENTS HAVE BEEN REVALUED EITHER – THE COMPARABLE AMOUNTS DETERMINED UNDER THE HISTORICAL COST ACCOUNTING RULES (i.e. the aggregate historical cost amount that would have been included had the **assets** not been revalued, reflecting any write-downs to **recoverable amount** that would have been necessary); OR THE DIFFERENCES BETWEEN THOSE AMOUNTS AND THE CORRESPONDING AMOUNTS ACTUALLY SHOWN IN THE BALANCE SHEET MUST BE SHOWN SEPARATELY IN THE BALANCE SHEET OR IN A NOTE TO THE ACCOUNTS. **6.31**

THE AGGREGATE AMOUNT OF LISTED INVESTMENTS INCLUDED UNDER EACH ITEM OF INVESTMENTS SHOWN IN THE BALANCE SHEET MUST BE DISCLOSED. FOR EACH ITEM WHICH INCLUDES LISTED INVESTMENTS, THE FOLLOWING MUST BE DISCLOSED: **6.32**

(A) THE AGGREGATE MARKET VALUE OF THE LISTED INVESTMENTS WHERE IT DIFFERS FROM THEIR BALANCE SHEET AMOUNT; AND

(B) BOTH THE MARKET VALUE AND THE STOCK EXCHANGE VALUE OF ANY INVESTMENTS, OF WHICH THE MARKET VALUE IS TAKEN AS BEING HIGHER THAN THE STOCK EXCHANGE VALUE.

WHERE THE COMPANY HAS AT THE END OF THE **FINANCIAL YEAR** A SIGNIFICANT HOLDING IN AN UNDERTAKING (WHICH IS NOT A SUBSIDIARY UNDERTAKING OF THE COMPANY) WHICH REPRESENTS 20% OR MORE OF THE NOMINAL VALUE OF ANY CLASS OF SHARES IN THE UNDERTAKING, OR MORE THAN 20% OF THE BOOK VALUE OF THE INVESTING COMPANY'S TOTAL ASSETS, THE FOLLOWING MUST BE STATED IN RELATION TO THAT UNDERTAKING:*†‡ **6.33**

**If the directors of the company are of opinion the number of undertakings in respect of which the company is required to disclose information is such that compliance would result in information of excessive length being given, the information need only be given in respect of the undertakings principally affecting the figures shown in the company's annual accounts. Where the disclosures are limited in this way, the notes shall include a statement that the information is given only with respect to such undertakings and full details must be annexed to the company's next annual return.*

†*INFORMATION NEED NOT BE DISCLOSED WITH RESPECT TO AN UNDERTAKING WHICH IS ESTABLISHED UNDER THE LAW OF A COUNTRY OUTSIDE THE UNITED KINGDOM OR CARRIES ON BUSINESS OUTSIDE THE UNITED KINGDOM, IF IN THE OPINION OF THE DIRECTORS OF THE COMPANY THE DISCLOSURE WOULD BE SERIOUSLY PREJUDICIAL TO THE BUSINESS OF THAT UNDERTAKING, OR TO THE BUSINESS OF THE COMPANY OR ANY OF ITS SUBSIDIARY UNDERTAKINGS, AND THE SECRETARY OF STATE AGREES THAT THE INFORMATION NEED NOT BE DISCLOSED. WHERE ADVANTAGE IS TAKEN OF THIS, THAT FACT SHALL BE STATED IN A NOTE TO THE COMPANY'S ANNUAL ACCOUNTS. THIS STATUTORY EXEMPTION IS NOT AVAILABLE IN THE REPUBLIC OF IRELAND.*

‡*Disclosure requirements for holdings in subsidiary undertakings are set out in paragraphs 15.17*

(A) THE NAME OF THE UNDERTAKING;

(B) IF THE UNDERTAKING IS INCORPORATED OUTSIDE THE UNITED KINGDOM, THE COUNTRY IN WHICH IT IS INCORPORATED;

(C) IF IT IS UNINCORPORATED, THE ADDRESS OF ITS PRINCIPAL PLACE OF BUSINESS;

(D) THE IDENTITY AND PROPORTION OF THE NOMINAL VALUE OF EACH CLASS OF SHARES HELD;

(E) THE AGGREGATE AMOUNT OF THE CAPITAL AND RESERVES OF THE UNDERTAKING AS AT THE END OF THE MOST RECENT **FINANCIAL YEAR** ENDING WITH OR BEFORE THAT OF THE INVESTING COMPANY; AND

(F) ITS PROFIT OR LOSS FOR THAT YEAR.

Revaluation reserve

6.34 GAINS AND LOSSES ARISING ON THE REVALUATION OF ASSETS that have been **recognised** in the statement of **total recognised gains and losses** MUST BE CREDITED, OR DEBITED, TO A SEPARATE REVALUATION RESERVE.

6.35 AMOUNTS MAY BE TRANSFERRED FROM THE REVALUATION RESERVE TO THE PROFIT AND LOSS ACCOUNT WHEN THEY ARE REALISED. For **tangible fixed assets**, this will normally result in an annual transfer from the revaluation reserve to the profit and loss account over the **useful economic life** of the **asset** (i.e. in line with the **depreciation** charge). Realisation may also occur on the eventual disposal of the **asset**.

6.36 THE TREATMENT FOR TAXATION PURPOSES OF AMOUNTS CREDITED OR DEBITED TO THE REVALUATION RESERVE MUST BE DISCLOSED IN A NOTE TO THE ACCOUNTS.

Depreciation

6.37 Paragraphs 6.38-6.43 apply to all **tangible fixed assets** other than **investment properties**.

6.38 The cost (or revalued amount) less estimated **residual value** of a **tangible fixed asset** shall be depreciated on a systematic basis over its **useful economic life**. The **depreciation** method used shall reflect as fairly as possible the pattern in which the asset's economic benefits are consumed by the entity. The **depreciation** charge for each period shall be **recognised** as an expense in the profit and loss account unless it is permitted to be included in the carrying amount of another **asset**.

6.39 Where a **tangible fixed asset** comprises two or more major components with substantially different **useful economic lives**, each component shall be accounted for separately for **depreciation** purposes and depreciated over its individual **useful economic life**. With certain exceptions, such as sites used for extractive purposes or landfill, land has an unlimited life and therefore is not depreciated.

6.40 The **useful economic lives** and **residual values** of **tangible fixed assets** shall be reviewed regularly and, when necessary, revised. On revision, the carrying amount of the **tangible fixed asset** at the date of revision less the revised **residual value** shall be depreciated over the revised remaining **useful economic life**.

6.41 A change from one method of providing **depreciation** to another is permissible only on the grounds that the new method will give a fairer presentation of the results and of the financial position. Such a change does not, however, constitute a change of **accounting policy**; the carrying amount of the **tangible fixed asset** is depreciated using the revised method over the remaining **useful economic life**, beginning in the period in which the change is made.

The following shall be disclosed in the financial statements for (1) land and buildings and (2) other **tangible fixed assets** in aggregate: 6.42

(a) the **depreciation** methods used;
(b) the **useful economic lives** or the **depreciation** rates used; and
(c) where material, the financial effect of a change during the period in either the estimate of **useful economic lives** or the estimate of **residual values**.

Where there has been a change in the **depreciation** method used, the effect, if material, shall be disclosed in the period of change. The reason for the change shall also be disclosed. 6.43

Write-downs to recoverable amount

Paragraphs 6.45-6.48 apply to capitalised goodwill and all fixed assets (i.e. **tangible fixed assets**, **intangible assets** and investments) except **investment properties** and financial instruments (other than investments in subsidiaries, associates and joint ventures). 6.44

Fixed assets and goodwill shall be carried in the balance sheet at no more than **recoverable amount**. If the net book amount of a fixed asset or goodwill is considered not to be recoverable in full at the balance sheet date (perhaps as a result of obsolescence or a fall in demand for a product), the net book amount shall be written down to the estimated **recoverable amount**, which shall then be written off over the remaining **useful economic life** of the asset.* 6.45

****Editor's note**: With effect for accounting periods beginning on or after 1 January 2015 this is replaced with:*

Fixed assets and goodwill shall be carried in the balance sheet at no more than recoverable amount. If the net book amount of a fixed asset or goodwill is considered not to be recoverable in full at the balance sheet date, the net book amount shall be written down to the estimated recoverable amount, which shall then be written off over the remaining useful economic life of the asset.

and the following paragraphs are added:

6.45A At each reporting date an assessment shall be carried out of whether there is any indication that an asset should be written down (ie whether its carrying amount is more than its recoverable amount). If any such indication exists, the recoverable amount of the asset shall be estimated. If there is no indication that an asset should be written down, it is not necessary to estimate the recoverable amount.

6.45B In assessing whether there is any indication that an asset should be written down, the following might be considered:

(a) During the period, an asset's market value has declined significantly more than would be expected as a result of the passage of time or normal use.
(b) Significant changes with an adverse effect on an asset, or the entity, have taken place during the period, or will take place in the near future, (for example external factors such as technological, market, economic or legal changes or internal factors such as the asset becoming idle, or plans to dispose of an asset before the previously expected date).
(c) Market interest rates have increased during the period, and those increases are likely to affect materially the asset's recoverable amount.
(d) Evidence is available of obsolescence or physical damage of an asset.
(e) Evidence is available from internal reporting that indicates that operating results or cash flows from the use of the asset are, or will be, worse than expected.

6.45C If there is an indication that an asset should be written down, this may indicate that the entity should review the remaining useful economic life, the depreciation method or the residual value of the asset and adjust it in accordance with paragraph 6.40 even if no loss is recognised for writing down the asset.

6.46 If the **recoverable amount** of a **tangible fixed asset** or investment subsequently increases as a result of a change in economic conditions or in the expected use of the asset, the net book amount shall be written back to the lower of **recoverable amount** and the amount at which the asset would have been recorded had the original write-down not been made.

6.47 If the **recoverable amount** of an **intangible asset** or capitalised goodwill subsequently increases, the net book amount shall be written back only if an external event caused the original write-down and subsequent external events clearly and demonstrably reverse the effects of that event in a way that was not foreseen when the original write-down was calculated.

6.48 Write-downs (and any reversals) to **recoverable amount** shall be charged (or credited) in the profit and loss account for the period. However, write-downs of revalued **tangible fixed assets** that reverse previous revaluation gains simply as a result of changing market prices shall instead be **recognised** in the statement of **total recognised gains and losses**, to the extent that the carrying amount of the asset is greater than its depreciated historical cost. ANY AMOUNTS WHICH ARE NOT SHOWN IN THE PROFIT AND LOSS ACCOUNT MUST BE DISCLOSED (EITHER SEPARATELY OR IN AGGREGATE) IN A NOTE TO THE ACCOUNTS.

6.49 WHERE FIXED ASSETS ARE NOT ACTUALLY REVALUED IN THE BALANCE SHEET BUT THEIR VALUE IS CONSIDERED BY THE **DIRECTORS**, A NOTE TO THE ACCOUNTS MUST STATE THE FOLLOWING:

(A) THAT THE **DIRECTORS** HAVE CONSIDERED THE VALUE OF SOME OR ALL OF THE FIXED ASSETS OF THE COMPANY, WITHOUT ACTUALLY REVALUING THOSE ASSETS;

(B) THAT THE **DIRECTORS** ARE SATISFIED THAT THE AGGREGATE VALUE OF THOSE ASSETS AT THE TIME IN QUESTION IS OR WAS NOT LESS THAN THE AGGREGATE AMOUNT AT WHICH THEY WERE THEN STATED IN THE COMPANY'S ACCOUNTS; AND

(C) THE ASSETS AFFECTED ARE ACCORDINGLY STATED IN THE ACCOUNTS ON THE BASIS THAT A REVALUATION OF THE COMPANY'S FIXED ASSETS TOOK PLACE AT THAT TIME.

Investment properties

6.50 **Investment properties** shall not be subject to periodic charges for **depreciation** except for properties held on lease, which shall be **depreciated** at least over the period when the unexpired term is 20 years or less.

6.51 **Investment properties** shall be included in the balance sheet at their market value and the carrying value shall be displayed prominently either on the face of the balance sheet or in the notes.

6.52 The names of the persons making the valuation, or particulars of their qualifications, shall be disclosed together with the bases of valuation used by them. If a person making a valuation is an employee or officer of the company or group that owns the property this fact shall be disclosed.

6.53 Changes in the market value of **investment properties** shall not be taken to the profit and loss account but shall be taken to the statement of **total recognised gains and losses** (being a movement on an investment revaluation reserve), unless a deficit (or its reversal) on an individual **investment property** is expected to be permanent, in which case it shall be charged (or credited) in the profit and loss account of the period.

Government grants*

Subject to paragraph 6.55, **government grants** shall be **recognised** in the profit and loss account so as to match them with the expenditure towards which they are intended to contribute. To the extent that the grant is made as a contribution towards expenditure on a fixed asset, in principle it may be deducted from the purchase price or production cost of that asset. However, the option to deduct **government grants** from the purchase price or production costs of fixed assets is not available to companies governed by the accounting and reporting requirements of UK **companies legislation.** In such cases, the amount so deferred shall be treated as deferred income. **6.54**

A **government grant** shall not be **recognised** in the profit and loss account until the conditions for its receipt have been complied with and there is reasonable assurance that the grant will be received. **6.55**

Potential liabilities to repay grants either in whole or in part in specified circumstances shall be provided for only to the extent that repayment is probable. The repayment of a **government grant** shall be accounted for by setting off the repayment against any unamortised deferred income relating to the grant. Any excess shall be charged immediately to the profit and loss account. **6.56**

The following information shall be disclosed in the financial statements: **6.57**

(a) the effects of **government grants** on the results for the period and/or the financial position of the entity; and
(b) where the results of the period are affected materially by the receipt of forms of **government** assistance other than grants, the nature of that assistance and, to the extent that the effects on the financial statements can be measured, an estimate of those effects.

7 LEASES

Hire purchase and leasing

Those **hire purchase contracts** which are of a financing nature shall be accounted for on a basis similar to that set out below for **finance leases**. Conversely, other **hire purchase contracts** shall be accounted for on a basis similar to that set out below for **operating leases.** **7.1**

Accounting by lessees

A **finance lease** shall be recorded in the balance sheet of a lessee as an asset and as an **obligation** to pay future rentals. At the **inception** of the lease the sum to be recorded both as an asset and as a liability shall normally be the **fair value** of the asset. **7.2**

In those cases where the **fair value** of the asset does not give a realistic estimate of the cost to the lessee of the asset and of the **obligation** entered into, a better estimate shall be used. In principle this shall approximate to the present value of the **minimum lease payments**, derived by discounting them at the interest rate implicit in the lease. An example of where this might be used would be where the lessee has benefited from grants and capital allowances that enable the **minimum lease payments** under a **7.3**

* *Additional specific legal requirements relating to government grants in the Republic of Ireland are included in the derivation tables on the ASB website.*

finance lease to be adjusted to a total that is less than the **fair value** of the asset. A negative **finance charge** shall not be shown.

7.4 The total **finance charge** under a **finance lease** shall be allocated to accounting periods during the **lease term** so as to produce a constant periodic rate of charge on the remaining balance of the **obligation** for each accounting period, or a reasonable approximation thereto. The straight-line method may provide such a reasonable approximation.

7.5 The rental under an **operating lease** shall be charged on a straight-line basis over the **lease term** even if the payments are not made on such a basis, unless another systematic and rational basis is more appropriate.

7.6 Incentives to sign a lease, in whatever form they may take, shall be spread by the lessee on a straight-line basis over the **lease term** or, if shorter than the full **lease term**, over the period to the review date on which the rent is first expected to be adjusted to the prevailing market rate.

7.7 An **asset** leased under a **finance lease** shall be depreciated over the shorter of the **lease term** or its useful life. However, in the case of a **hire purchase contract** that has the characteristics of a **finance lease** the asset shall be depreciated over its useful life.

Accounting by lessors

7.8 The amount due from the lessee under a **finance lease** shall be recorded in the balance sheet of a lessor as a debtor at the amount of the **net investment** in the lease after making provisions for items such as bad and doubtful rentals receivable.

7.9 The total **gross earnings** under **finance leases** shall be **recognised** on a systematic and rational basis. This will normally be a constant periodic rate of return on the lessor's **net investment**.

7.10 Rental income from an **operating lease** shall be **recognised** on a straight-line basis over the period of the lease, even if the payments are not made on such a basis, unless another systematic and rational basis is more representative of the time pattern in which the benefit from the **leased** asset is receivable.

7.11 An asset held for use in **operating leases** by a lessor shall be recorded as a fixed **asset** and **depreciated** over its useful life.

Manufacturer/dealer lessor

7.12 A manufacturer or dealer lessor shall not **recognise** a selling profit under an **operating lease**. The selling profit under a **finance lease** shall be restricted to the excess of the **fair value** of the **asset** over the manufacturer's or dealer's cost less any grants receivable by the manufacturer or dealer towards the purchase, construction or use of the **asset**.

Sale and leaseback transactions – accounting by the seller/lessee

7.13 In a sale and leaseback transaction that results in a **finance lease**, any apparent profit or loss (i.e. the difference between the sale price and the previous carrying value) shall be deferred and amortised in the financial statements of the seller/lessee over the shorter of the **lease term** and the useful life of the **asset**.

If the leaseback is an **operating lease**: 7.14

(a) any profit or loss shall be **recognised** immediately, provided it is clear that the transaction is established at **fair value**;
(b) if the sale price is below **fair value** any profit or loss shall be **recognised** immediately, except that if the apparent loss is compensated for by future rentals at below market price it shall to that extent be deferred and amortised over the remainder of the **lease term** (or, if shorter, the period during which the reduced rentals are chargeable); or
(c) if the sale price is above **fair value**, the excess over **fair value** shall be deferred and amortised over the shorter of the remainder of the **lease term** and the period to the next rent review (if any).

Sale and leaseback transactions – accounting by the buyer/lessor

A buyer/lessor shall account for a sale and leaseback in the same way as other leases are accounted for, i.e. using the methods set out in paragraphs 7.8-7.12. 7.15

Disclosure by lessees

Disclosure shall be made of: 7.16

(a) either:

 (i) the gross amounts of **assets** that are held under **finance leases** together with the related accumulated **depreciation** for (1) land and buildings and (2) other fixed **assets** in aggregate; or
 (ii) alternatively to being shown separately from that in respect of owned fixed **assets**, the information in (i) above may be integrated with it, such that the totals of gross amount, accumulated **depreciation**, net amount and **depreciation** allocated for the period for (1) land and buildings and (2) other fixed assets in aggregate for **assets** held under **finance leases** are included with similar amounts for owned fixed **assets**. Where this alternative treatment is adopted, the net amount of **assets** held under **finance leases** and the amount of **depreciation** allocated for the period in respect of **assets** under **finance leases** included in the overall total shall be disclosed separately.

(b) the amounts of **obligations** related to **finance leases** (net of **finance charges** allocated to future periods). These shall be disclosed separately from other **obligations** and liabilities, either on the face of the balance sheet or in the notes to the accounts.
(c) the amount of any commitments existing at the balance sheet date in respect of **finance leases** that have been entered into but whose **inception** occurs after the year end.

In respect of **operating leases**, the lessee shall disclose the payments that it is committed to make during the next year, analysed into those in which the commitment expires within that year, those expiring in the second to fifth years inclusive, and those expiring over five years from the balance sheet date. 7.17

Disclosure by lessors

Disclosure shall be made of: 7.18

(a) the gross amounts of **assets** held for use in **operating leases** and the related accumulated **depreciation** charges;

(b) the cost of assets acquired, whether by purchase or **finance lease**, for the purpose of letting under **finance leases**; and
(c) the **net investment** in (i) **finance leases** and (ii) **hire purchase contracts** at each balance sheet date.

8 CURRENT ASSETS

*Stocks and long-term contracts**

8.1 The amount at which stocks are stated in the financial statements shall be the total of the lower of cost and **net realisable value** of the separate items of stock or of groups of similar items.

8.2 WHERE THERE IS NO RECORD OF THE PURCHASE PRICE OR PRODUCTION COST OF STOCK THE VALUE ASCRIBED MUST BE THE EARLIEST AVAILABLE RECORD OF ITS VALUE. PARTICULARS MUST BE GIVEN OF ANY CASE WHERE THE PURCHASE PRICE OR PRODUCTION COST OF ANY ASSET IS FOR THE FIRST TIME DETERMINED IN THIS WAY.

8.3 FINANCE COSTS (SUCH AS INTEREST) THAT ARE DIRECTLY ATTRIBUTABLE TO THE ACQUISITION, CONSTRUCTION OR PRODUCTION OF STOCK MAY BE INCLUDED AS PART OF THE COST. IN SUCH CIRCUMSTANCES, THE NOTES TO THE ACCOUNTS MUST DISCLOSE THAT FINANCE COSTS ARE INCLUDED IN DETERMINING THE COST OF THE **ASSET** AND THE AMOUNT OF FINANCE COSTS SO INCLUDED.

8.4 WHERE STOCKS ARE CONSTANTLY BEING REPLACED AND THEIR VALUE IS NOT MATERIAL TO ASSESSING THE COMPANY'S STATE OF AFFAIRS AND THEIR QUANTITY, VALUE AND COMPOSITION ARE NOT SUBJECT TO MATERIAL VARIATION, THEY MAY BE INCLUDED AT A FIXED QUANTITY AND VALUE.

8.5 DISTRIBUTION COSTS MAY NOT BE INCLUDED IN THE PRODUCTION COSTS OF STOCKS.

8.6 **Long-term contracts** shall be assessed on a contract-by-contract basis and reflected in the profit and loss account by recording turnover and related costs as contract activity progresses. Turnover is ascertained in a manner appropriate to the stage of completion of the contract, the business and the industry in which it operates.

8.7 Where it is considered that the outcome of a **long-term contract** can be assessed with reasonable certainty before its conclusion, the prudently calculated **attributable profit** shall be **recognised** in the profit and loss account as the difference between the reported turnover and related costs for that contract.

8.8 **Long-term contracts** shall be disclosed in the balance sheet as follows:

(a) The amount by which recorded turnover is in excess of payments on account shall be classified as 'amounts recoverable on contracts' and separately disclosed within debtors.
(b) The balance of payments on account (in excess of the amounts (i) matched with turnover and (ii) offset against **long-term contract** balances) shall be classified as payments on account and separately disclosed within creditors.
(c) The amount of **long-term contracts**, at costs incurred, net of amounts transferred to cost of sales, after deducting **foreseeable losses** and payments on account not matched with turnover, shall be classified as 'long-term contract

**Guidance on the practical considerations of arriving at amounts at which stocks and long-term contracts are stated in financial statements is given in Appendix III.*

balances' and separately disclosed within the balance sheet heading 'stocks'. The balance sheet note shall disclose separately the balances of:

(i) net cost less **foreseeable losses**; and
(ii) applicable payments on account.

(d) The amount by which the provision or accrual for **foreseeable losses** exceeds the costs incurred (after transfers to cost of sales) shall be included within either 'provisions for liabilities' or 'creditors' as appropriate.

*Consignment stock**

Where **consignment stock** is in substance an **asset** of the dealer, the stock shall be **recognised** as such on the dealer's balance sheet, together with a corresponding liability to the manufacturer. Any deposit shall be deducted from the **liability** and the excess classified as a trade creditor. Where stock is not in substance an **asset** of the dealer, the stock shall not be included on the dealer's balance sheet until the transfer of title has crystallised. Any deposit shall be included under 'other debtors'. **8.9**

Debt factoring†

Where the entity has transferred to the factor all significant benefits (i.e. the future cash flows from payment by the debtors) and all significant risks (i.e. slow payment risk and the risk of bad debts) relating to the debts, and has no **obligation** to repay the factor, the debts shall be removed from the entity's balance sheet and no **liability** shall be shown in respect of the proceeds received from the factor. A profit or loss shall be **recognised,** calculated as the difference between the carrying amount of the debts and the proceeds received. **8.10**

Where the entity has retained significant benefits and risks relating to factored debts, and all the following conditions are met: **8.11**

(a) there is absolutely no doubt that the entity's exposure to loss is limited to a fixed monetary amount (e.g. because there is no recourse or such recourse has a fixed monetary ceiling);
(b) amounts received from the factor are secured only on the debts factored;
(c) the debts factored are capable of separate identification;
(d) the debt factor has no recourse to other debts or assets;
(e) the entity has no right to reacquire the debts in the future;
(f) the factor has no right to return the debts even in the event of the cessation of the factoring agreement,

then the factored debts shall be shown gross (after providing for bad debts, credit protection charges and any accrued interest) separately on the face of the balance sheet. Any amounts received from the factor in respect of those debts, to the extent that they are not returnable, shall be shown as deductions therefrom on the face of the balance sheet (a 'linked presentation'). The financial statements shall include a note stating that the entity is not required to support bad debts in respect of factored debts and that the factors have stated in writing that they will not seek recourse other than out of factored debts. The interest element of the factor's charges shall be

**A table illustrating the considerations affecting the treatment of consignment stock is given in Appendix III.*

†Similar arrangements, such as invoice discounting, shall be accounted for in the same way as debt factoring. A table illustrating the considerations affecting the treatment of debt factoring is given in Appendix III.

recognised as it accrues and included in the profit and loss account with other interest charges.

8.12 In all other cases a separate presentation shall be adopted. A gross **asset** (equivalent in amount to the gross amount of the debts) shall be shown on the balance sheet of the entity within **assets** and a corresponding **liability** in respect of the proceeds received from the factor shall be shown within **liabilities**. The interest element of the factor's charges and other factoring costs shall be **recognised** as they accrue and included in the profit and loss account with other interest charges.

Current asset investments

8.13 CURRENT ASSET INVESTMENTS MUST INITIALLY BE STATED IN THE FINANCIAL STATEMENTS AT THE LOWER OF COST AND NET REALISABLE VALUE. ALTERNATIVELY, THEY MAY BE MEASURED AT THEIR CURRENT COST. Gains and losses shall be **recognised** (in the profit and loss account or statement of **total recognised gains and losses**) using the same basis applied to **tangible fixed assets** in paragraphs 6.25 and 6.26 above.

8.14 WHERE LISTED SHARES ARE HELD AS A CURRENT ASSET INVESTMENT, THE FOLLOWING INFORMATION MUST BE DISCLOSED:

(A) THE AGGREGATE MARKET VALUE OF THOSE INVESTMENTS WHERE IT DIFFERS FROM THEIR BALANCE SHEET AMOUNT; AND
(B) BOTH THE MARKET VALUE AND THE STOCK EXCHANGE VALUE OF ANY INVESTMENTS, OF WHICH THE MARKET VALUE IS TAKEN AS BEING HIGHER THAN THE STOCK EXCHANGE VALUE.

Start-up costs and pre-contract costs

8.15 **Start-up costs** shall be accounted for on a basis consistent with the accounting treatment of similar costs incurred as part of the entity's on-going activities. In cases where there are no such similar costs, **start-up** costs that do not meet the criteria for **recognition** as **assets** under another specific requirement of the FRSSE shall be **recognised** as an expense when they are incurred. They shall not be carried forward as an **asset**.

8.16 **Pre-contract costs** shall be expensed as incurred, except that **directly attributable costs** shall be **recognised** as an **asset** when it is virtually certain that a contract will be obtained and the contract is expected to result in future net cash inflows with a present value no less than all amounts **recognised** as an **asset**. Costs incurred before the **asset recognition** criteria are met shall not be **recognised** as an **asset**.

9 TAXATION

General

9.1 **Tax** (current and **deferred**) shall be **recognised** in the profit and loss account, except to the extent that it is attributable to a gain or loss that is or has been **recognised** directly in the statement of **total recognised gains and losses** (in which case the tax shall also be **recognised** directly in that statement).

9.2 The material components of the (current and **deferred**) **tax** charge (or credit) for the period shall be disclosed separately.

Any special circumstances that affect the overall tax charge or credit for the period, or may affect those of future periods, shall be disclosed by way of a note to the profit and loss account and their individual effects quantified. The effects of a fundamental change in the basis of taxation shall be included in the tax charge or credit for the period and separately disclosed on the face of the profit and loss account. 9.3

Deferred tax

Deferred tax shall be **recognised** in respect of all **timing differences** that have originated but not reversed by the balance sheet date; however, **deferred tax** shall not be **recognised** on: 9.4

(a) revaluation gains and losses unless, by the balance sheet date, the entity has entered into a binding agreement to sell the **asset** and has revalued the **asset** to the selling price; or
(b) taxable gains arising on revaluations or sales if it is more likely than not that the gain will be rolled over into a replacement **asset**.

Unrelieved tax losses and other **deferred tax assets** shall be **recognised** only to the extent that it is more likely than not that they will be recovered against the reversal of **deferred tax liabilities** or other future taxable profits (the very existence of unrelieved tax losses is strong evidence that there may not be 'other future taxable profits' against which the losses will be relieved). 9.5

Deferred tax shall be **recognised** when the tax allowances for the cost of a fixed **asset** are received before or after the **depreciation** of the fixed **asset** is **recognised** in the profit and loss account. However, if and when all conditions for retaining the tax allowances have been met, the **deferred tax** shall be reversed. 9.6

Deferred tax shall not be **recognised** on **permanent differences**. 9.7

Deferred tax shall be measured at the average tax rates that would apply when the **timing differences** are expected to reverse, based on tax rates and laws that have been enacted by the balance sheet date. 9.8

The discounting of **deferred tax assets** and **liabilities** is not required. However, if an entity does adopt a policy of discounting, all **deferred tax** balances that have been measured by reference to undiscounted cash flows and for which the impact of discounting is material shall be discounted. Where discounting is used, the unwinding of the discount shall be shown as a component of the tax charge and disclosed separately. 9.9

The **deferred tax** balance and its material components shall be disclosed. 9.10

The movement between the opening and closing net **deferred tax** balances, and the material components of this movement, shall be disclosed. 9.11

If **assets** have been revalued, or if their market values have been disclosed in a note, the amount of tax that would be payable or recoverable if the **assets** were sold at the values shown shall be disclosed. 9.12

Tax on dividends

9.13 Outgoing dividends and similar amounts payable shall be **recognised** at an amount that includes any **withholding tax** but excludes other taxes, such as attributable **tax credits**.

9.14 Incoming dividends and similar income receivable shall be **recognised** at an amount that includes any **withholding tax** but excludes other taxes, such as attributable **tax credits**. Any **withholding tax** suffered shall be shown as part of the tax charge.

Value added tax (VAT)

9.15 Turnover shown in the profit and loss account shall exclude either VAT on taxable outputs or VAT imputed under the flat rate VAT scheme. Irrecoverable VAT allocable to fixed **assets** and to other items disclosed separately in the financial statements shall be included in their cost where practicable and material.

10 PENSIONS

10.1 The cost of a **defined contribution scheme** is equal to the contributions payable to the scheme for the accounting period. The cost shall be **recognised** within operating profit in the profit and loss account.

10.2 PARTICULARS MUST BE GIVEN OF ANY PENSION COMMITMENTS INCLUDED UNDER ANY PROVISION SHOWN IN THE COMPANY'S BALANCE SHEET AND ANY SUCH COMMITMENTS FOR WHICH NO PROVISION HAS BEEN MADE. WHERE ANY SUCH COMMITMENT RELATES WHOLLY OR PARTLY TO PENSIONS PAYABLE TO PAST **DIRECTORS** OF THE COMPANY, SEPARATE PARTICULARS MUST BE GIVEN OF THAT COMMITMENT, SO FAR AS IT RELATES TO SUCH PENSIONS.

10.3 The following disclosures shall be made in respect of a **defined contribution scheme**:

(a) the nature of the scheme (i.e. defined contribution);
(b) the cost for the period; and
(c) any outstanding or prepaid contributions at the balance sheet date.

10.4 An employer participating in a **defined benefit scheme** shall refer to Appendix II 'Accounting for retirement benefits: defined benefit schemes'.

11 PROVISIONS, CONTINGENT LIABILITIES AND CONTINGENT ASSETS

11.1 The requirements in paragraphs 11.2-11.8 do not apply to pensions, **deferred tax** and leases, which are covered by more specific requirements of the FRSSE.

Provisions

11.2 A **provision** shall be **recognised** when, and only when, it is probable (i.e. more likely than not) that a present **obligation** exists, as a result of a past event, and that it will require a transfer of economic benefits in settlement that can be estimated reliably. The amount **recognised** as a **provision** shall be the best estimate of the expenditure required to settle the **obligation** at the balance sheet date. Where the effect of the time value of money is material, the amount of a **provision** shall be the present value of the expenditures expected to be required to settle the **obligation**. Where discounting is used, the unwinding of the discount shall be shown as other finance costs adjacent to interest.*

Where some or all of the expenditure required to settle a **provision** may be reimbursed by another party (e.g. through an insurance claim), the reimbursement shall be **recognised**, as a separate **asset**, only when it is virtually certain to be received if the entity settles the **obligation**. In the profit and loss account, the expense relating to the **provision** may be presented net of the recovery. Gains from the expected disposal of **assets** shall be excluded from the measurement of a provision. **11.3**

Provisions shall be reviewed at each balance sheet date and adjusted to reflect the current best estimate. **11.4**

A **provision** shall be used only for expenditures for which the **provision** was originally **recognised**. **11.5**

FOR EACH CLASS OF **PROVISION** THE FOLLOWING INFORMATION MUST BE PROVIDED: **11.6**

(A) THE AMOUNT OF THE **PROVISION** AT THE BEGINNING AND THE END OF THE **FINANCIAL YEAR**;
(B) ANY AMOUNTS TRANSFERRED TO OR FROM THE **PROVISION** DURING THE YEAR;
(C) THE SOURCE AND APPLICATION OF THE AMOUNTS TRANSFERRED; AND
(D) PARTICULARS OF EACH MATERIAL **PROVISION** INCLUDED UNDER 'OTHER PROVISIONS' IN THE COMPANY'S BALANCE SHEET IN ANY CASE WHERE THE AMOUNT OF THAT **PROVISION** IS MATERIAL.

THE DISCLOSURES SET OUT ABOVE ARE NOT REQUIRED WHERE THE MOVEMENT CONSISTS OF THE APPLICATION OF A **PROVISION** FOR THE PURPOSE FOR WHICH IT WAS ESTABLISHED.

Contingent liabilities and contingent assets

Contingent liabilities and **contingent assets** shall not be **recognised.** **11.7**

The following shall be disclosed for **contingent liabilities**, except where their existence is remote, and for probable **contingent assets**: **11.8**

(a) a brief description of the nature of the contingent item; and
(b) where practicable, an estimate of its financial effect; and
(C) ITS LEGAL NATURE.

DETAILS MUST BE PROVIDED WHERE ANY VALUABLE SECURITY HAS BEEN PROVIDED BY THE COMPANY IN CONNECTION WITH A **CONTINGENT LIABILITY** AND IF SO, WHAT. **11.9**

WHERE PRACTICABLE, THE AGGREGATE AMOUNT, OR ESTIMATED AMOUNT, OF CONTRACTS FOR CAPITAL EXPENDITURE NOT PROVIDED FOR MUST BE DISCLOSED. DETAILS OF ANY OTHER FINANCIAL COMMITMENTS NOT PROVIDED FOR WHICH ARE RELEVANT TO ASSESSING THE COMPANY'S STATE OF AFFAIRS MUST ALSO BE DISCLOSED. **11.10**

PARTICULARS MUST BE GIVEN OF ANY CHARGE ON THE ASSETS OF THE COMPANY TO SECURE THE LIABILITIES OF ANY OTHER PERSON, INCLUDING WHERE PRACTICABLE, THE AMOUNT SECURED. **11.11**

**There are a number of acceptable methods of discounting, and the appropriate discount rate depends on the method adopted. However, if cash flows are expressed in future prices and have been adjusted for risk, it will be appropriate to discount them at a risk-free rate such as a market rate on relevant government bonds. An illustrative example of a provision calculated using discounting is given in Appendix III.*

12 FINANCIAL INSTRUMENTS, SHARE CAPITAL AND SHARE-BASED PAYMENTS

General

12.1 A **financial instrument**, or its component parts, shall be classified as a **financial liability**, a **financial asset** or an **equity instrument** in accordance with the substance of the contractual arrangement rather than its legal form. Some **financial instruments** take the legal form of equity but are **liabilities** in substance and others may combine features associated with **equity instruments** and features associated with **financial liabilities**. For example a preference share that provides for mandatory redemption by the issuer for a fixed or determinable amount at a fixed or determinable future date, or gives the holder the right to require the issuer to redeem the instrument at or after a particular date for a fixed or determinable amount, is a **financial liability**.

12.2 The **finance costs** of **borrowings** shall be allocated to periods over the **term** of the **borrowings** at a constant rate on the carrying amount. All **finance costs** shall be charged in the profit and loss account.

12.3 **Borrowings** shall be initially stated in the balance sheet at the **fair value** of consideration received. The carrying amount of **borrowings** shall be increased by the **finance cost** in respect of the reporting period and reduced by payments made in respect of the **borrowings** in that period.

12.4 Where an **arrangement fee** is such as to represent a significant additional cost of finance when compared with the interest payable over the life of the instrument, the treatment set out in paragraph 12.2 shall be followed. Where this is not the case it shall be charged in the profit and loss account immediately it is incurred.

12.5 THE AMOUNT OF ANY CONVERTIBLE DEBT ISSUED MUST BE SEPARATELY DISCLOSED FROM OTHER LIABILITIES.

12.6 Dividends relating to a **financial instrument** or a component that is a **financial liability** shall be recognised as expense in profit or loss. Distributions to holders of an **equity instrument** shall be debited by the entity directly to equity, net of any related income tax benefit. If an entity declares dividends after the balance sheet date, the dividends shall not be **recognised** as a **liability** at the balance sheet date.

12.7 THE NOTES TO THE ACCOUNTS MUST STATE:

(A) THE AGGREGATE AMOUNT OF DIVIDENDS PAID IN THE FINANCIAL YEAR (OTHER THAN THOSE FOR WHICH A LIABILITY EXISTED AT THE IMMEDIATELY PRECEDING BALANCE SHEET DATE);

(B) THE AGGREGATE AMOUNT OF DIVIDENDS THAT THE COMPANY IS LIABLE TO PAY AT THE BALANCE SHEET DATE; AND

(C) THE AGGREGATE AMOUNT OF DIVIDENDS THAT ARE PROPOSED BEFORE THE DATE OF APPROVAL OF THE ACCOUNTS, AND NOT OTHERWISE DISCLOSED UNDER PARAGRAPH (A) OR (B) ABOVE.

12.8 IF ANY FIXED CUMULATIVE DIVIDENDS ON THE COMPANY'S SHARES ARE IN ARREARS, THE AMOUNT OF THE ARREARS AND THE PERIOD FOR WHICH EACH CLASS OF DIVIDENDS IS IN ARREARS MUST BE DISCLOSED.

The company's share capital

THE FOLLOWING INFORMATION MUST BE DISCLOSED WITH RESPECT TO THE COMPANY'S SHARE CAPITAL: **12.9**

(A) WHERE SHARES OF MORE THAN ONE CLASS HAVE BEEN ALLOTTED, THE NUMBER AND AGGREGATE NOMINAL VALUE OF SHARES OF EACH CLASS ALLOTTED;

(B) FOR ANY PART OF THE ALLOTTED SHARE CAPITAL THAT CONSISTS OF REDEEMABLE SHARES:

(I) THE EARLIEST AND LATEST DATES ON WHICH THE COMPANY HAS THE POWER TO REDEEM THOSE SHARES;

(II) WHETHER THOSE SHARES MUST BE REDEEMED IN ANY EVENT OR ARE LIABLE TO BE REDEEMED AT THE OPTION OF THE COMPANY OR OF THE SHAREHOLDER; AND

(III) WHETHER ANY (AND, IF SO, WHAT) PREMIUM IS PAYABLE ON REDEMPTION.

IF THE COMPANY HAS ALLOTTED ANY SHARES DURING THE PERIOD, THE FOLLOWING INFORMATION MUST BE DISCLOSED: **12.10**

(A) THE CLASSES OF SHARES ALLOTTED; AND

(B) FOR EACH CLASS, THE NUMBER ALLOTTED, THEIR AGGREGATE NOMINAL VALUE, AND THE CONSIDERATION RECEIVED BY THE COMPANY FOR THE ALLOTMENT.

THE AMOUNT OF ALLOTTED SHARE CAPITAL AND THE AMOUNT OF CALLED UP SHARE CAPITAL WHICH HAS BEEN PAID UP MUST BE SEPARATELY DISCLOSED. **12.11**

THE NUMBER, DESCRIPTION AND AMOUNT OF SHARES IN THE COMPANY HELD BY OR ON BEHALF OF ITS **SUBSIDIARY UNDERTAKINGS** MUST BE DISCLOSED UNLESS THE SUBSIDIARY UNDERTAKING IS CONCERNED AS A PERSONAL REPRESENTATIVE OR A TRUSTEE. **12.12**

Share Based Payments

An entity which undertakes **share-based payment arrangements**, including transactions with **employees or others providing similar services** shall account for them as follows. **12.13**

Cash-settled share-based payment transactions

(a) **An entity shall recognise** the goods or services received or acquired when it obtains the goods or as the services are received. If the goods or services received or acquired do not qualify for recognition as **assets**, they shall be **recognised** as expenses. The entity shall **recognise** a corresponding **liability.**

(b) **The amount of the goods or services and the corresponding liability recognised** shall be the best estimate of the expenditure required to settle the **liability** at the balance sheet date. The **liability** shall be remeasured at each balance sheet date and at the date of settlement.

(c) Information shall be disclosed in a note to describe the principal terms and conditions of cash settled share-based payment transactions that exist during the period, including their current and potential financial effect.

Equity-settled share-based payment arrangements

(d) Information shall be disclosed in a note to describe the principal terms and conditions of any equity settled share-based payment arrangements that exist during the period including, the number of shares and the number of employees and others potentially involved, the grant date, any performance conditions and over what periods these apply and, where applicable, any option exercise prices.

12.14 Where the terms of the arrangement provide the counterparty with the choice of whether the entity settles the transaction in cash (or other assets) or by issuing **equity instruments**, the transaction, shall be accounted for as a cash-settled transaction in accordance with paragraph 12.13 (a) to (c) above. The liability shall be measured at the best estimate of the amount required to settle it at the balance sheet date if the counterparty were to opt for cash settlement. If the obligation is eventually settled by the issue of equity instruments, the liability previously recognised should be treated as the proceeds of issue of those instruments.

12.15 Where the entity and not the counterparty has the choice of settlement method, the arrangement shall be treated as either an equity settled transaction in accordance with paragraph 12.13(d) or a cash settled transaction in accordance with paragraph 12.13 (a) to (c), as appropriate in the entity's circumstances.

13 FOREIGN CURRENCY TRANSLATION

Transactions in foreign currencies

13.1 WHERE SUMS ORIGINALLY DENOMINATED IN FOREIGN CURRENCIES HAVE BEEN BROUGHT INTO ACCOUNT UNDER ANY ITEMS SHOWN IN THE BALANCE SHEET OR PROFIT AND LOSS ACCOUNT, THE BASIS ON WHICH THOSE SUMS HAVE BEEN TRANSLATED INTO **LOCAL CURRENCY** MUST BE DISCLOSED.

13.2 Subject to the provisions of paragraphs 13.4 and 13.6 each **asset**, **liability**, revenue or cost arising from a transaction denominated in a foreign currency shall be translated into the **local currency** at the **exchange rate** in operation on the date on which the transaction occurred; if the rates do not fluctuate significantly, an average rate for a period may be used as an approximation. Where the transaction is to be settled at a contracted rate, that rate shall be used. Where a trading transaction is covered by a related or matching **forward contract**, the rate of exchange specified in that contract may be used.

13.3 Subject to the special provisions of paragraph 13.6, which relate to the treatment of foreign equity investments financed by foreign currency **borrowings**, no subsequent **translations** shall normally be made once non-monetary **assets** have been translated and recorded.

13.4 At each balance sheet date, monetary **assets** and **liabilities** denominated in a foreign currency shall be translated by using the **closing rate** or, where appropriate, the rates of exchange fixed under the terms of the relevant transactions. Where there are related or matching **forward contracts** in respect of trading transactions, the rates of exchange specified in those contracts may be used.

13.5 All exchange gains or losses on settled transactions and unsettled **monetary items** shall be reported as part of the profit or loss for the period from **ordinary activities**.

13.6 Where a company has used foreign currency **borrowings** to finance, or to provide a hedge against, its foreign equity investments and the conditions set out in this paragraph apply, the equity investments may be denominated in the appropriate foreign currencies and the carrying amounts translated at the end of each accounting period at **closing rates** for inclusion in the investing company's financial statements. Where investments are treated in this way, any exchange differences arising shall be taken to reserves and the exchange gains or losses on the foreign currency **borrowings** shall then be offset, as a reserve movement, against these exchange differences. The conditions that must apply are as follows:

(a) in any accounting period, exchange gains or losses arising on the **borrowings** may be offset only to the extent of exchange differences arising on the equity investments;
(b) the foreign currency **borrowings**, whose exchange gains or losses are used in the offset process, shall not exceed, in the aggregate, the total amount of cash that the investments are expected to be able to generate, whether from profits or otherwise; and
(c) the accounting treatment adopted shall be applied consistently from period to period.

Incorporating accounts of foreign entities

When preparing accounts for a company and its **foreign entities** (which includes the incorporation of the results of associated companies or foreign branches into those of an investing company) the **closing rate/net investment** method of translating the **local currency** financial statements shall normally be used. 13.7

Exchange differences arising from the retranslation of the opening **net investment** in a **foreign entity** at the **closing rate** shall be recorded as a movement on reserves. 13.8

The profit and loss account of a **foreign entity** accounted for under the **closing rate/ net investment** method shall be translated at the **closing rate** or at an average rate for the period. Where an average rate is used, the difference between the profit and loss account translated at an average rate and at the **closing rate** shall be recorded as a movement on reserves. The average rate used shall be calculated by the method considered most appropriate for the circumstances of the **foreign entity**. 13.9

In those circumstances where the trade of the **foreign entity** is more dependent on the economic environment of the investing company's currency than that of its own reporting currency, the transactions of the foreign operation shall be reported as though all of its transactions had been entered into by the investing company itself in its own currency, as stated in paragraphs 13.2-13.5. 13.10

The method used for translating the financial statements of each **foreign entity** shall be applied consistently from period to period unless its financial and other operational relationships with the investing company change. 13.11

Where foreign currency **borrowings** have been used to finance, or provide a hedge against, group equity investments in **foreign entities**, exchange gains or losses on the **borrowings**, which would otherwise have been taken to the profit and loss account, may be offset as reserve movements against exchange differences arising on the retranslation of the **net investments** provided that: 13.12

(a) the relationships between the investing company and the **foreign entities** concerned justify the use of the **closing rate** method for consolidation purposes;
(b) in any accounting period, the exchange gains and losses arising on foreign currency **borrowings** are offset only to the extent of the exchange differences arising on the **net investments** in **foreign entities**;
(c) the foreign currency **borrowings**, whose exchange gains or losses are used in the offset process, shall not exceed, in the aggregate, the total amount of cash that the **net investments** are expected to be able to generate, whether from profits or otherwise; and

(d) the accounting treatment is applied consistently from period to period.

Where the provisions of paragraph 13.6 have been applied in the investing company's financial statements to a foreign equity investment that is neither a subsidiary nor an associated company, the same offset procedure may be applied in the **consolidated financial statements**.

14 POST BALANCE SHEET EVENTS

14.1 An entity shall adjust the amounts **recognised** in its financial statements to reflect adjusting **events after the balance sheet date**.

14.2 An entity shall not adjust the amounts **recognised** in its financial statements to reflect non-adjusting **events after the balance sheet date**.

14.3 If non-adjusting **events after the balance sheet date** are material, non-disclosure could influence the economic decisions of users taken on the basis of the financial statements. Accordingly, an entity shall disclose the following for each material category of non-adjusting event after the balance sheet date:

(a) the nature of the event; and

(b) an estimate of its financial effect, or a statement that such an estimate cannot be made.

14.4 The date on which the financial statements are approved for issue and who gave that approval shall be disclosed in the financial statements.

15 RELATED PARTY DISCLOSURES

15.1 Where the reporting entity:

(a) purchases, sells or transfers goods and other **assets** or **liabilities**; or
(b) renders or receives services; or
(c) provides or receives finance or financial support; (irrespective of whether a price is charged) to, from or on behalf of a **related party**, then such material* transactions shall be disclosed, including:

(i) the names of the transacting **related parties**;
(ii) a description of the relationship between the parties;
(iii) a description of the transactions;
(iv) the amounts involved;
(v) any other elements of the transactions necessary for an understanding of the financial statements;
(vi) the amounts due to or from **related parties** at the balance sheet date and provisions for doubtful debts due from such parties at that date; and
(vii) amounts written off in the period in respect of debts due to or from **related parties**.

15.2 Personal guarantees given by **directors** in respect of **borrowings** by the reporting entity shall be disclosed in the notes to the financial statements.

**The materiality of a related party transaction shall be judged in terms of its significance to the reporting entity.*

AMOUNTS INCLUDED IN THE PROFIT AND LOSS ACCOUNT UNDER 'INVESTMENT INCOME' AND 'OTHER INTEREST RECEIVABLE AND SIMILAR INCOME' THAT WERE RECEIVED, OR ARE RECEIVABLE FROM GROUP UNDERTAKINGS, MUST BE SHOWN SEPARATELY. **15.3**

AMOUNTS INCLUDED IN THE PROFIT AND LOSS ACCOUNT UNDER 'INTEREST PAYABLE AND SIMILAR CHARGES' PAID, OR PAYABLE, TO GROUP UNDERTAKINGS, MUST BE SHOWN SEPARATELY. **15.4**

COMMITMENTS WHICH ARE UNDERTAKEN ON BEHALF OF OR FOR THE BENEFIT OF (A) ANY PARENT UNDERTAKING OR FELLOW **SUBSIDIARY UNDERTAKING**, OR (B) ANY **SUBSIDIARY UNDERTAKING** OF THE COMPANY, MUST BE DISCLOSED SEPARATELY FROM THOSE COMMITMENTS DISCLOSED UNDER PARAGRAPHS 10.2 AND 11.8 TO 11.11, AND COMMITMENTS UNDERTAKEN UNDER (A) MUST BE DISCLOSED SEPARATELY FROM THOSE UNDERTAKEN UNDER (B). **15.5**

Other transactions with **related parties** may be disclosed on an aggregated basis (aggregation of similar transactions by type of **related party**) unless disclosure of an individual transaction, or connected transactions, is necessary for an understanding of the impact of the transactions on the financial statements of the reporting entity or is required by law. **15.6**

Disclosure, as a **related party** transaction, is not required of: **15.7**

(a) pension contributions paid to a pension fund;
(b) emoluments in respect of services as an employee of the reporting entity; or
(c) transactions with the parties listed below simply as a result of their role as:

  (i) providers of finance in the course of their business in that regard;
  (ii) utility companies;
  (iii) **government** departments and their sponsored bodies; or
  (iv) a customer, supplier, franchiser, distributor or general agent.*

When the reporting entity is controlled by another party, there shall be disclosure of the **related party** relationship and the name of that party and, if different, that of the ultimate controlling party. If the controlling party or ultimate controlling party of the reporting entity is not known, that fact shall be disclosed. This information shall be disclosed irrespective of whether any transactions have taken place between the controlling parties and the reporting entity. **15.8**

WHERE THE COMPANY IS A **SUBSIDIARY UNDERTAKING**, THE FOLLOWING INFORMATION MUST BE GIVEN WITH RESPECT TO THE COMPANY (IF ANY) REGARDED BY THE DIRECTORS AS BEING THE COMPANY'S ULTIMATE PARENT COMPANY: **15.9**

(A) THE NAME OF THAT COMPANY; AND
(B) ITS COUNTRY OF INCORPORATION IF OUTSIDE THE UNITED KINGDOM AND IF KNOWN TO THE DIRECTORS.

****Editor's note****: *With effect for accounting periods beginning on or after 1 January 2015 the following is added:*

(d) related party transactions entered into between two or more members of a group, provided that any subsidiary which is a party to the transaction is wholly owned by such a member.

Parent undertaking drawing up accounts for larger group*

15.10 WHERE THE COMPANY IS A **SUBSIDIARY UNDERTAKING**, THE FOLLOWING INFORMATION MUST BE GIVEN WITH RESPECT TO THE PARENT UNDERTAKING OF:

(A) THE LARGEST GROUP OF WHICH IT IS A MEMBER FOR WHICH GROUP ACCOUNTS ARE DRAWN UP; AND

(B) THE SMALLEST SUCH GROUP OF UNDERTAKINGS:

(I) THE NAME OF THE PARENT UNDERTAKING;

(II) THE COUNTRY OF INCORPORATION, IF OUTSIDE THE UNITED KINGDOM;

(III) IF UNINCORPORATED, THE ADDRESS OF ITS PRINCIPAL PLACE OF BUSINESS; AND

(IV) IF COPIES OF EITHER OF THE GROUP ACCOUNTS REFERRED TO IN (A) OR (B) ABOVE ARE AVAILABLE TO THE PUBLIC, THE ADDRESS FROM WHICH THEY MAY BE OBTAINED.

Directors' benefits: advances, credit and guarantees

15.11 INFORMATION ABOUT THE FOLLOWING DIRECTORS' BENEFITS MUST BE PROVIDED IN THE NOTES TO THE ACCOUNTS. FOR THE PURPOSES OF THIS SECTION, THE DIRECTORS OF A COMPANY ARE THE PERSONS WHO WERE A DIRECTOR AT ANY TIME IN THE FINANCIAL YEAR TO WHICH THE ACCOUNTS RELATE:

(A) ADVANCES AND CREDITS GRANTED BY THE COMPANY TO ITS DIRECTORS; AND

(B) GUARANTEES OF ANY KIND ENTERED INTO BY THE COMPANY ON BEHALF OF ITS DIRECTORS.

15.12 THE INFORMATION REQUIRED FOR AN ADVANCE OR CREDIT IS AS FOLLOWS:

(A) ITS AMOUNT;

(B) AN INDICATION OF THE INTEREST RATE;

(C) ITS MAIN CONDITIONS; AND

(D) ANY AMOUNTS REPAID.

15.13 THE INFORMATION REQUIRED FOR A GUARANTEE IS AS FOLLOWS:

(A) ITS MAIN TERMS;

(B) THE AMOUNT OF THE MAXIMUM LIABILITY THAT MAY BE INCURRED BY THE COMPANY (OR ITS SUBSIDIARY); AND

(C) ANY AMOUNT PAID AND ANY LIABILITY INCURRED BY THE COMPANY (OR ITS SUBSIDIARY) FOR THE PURPOSE OF FULFILLING THE GUARANTEE (INCLUDING ANY LOSS INCURRED BY REASON OF ENFORCEMENT OF THE GUARANTEE).

15.14 THERE MUST ALSO BE DISCLOSED IN THE NOTES TO THE ACCOUNTS THE TOTALS OF AMOUNTS STATED UNDER PARAGRAPHS 15.12(A); 15.12(D); 15.13(B) AND 15.13(C) ABOVE.

15.15 THE REQUIREMENTS OF THIS SECTION APPLY IN RELATION TO EVERY ADVANCE, CREDIT OR GUARANTEE SUBSISTING AT ANY TIME IN THE FINANCIAL YEAR TO WHICH THE ACCOUNTS RELATE:

(A) WHENEVER IT WAS ENTERED INTO;

**INFORMATION NEED NOT BE DISCLOSED WITH RESPECT TO AN UNDERTAKING WHICH IS ESTABLISHED UNDER THE LAW OF A COUNTRY OUTSIDE THE UNITED KINGDOM OR CARRIES ON BUSINESS OUTSIDE THE UNITED KINGDOM, IF IN THE OPINION OF THE DIRECTORS OF THE COMPANY THE DISCLOSURE WOULD BE SERIOUSLY PREJUDICIAL TO THE BUSINESS OF THAT UNDERTAKING, OR TO THE BUSINESS OF THE COMPANY OR ANY OF ITS SUBSIDIARY UNDERTAKINGS, AND THE SECRETARY OF STATE AGREES THAT THE INFORMATION NEED NOT BE DISCLOSED. WHERE ADVANTAGE IS TAKEN OF THIS EXEMPTION, THAT FACT SHALL BE STATED IN A NOTE TO THE COMPANY'S ANNUAL ACCOUNTS. This statutory exemption is not available in the Republic of Ireland.*

(B) WHETHER OR NOT THE PERSON WAS A DIRECTOR OF THE COMPANY IN QUESTION AT THE TIME IT WAS ENTERED INTO; AND

(C) IN THE CASE OF AN ADVANCE, CREDIT OR GUARANTEE INVOLVING A SUBSIDIARY UNDERTAKING OF THAT COMPANY, WHETHER OR NOT THAT UNDERTAKING WAS SUCH A SUBSIDIARY UNDERTAKING AT THE TIME IT WAS ENTERED INTO.

Subsidiary undertakings

THE FOLLOWING INFORMATION MUST BE GIVEN WHERE AT THE END OF THE **FINANCIAL YEAR** THE COMPANY HAS **SUBSIDIARY UNDERTAKINGS**: 15.16

(A) THE NAME OF EACH **SUBSIDIARY UNDERTAKING** MUST BE STATED; AND

(B) WITH RESPECT TO EACH **SUBSIDIARY UNDERTAKING** IF IT IS INCORPORATED OUTSIDE THE UNITED KINGDOM, THE COUNTRY IN WHICH IT IS INCORPORATED; IF IT IS UNINCORPORATED, THE ADDRESS OF ITS PRINCIPAL PLACE OF BUSINESS.

Holdings in subsidiary undertakings*

THERE MUST BE STATED IN RELATION TO SHARES OF EACH CLASS HELD BY THE COMPANY IN A **SUBSIDIARY UNDERTAKING** – 15.17

(A) THE IDENTITY OF THE CLASS; AND

(B) THE PROPORTION OF THE NOMINAL VALUE OF THE SHARES OF THAT CLASS REPRESENTED BY THOSE SHARES.

THE SHARES HELD BY THE COMPANY ITSELF MUST BE DISTINGUISHED FROM THOSE ATTRIBUTED TO THE COMPANY WHICH ARE HELD BY OR ON BEHALF OF A SUBSIDIARY UNDERTAKING.

Financial information about subsidiary undertakings

THERE MUST BE DISCLOSED WITH RESPECT TO EACH **SUBSIDIARY UNDERTAKING** – 15.18

(A) THE AGGREGATE AMOUNT OF ITS CAPITAL AND RESERVES AS AT THE END OF ITS RELEVANT **FINANCIAL YEAR**; AND

(B) ITS PROFIT OR LOSS FOR THAT YEAR.

THAT INFORMATION NEED NOT BE GIVEN IF: 15.19

(A) THE COMPANY IS EXEMPT BY VIRTUE OF SECTION 400 AND 401 OF THE COMPANIES ACT 2006 FROM THE REQUIREMENT TO PREPARE GROUP ACCOUNTS;

(B) THE COMPANY'S INVESTMENT IN THE **SUBSIDIARY UNDERTAKING** IS INCLUDED IN THE COMPANY'S ACCOUNTS BY WAY OF THE EQUITY METHOD OF VALUATION;

(C) THE **SUBSIDIARY UNDERTAKING** IS NOT REQUIRED BY ANY PROVISION OF THE COMPANIES ACT 2006 TO DELIVER A COPY OF ITS BALANCE SHEET FOR ITS RELEVANT **FINANCIAL YEAR** AND DOES NOT OTHERWISE PUBLISH THAT BALANCE SHEET IN THE UNITED KINGDOM OR ELSEWHERE, AND THE COMPANY'S HOLDING IS LESS THAN 50 PER CENT OF THE NOMINAL VALUE OF THE SHARES IN THE UNDERTAKING; OR

(D) IT IS NOT MATERIAL.

THE "RELEVANT **FINANCIAL YEAR**" OF A **SUBSIDIARY UNDERTAKING** IS – 15.20

(A) IF ITS **FINANCIAL YEAR** ENDS WITH THAT OF THE COMPANY, THAT YEAR; AND

(B) IF NOT, ITS **FINANCIAL YEAR** ENDING LAST BEFORE THE END OF THE COMPANY'S **FINANCIAL YEAR**.

**Disclosure requirements for holdings in undertakings other than subsidiary undertakings are set out in paragraph 6.33*

Membership of certain undertakings

15.21 THE FOLLOWING INFORMATION MUST BE GIVEN WHERE AT THE END OF THE **FINANCIAL YEAR** THE COMPANY IS A MEMBER OF A **QUALIFYING UNDERTAKING**:

(A) THE NAME AND LEGAL FORM OF THE UNDERTAKING; AND

(B) THE ADDRESS OF THE UNDERTAKING'S REGISTERED OFFICE (WHETHER IN OR OUTSIDE THE UNITED KINGDOM) OR, IF IT DOES NOT HAVE SUCH AN OFFICE, ITS HEAD OFFICE (WHETHER IN OR OUTSIDE THE UNITED KINGDOM).

15.22 WHERE THE UNDERTAKING IS A QUALIFYING PARTNERSHIP THERE MUST ALSO BE STATED EITHER –

(A) THAT A COPY OF THE LATEST ACCOUNTS OF THE UNDERTAKING HAS BEEN OR IS TO BE APPENDED TO THE COPY OF THE COMPANY'S ACCOUNTS SENT TO THE REGISTRAR UNDER SECTION 444 OF THE COMPANIES ACT 2006; OR

(B) THE NAME OF AT LEAST ONE BODY CORPORATE (WHICH MAY BE THE COMPANY) IN WHOSE GROUP ACCOUNTS THE UNDERTAKING HAS BEEN OR IS TO BE DEALT WITH ON A CONSOLIDATED BASIS.

15.23 INFORMATION OTHERWISE REQUIRED BY PARAGRAPH 15.21 ABOVE NEED NOT BE GIVEN IF IT IS NOT MATERIAL.

15.24 INFORMATION OTHERWISE REQUIRED BY PARAGRAPH 15.22 (B) ABOVE NEED NOT BE GIVEN IF THE NOTES TO THE COMPANY'S ACCOUNTS DISCLOSE THAT THE COMPANY IS EXEMPT BECAUSE THE PARTNERSHIP IS DEALT WITH ON A CONSOLIDATED BASIS IN GROUP ACCOUNTS PEPARED BY (I) A MEMBER OF THE PARTNERSHIP ESTABLISHED UNDER LAW, OR (II) A PARENT UNDERTAKING OF SUCH A MEMBER.

16 CONSOLIDATED FINANCIAL STATEMENTS

16.1 IF AT THE END OF A FINANCIAL YEAR A COMPANY SUBJECT TO THE SMALL COMPANIES REGIME IS A PARENT COMPANY, THE DIRECTORS, AS WELL AS PREPARING INDIVIDUAL ACCOUNTS FOR THE YEAR, MAY PREPARE GROUP ACCOUNTS FOR THE YEAR.

16.2 Where the reporting entity is preparing **consolidated financial statements**, it should regard as standard the accounting practices and disclosure requirements set out in FRSs 2, 6, 7 and, as they apply in respect of **consolidated financial statements**, FRSs 5, 9, 10*, 11 and 28. Where the reporting entity is part of a group that prepares publicly available **consolidated financial statements**, it is entitled to the exemptions given in FRS 8 paragraph 3(a)-(c).†

**FRS 10 and, as directed by FRS 10, FRS 11 need be applied only in respect of purchased goodwill arising on consolidation.*

†***Editor's note**: With effect for accounting periods beginning on or after 1 January 2015 this is replaced with:*

Where the reporting entity is preparing consolidated financial statements, it should have regard to paragraph 5 of the Status of the FRSSE as a means of developing its policies and practices for the preparation of its consolidated financial statements.

Form and content of small group accounts*

WHERE A SMALL COMPANY HAS PREPARED INDIVIDUAL ACCOUNTS IN ACCORDANCE WITH THE LEGAL REQUIREMENTS REFLECTED IN THE FRSSE AND IS PREPARING GROUP ACCOUNTS IN RESPECT OF THE SAME YEAR PARAGRAPHS 16.4 TO 16.8 APPLY. **16.3**

IN PREPARING GROUP ACCOUNTS, A COMPANY MUST HAVE REGARD TO THE LEGAL REQUIREMENTS REFLECTED IN THE FRSSE AND THE PROVISIONS OF SCHEDULE 6 OF THE SMALL COMPANIES AND GROUPS (ACCOUNTS AND DIRECTORS' REPORT) REGULATIONS 2008 (SI 2008/409). ANY REFERENCES IN THAT SCHEDULE TO COMPLIANCE WITH THE PROVISIONS OF 'SCHEDULE 6' SHALL BE CONSTRUED AS REFERENCES TO THE LEGAL REQUIREMENTS REFLECTED IN THE FRSSE. **16.4**

IN PREPARING GROUP ACCOUNTS, DETAILS MUST BE SHOWN IN THE NOTES TO THE GROUP ACCOUNTS OF: **16.5**

(A) ADVANCES AND CREDITS GRANTED TO THE DIRECTORS OF THE PARENT COMPANY, BY THAT COMPANY, OR BY ANY OF ITS SUBSIDIARY UNDERTAKINGS; AND

(B) GUARANTEES OF ANY KIND ENTERED INTO ON BEHALF OF THE DIRECTORS OF THE PARENT COMPANY, BY THAT COMPANY OR BY ANY OF ITS SUBSIDIARY UNDERTAKINGS.

THE BALANCE SHEET FORMAT SET OUT IN PARAGRAPH 2.27 SHALL BE MODIFIED AS FOLLOWS. FOR ITEM B.III 'INVESTMENTS' SUBSTITUTE: **16.6**

"B.III INVESTMENTS

1. SHARES IN GROUP UNDERTAKINGS
2. INTERESTS IN ASSOCIATED UNDERTAKINGS
3. OTHER PARTICIPATING INTERESTS
4. LOANS TO GROUP UNDERTAKINGS AND UNDERTAKINGS IN WHICH A PARTICIPATING INTEREST IS HELD
5. OTHER INVESTMENTS OTHER THAN LOANS
6. OTHERS."

THE PROFIT AND LOSS ACCOUNT FORMAT SET OUT IN PARAGRAPH 2.29 SHALL BE MODIFIED BY REPLACING THE ITEM HEADED "INCOME FROM PARTICIPATING INTERESTS"† BY TWO ITEMS: INCOME FROM INTERESTS IN ASSOCIATED UNDERTAKINGS" AND "INCOME FROM OTHER PARTICIPATING INTERESTS". **16.7**

WHERE GROUP ACCOUNTS ARE PREPARED THE BALANCE SHEET MUST CONTAIN IN A PROMINENT POSITION ON THE BALANCE SHEET, ABOVE THE SIGNATURE REQUIRED BY PARAGRAPH 2.30, THAT THEY ARE PREPARED IN ACCORDANCE WITH THE SPECIAL PROVISIONS IN PART 15 OF THE COMPANIES ACT 2006 RELATING TO SMALL COMPANIES. **16.8**

17 DIRECTORS' REMUNERATION

THE OVERALL TOTAL OF THE FOLLOWING ITEMS MUST BE DISCLOSED IN RESPECT OF DIRECTORS' REMUNERATION: **17.1**

(A) THE OVERALL AMOUNT OF REMUNERATION PAID TO OR RECEIVABLE BY **DIRECTORS** IN RESPECT OF **QUALIFYING SERVICES**;

**There are no special provisions in Republic of Ireland company law that relate to the preparation of group accounts by small companies. See Apendix I.*

†That is item 8 in format 1 and item 10 in format 2

(B) THE OVERALL AMOUNT OF MONEY PAID TO OR RECEIVABLE BY **DIRECTORS** AND THE NET VALUE OF ASSETS (OTHER THAN MONEY, SHARE OPTIONS OR SHARES) RECEIVED OR RECEIVABLE BY DIRECTORS, UNDER LONG TERM INCENTIVE SCHEMES IN RESPECT OF QUALIFYING SERVICES; AND

(C) THE OVERALL VALUE OF ANY COMPANY CONTRIBUTIONS PAID, OR TREATED AS PAID, TO A **PENSION SCHEME** IN RESPECT OF **DIRECTORS' QUALIFYING SERVICES** AND BY REFERENCE TO WHICH THE RATE OR AMOUNT OF ANY MONEY PURCHASE BENEFITS THAT MAY BECOME PAYABLE WILL BE CALCULATED.

IN THE CASE OF **MONEY PURCHASE SCHEMES** AND **DEFINED BENEFIT SCHEMES**, DISCLOSE THE NUMBER OF **DIRECTORS** (IF ANY) TO WHOM **RETIREMENT BENEFITS** ARE ACCRUING IN RESPECT OF **QUALIFYING SERVICES**.

17.2 DISCLOSURE MUST BE PROVIDED OF THE AGGREGATE AMOUNTS OF ANY COMPENSATION TO **DIRECTORS** OR PAST **DIRECTORS** IN RESPECT OF LOSS OF OFFICE, INCLUDING BENEFITS OTHER THAN IN CASH, AND THE ESTIMATED MONEY VALUE OF SUCH BENEFITS AND THEIR NATURE.

17.3 DISCLOSURE MUST BE PROVIDED OF THE AGGREGATE AMOUNT OF ANY CONSIDERATION PAID TO, OR RECEIVABLE BY, THIRD PARTIES* FOR MAKING AVAILABLE THE SERVICES OF ANY PERSON:

(A) AS A **DIRECTOR** OF THE COMPANY; OR

(B) WHILE **DIRECTOR** OF THE COMPANY, AS **DIRECTOR** OF ANY SUBSIDIARY UNDERTAKING, OR OTHERWISE IN CONNECTION WITH THE MANAGEMENT OF THE AFFAIRS OF THE COMPANY OR ANY OF ITS **SUBSIDIARY UNDERTAKINGS**.

THE REFERENCE TO CONSIDERATION INCLUDES BENEFITS OTHER THAN IN CASH AND THE ESTIMATED MONEY VALUE OF SUCH BENEFITS AND THEIR NATURE MUST BE DISCLOSED.

18 THE DIRECTORS' REPORT

Introduction

18.1 THE DIRECTORS OF A COMPANY MUST PREPARE A DIRECTORS' REPORT FOR EACH INDIVIDUAL FINANCIAL YEAR OF THE COMPANY. THE FOLLOWING DISCLOSURES MUST BE PROVIDED IN THE DIRECTORS' REPORT:

(A) THE PRINCIPAL ACTIVITIES OF THE COMPANY;

(B) DETAILS OF THE COMPANY'S **DIRECTORS**;

(C) POLITICAL DONATIONS AND EXPENDITURE;

(D) CHARITABLE DONATIONS;

(E) ACQUISITION OF OWN SHARES; AND

(F) EMPLOYMENT, ETC OF DISABLED PERSONS.

*THIRD PARTIES ARE PERSONS OTHER THAN (1) THE DIRECTOR HIMSELF OR A PERSON CONNECTED WITH HIM OR BODY CORPORATE CONTROLLED BY HIM, AND (2) THE COMPANY OR ANY OF ITS SUBSIDIARY UNDERTAKINGS. *Sections 252 and 253 of the 2006 Companies Act define what is meant by "Persons connected with a director" and "Member of the **director's family**". Amounts paid to or receivable by a person connected with a director, or a body corporate controlled by a director, shall be included instead within the disclosures set out in paragraph 17.1.*

A DIRECTOR OF A COMPANY IS LIABLE TO COMPENSATE THE COMPANY FOR ANY UNTRUE OR MISLEADING STATEMENT IN THE DIRECTORS' REPORT OR ANY OMISSION FROM IT IF HE KNEW THE STATEMENT TO BE UNTRUE OR MISLEADING OR HE KNEW THE OMISSION TO BE DISHONEST CONCEALMENT OF A MATERIAL FACT. **18.2**

WHERE THE COMPANY IS A PARENT AND CHOOSES TO PREPARE GROUP ACCOUNTS, THE DIRECTORS' REPORT MUST BE A GROUP REPORT RELATING TO THE UNDERTAKINGS INCLUDED IN THE CONSOLIDATION. **18.3**

The principal activities of the company

THE REPORT MUST STATE THE PRINCIPAL ACTIVITIES OF THE COMPANY AND ITS SUBSIDIARIES DURING THE YEAR. These activities will be the various classes of business in which the company operates. **18.4**

Details of the company's directors

THE REPORT MUST STATE THE NAMES OF THE PERSONS WHO, AT ANY TIME DURING THE **FINANCIAL YEAR**, WERE **DIRECTORS** OF THE COMPANY. **18.5**

Disclosure of qualifying third party indemnity provisions

IF, WHEN A DIRECTORS' REPORT IS APPROVED, ANY QUALIFYING THIRD PARTY INDEMNITY PROVISION (WHETHER MADE BY THE COMPANY OR OTHERWISE) IS IN FORCE OR WAS IN FORCE DURING THE FINANCIAL YEAR FOR THE BENEFIT OF ONE OR MORE DIRECTORS OF THE COMPANY (OR OF AN ASSOCIATED COMPANY), THE REPORT MUST STATE THAT ANY SUCH PROVISION IS OR WAS IN FORCE. **18.6**

Political donations and expenditure and charitable donations

IF THE COMPANY OR THE COMPANY AND ITS SUBSIDIARIES, HAS IN THE **FINANCIAL YEAR** MADE ANY POLITICAL DONATION TO ANY POLITICAL PARTY OR OTHER POLITICAL ORGANISATION, OR MADE ANY POLITICAL DONATION TO ANY INDEPENDENT ELECTION CANDIDATE, OR INCURRED ANY POLITICAL EXPENDITURE, AND THE AMOUNT OF THE DONATION OR EXPENDITURE OR (AS THE CASE MAY BE) THE AGGREGATE AMOUNT OF ALL DONATIONS AND EXPENDITURE EXCEEDED £2,000, THEN THE DIRECTORS' REPORT MUST DISCLOSE THE FOLLOWING PARTICULARS: **18.7**

(A) FOR POLITICAL DONATIONS – THE NAME OF EACH POLITICAL PARTY, OTHER POLITICAL ORGANISATION OR INDEPENDENT ELECTION CANDIDATE TO WHOM SUCH A DONATION HAS BEEN MADE AND THE TOTAL AMOUNT GIVEN TO THAT PARTY, ORGANISATION OR CANDIDATE BY WAY OF SUCH DONATIONS IN THE FINANCIAL YEAR; AND

(B) FOR POLITICAL EXPENDITURE – THE TOTAL AMOUNT INCURRED BY WAY OF SUCH EXPENDITURE IN THE FINANCIAL YEAR.

IF THE COMPANY, OR THE COMPANY AND ITS SUBSIDIARIES MADE ANY CONTRIBUTION TO A NON-EU POLITICAL PARTY, THE DIRECTORS' REPORT MUST CONTAIN A STATEMENT OF THE AMOUNT OF THE CONTRIBUTION OR, IF IT HAS MADE TWO OR MORE SUCH CONTRIBUTIONS IN THE YEAR, A STATEMENT OF THE TOTAL AMOUNT OF THE CONTRIBUTIONS. **18.8**

IF THE COMPANY, OR THE COMPANY AND ITS SUBSIDIARIES, HAS IN THE FINANCIAL YEAR GIVEN MONEY FOR CHARITABLE PURPOSES AND THE MONEY GIVEN EXCEEDS £2,000 THE AMOUNT GIVEN FOR EACH OF THE PURPOSES FOR WHICH MONEY HAS BEEN GIVEN MUST BE DISCLOSED. **18.9**

*Acquisition of own shares**

18.10 WHERE THE COMPANY ACQUIRES ITS OWN SHARES, EITHER BY PURCHASE OR ACQUISITION BY FORFEITURE, THE DIRECTORS' REPORT MUST STATE:

(A) THE NUMBER AND NOMINAL VALUE OF SHARES PURCHASED, THE AGGREGATE CONSIDERATION PAID FOR THE SHARES AND THE REASONS FOR THE PURCHASE;
(B) THE NUMBER AND NOMINAL VALUE OF SHARES ACQUIRED;
(C) THE MAXIMUM NUMBER AND NOMINAL VALUE OF SHARES ACQUIRED OR CHARGED DURING THE YEAR; AND
(D) THE NUMBER AND NOMINAL VALUE OF SUCH SHARES ACQUIRED WHICH WERE DISPOSED OF IN THE YEAR. THE AMOUNT OF MONEY RECEIVED SHALL BE DISCLOSED WHERE THE SHARES WERE DISPOSED OF FOR MONEY.

IN EACH OF THE ABOVE CASES, THE PERCENTAGE OF THE CALLED-UP SHARE CAPITAL WHICH THEY REPRESENT AND, IN EACH CASE WHERE SHARES HAVE BEEN CHARGED, THE AMOUNT OF THE CHARGE MUST BE STATED.

Employment, etc of disabled persons

18.11 WHERE THE AVERAGE NUMBER OF EMPLOYEES EXCEEDS 250 THE DIRECTORS' REPORT MUST INCLUDE A STATEMENT DESCRIBING THE POLICY WHICH THE COMPANY HAS ADOPTED FOR:

(A) GIVING FULL AND FAIR CONSIDERATION TO APPLICATIONS FOR EMPLOYMENT BY DISABLED PERSONS, HAVING REGARD TO THEIR PARTICULAR APTITUDES AND ABILITIES;
(B) CONTINUING EMPLOYMENT AND APPROPRIATE TRAINING FOR EMPLOYEES OF THE COMPANY WHO BECAME DISABLED DURING THE PERIOD WHEN THEY WERE EMPLOYED BY THE COMPANY; AND
(C) OTHERWISE FOR THE TRAINING, CAREER DEVELOPMENT AND PROMOTION OF DISABLED PERSONS EMPLOYED BY THE COMPANY.

Statement as to disclosure of information to auditors

18.12 WHERE A SMALL COMPANY CHOOSES NOT TO TAKE ADVANTAGE OF THE EXEMPTION IN THE 2006 COMPANIES ACT RELATING TO THE AUDIT OF ACCOUNTS, THE DIRECTORS' REPORT MUST CONTAIN A STATEMENT THAT, SO FAR AS EACH OF THE DIRECTORS AT THE TIME THE REPORT IS APPROVED ARE AWARE:

(A) THERE IS NO RELEVANT AUDIT INFORMATION OF WHICH THE COMPANY'S AUDITORS ARE UNAWARE; AND
(B) THE DIRECTORS HAVE TAKEN ALL STEPS THAT THEY OUGHT TO HAVE TAKEN TO MAKE THEMSELVES AWARE OF ANY RELEVANT AUDIT INFORMATION AND TO ESTABLISH THAT THE AUDITORS ARE AWARE OF THAT INFORMATION.

Approval and signing of the directors' report

18.13 THE DIRECTORS' REPORT MUST BE APPROVED BY THE BOARD OF **DIRECTORS** AND SIGNED ON BEHALF OF THE BOARD BY A **DIRECTOR** OR THE SECRETARY OF THE COMPANY. EVERY COPY

**THESE DISCLOSURE REQUIREMENTS APPLY WHERE OWN SHARES ARE: (I) PURCHASED BY THE COMPANY OR ACQUIRED BY THE COMPANY BY FORFEITURE OR SURRENDER IN LIEU OF FORFEITURE; (II) ACQUIRED BY THE COMPANY OTHERWISE THAN FOR VALUABLE CONSIDERATION; (III) ACQUIRED BY A NOMINEE OF THE COMPANY WITHOUT FINANCIAL ASSISTANCE FROM THE COMPANY, OR BY ANY PERSON WITH FINANCIAL ASSISTANCE FROM THE COMPANY, AND, IN EITHER CASE, THE COMPANY HAS A BENEFICIAL INTEREST IN THE SHARES; OR (IV) MADE SUBJECT TO A LIEN OR CHARGE UNDER S150 OR S6(3) OF THE CONSEQUENTIAL PROVISIONS ACT 1985.*

OF THE DIRECTORS' REPORT WHICH IS PUBLISHED BY OR ON BEHALF OF THE BOARD MUST STATE THE NAME OF THE PERSON WHO SIGNED IT ON BEHALF OF THE BOARD.

THE COPY OF THE DIRECTORS' REPORT WHICH IS DELIVERED TO THE REGISTRAR MUST STATE THE NAME OF THE PERSON WHO SIGNED IT ON BEHALF OF THE BOARD. **18.14**

IF THE DIRECTORS' REPORT IS PREPARED IN ACCORDANCE WITH THE SMALL COMPANIES REGIME, IT MUST CONTAIN A STATEMENT TO THAT EFFECT IN A PROMINENT POSITION ABOVE THE SIGNATURE. **18.15**

IF A DIRECTORS' REPORT IS APPROVED THAT DOES NOT COMPLY WITH THE REQUIREMENTS OF THE COMPANIES ACT 2006, THEN EVERY DIRECTOR OF THE COMPANY WHO KNEW THAT IT DID NOT COMPLY OR WAS RECKLESS AS TO WHETHER IT COMPLIED AND FAILED TO TAKE REASONABLE STEPS TO SECURE COMPLIANCE WITH THOSE REQUIREMENTS OR, AS THE CASE MAY BE, TO PREVENT THE REPORT FROM BEING APPROVED, COMMITS AN OFFENCE AND IS LIABLE TO A FINE. **18.16**

19 DATE FROM WHICH EFFECTIVE AND TRANSITIONAL ARRANGEMENTS

The accounting practices set out in this Financial Reporting Standard for Smaller Entities (effective April 2008) shall be regarded as standard in respect of financial statements relating to accounting periods beginning on or after 6 April 2008. Earlier application is not permitted.*† **19.1**

Transitional arrangements – goodwill

All goodwill that was eliminated against reserves in accordance with an **accounting policy** permitted until 23 March 1999 may remain eliminated against reserves thereafter.‡ Alternatively, in its first accounting period beginning on or after 23 March 1999, an entity may reinstate by prior period adjustment all goodwill previously eliminated against reserves. **19.2**

Transitional arrangements – tangible fixed assets

Where, for its first accounting period ending on or after 23 March 2000, an entity does not adopt an **accounting policy** of revaluation, but the carrying amount of its **tangible fixed assets** reflects previous revaluations, it may: **19.3**

(a) retain the book amounts. In these circumstances the entity shall disclose the fact that the transitional provisions of the FRSSE are being followed and that the valuation has not been updated and give the date of the last revaluation; or

(b) restate the carrying amount of the **tangible fixed assets** to historical cost (less restated accumulated **depreciation**), as a change in **accounting policy**.

**Earlier application is not being permitted because of the need for accounts prepared in accordance with the FRSSE for accounting periods commencing on or before 5 April 2006 to comply with the requirements of company law, as set out in the Companies Act 1985 and consequently the FRSSE (effective January 2007) remains applicable.*

†***Editor's note**: With effect for accounting periods beginning on or after 1 January 2015 this is replaced with:*

The accounting practices set out in this Financial Reporting Standard for Smaller Entities (effective January 2015) shall be regarded as standard in respect of financial statements relating to accounting periods beginning on or after 1 January 2015. Earlier application is permitted.

‡*The treatment of such amounts on disposal of a business is set out in paragraph 3.7.*

19.4 Where, for its first accounting period ending on or after 23 March 2000, an entity separates **tangible fixed assets** into different components with significantly different useful economic lives for **depreciation** purposes, the changes shall be dealt with as a prior period adjustment, as a change in **accounting policy**. Other revisions to the useful economic lives and **residual values** of **tangible fixed assets** are not the result of a change in **accounting policy** and shall be treated in accordance with paragraph 6.40 and not as **prior period adjustments**.

20 WITHDRAWAL OF THE FRSSE (EFFECTIVE JANUARY 2007)

20.1 The Financial Reporting Standard for Smaller Entities (effective April 2008) supersedes the FRSSE (effective January 2007).*

***Editor's note**: With effect for accounting periods beginning on or after 1 January 2015 this is replaced with:*

The Financial Reporting Standard for Smaller Entities (effective January 2015) supersedes the FRSSE (effective April 2008).

C – Definitions

The following definitions shall apply in the FRSSE and in particular in the Statement of Standard Accounting Practice set out in sections 1-20 of Part B.

Accounting policies:-

Those principles, bases, conventions, rules and practices applied by an entity that specify how the effects of transactions and other events are to be reflected in its financial statements through:

(i) **recognising**;
(ii) selecting measurement bases for; and
(iii) presenting

assets, **liabilities**, gains, losses and changes to shareholders' funds. Accounting policies do not include **estimation techniques.**

Accounting policies define the process whereby transactions and other events are reflected in financial statements. For example, an accounting policy for a particular type of expenditure may specify whether an **asset** or a loss is to be **recognised**; the basis on which it is to be measured; and where in the profit and loss account or balance sheet it is to be presented.

Actuarial gains and losses:-

Changes in actuarial deficits or surpluses that arise because events have not coincided with the actuarial assumptions made for the last valuation or because the actuarial assumptions have changed.

Applied research:-

Original or critical investigation undertaken in order to gain new scientific or technical knowledge and directed towards a specific practical aim or objective.

Arrangement fees:-

The costs that are incurred directly in connection with the issue of a **capital instrument**, i.e. those costs that would not have been incurred if the specific instrument in question had not been issued.

Assets:-

Rights or other access to future economic benefits controlled by an entity as a result of past transactions or events.

Attributable profit (on long-term contracts):-

That part of the total profit currently estimated to arise over the duration of the contract, after allowing for estimated remedial and maintenance costs and increases in costs so far as not recoverable under the terms of the contract, that fairly reflects the profit attributable to that part of the work performed at the accounting date. (There can be no attributable profit until the profitable outcome of the contract can be assessed with reasonable certainty.)

Borrowings:-

Capital instruments that are classified as **liabilities**.

Capital instruments:-

All instruments that are issued (or arrangements entered into) by reporting entities as a means of raising finance, including shares, debentures, loans and debt instruments, options and warrants that give the holder the right to subscribe for or obtain capital instruments. In the case of **consolidated financial statements** the term includes capital instruments issued by subsidiaries except those that are held by another member of the group that is included in the consolidation.

Cash-settled share-based payment transaction:-

A **share-based payment transaction** in which the entity acquires goods or services by incurring a **liability** to transfer cash or other **assets** to the supplier of those goods or services for amounts that are based on the price (or value) of the entity's shares or other **equity instruments** of the entity.

Close family:-

Close members of the family of an individual are those family members, or members of the same household, who may be expected to influence, or be influenced by, that person in their dealings with the reporting entity.*

Closing rate:-

The closing rate is the **exchange rate** for spot transactions ruling at the balance sheet date and is the mean of the buying and selling rates at the close of business on the day for which the rate is to be ascertained.

Companies legislation:-

(a) In the United Kingdom, the Companies Act 2006; and
(b) in the Republic of Ireland, the Companies Acts 1963-2003 and all other Regulations to be read as one with the Companies Acts.

Consignment stock:-

Consignment stock is stock held by one party (the 'dealer') but legally owned by another (the 'manufacturer'), on terms that give the dealer the right to sell the stock in the normal course of its business or, at its option, to return it unsold to the legal owner.

***Editor's note**: With effect for accounting periods beginning on or after 1 January 2015 this is replaced with:*

Close members of the family of a person:-

Close members of the family of a person are those family members who may be expected to influence, or be influenced by, that person in their dealings with the entity and include:
(a) that person's children and spouse or domestic partner;
(b) children of that person's spouse or domestic partner; and
(c) dependents of that person or that person's spouse or domestic partner.

Consolidated financial statements:-

The financial statements of a group prepared by consolidation. A group is a parent undertaking and its subsidiary undertakings. Consolidation is the process of adjusting and combining financial information from the individual financial statements of a parent undertaking and its subsidiary undertakings to prepare consolidated financial statements that present financial information for the group as a single economic entity.

Contingent asset:-

A possible **asset** that arises from past events and whose existence will be confirmed only by the occurrence of one or more uncertain future events not wholly within the entity's control.

Contingent liability:-

(a) A possible **obligation** that arises from past events and whose existence will be confirmed only by the occurrence of one or more uncertain future events not wholly within the entity's control; or

(b) an **obligation** at the balance sheet date that arises from past events but is not **recognised** as a **provision** because:

  (i) it is not probable that a transfer of economic benefits will be required to settle the **obligation**; or

  (ii) the amount of the **obligation** cannot be measured with sufficient **reliability**.

Cost (of stock):-

Cost is defined as being that expenditure which has been incurred in the normal course of business in bringing the product or service to its present location and condition. This expenditure should include, in addition to cost of purchase, such costs of conversion (including, for example, attributable overheads) as are appropriate to that location and condition. BORROWING COSTS THAT ARE DIRECTLY ATTRIBUTABLE TO THE ACQUISITION, CONSTRUCTION OR PRODUCTION OF STOCK MAY BE INCLUDED AS PART OF THE COST.

Current service cost:-

The increase in the present value of the **scheme liabilities** expected to arise from employee service in the current period.

Current tax:-

The amount of tax estimated to be payable or recoverable in respect of the taxable profit or loss for a period, along with adjustments to estimates in respect of previous periods.

Curtailment:-

An event that reduces the expected years of future service of present employees or reduces for a number of employees the accrual of defined benefits for some or all of their future service.

Deferred tax:-

Estimated future tax consequences of transactions and events **recognised** in the financial statements of the current and previous periods.

Defined benefit scheme:-

A pension or other **retirement benefit** scheme other than a **defined contribution scheme**. Normally, the scheme rules define the benefits independently of the contributions payable, and the benefits are not directly related to the investments of the scheme.

Defined contribution scheme:-

A pension or other **retirement benefit** scheme into which an employer pays regular contributions fixed as an amount or as a percentage of pay. The employer will have no legal or constructive **obligation** to pay further contributions if the scheme does not have sufficient **assets** to pay all employee benefits relating to employee service in the current and prior periods.

Depreciation:-

The measure of the cost or revalued amount of the economic benefits of a fixed **asset** that have been consumed during the period. Consumption includes the wearing out, using up or other reduction in the **useful economic life** of a fixed **asset** whether arising from use, effluxion of time or obsolescence through either changes in technology or demand for the goods and services produced by the **asset**.

Development:-

Use of scientific or technical knowledge in order to produce new or substantially improved materials, devices, products or services, to install new processes or systems before the commencement of commercial production or commercial applications, or to improve substantially those already produced or installed.

Directly attributable costs:-

The costs that relate directly to securing the specific contract after the asset recognition criteria for **pre-contract costs** are met, if they can be separately identified and measured reliably.

Directors:-

The directors of a company or other body, the partners, proprietors, committee of management or trustees of other forms of entity, or equivalent persons responsible for directing the entity's affairs and preparing its financial statements.

DIRECTOR'S FAMILY:-

THE MEMBERS OF A DIRECTOR'S FAMILY ARE;

(A) THE DIRECTOR'S SPOUSE OR CIVIL PARTNER;
(B) ANY OTHER PERSON (WHETHER OF A DIFFERENT SEX OR THE SAME SEX) WITH WHOM THE DIRECTOR LIVES AS PARTNER IN AN ENDURING FAMILY RELATIONSHIP;
(C) THE DIRECTOR'S CHILDREN OR STEP-CHILDREN;

(D) ANY CHILDREN OR STEP-CHILDREN OF A PERSON WITHIN PARAGRAPH (B) (AND WHO ARE NOT CHILDREN OR STEP-CHILDREN OF THE DIRECTOR) WHO LIVE WITH THE DIRECTOR AND HAVE NOT ATTAINED THE AGE OF 18; AND
(E) THE DIRECTOR'S PARENTS.

IT EXCLUDES A PERSON WHO IS A DIRECTOR OF THE COMPANY.

Employees and others providing similar services:-

Individuals who render personal services to the entity and either (a) the individuals are regarded as employees for legal or tax purposes, (b) the individuals work for the entity under its direction in the same way as individuals who are regarded as employees for legal or tax purposes, or (c) the services rendered are similar to those rendered by employees. For example, the term encompasses all management personnel, i.e. those persons having authority and responsibility for planning, directing and controlling the activities of the entity, including non-executive directors.

Equity instrument:-

Any contract that evidences a residual interest in the assets of an entity after deducting all of its liabilities.

Equity instrument granted:-

The right (conditional or unconditional) to an equity instrument of the entity conferred by the entity on another party, under a share-based payment arrangement.

Equity-settled share-based payment transaction:-

A **share-based payment transaction** in which the entity receives goods or services as consideration for **equity instruments** of the entity (including shares or share options).

Estimation techniques:-

The methods adopted by an entity to arrive at estimated monetary amounts, corresponding to the measurement bases selected, for **assets, liabilities**, gains, losses and changes to shareholders' funds.

Estimation techniques implement the measurement aspects of **accounting policies**. An **accounting policy** will specify the basis on which an item is to be measured; where there is uncertainty over the monetary amount corresponding to that basis, the amount will be arrived at by using an estimation technique.

Estimation techniques include, for example:-

(a) methods of **depreciation**, such as straight-line and reducing balance, applied in the context of a particular measurement basis, used to estimate the proportion of the economic benefits of a tangible fixed asset consumed in a period; and
(b) different methods used to estimate the proportion of trade debts that will not be recovered, particularly where such methods consider a population as a whole rather than individual balances.

Events after the balance sheet date:-

Those events, both favourable and unfavourable, that occur between the balance sheet date and the date when financial statements are authorised for issue. Two types of events can be identified:

Adjusting events

(a) those that provide evidence of conditions that existed at the balance sheet date; and

Non-adjusting events

(b) those that are indicative of conditions that arose after the balance sheet date.

Exceptional items:-

Material items that derive from events or transactions that fall within the **ordinary activities** of the reporting entity and individually or, if of a similar type, in aggregate need to be disclosed by virtue of their size or incidence if the financial statements are to give a true and fair view.

Exchange rate:-

An exchange rate is a rate at which two currencies may be exchanged for each other at a particular point in time; different rates apply for spot and forward transactions.

Exchange transaction:-

A transaction in which one party supplies goods or services to another party in exchange for a consideration, usually monetary.

Fair value:-

Fair value is the amount at which an **asset** or **liability** could be exchanged in an arm's length transaction between informed and willing parties, other than in a forced or liquidation sale, less, where applicable, any grants receivable towards the purchase or use of an **asset**.

Finance charge (on a lease):-

The finance charge is the amount borne by the lessee over the **lease term**, representing the difference between the total of the **minimum lease payments** (including any residual amounts guaranteed by the lessee) and the amount at which the lessee records the leased asset at the **inception** of the lease.

Finance costs (of a capital instrument):-

The difference between the net proceeds of a **capital instrument** and the total amount of the payments (or other transfer of economic benefits) that the issuer may be required to make in respect of the instrument other than **arrangement fees**.

Finance lease:-

A finance lease is a lease that transfers substantially all the risks and rewards of ownership of an asset to the lessee. It should be presumed that such a transfer of risks and rewards occurs if at the **inception** of a lease the present value of the **minimum**

lease payments, including any initial payment, amounts to substantially all (normally 90 per cent or more) of the **fair value** of the leased asset. The present value should be calculated by using the interest rate implicit in the lease. If the **fair value** of the asset is not determinable an estimate thereof should be used.

Financial asset:-

Any asset that is:

(a) cash;
(b) an equity instrument of another entity;
(c) a contractual right:
  (i) to receive cash or another financial asset from another entity; or
  (ii) to exchange financial assets or financial liabilities with another entity under conditions that are potentially favourable to the entity; or
(d) a contract that will or may be settled in the entity's own equity instruments and is:
  (i) a non-derivative for which the entity is or may be obliged to receive a variable number of the entity's own equity instruments; or
  (ii) a derivative that will or may be settled other than by the exchange of a fixed amount of cash or another financial asset for a fixed number of the entity's own equity instruments. For this purpose the entity's own equity instruments do not include instruments that are themselves contracts for the future receipt or delivery of the entity's own equity instruments.

Financial instrument:-

Any contract that gives rise to a **financial asset** of one entity and a **financial liability** or equity instrument of another entity.

Financial liability:-

Any liability that is:

(a) a contractual obligation:
  (i) to deliver cash or another financial asset to another entity; or
  (ii) to exchange financial assets or financial liabilities with another entity under conditions that are potentially unfavourable to the entity; or
(b) a contract that will or may be settled in the entity's own equity instruments and is:
  (i) a non-derivative for which the entity is or may be obliged to deliver a variable number of the entity's own equity instruments; or
  (ii) a derivative that will or may be settled other than by the exchange of a fixed amount of cash or another financial asset for a fixed number of the entity's own equity instruments. For this purpose the entity's own equity instruments do not include instruments that are themselves contracts for the future receipt or delivery of the entity's own equity instruments.

FINANCIAL YEAR:-

A COMPANY'S **FINANCIAL YEAR** BEGINS WITH THE FIRST DAY OF ITS ACCOUNTING REFERENCE PERIOD AND ENDS WITH THE LAST DAY OF THAT PERIOD OR SUCH OTHER DATE, NOT MORE THAN SEVEN DAYS BEFORE OR AFTER THE END OF THAT PERIOD, AS THE **DIRECTORS** MAY DETERMINE.

Foreign entity:-

A foreign entity is a subsidiary, associated company or branch whose operations are based in a country other than that of the investing company or whose **assets** and **liabilities** are denominated mainly in a foreign currency.

Foreseeable losses (on a long-term contract):-

Losses that are currently estimated to arise over the duration of the contract (after allowing for estimated remedial and maintenance costs and increases in costs so far as not recoverable under the terms of the contract). This estimate is required irrespective of:

(a) whether work has yet commenced on such contracts;
(b) the proportion of work carried out at the accounting date; or
(c) the amount of profits expected to arise on other contracts.

Forward contract:-

A forward contract is an agreement to exchange different currencies at a specified future date and at a specified rate. The difference between the specified rate and the spot rate ruling on the date the contract was entered into is the discount or premium on the forward contract.

Government:-

Government includes government and inter-governmental agencies and similar bodies whether local, national or international.

Government grants:-

Government grants are assistance by **government** in the form of cash or transfers of assets to an entity in return for past or future compliance with certain conditions relating to the operating activities of the entity.

Grant date for share-based payment arrangements:-

The date at which the entity and another party (including an employee) agree to a share-based payment arrangement, being when the entity and the counterparty have a shared understanding of the terms and conditions of the arrangement. At grant date the entity confers on the counterparty the right to cash, other **assets**, or **equity instruments** of the entity, provided the specified vesting conditions, if any, are met. If that agreement is subject to an approval process (for example, by shareholders), grant date is the date when that approval is obtained.

Gross earnings (from a lease):-

Gross earnings comprise the lessor's gross finance income over the **lease term**, representing the difference between its gross investment in the lease and the cost of the leased **asset** less any grants receivable towards the purchase or use of the **asset**.

Hire purchase contract:-

A hire purchase contract is a contract for the hire of an **asset** that contains a **provision** giving the hirer an option to acquire legal title to the **asset** upon the fulfilment of certain conditions stated in the contract.

Identifiable assets and liabilities:-

Identifiable assets and liabilities are the **assets** and **liabilities** of an entity that are capable of being disposed of or settled separately, without disposing of a business of the entity.

Inception (of a lease):-

The inception of a lease is the earlier of the time the asset is brought into use and the date from which rentals first accrue.

Intangible assets:-

Intangible assets are non-financial fixed **assets** that do not have physical substance but are **identifiable** and are controlled by the entity through custody or legal rights.

Interest cost:-

The expected increase during the period in the present value of the **scheme liabilities** because the benefits are one period closer to **settlement**.

Investment property:-

An investment property is an interest in land and/or buildings:

(a) in respect of which construction work and development have been completed; and

(b) which is held for its investment potential, any rental income being negotiated at arm's length, but excluding:

 (i) a property that is owned and occupied by a company for its own purposes; and

 (ii) a property let to and occupied by another group company.*

Lease term:-

The lease term is the period for which the lessee has contracted to lease the **asset** and any further terms for which the lessee has the option to continue to lease the **asset** with or without further payment, which option it is reasonably certain at the **inception** of the lease that the lessee will exercise.

Liabilities:-

An entity's **obligations** to transfer economic benefits as a result of past transactions or events.

***Editor's note**: *With effect for accounting periods beginning on or after 1 January 2015 the following definition is inserted:*

Key management personnel:-

Key management personnel are those persons having authority and responsibility for planning, directing and controlling the activities of the entity, directly or indirectly, including any director (whether executive or otherwise) of that entity.

Local currency:-

An entity's local currency is the currency of the primary economic environment in which it operates and generates net cash flows.

Long-term contract:-

A contract entered into for the design, manufacture or construction of a single substantial **asset** or the provision of a service (or of a combination of **assets** or services that together constitute a single project) where the time taken substantially to complete the contract is such that the contract activity falls into different accounting periods. A contract that is required to be accounted for as long-term by the FRSSE will usually extend for a period exceeding one year. However, a duration exceeding one year is not an essential feature of a long-term contract. Some contracts with a shorter duration than one year should be accounted for as long-term contracts if they are sufficiently material to the activity of the period that not to record turnover and **attributable profit** would lead to distortion of the period's turnover and results such that the financial statements would not give a true and fair view, provided that the policy is applied consistently within the reporting entity and from year to year.

Minimum lease payments:-

The minimum lease payments are the minimum payments over the remaining part of the **lease term** (excluding charges for services and taxes to be paid by the lessor) and:

(a) in the case of the lessee any residual amounts guaranteed by it or by a party related to it; or
(b) in the case of the lessor any residual amounts guaranteed by the lessee or by an independent third party.

Monetary items:-

Monetary items are money held and amounts to be received or paid in money and should be categorised as either short-term or long-term. Short-term monetary items are those that fall due within one year of the balance sheet date.

MONEY PURCHASE SCHEME:-

A **DEFINED CONTRIBUTION SCHEME** UNDER WHICH ALL OF THE BENEFITS THAT MAY BECOME PAYABLE ARE CALCULATED BY REFERENCE TO THE PAYMENTS MADE OR TREATED AS MADE BY THE SCHEME MEMBER AND WHICH ARE NOT AVERAGE SALARY BENEFITS.

Net investment (in a foreign entity):-

The net investment that a company has in a **foreign entity** is its effective equity stake and comprises its proportion of such **foreign entity's** net assets; in appropriate circumstances, intragroup loans and other deferred balances may be regarded as part of the effective equity stake.

Net investment (in a lease):-

The net investment in a lease at a point in time comprises:

(a) the gross investment in a lease (i.e. the total of the **minimum lease payments** and that portion of the **residual value** of the **leased asset**, the realisation of which by the lessor is not assured or is guaranteed solely by a party related to the lessor); less

(b) **gross earnings** allocated to future periods.

Net realisable value (of fixed assets):-

Net realisable value of a fixed asset is the amount at which the asset could be disposed of, less any direct selling costs.

Net realisable value (of stocks and long-term contracts):-

The actual or estimated selling price (net of trade but before settlement discounts) less:

(a) all further costs to completion; and
(b) all costs to be incurred in marketing, selling and distributing.

Obligation:-

An obligation may be either a legal obligation (derived, for example, from a contract or legislation) or a constructive obligation, where the entity has indicated to other parties that it will accept certain responsibilities and has created valid expectations in those other parties that it will discharge those responsibilities.

Operating lease:-

An operating lease is a lease other than a **finance lease**.

Ordinary activities:-

Any activities that are undertaken by a reporting entity as part of its business and such related activities in which the reporting entity engages in furtherance of, incidental to, or arising from, these activities. Ordinary activities include the effects on the reporting entity of any event in the various environments in which it operates, including the political, regulatory, economic and geographical environments, irrespective of the frequency or unusual nature of the events.

Past service cost:-

The increase in the present value of the **scheme liabilities** related to employee service in prior periods arising in the current period as a result of the introduction of, or improvement to, **retirement benefits.**

Pension schemes:-

A pension scheme is an arrangement (other than accident insurance) to provide pension and/or other benefits for members on leaving service or retiring and, after a *member's death*, for his/her dependants.

Performance:-

The fulfilment of the seller's contractual **obligations** to a customer through the supply of goods and services.

Permanent differences:-

Differences between an entity's taxable profits and its results as stated in the financial statements that arise because certain types of income and expenditure are non-taxable or disallowable, or because certain tax charges or allowances have no corresponding amount in the financial statements.

Pre-contract costs:-

The costs of tendering for and securing contracts to supply products or services.

Prior period adjustments:-

Material adjustments applicable to prior periods arising from changes in **accounting policies** or from the correction of fundamental errors. They do not include normal recurring adjustments or corrections of accounting estimates made in prior periods.

Projected unit method:-

An accrued benefits valuation method in which the **scheme liabilities** make allowance for projected earnings. An accrued benefits valuation method is a valuation method in which the **scheme liabilities** at the valuation date relate to:

(a) the benefits for pensioners and deferred pensioners (i.e. individuals who have ceased to be active members but are entitled to benefits payable at a later date) and their dependants, allowing where appropriate for future increases; and
(b) the accrued benefits for members in service on the valuation date.

The accrued benefits are the benefits for service up to a given point in time, whether vested rights or not. Guidance on the projected unit method is given in the Guidance Note GN26 issued by the Faculty and Institute of Actuaries.

Provision:-

A **liability** of uncertain timing or amount.*

Purchased goodwill:-

Purchased goodwill is goodwill that is established as a result of the purchase of a business accounted for as an acquisition. It represents the difference between the cost of the acquired business and the aggregate of the **fair values** recorded for the **identifiable assets and liabilities** acquired. Positive goodwill arises when the acquisition cost exceeds the aggregate **fair values** of the **identifiable assets and liabilities**. Negative goodwill arises when the aggregate **fair values** of the **identifiable assets and liabilities** of the entity exceed the acquisition cost.

***Editor's note**: With effect for accounting periods beginning on or after 1 January 2015 the following definition is inserted:*

Public benefit entity:-

An entity whose primary objective is to provide goods or services for the general public, community or social benefit and where any equity is provided with a view to supporting the entity's primary objectives rather than with a view to providing a financial return to equity providers, shareholders or members.

Pure (or basic) research:-

Experimental or theoretical work undertaken primarily to acquire new scientific or technological knowledge for its own sake rather than directed towards any specific aim or application.

QUALIFYING SERVICES:-

SERVICES AS A DIRECTOR OF THE COMPANY OR SERVICES WHILE DIRECTOR OF THE COMPANY AND AS DIRECTOR OF ANY OF ITS SUBSIDIARY UNDERTAKINGS OR OTHERWISE IN CONNECTION WITH THE MANAGEMENT OF THE AFFAIRS OF THE COMPANY OR ANY OF ITS SUBSIDIARIES.

QUALIFYING THIRD PARTY INDEMNITY PROVISION:-

A PROVISION BY WHICH A COMPANY DIRECTLY OR INDIRECTLY PROVIDES AN INDEMNITY FOR A DIRECTOR OF THE COMPANY OR AN ASSOCIATED COMPANY WHICH SATISFIES THE FOLLOWING THREE CONDITIONS:

(A) THE PROVISION DOES NOT PROVIDE ANY INDEMNITY AGAINST ANY LIABILITY INCURRED BY THE DIRECTOR TO THE COMPANY OR ANY ASSOCIATED COMPANY;

(B) THE PROVISION DOES NOT PROVIDE ANY INDEMNITY AGAINST ANY LIABILITY INCURRED BY THE DIRECTOR TO PAY A FINE IMPOSED BY CRIMINAL PROCEEDINGS OR PAY A PENALTY TO A REGULATORY AUTHORITY IN RESPECT OF NON-COMPLIANCE;

(C) THE PROVISION DOES NOT PROVIDE ANY INDEMNITY AGAINST ANY LIABILITY INCURRED BY THE DIRECTOR (I) IN DEFENDING ANY CRIMINAL PROCEEDINGS IN WHICH HE IS CONVICTED OR (II) IN DEFENDING ANY CIVIL PROCEEDINGS BROUGHT BY THE COMPANY OR AN ASSOCIATED COMPANY IN WHICH JUDGEMENT IS GIVEN AGAINST HIM, OR (III) IN WHICH THE COURT REFUSES TO GRANT RELIEF IN CONNECTION WITH ANY APPLICATION UNDER THE FOLLOWING PROVISIONS: ACQUISITION OF SHARES BY INNOCENT NOMINEE, OR GENERAL POWER TO GRANT RELIEF IN CSE OF HONEST AND REASONABLE CONDUCT.

QUALIFYING UNDERTAKING:-

A QUALIFYING PARTNERSHIP OR AN UNLIMITED COMPANY EACH OF WHOSE MEMBERS IS (I) A LIMITED COMPANY, OR (II) ANOTHER UNLIMITED COMPANY EACH OF WHOSE MEMBERS IS A LIMITED COMPANY, OR (III) A SCOTTISH PARTNERSHIP EACH OF WHOSE MEMBERS IS A LIMITED COMPANY.

THIS INCLUDES ANY COMPARABLE UNDERTAKING INCORPORATED IN OR FORMED UNDER THE LAW OF ANY COUNTRY OR TERRITORY OUTSIDE UNITED KINGDOM.

Recognised:-

Recognition is the process of incorporating an item into the primary financial statements under the appropriate heading. It involves depiction of the item in words and by a monetary amount and inclusion of that amount in the statement totals.

Recoverable amount:-

Recoverable amount of an **asset** is the higher of the amounts that can be obtained from selling the **asset** (i.e. **net realisable value**) or continuing to use the **asset** in the business (i.e. value in use). Value in use is calculated as the present value of the future cash flows* obtainable as a result of the **asset's** continued use (including those resulting from its ultimate disposal), or a reasonable estimate thereof.

Regular (pension) cost:-

The consistent ongoing cost **recognised** under the actuarial method used.

Related parties:-

Two or more parties are related parties when at any time during the financial period:

(a) one party has direct or indirect control of the other party; or
(b) the parties are subject to common control from the same source; or
(c) one party has significant influence over the financial and operating policies of the other party. Significant influence would occur if that other party is inhibited from pursuing its own separate interests.

For the avoidance of doubt, related parties of the reporting entity include the following:

(i) parent undertakings, subsidiary and fellow subsidiary undertakings;
(ii) associates and joint ventures;
(iii) investors with significant influence and their **close families**; and
(iv) **directors** of the reporting entity and of its parent undertakings and their **close families**.†

Reliability:-

Financial information is reliable if:

(a) it can be depended upon by users to represent faithfully what it either purports to represent or could reasonably be expected to represent, and therefore reflects the substance of the transactions and other events that have taken place;
(b) it is free from deliberate or systematic bias (i.e. it is neutral);

**This calculation may not be relevant for fixed assets held by charities and other not-for-profit entities, where they are not held for the purpose of generating cash flows.*

†***Editor's note****: With effect for accounting periods beginning on or after 1 January 2015 this is replaced with:*

A related party is a person or entity that is related to the entity that is preparing its financial statements (in this Standard referred to as the 'reporting entity').

(a) A person or a close member of that person's family is related to a reporting entity if that person:
  (i) has control or joint control over the reporting entity;
  (ii) has significant influence over the reporting entity; or
(b) is a member of the key management personnel of the reporting entity or of a parent of the reporting entity. An entity is related to a reporting entity if any of the following conditions applies:
  (i) The entity and the reporting entity are members of the same group (which means that each parent, subsidiary and fellow subsidiary is related to the others).
  (ii) One entity is an associate or joint venture of the other entity (or an associate or joint venture of a member of a group of which the other entity is a member).
  (iii) Both entities are joint ventures of the same third party.
  (iv) One entity is a joint venture of a third entity and the other entity is an associate of the third entity.
  (v) The entity is a retirement benefit scheme for the benefit of employees of either the reporting entity or an entity related to the reporting entity. If the reporting entity is itself such a scheme, the sponsoring employers are also related to the reporting entity.
  (vi) The entity is controlled or jointly controlled by a person identified in (a).
  (vii) A person identified in (a)(i) has significant influence over the entity or is a member of the key management personnel of the entity (or of a parent of the entity).

(c) it is free from material error;
(d) it is complete within the bounds of materiality; and
(e) under conditions of uncertainty, it has been prudently prepared (i.e. a degree of caution has been applied in exercising judgement and making the necessary estimates).

Research and development expenditure:-

Research and development expenditure means expenditure falling into one or more of the broad categories of **pure (or basic) research**, **applied research** and **development** (except to the extent that it relates to locating or exploiting oil, gas or mineral deposits or is reimbursable by third parties either directly or under the terms of a firm contract to develop and manufacture at an agreed price calculated to reimburse both elements of expenditure).

Residual value:-

Residual value is the realisable value of an **asset** at the end of its **useful economic life**, based on prices prevailing at the date of acquisition or revaluation, where this has taken place. Residual values do not take account of future price changes Realisation costs should be deducted in arriving at the residual value.

Retirement benefits:-

All forms of consideration given by an employer in exchange for services rendered by employees that are payable after the completion of employment. Retirement benefits do not include termination benefits payable as a result of either (i) an employer's decision to terminate an employee's employment before the normal retirement date or (ii) an employee's decision to accept voluntary redundancy in exchange for those benefits, because these are not given in exchange for services rendered by employees.

Right to consideration:-

A seller's right to the amount received or receivable in exchange for its **performance**. This right does not necessarily correspond to amounts falling due in accordance with a schedule of stage payments which may be specified in a contractual arrangement. Whilst stage payments will often be timed to coincide with **performance**, they may not correspond exactly. Stage payments reflect only the agreed timing of payment, whereas a right to consideration arises through the seller's **performance**.

Scheme liabilities:-

The **liabilities** of a defined benefit scheme for outgoings due after the valuation date. Scheme liabilities measured using the **projected unit method** reflect the benefits that the employer is committed to provide for service up to the valuation date.

Settlement:-

An irrevocable action that relieves the employer (or the **defined benefit scheme**) of the primary responsibility for a pension **obligation** and eliminates significant risks relating to the **obligation** and the **assets** used to effect the settlement.

Share-based payment transaction:-

A transaction in which the entity receives goods or services as consideration for **equity instruments** of the entity (including shares or share options), or acquires goods or services by incurring **liabilities** to the supplier of those goods or services for amounts that are based on the price of the entity's shares or other **equity instruments** of the entity.

Social security costs:-

Any contributions by the entity to any state social security or pension scheme, fund or arrangement.

Start-up costs:-

Costs arising from those one-time activities related to opening a new facility, introducing a new product or service, conducting business in a new territory, conducting business with a new class of customer, initiating a new process in an existing facility, starting some new operation and similar items. They include costs of relocating or reorganising part or all of an entity, costs related to organising a new entity, and expenses and losses incurred both before and after opening.

*Subsidiary undertakings**

An undertaking is a subsidiary of a parent undertaking where the parent:

(a) holds a majority of the voting rights in the undertaking; or
(b) is a member of the undertaking and has the right to appoint or remove a majority of its board of directors; or
(c) has the right to exercise a dominant influence over the undertaking by virtue of provisions contained in its memorandum or articles or by virtue of a control contract; or
(d) is a member of the undertaking and controls alone, pursuant to an agreement with other shareholders or members, a majority of the voting rights in the undertaking; or
(e) has the power to exercise, or actually exercises, dominant influence or control over the undertaking; or
(f) the parent and the subsidiary undertaking are managed on a unified basis.

Tangible fixed ***assets:-***

Assets that have physical substance and are held for use in the production or supply of goods or services, for rental to others, or for administrative purposes on a continuing basis in the reporting entity's activities.

Tax credit:-

The tax credit given under UK legislation to the recipient of a dividend from a UK company.

Term (of a capital instrument):-

The period from the date of issue of the **capital instrument** to the date at which it will expire, be redeemed, or be cancelled. If either party has the option to require the instrument to be redeemed or cancelled and, under the terms of the instrument, it is uncertain whether such an option will be exercised, the term should be taken to end on the earliest date at which the instrument would be redeemed or cancelled on exercise of such an option. If either party has the right to extend the period of an

**In case of doubt, reference should be made to the full definition in section 1162 of the Companies Act 2006.*

instrument, the term should not include the period of the extension if there is a genuine commercial possibility that the period will not be extended.

Timing differences:-

Differences between taxable profits and the results as stated in the financial statements that arise from the inclusion of gains and losses in tax assessments in periods different from those in which they are **recognised** in financial statements. For example, a timing difference would arise when tax allowances for the cost of a fixed asset are accelerated or decelerated, i.e. received before or after the **depreciation** of the fixed asset is **recognised** in the profit and loss account.

Total recognised gains and losses:-

The total of all gains and losses of the reporting entity that are **recognised** in a period and are attributable to the shareholders.

Translation:-

Translation is the process whereby financial data denominated in one currency are expressed in terms of another currency. It includes both the expression of individual transactions in terms of another currency and the expression of a complete set of financial statements prepared in one currency in terms of another currency.

Useful economic life:-

The useful economic life of a tangible fixed asset is the period over which the entity expects to derive economic benefit from that asset.

Withholding tax:-

Tax on dividends or other income that is deducted by the payer of the income and paid to the tax authorities wholly on behalf of the recipient.

D – Voluntary disclosures

The disclosures below are not mandatory and do not form part of the Statement of Standard Accounting Practice. The Board, however, encourages reporting entities voluntarily to include the following disclosures in their financial statements.

CASH FLOW INFORMATION*

1 Reporting entities are encouraged, but not required, to provide a cash flow statement using the indirect method as explained below.†

2 The indirect method starts with operating profit (which is normally profit before income from shares in group undertakings) and adjusts it for non-cash charges and credits to reconcile it with cash generated from operations. Other sources and applications of cash are shown to arrive at total cash generated (or utilised) in the period.

3 Cash is taken as 'cash at bank and in hand' less overdrafts repayable on demand, which should be reconciled to the balance sheet.

4 Cash flows are shown net of any attributable value added tax or other sales tax unless the tax is irrecoverable by the reporting entity.

5 It is recommended that material transactions not resulting in movements of cash of the reporting entity are disclosed by way of note, if disclosure is necessary for an understanding of the underlying transactions.

**The Board's reasoning for including a voluntary recommendation for cash flow information is set out in Appendix IV.*

†An illustrative example of a cash flow statement using the indirect method is given in Appendix III.

E – Adoption of the FRSSE (effective April 2008) by the Board

The Financial Reporting Standard for Smaller Entities (effective April 2008) was approved for issue by a vote of ten out of the eleven members of the Accounting Standards Board. Kenneth Lever abstained from voting in accordance with the Board's agreed procedure for newly appointed members.

Ian Mackintosh	Chairman
David Loweth	Technical Director
Nick Anderson	
Michael Ashley	
Edward Beale	
Marisa Cassoni	
Peter Elwin	
Robert Overend	
Andy Simmonds	
Geoffrey Whittington	

Appendix I
Note on legal requirements for companies

THE UNITED KINGDOM

Companies Act 2006, sections 382 to 384

1 The definition of a small company is contained in sections 382 and 383 of the Companies Act 2006. The qualifying conditions are met by a company in a year in which it does not exceed two or more of the following criteria:

Turnover	£6,500,000
Balance sheet total	£3,260,000
Average number of employees	50

For any company, other than a newly incorporated company, to qualify as small, the qualifying conditions must be met for two consecutive years. A company will cease to qualify as small if it fails to meet the qualifying conditions for two consecutive years. However, if a company which qualified as small in one period no longer meets the criteria for small in the next period, the company may continue to claim the exemption available in the next period. If that company then reverts back to being small by meeting the criteria, the exemption will continue uninterrupted.

2 Certain companies are excluded by section 384 from the 'small company' criteria for reasons of public interest. These are any entity that is, or is in a group that includes:

(a) a public company;
(b) a small company that is an authorised insurance company, a banking company, an e-money issuer, a MifId investment firm or a UCITS management company or a company that carries on insurance market activity;
(c) a body corporate (other than a company) whose shares are admitted to trading on a regulated market in an EEA State; or
(d) a person (other than a small company) who has permission under Part 4 of the Financial Services and Markets Act 2000 to carry on a regulated activity.

3 A parent company shall not be treated as qualifying as a small company in relation to a financial year unless the group headed by it qualifies as a small group.

4 The definition of a small group is contained in section 383. The qualifying conditions are met by a group in a year in which it does not exceed two or more of the following criteria:

Aggregate turnover	£6,500,000 net (or £7,800,000 gross)
Aggregate balance sheet total	£3,260,000 net (or £3,900,000 gross)
Aggregate number of employees	50

'Net' means after the set-offs and other adjustments required by Schedule 6 of the Small Companies and Groups (Accounts and Directors' Report) Regulations 2008 in the case of group accounts, and 'gross' means without those set-offs and adjustments. A company may satisfy the relevant requirements on the basis of either the net or the gross figure.*

REPUBLIC OF IRELAND

The following table shows the references in companies legislation in the Republic of Ireland that correspond to the references in paragraphs 1-4 above. 5

UNITED KINGDOM	REPUBLIC OF IRELAND
Sections 382 and 383	Companies (Amendment) Act 1986, sections 2, 8 and 9
Sections 384	No equivalent
The Small Companies and Groups (Accounts and Directors' Report) Regulations 2008	No equivalent

The qualifying conditions for the definition of a small company may be met by a company in a year in which it does not exceed two or more of the following criteria:

Turnover	€3.81 million
Balance sheet total	€1.9 million
Average number of employees	50

The FRSSE can be applied to those companies meeting the criteria as set out in the Republic of Ireland Companies Acts that allow them to be treated as "small" for the purposes of filing information with the Companies Registration Office. Small groups are not defined in Republic of Ireland legislation. However, in the Republic of Ireland, for the purposes of the FRSSE, small groups should meet, on a consolidated basis, the same legal conditions as are required for small companies. If a group does not qualify as small, then the parent undertaking of that group, even if it qualifies as a small company under Republic of Ireland legislation, is not entitled to adopt the FRSSE.

DERIVATION TABLES FOR LEGAL REQUIREMENTS REFERRED TO IN THE FRSSE

Derivation tables for all the legal requirements referred to in the FRSSE are available from the ASB website at www.frc.org.uk/asb/technical/frsse.cfm in the derivation tables which indicates the source of company law in the United Kingdom and the Republic of Ireland. 6

Republic of Ireland users of the FRSSE should note that the requirements of company law as shown in SMALL CAPITALS in the text of the FRSSE relate to UK company law as applicable to small companies. The corresponding reference to Republic of Ireland companies legislation is shown in Table 1 of the derivation tables . However, Republic of Ireland users should note that the detail of the Republic of Ireland legal requirements in many cases differs from UK company law. 7

**Reference should also be made to Schedule 6 of the Large and Medium-sized Companies and Groups (Accounts and Reports) Regulations 2008 because it is possible that after the set-offs and other adjustments required by that Schedule, a group which started off large or medium-sized could become small.*

8 In addition, there are a number of Republic of Ireland legal requirements that are not reflected in the FRSSE. There is no equivalent to the Small Companies and Groups (Accounts and Directors' Report) Regulations 2008 providing certain exemptions for small companies when preparing annual accounts for shareholders. Exemptions from company law requirements for small companies in the Republic of Ireland are limited and relate primarily to information that must be filed with the Companies Registration Office. These additional requirements are referenced in Table 2 of the derivation tables.

9 There are no special provisions in Republic of Ireland company law that relate to the preparation of group accounts by small entities. The general requirement for the preparation of group accounts is contained in section 150 of the Companies Act 1963. Regulation 7 of the EC (Companies: Group Accounts) Regulations 1992, SI 201/1992, contains an exemption from the requirement to prepare group accounts for certain undertakings to whom the above Regulation applies. The legal references are given in Table 2 of the derivation tables.

10 Republic of Ireland users should refer to the underlying legislation when using the FRSSE. The Republic of Ireland legal requirements set out in the derivation tables are intended to reflect company law as applicable to accounting periods beginning on or after 6 April 2008.

STATUS OF THE FRSSE

11 Legal advice has been obtained that in accounting standards smaller entities may properly be allowed exemptions or different treatment provided that such differences are justified on rational grounds. The Board will have regard to the criteria given in the 'Status of the FRSSE' section in determining whether such rational grounds exist.

12 The summary of advice regarding the status of the FRSSE given by Richard Sykes QC in December 1995 is reproduced below:

"I do not see any conflict with the law or likely weakening of the authority of ASB or FRRP* as respects the upholding of Standards provided that

(i) the treatment required by the FRSSE is the same as that required by existing Standards or is a simplified version of that treatment; or

(ii) in a case where a future Standard calls for a new treatment for Big GAAP† Companies only and which is also likely to be significant to small companies, ASB is able to justify on rational grounds any lack of a change in treatment for smaller entities when the FRSSE is in due course revised;

(iii) in a case where in the future the FRSSE requires a treatment which is materially different from then existing Standards on a significant matter ASB is able to justify on rational grounds such different treatment in the case of smaller entities.

(iv) it is recognised that the starting point for deciding how a smaller entity will account for something not covered by the FRSSE will be existing practice and that the smaller entity must be able to justify its departure from such practice on rational grounds related to its size. Where the matter is covered by a Big GAAP Standard, that Standard would provide the obvious source in determining existing practice.

**Financial Reporting Review Panel.*

†Generally accepted accounting practice.

Rational grounds for justifying different treatments might include:

(i) the different nature of entities;
(ii) particularly if the different treatment is in the area of disclosure, the different users of their financial statements; and
(iii) established practices existing at the time of issue of a Standard or FRSSE revision."

Appendix II
Accounting for retirement benefits: defined benefit schemes

1 The following requirements should be regarded as standard:

(a) **Assets** in a **defined benefit scheme** should be measured at their **fair value** at the balance sheet date.

(b) **Defined benefit scheme liabilities** should be measured on an actuarial basis using the **projected unit method**. The **scheme liabilities** comprise both any benefits promised under the formal terms of the scheme and any constructive **obligations** for further benefits.

(c) The assumptions underlying the valuation should be mutually compatible and lead to the best estimate of the future cash flows that will arise under the **scheme liabilities**. The assumptions are ultimately the responsibility of the **directors** (or equivalent) but should be set upon advice given by an actuary. Any assumptions that are affected by economic conditions (financial assumptions) should reflect market expectations at the balance sheet date.

(d) **Defined benefit scheme liabilities** should be discounted at the current rate of return on a high quality corporate bond of equivalent currency and term.

(e) Full actuarial valuations by a professionally qualified actuary should be obtained for a **defined benefit scheme** at intervals not exceeding three years. The actuary should review the most recent actuarial valuation at the balance sheet date and update it to reflect current conditions.

(f) The surplus/deficit in a **defined benefit scheme** is the excess/shortfall of the value of the **assets** in the scheme over/below the present value of the **scheme liabilities**. The employer should **recognise** an **asset** to the extent that it is able to recover a surplus either through reduced contributions in the future or through refunds from the scheme. The employer should **recognise** a **liability** to the extent that it reflects its legal or constructive **obligation**.

(g) Any unpaid contributions to the scheme should be presented in the balance sheet as a creditor due within one year. The defined benefit **asset** or **liability** should be presented separately on the face of the balance sheet:

   (i) in balance sheets of the type prescribed for small companies in the United Kingdom by the Small Companies and Groups (Accounts and Directors' Report) Regulations 2008*, format 1 after item J Accruals and deferred income but before item K Capital and reserves; and

   (ii) in balance sheets of the type prescribed for small companies in the United Kingdom by the Small Companies and Groups (Accounts and Directors' Report) Regulations 2008, format 2: any **asset** after ASSETS item D Prepayments and accrued income and any **liability** after LIABILITIES item D Accruals and deferred income.

(h) The **deferred tax** relating to the defined benefit **asset** or **liability** should be offset against the defined benefit **asset** or **liability** and not included with other **deferred tax assets** or **liabilities**:

(i) The components of the change in the defined benefit **asset** or **liability** (other than those arising from contributions to the scheme) should be presented separately in the performance statements as follows:

***There is no equivalent to Statutory Instrument 2008/409* 'The Small Companies and Groups (Accounts and Directors Report) Regulations 2008' *in companies legislation in the Republic of Ireland. See the derivation table on the ASB website for Republic of Ireland legal requirements.*

(i) the **current service cost** should be included within operating profit in the profit and loss account;
(ii) the net of the **interest cost** and the expected return on assets should be included as other finance costs (or income) adjacent to interest;
(iii) **actuarial gains and losses** should be **recognised** in the statement of **total recognised gains and losses**;
(iv) **past service costs** should be **recognised** in the profit and loss account in the period in which the increases in benefit vest; and
(v) losses arising on a **settlement** or **curtailment** should be **recognised** in the profit and loss account when the employer becomes demonstrably committed to the transaction (gains should only be **recognised** once all parties whose consent is required are irrevocably committed).

(j) The following disclosures should be made in respect of a **defined benefit scheme**:
(i) the nature of the scheme (i.e. **defined benefit**);
(ii) the date of the most recent full actuarial valuation on which the amounts in the financial statements are based. If the actuary is an employee or officer of the reporting entity, or of the group of which it is a member, this fact should be disclosed;
(iii) the contribution made in respect of the accounting period and any agreed contribution rates for future years; and
(iv) for closed schemes and those in which the age profile of the active membership is rising significantly, the fact that under the **projected unit method** the **current service cost** will increase as the members of the scheme approach retirement.

(k) The **fair value** of the scheme **assets**, the present value of the scheme **liabilities** based on the accounting assumptions and the resulting surplus or deficit should be disclosed in a note to the financial statements. Where the **asset** or **liability** in the balance sheet differs from the surplus or deficit in the scheme, an explanation of the difference should be given. An analysis of the movements during the period in the surplus or deficit in the scheme should be given.

Appendix III
Illustrative examples and practical considerations

This Appendix contains illustrative examples and practical considerations for general guidance and does not form part of the Financial Reporting Standard. The best form of reporting will depend on individual circumstances.

Example: Statement of total recognised gains and losses

	2002	2001 as restated
	£	£
Profit for the financial year	29,000	7,000
Unrealised surplus on revaluation of property	4,000	6,000
Unrealised (loss) /gain on trade investment	(3,000)	7,000
Total recognised gains and losses relating to the year	30,000	20,000
Prior year adjustment (as explained in note x)	(10,000)	
Total gains and losses recognised since last annual report	20,000	

Example: Disclosure – defined contribution pension scheme

The company operates a defined contribution pension scheme. The assets of the scheme are held separately from those of the company in an independently administered fund. The pension cost charge represents contributions payable by the company to the fund and amounted to £50,000 (2001 £45,000). Contributions totalling £2,500 (2001 £1,500) were payable to the fund at the year-end and are included in creditors.

Example: Disclosure – defined benefit pension scheme*

The company operates a pension scheme providing benefits based on final pensionable pay. The assets of the scheme are held separately from those of the company, being invested with insurance companies.

The contributions are determined by a qualified actuary on the basis of triennial valuations using the projected unit method. The most recent valuation was as at 31 December 2005 which has been updated to reflect conditions at the balance sheet date. The assumptions that have the most significant effect on the results of the valuation are those relating to the rate of return on investments and the rate of increase in salaries and pensions. It was assumed that the investment returns would

**This example reflects the disclosure requirements of paragraph 1 of Appendix II.*

be 6 per cent per year, that salary increases would average 4 per cent per year and that present and future pensions would increase at the rate of 3 per cent per year.

The pension charge for the year was £46,000 (2005 £25,000). This included £12,000 (2005 £nil) in respect of past service costs. The contributions of the company and employees will remain at 10 per cent and 5 per cent of earnings respectively.

The defined benefit scheme is closed to new members and so under the projected unit method the current service cost would be expected to increase over time as members of the scheme approach retirement.

Value of scheme assets and liabilities	2006	2005
	£	£
Market value of assets	1,488,000	962,000
Present value of scheme liabilities	(1,009,000)	(758,000)
Pension scheme surplus/(deficit)	479,000	204,000
Related deferred tax asset/(liability)	(144,000)	(61,000)
Net pension scheme asset/(liability)	335,000	143,000

Movements in year	2006	2005
	£	£
Pension scheme surplus/(deficit) at beginning of year	204,000	92,000
Current service cost	(34,000)	(25,000)
Cash contribution	25,000	35,000
Past service costs	(12,000)	0
Other finance income	20,000	11,000
Actuarial gain	276,000	91,000
Pension scheme surplus/(deficit) at end of year	479,000	204,000

PRACTICAL CONSIDERATIONS: STOCKS AND LONG-TERM CONTRACTS

Many of the problems involved in arriving at the amount at which stocks and long-term contracts are stated in financial statements are of a practical nature rather than resulting from matters of principle. The following paragraphs discuss some particular areas in which difficulty may be encountered.

The allocation of overheads

Production overheads are included in the cost of conversion together with direct labour, direct expenses and subcontracted work. This inclusion is a necessary corollary of the principle that expenditure should be included to the extent to which it has been incurred in bringing the product 'to its present location and condition'. However, all abnormal conversion costs (such as exceptional spoilage, idle capacity 1 and other losses) that are avoidable under normal operating conditions need, for the same reason, to be excluded.

2 Where firm sales contracts have been entered into for the provision of goods or services to customer's specification, overheads relating to design, and marketing and selling costs incurred before manufacture, may be included in arriving at cost.

3 The costing methods adopted by a business are usually designed to ensure that all direct material, direct labour, direct expenses and subcontracted work are identified and charged on a reasonable and consistent basis, but problems arise on the allocation of overheads, which must usually involve the exercise of personal judgement in the selection of an appropriate convention.

4 The classification of overheads necessary to achieve this allocation takes the function of the overhead as its distinguishing characteristic (e.g. whether it is a function of production, marketing, selling or administration), rather than whether the overhead tends to vary with time or with volume.

5 The costs of general management, as distinct from functional management, are not directly related to current production and are, therefore, excluded from the cost of conversion and, hence, from the cost of stocks and long-term contracts.

6 In the case of smaller organisations whose management may be involved in the daily administration of each of the various functions, particular problems may arise in practice in distinguishing these general management overheads. In such organisations the costs of management may fairly be allocated on suitable bases to the functions of production, marketing, selling and administration.

7 Problems may also arise in allocating the costs of central service departments, the allocation of which should depend on the function or functions that the department is serving. For example, the accounts department will normally support the following functions:

(a) production – by paying direct and indirect production wages and salaries, by controlling purchases and by preparing periodic financial statements for the production units;
(b) marketing and distribution – by analysing sales and by controlling the sales ledger;
(c) general administration – by preparing management accounts and annual financial statements and budgets, by controlling cash resources and by planning investments.

Only those costs of the accounts department that can reasonably be allocated to the production function fall to be included in the cost of conversion.

8 The allocation of overheads included in the valuation of stocks and long-term contracts needs to be based on the company's normal level of activity, taking one year with another. The governing factor is that the cost of unused capacity should be written off in the current year. In determining what constitutes 'normal' the following factors need to be considered:

(a) the volume of production that the production facilities are intended by their designers and by management to produce under the working conditions (e.g. single or double shift) prevailing during the year;
(b) the budgeted level of activity for the year under review and for the ensuing year;
(c) the level of activity achieved both in the year under review and in previous years.

Although temporary changes in the load of activity may be ignored, persistent variation should lead to revision of the previous norm.

Where management accounts are prepared on a marginal cost basis, it will be necessary to add to the figure of stocks so arrived at the appropriate proportion of those production overheads not already included in the marginal cost. 9

The adoption of a conservative approach to the valuation of stocks and long-term contracts has sometimes been used as one of the reasons for omitting selected production overheads. In so far as the circumstances of the business require an element of prudence in determining the amount at which stocks and long-term contracts are stated, this needs to be taken into account in the determination of net realisable value and not by the exclusion from cost of selected overheads. 10

METHODS OF COSTING

It is frequently not practicable to relate expenditure to specific units of stocks and long-term contracts. The ascertainment of the nearest approximation to cost gives rise to two problems: 11

(a) the selection of an appropriate method for relating costs to stocks and long-term contracts (e.g. job costing, batch costing, process costing, standard costing);
(b) the selection of an appropriate method for calculating the related costs where a number of identical items have been purchased or made at different times (e.g. unit cost, average cost or 'first in, first out' (FIFO)).

In selecting the methods referred to in paragraph 11(a) and (b), management must exercise judgement to ensure that the methods chosen provide the fairest practicable approximation to cost. Furthermore, where standard costs are used they need to be reviewed frequently to ensure that they bear a reasonable relationship to actual costs obtaining during the period. Methods such as base stock and 'last in, first out' (LIFO) are not usually appropriate methods of stock valuation because they often result in stocks being stated in the balance sheet at amounts that bear little relationship to recent cost levels. When this happens, not only is the presentation of current assets misleading, but there is potential distortion of subsequent results if stock levels reduce and out-of-date costs are drawn into the profit and loss account. 12

The method of arriving at cost by applying the latest purchase price to the total number of units in stock is unacceptable in principle because it is not necessarily the same as actual cost and, in times of rising prices, will result in the taking of a profit that has not been realised. 13

One method of arriving at cost, in the absence of a satisfactory costing system, is the use of selling price less an estimated profit margin. This is acceptable only if it can be demonstrated that the method gives a reasonable approximation of the actual cost. 14

In industries where the cost of minor by-products is not separable from the cost of the principal products, stocks of such by-products may be stated in accounts at their net realisable value. In this case the costs of the main products are calculated after deducting the net realisable value of the by-products. 15

The determination of net realisable value

16 The initial calculation of provisions to reduce stocks from cost to net realisable value may often be made by the use of formulae based on predetermined criteria. The formulae normally take account of the age, movements in the past, expected future movements and estimated scrap values of the stock, as appropriate. Whilst the use of such formulae establishes a basis for making a provision that can be consistently applied, it is still necessary for the results to be reviewed in the light of any special circumstances that cannot be anticipated in the formulae, such as changes in the state of the order book.

17 Where a provision is required to reduce the value of finished goods below cost, the stocks of the parts and subassemblies held for the purpose of the manufacture of such products, together with stocks on order, need to be reviewed to determine if provision is also required against such items.

18 Where stocks of spares are held for sale, special consideration of the factors in paragraph 16 will be required in the context of:

(a) the number of units sold to which they are applicable;
(b) the estimated frequency with which a replacement spare is required;
(c) the expected useful life of the unit to which they are applicable.

19 Events occurring between the balance sheet date and the date of completion of the financial statements need to be considered in arriving at the net realisable value at the balance sheet date (e.g. a subsequent reduction in selling prices). However, no reduction falls to be made when the realisable value of material stocks is less than the purchase price, provided that the goods into which the materials are to be incorporated can still be sold at a profit after incorporating the materials at cost price.

The application of net realisable value

20 The principal situations in which net realisable value is likely to be less than cost are where there has been:

(a) an increase in costs or a fall in selling price;
(b) physical deterioration of stocks;
(c) obsolescence of products;
(d) a decision as part of a company's marketing strategy to manufacture and sell products at a loss;
(e) errors in production or purchasing.

Furthermore, when stocks are held that are unlikely to be sold within the turnover period normal in that company (i.e. excess stocks), the impending delay in realisation increases the risk that the situations outlined in (a)-(c) above may occur before the stocks are sold and needs to be taken into account in assessing net realisable value.

Long-term contracts

21 In ascertaining costs of long-term contracts it is not normally appropriate to include interest payable on borrowed money. However, in circumstances where sums borrowed can be identified as financing specific long-term contracts, it may be appropriate to include such related interest in cost, in which circumstances the inclusion of interest and the amount of interest so included should be disclosed in a note to the financial statements.

In some businesses, long-term contracts for the supply of services or manufacture and supply of goods exist where the prices are determined and invoiced according to separate parts of the contract. In these businesses the most appropriate method of reflecting profits on each contract is usually to match costs against performance of the separable parts of the contract, treating each such separable part as a separate contract. In such instances, however, future revenues from the contract need to be compared with future estimated costs and provision made for any foreseen loss. **22**

Turnover (ascertained in a manner appropriate to the industry, the nature of the contracts concerned and the contractual relationship with the customer) and related costs should be recorded in the profit and loss account as contract activity progresses. Turnover may sometimes be ascertained by reference to valuation of the work carried out to date. In other cases, there may be specific points during a contract at which individual elements of work done with separately ascertainable sales and values and costs can be identified and appropriately recorded as turnover (e.g. because delivery or customer acceptance has taken place. **23**

In determining whether the stage has been reached at which it is appropriate to recognise profit, account should be taken of the nature of the business concerned. It is necessary to define the earliest point for each particular contract before which no profit is taken up, the overriding principle being that there can be no attributable profit until the outcome of a contract can reasonably be foreseen. Of the profit that in the light of all the circumstances can be foreseen with a reasonable degree of certainty to arise on completion of the contract, there should be regarded as earned to date only that part which prudently reflects the amount of work performed to date. The method used for taking up such profit needs to be consistently applied. **24**

In calculating the total estimated profit on the contract, it is necessary to take into account not only the total costs to date and the total estimated further costs to completion (calculated by reference to the same principles as were applied to cost to date) but also the estimated future costs of rectification and guarantee work, and any other future work to be undertaken under the terms of the contract. These are then compared with the total sales value of the contract. In considering future costs, it is necessary to have regard to likely increases in wages and salaries, to likely increases in the price of raw materials and to rises in general overheads, so far as these items are not recoverable from the customer under the terms of the contract. **25**

Where approved variations have been made to a contract in the course of it and the amount to be received in respect of these variations has not yet been settled and is likely to be a material factor in the outcome, it is necessary to make a conservative estimate of the amount likely to be received and this is then treated as part of the total sales value. On the other hand, allowance needs to be made for foreseen claims or penalties payable arising out of delays in completion or from other causes. **26**

The settlement of claims arising from circumstances not envisaged in the contract or arising as an indirect consequence of approved variations is subject to a high level of uncertainty relating to the outcome of future negotiations. In view of this, it is generally prudent to recognise receipts in respect of such claims only when negotiations have reached an advanced stage and there is sufficient evidence of the acceptability of the claim in principle to the purchaser, with an indication of the amount involved also being available. **27**

The amounts to be included in the year's profit and loss account will be both the appropriate amount of turnover and the associated costs of achieving that turnover, to the extent that these amounts exceed corresponding amounts recognised in previous years. The estimated outcome of a contract that extends over several **28** accounting years will nearly always vary in the light of changes in circumstances and for this reason the result of the year will not necessarily represent the proportion of the total profit on the contract that is appropriate to the amount of work carried out in the period; it may also reflect the effect of changes in circumstances during the year that affect the total profit estimated to accrue on completion.

PRACTICAL CONSIDERATIONS – CONSIGNMENT STOCK

29 In determining whether consignment stock is in substance an asset of the dealer, it is necessary to identify whether the dealer has access to the benefits of the stock and exposure to the risks inherent in those benefits. Therefore, to assist in using paragraph 8.9 of the FRSSE, the following table is provided.

Indications that the stock is not an asset of the dealer at delivery	Indications that the stock is an asset of the dealer at delivery
The manufacturer can require the dealer to return stock (or to transfer stock to another dealer) without compensation *or* Penalty paid by the dealer to prevent returns/transfers of stock at the manufacturer's request.	The manufacturer cannot require the dealer to return or transfer stock *or* Financial incentives given to persuade the dealer to transfer stock at the manufacturer's request.
The dealer has unfettered right to return stock to the manufacturer without penalty and actually exercises the right in practice.	The dealer has no right to return stock or is commercially compelled not to exercise its right of return.
The manufacturer bears obsolescence risk, e.g.: - obsolete stock is returned to the manufacturer without penalty *or* - financial incentives given by the manufacturer to prevent stock being returned to it (e.g. on model change or if it becomes obsolete).	The dealer bears obsolescence risk, e.g.: - penalty charged if the dealer returns stock to the manufacturer *or* - obsolete stock cannot be returned to the manufacturer and no compensation is paid by the manufacturer for losses due to obsolescence.
Stock transfer price charged by the manufacturer is based on the manufacturer's list price at date of transfer of legal title.	Stock transfer price charged by the manufacturer is based on the manufacturer's list price at date of delivery.
The manufacturer bears slow movement risk, e.g.: - transfer price set independently of time for which the dealer holds stock, and there is no deposit.	The dealer bears slow movement risk, e.g.: - the dealer is effectively charged interest as transfer price or other payments to the manufacturer vary with time for which the dealer holds stock *or* - the dealer makes a substantial interest-free deposit that varies with the levels of stock held.

PRACTICAL CONSIDERATIONS – DEBT FACTORING

To assist in using paragraphs 8.10-8.12 of the FRSSE, the following table is provided. 30

Indications that derecognition is appropriate (debts are not an asset of the seller)	Indications that a linked presentation is appropriate	Indications that a separate presentation is appropriate (debts are an asset of the seller)
Transfer is for a single, non-returnable fixed sum.	Some non-returnable proceeds received, but the seller has rights to further sums from the factor (or vice versa) whose amount depends on whether or when debtors pay.	Finance cost varies with speed of collection of debts, e.g.: - by adjustment to consideration for original transfer *or* - subsequent transfers priced to recover costs of earlier transfers.
There is no recourse to the seller for losses.	There is either no recourse for losses, or such recourse has a fixed monetary ceiling.	There is full recourse to the seller for losses.
The factor is paid all amounts received from the factored debts (and no more). The seller has no rights to further sums from the factor.	The factor is paid only out of amounts collected from the factored debts, and the seller has no right or obligation to repurchase debts.	The seller is required to repay amounts received from the factor on or before a set date, regardless of timing or amounts of collections from debtors.

PRACTICAL CONSIDERATIONS – BILL AND HOLD ARRANGEMENTS

Under a bill and hold arrangement, a seller enters into a contractual arrangement with a customer for the supply of goods where there is transfer of title but physical delivery is deferred to a later date. 31

Analysis

The purpose of the analysis below is to determine whether, in the circumstances described in paragraph 37, the seller should: 32

(a) recognise turnover and a **right to consideration**; or
(b) continue to recognise the goods as stock.

In accordance with the general principles set out in Section 4 of the FRSSE the goods cease to be assets of the seller and become assets of the customer (and in exchange the seller obtains the **right to consideration**) when the seller transfers to the customer access to the significant benefits relating to the goods and exposure to the risks inherent in those benefits. From the customer's perspective, the principal benefits and risks include: 33

Benefits

(a) the right to obtain the goods as and when required;
(b) the sole right to the goods for their sale to a third party and the future cash flows from such a sale; and
(c) insulation from changes in prices charged by the seller (e.g. because the seller has revised its standard price list).

Risks

(a) slow movement, resulting in increased costs of financing and holding of the goods, and an increased risk of obsolescence; and
(b) being compelled to take delivery of goods that have become obsolete or not readily saleable, resulting in no onward sale or a sale at a reduced price.

34 In order for the seller to have the right to recognise changes in its assets or liabilities, and turnover, arising from its **right to consideration** in respect of the bill and hold arrangement, the terms of the contractual arrangement between the seller and the customer should include all of the following characteristics:

(a) the goods should be complete and ready for delivery;
(b) the seller should not have retained any significant **performance obligations** other than the safekeeping of the goods and their shipment when the customer requests this;
(c) subject to any rights of return, the seller should have obtained the **right to consideration** regardless of whether the goods are shipped, at the customer's request, to its delivery address. Where rights of return are granted, particular consideration is required of the commercial substance of the related sales, especially the transfer of risk. Rights of return are addressed at paragraphs 43-53 below;
(d) the goods should be identified separately from the seller's other stock and should not be capable of being used to fill other orders that are received between the date of the bill and hold sale and shipment of the goods to the customer; and
(e) the bill and hold terms should be in accordance with the commercial objectives of the customer and not the seller. For example, where the delay in the delivery of the goods is to meet the customer's need for flexibility in the timing and location of delivery, and the conditions set out in paragraphs (a) to (d) above are met, it will be appropriate for the seller to recognise changes in assets or liabilities, and turnover.

Accounting

Substance of the transaction is that the goods represent an asset of the customer

35 Where it is concluded that the stock is an asset of the customer, resulting in the seller having a **right to consideration**, the seller should recognise the related changes in its assets or liabilities, and turnover.

Substance of the transaction is that the goods represent an asset of the seller

36 Where it is concluded that the stock remains an asset of the seller, it should be retained on the seller's balance sheet. Any amounts received from the customer should be included within creditors in accordance with paragraph 4.2 of the FRSSE.

PRACTICAL CONSIDERATIONS – SALES WITH RIGHTS OF RETURN

Features

The terms of contractual arrangements may allow customers to return goods that they have purchased and obtain a refund or release from the **obligation** to pay. 37

Rights of return may be included explicitly or implicitly within contractual arrangements. Alternatively, they may arise through statutory requirements. 38

Analysis

The purpose of the analysis below is to determine the effect of rights of return on a seller's recognition of changes in its assets or liabilities, and turnover. 39

The inclusion of rights of return in a contractual arrangement may affect both the quantification of the seller's **right to consideration**, compared to an otherwise identical arrangement which does not have these rights, and the point at which the seller should recognise that right. This is because rights of return give rise to a contractual **obligation** on the part of the seller to transfer economic benefits to its customer and in some cases oblige the seller to defer recognition of the sales transaction so long as substantially all of the risks associated with the goods are retained. 40

The seller's recognition of its **right to consideration** and contractual **obligation** to transfer economic benefits to its customer in respect of rights of return are linked transactions. In consequence, changes in the seller's assets or liabilities should reflect the loss expected to arise from the rights of return. Turnover should exclude the sales value of estimated returns. 41

A seller will generally be able to estimate reliably the sales value of returns, having regard to risk, which may be less than its maximum potential **obligation**. It will generally be possible to derive a **reliable** estimate from historical experience of the amount of comparable goods returned as a proportion of comparable sales. 42

If a seller is unable to estimate reliably the expected value of returns, the maximum potential amount should be calculated in accordance with the terms of its contractual arrangement with the customer and excluded from turnover. 43

In some cases, the risk of return may be so significant that substantially all of the risks associated with the goods are retained by the seller and accordingly the seller does not have the **right to consideration**. In such circumstances the seller should not recognise any changes in its assets or liabilities, and turnover, from the transaction. Any amounts received from the customer should be accounted for as a payment in advance, in accordance with paragraph 4.2 of the FRSSE. 44

Accounting

A seller should record changes in its assets or liabilities, and turnover, to the extent that its **performance** has earned it the **right to consideration**, taking account of any expected loss. The amount recorded as turnover should exclude the sales value of estimated returns from the total sales value of the goods supplied to customers. 45

46 At each reporting date, the seller should review its estimate of returns, having regard to changes in expectations and the expiry of contractual rights of return. Subsequent adjustments to the estimate should be recorded within revenue.

47 Where a seller has been precluded from recognising changes in its assets or liabilities, and turnover, because substantially all of the risks associated with the goods are retained and so it has not earned the **right to consideration**, it should recognise these changes and turnover on the earlier of the dates on which:

(a) it is capable of estimating the level of returns with **reliability**; and
(b) the right of return expires or is surrendered.

PRACTICAL CONSIDERATIONS – PRESENTATION OF TURNOVER AS PRINCIPAL OR AS AGENT

Features

48 A seller may act on its own account when contracting with its customers for the supply of goods in return for the right to consideration. In such transactions the seller is frequently referred to as a principal.

49 Alternatively, a seller may act as an intermediary, earning a fee or commission in return for arranging the provision of goods or services on behalf of a principal. In such transactions, the seller is frequently referred to as an agent.

Analysis

50 The purpose of the analysis below is to determine whether a seller obtains the right to consideration by performing its contractual obligations:

(a) as principal in an exchange transaction with its customer; or
(b) as agent in relation to a transaction between its principal and the principal's customer.

51 The general principles of the standard require that, in order for a seller to account for exchange transactions as principal, it should normally have exposure to all significant benefits and risks associated with at least one of the following:

(a) Selling price: the ability, within economic constraints, to establish the selling price with the customer, either directly or, where the selling price of an item is fixed, indirectly by providing additional goods or services or adjusting the terms of a linked transaction; or
(b) Stock: exposure to the risks of damage, slow movement and obsolescence, and changes in suppliers' prices.

52 Where the seller has not disclosed that it is acting as agent, there is a rebuttable presumption that it is acting as principal.

53 Additional factors which indicate that a seller may be acting as principal include:

(a) performance of part of the services, or modification to the goods supplied;
(b) assumption of credit risk; and
(c) discretion in supplier selection.

54 In contrast, where a seller acts as agent it will not normally be exposed to the majority of the benefits and risks associated with the exchange transaction. Agency arrangements will typically include the following characteristics:

(a) the seller has disclosed the fact that it is acting as agent;
(b) once the seller has confirmed its customer's order with a third party, the seller will normally have no further involvement in the performance of the ultimate supplier's contractual obligations;
(c) the amount that the seller earns is predetermined, being either a fixed fee per transaction or a stated percentage of the amount billed to the customer; and
(d) the seller bears no stock or credit risk, other than in circumstances where it receives additional consideration from the ultimate supplier in return for its assumption of this risk.

Accounting

Seller acts as principal

Where the substance of a transaction is that the seller acts as principal, it should report turnover based on the gross amount received or receivable in return for its performance under the contractual arrangement. **55**

Seller acts as agent

Where the substance of a transaction is that the seller acts as agent, it should report as turnover the commission or other amounts received or receivable in return for its performance under the contractual arrangement. Any amounts received or receivable from the customer that are payable to the principal should not be included in the agent's turnover. **56**

Illustrations

A seller acts as a building contractor for the construction of a new office block. An analysis of the arrangement shows that the terms of the seller's contract with its customer include a negotiated selling price, credit risk for amounts due from the customer, primary responsibility for the construction and quality of the new building and discretion as to whether it carries out the work itself or employs subcontractors. The seller is acting as principal and should account for the gross amount of turnover, regardless of whether it carries out the work itself or employs subcontractors to carry out part or all of the construction activities. **57**

A seller acts as an online retailer from a website, where it advertises holidays. An analysis of the arrangement shows that it acts as an intermediary between its customers and the ultimate sellers of the holidays and that it does not set the selling price. Its contractual terms of business include an exclusion of any liability to its customers once they have been put in touch with the ultimate sellers. The seller is paid a fee for each customer that purchases a holiday from an ultimate seller and has no involvement in the transaction after it has put the customer in touch with the ultimate seller. The seller is acting as agent and its turnover should include only the fees it receives from the ultimate seller. **58**

A department store provides space for concessionaires to sell products and receives a fixed amount of rental income from the concessionaire. An analysis of the factors discussed in paragraphs 57-60 shows that the concessionaire is acting as principal in an exchange transaction with its customers and is entitled to the amounts received from the sale of the goods and services. In these circumstances, the concessionaire should include within its turnover the amounts received or receivable in respect of the **59** sale of the goods and services. The department store should not include within its turnover the value of the concessionaire's sales.

Disclosure – seller acts as agent

60 Where a seller acts as agent, it is encouraged, where practicable, to disclose the gross value of sales throughput as additional, non-statutory information. Where such disclosure is given, a brief explanation of the relationship of recognised turnover to the gross value of sales throughput should be given.

PRACTICAL CONSIDERATIONS – CLASSIFICATION OF PREFERENCE SHARES

61 Paragraph 12.1 of the FRSSE provides an example of a preference share that is classified as a financial liability. The following analysis provides further guidance on the classification of preference shares as financial liabilities or equity instruments.

Illustrative features of preference shares

62 A company issues preference shares that:

- carry a fixed right to cumulative dividends;
- have the same voting rights as the ordinary shares;
- the issuer is under no obligation to redeem these shares (but may be able to choose to redeem them); and
- in a formal winding up the preference shares rank above the ordinary shares and receive par value.

Analysis

63 In determining whether the preference shares are a financial liability or an equity instrument the issuer will need to assess the particular rights attaching to the shares.

64 In the straightforward case where the preference shares provide for redemption on a set date they would be classified as financial liabilities. The classification is clear from looking at the rights attached to the shares i.e. at the set redemption date the issuer has an obligation to transfer financial assets to the holder of the preference shares.

65 For preference shares that the issuer is not obliged to redeem the appropriate classification is determined by the other rights that attach to them i.e. based on an assessment of the substance of the contractual arrangements and by reference to the definitions of financial liabilities and equity instruments. Therefore only when the distributions to the holders of the preference shares are at the discretion of the issuer will such shares be classified as equity instruments. It should be noted there is a difference between an expectation of dividend payments and an obligation.

66 One feature of the above preference shares is that the holders are entitled to fixed rights to cumulative dividends which are not at the discretion of the issuer. This would indicate that the issuer has an obligation to transfer financial assets to the holders of the preference shares. The shares would therefore be classified as financial liabilities*.

**In arriving at this conclusion, it is assumed that the dividend represents a market rate of return and that the instrument was issued at fair value.*

EXAMPLE: CASH FLOW STATEMENT

Entities are encouraged, but not required, to report some cash flow information using the indirect method. An example of a presentation of an indirect method of cash flow statement is given below, as an indication of the type of statements that smaller entities may wish to include in their financial statements. Comparative figures are not shown in the example.

	£	£
Cash generated from operations		
Operating profit/(loss)	**(5,050)**	
Reconciliation to cash generated from operations:		
Depreciation	245	
Increase in stocks	(194)	
Decrease in trade debtors	67,440	
Decrease in trade creditors	(4,678)	
Increase in other creditors	3,127	
		60,890
Cash from other sources		
Interest received	150	
Issues of shares for cash	5,500	
New long-term bank borrowings	4,500	
Proceeds from sale of tangible fixed assets	50	
		10,200
Application of cash		
Interest paid	(3,000)	
Tax paid	(29,220)	
Dividends paid	(10,000)	
Purchase of fixed assets	(10,500)	
Repayment of amounts borrowed	(3,000)	
		(55,720)
Net increase in cash		**15,370**
Cash at bank and in hand less overdrafts at beginning of year		(4,321)
Cash at bank and in hand less overdrafts at end of year		**11,049**
Consisting of:		
Cash at bank and in hand		11,549
Overdrafts included in 'bank loans and overdrafts falling due within one year'		(500)
		11,049

Major non-cash transactions: finance leases

During the year the company entered into finance lease arrangements in respect of assets with a total capital value at the inception of the leases of £2,850.

EXAMPLE: DISCOUNTING WHEN MAKING A PROVISION

A company faces a fine for operating without due regard to safety legislation. The company has been notified of the case and expects to lose it but does not expect the fine (of £100,000) to be payable for five years. How much should be provided for if the amount and timing of the fine is assumed to be certain and the market rate on relevant government bonds is 5 per cent?

The discounted amount for the payment of £100,000 to be made in five years' time is:

$$\frac{£100,000}{(1+(5/100))^5} = £78,353$$

Therefore, in the current year £78,353 is recorded as an expense and a provision in the company's books, rather than £100,000.

In the subsequent years the discount will unwind, increasing the amount of the provision and resulting in a debit to the profit and loss account (shown as a financial expense separate from interest) as follows:

		£
year 1	(78,353 × 5%)	3,918
year 2	((78,353 + 3,918) × 5%)	4,113
year 3	etc	4,319
year 4	etc	4,535
year 5	etc	4,762
		21,647
Add amount originally recorded		78,353
Total provision at end of year 5		100,000

Appendix IV
The development of the FRSSE

For many years there has been different reporting by different types of company: the requirements for listed public companies have been more onerous than for private companies and those for larger companies more onerous than for smaller companies. In particular, the provisions of the EC Fourth and Seventh Company Law Directives have been adopted in the UK and the Republic of Ireland, through which the disclosure requirements for large, medium-sized and small companies have been varied, allowing small companies more extensive exemptions both in the abbreviated accounts to be filed with the registrar of companies and in the statutory accounts for shareholders. 1

The application of accounting standards for smaller companies has also been an issue for standard-setters. The Board, prompted by the concern to reduce burdens on business, asked the Consultative Committee of Accountancy Bodies (CCAB) to establish a Working Party to examine the issue and to undertake wide consultation with a view to recommending criteria for exempting certain types of entity from accounting standards on the grounds of size or relative lack of public interest. 2

The CCAB Working Party published a Consultative Document in November 1994. This proposed that the Board should exempt all entities that met the Companies Act definition of a small company from compliance with all but the five accounting standards and the UITF Abstract noted below, which would continue to apply. 3

SSAP 4	'Accounting for government grants'
SSAP 9	'Stocks and long-term contracts'
SSAP 13	'Accounting for research and development'
SSAP 17	'Accounting for post balance sheet events'
SSAP 18	'Accounting for contingencies'
UITF Abstract 7	'True and fair view override disclosures'.

Comments in response to that Consultative Document supported the use of the small companies threshold and a change in the present system whereby small entities were required to comply with almost all accounting standards. However, there was no clear support for the proposal of piecemeal application of a limited number of standards. Analysis of the comments identified a number of recurrent themes, including the need for guidance on measurement issues and the suggestion that a codification of all standards should be undertaken as well as a comprehensive review of those standards that were perceived as needing revision or updating, particularly in the context of their application to smaller entities. On the latter point, the amount of time needed for this codification and review was recognised, as was the observation that it might not provide a complete solution for the issues faced by smaller entities. 4

Prompted by the comments received, the proposals in the DTI's Consultative Document 'Accounting Simplifications' published in May 1995 and the wish to focus on the needs of smaller entities, the CCAB Working Party proposed in its Paper 5

'Designed to fit', published in December 1995, that there should be a specific Financial Reporting Standard for Smaller Entities. To demonstrate that this approach was feasible, practical and capable of delivering benefits to those involved with financial statements for smaller entities, a draft FRSSE was included in 'Designed to fit'.

6 Letters of comment received in response to 'Designed to fit' indicated general support for a FRSSE that would apply to small companies and groups, as defined in companies legislation. Accordingly, the CCAB Working Party recommended to the Board that it should publish, as part of its due process, an Exposure Draft containing the proposed FRSSE, amended as appropriate to incorporate comments made on the draft contained in 'Designed to fit'.

7 The Board, largely accepting the CCAB Working Party's recommendations, duly published an Exposure Draft of the proposed FRSSE in December 1996, based on the proposals in 'Designed to fit', but with three main differences. First, the proposed FRSSE in the Exposure Draft was capable of application to small groups, unlike the proposals in 'Designed to fit'. Secondly, guidance on debt factoring arrangements was included in the Exposure Draft. Lastly, the requirement in 'Designed to fit' for a summarised cash flow statement was omitted. This led to the issue of the FRSSE in November 1997.

LINK WITH COMPANIES LEGISLATION

8 The FRSSE is linked with accounts drawn up in Great Britain under Schedule 8 to the Companies Act 1985* for the following reasons:

(a) it allows the establishment of a clearly distinguishable regime, i.e. the relevant statutory Schedule and the FRSSE. The importance of this was enhanced by the implementation of the Companies Act 1985 (Accounts of Small and Medium-Sized Companies and Minor Accounting Amendments) Regulations 1997 (SI 1997/220), which established a revised Schedule 8, containing all of the provisions applying to small companies; and

(b) it creates the link with the Schedule 8 provisions on a true and fair view, which may be of assistance to standard-setters and others in justifying different disclosure and any simplified measurement regime.

MATTERS CONSIDERED IN THE DEVELOPMENT OF THE FRSSE ISSUED IN NOVEMBER 1997

Application to small groups

9 Small groups are not required by law to prepare consolidated accounts, and therefore in practice not many do so, at least on a statutory basis. The Board, however, agreed that it would be unfair to those small groups that voluntarily prepare group accounts, if they were not able to take advantage of the provisions in the FRSSE. To import all the necessary requirements from accounting standards and UITF Abstracts into the FRSSE to deal with consolidated accounts would have added substantially to its length and complexity, even though it would have been of interest to only a small percentage of entities. Accordingly, the Board preferred to extend the FRSSE in certain areas and then require small groups adopting the FRSSE to follow those accounting standards and UITF Abstracts that deal with consolidated

**The equivalent legislation in Northern Ireland is Schedule 8 to the Companies (Northern Ireland) Order 1986. There is no equivalent to Schedule 8 in companies legislation in the Republic of Ireland. See the derivation table on the ASB website for Republic of Ireland legal requirements.*

financial statements. This approach was supported by the majority of respondents to the Exposure Draft commenting on the matter.

Cash flow statements

Consistently with the views of the majority of respondents to 'Designed to fit', the Exposure Draft did not propose any cash flow disclosures based on FRS 1 (Revised 1996) 'Cash Flow Statements'. The majority of respondents to the Exposure Draft supported the deletion of the cash flow requirements. However, given that management of cash is fundamental to the success of small businesses, the Board agreed with the minority of respondents, mainly representing users of the financial statements, that a cash flow statement is important. It provides a useful focus for discussions with management, as well as a reference point for subsequent more detailed analysis that users might require. Despite this, the Board recognised the difficulty of mandating a cash flow requirement when, previously, small entities had been exempt from such a requirement. Furthermore, the Board acknowledged that a cash flow format based on FRS 1 (Revised 1996) was not necessarily suitable or appropriate for smaller businesses. 10

The Board, therefore, while not mandating cash flow statements, strongly encourages smaller entities to provide such a statement voluntarily. Consultations suggested that it would be preferable to advocate only one method of cash flow presentation, for consistency and comparability. The direct method of cash flow statement, in a format similar to an entity's own cash forecasts and management accounts, may provide a link between management's cash projections and the financial statements. However, the indirect method is helpful in understanding the connection between the cash generated during a period and the resulting profit. Following consultation, the Board encourages the presentation of a cash flow statement using the indirect method as it is generally held to be more useful and better understood by many users of financial statements, as well as less costly to prepare. 11

Related party disclosures

About half of the respondents to the Board's Exposure Draft of the FRSSE believed that the FRSSE should not include any of the provisions from FRS 8 'Related Party Disclosures'. They argued that they were unnecessary, given that Parts II and III of Schedule 6 to the Companies Act 1985 require the disclosure of dealings in favour of directors and connected persons. Furthermore, if there was a material transaction with a related party, possibly executed at other than fair value, then, where there was any doubt whether applying any provision of the FRSSE would be sufficient to give a true and fair view, adequate explanation in the notes to the accounts of the transaction or arrangement concerned and the treatment adopted would be required (paragraph 2.5). 12

The Board, however, shared the view of the other respondents that related party disclosures are needed for a proper understanding of an entity's operations and for a true and fair view, given that material related party transactions are generally more prevalent in smaller businesses. It also noted that, in respect of dealings in favour of directors and connected persons, the statutory provisions apply equally to companies of all sizes and although the provisions overlapped the disclosure requirements in FRS 8 in many respects, the FRS was broader in scope and, in particular, expressed more clearly than the Act the spirit of Schedule 6. It also clarified, to the benefit of both preparers and auditors, the disclosures necessary to meet the fundamental requirement that accounts should give a true and fair view. 13

14 The Board, however, accepted that the full requirements of FRS 8 were unduly onerous and could be reduced for smaller entities, without compromising the benefit of the disclosures. Accordingly, the FRSSE requires that only those related party transactions that are material to the reporting entity need be disclosed in the notes to the financial statements, even though the FRS requires the disclosure of some transactions that are material only in relation to the other related party.

FRS 5

15 The FRSSE requires regard to be had to the substance of any arrangement or transaction, or series of such, into which an entity has entered. But it does not contain the extensive discussion in FRS 5 'Reporting the Substance of Transactions' on reflecting the substance of transactions. This is because small entities generally do not enter into complex transactions. However, the Board was advised that debt factoring and consignment stock may be a common feature of such entities and accordingly the provisions, principally in FRS 5's Application Notes, are likely to be of value to small entities. The relevant guidance in FRS 5 has therefore been included in the FRSSE.

SUBSEQUENT AMENDMENTS TO THE FRSSE

The FRSSE (effective March 1999)

16 On issuing the FRSSE, the Board acknowledged that it would need to be revised and updated periodically to reflect developments in financial reporting. The first such revision was issued in December 1998, and incorporated the relevant aspects of FRSs 9-11 and UITF Abstracts 18-22. The main changes were to align the requirements for entities applying the FRSSE with the basic measurement requirements of FRS 10 'Goodwill and Intangible Assets', which was issued in December 1997, and FRS 11 'Impairment of Fixed Assets and Goodwill', which was issued in July 1998.

17 The measurement requirements in the FRSSE were simplified, compared with those of FRS 10 and FRS 11, by:

- setting 20 years as a maximum, rather than a presumed maximum that may be rebutted, for the useful economic lives assigned to intangible assets and goodwill arising on the acquisition of unincorporated businesses, thereby removing the need for annual exercises to forecast and discount future cash flows;
- removing the exception that allows recognition of internally developed intangible assets with market values and revaluation of any intangible asset with a market value;
- omitting the detailed requirements for calculating value in use (as part of recoverable amount) and the subsequent monitoring of cash flows for five years following an impairment review where recoverable amount has been based on value in use.

18 The Board acknowledged that in principle the options for smaller entities applying the FRSSE would be more restricted than those for entities applying FRS 10. However, the Board is of the opinion that it would not, in practice, be restricting the options, as smaller entities would rarely be in a position to take advantage of them. The Board has not incorporated the detailed requirements from FRS 11 in the FRSSE, in order to allow smaller entities greater flexibility by enabling simpler calculations to be used where appropriate, given that detailed cash flow projections of smaller businesses are often not readily available.

The FRSSE (effective March 2000)

The second revision of the FRSSE was issued in December 1999. It incorporated the relevant aspects, modified and simplified where appropriate for smaller entities, of the four Financial Reporting Standards (FRSs 12-15) that were issued between July 1998 and June 1999. **19**

The main changes were to update and add to the material relating to provisions and fixed assets, to reflect the issue of FRSs 12 'Provisions, contingent liabilities and contingent assets' and 15 'Tangible fixed assets'. FRSs 13 and 14, which deal with financial instruments and earnings per share, respectively, were not addressed. **20**

The detailed rules of FRS 12 relating to discounting were omitted from the FRSSE, as were the majority of the disclosure requirements. The requirements of FRS 15 were also simplified for inclusion in the FRSSE, particularly those relating to revaluations and the disclosure requirements. **21**

The FRSSE (effective June 2002)

The third revision of the FRSSE was issued in December 2001. It incorporated the relevant aspects, modified and simplified where appropriate for smaller entities of the four Financial Reporting Standards (FRSs 16-19) that were issued between July 1999 and June 2001. **22**

The main changes were to update the requirements relating to current and deferred tax to reflect the issue of FRS 16 'Current tax' and FRS 19 'Deferred tax'. The requirement for discounting of deferred tax balances in FRS 19 was not included and a number of presentational and disclosure requirements were omitted. **23**

A new Appendix II was added to the FRSSE setting out the requirements for accounting for defined benefit schemes included in FRS 17 'Retirement benefits'. Some of the requirements of FRS 18 'Accounting policies' were incorporated into the FRSSE to ensure the framework underpinning the definition, selection and disclosure of accounting policies by FRSSE entities is consistent with that applied by other companies. **24**

The FRSSE (effective January 2005)

The fourth edition of the FRSSE was issued in April 2005. In developing this revision, the Board considered the relevant aspects, modified and simplified as appropriate for smaller entities, of the two Financial Reporting Standards (FRS 20 and 21), amendments to FRS 5 and FRS 17 and eight UITF Abstracts (UITF Abstracts 31 to 38) that were issued between June 2001 and November 2004. The Board also considered the requirements of relevant companies legislation. **25**

The main changes were to update the requirements for post balance sheet events to be consistent with FRS 21 and to incorporate the principles on revenue recognition from Application Note G to FRS 5. Specific guidance on "bill and hold arrangements", "sales with rights of return" and "presentation of turnover as principal or as agent" were also included in Appendix III as these are transactions commonly undertaken by smaller entities. An additional disclosure example for a defined contribution pension scheme was also included in Appendix III. **26**

The Board decided not to introduce any of the requirements from FRS 20 (IFRS 2) Share-based Payment into the FRSSE but proposed to consider further in a future update. It also decided not to reflect the requirements of UITF Abstracts 31 to 38 **27** other than UITF Abstract 34 "Pre-contract costs" which deals with the costs incurred in bidding for and securing contracts to supply goods or services of the FRSSE. The Board also incorporated the requirements of UITF Abstract 40 as guidance in Appendix III.

The FRSSE (effective January 2007)

28 The amendments made to the January 2005 version of the FRSSE are largely based upon those proposed in the Exposure Draft on amending the FRSSE that was published in April 2006. In developing this revision, the Board was again advised by its specialist Committee on Accounting for Smaller Entities (CASE).

29 This fifth edition of the FRSSE was published in January 2007 and incorporates the relevant aspects, modified and simplified where appropriate for smaller entities, of the eight new Financial Reporting Standards (FRS 22 to FRS 29), two amendments to FRSs (FRS 2 and FRS 26) and two UITF Abstracts (UITF 39 and UITF 40) that have been issued since October 2004, when the last Exposure Draft of amendments to the FRSSE was published. It also considers FRS 20 "Share-based payment", which was not addressed in the last amendment of the FRSSE, and changes in the company law financial reporting requirements affecting smaller entities.

30 The main question asked by the Board in publishing the Exposure Draft was whether the FRSSE should require smaller entities to apply the key principles of FRS20 for share-based payment arrangements. The majority of respondents argued against this proposal on the grounds that share-based payments were relatively uncommon for smaller entities and that the costs of complying with FRS20 are likely to outweigh the benefits obtained by users of small company accounts. The Board acknowledged these arguments and accepted CASE's proposals that cash settled transactions should be reported at the entity's best estimate of the expenditure required to settle the liability at the balance sheet date and that equity settled arrangements should be reported on a disclosure only basis.

31 The other main issue arising from consultation relates to the FRS 25 requirements for classifying capital instruments as either debt or equity. Respondents commented this was a difficult issue for smaller entities, particularly in terms of preference shares, and one where illustrative guidance in the FRSSE would be welcomed. The FRSSE (effective January 2007) therefore includes working examples that are intended to assist smaller entities in applying the presentation requirements of FRS 25.

32 A number of other minor changes have been made to the FRSSE (effective January 2007) to reflect recent changes in company law and to make some presentational changes. The most significant presentational change has been to remove Appendices V to VII, thereby helping to make the FRSSE a more manageable document. The Board acknowledges that smaller entities find the derivation information included in these Appendices helpful and is. therefore committed to making it freely available on the ASB website.

The FRSSE (effective April 2008)

33 The amendments made to the FRSSE (effective January 2007) reflect the impact of the Companies Act 2006. The Board decided to issue an updated version of the FRSSE to ensure it continued to accurately reflect company law requirements, as set out in the Companies Act 2006. Updating the FRSSE would also ensure that it retains is usefulness as a "one stop shop". In issuing this version of the FRSSE (effective April 2008), the Board was advised by its Committee on Accounting for Smaller Entities (CASE).

In carrying out a review of the FRSSE (effective January 2007) there were two amendments to accounting standards to consider and five new UITF Abstracts. The Board decided that it was not necessary, at this stage, to update the accounting requirements of the FRSSE for these developments. **34**

The impact of the Companies Act 2006 is not significant in terms of smaller company accounting, although there are some substantive changes. These include increases to the thresholds for companies qualifying as small and increases in the thresholds for reporting political and charitable donations. Further detail on these changes is provided in Appendix V.* **35**

The derivation table available on the ASB website provides a full cross-reference between the Companies Act 2006 and the legislative requirements set out in the FRSSE (effective April 2008). It also retains separate columns showing the equivalent references for the FRSSE (effective January 2007) to the 1985 Companies Act and relevant legislation in Northern Ireland and the Republic of Ireland. The Companies Act 2006 represents United Kingdom legislation, unlike the Companies Act 1985 which only covered Great Britain. For this reason, the FRSSE (effective April 2008) does not require separate derivations for Northern Ireland. **36**

There have been no changes to the legal requirements in the Republic of Ireland. **37**

RELATIONSHIP WITH OTHER ASB DOCUMENTS†

The FRSSE is designed to provide smaller entities with a single accounting standard that is focused on their particular circumstances. Smaller entities that choose to **38**

* ***Editor's note**: With effect for accounting periods beginning on or after 1 January 2015 the final sentence of this paragraph is deleted.*

† ***Editor's note**: With effect for accounting periods beginning on or after 1 January 2015 paragraphs 38 and 39 are replaced with the following:*

The FRSSE (effective January 2015)

38 In November 2012 the FRC amended the FRSSE as a consequence of the significant changes that were made to UK and Republic of Ireland financial reporting standards at this date. In November 2012 the FRC revised extant Financial Reporting Standards, withdrawing its existing financial reporting standards and supplementary literature from 1 January 2015 and replacing them with revised financial reporting requirements, based on International Financial Reporting Standards (for example, the IFRS for SMEs was used as a basis for FRS 102 *The Financial Reporting Standard applicable in the UK and Republic of Ireland*). The FRSSE (effective April 2008) was amended as a consequence of these changes.

39 The consequential amendments to the FRSSE were to update references in the FRSSE (effective April 2008) to accounting standards that were withdrawn or for greater consistency with legislation. In addition, the FRC explained that where an entity applying the FRSSE undertakes a new transaction for which it has no existing accounting policy it should have regard to FRS 102, not as a mandatory document but as a means of establishing current practice. The FRC removed the reference to the accounting standards applicable to consolidated financial statements because the general requirements in the FRSSE for developing accounting policies for transactions or events that are not dealt with in the FRSSE are equally applicable to consolidated financial statements.

40 The FRC made two further amendments to the FRSSE:

(a) it introduced a requirement which is consistent with the EU Directives, that if an entity is unable to make a reliable estimate of the useful life of goodwill or intangible assets, the life shall be presumed not to exceed five years.

(b) it clarified that an entity shall assess annually whether there is any indicationthat an asset should be written down. This will assist entities applying the existing requirement for fixed assets and goodwill to be carried at no more than their recoverable amount.

These amendments relate to applying existing company law requirements.

adopt the FRSSE are exempt from other accounting standards and UITF Abstracts (with certain exceptions for those small groups preparing consolidated financial statements). The Board accepts that the FRSSE is not comprehensive and that there may be issues of general application on which guidance will be sought. Preparers may come across transactions on which accounting guidance is not provided in the FRSSE. This raises the question of whether, in the absence of guidance within the FRSSE, preparers and auditors would be required to follow all SSAPs, other FRSs and UITF Abstracts to the extent that they provide guidance on transactions of relevance to the smaller entity. The Board's view, formulated after consultation with legal advisers and others, is that users expect financial statements to be prepared using accepted practice. If a practice was clearly established and accepted, it should be followed unless there were good reasons to depart from it. Accordingly, preparers and auditors should have regard to SSAPs, FRSs and UITF Abstracts, not as mandatory documents, but as a means of establishing current practice.

39 Some respondents asked that there should be specific cross-references within the FRSSE to SSAPs, other FRSs and UITF Abstracts. The Board rejected this suggestion because the inclusion of cross-references would lead to preparers and auditors having to consider those other pronouncements in all cases, as well as the FRSSE, thereby lengthening checklists and adding to the burden. Furthermore, it is recognised that as new FRSs are issued that amend generally accepted accounting practice as it applies to larger entities, it may not be appropriate for such rules to apply to smaller entities. An example that has been frequently cited, but on which the Board has not established a firm position, is that some of the likely proposals on marking to market fixed interest instruments, while appropriate for larger entities, would not be appropriate for smaller entities. Because generally accepted accounting practice had not been established for all in this area then there would not be an expectation that smaller entities should have regard to such a new rule.

41 The FRSSE is designed to provide smaller entities with a single accounting standard that is focused on their particular circumstances. Smaller entities that choose to adopt the FRSSE are exempt from other accounting standards. The FRC accepts that the FRSSE is not comprehensive and that there may be issues of general application on which guidance will be sought. Preparers may come across transactions on which accounting guidance is not provided in the FRSSE. This raises the question of whether, in the absence of guidance within the FRSSE, preparers would be required to follow FRS 102 *The Financial Reporting Standard applicable in the UK and Republic of Ireland* to the extent that it provides guidance on transactions of relevance to the smaller entity. The FRC's view, formulated after consultation with legal advisers and others, is that users expect financial statements to be prepared using accepted practice. If a practice was clearly established and accepted, it should be followed unless there were good reasons to depart from it. Accordingly, preparers should have regard to FRSs (including FRS 102 *The Financial Reporting Standard applicable in the UK and Republic of Ireland*), not as mandatory documents, but as a means of establishing current practice.

42 In relation to earlier versions of the FRSSE, some respondents asked that there should be specific cross references within the FRSSE to SSAPs, other FRSs and UITF Abstracts (the equivalent cross references would now be to FRS 102 *The Financial Reporting Standard applicable in the UK and Republic of Ireland*). The FRC rejected this suggestion because the inclusion of cross-references would lead to preparers having to consider those other pronouncements in all cases, as well as the FRSSE, thereby lengthening checklists and adding to the burden. Furthermore, it is recognised that as new FRSs are issued (including introducing FRS 102 The Financial Reporting Standard applicable in the UK and Republic of Ireland) that amend generally accepted accounting practice as it applies to larger entities, it may not be appropriate for such rules to apply to smaller entities.

Appendix V*
Amendment to the FRSSE (effective January 2007)

In publishing this updated version of the Financial Reporting Standard for Smaller Entities (effective April 2008), the Board was advised by its specialist Committee on Accounting for Smaller Entities (CASE). 1

Accounting developments

Although no new accounting standards have been issued since the last Exposure Draft of amendments to the FRSSE was published in April 2006, there have been amendments to two FRSs and five new UITF Abstracts that have been issued. These are listed below. 2

Amendments to FRSs and UITF abstracts	*Title*	*Issued*
Amendment to FRS 3	Reporting Financial Performance	January 2007
Amendment to FRS17	Retirement benefits	July 2007
UITF Abstract 41	(IFRIC Interpretation 8) Scope of FRS 20 (IFRS 2)	April 2006
UITF Abstract 42	(IFRIC Interpretation 9) Reassessment of embedded derivatives	April 2006
UITF Abstract 43	The interpretation of equivalence for the purposes of section 228A of the Companies Act 1985	October 2006
UITF Abstract 44	(IFRIC Interpretation 11) FRS 20 (IFRS 2) Group and Treasury Share Transactions	February 2007
UITF Abstract 45	(IFRIC Interpretation 6) Liabilities arising from participating in a specific market – Waste, electrical and electronic equipment	February 2007

The Board agreed not to update the FRSSE at this stage for these accounting developments. 3

Legal developments

The main issue considered by the Board and CASE in reviewing the FRSSE (effective January 2007) was the impact of the Companies Act 2006 (the 2006 Act). The Board agreed that it was necessary for the FRSSE to be updated to reflect the 2006 Act, particularly in view of the need to ensure the FRSSE remains up to date 4

****Editor's note**: With effect for accounting periods beginning on or after 1 January 2015 Appendix V is deleted in its entirety.*

and retains its usefulness as a "one stop shop". The Board also agreed that the derivation table that is maintained on the ASB website should be updated to reflect the requirements of the 2006 Act (available at http://www.frc.org.uk/asb/technical/frsse.cfm).

5 The main impact of the 2006 Act is to set out the accounting and reporting requirements for small companies in a separate Regulation (SI 2008/409 *'The Small Companies and Groups (Accounts and Directors' Report) Regulations 2008)*. Importantly, this is largely a tidying-up exercise with few substantive changes made to the legal requirements for small company accounts. There have however been some changes, for example the 2006 Act covers the United Kingdom (so is now applicable to Northern Ireland, plus references to accounting requirements that the 1985 Act states companies "**shall**" follow have been replaced in the 2006 Act by the term "**must**".

6 The requirements for small company accounts and reports are set out in sections 381 to 384 of the 2006 Act, including the qualifying conditions for companies and groups qualifying as small. These conditions include thresholds for turnover and the balance sheet and these have been increased by 20 per cent by Statutory Instrument 2008/393 '*The Companies Act 2006 (Amendment) (Accounts and Reports) Regulations 2008*'. The option to prepare group accounts is retained in section 399 of the 2006 Act, although SI 2008/393 also increases the thresholds for companies to qualify as a small group.

7 Importantly, the 2006 Act provides the Secretary of State with the power to make Regulations covering the accounting requirements and these are largely reflected in Statutory Instrument 2008/409 '*The Small Companies and Groups (Accounts and Directors' Report) Regulations 2008*'. This includes a small number of changes that have been reflected in the updated FRSSE (effective April 2008), as reflected in the following table (which includes references both to the relevant paragraph of the FRSSE and the relevant part of the 2006 Act).

CHANGES TO FRSSE ARISING FROM 2006 COMPANIES ACT

FRSSE paragraph	Description of change in legal requirements	2006 Act reference
Para 9 on pages 11 and 12	Revised scope to reflect amended eligibility criteria. This is a detailed matter limiting the scope for small investment firms and entities such as e-money issuers to use the FRSSE	s 384 (1) and (2)
2.31 and 18.13	Remove reference to accounts being laid before the company in general meeting – as no longer a requirement for private company to have an AGM.	s 433 (1)
2.39	Requirement to disclose details of any liability limitation agreement (where accounts subject to audit)	Reg 2008/489* para 8
12.9	Delete requirement to disclose authorised share capital	n/a
15.9	Additional text on disclosing country of incorporation if outside the UK "if known to directors"	Reg 2008/409*, Sch 2, para 10
15.11 to 15.15	Changed text for transactions with directors – 'loans, quasi-loans, credit transactions and guarantees' now referred to as 'advances, credits and guarantees'.	s 413
16.5	Requirement to show details in group accounts of directors' benefits.	s 413(2)
16.7	Insert modification for P&L Account when preparing group accounts	Reg 2008/409, Sch 6, para 1 (3)
17.1	Use of term directors' "remuneration" instead of emoluments	Reg 2008/409, Sch 3, para 1
18.1	Separate out political donations from charitable donations	Reg 2008/409, Sch 5
18.3	New text confirming that where the company is a parent, and chooses to prepare group accounts, the directors' report must be a group report	s 415
18.5	Delete text for Directors' interests – as no longer a requirement to *maintain* a Register of Interests	n/a

FRSSE paragraph	Description of change in legal requirements	2006 Act reference
18.7 to 18.9	Insert new requirement for disclosures regards Independent election candidates Insert £2,000 threshold (to reflect increase for disclosure from £200 in 1985 Act)	Reg 2008/409, Sch 5, para 2 (a) (ii) Reg 2008/409, Sch 5, para 3
Definitions page 100	New definition for director's family	s 253
App I pages 125 and 126	Insert new thresholds for companies and groups to qualify as small Insert new text for companies that are excluded from small company criteria Delete separate paragraph on Northern Ireland	s 382 (3) and Reg 2008/393* s 384 (1) and (2)

- *Statutory Instrument 2008/489 'The Companies (Disclosure of Auditor Remuneration and Liability Limitation Agreements) Regulations 2008.
- *Statutory Instrument 2008/409 'The Small Companies and Groups (Accounts and Directors' Report) Regulations 2008.
- *Statutory Instrument 2008/393 'The Companies Act 2006 (Amendment) (Accounts and Reports) Regulations 2008.

Other changes

8 The effective date has been updated to reflect the coming into force on 6 April 2008 of the accounting and reporting requirements for small companies under the 2006 Act. The effective date for the FRSSE (effective April 2008) is therefore for accounting periods beginning on or after 6 April 2008. To ensure that small company accounts comply with legal requirements, earlier adoption is not permitted.

9 There is a new definition for Director's family, to reflect new text that is used in the 2006 Act. A number of other consequential minor amendments have also been made.

Consultation

10 The Board decided that it would not be necessary to consult on this update to the FRSSE (effective April 2008) because no changes are being made to the GAAP based accounting requirements.

11 The Board expects that any further update to the FRSSE, including the accounting requirements, will arise as a result of its proposals to converge UK GAAP with International Financial Reporting Standards. The Board is currently finalising its plans for convergence and will be consulting on these, including proposals for small company accounting, in the near future.

FRS 100
Application of Financial Reporting Requirements

Contents

Summary

Financial Reporting Standard 100
Application of Financial Reporting Requirements

Objective
Scope
Abbreviations and definitions
Basis of preparation of financial statements
Application of statements of recommended practice
Statement of compliance
Date from which effective and transitional arrangements
Withdrawal of current accounting standards
Consequential amendments to the FRSSE

Application Guidance

The interpretation of equivalence

Approval by the FRC

The Accounting Council's Advice to the FRC to issue FRS 100

Appendices

I Glossary
II Note on legal requirements
III Previous consultations
IV Republic of Ireland (RoI) legal references

Summary

(i) In 2012 and 2013 the Financial Reporting Council (FRC) revised financial reporting standards for the United Kingdom and Republic of Ireland. The revision fundamentally reformed financial reporting, replacing almost all extant standards with three Financial Reporting Standards:

FRS 100 *Application of Financial Reporting Requirements*;
FRS 101 *Reduced Disclosure Framework*; and
FRS 102 *The Financial Reporting Standard applicable in the UK and Republic of Ireland.*

(ii) The revisions made by the FRC followed a sustained and detailed period of consultation. The FRC made these fundamental changes recognising that the introduction of International Financial Reporting Standards for listed groups in 2002 (with application from 2005) called into question the need for two sets of financial reporting standards. Evidence from consultation supported a move towards an international-based framework for financial reporting, but one that was proportionate to the needs of preparers and users.

(iii) The FRC's overriding objective in setting accounting standards is to enable users of accounts to receive high-quality understandable financial reporting proportionate to the size and complexity of the entity and users' information needs.

(iv) In meeting this objective, the FRC aims to provide succinct financial reporting standards that:

(a) have consistency with international accounting standards through the application of an IFRS-based solution unless an alternative clearly better meets the overriding objective;
(b) reflect up-to-date thinking and developments in the way entities operate and the transactions they undertake;
(c) balance consistent principles for accounting by all UK and Republic of Ireland entities with practical solutions, based on size, complexity, public interest and users' information needs;
(d) promote efficiency within groups; and
(e) are cost-effective to apply.

(v) The requirements in this Financial Reporting Standard (FRS) take into consideration the findings from the consultations on the future of financial reporting in the UK and Republic of Ireland that took place between 2002 and 2012.

(vi) This FRS sets out the financial reporting requirements for UK and Republic of Ireland entities. Financial statements (whether consolidated financial statements or individual financial statements) that are within the scope of this FRS must be prepared in accordance with the following requirements:

(a) If the financial statements are those of an entity that is eligible to apply the Financial Reporting Standard for Smaller Entities (FRSSE), they may be prepared in accordance with that standard.
(b) If the financial statements are those of an entity that is not eligible to apply the FRSSE, or of an entity that is eligible to apply the FRSSE but chooses not to do so, they must be prepared in accordance with FRS 102, EU-adopted IFRS or, if the financial statements are the individual financial statements of a qualifying entity, FRS 101*.

**Under company law in the Republic of Ireland, certain companies are permitted to prepare Companies Act accounts using a financial reporting framework based on accounting standards other than those issued by the FRC. Please refer to Appendix IV for further details.*

(vii) FRS 101 sets out a reduced disclosure framework which addresses the financial reporting requirements and disclosure exemptions for the individual financial statements of subsidiaries and ultimate parents that otherwise apply the recognition, measurement and disclosure requirements of EU-adopted IFRS.

(viii) FRS 102 is a single financial reporting standard that applies to the financial statements of entities that are not applying EU-adopted IFRS, FRS 101 or the FRSSE.

(ix) The FRSSE sets out the financial reporting requirements for smaller entities as defined by company law and entities which are not companies but would otherwise meet the criteria of a small company.

Financial Reporting Standard 100
Application of Financial Reporting Requirements

OBJECTIVE

1 The objective of this Financial Reporting Standard (FRS) is to set out the applicable financial reporting framework for entities preparing financial statements in accordance with legislation, regulations or accounting standards applicable in the United Kingdom and Republic of Ireland.

SCOPE

2 This FRS applies to financial statements that are intended to give a true and fair view of the assets, liabilities, financial position and profit or loss for a period.

ABBREVIATIONS AND DEFINITIONS

3 The terms **Act**, **date of transition**, **EU-adopted IFRS**, **financial institution**, **FRS 100**, **FRS 101**, **FRS 102**, **FRSSE**, **IAS Regulation**, **IFRS**, **individual financial statements**, **public benefit entity**, **qualifying entity**, **Regulations** and **SORP** are defined in the glossary included as Appendix I to this FRS.

BASIS OF PREPARATION OF FINANCIAL STATEMENTS

4 Financial statements (whether consolidated financial statements or individual financial statements) that are within the scope of this FRS, and that are not required by the IAS Regulation or other legislation or regulation to be prepared in accordance with EU-adopted IFRS, must be prepared in accordance with the following requirements:

(a) If the financial statements are those of an entity that is eligible to apply the FRSSE*, they may be prepared in accordance with that standard;

(b) If the financial statements are those of an entity that is not eligible to apply the FRSSE, or of an entity that is eligible to apply the FRSSE but chooses not to do so, they must† be prepared in accordance with FRS 102, EU-adopted IFRS‡ or, if the financial statements are the individual financial statements of a qualifying entity, FRS 101.§

**The eligibility criteria for applying the FRSSE are set out in paragraph 8 of the FRSSE. One of the criteria is that the entity must be 'small' as defined in company law. Turnover and balance sheet total should be measured in accordance with the FRSSE for the purposes of establishing whether the entity is 'small'; the measurement of turnover and balance sheet total in accordance with FRS 101 or FRS 102 need not be considered.*

†Under company law in the Republic of Ireland, certain companies are permitted to prepare Companies Act accounts using a financial reporting framework based on accounting standards other than those issued by the FRC. Please refer to Appendix IV for further details.

‡Some entities are prohibited from applying EU-adopted IFRS, for example section 395(2) of the Act states that 'the individual accounts of a company that is a charity must be Companies Act individual accounts', and section 403(3) of the Act mirrors this for the group accounts of a parent company that is a charity.

§Individual accounts that are prepared by a company in accordance with FRS 101 or FRS 102 are Companies Act individual accounts (section 395(1)(a) of the Act), whereas individual accounts that are prepared by a company in accordance with EU-adopted IFRS are IAS individual accounts (section 395(1)(b) of the Act).

APPLICATION OF STATEMENTS OF RECOMMENDED PRACTICE (SORPS)

If an entity's financial statements are prepared in accordance with the FRSSE or FRS 102, SORPs will apply in the circumstances set out in those standards. **5**

When a SORP applies, the entity should state in its financial statements the title of the SORP and whether its financial statements have been prepared in accordance with the SORP's provisions that are currently in effect*. In the event of a departure from those provisions, the entity should give a brief description of how the financial statements depart from the recommended practice set out in the SORP, which shall include: **6**

(a) for any treatment that is not in accordance with the SORP, the reasons why the treatment adopted is judged more appropriate to the entity's particular circumstances; and
(b) brief details of any disclosures recommended by the SORP that have not been provided, and the reasons why they have not been provided.

SORPs recommend particular accounting treatments and disclosures with the aim of narrowing areas of difference and variety between comparable entities. Compliance with a SORP that has been generally accepted by an industry or sector leads to enhanced comparability between the financial statements of entities in that industry or sector. Comparability is further enhanced if users are made aware of the extent to which an entity complies with a SORP, and the reasons for any departures. The effect of a departure from a SORP need not be quantified, except in those rare cases where such quantification is necessary for the entity's financial statements to give a true and fair view. **7**

Entities whose financial statements do not fall within the scope of a SORP may, if the SORP is otherwise relevant to them, nevertheless choose to comply with the SORP's recommendations when preparing financial statements, provided that the SORP does not conflict with the requirements of the framework adopted. Where this is the case, entities are encouraged to disclose that fact. **8**

STATEMENT OF COMPLIANCE

Where an entity prepares its financial statements in accordance with FRS 101, FRS 102 or the FRSSE, it shall include a statement of compliance in the notes to the financial statements in accordance with the requirements set out in the relevant standard. **9**

DATE FROM WHICH EFFECTIVE AND TRANSITIONAL ARRANGEMENTS

An entity shall apply this FRS for accounting periods beginning on or after 1 January 2015. Early application of this FRS is permitted subject to the early application provisions set out in FRS 101, FRS 102 and the FRSSE (effective January 2015). If an entity applies this FRS before 1 January 2015 it shall disclose that fact. **10**

On first-time application of this FRS, or when an entity changes the basis of preparation of its financial statements within the requirements of this FRS, it shall apply the transitional arrangements relevant to its circumstances as follows: **11**

**The provisions of a SORP will cease to have effect, for example, to the extent that they conflict with a more recent financial reporting standard.*

(a) An entity transitioning to EU-adopted IFRS shall apply the transitional arrangements set out in IFRS 1 *First-time Adoption of International Financial Reporting Standards* as adopted by the EU.
(b) A qualifying entity transitioning to FRS 101 shall, unless it is applying EU-adopted IFRS prior to the date of transition (see paragraph 12), apply the requirements of paragraphs 6 to 33 of IFRS 1 as adopted by the EU including the relevant appendices; references to IFRSs in IFRS 1 are interpreted to mean EU-adopted IFRS as amended in accordance with paragraph 5(b) of FRS 101.
(c) An entity transitioning to FRS 102 shall apply the transitional arrangements set out in that standard.
(d) An entity transitioning to the FRSSE shall apply the transitional arrangements set out in the FRSSE.

12 A qualifying entity applying EU-adopted IFRS prior to the date of transition to FRS 101 will then be preparing Companies Act individual accounts in accordance with section 395(1)(a) of the Act and thus will no longer be preparing IAS individual accounts in accordance with section 395(1)(b) of the Act.* It shall consider whether amendments are required to comply with paragraph 5(b) of FRS 101, but it does not reapply the provisions of IFRS 1. Where amendments to the recognition, measurement and disclosure requirements of EU-adopted IFRS in accordance with paragraph 5(b) of FRS 101 are required, the entity shall determine whether the amendments have a material effect on the first financial statements presented. Where there is:

(a) no material effect, the qualifying entity shall disclose that it has undergone transition to FRS 101 and a brief narrative of the disclosure exemptions adopted, for all periods presented; or
(b) a material effect, the qualifying entity's first financial statements shall include:
    (i) a description of the nature of each material change in accounting policy;
    (ii) reconciliations of its equity determined in accordance with EU-adopted IFRS to its equity determined in accordance with FRS 101 for both the date of transition to FRS 101 and for the end of the latest period presented in the entity's most recent annual financial statements prepared in accordance with EU-adopted IFRS; and
    (iii) a reconciliation of the profit or loss determined in accordance with EU-adopted IFRS to its profit or loss determined in accordance with FRS 101 for the latest period presented in the entity's most recent annual financial statements prepared in accordance with EU-adopted IFRS.

13 Where paragraph 12(b) applies but it is impracticable to apply the amendments retrospectively, a qualifying entity shall apply the amendments to the earliest period for which it is practicable to do so, and it shall identify the data presented for prior periods that are not comparable with data for the period in which it prepares its first financial statements that conform with the reduced disclosure framework set out in FRS 101.

WITHDRAWAL OF CURRENT ACCOUNTING STANDARDS

14 The following SSAPs, FRSs and UITF Abstracts are superseded on the early application of this FRS. These SSAPs, FRSs and UITF Abstracts will be withdrawn for accounting periods beginning on or after 1 January 2015.

SSAP 4	*Accounting for government grants;*
SSAP 5	*Accounting for value added tax;*

**Further relevant information can be found at paragraph A2.14 of Appendix II.*

SSAP 9	*Stocks and long-term contracts*;
SSAP 13	*Accounting for research and development*;
SSAP 19	*Accounting for investment properties*;
SSAP 20	*Foreign currency translation*;
SSAP 21	*Accounting for leases and hire purchase contracts; including the Guidance Notes on SSAP 21*;
SSAP 25	*Segmental reporting*;
FRS 1	*Cash flow statements (revised 1996)*;
FRS 2	*Accounting for subsidiary undertakings*;
FRS 3	*Reporting financial performance*;
FRS 4	*Capital instruments*;
FRS 5	*Reporting the substance of transactions*;
FRS 6	*Acquisitions and mergers*;
FRS 7	*Fair values in acquisition accounting*;
FRS 8	*Related party disclosures*;
FRS 9	*Associates and joint ventures*;
FRS 10	*Goodwill and intangible assets*;
FRS 11	*Impairment of fixed assets and goodwill*;
FRS 12	*Provisions, contingent liabilities and contingent assets*;
FRS 13	*Derivatives and other financial instruments: disclosures*;
FRS 15	*Tangible fixed assets*;
FRS 16	*Current tax*;
FRS 17	*Retirement benefits*;
FRS 18	*Accounting policies*;
FRS 19	*Deferred tax*;
FRS 20 (IFRS 2)	*Share-based payment*;
FRS 21 (IAS 10)	*Events after the balance sheet date*;
FRS 22 (IAS 33)	*Earnings per share*;
FRS 23 (IAS 21)	*The effects of changes in foreign exchange rates*;
FRS 24 (IAS 29)	*Financial reporting in hyperinflationary economies*;
FRS 25 (IAS 32)	*Financial instruments: Presentation*;
FRS 26 (IAS 39)	*Financial instruments: Recognition and Measurement*;
FRS 28	*Corresponding amounts*;
FRS 29 (IFRS 7)	*Financial instruments: Disclosures*;
FRS 30	*Heritage assets*;
UITF Abstract 4:	*Presentation of long-term debtors in current assets*;
UITF Abstract 5:	*Transfers from current assets to fixed assets*;
UITF Abstract 9:	*Accounting for operations in hyper-inflationary economies;*
UITF Abstract 11:	*Capital instruments: Issuer call options*;
UITF Abstract 15:	*Disclosure of substantial acquisitions (Revised 1999)*;
UITF Abstract 19:	*Tax on gains and losses on foreign currency borrowings that hedge an investment in a foreign enterprise*;
UITF Abstract 21:	*Accounting issues arising from the proposed introduction of the euro*;
UITF Abstract 22:	*The acquisition of a Lloyd's business*;
UITF Abstract 23:	*Application of the transitional rules in FRS 15*;
UITF Abstract 24:	*Accounting for start-up costs*;
UITF Abstract 25:	*National Insurance contributions on share option gains*;
UITF Abstract 26:	*Barter transactions for advertising*;
UITF Abstract 27:	*Revision to estimates of the useful economic life of goodwill and intangible assets*;
UITF Abstract 28:	*Operating lease incentives*;
UITF Abstract 29:	*Website development costs*;
UITF Abstract 31:	*Exchanges of businesses or other non-monetary assets for an interest in a subsidiary, joint venture or associate*;

UITF Abstract 32: *Employee benefit trusts and other intermediate payment arrangements*;
UITF Abstract 34: *Pre-contract costs*;
UITF Abstract 35: *Death-in-service and incapacity benefits*;
UITF Abstract 36: *Contracts for sales of capacity*;
UITF Abstract 38: *Accounting for ESOP trusts*;
UITF Abstract 39: *(IFRIC Interpretation 2) Members' shares in co-operative entities and similar instruments*;
UITF Abstract 40: *Revenue recognition and service contracts*;
UITF Abstract 41: *(IFRIC Interpretation 8) Scope of FRS 20 (IFRS 2)*;
UITF Abstract 42: *(IFRIC Interpretation 9) Reassessment of embedded derivatives*;
UITF Abstract 43: *The interpretation of equivalence for the purposes of section 228A of the Companies Act 1985*;
UITF Abstract 44: *(IFRIC Interpretation 11) FRS 20 (IFRS 2) Group and Treasury Share Transactions*;
UITF Abstract 45: *(IFRIC Interpretation 6) Liabilities arising from participating in a specific market – Waste electrical and electronic equipment*;
UITF Abstract 46: *(IFRIC Interpretation 16) Hedges of a net investment in a foreign operation;*
UITF Abstract 47: *(IFRIC Interpretation 19) Extinguishing financial liabilities with equity instruments;* and
UITF Abstract 48: *Accounting implications of the replacement of the retail prices index with the consumer prices index for retirement benefits.*

15 The following statements are also withdrawn:

Statement of Principles for Financial Reporting;
Statement of Principles for Financial Reporting – Interpretation for public benefit entities; and
Reporting Statement: Retirement Benefits – Disclosures.

CONSEQUENTIAL AMENDMENTS TO THE FRSSE

16 Not reproduced, as all changes have been reflected in this volume.

Application Guidance: The Interpretation of Equivalence

This application guidance forms an integral part of FRS 100

INTRODUCTION

Section 401 of the Act exempts, subject to certain conditions, an intermediate parent from the requirement to prepare consolidated financial statements where its parent is not established under the law of an EEA state. Section 401 states that: **AG1**

(2) Exemption is conditional upon compliance with all of the following conditions—

(a) the company and all of its subsidiary undertakings must be included in consolidated accounts for a larger group drawn up to the same date, or to an earlier date in the same financial year, by a parent undertaking;

(b) those accounts and, where appropriate, the group's annual report, must be drawn up—

(i) in accordance with the provisions of the Seventh Directive (83/349/EEC) (as modified, where relevant, by the provisions of the Bank Accounts Directive (86/635/EEC) or the Insurance Accounts Directive (91/674/EEC)), or

(ii) in a manner ***equivalent*** *to consolidated accounts and consolidated annual reports so drawn up;...* (emphasis added)

FRS 101 and FRS 102 permit certain exemptions from disclosures, but those exemptions are in some cases subject to **equivalent** disclosures being included in the consolidated financial statements of the group in which the entity is consolidated. **AG2**

This Application Guidance provides guidance on interpreting the meaning of equivalence in the two circumstances set out above. **AG3**

SECTION 401 OF THE COMPANIES ACT 2006

Use of the exemption in section 401 requires an analysis of a particular set of consolidated financial statements to determine whether they are drawn up in a manner equivalent to consolidated financial statements that are in accordance with the Seventh Directive*. This Application Guidance aims to assist entities in adopting a consistent approach to this issue. In the absence of this guidance, companies and their auditors might feel obliged to take an overly cautious approach in response to uncertainty about whether the exemptions can be used. **AG4**

It is generally accepted that the reference to equivalence in section 401 of the Act does not mean compliance with every detail of the Seventh Directive. When assessing whether consolidated financial statements of a higher non-EEA parent are drawn up in a manner equivalent to consolidated financial statements drawn up in accordance with the Seventh Directive, it is necessary to consider whether they meet the basic requirements of the Fourth and Seventh Directives; in particular the requirement to give a true and fair view, without implying strict conformity with each and every **AG5**

**The Seventh Directive deals with consolidated accounts and applies most of the requirements of the Fourth Directive (78/660/EEC) to those consolidated accounts. Consideration of equivalence with the Seventh Directive therefore requires consideration of equivalence with the relevant provisions of the Fourth Directive. References in this Application Guidance to accounts being prepared in accordance with the Seventh Directive include, where appropriate, compliance with the relevant provisions of the Fourth Directive.*

provision. A qualitative approach is more in keeping with the deregulatory nature of the exemption than a requirement to consider the detailed requirements on a checklist basis.

AG6 The consequences of adopting the principle in paragraph AG5 are that consolidated financial statements of the higher parent will meet the test of equivalence in the Seventh Directive if they:

(a) give a true and fair view and comply with FRS 102;
(b) are prepared in accordance with EU-adopted IFRS;
(c) are prepared in accordance with IFRS, subject to the consideration of the reasons for any failure by the European Commission to adopt a standard or interpretation; and
(d) are prepared using other GAAPs which are closely related to IFRS, subject to consideration of the effect of any differences from EU-adopted IFRS.

Consolidated financial statements of the higher parent prepared using:

(e) other GAAPs should be assessed for equivalence with the Seventh Directive based on the particular facts, including the similarities to and differences from the Seventh Directive (see paragraph AG7); and
(f) the IFRS for SMEs shall be assessed for equivalence with the Seventh Directive where the following factors are considered:
    (i) applying the disclosure requirements for extraordinary items;
    (ii) requiring additional disclosures for financial liabilities that were held at fair value but were neither held as part of a trading portfolio nor a derivative;
    (iii) shortening the presumed life of goodwill from 10 to not exceeding five years, where an entity is unable to make a reliable estimate of the useful life;
    (iv) recognising negative goodwill in the income statement only when it meets the definition of a realised profit;
    (v) replacing the prohibition on reversal of impairment losses of goodwill with a requirement to reverse the loss if, and only if, the reasons for the impairment cease to apply; and
    (vi) removing the requirement for unpaid called-up share capital to be recognised as an offset to equity.

AG7 A mechanism to determine the equivalence of the Generally Accepted Accounting Principles (GAAP) from third countries was established in 2007. Accordingly, the European Commission adopted a Decision and Regulation which identified as equivalent to IFRS the US GAAP, the Japanese GAAP, and accepted financial statements using the GAAP of China, Canada, India and South Korea within the EU on a temporary basis until 31 December 2011. In accordance with relevant EU legislation the European Commission has been updating the European Parliament at regular intervals on the progress made by these countries with their respective programmes to converge their GAAP with IFRS*.

**As set out in a European Commission Staff Working Paper* State of play on convergence between International Financial Reporting Standards (IFRS) and third country national Generally Accepted Accounting Principles (GAAP) *(Ref: SEC(2011) 911 final)*.

This decision was amended on 11 April 2012* to state that from 1 January 2012, with regard to annual consolidated financial statements and half-yearly consolidated financial statements, the following standards shall be considered as equivalent to IFRS adopted pursuant to Regulation (EC) No 1606/2002:

(a) GAAP of the People's Republic of China;
(b) GAAP of Canada; and
(c) GAAP of the Republic of Korea.

Further, third country issuers shall be permitted to prepare their annual consolidated financial statements and half-yearly consolidated financial statements in accordance with the Generally Accepted Accounting Principles of the Republic of India for financial years starting before 1 January 2015.

EQUIVALENT DISCLOSURES ARE INCLUDED IN THE CONSOLIDATED FINANCIAL STATEMENTS OF THE GROUP

In deciding whether the consolidated financial statements of the parent provide disclosures which are equivalent to the requirements of EU-adopted IFRS or FRS 102, from which relief is provided in paragraphs 8 to 9 of FRS 101 and paragraphs 1.12 to 1.13 of FRS 102 respectively, it is necessary to consider whether the consolidated financial statements of the parent provide disclosures that meet the basic disclosure requirements of the relevant standard or interpretation issued (or adopted) by the relevant standard setter, without requiring strict conformity with each and every disclosure. This assessment should be based on the particular facts, including the similarities to and differences from the requirements of the relevant standard from which relief is provided. **AG8**

The concept of 'equivalence' described in paragraph AG8 is intended to be aligned to that described for section 401 of the Act. **AG9**

Disclosure exemptions for subsidiaries are permitted where the relevant disclosure requirements are met in the consolidated financial statements, even where the disclosures are made in aggregate or in an abbreviated form. If, however, no disclosure is made in the consolidated financial statements on the grounds of materiality, the relevant disclosures should be made at the subsidiary level if material in those financial statements. **AG10**

**Commission Implementing Decision of 11 April 2012 amending Decision 2008/961/EC on the use by third countries' issuers of securities of certain third country's national accounting standards and International Financial Reporting Standards to prepare their consolidated financial statements (Ref: 2012/194/EU).*

Approval by the FRC

Financial Reporting Standard 100 *Application of Financial Reporting Requirements* was approved for issue by the Board of the Financial Reporting Council on 1 November 2012, following its consideration of the Accounting Council's advice for this FRS.

The Accounting Council's Advice to the FRC to issue FRS 100

INTRODUCTION

1 This report provides an overview of the main issues which have been considered by the Accounting Council in advising the Financial Reporting Council (FRC) to issue FRS 100 *Application of Financial Reporting Requirements.* The FRC, in accordance with the Statutory Instrument *Statutory Auditors (Amendment of Companies Act 2006 and Delegation of Functions etc) Order 2012* (SI 2012/1741), is the prescribed body for issuing accounting standards in the UK. *The Foreword to Accounting Standards* sets out the application of accounting standards in the Republic of Ireland.

2 In accordance with *FRC Codes and Standards: procedures*, any proposal to issue, amend or withdraw a code or standard is put to the FRC with the full advice of the relevant Councils and/or the Codes & Standards Committee. Ordinarily, the FRC will only reject the advice put to it where:

- it is apparent that a significant group of stakeholders has not been adequately consulted;
- the necessary assessment of the impact of the proposal has not been completed, including an analysis of costs and benefits;
- insufficient consideration has been given to the timing or cost of implementation; or
- the cumulative impact of a number of proposals would make the adoption of an otherwise satisfactory proposal inappropriate.

3 The FRC has established the Accounting Council as the relevant Council to assist it in the setting of accounting standards.

ADVICE

4 The Accounting Council is advising the FRC to issue:

FRS 100 *Application of Financial Reporting Requirements*; and
FRS 101 *Reduced Disclosure Framework*.

5 FRS 102 *The Financial Reporting Standard Applicable in the UK and Republic of Ireland* completes the new suite of financial reporting standards. The Accounting Council will provide its advice to the FRC on FRS 102 in that standard.

BACKGROUND

6 Accounting standards were formerly developed by the Accounting Standards Board (ASB). The ASB commenced its project to update accounting standards in 2002; Appendix III provides a history of the previous consultations and a summary of how the overall proposals have developed.*

7 The ASB (and subsequently the Accounting Council) gave careful consideration to the project's objective and intended effects during its consultations on updating

**References in this section and Appendix III are made to the FRC, ASB or Accounting Council, as appropriate in terms of the time period and context of the reference.*

accounting standards. In developing the requirements in this FRS, FRS 101 and FRS 102, the overriding objective is:

> *To enable users of accounts to receive high-quality understandable financial reporting proportionate to the size and complexity of the entity and users' information needs.*

8 In achieving this objective, the ASB decided (and the Accounting Council subsequently agreed) that it should provide succinct financial reporting standards that:

- have consistency with global accounting standards through the application of an IFRS-based solution unless an alternative clearly better meets the overriding objective;
- reflect up-to-date thinking and developments in the way businesses operate and the transactions they undertake;
- balance consistent principles for accounting by all UK and Republic of Ireland entities with practical solutions, based on size, complexity, public interest and users' information needs;
- promote efficiency within groups; and
- are cost-effective to apply.

9 The requirements in this FRS were principally consulted on in two exposure drafts; FRED 43 *Application of Financial Reporting Requirements* issued in October 2010, and FRED 46 *Application of Financial Reporting Requirements* (revised) issued in January 2012.

A DIFFERENTIAL FINANCIAL REPORTING SYSTEM AND THE ELIMINATION OF 'PUBLIC ACCOUNTABILITY'

10 In the early stages of developing this FRS, the ASB consulted on whether to introduce a differential financial reporting system. A differential system requires an entity to apply specified accounting standards as prescribed based on the size, nature or other differentiating feature of the entity. FRED 43 set out proposals for a differential financial reporting system based on three tiers of entities using public accountability and size as differentiators. The proposals in FRED 43 would have extended the application of EU-adopted IFRS to those entities with public accountability*. Whilst there was some support for a differential financial reporting system, entities that would be required to apply EU-adopted IFRS did not support the proposal, principally on the basis of costs and benefits.

11 The ASB gave careful consideration to the concerns raised and concluded that public accountability (and therefore the differential financial reporting system) could be eliminated if it were to extend the proposals by including additional requirements in FRED 44 *Financial Reporting Standard for Medium-sized Entities* for entities with publicly traded debt or equity, and for financial institutions, so that the proposals in that FRED applied to a broader group of entities. FRED 44 proposed to replace the majority of extant financial reporting standards with a single standard based on the International Financial Reporting Standard for Small and Medium-sized Entities

**FRED 43 defined an entity as having public accountability if:*

(a) as at the reporting date, its debt or equity instruments are traded in a public market or it is in the process of issuing such instruments for trading in a public market (a domestic or foreign stock exchange or an over-the-counter market, including local and regional markets); or

(b) as one of its primary businesses, it holds assets in a fiduciary capacity for a broad group of outsiders and/or it is a deposit taking entity for a broad group of outsiders. This is typically the case for banks, credit unions, insurance companies, securities brokers/dealers, mutual funds or investment banks.

(IFRS for SMEs). As a consequence, FRED 44 was revised and FRED 48 issued, which addressed a broader group of entities including those previously considered to have public accountability, single entities listed on a regulated market, entities listed on a non-regulated market and additional disclosure requirements for financial instruments held by financial institutions.

Respondents to FRED 46 supported the removal of the public accountability criteria and the Accounting Council agreed to advise the FRC not to extend the application of EU-adopted IFRS beyond that already required by company law or other legislation or regulation. **12**

Once this FRS becomes effective, there will be five FRSs applicable in the UK and Republic of Ireland: **13**

- FRS 100 *Application of Financial Reporting Requirements;*
- FRS 101 *Reduced Disclosure Framework*;
- FRS 102 *The Financial Reporting Standard applicable in the UK and Republic of Ireland*;
- *Financial Reporting Standard for Smaller Entities* (effective January 2015) (the FRSSE); and
- FRS 27 *Life assurance*.*

FRS 101 *REDUCED DISCLOSURE FRAMEWORK*

FRS 101 was developed in response to concerns that arose from earlier consultations (see Appendix III). Respondents to those consultations (and particularly the 2009 Policy Proposal) noted that a move to the IFRS for SMEs for subsidiaries of entities that apply EU-adopted IFRS would require recognition and measurement differences to be monitored and maintained at group level, and yet the alternative of a move to EU-adopted IFRS would increase disclosure in comparison to current accounting standards. The ASB therefore developed a reduced disclosure framework to address these concerns. **14**

Further details regarding the development of FRS 101 are located in the Accounting Council's Advice to the FRC accompanying that FRS. **15**

FRS 102 *THE FINANCIAL REPORTING STANDARD APPLICABLE IN THE UK AND REPUBLIC OF IRELAND*

FRS 102 will replace the majority of current accounting standards applicable in the UK and Republic of Ireland with a single FRS based on the IFRS for SMEs. Details of the development of FRS 102 will be set out in the Accounting Council's Advice to the FRC accompanying that FRS. One member of the Accounting Council considers that the level of input from users does not constitute adequate consultation, despite extensive efforts at outreach, and holds an alternative view on aspects of the Accounting Council's expected advice on FRS 102. **16**

THE FINANCIAL REPORTING STANDARD FOR SMALLER ENTITIES (FRSSE)

The Accounting Council advises the FRC (consistent with FREDs 43 and 46) to retain the FRSSE for a period following the application of FRS 102, with a view to consulting again on the FRSSE's future in the short to medium term. **17**

**At the time of approving this advice consideration is being given to updating FRS 27.*

18 The eligibility criteria for applying the FRSSE are set out in paragraph 8 of the FRSSE. One of the criteria is that the entity must be 'small' as defined in company law. Turnover and balance sheet total should be measured in accordance with the FRSSE for the purposes of establishing whether the entity is 'small'; the measurement of turnover and balance sheet total in accordance with FRS 101 or FRS 102 need not be considered.

19 The Accounting Council also advises the FRC to undertake further consultation to address the implications for the FRSSE of:

(a) the European Commission proposals arising from its review of the EU Accounting Directives (an initial proposed Directive was issued in October 2011); and
(b) the Directive on annual accounts of micro-entities that was approved by the European Council in February 2012.

20 The amendments to the FRSSE set out in this FRS arise as a consequence of withdrawing current accounting standards.

STATEMENTS OF RECOMMENDED PRACTICE (SORPS)

21 In its 2009 Policy Proposal, the ASB's recommendation was to remove almost all of the SORPs. Respondents to the Policy Proposal questioned this and many noted that SORPs contribute to improving the quality of financial reporting in the UK. Instead FRED 43 proposed to streamline the number of SORPs in existence. Respondents to FRED 43 were supportive of this revised proposal. The decision, however, to eliminate the definition of public accountability and thereby broaden the scope of entities eligible to apply FRS 102 had a consequential impact on the SORPs (for example, pension funds would no longer be required to apply EU-adopted IFRS), so the ASB amended its proposals again in FRED 48.

22 The proposals in FRED 48 received support and the Accounting Council is now advising the FRC that they be taken forward, as follows:

SORP	Accounting Council Advice
Accounting for insurance business	A separate consultation will be undertaken on the accounting for insurance
Accounting for oil & gas	The SORP-making body has indicated that they do not believe that it would make sense to update the 2001 SORP
Authorised funds	Update to be based on FRS 102
Banking segments	Withdraw
Charities	Update to be based on FRS 102
Financial reports of pension funds	Update for consistency with FRS 102 to supplement Section 34 of FRS 102
Further and higher education	Update to be based on FRS 102
Investment companies	Update to be based on FRS 102
Leasing	Withdraw
Limited liability partnerships	Update to be based on FRS 102
Registered social housing providers	Update to be based on FRS 102

In response to a request for clarification as to the role of the SORPs, the Accounting Council is advising the FRC that a reference to the application of SORPs be included in this FRS and in Section 10 *Accounting policies, estimates and errors* of FRS 102, to note that they are a source of guidance on accounting policies. 23

CLARIFICATION OF EQUIVALENCE

FRS 101 and FRS 102 permit certain exemptions from disclosures, which are in some cases subject to equivalent disclosures being included in the consolidated financial statements of the group in which the entity is consolidated. Clarification on interpreting the meaning of the term equivalence is included in Application Guidance I of this FRS. 24

WITHDRAWN PUBLICATIONS

Paragraph 14 of this FRS sets out the withdrawal of current accounting standards. For the avoidance of doubt, the Accounting Council (and FRC) will also not proceed with developing the following superseded Financial Reporting Exposure Drafts (FREDs): 25

Leases: Implementation of a new approach
IASB Exposure draft of a proposed IFRS for small and medium-sized entities (Issued April 2007)

FRED 22 *Revision of FRS 3 Reporting financial performance*
FRED 28 *Inventories: Construction and service contracts*
FRED 29 *Property, plant and equipment: Borrowing costs*
FRED 32 *Disposal of non-current assets and presentation of discontinued operations*
FRED 36 *Business combinations*
FRED 37 *Intangible assets (IAS 38) and FRED 38 Impairment of assets (IAS 36)*
FRED 39 *Amendments to FRS 12 Provisions, contingent liabilities and contingent assets and FRS 17 Retirement benefits*
FRED 43 *Application of Financial Reporting Requirements*
FRED 44 *The Financial Reporting Standards for Medium-sized Entities*
FRED 45 *The Financial Reporting Standard for Public Benefit Entities*

EFFECTIVE DATE AND EARLY APPLICATION

In reassessing the effective date as proposed in FREDs 46 to 48, the Accounting Council supports the previous view of the ASB that application should be deferred to January 2015 for the following reasons: 26

(a) although the revisions to the ASB's original proposals should ease the transition, an 18 month period between the publication of the final standard and effective date should be retained as there are significant changes to the accounting requirements for financial instruments; and
(b) the effective date should take into consideration the process of updating the SORPs.

This decision was reassessed by the Accounting Council when it considered the responses to FREDs 46 to 48. It decided that it was not necessary to have the same early application provisions for FRS 101, FRS 102 and the FRSSE (effective January 2015) and that specific requirements relating to early application should be set out separately in each standard. 27

APPROVAL OF THIS ADVICE

28 This advice to the FRC was approved by the nine members of the Accounting Council on 25 October 2012. The Accounting Council is comprised of the following members:

Roger Marshall (Chair of the Accounting Council)
Nick Anderson
Dr Richard Barker
Edward Beale
Peter Elwin
Ken Lever
Robert Overend
Andy Simmonds
Pauline Wallace

Appendix I: Glossary

Act	The Companies Act 2006.
date of transition	The beginning of the earliest period for which an entity presents full comparative information under a given standard in its first financial statements that comply with that standard.
EU-adopted IFRS	**IFRS** that have been adopted in the European Union in accordance with EU Regulation 1606/2002.
financial institution	Any of the following: (a) a bank which is: (i) a firm with a Part IV permission* which includes accepting deposits and: (a) which is a credit institution; or (b) whose Part IV permission includes a requirement that it complies with the rules in the General Prudential sourcebook and the Prudential sourcebook for Banks, Building Societies and Investment Firms relating to banks, but which is not a building society, a friendly society or a credit union; (ii) an EEA bank which is a full credit institution; (b) a building society which is defined in section 119(1) of the Building Societies Act 1986 as a building society incorporated (or deemed to be incorporated) under that act; (c) a credit union, being a body corporate registered under the Industrial and Provident Societies Act 1965 as a credit union in accordance with the Credit Unions Act 1979, which is an authorised person; (d) custodian bank, broker-dealer or stockbroker; (e) an entity that undertakes the business of effecting or carrying out insurance contracts, including general and life assurance entities; (f) an incorporated friendly society incorporated under the Friendly Societies Act 1992 or a registered friendly society registered under section 7(1)(a) of the Friendly Societies Act 1974 or any enactment which it replaced, including any registered branches; (g) an investment trust, Irish Investment Company†, venture capital trust, mutual fund, exchange traded fund, unit trust, open-ended investment company (OEIC); (h) a retirement benefit plan; or

**As defined in section 40(4) of the Financial Services and Markets Act 2000 or references to equivalent provisions of any successor legislation.*

†An Irish Investment Company is a corporate vehicle as defined by section 47(3) of the Companies (Amendment) Act 1983 and paragraph 58 of the Schedule to the Companies (Amendment) Act 1986, and regulated by the Central Bank of Ireland.

	(i) any other entity whose principal activity is to generate wealth or manage risk through financial instruments. This is intended to cover entities that have business activities similar to those listed above but are not specifically included in the list above. A parent entity whose sole activity is to hold investments in other group entities is not a financial institution.
FRS 100	FRS 100 *Application of Financial Reporting Requirements*
FRS 101	FRS 101 *Reduced Disclosure Framework*
FRS 102	FRS 102 *The Financial Reporting Standard applicable in the UK and Republic of Ireland*
FRSSE	The extant version* of the *Financial Reporting Standard for Smaller Entities*
IAS Regulation	EU Regulation 1606/2002.
IFRS	Standards and interpretations issued (or adopted) by the International Accounting Standards Board (IASB). They comprise: (a) International Financial Reporting Standards; (b) International Accounting Standards; and (c) Interpretations developed by the IFRS Interpretations Committee (the Interpretations Committee) or the former Standing Interpretations Committee (SIC).
individual financial statements	The accounts that are required to be prepared by an entity in accordance with the **Act** or relevant legislation, for example: (a) 'individual accounts', as set out in section 394 of the Act; (b) 'statement of accounts', as set out in section 132 of the Charities Act 2011; or (c) 'individual accounts', as set out in section 72A of the Building Societies Act 1986. Separate financial statements are included in the meaning of this term.
public benefit entity	An entity whose primary objective is to provide goods or services for the general public, community or social benefit and where any equity is provided with a view to supporting the entity's primary objectives rather than with a view to providing a financial return to equity providers, shareholders or members.
qualifying entity (for the purposes	A member of a group where the parent of that group prepares publicly available consolidated financial statements which are intended to give a true and fair view (of the assets,

**At the date of issue of this FRS, the extant version of the FRSSE is the* Financial Reporting Standard for Smaller Entities (effective April 2008). *The* Financial Reporting Standard for Smaller Entities (effective January 2015) *will replace it as the extant standard from 1 January 2015.*

of FRS 100 and FRS 101)	liabilities, financial position and profit or loss) and that member is included in the consolidation†. A charity may not be a qualifying entity.
Regulations	The Large and Medium-sized Companies and Groups (Accounts and Reports) Regulations 2008 (SI 2008/410).
Statement of Recommended Practice (SORP)	An extant Statement of Recommended Practice developed in accordance with *SORPs: Policy and Code of Practice*. SORPs recommend accounting practices for specialised industries or sectors. They supplement accounting standards and other legal and regulatory requirements in the light of the special factors prevailing or transactions undertaken in a particular industry or sector.

†*As set out in section 474(1) of the Act.*

Appendix II: Note on Legal Requirements

INTRODUCTION

A2.1 This appendix provides an overview of how the requirements in FRS 100 address United Kingdom company law requirements. It is therefore written from the perspective of a company to which the Companies Act 2006 applies*. Appendix IV contains the Republic of Ireland legal references.

A2.2 Many entities that are not constituted as companies apply accounting standards promulgated by the FRC for the purposes of preparing financial statements that present a true and fair view. A brief consideration of the legal framework for some other entities can be found at A2.20 and A2.21. For those entities that are within the scope of a SORP, the relevant SORP may provide more details on the legal framework.

A2.3 References to the Act in this appendix are to the *Companies Act 2006*. References to the Regulations are to *The Large and Medium-sized Companies and Groups (Accounts and Reports) Regulations 2008* (SI 2008/410).

APPLICABLE ACCOUNTING FRAMEWORK

A2.4 Group accounts of certain parent entities (those with securities admitted for trading on a regulated market in an EU Member State) are required by Article 4 of EU Regulation 1606/2002 (IAS Regulation) to be prepared in accordance with EU-adopted IFRS.

A2.5 All other entities, except those that are eligible to apply the *Financial Reporting Standard for Smaller Entities* (effective January 2015) (FRSSE), must apply either FRS 102 *The Financial Reporting Standard applicable in the UK and Republic of Ireland*, EU-adopted IFRS or, for financial statements that are the individual financial statements of a qualifying entity, FRS 101 *Reduced Disclosure Framework*†.

A2.6 Section 395(1) of the Act states:

> "A company's individual accounts may be prepared—
>
> (a) in accordance with section 396 ("Companies Act individual accounts"), or
> (b) in accordance with international accounting standards ("IAS individual accounts")."

Section 403(2) of the Act states:

> "The group accounts of other companies may be prepared—
>
> (a) in accordance with section 404 ("Companies Act group accounts"), or
> (b) in accordance with international accounting standards ("IAS group accounts")."

**Some charities are also companies, and are therefore required to apply the requirements of both the Companies Act 2006 and the Charities Act 2011.*

†*Under company law in the Republic of Ireland, certain companies are permitted to prepare Companies Act accounts using a financial reporting framework based on accounting standards other than those issued by the FRC. Please refer to Appendix IV for further details.*

Accounts prepared in accordance with EU-adopted IFRS are therefore within the scope of the IAS Regulation. All other accounts are classified as either 'Companies Act individual accounts', including those of qualifying entities applying FRS 101, or 'Companies Act group accounts' and are therefore required to comply with the applicable provisions of Parts 15 and 16 of the Act and with the Regulations. A2.7

Financial reporting by small entities

Entities that are eligible, in accordance with the Act (or by analogy), to apply the small companies regime may apply the FRSSE (which includes all relevant extracts of company law) or may elect to apply either FRS 102, EU-adopted IFRS or, for financial statements that are the individual financial statements of a qualifying entity, FRS 101. The conditions applicable to the small companies regime are contained in sections 381 to 384 of the Act. The qualifying conditions are met by a company in a year in which it does not exceed two or more of the following limits: A2.8

Turnover	£6,500,000
Balance sheet total	£3,260,000
Average number of employees	50

For any company, other than a newly incorporated company, to qualify as small, the qualifying conditions must be met for two consecutive years*. A company will cease to qualify as small if it fails to meet the qualifying conditions for two consecutive years. A2.9

Certain companies are excluded by section 384 of the Act from the small companies regime and may not apply the FRSSE†. These companies are those that meet any of the following conditions or are part of an ineligible group, which is, or was at any time during the financial year, a group with a member meeting one of the conditions: A2.10

(a) a public company;
(b) a company that is an authorised insurance company, a banking company, an e-money issuer, a MiFID investment firm or a UCITS management company or a company that carries on insurance market activity;
(c) a body corporate (other than a company) whose shares are admitted to trading on a regulated market in an EEA State; or
(d) a person (other than a small company) who has permission under Part 4 of the Financial Services and Markets Act 2000 to carry on a regulated activity.

A parent company shall not be treated as qualifying as a small company in relation to a financial year unless the group headed by it qualifies as a small group. A2.11

The conditions applicable to a small group are contained in section 383 of the Act. The qualifying criteria are met by a group in a year in which it does not exceed two or more of the following limits‡: A2.12

**An entity will continue to qualify as small in the first financial year in which it does not meet the size criteria, if it met the qualifying conditions in the preceding year and qualified as small in relation to that year.*

†In addition, the FRSSE is not available to companies preparing individual or group accounts in accordance with the fair value rules. The FRSSE does, however, permit revaluation of fixed assets (including investments) using the alternative accounting rules.

‡'Net' means after any set-offs and other adjustments required by Schedule 6 to the Small Companies and Groups (Accounts and Directors' Report) Regulations 2008 (SI 2008/409) in the case of group accounts, and 'gross' means without those set-offs and other adjustments. A company may satisfy any relevant requirement on the basis of either the net or the gross figure.

Aggregate turnover	£6,500,000 net (or £7,800,000 gross)
Aggregate balance sheet total	£3,260,000 net (or £3,900,000 gross)
Aggregate number of employees	50

Financial reporting by charitable companies

A2.13 Section 395(2) of the Act states that 'the individual accounts of a company that is a charity must be Companies Act individual accounts', and section 403(3) of the Act mirrors this for a parent company that is a charity.

Moving between IAS accounts and Companies Act accounts

A2.14 Sections 395 and 403 of the Act restrict an entity's ability to move from preparing IAS individual accounts to preparing Companies Act individual accounts and from preparing IAS group accounts to preparing Companies Act group accounts respectively. A company or group is permitted to switch from IAS accounts to Companies Act accounts preparation:

(a) if there is a 'relevant change in circumstance' (as defined in the Act); or
(b) for financial years ending on or after 1 October 2012, for a reason other than a relevant change of circumstance, once in a five year period.*

A2.15 For example, provided the condition in section 395(4A) is met, a subsidiary company which previously prepared IAS individual accounts is permitted to move to preparing Companies Act individual accounts in applying FRS 101 or FRS 102, providing it is also complying with other requirements of the Act, such as those relating to consistency of financial reporting within groups

Consistency of financial reporting within groups

A2.16 Section 407 of the Act requires that the directors of the parent company secure that individual accounts of a parent company and each of its subsidiaries† are prepared using the same financial reporting framework, except to the extent that in the directors' opinion there are good reasons for not doing so.

In addition, consistency is not required in the following situations:

(a) when the parent company does not prepare consolidated accounts; or
(b) when some subsidiaries are charities (consistency is not needed between the framework used for these and for other subsidiaries).

Where the directors of a parent company prepare IAS group accounts and IAS individual accounts, there only has to be consistency across the individual financial statements of the subsidiaries.

A2.17 All companies, other than those which elect or are required to prepare IAS individual accounts in accordance with law, prepare Companies Act individual accounts.

* *The Companies and Limited Liability Partnership (Accounts and Audit Exemptions and Change of Accounting Framework) Regulations 2012 (SI 2012/2301).*

† *This only applies to accounts of subsidiaries that are required to be prepared under Part 15 of the Act.*

APPLICABILITY OF UK COMPANY LAW TO ENTITIES PREPARING IAS ACCOUNTS

Entities that prepare IAS accounts, either voluntarily or because they are required to do so by law, only need apply certain sections of the Act as it relates to financial reporting. They are not required to comply with Schedules 1 and 6 to the Regulations (for companies and groups), nor with Schedules 2 or 3 (for banks and insurance companies). Schedules 4, 5, 7 and 8 to the Regulations are, however, still applicable. **A2.18**

The sections of parts 15 and 16 of the Act that contain financial reporting requirements applying to IAS accounts (as well as to Companies Act accounts) are as follows: **A2.19**

Section 410A	*Off-balance sheet arrangements*;
Section 411	*Employee numbers and costs*;
Section 412	*Directors' benefits: Remuneration*;
Section 413	*Directors' benefits: Advances, credit and guarantees*;
Sections 415 to 419	*Directors' Report*;
Sections 420 to 421	*Directors' Remuneration Report*; and
Section 494	*Services provided by auditor and associates and related remuneration*

ENTITIES NOT SUBJECT TO COMPANY LAW

Many entities that may apply FRS 102 are not companies, but are nevertheless required by their governing legislation or other regulation or requirement, to prepare financial statements that present a true and fair view of the financial performance and financial position of the reporting entity. However, the FRC sets accounting standards within the framework of the Act and therefore it is the company law requirements that the FRC primarily considered when developing FRS 102. Entities preparing financial statements within other legal frameworks will need to satisfy themselves that FRS 102 does not conflict with any relevant legal obligations. **A2.20**

However, the FRC notes the following: **A2.21**

Legislation	Overview of requirements
Building Societies Act 1986	The annual accounts of a building society shall give a true and fair of the income and expenditure for the year and the balance sheet shall give a true and fair view of the state of affairs of the society at the end of the financial year. Regulations make further requirements about the form and content of building society accounts, which do not appear inconsistent with the requirement of FRS 102.
Charity law in England and Wales: Charities Act 2011 and regulations made thereunder	All charities are required to prepare accounts. The regulations require financial statements (other than cash-based receipts and payments accounts prepared by smaller charities) to present a true and fair view of the incoming resources, application of resources and the balance sheet, and to be prepared in accordance with the SORP. However company charities prepare their accounts in accordance with UK company law to give a 'true and fair view'.

Legislation	Overview of requirements
	The Charities SORP 2005 requires the application of accounting standards and is compatible with the legal requirements, clarifying how they apply to accounting by charities. The SORP will be updated to reflect the requirements of FRS 102. UK Company law prohibits charities from preparing IAS accounts.
Charity law in Scotland: Charities and Trustee Investments Act (Scotland) 2005 and regulations made thereunder	All charities are required to prepare accounts. The regulations require financial statements (other than cash-based receipts and payments accounts prepared by smaller charities) to present a true and fair view of the incoming resources, application of resources and the balance sheet, and to be prepared in accordance with the SORP. These regulations apply equally to company charities.
Charity law in Northern Ireland: Charities Act (Northern Ireland) 2008	The Charities Act 2008 has yet to come fully into effect. The Act provides for all charities to prepare accounts. The Act provides for regulations concerning the financial statements. The financial statements other than cash-based receipts and payments accounts prepared by smaller charities are to present a true and fair view of the incoming resources, application of resources and the balance sheet. However company charities prepare their accounts in accordance with UK company law to give a 'true and fair view'.
Friendly and Industrial and Provident Societies Act 1968	Every Society shall prepare a revenue account and a balance sheet giving a true and fair view of the income and expenditure and state of affairs of the Society. FRS 102 does not appear to give rise to any legal conflicts for Societies. However, Societies often carry out activities that are regulated and may be required to comply with additional regulations on top of the legal requirements and accounting standards. Some Societies fall within the scope of SORPs, which will be updated to reflect the requirements of FRS 102.
Friendly Societies Act 1992	Every society shall prepare a balance sheet and an income and expenditure account for each financial year giving a true and fair view of the affairs of the society and its income and expenditure for the year. The Regulations* make further requirements about the form and content of friendly society accounts, which do not appear inconsistent with the requirements of FRS 102.

**The Friendly Societies (Accounts and Related Provisions) Regulations 1994 (as amended).*

Legislation	Overview of requirements
The Occupational Pension Schemes (Requirement to obtain Audited Accounts and a Statement from the Auditor) Regulations 1996	The accounts of pension funds within the scope of the regulations should show a true and fair view of the transactions during the year, assets held at the end of the year and liabilities of the scheme, other than those to pay pensions and benefits. FRS 102 includes retirement benefit plans as a specialised activity.

Appendix III: Previous Consultations

HISTORY OF PREVIOUS CONSULTATIONS

A3.1 The requirements in FRSs 100 to 102 are the outcome of a lengthy and extensive consultation. The FRC (and formerly the ASB) together with the Department for Business, Innovation and Skills have consulted on the future of accounting standards in the UK and Republic of Ireland (RoI) over a ten-year period.

Table 1 – Consultations conducted

Year	Consultation
2002	DTI* consults on adoption of IAS Regulation
2004	Discussion Paper – Strategy for Convergence with IFRS
2005	Exposure Draft – Policy Statement: The Role of the ASB
2006	Public Meeting and Proposals for Comment
2006	Press Notice seeking views
2007	Consultation Paper – Proposed IFRS for SMEs
2009	Consultation Paper – Policy Proposal: The future of UK GAAP
2010	Request for Responses – Development of the Impact Assessment
2010	Financial Reporting Exposure Drafts 43 and 44
2011	Financial Reporting Exposure Draft 45
2012	Financial Reporting Exposure Drafts 46, 47 and 48

2004

A3.2 In 2004 the Discussion Paper contained two key elements underpinning the proposals: firstly that UK and Republic of Ireland (RoI) accounting standards should be based on IFRS and secondly that a phased approach to the introduction of the standards should be adopted.

A3.3 The ASB embarked on the phased approach and issued a number of standards based on IFRS. The majority of respondents agreed with a framework based on IFRS, and although supportive overall, the response to the phased approach was mixed.

2005

A3.4 In its 2005 Exposure Draft (2005 ED) of a Policy Statement *Accounting standard-setting in a changing environment: The role of the Accounting Standards Board*, amongst other aspects of its role, the ASB identified its intention to converge with IFRS by implementing new IFRS in the UK as soon as possible. It also proposed to

**The Department of Trade and Industry (DTI) was a United Kingdom government department which was replaced with the announcement of the creation of the Department for Business, Enterprise and Regulatory Reform and the Department for Innovation, Universities and Skills on 28 June 2007, which were themselves merged into the Department for Business, Innovation and Skills (BIS) on 6 June 2009.*

continue the phased approach to adopting UK accounting standards based on older IFRSs, but recognised there was little case for being more prescriptive than IFRS.

Although the ASB had, in the 2005 ED, wanted to move the debate on to how it would seek to influence the IASB's agenda, respondents' main concern remained about convergence. In 2005, the ASB issued an exposure draft proposing the IASB's standard on Business Combinations be adopted in the UK and RoI. This exposure draft highlighted the complexity of a mixed set of UK accounting standards, with some based on IFRSs and others developed independently by the ASB. The majority of respondents continued to agree with the aim of basing UK accounting standards on IFRS, but a broader set of views on how to achieve this was emerging. **A3.5**

As time progressed the ASB formed the view that convergence by adopting certain IFRSs was not meeting the needs of its constituents, which no longer included quoted groups. The ASB was concerned about the complexity of certain IFRSs, and it noted that introducing them piecemeal created complications and anomalies within the body of current FRSs. This arose because IFRS-based standards were not an exact replacement for current FRSs and many consequential amendments were required to 'fit' each replacement IFRS-based standard into the existing body of UK FRS. The ASB agreed to continue with its convergence programme, but decided to re-examine how to achieve this. **A3.6**

2006

The ASB published revised proposals to be discussed at the 2006 public meeting. By this time the IASB had started its IFRS for SMEs project, and the ASB decided this might have a role as one of the tiers in the UK financial reporting framework. The ASB proposed a 'big bang' with new IFRS-based UK accounting standards mandatory from a single date, 1 January 2009. The ASB's proposal was for a three-tier system, with Tier 1 being EU-adopted IFRS, and the other two tiers being developed as the IASB progressed with its project on the IFRS for SMEs. **A3.7**

Those attending the public meeting supported the aim of basing UK and RoI accounting standards on IFRS and adapting them to ensure they were appropriate for the entities applying them. **A3.8**

Taking this feedback into account, later in 2006 the ASB issued a Press Notice (PN 289) seeking views on its current thinking: **A3.9**

(a) All quoted and publicly accountable companies should apply EU-adopted IFRS.
(b) The FRSSE should be retained and extended to include medium-sized entities.
(c) UK subsidiaries of groups applying full IFRS should apply EU-adopted IFRS, but with reduced disclosure requirements.
(d) No firm decision on the remainder (Tier 2), but options included extending the FRSSE, extending full IFRS, maintaining separate UK accounting standards or some combination of these.

The responses were mixed, but there was agreement that whatever the solution, it should be based on IFRS and there should be different reporting tiers to ensure proportionality. **A3.10**

2007

A3.11 The IASB published an exposure draft of its IFRS for SMEs in early 2007; shortly afterwards the ASB published its own consultation paper. This sought views on how the IFRS for SMEs might fit into the future UK financial reporting framework, for example whether it might be appropriate for Tier 2, with the FRSSE continuing for those eligible for the small companies' regime.

A3.12 Feedback on the IFRS for SMEs was largely positive: it would be suitable for Tier 2, it was international, it was compatible with IFRS, and it represented a significant simplification. Overall, it was seen as a workable alternative to IFRS. In addition, respondents wanted to retain the FRSSE (because it reduces the regulatory burden on smaller entities) and to give subsidiaries the option of applying the IFRS for SMEs as well as a reduced disclosure regime if applying full IFRS.

2009

A3.13 The IFRS for SMEs was published in 2009, allowing the ASB to further develop its proposals in the Consultation Paper *Policy Proposal: The future of UK GAAP*. The proposals were largely consistent with the cumulative results of the preceding consultations and included:

(a) a move to an IFRS-based framework;
(b) a three-tier approach;
(c) publicly accountable entities would be Tier 1 and would apply EU-adopted IFRS;
(d) small companies would be Tier 3 and continue to apply the FRSSE; and
(e) other entities would be Tier 2 and should apply a UK and RoI accounting standard based on the IFRS for SMEs.

A3.14 The only significant proposal that was inconsistent with respondents' previous comments was that subsidiaries should simply apply the requirement of the tier they individually met – respondents had wanted subsidiaries to be able to take advantage of disclosure exemptions, and at that time the ASB had yet to be convinced that significant cost savings were available from a reduced disclosure framework. Taking into account the feedback received, this proposal was subsequently reversed and the reduced disclosure framework was incorporated into FREDs 43 and then 46, and it is now set out in FRS 101.

A3.15 In addition to the many useful and detailed points made, some common themes included general agreement that change was needed to UK accounting standards and that there was support for many of the changes proposed in the consultation paper.

2010 onwards

A3.16 The request for responses to aid development of the Impact Assessment focused on obtaining feedback on the expected costs, benefits and impact of the proposals subsequently set out in FREDs 43 and 44, rather than on the accounting principles. As the focus was on costs and benefits no specific question was asked about the principle of the proposed introduction of an IFRS-based framework, but nevertheless respondents commented on this: of the 32 responses received only 12.5% did not agree with the introduction of an IFRS-based framework.

A3.17 FRED 43 and 44 issued in October 2010 set out the draft suggested text for two new accounting standards that would replace the majority of extant Financial Reporting

Standards (current FRS) in the UK and RoI. The ASB issued a supplementary FRED addressing specific needs of public benefit entities (FRED 45) in March 2011. The ASB then updated FREDs 43, 44 and 45, replacing them with the revised FREDs 46, 47 and 48 in January 2012, by eliminating the concept of public accountability and by introducing a number of accounting treatment options that are available in EU-adopted IFRS. The Accounting Council's advice to the FRC to issue FRSs 100 to 102 includes more discussion of the feedback received on FREDs 43 to 48 and how the proposals have been refined and developed into the standards.

HOW HAVE THE PROPOSALS BEEN DEVELOPED?

As set out above, the FRC, the Accounting Council (and previously the ASB) have consulted regularly on the future of financial reporting in the UK and RoI. Over the consultations the ASB's (and the Accounting Council's) thinking has evolved based on careful consideration of the feedback at each stage. Whilst responses were sometimes mixed, there has been agreement that: **A3.18**

(a) current FRS, which are a mixture of Statements of Standard Accounting Practice (SSAPs) issued by the Consultative Committee of Accounting Bodies, FRSs developed and issued by the ASB and IFRS-based standards issued by the ASB to converge with international standards, are an uncomfortable mismatch that lack strong underlying principles or cohesion; and

(b) whatever the solution, it should be based on IFRS and there should be different reporting tiers to ensure proportionality.

During the consultation process to date, the Accounting Council and formerly the ASB have been guided by the following principles: **A3.19**

(a) The framework must be fit for purpose, so that each entity required to produce true and fair financial statements under UK and RoI law will deliver financial statements that are suited to the needs of its primary users. The Accounting Council has kept in close contact with constituent users on this point, including investors, creditor institutions and the tax authorities.

(b) The framework must be proportionate, so that preparing entities are not unduly burdened by costs that outweigh the benefit to them and to the primary users of information in their financial statements. The FRC believes that the proposals will produce a lower cost regime, while enhancing user benefits. It has carried out a consultation stage impact assessment with input from interested parties, and will continue to assess cost-benefit issues.

(c) The framework must be in line with UK company law. This determines which entities must produce true and fair financial statements. Exemptions within the law have generally been retained. The detailed requirements of the Companies Act 2006 are driven to a great extent by the European Accounting Directives, which are being revised*.

(d) The framework must be future-proofed, where possible. The FRC will continue to monitor the situation and has sovereignty over UK accounting standards (subject to the law). Changes to the Accounting Directives may lead to further developments, for example the European Council and European Parliament decision to permit Member States an option to treat micro-entities as a separate category of Company and exempt them from certain accounting requirements.

**The EU's consultation process on review of the Accounting Directives is summarised at http://ec.europa.eu/internal_market/accounting/sme_accounting/review_directives_en.htm*

SUMMARY OF OUTREACH

A3.20 During the development and throughout the consultation period of FREDs 43 to 48, the ASB undertook an extensive programme of outreach aimed at raising awareness of the proposals and to address the view (held by some) that previous consultations had not gathered sufficient evidence to support and test the assumptions made.

A3.21 As part of the outreach programme to obtain both formal and informal feedback, a series of meetings and events took place with users, including with lenders to small and medium-sized entities. Lenders noted that financial statements are an important part of their decision-making process when considering whether to provide finance and, whilst a decision to provide finance is not based on financial statements alone, they provide useful information and verification to the lender.

A3.22 Although the ASB and the Accounting Council employed their best efforts to obtain feedback from users (a constituent group historically difficult to engage with formally) it is disappointing that limited formal responses were received and the Accounting Council has not been more successful in obtaining input from users.

A3.23 In addition, a review was made of academic research that addressed the users of the financial statements of small and medium-sized entities. The conclusion drawn from the research was that many entities requested financial statements from Companies House when considering whether to trade with another entity. The European Federation of Accountants and Auditors (EFAA) issued, in May 2011, a statement that identified the users of financial statements, noting who the users of SMEs' financial statements are and that information on the public record assists all users of financial statements of SMEs by providing, in an efficient manner, basic information that protects their rights.

A3.24 The ASB considered that the outreach programme had gleaned information from people who would not normally submit formal responses to a consultation and provided very useful information that could be used in developing the next stage of the project. The ASB noted that whilst this information was not part of the public record, as are formal consultation responses, it could use the information to assist in developing the revised FREDs 46 to 48, supplementing information contained in responses, and would seek further comment in the next stage of its deliberations.

A3.25 The Accounting Council continued the work of the ASB in finalising FRSs 100 to 102. The responses to FREDs 46 to 48 were analysed and discussed, and engagements were conducted to take into account the views and suggestions of all relevant associations and contacts. Respondents and outreach contacts were satisfied with FREDs 46 to 48, and many of the response letters were forthcoming in their overall praise for the proposals. A significant number of constituents anticipated cost savings arising from the application of FRS 101. Many respondents considered that FRS 102 would improve UK accounting standards, in particular by introducing requirements for accounting for financial instruments. Further they considered that the improvements will be achieved in a way that will be proportionate to the needs of users, and that once the transition phase has been overcome, it will have the effect of reducing the reporting burden on those UK companies that adopt it.

Appendix IV: Republic of Ireland (RoI) Legal References

INTRODUCTION

The table below outlines the provisions in the Companies Acts 1963 to 2012 and related Regulations which implement EC Accounting Directives (Irish company law), corresponding to the provisions of the UK *Companies Act 2006* (the 2006 Act) and the UK *Large and Medium-sized Companies and Groups (Accounts and Reports) Regulations 2008* (the 2008 Regulations) (SI 2008/410) referred to in this FRS. A4.1

The principal Irish companies' legislation referred to in the table below is: A4.2

- The Companies Act 1963 (1963 Act);
- The Companies (Amendment) Act 1986 (1986 Act);
- The Companies Act 1990 (1990 Act);
- The Companies (Amendment) (No. 2) Act 1999 (1999 Act);
- The European Communities (Companies: Group Accounts) Regulations 1992 – S.I. No. 201 of 1992 (Group Accounts Regulations 1992 or GAR 1992);
- The European Communities (Credit Institutions: Accounts) Regulations 1992 – S.I. No. 294 of 1992 (Credit Institutions Regulations 1992 or CIR 1992);
- The European Communities (Insurance Undertakings: Accounts) Regulations 1996 – S.I. No. 23 of 1996 (Insurance Undertakings Regulations 1996 or IUR 1996);
- The European Communities (Directive 2006/46/EC) Regulations, 2009 – S.I. No. 450 of 2009.

Where general references are made in this FRS to the '2006 Act', 'Companies Act 2006 ('and the Regulations')', 'the Companies Act', 'the Act', 'the Large and Medium-sized Companies and Groups (Accounts and Reports) Regulations 2008', 'the 2008 Regulations' and 'the Regulations', readers should refer, in an Irish context, to the relevant sections and paragraphs of the Irish companies' legislation listed above. Such general references are not included in the table below. References in the text to 'IAS accounts' are equivalent to 'IFRS accounts' in Irish company law. A4.3

The following Irish legislation is also referenced in the table below: A4.4

- The Building Societies Act 1989;
- The Credit Union Act 1997;
- The Central Bank Act 1971;
- The Charities Act 2009;
- The Industrial and Provident Societies (Amendment) Act 1978;
- The Electoral Act 1997;
- The Friendly Societies Acts 1896 to 1977;
- The Friendly Societies (Amendment) Act 1977;
- The Friendly Societies Regulations 1988 – S.I. No. 74 of 1988;
- The Pensions Act 1990; and
- The Occupational Pension Schemes (Disclosure of Information) Regulations 2006 – S.I. No. 301 of 2006.

COMPANIES ACT ACCOUNTS UNDER IRISH COMPANY LAW

Certain companies are permitted under Irish company law to prepare their Companies Act accounts under a financial reporting framework based on accounting standards other than those issued by the Financial Reporting Council (FRC) and A4.5

promulgated by the Institute of Chartered Accountants in Ireland in respect of their application in the Republic of Ireland. Specifically:

- Pursuant to the Companies (Miscellaneous Provisions) Act 2009, as amended by the Companies (Amendment) Act 2012, relevant parent undertakings are permitted to prepare 'Companies Act individual accounts' and/or 'Companies Act group accounts' in accordance with US GAAP, as modified to ensure consistency with Irish company law.
- Investment companies subject to Part XIII of the Companies Act 1990 or the European Communities (Undertakings for Collective Investment in Transferable Securities) Regulations 2011 may adopt an alternative body of accounting standards, being standards which apply in the United States of America, Canada or Japan in preparing 'Companies Act individual accounts'.

Such companies, therefore, may adopt standards other than those issued by the FRC in preparing Companies Act accounts under Irish company law.

SMALL COMPANIES UNDER IRISH COMPANY LAW

A4.6 There is no equivalent to the UK *small companies regime* (see Sections 381 to 384 of the 2006 Act) in Irish company law. Section 8 of the Companies (Amendment) Act 1986 (as amended by the European Union (Accounts) Regulations 2012 (S.I. No. 304 of 2012) defines small companies for the purposes of Irish company law. However, whilst Sections 10 and 12 provide certain exemptions for such companies in relation to their financial statements filed with the Registrar of Companies, there are no exemptions for individual or group accounts prepared for members. Under Section 8 (as amended) the qualifying conditions for a company to be treated as a small company in respect of any financial year are as follows:

- The amount of turnover for that year does not exceed €8,800,000;
- The balance sheet total for that year does not exceed €4,400,000; and
- Average number of employees does not exceed 50.

A4.7 Except for companies in their first financial year, Section 8(1)(a) provides that companies qualify to be treated as small if, in respect of that year and the financial year immediately preceding that year, the company satisfies at least two of the above criteria. Section 9 provides that where a company has qualified as small, it continues to be so qualified until it does not meet two of the above three criteria for two consecutive years. Similarly, where a company no longer qualifies as small, two consecutive years of meeting two of the three criteria are required to qualify again as small.

A4.8 The following do not qualify as small under Irish company law:

- Companies subject to the European Communities (Credit Institutions: Accounts) Regulations 1992;
- Companies subject to the European Communities (Insurance Undertakings: Accounts) Regulations 1996; and
- Private companies whose securities are admitted to trading on a regulated market.

SIZE EXEMPTIONS FROM THE PREPARATION OF GROUP ACCOUNTS UNDER IRISH COMPANY LAW

A4.9 An Irish parent company within the scope of the European Communities (Companies: Group Accounts) Regulations 1992 is exempt from the requirement to prepare group accounts if it, together with its subsidiaries, meets the size and other criteria set out in Regulation 7 of those regulations. The size criteria in summary require that the parent and subsidiaries together meet two of the following three conditions:

- The amount of turnover for that year does not exceed €15,236,858;
- The balance sheet total for that year does not exceed €7,618,428; and
- Average number of employees does not exceed 250.

Except for the year in which a company becomes a parent undertaking, the exemption can only be availed of if two of the three conditions are met in respect of the financial year and the immediately preceding financial year. **A4.10**

Exemptions from preparing group accounts on the basis of size, in accordance with Regulation 7 of the European Communities (Companies: Group Accounts) Regulations 1992, are only available to parent companies that are private companies and are not available to parent companies subject to the European Communities (Credit Institutions: Accounts) Regulations 1992 or the European Communities (Insurance Undertakings: Accounts) Regulations 1996. **A4.11**

OTHER NOTES

The table below is intended as a reference guide to the corresponding or similar provisions in Irish company law and does not purport to be complete. Readers should note that not all Irish provisions are equivalent to the corresponding UK provisions and are advised to refer to the Irish legislation for an understanding of relevant requirements. Readers should also be aware that various sections and paragraphs referenced below have been amended by subsequent legislation and readers should ensure that they refer to such amended text where applicable. **A4.12**

Summary

Paragraph	UK References	RoI References					
	2006 Act and the 2008 Regulations (unless otherwise stated)	1963 Act	1986 Act	1990 Act	GAR 1992	CIR 1992	IUR 1996
ix	'smaller entities as defined by company law'	There are no equivalent provisions in Irish company law to the UK *small companies regime* or to the Small Companies and Groups (Accounts and Directors' Report) Regulations 2008. Small companies are defined in Section 8 of the 1986 Act. Please refer to the note above in the introduction to this table.					

FRS 100 Application Of Financial Reporting Requirements

	UK References	RoI References					
Paragraph	**2006 Act and the 2008 Regulations (unless otherwise stated)**	**1963 Act**	**1986 Act**	**1990 Act**	**GAR 1992**	**CIR 1992**	**IUR 1996**
4(a) (Footnote 2)	'smaller entities as defined by company law'	There are no equivalent provisions in Irish company law to the UK *small companies regime* or to the Small Companies and Groups (Accounts and Directors' Report) Regulations 2008. Small companies are defined in Section 8 of the 1986 Act. Please refer to the note above in the introduction to this table.					
4(b) (Footnote 3)	Sections 395(2) and 403(3)	There are no directly equivalent provisions in Irish company law to Sections 395(2) and 403(3), although Sections 148(3) and 150(4) respectively of the 1963 Act do require certain categories of entities to prepare 'Companies Act individual accounts' or 'Companies Act group accounts', including those *'not trading for the acquisition of gain by members'*.					
4(b) (Footnote 4) and 12	Section 395(1)(a)	Section 148(2)(a)				Regulation 5(1)	Regulation 5(1)
4(b) (Footnote 4) and 12	Section 395(1)(b)	Section 148(2)(b)				Regulation 5(1)	Regulation 5(1)

Application Guidance: The interpretation of equivalence

	UK References	RoI References					
Paragraph	**2006 Act and the 2008 Regulations (unless otherwise stated)**	**1963 Act**	**1986 Act**	**1990 Act**	**GAR 1992**	**CIR 1992**	**IUR 1996**
AG1 / AG4 / AG5 / AG6 / AG9	Section 401				Regulation 9A	Regulation 8A	Regulation 12A
AG1	Section 401(2)				Regulation 9A(3)	Regulation 8A(3)	Regulation 12A(3)

Appendix I: Glossary

	UK References	RoI References					
Paragraph	**2006 Act and the 2008 Regulations (unless otherwise stated)**	**1963 Act**	**1986 Act**	**1990 Act**	**GAR 1992**	**CIR 1992**	**IUR 1996**
'Financial institution' and footnote 15	Part IV permission; Section 40(4) of the Financial Services and Markets Act 2000	There is no equivalent legislation in Ireland to the Financial Services and Markets Act 2000. Banks in Ireland are licensed under Section 9 of the Central Bank Act 1971.					
'Financial institution'	Section 119(1) of the Building Societies Act 1986	Section 2(1) of the Building Societies Act 1989					
'Financial institution'	Industrial and Provident Societies Act 1965 and Credit Unions Act 1979	Credit Unions Act 1997					
'Financial institution'	Friendly Societies Act 1992; section 7(1)(a) of the Friendly Societies Act 1974	Friendly Societies Acts 1896 to 1977					
'Individual financial statements'	Section 394	Section 148					

	UK References	RoI References					
Paragraph	**2006 Act and the 2008 Regulations (unless otherwise stated)**	**1963 Act**	**1986 Act**	**1990 Act**	**GAR 1992**	**CIR 1992**	**IUR 1996**
'Individual financial statements'	Section 132 of the Charities Act 2011	Section 48 of the Charities Act 2009 provides that all charities are to prepare an annual statement of accounts, the form and content of which can be prescribed by regulations of the Minister. Section 48 is, at the date of publication of this FRS, not commenced and no regulations regarding the form and content of charities' annual statements of accounts have been published. Charity companies are required to prepare financial statements which give a true and fair view in accordance with the Companies Acts. Sections 148(3) and 150(4) of the 1963 Act require that companies "*not trading for the acquisition of gain by the members*" must prepare Companies Act accounts (i.e. not IFRS accounts), and this definition may apply to many Irish charity companies.					
'Individual financial statements'	Section 72A of the Building Societies Act 1986	Section 77 of the Building Societies Act 1989 requires the preparation of (a) an income and expenditure account giving a true and fair view of its income and expenditure for that year, (b) a balance sheet giving a true and fair view of the state of its affairs as at the end of that year, and (c) a statement of the source and application of funds giving a true and fair view of the manner in which its business has been financed and in which its financial resources have been used during that year.					
'Qualifying entity' (Footnote 18)	S474(1) of the Act				Regulation 3(1)	Paragraph 1 of part IV of the Schedule	

Appendix II: Note on legal requirements

	UK References	RoI References					
Paragraph	**2006 Act and the 2008 Regulations (unless otherwise stated)**	**1963 Act**	**1986 Act**	**1990 Act**	**GAR 1992**	**CIR 1992**	**IUR 1996**
A2.1 (Footnote 19)	Charities Act 2011	Charities Act 2009, Section 48 provides that all charities are to prepare an annual statement of accounts, the form and content of which can be prescribed by regulations of the Minister. Section 48 is, at the date of publication of this FRS, not commenced and no regulations regarding the form and content of charities' annual statements of accounts have been produced. Charity companies are required to prepare financial statements which give a true and fair view in accordance with the Companies Acts. Sections 148(3) and 150(4) of the 1963 Act requires that companies '*not trading for the acquisition of gain by the members*' must prepare Companies Act accounts (i.e. not IFRS accounts), and this definition may apply to many Irish charity companies.					
A2.6	Section 395(1)	Section 148(2)				Regulation 5	Regulation 5
A2.6	Section 396	Section 149	Section 3			Regulation 5	Regulation 5
A2.6	Section 403(2)	Section 150(3)					
A2.6	Section 404	Section 150A and 151			Regulation 14	Regulation 7	Regulation 10

	UK References	RoI References					
Paragraph	**2006 Act and the 2008 Regulations (unless otherwise stated)**	**1963 Act**	**1986 Act**	**1990 Act**	**GAR 1992**	**CIR 1992**	**IUR 1996**
A2.7	'Parts 15 and 16 of the Act and with the Regulations'	Sections 148, 149, 150, 150A, 150C, 151, 152, 153, 156, 161D and 191	Sections 3 to 6, 16, 16A and 17 and the Schedule	Sections 41-43 and Section 63	Regulations 2 to 35 and the Schedule	Regulations 2, 5, 7, 8, 8A, 9 and 10 and the Schedule	Regulations 2, 5, 6, 7, 8, 10, 11, 12, 12A and 13 and the Schedule
		See also section 33(4) of the Companies (Amendment) (No.2) Act 1999					
A2.8	'*the small companies regime*' and Sections 381-384	There are no equivalent provisions in Irish company law to the UK *small companies regime* or to the Small Companies and Groups (Accounts and Directors' Report) Regulations 2008. Small companies are defined in Section 8 of the 1986 Act. Please refer to the note above in the introduction to this table.					
A2.10	Section 384 and '*the small companies regime*'	There are no equivalent provisions in Irish company law to the UK *small companies regime*. Section 2 of the 1986 Act sets out which companies cannot qualify as small under Section 8 of the 1986 Act and cannot, therefore, avail of the filing exemptions under Sections 10 and 12 or apply the FRSSE in preparing their financial statements. Please refer to the note above in the introduction to this table.					
A2.10	Part 4 of the FSMA 2000 (companies excluded from the *small companies regime*)	There is no equivalent legislation in Ireland to the Financial Services and Markets Act 2000. There are also no equivalent provisions in Irish company law to the UK *small companies regime* or to the Small Companies and Groups (Accounts and Directors' Report) Regulations 2008. Small companies are defined in Section 8 of the 1986 Act. Please refer to the note above in the introduction to this table.					
A2.12	Section 383	There is no equivalent provision in Irish company law dealing with the criteria for a small parent company or a definition of small groups.					

	UK References	RoI References					
Paragraph	**2006 Act and the 2008 Regulations (unless otherwise stated)**	**1963 Act**	**1986 Act**	**1990 Act**	**GAR 1992**	**CIR 1992**	**IUR 1996**
A2.12 and footnote 23	Schedule 6 of the Small companies and Groups (Accounts and Directors' Report) Regulations 2008	There are no equivalent provisions in Irish company law to the UK *small companies regime* or to the Small Companies and Groups (Accounts and Directors' Report) Regulations 2008. Small companies are defined in Section 8 of the 1986 Act. Please refer to the note above in the introduction to this table.					
A2.13	Sections 395(2) and 403(3)	There are no directly equivalent provisions in Irish company law to Sections 395(2) and 403(3), although Sections 148(3) and 150(4) respectively of the 1963 Act do require certain categories of companies to prepare 'Companies Act individual accounts' or 'Companies Act group accounts', including those '*not trading for the acquisition of gain by members*'.					
A2.14 and footnote 24	Sections 395 and 403	Sections 148(5) and 150(6) allow a company to switch from IFRS accounts to Companies Act accounts, for individual accounts and group accounts respectively, where there is a 'relevant change in circumstance'. As at the date of publication of this FRS, there are no equivalent provisions in Irish company law to sections 395(4A) and 403(5A), providing for the ability of companies to switch from IFRS accounts to Companies Act accounts every five years for reasons other than a relevant change in circumstance.					
A2.15	Section 395(4A)	As at the date of publication of this FRS, there are no equivalent provisions in Irish company law providing for the ability of companies to switch from IFRS accounts to Companies Act accounts every five years for reasons other than a relevant change in circumstance.					
A2.16	Section 407	Section 150C					

	UK References	RoI References					
Paragraph	**2006 Act and the 2008 Regulations (unless otherwise stated)**	**1963 Act**	**1986 Act**	**1990 Act**	**GAR 1992**	**CIR 1992**	**IUR 1996**
A2.16 (Footnote 25)	'Accounts of subsidiaries that are required to be prepared under Part 15 of the Act.'	Section 148				Regulation 5	Regulation 5
A2.18	Entities preparing IAS accounts either voluntarily or because they are required to do so by law: ● only need apply certain sections of the Act as it relates to financial reporting; and ● are not required to comply with Schedules 1 and 6 (for companies and groups) nor with Schedules 2 or 3 (for bank and insurance companies).	Companies that prepare IFRS accounts either voluntarily or because they are required to do so in accordance with Sections 148 (individual accounts) and 150 (group accounts) of the 1963 Act, are not required to comply with the detailed accounting requirements of the Companies Acts 1963-2012 (and related Regulations), save for certain disclosures as detailed in Section 149(A)(1)(b) and Section 150B(2) of the 1963 Act. Regulations 5(1B) and 7(5) of the CIR 1992 set out the required disclosures for the IFRS accounts of credit institutions and regulations 5(1B) and 10(5) of the IUR 1996 set out the required disclosures for the IFRS accounts of insurance undertakings.					

	UK References	RoI References					
Paragraph	**2006 Act and the 2008 Regulations (unless otherwise stated)**	**1963 Act**	**1986 Act**	**1990 Act**	**GAR 1992**	**CIR 1992**	**IUR 1996**
A2.18	Schedules 4,5, 7 and 8 are still applicable to 'IAS accounts'	Please refer to the references to these Schedules below. Readers should refer to Sections 149(a)(1)(b) and 150B(2) of the 1963 Act as the additional disclosure requirements for IFRS accounts in UK and Irish company law are not the same in all cases.					
A2.18	Schedule 4 (application to IAS accounts)		Section 16 and 16A		Paragraphs 18 to 22 of Part 2 of the Schedule	Regulation 10 and Part III of the Schedule	Paragraphs 32-36 of Part IV of the Schedule
A2.18	Schedule 5 (application to IAS accounts)	Section 191	Paragraph 39(6) of Part IV of the Schedule		Paragraph 16 of Part 2 of the Schedule	Paragraph 74(4) of Part I and paragraph 1 of Part II of the Schedule	Paragraph 21(e) of Part III and paragraph 1 of Part IV of the Schedule
A2.18	Schedule 7	Sections 158	Sections 13 and 14	Section 63	Regulation 37	Regulations 11 and 11A	Regulations 14 and 14A
A2.18	Schedule 8	Section 191 of the 1963 Act sets out the disclosure requirements with regard to directors' salaries and payments. There are no specific requirements with regard to the disclosure of directors' remuneration for quoted companies in Irish company law. However, the Listing Rules of the Irish Stock Exchange contain further requirements in this regard.					

	UK References	RoI References					
Paragraph	**2006 Act and the 2008 Regulations (unless otherwise stated)**	**1963 Act**	**1986 Act**	**1990 Act**	**GAR 1992**	**CIR 1992**	**IUR 1996**
A2.19	Various sections of Parts 15 and 16 of the Act that contain financial reporting requirements applying to 'IAS accounts'	Companies that prepare 'IFRS accounts' in accordance with Sections 149 (individual accounts) and 150 (group accounts) of the 1963 Act, are not required to comply with the detailed accounting requirements of the Companies Acts 1963-2012 (and related Regulations), save for certain disclosures as detailed in Section 149(A)(1)(b) and Section 150B(2). Regulations 5(1B) and 7(5) of the CIR 1992 set out the required disclosures for the IFRS accounts of credit institutions and regulations 5(1B) and 10(5) of the IUR 1996 set out the required disclosures for the IFRS accounts of insurance undertakings.					
A2.19	Section 410A	Sections 149A(1)(b)(xii) and 150B(2)(l) applying Section 7(1)(a) of SI 450 of 2009	Paragraph 36A of Part IV of the Schedule, (pursuant to Section 149A(1)(b)(xii) of the 1963 Act)			Regulation 5(1B)(l) applying paragraph 66A of Part I of the Schedule and Regulation 7(5)(l) applying Section 7A(2)(a) of Part II of the Schedule	Regulation 5(1B)(k) applying paragraph 19A of Part III of the Schedule and Regulation 10(5)(k) applying paragraph 37(a) of Part IV, of the Schedule

	UK References	RoI References					
Paragraph	**2006 Act and the 2008 Regulations (unless otherwise stated)**	**1963 Act**	**1986 Act**	**1990 Act**	**GAR 1992**	**CIR 1992**	**IUR 1996**
A2.19	Section 411	Section 149A(1)(b)(ix) and Section 150B(2)(e)	Paragraph 42 of Part IV of the Schedule, (pursuant to Section 149A(1)(b)(ix) of the 1963 Act)		Paragraph 15 of Part 2 of the Schedule (pursuant to Section 150B(2)(e) of the 1963 Act)	Regulations 5(1B)(e) and 7(5)(e) applying paragraph 77 of Part I of the Schedule	Regulation 5(1B)(e) applying paragraph 27 of Part III of the Schedule and Regulation 10(5)(e) applying paragraph 29 of Part IV of the Schedule
A2.19	Section 412	Sections 149A(1)(b)(i) and 150B(2)(a) applying Section 191	Paragraph 39(6) of Part IV of the Schedule (pursuant to Section 149A(1)(b)(i) of the 1963 Act)		Paragraph 16 of Part 2 of the Schedule (pursuant to Section 150(2)(a) of the 1963 Act)	Regulation 5(1B)(a) applying paragraph 74(4) of Part I of the Schedule and Regulation 7(5)(a) applying paragraph 4 of Part IV of the Schedule	Regulation 5(1B)(a) applying paragraph 21(e) of Part III of the Schedule and Regulation 10(5)(a) applying paragraph 30(1) of Part IV of the Schedule

	UK References	RoI References					
Paragraph	2006 Act and the 2008 Regulations (unless otherwise stated)	1963 Act	1986 Act	1990 Act	GAR 1992	CIR 1992	IUR 1996
A2.19	Section 413			Sections 41 to 43			
A2.19	Sections 415-419	Section 158	Sections 13 and 14	Section 63	Regulation 37	Regulations 11 and 11A	Regulations 14 and 14A
		Sections 26 and 46 of the Electoral Act 1997 also require disclosures in respect of political donations to be provided in the directors' report.					
A2.19	Sections 420-421	Section 191 of the 1963 Act sets out the disclosure requirements with regard to directors' salaries and payments. There are no specific requirements with regard to the disclosure of directors' remuneration for quoted companies in Irish company law. However, the Listing Rules of the Irish Stock Exchange contain further requirements in this regard.					
A2.19	Section 494	Section 161D					
A2.21	Building Societies Act 1986	Building Societies Act 1989, Part VII, Section 77(1)					
A2.21	Charities Act 2011 and regulations made thereunder	Section 48 of the Charities Act, 2009 provides that all charities are to prepare an annual statement of accounts, the form and content of which can be prescribed by regulations of the Minister. Section 48 is, as of the date of publication of this FRS, not commenced and no regulations regarding the form and content of charities' annual statements of accounts have been published. Charity companies are required to prepare financial statements which give a true and fair view in accordance with the Companies Acts. Sections 148(3) and 150(4) of the 1963 Act requires that companies *'not trading for the acquisition of gain by the members'* must prepare Companies Act accounts (i.e. not IFRS accounts) and this definition may apply to many Irish charity companies.					

	UK References	RoI References					
Paragraph	**2006 Act and the 2008 Regulations (unless otherwise stated)**	**1963 Act**	**1986 Act**	**1990 Act**	**GAR 1992**	**CIR 1992**	**IUR 1996**
A2.21	Friendly and Industrial and Provident Societies Act 1968	Section 30 of part IV of the Industrial and Provident Societies (Amendment) Act, 1978; Regulation 4 of the Friendly Societies Regulations 1988, pursuant to Section 3 of the Friendly Societies (Amendment) Act 1977					
A2.21 and footnote 26	Friendly Societies Act 1992 and the Friendly Societies (Accounts and Related Provisions) Regulations 1994 (as amended)	Regulation 4 of the Friendly Societies Regulations 1988, pursuant to Section 3 of the Friendly Societies (Amendment) Act 1977					
A2.21	The Occupational Pension Schemes (Requirement to obtain Audited Accounts and a Statement from the Auditor) Regulations 1996	Section 56 of the Pensions Act 1990; Regulation 5 and paragraphs 1 and 2(a)(ii) of Schedule A of the Occupational Pension Schemes (Disclosure of Information) Regulations 2006					

Appendix III: Previous consultations

	UK References	RoI References					
Paragraph	**2006 Act and the 2008 Regulations (unless otherwise stated)**	**1963 Act**	**1986 Act**	**1990 Act**	**GAR 1992**	**CIR 1992**	**IUR 1996**
Para. A3.11	'*small companies regime*'	There are no equivalent provisions in Irish company law to the UK *small companies regime* or to the Small Companies and Groups (Accounts and Directors' Report) Regulations 2008. Small companies are defined in Section 8 of the 1986 Act. Please refer to the note above in the introduction to this table.					

FRS 101
Reduced Disclosure Framework
Disclosure exemptions from EU-adopted IFRS for qualifying entities

Contents

Summary

Financial Reporting Standard 101
Reduced Disclosure Framework

Objective
Scope
Abbreviations and definitions
Reduced disclosures for subsidiaries and ultimate parents
Statement of compliance
Date from which effective and transitional arrangements

Application guidance

Amendments to International Financial Reporting Standards as adopted in the European Union for compliance with the Act and the Regulations

Approval by the FRC

The Accounting Council's Advice to the FRC to issue FRS 101

Appendices

I Glossary
II Note on legal requirements
III Previous consultations
IV Republic of Ireland (RoI) legal references

Summary

(i) In 2012 and 2013 the Financial Reporting Council (FRC) revised financial reporting standards in the United Kingdom and Republic of Ireland. The revisions fundamentally reformed financial reporting, replacing almost all extant standards with three Financial Reporting Standards:

FRS 100 *Application of Financial Reporting Requirements;*
FRS 101 *Reduced Disclosure Framework*; and
FRS 102 *The Financial Reporting Standard applicable in the UK and Republic of Ireland.*

(ii) The revisions made by the FRC followed a sustained and detailed period of consultation. The FRC made these fundamental changes recognising that the introduction of International Financial Reporting Standards for listed groups in 2002 (with application from 2005) called into question the need for two sets of financial reporting standards. Evidence from consultation supported a move towards an international-based framework for financial reporting, but one that was proportionate to the needs of preparers and users.

(iii) The FRC's overriding objective in setting accounting standards is to enable users of accounts to receive high-quality understandable financial reporting proportionate to the size and complexity of the entity and users' information needs.

(iv) In meeting this objective, the FRC aims to provide succinct financial reporting standards that:

(a) have consistency with international accounting standards through the application of an IFRS-based solution unless an alternative clearly better meets the overriding objective;
(b) reflect up-to-date thinking and developments in the way entities operate and the transactions they undertake;
(c) balance consistent principles for accounting by all UK and Republic of Ireland entities with practical solutions, based on size, complexity, public interest and users' information needs;
(d) promote efficiency within groups; and
(e) are cost-effective to apply.

(v) The requirements in this Financial Reporting Standard (FRS) take into consideration the findings from the consultations on the future of financial reporting in the UK and Republic of Ireland that took place between 2002 and 2012.

(vi) This FRS sets out a reduced disclosure framework which addresses the financial reporting requirements and disclosure exemptions for the individual financial statements of subsidiaries and ultimate parents that otherwise apply the recognition, measurement and disclosure requirements of EU-adopted IFRS. It is envisaged that the provision of these disclosure exemptions could result in cost savings in the preparation of financial statements of subsidiaries and ultimate parents, without reducing the quality of financial reporting.

(vii) Disclosure exemptions are available to a qualifying entity, as defined in the glossary to this FRS, in its individual financial statements (but not in consolidated financial statements which it is required or voluntarily chooses to prepare). However, a qualifying entity which is a financial institution is not exempt from the disclosure requirements of IFRS 7 *Financial Instruments: Disclosures*, IFRS 13 *Fair Value Measurement* to the extent that they apply to financial instruments, and paragraphs 134 to 136 of IAS 1 *Presentation of Financial Statements*.

(viii) A qualifying entity may apply the reduced disclosure framework regardless of whether the financial reporting framework applied in the consolidated financial statements of the group is based on standards and interpretations issued (or adopted) by the International Accounting Standards Board.

(ix) Financial statements prepared by a qualifying entity in accordance with this FRS are not IAS Accounts as defined in section 395(1)(b) of the Companies Act 2006 (the Act) but are Companies Act accounts. Therefore the entity must comply with the Act and the Regulations and where applicable make amendments to EU-adopted IFRS requirements.

(x) Disclosure exemptions are also available to qualifying entities applying the recognition and measurement principles of FRS 102; the relevant financial reporting requirements and disclosure exemptions are set out in that FRS.

Financial Reporting Standard 101
Reduced Disclosure Framework
Disclosure exemptions from EU-adopted IFRS for qualifying entities

OBJECTIVE

1 The objective of this Financial Reporting Standard (FRS) is to set out the disclosure exemptions (a reduced disclosure framework) for the individual financial statements of subsidiaries, including intermediate parents, and ultimate parents that otherwise apply the recognition, measurement and disclosure requirements of EU-adopted IFRS.

SCOPE

2 This FRS may be applied to the individual financial statements of a qualifying entity, as defined in the glossary, that are intended to give a true and fair view of the assets, liabilities, financial position and profit or loss for a period.

3 A qualifying entity which is required to prepare consolidated financial statements (for example, if the entity is required by section 399 of the Act to prepare group accounts, and is not entitled to any of the exemptions in sections 400 to 402 of the Act), or which voluntarily chooses to do so, may not apply this FRS in its consolidated financial statements.

ABBREVIATIONS AND DEFINITIONS

4 The terms **Act**, **date of transition**, **EU-adopted IFRS**, **financial institution**, **FRS 100**, **FRS 101**, **FRS 102**, **FRSSE**, **IAS Regulation**, **IFRS**, **individual financial statements**, **public benefit entity**, **qualifying entity** and **Regulations** are defined in the glossary included as Appendix I to this FRS.

REDUCED DISCLOSURES FOR SUBSIDIARIES AND ULTIMATE PARENTS

5 A qualifying entity applying this FRS to its individual financial statements may take advantage of the disclosure exemptions in paragraphs 8 to 9, in accordance with paragraphs 6 to 7, provided that:

(a) Its shareholders have been notified in writing about, and do not object to, the use of the disclosure exemptions. Objections to the use of the disclosure exemptions may be served on the qualifying entity, in accordance with reasonable specified timeframes and format requirements, by a shareholder that is the immediate parent of the entity, or by a shareholder or shareholders holding in aggregate 5% or more of the total allotted shares in the entity or more than half of the allotted shares in the entity that are not held by the immediate parent.

(b) It otherwise applies as its financial reporting framework the recognition, measurement and disclosure requirements of EU-adopted IFRS, but makes amendments to EU-adopted IFRS requirements where necessary in order to comply with the Act and the Regulations, given that the financial statements that it prepares are Companies Act accounts as defined in section 395(1)(a) of the Act, not IAS accounts as defined in section 395(1)(b) of the Act. Application Guidance I to this FRS sets out the necessary amendments.

(c) It discloses in the notes to its financial statements:

(i) a brief narrative summary of the disclosure exemptions adopted; and
(ii) the name of the parent* of the group in whose consolidated financial statements its financial statements are consolidated, and from where those financial statements may be obtained.

A qualifying entity which is not a financial institution may take advantage in its individual financial statements of the disclosure exemptions set out in paragraphs 8 to 9 of this FRS. In relation to paragraphs 8(d) and (e), for financial liabilities that are held at fair value that are part of a trading portfolio or are derivatives, the qualifying entity can take advantage of those exemptions. Where the qualifying entity has financial instruments held at fair value subject to the requirements of section 36(4) of Schedule 1 to the Regulations, it must apply the disclosure requirements† of paragraphs 8(e), 9(c), 10, 11, 17, 20(a)(i), 25, 26, 28, 29, 30, 31 of IFRS 7 and paragraph 93 of IFRS 13 to those financial instruments held at fair value. For accounting periods beginning before 1 January 2013, paragraph 93 of IFRS 13 should be replaced with paragraphs 27, 27A and 27B of IFRS 7. **6**

A qualifying entity which is a financial institution may take advantage in its individual financial statements of the disclosure exemptions set out in paragraphs 8 to 9 of this FRS, except for: **7**

(a) the disclosure exemptions from IFRS 7 *Financial Instruments: Disclosures* (see paragraph 8(d));
(b) the disclosure exemptions from IFRS 13 *Fair Value Measurement* (see paragraph 8(e)) to the extent that they apply to financial instruments‡; and
(c) the disclosure exemptions from paragraphs 134 to 136 of IAS 1 *Presentation of Financial Statements* (see paragraph 8(g)).

A qualifying entity may take advantage of the following disclosure exemptions, from when the relevant standard is applied§: **8**

(a) The requirements of paragraphs 45(b) and 46 to 52 of IFRS 2 *Share-based Payment*, provided that for a qualifying entity that is:

(i) a subsidiary, the share-based payment arrangement concerns equity instruments of another group entity;
(ii) an ultimate parent, the share-based payment arrangement concerns its own equity instruments and its separate financial statements are presented alongside the consolidated financial statements of the group;

and, in both cases, provided that equivalent disclosures are included in the consolidated financial statements of the group in which the entity is consolidated.

**The parent identified in the definition of the term 'qualifying entity' (see the glossary included as Appendix I to this FRS).*

†Note, however, that the requirements in paragraph 6 are applicable to public benefit entities and other entities that are a qualifying entity, not just to companies that are a qualifying entity.

‡A qualifying entity that is a financial institution may take advantage in its individual financial statements of the disclosure exemptions from IFRS 13 (see paragraph 8(e)) to the extent that they apply to assets and liabilities other than financial instruments.

§Where a paragraph within a given standard cross-refers to an exempted paragraph listed above, the qualifying entity is permitted to still take the exemption.

(b) The requirements of paragraphs 62, B64(d), B64(e), B64(g), B64(h), B64(j) to B64(m), B64(n)(ii), B64(o)(ii), B64(p), B64(q)(ii), B66 and B67 of IFRS 3 *Business Combinations* provided that equivalent disclosures are included in the consolidated financial statements of the group in which the entity is consolidated.

(c) The requirements of paragraph 33(c) of IFRS 5 *Non-current Assets Held for Sale and Discontinued Operations* provided that equivalent disclosures are included in the consolidated financial statements of the group in which the entity is consolidated.

(d) The requirements of IFRS 7 *Financial Instruments: Disclosures*, provided that equivalent disclosures are included in the consolidated financial statements of the group in which the entity is consolidated.

(e) The requirements of paragraphs 91 to 99 of IFRS 13 *Fair Value Measurement*, provided that equivalent disclosures are included in the consolidated financial statements of the group in which the entity is consolidated.

(f) The requirement in paragraph 38 of IAS 1 *Presentation of Financial Statements* to present comparative information in respect of:
   (i) paragraph 79(a)(iv) of IAS 1;
   (ii) paragraph 73(e) of IAS 16 *Property, Plant and Equipment*;
   (iii) paragraph 118(e) of IAS 38 *Intangible Assets*;
   (iv) paragraphs 76 and 79(d) of IAS 40 *Investment Property*; and
   (v) paragraph 50 of IAS 41 *Agriculture*.

(g) The requirements of paragraphs 10(d), 10(f), 16, 38A, 38B, 38C, 38D, 40A, 40B, 40C, 40D, 111 and 134 to 136 of IAS 1 *Presentation of Financial Statements*.
For accounting periods beginning before 1 January 2013, paragraphs 38A, 38B, 38C, 38D, 40A, 40B, 40C and 40D of IAS 1 (effective 1 January 2013) should be replaced with paragraphs 39 and 40 of IAS 1 (effective 1 January 2009).

(h) The requirements of IAS 7 *Statement of Cash Flows*.

(i) The requirements of paragraphs 30 and 31 of IAS 8 *Accounting Policies, Changes in Accounting Estimates and Errors*.

(j) The requirements of paragraph 17 of IAS 24 *Related Party Disclosures*.

(k) The requirements in IAS 24 *Related Party Disclosures* to disclose related party transactions entered into between two or more members of a group, provided that any subsidiary which is a party to the transaction is wholly owned by such a member.

(l) The requirements of paragraphs 134(d) to 134(f) and 135(c) to 135(e) of IAS 36 *Impairment of Assets*, provided that equivalent disclosures are included in the consolidated financial statements of the group in which the entity is consolidated.

9 Reference should be made to the Application Guidance to FRS 100 in deciding whether the consolidated financial statements of the group provide disclosures which are equivalent to the requirements of EU-adopted IFRS, from which relief is provided in paragraph 8 of this FRS.

STATEMENT OF COMPLIANCE

10 Where a qualifying entity prepares its financial statements in accordance with FRS 101, it shall state in the notes to the financial statements: '*These financial statements were prepared in accordance with Financial Reporting Standard 101 Reduced Disclosure Framework*.' The financial statements of such an entity do not comply with all of the requirements of EU-adopted IFRSs and should not therefore contain the unreserved statement of compliance set out in paragraph 3 of IFRS 1 *First-time*

Adoption of International Financial Reporting Standards and paragraph 16 of IAS 1 *Presentation of Financial Statements*.

DATE FROM WHICH EFFECTIVE AND TRANSITIONAL ARRANGEMENTS

A qualifying entity may apply this FRS for accounting periods beginning on or after 1 January 2015. Early application of this FRS is permitted. If an entity applies this FRS before 1 January 2015 it shall disclose that fact. **11**

Application Guidance: Amendments to International Financial Reporting Standards as Adopted in the European Union for Compliance with the Act and the Regulations

This application guidance forms an integral part of FRS 101

AG1 In accordance with the Act, an entity may prepare Companies Act accounts or IAS accounts. A qualifying entity which applies FRS 101 prepares Companies Act accounts. This Application Guidance to FRS 101 sets out amendments to EU-adopted IFRS that are necessary to achieve compliance with the Act and related Regulations (deleted text is struck through and inserted text is underlined):

(a) Paragraph D16 of IFRS 1 *First-time Adoption of International Financial Reporting Standards* is amended as follows:
If a subsidiary becomes a first-time adopter later than its parent, the subsidiary shall, in its financial statements, measure its assets and liabilities at either:

(a) the carrying amounts that would be included in the parent's consolidated financial statements, based on the parent's date of transition to IFRSs, if no adjustments were made for consolidation procedures and for the effects of the business combination in which the parent acquired the subsidiary; or

(b) the carrying amounts required by the rest of this IFRS, based on the subsidiary's date of transition to IFRSs. These carrying amounts could differ from those described in (a):

(i) when the exemptions in this IFRS result in measurements that depend on the date of transition to IFRSs;

(ii) when the accounting policies used in the subsidiary's financial statements differ from those in the consolidated financial statements. For example, the subsidiary may use as its accounting policy the cost model in IAS 16 *Property, Plant and Equipment*, whereas the group may use the revaluation model.

A similar election is available to an associate or joint venture that becomes a first-time adopter later than an entity that has significant influence or joint control over it.

A qualifying entity that applies this provision must ensure that its assets and liabilities are measured in compliance with FRS 101.

(b) Paragraph D17 of IFRS 1 *First-time Adoption of International Financial Reporting Standards* is amended as follows:
However, if an entity becomes a first-time adopter later than its subsidiary (or associate or joint venture) the entity shall, in its consolidated financial statements, measure the assets and liabilities of the subsidiary (or associate or joint venture) at the same carrying amounts as in the financial statements of the subsidiary (or associate or joint venture), after adjusting for consolidation and equity accounting adjustments and for the effects of the business combination in which the entity acquired the subsidiary. Similarly, if a parent becomes a first-time adopter for its separate financial statements earlier or later than for its consolidated financial statements, it shall measure its assets and liabilities at the same amounts in both financial statements, except for consolidation adjustments.

A qualifying entity that applies this provision must ensure that its assets and liabilities are measured in compliance with FRS 101.

(c) Paragraph 34 of IFRS 3 *Business Combinations* is amended as follows:
Occasionally, an acquirer will make a bargain purchase, which is a business combination in which the amount in paragraph 32(b) exceeds the aggregate of the amounts specified in paragraph 32(a). If that excess remains after applying the requirements in paragraph 36, the acquirer shall recognise and separately disclose the resulting ~~gain in profit or loss~~ excess on the face of the statement of financial position on the acquisition date, immediately below goodwill, and followed by a subtotal of the net amount of goodwill and the excess. The ~~gain~~ excess shall be attributed to the acquirer. Subsequently, the excess up to the fair value of the non-monetary assets acquired shall be recognised in profit or loss in the periods in which the non-monetary assets are recovered. Any excess exceeding the fair value of non-monetary assets acquired shall be recognised in profit or loss in the periods expected to be benefited.

(d) Paragraphs 39 and 40 of IFRS 3 *Business Combinations* are amended as follows:

39 ~~The consideration the acquirer transfers in exchange for the acquiree includes any asset or liability resulting from a contingent consideration arrangement (see paragraph 37). The acquirer shall recognise the acquisition-date fair value of contingent consideration as part of the consideration transferred in exchange for the acquiree.~~ When a business combination agreement provides for an adjustment to the cost of the combination contingent on future events, the acquirer shall include the estimated amount of that adjustment in the cost of the combination at the acquisition date if the adjustment is probable and can be measured reliably.

40 ~~The acquirer shall classify an obligation to pay contingent consideration as a liability or as equity on the basis of the definitions of an equity instrument and a financial liability in paragraph 11 of IAS 32 Financial Instruments: Presentation, or other applicable IFRSs. The acquirer shall classify as an asset a right to the return of previously transferred consideration if specified conditions are met. Paragraph 58 provides guidance on the subsequent accounting for contingent consideration.~~ However, if the potential adjustment is not recognised at the acquisition date but subsequently becomes probable and can be measured reliably, the additional consideration shall be treated as an adjustment to the cost of the combination.

(e) Paragraph 58 of IFRS 3 *Business Combinations* is deleted.

(f) Without amending paragraph B63(a) of IFRS 3 *Business Combinations,* its requirement shall be read in conjunction with paragraph A2.8 of this standard.

(g) Paragraph 33 of IFRS 5 *Non-current Assets Held for Sale and Discontinued Operations* is amended as follows:
An entity shall disclose:

(a) a single amount in the statement of comprehensive income comprising the total of:
(i) the post-tax profit or loss of discontinued operations and
(ii) the post-tax gain or loss recognised on the measurement to fair value less costs to sell or on the disposal of the assets or disposal group(s) constituting the discontinued operation.

(b) an analysis of the single amount in (a) into:
(i) the revenue, expenses and pre-tax profit or loss of discontinued operations;

(ii) the related income tax expense as required by paragraph 81(h) of IAS 12;

(iii) the gain or loss recognised on the measurement to fair value less costs to sell or on the disposal of the assets or disposal group(s) constituting the discontinued operation; and

(iv) the related income tax expense as required by paragraph 81(h) of IAS 12.

The analysis ~~may be~~ shall be presented in ~~the notes or in the statement of comprehensive income. If it is presented~~ ~~In~~ the statement of comprehensive income ~~it shall be presented~~ in a ~~section~~ column identified as relating to discontinued operations, ie separately from continuing operations; a total column shall also be presented. The analysis is not required for disposal groups that are newly acquired subsidiaries that meet the criteria to be classified as held for sale on acquisition (see paragraph 11).

(c) the net cash flows attributable to the operating, investing and financing activities of discontinued operations. These disclosures may be presented either in the notes or in the financial statements. These disclosures are not required for disposal groups that are newly acquired subsidiaries that meet the criteria to be classified as held for sale on acquisition (see paragraph 11).

(d) the amount of income from continuing operations and from discontinued operations attributable to owners of the parent. These disclosures ~~may be~~ are presented ~~either in the notes or~~ in the statement of comprehensive income.

(h) Paragraph 53A and corresponding footnote is inserted into IAS 1 *Presentation of Financial Statements* as follows:

Statement of financial position

Information to be presented in the statement of financial position

53A A qualifying entity shall comply with the balance sheet format requirements of the Act* instead of paragraphs 54 to 76 of IAS 1 *Presentation of Financial Statements*, unless the entity elects to apply those paragraphs and the resulting statement of financial position complies with the balance sheet format requirements of the Act.

[Footnote text]

* An entity shall apply, as required by company law, either Part 1 'General Rules and Formats' of Schedule 1 to the Regulations; Part 1 'General Rules and Formats' of Schedule 2 to the Regulations; Part 1 'General Rules and Formats' of Schedule 3 to the Regulations; or Part 1 'General Rules and Formats' of Schedule 1 to the LLP Regulations.

(i) Paragraph 81C and corresponding footnote is inserted into IAS 1 *Presentation of Financial Statements* as follows:

Information to be presented in profit or loss

81C A qualifying entity shall present the components of profit or loss in the statement of comprehensive income (in either the single statement or two statement approach) in accordance with the profit and loss account format requirements of the Act* instead of paragraphs 82 and 84 to 86 of IAS 1 *Presentation of Financial Statements*. The entity may elect to apply the requirements of those paragraphs so long as the resulting statement of comprehensive income complies with the profit and loss account format requirements of the Act.

[Footnote text]

* An entity shall apply, as required by company law, either Part 1 'General Rules and Formats' of Schedule 1 to the Regulations; Part 1 'General Rules and Formats' of Schedule 2 to the Regulations; Part 1 'General Rules and Formats' of Schedule 3 to the Regulations; or Part 1 'General Rules and Formats' of Schedule 1 to the LLP Regulations.

(j) Paragraph 87 of IAS 1 *Presentation of Financial Statements* is amended and paragraph 87A is inserted into IAS 1 as follows:

87 ~~An entity shall not present any items of income or expense as extraordinary items, in the statement(s) presenting profit or loss and other comprehensive or in the notes.~~Ordinary activities are any activities which are undertaken by a reporting entity as part of its business and such related activities in which the reporting entity engages in furtherance of, incidental to, or arising from, these activities. Ordinary activities include any effects on the reporting entity of any event in the various environments in which it operates, including the political, regulatory, economic and geographical environments, irrespective of the frequency or unusual nature of the events.

87A Extraordinary items are material items possessing a high degree of abnormality which arise from events or transactions that fall outside the ordinary activities of the reporting entity and which are not expected to recur. They do not include items occurring within the entity's ordinary activities that are required to be disclosed by IAS 1.97, nor do they include prior period items merely because they relate to a prior period.

(k) Paragraph 88 of IAS 1 *Presentation of Financial Statements* is amended as follows:

An entity shall recognise all items of income and expense arising in a period in profit or loss unless an IFRS requires or permits otherwise, or unless prohibited by the Act.

(l) Paragraph 28 of IAS 16 *Property, Plant and Equipment* is deleted.

(m) Paragraph 24 of IAS 20 *Accounting for Government Grants and Disclosure of Government Assistance* is amended as follows:

Government grants related to assets, including non-monetary grants at fair value, shall be presented in the statement of financial position ~~either~~ by setting up the grant as deferred income ~~or by deducting the grant in arriving at the carrying amount of the asset~~.

(n) Paragraph 25 of IAS 20 *Accounting for Government Grants and Disclosure of Government Assistance* is deleted.

(o) Paragraph 26 of IAS 20 *Accounting for Government Grants and Disclosure of Government Assistance* is amended as follows:

~~One method recognises the~~ The grant is recognised as deferred income that is recognised in profit or loss on a systematic basis over the useful life of the asset.

(p) Paragraph 27 of IAS 20 *Accounting for Government Grants and Disclosure of Government Assistance* is deleted.

(q) Paragraph 28 of IAS 20 *Accounting for Government Grants and Disclosure of Government Assistance* is amended as follows:

The purchase of assets and the receipt of related grants can cause major movements in the cash flow of an entity. For this reason and in order to show the gross investment in assets, such movements are ~~often~~ disclosed as separate items in the statement of cash flows ~~regardless of whether or not the grant is deducted from the related asset for presentation purposes in the statement of financial position~~.

(r) Paragraph 29 of IAS 20 *Accounting for Government Grants and Disclosure of Government Assistance* is amended as follows:

Grants related to income are presented as part of profit or loss, either separately or under a general heading such as 'Other income'; ~~alternatively,~~ they are not deducted in reporting the related expense.

(s) Paragraph 124 of IAS 36 *Impairment of Assets* is amended as follows:

An impairment loss recognised for goodwill shall ~~not~~ be reversed in a subsequent period if, and only if, the reasons for the impairment loss have ceased to apply.

Approval by the FRC

Financial Reporting Standard 101 *Reduced Disclosure Framework* was approved for issue by the Board of the Financial Reporting Council on 1 November 2012, following its consideration of the Accounting Council's advice for this FRS.

The Accounting Council's Advice to the FRC to issue FRS 101

INTRODUCTION

1 This report provides an overview of the main issues which have been considered by the Accounting Council in advising the Financial Reporting Council (FRC) to issue FRS 101 *Reduced Disclosure Framework*. The FRC, in accordance with the Statutory Instrument *Statutory Auditors (Amendment of Companies Act 2006 and Delegation of Functions etc) Order 2012* (SI 2012/1741), is the prescribed body for issuing accounting standards in the UK. *The Foreword to Accounting Standards* sets out the application of accounting standards in the Republic of Ireland.

2 In accordance with FRC *Codes and Standards: procedures*, any proposal to issue, amend or withdraw a code or standard is put to the FRC with the full advice of the relevant Councils and/or the Codes & Standards Committee. Ordinarily, the FRC will only reject the advice put to it where:

- it is apparent that a significant group of stakeholders has not been adequately consulted;
- the necessary assessment of the impact of the proposal has not been completed, including an analysis of costs and benefits;
- insufficient consideration has been given to the timing or cost of implementation; or
- the cumulative impact of a number of proposals would make the adoption of an otherwise satisfactory proposal inappropriate.

3 The FRC has established the Accounting Council as the relevant Council to assist it in the setting of accounting standards.

ADVICE

4 The Accounting Council is advising the FRC to issue:

FRS 100 *Application of Financial Reporting Requirements*; and
FRS 101 *Reduced Disclosure Framework*.

5 FRS 102 *The Financial Reporting Standard Applicable in the UK and Republic of Ireland* completes the new suite of financial reporting standards. The Accounting Council will provide its advice to the FRC on FRS 102 in that standard.

BACKGROUND

6 Accounting standards were formerly developed by the Accounting Standards Board (ASB). The ASB commenced its project to update accounting standards in 2002; Appendix III provides a history of the previous consultations and a summary of how the overall proposals have developed*.

7 FRS 101 was developed in response to concerns that arose from earlier consultations (see Appendix III). Respondents to those consultations (and particularly the 2009 Policy Proposal) noted that a move to the IFRS for SMEs for subsidiaries of entities that apply EU-adopted IFRS would require recognition and measurement

**References in this section and Appendix III are made to the FRC, ASB or Accounting Council, as appropriate in terms of the time period and context of the reference.*

differences to be monitored and maintained at group level, and yet the alternative of a move to EU-adopted IFRS would increase disclosure in comparison to current accounting standards. The ASB therefore developed a reduced disclosure framework to address these concerns.

THE REDUCED DISCLOSURE FRAMEWORK PRINCIPLES

In developing the reduced disclosure framework, the ASB set principles for determining which of the disclosure requirements in EU-adopted IFRS should be applied by qualifying entities. Setting principles provides a structure for future amendments to the reduced disclosure framework as new and revised IFRSs are adopted in the EU. The principles are specific to qualifying entities, so the impact on preparers and users of qualifying entity individual financial statements is a common theme to be considered in applying the principles. The agreed principles, which were first introduced when FRED 47 *Reduced Disclosure Framework* was issued, are as follows: **8**

(1) Relevance:
Does the disclosure requirement provide information that is capable of making a difference to the decisions made by the users of the financial statements of a qualifying entity?

(2) Cost constraint on useful financial reporting:
Does the disclosure requirement impose costs on the preparers of the financial statements of a qualifying entity that are not justified by the benefits to the users of those financial statements?

(3) Avoid gold plating:
Does the disclosure requirement override an existing exemption provided by company law in the UK?

The Accounting Council is advising the FRC to adopt these principles. **9**

THE SCOPE OF THE REDUCED DISCLOSURE FRAMEWORK

The reduced disclosure framework was first proposed in FRED 43 *Application of Financial Reporting Requirements*, and revised proposals were issued in FRED 47. FRED 43 proposed that qualifying subsidiaries could apply the reduced disclosure framework. The scope of the framework was extended beyond subsidiaries in FRED 47, so that the ultimate parent of a group may take advantage of the disclosure framework in its individual financial statements. Intermediate parents are subsidiaries and so were already included within the scope of the reduced disclosure framework. **10**

The ASB decided, in clarifying the scope of the reduced disclosure framework in FRED 47, that a qualifying entity which is required to prepare consolidated financial statements (for example, if the entity is required by section 399 of the Act to prepare group accounts, and is not entitled to any of the exemptions in sections 400 to 402 of the Act), or a qualifying entity which voluntarily chooses to prepare consolidated financial statements, should not be permitted to apply the reduced disclosure framework in its consolidated financial statements. The ASB recognised that entities which are required or voluntarily choose to prepare consolidated financial statements generally have users with greater information requirements than the users of entities which only prepare individual financial statements. The ASB's decision not to extend the reduced disclosure framework to consolidated financial statements was questioned by a few respondents to FRED 47. The Accounting Council noted that the concerns raised were industry-specific and held the view previously identified that users of these financial statements had greater information requirements. The **11**

Accounting Council is therefore advising the FRC that the scope of the FRS remains unchanged from that proposed in FRED 47.

APPLICATION OF THE REDUCED DISCLOSURE FRAMEWORK TO FINANCIAL INSTITUTIONS

12 FRED 43 proposed that a subsidiary with public accountability should not be permitted to apply the reduced disclosure framework (see the Accounting Council's Advice to the FRC for FRS 100). With the elimination of 'public accountability' as a differentiator for a financial reporting system in FRED 46 (which replaced FRED 43), the ASB reconsidered which entities should be eligible to apply the reduced disclosure framework.

13 FRED 47 proposed consistent disclosure requirements for financial institutions, between those financial institutions that would be required to provide additional disclosures in accordance with FRED 48 and those financial institutions that are a qualifying entity taking advantage of the reduced disclosure framework. The ASB sought views on whether qualifying entities which are financial institutions should:

(a) provide disclosures required by IFRS 7 *Financial Instrument: Disclosures* and the disclosure requirements of IFRS 13 *Fair Value Measurement*; or

(b) provide disclosures required by IFRS 7 except for paragraphs 6, 7, 9(b), 16, 27A, 31, 33, 36, 37, 38, 39, 40 and 41 (this would provide consistency with disclosures required by FRED 48), and from paragraphs 92 to 99 of IFRS 13 (all disclosure requirements except the disclosure objectives).

14 Respondents had mixed views. Some held the view that a qualifying entity that is a financial institution should be permitted some exemptions from financial instrument disclosures in line with those in FRED 48, but others constituents disagreed on the basis that financial instruments are a significant part of the business for financial institutions and that those entities should provide an appropriate level of disclosure. The Accounting Council is advising the FRC that there should be no exemptions from IFRS 7 for financial institutions. This is also simple to apply and ensures financial institutions provide appropriate disclosure about their financial instruments.

15 Some respondents noted that there was an inconsistency in the application of the disclosure requirements in IFRS 13 between financial institutions and other entities. The inconsistency arose because financial institutions were required to provide disclosures for assets and liabilities held at fair value that are not financial instruments whereas other entities were exempt. The Accounting Council therefore considers that FRS 101 should clarify that a qualifying entity which is a financial institution is restricted from taking advantage of the disclosure exemptions from IFRS 13 only to the extent that they apply to financial instruments.

16 The Accounting Council is also advising the FRC that financial institutions should not be permitted to take advantage of the exemption from applying the capital disclosure requirements in IAS 1 *Presentation of Financial Statements*. Responses to FRED 47 had noted that capital disclosures provide relevant information for financial institutions.

RELATED PARTY EXEMPTION FOR THE REDUCED DISCLOSURE FRAMEWORK

17 In issuing FRED 47 the ASB decided to include an exemption in the reduced disclosure framework from disclosing a related party transaction in accordance with

IAS 24 *Related Party Disclosures* where the related party transaction was entered into between two or more members of a group, provided that any subsidiary which is a party to a transaction is wholly owned by such a member. This exemption is consistent with company law and was well-received by constituents; the Accounting Council advises the FRC to carry the exemption forward into FRS 101. The exemption set out in paragraph 8(k) of FRS 101 should only be applied where all subsidiaries which are a party to the transaction are wholly owned by a member of the group. The provision of this exemption is in line with principle 3 in paragraph 8 of this report.

EXTENSION OF THE REDUCED DISCLOSURE FRAMEWORK TO RECENTLY ISSUED INTERNATIONAL FINANCIAL REPORTING STANDARDS AND AMENDMENTS

The reduced disclosure framework principles (see paragraph 7) were applied in FRED 47 to those IFRSs issued or amended in 2011, including: **18**

(a) IFRS 9 *Financial Instruments* (as revised in 2011);
(b) IFRS 10 *Consolidated Financial Statements*;
(c) IFRS 11 *Joint Arrangements*;
(d) IFRS 12 *Disclosure of Interests in Other Entities*;
(e) IFRS 13 *Fair Value Measurement*;
(f) IAS 1 *Presentation of Financial Statements* (as revised in 2011);
(g) IAS 19 *Employee Benefits* (as revised in 2011);
(h) IAS 27 *Separate Financial Statements* (as revised in 2011); and
(i) IAS 28 *Investments in Associates and Joint Ventures* (as revised in 2011).

The Accounting Council subsequently considered the application of the reduced disclosure framework principles to *Annual Improvements to IFRSs 2009-2011 Cycle* which was issued by the IASB in May 2012. The application of the reduced disclosure framework principles leads the Accounting Council to advise the FRC (paragraph 8(g) of FRS 101) to provide disclosure exemptions from paragraphs 38A, 38B, 38C, 38D, 40A, 40B, 40C and 40D of IAS 1 *Presentation of Financial Statements*. Paragraphs 38A, 38B, 38C and 38D are concerned with comparative information in respect of the preceding period, and paragraphs 40A, 40B, 40C and 40D are concerned with a statement of financial position as at the beginning of the preceding period. **19**

The Accounting Council advises the FRC to update FRS 101 at regular intervals, to ensure that the disclosure framework maintains consistency with EU-adopted IFRS. **20**

THE PRECEDENCE OF THE COMPANIES ACT

The presentation requirements applicable to the statement of financial position and the statement of comprehensive income in IAS 1 have been amended in the Application Guidance of FRS 101 to clarify that a qualifying entity must comply with the company law format requirements. The Accounting Council advises the FRC to reconsider the format requirements of FRS 101 should the Government decide to amend company law at a future date. **21**

APPROVAL OF THIS ADVICE

22 This advice to the FRC was approved by the nine members of the Accounting Council on 25 October 2012. The Accounting Council is comprised of the following members:

Roger Marshall (Chair of the Accounting Council)
Nick Anderson
Dr Richard Barker
Edward Beale
Peter Elwin
Ken Lever
Robert Overend
Andy Simmonds
Pauline Wallace

Appendix I: Glossary

Act	The Companies Act 2006.
date of transition	The beginning of the earliest period for which an entity presents full comparative information under a given standard in its first financial statements that comply with that standard.
EU-adopted IFRS	**IFRS** that have been adopted in the European Union in accordance with EU Regulation 1606/2002.
financial institution	Any of the following: (a) a bank which is: (i) a firm with a Part IV permission* which includes accepting deposits and: (a) which is a credit institution; or (b) whose Part IV permission includes a requirement that it complies with the rules in the General Prudential sourcebook and the Prudential sourcebook for Banks, Building Societies and Investment Firms relating to banks, but which is not a building society, a friendly society or a credit union; (ii) an EEA bank which is a full credit institution; (b) a building society which is defined in section 119(1) of the Building Societies Act 1986 as a building society incorporated (or deemed to be incorporated) under that act; (c) a credit union, being a body corporate registered under the Industrial and Provident Societies Act 1965 as a credit union in accordance with the Credit Unions Act 1979, which is an authorised person; (d) custodian bank, broker-dealer or stockbroker; (e) an entity that undertakes the business of effecting or carrying out insurance contracts, including general and life assurance entities; (f) an incorporated friendly society incorporated under the Friendly Societies Act 1992 or a registered friendly society registered under section 7(1)(a) of the Friendly Societies Act 1974 or any enactment which it replaced, including any registered branches; (g) an investment trust, Irish Investment Company†, venture capital trust, mutual fund, exchange traded fund, unit trust, open-ended investment company (OEIC); (h) a retirement benefit plan; or

**As defined in section 40(4) of the Financial Services and Markets Act 2000 or references to equivalent provisions of any successor legislation.*

†An Irish Investment Company is a corporate vehicle as defined by section 47(3) of the Companies (Amendment) Act 1983 and paragraph 58 of the Schedule to the Companies (Amendment) Act 1986, and regulated by the Central Bank of Ireland.

	(i) any other entity whose principal activity is to generate wealth or manage risk through financial instruments. This is intended to cover entities that have business activities similar to those listed above but are not specifically included in the list above. A parent entity whose sole activity is to hold investments in other group entities is not a financial institution.
FRS 100	FRS 100 *Application of Financial Reporting Requirements*
FRS 101	FRS 101 *Reduced Disclosure Framework*
FRS 102	FRS 102 *The Financial Reporting Standard applicable in the UK and Republic of Ireland*
FRSSE	The extant version* of the *Financial Reporting Standard for Smaller Entities*
IAS Regulation	EU Regulation 1606/2002.
IFRS	Standards and interpretations issued (or adopted) by the International Accounting Standards Board (IASB). They comprise: (a) International Financial Reporting Standards; (b) International Accounting Standards; and (c) Interpretations developed by the IFRS Interpretations Committee (the Interpretations Committee) or the former Standing Interpretations Committee (SIC).
individual financial statements	The accounts that are required to be prepared by an entity in accordance with the Act or relevant legislation, for example: (a) 'individual accounts', as set out in section 394 of the Act; (b) 'statement of accounts', as set out in section 132 of the Charities Act 2011; or (c) 'individual accounts', as set out in section 72A of the Building Societies Act 1986. Separate financial statements are included in the meaning of this term.
public benefit entity	An entity whose primary objective is to provide goods or services for the general public, community or social benefit and where any equity is provided with a view to supporting the entity's primary objectives rather than with a view to providing a financial return to equity providers, shareholders or members.

**At the date of issue of this FRS, the extant version of the FRSSE is the Financial Reporting Standard for Smaller Entities (effective April 2008).* The *Financial Reporting Standard for Smaller Entities (effective January 2015)* will replace it as the extant standard from 1 January 2015.

qualifying entity	A member of a group where the parent of that group prepares publicly available consolidated financial statements which are intended to give a true and fair view (of the assets, liabilities, financial position and profit or loss) and that member is included in the consolidation*. A charity may not be a qualifying entity.
Regulations	The Large and Medium-sized Companies and Groups (Accounts and Reports) Regulations 2008 (SI 2008/410).

**As set out in section 474(1) of the Act.*

Appendix II: Note on Legal Requirements

INTRODUCTION

A2.1 This appendix provides an overview of how the requirements in FRS 101 address United Kingdom company law requirements. It is therefore written from the perspective of a company to which the Companies Act 2006 applies. Appendix IV contains Republic of Ireland legal references.

A2.2 References to the Act in this appendix are to the *Companies Act 2006*. References to the Regulations are to *The Large and Medium-sized Companies and Groups (Accounts and Reports) Regulations 2008* (SI 2008/410). References to specific provisions are to Schedule 1 to the Regulations; entities applying Schedules 2 or 3 should read them as referring to the equivalent paragraph in those schedules.

COMPANIES ACT ACCOUNTS

A2.3 Accounts prepared in accordance with EU-adopted IFRS are 'IAS accounts', and are within the scope of EU Regulation 1606/2002 (IAS Regulation). Where a qualifying entity prepares accounts in accordance with FRS 101, it prepares Companies Act accounts as referred to in section 395 of the Act. Those accounts must comply with the applicable provisions of Parts 15 and 16 of the Act and with the Regulations.

APPLICABLE ACCOUNTING FRAMEWORK

Consistency of financial reporting within groups

A2.4 Section 407 of the Act requires that the directors of the parent company secure that individual accounts of a parent company and each of its subsidiaries are prepared using the same financial reporting framework, except to the extent that in the directors' opinion there are good reasons for not doing so.

In addition, consistency is not required in the following situations:

(a) when the parent company does not prepare consolidated accounts; or
(b) when some subsidiaries are charities (consistency is not needed between the framework used for these and for other subsidiaries).

Where the directors of a parent company prepare IAS group accounts and IAS individual accounts, there only has to be consistency across the individual financial statements of the subsidiaries.

A2.5 All companies, other than those which elect or are required to prepare IAS individual accounts in accordance with the Act, prepare Companies Act individual accounts.

Financial instruments measured at fair value

A2.6 All preparers of Companies Act accounts must comply with the requirements of paragraph 36 of Schedule 1 to the Regulations*, which provides that:

**The Small Companies and Groups (Accounts and Directors' Report) Regulations 2008 (SI 2008/409) contain an identical provision for companies subject to the small companies regime*

(1) Subject to sub-paragraphs (2) to (5), financial instruments (including derivatives) may be included at fair value.

(2) Sub-paragraph (1) does not apply to financial instruments that constitute liabilities unless—

(a) they are held as part of a trading portfolio,
(b) they are derivatives, or
(c) they are financial instruments falling within sub-paragraph (4).

(3) Unless they are financial instruments falling within sub-paragraph (4), sub-paragraph (1) does not apply to—

(a) financial instruments (other than derivatives) held to maturity,
(b) loans and receivables originated by the company and not held for trading purposes,
(c) interests in subsidiary undertakings, associated undertakings and joint ventures,
(d) equity instruments issued by the company,
(e) contracts for contingent consideration in a business combination, or
(f) other financial instruments with such special characteristics that the instruments, according to generally accepted accounting principles or practice, should be accounted for differently from other financial instruments.

(4) Financial instruments that may be included in accounts at fair value, under international accounting standards adopted by the European Commission on or before 5th September 2006 in accordance with the IAS Regulation, may be so included provided that the disclosures required by such accounting standards are made.
[...]

A qualifying entity taking advantage of the reduced disclosure framework in FRS 101 must comply with the fair value measurement requirements applicable to financial instruments under the Regulations. Therefore, the qualifying entity must, for example, make all IFRS disclosures required for financial instruments held at fair value subject to the requirements of section 36(4) of Schedule 1 to the Regulations as set out in paragraph 6 of FRS 101. **A2.7**

Non-amortisation of goodwill

A qualifying entity preparing accounts in accordance with FRS 101 may have recognised goodwill which, in accordance with IFRS 3 *Business Combinations*, is not amortised. The non-amortisation of goodwill conflicts with paragraph 22 of Schedule 1 to the Regulations, which requires acquired goodwill to be reduced by provisions for depreciation calculated to write off the amount systematically over a period chosen by the directors, not exceeding its useful economic life. As such, the non-amortisation of goodwill will usually be a departure, for the overriding purpose of giving a true and fair view, from the requirement of paragraph 22 of Schedule 1 to the Regulations. In this circumstance there will need to be given in the notes to the accounts 'particulars of the departure, the reasons for it and its effect' (paragraph 10(2) of Schedule 1 to the Regulations). This is not a new instance of the use of the 'true and fair override' as paragraph 18 of FRS 10 *Goodwill and intangible assets* noted that it would have been required by companies applying paragraph 17 of FRS 10 which states 'Where goodwill and intangible assets are regarded as having indefinite useful economic lives, they should not be amortised.' **A2.8**

Presentation and formats

A2.9 A qualifying entity preparing accounts in accordance with FRS 101 must comply with the company law format requirements applicable to the statement of financial position and the statement of comprehensive income. The format and presentation requirements of IAS 1 *Presentation of Financial Statements* may conflict with those in company law because of the following:

(a) Differences in the definition of 'fixed assets'* (the term used in the Regulations) and 'non-current assets' (the term used in EU-adopted IFRS).
(b) Differences in the definition of 'current assets' as the term is used in the Regulations and EU-adopted IFRS.
(c) Differences in the definition of 'creditors falling due within or after one year' (the terms used in the Regulations) and 'current and non-current liabilities' (the term used in EU-adopted IFRS). Under the Act a loan is treated as due for repayment on the earliest date on which a lender could require repayment, whilst under EU-adopted IFRS the due date is based on when the entity expects to settle the liability or has no unconditional right to defer payment.
(d) The Act requires presentation of debtors falling due after more than one year within current assets. Under EU-adopted IFRS those items would be presented in non-current assets. UITF Abstract 4 *Presentation of long-term debtors in current assets* (the UITF's consensus is reproduced below in paragraph A2.10) addressed the inclusion of debtors due after more than one year within 'current assets'.

A2.10 In relation to paragraph A2.9(d), in most cases it will be satisfactory to disclose the size of debtors due after more than one year in the notes to the accounts. There will be some instances, however, where the amount is so material in the context of the total net current assets that in the absence of disclosure of the debtors due after more than one year on the face of the balance sheet readers may misinterpret the accounts. In such circumstances, the amount should be disclosed on the face of the balance sheet within current assets.

A2.11 The Regulations require the separate disclosure of extraordinary items in the profit and loss account. A qualifying entity preparing financial statements in accordance with FRS 101 must therefore disclose items that are deemed to be extraordinary items separately in the statement of comprehensive income. Entities should note that extraordinary items are extremely rare as they relate to highly abnormal events or transactions.

Realised profits

A2.12 Paragraph 13(a) of Schedule 1 to the Regulations requires that only profits realised at the balance sheet date are included in the profit and loss account, a requirement modified from that in Article 3.1(c)(aa) of the Fourth Directive† which refers to profits 'made' at the balance sheet date.

A2.13 Paragraph 39 of Schedule 1 to the Regulations allows that investment property and living animals and plants that may under international accounting standards be held at fair value, may also be held at fair value in Companies Act accounts.

**Assets of an entity which are intended for use on a continuing basis in the entity's activities.*

†*European Commission, Council Directive 78/660/EEC.*

Paragraph 40(2) of Schedule 1 to the Regulations then requires that, in general, movements in the value of financial instruments, investment properties or living animals or plants are recognised in the profit and loss account, notwithstanding the usual restrictions allowing only realised profits and losses to be included in the profit and loss account. Paragraph 40 of Schedule 1 to the Regulations thereby overrides the requirements of Paragraph 13(a) of Schedule 1. **A2.14**

Entities measuring investment properties, living animals or plants, or financial instruments at fair value should note that they may transfer such amounts to a separate non-distributable reserve instead of carrying them forward in retained earnings but are not required to do so. Presenting fair value movements that are not distributable profits in a separate reserve may assist with the identification of profits available for that purpose. **A2.15**

Entities should also continue to note that whether profits are available for distribution must be determined in accordance with applicable law. Entities may also refer to the Technical Release 02/10 *Guidance on Realised and Distributable Profits under the Companies Act 2006* issued by the Institute of Chartered Accountants in England and Wales and the Institute of Chartered Accountants of Scotland or any successor document, to determine profits available for distribution. **A2.16**

Table I
Areas for consideration by a qualifying entity preparing accounts in accordance with FRS 101 *Reduced Disclosure Framework*, in order to ensure compliance with the Act

IFRS	Explanation/potential issues	Amendment to EU-adopted IFRS
IFRS 1	*Assets and liabilities of a parent or subsidiaries* IFRS 1 provides an option for a subsidiary which becomes a first-time adopter later than its parent, which allows the subsidiary to measure its assets and liabilities at the carrying amounts that would be included in the parent's consolidated financial statements, based on the parent's date of transition to IFRS (D16). Under IFRS 1, if a parent becomes a first-time adopter later than in its consolidated financial statements, it shall measure its assets and liabilities at the same carrying amounts as in the consolidated financial statements (D17). Entities preparing their financial statements in accordance with FRS 101 must comply with the measurement requirements of the Act, which may be inconsistent with those of EU-adopted IFRS applied in the consolidated financial statements.	Restricted the application of the first-time adoption options in IFRS 1 D16 and D17 to situations where the measurement of assets and liabilities in the subsidiary's or parent's individual financial statements based on the consolidated financial statements would comply with FRS 101.

IFRS	Explanation/potential issues	Amendment to EU-adopted IFRS
IFRS 3	*Negative goodwill* IFRS 3 requires that negative goodwill is recognised as a gain in profit or loss at the acquisition date (IFRS 3.34). The Act does not contain accounting requirements for a negative consolidation difference subsequent to recognition. Nevertheless, the Seventh Directive* sets out conditions under which a negative consolidation difference may be transferred to the profit and loss account. The conditions under the Seventh Accounting Directive may be inconsistent with the recognition requirements for negative goodwill under EU-adopted IFRS.	Amended IFRS 3.34 to align with FRS 102, Section 19 *Business Combinations and Goodwill*, paragraph 19.24.
	Contingent consideration IFRS 3 requires the measurement of contingent consideration at fair value. Contingent consideration classified as a financial asset or liability is remeasured at fair value with fair value movements recognised in profit or loss (IFRS 3.58). The Regulations do not permit measurement at fair value of contingent consideration that is a financial instrument (the exemption of paragraph 36(4) of Schedule 1 to the Regulations does not apply) unless it is a derivative.	Amended IFRS 3.39 and IFRS 3.40 to align with FRS 102, Section 19 *Business Combinations and Goodwill*, paragraphs 19.12 and 19.13. Deleted IFRS 3.58.
IFRS 5	*Analysis of results of discontinued operation* IFRS 5 allows the analysis of post-tax results of discontinued operations to be presented on the face of the statement of comprehensive income or in the notes (IFRS 5.33). The Regulations require an entity to show totals for turnover, profit or loss before taxation and tax arising from ordinary activities on the face of the profit and loss account.	Removed the option in IFRS 5.33 to present the analysis in the notes to the accounts. The information must be presented on the face of the statement of comprehensive income in a columnar format.

* European Commission, Council Directive 83/349/EEC.

IFRS	Explanation/potential issues	Amendment to EU-adopted IFRS
IAS 1	*Formats* The format requirements applicable under IAS 1 and those under the Regulations may be incompatible.	IAS 1.53A and IAS 1.81C are inserted to disapply IAS 1.54 to IAS 1.76, IAS 1.82 and IAS 1.84 to IAS 1.86, unless the application of these requirements complies with the Regulations.
	Extraordinary items IAS 1 does not permit the presentation of extraordinary items (IAS 1.87) however, the Regulations require it.	Amended IAS 1.87 to remove the prohibition and inserted IAS 1.87A to include the definition of extraordinary items consistent with that in FRS 102, Section 5 *Statement of comprehensive income and income statement*, paragraph 5.10A.
	Realised profits IAS 1 requires the recognition of all income and expenses in profit or loss, unless otherwise required or permitted by an IFRS (IAS 1.88). The Regulations require that only profits realised at the balance sheet date are included in the profit and loss account (see paragraphs A2.12 to A2.15 above).	Amended IAS 1.88 to clarify the precedence of the Act.
IAS 16	*Government grants* IAS 16.28 permits the carrying amount of property, plant and equipment to be reduced by government grants in accordance with IAS 20. Off-setting of items that represent assets against items that represent liabilities is prohibited under the Regulations, unless specifically permitted or required. This option in EU-adopted IFRS is not compliant with the Regulations.	Deleted IAS 16.28.

IFRS	Explanation/potential issues	Amendment to EU-adopted IFRS
IAS 20	*Balance sheet off-setting* IAS 20.24 contains an option which permits government grants related to assets to be deducted in arriving at the carrying amount of the asset. Off-setting of items that represent assets against items that represent liabilities is prohibited under the Regulations, unless specifically permitted or required. This option in EU-adopted IFRS is not compliant with the Regulations.	Amended IAS 20.24, IAS 20.26, IAS 20.28 and deleted IAS 20.25 and IAS 20.27 to remove the off-set option.
	Profit and loss account off-setting IAS 20.29 contains an option which permits grants related to income to be deducted in reporting the related expense. Off-setting of items that represent income against items that represent expenditure is prohibited under the Regulations, unless specifically permitted or required. This option in EU-adopted IFRS is not compliant with the Regulations.	Amended IAS 20.29 to remove the off-set option.
IAS 36	*Reversal of impairment of goodwill* IAS 36 prohibits the reversal of impairment losses recognised on goodwill (IAS 36.124). The Regulations require the reversal of a provision for diminution in value of a fixed asset, if the reason for the provision has ceased to exist.	Amended IAS 36.124 and aligned with the requirement in FRS 102, Section 27 *Impairment of assets*, paragraph 27.28.

Appendix III: Previous Consultations

HISTORY OF PREVIOUS CONSULTATIONS

A3.1 The requirements in FRSs 100 to 102 are the outcome of a lengthy and extensive consultation. The FRC (and formerly the ASB) together with the Department for Business, Innovation and Skills have consulted on the future of accounting standards in the UK and Republic of Ireland (RoI) over a ten year period.

Table 1 – Consultations conducted

YEAR	CONSULTATION
2002	DTI* consults on adoption of IAS Regulation
2004	Discussion Paper – Strategy for Convergence with IFRS
2005	Exposure Draft – Policy Statement: The Role of the ASB
2006	Public Meeting and Proposals for Comment
2006	Press Notice seeking views
2007	Consultation Paper – Proposed IFRS for SMEs
2009	Consultation Paper – Policy Proposal: The future of UK GAAP
2010	Request for Responses – Development of the Impact Assessment
2010	Financial Reporting Exposure Drafts 43 and 44
2011	Financial Reporting Exposure Draft 45
2012	Financial Reporting Exposure Drafts 46, 47 and 48

2004

A3.2 In 2004 the Discussion Paper contained two key elements underpinning the proposals: firstly that UK and Republic of Ireland (RoI) accounting standards should be based on IFRS and secondly that a phased approach to the introduction of the standards should be adopted.

A3.3 The ASB embarked on the phased approach and issued a number of standards based on IFRS. The majority of respondents agreed with a framework based on IFRS, and although supportive overall, the response to the phased approach was mixed.

2005

A3.4 In its 2005 Exposure Draft (2005 ED) of a Policy Statement *Accounting standard-setting in a changing environment: The role of the Accounting Standards Board*, amongst other aspects of its role, the ASB identified its intention to converge with IFRS by implementing new IFRS in the UK as soon as possible. It also proposed to

**The Department of Trade and Industry (DTI) was a United Kingdom government department which was replaced with the announcement of the creation of the Department for Business, Enterprise and Regulatory Reform and the Department for Innovation, Universities and Skills on 28 June 2007, which were themselves merged into the Department for Business, Innovation and Skills (BIS) on 6 June 2009.*

continue the phased approach to adopting UK accounting standards based on older IFRSs, but recognised there was little case for being more prescriptive than IFRS.

Although the ASB had, in the 2005 ED, wanted to move the debate on to how it would seek to influence the IASB's agenda, respondents' main concern remained about convergence. In 2005, the ASB issued an exposure draft proposing the IASB's standard on Business Combinations be adopted in the UK and RoI. This exposure draft highlighted the complexity of a mixed set of UK accounting standards, with some based on IFRSs and others developed independently by the ASB. The majority of respondents continued to agree with the aim of basing UK accounting standards on IFRS, but a broader set of views on how to achieve this was emerging. **A3.5**

As time progressed the ASB formed the view that convergence by adopting certain IFRSs was not meeting the needs of its constituents, which no longer included quoted groups. The ASB was concerned about the complexity of certain IFRSs, and it noted that introducing them piecemeal created complications and anomalies within the body of current FRSs. This arose because IFRS-based standards were not an exact replacement for current FRSs and many consequential amendments were required to 'fit' each replacement IFRS-based standard into the existing body of UK FRS. The ASB agreed to continue with its convergence programme, but decided to re-examine how to achieve this. **A3.6**

2006

The ASB published revised proposals to be discussed at the 2006 public meeting. By this time the IASB had started its IFRS for SMEs project, and the ASB decided this might have a role as one of the tiers in the UK financial reporting framework. The ASB proposed a 'big bang' with new IFRS-based UK accounting standards mandatory from a single date, 1 January 2009. The ASB's proposal was for a three-tier system, with Tier 1 being EU-adopted IFRS, and the other two tiers being developed as the IASB progressed with its project on the IFRS for SMEs. **A3.7**

Those attending the public meeting supported the aim of basing UK and RoI accounting standards on IFRS and adapting them to ensure they were appropriate for the entities applying them. **A3.8**

Taking this feedback into account, later in 2006 the ASB issued a Press Notice (PN 289) seeking views on its current thinking: **A3.9**

(a) All quoted and publicly accountable companies should apply EU-adopted IFRS.
(b) The FRSSE should be retained and extended to include medium-sized entities.
(c) UK subsidiaries of groups applying full IFRS should apply EU-adopted IFRS, but with reduced disclosure requirements.
(d) No firm decision on the remainder (Tier 2), but options included extending the FRSSE, extending full IFRS, maintaining separate UK accounting standards or some combination of these.

The responses were mixed, but there was agreement that whatever the solution, it should be based on IFRS and there should be different reporting tiers to ensure proportionality. **A3.10**

2007

A3.11 The IASB published an exposure draft of its IFRS for SMEs in early 2007; shortly afterwards the ASB published its own consultation paper. This sought views on how the IFRS for SMEs might fit into the future UK financial reporting framework, for example whether it might be appropriate for Tier 2, with the FRSSE continuing for those eligible for the small companies' regime.

A3.12 Feedback on the IFRS for SMEs was largely positive: it would be suitable for Tier 2, it was international, it was compatible with IFRSs, and it represented a significant simplification. Overall, it was seen as a workable alternative to IFRS. In addition, respondents wanted to retain the FRSSE (because it reduces the regulatory burden on smaller entities) and to give subsidiaries the option of applying the IFRS for SMEs as well as a reduced disclosure regime if applying full IFRS.

2009

A3.13 The IFRS for SMEs was published in 2009, allowing the ASB to further develop its proposals in the Consultation Paper *Policy Proposal: The future of UK GAAP*. The proposals were largely consistent with the cumulative results of the preceding consultations and included:

(a) a move to an IFRS-based framework;
(b) a three-tier approach;
(c) publicly accountable entities would be Tier 1 and would apply EU-adopted IFRS;
(d) small companies would be Tier 3 and continue to apply the FRSSE; and
(e) other entities would be Tier 2 and should apply a UK and RoI accounting standard based on the IFRS for SMEs.

A3.14 The only significant proposal that was inconsistent with respondents' previous comments was that subsidiaries should simply apply the requirement of the tier they individually met – respondents had wanted subsidiaries to be able to take advantage of disclosure exemptions, and at that time the ASB had yet to be convinced that significant cost savings were available from a reduced disclosure framework. Taking into account the feedback received, this proposal was subsequently reversed and the reduced disclosure framework was incorporated into FREDs 43 and then 46, and it is now set out in FRS 101.

A3.15 In addition to the many useful and detailed points made, some common themes included general agreement that change was needed to UK accounting standards and that there was support for many of the changes proposed in the consultation paper.

2010 onwards

A3.16 The request for responses to aid development of the Impact Assessment focused on obtaining feedback on the expected costs, benefits and impact of the proposals subsequently set out in FREDs 43 and 44, rather than on the accounting principles. As the focus was on costs and benefits no specific question was asked about the principle of the proposed introduction of an IFRS-based framework, but nevertheless respondents commented on this: of the 32 responses received only 12.5% did not agree with the introduction of an IFRS-based framework.

A3.17 FREDs 43 and 44 issued in October 2010 set out the draft suggested text for two new accounting standards that would replace the majority of extant Financial Reporting

Standards (current FRS) in the UK and RoI. The ASB issued a supplementary FRED addressing specific needs of public benefit entities (FRED 45) in March 2011. The ASB then updated FREDs 43, 44 and 45, replacing them with the revised FREDs 46, 47 and 48 in January 2012, by eliminating the concept of public accountability and by introducing a number of accounting treatment options that are available in EU-adopted IFRS. The Accounting Council's advice to the FRC to issue FRSs 100 to 102 includes more discussion of the feedback received on FREDs 43 to 48 and how the proposals have been refined and developed into the standards.

HOW HAVE THE PROPOSALS BEEN DEVELOPED?

As set out above, the FRC, the Accounting Council (and previously the ASB) have consulted regularly on the future of financial reporting in the UK and RoI. Over the consultations the ASB's (and the Accounting Council's) thinking has evolved based on careful consideration of the feedback at each stage. Whilst responses were sometimes mixed, there has been agreement that: **A3.18**

(a) current FRS, which are a mixture of Statements of Standard Accounting Practice (SSAPs) issued by the Consultative Committee of Accounting Bodies, FRSs developed and issued by the ASB and IFRS-based standards issued by the ASB to converge with international standards, are an uncomfortable mismatch that lack strong underlying principles or cohesion; and
(b) whatever the solution, it should be based on IFRS and there should be different reporting tiers to ensure proportionality.

During the consultation process to date, the Accounting Council and formerly the ASB have been guided by the following principles: **A3.19**

(a) The framework must be fit for purpose, so that each entity required to produce true and fair financial statements under UK and RoI law will deliver financial statements that are suited to the needs of its primary users. The Accounting Council has kept in close contact with constituent users on this point, including investors, creditor institutions and the tax authorities.
(b) The framework must be proportionate, so that preparing entities are not unduly burdened by costs that outweigh the benefit to them and to the primary users of information in their financial statements. The FRC believes that the proposals will produce a lower cost regime, while enhancing user benefits. It has carried out a consultation stage impact assessment with input from interested parties, and will continue to assess cost-benefit issues.
(c) The framework must be in line with UK company law. This determines which entities must produce true and fair financial statements. Exemptions within the law have generally been retained. The detailed requirements of the Companies Act 2006 are driven to a great extent by the European Accounting Directives, which are being revised*.
(d) The framework must be future-proofed, where possible. The FRC will continue to monitor the situation and has sovereignty over UK accounting standards (subject to the law). Changes to the Accounting Directives may lead to further developments, for example the European Council and European Parliament decision to permit Member States an option to treat micro-entities as a separate category of Company and exempt them from certain accounting requirements.

**The EU's consultation process on review of the Accounting Directives is summarised at http://ec.europa.eu/internal_market/accounting/sme_accounting/review_directives_en.htm.*

SUMMARY OF OUTREACH

A3.20 During the development and throughout the consultation period of FREDs 43 to 48, the ASB undertook an extensive programme of outreach aimed at raising awareness of the proposals and to address the view (held by some) that previous consultations had not gathered sufficient evidence to support and test the assumptions made.

A3.21 As part of the outreach programme to obtain both formal and informal feedback, a series of meetings and events took place with users, including with lenders to small and medium-sized entities. Lenders noted that financial statements are an important part of their decision-making process when considering whether to provide finance and, whilst a decision to provide finance is not based on financial statements alone, they provide useful information and verification to the lender.

A3.22 Although the ASB and the Accounting Council employed their best efforts to obtain feedback from users (a constituent group historically difficult to engage with formally) it is disappointing that limited formal responses were received and the Accounting Council has not been more successful in obtaining input from users.

A3.23 In addition, a review was made of academic research that addressed the users of the financial statements of small and medium-sized entities. The conclusion drawn from the research was that many entities requested financial statements from Companies House when considering whether to trade with another entity. The European Federation of Accountants and Auditors (EFAA) issued, in May 2011, a statement that identified the users of financial statements, noting who the users of SMEs' financial statements are and that information on the public record assists all users of financial statements of SMEs by providing, in an efficient manner, basic information that protects their rights.

A3.24 The ASB considered that the outreach programme had gleaned information from people who would not normally submit formal responses to a consultation and provided very useful information that could be used in developing the next stage of the project. The ASB noted that whilst this information was not part of the public record, as are formal consultation responses, it could use the information to assist in developing the revised FREDs 46 to 48, supplementing information contained in responses, and would seek further comment in the next stage of its deliberations.

A3.25 The Accounting Council continued the work of the ASB in finalising FRSs 100 to 102. The responses to FREDs 46 to 48 were analysed and discussed, and engagements were conducted to take into account the views and suggestions of all relevant associations and contacts. Respondents and outreach contacts were satisfied with FREDs 46 to 48, and many of the response letters were forthcoming in their overall praise for the proposals. A significant number of constituents anticipated cost savings arising from the application of FRS 101. Many respondents considered that FRS 102 would improve UK accounting standards, in particular by introducing requirements for accounting for financial instruments. Further they considered that the improvements will be achieved in a way that will be proportionate to the needs of users, and that once the transition phase has been overcome, it will have the effect of reducing the reporting burden on those UK companies that adopt it.

Appendix IV: Republic of Ireland (RoI) Legal References

INTRODUCTION

A4.1 The table below outlines the provisions in the Companies Acts 1963 to 2012 and related Regulations which implement EC Accounting Directives (Irish company law), corresponding to the provisions of the UK *Companies Act 2006* (the 2006 Act) and the UK *Large and Medium-sized Companies and Groups (Accounts and Reports) Regulations 2008* (the 2008 Regulations) (SI 2008/410) referred to in this FRS.

A4.2 The principal Irish companies' legislation referred to in the table below is:

- The Companies Act 1963 (1963 Act);
- The Companies (Amendment) Act 1986 (1986 Act);
- The Companies Act 1990 (1990 Act);
- The Companies (Amendment) (No. 2) Act 1999 (1999 Act);
- The European Communities (Companies: Group Accounts) Regulations 1992 – S.I. No. 201 of 1992 (Group Accounts Regulations 1992 or GAR 1992);
- The European Communities (Credit Institutions: Accounts) Regulations 1992 – S.I. No. 294 of 1992 (Credit Institutions Regulations 1992 or CIR 1992);
- The European Communities (Insurance Undertakings: Accounts) Regulations 1996 – S.I. No. 23 of 1996 (Insurance Undertakings Regulations 1996 or IUR 1996).

A4.3 Where general references are made in this FRS to the '2006 Act', 'Companies Act 2006 (and the Regulations)', 'the Companies Act', 'the Act', 'the Large and Medium-sized Companies and Groups (Accounts and Reports) Regulations 2008', 'the 2008 Regulations' and 'the Regulations', readers should refer, in an Irish context, to the relevant sections and paragraphs of the Irish companies' legislation listed above. Such general references are not included in the table below. References in the text to 'IAS accounts' are equivalent to 'IFRS accounts' in Irish company law.

A4.4 The following Irish legislation is also referenced in the table below:

- The Building Societies Act 1989;
- The Credit Union Act 1997;
- The Central Bank Act 1971;
- The Charities Act 2009;
- The Friendly Societies Acts 1896 to 1977.

COMPANIES ACT ACCOUNTS UNDER IRISH COMPANY LAW

A4.5 Certain companies are permitted under Irish company law to prepare their Companies Act accounts under a financial reporting framework based on accounting standards other than those issued by the Financial Reporting Council (FRC) and promulgated by the Institute of Chartered Accountants in Ireland in respect of their application in the Republic of Ireland. Specifically:

- Pursuant to the Companies (Miscellaneous Provisions) Act 2009, as amended by the Companies (Amendment) Act 2012, relevant parent undertakings are permitted to prepare 'Companies Act individual accounts' and/or 'Companies Act group accounts' in accordance with US GAAP, as modified to ensure consistency with Irish company law.
- Investment companies subject to Part XIII of the Companies Act 1990 or the European Communities (Undertakings for Collective Investment in Transferable Securities) Regulations 2011 may adopt an alternative body of accounting

standards, being standards which apply in the United States of America, Canada or Japan in preparing 'Companies Act individual accounts'.

Such companies, therefore, may adopt standards other than those issued by the FRC in preparing Companies Act accounts under Irish company law.

SMALL COMPANIES UNDER IRISH COMPANY LAW

A4.6 There is no equivalent to the UK *small companies regime* (see Sections 381 to 384 of the 2006 Act) in Irish company law. Section 8 of the Companies (Amendment) Act 1986 (as amended by the European Union (Accounts) Regulations 2012 (S.I. No. 304 of 2012)) defines small companies for the purposes of Irish law. However, whilst Sections 10 and 12 provide certain exemptions for such companies in relation to their financial statements filed with the Registrar of Companies, there are no exemptions for individual or group accounts prepared for members. Under Section 8 (as amended) the qualifying conditions for a company to be treated as a small company in respect of any financial year are as follows:

- The amount of turnover for that year does not exceed €8,800,000;
- The balance sheet total for that year does not exceed €4,400,000; and
- Average number of employees does not exceed 50.

A4.7 Except for companies in their first financial year, Section 8(1)(a) provides that companies qualify to be treated as small if, in respect of that year and the financial year, immediately preceding that year, the company satisfies at least two of the above criteria. Section 9 provides that where a company has qualified as small, it continues to be so qualified until it does not meet two of the above three criteria for two consecutive years. Similarly, where a company no longer qualifies as small, two consecutive years of meeting two of the three criteria are required to qualify again as small.

A4.8 The following do not qualify as small under Irish company law:

- Companies subject to the European Communities (Credit Institutions: Accounts) Regulations 1992;
- Companies subject to the European Communities (Insurance Undertakings: Accounts) Regulations 1996; and
- Private companies whose securities are admitted to trading on a regulated market.

OTHER NOTES

A4.9 As noted in paragraph A2.2 of this FRS, while the UK company law references are made to Schedule 1 to the 2008 Regulations, entities applying Schedules 2 (banking companies) or 3 (insurance companies) to those Regulations should read them as referring to the equivalent paragraphs in those Schedules. In the table below, the corresponding or similar provisions in Irish company law are specifically set out.

A4.10 As this FRS does not apply to the preparation of consolidated financial statements (see paragraph 3 of this FRS), readers should note that, with a number of specific exceptions, there are no references included in the table below to the Group Accounts Regulations, 1992 or other legislative provisions pertaining to group accounts. The exceptions relate to paragraphs dealing with the scope of the standard and the definitions of qualifying entities.

The table below is intended as a reference guide to the corresponding or similar provisions in Irish company law and does not purport to be complete. Readers should note that not all Irish provisions are equivalent to the corresponding UK provisions and are advised to refer to the Irish legislation for an understanding of relevant requirements. Readers should also be aware that various sections and paragraphs referenced below have been amended by subsequent legislation and readers should ensure that they refer to such amended text where applicable. **A4.11**

Summary

	UK References	ROI References				
Paragraph	**2006 Act and the 2008 Regulations (unless otherwise stated)**	**1963 Act**	**1986 Act**	**GAR 1992**	**CIR 1992**	**IUR 1996**
ix	Section 395(1)(b)	Section 148(2)(b)			Regulation 5(1)	Regulation 5(1)

Financial Reporting Standard 101 *Reduced Disclosure Framework*

	UK References	ROI References				
Paragraph	**2006 Act and the 2008 Regulations (unless otherwise stated)**	**1963 Act**	**1986 Act**	**GAR 1992**	**CIR 1992**	**IUR 1996**
3	Section 399	Section 150(1)		Regulations 5 and 7	Regulation 7(3)	Regulation 10(3)
3	Sections 400 to 401			Regulations 8, 9 and 9A	Regulations 8 and 8A	Regulations 12 and 12A
3	Section 402	Section 150(1A)*			Paragraph 2 of Part II to the Schedule	Regulation 10(1A)*
		*Section 150(1A) of the 1963 Act and Regulation 10(1A) of the IUR 1996 contain an exemption from preparing group accounts which is similar but not identical to Section 402.				

Paragraph	UK References	ROI References				
	2006 Act and the 2008 Regulations (unless otherwise stated)	**1963 Act**	**1986 Act**	**GAR 1992**	**CIR 1992**	**IUR 1996**
5(b)	Section 395(1)(a)	Section 148(2)(a)			Regulation 5(1)	Regulation 5(1)
5(b)	Section 395(1)(b)	Section 148(2)(b)			Regulation 5(1)	Regulation 5(1)
6	Paragraph 36(4) of Schedule 1 to the Regulations		Paragraph 22AA of Part IIIA of the Schedule		Paragraphs 46A(4A) and 46A(4B) of Part I of the Schedule	

Application Guidance: Amendments to International Financial Reporting Standards as adopted in the European Union for compliance with the Act and the Regulations

	UK References	ROI References				
Paragraph	**2006 Act and the 2008 Regulations (unless otherwise stated)**	**1963 Act**	**1986 Act**	**GAR 1992**	**CIR 1992**	**IUR 1996**
AG1	'Companies Act accounts or IAS accounts'	Sections 148, 149, 149A, 150, 150A and 150B				
AG1(h) and footnote AG1(i) and footnote	Part 1 'General Rules and Formats' of Schedule 1 to the Regulations		Part I of the Schedule			
AG1(h) and footnote AG1(i) and footnote	Part 1 'General Rules and Formats' of Schedule 2 to the Regulations				Chapter 1 of Part I of the Schedule	
AG1(h) and footnote AG1(i) and footnote	Part 1 'General Rules and Formats' of Schedule 3 to the Regulations					Part I of the Schedule
AG1(h) and footnote AG1(i) and footnote	Part 1 'General Rules and Formats' of Schedule 1 to the LLP Regulations	No equivalent LLP legislation in Ireland.				

The Accounting Council's Advice to the FRC to issue FRS 101

	UK References	ROI References				
Paragraph	**2006 Act and the 2008 Regulations (unless otherwise stated)**	**1963 Act**	**1986 Act**	**GAR 1992**	**CIR 1992**	**IUR 1996**
11	Section 399	Section 150(1)		Regulations 5 and 7	Regulation 7(3)	Regulation 10(3)
11	Sections 400 to 401			Regulations 8, 9 and 9A	Regulations 8 and 8A	Regulations 12 and 12A
11	Section 402	Section 150(1A)*			Paragraph 2 of Part II to the Schedule	Regulation 10(1A)*
		*Section 150(1A) of the 1963 Act and Regulation 10(1A) of the IUR 1996 contain an exemption from preparing group accounts which is similar but not identical to Section 402.				

Appendix I: Glossary

	UK References	ROI References				
Paragraph	**2006 Act and the 2008 Regulations (unless otherwise stated)**	**1963 Act**	**1986 Act**	**GAR 1992**	**CIR 1992**	**IUR 1996**
'Financial institution' and footnote 6	Part IV permission; Section 40(4) of the Financial Services and Markets Act 2000	There is no equivalent legislation in Ireland to the Financial Services and Markets Act 2000. Banks in Ireland are licensed under Section 9 of the Central Bank Act 1971.				
'Financial institution'	Section 119(1) of the Building Societies Act 1986	Section 2(1) of the Building Societies Act 1989				
'Financial institution'	Industrial and Provident Societies Act 1965 and Credit Unions Act 1979	Credit Unions Act 1997				
'Financial institution'	Friendly Societies Act 1992; section 7(1)(a) of the Friendly Societies Act 1974	Friendly Societies Acts 1896 to 1977				
'Individual financial statements'	Section 394	Section 148				

	UK References	ROI References				
Paragraph	2006 Act and the 2008 Regulations (unless otherwise stated)	1963 Act	1986 Act	GAR 1992	CIR 1992	IUR 1996
'Individual financial statements'	Section 132 of the Charities Act 2011	Section 48 of the Charities Act 2009 provides that all charities are to prepare an annual statement of accounts, the form and content of which can be prescribed by regulations of the Minister. Section 48 is, at the date of publication of this FRS, not commenced and no regulations regarding the form and content of charities' annual statements of accounts have been published. Charity companies are required to prepare financial statements which give a true and fair view in accordance with the Companies Acts. Sections 148(3) and 150(4) of the 1963 Act require that companies "*not trading for the acquisition of gain by the members*" must prepare Companies Act accounts (i.e. not IFRS accounts), and this definition may apply to many Irish charity companies.				
'Individual financial statements'	Section 72A of the Building Societies Act 1986	Section 77 of the Building Societies Act 1989 requires the preparation of (a) an income and expenditure account giving a true and fair view of its income and expenditure for that year, (b) a balance sheet giving a true and fair view of the state of its affairs as at the end of that year, and (c) a statement of the source and application of funds giving a true and fair view of the manner in which its business has been financed and in which its financial resources have been used during that year.				
'Qualifying entity' (Footnote 9)	S474(1) of the Act			Regulation 3(1)	Paragraph 1 of part IV of the Schedule	

Appendix II: Note on legal requirements

	UK References	ROI References				
Paragraph	**2006 Act and the 2008 Regulations (unless otherwise stated)**	**1963 Act**	**1986 Act**	**GAR 1992**	**CIR 1992**	**IUR 1996**
A2.2	Schedule 1 to the Regulations		Sections 4, 5 and 6 and the Schedule			
A2.2	Schedule 2 to the Regulations				Part I of the Schedule	
A2.2	Schedule 3 to the Regulations					Regulations 6, 7 and 8 and Parts I, II and III of the Schedule
A2.3	'Companies Act accounts' required to comply with Parts 15 and 16 of the Act and [with] the Regulations	Sections 148, 149,150C, 156, 161D and 191	Sections 3 to 6, 16, 16A and 17 and the Schedule		Regulations 2, 5 and 10 and Parts I, IIIA and IV of the Schedule	Regulations 2, 5, 6, 7 and 8 and Parts I, II and III of the Schedule
		See also sections 41, 43 and 63 of the Companies Act 1990 and section 33(4) of the Companies (Amendment)(No.2) Act 1999 (as amended)				
A2.3	Section 395	Section 148			Regulation 5(1)	Regulation 5(1)
A2.4	Section 407	Section 150C				

	UK References	ROI References				
Paragraph	**2006 Act and the 2008 Regulations (unless otherwise stated)**	**1963 Act**	**1986 Act**	**GAR 1992**	**CIR 1992**	**IUR 1996**
A2.6	Paragraph 36 of Schedule 1 to the Regulations		Paragraphs 22A and 22AA of Part IIIA the Schedule		Paragraph 46A of Part I of the Schedule	
A2.6 (Footnote 10)	The Small Companies and Groups (Accounts and Directors Report) Regulations 2008 (SI 2008/409)	There is no equivalent in Irish company law to the UK *small companies regime* or to the Small Companies and Groups (Accounts and Directors' Report) Regulations 2008. Small companies are defined in Section 8 of the 1986 Act. Please refer to the note in the introduction above. The above references to paragraphs 22A and 22AA of Part IIIA the Schedule to the 1986 act and paragraph 46A of Part I of the Schedule to the CIR 1992 apply equally to small companies as to large and medium-sized companies in Ireland.				
A2.7	Fair value measurement requirements applicable to financial instruments under the Regulations		Part IIIA of the Schedule		Paragraphs 46A, 46B, 46C and 46D of Part I of the Schedule	
A2.7	Paragraph 36(4) of Schedule 1 to the Regulations.		Paragraph 22AA of Part IIIA of the Schedule		Paragraphs 46A(4A) and 46A(4B) of Part I of the Schedule	

Paragraph	UK References	ROI References				
	2006 Act and the 2008 Regulations (unless otherwise stated)	**1963 Act**	**1986 Act**	**GAR 1992**	**CIR 1992**	**IUR 1996**
A2.8	Paragraph 22 of Schedule 1 to the Regulations		Paragraph 9 of Part II of the Schedule		Paragraph 28 of Part I of the Schedule	Paragraph 4 of Part II of the Schedule
A2.8	Paragraph 10(2) of Schedule 1 to the Regulations		Section 6		Paragraph 22 of Part I of the Schedule	Regulation 8
A2.12 and A2.14	Paragraph 13(a) of Schedule 1 to the Regulations		Section 5(c)(i)		Paragraph 19(a) of Part I of the Schedule	Regulation 7(c)(i)
A2.13	Paragraph 39 of Schedule 1 to the Regulations		Paragraph 22CA of Part IIIA of the Schedule		Paragraph 46BA of Part I of the Schedule	
A2.14	Paragraphs 40 and 40(2) of Schedule 1 to the Regulations		Paragraph 22D and 22D(2) of Part IIIA of the Schedule		Paragraph 46C and 46C(1) of Part I of the Schedule	

Appendix II: Table 1 – Areas for consideration by a qualifying entity preparing accounts in accordance with FRS 101 *Reduced Disclosure Framework*, in order to ensure compliance with the Act

	UK References	**ROI References**				
Paragraph	**2006 Act and the 2008 Regulations (unless otherwise stated)**	**1963 Act**	**1986 Act**	**GAR 1992**	**CIR 1992**	**IUR 1996**
IFRS 3	Paragraph 36(4) of Schedule 1 to the Regulations		Paragraph 22AA of Part IIIA of the Schedule		Paragraphs 46A(4A) and 46A(4B) of Part I of the Schedule	

Appendix III: Previous consultations

	UK References	**ROI References**				
Paragraph	**2006 Act and the 2008 Regulations (unless otherwise stated)**	**1963 Act**	**1986 Act**	**GAR 1992**	**CIR 1992**	**IUR 1996**
A3.11	'*small companies regime*'	There are no equivalent provisions in Irish law to the UK *small companies regime* or to the Small Companies and Groups (Accounts and Directors' Report) Regulations 2008. Small companies are defined in Section 8 of the 1986 Act. Please refer to the note above in the introduction to this table.				

FRS 102
The Financial Reporting Standard applicable in the UK and Republic of Ireland

References in this document to FRS 103 *Insurance Contracts* will not have effect until FRS 103 has been issued by the FRC.

Contents

Summary

Financial Reporting Standard 102
Financial Reporting Standard applicable in the UK and Republic of Ireland

1 Scope
2 Concepts and Pervasive Principles
3 Financial Statement Presentation
4 Statement of Financial Position
5 Statement of Comprehensive Income and Income Statement
Appendix: Example showing presentation of discontinued operations
6 Statement of Changes in Equity and Statement of Income and Retained Earnings
7 Statement of Cash Flows
8 Notes to the Financial Statements
9 Consolidated and Separate Financial Statements
10 Accounting Policies, Estimates and Errors
11 Basic Financial Instruments
12 Other Financial Instruments Issues
13 Inventories
14 Investments in Associates
15 Investments in Joint Ventures
16 Investment Property
17 Property, Plant and Equipment
18 Intangible Assets other than Goodwill
19 Business Combinations and Goodwill
20 Leases
21 Provisions and Contingencies
Appendix: Examples of recognising and measuring provisions
22 Liabilities and Equity
Appendix: Example of the issuer's accounting for convertible debt
23 Revenue
Appendix: Examples of revenue recognition
24 Government Grants
25 Borrowing Costs
26 Share-based Payment
27 Impairment of Assets
28 Employee Benefits
29 Income Tax
30 Foreign Currency Translation
31 Hyperinflation

32 Events after the End of the Reporting Period
33 Related Party Disclosures
34 Specialised Activities
Agriculture
Extractive Activities
Service Concession Arrangements
Financial Institutions
Retirement Benefit Plans: Financial Statements
Heritage Assets
Funding Commitments
Incoming Resources from Non-exchange Transactions
Public Benefit Entity Combinations
Public Benefit Entity Concessionary Loans
Appendix A: Guidance on funding commitments
Appendix B: Guidance on incoming resources from non-exchange transactions
35 Transition to this FRS

Approval by the FRC

The Accounting Council's Advice to the FRC to issue FRS 102

Appendices

I Glossary
II Significant Differences Between FRS 102 and the IFRS for SMEs
III Table of Equivalence for UK Companies Act terminology
IV Note on Legal Requirements
V Previous Consultations
VI Republic of Ireland (RoI) Legal References

Summary

(i) In 2012 and 2013 the Financial Reporting Council (FRC) revised financial reporting standards in the United Kingdom and Republic of Ireland. The revisions fundamentally reformed financial reporting, replacing almost all extant standards with three Financial Reporting Standards:

FRS 100 *Application of Financial Reporting Requirements*;
FRS 101 *Reduced Disclosure Framework*; and
FRS 102 *The Financial Reporting Standard applicable in the UK and Republic of Ireland.*

(ii) The revisions made by the FRC followed a sustained and detailed period of consultation. The FRC made these fundamental changes recognising that the introduction of International Financial Reporting Standards for listed groups in 2002 (with application from 2005) called into question the need for two sets of financial reporting standards. Evidence from consultation supported a move towards an international-based framework for financial reporting, but one that was proportionate to the needs of preparers and users.

(iii) The FRC's overriding objective in setting accounting standards is to enable users of accounts to receive high-quality understandable financial reporting proportionate to the size and complexity of the entity and users' information needs.

(iv) In meeting this objective, the FRC aims to provide succinct financial reporting standards that:

(a) have consistency with international accounting standards through the application of an IFRS-based solution unless an alternative clearly better meets the overriding objective;
(b) reflect up-to-date thinking and developments in the way entities operate and the transactions they undertake;
(c) balance consistent principles for accounting by all UK and Republic of Ireland entities with practical solutions, based on size, complexity, public interest and users' information needs;
(d) promote efficiency within groups; and
(e) are cost-effective to apply.

(v) The requirements in this Financial Reporting Standard (FRS) take into consideration the findings from the previous consultations on the future of financial reporting in the UK and Republic of Ireland that took place between 2002 and 2012.

(vi) This FRS is a single financial reporting standard that applies to the financial statements of entities that are not applying EU-adopted IFRS, FRS 101 or the FRSSE*.

THE FINANCIAL REPORTING STANDARD APPLICABLE IN THE UK AND REPUBLIC OF IRELAND AND THE IFRS FOR SMES

(vii) This FRS aims to provide entities with succinct financial reporting requirements. The requirements in this FRS are based on the International Accounting Standards Board's (IASB) International Financial Reporting Standard for Small and Medium-sized Entities (IFRS for SMEs) issued in 2009. The IFRS for SMEs is intended to apply to the general purpose financial

**This FRS does not, however apply to the preparation of 'Companies Act accounts' of certain companies under company law in the Republic of Ireland. Please refer to Appendix VI for further details.*

statements of, and other financial reporting by, entities that in many countries are referred to by a variety of terms including 'small and medium-sized', 'private' and 'non-publicly accountable'.

(viii) The Accounting Standards Board (ASB)* first consulted on the use of the IFRS for SMEs to replace extant Financial Reporting Standards in the United Kingdom and Republic of Ireland in 2006. In 2010 the ASB issued a financial reporting exposure draft (FRED 44 *Financial Reporting Standard for Medium-sized Entities*) proposing the application of the IFRS for SMEs to entities that did not have public accountability and were not eligible to apply the FRSSE. Entities with public accountability would have been required to apply EU-adopted IFRS; respondents to the proposals were not supportive of the extension of the application of EU-adopted IFRS. Based on this feedback, the ASB decided to amend the IFRS for SMEs so that it is relevant to a broader group of preparers and users.

(ix) The IFRS for SMEs is a simplification of the principles in IFRS for recognising and measuring assets, liabilities, income and expenses; in most cases it includes only the simpler accounting treatment where IFRS permit accounting options, it contains fewer disclosures and it is drafted more succinctly than IFRS. Whilst respondents to FRED 44 welcomed simplification, many did not support the removal of accounting options where those options were permitted in extant FRS. As a consequence, the ASB amended the IFRS for SMEs to include accounting options in current FRS and permitted by IFRS, but not included in the IFRS for SMEs.

(x) The ASB also issued FRED 45 *Financial Reporting Standard for Public Benefit Entities* in 2011 that addressed the accounting for some transactions and circumstances that are common to public benefit entities. Respondents to FRED 45 noted that it was difficult to identify when the requirements in the FRED should be applied. The ASB consequently decided to combine the requirements of FREDs 44 and 45 into one FRS.

(xi) The FRC has thus modified the IFRS for SMEs substantially, both in terms of the scope of entities eligible to apply it and in terms of the accounting treatments provided. To reflect this wider scope the proposed name of the standard was revised to FRS 102 *Financial Reporting Standard applicable in the UK and Republic of Ireland.*

(xii) FRS 102 is designed to apply to the general purpose financial statements and financial reporting of entities including those that are not constituted as companies and those that are not profit-oriented. General purpose financial statements are intended to focus on the common information needs of a wide range of users; shareholders, lenders, other creditors, employees and members of the public, for example.

ORGANISATION OF FRS 102

(xiii) FRS 102 is organised by topic with each topic presented in a separate numbered section. Cross-references to paragraphs are identified by section followed by paragraph number. Paragraph numbers are in the form of xx.yy, where xx is the section number and yy is the sequential paragraph number within that section. Those paragraphs that apply solely to public benefit entities are identified by the prefix 'PBE'†. In order to maintain consistency with the

**The Financial Reporting Council (FRC) became the prescribed body for issuing accounting standards on 2 July 2012; the prescribed body was previously the Accounting Standards Board (ASB). References in this section and Appendix V are made to the FRC, ASB or Accounting Council, as appropriate in terms of the time period and context of the reference.*

†*In some cases 'PBE' prefixed paragraphs also apply to other entities in a public benefit entity group.*

paragraph numbering of the IFRS for SMEs, when a paragraph from the IFRS for SMEs has been deleted and not replaced with an alternative paragraph, the phrase [not used] is given. In examples that include monetary amounts, the measuring unit is Currency Unit (abbreviated as CU).

(xiv) All the paragraphs of FRS 102 have equal authority. Some sections include appendices of implementation guidance or examples. Some of these are an integral part of the FRS while others provide guidance concerning its application; each specifies its status.

(xv) This FRS is set out in Sections 1 to 35 and the Glossary (Appendix I). Terms defined in the Glossary are in **bold type** the first time they appear in each section and sub-section within Section 34.

FRS 102
The Financial Reporting Standard applicable in the UK and Republic of Ireland

Section 1
Scope

SCOPE OF THIS FINANCIAL REPORTING STANDARD

This FRS applies to **financial statements** that are intended to give a true and fair view of a reporting entity's **financial position** and **profit or loss** (or **income and expenditure**) for a period. 1.1

The requirements of this FRS are applicable to **public benefit entities** and other entities, not just to companies. However, those paragraph numbers prefixed with 'PBE' shall only be applied by public benefit entities, and shall not be applied directly, or by analogy, by entities that are not public benefit entities, other than, where specifically directed, entities within a **public benefit entity group**. 1.2

BASIS OF PREPARATION OF FINANCIAL STATEMENTS

As stated in **FRS 100**, an entity that is required by the **IAS Regulation** (or other legislation or regulation) to prepare **consolidated financial statements** in accordance with **EU-adopted IFRS** must do so. The **individual financial statements** of such an entity, or the individual financial statements or consolidated financial statements of any other entity within the scope of FRS 100, must be prepared in accordance with the following requirements: 1.3

(a) If the financial statements are those of an entity that is eligible to apply the **FRSSE***, they may be prepared in accordance with that standard.

(b) If the financial statements are those of an entity that is not eligible to apply the FRSSE, or of an entity that is eligible to apply the FRSSE but chooses not to do so, they must† be prepared in accordance with this FRS, EU-adopted IFRS or **FRS 101**‡.

An entity whose **ordinary shares** or **potential ordinary shares** are **publicly traded**, or that files, or is in the process of filing, its financial statements with a securities commission or other regulatory organisation for the purpose of issuing ordinary shares in a public market, or an entity that chooses to disclose earnings per share, shall apply IAS 33 *Earnings per Share* (as adopted in the EU). 1.4

**The eligibility criteria for applying the FRSSE are set out in paragraph 8 of the FRSSE. One of the criteria is that the entity must be 'small' as defined in company law. Turnover and balance sheet total should be measured in accordance with the FRSSE for the purposes of establishing whether the entity is 'small'; the measurement of turnover and balance sheet total in accordance with FRS 101 or FRS 102 need not be considered.*

†Under company law in the Republic of Ireland, certain companies are permitted to prepare 'Companies Act accounts' using accounting standards other than those issued by the FRC. Please refer to Appendix VI for further details.

‡Individual financial statements that are prepared by a company in accordance with FRS 101 or FRS 102 are Companies Act individual accounts (section 395(1)(a) of the Act), whereas those prepared in accordance with EU-adopted IFRS are IAS individual accounts (section 395(1)(b) of the Act).

1.5 An entity whose debt or equity instruments are publicly traded, or that files, or is in the process of filing, its financial statements with a securities commission or other regulatory organisation for the purpose of issuing any class of instruments in a public market, or an entity that chooses to provide information described as segment information, shall apply IFRS 8 *Operating Segments* (as adopted in the EU). If an entity discloses disaggregated information, but the information does not comply with the requirements of IFRS 8, it shall not describe the information as segment information.

1.6 An entity shall apply FRS 103 *Insurance Contracts* to:

(a) **insurance contracts** (including **reinsurance contracts**) that it issues and reinsurance contracts that it holds; and
(b) **financial instruments** with a **discretionary participation feature** that it issues.

1.7 When applying IAS 33, IFRS 8 and IFRS 6 *Exploration for and Evaluation of Mineral Resources* (see paragraph 34.11), references made to other IFRSs within those standards shall be taken to be references to the relevant section or paragraph in this FRS.

REDUCED DISCLOSURES FOR SUBSIDIARIES (AND ULTIMATE PARENTS)

1.8 A **qualifying entity** (for the purposes of this FRS) which is not a **financial institution** may take advantage in its individual financial statements of the disclosure exemptions set out in paragraph 1.12. In relation to paragraph 1.12(c) for **financial liabilities** that are held at **fair value** that are either part of a trading portfolio or are **derivatives**, the qualifying entity can take advantage of those exemptions. Where the qualifying entity has financial instruments held at fair value subject to the requirements of paragraph 36(4) of Schedule 1 to the **Regulations**, it must apply the disclosure requirements of Section 11 *Basic Financial Instruments* to those financial instruments held at fair value.

1.9 A qualifying entity (for the purposes of this FRS) which is a financial institution may take advantage in its individual financial statements of the disclosure exemptions set out in paragraph 1.12, except for the disclosure exemptions from Section 11 and Section 12 *Other Financial Instruments Issues*.

1.10 A qualifying entity (for the purposes of this FRS) which is required to prepare consolidated financial statements (for example, if the entity is required by section 399 of the **Act** to prepare consolidated financial statements, and is not entitled to any of the exemptions in sections 400 to 402 of the Act), or which voluntarily chooses to do so, may not take advantage of the disclosure exemptions set out in paragraph 1.12 in its consolidated financial statements.

1.11 A qualifying entity (for the purposes of this FRS) may take advantage of the disclosure exemptions in paragraph 1.12, in accordance with paragraphs 1.8 to 1.10, provided that:

(a) Its shareholders have been notified in writing about, and do not object to, the use of the disclosure exemptions. Objections to the use of the disclosure exemptions may be served on the qualifying entity, in accordance with reasonable specified timeframes and format requirements, by a shareholder that is the immediate **parent** of the entity, or by a shareholder or shareholders holding in aggregate 5 per cent or more of the total allotted shares in the entity or more than half of the allotted shares in the entity that are not held by the immediate parent.

(b) It otherwise applies the **recognition**, **measurement** and disclosure requirements of this FRS.

(c) It discloses in the **notes** to its financial statements:

(i) a brief narrative summary of the disclosure exemptions adopted; and

(ii) the name of the parent* of the **group** in whose consolidated financial statements its financial statements are consolidated, and from where those financial statements may be obtained.

A qualifying entity (for the purposes of this FRS) may take advantage of the following disclosure exemptions: **1.12**

(a) The requirements of Section 4 *Statement of Financial Position* paragraph 4.12(a)(iv).

(b) The requirements of Section 7 *Statement of Cash Flows* and Section 3 *Financial Statement Presentation* paragraph 3.17(d).

(c) The requirements of Section 11 paragraphs 11.39 to 11.48A and Section 12 paragraphs 12.26 to 12.29 providing the equivalent disclosures required by this FRS are included in the consolidated financial statements of the group in which the entity is consolidated.

(d) The requirements of Section 26 *Share-based Payment* paragraphs 26.18(b), 26.19 to 26.21 and 26.23, provided that for a qualifying entity that is:

(i) a **subsidiary**, the share-based payment arrangement concerns equity instruments of another group entity;

(ii) an ultimate parent, the share-based payment arrangement concerns its own equity instruments and its **separate financial statements** are presented alongside the consolidated financial statements of the group;

and, in both cases, provided that the equivalent disclosures required by this FRS are included in the consolidated financial statements of the group in which the entity is consolidated.

(e) The requirement of Section 33 *Related Party Disclosures* paragraph 33.7.

Reference shall be made to the Application Guidance to FRS 100 in deciding whether the consolidated financial statements of the parent provide disclosures which are equivalent to the requirements of this FRS (ie the full requirements of this FRS when not applying the disclosure exemptions) from which relief is provided in paragraph 1.12. **1.13**

DATE FROM WHICH EFFECTIVE AND TRANSITIONAL ARRANGEMENTS

An entity shall apply this FRS for accounting periods beginning on or after 1 January 2015. Early application is permitted for accounting periods ending on or after 31 December 2012. For entities that are within the scope of a SORP, early application is permitted for accounting periods ending on or after 31 December 2012 providing it does not conflict with the requirements of a current SORP or legal requirements for the preparation of financial statements. If an entity applies this FRS before 1 January 2015 it shall disclose that fact. **1.14**

**The parent identified in the definition of the term 'qualifying entity'.*

Section 2
Concepts and Pervasive Principles

SCOPE OF THIS SECTION

2.1 This section describes the **objective of financial statements** of entities within the scope of this FRS and the qualities that make the information in the **financial statements** of entities within the scope of this FRS useful. It also sets out the concepts and basic principles underlying the financial statements of entities within the scope of this FRS.

2.1A Although this section sets out the concepts and pervasive principles underlying financial statements, in some circumstances there may be inconsistencies between the concepts and principles in this section of the FRS and the specific requirements of another section. In these circumstances the specific requirements of the other section within the FRS take precedence over this section.

OBJECTIVE OF FINANCIAL STATEMENTS

2.2 The objective of financial statements is to provide information about the **financial position**, **performance** and **cash flows** of an entity that is useful for economic decision-making by a broad range of users who are not in a position to demand reports tailored to meet their particular information needs.

2.3 Financial statements also show the results of the stewardship of management—the accountability of management for the resources entrusted to it.

QUALITATIVE CHARACTERISTICS OF INFORMATION IN FINANCIAL STATEMENTS

Understandability

2.4 The information provided in financial statements should be presented in a way that makes it comprehensible by users who have a reasonable knowledge of **business** and economic activities and accounting and a willingness to study the information with reasonable diligence. However, the need for **understandability** does not allow relevant information to be omitted on the grounds that it may be too difficult for some users to understand.

Relevance

2.5 The information provided in financial statements must be relevant to the decision-making needs of users. Information has the quality of **relevance** when it is capable of influencing the economic decisions of users by helping them evaluate past, present or future events or confirming, or correcting, their past evaluations.

Materiality

2.6 Information is **material**—and therefore has relevance—if its omission or misstatement, individually or collectively, could influence the economic decisions of users taken on the basis of the financial statements. Materiality depends on the size and nature of the omission or misstatement judged in the surrounding circumstances. The size or nature of the item, or a combination of both, could be the determining factor. However, it is inappropriate to make, or leave uncorrected, immaterial departures from this FRS to achieve a particular presentation of an entity's financial position, financial performance or cash flows.

Reliability

The information provided in financial statements must be reliable. Information is reliable when it is free from material **error** and bias and represents faithfully that which it either purports to represent or could reasonably be expected to represent. Financial statements are not free from bias (ie not neutral) if, by the selection or presentation of information, they are intended to influence the making of a decision or judgement in order to achieve a predetermined result or outcome. **2.7**

Substance over form

Transactions and other events and conditions should be accounted for and presented in accordance with their substance and not merely their legal form. This enhances the **reliability** of financial statements. **2.8**

Prudence

The uncertainties that inevitably surround many events and circumstances are acknowledged by the disclosure of their nature and extent and by the exercise of **prudence** in the preparation of the financial statements. Prudence is the inclusion of a degree of caution in the exercise of the judgements needed in making the estimates required under conditions of uncertainty, such that **assets** or **income** are not overstated and **liabilities** or **expenses** are not understated. However, the exercise of prudence does not allow the deliberate understatement of assets or income, or the deliberate overstatement of liabilities or expenses. In short, prudence does not permit bias. **2.9**

Completeness

To be reliable, the information in financial statements must be complete within the bounds of materiality and cost. An omission can cause information to be false or misleading and thus unreliable and deficient in terms of its relevance. **2.10**

Comparability

Users must be able to compare the financial statements of an entity through time to identify trends in its financial position and performance. Users must also be able to compare the financial statements of different entities to evaluate their relative financial position, performance and cash flows. Hence, the **measurement** and display of the financial effects of like transactions and other events and conditions must be carried out in a consistent way throughout an entity and over time for that entity, and in a consistent way across entities. In addition, users must be informed of the **accounting policies** employed in the preparation of the financial statements, and of any changes in those policies and the effects of such changes. **2.11**

Timeliness

To be relevant, financial information must be able to influence the economic decisions of users. **Timeliness** involves providing the information within the decision time frame. If there is undue delay in the reporting of information it may lose its **2.12** relevance. Management may need to balance the relative merits of timely reporting and the provision of reliable information. In achieving a balance between relevance and reliability, the overriding consideration is how best to satisfy the needs of users in making economic decisions.

Balance between benefit and cost

2.13 The benefits derived from information should exceed the cost of providing it. The evaluation of benefits and costs is substantially a judgemental process. Furthermore, the costs are not necessarily borne by those users who enjoy the benefits, and often the benefits of the information are enjoyed by a broad range of external users.

2.14 Financial reporting information helps capital providers make better decisions, which results in more efficient functioning of capital markets and a lower cost of capital for the economy as a whole. Individual entities also enjoy benefits, including improved access to capital markets, favourable effect on public relations, and perhaps lower costs of capital. The benefits may also include better management decisions because financial information used internally is often based at least partly on information prepared for general purpose financial reporting purposes.

FINANCIAL POSITION

2.15 The financial position of an entity is the relationship of its assets, liabilities and **equity** as of a specific date as presented in the **statement of financial position**. These are defined as follows:

(a) An asset is a resource controlled by the entity as a result of past events and from which future economic benefits are expected to flow to the entity.
(b) A liability is a present obligation of the entity arising from past events, the settlement of which is expected to result in an outflow from the entity of resources embodying economic benefits.
(c) Equity is the residual interest in the assets of the entity after deducting all its liabilities.

2.16 Some items that meet the definition of an asset or a liability may not be recognised as assets or liabilities in the statement of financial position because they do not satisfy the criteria for **recognition** in paragraphs 2.27 to 2.32. In particular, the expectation that future economic benefits will flow to or from an entity must be sufficiently certain to meet the probability criterion before an asset or liability is recognised.

Assets

2.17 The future economic benefit of an asset is its potential to contribute, directly or indirectly, to the flow of **cash** and **cash equivalents** to the entity. Those cash flows may come from using the asset or from disposing of it.

2.18 Many assets, for example **property, plant and equipment**, have a physical form. However, physical form is not essential to the existence of an asset. Some assets are intangible.

2.19 In determining the existence of an asset, the right of ownership is not essential. Thus, for example, property held on a **lease** is an asset if the entity controls the benefits that are expected to flow from the property.

Liabilities

An essential characteristic of a liability is that the entity has a present obligation to act or perform in a particular way. The obligation may be either a legal obligation or a **constructive obligation**. A legal obligation is legally enforceable as a consequence of a binding contract or statutory requirement. A constructive obligation is an obligation that derives from an entity's actions when: 2.20

(a) by an established pattern of past practice, published policies or a sufficiently specific current statement, the entity has indicated to other parties that it will accept certain responsibilities; and
(b) as a result, the entity has created a valid expectation on the part of those other parties that it will discharge those responsibilities.

The settlement of a present obligation usually involves the payment of cash, transfer of other assets, provision of services, the replacement of that obligation with another obligation, or conversion of the obligation to equity. An obligation may also be extinguished by other means, such as a creditor waiving or forfeiting its rights. 2.21

Equity

Equity is the residual interest in the assets of the entity after deducting all its liabilities. It may be sub-classified in the statement of financial position. For example, in a corporate entity, sub-classifications may include funds contributed by shareholders, retained earnings and **gains** or losses recognised in **other comprehensive income**. 2.22

PERFORMANCE

Performance is the relationship of the income and expenses of an entity during a **reporting period**. This FRS permits entities to present performance in a single financial statement (a **statement of comprehensive income**) or in two financial statements (an **income statement** and a statement of comprehensive income). **Total comprehensive income** and **profit or loss** are frequently used as measures of performance or as the basis for other measures, such as return on investment or earnings per share. Income and expenses are defined as follows: 2.23

(a) Income is increases in economic benefits during the reporting period in the form of inflows or enhancements of assets or decreases of liabilities that result in increases in equity, other than those relating to contributions from equity investors.
(b) Expenses are decreases in economic benefits during the reporting period in the form of outflows or depletions of assets or incurrences of liabilities that result in decreases in equity, other than those relating to distributions to equity investors.

The recognition of income and expenses results directly from the recognition and measurement of assets and liabilities. Criteria for the recognition of income and expenses are discussed in paragraphs 2.27 to 2.32. 2.24

Income

The definition of income encompasses both **revenue** and gains. 2.25

(a) Revenue is income that arises in the course of the ordinary activities of an entity and is referred to by a variety of names including sales, fees, interest, dividends, royalties and rent.
(b) Gains are other items that meet the definition of income but are not revenue. When gains are recognised in the statement of comprehensive income, they are usually displayed separately because knowledge of them is useful for making economic decisions.

Expenses

2.26 The definition of expenses encompasses losses as well as those expenses that arise in the course of the ordinary activities of the entity.

(a) Expenses that arise in the course of the ordinary activities of the entity include, for example, cost of sales, wages and **depreciation**. They usually take the form of an outflow or depletion of assets such as cash and cash equivalents, **inventory**, or property, plant and equipment.
(b) Losses are other items that meet the definition of expenses and may arise in the course of the ordinary activities of the entity. When losses are recognised in the statement of comprehensive income, they are usually presented separately because knowledge of them is useful for making economic decisions.

RECOGNITION OF ASSETS, LIABILITIES, INCOME AND EXPENSES

2.27 Recognition is the process of incorporating in the statement of financial position or statement of comprehensive income an item that meets the definition of an asset, liability, equity, income or expense and satisfies the following criteria:

(a) it is **probable** that any future economic benefit associated with the item will flow to or from the entity; and
(b) the item has a cost or value that can be measured reliably.

2.28 The failure to recognise an item that satisfies those criteria is not rectified by disclosure of the accounting policies used or by **notes** or explanatory material.

The probability of future economic benefit

2.29 The concept of probability is used in the first recognition criterion to refer to the degree of uncertainty that the future economic benefits associated with the item will flow to or from the entity. Assessments of the degree of uncertainty attaching to the flow of future economic benefits are made on the basis of the evidence relating to conditions at the end of the reporting period available when the financial statements are prepared. Those assessments are made individually for individually significant items, and for a group for a large population of individually insignificant items.

Reliability of measurement

2.30 The second criterion for the recognition of an item is that it possesses a cost or value that can be measured with reliability. In many cases, the cost or value of an item is known. In other cases it must be estimated. The use of reasonable estimates is an essential part of the preparation of financial statements and does not undermine their reliability. When a reasonable estimate cannot be made, the item is not recognised in the financial statements.

An item that fails to meet the recognition criteria may qualify for recognition at a later date as a result of subsequent circumstances or events. **2.31**

An item that fails to meet the criteria for recognition may nonetheless warrant disclosure in the notes or explanatory material or in supplementary schedules. This is appropriate when knowledge of the item is relevant to the evaluation of the financial position, performance and changes in financial position of an entity by the users of financial statements. **2.32**

MEASUREMENT OF ASSETS, LIABILITIES, INCOME AND EXPENSES

Measurement is the process of determining the monetary amounts at which an entity measures assets, liabilities, income and expenses in its financial statements. Measurement involves the selection of a basis of measurement. This FRS specifies which measurement basis an entity shall use for many types of assets, liabilities, income and expenses. **2.33**

Two common measurement bases are historical cost and **fair value**: **2.34**

(a) For assets, historical cost is the amount of cash or cash equivalents paid or the fair value of the consideration given to acquire the asset at the time of its acquisition. For liabilities, historical cost is the amount of proceeds of cash or cash equivalents received or the fair value of non-cash assets received in exchange for the obligation at the time the obligation is incurred, or in some circumstances (for example, **income tax**) the amounts of cash or cash equivalents expected to be paid to settle the liability in the normal course of business. Amortised historical cost is the historical cost of an asset or liability plus or minus that portion of its historical cost previously recognised as an expense or income.

(b) Fair value is the amount for which an asset could be exchanged, a liability settled, or an equity instrument granted could be exchanged, between knowledgeable, willing parties in an arm's length transaction. In the absence of any specific guidance provided in the relevant section of this FRS, where fair value measurement is permitted or required the guidance in paragraphs 11.27 to 11.32 shall be applied.

PERVASIVE RECOGNITION AND MEASUREMENT PRINCIPLES

The requirements for recognising and measuring assets, liabilities, income and expenses in this FRS are based on pervasive principles that are derived from the IASB *Framework for the Preparation and Presentation of Financial Statements** and from **EU-adopted IFRS**. In the absence of a requirement in this FRS that applies specifically to a transaction or other event or condition, paragraph 10.4 provides guidance for making a judgement and paragraph 10.5 establishes a hierarchy for an entity to follow in deciding on the appropriate accounting policy in the circumstances. The second level of that hierarchy requires an entity to look to the definitions, recognition criteria and measurement concepts for assets, liabilities, income and expenses and the pervasive principles set out in this section. **2.35**

**In 2010 the IASB issued the* Conceptual Framework for Financial Reporting, *which superseded the* Framework for the Preparation and Presentation of Financial Statements.

ACCRUAL BASIS

2.36 An entity shall prepare its financial statements, except for cash flow information, using the **accrual basis** of accounting. On the accrual basis, items are recognised as assets, liabilities, equity, income or expenses when they satisfy the definitions and recognition criteria for those items.

RECOGNITION IN FINANCIAL STATEMENTS

Assets

2.37 An entity shall recognise an asset in the statement of financial position when it is probable that the future economic benefits will flow to the entity and the asset has a cost or value that can be measured reliably. An asset is not recognised in the statement of financial position when expenditure has been incurred for which it is considered not probable that economic benefits will flow to the entity beyond the current reporting period. Instead such a transaction results in the recognition of an expense in the statement of comprehensive income (or in the income statement, if presented).

2.38 An entity shall not recognise a **contingent asset** as an asset. However, when the flow of future economic benefits to the entity is virtually certain, then the related asset is not a contingent asset, and its recognition is appropriate.

Liabilities

2.39 An entity shall recognise a liability in the statement of financial position when:

(a) the entity has an obligation at the end of the reporting period as a result of a past event;

(b) it is probable that the entity will be required to transfer resources embodying economic benefits in settlement; and

(c) the settlement amount can be measured reliably.

2.40 A **contingent liability** is either a possible but uncertain obligation or a present obligation that is not recognised because it fails to meet one or both of the conditions (b) and (c) in paragraph 2.39. An entity shall not recognise a contingent liability as a liability, except for contingent liabilities of an acquiree in a **business combination** (see Section 19 *Business Combinations and Goodwill*).

Income

2.41 The recognition of income results directly from the recognition and measurement of assets and liabilities. An entity shall recognise income in the statement of comprehensive income (or in the income statement, if presented) when an increase in future economic benefits related to an increase in an asset or a decrease of a liability has arisen that can be measured reliably.

Expenses

2.42 The recognition of expenses results directly from the recognition and measurement of assets and liabilities. An entity shall recognise expenses in the statement of comprehensive income (or in the income statement, if presented) when a decrease in future economic benefits related to a decrease in an asset or an increase of a liability has arisen that can be measured reliably.

Total comprehensive income and profit or loss

Total comprehensive income is the arithmetical difference between income and expenses. It is not a separate element of financial statements, and a separate recognition principle is not needed for it. **2.43**

Profit or loss is the arithmetical difference between income and expenses other than those items of income and expense that this FRS classifies as items of other comprehensive income. It is not a separate element of financial statements, and a separate recognition principle is not needed for it. **2.44**

Generally this FRS does not allow the recognition of items in the statement of financial position that do not meet the definition of assets or of liabilities regardless of whether they result from applying the notion commonly referred to as the 'matching concept' for measuring profit or loss. **2.45**

MEASUREMENT AT INITIAL RECOGNITION

At initial recognition, an entity shall measure assets and liabilities at historical cost unless this FRS requires initial measurement on another basis such as fair value. **2.46**

SUBSEQUENT MEASUREMENT

Financial assets and financial liabilities

An entity measures basic **financial assets** and basic **financial liabilities** at **amortised cost** less impairment except for: **2.47**

(a) investments in non-convertible preference shares and non-puttable ordinary and preference shares that are **publicly traded** or whose fair value can otherwise be measured reliably, which are measured at fair value with changes in fair value recognised in profit or loss; and
(b) any financial instruments that upon their initial recognition were designated by the entity as at fair value through profit or loss.

An entity generally measures all other financial assets and financial liabilities at fair value, with changes in fair value recognised in profit or loss, unless this FRS requires or permits measurement on another basis such as cost or amortised cost. **2.48**

Non-financial assets

Most non-financial assets that an entity initially recognised at historical cost are subsequently measured on other measurement bases. For example: **2.49**

(a) An entity measures property, plant and equipment using either the cost model or the revaluation model.
(b) An entity measures inventories at the lower of cost and selling price less costs to complete and sell.

Measurement of assets at amounts lower than initial historical cost is intended to ensure that an asset is not measured at an amount greater than the entity expects to recover from the sale or use of that asset.

2.50 For certain types of non-financial assets, this FRS permits or requires measurement at fair value. For example:

(a) Investments in **associates** and **joint ventures** that an entity measures at fair value (see paragraphs 14.4(b) and 14.4B, and 15.9(b) and 15.9B respectively).
(b) **Investment property** that an entity measures at fair value (see paragraph 16.7).
(c) **Biological assets** that an entity measures at fair value less estimated costs to sell in accordance with the fair value model (see paragraph 34.3A(a)) and **agricultural produce** that an entity measures, at the point of harvest, at fair value less estimated costs to sell in accordance with either the fair value model (see paragraph 34.3A(a)) or cost model (see paragraph 34.9).
(d) Property, plant and equipment that an entity measures in accordance with the revaluation model (see paragraph 17.15B).
(e) **Intangible assets** that an entity measures in accordance with the revaluation model (see paragraph 18.18B).

Liabilities other than financial liabilities

2.51 Most liabilities other than financial liabilities are measured at the best estimate of the amount that would be required to settle the obligation at the **reporting date**.

OFFSETTING

2.52 An entity shall not offset assets and liabilities, or income and expenses, unless required or permitted by an FRS.

(a) Measuring assets net of valuation allowances (for example, allowances for inventory obsolescence and allowances for uncollectible receivables) is not offsetting.
(b) If an entity's normal **operating activities** do not include buying and selling **fixed assets**, including investments and operating assets, then the entity reports gains and losses on disposal of such assets by deducting from the proceeds on disposal the **carrying amount** of the asset and related selling expenses.

Section 3
Financial Statement Presentation

SCOPE OF THIS SECTION

This section explains **fair presentation** of **financial statements**, what compliance with this FRS requires, and what is a complete set of financial statements. **3.1**

FAIR PRESENTATION

Financial statements shall present fairly the **financial position**, financial **performance** and **cash flows** of an entity. Fair presentation requires the faithful representation of the effects of transactions, other events and conditions in accordance with the definitions and **recognition** criteria for **assets**, **liabilities**, **income** and **expenses** set out in Section 2 *Concepts and Pervasive Principles*. **3.2**

(a) The application of this FRS, with additional disclosure when necessary, is presumed to result in financial statements that achieve a fair presentation of the financial position, financial performance and cash flows of entities within the scope of this FRS.

(b) [Not used]

The additional disclosures referred to in (a) are necessary when compliance with the specific requirements in this FRS is insufficient to enable users to understand the effect of particular transactions, other events and conditions on the entity's financial position and financial performance.

COMPLIANCE WITH THIS FRS

An entity whose financial statements comply with this FRS shall make an explicit and unreserved statement of such compliance in the **notes**. Financial statements shall not be described as complying with this FRS unless they comply with all the requirements of this FRS. **3.3**

A **public benefit entity** that applies the 'PBE' prefixed paragraphs shall make an explicit and unreserved statement that it is a public benefit entity. **PBE3.3A**

In the extremely rare circumstances when management concludes that compliance with this FRS would be so misleading that it would conflict with the **objective of financial statements** of entities within the scope of this FRS set out in Section 2, the entity shall depart from that requirement in the manner set out in paragraph 3.5. **3.4**

When an entity departs from a requirement of this FRS in accordance with paragraph 3.4, or from a requirement of applicable legislation, it shall disclose the following: **3.5**

(a) that management has concluded that the financial statements present fairly the entity's financial position, financial performance and cash flows;

(b) that it has complied with this FRS or applicable legislation, except that it has departed from a particular requirement of this FRS or applicable legislation to *achieve a fair presentation*; and

(c) the nature of the departure, including the treatment that this FRS or applicable legislation would require, the reason why that treatment would be so misleading in the circumstances that it would conflict with the objective of financial statements set out in Section 2, and the treatment adopted*.

3.6 When an entity has departed from a requirement of this FRS or applicable legislation in a prior period, and that departure affects the amounts recognised in the financial statements for the current period, it shall make the disclosures set out in paragraph 3.5(c).

3.7 [Not used]

GOING CONCERN

3.8 When preparing financial statements, the management of an entity using this FRS shall make an assessment of the entity's ability to continue as a **going concern**. An entity is a going concern unless management either intends to liquidate the entity or to cease trading, or has no realistic alternative but to do so. In assessing whether the going concern assumption is appropriate, management takes into account all available information about the future, which is at least, but is not limited to, twelve months from the date when the financial statements are authorised for issue.

3.9 When management is aware, in making its assessment, of **material** uncertainties related to events or conditions that cast significant doubt upon the entity's ability to continue as a going concern, the entity shall disclose those uncertainties. When an entity does not prepare financial statements on a going concern basis, it shall disclose that fact, together with the basis on which it prepared the financial statements and the reason why the entity is not regarded as a going concern.

FREQUENCY OF REPORTING

3.10 An entity shall present a complete set of financial statements (including comparative information as set out in paragraph 3.14) at least annually. When the end of an entity's **reporting period** changes and the annual financial statements are presented for a period longer or shorter than one year, the entity shall disclose the following:

(a) that fact;
(b) the reason for using a longer or shorter period; and
(c) the fact that comparative amounts presented in the financial statements (including the related notes) are not entirely comparable.

CONSISTENCY OF PRESENTATION

3.11 An entity shall retain the presentation and classification of items in the financial statements from one period to the next unless:

(a) it is apparent, following a significant change in the nature of the entity's operations or a review of its financial statements, that another presentation or classification would be more appropriate having regard to the criteria for the selection and application of **accounting policies** in Section 10 *Accounting Policies, Estimates and Errors*; or

For companies sections 396(5) and 404(5) of the Companies Act 2006 require that 'If in special circumstances compliance with any of [the Regulations and any other provisions made by or under the Act] is inconsistent with the requirement to give a true and fair view, the directors must depart from that provision to the extent necessary to give a true and fair view. Particulars of any such departure, the reasons for it and its effect must be given in a note to the accounts.'

(b) this FRS, or another applicable FRS or FRC Abstract, requires a change in presentation.

When the presentation or classification of items in the financial statements is changed, an entity shall reclassify comparative amounts unless the reclassification is **impracticable**. When comparative amounts are reclassified, an entity shall disclose the following: 3.12

(a) the nature of the reclassification;
(b) the amount of each item or class of items that is reclassified; and
(c) the reason for the reclassification.

If it is impracticable to reclassify comparative amounts, an entity shall disclose why reclassification was not practicable. 3.13

COMPARATIVE INFORMATION

Except when this FRS permits or requires otherwise, an entity shall present comparative information in respect of the preceding period for all amounts presented in the current period's financial statements. An entity shall include comparative information for narrative and descriptive information when it is relevant to an understanding of the current period's financial statements. 3.14

MATERIALITY AND AGGREGATION

An entity shall present separately each material class of similar items. An entity shall present separately items of a dissimilar nature or function unless they are immaterial. 3.15

Financial statements result from processing large numbers of transactions or other events that are aggregated into classes according to their nature or function. The final stage in the process of aggregation and classification is the presentation of condensed and classified data, which form line items in the financial statements. If a line item is not individually material, it is aggregated with other items either in those statements or in the notes. An item that may not warrant separate presentation in those statements may warrant separate presentation in the notes. 3.16

An entity need not provide a specific disclosure required by this FRS if the information is not material. 3.16A

COMPLETE SET OF FINANCIAL STATEMENTS

A complete set of financial statements of an entity shall include all of the following: 3.17

(a) a **statement of financial position** as at the **reporting date**;
(b) either:
    (i) a single **statement of comprehensive income** for the reporting period displaying all items of income and expense recognised during the period including those items recognised in determining **profit or loss** (which is a subtotal in the statement of comprehensive income) and items of **other comprehensive income**; or
    (ii) a separate **income statement** and a separate statement of comprehensive income. If an entity chooses to present both an income statement and a statement of comprehensive income, the statement of comprehensive income begins with profit or loss and then displays the items of other comprehensive income;

(c) a **statement of changes in equity** for the reporting period;
(d) a **statement of cash flows** for the reporting period; and
(e) notes, comprising a summary of significant accounting policies and other explanatory information.

3.18 If the only changes to **equity** during the periods for which financial statements are presented arise from profit or loss, payment of dividends, corrections of prior period **errors**, and changes in accounting policy, the entity may present a single **statement of income and retained earnings** in place of the statement of comprehensive income and statement of changes in equity (see paragraph 6.4).

3.19 If an entity has no items of other comprehensive income in any of the periods for which financial statements are presented, it may present only an income statement, or it may present a statement of comprehensive income in which the 'bottom line' is labelled 'profit or loss'.

3.20 Because paragraph 3.14 requires comparative amounts in respect of the previous period for all amounts presented in the financial statements, a complete set of financial statements means that an entity shall present, as a minimum, two of each of the required financial statements and related notes.

3.21 In a complete set of financial statements, an entity shall present each financial statement with equal prominence.

3.22 An entity may use titles for the financial statements other than those used in this FRS as long as they are not misleading.

IDENTIFICATION OF THE FINANCIAL STATEMENTS

3.23 An entity shall clearly identify each of the financial statements and the notes and distinguish them from other information in the same document. In addition, an entity shall display the following information prominently, and repeat it when necessary for an understanding of the information presented:

(a) the name of the reporting entity and any change in its name since the end of the preceding reporting period;
(b) whether the financial statements cover the individual entity or a group of entities;
(c) the date of the end of the reporting period and the period covered by the financial statements;
(d) the **presentation currency**, as defined in Section 30 *Foreign Currency Translation*; and
(e) the level of rounding, if any, used in presenting amounts in the financial statements.

3.24 An entity shall disclose the following in the notes:

(a) the legal form of the entity, its country of incorporation and the address of its registered office (or principal place of business, if different from the registered office); and
(b) a description of the nature of the entity's operations and its principal activities, unless this is disclosed in the business review (or similar statement) accompanying the financial statements.

PRESENTATION OF INFORMATION NOT REQUIRED BY THIS FRS

This FRS does not address presentation of **interim financial reports**. An entity that prepares such reports shall describe the basis for preparing and presenting the information. 3.25

Section 4
Statement of Financial Position

SCOPE OF THIS SECTION

4.1 This section sets out the information that is to be presented in a **statement of financial position** and how to present it. The statement of financial position (which is referred to as the balance sheet in the **Act**) presents an entity's **assets, liabilities** and **equity** as of a specific date—the end of the **reporting period**. This section applies to all entities, whether or not they report under the Act. Entities that do not report under the Act should comply with the requirements of this section, and with the **Regulations** (or, where applicable, the **LLP Regulations**) where referred to in this section, except to the extent that these requirements are not permitted by any statutory framework under which such entities report.

INFORMATION TO BE PRESENTED IN THE STATEMENT OF FINANCIAL POSITION

4.2 An entity shall present a statement of financial position in accordance with one of the following requirements for a balance sheet:

(a) Part 1 *General Rules and Formats* of Schedule 1 to the Regulations.
(b) Part 1 *General Rules and Formats* of Schedule 2 to the Regulations.
(c) Part 1 *General Rules and Formats* of Schedule 3 to the Regulations.
(d) Part 1 *General Rules and Formats* of Schedule 1 to the LLP Regulations.

The consolidated statement of financial position of a **group** shall be presented in accordance with the requirements for a consolidated balance sheet in Schedule 6 to the Regulations or Schedule 3 to the LLP Regulations.

4.3 An entity shall present additional line items, headings and subtotals in the statement of financial position when such presentation is relevant to an understanding of the entity's **financial position**.

Debtors due after more than one year

4.4 [Not used]

4.4A In instances where the amount of debtors due after more than one year is so **material** in the context of the total net current assets that in the absence of disclosure of the debtors due after more than one year on the face of the statement of financial position readers may misinterpret the **financial statements**, the amount should be disclosed on the face of the statement of financial position within **current assets**. In most cases it will be satisfactory to disclose the amount due after more than one year in the **notes** to the financial statements.

4.5 [Not used]

4.6 [Not used]

Creditors: amounts falling due within one year

An entity shall classify a creditor as due within one year when the entity does not have an unconditional right, at the end of the reporting period, to defer settlement of the creditor for at least twelve months after the **reporting date**. **4.7**

[Not used] **4.8**

INFORMATION TO BE PRESENTED EITHER IN THE STATEMENT OF FINANCIAL POSITION OR IN THE NOTES

[Not used] **4.9**

[Not used] **4.10**

[Not used] **4.11**

An entity with share capital shall disclose the following, either in the statement of financial position or in the notes: **4.12**

(a) For each class of share capital:

(i) [Not used]
(ii) The number of shares issued and fully paid, and issued but not fully paid.
(iii) Par value per share, or that the shares have no par value.
(iv) A reconciliation of the number of shares outstanding at the beginning and at the end of the period. This reconciliation need not be presented for prior periods.
(v) The rights, preferences and restrictions attaching to that class including restrictions on the distribution of dividends and the repayment of capital.
(vi) Shares in the entity held by the entity or by its **subsidiaries**, **associates**, or **joint ventures**.
(vii) Shares reserved for issue under options and contracts for the sale of shares, including the terms and amounts.

(b) A description of each reserve within equity.

An entity without share capital, such as a partnership or trust, shall disclose information equivalent to that required by paragraph 4.12(a), showing changes during the period in each category of equity, and the rights, preferences and restrictions attaching to each category of equity. **4.13**

INFORMATION TO BE PRESENTED IN THE NOTES

If, at the reporting date, an entity has a binding sale agreement for a major disposal of assets, or a **disposal group**, the entity shall disclose the following information: **4.14**

(a) a description of the asset(s) or the disposal group;
(b) a description of the facts and circumstances of the sale; and
(c) the **carrying amount** of the assets or, for a disposal group, the carrying amounts of the underlying assets and liabilities.

Section 5
Statement of Comprehensive Income and Income Statement

SCOPE OF THIS SECTION

5.1 This section requires an entity to present its **total comprehensive income** for a period—ie its financial **performance** for the period—in one or two statements. It sets out the information that is to be presented in those statements and how to present it. This section applies to all entities, whether or not they report under the **Act**. Entities that do not report under the Act should comply with the requirements of this section, and with the **Regulations** (or, where applicable, the **LLP Regulations**) where referred to in this section, except to the extent that these requirements are not permitted by any statutory framework under which such entities report. If an entity meets specified conditions and chooses to do so, it may present a **statement of income and retained earnings** as set out in Section 6 *Statement of Change in Equity and Statement of Income and Retained Earnings.*

PRESENTATION OF TOTAL COMPREHENSIVE INCOME

5.2 An entity shall present its total comprehensive income for a period either:

(a) in a single **statement of comprehensive income**, in which case the statement of comprehensive income presents all items of **income** and **expense** recognised in the period; or

(b) in two statements—an **income statement** (which is referred to as the profit and loss account in the Act) and a statement of comprehensive income—in which case the income statement presents all items of income and expense recognised in the period except those that are recognised in total comprehensive income outside of **profit or loss** as permitted or required by this FRS.

5.3 A change from the single-statement approach to the two-statement approach, or vice versa, is a change in **accounting policy** to which Section 10 *Accounting Policies, Estimates and Errors* applies.

Single-statement approach

5.4 [Not used]

5.5 An entity shall present, in the statement of comprehensive income, the items to be included in a profit and loss account in accordance with one of the following requirements:

(a) Part 1 *General Rules and Formats* of Schedule 1 to the Regulations;
(b) Part 1 *General Rules and Formats* of Schedule 2 to the Regulations;
(c) Part 1 *General Rules and Formats* of Schedule 3 to the Regulations; or
(d) Part 1 *General Rules and Formats* of Schedule 1 to the LLP Regulations.

The consolidated statement of comprehensive income of a **group** shall be presented in accordance with the requirements for a consolidated profit and loss account of Schedule 6 to the Regulations or Schedule 3 to the LLP Regulations.

5.5A In addition an entity shall include, in the statement of comprehensive income, line items that present the following amounts for the period:

(a) Classified by nature (excluding amounts in (b)), the components of **other comprehensive income** recognised as part of total comprehensive income outside profit or loss as permitted or required by this FRS. An entity may present the components of other comprehensive income either:

(i) net of related tax effects; or
(ii) before the related tax effects with one amount shown for the aggregate amount of **income tax** relating to those components.

(b) Its share of the other comprehensive income of **associates** and **jointly controlled entities** accounted for by the equity method.
(c) Total comprehensive income.

An entity shall present the following items as allocations of profit or loss and other comprehensive income in the statement of comprehensive income for the period: **5.6**

(a) Profit or loss for the period attributable to:

(i) **non-controlling interest**; and
(ii) **owners** of the **parent**.

(b) Total comprehensive income for the period attributable to:

(i) non-controlling interest; and
(ii) owners of the parent.

Two-statement approach

Under the two-statement approach, an entity shall present in an income statement, the items to be included in a profit and loss account in accordance with one of the following requirements: **5.7**

(a) Part 1 *General Rules and Formats* of Schedule 1 to the Regulations;
(b) Part 1 *General Rules and Formats* of Schedule 2 to the Regulations;
(c) Part 1 *General Rules and Formats* of Schedule 3 to the Regulations; or
(d) Part 1 *General Rules and Formats* of Schedule 1 to the LLP Regulations.

The consolidated income statement of a group shall be presented in accordance with the requirements for a consolidated profit and loss account of Schedule 6 to the Regulations or Schedule 3 to the LLP Regulations.

If an entity presents profit or loss in an income statement, it shall present the information required in paragraph 5.6(a) in that statement. **5.7A**

The statement of comprehensive income shall begin with profit or loss as its first line and shall display, as a minimum, line items that present the amounts in paragraphs 5.5A and 5.6(b) for the period. **5.7B**

Requirements applicable to both approaches

In addition to the requirements of paragraphs 5.5 or 5.7, as a minimum, **turnover** must be presented on the face of the income statement (or statement of comprehensive income if presented). **5.7C**

An entity shall also disclose on the face of the income statement (or statement of comprehensive income if presented) an amount comprising the total of: **5.7D**

(a) the post-tax profit or loss of **discontinued operations**; and
(b) the post-tax gain or loss attributable to the impairment or on the disposal of the **assets** or **disposal group(s)** constituting discontinued operations.

A line-by-line analysis shall be presented in the income statement (or statement of comprehensive income if presented), in a column identified as relating to discontinued operations, ie separately from continuing operations; a total column shall also be presented.

5.7E An entity shall re-present the disclosures in paragraph 5.7D for prior periods presented in the **financial statements** so that the disclosures relate to all operations that have been discontinued by the end of the **reporting period** for the latest period presented.

5.8 Under this FRS, the effects of corrections of **material errors** and changes in accounting policies are presented as retrospective adjustments of prior periods rather than as part of profit or loss in the period in which they arise (see Section 10).

5.9 An entity shall present additional line items, headings and subtotals in the statement of comprehensive income (and in the income statement, if presented), when such presentation is relevant to an understanding of the entity's financial performance.

5.9A When items included in total comprehensive income are material, an entity shall disclose their nature and amount separately, in the statement of comprehensive income (and in the income statement, if presented) or in the **notes**.

5.9B This FRS does not require disclosure of 'operating profit'. However, if an entity elects to disclose the results of **operating activities** the entity should ensure that the amount disclosed is representative of activities that would normally be regarded as 'operating'. For example, it would be inappropriate to exclude items clearly related to operations (such as inventory write-downs and restructuring and relocation expenses) because they occur irregularly or infrequently or are unusual in amount. Similarly, it would be inappropriate to exclude items on the grounds that they do not involve **cash flows**, such as **depreciation** and **amortisation** expenses.

Ordinary activities and extraordinary items

5.10 Ordinary activities are any activities which are undertaken by a reporting entity as part of its business and such related activities in which the reporting entity engages in furtherance of, incidental to, or arising from, these activities. Ordinary activities include any effects on the reporting entity of any event in the various environments in which it operates, including the political, regulatory, economic and geographical environments, irrespective of the frequency or unusual nature of the events.

5.10A Extraordinary items are material items possessing a high degree of abnormality which arise from events or transactions that fall outside the ordinary activities of the reporting entity and which are not expected to recur. The additional line items required to be presented by paragraph 5.9 and material items required to be disclosed by paragraph 5.9A, are not extraordinary items when they arise from the ordinary activities of the entity. Extraordinary items do not include prior period items merely because they relate to a prior period.

ANALYSIS OF EXPENSES

5.11 Unless otherwise required under the Regulations, an entity shall present an analysis of expenses using a classification based on either the nature of expenses or the function of expenses within the entity, whichever provides information that is reliable and more relevant.

Analysis by nature of expense

(a) Under this method of classification, expenses are aggregated in the statement of comprehensive income (or in the income statement, under the two-statement approach) according to their nature (eg depreciation, raw materials and consumables and staff costs), and are not reallocated among various functions within the entity.

Analysis by function of expense

(b) Under this method of classification, expenses are aggregated according to their function as part of cost of sales or, for example, the costs of distribution or administrative activities.

Appendix to Section 5

EXAMPLE SHOWING PRESENTATION OF DISCONTINUED OPERATIONS

This appendix accompanies, but is not part of, Section 5. It provides guidance on applying the requirements of Section 5 paragraph 5.7D for presenting discontinued operations. The example illustrates the presentation of comprehensive income in a single statement and the classification of expenses within profit by function. A columnar format is used in order to present a single line item as required by paragraph 5.7D, while still complying with the requirements of the Act to show totals for ordinary activities of items such as turnover, profit or loss before taxation and tax.

Statement of comprehensive income

for the year ended 31 December 20X1

	20X1			20X0		
	Continuing operations	**Discontinued operations**	**Total**	Continuing operations (as restated)	Discontinued operations (as restated)	Total
	CU	**CU**	**CU**	CU	CU	CU
Turnover	**4,200**	**1,232**	**5,432**	3,201	1,500	4,701
Cost of Sales	**(2,591)**	**(1,104)**	**(3,695)**	(2,281)	(1,430)	(3,711)
Gross profit	**1,609**	**128**	**1,737**	920	70	990
Administrative expenses	**(452)**	**(110)**	**(562)**	(418)	(120)	(538)
Other operating income	**212**	–	**212**	198	–	198
Profit on disposal of operations	–	**301**	**301**	–	–	–
Operating profit	**1,369**	**319**	**1,688**	700	(50)	650
Interest receivable and similar income	**14**	–	**14**	16	–	16
Interest payable and similar charges	**(208)**	–	**(208)**	(208)	–	(208)
Profit on ordinary activities before tax	**1,175**	**319**	**1,494**	508	(50)	458
Taxation	**(390)**	**(4)**	**(394)**	(261)	3	(258)
Profit on ordinary activities after taxation and profit for the financial year	**785**	**315**	**1,100**	247	(47)	200
Other comprehensive income						
Actuarial losses on defined benefit pension plans			**(108)**			(68)
Deferred tax movement relating to actuarial losses			**28**			18
Total comprehensive income for the year			**1,020**			150

Section 6
Statement of Changes in Equity and Statement of Income and Retained Earnings

SCOPE OF THIS SECTION

This section sets out requirements for presenting the changes in an entity's **equity** for a period, either in a statement of changes in equity or, if specified conditions are met and an entity chooses, in a **statement of income and retained earnings**. 6.1

STATEMENT OF CHANGES IN EQUITY

Purpose

The statement of changes in equity presents an entity's **profit or loss** for a **reporting period**, **other comprehensive income** for the period, the effects of changes in **accounting policies** and corrections of **material errors** recognised in the period, and the amounts of investments by, and dividends and other distributions to, equity investors during the period. 6.2

Information to be presented in the statement of changes in equity

An entity shall present a statement of changes in equity showing in the statement: 6.3

(a) **total comprehensive income** for the period, showing separately the total amounts attributable to **owners** of the **parent** and to **non-controlling interests**;
(b) for each component of equity, the effects of **retrospective application** or retrospective restatement recognised in accordance with Section 10 *Accounting Policies, Estimates and Errors*; and
(c) for each component of equity, a reconciliation between the **carrying amount** at the beginning and the end of the period, separately disclosing changes resulting from:
    (i) profit or loss;
    (ii) other comprehensive income; and
    (iii) the amounts of investments by, and dividends and other distributions to, owners, showing separately issues of shares, purchase of own share transactions, dividends and other distributions to owners, and changes in ownership interests in **subsidiaries** that do not result in a loss of **control**.

Information to be presented in the statement of changes in equity or in the notes

For each component of equity, an entity shall present, either in the statement of changes in equity or in the **notes**, an analysis of other comprehensive income by item (see paragraph 6.3(c)(ii)). 6.3A

STATEMENT OF INCOME AND RETAINED EARNINGS

Purpose

The statement of income and retained earnings presents an entity's profit or loss and changes in retained earnings for a reporting period. Paragraph 3.18 permits an entity to present a statement of income and retained earnings in place of a **statement of comprehensive income** and a statement of changes in equity if the only changes to its equity during the periods for which **financial statements** are presented arise from 6.4

profit or loss, payment of dividends, corrections of prior period material errors, and changes in accounting policy.

Information to be presented in the statement of income and retained earnings

6.5 An entity shall present, in the statement of income and retained earnings, the following items in addition to the information required by Section 5 *Statement of Comprehensive Income and Income Statement*:

(a) retained earnings at the beginning of the reporting period;
(b) dividends declared and paid or payable during the period;
(c) restatements of retained earnings for corrections of prior period material errors;
(d) restatements of retained earnings for changes in accounting policy; and
(e) retained earnings at the end of the reporting period.

Section 7
Statement of Cash Flows

SCOPE OF THIS SECTION

This section sets out the information that is to be presented in a **statement of cash flows** and how to present it. The statement of cash flows provides information about the changes in **cash** and **cash equivalents** of an entity for a **reporting period**, showing separately changes from **operating activities, investing activities** and **financing activities**. 7.1

This section and paragraph 3.17(d) do not apply to: 7.1A

(a) mutual life assurance companies;
(b) **retirement benefit plans**; or
(c) investment funds that meet all the following conditions:
 (i) substantially all of the entity's investments are highly liquid;
 (ii) substantially all of the entity's investments are carried at market value; and
 (iii) the entity provides a statement of changes in net assets.

CASH EQUIVALENTS

Cash equivalents are short-term, highly liquid investments that are readily convertible to known amounts of cash and that are subject to an insignificant risk of changes in value. Therefore, an investment normally qualifies as a cash equivalent only when it has a short maturity of, say, three months or less from the date of acquisition. Bank overdrafts are normally considered financing activities similar to borrowings. However, if they are repayable on demand and form an integral part of an entity's cash management, bank overdrafts are a component of cash and cash equivalents. 7.2

INFORMATION TO BE PRESENTED IN THE STATEMENT OF CASH FLOWS

An entity shall present a statement of cash flows that presents **cash flows** for a reporting period classified by operating activities, investing activities and financing activities. 7.3

Operating activities

Operating activities are the principal revenue-producing activities of the entity. Therefore, cash flows from operating activities generally result from the transactions and other events and conditions that enter into the determination of **profit or loss**. Examples of cash flows from operating activities are: 7.4

(a) cash receipts from the sale of goods and the rendering of services;
(b) cash receipts from royalties, fees, commissions and other revenue;
(c) cash payments to suppliers for goods and services;
(d) cash payments to and on behalf of employees;
(e) cash payments or refunds of **income tax**, unless they can be specifically identified with financing and investing activities;
(f) cash receipts and payments from investments, loans and other contracts held for dealing or trading purposes, which are similar to **inventory** acquired specifically for resale; and

(g) cash advances and loans made to other parties by **financial institutions**.

Some transactions, such as the sale of an item of plant by a manufacturing entity, may give rise to a **gain** or loss that is included in profit or loss. However, the cash flows relating to such transactions are cash flows from investing activities.

Investing activities

7.5 Investing activities are the acquisition and disposal of long-term assets and other investments not included in cash equivalents. Examples of cash flows arising from investing activities are:

(a) cash payments to acquire **property, plant and equipment** (including self-constructed property, plant and equipment), **intangible assets** and other long-term assets. These payments include those relating to capitalised development costs and self-constructed property, plant and equipment;
(b) cash receipts from sales of property, plant and equipment, intangibles and other long-term assets;
(c) cash payments to acquire **equity** or debt instruments of other entities and interests in **joint ventures** (other than payments for those instruments classified as cash equivalents or held for dealing or trading);
(d) cash receipts from sales of equity or debt instruments of other entities and interests in joint ventures (other than receipts for those instruments classified as cash equivalents or held for dealing or trading);
(e) cash advances and loans made to other parties (except those made by financial institutions – see paragraph 7.4(g));
(f) cash receipts from the repayment of advances and loans made to other parties;
(g) cash payments for futures contracts, forward contracts, option contracts and swap contracts, except when the contracts are held for dealing or trading, or the payments are classified as financing activities; and
(h) cash receipts from futures contracts, forward contracts, option contracts and swap contracts, except when the contracts are held for dealing or trading, or the receipts are classified as financing activities.

When a contract is accounted for as a hedge (see Section 12 *Other Financial Instruments Issues*), an entity shall classify the cash flows of the contract in the same manner as the cash flows of the item being hedged.

Financing activities

7.6 Financing activities are activities that result in changes in the size and composition of the contributed equity and borrowings of an entity. Examples of cash flows arising from financing activities are:

(a) cash proceeds from issuing shares or other equity instruments;
(b) cash payments to **owners** to acquire or redeem the entity's shares;
(c) cash proceeds from issuing debentures, loans, notes, bonds, mortgages and other short-term or long-term borrowings;
(d) cash repayments of amounts borrowed; and
(e) cash payments by a lessee for the reduction of the outstanding **liability** relating to a **finance lease**.

REPORTING CASH FLOWS FROM OPERATING ACTIVITIES

An entity shall present cash flows from operating activities using either: **7.7**

(a) the indirect method, whereby profit or loss is adjusted for the effects of non-cash transactions, any deferrals or accruals of past or future operating cash receipts or payments, and items of **income** or **expense** associated with investing or financing cash flows; or

(b) the direct method, whereby major classes of gross cash receipts and gross cash payments are disclosed.

Indirect method

Under the indirect method, the net cash flow from operating activities is determined by adjusting profit or loss for the effects of: **7.8**

(a) changes during the period in inventories and operating receivables and payables;

(b) non-cash items such as **depreciation**, **provisions**, **deferred tax**, accrued income (expenses) not yet received (paid) in cash, unrealised foreign currency gains and losses, undistributed profits of **associates**, and **non-controlling interests**; and

(c) all other items for which the cash effects relate to investing or financing.

Direct method

Under the direct method, net cash flow from operating activities is presented by disclosing information about major classes of gross cash receipts and gross cash payments. Such information may be obtained either: **7.9**

(a) from the accounting records of the entity; or

(b) by adjusting sales, cost of sales and other items in the **statement of comprehensive income** (or the **income statement**, if presented) for:
   (i) changes during the period in inventories and operating receivables and payables;
   (ii) other non-cash items; and
   (iii) other items for which the cash effects are investing or financing cash flows.

REPORTING CASH FLOWS FROM INVESTING AND FINANCING ACTIVITIES

An entity shall present separately major classes of gross cash receipts and gross cash payments arising from investing and financing activities, except to the extent that net presentation is permitted by paragraphs 7.10A to 7.10E. The aggregate cash flows arising from acquisitions and from disposals of **subsidiaries** or other business units shall be presented separately and classified as investing activities. **7.10**

REPORTING CASH FLOWS ON A NET BASIS

Cash flows arising from the following operating, investing or financing activities may be reported on a net basis: **7.10A**

(a) cash receipts and payments on behalf of customers when the cash flows reflect the activities of the customer rather than those of the entity; and

(b) cash receipts and payments for items in which the turnover is quick, the amounts are large, and the maturities are short.

7.10B Examples of cash receipts and payments referred to in paragraph 7.10A(a) are:

(a) the acceptance and repayment of demand deposits of a bank;
(b) funds held for customers by an investment entity; and
(c) rents collected on behalf of, and paid over to, the owners of properties.

7.10C Examples of cash receipts and payments referred to in paragraph 7.10A(b) are advances made for, and the repayment of:

(a) principal amounts relating to credit card customers;
(b) the purchase and sale of investments; and
(c) other short-term borrowings, for example, those which have a maturity period of three months or less.

7.10D Financial institutions may report cash flows described in paragraph 34.33 on a net basis.

7.10E A financial institution that undertakes the business of effecting or carrying out **insurance contracts**, other than mutual life assurance companies scoped out of this section in paragraph 7.1A(a), should include the cash flows of their long-term business only to the extent of cash transferred and available to meet the obligations of the company or group as a whole.

FOREIGN CURRENCY CASH FLOWS

7.11 An entity shall record cash flows arising from transactions in a foreign currency in the entity's **functional currency** by applying to the foreign currency amount the exchange rate between the functional currency and the foreign currency at the date of the cash flow or an exchange rate that approximates the actual rate (for example, a weighted average exchange rate for the period).

7.12 An entity shall translate cash flows of a foreign subsidiary at the exchange rate between the entity's functional currency and the foreign currency at the date of the cash flow or at an exchange rate that approximates the actual rate (for example, a weighted average exchange rate for the period).

7.13 Unrealised gains and losses arising from changes in foreign currency exchange rates are not cash flows. However, to reconcile cash and cash equivalents at the beginning and the end of the period, the effect of exchange rate changes on cash and cash equivalents held or due in a foreign currency must be presented in the statement of cash flows. Therefore, the entity shall remeasure cash and cash equivalents held during the reporting period (such as amounts of foreign currency held and foreign currency bank accounts) at period-end exchange rates. The entity shall present the resulting unrealised gain or loss separately from cash flows from operating, investing and financing activities.

INTEREST AND DIVIDENDS

7.14 An entity shall present separately cash flows from interest and dividends received and paid. The entity shall classify these cash flows consistently from period to period as operating, investing or financing activities.

7.15 An entity may classify interest paid and interest and dividends received as operating cash flows because they are included in profit or loss. Alternatively, the entity may classify interest paid and interest and dividends received as financing cash flows and investing cash flows respectively, because they are costs of obtaining financial resources or returns on investments.

An entity may classify dividends paid as a financing cash flow because they are a cost of obtaining financial resources. Alternatively, the entity may classify dividends paid as a component of cash flows from operating activities because they are paid out of operating cash flows. **7.16**

INCOME TAX

An entity shall present separately cash flows arising from income tax and shall classify them as cash flows from operating activities unless they can be specifically identified with financing and investing activities. When tax cash flows are allocated over more than one class of activity, the entity shall disclose the total amount of taxes paid. **7.17**

NON-CASH TRANSACTIONS

An entity shall exclude from the statement of cash flows investing and financing transactions that do not require the use of cash or cash equivalents. An entity shall disclose such transactions elsewhere in the **financial statements** in a way that provides all the relevant information about those investing and financing activities. **7.18**

Many investing and financing activities do not have a direct impact on current cash flows even though they affect the capital and asset structure of an entity. The exclusion of non-cash transactions from the statement of cash flows is consistent with the objective of a statement of cash flows because these items do not involve cash flows in the current period. Examples of non-cash transactions are: **7.19**

(a) the acquisition of assets either by assuming directly related liabilities or by means of a finance lease;
(b) the acquisition of an entity by means of an equity issue; and
(c) the conversion of debt to equity.

COMPONENTS OF CASH AND CASH EQUIVALENTS

An entity shall present the components of cash and cash equivalents and shall present a reconciliation of the amounts presented in the statement of cash flows to the equivalent items presented in the **statement of financial position**. However, an entity is not required to present this reconciliation if the amount of cash and cash equivalents presented in the statement of cash flows is identical to the amount similarly described in the statement of financial position. **7.20**

Entities applying Part 1 *General Rules and Formats* of Schedule 2 to the **Regulations** should include as cash, only cash and balances at central banks and loans and advances to banks repayable on demand. **7.20A**

OTHER DISCLOSURES

An entity shall disclose, together with a commentary by management, the amount of significant cash and cash equivalent balances held by the entity that are not available for use by the entity. Cash and cash equivalents held by an entity may not be available for use by the entity because of, among other reasons, foreign exchange controls or legal restrictions. **7.21**

Section 8
Notes to the Financial Statements

SCOPE OF THIS SECTION

8.1 This section sets out the principles underlying information that is to be presented in the **notes** to the **financial statements** and how to present it. Notes contain information in addition to that presented in the **statement of financial position**, **statement of comprehensive income** (if presented), **income statement** (if presented), combined **statement of income and retained earnings** (if presented), **statement of changes in equity** (if presented), and **statement of cash flows**. Notes provide narrative descriptions or disaggregations of items presented in those statements and information about items that do not qualify for **recognition** in those statements. In addition to the requirements of this section, nearly every other section of this FRS requires disclosures that are normally presented in the notes.

STRUCTURE OF THE NOTES

8.2 The notes shall:

(a) present information about the basis of preparation of the financial statements and the specific **accounting policies** used, in accordance with paragraphs 8.5 to 8.7;
(b) disclose the information required by this FRS that is not presented elsewhere in the financial statements; and
(c) provide information that is not presented elsewhere in the financial statements but is relevant to an understanding of any of them.

8.3 An entity shall, as far as practicable, present the notes in a systematic manner. An entity shall cross-reference each item in the financial statements to any related information in the notes.

8.4 An entity normally presents the notes in the following order:

(a) a statement that the financial statements have been prepared in compliance with this FRS (see paragraph 3.3);
(b) a summary of significant accounting policies applied (see paragraph 8.5);
(c) supporting information for items presented in the financial statements, in the sequence in which each statement and each line item is presented; and
(d) any other disclosures.

DISCLOSURE OF ACCOUNTING POLICIES

8.5 An entity shall disclose the following in the summary of significant accounting policies:

(a) the measurement basis (or bases) used in preparing the financial statements; and
(b) the other accounting policies used that are relevant to an understanding of the financial statements.

INFORMATION ABOUT JUDGEMENTS

8.6 An entity shall disclose, in the summary of significant accounting policies or other notes, the judgements, apart from those involving estimations (see paragraph 8.7), that management has made in the process of applying the entity's accounting policies and that have the most significant effect on the amounts recognised in the financial statements.

INFORMATION ABOUT KEY SOURCES OF ESTIMATION UNCERTAINTY

An entity shall disclose in the notes information about the key assumptions concerning the future, and other key sources of estimation uncertainty at the reporting date, that have a significant risk of causing a **material** adjustment to the **carrying amounts** of **assets** and **liabilities** within the next financial year. In respect of those assets and liabilities, the notes shall include details of: **8.7**

(a) their nature; and
(b) their carrying amount as at the end of the **reporting period**.

Section 9
Consolidated and Separate Financial Statements

SCOPE OF THIS SECTION

9.1 This section applies to all **parents** that present **consolidated financial statements** (which are referred to as group accounts in the **Act**) intended to give a true and fair view of the **financial position** and **profit or loss** (or **income and expenditure**) of their **group**, whether or not they report under the Act. Parents that do not report under the Act should comply with the requirements of this section, and of the Act where referred to in this section, except to the extent that these requirements are not permitted by any statutory framework under which such entities report. This section also includes guidance on **individual financial statements** and **separate financial statements.**

REQUIREMENT TO PRESENT CONSOLIDATED FINANCIAL STATEMENTS

9.2 Except as permitted or required by paragraph 9.3, a parent entity shall present consolidated financial statements in which it consolidates all its investments in **subsidiaries** in accordance with this FRS. A parent entity need only prepare consolidated accounts under the Act if it is a parent at the year end.

9.3 A parent is exempt from the requirement to prepare consolidated financial statements on any one of the following grounds:

(a) The parent is a wholly-owned subsidiary and its immediate parent is established under the law of an EEA State. Exemption is conditional on compliance with certain further conditions set out in section 400(2) of the Act.
(b) The parent is a majority-owned subsidiary and meets all the conditions for exemption as a wholly-owned subsidiary set out in section 400(2) of the Act as well as the additional conditions set out in section 400(1)(b) of the Act.
(c) The parent is a wholly-owned subsidiary of another entity and that parent is not established under the law of an EEA State. Exemption is conditional on compliance with certain further conditions set out in section 401(2) of the Act.
(d) The parent is a majority-owned subsidiary and meets all of the conditions for exemption as a wholly-owned subsidiary set out in section 401(2) of the Act as well as the additional conditions set out in section 401(1)(b) of the Act.
(e) The parent, and group headed by it, qualify as small as set out in section 383 of the Act and the group is not ineligible as set out in section 384 of the Act.
(f) All of the parent's subsidiaries are required to be excluded from consolidation by paragraph 9.9.
(g) For parents not reporting under the Act, if its statutory framework does not require the preparation of consolidated financial statements.

In sub-paragraphs (a) to (d), the parent is not exempt if any of its securities are admitted to trading on a regulated market of any EEA State within the meaning of Directive 2004/39/EC.

9.4 A subsidiary is an entity that is controlled by the parent. **Control** is the power to govern the financial and operating policies of an entity so as to obtain benefits from its activities.

9.5 Control is presumed to exist when the parent owns, directly or indirectly through subsidiaries, more than half of the voting power of an entity. That presumption may be overcome in exceptional circumstances if it can be clearly demonstrated that such ownership does not constitute control. Control also exists when the parent owns half or less of the voting power of an entity but it has:

(a) power over more than half of the voting rights by virtue of an agreement with other investors;
(b) power to govern the financial and operating policies of the entity under a statute or an agreement;
(c) power to appoint or remove the majority of the members of the board of directors or equivalent governing body and control of the entity is by that board or body; or
(d) power to cast the majority of votes at meetings of the board of directors or equivalent governing body and control of the entity is by that board or body.

Control can also be achieved by having options or convertible instruments that are currently exercisable or by having an agent with the ability to direct the activities for the benefit of the controlling entity. **9.6**

Control can also exist when the parent has the power to exercise, or actually exercises, dominant influence or control over the undertaking or it and the undertaking are managed on a unified basis. **9.6A**

[Not used] **9.7**

A subsidiary is not excluded from consolidation because its business activities are dissimilar to those of the other entities within the consolidation. Relevant information is provided by consolidating such subsidiaries and disclosing additional information in the consolidated financial statements about the different business activities of subsidiaries. **9.8**

A subsidiary is not excluded from consolidation because the information necessary for the preparation of consolidated financial statements cannot be obtained without disproportionate **expense** or undue delay, unless its inclusion is not **material** (individually or collectively for more than one subsidiary) for the purposes of giving a true and fair view in the context of the group. **9.8A**

A subsidiary shall be excluded from consolidation where: **9.9**

(a) severe long-term restrictions substantially hinder the exercise of the rights of the parent over the **assets** or management of the subsidiary; or
(b) the interest in the subsidiary is **held exclusively with a view to subsequent resale**; and the subsidiary has not previously been consolidated in the consolidated financial statements prepared in accordance with this FRS.

A subsidiary excluded from consolidation on the grounds set out in paragraph 9.9(a) shall be measured using an accounting policy selected by the parent in accordance with paragraph 9.26, except where the parent still exercises a significant influence over the subsidiary. If this is the case, the parent should treat the subsidiary as an associate using the equity method set out in paragraph 14.8. **9.9A**

A subsidiary excluded from consolidation on the grounds set out in paragraph 9.9(b) which is: **9.9B**

(a) **held as part of an investment portfolio** shall be measured at **fair value** with changes in fair value recognised in profit or loss;* or
(b) not held as part of an investment portfolio shall be measured using an **accounting policy** selected by the parent in accordance with paragraph 9.26.

SPECIAL PURPOSE ENTITIES

9.10 An entity may be created to accomplish a narrow objective (eg to effect a **lease**, undertake **research** and **development** activities, securitise **financial assets** or facilitate employee shareholdings under remuneration schemes, such as Employee Share Ownership Plans (ESOPs)). Such a special purpose entity (SPE) may take the form of a corporation, trust, partnership or unincorporated entity. Often, SPEs are created with legal arrangements that impose strict requirements over the operations of the SPE.

9.11 Except as permitted or required by paragraph 9.3, a parent entity shall prepare consolidated financial statements that include the entity and any SPEs that are controlled by that entity. In addition to the circumstances described in paragraph 9.5, the following circumstances may indicate that an entity controls a SPE (this is not an exhaustive list):

(a) the activities of the SPE are being conducted on behalf of the entity according to its specific business needs;
(b) the entity has the ultimate decision-making powers over the activities of the SPE even if the day-to-day decisions have been delegated;
(c) the entity has rights to obtain the majority of the benefits of the SPE and therefore may be exposed to risks incidental to the activities of the SPE; and
(d) the entity retains the majority of the residual or ownership risks related to the SPE or its assets.

9.12 Paragraphs 9.10 and 9.11 do not apply to **post-employment benefit plans** or other long-term employee benefit plans to which Section 28 *Employee Benefits* applies. A special purpose entity that is an intermediate payment arrangement shall be accounted for in accordance with paragraphs 9.33 to 9.38.

CONSOLIDATION PROCEDURES

9.13 The consolidated financial statements present financial information about the group as a single economic entity. In preparing consolidated financial statements, an entity shall:

(a) combine the **financial statements** of the parent and its subsidiaries line by line by adding together like items of assets, **liabilities**, **equity**, **income** and expenses;
(b) eliminate the **carrying amount** of the parent's investment in each subsidiary and the parent's portion of equity of each subsidiary;
(c) measure and present **non-controlling interest** in the profit or loss of consolidated subsidiaries for the **reporting period** separately from the interest of the **owners** of the parent; and
(d) measure and present non-controlling interest in the net assets of consolidated subsidiaries separately from the parent shareholders' equity in them. Non-controlling interest in the net assets consists of:

(i) the amount of the non-controlling interest's share in the net amount of the identifiable assets, liabilities and contingent liabilities recognised and

**Additional disclosures may need to be provided in accordance with company law (see Appendix IV, paragraph A4.17).*

measured in accordance with Section 19 *Business Combinations and Goodwill* at the date of the original combination; and

(ii) the non-controlling interest's share of changes in equity since the date of the combination.

The proportions of profit or loss and changes in equity allocated to the owners of the parent and to the non-controlling interest are determined on the basis of existing ownership interests and do not reflect the possible exercise or conversion of options or convertible instruments. **9.14**

Intragroup balances and transactions

Intragroup balances and transactions, including income, expenses and dividends, are eliminated in full. Profits and losses resulting from intragroup transactions that are recognised in assets, such as **inventory** and **property, plant and equipment**, are eliminated in full. Intragroup losses may indicate an impairment that requires **recognition** in the consolidated financial statements (see Section 27 *Impairment of Assets*). Section 29 *Income Tax* applies to **timing differences** that arise from the elimination of profits and losses resulting from intragroup transactions. **9.15**

Uniform reporting date and reporting period

The financial statements of the parent and its subsidiaries used in the preparation of the consolidated financial statements shall be prepared as of the same **reporting date**, and for the same reporting period, unless it is **impracticable** to do so. Where the reporting date and reporting period of a subsidiary are not the same as the parent's reporting date and reporting period, the consolidated financial statements must be made up: **9.16**

(a) from the financial statements of the subsidiary as of its last reporting date before the parent's reporting date, adjusted for the effects of significant transactions or events that occur between the date of those financial statements and the date of the consolidated financial statements, provided that reporting date is no more than three months before that of the parent; or
(b) from interim financial statements prepared by the subsidiary as at the parent's reporting date.

Uniform accounting policies

Consolidated financial statements shall be prepared using uniform accounting policies for like transactions and other events and conditions in similar circumstances. If a member of the group uses accounting policies other than those adopted in the consolidated financial statements for like transactions and events in similar circumstances, appropriate adjustments are made to its financial statements in preparing the consolidated financial statements. **9.17**

ACQUISITION AND DISPOSAL OF SUBSIDIARIES

The income and expenses of a subsidiary are included in the consolidated financial statements from the **acquisition date**, except when a **business combination** is accounted for by using the merger accounting method under Section 19 or, for certain public benefit entity combinations, Section 34 *Specialised Activities*. The income and expenses of a subsidiary are included in the consolidated financial statements until the date on which the parent ceases to control the subsidiary. A parent may cease to **9.18** control a subsidiary with or without a change in absolute or relative ownership levels. This could occur, for example, when a subsidiary becomes subject to the control of a government, court, administrator or regulator.

Disposal – where control is lost

9.18A Where a parent ceases to control a subsidiary, a **gain** or loss is recognised in the consolidated statement of comprehensive income (or in the **income statement**, if presented) calculated as the difference between:

(a) the proceeds from the disposal (or the event that resulted in the loss of control); and

(b) the proportion of the carrying amount of the subsidiary's net assets, including any related **goodwill**, disposed of (or lost) as at the date of disposal (or date control is lost).

The cumulative amount of any exchange differences that relate to a foreign subsidiary recognised in equity in accordance with Section 30 *Foreign Currency Translation* is not recognised in profit or loss as part of the gain or loss on disposal of the subsidiary and shall be transferred directly to retained earnings.

9.18B The gain or loss arising on the disposal shall also include those amounts that have been recognised in **other comprehensive income** in relation to that subsidiary, where those amounts are required to be reclassified to profit or loss upon disposal in accordance with other sections of this FRS. Amounts that are not required to be reclassified to profit or loss upon disposal of the related assets or liabilities in accordance with other sections of this FRS shall be transferred directly to retained earnings.

9.19 If an entity ceases to be a subsidiary but the investor (former parent) continues to hold:

(a) an investment that is not an **associate** (see paragraph 9.19(b)) or a **jointly controlled entity** (see paragraph 9.19(c)), that investment shall be accounted for as a financial asset in accordance with Section 11 *Basic Financial Instruments* or Section 12 *Other Financial Instruments Issues* from the date the entity ceases to be a subsidiary;

(b) an associate, that associate shall be accounted for in accordance with Section 14 *Investments in Associates*; or

(c) a jointly controlled entity, that jointly controlled entity shall be accounted for in accordance with Section 15 *Investments in Joint Ventures*.

The carrying amount of the net assets (and goodwill) attributable to the investment at the date that the entity ceases to be a subsidiary shall be regarded as the cost on initial **measurement** of the financial asset, investment in associate or jointly controlled entity, as appropriate. In applying the equity method to investments in associate or jointly controlled entities as required in sub-paragraphs (b) and (c) above, paragraph 14.8(c) shall not be applied.

Disposal – where control is retained

9.19A Where a parent reduces its holding in a subsidiary and control is retained, it shall be accounted for as a transaction between equity holders and the resulting change in non-controlling interest shall be accounted for in accordance with paragraph 22.19. No gain or loss shall be recognised at the date of disposal.

Acquisition – Control achieved in stages

Where a parent acquires control of a subsidiary in stages, the transaction shall be accounted for in accordance with paragraphs 19.11A and 19.14 applied at the date control is achieved. **9.19B**

Acquisition – Increasing a controlling interest in a subsidiary

Where a parent increases its controlling interest in a subsidiary, the identifiable assets and liabilities and a **provision** for **contingent liabilities** of the subsidiary shall not be revalued to fair value and no additional goodwill shall be recognised at the date the controlling interest is increased. **9.19C**

The transaction shall be accounted for as a transaction between equity holders and the resulting change in non-controlling interest shall be accounted for in accordance with paragraph 22.19. **9.19D**

NON-CONTROLLING INTEREST IN SUBSIDIARIES

An entity shall present non-controlling interest in the consolidated statement of financial position within equity, separately from the equity of the owners of the parent. **9.20**

An entity shall disclose non-controlling interest in the profit or loss of the group separately in the **statement of comprehensive income** (or income statement, if presented). **9.21**

Profit or loss and each component of other comprehensive income shall be attributed to the owners of the parent and to non-controlling interest. **Total comprehensive income** shall be attributed to the owners of the parent and to non-controlling interest even if this results in non-controlling interest having a deficit balance. **9.22**

DISCLOSURES IN CONSOLIDATED FINANCIAL STATEMENTS

The following disclosures shall be made in consolidated financial statements: **9.23**

(a) the fact that the statements are consolidated financial statements;
(b) the basis for concluding that control exists when the parent does not own, directly or indirectly through subsidiaries, more than half of the voting power;
(c) any difference in the reporting date of the financial statements of the parent and its subsidiaries used in the preparation of the consolidated financial statements;
(d) the nature and extent of any significant restrictions (eg resulting from borrowing arrangements or regulatory requirements) on the ability of subsidiaries to transfer funds to the parent in the form of cash dividends or to repay loans; and
(e) the name of any subsidiary excluded from consolidation and the reason for exclusion.

INDIVIDUAL AND SEPARATE FINANCIAL STATEMENTS

Preparation of individual and separate financial statements

The requirements for the preparation of individual financial statements are set out in the Act or other statutory framework. **9.23A**

9.24 Separate financial statements are those prepared by a parent in which the investments in subsidiaries, associates or jointly controlled entities are accounted for either at cost or fair value rather than on the basis of the reported results and net assets of the investees. Separate financial statements are included within the meaning of individual financial statements.

9.25 An entity that is not a parent shall account for any investments in associates and any interests in jointly controlled entities in accordance with paragraph 14.4 or 15.9, as appropriate in its individual financial statements.

Accounting policy election in separate financial statements

9.26 When an entity that is a parent prepares separate financial statements and describes them as conforming to this FRS, those financial statements shall comply with all of the requirements of this FRS. The parent shall select and adopt a policy of accounting for its investments in subsidiaries, associates and jointly controlled entities either:

(a) at cost less impairment;
(b) at fair value with changes in fair value recognised in other comprehensive income in accordance with paragraphs 17.15E and 17.15F; or
(c) at fair value with changes in fair value recognised in profit or loss (paragraphs 11.27 to 11.32 provide guidance on fair value).

The entity shall apply the same accounting policy for all investments in a single class (subsidiaries, associates or jointly controlled entities), but it can elect different policies for different classes.

9.26A A parent that is exempt in accordance with paragraph 9.3 from the requirement to present consolidated financial statements, and presents separate financial statements as its only financial statements, shall account for its investments in subsidiaries, associates and jointly controlled entities in accordance with paragraph 9.26.

Disclosures in separate financial statements

9.27 When a parent prepares separate financial statements, those separate financial statements shall disclose:

(a) that the statements are separate financial statements; and
(b) a description of the methods used to account for the investments in subsidiaries, jointly controlled entities and associates.

9.27A A parent that uses one of the exemptions from presenting consolidated financial statements (described in paragraph 9.3) shall disclose the grounds on which the parent is exempt.

9.27B When a parent adopts a policy of accounting for its investments in subsidiaries, associates or jointly controlled entities at fair value with changes in fair value recognised in profit or loss, it must comply with the requirements of paragraph 36(4) of Schedule 1 to the **Regulations** by applying the disclosure requirements of Section 11 *Basic Financial Instruments* to those investments.

9.28 [Not used]

9.29 [Not used]

[Not used] **9.30**

EXCHANGES OF BUSINESSES OR OTHER NON-MONETARY ASSETS FOR AN INTEREST IN A SUBSIDIARY, JOINTLY CONTROLLED ENTITY OR ASSOCIATE

Where a reporting entity exchanges a **business**, or other non-monetary assets, for an interest in another entity, and that other entity thereby becomes a subsidiary, **jointly controlled entity** or associate of the reporting entity, the following accounting treatment shall apply in the consolidated financial statements of the reporting entity: **9.31**

(a) To the extent that the reporting entity retains an ownership interest in the business, or other non-monetary assets, exchanged, even if that interest is then held through the other entity, that retained interest, including any related goodwill, is treated as having been owned by the reporting entity throughout the transaction and should be included at its pre-transaction carrying amount.

(b) Goodwill should be recognised as the difference between:

    (i) the fair value of the consideration given; and
    (ii) the fair value of the reporting entity's share of the pre-transaction identifiable net assets of the other entity.

    The consideration given for the interest acquired in the other entity will include that part of the business, or other non-monetary assets, exchanged and no longer owned by the reporting entity. The consideration may also include **cash** or monetary assets to achieve equalisation of values. Where it is difficult to value the consideration given, the best estimate of its value may be given by valuing what is acquired.

(c) To the extent that the fair value of the consideration received by the reporting entity exceeds the carrying value of the part of the business, or other non-monetary assets exchanged and no longer owned by the reporting entity, and any related goodwill together with any cash given up, the reporting entity should recognise a gain. Any unrealised gain arising on the exchange shall be recognised in other comprehensive income.

(d) To the extent that the fair value of the consideration received by the reporting entity is less than the carrying value of the part of the business, or other non-monetary assets no longer owned by the reporting entity, and any related goodwill, together with any cash given up, the reporting entity should recognise a loss. This loss should be recognised either as an impairment in accordance with Section 27 *Impairment of Assets* or, for any loss remaining after an impairment review of the relevant assets, in profit or loss.

No gain or loss should be recognised in those rare cases where the artificiality or lack of substance of the transaction is such that a gain or loss on the exchange could not be justified. Where a gain or loss on the exchange is not taken into account because the transaction is artificial or has no substance, the circumstances should be explained. **9.32**

INTERMEDIATE PAYMENT ARRANGEMENTS

Intermediate payment arrangements may take a variety of forms: **9.33**

(a) The intermediary is usually established by a sponsoring entity and constituted as a trust, although other arrangements are possible.

(b) The relationship between the sponsoring entity and the intermediary may take different forms. For example, when the intermediary is constituted as a trust, the sponsoring entity will not have a right to direct the intermediary's activities.

However, in these and other cases the sponsoring entity may give advice to the intermediary or may be relied on by the intermediary to provide the information it needs to carry out its activities. Sometimes, the way the intermediary has been set up gives it little discretion in the broad nature of its activities.

(c) The arrangements are most commonly used to pay employees, although they are sometimes used to compensate suppliers of goods and services other than employee services. Sometimes the sponsoring entity's employees and other suppliers are not the only beneficiaries of the arrangement. Other beneficiaries may include past employees and their dependants, and the intermediary may be entitled to make charitable donations.

(d) The precise identity of the persons or entities that will receive payments from the intermediary, and the amounts that they will receive, are not usually agreed at the outset.

(e) The sponsoring entity often has the right to appoint or veto the appointment of the intermediary's trustees (or its directors or the equivalent).

(f) The payments made to the intermediary and the payments made by the intermediary are often cash payments but may involve other transfers of value.

Examples of intermediate payment arrangements are employee share ownership plans (ESOPs) and employee benefit trusts that are used to facilitate employee shareholdings under remuneration schemes. In a typical employee benefit trust arrangement for share-based payments, an entity makes payments to a trust or guarantees borrowing by the trust, and the trust uses its funds to accumulate assets to pay the entity's employees for services the employees have rendered to the entity.

Although the trustees of an intermediary must act at all times in accordance with the interests of the beneficiaries of the intermediary, most intermediaries (particularly those established as a means of remunerating employees) are specifically designed so as to serve the purposes of the sponsoring entity, and to ensure that there will be minimal risk of any conflict arising between the duties of the trustees of the intermediary and the interest of the sponsoring entity, such that there is nothing to encumber implementation of the wishes of the sponsoring entity in practice. Where this is the case, the sponsoring entity has de facto control.

Accounting for intermediate payment arrangements

9.34 When a sponsoring entity makes payments (or transfers assets) to an intermediary, there is a rebuttable presumption that the entity has exchanged one asset for another and that the payment itself does not represent an immediate expense. To rebut this presumption at the time the payment is made to the intermediary, the entity must demonstrate:

(a) it will not obtain future economic benefit from the amounts transferred; or

(b) it does not have control of the right or other access to the future economic benefit it is expected to receive.

9.35 Where a payment to an intermediary is an exchange by the sponsoring entity of one asset for another, any assets that the intermediary acquires in a subsequent exchange transaction will also be under the control of the entity. Accordingly, assets and liabilities of the intermediary shall be accounted for by the sponsoring entity as an extension of its own business and recognised in its own individual financial statements. An asset will cease to be recognised as an asset of the sponsoring entity when, for example, the asset of the intermediary vests unconditionally with identified beneficiaries.

A sponsoring entity may distribute its own equity instruments, or other equity instruments, to an intermediary in order to facilitate employee shareholdings under a remuneration scheme. Where this is the case and the sponsoring entity has control, or de facto control, of the assets and liabilities of the intermediary, the commercial effect is that the sponsoring entity is, for all practical purposes, in the same position as if it had purchased the shares directly. **9.36**

Where an intermediary holds the sponsoring entity's equity instruments, the sponsoring entity shall account for the equity instruments as if it had purchased them directly. The sponsoring entity shall account for the assets and liabilities of the intermediary in its individual financial statements as follows: **9.37**

(a) The consideration paid for the equity instruments of the sponsoring entity shall be deducted from equity until such time that the equity instruments **vest** unconditionally with employees.
(b) Consideration paid or received for the purchase or sale of the sponsoring entity's own equity instruments shall be shown as separate amounts in the **statement of changes in equity**.
(c) Other assets and liabilities of the intermediary shall be recognised as assets and liabilities of the sponsoring entity.
(d) No gain or loss shall be recognised in profit or loss or other comprehensive income on the purchase, sale, issue or cancellation of the entity's own equity instruments.
(e) Finance costs and any administration expenses shall be recognised on an accruals basis rather than as funding payments are made to the intermediary.
(f) Any dividend income arising on the sponsoring entity's own equity instruments shall be excluded from profit or loss and deducted from the aggregate of dividends paid.

Disclosures in individual and separate financial statements

When a sponsoring entity recognises the assets and liabilities held by an intermediary, it should disclose sufficient information in the **notes** to its financial statements to enable users to understand the significance of the intermediary and the arrangement in the context of the sponsoring entity's financial statements. This should include: **9.38**

(a) a description of the main features of the intermediary including the arrangements for making payments and for distributing equity instruments;
(b) any restrictions relating to the assets and liabilities of the intermediary;
(c) the amount and nature of the assets and liabilities held by the intermediary, which have not yet vested unconditionally with the beneficiaries of the arrangement;
(d) the amount that has been deducted from equity and the number of equity instruments held by the intermediary, which have not yet vested unconditionally with the beneficiaries of the arrangement;
(e) for entities that have their equity instruments listed or **publicly traded** on a stock exchange or market, the market value of the equity instruments held by the intermediary which have not yet vested unconditionally with employees;
(f) the extent to which the equity instruments are under option to employees, or have been conditionally gifted to them; and
(g) the amount that has been deducted from the aggregate dividends paid by the sponsoring entity.

Section 10
Accounting Policies, Estimates and Errors

SCOPE OF THIS SECTION

10.1 This section provides guidance for selecting and applying the **accounting policies** used in preparing **financial statements**. It also covers **changes in accounting estimates** and corrections of **errors** in prior period financial statements.

SELECTION AND APPLICATION OF ACCOUNTING POLICIES

10.2 Accounting policies are the specific principles, bases, conventions, rules and practices applied by an entity in preparing and presenting financial statements.

10.3 If an FRS or FRC Abstract specifically addresses a transaction, other event or condition, an entity shall apply that FRS or FRC Abstract. However, the entity need not follow a requirement in an FRS or FRC Abstract if the effect of doing so would not be **material**.

10.4 If an FRS or FRC Abstract does not specifically address a transaction, other event or condition, an entity's management shall use its judgement in developing and applying an accounting policy that results in information that is:

(a) relevant to the economic decision-making needs of users; and
(b) reliable, in that the financial statements:
   (i) represent faithfully the **financial position**, financial **performance** and **cash flows** of the entity;
   (ii) reflect the economic substance of transactions, other events and conditions, and not merely the legal form;
   (iii) are neutral, ie free from bias;
   (iv) are prudent; and
   (v) are complete in all material respects.

10.5 In making the judgement described in paragraph 10.4, management shall refer to and consider the applicability of the following sources in descending order:

(a) the requirements and guidance in an FRS or FRC Abstract dealing with similar and related issues;
(b) where an entity's financial statements are within the scope of a **Statement of Recommended Practice (SORP)** the requirements and guidance in that SORP dealing with similar and related issues; and
(c) the definitions, **recognition** criteria and measurement concepts for **assets**, **liabilities**, **income** and **expenses** and the pervasive principles in Section 2 *Concepts and Pervasive Principles*.

10.6 In making the judgement described in paragraph 10.4, management may also consider the requirements and guidance in **EU-adopted IFRS** dealing with similar and related issues. Paragraphs 1.4 to 1.7 require certain entities to apply IAS 33 *Earnings per Share* (as adopted in the EU) , IFRS 8 *Operating Segments* (as adopted in the EU) or IFRS 6 *Exploration for and Evaluation of Mineral Resources*.

CONSISTENCY OF ACCOUNTING POLICIES

10.7 An entity shall select and apply its accounting policies consistently for similar transactions, other events and conditions, unless an FRS or FRC Abstract specifically requires or permits categorisation of items for which different policies may be appropriate. If an FRS or FRC Abstract requires or permits such categorisation, an appropriate accounting policy shall be selected and applied consistently to each category.

CHANGES IN ACCOUNTING POLICIES

An entity shall change an accounting policy only if the change: **10.8**

(a) is required by an FRS or FRC Abstract; or
(b) results in the financial statements providing reliable and more relevant information about the effects of transactions, other events or conditions on the entity's financial position, financial performance or cash flows.

The following are not changes in accounting policies: **10.9**

(a) the application of an accounting policy for transactions, other events or conditions that differ in substance from those previously occurring;
(b) the application of a new accounting policy for transactions, other events or conditions that did not occur previously or were not material; and
(c) a change to the cost model when a reliable measure of **fair value** is no longer available (or vice versa) for an asset that an FRS or FRC Abstract would otherwise require or permit to be measured at fair value.

If an FRS or FRC Abstract allows a choice of accounting treatment (including the measurement basis) for a specified transaction or other event or condition and an entity changes its previous choice, that is a change in accounting policy. **10.10**

The initial application of a policy to revalue assets in accordance with Section 17 *Property, Plant and Equipment* or Section 18 *Intangible Assets other than Goodwill* is a change in accounting policy to be dealt with as a revaluation in accordance with those sections, rather than in accordance with paragraphs 10.11 and 10.12. **10.10A**

Applying changes in accounting policies

An entity shall account for changes in accounting policy as follows: **10.11**

(a) an entity shall account for a change in accounting policy resulting from a change in the requirements of an FRS or FRC Abstract in accordance with the transitional provisions, if any, specified in that amendment;
(b) when an entity has elected to follow IAS 39 *Financial Instruments: Recognition and Measurement* and/or IFRS 9 *Financial Instruments* instead of following Section 11 *Basic Financial Instruments* and Section 12 *Other Financial Instruments Issues* as permitted by paragraph 11.2, and the requirements of IAS 39 and/or IFRS 9 change, the entity shall account for that change in accounting policy in accordance with the transitional provisions, if any, specified in the revised IAS 39 and/or IFRS 9; and
(c) when an entity is required or has elected to follow IAS 33 *Earnings per Share*, IFRS 8 *Operating Segments* or IFRS 6 *Exploration for and Evaluation of Mineral Resources* and the requirements of those standards change, the entity shall account for that change in accounting policy in accordance with the transitional provisions, if any, specified in those standards as amended; and
(d) an entity shall account for all other changes in accounting policy retrospectively (see paragraph 10.12).

Retrospective application

10.12 When a change in accounting policy is applied retrospectively in accordance with paragraph 10.11, the entity shall apply the new accounting policy to comparative information for prior periods to the earliest date for which it is practicable, as if the new accounting policy had always been applied. When it is **impracticable** to determine the individual-period effects of a change in accounting policy on comparative information for one or more prior periods presented, the entity shall apply the new accounting policy to the **carrying amounts** of assets and liabilities as at the beginning of the earliest period for which **retrospective application** is practicable, which may be the current period, and shall make a corresponding adjustment to the opening balance of each affected component of **equity** for that period.

DISCLOSURE OF A CHANGE IN ACCOUNTING POLICY

10.13 When an amendment to an FRS or FRC Abstract has an effect on the current period or any prior period, or might have an effect on future periods, an entity shall disclose the following:

(a) the nature of the change in accounting policy;

(b) for the current period and each prior period presented, to the extent practicable, the amount of the adjustment for each financial statement line item affected;

(c) the amount of the adjustment relating to periods before those presented, to the extent practicable; and

(d) an explanation if it is impracticable to determine the amounts to be disclosed in (b) or (c) above.

Financial statements of subsequent periods need not repeat these disclosures.

10.14 When a voluntary change in accounting policy has an effect on the current period or any prior period, an entity shall disclose the following:

(a) the nature of the change in accounting policy;

(b) the reasons why applying the new accounting policy provides reliable and more relevant information;

(c) to the extent practicable, the amount of the adjustment for each financial statement line item affected, shown separately:

(i) for the current period;
(ii) for each prior period presented; and
(iii) in the aggregate for periods before those presented; and

(d) an explanation if it is impracticable to determine the amounts to be disclosed in (c) above.

Financial statements of subsequent periods need not repeat these disclosures.

CHANGES IN ACCOUNTING ESTIMATES

10.15 A **change in accounting estimate** is an adjustment of the carrying amount of an asset or a liability, or the amount of the periodic consumption of an asset, that results from the assessment of the present status of, and expected future benefits and obligations associated with, assets and liabilities. Changes in accounting estimates result from new information or new developments and, accordingly, are not corrections of errors. When it is difficult to distinguish a change in an accounting policy from a change in an accounting estimate, the change is treated as a change in an accounting estimate.

An entity shall recognise the effect of a change in an accounting estimate, other than a change to which paragraph 10.17 applies, **prospectively** by including it in **profit or loss** in: **10.16**

(a) the period of the change, if the change affects that period only; or
(b) the period of the change and future periods, if the change affects both.

To the extent that a change in an accounting estimate gives rise to changes in assets and liabilities, or relates to an item of equity, the entity shall recognise it by adjusting the carrying amount of the related asset, liability or equity item in the period of the change. **10.17**

Disclosure of a change in estimate

An entity shall disclose the nature of any change in an accounting estimate and the effect of the change on assets, liabilities, income and expense for the current period. If it is practicable for the entity to estimate the effect of the change in one or more future periods, the entity shall disclose those estimates. **10.18**

CORRECTIONS OF PRIOR PERIOD ERRORS

Prior period errors are omissions from, and misstatements in, an entity's financial statements for one or more prior periods arising from a failure to use, or misuse of, reliable information that: **10.19**

(a) was available when financial statements for those periods were authorised for issue; and
(b) could reasonably be expected to have been obtained and taken into account in the preparation and presentation of those financial statements.

Such errors include the effects of mathematical mistakes, mistakes in applying accounting policies, oversights or misinterpretations of facts, and fraud. **10.20**

To the extent practicable, an entity shall correct a material prior period error retrospectively in the first financial statements authorised for issue after its discovery by: **10.21**

(a) restating the comparative amounts for the prior period(s) presented in which the error occurred; or
(b) if the error occurred before the earliest prior period presented, restating the opening balances of assets, liabilities and equity for the earliest prior period presented.

When it is impracticable to determine the period-specific effects of a material error on comparative information for one or more prior periods presented, the entity shall restate the opening balances of assets, liabilities and equity for the earliest period for which retrospective restatement is practicable (which may be the current period). **10.22**

Disclosure of prior period errors

An entity shall disclose the following about material prior period errors: **10.23**

(a) the nature of the prior period error;

(b) for each prior period presented, to the extent practicable, the amount of the correction for each financial statement line item affected;
(c) to the extent practicable, the amount of the correction at the beginning of the earliest prior period presented; and
(d) an explanation if it is not practicable to determine the amounts to be disclosed in (b) or (c) above.

Financial statements of subsequent periods need not repeat these disclosures.

Section 11
Basic Financial Instruments

SCOPE OF SECTIONS 11 AND 12

Section 11 *Basic Financial Instruments* and Section 12 *Other Financial Instruments Issues* together deal with recognising, derecognising, measuring and disclosing **financial instruments (financial assets** and **financial liabilities**). Section 11 applies to basic financial instruments and is relevant to all entities. Section 12 applies to other, more complex financial instruments and transactions. If an entity enters into only basic financial instrument transactions then Section 12 is not applicable. However, even entities with only basic financial instruments shall consider the scope of Section 12 to ensure they are exempt. **11.1**

Public benefit entities and other members of a **public benefit entity group** that make or receive **public benefit entity concessionary loans** shall refer to the relevant paragraphs of Section 34 *Specialised Activities* for the accounting requirements for such loans. **PBE11.1A**

ACCOUNTING POLICY CHOICE

An entity shall choose to apply either: **11.2**

(a) the provisions of both Section 11 and Section 12 in full; or

(b) the **recognition** and **measurement** provisions of IAS 39 *Financial Instruments: Recognition and Measurement* (as adopted for use in the EU) and the disclosure requirements of Sections 11 and 12; or

(c) the recognition and measurement provisions of IFRS 9 *Financial Instruments* and/or IAS 39 (as amended following the publication of IFRS 9) and the disclosure requirements of Sections 11 and 12;

to account for all of its financial instruments. Where an entity chooses (b) or (c) it applies the scope of the relevant standard to its financial instruments. An entity's choice of (a), (b) or (c) is an **accounting policy** choice. Paragraphs 10.8 to 10.14 contain requirements for determining when a change in accounting policy is appropriate, how such a change should be accounted for and what information should be disclosed about the change.

INTRODUCTION TO SECTION 11

A financial instrument is a contract that gives rise to a financial asset of one entity and a financial liability or equity instrument of another entity. **11.3**

[Not used] **11.4**

Basic financial instruments within the scope of Section 11 are those that satisfy the conditions in paragraph 11.8. Examples of financial instruments that normally satisfy those conditions include: **11.5**

(a) **cash**;

(b) demand and fixed-term deposits when the entity is the depositor, eg bank accounts;

(c) commercial paper and commercial bills held;

(d) accounts, notes and loans receivable and payable;

(e) bonds and similar debt instruments;

(f) investments in non-convertible preference shares and non-puttable ordinary and preference shares; and

(g) commitments to receive a loan and commitments to make a loan to another entity that meet the conditions of paragraph 11.8(c).

11.6 Examples of financial instruments that do not normally satisfy the conditions in paragraph 11.8, and are therefore within the scope of Section 12, include:

(a) asset-backed securities, such as collateralised mortgage obligations, repurchase agreements and securitised packages of receivables;
(b) options, rights, warrants, futures contracts, forward contracts and interest rate swaps that can be settled in cash or by exchanging another financial instrument;
(c) financial instruments that qualify and are designated as **hedging instruments** in accordance with the requirements in Section 12; and
(d) commitments to make a loan to another entity and commitments to receive a loan, if the commitment can be settled net in cash.
(e) [not used]

SCOPE OF SECTION 11

11.7 Section 11 applies to all financial instruments meeting the conditions of paragraph 11.8 except for the following:

(a) Investments in **subsidiaries, associates** and **joint ventures** that are accounted for in accordance with Section 9 *Consolidated and Separate Financial Statements*, Section 14 *Investments in Associates* or Section 15 *Investments in Joint Ventures*.
(b) Financial instruments that meet the definition of an entity's own equity and the equity component of **compound financial instruments** issued by the reporting entity that contain both a **liability** and an equity component (see Section 22 *Liabilities and Equity)*.
(c) **Leases**, to which Section 20 *Leases* applies. However, the **derecognition** requirements in paragraphs 11.33 to 11.35 and impairment accounting requirements in paragraphs 11.21 to 11.26 apply to derecognition and impairment of receivables recognised by a lessor and the derecognition requirements in paragraphs 11.36 to 11.38 apply to payables recognised by a lessee arising under a **finance lease**. Section 12 applies to leases with characteristics specified in paragraph 12.3(f).
(d) Employers' rights and obligations under employee benefit plans, to which Section 28 *Employee Benefits* applies, although paragraphs 11.27 to 11.32 do apply in determining the **fair value** of **plan assets**.
(e) Financial instruments, contracts and obligations to which Section 26 *Share-based Payment* applies, and contracts within the scope of paragraph 12.5.
(f) **Insurance contracts** (including **reinsurance contracts**) that the entity issues and reinsurance contracts that the entity holds (see FRS 103 *Insurance Contracts*).
(g) Financial instruments issued by an entity with a **discretionary participation feature** (see FRS 103 *Insurance Contracts*).
(h) Reimbursement assets accounted for in accordance with Section 21 *Provisions and Contingencies*.
(i) **Financial guarantee contracts** (see Section 21).

A reporting entity that issues the financial instruments set out in (f) or (g) or holds the financial instruments in (f) is required by paragraph 1.6 of this FRS to apply FRS 103 to those financial instruments.

BASIC FINANCIAL INSTRUMENTS

11.8 An entity shall account for the following financial instruments as basic financial instruments in accordance with Section 11:

(a) cash;
(b) a debt instrument (such as an account, note, or loan receivable or payable) that meets the conditions in paragraph 11.9;
(c) commitments to receive or make a loan to another entity that:

 (i) cannot be settled net in cash; and
 (ii) when the commitment is executed, are expected to meet the conditions in paragraph 11.9; and

(d) an investment in non-convertible preference shares and non-puttable **ordinary shares** or preference shares.

A debt instrument that satisfies all of the conditions in (a) to (d) below shall be accounted for in accordance with Section 11: **11.9**

(a) Returns to the holder are:

 (i) a fixed amount;
 (ii) a fixed rate of return over the life of the instrument;
 (iii) a variable return that, throughout the life of the instrument, is equal to a single referenced quoted or observable interest rate (such as LIBOR); or
 (iv) some combination of such fixed rate and variable rates (such as LIBOR plus 200 basis points), provided that both the fixed and variable rates are positive (eg an interest rate swap with a positive fixed rate and negative variable rate would not meet this criterion). For fixed and variable rate interest returns, interest is calculated by multiplying the rate for the applicable period by the principal amount outstanding during the period.

(b) There is no contractual provision that could, by its terms, result in the holder losing the principal amount or any interest attributable to the current period or prior periods. The fact that a debt instrument is subordinated to other debt instruments is not an example of such a contractual provision.
(c) Contractual provisions that permit the issuer (the borrower) to prepay a debt instrument or permit the holder (the lender) to put it back to the issuer before maturity are not contingent on future events other than to protect:

 (i) the holder against the credit deterioration of the issuer (eg defaults, credit downgrades or loan covenant violations), or a change in control of the issuer; or
 (ii) the holder or issuer against changes in relevant taxation or law.

(d) There are no conditional returns or repayment provisions except for the variable rate return described in (a) and prepayment provisions described in (c).

Examples of financial instruments that would normally satisfy the conditions in paragraph 11.9 are: **11.10**

(a) trade accounts and notes receivable and payable, and loans from banks or other third parties;
(b) accounts payable in a foreign currency. However, any change in the account payable because of a change in the exchange rate is recognised in **profit or loss** as required by paragraph 30.10;
(c) loans to or from subsidiaries or associates that are due on demand; and
(d) a debt instrument that would become immediately receivable if the issuer defaults on an interest or principal payment (such a provision does not violate the conditions in paragraph 11.9).

Examples of financial instruments that do not satisfy the conditions in paragraph 11.9 (and are therefore within the scope of Section 12) include: **11.11**

(a) an investment in another entity's equity instruments other than non-convertible preference shares and non-puttable ordinary and preference shares (see paragraph 11.8(d));
(b) an interest rate swap that returns a **cash flow** that is positive or negative, or a forward commitment to purchase a commodity or financial instrument that is capable of being cash-settled and that, on settlement, could have positive or negative cash flow, because such swaps and forwards do not meet the condition in paragraph 11.9(a);
(c) options and forward contracts, because returns to the holder are not fixed and the condition in paragraph 11.9(a) is not met; and
(d) investments in convertible debt, because the return to the holder can vary with the price of the issuer's equity shares rather than just with market interest rates.
(e) [not used]

INITIAL RECOGNITION OF FINANCIAL ASSETS AND LIABILITIES

11.12 An entity shall recognise a financial asset or a financial liability only when the entity becomes a party to the contractual provisions of the instrument.

INITIAL MEASUREMENT

11.13 When a financial asset or financial liability is recognised initially, an entity shall measure it at the transaction price (including **transaction costs** except in the initial measurement of financial assets and liabilities that are measured at fair value through profit or loss) unless the arrangement constitutes, in effect, a financing transaction. A financing transaction may take place in connection with the sale of goods or services, for example, if payment is deferred beyond normal business terms or is financed at a rate of interest that is not a market rate. If the arrangement constitutes a financing transaction, the entity shall measure the financial asset or financial liability at the **present value** of the future payments discounted at a market rate of interest for a similar debt instrument.

Examples – financial assets	
1	For a long-term loan made to another entity, a receivable is recognised at the present value of cash receivable (including interest payments and repayment of principal) from that entity.
2	For goods sold to a customer on short-term credit, a receivable is recognised at the undiscounted amount of cash receivable from that entity, which is normally the invoice price.
3	For an item sold to a customer on two-years interest-free credit, a receivable is recognised at the current cash sale price for that item (in financing transactions conducted on an arm's length basis the cash sales price would normally approximate to the present value). If the current cash sale price is not known, it may be estimated as the present value of the cash receivable discounted using the **prevailing market rate(s)** of interest for a similar receivable.
4	For a cash purchase of another entity's ordinary shares, the investment is recognised at the amount of cash paid to acquire the shares.

Examples – financial liabilities	
1	For a loan received from a bank, a payable is recognised initially at the present value of cash payable to the bank (eg including interest payments and repayment of principal).
2	For goods purchased from a supplier on short-term credit, a payable is recognised at the undiscounted amount owed to the supplier, which is normally the invoice price.

SUBSEQUENT MEASUREMENT

At the end of each **reporting period**, an entity shall measure financial instruments as follows, without any deduction for transaction costs the entity may incur on sale or other disposal: **11.14**

(a) Debt instruments that meet the conditions in paragraph 11.8(b) shall be measured at **amortised cost** using the **effective interest method**. Paragraphs 11.15 to 11.20 provide guidance on determining amortised cost using the effective interest method. Debt instruments that are payable or receivable within one year shall be measured at the undiscounted amount of the cash or other consideration expected to be paid or received (ie net of impairment—see paragraphs 11.21 to 11.26) unless the arrangement constitutes, in effect, a financing transaction (see paragraph 11.13). If the arrangement constitutes a financing transaction, the entity shall measure the debt instrument at the present value of the future payments discounted at a market rate of interest for a similar debt instrument.

(b) Debt instruments that meet the conditions in paragraph 11.8(b) may upon their initial recognition be designated by the entity as at fair value through profit or loss (paragraphs 11.27 to 11.32 provide guidance on fair value) provided doing so results in more relevant information, because either:

  (i) it eliminates or significantly reduces a measurement or recognition inconsistency (sometimes referred to as 'an accounting mismatch') that would otherwise arise from measuring assets or debt instruments or recognising the **gains** and losses on them on different bases; or

  (ii) a group of debt instruments or financial assets and debt instruments is managed and its performance is evaluated on a fair value basis, in accordance with a documented risk management or investment strategy, and information about the group is provided internally on that basis to the entity's **key management personnel** (as defined in Section 33 *Related Party Disclosures*, paragraph 33.6), for example members of the entity's board of directors and its chief executive officer.

(c) Commitments to receive a loan and to make a loan to another entity that meet the conditions in paragraph 11.8(c) shall be measured at cost (which sometimes is nil) less impairment.

(d) Investments in non-convertible preference shares and non-puttable ordinary shares or preference shares shall be measured as follows (paragraphs 11.27 to 11.32 provide guidance on fair value):

  (i) if the shares are **publicly traded** or their fair value can otherwise be measured reliably, the investment shall be measured at fair value with changes in fair value recognised in profit or loss; and

  (ii) all other such investments shall be measured at cost less impairment.

Impairment or uncollectability must be assessed for financial assets in (a), (c) and (d)(ii) above. Paragraphs 11.21 to 11.26 provide guidance.

Amortised cost and effective interest method

11.15 The amortised cost of a financial asset or financial liability at each **reporting date** is the net of the following amounts:

(a) the amount at which the financial asset or financial liability is measured at initial recognition;
(b) minus any repayments of the principal;
(c) plus or minus the cumulative amortisation using the effective interest method of any difference between the amount at initial recognition and the maturity amount;
(d) minus, in the case of a financial asset, any reduction (directly or through the use of an allowance account) for impairment or uncollectability.

Financial assets and financial liabilities that have no stated interest rate (and do not constitute a financing transaction) and are classified as payable or receivable within one year are initially measured at an undiscounted amount in accordance with paragraph 11.14(a). Therefore, (c) above does not apply to them.

11.16 The effective interest method is a method of calculating the amortised cost of a financial asset or a financial liability (or a group of financial assets or financial liabilities) and of allocating the interest income or interest expense over the relevant period. The **effective interest rate** is the rate that exactly discounts estimated future cash payments or receipts through the expected life of the financial instrument or, when appropriate, a shorter period, to the **carrying amount** of the financial asset or financial liability. The effective interest rate is determined on the basis of the carrying amount of the financial asset or liability at initial recognition. Under the effective interest method:

(a) the amortised cost of a financial asset (liability) is the present value of future cash receipts (payments) discounted at the effective interest rate; and
(b) the interest expense (income) in a period equals the carrying amount of the financial liability (asset) at the beginning of a period multiplied by the effective interest rate for the period.

11.17 When calculating the effective interest rate, an entity shall estimate cash flows considering all contractual terms of the financial instrument (eg prepayment, call and similar options) and known credit losses that have been incurred, but it shall not consider possible future credit losses not yet incurred.

11.18 When calculating the effective interest rate, an entity shall amortise any related fees, finance charges paid or received (such as 'points'), transaction costs and other premiums or discounts over the expected life of the instrument, except as follows. The entity shall use a shorter period if that is the period to which the fees, finance charges paid or received, transaction costs, premiums or discounts relate. This will be the case when the variable to which the fees, finance charges paid or received, transaction costs, premiums or discounts relate is repriced to market rates before the expected maturity of the instrument. In such a case, the appropriate amortisation period is the period to the next such repricing date.

11.19 For variable rate financial assets and variable rate financial liabilities, periodic re-estimation of cash flows to reflect changes in market rates of interest alters the effective interest rate. If a variable rate financial asset or variable rate financial liability is recognised initially at an amount equal to the principal receivable or payable at maturity, re-estimating the future interest payments normally has no significant effect on the carrying amount of the asset or liability.

If an entity revises its estimates of payments or receipts, the entity shall adjust the carrying amount of the financial asset or financial liability (or group of financial instruments) to reflect actual and revised estimated cash flows. The entity shall recalculate the carrying amount by computing the present value of estimated future cash flows at the financial instrument's original effective interest rate. The entity shall recognise the adjustment as **income** or **expense** in profit or loss at the date of the revision. 11.20

Example of determining amortised cost for a five-year loan using the effective interest method

On 1 January 20X0, an entity acquires a bond for Currency Units (CU)900, incurring transaction costs of CU50. Interest of CU40 is receivable annually, in arrears, over the next five years (31 December 20X0 to 31 December 20X4). The bond has a mandatory redemption of CU1100 on 31 December 20X4.

Year	Carrying amount at beginning of period	Interest income at 6.9583%*	Cash inflow	Carrying amount at end of period
	CU	CU	CU	CU
20X0	950.00	66.11	(40.00)	976.11
20X1	976.11	67.92	(40.00)	1,004.03
20X2	1,004.03	69.86	(40.00)	1,033.89
20X3	1,033.89	71.94	(40.00)	1,065.83
20X4	1,065.83	74.16	(40.00)	1,100.00
			(1,100.00)	0

* The effective interest rate of 6.9583 per cent is the rate that discounts the expected cash flows on the bond to the initial carrying amount:

$40/(1.069583)^1 + 40/(1.069583)^2 + 40/(1.069583)^3 + 40/(1.069583)^4 + 1{,}140/(1.069583)^5 = 950$

Impairment of financial instruments measured at cost or amortised cost

Recognition

At the end of each reporting period, an entity shall assess whether there is objective evidence of impairment of any financial assets that are measured at cost or amortised cost. If there is objective evidence of impairment, the entity shall recognise an **impairment loss** in profit or loss immediately. 11.21

Objective evidence that a financial asset or group of assets is impaired includes observable data that come to the attention of the holder of the asset about the following loss events: 11.22

(a) significant financial difficulty of the issuer or obligor;
(b) a breach of contract, such as a default or delinquency in interest or principal payments;
(c) the creditor, for economic or legal reasons relating to the debtor's financial difficulty, granting to the debtor a concession that the creditor would not otherwise consider;

(d) it has become **probable** that the debtor will enter bankruptcy or other financial reorganisation; and
(e) observable data indicating that there has been a measurable decrease in the estimated future cash flows from a group of financial assets since the initial recognition of those assets, even though the decrease cannot yet be identified with the individual financial assets in the group, such as adverse national or local economic conditions or adverse changes in industry conditions.

11.23 Other factors may also be evidence of impairment, including significant changes with an adverse effect that have taken place in the technological, market, economic or legal environment in which the issuer operates.

11.24 An entity shall assess the following financial assets individually for impairment:
(a) all equity instruments regardless of significance; and
(b) other financial assets that are individually significant.

An entity shall assess other financial assets for impairment either individually or grouped on the basis of similar **credit risk** characteristics.

Measurement

11.25 An entity shall measure an impairment loss on the following instruments measured at cost or amortised cost as follows:

(a) For an instrument measured at amortised cost in accordance with paragraph 11.14(a), the impairment loss is the difference between the asset's carrying amount and the present value of estimated cash flows discounted at the asset's original effective interest rate. If such a financial instrument has a variable interest rate, the discount rate for measuring any impairment loss is the current effective interest rate determined under the contract.
(b) For an instrument measured at cost less impairment in accordance with paragraph 11.14(c) and (d)(ii) the impairment loss is the difference between the asset's carrying amount and the best estimate (which will necessarily be an approximation) of the amount (which might be zero) that the entity would receive for the asset if it were to be sold at the reporting date.

Reversal

11.26 If, in a subsequent period, the amount of an impairment loss decreases and the decrease can be related objectively to an event occurring after the impairment was recognised (such as an improvement in the debtor's credit rating), the entity shall reverse the previously recognised impairment loss either directly or by adjusting an allowance account. The reversal shall not result in a carrying amount of the financial asset (net of any allowance account) that exceeds what the carrying amount would have been had the impairment not previously been recognised. The entity shall recognise the amount of the reversal in profit or loss immediately.

Fair value

11.27 Paragraph 11.14(b) and other sections of this FRS make reference to the fair value guidance in paragraphs 11.27 to 11.32, including Section 9 *Consolidated and Separate Financial Statements*, Section 12 *Other Financial Instruments Issues*, Section 13 *Inventories*, Section 14 *Investments in Associates*, Section 15 *Investments in Joint Ventures*, Section 16 *Investment Property*, Section 17 *Property, Plant and Equipment*,

Section 18 *Intangible Assets other than Goodwill*, Section 27 *Impairment of Assets*, Section 28 *Employee Benefits* (in relation to plan assets) and Section 34 *Specialised Activities*. In applying the fair value guidance to assets or liabilities accounted for in accordance with those sections, the reference to ordinary shares or preference shares in these paragraphs should be read to include the types of assets and liabilities addressed in those sections.

Paragraph 11.14(d)(i) requires an investment in non-convertible preference shares and non-puttable ordinary shares or preference shares to be measured at fair value if the shares are publicly traded or if their fair value can otherwise be measured reliably. An entity shall use the following hierarchy to estimate the fair value of the shares:

(a) The best evidence of fair value is a quoted price for an identical asset in an **active market**. Quoted in an active market in this context means quoted prices are readily and regularly available and those prices represent actual and regularly occurring market transactions on an arm's length basis. The quoted price is usually the current bid price.
(b) When quoted prices are unavailable, the price of a recent transaction for an identical asset provides evidence of fair value as long as there has not been a significant change in economic circumstances or a significant lapse of time since the transaction took place. If the entity can demonstrate that the last transaction price is not a good estimate of fair value (eg because it reflects the amount that an entity would receive or pay in a forced transaction, involuntary liquidation or distress sale), that price is adjusted.
(c) If the market for the asset is not active and recent transactions of an identical asset on their own are not a good estimate of fair value, an entity estimates the fair value by using a valuation technique. The objective of using a valuation technique is to estimate what the transaction price would have been on the measurement date in an arm's length exchange motivated by normal business considerations.

Valuation technique

Valuation techniques include using recent arm's length market transactions for an identical asset between knowledgeable, willing parties, if available, reference to the current fair value of another asset that is substantially the same as the asset being measured, discounted cash flow analysis and option pricing models. If there is a valuation technique commonly used by market participants to price the asset and that technique has been demonstrated to provide reliable estimates of prices obtained in actual market transactions, the entity uses that technique. **11.28**

The objective of using a valuation technique is to establish what the transaction price would have been on the measurement date in an arm's length exchange motivated by normal business considerations. Fair value is estimated on the basis of the results of a valuation technique that makes maximum use of market inputs, and relies as little as possible on entity-determined inputs. A valuation technique would be expected to arrive at a reliable estimate of the fair value if: **11.29**

(a) it reasonably reflects how the market could be expected to price the asset; and
(b) the inputs to the valuation technique reasonably represent market expectations and measures of the risk return factors inherent in the asset.

No active market

11.30 The fair value of ordinary shares or preference shares that do not have a quoted market price in an active market is reliably measurable if:

(a) the variability in the range of reasonable fair value estimates is not significant for that asset; or

(b) the probabilities of the various estimates within the range can be reasonably assessed and used in estimating fair value.

11.31 There are many situations in which the variability in the range of reasonable fair value estimates of assets that do not have a quoted market price is likely not to be significant. Normally it is possible to estimate the fair value of ordinary shares or preference shares that an entity has acquired from an outside party. However, if the range of reasonable fair value estimates is significant and the probabilities of the various estimates cannot be reasonably assessed, an entity is precluded from measuring the ordinary shares or preference shares at fair value.

11.32 If a reliable measure of fair value is no longer available for an asset measured at fair value (eg ordinary shares or preference shares measured at fair value through profit or loss), its carrying amount at the last date the asset was reliably measurable becomes its new cost. The entity shall measure the ordinary shares or preference shares at this cost amount less impairment until a reliable measure of fair value becomes available.

DERECOGNITION OF A FINANCIAL ASSET

11.33 An entity shall derecognise a financial asset only when:

(a) the contractual rights to the cash flows from the financial asset expire or are settled, or

(b) the entity transfers to another party substantially all of the risks and rewards of ownership of the financial asset, or

(c) the entity, despite having retained some significant risks and rewards of ownership, has transferred control of the asset to another party and the other party has the practical ability to sell the asset in its entirety to an unrelated third party and is able to exercise that ability unilaterally and without needing to impose additional restrictions on the transfer. In this case, the entity shall:

   (i) derecognise the asset; and

   (ii) recognise separately any rights and obligations retained or created in the transfer.

The carrying amount of the transferred asset shall be allocated between the rights or obligations retained and those transferred on the basis of their relative fair values at the transfer date. Newly created rights and obligations shall be measured at their fair values at that date. Any difference between the consideration received and the amounts recognised and derecognised in accordance with this paragraph shall be recognised in profit or loss in the period of the transfer.

11.34 If a transfer does not result in derecognition because the entity has retained significant risks and rewards of ownership of the transferred asset, the entity shall continue to recognise the transferred asset in its entirety and shall recognise a financial liability for the consideration received. The asset and liability shall not be offset. In subsequent periods, the entity shall recognise any income on the transferred asset and any expense incurred on the financial liability.

If a transferor provides non-cash collateral (such as debt or equity instruments) to the transferee, the accounting for the collateral by the transferor and the transferee depends on whether the transferee has the right to sell or repledge the collateral and on whether the transferor has defaulted. The transferor and transferee shall account for the collateral as follows: **11.35**

(a) If the transferee has the right by contract or custom to sell or repledge the collateral, the transferor shall reclassify that asset in its **statement of financial position** (eg as a loaned asset, pledged equity instruments or repurchase receivable) separately from other assets.
(b) If the transferee sells collateral pledged to it, it shall recognise the proceeds from the sale and a liability measured at fair value for its obligation to return the collateral.
(c) If the transferor defaults under the terms of the contract and is no longer entitled to redeem the collateral, it shall derecognise the collateral, and the transferee shall recognise the collateral as its asset initially measured at fair value or, if it has already sold the collateral, derecognise its obligation to return the collateral.
(d) Except as provided in (c), the transferor shall continue to carry the collateral as its asset, and the transferee shall not recognise the collateral as an asset.

Example: Transfer that qualifies for derecognition

An entity sells a group of its accounts receivable to a bank at less than their face amount. The entity continues to handle collections from the debtors on behalf of the bank, including sending monthly statements, and the bank pays the entity a market-rate fee for servicing the receivables. The entity is obliged to remit promptly to the bank any and all amounts collected, but it has no obligation to the bank for slow payment or non-payment by the debtors. In this case, the entity has transferred to the bank substantially all of the risks and rewards of ownership of the receivables. Accordingly, it removes the receivables from its statement of financial position (ie derecognises them), and it shows no liability in respect of the proceeds received from the bank. The entity recognises a loss calculated as the difference between the carrying amount of the receivables at the time of sale and the proceeds received from the bank. The entity recognises a liability to the extent that it has collected funds from the debtors but has not yet remitted them to the bank.

Example: Transfer that does not qualify for derecognition

The facts are the same as the preceding example except that the entity has agreed to buy back from the bank any receivables for which the debtor is in arrears as to principal or interest for more than 120 days.

In this case, the entity has retained the risk of slow payment or non-payment by the debtors—a significant risk with respect to receivables. Accordingly, the entity does not treat the receivables as having been sold to the bank, and it does not derecognise them. Instead, it treats the proceeds from the bank as a loan secured by the receivables. The entity continues to recognise the receivables as an asset until they are collected or written off as uncollectible.

DERECOGNITION OF A FINANCIAL LIABILITY

11.36 An entity shall derecognise a financial liability (or a part of a financial liability) only when it is extinguished—ie when the obligation specified in the contract is discharged, is cancelled or expires.

11.37 If an existing borrower and lender exchange financial instruments with substantially different terms, the entities shall account for the transaction as an extinguishment of the original financial liability and the recognition of a new financial liability. Similarly, an entity shall account for a substantial modification of the terms of an existing financial liability or a part of it (whether or not attributable to the financial difficulty of the debtor) as an extinguishment of the original financial liability and the recognition of a new financial liability.

11.38 The entity shall recognise in profit or loss any difference between the carrying amount of the financial liability (or part of a financial liability) extinguished or transferred to another party and the consideration paid, including any non-cash assets transferred or liabilities assumed.

PRESENTATION

11.38A A financial asset and a financial liability shall be offset and the net amount presented in the statement of financial position when, and only when, an entity:

(a) currently has a legally enforceable right to set off the recognised amounts; and
(b) intends either to settle on a net basis, or to realise the asset and settle the liability simultaneously.

DISCLOSURES

11.39 The disclosures below make reference to disclosures for financial liabilities measured at fair value through profit or loss. Entities that have only basic financial instruments (and therefore do not apply Section 12), and have not chosen to designate financial instruments as at fair value through profit or loss (in accordance with paragraph 11.14(b)) will not have any financial liabilities measured at fair value through profit or loss and hence will not need to provide such disclosures.

Disclosure of accounting policies for financial instruments

11.40 In accordance with paragraph 8.5, an entity shall disclose, in the summary of significant accounting policies, the measurement basis (or bases) used for financial instruments and the other accounting policies used for financial instruments that are relevant to an understanding of the **financial statements**.

Statement of financial position – categories of financial assets and financial liabilities

11.41 An entity shall disclose the carrying amounts of each of the following categories of financial assets and financial liabilities at the reporting date, in total, either in the statement of financial position or in the **notes**:

(a) financial assets measured at fair value through profit or loss (paragraphs 11.14(b), 11.14(d)(i), 12.8 and 12.9);
(b) financial assets that are debt instruments measured at amortised cost (paragraph 11.14(a));

(c) financial assets that are equity instruments measured at cost less impairment (paragraphs 11.14(d)(ii), 12.8 and 12.9);
(d) financial liabilities measured at fair value through profit or loss (paragraphs 11.14(b), 12.8 and 12.9). Financial liabilities that are not held as part of a trading portfolio and are not **derivatives** shall be shown separately;
(e) financial liabilities measured at amortised cost (paragraph 11.14(a)); and
(f) loan commitments measured at cost less impairment (paragraph 11.14(c)).

An entity shall disclose information that enables users of its financial statements to evaluate the significance of financial instruments for its **financial position** and **performance**. For example, for long-term debt such information would normally include the terms and conditions of the debt instrument (such as interest rate, maturity, repayment schedule, and restrictions that the debt instrument imposes on the entity). **11.42**

For all financial assets and financial liabilities measured at fair value, the entity shall disclose the basis for determining fair value, eg quoted market price in an active market or a valuation technique. When a valuation technique is used, the entity shall disclose the assumptions applied in determining fair value for each class of financial assets or financial liabilities. For example, if applicable, an entity discloses information about the assumptions relating to prepayment rates, rates of estimated credit losses, and interest rates or discount rates. **11.43**

If a reliable measure of fair value is no longer available for ordinary or preference shares measured at fair value through profit or loss, the entity shall disclose that fact. **11.44**

Derecognition

If an entity has transferred financial assets to another party in a transaction that does not qualify for derecognition (see paragraphs 11.33 to 11.35), the entity shall disclose the following for each class of such financial assets: **11.45**

(a) the nature of the assets;
(b) the nature of the risks and rewards of ownership to which the entity remains exposed; and
(c) the carrying amounts of the assets and of any associated liabilities that the entity continues to recognise.

Collateral

When an entity has pledged financial assets as collateral for liabilities or **contingent liabilities**, it shall disclose the following: **11.46**

(a) the carrying amount of the financial assets pledged as collateral; and
(b) the terms and conditions relating to its pledge.

Defaults and breaches on loans payable

For **loans payable** recognised at the reporting date for which there is a breach of terms or default of principal, interest, sinking fund, or redemption terms that has not been remedied by the reporting date, an entity shall disclose the following: **11.47**

(a) details of that breach or default;
(b) the carrying amount of the related loans payable at the reporting date; and
(c) whether the breach or default was remedied, or the terms of the loans payable were renegotiated, before the financial statements were authorised for issue.

Items of income, expense, gains or losses

11.48 An entity shall disclose the following items of income, expense, gains or losses:

(a) income, expense, net gains or net losses, including changes in fair value, recognised on:

(i) financial assets measured at fair value through profit or loss;

(ii) financial liabilities measured at fair value through profit or loss (with separate disclosure of movements on those which are not held as part of a trading portfolio and are not derivatives);

(iii) financial assets measured at amortised cost; and

(iv) financial liabilities measured at amortised cost;

(b) total interest income and total interest expense (calculated using the effective interest method) for financial assets or financial liabilities that are not measured at fair value through profit or loss; and

(c) the amount of any impairment loss for each class of financial asset. A class of financial asset is a grouping that is appropriate to the nature of the information disclosed and that takes into account the characteristics of the financial assets.

Financial instruments at fair value through profit or loss

11.48A The following disclosures are required only for financial instruments at fair value through profit or loss that are not held as part of a trading portfolio and are not derivatives:

(a) The amount of change, during the period and cumulatively, in the fair value of the financial instrument that is attributable to changes in the credit risk of that instrument, determined either:

(i) as the amount of change in its fair value that is not attributable to changes in market conditions that give rise to **market risk**; or

(ii) using an alternative method the entity believes more faithfully represents the amount of change in its fair value that is attributable to changes in the credit risk of the instrument.

(b) The method used to establish the amount of change attributable to changes in own credit risk, or, if the change cannot be measured reliably or is not **material**, that fact.

(c) The difference between the financial liability's carrying amount and the amount the entity would be contractually required to pay at maturity to the holder of the obligation.

(d) If an instrument contains both a liability and an equity feature, and the instrument has multiple features that substantially modify the cash flows and the values of those features are interdependent (such as a callable convertible debt instrument), the existence of those features.

(e) Any difference between the fair value at initial recognition and the amount that would be determined at that date using a valuation technique, and the amount recognised in profit or loss.

(f) Information that enables users of the entity's financial statements to evaluate the nature and extent of relevant risks arising from financial instruments to which the entity is exposed at the end of the reporting period. These risks typically include, but are not limited to, credit risk, **liquidity risk** and market risk. The disclosure should include both the entity's exposure to each type of risk and how it manages those risks.

Financial institutions

A **financial institution** (other than a **retirement benefit plan**) shall, in addition, apply the requirements of paragraph 34.17. **11.48B**

A retirement benefit plan shall, in addition, apply the requirements of paragraphs 34.39 to 34.48. **11.48C**

Section 12
Other Financial Instruments Issues

SCOPE OF SECTIONS 11 AND 12

12.1 Section 11 *Basic Financial Instruments* and Section 12 *Other Financial Instruments Issues* together deal with recognising, derecognising, measuring, and disclosing **financial instruments** (**financial assets** and **financial liabilities**). Section 11 applies to basic financial instruments and is relevant to all entities. Section 12 applies to other, more complex financial instruments and transactions. If an entity enters into only basic financial instrument transactions then Section 12 is not applicable. However, even entities with only basic financial instruments shall consider the scope of Section 12 to ensure they are exempt.

PBE12.1A **Public benefit entities** or other members of a **public benefit entity group** that make or receive **public benefit entity concessionary loans** shall refer to the relevant paragraphs of Section 34 *Specialised Activities* for the accounting requirements for such loans.

ACCOUNTING POLICY CHOICE

12.2 An entity shall choose to apply either:

(a) the provisions of both Section 11 and Section 12 in full; or
(b) the **recognition** and **measurement** provisions of IAS 39 *Financial Instruments: Recognition and Measurement* (as adopted for use in the EU) and the disclosure requirements of Sections 11 and 12; or
(c) the recognition and measurement provisions of IFRS 9 *Financial Instruments* and/or IAS 39 (as amended following the publication of IFRS 9) and the disclosure requirements of Sections 11 and 12;

to account for all of its financial instruments. Where an entity chooses (b) or (c) it applies the scope of the relevant standard to its financial instruments. An entity's choice of (a), (b) or (c) is an **accounting policy** choice. Paragraphs 10.8 to 10.14 contain requirements for determining when a change in accounting policy is appropriate, how such a change should be accounted for and what information should be disclosed about the change in accounting policy.

SCOPE OF SECTION 12

12.3 Section 12 applies to all financial instruments except the following:

(a) Those covered by Section 11.
(b) Investments in **subsidiaries** (see Section 9 *Consolidated and Separate Financial Statements*), **associates** (see Section 14 *Investments in Associates*) and **joint ventures** (see Section 15 *Investments in Joint Ventures*).
(c) Employers' rights and obligations under employee benefit plans (see Section 28 *Employee Benefits*).
(d) **Insurance contracts** (including **reinsurance contracts**) that the entity issues and reinsurance contracts that the entity holds (see FRS 103 *Insurance Contracts*).
(e) Financial instruments that meet the definition of an entity's own **equity** and the equity component of **compound financial instruments** issued by the reporting entity that contain both a **liability** and an equity component (see Section 22 *Liabilities and Equity*).
(f) **Leases** (see Section 20 *Leases*) unless the lease could, as a result of non-typical contractual terms, result in a loss to the lessor or the lessee.

(g) Contracts for contingent consideration in a **business combination** (see Section 19 *Business Combinations and Goodwill*). This exemption applies only to the acquirer.
(h) Any forward contract between an acquirer and a selling shareholder to buy or sell an acquiree that will result in a business combination at a future **acquisition date**. The term of the forward contract should not exceed a reasonable period normally necessary to obtain any required approvals and to complete the transaction.
(i) Financial instruments, contracts and obligations to which Section 26 Share-based Payment applies, except for contracts within the scope of paragraph 12.5.
(j) Financial instruments issued by an entity with a **discretionary participation feature** (see FRS 103).
(k) Reimbursement assets accounted for in accordance with Section 21 *Provisions and Contingencies*.
(l) **Financial guarantee contracts** (see Section 21).

A reporting entity that issues the financial instruments set out in (d) or (j) or holds the financial instruments set out in (d) is required by paragraph 1.6 to apply FRS 103 to those financial instruments.

Most contracts to buy or sell a non-financial item such as a commodity, **inventory**, or **property, plant and equipment** are excluded from this section because they are not financial instruments. However, this section applies to all contracts that impose risks on the buyer or seller that are not typical of contracts to buy or sell non-financial items. For example, this section applies to contracts that, as a result of its contractual terms, could result in a loss to the buyer or seller that is unrelated to changes in the price of the non-financial item, changes in foreign exchange rates, or a default by one of the counterparties. **12.4**

In addition to the contracts described in paragraph 12.4, this section applies to contracts to buy or sell non-financial items if the contract can be settled net in **cash** or another financial instrument, or by exchanging financial instruments as if the contracts were financial instruments, with the following exception: contracts that were entered into and continue to be held for the purpose of the receipt or delivery of a non-financial item in accordance with the entity's expected purchase, sale or usage requirements are not financial instruments for the purposes of this section. **12.5**

INITIAL RECOGNITION OF FINANCIAL ASSETS AND LIABILITIES

An entity shall recognise a financial asset or a financial liability only when the entity becomes a party to the contractual provisions of the instrument. **12.6**

INITIAL MEASUREMENT

When a financial asset or financial liability is recognised initially, an entity shall measure it at its **fair value**, which is normally the transaction price (including **transaction costs** except in the initial measurement of financial assets and liabilities that are measured at fair value through profit or loss). If payment for an asset is deferred beyond normal business terms or is financed at a rate of interest that is not a market rate, the entity shall initially measure the asset at the **present value** of the future payments discounted at a market rate of interest for a similar debt instrument. **12.7**

SUBSEQUENT MEASUREMENT

12.8 At the end of each **reporting period**, an entity shall measure all financial instruments within the scope of Section 12 at fair value and recognise changes in fair value in **profit or loss**, except as follows:

(a) investments in equity instruments that are not **publicly traded** and whose fair value cannot otherwise be measured reliably and contracts linked to such instruments that, if exercised, will result in delivery of such instruments, shall be measured at cost less impairment; and

(b) **hedging instruments** in a designated hedging relationship accounted for in accordance with paragraph 12.23.

12.9 If a reliable measure of fair value is no longer available for an equity instrument (or a contract linked to such an instrument) that is not publicly traded but is measured at fair value through profit or loss, its fair value at the last date the instrument was reliably measurable is treated as the cost of the instrument. The entity shall measure the instrument at this cost amount less impairment until a reliable measure of fair value becomes available.

FAIR VALUE

12.10 An entity shall apply the guidance on fair value in paragraphs 11.27 to 11.32 to fair value measurements in accordance with this section as well as for fair value measurements in accordance with Section 11.

12.11 The fair value of a financial liability that is due on demand is not less than the amount payable on demand, discounted from the first date that the amount could be required to be paid.

12.12 An entity shall not include transaction costs in the initial measurement of financial assets and liabilities that will be measured subsequently at fair value through profit or loss.

IMPAIRMENT OF FINANCIAL INSTRUMENTS MEASURED AT COST OR AMORTISED COST

12.13 An entity shall apply the guidance on impairment of a financial instrument measured at cost in paragraphs 11.21 to 11.26 to financial instruments measured at cost less impairment in accordance with this section.

DERECOGNITION OF A FINANCIAL ASSET OR FINANCIAL LIABILITY

12.14 An entity shall apply the **derecognition** requirements in paragraphs 11.33 to 11.38 to financial assets and financial liabilities to which this section applies.

HEDGE ACCOUNTING

12.15 If specified criteria are met, an entity may designate a hedging relationship between a hedging instrument and a **hedged item** in such a way as to qualify for hedge accounting.

12.16 To qualify for hedge accounting, an entity shall comply with all of the following conditions:

(a) the entity designates and documents the hedging relationship so that the risk being hedged, the hedged item and the hedging instrument are clearly identified and the risk in the hedged item is the risk being hedged with the hedging instrument;
(b) the hedged risk is one of the risks specified in paragraph 12.17;
(c) the hedging instrument is as specified in paragraph 12.18; and
(d) the entity expects the hedging instrument to be highly effective in offsetting the designated hedged risk. The **effectiveness of a hedge** is the degree to which changes in the fair value or **cash flows** of the hedged item that are attributable to the hedged risk are offset by changes in the fair value or cash flows of the hedging instrument.

This FRS permits hedge accounting only for the following risks: **12.17**

(a) interest rate risk and foreign exchange risk of a debt instrument measured at **amortised cost**;
(b) foreign exchange and interest rate risk in a **firm commitment** or a **highly probable forecast transaction**;
(c) price risk of a commodity that the entity holds or price risk in a firm commitment or highly probable forecast transaction to purchase or sell a commodity; and
(d) foreign exchange risk in a **net investment in a foreign operation**.

This FRS permits hedge accounting only if the hedging instrument meets all of the following terms and conditions: **12.18**

(a) it is an interest rate swap, a foreign currency swap, a cross currency interest rate swap, a forward or future foreign currency exchange contract, a forward or future commodity exchange contract, or any financial instrument used to hedge foreign exchange risk in a foreign operation; provided it is expected to be highly effective in offsetting the designated hedged risk(s) as identified in paragraph 12.17;
(b) it involves a party external to the reporting entity (ie external to the **group**, segment or individual entity being reported on);
(c) its **notional amount** is equal to the designated amount of the principal or notional amount of the hedged item;
(d) it has a specified maturity date not later than:

    (i) the maturity of the financial instrument being hedged;
    (ii) the expected settlement of the commodity purchase or sale commitment; or
    (iii) the later of the occurrence and settlement of the highly probable forecast foreign currency or commodity transaction being hedged; and

(e) it has no prepayment, early termination or extension features other than at fair value.

Hedge of fixed interest rate risk or foreign exchange risk of a recognised financial instrument or commodity price risk in a firm commitment or of a commodity held

If the conditions in paragraph 12.16 are met and the hedged risk is the exposure to a fixed interest rate risk or foreign exchange risk of a debt instrument measured at amortised cost or the commodity price risk of a commodity that it holds or has a firm commitment, the entity shall: **12.19**

(a) recognise the hedging instrument as an **asset** or liability and the change in the fair value of the hedging instrument in profit or loss; and

(b) recognise the change in the fair value of the hedged item related to the hedged risk in profit or loss and as an adjustment to the **carrying amount** of the hedged item.

12.20 If the hedged risk is the fixed interest rate risk of a debt instrument measured at amortised cost, the entity shall recognise the periodic net cash settlements on the interest rate swap that is the hedging instrument in profit or loss in the period in which the net settlements accrue.

12.21 The entity shall discontinue the hedge accounting specified in paragraph 12.19 if:

(a) the hedging instrument expires or is sold or terminated;
(b) the hedge no longer meets the conditions for hedge accounting specified in paragraph 12.16; or
(c) the entity revokes the designation.

12.22 If hedge accounting is discontinued and the hedged item is an asset or liability carried at amortised cost that has not been derecognised, any **gains** or losses recognised as adjustments to the carrying amount of the hedged item are amortised into profit or loss using the **effective interest method** over the remaining life of the hedged instrument.

Hedge of variable interest rate risk or foreign exchange risk of a recognised financial instrument, foreign exchange risk or interest rate risk in a firm commitment or highly probable forecast transaction or commodity price risk in a highly probable forecast transaction, or foreign exchange risk in a net investment in a foreign operation

12.23 If the conditions in paragraph 12.16 are met and the hedged risk is:

(a) the variable interest rate risk or foreign exchange risk in a debt instrument measured at amortised cost;
(b) the foreign exchange risk or interest rate risk in a firm commitment or a highly probable forecast transaction;
(c) the commodity price risk in a highly probable forecast transaction; or
(d) the foreign exchange risk in a net investment in a foreign operation;

the entity shall recognise in **other comprehensive income** the portion of the change in the fair value of the hedging instrument that was effective in offsetting the change in the fair value or expected cash flows of the hedged item. The entity shall recognise in profit or loss any excess (in absolute terms) of the cumulative change in fair value of the hedging instrument since inception of the hedge over the cumulative change in the fair value of the expected cash flows of the hedged item since inception of the hedge (sometimes called hedge ineffectiveness). The hedging gain or loss recognised in other comprehensive income shall be reclassified to profit or loss when the hedged item is recognised in profit or loss or when the hedging relationship ends. However, the cumulative amount of any exchange differences that relate to a hedge of a net investment in a foreign operation recognised in other comprehensive income shall not be reclassified to profit or loss on disposal or partial disposal of the foreign operation.

12.24 If the hedged risk is the variable interest rate risk in a debt instrument measured at amortised cost, the entity shall subsequently recognise in profit or loss the periodic net cash settlements from the interest rate swap that is the hedging instrument in the period in which the net settlements accrue.

The entity shall discontinue the hedge accounting specified in paragraph 12.23 if: **12.25**

(a) the hedging instrument expires, is sold or terminated;
(b) the hedge no longer meets the criteria for hedge accounting in paragraph 12.16;
(c) in a hedge of a forecast transaction, the forecast transaction is no longer highly probable; or
(d) the entity revokes the designation.

If the forecast transaction is no longer expected to take place or if the hedged debt instrument measured at amortised cost is derecognised, any gain or loss on the hedging instrument that was recognised in other comprehensive income shall be reclassified from other comprehensive income to profit or loss.

PRESENTATION

A financial asset and a financial liability shall be offset and the net amount presented in the **statement of financial position** when, and only when, an entity: **12.25A**

(a) currently has a legally enforceable right to set off the recognised amounts; and
(b) intends either to settle on a net basis, or to realise the asset and settle the liability simultaneously.

DISCLOSURES

An entity applying this section shall make all of the disclosures required in Section 11 incorporating in those disclosures, financial instruments that are within the scope of this section as well as those within the scope of Section 11. For financial instruments in the scope of this section that are not held as part of a trading portfolio and are not **derivative** instruments, an entity shall provide additional disclosures as set out in paragraph 11.48A. In addition, if the entity uses hedge accounting, it shall make the additional disclosures in paragraphs 12.27 to 12.29. **12.26**

An entity shall disclose the following separately for hedges of each of the four types of risks described in paragraph 12.17: **12.27**

(a) a description of the hedge;
(b) a description of the financial instruments designated as hedging instruments and their fair values at the **reporting date**; and
(c) the nature of the risks being hedged, including a description of the hedged item.

If an entity uses hedge accounting for a hedge as described in paragraphs 12.19 to 12.22 it shall disclose the following: **12.28**

(a) the amount of the change in fair value of the hedging instrument recognised in profit or loss for the period.
(b) the amount of the change in fair value of the hedged item recognised in profit or loss for the period.

If an entity uses hedge accounting for a hedge as described in paragraphs 12.23 to 12.25 it shall disclose the following: **12.29**

(a) the periods when the cash flows are expected to occur and when they are expected to affect profit or loss;
(b) a description of any forecast transaction for which hedge accounting had previously been used, but which is no longer expected to occur;
(c) the amount of the change in fair value of the hedging instrument that was recognised in other comprehensive income during the period (paragraph 12.23);

(d) the amount that was reclassified from other comprehensive income to profit or loss for the period (paragraphs 12.23 and 12.25); and
(e) the amount of any excess of the fair value of the hedging instrument over the change in the fair value of the expected cash flows that was recognised in profit or loss for the period (paragraph 12.24).

Section 13
Inventories

SCOPE OF THIS SECTION

This section sets out the principles for recognising and measuring **inventories**. Inventories are **assets**: 13.1

(a) held for sale in the ordinary course of business;
(b) in the process of production for such sale; or
(c) in the form of materials or supplies to be consumed in the production process or in the rendering of services.

This section applies to all inventories, except: 13.2

(a) work in progress arising under **construction contracts**, including directly related service contracts (see Section 23 *Revenue*);
(b) **financial instruments** (see Section 11 *Basic Financial Instruments* and Section 12 *Other Financial Instruments Issues*); and
(c) **biological assets** related to **agricultural activity** and **agricultural produce** at the point of harvest (see Section 34 *Specialised Activities*).

This section does not apply to the **measurement** of inventories measured at **fair value less costs to sell** through **profit or loss** at each reporting date. 13.3

MEASUREMENT OF INVENTORIES

An entity shall measure inventories at the lower of **cost** and estimated selling price less costs to complete and sell. 13.4

Inventories held for distribution at no or nominal consideration shall be measured at cost adjusted, when applicable, for any loss of **service potential**. 13.4A

COST OF INVENTORIES

An entity shall include in the cost of inventories all costs of purchase, costs of conversion and other costs incurred in bringing the inventories to their present location and condition. 13.5

Where inventories are acquired through a **non-exchange transaction**, their cost shall be measured at their **fair value** as at the date of acquisition. For **public benefit entities** and entities within a **public benefit entity group**, this requirement only applies to inventories that are recognised as a result of the requirements for incoming resources from non-exchange transactions as prescribed in Section 34 *Specialised Activities*. 13.5A

COSTS OF PURCHASE

The costs of purchase of inventories comprise the purchase price, import duties and other taxes (other than those subsequently recoverable by the entity from the taxing authorities), and transport, handling and other costs directly attributable to the acquisition of finished goods, materials and services. Trade discounts, rebates and other similar items are deducted in determining the costs of purchase. 13.6

An entity may purchase inventories on deferred settlement terms. In some cases, the arrangement effectively contains an unstated financing element, for example, a difference between the purchase price for normal credit terms and the deferred 13.7

settlement amount. In these cases, the difference is recognised as interest expense over the period of the financing and is not added to the cost of the inventories unless the inventory is a **qualifying asset** (see Section 25 *Borrowing Costs)* and the entity adopts a policy of capitalisation of borrowing costs.

COSTS OF CONVERSION

13.8 The costs of conversion of inventories include costs directly related to the units of production, such as direct labour. They also include a systematic allocation of fixed and variable production overheads that are incurred in converting materials into finished goods. Fixed production overheads are those indirect costs of production that remain relatively constant regardless of the volume of production, such as **depreciation** and maintenance of factory buildings and equipment, and the cost of factory management and administration. Variable production overheads are those indirect costs of production that vary directly, or nearly directly, with the volume of production, such as indirect materials and indirect labour.

13.8A Production overheads include the costs for obligations (recognised and measured in accordance with Section 21 *Provisions and Contingencies*) for dismantling, removing and restoring a site on which an item of **property, plant and equipment** is located that are incurred during the **reporting period** as a consequence of having used that item of property, plant and equipment to produce inventory during that period.

ALLOCATION OF PRODUCTION OVERHEADS

13.9 An entity shall allocate fixed production overheads to the costs of conversion on the basis of the normal capacity of the production facilities. Normal capacity is the production expected to be achieved on average over a number of periods or seasons under normal circumstances, taking into account the loss of capacity resulting from planned maintenance. The actual level of production may be used if it approximates normal capacity. The amount of fixed overhead allocated to each unit of production is not increased as a consequence of low production or idle plant. Unallocated overheads are recognised as an **expense** in the period in which they are incurred. In periods of abnormally high production, the amount of fixed overhead allocated to each unit of production is decreased so that inventories are not measured above cost. Variable production overheads are allocated to each unit of production on the basis of the actual use of the production facilities.

JOINT PRODUCTS AND BY-PRODUCTS

13.10 A production process may result in more than one product being produced simultaneously. This is the case, for example, when joint products are produced or when there is a main product and a by-product. When the costs of raw materials or conversion of each product are not separately identifiable, an entity shall allocate them between the products on a rational and consistent basis. The allocation may be based, for example, on the relative sales value of each product either at the stage in the production process when the products become separately identifiable, or at the completion of production. Most by-products, by their nature, are immaterial. When this is the case, the entity shall measure them at selling price less costs to complete and sell and deduct this amount from the cost of the main product. As a result, the **carrying amount** of the main product is not materially different from its cost.

OTHER COSTS INCLUDED IN INVENTORIES

An entity shall include other costs in the cost of inventories only to the extent that they are incurred in bringing the inventories to their present location and condition. **13.11**

Paragraph 12.19(b) provides that, in some circumstances, the change in the fair value of the **hedging instrument** in a hedge of fixed interest rate risk or commodity price risk of a commodity held adjusts the carrying amount of the commodity. **13.12**

COSTS EXCLUDED FROM INVENTORIES

Examples of costs excluded from the cost of inventories and recognised as expenses in the period in which they are incurred are: **13.13**

(a) abnormal amounts of wasted materials, labour or other production costs;
(b) storage costs, unless those costs are necessary during the production process before a further production stage;
(c) administrative overheads that do not contribute to bringing inventories to their present location and condition; and
(d) selling costs.

COST OF INVENTORIES OF A SERVICE PROVIDER

To the extent that service providers have inventories, they measure them at the costs of their production. These costs consist primarily of the labour and other costs of personnel directly engaged in providing the service, including supervisory personnel, and attributable overheads. Labour and other costs relating to sales and general administrative personnel are not included but are recognised as expenses in the period in which they are incurred. The cost of inventories of a service provider does not include profit margins or non-attributable overheads that are often factored into prices charged by service providers. **13.14**

COST OF AGRICULTURAL PRODUCE HARVESTED FROM BIOLOGICAL ASSETS

Section 34 requires that inventories comprising agricultural produce that an entity has harvested from its biological assets should be measured on initial **recognition,** at the point of harvest, at either their fair value less estimated costs to sell or the lower of cost and estimated selling price less costs to complete and sell. This becomes the cost of the inventories at that date for application of this section. **13.15**

TECHNIQUES FOR MEASURING COST, SUCH AS STANDARD COSTING, RETAIL METHOD AND MOST RECENT PURCHASE PRICE

An entity may use techniques such as the standard cost method, the retail method or most recent purchase price for measuring the cost of inventories if the result approximates cost. Standard costs take into account normal levels of materials and supplies, labour, efficiency and capacity utilisation. They are regularly reviewed and, if necessary, revised in the light of current conditions. The retail method measures cost by reducing the sales value of the inventory by the appropriate percentage gross margin. **13.16**

COST FORMULAS

13.17 An entity shall measure the cost of inventories of items that are not ordinarily interchangeable and goods or services produced and segregated for specific projects by using specific identification of their individual costs.

13.18 An entity shall measure the cost of inventories, other than those dealt with in paragraph 13.17, by using the first-in, first-out (FIFO) or weighted average cost formula. An entity shall use the same cost formula for all inventories having a similar nature and use to the entity. For inventories with a different nature or use, different cost formulas may be justified. The last-in, first-out method (LIFO) is not permitted by this FRS.

IMPAIRMENT OF INVENTORIES

13.19 Paragraphs 27.2 to 27.4 require an entity to assess at the end of each reporting period whether any inventories are impaired, ie the carrying amount is not fully recoverable (eg because of damage, obsolescence or declining selling prices). If an item (or group of items) of inventory is impaired, those paragraphs require the entity to measure the inventory at its selling price less costs to complete and sell, and to recognise an **impairment loss**. Those paragraphs also require a reversal of a prior impairment in some circumstances.

RECOGNITION AS AN EXPENSE

13.20 When inventories are sold, the entity shall recognise the carrying amount of those inventories as an expense in the period in which the related **revenue** is recognised.

13.20A When inventories held for distribution at no or nominal consideration are distributed, the carrying amount of those inventories shall be recognised as an expense.

13.21 Some inventories may be allocated to other asset accounts, for example, inventory used as a component of self-constructed property, plant or equipment. Inventories allocated to another asset in this way are accounted for subsequently in accordance with the section of this FRS relevant to that type of asset.

DISCLOSURES

13.22 An entity shall disclose the following:

(a) the **accounting policies** adopted in measuring inventories, including the cost formula used;
(b) the total carrying amount of inventories and the carrying amount in classifications appropriate to the entity;
(c) the amount of inventories recognised as an expense during the period;
(d) impairment losses recognised or reversed in profit or loss in accordance with Section 27; and
(e) the total carrying amount of inventories pledged as security for **liabilities**.

Section 14
Investments in Associates

SCOPE OF THIS SECTION

This section applies to accounting for **associates** in **consolidated financial statements**. This section also applies to accounting for investments in associates in the **individual financial statements** of an investor that is not a **parent**. An entity that is a parent shall account for its investments in associates in its **separate financial statements** in accordance with paragraphs 9.26 and 9.26A, as appropriate. 14.1

ASSOCIATES DEFINED

An associate is an entity, including an unincorporated entity such as a partnership, over which the investor has **significant influence** and that is neither a **subsidiary** nor an interest in a **joint venture**. 14.2

Significant influence is the power to participate in the financial and operating policy decisions of the associate but is not **control** or **joint control** over those policies. 14.3

(a) If an investor holds, directly or indirectly (eg through subsidiaries), 20 per cent or more of the voting power of the associate, it is presumed that the investor has significant influence, unless it can be clearly demonstrated that this is not the case.
(b) Conversely, if the investor holds, directly or indirectly (eg through subsidiaries), less than 20 per cent of the voting power of the associate, it is presumed that the investor does not have significant influence, unless such influence can be clearly demonstrated.
(c) A substantial or majority ownership by another investor does not preclude an investor from having significant influence.

MEASUREMENT—ACCOUNTING POLICY ELECTION

An investor that is not a parent but that has an investment in one or more associates shall, in its individual financial statements, account for all of its investments in associates using either: 14.4

(a) the cost model in accordance with paragraphs 14.5 to 14.6;
(b) [not used]
(c) the fair value model in accordance with paragraphs 14.9 to 14.10A; or
(d) at fair value with changes in fair value recognised in profit or loss (paragraphs 11.27 to 11.32 provide guidance on fair value).

An investor that is a parent shall, in its consolidated financial statements, account for all of its investments in associates using the equity method in accordance with paragraph 14.8, except as required by paragraph 14.4B. 14.4A

Where an investor is a parent and has an associate that is **held as part of an investment portfolio**, the associate shall be measured at **fair value** with changes in fair value recognised in **profit or loss** in the consolidated financial statements. 14.4B

Cost model

14.5 An investor that is not a parent, that chooses to adopt the cost model, shall measure its investments in associates at cost less any accumulated **impairment losses** recognised in accordance with Section 27 *Impairment of Assets*.

14.6 The investor shall recognise dividends and other distributions received from the investment as **income** without regard to whether the distributions are from accumulated profits of the associate arising before or after the date of acquisition.

14.7 [Not used]

Equity method

14.8 Under the equity method of accounting, an equity investment is initially recognised at the transaction price (including **transaction costs**) and is subsequently adjusted to reflect the investor's share of the profit or loss, **other comprehensive income** and **equity** of the associate.

(a) *Distributions and other adjustments to carrying amount.* Distributions received from the associate reduce the **carrying amount** of the investment. Adjustments to the carrying amount may also be required as a consequence of changes in the associate's equity arising from items of other comprehensive income.

(b) *Potential voting rights.* Although potential voting rights are considered in deciding whether significant influence exists, an investor shall measure its share of profit or loss and other comprehensive income of the associate and its share of changes in the associate's equity on the basis of present ownership interests. Those measurements shall not reflect the possible exercise or conversion of potential voting rights.

(c) *Implicit goodwill and fair value adjustments.* On acquisition of the investment in an associate, an investor shall account for any difference (whether positive or negative) between the cost of acquisition and the investor's share of the fair values of the net identifiable assets of the associate in accordance with paragraphs 19.22 to 19.24. An investor shall adjust its share of the associate's profits or losses after acquisition to account for additional **depreciation** or **amortisation** of the associate's depreciable or amortisable assets (including **goodwill**) on the basis of the excess of their fair values over their carrying amounts at the time the investment was acquired.

(d) *Impairment.* If there is an indication that an investment in an associate may be impaired, an investor shall test the entire carrying amount of the investment for impairment in accordance with Section 27 as a single **asset**. Any goodwill included as part of the carrying amount of the investment in the associate is not tested separately for impairment but, rather, as part of the test for impairment of the investment as a whole.

(e) *Investor's transactions with associates.* The investor shall eliminate unrealised profits and losses resulting from upstream (associate to investor) and downstream (investor to associate) transactions to the extent of the investor's interest in the associate. Unrealised losses on such transactions may provide evidence of an impairment of the asset transferred.

(f) *Date of associate's financial statements.* In applying the equity method, the investor shall use the **financial statements** of the associate as of the same date as the financial statements of the investor unless it is **impracticable** to do so. If it is impracticable, the investor shall use the most recent available financial statements of the associate, with adjustments made for the effects of any significant transactions or events occurring between the accounting period ends.

(g) *Associate's accounting policies.* If the associate uses **accounting policies** that differ from those of the investor, the investor shall adjust the associate's financial statements to reflect the investor's accounting policies for the purpose of applying the equity method unless it is impracticable to do so.

(h) *Losses in excess of investment.* If an investor's share of losses of an associate equals or exceeds the carrying amount of its investment in the associate, the investor shall discontinue recognising its share of further losses. After the investor's interest is reduced to zero, the investor shall recognise additional losses by a **provision** (see Section 21 *Provisions and Contingencies*) only to the extent that the investor has incurred legal or **constructive obligations** or has made payments on behalf of the associate. If the associate subsequently reports profits, the investor shall resume recognising its share of those profits only after its share of the profits equals the share of losses not recognised.

(i) *Discontinuing the equity method.* An investor shall cease using the equity method from the date that significant influence ceases and, provided the associate does not become a subsidiary in accordance with *Section 19 Business Combinations and Goodwill* or a joint venture in accordance with Section 15 *Investments in Joint Ventures*, shall account for the investment as follows:

  (i) If the investor loses significant influence over an associate as a result of a full or partial disposal, it shall derecognise that associate and recognise in profit or loss the difference between the proceeds from the disposal and the carrying amount of the investment in the associate relating to the proportion disposed of or lost at the date significant influence is lost. The investor shall account for any retained interest using Section 11 *Basic Financial Instruments* or Section 12 *Other Financial Instruments Issues*, as appropriate. The carrying amount of the investment at the date that it ceases to be an associate shall be regarded as its cost on initial **measurement** as a **financial asset**; and

  (ii) If an investor loses significant influence for reasons other than a partial disposal of its investment, the investor shall regard the carrying amount of the investment at that date as a new cost basis and shall account for the investment using Sections 11 or 12, as appropriate.

The gain or loss arising on the disposal shall also include those amounts that have been recognised in **other comprehensive income** in relation to that associate where those amounts are required to be reclassified to profit or loss upon disposal in accordance with other sections of this FRS. Amounts that are not required to be reclassified to profit or loss upon disposal of the related assets or liabilities in accordance with other sections of this FRS shall be transferred directly to retained earnings.

Fair value model

When an investment in an associate is recognised initially, an investor that is not a parent, that chooses to adopt the fair value model, shall measure it at the transaction price. **14.9**

At each reporting date, an investor that is not a parent, that chooses to adopt the fair value model, shall measure its investments in associates at fair value, with changes in fair value recognised in other comprehensive income in accordance with paragraphs 17.15E and 17.15F, using the fair value guidance in paragraphs 11.27 to 11.32. An investor using the fair value model shall use the cost model for any investment in an associate for which it is impracticable to measure fair value reliably without undue cost or effort. **14.10**

14.10A The investor shall recognise dividends and other distributions received from the investment as income without regard to whether the distributions are from accumulated profits of the associate arising before or after the date of acquisition.

PRESENTATION IN INDIVIDUAL AND CONSOLIDATED FINANCIAL STATEMENTS

14.11 Unless otherwise required under the Regulations, an investor shall classify investments in associates as **fixed assets**.

DISCLOSURES IN INDIVIDUAL AND CONSOLIDATED FINANCIAL STATEMENTS

14.12 The financial statements shall disclose:

(a) the accounting policy for investments in associates;
(b) the carrying amount of investments in associates; and
(c) the fair value of investments in associates accounted for using the equity method for which there are published price quotations.

14.13 For investments in associates accounted for in accordance with the cost model, an investor shall disclose the amount of dividends and other distributions recognised as income.

14.14 For investments in associates accounted for in accordance with the equity method, an investor shall disclose separately its share of the profit or loss of such associates and its share of any **discontinued operations** of such associates.

14.15 For investments in associates accounted for in accordance with the fair value model, an investor shall make the disclosures required by paragraphs 11.43 and 11.44.

14.15A The individual financial statements of an investor that is not a parent shall disclose summarised financial information about the investments in the associates, along with the effect of including those investments as if they had been accounted for using the equity method. Investing entities that are exempt from preparing consolidated financial statements, or would be exempt if they had subsidiaries, are exempt from this requirement.

Section 15
Investments in Joint Ventures

SCOPE OF THIS SECTION

This section applies to accounting for **joint ventures** in **consolidated financial statements**, for investments in joint ventures in the **individual financial statements** of a **venturer** that is not a **parent**, and for investment in **jointly controlled operations** and **jointly controlled assets** in the **separate financial statements** of a venturer that is a parent. A venturer that is a parent shall account for interests in **jointly controlled entities** in its **separate financial statements** in accordance with paragraphs 9.26 and 9.26A, as appropriate. 15.1

JOINT VENTURES DEFINED

Joint control is the contractually agreed sharing of **control** over an economic activity, and exists only when the strategic financial and operating decisions relating to the activity require the unanimous consent of the parties sharing control (the venturers). 15.2

A joint venture is a contractual arrangement whereby two or more parties undertake an economic activity that is subject to joint control. Joint ventures can take the form of jointly controlled operations, jointly controlled assets, or jointly controlled entities. 15.3

JOINTLY CONTROLLED OPERATIONS

The operation of some joint ventures involves the use of the **assets** and other resources of the venturers rather than the establishment of a corporation, partnership or other entity, or a financial structure that is separate from the venturers themselves. Each venturer uses its own **property, plant and equipment** and carries its own **inventories**. It also incurs its own **expenses** and **liabilities** and raises its own finance, which represent its own obligations. The joint venture activities may be carried out by the venturer's employees alongside the venturer's similar activities. The joint venture agreement usually provides a means by which the **revenue** from the sale of the joint product and any expenses incurred in common are shared among the venturers. 15.4

In respect of its interests in jointly controlled operations, a venturer shall recognise in its **financial statements**: 15.5

(a) the assets that it controls and the liabilities that it incurs; and
(b) the expenses that it incurs and its share of the **income** that it earns from the sale of goods or services by the joint venture.

JOINTLY CONTROLLED ASSETS

Some joint ventures involve the joint control, and often the joint ownership, by the venturers of one or more assets contributed to, or acquired for the purpose of, the joint venture and dedicated to the purposes of the joint venture. 15.6

In respect of its interest in a jointly controlled asset, a venturer shall recognise in its financial statements: 15.7

(a) its share of the jointly controlled assets, classified according to the nature of the assets;
(b) any liabilities that it has incurred;

(c) its share of any liabilities incurred jointly with the other venturers in relation to the joint venture;
(d) any income from the sale or use of its share of the output of the joint venture, together with its share of any expenses incurred by the joint venture; and
(e) any expenses that it has incurred in respect of its interest in the joint venture.

JOINTLY CONTROLLED ENTITIES

15.8 A jointly controlled entity is a joint venture that involves the establishment of a corporation, partnership or other entity in which each venturer has an interest. The entity operates in the same way as other entities, except that a contractual arrangement between the venturers establishes joint control over the economic activity of the entity.

Measurement—accounting policy election

15.9 A venturer that is not a parent but has one or more interests in jointly controlled entities shall, in its individual financial statements, account for all of its interests in jointly controlled entities using either:
(a) the cost model in accordance with paragraphs 15.10 to 15.11;
(b) [not used]
(c) the fair value model in accordance with paragraphs 15.14 to 15.15A; or
(d) at fair value with changes in fair value recognised in profit or loss (paragraphs 11.27 to 11.32 provide guidance on fair value).

15.9A A venturer that is a parent shall, in its consolidated financial statements, account for all of its investments in jointly controlled entities using the equity method in accordance with paragraph 15.13, except as required by paragraph 15.9B.

15.9B A venturer that is a parent shall measure its investments in jointly controlled entities **held as part of an investment portfolio** at **fair value** with changes in fair value recognised in **profit or loss** in the consolidated financial statements.

Cost model

15.10 A venturer that is not a parent, that chooses to adopt the cost model, shall measure its investments in jointly controlled entities, at cost less any accumulated **impairment losses** recognised in accordance with Section 27 *Impairment of Assets*.

15.11 The venturer shall recognise distributions received from the investment as income without regard to whether the distributions are from accumulated profits of the jointly controlled entity arising before or after the date of acquisition.

15.12 [Not used]

Equity method

15.13 A venturer shall measure its investments in jointly controlled entities by the equity method using the procedures in accordance with paragraph 14.8 (substituting 'joint control' where that paragraph refers to 'significant influence', and 'jointly controlled entity' where that paragraph refers to 'associate').

Fair value model

When an investment in a jointly controlled entity is recognised initially, a venturer that is not a parent, that chooses to adopt the fair value model, shall measure it at the transaction price. 15.14

At each reporting date, a venturer that is not a parent, that chooses to adopt the fair value model, shall measure its investments in jointly controlled entities at fair value using the fair value guidance in paragraphs 11.27 to 11.32. Changes in fair value shall be recognised in accordance with paragraphs 17.15E and 17.15F. A venturer using the fair value model shall use the cost model for any investment in a jointly controlled entity for which it is **impracticable** to measure fair value reliably without undue cost or effort. 15.15

The venturer shall recognise dividends and other distributions received from the investment as income without regard to whether the distributions are from accumulated profits of the jointly controlled entity arising before or after the date of acquisition. 15.15A

TRANSACTIONS BETWEEN A VENTURER AND A JOINT VENTURE

When a venturer contributes or sells assets to a joint venture, **recognition** of any portion of a **gain** or loss from the transaction shall reflect the substance of the transaction. While the assets are retained by the joint venture, and provided the venturer has transferred the significant risks and rewards of ownership, the venturer shall recognise only that portion of the gain or loss that is attributable to the interests of the other venturers. The venturer shall recognise the full amount of any loss when the contribution or sale provides evidence of an impairment loss. 15.16

When a venturer purchases assets from a joint venture, the venturer shall not recognise its share of the profits of the joint venture from the transaction until it resells the assets to an independent party. A venturer shall recognise its share of the losses resulting from these transactions in the same way as profits except that losses shall be recognised immediately when they represent an impairment loss. 15.17

IF INVESTOR DOES NOT HAVE JOINT CONTROL

An investor in a joint venture that does not have joint control shall account for that investment in accordance with Section 11 *Basic Financial Instruments* or Section 12 *Other Financial Instruments Issues* or, if it has **significant influence** in the joint venture, in accordance with Section 14 *Investments in Associates*. 15.18

DISCLOSURES IN INDIVIDUAL AND CONSOLIDATED FINANCIAL STATEMENTS

The financial statements shall disclose the following: 15.19

(a) the **accounting policy** for recognising investments in jointly controlled entities;
(b) the **carrying amount** of investments in jointly controlled entities;
(c) the fair value of investments in jointly controlled entities accounted for using the equity method for which there are published price quotations; and
(d) the aggregate amount of its commitments relating to joint ventures, including its share in the capital commitments that have been incurred jointly with other

venturers, as well as its share of the capital commitments of the joint ventures themselves.

15.20 For jointly controlled entities accounted for in accordance with the equity method, the venturer shall disclose separately its share of the profit or loss of such investments and its share of any **discontinued operations** of such jointly controlled entities.

15.21 For jointly controlled entities accounted for in accordance with the fair value model, the venturer shall make the disclosures required by paragraphs 11.43 and 11.44.

15.21A The individual financial statements of a venturer that is not a parent shall disclose summarised financial information about the investments in the jointly controlled entities, along with the effect of including those investments as if they had been accounted for using the equity method. Investing entities that are exempt from preparing consolidated financial statements, or would be exempt if they had subsidiaries, are exempt from this requirement.

Section 16
Investment Property

SCOPE OF THIS SECTION

This section applies to accounting for investments in land or buildings that meet the definition of **investment property** in paragraph 16.2 and some property interests held by a lessee under an **operating lease** (see paragraph 16.3) that are treated like investment property. Only investment property whose **fair value** can be measured reliably without undue cost or effort on an on-going basis is accounted for in accordance with this section at fair value through **profit or loss**. All other investment property is accounted for as **property, plant and equipment** using the cost model in Section 17 *Property, Plant and Equipment* and remains within the scope of Section 17 unless a reliable measure of fair value becomes available and it is expected that fair value will be reliably measurable on an on-going basis. **16.1**

DEFINITION AND INITIAL RECOGNITION OF INVESTMENT PROPERTY

Investment property is property (land or a building, or part of a building, or both) held by the owner or by the lessee under a **finance lease** to earn rentals or for capital appreciation or both, rather than for: **16.2**

(a) use in the production or supply of goods or services or for administrative purposes; or
(b) sale in the ordinary course of business.

A property interest that is held by a lessee under an operating lease may be classified and accounted for as investment property using this section if, and only if, the property would otherwise meet the definition of an investment property and the lessee can measure the fair value of the property interest without undue cost or effort on an on-going basis. This classification alternative is available on a property-by-property basis. **16.3**

Property held primarily for the provision of social benefits, eg social housing held by a **public benefit entity**, shall not be classified as investment property and shall be accounted for as property, plant and equipment in accordance with Section 17. **16.3A**

Mixed use property shall be separated between investment property and property, plant and equipment. However, if the fair value of the investment property component cannot be measured reliably without undue cost or effort, the entire property shall be accounted for as property, plant and equipment in accordance with Section 17. **16.4**

MEASUREMENT AT INITIAL RECOGNITION

An entity shall measure investment property at its cost at initial **recognition**. The cost of a purchased investment property comprises its purchase price and any directly attributable expenditure such as legal and brokerage fees, property transfer taxes and other transaction costs. If payment is deferred beyond normal credit terms, the cost is the **present value** of all future payments. An entity shall determine the cost of a self-constructed investment property in accordance with paragraphs 17.10 to 17.14. **16.5**

The initial cost of a property interest held under a **lease** and classified as an investment property shall be as prescribed for a finance lease by paragraphs 20.9 and **16.6**

20.10, even if the lease would otherwise be classified as an operating lease if it was in the scope of Section 20 *Leases*. In other words, the **asset** is recognised at the lower of the fair value of the property and the present value of the **minimum lease payments**. An equivalent amount is recognised as a **liability** in accordance with paragraphs 20.9 and 20.10. Any premium paid for a lease is treated as part of the minimum lease payments for this purpose, and is therefore included in the cost of the asset, but is excluded from the liability.

MEASUREMENT AFTER RECOGNITION

16.7 Investment property whose fair value can be measured reliably without undue cost or effort shall be measured at fair value at each **reporting date** with changes in fair value recognised in profit or loss. If a property interest held under a lease is classified as investment property, the item accounted for at fair value is that interest and not the underlying property. Paragraphs 11.27 to 11.32 provide guidance on determining fair value. An entity shall account for all other investment property as property, plant and equipment using the cost model in Section 17.

TRANSFERS

16.8 If a reliable measure of fair value is no longer available without undue cost or effort for an item of investment property measured using the fair value model, the entity shall thereafter account for that item as property, plant and equipment in accordance with Section 17 until a reliable measure of fair value becomes available. The **carrying amount** of the investment property on that date becomes its cost under Section 17. Paragraph 16.10(e)(iii) requires disclosure of this change. It is a change of circumstances and not a change in **accounting policy**.

16.9 Other than as required by paragraph 16.8, an entity shall transfer a property to, or from, investment property only when the property first meets, or ceases to meet, the definition of investment property.

DISCLOSURES

16.10 An entity shall disclose the following for all investment property accounted for at fair value through profit or loss (paragraph 16.7):

(a) the methods and significant assumptions applied in determining the fair value of investment property;

(b) the extent to which the fair value of investment property (as measured or disclosed in the **financial statements**) is based on a valuation by an independent valuer who holds a recognised and relevant professional qualification and has recent experience in the location and class of the investment property being valued. If there has been no such valuation, that fact shall be disclosed;

(c) the existence and amounts of restrictions on the realisability of investment property or the remittance of **income** and proceeds of disposal;

(d) contractual obligations to purchase, construct or develop investment property or for repairs, maintenance or enhancements; and

(e) a reconciliation between the carrying amounts of investment property at the beginning and end of the period, showing separately:

  (i) additions, disclosing separately those additions resulting from acquisitions through **business combinations**;

  (ii) net gains or losses from fair value adjustments;

(iii) transfers to property, plant and equipment when a reliable measure of fair value is no longer available without undue cost or effort (see paragraph 16.8);
(iv) transfers to and from **inventories** and owner-occupied property; and
(v) other changes.

This reconciliation need not be presented for prior periods.

In accordance with Section 20 *Leases*, an entity shall provide all relevant disclosures required in that section about leases into which it has entered. **16.11**

Section 17
Property, Plant and Equipment

SCOPE

17.1 This section applies to the accounting for **property**, **plant and equipment** and to **investment property** whose **fair value** cannot be measured reliably without undue cost or effort. Section 16 *Investment Property* applies to investment property whose fair value can be measured reliably without undue cost or effort.

17.2 Property, plant and equipment are tangible assets that:

(a) are held for use in the production or supply of goods or services, for rental to others, or for administrative purposes; and
(b) are expected to be used during more than one period;

17.3 Property, plant and equipment does not include:

(a) **biological assets** related to **agricultural activity** (see Section 34 *Specialised Activities*) or **heritage assets** (see Section 34); or
(b) mineral rights and mineral reserves, such as oil, natural gas and similar non-regenerative resources (see Section 34).

RECOGNITION

17.4 An entity shall apply the **recognition** criteria in paragraph 2.27 in determining whether to recognise an item of property, plant or equipment. Therefore, the entity shall recognise the cost of an item of property, plant and equipment as an **asset** if, and only if:

(a) it is **probable** that future economic benefits associated with the item will flow to the entity; and
(b) the cost of the item can be measured reliably.

17.5 Spare parts and servicing equipment are usually carried as **inventory** and recognised in **profit or loss** as consumed. However, major spare parts and stand-by equipment are property, plant and equipment when an entity expects to use them during more than one period. Similarly, if the spare parts and servicing equipment can be used only in connection with an item of property, plant and equipment, they are considered property, plant and equipment.

17.6 Parts of some items of property, plant and equipment may require replacement at regular intervals (eg the roof of a building). An entity shall add to the **carrying amount** of an item of property, plant and equipment the cost of replacing part of such an item when that cost is incurred if the replacement part is expected to provide incremental future benefits to the entity. The carrying amount of those parts that are replaced is derecognised in accordance with paragraphs 17.27 to 17.30. Paragraph 17.16 provides that if the major components of an item of property, plant and equipment have significantly different patterns of consumption of economic benefits, an entity shall allocate the initial cost of the asset to its major components and depreciate each such component separately over its **useful life**.

17.7 A condition of continuing to operate an item of property, plant and equipment (eg a bus) may be performing regular major inspections for faults regardless of whether parts of the item are replaced. When each major inspection is performed, its cost is recognised in the carrying amount of the item of property, plant and equipment as a replacement if the recognition criteria are satisfied. Any remaining carrying amount of the cost of the previous major inspection (as distinct from physical parts) is derecognised. This is done regardless of whether the cost of the previous major inspection was identified in the transaction in which the item was acquired or constructed. If necessary, the estimated cost of a future similar inspection may be used as an indication of what the cost of the existing inspection component was when the item was acquired or constructed.

Land and buildings are separable assets, and an entity shall account for them separately, even when they are acquired together. **17.8**

MEASUREMENT AT INITIAL RECOGNITION

An entity shall measure an item of property, plant and equipment at initial recognition at its cost. **17.9**

Elements of cost

The cost of an item of property, plant and equipment comprises all of the following: **17.10**

(a) Its purchase price, including legal and brokerage fees, import duties and non-refundable purchase taxes, after deducting trade discounts and rebates.
(b) Any costs directly attributable to bringing the asset to the location and condition necessary for it to be capable of operating in the manner intended by management. These can include the costs of site preparation, initial delivery and handling, installation and assembly, and testing of functionality.
(c) The initial estimate of the costs, recognised and measured in accordance with Section 21 *Provisions and Contingencies,* of dismantling and removing the item and restoring the site on which it is located, the obligation for which an entity incurs either when the item is acquired or as a consequence of having used the item during a particular period for purposes other than to produce inventories during that period.
(d) Any **borrowing costs** capitalised in accordance with paragraph 25.2.

The following costs are not costs of an item of property, plant and equipment, and an entity shall recognise them as an **expense** when they are incurred: **17.11**

(a) costs of opening a new facility;
(b) costs of introducing a new product or service (including costs of advertising and promotional activities);
(c) costs of conducting business in a new location or with a new class of customer (including costs of staff training); and
(d) administration and other general overhead costs.

The **income** and related expenses of incidental operations during construction or development of an item of property, plant and equipment are recognised in profit or loss if those operations are not necessary to bring the item to its intended location and operating condition. **17.12**

Measurement of cost

The cost of an item of property, plant and equipment is the cash price equivalent at the recognition date. If payment is deferred beyond normal credit terms, the cost is the **present value** of all future payments. **17.13**

Exchanges of assets

17.14 An item of property, plant or equipment may be acquired in exchange for a non-monetary asset or assets, or a combination of monetary and non-monetary assets. An entity shall measure the cost of the acquired asset at fair value unless:

(a) the exchange transaction lacks commercial substance; or
(b) the fair value of neither the asset received nor the asset given up is reliably measurable. In that case, the asset's cost is measured at the carrying amount of the asset given up.

MEASUREMENT AFTER INITIAL RECOGNITION

17.15 An entity shall measure all items of property, plant and equipment after initial recognition using the cost model (in accordance with paragraph 17.15A) or the revaluation model (in accordance with paragraphs 17.15B to 17.15F). Where the revaluation model is selected, this shall be applied to all items of property, plant and equipment in the same class (ie having a similar nature, function or use in the business). An entity shall recognise the costs of day-to-day servicing of an item of property, plant and equipment in profit or loss in the period in which the costs are incurred.

Cost model

17.15A Under the cost model, an entity shall measure an item of property, plant and equipment at cost less any accumulated **depreciation** and any accumulated **impairment losses.**

Revaluation model

17.15B Under the revaluation model, an item of property, plant and equipment whose fair value can be measured reliably shall be carried at a revalued amount, being its fair value at the date of revaluation less any subsequent accumulated depreciation and subsequent accumulated impairment losses. Revaluations shall be made with sufficient regularity to ensure that the carrying amount does not differ materially from that which would be determined using fair value at the end of the **reporting period**.

17.15C The fair value of land and buildings is usually determined from market-based evidence by appraisal that is normally undertaken by professionally qualified valuers. The fair value of items of plant and equipment is usually their market value determined by appraisal. Paragraphs 11.27 to 11.32 provide further guidance on determining fair value.

17.15D If there is no market-based evidence of fair value because of the specialised nature of the item of property, plant and equipment and the item is rarely sold, except as part of a continuing business, an entity may need to estimate fair value using an income or a **depreciated replacement cost** approach.

Reporting gains and losses on revaluations

17.15E If an asset's carrying amount is increased as a result of a revaluation, the increase shall be recognised in **other comprehensive income** and accumulated in **equity**. However, the increase shall be recognised in profit or loss to the extent that it reverses a revaluation decrease of the same asset previously recognised in profit or loss.

The decrease of an asset's carrying amount as a result of a revaluation shall be recognised in other comprehensive income to the extent of any previously recognised revaluation increase accumulated in equity, in respect of that asset. If a revaluation decrease exceeds the accumulated revaluation gains accumulated in equity in respect of that asset, the excess shall be recognised in **profit or loss**. **17.15F**

DEPRECIATION

If the major components of an item of property, plant and equipment have significantly different patterns of consumption of economic benefits, an entity shall allocate the initial cost of the asset to its major components and depreciate each such component separately over its useful life. Other assets shall be depreciated over their useful lives as a single asset. There are some exceptions, such as land which generally has an unlimited useful life and therefore is not usually depreciated. **17.16**

The depreciation charge for each period shall be recognised in profit or loss unless another section of this FRS requires the cost to be recognised as part of the cost of an asset. For example, the depreciation of manufacturing property, plant and equipment is included in the costs of inventories (see Section 13 *Inventories*). **17.17**

DEPRECIABLE AMOUNT AND DEPRECIATION PERIOD

An entity shall allocate the **depreciable amount** of an asset on a systematic basis over its useful life. **17.18**

Factors such as a change in how an asset is used, significant unexpected wear and tear, technological advancement, and changes in market prices may indicate that the **residual value** or useful life of an asset has changed since the most recent annual **reporting date**. If such indicators are present, an entity shall review its previous estimates and, if current expectations differ, amend the residual value, depreciation method or useful life. The entity shall account for the change in residual value, depreciation method or useful life as a change in an accounting estimate in accordance with paragraphs 10.15 to 10.18. **17.19**

Depreciation of an asset begins when it is available for use, ie when it is in the location and condition necessary for it to be capable of operating in the manner intended by management. Depreciation of an asset ceases when the asset is derecognised. Depreciation does not cease when the asset becomes idle or is retired from active use unless the asset is fully depreciated. However, under usage methods of depreciation the depreciation charge can be zero while there is no production. **17.20**

An entity shall consider all the following factors in determining the useful life of an asset: **17.21**

(a) The expected usage of the asset. Usage is assessed by reference to the asset's expected capacity or physical output.
(b) Expected physical wear and tear, which depends on operational factors such as the number of shifts for which the asset is to be used and the repair and maintenance programme, and the care and maintenance of the asset while idle.
(c) Technical or commercial obsolescence arising from changes or improvements in production, or from a change in the market demand for the product or service output of the asset.

(d) Legal or similar limits on the use of the asset, such as the expiry dates of related **leases**.

DEPRECIATION METHOD

17.22 An entity shall select a depreciation method that reflects the pattern in which it expects to consume the asset's future economic benefits. The possible depreciation methods include the straight-line method, the diminishing balance method and a method based on usage such as the units of production method.

17.23 If there is an indication that there has been a significant change since the last annual reporting date in the pattern by which an entity expects to consume an asset's future economic benefits, the entity shall review its present depreciation method and, if current expectations differ, change the depreciation method to reflect the new pattern. The entity shall account for the change as a change in an accounting estimate in accordance with paragraphs 10.15 to 10.18.

IMPAIRMENT

Recognition and measurement of impairment

17.24 At each reporting date, an entity shall apply Section 27 *Impairment of Assets* to determine whether an item or group of items of property, plant and equipment is impaired and, if so, how to recognise and measure the impairment loss. That section explains when and how an entity reviews the carrying amount of its assets, how it determines the **recoverable amount** of an asset, and when it recognises or reverses an impairment loss.

Compensation for impairment

17.25 An entity shall include in profit or loss, compensation from third parties for items of property, plant and equipment that were impaired, lost or given up only when the compensation is virtually certain.

Property, plant and equipment held for sale

17.26 Paragraph 27.9(f) states that a plan to dispose of an asset before the previously expected date is an indicator of impairment that triggers the calculation of the asset's recoverable amount for the purpose of determining whether the asset is impaired.

DERECOGNITION

17.27 An entity shall derecognise an item of property, plant and equipment:

(a) on disposal; or

(b) when no future economic benefits are expected from its use or disposal.

17.28 An entity shall recognise the **gain** or loss on the **derecognition** of an item of property, plant and equipment in profit or loss when the item is derecognised (unless Section 20 *Leases* requires otherwise on a sale and leaseback). The entity shall not classify such gains as **revenue**.

In determining the date of disposal of an item, an entity shall apply the criteria in Section 23 *Revenue* for recognising revenue from the sale of goods. Section 20 applies to disposal by a sale and leaseback. **17.29**

An entity shall determine the gain or loss arising from the derecognition of an item of property, plant and equipment as the difference between the net disposal proceeds, if any, and the carrying amount of the item. **17.30**

DISCLOSURES

An entity shall disclose the following for each class of property, plant and equipment: **17.31**

(a) the measurement bases used for determining the gross carrying amount;
(b) the depreciation methods used;
(c) the useful lives or the depreciation rates used;
(d) the gross carrying amount and the accumulated depreciation (aggregated with accumulated impairment losses) at the beginning and end of the reporting period;
(e) a reconciliation of the carrying amount at the beginning and end of the reporting period showing separately:
   (i) additions;
   (ii) disposals;
   (iii) acquisitions through **business combinations**;
   (iv) revaluations;
   (v) transfers to or from investment property if a reliable measure of fair value becomes available or unavailable (see paragraph 16.8);
   (vi) impairment losses recognised or reversed in profit or loss in accordance with Section 27 *Impairment of Assets*;
   (vii) depreciation; and
   (viii) other changes.

This reconciliation need not be presented for prior periods.

The entity shall also disclose the following: **17.32**

(a) the existence and carrying amounts of property, plant and equipment to which the entity has restricted title or that is pledged as security for **liabilities**; and
(b) the amount of contractual commitments for the acquisition of property, plant and equipment.

If items of property, plant and equipment are stated at revalued amounts, the following shall be disclosed: **17.32A**

(a) the effective date of the revaluation;
(b) whether an independent valuer was involved;
(c) the methods and significant assumptions applied in estimating the items' fair values; and
(d) for each revalued class of property, plant and equipment, the carrying amount that would have been recognised had the assets been carried under the cost model.

Section 18
Intangible Assets other than Goodwill

SCOPE OF THIS SECTION

18.1 This section applies to accounting for all **intangible assets** other than **goodwill** (see Section 19 *Business Combinations and Goodwill*) and intangible assets held by an entity for sale in the ordinary course of business (see Section 13 *Inventories* and Section 23 *Revenue*).

18.1A This section does not apply to the accounting for **deferred acquisition costs** and intangible assets arising from contracts in the scope of FRS 103 *Insurance Contracts*, except for the disclosure requirements in this section which apply to intangible assets arising from contracts in the scope of FRS 103.

18.2 An intangible asset is an identifiable non-monetary asset without physical substance. Such an **asset** is identifiable when:

(a) it is separable, ie capable of being separated or divided from the entity and sold, transferred, licensed, rented or exchanged, either individually or together with a related contract, asset or **liability**; or

(b) it arises from contractual or other legal rights, regardless of whether those rights are transferable or separable from the entity or from other rights and obligations.

18.3 This section does not apply to the following:

(a) **financial assets** (see Section 11 *Basic Financial Instruments* and Section 12 *Other Financial Instruments Issues*);

(b) **heritage assets** (see Section 34 *Specialised Activities*); or

(c) mineral rights and mineral reserves, such as oil, natural gas and similar non-regenerative resources (see Section 34).

RECOGNITION

General principle for recognising intangible assets

18.4 An entity shall apply the **recognition** criteria in paragraph 2.27 in determining whether to recognise an intangible asset. Therefore, the entity shall recognise an intangible asset as an asset if, and only if:

(a) it is **probable** that the expected future economic benefits that are attributable to the asset will flow to the entity; and

(b) the cost or value of the asset can be measured reliably.

18.5 An entity shall assess the probability of expected future economic benefits using reasonable and supportable assumptions that represent management's best estimate of the economic conditions that will exist over the **useful life** of the asset.

18.6 An entity uses judgement to assess the degree of certainty attached to the flow of future economic benefits that are attributable to the use of the asset on the basis of the evidence available at the time of initial recognition, giving greater weight to external evidence.

18.7 The probability recognition criterion in paragraph 18.4(a) is always considered satisfied for intangible assets that are separately acquired.

Acquisition as part of a business combination

An intangible asset acquired in a **business combination** is normally recognised as an asset because its **fair value** can be measured with sufficient **reliability**. However, an intangible asset acquired in a business combination is not recognised when it arises from legal or other contractual rights and there is no history or evidence of exchange transactions for the same or similar assets, and otherwise estimating fair value would be dependent on immeasurable variables. **18.8**

Internally generated intangible assets

To assess whether an internally generated intangible asset meets the criteria for recognition, an entity classifies the generation of the asset into: **18.8A**

(a) a **research** phase; and
(b) a **development** phase.

If an entity cannot distinguish the research phase from the development phase of an internal project to create an intangible asset, the entity treats the expenditure on that project as if it were incurred in the research phase only. **18.8B**

*An entity shall recognise expenditure on the following items as an **expense** and shall not recognise such expenditure as intangible assets: **18.8C**

(a) Internally generated brands, logos, publishing titles, customer lists and items similar in substance.
(b) Start-up activities (ie start-up costs), which include establishment costs such as legal and secretarial costs incurred in establishing a legal entity, expenditure to open a new facility or business (ie pre-opening costs) and expenditure for starting new operations or launching new products or processes (ie pre-operating costs).
(c) Training activities.
(d) Advertising and promotional activities (unless it meets the definition of **inventories held for distribution at no or nominal consideration** (see paragraph 13.4A)).
(e) Relocating or reorganising part or all of an entity.
(f) Internally generated goodwill.

†Paragraph 18.8C does not preclude recognising a prepayment as an asset when payment for goods or services has been made in advance of the delivery of the goods or the rendering of the services. **18.8D**

Research phase

No intangible asset arising from research (or from the research phase of an internal project) shall be recognised. Expenditure on research (or on the research phase of an internal project) shall be recognised as an expense when it is incurred. **18.8E**

In the research phase of an internal project, an entity cannot demonstrate that an intangible asset exists that will generate probable future economic benefits. **18.8F**

Examples of research activities are: **18.8G**

****Is paragraph 18.15 in the IFRS for SMEs.***

†Is paragraph 18.16 in the IFRS for SMEs.

(a) Activities aimed at obtaining new knowledge.
(b) The search for, evaluation and final selection of, applications of research findings and other knowledge.
(c) The search for alternatives for materials, devices, products, processes, systems or services.
(d) The formulation, design, evaluation and final selection of possible alternatives for new or improved material, devices, projects, processes, systems or services.

Development phase

18.8H An entity may recognise an intangible asset arising from development (or from the development phase of an internal project) if, and only if, an entity can demonstrate all of the following:

(a) The technical feasibility of completing the intangible asset so that it will be available for use or sale.
(b) Its intention to complete the intangible asset and use or sell it.
(c) Its ability to use or sell the intangible asset.
(d) How the intangible asset will generate probable future economic benefits. Among other things, the entity can demonstrate the existence of a market for the output of the intangible asset or the intangible asset itself or, if it is to be used internally, the usefulness of the intangible asset.
(e) The availability of adequate technical, financial and other resources to complete the development and to use or sell the intangible asset.
(f) Its ability to measure reliably the expenditure attributable to the intangible asset during its development.

18.8I In the development phase of an internal project, an entity can, in some instances, identify an intangible asset and demonstrate that the asset will generate probable future economic benefits. This is because the development phase of a project is further advanced than the research phase.

18.8J Examples of development activities are:

(a) The design, construction and testing of pre-production or pre-use prototypes and models.
(b) The design of tools, jigs, moulds and dies involving new technology.
(c) The design, construction and operation of a pilot plant that is not of a scale economically feasible for commercial production.
(d) The design, construction and testing of a chosen alternative for new or improved materials, devices, products, processes, systems or services.

18.8K Where an entity adopts a policy of capitalising expenditure in the development phase that meets the conditions of paragraph 18.8H, that policy shall be applied consistently to all expenditure that meets the requirements of paragraph 18.8H. Expenditure that does not meet the conditions of paragraph 18.8H is expensed as incurred.

INITIAL MEASUREMENT

18.9 An entity shall measure an intangible asset initially at cost.

Separate acquisition

The cost of a separately acquired intangible asset comprises: **18.10**

(a) its purchase price, including import duties and non-refundable purchase taxes, after deducting trade discounts and rebates; and
(b) any directly attributable cost of preparing the asset for its intended use.

Internally generated intangible assets

The cost of an internally generated intangible asset for the purpose of paragraph 18.9 is the sum of expenditure incurred from the date when the intangible asset first meets the recognition criteria in paragraphs 18.4 and 18.8H. **18.10A**

The cost of an internally generated intangible asset comprises all directly attributable costs necessary to create, produce and prepare the asset to be capable of operating in the manner intended by management. Examples of directly attributable costs are: **18.10B**

(a) costs of materials and services used or consumed in generating the intangible asset;
(b) costs of **employee benefits** (as defined in Section 28 *Employee Benefits*) arising from the generation of the intangible asset;
(c) fees to register a legal right; and
(d) **amortisation** of patents and licences that are used to generate the intangible asset.

Section 25 *Borrowing Costs* specifies criteria for the recognition of interest as an element of the cost of an internally generated intangible asset.

Acquisition as part of a business combination

If an intangible asset is acquired in a business combination, the cost of that intangible asset is its fair value at the **acquisition date**. **18.11**

Acquisition by way of a grant

If an intangible asset is acquired by way of a grant, the cost of that intangible asset is its fair value at the date the grant is received or receivable in accordance with Section 24 *Government Grants*. **18.12**

Exchanges of assets

An intangible asset may be acquired in exchange for a non-monetary asset or assets, or a combination of monetary and non-monetary assets. An entity shall measure the cost of such an intangible asset at fair value unless: **18.13**

(a) the exchange transaction lacks commercial substance; or
(b) the fair value of neither the asset received nor the asset given up is reliably measurable. In that case, the asset's cost is measured at the **carrying amount** of the asset given up.

[Replaced by paragraph 18.8A] **18.14**

[Moved to paragraph 18.8C] **18.15**

18.16 [Moved to paragraph 18.8D]

PAST EXPENSES NOT TO BE RECOGNISED AS AN ASSET

18.17 Expenditure on an intangible item that was initially recognised as an expense shall not be recognised at a later date as part of the cost of an asset.

MEASUREMENT AFTER INITIAL RECOGNITION

18.18 An entity shall measure intangible assets after initial recognition using the cost model (in accordance with paragraph 18.18A) or the revaluation model (in accordance with paragraphs 18.18B to 18.18H). Where the revaluation model is selected, this shall be applied to all intangible assets in the same class. If an intangible asset in a class of revalued intangible assets cannot be revalued because there is no **active market** for this asset, the asset shall be carried at its cost less any accumulated amortisation and impairment losses.

Cost model

18.18A Under the cost model, an entity shall measure its assets at cost less any accumulated amortisation and any accumulated **impairment losses**. The requirements for amortisation are set out in paragraphs 18.19 to 18.24.

Revaluation model

18.18B Under the revaluation model, an intangible asset shall be carried at a revalued amount, being its fair value at the date of revaluation less any subsequent accumulated amortisation and subsequent accumulated impairment losses, provided that the fair value can be determined by reference to an active market. The requirements for amortisation are set out in paragraphs 18.19 to 18.24.

18.18C The revaluation model does not allow:

(a) the revaluation of intangible assets that have not previously been recognised as assets; or
(b) the initial recognition of intangible assets at amounts other than cost.

18.18D Revaluations shall be made with sufficient regularity to ensure that the carrying amount does not differ materially from that which would be determined using fair value at the end of the **reporting period**.

18.18E If the fair value of a revalued intangible asset can no longer be determined by reference to an active market in accordance with the requirements of paragraph 18.18B, the carrying amount of the asset shall be its revalued amount at the date of the last revaluation by reference to the active market, less any subsequent accumulated amortisation and any subsequent accumulated impairment losses.

18.18F The revaluation model is applied after an asset has been initially recognised at cost. However, if only part of the cost of an intangible asset is recognised as an asset because the asset did not meet the criteria for recognition until part of the way through the process (see paragraph 18.10A), the revaluation model may be applied to the whole of that asset.

Reporting gains and losses on revaluations

If an asset's carrying amount is increased as a result of a revaluation, the increase shall be recognised in **other comprehensive income** and accumulated in **equity**. However, the increase shall be recognised in **profit or loss** to the extent that it reverses a revaluation decrease of the same asset previously recognised in profit or loss. **18.18G**

The decrease of an asset's carrying amount as a result of a revaluation shall be recognised in other comprehensive income to the extent of any previously recognised revaluation increase accumulated in equity, in respect of that asset. If a revaluation decrease exceeds the accumulated revaluation gains recognised in equity in respect of that asset, the excess shall be recognised in profit or loss. **18.18H**

AMORTISATION OVER USEFUL LIFE

For the purpose of this FRS, all intangible assets shall be considered to have a finite useful life. The useful life of an intangible asset that arises from contractual or other legal rights shall not exceed the period of the contractual or other legal rights, but may be shorter depending on the period over which the entity expects to use the asset. If the contractual or other legal rights are conveyed for a limited term that can be renewed, the useful life of the intangible asset shall include the renewal period(s) only if there is evidence to support renewal by the entity without significant cost. **18.19**

If an entity is unable to make a reliable estimate of the useful life of an intangible asset, the life shall not exceed five years. **18.20**

Amortisation period and amortisation method

An entity shall allocate the **depreciable amount** of an intangible asset on a systematic basis over its useful life. The amortisation charge for each period shall be recognised in profit or loss, unless another section of this FRS requires the cost to be recognised as part of the cost of an asset. For example, the amortisation of an intangible asset may be included in the costs of **inventories** or **property, plant and equipment**. **18.21**

Amortisation begins when the intangible asset is available for use, ie when it is in the location and condition necessary for it to be usable in the manner intended by management. Amortisation ceases when the asset is derecognised. The entity shall choose an amortisation method that reflects the pattern in which it expects to consume the asset's future economic benefits. If the entity cannot determine that pattern reliably, it shall use the straight-line method. **18.22**

Residual value

An entity shall assume that the **residual value** of an intangible asset is zero unless: **18.23**

(a) there is a commitment by a third party to purchase the asset at the end of its useful life; or

(b) there is an active market for the asset and:

 (i) residual value can be determined by reference to that market; and

 (ii) it is probable that such a market will exist at the end of the asset's useful life.

Review of amortisation period and amortisation method

18.24 Factors such as a change in how an intangible asset is used, technological advancement, and changes in market prices may indicate that the residual value or useful life of an intangible asset has changed since the most recent annual **reporting date**. If such indicators are present, an entity shall review its previous estimates and, if current expectations differ, amend the residual value, amortisation method or useful life. The entity shall account for the change in residual value, amortisation method or useful life as a change in an accounting estimate in accordance with paragraphs 10.15 to 10.18.

RECOVERABILITY OF THE CARRYING AMOUNT—IMPAIRMENT LOSSES

18.25 To determine whether an intangible asset is impaired, an entity shall apply Section 27 *Impairment of Assets*. That section explains when and how an entity reviews the carrying amount of its assets, how it determines the **recoverable amount** of an asset, and when it recognises or reverses an impairment loss.

RETIREMENTS AND DISPOSALS

18.26 An entity shall derecognise an intangible asset, and shall recognise a **gain** or loss in profit or loss:

(a) on disposal; or
(b) when no future economic benefits are expected from its use or disposal.

DISCLOSURES

18.27 An entity shall disclose the following for each class of intangible assets:

(a) the useful lives or the amortisation rates used and the reasons for choosing those periods;
(b) the amortisation methods used;
(c) the gross carrying amount and any accumulated amortisation (aggregated with accumulated impairment losses) at the beginning and end of the reporting period;
(d) the line item(s) in the **statement of comprehensive income** (or in the **income statement**, if presented) in which any amortisation of intangible assets is included; and
(e) a reconciliation of the carrying amount at the beginning and end of the reporting period showing separately:

  (i) additions, indicating separately those from internal development and those acquired separately;
  (ii) disposals;
  (iii) acquisitions through business combinations;
  (iv) revaluations;
  (v) amortisation;
  (vi) impairment losses; and
  (vii) other changes.

This reconciliation need not be presented for prior periods.

An entity shall also disclose: **18.28**

(a) a description, the carrying amount and remaining amortisation period of any individual intangible asset that is **material** to the entity's **financial statements**;
(b) for intangible assets acquired by way of a grant and initially recognised at fair value (see paragraph 18.12):
   (i) the fair value initially recognised for these assets; and
   (ii) their carrying amounts.
(c) the existence and carrying amounts of intangible assets to which the entity has restricted title or that are pledged as security for liabilities; and
(d) the amount of contractual commitments for the acquisition of intangible assets.

An entity shall disclose the aggregate amount of research and development expenditure recognised as an expense during the period (ie the amount of expenditure incurred internally on research and development that has not been capitalised as an intangible asset or as part of the cost of another asset that meets the recognition criteria in this FRS). **18.29**

If intangible assets are accounted for at revalued amounts, an entity shall disclose the following: **18.29A**

(a) the effective date of the revaluation;
(b) whether an independent valuer was involved;
(c) the methods and significant assumptions applied in estimating the assets' fair values; and
(d) for each revalued class of intangible assets, the carrying amount that would have been recognised had the assets been carried under the cost model.

Section 19
Business Combinations and Goodwill

SCOPE OF THIS SECTION

19.1 This section applies to accounting for **business combinations**. It provides guidance on identifying the acquirer, measuring the cost of the business combination, and allocating that cost to the **assets** acquired and **liabilities** and **provisions** for **contingent liabilities** assumed. It also addresses accounting for **goodwill** both at the time of a business combination and subsequently.

19.2 This section specifies the accounting for all business combinations except:

(a) the formation of a **joint venture**; and
(b) acquisition of a group of assets that does not constitute a **business**.

PBE19.2A In addition, **public benefit entities** shall consider the requirements of Section 34 *Specialised Activities* in accounting for **public benefit entity combinations**.

BUSINESS COMBINATIONS DEFINED

19.3 A business combination is the bringing together of separate entities or businesses into one reporting entity. The result of nearly all business combinations is that one entity, the acquirer, obtains **control** of one or more other businesses, the acquiree. The **acquisition date** is the date on which the acquirer obtains control of the acquiree.

19.4 A business combination may be structured in a variety of ways for legal, taxation or other reasons. It may involve the purchase by an entity of the **equity** of another entity, the purchase of all the net assets of another entity, the assumption of the liabilities of another entity, or the purchase of some of the net assets of another entity that together form one or more businesses.

19.5 A business combination may be effected by the issue of equity instruments, the transfer of **cash**, **cash equivalents** or other assets, or a mixture of these. The transaction may be between the shareholders of the combining entities or between one entity and the shareholders of another entity. It may involve the establishment of a new entity to control the combining entities or net assets transferred, or the restructuring of one or more of the combining entities.

PURCHASE METHOD

19.6 All business combinations shall be accounted for by applying the purchase method, except for:

(a) **group reconstructions** which may be accounted for by using the merger accounting method (see paragraphs 19.27 to 19.33); and
(b) public benefit entity **combinations that are in substance a gift** or that are a **merger** which shall be accounted for in accordance with Section 34 *Specialised Activities*.

19.7 Applying the purchase method involves the following steps:

(a) identifying an acquirer;
(b) measuring the cost of the business combination; and
(c) allocating, at the acquisition date, the cost of the business combination to the assets acquired and liabilities and provisions for contingent liabilities assumed.

Identifying the acquirer

An acquirer shall be identified for all business combinations accounted for by applying the purchase method. The acquirer is the combining entity that obtains control of the other combining entities or businesses. 19.8

Control is the power to govern the financial and operating policies of an entity or business so as to obtain benefits from its activities. Control of one entity by another is described in Section 9 *Consolidated and Separate Financial Statements*. 19.9

Although it may sometimes be difficult to identify an acquirer, there are usually indications that one exists. For example: 19.10

(a) If the **fair value** of one of the combining entities is significantly greater than that of the other combining entity, the entity with the greater fair value is likely to be the acquirer.
(b) If the business combination is effected through an exchange of voting ordinary equity instruments for cash or other assets, the entity giving up cash or other assets is likely to be the acquirer.
(c) If the business combination results in the management of one of the combining entities being able to dominate the selection of the management team of the resulting combined entity, the entity whose management is able so to dominate is likely to be the acquirer.

Cost of a business combination

The acquirer shall measure the cost of a business combination as the aggregate of: 19.11

(a) the fair values, at the acquisition date, of assets given, liabilities incurred or assumed, and equity instruments issued by the acquirer, in exchange for control of the acquiree; plus
(b) any costs directly attributable to the business combination.

Where control is achieved following a series of transactions, the cost of the business combination is the aggregate of the fair values of the assets given, liabilities assumed and equity instruments issued by the acquirer at the date of each transaction in the series. 19.11A

Adjustments to the cost of a business combination contingent on future events

When a business combination agreement provides for an adjustment to the cost of the combination contingent on future events, the acquirer shall include the estimated amount of that adjustment in the cost of the combination at the acquisition date if the adjustment is **probable** and can be measured reliably. 19.12

However, if the potential adjustment is not recognised at the acquisition date but subsequently becomes probable and can be measured reliably, the additional consideration shall be treated as an adjustment to the cost of the combination. 19.13

Allocating the cost of a business combination to the assets acquired and liabilities and contingent liabilities assumed

The acquirer shall, at the acquisition date, allocate the cost of a business combination by recognising the acquiree's identifiable assets and liabilities and a provision for those contingent liabilities (that satisfy the **recognition** criteria in paragraph 19.20) at 19.14

their fair values at that date, except for the items specified in paragraphs 19.15A to 19.15C. Any difference between the cost of the business combination and the acquirer's interest in the net amount of the identifiable assets, liabilities and provisions for contingent liabilities so recognised shall be accounted for in accordance with paragraphs 19.22 to 19.24.

19.15 Except for the items specified in paragraphs 19.15A to 19.15C, the acquirer shall recognise separately the acquiree's identifiable assets, liabilities and contingent liabilities at the acquisition date only if they satisfy the following criteria at that date:

(a) In the case of an asset other than an **intangible asset**, it is probable that any associated future economic benefits will flow to the acquirer, and its fair value can be measured reliably.
(b) In the case of a liability other than a contingent liability, it is probable that an outflow of resources will be required to settle the obligation, and its fair value can be measured reliably.
(c) In the case of an intangible asset or a contingent liability, its fair value can be measured reliably.

19.15A The acquirer shall recognise and measure a **deferred tax asset** or **liability** arising from the assets acquired and liabilities assumed in accordance with Section 29 *Income Tax*.

19.15B The acquirer shall recognise and measure a liability (or asset, if any) related to the acquiree's employee benefit arrangements in accordance with Section 28 *Employee Benefits*.

19.15C The acquirer shall recognise and measure a share-based payment in accordance with Section 26 *Share-based Payment*.

19.16 The acquirer's **statement of comprehensive income** shall incorporate the acquiree's profits or losses after the acquisition date by including the acquiree's **income** and **expenses** based on the cost of the business combination to the acquirer. For example, depreciation expense included after the acquisition date in the acquirer's statement of comprehensive income that relates to the acquiree's depreciable assets shall be based on the fair values of those depreciable assets at the acquisition date, ie their cost to the acquirer.

19.17 Application of the purchase method starts from the acquisition date, which is the date on which the acquirer obtains control of the acquiree. Because control is the power to govern the financial and operating policies of an entity or business so as to obtain benefits from its activities, it is not necessary for a transaction to be closed or finalised at law before the acquirer obtains control. All pertinent facts and circumstances surrounding a business combination shall be considered in assessing when the acquirer has obtained control.

19.18 In accordance with paragraph 19.14, the acquirer recognises separately only the identifiable assets, liabilities and contingent liabilities of the acquiree that existed at the acquisition date and satisfy the recognition criteria in paragraph 19.15 (except for the items specified in paragraphs 19.15A to 19.15C). Therefore:

(a) the acquirer shall recognise liabilities for terminating or reducing the activities of the acquiree as part of allocating the cost of the combination only to the extent that the acquiree has, at the acquisition date, an existing liability for restructuring recognised in accordance with Section 21 *Provisions and Contingencies*; and

(b) the acquirer, when allocating the cost of the combination, shall not recognise liabilities for future losses or other costs expected to be incurred as a result of the business combination.

If the initial accounting for a business combination is incomplete by the end of the **reporting period** in which the combination occurs, the acquirer shall recognise in its **financial statements** provisional amounts for the items for which the accounting is incomplete. Within twelve months after the acquisition date, the acquirer shall retrospectively adjust the provisional amounts recognised as assets and liabilities at the acquisition date (ie account for them as if they were made at the acquisition date) to reflect new information obtained. Beyond twelve months after the acquisition date, adjustments to the initial accounting for a business combination shall be recognised only to correct a **material error** in accordance with Section 10 *Accounting Policies, Estimates and Errors*. **19.19**

Contingent liabilities

Paragraph 19.15(c) specifies that the acquirer recognises separately a provision for a contingent liability of the acquiree only if its fair value can be measured reliably. If its fair value cannot be measured reliably: **19.20**

(a) there is a resulting effect on the amount recognised as goodwill or the amount accounted for in accordance with paragraph 19.24; and
(b) the acquirer shall disclose the information about that contingent liability as required by Section 21.

After their initial recognition, the acquirer shall measure contingent liabilities that are recognised separately in accordance with paragraph 19.15(c) at the higher of: **19.21**

(a) the amount that would be recognised in accordance with Section 21; and
(b) the amount initially recognised less amounts previously recognised as **revenue** in accordance with Section 23 *Revenue*.

Goodwill

The acquirer shall, at the acquisition date: **19.22**

(a) recognise goodwill acquired in a business combination as an asset; and
(b) initially measure that goodwill at its cost, being the excess of the cost of the business combination over the acquirer's interest in the net amount of the identifiable assets, liabilities and contingent liabilities recognised and measured in accordance with paragraphs 19.15, 19.15A to 19.15C.

After initial recognition, the acquirer shall measure goodwill acquired in a business combination at cost less accumulated **amortisation** and accumulated **impairment losses**: **19.23**

(a) An entity shall follow the principles in paragraphs 18.19 to 18.24 for amortisation of goodwill. Goodwill shall be considered to have a finite **useful life**, and shall be amortised on a systematic basis over its life. If an entity is unable to make a reliable estimate of the useful life of goodwill, the life shall not exceed five years.
(b) An entity shall follow Section 27 *Impairment of Assets* for recognising and measuring the impairment of goodwill.

Excess over cost of acquirer's interest in the net fair value of acquiree's identifiable assets, liabilities and contingent liabilities

19.24 If the acquirer's interest in the net amount of the identifiable assets, liabilities and provisions for contingent liabilities recognised in accordance with paragraph 19.14 exceeds the cost of the business combination (also referred to as 'negative goodwill'), the acquirer shall:

(a) Reassess the identification and **measurement** of the acquiree's assets, liabilities and provisions for contingent liabilities and the measurement of the cost of the combination.
(b) Recognise and separately disclose the resulting excess on the face of the **statement of financial position** on the acquisition date, immediately below goodwill, and followed by a subtotal of the net amount of goodwill and the excess.
(c) Recognise subsequently the excess up to the fair value of non-monetary assets acquired in profit or loss in the periods in which the non-monetary assets are recovered. Any excess exceeding the fair value of non-monetary assets acquired shall be recognised in profit or loss in the periods expected to be benefited.

DISCLOSURES

For business combinations effected during the reporting period

19.25 For each business combination, excluding any group reconstructions, that was effected during the period, the acquirer shall disclose the following:

(a) the names and descriptions of the combining entities or businesses;
(b) the acquisition date;
(c) the percentage of voting equity instruments acquired;
(d) the cost of the combination and a description of the components of that cost (such as cash, equity instruments and debt instruments);
(e) the amounts recognised at the acquisition date for each class of the acquiree's assets, liabilities and contingent liabilities, including goodwill;
(f) [not used]
(g) the useful life of goodwill, and if this exceeds five years, supporting reasons for this; and
(h) the periods in which the excess recognised in accordance with paragraph 19.24 will be recognised in profit or loss.

19.25A The acquirer shall disclose, separately for each material business combination that occurred during the reporting period, the amounts of revenue and profit or loss of the acquiree since the acquisition date included in the consolidated statement of comprehensive income for the reporting period. The disclosure may be provided in aggregate for business combinations that occurred during the reporting period which, individually, are not material.

For all business combinations

19.26 An acquirer shall disclose a reconciliation of the **carrying amount** of goodwill at the beginning and end of the reporting period, showing separately:

(a) changes arising from new business combinations;
(b) amortisation;
(c) impairment losses;
(d) disposals of previously acquired businesses; and

(e) other changes.

This reconciliation need not be presented for prior periods.

An acquirer shall disclose a reconciliation of the carrying amount of the excess recognised in accordance with paragraph 19.24 at the beginning and end of the reporting period, showing separately: **19.26A**

(a) changes arising from new business combinations;
(b) amounts recognised in profit or loss in accordance with paragraph 19.24(c);
(c) disposals of previously acquired businesses; and
(d) other changes.

This reconciliation need not be presented for prior periods.

GROUP RECONSTRUCTIONS

Group reconstructions may be accounted for by using the merger accounting method provided: **19.27**

(a) the use of the merger accounting method is not prohibited by company law or other relevant legislation;
(b) the ultimate equity holders remain the same, and the rights of each equity holder, relative to the others, are unchanged; and
(c) no **non-controlling interest** in the net assets of the **group** is altered by the transfer.

Applicability to various structures of business combinations

The provisions of paragraphs 19.29 to 19.33, which are explained by reference to an acquirer or issuing entity that issues shares as consideration for the transfer to it of shares in the other parties to the combination, should also be read so as to apply to other arrangements that achieve similar results. **19.28**

Merger accounting method

With the merger accounting method the carrying values of the assets and liabilities of the parties to the combination are not required to be adjusted to fair value, although appropriate adjustments shall be made to achieve uniformity of **accounting policies** in the combining entities. **19.29**

The results and cash flows of all the combining entities shall be brought into the financial statements of the combined entity from the beginning of the financial year in which the combination occurred, adjusted so as to achieve uniformity of accounting policies. The comparative information shall be restated by including the **total comprehensive income** for all the combining entities for the previous reporting period and their statement of financial position for the previous **reporting date**, adjusted as necessary to achieve uniformity of accounting policies. **19.30**

The difference, if any, between the nominal value of the shares issued plus the fair value of any other consideration given, and the nominal value of the shares received in exchange shall be shown as a movement on other reserves in the **consolidated financial statements**. Any existing balances on the share premium account or capital redemption reserve of the new subsidiary shall be brought in by being shown as a **19.31** movement on other reserves. These movements shall be shown in the **statement of changes in equity**.

19.32 Merger expenses are not to be included as part of this adjustment, but shall be charged to the statement of comprehensive income as part of profit or loss of the combined entity at the effective date of the group reconstruction.

Disclosures

19.33 For each group reconstruction, that was effected during the period, the combined entity shall disclose the following:

(a) the names of the combining entities (other than the reporting entity);
(b) whether the combination has been accounted for as an acquisition or a merger; and
(c) the date of the combination.

Section 20
Leases

SCOPE OF THIS SECTION

This section covers accounting for all **leases** other than: 20.1

(a) leases to explore for or use minerals, oil, natural gas and similar non-regenerative resources (see Section 34 *Specialised Activities*);
(b) licensing agreements for such items as motion picture films, video recordings, plays, manuscripts, patents and copyrights (see Section 18 *Intangible Assets other than Goodwill*);
(c) **measurement** of property held by lessees that is accounted for as **investment property** and measurement of investment property provided by lessors under **operating leases** (see Section 16 *Investment Property*);
(d) measurement of **biological assets** held by lessees under **finance leases** and biological assets provided by lessors under operating leases (see Section 34); and
(e) leases that could lead to a loss to the lessor or the lessee as a result of non-typical contractual terms (see paragraph 12.3(f)).
(f) [not used]

This section applies to agreements that transfer the right to use **assets** even though substantial services by the lessor may be called for in connection with the operation or maintenance of such assets. This section does not apply to agreements that are contracts for services that do not transfer the right to use assets from one contracting party to the other. 20.2

Some arrangements do not take the legal form of a lease but convey rights to use assets in return for payments. Examples of arrangements in which one entity (the supplier) may convey a right to use an asset to another entity (the purchaser), often together with related services, may include outsourcing arrangements, telecommunication contracts that provide rights to capacity and take-or-pay contracts. 20.3

Determining whether an arrangement is, or contains, a lease shall be based on the substance of the arrangement and requires an assessment of whether: 20.3A

(a) fulfilment of the arrangement is dependent on the use of a specific asset or assets. Although a specific asset may be explicitly identified in an arrangement, it is not the subject of a lease if fulfilment of the arrangement is not dependent on the use of the specified asset. An asset is implicitly specified if, for example, the supplier owns or leases only one asset with which to fulfil the obligation and it is not economically feasible or practicable for the supplier to perform its obligation through the use of alternative assets; and
(b) the arrangement conveys a right to use the asset. This will be the case where the arrangement conveys to the purchaser the right to control the use of the underlying asset.

CLASSIFICATION OF LEASES

A lease is classified as a finance lease if it transfers substantially all the risks and rewards incidental to ownership. A lease is classified as an operating lease if it does not transfer substantially all the risks and rewards incidental to ownership. 20.4

Whether a lease is a finance lease or an operating lease depends on the substance of the transaction rather than the form of the contract. Examples of situations that 20.5

individually or in combination would normally lead to a lease being classified as a finance lease are:

(a) the lease transfers ownership of the asset to the lessee by the end of the **lease term**;
(b) the lessee has the option to purchase the asset at a price that is expected to be sufficiently lower than the **fair value** at the date the option becomes exercisable for it to be reasonably certain, at the **inception of the lease**, that the option will be exercised;
(c) the lease term is for the major part of the economic life of the asset even if title is not transferred;
(d) at the inception of the lease the **present value** of the **minimum lease payments** amounts to at least substantially all of the fair value of the leased asset; and
(e) the leased assets are of such a specialised nature that only the lessee can use them without major modifications.

20.6 Indicators of situations that individually or in combination could also lead to a lease being classified as a finance lease are:

(a) if the lessee can cancel the lease, the lessor's losses associated with the cancellation are borne by the lessee;
(b) **gains** or losses from the fluctuation in the **residual value** of the leased asset accrue to the lessee (eg in the form of a rent rebate equalling most of the sales proceeds at the end of the lease); and
(c) the lessee has the ability to continue the lease for a secondary period at a rent that is substantially lower than market rent.

20.7 The examples and indicators in paragraphs 20.5 and 20.6 are not always conclusive. If it is clear from other features that the lease does not transfer substantially all risks and rewards incidental to ownership, the lease is classified as an operating lease. For example, this may be the case if ownership of the asset is transferred to the lessee at the end of the lease for a variable payment equal to the asset's then fair value, or if there are **contingent rents**, as a result of which the lessee does not have substantially all risks and rewards incidental to ownership.

20.8 Lease classification is made at the inception of the lease and is not changed during the term of the lease unless the lessee and the lessor agree to change the provisions of the lease (other than simply by renewing the lease), in which case the lease classification shall be re-evaluated.

FINANCIAL STATEMENTS OF LESSEES: FINANCE LEASES

Initial recognition

20.9 At the **commencement of the lease term**, a lessee shall recognise its rights of use and obligations under finance leases as assets and **liabilities** in its **statement of financial position** at amounts equal to the fair value of the leased asset or, if lower, the present value of the minimum lease payments, determined at the inception of the lease. Any initial direct costs of the lessee (incremental costs that are directly attributable to negotiating and arranging a lease) are added to the amount recognised as an asset.

20.10 The present value of the minimum lease payments shall be calculated using the **interest rate implicit in the lease**. If this cannot be determined, the **lessee's incremental borrowing rate** shall be used.

Subsequent measurement

A lessee shall apportion minimum lease payments between the finance charge and the reduction of the outstanding liability using the **effective interest method** (see paragraphs 11.15 to 11.20). The lessee shall allocate the finance charge to each period during the lease term so as to produce a constant periodic rate of interest on the remaining balance of the liability. A lessee shall charge contingent rents as **expenses** in the periods in which they are incurred. **20.11**

A lessee shall depreciate an asset leased under a finance lease in accordance with Section 17 *Property, Plant and Equipment*. If there is no reasonable certainty that the lessee will obtain ownership by the end of the lease term, the asset shall be fully depreciated over the shorter of the lease term and its **useful life**. A lessee shall also assess at each **reporting date** whether an asset leased under a finance lease is impaired (see Section 27 *Impairment of Assets*). **20.12**

Disclosures

A lessee shall make the following disclosures for finance leases: **20.13**

(a) for each **class of asset**, the net **carrying amount** at the end of the **reporting period**;
(b) the total of future minimum lease payments at the end of the reporting period, for each of the following periods:
    (i) not later than one year;
    (ii) later than one year and not later than five years; and
    (iii) later than five years; and
(c) a general description of the lessee's significant leasing arrangements including, for example, information about contingent rent, renewal or purchase options and escalation clauses, subleases, and restrictions imposed by lease arrangements.

In addition, the requirements for disclosure about assets in accordance with Sections 17 and 27 apply to lessees for assets leased under finance leases. **20.14**

FINANCIAL STATEMENTS OF LESSEES: OPERATING LEASES

Recognition and measurement

A lessee shall recognise lease payments under operating leases (excluding costs for services such as insurance and maintenance) as an expense over the lease term on a straight-line basis unless either: **20.15**

(a) another systematic basis is representative of the time pattern of the user's benefit, even if the payments are not on that basis; or
(b) the payments to the lessor are structured to increase in line with expected general inflation (based on published indexes or statistics) to compensate for the lessor's expected inflationary cost increases. If payments to the lessor vary because of factors other than general inflation, then this condition (b) is not met.

Example of applying paragraph 20.15(b):	
X operates in a jurisdiction in which the consensus forecast by local banks is that the general price level index, as published by the government, will increase by an average of 10 per cent annually over the next five years. X leases some office space from Y for five years under an operating lease. The lease payments are structured to reflect the expected 10 per cent annual general inflation over the five-year term of the lease as follows:	
Year 1	CU100,000
Year 2	CU110,000
Year 3	CU121,000
Year 4	CU133,000
Year 5	CU146,000
X recognises annual rent expense equal to the amounts owed to the lessor as shown above. If the escalating payments are not clearly structured to compensate the lessor for expected inflationary cost increases based on published indexes or statistics, then X recognises annual rent expense on a straight-line basis: CU122,000 each year (sum of the amounts payable under the lease divided by five years).	

20.15A A lessee shall recognise the aggregate benefit of **lease incentives** as a reduction to the expense recognised in accordance with paragraph 20.15 over the lease term, on a straight-line basis unless another systematic basis is representative of the time pattern of the lessee's benefit from the use of the leased asset. Any costs incurred by the lessee (for example costs for termination of a pre-existing lease, relocation or leasehold improvements) shall be accounted for in accordance with the applicable section of this FRS.

20.15B Where an operating lease becomes an **onerous contract** an entity shall also apply Section 21 *Provisions and Contingencies*.

Disclosures

20.16 A lessee shall make the following disclosures for operating leases:

(a) the total of future minimum lease payments under non-cancellable operating leases for each of the following periods:

(i) not later than one year;
(ii) later than one year and not later than five years; and
(iii) later than five years; and

(b) lease payments recognised as an expense.
(c) [not used]

FINANCIAL STATEMENTS OF LESSORS: FINANCE LEASES

Initial recognition and measurement

20.17 A lessor shall recognise assets held under a finance lease in its statement of financial position and present them as a receivable at an amount equal to the net investment in the lease. The **net investment in a lease** is the lessor's **gross investment in the lease**

discounted at the interest rate implicit in the lease. The gross investment in the lease is the aggregate of:

(a) the minimum lease payments receivable by the lessor under a finance lease; and
(b) any unguaranteed residual value accruing to the lessor.

For finance leases other than those involving manufacturer or dealer lessors, initial direct costs (costs that are incremental and directly attributable to negotiating and arranging a lease) are included in the initial measurement of the finance lease receivable and reduce the amount of **income** recognised over the lease term. **20.18**

Subsequent measurement

The **recognition** of finance income shall be based on a pattern reflecting a constant periodic rate of return on the lessor's net investment in the finance lease. Lease payments relating to the period, excluding costs for services, are applied against the gross investment in the lease to reduce both the principal and the unearned finance income. If there is an indication that the estimated unguaranteed residual value used in computing the lessor's gross investment in the lease has changed significantly, the income allocation over the lease term is revised, and any reduction in respect of amounts accrued is recognised immediately in **profit or loss**. **20.19**

Manufacturer or dealer lessors

Manufacturers or dealers often offer to customers the choice of either buying or leasing an asset. A finance lease of an asset by a manufacturer or dealer lessor gives rise to two types of income: **20.20**

(a) profit or loss equivalent to the profit or loss resulting from an outright sale of the asset being leased, at normal selling prices, reflecting any applicable volume or trade discounts; and
(b) finance income over the lease term.

The sales **revenue** recognised at the commencement of the lease term by a manufacturer or dealer lessor is the fair value of the asset or, if lower, the present value of the minimum lease payments accruing to the lessor, computed at a market rate of interest. The cost of sale recognised at the commencement of the lease term is the cost, or carrying amount if different, of the leased asset less the present value of the unguaranteed residual value. The difference between the sales revenue and the cost of sale is the selling profit, which is recognised in accordance with the entity's policy for outright sales. **20.21**

If artificially low rates of interest are quoted, selling profit shall be restricted to that which would apply if a market rate of interest were charged. Costs incurred by manufacturer or dealer lessors in connection with negotiating and arranging a lease shall be recognised as an expense when the selling profit is recognised. **20.22**

Disclosures

A lessor shall make the following disclosures for finance leases: **20.23**

(a) a reconciliation between the gross investment in the lease at the end of the reporting period, and the present value of minimum lease payments receivable at the end of the reporting period. In addition, a lessor shall disclose the gross investment in the lease and the present value of minimum lease payments receivable at the end of the reporting period, for each of the following periods:

(i) not later than one year;
(ii) later than one year and not later than five years; and
(iii) later than five years;

(b) unearned finance income;

(c) the unguaranteed residual values accruing to the benefit of the lessor;

(d) the accumulated allowance for uncollectible minimum lease payments receivable;

(e) contingent rents recognised as income in the period; and

(f) a general description of the lessor's significant leasing arrangements, including, for example, information about contingent rent, renewal or purchase options and escalation clauses, subleases, and restrictions imposed by lease arrangements.

FINANCIAL STATEMENTS OF LESSORS: OPERATING LEASES

Recognition and measurement

20.24 A lessor shall present assets subject to operating leases in its statement of financial position according to the nature of the asset.

20.25 A lessor shall recognise lease income from operating leases (excluding amounts for services such as insurance and maintenance) in profit or loss on a straight-line basis over the lease term, unless either:

(a) another systematic basis is representative of the time pattern of the lessee's benefit from the leased asset, even if the receipt of payments is not on that basis; or

(b) the payments to the lessor are structured to increase in line with expected general inflation (based on published indexes or statistics) to compensate for the lessor's expected inflationary cost increases. If payments to the lessor vary according to factors other than inflation, then condition (b) is not met.

20.25A A lessor shall recognise the aggregate cost of lease incentives as a reduction to the income recognised in accordance with paragraph 20.25 over the lease term on a straight-line basis, unless another systematic basis is representative of the time pattern over which the lessor's benefit from the leased asset is diminished.

20.26 A lessor shall recognise as an expense, costs, including **depreciation**, incurred in earning the lease income. The depreciation policy for depreciable leased assets shall be consistent with the lessor's normal depreciation policy for similar assets.

20.27 A lessor shall add to the carrying amount of the leased asset any initial direct costs it incurs in negotiating and arranging an operating lease and shall recognise such costs as an expense over the lease term on the same basis as the lease income.

20.28 To determine whether a leased asset has become impaired, a lessor shall apply Section 27.

20.29 A manufacturer or dealer lessor does not recognise any selling profit on entering into an operating lease because it is not the equivalent of a sale.

Disclosures

A lessor shall disclose the following for operating leases: 20.30

(a) the future minimum lease payments under non-cancellable operating leases for each of the following periods:
  (i) not later than one year;
  (ii) later than one year and not later than five years; and
  (iii) later than five years;
(b) total contingent rents recognised as income; and
(c) a general description of the lessor's significant leasing arrangements, including, for example, information about contingent rent, renewal or purchase options and escalation clauses, and restrictions imposed by lease arrangements.

In addition, the requirements for disclosure about assets in accordance with Sections 17 and 27 apply to lessors for assets provided under operating leases. 20.31

SALE AND LEASEBACK TRANSACTIONS

A sale and leaseback transaction involves the sale of an asset and the leasing back of the same asset. The lease payment and the sale price are usually interdependent because they are negotiated as a package. The accounting treatment of a sale and leaseback transaction depends on the type of lease. 20.32

Sale and leaseback transaction results in a finance lease

If a sale and leaseback transaction results in a finance lease, the seller-lessee shall not recognise immediately, as income, any excess of sales proceeds over the carrying amount. Instead, the seller-lessee shall defer such excess and amortise it over the lease term. 20.33

Sale and leaseback transaction results in an operating lease

If a sale and leaseback transaction results in an operating lease, and it is clear that the transaction is established at fair value, the seller-lessee shall recognise any profit or loss immediately. If the sale price is below fair value, the seller-lessee shall recognise any profit or loss immediately unless the loss is compensated for by future lease payments at below market price. In that case the seller-lessee shall defer and amortise such loss in proportion to the lease payments over the period for which the asset is expected to be used. If the sale price is above fair value, the seller-lessee shall defer the excess over fair value and amortise it over the period for which the asset is expected to be used. 20.34

Disclosures

Disclosure requirements for lessees and lessors apply equally to sale and leaseback transactions. The required description of significant leasing arrangements includes description of unique or unusual provisions of the agreement or terms of the sale and leaseback transactions. 20.35

Section 21
Provisions and Contingencies

SCOPE OF THIS SECTION

21.1 This section applies to all **provisions** (ie **liabilities** of uncertain timing or amount), **contingent liabilities** and **contingent assets** except those provisions covered by other sections of this FRS. Where those other sections contain no specific requirements to deal with contracts that have become onerous, this section applies to those contracts.

21.1A This section applies to **financial guarantee contracts** unless:

(a) an entity has chosen to apply IAS 39 *Financial Instruments: Recognition and Measurement* and/or IFRS 9 *Financial Instruments* to its **financial instruments** (see paragraphs 11.2 and 12.2); or
(b) an entity has elected under FRS 103 *Insurance Contracts* to continue the application of insurance contract accounting.

21.1B This section does not apply to financial instruments (including loan commitments) that are within the scope of Section 11 *Basic Financial Instruments* and 12 *Other Financial Instrument Issues*. This section does not apply to **insurance contracts** (including **reinsurance contracts**) that an entity issues and reinsurance contracts that the entity holds, or financial instruments issued by an entity with a **discretionary participation feature** that are within the scope of FRS 103 *Insurance Contracts*.

21.2 The requirements in this section do not apply to executory contracts unless they are **onerous contracts**. Executory contracts are contracts under which neither party has performed any of its obligations or both parties have partially performed their obligations to an equal extent.

21.3 The word 'provision' is sometimes used in the context of such items as **depreciation**, impairment of **assets**, and uncollectible receivables. Those are adjustments of the **carrying amounts** of assets, rather than **recognition** of liabilities, and therefore are not covered by this section.

INITIAL RECOGNITION

21.4 An entity shall recognise a provision only when:

(a) the entity has an obligation at the **reporting date** as a result of a past event;
(b) it is **probable** (ie more likely than not) that the entity will be required to transfer economic benefits in settlement; and
(c) the amount of the obligation can be estimated reliably.

21.5 The entity shall recognise the provision as a liability in the **statement of financial position** and shall recognise the amount of the provision as an **expense**, unless another section of this FRS requires the cost to be recognised as part of the cost of an asset such as **inventories** or **property, plant and equipment**.

21.6 The condition in paragraph 21.4(a) means that the entity has no realistic alternative to settling the obligation. This can happen when the entity has a legal obligation that can be enforced by law or when the entity has a **constructive obligation** because the past event (which may be an action of the entity) has created valid expectations in other parties that the entity will discharge the obligation. Obligations that will arise from the entity's future actions (ie the future conduct of its business) do not satisfy the condition in paragraph 21.4(a), no matter how likely they are to occur and even if they are contractual. To illustrate, because of commercial pressures or legal requirements, an entity may intend or need to carry out expenditure to operate in a particular way in the future (for example, by fitting smoke filters in a particular type of factory). Because the entity can avoid the future expenditure by its future actions, for example by changing its method of operation or selling the factory, it has no present obligation for that future expenditure and no provision is recognised.

INITIAL MEASUREMENT

An entity shall measure a provision at the best estimate of the amount required to settle the obligation at the reporting date. The best estimate is the amount an entity would rationally pay to settle the obligation at the end of the **reporting period** or to transfer it to a third party at that time. **21.7**

(a) When the provision involves a large population of items, the estimate of the amount reflects the weighting of all possible outcomes by their associated probabilities. The provision will therefore be different depending on whether the probability of a loss of a given amount is, for example, 60 per cent or 90 per cent. Where there is a continuous range of possible outcomes, and each point in that range is as likely as any other, the mid-point of the range is used.

(b) When the provision arises from a single obligation, the individual most likely outcome may be the best estimate of the amount required to settle the obligation. However, even in such a case, the entity considers other possible outcomes. When other possible outcomes are either mostly higher or mostly lower than the most likely outcome, the best estimate will be a higher or lower amount.

When the effect of the time value of money is **material**, the amount of a provision shall be the **present value** of the amount expected to be required to settle the obligation. The discount rate (or rates) shall be a pre-tax rate (or rates) that reflect(s) current market assessments of the time value of money and risks specific to the liability. The risks specific to the liability shall be reflected either in the discount rate or in the estimation of the amounts required to settle the obligation, but not both.

An entity shall exclude **gains** from the expected disposal of assets from the **measurement** of a provision. **21.8**

When some or all of the amount required to settle a provision may be reimbursed by another party (eg through an insurance claim), the entity shall recognise the reimbursement as a separate asset only when it is virtually certain that the entity will receive the reimbursement on settlement of the obligation. The amount recognised for the reimbursement shall not exceed the amount of the provision. The reimbursement receivable shall be presented in the statement of financial position as an asset and shall not be offset against the provision. In the **statement of comprehensive income** (or in the **income statement**, if presented) the expense relating to a provision may be presented net of the amount recognised for a reimbursement. **21.9**

SUBSEQUENT MEASUREMENT

An entity shall charge against a provision only those expenditures for which the provision was originally recognised. **21.10**

An entity shall review provisions at each reporting date and adjust them to reflect the current best estimate of the amount that would be required to settle the obligation at that reporting date. Any adjustments to the amounts previously recognised shall be recognised in **profit or loss** unless the provision was originally recognised as part of **21.11** the cost of an asset (see paragraph 21.5). When a provision is measured at the present value of the amount expected to be required to settle the obligation, the unwinding of the discount shall be recognised as a finance cost in profit or loss in the period it arises.

ONEROUS CONTRACTS

21.11A If an entity has an **onerous contract**, the present obligation under the contract shall be recognised and measured as a provision (see Example 2 of the Appendix to this section).

FUTURE OPERATING LOSSES

21.11B Provisions shall not be recognised for future operating losses (see Example 1 of the Appendix to this section).

RESTRUCTURING

21.11C A **restructuring** gives rise to a constructive obligation only when an entity:

(a) has a detailed formal plan for the restructuring identifying at least:
  - (i) the business or part of a business concerned;
  - (ii) the principal locations affected;
  - (iii) the location, function, and approximate number of employees who will be compensated for terminating their services;
  - (iv) the expenditures that will be undertaken; and
  - (v) when the plan will be implemented; and

(b) has raised a valid expectation in those affected that it will carry out the restructuring by starting to implement that plan or announcing its main features to those affected by it.

21.11D An entity recognises a provision for restructuring costs only when it has a legal or constructive obligation at the reporting date to carry out the restructuring.

CONTINGENT LIABILITIES

21.12 A contingent liability is either a possible but uncertain obligation or a present obligation that is not recognised because it fails to meet one or both of the conditions (b) and (c) in paragraph 21.4. An entity shall not recognise a contingent liability as a liability, except for provisions for contingent liabilities of an acquiree in a **business combination** (see paragraphs 19.20 and 19.21). Disclosure of a contingent liability is required by paragraph 21.15 unless the possibility of an outflow of resources is remote. When an entity is jointly and severally liable for an obligation, the part of the obligation that is expected to be met by other parties is treated as a contingent liability.

CONTINGENT ASSETS

21.13 An entity shall not recognise a contingent asset as an asset. Disclosure of a contingent asset is required by paragraph 21.16 when an inflow of economic benefits is probable. However, when the flow of future economic benefits to the entity is virtually certain, then the related asset is not a contingent asset, and its recognition is appropriate.

DISCLOSURES

Disclosures about provisions

For each class of provision, an entity shall disclose the following: **21.14**

(a) a reconciliation showing:

 (i) the carrying amount at the beginning and end of the period;
 (ii) additions during the period, including adjustments that result from changes in measuring the discounted amount;
 (iii) amounts charged against the provision during the period; and
 (iv) unused amounts reversed during the period;

(b) a brief description of the nature of the obligation and the expected amount and timing of any resulting payments;
(c) an indication of the uncertainties about the amount or timing of those outflows; and
(d) the amount of any expected reimbursement, stating the amount of any asset that has been recognised for that expected reimbursement.

Comparative information for prior periods is not required.

Disclosures about contingent liabilities

Unless the possibility of any outflow of resources in settlement is remote, an entity shall disclose, for each class of contingent liability at the reporting date, a brief description of the nature of the contingent liability and, when practicable: **21.15**

(a) an estimate of its financial effect, measured in accordance with paragraphs 21.7 to 21.11;
(b) an indication of the uncertainties relating to the amount or timing of any outflow; and
(c) the possibility of any reimbursement.

If it is **impracticable** to make one or more of these disclosures, that fact shall be stated.

Disclosures about contingent assets

If an inflow of economic benefits is probable (more likely than not) but not virtually certain, an entity shall disclose a description of the nature of the contingent assets at the end of the reporting period, and, when practicable, an estimate of their financial effect, measured using the principles set out in paragraphs 21.7 to 21.11. If it is impracticable to make this disclosure, that fact shall be stated. **21.16**

Prejudicial disclosures

In extremely rare cases, disclosure of some or all of the information required by paragraphs 21.14 to 21.16 can be expected to prejudice seriously the position of the entity in a dispute with other parties on the subject matter of the provision, contingent liability or contingent asset. In such cases, an entity need not disclose the information, but shall disclose the general nature of the dispute, together with the fact that, and reason why, the information has not been disclosed. **21.17**

Disclosure about financial guarantee contracts

21.17A An entity shall disclose the nature and business purpose of the financial guarantee contracts it has issued. If applicable, an entity shall also provide the disclosures required by paragraphs 21.14 and 21.15.

Appendix to Section 21

EXAMPLES ON RECOGNISING AND MEASURING PROVISIONS

This appendix accompanies, but is not part of, Section 21. It provides guidance for applying the requirements of Section 21 in recognising and measuring provisions.

All of the entities in the examples in this appendix have 31 December as their reporting date. In all cases, it is assumed that a reliable estimate can be made of any outflows expected. In some examples the circumstances described may have resulted in impairment of the assets; this aspect is not dealt with in the examples. References to 'best estimate' are to the present value amount, when the effect of the time value of money is material.

Example 1 Future operating losses

An entity determines that it is probable that a segment of its operations will incur future operating losses for several years. **21A.1**

Present obligation as a result of a past obligating event: There is no past event that obliges the entity to pay out resources.

Conclusion: The entity does not recognise a provision for future operating losses. Expected future losses do not meet the definition of a liability. The expectation of future operating losses may be an indicator that one or more assets are impaired (see Section 27 *Impairment of Assets).*

Example 2 Onerous contracts

An onerous contract is one in which the unavoidable costs of meeting the obligations under the contract exceed the economic benefits expected to be received under it. The unavoidable costs under a contract reflect the least net cost of exiting from the contract, which is the lower of the cost of fulfilling it and any compensation or penalties arising from failure to fulfil it. For example, an entity may be contractually required under an operating lease to make payments to lease an asset for which it no longer has any use. **21A.2**

Present obligation as a result of a past obligating event: The entity is contractually required to pay out resources for which it will not receive commensurate benefits.

Conclusion: If an entity has a contract that is onerous, the entity recognises and measures the present obligation under the contract as a provision.

Example 3 Restructurings

[Moved to paragraph 21.11C] **21A.3**

Example 4 Warranties

A manufacturer gives warranties at the time of sale to purchasers of its product. Under the terms of the contract for sale, the manufacturer undertakes to make good, by repair or replacement, manufacturing defects that become apparent within three **21A.4** years from the date of sale. On the basis of experience, it is probable (ie more likely than not) that there will be some claims under the warranties.

Present obligation as a result of a past obligating event: The obligating event is the sale of the product with a warranty, which gives rise to a legal obligation.

An outflow of resources embodying economic benefits in settlement: Probable for the warranties as a whole.

Conclusion: The entity recognises a provision for the best estimate of the costs of making good under the warranty products sold before the reporting date.

Illustration of calculations:

In 20X0, goods are sold for CU1,000,000. Experience indicates that 90 per cent of products sold require no warranty repairs; 6 per cent of products sold require minor repairs costing 30 per cent of the sale price; and 4 per cent of products sold require major repairs or replacement costing 70 per cent of sale price. Therefore estimated warranty costs are:

CU1,000,000 × 90% × 0 =	CU0
CU1,000,000 × 6% × 30% =	CU18,000
CU1,000,000 × 4% × 70% =	CU28,000
Total	CU46,000

The expenditures for warranty repairs and replacements for products sold in 20X0 are expected to be made 60 per cent in 20X1, 30 per cent in 20X2, and 10 per cent in 20X3, in each case at the end of the period. Because the estimated cash flows already reflect the probabilities of the cash outflows, and assuming there are no other risks or uncertainties that must be reflected, to determine the present value of those cash flows the entity uses a 'risk-free' discount rate based on government bonds with the same term as the expected cash outflows (6 per cent for one-year bonds and 7 per cent for two-year and three-year bonds). Calculation of the present value, at the end of 20X0, of the estimated cash flows related to the warranties for products sold in 20X0 is as follows:

Year		Expected cash payments (CU)	Discount rate	Discount factor	Present value (CU)
1	60% × CU46,000	27,600	6%	0.9434 (at 6% for 1 year)	26,038
2	30% × CU46,000	13,800	7%	0.8734 (at 7% for 2 years)	12,053
3	10% × CU46,000	4,600	7%	0.8163 (at 7% for 3 years)	3,755
Total					41,846

The entity will recognise a warranty obligation of CU41,846 at the end of 20X0 for products sold in 20X0.

Example 5 Refunds policy

A retail store has a policy of refunding purchases by dissatisfied customers, even though it is under no legal obligation to do so. Its policy of making refunds is generally known. **21A.5**

Present obligation as a result of a past obligating event: The obligating event is the sale of the product, which gives rise to a constructive obligation because the conduct of the store has created a valid expectation on the part of its customers that the store will refund purchases.

An outflow of resources embodying economic benefits in settlement: Probable that a proportion of goods will be returned for refund.

Conclusion: The entity recognises a provision for the best estimate of the amount required to settle the refunds.

Example 6 Closure of a division: no implementation before end of reporting period

On 12 December 20X0 the board of an entity decided to close down a division. Before the end of the reporting period (31 December 20X0) the decision was not communicated to any of those affected and no other steps were taken to implement the decision. **21A.6**

Present obligation as a result of a past obligating event: There has been no obligating event, and so there is no obligation.

Conclusion: The entity does not recognise a provision.

Example 7 Closure of a division: communication and implementation before end of reporting period

On 12 December 20X0 the board of an entity decided to close a division making a particular product. On 20 December 20X0 a detailed plan for closing the division was agreed by the board, letters were sent to customers warning them to seek an alternative source of supply, and redundancy notices were sent to the staff of the division. **21A.7**

Present obligation as a result of a past obligating event: The obligating event is the communication of the decision to the customers and employees, which gives rise to a constructive obligation from that date, because it creates a valid expectation that the division will be closed.

An outflow of resources embodying economic benefits in settlement: Probable.

Conclusion: The entity recognises a provision at 31 December 20X0 for the best estimate of the costs that would be incurred to close the division at the reporting date.

Example 8 Staff retraining as a result of changes in the income tax system

21A.8 The government introduces changes to the income tax system. As a result of those changes, an entity in the financial services sector will need to retrain a large proportion of its administrative and sales workforce in order to ensure continued compliance with tax regulations. At the end of the reporting period, no retraining of staff has taken place.

Present obligation as a result of a past obligating event: The tax law change does not impose an obligation on an entity to do any retraining. An obligating event for recognising a provision (the retraining itself) has not taken place.

Conclusion: The entity does not recognise a provision.

Example 9 A court case

21A.9 A customer has sued Entity X, seeking damages for injury the customer allegedly sustained from using a product sold by Entity X. Entity X disputes liability on grounds that the customer did not follow directions in using the product. Up to the date the board authorised the financial statements for the year to 31 December 20X1 for issue, the entity's lawyers advise that it is probable that the entity will not be found liable. However, when the entity prepares the financial statements for the year to 31 December 20X2, its lawyers advise that, owing to developments in the case, it is now probable that the entity will be found liable.

(a) At 31 December 20X1
Present obligation as a result of a past obligating event: On the basis of the evidence available when the financial statements were approved, there is no obligation as a result of past events.
Conclusion: No provision is recognised. The matter is disclosed as a contingent liability unless the probability of any outflow is regarded as remote.

(b) At 31 December 20X2
Present obligation as a result of a past obligating event: On the basis of the evidence available, there is a present obligation. The obligating event is the sale of the product to the customer.
An outflow of resources embodying economic benefits in settlement: Probable.
Conclusion: A provision is recognised at the best estimate of the amount to settle the obligation at 31 December 20X2, and the expense is recognised in profit or loss. It is not a correction of an error in 20X1 because, on the basis of the evidence available when the 20X1 financial statements were approved, a provision should not have been recognised at that time.

Section 22
Liabilities and Equity

SCOPE OF THIS SECTION

This section establishes principles for classifying **financial instruments** as either **liabilities** or **equity** and deals with the accounting for **compound financial instruments**. It also addresses the issue of equity instruments and distributions to individuals or other parties acting in their capacity as investors in equity instruments (ie in their capacity as **owners**) and the accounting for purchases of own equity. This section also deals with the accounting for **non-controlling interests** in **consolidated financial statements**. Section 26 *Share-based Payment* addresses accounting for a transaction in which the entity receives goods or services (including employee services) as consideration for its equity instruments (including shares or **share options**) from employees and other vendors acting in their capacity as vendors of goods and services. **22.1**

This section shall be applied to all types of financial instruments except: **22.2**

(a) Investments in **subsidiaries**, **associates** and **joint ventures** that are accounted for in accordance with Section 9 *Consolidated and Separate Financial Statements*, Section 14 *Investments in Associates* or Section 15 *Investments in Joint Ventures*.
(b) Employers' rights and obligations under employee benefit plans, to which Section 28 *Employee Benefits* applies.
(c) Contracts for contingent consideration in a **business combination** (see Section 19 *Business Combinations and Goodwill*). This exemption applies only to the acquirer.
(d) Financial instruments, contracts and obligations under **share-based payment transactions** to which Section 26 applies, except that paragraphs 22.3 to 22.6 shall be applied to **treasury shares** issued, purchased, sold, transferred or cancelled in connection with employee share option plans, employee share purchase plans, and all other share-based payment arrangements.
(e) **Insurance contracts** (including **reinsurance contracts**) that an entity issues and reinsurance contracts that it holds (see FRS 103 *Insurance Contracts*).
(f) Financial instruments with a **discretionary participation feature** that an entity issues (see FRS 103).
(g) **Financial guarantee contracts** (see Section 21 *Provisions and Contingencies*).

A reporting entity that issues the financial instruments set out in (e) and (f) or holds the financial instruments set out (e) is required by paragraph 1.6 to apply FRS 103 to those financial instruments.

CLASSIFICATION OF AN INSTRUMENT AS LIABILITY OR EQUITY

Equity is the residual interest in the **assets** of an entity after deducting all its liabilities. Equity includes investments by the owners of the entity, plus additions to those investments earned through profitable operations and retained for use in the entity's operations, minus reductions to owners' investments as a result of unprofitable operations and distributions to owners. **22.3**

A **financial liability** is any liability that is:

(a) a contractual obligation:

(i) to deliver **cash** or another **financial asset** to another entity; or

(ii) to exchange financial assets or financial liabilities with another entity under conditions that are potentially unfavourable to the entity; or

(b) a contract that will or may be settled in the entity's own equity instruments and:

(i) under which the entity is or may be obliged to deliver a variable number of the entity's own equity instruments; or

(ii) which will or may be settled other than by the exchange of a fixed amount of cash or another financial asset for a fixed number of the entity's own equity instruments. For this purpose the entity's own equity instruments do not include instruments that are themselves contracts for the future receipt or delivery of the entity's own equity instruments.

22.3A A financial instrument, where the issuer does not have the unconditional right to avoid settling in cash or by delivery of another financial asset (or otherwise to settle it in such a way that it would be a financial liability) and where settlement is dependent on the occurrence or non-occurrence of uncertain future events beyond the control of the issuer and the holder, is a financial liability of the issuer unless:

(a) the part of the contingent settlement provision that could require settlement in cash or another financial asset (or otherwise in such a way that it would be a financial liability) is not genuine;

(b) the issuer can be required to settle the obligation in cash or another financial asset (or otherwise to settle it in such a way that it would be a financial liability) only in the event of liquidation of the issuer; or

(c) the instrument has all the features and meets the conditions in paragraph 22.4.

22.4 Some financial instruments that meet the definition of a liability are classified as equity because they represent the residual interest in the net assets of the entity:

(a) A puttable instrument is a financial instrument that gives the holder the right to sell that instrument back to the issuer for cash or another financial asset or is automatically redeemed or repurchased by the issuer on the occurrence of an uncertain future event or the death or retirement of the instrument holder. A puttable instrument that has all of the following features is classified as an equity instrument:

(i) It entitles the holder to a pro rata share of the entity's net assets in the event of the entity's liquidation. The entity's net assets are those assets that remain after deducting all other claims on its assets.

(ii) The instrument is in the class of instruments that is subordinate to all other classes of instruments.

(iii) All financial instruments in the class of instruments that is subordinate to all other classes of instruments have identical features.

(iv) Apart from the contractual obligation for the issuer to repurchase or redeem the instrument for cash or another financial asset, the instrument does not include any contractual obligation to deliver cash or another financial asset to another entity, or to exchange financial assets or financial liabilities with another entity under conditions that are potentially unfavourable to the entity, and it is not a contract that will or may be settled in the entity's own equity instruments as set out in paragraph 22.3(b) of the definition of a financial liability.

(v) The total expected **cash flows** attributable to the instrument over the life of the instrument are based substantially on the **profit or loss**, the change in the recognised net assets or the change in the **fair value** of the recognised and unrecognised net assets of the entity over the life of the instrument (excluding any effects of the instrument).

(b) Instruments, or components of instruments, that are subordinate to all other classes of instruments are classified as equity if they impose on the entity an obligation to deliver to another party a pro rata share of the net assets of the entity only on liquidation.

The following are examples of instruments that are either classified as liabilities or equity: **22.5**

(a) An instrument of the type described in paragraph 22.4(b) is classified as a liability if the distribution of net assets on liquidation is subject to a maximum amount (a ceiling). For example, if on liquidation the holders of the instrument receive a pro rata share of the net assets, but this amount is limited to a ceiling and the excess net assets are distributed to a charity organisation or the government, the instrument is not classified as equity.

(b) A puttable instrument is classified as equity if, when the put option is exercised, the holder receives a pro rata share of the net assets of the entity determined by:

   (i) dividing the entity's net assets on liquidation into units of equal amounts; and

   (ii) multiplying that amount by the number of the units held by the financial instrument holder.

   However, if the holder is entitled to an amount measured on some other basis the instrument is classified as a liability.

(c) An instrument is classified as a liability if it obliges the entity to make payments to the holder before liquidation, such as a mandatory dividend.

(d) A puttable instrument that is classified as equity in a subsidiary's **financial statements** is classified as a liability in the consolidated financial statements.

(e) A preference share that provides for mandatory redemption by the issuer for a fixed or determinable amount at a fixed or determinable future date, or gives the holder the right to require the issuer to redeem the instrument at or after a particular date for a fixed or determinable amount, is a financial liability.

Members' shares in co-operative entities and similar instruments are equity if: **22.6**

(a) the entity has an unconditional right to refuse redemption of the members' shares; or

(b) redemption is unconditionally prohibited by local law, regulation or the entity's governing charter.

ORIGINAL ISSUE OF SHARES OR OTHER EQUITY INSTRUMENTS

An entity shall recognise the issue of shares or other equity instruments as equity when it issues those instruments and another party is obliged to provide cash or other resources to the entity in exchange for the instruments. **22.7**

(a) [Not used]

(b) If the entity receives the cash or other resources before the equity instruments are issued, and the entity cannot be required to repay the cash or other resources received, the entity shall recognise the corresponding increase in equity to the extent of consideration received.

(c) To the extent that the equity instruments have been subscribed for but not issued (or called up), and the entity has not yet received the cash or other resources, the entity shall not recognise an increase in equity.

An entity shall measure the equity instruments at the fair value of the cash or other resources received or receivable, net of direct costs of issuing the equity instruments. **22.8**

If payment is deferred and the time value of money is **material**, the initial **measurement** shall be on a **present value** basis.

22.9 An entity shall account for the **transaction costs** of an equity transaction as a deduction from equity, net of any related income tax benefit.

22.10 How the increase in equity arising on the issue of shares or other equity instruments is presented in the **statement of financial position** is determined by applicable laws. For example, the par value (or other nominal value) of shares and the amount paid in excess of par value may be presented separately.

EXERCISE OF OPTIONS, RIGHTS AND WARRANTS

22.11 An entity shall apply the principles in paragraphs 22.7 to 22.10 to equity issued by means of exercise of options, rights, warrants and similar equity instruments.

CAPITALISATION OR BONUS ISSUES OF SHARES AND SHARE SPLITS

22.12 A capitalisation or bonus issue (sometimes referred to as a stock dividend) is the issue of new shares to shareholders in proportion to their existing holdings. For example, an entity may give its shareholders one dividend or bonus share for every five shares held. A share split (sometimes referred to as a stock split) is the dividing of an entity's existing shares into multiple shares. For example, in a share split, each shareholder may receive one additional share for each share held. In some cases, the previously outstanding shares are cancelled and replaced by new shares. Capitalisation and bonus issues and share splits do not change total equity. An entity shall reclassify amounts within equity as required by applicable laws.

CONVERTIBLE DEBT OR SIMILAR COMPOUND FINANCIAL INSTRUMENTS

22.13 On issuing convertible debt or similar compound financial instruments that contain both a liability and an equity component, an entity shall allocate the proceeds between the liability component and the equity component. To make the allocation, the entity shall first determine the amount of the liability component as the fair value of a similar liability that does not have a conversion feature or similar associated equity component. The entity shall allocate the residual amount as the equity component. Transaction costs shall be allocated between the debt component and the equity component on the basis of their relative fair values.

22.14 The entity shall not revise the allocation in a subsequent period.

22.15 In periods after the instruments were issued, the entity shall account for the liability component as a financial instrument in accordance with Section 11 *Basic Financial Instruments* or Section 12 *Other Financial Instruments Issues* as appropriate. The appendix to this section illustrates the issuer's accounting for convertible debt where the liability component is a basic financial instrument.

TREASURY SHARES

22.16 Treasury shares are the equity instruments of an entity that have been issued and subsequently reacquired by the entity. An entity shall deduct from equity the fair value of the consideration given for the treasury shares. The entity shall not recognise a **gain** or loss in profit or loss on the purchase, sale, transfer or cancellation of treasury shares.

DISTRIBUTIONS TO OWNERS

An entity shall reduce equity for the amount of distributions to its owners (holders of its equity instruments). **22.17**

An entity shall disclose the fair value of any non-cash assets that have been distributed to its owners during the **reporting period**, except when the non-cash assets are ultimately controlled by the same parties both before and after the distribution. **22.18**

NON-CONTROLLING INTEREST AND TRANSACTIONS IN SHARES OF A CONSOLIDATED SUBSIDIARY

In the consolidated financial statements, a non-controlling interest in the net assets of a subsidiary is included in equity. An entity shall treat changes in a parent's controlling interest in a subsidiary that do not result in a loss of **control** as transactions with equity holders in their capacity as equity holders. Accordingly, the **carrying amount** of the non-controlling interest shall be adjusted to reflect the change in the parent's interest in the subsidiary's net assets. Any difference between the amount by which the non-controlling interest is so adjusted and the fair value of the consideration paid or received, if any, shall be recognised directly in equity and attributed to equity holders of the parent. An entity shall not recognise a gain or loss on these changes. Also, an entity shall not recognise any change in the carrying amounts of assets (including goodwill) or liabilities as a result of such transactions. **22.19**

Appendix to Section 22

EXAMPLE OF THE ISSUER'S ACCOUNTING FOR CONVERTIBLE DEBT

The appendix accompanies, but is not part of, Section 22. It provides guidance for applying the requirements of paragraphs 22.13 to 22.15.

On 1 January 20X5 an entity issues 500 convertible bonds. The bonds are issued at par with a face value of CU100 per bond and are for a five-year term, with no transaction costs. The total proceeds from the issue are CU50,000. Interest is payable annually in arrears at an annual interest rate of 4 per cent. Each bond is convertible, at the holder's discretion, into 25 ordinary shares at any time up to maturity. At the time the bonds are issued, the market interest rate for similar debt that does not have the conversion option is 6 per cent.

When the instrument is issued, the liability component must be valued first, and the difference between the total proceeds on issue (which is the fair value of the instrument in its entirety) and the fair value of the liability component is assigned to the equity component. The fair value of the liability component is calculated by determining its present value using the discount rate of 6 per cent. The calculations and journal entries are illustrated below:

	CU
Proceeds from the bond issue (A)	50,000
Present value of principal at the end of five years (see calculations below)	37,363
Present value of interest payable annually in arrears for five years	8,425
Present value of liability, which is the fair value of liability component (B)	45,788
Residual, which is the fair value of the equity component (A) – (B)	4,212

The issuer of the bonds makes the following journal entry at issue on 1 January 20X5:

Dr Cash	CU50,000	
Cr Financial Liability – Convertible bond		CU45,788
Cr Equity		CU4,212

The CU4,212 represents a discount on issue of the bonds, so the entry could also be shown 'gross':

Dr Cash	CU50,000	
Dr Financial Liability – Convertible bond discount	CU4,212	
Cr Financial Liability – Convertible bond		CU50,000
Cr Equity		CU4,212

After issue, the issuer will amortise the bond discount according to the following table:

	(a) Interest payment CU	(b) Total interest expense = 6% x (e) CU	(c) Amortisation of bond discount = (b) – (a) CU	(d) Bond discount = (d) – (c) CU	(e) Net liability = 50,000 – (d) CU
1/1/20X5				4,212	45,788
31/12/20X5	2,000	2,747	747	3,465	46,535
31/12/20X6	2,000	2,792	792	2,673	47,327
31/12/20X7	2,000	2,840	840	1,833	48,167
31/12/20X8	2,000	2,890	890	943	49,057
31/12/20X9	2,000	2,943	943	0	50,000
Totals	10,000	14,212	4,212		

At the end of 20X5, the issuer would make the following journal entry:

Dr Interest expense	CU2,747	
Cr Bond discount		CU747
Cr Cash		CU2,000

Calculations

Present value of principal of CU50,000 at 6 per cent

$CU50{,}000/(1.06)^5 = 37{,}363$

Present value of the interest annuity of CU2,000 (= CU50,000 × 4 per cent) payable at the end of each of five years

The CU2,000 annual interest payments are an annuity: a cash flow stream with a limited number (n) of periodic payments (C), receivable at dates 1 to n. To calculate the present value of this annuity, future payments are discounted by the periodic rate of interest (i) using the following formula:

$PV = C/i \times [1 - 1/(1+i)^n]$

Therefore, the present value of the CU2,000 interest payments is $(2{,}000/.06) \times [1 - [(1/1.06)^5] = 8{,}425$

This is equivalent to the sum of the present values of the five individual CU2,000 payments, as follows:

	CU
Present value of interest payment at 31 December 20X5 = 2,000/1.06	1,887
Present value of interest payment at 31 December 20X6 = $2,000/1.06^2$	1,780
Present value of interest payment at 31 December 20X7 = $2,000/1.06^3$	1,679
Present value of interest payment at 31 December 20X8 = $2,000/1.06^4$	1,584
Present value of interest payment at 31 December 20X9 = $2,000/1.06^5$	1,495
Total	8,425

Yet another way to calculate this is to use a table of present value of an ordinary annuity in arrears, five periods, interest rate of 6 per cent per period. (Such tables are easily found on the Internet.) The present value factor is 4.2124. Multiplying this by the annuity payment of CU2,000 determines the present value of CU8,425.

Section 23
Revenue

SCOPE OF THIS SECTION

This section shall be applied in accounting for **revenue** arising from the following transactions and events: 23.1

(a) the sale of goods (whether produced by the entity for the purpose of sale or purchased for resale);
(b) the rendering of services;
(c) **construction contracts** in which the entity is the contractor; and
(d) the use by others of entity assets yielding interest, royalties or dividends.

Revenue or other income arising from some transactions and events is dealt with in other sections of this FRS: 23.2

(a) lease agreements (see Section 20 *Leases*);
(b) dividends and other income arising from investments that are accounted for using the equity method (see Section 14 *Investments in Associates* and Section 15 *Investments in Joint Ventures*);
(c) changes in the **fair value** of **financial assets** and **financial liabilities** or their disposal (see Section 11 *Basic Financial Instruments* and Section 12 *Other Financial Instruments Issues*);
(d) changes in the fair value of **investment property** (see Section 16 *Investment Property*);
(e) initial **recognition** and changes in the fair value of **biological assets** related to **agricultural activity** (see Section 34 *Specialised Activities*); and
(f) initial recognition of **agricultural produce** (see Section 34).

This section excludes revenue or other income arising from transactions and events dealt with in FRS 103 *Insurance Contracts*. 23.2A

MEASUREMENT OF REVENUE

An entity shall measure revenue at the fair value of the consideration received or receivable. The fair value of the consideration received or receivable takes into account the amount of any trade discounts, prompt settlement discounts and volume rebates allowed by the entity. 23.3

An entity shall include in revenue only the gross inflows of economic benefits received and receivable by the entity on its own account. An entity shall exclude from revenue all amounts collected on behalf of third parties such as sales taxes, goods and services taxes and value added taxes. In an agency relationship, an entity (the **agent**) shall include in revenue only the amount of its commission. The amounts collected on behalf of the **principal** are not revenue of the entity. 23.4

Deferred payment

When the inflow of **cash** or **cash equivalents** is deferred, and the arrangement constitutes in effect a financing transaction, the fair value of the consideration is the **present value** of all future receipts determined using an **imputed rate of interest**. A financing transaction arises when, for example, an entity provides interest-free credit to the buyer or accepts a note receivable bearing a below-market interest rate from 23.5

the buyer as consideration for the sale of goods. The imputed rate of interest is the more clearly determinable of either:

(a) the prevailing rate for a similar instrument of an issuer with a similar credit rating; or
(b) a rate of interest that discounts the nominal amount of the instrument to the current cash sales price of the goods or services.

An entity shall recognise the difference between the present value of all future receipts and the nominal amount of the consideration as interest revenue in accordance with paragraphs 23.28 and 23.29 and Section 11.

Exchanges of goods or services

23.6 An entity shall not recognise revenue:

(a) when goods or services are exchanged for goods or services that are of a similar nature and value; or
(b) when goods or services are exchanged for dissimilar goods or services but the transaction lacks commercial substance.

23.7 An entity shall recognise revenue when goods are sold or services are exchanged for dissimilar goods or services in a transaction that has commercial substance. In that case, the entity shall measure the transaction:

(a) at the fair value of the goods or services received adjusted by the amount of any cash or cash equivalents transferred;
(b) if the amount under (a) cannot be measured reliably, then at the fair value of the goods or services given up adjusted by the amount of any cash or cash equivalents transferred; or
(c) if the fair value of neither the goods or services received nor the goods or services given up can be measured reliably, then at the **carrying amount** of the goods or services given up adjusted by the amount of any cash or cash equivalents transferred.

IDENTIFICATION OF THE REVENUE TRANSACTION

23.8 An entity usually applies the revenue recognition criteria in this section separately to each transaction. However, an entity applies the recognition criteria to the separately identifiable components of a single transaction when necessary to reflect the substance of the transaction. For example, an entity applies the recognition criteria to the separately identifiable components of a single transaction when the selling price of a product includes an identifiable amount for subsequent servicing. Conversely, an entity applies the recognition criteria to two or more transactions together when they are linked in such a way that the commercial effect cannot be understood without reference to the series of transactions as a whole. For example, an entity applies the recognition criteria to two or more transactions together when it sells goods and, at the same time, enters into a separate agreement to repurchase the goods at a later date, thus negating the substantive effect of the transaction.

23.9 Sometimes, as part of a sales transaction, an entity grants its customer a loyalty award that the customer may redeem in the future for free or discounted goods or services. In this case, in accordance with paragraph 23.8, the entity shall account for the award credits as a separately identifiable component of the initial sales transaction. The entity shall allocate the fair value of the consideration received or receivable in respect of the initial sale between the award credits and the other components of the sale. The consideration allocated to the award credits shall be measured by reference to their fair value, ie the amount for which the award credits could be sold separately.

SALE OF GOODS

An entity shall recognise revenue from the sale of goods when all the following conditions are satisfied: **23.10**

(a) the entity has transferred to the buyer the significant risks and rewards of ownership of the goods;
(b) the entity retains neither continuing managerial involvement to the degree usually associated with ownership nor effective control over the goods sold;
(c) the amount of revenue can be measured reliably;
(d) it is **probable** that the economic benefits associated with the transaction will flow to the entity; and
(e) the costs incurred or to be incurred in respect of the transaction can be measured reliably.

The assessment of when an entity has transferred the significant risks and rewards of ownership to the buyer requires an examination of the circumstances of the transaction. In most cases, the transfer of the risks and rewards of ownership coincides with the transfer of the legal title or the passing of possession to the buyer. This is the case for most retail sales. In other cases, the transfer of risks and rewards of ownership occurs at a time different from the transfer of legal title or the passing of possession. **23.11**

An entity does not recognise revenue if it retains significant risks and rewards of ownership. Examples of situations in which the entity may retain the significant risks and rewards of ownership are: **23.12**

(a) when the entity retains an obligation for unsatisfactory performance not covered by normal warranties;
(b) when the receipt of the revenue from a particular sale is contingent on the buyer selling the goods;
(c) when the goods are shipped subject to installation and the installation is a significant part of the contract that has not yet been completed; and
(d) when the buyer has the right to rescind the purchase for a reason specified in the sales contract, or at the buyer's sole discretion without any reason, and the entity is uncertain about the probability of return.

If an entity retains only an insignificant risk of ownership, the transaction is a sale and the entity recognises the revenue. For example, a seller recognises revenue when it retains the legal title to the goods solely to protect the collectability of the amount due. Similarly an entity recognises revenue when it offers a refund if the customer finds the goods faulty or is not satisfied for other reasons, and the entity can estimate the returns reliably. In such cases, the entity recognises a **provision** for returns in accordance with Section 21 *Provisions and Contingencies*. **23.13**

RENDERING OF SERVICES

When the outcome of a transaction involving the rendering of services can be estimated reliably, an entity shall recognise revenue associated with the transaction by reference to the stage of completion of the transaction at the end of the **reporting period** (sometimes referred to as the percentage of completion method). The outcome **23.14** of a transaction can be estimated reliably when all the following conditions are satisfied:

(a) the amount of revenue can be measured reliably;
(b) it is probable that the economic benefits associated with the transaction will flow to the entity;
(c) the stage of completion of the transaction at the end of the reporting period can be measured reliably; and
(d) the costs incurred for the transaction and the costs to complete the transaction can be measured reliably.

Paragraphs 23.21 to 23.27 provide guidance for applying the percentage of completion method.

23.15 When services are performed by an indeterminate number of acts over a specified period of time, an entity recognises revenue on a straight-line basis over the specified period unless there is evidence that some other method better represents the stage of completion. When a specific act is much more significant than any other act, the entity postpones recognition of revenue until the significant act is executed.

23.16 When the outcome of the transaction involving the rendering of services cannot be estimated reliably, an entity shall recognise revenue only to the extent of the **expenses** recognised that are recoverable.

CONSTRUCTION CONTRACTS

23.17 When the outcome of a construction contract can be estimated reliably, an entity shall recognise contract revenue and contract costs associated with the construction contract as revenue and expenses respectively by reference to the stage of completion of the contract activity at the end of the reporting period (often referred to as the percentage of completion method). Reliable estimation of the outcome requires reliable estimates of the stage of completion, future costs and collectability of billings. Paragraphs 23.21 to 23.27 provide guidance for applying the percentage of completion method.

23.18 The requirements of this section are usually applied separately to each construction contract. However, in some circumstances, it is necessary to apply this section to the separately identifiable components of a single contract or to a group of contracts together in order to reflect the substance of a contract or a group of contracts.

23.19 When a contract covers a number of **assets**, the construction of each asset shall be treated as a separate construction contract when:

(a) separate proposals have been submitted for each asset;
(b) each asset has been subject to separate negotiation, and the contractor and customer are able to accept or reject that part of the contract relating to each asset; and
(c) the costs and revenues of each asset can be identified.

23.20 A group of contracts, whether with a single customer or with several customers, shall be treated as a single construction contract when:

(a) the group of contracts is negotiated as a single package;
(b) the contracts are so closely interrelated that they are, in effect, part of a single project with an overall profit margin; and
(c) the contracts are performed concurrently or in a continuous sequence.

PERCENTAGE OF COMPLETION METHOD

This method is used to recognise revenue from rendering services (see paragraphs 23.14 to 23.16) and from construction contracts (see paragraphs 23.17 to 23.20). An entity shall review and, when necessary, revise the estimates of revenue and costs as the service transaction or construction contract progresses. **23.21**

An entity shall determine the stage of completion of a transaction or contract using the method that measures most reliably the work performed. Possible methods include: **23.22**

(a) the proportion that costs incurred for work performed to date bear to the estimated total costs. Costs incurred for work performed to date do not include costs relating to future activity, such as for materials or prepayments;
(b) surveys of work performed; and
(c) completion of a physical proportion of the contract work or the completion of a proportion of the service contract.

Progress payments and advances received from customers often do not reflect the work performed.

An entity shall recognise costs that relate to future activity on the transaction or contract, such as for materials or prepayments, as an asset if it is probable that the costs will be recovered. **23.23**

An entity shall recognise as an expense immediately any costs whose recovery is not probable. **23.24**

When the outcome of a construction contract cannot be estimated reliably: **23.25**

(a) an entity shall recognise revenue only to the extent of contract costs incurred that it is probable will be recoverable; and
(b) the entity shall recognise contract costs as an expense in the period in which they are incurred.

When it is probable that total contract costs will exceed total contract revenue on a construction contract, the expected loss shall be recognised as an expense immediately, with a corresponding provision for an **onerous contract** (see Section 21). **23.26**

If the collectability of an amount already recognised as contract revenue is no longer probable, the entity shall recognise the uncollectible amount as an expense rather than as an adjustment of the amount of contract revenue. **23.27**

INTEREST, ROYALTIES AND DIVIDENDS

An entity shall recognise revenue arising from the use by others of entity assets yielding interest, royalties and dividends on the bases set out in paragraph 23.29 when: **23.28**

(a) it is probable that the economic benefits associated with the transaction will flow to the entity; and
(b) the amount of the revenue can be measured reliably.

An entity shall recognise revenue on the following bases: **23.29**

(a) Interest shall be recognised using the **effective interest method** as described in paragraphs 11.15 to 11.20. When calculating the **effective interest rate**, an entity shall include any related fees, finance charges paid or received (such as 'points'), **transaction costs** and other premiums or discounts.

(b) Royalties shall be recognised on an **accrual basis** in accordance with the substance of the relevant agreement.

(c) Dividends shall be recognised when the shareholder's right to receive payment is established.

DISCLOSURES

General disclosures about revenue

23.30 An entity shall disclose:

(a) the **accounting policies** adopted for the recognition of revenue, including the methods adopted to determine the stage of completion of transactions involving the rendering of services; and

(b) the amount of each category of revenue recognised during the period, showing separately, at a minimum, revenue arising from:

(i) the sale of goods;
(ii) the rendering of services;
(iii) interest;
(iv) royalties;
(v) dividends;
(vi) commissions;
(vii) grants; and
(viii) any other significant types of revenue.

Disclosures relating to revenue from construction contracts

23.31 An entity shall disclose the following:

(a) the amount of contract revenue recognised as revenue in the period;
(b) the methods used to determine the contract revenue recognised in the period; and
(c) the methods used to determine the stage of completion of contracts in progress.

23.32 An entity shall present:

(a) the gross amount due from customers for contract work, as an asset; and
(b) the gross amount due to customers for contract work, as a **liability**.

Appendix to Section 23

EXAMPLES OF REVENUE RECOGNITION UNDER THE PRINCIPLES IN SECTION 23

This appendix accompanies, but is not part of, Section 23. It provides guidance for applying the requirements of Section 23 in recognising revenue.

The following examples focus on particular aspects of a transaction and are not a comprehensive discussion of all the relevant factors that might influence the recognition of revenue. The examples generally assume that the amount of revenue can be measured reliably, it is probable that the economic benefits will flow to the entity and the costs incurred or to be incurred can be measured reliably. **23A.1**

SALE OF GOODS

The law in different countries may cause the recognition criteria in Section 23 to be met at different times. In particular, the law may determine the point in time at which the entity transfers the significant risks and rewards of ownership. Therefore, the examples in this appendix need to be read in the context of the laws relating to the sale of goods in the country in which the transaction takes place. **23A.2**

Example 1 'Bill and hold' sales, in which delivery is delayed at the buyer's request but the buyer takes title and accepts billing

The seller recognises revenue when the buyer takes title, provided: **23A.3**

(a) it is probable that delivery will be made;
(b) the item is on hand, identified and ready for delivery to the buyer at the time the sale is recognised;
(c) the buyer specifically acknowledges the deferred delivery instructions; and
(d) the usual payment terms apply.

Revenue is not recognised when there is simply an intention to acquire or manufacture the goods in time for delivery.

Example 2 Goods shipped subject to conditions: installation and inspection

The seller normally recognises revenue when the buyer accepts delivery, and installation and inspection are complete. However, revenue is recognised immediately upon the buyer's acceptance of delivery when: **23A.4**

(a) the installation process is simple, for example the installation of a factory-tested television receiver that requires only unpacking and connection of power and antennae; or
(b) the inspection is performed only for the purposes of final determination of contract prices, for example, shipments of iron ore, sugar or soya beans.

Example 3 Goods shipped subject to conditions: on approval when the buyer has negotiated a limited right of return

If there is uncertainty about the possibility of return, the seller recognises revenue when the shipment has been formally accepted by the buyer or the goods have been delivered and the time period for rejection has elapsed. **23A.5**

Example 4 Goods shipped subject to conditions: consignment sales under which the recipient (buyer) undertakes to sell the goods on behalf of the shipper (seller)

23A.6 The shipper recognises revenue when the goods are sold by the recipient to a third party.

Example 5 Goods shipped subject to conditions: cash on delivery sales

23A.7 The seller recognises revenue when delivery is made and cash is received by the seller or its agent.

Example 6 Layaway sales under which the goods are delivered only when the buyer makes the final payment in a series of instalments

23A.8 The seller recognises revenue from such sales when the goods are delivered. However, when experience indicates that most such sales are consummated, revenue may be recognised when a significant deposit is received, provided the goods are on hand, identified and ready for delivery to the buyer.

Example 7 Orders when payment (or partial payment) is received in advance of delivery for goods not currently held in inventory, for example, the goods are still to be manufactured or will be delivered direct to the buyer from a third party

23A.9 The seller recognises revenue when the goods are delivered to the buyer.

Example 8 Sale and repurchase agreements (other than swap transactions) under which the seller concurrently agrees to repurchase the same goods at a later date, or when the seller has a call option to repurchase, or the buyer has a put option to require the repurchase, by the seller, of the goods

23A.10 For a sale and repurchase agreement on an asset other than a financial asset, the seller must analyse the terms of the agreement to ascertain whether, in substance, the risks and rewards of ownership have been transferred to the buyer. If they have been transferred, the seller recognises revenue. When the seller has retained the risks and rewards of ownership, even though legal title has been transferred, the transaction is a financing arrangement and does not give rise to revenue. For a sale and repurchase agreement on a financial asset, the derecognition provisions of Section 11 apply.

Example 9 Sales to intermediate parties, such as distributors, dealers or others for resale

23A.11 The seller generally recognises revenue from such sales when the risks and rewards of ownership have been transferred. However, when the buyer is acting, in substance, as an agent, the sale is treated as a consignment sale.

Example 10 Subscriptions to publications and similar items

23A.12 When the items involved are of similar value in each time period, the seller recognises revenue on a straight-line basis over the period in which the items are dispatched. When the items vary in value from period to period, the seller recognises revenue on the basis of the sales value of the item dispatched in relation to the total estimated sales value of all items covered by the subscription.

Example 11 Instalment sales, under which the consideration is receivable in instalments

The seller recognises revenue attributable to the sales price, exclusive of interest, at the date of sale. The sale price is the present value of the consideration, determined by discounting the instalments receivable at the imputed rate of interest. The seller recognises the interest element as revenue using the effective interest method. **23A.13**

Example 12 Agreements for the construction of real estate

An entity that undertakes the construction of real estate, directly or through sub-contractors, and enters into an agreement with one or more buyers before construction is complete, shall account for the agreement using the percentage of completion method, only if: **23A.14**

(a) the buyer is able to specify the major structural elements of the design of the real estate before construction begins and/or specify major structural changes once construction is in progress (whether it exercises that ability or not); or
(b) the buyer acquires and supplies construction materials and the entity provides only construction services.

If the entity is required to provide services together with construction materials in order to perform its contractual obligation to deliver real estate to the buyer, the agreement shall be accounted for as the sale of goods. In this case, the buyer does not obtain control or the significant risks and rewards of ownership of the work in progress in its current state as construction progresses. Rather, the transfer occurs only on delivery of the completed real estate to the buyer. **23A.15**

Example 13 Sale with customer loyalty award

An entity sells product A for CU100. Purchasers of product A get an award credit enabling them to buy product B for CU10. The normal selling price of product B is CU18. The entity estimates that 40 per cent of the purchasers of product A will use their award to buy product B at CU10. The normal selling price of product A, after taking into account discounts that are usually offered but that are not available during this promotion, is CU95. **23A.16**

The fair value of the award credit is 40 per cent × [CU18 – CU10] = CU3.20. The entity allocates the total revenue of CU100 between product A and the award credit by reference to their relative fair values of CU95 and CU3.20 respectively. Therefore: **23A.17**

(a) Revenue for product A is CU100 × [CU95 / (CU95 + CU3.20)] = CU96.74
(b) Revenue for product B is CU100 × [CU3.20 / (CU95 + CU3.20)] = CU3.26

RENDERING OF SERVICES

Example 14 Installation fees

The seller recognises installation fees as revenue by reference to the stage of completion of the installation, unless they are incidental to the sale of a product, in which case they are recognised when the goods are sold. **23A.18**

Example 15 Servicing fees included in the price of the product

When the selling price of a product includes an identifiable amount for subsequent servicing (eg after sales support and product enhancement on the sale of software), **23A.19** the seller defers that amount and recognises it as revenue over the period during which the service is performed. The amount deferred is that which will cover the expected costs of the services under the agreement, together with a reasonable profit on those services.

Example 16 Advertising commissions

23A.20 Media commissions are recognised when the related advertisement or commercial appears before the public. Production commissions are recognised by reference to the stage of completion of the project.

Example 17 Insurance agency commissions

23A.21 Insurance agency commissions received or receivable that do not require the agent to render further service are recognised as revenue by the agent on the effective commencement or renewal dates of the related policies. However, when it is probable that the agent will be required to render further services during the life of the policy, the agent defers the commission, or part of it, and recognises it as revenue over the period during which the policy is in force.

Example 17A Financial services fees

23A.21A The recognition of revenue for financial service fees depends on the purposes for which the fees are assessed and the basis of accounting for any associated financial instrument. The description of fees for financial services may not be indicative of the nature and substance of the services provided. Therefore it is necessary to distinguish between fees that are an integral part of the effective interest rate of a financial instrument, fees that are earned as services are provided, and fees that are earned on the execution of a significant act.

Example 18 Admission fees

23A.22 The seller recognises revenue from artistic performances, banquets and other special events when the event takes place. When a subscription to a number of events is sold, the seller allocates the fee to each event on a basis that reflects the extent to which services are performed at each event.

Example 19 Tuition fees

23A.23 The seller recognises revenue over the period of instruction.

Example 20 Initiation, entrance and membership fees

23A.24 Revenue recognition depends on the nature of the services provided. If the fee permits only membership, and all other services or products are paid for separately, or if there is a separate annual subscription, the fee is recognised as revenue when no significant uncertainty about its collectability exists. If the fee entitles the member to services or publications to be provided during the membership period, or to purchase goods or services at prices lower than those charged to non-members, it is recognised on a basis that reflects the timing, nature and value of the benefits provided.

FRANCHISE FEES

Franchise fees may cover the supply of initial and subsequent services, equipment and other tangible assets, and know-how. Accordingly, franchise fees are recognised as revenue on a basis that reflects the purpose for which the fees were charged. The following methods of franchise fee recognition are appropriate. **23A.25**

Example 21 Franchise fees: Supplies of equipment and other tangible assets

The franchisor recognises the fair value of the assets sold as revenue when the items are delivered or title passes. **23A.26**

Example 22 Franchise fees: Supplies of initial and subsequent services

The franchisor recognises fees for the provision of continuing services, whether part of the initial fee or a separate fee, as revenue as the services are rendered. When the separate fee does not cover the cost of continuing services together with a reasonable profit, part of the initial fee, sufficient to cover the costs of continuing services and to provide a reasonable profit on those services, is deferred and recognised as revenue as the services are rendered. **23A.27**

The franchise agreement may provide for the franchisor to supply equipment, inventories, or other tangible assets at a price lower than that charged to others or a price that does not provide a reasonable profit on those sales. In these circumstances, part of the initial fee, sufficient to cover estimated costs in excess of that price and to provide a reasonable profit on those sales, is deferred and recognised over the period the goods are likely to be sold to the franchisee. The balance of an initial fee is recognised as revenue when performance of all the initial services and other obligations required of the franchisor (such as assistance with site selection, staff training, financing and advertising) has been substantially accomplished. **23A.28**

The initial services and other obligations under an area franchise agreement may depend on the number of individual outlets established in the area. In this case, the fees attributable to the initial services are recognised as revenue in proportion to the number of outlets for which the initial services have been substantially completed. **23A.29**

If the initial fee is collectible over an extended period and there is a significant uncertainty that it will be collected in full, the fee is recognised as cash instalments are received. **23A.30**

Example 23 Franchise fees: Continuing franchise fees

Fees charged for the use of continuing rights granted by the agreement, or for other services provided during the period of the agreement, are recognised as revenue as the services are provided or the rights used. **23A.31**

Example 24 Franchise fees: Agency transactions

Transactions may take place between the franchisor and the franchisee that, in substance, involve the franchisor acting as agent for the franchisee. For example, the franchisor may order supplies and arrange for their delivery to the franchisee at no profit. Such transactions do not give rise to revenue. **23A.32**

Example 25 Fees from the development of customised software

23A.33 The software developer recognises fees from the development of customised software as revenue by reference to the stage of completion of the development, including completion of services provided for post-delivery service support.

INTEREST, ROYALTIES AND DIVIDENDS

Example 26 Licence fees and royalties

23A.34 The licensor recognises fees and royalties paid for the use of an entity's assets (such as trademarks, patents, software, music copyright, record masters and motion picture films) in accordance with the substance of the agreement. As a practical matter, this may be on a straight-line basis over the life of the agreement, for example, when a licensee has the right to use specified technology for a specified period of time.

23A.35 An assignment of rights for a fixed fee or non-refundable guarantee under a non-cancellable contract that permits the licensee to exploit those rights freely and the licensor has no remaining obligations to perform is, in substance, a sale. An example is a licensing agreement for the use of software when the licensor has no obligations after delivery. Another example is the granting of rights to exhibit a motion picture film in markets in which the licensor has no control over the distributor and expects to receive no further revenues from the box office receipts. In such cases, revenue is recognised at the time of sale.

23A.36 In some cases, whether or not a licence fee or royalty will be received is contingent on the occurrence of a future event. In such cases, revenue is recognised only when it is probable that the fee or royalty will be received, which is normally when the event has occurred.

Section 24
Government Grants

SCOPE OF THIS SECTION

This section specifies the accounting for all **government grants**. A government grant is assistance by government in the form of a transfer of resources to an entity in return for past or future compliance with specified conditions relating to the **operating activities** of the entity. **24.1**

Government grants exclude those forms of government assistance that cannot reasonably have a value placed upon them and transactions with government that cannot be distinguished from the normal trading transactions of the entity. **24.2**

This section does not cover government assistance that is provided for an entity in the form of benefits that are available in determining **taxable profit (tax loss)**, or are determined or limited on the basis of income tax liability. Examples of such benefits are income tax holidays, investment tax credits, accelerated depreciation allowances and reduced income tax rates. Section 29 *Income Tax* covers accounting for taxes based on **income**. **24.3**

RECOGNITION AND MEASUREMENT

Government grants, including non-monetary grants shall not be recognised until there is reasonable assurance that: **24.3A**

(a) the entity will comply with the conditions attaching to them; and
(b) the grants will be received.

An entity shall recognise grants either based on the performance model or the accrual model. This policy choice shall be applied on a class-by-class basis. **24.4**

An entity shall measure grants at the **fair value** of the **asset** received or receivable. **24.5**

Where a grant becomes repayable it shall be recognised as a **liability** when the repayment meets the definition of a liability. **24.5A**

Performance model

An entity applying the performance model shall recognise grants as follows: **24.5B**

(a) A grant that does not impose specified future **performance-related conditions** on the recipient is recognised in income when the grant proceeds are received or receivable.
(b) A grant that imposes specified future performance-related conditions on the recipient is recognised in income only when the performance-related conditions are met.
(c) Grants received before the **revenue recognition** criteria are satisfied are recognised as a liability.

Accrual model

An entity applying the accrual model shall classify grants either as a grant relating to revenue or a grant relating to assets. **24.5C**

24.5D Grants relating to revenue shall be recognised in income on a systematic basis over the periods in which the entity recognises the related costs for which the grant is intended to compensate.

24.5E A grant that becomes receivable as compensation for **expenses** or losses already incurred or for the purpose of giving immediate financial support to the entity with no future related costs shall be recognised in income in the period in which it becomes receivable.

24.5F Grants relating to assets shall be recognised in income on a systematic basis over the expected **useful life** of the asset.

24.5G Where part of a grant relating to an asset is deferred it shall be recognised as deferred income and not deducted from the **carrying amount** of the asset.

DISCLOSURES

24.6 An entity shall disclose the following:

(a) the **accounting policy** adopted for grants in accordance with paragraph 24.4;
(b) the nature and amounts of grants recognised in the **financial statements**;
(c) unfulfilled conditions and other contingencies attaching to grants that have been recognised in income; and
(d) an indication of other forms of government assistance from which the entity has directly benefited.

24.7 For the purpose of the disclosure required by paragraph 24.6(d), government assistance is action by government designed to provide an economic benefit specific to an entity or range of entities qualifying under specified criteria. Examples include free technical or marketing advice, the provision of guarantees, and loans at nil or low interest rates.

Section 25
Borrowing Costs

SCOPE OF THIS SECTION

This section specifies the accounting for **borrowing costs**. Borrowing costs are interest and other costs that an entity incurs in connection with the borrowing of funds. Borrowing costs include: **25.1**

(a) interest expense calculated using the **effective interest method** as described in Section 11 *Basic Financial Instruments*;
(b) finance charges in respect of **finance leases** recognised in accordance with Section 20 *Leases*; and
(c) exchange differences arising from foreign currency borrowings to the extent that they are regarded as an adjustment to interest costs.

RECOGNITION

An entity may adopt a policy of capitalising borrowing costs that are directly attributable to the acquisition, construction or production of a **qualifying asset** as part of the cost of that **asset**. Where an entity adopts a policy of capitalisation of borrowing costs, it shall be applied consistently to a class of qualifying assets. Where an entity does not adopt a policy of capitalising borrowing costs, all borrowing costs shall be recognised as an **expense** in **profit or loss** in the period in which they are incurred. **25.2**

The borrowing costs that are directly attributable to the acquisition, construction or production of a qualifying asset are those borrowing costs that would have been avoided if the expenditure on the qualifying asset had not been made. **25.2A**

To the extent that an entity borrows funds specifically for the purpose of obtaining a qualifying asset, the entity shall determine the amount of borrowing costs eligible for capitalisation as the actual borrowing costs incurred on that borrowing during the period less any investment income on the temporary investment of those borrowings. **25.2B**

To the extent that funds applied to obtain a qualifying asset form part of the entity's general borrowings, the amount of borrowing costs eligible for capitalisation are determined by applying a capitalisation rate to the expenditure on that asset. For this purpose the expenditure on the asset is the average **carrying amount** of the asset during the period, including borrowing costs previously capitalised. The capitalisation rate used in an accounting period shall be the weighted average of rates applicable to the entity's general borrowings that are outstanding during the period. This excludes borrowings by the entity that are specifically for the purpose of obtaining other qualifying assets. The amount of borrowing costs that an entity capitalises during a period shall not exceed the amount of borrowing costs it incurred during that period. **25.2C**

An entity shall: **25.2D**

(a) capitalise borrowing costs as part of the cost of a qualifying asset from the point when it first incurs both expenditure on the asset and borrowing costs, and undertakes activities necessary to prepare the asset for its intended use or sale;
(b) suspend capitalisation during extended periods where active development of the asset has paused; and

(c) cease capitalisation when substantially all the activities necessary to prepare the qualifying asset for its intended use or sale are complete.

DISCLOSURES

25.3 Paragraph 5.5 sets out the presentation requirements for items of profit or loss, including interest payable. Paragraph 11.48(b) requires disclosure of total interest expense (using the effective interest method) for **financial liabilities** that are not at fair value through profit or loss. When a policy of capitalising borrowing costs is not adopted, this section does not require any additional disclosure.

25.3A Where a policy of capitalisation is adopted, an entity shall disclose:

(a) the amount of borrowing costs capitalised in the period; and
(b) the capitalisation rate used.

Section 26
Share-based Payment

SCOPE OF THIS SECTION

This section specifies the accounting for all **share-based payment transactions** including: **26.1**

(a) **equity-settled share-based payment transactions**, in which the entity:
 (i) receives goods or services as consideration for its own equity instruments (including shares or **share options**); or
 (ii) receives goods or services but has no obligation to settle the transaction with supplier;

(b) **cash-settled share-based payment transactions**, in which the entity acquires goods or services by incurring a **liability** to transfer **cash** or other assets to the supplier of those goods or services for amounts that are based on the price (or value) of the entity's shares or other equity instruments of the entity or another group entity; and

(c) transactions in which the entity receives or acquires goods or services and the terms of the arrangement provide either the entity or the supplier of those goods or services with a choice of whether the entity settles the transaction in cash (or other assets) or by issuing equity instruments.

A share-based payment transaction may be settled by another group entity (or a shareholder of any group entity) on behalf of the entity receiving or acquiring the goods or services. Paragraph 26.1 also applies to an entity that: **26.1A**

(a) receives goods or services when another entity in the same group (or shareholder of any group entity) has the obligation to settle the share-based payment transaction; or

(b) has an obligation to settle a share-based payment transaction when another entity in the same group receives the goods or services

unless the transaction is clearly for a purpose other than payment for goods or services supplied to the entity receiving them.

Cash-settled share-based payment transactions include share appreciation rights. For example, an entity might grant share appreciation rights to employees as part of their remuneration package, whereby the employees will become entitled to a future cash payment (rather than an equity instrument), based on the increase in the entity's share price from a specified level over a specified period of time. Or an entity might grant to its employees a right to receive a future cash payment by granting to them a right to shares (including shares to be issued upon the exercise of share options) that are redeemable, either mandatorily (eg upon cessation of employment) or at the employee's option. **26.2**

RECOGNITION

An entity shall recognise the goods or services received or acquired in a share-based payment transaction when it obtains the goods or as the services are received. The entity shall recognise a corresponding increase in **equity** if the goods or services were received in an equity-settled share-based payment transaction, or a liability if the goods or services were acquired in a cash-settled share-based payment transaction. **26.3**

26.4 When the goods or services received or acquired in a share-based payment transaction do not qualify for **recognition** as assets, the entity shall recognise them as **expenses**.

RECOGNITION WHEN THERE ARE VESTING CONDITIONS

26.5 If the share-based payments granted to employees **vest** immediately, the employee is not required to complete a specified period of service before becoming unconditionally entitled to those share-based payments. In the absence of evidence to the contrary, the entity shall presume that services rendered by the employee as consideration for the share-based payments have been received. In this case, on **grant date** the entity shall recognise the services received in full, with a corresponding increase in equity or liabilities.

26.6 If the share-based payments do not vest until the employee completes a specified period of service, the entity shall presume that the services to be rendered by the counterparty as consideration for those share-based payments will be received in the future, during the vesting period. The entity shall account for those services as they are rendered by the employee during the vesting period, with a corresponding increase in equity or liabilities.

MEASUREMENT OF EQUITY-SETTLED SHARE-BASED PAYMENT TRANSACTIONS

Measurement principle

26.7 For equity-settled share-based payment transactions, an entity shall measure the goods or services received, and the corresponding increase in equity, at the **fair value** of the goods or services received, unless that fair value cannot be estimated reliably. If the entity cannot estimate reliably the fair value of the goods or services received, the entity shall measure their value, and the corresponding increase in equity, by reference to the fair value of the equity instruments granted measured in accordance with paragraphs 26.10 and 26.11. To apply this requirement to transactions with employees and others providing similar services, the entity shall measure the fair value of the services received by reference to the fair value of the equity instruments granted, because typically it is not possible to estimate reliably the fair value of the services received.

26.8 For transactions with employees (including others providing similar services), the fair value of the equity instruments shall be measured at grant date. For transactions with parties other than employees, the measurement date is the date when the entity obtains the goods or the counterparty renders service.

26.9 A grant of equity instruments might be conditional on employees satisfying specified **vesting conditions** related to service or performance. An example of a vesting condition relating to service is where a grant of shares or share options is conditional on the employee remaining in the entity's employ for a specified period of time. Examples of vesting conditions relating to performance are where a grant of shares or share options is conditional on the entity achieving a specified growth in profit (an example of a non-market condition) or a specified increase in the entity's share price (an example of a **market condition**). All vesting conditions related solely to employee service or to a non-market performance condition shall be taken into account when estimating the number of equity instruments expected to vest. Subsequently, the entity shall revise that estimate, if necessary, if new information indicates that the number of equity instruments expected to vest differs from previous estimates. On the vesting date, the entity shall revise the estimate to equal the number of equity instruments that ultimately vested. All market conditions and non-vesting conditions shall be taken into account when estimating the fair value of the shares or share options at the measurement date, with no subsequent adjustment irrespective of the outcome of the market or non-vesting condition, provided that all other vesting conditions are satisfied.

Shares

An entity shall measure the fair value of shares (and the related goods or services received) using the following three-tier measurement hierarchy: **26.10**

(a) If an observable market price is available for the equity instruments granted, use that price.
(b) If an observable market price is not available, measure the fair value of equity instruments granted using entity-specific observable market data such as:

(i) a recent transaction in the entity's shares; or
(ii) a recent independent fair valuation of the entity or its principal assets.

(c) If an observable market price is not available and obtaining a reliable **measurement** of fair value under (b) is **impracticable**, indirectly measure the fair value of the shares using a valuation method that uses market data to the greatest extent practicable to estimate what the price of those equity instruments would be on the grant date in an arm's length transaction between knowledgeable, willing parties. The entity's directors shall use their judgement to apply a generally accepted valuation methodology for valuing equity instruments that is appropriate to the circumstances of the entity.

Share options and equity-settled share appreciation rights

An entity shall measure the fair value of share options and equity-settled share appreciation rights (and the related goods or services received) using the following three-tier measurement hierarchy: **26.11**

(a) If an observable market price is available for the equity instruments granted, use that price.
(b) If an observable market price is not available, measure the fair value of share options and share appreciation rights granted using entity-specific observable market data such as for a recent transaction in the share options.
(c) If an observable market price is not available and obtaining a reliable measurement of fair value under (b) is impracticable, indirectly measure the fair value of share options or share appreciation rights using an alternative valuation methodology such as an option pricing model. The inputs for an option pricing model (such as the weighted average share price, exercise price, expected volatility, option life, expected dividends and the risk-free interest rate) shall use market data to the greatest extent possible. Paragraph 26.10 provides guidance on determining the fair value of the shares used in determining the weighted average share price. The entity shall derive an estimate of expected volatility consistent with the valuation methodology used to determine the fair value of the shares.

Modifications to the terms and conditions on which equity instruments were granted

If an entity modifies the vesting conditions in a manner that is beneficial to the employee, for example, by reducing the exercise price of an option or reducing the **26.12** vesting period or by modifying or eliminating a performance condition, the entity shall take the modified vesting conditions into account in accounting for the share-based payment transaction, as follows:

(a) If the modification increases the fair value of the equity instruments granted (or increases the number of equity instruments granted) measured immediately before and after the modification, the entity shall include the incremental fair value granted in the measurement of the amount recognised for services received as consideration for the equity instruments granted. The incremental fair value granted is the difference between the fair value of the modified equity instrument and that of the original equity instrument, both estimated as at the date of the modification. If the modification occurs during the vesting period, the incremental fair value granted is included in the measurement of the amount recognised for services received over the period from the modification date until the date when the modified equity instruments vest, in addition to the amount based on the grant date fair value of the original equity instruments, which is recognised over the remainder of the original vesting period.
(b) If the modification reduces the total fair value of the share-based payment arrangement, or apparently is not otherwise beneficial to the employee, the entity shall nevertheless continue to account for the services received as consideration for the equity instruments granted as if that modification had not occurred.

Cancellations and settlements

26.13 An entity shall account for a cancellation or settlement of an equity-settled share-based payment award as an acceleration of vesting, and therefore shall recognise immediately the amount that otherwise would have been recognised for services received over the remainder of the vesting period.

CASH-SETTLED SHARE-BASED PAYMENT TRANSACTIONS

26.14 For cash-settled share-based payment transactions, an entity shall measure the goods or services acquired and the liability incurred at the fair value of the liability. Until the liability is settled, the entity shall remeasure the fair value of the liability at each **reporting date** and at the date of settlement, with any changes in fair value recognised in **profit or loss** for the period.

SHARE-BASED PAYMENT TRANSACTIONS WITH CASH ALTERNATIVES

26.15 Some share-based payment transactions give either the entity or the counterparty a choice of settling the transaction in cash (or other assets) or by transfer of equity instruments. In such a case, the entity shall account for the transaction as a cash-settled share-based payment transaction unless either:

(a) the entity has a past practice of settling by issuing equity instruments; or
(b) the option has no commercial substance because the cash settlement amount bears no relationship to, and is likely to be lower in value than, the fair value of the equity instrument.

In circumstances (a) and (b), the entity shall account for the transaction as an equity-settled share-based payment transaction in accordance with paragraphs 26.7 to 26.13.

GROUP PLANS

If a share-based payment award is granted by an entity to the employees of one or more members in the **group**, the members are permitted, as an alternative to the treatment set out in paragraphs 26.3 to 26.15, to recognise and measure the share-based payment expense on the basis of a reasonable allocation of the expense for the group. **26.16**

GOVERNMENT-MANDATED PLANS

Some jurisdictions have programmes established under law by which equity investors (such as employees) are able to acquire equity without providing goods or services that can be specifically identified (or by providing goods or services that are clearly less than the fair value of the equity instruments granted). This indicates that other consideration has been or will be received (such as past or future employee services). These are equity-settled share-based payment transactions within the scope of this section. The entity shall measure the unidentifiable goods or services received (or to be received) as the difference between the fair value of the share-based payment and the fair value of any identifiable goods or services received (or to be received) measured at the grant date. **26.17**

DISCLOSURES

An entity shall disclose the following information about the nature and extent of share-based payment arrangements that existed during the period: **26.18**

(a) A description of each type of share-based payment arrangement that existed at any time during the period, including the general terms and conditions of each arrangement, such as vesting requirements, the maximum term of options granted, and the method of settlement (eg whether in cash or equity). An entity with substantially similar types of share-based payment arrangements may aggregate this information.

(b) The number and weighted average exercise prices of share options for each of the following groups of options:

  (i) outstanding at the beginning of the period;
  (ii) granted during the period;
  (iii) forfeited during the period;
  (iv) exercised during the period;
  (v) expired during the period;
  (vi) outstanding at the end of the period; and
  (vii) exercisable at the end of the period.

For equity-settled share-based payment arrangements, an entity shall disclose information about how it measured the fair value of goods or services received or the value of the equity instruments granted. If a valuation methodology was used, the entity shall disclose the method and its reason for choosing it. **26.19**

For cash-settled share-based payment arrangements, an entity shall disclose information about how the liability was measured. **26.20**

For share-based payment arrangements that were modified during the period, an entity shall disclose an explanation of those modifications. **26.21**

If the entity is part of a group share-based payment plan, and it recognises and measures its share-based payment expense on the basis of a reasonable allocation of **26.22** the expense recognised for the group, it shall disclose that fact and the basis for the allocation (see paragraph 26.16).

26.23 An entity shall disclose the following information about the effect of share-based payment transactions on the entity's profit or loss for the period and on its **financial position**:

(a) the total expense recognised in profit or loss for the period; and
(b) the total **carrying amount** at the end of the period for liabilities arising from share-based payment transactions.

Section 27
Impairment of Assets

OBJECTIVE AND SCOPE

An **impairment loss** occurs when the **carrying amount** of an **asset** exceeds its **recoverable amount**. This section shall be applied in accounting for the impairment of all assets other than the following, for which other sections of this FRS establish impairment requirements: 27.1

(a) assets arising from **construction contracts** (see Section 23 *Revenue*);
(b) **deferred tax assets** (see Section 29 *Income Tax*);
(c) assets arising from **employee benefits** (see Section 28 *Employee Benefits*);
(d) **financial assets** within the scope of Section 11 *Basic Financial Instruments* or Section 12 *Other Financial Instruments Issues*;
(e) **investment property** measured at **fair value** (see Section 16 *Investment Property*); and
(f) **biological assets** related to **agricultural activity** measured at fair value less estimated costs to sell (see Section 34 *Specialised Activities*).

This section shall not apply in accounting for the impairment of **deferred acquisition costs** and **intangible assets** arising from contracts within the scope of FRS 103 *Insurance Contracts*. 27.1A

IMPAIRMENT OF INVENTORIES

Selling price less costs to complete and sell

An entity shall assess at each **reporting date** whether any **inventories** are impaired. The entity shall make the assessment by comparing the carrying amount of each item of inventory (or group of similar items – see paragraph 27.3) with its selling price less costs to complete and sell. If an item of inventory (or group of similar items) is impaired, the entity shall reduce the carrying amount of the inventory (or the group) to its selling price less costs to complete and sell. That reduction is an impairment loss and it is recognised immediately in **profit or loss**. 27.2

If it is **impracticable** to determine the selling price less costs to complete and sell for inventories item by item, the entity may group items of inventory relating to the same product line that have similar purposes or end uses and are produced and marketed in the same geographical area for the purpose of assessing impairment. 27.3

Reversal of impairment

An entity shall make a new assessment of selling price less costs to complete and sell at each subsequent reporting date. When the circumstances that previously caused inventories to be impaired no longer exist or when there is clear evidence of an increase in selling price less costs to complete and sell because of changed economic circumstances, the entity shall reverse the amount of the impairment (ie the reversal is limited to the amount of the original impairment loss) so that the new carrying amount is the lower of the cost and the revised selling price less costs to complete and sell. 27.4

IMPAIRMENT OF ASSETS OTHER THAN INVENTORIES

General principles

27.5 If, and only if, the recoverable amount of an asset is less than its carrying amount, the entity shall reduce the carrying amount of the asset to its recoverable amount. That reduction is an impairment loss. Paragraphs 27.11 to 27.20A provide guidance on measuring recoverable amount.

27.6 An entity shall recognise an impairment loss immediately in profit or loss, unless the asset is carried at a revalued amount in accordance with another section of this FRS (for example, in accordance with the revaluation model in Section 17 *Property, Plant and Equipment*). Any impairment loss of a revalued asset shall be treated as a revaluation decrease in accordance with that other section.

Indicators of impairment

27.7 An entity shall assess at each reporting date whether there is any indication that an asset may be impaired. If any such indication exists, the entity shall estimate the recoverable amount of the asset. If there is no indication of impairment, it is not necessary to estimate the recoverable amount.

27.8 If it is not possible to estimate the recoverable amount of the individual asset, an entity shall estimate the recoverable amount of the **cash-generating unit** to which the asset belongs. This may be the case because measuring recoverable amount requires forecasting **cash flows**, and sometimes individual assets do not generate cash flows by themselves. An asset's cash-generating unit is the smallest identifiable group of assets that includes the asset and generates cash inflows that are largely independent of the cash inflows from other assets or groups of assets.

27.9 In assessing whether there is any indication that an asset may be impaired, an entity shall consider, as a minimum, the following indications:

External sources of information

(a) During the period, an asset's market value has declined significantly more than would be expected as a result of the passage of time or normal use.
(b) Significant changes with an adverse effect on the entity have taken place during the period, or will take place in the near future, in the technological, market, economic or legal environment in which the entity operates or in the market to which an asset is dedicated.
(c) Market interest rates or other market rates of return on investments have increased during the period, and those increases are likely to affect materially the discount rate used in calculating an asset's **value in use** and decrease the asset's **fair value less costs to sell**.
(d) The carrying amount of the net assets of the entity is more than the estimated fair value of the entity as a whole (such an estimate may have been made, for example, in relation to the potential sale of part or all of the entity).

Internal sources of information

(e) Evidence is available of obsolescence or physical damage of an asset.
(f) Significant changes with an adverse effect on the entity have taken place during the period, or are expected to take place in the near future, in the extent to

which, or manner in which, an asset is used or is expected to be used. These changes include the asset becoming idle, plans to discontinue or restructure the operation to which an asset belongs, plans to dispose of an asset before the previously expected date, and reassessing the **useful life** of an asset as finite rather than indefinite.

(g) Evidence is available from internal reporting that indicates that the economic performance of an asset is, or will be, worse than expected. In this context economic performance includes operating results and cash flows.

If there is an indication that an asset may be impaired, this may indicate that the **27.10**
entity should review the remaining useful life, the **depreciation (amortisation)** method or the **residual value** for the asset and adjust it in accordance with the section of this FRS applicable to the asset (eg Section 17 *Property, Plant and Equipment* and Section 18 *Intangible Assets other than Goodwill*), even if no impairment loss is recognised for the asset.

Measuring recoverable amount

The recoverable amount of an asset or a cash-generating unit is the higher of its fair **27.11**
value less costs to sell and its value in use. If it is not possible to estimate the recoverable amount of an individual asset, references to an asset in paragraphs 27.12 to 27.20A should be read as references also to an asset's cash-generating unit.

It is not always necessary to determine both an asset's fair value less costs to sell and **27.12**
its value in use. If either of these amounts exceeds the asset's carrying amount, the asset is not impaired and it is not necessary to estimate the other amount.

If there is no reason to believe that an asset's value in use materially exceeds its fair **27.13**
value less costs to sell, the asset's fair value less costs to sell may be used as its recoverable amount. This will often be the case for an asset that is held for disposal.

Fair value less costs to sell

Fair value less costs to sell is the amount obtainable from the sale of an asset in an **27.14**
arm's length transaction between knowledgeable, willing parties, less the costs of disposal. The best evidence of the fair value less costs to sell of an asset is a price in a binding sale agreement in an arm's length transaction or a market price in an **active market**. If there is no binding sale agreement or active market for an asset, fair value less costs to sell is based on the best information available to reflect the amount that an entity could obtain, at the reporting date, from the disposal of the asset in an arm's length transaction between knowledgeable, willing parties, after deducting the costs of disposal. In determining this amount, an entity considers the outcome of recent transactions for similar assets within the same industry.

When determining an asset's fair value less costs to sell, consideration shall be given **27.14A**
to any restrictions imposed on that asset. Costs to sell shall also include the cost of obtaining relaxation of a restriction where necessary in order to enable the asset to be sold. If a restriction would also apply to any potential purchaser of an asset, the fair value of the asset may be lower than that of an asset whose use is not restricted.

Value in use

Value in use is the **present value** of the future cash flows expected to be derived from **27.15**
an asset. This present value calculation involves the following steps:

(a) estimating the future cash inflows and outflows to be derived from continuing use of the asset and from its ultimate disposal; and
(b) applying the appropriate discount rate to those future cash flows.

27.16 The following elements shall be reflected in the calculation of an asset's value in use:

(a) an estimate of the future cash flows the entity expects to derive from the asset;
(b) expectations about possible variations in the amount or timing of those future cash flows;
(c) the time value of money, represented by the current market risk-free rate of interest;
(d) the price for bearing the uncertainty inherent in the asset; and
(e) other factors, such as illiquidity, that market participants would reflect in pricing the future cash flows the entity expects to derive from the asset.

27.17 In measuring value in use, estimates of future cash flows shall include:

(a) projections of cash inflows from the continuing use of the asset;
(b) projections of cash outflows that are necessarily incurred to generate the cash inflows from continuing use of the asset (including cash outflows to prepare the asset for use) and can be directly attributed, or allocated on a reasonable and consistent basis, to the asset; and
(c) net cash flows, if any, expected to be received (or paid) for the disposal of the asset at the end of its useful life in an arm's length transaction between knowledgeable, willing parties.

The entity may wish to use any recent financial budgets or forecasts to estimate the cash flows, if available. To estimate cash flow projections beyond the period covered by the most recent budgets or forecasts an entity may wish to extrapolate the projections based on the budgets or forecasts using a steady or declining growth rate for subsequent years, unless an increasing rate can be justified.

27.18 Estimates of future cash flows shall not include:

(a) cash inflows or outflows from **financing activities**; or
(b) income tax receipts or payments.

27.19 Future cash flows shall be estimated for the asset in its current condition. Estimates of future cash flows shall not include estimated future cash inflows or outflows that are expected to arise from:

(a) a future restructuring to which an entity is not yet committed; or
(b) improving or enhancing the asset's performance.

27.20 The discount rate (rates) used in the present value calculation shall be a pre-tax rate (rates) that reflect(s) current market assessments of:

(a) the time value of money; and
(b) the risks specific to the asset for which the future cash flow estimates have not been adjusted.

The discount rate (rates) used to measure an asset's value in use shall not reflect risks for which the future cash flow estimates have been adjusted, to avoid double-counting.

27.20A For assets held for their **service potential**, a cash flow driven valuation (such as value in use) may not be appropriate. In these circumstances **value in use (in respect of assets held for their service potential)** is determined by the present value of the asset's remaining service potential plus the net amount the entity will receive from its disposal. In some cases this may be taken to be costs avoided by possession of the asset. Therefore, **depreciated replacement cost**, may be a suitable measurement model but other approaches may be used where more appropriate.

Recognising and measuring an impairment loss for a cash-generating unit

An impairment loss shall be recognised for a cash-generating unit if, and only if, the recoverable amount of the unit is less than the carrying amount of the unit. The impairment loss shall be allocated to reduce the carrying amount of the assets of the unit in the following order: **27.21**

(a) first, to reduce the carrying amount of any **goodwill** allocated to the cash-generating unit; and
(b) then, to the other assets of the unit pro rata on the basis of the carrying amount of each asset in the cash-generating unit.

However, an entity shall not reduce the carrying amount of any asset in the cash-generating unit below the highest of: **27.22**

(a) its fair value less costs to sell (if determinable);
(b) its value in use (if determinable); and
(c) zero.

Any excess amount of the impairment loss that cannot be allocated to an asset because of the restriction in paragraph 27.22 shall be allocated to the other assets of the unit pro rata on the basis of the carrying amount of those other assets. **27.23**

ADDITIONAL REQUIREMENTS FOR IMPAIRMENT OF GOODWILL

Goodwill, by itself, cannot be sold. Nor does it generate cash flows to an entity that are independent of the cash flows of other assets. As a consequence, the fair value of goodwill cannot be measured directly. Therefore, the fair value of goodwill must be derived from **measurement** of the fair value of the cash-generating unit(s) of which the goodwill is a part. **27.24**

For the purpose of impairment testing, goodwill acquired in a **business combination** shall, from the **acquisition date**, be allocated to each of the acquirer's cash-generating units that are expected to benefit from the synergies of the combination, irrespective of whether other assets or **liabilities** of the acquiree are assigned to those units. **27.25**

Part of the recoverable amount of a cash-generating unit is attributable to the **non-controlling interest** in goodwill. For the purpose of impairment testing of a non-wholly-owned cash-generating unit with goodwill, the carrying amount of that unit is notionally adjusted, before being compared with its recoverable amount, by grossing up the carrying amount of goodwill allocated to the unit to include the goodwill attributable to the non-controlling interest. This notionally adjusted carrying amount is then compared with the recoverable amount of the unit to determine whether the cash-generating unit is impaired. **27.26**

If goodwill cannot be allocated to individual cash-generating units (or groups of cash-generating units) on a non-arbitrary basis, then for the purposes of testing goodwill the entity shall test the impairment of goodwill by determining the recoverable amount of either: **27.27**

(a) the acquired entity in its entirety, if the goodwill relates to an acquired entity that has not been integrated. Integrated means the acquired **business** has been restructured or dissolved into the reporting entity or other **subsidiaries;** or
(b) the entire group of entities, excluding any entities that have not been integrated, if the goodwill relates to an entity that has been integrated.

In applying this paragraph, an entity will need to separate goodwill into goodwill relating to entities that have been integrated and goodwill relating to entities that have not been integrated. Also the entity shall follow the requirements for cash-generating units in this section when calculating the recoverable amount of, and allocating impairment losses and reversals to assets belonging to, the acquired entity or group of entities.

Reversal of an impairment loss

27.28 An impairment loss recognised for all assets, including goodwill, shall be reversed in a subsequent period if and only if the reasons for the impairment loss have ceased to apply.

27.29 An entity shall assess at each reporting date whether there is any indication that an impairment loss recognised in prior periods may no longer exist or may have decreased. Indications that an impairment loss may have decreased or may no longer exist are generally the opposite of those set out in paragraph 27.9. If any such indication exists, the entity shall determine whether all or part of the prior impairment loss should be reversed. The procedure for making that determination will depend on whether the prior impairment loss on the asset was based on:

(a) the recoverable amount of that individual asset (see paragraph 27.30); or
(b) the recoverable amount of the cash-generating unit to which the asset belongs (see paragraph 27.31).

Reversal where recoverable amount was estimated for an individual impaired asset

27.30 When the prior impairment loss was based on the recoverable amount of the individual impaired asset, the following requirements apply:

(a) The entity shall estimate the recoverable amount of the asset at the current reporting date.
(b) If the estimated recoverable amount of the asset exceeds its carrying amount, the entity shall increase the carrying amount to recoverable amount, subject to the limitation described in (c) below. That increase is a reversal of an impairment loss. The entity shall recognise the reversal immediately in profit or loss unless the asset is carried at revalued amount in accordance with another section of this FRS (for example, the revaluation model in Section 17 *Property, plant and equipment*). Any reversal of an impairment loss of a revalued asset shall be treated as a revaluation increase in accordance with the relevant section of this FRS.
(c) The reversal of an impairment loss shall not increase the carrying amount of the asset above the carrying amount that would have been determined (net of amortisation or depreciation) had no impairment loss been recognised for the asset in prior years.
(d) After a reversal of an impairment loss is recognised, the entity shall adjust the depreciation (amortisation) charge for the asset in future periods to allocate the asset's revised carrying amount, less its residual value (if any), on a systematic basis over its remaining useful life.

Reversal when recoverable amount was estimated for a cash-generating unit

When the original impairment loss was based on the recoverable amount of the cash-generating unit to which the asset, including goodwill belongs, the following requirements apply: **27.31**

(a) The entity shall estimate the recoverable amount of that cash-generating unit at the current reporting date.
(b) If the estimated recoverable amount of the cash-generating unit exceeds its carrying amount, that excess is a reversal of an impairment loss. The entity shall allocate the amount of that reversal to the assets of the unit, pro rata with the carrying amounts of those assets and goodwill in the order set out below, subject to the limitation described in (c) below. Those increases in carrying amounts shall be treated as reversals of impairment losses and recognised immediately in profit or loss unless an asset is carried at revalued amount in accordance with another section of this FRS (for example, the revaluation model in Section 17 *Property, plant and equipment*). Any reversal of an impairment loss of a revalued asset shall be treated as a revaluation increase in accordance with the relevant section of this FRS.

    (i) First the assets (other than goodwill) of the unit pro rata on the basis of the carrying amount of each asset in the cash-generating unit; and
    (ii) then to any goodwill allocated to the cash-generating unit.

(c) In allocating a reversal of an impairment loss for a cash-generating unit, the reversal shall not increase the carrying amount of any asset above the lower of:

    (i) its recoverable amount; and
    (ii) the carrying amount that would have been determined (net of amortisation or depreciation) had no impairment loss been recognised for the asset in prior periods.

(d) Any excess amount of the reversal of the impairment loss that cannot be allocated to an asset because of the restriction in (c) above shall be allocated pro rata to the other assets of the cash-generating unit.
(e) After a reversal of an impairment loss is recognised, if applicable, the entity shall adjust the depreciation (amortisation) charge for each asset in the cash-generating unit in future periods to allocate the asset's revised carrying amount, less its residual value (if any), on a systematic basis over its remaining useful life.

DISCLOSURES

An entity shall disclose the following for each **class of assets** indicated in paragraph 27.33: **27.32**

(a) the amount of impairment losses recognised in profit or loss during the period and the line item(s) in the **statement of comprehensive income** (or in the **income statement**, if presented) in which those impairment losses are included; and
(b) the amount of reversals of impairment losses recognised in profit or loss during the period and the line item(s) in the statement of comprehensive income (or in the income statement, if presented) in which those impairment losses are reversed.

An entity shall disclose the information required by paragraph 27.32 for each of the following classes of asset: **27.33**

(a) inventories;

(b) **property, plant and equipment** (including investment property accounted for by the cost method);
(c) goodwill;
(d) **intangible assets** other than goodwill;
(e) investments in **associates**; and
(f) investments in **joint ventures**.

27.33A An entity shall disclose a description of the events and circumstances that led to the **recognition** or reversal of the impairment loss.

Section 28
Employee Benefits

SCOPE OF THIS SECTION

Employee benefits are all forms of consideration given by an entity in exchange for service rendered by employees, including directors and management. This section applies to all employee benefits, except for **share-based payment transactions**, which are covered by Section 26 *Share-based Payment*. Employee benefits covered by this section will be one of the following four types: **28.1**

(a) short-term employee benefits, which are employee benefits (other than **termination benefits**) that are expected to be settled wholly before twelve months after the end of the **reporting period** in which the employees render the related service;
(b) **post-employment benefits**, which are employee benefits (other than termination benefits and short-term employee benefits) that are payable after the completion of employment;
(c) other long-term employee benefits, which are all employee benefits, other than short-term employee benefits, post-employment benefits and termination benefits; or
(d) termination benefits, which are employee benefits provided in exchange for the termination of an employee's employment as a result of either:
    (i) an entity's decision to terminate an employee's employment before the normal retirement date; or
    (ii) an employee's decision to accept voluntary redundancy in exchange for those benefits.

[Not used] **28.2**

GENERAL RECOGNITION PRINCIPLE FOR ALL EMPLOYEE BENEFITS

An entity shall recognise the cost of all employee benefits to which its employees have become entitled as a result of service rendered to the entity during the reporting period: **28.3**

(a) As a **liability**, after deducting amounts that have been paid either directly to the employees or as a contribution to an employee benefit fund*. If the amount paid exceeds the obligation arising from service before the **reporting date**, an entity shall recognise that excess as an asset to the extent that the prepayment will lead to a reduction in future payments or a cash refund.
(b) As an **expense**, unless another section of this FRS requires the cost to be recognised as part of the cost of an asset such as **inventories** (for example in accordance with paragraph 13.8) or **property, plant and equipment** (in accordance with paragraph 17.10).

**Contributions to an employee benefit fund that is an intermediate payment arrangement shall be accounted for in accordance with paragraphs 9.33 to 9.38, and as a result if the employer is a sponsoring entity the assets and liabilities of the intermediary will be accounted for by the sponsoring entity as an extension of its own business. In which case the payment to the employee benefit fund does not extinguish the liability of the employer.*

SHORT-TERM EMPLOYEE BENEFITS

Examples

28.4 Short-term employee benefits include items such as the following, if expected to be settled wholly before 12 months after the end of the annual reporting period in which the employees render the related service:

(a) wages, salaries and social security contributions;
(b) paid annual leave and paid sick leave;
(c) profit-sharing and bonuses; and
(d) non-monetary benefits (such as medical care, housing, cars and free or subsidised goods or services) for current employees.

Measurement of short-term benefits generally

28.5 When an employee has rendered service to an entity during the reporting period, the entity shall measure the amounts recognised in accordance with paragraph 28.3 at the undiscounted amount of short-term employee benefits expected to be paid in exchange for that service.

Recognition and measurement: Short-term compensated absences

28.6 An entity may compensate employees for absence for various reasons including annual leave and sick leave. Some short-term compensated absences accumulate—they can be carried forward and used in future periods if the employee does not use the current period's entitlement in full. Examples include annual leave and sick leave. An entity shall recognise the expected cost of **accumulating compensated absences** when the employees render service that increases their entitlement to future compensated absences. The entity shall measure the expected cost of accumulating compensated absences at the undiscounted additional amount that the entity expects to pay as a result of the unused entitlement that has accumulated at the end of the reporting period. The entity shall present this amount as falling due within one year at the reporting date.

28.7 An entity shall recognise the cost of other (non-accumulating) compensated absences when the absences occur. The entity shall measure the cost of non-accumulating compensated absences at the undiscounted amount of salaries and wages paid or payable for the period of absence.

Recognition: Profit-sharing and bonus plans

28.8 An entity shall recognise the expected cost of profit-sharing and bonus payments only when:

(a) the entity has a present legal or **constructive obligation** to make such payments as a result of past events (this means that the entity has no realistic alternative but to make the payments); and
(b) a reliable estimate of the obligation can be made.

POST-EMPLOYMENT BENEFITS: DISTINCTION BETWEEN DEFINED CONTRIBUTION PLANS AND DEFINED BENEFIT PLANS

Post-employment benefits include, for example: **28.9**

(a) retirement benefits, such as pensions; and
(b) other post-employment benefits, such as post-employment life insurance and post-employment medical care.

Arrangements whereby an entity provides post-employment benefits are **post-employment benefit plans**. An entity shall apply this section to all such arrangements whether or not they involve the establishment of a separate entity to receive contributions and to pay benefits. In some cases, these arrangements are imposed by law rather than by action of the entity. In some cases, these arrangements arise from actions of the entity even in the absence of a formal, documented plan.

Post-employment benefit plans are classified as either **defined contribution plans** or **defined benefit plans**, depending on their principal terms and conditions: **28.10**

(a) Defined contribution plans are post-employment benefit plans under which an entity pays fixed contributions into a separate entity (a fund) and has no legal or constructive obligation to pay further contributions or to make direct benefit payments to employees if the fund does not hold sufficient assets to pay all employee benefits relating to employee service in the current and prior periods. Thus, the amount of the post-employment benefits received by the employee is determined by the amount of contributions paid by an entity (and perhaps also the employee) to a post-employment benefit plan or to an insurer, together with investment returns arising from the contributions.
(b) Defined benefit plans are post-employment benefit plans other than defined contribution plans. Under defined benefit plans, the entity's obligation is to provide the agreed benefits to current and former employees, and actuarial risk (that benefits will cost more or less than expected) and investment risk (that returns on assets set aside to fund the benefits will differ from expectations) are borne, in substance, by the entity. If actuarial or investment experience is worse than expected, the entity's obligation may be increased, and vice versa if actuarial or investment experience is better than expected.

Multi-employer plans and state plans

Multi-employer plans and **state plans** are classified as defined contribution plans or defined benefit plans on the basis of the terms of the plan, including any constructive obligation that goes beyond the formal terms. However, if sufficient information is not available to use defined benefit accounting for a multi-employer plan that is a defined benefit plan, an entity shall account for the plan in accordance with paragraphs 28.13 and 28.13A as if it was a defined contribution plan and make the disclosures required by paragraphs 28.40 and 28.40A. An entity shall account for a state plan in the same way as for a multi-employer plan. **28.11**

Where an entity participates in a defined benefit plan, which is a multi-employer plan that in accordance with paragraph 28.11 is accounted for as if the plan were a defined contribution plan, and the entity has entered into an agreement with the multi-employer plan that determines how the entity will fund a deficit, the entity shall recognise a liability for the contributions payable that arise from the agreement (to the extent that they relate to the deficit) and the resulting expense in **profit or loss** in accordance with paragraphs 28.13 and 28.13A. **28.11A**

Insured benefits

28.12 An entity may pay insurance premiums to fund a post-employment benefit plan. The entity shall treat such a plan as a defined contribution plan unless the entity has a legal or constructive obligation either:

(a) to pay the employee benefits directly when they become due; or
(b) to pay further amounts if the insurer does not pay all future employee benefits relating to employee service in the current and prior periods.

A constructive obligation could arise indirectly through the plan, through the mechanism for setting future premiums, or through a **related party** relationship with the insurer. If the entity retains such a legal or constructive obligation, the entity shall treat the plan as a defined benefit plan.

POST-EMPLOYMENT BENEFITS: DEFINED CONTRIBUTION PLANS

Recognition and measurement

28.13 An entity shall recognise the contribution payable for a period:

(a) As a liability, after deducting any amount already paid. If contribution payments exceed the contribution due for service before the reporting date, an entity shall recognise that excess as an asset to the extent that the prepayment will lead to a reduction in future payments or a cash refund.
(b) As an expense, unless another section of this FRS requires the cost to be recognised as part of the cost of an asset such as inventories or property, plant and equipment.

28.13A When contributions to a defined contribution plan (or a defined benefit plan which, in accordance with paragraph 28.11, is accounted for as a defined contribution plan) are not expected to be settled wholly within 12 months after the end of the reporting period in which the employees render the related service, the liability shall be measured at the **present value** of the contributions payable using the methodology for selecting a discount rate specified in paragraph 28.17. The unwinding of the discount shall be recognised as a finance cost in profit or loss in the period in which it arises.

POST-EMPLOYMENT BENEFITS: DEFINED BENEFIT PLANS

Recognition

28.14 In applying the general **recognition** principle in paragraph 28.3 to defined benefit plans, an entity shall recognise:

(a) a liability for its obligations under defined benefit plans net of **plan assets**—its '**net defined benefit liability**' (see paragraphs 28.15 to 28.22); and
(b) the net change in that liability during the period as the cost of its defined benefit plans during the period (see paragraphs 28.23 to 28.27).

Measurement of the net defined benefit liability

28.15 An entity shall measure the net defined benefit liability for its obligations under defined benefit plans at the net total of the following amounts:

(a) the present value of its obligations under defined benefit plans (its **defined benefit obligation**) at the reporting date (paragraphs 28.16 to 28.21A provide guidance for measuring this obligation); minus
(b) the **fair value** at the reporting date of plan assets (if any) out of which the obligations are to be settled. Paragraphs 11.27 to 11.32 establish requirements for determining the fair values of those plan assets, except that, if the asset is an insurance policy that exactly matches the amount and timing of some or all of the benefits payable under the plan, the fair value of the asset is deemed to be the present value of the related obligation.

Inclusion of both vested and unvested benefits

The present value of an entity's obligations under defined benefit plans at the reporting date shall reflect the estimated amount of benefit that employees have earned in return for their service in the current and prior periods, including benefits that are not yet **vested** (see paragraph 28.26) and including the effects of benefit formulas that give employees greater benefits for later years of service. This requires the entity to determine how much benefit is attributable to the current and prior periods on the basis of the plan's benefit formula and to make estimates (**actuarial assumptions**) about demographic variables (such as employee turnover and mortality) and financial variables (such as future increases in salaries and medical costs) that influence the cost of the benefit. The actuarial assumptions shall be unbiased (neither imprudent nor excessively conservative), mutually compatible, and selected to lead to the best estimate of the future **cash flows** that will arise under the plan. **28.16**

Discounting

An entity shall measure its defined benefit obligation on a discounted present value basis. The entity shall determine the rate used to discount the future payments by reference to market yields at the reporting date on high quality corporate bonds. In countries with no deep market in such bonds, the entity shall use the market yields (at the reporting date) on government bonds. The currency and term of the corporate bonds or government bonds shall be consistent with the currency and estimated period of the future payments. **28.17**

Actuarial valuation method

An entity shall use the **projected unit credit method** to measure its defined benefit obligation and the related expense. If defined benefits are based on future salaries, the projected unit credit method requires an entity to measure its defined benefit obligations on a basis that reflects estimated future salary increases. Additionally, the projected unit credit method requires an entity to make various actuarial assumptions in measuring the defined benefit obligation, including discount rates, employee turnover, mortality, and (for defined benefit medical plans) medical cost trend rates. **28.18**

[Not used] **28.19**

This FRS does not require an entity to engage an independent actuary to perform the comprehensive actuarial valuation needed to calculate its defined benefit obligation. Nor does it require that a comprehensive actuarial valuation must be done annually. In the periods between comprehensive actuarial valuations, if the principal actuarial assumptions have not changed significantly the defined benefit obligation can be measured by adjusting the prior period measurement for changes in employee demographics such as number of employees and salary levels. **28.20**

Plan introductions, changes, curtailments and settlements

28.21 If a defined benefit plan has been introduced or the benefits have changed in the current period, the entity shall increase or decrease its net defined benefit liability to reflect the change, and shall recognise the increase (decrease) as an expense (**income**) in measuring **profit or loss** in the current reporting period.

28.21A If a defined benefit plan has been curtailed (ie benefits or group of covered employees are reduced) or settled (the relevant part of the employer's obligation is completely discharged) in the current period, the defined benefit obligation shall be decreased or eliminated, and the entity shall recognise the resulting **gain** or loss in profit or loss in the current period.

Defined benefit plan asset

28.22 If the present value of the defined benefit obligation at the reporting date is less than the fair value of plan assets at that date, the plan has a surplus. An entity shall recognise a plan surplus as a defined benefit plan asset only to the extent that it is able to recover the surplus either through reduced contributions in the future or through refunds from the plan.

Cost of a defined benefit plan

28.23 An entity shall recognise the cost of a defined benefit plan, except to the extent that another section of this FRS requires part or all of the cost to be recognised as part of the cost of an asset, as follows:

(a) the change in the net defined benefit liability arising from employee service rendered during the reporting period in profit or loss;
(b) net interest on the net defined benefit liability during the reporting period in profit or loss;
(c) the cost of plan introductions, benefit changes, curtailments and settlements in profit or loss (see paragraphs 28.21 and 28.21A); and
(d) remeasurement of the net defined benefit liability in **other comprehensive income**.

Some defined benefit plans require employees or third parties to contribute to the cost of the plan. Contributions by employees reduce the cost of the benefits to the entity.

28.24 The net interest on the net defined benefit liability shall be determined by multiplying the net defined benefit liability by the discount rate in paragraph 28.17, both as determined at the start of the annual reporting period, taking account of any changes in the net defined benefit liability during the period as a result of contribution and benefit payments.

28.24A The net interest on the net defined benefit liability can be viewed as comprising interest cost on the defined benefit obligation and interest income on plan assets excluding the effect of any surplus that is not recoverable in accordance with paragraph 28.22.

28.24B Interest income on plan assets, excluding the effect of any surplus that is not recoverable in accordance with paragraph 28.22, is a component of the return on plan assets, and is determined by multiplying the fair value of the plan assets by the discount rate specified in paragraph 28.17 both as determined at the start of the annual reporting period, taking account of any changes in the plan assets held during the period as a result of contribution and benefit payments. The difference between the interest income on plan assets and the return on plan assets is included in the remeasurement of the net defined benefit liability.

Remeasurement of the net defined benefit liability comprises: **28.25**

(a) **actuarial gains and losses**; and
(b) the return on plan assets, excluding amounts included in net interest on the net defined benefit liability.

Remeasurement of the net defined benefit liability recognised in other comprehensive income shall not be reclassified to profit or loss in a subsequent period. **28.25A**

Employee service gives rise to an obligation under a defined benefit plan even if the benefits are conditional on future employment (in other words, they are not yet vested). Employee service before the vesting date gives rise to a constructive obligation because, at each successive reporting date, the amount of future service that an employee will have to render before becoming entitled to the benefit is reduced. In measuring its defined benefit obligation, an entity considers the probability that some employees may not satisfy vesting requirements. Similarly, although some post-employment benefits (such as post-employment medical benefits) become payable only if a specified event occurs when an employee is no longer employed (such as an illness), an obligation is created when the employee renders service that will provide entitlement to the benefit if the specified event occurs. The probability that the specified event will occur affects the **measurement** of the obligation, but does not determine whether the obligation exists. **28.26**

If defined benefits are reduced for amounts that will be paid to employees under government-sponsored plans, an entity shall measure its defined benefit obligations on a basis that reflects the benefits payable under the government plans, but only if: **28.27**

(a) those plans were enacted before the reporting date; or
(b) past history, or other reliable evidence, indicates that those state benefits will change in some predictable manner, for example, in line with future changes in general price levels or general salary levels.

Reimbursements

If an entity is virtually certain that another party will reimburse some or all of the expenditure required to settle a defined benefit obligation, the entity shall recognise its right to reimbursement as a separate asset. An entity shall treat that asset in the same way as plan assets. **28.28**

OTHER LONG-TERM EMPLOYEE BENEFITS

Other long-term employee benefits include items such as the following, if not expected to be settled wholly before 12 months after the end of the annual reporting period in which the employees render the related service: **28.29**

(a) long-term paid absences such as long-service or sabbatical leave;
(b) other long-service benefits;
(c) long-term disability benefits;
(d) profit-sharing and bonuses; and
(e) deferred remuneration.

28.30 An entity shall recognise a liability for other long-term employee benefits measured at the net total of the following amounts:

(a) the present value of the benefit obligation at the reporting date (calculated using the methodology for selecting a discount rate in paragraph 28.17); minus
(b) the fair value at the reporting date of plan assets (if any) out of which the obligations are to be settled directly.

An entity shall recognise the change in the liability in profit or loss, except to the extent that this FRS requires or permits their inclusion in the cost of an asset.

TERMINATION BENEFITS

28.31 An entity may be committed, by legislation, by contractual or other agreements with employees or their representatives or by a constructive obligation based on business practice, custom or a desire to act equitably, to make payments (or provide other benefits) to employees when it terminates their employment. Such payments are termination benefits.

Recognition

28.32 Because termination benefits do not provide an entity with future economic benefits, an entity shall recognise them as an expense in profit or loss immediately.

28.33 When an entity recognises termination benefits, the entity may also have to account for a curtailment of retirement benefits or other employee benefits.

28.34 An entity shall recognise termination benefits as a liability and an expense only when the entity is demonstrably committed either:

(a) to terminate the employment of an employee or group of employees before the normal retirement date; or
(b) to provide termination benefits as a result of an offer made in order to encourage voluntary redundancy.

28.35 An entity is demonstrably committed to a termination only when the entity has a detailed formal plan for the termination* and is without realistic possibility of withdrawal from the plan.

Measurement

28.36 An entity shall measure termination benefits at the best estimate of the expenditure that would be required to settle the obligation at the reporting date. In the case of an offer made to encourage voluntary redundancy, the measurement of termination benefits shall be based on the number of employees expected to accept the offer.

28.37 When termination benefits are due more than 12 months after the end of the reporting period, they shall be measured at their discounted present value using the methodology for selecting a discount rate specified in paragraph 28.17.

** An example of the features of a detailed formal plan for restructuring, which may include termination benefits, is given in paragraph 21.11C.*

GROUP PLANS

Where an entity participates in a defined benefit plan that shares risks between entities under common control it shall obtain information about the plan as a whole measured in accordance with this FRS on the basis of assumptions that apply to the plan as a whole. If there is a contractual agreement or stated policy for charging the net defined benefit cost of a defined benefit plan as a whole measured in accordance with this FRS to individual group entities, the entity shall, in its **individual financial statements**, recognise the net defined benefit cost of a defined benefit plan so charged. If there is no such agreement or policy, the net defined benefit cost of a defined benefit plan shall be recognised in the individual financial statements of the group entity which is legally responsible for the plan. The other group entities shall, in their individual financial statements, recognise a cost equal to their contribution payable for the period. **28.38**

DISCLOSURES

Disclosures about short-term employee benefits

This section does not require specific disclosures about short-term employee benefits. **28.39**

Disclosures about defined contribution plans

An entity shall disclose the amount recognised in profit or loss as an expense for defined contribution plans. **28.40**

If an entity treats a defined benefit multi-employer plan as a defined contribution plan because sufficient information is not available to use defined benefit accounting (see paragraph 28.11) it shall: **28.40A**

(a) disclose the fact that it is a defined benefit plan and the reason why it is being accounted for as a defined contribution plan, along with any available information about the plan's surplus or deficit and the implications, if any, for the entity;
(b) include a description of the extent to which the entity can be liable to the plan for other entities' obligations under the terms and conditions of the multi-employer plan; and
(c) disclose how any liability recognised in accordance with paragraph 28.11A has been determined.

Disclosures about defined benefit plans

An entity shall disclose the following information about defined benefit plans (except for any defined multi-employer benefit plans that are accounted for as a defined contribution plan in accordance with paragraphs 28.11 and 28.11A, for which the disclosures in paragraphs 28.40 and 28.40A apply instead). If an entity has more than one defined benefit plan, these disclosures may be made in aggregate, separately for each plan, or in such groupings as are considered to be the most useful: **28.41**

(a) A general description of the type of plan, including **funding** policy.
(b) [Not used]
(c) [Not used]
(d) The date of the most recent comprehensive actuarial valuation and, if it was not as of the reporting date, a description of the adjustments that were made to measure the defined benefit obligation at the reporting date.

(e) A reconciliation of opening and closing balances for each of the following:

 (i) the defined benefit obligation;
 (ii) the fair value of plan assets; and
 (iii) any reimbursement right recognised as an asset.

(f) Each of the reconciliations in paragraph 28.41(e) shall show each of the following, if applicable:

 (i) the change in the defined benefit liability arising from employee service rendered during the reporting period in profit or loss;
 (ii) interest income or expense;
 (iii) remeasurement of the defined benefit liability, showing separately actuarial gains and losses and the return on plan assets less amounts included in (ii) above; and
 (iv) plan introductions, changes, curtailments and settlements.

(g) The total cost relating to defined benefit plans for the period, disclosing separately the amounts:

 (i) recognised in profit or loss as an expense; and
 (ii) included in the cost of an asset.

(h) For each major class of plan assets, which shall include, but is not limited to, equity instruments, debt instruments, property, and all other assets, the percentage or amount that each major class constitutes of the fair value of the total plan assets at the reporting date.

(i) The amounts included in the fair value of plan assets for:

 (i) each class of the entity's own **financial instruments**; and
 (ii) any property occupied by, or other assets used by, the entity.

(j) The return on plan assets.

(k) The principal actuarial assumptions used, including, when applicable:

 (i) the discount rates;
 (ii) [not used]
 (iii) the expected rates of salary increases;
 (iv) medical cost trend rates; and
 (v) any other **material** actuarial assumptions used.

The reconciliations in (e) and (f) above need not be presented for prior periods.

28.41A If an entity participates in a defined benefit plan that shares risks between entities under common control (see paragraph 28.38) it shall disclose the following information:

(a) The contractual agreement or stated policy for charging the cost of a defined benefit plan or the fact that there is no policy.

(b) The policy for determining the contribution to be paid by the entity.

(c) If the entity accounts for an allocation of the net defined benefit cost, all the information required in paragraph 28.41.

(d) If the entity accounts for the contributions payable for the period, the information about the plan as a whole required by paragraph 28.41(a), (d), (h) and (i).

This information can be disclosed by cross-reference to disclosures in another group entity's **financial statements** if:

(i) that group entity's financial statements separately identify and disclose the information required about the plan; and

(ii) that group entity's financial statements are available to users of the financial statements on the same terms as the financial statements of the entity and at the same time as, or earlier than, the financial statements of the entity.

Disclosures about other long-term benefits

For each category of other long-term benefits that an entity provides to its employees, the entity shall disclose the nature of the benefit, the amount of its obligation and the extent of funding at the reporting date. **28.42**

Disclosures about termination benefits

For each category of termination benefits that an entity provides to its employees, the entity shall disclose the nature of the benefit, its **accounting policy**, and the amount of its obligation and the extent of funding at the reporting date. **28.43**

When there is uncertainty about the number of employees who will accept an offer of termination benefits, a **contingent liability** exists. Section 21 *Provisions and Contingencies* requires an entity to disclose information about its contingent liabilities unless the possibility of an outflow in settlement is remote. **28.44**

Section 29
Income Tax

SCOPE OF THIS SECTION

29.1 For the purpose of this FRS, **income tax** includes all domestic and foreign taxes that are based on **taxable profit**. Income tax also includes taxes, such as withholding taxes, that are payable by a **subsidiary, associate** or **joint venture** on distributions to the reporting entity.

29.2 This section covers accounting for income tax. It requires an entity to recognise the current and future tax consequences of transactions and other events that have been recognised in the **financial statements**. These recognised tax amounts comprise **current tax** and **deferred tax**. Current tax is tax payable (refundable) in respect of the taxable profit (tax loss) for the current period or past **reporting periods**. Deferred tax represents the future tax consequences of transactions and events recognised in the financial statements of the current and previous periods. This section also requires that deferred tax is recognised in respect of **assets** (other than **goodwill**) and **liabilities** recognised as a result of a **business combination**.

29.2A This section also covers accounting for value added tax (VAT) and other similar sales taxes, which are not income taxes.

RECOGNITION AND MEASUREMENT OF CURRENT TAX

29.3 An entity shall recognise a current tax liability for tax payable on taxable profit for the current and past periods. If the amount of tax paid for the current and past periods exceeds the amount of tax payable for those periods, the entity shall recognise the excess as a current tax asset.

29.4 An entity shall recognise a current tax asset for the benefit of a tax loss that can be carried back to recover tax paid in a previous period.

29.5 An entity shall measure a current tax liability (asset) at the amounts of tax it expects to pay (recover) using the tax rates and laws that have been enacted or **substantively enacted** by the **reporting date**.

RECOGNITION OF DEFERRED TAX

Timing differences

29.6 Deferred tax shall be recognised in respect of all **timing differences** at the reporting date, except as otherwise required by paragraphs 29.7 to 29.9 and 29.11 below. Timing differences are differences between taxable profits and **total comprehensive income** as stated in the financial statements that arise from the inclusion of **income** and **expenses** in tax assessments in periods different from those in which they are recognised in financial statements.

29.7 Unrelieved tax losses and other **deferred tax assets** shall be recognised only to the extent that it is **probable** that they will be recovered against the reversal of **deferred tax liabilities** or other future taxable profits (the very existence of unrelieved tax losses is strong evidence that there may not be other future taxable profits against which the losses will be relieved).

Deferred tax shall be recognised when the tax allowances for the cost of a **fixed asset** are received before or after the **depreciation** of the fixed asset is recognised in **profit or loss**. If and when all conditions for retaining the tax allowances have been met, the deferred tax shall be reversed. **29.8**

Deferred tax shall be recognised when income or expenses from a subsidiary, associate, branch, or interest in joint venture have been recognised in the financial statements, and will be assessed to or allowed for tax in a future period, except where: **29.9**

(a) the reporting entity is able to control the reversal of the timing difference; and
(b) it is probable that the timing difference will not reverse in the foreseeable future.

Such timing differences may arise, for example, where there are undistributed profits in a subsidiary, associate, branch or interest in a joint venture.

Permanent differences

Permanent differences arise because certain types of **income** and expenses are non-taxable or disallowable, or because certain tax charges or allowances are greater or smaller than the corresponding income or expense in the financial statements. Deferred tax shall not be recognised on permanent differences except for circumstances set out in paragraph 29.11. **29.10**

Business combinations

When the amount that can be deducted for tax for an asset (other than goodwill) that is recognised in a business combination is less (more) than the value at which it is recognised, a deferred tax liability (asset) shall be recognised for the additional tax that will be paid (avoided) in respect of that difference. Similarly, a deferred tax asset (liability) shall be recognised for the additional tax that will be avoided (paid) because of a difference between the value at which a liability is recognised and the amount that will be assessed for tax. The amount attributed to goodwill shall be adjusted by the amount of deferred tax recognised. **29.11**

MEASUREMENT OF DEFERRED TAX

An entity shall measure a deferred tax liability (asset) using the tax rates and laws that have been enacted or substantively enacted by the reporting date that are expected to apply to the reversal of the timing difference except for the cases dealt with in paragraphs 29.15 and 29.16 below. **29.12**

When different tax rates apply to different levels of taxable profit, an entity shall measure deferred tax expense (income) and related deferred tax liabilities (assets) using the average enacted or substantively enacted rates that it expects to be applicable to the taxable profit (tax loss) of the periods in which it expects the deferred tax asset to be realised or the deferred tax liability to be settled. **29.13**

In some jurisdictions, income taxes are payable at a higher or lower rate if part or all of the profit or retained earnings is paid out as a dividend to shareholders of the entity. In other jurisdictions, income taxes may be refundable or payable if part or all of the profit or retained earnings is paid out as a dividend to shareholders of the entity. In both of those circumstances, an entity shall measure current and deferred taxes at the tax rate applicable to undistributed profits until the entity recognises a **29.14** liability to pay a dividend. When the entity recognises a liability to pay a dividend, it shall recognise the resulting current or deferred tax liability (asset), and the related **tax expense** (income).

29.15 Deferred tax relating to a non-depreciable asset that is measured using the revaluation model in Section 17 *Property, Plant and Equipment* shall be measured using the tax rates and allowances that apply to the sale of the asset.

29.16 Deferred tax relating to **investment property** that is measured at **fair value** in accordance with Section 16 *Investment Property* shall be measured using the tax rates and allowances that apply to sale of the asset, except for investment property that has a limited **useful life** and is held within a business model whose objective is to consume substantially all of the economic benefits embodied in the property over time.

MEASUREMENT OF BOTH CURRENT AND DEFERRED TAX

29.17 An entity shall not discount current or deferred tax assets and liabilities.

WITHHOLDING TAX ON DIVIDENDS

29.18 When an entity pays dividends to its shareholders, it may be required to pay a portion of the dividends to taxation authorities on behalf of shareholders. Outgoing dividends and similar amounts payable shall be recognised at an amount that includes any withholding tax but excludes other taxes, such as attributable tax credits.

29.19 Incoming dividends and similar income receivable shall be recognised at an amount that includes any withholding tax but excludes other taxes, such as attributable tax credits. Any withholding tax suffered shall be shown as part of the tax charge.

VALUE ADDED TAX ('VAT') AND OTHER SIMILAR SALES TAXES

29.20 **Turnover** shown in profit or loss shall exclude VAT and other similar sales taxes on taxable outputs and VAT imputed under the flat rate VAT scheme. Expenses shall exclude recoverable VAT and other similar recoverable sales taxes. Irrecoverable VAT allocable to fixed assets and to other items disclosed separately in the financial statements shall be included in their cost where practicable and **material**.

PRESENTATION

Allocation in comprehensive income and equity

29.21 An entity shall present changes in a current tax liability (asset) and changes in a deferred tax liability (asset) as tax expense (income) with the exception of those changes arising on the initial **recognition** of a business combination which shall be dealt with in accordance with paragraph 29.11.

29.22 An entity shall present tax expense (income) in the same component of **total comprehensive income** (ie continuing or **discontinued operations**, and profit or loss or **other comprehensive income**) or **equity** as the transaction or other event that resulted in the tax expense (income).

Presentation in the statement of financial position

An entity shall present deferred tax liabilities within provisions for liabilities and deferred tax assets within debtors. **29.23**

Offsetting

An entity shall offset current tax assets and current tax liabilities, if and only if, it has a legally enforceable right to set off the amounts and it intends either to settle on a net basis or to realise the asset and settle the liability simultaneously. **29.24**

An entity shall offset deferred tax assets and deferred tax liabilities if, and only if: **29.24A**

(a) the entity has a legally enforceable right to set off current tax assets against current tax liabilities; and
(b) the deferred tax assets and deferred tax liabilities relate to income taxes levied by the same taxation authority on either the same taxable entity or different taxable entities which intend either to settle current tax liabilities and assets on a net basis, or to realise the assets and settle the liabilities simultaneously, in each future period in which significant amounts of deferred tax liabilities or assets are expected to be settled or recovered.

DISCLOSURES

An entity shall disclose information that enables users of its financial statements to evaluate the nature and financial effect of the current and deferred tax consequences of recognised transactions and other events. **29.25**

An entity shall disclose separately the major components of tax expense (income). Such components of tax expense (income) may include: **29.26**

(a) current tax expense (income);
(b) any adjustments recognised in the period for current tax of prior periods;
(c) the amount of deferred tax expense (income) relating to the origination and reversal of timing differences;
(d) the amount of deferred tax expense (income) relating to changes in tax rates or the imposition of new taxes;
(e) adjustments to deferred tax expense (income) arising from a change in the tax status of the entity or its shareholders; and
(f) the amount of tax expense (income) relating to changes in **accounting policies** and **material errors** (see Section 10 *Accounting Policies, Estimates and Errors*).

An entity shall disclose the following separately: **29.27**

(a) the aggregate current and deferred tax relating to items that are recognised as items of other comprehensive income or equity;
(b) a reconciliation between:

    (i) the tax expense (income) included in profit or loss; and
    (ii) the profit or loss on ordinary activities before tax multiplied by the applicable tax rate;

(c) the amount of the net reversal of deferred tax assets and deferred tax liabilities expected to occur during the year beginning after the **reporting period** together with a brief explanation for the expected reversal;
(d) an explanation of changes in the applicable tax rate(s) compared with the previous reporting period;

(e) the amount of deferred tax liabilities and deferred tax assets at the end of the reporting period for each type of timing difference and the amount of unused tax losses and tax credits;

(f) the expiry date, if any, of timing differences, unused tax losses and unused tax credits; and

(g) in the circumstances described in paragraph 29.14, an explanation of the nature of the potential income tax consequences that would result from the payment of dividends to its shareholders.

Section 30
Foreign Currency Translation

SCOPE OF THIS SECTION

An entity can conduct foreign activities in two ways. It may have transactions in foreign currencies or it may have **foreign operations**. In addition, an entity may present its **financial statements** in a foreign currency. This section prescribes how to include foreign currency transactions and foreign operations in the financial statements of an entity and how to translate financial statements into a **presentation currency**. Hedge accounting of foreign currency items is dealt with in Section 12 *Other Financial Instruments Issues*. **30.1**

FUNCTIONAL CURRENCY

Each entity shall identify its **functional currency**. An entity's functional currency is the currency of the primary economic environment in which the entity operates. **30.2**

The primary economic environment in which an entity operates is normally the one in which it primarily generates and expends **cash**. Therefore, the following are the most important factors an entity considers in determining its functional currency: **30.3**

(a) the currency:
   (i) that mainly influences sales prices for goods and services (this will often be the currency in which sales prices for its goods and services are denominated and settled); and
   (ii) of the country whose competitive forces and regulations mainly determine the sales prices of its goods and services; and

(b) the currency that mainly influences labour, material and other costs of providing goods or services (this will often be the currency in which such costs are denominated and settled).

The following factors may also provide evidence of an entity's functional currency: **30.4**

(a) the currency in which funds from **financing activities** (issuing debt and equity instruments) are generated; and
(b) the currency in which receipts from **operating activities** are usually retained.

The following additional factors are considered in determining the functional currency of a foreign operation, and whether its functional currency is the same as that of the reporting entity (the reporting entity, in this context, being the entity that has the foreign operation as its **subsidiary**, branch, **associate** or **joint venture**): **30.5**

(a) Whether the activities of the foreign operation are carried out as an extension of the reporting entity, rather than being carried out with a significant degree of autonomy. An example of the former is when the foreign operation only sells goods imported from the reporting entity and remits the proceeds to it. An example of the latter is when the operation accumulates cash and other **monetary items**, incurs **expenses**, generates **income** and arranges borrowings, all *substantially in its* local currency.
(b) Whether transactions with the reporting entity are a high or a low proportion of the foreign operation's activities.
(c) Whether **cash flows** from the activities of the foreign operation directly affect the cash flows of the reporting entity and are readily available for remittance to it.

(d) Whether cash flows from the activities of the foreign operation are sufficient to service existing and normally expected debt obligations without funds being made available by the reporting entity.

REPORTING FOREIGN CURRENCY TRANSACTIONS IN THE FUNCTIONAL CURRENCY

Initial recognition

30.6 A foreign currency transaction is a transaction that is denominated or requires settlement in a foreign currency, including transactions arising when an entity:

(a) buys or sells goods or services whose price is denominated in a foreign currency;
(b) borrows or lends funds when the amounts payable or receivable are denominated in a foreign currency; or
(c) otherwise acquires or disposes of **assets**, or incurs or settles **liabilities**, denominated in a foreign currency.

30.7 An entity shall record a foreign currency transaction, on initial **recognition** in the functional currency, by applying to the foreign currency amount the spot exchange rate between the functional currency and the foreign currency at the date of the transaction.

30.8 The date of a transaction is the date on which the transaction first qualifies for recognition in accordance with this FRS. For practical reasons, a rate that approximates the actual rate at the date of the transaction is often used, for example, an average rate for a week or a month might be used for all transactions in each foreign currency occurring during that period. However, if exchange rates fluctuate significantly, the use of the average rate for a period is inappropriate.

Reporting at the end of the subsequent reporting periods

30.9 At the end of each **reporting period**, an entity shall:

(a) translate foreign currency monetary items using the **closing rate**;
(b) translate non-monetary items that are measured in terms of historical cost in a foreign currency using the exchange rate at the date of the transaction; and
(c) translate non-monetary items that are measured at **fair value** in a foreign currency using the exchange rates at the date when the fair value was determined.

30.10 An entity shall recognise, in **profit or loss** in the period in which they arise, exchange differences arising on the settlement of monetary items or on translating monetary items at rates different from those at which they were translated on initial recognition during the period or in previous periods, except as described in paragraph 30.13.

30.11 When another section of this FRS requires a **gain** or loss on a non-monetary item to be recognised in **other comprehensive income**, an entity shall recognise any exchange component of that gain or loss in other comprehensive income. Conversely, when a gain or loss on a non-monetary item is recognised in profit or loss, an entity shall recognise any exchange component of that gain or loss in profit or loss.

NET INVESTMENT IN A FOREIGN OPERATION

An entity may have a monetary item that is receivable from or payable to a foreign operation. An item for which settlement is neither planned nor likely to occur in the foreseeable future is, in substance, a part of the entity's net investment in that foreign operation, and is accounted for in accordance with paragraph 30.13. Such monetary items may include long-term receivables or loans. They do not include trade receivables or trade payables. **30.12**

Exchange differences arising on a monetary item that forms part of a reporting entity's **net investment in a foreign operation** shall be recognised in profit or loss in the **separate financial statements** of the reporting entity or the **individual financial statements** of the foreign operation, as appropriate. In the financial statements that include the foreign operation and the reporting entity (eg **consolidated financial statements** when the foreign operation is a subsidiary), such exchange differences shall be recognised in other comprehensive income and accumulated in **equity**. They shall not be recognised in profit or loss on disposal of the net investment. **30.13**

CHANGE IN FUNCTIONAL CURRENCY

When there is a change in an entity's functional currency, the entity shall apply the translation procedures applicable to the new functional currency prospectively from the date of the change. **30.14**

As noted in paragraphs 30.2 to 30.5, the functional currency of an entity reflects the underlying transactions, events and conditions that are relevant to the entity. Accordingly, once the functional currency is determined, it can be changed only if there is a change to those underlying transactions, events and conditions. For example, a change in the currency that mainly influences the sales prices of goods and services may lead to a change in an entity's functional currency. **30.15**

The effect of a change in functional currency is accounted for prospectively. In other words, an entity translates all items into the new functional currency using the exchange rate at the date of the change. The resulting translated amounts for non-monetary items are treated as their historical cost. **30.16**

USE OF A PRESENTATION CURRENCY OTHER THAN THE FUNCTIONAL CURRENCY

Translation to the presentation currency

An entity may present its financial statements in any currency (or currencies). If the presentation currency differs from the entity's functional currency, the entity shall translate its items of income and expense and **financial position** into the presentation currency. For example, when a **group** contains individual entities with different functional currencies, the items of income and expense and financial position of each entity are expressed in a common currency so that consolidated financial statements may be presented. **30.17**

An entity whose functional currency is not the currency of a hyperinflationary economy shall translate its results and financial position into a different presentation currency using the following procedures: **30.18**

(a) assets and liabilities for each **statement of financial position** presented (ie including comparatives) shall be translated at the closing rate at the date of that statement of financial position;

(b) income and expenses for each **statement of comprehensive income** (ie including comparatives) shall be translated at exchange rates at the dates of the transactions; and
(c) all resulting exchange differences shall be recognised in other comprehensive income.

30.19 For practical reasons, an entity may use a rate that approximates the exchange rates at the dates of the transactions, for example an average rate for the period to translate income and expense items. However, if exchange rates fluctuate significantly, the use of the average rate for a period is inappropriate.

30.20 The exchange differences referred to in paragraph 30.18(c) result from:

(a) translating income and expenses at the exchange rates at the dates of the transactions and assets and liabilities at the closing rate; and
(b) translating the opening net assets at a closing rate that differs from the previous closing rate.

When the exchange differences relate to a foreign operation that is consolidated but not wholly-owned, accumulated exchange differences arising from translation and attributable to the **non-controlling interest** are allocated to, and recognised as part of, non-controlling interest in the consolidated statement of financial position.

30.21 An entity whose functional currency is the currency of a hyperinflationary economy shall adjust its results and financial position using the procedures specified in Section 31 *Hyperinflation* before applying the requirements of this section.

Translation of a foreign operation into the investor's presentation currency

30.22 In incorporating the assets, liabilities, income and expenses of a foreign operation with those of the reporting entity, the entity shall follow normal consolidation procedures, such as the elimination of intragroup balances and intragroup transactions of a subsidiary (see Section 9 *Consolidated and Separate Financial Statements*) and the translation procedures set out in paragraphs 30.17 to 30.21. An intragroup monetary asset (or liability), whether short-term or long-term, cannot be eliminated against the corresponding intragroup liability (or asset) without showing the results of currency fluctuations in the consolidated financial statements. This is because the monetary item represents a commitment to convert one currency into another and exposes the reporting entity to a gain or loss through currency fluctuations. Accordingly, in the consolidated financial statements, a reporting entity continues to recognise such an exchange difference in profit or loss or, if it arises from the circumstances described in paragraph 30.13, the entity shall recognise it in other comprehensive income.

30.23 Any **goodwill** arising on the acquisition of a foreign operation and any fair value adjustments to the **carrying amounts** of assets and liabilities arising on the acquisition of that foreign operation shall be treated as assets and liabilities of the foreign operation. Thus, they shall be expressed in the functional currency of the foreign operation and shall be translated at the closing rate in accordance with paragraph 30.18.

DISCLOSURES

30.24 In paragraphs 30.26 and 30.27, references to functional currency apply, in the case of a group, to the functional currency of the **parent**.

An entity shall disclose the following: **30.25**

(a) the amount of exchange differences recognised in profit or loss during the period, except for those arising on **financial instruments** measured at fair value through profit or loss in accordance with Sections 11 *Basic Financial Instruments* and Section 12.

(b) the amount of exchange differences arising during the period and classified in equity at the end of the period.

An entity shall disclose the currency in which the financial statements are presented. When the presentation currency is different from the functional currency, an entity shall state that fact and shall disclose the functional currency and the reason for using a different presentation currency. **30.26**

When there is a change in the functional currency of either the reporting entity or a significant foreign operation, the entity shall disclose that fact and the reason for the change in functional currency. **30.27**

Section 31
Hyperinflation

SCOPE OF THIS SECTION

31.1 This section applies to an entity whose **functional currency** is the currency of a hyperinflationary economy. It requires such an entity to prepare **financial statements** that have been adjusted for the effects of hyperinflation.

HYPERINFLATIONARY ECONOMY

31.2 This section does not establish an absolute rate at which an economy is deemed hyperinflationary. An entity shall make that judgement by considering all available information including, but not limited to, the following possible indicators of hyperinflation:

(a) The general population prefers to keep its wealth in non-monetary assets or in a relatively stable foreign currency. Amounts of local currency held are immediately invested to maintain purchasing power.
(b) The general population regards monetary amounts not in terms of the local currency but in terms of a relatively stable foreign currency. Prices may be quoted in that currency.
(c) Sales and purchases on credit take place at prices that compensate for the expected loss of purchasing power during the credit period, even if the period is short.
(d) Interest rates, wages and prices are linked to a price index.
(e) The cumulative inflation rate over three years is approaching, or exceeds, 100 per cent.

MEASURING UNIT IN THE FINANCIAL STATEMENTS

31.3 All amounts in the financial statements of an entity whose functional currency is the currency of a hyperinflationary economy shall be stated in terms of the measuring unit current at the end of the **reporting period**. The comparative information for the previous period required by paragraph 3.14, and any information presented in respect of earlier periods, shall also be stated in terms of the measuring unit current at the **reporting date**.

31.4 The restatement of financial statements in accordance with this section requires the use of a general price index that reflects changes in general purchasing power. In most economies there is a recognised general price index, normally produced by the government, that entities will follow.

PROCEDURES FOR RESTATING HISTORICAL COST FINANCIAL STATEMENTS

Statement of financial position

31.5 **Statement of financial position** amounts not expressed in terms of the measuring unit current at the end of the reporting period are restated by applying a general price index.

31.6 **Monetary items** are not restated because they are expressed in terms of the measuring unit current at the end of the reporting period. Monetary items are money held and items to be received or paid in money.

Assets and **liabilities** linked by agreement to changes in prices, such as index-linked bonds and loans, are adjusted in accordance with the agreement and presented at this adjusted amount in the restated statement of financial position. **31.7**

All other assets and liabilities are non-monetary: **31.8**

(a) Some non-monetary items are carried at amounts current at the end of the reporting period, such as net realisable value and **fair value**, so they are not restated. All other non-monetary assets and liabilities are restated.

(b) Most non-monetary items are carried at cost or cost less **depreciation**; hence they are expressed at amounts current at their date of acquisition. The restated cost, or cost less depreciation, of each item is determined by applying to its historical cost and accumulated depreciation the change in a general price index from the date of acquisition to the end of the reporting period.

(c) The restated amount of a non-monetary item is reduced, in accordance with Section 27 *Impairment of Assets*, when it exceeds its **recoverable amount**.

At the beginning of the first period of application of this section, the components of **equity**, except retained earnings, are restated by applying a general price index from the dates the components were contributed or otherwise arose. Restated retained earnings are derived from all the other amounts in the restated statement of financial position. **31.9**

At the end of the first period and in subsequent periods, all components of owners' equity are restated by applying a general price index from the beginning of the period or the date of contribution, if later. The changes for the period in owners' equity are disclosed in accordance with Section 6 *Statement of Changes in Equity and Statement of Income and Retained Earnings*. **31.10**

Statement of comprehensive income and income statement

All items in the **statement of comprehensive income** (and in the **income statement**, if presented) shall be expressed in terms of the measuring unit current at the end of the reporting period. Therefore, all amounts need to be restated by applying the change in the general price index from the dates when the items of **income** and **expenses** were initially recognised in the financial statements. If general inflation is approximately even throughout the period, and the items of income and expense arose approximately evenly throughout the period, an average rate of inflation may be appropriate. **31.11**

Statement of cash flows

An entity shall express all items in the **statement of cash flows** in terms of the measuring unit current at the end of the reporting period. **31.12**

Gain or loss on net monetary position

In a period of inflation, an entity holding an excess of monetary assets over monetary liabilities loses purchasing power, and an entity with an excess of monetary liabilities over monetary assets gains purchasing power, to the extent the assets and liabilities are not linked to a price level. An entity shall include in **profit or loss** the **gain** or loss on the net monetary position. An entity shall offset the adjustment to those assets and liabilities linked by agreement to changes in prices made in accordance with paragraph 31.7 against the gain or loss on net monetary position. **31.13**

Economies ceasing to be hyperinflationary

31.14 When an economy ceases to be hyperinflationary and an entity discontinues the preparation and presentation of financial statements prepared in accordance with this section, it shall treat the amounts expressed in the **presentation currency** at the end of the previous reporting period as the basis for the **carrying amounts** in its subsequent financial statements.

DISCLOSURES

31.15 An entity to which this section applies shall disclose the following:

(a) the fact that financial statements and other prior period data have been restated for changes in the general purchasing power of the functional currency;

(b) the identity and level of the price index at the reporting date and changes during the current reporting period and the previous reporting period; and

(c) amount of gain or loss on monetary items.

Section 32
Events after the End of the Reporting Period

SCOPE OF THIS SECTION

This section defines events after the end of the **reporting period** and sets out principles for recognising, measuring and disclosing those events. **32.1**

EVENTS AFTER THE END OF THE REPORTING PERIOD DEFINED

Events after the end of the reporting period are those events, favourable and unfavourable, that occur between the end of the reporting period and the date when the **financial statements** are authorised for issue. There are two types of events: **32.2**

(a) those that provide evidence of conditions that existed at the end of the reporting period (adjusting events after the end of the reporting period); and
(b) those that are indicative of conditions that arose after the end of the reporting period (non-adjusting events after the end of the reporting period).

Events after the end of the reporting period include all events up to the date when the financial statements are authorised for issue, even if those events occur after the public announcement of **profit or loss** or other selected financial information. **32.3**

RECOGNITION AND MEASUREMENT

Adjusting events after the end of the reporting period

An entity shall adjust the amounts recognised in its financial statements, including related disclosures, to reflect adjusting events after the end of the reporting period. **32.4**

The following are examples of adjusting events after the end of the reporting period that require an entity to adjust the amounts recognised in its financial statements, or to recognise items that were not previously recognised: **32.5**

(a) The settlement after the end of the reporting period of a court case that confirms that the entity had a present obligation at the end of the reporting period. The entity adjusts any previously recognised **provision** related to this court case in accordance with Section 21 *Provisions and Contingencies* or recognises a new provision. The entity does not merely disclose a **contingent liability**. Rather, the settlement provides additional evidence to be considered in determining the provision that should be recognised at the end of the reporting period in accordance with Section 21.
(b) The receipt of information after the end of the reporting period indicating that an **asset** was impaired at the end of the reporting period, or that the amount of a previously recognised **impairment loss** for that asset needs to be adjusted. For example:
    (i) the bankruptcy of a customer that occurs after the end of the reporting period usually confirms that a loss existed at the end of the reporting period on a trade receivable and that the entity needs to adjust the **carrying amount** of the trade receivable; and
    (ii) the sale of **inventories** after the end of the reporting period may give evidence about their selling price at the end of the reporting period for the purpose of assessing impairment at that date.

(c) The determination after the end of the reporting period of the cost of assets purchased, or the proceeds from assets sold, before the end of the reporting period.
(d) The determination after the end of the reporting period of the amount of profit-sharing or bonus payments, if the entity had a legal or **constructive obligation** at the end of the reporting period to make such payments as a result of events before that date (see Section 28 *Employee Benefits*).
(e) The discovery of fraud or **errors** that show that the financial statements are incorrect.

Non-adjusting events after the end of the reporting period

32.6 An entity shall not adjust the amounts recognised in its financial statements to reflect non-adjusting events after the end of the reporting period.

32.7 Examples of non-adjusting events after the end of the reporting period include:

(a) A decline in market value of investments between the end of the reporting period and the date when the financial statements are authorised for issue. The decline in market value does not normally relate to the condition of the investments at the end of the reporting period, but reflects circumstances that have arisen subsequently. Therefore, an entity does not adjust the amounts recognised in its financial statements for the investments. Similarly, the entity does not update the amounts disclosed for the investments as at the end of the reporting period, although it may need to give additional disclosure in accordance with paragraph 32.10.
(b) An amount that becomes receivable as a result of a favourable judgement or settlement of a court case after the **reporting date** but before the financial statements are authorised for issued. This would be a **contingent asset** at the reporting date (see paragraph 21.13), and disclosure may be required by paragraph 21.16. However, agreement on the amount of damages for a judgement that was reached before the reporting date, but was not previously recognised because the amount could not be measured reliably, may constitute an adjusting event.

Further examples of non-adjusting events are set out in paragraph 32.11.

Going concern

32.7A An entity shall not prepare its financial statements on a **going concern** basis if management determines after the reporting period either that it intends to liquidate the entity or to cease trading, or that it has no realistic alternative but to do so.

32.7B Deterioration in operating results and **financial position** after the reporting period may indicate a need to consider whether the going concern assumption is still appropriate. If the going concern assumption is no longer appropriate, the effect is so pervasive that this section requires a fundamental change in the basis of accounting, rather than an adjustment to the amounts recognised within the original basis of accounting and therefore the disclosure requirements of paragraph 3.9 apply.

Dividends

32.8 If an entity declares dividends to holders of its equity instruments after the end of the reporting period, the entity shall not recognise those dividends as a **liability** at the end of the reporting period because no obligation exists at that time. The amount of the dividend may be presented as a segregated component of retained earnings at the end of the reporting period.

DISCLOSURE

Date of authorisation for issue

An entity shall disclose the date when the financial statements were authorised for issue and who gave that authorisation. If the entity's **owners** or others have the power to amend the financial statements after issue, the entity shall disclose that fact. **32.9**

Non-adjusting events after the end of the reporting period

An entity shall disclose the following for each category of non-adjusting event after the end of the reporting period: **32.10**

(a) the nature of the event; and
(b) an estimate of its financial effect or a statement that such an estimate cannot be made.

The following are examples of non-adjusting events after the end of the reporting period that would generally result in disclosure. The disclosures will reflect information that becomes known after the end of the reporting period but before the financial statements are authorised for issue: **32.11**

(a) a major **business combination** or disposal of a major **subsidiary**;
(b) announcement of a plan to discontinue an operation;
(c) major purchases of assets, disposals or plans to dispose of assets, or expropriation of major assets by government;
(d) the destruction of a major production plant by a fire;
(e) announcement, or commencement of the implementation, of a major restructuring;
(f) issues or repurchases of an entity's debt or equity instruments;
(g) abnormally large changes in asset prices or foreign exchange rates;
(h) changes in tax rates or tax laws enacted or announced that have a significant effect on current and **deferred tax assets and liabilities**;
(i) entering into significant commitments or contingent liabilities, for example, by issuing significant guarantees; and
(j) commencement of major litigation arising solely out of events that occurred after the end of the reporting period.

Section 33
Related Party Disclosures

SCOPE OF THIS SECTION

33.1 This section requires an entity to include in its **financial statements** the disclosures necessary to draw attention to the possibility that its **financial position** and **profit or loss** have been affected by the existence of **related parties** and by transactions and outstanding balances with such parties.

33.1A Disclosures need not be given of transactions entered into between two or more members of a **group**, provided that any **subsidiary** which is a party to the transaction is wholly owned by such a member.

RELATED PARTY DEFINED

33.2 A related party is a person or entity that is related to the entity that is preparing its financial statements (the reporting entity).

(a) A person or a **close member of that person's family** is related to a reporting entity if that person:

(i) has **control** or **joint control** over the reporting entity;
(ii) has **significant influence** over the reporting entity; or
(iii) is a member of the **key management personnel** of the reporting entity or of a **parent** of the reporting entity.

(b) An entity is related to a reporting entity if any of the following conditions apply:

(i) the entity and the reporting entity are members of the same group (which means that each parent, subsidiary and fellow subsidiary is related to the others).
(ii) one entity is an **associate** or **joint venture** of the other entity (or an associate or joint venture of a member of a group of which the other entity is a member).
(iii) both entities are joint ventures of the same third party.
(iv) one entity is a joint venture of a third entity and the other entity is an associate of the third entity.
(v) the entity is a **post-employment benefit plan** for the benefit of employees of either the reporting entity or an entity related to the reporting entity. If the reporting entity is itself such a plan, the sponsoring employers are also related to the reporting entity.
(vi) the entity is controlled or jointly controlled by a person identified in (a).
(vii) a person identified in (a)(i) has significant influence over the entity or is a member of the key management personnel of the entity (or of a parent of the entity).

33.3 In considering each possible related party relationship, an entity shall assess the substance of the relationship and not merely the legal form.

33.4 In the context of this FRS, the following are not related parties:

(a) Two entities simply because they have a director or other member of key management personnel in common or because a member of key management personnel of one entity has significant influence over the other entity.
(b) Two **venturers** simply because they share joint control over a joint venture.

(c) Any of the following simply by virtue of their normal dealings with an entity (even though they may affect the freedom of action of an entity or participate in its decision-making process):

(i) providers of finance;
(ii) trade unions;
(iii) public utilities; and
(iv) government departments and agencies.

(d) A customer, supplier, franchisor, distributor or general agent with whom an entity transacts a significant volume of business, merely by virtue of the resulting economic dependence.

In the definition of a related party, an associate includes subsidiaries of the associate and a joint venture includes subsidiaries of the joint venture. Therefore, for example, an associate's subsidiary and the investor that has significant influence over the associate are related to each other. 33.4A

DISCLOSURES

Disclosure of parent-subsidiary relationships

Relationships between a parent and its subsidiaries shall be disclosed irrespective of whether there have been **related party transactions**. An entity shall disclose the name of its parent and, if different, the ultimate controlling party. If neither the entity's parent nor the ultimate controlling party produces financial statements available for public use, the name of the next most senior parent that does so (if any) shall also be disclosed. 33.5

Disclosure of key management personnel compensation

Key management personnel are those persons having authority and responsibility for planning, directing and controlling the activities of the entity, directly or indirectly, including any director (whether executive or otherwise) of that entity. Compensation includes all **employee benefits** (as defined in Section 28 *Employee Benefits*) including those in the form of share-based payments (see Section 26 *Share-based Payment*). Employee benefits include all forms of consideration paid, payable or provided by the entity, or on behalf of the entity (eg by its parent or by a shareholder), in exchange for services rendered to the entity. It also includes such consideration paid on behalf of a parent of the entity in respect of goods or services provided to the entity. 33.6

An entity shall disclose key management personnel compensation in total. 33.7

Disclosure of related party transactions

A related party transaction is a transfer of resources, services or obligations between a reporting entity and a related party, regardless of whether a price is charged. Examples of related party transactions that are common to entities within the scope of this FRS include, but are not limited to: 33.8

(a) transactions between an entity and its principal **owner(s)**;
(b) transactions between an entity and another entity when both entities are under the common control of a single entity or person; and

(c) transactions in which an entity or person that controls the reporting entity incurs **expenses** directly that otherwise would have been borne by the reporting entity.

33.9 If an entity has related party transactions, it shall disclose the nature of the related party relationship as well as information about the transactions, outstanding balances and commitments necessary for an understanding of the potential effect of the relationship on the financial statements. Those disclosure requirements are in addition to the requirements in paragraph 33.7 to disclose key management personnel compensation. At a minimum, disclosures shall include:

(a) The amount of the transactions.
(b) The amount of outstanding balances and:
  (i) their terms and conditions, including whether they are secured, and the nature of the consideration to be provided in settlement; and
  (ii) details of any guarantees given or received.

(c) Provisions for uncollectible receivables related to the amount of outstanding balances.
(d) The expense recognised during the period in respect of bad or doubtful debts due from related parties.

Such transactions could include purchases, sales, or transfers of goods or services, **leases**, guarantees and settlements by the entity on behalf of the related party or vice versa.

33.10 An entity shall make the disclosures required by paragraph 33.9 separately for each of the following categories:

(a) entities with control, joint control or significant influence over the entity;
(b) entities over which the entity has control, joint control or significant influence;
(c) key management personnel of the entity or its parent (in the aggregate); and
(d) other related parties.

33.11 An entity is exempt from the disclosure requirements of paragraph 33.9 in relation to:

(a) a **state** (a national, regional or local government) that has control, joint control or significant influence over the reporting entity; and
(b) another entity that is a related party because the same state has control, joint control or significant influence over both the reporting entity and the other entity.

However, the entity must still disclose a parent-subsidiary relationship as required by paragraph 33.5.

33.12 The following are examples of transactions that shall be disclosed if they are with a related party:

(a) purchases or sales of goods (finished or unfinished);
(b) purchases or sales of property and other **assets**;
(c) rendering or receiving of services;
(d) leases;
(e) transfers of **research** and **development**;
(f) transfers under licence agreements;
(g) transfers under finance arrangements (including loans and equity contributions in **cash** or in kind);
(h) provision of guarantees or collateral;

(i) settlement of **liabilities** on behalf of the entity or by the entity on behalf of another party; and
(j) participation by a parent or subsidiary in a **defined benefit plan** that shares risks between group entities.

An entity shall not state that related party transactions were made on terms
equivalent to those that prevail in arm's length transactions unless such terms can be 33.13
substantiated.

An entity may disclose items of a similar nature in the aggregate except when
separate disclosure is necessary for an understanding of the effects of related party 33.14
transactions on the financial statements of the entity.

Section 34
Specialised Activities

SCOPE OF THIS SECTION

34.1 This section sets out the financial reporting requirements for entities applying this FRS involved in the following types of specialised activities:

(a) Agriculture (see paragraphs 34.2 to 34.10A);
(b) Extractive Activities (see paragraphs 34.11 to 34.11C);
(c) Service Concession Arrangements (see paragraphs 34.12 to 34.16A);
(d) Financial Institutions (see paragraphs 34.17 to 34.33);
(e) Retirement Benefit Plans: Financial Statements (see paragraphs 34.34 to 34.48);
(f) Heritage Assets (see paragraphs 34.49 to 34.56);
(g) Funding Commitments (see paragraphs 34.57 to 34.63);
(h) Incoming Resources from Non-Exchange Transactions (see paragraphs 34.64 to 34.74);
(i) Public Benefit Entity Combinations (see paragraphs 34.75 to 34.86); and
(j) Public Benefit Entity Concessionary Loans (see paragraphs 34.87 to 34.97).

AGRICULTURE

34.2 An entity using this FRS that is engaged in **agricultural activity** shall determine an **accounting policy** for each class of **biological asset** and its related **agricultural produce.**

Recognition

34.3 An entity shall recognise a biological asset or an item of agricultural produce when, and only when:

(a) the entity controls the **asset** as a result of past events;
(b) it is **probable** that future economic benefits associated with the asset will flow to the entity; and
(c) the **fair value** or cost of the asset can be measured reliably.

Measurement

34.3A For each class of biological asset and its related agricultural produce an entity shall choose as its accounting policy either:

(a) the fair value model set out in paragraphs 34.4 to 34.7A; or
(b) the cost model set out in paragraphs 34.8 to 34.10A.

34.3B If an entity has chosen the fair value model for a class of biological asset and its related agricultural produce, it shall not subsequently change its accounting policy to the cost model.

Measurement – fair value model

34.4 An entity applying the fair value model shall measure a biological asset on initial **recognition** and at each **reporting date** at its **fair value less costs to sell**. Changes in fair value less costs to sell shall be recognised in **profit or loss**.

34.5 Agricultural produce harvested from an entity's biological assets shall be measured at the point of harvest at its fair value less costs to sell. Such **measurement** is the cost at that date when applying Section 13 *Inventories* or another applicable section of this FRS.

In determining fair value, an entity shall consider the following: **34.6**

(a) If an **active market** exists for a biological asset or agricultural produce in its present location and condition, the quoted price in that market is the appropriate basis for determining the fair value of that asset. If an entity has access to different active markets, the entity shall use the price existing in the market that it expects to use.
(b) If an active market does not exist, an entity uses one or more of the following, when available, in determining fair value:
   (i) the most recent market transaction price, provided that there has not been a significant change in economic circumstances between the date of that transaction and the end of the **reporting period**;
   (ii) market prices for similar assets with adjustment to reflect differences; and
   (iii) sector benchmarks such as the value of an orchard expressed per export tray, bushel, or hectare, and the value of cattle expressed per kilogram of meat.
(c) In some cases, the information sources listed in (b) may suggest different conclusions as to the fair value of a biological asset or an item of agricultural produce. An entity considers the reasons for those differences, to arrive at the most reliable estimate of fair value within a relatively narrow range of reasonable estimates.
(d) In some circumstances, fair value may be readily determinable even though market determined prices or values are not available for a biological asset in its present condition. An entity shall consider whether the **present value** of expected net cash flows from the asset discounted at a current market determined rate results in a reliable measure of fair value.

If the fair value of a biological asset cannot be measured reliably, the entity shall apply the cost model to that biological asset in accordance with paragraphs 34.8 and 34.10A until such time that the fair value can be reliably measured. **34.6A**

Disclosures – fair value model

An entity shall disclose the following for each class of biological asset measured using the fair value model: **34.7**

(a) A description of each class of biological asset.
(b) The methods and significant assumptions applied in determining the fair value of each class of biological asset.
(c) A reconciliation of changes in the **carrying amount** of each class of biological asset between the beginning and the end of the current period. The reconciliation shall include:
   (i) the **gain** or loss arising from changes in fair value less costs to sell;
   (ii) increases resulting from purchases;
   (iii) decreases attributable to sales;
   (iv) decreases resulting from harvest;
   (v) increases resulting from **business combinations**; and
   (vi) other changes.

This reconciliation need not be presented for prior periods.

34.7A If an entity measures any individual biological assets at cost in accordance with paragraph 34.6A, it shall explain why fair value cannot be reliably measured. If the fair value of such a biological asset becomes reliably measurable during the current period an entity shall explain why fair value has become reliably measurable and the effect of the change.

34.7B An entity shall disclose the methods and significant assumptions applied in determining the fair value at the point of harvest of each class of agricultural produce.

Measurement – cost model

34.8 An entity applying the cost model shall measure biological assets at cost less any accumulated **depreciation** and any accumulated **impairment losses**.

34.9 In applying the cost model, agricultural produce harvested from an entity's biological assets shall be measured at the point of harvest at either:

(a) the lower of cost and estimated selling price less costs to complete and sell; or
(b) its fair value less costs to sell. Any gain or loss arising on initial recognition of agricultural produce at fair value less costs to sell shall be included in profit or loss for the period in which it arises.

Such measurement is the cost at that date when applying Section 13 or another applicable section of this FRS.

Disclosures – cost model

34.10 An entity shall disclose the following for each class of biological asset measured using the cost model:

(a) a description of each class of biological asset;
(b) [not used]
(c) the depreciation method used;
(d) the useful lives or the depreciation rates used; and
(e) a reconciliation of changes in the carrying amount of each class of biological asset between the beginning and the end of the current period. The reconciliation shall include:

  (i) increases resulting from purchases;
  (ii) decreases attributable to sales;
  (iii) decreases resulting from harvest;
  (iv) increases resulting from business combinations;
  (v) impairment losses recognised or reversed in profit or loss in accordance with Section 27 *Impairment of Assets;* and
  (vi) other changes.

This reconciliation need not be presented for prior periods.

34.10A An entity shall disclose, for any agricultural produce measured at fair value less costs to sell, the methods and significant assumptions applied in determining the fair value at the point of harvest of each class of agricultural produce.

EXTRACTIVE ACTIVITIES

An entity using this FRS that is engaged in the exploration for and/or evaluation of mineral resources (extractive activities) shall apply the requirements of IFRS 6 *Exploration for and Evaluation of Mineral Resources*. **34.11**

When applying the requirements of IFRS 6, references made to other IFRSs within that standard shall be taken to be references to the relevant section or paragraph within this FRS. **34.11A**

Notwithstanding the requirements of paragraph 34.11A, when applying paragraph 21 of IFRS 6, a **cash-generating unit** or group of cash-generating units shall be no larger than an **operating segment** and the reference to IFRS 8 *Operating Segments* shall be ignored. **34.11B**

On first-time adoption of this FRS if it is not practical to apply a particular requirement of paragraph 18 of IFRS 6 to previous comparative amounts an entity shall disclose that fact. **34.11C**

SERVICE CONCESSION ARRANGEMENTS

A **service concession arrangement** is an arrangement whereby a public sector body, or a **public benefit entity** (the grantor) contracts with a private sector entity (the operator) to construct (or upgrade), operate and maintain **infrastructure assets** for a specified period of time (concession period). The operator is paid for its services over the period of the arrangement. A common feature of a service concession arrangement is the public service nature of the obligation undertaken by the operator, whereby the arrangement contractually obliges the operator to provide services to, or on behalf of, the grantor for the benefit of the public. **34.12**

Specifically an arrangement is a service concession arrangement when the following conditions apply: **34.12A**

(a) the grantor controls or regulates what services the operator must provide using the infrastructure assets, to whom, and at what price; and
(b) the grantor controls, through ownership, beneficial entitlement or otherwise, any significant **residual interest** in the assets at the end of the term of the arrangement.

Where the infrastructure assets have no significant **residual value** at the end of the term of the arrangement (ie the arrangement is for its entire useful life), then the arrangement shall be accounted for as a service concession if the conditions in (a) are met.

For the purpose of condition (b), the grantor's control over any significant residual interest should both restrict the operator's practical ability to sell or pledge the infrastructure assets and give the grantor a continuing right of use throughout the concession period.

A service concession arrangement shall be accounted for in accordance with the requirements of paragraphs 34.12E to 34.16A. **34.12B**

A service concession arrangement may contain a group of contracts and sub-arrangements as elements of the service concession arrangement as a whole. Such an arrangement shall be treated as a whole when the group of contracts and sub-arrangements are linked in such a way that the commercial effect cannot be **34.12C** understood without reference to them as a whole. Accordingly, the contractual terms of certain contracts or arrangements may meet both the scope requirements of paragraphs 34.12 and 34.12A, and Section 20 *Leases*. Where this is the case, the requirements of this section shall prevail.

34.12D Where an arrangement does not meet the requirements of paragraphs 34.12 and 34.12A, it shall be accounted for in accordance with Section 17 *Property, Plant and Equipment*, Section 18 *Intangible Assets other than Goodwill*, Section 20 or Section 23 *Revenue*, based on the nature of the arrangement.

Accounting by grantors – Finance lease liability model

34.12E The infrastructure assets shall be recognised as **assets** of the grantor together with a **liability** for its obligations under the service concession arrangement.

34.12F The grantor shall initially recognise the infrastructure assets and associated liability in accordance with paragraphs 20.9 and 20.10. If as a result of applying paragraphs 20.9 and 20.10 the grantor has not recognised a liability to make payments to the operator, it shall not recognise the infrastructure assets.

34.12G The liability shall be recognised as a finance lease liability and subsequently accounted for in accordance with paragraph 20.11.

34.12H The infrastructure assets shall be recognised as **property, plant and equipment** or as **intangible assets**, as appropriate, and subsequently accounted for in accordance with Section 17 or Section 18.

Accounting by operators

Treatment of the operator's rights over the infrastructure

34.12I Infrastructure assets shall not be recognised as property, plant and equipment by the operator because the contractual service arrangement does not convey the right to control the use of the public service assets to the operator. The operator has access to operate the infrastructure to provide the public service on behalf of the grantor in accordance with the terms specified in the arrangement.

Recognition and measurement of consideration

34.13 There are two principal categories of service concession arrangements:

(a) In one, the operator receives a **financial asset** - an unconditional contractual right to receive a specified or determinable amount of **cash** or another financial asset from, or at the direction of, the grantor in return for constructing (or upgrading) the infrastructure assets, and then operating and maintaining the asset for a specified period of time. This category includes guarantees by the grantor to pay for any shortfall between amounts received from users of the public service and specified or determinable amounts.

(b) In the other, the operator receives an **intangible asset** - a right to charge for use of the infrastructure assets that it constructs (or upgrades) and then operates and maintains for a specified period of time. A right to charge users is not an unconditional right to receive cash because the amounts are contingent on the extent to which the public uses the service.

Sometimes, a single arrangement may contain both types: to the extent that the grantor has given an unconditional guarantee of payment for the construction (or upgrade) of the infrastructure assets, the operator has a financial asset; to the extent that the operator receives a right to charge the public for using the service the operator has an intangible asset.

Accounting – financial asset model

The operator shall recognise a financial asset to the extent that it has an unconditional contractual right to receive cash or another financial asset from, or at the direction of, the grantor for the construction (or upgrade) services. The operator shall initially recognise the financial asset at fair value for the consideration received or receivable, based on the fair value of the construction (or upgrade) services provided. Thereafter, it shall account for the financial asset in accordance with Section 11 *Basic Financial Instruments* and Section 12 *Other Financial Instruments Issues*. **34.14**

Accounting – intangible asset model

The operator shall recognise an intangible asset to the extent that it receives a right (a licence) to charge users of the public service. The operator shall initially recognise the intangible asset at fair value for the consideration received or receivable, based on the fair value of the construction (or upgrade) services provided. Thereafter, it shall account for the intangible asset in accordance with Section 18. **34.15**

Operating services

The operator shall account for **revenue** in accordance with Section 23 for the operating services it performs. **34.16**

Borrowing costs

Borrowing costs attributable to the arrangement shall be recognised as an **expense**, in accordance with Section 25 *Borrowing Costs*, in the period in which they are incurred unless the operator has an intangible asset. In this case borrowing costs attributable to the arrangement may be capitalised in accordance with Section 25 where a policy of capitalisation has been adopted in accordance with that section. **34.16A**

FINANCIAL INSTITUTIONS

A **financial institution** (other than a **retirement benefit plan**) applying this FRS shall, in addition to the disclosure requirements in Section 11 *Basic Financial Instruments* and Section 12 *Other Financial Instruments Issues*, provide the disclosures in paragraphs 34.19 to 34.33. The disclosures in paragraphs 34.19 to 34.33 are required to be provided in: **34.17**

(a) the **individual financial statements** of a financial institution (other than a retirement benefit plan); and

(b) the **consolidated financial statements** of a **group** containing a financial institution (other than a retirement benefit plan) when the **financial instruments** held by the financial institution are **material** to the group. Where this is the case, the disclosures apply regardless of whether the principal activity of the group is being a financial institution or not. The disclosures in paragraphs 34.19 to 34.33 only need to be given in respect of financial instruments held by entities within the group that are financial institutions (other than retirement benefit plans).

34.18 A retirement benefit plan shall provide the disclosures in paragraphs 34.35 to 34.48 of this FRS.

Disclosures

Significance of financial instruments for financial position and performance

34.19 A financial institution shall disclose information that enables users of its **financial statements** to evaluate the significance of financial instruments for its **financial position** and **performance**.

34.20 A financial institution shall disclose a disaggregation of the **statement of financial position** line item by class of financial instrument. A class is a grouping of financial instruments that is appropriate to the nature of the information disclosed and that takes into account the characteristics of those financial instruments.

Impairment

34.21 Where a financial institution uses a separate allowance account to record impairments, it shall disclose a reconciliation of changes in that account during the period for each class of **financial asset**.

Fair value

34.22 For financial instruments held at **fair value** in the statement of financial position, a financial institution shall disclose for each class of financial instrument, an analysis of the level in the fair value hierarchy (as set out in paragraph 11.27) into which the fair value measurements are categorised.

Nature and extent of risks arising from financial instruments

34.23 A financial institution shall disclose information that enables users of its financial statements to evaluate the nature and extent of **credit risk**, **liquidity risk** and **market risk** arising from financial instruments to which the financial institution is exposed at the end of the **reporting period**.

34.24 For each type of risk arising from financial instruments, a financial institution shall disclose:

(a) the exposures to risk and how they arise;
(b) its objectives, policies and processes for managing the risk and the methods used to measure the risk; and
(c) any changes in (a) or (b) from the previous period.

Credit risk

34.25 A financial institution shall disclose by class of financial instrument:

(a) The amount that best represents its maximum exposure to credit risk at the end of the reporting period. This disclosure is not required for financial instruments whose **carrying amount** best represents the maximum exposure to credit risk.

(b) A description of collateral held as security and of other credit enhancements, and the extent to which these mitigate credit risk.
(c) The amount by which any related credit **derivatives** or similar instruments mitigate that maximum exposure to credit risk.
(d) Information about the credit quality of **financial assets** that are neither past due nor impaired.

A financial institution shall provide, by class of financial asset, an analysis of: **34.26**

(a) the age of financial assets that are past due as at the end of the reporting period but not impaired; and
(b) the financial assets that are individually determined to be impaired as at the end of the reporting period, including the factors the financial institution considered in determining that they are impaired.

When a financial institution obtains financial or non-financial assets during the period by taking possession of collateral it holds as security or calling on other credit enhancements (eg guarantees), and such **assets** meet the **recognition** criteria in other sections, a financial institution shall disclose: **34.27**

(a) the nature and carrying amount of the assets obtained; and
(b) when the assets are not readily convertible into **cash**, its policies for disposing of such assets or for using them in its operations.

Liquidity risk

A financial institution shall provide a maturity analysis for **financial liabilities** that shows the remaining contractual maturities at undiscounted amounts separated between derivative and non-derivative financial liabilities. **34.28**

Market risk

A financial institution shall provide a sensitivity analysis for each type of market risk (eg interest rate risk, currency risk, other price risk) it is exposed to, showing the impact on **profit or loss** and **equity**. Details of the methods and assumptions used should be provided. **34.29**

If a financial institution prepares a sensitivity analysis, such as value-at-risk, that reflects interdependencies between risk variables (eg interest rates and exchange rates) and uses it to manage **financial risks**, it may use that sensitivity analysis instead. **34.30**

Capital

A financial institution shall disclose information that enables users of its financial statements to evaluate the entity's objectives, policies and processes for managing capital. A financial institution shall disclose the following: **34.31**

(a) Qualitative information about its objectives, policies and processes for managing capital, including:
  (i) a description of what it manages as capital;
  (ii) when an entity is subject to externally imposed capital requirements, the nature of those requirements and how those requirements are incorporated into the management of capital; and
  (iii) how it is meeting its objectives for managing capital.

(b) Summary quantitative data about what it manages as capital. Some entities regard some financial liabilities (eg some forms of subordinated debt) as part of capital. Other entities regard capital as excluding some components of equity (eg components arising from cash flow hedges).
(c) Any changes in (a) and (b) from the previous period.
(d) Whether during the period it complied with any externally imposed capital requirements to which it is subject.
(e) When the entity has not complied with such externally imposed capital requirements, the consequences of such non-compliance.

A financial institution bases these disclosures on the information provided internally to **key management personnel**.

34.32 A financial institution may manage capital in a number of ways and be subject to a number of different capital requirements. For example, a conglomerate may include entities that undertake insurance activities and banking activities and those entities may operate in several jurisdictions. When an aggregate disclosure of capital requirements and how capital is managed would not provide useful information or would distort a financial statement user's understanding of the financial institution's capital resources, the financial institution shall disclose separate information for each capital requirement to which the entity is subject.

Reporting cash flows on a net basis

34.33 A financial institution that presents a statement of cash flow in accordance with Section 7 *Statement of Cash Flows* may report cash flows arising from each of the following activities on a net basis:

(a) cash receipts and payments for the acceptance and repayment of deposits with a fixed maturity date;
(b) the placement of deposits with and withdrawal of deposits from other financial institutions; and
(c) cash advances and loans made to customers and the repayment of those advances and loans.

This paragraph does not impose a requirement to produce a cash flow statement.

RETIREMENT BENEFIT PLANS: FINANCIAL STATEMENTS

34.34 An entity applying this FRS that is a **retirement benefit plan** shall also apply the requirements of paragraphs 34.35 to 34.48. A retirement benefit plan may be a **defined benefit plan**, a **defined contribution plan**, or have both defined benefit and defined contribution elements. The **financial statements** shall distinguish between defined benefit and defined contribution elements, where **material**.

Requirements applicable to both defined benefit plans and defined contribution plans

34.35 A retirement benefit plan need not comply with the requirements of paragraph 3.17. The financial statements of a retirement benefit plan shall contain as part of the financial statements:

(a) a statement of changes in **net assets available for benefits** (which can also be called a Fund Account) (see paragraph 34.37);

(b) a statement of net assets available for benefits (see paragraph 34.38); and
(c) **notes**, comprising a summary of significant **accounting policies** and other explanatory information.

At each **reporting date**, the net assets available for benefits shall be measured in accordance with paragraph 28.15(b). Changes in fair value shall be recognised in the statements of changes in net assets available for benefits. **34.36**

Statement of changes in net assets available for benefits (Fund Account)

The financial statements of a retirement benefit plan, whether defined contribution or defined benefit, shall present the following in the statement of changes in net assets available for benefits: **34.37**

(a) employer contributions;
(b) employee contributions;
(c) investment income such as interest and dividends;
(d) other income;
(e) benefits paid or payable (analysed, for example, as retirement, death and disability benefits, and lump sum payments);
(f) administrative expenses;
(g) other expenses;
(h) taxes on income;
(i) profits and losses on disposal of investments and changes in value of investments; and
(j) transfers from and to other plans.

Statement of net assets available for benefits

The financial statements of a retirement benefit plan, whether defined contribution or defined benefit, shall present the following in the statement of net assets available for benefits: **34.38**

(a) **assets** at the end of the period suitably classified; and
(b) **liabilities** other than the actuarial **present value** of promised retirement benefits.

The basis of valuation of assets shall be presented in the notes to the financial statements.

Disclosures

Assets other than financial instruments held at fair value

Where a retirement benefit plan holds assets other than financial instruments at fair value in accordance with paragraph 34.36, it shall apply the disclosure requirements of the relevant section of this FRS, for example in relation to **investment property** it shall provide the disclosures required by paragraph 16.10. **34.39**

Significance of financial instruments for financial position and performance

A retirement benefit plan shall disclose information that enables users of its financial statements to evaluate the significance of financial instruments for its **financial position** and **performance**. **34.40**

34.41 A retirement benefit plan shall disclose a disaggregation of the statement of net assets available for benefits by class of financial instrument. A class is a grouping of financial instruments that is appropriate to the nature of the information disclosed and that takes into account the characteristics of those financial instruments.

Fair value

34.42 For financial instruments held at fair value in the statement of net assets available for benefits, a retirement benefit plan shall disclose for each class of financial instrument, an analysis of the level in the fair value hierarchy (as set out in paragraph 11.27) into which the fair value measurements are categorised.

Nature and extent of risks arising from financial instruments

34.43 A retirement benefit plan shall disclose information that enables users of its financial statements to evaluate the nature and extent of **credit risk** and **market risk** arising from financial instruments to which the retirement benefit plan is exposed at the end of the **reporting period**.

34.44 For each type of credit and market risk arising from financial instruments, a retirement benefit plan shall disclose:

(a) the exposures to risk and how they arise;
(b) its objectives, policies and processes for managing the risk and the methods used to measure the risk; and
(c) any changes in (a) or (b) from the previous period.

In relation to credit risk, a retirement benefit plan shall, in addition, provide the disclosures set out in paragraphs 34.45 and 34.46.

Credit risk

34.45 A retirement benefit plan shall disclose by class of financial instrument:

(a) The amount that best represents its maximum exposure to credit risk at the end of the reporting period. This disclosure is not required for financial instruments whose **carrying amount** best represents the maximum exposure to credit risk.
(b) A description of collateral held as security and of other credit enhancements, and the extent to which these mitigate credit risk.
(c) The amount by which any related credit **derivatives** or similar instruments mitigate that maximum exposure to credit risk.
(d) Information about the credit quality of financial assets that are neither past due nor impaired.

34.46 When a retirement benefit plan obtains financial or non-financial assets during the period by taking possession of collateral it holds as security or calling on other credit enhancements (eg guarantees), and such assets meet the **recognition** criteria in other sections, a retirement benefit plan shall disclose:

(a) the nature and carrying amount of the assets obtained; and
(b) when the assets are not readily convertible into **cash**, its policies for disposing of such assets or for retaining them.

Defined benefit plans – actuarial liabilities

A defined benefit plan is not required to recognise a liability in relation to the promised retirement benefits. **34.47**

A defined benefit plan shall disclose, in a report alongside the financial statements, information regarding the actuarial present value of promised retirement benefits including: **34.48**

(a) a statement of the actuarial present value of promised retirement benefits, based on the most recent valuation of the scheme;
(b) the date of the most recent valuation of the scheme; and
(c) the significant actuarial assumptions made and the method used to calculate the actuarial present value of promised retirement benefits.

HERITAGE ASSETS

All **heritage assets** shall be accounted for in accordance with the requirements of paragraphs 34.50 to 34.56. These paragraphs do not apply to **investment property**, **property, plant and equipment** or **intangible assets** which fall within the scope of Section 16 *Investment Properties*, Section 17 *Property, Plant and Equipment and Section 18 Intangible Assets other than Goodwill.* **34.49**

Works of art and similar objects are sometimes held by commercial entities but are not heritage assets because they are not maintained principally for their contribution to knowledge and culture. These assets shall therefore be accounted for in accordance with Section 17. Heritage assets used by the entity itself, for example historic buildings used for teaching by education establishments, shall also be accounted for in accordance with Section 17. This is based on the view that an operational perspective is likely to be most relevant for most users of **financial statements**. However, entities that use historic buildings and similar assets may wish to consider whether it is appropriate to apply the disclosures required by paragraphs 34.55 and 34.56. **34.50**

Recognition and measurement

An entity shall recognise and measure heritage assets in accordance with Section 17 (ie using the cost model or revaluation model), subject to the requirements set out in paragraphs 34.52 to 34.53 below. **34.51**

Heritage assets shall be recognised in the **statement of financial position** separately from other assets. **34.52**

Where heritage assets have previously been capitalised or are recently purchased, information on the cost or value of the asset will be available. Where this information is not available, and cannot be obtained at a cost which is commensurate with the benefits to users of the financial statements, the assets shall not be recognised in the statement of financial position, but must be disclosed in accordance with the requirements below. **34.53**

At each **reporting date**, an entity shall apply Section 27 *Impairment of Assets* to determine whether a heritage asset is impaired and, if so, how to recognise and measure the **impairment loss**. A heritage asset may be impaired, for example where it has suffered physical deterioration, breakage or doubts arise as to its authenticity. **34.54**

Disclosure

34.55 An entity shall disclose the following for all heritage assets it holds:

(a) An indication of the nature and scale of heritage assets held by the entity.

(b) The policy for the acquisition, preservation, management and disposal of heritage assets (including a description of the records maintained by the entity of its collection of heritage assets and information on the extent to which access to the assets is permitted).

(c) The **accounting policies** adopted for heritage assets, including details of the measurement bases used.

(d) For heritage assets that have not been recognised in the statement of financial position, the **notes** to the financial statements shall:

(i) explain the reasons why;
(ii) describe the significance and nature of those assets; and
(iii) disclose information that is helpful in assessing the value of those heritage assets.

(e) Where heritage assets are recognised in the statement of financial position the following disclosure is required:

(i) the **carrying amount** of heritage assets at the beginning of the **reporting period** and the reporting date, including an analysis between classes or groups of heritage assets recognised at cost and those recognised at valuation; and
(ii) where assets are recognised at valuation, sufficient information to assist in understanding the valuation being recognised (date of valuation, method used, whether carried out by external valuer and if so their qualification and any significant limitations on the valuation).

(f) A summary of transactions relating to heritage assets for the reporting period and each of the previous four reporting periods disclosing:

(i) the cost of acquisitions of heritage assets;
(ii) the value of heritage assets acquired by donations;
(iii) the carrying amount of heritage assets disposed of in the period and proceeds received; and
(iv) any impairment recognised in the period.

The summary shall show separately those transactions included in the statement of financial position and those that are not.

(g) In exceptional circumstances where it is **impracticable** to obtain a valuation of heritage assets acquired by donation the reason shall be stated.

Disclosures can be aggregated for groups or classes of heritage assets, provided this does not obscure significant information.

34.56 Where it is impracticable to do so, the disclosures required by paragraph 34.55(f) need not be given for any accounting period earlier than the previous comparable period, and a statement to the effect that it is impracticable shall be made.

FUNDING COMMITMENTS

34.57 An entity that commits to provide resources to other entities shall apply the requirements of paragraphs 34.58 to 34.63 and the accompanying guidance at Appendix A to this section, except for commitments to make a loan to which entities shall apply Section 11 *Basic Financial Instruments* or Section 12 *Other Financial Instrument Issues*, as applicable.

When applying these paragraphs, the requirements of Section 2 *Concepts and Pervasive Principles* and Section 21 *Provisions and Contingencies* shall also be taken into consideration. 34.58

Recognition

An entity shall recognise a **liability** and, usually, a corresponding **expense**, when it has made a commitment that it will provide resources to another party, if, and only if: 34.59

(a) the definition and **recognition** criteria for a liability have been satisfied;
(b) the obligation (which may be a **constructive obligation**) is such that the entity cannot realistically withdraw from it; and
(c) the entitlement of the other party to the resources does not depend on the satisfaction of **performance-related conditions**.

Commitments that are performance-related will be recognised when those performance-related conditions are met. 34.60

Measurement

An entity shall measure any recognised liability at the **present value** of the resources committed. 34.61

Disclosure

An entity that has made a commitment shall disclose the following: 34.62

(a) the commitment made;
(b) the time-frame of that commitment;
(c) any performance-related conditions attached to that commitment; and
(d) details of how that commitment will be funded.

The above disclosures may be made in aggregate, providing that such aggregation does not obscure significant information. However, separate disclosure shall be made for recognised and unrecognised commitments. 34.63

INCOMING RESOURCES FROM NON-EXCHANGE TRANSACTIONS

The accounting for **government grants** is addressed in Section 24 *Government Grants.* PBE34.64

Paragraphs PBE34.67 to PBE34.74 and the accompanying guidance at Appendix B to this section apply to other resources received from **non-exchange transactions** by **public benefit entities** or entities within a **public benefit entity group.** A non-exchange transaction is a transaction whereby an entity receives value from another entity without directly giving approximately equal value in exchange or gives value to another entity without directly receiving approximately equal value in exchange. PBE34.65

Non-exchange transactions include, but are not limited to, donations (of **cash**, goods, and services) and legacies. PBE34.66

Recognition and measurement

PBE34.67 An entity shall recognise receipts of resources from non-exchange transactions as follows:

(a) Transactions that do not impose specified future performance-related conditions on the recipient are recognised in **income** when the resources are received or receivable.
(b) Transactions that do impose specified future performance-related conditions on the recipient are recognised in income only when the performance-related conditions are met.
(c) Where resources are received before the **revenue recognition** criteria are satisfied, a **liability** is recognised.

PBE34.68 The existence of a **restriction** does not prohibit a resource from being recognised in income when receivable.

PBE34.69 When applying the requirements of paragraph PBE34.67, an entity must take into consideration whether the resource can be measured reliably and whether the benefits of recognising the resource outweigh the costs.

PBE34.70 Therefore, where it is not practicable to estimate the value of the resource with sufficient **reliability**, the income shall be included in the financial period when the resource is sold.

PBE34.71 An entity shall recognise a liability for any resource that has previously been received and recognised in income when, as a result of a subsequent failure to meet restrictions or performance-related conditions attached to it, repayment becomes **probable**.

PBE34.72 Donations of services that can be reasonably quantified will usually result in the recognition of income and an **expense**. An **asset** will be recognised only when those services are used for the production of an asset and the services received will be capitalised as part of the cost of that asset.

PBE34.73 An entity shall measure incoming resources from non-exchange transactions as follows:

(a) Donated services and facilities, that would otherwise have been purchased, shall be measured at the value to the entity.
(b) All other incoming resources from non-exchange transactions shall be measured at the **fair value** of the resources received or receivable.

Disclosure

PBE34.74 An entity shall disclose the following:

(a) the nature and amounts of resources receivable from non-exchange transactions recognised in the **financial statements**;
(b) any unfulfilled conditions or other contingencies attaching to resources from non-exchange transactions that have not been recognised in income; and
(c) an indication of other forms of resources from non-exchange transactions from which the entity has benefited.

PUBLIC BENEFIT ENTITY COMBINATIONS

Paragraphs PBE34.76 to PBE34.86 apply only to **public benefit entities** for the following categories of **entity combinations** which involve a whole entity or parts of an entity combining with another entity: **PBE34.75**

(a) combinations at nil or nominal consideration which are in substance a gift; and
(b) combinations which meet the definition and criteria of a **merger**.

Combinations which are determined to be acquisitions shall be accounted for in accordance with Section 19 *Business Combinations and Goodwill*. **PBE34.76**

Combinations that are in substance a gift

Accounting treatment and disclosure

A **combination that is in substance a gift** shall be accounted for in accordance with Section 19 except for the matters addressed in paragraphs PBE34.78 and PBE34.79 below. **PBE34.77**

Any excess of the **fair value** of the **assets** received over the fair value of the **liabilities** assumed is recognised as a **gain** in **income and expenditure**. This gain represents the gift of the value of one entity to another and shall be recognised as income. **PBE34.78**

Any excess of the fair value of the liabilities assumed over the fair value of the assets received is recognised as a loss in income and expenditure. This loss represents the net obligations assumed, for which the receiving entity has not received a financial reward and shall be recognised as an **expense**. **PBE34.79**

Combinations that are a merger

An entity combination that is a merger shall apply merger accounting as prescribed below. **PBE34.80**

Any entity combination which is neither a combination that is in substance a gift nor a merger shall be accounted for as an acquisition in accordance with Section 19. **PBE34.81**

Accounting treatment

Under merger accounting the carrying value of the assets and liabilities of the parties to the combination are not adjusted to fair value, although adjustments shall be made to achieve uniformity of **accounting policies** across the combining entities. **PBE34.82**

The results and **cash flows** of all the combining entities shall be brought into the **financial statements** of the newly formed entity from the beginning of the financial period in which the merger occurs. **PBE34.83**

The comparative amounts shall be restated by including the results for all the combining entities for the previous accounting period and their **statement of financial positions** for the previous **reporting date**. The comparative figures shall be marked as 'combined' figures. **PBE34.84**

All costs associated with the merger shall be charged as an expense in the period incurred. **PBE34.85**

Disclosure

PBE34.86 For each entity combination accounted for as a merger in the **reporting period** the following shall be disclosed in the newly formed entity's financial statements:

(a) the names and descriptions of the combining entities or businesses;
(b) the date of the merger;
(c) an analysis of the principal components of the current year's **total comprehensive income** to indicate:

(i) the amounts relating to the newly formed merged entity for the period after the date of the merger; and
(ii) the amounts relating to each party to the merger up to the date of the merger.

(d) an analysis of the previous year's total comprehensive income between each party to the merger;
(e) the aggregate carrying value of the net assets of each party to the merger at the date of the merger; and
(f) the nature and amount of any significant adjustments required to align accounting policies and an explanation of any further adjustments made to net assets as a result of the merger.

PUBLIC BENEFIT ENTITY CONCESSIONARY LOANS

PBE34.87 Paragraphs PBE34.89 to PBE34.97 address the **recognition**, **measurement** and disclosure of **public benefit entity concessionary loan** arrangements within the **financial statements** of **public benefit entities** or entities within a **public benefit entity group** making or receiving public benefit entity concessionary loans. These paragraphs apply to public benefit entity concessionary loan arrangements only and are not applicable to loans which are at a market rate or to other commercial arrangements.

PBE34.88 Public benefit entity concessionary loans are loans made or received between a public benefit entity or an entity within the public benefit entity group, and another party at below the **prevailing market rate** of interest that are not repayable on demand and are for the purposes of furthering the objectives of the public benefit entity or public benefit entity **parent**.

Accounting treatment

PBE34.89 Entities making or receiving public benefit entity concessionary loans shall use either:

(a) the recognition, measurement and disclosure requirements in Section 11 *Basic Financial Instruments* or Section 12 *Other Financial Instruments Issues* (for example, Section 11 requires initial measurement at **fair value** and subsequent measurement at **amortised cost** using the **effective interest method**); or
(b) the accounting treatment set out in paragraphs PBE34.90 to PBE34.97 below.

A public benefit entity or an entity within a public benefit entity group shall apply the same **accounting policy** to concessionary loans both made and received.

Initial measurement

PBE34.90 A public benefit entity or an entity within a public benefit entity group making or receiving concessionary loans shall initially measure these arrangements at the amount received or paid and recognise them in the **statement of financial position**.

Subsequent measurement

In subsequent years, the **carrying amount** of concessionary loans in the financial statements shall be adjusted to reflect any accrued interest payable or receivable. **PBE34.91**

To the extent that a loan that has been made is irrecoverable, an **impairment loss** shall be recognised in **income and expenditure**. **PBE34.92**

Presentation and disclosure

The entity shall present concessionary loans made and concessionary loans received either as a separate line items on the face of the statement of financial position or in the **notes** to the financial statements. **PBE34.93**

Concessionary loans shall be presented separately between amounts repayable or receivable within one year and amounts repayable or receivable after more than one year. **PBE34.94**

The entity shall disclose in the summary of significant accounting policies the measurement basis used for concessionary loans and any other accounting policies which are relevant to the understanding of these transactions within the financial statements. **PBE34.95**

The entity shall disclose the following: **PBE34.96**

(a) the terms and conditions of concessionary loan arrangements, for example the interest rate, any security provided and the terms of the repayment; and
(b) the value of concessionary loans which have been committed but not taken up at the year end.

Concessionary loans made or received shall be disclosed separately. However multiple loans made or received may be disclosed in aggregate, providing that such aggregation does not obscure significant information. **PBE34.97**

Appendix A to Section 34

GUIDANCE ON FUNDING COMMITMENTS (paragraphs 34.57 to 34.63)

This guidance is an integral part of the Standard.

34A.1 Entities often make commitments to provide cash or other resources to other entities. In such a case, it is necessary to determine whether the commitment should be recognised as a liability. The definition of a liability requires that there be a present obligation, and not merely an expectation of a future outflow.

34A.2 A general statement that the entity intends to provide resources to certain classes of potential beneficiaries in accordance with its objectives does not in itself give rise to a liability, as the entity may amend or withdraw its policy, and potential beneficiaries do not have the ability to insist on their fulfilment. Similarly, a promise to provide cash conditional on the receipt of future income in itself may not give rise to a liability where the entity cannot be required to fulfil it if the future income is not received and it is probable that the economic benefits will not be transferred.

34A.3 A liability is recognised only for a commitment that gives the recipient a valid expectation that payment will be made and from which the grantor cannot realistically withdraw. One of the implications of this is that a liability only exists where the commitment has been communicated to the recipient.

34A.4 Commitments are not recognised if they are subject to performance-related conditions. In such a case, the entity is required to fulfil its commitment only when the performance-related conditions are met and no liability exists until that time.

34A.5 A commitment may contain conditions that are not performance-related conditions. For example, a requirement to provide an annual financial report to the grantor may serve mainly as an administrative tool because failure to comply would not release the grantor from its commitment. This may be distinguished from a requirement to submit a detailed report for review and consideration by the grantor of how funds will be utilised in order to secure payment. A mere restriction on the specific purpose for which funds are to be used does not in itself constitute a performance-related condition.

34A.6 For funding commitments that are not recognised, it is important that full and informative disclosures are made of their existence and of the sources of funding for these unrecognised commitments.

Appendix B to Section 34

GUIDANCE ON INCOMING RESOURCES FROM NON-EXCHANGE TRANSACTIONS (paragraphs 34.64 to 34.74)

This guidance is an integral part of the Standard.

Recognition

The receipt of resources will usually result in an entity recognising an asset and corresponding income for the fair value of resources when those resources become received or receivable. Instances when this may differ include where: **PBE34B.1**

(a) an entity received those resources in the form of services (see paragraphs PBE34B.8 to PBE34B.12); or

(b) there are performance-related conditions attached to the resources, which have yet to be fulfilled (see paragraphs PBE34B.13 to PBE34B.14).

Resources shall only be recognised when the fair value of the incoming resources can be measured reliably. **PBE34B.2**

The concepts of materiality (see paragraph 2.6), and balance between benefit and cost (see paragraph 2.13) should be considered when deciding which resources received shall be recognised in the financial statements. **PBE34B.3**

When it is impracticable to recognise resources from non-exchange transactions, the income is recognised in the period in which the resources are sold or distributed. The most common example is that of high volume, low value second-hand goods donated for resale. **PBE34B.4**

Legacies

Donations in the form of legacies are recognised when it is probable that the legacy will be received and its value can be measured reliably. These criteria will normally be met following probate once the executor(s) of the estate has established that there are sufficient assets in the estate, after settling liabilities, to pay the legacy. **PBE34B.5**

Evidence that the executor(s) has determined that a payment can be made, may arise on the agreement of the estate's accounts or notification that payment will be made. Where notification is received after the year-end but it is clear that the executor(s) has agreed prior to the year-end that the legacy can be paid, the legacy is accrued in the financial statements. The certainty and measurability of the receipt may be affected by subsequent events such as valuations and disputes. **PBE34B.6**

Entities that are in receipt of numerous immaterial legacies for which individual identification would be burdensome may take a portfolio approach. **PBE34B.7**

Services

Donated services that can be reasonably quantified shall be recognised in the financial statements when they are received. **PBE34B.8**

PBE34B.9 Donated services that are consumed immediately are usually recognised as an expense. However, there may be circumstances when a service is used in the production of an asset, for example erecting a building. In these cases, the associated donated service (eg plumbing and electrical services) would be recognised as a part of the cost of that asset.

PBE34B.10 Donated services that can be reasonably quantified include donated facilities, such as office accommodation, services that would otherwise have been purchased and services usually provided by an individual or an entity as part of their trade or profession for a fee.

PBE34B.11 It is expected that contributions made by volunteers cannot be reasonably quantified and therefore these services shall not be recognised.

PBE34B.12 Paragraph PBE34.74(c) requires an entity to disclose other forms of resources from non-exchange transactions from which the entity has benefited. This will include the disclosure of unrecognised volunteer services.

Performance-related conditions

PBE34B.13 Some resources are given with performance-related conditions attached which require the recipient to use the resources to provide a specified level of service in order to be entitled to retain the resources. An entity will not recognise income from those resources until these performance-related conditions have been met.

PBE34B.14 However, some requirements are stated so broadly that they do not actually impose a performance-related condition on the recipient. In these cases the recipient will recognise income on receipt of the transfer of resources.

Measurement

PBE34B.15 Paragraph PBE34.73(a) requires donated services and facilities to be measured at the value to the entity. This requirement only applies to those services and facilities that would otherwise have been purchased by the entity. The value placed on these services and facilities should be the estimated value to the entity of the service or facility received, this will be the price the entity estimates it would pay in the open market for a service or facility of equivalent utility to the entity.

PBE34B.16 Paragraph PBE34.73(b) requires resources received or receivable, that are not services or facilities, to be measured at their fair value. These fair values are usually the price that the entity would have to pay on the open market for an equivalent resource.

PBE34B.17 When there is no direct evidence of an open market value for an equivalent item a value may be derived from sources such as:

(a) the cost of the item to the donor; or
(b) in the case of goods that are expected to be sold, the estimated resale value (which may reflect the amount actually realised) after deducting the cost to sell the goods.

PBE34B.18 Donated services are recognised as income and an equivalent amount shall be recognised as an expense in income and expenditure, unless the expense can be capitalised as part of the cost of an asset.

Section 35
Transition to this FRS

SCOPE OF THIS SECTION

This section applies to a **first-time adopter of this FRS**, regardless of whether its previous accounting framework was **EU-adopted IFRS** or another set of generally accepted accounting principles (GAAP) such as its national accounting standards, or another framework such as the local income tax basis. **35.1**

Notwithstanding the requirements in paragraphs 35.3 and 35.4, an entity that has applied **FRS 102** in a previous **reporting period**, but whose most recent previous annual **financial statements** did not contain an explicit and unreserved statement of compliance with this FRS, must either apply this section or else apply FRS 102 retrospectively in accordance with Section 10 *Accounting Policies, Changes in Estimates and Errors* as if the entity had never stopped applying this FRS. **35.2**

FIRST-TIME ADOPTION

A first-time adopter of this FRS shall apply this section in its first financial statements that conform to this FRS. **35.3**

An entity's first financial statements that conform to this FRS are the first financial statements* in which the entity makes an explicit and unreserved statement in those financial statements of compliance with this FRS. Financial statements prepared in accordance with this FRS are an entity's first such financial statements if, for example, the entity: **35.4**

(a) did not present financial statements for previous periods;
(b) presented its most recent previous financial statements under previous UK and Republic of Ireland requirements that are therefore not consistent with this FRS in all respects; or
(c) presented its most recent previous financial statements in conformity with EU-adopted IFRS.

Paragraph 3.17 defines a complete set of financial statements. **35.5**

Paragraph 3.14 requires an entity to disclose, in a complete set of financial statements, comparative information in respect of the preceding period for all amounts presented in the financial statements, as well as specified comparative narrative and descriptive information. An entity may present comparative information in respect of more than one preceding period. Therefore, an entity's **date of transition** to this FRS is the beginning of the earliest period for which the entity presents full comparative information in accordance with this FRS in its first financial statements that comply with this FRS. **35.6**

PROCEDURES FOR PREPARING FINANCIAL STATEMENTS AT THE DATE OF TRANSITION

Except as provided in paragraphs 35.9 to 35.11B, an entity shall, in its opening **statement of financial position** as of its date of transition to this FRS (ie the beginning of the earliest period presented): **35.7**

(a) recognise all **assets** and **liabilities** whose **recognition** is required by this FRS;

**This excludes interim financial statements.*

(b) not recognise items as assets or liabilities if this FRS does not permit such recognition;
(c) reclassify items that it recognised under its previous financial reporting framework as one type of asset, liability or component of **equity**, but are a different type of asset, liability or component of equity under this FRS; and
(d) apply this FRS in measuring all recognised assets and liabilities.

This section does not require the opening statement of financial position to be presented.

35.8 The **accounting policies** that an entity uses in its opening statement of financial position under this FRS may differ from those that it used for the same date using its previous financial reporting framework. The resulting adjustments arise from transactions, other events or conditions before the date of transition to this FRS. Therefore, an entity shall recognise those adjustments directly in retained earnings (or, if appropriate, another category of equity) at the date of transition to this FRS.

35.9 On first-time adoption of this FRS, an entity shall not retrospectively change the accounting that it followed under its previous financial reporting framework for any of the following transactions:

(a) ***Derecognition** of **financial assets** and **financial liabilities***:
Financial assets and liabilities derecognised under an entity's previous accounting framework before the date of transition shall not be recognised upon adoption of this FRS. Conversely, for financial assets and liabilities that would have been derecognised under this FRS in a transaction that took place before the date of transition, but that were not derecognised under an entity's previous accounting framework, an entity may choose:

(i) to derecognise them on adoption of this FRS; or
(ii) to continue to recognise them until disposed of or settled.

(b) *Hedge accounting*:
An entity shall not change its hedge accounting before the date of transition to this FRS for hedging relationships that no longer exist at the date of transition. For hedging relationships that exist at the date of transition, the entity shall follow the hedge accounting requirements of Section 12 *Other Financial Instruments Issues*, including the requirements for discontinuing hedge accounting for hedging relationships that do not meet the conditions of Section 12.
(c) *Accounting estimates*.
(d) ***Discontinued operations***.
(e) *Measuring **non-controlling interests***:
The requirements:

(i) to allocate **profit or loss** and **total comprehensive income** between non-controlling interest and **owners** of the **parent**;
(ii) for accounting for changes in the parent's ownership interest in a subsidiary that do not result in a loss of control; and
(iii) for accounting for a loss of control over a subsidiary

shall be applied prospectively from the date of transition to this FRS (or from such earlier date as this FRS is applied to restate **business combinations**—see paragraph 35.10(a)).

35.10 An entity may use one or more of the following exemptions in preparing its first financial statements that conform to this FRS:

(a) ***Business combinations, including group reconstructions***

A first-time adopter may elect not to apply Section 19 *Business Combinations and Goodwill* to business combinations that were effected before the date of transition to this FRS. However, if a first-time adopter restates any business combination to comply with Section 19, it shall restate all later business combinations. If a first time adopter does not apply Section 19 retrospectively, the first-time adopter shall recognise and measure all its assets and liabilities acquired or assumed in a past business combination at the date of transition to this FRS in accordance with paragraphs 35.7 to 35.9 or if applicable, with paragraphs 35.10(b) to (r) except for:

(i) **intangible assets** other than **goodwill** – intangible assets subsumed within goodwill shall not be separately recognised; and
(ii) goodwill - no adjustment shall be made to the carrying value of goodwill.

(b) ***Share-based payment transactions***

A first-time adopter is not required to apply Section 26 *Share-based Payment* to equity instruments that were granted before the date of transition to this FRS, or to liabilities arising from share-based payment transactions that were settled before the date of transition to this FRS. Except that a first-time adopter previously applying FRS 20 *(IFRS 2) Share-based Payment* or IFRS 2 *Share-based Payment* shall, in relation to equity instruments that were granted before the date of transition to this FRS, apply either FRS 20 / IFRS 2 (as applicable) or Section 26 of this FRS at the date of transition.

(c) ***Fair value as deemed cost***

A first-time adopter may elect to measure an:

(i) item of **property, plant and equipment**;
(ii) **investment property**; or
(iii) intangible asset which meets the recognition criteria and the criteria for revaluation in Section 18 *Intangible Assets other than Goodwill*

on the date of transition to this FRS at its **fair value** and use that fair value as its **deemed cost** at that date.

(d) ***Revaluation as deemed cost***

A first-time adopter may elect to use a previous GAAP revaluation of an:

(i) item of property, plant and equipment;
(ii) investment property; or
(iii) intangible asset which meets the recognition criteria and the criteria for revaluation in Section 18 *Intangible Assets other than Goodwill*

at, or before, the date of transition to this FRS as its deemed cost at the revaluation date.

(e) [Not used]

(f) ***Individual and separate financial statements***

When an entity prepares individual or **separate financial statements**, paragraphs 9.26, 14.4 and 15.9 require the entity to account for its investments in **subsidiaries**, **associates**, and **jointly controlled entities** either at cost less impairment or at fair value.

If a first-time adopter measures such an investment at cost, it shall measure that investment at one of the following amounts in its individual or separate opening statement of financial position, as appropriate, prepared in accordance with this FRS:

(i) cost determined in accordance with Section 9 *Consolidated and Separate Financial Statements*, Section 14 *Investments in Associates* or Section 15 *Investments in Joint Ventures*; or

(ii) deemed cost, which shall be the **carrying amount** at the date of transition as determined under the entity's previous GAAP.

(g) ***Compound financial instruments***

Paragraph 22.13 requires an entity to split a **compound financial instrument** into its liability and equity components at the date of issue. A first-time adopter need not separate those two components if the liability component is not outstanding at the date of transition to this FRS.

(h) [Not used]

(i) ***Service concession arrangements – Accounting by operators***

A first-time adopter is not required to apply paragraphs 34.12E to 34.16A to **service concession arrangements** that were entered into before the date of transition to this FRS. Such service concession arrangements shall continue to be accounted for using the same accounting policies being applied at the date of transition to this FRS.

(j) ***Extractive activities***

A first-time adopter that under a previous GAAP accounted for exploration and development costs for oil and gas properties in the development or production phases, in cost centres that included all properties in a large geographical area may elect to measure oil and gas assets at the date of transition to this FRS on the following basis:

(i) Exploration and evaluation assets at the amount determined under the entity's previous GAAP.

(ii) Assets in the development or production phases at the amount determined for the cost centre under the entity's previous GAAP. The entity shall allocate this amount to the cost centre's underlying assets pro rata using reserve volumes or reserve values as of that date.

The entity shall test exploration and evaluation assets and assets in the development and production phases for impairment at the date of transition to this FRS in accordance with Section 34 *Specialised Activities* or Section 27 *Impairment of Assets* of this FRS respectively, and if necessary, reduce the amount determined in accordance with (i) or (ii) above. For the purposes of this paragraph, oil and gas assets comprise only those assets used in the exploration, evaluation, development or production of oil and gas.

(k) ***Arrangements containing a lease***

A first-time adopter may elect to determine whether an arrangement existing at the date of transition to this FRS contains a **lease** (see paragraph 20.3A) on the basis of facts and circumstances existing at that date, rather than when the arrangement was entered into.

(l) ***Decommissioning liabilities included in the cost of property, plant and equipment***

Paragraph 17.10(c) states that the cost of an item of property, plant and equipment includes the initial estimate of the costs of dismantling and removing the item and restoring the site on which it is located, the obligation for which an entity incurs either when the item is acquired or as a consequence of having used the item during a particular period for purposes other than to produce **inventories** during that period. A first-time adopter may elect to measure this component of the cost of an item of property, plant and equipment at the date of transition to this FRS, rather than on the date(s) when the obligation initially arose.

(m) ***Dormant companies****

A company within the Companies Act definition of a dormant company may elect to retain its accounting policies for reported assets, liabilities and equity at

**Irish company law does not contain an equivalent definition.*

the date of transition to this FRS until there is any change to those balances or the company undertakes any new transactions.

(n) ***Deferred development costs as a deemed cost***

A first-time adopter may elect to measure the carrying amount at the date of transition to this FRS for development costs deferred in accordance with SSAP 13 *Accounting for research and development* as its deemed cost at that date.

(o) ***Borrowing costs***

An entity electing to adopt an accounting policy of capitalising **borrowing costs** as part of the cost of a **qualifying asset** may elect to treat the date of transition to this FRS as the date on which capitalisation commences.

(p) ***Lease incentives***

A first-time adopter is not required to apply paragraphs 20.15A and 20.25A to **lease incentives** provided the term of the lease commenced before the date of transition to this FRS. The first-time adopter shall continue to recognise any residual benefit or cost associated with these lease incentives on the same basis as that applied at the date of transition to this FRS.

(q) ***Public benefit entity combinations***

A first-time adopter may elect not to apply paragraphs PBE34.75 to PBE34.86 relating to **public benefit entity combinations** to combinations that were effected before the date of transition to this FRS. However, if on first-time adoption a **public benefit entity** restates any entity combination to comply with this section, it shall restate all later entity combinations.

(r) ***Assets and liabilities of subsidiaries, associates and joint ventures***

If a subsidiary becomes a first-time adopter later than its parent, the subsidiary shall in its financial statements measure its assets and liabilities at either:

(i) the carrying amounts that would be included in the parent's **consolidated financial statements**, based on the parent's date of transition to this FRS, if no adjustments were made for consolidation procedures and for the effects of the business combination in which the parent acquired the subsidiary; or

(ii) the carrying amounts required by the rest of this FRS, based on the subsidiary's date of transition to this FRS. These carrying amounts could differ from those described in (i) when:

(a) the exemptions in this FRS result in measurements that depend on the date of transition to this FRS; or

(b) the accounting policies used in the subsidiary's financial statements differ from those in the consolidated financial statements. For example, the subsidiary may use as its accounting policy the cost model in Section 17 *Property, Plant and Equipment*, whereas the **group** may use the revaluation model.

A similar election is available to an associate or **joint venture** that becomes a first-time adopter later than an entity that has **significant influence** or **joint control** over it.

However, if an entity becomes a first-time adopter later than its subsidiary (or associate or joint venture) the entity shall, in its consolidated financial statements, measure the assets and liabilities of the subsidiary (or associate or joint venture) at the same carrying amounts as in the financial statements of the subsidiary (or associate or joint venture), after adjusting for consolidation (and equity accounting) adjustments and for the effects of the business combination *in which* the entity acquired the subsidiary (or transaction in which it acquired the associate or joint venture). Similarly, if a parent becomes a first-time adopter for its separate financial statements earlier or later than for its consolidated financial statements, it shall measure its assets and liabilities at the same amounts in both financial statements, except for consolidation adjustments.

(s) ***Designation of previously recognised financial instruments***
This FRS permits a financial instrument (provided it meets certain criteria) to be designated on initial recognition as a financial asset or financial liability at fair value through profit or loss. Despite this an entity is permitted to designate, at the date of transition to this FRS, any financial asset or financial liability at fair value through profit or loss provided the asset or liability meets the criteria in paragraph 11.14(b) at that date.

35.11 If it is **impracticable** for an entity to restate the opening statement of financial position at the date of transition for one or more of the adjustments required by paragraph 35.7, the entity shall apply paragraphs 35.7 to 35.10 for such adjustments in the earliest period for which it is practicable to do so, and shall identify the data presented for prior periods that are not comparable with data for the period in which it prepares its first financial statements that conform to this FRS. If it is impracticable for an entity to provide any disclosures required by this FRS for any period before the period in which it prepares its first financial statements that conform to this FRS, the omission shall be disclosed.

35.11A Where applicable to the transactions, events or arrangements affected by applying these exemptions, an entity may continue to use the exemptions that are applied at the date of transition to this FRS when preparing subsequent financial statements, until such time when the assets and liabilities associated with those transactions, events or arrangements are derecognised.

35.11B Where there is subsequently a significant change in the circumstances or conditions associated with transactions, events or arrangements that existed at the date of transition, to which an exemption has been applied, an entity shall reassess the appropriateness of applying that exemption in preparing subsequent financial statements in order to maintain **fair presentation** in accordance with Section 3 *Financial Statement Presentation*.

DISCLOSURES

Explanation of transition to this FRS

35.12 An entity shall explain how the transition from its previous financial reporting framework to this FRS affected its reported **financial position** and financial **performance**.

Reconciliations

35.13 To comply with paragraph 35.12, an entity's first financial statements prepared using this FRS shall include:

(a) A description of the nature of each change in accounting policy.

(b) Reconciliations of its equity determined in accordance with its previous financial reporting framework to its equity determined in accordance with this FRS for both of the following dates:

(i) the date of transition to this FRS; and

(ii) the end of the latest period presented in the entity's most recent annual financial statements determined in accordance with its previous financial reporting framework.

(c) A reconciliation of the profit or loss determined in accordance with its previous financial reporting framework for the latest period in the entity's most recent annual financial statements to its profit or loss determined in accordance with this FRS for the same period.

If an entity becomes aware of **errors** made under its previous financial reporting framework, the reconciliations required by paragraphs 35.13(b) and (c) shall, to the extent practicable, distinguish the correction of those errors from changes in accounting policies. **35.14**

If an entity did not present financial statements for previous periods, it shall disclose that fact in its first financial statements that conform to this FRS. **35.15**

Approval by the FRC

Financial Reporting Standard 102 *The Financial Reporting Standard applicable in the UK and Republic of Ireland* was approved for issue by the Financial Reporting Council on 5 March 2013, following its consideration of the Accounting Council's Advice for this FRS.

The Accounting Council's Advice to the FRC to issue FRS 102

INTRODUCTION

This report provides an overview of the main issues that have been considered by the Accounting Council in advising the Financial Reporting Council (FRC) to issue FRS 102 *The Financial Reporting Standard applicable in the UK and Republic of Ireland*. The FRC, in accordance with the Statutory Auditors (Amendment of Companies Act 2006 and Delegation of Functions etc) Order 2012 (SI 2012/1741), is the prescribed body for issuing accounting standards in the UK. The Foreword to Accounting Standards sets out the application of accounting standards in the Republic of Ireland. 1

In accordance with the *FRC Codes and Standards: procedures*, any proposal to issue, amend or withdraw a code or standard is put to the FRC Board with the full advice of the relevant Councils and/or the Codes & Standards Committee. Ordinarily, the FRC Board will only reject the advice put to it where: 2

- it is apparent that a significant group of stakeholders has not been adequately consulted;
- the necessary assessment of the impact of the proposal has not been completed, including an analysis of costs and benefits;
- insufficient consideration has been given to the timing or cost of implementation; or
- the cumulative impact of a number of proposals would make the adoption of an otherwise satisfactory proposal inappropriate.

The FRC has established the Accounting Council as the relevant Council to assist it in the setting of accounting standards. 3

ADVICE

All but one member of the Accounting Council is advising the FRC to issue FRS 102 *The Financial Reporting Standard Applicable in the UK and Republic of Ireland*. 4

One member of the Accounting Council, Edward Beale, does not agree with some aspects of the Accounting Council's advice and his dissenting view is set out in the appendix to the Accounting Council's Advice. 5

FRS 100 *Application of Financial Reporting Requirements* and FRS 101 *Reduced Disclosure Framework* which are also part of this suite of financial reporting standards were issued by the FRC in November 2012. The Accounting Council's advice to the FRC on those standards is contained in those standards. 6

BACKGROUND

Accounting standards were formerly developed by the Accounting Standards Board (ASB). The ASB commenced its project to update accounting standards in 2002; Appendix V provides a history of the previous consultations and a summary of how the overall proposals have developed.* 7

FRS 102 was developed from the IASB's IFRS for SMEs to replace the majority of UK accounting standards in a single volume. 8

*** *References in this section and Appendix V are made to the FRC, ASB or Accounting Council, as appropriate in terms of the time period and context of the reference.***

OBJECTIVE

9 During its consultations on updating accounting standards, the ASB (and subsequently the FRC) gave careful consideration to its objective and the intended effects. In developing the requirements in this FRS, FRS 100 and FRS 101, the overriding objective is:

> To enable users of accounts to receive high-quality understandable financial reporting proportionate to the size and complexity of the entity and users' information needs.

10 In achieving this objective, the Accounting Council decided (and the FRC subsequently adopted this decision) that it should provide succinct financial reporting standards that:

- have consistency with global accounting standards through the application of an IFRS-based solution unless an alternative clearly better meets the overriding objective;
- reflect up-to-date thinking and developments in the way businesses operate and the transactions they undertake;
- balance consistent principles for accounting by all UK and Republic of Ireland entities with practical solutions, based on size, complexity, public interest and users' information needs;
- promote efficiency within groups; and
- are cost-effective to apply.

11 The requirements in this FRS were principally consulted on in four exposure drafts:

- FRED 44 *Financial Reporting Standard for Medium-sized Entitles* issued in October 2010;
- FRED 45 *Financial Reporting Standard for Public Benefit Entities* issued in March 2011;
- FRED 48 *Financial Reporting Standard applicable in the UK and Republic of Ireland* issued in January 2012; and
- Amendment to FRED 48 issued in October 2012.

CONSULTATION WITH STAKEHOLDERS

12 The Accounting Council has obtained feedback from stakeholders throughout the project in a variety of ways. Appendix V sets out a history of the consultation on this project. In addition to formal consultation through exposure drafts, and previous consultation papers, feedback has been obtained through an extensive programme of outreach aimed at raising awareness of the proposals and to address the view (held by some) that earlier consultations had not gathered sufficient evidence to support and test its assumptions.

13 The Accounting Council recognised that sometimes stakeholders who will be affected by the outcome of a proposal can be difficult to engage in formal, written consultation. As a result, and in accordance with the principles of Better Regulation it developed an outreach programme that would reach beyond those stakeholders that typically respond to Exposure Drafts.

14 As part of the outreach programme a series of meetings and events took place with lenders to small and medium-sized entities. Lenders noted that financial statements are an important part of their decision-making process when considering providing

finance and whilst a decision to provide finance is not based on financial statements alone, they provide useful information and verification to the lender.

In addition, a review was made of academic research that addressed the users of small and medium-sized entities' financial statements. The conclusion drawn from the research was that many entities requested financial statements from Companies House when considering whether to trade with another entity. The European Federation of Accountants and Auditors (EFAA) issued in May 2011 a statement that identified the users of financial statements noting who the users of SMEs financial statements are and that information on the public record assists all users of financial statements of SMEs by providing, in an efficient manner, basic information that protects their rights. **15**

The Accounting Council considers that the outreach programme, across the project as a whole, has gleaned information from stakeholders who would not normally submit formal responses to a consultation and provided very useful information. The Accounting Council noted that whilst this information was not part of the public record, as formal consultation responses are, it could use the information to assist in finalising the standards, which supplemented the information contained in formal responses. **16**

Consultation with stakeholders carried out by others

In addition to the consultation and outreach work carried out by the Accounting Council itself, the Accounting Council notes that some respondents, notably the accountancy institutes, conducted their own outreach amongst their members in determining their responses to the exposure drafts. **17**

Classification of respondents

When analysing responses to consultations it has been the Accounting Council's practice to classify respondents into a number of standard categories in order to determine whether similar views are consistently held by a particular category of respondents. This classification is set out in the Feedback Statement that accompanies this FRS. **18**

The classification of respondents only allows respondents to be classified to a single category and is based on the main perspective articulated in the response. However, the Accounting Council notes that many people that are interested in financial reporting and respond to consultations have a number of different perspectives, for example those that prepare financial statements often also use the financial statements of customers, suppliers and competitors in making decisions about running their business. **19**

Therefore, there is an inherent limitation in the classification of respondents, which tends to underestimate the number of users of financial statements that have responded. **20**

USING THE IFRS FOR SMEs AS A BASIS

Set out in Appendix V is a history of previous consultations. The ASB first started to consider the future of UK and Republic of Ireland accounting standards following the EU decision to require consolidated accounts of listed companies to comply with IFRS. The long held view is that there can be no justification for two different sets of **21** accounting standards in the UK. Consequently, throughout the various consultations it has been proposed that the new accounting standards should have consistency with global accounting standards; this has continually been supported by the majority of respondents. Therefore the Accounting Council has proceeded with the project on this basis. The Impact Assessment accompanying this standard sets out alternative strategic options that the Accounting Council considered in framing the project (including UK accounting standards not based on IFRS), but taking into account consultation responses these were rejected. Therefore the Accounting Council developed the standard within the strategic context of an IFRS-based solution.

22 The Accounting Council noted that the IFRS for SMEs:

- is a way of achieving a consistent accounting framework, as it is a simplification of IFRS;
- was developed by the IASB and published in 2009, reflecting more up-to-date thinking and developments than current FRS, especially for financial instruments;
- is a single book setting out clear accounting requirements; and
- is a cost effective way of updating current FRS.

23 The Accounting Council noted that one of the most significant changes being introduced in this standard is the changes to the recognition, measurement and disclosures related to financial instruments. Current FRSs contain limited requirements on accounting for financial instruments for unlisted entities or those that do not apply the fair value accounting rules. Entities use derivatives to manage risk and it is important that financial statements recognise and provide disclosures about the effect of those instruments on the entity's performance and position. The Accounting Council believes that the approach under current FRSs, where derivatives are not recognised, does not adequately reflect the risks arising from financial instruments. FRS 102 will lead to an improvement in accounting for financial instruments.

24 The Accounting Council adopted guidelines for developing this standard from the IFRS for SMEs, and noted that some pragmatism was required in determining when it would be appropriate to diverge from the IFRS for SMEs. The objective is high-quality understandable financial reporting, and the standard needs to work within the legal framework in the UK and Republic of Ireland, including enabling the provisions of company law to be adhered to. The guidelines also balance high-quality understandable financial reporting and cost effective application. The high degree of support from respondents for the strategic thrust of the approach to developing the new standards suggested that respondents were prepared to balance high-quality financial reporting and costs/benefits. The Accounting Council therefore concluded that its objective and guidelines for making changes to the IFRS for SMEs should be:

In amending the IFRS for SMEs for application in the UK and Republic of Ireland (RoI) the FRC maintains its commitment to:

(a) ensuring high-quality financial reporting by UK and RoI entities applying FRS 102;
(b) operate under an international accounting framework; and
(c) acknowledge that users' preference for consistent financial reporting must be balanced with costs to preparers.

The guidelines when considering amendments to the IFRS for SMEs are:

(a) changes should be made to permit accounting treatments that exist in FRSs at the transition date that align with EU-adopted IFRS;
(b) changes should be consistent with EU-adopted IFRS unless a non-IFRS-based solution clearly better meets the objective of providing high-quality understandable financial reporting proportionate to the size and complexity of the entity and the users' information needs. In these cases elements of an IFRS-based solution may nevertheless be retained;
(c) use should be made, where possible, of existing exemptions in company law to avoid gold-plating; and
(d) changes should be made to provide clarification, by reference to EU-adopted IFRS, that will avoid unnecessary diversity in practice.

The Accounting Council noted that by providing clarifications within FRS 102 when compared with the IFRS for SMEs it could avoid unnecessary diversity in practice. Similarly, whilst maintaining its commitment to high-quality financial reporting and a global framework, the Accounting Council determined that it should amend the IFRS for SMEs by reference to EU-adopted IFRS. 25

AMENDMENTS MADE TO THE IFRS FOR SMES IN DEVELOPING FRS 102

In developing FRS 102 from the IFRS for SMEs, the Accounting Council advises that a number of amendments should be made to the IFRS for SMEs. The following table identifies the more significant amendments and which of the guidelines were applied in making those amendments. Where an amendment is marked ✓✓ it indicates that the amendment is as a consequence of the decision that the scope of FRS 102 is different from that of the IFRS for SMEs. 26

Amendment	**Guideline**				**Law**
	a)	**b)**	**c)**	**d)**	
Scope					
Elimination of public accountability		✓			
Cross-references to IFRS 8 and IAS 33 for listed entities.				✓✓	
Definition of a financial institution				✓	
Inclusion of public benefit entities		✓			
Presentation					
True and fair override					✓
Statement of financial position					✓
Statement of comprehensive income, including discontinued operations					✓
Statement of changes in equity	✓				

Amendment	Guideline				Law
	a)	b)	c)	d)	
Consolidated financial statements					
Consistency with the Act					✓
ESOPs		✓			
Subsidiaries held exclusively for resale, including in an investment portfolio	✓				
Changes in stake and gains or losses on disposals	✓			✓	✓
Exchanges of businesses for interests in another business (was UITF Abstract 31)				✓	
Accounting policies					
Clarification of when to refer to a SORP in developing accounting policies		✓			
Financial instruments					
Disclosures required by financial institutions (might be considered an expansion of paragraph 11.42 for those entities)				✓✓	
Treatment of loan covenants for determining whether an instrument is basic	✓				
Disclosures for certain financial instruments required by law					✓
Hedge accounting is permitted for a net investment in a foreign operation and in respect of foreign exchange risks in a debt instrument measured at amortised cost	✓	✓			
Borrowing costs may be capitalised in certain circumstances	✓				
Public benefit entities can account for concessionary loans at transaction amount		✓✓			
Fair value option	✓				
Option to apply IAS 39 or IFRS 9 recognition and measurement requirements	✓				
Financial guarantee contracts scoped out of financial instrument accounting		✓			
Property, plant and equipment					
Revaluation	✓				

Amendment	**Guideline**				**Law**
	a)	**b)**	**c)**	**d)**	
Intangible assets					
Capitalisation of development costs					
Revaluation after initial recognition	✓				
Where unable to make a reliable estimate of useful life, it should not exceed 5 years.					✓
Business combinations and goodwill					
Permit merger accounting for group reconstructions			✓		
Permit merger accounting by public benefit entities		✓✓			
Where unable to make a reliable estimate of useful life of goodwill, it should not exceed 5 years.					✓
Leases					
Clarification of definitions				✓	
Clarification of scope for 'arrangements that contain a lease'				✓	
Liabilities and equity					
Clarification of whether an instrument is a financial liability or equity in certain circumstances				✓	
Only disclosure required for non-cash distributions to owners		✓			
Grants					
Introduction of accrual method as an option for accounting for government grants	✓				
Share-based payment					
Clarification that option pricing models are not required particularly for unquoted shares				✓	
Share-based payments granted by another group entity				✓	

Amendment	**Guideline**				**Law**
	a)	**b)**	**c)**	**d)**	
Employee benefits					
Presentation of the cost of a defined benefit pension is consistent with IAS 19's 2011 amendments.		✓			
Recognition of liability by entities in multi-employer schemes with a schedule of funding for a deficit				✓	
Income tax					
Timing differences plus approach		✓			
Revised disclosure requirements		✓			
Guidance on accounting for VAT				✓	
Related party disclosures					
Disclosure exemption for wholly-owned entities			✓		
Specialised activities					
Agriculture – permit historical cost model for biological assets.		✓			
Extractive industries – refer to IFRS 6	✓				
Service concession arrangements – grantors				✓✓	
Service concession arrangements – operators				✓	
Retirement benefit plans		✓			
Heritage assets		✓			
Funding commitments				✓✓	
PBE – incoming resources from non-exchange transactions (including performance-related conditions and restrictions)		✓✓			

Scope of FRS 102

27 In an earlier consultation the Accounting Council proposed a differential financial reporting system based on three tiers of entities using public accountability as a differentiator, which would have required some entities to apply EU-adopted IFRS that would not otherwise have been required to do so. Several concerns were noted about this; the more significant include:

(a) the costs for those entities that would be required to apply EU-adopted IFRS could not be justified in relation to the benefit to users of those entities financial statements;
(b) inconsistencies in the recognition and measurement requirements between EU-adopted IFRS and the proposals at the time for FRS 102 would reduce comparability between entities; and
(c) the application guidance addressing the definition of public accountability remained unclear despite the guidance being developed further from the Policy Proposal.

The Accounting Council wanted to address the concerns from respondents that the costs for those entities that would be required to apply EU-adopted IFRS could not be justified in relation to the benefit to users of those entities' financial statements. As a result it proposed eliminating public accountability as a differentiator and determined that FRS 102 should be applied by entities that were not required to apply EU-adopted IFRS, nor were eligible and chose to apply the FRSSE. Respondents agreed with this approach. **28**

As a consequence various entities that are outside the scope of the IFRS for SMEs are within the scope of FRS 102, typically these are financial institutions. **29**

The Accounting Council noted that a significant number of public benefit entities apply UK accounting standards, and would be within the scope of FRS 102. **30**

Consequences of the scope of FRS 102

As the scope of FRS 102 is wider than the scope of the IFRS for SMEs, there are areas not addressed in the IFRS for SMEs that might be relevant to the broader group of entities applying FRS 102. **31**

In considering these areas the Accounting Council reflected on users' needs for additional information relevant to entities that are listed but not on a regulated market, ie those entities that were in part (a) of the definition of public accountability but were not required by EU Regulation to apply EU-adopted IFRS. This identified that earnings per share, operating segments and accounting for insurance contracts were not addressed in the IFRS for SMEs and accounting requirements would need to be set in these areas. **32**

The Accounting Council, however, noted that in addressing the needs of this broader group of entities it should not lose sight of its objective to provide succinct financial reporting standards. Consequently, consideration was given to whether entities listed on a non-regulated market could apply EU-adopted IFRS for the areas identified by including cross references to EU-adopted IFRS in FRS 102 rather than setting out the requirements in the FRS itself. **33**

The Accounting Council broadly termed as financial institutions those entities that, in accordance with FRED 43 were within the scope of part (b) of the definition of public accountability, (ie entities that hold assets in a fiduciary capacity or take deposits, including credit unions, building societies and investment entities). In considering the users' needs for financial information on financial institutions the Accounting Council noted that FRS 102 set out improvements from current FRS, for the recognition and measurement of financial instruments, however, it had limited specific disclosure requirements for financial instruments. The Accounting Council decided that if it were to eliminate the definition of public accountability it would need to address the disclosure requirements for financial institutions, noting **34** that financial instruments are central to the business model of these entities and how such entities generate wealth and manage risk.

35 Having identified that it would need to improve the disclosure requirements for financial institutions, if it were to remove the definition of public accountability, the Accounting Council sought to find a clear definition of a financial institution. Various options were considered including whether to retain part (b) of the definition of publicly accountable, however this approach was rejected because it did not address the application difficulties raised by respondents to FRED 43.

36 The second option considered was to use the definition in section 467(1) of the Companies Act 2006; one advantage was that this was in part basing the definition on whether the entity was regulated or not.

37 The third option was simply to list the types of entity which should provide additional disclosures for financial instruments. In this regard the Accounting Council gave consideration to its previous accounting standard FRS 13 *Derivatives and Financial Instrument: Disclosures*, which applied a differential disclosure regime depending on the category of entity. On balance the Accounting Council decided that a list of entities provided the clearest approach to determine which entities should be defined as financial institutions. However, the Accounting Council also agreed with some respondents to FRED 48 that a principle behind entities selected for inclusion on the list should be articulated. As a result the Accounting Council added a final item to the list, intended to capture any entities similar to those listed above, which would also add an element of future-proofing to the definition. The Accounting Council advises that a parent entity whose sole activity is to hold investments in other group entities is not a financial institution, but notes that a subsidiary entity engaged solely in treasury activities for the group as a whole is likely to meet the definition of a financial institution.

38 Having undertaken the analysis above, it was concluded that public accountability could be eliminated and FRS 102 could apply to a broader group of entities than the IFRS for SMEs. To address the users' information needs for entities listed on a non-regulated market, FRS 102 includes cross-referencing to EU-adopted IFRS and additional disclosure requirements have been inserted for financial instruments held by financial institutions.

39 The Accounting Council observed that if it were to require a financial institution applying FRS 102 to disclose additional information regarding its financial instruments, it also needed to consider its proposals for reduced disclosures. It decided that financial institutions applying reduced disclosures would not be permitted exemptions from the additional disclosures for financial institutions.

40 The Accounting Council considered whether broadening the scope of FRS 102 would increase the pressure to update the standard (in line with changes being made to full IFRS) more frequently than on a three-year cycle. The Accounting Council agreed that there may be circumstances where FRS 102 would require updating in an interim period between the three-year cycles, but where this occurred the amendments proposed should be limited.

Presentation

41 The Accounting Council considered feedback to FRED 44 and to the draft case studies prepared by its staff that were posted on its website that addressed the interaction between FRED 44 and the presentation formats required by company

law. The Accounting Council noted that there were specific conflicts between the IFRS for SMEs and the formats, specifically the definition of current assets differed between the two sets of requirements.

The Accounting Council considered whether to replicate the requirements set out in company law for the information to be presented in the statement of financial position and the income statement, but was concerned that this would add clutter to FRS 102 which was not consistent with its objectives. However, it needed to work within company law and whilst it had encouraged changes to simplify the Accounting Directives it was unlikely such change would take place in the near future. The Accounting Council decided that it should promote only formats already determined in company law. This would have the consequence of all entities being required to comply with the company law formats, promoting consistency amongst all those preparing financial statements intended to give a true and fair view. **42**

In amending the IFRS for SMEs to include the Companies Act formats, it was noted that the ASB had had a long-standing policy that company law formats on their own were not sufficient and should be supplemented to highlight a range of important components of financial performance to aid users' understanding of the performance of the entity. Therefore some requirements from FRS 3 *Reporting Financial Performance*, notably covering acquisitions, exceptional items and discontinued operations need to be factored in. The IFRS for SMEs was amended so that FRS 102 includes: **43**

(a) the disclosure of post-acquisition revenue and profit or loss of an acquiree in a business combination in the notes to the financial statements;
(b) no mandatory requirement to disclose an operating profit line but guidance, based on IAS 1 *Presentation of Financial Statements*, on matters to consider where entities choose to present operating profit; and
(c) the inclusion of an explicit requirement to disclose material items.

The existing FRS 3 requirement to show separately on the face of the profit and loss account: profits or losses on sale or termination of an operation; costs of a fundamental reorganisation materially affecting the operation and profits; and losses on disposal of fixed assets (all of which would still have to be disclosed where material) has not been included. **44**

The Accounting Council advises that, in view of the company law requirement that turnover includes the turnover from discontinued operations, a practical way of presenting this and the post-tax profit or loss on discontinued operations would be for the information about discontinued operations to be presented via a columnar approach. An example illustrating this is set out in FRS 102. **45**

Consolidated financial statements

Definitions of control, parent and subsidiary

The Accounting Council notes that the definitions of control, parent and subsidiary included in FRS 102 are consistent with the IFRS for SMEs (and based on EU-adopted IFRS prior to the issuing of IFRS 10 *Consolidated Financial Statements*), but differ from those used in current FRS. Some respondents queried whether the definitions should be based on company law. The Accounting Council rejected this suggestion, but noted that by using the IFRS for SMEs definitions (consistently with its objective and guidelines), it was widening the application of control to include certain special purpose entities within the definition of a group. However, as noted below, the Accounting Council advises that this should not include employee benefit **46** trusts and ESOPs (which should continue to be accounted for as if they are assets and liabilities of the sponsoring entity).

Employee benefit trusts, ESOPs and similar arrangements

47 In clarifying the requirements for consolidation, including considering consistency with company law requirements, the Accounting Council noted that the accounting treatment for employee benefit trusts, ESOPs or similar arrangements would give rise to a change in accounting from current FRS. The removal of UITF Abstract 38 *Accounting for ESOP trusts* would mean that such arrangements would no longer be included in individual financial statements but only in consolidated financial statements. Further, for an entity with such an arrangement, which is not a parent entity, a change in accounting requirements would lead to the preparation of 'group' financial statements where they would otherwise not have been required. Therefore the Accounting Council decided to retain the accounting treatment from UITF Abstract 32 *Employee benefit trusts and other intermediate payment arrangements* which are included in Section 9 *Consolidated and Separate Financial Statements* of FRS 102.

Investment entities exemption from consolidation

48 In September 2011 the IASB issued an exposure draft proposing to exempt qualifying investment entities from consolidating their investments. The accounting requirements were finalised and published as an amendment to IFRS 10 *Consolidated Financial Statements*, IFRS 12 *Disclosure of Interests in Other Entities* and IAS 27 *Separate Financial Statements* in October 2012. The Accounting Council noted that without a similar exemption in FRS 102, investment entities eligible to apply FRS 102, would need to elect to prepare EU-adopted IFRS in order to take advantage of the exemption. The Accounting Council did not consider this to be a logical or meaningful outcome and therefore sought to find a solution.

49 Section 405(3) of the Companies Act sets out the circumstances in which a subsidiary may be excluded from consolidation and the Accounting Council must work within these requirements. Section 405(3) permits a subsidiary to be excluded from consolidation on the following grounds:

(a) severe long-term restrictions substantially hinder the exercise of the rights of the parent company over the assets or management of that subsidiary;
(b) the information necessary for the preparation of group accounts cannot be obtained without disproportion expense or undue delay; or
(c) the interest of the parent company is held exclusively with a view to subsequent resale.

50 Taking into account the IASB's publication of *Investment Entities* (Amendments to IFRS 10, IFRS 12 and IAS 27) in October 2012, the Accounting Council advises that the definition of an interest held exclusively with a view to subsequent resale should include interests held as part of an investment portfolio.

51 FRS 102 permits that subsidiaries excluded from consolidation may be measured at fair value through profit or loss. This is a departure from the requirements of the Companies Act for the overriding purpose of giving a true and fair view in the consolidated financial statements.

Changes in stake and gains or losses on disposals

The Accounting Council noted that the requirements of the IFRS for SMEs in relation to changes in stake and gains and losses on disposals were not entirely coherent being based partly on IFRS 3 *Business combinations* (issued 2004) and partly on IFRS 3 *Business combinations* (revised 2008), and further some of the requirements are not consistent with company law provisions on the recognition of unrealised gains. 52

The Accounting Council considered that a coherent model for increases and decreases in stakes held in another entity was required, and that it must be consistent with company law. As a result the requirements of Section 9 *Consolidated and Separate Financial Statements* and Section 19 *Business Combinations and Goodwill* are now based on IFRS 3 (issued 2004), providing an IFRS-based solution that is consistent with company law. 53

Distribution of non-cash assets to owners

The Accounting Council had also been asked to clarify that the distribution of non-cash assets to owners did not apply to distributions within groups. In considering this requirement, the Accounting Council noted a distinction between the disposal of an asset at fair value followed by a distribution to shareholders of the profit, and making a distribution of the asset to shareholders. In its view, a distribution to shareholders does not generate a profit, whereas a disposal does generate a profit that may then be distributed to shareholders. The Accounting Council decided, given it did not support the accounting requirement, to remove the requirement in the IFRS for SMEs to recognise a liability to pay a dividend for a non-cash asset at fair value and to require disclosure of the fair value of the assets distributed to shareholders. 54

Financial instruments

In FREDs 43 and 44 the ASB noted that current FRSs were in need of updating and that they permitted certain transactions not to be recorded. Sections 11 *Basic Financial Instruments* and 12 *Other Financial Instruments Issues* of FRED 44 proposed to address these weaknesses in current FRS. The Accounting Council noted that the IFRS for SMEs has simplified the accounting for financial instruments when compared with IAS 39 *Financial Instruments: Recognition and Measurement*, whilst generally achieving similar accounting. However, there will be areas where those familiar with IAS 39 will need to take care to ensure compliance with FRS 102, for example the hierarchy to be used in determining the fair value of an asset set out in paragraph 11.27 is not the same as the 'fair value hierarchy' set out in IAS 39. 55

The Accounting Council carefully considered the views of respondents to FRED 44 concerning the proposed accounting for financial instruments set out in the FRED. 56

The Accounting Council noted the concern, primarily from the social housing sector, that recognition of derivatives used for hedging purposes at fair value may result in volatility in profit or loss. It considered carefully the requirement to recognise derivatives at fair value but noted that any changes to the financial instrument proposals should be consistent with the guidelines for amending the IFRS for SMEs. The Accounting Council concluded that it would not be consistent with the objective of providing high-quality information, or the guidelines for amending the IFRS for SMEs, to change the recognition requirements for derivatives. Recognition of 57 derivatives, and associated disclosure, will provide relevant information to users about the risks an entity has in relation to its financial instruments.

Impact of the IASB hedge accounting and impairment projects

58 The requirements for hedge accounting and impairment of financial assets in FRS 102 are based on the requirements of IAS 39. The IASB is currently reviewing hedge accounting and impairment requirements (including developing an 'expected loss' model for the recognition of impairments of financial assets) and the Accounting Council is reluctant to propose new accounting requirements in respect of these areas before the IASB's projects are finalised in IFRS 9 *Financial Instruments*. The Accounting Council is concerned that doing so would risk financial instruments requirements in FRS 102 being out of line with both IFRS 9 and IAS 39. Simultaneously, the Accounting Council believes that the next scheduled amendment date for FRS 102 is too far in the future and consequential amendments to FRS 102 may therefore be untimely for entities that would like to apply the new IFRS 9 accounting requirements without undue delay. For that reason the Accounting Council agreed that a proposed amendment to FRS 102 would be issued for public consultation once the IASB has completed the hedge accounting and impairment projects and IFRS 9 has been updated; it is likely that there will be two separate exposure drafts, one addressing each topic. The Accounting Council intends to make amendments to FRS 102 (should the consultation determine this is appropriate) prior its effective date, although the exact timetable of any possible amendment is dependent upon when the IASB completes the impairment and hedge accounting requirements in IFRS 9.

Financial instruments accounting policy choices

59 In order to allow entities applying FRS 102 maximum flexibility, entities have a choice of either:

(a) applying the requirements of Sections 11 and 12 of FRS 102;
(b) applying the recognition and measurement requirements in IAS 39 (as adopted for use in the EU) as the standard applies prior to the application of IFRS 9; or
(c) applying IFRS 9 (as far as it has replaced the requirements in IAS 39) and IAS 39 (as far it remains applicable if IFRS 9 is applied).

By providing these accounting policy choices entities have the flexibility to apply the accounting requirements of IFRS 9 without delay should they wish to do so*. Entities that elect to account for financial instruments by applying the requirements of Sections 11 and 12, especially those entities that choose to apply FRS 102 before its effective date, may be required to change their accounting for financial instruments should some of the requirements in Sections 11 and 12 be amended for consistency with the principles of IFRS 9 in respect of hedge and impairment accounting, once those have been determined.

Disclosures by financial institutions

60 Having defined financial institutions, the Accounting Council advises that additional disclosures should be provided for the financial instruments held by these entities. It developed a proportionate set of disclosures for financial institutions, using IFRS 7 *Financial Instruments: Disclosures* as the basis.

**As FRS 102 is a UK and Republic of Ireland accounting standard, IFRS 9 can be applied through FRS 102 in advance of EU endorsement.*

Fair value option

A number of respondents to FRED 48 noted that bonds within the scope of Section 11 must be measured at amortised cost, even if they are managed on a fair value basis or their measurement at amortised cost introduces measurement differences, and suggested that an option to measure such items at fair value should be permitted in FRS 102. The Accounting Council agreed that, consistently with EU-adopted IFRS, an option should be available to designate financial assets and liabilities to be measured at fair value through profit or loss. **61**

Hedge accounting

In light of the comments received in response to FREDs 44 and 48, and in order to reduce inconsistencies with EU-adopted IFRS, the Accounting Council advises that hedge accounting of a net investment in a foreign operation in consolidated financial statements be permitted and that entities are permitted to hedge foreign exchange risk arising in a debt instrument measured at amortised cost. Consistently with EU-adopted IFRS the Accounting Council also advises that hedge accounting of a net investment in a foreign operation should not be permitted in the separate financial statements of a parent. **62**

Financial guarantee contracts

Respondents to FRED 48 asked for clarification of the accounting requirements for financial guarantee contracts. The accounting for financial guarantee contracts is within the scope of Section 21 *Provisions and Contingencies* unless an entity has chosen to apply IAS 39 and/or IFRS 9, or has an existing accounting policy of insurance contract accounting for financial guarantee contracts and chooses to continue to apply that policy under FRS 103 *Insurance Contracts*. **63**

Group reconstructions

The Accounting Council advises that FRS 102 should retain the current accounting permitted by FRS 6 *Acquisitions and mergers* for group reconstructions. The Accounting Council noted that whilst EU-adopted IFRS does not provide accounting requirements for the accounting for business combinations under common control the accounting provided by FRS 6 is well understood and provides useful requirements. It therefore decided to carry forward these requirements into FRS 102. In practice, the Accounting Council does not expect the introduction of FRS 102 to change the accounting for group reconstructions. For example, where a combination is effected by using a newly formed parent company to hold the shares of each of the parties to a combination, the accounting treatment depends on the substance of the business combination being effected. **64**

Leases

Leases are accounted for in accordance with the requirements of Section 20 *Leases*, except for those leases falling within the scope of Section 12, which are those that could result in a loss to the lessor or the lessee as a result of non-typical contractual terms, for example these that are unrelated to: **65**

(a) changes in the price of the leased asset;
(b) changes in foreign exchange rates; or
(c) a default by one of the counterparties.

66 The Accounting Council notes that the reference to 'changes in the price of the leased asset' is framed widely and in practice it does not expect many leases to fall within the scope of Section 12.

Grants

67 A number of respondents, particularly from the public benefit entity sector, raised concerns about the proposed changes to the recognition requirements for grants received from government and other bodies. The proposals in FRED 44 based the recognition of income from grants on when an entity fulfilled the performance criteria stipulated in the grant. This would have been a change from both current FRS and EU-adopted IFRS which attempt to match grant income with the related expenditure. The Accounting Council observed that the IFRS for SMEs used an approach not in current EU-adopted IFRSs.

68 The Accounting Council reviewed the concerns of entities noting that it could amend the performance criterion approach to provide application guidance on performance outcome. This approach would require a research project to be undertaken and cause delay to the finalisation of FRS 102. An alternative was to amend the requirements in the IFRS for SMEs so that they were consistent with EU-adopted IFRS and defer a research project on the accounting for grants until after the publication of FRS 102. However, respondents also noted that some entities, mainly in the public benefit entity sector, currently recognised income from grants on the basis of performance criteria and that reverting to the requirements of EU-adopted IFRS (which is similar to current FRS) would introduce a change for these entities. The Accounting Council did not wish to implement a change for entities that might be reversed when it subsequently undertook a research project on grant accounting. It therefore concluded it should allow entities a choice between the accounting requirements of the IFRS for SMEs and those in EU-adopted IFRS.

69 The Accounting Council recognises that the respondents to FRED 44 highlighted an inconsistency in current practice and that the solution in FRS 102 is therefore, an interim solution until completion on a research project is undertaken.

70 Respondents have further commented that as Section 24 *Government Grants* is restricted to government grants, grants received by public benefit entities from other sources will be accounted for in accordance with Section 34 *Specialised Activities: Incoming Resources from Non-Exchange Transactions*, and there is now the possibility that the accounting for grants depends on the source of the grant, rather than whether or not the underlying terms and conditions of the grants differ. Whilst this is not ideal, the Accounting Council advises permitting the accrual model for government grants in accordance with its guidelines for amending the IFRS for SMEs as an interim solution to avoid changes in accounting that might be reversed in the future.

71 For those entities that apply the performance model to capital grants, either as an accounting policy choice for government grants, or through applying Section 34 to grants from other sources, the Accounting Council notes that there may be a change from current accounting practice, which may lead to greater volatility in the income statement. The effect of this volatility can be explained in the notes to the financial statements.

Share-based payment

The Accounting Council noted that at present entities in the UK and Republic of Ireland* that enter into share-based payment transactions are required to apply FRS 20 (IFRS 2) *Share-based Payment*. However, for unlisted entities it can be difficult to apply option pricing models and therefore the benefits outweigh the costs. As a result the Accounting Council advises that directors apply judgement by using models that are appropriate to the entity's circumstance. The Accounting Council considers that this provides a cost effective way of recognising the cost of share-based payments. **72**

Employee benefits

The Accounting Council noted that the requirements of FRS 17 *Retirement benefits* are broadly consistent with the equivalent requirements of IAS 19 *Employee Benefits*, which form the basis of the IFRS for SMEs in this area, including the principles for the measurement of the net defined benefit liability and the recognition of plan deficits and surpluses. The disclosure requirements of FRS 102 for defined benefit pension plans are reduced when compared with those in FRS 17. **73**

Cost of a defined benefit plan

Respondents noted that the presentation requirements for post-employment benefit plans were not clear in FRED 44. Specifically a request was made to clarify where the difference between the actual return on plan assets and expected return on plan assets should be presented. The Accounting Council, in considering this request, noted that the presentation requirements in IAS 19 had been amended in 2011. The amendments to IAS 19 were consistent with the ASB's recommendations in its report following the consultation document *The Financial Reporting of Pensions*. In view of this, the Accounting Council decided to update FRS 102 to be consistent with the revised IAS 19, which requires an entity to recognise the net change in the defined benefit liability as follows: **74**

(a) the change in the defined benefit liability arising from employee service rendered during the reporting period in profit or loss;
(b) net interest on the net defined benefit liability in profit or loss; and
(c) remeasurement of the net defined benefit liability in other comprehensive income.

In advising this amendment, the Accounting Council also noted that the accounting requirements in the IFRS for SMEs for group pension plan arrangements were more stringent than those set out in IAS 19 (revised 2011). The Accounting Council therefore decided to update these requirements to be consistent with the IAS 19 (revised 2011). **75**

Group defined benefit pension plans

Consistently with IAS 19 (revised 2011) paragraph 28.38 of FRS 102 requires entities participating in a group defined benefit pension plan to recognise the net defined benefit cost in their individual financial statements where a relevant agreement or policy exists. Otherwise the entity that is legally responsible for the group pension plan will recognise the entire net defined benefit cost in its individual financial statements. The Accounting Council noted that although this paragraph only refers **76**

**Other than those applying the FRSSE.*

explicitly to the cost of the pension plan, the net defined benefit cost is calculated by reference to both the defined benefit obligation and the fair value of plan assets. Therefore paragraph 28.38 does require the recognition of the relevant net defined benefit liability in the individual financial statements of any group entities recognising a net defined benefit cost.

Multi-employer defined benefit plans

77 In October 2012 the FRC issued an exposure draft of proposed amendments to FRED 48, including amendments to Section 28 *Employee Benefits*. These amendments related to multi-employer defined benefit plans that are accounted for as defined contribution plans. The Accounting Council is aware that diversity in accounting practice had arisen in relation to entities who participate in a defined benefit multi-employer plan, who account for that plan as a defined contribution plan and who have entered into a funding agreement for future payments relating to past service liabilities, to recognise a liability in relation to the deficit in the plan in their financial statements.

78 Consistently with the guidelines for amending the IFRS for SMEs, the Accounting Council advises incorporating the relevant requirement from IAS 19 and notes that the IASB's basis for conclusions said that 'In relation to the funding of a deficit, [...] this principle [is] consistent with the recognition of a provision in accordance with IAS 37.'

79 The Accounting Council also advises clarifying the measurement requirements for such a liability. In the circumstances that the entity has entered into a funding agreement for future payments relating to past service it shall recognise those future payments as a liability, discounted using the methodology for selecting a discount rate for post-employment benefit liabilities. The Accounting Council debated whether the discount rate should alternatively be based on the entity's cost of capital, but decided to advise the use of a rate consistent with the methodology used for accounting for other pension liabilities.

80 The Accounting Council noted that some respondents to the exposure draft disagreed with the proposed amendment or requested a delay in implementation, but the Accounting Council believes that where participants in a multi-employer defined benefit pension plan have entered into an agreement to fund a deficit, and have applied defined contribution accounting, a liability exists and its recognition provides useful information to users.

81 Some respondents suggested that FRS 102 should also address situations where a multi-employer pension plan was in surplus, and entered into an agreement to distribute that surplus to the participating employers. Although the Accounting Council noted that this is addressed in IAS 19, it expected that the situation would arise rarely in practice, and considered that entities would be able to determine the appropriate accounting using the principles set out in FRS 102. Therefore it does not advise making an amendment for this.

Income tax

82 In FRED 44 the ASB proposed using the text of IAS 12 *Income Taxes* in place of the IFRS for SMEs section on income tax. The ASB had amended the tax section of the IFRS for SMEs because it had been based on proposals subsequently abandoned by the IASB and therefore the IFRS for SMEs was not consistent with full IFRS. Respondents to the Policy Proposal had not supported retaining the IFRS for SMEs requirements in this area. Respondents to FRED 44 had accepted that the IFRS for SMEs treatment could not be used, but did not support the ASB's proposal to replace the tax section with IAS 12.

In developing FRED 48 the ASB considered what would be the most suitable alternative, and took into account the findings of its research work with EFRAG in developing the Discussion Paper *Improving the Financial Reporting of Income Tax* (issued in December 2011), as well as its commitment to an IFRS-based solution and the requirements of FRS 19 *Deferred Tax* from which entities would be transitioning. It set out an alternative approach that based the recognition requirements on timing differences, with additional recognition requirements for certain temporary differences that are not timing differences, which was referred to as a 'timing differences plus' approach. The advantages of this approach seemed to be that it would: **83**

(a) provide useful information to users of financial statements; and
(b) provide the simple solution preparers were looking for that was close to current FRS and that would give the same answers as IFRSs in most cases.

Most respondents supported the 'timing differences plus' approach, which has therefore been retained in FRS 102. **84**

The most significant change to the requirements in current FRS is that the proposed approach requires the recognition of the deferred tax implications of the revaluation of assets. Gains and losses recognised on a revaluation are timing differences and the tax effects should be recognised. Such a requirement is consistent with IAS 12 and the IFRS for SMEs. **85**

Another significant change from current FRS is that discounting of current and deferred tax is not allowed which is consistent with the IFRS for SMEs. **86**

Under IAS 12 deferred tax is not generally recognised on the initial recognition of an asset, except that of assets and liabilities arising from a business combination. No specific exception for this is necessary under the 'timing differences plus' approach as no timing difference arises. The proposed treatment is therefore consistent in this respect with IAS 12. **87**

A pure timing difference approach does not provide complete consistency with the requirements of IAS 12. In particular, IAS 12 requires that deferred tax is recognised in respect of the difference between the amount recognised on a business combination for assets and liabilities (other than goodwill) and the amount that will be allowed for or assessed to tax in respect of such assets and liabilities. These differences are not timing differences. In order to maintain consistency with IFRS on this major issue, the Accounting Council agreed to supplement the timing difference approach with a requirement to recognise deferred tax on business combinations. **88**

However, the 'timing differences plus' approach adopted in FRS 102 does not ensure complete consistency with the requirements of IAS 12. For example FRS 102 does not permit the recognition of deferred tax: **89**

(a) where the tax deduction (or estimated future deduction) for share-based payment exceeds the cumulative amount of the related remuneration expense; and
(b) in some cases, where the tax basis of an asset is changed, for example where legislation changes the amount of future tax relief relating to the asset.

The Accounting Council considered, however, that the differences from IAS 12 were likely to be relatively rare and that in such cases the relevance of the information produced in accordance with IAS 12 was unclear. **90**

91 The proposed disclosure requirements have been reviewed in the light of comments on FRED 48. In particular the requirement to disclose differences between the current tax charge and a standard rate of tax for the next three years has been replaced by a requirement to disclose expected net reversals of timing differences for the next year. The requirement to disclose is on a net basis, which takes account of both the reversal of existing timing differences and the origination of new ones. The net basis provides information that is relevant to the entity's future cash flows, and hence is more relevant than disclosure on a gross basis. The Accounting Council considers that the additional benefit of disclosure on a net basis outweighed the cost to preparers of forecasting future new timing differences.

Related party disclosures

92 In response to feedback from respondents, the Accounting Council advises that the company law exemption from disclosing intra-group related party transactions should be included in FRS 102.

93 Some respondents raised the issue of a possible exemption from the disclosure of outstanding balances as well as transactions. However, the Accounting Council noted that there is a separate legal requirement, in relation to the format of the balance sheet which requires disclosure of outstanding balances in aggregate for group undertakings and, separately, for undertakings in which the company has a participating interest. As Section 33 *Related Party Disclosures* requires disclosure in aggregate for a category of related parties, one of which is 'entities over which the entity has control, joint control or significant influence' this should be met by compliance with the requirements of Section 4 *Statement of Financial Position*. As a result it is not possible to provide an effective exemption from the disclosure of outstanding balances with group undertakings.

Specialised activities

Agriculture

94 The IFRS for SMEs includes guidance for specialised activities including agriculture. The proposed requirements for agriculture are a predominately fair value model and are based on IAS 41 *Agriculture*. Respondents questioned the proposed requirements noting that current FRSs do not set out accounting requirements and although the proposals included an exemption from applying fair value where there is undue cost or effort, the fair value information is inconsistent with the way most agricultural businesses are managed and would not benefit the users of financial statements.

95 The Accounting Council evaluated the comments raised and advises that entities engaged in agricultural activities should be permitted an accounting policy choice for their biological assets, between the cost model and fair value model set out in the IFRS for SMEs.

96 The Accounting Council noted that both the cost model and the fair value model, as set out in the IFRS for SMEs, require agricultural produce to be measured at the point of harvest at fair value less costs to sell. However, it considered that respondents in favour of the cost model would have expected the cost model to mean that both biological assets and agricultural produce would be measured at cost.

97 The Accounting Council noted that agricultural produce should be capable of measurement at fair value without undue cost or effort, and should provide more relevant information to users. However, it noted that respondents argued that

agricultural businesses often manage their business on the basis of cost information and advises that agricultural produce should be permitted to be measured at cost. The Accounting Council advises limiting the use of the cost model for agricultural produce to those entities that have chosen the cost model for biological assets; however these entities should also have the option of using the fair value model for agricultural produce.

Extractive activities

Respondents noted that the requirements of the IFRS for SMEs in relation to extractive activities were not consistent with IFRS 6 *Exploration for and Evaluation of Mineral Resources*, and the application of the IFRS for SMEs requirements, in conjunction with other elements of FRS 102 would significantly change accounting practices for entities engaged in extractive activities. It would be likely that no assets could be recognised from the costs of exploration activities, yet entities applying EU-adopted IFRS would be permitted to recognise such assets. **98**

The Accounting Council agreed that entities applying FRS 102 should not be prohibited from applying accounting policies that are available to those entities applying EU-adopted IFRS, and advises that the requirements of IFRS 6 are incorporated into FRS 102 by cross reference. **99**

Service concession arrangements

Respondents raised two main issues relating to the accounting for service concession arrangements. The first was that the requirements of the IFRS for SMEs in relation to the accounting by operators had been over-simplified when compared with IFRIC 12 *Service Concession Arrangements*. The Accounting Council agreed and FRS 102 includes additional clarification of the principles of accounting by operators for service concession arrangements, which were developed from IFRIC 12. **100**

The second issue related to grantors, with some respondents noting that grantors might be within the scope of FRS 102. This was addressed in the October 2012 exposure draft of proposed amendments to FRED 48 issued by the FRC. **101**

EU-adopted IFRS does not address accounting by grantors of service concession arrangements; grantors are expected to be outside the scope of EU-adopted IFRS. As a result, and consistently with the guidelines for amending the IFRS for SMEs, the Accounting Council sought to develop accounting for grantors that is consistent with the principles underpinning the accounting by operators of service concession arrangements, which is set out in IFRIC 12. The scope of IFRIC 12 is such that the grantor controls the residual interest in the infrastructure asset, and therefore for service concession arrangements meeting the definition in FRS 102, the Accounting Council advises that the grantor recognises its interest in the infrastructure asset usually as property, plant and equipment, with a corresponding liability measured using a finance lease model. **102**

The Accounting Council noted that the International Public Sector Accounting Standards Board (IPSASB) has issued a standard IPSAS 32 *Service Concession Arrangements: Grantor*, which includes two models for accounting by the grantor, depending on the terms of the arrangement with the operator. In addition to the finance lease model advised by the Accounting Council, IPSAS 32 includes a 'grant of right to the operator model' which applies to 'user-pays' arrangements. The Accounting Council does not advise the application of this model because it appears to result in the recognition as liabilities of amounts that may not meet the definition **103** of a liability. However, some respondents to the exposure draft suggested that this model should be permitted. The Accounting Council advises that further research should be carried out on the most appropriate accounting for user-pays service concession arrangements, but that this should not delay the issue of FRS 102.

104 The Accounting Council considered whether transitional provisions should be available for grantors. It noted that for some grantors, the proposals would result in recognising assets and liabilities for the infrastructure assets that are not presently recognised. It considered that this provides more relevant information to users, and therefore advises the FRC that transitional provisions should not be available. As a result grantors will not be permitted to apply the transitional exemptions that are available to operators, as set out in FRS 102 paragraph 35.10(i), by analogy.

Retirement benefit plans

105 FRED 43 proposed that retirement benefit plans were publicly accountable and therefore should apply EU-adopted IFRS, but having decided to eliminate the definition of publicly accountable, retirement benefit plans are now within the scope of FRS 102, yet the IFRS for SMEs contains no specific provisions for retirement benefit plans.

106 The Accounting Council considered whether to direct retirement benefit plans to IAS 26 *Accounting and Reporting by Retirement Benefit Plans* and request that the Statement of Recommended Practice (SORP) *Financial Reports of Pension Schemes* be updated to be consistent with IAS 26. This option was, however, rejected based on feedback which suggested that the application of IAS 26 would be difficult for two reasons:

(a) legal accounting and reporting requirements in the UK are different to those in IAS 26; and
(b) IAS 26 itself makes references to other IFRSs and the interaction between these references and FRS 102 would be complicated.

A further complication would arise as the SORP would also provide application guidance for retirement benefit plans.

107 Following this feedback the Accounting Council decided to develop, as part of the specialised activities section, accounting requirements for retirement benefit plans financial statements that could be supplemented by the SORP.

108 In developing the proposals, the Accounting Council considered the issue of whether the financial statements of retirement benefit plans need to provide disclosure regarding the pension liabilities and the related funding of the plan. Following feedback from respondents, the Accounting Council decided that such information should not be recognised in the financial statements, but provided alongside it, as is currently the case.

109 The Accounting Council advises that because of the way in which retirement benefit plans use financial instruments they should be considered to be financial institutions. However, not all of the disclosure requirements for financial institutions are relevant to retirement benefit plans and it will be more user-friendly to have all requirements in one place. Therefore Section 34 sets out all the requirements for retirement benefit plans in one sub-section.

Insurance contracts

FRED 48 proposed that entities with insurance contracts should apply IFRS 4 *Insurance Contracts* to those contracts. In addition, insurance-related contracts not meeting the definition of an insurance contract shall usually be accounted for as financial instruments in accordance with Sections 11 and 12. **110**

The FRC also has FRS 27 *Life Assurance* in issue. The Accounting Council debated the various options for setting out the requirements for entities engaged in insurance business, and decided that it should advise the FRC to issue a separate accounting standard on insurance contracts, FRS 103 *Insurance Contracts*. An exposure draft of this standard will be available after FRS 102 has been issued, but FRS 102 cross-refers to it. The Accounting Council's Advice to the FRC to issue FRS 103 will be set out in that standard. **111**

Other options available in EU-adopted IFRS

Respondents to FRED 44, in general, supported the use of the IFRS for SMEs as a base for a future financial reporting standard in the UK and Republic of Ireland. There were, however, concerns raised that would require careful consideration, most notably the removal of certain accounting treatments (options) that are available in current FRSs and EU-adopted IFRS but were not proposed in FRED 44. **112**

Responses from the housing associations particularly focused on how the removal of options might have behavioural implications that the Accounting Council should take into consideration. The housing associations noted that: **113**

(a) the removal of the options would reduce comparability between entities that apply EU-adopted IFRS and those applying FRED 44 for entities operating in the same market, for example entities applying FRED 44 would not be permitted to revalue property, plant and equipment whereas entities applying EU-adopted IFRS could; and
(b) the inability to include borrowing costs as part of the costs of property, plant and equipment may cause some housing associations to breach terms and conditions of current financing arrangements; this gave potential for banks and other lenders to renegotiate existing financing arrangements but at a higher cost of capital.

Other respondents noted that removal of the accounting options was potentially an over-simplification for the UK and Republic of Ireland. These respondents noted the IFRS for SMEs had been developed by the IASB for countries that had a less developed financial reporting framework than the UK and Republic of Ireland. They considered that as options existed in current FRSs the simplification had not been justified by the Accounting Council. **114**

A further view put forward by respondents was that retaining the options that existed in current FRS would reduce transition costs and ease transition between the different standards and also with EU-adopted IFRS. **115**

Application of the guidelines permitted the introduction of accounting options that exist in current FRS and EU-adopted IFRS that respondents had highlighted as reducing comparability. FRS 102 therefore includes accounting options for: **116**

(a) capitalisation of borrowing costs;
(b) revaluation of property, plant and equipment and intangible assets; and
(c) capitalisation of development costs, in certain circumstances.

Providing clarifications in FRS 102

117 Having agreed guidelines that include making amendments to the IFRS for SMEs to provide clarifications, the Accounting Council considered relevant requests from respondents. Some clarifications were made by reference to EU-adopted IFRS (see column (d) of the table at paragraph 26 of the Accounting Council's Advice), others were made by reference to current FRS, for example whether there is an interaction with company law. As a result a number of clarifications have been made, examples include:

(a) disclosure requirements for discontinued operations;
(b) treatment of loan covenants, so that the treatment is consistent with IFRS 9 *Financial Instruments*;
(c) financial instruments that would be equity under IAS 32 *Financial Instruments: Presentation* are not liabilities, when an entity is required to prepare consolidated financial statements;
(d) when an investor that is not a parent but has an investment in one or more associates and/or jointly controlled entities shall account for its investments and/or jointly controlled entities using either cost or fair value;
(e) the presumed life for goodwill, in particular when an entity is otherwise unable to make a reliable estimate shall not be in excess of five years and thereby consistent with company law. The same also applies to intangible assets;
(f) accounting treatment for group share-based payments where the award is granted by the parent or another group entity; and
(g) that option pricing models are not required for the value of shared-based payments, particularly for unquoted shares or share options.

Other matters

118 The Accounting Council considered whether to provide guidance for the term 'undue cost or effort' where respondents had sought clarification. The Accounting Council noted that Section 2 *Concepts and Pervasive Principles* discussed the balance between benefit and cost and that no further clarification was required.

The retention of Urgent Issue Task Force (UITF) Abstracts

119 FREDs 43 and 44 proposed to withdraw all UITF Abstracts except UITF Abstract 43 *The Interpretation of equivalence for the purposes of section 228A of the Companies Act*. Respondents to the FRED proposed that in addition to UITF Abstract 43, other UITF Abstracts should be retained. The Accounting Council gave consideration to this request and noted that rather than retain UITF Abstracts, consistent with its objective to provide succinct financial reporting standards, it should incorporate any guidance into FRS 102.

120 Based on feedback the Accounting Council advises that the following accounting requirements of UITF Abstracts are retained by incorporation, as follows:

UITF Abstract		**Action**
4	*Presentation of long-term debtors in current assets*	Incorporated into the legal appendix.
31	*Exchange of businesses or other non-monetary assets for an interest in a subsidiary, joint venture or associate*	Additional paragraphs 9.31 and 9.32 are inserted.
32	*Employee benefit trusts and other intermediate payment arrangements*	Additional paragraphs are inserted into Section 9.
43	*The interpretation of equivalence for the purposes of section 228A of the Companies Act 1985*	The guidance has been updated and included as application guidance to FRS 100.

The Accounting Council decided to advise the withdrawal of UITF Abstract 48 *Accounting implications of the replacement of the retail prices index with the consumer prices index for retirement benefits* as the circumstance it addressed were related to a one time period which has now expired. **121**

Interaction with company law

The Accounting Council gave careful consideration to the comments received to its draft legal appendix set out in FREDs 44 and 48. The Accounting Council agreed with respondents' views that the appendix should address entities that are not companies. **122**

The Accounting Council also considered whether it should retain, as proposed in FRED 44, accounting options that had been removed because the option conflicted with company law, where an entity that is not a company would not be restricted in the same way as a company. For example, SSAP 4 Accounting for *government grants* contained an option that was not permitted by the company law. **123**

The Accounting Council confirmed the position it had taken in developing FRED 44 that options that existed in the IFRS for SMEs, but not permitted by company law, should be removed. This would promote consistency between reporting entities regardless of the legal framework under which they operate. **124**

Public benefit entities (PBEs)

The Consultation Paper *Policy Proposal: The Future of UK GAAP* (issued in 2009) set out 10 issues that could be included in a Public Benefit Entities (PBEs) specific standard. However, these 10 issues were refined to six which were deemed to be those most significant and relevant to the PBE sectors that were not satisfactorily addressed by the IFRS for SMEs. These six issues were: **125**

(a) Concessionary loans;
(b) Property held for the provision of social benefits;
(c) Entity combinations;
(d) Impairment of assets: public benefit considerations;
(e) Funding commitments; and
(f) Incoming resources from non-exchange transactions.

Concessionary loans

126 Paragraphs have been inserted into Section 34 *Specialised Activities* to address the accounting requirements for PBEs making and receiving concessionary loans.

127 There are two main accounting treatments to consider when determining the basis for the measurement of concessionary loans; the amount paid or received, and fair value. This has been the subject of significant discussion and debate by the Accounting Council, taking into account the information that users of PBE accounts may consider useful and the difficulties that may arise for smaller organisations in measuring concessionary loans at fair value.

128 Accounting for concessionary loans at the amount paid or received rather than fair value is not consistent with the accounting requirements set out in either Section 11 of FRS 102, EU-adopted IFRS or IPSAS 29 *Financial Instruments: Recognition and Measurement* (which require that such arrangements are measured and recognised in the financial statements at their fair value).

129 Nevertheless the Accounting Council advises that due to the difficulties that smaller PBEs may face with using fair value, PBEs that make or receive concessionary loans may have the option of measuring such loans at either the amount paid or received or at fair value. However, PBEs that make and receive concessionary loans must apply the same measurement method to both. Further the Accounting Council proposes that the same accounting may be applied by other wholly-owned entities in a public benefit entity group, to eliminate the need to restate concessionary loans made or received for the purposes of furthering the PBEs objectives on consolidation.

130 Presentation and disclosure of concessionary loan arrangements are an important part of the proposals for concessionary loans and the Accounting Council concluded that the disclosure requirements in FRS 102 will provide sufficient information to understand and interpret the impact of this type of transaction on the financial statements.

Property held for the provision of social benefits

131 Subsequent to FRED 45, the Accounting Council decided that the requirements for property held for the provision of social benefits should apply to all entities applying FRS 102 and should not be restricted to PBEs.

132 Consideration was given as to whether properties that are held for the provision of social benefits meet the definition of an investment property. The definition of investment property in paragraph 16.2 of FRS 102, excludes properties held for use in the production or supply of goods and services or for administrative purposes. A property held to earn rentals and/or for capital appreciation, but not used in the production or supply of goods or services, meets this definition. The Accounting Council noted that although many PBEs that engage in the provision of social housing receive rental income, their primary purpose is to provide social benefits.

133 Provision of social housing is akin to supplying a service and therefore, property held for the primary purpose of providing social benefits should be excluded from the scope of investment property and be accounted for as property, plant and equipment.

The Accounting Council acknowledges that PBEs may hold 'investment properties' which are not held primarily to provide social benefits and will return market value rentals and/or are held for their capital appreciation. FRS 102 requires those properties to be accounted for as investment properties. **134**

Public benefit entity combinations

In considering the issue of entity combinations involving two or more public benefit entities, the Accounting Council noted that there is some debate over whether the use of acquisition accounting for all combinations would be appropriate. In particular whether acquisition accounting reflects the substance of a transaction if there is a gift of one entity to another in a combination at nil or nominal consideration, or where two or more organisations genuinely merge to form a new entity. **135**

Where there is a combination of entities at nil or nominal consideration which is in substance a gift, it is appropriate to follow the same accounting principles as donations of assets (as set out in Section 34 *Specialised Activities: Incoming Resources from Non-Exchange Transactions*) by recognising the fair value of the assets received and liabilities assumed as a gain or loss in income and expenditure. **136**

Accounting for combinations that meet the definition of a merger requires a different methodology to acquisition accounting in order to reflect the true substance of the transaction. Whilst it is not anticipated that all combinations involving two or more public benefit entities are mergers or that merger accounting will generally be applicable to such combinations it is considered appropriate to retain merger accounting in certain circumstances. In considering this matter it was noted that the accounting requirements for PBEs in some jurisdictions, for example, the US and Australia have recently been reviewed and noted that merger accounting has been retained for the public and not-for-profit sectors. **137**

In retaining merger accounting, the Accounting Council considered the criteria to be met for a merger. The criteria set out in FRS 6 *Acquisitions and Mergers* provided a starting point, but are framed in the context of the commercial sector and therefore the criteria have been adapted to make them more appropriate for public benefit entities. In particular, a criterion has been added to include consideration of the impact of the combination on beneficiaries and the benefits to which they are entitled. **138**

One specific concern highlighted in relation to the requirements of FRS 6, is the need to restate comparatives by adding together the previous periods' reported figures of each of the combining entities. This does not reflect the substance of the transaction as the historical parties which formed the entity did not exist in the previous accounting period and therefore FRS 102 requires that comparatives are marked as 'combined' to make it clear that they are a combination of previously reported figures for the combining entities. **139**

Impairment of assets

FRS 102 requires impaired assets to be measured at the lower of their fair value less costs to sell and their value in use. In a for-profit context, value in use is determined by measuring the present value of the cash flows derived from the asset. However, often PBE assets are held for their service potential rather than their ability to generate cash flows. In such a case it is sometimes impossible to determine value in use by reference to cash flows and it is more appropriate to regard value in use as the present value of future service potential rather than cash flows. **140**

141 International Public Sector Accounting Standard (IPSAS) 21 *Impairment of Non-Cash Generating Assets* permits value in use to be determined by any of three approaches:

(a) depreciated replacement cost (DRC);
(b) restoration cost; and
(c) the service units approach.

Restoration cost and the service units approach are applications of DRC as DRC is used as the starting point. DRC reflects the cash outflows that are saved through ownership of an asset and is likely to be widely applicable and appropriate for PBEs. Therefore FRS 102 permits a service potential driven valuation to be used for assets held for their service potential.

142 The use of DRC is not mandated; other methods that value service potential rather than cash flows may be used if those methods are more appropriate in those particular circumstances.

143 FRED 45 only allowed this alternative valuation method for PBEs, however subsequent to that consultation, the Accounting Council advises that any entity that holds an asset for service potential can use a service potential valuation method. It is not expected that, for example, headquarters buildings that do not generate cash flows independently of other assets or groups of assets but nevertheless contribute to the cash-generating activities of the entity, will usually be measured on the basis of their service potential.

144 The Accounting Council also discussed whether a restriction on the use of an asset would affect its fair value. As an asset's fair value is based on the amount that an entity could obtain, restrictions might impact on the fair value where they prevent a purchaser from using the asset for another purpose that would be more valuable than that required by the restriction. In addition, the costs to sell should include the costs of breaking the restriction.

145 Another issue for discussion was indicators of impairment. Although the indicators provided in FRS 102 are mainly linked to the expected cash flow of an asset and as such may not necessarily be relevant to some PBE assets, the Accounting Council considered that they must, as a minimum, be considered by PBEs as possible indicators of impairment.

146 In addition, the Accounting Council noted that other accounting literature (eg IPSAS 21 and SORPs) identified other indicators of impairment including:

(a) cessation, or near cessation of the demand or need for services provided by the asset;
(b) social, demographic or environmental changes resulting in a reduction of beneficiaries; and
(c) a major loss of key employees associated with particular activities.

147 The Accounting Council concluded that it would not be appropriate to include these indicators in FRS 102, as they are not exclusively relevant to PBEs and because the indicators given in FRS 102 will continue to apply to PBEs. Therefore, their inclusion would make such entities subject to a confusing list of overlapping indicators. The indicators given in FRS 102 are merely minimum requirements, and recognition of an impairment loss is required irrespective of whether any of the given indicators are met.

The Accounting Council also considered whether to specify that an indicator of impairment was present where an asset's service potential was not fully utilised and noted that an entity may require standby or surplus capacity to ensure that it has adequate capacity to provide services at all times. For example, a building that provides accommodation for the homeless may not be used to full capacity during the summer months but is utilised fully during winter. In this circumstance, the surplus capacity is part of the required service potential of the asset and the asset is not impaired. For this reason, it was concluded that it would be inappropriate to specify that the unutilised capacity should be treated as an indicator of impairment. **148**

Funding commitments

The Accounting Council also discussed when to recognise a commitment to provide funding in a non-exchange transaction. The *Statement of Principles: Interpretation for Public Benefit Entities* previously addressed this issue, and it was considered necessary to incorporate these details into FRS 102 to be used in conjunction with Sections 2 *Concepts and Pervasive Principles* and 21 *Provisions and Contingencies*. **149**

The issue was identified as being particularly important because many PBEs provide funding on an on-going basis and there is little guidance on how such multi-year commitments should be recognised. **150**

The Accounting Council considered when a liability for such a commitment should be recognised and determined that an entity would only recognise a liability if the commitment to provide funding was made unconditionally, and the grantor could not realistically withdraw from the commitment. In this situation, an entity would recognise a liability for the present value of the total funding promised. **151**

As this is an application of the principles in Sections 2 and 21, the Accounting Council advises that the requirements for funding commitments should apply to all entities and not just PBEs. **152**

Incoming resources from non-exchange transactions

The receipt of resources from non-exchange transactions is an inflow of resources that is highly significant for many PBEs: the receipt of donations, grants and legacies from non-exchange transactions are a major source of their funding and this issue is not addressed in the IFRS for SMEs apart from in Section 24 *Government Grants*. **153**

The Accounting Council considered that for PBE financial statements to be complete, they should reflect the benefit that the inflow of these resources had to the entity. FRS 102 requires, in principle, PBEs to value the resources they receive from non-exchange transactions at their fair value. The Accounting Council discussed whether using fair value would overstate the value of a donation where the entity is unable to exploit fully an asset, and the equivalent service potential could be derived from a lower value asset. Being able to achieve the same service potential from a lower value asset might suggest that the value of the donated asset should be at the lower value. However, FRS 102 requires donated assets to be valued at their fair value. This reflects that the circumstances described above would rarely occur. In many cases, an entity would be able to sell the donated asset and if appropriate, purchase a cheaper asset with the equivalent service potential. **154**

Incorporating an exception for donated assets which may not be fully exploited would make the application of FRS 102 more onerous, as it would require all entities in receipt of donated assets (except those intended for resale) to consider whether **155** they would be able to exploit the asset fully. This would be subjective and may incur the risk of understatement of the value of donated assets.

156 The Accounting Council noted that where goods are donated for subsequent sale (for example donations to charity shops), it could be argued that the donated goods should be valued only when they are sold. This is not consistent with the accruals concept which requires the financial statements to recognise goods when they are received. However, the Accounting Council advises, on pragmatic grounds, that donated goods should only be recognised as income on receipt when the item is material, can be measured reliably and if the benefits of recognising the item outweigh the costs. Further the Accounting Council proposes that the same accounting may be applied by other wholly-owned entities in a public benefit entity group, to eliminate the need to restate goods donated for subsequent sale on consolidation (for example where a charity operates it shops through a subsidiary that is a non-charitable company).

157 FRS 102 requires donated services that would otherwise have been purchased to be accounted for at their estimated value to the recipient. This is a pragmatic solution recognising that there are potential issues in determining a value for volunteer services and their contribution to the organisation and notes that quantifying this type of service may not be practicable. There is an argument to suggest that valuing volunteer services could be measured by reference to a metric such as the minimum wage, however this measure does not take into consideration an organisation's requirements for volunteers. In addition, this would be attributing an arbitrary value onto a volunteer's time which may not be reflective of their skills, experience or role and to determine a different method of valuation would be very subjective.

158 However, when a service is provided voluntarily for which the entity would otherwise have to pay (eg legal or financial advice) the value of that service should be recognised in the financial statements where, as will usually be the case, its value can be reasonably quantified.

Other PBE issues

159 The Accounting Council discussed the issue of reporting entity control and the indicators of control that may be specific to the PBE sectors. The indicators of control set out in Section 9 *Consolidated and Separate Financial Statements* of FRS 102 focus on benefits, and in the PBE sectors benefit can be in the form of indirect benefit through a PBE's beneficiaries or benefit which furthers a PBE's activities. Following discussion of these issues the Accounting Council advises that FRS 102 can be interpreted and applied to PBEs and therefore no separate guidance for PBEs is considered necessary.

160 A number of additional topics were identified through the development of FRS 102, which may be considered in the future and as possible updates to FRS 102. The following table summarises these subjects:

Narrative Reporting	To consider narrative reporting requirements for public benefit entities and any specific matters.
Fresh Start Accounting	To consider the concept of fresh start accounting as an alternative accounting treatment for entity combinations where the effect of a combination is to create a new entity that cannot be reasonably portrayed as the enlargement of a pre-existing party.

Social Benefit Obligations	To consider if and how social benefit obligations should be recognised and measured in the financial statements. The International Public Sector Accounting Standards Board currently have a project addressing this issue and it is likely to be most productive to await the outcome of that work.
Fund Accounting	To consider how fund accounting would be applied in accordance with the requirements of FRS 102 for segmental reporting.

Transition to FRS 102

The Accounting Council noted that FRS 102 does not permit goodwill to have an indefinite useful life, unlike current FRS. On transition to FRS 102 entities that previously determined that goodwill had an indefinite useful life will need to reassess goodwill to determine its remaining useful life, and subsequently amortise the goodwill over that period. **161**

Effective date

FREDs 43 and 44 proposed an effective date for accounting periods beginning on or after 1 July 2013, with early application being permitted. Respondents' views regarding the proposals were very mixed with some calling for earlier adoption and others for deferral of the proposals. **162**

The Accounting Council took into consideration its decision that FRS 102 would apply to a broader scope of entities and its revised guidelines for amending the IFRS for SMEs in relation to the effective date. The Accounting Council noted that: **163**

(a) Although the revisions to its original proposals should ease the transition, an 18 month period between the publication of the final standard and effective date should be retained as there are significant changes to the accounting requirements for financial instruments.
(b) The IASB's decision to revise the effective date of IFRS 9 *Financial Instruments* to 2015. The ASB noted that entities that apply current FRS without FRS 26, who wished to move to the proposed reduced disclosure framework would not be able to apply IFRS 9 until it was adopted by the EU. Consequently such entities would need to apply IAS 39 *Financial Instruments: Recognition and Measurement* for an interim period. The costs associated with these changes were not justifiable.
(c) The effective date needed to take into consideration the updating of the SORPs that is required.

The Accounting Council advises that the effective date of FRS 102 should be accounting periods beginning on or after 1 January 2015. **164**

The Accounting Council also considered whether to permit early application of FRS 102. It noted that as FRS 102 represents an improvement in financial reporting it would not be appropriate to prevent early application of its requirements. However, the Accounting Council advises that early application of FRS 102 should not be permitted for accounting periods before those ending on or after 31 December 2012, which is consistent with the first date at which it is likely to be practical for entities applying FRS 101 to apply that standard. **165**

166 The Accounting Council also considered the early application of FRS 102 by entities that are within the scope of a SORP. It noted that most of the SORPs require updating for consistency with FRS 102, and for charities there are legal requirements relating to the application of the SORP. The Accounting Council therefore advises that early application should be permitted for entities applying a SORP provided that FRS 102 does not conflict with the requirements of a current SORP or legal requirements for the preparation of financial statements.

APPROVAL OF THIS ADVICE

167 This advice to the FRC was approved by eight of the nine members of the Accounting Council on 17 January 2013. Mr Beale dissented from the approval of the advice and his dissenting view is set out in the Appendix to the Accounting Council's advice. The Accounting Council is comprised of the following members:

Roger Marshall (Chair of the Accounting Council)
Nick Anderson
Dr Richard Barker
Edward Beale
Peter Elwin
Ken Lever
Robert Overend
Andy Simmonds
Pauline Wallace

Appendix to the Accounting Council's Advice to the FRC to issue FRS 102

DISSENTING VIEW OF MR BEALE

Mr Beale agrees that it is fundamental that financial statements should provide useful information to users, who are defined as being: investors not involved in management, customers and suppliers, including suppliers of capital and of non-equity finance. He agrees with the Accounting Council that it is disappointing that despite extensive outreach activities, the Accounting Council has not received more feedback from users, both formal and informal, on whether or not financial statements prepared in accordance with FRS 102 will meet their information needs. 1

Mr Beale does not believe that the consultation responses from industry representative bodies*, and from organisations which are both preparers and users, can be considered to be input from users since these responses are from a preparer perspective. 2

The informal input received by the FRC staff supports FRS 102 as drafted, and is generally consistent with the input from preparers and industry representative bodies. However, this informal input is inconsistent with the five† formal consultation responses received from users and the informal input received personally by Mr Beale. This inconsistency in the content of informal input may be due to the informal input received by FRC staff being from providers of non-equity finance whereas the informal input received by Mr Beale has been from directors (who are both users and preparers) and investors. 3

This informal input received by FRC staff in relation to FRS 102 differs from comments that FRC staff have recently received on other projects: 4

(a) from credit analysts and bond fund managers in relation to the financial statements of listed entities‡ (that there is not sufficient forward looking information on cash flows and challenging the usefulness of fair value); and

(b) as part of the Financia Reporting Laboratory's work on a single figure for remuneration§ (regarding valuation of equity incentives and pension costs).

In Mr Beale's experience users are concerned with issues identified by the FRC in *Louder than Words*¶¶, which they believe have not been adequately addressed in FRS 102. In his analysis, the common thread behind these user concerns is a desire for clearer, more understandable, information, from which they can derive better predictions about future cash flows on a going concern basis, even at the expense of further divergence from IFRS. Understandability is crucial to confidence in the integrity of financial reporting and thus maximising the benefits from accounts. Despite the importance of mantaining consistency with IFRS, Mr Beale believes 5

**Some of which have been classified in the Feedback Statements as 'user representative bodies'.*

†*Four of these formal consultation responses are from users connected to Mr Beale and include three responses to FREDs 43 and 44, of which two were formally classified as being from preparers and one from an academic.*

‡*http://www.frc.org.uk/getattachment/b0ef085-b542-4eaf-bc36-d52e26eb3833/How-credit-analysts-view-and-use-the-financial-statements.aspx*

§*http://frc.org.uk/getattachment/5310093d-c92-45e1-8106-278ae7ac1a4b/A-single-figure-for-remuneration.aspx*

¶¶*http://www.frc.org.uk/getattachment/7d952925-74ea-4deb-b659-e9242b09f2fa/Louder-than-words.aspx*

that the FRC should not be issuing new accounting standards perpetuating problems identified in existing standards.

6 In particular Mr Beale believes that there are significant further opportunities to improve the balance between costs and benefits in the sections of FRS 102 dealing with: Financial Instruments, Deferred Tax, Defined Benefit Pension Schemes, and Equity Settled Share-based Payments. This is discussed further below. In his view FRS 102 could have achieved clearer reporting in the above areas by departing further from the IFRS for SMEs, thus better meeting users' needs for high-quality financial information in line with the overriding objective.

7 The FRC needs to consider whether the extensive outreach activities undertaken constitute 'adequate consultation'. In Mr Beale's opinion the determination of 'adequate consultation' should be based on the outcome from the consultation process and, regrettably, there has been virtually no formal input from the people who will be using accounts prepared under FRS 102. Based on the consultation responses from users and the informal input from users that he has received, Mr Beale is advising that the FRC defer approval of FRS 102 until it has a better understanding of the degree of support from users, and in the meantime to work on improving the balance between costs and benefits in the areas outlined above.

8 In Mr Beale's experience, users do not consider UK GAAP to be in need of urgent replacement, and will not be concerned about any delays to FRS 102 necessary to determine the degree of user support and resolve any outstanding issues.

Further opportunities to improve the balance between costs and benefits

9 There are two issues of principle underpinning the areas of FRS 102 that, in Mr Beale's opinion, can be significantly improved:

(a) Since the purpose of accounts is to supply useful information to users, the most important concepts underpinning accounting standards should be 'relevance' (include information that is useful to users) and its converse, 'materiality' (exclude information that is not useful). All other accounting concepts should clearly be subsidiary to these. Such an emphasis on the priority attributable to 'relevance' and 'materiality' will promote measurement of assets and liabilities in a manner that conveys useful information to users, and will normally exclude mark to model valuations, and limit application of fair value elsewhere.

(b) At present some assets and liabilities are revalued, and some unrealised profits are taken to earnings. To ensure a principled base for accounting standards the FRC needs to determine general principles covering (i) when it is appropriate for assets and liabilities to be revalued, and (ii) whether unrealised profits arising from revaluations should be recognised in earnings or as a movement in reserves. A consistent approach to revaluation of items such as fixed assets and financial instruments, and a consistent approach to profit recognition, cannot be achieved without such principles. In his opinion, for the purposes of FRS 102: assets should be revalued when there is a sufficiently liquid market for their market value to be determined reliably, or when an impairment provision is necessary; liabilities should only be revalued when there are changes to the amount required to settle them when they fall due; and unrealised profits should not be included within earnings, except for profits on liquid investments.

In Mr Beale's opinion, opportunities to significantly improve the balance of costs and benefits within FRS 102 exist in four areas, two of general application: financial instruments, and deferred tax; and two of more limited application: equity settled share based payments and defined benefit pension schemes. These are summarised below.

FINANCIAL INSTRUMENTS

Current FRSs have been criticised in that they allow certain financial instruments not to be recorded. Such criticism is incorrect in that the existence of, and details about, these financial instruments should (where 'material') be recorded in the notes to the accounts. This criticism has been used by some to justify moving to an IFRS based approach to accounting for financial instruments, which has been widely criticised, and which is not the most cost effective approach to providing users of accounts with the information that they desire. **10**

Many different assets and liabilities fall within the definition of financial instruments and attempting to deal with all of these in the same manner introduces unnecessary complexity. The two sections on financial instruments include three to four pages of rules on which section should be applied, and are written in a language which is in places very difficult for people not accustomed to IFRS to understand. These sections have also been drafted to cater for financial institutions as well as ordinary businesses, and this exacerbates the difficulty that non-experts will have in applying them. Preparers of accounts will generally only refer to accounting standards once a year in the lead up to preparation of their annual accounts. FRS 102 needs to be readily understandable for such preparers, and there is a risk that if accounting standards are not sufficiently accessible they will be applied in a manner that generates unnecessary complexity and clutter. **11**

The two sections on financial instruments should be redrafted in language that is understandable to the normal businessperson and is not the preserve of experts. Redrafting of these sections should focus on the information that users need relating to ordinary businesses, with additional requirements for financial institutions dealt with in the section for specialised activities, by expanding the part relating to financial institutions, and which can in turn refer to IAS 39 *Financial Instruments: Recognition and Measurement*, IFRS 7 *Financial Instruments: Disclosure* and IFRS 9 *Financial Instruments* where appropriate. **12**

Users need different 'information sets' on financial instruments that are: fixed assets, current assets and liabilities; and FRS 102 should consider financial instruments in these three categories, rather than trying to cover all three categories with one set of rules. Prudence should be incorporated where necessary so that the treatment of assets is not necessarily the mirror of the treatment of liabilities. **13**

Financial assets

For normal businesses, financial assets should be carried at fair value when the principles for revaluation set out above are met, and failing that at cost less any necessary impairment provision. Income should be recognised in a prudent manner: as it is earned (eg interest on a daily basis), or when it can be reliably measured (eg dividends). **14**

Circumstances may arise which cause the valuation basis of financial assets to change, but such situations are unlikely to occur frequently outside financial institutions. Where they do occur, the consequences of reclassifications can be made obvious to users of accounts through note disclosures. Strict anti-abuse rules are not necessary. A clear analysis in the notes can highlight where reclassification is potentially being abused to manage earnings, so that users can discuss their concerns **15** with management, auditors or regulators as appropriate. Any additional requirements considered necessary for financial institutions can be dealt with in the section for specialised activities.

Financial liabilities

16 When a financial liability is included in the balance sheet at a value which is different from the amount required to settle the liability when it falls due, disclosure of amount of principal repayable is necessary, so that users can understand the underlying cash flow. The notes then show two different values for the same liability. This duplication of valuation bases creates extra cost to both preparers and users of accounts and risks causing confusion. Confusion can be minimised by using the settlement value in the statement of financial position, rather than fair values or amortised cost, recognising deferred financing costs where necessary, and providing information in the notes about financing costs and settlement dates. Interested users will then have the information necessary to perform their own comparisons with other businesses, as well as clearer information on the business's funding requirements.

17 The above approach to liabilities could lead to extensive disclosures for financial institutions and others where there are a large number of different types of financial liability. The section on specialised activities should set out an approach for the aggregation of necessary disclosures and allow an opt into IFRS 9/IAS 39.

Impairment of financial assets

18 Impairment provisions are only allowed in FRS 102 where there is 'objective evidence' of impairment. Businesses are not allowed to make provision for expected losses, even where there is past experience supporting the likelihood of such losses. Expected loss provisions should be allowed now, before IFRS 9 has been updated, to avoid assets being overvalued. A clear analysis in the notes will highlight where impairment provisions are potentially being abused to manage earnings, so that users can discuss their concerns with management, auditors or regulators as appropriate. Additional requirements may be imposed on financial institutions through the section on specialised activities.

Hedging

19 Hedge accounting is only permitted in FRS 102 if 'specified criteria' are met. In the past similar restrictions have led to businesses not hedge accounting for financial instruments acquired, or entered into, for hedging purposes. The purpose of accounting standards is not to promote good management but good reporting. Accounting standards are not the appropriate way to attempt to stop the miss-selling, or miss-buying, of derivatives. There needs to be transparency over hedges entered into so that the effect of hedges in managing risk can be understood by users of accounts. This can be achieved by linked accounting for hedges and items being hedged, so that accounting faithfully represents the underlying commercial activity.

20 Concerns over earnings management can be alleviated by disclosure of the impact on earnings of hedges closed out in a different period to the risk that they purported to hedge. Businesses other than financial institutions should be able to allay concerns over the effectiveness of hedges by explaining how their limited number of material risks are being hedged. Financial institutions may have too many hedges to be able to

provide this information in a meaningful manner and an alternative approach for such businesses should be set out in the section on specialised activities.

DEFERRED TAX

As the recent ASB/EFRAG discussion paper on tax identified, users want to know how future tax payments will differ from the amount calculated by applying the standard tax rate to future profits. This difference will be in part due to future actions and in part due to past actions. **21**

The section of FRS 102 on deferred tax is not predicated on a going concern basis, and in effect identifies the impact on future tax payments if the business ceases trading. As such, except for the disclosure of amounts expected to reverse in the next period, the approach in FRS 102 is of little relevance to most users and will create disclosures which will generally be ignored by users. **22**

The disclosure required by FRS 102 of the amount of the deferred tax provision which will be released in the next period is of limited usefulness. This is only part of the difference between expected tax cost and standard tax rate. Prediction of the element due to future actions is not currently required. **23**

The information that users need can best be provided by way of disclosure of the expected future tax rate and any other material information that may influence future tax payments, eg losses carried forward. A deferred tax provision should not be made because this does not provide useful information in a cost effective manner. The exception to this is that the logic behind revaluing certain items dictates that, for consistency, the tax impact of such revaluations needs to be recognised too. **24**

EQUITY SETTLED SHARE-BASED PAYMENTS

As identified by the recent financial reporting laboratory work on valuation of remuneration, users do not understand the complex models used to value equity settled share based payments. The cost of creating these values is therefore wasted. **25**

These valuation models also generate a substantial amount of clutter when trying to explain how the valuation is arrived at. **26**

It should also be noted that the standard valuation models assume liquid markets and negligible spreads. These assumptions are not appropriate for the types of businesses that will be applying FRS 102. Given the lack of guidance in FRS 102, and the complexity of the valuation models, in Mr Beale's opinion it is highly likely that preparers will use inappropriate valuation models, or use valuation models in inappropriate ways, and that users will not have enough knowledge to identify this. **27**

Unless there is a liquid market to provide a relevant value for equity settled share based payments, their existence should be disclosed in the notes to the accounts, and there should be no notional cost in the income statement. **28**

DEFINED BENEFIT PENSION SCHEMES

The information relating to defined benefit pension schemes that users need is: the current cost of providing the benefit, the expected additional payments required to make good any funding deficit (or payment holiday because of funding surpluses) and an explanation of the contingent liability in respect of potential future funding shortfalls. **29**

30 At present there is a requirement to prepare a fund valuation solely for accounting purposes and then to consolidate the net assets or, more usually, liabilities of the fund. Changes in the net assets/liabilities are then split into three parts and recognised in operating costs, financing costs and other comprehensive income. This is supplemented by extensive disclosures. However, the disclosures do not require information about the uncertainties or sensitivities attached to the valuation inputs eg the time periods over which payments out of the fund will be made, discount and inflation rates, and other risks inherent in the fund.

31 Most users do not understand pension scheme valuations. They see fund valuations which are massively volatile, and perceive most current requirements as adding to clutter and generating additional preparation costs for no benefit.

32 Clutter could be reduced by not consolidating the pension fund, but instead disclosing the level of normal contributions being made and providing for contributions required to make good any funding shortfall. Changes in this liability to make good any funding shortfall should be expensed and explained. In addition disclosures should be made describing the contingent liability to fund any future increases in fund deficits. Those users who do understand pension scheme valuations can obtain the more detailed information that they are likely to want about pension scheme funding from the fund valuation prepared for that purpose, which should be made available on demand or on a web site. Such an approach would save the costs associated with preparing a valuation solely for accounting purposes as well as reducing clutter in the accounts.

TRAINING COSTS

33 Maintaining limited UK GAAP differences from IFRS will marginally increase the cost of training accountants, but should improve their employability, and will increase the challenge on the IASB to further improve IFRS, thereby improving the balance between benefits and costs overall.

Appendix I: Glossary

This glossary is an integral part of the Standard.

accounting policies	The specific principles, bases, conventions, rules and practices applied by an entity in preparing and presenting **financial statements.**
accrual basis (of accounting)	The effects of transactions and other events are recognised when they occur (and not as **cash** or its equivalent is received or paid) and they are recorded in the accounting records and reported in the **financial statements** of the periods to which they relate.
accumulating compensated absences	Compensated absences that are carried forward and can be used in future periods if the current period's entitlement is not used in full.
acquisition date	The date on which the acquirer obtains **control** of the acquiree.
Act	The Companies Act 2006
active market	A market in which all the following conditions exist: (a) the items traded in the market are homogeneous; (b) willing buyers and sellers can normally be found at any time; and (c) prices are available to the public.
actuarial assumptions	An entity's unbiased and mutually compatible best estimates of the demographic and financial variables that will determine the ultimate cost of providing post-employment benefits.
actuarial gains and losses	Changes in the **present value** of the **defined benefit obligation** resulting from: (a) experience adjustments (the effects of differences between the previous **actuarial assumptions** and what has actually occurred); and (b) the effects of changes in actuarial assumptions.
agent	An entity is acting as an agent when it does not have exposure to the significant risks and rewards associated with the sale of goods or the rendering of services. One feature indicating that an entity is acting as an agent is that the amount the entity earns is predetermined, being either a fixed fee per transaction or a stated percentage of the amount billed to the customer.
agricultural activity	The management by an entity of the biological transformation of **biological assets** for sale, into agricultural produce or into additional biological assets.

agricultural produce	The harvested product of the entity's **biological assets**.
amortisation	The systematic allocation of the **depreciable amount** of an **asset** over its **useful life**.
amortised cost (of a financial asset or financial liability)	The amount at which the **financial asset** or **financial liability** is measured at initial **recognition** minus principal repayments, plus or minus the cumulative **amortisation** using the **effective interest method** of any difference between that initial amount and the maturity amount, and minus any reduction (directly or through the use of an allowance account) for impairment or uncollectability.
asset	A resource controlled by the entity as a result of past events and from which future economic benefits are expected to flow to the entity.
asset held by a long-term employee benefit fund	An **asset** (other than non-transferable financial instruments issued by the reporting entity) that: (a) is held by an entity (a fund) that is legally separate from the reporting entity and exists solely to pay or fund **employee benefits**; and (b) is available to be used only to pay or fund employee benefits, is not available to the reporting entity's own creditors (even in bankruptcy), and cannot be returned to the reporting entity, unless either: (i) the remaining assets of the fund are sufficient to meet all the related employee benefit obligations of the plan or the reporting entity; or (ii) the assets are returned to the reporting entity to reimburse it for employee benefits already paid.
associate	An entity, including an unincorporated entity such as a partnership, over which the investor has **significant influence** and that is neither a **subsidiary** nor an interest in a **joint venture**.
biological asset	A living animal or plant.
borrowing costs	Interest and other costs incurred by an entity in connection with the borrowing of funds.
business	An integrated set of activities and **assets** conducted and managed for the purpose of providing: (a) a return to investors; or (b) lower costs or other economic benefits directly and proportionately to policyholders or participants. A business generally consists of inputs, processes applied to those inputs, and resulting outputs that are, or will be, used to generate **revenues**. If **goodwill** is present in a transferred set of activities and assets, the transferred set shall be presumed to be a business.

business combination	The bringing together of separate entities or **businesses** into one reporting entity.
carrying amount	The amount at which an **asset** or **liability** is recognised in the **statement of financial position**.
cash	Cash on hand and demand deposits.
cash equivalents	Short-term, highly liquid investments that are readily convertible to known amounts of **cash** and that are subject to an insignificant risk of changes in value.
cash flows	Inflows and outflows of **cash** and **cash equivalents**.
cash-generating unit	The smallest identifiable group of **assets** that generates cash inflows that are largely independent of the cash inflows from other assets or groups of assets.
cash-settled share-based payment transaction	A **share-based payment transaction** in which the entity acquires goods or services by incurring a **liability** to transfer **cash** or other **assets** to the supplier of those goods or services for amounts that are based on the price (or value) of the entity's shares or other equity instruments of the entity or another group entity.
change in accounting estimate	An adjustment of the **carrying amount** of an **asset** or a **liability**, or the amount of the periodic consumption of an asset, that results from the assessment of the present status of, and expected future benefits and obligations associated with, assets and liabilities. Changes in accounting estimates result from new information or new developments and, accordingly, are not corrections of **errors**.
class of assets	A grouping of **assets** of a similar nature and use in an entity's operations.
close members of the family of a person	Those family members who may be expected to influence, or be influenced by, that person in their dealings with the entity including: (a) that person's children and spouse or domestic partner; (b) children of that person's spouse or domestic partner; and (c) dependants of that person or that person's spouse or domestic partner.
closing rate	The spot exchange rate at the end of the **reporting period**
combination that is in substance is a gift	A combination carried out at nil or nominal consideration that is not a fair value exchange but in substance the gift of one entity to another.
commencement of lease term	The date from which the lessee is entitled to exercise its right to use the leased asset. It is the date of initial **recognition** of

	the **lease** (ie the recognition of the **assets**, **liabilities**, **income** or **expenses** resulting from the lease, as appropriate).
component of an entity	Operations and **cash flows** that can be clearly distinguished, operationally and for financial reporting purposes, from the rest of the entity.
compound financial instrument	A financial instrument that, from the issuer's perspective, contains both a **liability** and an **equity** element.
consolidated financial statements	The financial statements of a **parent** and its **subsidiaries** presented as those of a single economic entity.
construction contract	A contract specifically negotiated for the construction of an **asset** or a combination of assets that are closely interrelated or interdependent in terms of their design, technology and function or their ultimate purpose or use.
constructive obligation	An obligation that derives from an entity's actions where: (a) by an established pattern of past practice, published policies or a sufficiently specific current statement, the entity has indicated to other parties that it will accept certain responsibilities; and (b) as a result, the entity has created a valid expectation on the part of those other parties that it will discharge those responsibilities.
contingent asset	A possible **asset** that arises from past events and whose existence will be confirmed only by the occurrence or non-occurrence of one or more uncertain future events not wholly within the control of the entity.
contingent liability	(a) a possible obligation that arises from past events and whose existence will be confirmed only by the occurrence or non-occurrence of one or more uncertain future events not wholly within the control of the entity; or (b) a present obligation that arises from past events but is not recognised because: (i) it is not **probable** that an outflow of resources embodying economic benefits will be required to settle the obligation; or (ii) the amount of the obligation cannot be measured with sufficient **reliability**.
contingent rent	That portion of the lease payments that is not fixed in amount but is based on the future amount of a factor that changes other than with the passage of time (eg percentage of future sales, amount of future use, future price indices, and future market rates of interest).

control (of an entity)	The power to govern the financial and operating policies of an entity so as to obtain benefits from its activities.
credit risk	The risk that one party to a financial instrument will cause a financial loss for the other party by failing to discharge an obligation.
current assets	**Assets** of an entity which are not intended for use on a continuing basis in the entity's activities.
current tax	The amount of income tax payable (refundable) in respect of the taxable profit (tax loss) for the current period or past **reporting periods**.
date of transition	The beginning of the earliest period for which an entity presents full comparative information in a given standard in its first **financial statements** that comply with that standard.
deemed cost	An amount used as a surrogate for cost or depreciated cost at a given date. Subsequent **depreciation** or **amortisation** assumes that the entity had initially recognised the **asset** or **liability** at the given date and that its cost was equal to the deemed cost.
deferred acquisition costs	Costs arising from the conclusion of **insurance contracts** that are incurred during a **reporting period** but which relate to a subsequent reporting period.
deferred tax	Income tax payable (recoverable) in respect of the **taxable profit (tax loss)** for future **reporting periods** as a result of past transactions or events.
deferred tax assets	Income tax recoverable in future **reporting periods** in respect of: (a) future tax consequences of transactions and events recognised in the **financial statements** of the current and previous periods; (b) the carry forward of unused tax losses; and (c) the carry forward of unused tax credits.
deferred tax liabilities	Income tax payable in future **reporting periods** in respect of future tax consequences of transactions and events recognised in the **financial statements** of the current and previous periods.
defined benefit obligation (present value of)	The **present value**, without deducting any **plan assets**, of expected future payments required to settle the obligation resulting from employee service in the current and prior periods.
defined benefit plans	**Post-employment benefit plans** other than **defined contribution plans**.

defined contribution plans	**Post-employment benefit plans** under which an entity pays fixed contributions into a separate entity (a fund) and has no legal or **constructive obligation** to pay further contributions or to make direct benefit payments to employees if the fund does not hold sufficient **assets** to pay all **employee benefits** relating to employee service in the current and prior periods.
depreciable amount	The cost of an **asset**, or other amount substituted for cost (in the **financial statements**), less its residual value.
depreciated replacement cost	The most economic cost required for the entity to replace the **service potential** of an **asset** (including the amount that the entity will receive from its disposal at the end of its **useful life**) at the **reporting date**.
depreciation	The systematic allocation of the **depreciable amount** of an **asset** over its **useful life.**
derecognition	The removal of a previously recognised **asset** or **liability** from an entity's **statement of financial position**.
derivative	A financial instrument or other contract with all three of the following characteristics: (a) its value changes in response to the change in a specified interest rate, financial instrument price, commodity price, foreign exchange rate, index of prices or rates, credit rating or credit index, or other variable (sometimes called the 'underlying'), provided in the case of a non-financial variable that the variable is not specific to a party to the contract; (b) it requires no initial net investment or an initial net investment that is smaller than would be required for other types of contracts that would be expected to have a similar response to changes in market factors; and (c) it is settled at a future date.
development	The application of **research** findings or other knowledge to a plan or design for the production of new or substantially improved materials, devices, products, processes, systems or services before the start of commercial production or use.
discontinued operation	A **component of an entity** that has been disposed of and: (a) represented a separate major line of **business** or geographical area of operations; (b) was part of a single co-ordinated plan to dispose of a separate major line of business or geographical area of operations; or (c) was a **subsidiary** acquired exclusively with a view to resale.
discretionary participation feature	A contractual right to receive, as a supplement to guaranteed benefits, additional benefits: (a) that are likely to be a significant portion of the total contractual benefits;

	(b) whose amount or timing is contractually at the discretion of the issuer; and (c) that are contractually based on: (i) the performance of a specified pool of contracts or a specified type of contract; (ii) realised and/or unrealised investment returns on a specified pool of **assets** held by the issuer; or (iii) the **profit or loss** of the company, fund or other entity that issues the contract.
disposal group	A group of **assets** to be disposed of, by sale or otherwise, together as a group in a single transaction, and **liabilities** directly associated with those assets that will be transferred in the transaction. The group includes **goodwill** acquired in a **business combination** if the group is a **cash-generating unit** to which goodwill has been allocated in accordance with the requirements of paragraphs 27.24 to 27.27 of this FRS.
effective interest method	A method of calculating the **amortised cost** of a **financial asset** or a **financial liability** (or a group of financial assets or financial liabilities) and of allocating the interest income or interest expense over the relevant period.
effective interest rate	The rate that exactly discounts estimated future cash payments or receipts through the expected life of the financial instrument or, when appropriate, a shorter period to the **carrying amount** of the **financial asset** or **financial liability**.
effectiveness of a hedge	The degree to which changes in the **fair value** or **cash flows** of the **hedged item** that are attributable to a hedged risk are offset by changes in the fair value or cash flows of the **hedging instrument**.
employee benefits	All forms of consideration given by an entity in exchange for service rendered by employees.
entity combination	See **business combination**.
equity	The residual interest in the **assets** of the entity after deducting all its **liabilities**.
equity-settled share-based payment transaction	A **share-based payment transaction** in which the entity: (a) receives goods or services as consideration for its own equity instruments (including shares or **share options**); or (b) receives goods or services but has no obligation to settle the transaction with the supplier.
errors	Omissions from, and misstatements in, the entity's **financial statements** for one or more prior periods arising from a failure to use, or misuse of, reliable information that: (a) was available when financial statements for those periods were authorised for issue; and

	(b) could reasonably be expected to have been obtained and taken into account in the preparation and presentation of those financial statements.
expenses	Decreases in economic benefits during the **reporting period** in the form of outflows or depletions of **assets** or incurrences of **liabilities** that result in decreases in **equity**, other than those relating to distributions to equity investors.
EU-adopted IFRS	IFRS that have been adopted in the European Union in accordance with EU Regulation 1606/2002.
fair presentation	Faithful representation of the effects of transactions, other events and conditions in accordance with the definitions and **recognition** criteria for **assets**, **liabilities**, **income** and **expenses** unless the override stated in paragraph 3.4 applies.
fair value	The amount for which an **asset** could be exchanged, a **liability** settled, or an equity instrument granted could be exchanged, between knowledgeable, willing parties in an arm's length transaction. In the absence of any specific guidance provided in the relevant section of this FRS, the guidance in paragraphs 11.27 to 11.32 shall be used in determining fair value.
fair value less costs to sell	The amount obtainable from the sale of an **asset** or **cash-generating unit** in an arm's length transaction between knowledgeable, willing parties, less the costs of disposal.
finance lease	A **lease** that transfers substantially all the risks and rewards incidental to ownership of an **asset**. Title may or may not eventually be transferred. A lease that is not a finance lease is an operating lease.
financial asset	Any **asset** that is: (a) **cash**; (b) an equity instrument of another entity; (c) a contractual right: (i) to receive cash or another financial asset from another entity, or (ii) to exchange financial assets or **financial liabilities** with another entity under conditions that are potentially favourable to the entity; or (d) a contract that will or may be settled in the entity's own equity instruments and: (i) under which the entity is or may be obliged to receive a variable number of the entity's own equity instruments; or (ii) that will or may be settled other than by the exchange of a fixed amount of cash or another financial asset for a fixed number of the entity's own equity instruments. For this purpose the entity's own equity instruments do not include instruments that are themselves contracts for the

	future receipt or delivery of the entity's own equity instruments.
financial guarantee contract	A contract that requires the issuer to make specified payments to reimburse the holder for a loss it incurs because a specified debtor fails to make payments when due in accordance with the original or modified terms of a debt instrument.
financial institution	Any of the following: (a) a bank which is: (i) a firm with a Part IV permission* which includes accepting deposits and: (a) which is a credit institution; or (b) whose Part IV permission includes a requirement that it complies with the rules in the General Prudential sourcebook and the Prudential sourcebook for Banks, Building Societies and Investment Firms relating to banks, but which is not a building society, a friendly society or a credit union; (ii) an EEA bank which is a full credit institution; (b) a building society which is defined in section 119(1) of the Building Societies Act 1986 as a building society incorporated (or deemed to be incorporated) under that act; (c) a credit union, being a body corporate registered under the Industrial and Provident Societies Act 1965 as a credit union in accordance with the Credit Unions Act 1979, which is an authorised person; (d) custodian bank, broker-dealer or stockbroker; (e) an entity that undertakes the business of effecting or carrying out **insurance contracts**, including general and life assurance entities; (f) an incorporated friendly society incorporated under the Friendly Societies Act 1992 or a registered friendly society registered under section 7(1)(a) of the Friendly Societies Act 1974 or any enactment which it replaced, including any registered branches; (g) an investment trust, Irish Investment Company†, venture capital trust, mutual fund, exchange traded fund, unit trust, open-ended investment company (OEIC); (h) a **retirement benefit plan**; or (i) any other entity whose principal activity is to generate wealth or manage risk through financial instruments. This is intended to cover entities that have business

**As defined in section 40(4) of the Financial Services and Markets Act 2000 or references to equivalent provisions of any successor legislation.*

†An Irish Investment Company is a corporate vehicle as defined by section 47(3) of the Companies (Amendment) Act 1983 and paragraph 58 of the Schedule to the Companies (Amendment) Act 1986, and regulated by the Central Bank of Ireland.

	activities similar to those listed above but are not specifically included in the list above. A **parent** entity whose sole activity is to hold investments in other group entities is not a financial institution.
financial instrument	A contract that gives rise to a **financial asset** of one entity and a **financial liability** or equity instrument of another entity.
financial liability	Any **liability** that is: (a) a contractual obligation: (i) to deliver **cash** or another **financial asset** to another entity; or (ii) to exchange financial assets or financial liabilities with another entity under conditions that are potentially unfavourable to the entity, or (b) a contract that will or may be settled in the entity's own equity instruments and: (i) under which the entity is or may be obliged to deliver a variable number of the entity's own equity instruments; or (ii) will or may be settled other than by the exchange of a fixed amount of cash or another financial asset for a fixed number of the entity's own equity instruments. For this purpose the entity's own equity instruments do not include instruments that are themselves contracts for the future receipt or delivery of the entity's own equity instruments.
financial position	The relationship of the **assets**, **liabilities** and **equity** of an entity as reported in the **statement of financial position**.
financial statements	Structured representation of the **financial position**, financial **performance** and **cash flows** of an entity.
financial risk	The risk of a possible future change in one or more of a specified interest rate, financial instrument price, commodity price, foreign exchange rate, index of prices or rates, credit rating or credit index or other variable, provided in the case of a non-financial variable that the variable is not specific to a party to the contract.
financing activities	Activities that result in changes in the size and composition of the contributed **equity** and borrowings of the entity.
firm commitment	A binding agreement for the exchange of a specified quantity of resources at a specified price on a specified future date or dates.
first-time adopter of this FRS	An entity that presents its first annual **financial statements** that conform to this FRS, regardless of whether its previous accounting framework was **EU-adopted IFRS** or another set of accounting standards.

fixed assets	**Assets** of an entity which are intended for use on a continuing basis in the entity's activities.
forecast transaction	An uncommitted but anticipated future transaction.
foreign operation	An entity that is a **subsidiary, associate, joint venture** or branch of a reporting entity, the activities of which are based or conducted in a country or currency other than those of the reporting entity.
FRS 100	FRS 100 *Application of Financial Reporting Requirements.*
FRS 101	FRS 101 *Reduced Disclosure Framework*
FRS 102	FRS 102 *The Financial Reporting Standard applicable in the UK and Republic of Ireland*
FRS 103	FRS 103 *Insurance Contracts*
FRSSE	The extant version* of the *Financial Reporting Standard for Smaller Entities.*
functional currency	The currency of the primary economic environment in which the entity operates.
funding (of post-employment benefits)	Contributions by an entity, and sometimes its employees, into an entity, or fund, that is legally separate from the reporting entity and from which the **employee benefits** are paid.
gains	Increases in economic benefits that meet the definition of **income** but are not **revenue.**
general purpose financial statements (generally referred to simply as financial statements)	**Financial statements** directed to the general financial information needs of a wide range of users who are not in a position to demand reports tailored to meet their particular information needs.
going concern	An entity is a going concern unless management either intends to liquidate the entity or to cease trading, or has no realistic alternative but to do so.

**At the date of issue of this FRS, the extant version of the FRSSE is the Financial Reporting Standard for Smaller Entities (effective April 2008).* The *Financial Reporting Standard for Smaller Entities (effective January 2015)* will replace it as the extant standard from 1 January 2015.

goodwill	Future economic benefits arising from **assets** that are not capable of being individually identified and separately recognised.
government grant	Assistance by government in the form of a transfer of resources to an entity in return for past or future compliance with specified conditions relating to the **operating activities** of the entity. Government refers to government, government agencies and similar bodies whether local, national or international.
grant date	The date at which the entity and another party (including an employee) agree to a share-based payment arrangement, being when the entity and the counterparty have a shared understanding of the terms and conditions of the arrangement. At grant date the entity confers on the counterparty the right to **cash**, other **assets**, or equity instruments of the entity, provided the specified vesting conditions, if any, are met. If that agreement is subject to an approval process (for example, by shareholders), grant date is the date when that approval is obtained.
gross investment in a lease	The aggregate of: (a) the **minimum lease payments** receivable by the lessor under a **finance lease**; and (b) any unguaranteed **residual value** accruing to the lessor.
group	A **parent** and all its **subsidiaries**.
group reconstruction	Any one of the following arrangements: (a) the transfer of an equity holding in a **subsidiary** from one group entity to another; (b) the addition of a new **parent** entity to a **group**; (c) the transfer of equity holdings in one or more subsidiaries of a group to a new entity that is not a group entity but whose equity holders are the same as those of the group's parent; or (d) the combination into a group of two or more entities that before the combination had the same equity holders.
hedged item	For the purpose of special hedge accounting under Section 12 of this FRS, a hedged item is: (a) interest rate risk of a debt instrument measured at **amortised cost**; (b) foreign exchange or interest rate risk in a **firm commitment** or a **highly probable forecast transaction**; (c) price risk of a commodity that the entity holds or price risk in a firm commitment or highly probable forecast transaction to purchase or sell a commodity; or (d) foreign exchange risk in a **net investment in a foreign operation**.

hedging instrument	For the purpose of special hedge accounting under Section 12 of this FRS, a hedging instrument is a financial instrument that meets all of the following terms and conditions: (a) it is an interest rate swap, a foreign currency swap, a cross currency interest rate swap, a forward or future foreign currency exchange contract, a forward or future commodity exchange contract, or any financial instrument used to hedge foreign exchange risk in a **net investment in a foreign operation**; provided it is expected to be highly effective in offsetting the designated hedged risk(s) identified in paragraph 12.17. (b) it involves a party external to the reporting entity (ie external to the **group**, segment or individual entity being reported on). (c) its **notional amount** is equal to the designated amount of the principal or notional amount of the **hedged item**. (d) it has a specified maturity date not later than (i) the maturity of the financial instrument being hedged, (ii) the expected settlement of the commodity purchase or sale commitment, or (iii) the later of the occurrence and settlement of the **highly probable** forecast foreign currency or commodity transaction being hedged. (e) it has no prepayment, early termination or extension features other than at **fair value**. An entity that chooses to apply IAS 39 *Financial Instruments: Recognition and Measurement* (as adopted in the EU) in accounting for financial instruments shall apply the definition of a hedging instrument in that standard rather than this definition.
held exclusively with a view to subsequent resale	An interest: (a) for which a purchaser has been identified or is being sought, and which is reasonably expected to be disposed of within approximately one year of its date of acquisition; or (b) that was acquired as a result of the enforcement of a security, unless the interest has become part of the continuing activities of the **group** or the holder acts as if it intends the interest to become so; or (c) which is **held as part of an investment portfolio**.
held as part of an investment portfolio	An interest is held as part of an investment portfolio if its value to the investor is through **fair value** as part of a directly or indirectly held basket of investments rather than as media through which the investor carries out **business**. A basket of investments is indirectly held if an investment fund holds a single investment in a second investment fund which, in turn, holds a basket of investments.

heritage assets	Tangible and **intangible assets** with historic, artistic, scientific, technological, geophysical, or environmental qualities that are held and maintained principally for their contribution to knowledge and culture.
highly probable	Significantly more likely than **probable**.
IAS Regulation	EU Regulation 1606/2002.
IFRS (International Financial Reporting Standards)	Standards and interpretations issued (or adopted) by the International Accounting Standards Board (IASB). They comprise: (a) International Financial Reporting Standards; (b) International Accounting Standards; and (c) Interpretations developed by the IFRS Interpretations Committee (IFRIC) or the former Standing Interpretations Committee (SIC).
impairment loss	The amount by which the **carrying amount** of an **asset** exceeds: (a) in the case of **inventories**, its selling price less costs to complete and sell; or (b) in the case of other assets, its **recoverable amount**.
impracticable	Applying a requirement is impracticable when the entity cannot apply it after making every reasonable effort to do so.
imputed rate of interest	The more clearly determinable of either: (a) the prevailing rate for a similar instrument of an issuer with a similar credit rating; or (b) a rate of interest that discounts the nominal amount of the instrument to the current cash sales price of the goods or services.
inception of the lease	The earlier of the date of the lease agreement and the date of commitment by the parties to the principal provisions of the **lease**.
income	Increases in economic benefits during the **reporting period** in the form of inflows or enhancements of **assets** or decreases of **liabilities** that result in increases in **equity**, other than those relating to contributions from equity investors.
income and expenditure	The total of **income** less **expenses**, excluding the components of **other comprehensive income**. In the for-profit sector this is known as **profit or loss.**
income statement	**Financial statement** that presents all items of **income** and **expense** recognised in a **reporting period**, excluding the items of **other comprehensive income** (referred to as the profit and loss account in the **Act**).

income tax	All domestic and foreign taxes that are based on **taxable profits**. Income tax also includes taxes, such as withholding taxes, that are payable by a **subsidiary**, **associate** or **joint venture** on distributions to the reporting entity.
individual financial statements	The accounts that are required to be prepared by an entity in accordance with the Act or relevant legislation, for example: (a) 'individual accounts', as set out in section 394 of the Act; (b) 'statement of accounts', as set out in section 132 of the Charities Act 2011; or (c) 'individual accounts', as set out in section 72A of the Building Societies Act 1986. **Separate financial statements** are included in the meaning of this term.
infrastructure assets	Infrastructure for public services, such as roads, bridges, tunnels, prisons, hospitals, airports, water distribution facilities, energy supply and telecommunications networks.
insurance contract	A contract under which one party (the insurer) accepts significant insurance risk from another party (the policyholder) by agreeing to compensate the policyholder if a specified uncertain future event (the insured event) adversely affects the policyholder.
intangible asset	An identifiable non-monetary asset without physical substance. Such an **asset** is identifiable when: (a) it is separable, ie capable of being separated or divided from the entity and sold, transferred, licensed, rented or exchanged, either individually or together with a related contract, asset or **liability**; or (b) it arises from contractual or other legal rights, regardless of whether those rights are transferable or separable from the entity or from other rights and obligations.
interest rate implicit in the lease	The discount rate that, at the **inception of the lease**, causes the aggregate **present value** of: (a) the **minimum lease payments**; and (b) the unguaranteed **residual value** to be equal to the sum of: (i) the **fair value** of the leased asset; and (ii) any initial direct costs of the lessor.
interim financial report	A financial report containing either a complete set of **financial statements** or a set of condensed financial statements for an **interim period**.
interim period	A financial **reporting period** shorter than a full financial year.
intrinsic value	The difference between the fair value of the shares to which the counterparty has the (conditional or unconditional) right to subscribe or which it has the right to receive, and the price (if any) the counterparty is (or will be) required to pay for

	those shares. For example, a share option with an exercise price of CU15, on a share with a fair value of CU20, has an intrinsic value of CU5.
inventories	**Assets**: (a) held for sale in the ordinary course of business; (b) in the process of production for such sale; or (c) in the form of materials or supplies to be consumed in the production process or in the rendering of services.
inventories held for distribution at no or nominal consideration	**Assets** that are: (a) held for distribution at no or nominal consideration in the ordinary course of operations; (b) in the process of production for distribution at no or nominal consideration in the ordinary course of operations; or (c) in the form of material or supplies to be consumed in the production process or in the rendering of services at no or nominal consideration.
investing activities	The acquisition and disposal of long-term assets and other investments not included in **cash equivalents**.
investment property	Property (land or a building, or part of a building, or both) held by the owner or by the lessee under a **finance lease** to earn rentals or for capital appreciation or both, rather than for: (a) use in the production or supply of goods or services or for administrative purposes, or (b) sale in the ordinary course of **business**.
joint control	The contractually agreed sharing of **control** over an economic activity. It exists only when the strategic financial and operating decisions relating to the activity require the unanimous consent of the parties sharing control (the **venturers**).
joint venture	A contractual arrangement whereby two or more parties undertake an economic activity that is subject to **joint control**. Joint ventures can take the form of jointly controlled operations, jointly controlled assets, or **jointly controlled entities**.
jointly controlled entity	A **joint venture** that involves the establishment of a corporation, partnership or other entity in which each **venturer** has an interest. The entity operates in the same way as other entities, except that a contractual arrangement between the venturers establishes **joint control** over the economic activity of the entity.
key management personnel	Those persons having authority and responsibility for planning, directing and controlling the activities of the entity, directly or indirectly, including any director (whether executive or otherwise) of that entity.

lease	An agreement whereby the lessor conveys to the lessee in return for a payment or series of payments the right to use an **asset** for an agreed period of time.
lease incentives	Incentives provided by the lessor to the lessee to enter into a new or renew an operating lease. Examples of such incentives include up-front cash payments to the lessee, the reimbursement or assumption by the lessor of costs of the lessee (such as relocation costs, leasehold improvements and costs associated with pre-existing lease commitments of the lessee), or initial periods of the **lease** provided by the lessor rent-free or at a reduced rent.
lease term	The non-cancellable period for which the lessee has contracted to **lease** the **asset** together with any further terms for which the lessee has the option to continue to lease the asset, with or without further payment, when at the **inception of the lease** it is reasonably certain that the lessee will exercise the option.
lessee's incremental borrowing rate (of interest)	The rate of interest the lessee would have to pay on a similar **lease** or, if that is not determinable, the rate that, at the **inception of the lease**, the lessee would incur to borrow over a similar term, and with a similar security, the funds necessary to purchase the **asset**.
liability	A present obligation of the entity arising from past events, the settlement of which is expected to result in an outflow from the entity of resources embodying economic benefits.
liquidity risk	The risk that an entity will encounter difficulty in meeting obligations associated with **financial liabilities** that are settled by delivering **cash** or another **financial asset**.
LLP Regulations	The Large and Medium-sized Limited Liability Partnerships (Accounts) Regulations 2008 (SI 2008/1913).
loans payable	**Financial liabilities** other than short-term trade payables on normal credit terms.
market condition	A condition upon which the exercise price, vesting or exercisability of an equity instrument depends that is related to the market price of the entity's equity instruments, such as attaining a specified share price or a specified amount of **intrinsic value** of a **share option**, or achieving a specified target that is based on the market price of the entity's equity instruments relative to an index of market prices of equity instruments of other entities.
market risk	The risk that the **fair value** or future **cash flows** of a financial instrument will fluctuate because of changes in market prices. Market risk comprises three types of risk: currency risk, interest rate risk and other price risk.

	Interest rate risk – the risk that the fair value or future cash flows of a financial instrument will fluctuate because of changes in market interest rates. Currency risk – the risk that the fair value or future cash flows of a financial instrument will fluctuate because of changes in foreign exchange rates. Other price risk – the risk that the fair value or future cash flows of a financial instrument will fluctuate because of changes in market prices (other than those arising from interest rate risk or currency risk), whether those changes are caused by factors specific to the financial instrument or its issuer, or factors affecting all similar financial instruments traded in the market.
material	Omissions or misstatements of items are material if they could, individually or collectively, influence the economic decisions of users taken on the basis of the **financial statements**. Materiality depends on the size and nature of the omission or misstatement judged in the surrounding circumstances. The size or nature of the item, or a combination of both, could be the determining factor.
measurement	The process of determining the monetary amounts at which the elements of the **financial statements** are to be recognised and carried in the **statement of financial position** and **statement of comprehensive income**.
merger	An **entity combination** that results in the creation of a new reporting entity formed from the combining parties, in which the controlling parties of the combining entities come together in a partnership for the mutual sharing of risks and benefits of the newly formed entity and in which no party to the combination in substance obtains **control** over any other, or is otherwise seen to be dominant. All of the following criteria must be met for an entity combination to meet the definition of a merger: (a) no party to the combination is portrayed as either acquirer or acquiree, either by its own board or management or by that of another party to the combination; (b) there is no significant change to the classes of beneficiaries of the combining entities or the purpose of the benefits provided as a result of the combination; and (c) all parties to the combination, as represented by the members of the board, participate in establishing the management structure of the combined entity and in selecting the management personnel, and such decisions are made on the basis of a consensus between the parties to the combination rather than purely by exercise of voting rights.

minimum lease payments	The payments over the **lease term** that the lessee is or can be required to make, excluding **contingent rent**, costs for services and taxes to be paid by and reimbursed to the lessor, together with: (a) for a lessee, any amounts guaranteed by the lessee or by a party related to the lessee; or (b) for a lessor, any **residual value** guaranteed to the lessor by: (i) the lessee; (ii) a party related to the lessee; or (iii) a third party unrelated to the lessor that is financially capable of discharging the obligations under the guarantee. However, if the lessee has an option to purchase the **asset** at a price that is expected to be sufficiently lower than **fair value** at the date the option becomes exercisable for it to be reasonably certain, at the **inception of the lease**, that the option will be exercised, the minimum lease payments comprise the minimum payments payable over the lease term to the expected date of exercise of this purchase option and the payment required to exercise it.
monetary items	Units of currency held and **assets** and **liabilities** to be received or paid in a fixed or determinable number of units of currency.
multi-employer (benefit) plans	**Defined contribution plans** (other than **state plans**) or **defined benefit plans** (other than state plans) that: (a) pool the **assets** contributed by various entities that are not under common control, and (b) use those assets to provide benefits to employees of more than one entity, on the basis that contribution and benefit levels are determined without regard to the identity of the entity that employs the employees concerned.
net assets available for benefits	The **assets** of a plan less **liabilities** other than the actuarial **present value** of promised retirement benefits
net defined benefit liability	The **present value** of the **defined benefit obligation** at the **reporting date** minus the **fair value** at the reporting date of **plan assets** (if any) out of which the obligations are to be settled.
net investment in a foreign operation	The amount of the reporting entity's interest in the net assets of that operation.
net investment in a lease	The **gross investment in a lease** discounted at the **interest rate implicit in the lease**.

non-controlling interest	The **equity** in a **subsidiary** not attributable, directly or indirectly, to a **parent**.
non-exchange transaction	A transaction whereby an entity receives value from another entity without directly giving approximately equal value in exchange, or gives value to another entity without directly receiving approximately equal value in exchange.
notes (to financial statements)	Notes contain information in addition to that presented in the **statement of financial position**, **statement of comprehensive income**, **income statement** (if presented), combined **statement of income and retained earnings** (if presented), **statement of changes in equity** and **statement of cash flows**. Notes provide narrative descriptions or disaggregations of items presented in those statements and information about items that do not qualify for **recognition** in those statements.
notional amount	The quantity of currency units, shares, bushels, pounds or other units specified in a financial instrument contract.
objective of financial statements	To provide information about the **financial position**, **performance** and **cash flows** of an entity that is useful for economic decision-making by a broad range of users who are not in a position to demand reports tailored to meet their particular information needs.
onerous contract	A contract in which the unavoidable costs of meeting the obligations under the contract exceed the economic benefits expected to be received under it.
operating activities	The principal revenue-producing activities of the entity and other activities that are not investing or **financing activities**.
operating lease	A **lease** that does not transfer substantially all the risks and rewards incidental to ownership. A lease that is not an operating lease is a **finance lease**.
operating segment	An operating segment is a **component of an entity**: (a) that engages in business activities from which it may earn **revenues** and incur **expenses** (including revenues and expenses relating to transactions with other components of the same entity); (b) whose operating results are regularly reviewed by the entity's chief operating decision maker to make decisions about resources to be allocated to the segment and assess its **performance**; and (c) for which discrete financial information is available.
ordinary share	An equity instrument that is subordinate to all other classes of equity instrument.

other comprehensive income	Items of **income** and **expense** (including reclassification adjustments) that are not recognised in **profit or loss** as required or permitted by this FRS.
owners	Holders of instruments classified as **equity**.
parent	An entity that has one or more **subsidiaries**.
performance	The relationship of the **income** and **expenses** of an entity, as reported in the **statement of comprehensive income**.
performance-related condition	A condition that requires the performance of a particular level of service or units of output to be delivered, with payment of, or entitlement to, the resources conditional on that performance.
permanent differences	Differences between an entity's **taxable profits** and its **total comprehensive income** as stated in the **financial statements**, other than **timing differences**.
plan assets (of an employee benefit plan)	(a) **assets held by a long-term employee benefit fund**; and (b) **qualifying insurance policies**.
post-employment benefits	**Employee benefits** (other than **termination benefits** and short-term employee benefits) that are payable after the completion of employment.
post-employment benefit plans	Formal or informal arrangements under which an entity provides **post-employment benefits** for one or more employees.
potential ordinary share	A financial instrument or other contract that may entitle its holder to **ordinary shares**.
present value	A current estimate of the present discounted value of the future net **cash flows** in the normal course of **business**.
presentation currency	The currency in which the **financial statements** are presented.
prevailing market rate	The rate of interest that would apply to the entity in an open market for a similar financial instrument.
principal	An entity is acting as a principal when it has exposure to the significant risks and rewards associated with the sale of goods or the rendering of services. Features that indicate that an entity is acting as a principal include: (a) the entity has the primary responsibility for providing the goods or services to the customer or for fulfilling the order, for example by being responsible for the

	acceptability of the products or services ordered or purchased by the customer; (b) the entity has inventory risk before or after the customer order, during shipping or on return; (c) the entity has latitude in establishing prices, either directly or indirectly, for example by providing additional goods or services; and (d) the entity bears the customer's credit risk for the amount receivable from the customer.
probable	More likely than not.
profit or loss	The total of **income** less **expenses**, excluding the components of **other comprehensive income**.
projected unit credit method	An actuarial valuation method that sees each period of service as giving rise to an additional unit of benefit entitlement and measures each unit separately to build up the final obligation (sometimes known as the accrued benefit method pro-rated on service or as the benefit/years of service method).
property, plant and equipment	Tangible assets that: (a) are held for use in the production or supply of goods or services, for rental to others, or for administrative purposes, and (b) are expected to be used during more than one period.
prospectively (applying a change in accounting policy)	Applying the new **accounting policy** to transactions, other events and conditions occurring after the date as at which the policy is changed.
provision	A **liability** of uncertain timing or amount.
prudence	The inclusion of a degree of caution in the exercise of the judgements needed in making the estimates required under conditions of uncertainty, such that **assets** or **income** are not overstated and **liabilities** or **expenses** are not understated.

public benefit entity	An entity whose primary objective is to provide goods or services for the general public, community or social benefit and where any **equity** is provided with a view to supporting the entity's primary objectives rather than with a view to providing a financial return to equity providers, shareholders or members.*
public benefit entity concessionary loan	A loan made or received between a **public benefit entity** or an entity within a **public benefit entity group** and another party: (a) at below the **prevailing market rate** of interest; (b) that is not repayable on demand; and (c) is for the purposes of furthering the objectives of the public benefit entity or public benefit entity **parent**.
public benefit entity group	A **public benefit entity parent** and all of its wholly-owned **subsidiaries**.
publicly traded (debt or equity instruments)	Traded, or in process of being issued for trading, in a public market (a domestic or foreign stock exchange or an over-the-counter market, including local and regional markets).
qualifying asset	An **asset** that necessarily takes a substantial period of time to get ready for its intended use or sale. Depending on the circumstances any of the following may be qualifying assets: (a) **inventories**; (b) manufacturing plants; (c) power generation facilities; (d) **intangible assets**; and (e) **investment properties**. **Financial assets**, and inventories that are produced over a short period of time, are not qualifying assets. Assets that are ready for their intended use or sale when acquired are not qualifying assets.

**The term 'public benefit entity' does not necessarily imply that the purpose of the entity is for the benefit of the public as a whole. For example, many PBEs exist for the direct benefit of a particular group of people, although it is possible that society as a whole also benefits indirectly. The important factor is what the primary purpose of such an entity is, and that it does not exist primarily to provide economic benefit to its investors. Organisations such as mutual insurance companies, other mutual co-operative entities and clubs that provide dividends or other economic benefits directly and proportionately to their owners, members or participants are not PBEs.*

Some PBEs undertake certain activities that are intended to make a surplus in order to fund their primary activities. Consideration should be given to the primary purpose of an entity's (or group's) activities in assessing whether it meets the definition of a PBE.

PBEs may have received contributions in the form of equity, even though the entity does not have a primary profit motive. However, because of the fundamental nature of public benefit entities, any such contributions are made by the equity holders of the entity primarily to enable the provision of goods or services to beneficiaries rather than with a view to a financial return for themselves. This is different from the position of lenders; loans do not fall into the category of equity.

qualifying entity (for the purposes of this FRS)	A member of a **group** where the **parent** of that group prepares publicly available **consolidated financial statements** which are intended to give a true and fair view (of the **assets**, **liabilities**, **financial position** and **profit or loss**) and that member is included in the consolidation*.
qualifying insurance policies	An insurance policy† issued by an insurer that is not a **related party** of the reporting entity, if the proceeds of the policy: (a) can be used only to pay or fund **employee benefits** under a **defined benefit plan**; and (b) are not available to the reporting entity's own creditors (even in bankruptcy) and cannot be paid to the reporting entity, unless either: (i) the proceeds represent surplus **assets** that are not needed for the policy to meet all the related employee benefit obligations; or (ii) the proceeds are returned to the reporting entity to reimburse it for employee benefits already paid.
recognition	The process of incorporating in the **statement of financial position** or **statement of comprehensive income** an item that meets the definition of an asset, liability, equity, income or expense and satisfies the following criteria: (a) it is **probable** that any future economic benefit associated with the item will flow to or from the entity; and (b) the item has a cost or value that can be measured with **reliability**.
recoverable amount	The higher of an **asset's** (or **cash-generating unit's**) **fair value less costs to sell** and its value in use.
Regulations	The Large and Medium-sized Companies and Groups (Accounts and Reports) Regulations 2008 (SI 2008/410).
reinsurance contract	An **insurance contract** issued by one insurer (the reinsurer) to compensate another insurer (the cedant) for losses on one or more contracts issued by the cedant.
related party	A related party is a person or entity that is related to the entity that is preparing its **financial statements** (the reporting entity). (a) A person or a close member of that person's family is related to a reporting entity if that person: (i) has **control** or **joint control** over the reporting entity; (ii) has **significant influence** over the reporting entity; or (iii) is a member of the **key management personnel** of the reporting entity or of a **parent** of the reporting entity. (b) An entity is related to a reporting entity if any of the following conditions apply:

**As set out in section 474(1) of the Act.*

†*A qualifying insurance policy is not necessarily an insurance contract.*

	(i) the entity and the reporting entity are members of the same **group** (which means that each parent, **subsidiary** and fellow subsidiary is related to the others). (ii) one entity is an **associate** or **joint venture** of the other entity (or of a member of a group of which the other entity is a member). (iii) both entities are joint ventures of the same third entity. (iv) one entity is a joint venture of a third entity and the other entity is an associate of the third entity. (v) the entity is a **post-employment benefit plan** for the benefit of employees of either the reporting entity or an entity related to the reporting entity. If the reporting entity is itself such a plan, the sponsoring employers are also related to the reporting entity. (vi) the entity is controlled or jointly controlled by a person identified in (a). (vii) a person identified in (a)(i) has significant influence over the entity or is a member of the key management personnel of the entity (or of a parent of the entity).
related party transaction	A transfer of resources, services or obligations between a reporting entity and a **related party**, regardless of whether a price is charged.
relevance	The quality of information that allows it to influence the economic decisions of users by helping them evaluate past, present or future events or confirming, or correcting, their past evaluations.
reliability	The quality of information that makes it free from **material error** and bias and represents faithfully that which it either purports to represent or could reasonably be expected to represent.
reporting date	The end of the latest period covered by **financial statements** or by an interim financial report.
reporting period	The period covered by **financial statements** or by an **interim financial report**.
research	Original and planned investigation undertaken with the prospect of gaining new scientific or technical knowledge and understanding.
residual value (of an asset)	The estimated amount that an entity would currently obtain from disposal of an **asset**, after deducting the estimated costs of disposal, if the asset were already of the age and in the condition expected at the end of its **useful life**.

restriction	A requirement that limits or directs the purposes for which a resource may be used that does not meet the definition of a **performance-related condition**.
restructuring	A restructuring is a programme that is planned and controlled by management and materially changes either: (a) the scope of a business undertaken by an entity; or (b) the manner in which that business is conducted.
retirement benefit plan	Arrangements whereby an entity provides benefits for employees on or after termination of service (either in the form of an annual **income** or as a lump sum) when such benefits, or the contributions towards them, can be determined or estimated in advance of retirement from the provisions of a document or from the entity's practice.
retrospective application (of an accounting policy)	Applying a new **accounting policy** to transactions, other events and conditions as if that policy had always been applied.
revenue	The gross inflow of economic benefits during the period arising in the course of the ordinary activities of an entity when those inflows result in increases in **equity**, other than increases relating to contributions from equity participants.
separate financial statements	Those presented by a **parent** in which the investments in **subsidiaries, associates** or **jointly controlled entities** are accounted for either at cost or **fair value** rather than on the basis of the reported results and net assets of the investees. Separate financial statements are included within the meaning of **individual financial statements**.
service concession arrangement	An arrangement whereby a public sector body or a **public benefit entity** (the grantor) contracts with a private sector entity (the operator) to construct (or upgrade), operate and maintain **infrastructure assets** for a specified period of time (the concession period).
service potential	The economic utility of an **asset**, based on the total benefit expected to be derived by the entity from use (and/or through sale) of the asset.
share-based payment transaction	A transaction in which the entity: (a) receives goods or services (including employee services) as consideration for its own equity instruments (including shares or **share options**); or (b) receives goods or services but has no obligation to settle the transaction with supplier; or (c) acquires goods or services by incurring **liabilities** to the supplier of those goods or services for amounts that are based on the price (or value) of the entity's shares or other equity instruments of the entity or another group entity.

share option	A contract that gives the holder the right, but not the obligation, to subscribe to the entity's shares at a fixed or determinable price for a specific period of time.
significant influence	Significant influence is the power to participate in the financial and operating policy decisions of the **associate** but is not **control** or **joint control** over those policies.
Statement of Recommended Practice (SORP)	An extant Statement of Recommended Practice developed in accordance with *SORPs: Policy and Code of Practice*. SORPs recommend accounting practices for specialised industries or sectors. They supplement accounting standards and other legal and regulatory requirements in the light of the special factors prevailing or transactions undertaken in a particular industry or sector.
state	A national, regional, or local government.
state (employee benefit) plan	Employee benefit plans established by legislation to cover all entities (or all entities in a particular category, for example a specific industry) and operated by national or local government or by another body (for example an autonomous agency created specifically for this purpose) which is not subject to control or influence by the reporting entity.
statement of cash flows	**Financial statement** that provides information about the changes in **cash** and **cash equivalents** of an entity for a period, showing separately changes during the period from operating, investing and **financing activities**.
statement of comprehensive income	**Financial statement** that presents all items of **income** and **expense** recognised in a period, including those items recognised in determining **profit or loss** (which is a subtotal in the statement of comprehensive income) and items of **other comprehensive income**. If an entity chooses to present both an **income statement** and a statement of comprehensive income, the statement of comprehensive income begins with profit or loss and then displays the items of other comprehensive income.
statement of financial position	**Financial statement** that presents the relationship of an entity's **assets**, **liabilities** and **equity** as of a specific date (referred to as the balance sheet in the **Act**).
statement of income and retained earnings	**Financial statement** that presents the **profit or loss** and changes in retained earnings for a **reporting period**.
subsidiary	An entity, including an unincorporated entity such as a partnership, that is **controlled** by another entity (known as the **parent**).

substantively enacted	Tax rates shall be regarded as substantively enacted when the remaining stages of the enactment process historically have not affected the outcome and are unlikely to do so. A UK tax rate shall be regarded as having been substantively enacted if it is included in either: (a) a Bill that has been passed by the House of Commons and is awaiting only passage through the House of Lords and Royal Assent; or (b) a resolution having statutory effect that has been passed under the Provisional Collection of Taxes Act 1968. (Such a resolution could be used to collect taxes at a new rate before that rate has been enacted. In practice, corporation tax rates are now set a year ahead to avoid having to invoke the Provisional Collection of Taxes Act for the quarterly payment system.) A Republic of Ireland tax rate can be regarded as having been substantively enacted if it is included in a Bill that has been passed by the Dail.
tax expense	The aggregate amount included in **total comprehensive income** or **equity** for the **reporting period** in respect of **current tax** and **deferred tax**.
taxable profit (tax loss)	The profit (loss) for a **reporting period** upon which income taxes are payable or recoverable, determined in accordance with the rules established by the taxation authorities. Taxable profit equals taxable income less amounts deductible from taxable income.
termination benefits	**Employee benefits** provided in exchange for the termination of an employee's employment as a result of either: (a) an entity's decision to terminate an employee's employment before the normal retirement date; or (b) an employee's decision to accept voluntary redundancy in exchange for those benefits.
timing differences	Differences between **taxable profits** and **total comprehensive income** as stated in the **financial statements** that arise from the inclusion of **income** and **expenses** in tax assessments in periods different from those in which they are recognised in financial statements.
timeliness	Providing the information in **financial statements** within the decision time frame.
total comprehensive income	The change in **equity** during a period resulting from transactions and other events, other than those changes resulting from transactions from equity participants (equal to the sum of **profit or loss** and **other comprehensive income**).
transaction costs (financial instruments)	Incremental costs that are directly attributable to the acquisition, issue or disposal of a **financial asset** or **financial liability**, or the issue or reacquisition of an entity's **own equity**

	instrument. An incremental cost is one that would not have been incurred if the entity had not acquired, issued or disposed of the financial asset or financial liability, or had not issued or reacquired its own equity instrument.
treasury shares	An entity's own equity instruments, held by that entity or other members of the consolidated group.
turnover	The amounts derived from the provision of goods and services falling within the entity's ordinary activities, after deduction of: (a) trade discounts; (b) value added tax; and (c) any other taxes based on the amounts so derived.
understandability	The presentation of information in a way that makes it comprehensible by users who have a reasonable knowledge of **business** and economic activities and accounting and a willingness to study the information with reasonable diligence.
useful life	The period over which an **asset** is expected to be available for use by an entity or the number of production or similar units expected to be obtained from the asset by an entity.
value in use	The **present value** of the future **cash flows** expected to be derived from an **asset** or **cash-generating unit**.
value in use (in respect of assets held for their service potential)	When the future economic benefits of an **asset** are not primarily dependent on the asset's ability to generate net cash inflows, **value in use** (in respect of assets held for their **service potential**) is the **present value** to the entity of the asset's remaining service potential if it continues to be used, plus the net amount that the entity will receive from its disposal at the end of its **useful life**.
venturer	A party to a **joint venture** that has **joint control** over that joint venture.
vest	Become an entitlement. Under a share-based payment arrangement, a counterparty's right to receive **cash**, other **assets** or equity instruments of the entity vests when the counterparty's entitlement is no longer conditional on the satisfaction of any vesting conditions.
vested benefits	Benefits, the rights to which, under the conditions of a **retirement benefit plan**, are not conditional on continued employment.

Appendix II: Significant Differences Between FRS 102 and the IFRS for SMEs

Section		Changes to the IFRS for SMEs
1	Scope of this FRS	This section of the IFRS for SMEs has been replaced. The IFRS for SMEs applies to small and medium sized entities that do not have public accountability and publish general purpose financial statements. FRS 100 *Application of Financial Reporting Requirements* sets out the scope of entities applying this FRS.
2	Concepts and Pervasive Principles	No significant changes.
3	Financial Statement Presentation	The requirements in paragraph 3.7 are deleted and requirements set out in the Act are referred to for the use of the true and fair override. Paragraph 3.16 is amended to clarify the role of materiality in the preparation of financial statements. Paragraph 3.16A is inserted to specify that disclosures are not required if the information is not material.
4	Statement of Financial Position	The requirements of this section have predominantly been removed and replaced by the requirements set out in the Act. Entities that do not report under the Act comply with the requirements of this section, and of the Regulations, except to the extent that these requirements are not permitted by any statutory framework under which such entities report.
5	Statement of Comprehensive Income and Income Statement	The requirements of this section have predominantly been removed and replaced by the requirements set out in the Act. Entities that do not report under the Act comply with the requirements of this section and of the Regulations except to the extent that these requirements are not permitted by any statutory framework under which such entities report. Paragraph 5.10 has been amended and paragraph 5.10A is inserted to comply with the Act and includes the definition of an extraordinary item.
6	Statement of Changes in Equity and Statement of Income and Retained Earnings	Paragraph 6.3A is inserted to require presentation for each component of equity an analysis of other comprehensive income by item, either in the notes, or in the statement of changes in equity.

Section		Changes to the IFRS for SMEs
7	Statement of Cash Flows	The scope of this section is amended to exclude mutual life assurance companies, pension funds and certain investment funds. Paragraphs 7.10A to 7.10E are inserted to require the reporting of cash flows on a net basis in some circumstances. Paragraphs 7.11 and 7.12 are amended to provide some relaxation of the exchange rates permitted to be used.
8	Notes to the Financial Statements	No significant changes.
9	Consolidated and Separate Financial Statements	The scope of this section is amended to clarify that it applies to all parent entities that present consolidated financial statements intended to give a true and fair view. The requirements to present consolidated financial statements are amended to comply with the Act. Paragraph 9.9 requires a subsidiary that is held exclusively with a view to subsequent resale because it is held as part of an investment portfolio, to be excluded from consolidation. Such subsidiaries are required to be measured at fair value with changes recognised in profit or loss. This exemption is required irrespective of whether the subsidiary was previously consolidated under previous GAAP, prior to transition to FRS 102. In addition paragraphs 14.4B and 15.9B are inserted to require an investor that has investments in associates or jointly controlled entities that are held as part of an investment portfolio to measure those investments at fair value with the changes recognised in profit or loss in their consolidated financial statements. Clarification is added to paragraph 9.10 that Employee Share Ownership Plans and similar arrangements are Special Purpose Entities. Paragraph 9.16 is amended to comply with paragraph 2(2) of Schedule 6 to the Regulations in order to require a subsidiary's financial statements, which are included in the consolidated financial statements, to be for the same reporting period (financial year) and as at the same reporting date (year-end). Where it is not practicable to align the subsidiary's reporting date (year-end) with the parent's, paragraph 9.16 has been amended to specify which financial

Section		Changes to the IFRS for SMEs
		statements of the subsidiary are permitted to be used in the consolidation. Paragraphs 9.18A and 9.18B are inserted to clarify the treatment of a disposal where control is lost. Paragraph 9.19A is inserted to clarify the treatment of the disposal where control is retained. Paragraph 9.19B is inserted to clarify the treatment of an acquisition made in stages. Paragraphs 9.19C and 9.19D are inserted to clarify the treatment of non-controlling interest when a parent changes its holding in a subsidiary but control is retained. Paragraphs 9.23A to 9.25 are amended to clarify the distinction between the individual financial statements and separate financial statements and that the Act specifies when individual financial statements are required to be prepared. Paragraphs 9.28 to 9.30 relating to combined financial statements are deleted. Paragraphs 9.31 and 9.32 provide guidance on exchanges of businesses or other non-monetary assets for an interest in a subsidiary, joint venture or associate. This guidance was previously contained in UITF Abstract 31 *Exchanges of businesses or other non-monetary assets for an interest in a subsidiary, joint venture or associate.* Paragraphs 9.33 to 9.38 are inserted to provide guidance on the accounting treatment for intermediate payment arrangements. These were previously contained in UITF Abstract 32 *Employee benefit trusts and other intermediate payment arrangements.*
10	Accounting Policies, Estimates and Errors	Paragraph 10.5 clarifies when an entity is required to refer to SORPs in developing an accounting policy. Paragraph 10.10A is inserted to bring the accounting treatment for changes in accounting policy relating to property, plant and equipment (Section 17) and intangible assets (Section 18) in line with IAS 10 *Accounting Policies, Estimate and Errors.*
11	Basic Financial Instruments	The scope of section 11 is amended to clarify that certain financial instruments are not within its scope.

Section		Changes to the IFRS for SMEs
		Paragraph 11.9(c) is amended to clarify that contractual prepayment provisions which are contingent future events exclude those which protect the holder from credit deterioration or tax changes. Paragraph 11.14(b) is inserted to clarify that entities may choose to designate debt instruments as fair value through profit or loss under certain circumstances. Paragraph 11.38A is inserted to allow offsetting of certain financial assets and financial liabilities in the statement of financial position. Paragraph 11.48A is inserted to provide disclosures required in accordance with the Regulations for financial instruments that are not held as part of a trading portfolio and are not derivatives. Paragraphs 11.48B and 11.48C require additional disclosures for financial institutions.
12	Other Financial Instruments Issues	The scope of Section 12 is amended to exclude financial instruments issued by an entity with a discretionary participation feature, reimbursement assets and financial guarantee contracts. Paragraph 12.23 clarifies that the cumulative amount of foreign exchange differences relating to a hedge of a net investment in a foreign operation are not reclassified to profit or loss on disposal or partial disposal. Paragraph 12.25A is inserted to allow offsetting of certain financial assets and financial liabilities in the statement of financial position. Paragraph 12.26 is amended to comply with requirements set out in the Act.
13	Inventories	Paragraphs 13.4A and 13.20A are inserted to provide guidance on inventories held for distribution at no or nominal consideration. Paragraph 13.5A is inserted to provide guidance on inventory acquired through non-exchange transactions. Paragraph 13.8A is inserted to clarify the treatment for provisions made against dismantling and restoration costs (of PPE) in the cost of inventory.

Section		Changes to the IFRS for SMEs
		Paragraph 13.15 is amended to allow for the inclusion of a cost model for agricultural produce in Section 34 *Specialised Activities*.
14	Investments in Associates	The scope of this section is amended to clarify its application to consolidated financial statements and to the financial statements of an entity that is not a parent but which holds investments in associates. Paragraph 14.4(b) of the IFRS for SMEs is deleted as the equity method of accounting for investments in associates in individual financial statements is not compliant with company law. Paragraph 14.4(d) is inserted to allow non-parent investors to account for investments in associates at fair value with changes recognised in profit or loss. Paragraphs 14.4B is inserted to require an investor that is a parent which has investments in associates that are held as part of an investment portfolio to measure those investments at fair value with the changes recognised in profit or loss in their consolidated financial statements. Paragraph 14.9 is amended to require transaction costs to be included as part of the transaction price on initial recognition. Paragraph 14.10 is amended to require changes in fair value to be recognised through other comprehensive income, in accordance with paragraphs 17.15E and 17.15F, when the fair value model is applied, rather than through profit or loss. Paragraph 14.15A is inserted to provide information about associates held by entities that are not parents.
15	Investments in Joint Ventures	The scope of this section is amended to clarify its application to consolidated financial statements and to the financial statements of a venturer that is not a parent. Paragraph 15.9(b) of the IFRS for SMEs is deleted as the equity method of accounting for interests in jointly controlled entities in individual financial statements is not compliant with company law. Paragraph 15.9(d) is inserted to allow non-parent investors to account for investments in jointly controlled entities at fair value with the changes recognised in profit or loss.

Section		**Changes to the IFRS for SMEs**
		Paragraph 15.9B is inserted to require an investor that is a parent which has investments in jointly controlled entities that are held as part of an investment portfolio to measure those investments at fair value with the changes recognised in profit or loss in their consolidated financial statements. Paragraph 15.14 is amended to require transaction costs to be included as part of the transaction price on initial recognition. Paragraph 15.15 is amended to require changes in fair value to be recognised through other comprehensive income, in accordance with paragraphs 17.15E and 17.15F, when the fair value model is applied, rather than through profit or loss. Paragraph 15.21A is inserted to provide information about associates held by entities that are not parents.
16	Investment Property	No significant changes.
17	Property, Plant and Equipment	Section 17 is amended to provide, after initial recognition, that an entity may use the cost model or revaluation model.
18	Intangible Assets other than Goodwill	Section 18 is amended to permit entities to recognise intangible assets that result from expenditure incurred on the internal development of an intangible item (subject to certain criteria). The section provides guidance on what comprises the cost of an internally generated intangible asset and the criteria for initial recognition. The section is also amended to provide, after initial recognition, that an entity may use the cost model or revaluation model.
19	Business Combinations and Goodwill	Section 19 is amended to permit the use of merger accounting method for group reconstructions. The merger method is set out in paragraphs 19.29 to 19.33. Paragraphs 19.15A to 19.15C are inserted to provide guidance on the treatment of deferred tax assets or liabilities, employee benefit arrangements and share-based payments of a subsidiary on acquisition. Paragraph 19.23(a) is amended to comply with company law such that, where an entity is unable to make a reliable estimate of the useful life of goodwill, the life shall be presumed not to exceed

Section		Changes to the IFRS for SMEs
		five years rather than 10 years as set out in the IFRS for SMEs. Paragraph 19.24 is amended and paragraph 19.26A is inserted to comply with the requirements of the Act for bargain purchases (negative goodwill).
20	Leases	The scope of Section 20 is amended to include operating leases that are onerous within its scope. Paragraphs 20.15A and 20.25A are inserted to clarify the treatment of operating lease incentives for lessees and lessors respectively. Paragraph 20.15B is inserted to provide guidance on the treatment of onerous operating lease contracts.
21	Provisions and Contingencies	The scope of Section 21 is amended to include financial guarantee contracts. Paragraph 21.17A is inserted to provide guidance on the accounting treatment of financial guarantee contracts.
22	Liabilities and Equity	Paragraph 22.3A is inserted to clarify that a financial instrument where the issuer does not have the unconditional right to avoid settling in cash or by delivery of another financial asset (or otherwise to settle it in such a way that it would be a financial liability); and where settlement is dependent on the occurrence or non-occurrence of uncertain future events beyond the control of the issuer and the holder, is a financial liability of the issuer unless specific circumstances apply. The requirement for an entity to recognise a liability at fair value when non-cash assets are distributed to owners is removed and only disclosure is required in paragraph 22.18.
23	Revenue	No significant changes.
24	Government Grants	Paragraphs 24.5C to 24.5G are inserted to allow an additional model of accounting for grants (the accrual model). The model permits entities to recognise grant income on a systematic basis over the period in which the entity recognises the related costs for which the grant is intended to compensate.

Section		Changes to the IFRS for SMEs
25	Borrowing Costs	Section 25 is amended to allow an option that permits entities to capitalise borrowing costs that are directly attributable to the acquisition, construction or production of a qualifying asset.
26	Share-based Payment	The definition of equity-settled share based payments has been amended to align with the revised IFRS 2 definition. It is clarified that option pricing models do not have to be applied in all circumstances.
27	Impairment of Assets	Paragraph 27.20A is inserted to provide guidance on the treatment of impairments on assets held for their service potential. Paragraph 27.31 is amended to allow the reversal of impairment losses against goodwill. Paragraph 27.33A is inserted to include a descriptive disclosure requirement of the events and circumstances that led to the recognition or reversal of the impairment loss.
28	Employee Benefits	The presentation of the cost of a defined benefit plan and the accounting for group plans have been amended to be consistent with the requirements of IAS *19 Employee Benefits* as amended in 2011. Paragraph 28.11A is inserted to require the recognition of a liability on a defined benefit multi-employer plan, which is accounted as defined contribution scheme, where funding of a deficit has been agreed. Paragraph 28.19 is deleted to remove the option to use a simplified valuation method in measuring the liability.
29	Income Tax	Section 29 of the IFRS for SMEs has been entirely replaced with revised requirements.
30	Foreign Currency Translation	No significant changes.
31	Hyperinflation	No significant changes.
32	Events after the End of the Reporting Period	Paragraphs 32.7A and 32.7B are inserted to provide guidance on the impact of changes in an entity's going concern status.
33	Related Party Disclosures	Paragraph 33.1A is inserted to include the exemption from disclosure of related party

Section		Changes to the IFRS for SMEs
		transactions for wholly-owned entities available in the Act.
34	Specialised Activities	Agriculture – this sub-section is amended to allow the option to hold biological assets and agricultural produce at cost. Extractives – this sub-section has been amended to require application of IFRS 6. Service concession arrangements – this sub-section is amended to provide clarify the accounting by operators and provide guidance to grantors. The following additional sub-sections are inserted: Financial Institutions; Retirement Benefit Plans: Financial Statements; Heritage Assets; Funding Commitments; Incoming Resources from Non-Exchange Transactions; Public Benefit Entity Combinations; and Public Benefit Entity Concessionary Loans.
35	Transition to this FRS	Amendments to this section reflect the changes in preceding sections.

Appendix III: Table of Equivalence for UK Companies Act Terminology

The following table compares company law terminology with broadly equivalent terminology used in FRS 102. In some cases there are minor differences between the broadly equivalent definitions, which are also summarised below.

Company law terminology	**FRS 102 terminology**
Accounting reference date	Reporting date
Accounts	Financial statements
Associated undertaking	Associate
Balance sheet	Statement of financial position
Capital and reserves	Equity
Cash at bank and in hand	Cash*
Debtors	Trade receivables
Diminution in value [of assets]	Impairment
Financial year	Reporting period
Group [accounts]	Consolidated [financial statements]
IAS	EU-adopted IFRS
Individual [accounts]	Individual [financial statements]
Interest payable and similar charges	Finance costs
Interest receivable and similar income	Finance income/Investment income
Minority interests	Non-controlling interest
Net realisable value [of any current asset]	Estimated selling price less costs to complete and sell
Parent undertaking	Parent
Profit and loss account	Income statement (under the two-statement approach) Part of the statement of comprehensive income (under the single- statement approach)
Related undertakings†	Subsidiaries, associates and joint ventures
Stocks	Inventories

**FRS 102 requires the cash flow statement to reconcile the movement in 'cash and cash equivalents'. Disclosure is required of reconciliation between amounts presented in the statement of financial position (ie cash) and 'cash and cash equivalents'.*

†This would also include entities in which a company has at least a 20% holding, but which are not a subsidiary, joint venture or an associate. A shareholding of 20% is presumed to give significant influence to the holder, such that the investment would be classified as an associate, therefore in practice there are unlikely to be many related undertakings that are not subsidiaries, joint ventures or associates.

Company law terminology	FRS 102 terminology
Subsidiary undertaking	Subsidiary
Tangible assets	Includes: Property, plant equipment; Investment property
Trade creditors	Trade payables

Appendix IV: Note on Legal Requirements

INTRODUCTION

This appendix provides an overview of how the requirements in FRS 102 address United Kingdom company law requirements. It is therefore written from the perspective of a company to which the Companies Act 2006 applies*. Appendix VI contains the Republic of Ireland legal references. **A4.1**

Many entities that are not constituted as companies apply accounting standards promulgated by the FRC for the purposes of preparing financial statements that present a true and fair view†. A brief consideration of the legal framework for some other entities can be found at A4.41 and A4.42. For those entities that are within the scope of a Statement of Recommended Practice (SORP), the relevant SORP will provide more details on the legal framework. **A4.2**

References to the Act in this appendix are to the *Companies Act 2006*. References to the Regulations are to *The Large and Medium-sized Companies and Groups (Accounts and Reports) Regulations 2008* (SI 2008/410). References to specific provisions are to Schedule 1 to the Regulations; entities applying Schedules 2, 3 or 6 should read them as referring to the equivalent paragraph in those schedules. **A4.3**

APPLICABLE ACCOUNTING FRAMEWORK

Group accounts of certain parent entities (those with securities admitted to trading on a regulated market in an EU Member State) are required by Article 4 of EU Regulation 1606/2002 (IAS Regulation) to be prepared in accordance with EU-adopted IFRS. **A4.4**

All other entities, except those that are eligible to apply the *Financial Reporting Standard for Smaller Entities* (effective January 2015) (FRSSE), must apply‡ either FRS 102 *The Financial Reporting Standard applicable in the UK and Republic of Ireland*, EU-adopted IFRS or FRS 101 (if the financial statements are the individual financial statements of a qualifying entity eligible to apply FRS 101 *Reduced Disclosure Framework*). **A4.5**

Section 395(1) of the Act states: **A4.6**

> 'A company's individual accounts may be prepared—
>
> (a) in accordance with section 396 ("Companies Act individual accounts"), or
> (b) in accordance with international accounting standards ("IAS individual accounts").'

**Some charities are also companies, and are therefore required to apply the requirements of both the Companies Act 2006 and the Charities Act 2011.*

†*More information about the 'true and fair' concept can be found on the FRC's website at http://www.frc.org.uk/Our-Work/Codes-Standards/Accounting-and-Reporting-Policy/True-and-Fair.aspx.*

‡*Under company law in the Republic of Ireland, certain entities are permitted to prepare Companies Act accounts using accounting standards other than those issued by the FRC. Please refer to Appendix VI for further details.*

Section 403(2) of the Act states:

'The group accounts of other companies may be prepared—

(a) in accordance with section 404 ("Companies Act group accounts"), or
(b) in accordance with international accounting standards ("IAS group accounts").'

A4.7 Accounts prepared in accordance with FRS 102 are classified as either 'Companies Act individual accounts', including those of qualifying entities applying FRS 102, or 'Companies Act group accounts' and are therefore required to comply with the applicable provisions of Parts 15 and 16 of the Act and with the Regulations.

Consistency of financial reporting within groups

A4.8 Section 407 of the Act requires that the directors of the parent company secure that individual accounts of a parent company and each of its subsidiaries are prepared using the same financial reporting framework, except to the extent that in the directors' opinion there are good reasons for not doing so.

In addition, consistency is not required in the following situations:

(a) when the parent company does not prepare consolidated financial statements; or
(b) when some subsidiaries are charities (consistency is not needed between the framework used for these and for other subsidiaries).

Where the directors of a parent company prepare IAS group accounts and IAS individual accounts, there only has to be consistency across the individual financial statements of the subsidiaries.

A4.9 All companies, other than those which elect or are required to prepare IAS individual accounts in accordance with the Act, prepare Companies Act individual accounts.

APPLICATION OF FRS 102

Compliance with company law

A4.10 The FRS has been developed for application in the UK and Republic of Ireland, using the IFRS for SMEs as a basis. Part of that development process included making amendments to the IFRS for SMEs to ensure compliance with the Act and the Regulations. For example, changes were made to eliminate options that are not permitted by company law. However, FRS 102 is not intended to be a one-stop-shop for all accounting and legal requirements, and although the FRC believes the FRS 102 is not inconsistent with company law, compliance with FRS 102 alone will often be insufficient to ensure compliance with all the disclosure requirements set out in the Act and the Regulations. As a result preparers will continue to be required to have regard to the requirements of company law in addition to accounting standards.

A4.11 This appendix does not list every legal requirement, but instead focuses on those areas where greater judgement might be required in determining compliance with the law.

Financial instruments measured at fair value

All preparers of Companies Act accounts must comply with the requirements of paragraph 36 of Schedule 1 to the Regulations, which provides that: **A4.12**

'(1) Subject to sub-paragraphs (2) to (5), financial instruments (including derivatives) may be included at fair value.

(2) Sub-paragraph (1) does not apply to financial instruments that constitute liabilities unless—

a. they are held as part of a trading portfolio,
b. they are derivatives, or
c. they are financial instruments falling within sub-paragraph (4).

(3) Unless they are financial instruments falling within sub-paragraph (4), sub-paragraph (1) does not apply to –

a. financial instruments (other than derivatives) held to maturity,
b. loans and receivables originated by the company and not held for trading purposes,
c. interests in subsidiary undertakings, associated undertakings and joint ventures,
d. equity instruments issued by the company,
e. contracts for contingent consideration in a business combination, or
f. other financial instruments with such special characteristics that the instruments, according to generally accepted accounting principles or practice, should be accounted for differently from other financial instruments.

(4) Financial instruments that, under international accounting standards adopted by the European Commission on or before 5th September 2006 in accordance with the IAS Regulation, may be included in accounts at fair value, may be so included, provided that the disclosures required by such accounting standards are made.

(5) [...]'

An entity applying this FRS and holding financial instruments measured at fair value either in accordance with Sections 11 *Basic Financial Instruments* or 12 *Other Financial Instruments Issues* may be required to provide the disclosures required by paragraph 36(4) of Schedule 1 to the Regulations. The disclosures as required by paragraph 36(4) have been incorporated into Section 11. Some of the Section 11 disclosure requirements apply to all financial instruments measured at fair value, whilst others (see paragraph 11.48A of FRS 102) apply only to financial instruments that are not held as part of a trading portfolio and are not derivatives. The disclosure requirements of paragraph 11.48A will predominantly apply to certain financial liabilities, however, there may be instances where paragraph 36(3) of Schedule 1 to the Regulations requires that the disclosures must also be provided in relation to financial assets, for example investments in subsidiaries, associates or jointly controlled entities measured at fair value (see paragraph 9.27B of FRS 102). **A4.13**

Requirement to present financial statements

FRS 102 does not prescribe which entities prepare financial statements and preparers should apply the requirements of the Act in determining whether financial statements (either individual or consolidated) are required. FRS 102 sets out the requirements for a complete set of financial statements that present fairly the financial position, financial performance and cash flows of an entity, where these are required by law, or other regulation or requirement. **A4.14**

A4.15 A parent company preparing consolidated financial statements under section 434(2) of the Act must publish its company financial statements together with the consolidated financial statements, although section 408 of the Act provides an exemption from including the company's individual profit and loss account.

Subsidiaries excluded from consolidation

A4.16 Paragraph 9.9(b) of Section 9 *Consolidated and Separate Financial Statements* requires a group to exclude subsidiaries from consolidation on the grounds that they are held exclusively with a view to subsequent resale. By defining 'held exclusively with a view to subsequent resale' in FRS 102 to include those interests that are held as part of an investment portfolio, subsidiaries held as part of such an investment portfolio are excluded from consolidation in accordance with section 405(3) of the Act and an entity will not need to apply the true and fair override in this circumstance.

A4.17 Paragraph 9.9B(a) requires a group to measure subsidiaries excluded from consolidation by virtue of paragraph 9.9(b) and held as part of an investment portfolio, at fair value through profit or loss. The measurement at fair value through profit and loss is a departure from the requirements of paragraph 36 of Schedule 1 to the Regulations, for the overriding purpose of giving a true and fair view in the consolidated financial statements. In this circumstance, entities must provide in the notes to the financial statements the 'particulars of the departure, the reasons for it and its effect' (paragraph 10(2) of Schedule 1 to the Regulations).

Calculation of goodwill where a business combination is achieved in stages

A4.18 Paragraph 9 of Schedule 6 to the Regulations sets out the requirements for the acquisition method of accounting, which results in goodwill (or negative goodwill) being calculated as the difference between:

(a) the fair value of the group's share of identifiable assets and liabilities of the subsidiary at the date control is achieved; and
(b) the total acquisition cost of the interests held by the group in that subsidiary.

This applies even where part of the acquisition cost arises from purchases at earlier dates.

A4.19 In most cases, this method provides a practical means of applying acquisition accounting because it does not require retrospective assessments of the fair value of the identifiable assets and liabilities of the subsidiary. In certain circumstances, however, not using fair values at the dates of earlier purchases while using acquisition costs which in part relate to earlier purchases may result in accounting that is inconsistent with the way the investment has been treated previously and, for that reason, may fail to give a true and fair view.

A4.20 For example, an undertaking that has been treated as an associate may then be acquired by that group as a subsidiary. Using the method required by the Regulations and paragraph 9.19B of FRS 102 to calculate goodwill on such an acquisition has the effect that the group's share of profits or losses and reserve movements of its associate becomes reclassified as goodwill (usually negative goodwill). A similar problem may arise where the group has substantially restated its investment in an undertaking that subsequently becomes its subsidiary. For example, where such an investment has been written down because it is impaired, the effect of applying the

Regulations' method of acquisition accounting would be to increase reserves and create an asset (goodwill).

In the rare cases where the method for calculating goodwill set out in the Regulations and in paragraph 9.19B of FRS 102 would be misleading, the goodwill should be calculated as the sum of goodwill arising from each purchase of an interest in the relevant undertaking adjusted as necessary for any subsequent impairment. Goodwill arising on each purchase should be calculated as the difference between the cost of that purchase and the fair value at the date of that purchase of the identifiable assets and liabilities attributable to the interest purchased. The difference between the goodwill calculated using this method and that calculated using the method provided by the Regulations and FRS 102 is shown in reserves. Section 404(5) of the Act sets out the disclosures required in cases where the statutory requirement is not applied. Paragraph 3.5 of FRS 102 sets out the disclosures when an entity departs from a requirement of FRS 102 or from a requirement of applicable legislation. **A4.21**

Netting

FRS 102 permits an expense relating to a provision to be presented net of the amount recognised for a reimbursement (which may only be recognised if it is virtually certain it will be received) (see paragraph 21.9 of FRS 102). Paragraph 8 of Schedule 1 to the Regulations requires that 'Amounts in respect of items representing assets or income may not be set off against amounts in respect of items representing liabilities or expenditure (as the case may be), or vice versa.' The reimbursement asset is recognised separately from the underlying obligation to reflect the fact that the entity often will continue to be liable if the third party from which the reimbursement is due fails to pay. On the other hand, the net presentation in the income statement reflects the cost to the entity and net presentation therefore does not conflict with the Regulation. **A4.22**

FRS 102 requires that a financial asset and financial liability are offset and the net amount presented in the statement of financial position, if certain criteria are met (see paragraph 11.38A of FRS 102). The net presentation does not conflict with paragraph 8 of Schedule 1 to the Regulations, because provided the criteria for the net presentation are met, the presentation reflects the expected net cash flows from settling two or more separate financial instruments. **A4.23**

Recording investments at cost

Paragraph 9.26 of FRS 102 requires that in an investor's separate financial statements its investments in subsidiaries are accounted for at cost less impairment, or at fair value. Where the cost model is applied, sections 611 to 615 of the Act set out the treatment where 'merger relief' or 'group reconstruction relief' are available. These reliefs reduce the amount required to be included in share premium; they also (in section 615) allow the initial carrying amount to be adjusted downwards so it is equal to either the previous carrying amount of the investment in the transferor's books or the nominal value of the shares issued, depending on which relief applies. If the fair value model in paragraph 9.26 is used, then the relief in section 615 is not available, so the investment's carrying value may not be reduced, although the provisions in sections 611 and 612 remain relevant in respect of amounts required to be recorded in share premium. **A4.24**

Realised profits

A4.25 Paragraph 13(a) of Schedule 1 to the Regulations requires that only profits realised at the reporting date are included in profit or loss, a requirement modified from that in Article 31.1(c)(aa) of the Fourth Directive which refers to profits 'made' at the balance sheet date.

A4.26 Paragraph 36(4) and paragraph 39 of Schedule 1 to the Regulations allow that financial instruments, investment property, and living animals and plants that may under international accounting standards be held at fair value, may also be held at fair value in Companies Act accounts.

A4.27 Paragraph 40(2) of Schedule 1 to the Regulations then requires that movements in the value of financial instruments, investment properties, and living animals and plants are recognised in the profit and loss account, notwithstanding the usual restrictions allowing only realised profits and losses to be included in the profit and loss account. Paragraph 40 of Schedule 1 to the Regulations thereby overrides the requirements of paragraph 13(a) of Schedule 1.

A4.28 Entities measuring financial instruments, investment properties, and living animals and plants at fair value should note that they may transfer such amounts to a separate non-distributable reserve, instead of a transfer to retained earnings, but are not required to do so. Presenting fair value movements, that are not distributable profits, in the separate reserve may assist with the identification of profits available for that purpose.

A4.29 The determination of profits available for distribution is a complex area where accounting and company law interface. In determining profits available for distribution an entity may refer to Technical Release 02/10 *Guidance on realised and distributable profits under the Companies Act 2006* issued by the Institute of Chartered Accountants in England and Wales and the Institute of Chartered Accountants of Scotland, or any successor document, to determine profits available for distribution..

Merger accounting

A4.30 Paragraph 10 of Schedule 6 to the Regulations permits the use of merger accounting in certain circumstances. FRS 102 requires the application of the purchase method of accounting for all business combinations within the scope of Section 19 *Business Combinations and Goodwill*, other than group reconstructions. Paragraph 19.27 permits merger accounting for group reconstructions. Section 34 *Specialised Activities* requires that combinations by public benefit entities meeting certain criteria are accounted for as a merger. FRS 102 therefore restricts the circumstances in which merger accounting may be applied.

Treasury shares

A4.31 Paragraph 22.16 of FRS 102 sets out the accounting requirements when an entity purchases its own equity instruments (ie treasury shares).

A4.32 Companies subject to the Act, need to comply with the accounting requirements of paragraph 22.16 as well as with the requirements of the Act when they purchase their own equity and hold it in treasury (Sections 690 to 708 and 724 to 732, respectively).

Measurement of investments in associates and jointly controlled entities for an investor, which is not a parent

Paragraph 36 of Schedule 1 to the Regulations sets out the fair value accounting rules and permits investments in associates and joint ventures to be measured at fair value through profit or loss only where they are permitted to be treated as financial instruments in accordance with IAS Regulation. EU-adopted IFRS does allow investments in subsidiaries, associates and jointly controlled entities to be measured in accordance with IAS 39 *Financial Instruments Recognition and Measurement* within separate financial statements (as set out in IAS 27 *Consolidated and Separate Financial Statements*). **A4.33**

Therefore, where the fair value model is applied by an investor, changes in fair value may be recognised through profit or loss, or other comprehensive income. Under the alternative accounting rules set out in Section C of Schedule 1 to the Regulations, the initial recognition of the investment must include any expenses that are incidental to the acquisition of the investment. **A4.34**

Measurement of inventories held for distribution at no or nominal value

Paragraph 24(1) of Schedule 1 to the Regulations requires that if the net realisable value of any current asset is lower than its purchase price or production cost, the amount to be included in respect of that asset must be the net realisable value. However, paragraph 32(5) permits stocks to be included at their current cost, when applying the alternative accounting rules. **A4.35**

Inventories held for distribution at no or nominal value include items that might be distributed to beneficiaries by public benefit entities and items such as advertising and promotional material. As the items will be distributed at no or nominal cost, the net realisable value will usually be lower than the purchase price. **A4.36**

However, paragraph 13.4A of FRS 102 requires inventories held for distribution at no or nominal cost to be measured at cost. Although the alternative accounting rules require measurement at current cost, for inventories held for distribution at no or nominal value, there is unlikely to be a significant difference between cost and current cost. **A4.37**

Accounts formats

Sections 4 and 5 of FRS 102 require entities to apply one of the profit and loss account and balance sheet formats set out in the Regulations and LLP Regulations, when preparing their statement of comprehensive income (single-statement approach) or income statement (two-statement approach) and statement of financial position, respectively. **A4.38**

Discontinued operations

FRS 102 requires an entity with discontinued operations to provide an analysis between continuing operations and discontinued operations of each of the line items on the face of the statement of comprehensive income, or income statement, up to and including post-tax profit or loss for the period and illustrates this presentation in a columnar format. This is in order to present the post-tax results of those operations, combined with the profit or loss on their disposal, as a single line item while **A4.39** still complying with the requirement of company law to show totals for ordinary activities of items such as turnover, profit or loss before taxation and tax.

Long-term debtors

A4.40 UITF Abstract 4 *Presentation of long-term debtors in current assets* addressed the inclusion of debtors due after more than one year within 'current assets'; that UITF consensus has been withdrawn, but its conclusions remain valid and have been included in paragraph 4.4A of FRS 102.

Entities not subject to company law

A4.41 Many entities that apply FRS 102 are not companies, but are nevertheless required by their governing legislation, or other regulation or requirement to prepare financial statements that present a true and fair view of the financial performance and financial position of the reporting entity. However, the FRC sets accounting standards within the framework of the Act and therefore it is the company law requirements that the FRC primarily considered when developing FRS 102. Entities preparing financial statements within other legal frameworks will need to satisfy themselves that FRS 102 does not conflict with any relevant legal obligations.

A4.42 However, the FRC notes the following:

Legislation	**Overview of requirements**
Building Societies Act 1986	The annual accounts of a building society shall give a true and fair of the income and expenditure for the year and the balance sheet shall give a true and fair view of the state of affairs of the society at the end of the financial year. Regulations make further requirements about the form and content of building society accounts, which do not appear inconsistent with the requirement of FRS 102.
Charity law in England and Wales: Charities Act 2011 and regulations made thereunder	All charities are required to prepare accounts. The regulations require financial statements (other than cash-based receipts and payments accounts prepared by smaller charities) to present a true and fair view of the incoming resources, application of resources and the balance sheet, and to be prepared in accordance with the SORP. However company charities prepare their accounts in accordance with UK company law to give a 'true and fair view'. The Charities SORP 2005 requires the application of accounting standards and is compatible with the legal requirements, clarifying how they apply to accounting by charities. The SORP will be updated to reflect the requirements of FRS 102. UK company law prohibits charities from preparing IAS accounts.

Legislation	**Overview of requirements**
Charity law in Scotland: Charities and Trustee Investments Act (Scotland) 2005 and regulations made thereunder	All charities are required to prepare accounts. The regulations require financial statements (other than cash-based receipts and payments accounts prepared by smaller charities) to present a true and fair view of the incoming resources, application of resources and the balance sheet, and to be prepared in accordance with the SORP. These regulations apply equally to company charities.
Charity law in Northern Ireland: Charities Act (Northern Ireland) 2008	The Charities Act 2008 has yet to come fully into effect. The Act provides for all charities to prepare accounts. The Act provides for regulations concerning the financial statements. The financial statements other than cash-based receipts and payments accounts prepared by smaller charities are to present a true and fair view of the incoming resources, application of resources and the balance sheet. However company charities prepare their accounts in accordance with UK company law to give a 'true and fair view'.
Friendly and Industrial and Provident Societies Act 1968	Every Society shall prepare a revenue account and a balance sheet giving a true and fair view of the income and expenditure and state of affairs of the Society. FRS 102 does not appear to give rise to any legal conflicts for Societies. However, Societies often carry out activities that are regulated and may be required to comply with additional regulations on top of the legal requirements and accounting standards. Some Societies fall within the scope of SORPs, which may be updated to reflect the requirements of FRS 102.
Friendly Societies Act 1992	Every society shall prepare a balance sheet and an income and expenditure account for each financial year giving a true and fair view of the affairs of the society and its income and expenditure for the year. The Regulations* make further requirements about the form and content of friendly society accounts, which do not appear inconsistent with the requirements of FRS 102.

**The Friendly Societies (Accounts and Related Provisions) Regulations 1994 (as amended).*

Legislation	Overview of requirements
The Occupational Pension Schemes (Requirement to obtain Audited Accounts and a Statement from the Auditor) Regulations 1996	The accounts of pension funds within the scope of the regulations should show a true and fair view of the transactions during the year, assets held at the end of the year and liabilities of the scheme, other than those to pay pensions and benefits. FRS 102 includes retirement benefit plans as a specialised activity.

Appendix V: Previous Consultations

The requirements in FRSs 100 to 102 are the outcome of a lengthy and extensive consultation. The FRC (and formerly the ASB) together with the Department for Business, Innovation and Skills have consulted on the future of accounting standards in the UK and Republic of Ireland (RoI) over a ten-year period. **A5.1**

Table 1 – Consultations conducted

Year	Consultation
2002	DTI* consults on adoption of IAS Regulation
2004	Discussion Paper – Strategy for Convergence with IFRS
2005	Exposure Draft – Policy Statement: The Role of the ASB
2006	Public Meeting and Proposals for Comment
2006	Press Notice seeking views
2007	Consultation Paper – Proposed IFRS for SMEs
2009	Consultation Paper – Policy Proposal: The future of UK GAAP
2010	Request for Responses – Development of the Impact Assessment
2010	Financial Reporting Exposure Drafts 43 and 44
2011	Financial Reporting Exposure Draft 45
2012	Financial Reporting Exposure Drafts 46, 47 and 48
2012	Financial Reporting Exposure Draft: Amendment to FRED 48

2004

In 2004 the Discussion Paper contained two key elements underpinning the proposals: firstly that UK and Republic of Ireland (RoI) accounting standards should be based on IFRS and secondly that a phased approach to the introduction of the standards should be adopted. **A5.2**

The ASB embarked on the phased approach and issued a number of standards based on IFRS. The majority of respondents agreed with a framework based on IFRS, and although supportive overall, the response to the phased approach was mixed. **A5.3**

2005

In its 2005 Exposure Draft (2005 ED) of a Policy Statement *Accounting standard-setting in a changing environment: The role of the Accounting Standards Board*, amongst other aspects of its role, the ASB identified its intention to converge with IFRS by implementing new IFRS in the UK as soon as possible. It also proposed to **A5.4**

**The Department of Trade and Industry (DTI) was a United Kingdom government department which was replaced with the announcement of the creation of the Department for Business, Enterprise and Regulatory Reform and the Department for Innovation, Universities and Skills on 28 June 2007, which were themselves merged into the Department for Business, Innovation and Skills (BIS) on 6 June 2009.*

continue the phased approach to adopting UK accounting standards based on older IFRSs, but recognised there was little case for being more prescriptive than IFRS.

A5.5 Although the ASB had, in the 2005 ED, wanted to move the debate on to how it would seek to influence the IASB's agenda, respondents' main concern remained about convergence. In 2005, the ASB issued an exposure draft proposing the IASB's standard on Business Combinations be adopted in the UK and RoI. This exposure draft highlighted the complexity of a mixed set of UK accounting standards, with some based on IFRSs and others developed independently by the ASB. The majority of respondents continued to agree with the aim of basing UK accounting standards on IFRS, but a broader set of views on how to achieve this was emerging.

A5.6 As time progressed the ASB formed the view that convergence by adopting certain IFRSs was not meeting the needs of its constituents, which no longer included quoted groups. The ASB was concerned about the complexity of certain IFRSs, and it noted that introducing them piecemeal created complications and anomalies within the body of current FRSs. This arose because IFRS-based standards were not an exact replacement for current FRSs and many consequential amendments were required to 'fit' each replacement IFRS-based standard into the existing body of UK FRS. The ASB agreed to continue with its convergence programme, but decided to re-examine how to achieve this.

2006

A5.7 The ASB published revised proposals to be discussed at the 2006 public meeting. By this time the IASB had started its IFRS for SMEs project, and the ASB decided this might have a role as one of the tiers in the UK financial reporting framework. The ASB proposed a 'big bang' with new IFRS-based UK accounting standards mandatory from a single date, 1 January 2009. The ASB's proposal was for a three-tier system, with Tier 1 being EU-adopted IFRS, and the other two tiers being developed as the IASB progressed with its project on the IFRS for SMEs.

A5.8 Those attending the public meeting supported the aim of basing UK and RoI accounting standards on IFRS and adapting them to ensure they were appropriate for the entities applying them.

A5.9 Taking this feedback into account, later in 2006 the ASB issued a Press Notice (PN 289) seeking views on its current thinking:

(a) All quoted and publicly accountable companies should apply EU-adopted IFRS.
(b) The FRSSE should be retained and extended to include medium-sized entities.
(c) UK subsidiaries of groups applying full IFRS should apply EU-adopted IFRS, but with reduced disclosure requirements.
(d) No firm decision on the remainder (Tier 2), but options included extending the FRSSE, extending full IFRS, maintaining separate UK accounting standards or some combination of these.

A5.10 The responses were mixed, but there was agreement that whatever the solution, it should be based on IFRS and there should be different reporting tiers to ensure proportionality.

2007

The IASB published an exposure draft of its IFRS for SMEs in early 2007; shortly afterwards the ASB published its own consultation paper. This sought views on how the IFRS for SMEs might fit into the future UK financial reporting framework, for example whether it might be appropriate for Tier 2, with the FRSSE continuing for those eligible for the small companies' regime. **A5.11**

Feedback on the IFRS for SMEs was largely positive: it would be suitable for Tier 2, it was international, it was compatible with IFRS, and it represented a significant simplification. Overall, it was seen as a workable alternative to IFRS. In addition, respondents wanted to retain the FRSSE (because it reduces the regulatory burden on smaller entities) and to give subsidiaries the option of applying the IFRS for SMEs as well as a reduced disclosure regime if applying full IFRS. **A5.12**

2009

The IFRS for SMEs was published in 2009, allowing the ASB to further develop its proposals in the Consultation Paper *Policy Proposal: The future of UK GAAP*. The proposals were largely consistent with the cumulative results of the preceding consultations and included: **A5.13**

(a) a move to an IFRS-based framework;
(b) a three-tier approach;
(c) publicly accountable entities would be Tier 1 and would apply EU-adopted IFRS;
(d) small companies would be Tier 3 and continue to apply the FRSSE; and
(e) other entities would be Tier 2 and should apply a UK and RoI accounting standard based on the IFRS for SMEs.

The only significant proposal that was inconsistent with respondents' previous comments was that subsidiaries should simply apply the requirement of the tier they individually met – respondents had wanted subsidiaries to be able to take advantage of disclosure exemptions, and at that time the ASB had yet to be convinced that significant cost savings were available from a reduced disclosure framework. Taking into account the feedback received, this proposal was subsequently reversed and the reduced disclosure framework was incorporated into FREDs 43 and then 46, and it is now set out in FRS 101. **A5.14**

In addition to the many useful and detailed points made, some common themes included general agreement that change was needed to UK accounting standards and that there was support for many of the changes proposed in the consultation paper. **A5.15**

2010 onwards

The request for responses to aid development of the Impact Assessment focused on obtaining feedback on the expected costs, benefits and impact of the proposals subsequently set out in FREDs 43 and 44, rather than on the accounting principles. As the focus was on costs and benefits no specific question was asked about the principle of the proposed introduction of an IFRS-based framework, but nevertheless respondents commented on this: of the 32 responses received only 12.5 per cent did not agree with the introduction of an IFRS-based framework. **A5.16**

FRED 43 and 44 issued in October 2010 set out the draft suggested text for two new accounting standards that would replace the majority of extant Financial Reporting **A5.17**

Standards (current FRS) in the UK and RoI. The ASB issued a supplementary FRED addressing specific needs of public benefit entities (FRED 45) in March 2011. The ASB then updated FREDs 43, 44 and 45, replacing them with the revised FREDs 46, 47 and 48 in January 2012, by eliminating the concept of public accountability and by introducing a number of accounting treatment options that are available in EU-adopted IFRS. The Accounting Council's advice to the FRC to issue FRSs 100 to 102 includes more discussion of the feedback received on FREDs 43 to 48 and how the proposals have been refined and developed into the standards.

HOW HAVE THE PROPOSALS BEEN DEVELOPED?

A5.18 As set out above, the FRC, the Accounting Council (and previously the ASB) have consulted regularly on the future of financial reporting in the UK and RoI. Over the consultations the ASB's (and the Accounting Council's) thinking has evolved based on careful consideration of the feedback at each stage. Whilst responses were sometimes mixed, there has been agreement that:

(a) current FRS, which are a mixture of Statements of Standard Accounting Practice (SSAPs) issued by the Consultative Committee of Accounting Bodies, FRSs developed and issued by the ASB and IFRS-based standards issued by the ASB to converge with international standards, are an uncomfortable mismatch that lack strong underlying principles or cohesion; and

(b) whatever the solution, it should be based on IFRS and there should be different reporting tiers to ensure proportionality.

A5.19 During the consultation process to date, the Accounting Council and formerly the ASB have been guided by the following principles:

(a) The framework must be fit for purpose, so that each entity required to produce true and fair financial statements under UK and RoI law will deliver financial statements that are suited to the needs of its primary users. The Accounting Council has kept in close contact with constituent users on this point, including investors, creditor institutions and the tax authorities.

(b) The framework must be proportionate, so that preparing entities are not unduly burdened by costs that outweigh the benefit to them and to the primary users of information in their financial statements. The FRC believes that the proposals will produce a lower cost regime, while enhancing user benefits. It has carried out a consultation stage impact assessment with input from interested parties, and will continue to assess cost-benefit issues.

(c) The framework must be in line with UK company law. This determines which entities must produce true and fair financial statements. Exemptions within the law have generally been retained. The detailed requirements of the Companies Act 2006 are driven to a great extent by the European Accounting Directives, which are being revised*.

(d) The framework must be future-proofed, where possible. The FRC will continue to monitor the situation and has sovereignty over UK accounting standards (subject to the law). Changes to the Accounting Directives may lead to further developments, for example the European Council and European Parliament decision to permit Member States an option to treat micro-entities as a separate category of Company and exempt them from certain accounting requirements.

**The EU's consultation process on review of the Accounting Directives is summarised at http://ec.europa.eu/internal_market/ accounting/sme_accounting/review_directives_en.htm*

SUMMARY OF OUTREACH

During the development and throughout the consultation period of FREDs 43 to 48, the ASB undertook an extensive programme of outreach aimed at raising awareness of the proposals and to address the view (held by some) that previous consultations had not gathered sufficient evidence to support and test the assumptions made. **A5.20**

As part of the outreach programme to obtain both formal and informal feedback, a series of meetings and events took place with users, including with lenders to small and medium-sized entities. Lenders noted that financial statements are an important part of their decision-making process when considering whether to provide finance and, whilst a decision to provide finance is not based on financial statements alone, they provide useful information and verification to the lender. **A5.21**

Although the ASB and the Accounting Council employed their best efforts to obtain feedback from users (a constituent group historically difficult to engage with formally) it is disappointing that limited formal responses were received and the Accounting Council has not been more successful in obtaining input from users. **A5.22**

In addition, a review was made of academic research that addressed the users of the financial statements of small and medium-sized entities. The conclusion drawn from the research was that many entities requested financial statements from Companies House when considering whether to trade with another entity. The European Federation of Accountants and Auditors (EFAA) issued, in May 2011, a statement that identified the users of financial statements, noting who the users of SMEs' financial statements are and that information on the public record assists all users of financial statements of SMEs by providing, in an efficient manner, basic information that protects their rights. **A5.23**

The ASB considered that the outreach programme had gleaned information from people who would not normally submit formal responses to a consultation and provided very useful information that could be used in developing the next stage of the project. The ASB noted that whilst this information was not part of the public record, as are formal consultation responses, it could use the information to assist in developing the revised FREDs 46 to 48, supplementing information contained in responses, and would seek further comment in the next stage of its deliberations. **A5.24**

The Accounting Council continued the work of the ASB in finalising FRSs 100 to 102. The responses to FREDs 46 to 48 were analysed and discussed, and engagements were conducted to take into account the views and suggestions of all relevant associations and contacts. Respondents and outreach contacts were satisfied with FREDs 46 to 48, and many of the response letters were forthcoming in their overall praise for the proposals. A significant number of constituents anticipated cost savings arising from the application of FRS 101. Many respondents considered that FRS 102 would improve UK accounting standards, in particular by introducing requirements for accounting for financial instruments. Further they considered that the improvements will be achieved in a way that will be proportionate to the needs of users, and that once the transition phase has been overcome, it will have the effect of reducing the reporting burden on those UK companies that adopt it. **A5.25**

Appendix VI: Republic of Ireland (RoI) Legal References

INTRODUCTION

A6.1 The table below outlines the provisions in the Companies Acts 1963 to 2012 and related Regulations which implement EC Accounting Directives (Irish company law), corresponding to the provisions of the UK *Companies Act 2006* (the 2006 Act) and the UK *Large and Medium-sized Companies and Groups (Accounts and Reports) Regulations 2008* (the 2008 Regulations) (SI 2008/410) referred to in this FRS.

A6.2 The principal Irish companies' legislation referred to in the table below is:

- The Companies Act 1963 (1963 Act);
- The Companies (Amendment) Act 1983 (1983 Act);
- The Companies (Amendment) Act 1986 (1986 Act);
- The Companies Act 1990 (1990 Act);
- The Companies (Amendment) (No 2) Act 1999;
- The European Communities (Companies: Group Accounts) Regulations 1992 – S.I. No. 201 of 1992 (Group Accounts Regulations 1992 or GAR 1992);
- The European Communities (Credit Institutions: Accounts) Regulations 1992 – S.I. No. 294 of 1992 (Credit Institutions Regulations 1992 or CIR 1992);
- The European Communities (Insurance Undertakings: Accounts) Regulations 1996 – S.I. No. 23 of 1996 (Insurance Undertakings Regulations 1996 or IUR 1996).

A6.3 General references are made in this FRS to UK legislation such as the '2006 Act', 'Companies Act 2006 ('and the Regulations')', 'the Companies Act', 'the Act', 'the Large and Medium-sized Companies and Groups (Accounts and Reports) Regulations, 2008', 'the 2008 Regulations' and 'the Regulations'. In an Irish context reference should be made to the relevant sections and paragraphs of Irish companies' legislation. Such general references are not dealt with in the table below. References in the text to 'IAS accounts' are equivalent to 'IFRS accounts' in Irish company law.

A6.4 The following Irish legislation is also referenced in the table below:

- The Building Societies Act 1989;
- The Credit Union Acts 1997 to 2012;
- The Central Bank Act 1971;
- The Charities Act 2009;
- The Friendly Societies Acts 1896 to 1977;
- The Friendly Societies (Amendment) Act 1977;
- The Friendly Societies Regulations 1988 – S.I. No. 74 of 1988;
- The Industrial and Provident Societies (Amendment) Act 1978;
- The Pensions Act 1990; and
- The Occupational Pension Schemes (Disclosure of Information) Regulations 2006 – S.I. No. 301 of 2006.

COMPANIES ACT ACCOUNTS UNDER IRISH COMPANY LAW

A6.5 Certain companies are permitted under Irish company law to prepare their Companies Act accounts using accounting standards other than those issued by the Financial Reporting Council (FRC) and promulgated by the Institute of Chartered Accountants in Ireland in respect of their application in the Republic of Ireland. Specifically:

- Pursuant to the Companies (Miscellaneous Provisions) Act 2009, as amended by the Companies (Amendment) Act 2012, relevant parent undertakings are permitted to prepare 'Companies Act individual accounts' and/or 'Companies Act group accounts' in accordance with US GAAP, as modified to ensure consistency with Irish company law.

- Investment companies subject to Part XIII of the Companies Act 1990 or the European Communities (Undertakings for Collective Investment in Transferable Securities) Regulations 2011 may adopt an alternative body of accounting standards, being standards which apply in the United States of America, Canada or Japan in preparing 'Companies Act individual accounts'.

Such companies, therefore, may adopt standards other than those issued by the FRC in preparing Companies Act accounts under Irish company law. **A6.6**

SMALL COMPANIES UNDER IRISH COMPANY LAW

There is no equivalent to the UK *small companies regime* (see Sections 381 to 384 of the 2006 Act) in Irish company law. Section 8 of the Companies (Amendment) Act 1986 (as amended by the European Union (Accounts) Regulations 2012 (S.I. No. 304 of 2012)) defines small companies for the purposes of Irish company law. However, whilst Sections 10 and 12 provide certain exemptions for such companies in relation to their financial statements that are filed with the Registrar of Companies, there are no exemptions for individual or group accounts prepared for members. Under Section 8 (as amended) the qualifying conditions for a company to be treated as a small company in respect of any financial year are as follows: **A6.7**

- The amount of turnover for that year does not exceed €8,800,000;
- The balance sheet total for that year does not exceed €4,400,000; and
- Average number of employees does not exceed 50.

Except for companies in their first financial year, Section 8(1)(a) provides that companies qualify to be treated as small if, in respect of that year and the financial year immediately preceding that year, the company satisfies at least two of the above criteria. Section 9 provides that where a company has qualified as small, it continues to be so qualified until it does not meet two of the above three criteria for two consecutive years. Similarly, where a company no longer qualifies as small, two consecutive years of meeting two of the three criteria are required to qualify again as small. **A6.8**

The following do not qualify as small under Irish company law: **A6.9**

- Companies subject to the European Communities (Credit Institutions: Accounts) Regulations 1992;
- Companies subject to the European Communities (Insurance Undertakings: Accounts) Regulations 1996;
- Private companies whose securities are admitted to trading on a regulated market.

SIZE EXEMPTIONS FROM THE PREPARATION OF GROUP ACCOUNTS UNDER IRISH COMPANY LAW

An Irish parent company within the scope of the European Communities (Companies: Group Accounts) Regulations 1992 is exempt from the requirement to prepare group accounts if it, together with its subsidiaries, meets the size and other criteria set out in Regulation 7 of those Regulations. The size criteria in summary require that the parent and subsidiaries together meet two of the following three conditions: **A6.10**

- The amount of turnover for that year does not exceed €15,236,858;
- The balance sheet total for that year does not exceed €7,618,428; and

- Average number of employees does not exceed 250.

A6.11 Except for the year in which a company becomes a parent undertaking, the exemption can only be availed of if two of the three conditions are met in respect of the financial year and the immediately preceding financial year.

A6.12 Exemptions from preparing group accounts on the basis of size, in accordance with Regulation 7 of the European Communities (Companies: Group Accounts) Regulations 1992, are only available to parent companies that are private companies and are not available to parent companies subject to the European Communities (Credit Institutions: Accounts) Regulations 1992 or the European Communities (Insurance Undertakings: Accounts) Regulations 1996.

MERGER ACCOUNTING

A6.13 As there is currently no legislative equivalent to merger relief in the Republic of Ireland, no relief from the requirement of Section 62(1) to establish a share premium account is available. Section 149(5) provides that pre-acquisition profits of an acquired subsidiary may not, for any purpose, be treated in the holding company's accounts as revenue profits. Section 149(5) contains a provision that, where the directors and auditors are satisfied and so certify that it would be fair and reasonable and would not prejudice the rights and interests of any person, the profits or losses attributable to any shares in a subsidiary may be treated in a manner otherwise than in accordance with this subsection.

A6.14 Accordingly, in considering whether merger accounting may be applied, directors and auditors should consider the consequences of providing such certification.

OTHER NOTES

A6.15 As noted in paragraph A4.3 of Appendix IV of this FRS, while the UK company law references are made to Schedule 1 to the 2008 Regulations, UK entities applying Schedules 2 (banking companies), 3 (insurance companies) or 6 (Companies Act group accounts) to those Regulations should read them as referring to the equivalent paragraphs in those Schedules. In the table below, the corresponding or similar provisions in Irish company law are specifically set out.

A6.16 The table below is intended as a reference guide to the corresponding or similar provisions in Irish company law and does not purport to be complete. It should be noted that not all Irish legal provisions are equivalent to the corresponding UK legal provisions and reference should be made to the Irish legislation for an understanding of relevant requirements. In some cases reference may need to be made to other parts of Irish company law.

SECTION 1: SCOPE

	UK References	RoI References						
Paragraph	**2006 Act and the 2008 Regulations (unless otherwise stated)**	**1963 Act**	**1983 Act**	**1986 Act**	**1990 Act**	**GAR 1992**	**CIR 1992**	**IUR 1996**
1.3(b) (Footnote 6)	Section 395(1)(a)	Section 148(2)(a)					Regulation 5(1)	Regulation 5(1)
1.3(b) (Footnote 6)	Section 395(1)(b)	Section 148(2)(b)					Regulation 5(1)	Regulation 5(1)
1.8	Paragraph 36(4) of Schedule 1			Paragraph 22AA of Part IIIA of the Schedule		Regulation 15 (applying the Schedule to the 1986 Act)	Paragraphs 46A(4A) and 46A(4B) of Part I and paragraph 1 of Part II of the Schedule	
1.10	Section 399	Section 150(1)				Regulations 5 and 7	Regulation 7(3)	Regulation 10(3)
1.10	Sections 400 to 401					Regulations 8, 9 and 9A	Regulations 8 and 8A	Regulations 12 and 12A

SECTION 1: SCOPE (contd.)

	UK References	RoI References						
Paragraph	**2006 Act and the 2008 Regulations (unless otherwise stated)**	**1963 Act**	**1983 Act**	**1986 Act**	**1990 Act**	**GAR 1992**	**CIR 1992**	**IUR 1996**
1.10	Section 402	Section 150(1A)*					Paragraph 2 of Part II of the Schedule	Regulation 10(1A)*
		*Section 150(1A) of the 1963 Act and Regulation 10(1A) of the IUR 1996 contain an exemption from preparing group accounts which is similar but not identical to Section 402.						

SECTION 3: FINANCIAL STATEMENT PRESENTATION

	UK References	RoI References						
Paragraph	**2006 Act and the 2008 Regulations (unless otherwise stated)**	**1963 Act**	**1983 Act**	**1986 Act**	**1990 Act**	**GAR 1992**	**CIR 1992**	**IUR 1996**
3.5 (Footnote 9)	Section 396(5)			Section 3(1)(d) and (e)		Regulation 14(3) and (4)	Regulation 5(1A)(d) and (e) and Regulation 7(7)(d) and (e)	Regulation 5(1A)(d) and (e) and Regulation 10(7)(d) and (e)

SECTION 4: STATEMENT OF FINANCIAL POSITION and SECTION 5: STATEMENT OF COMPREHENSIVE INCOME AND INCOME STATEMENT

	UK References	RoI References						
Paragraph	**2006 Act and the 2008 Regulations (unless otherwise stated)**	**1963 Act**	**1983 Act**	**1986 Act**	**1990 Act**	**GAR 1992**	**CIR 1992**	**IUR 1996**
4.2, 5.5 and 5.7	Part 1 *General Rules and Formats* of Schedule 1 to the Regulations			Part 1 of the Schedule				
4.2, 5.5 and 5.7	Part 1 *General Rules and Formats* of Schedule 2 to the Regulations						Chapter 1 of Part I of the Schedule	
4.2, 5.5 and 5.7	Part 1 *General Rules and Formats* of Schedule 3 to the Regulations							Part I of the Schedule

SECTION 4: STATEMENT OF FINANCIAL POSITION and SECTION 5: STATEMENT OF COMPREHENSIVE INCOME AND INCOME STATEMENT (contd.)

	UK References	**RoI References**						
Paragraph	**2006 Act and the 2008 Regulations (unless otherwise stated)**	**1963 Act**	**1983 Act**	**1986 Act**	**1990 Act**	**GAR 1992**	**CIR 1992**	**IUR 1996**
4.2, 5.5 and 5.7	Schedule 6 to the Regulations					Regulation 15 (applying the Schedule to the 1986 Act)	Paragraph 1 of Part II of the Schedule (applying Part I of the Schedule)	Paragraph 1 of Part IV of the Schedule (applying Part I of the Schedule)
4.2, 5.5 and 5.7	Schedule 1 and Schedule 3 to the LLP Regulations	There is no equivalent Irish LLP legislation.						

SECTION 7: STATEMENT OF CASH FLOWS

	UK References	RoI References						
Paragraph	**2006 Act and the 2008 Regulations (unless otherwise stated)**	**1963 Act**	**1983 Act**	**1986 Act**	**1990 Act**	**GAR 1992**	**CIR 1992**	**IUR 1996**
7.20A	Part 1 *General Rules and Formats* of Schedule 2 to the Regulations						Chapter 1 of Part I of the Schedule	

SECTION 9: CONSOLIDATED AND SEPARATE FINANCIAL STATEMENTS

	UK References	RoI References						
Paragraph	**2006 Act and the 2008 Regulations (unless otherwise stated)**	**1963 Act**	**1983 Act**	**1986 Act**	**1990 Act**	**GAR 1992**	**CIR 1992**	**IUR 1996**
9.3(a) and (b)	Section 400(2)					Regulations 8(3) and 9	Regulation 8(3)	Regulation 12(3)
9.3(b)	Section 400(1)(b)					Regulations 8(1) and 9	Regulations 8(1), (2) and (6)	Regulations 12(1), (2) and (6)
9.3(c) and (d)	Section 401(2)					Regulation 9A(3)	Regulation 8A(3)	Regulation 12A(3)
9.3(d)	Section 401(1)(b)					Regulation 9A(1)(b)	Regulation 8A(1)(b)	Regulation 12A(1)(b)
9.3(e)	Section 383	Please refer to the note above in the introduction to this table - Size exemptions from the preparation of group accounts under Irish company law.						
9.3(e)	Section 384	Please refer to the note above in the introduction to this table - Size exemptions from the preparation of group accounts under Irish company law.						

SECTION 9: CONSOLIDATED AND SEPARATE FINANCIAL STATEMENTS (contd.)

	UK References	RoI References						
Paragraph	**2006 Act and the 2008 Regulations (unless otherwise stated)**	**1963 Act**	**1983 Act**	**1986 Act**	**1990 Act**	**GAR 1992**	**CIR 1992**	**IUR 1996**
9.27B	Paragraph 36(4) of Schedule 1 to the Regulations			Paragraph 22AA of Part IIIA of the Schedule		Regulation 15 (applying the Schedule to the 1986 Act)	Paragraphs 46A(4A) and 46A(4B) of Part I and paragraph 1 of Part II of the Schedule	

SECTION 35: TRANSITION TO THIS FRS

	UK References	RoI References						
Paragraph	**2006 Act and the 2008 Regulations (unless otherwise stated)**	**1963 Act**	**1983 Act**	**1986 Act**	**1990 Act**	**GAR 1992**	**CIR 1992**	**IUR 1996**
35.10(m)	Companies Act definition of a dormant company	There is no equivalent definition in Irish company law.						

THE ACCOUNTING COUNCIL'S ADVICE TO THE FRC TO ISSUE FRS 102

	UK References	**RoI References**						
Paragraph	**2006 Act and the 2008 Regulations (unless otherwise stated)**	**1963 Act**	**1983 Act**	**1986 Act**	**1990 Act**	**GAR 1992**	**CIR 1992**	**IUR 1996**
36	Section 467(1)			Sections 2 and 8				
49	Section 405(3)					Regulation 11	Paragraph 2(3) of Part II of the Schedule	Paragraph 2(3) of Part IV of the Schedule

APPENDIX I: GLOSSARY

	UK References	RoI References						
Paragraph	**2006 Act and the 2008 Regulations (unless otherwise stated)**	**1963 Act**	**1983 Act**	**1986 Act**	**1990 Act**	**GAR 1992**	**CIR 1992**	**IUR 1996**
'financial institution' and footnote 25	Part IV permission; Section 40(4) of the Financial Services and Markets Act 2000	There is no equivalent legislation in Ireland to the Financial Services and Markets Act 2000. Banks in Ireland are licensed under Section 9 of the Central Bank Act 1971.						
'financial institution'	Section 119(1) of the Building Societies Act 1986	Section 2(1) of the Building Societies Act 1989						
'financial institution'	Industrial and Provident Societies Act 1965 and Credit Unions Act 1979	Credit Union Acts 1997 to 2012						

APPENDIX I: GLOSSARY (contd.)

	UK References	**RoI References**						
Paragraph	**2006 Act and the 2008 Regulations (unless otherwise stated)**	**1963 Act**	**1983 Act**	**1986 Act**	**1990 Act**	**GAR 1992**	**CIR 1992**	**IUR 1996**
'financial institution'	Friendly Societies Act 1992; section 7(1)(a) of the Friendly Societies Act 1974	Friendly Societies Acts 1896 to 1977						
'individual financial statements'	Section 394	Section 148						
'individual financial statements'	Section 132 of the Charities Act 2011	Section 48 of the Charities Act 2009 provides that all charities are to prepare an annual statement of accounts, the form and content of which can be prescribed by Regulations of the Minister. Section 48 is, at the date of publication of this FRS, not commenced and no Regulations regarding the form and content of charities' annual statements of accounts have been published. Charity companies are required to prepare financial statements which give a true and fair view in accordance with the Companies Acts. Sections 148(3) and 150(4) of the 1963 Act require that companies "not trading for the acquisition of gain by the members" must prepare Companies Act accounts (ie not IFRS accounts), and this definition may apply to many Irish charity companies.						

APPENDIX I: GLOSSARY (contd.)

	UK References	RoI References						
Paragraph	**2006 Act and the 2008 Regulations (unless otherwise stated)**	**1963 Act**	**1983 Act**	**1986 Act**	**1990 Act**	**GAR 1992**	**CIR 1992**	**IUR 1996**
'individual financial statements'	Section 72A of the Building Societies Act 1986	Section 77 of the Building Societies Act 1989 requires the preparation of (a) an income and expenditure account giving a true and fair view of its income and expenditure for that year, (b) a balance sheet giving a true and fair view of the state of its affairs as at the end of that year, and (c) a statement of the source and application of funds giving a true and fair view of the manner in which its business has been financed and in which its financial resources have been used during that year.						
'LLP Regulations'	The Large and Medium-sized Limited Liability Partnerships (Accounts) Regulations 2008 (SI 2008/ 1913)	There is no equivalent Irish LLP legislation						
'qualifying entity' (footnote 29)	Section 474(1)					Regulation 3(1)	Paragraph 1 of Part IV of the Schedule	

APPENDIX II: SIGNIFICANT DIFFERENCES BETWEEN FRS 102 AND THE IFRS FOR SMEs

	UK References	RoI References						
Paragraph	**2006 Act and the 2008 Regulations (unless otherwise stated)**	**1963 Act**	**1983 Act**	**1986 Act**	**1990 Act**	**GAR 1992**	**CIR 1992**	**IUR 1996**
Section 9	Paragraph 2(2) of Schedule 6 to the Regulations					Regulation 26(2)	Paragraph 3(3) of Part II of the Schedule	Paragraph 3(3) of Part IV of the Schedule
Section 9	Paragraph 13(a) of Schedule 1 to the Regulations			Section 5(c)(i)		Regulation 28 (applying Section 5 of the 1986 Act)	Paragraph 19(a) of Part I and paragraph 1 of Part II of the Schedule	Regulation 7(c)(i) and paragraph 13 of Part IV of the Schedule
Sections 14 and 15	Paragraph 27 of Schedule 1 to the Regulations			Paragraph 14 of Part II of the Schedule		Regulation 15 (applying the Schedule to the 1986 Act)	Paragraph 36 of Part I of the Schedule and paragraph 1 of Part II of the Schedule	Paragraphs 7 to 8 of Part II of the Schedule and paragraph 13 of Part IV of the Schedule

APPENDIX II: SIGNIFICANT DIFFERENCES BETWEEN FRS 102 AND THE IFRS FOR SMEs (cont.)

	UK References	RoI References						
Paragraph	**2006 Act and the 2008 Regulations (unless otherwise stated)**	**1963 Act**	**1983 Act**	**1986 Act**	**1990 Act**	**GAR 1992**	**CIR 1992**	**IUR 1996**
Sections 14 and 15	Section C of Schedule 1 to the Regulations			Part III of the Schedule		Regulation 15 (applying the Schedule to the 1986 Act)	Paragraphs 39 to 44 of Part I of the Schedule and paragraph 1 of Part II of the Schedule	Chapter 2 of Part II of the Schedule and paragraph 13 of Part IV of the Schedule
Sections 14 and 15	Paragraph 36 of Schedule 1 to the Regulations			Paragraphs 22A and 22AA of Part IIIA of the Schedule		Regulation 15 (applying the Schedule to the 1986 Act)	Paragraph 46A of Part I and paragraph 1 of Part II of the Schedule	

APPENDIX IV: NOTE ON LEGAL REQUIREMENTS

	UK References	RoI References						
Paragraph	**2006 Act and the 2008 Regulations (unless otherwise stated)**	**1963 Act**	**1983 Act**	**1986 Act**	**1990 Act**	**GAR 1992**	**CIR 1992**	**IUR 1996**
A4.1 (Footnote 33)	Charities Act 2011 and Regulations made thereunder	Section 48 of the Charities Act 2009 provides that all charities are to prepare an annual statement of accounts, the form and content of which can be prescribed by Regulations of the Minister. Section 48 is, at the date of publication of this FRS, not commenced and no Regulations regarding the form and content of charities' annual statements of accounts have been published. Charity companies are required to prepare financial statements which give a true and fair view in accordance with the Companies Acts. Sections 148(3) and 150(4) of the 1963 Act require that companies "not trading for the acquisition of gain by the members" must prepare Companies Act accounts (ie not IFRS accounts), and this definition may apply to many Irish charity companies.						
A4.3	Schedule 1 to the Regulations			Sections 4, 5 and 6 and the Schedule				
A4.3	Schedule 2 to the Regulations						Part I of the Schedule	

APPENDIX IV: NOTE ON LEGAL REQUIREMENTS (cont.)

	UK References	RoI References						
Paragraph	**2006 Act and the 2008 Regulations (unless otherwise stated)**	**1963 Act**	**1983 Act**	**1986 Act**	**1990 Act**	**GAR 1992**	**CIR 1992**	**IUR 1996**
A4.3	Schedule 3 to the Regulations							Regulations 6, 7 and 8 and Parts I, II and III of the Schedule
A4.3	Schedule 6 to the Regulations					Regulations 15 to 35 & the Schedule	Part II of the Schedule	Regulations 6, 7, 8 and 10 and Parts I, II and III, as modified by Part IV of the Schedule
A4.6	Section 395(1)	Section 148(2)					Regulation 5	Regulation 5
A4.6	Section 396	Section 149		Section 3			Regulation 5	Regulation 5
A4.6	Section 403(2)	Section 150(3)						
A4.6	Section 404	Section 150A and 151				Regulation 14	Regulation 7	Regulation 10

APPENDIX IV: NOTE ON LEGAL REQUIREMENTS (cont.)

	UK References	RoI References						
Paragraph	**2006 Act and the 2008 Regulations (unless otherwise stated)**	**1963 Act**	**1983 Act**	**1986 Act**	**1990 Act**	**GAR 1992**	**CIR 1992**	**IUR 1996**
A4.7	'Accounts prepared in accordance with FRS 102 are ...required to comply with the applicable provisions of Parts 15 and 16 of the Act and with the Regulations'	Sections 148, 149, 150, 150A, 150C, 151, 152, 153, 156, 161D and 191 See also Section 33(4) of the Companies (Amendment) (No.2) Act 1999		Sections 3 to 6, 16, 16A and 17 and the Schedule	Sections 41 to 43 and Section 63	Regulations 2 to 35 and the Schedule	Regulations 2, 5, 7, 8, 8A, 9 and 10 and the Schedule	Regulations 2, 5, 6, 7, 8, 10, 11, 12, 12A and 13 and the Schedule
A4.8	Section 407	Section 150C						

APPENDIX IV: NOTE ON LEGAL REQUIREMENTS (contd.)

	UK References	RoI References						
Paragraph	**2006 Act and the 2008 Regulations (unless otherwise stated)**	**1963 Act**	**1983 Act**	**1986 Act**	**1990 Act**	**GAR 1992**	**CIR 1992**	**IUR 1996**
A4.12	Paragraph 36 of Schedule 1 to the Regulations			Paragraphs 22A and 22AA of Part IIIA of the Schedule		Regulation 15 (applying the Schedule to the 1986 Act)	Paragraph 46A of Part I of the Schedule and paragraph 1 of Part II of the Schedule	
A4.13	Paragraph 36(4) of Schedule 1 to the Regulations			Paragraph 22AA of Part IIIA of the Schedule		Regulation 15 (applying the Schedule to the 1986 Act)	Paragraphs 46A(4A) and 46A(4B) of Part I and paragraph 1 of Part II of the Schedule	
A4.13	Paragraph 36(3) of Schedule 1 to the Regulations			Paragraph 22A(3) of Part IIIA of the Schedule		Regulation 15 (applying the Schedule to the 1986 Act)	Paragraph 46A(4) of Part I and paragraph 1 of Part II of the Schedule	

APPENDIX IV: NOTE ON LEGAL REQUIREMENTS (contd.)

	UK References	RoI References						
Paragraph	**2006 Act and the 2008 Regulations (unless otherwise stated)**	**1963 Act**	**1983 Act**	**1986 Act**	**1990 Act**	**GAR 1992**	**CIR 1992**	**IUR 1996**
A4.15	Section 434(2)			Section 19(3A)			Regulation 6(4)	Regulation 9(4)
A4.15	Section 408	Sections 148(8) and (9)		Sections 7(1A) and (1B)				
A4.16	Section 405(3)					Regulation 11	Paragraph 2(3) of Part II of the Schedule	Paragraph 2(3) of Part IV of the Schedule
A4.17	Paragraph 36 of Schedule 1 to the Regulations			Paragraphs 22A and 22AA of Part IIIA of the Schedule		Regulation 15 (applying the Schedule to the 1986 Act)	Paragraph 46A of Part I and paragraph 1 of Part II of the Schedule	
A4.17	Paragraph 10(2) of Schedule 1 to the Regulations			Section 6		Regulation 28 (applying Section 6 of the 1986 Act)	Paragraph 22 of Part I and paragraph 1 of Part II of the Schedule	Regulation 8

APPENDIX IV: NOTE ON LEGAL REQUIREMENTS (contd.)

	UK References	**RoI References**						
Paragraph	**2006 Act and the 2008 Regulations (unless otherwise stated)**	**1963 Act**	**1983 Act**	**1986 Act**	**1990 Act**	**GAR 1992**	**CIR 1992**	**IUR 1996**
A4.18	Paragraph 9 of Schedule 6 to the Regulations					Regulation 19	Paragraph 10 of Part II of the Schedule	Paragraph 9 of Part IV of the Schedule
A4.21	Section 404(5)					Regulation 14(3) and (4)	Regulation 7(7)(d) and (e)	Regulation 10(7)(d) and (e)
A4.22 and A4.23	Paragraph 8 of Schedule 1 to the Regulations			Section 4(11)		Regulation 15 (applying Section 4 of the 1986 Act)	Paragraph 5 of Part I and paragraph 1 of Part II of the Schedule	Regulation 6(9) and paragraph 3(1) of Part IV of the Schedule
A4.24	Sections 611-615	There are no corresponding Irish provisions to Sections 611-615 (group reconstruction and merger relief)						

APPENDIX IV: NOTE ON LEGAL REQUIREMENTS (contd.)

	UK References	RoI References						
Paragraph	**2006 Act and the 2008 Regulations (unless otherwise stated)**	**1963 Act**	**1983 Act**	**1986 Act**	**1990 Act**	**GAR 1992**	**CIR 1992**	**IUR 1996**
A4.25 and A4.27	Paragraph 13(a) of Schedule 1 to the Regulations			Section 5(c)(i)		Regulation 28 (applying Section 5 of the 1986 Act)	Paragraph 19(a) of Part I and paragraph 1 of Part II of the Schedule	Regulation 7(c)(i) and paragraph 13 of Part IV of the Schedule
A4.26	Paragraph 36(4) of Schedule 1 to the Regulations			Paragraph 22AA of Part IIIA of the Schedule		Regulation 15 (applying the Schedule to the 1986 Act)	Paragraphs 46A(4A) and 46A(4B) of Part I and paragraph 1 of Part II of the Schedule	
A4.26	Paragraph 39 of Schedule 1 to the Regulations			Paragraph 22CA of Part IIIA of the Schedule		Regulation 15 (applying the Schedule to the 1986 Act)	Paragraph 46BA of Part I and paragraph 1 of Part II of the Schedule	

APPENDIX IV: NOTE ON LEGAL REQUIREMENTS (contd.)

	UK References	**RoI References**						
Paragraph	**2006 Act and the 2008 Regulations (unless otherwise stated)**	**1963 Act**	**1983 Act**	**1986 Act**	**1990 Act**	**GAR 1992**	**CIR 1992**	**IUR 1996**
A4.27	Paragraphs 40 and 40(2) of Schedule 1 to the Regulations			Sections 22D and 22D(2) of Part IIIA of the Schedule		Regulation 15 (applying the Schedule to the 1986 Act)	Paragraphs 46C and 46C(1) of Part I and paragraph 1 of Part II of the Schedule	
A4.30	Paragraph 10 of Schedule 6 to the Regulations	Sections 62 and 149(5)*				Regulation 21	Paragraph 11 of Part II of the Schedule	Paragraph 10 of Part IV of the Schedule
		*Please refer to the note above in the introduction to this table – merger accounting						
A4.32	Sections 690 to 708	Section 72			Part XI			
A4.32	Sections 724 to 732		Section 43A		Section 209			

APPENDIX IV: NOTE ON LEGAL REQUIREMENTS (contd.)

	UK References	**RoI References**						
Paragraph	**2006 Act and the 2008 Regulations (unless otherwise stated)**	**1963 Act**	**1983 Act**	**1986 Act**	**1990 Act**	**GAR 1992**	**CIR 1992**	**IUR 1996**
A4.33	Paragraph 36 of Schedule 1 to the Regulations			Paragraphs 22A and 22AA of Part IIIA of the Schedule		Regulation 15 (applying the Schedule to the 1986 Act)	Paragraph 46A of Part I and paragraph 1 of Part II of the Schedule	
A4.34	Section C of Schedule 1 to the Regulations			Part III of the Schedule		Regulation 15 (applying the Schedule to the 1986 Act)	Section B of Chapter II of Part I of the Schedule and paragraph 1 of Part II of the Schedule	Chapter 2 of Part II of the Schedule
A4.35	Paragraph 24(1) of Schedule 1 to the Regulations			Paragraph 11(1) of the Schedule		Regulation 15 (applying the Schedule to the 1986 Act)	Paragraph 33(1) of Part I of the Schedule and paragraph 1 of Part II of the Schedule	Paragraph 5(2) of Part II of the Schedule and paragraph 13 of Part IV of the Schedule

APPENDIX IV: NOTE ON LEGAL REQUIREMENTS (contd.)

	UK References	**RoI References**						
Paragraph	**2006 Act and the 2008 Regulations (unless otherwise stated)**	**1963 Act**	**1983 Act**	**1986 Act**	**1990 Act**	**GAR 1992**	**CIR 1992**	**IUR 1996**
A4.35	Paragraph 32(5) of Schedule 1 to the Regulations			Paragraph 19(5) of the Schedule		Regulation 15 (applying the Schedule to the 1986 Act)	Paragraph 41(4) of Part I of the Schedule and paragraph 1 of Part II of the Schedule	Paragraph 15(2) of Part II of the Schedule and paragraph 13 of Part IV of the Schedule
A4.38	LLP Regulations	There is no equivalent Irish LLP legislation.						
A4.42	Building Societies Act 1986	Building Societies Act 1989, Part VII, Section 77(1)						
A4.42	Charities Act 2011 and Regulations made thereunder	Section 48 of the Charities Act 2009 provides that all charities are to prepare an annual statement of accounts, the form and content of which can be prescribed by Regulations of the Minister. Section 48 is, at the date of publication of this FRS, not commenced and no Regulations regarding the form and content of charities' annual statements of accounts have been published. Charity companies are required to prepare financial statements which give a true and fair view in accordance with the Companies Acts. Sections 148(3) and 150(4) of the 1963 Act require that companies "not trading for the acquisition of gain by the members" must prepare Companies Act accounts (ie not IFRS accounts), and this definition may apply to many Irish charity companies.						

APPENDIX IV: NOTE ON LEGAL REQUIREMENTS (contd.)

	UK References	RoI References						
Paragraph	**2006 Act and the 2008 Regulations (unless otherwise stated)**	**1963 Act**	**1983 Act**	**1986 Act**	**1990 Act**	**GAR 1992**	**CIR 1992**	**IUR 1996**
A4.42	Friendly and Industrial and Provident Societies Act 1968	Section 30 of Part IV of the Industrial and Provident Societies (Amendment) Act, 1978; Regulation 4 of the Friendly Societies Regulations 1988, pursuant to Section 3 of the Friendly Societies (Amendment) Act 1977						
A4.42 and Footnote 36	Friendly Societies Act 1992 and Friendly Societies (Accounts and Related Provisions) Regulations 1994 (as amended)	Regulation 4 of the Friendly Societies Regulations 1988, pursuant to Section 3 to the Friendly Societies (Amendment) Act 1977						

APPENDIX IV: NOTE ON LEGAL REQUIREMENTS (contd.)

	UK References	RoI References						
Paragraph	**2006 Act and the 2008 Regulations (unless otherwise stated)**	**1963 Act**	**1983 Act**	**1986 Act**	**1990 Act**	**GAR 1992**	**CIR 1992**	**IUR 1996**
A4.42	The Occupational Pension Schemes (Requirement to obtain Audited Accounts and a Statement from the Auditor) Regulations 1996	Section 56 of the Pensions Act 1990; Regulation 5 and paragraphs 1 and 2(a)(ii) of Schedule A to the Occupational Pension Schemes (Disclosure of Information) Regulations 2006.						

APPENDIX V: PREVIOUS CONSULTATIONS

	UK References	**RoI References**						
Paragraph	**2006 Act and the 2008 Regulations (unless otherwise stated)**	**1963 Act**	**1983 Act**	**1986 Act**	**1990 Act**	**GAR 1992**	**CIR 1992**	**IUR 1996**
A5.11	'small companies' regime'	There are no equivalent provisions in Irish company law to the UK small companies regime or to the Small Companies and Groups (Accounts and Directors' Report) Regulations 2008. Small companies are defined in Section 8 of the 1986 Act. Please refer to the note above in the introduction to this table.						

Part Four

Statements by the Accounting Standards Board

Reporting Statement: Operating and financial review

Contents

Paragraphs

REPORTING STATEMENT: OPERATING AND FINANCIAL REVIEW (OFR)	
INTRODUCTION	**1-5**
SUMMARY	**a-g**
OBJECTIVE	**1**
SCOPE	**2**
DEFINITIONS	**3**
PRINCIPLES	**4-25**
DISCLOSURE FRAMEWORK	**26-74**
Details of particular matters	**28-29**
The nature, objectives and strategies of the business	**30-42**
Current and future development and performance	**43-49**
Resources	**50-51**
Risks and uncertainties	**52-56**
Relationships	**57-59**
Financial position	**60-74**
KEY PERFORMANCE INDICATORS	**75-77**
OTHER MEASURES	**78**
SERIOUSLY PREJUDICIAL	**79**
STATEMENT OF COMPLIANCE	**80**
IMPLEMENTATION GUIDANCE	**IG1-IG35**

Reporting statement: Operating and Financial Review (OFR)

Introduction

1 The Accounting Standards Board (ASB) originally issued the Statement 'Operating and Financial Review' in July 1993. The Statement built on the foundations of existing best practice by providing a framework within which directors could discuss the main factors underlying the company's performance and financial position. The Statement was updated and a revised version issued in January 2003 to reflect later improvements in narrative reporting.

2 Following a recommendation in the final report of the Company Law Review (CLR) Steering Group (2001) and the Government response on the White Paper 'Modernising Company Law' (2002), the Government decided to require quoted companies to prepare and publish OFRs. In May 2004, the Government issued proposals on the detailed implementation of this new requirement in a consultation document 'Draft Regulations on the Operating and Financial Review and Directors' Report'. The consultation document contained draft secondary legislation to implement a new statutory OFR as well as certain provisions of the EU Accounts Modernisation Directive requiring an enhanced review of a company's business (the Business Review) in the directors' report. Following consultation, the final OFR Regulations were passed into law in March 2005, taking effect for financial years beginning on or after 1 April 2005.

3 The Government also gave the ASB a statutory power to make reporting standards for the OFR. In November 2004, the ASB issued Reporting Exposure Draft (RED) 1 'The Operating and Financial Review'. Following consultation, Reporting Standard (RS) 1 was issued in May 2005.

4 On 28 November 2005, the Chancellor of the Exchequer announced the Government's intention to remove the statutory requirement on quoted companies to publish OFRs, on the grounds that the central requirements of the Business Review are largely identical to those of the statutory OFR and the Government has a general policy not to impose regulatory requirements on UK businesses over and above the relevant EU Directive requirements. Regulations to repeal the requirement for the OFR were laid in December 2005 and came into force on 12 January 2006.

5 The statutory underpinning for RS 1 has been removed as a result of the removal of the statutory requirement for the OFR. As a consequence, RS 1 has now been formally withdrawn and the ASB has 'converted' RS 1 into a statement of best practice on the OFR, which is set out in this document. In preparing this statement, the ASB has sought to limit the changes to those required as a consequence of the repeal of the OFR legislation and to make the language consistent with a voluntary statement of best practice rather than a standard. Given the extensive consultation that took place in developing RS 1, and the need to continue to give entities guidance in preparing OFRs, the ASB is issuing this as a final Reporting Statement, rather than engaging in a further round of consultation.

Reporting statement: Operating and Financial Review (OFR)

Summary

The Reporting Statement is designed as a formulation and development of best practice; it is intended to have persuasive rather than mandatory force. This Statement has been written with quoted companies in mind, but is also applicable to any other entities that purport to prepare an OFR. **a**

The Reporting Statement recommends that directors prepare an OFR addressed to members, setting out their analysis of the business, with a forward-looking orientation in order to assist members to assess the strategies adopted by the entity and the potential for those strategies to succeed. The information disclosed in the OFR will also be of relevance to other stakeholders. The OFR should not, however, be seen as a replacement for other forms of reporting addressed to a wider stakeholder group. **b**

The Reporting Statement sets out a number of other principles regarded as best practice in the preparation of an OFR, namely that the review should: both complement and supplement the financial statements; be comprehensive and understandable; be balanced and neutral; and be comparable over time. **c**

The Reporting Statement sets out the key elements of the disclosure framework that directors should address in an OFR, including details on particular matters that should be disclosed to the extent necessary to meet the objective of the OFR. **d**

Those Key Performance Indicators (KPIs) judged by the directors to be effective in measuring the development, performance and position of the business of the entity should be disclosed, together with information that should enable members to understand and evaluate each KPI. **e**

The Reporting Statement recommends the inclusion of other measures and evidence to support the information included in the OFR. **f**

The Reporting Statement is accompanied by Implementation Guidance that provides illustrative examples of KPIs that might be disclosed in an OFR, as well as further guidance as to what is envisaged with regard to particular matters. **g**

Reporting statement: Operating and Financial Review (OFR)

OBJECTIVE

1 The objective of this Reporting Statement is to specify the best practice for an OFR, which should be a balanced and comprehensive analysis, consistent with the size and complexity of the business, of:

a. the development and performance of the business of the entity during the financial year;
b. the position of the entity at the end of the year;
c. the main trends and factors underlying the development, performance and position of the business of the entity during the financial year; and
d. the main trends and factors which are likely to affect the entity's future development, performance and position,

prepared so as to assist members to assess the strategies adopted by the entity and the potential for those strategies to succeed.

SCOPE

2 The Reporting Statement has been written with quoted companies in mind, but is also applicable to any other entities that purport to prepare an OFR.

DEFINITIONS

3 The following terms are used in this Reporting Statement with the meanings specified:

Directors

Reference to either "directors" or "board of directors" within the Reporting Statement is taken to be the entity's governing body where the entity is not a company.

Key Performance Indicators (KPIs)

KPIs are factors by reference to which the development, performance or position of the business of the entity can be measured effectively. They are quantified measurements that reflect the critical success factors of an entity and disclose progress towards achieving a particular objective or objectives.

Operating and Financial Review (OFR)

An OFR is a narrative explanation, provided in or accompanying the annual report, of the main trends and factors underlying the development, performance and position of an entity during the financial year covered by the financial statements, and those which are likely to affect the entity's future development, performance and position.

PRINCIPLES

The OFR should set out an analysis of the business through the eyes of the board of directors. 4

The OFR should reflect the directors' view of the business. Accordingly, the entity should disclose appropriate elements of information used in managing the entity, including its subsidiary undertakings. Where appropriate, the review may give greater emphasis to those matters which are significant to the entity and its subsidiary undertakings taken as a whole. Such matters may include issues specific to business segments where relevant to the understanding of the business as a whole. Directors should develop the presentation of their OFR in a way that complements the format of their annual report as a whole. 5

The OFR should focus on matters that are relevant to the interests of members. 6

Members' needs are paramount when directors consider what information should be contained in the OFR. Information in the OFR will also be of interest to users other than members, for example other investors, potential investors, creditors, customers, suppliers, employees and society more widely. The directors should consider the extent to which they should report on issues relevant to those other users where, because of those issues influence on the performance of the business and its value, they are also of significance to members. The OFR should not, however, be seen as a replacement for other forms of reporting addressed to a wider stakeholder group. 7

The OFR should have a forward-looking orientation, identifying those trends and factors relevant to the members' assessment of the current and future performance of the business and the progress towards the achievement of long-term business objectives. 8

The particular factors discussed should be those that have affected development, performance, and position during the financial year and those which are likely to affect the entity's future development, performance and position. 9

Given the nature of some forward-looking information, in particular elements that cannot be objectively verified but have been made in good faith, directors may want to include a statement in the OFR to treat such elements with caution, explaining the uncertainties underpinning such information. 10

The OFR should comment on the impact on future performance of significant events after the balance sheet date. 11

The OFR should also discuss predictive comments, both positive and negative, made in previous reviews whether or not these have been borne out by events. 12

The OFR should complement as well as supplement the financial statements, in order to enhance the overall corporate disclosure. 13

In complementing the financial statements, the OFR should provide useful financial and non-financial information about the business and its performance that is not reported in financial statements but which, the directors' judge, might be relevant to the members' evaluation of past results and assessment of future prospects. 14

In supplementing the financial statements, the OFR should where relevant: 15

- provide additional explanations of amounts recorded in the financial statements;

- explain the conditions and events that shaped the information contained in the financial statements.

Where amounts from the financial statements have been adjusted for inclusion in the OFR, that fact should be highlighted and a reconciliation provided.

16 **The OFR should be comprehensive and understandable.**

17 Directors should consider whether the omission of information might reasonably be expected to influence significantly the assessment made by members.

18 The recommendation for the OFR to be comprehensive does not mean that the OFR should cover all possible matters: the objective is quality, not quantity of content. It is neither possible nor desirable for a Reporting Statement to list all the elements that might need to be included, since these will vary depending on the nature and circumstances of the particular business and how the business is run.

19 Directors should consider the evidence underpinning the information to be included in the OFR. Where relevant, directors should explain the source of the information and the degree to which the information is objectively supportable, to allow members to assess the reliability of the information presented for themselves.

20 Directors should consider the key issues to include in the OFR that will provide members with focused and relevant information. The inclusion of too much information may obscure judgements and will not promote understanding. Where additional information is discussed elsewhere in the annual report, or in other reports, cross-referencing to those sources will assist members.

21 The OFR should be written in a clear and readily understandable style.

22 **The OFR should be balanced and neutral, dealing even-handedly with both good and bad aspects.**

23 The directors should ensure that the OFR retains balance and that members are not misled as a result of the omission of any information on unfavourable aspects.

24 **The OFR should be comparable over time.**

25 Disclosure should be sufficient for the members to be able to compare the information presented with similar information about the entity for previous financial years. Comparability enables identification of the main trends and factors, and their analysis, over successive financial years. Directors may wish to consider the extent to which the OFR is comparable with reviews prepared by other entities in the same industry or sector.

DISCLOSURE FRAMEWORK

26 Paragraphs 27 to 74 below set out a framework for the disclosures to be provided by directors in an OFR. This framework is not a template, nor should the elements in paragraph 27 be taken as headings that should be included within an OFR. Its purpose is to set out the key content elements that should be addressed within an OFR. It is for directors to consider how best to use the framework to structure the OFR and the precise content, including the level of detail to be disclosed, relating to the key elements, given the particular circumstances of the entity. These circumstances may include:

a. the industry or industries in which it operates;
b. the range of products, services or processes it offers;
c. the number of markets it serves.

The OFR should provide information to assist members to assess the strategies adopted by the entity and the potential for those strategies to succeed. The key elements of the disclosure framework recommended to achieve this are: 27

a. the nature of the business, including a description of the market, competitive and regulatory environment in which the entity operates, and the entity's objectives and strategies;
b. the development and performance of the business, both in the financial year under review and in the future;
c. the resources, principal risks and uncertainties and relationships that may affect the entity's long-term value; and
d. position of the business including a description of the capital structure, treasury policies and objectives and liquidity of the entity, both in the financial year under review and the future.

Details of particular matters

To the extent necessary to meet the recommendations set out in paragraph 27 above, the OFR should include information about: 28

a. environmental matters (including the impact of the business of the entity on the environment);
b. the entity's employees;
c. social and community issues;
d. persons with whom the entity has contractual or other arrangements with are essential to the business of the entity;
e. receipts from, and returns to, members of the entity in respect of shares held by them; and
f. all other matters the directors consider to be relevant.

For items (a) to (c) in paragraph 28, the OFR should, in particular, include: 29
a. the policies of the entity in each area mentioned; and
b. the extent to which those policies have been successfully implemented.

The nature, objectives and strategies of the business

The OFR should include a description of the business and the external environment in which it operates as context for the directors' discussion and analysis of performance and financial position. 30

A description of the business is recommended in order to provide members with an understanding of the industry or industries in which the entity operates, its main products, services, customers, business processes and distribution methods, the structure of the business, and its economic model, including an overview of the main operating facilities and their location. 31

Every entity is affected by its external environment. Depending on the nature of the business, the OFR should include discussion of matters such as the entity's major markets and competitive position within those markets and the significant features of the legal, regulatory, macro-economic and social environment that influence the business. For example, an entity may disclose the fact that it has significant 32 operations in a number of different countries, which could have an impact on the future development and performance of the business.

33 **The OFR should discuss the objectives of the business to generate or preserve value over the longer-term.**

34 Objectives will often be defined in terms of financial performance; however, objectives in non-financial areas should also be discussed where appropriate.

35 The nature of the industry will affect the directors' determination of an appropriate time perspective for reporting in the OFR. For example, a business that focuses on large long-term projects must carry out its strategic planning over the full project lifecycle, which may be 20 years or more. Furthermore, where a project has a long-term impact on the environment, this is likely to affect long-term value and should therefore determine the time perspective for reporting in the OFR. By contrast, a service industry with few physical assets and depending on the supply of particular employee skills for its source of competitive advantage, will plan over a period consistent with its ability to recruit, train and develop its staff, which may be much shorter.

36 **The OFR should set out the directors' strategies for achieving the objectives of the business.**

37 Disclosure of the directors' strategies is recommended in order for members to assess the current and past action undertaken by directors in respect of the stated objectives.

38 **To the extent necessary to meet the recommendations set out in paragraph 27 above, the OFR should include the key performance indicators, both financial and, where appropriate, non-financial, used by the directors to assess progress against their stated objectives.**

39 The KPIs disclosed should be those that the directors judge are effective in measuring the delivery of their strategies and managing their business. Regular measurement using KPIs should enable an entity to set and communicate its performance targets and to measure whether it is achieving them.

40 Comparability will be enhanced if the KPIs disclosed are accepted and widely used, either within the industry sector or more generally.

41 **Directors should also consider the extent to which other measures and evidence should be included in the OFR.**

42 These could be narrative evidence describing how the directors manage the business or quantified measures used to monitor the entity's external environment and/or progress towards the achievement of its objectives.

Current and future development and performance

43 **The OFR should describe the significant features of the development and performance of the business in the financial year covered by the financial statements, focusing on those business segments that are relevant to an understanding of the development and performance as a whole.**

Trends and factors in development and performance suggested by an analysis of the current and previous financial years should be highlighted. Development and performance should be described in the context of the strategic objectives of the business. 44

The OFR should cover significant aspects of the statements of financial performance and where appropriate should be linked to other aspects of performance. 45

The OFR should set out the directors' analysis of the effect on current development and performance of changes during the financial year in the industry or the external environment in which the business operates and of developments within the business. For example, changes in market conditions could have an impact on the development and performance of the entity during the period, as could the introduction, or announcement, of new products and services. 46

The OFR should analyse the main trends and factors that directors consider likely to impact future prospects. 47

The main trends and factors likely to affect the future development and performance will vary according to the nature of the business, but could include the development of known new products and services or the benefits expected from capital investment. The OFR should discuss the current level of investment expenditure together with planned future expenditure and should explain how that investment is directed to assist the achievement of business objectives. Any assumptions underlying the main trends and factors should be disclosed. 48

Directors should consider the potential future significance of issues in deciding whether or not to include an analysis of them in the OFR. 49

Resources

The OFR should include a description of the resources available to the entity and how they are managed. 50

The OFR should set out the key strengths and resources, tangible and intangible, available to the business, which will assist it in the pursuit of its objectives and, in particular, those items that are not reflected in the balance sheet. Depending on the nature of the business, these may include: corporate reputation and brand strength; natural resources; employees; research and development; intellectual capital; licences, patents, copyright and trademarks; and market position. 51

Principal risks and uncertainties

The OFR should include a description of the principal risks and uncertainties facing the entity, together with a commentary on the directors' approach to them. 52

While different industries and entities use different risk models or approaches for identifying and managing risk, all entities face and should disclose strategic, commercial, operational and financial risks where these may significantly affect the entity's strategies and development of the entity's value. 53

The principal risks and uncertainties facing entities will vary according to the nature of the business, although it is expected that some risks, such as reputational risk, will be common to all. 54

55 The description of the principal risks and uncertainties should cover both the exposure to negative consequences as well as potential opportunities. The directors' policy for managing principal risks should be disclosed.

56 The OFR should cover the principal risks and uncertainties necessary for an understanding of the objectives and strategies of the business, both where they constitute a significant external risk to the entity, and where the entity's impact on other parties through its activities, products or services, affects its performance. Directors should consider the full range of business risks.

Relationships

57 **To the extent necessary to meet the recommendations set out in paragraph 27 above, the OFR should include information about significant relationships with stakeholders other than members, which are likely, directly or indirectly, to influence the performance of the business and its value.**

58 Directors, in deciding what should be included in the OFR, should take a broad view in considering the extent to which the actions of stakeholders other than members can affect an entity's performance and thus its value. For example, for many entities, relationships with customers, suppliers, employees, contractors, lenders, creditors and regulators will be important, as will the entity's broader impact on society and the communities affected by its activities. Strategic alliances with other entities can also affect the performance of the entity and its value.

59 **Where necessary for an understanding of the business, the OFR should describe receipts from, and returns to, shareholders in relation to shares held by them. This should include a description of any distributions, capital raising and share repurchases.**

Financial position

60 **The OFR should contain an analysis of the financial position of the entity.**

61 The analysis, whilst based upon the financial statements, should comment on the events that have impacted the financial position of the entity during the financial year, and future factors that are likely to affect the financial position going forward. The analysis should supplement the disclosures required in accounting standards, in particular those required by FRS 25 (IAS 32) 'Financial Instruments: Disclosure and Presentation' or FRS 29 (IFRS 7) 'Financial Instruments: Disclosures'.

62 The OFR should highlight accounting policies set out in the notes to the financial statements and discuss those accounting policies that are critical to an understanding of the performance and financial position of the entity, focusing on those which have required the particular exercise of judgement in their application and to which the results are most sensitive. In addition, it should draw attention to the accounting policies which have changed during the financial year under review.

63 **The OFR should contain a discussion of the capital structure of the entity.**

64 This could include the balance between equity and debt, the maturity profile of debt, type of capital instruments used, currency, regulatory capital and interest rate structure. The discussion should include comments on short and longer-term funding plans to support the directors' strategies to achieve the entity's objectives. In addition, the discussion should comment on why the entity has adopted its particular capital structure.

The OFR should set out the entity's treasury policies and objectives. **65**

The OFR should also discuss the implementation of these policies in the financial year under review. **66**

The purpose and effect of major financing transactions undertaken up to the date of approval of the financial statements should be explained. The effect of interest costs on profits and the potential impact of interest rate changes should also be discussed. **67**

Cash flows

The OFR should discuss the cash inflows and outflows during the financial year, along with the entity's ability to generate cash, to meet known or probable cash requirements and to fund growth. **68**

Any discussion should supplement the information provided in the financial statements by, for example, commenting on any special factors that have influenced cash flows in the financial year and those that may have a significant effect on future cash flows. This could include, for example, the existence and timing of commitments for capital expenditures and other known or probable cash requirements. Where entities have cash that is surplus to future operating requirements and current levels of distribution, the discussion should include future plans for making use of the excess cash. **69**

Although segmental analysis of profit may be indicative of the cash flow generated by each segment, this will not always be so – for example, because of fluctuations in capital expenditure and depreciation. Where segmental cash flows are significantly out of line with segmental revenues or profits, this should be indicated and explained. **70**

Liquidity

The OFR should discuss the entity's current and prospective liquidity. Where relevant, this should include commentary on the level of borrowings, the seasonality of borrowing requirements (indicated by the peak level of borrowings during that period) and the maturity profile of both borrowings and undrawn committed borrowing facilities. **71**

The discussion on liquidity should discuss the ability of the entity to fund its current and future operations and stated strategies. **72**

The discussion should cover internal sources of liquidity, referring to any restrictions on the ability to transfer funds from one part of the group to meet the obligations of another part of the group, where these represent, or might foreseeably come to represent, a significant restraint on the group. Such constraints would include exchange controls and taxation consequences of transfers. **73**

Where the entity has entered into covenants in financing contracts which could have the effect of restricting the use of financing arrangements or credit facilities, and negotiations with the lenders on the operation of these covenants are taking place or are expected to take place, this fact should be indicated in the OFR. Where a breach of a covenant has occurred or is expected to occur, the OFR should give details of the measures taken or proposed to remedy the situation. **74**

KEY PERFORMANCE INDICATORS

75 **An entity should provide information that enables members to understand each KPI disclosed in the OFR.**

76 **For each KPI disclosed in the OFR:**

- **the definition and its calculation method should be explained;**
- **its purpose should be explained;**
- **the source of underlying data should be disclosed and, where relevant, assumptions explained;**
- **quantification or commentary on future targets should be provided;**
- **where information from the financial statements has been adjusted for inclusion in the OFR, that fact should be highlighted and a reconciliation provided;**
- **where available, corresponding amount for the financial year immediately preceding the current year should be disclosed; and**
- **any changes to KPIs should be disclosed and the calculation method used compared to previous financial years, including significant changes in the underlying accounting policies adopted in the financial statements, should be identified and explained.**

77 Quantification or commentary on future targets is about communicating the direction the entity is taking by, for example, setting out future strategies and goals.

OTHER PERFORMANCE INDICATORS

78 **Where a quantified measure, other than a KPI, is included, the OFR should disclose:**

- **the definition and its calculation method; and**
- **where available, corresponding amount for the financial year immediately preceding the current year.**

SERIOUSLY PREJUDICIAL

79 **Consistent with existing practice in informing the markets on such matters, no disclosure of information should be made about impending developments or about matters in the course of negotiation if the disclosure would, in the opinion of the directors, be seriously prejudicial to the interests of the entity.**

STATEMENT OF COMPLIANCE

80 **As this is a Reporting Statement of voluntary best practice, directors are not required to include in the annual report any formal confirmation that they have complied with this Reporting Statement. That said, as a matter of best practice, the OFR should include a statement as to whether it has been prepared in accordance with this Reporting Statement.**

Implementation guidance

This guidance accompanies, but is not part of, the Reporting Statement.

INTRODUCTION

This Implementation Guidance: IG1

a. Outlines some suggestions and illustrations of the content recommended to be covered in the OFR with regard to the disclosure framework as set out in paragraph 27 of the Reporting Statement, and related Key Performance Indicators (KPIs) (paragraphs 38 to 40).

b. Provides some further "signposting" guidance as to the areas directors should consider with regard to the particular matters identified in paragraph 28 (a)-(e) of the Reporting Statement.

The format used for the illustrative examples of KPIs featured in IG Examples 1-23 should not be taken as a template. Its purpose is simply to demonstrate the information that could be provided for a particular measure. It is not envisaged that the layout presented in the Implementation Guidance will be replicated by an entity preparing an OFR. It is for the directors to consider how best to present the information, perhaps by providing some of the details within in footnotes, or in a separate section of the OFR.

Furthermore, these suggestions are non-exhaustive. Many further KPIs exist within different industries.

In addition, the definitions and other criteria set out in IG Examples 1-23 are illustrative and should not be taken to imply generally accepted definitions or calculations.

CONTENT RELATED TO THE DISCLOSURE FRAMEWORK AND RELATED KPIS

The guidance in paragraphs IG11-IG35 suggests possible content envisaged for each element of the disclosure framework, whilst IG Examples 1-23 provide illustrative examples of KPIs and the disclosure recommended under paragraphs 75 and 76 of the Reporting Statement. IG2

Paragraph 27 of the Reporting Statement requires that the OFR should provide the information to assist members to assess the strategies adopted by the entity and the potential for those strategies to succeed. To this end, the Reporting Statement provides a disclosure framework which sets out the areas to be considered by directors in preparing their entity's OFR. As acknowledged in the Reporting Statement, it is for directors to consider how best to use the framework to structure the OFR. IG3

Paragraphs 75 and 76 set out the disclosure requirements relating to each KPI, which are dealt with in paragraphs 38 to 40 of the Reporting Statement. IG4

Whilst IG Examples 1-23 are expressed as KPIs, they could also be considered as examples of quantified other measures as set out in paragraphs 41 and 42 of the Reporting Statement. If any of these examples were disclosed as quantified other measures, then the recommended disclosure would only cover the measures definition, its calculation method and the corresponding amount as set out in paragraph 78 of the Reporting Statement. IG5

IG6 Other trends and factors monitored by the entity may also be considered quantified other measures, although they would not ever be KPIs as they are outside of the control of the entity. For example, an insurance company might monitor changing demographics as a key trend in the external operating environment, due to the impact of demographics on future demand for its products. Accordingly, in such circumstances, quantified demographic information would be included in the OFR as an example of a quantified other measure.

IG7 Definitions and other criteria set out in IG Examples 1-23 are illustrative and should not be taken to imply generally accepted definitions or calculations. They are simply provided to demonstrate the information that could be provided for a particular measure. It is important that the information provided in the OFR with regard to any KPIs or quantified other measures makes explicit the definition and precise calculation method used by the entity.

PARTICULAR MATTERS

IG8 **The guidance below includes some background material that might be useful to consider when developing an entity's OFR with regard to the specific "particular matters" set out in paragraph 28 (a)-(e) of the Reporting Statement. In addition, where the management of a particular matter has been identified as being essential to the successful implementation of a stated strategy or could have an effect on the entity's short or long-term value, the guidance provides some illustrations of areas that might be covered.**

IG9 **Paragraph 28 (a)-(e) of the Reporting Statement requires that, to the extent necessary to meet the requirements set out in paragraph 27 of the Reporting Statement, the OFR should include information about a number of particular matters, e.g. employees, and environment. As explained in paragraph 27 of the Reporting Statement, the OFR should provide the information necessary to assist members to assess the strategies adopted by the entity and the potential for those strategies to succeed. Accordingly, where the management of a particular matter could significantly affect the entity's ability to successfully implement its strategies or the entity's short or long-term value, that matter should be addressed within the OFR.**

IG10 **Paragraph 28 (a)-(e) contains a non-exhaustive list of topics that directors should consider for inclusion in their OFR to the extent necessary. Accordingly, paragraph 28 (f) provides a further recommendation that directors, to the extent necessary, include within the OFR "all other relevant matters." The directors should consider what other topics also should be included in the OFR, as these will be specific to the entity, its objectives and strategies, as well as dependent on the industry in which it operates.**

Nature, objectives and strategies of the business

IG11 The Reporting Statement recommends the provision of meaningful contextual information regarding the directors' objectives and strategies, along with a description of the business and its external environment, to assist members to assess the strategies adopted and the potential for those strategies to succeed.

IG12 Specifically, the OFR should set out the objectives of the business and the directors' strategies for generating or preserving value for members over the long term. A number of economic measures exist that are commonly used by companies in order to assess the company's ability to create value over time, and which are likely to be considered a KPI. These include:

- Return on capital employed.

- Incremental returns on investments.
- Economic profit type measures.
- Organic rates of growth and returns thereon.

IG Example 1: Return on capital employed (ROCE)

As an example of a measure of the creation of value, the recommended disclosure should incorporate the following:

- Definition and calculation: ROCE, measures the profit as a percentage of the total capital employed (invested) in the business.
- Purpose: The company's aim is to increase shareholder value. This is measured by the extent to which this goal has been achieved by using ROCE, as it is a measure of how well the money invested in the business is providing a return to investors.
- Source of underlying data: GAAP financial statement figures as adjusted below.
- Reconciliation of financial statement information:

  Operating result for calculation of ROCE =
  Operating result as per financial statements
  Plus interest from sales financing
  Capital employed =
  Intangible assets/property, plant and equipment
  Plus investments
  Plus accumulated goodwill amortisation
  Plus inventories
  Plus trade accounts receivable
  Plus other assets including prepaid expenses
  Less non-interesting bearing provisions/liabilities
- Quantified target: 10%.
- Quantified data: 2005 – Consolidated ROCE – 10.4%, 2004 – 10.2%, 2003 – 9.8%.
- No changes have been made to the source of data or calculation methods used.

IG Example 2: "Economic profit"

Economic profit is a further example of a measure that a company might use to quantify the creation of value. The recommended disclosure should incorporate the following:

- Definition and calculation: Economic profit, being a measure of capital adjusted profit. Based upon operating profit after tax, adjusted for one-off items and the cost of capital.
- Purpose: The company's key objective is to increase shareholder value, which is measured and managed using economic profit.
- Source of underlying data: GAAP financial statement figures as adjusted below.
- Quantified target: Economic profit for 2006 of £200 million, 2005 target was £150 million.
- Reconciliation of financial statement information:
  Profit after tax and minority interests, excluding goodwill amortisation =
  Operating profit after tax and minority interests
  Plus goodwill amortisation
  Less tax credit on goodwill
  Economic profit =
  Profit after tax and minority interests, excluding goodwill amortisation
  Less cost of capital
- Quantified data: 2005 – £160 million, 2004 – £145 million, 2003 – £140 million.
- No changes have been made to the source of data or calculation methods used.

Market positioning

IG13 Directors may also set their long term objectives around market positioning. In such cases, KPIs commonly used by the board, and accordingly included in the OFR might include:

- Market position.
- Market share.

IG Example 3: Market Share

For a company reporting market share as a KPI, the recommended disclosure should incorporate the following:

- Definition and calculation: Market share, being company revenue over estimated market revenue.
- Purpose: To assess how the company is performing in its particular market.
- Source of underlying data: No external verifiable source for market share exists; accordingly data are internal estimates.
- Quantified target: Achieve market share of 25% within 5 years.
- Quantified data: Five year trend data, 2001 – 17%, 2002 –18%, 2003 – 17%, 2004 – 19%, 2005 – 20%.
- No changes have been made to the source of data or calculation methods used.

Development, performance and position

The Reporting Statement recommends that the OFR should set out an historical and prospective analysis of the development, performance and position of the company. Whilst a number of the measures used to monitor the development, performance and position of the company may be traditional financial measures, directors often supplement these with other measures common to their industry to monitor their progress towards stated objectives. **IG14**

IG Example 4: Average revenue per user (customer)

A telecoms company may measure average revenue per user (ARPU) by types of product offerings as a KPI. By doing this, the directors are able to monitor customer buying patterns as this is a key factor that is likely to affect the development of future revenues. Recommended disclosure should incorporate the following information:

- Definition and calculation: Average revenue per user (ARPU) by major product segments, e.g. pre-pay and post-pay customers.
- Purpose: In the mobile network industry, ARPU is one of the key drivers for future revenue growth.
- Source of underlying data: Internal company data.
- Quantified target: To increase ARPU by 15% per annum for pre-pay customers and 5% per annum for post-pay customers.
- Quantified data: ARPU graph showing comparatives and percentage change year on year e.g. Pre-pay 2004 – £121, 2005 – £141, growth of 16.5%, Post-pay 2004 – £503, 2005 – £525, growth of 4.4%.
- No changes have been made to the source of data or calculation methods used.

IG Example 5: Number of subscribers

A pay TV company with an objective of achieving revenue growth may monitor the effectiveness of their actions and progress towards their goal through measuring of the number of subscribers as a KPI. Recommended disclosure should incorporate the following information:

- Definition and calculation: Number of subscribers by type of connection, i.e. direct to home (DTH) and cable.
- Purpose: In the pay TV industry, the level of subscribers is the key driver for future revenue growth.
- Source of underlying data: Internal company data.
- Quantified target: To increase the number of subscribers by 10% per annum for each type of connection.
- Quantified data: Table of number of subscribers and percentage increase from year to year e.g. 2005 – DTH 4,532 million, cable 3,241 million, 2004 – DTH 4,013, cable 3,004, growth of 12.9% and 7.9%.
- No changes have been made to the source of data or calculation methods used.

IG Example 6: Sales per square foot

A retail company with an objective of increasing revenues may monitor and measure revenue per square foot as a KPI. Recommended disclosure should incorporate the following information:

- Definition and calculation: Average revenue per square foot (£ per week), with square footage measured as store space excluding storage/delivery space, checkout and administrative space.
- Purpose: In the retail industry, sales per square foot is one of the key drivers for future revenue growth.
- Source of underlying data: Internal company data.
- Quantified target: To increase sales per square foot to £20 per square foot/ week.
- Quantified data: Graph showing weekly sales per square foot over the past five years, 2005 – £18.53, 2004 – £17.56, 2003 – £16.99, 2002 – £16.04, 2001 – £15.67
- No changes have been made to the source of data or calculation methods used.

IG Example 7: Percentage of revenue from new products

A consumer products company that has a strategy of providing innovation products to its customers may measure and monitor the percentage of revenue from new products as a KPI. Recommended disclosure should incorporate the following information:

- Definition and calculation: Percentage of revenue from new products = revenue from those products launched over the past two years over total revenue for the year.
- Purpose: In order to continue to grow in the fast paced market of consumer products, the company needs to ensure that it is continually renewing its product portfolio. One way of measuring success is to look at the percentage of revenue generated by new products.
- Source of underlying data: Internal company data.
- Quantified target: To achieve 35% of revenue from new products per annum.
- Quantified data: Percentage of revenue from new products, 2005 – 37%, 2004 – 33%, 2003 – 36%.
- No changes have been made to the source of data or calculation methods used.

IG Example 8: Number of products sold per customer

In the financial services industry, a company may have an objective to increase margins by increasing the number of products sold to existing customers. Directors may monitor the number of products sold per customer, or "customer penetration" rates as a KPI. Recommended disclosure should incorporate the following information:

- Definition and calculation: Customer penetration rates by geographic segment. Penetration rates are measured by taking the number of products sold to each customer on an annual basis.
- Purpose: Increasing customer penetration rates, leads to increased revenues without incurring significant customer handling costs.
- Source of underlying data: Company data from UK and South Africa.
- Quantified target: To increase customer penetration rates to 5.0 products per customer territory.
- Quantified data: Penetration, 2005 – UK 4.3, South Africa 4.9, 2004 – UK 4.5, South Africa 4.5, 2003 – UK 4.0, South Africa 4.1.
- No changes have been made to the source of data or calculation methods used.

IG Example 9: Products in the development pipeline

In the pharmaceutical industry, for example, future revenues may be greatly affected by the launch of new products from the company's product development pipeline. Directors may monitor number of products at each stage of development and the markets/timing for future launches as a KPI. Recommended disclosure should incorporate the following information:

- Definition and calculation: Product development pipeline being the key products currently under development, and the stage of development (Phase I, II or III). Phase I initial evaluation, Phase II determination of dose and initial evaluation of efficacy, Phase III large comparative study in patients to establish clinical benefit and safety.
- Purpose: In order to achieve a strategy of continuing growth, the company must have a productive product development pipeline.
- Source of underlying data: Company data.
- Quantified target: To have 5 new products launched annually.
- Quantified data: Phase I – 25 projects, Phase II – 18 projects, Phase III – 12 projects, number of new products launched this year 4. Detailed information for those projects in Phase III and those launched during the year, e.g. name of product, description, projected market launch dates by territory.
- No changes have been made to the source of data or calculation methods used.

IG Example 10: Cost per unit produced

The directors in a utility company may measure costs per unit produced as a KPI in order to monitor progress towards becoming a low cost producer. Recommended disclosure should incorporate the following information:

- Definition and calculation: Exploration and production finding and development unit costs, being costs per £ per boe (E&P F&D costs (£/boe)). Boe means barrel of oil equivalent, which is a standard method of equating oil, gas and natural gas liquids by converting gas and natural gas liquids to oil based on their relative energy contents.
- Purpose: One of the key drivers to strong economic returns is to reduce E&P F&D costs.
- Source of underlying data: Internal company data.
- Quantified target: To be in the top quartile of low cost producers in Europe as compared to benchmarking studies produced by Evaluate Energy for 2004.
- Quantified data: E&P F&D unit costs (£ per boe) graph showing comparatives for three years e.g. 2003 – 3.22, 2004 – 3.20, 2005 – 3.08.
- No changes have been made to the source of data or calculation methods used.

Resources, principal risks and uncertainties and relationships

IG15 The Reporting Statement recommends that the OFR should set out the resources, principal risks and uncertainties and relationships that may significantly affect the company's short and long-term value. A number of the examples highlighted in the Reporting Statement could be considered either resources, risks or a relationship, or all three. Key resources of an entity may also be key stakeholders and accordingly lead to risks and uncertainties.

IG16 The KPIs used by directors will be those used to monitor the effective management of their resources, risks and relationships, as these will be the areas that may significantly affect the company's short and long-term value.

Persons with whom the entity has relations

IG17 The decisions of those with whom the entity has relations – regulators, customers, suppliers, employees, community and society at large – can affect a company's prospective performance and accordingly its value. For example, in regulated sectors, the risk of non-compliance with regulatory requirements could lead to the loss of a licence to operate. Accordingly the effective management of these relationships could significantly impact on the success of the entity's strategies and affect the long-term value of the entity.

IG18 The directors should consider whether such relationships could have a significant impact. The directors could do this by seeking the answers to a number of key questions, such as:

a. How do our customers view the service we provide?
b. How do our employees' feel about the entity?
c. How do our suppliers view the entity?
d. How do our regulators view the entity?

IG19 For example, in considering the first question above, IG Example 11 provides an illustration of how an entity could measure the customers' relationship with the entity, by measuring "customer churn" rates as a KPI. Ultimately, the selection of appropriate customer measures will depend on the nature of the business and the strategies adopted by the board.

Areas of importance relating to employees, the community and society at large, including environmental matters, are addressed in paragraphs IG25-IG33. For other stakeholders with which the entity has relations, such as customers, suppliers, regulators, contractors and pensioners, some areas of interest might be: **IG20**

- Profile of the stakeholder and nature of the relationship (length of relationship, is it subject to contract, if so when does the contract expire).
- Level of dependency.
- Satisfaction with relationship – feedback results, levels of complaints, fines etc.

IG Example 11: "Customer churn"

In the telecoms industry, future prospects are greatly affected by the number of customers they can retain. Directors may monitor "customer churn" rates by the types of products offered as a KPI. Recommended disclosure should incorporate the following information:

- Definition and calculation: Churn rates by geographical market. Churn measured as the percentage of customers who do not renew their contract with the company at the end of the contract, over the total number of customers under that contract type.
- Purpose: Reducing churn rates means there is less pressure to increase customer acquisitions in order to improve revenues. Lower churn rates lead to direct savings in the form of savings in marketing, sales, installation and disconnection costs.
- Source of underlying data: Company data from UK, Germany and France.
- Quantified target: To reduce customer churn by 5% per annum in each territory.
- Quantified data: Churn rate, 2003 – UK 15%, Germany 18%, France 22%, 2002 – UK 14%, Germany 21%, France 25%, 2001 – UK 15%, Germany 24%, France 26%.
- No changes have been made to the source of data or calculation methods used.

Environmental matters

Environmental matters, particularly environmental risks and uncertainties, impact to some extent on all businesses, as they can affect investment decisions, consumer behaviour and Government policy. Poor management of energy, natural resources or waste can affect current performance; failure to plan for a future in which environmental factors are likely to be increasingly significant may risk the long-term future of the business. Proper attention to the environmental impacts of supply chains and products and to regulatory compliance of the company's own operations are both important for a business' public reputation and for its licence to operate. **IG21**

Environmental matters cover a very wide range of areas. The matters that will be of concern to a particular entity will vary depending on both the industry in which it operates and the strategies it has adopted. However, some consensus as to the generic environmental concerns facing all companies has been reached*, which might serve as a useful reference point for directors: **IG22**

**UN Conference on Trade and Development (2000) Integrating Environmental and Financial Performance at the Enterprise Level*

- Water use;
- Energy use;
- Waste;
- Climate change, including global warming contribution or emissions management;
- Ozone depleting substances.

IG23 Entities in industries that have a significant environmental footprint may set objectives and adopt strategies to specifically address key environmental risks, as illustrated in IG Examples 12 to 14. For others, whilst the management of environmental risks will impact the company's reputation, monitoring of performance in this area will not be considered a KPI. However, as set out in paragraph 19 of the Reporting Statement, the directors should support the information provided in the OFR with other evidence, for example consumption rates of scarce resources (energy and/or water) if this significantly impacts the entity's reputation, by providing the information recommended in paragraphs 41 and 42 of the Reporting Statement.

IG Example 12: Environmental spillage

A company involved in the transportation of hazardous materials may monitor "significant spills" as a KPI due to the potential impact of a spill on the reputation of the company. Recommended disclosure should incorporate the following information:

- Definition and calculation: Significant spills, being spills exceeding 100,000 litres.
- Purpose: To assess the effectiveness of the management of hazardous waste.
- Source of underlying data: All data from 100% controlled companies, representing 85% of the total group on a revenue basis.
- Quantified target: Reduce significant spills to below 10 per annum within 3 years.
- Quantified data: In 2005 there were 25 significant spills, in 2004 there were 30 spills, all due to leaking tanks.
- No changes have been made to the source of data or calculation methods used.

IG Example 13: CO_2 emissions

A company involved in energy production may monitor CO_2 equivalent emissions due to both potential fines and the impact of growing emissions on the reputation of the company. Recommended disclosure should incorporate the following information:

- Definition and calculation: CO_2 emissions, being on-site greenhouse gas emissions measured in million of tonnes of CO_2 equivalents (CO_2-e)
- Purpose: To assess the effectiveness of the management of the company's impact on greenhouse gas emissions.
- Source of underlying data: Data from 100% controlled companies within Europe and Africa, representing 95% of the company on a revenue basis.
- Quantified target: A 5% annual reduction in CO_2 equivalents
- Quantified data: 2005 CO_2-e 5.7, 2004 6.0, 2003 6.2
- No changes have been made to the source of data or calculation methods used.

IG Example 14: Waste

A retail group that promotes its 'green credentials' might monitor waste due to packaging, as this may impact on the reputation of the company. Recommended disclosure should incorporate the following information:

- Definition and calculation: Amount of waste (measured in kg) arising from packaging on each £1,000 of products we sell.
- Purpose: As the retail businesses in the group handle large amounts of packaging for transporting and presenting the goods sold, the group has established processes to minimise packaging waste.
- Source of underlying data: Data from all retail businesses in the group, representing 80% of the company on a revenue basis.
- Quantified target: To reduce the trend of increasing the amount of packaging to at least, or below, the levels in 2000, being 11.1kg packaging waste per £1,000 of sales.
- Quantified data: 2005 13.4, 2004 14.0, 2003 13.8, 2002 12.9, 2001, 12.1
- No changes have been made to the source of data or calculation methods used.

Employees

Employees may be a particularly key resource – and accordingly a key risk – for many entities. The strengths of a company's workforce and the ways it is managed can play a major role in both current and future company performance. Entities will need to be able to recruit and retain the staff they need to achieve their business strategies. Accordingly, the risks and uncertainties associated with the management of recruitment and retention of staff with the particular skills required for the entity's strategies could have a significant impact on the entity's future development and performance. For example, poor employment relationships can carry the risk of costly litigation, low workforce morale and ultimately affect company reputation. In addition, directors should consider their employment policies and practices and to assess which aspects are relevant to an understanding of the entity. For example, the degree to which the human resources of the entity represent a significant competitive advantage or are critical to a key product, service or process. **IG24**

The employee matters that will be of concern to directors will vary from entity to entity, depending on the industry in which the entity operates and the strategies it has adopted. **IG25**

In order to assess employee performance and development, the following areas, along with related performance measures, may be helpful: **IG26**

- Employee health and safety (which could also be considered a "social matter" see paragraph IG30) – details of RIDDOR (Reporting of injuries, diseases and dangerous occurrences regulations 1995), lost days to injury, levels of occupational related diseases in the workforce, compliance levels with working hours directives;
- Recruitment and retention – employee turnover, retention rates, remuneration policies, number of applicants per post, offer/acceptance statistics, levels of skills shortages;
- Training and development – hours spent on training, number of courses taken, leadership/career development;
- Morale/motivation – employee feedback results, absence rates, levels of employee engagement;

- Workforce performance and profile – employee productivity, revenue/profit per employee, diversity (see also IG30), number of professionally qualified employees.

IG27 IG Examples 15 and 16 provide some illustrations of where entities might set objectives relative to employees and monitor their progress as KPIs. Alternatively, the board may monitor employee measures to assess how effectively the entity is managing its employees' resources, development and performance to ensure that adequate resources are available to the entity, even though these performance measures are not considered KPIs. In such circumstances, it would be appropriate for the OFR to include these performance measures as other evidence, as set out in paragraphs 41 and 42 of the Reporting Statement.

IG Example 15: Employee morale

A professional services company may measure "employee satisfaction" in order to monitor employee morale, as decreasing levels of morale indicate higher levels of leavers in the future. Recommended disclosure should incorporate the following information:

- Definition and calculation: Employee satisfaction on a scale of 1 to 5 where 1 is low and 5 is high.
- Purpose: A professional services company needs to ensure it retains its best and brightest employees in order to properly service clients.
- Source of underlying data: Annual employee surveys in the UK, France and Germany, representing 85% of the total client facing employees.
- Quantified target: For 2006 to achieve a rating of 4.5, with the populations surveyed to cover at least 95% of client facing employees.
- Quantified data: Employee satisfaction graph showing comparatives e.g. 2004 – 4.1 rating, 2005 – 4.4 rating.
- Comparability: The 2004 survey results were based on surveys in the UK and France, representing 65% of total client facing employees.

IG Example 16: Employee health and safety

In an industry such as mining, where the "licence to operate" is based on effectively managing a myriad of issues, including health and safety, the directors may monitor "lost time injury frequency rate" as a KPI. Recommended disclosure should incorporate the following:

- Definition and calculation: Lost time injury frequency rate (LTIFR) – the number of lost-time injuries per million hours worked.
- Purpose: As the industry involves large equipment and working with hazardous materials, safety is a core value and a major priority.
- Source of underlying data: Injury data returns from 100% owned facilities only.
- Quantified target: To reduce LTIFR by 10% per annum.
- Quantified data: LTIFR table showing comparatives e.g. 2004 – 10 injuries/million hours worked, 2005 – 8.4 injuries/million hours worked.
- No changes have been made to the source of data or calculation methods used.

Social and community matters

The management of an entity's social and community matters can affect its reputation and licence to operate in a similar way to the management of environmental matters. Social concerns with regard to product safety, e.g. genetically modified foods, product responsibility, e.g. underage drinking or smoking, and the ethical management of the supply chain are all examples of issues that can significantly impact on the reputation of an entity. Furthermore, disregard for local community concerns can result in successful opposition to development applications. **IG28**

As with the other areas noted under particular matters, the areas that will be of concern to a particular entity will vary depending on both the industry in which it operates and the strategies it has adopted. **IG29**

Currently, there is no commonly held definition of social and community matters*, nor is there a common understanding of the generic issues. It is also the case that specific matters within the broad social and community category can change as new issues arise. However, areas that directors might want to consider include: **IG30**

- Public health issues, such as obesity, perceived safety issues related to high use of mobile phones, smoking;
- Employee health and safety (can also be considered an area under employees, see IG26);
- Social risks existing in the supply chain, for example the use of child labour and payments of "fair wages";
- Diversity in either the employee (see IG26) or customer base;
- Impact on the local community, for example noise, pollution, transport congestion (these areas could also link to environmental matters);
- Indigenous and human right issues relating to communities local to overseas operations.

Entities where reputation is a key concern might set objectives and adopt strategies that specifically address key social or community concerns, as illustrated in IG Examples 17 and 18. Alternatively, the monitoring of social and community matters may not be considered a KPI, however, directors will still monitor their performance in these areas. In such situations, it would be appropriate for the OFR to include these performance measures, as set out in paragraphs 41 and 42. **IG31**

**As noted in the International Organisation for Standardization (ISO) document 'Working Report on Social Responsibility' (2004), page 67.*

IG Example 17: Monitoring of social risks in the supply chain

A company that sources its branded products from overseas could face additional risks relating to stakeholder, in particular customer, concerns around local labour practices. In this situation, a company might have put in place a system to validate and monitor supply chain performance, specifically related to adherence to stated policies. The directors may monitor the extent of the programme and compliance rates as KPIs. Recommended disclosure should incorporate the following:

- Definition and calculation: Number of factories subject to ratings by independent accredited monitors, number of factories in each rating category, where one star signifies numerous severe non-compliance issues and four stars reflects those factories with no non-compliance issues.
- Purpose: Whilst the company has outsourced its supply chain, it wants to reassure customers that it has not outsourced its moral responsibility for the way its products are made. The objective is for all parts of the business – including suppliers – to share a common set of values and live up to them.
- Source of underlying data: Results of assessments made by accredited monitors in the current year.
- Quantified target: To increase the number of suppliers monitored by 20% per annum and reduce non-compliance to below 3%.
- Quantified data: Geographical split (for current year and prior year) of results for overseas suppliers, by Asia, Americas and Europe. Total factories in each of the four rating categories.
- No changes have been made to the source of data or calculation methods used.

IG Example 18: Noise infringements

An airport operator might want to measure the number of noise infringements as a KPI in order to monitor the success of its management of this "licence to operate" and reputational risk issue. Recommended disclosure should incorporate the following information:

- Definition and calculation: Number of noise infringements being the number of aircraft exceeding Department of Transport take-off noise limits.
- Purpose: Our ability to expand any airport is dependent on continuing support from local communities. If we fail to ensure aircraft using our airports comply with local noise limits, we are putting at risk future developments which are necessary given the growth in the airline industry in the country.
- Source of underlying data: Internal company data.
- Quantified target: Reduce noise infringements by 5% per annum.
- Quantified data: Annual noise infringements table showing comparatives, e.g. 2005 – 55, 2004 – 57, 2003 – 60, 2002 – 64, 2001 – 63.
- No changes have been made to the source of data or calculation methods used.

Receipts from, and returns to, shareholders

IG32 Paragraph 59 of the Reporting Statement recommends that the OFR should include information relating to receipts from, and returns to, shareholders. This would include details of, and the rationale behind, any of the following:

1. Receipts from shareholders resulting from capital raising activities;
2. Distribution via dividends or special dividends;
3. Return of capital by means of share repurchases and share reconstructions.

Other resources

Paragraph 50 of the Reporting Statement recommends that the OFR should include a description of the resources available to the entity and how they are managed. In addition to employee and customers already featured in IG Examples 11 to 13, other resources could include areas such as corporate reputation and brand strength; the condition of infrastructure; research and development; intellectual capital; licenses, patents, copyright and trademarks; market position and reserves of natural resources, as illustrated in IG Example 19. **IG33**

IG Example 19: Reserves

In an extractive industry, future revenues are greatly affected by the reserves controlled by the company. Accordingly, proven and probable reserves may be monitored by the directors as a KPI. Recommended disclosure should incorporate the following:

- Definition and calculation: Reserves are defined as those quantities of petroleum which are anticipated to be commercially recoverable from known accumulations from a given date forward. Reserves are reported net of the gas required for processing and transportation to the customer. The reporting process is in line with reserves definitions and resource classification systems published by the Society of Petroleum Engineers (SPE) and the World Petroleum Congress (WPC).
- Purpose: The most critical driver of growth of any oil and gas company is reserve replacement.
- Source of underlying data: Internal company data reviewed by an independent expert (who should be named, along with professional qualifications).
- Target: To replace current year's sales volume through reserve growth in the year.
- Quantified data:
  Proven at end of 2004 = 316, less production 57, add revisions 27, add exploration additions 41, Proven at end of 2005 = 327.
  Proven and probable at end of 2004 = 724, less production 57, add revisions -4, add exploration additions 69, Proven and probable at end of 2005 = 732.
- No changes have been made to the source of data or calculations methods used.

Other business risks

As set out in paragraph 52 of the Reporting Statement, the OFR should include a description of the principal risks and uncertainties facing the entity, together with a commentary on the directors' approach to them. In addition to risks related to environmental, social and community matters addressed in IG Examples 12 to 14, and 17 and 18, other risks might arise due to the external environment, dependencies on others, and the management of resources, both non-financial and financial, as illustrated in IG Examples 20 and 21. **IG34**

IG Example 20: Market risk

A bank might measure market risks arising from uncertainty about changes in market prices and rates, such as interest rates, equity prices, exchange rates, commodity prices) by using "value-at-risk" approaches as a KPI. Recommended disclosure should incorporate the following information:

- Definition and calculation: Value-at-risk (VaR) uses a Monte Carlo simulation process. Volatilities and correlations of market parameters are observed over the most recent twelve-month period and used on an unweighted basis. The VaR estimates are made at a 99% confidence level for a one-day time horizon.
- Purpose: Tracking the daily VaR allows the bank to derive a quantitative measure of market risk in order to monitor the risk profile it has taken on related to all market risk areas.
- Source of underlying data: VaR of trading units in the UK and of the units responsible for management of interest rate and foreign exchange risks of non-trading units.
- Target: The goal is not to exceed the limit set by the VaR calculation on any day of trading during any year.
- Quantified data: VaR histogram, showing the number of days VaR was at certain levels.
- No changes have been made to the source of data or calculation methods used.

IG Example 21: Business Continuity Management

A company providing computer services may monitor its compliance with business continuity plans. Recommended disclosure should incorporate the following information:

- Definition and calculation: Number of business units in each rating category, where an 'Pass' rating signifies full compliance with stated business continuity plans, whilst 'Fail' rating signifies numerous non-compliance issues.
- Purpose: As the provider of computer services, the company wishes to provide assurance of their ability to withstand events that would interrupt the provisions of such services.
- Source of underlying data: Data from all business units within the company.
- Quantified target: To achieve full compliance with stated business continuity plans, ie nil 'fail' ratings.
- Quantified data: 2005 98% Pass, 2% Fail, 2004 95% Pass, 5% Fail, 2003 93% Pass, 7% Fail.
- No changes have been made to the source of data or calculation methods used.

Financial position

IG35 The Reporting Statement recommends that the OFR should set out an analysis of the position of the entity both in the financial year and the future, including a description of the capital structure, treasury policies and objectives, and liquidity of the entity. Whilst a number of the measures used to monitor the position of the company may be traditional financial measures, directors often supplement these with other measures common to their industry to monitor their progress towards stated objectives. Such disclosures may include sensitivity analysis in respect of financial instrument disclosures.

IG Example 22: "Economic capital"

The directors of a financial institution may measure economic capital, in addition to regulatory capital, as a risk management tool and to monitor risk positions in individual business units. Recommended disclosure should incorporate the following information:

- Definition and calculation: Economic capital is the amount of capital that a transaction or business unit requires in order to support the economic risks it creates. A 99.95% confidence interval and a one-year time horizon are used to calculate economic capital. The economic capital calculation is subdivided into five distinct risk types: credit risk, market risk, transfer risk, business risk and operational risk.
- Purpose: The directors measure economic capital in order to monitor the efficient use of group's capital base.
- Source of underlying data: Internal company data.
- Quantified data: Economic capital for each business unit, reconciling to total economic capital for 2004 and 2005.
- No changes have been made to the source of data or calculation methods used.

IG Example 23: Cash conversion rate

To supplement the cash flow information provided in the financial statements, directors may measure operating profit cash conversion rates as a KPI. Recommended disclosure should incorporate the following information:

- Definition and calculation: Cash conversion rate being cash flow from operations as a percentage of operating profit.
- Purpose: One of the key drivers to strong economic returns is the ability to convert operating profits into cash.
- Source of underlying data: Internal company data.
- Quantified target: A minimum target of 85% cash conversion for any year.
- Quantified data: Cash conversion 2001 – 74%, 2002 – 101%, 2003 – 92%, 2004 – 85%, 2005 – 92%.
- No changes have been made to the source of data or calculation methods used.

Reporting Statement: Retirement Benefits – Disclosures

Contents

INTRODUCTION

SUMMARY

REPORTING STATEMENT 'RETIREMENT BENEFITS – DISCLOSURES'
Objective
Scope
Principles

ILLUSTRATIVE EXAMPLES OF DISCLOSURES

APPENDIX A: THE DEVELOPMENT OF THE REPORTING STATEMENT

Reporting Statement: Retirement Benefits – Disclosures

Introduction

This document sets out a Reporting Statement 'Retirement Benefits – Disclosures'. The Reporting Statement builds on Financial Reporting Standard (FRS) 17 'Retirement Benefits' (as amended in December 2006) and sets out additional disclosures that complement the disclosure requirements of FRS 17. It is a best practice guide and is not mandatory. **1**

The Accounting Standards Board (ASB) published FRS 17 in November 2000, although its full requirements only became mandatory for accounting periods beginning on or after 1 January 2005. Following its implementation, some commentators expressed a concern that the financial statements do not contain sufficient information in relation to defined benefit schemes to allow users of the financial statements to obtain a clear view of the risks and rewards arising from defined benefit schemes. **2**

In May 2006 the ASB issued for comment a Financial Reporting Exposure Draft (FRED) of a proposed amendment to FRS 17 and a draft Reporting Statement 'Retirement Benefits – Disclosures'. In finalising this document the ASB has taken into consideration the comments received in respect to the FRED. **3**

The ASB considered the amended FRS 17 addressed many, but not all, of the concerns of commentators and so decided to develop the Reporting Statement. As the amendment to FRS 17 replaced the disclosure requirements set out in the previous version of FRS 17 with those of International Accounting Standards (IAS) 19 'Employee Benefits' the ASB noted the Reporting Statement can be applied by entities adopting either UK or International Financial Reporting Standards (IFRS). **4**

The ASB was conscious that any additional disclosure requirements, beyond those set out in the amended FRS 17, should address the needs of users whilst not being cumbersome to preparers. The ASB is of the view a Reporting Statement which sets out principles for disclosure, rather than specific requirements, allows entities the flexibility to provide disclosures that are appropriate to their exposure to risks and rewards arising from defined benefit schemes. **5**

Summary

The Reporting Statement is designed as a formulation of best practice; it is intended to have persuasive rather than mandatory force. The Reporting Statement is written for any entity that operates or sponsors a defined benefit scheme. **a**

The Reporting Statement recommends that the directors provide disclosures in the notes to the financial statements that complement the disclosure requirements set out in FRS 17 'Retirement Benefits'. The extent of disclosure depends on the significance to the entity of its participation in defined benefit schemes and of its exposure to risk arising from those schemes. **b**

The Reporting Statement sets out six principles to be considered when providing disclosures for defined benefit schemes in the financial statements. The six areas addressed by the principles are: **c**

i the relationship between the entity and trustees (managers) of the defined benefit scheme;
ii the principal assumptions used to measure scheme liabilities;
iii the sensitivity of the principal assumptions used to measure the scheme liabilities;
iv how the liabilities arising from defined benefit schemes are measured;
v the future funding obligations in relation to the defined benefit scheme; and
vi the nature and extent of the risks arising from financial instruments held by the defined benefit scheme.

d The principles set out in the Reporting Statement aim to assist the users of financial statements in understanding the risks and rewards, and funding obligations, arising from defined benefit schemes.

Reporting Statement: Retirement Benefits – Disclosures

OBJECTIVE

The objective of this Reporting Statement is to recommend disclosures for defined benefit schemes such that: 1

a. the financial statements contain adequate disclosure of the cost of providing retirement benefits and the related gains, losses, assets and liabilities;
b. the users of financial statements can obtain a clear view of the risks and rewards arising from defined benefit schemes; and
c. the funding obligations of the entity in relation to liabilities of a defined benefit scheme are clearly identified.

SCOPE

This Reporting Statement may be applied to financial statements that are intended to give a true and fair view of a reporting entity's financial position and profit or loss (or income and expenditure) for a period the reporting entity operates or sponsors a defined benefit scheme. 2

DEFINITIONS

The following definitions shall apply in this Reporting Statement: 3

Accumulated Benefits Obligation – the liability calculated on the projected unit method as defined in FRS 17 'Retirement Benefits' where no allowance is made for projected earnings.

Cost of buying out scheme benefits – this cost is based on an actual insolvency amount where this is available, or estimated using a suitable method based on the guidance contained in Guidance Note 9 'Funding Defined Benefits – Presentation of Actuarial Advice' adopted by the Board of Actuarial Standards.

Duration of scheme liabilities – The duration of the scheme liabilities is a measure of how long on average it is until the benefits of the scheme fall due. This is the weighted average time to payment of the cash flows, weighted by the present value of the cash flows (ie on a discounted basis).

Duration is calculated by adding the results of multiplying the present value of each cash flow by the time it is received (paid) and then dividing by the total present value of all the cash flows.

PRINCIPLES

The financial statements should disclose information that enables the users of the financial statements to understand the relationship between the reporting entity and the trustees (managers) of defined benefit schemes. 4

FRS 17* 'Retirement Benefits', paragraph 76 (IAS 19 'Employee Benefits' paragraph 120), requires an employer to disclose information that enables users of 5

**As amended December 2006.*

financial statements to evaluate the nature of its defined benefits schemes and the financial effects of changes in those schemes during the period.

6 Many retirement benefit schemes are established as trusts. The basis of trust law is that one group (the trustees) hold assets for the benefit of another group (the beneficiaries). The relationship between the entity and the trust is normally governed by a trust deed and/or trust rules. In addition to trust law itself, the powers of trustees may be regulated by legislation. The powers conferred on trustees by regulation may enhance their authority compared to that of the trust deed and/or trust rules.

7 The relationship between the reporting entity and the trustees (managers) of the scheme will determine how an entity manages and arranges its affairs with regard to the defined benefit scheme, including: determination of the investment strategy for the assets held by the scheme, arrangements to determine principles for funding the scheme including how contribution levels to the scheme are agreed. The management and arrangement of affairs may be affected by the powers vested in the trustees (managers). The financial statements should explain significant and unusual powers that have been granted to the trustees (managers) of the scheme that could have a material financial effect on the reporting entity.

8 **The financial statements should include sufficient information about the principal assumptions the entity has used to measure scheme liabilities to allow users to understand the inherent uncertainties affecting the measurement of scheme liabilities. These assumptions should include, where this is not otherwise required by FRS 17 (or IAS 19), mortality rates.**

9 FRS 17 paragraph 77(m) (IAS 19 paragraph 120A(n)) requires the entity to disclose the principal actuarial assumptions used as at the balance sheet date. This Reporting Statement recommends, where otherwise not required, that the assumptions disclosed include mortality rates.

10 Information provided in the financial statements should communicate in a clear and effective manner the number of years post retirement it is anticipated pensions will be paid to members of the defined benefit scheme. Where the number of years assumed differs depending on geographical, demographical or other significant reasons, the different mortality rates should be separately disclosed.

11 Where it is anticipated a change in mortality rates could have a material effect on the measurement of the scheme liabilities a sensitivity analysis, as recommended by paragraph 12 of this Reporting Statement, should be provided.

12 **The financial statements should disclose a sensitivity analysis for the principal assumptions used to measure the scheme liabilities, showing how the measurement of scheme liabilities would have been affected by changes in the relevant assumption that were reasonably possible at the balance sheet date.**

For the purposes of this disclosure, all other assumptions should be held constant.

13 The inherent uncertainties affecting the measurement of scheme liabilities require the liabilities to be measured on an actuarial basis. This involves estimating the future cash flows arising under the scheme liabilities based on a number of actuarial assumptions. The measurement of scheme liabilities can be materially affected by changes in assumptions. The financial statements should disclose how changes in the assumptions could affect the measurement of scheme liabilities.

Where an entity chooses not to provide a sensitivity analysis, it may decide to provide alternative disclosures that provide greater information about the nature of scheme liabilities. Such information may include an analysis of liabilities between pensioners, deferred pensioners and employed members. 14

The financial statements should disclose information that enables users to understand the method of measurement used to measure scheme liabilities arising from defined benefit schemes. 15

FRS 17 requires defined benefit scheme liabilities to be measured on an actuarial basis using the projected unit method. The scheme liabilities should be discounted at a rate that reflects the time value of money and the characteristics of the liability (assumed to be the current rate of return of a high quality corporate bond). There are, however, alternative approaches to the measurement of defined benefit scheme liabilities*. 16

One such alternative approach is the cost of buying out benefits. In certain jurisdictions this amount may be disclosed to trustees (managers) and/or members of defined benefit schemes. Where the cost of buying out benefits is made available to trustees (managers) and/or members of defined benefit schemes it is recommended that the financial statements also disclose the cost of buying out benefits. 17

Another alternative approach for measuring defined benefit scheme liabilities is the accumulated benefits obligation (ABO). The ABO is similar to measuring defined benefit scheme liabilities using the projected unit method but does not take into consideration future salary increases. An entity may consider it useful to disclose the ABO when explaining how scheme liabilities are measured. 18

The financial statements should disclose information that enables the users of financial statements to understand the funding obligations (estimated where applicable) that the entity has in relation to defined benefit schemes. 19

FRS 17 paragraph 77(p) (IAS 19 paragraph 120A(q)) requires the employer's best estimate, as soon as it can reasonably be determined, of contributions expected to be paid to the scheme during the accounting period beginning after the balance sheet date. Scheme liabilities are, however, often of a long term nature and contributions expected to be paid in the next accounting period may not provide sufficient information to allow the users of the financial statements to understand how the scheme liabilities affect the economic resources available to the entity, including its cash flow. 20

The financial statements should disclose rates or amounts of contributions which have been agreed with the trustees (managers) of the scheme and are payable to the scheme by or on behalf of the reporting entity. 21

The funding requirements for defined benefit schemes are often regulated by legislation. An entity may be required or may choose to agree principles for funding scheme liabilities with the trustees (managers) of the scheme. The financial statements should disclose the funding principles the entity has agreed or operates with regard to defined benefit schemes. 22

**The measurement of defined benefit scheme liabilities is discussed in paragraphs 11 to 22 of The Development of the FRS to FRS 17 'Retirement Benefits'.*

23 Where a defined benefit scheme is in deficit* and the entity has entered into an agreement with the trustees (managers) of the scheme to make additional contributions to reduce or recover the deficit, in addition to normal levels of funding, the financial statements should disclose separately the additional contributions. The financial statements should also disclose separately the number of years over which it is anticipated the additional contributions will be paid to the defined benefit scheme in order to recover or reduce the deficit.

24 In order to evaluate the economic resources available to the entity, users of financial statements are particularly interested in the period of time over which the liabilities of the defined benefit scheme mature. A measure of this is the duration of scheme liabilities, which should be disclosed in the financial statements.

25 The duration of the scheme's liabilities may not alone provide users with information as to how the cash flows of defined benefit schemes fall due. In addition to the duration of liabilities, the financial statements should disclose information that allows users to understand the projected cash flows of defined benefit schemes. This information might usefully be presented in graphical form.

26 **The financial statements should disclose information that enables users of financial statements to evaluate the nature and extent of the risks and rewards arising from the financial instruments held by defined benefit schemes at the balance sheet date.**

27 For each type of risk arising from financial instruments held by defined benefit schemes, an entity may disclose:

a. the exposures to risk and how they arise;
b. the objectives, policies and processes undertaken by the defined benefits scheme or the entity for managing the risk and the methods used to measure the risk; and
c. any changes in (a) or (b) from the previous period.

28 An entity may disclose a sensitivity analysis, such as value-at-risk, for types of risks to which the defined benefit scheme is exposed. Where an entity discloses such sensitivity analysis it should also disclose the method and assumptions used in preparing this analysis and any changes from the previous period in the methods and assumptions used.

29 FRS 17 paragraph 77(i) (IAS 19 paragraph 120A(j)) requires an entity to disclose for each major category of scheme assets the percentage or amount that each major category constitutes of the fair value of the total scheme assets. It is recommended that this disclosure includes the expected rate of return assumed for each major category of scheme assets for the period presented.

30 The assumption made for the expected return on assets does not affect the valuation of the scheme assets because they are measured at fair value. It does, however, determine the amount to be recognised in the profit and loss account.

* *A deficit/surplus in a defined benefit scheme is the shortfall/excess of the value of the assets in the scheme below/over the present value of the scheme liabilities.*

Illustrative examples of disclosures

The following illustrations of possible disclosure examples for defined benefit schemes are provided for general guidance only and do not form part of the Reporting Statement. The disclosures provided should supplement those disclosures provided in accordance with FRS 17 and IAS 19.

Illustration 1 – Explanation of the relationship between the reporting entity and the trustees (managers) of the defined benefit scheme
(Paragraphs 4 to 7)

The pension scheme assets are held in a separate Trustee-administered fund to meet long-term pension liabilities to past and present employees. The trustees of the fund are required to act in the best interest of the fund's beneficiaries. The appointment of trustees to the fund is determined by the scheme's trust documentation. The Group has a policy that one-third of all trustees should be nominated by members of the fund, including at least one member by current pensioners.

*In addition to its statutory duties the board of trustees have been granted the power to 'call' for additional contributions in the event of certain circumstances. The circumstances in which the trustees can exercise this power include a disposal that accounts for more than 15% of the net assets, as reported in the consolidated Balance Sheet or when the funding position of the scheme falls below 65% of the scheme liabilities.

**This disclosure is also provided in accordance with FRS 12 'Provisions, Contingent Liabilities and Contingent Assets' and IAS 37 'Provisions, Contingent Liabilities and Contingent Assets'.*

Illustration 2 - Disclosure of principal assumptions
(Paragraphs 8 to 11)

Principal actuarial assumptions at the balance sheet date:

	UK		USA	
	2006	*2005*	*2006*	*2005*
Discount rate at 31 December	5%	5.7%	5.25%	6.25%
Expected return on plan assets at 31 December	5.4%	7.0%	6%	7.5%
Future salary increases	5%	4%	4.5%	3.8%
Future pension increases	3%	2%	2.9%	3.0%
Proportion of employees opting for early retirement	30%	30%	25%	25%

Investigations have been carried out within the past three years into the mortality experience of the Group's major schemes. These investigations concluded that the current mortality assumptions include sufficient allowance for future improvements in mortality rates. The assumed life expectations on retirement at age 65 are:

	UK		USA	
	2006	*2005*	*2006*	*2005*
Retiring today				
Males	20.1	20.1	19.5	19.5
Females	22.9	22.9	21.8	21.8
Retiring in 20 years				
Males	21.4	21.3	21.1	21.0
Females	24.1	24.0	23.0	23.0

Illustration 3 - Sensitivity analysis of the principal assumptions used to measure scheme liabilities
(Paragraphs 12 to 14)

The sensitivities regarding the principal assumptions used to measure the scheme liabilities are set out below:

Assumption	*Change in assumption*	*Impact on scheme liabilities*
Discount rate	Increase/decrease by 0.5%	Increase/decrease by 9.5%
Rate of inflation	Increase/decrease by 0.5%	Increase/decrease by 5.5%
Rate of salary growth	Increase/decrease by 0.5%	Increase/decrease by 3%
Rate of mortality	Increase by 1 year	Increase by 4.5%

Illustration 4 - How the liabilities arising from defined benefit schemes are measured (Paragraphs 15 to 18)

The Group provides retirement benefits to some of its former and approximately 60% of current employees through defined benefit schemes. The level of retirement benefit is principally based on salary earned in the last five years of employment.

The liabilities of the defined benefit scheme are measured by discounting the best estimate of future cash flows to be paid out by the scheme using the projected unit method. This amount is reflected in the deficit in the balance sheet*. The projected unit method is an accrued benefits valuation method in which the scheme liabilities make allowance for projected earnings. The accumulated benefit obligation is an actuarial measure of the present value of benefits for service already rendered but differs from the projected unit method in that it includes no assumption for future salary increases. At the balance sheet date the accumulated benefit obligation was £xm.

An alternative method of valuation to the projected unit method is a solvency basis, often estimated using the cost of buying out benefits at the balance sheet date with a suitable insurer. This amount represents the amount that would be required to settle the scheme liabilities at the balance sheet date rather than the Group continuing to fund the on-going liabilities of the scheme. The Group estimates the amount required to settle the scheme's liabilities at the balance sheet date is £xm.

**An entity that prepares financial statements in accordance with IAS 19 'Employee Benefits' should explain the method of recognition for actuarial gains and losses.*

Illustration 5 – Future funding obligations in relation to defined benefit schemes
(Paragraph 19 to 25)

The most recently completed triennial actuarial valuation of the Group's main retirement benefits fund was performed by an independent actuary for the trustees of the scheme and was carried out as at 31 December 2005. Following the valuation the Group's ordinary contributions rate increased, with effect from 1 January 2006, from 12.9% of pensionable salaries to 13.4% representing regular contributions. In addition the Group contributed a further £8m to the scheme as a contribution towards the current deficit. The Group has agreed with the trustees it will aim to eliminate the deficit over the next 8 years. The Group will monitor funding levels on an annual basis. The next triennial valuation is due to be completed as at 31 December 2008. The Group considers that the contribution rates agreed with trustees at the last valuation date are sufficient to eliminate the deficit over the agreed period and that regular contributions, which are based on service costs, will not increase significantly.

The Group has agreed the following funding objectives with trustees:

1. To return the on-going funding level of the scheme to 100% of the projected past service liabilities within a period of 8 years measured in accordance with FRS 17;
2. Once the funding level of the scheme is 100% of the projected past service liabilities to maintain funding at least at this level; and
3. To meet the liabilities of the scheme in the event that the scheme is wound-up.

The levels of contributions are based on the current service costs and the expected future cash flows of the defined benefit scheme. The Group estimates the present value of the duration of UK scheme liabilities on average fall due over Y years and foreign schemes over X years.

The benefits payable by the defined benefit scheme are expected to be paid as follows:

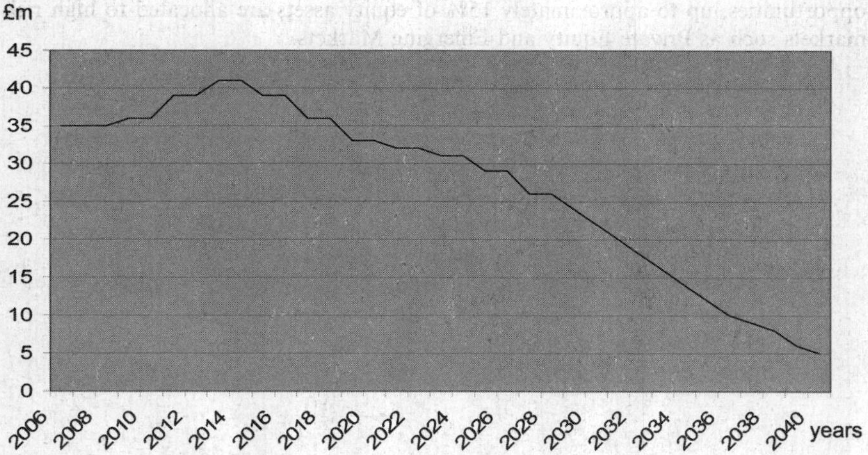

Illustration 6 – Nature and extent of the risks arising from financial instruments held by the defined benefit scheme
(Paragraphs 26 to 30)

At 31 December 2006 the scheme assets were invested in a diversified portfolio that consisted primarily of equity and debt securities. The fair value of the scheme assets as a percentage of total scheme assets and target allocations are set out below:

	Planned 2007	**2006**	**2005**
(as a percentage of total scheme assets)			
Equity securities	60	62	65
Debt	25	22	19
Property	10	9	12
Other	5	7	4

In conjunction with the trustees, the Group has recently conducted an asset-liability review for its major schemes. These studies are used to assist the trustees and the Group to determine the optimal long-term asset allocation with regard to the structure of liabilities within the scheme. The results of the study are used to assist the trustees in managing the volatility in the underlying investment performance and risk of a significant increase in the scheme deficit by providing information used to determine the pension schemes investment strategy.

The majority of the equities held by the scheme are in international blue chip entities. The aim is to hold a globally diversified portfolio of equities, with a target of 60% of equities being held in UK and Europe, 30% in US equities and the remainder in emerging markets. To maintain a wide range of diversification and to improve return opportunities, up to approximately 15% of equity assets are allocated to high risk markets such as Private Equity and Emerging Markets.

Appendix A
The development of the reporting statement

This development of the Reporting Statement accompanies, but is not part of the Reporting Statement.

INTRODUCTION

This development of the Reporting Statement summarises the Accounting Standards Board's (ASB) considerations in reaching its conclusions in the Reporting Statement for 'Retirement Benefits - Disclosures'. A1

BACKGROUND

The ASB published Financial Reporting Standard (FRS) 17 'Retirement Benefits' in November 2000, although its requirements have only become mandatory in full for accounting periods beginning on or after 1 January 2005. A2

Following the implementation of FRS 17 a number of comments concerning the accounting for pensions have arisen. In particular, there is a general concern that financial statements do not include sufficient information to allow users of the financial statements to obtain a clear view of the risks and rewards arising from defined benefit schemes. A3

In addition the UK legal and regulatory environment for retirement benefit schemes has changed significantly since FRS 17 was published, which could not have been anticipated when FRS 17 was developed. Regulatory changes arising from the Pensions Act 2004 include the following: A4

- establishment of The Pensions Regulator (TPR), a new regulator with significant new powers;
- the establishment of the Pension Protection Fund (PPF) to pay compensation to members of eligible defined benefits schemes where there is a qualifying insolvency event in relation to the employer; and
- a new statutory obligation on solvent companies to meet their pension obligations.

In October 2005 the ASB announced a research project into the financial reporting of pensions. The project is wide ranging and is reconsidering the fundamental principles of accounting for retirement benefits. The ASB aims to issue a Discussion Paper outlining its findings during 2007. A5

In December 2005 the Financial Reporting Council (FRC) published its Regulatory Strategy (version 2) and its Plan & Budget 2006/07. As part of its objective to promote high quality corporate reporting, the FRC undertook to review best practice for the disclosure of pension liabilities by UK companies in the context of the regulatory regime for UK pension schemes. A6

In view of comments received following the implementation of FRS 17 the ASB decided to undertake a review of disclosures for retirement benefit schemes as set out in FRS 17. The review was distinct from the wider research project and had a narrow focus on how disclosures for defined benefit schemes could be improved in the short-term giving particular consideration to the changes made in the UK regulatory regime. A7

APPROACH TO THE REVIEW

A8 To assist in its research project the ASB formed a Pensions Advisory Panel in the UK, with members who could provide a variety of expert perspectives on pensions accounting, including those of actuaries, regulators, auditors, the preparers and users of financial statements. In addition the research project is supported by a Working Group from the European Financial Reporting Advisory Group (EFRAG). The role of the Panel and the Working Group is to ensure that a number of knowledgeable points of view are fully considered. The ASB wished to progress the short-term review of disclosures as quickly as possibly and considered the Panel and the Working Group would provide a unique resource to assist the ASB in its short-term review. The Panel and Working Group agreed to assist the ASB in its short-term review. The ASB would like to thank the members of the Panel and Working Group for their contribution to the Reporting Statement.

A9 Following research on possible improvements to disclosures for defined benefit schemes a number of recommendations were made to the ASB for consideration. The ASB then considered how these recommendations could be implemented within the context of existing UK Financial Reporting Standards.

A10 In May 2006 the ASB issued a Financial Reporting Exposure Draft (FRED) that proposed to replace the disclosure requirements set out in FRS 17 with those of IAS 19 'Employee Benefits.' In addition the FRED set out a draft Reporting Statement which proposed disclosures that would complement those disclosures required by the amended FRS 17.

A11 Respondents to the FRED were generally in agreement with its proposals to replace the disclosure requirements of FRS 17 with those of IAS 19. In December 2006 the ASB published an amendment to FRS 17. Respondents, however, expressed mixed views in relation to the proposals set out in the draft Reporting Statement. These views have been considered in developing the Reporting Statement.

OBJECTIVE

A12 The objective of the Reporting Statement is to recommend disclosures that provide the users of financial statements with information, in addition to the disclosure required by the amended FRS 17 (or IAS 19), which enables them to evaluate the risks and rewards arising from defined benefit schemes including the funding requirements placed on the entity by those schemes.

SCOPE OF THE REPORTING STATEMENT

A13 In reaching its decision to issue a Reporting Statement the ASB gave due consideration to the needs of users of financial statements. The ASB was also conscious that any additional disclosure requirements, that went beyond those set out in the amended FRS 17, should not be cumbersome to preparers. Some respondents to the FRED, however, questioned the ASB's decision to propose a Reporting Statement. The ASB decided it should set out clearly its considerations in deciding to propose a Reporting Statement.

A14 When the ASB decided to propose a Reporting Statement it considered that the needs of the users of UK financial statements had been influenced by changes in the UK regulatory environment. However, it noted UK quoted entities generally apply International Financial Reporting Standards (IFRS) and therefore an amendment to the disclosure requirements in FRS 17 alone may not address the needs of users. The

ASB sought to find a solution which improved disclosures provided by UK entities whether the entity applied International or UK Financial Reporting Standards.

The ASB noted, in January 2006, it had published a non-mandatory Reporting Statement: 'Operating and Financial Review' which is a formulation of best practice and is intended to have persuasive rather than mandatory force. The ASB considered it could achieve its objective of improving disclosures for defined benefit schemes by publishing a Reporting Statement that addressed the disclosure requirements for defined benefit schemes. **A15**

In reaching its decision to publish a Reporting Statement the ASB gave due consideration to its strategy for convergence of UK Financial Reporting Standards with those of International Financial Reporting Standards. Although the ASB is still considering its convergence plan, it had previously stated*: **A16**

> *In general there is little case for UK accounting standards being more prescriptive than IFRS. However, the ASB will not, as a matter of policy, preclude the possibility of promulgating standards that go beyond IFRS where, in its judgement, the need for this is demonstrable.*

The ASB gave due consideration to this statement and decided that there was a clear demonstrable need to encourage improvements in the disclosure relating to defined benefit schemes.

During its redeliberation of the proposals in the draft Reporting Statement, the ASB reconsidered its decision to propose a Reporting Statement. The ASB affirmed its decision, noting that the amendment to FRS 17 alone would not address the needs of users and that the Reporting Statement was complementary to the amendment made to FRS 17. **A17**

Some respondents to the FRED expressed a concern that the role of the Reporting Statement was not clear. During its redeliberations the ASB noted that it had, in the past, issued not only the Reporting Statement – 'Operating and Financial Review' but it had also issued Statements on 'Interim Reports' and 'Preliminary Announcements'. These statements all specified that they were designed as a formulation and development of best practice and are intended to have persuasive rather than mandatory force. **A18**

The ASB considers that the role of the Reporting Statement is that of a best practice guide. The ASB also reaffirmed its early view that a Reporting Statement, which sets out principles for disclosure, rather than specific requirements, allows entities the flexibility to provide disclosures that are appropriate to their exposure to risks arising from defined benefit schemes. **A19**

PRINCIPLES

Relationship between the entity and trustees (managers) of the defined benefit scheme

The draft Reporting Statement proposed that the directors disclose information that enabled users of financial statements to understand the relationship between the entity (employer) and trustees (managers) of the defined benefit scheme. This **A20**

Draft Policy Statement (2005) – Accounting Standard Setting in a Changing Environment: the Role of the Accounting Standards Board.

information would allow users of financial statements to understand the extent to which an entity is able to influence arrangements with the scheme.

A21 In making this proposal the ASB was conscious of the importance of the independent role of trustees (managers) of many defined benefit schemes and how the extent of this independence might vary between individual schemes and between schemes in different legal jurisdictions. The ASB consider that the relationship between the trustees (managers) of defined benefit schemes and the reporting entity affects how an entity is able to manage its affairs with regard to the defined benefit scheme and, that users of financial statements would benefit from having a greater understanding of this relationship.

A22 A number of respondents were concerned that the proposals as set out in the draft Reporting Statement would lead to cumbersome disclosures that were complex and difficult to understand. These respondents considered that the level of complexity could lead to 'boilerplate' disclosures that provided very little information to the users of financial statements.

A23 Some respondents, however, accepted there was a need for greater disclosures regarding the relationship between the entity and trustees (managers) and considered the disclosures recommended in the draft Reporting Statement should focus on any 'out-of-the ordinary' powers of, or constraints on the trustees, or schemes for which the trustees' position differs significantly from that for other UK schemes.

A24 The ASB considered the alternative views of respondents. The ASB, however, retained its view that there was a need for financial statements to provide information that assisted a user to understand the relationship between the entity and the trustees (managers) of the scheme but agreed that the wording in the Reporting Statement should make clear that disclosure should address powers that were both significant and unusual in relation to the legal and regulatory framework to which the entity operated. It also noted that disclosure was only recommended where these powers could have a material financial affect on the reporting entity.

Principal assumptions used to measure scheme liabilities

A25 A particular concern highlighted by commentators in relation to the previous FRS 17 was the absence of the requirement to disclose mortality rates used to calculate scheme liabilities. In developing the FRED, issued in May 2006, the ASB noted that IAS 19 requires the principal actuarial assumptions of the scheme to be disclosed (and therefore requires disclosure of mortality rates where it is considered to be a principal assumption) whereas FRS 17 required only the principal financial assumptions to be disclosed. In the FRED the ASB decided, consistent with its policy of convergence, not to amend the text of IAS 19 (as adopted into FRS 17) to specify the disclosure of mortality rates but to recommend in the draft Reporting Statement that mortality rates be disclosed.

A26 Respondents to the FRED were generally in agreement with the proposal to disclose mortality rates. A number of respondents did, however, question the illustrative example set out in the draft Reporting Statement. Those that questioned the illustrative example noted that the example was not consistent with the recommendation in the draft Reporting Statement. The ASB thereby amended the illustrative example in the Reporting Statement.

The ASB, in amending the illustrative example in the Reporting Statement, also took into consideration the views of some respondents that too much emphasis was placed on the disclosure of mortality rates and that other assumptions may be significant. **A27**

In addition, some respondents asked for greater clarification as to how disclosures for mortality rates should be set out in the financial statements. In view of respondents' comments, the ASB considered whether it should provide more prescriptive guidance than that set out in the draft Reporting Statement. **A28**

In considering whether to provide more prescriptive guidance for the disclosure of mortality rates the ASB took into consideration the report issued by the Financial Reporting Review Panel which noted the inconsistency in disclosure of mortality rates gave rise to a lack of comparability between reporting entities. **A29**

The ASB was also mindful of the ongoing research project into pension accounting and considered it should not provide prescriptive guidance while the research work was ongoing. The ASB did, however, reiterate its earlier view that disclosure of the number of years post retirement (mortality rate) it is anticipated pensions will be paid to members of the scheme would provide more useful information to users of financial statements than details of a mortality standard table used, or details of a cohort factor, which may require a user to undertake further research to determine the actual number of years. **A30**

The ASB also noted that the 'Statement of Principles for Financial Reporting' notes that good presentation ensures that the essential messages of the financial statements are communicated clearly and effectively in a simple and straightforward manner as is possible. **A31**

The draft Reporting Statement also carried forward as a recommendation a requirement from the previous FRS 17 that where an entity has a closed scheme or a scheme in which the age profile of the active membership is rising significantly, the fact that under the projected unit method, the current service costs will increase as the members of the scheme approach retirement. The ASB took into consideration the views from respondents who considered the disclosure was misleading. In view of the comments received the ASB decided to remove the recommendation from the Reporting Statement. **A32**

Sensitivity analysis of the principal assumptions used to measure scheme liabilities

In developing the draft Reporting Statement the ASB had taken into consideration that the measurement of scheme liabilities is inherently uncertain and based on assumptions selected by the entity's managers (directors). The ASB also noted that neither the previous FRS 17 nor IAS 19 required a sensitivity analysis that disclosed the effect that changes in assumptions made to the measurement of scheme liabilities. The ASB decided to recommend in the draft Reporting Statement that the financial statements include a sensitivity analysis for the principal assumptions used to measure the scheme liabilities. **A33**

In forming this view the ASB gave due consideration to the views of some commentators that greater information should be provided about the defined benefit scheme to allow users to undertake their own sensitivity analysis, whilst others considered that the reporting entity should prepare the sensitivity analysis. The ASB considered these two views and concluded that a sensitivity analysis prepared by the reporting entity would provide more reliable information than an external user of the financial statements could prepare. **A34**

A35 Although respondents to this recommendation noted the benefit of the disclosure, some expressed a concern regarding the additional costs incurred in the preparation of the sensitivity analysis. They noted the additional costs might outweigh the benefits of disclosure.

A36 The ASB considered this concern but noted that the Reporting Statement is a best practice statement and is not mandatory. The ASB considered therefore the reporting entity should decide whether on cost/benefit or other grounds to include such an analysis. The ASB also considered that where an entity decided not to include a sensitivity analysis it could provide alternative disclosures that enable users to understand scheme liabilities.

How the liabilities arising from defined benefit schemes are measured

A37 The draft Reporting Statement recommends that the financial statements should disclose information that enable users to understand the nature of the liabilities arising from defined benefit schemes. In making this recommendation the ASB noted that FRS 17 requires scheme liabilities to be measured using the projected unit method. There are, however, alternative approaches to the measurement of defined benefit scheme liabilities*.

A38 In the draft Reporting Statement it was noted one alternative approach was the cost of buying out benefits with a suitable insurance entity at the balance sheet date.

A39 In setting out its proposals in the draft Reporting Statement the ASB considered a number of points of view on this disclosure. The ASB, noted that with the improved disclosures proposed in the draft Reporting Statement, users of financial statements may be able to estimate the cost of buying out scheme benefits with a suitable insurance entity at the Balance Sheet date. The ASB was concerned that this could give rise to a number of estimates being made that may be inaccurate. The ASB therefore decided to recommend disclosure of the cost of buying out scheme liabilities in the draft Reporting Statement but to specifically seek the views of constituents on whether this disclosure should be included in the final Reporting Statement.

A40 The majority of respondents to the draft Reporting Statement did not support the recommendation to disclose the cost of buying out scheme liabilities. The principal arguments put forward by these respondents were:

- users would misunderstand the disclosure, particularly regarding future funding requirements;
- this misunderstanding will lead to more scheme closures;
- there is limited actuarial guidance on how to calculate this amount – as a consequence the calculation is subjective;
- The Pension Regulator (TPR) had removed buy-out as a scheme trigger for funding regulations and therefore disclosure is inconsistent; and
- the insurance market is not sufficiently homogenous to assure reliable measurement.

These respondents supported the concerns the ASB had set out in The Development of the Draft Reporting Statement, namely:

**The measurement of defined benefit scheme liabilities is discussed in paragraphs 11 to 22 of The Development of the FRS to FRS 17 'Retirement Benefits'.*

- that the disclosure of a buy-out cost is not consistent with the going-concern concept;
- the buy-out cost may not be easily available for non-UK schemes; and
- the amount is merely an estimate and an active market does not exist for these obligations.

During its redeliberation of this proposal the ASB noted that in the UK under the Occupational Pension Schemes (Employer Debt) Regulations 2005 (SI 2005/678), the debt on the employer on the winding up of a pension scheme will be determined on a full buy-out basis. In addition the ASB noted: **A41**

(i) S224 of Pensions Act 2004 requires that the trustees or managers obtain valuations:

a. at intervals of not more than one year or, if they obtain actuarial reports for the intervening years, at intervals of not more than three years, and

b. in such circumstances and on such other occasions as may be prescribed.

(ii) summary funding statements disclose the buy-out amount.

The ASB considered the comment made by respondents that there was a lack of guidance on how to disclose the cost of buying out scheme liabilities. The ASB, however, noted that Guidance Note 9 'Funding Defined Benefits – Presentation of Actuarial Advice' as adopted by the Board of Actuarial Standards provided some guidance on how to calculate this amount. The Board therefore decided to specifically refer to the Guidance Note in the Reporting Statement. **A42**

The ASB took into consideration the views of respondents very carefully but could find no justification that information made available to members of defined benefit schemes and/or trustees (managers of schemes), should not be made available to members (investors) of the entity. However the ASB noted the concern of respondents and decided to amend the recommendation in the draft Reporting Statement to only recommend disclosure where the cost of buying out benefits is made available to trustees (managers) and/or members of defined benefit schemes. **A43**

In considering the comments from respondents regarding this disclosure the ASB noted that some commentators had highlighted that the illustrative example discussed the Accumulated Benefits Obligation (ABO) in addition to the amount that would be required to buy out benefits. Respondents had noted that it might be useful for users of financial statements to understand the effect on scheme liabilities arising from future salary growth assumptions but, that the Reporting Statement should define the terms and provide clarification that the term is a suitable alternative. The ASB agreed with respondents and amended the Reporting Statement accordingly. **A44**

Future funding obligations in relation to defined benefit schemes

The amended FRS 17 requires an entity to disclose details of any contributions agreed to be paid in the next accounting period to the defined benefit scheme. Scheme liabilities are, however, often of a long-term nature and contributions expected to be paid in the next accounting period may not provide sufficient information to allow the users of the financial statements to understand how the funding requirements for scheme liabilities impact the economic resources available to the entity, including its cash flow. In developing its proposals in the draft Reporting Statement the ASB, supported by the views of its Advisory Panel, considered that greater information regarding funding would allow users to evaluate how funding obligations affect an entity's economic resources. **A45**

A46 In recommending that greater information be provided regarding funding obligations the ASB considered the regulations introduced in the UK setting out a new funding regime for defined benefit schemes. The new funding regime proposes a partnership approach between employers and trustees (managers) of defined benefit schemes. The ASB formed the view that users of financial statements would gain from a greater understanding of agreements reached between the trustees (managers) of defined benefit schemes and the reporting entity regarding not only agreed contributions but also funding principles.

A47 The ASB gave consideration to the number of defined benefit schemes that are, at present, in deficit. Some entities have entered into agreements with the trustees (managers) of the defined benefit scheme to make additional ('special') contributions to the scheme in order to reduce the current level of deficit. These 'special' contributions are often separate from 'regular' contributions and are to be made over a specified period of years. The ASB considered that disclosure of both 'regular' and 'special' contributions would provide the users of financial statements with information about how an entity's cash flows are affected by 'regular' and 'special' contributions.

A48 Respondents to the draft Reporting Statement were generally in agreement with the need for greater information requiring funding obligations but were concerned that funding requirements are reviewed regularly between the entity and the trustees (managers) of retirement benefit schemes. They therefore considered that detailed funding projections may be misleading and would not provide useful information to users of financial statements. The Board took the views of respondents into consideration and decided that details of funding obligations should be of a narrative nature.

A49 In addition to understanding agreed contribution levels for defined benefit schemes, it was noted by some commentators that it is important also to understand how long on average the liabilities of a retirement benefit scheme mature. The Reporting Statement recommends that the financial statements should disclose the duration of the scheme liabilities.

A50 The Reporting Statement also recommends that information should be provided with regard to how the liabilities of the defined benefit scheme fall due. Some respondents questioned this recommendation, arguing that these are the cash flows of the scheme and are separate from those of the reporting entity. Consequentially, they had no direct impact on the cash flows of the entity and should not therefore be disclosed in the reporting entity's financial statements. The ASB, however, considered that the cash flow information provided useful information to users of financial statements as it allowed users to understand the profile of cash flows including peak cash flows. The ASB therefore decided to retain the disclosure but agreed a graphical presentation of the information may be of more use to users of financial statements.

Nature and extent of the risks arising from financial instruments held by the defined benefit scheme

A51 FRS 17 as amended requires scheme assets to be analysed only by class of asset. This classification does not enable users to evaluate the risks arising from financial assets or liabilities that might be held by the scheme. The Reporting Statement therefore recommends that the financial statements disclose information that enables users of financial statements to evaluate the nature and extent of the risks arising from the financial assets or liabilities held by the defined benefits scheme.

In making this recommendation the Board took into consideration the growing trend of 'Liability Driven Investment' which aims to reduce the risk by focusing on the significant risks and narrowing the range of possible outcomes, using financial instruments. A52

Statement: Half-yearly financial reports

(Issued July 2007)

Contents

	Paragraphs
INTRODUCTION	
SUMMARY	
STATEMENT 'HALF-YEARLY FINANCIAL REPORTS'	1–57
OBJECTIVE	1
SCOPE	2
HALF-YEARLY FINANCIAL REPORTS	
Role of the Half-yearly financial report	3–4
Timescale	5
Basis of presentation	6–10
Accounting policies	11–12
Changes in accounting policy and prior period adjustments	13–14
Annually determined income and expenditure	15–17
Seasonal revenues	18
Taxation	19-24
Foreign exchange	25
Valuation	26
Restoration of past losses	27
Materiality	28
Content of the Half-yearly financial report	29-33
Half-yearly management report	34–39
Profit and loss account	40
Acquisitions and discontinued operations	41–42
Segment information	43–44
Exceptional items	45–47
Earnings per share	48
Statement of total recognised gains and losses	49–50
Balance sheet	51
Cash flow statement	52–53
Corresponding amounts	54–55

Other disclosures 56–57

APPENDICES

A: THE LEGAL AND REGULATORY FRAMEWORK A1–A19

B: COMPLIANCE WITH INTERNATIONAL FINANCIAL REPORTING STANDARDS B1–B4

C: THE DEVELOPMENT OF THE STATEMENT 'HALF-YEARLY FINANCIAL REPORTS' C1–C14

Statement: Half-yearly financial reports

Introduction

1 This document sets out a statement 'Half-yearly financial reports', which is designed to provide guidance for any UK* entities that are required or voluntarily choose to prepare half-yearly financial reports, other than those required by the Disclosure and Transparency Rules (DTR)† of the Financial Services Authority (FSA) to apply International Accounting Standard (IAS) 34 'Interim Financial Reporting'. UK issuers not required to apply IAS 34 can satisfy the requirement in the DTR for the half-yearly financial reports by following the provisions of this statement.‡

2 As noted below, the DTR clarify that issuers can satisfy the requirement for half-yearly financial reports to give a true and fair view by a statement that they have been prepared in accordance with pronouncements by the Accounting Standards Board (ASB). The FSA has effectively mandated the use of this statement. The FSA rule is in all cases subject to the condition that the person making the 'true and fair' statement has reasonable grounds to be satisfied that the condensed§ set of financial statements prepared in accordance with the applicable set of accounting standards is not misleading.

3 This statement updates and replaces the ASB's September 1997 statement 'Interim Reports', which is now formally withdrawn.

Summary

a. This statement is designed to provide guidance for any UK and Irish entities that are required or voluntarily choose to prepare half-yearly financial reports, other than those required by the Disclosure and Transparency Rules (DTR) of the Financial Services Authority (FSA) and the Irish equivalent as laid out in legislation to apply International Accounting Standard (IAS) 34 'Interim Financial Reporting'.

b. It is intended to have persuasive rather than mandatory force. However, for UK issuers, subject to the DTR and, not required to apply IAS 34, the DTR make clear that the requirement for responsible persons to give an explicit statement that the condensed set of financial statements give a true and fair view can be satisfied by giving a statement that the condensed information has been prepared in accordance with pronouncements on interim reporting issued by the ASB. In effect this mandates such UK issuers, subject to the DTR, to apply this statement. The statement may also be applied by any other entities that purport to prepare half-yearly financial reports.

******The statement may also be applied by similar entities in the Republic of Ireland*

†*In the UK the Disclosure and Transparency Rules are now issued by the Financial Services Authority in its capacity as UK Regulatory Authority. In the Republic of Ireland, the half-yearly reporting requirements of the Transparency Directive are set out in the Transparency (Directive 2004/109/EC) Regulations 2007 and will replace section 6.9 ('Half-yearly reports') of the Irish Stock Exchange's Listing Rules.*

‡***Editor's note****: References to the Financial Services Authority in this Statement should now be read as references to the Financial Conduct Authority.*

§*The Transparency Directive replaces the term 'summarised' with the term 'condensed'.*

Irish issuers subject to the Transparency Directive are also effectively mandated to use this statement by virtue of section 8 (5)(d)(ii) of the Transparency (Directive 2004/109/EC) Regulations 2007 as outlined in paragraph A13 of Appendix A. c.

Statement: half-yearly financial reports

Objective

The objective of this statement is to outline the basis of presentation for half-yearly financial reports and define the content of half-yearly financial reports. The statement gives guidance on the content of half-yearly financial reports to assist shareholders to make a more informed assessment of the entity at a half-yearly stage. 1

Scope

This statement sets out guidance that may be applied by any UK entities that are required or voluntarily choose to prepare half-yearly financial reports, other than those required by the DTR to apply IAS 34. For UK issuers not required to apply IAS 34, the DTR make clear that the requirement for responsible persons to give an explicit statement that the condensed set of financial statements give a true and fair view can be satisfied by giving a statement that the condensed information has been prepared in accordance with pronouncements on interim reporting issued by the ASB. This statement sets out such a pronouncement. 2

Role of the half-yearly financial report

A condensed set of financial statements is a requirement of the Transparency Directive and DTR, mainly because the interval between annual reports is considered to be too long a period for users and specifically shareholders to be without financial information, particularly when developments are affecting trading conditions. 3

Half-yearly financial reports play an important role as a progress report in the continuing reporting process of the operating, financing and investing activities of a business. Like annual financial statements they fulfill a confirmatory and predictive function. Within the constraints of time and cost, half-yearly financial reports are designed to enable users to monitor the progress of a business from its financial position as stated in the last set of annual financial statements and to assess the impact of recent events on operating performance and financial position. Additionally, UK company law requires that a condensed set of financial statements provide a true and fair view. 4

Timescale

For information to be of value in updating users' knowledge of an entity it must be timely. The DTR require that entities make their half-yearly financial reports available within two months of the half-yearly period-end. 5

Basis of presentation

Half-yearly financial reports, like annual financial statements, are presented in respect of a distinct reporting period. A fair assessment of the progress of the 6 business can be made only if the half-yearly accounts are prepared on a consistent and comparable basis taking one reporting period with another.

7 Traditionally, two rather different methods have been used in the preparation of half-yearly reports: the 'integral method' and the 'discrete method'.

8 The integral method views the half-yearly period as a part of the larger annual reporting cycle. Its function is predominantly to predict and explain the financial information for the full financial year. Items are therefore recognised in half-yearly periods on the basis of estimating the total annual revenue and expenses and allocating accordingly.

9 Under the discrete method, the half-yearly period is treated as an accounting period distinct from the annual cycle. Incomplete transactions are treated according to the same principles as are applied at the year-end. This has the advantage that the elements of financial statements are defined in the same way as for the annual financial statements.

10 The Board continues to endorse an approach whereby items of income and expense are measured and recognised on a basis consistent with that used in the preparation of annual financial statements (the discrete method). Certain items of income and expenditure occur on an annual basis and these are considered in paragraphs 15-17 below.

Accounting policies

11 The DTR require that the accounting policies and presentation of figures in half-yearly financial reports are consistent with those in the annual financial statements. Accordingly, half-yearly financial reports should be prepared using the same measurement basis and adopting the same accounting principles and practices as are employed in the annual financial statements.

12 Half-yearly financial reports should include a statement that they are prepared on the basis of the accounting policies set out in the most recent set of annual financial statements. Half-yearly financial reports are often reviewed in conjunction with the previous year's financial statements and therefore their accounting policies need to be stated and explained only where they differ from those previously adopted.

Changes in accounting policy and prior period adjustments

13 When it is known at the time that half-yearly financial reports are prepared that an accounting policy change (or a presentation change) will be made in the annual accounts (including voluntary changes in accounting policy, not resulting from a new or revised accounting standard, UITF abstract or a change in companies legislation), the change should be implemented in the half-yearly financial reports rather than deferred to the year-end. This ensures that the half-yearly results are presented on the same basis as those for the full financial year. Where a known accounting policy change in the current year is not implemented in the half-yearly report an estimate of its effect should be disclosed; if that is not possible, an explanation of its affect should be included.

14 Following a change in accounting policy, the amounts for the current and prior periods should be stated on the basis of the new policies. The cumulative effect of the policy change on opening reserves (ie at the beginning of the financial year) should be disclosed at the foot of the statement of total recognised gains and losses of the

period. Similar disclosures should be made in respect of other prior period adjustments arising from the discovery of fundamental errors. A description should be given to help users understand the nature of each change or adjustment and the reasons for the change should be disclosed.

Annually determined income and expenditure

Certain items of income and expenditure are determined on a formal basis once a year when the full financial statements are prepared; examples include bonuses, profit-sharing arrangements, volume discounts, sales commissions and rent based on income or sales criteria. **15**

In each case it is necessary to determine whether an obligation to transfer economic benefits as a result of past transactions or events exists at the half-yearly period-end. Only if there is such an obligation (either contractual or constructive), should a provision be made at the period-end. An intention to transfer economic benefits is, by itself, not sufficient to recognise future costs and income in the half-yearly period. **16**

For example, a genuinely discretionary one-off bonus given at the end of the year would be recognised only in the second half-yearly financial report. On the other hand, a profit-related bonus paid at the year-end, although non contractual, would be recognised in the first half-yearly financial report, on the basis of profits earned in that half-year, if past practice indicated that there was a constructive obligation. Similarly, a contractual supplier's volume discount, based on an annual target for the year, would also be recognised in the first half-yearly report on the basis of a proportion of the expected annual discount. **17**

Seasonal revenues

A business is seasonal where there is a substantial and recurring variation between the levels of profit in the first half-yearly period compared to the second half-year. Fluctuating revenues of seasonal businesses are generally understood by the marketplace and it is appropriate to report them as they arise. **18**

Taxation

The half-yearly tax charge should be based on an estimate of the likely effective tax rate for the year, expressed as a percentage of the expected results for the year and then applied to the half-yearly profit or loss arising. This approach results in taxation, including permanent and timing tax differences, being recognised rateably over the year as a whole in common with other contractual, annually determined items of income and expenditure as noted in paragraphs 15 to 17. **19**

To the extent practicable and where more meaningful, a separate estimated effective annual tax rate should be determined for each material tax jurisdiction and applied individually to the half-yearly period pre-tax income of each jurisdiction. Similarly, if different income tax rates apply to different categories of income, to the extent practicable, a separate rate should be applied to each individual category of half-yearly period pre-tax income, where material. In many cases a weighted average of rates across jurisdictions or across categories of income may be a reasonable approximation of the effect of using more specific rates. **20**

Exceptional items are, by definition, material to the financial statements and can often distort the overall tax charge if the tax rate applying to the exceptional item differs significantly from the likely effective tax rate. Therefore, where material, the **21** tax effect of exceptional items should not be included in the likely effective annual tax rate but should be recognised in the same period(s) as the relevant exceptional item. In such circumstances, the estimated annual effective tax rate (excluding exceptional items) will be applied to the half-yearly profits or losses before exceptional items.

22 The half-yearly financial report should give a brief explanation of the basis of the effective tax rate.

23 The general approach of making an estimate of the effective tax rate for the year should be employed even where, for example, an entity's result in the first half-year is expected to be completely offset by its result in the second half-year. Even if the overall result is break-even, there will still be an effective tax rate (say 30 per cent). The full year's tax of nil is, conceptually, 30 per cent of no profit, rather than zero per cent. Thus that tax rate is applied to both profits and losses. However, a tax credit should be booked (and a deferred tax asset recognised) for half-yearly tax losses only if there is reasonable assurance that it will reverse in the foreseeable future (in accordance with Financial Reporting Standard (FRS) 19 'Deferred tax').

24 In determining the amount of tax losses to recognise in the half-yearly period, an estimate should be made of the utilisation expected over the whole tax year. The amount recognised in the half-yearly period should be proportional to the profit before tax of the half-yearly period and the estimated annual profit before tax, but limited to the amount recoverable for the year as a whole*

Foreign exchange

25 The profit and loss account of a foreign entity accounted for under the net investment or closing rate method should be translated for those applying SSAP20, either at the average rate for the half-yearly period, or at the closing rate at the end of that period, whichever is consistent with the company's accounting policy. For those entities applying FRS 23 the average rate should be used, in accordance with that FRS.

Valuation

26 Whether value changes of assets held at a valuation are recognised depends upon the nature of the assets and the difficulty of obtaining valuations. Revaluation would be necessary, for example, in respect of quoted stocks carried at market value, but not, as a matter of course, in respect of properties, where revaluations on the basis used in the previous annual financial statements would suffice, subject to the following:

(a) the most recent valuations available should be used;
(b) where valuations have been brought forward, without amendment from the previous annual accounts, a statement to that effect should be given; and
(c) where significant, the directors are encouraged to comment on price movements since the last valuation.

**For example, if there was a tax loss brought forward of £75,000; estimated first half-year taxable profits of £100,000; and an expected second half-year loss of £40,000; then tax losses of £60,000 would be absorbed in the first half of the year (being the maximum annual utilisation of tax losses brought forward, based on expected taxable profits to be set against second half-year tax losses of £40,000. This would result in a tax charge (at, say, an effective tax rate of 30%) of £12,000 in the first half-year and a tax credit of £12,000 in the second half-year, giving a nil overall tax charge for the year.*

Restoration of past losses

Additionally with regards to valuation, any impairment losses on acquired goodwill should be recognised if the acquired goodwill is deemed to have been impaired and the provision for those losses should not usually be reversed in a subsequent period, except in circumstances indicated in paragraph 44 of FRS 10. The same treatment should apply to provisions relating to investments in available-for-sale equity instruments and unquoted equity instruments that are not carried at fair value because their fair value cannot be reliably measured. **27**

Materiality

Consistently with the discrete approach, materiality should be assessed with reference to the results and financial position for the half-yearly period rather than in relation to expected results and financial position for the full year. **28**

Content of the half-yearly financial report

Half-yearly financial reports provide an update on the latest set of annual financial statements and, accordingly, should focus on new activities, events and circumstances. **29**

An informed assessment of financial position and performance does not focus solely on the profit (or loss) for the period, but requires comparison of information from the profit and loss account, statement of total recognised gains and losses, balance sheet and cash flow statement. Whilst not all information in the four primary statements is critical to such an analysis, it is useful to present the significant information within the context of the four statements, along with an interim management report that highlights and explains these elements in the context of events since the previous annual report and accounts. **30**

It is therefore recommended that a half-yearly financial report should include a half-yearly management report, condensed profit and loss account, statement of total recognised gains and losses, condensed balance sheet and condensed cash flow statement. **31**

Significant events and trends mentioned in the content of the half-yearly financial report should be supported by the underlying figures given either on the face of the primary statements or by way of note. Sufficient supplementary information should be given, where appropriate, to the nature of the company's business and as the directors see fit to permit an understanding of the significant items contained within the primary statements. **32**

The information should be presented in a concise manner, should be consistent and comparable with that previously reported (the annual report) and should facilitate comparison between like companies. **33**

Half-yearly management report

The DTR require half-yearly financial reports to include a half-yearly management report which must include at least an indication of important events that have occurred during the first six months of the financial year, their impact on the condensed set of financial statements and a description of the principal risks and uncertainties for the remaining six months of the year. Any additional material to be contained in the report, as outlined in the paragraphs below, should be considered in **34** the context of what is needed to meet the requirements of the DTR. The half-yearly management report is not intended to be as comprehensive as an operating and financial review (OFR), but should include any significant information enabling investors to make an informed assessment of the trend of the entity's activities and profit or loss. Half-yearly management reports should focus attention on areas of change since the last set of annual financial statements. A balanced narrative commentary that explains the reasons for significant movements in key performance indicators and indicates perceived trends within the business is an important feature of a half-yearly financial report, providing management with the opportunity to report on its stewardship of the business as a whole.

35 The half-yearly management report should disclose as major related parties' transactions, as a minimum:

(a) related parties' transactions that have taken place in the first half-year and have had a material effect on the financial position or the performance of the entity during the half-year;

(b) any changes in the related parties' transactions described in the last annual report that could have a material effect on the financial position or performance of the enterprise in the first half-year of the current financial year.

36 Attention should be drawn to events and changes within the period that are likely to have a significant effect on the succeeding period despite having had relatively little impact in the current period.

37 The commentary should describe the nature of any seasonal activity and, together with other disclosures, provide adequate information for the performance of the business and its financial position at the end of the period to be understood in the context of the annual cycle. The principles by which seasonal results are reflected in the half-yearly report should be stated, particularly where there are any expected changes in the effects of seasonality.

38 As well as referring to trading performance, the commentary should draw attention to the condensed balance sheet and cash flow statement. It should also highlight and explain significant changes since the last annual financial statements, particularly regarding movements in working capital, liquidity and net debt that are likely to be of value to users in their assessment of the business.

39 The commentary should explain any other matter that management thinks would help users to understand the report. This would include for example, where relevant:

- acquisitions and disposals of major fixed assets or investments during the period covered by the report;
- changes in estimates for liabilities, commitments and off balance sheet financial instruments since the previous year-end;
- material changes in capital structure or financing; and
- events arising after the end of the period covered by the half-year financial report.

Profit and loss account

40 A half-yearly financial report should include a condensed profit and loss account that should show each of the headings and subtotals included in the most recent annual financial statements. Additional line items should be included if, as a result of their omission, the half-yearly financial statements would give a misleading view of the profit or loss of the entity.

Acquisitions and discontinued operations

Turnover and operating profit of acquisitions and discontinued operations (as defined in FRS 3 'Reporting Financial Performance') should be disclosed separately on the face of the profit and loss account in the period in accordance with FRS 3. For this purpose, operations are regarded as discontinued when the sale or termination is completed either in the half-yearly period or before the earlier of two months after the end of the half-yearly period and the date on which the half-yearly financial report is approved. **41**

It may be appropriate to disclose separately, either by way of note or in the half-yearly management report, the results of operations which, although not discontinued, are in the process of discontinuing or are expected to be classified as discontinued in the current year's financial statements. Where it is not practicable to determine the post-acquisition results of an operation to the end of the half-yearly period, an indication should be given of the contribution of the acquisition to the turnover and operating profit of the continuing operations. **42**

Segment information

To improve the quality of trend analysis and comparability, an entity is required to present segmental information in its annual financial statements and, should adopt the same basis and business classifications in the half-yearly financial report. An entity should disclose: **43**

- segment turnover, distinguishing inter-segment sales if significant; and
- segment profit or loss as disclosed in the annual financial statements – normally profit or loss before accounting for interest, taxation and minority interests.

The basis of presentation of segment information in the half-yearly financial report should, where possible, be consistent with that to be used at the current year-end in order to assist users in making predictions that will be readily comparable with the annual results. Any significant differences in presentation from that used in the latest annual financial statements should be disclosed and explained. Where it is not possible to produce segment information consistent with that used at the current year-end, a statement to that effect should be made and an explanation given. **44**

Exceptional items

By definition, exceptional items are unusual in nature and significant in amount. They rarely extend over more than one year and it is not generally appropriate to allocate their effect to different parts of the reporting period. They should be recognised and disclosed in the profit and loss account of the half-yearly period in which they occur. Certain exceptional items should be shown separately after operating profit and before interest as required by paragraph 20 of FRS 3 'Reporting Financial Performance'. **45**

Other exceptional items should be charged or credited in arriving at the profit or loss on ordinary activities by inclusion under the statutory headings to which they relate. In addition, they should be disclosed and described by way of a note. **46**

The tax effects of exceptional items disclosed on the face of the profit and loss account, in accordance with paragraph 45 above, should be separately disclosed in the profit and loss account or a related note. **47**

Earnings per share

48 Listed companies should disclose earnings per share and, diluted earnings per share, expressed as pence per share. Basic earnings per share and, diluted earnings per share should be derived from the results for the half-yearly period and calculated and disclosed in the same manner as at the year-end. Entities that choose to present in their annual financial statements additional amounts per share based on another level of earnings, should also present them in their half-yearly financial report, calculated and disclosed in accordance with FRS 22 'Earnings per share'.

Statement of total recognised gains and losses

49 A statement of total recognised gains and losses should be included where gains or losses, other than profit or loss for the half-yearly period, as reported in the profit and loss account, are recognised in the period.

50 A reconciliation of movements in shareholders' funds is required only where movements other than those in the statement of total recognised gains and losses need to be explained.

Balance sheet

51 A condensed balance sheet (together with corresponding amounts) should show each of the headings and subtotals used in the balance sheet included in the most recent annual financial statements. Additional line items must be included if, as a result of their omission, the half-yearly financial statements would give a misleading view of the assets, liabilities and financial position of the entity.

Cash flow statement

52 Information on the amounts and sources of cash flows provides an additional perspective to the performance of an entity through the half-yearly period. Total amounts for the categories of cash flows specified by FRS 1 (Revised 1996) 'Cash Flow Statements' should be presented as follows:

- Net cash inflow/outflow from operating activities
- Returns on investments and servicing of finance
- Taxation
- Capital expenditure and financial investment
- Acquisitions and disposals
- Equity dividends paid
- Management of liquid resources
- Financing
- Increase/decrease in cash
- Dividends from joint ventures and associates.

53 A reconciliation of operating profit to operating cash flow should be given in sufficient detail for users to appreciate its chief components. A reconciliation should also be given of the movement of cash in the period to the movement in net debt, as required by FRS 1 'Cash flow statements' (Revised 1996), including the effect of movements on short-term and long-term borrowings, cash and other components of net debt, unless disclosed elsewhere.

Corresponding amounts

Corresponding amounts for the condensed profit and loss account, the statement of total recognised gains and losses and condensed cash flow statement should be presented for the corresponding half-yearly period and the previous full financial year. This provides a meaningful view of performance to date, particularly where the business is seasonal. Users may then compare amounts on a year-on-year basis, or use them in the evaluation of trends and estimations of annual results. **54**

Balance sheet information is included in half-yearly financial reports to highlight changes in key indicators of financial performance in the context of the entity's operating environment since the entity's last accounting year-end. The critical corresponding amounts are, therefore, those from the last annual financial statements, which may be accompanied by those from the previous corresponding half-yearly period to highlight the effect of seasonality. **55**

Other disclosures

Subject to the limited exceptions noted in this statement, disclosures demanded by Financial Reporting Standards and Statements of Standard Accounting Practice are not generally required in the presentation of half-yearly reports. **56**

There are, however, certain disclosures specific to half-yearly reports that are helpful to users in assessing the relevance and reliability with which the reports might be used. They are: **57**

- the period covered by the report;
- the date on which it is approved by the board of directors; and
- the extent to which the information it contains has been audited or reviewed.

Appendix A
The legal and regulatory framework

TRANSPARENCY DIRECTIVE

A1 The Transparency Directive (TD) (2004/109/EC) was published in the Official Journal in December 2004. The TD is designed to enhance transparency on EU capital markets by requiring regulated market issuers to produce periodic financial reports and shareholders in such companies to disclose major holdings. The Directive is a minimum harmonisation Directive which allows the home Member State of regulated market issuers to impose more stringent requirements than those set out in the Directive whilst restricting the host Member State to the minimum TD requirements. The Transparency Directive has to be implemented by all Member States no later than 20 January 2007.

A2 The TD introduces (in Article 5) more comprehensive requirements for half-yearly financial reports for regulated markets issuers, comprising a condensed set of financial statements prepared in accordance with the applicable accounting standards, a half-yearly management report and an appropriate statement of assurance from persons responsible in the issuer.

A3 Where an issuer is required to produce consolidated accounts, the condensed set of financial statements must be prepared in line with Regulation No 1606/2002 (on the application of International Accounting Standards). Where the issuer is not required to prepare consolidated accounts, the condensed financial statements must at least include a condensed balance sheet, and a condensed profit and loss account, prepared in line with the same principles applied to the annual financial accounts. In practice this requires publicly quoted entities using International Financial Reporting Standards (IFRS) as endorsed by the European Commission for their annual accounts (this is the great majority of UK public quoted entities), to produce half-yearly reports in accordance with IAS 34 'Interim Financial Reporting'. Those entities that continue to apply UK Financial Reporting Standards will be required to produce half-yearly reports in accordance with this statement.

A4 Article 5 of the Directive contains a requirement for each person making a responsibility statement to state that to the best of his or her knowledge the condensed set of financial statements 'give a true and fair view'.

A5 Article 5(6) notes that the Commission will adopt implementing measures (so-called 'Level 2' measures, see below) in order to take account of technical developments on financial markets and to ensure the uniform application of Article 5. This includes a commitment on the Commission to specify the minimum content of the condensed balance sheet and profit and loss account and explanatory notes on these accounts, where they are not prepared in accordance with IAS 34.

A6 Article 6 of the Directive requires issuers whose shares are admitted to trading on a regulated market to publish interim management statements for the first and third quarters of the year. The statement has to provide (a) an explanation of material events and transactions that have taken place during the relevant period and their impact on the financial position; and (b) a general description of the financial position and performance of the issuers.

LEVEL 2 MEASURES

Level 2 measures have been issued by the Commission in Directive 2007/14/EC. Article 3.2 of the implementing measures require that the condensed balance sheet and the condensed profit and loss account shall show each of the headings and subtotals included in the most recent annual financial statements of the issuer. Additional line items shall be included if, as a result of their omission, the half-yearly financial statements would give a misleading view of the assets, liabilities, financial position and profit or loss of the issuer. **A7**

In addition, the following comparative information shall be included: **A8**

(a) balance sheet at the end of the first half-year of the current financial year and comparative balance sheet as at the end of the immediate preceding financial year; and
(b) profit and loss account cumulatively for the first half-year of the current financial year, from two years after the date of entry into force of the Transparency Directive, comparative information for the comparable period for the preceding financial year.

The explanatory notes shall include the following: **A9**

(a) sufficient information to ensure the comparability of the condensed half-yearly financial statements with the annual financial statements; and
(b) sufficient information and explanations to ensure a user's proper understanding of any material changes in amounts and of any developments in the half-year period concerned, which are reflected in the balance sheet and the profit and loss account.

According to the Transparency Directive 2004/109/EC, a half-yearly management report should disclose as major related parties' transactions, as a minimum, the following: **A10**

(a) related parties' transactions that have taken place in the first six months of the current financial year and that have materially affected the financial position or the performance of the enterprise during the period; and
(b) any changes in the related parties' transactions described in the last annual report that could have a material effect on the financial position or performance of the enterprise in the first six months of the current financial year.

Where the issuer of shares is not required to prepare consolidated accounts, it shall disclose, as a minimum, the related parties' transactions referred to in the 4th Company Law Directive 78/660/EEC. **A11**

UK IMPLEMENTATION

The Financial Services Authority (FSA) is responsible for the implementation in the UK of the TD. The FSA has implemented the TD in full and has made no amendments to the provisions on half-yearly reports. FSA confirmation of the finalisation of the rules was made in April 2007 and include provisions in respect of half-yearly financial reporting. **A12**

REPUBLIC OF IRELAND IMPLEMENTATION

In the Republic of Ireland the Investment Funds Companies and Miscellaneous Provisions Act 2006 provides for, inter alia, the implementation of certain aspects of the TD. The half-yearly reporting requirements are set out in the Transparency **A13**

(Directive 2004/109/EC) Regulations 2007 ("The Regulations") and will replace section 6.9 ("Half-yearly reports") of the Irish Stock Exchange's Listing Rules. Section 6(3) of the Regulations state that the half-yearly financial report shall include:

(a) a condensed set of financial statements
(b) an interim management report, and
(c) responsibility statements.

Section 8(5)(c)(i) outlines the contents required to be contained in the responsibility statement. In order to satisfy these requirements, section 8(5)(d) states that a person making a responsibility statement shall include:

" ... a statement that the condensed set of financial statements have been prepared in accordance with:

(i) the international accounting standard applicable to the interim financial reporting adopted pursuant to the procedure provided for under Article 6 of Regulation (EC) No.1606/2002 of the European Parliament and of the Council of 19 July 2002; or
(ii) for Irish issuers not using IFRS, pronouncements on half-yearly reports issued by the Accounting Standards Board; or
(iii) for all other issuers not using IFRS, a national accounting standard relating to interim reporting, provided always that a person making such a statement has reasonable grounds to be satisfied that the condensed set of financial statements prepared in accordance with such a standard is not misleading."

REPUBLIC OF IRELAND LISTING RULES

A14 On 1 July 2005, the Irish Stock Exchange (ISE) ceased to use the UKLA Listing Rules as its base rule book and the ISE Listing Rules came into force. For issuers of equity securities, the ISE continues to maintain parity of listing standards with the FSA. Prior to implementation of the Transparency Directive in Ireland, listed companies produced half-yearly reports in accordance with the Listing Rules and in accordance with IAS 34 'Interim Financial Reporting'.

UK DISCLOSURE AND TRANSPARENCY RULES

A15 The Disclosure and Transparency Rules (DTR) are the rules which have been developed by the FSA for the UK implementation of the TD*. The rule which applies to half-yearly reporting is DTR 4.2.

A16 This rule requires that the half-yearly financial report must include:

(1) a condensed set of financial statements;
(2) a half-yearly management report; and
(3) a responsibility statement.

A17 If an issuer is required to prepare consolidated accounts, the condensed set of financial statements must be prepared in accordance with IAS 34 'Interim Financial Reporting'. Where issuers are not required to prepare consolidated accounts, the condensed set of financial statements must contain, as a minimum, the following:

(a) a condensed balance sheet;

****There is no DTR equivalent in the ROI as the requirements of the Transparency Directive are set out in legislation***

(b) a condensed profit and loss account; and
(c) explanatory notes on those accounts.

The DTR 'copy out' the requirements of the Level 2 measures, summarised in paragraphs A7 to A9 above. They also replicate the Listing Rules provision outlined in paragraph A13 above. **A18**

The half-yearly management report must include at least: **A19**

(1) an indication of important events that have occurred during the first half year of the financial year, and their impact on the condensed set of financial statements; and
(2) a description of the principal risks and uncertainties for the remaining half year of the financial year.

Appendix B
Compliance with international financial reporting standards

B1 Although the ASB's statement is drafted in the context of half-yearly financial reporting, whereas IAS 34 'Interim Financial Reporting' covers aspects relating to quarterly reporting in more detail, the key elements of the two pronouncements are consistent in all material respects.

B2 Like the ASB's statement, IAS 34 'Interim Financial Reporting' states that the same accounting recognition and measurement principles should be applied in the half-yearly report as are applied in the annual financial statements. IAS 34 also states that measurements for half-yearly reporting purposes should be made on a year-to-date basis, which ensures that an entity's frequency of reporting (annual, half-yearly, or quarterly) does not affect the measurement of its annual results. However, as a consequence, amounts reported in prior half-yearly periods of the current financial year may need to be remeasured at a later date, as new information becomes available. IAS 34 requires significant remeasurements of previously reported half-yearly data to be disclosed in the half-yearly report, or, if there is no separate half-yearly report for the final half-yearly period of the year, in a note to the annual financial statements.

B3 On 20 July 2006 the IFRIC issued an Interpretation IFRIC 10 'Interim Financial Reporting and Impairment'. The Interpretation addresses the apparent conflict between the requirements of IAS 34 Interim Financial Reporting and those on the recognition and reversal in financial statements of impairment losses on goodwill (set out in IAS 36 Impairment of Assets) and investments in equity instruments and in financial assets carried at cost (set out in IAS 39 Financial Instruments: Recognition and Measurement).

B4 IFRIC 10 states that any such impairment losses recognised in an interim financial statement must not be reversed in subsequent interim or annual financial statements. This statement (paragraph 27) includes a provision that such losses should not usually be reversed in a subsequent period, except in the circumstances indicated in paragraph 44 of FRS 10.

Appendix C
Development of the statement 'half-yearly financial reports'

The development of the statement accompanies, but is not part of the statement.

INTRODUCTION

This development to the statement summaries the Accounting Standards Board's (ASB) considerations in reaching its conclusions in updating this statement 'Half-yearly financial reports'. **C1**

This statement is designed to provide guidance for any UK* entities that are required or voluntarily choose to prepare half-yearly financial reports, other than those required by the Disclosure and Transparency Rules (DTR)† of the Financial Services Authority (FSA) to apply International Accounting Standard (IAS) 34 'Interim Financial Reporting'. UK issuers not required to apply IAS 34 can satisfy the requirement in the DTR for the half-yearly financial statements by following the provisions of this statement. **C2**

BACKGROUND

The ASB first issued a statement relating to interim reports in September 1997. The statement was developed following a recommendation by the Committee on the Financial Aspects of Corporate Governance (the Cadbury Committee) in 1992 that the ASB, in conjunction with the London Stock Exchange, should clarify the accounting principles to be adopted by companies when preparing interim reports. It also recommended that balance sheet information should be included as part of the interim report and suggested that the inclusion of cash flow information should also be considered‡. **C3**

In response to the Cadbury initiative, the Financial Reporting Committee of the Institute of Chartered Accountants in England and Wales undertook a project focusing on the accounting aspects of Interim reports. The project focused on the measurement basis and extent of disclosure required in Interim reports. The Committee published a Consultative Paper 'Interim Financial Reporting' in 1993 which led to a formal proposal being presented to the ASB. The 1997 Statement was developed from those proposals and presented its recommendations as best practice in the reporting of interim information. **C4**

At the time of the Statement, the then International Accounting Standards Committee (IASC) was developing a new International Accounting Standard (IAS) on **C5**

**The statement may also be applied by similar entities in the Republic of Ireland.*

†In the UK the Disclosure and Transparency Rules are now issued by the Financial Services Authority in its capacity as UK Regulatory Authority. In the Republic of Ireland, the half-yearly reporting requirements of the Transparency Directive will be set out in secondary legislation and, upon enactment of the legislation, will replace section 6.9 ('Half-yearly reports') of the Irish Stock Exchange's Listing Rules.

‡Furthermore in the Republic of Ireland, the Report of the Financial Reporting Commission published in 1992 (the Ryan Report) also advocating half-yearly financial reporting and recommended that interim reports should include details of items of an exceptional nature such as capital profits or losses, depreciation and interest charges, and segment data, together with a balance sheet in sufficient detail for the financial position to be assessed.

recognising, measuring and reporting interim financial information. IASC's initial proposals, published in September 1996 and its subsequent Exposure Draft E57, issued in August 1997, were considered by the ASB during the preparation of its 1997 Statement.

C6 In February 2007 the ASB issued an Exposure Draft (ED) of the Statement. Respondents to the ED were generally in agreement with the proposal to update the Statement and agreed that the changes made should be restricted to those made necessary by the developments outlined in paragraph C7 below. The respondents thought that the revised Statement would provide guidance for UK and Republic of Ireland (ROI) issuers not using IFRS who are required to produce half-yearly reports and, in the main considered that the guidance contained in this Statement is sufficient for its purpose. The ASB therefore decided to proceed with publication of this Statement.

REASONS FOR UPDATING THE STATEMENT

C7 The main development that led the ASB to conclude that it was necessary to update the statement occurred during 2006, when the FSA consulted on the UK implementation of the EU Transparency Directive (TD) (Directive 2004/109/EC). The TD was designed to enhance transparency on EU capital markets by requiring regulated market issuers to produce periodic financial reports and shareholders in such companies to disclose major holdings. The requirements of the TD had to be implemented by all Member States no later than 20 January 2007. In October 2006, the FSA published a policy statement 'PS 06/11 Implementation of the Transparency Directive – Feedback on CP06/4' setting out near-final rules of the implementation of the TD. FSA confirmation of the finalisation of the rules was made in April 2007 and include provisions in respect of half-yearly financial reporting.

C8 UK and ROI entities listed on a regulated market are required to prepare consolidated financial statements in accordance with European Union (EU) endorsed International Financial Reporting Standards (IFRS). UK and ROI listed entities preparing consolidated financial statements are required to prepare half-yearly reports in accordance with IAS 34. The FSA's Disclosure and Transparency Rules (DTR) also require half-yearly financial reports to be prepared in accordance with IAS 34. Other UK issuers have to apply UK Generally Accepted Accounting Practice (GAAP) to produce their half-yearly financial statements. Some respondents to CP06/4 highlighted the current uncertainty as to what constitutes 'UK GAAP' for entities not preparing half-yearly financial statements under IAS 34. The DTR refer to pronouncements on half-yearly financial reporting issued by the ASB. The decision to rename the Statement to 'Half-yearly Financial Reports' is in line with the wording of the DTR.

C9 DTR 4.2.10 clarifies that the requirement to provide a true and fair view in half-yearly financial statements is satisfied by a statement that the condensed set of financial statements have been prepared in accordance with IAS 34, or (for UK issuers not using IFRS) pronouncements on half-yearly reporting issued by the ASB, or (for all other issuers not using IFRS) a national accounting standard relating to half-yearly reporting. The ASB therefore decided to update its Statement, given that, for UK issuers not using IFRS, the FSA decision effectively mandated its use. The FSA rule is in all cases subject to the condition that the person making the 'true and fair' statement has reasonable grounds to be satisfied that the condensed set of financial statements prepared in accordance with the applicable set of accounting standards is not misleading. The FSA has noted in PS06/11 that it is aware that this may dilute the true and fair concept but retention of this wording is unavoidable given that it is in the text of the TD.

In ROI section 8(5)(d)(ii) of the Transparency (Directive 2004/109/EC) Regulations 2007 ("The Regulations") states that for Irish issuers not using IFRS, pronouncements on half-yearly reports issued by the ASB should be used in order to satisfy the true and fair view requirements of section 8(5)(c)(i) of the Regulations. Section 8(5)(e) further states that "This application of true and fair view has no effect on the interpretation of the true and fair view for annual accounts in accordance with the Fourth Council Directive 78/660/EEC of 25 July 1978 and the Seventh Council Directive 83/349/EEC of 13 June 1983, and Regulation (EC) No.1606/2002 of the European Parliament and of the Council of 19 July 2002." **C10**

Article 6 of the Directive requires issuers whose shares are admitted to trading on a regulated market to publish interim management statements for the first and third quarters of the year. The statement has to provide (a) an explanation of material events and transactions that have taken place during the relevant period and their impact on the financial position; and (b) a general description of the financial position and performance of the issuers. The FSA has simply 'copied-out' the TD's provisions on half-yearly management statements in the DTR and has not provided any additional guidance. The FSA's proposal not to provide any additional guidance was supported by respondents to the FSA's consultation. This statement is not intended to give guidance on the preparation of interim management statements. **C11**

The ASB gave consideration to the above matters and decided to update its Statement on Interim Reports and rename it 'Half-Yearly Financial Reports' to reflect the requirements of the DTR. **C12**

SUMMARY OF CHANGES MADE TO THE STATEMENT

The changes made to the statement take account of changes which have been effected since the Statement on Interim Reports was issued in 1997, as outlined in paragraph C7 above. To this extent it was necessary to update the statement to ensure that: **C13**

(a) it is consistent with all major aspects of IAS 34;
(b) it is consistent with the DTR; and
(c) it does not give rise to conflicting guidance.

In preparing this statement, the ASB has sought to make the minimum number of changes necessary in light of the developments, as set out in paragraph C7, including changes in terminology. The ASB adopted this approach in order to have revised guidance prepared in time for the first round of half-yearly financial reports that have to be prepared to meet the requirements of the TD and the DTR. The changes have: **C14**

- renamed the Statement, 'Half-Yearly Financial Reports';
- introduced a Summary and Objective paragraph to replace the previous Introduction;
- updated the wording of the standard to use language appropriate to IAS 34 and the DTR; and
- added an Appendix to reflect the current legal and regulatory framework.

Preliminary announcements

(Issued July 1998)

This Statement is designed as a formulation and development of best practice; it is intended to have persuasive rather than mandatory force and is not an accounting standard. In the interests of good financial reporting its use is commended by the Financial Reporting Council, the Hundred Group of Finance Directors, the London Stock Exchange and the Irish Stock Exchange.

Contents

	Paragraphs
Foreword by the Financial Reporting Council	
Introduction	
Preliminary announcements	1–50
Role of the preliminary announcement	1–3
Distribution	4–8
Timescale	9–10
Reliability	11–15
Accounting policies and prior year adjustments	16-18
Content	19–26
Management commentary	27–32
Final interim period	33–35
Profit and loss account	36–41
Acquisitions and discontinued operations	37
Segmental information	38
Taxation	39
Exceptional items	40
Earnings per share	41
Statement of total recognised gains and losses	42–43
Balance sheet	44
Cash flow statement	45–46
Comparative figures	47
Other disclosures	48–50

Foreword by the Financial Reporting Council

The Financial Reporting Council (FRC) recognises that, for listed companies, preliminary announcements play a key part in the annual financial reporting cycle, being the first public communication of companies' full-year results and year-end financial position. Preliminary announcements are relied upon to provide timely, sufficient and accurate information to ensure an orderly and efficient market.

Preliminary announcements form one of the focal points for investor interest, primarily because they confirm or update market expectations. Because of this, many companies are choosing to include more information in their preliminary announcements than is strictly required under the London Stock Exchange's Listing Rules – so that they convey the essential thrust of the full financial statements and the operating and financial review. This policy ensures that price-sensitive information is properly disseminated to the market and can therefore be openly discussed at analysts' briefings, which for many companies are playing an increasingly significant role in the public explanation of their performance and financial position.

The FRC believes that the Accounting Standards Board's Statement provides valuable guidance for directors wishing to embrace best practice when preparing their preliminary announcements. The FRC therefore welcomes the Board's Statement and encourages directors of all listed companies, and other such organisations as prepare preliminary announcements, to adopt its recommendations.

Sydney Lipworth

Sir Sydney Lipworth QC
Chairman, Financial Reporting Council
July 1998

Introduction

In the UK preliminary announcements are a requirement of the Listing Rules of the London Stock Exchange, under which listed companies are required to notify the Exchange of their preliminary statement of annual results and dividends (generally known as the preliminary announcement) without delay after board approval.* The Exchange requires companies to include in their preliminary announcement at least the items required by it for a half-yearly report (ie interim report), as well as any significant information necessary for the purpose of assessing the results being announced.

Preliminary announcements are companies' primary vehicle for the first public communication of their full-year results and year-end financial position to the markets. As such they often contain more information than the minimum required by the Exchange. This Statement provides voluntary guidance, which is intended to supplement the mandatory requirements of the Exchange, in respect of preliminary announcements.

The objective of the Statement is to improve the timeliness, quality, relevance and consistency of preliminary announcements within the constraints of reliability. Compliance with the Statement would both promote best practice within the context of the present reporting environment and increase comparability between preliminary announcements and previously published accounts.

Interim reports and preliminary announcements have much in common. They both communicate new information about the company's financial performance and position to the market, fulfilling confirmatory and predictive functions, although at different stages in the annual reporting cycle. The contents of interim reports and preliminary announcements, therefore, are likely to be similar. Accordingly, this Statement builds on the Statement of best practice 'Interim Reports' recently issued by the Accounting Standards Board.

Discussions about the role of preliminary announcements naturally lead to questions about their interaction with other year-end financial reports (ie the full report and accounts and summary financial statements). Indeed, comments on the exposure draft of this Statement included suggestions for reforming the year-end reporting package.

These ideas and the wider issues connected with the year-end financial reporting structure as a whole are being explored further by the Board, with the help of its working party.† This is intended to be a relatively long-term project to allow time for debate and future consultations on the overall reporting regime and for changes in practice to become accepted. In this context, the Board notes and welcomes the Government's announcement in March 1998 of its review of company law.

A similar position exists in the Republic of Ireland, since the Irish Stock Exchange has the same Listing Rules as the London Stock Exchange. All references to the Listing Rules of the London Stock Exchange should be taken as also including those of the Irish Stock Exchange. (Editor's note:** In the UK, the Listing Rules are now issued by the Financial Conduct Authority in its capacity as UK Listing Authority.)*

*†**Editor's note:** A Discussion Paper was published in February 2000 and is reproduced in Part Nine of this volume.*

SCOPE

The Statement recommends principles for the preparation of preliminary announcements which are intended to apply to all entities that are required by the Exchange to issue preliminary statements of annual results.

Preliminary Announcements

ROLE OF THE PRELIMINARY ANNOUNCEMENT

As the first external communication by companies of their financial performance and position for the financial year, the preliminary announcement plays a key part in the reporting cycle. It enables the market to assess whether the company's annual results have met, exceeded or fallen short of expectations. 1

To be of value in updating the market's knowledge of a company, preliminary announcements must be issued on a timely basis. Timely publication also helps to minimise the possibility of insider dealing. 2

The information in the preliminary announcement must be reliable and sufficient to permit an immediate, informed assessment of the company's overall performance. 3

DISTRIBUTION

Preliminary announcements tend to be targeted at financial analysts and institutional shareholders, as the persons or organisations most likely to influence a company's share price. 4

Under the Listing Rules of the Exchange, listed companies must notify the Exchange of their preliminary announcements. In turn, the Exchange disseminates the information given to it by electronic means using its Regulatory News Service. 5

It is not mandatory for preliminary announcements to be sent to shareholders; in practice, often only financial analysts and institutional shareholders receive them. Other shareholders are less likely to be in a position to take advantage of the information on a timely basis. However, in principle, to be equitable, all shareholders should be entitled, on request, to have access to the preliminary announcement as soon as it becomes available, although it should be noted that information required by the Exchange must not be given to another party before it has been notified to the Exchange. 6

Receiving a preliminary announcement after the market has reacted to that information is of limited use. In practical terms, apart from press advertisements, information can be made available to a wider audience contemporaneously, and at the earliest possible moment that it becomes available, only through the use of electronic means (eg the Internet). Companies are therefore strongly encouraged to make further use of electronic means as a way of disseminating financial information, and in particular the preliminary announcement, to a wider audience. 7

Notwithstanding the emerging use of the Internet, companies are encouraged to provide some means to ensure that all shareholders can, if they wish, readily obtain a copy of the preliminary announcement as soon as possible after its issue. There are various different methods (as well as electronic means) for achieving this and 8 companies should consider and adopt methods that are appropriate to their shareholder base. Examples include:

- press advertisements containing the essential details of the preliminary announcement;
- pre-registration schemes (for example with reply cards that could be sent out with interim reports);
- publicising an address or telephone number by which shareholders can obtain copies of the announcement;
- notifying shareholders (eg with the last interim report of the period) of the exact date that the announcement is expected to be issued, so that they can take appropriate action to receive the preliminary announcement if they choose to do so.

Some of the above arrangements may be particularly useful for shareholders in companies whose results are not reported in detail in the press.

TIMESCALE

9 The benefits of providing the market with early notification of the annual results need to be balanced against the practical problems of collecting and processing information at an acceptable cost and with the same reliability as is required of the full financial statements. With this balance in mind, companies should consider ways of accelerating their year-end reporting timetable, so that they can issue their preliminary announcement as soon as possible after the year-end. Whilst recognising that individual circumstances may make it impracticable for some companies to achieve, the Board nevertheless encourages companies to issue their preliminary announcements within 60 days of the year-end.

10 Furthermore, companies should issue the full report and accounts (and the summary financial statement, if prepared) as soon as practicable after the preliminary announcement has been issued.

RELIABILITY

11 To ensure reliability, the Exchange requires the company's auditors to agree with the release of the preliminary announcement. Therefore the directors should publish the preliminary announcement only when it has been approved by the board and agreement, as required by the Listing Rules, has been obtained from the auditors.* In addition, if the auditors' report on the full financial statements is likely to be qualified, the Listing Rules require details of the nature of the qualification to be given in the preliminary announcement.

12 There is an expectation that the information in a preliminary announcement will be consistent with that in the audited financial statements. To achieve this:

(a) the audit of the financial statements should be complete or at least at an advanced stage at the date of the preliminary announcement.

(b) all the figures appearing in the preliminary announcement should agree with the figures in the audited financial statements or in the draft financial statements on which the audit is at an advanced stage.

**Further guidance for auditors has been issued by the Auditing Practices Board in Bulletin 1998/7 'The auditors' association with preliminary announcements'.*

(c) the other information and commentary in the preliminary announcement should be consistent with the figures in the preliminary announcement and with the audited or draft financial statements.

The guidance in paragraph 12 above balances the need for timeliness and reliability. The overriding consideration is that the information in the preliminary announcement should be reliable and not subject to later alterations. The risk of later changes to the figures in the preliminary announcement is not completely extinguished unless the preliminary announcement is issued at the same time that the full financial statements are approved by the directors and the auditors have signed their opinion on them. **13**

Against this there lies the need for the timely publication of price-sensitive information once it is available, as evidenced in the Exchange's Listing Rules that the preliminary announcement must be notified to the Exchange without delay after board approval. It is accepted practice, therefore, that, where the reliability of the information in the announcement is not compromised, the main figures and highlights from the financial statements are issued as the preliminary announcement when the audit is at an advanced stage (ie when any outstanding audit matters are unlikely to have a material impact on the financial statements or disclosures in the preliminary announcement), but before the audit report on the financial statements has been signed. **14**

Section 240(3)(c) of the Companies Act 1985* requires companies to make a statement whether the company's auditors have made an audit report on the statutory accounts dealing with any financial year with which the non-statutory accounts (ie the preliminary announcement, in this case) purport to deal. To prevent misunderstandings about whether the underlying financial statements have been reported upon by the auditors, it would also be helpful if the preliminary announcement clearly stated that the audit report on the full financial statements has yet to be signed, if that is the case. **15**

ACCOUNTING POLICIES AND PRIOR YEAR ADJUSTMENTS

The accounting policies and presentation of figures in preliminary announcements should be consistent with those in the full financial statements, that have yet to be published. **16**

Preliminary announcements should include a statement that, subject to specified exceptions, they are prepared on the basis of the accounting policies as set out in the most recently published set of annual financial statements. Preliminary announcements are often reviewed in conjunction with the previous year's financial statements and therefore the accounting policies need to be stated and explained only where they differ from those adopted in the previous year's annual financial statements. **17**

Following a change in accounting policy, the amounts for the current and prior years should be stated on the basis of the new policies, consistently with the annual financial statements. The cumulative effect of the policy change on opening reserves (ie at the beginning of the financial year) should be disclosed at the foot of the statement of total recognised gains and losses of the year. Similar disclosures should be made in respect of other prior year adjustments arising from the discovery of **18**

**The equivalent legislation in Northern Ireland is Article 248(3)(c) in Part VIII of the Companies (Northern Ireland) Order 1986 and in the Republic of Ireland is section 19(2)(c) of the Companies (Amendment) Act 1986.*

fundamental errors. A description should be given to help users understand the nature of each change or adjustment.

CONTENT

19 Under the Listing Rules of the Exchange, a preliminary announcement must contain profit and loss information and any significant information necessary for the purpose of assessing the results being announced. Present practice, however, indicates a trend towards lengthier preliminary announcements and the disclosure of much more information than the minimum required by the Exchange.

20 The disclosure of more detailed information in preliminary announcements is driven by both demands from financial analysts and a desire on the part of companies to communicate effectively and efficiently with the market.

21 In addition, companies are keen to ensure that all price-sensitive information likely to be given at analysts' briefings is included in the preliminary announcement. By giving analysts more information, companies are also safeguarding against misunderstandings and misinterpretation of the information in the preliminary announcement, which would otherwise be detected only at a later date when the full report and accounts are published.

22 An informed assessment of financial position and performance requires comparison of information from the profit and loss account, statement of total recognised gains and losses, balance sheet and cash flow statement together with a narrative commentary that explains the primary statements in the context of events and trends since the previous annual report and accounts and the previous interim report.

23 It is therefore recommended that a preliminary announcement should include a narrative commentary, a summarised profit and loss account, a statement of total recognised gains and losses, a summarised balance sheet and a summarised cash flow statement.

24 Sufficient supplementary information should be given, where helpful, given the nature of the company's business, and as the directors see fit, to permit an understanding of the significant items contained within the primary statements. For example, in certain cases it may be useful to analyse fixed assets into component parts, provide more detail about the company's borrowings, or state the equity and non-equity interests in shareholders' funds, in accordance with FRS 4 'Capital Instruments'.

25 Significant events and trends mentioned in the commentary should be supported by the underlying figures given either on the face of the primary statements or by way of note.

26 The information should be presented in a succinct manner and should be consistent with that in the yet to be published full report and accounts and comparable with previously published reports.

MANAGEMENT COMMENTARY

27 An important feature of a preliminary announcement is a balanced narrative commentary that explains the reasons for significant movements in key indicators and indicates perceived trends within the business. The management commentary should enable users to appreciate the main factors influencing the company's performance

during the financial year and its position at the year-end. For example, gross margins are an important factor in the success of retailing businesses and should be adequately disclosed and explained in such cases.

Attention should also be drawn to events and changes within the year that are likely to have a significant effect on the succeeding year despite having had relatively little impact in the current year. **28**

The commentary is not intended to be as comprehensive as an operating and financial review (OFR). However, management should consider whether key issues normally referred to in the OFR should be included within the preliminary announcement (albeit in less detail and focusing on areas of change) in order to provide a balanced view and help users gain a better understanding of the company's business. **29**

The commentary should describe the nature of any seasonal activity and, together with other disclosures, provide adequate information for the performance of the business and its financial position at the end of the year to be assessed. **30**

As well as referring to trading performance, the commentary should draw attention to a summarised balance sheet and a cash flow statement and should highlight and explain significant changes since the last annual financial statements and interim report, particularly regarding movements in working capital, liquidity and net debt, that are likely to be of value to users in their assessment of the business. **31**

The commentary and/or notes to the preliminary announcement should explain any other matter that the directors think would help users to understand the report. This would include, for example, where relevant: **32**

- acquisitions and disposals of major fixed assets or investments during the year;
- changes in contingencies, commitments and off balance sheet financial instruments* since the previous year-end and/or half year-end;
- material changes in capital structure or financing;
- events arising after the end of the year;
- the effect of foreign exchange movements during the year;
- the impact of revised actuarial valuations on pension costs.

FINAL INTERIM PERIOD

The market normally tends to react only to new information arising from the final interim period (ie the second half or, if quarterly reporting is adopted, the fourth quarter of the year) that has not been previously reported upon. However, the preliminary announcement and the annual results have traditionally focused on the results for the year, generally without presenting or discussing the results for the final interim period of the year. This means that the results for this period are subsumed within those for the year and not generally reported to shareholders. **33**

It is, therefore, particularly important that the salient events and features of the final interim period are referred to and explained as part of the management commentary. **34**

Given the importance attached by users to the most current information, including adequate management commentary thereon, preparers are encouraged to comment specifically on the final interim period's results in the preliminary announcement. **35**

**The Board is reviewing the accounting treatment of off balance sheet financial instruments as part of its project on derivatives and other financial instruments.*

Separate presentation of the final interim period figures, together with their corresponding amounts, is also encouraged to the extent necessary to support the commentary and to facilitate an understanding of current performance. The extent of information on the final interim period will vary from company to company – in some cases a reference to the key figures in the narrative commentary will be sufficient. This may entail the disclosure and explanation of significant changes to previously reported interim figures for the current year (which would occur only if the change qualified as a prior period adjustment) and of significant changes in estimates of amounts in previously reported interim figures (which are recognised in the final interim period).

PROFIT AND LOSS ACCOUNT

36 A preliminary announcement should include a summarised profit and loss account that includes at least the following information where relevant (with separate identification of significant amounts relating to associates and joint ventures):

- Turnover
- Operating profit or loss
- Interest payable less interest receivable (net)
- Profit or loss on ordinary activities before tax
- Tax on profit or loss on ordinary activities
- Profit or loss on ordinary activities after tax
- Minority interests
- Profit or loss for the period
- Dividends paid and proposed.

Acquisitions and discontinued operations

37 Turnover and operating profit of acquisitions and discontinued operations (as defined in FRS 3 'Reporting Financial Performance') should be disclosed separately on the face of the profit and loss account in the period in accordance with FRS 3.

Segmental information

38 Segmental analysis of trading performance is often crucial to understanding the performance of a company or group. Therefore, where significant, segmental information should be disclosed in the preliminary announcement, for business and/or geographical classifications (using the same classifications as given in the full report and accounts for the year) as follows:

- segment turnover, distinguishing inter-segment sales if significant;
- segment profit or loss on the same basis as in the annual financial statements – normally profit or loss before accounting for interest, taxation and minority interests.

Taxation

39 Sufficient information should be given to understand any significant changes in the effective tax rate from the prior year. It may be necessary to analyse the tax charge into its significant components (eg UK and overseas tax; and/or current and deferred tax).

Exceptional items

Exceptional items should be disclosed in the preliminary announcement, either on the face of the profit and loss account or in a note in accordance with FRS 3, together with an adequate description. 40

Earnings per share

The Exchange requires listed companies to disclose earnings per share expressed as pence per share. Basic and diluted earnings per share should, therefore, be calculated and disclosed in the same manner as in the full financial statements. Companies that choose to present in their annual financial statements additional amounts per share based on another level of earnings should present them also in their preliminary announcements, in accordance with FRS 3. 41

STATEMENT OF TOTAL RECOGNISED GAINS AND LOSSES

A statement of total recognised gains and losses should be included where material gains or losses, other than profit or loss for the financial year as reported in the profit and loss account, are recognised in the period. 42

A reconciliation of movements in shareholders' funds should be included in the preliminary announcement only where movements other than those in the statement of total recognised gains and losses need to be explained. 43

BALANCE SHEET

A summarised balance sheet should highlight significant movements in key indicators of the company's financial position. For consistency, similar classifications to those used in the annual financial statements should be adopted. It is recommended that, for example, a Schedule 4 company or Schedule 4A* group should give at least the following balance sheet information: 44

- Fixed assets
- Current assets
  - Stocks
  - Debtors
  - Cash at bank and in hand
  - Other current assets
- Creditors: amounts falling due within one year
- Net current assets (liabilities)
- Total assets less current liabilities
- Creditors: amounts falling due after more than one year
- Provisions for liabilities and charges
- Capital and reserves
- Minority interests.

**In Great Britain, Schedule 4 or 4A to the Companies Act 1985; in Northern Ireland, Schedule 4 or 4A to the Companies (Northern Ireland) Order 1986; in the Republic of Ireland, the Schedule to the Companies (Amendment) Act 1986 and the Schedule to the European Communities (Companies: Group Accounts) Regulations 1992.*

CASH FLOW STATEMENT

45 **Cash flow information helps users to assess the company's liquidity, viability and financial adaptability. Therefore, total amounts for the categories of cash flows specified by FRS 1 (Revised 1996) 'Cash Flow Statements' should include, at least, the following headings:**

- **Net cash inflow/outflow from operating activities**
- **Dividends received from joint ventures and associates**
- **Returns on investments and servicing of finance**
- **Taxation**
- **Capital expenditure and financial investment**
- **Acquisitions and disposals**
- **Equity dividends paid**
- **Management of liquid resources**
- **Financing**
- **Increase/decrease in cash.**

46 **A reconciliation of operating profit to operating cash flow should be given in sufficient detail for users to appreciate its chief components. A reconciliation should also be given of the movement of cash in the period to the movement in net debt, as required by FRS 1 (Revised 1996), including the effect of movements on short-term and long-term borrowings, cash and other components of net debt, unless disclosed elsewhere in the preliminary announcement.**

COMPARATIVE FIGURES

47 **Comparative figures for the summarised profit and loss account, the statement of total recognised gains and losses, the summarised balance sheet and the summarised cash flow statement should be presented for the previous full financial year.**

OTHER DISCLOSURES

48 **Subject to the limited exceptions noted in this Statement, disclosures demanded by Financial Reporting Standards and Statements of Standard Accounting Practice are not generally required in the presentation of preliminary announcements.**

49 **The preliminary announcement should state:**

- **the period covered by the report;**
- **the date on which it is approved by the board of directors.**

50 **In Great Britain, the preliminary announcement should contain a statement that satisfies the provisions of section 240 of the Companies Act 1985* regarding the publication of non-statutory accounts.**

The equivalent legislation in Northern Ireland is Article 248 in Part VIII of the Companies (Northern Ireland) Order 1986 and in the Republic of Ireland is section 19 of the Companies (Amendment) Act 1986.

Part Five

UITF abstracts

Foreword to UITF abstracts

(Issued February 1994)

Contents

	Paragraph
Introduction	1–4
Authority of UITF Abstracts	5–7
Scope and application of UITF Abstracts	8–12
Compliance with UITF Abstracts	13–16
Applicability of a UITF Abstract to transactions entered into before the Abstract was issued	17
UITF Abstracts and the legal framework	18
Dissemination and implementation	19–21
Appendix	
Composition and procedures of the UITF (revised September 1995)	

Foreword to UITF abstracts

INTRODUCTION

1 This Foreword explains the authority, scope and application of the 'UITF Abstracts' issued by the Accounting Standards Board (ASB) that set out the consensus reached by its Urgent Issues Task Force (UITF) on particular issues. The composition and procedures of the UITF are set out in the Appendix to this Foreword.

2 The UITF's main role is to assist the ASB with important or significant accounting issues where there exists an accounting standard or a provision of companies legislation* (including the requirement to give a true and fair view) and where unsatisfactory or conflicting interpretations have developed or seem likely to develop. In such circumstances it operates by seeking a consensus as to the accounting treatment that should be adopted. Such a consensus is reached against the background of the ASB's declared aim of relying on principles rather than detailed prescription.

3 The UITF forms its view as to the appropriate accounting treatment for any particular issue within the framework of the law and the principles established in the accounting standards and other statements issued or adopted by the ASB. It also has due regard to international developments.

4 Given the standing of the UITF's membership, the ASB normally expects to accept the UITF's consensus, subject only to the ASB's overriding duty to ensure that nothing is done that conflicts with the law, accounting standards, or the ASB's present or future policy or plans. The rules of procedure have been designed accordingly.

AUTHORITY OF UITF ABSTRACTS

5 The establishment of the UITF and its aim of avoiding the development of unsatisfactory or conflicting interpretations of law or accounting standards have the strong support of the Consultative Committee of Accountancy Bodies (CCAB). The Councils of the CCAB bodies expect their members who assume responsibilities in respect of financial statements to observe UITF Abstracts until they are replaced by accounting standards or otherwise withdrawn by the ASB. The Councils have agreed that:

(a) where this responsibility is evidenced by the association of members' names with such financial statements in the capacity of directors or other officers other than auditors, the onus will be on them to ensure that the existence and purpose of UITF Abstracts are fully understood by fellow directors and other officers. Members should also use their best endeavours to ensure that UITF Abstracts are observed and that any significant departures found to be necessary are adequately disclosed and explained in the financial statements.

(b) where members act as auditors or reporting accountants, they should be in a position to justify significant departures to the extent that their concurrence with the departures is stated or implied. They are not, however, required to

References to companies legislation are to: in Great Britain, the Companies Act 1985; in Northern Ireland, the Companies (Northern Ireland) Order 1986; and in the Republic of Ireland, the Companies Acts 1963–90 and the European Communities (Companies: Group Accounts) Regulations 1992. ***Editor's note:* This should now be read as though it also referred to the Companies Act 2006.*

refer in their report to departures with which they concur, provided that adequate disclosure has been made in the notes to the financial statements.

The CCAB bodies, through appropriate committees, may enquire into apparent failures by their members to observe UITF Abstracts or to ensure adequate disclosure of significant departures. 6

The UITF notes the intention of the Institute of Chartered Accountants in Ireland of maintaining close liaison with the UITF on promulgating, with appropriate modifications for legal differences, UITF Abstracts for application in the Republic of Ireland. 7

SCOPE AND APPLICATION OF UITF ABSTRACTS

Directors of companies incorporated under companies legislation are required to prepare accounts that give a true and fair view of the state of affairs of the company, and where applicable the group, at the end of the financial year and of the profit or loss of the company or group for the financial year. 8

UITF Abstracts are applicable to financial statements of a reporting entity that are intended to give a true and fair view of its state of affairs at the balance sheet date and of its profit or loss (or income and expenditure) for the financial period ending on that date. UITF Abstracts need not be applied to immaterial items. Nothing in the UITF Abstracts is to be construed as amending or overriding the accounting standards or other statements adopted or issued by the ASB. 9

As with accounting standards it is important when applying UITF Abstracts to be guided by the spirit and reasoning behind them. The spirit and reasoning are set out in the individual UITF Abstracts (and are based on the ASB's Statement of Principles for Financial Reporting). UITF Abstracts are intended to be as concise as the nature of a particular topic allows rather than detailed rules dealing with every conceivable circumstance. 10

UITF Abstracts should be applied to United Kingdom and Republic of Ireland group financial statements (including any amounts relating to overseas entities that are included in those financial statements). UITF Abstracts are not intended to apply to financial statements of overseas entities prepared for local purposes. 11

Where UITF Abstracts prescribe information to be contained in financial statements, such requirements do not override exemptions from disclosure given by law to, and utilised by, certain types of entity. 12

COMPLIANCE WITH UITF ABSTRACTS

UITF Abstracts should be regarded as part of the corpus of practices forming the basis for determining what constitutes a true and fair view and should be read in conjunction with accounting standards. UITF Abstracts consequently may be taken into consideration by the Financial Reporting Review Panel (the Review Panel) in deciding whether financial statements call for review. 13

In the United Kingdom, the Review Panel and, in Great Britain the Department of Trade and Industry, in Northern Ireland the Department of Economic Development, have procedures for receiving and investigating complaints regarding the annual accounts of companies in respect of apparent departures from the accounting requirements of companies legislation including the requirement to give a true and 14 fair view. The Review Panel is authorised under the legislation to apply to the court for a declaration or declarator that the annual accounts of a company do not comply with the statutory requirements and an order requiring the directors of the company to prepare revised accounts. The Department of Trade and Industry and the Department of Economic Development have similar powers.*

15 The requirement to give a true and fair view may in special circumstances require a departure from UITF Abstracts. However, because UITF Abstracts are formulated with the objective of ensuring that the information resulting from their application faithfully represents the underlying commercial activity, the ASB envisages that only in exceptional circumstances will departure from the requirements of a UITF Abstract be necessary in order for the financial statements to give a true and fair view.

16 If in exceptional circumstances compliance with the requirements of a UITF Abstract is inconsistent with the requirement to give a true and fair view, the requirements of the UITF Abstract should be departed from to the extent necessary to give a true and fair view. In such cases informed and unbiased judgement should be used to devise an appropriate alternative treatment, which should be consistent with the economic and commercial characteristics of the circumstances concerned. Particulars of any material departure from a UITF Abstract, the reasons for it and its financial effects should be disclosed in the financial statements. The disclosure made should be equivalent to that given in respect of departures from specific accounting provisions of companies legislation.

APPLICABILITY OF A UITF ABSTRACT TO TRANSACTIONS ENTERED INTO BEFORE THE ABSTRACT WAS ISSUED

17 When a new UITF Abstract is issued the question arises whether its provisions should be applied to transactions that took place before the promulgation of the Abstract. The general policy of the ASB is that the provisions of UITF Abstracts should apply to all material transactions irrespective of the date at which they are entered into. The reasons for this policy are set out more fully in paragraphs 27–30 of the 'Foreword to Accounting Standards'. All references in those paragraphs to 'accounting standards' should in the present context be read as references to 'UITF Abstracts'.

UITF ABSTRACTS AND THE LEGAL FRAMEWORK

18 The status of UITF Abstracts in United Kingdom legislation is addressed in the Opinion by Miss Mary Arden QC† 'The true and fair requirement', which is published as an appendix to the 'Foreword to Accounting Standards' and should be read in conjunction with this Foreword.

DISSEMINATION AND IMPLEMENTATION

19 The UITF Abstracts are made publicly available by the ASB for the guidance of users, preparers and auditors of financial information. They include a discussion of the matter, the accounting issues identified, reference sources, and a summary of the UITF's deliberations, and clearly indicate what conclusion has been reached.

**In the Republic of Ireland the Department of Enterprise and Employment has powers to investigate generally the affairs of companies. The Review Panel does not operate in the Republic of Ireland.*

†*Now the Honourable Mrs Justice Arden.*

If the UITF is unable to reach a consensus, or if a consensus is not ratified by the ASB, an explanation of the circumstances will be published. **20**

A UITF Abstract takes effect from the effective date in the published Abstract, and is thereafter to be regarded as accepted practice in the area in question. Accordingly, all reporting entities will be expected to conform to it, if necessary by changing previously adopted accounting policies, unless the consensus explicitly states otherwise. **21**

Appendix
Composition and procedures of the UITF

(revised September 1995)

COMPOSITION

A1 The UITF is a committee of the ASB comprising a number of people of standing in the field of financial reporting. Its purpose is to enlist the experience and influence of its members to assist the ASB in its task of establishing and improving standards of financial accounting and reporting, for the benefit of users, preparers and auditors of financial information.

A2 The UITF consists of up to fifteen members experienced in the technicalities of financial reporting. The membership includes:

up to seven senior representatives from the largest accounting firms;

one member from a medium-sized or small accounting firm;

four members from industry or commerce; and

up to three further members chosen on a personal basis.

A3 The ASB may adjust the size and composition of the UITF from time to time.

A4 Members are appointed by the ASB for periods of up to two years. Membership is personal. Each member is entitled to appoint a named alternate; any such appointment and subsequent changes of appointment shall be notified to the Secretary of the ASB before the named alternate acts in the place of the member. The named alternate may attend and vote at any meetings that the member is unable to attend. If neither the member nor his named alternate is able to attend, the member may appoint another alternate to attend the meeting and shall inform the Secretary of the ASB in advance of the meeting, but such alternate does not have the right to vote.

A5 The office of Chairman of the UITF shall be held by the Chairman of the ASB.

A6 Members of the ASB are free to attend UITF meetings and have the right to speak, but do not have the right to vote.

A7 The Chairman may invite others to attend UITF meetings as observers.

ADMISSION OF ITEMS TO THE AGENDA

A8 Auditors and companies, and others with an interest in financial reporting, are invited to refer substantial new issues to the UITF where there is doubt about the most appropriate accounting treatment leading to a true and fair view and it is important that a standard treatment should be established before a precedent is set by practice.

A9 The Councils of the CCAB bodies invite their members to raise for possible consideration by the UITF any substantial accounting issues of general concern that arise in connection with the preparation and audit of financial statements. In raising such issues members should not disclose information of a confidential nature either directly or by implication to anyone likely to be aware of the background.

The UITF will not consider any issue that the ASB indicates falls within its own agenda unless specifically requested to do so by the ASB. **A10**

CONSULTATION

The urgent nature of the matters deal with by the UITF necessarily means that it is not possible for it to follow an extended consultation and due process procedure. The ASB therefore takes special measures to publicise the matters on the UITF's agenda. Preliminary decisions reached by the UITF are circulated for comment to recipients for the ASB Bulletin and to finance directors of listed companies. **A11**

QUORUM

The quorum for a meeting of the UITF is eleven voting members or their named alternates. **A12**

MEETINGS AND VOTING

Voting may take place either at meetings or by post. A consensus is necessary for the approval of an Abstract for ratification and issue by the ASB. **A13**

A consensus will have been attained at a meeting where not more than two voting members of the UITF, or their named alternates, present at the meeting dissent from the treatment proposed as the appropriate accounting practice for the matter in question. **A14**

A consensus will have been attained in a postal vote of the UITF where **A15**

(a) at least eleven of those eligible to participate in the vote (see below) return their votes by the relevant deadline and
(b) not more than two of those eligible to vote have registered, by the relevant deadline, a vote against the treatment proposed as the appropriate accounting practice for the matter in question. Participating in a postal vote is open only to those members and named alternates who were present at the last meeting of the UITF at which the topic was considered as an agenda item. Where a member was represented at that meeting by his named alternate, either he or the named alternate may register a vote.

When voting slips are dispatched for a postal vote, the Chairman of the UITF shall specify the deadline (being not less than seven calendar days from the date of dispatch) by which votes are to be returned. At his discretion the Chairman may, if the deadline has not yet been reached, extend it by up to seven further calendar days. If the Chairman is unable for any reason to specify the deadline, the deadline shall be specified by the Technical Director of the ASB. **A16**

A member of the UITF is expected to support any vote of his alternate and to agree to be bound by it. **A17**

The Chairman has no vote. **A18**

Meetings of the UITF shall be chaired by the Chairman of the UITF or in his absence the Technical Director of the ASB, or such other person as the Chairman may nominate, shall preside as chairman of the meeting. **A19**

RATIFICATION BY THE ASB

A20 As indicated in paragraph 4 of the 'Foreword to UITF Abstracts', the ASB will normally expect to accept the UITF's consensus. However, the ASB retains the right to decline to accept any consensus that it believes is contrary to law or to its extant or intended accounting standards. Where such a situation arises the ASB will set out its views to the UITF in writing for consideration as soon as practicable thereafter with the objective if possible of achieving a mutually acceptable solution.

A21 A consensus that has been ratified by the ASB will be published by the ASB as a UITF Abstract.

UITF abstract 4: Presentation of long-term debtors in current assets

(Issued July 1992)

THE ISSUE

Both for liabilities and for debtors the Companies Act requires a distinction to be drawn between the amounts payable or receivable within one year and those due to be settled or received after more than one year. Although the distinction is disclosed in the notes for each of the items forming part of debtors (including prepayments and accrued income if included in debtors), unlike in the case of liabilities it is not required to be carried through to the total of current assets nor to the significant Format 1 sub-total of net current assets (liabilities).* 1

In consequence, there is a certain imbalance between the items that the formats require to be classified under current assets or current liabilities. For example, a pension fund surplus (to the extent recognised in the balance sheet) could give rise to a prepayment forming part of net current assets (liabilities), whereas a deficiency would normally be shown as a provision under long-term liabilities.† In some cases the period expected to be required for recovery of such an asset may be considerable, perhaps in excess of ten years. Other examples of long-term debtor items include much of the trade debtors of lessors and deferred consideration in respect of the sale of an investment or other fixed asset. 2

APPLICATION TO SMALLER ENTITIES

Reporting entities applying the Financial Reporting Standard for Smaller Entities currently applicable are exempt from this Abstract. 2A

UITF CONSENSUS

In most cases it will be satisfactory to disclose the size of debtors due after more than one year in the notes to the accounts. There will be some instances, however, where the amount is so material in the context of the total net current assets that in the absence of disclosure of debtors due after more than one year on the face of the balance sheet readers may misinterpret the accounts. The Task Force have agreed that, in such circumstances, the amount should be disclosed on the face of the balance sheet. 3

DATE FROM WHICH EFFECTIVE

The disclosure required by this consensus should be adopted in financial statements relating to accounting periods ending on or after 23 August 1992, but earlier adoption is encouraged. 4

* ***Editor's note:*** *For accounting periods beginning on or after 6 April 2008 Schedule 4 to the Companies Act 1985 is replaced by Schedule 1 to the Large and Medium-sized Companies and Groups (Accounts and Reports) Regulations 2008 (SI 2008/410). The same issue arises.*

† *Under FRS 17 'Retirement benefits', the pension asset or liability will be shown separately rather than under these format headings. (**Editor's note:** FRS 17 came into effect fully with effect from 2005.)*

REFERENCES

Companies Act 1985 and Companies (Northern Ireland) Order 1986 – Schedule 4 Balance Sheet Formats 1 and 2 including notes 5 and 6.

Republic of Ireland – Companies (Amendment) Act 1986, the Schedule, Balance Sheet Formats 1 and 2 including note 4.

Statement of Standard Accounting Practice 21 – Accounting for leases and hire purchase contracts.

Statement of Standard Accounting Practice 24 – Accounting for pension costs.*

International Accounting Standard 13 – Presentation of Current Assets and Current Liabilities.†

***Editor's note:** *FRS 17 'Retirement benefits' superseded SSAP 24 fully with effect from 2005.*

†***Editor's note:** Replaced by IAS 1 (revised) 'Presentation of financial statements' issued August 1997. Further revised in December 2003.*

UITF abstract 5: Transfers from current assets to fixed assets

(Issued July 1992)

THE ISSUE

The Companies Act 1985 defines a fixed asset as one intended for use on a continuing basis in the company's activities and any which are not intended for such use are current assets (section 262(1)CA 1985). Where at a date subsequent to its original acquisition a current asset is retained for use on a continuing basis in the company's activities it becomes a fixed asset and the question arises as to the appropriate transfer value. An example is a property which is reclassified from trading properties to investment properties. 1

Of particular concern is the possibility that companies could avoid charging the profit and loss account with write-downs to net realisable value arising on unsold trading assets. This could be done by transferring the relevant assets from current assets to fixed assets at above net realisable value, as a result of which any later write down might be debited to revaluation reserve. 2

This abstract deals only with situations where current assets are included in the balance sheet at the lower of cost and net realisable value under paragraphs 22 and 23 of Schedule 4 to the Companies Act 1985. 3

The timing of the transfer of current assets to fixed assets should reflect the timing of management's change of intent and should not be backdated (for example to the start of the financial year). Since the date of the management decision is unlikely to correspond with the balance sheet date at which a full review of carrying values would be made, consideration must be given to the appropriate amounts at which such assets should be transferred at the time of transfer. 4

APPLICATION TO SMALLER ENTITIES

Reporting entities applying the Financial Reporting Standard for Smaller Entities currently applicable are exempt from this Abstract. 4A

UITF CONSENSUS

The Task Force reached a consensus that where assets are transferred from current to fixed, the current asset accounting rules should be applied up to the effective date of transfer, which is the date of management's change of intent. Consequently the transfer should be made at the lower of cost and net realisable value, and accordingly an assessment should be made of the net realisable value at the date of transfer and if this is less than its previous carrying value the diminution should be charged in the profit and loss account, reflecting the loss to the company while the asset was held as a current asset. 5

Whether assets are transferred at cost or at net realisable value in accordance with *paragraph 5 above, fixed asset* accounting rules will apply to the assets subsequent to the date of transfer. In cases where the transfer is at net realisable value, the asset should be accounted for as a fixed asset at a valuation (under the alternative accounting rules of the Act) as at the date of the transfer; at subsequent balance sheet dates it may or may not be revalued, but in either event the disclosure requirements appropriate to a valuation should be given. 6

DATE FROM WHICH EFFECTIVE

7 The accounting treatment required by this consensus should be adopted in financial statements relating to accounting periods ending on or after 23 December 1992, but earlier adoption is encouraged. In order to ensure consistency of treatment, corresponding amounts for preceding years should be restated where applicable.

REFERENCES

Companies Act 1985 Section 262(1) and Schedule 4 paragraphs 17 to 19, 22 to 23, 30 to 34 and 43.*

Northern Ireland—Companies (Northern Ireland) Order 1986, articles 229(1) and 270(1) and Schedule 4 paragraphs 17 to 19, 22 to 23, 30 to 34 and 43.

Republic of Ireland—Companies Act 1990 section 202(1) and the Companies (Amendment) Act 1986, the Schedule paragraphs 5 to 7, 10 to 11, 18 to 22, 30 and 60.

FRS 3 'Reporting Financial Performance'—paragraph 13.

Statement of Standard Accounting Practice 9—'Stocks and long-term contracts—paragraph 26.

Statement of Standard Accounting Practice 19—'Accounting for investment properties—paragraphs 11 and 13.

NOTE ON LEGAL REQUIREMENTS

The Task Force has been advised by leading Counsel that assets can be treated as having been transferred from current assets to fixed assets at a value equal to the lower of cost and net realisable value. Counsel indicated that the above advice is based on the assumption that where the transfer takes place at net realisable value, the asset will be accounted for as a fixed asset as at the date of transfer in accordance with the accounting rules in Schedule 4 to the Companies Act (that is, included at a current value rather than historical cost).

****Editor's note:*** *The various statutory references change with the introduction of the Companies Act 2006, which affects accounting for periods beginning on or after 6 April 2008. The various statutory references have changed as follows:*

Companies Act 1985 reference	***Companies Act 2006 reference***
Schedule 4	*Schedule 1 to the Large and Medium-sized Companies and Groups (Accounts and Reports) Regulations 2008 (SI 2008/410)*
Section 262 (1)	*Section 853*
Schedules 9 and 9A	*Schedules 2 and 3 to SI 2008/410*
Paragraphs 17 to 19 of Schedule 4	*Paragraphs 17 to 19 of Schedule 1 to SI 2008/410*
Paragraphs 22 to 23 of Schedule 4	*Paragraphs 23 to 24 of Schedule 1 to SI 2008/410*
Paragraphs 30 to 34 of Schedule 4	*Paragraphs 31 to 35 of Schedule 1 to SI 2008/410*
Paragraph 43 of Schedule 4	*Paragraph 52 of Schedule 1 to SI 2008/410*

UITF abstract 9: Accounting for operations in hyper-inflationary economies*

(Issued June 1993)

THE ISSUE

SSAP 20 'Foreign currency translation' states that 'where a foreign enterprise operates in a country in which a very high rate of inflation exists it may not be possible to present fairly in historical cost accounts the financial position of a foreign enterprise simply by a translation process. In such circumstances the local currency financial statements should be adjusted where possible to reflect current price levels before the translation process is undertaken'. However there is some uncertainty as to when and how this guidance should be applied in practice. 1

The overriding requirement to give a true and fair view of the profit or loss and state of affairs can be considered to require appropriate adjustments to be made where significant distortions arise from very high rates of inflation ('hyper-inflation'). Because it is a common condition, users of financial statements have developed tolerance for some inflation and in varying degrees allow for it in their analyses. The distortions caused by hyper-inflation may in practice be diluted by the relative rates of inflation in the reporting country and in other countries where the reporting entity operates, when taken together with the relative size of the operations in hyper-inflationary economies in the context of the reporting group. 2

The question of what constitutes hyper-inflation is necessarily judgmental. International Accounting Standard No.29 'Financial Reporting in Hyperinflationary Economies' describes a number of characteristics of the economic environment of a country which indicate hyper-inflation (see the Appendix to this Abstract). Failure to adjust for hyper-inflation before application of the SSAP 20 closing rate/net investment method of translation produces a significant debit to group reserves, whilst at the same time inflated profits are included in the group profit and loss account (whether from high interest income on deposits in a rapidly depreciating local currency or from trading operations at what could be considered unrealistically high profitability). 3

Methods adopted to eliminate distortions caused by hyper-inflation need to take account of the following factors: 4

(a) the lack of reliable and timely inflation indices in a number of hyper-inflationary economies can pose a major practical problem to adjusting local currency financial statements;

(b) it is necessary to have regard to the particular local circumstances as these can vary significantly between countries in terms of how real profitability should be measured.

APPLICATION TO SMALLER ENTITIES

Reporting entities applying the Financial Reporting Standard for Smaller Entities currently applicable are exempt from this Abstract. 4A

***Editor's note:** *For companies complying with FRS 24, UITF 9 is superseded. It remains in force for other companies.*

UITF CONSENSUS

5 The Task Force reached a consensus that adjustments are required where the distortions caused by hyper-inflation are such as to affect the true and fair view given by the group financial statements. In any event adjustments are required where the cumulative inflation rate over three years is approaching, or exceeds, 100% and the operations in the hyper-inflationary economies are material.

6 The Task Force considered that the following two methods of eliminating the distortions were consistent with SSAP 20 and therefore acceptable:

(a) adjusting the local currency financial statements to reflect current price levels before the translation process is undertaken, as suggested in paragraph 26 of SSAP 20. This includes taking any gain or loss on the net monetary position through the profit and loss account.

(b) using a relatively stable currency (which would not necessarily be sterling) as the functional currency (i.e., the currency of measurement) for the relevant foreign operations. For example in certain businesses operating in Latin American territories the US dollar acts effectively as the functional currency for business operations. The functional currency would in effect be the 'local currency' as defined in paragraph 39 of SSAP 20. In such circumstances, if the transactions are not recorded initially in that stable currency, they must first be remeasured into that currency by applying the temporal method described in SSAP 20 (but based on the dollar or other stable currency rather than sterling). The effect is that the movement between the original currency of record and the stable currency is used as a proxy for an inflation index.

7 If neither of the above methods is considered appropriate for material operations, then the reasons should be stated and alternative methods to eliminate the distortions should be adopted.

8 Where group operations in areas of hyper-inflation are material in the context of group results or net assets, the accounting policy adopted to eliminate the distortions of such inflation should be disclosed.

DATE FROM WHICH EFFECTIVE

9 The accounting treatment required by this consensus should be adopted in financial statements relating to accounting periods ending on or after 23 August 1993, but earlier adoption is encouraged. In order to ensure consistency of treatment, corresponding amounts for preceding years should be restated where applicable.

REFERENCES

Statement of Standard Accounting Practice 20 – Foreign Currency Translation – paragraphs 26, 39 and 55.

International Accounting Standard 29 – Financial Reporting in Hyper-inflationary Economies.

Appendix

Extract from IAS 29 'Financial Reporting in Hyper-inflationary Economies'

'3 This Statement does not establish an absolute rate at which hyperinflation is deemed to arise. It is a matter of judgement when restatement of financial statements in accordance with this Statement becomes necessary. Hyperinflation is indicated by characteristics of the economic environment of a country which include, but are not limited to, the following:

(a) the general population prefers to keep its wealth in nonmonetary assets or in a relatively stable foreign currency. Amounts of local currency held are immediately invested to maintain purchasing power;
(b) the general population regards monetary amounts not in terms of the local currency but in terms of a relatively stable foreign currency. Prices may be quoted in that currency;
(c) sales and purchases on credit take place at prices that compensate for the expected loss of purchasing power during the credit period, even if the period is short;
(d) interest rates, wages and prices are linked to a price index; and
(e) the cumulative inflation rate over three years is approaching, or exceeds, 100%'.

UITF abstract 11: Capital instruments: issuer call options*

(Issued September 1994)

THE ISSUE

1 The terms of a capital instrument sometimes include an issuer call option, that is, a right of the issuer (but not the investor) to redeem the instrument early, usually on the payment of a premium. Such an option is included primarily to preserve the financial flexibility of the issuer. The question arises as to the appropriate accounting for an instrument that includes an issuer call option following the issue of FRS 4 'Capital Instruments'.

2 FRS 4 requires the finance costs of debt and non-equity shares to be charged in the profit and loss account and allocated to periods over the term of the instrument at a constant rate on the carrying amount. Finance costs are defined as 'The difference between the net proceeds of an instrument and the total amount of the payments (or other transfers of economic benefits) that the issuer may be required to make in respect of the instrument' (paragraph 8). However, paragraph 16 states that 'If either party has the option to require the instrument to be redeemed or cancelled and, under the terms of the instrument, it is uncertain whether such an option will be exercised, the term should be taken to end on the earliest date at which the instrument would be redeemed or cancelled on exercise of such an option.' The Explanation of FRS 4 states that this is the case 'unless there is no genuine commercial possibility that the option will be exercised' (paragraph 73). This could be construed as requiring the accounting to be based on the assumption that the call option will be exercised and hence that the premium will be paid. Nevertheless, except in the special circumstances envisaged in paragraph 5 below, the amount payable under an issuer call option is not a payment 'that the issuer may be required to make in respect of the instrument' (part of the definition of 'finance costs' quoted above).

3 FRS 4 also contains a requirement that 'Gains and losses arising on the repurchase or early settlement of debt should be recognised in the profit and loss account in the period during which the repurchase or early settlement is made' (paragraph 32). Further, FRS 4 requires that where shares are redeemed, shareholders' funds should be reduced by the value of the consideration given (paragraph 39).

4 Issuers of instruments should not have to account for possible payments that they are not obliged to make, and may very well elect not to make. Payment of a premium on exercise of an issuer call option is a cost that stems directly from the decision to exercise the option and may therefore fairly be reported in the period in which exercise takes place.

5 Issuer call options as contemplated in this Abstract do not include those cases where the effective rate of interest (or the margin above a base rate by which interest is calculated) increases after the date at which the option is exercisable. In these cases the exercise price may be deemed to compensate the investor for forgoing such increased interest.

****Editor's note:** For companies complying with FRS 26, UITF 11 is superseded. It remains in force for other companies.*

APPLICATION TO SMALLER ENTITIES

Reporting entities applying the Financial Reporting Standard for Smaller Entities currently applicable are exempt from this Abstract. **5A**

UITF CONSENSUS

The Task Force reached a consensus that where an instrument includes a call option that can be exercised only by the issuer, the payment required on exercise of that option does not form part of the finance costs of the instrument in accordance with the requirements of FRS 4 'Capital Instruments'. In the case of debt, the gain or loss arising on any repurchase or early settlement will reflect the amount payable on exercise. In the case of shares, the amount payable on exercise will be used to reduce the amount of shareholders' funds. **6**

The Task Force noted that in the case of an instrument with an issuer call option exercise of which is uncertain, the term of the instrument, as defined in paragraph 16 of FRS 4, would end on the date that the option was exercisable. **7**

The Task Force agreed that, in accordance with paragraph 16 of FRS 4, this consensus should apply only to genuine options, and would not therefore apply to cases where, under the terms of the instrument, it was clear that the issuer would be commercially obliged to exercise its call option. An example of such a case would be where the terms of a debt instrument give the issuer the 'option' of early redemption but it is clear from the outset that in all conceivable circumstances it would be advantageous to the issuer to exercise the option rather than allow the debt to remain in issue. **8**

The Task Force also agreed that the consensus should not apply to those cases described in paragraph 5 above. The Task Force agreed that in those cases, 'the total amount of the payments . . . that the issuer may be required to make in respect of the instrument' must include the amount payable on exercise of the option. **9**

DATE FROM WHICH EFFECTIVE

The accounting treatment required by this abstract should be adopted in financial statements relating to accounting periods ending on or after 23 October 1994, but earlier adoption is encouraged. **10**

REFERENCES

Financial Reporting Standard 4 - Capital Instruments - paragraphs 8, 16, 32, 39 and 73.

UITF abstract 15: (revised 1999) Disclosure of substantial acquisitions

(Issued February 1999)

THE ISSUE

1 FRS 6 'Acquisitions and Mergers' specifies additional disclosures that are required in respect of substantial acquisitions. For listed companies, these disclosures are required for business combinations that are Class 1 or Super Class 1 transactions under the London Stock Exchange Listing Rules.*

2 The Listing Rules classify transactions by assessing their size relative to that of the company proposing to make the transaction. It does this by reference to whether any of a number of ratios (eg the assets of the target to those of the offeror) exceeds a given amount when expressed as a percentage. At the time FRS 6 was issued, Class 1 transactions were defined as those where the ratio exceeded 15 per cent, and Super Class 1 were those where the ratio exceeded 25 per cent. As a result of changes to the Listing Rules, Class 1 transactions are now defined as those where the ratio exceeds 25 per cent and the term 'Super Class 1' is no longer used.

3 For non-listed entities FRS 6 requires the disclosures in respect of substantial acquisitions where any of certain ratios exceeds 15 per cent.

APPLICATION TO SMALLER ENTITIES

4 Reporting entities applying the Financial Reporting Standard for Smaller Entities currently applicable are exempt from this Abstract.

UITF CONSENSUS

5 The UITF reached a consensus that, in order to retain the Accounting Standards Board's original intentions for FRS 6, the reference in paragraph 37(a) to Class 1 transactions should be interpreted as meaning those business combinations in which any of the ratios set out in the London Stock Exchange Listing Rules for the classification of transactions exceeds 15 per cent.

DATE FROM WHICH EFFECTIVE AND WITHDRAWAL OF UITF ABSTRACT 15 (as issued on 30 January 1996)

6 As this consensus maintains the status quo it is effective immediately.

7 This abstract supersedes UITF Abstract 15 (as issued on 30 January 1996) 'Disclosure of substantial acquisitions'.

References

Financial Reporting Standard 6 'Acquisitions and Mergers' paragraph 37.
The Listing Rules of the London Stock Exchange Chapter 10 'Transactions'.

***Editor's note:** *In the UK, the Listing Rules are now issued by the Financial Conduct Authority in its capacity as UK Listing Authority.*

UITF abstract 19: Tax on gains and losses on foreign currency borrowings that hedge an investment in a foreign enterprise

(Issued February 1998)

BACKGROUND

Where certain conditions are met, SSAP 20 'Foreign currency translation' permits certain gains and losses on foreign currency borrowings that have been used to finance or provide a hedge against equity investments in foreign enterprises to be reported as reserve movements. As a result of the subsequent introduction of FRS 3 'Reporting Financial Performance' these gains and losses are now reported in the statement of total recognised gains and losses.* 1

Until recently, neither the retranslation of the net investment in a foreign enterprise nor the gain or loss on foreign borrowings had any consequences for tax. Owing to recent changes in UK tax legislation this is no longer always the case and in some circumstances, for example where a matching election is not made for tax purposes, the gain or loss on retranslation of the borrowings is taxable. 2

THE ISSUES

The UITF considered how any tax effect of gains and losses on exchange differences on borrowings that are reported in the statement of total recognised gains and losses should be recognised. It concluded that such tax effects should also be reported in the statement of total recognised gains and losses. 3

The UITF considered the restrictions of SSAP 20 on the gains and losses that are dealt with in the statement of total recognised gains and losses. It concluded that the restriction that the gains and losses should not exceed the exchange differences on the equity investments (in individual accounts) or net investments in foreign enterprises (in consolidated accounts) should be applied after taking account of any tax charge or credit relating to the gain or loss on the borrowings. It noted that SSAP 20 also requires that the borrowings whose exchange gains and losses are dealt with in the statement of total recognised gains and losses should not exceed the amount of cash that the equity investment or net investment is expected to be able to generate, whether from profits or otherwise. The UITF believed that it would be consistent with its view on the restrictions on gains and losses that this test should also be performed on a net-of-tax basis.† 4

SSAP 20 also requires that the amount of exchange gains and losses on borrowings that are taken to the statement of total recognised gains and losses should be reported. The UITF concluded that it was necessary to disclose the amount of the related tax. 5

***Editor's note:** For companies complying with FRS 23 this paragraph now reads as follows:*
Where certain conditions are met, FRS 26 (IAS 39) 'Financial Instruments: Measurement' permits certain gains and losses on foreign currency borrowings that have been used to provide a hedge of net investments in foreign operations to be reported initially in the statement of total recognised gains and losses.

*†**Editor's note:** For companies complying with FRS 23 this paragraph is deleted.*

APPLICATION TO SMALLER ENTITIES

6 Reporting entities applying the Financial Reporting Standard for Smaller Entities currently applicable are exempt from this Abstract.

UITF CONSENSUS

7 The UITF reached a consensus that where exchange differences on foreign currency borrowings that have been used to finance, or provide a hedge against, equity investments in foreign enterprises are taken to reserves and reported in the statement of total recognised gains and losses, in accordance with paragraphs 51, 57 and 58 of SSAP 20 and paragraph 27 of FRS 3, tax charges or credits that are directly and solely attributable to such exchange differences should also be taken to reserves and reported in that statement.*†

8 The restriction on the amount of the gains or losses arising on the borrowings that are dealt with in the statement of total recognised gains and losses set out in paragraphs 51(a) and 57(b) of SSAP 20 should be applied after taking account of any tax charge or credit directly and solely attributable to the borrowings. Similarly, the comparison with the total amount of cash that the investments are expected to be able to generate and the exposure created by the borrowings (paragraphs 51(b) and 57(c) of SSAP 20) should be considered in after-tax terms.‡

9 The amount of tax charges and credits accounted for as described in paragraph 7 above should be disclosed, in addition to the gross amount of the exchange differences.

DATE FROM WHICH EFFECTIVE

10 The accounting treatment required by this consensus should be adopted in financial statements relating to accounting periods ending on or after 23 March 1998, but earlier adoption is encouraged.

REFERENCES

Statement of Standard Accounting Practice 20 'Foreign currency translation', paragraphs 51, 57, 58 and 60.

FRS 3 'Reporting Financial Performance', paragraph 27.

****Editor's note:*** *See also paragraph 6 of FRS 16 'Current tax'.*

†***Editor's note:*** *For companies complying with FRS 23 this paragraph now reads as follows:*
The UITF reached a consensus that where exchange differences on foreign currency borrowings that have been used to provide a hedge against a net investment in a foreign operation are taken to reserves and reported in the statement of total recognised gains and losses, in accordance with FRS 26, tax charges or credits that are directly and solely attributable to such exchange differences should also be taken to reserves and reported in that statement.

‡***Editor's note:*** *For companies complying with FRS 23 this paragraph is deleted.*

UITF abstract 21: Accounting issues arising from the proposed introduction of the euro

(Issued March 1998)

BACKGROUND

The advent of stage 3 of the Economic and Monetary Union (EMU) will necessitate significant expenditure by many business entities to adapt their operations and information systems to accommodate the single currency, the euro. This will be the case irrespective of whether a Member State participates in the single currency, since all those in, or trading with, participating Member States are potentially affected. 1

Entities will incur a variety of costs, which may include administrative planning, staff training, the provision of information to customers, modification of software and the adaptation of hardware, such as vending machines, retail outlets' cash registers or banks' automatic teller machines. 2

Apart from additional costs arising from the introduction of the euro there will be other consequences with potential accounting implications. For example, all foreign exchange differences that have arisen on balances denominated in participating currencies will become permanent and the exchange risk between currency units of participating Member States will disappear. 3

In June 1997 the European Commission published a paper 'Accounting for the introduction of the euro'. This Abstract is consistent with the relevant guidance included in that paper in relation to the euro. 4

THE ISSUES

The UITF has considered three issues: 5

(a) Should costs incurred in connection with the introduction of the euro be charged as an expense or capitalised as an asset and what disclosure is appropriate?

(b) What impact will the irrevocable locking of national currencies of participating Member States to the euro have on cumulative foreign exchange translation differences that have been recognised in periods before the introduction of the euro?

(c) What impact will the irrevocable locking of national currencies of participating Member States to the euro have on anticipatory hedging instruments existing at the date of introduction of the euro in respect of future transactions?

COSTS ASSOCIATED WITH THE INTRODUCTION OF THE EURO

Costs may be capitalised only if they give rise to an asset. Assets are defined in FRS 5 'Reporting the Substance of Transactions' as: 6

> 'Rights or other access to future economic benefits controlled by an entity as a result of past transactions or events.'

Many of the costs of preparing for the euro will not give rise to assets, for example the costs of staff training, giving information to customers etc. Where costs are incurred on adapting existing assets, it is necessary to assess whether the expenditure simply maintains the asset's originally assessed standard of performance or whether 7 the expenditure results in an enhancement of economic benefits by extending the service potential of the asset concerned. In the former case, there is no access to additional future economic benefits and the costs should be written off as incurred. In the latter case, the costs should be capitalised and depreciated over the asset's useful economic life.

8 Regarding the timing of recognition of a provision for costs associated with the introduction of the euro, the UITF noted that FRS 5 defines liabilities (of which provisions are one type) as 'An entity's obligations to transfer economic benefits as a result of past transactions or events.' One aspect of this is exemplified in FRED 14 (the Exposure Draft of a Financial Reporting Standard on accounting for provisions and contingencies, issued in June 1997). If the envisaged FRS* implements the proposals in FRED 14 a provision would be recognised when and only when an entity has a legal or constructive obligation to transfer economic benefits as a result of past events: the mere intention or even necessity to undertake expenditure related to the future would not be sufficient to give rise to an obligation. Thus costs associated with the introduction of the euro would be recognised in the accounting period in which the work is carried out and no provision would be made for estimated future costs.

9 A further issue concerns the disclosure of information regarding the nature and potential impact of the introduction of the euro, including the related costs incurred and likely to be incurred. In this connection the UITF believes that existing requirements, such as FRS 3 in respect of exceptional costs and companies legislation in respect of significant commitments (including revenue commitments), may apply in some cases. Where the potential impact is likely to be significant, the UITF recommends that entities should give disclosures as indicated in this Abstract.

10 This Abstract addresses the accounting for external and internal costs of the changeover to the euro.† It does not address the costs of modifying software or hardware produced for sale, nor does it address purchases of replacement software or hardware.

CUMULATIVE FOREIGN EXCHANGE TRANSLATION DIFFERENCES

11 Under the closing rate/net investment method of translating the financial statements of foreign entities, the amounts in the balance sheet of a foreign entity are translated into the reporting currency using the rate of exchange ruling at the balance sheet date. Translation differences arise if this rate differs from that ruling at the previous balance sheet date or at the date of any subsequent capital injection or reduction. Such translation differences are taken to reserves and reported in the statement of total recognised gains and losses in accordance with paragraph 53 of SSAP 20 'Foreign currency translation' and paragraph 27 of FRS 3 'Reporting financial performance'.

12 Where the parent undertaking and the subsidiary undertaking report at present in different national currencies of participating Member States the question arises as to what impact the irrevocable locking of national currencies of participating Member States to the euro will have on cumulative translation differences that have been recognised in periods before the introduction of the euro.

****Editor's note:** *FRS 12 'Provisions, Contingent Liabilities and Contingent Assets', issued September 1998, implemented these proposals of FRED 14.**

†*The entity and the country in which it reports may not, themselves, be changing over to the euro.*

FRS 3 makes it clear that the same gains and losses should not be recognised twice. The exchange differences have already been recognised through the statement of total recognised gains and losses and consequently there is no question of reporting them in the profit and loss account when such cumulative differences become permanent.* 13

ANTICIPATORY HEDGES EXISTING AT THE DATE OF INTRODUCTION OF THE EURO

Foreign exchange contracts (and other financial instruments) are often used to hedge currency risk. With the introduction of the euro the exchange risk between currency units of two participating Member States will disappear. The issue concerns the impact this would have on hedges of future transactions existing at the date the euro is introduced. 14

There is no accounting standard dealing with anticipatory hedges. The UITF considered the issue in the context of an entity with an accounting policy of deferring gains and losses on anticipatory hedges and recognising them in the profit and loss account in the same period as the related income or expense being hedged. The UITF concluded that the introduction of the euro would have no impact on the accounting treatment adopted at present and accordingly gains and losses would continue to be deferred.† 15

APPLICATION TO SMALLER ENTITIES

Reporting entities applying the Financial Reporting Standard for Smaller Entities currently applicable are exempt from this Abstract. However, where the impact of the changeover to the euro is likely to be significant, smaller entities are encouraged to consider the matters addressed in this Abstract. 16

UITF CONSENSUS

The UITF reached a consensus that the costs of making the necessary modifications to assets to deal with the euro should be written off to the profit and loss account except in those cases where (a) an entity already has an accounting policy to capitalise assets of the relevant type and (b) to the extent that the expenditure clearly results in an enhancement of an asset beyond that originally assessed rather than merely maintaining its service potential. Other costs associated with the introduction of the euro should also be written off to the profit and loss account. 17

Expenditure incurred in preparing for the changeover to the euro and regarded as exceptional should be disclosed in accordance with FRS 3. Particulars of commitments at the balance sheet date in respect of costs to be incurred (whether to be treated as capital or revenue) should be disclosed where they are regarded as relevant to assessing the entity's state of affairs. Where the potential impact is likely to be significant to the entity, the UITF recommends that other information and 18

***Editor's note:** For companies complying with FRS 23 this paragraph now reads as follows:*
Although the introduction of the euro will have made the exchange differences that have already been recognised through the statement of total recognised gains and losses permanent, there is no resulting change in their accounting treatment. It will not, for example, result in the cumulative differences being reported in the profit and loss account.

†***Editor's note:** For companies complying with FRS 23 this paragraph now reads as follows:*
Anticipatory hedges are dealt with in FRS 26. the introduction of the Euro would, under that standard, have no impact on the accounting treatment adopted for anticipatory hedges.

discussion should be given, including an indication of the total costs likely to be incurred. This information may be more appropriately located in the directors' report or any operating and financial review or other statement included in the annual report published by the entity.

19 Following the principle set out in FRS 3, cumulative foreign exchange translation differences recognised in the statement of total recognised gains and losses in accordance with SSAP 20 should remain in reserves after the introduction of the euro and should not be reported in the profit and loss account.*

20 Where gains and losses on financial instruments used as anticipatory hedges are at present deferred and matched with the related income or expense in a future period, the introduction of the euro should not alter this deferral and matching treatment.

DATE FROM WHICH EFFECTIVE

21 This consensus should be adopted as soon as practicable, but in any event for accounting periods ending on or after 23 March 1998.

REFERENCES

Legislation

Great Britain and Northern Ireland

Companies Act 1985 and Companies (Northern Ireland) Order 1986:
Schedule 4 – paragraph 50(5)
Schedule 8 – paragraph 46(5)
Schedule 9 – paragraph 66(3)
Schedule 9A – paragraph 70(5)

Republic of Ireland

Companies (Amendment) Act 1986: Schedule paragraph 36(6)
European Communities (Credit Institutions: Accounts) Regulations 1992: Schedule, Part 1, paragraph 66(4)
European Communities (Insurance Undertakings: Accounts) Regulations 1996: Schedule, Part III, paragraph 18(5)

Accounting Standards and ASB Statements

FRS 3 'Reporting Financial Performance' – paragraphs 2, 5, 19, 27 and 56
FRS 5 'Reporting the Substance of Transactions' – paragraphs 2 and 4
SSAP 20 'Foreign currency translation' – paragraphs 51, 53 and 57
ASB Statement 'Operating and Financial Review' – paragraphs 13–18.

***Editor's note:** *For companies complying with FRS 23 this paragraph now reads as follows:*
Cumulative foreign exchange translation differences recognised in the statement of total recognised gains and losses in accordance with FRS 23 should remain in reserves on the introduction of the euro; they should not be reported in the profit and loss account simply because of the euro's introduction.

Appendix
Further accounting issues arising from the introduction of the euro

(Issued August 1998)

The UITF has been asked for its views on how certain requirements should be applied in the context of the introduction of the euro. The opportunity has been taken to provide clarification in this Appendix, as many entities are likely to be affected, including some that are outside participating Member States. However, this Appendix deals mainly with issues that arise for those companies with a functional (or in SSAP 20's terms 'local') currency that is participating in monetary union. This Appendix has the same status as the Abstract itself.

Introduction

Although the euro had not been envisaged when SSAP 20 was published in 1983, the underlying principles of the SSAP nevertheless remain applicable following the introduction of the euro. It needs to be remembered that the introduction of the euro does not alter the reality that participating Member States had, in the periods before the introduction of the euro, exchange rates between themselves that were different from the fixed conversion rates applicable from 1 January 1999. Users of financial information therefore need to be aware that an exchange rate effect may be embodied in information related to periods before the introduction of the euro and that relationships between figures, although they may be stated in euro for the convenience of readers ('a convenience translation'), will vary depending on whether figures in the previous reporting currency were themselves the result of translation at the time. This aspect is considered further below (see question 1).

The following questions and answers elaborate on issues that have been raised.

1 What translation rate should be used where an entity chooses to provide a convenience translation of its financial statements, including comparative amounts in respect of accounting periods before the introduction of the euro?

The euro will be the continuation of each national currency of participating Member States from 1 January 1999. Where an entity presents a convenience translation of its financial statements into euro, including comparative amounts for accounting periods ending before the introduction of the euro, the original reporting currency amounts should be translated at that currency's conversion rate to the euro established at 1 January 1999. It is not appropriate to rework the translations underlying the preparation of the original financial statements in the relevant national currency of the Member State. For example, a French subsidiary of an Irish company may have had level profits for two consecutive years when expressed in francs. However, when expressed in punts the figures will have reflected the change in the punt/franc exchange rate over the two years and the profits expressed in punts are unlikely to be level. Translation of the franc figures into euro should be carried out by first translating them into punts at the exchange rates ruling at the relevant dates and then translating those figures into euro.

It would be helpful if the notes to the financial statements explained that the trends over the years are exactly the same as if the financial statements for all periods had been expressed in the previous national denomination. Expression of these historical amounts in euro does not eliminate or alter any translation effect that existed when they were originally reported in the currency of the Member State. The UITF recommends that entities should disclose the previous national denomination applicable when information on periods before 1 January 1999 is presented in euro.

2 What exchange rate should be used for financial statements with year-ends other than 31 December (for example, should the fixed conversion rates be anticipated in respect of balances at dates earlier than the date of introduction of the euro)?

The normal rules in SSAPS 17 and 20 should apply and exchange rate changes between the year-end (say September 1998) and 1 January 1999 should continue to be treated as non-adjusting events. At present it is possible for an exchange gain on an unsettled amount at a year-end to be recognised, although subsequently the gain could turn into a loss when the amount is settled. Both periods report what has happened in the relevant period. If, for example, a company with a September 1998 year-end includes in its assets and liabilities foreign currency amounts with participating Member States (amounts that may not be settled until after 1 January 1999) it would not be appropriate to record the balances at other than the closing rate at the end of September 1998.

3 Is any special treatment needed for apparent differences arising from the use of the temporal method as, for example, the same asset may be reported at a different euro figure in a subsidiary's own accounts and in the group accounts?

The temporal method is described in paragraphs 21-24 of SSAP 20. It is possible that there could be a different euro figure for the same asset (acquired before 1 January 1999) in a subsidiary's own accounts and in the group accounts, but this is a natural consequence of the temporal method, which preserves in group accounts the historical rates of exchange at which transactions were undertaken. If the functional currency of a subsidiary changes or becomes the same as the functional currency of its parent because exchange rates become fixed, it is not appropriate to restate prior year figures as if the functional currency had been different from what it actually was at the relevant time. If a revaluation of the asset was incorporated in the financial statements, it would be translated at the rate ruling at the date of revaluation. If that date were at or after the changeover to the euro the asset would appear in the financial statements of both the subsidiary and the group accounts at the same amount.

4 Does the introduction of the euro and the fixing of exchange rates mean that exchange gains on unsettled items (in respect of currencies of countries in participating Member States) become realised?

The UITF notes that the European Commission's paper 'Accounting for the introduction of the euro', published in June 1997, concludes that such gains should be treated as realised. However, SSAP 20 requires continuous recognition of gains and losses on all monetary items, even long-term ones, whether realised or not. There is no cause to recognise any further gain or loss when realisation takes place.

UITF abstract 22: The acquisition of a Lloyd's business

(Issued June 1998)

BACKGROUND

In accordance with the requirements of Lloyd's, Lloyd's syndicates adopt a fund basis of accounting, under which underwriting accounts are not closed for at least three years. Syndicates are managed by managing agents who are usually entitles, under the management agreement, to commissions equivalent to a shore in the syndicates' profits, which will not be known with certainty until the accounts are closed. 1

THE ISSUE

The issue concerns the recognition of assets and liabilities when a business such as a Lloyd's managing agent is acquired. FRS 7 'Fair Values in Acquisition Accounting' required that, on an acquisition, the assets and liabilities that are recognised 'should be those of the acquired entity that existed at the date of the acquisition' (paragraph 5). The issue is whether profit commissions receivable in respect of years that are not yet closed should be included in these assets. 2

One view is that such commissions should not be included. This is because they are inherently uncertain and would not be reflected in the agent's accounts (or those of its acquirer) until the syndicates' accounts are closed. If these commissions were included as assets on acquisition, there would be a hiatus in the amount of profit reported in the acquirer's accounts in the years following the acquisition. 3

Another view is that the commissions are clearly an asset of the acquired business. They will normally be reflected in the price paid to acquire the business. Supporters of this view point out that it is a basic principle of acquisition accounting that profits earned before the date of acquisition are not reported as post-acquisition profits. It is a normal consequence of accounting for the acquisition of a business with a long operating cycle (for example a life assurance business) that there is some discontinuity in the stream of reported profits, and Lloyd's simply provides an extreme example of this. 4

FRS 7 states that contingent assets are amongst the identifiable assets and liabilities recognised on an acquisition, and that assets and liabilities not normally recognised in accounts in the absence of an acquisition may be included in those assets. In particular, FRS 7 states that the recognition of an acquired contingent asset represents the expectation that the amount expended on its acquisition will be recovered, and does not anticipate a future gain. Recognition of an asset in respect of commissions receivable would be consistent with this view. 5

A similar issue arises in respect of the acquisition of Lloyd's members agents or Lloyd's corporate capital vehicles. The principles of FRS 7 would again require the identifiable assets and liabilities recognised to reflect an estimate of the profit or loss of the business that had arisen in respect of periods before the acquisition. 6

FRS 7 permits provisional valuations to be used if it has not been possible to complete the investigation of fair values by the date on which the first post-acquisition financial statements of the acquirer are approved by the directors. These provisional valuations should be amended if necessary in the next financial statements with a corresponding adjustment to goodwill. 7

APPLICATION TO SMALLER ENTITIES

8 Reporting entities applying the Financial Reporting Standard for Smaller Entities currently applicable are exempt from this Abstract.

UITF CONSENSUS

9 The UITF reached a consensus that, on the acquisition of a Lloyd's managing agent, the identifiable assets and liabilities to be recognised include all profit commissions receivable in respect of periods before the acquisition, including those relating to years that are not yet closed.

10 Such profit commissions receivable should be recognised at their fair value, based on the best estimate of the likely outcome based on profits earned before the date of acquisition.*

11 Similarly, the UITF reached a consensus that, on the acquisition of a business with analogous circumstances to those of a Lloyd's managing agent, such as a Lloyd's member agent or Lloyd's corporate capital vehicle, the identifiable assets and liabilities to be recognised should reflect an estimate of the profit or loss of the business that had arisen in respect of periods before the acquisition, including those relating to years that are not yet closed. The fair value of the acquired assets and liabilities should again be based on the best estimate of the likely outcome.

DATE FROM WHICH EFFECTIVE

12 The accounting treatment required by this consensus should be adopted in respect of acquisitions first accounted for in financial statements relating to accounting periods ending on or after 23 December 1998. Earlier adoption is encouraged but not required.

REFERENCES

Legislation

Great Britain and Northern Ireland

Companies Act 1985 and Companies (Northern Ireland) Order 1986
Schedule 4A paragraph 9†

Republic of Ireland

European Communities (Companies: Group Accounts) Regulations, 1992 Regulation 19

Accounting Standards

FRS 7 'Fair Values in Acquisition Accounting' paragraphs 5, 6, 15, 23-25 and 34-37.

Editor's note: *A Technical Release issued by the Institute of Chartered Accountants in England & Wales in January 1999 (Tech 1/99 – Accounting by Lloyd's Corporate Capital Vehicles) provides guidance on how this estimate should be made.*

†***Editor's note:*** *For accounting periods beginning on or after 6 April 2008 this changes to Paragraph 9 of Schedule 6 to the Large and Medium-sized Companies and Groups (Accounts and Reports) Regulations 2008 (SI 2008/410).*

UITF abstract 23: Application of the transitional rules in FRS 15

(Issued May 2000)

THE ISSUE

An issue has been raised on the application of paragraphs 106 and 108 of FRS 15 'Tangible fixed assets' and how widely the prior period adjustment approach may be used. The relevant basic requirement of FRS 15 is paragraph 83, which states: 1

'83 Where the tangible fixed asset comprises two or more major components with substantially different useful economic lives, each component should be accounted for separately for depreciation purposes and depreciated over its individual useful economic life.'

Paragraphs 36–41 also discuss the treatment of expenditure on components.

The transitional rules in paragraphs 106 and 108 are as follows: 2

'106 Except as provided for in paragraph 108, revisions to the useful economic lives and residual values of tangible fixed assets recognised on adoption of the FRS are not the result of a change in accounting policy and should be treated in accordance with paragraphs 93–96 [i.e. prospectively] and, not as prior period adjustments.'

'108 Where, on adoption of the FRS, entities separate tangible fixed assets into different components with significantly different useful economic lives for depreciation purposes, in accordance with paragraphs 36–41 and 83–85, the changes should be dealt with as prior period adjustments, as a change in accounting policy.'

Prior to the adoption of FRS 15 an entity may have based its depreciation policy on the whole of an asset, such as property, while recognising that certain components, such as lifts, had a substantially shorter life than the property as a whole: the cost of replacement of such components would have been provided for by means of a provision (prior to FRS 12) or written off as incurred. On adoption of FRS 15 an entity may at the same time (a) identify one or more separate components with significantly different useful economic lives from the remainder of the asset and (b) amend the residual value and/or economic useful life of the remainder of the asset. A typical example would be where the lifts within a building are to be treated as a separate component and depreciated separately and at the same time the building itself is to be depreciated for the first time. The question is whether the effect of both aspects can be combined into a single prior period adjustment under paragraph 108. 3

Since paragraph 106 is expressed as being subject to paragraph 108, it could be read as placing no limits on the extent to which prior period adjustments could be set up in respect of changes to depreciation rates on the introduction of component accounting. The UITF took the view that paragraph 108 should not be taken as disapplying paragraph 106 with regard to all elements of an asset in which one or more components had been identified on the adoption of FRS 15, but rather as introducing a limited exemption to deal with the situation discussed in paragraph 3 above. The UITF noted that paragraph 106 itself reflects the ongoing requirements for revisions of residual values and/or economic lives (set out in paragraphs 93–96) which is that they should be reflected prospectively over the remaining useful life of the asset. Allocating a shorter life to components of an asset does not itself involve changing the life/residual value placed previously on the asset as a whole. However, 4 reviewing the asset as a whole may also give rise to changes in the estimates of its life/residual value: such changes should be dealt with prospectively.

5 FRS 15 notes that land and buildings are separable components and are dealt with separately for accounting purposes, even when they are acquired together (paragraph 84). Where they had not previously been treated separately and there had been no charge for depreciation, any depreciation of the buildings component arising from the introduction of FRS 15 should be dealt with prospectively.

6 Before the adoption of FRS 12 'Provisions, contingent liabilities and contingent assets' and FRS 15, the fact that some components deteriorated faster than the asset as a whole might have been recognised by a provision for repairs and maintenance (including major refits or refurbishment and the replacement of major components) rather than by different depreciation rates on the components. On adoption of FRS 12 any such provision would have been eliminated by a prior period adjustment. It follows that it was necessary in FRS 15 to allow prior period treatment in respect of the corresponding adjustment resulting from recomputing cumulative depreciation by reference to components of an asset rather than the asset as a whole.

APPLICATION TO SMALLER ENTITIES

7 Reporting entities applying the Financial Reporting Standard for Smaller Entities currently applicable are exempt from this Abstract.

UITF CONSENSUS

8 The UITF reached a consensus that the prior period adjustment required by paragraph 108 of FRS 15, where components of an asset are identified, should be restricted to the effects of treating separately only those components in respect of which:

(a) any provision for repairs and maintenance (including replacement expenditure) was itself eliminated by prior period adjustment on adoption of FRS 12 or
(b) there has been a change from a previous policy of writing off as incurred relevant repairs and maintenance expenditure (including replacement expenditure) to a policy whereby such expenditure is capitalised because it replaces a separately depreciated component.

In particular, any prior period adjustment should not embrace any changes to the useful economic lives or residual values of the remainder of the asset.

DATE FROM WHICH EFFECTIVE

9 The accounting treatment required by this consensus should be adopted as soon as practicable, but in any event in financial statements relating to accounting periods ending on or after 23 March 2000 (the effective date of FRS 15).

REFERENCES

FRS 15 'Tangible fixed assets' – paragraphs 36–41, 83–4, 93–96, 106 and 108.
FRS 12 'Provisions, contingent liabilities and contingent assets' – paragraphs 14, 101 and Example 11 in Appendix III.

Appendix
Illustrative Example

Assume a building with a cost of £1 million, on which before FRS 15 no depreciation had been charged on the ground that any depreciation was immaterial. Inflation is ignored.

Ten years after the purchase of the building FRS 15 is adopted and the lifts within the building are identified as a separate component with a cost of £150,000 and a 20-year life. Assume (as an example of a paragraph 8 (a) situation) that a provision for the replacement of the lifts had been built up, amounting to £75,000 (10/20 2 £150,000). However, on the adoption of FRS 12 the provision is eliminated as a prior period adjustment.

Clearly the lifts have been in existence since the date of purchase and have always had a cost and a life (and possibly a residual value, assumed to be nil in this case).

On adoption of FRS 15 the lifts are formally recognised as a separate component in accordance with the standard and cumulative depreciation of £75,000 (being the difference between the amount of depreciation previously charged, i.e., nil in this case, and the recalculated amount) is charged in respect of that component by way of prior period adjustment in accordance with paragraph 108. In this case, this is equal and opposite to the prior period adjustment required on the adoption of FRS 12 (for simplicity it has been assumed that FRS 12 and FRS 15 were adopted at the same time, which may not have been the case in practice). This adjustment, of itself, should not result in revision of any depreciation previously charged in respect of the building excluding the lifts (nil in this example).

If (as an example of a paragraph 8 (b) situation) no provision had been made for replacement of the lifts, but the policy had been to write off as incurred the replacement of major components such as lifts, then the prior period adjustment on the adoption of FRS 15 would be £75,000 cumulative depreciation as above. When the lift is eventually replaced the new lift will be capitalised as it replaces a separately depreciated component.

In both examples above, any change to the life (or residual value) of the building as a whole should be accounted for prospectively under paragraph 106. Thus if the building was given a revised useful economic life of 50 years (i.e., a remaining useful economic life of 40 years) on adoption of FRS 15, the depreciation on the building (excluding the separately depreciated lift) would be accounted for prospectively, i.e., £21,250 per year (1/40 × £850,000).

UITF abstract 24: Accounting for start-up costs

(Issued June 2000)

THE ISSUE

1 The issue is whether start-up costs that cannot be included in the cost of a fixed asset may nevertheless be carried forward, for example as a prepayment, deferred expenditure or other kind of asset. FRS 15 'Tangible fixed assets' addresses the accounting for costs associated with a start-up or commissioning period. Paragraph 14 states that such costs should be included in the cost of a tangible fixed asset only where the asset is available for use but incapable of operating at normal levels without such a start-up or commissioning period.

2 FRS 15 includes a section on other start-up costs which notes that:

'there is no justification for regarding costs relating to other start-up periods [i.e., other than essential commissioning costs, which are regarded as part of the cost of the asset], where the asset is available for use but not yet operating at normal levels, for example because of a lack of demand, as part of the cost of the asset. An example is the start-up period of a new hotel or bookshop, which could operate at normal levels almost immediately, but for which experience teaches that demand will build up slowly and full utilisation or sales levels will be achieved only over a period of several months.' (paragraph 16)

FRS 15 does not specify how the costs of a start-up period that cannot be included in the cost of a tangible fixed asset should be accounted for.

3 This Abstract addresses whether an entity may apply an accounting treatment in respect of certain costs arising in a start-up period that differs from the treatment it would normally apply to similar costs incurred as part of its on-going activities. In particular, may costs that would usually be recognised as expenses when incurred be capitalised, or otherwise deferred, simply on the grounds that they relate to a new activity? Conversely, may costs that would usually be capitalised, or otherwise deferred, be recognised as expenses when incurred, simply on the grounds that they relate to a new activity?

4 For the purpose of this Abstract 'start-up costs' should be construed broadly so as to include costs arising from those one-time activities related to opening a new facility, introducing a new product or service, conducting business in a new territory, conducting business with a new class of customer, initiating a new process in an existing facility, starting some new operation and similar items. They include costs of relocating or reorganising part or all of an entity, costs related to organising a new entity, and expenses and losses incurred both before and after opening.

5 The UITF took the view that start-up costs should be treated in the same manner as similar costs incurred as part of the entity's on-going activities.

6 In the case of costs that are regarded as peculiar to a start-up activity, such that there are no similar costs incurred as part of the entity's on-going activities, the issue is whether the costs should be recognised as an asset or as an expense when incurred. Assets are defined as 'rights or other access to future economic benefits controlled by an entity as a result of past transactions or events'. Assets are recognised in financial statements only if certain criteria are met. The UITF took the view that, in general, start-up costs do not meet these criteria because the relationship between the expenditure and any future economic benefits that may be derived from that

expenditure is usually not sufficiently certain to warrant recognising start-up costs as assets and that, in particular, in most cases it is inappropriate to carry forward start-up costs as prepayments or deferred expenditure. Accordingly, the UITF concluded that start-up costs should be recognised as an expense when incurred unless they meet the specific conditions for recognition as assets under a relevant accounting standard, such as FRS 15, FRS 10 'Goodwill and intangible assets' or SSAP 13 'Accounting for research and development'.

The UITF noted that this conclusion is consistent with IAS 38 'Intangible Assets' paragraphs 56 and 57 and is similar to the requirements on start-up costs in the USA. 7

APPLICATION TO SMALLER ENTITIES

Reporting entities applying the Financial Reporting Standard for Smaller Entities currently applicable are exempt from this Abstract. 8

UITF CONSENSUS

The UITF reached a consensus that: 9

(a) start-up costs should be accounted for on a basis consistent with the accounting treatment of similar costs incurred as part of the entity's on-going activities; and

(b) in cases where there are no such similar costs, start-up costs that do not meet the criteria for recognition as assets under a relevant accounting standard, such as FRS 15 'Tangible fixed assets', FRS 10 'Goodwill and intangible assets' or SSAP 13 'Accounting for research and development', should be recognised as an expense when they are incurred. They should not be carried forward as an asset.

Where start-up costs meet the definition of exceptional items in FRS 3 'Reporting financial performance' they should be disclosed in accordance with that Standard. Entities are encouraged to give additional disclosures regarding start-up costs in accordance with paragraphs 16-18 of the ASB Statement 'Operating and Financial Review'. 10

DATE FROM WHICH EFFECTIVE

The accounting treatment required by this consensus should be adopted in financial statements relating to accounting periods ending on or after 23 July 2000, but earlier adoption is encouraged. 11

REFERENCES

ASB pronouncements

FRS 3 'Reporting financial performance' – paragraph 19
FRS 5 'Reporting the substance of transactions' – paragraphs 2 and 20
FRS 10 'Goodwill and intangible assets' – paragraph 14
FRS 15 'Tangible fixed assets' – paragraphs 14–16
SSAP 13 'Accounting for research and development' – paragraphs 25 and 26
ASB Statement 'Operating and financial review' – paragraphs 16–18

Other pronouncements

IAS 38 'Intangible assets' – paragraphs 56 and 57
AICPA (USA) Statement of Position 98–5 'Reporting on the costs of start-up activities'

UITF abstract 25: National Insurance contributions on share option gains

(Issued July 2000)

BACKGROUND

1 The Social Security Act 1998 introduced a National Insurance charge on UK employers on the gains made by employees upon exercise of options issued under unapproved share option schemes (i.e., those not approved by the Inland Revenue). The charge applies to options granted after 5 April 1999. The gain on which National Insurance contributions are payable is the difference between the share price at the date the options are exercised and the exercise price paid by the employee. This applies to those schemes where the shares are 'readily convertible assets', i.e., they can be sold on a stock exchange or there are arrangements in place that allow the employees to obtain cash for the shares.

THE ISSUE

2 The issue is whether the employer should accrue for the estimated liability between the grant date and the exercise date, which is when it becomes payable, and, if so, how the liability should be calculated.

3 FRS 12 'Provisions, contingent liabilities and contingent assets' requires a provision to be recognised when:

(a) an entity has a present obligation (legal or constructive) as a result of a past event;

(b) it is probable that a transfer of economic benefits will be required to settle the obligation; and

(c) a reliable estimate can be made of the amount of the obligation.

4 The UITF regards the granting of the option as the past event that gives rise to a present obligation to pay National Insurance when the option is exercised. By granting the option, the employer has exposed itself to an obligation to pay National Insurance, which exists independently of the employer's future actions. Only the amount payable is uncertain, as it is not possible to make a reliable estimate of what the employer's share price will be at a future date when the option may be exercised. However, when the amount of the obligation at an intervening balance sheet date is considered FRS 12 requires the amount recognised as a provision to be the best estimate of the expenditure required to settle the present obligation at the balance sheet date (paragraph 36). The market price of the shares provides a reliable basis for making such an estimate.

5 Where it is thought probable that a cash outflow will occur, a liability should be accrued over the performance period in respect of that probable future cash outflow, to the extent that the employees have performed their side of the arrangement. For example, if the terms of the arrangement require the employees to perform services over a three-year period, the liability should be accrued over that three-year period. The UITF therefore agreed that provision should be made systematically by reference to the market value of the shares at the balance sheet dates over the period from the date of grant to the end of the performance period; from that date to the date of actual exercise, the provision should be adjusted by reference to changes in market value. Where there is no performance period full provision should be made immediately. The performance period is the period during which the employee performs

the services necessary to become unconditionally entitled to the options, which may entail satisfying specified performance criteria or remaining in the company's employment for a specified period of time.

Legislation now before Parliament (the Child Support, Pensions and Social Security Bill) would permit the employer's National Insurance contributions to be recovered from or transferred to the employee. Where there is an agreement between employer and employee under which the employee agrees to reimburse all or part of the employer's National Insurance contributions, FRS 12 requires a provision for the full amount to be made and the expected reimbursement to be treated as a separate asset if receipt is virtually certain, with a net presentation permitted in the profit and loss account. Where there is a joint election by employer and employee under which the liability is formally transferred to the employee there is no liability to appear in the employer's accounts. 6

FRS 12 requires, for each class of provision, disclosure of an indication of the uncertainties about the amount or timing of the eventual transfer of economic benefits and, where necessary to provide adequate information, the major assumptions made concerning future events (paragraph 90). In the case of a provision for National Insurance on share options, disclosure of the share price and of the effect of a significant movement in that price may be necessary to provide a full understanding of these factors. 7

This Abstract addresses National Insurance contributions on share option gains. However, the principles apply to other analogous situations that give rise to employer's National Insurance liabilities. 8

APPLICATION TO SMALLER ENTITIES

Reporting entities applying the Financial Reporting Standard for Smaller Entities currently applicable are exempt from this Abstract. 9

UITF CONSENSUS

The UITF reached a consensus that provision should be made for National Insurance contributions on outstanding share options that are expected to be exercised. It should be calculated at the latest enacted National Insurance rate applied to the difference between the market value of the underlying shares at the balance sheet date and the option exercise price and allocated over the period from the date of grant* to the end of the performance period; from that date to the date of actual exercise the provision should be adjusted by using the current market value of the shares. Where there is no performance period full provision should be made immediately. 10

All amounts provided for in respect of National Insurance contributions in accordance with paragraph 10 should be charged to the profit and loss account, except insofar as they form part of staff costs capitalised under companies legislation and accounting standards. Any reimbursement by employees should be accounted for in accordance with paragraphs 56–61 of FRS 12. 11

****Editor's note:*** *See also UITF Abstract 30 'Date of award to employees of shares or rights to shares'.*

DATE FROM WHICH EFFECTIVE

12 The accounting treatment required by this consensus should be adopted in financial statements relating to accounting periods ending on or after 22 September 2000, but earlier adoption is encouraged.

REFERENCES AND LEGAL CONSIDERATIONS

FRS 12 'Provisions, contingent liabilities and contingent assets' – paragraphs 14, 36, 37, 56–61 and 90.

The effect of paragraph 94 of Schedule 4 to the Companies Act 1985* is that the National Insurance charge required by this Abstract is included as part of staff costs in the profit and loss account.†

The UITF has received legal advice that National Insurance contributions on share option gains do not constitute an expense of an issue of shares such as to allow the share premium account to be applied in writing off the expense in terms of the Companies Act 1985 section 130(2).‡

**In Northern Ireland – the Companies (Northern Ireland) Order 1986 Schedule 4 paragraph 92; in the Republic of Ireland – the Companies (Amendment) Act 1986 Schedule paragraph 74*

*†**Editor's note:** For accounting periods beginning on or after 6 April 2008 this changes to Paragraph 14 of Schedule 10 to the Large and Medium-sized Companies and Groups (Accounts and Reports) Regulations 2008 (SI 2008/410).*

‡In Northern Ireland – the Companies (Northern Ireland) Order 1986 Article 140; in the Republic Ireland – the Companies Act 1963 section 62(2)

Appendix
Illustrative example of the consensus in paragraphs 10 and 11

The company's year-end is 31 December.

A maximum of 10,000 share options are granted at 1 July 1999, when the market value is £1, at an exercise price of £1, dependent upon performance from 1 July 1999 to 30 June 2002. The options are exercisable from 1 July 2002 to 1 July 2003.

Employer's National Insurance contributions, currently at 12.2 per cent, are payable on exercise of the options.

31 December 1999
The market value of a share is £1.80. It is estimated that the maximum entitlement of options will be exercised.

National Insurance charge for the year: one-sixth of 12.2% of 10,000 x (£1.80 - £1) = £163.

31 December 2000
The market value of a share is £3.00. Again the full entitlement is expected to be exercised.

National Insurance cumulative charge: one-half of 12.2% of 10,000 x (£3.00 - £1) = £1,220
[Charge for the year : £1,220 - £163 = £1,057]

31 December 2001
The market value of a share is £2.80. It is now expected that only 8,000 share options will be exercised.

National Insurance cumulative charge: five-sixths of 12.2% x 8,000 x (£2.80 - £1) = £1,464
[Charge for the year: £1,464 - £1,220 = £244]

31 December 2002
The market value of a share is £2.20. Only 6,000 share options vested; none of these have been exercised.

National Insurance cumulative charge: 12.2% x 6,000 x (£2.20 - £1) = £878
[Credit for the year : £1,464 - £878 = £586]

31 December 2003
The 6,000 share options were exercised on 17 May 2003 when the market value of a share was £2.65.

The National Insurance liability was therefore: 12.2% x 6,000 x (£2.65 - £1) = £1,208
[Charge for the year: £1,208 - £878 = £330]

UITF abstract 26: Barter transactions for advertising

(Issued 9 November 2000)

THE ISSUE

1 An entity such as a publisher or broadcaster may agree to provide advertising in exchange for advertising services provided by its customer, rather than for a cash consideration. For example, it has recently become common for companies that provide commercial websites to display advertisements in exchange for advertising of their own services on another website. Such an exchange gives rise to the question of what amount, if any, should be included in reported turnover and expense.

2 Although this issue has no overall effect on the total profit or loss, it does affect the amount of turnover, which is often cited as a significant measure of performance for internet companies.

3 The recognition criteria in the Statement of Principles for Financial Reporting require (a) sufficient evidence and (b) measurement at a monetary amount with sufficient reliability. Where advertising services are provided for a cash consideration, the transaction evidences the value of the services provided. In contrast, where advertising is provided in exchange for advertising received, the arrangement provides little or no evidence of the value of the services provided.

4 The UITF decided that it would be appropriate to recognise turnover and costs in respect of barter transactions for advertising only if there is persuasive evidence of the value at which, if the advertising had not been exchanged, it would have been sold for cash in a similar transaction. The UITF believed that such circumstances would be rare.

5 The UITF noted that this conclusion is consistent with a recent consensus of the Emerging Issues Task Force in the USA (Accounting for Advertising Barter Transactions – Issue No 99-17).

6 This Abstract applies to barter transactions for advertising, whether on the internet, or on television, in magazines, on poster sites or by another medium.

7 FRS 5 'Reporting the substance of transactions' requires that, in determining the substance of a transaction to be reported, all its aspects and implications should be identified and greater weight given to those more likely to have commercial effect in practice. Accordingly, an arrangement should be regarded as a barter transaction where that fairly reflects its substance. This may be the case where a contract to provide advertising for a cash consideration is made on the understanding that a similar reciprocal contract is entered into. It may also be the case where the purchaser of advertising agrees to procure advertising services from another party in exchange rather than provide them itself.

8 This Abstract has been developed in the context of barter transactions for advertising. A distinctive feature of such transactions is that they involve little or no marginal cost. Application of this Abstract is not mandatory for barter transactions for services other than advertising, although its principles may be relevant to such transactions.

APPLICATION TO SMALLER ENTITIES

Reporting entities applying the Financial Reporting Standard for Smaller Entities currently applicable are exempt from this Abstract. 9

UITF CONSENSUS

The UITF reached a consensus that turnover and costs in respect of barter transactions for advertising should not be recognised unless there is persuasive evidence of the value at which, if the advertising had not been exchanged, it would have been sold for cash in a similar transaction. In these circumstances, that value should be included in turnover and costs. 10

Persuasive evidence of the value of advertising exchanged will exist only where it can be demonstrated that similar advertising has been sold for cash. This will be the case only where the entity has a history of selling similar advertising for cash, and where substantially all of the turnover from advertising within the accounting period is represented by cash sales. 11

To provide evidence of the value of advertising exchanged, cash sales of advertising must be similar in all significant respects. This requires that the cash sales are of advertising space in the same vehicle (for example, the same website or magazine) as that exchanged, and must have taken place within a reasonably short period of the exchange transaction (in no case more than six months before or after it). There must also be no other factors that would be expected to make the value of the advertising sold for cash significantly different from that exchanged. Specific factors to consider include: 12

- circulation, exposure, or saturation within an intended market;
- timing (time of day, day of week, daily, weekly, 24 hours a day/7 days a week, and season of the year);
- prominence (page on website, section of periodical, location on page, and size of advertisement);
- demographics of readers, viewers, or customers;
- duration (length of time advertising will be displayed).

The above list is not intended to be exhaustive.

Even where similar advertising has been sold for cash, it is necessary to consider whether in the light of all available information there is persuasive evidence of the value at which the advertising exchanged would have been sold if not exchanged. Specific factors that may be relevant include: 13

- the entity's practice in setting prices for the advertising it provides, and the circumstances in which discounts are offered;
- the probability that, if the advertising were not exchanged, a cash sale would have taken place;
- the value to the entity of the advertising received in exchange, and the evidence that the entity would have been willing to buy that advertising for cash if it had not been able to obtain it through an exchange transaction.

Entities should disclose in the notes to the financial statements the total amount of barter transactions for advertising that is included in turnover. Entities are encouraged to disclose information on the volume and type of such transactions and other kinds of barter transaction (whether or not included in turnover). 14

DATE FROM WHICH EFFECTIVE

15 The accounting treatment required by the consensus should be adopted in financial statements relating to accounting periods ending on or after 23 December 2000, but earlier adoption is encouraged.

REFERENCES

ASB pronouncements

FRS 5 'Reporting the Substance of Transactions' – paragraph 14

ASB Statement of Principles for Financial Reporting – Chapter 5

Other pronouncements

EITF Consensus (USA) 'Accounting for Advertising Barter Transactions' (Issue No 99–17)

UITF abstract 27: Revision to estimates of the useful economic life of goodwill and intangible assets

(Issued December 2000)

THE ISSUE

Paragraph 19 of FRS 10 states that 'There is a rebuttable presumption that the useful economic lives of purchased goodwill and intangible assets are limited to periods of 20 years or less.' Paragraph 33 states that 'The useful economic lives of goodwill and intangible assets should be reviewed at the end of each reporting period and revised if necessary. If a useful economic life is revised, the carrying value ... should be amortised over the revised remaining useful economic life.' 1

An entity may rebut the presumption because there is evidence that its goodwill (or intangible asset) has an indefinite life: in these circumstances no amortisation is charged. In a subsequent year, the entity may decide that it no longer wishes or is now unable to rebut the presumption. Amortisation over a period of up to 20 years from the date of acquisition would be necessary. The issue is whether such a change should be treated as a change of accounting policy (with a consequential prior period adjustment) or a change of useful economic life (and thus accounted for prospectively in accordance with paragraph 33 of FRS 10). 2

The UITF took the view that a decision not to rebut the presumption is not a change of accounting policy but rather a change in the way in which useful economic life is estimated. This is because the FRS does not allow a choice of policies; goodwill should be amortised unless its life is indefinite. What the FRS does allow is two different sets of assumptions for estimating useful economic life. The change referred to in paragraph 2 above is simply from one permitted way of estimating useful economic life to another, more prudent, one. 3

APPLICATION TO SMALLER ENTITIES

Reporting entities applying the Financial Reporting Standard for Smaller Entities currently applicable are exempt from this Abstract. 4

UITF CONSENSUS

The UITF reached a consensus that, other than on the initial implementation of FRS 10: 5

(a) where estimates of the useful economic lives of goodwill or intangible assets are revised, the carrying value should be amortised over the revised remaining useful economic life, as required by paragraph 33 of FRS 10; and
(b) this requirement applies equally where the presumption of a 20-year life has previously been rebutted, as it does to other revisions of estimates of the useful economic lives of goodwill and intangible assets.

DATE FROM WHICH EFFECTIVE

The accounting treatment required by this consensus should be adopted with immediate effect. Where applicable, corresponding amounts should be restated. 6

REFERENCES

FRS 10 'Goodwill and intangible assets' – paragraphs 19 and 33

UITF abstract 28: Operating lease incentives

(Issued February 2001)

THE ISSUE

In negotiating a new or renewed operating lease, a lessor may provide incentives for the lessee to enter into the agreement. Examples of such incentives are an up-front cash payment to the lessee or the reimbursement or assumption by the lessor of costs of the lessee (such as relocation costs, and costs associated with a pre-existing lease commitment of the lessee). Alternatively, initial periods of the lease term may be agreed to be rent-free or at a reduced rent. 1

The issue is how an incentive for an operating lease should be recognised in the financial statements of the lessee and of the lessor. 2

A payment (or other transfer of value) from a lessor to (or for the benefit of) a lessee should be regarded as a lease incentive when that fairly reflects its substance. A payment to reimburse a lessee for fitting-out costs should be regarded as a lease incentive where the fittings are suitable only for the lessee and accordingly do not add to the value of the property to the lessor. On the other hand, insofar as a reimbursement of expenditure enhances a property generally and causes commensurate benefit to flow to the lessor, it should be treated as reimbursement of expenditure on the property. For example, where the lifts in a building are to be renewed and a lease has only five years to run, a payment made by the lessor may not be an inducement to enter into a lease but payment for an improvement to the lessor's property. 3

This Abstract does not deal with incentives to surrender leases. However, such incentives should be examined to determine whether in substance the incentive relates to the new lease, particularly where the offer of the incentive is linked to an arrangement to vacate a property under lease from a different lessor. Such consideration should take into account the market rentals applicable to the old and new leases. If it is determined that the incentive, or part of it, relates in substance to the new lease, the provisions of this Abstract apply. 4

SSAP 21 'Accounting for leases and hire purchase contracts' does not deal specifically with accounting for lease incentives. However, it requires lessees to charge operating lease rentals 'on a straight-line basis over the lease term, even if the payments are not made on such a basis, unless another systematic and rational basis is more appropriate.' (paragraph 37) 5

As regards lessors, SSAP 21 requires that 'Rental income from an operating lease, excluding charges for services such as insurance and maintenance, should be recognised on a straight-line basis over the period of the lease, even if the payments are not made on such a basis, unless another systematic and rational basis is more representative of the time pattern in which the benefit from the leased asset is receivable.' (paragraph 43) 6

A lease may be structured in a way that accords with the cash flow needs of the lessee, for example by providing for rental reductions or payments from the lessor when certain costs are incurred by the lessee. An up-front incentive creates a presumption that the subsequent rentals are above the level acceptable to the parties in the market current at the time (even though they may be termed 'market rate'). This is because a lessor's main objective is to obtain the best rent available from the lessee for the property in question and the lessor has no interest in how a lessee spends any up-front incentive paid. 7

8 In accordance with the accruals concept, any incentive should be allocated to match the effect of the increased rentals payable in later periods, so that the financial statements reflect the true effective rental for the premises, irrespective of the particular cash flow arrangements agreed between the parties. The accounting treatment should be similar, however the arrangement is structured.

9 Many leases provide for periodic reviews whereby the rental can be adjusted to the prevailing market rate. In such a case it is necessary to recognise the incentive over the period in which, before taking account of the incentive, the rentals will be other than the market rate. This will generally be the period up to the first review date at which the rental being paid is expected to come into line with the prevailing market rate. Neither SSAP 21 nor the Guidance Notes specifically address the situation where rentals are periodically reviewed.

10 SSAP 19 'Accounting for investment properties' requires investment properties to be reported in the balance sheet at their open market value. That value should not include any amount that is reported as a separate asset, for example as accrued rent receivable, if there would be double-counting of assets. For example, a property might have a value of £20 million reflecting, in part, the rents on a lease that has been negotiated with a tenant. However, if a lease incentive (of say £1 million) was given as part of the negotiation of that rent, the open market value to be reported under investment properties would be £19 million, as the other £1 million would be reported as a separate asset.

11 Where a debtor is recognised in respect of an operating lease incentive, the requirements of UITF Abstract 4 'Presentation of long-term debtors in current assets' may be relevant.

APPLICATION TO SMALLER ENTITIES

12 Reporting entities applying the Financial Reporting Standard for Smaller Entities currently applicable are exempt from this Abstract.

UITF CONSENSUS

13 All incentives for the agreement of a new or renewed operating lease should be recognised as an integral part of the net payment agreed for the use of the leased asset, irrespective of the incentive's nature or form or the timing of payments.

Accounting by lessees

14 A lessee should recognise the aggregate benefit of incentives as a reduction of rental expense. The benefit should be allocated over the shorter of the lease term and a period ending on a date from which it is expected the prevailing market rental will be payable. The allocation should be on a straight-line basis unless another systematic basis is more representative of the time pattern of the lessee's benefit from the use of the leased asset.

Accounting by lessors

15 A lessor should recognise the aggregate cost of incentives as a reduction of rental income. The cost of the incentives should be allocated over the lease term or a shorter period ending on a date from which it is expected the prevailing market rental will be payable. The allocation should be on a straight-line basis unless another systematic

basis is more representative of the time pattern in which the benefit from the leased asset is receivable.

Where a building is accounted for as an investment property, the value at which it is stated in the balance sheet should not include any amount that is reported as a separate asset, for example, as accrued rent receivable. **16**

In accordance with normal accounting practice, an amount recognised as a debtor in respect of an operating lease incentive should be written down to the extent that it is not expected to be recovered. **17**

DATE FROM WHICH EFFECTIVE AND WITHDRAWAL OF UITF ABSTRACT 12

The accounting practices set out in this Abstract should be adopted for financial statements relating to accounting periods ending on or after 22 September 2001 (including corresponding amounts for the immediately preceding period) in respect of lease agreements commencing in the current or the preceding accounting period. Adoption in respect of earlier lease agreements is permitted but not required. **18**

This Abstract supersedes UITF Abstract 12 'Lessee accounting for reverse premiums and similar incentives'.* **19**

REFERENCES

ASB pronouncements

SSAP 19 'Accounting for investment properties', paragraph 11
SSAP 21 'Accounting for leases and hire purchase contracts', paragraphs 37 and 43
FRS 18 'Accounting Policies', paragraphs 26 and 27
UITF Abstract 4 'Presentation of long-term debtors in current assets'

IASC pronouncements

Standing Interpretations Committee, SIC-15 'Operating Leases - Incentives'
IAS 40 'Investment Property', paragraph 44†

**UITF Abstract 12 superseded that part of the guidance given in paragraph 16 of the Guidance Notes on SSAP 21 which suggests that the total rentals should be charged 'over the period in which the assets are in use'.*

†***Editor's note:*** *This is now paragraph 50 of IAS 40 as revised in December 2003.*

APPENDIX

Illustrative examples of the consensus in paragraphs 13-17

The examples each assume a lease for five years. It is assumed that a straight-line allocation basis is the most representative of the benefits. The accounting is illustrated from the perspective of the lessor. The lessee's expense would be equivalent to the lessor's income.

(a) First year rent-free, then four annual rentals of £500

Year	£ Income		£ Cash		£ Debtor	
	For year	Cumulative	Movement in year	Cumulative	Movement in year	Cumulative
1	400	400	—		400	400
2	400	800	500	500	(100)	300
3	400	1,200	500	1,000	(100)	200
4	400	1,600	500	1,500	(100)	100
5	400	2,000	500	2,000	(100)	—

(b) Cash incentive of £1,000 paid, and five rentals of £600

Year	£ Income		£ Cash		£ Debtor	
	For year	Cumulative	Movement in year	Cumulative	Movement in year	Cumulative
1			(1,000)		1,000	
			600		(600)	
	400	400		(400)	400	800
2			600		(600)	
	400	800		200	400	600
3			600		(600)	
	400	1,200		800	400	400
4			600		(600)	
	400	1,600		1,400	400	200
5			600		(600)	
	400	2,000		2,000	400	—

UITF abstract 29: Website development costs

(Issued February 2001)

THE ISSUE

Websites are used for a wide variety of business purposes, including promotion and advertising of products and services; taking orders for products or services; and selling access to information that is contained on the Website. Many companies incur significant costs in developing such Websites. 1

This Abstract addresses the accounting for the development costs of a Website for a company's own use: it does not address the accounting for the costs of developing a Website for another entity. 2

The costs of developing a Website include: 3

(a) *planning costs*—including, for example, the costs of undertaking feasibility studies, determining the objectives and functionalities of the Website, exploring ways of achieving the desired functionalities, identifying appropriate hardware and Web applications and selecting suppliers and consultants.

(b) *application and infrastructure development costs*—including the costs of obtaining and registering a domain name and of buying or developing hardware and operating software that relate to the functionality of the site (for example, updateable content management systems and e-commerce systems, including encryption software, and interfaces with other IT systems used by the entity).

(c) *design costs*—expenditure to develop the design and appearance of individual Website pages, including the creation of graphics.

(d) *content costs*—expenditure incurred on preparing, accumulating and posting the Website content.

Planning costs do not in themselves give rise to future economic benefits that are controlled by the entity. Such costs should not therefore be capitalised as an asset but should be charged to the profit and loss account as incurred. 4

In contrast, the remaining costs of Website development (paragraph 3(b)-(d)) could give rise to an asset, which should be capitalised if the relationship between the expenditure and the future economic benefits is sufficiently certain. 5

However, there is often substantial uncertainty regarding the viability, useful economic life and value of a Website. The UITF took the view that, in relation to amounts spent on the design and content of a Website (paragraph 3(c) and (d)), criteria should be established that ensured that the costs would be capitalised only to the extent that they created an enduring asset and there were reasonable grounds for supposing that future economic benefits in excess of the amounts capitalised would be generated by the Website. In the UITF's opinion, this would be the case only if the Website was capable of generating revenues directly, for example by enabling orders to be placed. 6

The UITF considered whether capitalised Website development costs should be regarded as tangible or as intangible fixed assets. It noted that Websites fitted neither classification perfectly. It also noted the statement in paragraph 2 of FRS 10 'Goodwill and Intangible Assets' that: 7

'Software development costs that are directly attributable to bringing a computer system or other computer-operated machinery into working condition for its intended use within the business are treated as part of the cost of the related hardware rather than as a separate intangible asset.'

8 The UITF decided that certain Website development costs were of the type that FRS 10 envisaged should be treated as tangible fixed assets. It took the view that the reference to the capitalisation of software development costs applied irrespective of whether the hardware on which the software ran was owned by the entity. It further decided that, in the interests of consistency and clarity, all Website development costs should be classified in the same way – separating the costs into tangible and intangible components could be difficult and would serve no practical purpose.

9 Website development costs are subject to the capitalisation, depreciation and impairment review requirements set out in FRS 15 and FRS 11 'Impairment of Fixed Assets and Goodwill'. They are not regarded as 'development costs' of the type referred to in companies legislation.*

APPLICATION TO SMALLER ENTITIES

10 Reporting entities applying the Financial Reporting Standard for Smaller Entities currently applicable are exempt from this Abstract.

UITF CONSENSUS

11 The UITF reached a consensus that:

(a) Website *planning* costs should be charged to the profit and loss account as incurred.
(b) subject to paragraph 12 below, *other Website development costs* should be capitalised as tangible fixed assets, in accordance with the requirements of FRS 15 'Tangible Fixed Assets'.
(c) expenditure to maintain or operate a Website once it has been developed should be charged to the profit and loss account as incurred, in accordance with the requirements of FRS 15.

12 *Design and content* development costs should be capitalised only to the extent that they lead to the creation of an enduring asset delivering benefits at least as great as the amount capitalised. This will be the case only to the extent that

(a) the expenditure is separately identifiable;
(b) the technical feasibility and commercial viability of the Website have been assessed with reasonable certainty in the light of factors such as likely market conditions (including competing products), public opinion, and possible legislation;
(c) the Website will generate sales or other revenues directly† and the expenditure makes an enduring contribution to the development of the revenue-generating capabilities of the Website;

In Great Britain, the Companies Act 1985; in Northern Ireland, the Companies (Northern Ireland) Order 1986; and in the Republic of Ireland, the Companies (Amendment) Act 1986.* ***Editor's note:* *This should now be read as though it also referred to the Companies Act 2006.*

†*For not-for-profit entities, an alternative measure of service potential may be more relevant, in which case paragraphs 12, 14 and 15 should be interpreted as permitting capitalisation only to the extent that the primary purpose of the Website is to provide a means of delivery of the specific services offered by the entity in fulfilment of its principal objectives.*

(d) there is a reasonable expectation that the present value of the future cash flows (ie future revenues less attributable costs) to be generated by the Website will be no less than the amounts capitalised in respect of that revenue-generating activity; and

(e) adequate resources exist, or are reasonably expected to be available, to enable the Website project to be completed and to meet any consequential need for increased working capital.

If there is insufficient evidence on which to base reasonable estimates of the economic benefits that will be generated in the period until the design and content are next updated, the costs of developing the design and content should be charged to the profit and loss account as incurred. **13**

Revenues that can be regarded as arising directly from the Website could include those attributable to orders placed via the Website, amounts paid by subscribers for access to information contained on the Website or advertising revenues obtained by selling advertising space on the Website. If a Website is used only for advertising or promotion of the entity's own products or services, it is unlikely to be possible to provide sufficient evidence to demonstrate that future sales or revenue will be generated directly by the Website. **14**

It is possible that revenues expected to arise directly from the Website will include some that would have been achieved by other means in the absence of the Website. In such circumstances, it will be necessary to consider whether other fixed assets have become impaired as a result of the development of the Website. **15**

As required by paragraph 8 of FRS 11 'Impairment of Fixed Assets and Goodwill', capitalised Website development costs should be reviewed for impairment if events or changes in circumstances indicate that the carrying amount may not be recoverable. **16**

Capitalised Website development costs should be depreciated over their estimated useful economic life, which should be selected and reviewed each period in accordance with the requirements of FRS 15. Given the rapid rate of technological innovation, the useful economic life of a Website is likely to be short. Further, where the design or content of a Website requires more frequent replacement than the Website as a whole, it may be appropriate to select a depreciation period for the cost of the design or content that is shorter than the depreciation period selected for the remainder of the asset. **17**

DATE FROM WHICH EFFECTIVE

The accounting treatment required by this Abstract should be adopted in financial statements relating to accounting periods ending on or after 23 March 2001, but earlier adoption is encouraged. **18**

REFERENCES

ASB pronouncements

FRS 10 'Goodwill and Intangible Assets' paragraph 2
FRS 11 'Impairment of Fixed Assets and Goodwill' paragraph 8
FRS 15 'Tangible Fixed Assets'

Other pronouncements

EITF (USA) Abstract No. 00-2 'Accounting for Web Site Development Costs' March 2000

UITF abstract 31: Exchanges of businesses or other non-monetary assets for an interest in a subsidiary, joint venture or associate

(Issued 18 October 2001

BACKGROUND

1 It is becoming increasingly common for reporting entities to exchange businesses for equity, for example by forming a joint venture combining one of their existing businesses with that of another entity. The UITF has been asked to develop guidance on certain issues that arise in accounting for such transactions.

THE ISSUES

2 This Abstract deals with the treatment in consolidated financial statements of transactions in which an entity (A) exchanges a business or other non-monetary assets for an interest in another entity (B) which thereby becomes A's subsidiary or which is or thereby becomes A's joint venture or associate. The Abstract does not prescribe the treatment of barter transactions in general.

3 The issues discussed in this Abstract are:

(a) should businesses or other non-monetary assets exchanged for an interest in a subsidiary, joint venture or associate be accounted for at fair value at the date of the transaction or at previous book values?

(b) how should any gain or loss arising on the transaction be reported?

4 The UITF has considered different approaches to these kinds of exchanges and has decided that they should be analysed in terms of net changes in ownership interests. For example, the exchange of a wholly-owned business for a 50 per cent interest in another entity which absorbs that business should be characterised as an exchange of that part of the business where ownership is wholly given up (the 50 per cent interest now belonging to the other party) for the 50 per cent ownership interest acquired in the other entity's pre-transaction business. Under this approach, any part of the business exchanged that is owned by the transferor both directly before the exchange and indirectly thereafter is treated as having been owned throughout the transaction, and therefore remains at book value. The consideration for the interest acquired in the entity will include that part of the business or non-monetary assets no longer owned by the transferor.* The assets acquired consist of the transferor's 50 per cent share in the pre-transaction net assets of the other entity. Where it is difficult to value the consideration given, the best estimate of its value may be given by valuing what is acquired.

5 The UITF noted that in acquisition accounting, accounting standards and companies legislation require the consideration to be stated at fair value and fair values to be ascribed to the separable assets and liabilities acquired, any difference arising being goodwill. This applies whether the investee is a subsidiary, an associate or a joint venture.

6 If the fair value of the consideration received exceeds the book value of the part of the business or non-monetary assets no longer owned by the transferor (and any related goodwill) together with any cash given up, the transferor will record a gain.

**The consideration may also include cash or monetary assets to achieve equalisation of values.*

In the reverse case, the transferor will record a loss. To the extent that the transferor group retains an interest in a business or non-monetary assets after a transaction covered by this Abstract, even if then held through a different subsidiary or a joint venture or associate, that interest should be included at its pre-transaction carrying amount. The assets acquired through the interest in the entity will be accounted for at fair value and any goodwill arising will be recorded.

The UITF noted that International Accounting Standards require recognition of the portion of a gain or loss attributable to the equity interests of other venturers when non-monetary assets are contributed to a jointly controlled entity in exchange for an equity interest in that entity (SIC-13 'Jointly Controlled Entities – Non-Monetary Contributions by Venturers'). This is subject to limited exceptions, one of which is where the non-monetary assets contributed are 'similar' to those contributed by the other venturers. However, the UITF noted the intended narrowness of the exception because 'similar' is restrictively defined to mean having a similar nature, a similar use in the same line of business and a similar fair value. **7**

The UITF concluded that the only exception to the use of fair values in the transactions covered by this Abstract would be rare cases where the transaction is artificial or has no substance such that a gain or loss would be recognised that could not be justified. For example, an exchange might purport to give rise to a recognisable gain even though the assets exchanged would be unlikely otherwise to be saleable. In such a case, no gain should be recognised. Where a gain or loss on exchange is not taken into account because of special circumstances, those circumstances should be explained. **8**

The UITF took the view that any unrealised gain arising on the transactions that are the subject of the Abstract should be reported in the statement of total recognised gains and losses. Where a loss arises, all relevant assets should first be reviewed for impairment with any impairment identified accounted for as required by FRS 11 'Impairment of Fixed Assets and Goodwill'. Any remaining loss should be recorded in the profit and loss account. Where an impairment has been identified, similar assets should also be reviewed for impairment. **9**

APPLICATION TO SMALLER ENTITIES

Reporting entities applying the Financial Reporting Standard for Smaller Entities currently applicable are exempt from this Abstract. **10**

UITF CONSENSUS

The UITF reached a consensus that where an entity (A) exchanges a business or other non-monetary assets for an interest in another entity (B), which thereby becomes A's subsidiary or which is or thereby becomes A's joint venture or associate, the following accounting treatment should apply in A's consolidated financial statements: **11**

(a) to the extent that A retains an ownership interest in a business or non-monetary assets exchanged for an interest in B after such a transaction, even if that business or non-monetary assets is then held through B as a subsidiary, joint venture or associate, that retained interest, including any related goodwill, should be included at its pre-transaction carrying amount.

(b) A's share of net assets acquired through its new interest in B should be accounted for at fair value, with the difference between these and the fair value of the consideration given being accounted for as goodwill.

(c) to the extent that the fair value of the consideration received by A exceeds the book value of the part of the business or non-monetary assets no longer owned by A (and any related goodwill*) together with any cash given up, A should recognise a gain. Any gain arising on the exchange that is not realised should be reported in A's statement of total recognised gains and losses.

(d) where the fair value of the consideration received by A is less than the book value of the part of the business or non-monetary assets no longer owned by A (and any related goodwill) together with any cash given up, A should recognise a loss, either as an impairment in accordance with FRS 11 or, for any loss remaining after an impairment review of the relevant assets, in A's profit and loss account.

12 No gain or loss should be recognised in those rare cases where the artificiality or lack of substance of the transaction is such that any gain or loss on the exchange could not be justified. Where a gain or loss on the exchange is not taken into account because the transaction is artificial or has no substance, the circumstances should be explained.

DATE FROM WHICH EFFECTIVE

13 The accounting treatment required by this Abstract should be adopted in respect of transactions first accounted for in financial statements relating to accounting periods commencing on or after 23 December 2001, but earlier adoption is encouraged.

REFERENCES

Legislation

Great Britain and Northern Ireland
Companies Act 1985 and Companies (Northern Ireland) Order 1986
Schedule 4A paragraph 9†

Republic of Ireland
European Communities (Companies: Group Accounts) Regulations 1992 Regulation 19

Accounting standards

FRS 2 'Accounting for Subsidiary Undertakings' paragraphs 51 and 91
FRS 6 'Acquisitions and Mergers' paragraph 20
FRS 7 'Fair Values in Acquisition Accounting' paragraph 26
FRS 9 'Associates and Joint Ventures' paragraph 31(a)
FRS 10 'Goodwill and Intangible Assets' paragraph 68

Other pronouncements
IASC Standing Interpretations Committee SIC-13 'Jointly Controlled Entities – Non-Monetary Contributions by Venturers'

**These amounts will include any related goodwill written off under SSAP 22 'Accounting for goodwill' and not reinstated in accordance with the transitional arrangements of FRS 10 'Goodwill and Intangible Assets'.*

†***Editor's note:*** *For accounting periods beginning on or after 6 April 2008 this changes to Paragraph 9 of Schedule 6 to the Large and Medium-sized Companies and Groups (Accounts and Reports) Regulations 2008 (SI 2008/410).*

UITF abstract 32: Employee benefit trusts and other intermediate payment arrangements

(Issued December 2001)

SCOPE

This Abstract deals with intermediate payment arrangements as described in paragraphs 2-3 below. Although employee share ownership plans (ESOPs) are an example of intermediate payment arrangements, this Abstract does not apply to them because there is already a UITF Abstract on the subject (UITF Abstract 13 'Accounting for ESOP Trusts'). Similarly, pension funds, another example of intermediate payment arrangements, are not dealt with in this Abstract because they are the subject of an accounting standard (FRS 17 'Retirement Benefits').* 1

BACKGROUND

In a typical employee benefit trust, an entity makes payments to a trust, the beneficiaries of which are to be the entity's employees, and the trust then uses assets accumulated from those payments to pay the entity's employees for some or all of the employee services they have rendered to the entity. 2

The arrangement described in paragraph 2 is only one example of an 'intermediate payment arrangement'. Such arrangements may take a variety of forms. 3

(a) Although the intermediary is usually constituted as a trust, other arrangements are possible.
(b) Although such arrangements are most commonly used to pay employees, they are sometimes used to compensate suppliers of goods and services other than employee services. Sometimes the sponsoring entity's employees and other suppliers are not the only beneficiaries of the arrangement. Other beneficiaries may include past employees and their dependants, and the intermediary may be entitled to make charitable donations.
(c) Usually, the precise identity of the persons or entities that will receive payments from the intermediary, and the amounts that they will receive, are not agreed at the outset.
(d) The relationship between the sponsoring entity and the intermediary may take different forms. For example, when the intermediary is constituted as a trust, the sponsoring entity will not have a right to direct the intermediary's activities. However, in these and other cases the sponsoring entity may give advice to the intermediary or may be relied on by the intermediary to provide the information it needs to carry out its activities. Sometimes, the way the intermediary has been set up gives it little discretion in the broad nature of its activities.
(e) Often, the sponsoring entity has the right to appoint or veto the appointment of the intermediary's trustees (or its directors or the equivalent).
(f) The payments made to the intermediary and the payments made by the intermediary are often cash payments but may involve other transfers of value.

THE ISSUES

This Abstract addresses two accounting issues that arise when intermediate payment arrangements are entered into: 4

Editor's note: *UITF 13 has now been replaced by UITF 38. FRS 17 came into force in 2005.*

(a) whether the sponsoring entity's payments to the intermediary represent an immediate expense of the entity; and
(b) if the payments do not represent an immediate expense, what is the nature and extent of the sponsoring entity's assets and liabilities after making the payment to the intermediary.

Does the sponsoring entity's payment to the intermediary represent an immediate expense?

5 Generally speaking, most expenses are incurred not when they are paid for but when a liability arises. For example, when an entity receives cleaning services the expense arises as it receives those services not when it pays for them, regardless of whether the services are paid for before they are received or after they have been received.

6 That is also the case for goods and services (including employee services) paid for through an intermediate payment arrangement. For example, with an employee benefit trust, generally speaking:

(a) the expense will be incurred when a liability for the employee costs arises. This will only coincidentally be when payment is made to the intermediary;
(b) the payment made by the intermediary will either settle a liability or will be made in advance of the liability arising (ie it will be a prepayment); and
(c) the payment made to the intermediary will involve the exchange of one asset for another.

7 A payment made to an intermediary will represent an immediate expense of the sponsoring entity only if the payment neither results in the acquisition of another asset (for example, restricted cash or a prepayment) nor settles a liability. Whether a payment involves the full or partial settlement of a liability is a matter of fact and is not considered in this Abstract. The Abstract focuses instead on whether the payment involves the acquisition of another asset.

8 An asset is defined in the Statement of Principles for Financial Reporting as a right or other access to future economic benefits that is controlled by the entity as a result of a past transaction or event. The attributes of an asset are therefore the access to future economic benefits and the control of that access.

(a) Future economic benefit can be obtained in a variety of forms. In the context of intermediate payment arrangements, probably the most common form the benefit takes is meeting some or all of the cost of goods or services provided to the sponsoring entity. That benefit can be the basis for an asset even though it is not capable of being turned into cash or of being distributed in a liquidation.
(b) Control comprises two abilities, the ability to direct and the ability to benefit from that direction. Although control is probably most visible when it is exerted through intervention and instruction on an ongoing day-to-day basis, it can be present in a variety of other guises. For example, even though a sponsoring entity of an intermediate payment arrangement involving a trust does not have the right to dictate to trustees how they should exercise their responsibilities under a trust, it may still, as Abstract 13 makes clear, have de facto control of that trust's assets and liabilities. Although Abstract 13 focuses on ESOP trusts, it is based upon the wider principles of FRS 5 'Reporting the Substance of Transactions' and its analysis, explanations and conclusions are relevant in analogous circumstances such as when other intermediate payment arrangements are involved.

FRS 5 requires that, when determining whether an entity has an asset, one should look beyond the structure of the transaction to consider its substance; in other words, consideration should be given to the commercial effect of the transaction in practice. Recognising that it is highly unusual for an entity to pay a significant amount to a third party without receiving something in return, the UITF takes the view that, when an entity transfers funds to an intermediary, there should be a rebuttable presumption that the sponsoring entity will obtain future economic benefit from the amounts transferred and that it has control of the rights or other access to those future economic benefits. **9**

To rebut this presumption at the time the payment is made to the intermediary, it will be necessary to demonstrate that either: **10**

(a) the sponsoring entity will not obtain future economic benefit from the amounts transferred. For example, it may be that the only beneficiaries of the intermediary are registered charities or a benevolent fund that is in no way linked to amounts otherwise due from the entity; or
(b) the sponsoring entity does not have control of the rights or other access to the future economic benefits it is expected to receive. This will involve evidence that the payments made by the intermediary are not habitually made in a way that is in accordance with the sponsoring entity's wishes.

The presumption of future economic benefit would not be rebutted where payments by the intermediary served to relieve the sponsoring entity from paying for such items as retirement benefit increases or benefits in kind (for example, medical insurance cover). **11**

The presumption of control would be rebutted at the time the payment is made to the intermediary if at that time the asset(s) transferred to the intermediary vest unconditionally in identified beneficiaries. **12**

If, and to the extent that, the sponsoring entity has obtained rights or other access to future economic benefit over which it has control through its payment to the intermediary, the payment will involve an exchange of one asset for another and no immediate expense will be incurred. **13**

If the sponsoring entity's payment to the intermediary does not represent an immediate expense, what is the nature and extent of its assets and liabilities after the payment?

As explained above, if a payment made by a sponsoring entity to an intermediary involves an exchange of one asset for another, that will be because, despite paying money to the intermediary, the sponsoring entity continues to have the benefit of that money and to have control of that benefit; in other words, the amount paid to the intermediary remains an asset of the sponsoring entity despite being in the intermediary's possession. That will remain the case if the intermediary then exchanges some or all of that amount for other assets. The UITF takes the view that, in such circumstances, the sponsoring entity has de facto control of the intermediary's assets and should, as a result, account for the intermediary as an extension of its own business. The intermediary's assets, and any liabilities that it has, should therefore be recognised as assets and liabilities of the sponsoring entity. The subsequent accounting for those assets and liabilities and for expense recognition should follow the normal accounting rules. Accordingly, an asset held by the intermediary would cease to be recognised as an asset of the sponsoring entity when, for example, it vests unconditionally in identified beneficiaries. **14**

15 Abstract 13 concludes that the assets and liabilities of most ESOP trusts are under the de facto control of the sponsoring company. The UITF is of the view that the reasoning that leads to that conclusion—and the conclusion itself—applies equally to the assets and liabilities of most employee benefit trusts.

APPLICATION TO SMALLER ENTITIES

16 Reporting entities applying the Financial Reporting Standard for Smaller Entities currently applicable are exempt from this Abstract.

UITF CONSENSUS

17 This UITF consensus applies to all intermediate payment arrangements other than those dealt with in Abstract 13 or FRS 17.*

18 The UITF reached a consensus that, when an entity transfers funds to an intermediary, there should be a rebuttable presumption that the sponsoring entity has exchanged one asset for another and that the payment itself does not represent an immediate expense.

19 Where a payment to an intermediary is an exchange by the sponsoring entity of one asset for another, any assets that the intermediary acquires in a subsequent exchange transaction will also be under the de facto control of the sponsoring entity. The intermediary's assets, and any liabilities that it has, should therefore be recognised as assets and liabilities of the sponsoring entity. The subsequent accounting for those assets and liabilities and for expense recognition should follow the normal accounting rules. Accordingly, an asset held by the intermediary would cease to be recognised as an asset of the sponsoring entity when, for example, it vests unconditionally in identified beneficiaries.

20 When an entity recognises the assets and liabilities held by an intermediary on its balance sheet, it should disclose sufficient information in the notes to its financial statements to enable readers to understand any restrictions relating to those assets and liabilities.

DATE FROM WHICH EFFECTIVE

21 The accounting treatment required by this Abstract should be adopted in financial statements relating to accounting periods ending on or after 23 December 2001, but earlier adoption is encouraged. Where applicable, corresponding amounts should be restated.

REFERENCES

ASB pronouncements

Statement of Principles for Financial Reporting, paragraphs 4.6 and 4.39
FRS 5 'Reporting the Substance of Transactions', paragraphs 14, 16, 20 and 54
FRS 17 'Retirement Benefits'
UITF Abstract 13 'Accounting for ESOP Trusts', paragraph 2(d) and the appendix†

****Editor's note:*** *UITF 13 has now been replaced by UITF 38. FRS 17 came into force in 2005.*

†***Editor's note:*** *UITF 13 has now been replaced by UITF 38.*

UITF abstract 34: Pre-contract costs

(Issued May 2002)

THE ISSUE

Entities in some industries incur significant costs in bidding for and securing contracts to supply products or services. Examples are entities that supply property and services under the Private Finance Initiative, Public-Private Partnerships, outsourcing and similar arrangements. Where a bid is successful, the entity will often have incurred significant costs before the contract is signed. There has been uncertainty over whether such costs should be recognised as an asset (and charged as expenses during the period of the contract) or charged as immediate expenses, and diverse accounting treatments have developed in practice. 1

The issues are: 2

(a) Should pre-contract costs be recognised as an asset?
(b) If so, how should the asset be measured?

This Abstract addresses the accounting by the supplier for the costs of tendering for and securing contracts (referred to herein as pre-contract costs). The Abstract applies to costs relating to contracts for the design, construction, manufacture or operation of assets or for the provision of services or a combination of assets and services. The Abstract does not, however, prescribe the accounting treatment of 3

(a) costs that are subject to the more specific requirements of accounting standards (such as FRS 4 *Capital Instruments*, FRS 10 *Goodwill and Intangible Assets*, FRS 15 *Tangible Fixed Assets* or SSAP 13 *Accounting for research and development*) or
(b) the costs of acquiring insurance policies in the financial statements of insurance entities (covered by Schedule 9A to the Companies Act 1985).

Prospective amendment: The draft FRS 'Financial Instruments: Disclosure and presentation' in FRED 30 'Financial Instruments: Disclosure and presentation, Recognition and measurement' supersedes FRS 4, following publication in final form.*

SHOULD PRE-CONTRACT COSTS BE RECOGNISED AS AN ASSET?

Assets are defined in the Statement of Principles for Financial Reporting as 'rights or other access to future economic benefits controlled by an entity as a result of past transactions or events'. An asset is recognised in financial statements only if there is sufficient evidence that the asset has been created (including, where appropriate, that a future inflow of benefit will occur) and it can be measured with sufficient reliability. 4

The UITF takes the view that pre-contract costs are not start-up costs covered by UITF Abstract 24 *Accounting for start-up costs*; rather they are part of the ongoing costs of obtaining contracts. The activity of bidding for contracts does not necessarily, however, give rise to rights or access to future economic benefits that are controlled by the entity. Control is defined in FRS 5 as 'the ability to obtain the future economic benefits relating to an asset and to restrict the access of others to those benefits'. Where it is merely possible that a contract will be awarded there is no control over future economic benefits, although there may well be an expectation that such benefits will accrue to the entity. 5

***Editor's note:** *FRED 30 became FRS 25.*

6 It follows that, at the stage where an entity has obtained the right to bid for a contract, it does not yet have an asset that should be recognised in the financial statements. That is the case even where a bid is part of a portfolio of bids that an entity undertakes in the expectation that at least some will result in profitable contracts. The recognition of an asset in the financial statements reflects an economically significant event, being the point at which control is obtained over the rights or access to future economic benefits from the award of a contract. Expenditure that is invested in tendering for a contract before that event occurs is not an asset that is recognised in financial statements.

7 The UITF took the view that, in this context, control does not arise before it is virtually certain that a contract will be awarded. Until the award of a contract is virtually certain there will not be sufficient evidence that an asset has been created. The exact point when the award of a contract becomes virtually certain – and pre-contract costs should be recognised as an asset – will depend on the particular circumstances of the case. The requirement for control means that only one competing bidder can recognise an asset that reflects rights or access to the future economic benefits from a contract. It would therefore be essential, but not necessarily sufficient, that there are no other bidders in competition – for example, where the entity has been appointed sole preferred bidder giving it exclusive rights to negotiate the contract terms with the purchaser. In addition, the award of the contract should be expected within a reasonable timescale and the proposed contractual arrangements should have been specified in sufficient detail to provide evidence that the pre-contract costs recognised as an asset will be recovered from the contract's net cash inflows. Virtual certainty is not achieved if the award of a contract is subject to uncertain future events not wholly within the control of the entity or the purchaser (such as the need for regulatory approval or the likelihood of legal challenge).

HOW SHOULD THE ASSET BE MEASURED?

8 The UITF takes the view that costs should be recognised as an asset only if they are directly attributable to a specific contract, can be separately identified and can be measured reliably.

9 The UITF considered three approaches to measuring an asset when the recognition criteria are met:

(i) Only pre-contract costs incurred from the date the asset recognition criteria are met are recognised as an asset. This means that pre-contract costs incurred before then (for example, during the competitive tendering stage) are recognised as expenses as incurred and are not subsequently reinstated as an asset.

(ii) All previously incurred pre-contract costs (ie including those charged as expenses in previous years' financial statements) are reinstated as part of the cost of the asset when the asset recognition criteria are met.

(iii) All pre-contract costs incurred within the accounting period in which the asset recognition criteria are met are recognised as part of the cost of the asset. This means that costs that have been charged as expenses in previous years' financial statements are not reinstated as part of the cost of the asset when the contract is obtained in a subsequent financial year.

10 Some commentators believe that all previously incurred pre-contract costs should be reinstated as part of the cost of the asset (and credited in the profit and loss account) when the asset recognition criteria are met. In their view, it is more meaningful to recognise as an asset all the costs that have been incurred in creating it than to recognise only those costs incurred in the later stages of the bid. Some proponents of that view believe that in essence an asset arises from the start of the bidding process but that full provision is made against the asset until there is sufficient certainty of recovery, when the provision is released. As noted earlier, the UITF took the view that no recognisable asset arises until there is virtual certainty that a contract will be awarded. Costs incurred before then are recognised as expenses, not as assets (or assets that are fully provided against); once an item is recognised as an expense in the profit and loss account, it is not subsequently credited in the profit and loss account in order to be charged as an expense again (as cost of sales) in future periods. The UITF also noted that International Accounting Standards do not allow costs incurred in securing a contract that are recognised as expenses when they are incurred to be recognised as part of the cost of an asset when the contract is obtained in a subsequent period.

Some other commentators agree that it is not appropriate to allow costs that have been recognised as expenses in previous accounting periods to be recognised as an asset in a subsequent period, but believe that all directly attributable costs incurred during the period in which the asset recognition criteria are met should be recognised as part of the cost of the asset. The UITF took the view that this approach too is inconsistent with the principles for asset recognition. Furthermore, under such a system the accounting information would lack comparability where the bidding process extended over more than one accounting period; that is because the amounts of costs reported as expenses or assets would vary depending on how early or late in the accounting period the asset recognition criteria were met. **11**

The UITF took the view that the approach in paragraph 9(i) is consistent with the criteria for asset recognition set out in paragraphs 4 to 7 above. Costs incurred before the event that gives rise to a recognisable asset in relation to the award of a contract are recognised as expenses because they do not meet the definition of an asset when they are incurred. **12**

Sometimes a consortium of bidders will form a special-purpose entity to undertake the contract and the consortium members may transfer pre-contract costs to that entity when the contract is signed. The amount recovered by a consortium member from the special-purpose entity at the inception of the contract may exceed the amount of pre-contract costs that have been recognised as an asset under the principles in this Abstract (as, for example, where the amount recovered takes account of pre-contract costs incurred before the asset recognition criteria were met). The accounting by the consortium members for the recovery of pre-contract costs from the special-purpose entity should reflect the principles in this Abstract (in particular, that costs incurred and written off as an expense before the asset recognition criteria are met are not subsequently reinstated as an asset), having regard to the substance of the arrangement. Where the special-purpose entity is an associate or joint venture, the recovery of an amount that exceeds the amount of pre-contract costs recognised as an asset does not result in an immediate gain in a consortium member's consolidated financial statements to the extent that the substance is a financing arrangement. This will usually be the case unless the original consortium members rearrange or dispose of their interests in the special-purpose entity. **13**

APPLICATION TO SMALLER ENTITIES

Reporting entities applying the Financial Reporting Standard for Smaller Entities currently applicable are exempt from this Abstract. **14**

UITF CONSENSUS

The UITF reached a consensus that: **15**

(a) Pre-contract costs should be recognised as expenses as incurred, except that directly attributable costs should be recognised as an asset when it is virtually certain that a contract will be obtained and the contract is expected to result in future net cash inflows (ie future revenues less attributable costs) with a present value no less than all amounts recognised as an asset.
(b) Costs incurred before the asset recognition criteria in (a) above are met should not be recognised as an asset then or later.
(c) Directly attributable costs are costs that relate directly to securing the specific contract after the asset recognition criteria in (a) above are met, if they can be separately identified and measured reliably.
(d) The accounting by consortium members for the recovery of pre-contract costs from a special-purpose entity should reflect the principles set out in (a) to (c) above.

DATE FROM WHICH EFFECTIVE

16 The accounting treatment required by this Abstract should be adopted in financial statements relating to accounting periods ending on or after 22 June 2002, but earlier adoption is encouraged.

REFERENCES

ASB pronouncements

Statement of Principles for Financial Reporting, Chapters 4 and 5
FRS 5 *Reporting the Substance of Transactions*, paragraphs 2 and 20
UITF Abstract 24 *Accounting for start-up costs*

Other pronouncements

IAS 11 'Construction Contracts', paragraph 21
IAS 38 'Intangible Assets', paragraphs 53-55 and 59*

Editor's note: *These have been moved to paragraphs 65-67 and 71 of IAS 38, as amended in March 2004.*

UITF abstract 35: Death-in-service and incapacity benefits

(Issued May 2002)

THE ISSUE

1 An issue has been raised on the application of paragraphs 73 and 74 of FRS 17 'Retirement Benefits'. The issue is how an entity should recognise the cost of providing death-in-service and incapacity benefits where the benefits are provided through a defined benefit pension scheme. Such benefits may include lump sum payments and pensions that become payable to employees' dependants.

2 The principles of FRS 17 view the obligation to pay pensions as covering the period of an employee's service; the scheme liability is an accrual at the reporting date of a portion of those total benefits. Those principles are reflected in the requirement in paragraphs 20 and 22 of FRS 17 for defined benefit scheme liabilities to be measured on an actuarial basis using the projected unit method. If those principles were applied to accounting for death-in-service and incapacity benefits that are provided through a defined benefit pension scheme, the scheme liability would include a portion of the estimated cost of paying benefits in respect of employees who are expected to die or become incapacitated between the reporting date and the date of leaving service.

3 Paragraphs 73 and 74 of FRS 17 are as follows:

73 A charge should be made to operating profit to reflect the expected cost of providing any death-in-service or incapacity benefits for the period. Any difference between that expected cost and amounts actually incurred should be treated as an actuarial gain or loss.

74 Where a scheme insures the death-in-service costs, the expected cost for the accounting period is simply the premium payable for the period. Where the costs are not insured, the expected cost reflects the probability of any employees dying in the period and the benefit that would then be paid out.

The effect of applying paragraphs 73 and 74 is that the liability for death-in-service and incapacity benefits would include the estimated cost of paying benefits only in respect of employees that have died or become incapacitated by the reporting date.

4 The UITF was asked to consider the application of these paragraphs where death-in-service and incapacity benefits are provided through a defined benefit pension scheme. The UITF took the view that where the costs of death-in-service and incapacity benefits are not insured and are provided through a defined benefit pension scheme, the scheme liability and the cost should be measured in accordance with paragraphs 20 and 22 of FRS 17, ie using the projected unit method. The effect is that the valuation of uninsured benefits reflects the current period's portion of the full benefits ultimately payable in respect of current members of the scheme; the cost of insured benefits is determined by the relevant insurance premiums. The UITF considered that, in valuing the scheme liability for a defined benefit pension scheme, the actuary will allow for the possibility that some employees will die or become incapacitated before they leave service (and that future pension payments will be reduced accordingly). The UITF concluded that it would be inappropriate for the benefits that would then become payable to be excluded from the valuation.

UITF CONSENSUS

5 The UITF reached a consensus that the cost of providing death-in-service and incapacity benefits should be recognised in accordance with paragraphs 73 and 74 of FRS 17, except where the benefits are provided through a defined benefit pension scheme and are not wholly insured, in which case the uninsured scheme liability and the cost for the accounting period should be measured by applying the principles in paragraphs 20 and 22 of FRS 17.

DATE FROM WHICH EFFECTIVE

6 The accounting treatment required by this consensus should be adopted as soon as practicable, but in any event in financial statements relating to accounting periods ending on or after 22 June 2002.

REFERENCES

FRS 17 'Retirement Benefits' – paragraphs 20, 22, 73, 74.

UITF abstract 36: Contracts for sales of capacity

(Issued March 2003)

THE ISSUE

1 Entities in some industries enter into contracts that convey the right to use some or all of the capacity of a physical asset. Examples are found in the telecommunications and electricity industries where entities buy and sell capacity on each others' networks. Whilst the capacity provider will retain ownership of the network assets, some contracts convey indefeasible rights of use (usually referred to as IRUs) to the buyer for an agreed period of time. Some contracts convey the right to use identifiable physical assets (or identifiable physical components of larger infrastructure assets); others convey the right to use a specified amount of capacity, defined in terms of an asset's output, rather than the right to use a specific physical item. The UITF decided that it should develop guidance on certain issues that arise in accounting for such transactions.

2 In this Abstract the parties to a contract that conveys a right of use are referred to as 'seller' and 'buyer', notwithstanding that analysis of the transaction may have the effect that the 'seller' continues to recognise the asset in its balance sheet.

3 The issues addressed in this Abstract are:

(a) Should the seller report the transaction as a sale (thereby derecognising an asset or a component of a larger asset), or should the seller continue to recognise existing assets in their entirety (thereby recognising income over the life of the contract)?

(b) In the performance statements, should the seller present gains and losses arising from the transaction as operating revenues and costs or as gains and losses on the disposal of fixed assets?

(c) How should transactions be accounted for where, rather than selling capacity for cash (or the right to receive cash), an entity exchanges capacity on its own network for capacity on another entity's network?

DERECOGNITION ISSUE

4 Contracts that convey rights of use are in many respects akin to leases. SSAP 21 *Accounting for leases and hire purchase contracts* defines a lease as:

> 'a contract between a lessor and a lessee for the hire of a specific asset. The lessor retains ownership of the asset but conveys the right to the use of the asset to the lessee for an agreed period of time in return for the payment of specified rentals. The term 'lease' as used in this statement also applies to other arrangements in which one party retains ownership of an asset but conveys the right to the use of the asset to another party for an agreed period of time in return for specified payments'.

From the lessor's perspective, SSAP 21 precludes accounting for the lease as a sale (thereby *derecognising the* asset that is the subject of the lease) unless the lease is a finance lease, ie 'a lease that transfers substantially all the risks and rewards of ownership of an asset to the lessee'. Assets held under operating leases should continue to be recognised in their entirety (as fixed assets) and rental income from the lease should be recognised (normally on a straight-line basis) over the period of the lease.

5 The derecognition principles in FRS 5 *Reporting the Substance of Transactions* (paragraph 22) require that a previously recognised asset should cease to be recognised (and should, therefore, be accounted for as an outright sale) where the transaction transfers (a) all significant rights or other access to benefits relating to that asset, and (b) all significant exposure to the risks inherent in those benefits. FRS 5 also addresses (in paragraph 23) special cases where transactions do not completely transfer all significant benefits and risks, but nonetheless result in a significant change in an entity's rights to benefits and exposure to risks. In such cases an entity needs to consider whether the description or monetary amount of the asset needs to be changed and also whether a liability needs to be recognised for any obligations assumed or risks retained. A contract that transfers an item for all of its life but where the seller retains some significant right to benefits or exposure to risk is an example of such special cases. Paragraph 24 of FRS 5 emphasises that where the amount of any resulting gain or loss is uncertain, full provision should be made for any probable loss but recognition of any gain, to the extent it is in doubt, should be deferred.

6 Derecognition of an asset by the seller and recognition of the same asset by the buyer implies that control is transferred to the buyer. Control is defined in FRS 5 as 'the ability to obtain the future economic benefits relating to an asset and to restrict the access of others to those benefits'.

7 It follows from the principles in FRS 5 and SSAP 21 that the criteria for derecognition in relation to a contract for rights of use cannot be satisfied unless a specific asset component can be identified as having been 'sold' to the buyer. The UITF considers that the purchaser's right of use should be exclusive and irrevocable, such that no other party, including the seller, would have the right to use the capacity that is the subject of the contract, even if the buyer is not using it. The term of the contract should be for a major part of the asset's useful economic life. An asset component might be tangibly separable (such as a specific cable or specific fibres) or the technology might allow an asset component to be intangibly separable (such as a specific wavelength); however, in either case the buyer's exclusivity must be guaranteed. If the seller had the right to perform its contractual obligations to deliver capacity by substituting other assets, the contract would not convey the right to use a specific asset and would not, therefore, qualify to be reported as the sale of an asset.

8 Where the capacity 'sold' is part of a larger infrastructure, it may be difficult to measure its cost or carrying value reliably, with the result that any gain or loss that would be recognised would be uncertain. Where the cost or carrying value cannot be measured reliably, the UITF takes the view that a specific asset component cannot be identified and the seller should not report the transaction as the sale of an asset.

9 In contracts for rights to use components of networks, the seller will often have some continuing involvement in making the asset available to the buyer, which may result in the seller retaining significant risks. In practical terms, this means there is no sale. The following are examples of risks that, if they are significant and are borne by the seller, serve as indicators that the seller should continue to recognise an asset in its entirety:

(a) risk of changes in asset value;
(b) risk of obsolescence or changes in technology;
(c) risk of damage;
(d) risk of unsatisfactory performance (arising, for example, from performance guarantees);

(e) risks relating to the seller's obligations to provide continuing access by operating and maintaining the assets (arising, for example, from exposure to costs that cannot be recovered from the buyer).

PERFORMANCE REPORTING ISSUE

As discussed above, some contracts for sales of capacity result in the seller continuing to recognise existing assets in their entirety. Income from the contract is then recognised over the life of the contract. Both income and expenses (including depreciation of the relevant fixed assets) are reported in operating results in accordance with FRS3 *Reporting Financial Performance*. **10**

Other contracts are reported as sales of assets. It is necessary to determine whether the asset that is the subject of such a contract is a fixed asset or a current asset (ie stock). The classification determines whether any gain or loss is reported as a profit or loss on the disposal of a fixed asset or whether the sale proceeds and the costs of sale are reported respectively as turnover and operating costs.* **11**

FRS 15's definition of tangible fixed assets refers to assets 'held for use in the production or supply of goods or services, for rental to others, or for administrative purposes on a continuing basis in the reporting entity's activities'. The business models of some entities include investment in capacity for resale as well as for use in the supply of services, such that similar assets may be held as current assets and fixed assets. The UITF takes the view that proceeds from disposals should not be reported in turnover unless the assets were designated as held for resale (and classified as stock) when they were acquired or on completion of construction. Capacity that was acquired or constructed to be used to supply ongoing services should not be transferred from fixed assets to stocks if capacity subsequently becomes surplus to the business' own requirements. **12**

If sales of assets are reported in operating results, and within the same reportable segment as the supply of ongoing services, the UITF takes the view that an analysis of turnover and profits should be clearly disclosed. **13**

EXCHANGE TRANSACTIONS

An entity may sell capacity on a network in exchange for receiving capacity on another entity's network. In some cases the two capacities are of a similar value and little or no cash is exchanged. In other cases, capacity is sold wholly or in part for cash (or the right to receive cash) and a separate agreement is entered into with the buyer at approximately the same time to purchase capacity of a similar value. Such cases are referred to in this Abstract as 'reciprocal transactions' where this reflects the substance of the transaction, even though the agreements may contain no reference to reciprocity. **14**

No accounting recognition should be given to transactions that are artificial or lacking in substance, which would be the case, for example, if exchange or reciprocal transactions were entered into for capacity for which the transacting parties had no current need and which would be unlikely otherwise to be saleable. Accordingly, in the following discussion it is assumed that there is a proper commercial rationale for **15**

**Treating proceeds of sale of fixed assets as turnover would contravene FRS 3. Paragraph 20 requires profit or losses on the disposal of fixed assets (except for marginal adjustments to depreciation) to be shown after operating profit.*

entering into exchange or reciprocal transactions and that they provide economic benefits to the transacting parties.

16 The derecognition issues considered in paragraphs 4 to 9 above are relevant in determining whether or not capacity provided in an exchange transaction should be accounted for as the sale of an asset or the provision of a service. If the appropriate treatment is to report the sale of an asset, the presentation issues considered in paragraphs 10 to 13 above are relevant in determining how recognised gains and losses, if any, should be presented in the performance statements. If continued recognition is the appropriate treatment, turnover, if any, is recognised over the life of the contract. Recognition of gains and turnover is, however, subject to the criteria set out below.

17 The recognition criteria in the *Statement of Principles for Financial Reporting* require (a) sufficient evidence and (b) measurement at a monetary amount with sufficient reliability. Where a contract to provide capacity is for a cash consideration, the transaction evidences the fair value of the asset or services provided. In contrast, measurement of the fair value of the asset or services provided (and received) is much more difficult where capacity is provided in exchange for capacity received. Where reciprocal transactions are entered into, an exchange of cash between the transacting parties for equal or substantially equal amounts does not provide reliable evidence of fair value. An exchange that involves part cash consideration does not provide reliable evidence of the fair value of the entire transaction.

18 The UITF decided that it would be appropriate to recognise turnover or gains in respect of exchange and reciprocal transactions only if fair value can be determined by reference to observable transactions in an active market, ie where the assets or services provided or received have a readily ascertainable market value as defined in FRS10 *Goodwill and Intangible Assets*.

APPLICATION TO SMALLER ENTITIES

19 Reporting entities applying the *Financial Reporting Standard for Smaller Entities* currently applicable are exempt from this Abstract.

UITF CONSENSUS

20 A seller of a right to use capacity should not report the transaction as the sale of an asset, or of a component of a larger asset, unless:

(a) the purchaser's right of use is exclusive and irrevocable;
(b) the asset component is specific and separable (such that the buyer's exclusivity is guaranteed and the seller has no right to substitute other assets);
(c) the term of the contract is for a major part of the asset's useful economic life;
(d) the attributable cost or carrying value can be measured reliably; and
(e) no significant risks, as indicated in paragraph 9, are retained by the seller.

21 Where a transaction is reported as the sale of an asset, the proceeds should be reported as turnover only if the assets were designated as held for resale (and classified as stock) when they were acquired or on completion of construction. Otherwise such transactions should be reported as disposals of fixed assets.

22 Where transactions are reported as asset sales in operating results, amounts included in turnover and profits from these transactions should be clearly disclosed.

Turnover or gains in respect of contracts to provide capacity in exchange for receiving capacity should be recognised only if the assets or services provided or received have a readily ascertainable market value. The same principle applies to reciprocal transactions to provide capacity entered into wholly or in part for a cash consideration. No accounting recognition should be given to transactions that are artificial or lacking in substance. **23**

DATE FROM WHICH EFFECTIVE

The accounting treatment required by this Abstract should be adopted in financial statements relating to accounting periods ending on or after 22 June 2003, but earlier adoption is encouraged. **24**

REFERENCES

ASB pronouncements

FRS 3 *Reporting Financial Performance*
FRS 5 *Reporting the Substance of Transactions* paragraphs 14, 21–25, 67–75
FRS 10 *Goodwill and Intangible Assets* paragraph 2
FRS 15 *Tangible Fixed Assets* paragraph 2
SSAP 21 *Accounting for leases and hire purchase contracts* paragraphs 14–15
UITF Abstract 26 *Barter transactions for advertising*
ASB *Statement of Principles for Financial Reporting* Chapter 5

UITF abstract 38
Accounting for ESOP trusts

(Issued December 2003)

INTRODUCTION

1 This Abstract supersedes UITF Abstract 13 'Accounting for ESOP trusts' (issued on 8 June 1995).

2 Abstract 13 addressed:

(a) the nature and extent of the sponsoring company's assets and liabilities that should be recognised under employee share ownership plans (ESOPs); and
(b) the timing of expense recognition under such arrangements.

3 This Abstract addresses issue (a) above. The principal change from Abstract 13 concerns the treatment of an interest in an entity's own shares arising through an ESOP trust. Abstract 13 required that such shares should be recognised as assets of the sponsoring entity. This Abstract reflects the principle in UITF Abstract 37 'Purchases and sales of own shares', which is consistent with International Financial Reporting Standards (IFRSs), that an entity that reacquires its own equity instruments should present them as a deduction in arriving at shareholders' funds rather than as assets.

4 This Abstract does not include any requirements concerning the recognition of the cost of awards to employees that take the form of shares or rights to shares. Those accounting requirements are dealt with in UITF Abstract 17 'Employee share schemes', which is amended by this Abstract. This Abstract does not include any requirements concerning the recognition of the cost of awards to employees that take the form of shares or rights to shares. Those accounting requirements are dealt with in FRS 20 (IFRS 2) Share-based Payment.*

THE ISSUE

5 ESOPs are designed to facilitate employee shareholdings and are often used as vehicles for distributing shares to employees under remuneration schemes.

6 The detailed structures of individual ESOPs are many and varied, as are the reasons for establishing them. However, the main features are often as follows:

(a) The ESOP trust provides a warehouse for the sponsoring company's shares, for example by acquiring and holding shares that are to be sold or transferred to employees in the future. The trustees may purchase the shares with finance provided by the sponsoring company (by way of cash contributions or loans), or by a third-party bank loan, or by a combination of the two. Loans from the company are usually interest-free. In other cases, the ESOP trust may subscribe directly for shares issued by the sponsoring company or acquire shares held as treasury shares.
(b) Where the ESOP trust borrows from a third party, the sponsoring company will usually guarantee the loan, ie it will be responsible for any shortfall if the trust's assets are insufficient to meet its debt repayment obligations. The company will also generally make regular contributions to the trust to enable the trust to meet its interest payments, ie to make good any shortfall between

Editor's note: *Amended by FRS 20.*

the dividend income of the trust (if any) and the interest payable. As part of this arrangement the trustees usually waive their right to dividends on the shares held by the trust.

(c) Shares held by the ESOP trust are distributed to employees through an employee share scheme. There are many different arrangements – these include: the purchase of shares by employees when exercising their share options under a share option scheme; the purchase of shares by the trustees of an approved profit-sharing scheme for allocation to employees under the rules of the scheme; or the transfer of shares to employees under some other incentive scheme.

(d) Although the trustees of the ESOP trust must act at all times in accordance with the interests of the beneficiaries under the trust, most ESOP trusts (particularly those established as a means of remunerating employees) are specifically designed so as to serve the purposes of the sponsoring company, and to ensure that there will be minimal risk of any conflict arising between the duties of the trustees and the interest of the company. Where this is so, the sponsoring company has de facto control and there will be nothing to encumber implementation of its wishes in practice.

FRS 5 'Reporting the Substance of Transactions' requires a reporting entity's financial statements to report the substance of the transactions into which it has entered (paragraph 14). In determining the substance of a transaction all its aspects and implications should be identified and greater weight given to those more likely to have a commercial effect in practice. To determine the substance of a transaction it is necessary to identify whether the transaction has given rise to new assets or liabilities for the reporting entity and whether it has changed the entity's existing assets or liabilities (paragraph 16). In the circumstances described above, the commercial effect is that the sponsoring company is, for all practical purposes, in the same position as if it had purchased the shares directly and it should account for them as such. As is explained below, shares of the company are presented in the balance sheet as a deduction in arriving at shareholders' funds, not as assets. 7

Where a company holds its own equity shares, IFRSs* require them to be accounted for as a deduction from equity in all circumstances; they should not be recognised as assets. The ASB's Statement of Principles for Financial Reporting is consistent with IFRSs in this regard. Paragraph 4.45 states "a purchase by a company of its own shares is an example of a return of capital and is therefore reflected in financial statements by reducing the amount of ownership interest". This accounting treatment of own shares is reflected in Abstract 37, which requires that consideration paid or received for the purchase or sale of an entity's own shares should be shown in the reconciliation of movements in shareholders' funds and that no gain or loss should be recognised in the profit and loss account or statement of total recognised gains and losses on the purchase, sale, or cancellation of an entity's own shares. The UITF takes the view that the same accounting treatment should apply where an entity's own shares are held by an ESOP trust. 8

APPLICATION TO SMALLER ENTITIES

Reporting entities applying the Financial Reporting Standard for Smaller Entities currently applicable are exempt from this Abstract. 9

**SIC-16 'Share Capital – Reacquired Own Equity Instruments (Treasury Shares)'.*

UITF CONSENSUS

10 The UITF reached a consensus that the sponsoring company of an ESOP trust should recognise the assets and liabilities of the trust in its own accounts whenever it has de facto control of those assets and liabilities. This will generally be the case when the trust is established in order to hold shares for an employee remuneration scheme and may be so in other circumstances. Where this consensus applies:

(a) Until such time as the company's own shares held by the ESOP trust vest unconditionally in employees, the consideration paid for the shares should be deducted in arriving at shareholders' funds.
(b) Other assets and liabilities (including borrowings) of the ESOP trust should be recognised as assets and liabilities of the sponsoring company.
(c) Consideration paid or received for the purchase or sale of the company's own shares in an ESOP trust should be shown as separate amounts in the reconciliation of movements in shareholders' funds.
(d) No gain or loss should be recognised in the profit and loss account or statement of total recognised gains and losses on the purchase, sale, issue or cancellation of the company's own shares.
(e) Finance costs and any administration expenses should be charged as they accrue and not as funding payments are made to the ESOP trust.
(f) Any dividend income arising on own shares should be excluded in arriving at profit before tax and deducted from the aggregate of dividends paid and proposed. The deduction should be disclosed if material. In accordance with the principles of FRS 22 (IAS 33) *Earnings per share*, the shares should be treated as if they were cancelled when calculating earnings per share.

11 Sufficient information should be disclosed in the financial statements of the sponsoring company to enable readers to understand the significance of the ESOP trust in the context of the sponsoring company. This should include:

(a) a description of the main features of the ESOP trust including the arrangements for distributing shares to employees;
(b) the amounts of reductions to shareholders' funds and the number and (for companies that have shares listed or publicly traded on a stock exchange or market) market value of shares held by the ESOP trust which have not yet vested unconditionally in employees; and
(c) the extent to which these shares are under option to employees, or have been conditionally gifted to them.

DATE FROM WHICH EFFECTIVE

12 The accounting treatment required by this Abstract should be adopted in financial statements relating to accounting periods ending on or after 22 June 2004, but earlier adoption is encouraged.

Corresponding amounts

13 Where applicable, corresponding balance sheet amounts should be restated to reclassify the company's own shares as deductions in arriving at shareholders' funds at the amount of the consideration paid for the shares. Amounts in the profit and loss account should also be restated, where applicable, for comparative periods presented.

WITHDRAWAL OF UITF ABSTRACT 13 (AS ISSUED ON 8 JUNE 1995)

This Abstract supersedes UITF Abstract 13 'Accounting for ESOP trusts' (issued on 8 June 1995). 14

AMENDMENT TO UITF ABSTRACT 17

[Withdrawn] 15

REFERENCES

ASB pronouncements
FRS 5 'Reporting the Substance of Transactions' – paragraphs 2, 4, 14, 16, 17, 20 and 46
Statement of Principles for Financial Reporting – Chapter 4
UITF Abstract 37 'Purchases and sales of own shares'

ASB exposure drafts
FRED 30 'Financial Instruments: Disclosure and Presentation' – paragraphs 29A-29B
FRED 31 'Share-based Payment' – Appendix E, paragraph E1

International Financial Reporting Standards
SIC-16 'Share Capital – Reacquired Own Equity Instruments (Treasury Shares)'

LEGAL CONSIDERATIONS

FRS 5 is not intended to affect the legal characterisation of a transaction, or to change the situation at law achieved by the parties to it (paragraph 46). Shares acquired by ESOP trusts and included in the balance sheet under this Abstract are not treasury shares as defined in the Companies Act 1985 (as amended by the Companies (Acquisition of Own Shares) (Treasury Shares) Regulations 2003) or as defined by the Companies Act 1990 in the Republic of Ireland. Nor does the inclusion of the shares in the company's balance sheet as a deduction in arriving at shareholders' funds imply that they have been purchased by the company as a matter of law or that they are required to be cancelled, which would be the consequence of such a purchase except for shares held as treasury shares (in Great Britain sections 162(2) and 160(4) of the Companies Act 1985).*

The UITF has received legal advice on the implications for companies' distributable profits when the accounting treatment required by this Abstract is followed. It has been advised that in Great Britain:

(a) Section 264 of the Companies Act 1985 provides that a public company may only make a distribution if, and to the extent that, this will not reduce the company's net assets to less than an amount equal to the aggregate of its called up share capital and undistributable reserves. Section 270 applies for the purposes of determining whether a distribution can be made without contravening

The corresponding references in Northern Ireland are to articles 172(2) and 170(4) of the Companies (Northern Ireland) Order 1986 and in the Republic of Ireland to sections 211(2) and 208(a) of the Companies Act 1990. The corresponding references for the Republic of Ireland indicate the provisions dealing with the same topic as the sections in the Companies Act 1985 and are not identical in all cases. The Republic of Ireland references should be consulted for further information.* ***Editor's note:* *For accounting periods beginning on or after 6 April 2008 treasury shares are covered by sections 724 to 732 of the Companies Act 2006, and distributable profits by, primarily, section 829 to 839 of that Act.*

sections 263, 264 or 265. It provides that the amount of a distribution which can be made is determined by reference, inter alia, to the company's assets and liabilities as stated in the company's accounts. These are normally the company's last annual accounts (but may be initial or interim accounts). As the effect of the accounting treatment required by this Abstract would be that, in drawing up the accounts in question, any shares held by an ESOP would be recorded as a deduction in arriving at shareholders' funds rather than as an asset, it follows that the relevant aggregate asset value for the purposes of the definition of net assets in section 264(2) would be reduced by a corresponding amount.

(b) In calculating a company's distributable profits, it is necessary to determine its "accumulated, realised profits so far as not previously utilised by distribution or capitalisation, less its accumulated, realised losses, so far as not previously written off in a reduction or reorganisation of capital duly made" (section 263(3) of the Companies Act 1985).

The acquisition of shares by an ESOP does not, of itself, affect the company's realised profits or realised losses. The accounting treatment required by this Abstract, which requires a deduction in arriving at shareholders' funds and that no gain or loss should be recognised in the profit and loss account, is consistent with this analysis. This analysis holds good notwithstanding that an acquisition of treasury shares, with which an acquisition of shares by an ESOP has similarities, involves a deduction from distributable profits.

Although the acquisition of shares by an ESOP will not, of itself, result in a realised profit or loss for the company concerned, a company will still need to consider other transactions with the ESOP, for example a loan to the ESOP to fund acquisitions of shares, and these may affect the company's realised profits and losses.

(c) In determining whether a company has sufficient distributable profits and net assets in order lawfully to pay a dividend to its shareholders, under section 270(2) of the Companies Act 1985 the relevant accounts are the company's own individual accounts and not its consolidated accounts.

Appendix I
Further explanation of consensus in terms of the principles of FRS 5

UITF Abstract 13 (issued on 8 June 1995)

The UITF's consensus in Abstract 13 required that the sponsoring company of an ESOP trust should recognise certain assets and liabilities of the trust as its own whenever it had de facto control of the shares held by the ESOP trust and bore their benefits or risks. Appendix 1 to Abstract 13 explained the consensus further in terms of the principles of FRS 5 and, in particular, the attributes of assets (as defined in FRS 5) which are access to future economic benefits and control of that access. The UITF concluded that, where the arrangements were such that the sponsoring company had de facto control, the ESOP trust fell within the consensus of Abstract 13. Moreover, the UITF noted that where an ESOP trust was established as a means of remunerating employees, the sponsoring company would generally bear the risks and many of the benefits of the shares held by the trust until such time as they vested unconditionally in employees (eg through gifts becoming unconditional or options being exercised).

Distinction between ESOP trusts and pension schemes

The UITF considered that the substance of ESOP trusts was different from that of pension schemes (where, under the requirements of FRS 17 'Retirement Benefits', the gross assets and liabilities of the scheme are not required to be included in the balance sheet) in that pension schemes have a longer time-frame and are wider in scope with the result that the obligations imposed by trust law and statute have a much greater commercial effect in practice.

The present Abstract

The UITF's consensus in this Abstract (Abstract 38) also requires the sponsoring company of an ESOP trust to recognise the assets and liabilities of the trust in its own accounts whenever it has de facto control of those assets and liabilities. In that respect, the requirements are unchanged from Abstract 13. However, whereas Abstract 13 required that a sponsoring company's own shares held by an ESOP trust should be recognised as assets of the company, this Abstract requires the company's own shares to be presented as a deduction in arriving at shareholders' funds rather than as assets. This change follows the changes to the accounting treatment of own shares in Abstract 37. Other assets and liabilities of an ESOP trust continue to be recognised as assets and liabilities of the sponsoring entity.

Appendix II
Illustrative examples

The examples do not form part of the Abstract and are given for illustrative purposes only. In particular, the period of service to which an employee benefit relates can be determined only having regard to all the facts and circumstances of any particular case. Whilst the examples illustrate how this question might be approached, they should not be regarded as definitive.

In examples 1-6 below it is assumed that the ESOP trust is established for the purpose of remunerating employees and that the sponsoring company has de facto control of the assets and liabilities held by the ESOP trust. The detailed legal arrangements are not discussed since the purpose of the examples is to focus on the accounting principles.

1 *The ESOP trust holds unallocated shares costing 100, funded by a bank loan. The sponsoring company undertakes to make contributions to the trust whenever the loan-to-value ratio falls below a set figure. At the reporting date market value is at least 100.*

The company deducts the consideration paid for the shares of 100 in arriving at shareholders' funds. The company also recognises a liability of 100. Interest expense is accrued in the usual way. The amount of the reduction to shareholders' funds (100) and the market value of the shares held are disclosed.

2 *As 1 but the market value of the shares falls to 80.*

The fall in the market value of the shares does not give rise to a recognised loss. The amount of the reduction to shareholders' funds (100) and the market value of the shares held is disclosed.

3 *As 1 but options are granted over the shares at 80, when the market value is 100.*

The company recognises an expense over the period to which the employee's performance relates, in accordance with FRS 20. The amount recognised as an expense is credited in arriving at shareholders' funds. The reduction to shareholders' funds of 100 in respect of the consideration paid for the shares, and the market value of the shares, are disclosed until the shares vest unconditionally in employees.

4 *As 3 but subsequent to the grant of the options the market value of the shares falls to 50.*

The accounting is the same as in Example 3. The fall in the market value of the shares does not give rise to a recognised loss.

5 *An annual profit share of 100 is paid to a profit-sharing share trust in order that it may buy and hold shares for specified employees for a tax-efficient period. Dividends on the shares are passed through to the employees.*

If the shares have vested unconditionally in the employees, they are not accounted for as the company's own shares since the shares are in substance those of the employees. If the entitlement will lapse in the event that the employees do not remain with the company for a specified period, the shares do not yet belong to the employees. The consideration paid for the shares is deducted in arriving at shareholders' funds and disclosed until the shares vest unconditionally in the employees.

[Withdrawn] 6

A company is a co-operative, owned by its employees. All of its shares are held in a trust for the benefit of the employees collectively and the trust receives dividends from the company which are distributed to employees in accordance with the provisions of the trust deed. The shares never vest in individual employees. The company does not have de facto control of the trust shares. 7

The shares held by the trust are not in substance the company's own shares and are not accounted for as such.

UITF abstract 39 (IFRIC Interpretation 2) Members' shares in co-operative entities and similar instruments

(Issued 10 February 2005)

Preface by the Urgent Issues Task Force

a This Abstract has the effect of implementing the International Accounting Standards Board's (IASB's) International Financial Reporting Interpretations Committee (IFRIC) Interpretation 2 'Members' Shares in Co-operative Entities and Similar Instruments' in the UK and the Republic of Ireland for entities preparing their financial statements in accordance with UK accounting standards.

b IFRIC 2 applies to financial instruments within the scope of IAS 32 'Financial Instruments: Disclosure and Presentation'. FRS 25 (IAS 32) 'Financial Instruments: Disclosure and Presentation' implemented the presentation requirements of IAS 32 for entities subject to UK accounting standards. The requirements, scope and effective date of Abstract 39 are identical to IFRIC 2 except that:

- entities applying the FRSSE will be exempt from the Abstract, and
- the effective date and transitional provisions have been amended to be consistent with FRS 25.

c This Abstract incorporates the text of IFRIC 2.* The text of IFRIC 2 contains various references to International Financial Reporting Standards (IFRSs). In this Abstract those references have been amended to enable the Interpretation to be applied in a UK context. The UITF believes that those amendments do not change the requirements of IFRIC 2 in any way.

**Deleted text has been struck through and inserted text is underlined.*

Contents

UITF abstract 39 (IFRIC Interpretation 2)
Members' Shares in Co-operative Entities and Similar Instruments

paragraphs

Background	**1-2**
Scope	**3-3A**
Issue	**4**
Consensus	**5-12**
Disclosure	**13**
Effective date	**14**
APPENDIX	
Examples of application of the consensus	
Example 1	**A2-A3**
Example 2	**A4-A5**
Example 3	**A6-A10**
Example 4	**A11-A13**
Example 5	**A14-A15**
Example 6	**A16-A17**
Example 7	**A18-A19**
BASIS FOR CONCLUSIONS ON IFRIC 2	

REFERENCES

- FRS 25 (IAS 32) *Financial Instruments: Disclosure and Presentation**
- FRS 26 (IAS 39) *Financial Instruments: Measurement*

BACKGROUND

1 Co-operatives and other similar entities are formed by groups of persons to meet common economic or social needs. National laws typically define a co-operative as a society endeavouring to promote its members' economic advancement by way of a joint business operation (the principle of self-help). Members' interests in a co-operative are often characterised as members' shares, units or the like, and are referred to below as 'members' shares'.

2 IAS 32 establishes principles for the classification of financial instruments as financial liabilities or equity. In particular, those principles apply to the classification of puttable instruments that allow the holder to put those instruments to the issuer for cash or another financial instrument. The application of those principles to members' shares in cooperative entities and similar instruments is difficult. Some of the International Accounting Standards Board's constituents have asked for help in understanding how the principles in IAS 32 apply to members' shares and similar instruments that have certain features, and the circumstances in which those features affect the classification as liabilities or equity.

SCOPE

3 This Abstract applies to financial instruments within the scope of FRS 25, including financial instruments issued to members of co-operative entities that evidence the members' ownership interest in the entity. This Abstract does not apply to financial instruments that will or may be settled in the entity's own equity instruments.

3A Reporting entities applying the Financial Reporting Standard for Smaller Entities currently applicable are exempt from this Abstract.

ISSUE

4 Many financial instruments, including members' shares, have characteristics of equity, including voting rights and rights to participate in dividend distributions. Some financial instruments give the holder the right to request redemption for cash or another financial asset, but may include or be subject to limits on whether the financial instruments will be redeemed. How should those redemption terms be evaluated in determining whether the financial instruments should be classified as liabilities or equity?

UITF CONSENSUS

5 The contractual right of the holder of a financial instrument (including members' shares in co-operative entities) to request redemption does not, in itself, require that financial instrument to be classified as a financial liability. Rather, the entity must consider all of the terms and conditions of the financial instrument in determining its classification as a financial liability or equity. Those terms and conditions include

**In December 2005, FRS 25 was amended as FRS 25* Financial Instruments: Presentation. *In August 2008 the ASB amended FRS 25 by requiring instruments to be classified as equity if those instruments have all the features and meet the conditions in paragraphs 16A and 16B or paragraphs 16C and 16D of FRS 25.*

relevant local laws, regulations and the entity's governing charter in effect at the date of classification, but not expected future amendments to those laws, regulations or charter.

Members' shares that would be classified as equity if the members did not have a right to request redemption are equity if either of the conditions described in paragraphs 7 and 8 is present or the members' shares have all the features and meet the conditions in paragraphs 16A and 16B or paragraphs 16C and 16D of FRS 25. Demand deposits, including current accounts, deposit accounts and similar contracts that arise when members act as customers are financial liabilities of the entity.* **6**

Members' shares are equity if the entity has an unconditional right to refuse redemption of the members' shares. **7**

Local law, regulation or the entity's governing charter can impose various types of prohibitions on the redemption of members' shares, eg unconditional prohibitions or prohibitions based on liquidity criteria. If redemption is unconditionally prohibited by local law, regulation or the entity's governing charter, members' shares are equity. However, provisions in local law, regulation or the entity's governing charter that prohibit redemption only if conditions-such as liquidity constraints-are met (or are not met) do not result in members' shares being equity. **8**

An unconditional prohibition may be absolute, in that all redemptions are prohibited. An unconditional prohibition may be partial, in that it prohibits redemption of members' shares if redemption would cause the number of members' shares or amount of paid-in capital from members' shares to fall below a specified level. Members' shares in excess of the prohibition against redemption are liabilities, unless the entity has the unconditional right to refuse redemption as described in paragraph 7 or the members' shares have all the features and meet the conditions in paragraphs 16A and 16B or paragraphs 16C and 16D of FRS 25. In some cases, the number of shares or the amount of paid-in capital subject to a redemption prohibition may change from time to time. Such a change in the redemption prohibition leads to a transfer between financial liabilities and equity.† **9**

At initial recognition, the entity shall measure its financial liability for redemption at fair value. In the case of members' shares with a redemption feature, the entity measures the fair value of the financial liability for redemption at no less than the maximum amount payable under the redemption provisions of its governing charter or applicable law discounted from the first date that the amount could be required to be paid (see example 3). **10**

As required by paragraph 35 of FRS 25, distributions to holders of equity instruments are recognised directly in equity, net of any income tax benefits. Interest, dividends and other returns relating to financial instruments classified as financial liabilities are expenses, regardless of whether those amounts paid are legally characterised as dividends, interest or otherwise. **11**

The Appendix, which is an integral part of the consensus, provides examples of the 12 application of this consensus. **12**

***Editor's note**: *Paragraph amended with effect for accounting periods beginning on or after 1 January 2010.*

†**Editor's note**: *Paragraph amended with effect for accounting periods beginning on or after 1 January 2010.*

DISCLOSURE

13 When a change in the redemption prohibition leads to a transfer between financial liabilities and equity, the entity shall disclose separately the amount, timing and reason for the transfer.

EFFECTIVE DATE

14 The effective date and transition requirements of this Abstract are the same as those for FRS 25 (paragraphs 96 to 97B). An entity shall apply this Interpretation Abstract for annual periods beginning on or after 1 January 2005. Earlier application is not permitted.

14A An entity shall apply the amendments in paragraphs 6, 9, A1 and A12 for annual periods beginning on or after 1 January 2010. If an entity applies *Puttable Financial Instruments and Obligations Arising on Liquidation* (Amendments to FRS 25), issued in August 2008, for an earlier period, the amendments in paragraphs 6, 9, A1 and A12 shall be applied for that earlier period.*

***Editor's note:** *Paragraph added in August 2008.*

Appendix
Examples of application of the consensus

This appendix is an integral part of the Abstract.

This appendix sets out seven examples of the application of the UITF consensus. The examples do not constitute an exhaustive list; other fact patterns are possible. Each example assumes that there are no conditions other than those set out in the facts of the example that would require the financial instrument to be classified as a financial liability and that the financial instrument does not have all the features or does not meet the conditions in paragraphs 16A and 16B or paragraphs 16C and 16D of FRS 25.* **A1**

UNCONDITIONAL RIGHT TO REFUSE REDEMPTION (paragraph 7)

Example 1

Facts

The entity's charter states that redemptions are made at the sole discretion of the entity. The charter does not provide further elaboration or limitation on that discretion. In its history, the entity has never refused to redeem members' shares, although the governing board has the right to do so. **A2**

Classification

The entity has the unconditional right to refuse redemption and the members' shares are equity. FRS 25 establishes principles for classification that are based on the terms of the financial instrument and notes that a history of, or intention to make, discretionary payments does not trigger liability classification. Paragraph AG26 of FRS 25 states: **A3**

> When preference shares are non-redeemable, the appropriate classification is determined by the other rights that attach to them. Classification is based on an assessment of the substance of the contractual arrangements and the definitions of a financial liability and an equity instrument. When distributions to holders of the preference shares, whether cumulative or non-cumulative, are at the discretion of the issuer, the shares are equity instruments. The classification of a preference share as an equity instrument or a financial liability is not affected by, for example:
>
> (a) a history of making distributions;
> (b) an intention to make distributions in the future;
> (c) a possible negative impact on the price of ordinary shares of the issuer if distributions are not made (because of restrictions on paying dividends on the ordinary shares if dividends are not paid on the preference shares);
> (d) the amount of the issuer's reserves;
> (e) an issuer's expectation of a profit or loss for a period; or
> (f) an ability or inability of the issuer to influence the amount of its profit or loss for the period.

****Editor's note****: Paragraph amended in August 2008.*

Example 2

Facts

A4 The entity's charter states that redemptions are made at the sole discretion of the entity. However, the charter further states that approval of a redemption request is automatic unless the entity is unable to make payments without violating local regulations regarding liquidity or reserves.

Classification

A5 The entity does not have the unconditional right to refuse redemption and the members' shares are a financial liability. The restrictions described above are based on the entity's ability to settle its liability. They restrict redemptions only if the liquidity or reserve requirements are not met and then only until such time as they are met. Hence, they do not, under the principles established in FRS 25, result in the classification of the financial instrument as equity. Paragraph AG25 of FRS 25 states:

> Preference shares may be issued with various rights. In determining whether a preference share is a financial liability or an equity instrument, an issuer assesses the particular rights attaching to the share to determine whether it exhibits the fundamental characteristic of a financial liability. For example, a preference share that provides for redemption on a specific date or at the option of the holder contains a financial liability because the issuer has an obligation to transfer financial assets to the holder of the share. *The potential inability of an issuer to satisfy an obligation to redeem a preference share when contractually required to do so, whether because of a lack of funds, a statutory restriction or insufficient profits or reserves, does not negate the obligation.* [Emphasis added]

PROHIBITIONS AGAINST REDEMPTION (PARAGRAPHS 8 AND 9)

Example 3

Facts

A6 A co-operative entity has issued shares to its members at different dates and for different amounts in the past as follows:

(a) 1 January 20x1 100,000 shares at CU10 each (CU1,000,000);
(b) 1 January 20x2 100,000 shares at CU20 each (a further CU2,000,000, so that the total for shares issued is CU3,000,000).

Shares are redeemable on demand at the amount for which they were issued.

A7 The entity's charter states that cumulative redemptions cannot exceed 20 per cent of the highest number of its members' shares ever outstanding. At 31 December 20x2 the entity has 200,000 of outstanding shares, which is the highest number of members' shares ever outstanding and no shares have been redeemed in the past. On 1 January 20x3 the entity amends its governing charter and increases the permitted level of cumulative redemptions to 25 per cent of the highest number of its members' shares ever outstanding.

Classification

Before the governing charter is amended

Members' shares in excess of the prohibition against redemption are financial liabilities. The co-operative entity measures this financial liability at fair value at initial recognition. Because these shares are redeemable on demand, the co-operative entity determines the fair value of such financial liabilities as required by paragraph 49 of FRS 26*, which states: 'The fair value of a financial liability with a demand feature (eg a demand deposit) is not less than the amount payable on demand ...' Accordingly, the co-operative entity classifies as financial liabilities the maximum amount payable on demand under the redemption provisions. **A8**

On 1 January 20x1 the maximum amount payable under the redemption provisions is 20,000 shares at CU10 each and accordingly the entity classifies CU200,000 as financial liability and CU800,000 as equity. However, on 1 January 20x2 because of the new issue of shares at CU20, the maximum amount payable under the redemption provisions increases to 40,000 shares at CU20 each. The issue of additional shares at CU20 creates a new liability that is measured on initial recognition at fair value. The liability after these shares have been issued is 20 per cent of the total shares in issue (200,000), measured at CU20, or CU800,000. This requires recognition of an additional liability of CU600,000. In this example no gain or loss is recognised. Accordingly the entity now classifies CU800,000 as financial liabilities and CU2,200,000 as equity. This example assumes these amounts are not changed between 1 January 20x1 and 31 December 20x2. **A9**

After the governing charter is amended

Following the change in its governing charter the co-operative entity can now be required to redeem a maximum of 25 per cent of its outstanding shares or a maximum of 50,000 shares at CU20 each. Accordingly, on 1 January 20x3 the co-operative entity classifies as financial liabilities an amount of CU1,000,000 being the maximum amount payable on demand under the redemption provisions, as determined in accordance with paragraph 49 of FRS 26. It therefore transfers on 1 January 20x3 from equity to financial liabilities an amount of CU200,000, leaving CU2,000,000 classified as equity. In this example the entity does not recognise a gain or loss on the transfer. **A10**

Example 4

Facts

Local law governing the operations of co-operatives, or the terms of the entity's governing charter, prohibit an entity from redeeming members' shares if, by redeeming them, it would reduce paid-in capital from members' shares below 75 per cent of the highest amount of paid-in capital from members' shares. The highest amount for a particular cooperative is CU1,000,000. At the balance sheet date the balance of paid-in capital is CU900,000. **A11**

****UITF footnote: The requirements illustrated in this example apply also to financial liabilities of entities that are applying FRS 4 'Capital Instruments' (as amended by FRS 25) rather than FRS 26.***

Classification

A12 In this case, CU750,000 would be classified as equity and CU150,000 would be classified as financial liabilities. In addition to the paragraphs already cited, paragraph 18(b) of FRS 25 states in part:

> ... a financial instrument that gives the holder the right to put it back to the issuer for cash or another financial asset (a 'puttable instrument') is a financial liability, except for those instruments classified as equity instruments in accordance with paragraphs 16A and 16B or paragraphs 16C and 16D. The financial instrument is a financial liability even when the amount of cash or other financial assets is determined on the basis of an index or other item that has the potential to increase or decrease. The existence of an option for the holder to put the instrument back to the issuer for cash or another financial asset means that the puttable instrument meets the definition of a financial liability, except for those instruments classified as equity instruments in accordance with paragraphs 16A and 16B or paragraphs 16C and 16D.*

A13 The redemption prohibition described in this example is different from the restrictions described in paragraphs 19 and AG25 of FRS 25. Those restrictions are limitations on the ability of the entity to pay the amount due on a financial liability, ie they prevent payment of the liability only if specified conditions are met. In contrast, this example describes an unconditional prohibition on redemptions beyond a specified amount, regardless of the entity's ability to redeem members' shares (eg given its cash resources, profits or distributable reserves). In effect, the prohibition against redemption prevents the entity from incurring any financial liability to redeem more than a specified amount of paid-in capital. Therefore, the portion of shares subject to the redemption prohibition is not a financial liability. While each member's shares may be redeemable individually, a portion of the total shares outstanding is not redeemable in any circumstances other than liquidation of the entity.

Example 5

Facts

A14 The facts of this example are as stated in example 4. In addition, at the balance sheet date, liquidity requirements imposed in the local jurisdiction prevent the entity from redeeming any members' shares unless its holdings of cash and short-term investments are greater than a specified amount. The effect of these liquidity requirements at the balance sheet date is that the entity cannot pay more than CU50,000 to redeem the members' shares.

Classification

A15 As in example 4, the entity classifies CU750,000 as equity and CU150,000 as a financial liability. This is because the amount classified as a liability is based on the entity's unconditional right to refuse redemption and not on conditional restrictions that prevent redemption only if liquidity or other conditions are not met and then only until such time as they are met. The provisions of paragraphs 19 and AG25 of FRS 25 apply in this case.

***Editor's note**: *Paragraph amended in August 2008.*

Example 6

Facts

The entity's governing charter prohibits it from redeeming members' shares, except to the extent of proceeds received from the issue of additional members' shares to new or existing members during the preceding three years. Proceeds from issuing members' shares must be applied to redeem shares for which members have requested redemption. During the three preceding years, the proceeds from issuing members' shares have been CU12,000 and no member's shares have been redeemed. **A16**

Classification

The entity classifies CU12,000 of the members' shares as financial liabilities. Consistently with the conclusions described in example 4, members' shares subject to an unconditional prohibition against redemption are not financial liabilities. Such an unconditional prohibition applies to an amount equal to the proceeds of shares issued before the preceding three years, and accordingly, this amount is classified as equity. However, an amount equal to the proceeds from any shares issued in the preceding three years is not subject to an unconditional prohibition on redemption. Accordingly, proceeds from the issue of members' shares in the preceding three years give rise to financial liabilities until they are no longer available for redemption of members' shares. As a result the entity has a financial liability equal to the proceeds of shares issued during the three preceding years, net of any redemptions during that period. **A17**

Example 7

Facts

The entity is a co-operative bank. Local law governing the operations of co-operative banks state that at least 50 per cent of the entity's total 'outstanding liabilities' (a term defined in the regulations to include members' share accounts) has to be in the form of members' paid-in capital. The effect of the regulation is that if all of a co-operative's outstanding liabilities are in the form of members' shares, it is able to redeem them all. On 31 December 20x1 the entity has total outstanding liabilities of CU200,000, of which CU125,000 represent members' share accounts. The terms of the members' share accounts permit the holder to redeem them on demand and there are no limitations on redemption in the entity's charter. **A18**

Classification

In this example members' shares are classified as financial liabilities. The redemption prohibition is similar to the restrictions described in paragraphs 19 and AG25 of FRS 25. The restriction is a conditional limitation on the ability of the entity to pay the amount due on a financial liability, ie they prevent payment of the liability only if specified conditions are met. More specifically, the entity could be required to redeem the entire amount of members' shares (CU125,000) if it repaid all of its other liabilities (CU75,000). Consequently, the prohibition against redemption does not prevent the entity from incurring a financial liability to redeem more than a specified number of members' shares or amount of paid-in capital. It allows the entity only to defer redemption until a condition is met, ie the repayment of other liabilities. Members' shares in this example are not subject to an unconditional prohibition against redemption and are therefore classified as financial liabilities. **A19**

Basis for Conclusions

This Basis for Conclusions accompanies, but is not part of, the Interpretation

ASB note: The IFRIC's Basis for Conclusions, which accompanies IFRIC 2, is set out below in full.

INTRODUCTION

BC1 This Basis for Conclusions summarises the IFRIC's considerations in reaching its consensus. Individual IFRIC members gave greater weight to some factors than to others.

BACKGROUND

BC2 In September 2001, the Standing Interpretations Committee instituted by the former International Accounting Standards Committee (IASC) published Draft Interpretation SIC D-34 *Financial Instruments – Instruments or Rights Redeemable by the Holder*. The Draft Interpretation stated: 'The issuer of a Puttable Instrument should classify the entire instrument as a liability.'

BC3 In 2001 the International Accounting Standards Board (IASB) began operations in succession to IASC. The IASB's initial agenda included a project to make limited amendments to the financial instruments standards issued by IASC. The IASB decided to incorporate the consensus from Draft Interpretation D-34 as part of those amendments. In June 2002 the IASB published an exposure draft of amendments to IAS 32 *Financial Instruments: Disclosure and Presentation* that incorporated the proposed consensus from Draft Interpretation D-34.

BC4 In their responses to the Exposure Draft and in their participation in public round-table discussions held in March 2003, representatives of co-operative banks raised questions about the application of the principles in IAS 32 to members' shares. This was followed by a series of meetings between IASB members and staff and representatives of the European Association of Co-operative Banks. After considering questions raised by the bank group, the IASB concluded that the principles articulated in IAS 32 should not be modified, but that there were questions about the application of those principles to cooperative entities that should be considered by the IFRIC.

BC5 In considering the application of IAS 32 to co-operative entities, the IFRIC recognised that a variety of entities operate as co-operatives and these entities have a variety of capital structures. The IFRIC decided that its proposed Interpretation should address some features that exist in a number of co-operatives. However, the IFRIC noted that its conclusions and the examples in the Interpretation are not limited to the specific characteristics of members' shares in European co-operative banks.

BASIS FOR CONSENSUS

BC6 Paragraph 15 of IAS 32 states:

> The issuer of a financial instrument shall classify the instrument, or its component parts, on initial recognition as a financial liability, a financial asset or an equity instrument in accordance with the *substance of the contractual*

> *arrangement* and the definitions of a financial liability, a financial asset and an equity instrument. [Emphasis added]

In many jurisdictions, local law or regulations state that members' shares are equity of the entity. However, paragraph 17 of IAS 32 states: **BC7**

> With the exception of the circumstances described in paragraphs 16A and 16B or paragraphs 16C and 16D, a critical feature in differentiating a financial liability from an equity instrument is *the existence of a contractual obligation of one party to the financial instrument (the issuer) either to deliver cash or another financial asset to the other party (the holder)* or to exchange financial assets or financial liabilities with the holder under conditions that are potentially unfavourable to the issuer. Although the holder of an equity instrument may be entitled to receive a pro rata share of any dividends or other distributions of equity, the issuer does not have a contractual obligation to make such distributions because it cannot be required to deliver cash or another financial asset to another party. [Emphasis added]*

Paragraphs cited in the examples in the Appendix and in the paragraphs above show that, under IAS 32, the terms of the contractual agreement govern the classification of a financial instrument as a financial liability or equity. If the terms of an instrument create an unconditional obligation to transfer cash or another financial asset, circumstances that might restrict an entity's ability to make the transfer when due do not alter the classification as a financial liability. If the terms of the instrument give the entity an unconditional right to avoid delivering cash or another financial asset, the instrument is classified as equity. This is true even if other factors make it likely that the entity will continue to distribute dividends or make or other payments. In view of those principles, the IFRIC decided to focus on circumstances that would indicate that the entity has the unconditional right to avoid making payments to a member who has requested that his or her shares be redeemed. **BC8**

The IFRIC identified two situations in which a co-operative entity has an unconditional right to avoid the transfer of cash or another financial asset. The IFRIC acknowledges that there may be other situations that may raise questions about the application of IAS 32 to members' shares. However, it understands that the two situations are often present in the contractual and other conditions surrounding members' shares and that interpretation of those two situations would eliminate many of the questions that may arise in practice. **BC9**

The IFRIC also noted that an entity assesses whether it has an unconditional right to avoid BC10 the transfer of cash or another financial asset on the basis of local laws, regulations and its governing charter in effect at the date of classification. This is because it is local laws, regulations and the governing charter in effect at the classification date, together with the terms contained in the instrument's documentation that constitute the terms and conditions of the instrument at that date. Accordingly, an entity does not take into account expected future amendments to local law, regulation or its governing charter. **BC10**

THE RIGHT TO REFUSE REDEMPTION (paragraph 7)

An entity may have the unconditional right to refuse redemption of a member's shares. If such a right exists, the entity does not have the obligation to transfer cash **BC11**

**Editor's note: Paragraph amended in August 2008.*

or another financial asset that IAS 32 identifies as a critical characteristic of a financial liability.

BC12 The IFRIC considered whether the entity's history of making redemptions should be considered in deciding whether the entity's right to refuse requests is, in fact, unconditional. The IFRIC observed that a history of making redemptions may create a reasonable expectation that all future requests will be honoured. However, holders of many equity instruments have a reasonable expectation that an entity will continue a past practice of making payments. For example, an entity may have made dividend payments on preference shares for decades. Failure to make those payments would expose the entity to significant economic costs, including damage to the value of its ordinary shares. Nevertheless, as outlined in IAS 32 paragraph AG26 (cited in paragraph A3), a holder's expectations about dividends do not cause a preferred share to be classified as a financial liability.

PROHIBITIONS AGAINST REDEMPTION (paragraphs 8 and 9)

BC13 An entity may be prohibited by law or its governing charter from redeeming members' shares if doing so would cause the number of members' shares, or the amount of paid-in capital from members' shares, to fall below a specified level. While each individual share might be puttable, a portion of the total shares outstanding is not.

BC14 The IFRIC concluded that conditions limiting an entity's ability to redeem members' shares must be evaluated sequentially. Unconditional prohibitions like those noted in paragraph 8 of the consensus prevent the entity from *incurring a liability* for redemption of all or some of the members' shares, regardless of whether it would otherwise be able to satisfy that financial liability. This contrasts with conditional prohibitions that prevent payments being made only if specified conditions-such as liquidity constraints-are met. Unconditional prohibitions prevent a liability from coming into existence, whereas the conditional prohibitions may only defer the payment of a liability already incurred. Following this analysis, an unconditional prohibition affects classification when an instrument subject to the prohibition is issued or when the prohibition is enacted or added to the entity's governing charter. In contrast, conditional restrictions such as those described in paragraphs 19 and AG25 of IAS 32 do not result in equity classification.

BC15 The IFRIC discussed whether the requirements in IAS 32 can be applied to the classification of members' shares as a whole subject to a partial redemption prohibition. IAS 32 refers to 'a financial instrument', 'a financial liability' and 'an equity instrument'. It does not refer to groups or portfolios of instruments. In view of this the IFRIC considered whether it could apply the requirements in IAS 32 to the classification of members' shares subject to partial redemption prohibitions. The application of IAS 32 to a prohibition against redeeming some portion of members' shares (eg 500,000 shares of an entity with 1,000,000 shares outstanding) is unclear.

BC16 The IFRIC noted that classifying a group of members' shares using the individual instrument approach could lead to misapplication of the principle of 'substance of the contract' in IAS 32. The IFRIC also noted that paragraph 23 of IAS 32 requires an entity that has entered into an agreement to purchase its own equity instruments to recognise a financial liability for the present value of the redemption amount (eg for the present value of the forward repurchase price, option exercise price or other redemption amount) even though the shares subject to the repurchase agreement are not individually identified. Accordingly, the IFRIC decided that for purposes of classification there are instances when IAS 32 does not require the individual instrument approach.

In many situations, looking at either individual instruments or all of the instruments governed by a particular contract would result in the same classification as financial liability or equity under IAS 32. Thus, if an entity is prohibited from redeeming any of its members' shares, the shares are not puttable and are equity. On the other hand, if there is no prohibition on redemption and no other conditions apply, members' shares are puttable and the shares are financial liabilities. However, in the case of partial prohibitions against redemption, the classification of members' shares governed by the same charter will differ, depending on whether such a classification is based on individual members' shares or the group of members' shares as a whole. For example, consider an entity with a partial prohibition that prevents it from redeeming 99 per cent of the highest number of members' shares ever outstanding. The classification based on individual shares considers each share to be potentially puttable and therefore a financial liability. This is different from the classification based on all of the members' shares. While each member's share may be redeemable individually, 99 per cent of the highest number of shares ever outstanding is not redeemable in any circumstances other than liquidation of the entity and therefore is equity. **BC17**

MEASUREMENT ON INITIAL RECOGNITION (paragraph 10)

The IFRIC noted that when the financial liability for the redemption of members' shares that are redeemable on demand is initially recognised, the financial liability is measured at fair value in accordance with paragraph 49 of IAS 39 *Financial Instruments: Recognition and Measurement*. Paragraph 49 states: 'The fair value of a financial liability with a demand feature (eg a demand deposit) is not less than the amount payable on demand, discounted from the first date that the amount could be required to be paid'. Accordingly, the IFRIC decided that the fair value of the financial liability for redemption of members' shares redeemable on demand is the maximum amount payable under the redemption provisions of its governing charter or applicable law. The IFRIC also considered situations in which the number of members' shares or the amount of paid-in capital subject to prohibition against redemption may change. The IFRIC concluded that a change in the level of a prohibition against redemption should lead to a transfer between financial liabilities and equity. **BC18**

SUBSEQUENT MEASUREMENT

Some respondents requested additional guidance on subsequent measurement of the liability for redemption of members' shares. The IFRIC noted that the focus of this Interpretation was on clarifying the classification of financial instruments rather than their subsequent measurement. Also, the IASB has on its agenda a project to address the accounting for financial instruments (including members' shares) that are redeemable at a pro rata share of the fair value of the residual interest in the entity issuing the financial instrument. The IASB will consider certain measurement issues in this project. The IFRIC was also informed that the majority of members' shares in co-operative entities are not redeemable at a pro rata share of the fair value of the residual interest in the cooperative entity thereby obviating the more complex measurement issues. In view of the above, the IFRIC decided not to provide additional guidance on measurement in the Interpretation. **BC19**

PRESENTATION

BC20 The IFRIC noted that entities whose members' shares are not equity could use the presentation formats included in paragraphs IE32 and IE33 of the Illustrative Examples with IAS 32.

ALTERNATIVES CONSIDERED

BC21 The IFRIC considered suggestions that:

(a) members' shares should be classified as equity until a member has requested redemption. That member's share would then be classified as a financial liability and this treatment would be consistent with local laws. Some commentators believe this is a more straightforward approach to classification.

(b) the classification of members' shares should incorporate the probability that members will request redemption. Those who suggest this view observe that experience shows this probability to be small, usually within 1-5 per cent, for some types of co-operative. They see no basis for classifying 100 per cent of the members' shares as liabilities on the basis of the behaviour of 1 per cent.

BC22 The IFRIC did not accept those views. Under IAS 32, the classification of an instrument as financial liability or equity is based on the 'substance of the contractual arrangement and the definitions of a financial liability, a financial asset and an equity instrument.' In paragraph BC7 of the Basis for Conclusions on IAS 32, the IASB observed:

> Although the legal form of such financial instruments often includes a right to the residual interest in the assets of an entity available to holders of such instruments, the inclusion of an option for the holder to put the instrument back to the entity for cash or another financial asset means that the instrument meets the definition of a financial liability. The classification as a financial liability is independent of considerations such as when the right is exercisable, how the amount payable or receivable upon exercise of the right is determined, and whether the puttable instrument has a fixed maturity.

BC23 The IFRIC also observed that an approach similar to that in paragraph BC21(a) is advocated in the Dissenting Opinion of one Board member on IAS 32. As the IASB did not adopt that approach its adoption here would require an amendment to IAS 32.

TRANSITION AND EFFECTIVE DATE (paragraph 14)

BC24 The IFRIC considered whether its Interpretation should have the same transition and effective date as IAS 32, or whether a later effective date should apply with an exemption from IAS 32 for members' shares in the interim. Some co-operatives may wish to amend their governing charter in order to continue their existing practice under national accounting requirements of classifying members' shares as equity. Such amendments usually require a general meeting of members and holding a meeting may not be possible before the effective date of IAS 32.

BC25 After considering a number of alternatives, the IFRIC decided against any exemption from the transition requirements and effective date in IAS 32. In reaching this conclusion, the IFRIC noted that it was requested to provide guidance on the application of IAS 32 when it is first adopted by co-operative entities, ie from 1 January 2005. Also, the vast majority of those who commented on the draft Interpretation did not object to the proposed effective date of 1 January 2005. Finally, the

IFRIC observed that classifying members' shares as financial liabilities before the date that the terms of these shares are amended will affect only 2005 financial statements, as first-time adopters are not required to apply IAS 32 to earlier periods. As a result, any effect of the Interpretation on first-time adopters is expected to be limited. Furthermore, the IFRIC noted that regulators are familiar with the accounting issues involved. A co-operative entity may be required to present members' shares as a liability until the governing charter is amended. The IFRIC understands that such amendments, if adopted, could be in place by mid-2005. Accordingly, the IFRIC decided that the effective date for the Interpretation would be annual periods beginning on or after 1 January 2005.

UITF abstract 40
Revenue recognition and service contracts

(Issued 10 March 2005)

BACKGROUND

1 Since the ASB issued Application Note G: Revenue Recognition, as an Amendment to FRS 5, 'Reporting the Substance of Transactions' ('Application Note G') in November 2003, questions have arisen about the accounting for revenue (ie turnover) from contracts to provide services, and the UITF has been asked to provide guidance. Although many of these requests specifically refer to services rendered by professional service firms (for example, firms of accountants and solicitors), the UITF believes the same principles should be applied in accounting for all service contracts. This Abstract therefore applies to all contracts for services.

THE ISSUES

2 The main point at issue, which this Abstract addresses, is when the applicable accounting literature requires or allows revenue to be recognised as contract activity progresses or on contract completion. In this Abstract, the term 'accounted for as a long-term contract' refers to the method described in SSAP 9 'Stocks and long-term contracts' of recognising revenue as contract activity progresses.

3 In some cases, it may be appropriate to treat a single contractual arrangement as two or more separate transactions, where there are distinguishable phases. This approach may only be adopted where the value of each element can be reliably estimated. Application Note G provides further guidance on this treatment (paragraphs G22-G28).

4 The contract terms and commercial substance of contracts for services vary considerably in practice, and it is therefore impracticable to provide definitive guidance for every situation. Each entity needs to develop an appropriate accounting policy, having regard to the requirements of this Abstract, Application Note G and SSAP 9. In some cases, a single approach will be appropriate for all contracts undertaken by an entity: in others, different approaches will be required for different classes of contracts.

Application Note G: general principles

5 Application Note G requires a seller to recognise revenue under an exchange transaction with a customer when, and to the extent that, the seller obtains a right to consideration in exchange for its performance*. At that time it recognises a new asset, usually a debtor (paragraph G4).

6 Application Note G also states that a seller may obtain a right to consideration when some, but not all, of its contractual obligations have been fulfilled. Where a seller has partially performed its contractual obligations, it recognises revenue to the extent

**Application Note G defines 'right to consideration' as 'A seller's right to the amount received or receivable in exchange for its performance. This right does not necessarily correspond to amounts falling due in accordance with a schedule of stage payments which may be specified in a contractual arrangement. Whilst stage payments will often be timed to coincide with performance, they may not correspond exactly. Stage payments reflect only the agreed timing of payment, whereas a right to consideration arises through the seller's performance'. The Application Note defines 'performance' as 'The fulfilment of the seller's contractual obligations to a customer through the supply of goods and services'.*

that it has obtained the right to consideration through its performance (paragraph G6).

Application Note G requires that the amount reported as revenue should be the fair value of the right to consideration: this will usually be based on the price specified in the contractual arrangement net of discounts, and any allowance for credit risk and other uncertainties (paragraph G7). **7**

Long-term contracts

SSAP 9 has been in issue for many years, and was last revised in 1988. SSAP 9 provides specific guidance on the accounting treatment of long-term contracts. It requires turnover (and related costs) to be recorded in the profit and loss account as contract activity progresses (paragraph 28). Turnover is ascertained in a manner appropriate to the stage of completion of the contract, the business and the industry in which it operates. Where the outcome of a contract can be assessed with reasonable certainty, the prudently calculated attributable profit should be recognised as the difference between turnover and the related costs. The excess of turnover over payments on account is reported as 'amounts recoverable on contracts' within debtors. **8**

Application Note G confirms that SSAP 9 should be applied in accounting for long-term contracts. It is consistent with, and does not amend, the requirements of SSAP 9. The guidance in Application Note G requires a seller to measure turnover in respect of long-term contracts by an assessment of the fair value of the goods or services provided to its reporting date as a proportion of the total fair value of the contract, noting that the guiding principle is to consider the stage of completion of the contractual obligations, which reflects the extent to which the seller has obtained the right to consideration (paragraph G18). The amount of turnover recognised may be derived from the proportion of costs incurred only where it provides evidence of the seller's performance and hence the extent to which it has obtained the right to consideration (paragraph G21). **9**

The definition of a long-term contract is set out in SSAP 9. It is: **10**

> *A contract entered into for the design, manufacture or construction of a single substantial asset or the provision of a service (or of a combination of assets or services which together constitute a single project) where the time taken substantially to complete the contract is such that the contract activity falls into different accounting periods. A contract that is required to be accounted for as long-term by this accounting standard will usually extend for a period exceeding one year. However, a duration exceeding one year is not an essential feature of a long-term contract. Some contracts with a shorter duration than one year should be accounted for as long-term contracts if they are sufficiently material to the activity of the period that not to record turnover and attributable profit would lead to distortion of the period's turnover and results such that the financial statements would not give a true and fair view, provided that the policy is applied consistently within the reporting entity and from year to year. (paragraph 22)*

The definition is clear that, in the case of contracts for assets, only those for 'a single substantial asset' are required to be accounted for as long-term contracts. Similarly, in the case of a contract for a combination of assets or services only those that 'constitute a single project' are required to be accounted for as long-term contracts. **11**

12 Thus contracts that require services to be provided on an ongoing basis rather than the provision of a single service (or a number of services that constitute a single project) do not fall to be accounted for as long-term contracts under SSAP 9. For example, a contract to provide repetitive services (such as general professional advice, accounting support, help desk support, maintenance or cleaning) on an ongoing basis should not be accounted for as a long-term contract.

13 The definition is clear that a contract for services that constitute a single project with duration of more than a year should be accounted for as a long-term contract. It is also clear that contracts with a shorter duration should be accounted for as long-term if contract activity falls into different accounting periods and a failure to reflect turnover and attributable profit would result in distortion of turnover and results, such that the financial statements would fail to give a true and fair view.*

14 Although SSAP 9 suggests that materiality should be judged in the context of turnover and attributable profit, other implications, for example the effect on reported assets and liabilities, may require that some contracts are accounted for as long-term contracts. The UITF takes the view that in considering whether contracts for services should be accounted for as long-term contracts, the aggregate effect of all such contracts on the financial statements as a whole should be considered.

15 As noted in SSAP 9, it is important that an entity applies its policy consistently to all similar contracts and from year to year.

Other contracts for services

16 The UITF takes the view that Application Note G requires all contracts for services to be accounted for in accordance with its general principles, including those stated in paragraphs 5 to 7 above. The overriding consideration is whether the seller has performed, or partially performed, its contractual obligations. If it has performed some, but not all, of its contractual obligations, it is required to recognise revenue to the extent that it has obtained the right to consideration through its performance.†

17 Revenue is recognised according to the substance of the seller's obligations under the contract (see paragraphs 18 to 20 for further explanation).

18 Where the substance of a transaction is that the seller's contractual obligations are performed gradually over time, revenue is recognised as contract activity progresses to reflect the seller's partial performance of its contractual obligations. This is the case where the substance of the obligation is either (i) to provide the services of staff, ie where the seller earns the right to consideration as each unit of time is worked or (ii) to require the seller to use its skills and expertise in carrying out acts that will take some time to perform, even when the output is encapsulated in a document, such as a report. In such cases, revenue is recognised to reflect the accrual of the right to consideration as contract activity progresses, by reference to valuation of the work performed as described in paragraph 9 above in relation to long-term contracts.

**The ASB's Statement 'Interim Reports' recommends that interim reports are prepared on the discrete method and notes that, under this method, incomplete transactions are treated according to the same principles as are applied at the year-end. Thus entities that prepare interim reports should consider the effect on their interim reports of not treating contracts as long-term contracts, even where they do not straddle the end of an annual accounting period.*

†This conclusion is broadly comparable to the requirements of IAS 18 'Revenue', which requires revenue from the rendering of services to be recognised by reference to the stage of completion of the transaction at the balance sheet date.

Thus, subject to the considerations in paragraph 20, in case (i) the amount of revenue may be derived from the time spent; in case (ii) the amount of revenue will reflect the fair value of the services provided as a proportion of the total fair value of the contract, which will reflect the time spent and the skills and expertise that have been provided.

Where the substance of a contract is that a right to consideration does not arise until the occurrence of a critical event, revenue is not recognised until that event occurs. This only applies where the right to consideration is conditional or contingent on a specified future event or outcome, the occurrence of which is outside the control of the seller. **19**

The amount of revenue recognised should reflect any uncertainties as to the amount which the customer will accept and be able to pay. It may be the case, for example, that even where the contract states that fees are to be calculated on a time basis, the customer will not accept that the time spent is reasonable. **20**

APPLICATION TO SMALLER ENTITIES

Reporting entities applying the Financial Reporting Standard for Smaller Entities currently applicable are exempt from this Abstract. **21**

UITF CONSENSUS

This UITF consensus applies to all contracts for services. **22**

Where there are distinguishable phases of a single contract it may be appropriate to account for the contract as two or more separate transactions, provided the value of each phase can be reliably estimated. **23**

Contracts for services should not be accounted for as long-term contracts unless they involve the provision of a single service, or a number of services that constitute a single project. **24**

A contract for services should be accounted for as a long-term contract where contract activity falls into different accounting periods and it is concluded that the effect is material. In determining whether contracts should be accounted for as long-term contracts, the aggregate effect of all such contracts on the financial statements as a whole should be considered. **25**

Where the substance of a contract is that the seller's contractual obligations are performed gradually over time, revenue should be recognised as contract activity progresses to reflect the seller's partial performance of its contractual obligations. The amount of revenue should reflect the accrual of the right to consideration as contract activity progresses by reference to value of the work performed. **26**

Where the substance of a contract is that a right to consideration does not arise until the occurrence of a critical event, revenue is not recognised until that event occurs. **27**

The amount of revenue recognised on any contract for services should reflect any uncertainties as to the amount that the customer will accept and pay. **28**

An entity should apply its policy consistently to all similar contracts and from year to year. **29**

DATE FROM WHICH EFFECTIVE

30 The accounting treatment required by this Abstract should be adopted in financial statements relating to accounting periods ending on or after 22 June 2005 but earlier adoption is encouraged. Where applicable, corresponding amounts should be restated.

References

SSAP 9 'Stocks and long-term contracts'
FRS 5 Application Note G 'Revenue Recognition'
FRS 18 'Accounting Policies'
International Accounting Standard 18 'Revenue'

UITF abstract 41 (IFRIC Interpretation 8) Scope of FRS 20 (IFRS 2)

(Issued 7 April 2006)

Preface by the Urgent Issues Task Force

This Abstract has the effect of implementing the International Accounting Standards Board's (IASB's) International Financial Reporting Interpretations Committee (IFRIC) Interpretation 8 'Scope of IFRS 2' in the UK and the Republic of Ireland for entities preparing their financial statements in accordance with UK accounting standards and, in doing so, are applying FRS 20 (IFRS 2) 'Share-based Payment'. **a**

FRS 20 implements IFRS 2 'Share-based Payment' for listed entities preparing their financial statements in accordance with UK accounting standards for accounting periods beginning on or after 1 January 2005 and for unlisted entities for accounting periods beginning on or after 1 January 2006. **b**

This Abstract incorporates the text of IFRIC 8. The text of IFRIC 8 contains various references to International Financial Reporting Standards (IFRSs). In this Abstract those references have been amended to enable the Interpretation to be applied in a UK context. The UITF believes that those amendments do not change the requirements of IFRIC 8 in any way. **c**

Contents

UITF abstract 41 (IFRIC Interpretation 8) Scope of FRS 20 (IFRS 2)

paragraphs

Background	**1-5**
Scope	**6**
Issue	**7**
Consensus	**8-12**
Effective date	**13**
Illustrative Example	
BASIS FOR CONCLUSIONS ON IFRIC 8	

REFERENCES

- FRS 3 *Reporting Financial Performance*
- FRS 20 (IFRS 2) *Share-based Payment*

BACKGROUND

FRS 20 applies to share based payment transactions in which the entity receives or 1
acquires goods or services. 'Goods' includes inventories, consumables, property, plant and equipment, intangible assets and other non financial assets (FRS 20, paragraph 5). Consequently, except for particular transactions excluded from its scope, FRS 20 applies to all transactions in which the entity receives non financial assets or services as consideration for the issue of equity instruments of the entity. FRS 20 also applies to transactions in which the entity incurs liabilities, in respect of goods or services received, that are based on the price (or value) of the entity's shares or other equity instruments of the entity.

In some cases, however, it might be difficult to demonstrate that goods or services 2
have been (or will be) received. For example, an entity may grant shares to a charitable organisation for nil consideration. It is usually not possible to identify the specific goods or services received in return for such a transaction. A similar situation might arise in transactions with other parties.

FRS 20 requires transactions in which share based payments are made to employees 3
to be measured by reference to the fair value of the share based payments at grant date (FRS 20, paragraph 11).* Hence, the entity is not required to measure directly the fair value of the employee services received.

For transactions in which share based payments are made to parties other than 4
employees, FRS 20 specifies a rebuttable presumption that the fair value of the goods or services received can be estimated reliably. In these situations, FRS 20 requires the transaction to be measured at the fair value of the goods or services at the date the entity obtains the goods or the counterparty renders service (FRS 20, paragraph 13). Hence, there is an underlying presumption that the entity is able to identify the goods or services received from parties other than employees. This raises the question of whether the FRS applies in the absence of identifiable goods or services. That in turn raises a further question: if the entity has made a share based payment and the identifiable consideration received (if any) appears to be less than the fair value of the share based payment, does this situation indicate that goods or services have been received, even though they are not specifically identified, and therefore that FRS 20 applies?

It should be noted that the phrase 'the fair value of the share based payment' refers 5
to the fair value of the particular share based payment concerned. For example, an entity might be required by government legislation to issue some portion of its shares to nationals of a particular country, which may be transferred only to other nationals of that country. Such a transfer restriction may affect the fair value of the shares concerned, and therefore those shares may have a fair value that is less than the fair value of otherwise identical shares that do not carry such restrictions. In this situation, if the question in paragraph 4 were to arise in the context of the restricted shares, the phrase 'the fair value of the share based payment' would refer to the fair value of the restricted shares, not the fair value of other, unrestricted shares.

***Under FRS 20, all references to employees include others providing similar services.**

SCOPE

6 FRS 20 applies to transactions in which an entity or an entity's shareholders have granted equity instruments* or incurred a liability to transfer cash or other assets for amounts that are based on the price (or value) of the entity's shares or other equity instruments of the entity. This Abstract applies to such transactions when the identifiable consideration received (or to be received) by the entity, including cash and the fair value of identifiable non-cash consideration (if any), appears to be less than the fair value of the equity instruments granted or liability incurred. However, this Abstract does not apply to transactions excluded from the scope of FRS 20 in accordance with paragraphs 3-6 of that FRS.

6A Reporting entities applying the Financial Reporting Standard for Smaller Entities currently applicable are exempt from this Abstract.

ISSUE

7 The issue addressed in the Abstract is whether FRS 20 applies to transactions in which the entity cannot identify specifically some or all of the goods or services received.

UITF CONSENSUS

8 FRS 20 applies to particular transactions in which goods or services are received, such as transactions in which an entity receives goods or services as consideration for equity instruments of the entity. This includes transactions in which the entity cannot identify specifically some or all of the goods or services received.

9 In the absence of specifically identifiable goods or services, other circumstances may indicate that goods or services have been (or will be) received, in which case FRS 20 applies. In particular, if the identifiable consideration received (if any) appears to be less than the fair value of the equity instruments granted or liability incurred, typically this circumstance indicates that other consideration (ie unidentifiable goods or services) has been (or will be) received.

10 The entity shall measure the identifiable goods or services received in accordance with FRS 20.

11 The entity shall measure the unidentifiable goods or services received (or to be received) as the difference between the fair value of the share based payment and the fair value of any identifiable goods or services received (or to be received).

12 The entity shall measure the unidentifiable goods or services received at the grant date. However, for cash settled transactions, the liability shall be remeasured at each reporting date until it is settled.

EFFECTIVE DATE

13 The accounting treatment required by this Abstract should be adopted in financial statements relating to accounting periods beginning on or after 1 May 2006, but earlier adoption is encouraged.

***These include equity instruments of the entity, the entity's parents and other entities in the same group as the entity.*

TRANSITION

An entity shall apply this Abstract retrospectively in accordance with the requirements of FRS 3, subject to the transitional provisions of FRS 20. **14**

ILLUSTRATIVE EXAMPLE

This example accompanies, but is not part of, UITF 41.

IE1 An entity granted shares with a total fair value of CU100,000* to parties other than employees who are from a particular section of the community (historically disadvantaged individuals), as a means of enhancing its image as a good corporate citizen. The economic benefits derived from enhancing its corporate image could take a variety of forms, such as increasing its customer base, attracting or retaining employees, or improving or maintaining its ability to tender successfully for business contracts.

IE2 The entity cannot identify the specific consideration received. For example, no cash was received and no service conditions were imposed. Therefore, the identifiable consideration (nil) is less than the fair value of the equity instruments granted (CU100,000).

IE3 Although the entity cannot identify any specific goods or services received, the circumstances indicate that goods or services have been (or will be) received, and therefore FRS 20 applies.

IE4 In this situation, because the entity cannot identify the specific goods or services received, the rebuttable presumption in paragraph 13 of FRS 20, that the fair value of the goods or services received can be estimated reliably, does not apply. The entity should instead measure the goods or services received by reference to the fair value of the equity instruments granted.

**In this example, monetary amounts are denominated in 'currency units' (CU).*

Basis for Conclusions on IFRIC Interpretation 8

This Basis for Conclusions accompanies, but is not part of, IFRIC 8.

ASB note: The IFRIC's Basis for Conclusions, which accompanies IFRIC 8, is set out below in full.

This Basis for Conclusions summarises the IFRIC's considerations in reaching its consensus. Individual IFRIC members gave greater weight to some factors than to others. **BC1**

IFRS 2 *Share-based Payment* applies to share-based payment transactions in which the entity receives or acquires goods or services. However, in some situations, it might be difficult to demonstrate that the entity has received goods or services. This raises the question of whether IFRS 2 applies to such transactions. **BC2**

This question arose in the context of particular transactions, similar to the transaction described in the Illustrative Example that accompanies the Interpretation. The IFRIC concluded that determining whether such transactions were within the scope of IFRS 2 raised a further question: if the entity has made a share-based payment and the identifiable consideration received (if any) appears to be less than the fair value of the share-based payment, does this situation indicate that goods or services have been received, even though those goods or services are not specifically identified, and therefore that IFRS 2 applies? **BC3**

The IFRIC noted that, when the International Accounting Standards Board developed IFRS 2, the Board concluded that the directors of an entity would expect to receive some goods or services in return for equity instruments issued (IFRS 2 paragraph BC37). This implies that it is not necessary to identify the specific goods or services received in return for the equity instruments granted to conclude that goods or services have been (or will be) received. Furthermore, paragraph 8 of the Standard establishes that it is not necessary for the goods or services received to qualify for recognition as an asset in order for the share-based payment to be within the scope of IFRS 2. In this case, the Standard requires the cost of the goods or services received or receivable to be recognised as expenses. **BC4**

Accordingly, the IFRIC concluded that the scope of IFRS 2 includes transactions in which the entity cannot identify some or all of the specific goods or services received. If the identifiable consideration received appears to be less than the fair value of the equity instruments granted or liability incurred, typically*, this circumstance indicates that other consideration (ie unidentifiable goods or services) has been (or will be) received. **BC5**

The IFRIC also noted that IFRS 2 presumes that the consideration received for share-based payments is consistent with the fair value of those share-based payments. For example, if the entity cannot estimate reliably the fair value of the goods or services received, IFRS 2 requires the entity to measure the fair value of the goods or services received by reference to the fair value of the share-based payment made to acquire those goods or services. **BC6**

**In some cases, the reason for the transfer would explain why no goods or services have been or will have been or will be received. For example, a principal shareholder, as part of estate planning, transfers some of his shares to a family member. In the absence of factors that indicate that the family member has provided, or is expected to provide, any goods or services to the entity in return for the shares, such a transaction would fall outside of the scope of IFRS 2 and thus this Interpretation.*

BC7 The IFRIC noted that it is neither necessary nor appropriate to measure the fair value of goods or services as well as the fair value of the share-based payment for every transaction in which the entity receives goods or non-employee services. However, when the identifiable consideration received appears to be less than the fair value of the share-based payment, measurement of both the goods or services received and the share-based payment may be necessary in order to measure the value of the unidentifiable goods or services received.

BC8 Paragraph 13 of IFRS 2 stipulates a rebuttable presumption that identifiable goods or services received can be reliably estimated. The IFRIC noted that goods or services that are unidentifiable cannot be reliably measured and that this rebuttable presumption is relevant only for identifiable goods or services.

BC9 The IFRIC noted that when the goods or services received are identifiable, the measurement principles in IFRS 2 should be applied. When the goods or services received are unidentifiable, the IFRIC concluded that the grant date is the most appropriate date for the purposes of providing a surrogate measure of the unidentifiable goods or services received (or to be received).

BC10 The IFRIC noted that some transactions include identifiable and unidentifiable goods or services. In this case, it would be necessary to measure the fair value of the unidentifiable goods or services received at the grant date and to measure the identifiable goods or services in accordance with IFRS 2.

BC11 For cash-settled transactions in which unidentifiable goods or services are received, it is necessary to remeasure the liability at each subsequent reporting date in order to be consistent with IFRS 2.

BC12 The IFRIC noted that the IFRS 2 requirements in respect of the recognition of the expense arising from share-based payments would apply to identifiable and unidentifiable goods or services. Therefore, the IFRIC decided not to issue additional guidance on this point.

BC13 When considering the transitional provisions relating to first time adopters applying the Interpretation, the IFRIC concluded that it was not necessary to amend IFRS 1 *First-Time Adoption of International Financial Reporting Standards*, because the Interpretation will have no effect unless IFRS 2 is effective.

UITF abstract 42 (IFRIC Interpretation 9) Reassessment of Embedded Derivatives

(Issued 7 April 2006)

Preface by the Urgent Issues Task Force

This Abstract has the effect of implementing the International Accounting Standards Board's (IASB's) International Financial Reporting Interpretations Committee (IFRIC) Interpretation 9 'Reassessment of Embedded Derivatives' in the UK and the Republic of Ireland for entities preparing their financial statements in accordance with UK accounting standards and, in doing so, are applying FRS 26 (IAS 39) 'Financial Instruments: Measurement'. **a**

FRS 26 implements IAS 39 'Financial Instruments: Recognition and Measurement' for listed entities* preparing their financial statements in accordance with UK accounting standards for accounting periods beginning on or after 1 January 2005, and for unlisted entities that adopt the fair value accounting rules in the Companies Act 1985, for accounting periods beginning on or after 1 January 2006. FRS 26 includes transition provisions for entities adopting the standard that are similar to those in IFRS 1 'First-time Adoption of International Financial Reporting Standards'. **b**

This Abstract incorporates the text of IFRIC 9. The text of IFRIC 9 contains various references to International Financial Reporting Standards (IFRSs). In this Abstract those references have been amended to enable the Interpretation to be applied in a UK context. The UITF believes that those amendments do not change the requirements of IFRIC 9 in any way. **c**

In September 2009 the Accounting Standards Board amended UITF Abstract 42 to incorporate changes made by the IASB to IFRIC 9 'Reassessment of Embedded Derivatives'. The amendments are applicable for annual periods ending on or after 31 December 2009. **d**

**Except for certain listed entities in the Republic of Ireland, for which the commencement date is 1 January 2006.*

Contents

UITF abstract 42 (IFRIC Interpretation 9) Reassessment of Embedded Derivatives

paragraphs

References

Background **1-2**

Scope **3-5**

Issue **6**

Consensus **7-8**

Effective date and transition **9**

BASIS FOR CONCLUSIONS ON IFRIC 9

REFERENCES

- FRS 26 (IAS 39) *Financial Instruments: Measurement*
- FRS 6 *Acquisitions and Mergers*

BACKGROUND

FRS 26 paragraph 10 describes an embedded derivative as 'a component of a hybrid (combined) instrument that also includes a non-derivative host contract-with the effect that some of the cash flows of the combined instrument vary in a way similar to a stand-alone derivative.' 1

FRS 26 paragraph 11 requires an embedded derivative to be separated from the host contract and accounted for as a derivative if, and only if: 2

(a) the economic characteristics and risks of the embedded derivative are not closely related to the economic characteristics and risks of the host contract;
(b) a separate instrument with the same terms as the embedded derivative would meet the definition of a derivative; and
(c) the hybrid (combined) instrument is not measured at fair value with changes in fair value recognised in profit or loss (ie a derivative that is embedded in a financial asset or financial liability at fair value through profit or loss is not separated).

SCOPE

Subject to paragraphs 4 and 5 below, this Abstract applies to all embedded derivatives within the scope of FRS 26. 3

This Abstract does not address remeasurement issues arising from a reassessment of embedded derivatives. 4

This Abstract does not address the acquisition of contracts with embedded derivatives in a business combination nor their possible reassessment at the date of acquisition*. 5

ISSUE

FRS 26 requires an entity, when it first becomes a party to a contract, to assess whether any embedded derivatives contained in the contract are required to be separated from the host contract and accounted for as derivatives under the Standard. This Abstract addresses the following issues: 6

(a) Does FRS 26 require such an assessment to be made only when the entity first becomes a party to the contract, or should the assessment be reconsidered throughout the life of the contract?

****Editor's note:*** *With effect for accounting periods beginning on or after 1 January 2010 this paragraph is amended to read:*

This Abstract does not apply to embedded derivatives in contracts acquired in:

(a) a business combination (as defined in FRS 6 'Acquisitions and mergers'); or
(b) [not used]
(c) the formation of a joint venture as defined in FRS 9 'Associates and joint ventures'

or their possible reassessment at the date of acquisition.

(b) Should a first-time adopter make its assessment on the basis of the conditions that existed when the entity first became a party to the contract, or those prevailing when the entity adopts FRS 26 for the first time?

UITF CONSENSUS

7 An entity shall assess whether an embedded derivative is required to be separated from the host contract and accounted for as a derivative when the entity first becomes a party to the contract. Subsequent reassessment is prohibited unless there is either (a) a change in the terms of the contract that significantly modifies the cash flows that otherwise would be required under the contract or (b) a reclassification of a financial asset out of the fair value through profit or loss category, in which cases an assessment is required. An entity determines whether a modification to cash flows is significant by considering the extent to which the expected future cash flows associated with the embedded derivative, the host contract or both have changed and whether the change is significant relative to the previously expected cash flows on the contract.

7A The assessment whether an embedded derivative is required to be separated from the host contract and accounted for as a derivative on reclassification of a financial asset out of the fair value through profit or loss category in accordance with paragraph 7 shall be made on the basis of the circumstances that existed on the later date of:

(a) when the entity first became a party to the contract; and
(b) a change in the terms of the contract that significantly modified the cash flows that otherwise would have been required under the contract.

For the purpose of this assessment paragraph 11(c) of FRS 26 shall not be applied (ie the hybrid (combined) contract shall be treated as if it had not been measured at fair value with changes in fair value recognised in profit or loss). If an entity is unable to make this assessment the hybrid (combined) contract shall remain classified as at fair value through profit or loss in its entirety.*

8 A first-time adopter shall assess whether an embedded derivative is required to be separated from the host contract and accounted for as a derivative on the basis of the conditions that existed at the later of the date it first became a party to the contract and the date a reassessment is required by paragraph 7.

EFFECTIVE DATE AND TRANSITION

9 The accounting treatment required by this Abstract should be adopted in financial statements related to accounting periods beginning on or after 1 June 2006, but earlier adoption is encouraged. The Abstract shall be applied retrospectively.

10 Embedded Derivatives (Amendments to UITF Abstract 42 and FRS 26) issued in September 2009 amended paragraph 7 and added paragraph 7A. An entity shall apply those amendments for annual periods ending on or after 31 December 2009. Earlier application is permitted.

11 Paragraph 5 was amended by 'Improvements to Financial Reporting Standards' issued in December 2009. An entity shall apply that amendment prospectively for annual periods beginning on or after 1 January 2010.

***Editor's note:** *Paragraph 7 was amended and 7A added in September 2009 with effect for accounting periods ending on or after 31 December 2009.*

Basis for Conclusions on IFRIC Interpretation 9

This Basis for Conclusions accompanies, but is not part of, IFRIC 9.

ASB note: The IFRIC's Basis for Conclusions, which accompanies IFRIC 9, is set out below in full.

INTRODUCTION

This Basis for Conclusions summarises the IFRIC's considerations in reaching its consensus. Individual IFRIC members gave greater weight to some factors than to others. **BC1**

As explained below, the IFRIC was informed that uncertainty existed over certain aspects of the requirements of IAS 39 *Financial Instruments: Recognition and Measurement* relating to the reassessment of embedded derivatives. The IFRIC published proposals on the subject in March 2005 as D15 *Reassessment of Embedded Derivatives* and developed IFRIC 9 after considering the thirty comment letters received. **BC2**

IAS 39 requires an entity, when it first becomes a party to a contract, to assess whether any embedded derivative contained in the contract needs to be separated from the host contract and accounted for as a derivative under the Standard. However, the issue arises whether IAS 39 requires an entity to continue to carry out this assessment after it first becomes a party to a contract, and if so, with what frequency. The Standard is silent on this issue and the IFRIC was informed that as a result there was a risk of divergence in practice. **BC3**

The question is relevant, for example, when the terms of the embedded derivative do not change but market conditions change and the market was the principal factor in determining whether the host contract and embedded derivative are closely related. Instances when this might arise are given in paragraph AG33(d) of IAS 39. Paragraph AG33(d) states that an embedded foreign currency derivative is closely related to the host contract provided it is not leveraged, does not contain an option feature, and requires payments denominated in one of the following currencies: **BC4**

(a) the functional currency of any substantial party to that contract;
(b) the currency in which the price of the related good or service that is acquired or delivered is routinely denominated in commercial transactions around the world (such as the US dollar for crude oil transactions); or
(c) a currency that is commonly used in contracts to purchase or sell non-financial items in the economic environment in which the transaction takes place (eg a relatively stable and liquid currency that is commonly used in local business transactions or external trade).

Any of the currencies specified in (a)-(c) above may change. Assume that when an entity first became a party to a contract, it assessed the contract as containing an embedded derivative that was closely related (because it was in one of the three categories in paragraph BC4) and hence not accounted for separately. Assume that subsequently market conditions change and that if the entity were to reassess the contract under the changed circumstances it would conclude that the embedded derivative is not closely related and therefore requires separate accounting. (The converse could also arise.) The issue is whether the entity should make such a reassessment. **BC5**

In 2009 the International Accounting Standards Board observed that the changes to the definition of a business combination in the revisions to IFRS 3 *Business* **BC5A**

Combinations (as revised in 2008) caused the accounting for the formation of a joint venture by the venturer to be within the scope of IFRIC 9. Similarly, the Board noted that common control transactions might raise the same issue depending on which level of the group reporting entity is assessing the combination.

BC5B The Board observed that during the development of the revised IFRS 3, it did not discuss whether it intended IFRIC 9 to apply to those types of transactions. The Board did not intend to change existing practice by including such transactions within the scope of IFRIC 9. Accordingly, in *Improvements to IFRSs* issued in April 2009, the Board amended paragraph 5 of IFRIC 9 to clarify that IFRIC 9 does not apply to embedded derivatives in contracts acquired in a combination between entities or businesses under common control or the formation of a joint venture.

BC5C Some respondents to the exposure draft *Post-implementation Revisions to IFRIC Interpretations* issued in January 2009 expressed the view that investments in associates should also be excluded from the scope of IFRIC 9. Respondents noted that paragraphs 20–23 of IAS 28 *Investments in Associates* state that the concepts underlying the procedures used in accounting for the acquisition of a subsidiary are also adopted in accounting for the acquisition of an investment in an associate.

BC5D In its redeliberations, the Board confirmed its previous decision that no scope exemption in IFRIC 9 was needed for investments in associates. However, in response to the comments received, the Board noted that reassessment of embedded derivatives in contracts held by an associate is not required by IFRIC 9 in any event. The investment in the associate is the asset the investor controls and recognises, not the underlying assets and liabilities of the associate.

REASSESSMENT OF EMBEDDED DERIVATIVES

BC6 The IFRIC noted that the rationale for the requirement in IAS 39 to separate embedded derivatives is that an entity should not be able to circumvent the recognition and measurement requirements for derivatives merely by embedding a derivative in a non-derivative financial instrument or other contract (for example, by embedding a commodity forward in a debt instrument). Changes in external circumstances (such as those set out in paragraph BC5) are not ways to circumvent the Standard. The IFRIC therefore concluded that reassessment was not appropriate for such changes.

BC7 The IFRIC noted that as a practical expedient IAS 39 does not require the separation of embedded derivatives that are closely related. Many financial instruments contain embedded derivatives. Separating all of these embedded derivatives would be burdensome for entities. The IFRIC noted that requiring entities to reassess embedded derivatives in all hybrid instruments could be onerous because frequent monitoring would be required. Market conditions and other factors affecting embedded derivatives would have to be monitored continuously to ensure timely identification of a change in circumstances and amendment of the accounting treatment accordingly. For example, if the functional currency of the counterparty changes during the reporting period so that the contract is no longer denominated in a currency of one of the parties to the contract, then a reassessment of the hybrid instrument would be required at the date of change to ensure the correct accounting treatment in future.

BC8 The IFRIC also recognised that although IAS 39 is silent on the issue of reassessment it gives relevant guidance when it states that for the types of contracts covered by paragraph AG33(b) the assessment of whether an embedded derivative is closely related is required only at inception. Paragraph AG33(b) states:

> An embedded floor or cap on the interest rate on a debt contract or insurance contract is closely related to the host contract, provided the cap is at or above the market rate of interest and the floor is at or below the market rate of interest *when the contract is issued*, and the cap or floor is not leveraged in relation to the host contract. Similarly, provisions included in a contract to purchase or sell an asset (eg a commodity) that establish a cap and a floor on the price to be paid or received for the asset are closely related to the host contract if both the cap and floor were out of the money *at inception* and are not leveraged. (Emphasis added).

The IFRIC also considered the implications of requiring subsequent reassessment. For example, assume that an entity, when it first becomes a party to a contract, separately recognises a host asset and an embedded derivative liability. If the entity were required to reassess whether the embedded derivative was to be accounted for separately and if the entity concluded some time after becoming a party to the contract that the derivative was no longer required to be separated, then questions of recognition and measurement would arise. In the above circumstances, the IFRIC identified the following possibilities: **BC9**

(a) the entity could remove the derivative from its balance sheet and recognise in profit or loss a corresponding gain or loss. This would lead to recognition of a gain or loss even though there had been no transaction and no change in the value of the total contract or its components.

(b) the entity could leave the derivative as a separate item in the balance sheet. The issue would then arise as to when the item was to be removed from the balance sheet. Should it be amortised (and, if so, how would the amortisation affect the effective interest rate of the asset), or should it be derecognised only when the asset is derecognised?

(c) the entity could combine the derivative (which is recognised at fair value) with the asset (which is recognised at amortised cost). This would alter both the carrying amount of the asset and its effective interest rate even though there had been no change in the economics of the whole contract. In some cases, it could also result in a negative effective interest rate.

The IFRIC noted that, under its view that subsequent reassessment is appropriate only when there has been a change in the terms of the contract that significantly modifies the cash flows that otherwise would be required by the contract, the above issues do not arise.

The IFRIC noted that IAS 39 requires an entity to assess whether an embedded derivative needs to be separated from the host contract and accounted for as a derivative when it first becomes a party to a contract. Consequently, if an entity purchases a contract that contains an embedded derivative it assesses whether the embedded derivative needs to be separated and accounted for as a derivative on the basis of conditions at that date. **BC10**

The IFRIC considered an alternative approach of making reassessment optional. It decided against this approach because it would reduce comparability of financial information. Also, the IFRIC noted that this approach would be inconsistent with the embedded derivative requirements in IAS 39 that either require or prohibit separation but do not give an option. Accordingly, the IFRIC concluded that reassessment should not be optional. **BC11**

Reassessment of embedded derivatives

BC11A Following the issue of *Reclassification of Financial Assets* (Amendments to IAS 39 and IFRS 7) in October 2008 constituents told the International Accounting Standards Board that there was uncertainty about the interaction between those amendments and IFRIC 9 regarding the assessment of embedded derivatives. Some of those taking part in the public round-table meetings held by the Board and the US Financial Accounting Standards Board in November and December 2008 in response to the global financial crisis also raised that issue. They asked the Board to consider further amendments to IFRSs to prevent any practice developing whereby, following reclassification of a financial asset, embedded derivatives that should be separately accounted for are not.

BC11B In accordance with paragraph 7 of IFRIC 9, assessment of the separation of an embedded derivative after an entity first became a party to the contract is prohibited unless there is a change in the terms of the contract that significantly modifies the cash flows that otherwise would be required under the contract. Constituents told the Board that some might interpret IFRIC 9 as prohibiting the separation of an embedded derivative on the reclassification of a hybrid (combined) financial asset out of the fair value through profit or loss category unless there is a concurrent change in its contractual terms.

BC11C The Board noted that when IFRIC 9 was issued, reclassifications out of the fair value through profit or loss category were prohibited and hence IFRIC 9 did not consider the possibility of such reclassifications.

BC11D The Board was clear that it did not intend the requirements to separate particular embedded derivatives from hybrid (combined) financial instruments to be circumvented as a result of the amendments to IAS 39 issued in October 2008. Therefore, the Board decided to clarify IFRIC 9 by amending paragraph 7.

BC11E The Board believes that unless assessment and separation of embedded derivatives is done when reclassifying hybrid (combined) financial assets out of the fair value through profit or loss category, structuring opportunities are created that the embedded derivative accounting requirements in IAS 39 were intended to prevent. This is because, by initially classifying a hybrid (combined) financial instrument as at fair value through profit or loss and later reclassifying it into another category, an entity can circumvent requirements for separation of an embedded derivative. The Board also noted that the only appropriate accounting for derivative instruments is to be included in the fair value through profit or loss category.

BC11F The Board decided also to clarify that an assessment on reclassification should be made on the basis of the circumstances that existed when the entity first became a party to the contract, or, if later, the date of a change in the terms of the contract that significantly modified the cash flows that otherwise would be required under the contract. This date is consistent with one of the stated purposes of embedded derivative accounting (ie preventing circumvention of the recognition and measurement requirements for derivatives) and provides some degree of comparability. Furthermore, because the terms of the embedded features in the hybrid (combined) financial instrument have not changed, the Board did not see a reason for arriving at an answer on separation different from what would have been the case at initial recognition of the hybrid (combined) contract (or a later date of a change in the terms of the contract). In addition, the Board clarified that paragraph 11(c) of IAS 39 should not be applied in assessing whether an embedded derivative requires separation. The Board noted that before reclassification the hybrid (combined) financial instrument is necessarily classified at fair value through profit or loss so that for the purpose of the assessment on reclassification this criterion is not relevant but would, if applied for assessments made in accordance with paragraph 7A of the Interpretation, always result in no embedded derivative being separated.

FIRST-TIME ADOPTERS OF IFRSS

In the Implementation Guidance with IFRS 1 *First-time Adoption of International Financial Reporting Standards, paragraph IG55 states*: **BC12**

> When IAS 39 requires an entity to separate an embedded derivative from a host contract, the initial carrying amounts of the components at the date when the instrument first satisfies the recognition criteria in IAS 39 reflect circumstances at that date (IAS 39, paragraph 11). If the entity cannot determine the initial carrying amounts of the embedded derivative and host contract reliably, it treats the entire combined contract as a financial instrument held for trading (IAS 39, paragraph 12). This results in fair value measurement (except when the entity cannot determine a reliable fair value, see IAS 39, paragraph 46(c)), with changes in fair value recognised in profit or loss.

This guidance reflects the principle in IFRS 1 that a first-time adopter should apply IFRSs as if they had been in place from initial recognition. This is consistent with the general principle used in IFRSs of full retrospective application of Standards. The IFRIC noted that the date of initial recognition referred to in paragraph IG55 is the date when the entity first became a party to the contract and not the date of first-time adoption of IFRSs. Accordingly, the IFRIC concluded that IFRS 1 requires an entity to assess whether an embedded derivative is required to be separated from the host contract and accounted for as a derivative on the basis of conditions at the date when the entity first became a party to the contract and not those at the date of first-time adoption. **BC13**

UITF abstract 43
The interpretation of equivalence for the purposes of section 228A of the Companies Act 1985*

(Issued 23 October 2006)

INTRODUCTION

1 With effect for accounting periods commencing on or after 1 January 2005, the Companies Act 1985 has been amended to include a new section 228A. This exempts, subject to certain conditions, an intermediate parent undertaking from the requirement to prepare consolidated accounts where its parent entity is not established under the law of an EEA state. The new exemption complements the well established exemption in section 228 for intermediate parent undertakings where the parent entity is established under the law of an EEA state.

2 Section 228A† states that:

"(2) *Exemption is conditional upon compliance with all of the following conditions:*

(a) that the company and all of its subsidiary undertakings are included in consolidated accounts for a larger group drawn up to the same date, or to an earlier date in the same financial year, by a parent undertaking;

(b) that those accounts and, where appropriate, the group's annual report, are drawn up in accordance with the provisions of the Seventh Directive (83/349/EEC) (where applicable as modified by the provisions of the Bank Accounts Directive (86/635/EEC) or the Insurance Accounts Directive (91/674/EEC)), or in a manner equivalent to consolidated accounts and consolidated annual reports so drawn up;

(c) . . ."

This Abstract provides guidance on interpretation of the underlined words. Questions have been raised as to whether financial statements drawn up in accordance with International Financial Reporting Standards (IFRS), US Generally Accepted Accounting Principles (GAAP) or other GAAPs meet the requirement for equivalence with the Seventh Directive. The UITF believes that guidance would be useful to reduce the likelihood of divergent practice emerging.

BACKGROUND

3 The requirements of section 228A are based on the EU Seventh Company Law Directive. No guidance has been issued at the EU level on the interpretation of the expression "in a manner equivalent" used in the legislation. It is understood that US GAAP is regularly treated as meeting the equivalence test in some of those countries that have implemented similar law based on the Seventh Directive.

***Editor's note:** For accounting periods beginning on or after 6 April 2008 this changes to section 401 of the Companies Act 2006.*

†*In the Republic of Ireland the wording of Regulation 9A of the European Communities (Companies: Group Accounts) Regulations 1992 is slightly different but the intention is the same and the underlined phrase is exactly the same.*

In the UK, the Department of Trade and Industry has stated in published guidance* that it considers that, in most circumstances, financial statements of a larger group prepared on the basis of IFRS would meet the equivalence test. In relation to US GAAP, Canadian GAAP and Japanese GAAP, the DTI guidance makes reference to the work that was being undertaken at the time that guidance was issued by the Committee of European Securities Regulators (CESR), in accordance with a mandate provided by the European Commission. 4

In June 2005, CESR published its recommendation to the European Commission on the equivalence of the GAAPs in the US, Canada and Japan (together the "third countries") with IFRS as adopted by the EU.† CESR's recommendation is that these three GAAPs, each taken as a whole, are equivalent to IFRS subject to certain caveats and additional disclosures. The CESR report does not deal with equivalence with the Seventh Directive, which is generally less prescriptive than IFRS, and the study was conducted for a different purpose in connection with the Prospectus Directive and the Transparency Directive. Nevertheless, it is expected that similar principles will apply to the consideration of equivalence between the Seventh Directive and third countries' GAAPs as apply to the consideration of equivalence between those GAAPs and IFRS. 5

THE ISSUE

Use of the exemption in section 228A requires an analysis of a particular set of consolidated accounts to determine whether they are drawn up in a manner equivalent to consolidated accounts that are in accordance with the Seventh Directive‡. However, whilst the analysis ultimately has to be on a case by case basis, it should be possible to identify some GAAPs that usually result in consolidated accounts being drawn up in a manner equivalent to the Seventh Directive. 6

The UITF believes that guidance would assist entities to adopt a consistent approach to this issue. In the absence of such guidance, companies and their auditors might feel obliged to take an overly cautious approach in response to uncertainty about whether the exemption can be used. This would result in unnecessary burdens on businesses in the UK and Republic of Ireland and might disadvantage them when compared to companies operating elsewhere in the EU. 7

General approach to assessing equivalence

It is generally accepted that the reference to equivalence in section 228A does not mean compliance with every detail of the Seventh Directive. The UITF believes that a qualitative approach, i.e. with a focus on compliance with the basic requirements of the Directive and in particular the requirement to give a true and fair view, is more in 8

**DTI, 'Guidance for British companies on changes to the accounting and reporting provisions of the Companies Act 1985', August 2005, paragraphs 5.3 to 5.6.*

†Technical advice on equivalence of certain third country GAAP and on description of certain third countries mechanisms of enforcement of financial information (Ref: CESR/05-230b). The European Commission has announced plans to postpone by two years implementation of the requirement for equivalence in the Prospectus and Transparency Directives and so the CESR guidance may not be implemented.

‡The Seventh Directive deals with consolidated accounts and applies most of the requirements of the Fourth Directive to those consolidated accounts. Consideration of equivalence with the Seventh Directive therefore requires consideration of equivalence with the relevant provisions of the Fourth Directive. References in this Abstract to accounts being prepared in accordance with the Seventh Directive include, where appropriate, compliance with the relevant provisions of the Fourth Directive.

keeping with the deregulatory nature of the exemption than a requirement to consider the detailed requirements on a checklist basis (see also paragraph 15 below).

UK accounting standards

9 Some entities have parents that are established in jurisdictions outside the EU and prepare consolidated accounts that give a true and fair view and comply with accounting standards applicable in the UK and Republic of Ireland. Those accounts will meet the requirement for equivalence.

IFRS adopted by the EU

10 The procedure for adoption of IFRS by the EU requires a standard to meet the basic requirements of the Fourth and Seventh Directives, including the requirement to give a true and fair view, without implying a strict conformity with each and every provision. Accounts prepared in accordance with IFRS as adopted by the EU will therefore always meet the test of equivalence.

IFRS

11 IFRS as issued by the IASB (i.e. without the qualifying "as adopted by the EU") will currently meet the test of equivalence. This is because there are no standards or interpretations issued by the IASB that conflict with the basic requirements of the Directives*. The fact that a standard or interpretation has not been adopted because of the time taken to complete the adoption process will not of itself indicate a lack of equivalence. However if, in future, the European Commission fails to adopt a standard on the grounds that it does not meet the basic requirements of either the Fourth or Seventh Directive, it will be necessary to consider whether the reasons for the failure to adopt the standard suggest that compliance with that standard will fail to give a true and fair view and will, therefore, fail the test of equivalence.

Accounting standards based on IFRS

12 There are some GAAPs (e.g. those in Australia, Hong Kong and South Africa) which are based on IFRS but may not correspond with IFRS in all respects. It is not practicable to give specific guidance on all of the increasing number of GAAPs that are based on, or are converging with, IFRS. In those cases where they are more restrictive than IFRS by eliminating choices, they will meet the test of equivalence for the purposes of section 228A. In other cases, it will be necessary to obtain an understanding of how they differ from IFRS and whether those differences might result in a departure from the basic requirements of the Fourth or Seventh Directives.

Accounting standards not based on IFRS

13 There are other GAAPs that are not based on IFRS. These include the third countries' GAAPs (i.e. US, Canadian and Japanese GAAPs) which were the subject of the CESR recommendation to the European Commission. CESR's recommendation was made from the perspective that investors' decisions should be unaffected by the use of different accounting standards. This test is not directly relevant to the

**The adoption of the Fair Value Amendment to IAS 39 has removed the possibility of a lack of equivalence through compliance with the "full" IAS 39 rather than the "carved out" version originally adopted by the EU.*

accounts of the higher parent required under section 228A because these will not be used for the purposes of investing in shares of the UK reporting entity - investors that are not part of the controlling interest have in any case a legal right to require consolidated accounts of the UK parent. However, an assessment of whether the third countries' GAAPs meet the section 228A equivalence test can be built upon the work of CESR.

The Fourth and Seventh Directives are generally less prescriptive than IFRS. For example, they do not prohibit merger accounting or include any particular requirements about how to account for share-based payments. The work undertaken by CESR in relation to equivalence with IFRS suggests that US GAAP, Canadian GAAP and Japanese GAAP will, in most cases, result in accounts that comply with the basic requirements of the Fourth and Seventh Directives. Some of the issues identified by CESR as resulting in a possible lack of equivalence between IFRS and the third countries' GAAPs are not relevant for the purposes of section 228A; however, two issues, namely the scope of consolidated accounts and the consistent use of accounting policies, are particularly relevant to assessing equivalence. **14**

The UITF believes that the basic requirement for a true and fair view includes the scope of consolidated accounts and consistent accounting policies. Therefore, meeting the test of equivalence is subject to ensuring both that the scope of entities included in the consolidated accounts is consistent with the Seventh Directive and that consistent accounting policies have been used for all entities included in the consolidated accounts. **15**

Scope of consolidated accounts

As a result of section 228A (2)(a) there is a specific requirement that the UK parent company and all of its subsidiary undertakings (as defined in the Act) are included in the consolidated accounts of the larger group. The requirement for undertakings outside of the UK sub-group is less stringent in that they need meet only the minimum requirements of the Seventh Directive assuming that the Member State options had been implemented in the least restrictive way. **16**

The text of Articles 1-3 of the Seventh Directive, which includes a definition of those undertakings that must be included in the consolidation, is set out in Appendix 1 to this Abstract for reference. Some parts of the definition in Article 1 are Member State options that cannot be regarded as mandatory requirements of the Directive. In particular, the requirement that an undertaking should be consolidated on the grounds of actual exercise of, or power to exercise, a dominant influence is a Member State option which was taken up in the UK but which need not be considered for the purpose of assessing equivalence. **17**

For example, some Special Purpose Entities would not have to be consolidated under the requirements of Article 1 even if they would have to be consolidated under UK GAAP. On the other hand, there may be cases where a third country's GAAP does not require the consolidation of an entity in circumstances where the Seventh Directive would do so. This would lead to a lack of equivalence for the purposes of section 228A where the effect on the consolidated accounts of the larger group is material to those accounts. **18**

Consistent accounting policies

The Seventh Directive includes a requirement that consolidated accounts should be drawn up on the basis of consistent accounting policies. There may be instances **19** where other GAAPs do not include such a requirement. This could lead to a lack of equivalence for the purposes of section 228A where the effect on the consolidated accounts of the larger group is material to those accounts.

Other differences

20 There are other areas of difference between the third countries' GAAPs and the Seventh Directive, for example in relation to the treatment of goodwill and negative goodwill. However, the requirements of IFRS 3 Business Combinations for goodwill and negative goodwill also differ from the detailed provisions of the Fourth and Seventh Directives. IFRS 3 has been adopted by the EU and therefore it may be considered that such differences are not material for the purpose of assessing equivalence.

Specialised industries

21 The UITF's consideration of this issue did not extend to those cases where the consolidated accounts of the larger group are prepared in accordance with specialised industry standards, including those that may be applicable to banks and insurance companies*. The UITF noted that some GAAPs include industry specific standards which grant exemptions from other standards. For example, US GAAP grants an exemption from the requirement to consolidate certain subsidiaries of some types of investment vehicle. Consideration should be given to whether the application of such industry specific standards will result in a lack of equivalence with the Directives.

Annual report

22 Section 228A (2)(b) imposes a condition that "where appropriate" the "annual report" of the larger group must be drawn up in accordance with the provisions of the Seventh Directive or in a manner equivalent to reports so drawn up. The term "annual report" is used in the section in the sense that it is used in the Directive and should be read as "Directors' report" in the UK context.

23 Section 228A does not provide further elaboration of the expression "where appropriate". Possible interpretations include "where the larger group prepares an annual report" or "where the larger group would be required to prepare an annual report under the Directive". The Directive provides that a Member State may waive the requirement for small companies to prepare an annual report. This Abstract does not provide guidance on the interpretation of the expression "where appropriate" as used in section 228A.

24 For ease of reference, the requirements of Article 46 of the Fourth Directive dealing with the contents of the annual report are set out in Appendix 2 to this Abstract. In keeping with the approach to equivalence of financial statements taken in this Abstract, any consideration of equivalence of the annual report would be at a high level rather than considering the detailed requirements on a checklist basis.

**In the case of banks and insurance companies the requirements of the Seventh Directive to be considered are those as modified, where appropriate, by the Bank Accounts Directive or the Insurance Accounts Directive.*

APPLICATION TO SMALLER ENTITIES

Reporting entities applying the Financial Reporting Standard for Smaller Entities are exempt from this Abstract*. **25**

UITF CONSENSUS

The UITF reached a consensus that for the purposes of section 228A of the Companies Act 1985: **26**

(a) when assessing whether consolidated accounts of a higher non-EEA parent are drawn up in a manner equivalent to consolidated accounts drawn up in accordance with the Seventh Directive, it is necessary to consider whether they meet the basic requirements of the Fourth and Seventh Directives, in particular the requirement to give a true and fair view, without implying strict conformity with each and every provision; and

(b) the consequences of adopting the principle in (a) above are:

(i) consolidated accounts of the higher parent that give a true and fair view and comply with accounting standards applicable in the UK and Republic of Ireland will meet the test of equivalence with the Seventh Directive;

(ii) consolidated accounts of the higher parent prepared in accordance with IFRS as adopted by the EU will meet the test of equivalence with the Seventh Directive;

(iii) consolidated accounts of the higher parent prepared in accordance with IFRS as issued by the IASB will meet the test of equivalence with the Seventh Directive subject to the consideration of the reasons for any failure by the European Commission to adopt a standard or interpretation;

(iv) consolidated accounts of the higher parent prepared using GAAPs which are closely related to IFRS will meet the test of equivalence with the Seventh Directive subject to consideration of the effect of any differences from IFRS as adopted by the EU;

(v) consolidated accounts of the higher parent prepared in accordance with US GAAP, Canadian GAAP and Japanese GAAP will normally meet the test of equivalence with the Seventh Directive subject to consideration of developments in those GAAPs following the date of issue of this Abstract and:

- ensuring the scope of entities included in those consolidated accounts is consistent with the Seventh Directive;
- ensuring that consistent accounting policies have been used for all entities included in those consolidated accounts; and
- evaluating the effect of any exemptions or modifications to the GAAPs allowed by specialised industry standards which have been applied in those consolidated accounts; and

(vi) consolidated accounts of the higher parent prepared using other GAAPs should be assessed for equivalence with the Seventh Directive based on the particular facts, including the similarities to, and differences from, the GAAPs considered specifically in this Abstract.

**Companies applying the Financial Reporting Standard for Smaller Entities will be entitled to the exemption from preparation of consolidated accounts for small groups in s248 and will not therefore have to rely on the exemption in s228A.*

DATE FROM WHICH EFFECTIVE

27 The interpretation of equivalence set out in this consensus for the purposes of section 228A should be adopted as soon as practicable.

REFERENCES

EU Directives

Seventh Directive 83/349/EEC

Fourth Directive 78/660/EEC

Legislation

Great Britain

Companies Act 1985 section 228A

Northern Ireland

The Companies (Northern Ireland) Order 1986 Article 236A

Republic of Ireland

The European Communities (Companies: Group Accounts) Regulations 1992 Regulation 9A

Appendix 1
Extract from the Seventh Directive concerning undertakings to beincluded in the consolidation

SECTION 1

Conditions for the preparation of consolidated accounts

Article 1

A Member State shall require any undertaking governed by its national law to draw up consolidated accounts and a consolidated annual report if that undertaking (a parent undertaking): 1

(a) has a majority of the shareholders' or members' voting rights in another undertaking (a subsidiary undertaking); or
(b) has the right to appoint or remove a majority of the members of the administrative, management or supervisory body of another undertaking (a subsidiary undertaking) and is at the same time a shareholder in or member of that undertaking; or
(c) has the right to exercise a dominant influence over an undertaking (a subsidiary undertaking) of which it is a shareholder or member, pursuant to a contract entered into with that undertaking or to a provision in its memorandum or articles of association, where the law governing that subsidiary undertaking permits its being subject to such contracts or provisions. A Member State need not prescribe that a parent undertaking must be a shareholder in or member of its subsidiary undertaking. Those Member States the laws of which do not provide for such contracts or clauses shall not be required to apply this provision; or
(d) is a shareholder in or member of an undertaking, and:

(aa) a majority of the members of the administrative, management or supervisory bodies of that undertaking (a subsidiary undertaking) who have held office during the financial year, during the preceding financial year and up to the time when the consolidated accounts are drawn up, have been appointed solely as a result of the exercise of its voting rights; or
(bb) controls alone, pursuant to an agreement with other shareholders in or members of that undertaking (a subsidiary undertaking), a majority of shareholders' or members' voting rights in that undertaking. The Member States may introduce more detailed provisions concerning the form and contents of such agreements.

The Member States shall prescribe at least the arrangements referred to in (bb) above.

They may make the application of (aa) above dependent upon the holding's representing 20 % or more of the shareholders' or members' voting rights. However, (aa) above shall not apply where another undertaking has the rights referred to in subparagraphs (a), (b) or (c) above with regard to that subsidiary undertaking.

Apart from the cases mentioned in paragraph 1 the Member States may require any undertaking governed by their national law to draw up consolidated accounts and a consolidated annual report if: 2

(a) that undertaking (a parent undertaking) has the power to exercise, or actually exercises, dominant influence or control over another undertaking (the subsidiary undertaking); or
(b) that undertaking (a parent undertaking) and another undertaking (the subsidiary undertaking) are managed on a unified basis by the parent undertaking.

Article 2

1 For the purposes of Article 1 (1) (a), (b) and (d), the voting rights and the rights of appointment and removal of any other subsidiary undertaking as well as those of any person acting in his own name but on behalf of the parent undertaking or of another subsidiary undertaking must be added to those of the parent undertaking.

2 For the purposes of Article 1 (1) (a), (b) and (d), the rights mentioned in paragraph 1 above must be reduced by the rights:

(a) attaching to shares held on behalf of a person who is neither the parent undertaking nor a subsidiary thereof; or
(b) attaching to shares held by way of security, provided that the rights in question are exercised in accordance with the instructions received, or held in connection with the granting of loans as part of normal business activities, provided that the voting rights are exercised in the interests of the person providing the security.

3 For the purposes of Article 1 (1) (a) and (d), the total of the shareholders' or members' voting rights in the subsidiary undertaking must be reduced by the voting rights attaching to the shares held by that undertaking itself by a subsidiary undertaking of that undertaking or by a person acting in his own name but on behalf of those undertakings.

Article 3

1 Without prejudice to Articles 13 and 15*, a parent undertaking and all of its subsidiary undertakings shall be undertakings to be consolidated regardless of where the registered offices of such subsidiary undertakings are situated.

2 For the purposes of paragraph 1 above, any subsidiary undertaking of a subsidiary undertaking shall be considered a subsidiary undertaking of the parent undertaking which is the parent of the undertakings to be consolidated.

**These Articles refer to circumstances in which the Directive permits an undertaking to be excluded from consolidated accounts.*

Appendix 2
Extract from the Fourth Directive dealing with contents of the annual report

Contents of the annual report

Article 46

(a) The annual report shall include at least a fair review of the development and performance of the company's business and of its position, together with a description of the principal risks and uncertainties that it faces. The review shall be a balanced and comprehensive analysis of the development and performance of the company's business and of its position, consistent with the size and complexity of the business; 1

(b) To the extent necessary for an understanding of the company's development, performance or position, the analysis shall include both financial and, where appropriate, non-financial key performance indicators relevant to the particular business, including information relating to environmental and employee matters;

(c) In providing its analysis, the annual report shall, where appropriate, include references to and additional explanations of amounts reported in the annual accounts.

The report shall also give an indication of: 2

(a) any important events that have occurred since the end of the financial year;
(b) the company's likely future development;
(c) activities in the field of research and development;
(d) the information concerning acquisitions of own shares prescribed by Article 22 (2) of Directive 77/91/EEC.
(e) the existence of branches of the company;
(f) in relation to the company's use of financial instruments and where material for the assessment of its assets, liabilities, financial position and profit or loss,

- the company's financial risk management objectives and policies, including its policy for hedging each major type of forecasted transaction for which hedge accounting is used, and
- the company's exposure to price risk, credit risk, liquidity risk and cash flow risk.

Member States may waive the obligation on companies covered by Article 11 to prepare annual reports, provided that the information referred to in Article 22 (2) of Directive 77/91/EEC concerning the acquisition by a company of its own shares is given in the notes to their accounts. 3

Member States may choose to exempt companies covered by Article 27 from the obligation in paragraph 1(b) above in so far as it relates to non-financial information. 4

UITF abstract 44 (IFRIC Interpretation 11) FRS 20 (IFRS 2) – Group and Treasury Share Transactions

(Issued 2 February 2007)

PREFACE BY THE URGENT ISSUES TASK FORCE

a This Abstract has the effect of implementing the International Accounting Standards [a] Board's (IASB's) International Financial Reporting Interpretations Committee (IFRIC) Interpretation 11 'IFRS 2 – Group and Treasury Share Transactions' in the UK and the Republic of Ireland for entities preparing their financial statements in accordance with UK accounting standards and, in doing so, are applying FRS 20 (IFRS 2) 'Share-based Payment'.

b FRS 20 implements IFRS 2 'Share-based Payment' for listed entities preparing their [b] financial statements in accordance with UK accounting standards for accounting periods beginning on or after 1 January 2005 and for unlisted entities for accounting periods beginning on or after 1 January 2006.

c This Abstract incorporates the text of IFRIC 11*. The text of IFRIC 11 contains various references to International Financial Reporting Standards (IFRSs). In this Abstract those references have been amended to enable the Interpretation to be applied in a UK context. The UITF believes that those amendments do not change the requirements of IFRIC 11 in any way.

***Deleted text has been struck through and inserted text is underlined.*

Contents

UITF Abstract 44 (IFRIC Interpretation 11)

FRS 20 (IFRS 2) – Group and Treasury Share Transactions

	paragraphs
References	
Issues	1-6
Consensus	7-11
Effective date	12
Transition	13
Illustrative Example	
BASIS FOR CONCLUSIONS ON IFRIC 11	

REFERENCES

- FRS 3 *Reporting Financial Performance*
- FRS 25 (IAS 32) *Financial Instruments: Presentation*
- FRS 20 (IFRS 2) *Share-based Payment*

ISSUES

1 This Abstract addresses two issues. The first is whether the following transactions should be accounted for as equity-settled or as cash-settled under the requirements of FRS 20:

(a) an entity grants to its employees rights to equity instruments of the entity (eg share options), and either chooses or is required to buy equity instruments (ie treasury shares) from another party, to satisfy its obligations to its employees; and

(b) an entity's employees are granted rights to equity instruments of the entity (eg share options), either by the entity itself or by its shareholders, and the shareholders of the entity provide the equity instruments needed.

2 The second issue concerns share-based payment arrangements that involve two or more entities within the same group. For example, employees of a subsidiary are granted rights to equity instruments of its parent as consideration for the services provided to the subsidiary. FRS 20 paragraph 3 states that:

> For the purposes of this IFRS, transfers of an entity's equity instruments by its shareholders to parties that have supplied goods or services to the entity (including employees) are share-based payment transactions, unless the transfer is clearly for a purpose other than payment for goods or services supplied to the entity. *This also applies to transfers of equity instruments of the entity's parent, or equity instruments of another entity in the same group as the entity, to parties that have supplied goods or services to the entity. [Emphasis added]*

However, FRS 20 does not give guidance on how to account for such transactions in the individual or separate financial statements of each group entity.

3 Therefore, the second issue addresses the following share-based payment arrangements:

(a) a parent grants rights to its equity instruments direct to the employees of its subsidiary: the parent (not the subsidiary) has the obligation to provide the employees of the subsidiary with the equity instruments needed; and

(b) a subsidiary grants rights to equity instruments of its parent to its employees: the subsidiary has the obligation to provide its employees with the equity instruments needed.

4 This Abstract also addresses how the share-based payment arrangements set out in paragraph 3 should be accounted for in the financial statements of the subsidiary that receives services from the employees.

5 There may be an arrangement between a parent and its subsidiary requiring the subsidiary to pay the parent for the provision of the equity instruments to the employees. This Abstract does not address how to account for such an intragroup payment arrangement.

Although this Abstract focuses on transactions with employees, it also applies to similar share-based payment transactions with suppliers of goods or services other than employees. 6

UITF CONSENSUS

Share-based payment arrangements involving an entity's own equity instruments (paragraph 1)

Share-based payment transactions in which an entity receives services as consideration for its own equity instruments shall be accounted for as equity-settled. This applies regardless of whether the entity chooses or is required to buy those equity instruments from another party to satisfy its obligations to its employees under the share-based payment arrangement. It also applies regardless of whether: 7

(a) the employee's rights to the entity's equity instruments were granted by the entity itself or by its shareholder(s); or
(b) the share-based payment arrangement was settled by the entity itself or by its shareholder(s).

Share-based payment arrangements involving equity instruments of the parent

A parent grants rights to its equity instruments to the employees of its subsidiary (paragraph 3(a))

Provided that the share-based arrangement is accounted for as equity-settled in the consolidated financial statements of the parent, the subsidiary shall measure the services received from its employees in accordance with the requirements applicable to equity-settled share-based payment transactions, with a corresponding increase recognised in equity as a contribution from the parent. 8

A parent may grant rights to its equity instruments to the employees of its subsidiaries, conditional upon the completion of continuing service with the group for a specified period. An employee of one subsidiary may transfer employment to another subsidiary during the specified vesting period without the employee's rights to equity instruments of the parent under the original share-based payment arrangement being affected. Each subsidiary shall measure the services received from the employee by reference to the fair value of the equity instruments at the date those rights to equity instruments were originally granted by the parent as defined in FRS 20 Appendix A, and the proportion of the vesting period served by the employee with each subsidiary. 9

Such an employee, after transferring between group entities, may fail to satisfy a vesting condition other than a market condition as defined in FRS 20 Appendix A, eg the employee leaves the group before completing the service period. In this case, each subsidiary shall adjust the amount previously recognised in respect of the services received from the employee in accordance with the principles in FRS 20 paragraph 19. Hence, if the rights to the equity instruments granted by the parent do not vest because of an employee's failure to meet a vesting condition other than a market condition, no amount is recognised on a cumulative basis for the services received from that employee in the financial statements of any subsidiary. 10

A subsidiary grants rights to equity instruments of its parent to its employees (paragraph 3(b))

11 The subsidiary shall account for the transaction with its employees as cash-settled. This requirement applies irrespective of how the subsidiary obtains the equity instruments to satisfy its obligations to its employees.

EFFECTIVE DATE

12 The accounting treatment required by this Abstract should be adopted in financial statements relating to accounting periods beginning or after 1 March 2007, but earlier adoption is encouraged.

TRANSITION

13 An entity shall apply this Abstract retrospectively in accordance with FRS 3, subject to the transitional provisions of FRS 20.

Illustrative Example

This Illustrative Example accompanies, but is not part of, the Abstract

A parent grants 200 share options to each of 100 employees of its subsidiary, conditional upon the completion of two years' service with the subsidiary. The fair value of the share options on grant date is CU30 each. At grant date, the subsidiary estimates that 80 per cent of the employees will complete the two-year service period. This estimate does not change during the vesting period. At the end of the vesting period, 81 employees complete the required two years of service. The parent does not require the subsidiary to pay for the shares needed to settle the grant of share options. **1E1**

The share-based payment transaction in the consolidated financial statements of the parent is accounted for as equity-settled in accordance with FRS 20. **1E2**

As required by paragraph 8 of the Abstract, over the two-year vesting period, the subsidiary measures the services received from the employees in accordance with the requirements applicable to equity-settled share-based payment transactions. Thus, the subsidiary measures the services received from the employees on the basis of the fair value of the share options at grant date. An increase in equity is recognised as a contribution from the parent in the financial statements of the subsidiary. **1E3**

The journal entries recorded by the subsidiary for each of the two years are as follows: **1E4**

Year 1		
Dr Remuneration expense (200 × 100 × 30 × 0.8 / 2)	CU240,000	
Cr Equity (Contribution from the parent)		CU240,000
Year 2		
Dr Remuneration expense (200 × 100 × 30 × 0.81 – 240,000)	CU246,000	
Cr Equity (Contribution from the parent)		CU246,000

Basis for Conclusions on IFRIC Interpretation 11

This Basis for Conclusions accompanies, but is not part of, IFRIC 11.

ASB note: The IFRIC's Basis for Conclusions, which accompanies IFRIC 11, is set out below in full.

INTRODUCTION

BC1 This Basis for Conclusions summarises the IFRIC's considerations in reaching its consensus. Individual IFRIC members gave greater weight to some factors than to others.

BC2 The IFRIC released draft Interpretation D17 IFRS 2 – Group and Treasury Share Transactions for public comment in May 2005. It received 40 letters in response.

CONSENSUS (PARAGRAPHS 7–11)

Share-based payment arrangements involving an entity's own equity instruments (paragraph 7)

BC3 D17 proposed that, regardless of whether the entity chooses or is required to buy the equity instruments needed from another party to settle the share-based payment arrangement, the share-based payment transactions should be accounted for as equity-settled. The IFRIC's rationale was that the consideration for the services received is equity instruments of the entity (rather than a liability to transfer cash or other assets). For the same reason, the IFRIC proposed in D17 that, regardless of whether the employees' rights to the entity's equity instruments were granted by the entity itself or by its shareholders, or whether the obligations under the share-based payment arrangement were settled by the entity itself or its shareholders, the share-based payment transactions should be accounted for as equity-settled.

BC4 Of the 40 respondents to D17, only a small number disagreed with D17's proposal to treat the transactions as equity-settled.

BC5 For the reason stated in paragraph BC3, the IFRIC reaffirmed its view that the share-based payment transactions specified in IFRIC 11 paragraph 1(a) and (b) should be accounted for as equity-settled.

BC6 Some respondents asked the IFRIC to clarify whether an entity should recognise a financial liability when the entity enters into a contractual arrangement to acquire its own equity instruments. The IFRIC noted that the relevant requirements in IAS 32 *Financial Instruments: Presentation* are clear. Therefore, the IFRIC decided not to explain those requirements in the Interpretation.

Share-based payment arrangements involving equity instruments of the parent (paragraphs 8–11)

BC7 D17 addressed the following share-based payment arrangements in which two or more entities in the same group are involved:

(a) a parent grants rights to its equity instruments direct to its subsidiary's employees; and

(b) an entity grants rights to equity instruments of its parent to its employees.

A parent grants rights to its equity instruments to the employees of its subsidiary (paragraph 8)

The IFRIC noted that paragraph 3 of IFRS 2 *Share-based Payment* requires an entity to recognise as share-based payment arrangements transfers of equity instruments of the entity's parent to parties that have supplied goods or services to the entity. However, the IFRIC observed that, for the purposes of the preparation of the financial statements of the subsidiary, the transaction described in paragraph BC7(a) does not meet the definition of either an equity-settled share-based payment transaction or a cash-settled share-based payment transaction. In this situation, the equity instruments granted are not the equity instruments of the subsidiary and the subsidiary has no obligation to transfer cash or other assets to the employees. **BC8**

Because the subsidiary does not have an obligation to deliver cash or other assets to the employees, the IFRIC proposed in D17 that it was not appropriate to account for the transaction as cash-settled in the financial statements of the subsidiary. Instead, the IFRIC suggested that the equity-settled basis was more consistent with the principles in IFRS 2. **BC9**

Of the 40 respondents to D17, only a small number disagreed that the transaction should be accounted for as equity-settled in the financial statements of the subsidiary. **BC10**

The IFRIC noted that the parent has an involvement in the arrangement by committing itself to provide the employees of the subsidiary with its equity instruments. To meet the requirement in IFRS 2 paragraph 3, the IFRIC believed that it was appropriate in this particular situation for the subsidiary in its own financial statements to apply the same measurement basis as the parent uses in its consolidated financial statements. Accordingly, the IFRIC concluded that, provided that the transaction is accounted for as equity-settled in the consolidated financial statements of the parent, the services received from the employees should be measured using the equity-settled basis in the financial statements of the subsidiary. Correspondingly, to reflect the parent's granting of rights to its equity instruments to the employees of the subsidiary, the IFRIC decided that the subsidiary should recognise in its equity a contribution from the parent equal to the amount at which the services from the employees are measured. **BC11**

The IFRIC discussed whether the Interpretation should address how to account for an intragroup payment arrangement requiring the subsidiary to pay the parent for the provision of the equity instruments to the employees. The IFRIC decided not to address that issue because it did not wish to widen the scope of the Interpretation to an issue that relates to the accounting for intragroup payment arrangements. **BC12**

A subsidiary grants rights to equity instruments of its parent to its employees (paragraph 11)

Although the subsidiary in the transaction described in paragraph BC7(b) has an obligation to its employees, the obligation is not determined on the basis of the price *of its own equity* instruments. Thus, the transaction does not meet the definition of a cash-settled share-based payment transaction in the financial statements of the subsidiary. In addition, because the equity instruments provided to the employees are not equity instruments of the subsidiary, the transaction does not meet the definition of an equity-settled share-based payment transaction either in the financial statements of the subsidiary. **BC13**

BC14 D17 proposed that the subsidiary should account for the transaction with its employees as cash-settled in its own financial statements. The rationale was that the cash-settled basis was more consistent with the principles in IFRS 2 because the subsidiary has an obligation to provide its employees with the equity instruments of the parent, which are treated as assets of the subsidiary when the subsidiary acquires them.

BC15 Many respondents to D17 disagreed with the proposed treatment. They disagreed that the accounting treatments for the two types of arrangement described in paragraph BC7 should depend on which entity grants to the employees rights to equity instruments of the parent. In their view, regardless of whether the parent or the subsidiary grants those rights to the employees, in most cases the parent is the one that supplies the equity instruments to settle the obligation. They believed that it was not appropriate to require the subsidiary to apply different accounting treatments to transactions with the same substance. They had concerns that different accounting treatments would give entities opportunities to structure their intragroup transactions in order to achieve desired accounting results.

BC16 The IFRIC noted that arrangements described in paragraph BC7(a) and (b) might be the same in the consolidated financial statements of the parent, and also from the perspective of the employees who receive the equity instruments. However, from the perspective of the subsidiary, the IFRIC observed that the two arrangements are different. The IFRIC noted that under arrangement (a) the parent, rather than the subsidiary, has the obligation to provide its employees with the equity instruments, whereas under arrangement (b) it is the subsidiary that has that obligation.

BC17 In addition, the IFRIC clarified that how the subsidiary acquires the equity instruments needed to meet its obligation to its employees is a separate transaction from its transaction with its employees.

BC18 For the above reasons, the IFRIC reaffirmed its view that the transaction with the employees described in paragraph BC7(b) should be accounted for as cash-settled in the financial statements of the subsidiary.

Transfers of employees between group entities (paragraphs 9 and 10)

BC19 The IFRIC noted that some share-based payment arrangements involve a parent granting rights to the employees of more than one subsidiary with a vesting condition that requires the employees to work for the group for a particular period. Sometimes, an employee of one subsidiary transfers employment to another subsidiary during the vesting period, without the employee's rights under the original share-based payment arrangements being affected. The IFRIC reasoned in D17 that the change of employment from one group entity to another does not represent a new grant of equity instruments, because the equity instruments were granted by the parent (not the individual subsidiary). Therefore, the IFRIC proposed in D17 that the subsidiary to which the employee transfers employment should measure the fair value of the services received from the employee by reference to the fair value of the equity instruments at the date those equity instruments were originally granted to the employee by the parent.

BC20 The respondents to D17 generally supported this proposed treatment. Some respondents also asked the IFRIC to clarify the following two points:

(a) whether the transfer of employees between group entities would be considered as a failure to satisfy a vesting condition in the financial statements of the subsidiary from which the employees transferred employment (ie whether that subsidiary should reverse the charge previously recognised in respect of the services received from such employees); and

(b) after the transfer of employment, if an employee leaves the group during the vesting period, whether each subsidiary should reverse the charge previously recognised in respect of the services from that employee during the vesting period.

The terms of the original share-based payment arrangement require the employees to work for the group, rather than for a particular group entity. Thus, the IFRIC in its redeliberations reaffirmed its view that the change of employment should not result in a new grant of equity instruments in the financial statements of the subsidiary to which the employees transferred employment. For the same reason, the IFRIC concluded that the transfer itself should not be treated as an employee's failure to satisfy a vesting condition. Thus, the transfer should not trigger any reversal of the charge previously recognised in respect of the services received from the employee in the financial statements of the subsidiary from which the employee transfers employment. **BC21**

The IFRIC noted that IFRS 2 paragraph 19 requires the cumulative amount recognised for goods or services as consideration for the equity instruments granted to be based on the number of equity instruments that eventually vest. Accordingly, on a cumulative basis, no amount is recognised for goods or services if the equity instruments do not vest because of failure to satisfy a vesting condition other than a market condition as defined in IFRS 2 Appendix A. Applying the principles in IFRS 2 paragraph 19, the IFRIC concluded that when the employee fails to satisfy a vesting condition other than a market condition, the services from that employee recognised in the financial statements of each subsidiary during the vesting period should be reversed. **BC22**

UITF abstract 45 (IFRIC Interpretation 6) Liabilities arising from Participating in a Specific Market – Waste Electrical and Electronic Equipment

(Issued 13 February 2007)

PREFACE BY THE URGENT ISSUES TASK FORCE

a This Abstract has the effect of implementing the International Accounting Standards Board's (IASB's) International Financial Reporting Interpretations Committee (IFRIC) Interpretation 6 'Liabilities arising from Participating in a Specific Market – Waste Electrical and Electronic Equipment' in the UK and the Republic of Ireland for entities preparing their financial statements in accordance with UK accounting standards.*

b This Abstract sets out guidance on the recognition of certain liabilities arising from the European Parliament and Council Directive on Waste Electrical and Electronic Equipment (2002/96/EC) ("the WEEE Directive"), which makes producers of electrical and electronic equipment responsible for financing certain waste management costs, including costs of collection, treatment, reuse, recovery and environmentally sound disposal.

c The UK Regulations implementing the WEEE Directive – S.l. 2006 No.3289 'The Waste Electrical and Electronic Equipment Regulations 2006' – were laid before Parliament on 12 December 2006 and entered into force on 2 January 2007.

d The Irish Regulations implementing the WEEE Directive – 'Waste Management (Waste Electrical and Electronic Equipment) Regulations 2005' (S.l. No. 340 of 2005) – came into effect in August 2005.

e The reference accounting standard for IFRIC 6 is IAS 37 'Provisions, Contingent Liabilities and Contingent Assets'. The relevant parts of IAS 37 are virtually identical to FRS 12 'Provisions, Contingent Liabilities and Contingent Assets'. This Abstract incorporates the text of IFRIC 6' and is accompanied by the IFRIC's Basis for Conclusions. The text of IFRIC 6 contains various references to International Financial Reporting Standards. In this Abstract those references have been amended to enable the Interpretation to be applied in a UK context. The UITF believes that those amendments do not change the requirements of IFRIC 6 in any way.

f The Consensus specifically provides guidance on the recognition of liabilities for waste management relating to 'historical household equipment' as specified in the WEEE Directive. Under the model for attributing costs in relation to historical household equipment, the obligation falls on producers who are currently participating in the market.

g Although the explicit scope of the Abstract is narrow, the principles in the Abstract should be applied by analogy when obligations are imposed in a similar way. As regards the WEEE Directive, therefore, entities should tailor their application of the Abstract to the details of the applicable national legislation. For example, under the UK Regulations, the same model of attributing waste management costs is applicable to all WEEE from private households (i.e. the Regulations do not distinguish historical waste and new waste). The principles of the Abstract are also relevant for

**Deleted text has been struck through and inserted text is underlined.*

other regulations that impose obligations in a way that is similar to the cost attribution model specified in the WEEE Directive.

REFERENCES

- FRS 12 *Provisions, Contingent Liabilities and Contingent Assets*

BACKGROUND

Paragraph 17 of FRS 12 specifies that an obligating event is a past event that leads to a present obligation that an entity has no realistic alternative to settling. 1

Paragraph 19 of FRS 12 states that provisions are recognised only for 'obligations arising from past events existing independently of an entity's future actions'. 2

The European Union's Directive on Waste Electrical and Electronic Equipment (WE&EE), which regulates the collection, treatment, recovery and environmentally sound disposal of waste equipment, has given rise to questions about when the liability for the decommissioning of WE&EE should be recognised. The Directive distinguishes between 'new' and 'historical' waste and between waste from private households and waste from sources other than private households. New waste relates to products sold after 13 August 2005. All household equipment sold before that date is deemed to give rise to historical waste for the purposes of the Directive. 3

The Directive states that the cost of waste management for historical household equipment should be borne by producers of that type of equipment that are in the market during a period to be specified in the applicable legislation of each Member State (the measurement period). The Directive states that each Member State shall establish a mechanism to have producers contribute to costs proportionately 'e.g. in proportion to their respective share of the market by type of equipment.' 4

Several terms used in the Abstract such as 'market share' and 'measurement period' may be defined very differently in the applicable legislation of individual Member States. For example, the length of the measurement period might be a year or only one month. Similarly, the measurement of market share and the formulae for computing the obligation may differ in the various national legislations. However, all of these examples affect only the measurement of the liability, which is not within the scope of the Abstract. 5

SCOPE

This Abstract provides guidance on the recognition, in the financial statements of producers, of liabilities for waste management under the EU Directive on WE&EE in respect of sales of historical household equipment. 6

The Abstract addresses neither new waste nor historical waste from sources other than private households. The liability for such waste management is adequately covered in FRS 12. However, if, in national legislation, new waste from private households is treated in a similar manner to historical waste from private households, the principles of the Abstract apply. 7

ISSUE

8 This Abstract addresses in the context of the decommissioning of WE&EE what constitutes the obligating event in accordance with paragraph 14(a) of FRS 12 for the recognition of a provision for waste management costs:

- the manufacture or sale of the historical household equipment? participation in the market during the measurement period?
- the incurrence of costs in the performance of waste management activities?

8A Reporting entities applying the Financial Reporting Standard for Smaller Entities currently applicable are exempt from this Abstract.

UITF CONSENSUS

9 Participation in the market during the measurement period is the obligating event in accordance with paragraph 14(a) of FRS 12. As a consequence, a liability for waste management costs for historical household equipment does not arise as the products are manufactured or sold. Because the obligation for historical household equipment is linked to participation in the market during the measurement period, rather than to production or sale of the items to be disposed of, there is no obligation unless and until a market share exists during the measurement period. The timing of the obligating event may also be independent of the particular period in which the activities to perform the waste management are undertaken and the related costs incurred.

EFFECTIVE DATE

10 The accounting treatment required by this Abstract should be adopted in financial statements relating to accounting periods ending on or after 22 June 2007 but earlier adoption is encouraged. Where applicable, corresponding amounts should be restated.

Basis for Conclusions on IFRIC 6

This Basis for Conclusions accompanies, but is not part of, IFRIC 6.

> *UITF note:* The IFRIC's Basis for Conclusions, which accompanies IFRIC 6, is set out below in full. Except as indicated byway of footnote, the paragraphs referred to in IAS 37 are identical to those in FRS 12.

This Basis for Conclusions summarises the IFRIC's considerations in reaching its consensus. Individual IFRIC members gave greater weight to some factors than to others. **BC1**

The IFRIC was informed that the European Union's Directive on Waste Electrical and Electronic Equipment (WE&EE) had given rise to questions about when a liability for the decommissioning of WE&EE for certain goods should be recognised. The IFRIC therefore decided to develop an Interpretation that would provide guidance regarding what constitutes an obligating event in the circumstances created by the Directive. **BC2**

The IFRIC's proposals were set out in Draft Interpretation D 10 *Liabilities arising from Participating in a Specific Market-Waste Electrical and Electronic Equipment,* which was published in November 2004.* The IFRIC received 22 comment letters on its proposals. **BC3**

The Directive indicates that it is participation in the market during the measurement period that triggers the obligation to meet the costs of waste management. **BC4**

For example, an entity selling electrical equipment in 20X4 has a market share of 4 per cent for that calendar year. It subsequently discontinues operations and is thus no longer in the market when the waste management costs for its products are allocated to those entities with market share in 20X7. With a market share of 0 per cent in 20X7, the entity's obligation is zero. However, if another entity enters the market for electronic products in 20X7 and achieves a market share of 3 per cent in that period, then that entity's obligation for the costs of waste management from earlier periods will be 3 per cent of the total costs of waste management allocated to 20X7, even though the entity was not in the market in those earlier periods and has not produced any of the products for which waste management costs are allocated to 20X7. **BC5**

The IFRIC concluded that the effect of the cost attribution model specified in the Directive is that the making of sales during the measurement period is the 'past event' that requires recognition of a provision under IAS 37 *Provisions, Contingent Liabilities and Contingent Assets* over the measurement period. Aggregate sales for the period determine the entity's obligation for a proportion of the costs of waste management allocated to that period. The measurement period is independent of the period when the cost allocation is notified to market participants. The timing of the obligating event may also be independent of the particular period in which the activities to peform the waste management are undertaken and the related costs incurred. Incurring costs in the performance of the waste management activities is a separate matter from incurring the obligation to share in the ultimate cost of those activities. **BC6**

* ~~*UITF footnote: A draft UITF Abstract was issued concurrently with Draft Interpretation D10 in Information Sheet 69.*~~

BC7 Some constituents asked the IFRIC to consider the effect of the following possible national legislation: the waste management costs for which a producer is responsible because of its participation in the market during a specified period (for example 20X6) are not based on the market share of the producer during that period but on the producer's participation in the market during a previous period (for example 20X5). The IFRIC noted that this affects only the measurement of the liability and that the obligating event is still participation in the market during 20X6.

BC8 The IFRIC considered whether its conclusion is undermined by the principle that the entity will continue to operate as a going concern. If the entity will continue to operate in the future, it treats the costs of doing so as future costs. For these future costs, paragraph 18 of IAS 37 emphasises that 'Financial statements deal with the financial position of an entity at the end of its reporting period and not its possible position in the future. Therefore, no provision is recognised for costs that need to be incurred to operate in the future.'

BC9 The IFRIC considered an argument that manufacturing or selling products for use in private households constitutes a past event that gives rise to a constructive obligation. Allocating waste management costs on the basis of market share would then be a matter of measurement rather than recognition. Supporters of this argument emphasise the definition of a constructive obligation in paragraph 10 of IAS 37* and point out that in determining whether past actions of an entity give rise to an obligation it is necessary to consider whether a change in practice is a realistic alternative. These respondents believed that when it would be necessary for an entity to take some unrealistic action in order to avoid the obligation then a constructive obligation exists and should be accounted for.

BC10 The IFRIC rejected this argument, concluding that a stated intention to participate in a market during a future measurement period does not create a constructive obligation for future waste management costs. In accordance with paragraph 19 of IAS 37, a provision can be recognised only in respect of an obligation that arises independently of the entity's future actions. For historical household equipment the obligation is created only by the future actions of the entity. If an entity has no market share in a measurement period, it has no obligation for the waste management costs relating to the products of that type which it had previously manufactured or sold and which otherwise would have created an obligation in that measurement period. This differentiates waste management costs, for example, from warranties (see Example 1 in Appendix C to IAS 37†), which represent a legal obligation even if the entity exits the market. Consequently, no obligation exists for the future waste management costs until the entity participates in the market during the measurement period.

**UITF footnote: Paragraph 2 of FRS 12 contains an identical definition of a constructive obligation.*

†*UITF footnote: Example 1 in Appendix III to FRS 12.*

UITF abstract 46 (IFRIC Interpretation 16) Hedges of a Net Investment in a Foreign Operation

(Issued 23 October 2008)

PREFACE BY THE URGENT ISSUES TASK FORCE

This Abstract has the effect of implementing the International Accounting Standards **a** a Board's (IASB's) International Financial Reporting Interpretations Committee (IFRIC) Interpretation 16 'Hedges of a Net Investment in a Foreign Operation' in the UK and Republic of Ireland. When implemented the Abstract will be applicable to entities preparing their financial statements in accordance with UK accounting standards and, in doing so, applying FRS 23 'The Effects of Changes in Foreign Exchange Rates' and FRS 26 'Financial Instruments: Recognition and Measurement'.

FRS 26 implements IAS 39 in UK GAAP for listed entities and those preparing their **b** b financial statements in accordance with the fair value accounting rules set out in the Companies Act 1985* for accounting periods beginning on or after 1 January 2005.

This Abstract incorporates the text of IFRIC 16. The text of IFRIC 16 contains **c** various references to International Financial Reporting Standards (IFRS). In this Abstract those references have been amended to enable the Interpretation to be applied in a UK context. The UITF believes that those amendments do not change the requirements of IFRIC 16.

**The Companies Act 1985 requirements were superseded from 6 April 2008 by Statutory Instrument 2008/410 which was issued under the Companies Act 2006 and now incorporates the equivalent fair value accounting rules.*

Contents

paragraphs

References

Background 1–6

Scope 7–8

Issues 9

Consensus 10–17

Nature of the hedged risk and amount of the hedged item for which a designated hedging relationship may be designated 10–13

Where the hedging instrument can be held 14–15

Disposal of a hedged foreign operation 16–17

Effective Date 18

Transition 19

Appendix

Application guidance

Illustrative Example

IFRIC'S Basis for Conclusions

REFERENCES

- FRS 3 *Reporting Financial Performance*
- FRS 23 (IAS 21) *The Effects of Changes in Foreign Exchange Rates*
- FRS 26 (IAS 39) *Financial Instruments: Recognition and Measurement*

BACKGROUND

Many reporting entities have investments in foreign operations (as defined in FRS 23 paragraph 8). Such foreign operations may be subsidiaries, associates, joint ventures or branches. FRS 23 requires an entity to determine the functional currency of each of its foreign operations as the currency of the primary economic environment of that operation. When translating the results and financial position of a foreign operation into a presentation currency, the entity is required to recognise foreign exchange differences in other comprehensive income until it disposes of the foreign operation. 1

Hedge accounting of the foreign currency risk arising from a net investment in a foreign operation will apply only when the net assets of that foreign operation are included in the financial statements.* The item being hedged with respect to the foreign currency risk arising from the net investment in a foreign operation may be an amount of net assets equal to or less than the carrying amount of the net assets of the foreign operation. 2

FRS 26 requires the designation of an eligible hedged item and eligible hedging instruments in a hedge accounting relationship. If there is a designated hedging relationship, in the case of a net investment hedge, the gain or loss on the hedging instrument that is determined to be an effective hedge of the net investment is recognised in other comprehensive income and is included with the foreign exchange differences arising on translation of the results and financial position of the foreign operation. 3

An entity with many foreign operations may be exposed to a number of foreign currency risks. This Abstract provides guidance on identifying the foreign currency risks that qualify as a hedged risk in the hedge of a net investment in a foreign operation. 4

FRS 26 allows an entity to designate either a derivative or a non-derivative financial instrument (or a combination of derivative and non-derivative financial instruments) as hedging instruments for foreign currency risk. This Abstract provides guidance on where, within a group, hedging instruments that are hedges of a net investment in a foreign operation can be held to qualify for hedge accounting. 5

FRS 23 and FRS 26 require cumulative amounts recognised in other comprehensive income relating to both the foreign exchange differences arising on translation of the results and financial position of the foreign operation and the gain or loss on the hedging instrument that is determined to be an effective hedge of the net investment to be reclassified from equity to profit or loss as a reclassification adjustment when the parent disposes of the foreign operation. This Abstract provides guidance on how an entity should determine the amounts to be reclassified from equity to profit or loss for both the hedging instrument and the hedged item. 6

**This will be the case for consolidated financial statements, financial statements in which investments are accounted for using the equity method, financial statements in which venturers' interests in joint ventures are proportionately consolidated and financial statements that include a branch.*

SCOPE

7 This Abstract applies to an entity that hedges the foreign currency risk arising from its net investments in foreign operations and wishes to qualify for hedge accounting in accordance with FRS 26. For convenience this Abstract refers to such an entity as a parent entity and to the financial statements in which the net assets of foreign operations are included as consolidated financial statements. All references to a parent entity apply equally to an entity that has a net investment in a foreign operation that is a joint venture, an associate or a branch.

8 This Abstract applies only to hedges of net investments in foreign operations; it should not be applied by analogy to other types of hedge accounting.

ISSUES

9 Investments in foreign operations may be held directly by a parent entity or indirectly by its subsidiary or subsidiaries. The issues addressed in this Abstract are:

(a) *the nature of the hedged risk and the amount of the hedged item for which a hedging relationship may be designated:*

(i) whether the parent entity may designate as a hedged risk only the foreign exchange differences arising from a difference between the functional currencies of the parent entity and its foreign operation, or whether it may also designate as the hedged risk the foreign exchange differences arising from the difference between the presentation currency of the parent entity's consolidated financial statements and the functional currency of the foreign operation;

(ii) if the parent entity holds the foreign operation indirectly, whether the hedged risk may include only the foreign exchange differences arising from differences in functional currencies between the foreign operation and its immediate parent entity, or whether the hedged risk may also include any foreign exchange differences between the functional currency of the foreign operation and any intermediate or ultimate parent entity (ie whether the fact that the net investment in the foreign operation is held through an intermediate parent affects the economic risk to the ultimate parent).

(b) *where in a group the hedging instrument can be held:*

(i) whether a qualifying hedge accounting relationship can be established only if the entity hedging its net investment is a party to the hedging instrument or whether any entity in the group, regardless of its functional currency, can hold the hedging instrument;

(ii) whether the nature of the hedging instrument (derivative or non-derivative) or the method of consolidation affects the assessment of hedge effectiveness.

(c) *what amounts should be reclassified from equity to profit or loss as reclassification adjustments on disposal of the foreign operation:*

(i) when a foreign operation that was hedged is disposed of, what amounts from the parent entity's foreign currency translation reserve in respect of the hedging instrument and in respect of that foreign operation should be reclassified from equity to profit or loss in the parent entity's consolidated financial statements;

(ii) whether the method of consolidation affects the determination of the amounts to be reclassified from equity to profit or loss.

UITF CONSENSUS

Nature of the hedged risk and amount of the hedged item for which a hedging relationship may be designated

Hedge accounting may be applied only to the foreign exchange differences arising between the functional currency of the foreign operation and the parent entity's functional currency. 10

In a hedge of the foreign currency risks arising from a net investment in a foreign operation, the hedged item can be an amount of net assets equal to or less than the carrying amount of the net assets of the foreign operation in the consolidated financial statements of the parent entity. The carrying amount of the net assets of a foreign operation that may be designated as the hedged item in the consolidated financial statements of a parent depends on whether any lower level parent of the foreign operation has applied hedge accounting for all or part of the net assets of that foreign operation and that accounting has been maintained in the parent's consolidated financial statements. 11

The hedged risk may be designated as the foreign currency exposure arising between the functional currency of the foreign operation and the functional currency of any parent entity (the immediate, intermediate or ultimate parent entity) of that foreign operation. The fact that the net investment is held through an intermediate parent does not affect the nature of the economic risk arising from the foreign currency exposure to the ultimate parent entity. 12

An exposure to foreign currency risk arising from a net investment in a foreign operation may qualify for hedge accounting only once in the consolidated financial statements. Therefore, if the same net assets of a foreign operation are hedged by more than one parent entity within the group (for example, both a direct and an indirect parent entity) for the same risk, only one hedging relationship will qualify for hedge accounting in the consolidated financial statements of the ultimate parent. A hedging relationship designated by one parent entity in its consolidated financial statements need not be maintained by another higher level parent entity. However, if it is not maintained by the higher level parent entity, the hedge accounting applied by the lower level parent must be reversed before the higher level parent's hedge accounting is recognised. 13

Where the hedging instrument can be held

A derivative or a non-derivative instrument (or a combination of derivative and non-derivative instruments) may be designated as a hedging instrument in a hedge of a net investment in a foreign operation. The hedging instrument(s) may be held by any entity or entities within the group, as long as the designation, documentation and effectiveness requirements of FRS 26 paragraph 88 that relate to a net investment hedge are satisfied. In particular, the hedging strategy of the group should be clearly documented because of the possibility of different designations at different levels of the group.* 14

For the purpose of assessing effectiveness, the change in value of the hedging instrument in respect of foreign exchange risk is computed by reference to the functional currency of the parent entity against whose functional currency the hedged risk is measured, in accordance with the hedge accounting documentation. 15

***Editor's note:** *Paragraph amended with effect for accounting periods beginning on or after 1 January 2010.*

Depending on where the hedging instrument is held, in the absence of hedge accounting the total change in value might be recognised in profit or loss, in other comprehensive income, or both. However, the assessment of effectiveness is not affected by whether the change in value of the hedging instrument is recognised in profit or loss or in other comprehensive income. As part of the application of hedge accounting, the total effective portion of the change is included in other comprehensive income. The assessment of effectiveness is not affected by whether the hedging instrument is a derivative or a non-derivative instrument or by the method of consolidation.

Disposal of a hedged foreign operation

16 When a foreign operation that was hedged is disposed of, the amount reclassified to profit or loss as a reclassification adjustment from the foreign currency translation reserve in the consolidated financial statements of the parent in respect of the hedging instrument is the amount that FRS 26 paragraph 102 requires to be identified. That amount is the cumulative gain or loss on the hedging instrument that was determined to be an effective hedge.

17 The amount reclassified to profit or loss from the foreign currency translation reserve in the consolidated financial statements of a parent in respect of the net investment in that foreign operation in accordance with FRS 23 paragraph 48 is the amount included in that parent's foreign currency translation reserve in respect of that foreign operation. In the ultimate parent's consolidated financial statements, the aggregate net amount recognised in the foreign currency translation reserve in respect of all foreign operations is not affected by the consolidation method. However, whether the ultimate parent uses the direct or the step-by-step method of consolidation* may affect the amount included in its foreign currency translation reserve in respect of an individual foreign operation. The use of the step-by-step method of consolidation may result in the reclassification to profit or loss of an amount different from that used to determine hedge effectiveness. This difference may be eliminated by determining the amount relating to that foreign operation that would have arisen if the direct method of consolidation had been used. Making this adjustment is not required by FRS 23. However, it is an accounting policy choice that should be followed consistently for all net investments.

EFFECTIVE DATE

18 An entity shall apply this Abstract for annual periods beginning on or after 1 October 2008. An entity shall apply the amendment to paragraph 14 made by 'Improvements to Financial Reporting Standards' issued in December 2009 for annual periods beginning on or after 1 January 2010. Earlier application of both is permitted. If an entity applies this Interpretation for a period beginning before 1 October 2008, or the amendment to paragraph 14 before 1 January 2010, it shall disclose that fact.

**The direct method is the method of consolidation in which the financial statements of the foreign operation are translated directly into the functional currency of the ultimate parent. The step-by-step method is the method of consolidation in which the financial statements of the foreign operation are first translated into the functional currency of any intermediate parent(s) and then translated into the functional currency of the ultimate parent (or the presentation currency if different).*

TRANSITION

FRS 3 specifies how an entity applies a change in accounting policy resulting from the initial application of an UITF Abstract. An entity is not required to comply with those requirements when first applying the Abstract. If an entity had designated a hedging instrument as a hedge of a net investment but the hedge does not meet the conditions for hedge accounting in this Abstract, the entity shall apply FRS 26 to discontinue that hedge accounting prospectively. **19**

Appendix
Application guidance

This appendix is an integral part of the Abstract.

AG1 This appendix illustrates the application of the Abstract using the corporate structure illustrated below. In all cases the hedging relationships described would be tested for effectiveness in accordance with FRS 26, although this testing is not discussed in this appendix. Parent, being the ultimate parent entity, presents its consolidated financial statements in its functional currency of euro (EUR). Each of the subsidiaries is wholly owned. Parent's £500 million net investment in Subsidiary B (functional currency pounds sterling (GBP)) includes the £159 million equivalent of Subsidiary B's US$300 million net investment in Subsidiary C (functional currency US dollars (USD)). In other words, Subsidiary B's net assets other than its investment in Subsidiary C are £341 million.

Nature of hedged risk for which a hedging relationship may be designated (paragraphs 10–13)

AG2 Parent can hedge its net investment in each of Subsidiaries A, B and C for the foreign exchange risk between their respective functional currencies (Japanese yen (JPY), pounds sterling and US dollars) and euro. In addition, Parent can hedge the USD/GBP foreign exchange risk between the functional currencies of Subsidiary B and Subsidiary C. In its consolidated financial statements, Subsidiary B can hedge its net investment in Subsidiary C for the foreign exchange risk between their functional currencies of US dollars and pounds sterling. In the following examples the designated risk is the spot foreign exchange risk because the hedging instruments are not derivatives. If the hedging instruments were forward contracts, Parent could designate the forward foreign exchange risk.

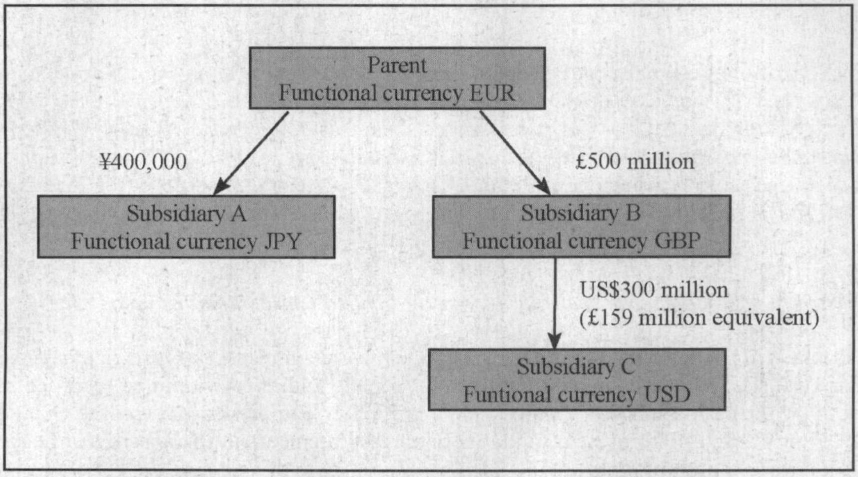

Amount of hedged item for which a hedging relationship may be designated (paragraphs 10–13)

AG3 Parent wishes to hedge the foreign exchange risk from its net investment in Subsidiary C. Assume that Subsidiary A has an external borrowing of US$300 million.

The net assets of Subsidiary A at the start of the reporting period are ¥400,000 million including the proceeds of the external borrowing of US$300 million.

The hedged item can be an amount of net assets equal to or less than the carrying amount of Parent's net investment in Subsidiary C (US$300 million) in its consolidated financial statements. In its consolidated financial statements Parent can designate the US$300 million external borrowing in Subsidiary A as a hedge of the EUR/USD spot foreign exchange risk associated with its net investment in the US$300 million net assets of Subsidiary C. In this case, both the EUR/USD foreign exchange difference on the US$300 million external borrowing in Subsidiary A and the EUR/USD foreign exchange difference on the US$300 million net investment in Subsidiary C are included in the foreign currency translation reserve in Parent's consolidated financial statements after the application of hedge accounting. **AG4**

In the absence of hedge accounting, the total USD/EUR foreign exchange difference on the US$300 million external borrowing in Subsidiary A would be recognised in Parent's consolidated financial statements as follows: **AG5**

- USD/JPY spot foreign exchange rate change, translated to euro, in profit or loss, and
- JPY/EUR spot foreign exchange rate change in other comprehensive income.

Instead of the designation in paragraph AG4, in its consolidated financial statements Parent can designate the US$300 million external borrowing in Subsidiary A as a hedge of the GBP/USD spot foreign exchange risk between Subsidiary C and Subsidiary B. In this case, the total USD/EUR foreign exchange difference on the US$300 million external borrowing in Subsidiary A would instead be recognised in Parent's consolidated financial statements as follows:

- the GBP/USD spot foreign exchange rate change in the foreign currency translation reserve relating to Subsidiary C,
- GBP/JPY spot foreign exchange rate change, translated to euro, in profit or loss, and
- JPY/EUR spot foreign exchange rate change in other comprehensive income.

Parent cannot designate the US$300 million external borrowing in Subsidiary A as a hedge of both the EUR/USD spot foreign exchange risk and the GBP/USD spot foreign exchange risk in its consolidated financial statements. A single hedging instrument can hedge the same designated risk only once. Subsidiary B cannot apply hedge accounting in its consolidated financial statements because the hedging instrument is held outside the group comprising Subsidiary B and Subsidiary C. **AG6**

Where in a group can the hedging instrument be held (paragraphs 14 and 15)?

As noted in paragraph AG5, the total change in value in respect of foreign exchange risk of the US$300 million external borrowing in Subsidiary A would be recorded in both profit or loss (USD/JPY spot risk) and other comprehensive income (EUR/JPY spot risk) in Parent's consolidated financial statements in the absence of hedge accounting. Both amounts are included for the purpose of assessing the effectiveness of the hedge designated in paragraph AG4 because the change in value of both the hedging instrument and the hedged item are computed by reference to the euro functional currency of Parent against the US dollar functional currency of Subsidiary C, in accordance with the hedge documentation. The method of consolidation (ie direct method or step-by-step method) does not affect the assessment of the effectiveness of the hedge. **AG7**

Amounts reclassified to profit or loss on disposal of a foreign operation (paragraphs 16 and 17)

AG8 When Subsidiary C is disposed of, the amounts reclassified to profit or loss in Parent's consolidated financial statements from its foreign currency translation reserve (FCTR) are:

(a) in respect of the US$300 million external borrowing of Subsidiary A, the amount that FRS 26 requires to be identified, ie the total change in value in respect of foreign exchange risk that was recognised in other comprehensive income as the effective portion of the hedge; and

(b) in respect of the US$300 million net investment in Subsidiary C, the amount determined by the entity's consolidation method. If Parent uses the direct method, its FCTR in respect of Subsidiary C will be determined directly by the EUR/USD foreign exchange rate. If Parent uses the step-by-step method, its FCTR in respect of Subsidiary C will be determined by the FCTR recognised by Subsidiary B reflecting the GBP/USD foreign exchange rate, translated to Parent's functional currency using the EUR/GBP foreign exchange rate. Parent's use of the step-by-step method of consolidation in prior periods does not require it to or preclude it from determining the amount of FCTR to be reclassified when it disposes of Subsidiary C to be the amount that it would have recognised if it had always used the direct method, depending on its accounting policy.

Hedging more than one foreign operation (paragraphs 11, 13 and 15)

AG9 The following examples illustrate that in the consolidated financial statements of Parent, the risk that can be hedged is always the risk between its functional currency (euro) and the functional currencies of Subsidiaries B and C. No matter how the hedges are designated, the maximum amounts that can be effective hedges to be included in the foreign currency translation reserve in Parent's consolidated financial statements when both foreign operations are hedged are US$300 million for EUR/USD risk and £341 million for EUR/GBP risk. Other changes in value due to changes in foreign exchange rates are included in Parent's consolidated profit or loss. Of course, it would be possible for Parent to designate US$300 million only for changes in the USD/GBP spot foreign exchange rate or £500 million only for changes in the GBP/EUR spot foreign exchange rate.

Parent holds both USD and GBP hedging instruments

AG10 Parent may wish to hedge the foreign exchange risk in relation to its net investment in Subsidiary B as well as that in relation to Subsidiary C. Assume that Parent holds suitable hedging instruments denominated in US dollars and pounds sterling that it could designate as hedges of its net investments in Subsidiary B and Subsidiary C. The designations Parent can make in its consolidated financial statements include, but are not limited to, the following:

(a) US$300 million hedging instrument designated as a hedge of the US$300 million of net investment in Subsidiary C with the risk being the spot foreign exchange exposure (EUR/USD) between Parent and Subsidiary C and up to £341 million hedging instrument designated as a hedge of £341 million of the net investment in Subsidiary B with the risk being the spot foreign exchange exposure (EUR/ GBP) between Parent and Subsidiary B.

(b) US$300 million hedging instrument designated as a hedge of the US$300 million of net investment in Subsidiary C with the risk being the spot foreign exchange exposure (GBP/USD) between Subsidiary B and Subsidiary C and up to £500 million hedging instrument designated as a hedge of £500 million of the net investment in Subsidiary B with the risk being the spot foreign exchange exposure (EUR/GBP) between Parent and Subsidiary B.

The EUR/USD risk from Parent's net investment in Subsidiary C is a different risk from the EUR/GBP risk from Parent's net investment in Subsidiary B. However, in the case described in paragraph AG10(a), by its designation of the USD hedging instrument it holds, Parent has already fully hedged the EUR/USD risk from its net investment in Subsidiary C. If Parent also designated a GBP instrument it holds as a hedge of its £500 million net investment in Subsidiary B, £159 million of that net investment, representing the GBP equivalent of its USD net investment in Subsidiary C, would be hedged twice for GBP/EUR risk in Parent's consolidated financial statements. **AG11**

In the case described in paragraph AG10(b), if Parent designates the hedged risk as the spot foreign exchange exposure (GBP/USD) between Subsidiary B and Subsidiary C, only the GBP/USD part of the change in the value of its US$300 million hedging instrument is included in Parent's foreign currency translation reserve relating to Subsidiary C. The remainder of the change (equivalent to the GBP/EUR change on £159 million) is included in Parent's consolidated profit or loss, as in paragraph AG5. Because the designation of the USD/GBP risk between Subsidiaries B and C does not include the GBP/EUR risk, Parent is also able to designate up to £500 million of its net investment in Subsidiary B with the risk being the spot foreign exchange exposure (GBP/EUR) between Parent and Subsidiary B. **AG12**

Subsidiary B holds the USD hedging instrument

Assume that Subsidiary B holds US$300 million of external debt the proceeds of which were transferred to Parent by an inter-company loan denominated in pounds sterling. Because both its assets and liabilities increased by £159 million, Subsidiary B's net assets are unchanged. Subsidiary B could designate the external debt as a hedge of the GBP/USD risk of its net investment in Subsidiary C in its consolidated financial statements. Parent could maintain Subsidiary B's designation of that hedging instrument as a hedge of its US$300 million net investment in Subsidiary C for the GBP/USD risk (see paragraph 13) and Parent could designate the GBP hedging instrument it holds as a hedge of its entire £500 million net investment in Subsidiary B. The first hedge, designated by Subsidiary B, would be assessed by reference to Subsidiary B's functional currency (pounds sterling) and the second hedge, designated by Parent, would be assessed by reference to Parent's functional currency (euro). In this case, only the GBP/USD risk from Parent's net investment in Subsidiary C has been hedged in Parent's consolidated financial statements by the USD hedging instrument, not the entire EUR/USD risk. Therefore, the entire EUR/ GBP risk from Parent's £500 million net investment in Subsidiary B may be hedged in the consolidated financial statements of Parent. **AG13**

However, the accounting for Parent's £159 million loan payable to Subsidiary B must also be considered. If Parent's loan payable is not considered part of its net investment in Subsidiary B because it does not satisfy the conditions in FRS 23 paragraph 15, the GBP/EUR foreign exchange difference arising on translating it would be included in Parent's consolidated profit or loss. If the £159 million loan payable to Subsidiary B is considered part of Parent's net investment, that net investment would be only £341 million and the amount Parent could designate as the hedged item for GBP/EUR risk would be reduced from £500 million to £341 million accordingly. **AG14**

AG15 If Parent reversed the hedging relationship designated by Subsidiary B, Parent could designate the US$300 million external borrowing held by Subsidiary B as a hedge of its US$300 million net investment in Subsidiary C for the EUR/USD risk and designate the GBP hedging instrument it holds itself as a hedge of only up to £341 million of the net investment in Subsidiary B. In this case the effectiveness of both hedges would be computed by reference to Parent's functional currency (euro). Consequently, both the USD/GBP change in value of the external borrowing held by Subsidiary B and the GBP/EUR change in value of Parent's loan payable to Subsidiary B (equivalent to USD/EUR in total) would be included in the foreign currency translation reserve in Parent's consolidated financial statements. Because Parent has already fully hedged the EUR/USD risk from its net investment in Subsidiary C, it can hedge only up to £341 million for the EUR/GBP risk of its net investment in Subsidiary B.

Illustrative example

This example accompanies, but is not part of, UITF Abstract 46.

Disposal of a foreign operation (paragraphs 16 and 17)

This example illustrates the application of paragraphs 16 and 17 in connection with the reclassification adjustment on the disposal of a foreign operation. **IE1**

Background

This example assumes the group structure set out in the application guidance and that Parent used a USD borrowing in Subsidiary A to hedge the EUR/USD risk of the net investment in Subsidiary C in Parent's consolidated financial statements. Parent uses the step-by-step method of consolidation. Assume the hedge was fully effective and the full USD/EUR accumulated change in the value of the hedging instrument before disposal of Subsidiary C is €24 million (gain). This is matched exactly by the fall in value of the net investment in Subsidiary C, when measured against the functional currency of Parent (euro). **IE2**

If the direct method of consolidation is used, the fall in the value of Parent's net investment in Subsidiary C of €24 million would be reflected totally in the foreign currency translation reserve relating to Subsidiary C in Parent's consolidated financial statements. However, because Parent uses the step-by-step method, this fall in the net investment value in Subsidiary C of €24 million would be reflected both in Subsidiary B's foreign currency translation reserve relating to Subsidiary C and in Parent's foreign currency translation reserve relating to Subsidiary B. **IE3**

The aggregate amount recognised in the foreign currency translation reserve in respect of Subsidiaries B and C is not affected by the consolidation method. Assume that using the direct method of consolidation, the foreign currency translation reserves for Subsidiaries B and C in Parent's consolidated financial statements are €62 million gain and €24 million loss respectively; using the step-by-step method of consolidation those amounts are €49 million gain and €11 million loss respectively. **IE4**

Reclassification

When the investment in Subsidiary C is disposed of, FRS 26 requires the full €24 million gain on the hedging instrument to be reclassified to profit or loss. Using the step-by-step method, the amount to be reclassified to profit or loss in respect of the net investment in Subsidiary C would be only €11 million loss. Parent could adjust the foreign currency translation reserves of both Subsidiaries B and C by €13 million in order to match the amounts reclassified in respect of the hedging instrument and the net investment as would have been the case if the direct method of consolidation had been used, if that was its accounting policy. An entity that had not hedged its net investment could make the same reclassification. **IE5**

Basis for Conclusions on IFRIC Interpretation 16

This Basis for Conclusions accompanies, but is not part of, IFRIC 16.

> *ASB note*: IFRIC's Basis for Conclusions, which accompanies IFRIC 16, is set out below in full.

INTRODUCTION

BC1 This Basis for Conclusions summarises the IFRIC's considerations in reaching its consensus. Individual IFRIC members gave greater weight to some factors than to others.

BACKGROUND

BC1 The IFRIC was asked for guidance on accounting for the hedge of a net investment in a foreign operation in the consolidated financial statements. Interested parties had different views of the risks eligible for hedge accounting purposes. One issue is whether the risk arises from the foreign currency exposure to the functional currencies of the foreign operation and the parent entity, or whether it arises from the foreign currency exposure to the functional currency of the foreign operation and the presentation currency of the parent entity's consolidated financial statements.

BC3 Concern was also raised about which entity within a group could hold a hedging instrument in a hedge of a net investment in a foreign operation and in particular whether the parent entity holding the net investment in a foreign operation must also hold the hedging instrument.

BC4 Accordingly, the IFRIC decided to develop guidance on the accounting for a hedge of the foreign currency risk arising from a net investment in a foreign operation.

BC5 The IFRIC published draft Interpretation D22 *Hedges of a Net Investment in a Foreign Operation* for public comment in July 2007 and received 45 comment letters in response to its proposals.

CONSENSUS

Hedged risk and hedged item

Functional currency versus presentation currency (paragraph 10)

BC6 The IFRIC received a submission suggesting that the method of consolidation can affect the determination of the hedged risk in a hedge of a net investment in a foreign operation. The submission noted that consolidation can be completed by either the direct method or the step-by-step method. In the direct method of consolidation, each entity within a group is consolidated directly into the ultimate parent entity's presentation currency when preparing the consolidated financial statements. In the step-by-step method, each intermediate parent entity prepares consolidated financial statements, which are then consolidated into its parent entity until the ultimate parent entity has prepared consolidated financial statements.

BC7 The submission stated that if the direct method was required, the risk that qualifies for hedge accounting in a hedge of a net investment in a foreign operation would arise only from exposure between the functional currency of the foreign operation and the presentation currency of the group. This is because each foreign operation is translated only once into the presentation currency. In contrast, the submission stated that if the step-by-step method was required, the hedged risk that qualifies for hedge accounting is the risk between the functional currencies of the foreign operation and the immediate parent entity into which the entity was consolidated. This is because each foreign operation is consolidated directly into its immediate parent entity.

In response to this, the IFRIC noted that IAS 21 *The Effects of Changes in Foreign Exchange Rates* does not specify a method of consolidation for foreign operations. Furthermore, paragraph BC18 of the Basis for Conclusions on IAS 21 states that the method of translating financial statements will result in the same amounts in the presentation currency regardless of whether the direct method or the step-by-step method is used. The IFRIC therefore concluded that the consolidation mechanism should not determine what risk qualifies for hedge accounting in the hedge of a net investment in a foreign operation. **BC8**

However, the IFRIC noted that its conclusion would not resolve the divergence of views on the foreign currency risk that may be designated as a hedge relationship in the hedge of a net investment in a foreign operation. The IFRIC therefore decided that an Interpretation was needed. **BC9**

The IFRIC considered whether the risk that qualifies for hedge accounting in a hedge of a net investment in a foreign operation arises from the exposure to the functional currency of the foreign operation in relation to the presentation currency of the group or the functional currency of the parent entity, or both. **BC10**

The answer to this question is important when the presentation currency of the group is different from an intermediate or ultimate parent entity's functional currency. If the presentation currency of the group and the functional currency of the parent entity are the same, the exchange rate being hedged would be identified as that between the parent entity's functional currency and the foreign operation's functional currency. No further translation adjustment would be required to prepare the consolidated financial statements. However, when the functional currency of the parent entity is different from the presentation currency of the group, a translation adjustment will be included in other comprehensive income to present the consolidated financial statements in a different presentation currency. The issue, therefore, is how to determine which foreign currency risk may be designated as the hedged risk in accordance with IAS 39 *Financial Instruments: Recognition and Measurement* in the hedge of a net investment in a foreign operation. **BC11**

The IFRIC noted the following arguments for permitting hedge accounting for a hedge of the presentation currency: **BC12**

(a) If the presentation currency of the group is different from the ultimate parent entity's functional currency, a difference arises on translation that is recognised in other comprehensive income. It is argued that a reason for allowing hedge accounting for a net investment in a foreign operation is to remove from the financial statements the fluctuations resulting from the translation to a presentation currency. If an entity is not allowed to use hedge accounting for the exposure to the presentation currency of the group when it is different from the functional currency of the parent entity, there is likely to be an amount included in other comprehensive income that cannot be offset by hedge accounting.

(b) IAS 21 requires an entity to reclassify from equity to profit or loss as a reclassification adjustment any foreign currency translation gains and losses included in other comprehensive income on disposal of a foreign operation. An amount in other comprehensive income arising from a different presentation currency is therefore included in the amount reclassified to profit or loss on disposal. The entity should be able to include the amount in a hedging relationship if at some stage it is recognised along with other reclassified translation amounts.

BC13 The IFRIC noted the following arguments for allowing an entity to designate hedging relationships solely on the basis of differences between functional currencies:

(a) The functional currency of an entity is determined on the basis of the primary economic environment in which that entity operates (ie the environment in which it generates and expends cash). However, the presentation currency is an elective currency that can be changed at any time. To present amounts in a presentation currency is merely a numerical convention necessary for the preparation of financial statements that include a foreign operation. The presentation currency will have no economic effect on the parent entity. Indeed, a parent entity may choose to present financial statements in more than one presentation currency, but can have only one functional currency.

(b) IAS 39 requires a hedging relationship to be effective in offsetting changes in fair values or cash flows attributable to the hedged risk. A net investment in a foreign operation gives rise to an exposure to changes in exchange rate risk for a parent entity. An economic exchange rate risk arises only from an exposure between two or more functional currencies, not from a presentation currency.

BC14 When comparing the arguments in paragraphs BC12 and BC13, the IFRIC concluded that the presentation currency does not create an exposure to which an entity may apply hedge accounting. The functional currency is determined on the basis of the primary economic environment in which the entity operates. Accordingly, functional currencies create an economic exposure to changes in cash flows or fair values; a presentation currency never will. No commentators on the draft Interpretation disagreed with the IFRIC's conclusion.

Eligible risk (paragraph 12)

BC15 The IFRIC considered which entity's (or entities') functional currency may be used as a reference point for the hedged risk in a net investment hedge. Does the risk arise from the functional currency of:

(a) the immediate parent entity that holds directly the foreign operation;

(b) the ultimate parent entity that is preparing its financial statements; or

(c) the immediate, an intermediate or the ultimate parent entity, depending on what risk that entity decides to hedge, as designated at the inception of the hedge?

BC16 The IFRIC concluded that the risk from the exposure to a different functional currency arises for any parent entity whose functional currency is different from that of the identified foreign operation. The immediate parent entity is exposed to changes in the exchange rate of its directly held foreign operation's functional currency. However, indirectly every entity up the chain of entities to the ultimate parent entity is also exposed to changes in the exchange rate of the foreign operation's functional currency.

BC17 Permitting only the ultimate parent entity to hedge its net investments would ignore the exposures arising on net investments in other parts of the entity. Conversely, permitting only the immediate parent entity to undertake a net investment hedge would imply that an indirect investment does not create a foreign currency exposure for that indirect parent entity.

The IFRIC concluded that a group must identify which risk (ie the functional currency of which parent entity and of which net investment in a foreign operation) is being hedged. The specified parent entity, the hedged risk and hedging instrument should all be designated and documented at the inception of the hedge relationship. As a result of comments received on the draft Interpretation, the IFRIC decided to emphasise that this documentation should also include the entity's strategy in undertaking the hedge as required by IAS 39. **BC18**

Amount of hedged item that may be hedged (paragraphs 11 and 13)

In the draft Interpretation the IFRIC noted that, in financial statements that include a foreign operation, an entity cannot hedge the same risk more than once. This comment was intended to remind entities that IAS 39 does not permit multiple hedges of the same risk. Some respondents asked the IFRIC to clarify the situations in which the IFRIC considered that the same risk was being hedged more than once. In particular, the IFRIC was asked whether the same risk could be hedged by different entities within a group as long as the amount of risk being hedged was not duplicated. **BC19**

In its redeliberations, the IFRIC decided to clarify that the carrying amount of the net assets of a foreign operation that may be hedged in the consolidated financial statements of a parent depends on whether any lower level parent of the foreign operation has hedged all or part of the net assets of that foreign operation and that accounting has been maintained in the parent's consolidated financial statements. An intermediate parent entity can hedge some or all of the risk of its net investment in a foreign operation in its own consolidated financial statements. However, such hedges will not qualify for hedge accounting at the ultimate parent entity level if the ultimate parent entity has also hedged the same risk. Alternatively, if the risk has not been hedged by the ultimate parent entity or another intermediate parent entity, the hedge relationship that qualified in the immediate parent entity's consolidated financial statements will also qualify in the ultimate parent entity's consolidated financial statements. **BC20**

In its redeliberations, the IFRIC also decided to add guidance to the Interpretation to illustrate the importance of careful designation of the amount of the risk being hedged by each entity in the group. **BC21**

Hedging instrument

Location of the hedging instrument (paragraph 14) and assessment of hedge effectiveness (paragraph 15)

The IFRIC discussed where in a group structure a hedging instrument may be held in a hedge of a net investment in a foreign operation. Guidance on the hedge of a net investment in a foreign operation was originally included in IAS 21. This guidance was moved to IAS 39 to ensure that the hedge accounting guidance included in paragraph 88 of IAS 39 would also apply to the hedges of net investments in foreign operations. **BC22**

The IFRIC concluded that any entity within the group, other than the foreign operation being hedged, may hold the hedging instrument, as long as the hedging instrument is effective in offsetting the risk arising from the exposure to the **BC23** functional currency of the foreign operation and the functional currency of the specified parent entity. The functional currency of the entity holding the instrument is irrelevant in determining effectiveness.

BC24 Paragraph BC24 was deleted and paragraphs BC24A–BC24D and paragraph BC40A added as a consequence of Improvements to IFRSs issued in April 2009.

BC24A Paragraph 14 of IFRIC 16 originally stated that the hedging instrument could not be held by the foreign operation whose net investment was being hedged. The restriction was included in draft Interpretation D22 (from which IFRIC 16 was developed) and attracted little comment from respondents. As originally explained in paragraph BC24, the IFRIC concluded, as part of its redeliberations, that the restriction was appropriate because the foreign exchange differences between the parent's functional currency and both the hedging instrument and the functional currency of the net investment would automatically be included in the group's foreign currency translation reserve as part of the consolidation process.

BC24B After IFRIC 16 was issued, it was brought to the attention of the International Accounting Standards Board that this conclusion was not correct. Without hedge accounting, part of the foreign exchange difference arising from the hedging instrument would be included in consolidated profit or loss. Therefore, in Improvements to IFRSs issued in April 2009, the Board amended paragraph 14 of IFRIC 16 to remove the restriction on the entity that can hold hedging instruments and deleted paragraph BC24.

BC24C Some respondents to the exposure draft Post-implementation Revisions to IFRIC Interpretations (ED/2009/1) agreed that a parent entity should be able to use a derivative held by the foreign operation being hedged as a hedge of the net investment in that foreign operation. However, those respondents recommended that the amendment should apply only to derivative instruments held by the foreign operation being hedged. They asserted that a nonderivative financial instrument would be an effective hedge of the net investment only if it were issued by the foreign operation in its own functional currency and this would have no foreign currency impact on the profit or loss of the consolidated group. Consequently, they thought that the rationale described in paragraph BC24B to support the amendment did not apply to non-derivative instruments.

BC24D In its redeliberations, the Board confirmed its previous decision that the amendment should not be restricted to derivative instruments. The Board noted that paragraphs AG13–AG15 of IFRIC 16 illustrate that a non-derivative instrument held by the foreign operation does not need to be considered to be part of the parent's net investment. As a result, even if it is denominated in the foreign operation's functional currency a non-derivative instrument could still affect the profit or loss of the consolidated group. Consequently, although it could be argued that the amendment was not required to permit non-derivative instruments to be designated as hedges, the Board decided that the proposal should not be changed.

BC25 The IFRIC also concluded that to apply the conclusion in paragraph BC23 when determining the effectiveness of a hedging instrument in the hedge of a net investment, an entity computes the gain or loss on the hedging instrument by reference to the functional currency of the parent entity against whose functional currency the hedged risk is measured, in accordance with the hedge documentation. This is the same regardless of the type of hedging instrument used. This ensures that the effectiveness of the instrument is determined on the basis of changes in fair value or cash flows of the hedging instrument, compared with the changes in the net investment as documented. Thus, any effectiveness test is not dependent on the functional currency of the entity holding the instrument. In other words, the fact that some of the change in the hedging instrument is recognised in profit or loss by one entity within the group and some is recognised in other comprehensive income by another does not affect the assessment of hedge effectiveness.

In the draft Interpretation the IFRIC noted Question F.2.14 in the guidance on implementing IAS 39, on the location of the hedging instrument, and considered whether that guidance could be applied by analogy to a net investment hedge. The answer to Question F.2.14 concludes: **BC26**

> IAS 39 does not require that the operating unit that is exposed to the risk being hedged be a party to the hedging instrument.

In its redeliberations, the IFRIC considered both the International Accounting Standards Board's amendment to IAS 21 in 2005 and the objective of hedging a net investment described in IAS 39 in addition to the guidance on implementing IAS 39. **BC27**

In 2005 the Board was asked to clarify which entity is the reporting entity in IAS 21 and therefore what instruments could be considered part of a reporting entity's net investment in a foreign operation. In particular, constituents questioned whether a monetary item must be transacted between the foreign operation and the reporting entity to be considered part of the net investment in accordance with IAS 21 paragraph 15, or whether it could be transacted between the foreign operation and any member of the consolidated group. **BC28**

In response the Board added IAS 21 paragraph 15A to clarify that, 'The entity that has a monetary item receivable from or payable to a foreign operation described in paragraph 15 may be any subsidiary of the group.' The Board explained its reasons for the amendment in paragraph BC25D of the Basis for Conclusions: **BC29**

> The Board concluded that the accounting treatment in the consolidated financial statements should not be dependent on the currency in which the monetary item is denominated, nor on which entity within the group conducts the transaction with the foreign operation.

Consistently with the Board's conclusion with respect to monetary items that are part of *the net investment*, the IFRIC concluded that monetary items (or derivatives) that are *hedging instruments* in a hedge of a net investment may be held by any entity within the group and the functional currency of the entity holding the monetary items can be different from those of either the parent or the foreign operation. The IFRIC, like the Board, agreed with constituents who noted that a hedging item denominated in a currency that is not the functional currency of the entity holding it does not expose the group to a greater foreign currency exchange difference than arises when the instrument is denominated in that functional currency. **BC30**

The IFRIC noted that its conclusions that the hedging instrument can be held by any entity in the group and that the foreign currency is determined at the relevant parent entity level have implications for the designation of hedged risks. As illustrated in paragraph AG5 of the application guidance, these conclusions make it possible for an entity to designate a hedged risk that is not apparent in the currencies of the hedged item or the foreign operation. This possibility is unique to hedges of net investments. Consequently, the IFRIC specified that the conclusions in the Interpretation should not be applied by analogy to other types of hedge accounting. **BC31**

The IFRIC also noted that the objective of hedge accounting as set out in IAS 39 is to achieve offsetting changes in the values of the *hedging instrument* and of the *net* **BC32** *investment* attributable to the hedged risk. Changes in foreign currency rates affect the value of the entire *net investment* in a foreign operation, not only the portion IAS 21 requires to be recognised in profit or loss in the absence of hedge accounting but also the portion recognised in other comprehensive income in the parent's consolidated financial statements. As noted in paragraph BC25, it is the total change in the hedging instrument as result of a change in the foreign currency rate with respect to the parent entity against whose functional currency the hedged risk is measured that is relevant, not the component of comprehensive income in which it is recognised.

Reclassification from other comprehensive income to profit or loss (paragraphs 16 and 17)

BC33 In response to requests from some respondents for clarification, the IFRIC discussed what amounts from the parent entity's foreign currency translation reserve in respect of both the hedging instrument and the foreign operation should be recognised in profit or loss in the parent entity's consolidated financial statements when the parent disposes of a foreign operation that was hedged. The IFRIC noted that the amounts to be reclassified from equity to profit or loss as reclassification adjustments on the disposition are:

(a) the cumulative amount of gain or loss on a hedging instrument determined to be an effective hedge that has been reflected in other comprehensive income (IAS 39 paragraph 102), and

(b) the cumulative amount reflected in the foreign currency translation reserve in respect of that foreign operation (IAS 21 paragraph 48).

BC34 The IFRIC noted that when an entity hedges a net investment in a foreign operation, IAS 39 requires it to identify the cumulative amount included in the group's foreign currency translation reserve as a result of applying hedge accounting, ie the amount determined to be an effective hedge. Therefore, the IFRIC concluded that when a foreign operation that was hedged is disposed of, the amount reclassified to profit or loss from the foreign currency translation reserve in respect of the hedging instrument in the consolidated financial statements of the parent should be the amount that IAS 39 requires to be identified.

Effect of consolidation method

BC35 Some respondents to the draft Interpretation argued that the method of consolidation creates a difference in the amounts included in the ultimate parent entity's foreign currency translation reserve for individual foreign operations that are held through intermediate parents. These respondents noted that this difference may become evident only when the ultimate parent entity disposes of a second tier subsidiary (ie an indirect subsidiary).

BC36 The difference becomes apparent in the determination of the amount of the foreign currency translation reserve that is subsequently reclassified to profit or loss. An ultimate parent entity using the direct method of consolidation would reclassify the cumulative foreign currency translation reserve that arose between its functional currency and that of the foreign operation. An ultimate parent entity using the step-by-step method of consolidation might reclassify the cumulative foreign currency translation reserve reflected in the financial statements of the intermediate parent, ie the amount that arose between the functional currency of the foreign operation and that of the intermediate parent, translated into the functional currency of the ultimate parent.

In its redeliberations, the IFRIC noted that the use of the step-by-step method of consolidation does create such a difference for an *individual* foreign operation although the aggregate net amount of foreign currency translation reserve for all the foreign operations is the same under either method of consolidation. At the same time, the IFRIC noted that the method of consolidation *should not* create such a difference for an individual foreign operation, on the basis of its conclusion that the economic risk is determined in relation to the ultimate parent's functional currency. **BC37**

The IFRIC noted that the amount of foreign currency translation reserve for an individual foreign operation determined by the direct method of consolidation reflects the economic risk between the functional currency of the foreign operation and that of the ultimate parent (if the parent's functional and presentation currencies are the same). However, the IFRIC noted that IAS 21 does not require an entity to use this method or to make adjustments to produce the same result. The IFRIC also noted that a parent entity is not precluded from determining the amount of the foreign currency translation reserve in respect of a foreign operation it has disposed of as if the direct method of consolidation had been used in order to reclassify the appropriate amount to profit or loss. However, it also noted that making such an adjustment on the disposal of a foreign operation is an accounting policy choice and should be followed consistently for the disposal of all net investments. **BC38**

The IFRIC noted that this issue arises when the net investment disposed of was not hedged and therefore is not strictly within the scope of the Interpretation. However, because it was a topic of considerable confusion and debate, the IFRIC decided to include a brief example illustrating its conclusions. **BC39**

Transition (paragraph 19)

In response to respondents' comments, the IFRIC clarified the Interpretation's transitional requirements. The IFRIC decided that entities should apply the conclusions in this Interpretation to existing hedging relationships on adoption and cease hedge accounting for those that no longer qualify. However, previous hedge accounting is not affected. This is similar to the transition requirements in IFRS 1 *First-time Adoption of International Financial Reporting Standards* paragraph 30, for relationships accounted for as hedges under previous GAAP. **BC40**

Effective date of amended paragraph 14

The Board amended paragraph 14 in April 2009. In ED/2009/01 the Board proposed that the amendment should be effective for annual periods beginning on or after 1 October 2008, at the same time as IFRIC 16. Respondents to the exposure draft were concerned that permitting application before the amendment was issued might imply that an entity could designate hedge relationships retrospectively, contrary to the requirements of IAS 39. Consequently, the Board decided that an entity should apply the amendment to paragraph 14 made in April 2009 for annual periods beginning on or after 1 July 2009. The Board also decided to permit early application but noted that early application is possible only if the designation, documentation and effectiveness requirements of paragraph 88 of IAS 39 and of IFRIC 16 are satisfied at the application date. **BC40A**

Summary of main changes from the draft Interpretation

The main changes from the IFRIC's proposals are as follows: **BC41**

(a) Paragraph 11 clarifies that the carrying amount of the net assets of a foreign operation that may be hedged in the consolidated financial statements of a parent depends on whether any lower level parent of the foreign operation has hedged all or part of the net assets of that foreign operation and that accounting has been maintained in the parent's consolidated financial statements.
(b) Paragraph 15 clarifies that the assessment of effectiveness is not affected by whether the hedging instrument is a derivative or a non-derivative instrument or by the method of consolidation.
(c) Paragraphs 16 and 17 and the illustrative example clarify what amounts should be reclassified from equity to profit or loss as reclassification adjustments on disposal of the foreign operation.
(d) Paragraph 19 clarifies transitional requirements.
(e) The appendix of application guidance was added to the Interpretation. Illustrative examples accompanying the draft Interpretation were removed.
(f) The Basis for Conclusions was changed to set out more clearly the reasons for the IFRIC's conclusions.

UITF Abstract 47 (IFRIC Interpretation 19) Extinguishing Financial Liabilities with Equity Instruments

(Issued 9 July 2010)

PREFACE BY THE URGENT ISSUES TASK FORCE

This Abstract has the effect of implementing the International Accounting Standards Board's (IASB's) International Financial Reporting Interpretations Committee (IFRIC) Interpretation 19 'Extinguishing Financial Liabilities with Equity Instruments' in the UK and Republic of Ireland. The Abstract applies to entities preparing their financial statements in accordance with UK accounting standards and applying FRS 26 (IAS 39) 'Financial Instruments: Recognition and Measurement'. **a**

FRS 26 implements IAS 39 in UK GAAP for listed entities and those preparing their financial statements in accordance with the fair value accounting rules set out in the The Large and Medium-sized Companies and Groups (Accounts and Reports) Regulations 2008 or The Large and Medium-sized Limited Liability Partnerships (Accounts) Regulations 2008. **b**

This Abstract incorporates the text of IFRIC 19. The text of IFRIC 19 contains various references to International Financial Reporting Standards (IFRS). In this Abstract those references have been amended to enable the Interpretation to be applied in a UK context. The UITF believes that those amendments do not change the requirements of IFRIC 19, but does draw the attention of users to the UK Legal Appendix which gives important information that must be taken into consideration in comlying with the requirements of the Abstract and the Companies Act 2006. **c**

The effective date for application of the Abstract is for annual periods beginning on or after 1 July 2010, with earlier application permitted. **d**

Contents

	paragraphs
References	
Background	**1**
Scope	**2–3**
Issues	**41**
Consensus	**5–11**
Effective Date and Transition	**12–13**
Appendix	
IFRIC Basis for Conclusions	
UITF Legal Appendix	

REFERENCES

- IASB *Framework for the Preparation and Presentation of Financial Statements*
- FRS 20 (IFRS 2) *Share-based Payment*
- FRS 18 Accounting Policies
- FRS 25 (IAS 32) *Financial Instruments: Presentation*
- FRS 26 (IAS 39) *Financial Instruments: Recognition and Measurement*

BACKGROUND

A debtor and creditor might renegotiate the terms of a financial liability with the result that the debtor extinguishes the liability fully or partially by issuing equity instruments to the creditor. These transactions are sometimes referred to as 'debt for equity swaps'. The UITF is issuing this Abstract following the IFRIC receiving requests for guidance on the accounting for such transactions and, as a result, issuing an Interpretation. 1

SCOPE

This Abstract addresses the accounting by an entity when the terms of a financial liability are renegotiated and result in the entity issuing equity instruments to a creditor of the entity to extinguish all or part of the financial liability. It does not address the accounting by the creditor. 2

An entity shall not apply this Abstract to transactions in situations where: 3

(a) the creditor is also a direct or indirect shareholder and is acting in its capacity as a direct or indirect existing shareholder.

(b) the creditor and the entity are controlled by the same party or parties before and after the transaction and the substance of the transaction includes an equity distribution by, or contribution to, the entity.

(c) extinguishing the financial liability by issuing equity shares is in accordance with the original terms of the financial liability.

This Abstract only applies to those entities within the scope of or who apply FRS 26 (IAS 39) *Financial Instruments: Recognition and Measurement*.

ISSUES

This Abstract addresses the following issues: 4

(a) Are an entity's equity instruments issued to extinguish all or part of a financial liability 'consideration paid' in accordance with paragraph 41 of FRS 26?

(b) How should an entity initially measure the equity instruments issued to extinguish such a financial liability?

(c) How should an entity account for any difference between the carrying amount of the financial liability extinguished and the initial measurement amount of the equity instruments issued?

UITF CONSENSUS

The issue of an entity's equity instruments to a creditor to extinguish all or part of a financial liability is consideration paid in accordance with paragraph 41 of FRS 26. An entity shall remove a financial liability (or part of a financial liability) from its balance sheet when, and only when, it is extinguished in accordance with paragraph 39 of FRS 26. 5

6 When equity instruments issued to a creditor to extinguish all or part of a financial liability are recognised initially, an entity shall measure them at the fair value of the equity instruments issued, unless that fair value cannot be reliably measured.

7 If the fair value of the equity instruments issued cannot be reliably measured then the equity instruments shall be measured to reflect the fair value of the financial liability extinguished. In measuring the fair value of a financial liability extinguished that includes a demand feature (eg a demand deposit), paragraph 49 of FRS 26 is not applied.

8 If only part of the financial liability is extinguished, the entity shall assess whether some of the consideration paid relates to a modification of the terms of the liability that remains outstanding. If part of the consideration paid does relate to a modification of the terms of the remaining part of the liability, the entity shall allocate the consideration paid between the part of the liability extinguished and the part of the liability that remains outstanding. The entity shall consider all relevant facts and circumstances relating to the transaction in making this allocation.

9 The difference between the carrying amount of the financial liability (or part of a financial liability) extinguished, and the consideration paid, shall be recognised in profit or loss, in accordance with paragraph 41 of FRS 26. The equity instruments issued shall be recognised initially and measured at the date the financial liability (or part of that liability) is extinguished.

10 When only part of the financial liability is extinguished, consideration shall be allocated in accordance with paragraph 8. The consideration allocated to the remaining liability shall form part of the assessment of whether the terms of that remaining liability have been substantially modified. If the remaining liability has been substantially modified, the entity shall account for the modification as the extinguishment of the original liability and the recognition of a new liability as required by paragraph 40 of FRS 26.

11 An entity shall disclose a gain or loss recognised in accordance with paragraphs 9 and 10 as a separate line item in profit or loss or in the notes.

EFFECTIVE DATE AND TRANSITION

12 An entity shall apply this Abstract for annual periods beginning on or after 1 July 2010. Earlier application is permitted. If an entity applies this Abstract for a period beginning before 1 July 2010, it shall disclose that fact.

13 An entity shall apply a change in accounting policy in accordance with FRS 18 Accounting Policies from the beginning of the earliest comparative period presented.

Appendix
Basis for Conclusion on IFRC Interpretation 19

This Basis for Conclusions accompanies, but is not part of, IFRIC 19.

ASB note: IFRIC's Basis for Conclusions, which accompanies IFRIC 19, is set out below in full.

Introduction

This Basis for Conclusions summarises the IFRIC's considerations in reaching its consensus. Individual IFRIC members gave greater weight to some factors than to others. **BC1**

The IFRIC received a request for guidance on the application of IAS 39 *Financial Instruments: Recognition and Measurement and IAS 32 Financial Instruments: Presentation* when an entity issues its own equity instruments to extinguish all or part of a financial liability. The question is how the entity should recognise the equity instruments issued.* **BC2**

The IFRIC noted that lenders manage loans to entities in financial difficulty in a variety of ways including one or more of the following: **BC3**

(a) selling the loans in the market to other investors/lenders;
(b) renegotiating the terms of the loan (eg extension of the maturity date or lower interest payments); or
(c) accepting the creditor's equity instruments in full or partial settlement of the liability (sometimes referred to as a 'debt for equity swap').

The IFRIC was informed that there was diversity in practice in how entities measure the equity instruments issued in full or partial settlement of a financial liability following renegotiation of the terms of the liability. Some recognise the equity instruments at the carrying amount of the financial liability and do not recognise any gain or loss in profit or loss. Others recognise the equity instruments at the fair value of either the liability extinguished or the equity instruments issued and recognise a difference between that amount and the carrying amount of the financial liability in profit or loss. **BC4**

In August 2009 the IFRIC published draft Interpretation D25 *Extinguishing Financial Liabilities with Equity Instruments* for public comment. It received 33 comment letters in response to the proposals. **BC5**

The IFRIC concluded that its Interpretation should address only the accounting by an entity when the terms of a financial liability are renegotiated and result in the entity issuing equity instruments to a creditor of the entity to extinguish part or all of the liability. It does not address the accounting by the creditor because other IFRSs already set out the relevant requirements. **BC6**

The IFRIC considered whether to provide guidance on transactions in which the creditor is also a direct or indirect shareholder and is acting in its capacity as an existing direct or indirect shareholder. The IFRIC concluded that the Interpretation should not address such transactions. It noted that determining whether the issue of **BC7**

**The equivalent UK references are FRS 26 (IAS 39)* Financial Instruments: Recognition and Measurement *and FRS 25 (IAS 32)* Financial Instruments: Presentation.

equity instruments to extinguish a financial liability in such situations is considered a transaction with an owner in its capacity as an owner would be a matter of judgement depending on the facts and circumstances.

BC8 In its redeliberations, the IFRIC clarified that transactions when the creditor and the entity are controlled by the same party or parties before and after the transaction are outside the scope of the Interpretation when the substance of the transaction includes an equity distribution by, or contribution to, the entity. The IFRIC acknowledged that the allocation of consideration between the extinguishment of all or part of a financial liability and the equity distribution or contribution components may not always be reliably measured.

BC9 Some respondents questioned whether the Interpretation should be applied to transactions when the extinguishment of the financial liability by issuing equity shares is in accordance with the original terms of the liability. In its redeliberations the IFRIC decided that these transactions should be excluded from the scope of the Interpretation, noting that IAS 32 includes specific guidance on those financial instruments.

Are an entity's equity instruments 'consideration paid'?

BC10 The IFRIC noted that IFRSs do not contain specific guidance on the measurement of an entity's equity instruments issued to extinguish all or part of a financial liability. Paragraph 41 of IAS 39 requires an entity to recognise in profit or loss the difference between the carrying amount of the financial liability extinguished and the consideration paid. That paragraph describes 'consideration paid' as including non-cash assets transferred, or liabilities assumed, and does not specifically mention equity instruments issued. Consequently, some are of the view that equity instruments are not 'consideration paid'.

BC11 Holders of this view believe that, because IFRSs are generally silent on how to measure equity instruments on initial recognition (see paragraph BC15), a variety of practices has developed. One such practice is to recognise the equity instruments issued at the carrying amount of the financial liability extinguished.

BC12 However, the IFRIC observed that both IFRS 2 *Share-based Payment** and IFRS 3 *Business Combinations*† make it clear that equity instruments are used as consideration to acquire goods and services as well as to obtain control of businesses.

BC13 The IFRIC also observed that the issue of equity instruments to extinguish a financial liability could be analysed as consisting of two transactions—first, the issue of new equity instruments to the creditor for cash and second, the creditor accepting payment of that amount of cash to extinguish the financial liability.

BC14 As a result of its analysis, the IFRIC concluded that the equity instruments issued to extinguish a financial liability are 'consideration paid' in accordance with paragraph 41 of IAS 39.

**The UK equivalent reference is FRS 20 (IFRS 2)* Share-based payment.

†*The UK equivalent reference is FRS 7* Fair Values in Acquisition Accounting.

How should the equity instruments be measured?

The IFRIC observed that although IFRSs do not contain a general principle for the initial recognition and measurement of equity instruments, guidance on specific transactions exists, including: **BC15**

(a) *initial recognition of compound instruments* (IAS 32). The amount allocated to the equity component is the residual after deducting the fair value of the financial liability component from the fair value of the entire compound instrument.
(b) *cost of equity transactions and own equity instruments ('treasury shares') acquired and reissued or cancelled* (IAS 32). No gain or loss is recognised in profit or loss on the purchase, sale, issue or cancellation of an entity's own equity instruments. These are transactions with an entity's owners in their capacity as owners.
(c) *equity instruments issued in share-based payment transactions* (IFRS 2). For equity-settled share-based payment transactions, the entity measures the goods or services received, and the corresponding increase in equity, directly, at the fair value of the goods or services received, unless that fair value cannot be estimated reliably. If the entity cannot estimate reliably the fair value of the goods or services received (eg transactions with employees), the entity measures their value, and the corresponding increase in equity, indirectly, by reference to the fair value of the equity instruments granted.
(d) *consideration transferred in business combinations* (IFRS 3). The total consideration transferred in a business combination is measured at fair value. It includes the acquisition-date fair values of any equity interests issued by the acquirer.

The IFRIC noted that the general principle of IFRSs is that equity is a residual and should be measured initially by reference to changes in assets and liabilities (the *Framework* and IFRS 2). IFRS 2 is clear that when goods or services are received in return for the issue of equity instruments, the increase in equity is measured directly at the fair value of the goods or services received. **BC16**

The IFRIC decided that the same principles should apply when equity instruments are issued to extinguish financial liabilities. However, the IFRIC was concerned that entities might encounter practical difficulties in measuring the fair value of both the equity instruments issued and the financial liability, particularly when the entity is in financial difficulty. Therefore, the IFRIC decided in D25 that equity instruments issued to extinguish a financial liability should be measured initially at the fair value of the equity instruments issued or the fair value of the liability extinguished, whichever is more reliably determinable. **BC17**

However, in response to comments received on D25, the IFRIC reconsidered whether the entity should initially measure equity instruments issued to a creditor to extinguish all or part of a financial liability at the fair value of the equity instruments issued or the fair value of the liability extinguished. The IFRIC noted that many respondents proposed that a preferred measurement basis should be determined to avoid an 'accounting choice' developing in practice, acknowledging that both measurement approaches would need to be used to identify which was more reliably determinable. **BC18**

Therefore the IFRIC decided to modify the proposal in D25 and identify a preferred measurement basis. In identifying this preferred measurement basis, the IFRIC noted that many respondents considered that the principles in IFRS 2 and the **BC19**

Framework referred to in paragraph BC16 support a measurement based on the fair value of the liability extinguished.

BC20 However, some respondents argued that the fair value of the equity issued should be the proposed measurement basis. They pointed out that this approach would be consistent with the consensus that the issue of an entity's equity instruments is consideration paid in accordance with paragraph 41 of IAS 39. They also argued that the fair value of the equity issued best reflects the total amount of consideration paid in the transaction, which may include a premium that the creditor requires to renegotiate the terms of the financial liability.

BC21 The IFRIC considered that the fair value of the equity issued should be the proposed measurement basis for the reasons described in paragraph BC20. Consequently the IFRIC concluded that an entity should initially measure equity instruments issued to a creditor to extinguish all or part of a financial liability at the fair value of the equity instruments issued, unless that fair value cannot be reliably measured. If the fair value of the equity instruments issued cannot be reliably measured then these equity instruments should initially be measured to reflect the fair value of the liability extinguished.

BC22 In redeliberations, the IFRIC noted that these transactions often take place in situations when the terms of the financial liability are breached and the liability becomes repayable on demand. The IFRIC agreed with comments received that paragraph 49 of IAS 39 is not applied in measuring the fair value of all or part of a financial liability extinguished in these situations. This is because the extinguishment transaction suggests that the demand feature is no longer substantive.

BC23 In response to comments, the IFRIC also clarified that the equity instruments issued should be recognised initially and measured at the date the financial liability (or part of that liability) is extinguished. This is consistent with paragraphs BC341 and BC342 of the Basis for Conclusions on IFRS 3, which discuss the views on whether equity instruments issued as consideration in a business combination should be measured at fair value at the agreement date or acquisition date, concluding that measurement should be at the acquisition date.

How should a difference between the carrying amount of the financial liability and the consideration paid be accounted for?

BC24 In accordance with paragraph 41 of IAS 39, the entity should recognise a gain or loss in profit or loss for any difference between the carrying amount of the financial liability extinguished and the consideration paid. This requirement is consistent with the *Framework's* discussion of income:

(a) Income is increases in economic benefits during the accounting period in the form of inflows or enhancements of assets or *decreases of liabilities that result in increases in equity*, other than those relating to contributions from equity participants. (paragraph 70(a)) (emphasis added)

(b) Gains represent other items that meet the definition of income and may, or may not, arise in the course of the ordinary activities of an entity. Gains represent increases in economic benefits ... (paragraph 75)

(c) Income may also result from the settlement of liabilities. For example, an entity may provide goods and services to a lender in settlement of an obligation to repay an outstanding loan. (paragraph 77)

Full extinguishment

The IFRIC noted that, as discussed in paragraph BC13, a transaction in which an entity issues equity instruments to extinguish a liability can be analysed as first, the issue of new equity instruments to the creditor for cash and second, the creditor accepting payment of that amount of cash to extinguish the financial liability. Consistently with paragraph BC24, when the creditor accepts cash to extinguish the liability, the entity should recognise a gain or loss in profit or loss. **BC25**

Similarly, the IFRIC noted that, in accordance with IAS 32, when an entity amends the terms of a convertible instrument to induce early conversion, the entity recognises in profit or loss the fair value of any additional consideration paid to the holder. Thus, the IFRIC concluded that when an entity settles an instrument by issuing its own equity instruments and that settlement is not in accordance with the original terms of the financial liability, the entity should recognise a gain or loss in profit or loss. **BC26**

As a result of its conclusions, the IFRIC decided that the entity should recognise a gain or loss in profit or loss. This gain or loss is equal to the difference between the carrying amount of the financial liability and the fair value of the equity instruments issued, or fair value of the liability extinguished if the fair value of the equity instruments issued cannot be reliably measured. **BC27**

Partial extinguishment

The IFRIC also observed that the restructuring of a financial liability can involve both the partial settlement of the liability by the issue of equity instruments to the creditor and the modification of the terms of the liability that remains outstanding. Therefore, the IFRIC decided that the Interpretation should also apply to partial extinguishments. In the case of a partial extinguishment, the discussion in paragraphs BC25–BC27 applies to the part of the liability extinguished. **BC28**

Many respondents requested clarification of the guidance on partial extinguishment included in D25. During its redeliberations, the IFRIC acknowledged that the issue of an entity's equity shares may reflect consideration paid for both the extinguishment of part of a financial liability and the modification of the terms of the part of the liability that remains outstanding. **BC29**

The IFRIC decided that to reflect this, an entity should allocate the consideration paid between the part of the liability extinguished and the part of the liability that remains outstanding. The entity would consider this allocation in determining the profit or loss to be recognised on the part of the liability extinguished and in its assessment of whether the terms of the remaining liability have been substantially modified. **BC30**

The IFRIC concluded that providing additional guidance on determining whether the terms of the part of the financial liability that remains outstanding has been substantially modified in accordance with paragraph 40 of IAS 39 was outside the scope of the Interpretation. **BC31**

Presentation

The IFRIC decided that an entity should disclose the gain or loss on the extinguishment of the financial liability by the issue of equity instruments as a separate **BC32** line item in profit or loss or in the notes. This requirement is consistent with the *Framework* and the requirements in other IFRSs, for example:

(a) When gains are recognised in the income statement, they are usually displayed separately because knowledge of them is useful for the purpose of making economic decisions. (paragraph 76 of the *Framework*)
(b) An entity shall present additional line items, headings and subtotals in the statement of comprehensive income and the separate income statement (if presented), when such presentation is relevant to an understanding of the entity's financial performance. (paragraph 85 of IAS 1 *Presentation of Financial Statements*)
(c) An entity shall disclose net gains or net losses on financial liabilities either in the statement of comprehensive income or in the notes. (paragraph 20 of IFRS 7 *Financial Instruments: Disclosures*)

Transition

BC33 The IFRIC decided that the Interpretation should be applied retrospectively even though it acknowledged that determining fair values retrospectively may be problematic. The IFRIC noted that IAS 8 *Accounting Policies, Changes in Accounting Estimates and Errors** provides guidance on circumstances in which retrospective application might be impracticable. The IFRIC concluded that it was preferable to require entities that could apply the Interpretation retrospectively to do so, rather than requiring all entities to apply it prospectively to future transactions. However, to simplify transition, the IFRIC also concluded that it should require retrospective application only from the beginning of the earliest comparative period presented because application to earlier periods would result only in a reclassification of amounts within equity.

Summary of main changes from the draft Interpretation

BC34 The main changes from the IFRIC's proposals in D25 are as follows:

(a) Paragraph 3 was added because the IFRIC identified specific transactions that are outside of the scope of the Interpretation.
(b) Paragraph 6 was modified to state that measurement should be based on the fair value of the equity instruments issued, unless that fair value cannot be reliably measured.
(c) Paragraph 7 was added to reflect the modification to paragraph 6. It also clarifies the intention of the IFRIC that in measuring the fair value of a financial liability extinguished that includes a demand feature (eg a demand deposit), paragraph 49 of IAS 39 is not applied.
(d) Paragraph 8 was added, and paragraph 10 was modified, to clarify how the Interpretation should be applied when only part of the financial liability is extinguished by the issue of equity instruments.
(e) Paragraph 9 was modified to state when the equity instruments issued should be initially measured.

**The UK equivalent references are FRS 18* 'Accounting Policies' *and FRS 3* 'Reporting Financial Performance'.

Urgent Issues Task Force

UK Legal Appendix: Extinguishing Financial Liabilities with Equity Instruments

The Abstract provides that an entity's equity instruments issued to a creditor to extinguish all or part of a financial liability is consideration paid in accordance with paragraph 41 of FRS 26 'Financial Instruments: Recognition and Measurement'. The equity instruments issued are recognised initially at fair value, unless the fair value cannot be reliably measured. 1

The Companies Act 2006 (the Act) makes certain provisions, regarding the payment for shares that must be taken into consideration in complying with the requirements of the Abstract and the Act. 2

Prohibition on issuing shares at a discount

Section 580 of the Act states that a company's shares must not be allotted at a discount. A company must ensure that the nominal value of the shares issued to extinguish the debt is such that the shares are not issued at a discount. This will be by reference to the face value of the debt (ie the liquidated sum that is released - see below), not the market value of the debt. 3

The Share Premium Account

Section 582 provides that shares allotted by a company and any premiums on them may be paid up in money or money's worth (including goodwill and know-how). Section 583 further provides that a share in a company is deemed paid up (as to its nominal value or any premium on it) in cash, or allotted for cash, if the consideration received for the allotment or payment up is a cash consideration. Section 583(3)(c) provides that cash consideration includes a release of a liability of the company for a liquidated sum. In the case where equity instruments extinguish debt, the consideration paid in terms of the Act is the liquidated sum amount (ie the face value of the debt). 4

The Act provides in section 610 that if a company issues shares at a premium, whether for cash or otherwise, a sum equal to the aggregate amount or value of the premiums on those shares must be transferred to "the share premium account". So, where the liquidated sum exceeds the nominal value of the shares issued then the excess must be recognised in the share premium account. 5

The Abstract requires that the difference between the consideration paid and the carrying amount of the financial liability is recognised in profit and loss. To comply with the Act and the Abstract it may be necessary to make a reserves transfer between the profit and loss reserve and the share premium account. 6

UITF Abstract 48

Accounting implications of the replacement of the retail prices index with the consumer prices index for retirement benefits

(Issued 17 December 2010)

The Issue

1 On 8 July 2010*, the Minister for Pensions announced the Government's intention to move to using the Consumer Prices Index (CPI) rather than the Retail Prices Index (RPI) as the inflation measure for determining the minimum pension increases to be applied to the statutory index-linked features of retirement benefits. The Government announced the next such annual inflation measure in December 2010. In general annual CPI increases have been lower than annual RPI increases and therefore the change has the potential to reduce pension Scheme liabilities.

2 The UITF has been requested to provide guidance on the accounting treatment of this change. The UITF agreed the Abstract should address three matters:

(i) whether there is a reduction in Scheme liabilities;

(ii) how the effect of a reduction in Scheme liabilities should be presented; and

(iii) when the effect of a reduction in Scheme liabilities should be recognised.

Scope

3 This Abstract applies to retirement benefits within the scope of FRS 17 'Retirement Benefits'.

Consensus

Whether there is a reduction in Scheme liabilities

4 The Government's announcement to replace RPI with CPI for the statutory minimum increase in pensions in defined benefit schemes has the potential to reduce Scheme liabilities. Whether there is a reduction in Scheme liabilities depends on facts and circumstances.

How the effect of a reduction in Scheme liabilities should be presented

5 In accordance with FRS 17 a change in the Scheme liabilities arising from a change in benefit is part of non-periodic pension costs and is recognised in the profit and loss account. In contrast a change in the Scheme liabilities arising from a change in an assumption is part of actuarial gains and losses and is recognised in the statement of total recognised gains and losses.

6 The UITF reached a consensus that the presentation of a reduction in Scheme liabilities is dependent on whether the obligation is to pay benefits with increases based on RPI, or more generally with inflation–linked increases. Paragraph 20 of FRS 17 states that Scheme liabilities comprise benefits promised under the formal terms of the scheme and any constructive obligation for further benefits where a public statement or past practice by the employer has created a valid expectation in

**For public sector schemes the announcement was made on 22 June 2010 as part of the Emergency Budget.*

the employees that such benefits will be granted. An employer's public statement or past practice gives rise to a constructive obligation where the entity has created a valid expectation that it will pay certain employee benefits.

Where the obligation is to pay benefit increases based on RPI the UITF reached a consensus that the change in Scheme liabilities is a change in benefit and gives rise to a past service cost in accordance with FRS 17. An entity may need to apply judgement in determining if it has an obligation to pay benefits based on RPI in accordance with the provisions of paragraph 20 of FRS 17. **7**

The UITF reached a consensus that if there is no obligation to pay benefit increases based on RPI then a change to CPI is a change in the financial assumption about inflation used to measure the Scheme liabilities and represents an actuarial gain or loss in accordance with FRS 17. **8**

When the effects of a reduction in Scheme liabilities should be recognised

The UITF reached a consensus that where the obligation is to pay benefit increases based on RPI the past service cost should be recognised in the accounting period when any necessary consultations have been concluded or employees' valid expectations have been changed. An entity may need to apply judgement in determining when employees' expectations have been changed. **9**

The UITF reached a consensus that if there is no obligation to pay benefit increases based on RPI an entity should use financial assumptions to measure Scheme liabilities that reflect market expectations at the balance sheet date, in accordance with paragraph 23 of FRS 17. A ministerial announcement, as, for example, that made in July 2010*, will form a reasonable basis for a change in market expectations regarding inflation to be assumed in calculating pension obligations under FRS 17. **10**

Disclosure

The UITF reached a consensus that an entity should provide disclosures that explain the effect of changes in the Scheme liabilities arising from the replacement of RPI with CPI, consistent with objective of FRS 17 of ensuring that the financial statements contain adequate disclosure of the cost of providing retirement benefits and the related gains, losses, assets and liabilities. **11**

Date from which effective

The accounting treatment required by this consensus should be adopted with immediate effect. **12**

Reference Literature

FRS 17 'Retirement Benefits'

**For public sector schemes the announcement was made on 22 June 2010 as part of the Emergency Budget.*

Appendix: Development of the Abstract: Accounting implications of the replacement of the retail prices index with the consumer prices index for retirement benefits

The Development of the Abstract accompanies, but is not part of Abstract 48.

Introduction

A1 This Appendix sets out the UITF's considerations in developing the Abstract: 'Accounting implications of the replacement of the Retail Prices Index with the Consumer Prices Index for Retirement Benefits'.

A2 The UITF received a request to provide guidance on the implications of the Government's announced intention to replace the Retail Prices Index (RPI) with the Consumer Prices Index (CPI) for the minimum increase in pensions in defined benefit schemes. The minimum increase in pensions in defined benefit schemes is set annually by the Government in a Statutory Instrument. The Government has announced that the calculation of that number (previously based on RPI) would in future be based on CPI. In general annual CPI increases have been lower than annual RPI increases. The change therefore has the potential to reduce pension Scheme liabilities.

Is an Abstract needed?

A3 The UITF reached agreement that an Abstract could provide useful guidance to preparers and auditors and bring consistency in application for users. The UITF noted that whilst there is an urgent need for guidance it must adhere to UITF due process. Adherence to due process would have the effect that definitive guidance could not be published until near the end of 2010. As part of its due process the UITF issued a draft Abstract for comment, as an Information Sheet, placing the UITF's provisional thinking into the public domain in October 2010.

Scope

A4 In developing the Abstract the UITF considered its scope. It noted that the issue related to the application of FRS 17 'Retirement Benefits'. It was, however, noted that entities preparing financial statements in accordance with international accounting standards may also need guidance.

A5 The UITF considered whether to refer the issue to the IFRS Interpretations Committee (IFRS IC) but decided the issue is specific to the UK and consequently is unlikely to meet the IFRS IC agenda criteria. In addition the IFRS IC may be unable to respond to the urgent need for guidance in the UK. The UITF is, however, mindful not to interpret international accounting standards.

A6 The UITF noted that entities applying paragraphs 10 to 12 of International Accounting Standard 8 'Accounting Policies, Changes in Accounting Estimates and Errors' may refer to the Abstract as a source of guidance in developing an accounting policy.

A7 Some respondents to the draft Abstract noted that in 2007 the IFRS IC (then known as the International Financial Reporting Interpretations Committee (IFRIC)) considered the question of how a change made by a Government should be accounted for. The IFRS IC did not take the matter on to its agenda but noted that the accounting for changes caused by Government should be the same as for changes made by an employer. It further noted that, in some circumstances, it might be difficult to determine whether the change affects either actuarial assumptions or benefits payable and noted that judgement is required. The UITF noted that this agenda decision is also a source of guidance for entities applying international accounting standards in developing an accounting policy.

During consideration of comments received to its draft Abstract the UITF noted that some respondents requested clarification as to whether the Abstract applies to both public and private sector retirement benefit schemes. The UITF noted that FRS 17 does not make a distinction between these schemes but agreed to clarify that the Abstract applies to all retirement benefits within the scope of FRS 17. **A8**

Whether there is a change in Scheme liabilities

The Government announcement to replace RPI with CPI for the minimum increase in pensions in defined benefit schemes has the potential to reduce Scheme liabilities. Whether there is a reduction in Scheme liabilities depends on facts and circumstances. **A9**

How the effect of a reduction in Scheme liabilities should be presented

In relation to the presentation of the reduction in Scheme liabilities the UITF noted a distinction between changes in benefits when the benefits are based on RPI compared to changes in benefits linked more generally to inflation. The UITF noted that where the benefit is based on RPI (i.e. there is a specific link to RPI) a change in the benefit entitlement may require amendment to the formal terms of the scheme or a change in the expectations of members, for example by some form of communication. In contrast, where there is an unspecified measure of inflation the CPI measure can be applied without further action. **A10**

The UITF noted that the distinction between changes in benefits arising when an obligation is based on RPI, compared to changes in benefits linked more generally to inflation, should be considered in terms of whether the obligation to the member is being changed. **A11**

The UITF reached a consensus that where there is a change in the obligation to the member, there is a benefit change. Where the obligation to the member is not changed, any change in the Scheme liabilities arises from a change in assumptions applied in measuring the liability arising from the unchanged benefit. The key to the accounting is whether there is a change in the obligation to the members. **A12**

The UITF noted that paragraph 20 of FRS 17 provides that Scheme liabilities comprise both any benefits promised under the formal terms of the scheme and any constructive obligation for further benefits where a public statement or past practice by the employer has created a valid expectation in the employees that such benefit will be granted. The UITF noted that an entity may need to apply judgement in determining if it has an obligation to pay benefits based on RPI. An obligation may exist where RPI is not embedded into the formal terms of the scheme but where associated literature makes reference to RPI or where the general understanding of scheme members is that increases would be calculated using RPI. The nature of any obligation to members may vary and will depend on a number of factors, including the nature and content of the employer's communications with members. **A13**

In its draft Abstract the UITF noted that the replacement of RPI with CPI as the inflation measure for determining minimum pension increases could give rise to a **A14** reduction in Scheme liabilities. Respondents to the draft Abstract noted that FRS 17 discusses a past service cost only in relation to an increase in Scheme liabilities; that is FRS 17 does not specifically address the circumstance of a negative past service cost. The UITF accepted this point but could see no reason why a negative past service cost should be treated differently from the provision set out in FRS 17 for a past service cost.

When the effect of a reduction in Scheme liabilities should be recognised

A15 The UITF noted that the nature of the change determines the period in which the effect of the reduction in Scheme liabilities is recognised.

A16 Where there is a change in benefit this is a past service cost and should be presented in the period in which the change occurs. It was agreed that changes in benefits could not be anticipated and could only be recognised when the benefit obligation was altered.

A17 Where a trust deed specifies that the obligation to pay benefits is linked to RPI the obligation cannot be reduced or amended to be linked to CPI without the agreement of members. Such a change gives rise to a past service cost in accordance with FRS 17 and the effect of the reduction in Scheme liabilities is recognised in the period agreement is reached.

A18 Where the entity has a constructive obligation to pay benefits linked to RPI this also gives rise to a past service cost in accordance with FRS 17. The effect of the reduction in Scheme liabilities is recognised in the period the obligation is altered, that is when employee's valid expectations have been changed.

Where there is a change in a financial assumption, in accordance with paragraph 23 of A19 FRS 17, the assumptions should reflect market expectations at the balance sheet date. Accordingly the change should be reported in the period in which the Government announcement was made.

Disclosures

In its draft Abstract the UITF did not discuss the need to make specific disclosures, A20 however, some respondents to the draft Abstract noted that in view of the level of judgement required it is important for entities to make clear disclosures about the accounting treatment they have adopted and how they have applied the changes in the financial statements. The UITF agreed and noted that one of the objectives of FRS 17 is that financial statements contain adequate disclosure of the cost of providing retirement benefits and the related gains, losses, assets and liabilities. The UITF decided to specify in the Abstract that an entity should disclose the effect of changes in Scheme liabilities of the change arising from replacing the RPI with CPI.

Part Six

Statements of Recommended Practice

INTRODUCTORY NOTE

Statements of Recommended Practice ('SORPs') have been issued since 1986. As stated in the Explanatory Foreword to SORPs issued by the Accounting Standards Committee in May 1986

> 'Statements of Recommended Practice ('SORPs') are developed in the public interest and set out current best accounting practice. The primary aims in issuing SORPs are to narrow the areas of difference and variety in the accounting treatment of the matters with which they deal and to enhance the usefulness of published accounting information. SORPs are issued on subjects on which it is not considered appropriate to issue an accounting standard at the time.'

That Explanatory Foreword also noted that

> 'SORPs will always take account of the principles laid down in accounting standards. They can never be taken as authority to depart from the requirements imposed by accounting standards, nor to extend the scope of accounting standards to include entities or circumstances which are otherwise excluded from specific accounting standards or accounting standards in general.
>
> It is recognised in the *(Explanatory) Foreword* to accounting standards that it would be impracticable for accounting standards to cater for all situations. In applying a modified or alternative treatment it is important to have regard to the spirit of and reasoning behind any relevant accounting standards. The recommendations contained in SORPs will always have regard to this spirit and reasoning. They may, therefore, be indicative of the treatment which should be adopted in a situation not specifically catered for by accounting standards'.

The ASC developed and issued two SORPs, 'Pension scheme accounts' and 'Accounting by charities', together with the Explanatory foreword referred to above. These were not adopted by the ASB and both SORPs have now been replaced by updated documents (see below). In addition, as at 31 July 1990, the date the ASC retired, the following SORPs had been 'franked' by the ASC:

	Issuing body	*Issued*
Disclosures about oil and gas exploration and production activities	OIAC	April 1986
Accounting for oil and gas exploration and development activities	OIAC	June 2001
Accounting for abandonment costs	OIAC	June 1988

(These SORPs were replaced by a revised SORP published in January 2000 — see below.)

Accounting for securities by banks	BBA/IBF	July 1990

(Subsequently withdrawn.)

Accounting for insurance business	ABI	May 1990

(This SORP was replaced by a revised SORP published in January 1999 – see below.)

The ASC also franked two SORPs on local authority accounting and one on accounting in UK universities, but these have been superseded respectively by the Code of Practice on Local Authority Accounting in Great Britain and the SORP on Accounting in Higher Education Institutions (see below).

The ASB announced in 1990 that it would not issue its own SORPs. In the event that the ASB's own authority is required to standardise practice within a specialised industry, the ASB's preference is to issue an industry standard. The ASB issued a policy statement for the development of SORPs in 1990, which was updated in 1994. In July 2000 this policy statement was superseded by the ASB statement 'SORPs: Policy and code of practice', which is reproduced after this note. Briefly, in respect of SORPs developed in accordance with ASB guidelines by bodies recognised by the ASB for that purpose, the ASB will give a statement confirming, as appropriate, that the SORP does not appear to contain any fundamental points of principle that are unacceptable in the context of current accounting practice or to conflict with an accounting standard or the ASB's plans for future standards.

Under these arrangements the following SORPs are in issue:

	Issuing body	*Issued*
Accounting for oil and gas exploration, development, production and decommissioning activities	OIAC	June 2001
(Available from: Portland Press Ltd Commerce Way Whitehill Industrial Estate Colchester CO2 8HP)		
Authorised Funds	IMA	October 2010
(Available from: The Investment Management Association 65 Kingsway London WC2B 6TD)		
Banking		
Segmental reporting	BBA/IBF	January 1993
(Available from: British Bankers' Association Pinners Hall 105–108 Old Broad Street London EC2N 1EX *and* Irish Bankers Federation Nassau House Nassau Street Dublin 2.)		
Accounting by Registered Social Housing Providers	NHF/ SFHA/ WFHA	March 2010
(Available from: National Housing Federation Lion Court 25 Procter Street London WC1V 6NY.)		

Accounting for Further and Higher Education (Available from: Universities UK Woburn House 20 Tavistock Square London WC1H 9HQ.)	UUK	October 2007
Accounting and Reporting by Charities (Available from: Charity Commission First Contact PO Box 1227 Liverpool L69 3UG.)	Charity Commission	May 2008
Financial Reports of Pension Schemes (Available from: Croner CCH Ltd 145 London Road Kingston upon Thames KT2 6SR.)	PRAG	May 2007
Financial Statements of Investment Trust Companies and Venture Capital Trusts (Available from: Association of Investment Companies 9th Floor 24 Chiswell Street London EC1Y 4YY.)	AITC	January 2009
Accounting for Insurance Business (Available from: Association of British Insurers 51 Gresham Street London EC2V 7HQ.)	ABI	December 2006
Accounting issues in the asset finance and leasing industry (Available from: Finance and Leasing Association Imperial House 15–19 Kingsway London WC2B 6UN.)	FLA	April 2000
Limited Liability Partnerships (Available from: CCAB PO Box 433 Chartered Accountant's Hall Moorgate Place London EC2P 2BJ.)	CCAB	March 2010

SORPs: Policy and Code of Practice

(Issued July 2000)

INTRODUCTION

Statements of Recommended Practice (SORPs) are recommendations on accounting practices for specialised industries or sectors. They supplement accounting standards and other legal and regulatory requirements in the light of the special factors prevailing or transactions undertaken in a particular industry or sector. SORPs are issued not by the Accounting Standards Board (ASB) but by industry or sectoral bodies recognised for the purpose by the ASB. (Bodies that have been recognised by the ASB for the purpose of producing a SORP or SORPs for an industry or sector are designated 'SORP-making bodies' in this document.)

To secure such recognition, SORP-making bodies are expected to meet criteria laid down by the ASB and to develop their SORP proposals in conformity with the ASB's code of practice. A SORP is required to carry a statement by the ASB confirming, as appropriate, that the SORP does not appear to contain any fundamental points of principle that are unacceptable in the context of current accounting practice or to conflict with an accounting standard or the ASB's plans for future standards. To assist in dealing with proposals for SORPs the ASB has two specialist advisory committees – the Financial Sector and Other Special Industries Committee and the Public Sector and Not-for-profit Committee.

POLICY FOR SORPS

The ASB has adopted the following policy in respect of SORPs:

a The ASB will recognise bodies for the purpose of issuing SORPs. Bodies will not be recognised unless the following conditions are met:

(i) The industry or sector has special accounting or financial reporting problems that require the clarification of accounting standards or interpretation (within the principles of the standards).

(ii) The body represents the whole or a major part of a significant industry or sector for the purposes of financial reporting within the relevant jurisdiction.

(iii) The body shares the ASB's aim of advancing and maintaining standards of financial reporting in the public interest.

(iv) The body agrees to abide by the ASB's code of practice for bodies recognised for issuing SORPs.

(v) Where an industry or sector is regulated or financed by another body, the regulator or financing body is content for the body seeking recognition by the ASB to promulgate SORPs for that industry or sector.

The ASB will, at its discretion, withdraw recognition if it appears that these conditions are no longer met, or if the recognised body fails to comply with the spirit of the code of practice. (This would include circumstances in which a SORP-making body publishes a SORP or similar guidance without securing the approval of the ASB.) The ASB may publicise the withdrawal of recognition if it believes publicity is necessary or desirable.

b SORPs issued by SORP-making bodies will include a statement by the ASB that:

(i) outlines the limited nature of the review the ASB has undertaken; and

(ii) confirms that the SORP does not appear to contain any fundamental points of principle that are unacceptable in the context of current accounting practice or to conflict with an accounting standard or the ASB's plans for future standards.

A pro-forma statement is as follows: c

'The ASB's Statement on the SORP

The aims of the Accounting Standards Board (the ASB) are to establish and improve standards of financial accounting and reporting, for the benefit of users, preparers, and auditors of financial information. To this end, the ASB issues accounting standards that are primarily applicable to general purpose company financial statements. In particular industries or sectors, further guidance may be required in order to implement accounting standards effectively. This guidance is issued, in the form of Statements of Recommended Practice (SORPs), by bodies recognised for the purpose by the ASB.

The XYZ Association (the Association) has confirmed that it shares the ASB's aim of advancing and maintaining standards of financial reporting in the public interest and has been recognised by the ASB for the purpose of issuing SORPs. As a condition of recognition, the Association has agreed to follow the ASB's code of practice for bodies recognised for issuing SORPs.

The code of practice sets out procedures to be followed in the development of SORPs. These procedures do not include a comprehensive review of the proposed SORP by the ASB, but a review of limited scope is performed.

On the basis of its review, the ASB has concluded that the SORP has been developed in accordance with the ASB's code of practice and does not appear to contain any fundamental points of principle that are unacceptable in the context of current accounting practice or to conflict with an accounting standard or the ASB's present plans for future standards.

Dated day/month/year'

The ASB will vary its statement to fit the circumstances of individual cases. d

The ASB will not necessarily make a statement on an exposure draft, but may require a statement to be included indicating areas of overlap with its own work and any reservations that it would find necessary to make if the material were carried through to a final SORP. e

In making a statement on a particular SORP, the ASB in no way guarantees that it will not in time produce a subsequent pronouncement that will supersede, and may contradict, that SORP. f

The ASB has appointed committees to advise it on whether to recognise bodies that wish to develop SORPs and on whether the ASB's statement should be given in respect of individual proposed SORPs. The committees include independent experts and are serviced by the ASB's technical staff and secretariat. The committees monitor adherence to the code of practice and ensure that the ASB is apprised of any issues of fundamental importance that come to their attention. The committees are not required to undertake a comprehensive review of proposed SORPs but only such review as is necessary to enable the ASB to make its statement. g

Code of Practice on the Development of SORPs

PRIMARY CONSIDERATIONS

1 Before beginning a new SORP project, a SORP-making body must seek approval from the ASB. This will ensure that the proposed project does not overlap with an ASB project or address a matter that the ASB would prefer to deal with itself.

2 SORPs should be developed in the context of current accounting practice. In particular, it should be recognised that SORPs cannot override the provisions of the law, accounting standards or UITF Abstracts. It should also be noted that failure to update a SORP does not exempt reporting entities from following, from their effective date, accounting standards or UITF Abstracts issued after the publication of a SORP (except for those entities that operate in the public sector under specific legislative regimes that would prevent or exempt them from doing so). When provisions of a SORP conflict with a more recent accounting standard or UITF Abstract, those provisions cease to have effect.*

3 The SORP should state, in a prominent position, the latest date up to which extant accounting standards and other pronouncements were considered in the development of the SORP. For SORPs that give comprehensive guidance on the preparation of financial statements, it is helpful to append a full list of accounting standards and other pronouncements extant at the date of publication of the SORP, with some indication of their relevance to the industry or sector and how each has been dealt with in the SORP. For specialised SORPs, only related standards would need to be mentioned.

4 A SORP should state its scope by indicating the types of entity to whose financial statements the SORP is intended to apply. Where the SORP-making body is aware that entities to which the SORP applies may also fall within the scope of another SORP, it will be useful to indicate which SORP should be applied (it will usually be appropriate to suggest that an entity should follow the SORP with the more specific application).†

5 A SORP should aim to reduce areas of difference of accounting treatments within the industry or sector by recommending a preferred accounting treatment. It should also seek, where practicable and appropriate, to adopt an approach to accounting in the industry or sector that is consistent with the approach taken in similar industries or sectors.

**In order to clarify the position of the SORP with reference to accounting standards and UITF Abstracts, SORP-making bodies should, where appropriate, include in their SORP a paragraph along the following lines:*

'Entities following this SORP should apply all extant accounting standards, UITF Abstracts and legislation [as specified]. When an accounting standard, UITF Abstract or legislation [as specified] is issued after publication of the most recent edition of the SORP, any provisions of the SORP that conflict with the new standard, UITF Abstract or legislation cease to have effect.'

†*In these situations, consultation will be necessary with the ASB and the other relevant SORP-making body.*

DEVELOPMENT OF A SORP

Working parties

Drafting of the SORP must be undertaken either by the SORP-making body itself or by a working party of the SORP-making body. In either case the process should ensure the participation of representatives of the industry or sector concerned, independent outsiders on behalf of the wider public interest and, where possible, users of financial statements, and have sufficient technical accounting support. The arrangements proposed (including membership of any working party), and any changes in those arrangements, should be notified in advance to the ASB, so that the ASB may satisfy itself that these requirements are met. **6**

Where the ASB's approval of the arrangements is premised on the use of a working party including representatives of outside interests, the SORP-making body should normally expect to accept the recommendations of its working party. Where in such cases a draft of a proposed SORP or exposure draft submitted to the ASB has, at the request of the SORP-making body, been changed from the text recommended by the working party, the change and the reason for it should be notified to the ASB. **7**

Due process

The SORP-making body should conduct its proceedings in a spirit of openness and follow due process involving wide consultation. In addition to organisations and individuals in the industry or sector concerned, those to be invited to comment should normally include member bodies of the CCAB, auditors actively involved in the industry or sector and relevant regulators and Government departments. **8**

Before publishing the final SORP, the SORP-making body should invite public comment, normally by means of a published exposure draft, allowing a reasonable period for comments. The ASB will wish to be satisfied that the period given for responses allows due process; a minimum period of three months should be given, although, where a case can be made, a shorter period may be acceptable. **9**

Comments may also be sought on a published statement of intent: however, it will not be acceptable to dispense with publication of an exposure draft, even following the publication of a statement of intent. The SORP-making body should attempt to secure publicity for its exposure drafts and statements of intent in journals specialising in the relevant industry or sector and in accountancy journals. **10**

During development of a SORP (or its revision) it is the responsibility of the SORP-making body to identify potential divergences from accounting standards and inform the ASB of them at an early stage. **11**

All exposure drafts and final SORPs should be presented to the relevant ASB committee for comment before publication. At each pre-publication stage sufficient time should be given to the committee to allow any necessary changes to be determined and incorporated. **12**

The ASB will wish to be satisfied that public comments have been appropriately invited and considered. Before publishing the SORP the SORP-making body should provide the ASB with copies of the comment letters, a summary or analysis of the main comments and an indication of how they have been dealt with, in sufficient time to allow any necessary changes to be incorporated. **13**

14 The invitation to comment included in exposure drafts should state that comments will be regarded as on the public record, unless confidentiality is requested. Copies of comments that are on the public record should be made available on request at a reasonable charge.

The ASB's statement on the SORP

15 Written permission should be obtained from the ASB for inclusion of the ASB statement in a SORP. The ASB's statement should be included in a prominent place in each SORP. No other reference to the ASB should be made without prior written approval from the ASB.

REVIEW OF SORPs

16 The SORP-making body should keep under review all the SORPs for which it is responsible. In particular, the body should consider:

- any implications for the SORPs of new and proposed accounting standards. In the interests of the SORP-making body and its constituency any divergences must be notified to the ASB as soon as is practicable.
- any evidence of widespread failure in the relevant industry or sector to follow any part of the guidance in a SORP that has come to the attention of the SORP-making body.
- any developments in the industry or sector that suggest that further guidance on accounting matters is desirable.

17 The body should report to the ASB, at least annually, the results of such a review. The report should confirm that the body continues to comply with this code of practice and state whether, in the light of the review, it proposes to revise any of the SORPs for which it is responsible.

ADDITIONAL GUIDANCE

18 It will not normally be necessary for a SORP-making body to supplement a SORP with further guidance. Any material that a SORP-making body proposes to issue formally, offering an interpretation of accounting standards that is likely to lead to widespread acceptance as industry or sectoral practice, should be included in the SORP or should be submitted to the same due process and scrutiny procedures as the SORP, including review by the ASB and its relevant committees.

19 There are, however, three circumstances where the publication of further guidance outside the SORP may be desirable:

(a) when urgent guidance is required on a new accounting standard or other relevant publication issued since the SORP was published. Normally, such guidance should subsequently be incorporated into a revised version of the SORP.

(b) when further guidance is required to interpret the requirements of the SORP within a particular subsector.

(c) when informal guidance on application of the SORP is necessary in order to aid practitioners.

20 In the situations described in paragraph 19(a) and (b), the SORP-making body should notify the ASB, explaining what guidance is proposed. The ASB may, if appropriate, confirm that it has no objection to the proposed guidance and require a

reference to the ASB to be included in the guidance. The guidance should not be published without the agreement of the ASB.

In the situation described in paragraph 19(a), where it is clear that guidance on a major issue is needed and cannot be delayed until revision of the SORP, the SORP-making body should attempt to follow all due process as required for the revision of a SORP. Where full due process has been followed, including review by the ASB and its relevant committees, then the 'ASB's statement on the SORP' may be attached to the guidance, giving it the same authority as the SORP. **21**

In the situations described in paragraph 19(b) and (c), a SORP-making body should ensure that the authority of any such material in relation to the SORP is clearly indicated, and in particular state whether it has been reviewed by the ASB. A pro-forma statement for cases where the ASB has not carried out a review is as follows: **22**

'The overall aim of the [additional guidance] is to assist practitioners in the preparation of statements of accounts. It does not form part of the [dated SORP], nor has it been reviewed by the ASB. It attempts to explain and illustrate what is required by the [dated SORP], but does not carry the authority of the SORP'.

RIGHT TO REPRODUCE

The SORP-making body shall grant the ASB the unrestricted right to reproduce in full any SORPs it has developed without being subject to any financial charge. **23**

Part Seven

ICAEW Accounting Recommendations

[TECH 03/08]
Guidance on materiality in financial reporting by UK entities

Guidance on materiality in financial reporting by UK entities, published in June 2008 by the Institute of Chartered Accountants in England and Wales.

Contents

	Paragraphs
Introduction	
Scope	1 – 4
Definition of materiality	5
General considerations	6 – 8
Applications of materiality	9 - 17
Users	18 – 22
Determinants of materiality	23 – 25
Size	26 – 27
Nature	28 – 31
Circumstances	32 – 35
Half-yearly statements	36
Making decisions about materiality	37 – 42
Evidencing decisions	43

This Technical Release provides general guidance and does not purport to deal with all possible questions and issues that may arise in any given situation. The Institute and the authors do not accept responsibility for loss caused to any person who acts or refrains from acting in reliance on the material in this publication, whether such loss is caused by negligence or otherwise.

Introduction

The principles of Tech 32/96 'The interpretation of materiality in financial reporting' were still sound and relevant more than 10 years after it was first published. However, many of its references to UK literature were no longer current and it did not deal at all with IFRS. The Financial Reporting Committee of the Institute's Financial Reporting Faculty has therefore updated the guidance to take account of the latest UK literature and IFRS, and to make sure that its principles remain in line with the latest thinking on materiality. This will help to minimise divergent practices in the application of materiality judgements in the preparation of financial statements.

A draft of the revised guidance was published for comment as Tech 01/07 in June 2007. Tech 03/08 has been finalised in the light of comments received. References to Company Law, Accounting and Auditing Standards and other accounting, auditing and regulatory literature and material are correct as at 9 June 2008.

Guidance on materiality in financial reporting by UK entities

Scope

This guidance is for preparers of financial statements ('preparers'). It considers the issue of materiality in financial reporting, including the relevant discussion in the *Statement of Principles for Financial Reporting* ('*Statement of Principles*') issued by the Accounting Standards Board ('ASB') in December 1999. It is intended to help with the practical application of the definitions and explanations of materiality. As the principles underlying the *Statement of Principles* and the *Framework for the Preparation and Presentation of Financial Statements* ('*Framework*') adopted by the International Accounting Standards Board ('IASB') in April 2001 are consistent, it may also be useful in relation to financial statements prepared under IFRS. 1

This guidance refers primarily to the financial statements of commercial entities reporting in compliance with companies legislation and therefore intended to give a true and fair view*. However, its principles can be applied more generally to financial statements prepared by other organisations (eg, charities, pension schemes, government departments, local authorities and public sector businesses)†, although the assessment of users' needs may vary (see paragraphs 20, 22, 38 and 39 below). 2

The principles set out in this guidance may also be relevant to other information, such as that provided in an operating and financial review, a business review, a half-yearly report, interim management statements, information about post balance sheet events or in corporate governance disclosures. 3

Auditors apply similar concepts in arriving at judgements about materiality, but are subject to separate guidance issued by the Auditing Practices Board ('APB'). Audit aspects of materiality are therefore not addressed in this guidance. 4

**The Companies Act 2006 s393 requires that the directors of a company must be satisfied that their accounts prepared in compliance with the Act give a true and fair view, irrespective of the accounting framework used. The Companies Act 1985 s262(2A) provides in relation to financial statements prepared under IAS that references in the relevant part of the Act to financial statements giving a true and fair view are references to their achieving a fair presentation. See also paragraph 8.2 of the Department of Trade and Industry's (now the Department for Business, Enterprise and Regulatory Reform's)* Guidance for British Companies on Changes to the Accounting and Reporting Provisions of the Companies Act 1985 *(revised August 2005). See also the Opinion of 21 April 2008 by Martin Moore QC, referenced in FRC Press Notice 222* Relevance of 'True and Fair' concept confirmed *(http://www.frc.org.uk/press/pub1615.html).*

†*The ASB published its* Statement of Principles for Financial Reporting: Proposed Interpretation for Public Benefit Entities *in June 2007, which includes a discussion of materiality (see paragraphs 15-19 of Chapter 3).*

Definition of materiality

5 The concept of materiality is fundamental to the reporting of information. The ASB's *Statement of Principles** defines and explains it as follows:

3.28 Materiality is the final test of what information should be given in a particular set of financial statements. While the paragraphs above describe the characteristics that, if present, will mean that the usefulness of the financial information has been maximised, the materiality test asks whether the resulting information content is of such significance as to require its inclusion in the financial statements.

3.29 Materiality is therefore a threshold quality that is demanded of all information given in the financial statements. Furthermore, when immaterial information is given in the financial statements, the resulting clutter can impair the understandability of the other information provided. In such circumstances, the immaterial information will need to be excluded.

3.30 An item of information is material to the financial statements if its misstatement or omission might reasonably be expected to influence the economic decisions of users of those financial statements, including their assessments of management's stewardship.

3.31 Whether information is material will depend on the size and nature of the item in question judged in the particular circumstances of the case. The principal factors to be taken into account are set out below. It will usually be a combination of these factors, rather than any one in particular, that will determine materiality.

(a) The item's size is judged in the context both of the financial statements as a whole and of the other information available to users that would affect their evaluation of the financial statements. This includes, for example, considering how the item affects the evaluation of trends and similar considerations.

(b) Consideration is given to the item's nature in relation to:

(i) the transactions or other events giving rise to it;

(ii) the legality, sensitivity, normality and potential consequences of the event or transaction;

(iii) the identity of the parties involved; and

(iv) the particular headings and disclosures that are affected.

If there are two or more similar items, the materiality of the items in aggregate as well as of the items individually needs to be considered.

General considerations

6 Materiality depends on an item's size, nature and circumstances. Dependence on size means that materiality is quantifiable in financial terms. However, the nature and

**Materiality is independent of any particular accounting framework. The* Statement of Principles *was developed from the IASB's* Framework, *which in turn drew on work carried out by the US Financial Accounting Standards Board (FASB) in relation to its conceptual framework project. The principles underlying the* Statement *and* Framework *are therefore consistent. The IASB and FASB are currently working on a joint project to develop a common conceptual framework. The guidance in this Technical Release may ultimately need to be revisited in the light of the IASB/FASB project.*

Paragraphs 29 and 30 of the Framework *deal with materiality in the context of relevance (see footnote 13 below). Paragraph 11 of IAS 1* Presentation of Financial Statements */ paragraph 7 of IAS 1 (Revised) states in relation to materiality that:*

Omissions or misstatements of items are material if they could, individually or collectively, influence the economic decisions of users taken / that users make on the basis of the financial statements. Materiality depends on the size and nature of the omission or misstatement judged in the surrounding circumstances. The size or nature of the item, or a combination of both, could be the determining factor.

circumstances of an item are qualitative matters and so materiality is not capable of general mathematical definition. Because judgement is required to determine materiality, different people may have different views about whether an item is material. Materiality will often be indicated by a range of potential values with the eventual treatment of a particular item depending upon a full consideration of the information involved and how it will be used.

Judgements about materiality ultimately depend on how information could influence the economic decisions of users of financial statements or other information ('users')*. According to Chapter One of the *Statement of Principles*: 7

> *The objective of financial statements is to provide information about the reporting entity's financial performance and financial position that is useful to a wide range of users for assessing the stewardship† of the entity's management and for making economic decisions.‡*

There is a role for guidelines in reaching consistent and properly considered conclusions. Nevertheless, if preparers are to be responsive to users, they should not substitute the mechanical application of rules and formulae for careful consideration of how information could influence or enhance users' economic decisions, such as whether to hold or sell investments or whether to reappoint or replace management. Preparers should also appreciate that information often has economic effects without changing economic decisions. For example, in preparing financial statements to be used to value a business for an acquisition, a relatively minor adjustment may alter the purchase price without changing the decision to proceed with the acquisition. 8

Applications of materiality

In financial reporting, the concept of materiality is applied to, inter alia, tolerances, uncertainties, differences and errors, in relation to: 9

(a) classes of transaction;
(b) account balances;
(c) disclosures; and
(d) the financial statements as a whole.

In maintaining accounting records relating to individual transactions with other parties, accuracy and precision are essential and therefore the concept of materiality does not apply.§ Other items are recorded in accounting records based on best estimates of the outcomes of future events, fair values and the appropriate allocation of costs and revenues to different activities and periods. Such estimates are subjective and the concept of materiality is applied in determining appropriate precision tolerances that reflect the nature of the items involved. 10

**The US Supreme Court has stated that an omitted fact is generally considered to be material if there is a substantial likelihood that a reasonable investor would have viewed its disclosure as significantly altering the 'total mix' of available information (TSC Industries, Inc. v. Northway, Inc., 426 US 438 [1976]).*

†*Stewardship is discussed in paragraph 22 below.*

‡*This is expressed in paragraph 12 of the* Framework *as: 'The objective of financial statements is to provide information about the financial position, performance and changes in financial position of an entity that is useful to a wide range of users in making economic decisions.'*

§*The legal requirement to maintain accounting records is in Companies Act 2006 s386 and Companies Act 1985 s221.*

11 The application of materiality thresholds and tolerances is fundamental to the internal and external reporting that underpins corporate governance, the management of commercial risk and business decision-making. Managements require internal reports which highlight relevant matters and omit irrelevant detail and they supplement basic accounting records with management systems and controls which, amongst other things:

(a) summarise information from the accounting records which might be material in aggregate; and
(b) prevent and detect material misstatement of that information.

12 For internal and external financial reporting purposes it is conventional to apply low thresholds for accumulating information so that similar items can be considered in aggregate against a chosen level of materiality as the time for reporting approaches. The use of lower thresholds helps ensure that cumulative omissions (including those accumulating over more than one year) and other errors do not lead to an overall material misstatement. It is also conventional to select a monetary unit, such as a pound or a thousand pounds, and to round to the nearest unit. The chosen unit is set sufficiently low to ensure that the resulting loss of precision and detail is clearly immaterial, trivial or inconsequential.

13 In assessing the materiality of errors, account should be taken of the effect on both the balance sheet and the profit and loss account, including the effect of uncorrected errors in past years and the effect on trends.*

14 In the context of external reporting, legislation and regulations for different types of organisation contain requirements to report particular accounting and other information. Legislation and regulations usually specifically describe such requirements as applying only when a materiality condition is satisfied: for example, the need to include a line item shown in the accounts formats in companies legislation.

15 Application of the concept of materiality is also explicitly permitted under financial reporting standards of the ASB and the IASB and their respective interpretations ('financial reporting standards') and companies legislation in a variety of circumstances.

16 Many materiality decisions are called for in the application of financial reporting standards. Even where preparers decide to apply an individual provision of a standard – eg, in relation to measurement – they are not necessarily committed to apply all the other provisions of the standard: eg, to make specified disclosures which are immaterial†. The importance of such decisions is clear from paragraph 20 of the ASB's *Foreword to Accounting Standards* which states that the Financial Reporting Review Panel (FRRP) is concerned with material departures from financial reporting standards or the accounting provisions of companies legislation where such a departure results in the financial statements in question not giving a true and fair view. (The FRRP considers financial statements prepared both under UK GAAP and IFRS.)

**Correction of errors is dealt with in FRS 3* Reporting Financial Performance *and IAS 8* Accounting Policies, Changes in Accounting Estimates and Errors.

†*Paragraph 31 of IAS 1 states that, 'Applying the concept of materiality means that a specific disclosure requirement in a Standard or an Interpretation need not be satisfied if the information is not material.' This is rephrased in paragraph 31 of IAS 1 (Revised) as 'An entity need not provide a specific disclosure required by an IFRS if the information is not material'.*

In respect of other disclosures required by legislation rather than by standards (for example, directors' emoluments, auditor remuneration, staff costs), application of the concept of materiality is neither specifically permitted nor forbidden by the relevant legislation. These disclosures are required principally for accountability purposes and materiality should be assessed in that light (see also paragraph 27 below). **17**

Users

The primary focus of the *Statement of Principles* is on those financial statements that are intended to give a true and fair view of the reporting entity's financial performance and financial position. For most entities, those statements will be their full annual financial statements to be laid before the members as a body. **18**

The *Statement of Principles* regards financial statements as providing information that is useful to a wide range of external users.* It notes a rebuttable presumption that '...financial statements that focus on the interest that investors have in the reporting entity's financial performance and financial position will, in effect, also be focusing on the common interest that all users have in that entity's financial performance and financial position.' Such users include actual and potential investors, employees, lenders, suppliers and other trade creditors, governments and their agencies, and members of the public with access to financial statements. In making judgements on materiality, preparers should therefore be concerned with identifying relevant users. Identifying groups of users for the purpose of making reporting decisions does not itself involve acknowledging a legal duty of care to such groups. **19**

The expectation that preparers will address the needs of a wide range of users is mitigated by the Boards' assertions in the *Statement of Principles* and the *Framework* that: **20**

(a) not all the information needs of all users can be met by financial statements (*Statement of Principles* paragraph 1.8 and *Framework* paragraph 10);
(b) financial statements that focus on the interest that investors have in the reporting entity's financial performance and financial position will, in effect, be focusing on the interest that all users have (*Statement of Principles* paragraph 1.11 and, in different terms, *Framework* paragraph 10);
(c) users can be assumed to have a reasonable knowledge of business and economic activities and accounting and a willingness to study information with reasonable diligence (*Statement of Principles* paragraph 3.27(c) and *Framework* paragraph 25).

It is therefore envisaged that judgements about materiality can generally be made on the basis of the needs of classes of knowledgeable and diligent users who are reasonable in their use of and reliance on financial statements and other information. Such users recognise the inherent limitations of financial statements and other information requiring the use of estimates and the consideration of future events. It is also important when there are large numbers of users in a group to consider representative users. Preparers should not seek to address a single hypothetical user, especially one on the brink of making a decision to buy or sell, whose decision might be changed by even a small change in a reported number or disclosure. **21**

**The* Framework *states that 'The objective of financial statements is to provide information about the financial position, performance and changes in financial position of an entity that is useful to a wide range of users in making economic decisions.' (paragraph 12).*

22 The ASB (and IASB) identify providers of risk capital as the primary users of financial statements. Consequently, in considering materiality, preparers are expected to focus on the relevance of information to the assessment of financial performance, position and adaptability and management's discharge of its stewardship responsibilities (referred to generally in this guidance as 'accountability'). In entities where the provision of risk capital is of reduced importance (eg, charities, pension schemes and government bodies), the same broad financial and accountability issues are still likely to be of most interest to the relevant primary user groups.

Determinants of materiality

23 The determinants of the materiality of an item are its size and nature as judged in the 'particular circumstances of the case' (see the *Statement of Principles)* or 'surrounding circumstances' (see paragraph 11 of IAS 1).* The tests are both quantitative and qualitative, and where the nature and circumstances are of sufficient importance it is these qualitative aspects, rather than considerations of the relative size of an item alone, that determines whether an item falls to be separately disclosed. Judgements are applied consistently within the period and from one period to the next.

24 It may be that an item should be brought to the attention of users due to its nature or the circumstances of its arising, notwithstanding that the amount might not otherwise be regarded as material. Criteria that might apply when deciding whether separate disclosure of an item is needed include the assessment of an item's nature in relation to the matters set out in paragraph 28 below.

25 Examples of such items include unlawful transactions, fines†, penalties and illegal dividends. Further examples of qualitative items would include the inadequate or improper description of an accounting policy when it is likely that a user of the financial statements would be misled by the description, and failure to disclose a breach of regulatory requirements when it is likely that the consequent imposition of regulatory restrictions will significantly impair operating capability.

Size

26 The size of an item recognised in primary financial statements can only be expressed in terms of monetary value. In considering the materiality of uncertainties and contingencies, preparers therefore have to make best estimates of the potential monetary amounts involved, taking into account the likelihood of crystallisation. In considering the materiality of related party transactions for which no price is charged, preparers should have regard to the potential monetary amounts involved.

27 Whilst the quantification of materiality is fundamental and unavoidable, materiality can never be judged purely on the basis of absolute size .

- £1 million is a large amount but in relation to a potential misstatement of sales by a large multinational, it is likely to be immaterial.

**The* Framework *judges the 'relevance' of an item by reference to its materiality and, separately, its nature: 'Information is material if its omission or misstatement could influence the economic decisions of users taken on the basis of the financial statements. Materiality depends on the size of the item or error judged in the particular circumstances of its omission or misstatement.' (paragraph 30) The* Statement of Principles *does not subsume 'nature' within relevance; it states that 'information is relevant if it has the ability to influence the economic decisions of users and is provided in time to influence those decisions.' (paragraph 3.2).*

†*See FRRP Press Notice 51 dated 12 May 1998 (http://www.frc.org.uk/frrp/press/pub0110.html).*

- Conversely, in some cases the nature and circumstances of an item can be of such importance to users that a size threshold is of little practical significance in determining materiality. For example, £10,000 is a comparatively small amount but it might be seen as material, even for a large multinational, if it relates to a benefit-in-kind which has been wrongly omitted from the disclosure of directors' remuneration.

The latter point may be particularly relevant where management accountability or corporate governance are at issue or in the context of disclosures in financial statements required by legislation (see paragraph 17 above).

Nature

The nature of an item is characterised by: 28

(a) the transactions or other events giving rise to it;
(b) the legality, sensitivity, normality and potential consequences of the event or transaction;
(c) the identity of the parties involved; and
(d) the account captions and disclosure notes affected.

Particular care should be taken not to offset items which are different in nature when they might be material if considered separately; eg, an unrecorded sale and the related cost of sale, or an item and its tax effect. Conversely, the materiality of items of a similar nature should be considered in aggregate; eg, if a number of sales have not been recorded, their materiality should be considered in aggregate. 29

The *Statement of Principles* states that, 'In requiring information provided by financial statements to represent faithfully what it purports to represent and to be neutral, there is an implication that the information is complete and free from error – at least within the bounds of materiality. Information that contains a material error or *has been omitted for reasons other than materiality* can cause the financial statements to be false or misleading and thus unreliable and deficient in terms of their relevance' (paragraph 3.16, emphasis in italics added). Creating immaterial errors deliberately or selectively correcting immaterial errors in order to influence a trend is not in accordance with UK GAAP.* 30

This is also an issue that has been highlighted in other relevant literature. For example, the APB's *Aggressive Earnings Management*† states that 'as a matter of principle the APB believes that directors and management should correct all misstatements identified by the auditors' (paragraph 35); and 'auditors consider whether judgements and decisions made by the directors and management ... could be part of a pattern of bias, even though individually they may appear reasonable, to avoid the financial statements reflecting the underlying reality' (paragraph 47). 31

Circumstances

The materiality of information can only be judged in relation to its ultimate impact, *or potential impact*, on users. Consequently, the materiality of a given item of a given 32

**See also paragraph 41 of IAS 8, which makes it clear that 'financial statements do not comply with IFRSs if they contain ... immaterial errors made intentionally to achieve a particular presentation of an entity's financial position, financial performance or cash flows.'*

†*http://www.frc.org.uk/images/uploaded/documents/aggrressive.pdf [sic]*

size will depend on the context of the accounting and other information available to users.

33 The immediate context of an item is the entity's financial statements. Some financial reporting standards and related guidance contain explicit references to the appropriate context in which to judge materiality and look beyond the immediate disclosures and captions affected by an item. It might be appropriate to focus on one or more of the following:

(a) individual disclosures;
(b) primary statement captions and subtotals;
(c) the relevant primary financial statement as a whole;
(d) the financial statements as a whole; and
(e) the entity's financial position or the scale of its operations as indicated by the financial statements.

34 Paragraph 20 of the Explanation of FRS 8 *Related Party Disclosures* provides additional guidance. It indicates that the materiality of related party transactions is to be judged not only in the broader context of the reporting entity but also in relation to an individual related party; eg, where that party is a director, key manager or some other accountable person. (This does not apply in the FRSSE, which is silent on the issue.)* If the disclosure of a related party transaction is considered to be sensitive (eg, for tax reasons or the nature of the transaction) this is likely to affect consideration of the transaction's materiality if disclosure might be expected to influence the users of the financial statements.

35 The financial statements of a single period for a single entity are of limited value and users generally consider such information in a wider context. It will therefore often be appropriate for preparers to modify their views on the materiality of an item in the light of:

(a) comparative figures and trend information;
(b) expectations including, where relevant, projections and forecasts;
(c) the financial statements of comparable entities; and
(d) economic and industry background information.

Half-yearly statements

36 The ASB Statement *Half-Yearly Financial Reports (July 2007)* states that 'materiality should be assessed by reference to the results and financial position for the half-yearly period rather than in relation to expected results and financial position for the full year' (paragraph 28).† Interim measurements of financial data may rely on estimates to a greater extent than annual measurements and this may be relevant when making assessments of materiality at half-yearly or other interim dates.

Making decisions about materiality

37 Prescriptive rules which seek to reflect how users make decisions cannot address all situations and relieve preparers of the need to apply judgement. Preparers may wish to develop and maintain guidelines for their own organisation which reflect their

**IAS 24* Related Party Disclosures *is silent on this issue. The ASB has published FRED 41 proposing to replace FRS 8 with an accounting standard based on IAS 24, and is therefore also silent on this issue.*

†*IAS 34* Interim Financial Reporting *similarly states that 'materiality shall be assessed in relation to the interim period financial data' (paragraph 23).*

consideration of users and the size, nature and circumstances of individual items within the financial statements. Such guidelines provide relatively objective rebuttable presumptions against which subsequent judgements about particular situations can be gauged. Preparers may have regard to the increasing precision with which materiality can be expressed during the course of preparation of financial statements. An important overall test of the appropriateness of decisions about materiality is to consider whether the resulting financial statements give a true and fair view as required by companies legislation and the regulations for many different types of entity.*

Materiality guidelines can be derived from answering the following questions: **38**

(a) who are the relevant users?
(b) what are their decision-making needs?
(c) what types of financial information are likely to influence the decisions of the users? (For example, users of financial statements of a nonprofit organisation and users of financial statements of a commercial trading entity may focus on different information.)
(d) for a given item, what is the appropriate context for assessing its materiality?
(e) in what range of values do items become critical in terms of materiality?
(f) how should particular items in these critical ranges be decided and reported?

Preparers' perceptions of users' needs can be based on: **39**

(a) general discussions with users and other information relating to users' expectations gathered as a result of a company's corporate governance procedures;
(b) observing users' responses to information, eg, press or analyst comment on particular disclosures, numbers, ratios or trends and the effects on decisions to hold or sell investments or to reappoint or replace management;
(c) the impact on market prices of specific items of news; and
(d) their own reactions and attitudes as users of financial information in similar situations.

In some cases the approach will be relatively straightforward. Where a company's bank facility is dependent on compliance with covenants based upon financial statements, the users of those statements include investors, bankers and creditors with an interest in knowing whether the covenants are violated.† Their decision-making needs will at least cover the figures that are used in the covenant calculations. An item will be judged material if it will make a difference in triggering non-compliance with a covenant or in ensuring that a covenant is satisfied. **40**

At certain critical thresholds, an assessment of users' needs will indicate a requirement for very low levels of materiality and potentially unrealistic demands for accuracy; eg, where trends reverse, profits become losses, technical insolvency occurs, or compliance with debt covenants is in doubt. In these circumstances, preparers should: **41**

**The Companies Act 2006 requires a true and fair view for financial statements prepared both under UK GAAP and IAS.*

†*Paragraph 18 of FRS 29 (IFRS 7)* Financial Instruments: Disclosures *and IFRS 7* Financial Instruments: Disclosures *require specified disclosures about defaults that occur during the period. Paragraph 67 of IAS 1 / paragraph 76 of IAS 1 (Revised) and FRS 21 (IAS 10)* Events after the balance sheet date *are relevant for disclosures of defaults that occur between the balance sheet date and the date the financial statements are authorised. (Paragraph 67 of IAS 1 / paragraph 76 of IAS 1 (Revised) sets out specified disclosures regarding the latter.)*

(a) adopt an even-handed approach in areas where the required degree of accuracy is difficult to achieve so that there is perceived to be an equal chance of mistakenly falling on either side of a critical divide;
(b) be particularly sensitive to the potentially misleading cumulative effect of individually immaterial items or errors (see paragraph 13 above); and
(c) consider whether the reliability of the information in relation to its potential use is such that the information should be accompanied by a clear statement of the circumstances of its preparation and its inherent limitations (see paragraph 26 above).*

42 On the basis of experience, a preparer might reasonably decide to attach particular importance to the materiality of items in a company's financial statements in the context of the trend of earnings and the margins of other companies in the same sector. Such considerations might be particularly appropriate in situations of marginal or break-even profitability.

Evidencing decisions

43 It may be appropriate for those preparing financial statements, whether as individuals or, collectively, as a body charged with governance, formally to document, for their own purposes, and commensurate with the size and complexity of the entity in the prevailing circumstances, their principles, policies and guidelines with regard to materiality and the main decisions they have taken. Such steps may be useful in appropriate circumstances in dealings with Regulators such as the FRRP.

**See also paragraph 113 of IAS 1 / paragraph 122 of IAS 1 (Revised), which requires disclosure of significant judgements made in applying the entity's accounting policies; and paragraph 116 of IAS 1 / paragraph 125 of IAS 1, which requires disclosure of assumptions about the future and other major sources of estimation uncertainty that have a significant risk of causing material adjustments in the next financial year.*

[TECH 02/10]
Guidance on the determination of realised profits and losses in the context of distributions under the Companies Act 2006

Guidance on realised and distributable profits under the Companies Act 2006 issued by the Institute of Chartered Accountants in England and Wales and the Institute of Chartered Accountants of Scotland (the Institutes) in October 2010.

Contents

	Paragraph
1. Introduction	**1.1 - 1.10**
2. The legal framework	**2.1 - 2.52**
The common law	**2.1 - 2.2**
Fiduciary and other duties and volatility	**2.3 - 2.5**
Definition of a distribution for Part 23 of the 2006 Act	**2.6**
Profits available for distribution	**2.7 - 2.8E**
Distributions in kind: Meaning	**2.8F**
Distributions in kind: Treatment of unrealised profits	**2.9 – 2.9A**
Distributions in kind; Determination of amount	**2.9B – 2.9F**
Distributions in kind: Effect of IFRIC 17	**2.9G – 2.9O**
Date of distribution	**2.10 – 2.10A**
Merger relief and group reconstruction relief	**2.11**
Relevant accounts	**2.12 – 2.24**
General	**2.12 – 2.18**
Annual accounts – all companies	**2.19**
Initial and interim accounts – public companies	**2.20 – 2.23**
Initial and interim accounts – private companies	**2.24**
Disclosure of distributable profits	**2.25 – 2.27**
Subsequent events	**2.28 – 2.29**
Public companies	**2.30 – 2.31**
Provisions	**2.31A – 2.34I**
The general rule and the exception	**2.31A – 2.34**
Application of the exception under IFRSs	**2.34A – 2.34I**
Asset revaluations	**2.35 – 2.37**
Development costs	**2.38 – 2.39**
Treasury shares	**2.40 – 2.43**
Section 832 – Investment companies	**2.44 – 2.47A**
Section 843 – Long term insurance business	**2.47B – 2.53**

3. Realised profits	**3.1 – 3.75**
General	**3.1 – 3.2**
Principles of realisation	**3.3 – 3.6**
Definitions	**3.7 – 3.13**
Profit	**3.8**
Realised profit	**3.9 – 3.9B**
Realised loss	**3.10**
Qualifying consideration	**3.11**
Readily convertible to cash	**3.12 – 3.13**
Application	**3.14 – 3.27**
Instances of realised profit	**3.14**
Instances of realised loss	**3.15**
Deferred tax	**3.17**
Exchange of assets ("top-slicing")	**3.18**
Hedging	**3.19 – 3.20**
Foreign exchange profits and losses	**3.21 – 3.21B**
Goodwill in an individual company	**3.22 – 3.23D**
Negative goodwill in an individual company	**3.24 – 3.27**
Changes in circumstances including changes in accounting policies and on the adoption of IFRSs	**3.28 – 3.42**
Introduction	**3.28 – 3.29**
Timing of the effect of changes in accounting policies on distributable profits	**3.30 – 3.37**
Realised profits that have been distributed and are subsequently eliminated by a change of circumstances (including a change of accounting policy)	**3.38 – 3.40**
Effect of errors	**3.41 – 3.42**
Application of the linkage etc principle in paragraph 3.5	**3.43 – 3.75**
4. Fair value accounting	**4.1 – 4.33**
Introduction	**4.1**
Guidance on the application of "readily convertible to cash"	**4.2 – 4.22**
Financial instruments	**4.2 – 4.4**
Close out	**4.5 – 4.7**
Embedded derivatives	**4.8**
Top-slicing	**4.9**
Unquoted equity investments	**4.10**
Strategic investments	**4.11 – 4.12**
Hedge relationship in group situation	**4.12A**
Investment properties	**4.13**
Own credit	**4.14 – 4.15**
Block discounts for securities traded on an active market	**4.16 – 4.22**
Available-for-sale financial assets and the fair value reserve	**4.23 – 4.25**
Fair value option	**4.26 – 4.28**
Losses	**4.29 – 4.33**
5. Hedge accounting	**5.1 – 5.18**
Hedge relationships in individual companies	**5.1 – 5.1A**
Fair value hedge accounting	**5.2 – 5.6**
Cash flow hedge accounting	**5.7 – 5.9**
Net investment hedge accounting	**5.10 – 5.11**
Transition from SSAP 20 – Hedge accounting for foreign equity investments	**5.12 – 5.18**
Hedge relationship in group situations	**5.19 – 5.22**

6. Issues arising from IAS 32 (and its equivalent, FRS 25) **6.1 – 6.87**

Introduction **6.1 – 6.6**
Assumptions **6.6A – 6.6C**
Principles – General 6.7 – 6.23
Principles – Impact of Section 831 for public companies **6.24 – 6.40**
Examples **6.41 – 6.87**
Example 1 – Forward contract to repurchase own equity shares **6.46 – 6.50**
Example 2 – Written option to repurchase own equity shares **6.51 – 6.53**
Example 3 – Forward contract to issue own equity shares **6.54 – 6.56**
Example 4 – Written option to issue own equity shares **6.57 – 6.58**
Example 5 – Convertible debt **6.59 – 6.61**
Example 6 – Preference shares presented as liabilities **6.62 – 6.70**
Example 7 – Mandatorily redeemable preference shares **6.71 – 6.77**
Example 8 – Convertible redeemable preference shares **6.78 – 6.87**

7. Employee share schemes **7.1 – 7.56**

ESOP trusts **7.1 – 7.45**
Introduction **7.1 – 7.3**
ESOP trusts under UK GAAP **7.4 – 7.5**
ESOP trusts under IFRSs **7.6 – 7.7**
Note of legal considerations attached to Abstract 38 **7.8**
Effect of deduction within equity on distributable profits **7.9 – 7.11**
Effect on section 831 restriction on purchase of own shares for a public company **7.12 – 7.21**
Effect on section 831 restriction on subscription for own shares for a public company **7.22 – 7.24**
The effect of the financial assistance rules in relation to a public company **7.25 – 7.31**
Purchase by an ESOP trust of shares held as treasury shares by a listed public company **7.33 – 7.35**
Effect on distributable profits for a public company when proceeds are received for sale of shares by an ESOP trust **7.36**
Realised loss when shares held by an ESOP trust are transferred to employees – where shares originally acquired externally **7.37 – 7.40**
Realised loss when shares held by an ESOP trust are transferred to employees – where shares originally subscribed **7.41**
Whether a profit on disposal of shares by an ESOP trust is a realised and distributable profit from the perspective of the sponsoring company **7.42 – 7.45**
Expenses for share-based payments required by IFRS 2 and FRS 20 **7.46 – 7.52**
Intra-group recharges for share-based payments **7.53 – 7.56**

8. Retirement benefit schemes **8.1 – 8.26**

Introduction **8.1 – 8.2**
Defined contribution schemes **8.3**
Multi-employer schemes **8.4**
Defined benefit schemes **8.5 – 8.26**
Summary **8.5 – 8.5A**
General principles **8.6 – 8.18**
Acquisition of an unincorporated business **8.19 – 8.20A**
Deferred tax **8.21 – 8.24**
Companies with more than one scheme **8.25 – 8.26**

9. Intra-group transactions	**9.1 – 9.44**
Introduction	**9.1 – 9.3**
Cash pooling arrangements and group treasury functions	**9.4**
Dividends	**9.5 – 9.27**
Dividend received or receivable on an investment in a subsidiary	**9.5**
Accrual of intra-group dividends payable and receivable	**9.6 – 9.18**
Dividend by a subsidiary to a parent which provides or reinvests the funds in the subsidiary	**9.19**
Dividends received out of pre-acquisition profits	**9.20 – 9.27**
Sale of an asset by a parent to its subsidiary	**9.28**
Sale of an asset by a subsidiary to a parent followed by a dividend to the parent of the resulting profit	**9.29 – 9.30**
Sale of an asset by a subsidiary to a fellow subsidiary followed by a dividend to the parent of the resulting profit	**9.31 – 9.32**
Dividend in kind	**9.33**
Return of capital contribution	**9.34**
Transfer of an asset for consideration followed by wavier of the resulting inter-company debt	**9.34A**
Debits within equity arising on group reconstructions	**9.35 – 9.42**
Merger relief and group reconstruction relief	**9.43 – 9.44D**
10. Miscellaneous issues	**10.1 – 10.64**
IAS 27, IAS 28 and IAS 31 – Separate financial statements	**10.1 – 10.6**
IFRS 1 – Fair value or revaluation as deemed cost	**10.17 – 10.20**
IFRS 1 and IAS 16 – Changes to depreciation policies	**10.21 – 10.22**
IFRS 1 – Deferred tax on business combinations	**10.23 – 10.25**
IFRS 1 – Past capitalisation of revaluation reserve	**10.26 – 10.35**
Investment properties and property, plant and equipment	**10.27 – 10.32**
Investments in subsidiaries	**10.33 – 10.35**
IAS 11 – Accounting for construction contracts	**10.36 – 10.38**
IAS 12 – Income taxes – Deferred tax	**10.39 – 10.43**
IAS 16 – Property, plant and equipment – asset swaps	**10.44 – 10.51**
IAS 18 – Revenue – Barter transactions	**10.52 – 10.56**
IFRIC 12 service concession arrangements	**10.65 – 10.68**
IFRIC 5 Decommissioning funds	**10.69 – 10.72**
Section 846 and replacement assets	**10.73 – 10.76**
Section 846 and fungible assets	**10.77 – 10.82**
11 Foreign currency share capital and use of presentation currencies	**11.1 – 11.38**
Introduction	**11.1 – 11.5**
Principles	**11.6 –11.38**
12 Cash box structures	**12.1 – 12.35**
Introduction to the cash box share issue method	**12.1**
Brief details	**12.2**
No share premium account?	**12.3**
Accounting entries	**12.4**
The framework for considering whether the reserve is a realised profit?	**12.6**
Prior to considering the use of the funds	**12.7**
Questions of the use of the funds	**12.8 – 12.11**
Should linkage be considered?	**12.12 – 12.14**

Conclusion as to framework to be employed in the assessment of realisation **12.15**
The effect of the application of paragraph 3.5 **12.16**
Recapitalisation of the company for regulatory reasons **12.17 – 12.19**
Recapitalisation of a subsidiary company, with equity, for regulatory reasons **12.20 – 12.21**
Recapitalisation of a subsidiary company, with equity, out of commercial necessity **12.22 – 12.23**
Recapitalisation of a subsidiary company, with inter-company debt, out of commercial necessity **12.24 – 12.25**
Repayment of the company's own debt **12.26 – 12.28**
Raising cash to be used to fund possible, unspecified acquisitions **12.29**
Using the cash received to fund a specific acquisition – where the placing and acquisition are inter-conditional **12.31 – 12.33**
Other acquisition funding cases **12.34**
Disclosure **12.35**

Examples of the application of sections 845 and 846 **Appendix 1**

Numerical illustrations for section 6 **Appendix 2**

Note of legal considerations reproduced from UITF – Abstract 38 **Appendix 3**

Numerical illustrations for section 8 **Appendix 4**

Illustrative examples of the effect of the principles relating to foreign currency set out in section 11 **Appendix 5**

Foreign currency branch examples **Appendix 6**

Illustrative examples of a company's position in several scenarios for capital reductions where there have been movements in the exchange rate between the functional currency and foreign share capital currency **Appendix 7**

Example of application of section 846 to fungible assets **Appendix 8**

Example of application of 3.11(e) for distribution by set off **Appendix 9**

1. INTRODUCTION 1.1 – 1.10

1.1 This Technical Release provides guidance on realised and distributable profits under the Companies Act 2006 (the Act). Its purpose is to identify, interpret and apply the principles relating to the determination of realised profits and losses for the purposes of making distributions under the Act. It is based on the guidance originally issued as TECH 01/09 in June 2009 but includes some significant additional material, the draft version of which was issued for comment as TECH 03/09 in December 2009. For the convenience of users, paragraph numbering has been kept consistent with TECH 01/09 so far as possible and consequently some paragraph numbers are not used where material has been deleted or moved.

1.2 Comments received on TECH 03/09 were generally supportive of the proposals and did not raise any major issues of principle. Some drafting improvements have been made in the light of comments received.

1.3 The more significant changes made from the proposals in TECH 03/09 are as follows:

(a) for profits arising from remeasurement of acquired liabilities prior to settlement, TECH 03/09 set out three options for consideration. None of the responses supported the approach in its paragraph 9.9 that such profits would be realised without any restrictions. Responses were divided between those supporting the 'readily convertible to cash' approach in its paragraph 9.7, which is consistent with the underlying principles of realisation established in previous guidance, and those supporting a departure from that approach in paragraph 9.8 which looked to whether qualifying consideration was received when the liability was assumed. The 9.7 approach is in effect an application of existing guidance and, as the Institutes have concluded that the level of support for the approach set out in paragraph 9.8 did not amount to sufficient to change 'generally accepted practice', this guidance therefore reflects the conclusion that a realised profit will arise on remeasurement of an acquired liability only when that profit is readily convertible to cash (as defined in paragraph 3.12);

(b) for goodwill written off to reserves, TECH 03/09 proposed a single approach to realisation which would have been independent of the accounting framework adopted. However, several of the responses suggested that it would be more appropriate to apply the principles of the accounting framework actually used to prepare the financial statements. This approach has been adopted in this technical release. A consequence of this decision is that in some cases goodwill written off to reserves that had been treated as a realised loss on the basis of notional amortisation in accordance with SSAP 22 or FRS 10 will no longer be treated as a realised loss on transition to IFRSs, because the impairment model is applied and there has been no impairment;

(c) for distributions settled by set-off, TECH 03/09 proposed two possible approaches. The approach proposed in paragraph 8.12, which was to add a new paragraph 3.11(e) to the definition of qualifying consideration, received most support and has been adopted in this technical release; and

(d) additional guidance has been added to address the treatment of reimbursement assets arising in connection with IFRIC 5 'Rights to Interests arising from Decommissioning, Restoration and Environmental Rehabilitation Funds' (see 10.69 to 10.72).

1.4 This Technical Release reflects accounting standards in issue at 1 June 2010. It does not provide guidance on how transactions and arrangements should be accounted for. However, it has been necessary to make assumptions about accounting treatments while providing guidance on the impact on realised and distributable profits.

This Technical Release represents generally accepted practice at 1 June 2010. Whilst many of the revisions to TECH 01/09 made by this TECH 02/10 represent principles that were generally accepted prior to that date, the revisions introduced now should not be used to question the lawfulness of distributions made at an earlier date. However, balances on reserves will need to be re-examined in the light of the guidance and the position should be re-assessed before a distribution is made. **1.5**

English and Scottish Counsel have confirmed that the guidance is consistent with the law at 1 June 2010. Counsel accept no responsibility (other than to the Institutes) in relation to advice ascribed to them in this guidance. **1.6**

The Act permits companies to prepare their individual accounts using UK GAAP or EU-adopted IFRSs. This guidance applies to companies reporting under both UK GAAP and EU-adopted IFRSs except where otherwise stated. The guidance has been written on the basis of "full" IFRSs as issued by the IASB except where otherwise stated but should be equally applicable to EU-adopted IFRSs. No reference is made to IFRS 9 'Financial instruments', which has not yet been adopted by the EU. Similarly, no consideration has been given to issues that may arise from use of the IFRS for SMEs, **1.7**

In the case of converged standards, reference to an IFRS or IAS should be read as applying to the equivalent UK standard unless the context requires otherwise. The guidance uses the IFRS terminology "in profit or loss". In the context of UK GAAP, this should be read as meaning "in the profit and loss account". References to the 'Accounting Regulations' are to the Large and Medium-sized Companies and Groups (Accounts and Reports) Regulations 2008 (SI 2008/410) and to the Small Companies and Groups (Accounts and Directors' Report) Regulations 2008 (SI 2008/409) as appropriate. **1.8**

The revised version of IAS 1 issued in 2007 makes some changes of terminology, for example referring to a statement of financial position instead of a balance sheet. It also introduced a requirement for a statement of comprehensive income which may be presented either as a single statement or as an income statement together with a separate statement showing other comprehensive income. For simplicity and consistency with UK GAAP, the previous terminology has been retained in this guidance. **1.9**

Companies should consider taking their own legal advice, particularly in relation to any matters not covered by this guidance. **1.10**

2. THE LEGAL FRAMEWORK 2.1 – 2.53

Introduction

The legal framework relating to the determination of realised profits and losses and of profits available for distribution consists of two elements: common law and statutory provisions. **2.1**

Those aspects of the Act that deal with matters other than those relating to the form and content of accounts continue to apply when accounts are prepared under IFRSs. All of the rules on capital maintenance in the Act therefore continue to apply. That is to say, the legal rules regarding shares (and the share premium account) continue to **2.1AA** control, for example, payments in respect of those shares even though the shares (and related share premium) may be presented as liabilities in the accounts. For example, the ability to pay dividends on preference shares is still determined by reference to the availability of distributable profits even if those dividends are reported as an expense in accordance with IFRSs.

The common law

2.1A The 2006 Act codifies the general duties of directors under common law. However, this does not render obsolete the rules in relation to capital maintenance or duties in relation to creditors of the company which remain relevant.

2.1B Under sections 851 and 852, any restrictions in common law or imposed by the company's articles on the sums available for distribution or the cases in which a distribution may be made, take precedence over the statutory provisions. Section 851(2) makes an exception to this rule. It provides that the amount of any distribution in kind is established by the statutory rules in sections 845 and 846 (see 2.9 – 2.9F below) and not by the applicable common law rules.

2.2 Under common law, a company cannot lawfully make a distribution out of capital. Thus, the directors must consider, both at the time of proposing the distribution and at the time it is made (see paragraph 2.10 below), whether the company, subsequent to the balance sheet date to which the 'relevant accounts' were prepared, has incurred losses that have eroded its profits available for distribution (the 'capital maintenance rule'). Guidance on the application of the capital maintenance rule to the introduction of a new accounting standard is given at 3.30 and 3.31 below. It is not practicable to give further guidance on the application of the capital maintenance rule in this Technical Release: appropriate advice will have to be taken to deal with specific circumstances.

Fiduciary and other duties and volatility

2.3 In addition, directors are subject to fiduciary and other duties in the exercise of the powers conferred on them. Examples of fiduciary and other duties include the obligation on directors to safeguard the company's assets and take reasonable steps to ensure that the company is in a position to settle its debts as they fall due. Directors must therefore specifically consider whether the company will still be solvent following a proposed distribution. Thus, directors should consider both the immediate cash flow implications of a distribution and the continuing ability of the company to pay its debts as they fall due. In reaching their decision they must take into account any change in the financial position of the company after the balance sheet date of the relevant accounts and the future cash needs of the company.

2.4 In the context of fair value accounting, volatility is an aspect where directors will need to consider their duties. The fair value of financial instruments may be volatile even though such fair value is properly determined in accordance with IAS 39 *Financial Instruments: Recognition and Measurement* (subsequently referred to as IAS 39 for brevity). Directors should consider, as a result of their duties, whether it is prudent to distribute profits arising from changes in the fair values of financial instruments considered to be volatile, even though they may otherwise be realised profits in accordance with this guidance.

2.5 Similarly, IAS 39 is based on a "mixed measurement model" whereby some financial instruments may be included at fair value while others may be included on an amortised cost basis. This may, in some cases, lead to volatility in the profit or loss for the period. For example, an asset and a liability may provide an economic hedge but if the asset is measured at fair value and the liability is not, a profit may be reported on one but a loss not reported on the other. Although such profits may be realised profits in accordance with this guidance, directors should consider, as a result of their duties, whether it would be prudent to distribute them.

Definition of a distribution for Part 23 of the 2006 Act

A "distribution" is defined by section 829 as every description of distribution of a company's assets to its members, whether in cash or otherwise, subject to the following exceptions: **2.6**

(a) an issue of shares as fully or partly paid bonus shares;
(b) the reduction of share capital;

(i) by extinguishing or reducing the liability of any of the members on any of the company's shares in respect of share capital not paid up; or
(ii) by repaying paid up share capital;

(c) the redemption or purchase of any of the company's own shares out of capital (including the proceeds of any fresh issue of shares) or out of unrealised profits in accordance with Chapter 3, 4 or 5 of Part 18; and
(d) a distribution of assets to members of the company on its winding-up.

Profits available for distribution

A company may make a distribution only out of profits available for that purpose (section 830(1)) (the common law position is set out in paragraph 2.2). A company's profits available for distribution are its accumulated, realised profits (so far as not previously distributed or capitalised) less its accumulated, realised losses (so far as not previously written off in a reduction or reorganisation of its share capital) (section 830(2)). Thus realised losses may not be offset against unrealised profits. Section 831 imposes a further restriction on public companies (see paragraph 2.30 below). **2.7**

Section 853(4) of the Act provides that references to realised profits and realised losses are to such profits or losses as fall to be treated as realised in accordance with principles generally accepted at the time when the accounts are prepared, with respect to the determination for accounting purposes of realised profits or losses. Section 3 below provides guidance on the application of this requirement. **2.8**

In addition, The Companies (Reduction of Share Capital) Order 2008 SI 2008/1915 ("the Order) specifies the cases in which a reserve arising from a reduction in a company's capital (ie share capital, share premium account, capital redemption reserve or redenomination reserve)* is to be treated as a realised profit as a matter of law. The Order also disapplies the general prohibition in section 654 on the distribution of a reserve arising from a reduction of capital. The Order provides that: **2.8A**

(a) if an unlimited company reduces its capital, a reserve arising from the reduction is treated as a realised profit;
(b) if a private company limited by shares reduces its capital and the reduction is supported by a solvency statement but has not been subject to an application to

**The Order refers only to share capital but section 11 of the Interpretation Act 1978 makes it plain that where an Act contains power to promote subordinate legislation, words used in that subordinate legislation have the same meaning as in the main Act. Subject to certain exceptions, the provisions of the Companies Act 2006 relating to the reduction of a company's share capital apply to any share premium account, capital redemption reserve or redenomination reserve as if they were part of paid up share capital (sections 610(4), 628(3) and 733(6)).*

the court for an order confirming it, the reserve arising from the reduction is treated as a realised profit; and

(c) if a limited company having a share capital reduces its capital and the reduction is confirmed by order of court, the reserve arising from the reduction is treated as a realised profit unless the court orders otherwise.

These provisions are without prejudice to any contrary provisions of an order or undertaking given to the court, the resolution for, or any other resolution relevant to, the reduction of capital, or the company's memorandum or articles of association. These provisions came into effect on 1 October 2008. In accordance with The Companies Act 2006 (Commencement No.7, Transitional Provisions and Savings) Order 2008, they apply irrespective of when the reduction in capital occurred or when the reserve arose. They therefore apply to capital reductions made under the 1985 Act and those made by unlimited companies.

2.8B Section 654 and the Order are concerned with the status of any reserve arising from the reduction of a company's capital. They do not apply to the extent that a reduction of capital takes the form of a payment to shareholders so that no reserve arises.

2.8C Section 654 and the Order do not differentiate between a reduction of foreign currency share capital and other reductions. Thus the Order applies to such cases and the reserve arising in such cases will, subject to the requirements of the Order, be a realised profit. The amount of the realised profit arising may not be the same as the amount of the reduction due to exchange movements because the reduction is calculated by reference to rates of exchange at the date of the reduction. For example, where there is a reduction of capital with no payment to shareholders, although the reduction is calculated by reference to the exchange rates at the date of the reduction, the amount of the realised profit arising will be equal to the nominal value of the shares translated at the exchange rate ruling when the shares were issued. Section 11 explains the issues in detail.

2.8D Section 662 is concerned with the duty of a public company to cancel any shares in itself that it holds when shares are forfeited, or surrendered to the company in lieu of forfeiture, in pursuance of the Articles, for failure to pay any sums payable in respect of the shares (and certain other situations). Unless the shares are disposed of within three years of the forfeiture or surrender, the company must cancel the shares and diminish the amount of the company's share capital by the nominal value of the shares cancelled. Section 662(4) provides that the directors of a company may take any steps necessary to enable the company to comply with this requirement without complying with the requirements of chapter 10 of Part 17 of the Act in relation to reductions of capital.

2.8E A reserve arising from a capital reduction under section 662 will not be a distributable reserve because of the restriction imposed by section 654 (see 2.8A above). Section 654 is not disapplied by section 662(4) because Section 654 is not in chapter 10 of Part 17 of the Act, neither is it disapplied in these circumstances by the Order*.

Distributions in kind: Meaning

2.8F Sections 845 and 846 make provision for a distribution consisting of or including, or treated as arising in consequence of, the sale, transfer or other disposition by a

**The Institutes believe that this may be as a result of an oversight in drafting the Order and have drawn the matter to the attention of the Department for Business, Innovation & Skills.*

company of a non-cash asset (referred to in this guidance as a 'distribution in kind'). A waiver of an amount receivable from a parent is considered as a distribution in kind, being an "other disposition", of that receivable.

Distributions in kind: Treatment of unrealised profits

Section 846 provides that where a company makes a distribution in kind and any part of the amount at which the asset is stated in the accounts relevant to the distribution represents an unrealised profit, that profit is to be treated as realised for the purposes of the distribution. Thus if a company wishes to distribute in kind an asset with a historical cost of £100 and which is in the books at £130 (with the surplus in the revaluation reserve), the surplus of £30 is treated as realised for this purpose and only £100 of other realised profits are needed. However, if the surplus has been capitalised, it is no longer available for this purpose and other realised profits of £130 would be needed to cover the proposed distribution. **2.9**

The application of section 846 to replacement assets is considered at 10.73 below. The application of section 846 to fungible assets is considered at 10.77 below. **2.9A**

Distributions in kind: Determination of amount

Section 845 was a new provision in the 2006 Act (not in the 1985 Act) which removed doubts arising from the decision in *Aveling Barford Ltd v Perion Ltd* [1989] BCLC 626 in relation to the amount of the distribution of a non-cash asset. Section 845 applies where: **2.9B**

(a) at the time of the disposition of the asset, the company has profits available for distribution; and
(b) if the amount of the distribution were to be determined in accordance with the section, the company could make the distribution without contravening Part 23.

Where section 845 applies, the amount of any distribution consisting of or arising from the sale, transfer or other disposition by the company of a non-cash asset should be calculated by reference to the value at which that asset is included in the company's accounts (ie its book value) as follows. If an asset is transferred for a consideration not less than its book value, the amount of the distribution is zero, but if the asset is transferred for a consideration less than its book value, the amount of the distribution is equal to that shortfall, which will therefore need to be covered by distributable profits. **2.9C**

In determining whether a company has profits available for distribution for the purposes of section 845, section 845(3) provides that the company's profits available for distribution are treated as increased by the amount (if any) by which the amount or value of any consideration for the disposition exceeds the book value of the asset. In this context, distributable profits may be 'treated as increased' from a negative starting point*. However, to apply section 845, a company must have profits available for distribution after any adjustment in accordance with section 845(3). This requirement is not met by a nil balance. There must be a positive balance even if it is only 1p. **2.9D**

**Legal interpretation of an amount being 'increased' in other contexts may be restricted to being increased from a lower amount but not from zero or below. However, in the context of section 845, such an interpretation would render sub-section (3) redundant and therefore this does not appear to be the intention of the legislation. Therefore, in this case, profits may be treated as increased from a negative starting point.*

2.9E The references to consideration in section 845 are not restricted to consideration that would meet the definition of 'qualifying consideration' in this guidance.

2.9F Appendix 1 sets out illustrative worked examples of a transfer of an asset applying section 845.

Distributions in kind: Effect of IFRIC 17

2.9G The amount of a distribution in kind for legal purposes will be the book value of the asset to be distributed, provided that this amount is available for distribution, because of the application of section 845 (see 2.9A to 2.9F above).

2.9H There are no requirements in UK GAAP about accounting for distributions in kind. UK companies have almost invariably accounted for such distributions based on the book value of the asset in question. It has also been acceptable to account for such a distribution based on the fair value of the asset and recognise a profit on disposal. This treatment has been used occasionally.

2.9I In December 2008, the IASB published IFRIC 17 *Distributions of Non-cash Assets to Owners*. It is to be applied prospectively (ie no restatement of prior periods is required) for annual periods beginning on or after 1 July 2009.The scope of IFRIC 17 excludes certain distributions, including those where the non-cash asset is controlled by the same party or parties before and after the distribution (e.g. intra-group transactions). It applies to a distribution that gives owners a choice of receiving either non-cash assets or a cash alternative. The ASB has stated (in UITF Information Sheet 88) that it has no plans to issue an Abstract based on IFRIC 17 because it has decided that the current accounting under UK GAAP is adequate.

2.9J IFRIC 17 requires that, when accounting for a distribution of a non-cash asset, the distribution is measured at the fair value of the asset in question. The difference between the fair value of the asset and its book value is subsequently recognised in profit or loss when the distribution is settled. This will be a significant change of practice and may, in certain circumstances, have an adverse impact on the ability of a public company to make a distribution for the reasons explained below.

2.9K IFRIC 17 requires the recognition of a liability to make the distribution when it is appropriately authorised and no longer at the discretion of the entity. In most cases this means that the liability, which will usually exceed in amount the carrying value of the asset to be distributed, will be recognised before the distribution is settled. It will not be possible to revalue the asset to fair value prior to settlement in most cases. For example, investments in subsidiaries are usually carried on the historical cost basis and it would not be regarded as acceptable to revalue, in isolation, a particular investment. Nor is it possible to anticipate the 'profit' on disposal as this arises only on 'settlement' which must necessarily be later (if only momentarily).

2.9L If relevant accounts are drawn up after the liability has arisen but before settlement, they will include the liability for the distribution and consequentially reduced net assets. That reduction will be larger than that which will ultimately arise once the distribution is settled. The profit reverses some of the reduction to leave net assets reduced overall only by the book value of the distributed asset.

2.9M The debit entry arising from recognition of a liability in accordance with IFRIC 17 is an advance recognition of an unsettled distribution obligation and is not a realised loss. The fact that it is recognised at an amount greater than the distribution measured under section 845, therefore, does not affect the ability of a private company to make a distribution.

For a public company, the temporary adverse impact on the company's net assets will have an adverse impact on its ability to make a distribution which is based on those relevant accounts (e.g. a proposed final dividend) because of the net asset test in section 831. However, it will not affect the company's ability to make the non-cash distribution in question because that distribution will have been made when it was approved (see 2.10 below) and is based on earlier relevant accounts. **2.9N**

The test in section 831 is a statutory one which applies to the amounts shown in the "relevant accounts" for the purposes of the distribution. There is no need to update these amounts on an ongoing basis throughout the year other than for earlier distributions as required by section 840. Therefore, the issue arises only when the 'relevant accounts' are drawn up to a date between the date of approval of the distribution and when it is settled. Provided that the period between approval and settlement does not straddle the company's year end, this issue is thus unlikely to cause a problem in practice. **2.9O**

Date of distribution

A distribution is made when it becomes a legally binding liability of the company, regardless of the date on which it is to be settled. In the case of a final dividend, this will be when it is declared by the company in general meeting or, for private companies, by the members passing a written resolution. In the case of an interim dividend authorised under common articles of association (e.g. 1985 Act Table A), normally no legally binding liability is established prior to payment being made of the dividend. In such a case, a distribution is made only when the dividend is paid. However, in the case of an interim dividend, steps may be taken to establish a legally binding liability at an earlier date. See 9.6 to 9.18 below concerning how such a liability may be established. That guidance is written in the context of intra-group transactions. However, the guidance may also be relevant in other cases. **2.10**

Distributable profits are consumed when a distribution is made in accordance with the previous paragraph. After that time, a shareholder's right to any unpaid dividend is as a creditor of the company rather than as a shareholder*. **2.10A**

Merger relief and group reconstruction relief

Where the company has entered into a transaction which gives rise to group reconstruction relief or merger relief under sections 611 or 612, it may choose under section 615 to disregard any amount that would otherwise have been included in the share premium account in determining the amount at which the acquired asset is stated in the company's balance sheet. Subject to the rules in accounting standards, the asset may therefore be stated at the nominal value of the shares issued together with any minimum premium value recognised when applying group reconstruction relief. However, it is also possible to record the asset acquired at fair value and to credit the amount of that relief to another reserve (often called a merger reserve)†. In such a case, that reserve is in law a profit and is initially treated as unrealised but becomes realised in a manner similar to a revaluation reserve. Thus, provided the **2.11**

**Section 74(2)(f) of the Insolvency Act 1986 provides that a sum due to a member in his character of a member by way of dividends etc is subordinated in a liquidation to the claims of other creditors.*

†As explained at 9.44B below, a third basis of measurement may be required when applying IAS 27 as revised in May 2008.

merger reserve is not capitalised (by way of a bonus issue of shares), the decision as to whether or not to record the merger reserve should not overall have any effect on the level of the company's realised profits. The accounting choice referred to in this paragraph may be restricted by the application of accounting standards. This is considered further at 9.43 to 9.44D below.

Relevant accounts

General

2.12 Under both the Act and common law, distributions are made by individual companies and not by groups. The group accounts are therefore not relevant for the purpose of determining a company's profits available for distribution (see 10.1 to 10.3 below). The status of accounts prepared in accordance with IAS 28 or IAS 31 (ie using equity accounting) where a company has an associate or jointly controlled entity but has no subsidiaries is considered at 10.4 below.

2.13 Whether or not a distribution may be made within the terms of the Act is determined by reference to a company's 'relevant accounts'. Where it is proposed to make a distribution during the company's first accounting reference period or before any accounts have been circulated, initial accounts must be prepared. In all other cases the relevant accounts are its last annual accounts that were circulated to members* or interim accounts, if the proposed distribution cannot be justified by reference to the last annual accounts.

2.14 The items in these accounts to which reference is made in determining the amount of a distribution which may be made are listed in section 836(1) as profits, losses, assets, liabilities, provisions†, share capital and reserves (including undistributable reserves). Thus, valuations or contingencies referred to in notes to the financial statements, but not incorporated in the balance sheet, do not affect the amount of realised profit calculated by reference to the relevant accounts. For example, if the relevant accounts record an unrealised profit but state in a note that, as a consequence of an event subsequent to the balance sheet date, the profit has become realised, interim accounts must nevertheless be prepared before a distribution can be made out of these profits.

2.15 Similarly, disclosures about the impact of future changes of accounting policy, such as those required by IAS 8(30), do not affect the amount of realised profit calculated by reference to the relevant accounts. However, they may be relevant to the application of the common law on capital maintenance where a distribution is to be made in the period in relation to which the change of policy will be implemented (see 3.30 and 3.31 below).

2.16 In practice it may not be sufficient to determine the amount of realised profits simply by examining the relevant accounts as further enquiries may be necessary as to the composition of the various reserves included in the balance sheet. For example, certain reserves may include both realised and unrealised profits. As there is no legal requirement for a company to distinguish in its accounts between distributable and non distributable profits as such (see 2.25 to 2.27 below), companies should keep

**Where a company circulates to members a summary financial statement, the relevant accounts are the full accounts from which the summary financial statement was derived.*

†Provisions are defined for this purpose in section 836(1) as, in the case of Companies Act accounts, provisions of any kind specified for this purpose by regulations under section 396 and, in the case of IAS accounts, provisions of any kind.

sufficient records to enable them to distinguish between those profits which are available for distribution and those which are not.

Under section 395, a company's individual accounts must be prepared either as "Companies Act individual accounts" or as "IAS individual accounts". Thus, the relevant accounts will be either its "Companies Act individual accounts" or "IAS individual accounts", depending on the choice made by the company. It follows that when a company elects to prepare its statutory individual accounts in accordance with EU-adopted IFRSs, it is the amounts stated in those accounts that are relevant for the purposes of justifying a distribution. **2.17**

The detailed requirements for relevant accounts (annual, interim or initial) are summarised in the following paragraphs. **2.18**

Annual accounts – all companies

If the company's last annual accounts constitute the relevant accounts they must be prepared under Part 15 of the Act (Accounts and Reports) and comply with the requirements of section 837. Such accounts may be either "Companies Act individual accounts" or "IAS individual accounts" (see 2.17 above). The requirements of section 837 are that: **2.19**

(a) the accounts must have been properly prepared in accordance with the Act (including the requirement in section 393 that they must not be approved unless the directors are satisfied that they give a true and fair view of the assets, liabilities, financial position and profit or loss of the company), subject only to matters not material for determining the lawfulness of a distribution;
(b) the accounts must have been circulated to members in accordance with section 423*;
(c) the accounts must be accompanied, where applicable, by the report of the auditors under section 495; and
(d) if the report of the auditors is qualified, the auditors must state in writing whether in their opinion the matters in respect of which their report is qualified is material for determining the lawfulness of the distribution. The statement by the auditors, which can be subsequent to the report, must be laid before the company in general meeting in the case of a public company, or be circulated to members in accordance with section 423 in the case of a private company.

The last two sub-paragraphs do not apply where the directors of the company have taken advantage of the audit exemption conferred by sections 477(1) or 480(1).

Initial and interim accounts – public companies

Sections 838 and 839 respectively provide that interim and initial accounts of a public company must have been 'properly prepared', or have been properly prepared subject only to matters that are not material for determining, by reference to those accounts, whether the proposed distribution would contravene sections 830 or 831. A copy of the interim and initial accounts must have been delivered to the Registrar of Companies before the distribution is made (ie before the date of the distribution – see 2.10 above). **2.20**

**Where a company circulates to members a summary financial statement, the relevant accounts are the full accounts from which the summary financial statement was derived.*

2.21 'Properly prepared' means that the accounts must comply with sections 395 to 397 which includes the true and fair requirement in relation to Companies Act accounts* and the requirement to apply EU-adopted IFRSs in relation to IAS accounts. These requirements are to be applied with such modifications as are necessary because the accounts are prepared otherwise than in respect of an accounting reference period. In the case of interim accounts, the balance sheet must be signed in accordance with section 414. There is no equivalent statutory requirement for initial accounts to be signed in accordance with section 414 but, in practice, the auditors will require the accounts to be approved and signed by the directors before the report of the auditors can be signed.

2.22 In requiring the interim and initial accounts to be 'properly prepared', or to be properly prepared except for matters which are not relevant in determining whether a proposed dividend would be lawful under the Act, the legislation permits a public company to omit information which is not relevant in determining whether a distribution would be lawful under the Act. In practice, therefore, interim or initial accounts will consist of a balance sheet and profit and loss account but the notes may be restricted to those matters that are relevant to a distribution. Corresponding amounts for the previous financial year would not be relevant.

2.23 Interim accounts are not required to be audited. However, initial accounts of a public company must be accompanied by a report by the auditors stating whether, in their opinion, the accounts have been 'properly prepared'. If their report is qualified (which would be the case if the company chooses to prepare initial accounts which do not give a true and fair view, as described in paragraph 2.22 above), the auditors must make an additional statement which states whether, in their opinion, the matters in respect of which their report is qualified is material for determining, by reference to the initial accounts, whether the distribution would contravene sections 830 or 831. A copy of the auditors' statement must also have been laid before the company in general meeting and delivered to the Registrar of Companies.

Initial and interim accounts – private companies

2.24 The requirements of sections 838 and 839 regarding the form and content of interim and initial accounts of public companies do not apply to private companies. Instead, the only requirement for private companies flows from the general definition at the start of those sections of interim or initial accounts as those necessary to enable a reasonable judgement to be made as to profits, losses, assets and liabilities, provisions, and share capital and reserves. Reliable management accounts which deal with these matters will often satisfy this requirement. However, management accounts sometimes do not deal with all relevant matters. For example, they may exclude tax. In these cases, appropriate adjustments need to be made to the management accounts.

Disclosure of distributable profits

2.25 There is no requirement under law or accounting standards for financial statements to distinguish between realised profits and unrealised profits or between distributable profits and non-distributable profits. Paragraph 2.16 above draws attention to the

**There is no statutory requirement for interim and initial accounts to give a true and fair view when they are prepared under IFRSs because section 393, which imposes an overarching requirement for annual accounts to give a true and fair view, does not apply for this purpose. However, the requirements of IAS 1 impose a similar requirement to 'present fairly'.*

need for companies to maintain sufficient records to enable them to distinguish between those profits that are available for distribution and those which are not.

The guidance at 2.16 above is likely to be of greater significance when reporting under IFRSs or using the fair value accounting rules under UK GAAP than has previously been the case. One reason for this is that the restriction in the Accounting Regulations that only profits realised at the balance sheet date may be included in the profit and loss account does not apply in these cases. **2.26**

It may be thought helpful to users of financial statements if there is an indication of which reserves are distributable but, as noted above, there is no legal requirement to do so. In some cases, there may be practical difficulties with providing such an analysis. For example, there may be uncertainties about whether certain profits are realised or unrealised. There is generally no need for directors to form a view on whether profits are realised unless they intend to utilise them to make a distribution. **2.27**

Subsequent events

Under common law, a company cannot lawfully make a distribution out of capital. Therefore it may be necessary to take into account losses incurred after the balance sheet date (see 2.2 above). **2.28**

One or more distributions may already have been made by reference to a particular set of accounts; for example, an interim dividend or a purchase of own shares. In determining the lawfulness of any proposed further distribution by reference to the same accounts, the directors must take account of any such distributions (section 840(1)). **2.29**

Public companies

A further restriction is placed on distributions by public companies (section 831). A public company may make a distribution only if, after giving effect to such distribution, the amount of its net assets (as defined in section 831(2)) is not less than the aggregate of its called up share capital and undistributable reserves as shown in the relevant accounts. **2.30**

Under section 831(4) the following are undistributable reserves: **2.31**

(a) share premium account (see also section 610);
(b) capital redemption reserve (see also section 733);
(c) the excess of accumulated unrealised profits, so far as not previously utilised by capitalisation, over the accumulated unrealised losses, so far as not previously written off in a reduction or reorganisation of its share capital; and
(d) any other reserve which the company is prohibited from distributing by any enactment (e.g. a redenomination reserve arising under section 628), or by its articles of association (or equivalent).

This means that, in calculating the amount available for distribution, a public company must reduce the amount of its net realised profits available for distribution by the amount of its net unrealised losses. The effects of this rule in relation to holdings of own shares through an ESOP trust and in relation to the presentation of shares as liabilities in the balance sheet are addressed at 7.12 *et seq* and 6.24 *et seq* respectively.

Provisions

The general rule and the exception

2.31A Section 841(2) states that for the purposes of Part 23, the following are treated as realised losses:

- in the case of Companies Act accounts, provisions of a kind specified for the purpose in regulations under section 396 (other than revaluation provisions); and
- in the case of IAS accounts, provisions of any kind (except revaluation provisions).

The Accounting Regulations* state that references to provisions for depreciation or diminution in value of assets are to any amounts written off by way of providing for depreciation or diminution in value of assets. It also states that references to provisions for liabilities (or, in the case of insurance companies to provisions for other risks), are to any amounts retained as reasonably necessary for the purpose of providing for any liability, the nature of which is clearly defined and which is either likely to be incurred, or certain to be incurred but uncertain as to the amount or as to the date on which it will arise.

2.32 The general rule is therefore that any provision (including one for depreciation or diminution in value as well as provisions for liabilities, charges or losses) is treated as a realised loss.

2.33 As an exception to the general rule, a 'revaluation provision' which is a provision for diminution in value of a fixed asset appearing on a revaluation of all the fixed assets (other than goodwill) (section 841(3)) is not treated as a realised loss. However, this exception would not apply where the fixed asset has been sold or scrapped, because in these circumstances any loss would need to be reclassified as realised. Furthermore, unrealised losses which exceed unrealised profits are relevant to a public company in determining the amount available for distribution as the requirements of section 831 (Restrictions on the distribution of assets) referred to at 2.30 above must be satisfied.

2.34 For the exception in 2.33 above to apply, it is not necessary for a revaluation of all the fixed assets to be recorded in the accounts. Section 841(4) provides that a revaluation of all the fixed assets is treated as having taken place if (1) the directors consider the value of any assets that have not actually been revalued, (2) they are satisfied that the aggregate value of those assets is not less than that stated in the company's accounts and (3) the notes to the accounts include a statement to that effect. The notes to the accounts should also state that amounts are stated in the accounts on the basis that a revaluation of fixed assets is treated as having taken place.

2.34AA Application of the exception in section 841 for revaluation provisions is not restricted to those circumstances where there is an offsetting unrealised profit (recognised or not). Where all of the assets are actually revalued, section 841 treats the provision as a revaluation provision without any additional restrictions.

2.34AB Where the assets, other than the impaired one, are not actually revalued but their value is 'considered' in accordance with section 841, the directors must be satisfied that the aggregate value of those assets (ie the ones not actually revalued) at the time of their consideration was not less than the aggregate amount at which they were

**Schedule 7 to SI 2008/409 and Schedule 9 to SI 2008/410.*

stated in the accounts. This does not impose any substantive additional restriction because financial reporting requirements ensure that an asset is not stated at a carrying amount which is higher than its value.

An unlawful return of capital might arise if a company makes a distribution out of accumulated realised profits without deducting an impairment loss which is treated as a revaluation provision in circumstances where there is an absence of any upside on other assets. The company may have made a distribution which results in its assets being less than its capital under common law (see 2.2 above). In the case of a public company, a distribution would never be possible under the statutory provisions in these circumstances because of section 831 (see 2.30 above). **2.34AC**

Application of the exception under IFRSs

Due to changes in accounting methods and choices as between cost and valuation, effected by the implementation of IFRSs, the question might arise as to whether the exception provided for by section 841(2) continues to be capable of use under IFRSs. The following paragraphs explain questions that might arise and the conclusion that the exception does continue to be capable of use under IFRSs. **2.34A**

For example, using section 841, an impairment write down of one subsidiary may be offset by an increase in value of another subsidiary for the purposes of determining profits available for distribution (although the impairment would still have to be recorded in the profit and loss account for financial reporting purposes). Another example is where financial assets are regarded as fixed assets, such as in the case of investment companies, and any decrease in the fair value of investments may be offset by any increase in the fair value of other investments for the purposes of determining profits available for distribution (even though certain increases in fair value might be treated as unrealised for the purposes of this guidance). However, as noted at 2.34AA above, the application of the exception in section 841 is not restricted to circumstances where there is an offsetting unrealised profit. **2.34C**

Definition of "fixed assets"

The definition of a "revaluation provision" (see 2.33 above) uses the term "fixed assets" which are defined in section 853(6) as meaning assets of a company which are intended for use on a continuing basis in the company's activities. This term is not used in IFRSs. "Non-current assets" as defined in IAS 1 will not correspond with "fixed assets" as defined in section 853(6), for example because the former may include long term debtors. **2.34D**

For the purposes of applying section 841, fixed assets are those assets that meet the section 853(6) definition of "fixed assets". As noted above, in "IAS individual accounts", these will not necessarily correspond with those presented as non-current assets in the relevant accounts. However, there is nothing in section 841 that requires the fixed assets to be shown in the balance sheet as such for the section to be applied. **2.34E**

Ability to revalue assets

Investments in subsidiaries present a particular issue in the context of section 841 and IFRSs. Under IFRSs, only two accounting policies are available for investments in subsidiaries that are not classified as held for sale: **2.34F**

(a) cost (see 9.22 below); or
(b) in accordance with IAS 39, which requires such investments to be maintained at fair value.

In practice, fair value under (b) above may be precluded because the range of reasonable fair value estimates is significant and the probabilities of the various estimates cannot reasonably be assessed (see IAS 39, AG 80-81). IAS 39 requires such investments to be carried at cost. Even where a fair value policy is possible, it will require valuations to be obtained each time a balance sheet is drawn up. This is unattractive to most companies. Most companies, therefore, hold subsidiaries at cost. The issue that arises is whether it is possible to apply the exception for "revaluation provisions" in section 841 in circumstances where the accounting policy is cost (either through choice or because IAS 39 does not permit the assets to be revalued).

2.34G Any assessment of the value of an asset can be described, for the purpose of the exception in section 841, as a revaluation, even if it is not in accordance with relevant accounting standards. In particular, the consideration of the value of an asset for the purposes of an impairment review could be described as a revaluation in this broad sense. Accordingly, section 841 does not use the term "revaluation" as meaning a revaluation in accordance with relevant accounting standards. However, depreciation of an asset is not consideration of the value of an asset for the purposes of section 841.

2.34H It is also relevant that, for the purposes of a revaluation of all the fixed assets (or all other than goodwill) under section 841, the assets do not have to be included in the balance sheet at their revalued amounts nor do they have to be permitted to be included in the balance sheet at a valuation. In accordance with section 841(4), "for the purposes of sub-sections (2) and (3) any consideration by the directors of the value at a particular time of a fixed asset is treated as a revaluation" (subject to the requirements of sub-section (4)). Section 841(4) refers to "any consideration by the directors of the value ....." without any explicit requirement for that value to be determined on a basis that would be permitted for inclusion in the balance sheet.

2.34I In conclusion, it is possible to apply the exception for "revaluation provisions" in section 841 in circumstances where the accounting policy is cost (either through choice or because IAS 39 does not permit the assets to be revalued).

Asset revaluations

2.35 Special considerations apply where a fixed asset has been revalued and an unrealised profit is recorded. Where a sum written off or retained for depreciation on or after the revaluation exceeds that which would have been charged if the unrealised profit had not been made, the excess does not give rise overall to a realised loss as there is a corresponding realisation of the related revaluation surplus, to the extent that that surplus has not previously been capitalised (section 841(5)). This means that the loss arising on the depreciation of revalued fixed assets is, in effect, calculated for distribution purposes by using historical cost principles, except to the extent that the surplus has previously been capitalised.

2.36 If an asset is revalued downwards below its recoverable amount, as defined in FRS 11 or IAS 36, then the difference between that revalued amount and recoverable amount is treated as an unrealised loss as it reflects a revaluation adjustment rather than a provision as defined in section 841*. Such a loss would become realised in the event of a subsequent scrapping, disposal or impairment of the asset.

**FRS 15(70) states that where it can be demonstrated that recoverable amount is greater than the revalued amount, the difference between recoverable amount and the revalued amount is clearly not an impairment and should therefore be recognised in the statement of total recognised gains and losses as a valuation adjustment, rather than the profit and loss account.*

Under IAS 16, any revaluation loss that exceeds an existing revaluation surplus will be recognised as an expense in the income statement. Under FRS 15, such a loss would be recognised in the Statement of Total Recognised Gains and Losses to the extent that the asset's recoverable amount was greater than its revalued amount. Also, under FRS 15, where an impairment loss on a revalued asset is caused by a clear consumption of economic benefits, the loss will be taken to the profit and loss account. Under IAS 16, it will be taken to equity to the extent that there is a revaluation surplus relating to the asset. Consequently, losses may be reported differently under IFRSs and UK GAAP but the effect on accumulated realised profits will be the same. **2.37**

Development costs

Section 844 requires that development costs shown as an asset should be treated as a realised loss, except where the directors justify the costs carried forward being treated as an asset. This would be the case if the costs are carried forward in accordance with applicable accounting standards. The justification must be included in a note to the accounts (section 844(3)). **2.38**

[Moved to 2.1AA] **2.39**

Treasury shares

Sections 724 to 732 of the Act relax, in some circumstances, the requirement that when a company purchases its own shares they are automatically cancelled. They allow certain public companies that purchase their own "qualifying shares" out of distributable profits the option of holding them "in treasury" (ie un-cancelled) for sale at a later date (which must be for cash) or transferring them for the purposes of, or pursuant to, an employee share scheme. The treasury shares may also be cancelled at a later date. Only "qualifying shares" may be held in treasury. Qualifying shares are shares which are included in the Official List, traded on AIM, officially listed in another EEA* state or traded on a regulated market established in an EEA state. In all other cases, shares purchased are cancelled by the automatic operation of the law in accordance with section 706. **2.40**

Any purchase of shares to be held in treasury has to be made out of distributable profits which will be reduced by the amount of the purchase price. **2.41**

The Act specifies how the proceeds of sale of any treasury shares for cash affects distributable profits. Where the proceeds of sale are equal to or less than the purchase price paid by the company for the shares, the proceeds should be treated as realised profits (ie to reverse the original reduction in realised profits up to the purchase price paid). Where the proceeds of sale exceed the purchase price paid by the company for the shares, that part of the proceeds that is equal to the purchase price paid should be treated as a realised profit of the company. A sum equal to the excess should be transferred to the share premium account (ie so that the purchase and sale of shares cannot create an overall increase in realised profits). For these purposes, section 731(4) provides that the purchase price paid by the company for the shares should be determined by the application of a weighted average price method. **2.42**

**The European Economic Area (EEA) comprises the European Union together with Norway, Iceland and Liechtenstein.*

2.43 Investments in own shares through an ESOP trust are not treasury shares as a matter of law. The distributable profit implications of shares held by an ESOP trust are considered in section 7 of this guidance. The purchase by an ESOP trust of shares held as treasury shares is considered at 7.33 to 7.35.

Section 832 – Investment companies

2.44 Investment companies are defined in section 833. Under section 832 they are permitted, subject to meeting certain requirements in section 832(5), to make distributions in circumstances, described in the following paragraph, which would not be permitted for other public companies under section 831. However, section 832 is an alternative rather than additional test for investment companies. Accordingly, an investment company may make a distribution in accordance with section 832 regardless of whether it would meet the tests in section 831 and, although possibly more rarely, *vice versa*. However, an investment company's articles must prohibit the distribution of capital profits (see section 833(2)(c)) and the application of section 831 cannot override this.

2.44A An investment company may make distributions at any time out of its accumulated realised revenue profits, so far as not previously utilised by a distribution or capitalisation, less its accumulated revenue losses (whether realised or unrealised), so far as not previously written off in a reduction or reorganisation of capital duly made:

- if at that time the amount of its assets is at least equal to one and a half times the aggregate of its liabilities to creditors;
- if, and to the extent that, the distribution does not reduce that amount to less than one and a half times that aggregate; and
- the conditions set out in section 832(5) are met.

2.45 In most circumstances, these rules allow an investment company to ignore capital losses, whether realised or unrealised, when making a distribution.

2.46 As noted at 6.24 *et seq* in relation to section 831, the presentation of financial instruments in accordance with the substance of their contractual terms under IFRSs may affect the amount of a company's liabilities as stated in its relevant accounts. In particular, where all or part of the amount attributable to preference shares is presented as a liability, total liabilities will be increased by that amount. The amount of a company's assets is unaffected by the reclassification of shares as liabilities.

2.47 However, section 832 refers to "liabilities to creditors". Although "creditors" is not defined for this purpose in the Act, this amount excludes amounts in respect of share capital and share premium that have been presented as liabilities. It also excludes other amounts due to shareholders in their capacity as such including accruals for dividends and redemption premiums that have been presented as expenses in the income statement and liabilities in the balance sheet. It would not, however, exclude general accruals, deferred income or deferred tax.

2.47A Ordinary dividends are accrued in the balance sheet only in those rare cases where they are legally binding liabilities at the balance sheet date (see 2.10 above). However, a shareholder's right to any unpaid dividend is as a creditor of the company rather than as a shareholder (see 2.10A above). Therefore, any such liability is a liability to creditors for the purposes of section 832.

Section 843 – Long term insurance business

The normal rules of the Act (ie the section 830 requirement for realised profits and the section 831 net assets rule) apply to insurance companies. However, for the purposes of determining whether there is a realised profit, the section 853(4) definition of realised profits, as being determined by reference to generally accepted accounting principles, is displaced in favour of special rules in the case of long-term insurance business. **2.47B**

Section 843 sets out special rules that apply to an authorised insurance company (as defined in section 1165), other than an insurance special purpose vehicle (as defined in section 843(8)), carrying on long-term insurance business. An amount included in the relevant part of the company's balance sheet is treated as a realised profit if it: **2.48**

- represents a surplus in the fund or funds maintained by it in respect of its long-term business (as defined in sub-section (7) and which includes both with-profits life business and other life business); and
- has not been allocated to policyholders or, as the case may be, carried forward unappropriated in accordance with asset identification rules made under section 142(2) of the Financial Services and Markets Act 2000.

For this purpose the relevant part of the balance sheet is that part of the balance sheet that represents accumulated profit or loss. A surplus in the fund or funds maintained by the company in respect of its long-term business means an excess of the assets representing that fund or those funds over the liabilities of the company attributable to its long-term business, as shown by an actuarial investigation. **2.49**

A deficit in the fund or funds maintained by the company in respect of its long-term business is treated as a realised loss. For this purpose, a deficit in any such fund or funds means an excess of the liabilities of the company attributable to its long-term business over the assets representing that fund or those funds, as shown by an actuarial investigation. **2.50**

Subject to this, any profit or loss arising in the company's long-term business is left out of account when determining realised profits and losses. **2.51**

For the purpose of these requirements, an actuarial investigation means an investigation made into the financial condition of an authorised insurance company in respect of its long-term business, by an actuary appointed as actuary to the company: **2.52**

- carried out once every period of twelve months in accordance with Rules made under Part 10 of the Financial Services and Markets Act 2000; or
- carried out in accordance with a requirement imposed by section 166 of that Act.

Much of the guidance in this Technical Release relates to the identification of generally accepted principles as to the determination of realised profits and losses in relation to section 853(4). To that extent, it is inapplicable to long-term insurance business of authorised insurance companies (other than special purpose vehicles) to which the above mentioned special rule applies instead. It should not be overlooked, however, that where such a company is a public company, it must also have regard to the section 831 net assets test. **2.53**

3. REALISED PROFITS 3.1 – 3.75

General

3.1 Section 830(2) of the Act defines a company's profits available for distribution as 'its accumulated, realised profits, so far as not previously utilised by distribution or capitalisation, less its accumulated, realised losses, so far as not previously written off in a reduction or reorganisation of capital duly made'. Realised profits and realised losses are defined as 'such profits or losses of the company as fall to be treated as realised in accordance with principles generally accepted at the time when the accounts are prepared, with respect to the determination for accounting purposes of realised profits or losses' (section 853(4)). It is apparent from the use of the words 'at the time when the accounts are prepared' that the concept of a realised profit is intended to be dynamic, changing with the development of generally accepted accounting principles, as well as bringing within the definition profits which might not in ordinary language be called realised.

3.2 The determination of a company's profits available for distribution is derived from what is recorded in its accounts which are relevant for this purpose (see 2.12 above). It is fundamental for this purpose that the company's accounts have been properly prepared in accordance with the law and generally accepted accounting principles. Profits available for distribution may include amounts reported outside the profit and loss account (ie in the Statement of Total Recognised Gains and Losses or Reconciliation of Movements in Shareholders' Funds and their equivalents under IFRSs).

Principles of realisation

3.3 It is generally accepted that profits shall be treated as realised for the purpose of applying the definition of realised profits in companies legislation only when realised in the form of cash or of other assets the ultimate cash realisation of which can be assessed with reasonable certainty. In this context, "realised" may encompass profits relating to assets that are readily realisable. This would embrace profits and losses resulting from the recognition of changes in fair values, in accordance with relevant accounting standards, to the extent that they are readily convertible to cash.

3.4 The principles of realisation set out in this guidance are consistent with the notion of realisation as expressed in FRS 18. They are, however, relevant irrespective of whether the relevant accounts are prepared under UK GAAP or under IFRSs. The guidance also recognises that certain amounts may, as a matter of law, be profits (see 3.8(b) below).

3.5 In assessing whether a company has a realised profit, transactions and arrangements should not be looked at in isolation. A realised profit will arise only where the overall commercial effect on the company is such that the definition of realised profit set out in this guidance is met.

3.5A Thus, for example, a group or series of transactions or arrangements should be viewed as a whole, particularly if they are artificial, linked (whether legally or otherwise) or circular or any combination of these. The principle in paragraph 3.5 is likely to be of particular relevance for, but not limited to, intra-group transactions which are considered in section 9 of this guidance. Further guidance on the application of the principle in paragraph 3.5 is set out at 3.43 to 3.75 below. The specific circumstances of 'cash box structures' are addressed in section 12.

A profit previously regarded as unrealised becomes realised when the relevant criteria set out in this guidance are met (for example, a revaluation surplus becomes realised when the related asset is sold for 'qualifying consideration'). Similarly, a profit previously regarded as realised becomes unrealised when the criteria set out in this guidance cease to be met. This is considered more fully at 3.28 to 3.29C below. 3.6

Definitions

The definitions which follow should be read in conjunction with the principles of realisation as well as the guidance on their interpretation set out in this Technical Release. 3.7

Profit

'Profit' for the purpose of section 853(4) comprises: 3.8

(a) 'gains', as defined in the Accounting Standards Board's 'Statement of Principles for Financial Reporting' and 'income' as defined in the International Accounting Standards Board's 'Framework' which both convey (with different wording) increases in ownership interest not resulting from contributions from owners; and
(b) other amounts which are profits as a matter of law, or which are treated as profits, including:

    (i) gratuitous contributions of assets from owners in their capacity as such; and
    (ii) an amount taken to a so-called 'merger reserve' reflecting the extent that relief is obtained under sections 611 or 612 of the Act from the requirement to recognise a share premium account.

Realised profit

A profit is realised, as a matter of generally accepted accounting practice, where it arises from: 3.9

(a) a transaction where the consideration received by the company is 'qualifying consideration'; or
(b) an event which results in 'qualifying consideration' being received by the company in circumstances where no consideration is given by the company; or
(c) the recognition in the financial statements of a change in fair value, in those cases where fair value has been determined in accordance with measurement guidance in the relevant accounting standards or company law, and to the extent that the change recognised is readily convertible to cash; or
(d) the translation of:

    (i) a monetary asset which comprises qualifying consideration; or
    (ii) a liability,

    denominated in a foreign currency; or
(e) the reversal of a loss previously regarded as realised; or
(f) a profit* previously regarded as unrealised (such as amounts taken to a revaluation reserve, merger reserve or other similar reserve) becoming realised as a result of:

**Where the related profit has been capitalised, it will not be available for transfer from unrealised profit to realised profit.*

(i) consideration previously received by the company becoming 'qualifying consideration'; or
(ii) the related asset being disposed of in a transaction where the consideration received by the company is 'qualifying consideration'; or
(iii) a realised loss being recognised on the scrapping or disposal of the related asset; or
(iv) a realised loss being recognised on the write-down for depreciation, amortisation, diminution in value or impairment of the related asset*;
(v) the distribution in kind of the asset to which the unrealised profit relates; or
(vi) the receipt of a dividend in the form of qualifying consideration when no profit is recognised because the dividend is deducted from the book value of the investment to which the unrealised profit relates (e.g. as required by IAS 27 before its amendment in May 2008† in the case of dividends out of pre-acquisition profits of subsidiaries) (see 9.22 *et seq* below),

in which case the appropriate proportion‡ of the related unrealised profit becomes a realised profit; or

(g) the remeasurement of a liability, to the extent that the change recognised is readily convertible to cash (see 3.9B below).

3.9A In addition, as explained at 2.8A, The Companies (Reduction of Share Capital) Order 2008 SI 2008/1915 specifies the cases in which a reserve arising from a reduction in a company's share capital is to be treated as a realised profit as a matter of law.

3.9B A profit arising on the remeasurement of a liability will often be the reversal of a realised loss, a foreign currency translation gain or a fair value gain, and may therefore be a realised profit in accordance with 3.9(c), (d) or (e), Paragraph 3.9(g) will be relevant in other cases such as that of a defined benefit pension liability assumed for consideration either in a separate transaction or as part of a business combination. In such a case the profit is only a realised profit in those rare cases where the change in value is readily convertible to cash as defined at 3.12 below.

Realised loss

3.10 Losses should be regarded as realised losses except to the extent that the law, accounting standards or this guidance provide otherwise. The statutory position is set out in section 2 of this guidance.

Qualifying consideration

3.11 Qualifying consideration comprises:

(a) cash; or
(b) an asset that is readily convertible to cash; or

**If the write down is subsequently reversed, an equal amount of profit should be regarded as becoming unrealised. In other words, the amount of profit regarded as becoming realised is equal to the cumulative* amount of any write down treated as a realised loss.

†*Amendments to IFRS 1 First-time Adoption of IFRSs and IAS 27 Consolidated and Separate Financial Statements: Cost of an Investment in a Subsidiary, Jointly Controlled Entity or Associate.*

‡*In the case of (iii) and (iv), the loss is treated as a realised loss under paragraph 3.15 of this guidance. However, part of this realised loss is compensated by a reclassification from unrealised to realised profit.*

consideration received is in the form of qualifying consideration. This approach is sometimes referred to as 'top-slicing'. (Example: fair value of consideration received is 10, of which 4 is cash and 6 is freehold property. If the depreciated historical cost of the asset sold is 5, the total gain is 5 but the realised profit is limited to 4.)

Hedging

Where hedge accounting is obtained in accordance with the relevant accounting standards, it is necessary to consider the combined effect of both sides of the hedging relationship to determine whether there is a realised profit or loss in accordance with the criteria in this guidance. **3.19**

Application of this principle in the context of hedge relationships within the individual financial statements of a company is considered at 5.1 to 5.18 of this guidance. Consideration of the effects of hedge relationships where the hedging instrument and the hedged item are held by different group companies is considered at 5.19 to 5.22. **3.20**

Foreign exchange profits and losses

Paragraph 65 of SSAP 20 Foreign currency translation, which was issued in 1983, states that 'the application of paragraph 50 of this statement may result in unrealised exchange gains on unsettled long-term monetary items being taken to the profit and loss account'. Since then, however, the currency markets have become more sophisticated and companies have significantly more flexibility to crystallise exchange profits on long-term monetary items. Consequently, unless there are doubts as to the convertibility or marketability of the currency in question, foreign exchange profits arising on the retranslation of monetary items are realised, irrespective of the maturity date of the monetary item. **3.21**

This has become generally accepted practice even though the exchange difference may not be 'readily convertible to cash' at the balance sheet date. However, a profit on retranslation of a monetary asset will not be a realised profit where the underlying balance on which the exchange difference arises does not itself meet the definition of 'qualifying consideration'. For example, this may be the case for some long-term inter-company balances within groups. **3.21A**

The position regarding exchange differences reported in a separate component of equity (ie not in the income statement) is considered at 5.7 below in relation to cash flow hedge accounting; and in relation to the translation of branches into the company's functional currency, the translation of the whole of a company's accounts from the company's functional currency to a presentation currency and questions of mismatch with the currency of denomination of shares are considered in section 11. **3.21B**

Goodwill in an individual company

Where goodwill arises in a company's individual accounts (which would be the case, for example, where the company has purchased an unincorporated business) the goodwill will become a realised loss as the goodwill is amortised or written down for impairment in accordance with relevant accounting standards. **3.22**

For periods ending before 23 December 1998, purchased goodwill may have been accounted for under SSAP 22 "Accounting for goodwill" by immediate elimination against reserves. Such goodwill may have remained eliminated against reserves under UK GAAP under the transitional provisions of FRS 10. Such goodwill should be **3.23** regarded as a realised loss to the extent that, had it always been recognised as an asset, it would have been amortised or impaired in accordance with FRS 10.

3.23A If the business to which the acquired goodwill relates is disposed of or closed, FRS 10 requires the profit or loss on disposal to include the goodwill previously taken to reserves to the extent that it has not previously been charged to the profit and loss account. Notional amortisation or impairment for the purposes of calculating realised profits does not affect this financial reporting requirement. However, the effect of the disposal on realised profits is therefore net of any amount already treated as a realised loss in accordance with this guidance.

3.23B Goodwill may also have remained eliminated against reserves on transition to IFRSs in accordance with IFRS 1. Such goodwill should be regarded as a realised loss to the extent that, had it always been recognised as an asset under IFRSs, it would have been impaired in accordance with IFRS 3 and IAS 36. This is unaffected by any amounts of notional amortisation in accordance with FRS 10 that might have been treated as realised losses prior to transition to IFRSs.

3.23C When applying IFRSs, goodwill previously written off to reserves is not taken into account in any profit or loss on subsequent disposal. However, any goodwill written off to reserves that has not previously been treated as a realised loss will become realised as a result of the disposal.

3.23D Companies not wishing to make these assessments may prudently opt to regard the entire amount of goodwill written off to reserves as a realised loss.

Negative goodwill in an individual company

3.24 The following guidance on negative goodwill applies under UK GAAP and IFRSs unless otherwise stated. Neither IFRS 3 nor IFRS 3 Revised (subsequently together referred to as IFRS 3) uses the term "negative goodwill" but instead they describe that concept using different words. For simplicity, such an amount is described in this guidance as negative goodwill.

3.25 Negative goodwill up to the fair values of the non-monetary assets acquired should be treated as being realised in the periods in which the non-monetary assets are recovered, whether through depreciation or sale. Where the negative goodwill exceeds the value of the non-monetary assets, this excess should be treated as being realised in the periods expected to benefit. However, negative goodwill should not be treated as a realised profit in the case of a sale of the non-monetary assets where the consideration received is not qualifying consideration.

3.26 Under UK GAAP, negative goodwill recognised in the profit and loss account in accordance with FRS 10 therefore represents a realised profit except in the case of a sale of the non-monetary assets where the consideration received is not qualifying consideration. Where negative goodwill was accounted for under SSAP 22 in the accounts of an individual company, it would have been regarded initially as an unrealised profit. It will become a realised profit on the same basis as if it had been negative goodwill accounted for under FRS 10.

3.27 IFRS 3 requires the immediate recognition of negative goodwill as a profit for financial reporting purposes but this does not accelerate the realisation of negative goodwill which is as set out at 3.25 above irrespective of the accounting framework adopted.

Changes in circumstances including changes in accounting policies and on the adoption of IFRSs

Introduction

The treatment of a retained profit or loss as realised (or unrealised), or the recognition of an item as a profit or loss or an asset or liability, may change subsequent to its original recognition as a result of: **3.28**

(a) a change in the principles of realisation; or
(b) a change in the law or in accounting standards or interpretations, either through an express reference to the realisation or otherwise of the profit or loss or, more commonly, through a change in the recognition or measurement of assets, liabilities, income or expenses. A company adopting IFRSs for the first time will, in effect, be making a number of changes in accounting policies; or
(c) some other change in circumstance such that what was originally qualifying consideration under paragraph 3.11(d) is no longer so, for example, where a receivable was initially regarded as qualifying consideration but circumstances change such that there is now no expectation that the receivable will be settled in the form of qualifying consideration.

Although the effect of these changes may be to reduce or even eliminate a company's net realised profits, that would not render unlawful a distribution already made out of realised profits determined by reference to 'relevant accounts' which had been prepared in accordance with generally accepted accounting principles applicable to those accounts (this is subject to paragraphs 3.30 and 3.31 below). This is because the Act defines realised profits and losses for determining the lawfulness of a distribution as 'such profits and losses of the company as fall to be treated as realised in accordance with principles generally accepted at the time when the accounts are prepared, with respect to the determination for accounting purposes of realised profits or losses' (section 853(4), emphasis added). **3.29**

The circumstances described in paragraph 3.28(c) do not extend to the case of "an asset that is readily convertible to cash" (which is "qualifying consideration" under paragraph 3.11(b)). Such assets are, when received, regarded as being so highly liquid as to be treated as equivalent to cash. That is to say, the initial determination that a profit is a realised one is, if based on the qualifying consideration's being cash or "an asset that is readily convertible to cash", definitive and unchangeable. Thus, for example, if changes in the market for a financial asset mean that from a certain point in time the asset no longer meets the "readily convertible to cash" test, then prior fair value movements – whether profits or losses – remain as realised. **3.29A**

This would be relevant if, for example, the financial asset were reclassified out of a fair value category under the amendment to IAS 39 of November 2008. To the extent that the last fair value includes amounts originally determined to be realised profits, they remain so. It is as if the profits were realised in cash and re-invested (outside of the principle in paragraph 3.5) into the financial asset in question. In such a reclassification case, it may of course be the case that the market changed, so as no longer to meet the "readily convertible to cash" test, at an earlier date than the reclassification. In such a case the financial asset's carrying value may include realised profits and unrealised profits. Whilst the realised profits will retain that status going forward, the unrealised profits are capable at some future date of changing to realised profits under paragraph 3.9(f). **3.29B**

It would be open to a company, instead of splitting the fair value movement since inception into movements that were and were not readily convertible to cash, to **3.29C** make a shortcut, prudent assumption that if there are cumulative net gains since inception, they are regarded as unrealised.

Timing of the effect of changes in accounting policies on distributable profits

3.30 The effects of the introduction of a new accounting standard or on the adoption of IFRSs become relevant to the application of the common law capital maintenance rule only in relation to distributions accounted for in periods in which the change will first be recognised in the accounts. Where items will fall to be treated as liabilities under a new standard in a period after the period in which the dividend is accounted for, directors do not have to pay regard to such future liabilities merely because they are disclosed in the notes to the accounts.

3.31 Where the directors are considering the payment of an interim dividend in respect of a financial year, and a new accounting standard may, for example, lead to items being recognised as liabilities in the accounts for that year, the directors must, under common law, have regard to the effect of these liabilities on the expected level of profits available for distribution at the end of the financial year when determining the lawfulness of the interim dividend.

3.32 For example, for a company adopting IFRSs for its individual accounts in 2010 the position is as follows:

- any final dividend for 2009 will not be provided in the 2009 UK GAAP accounts and will first be accounted for in the 2010 accounts. Such a dividend would therefore have to have regard to the effect of adoption of IFRSs even though the "relevant accounts" may still be those for 2009 prepared under UK GAAP;
- any interim dividend paid during 2010 would have to have regard to the effect of adoption of IFRSs even though the "relevant accounts" may still be those for 2009 prepared under UK GAAP; and
- the 2010 accounts prepared under IFRSs would be the relevant accounts for the purposes of the final dividend approved by shareholders in 2011. The effect of a change in accounting policy known to be adopted in 2011 needs to be taken into account in determining the dividend to be approved by shareholders in 2011. The dividend will be recognised in the 2011 accounts.

3.33 The considerations set out above apply to all dividends whether in respect of shares classified as equity or shares classified as debt (or partly shares and partly debt as a compound instrument) under either IFRSs or UK GAAP.

3.34 If the effect of a new accounting standard or guidance on profits which fall to be treated as realised is to increase the company's accumulated profits and the company wishes to distribute an amount in excess of that which could be determined by reference to what would otherwise constitute the company's 'relevant accounts', the company is required to prepare interim accounts complying with the new accounting standard or guidance. Where a public company is in this position, those interim accounts are required to be delivered to the Registrar under section 838.

3.35 For the purposes of a dividend made by reference, under statute, to UK GAAP relevant accounts, but at a time when the foregoing guidance requires the effect of a current year changeover to IFRSs to be considered, the directors will need to understand the consequences of adopting IFRSs for the company's profits available for distribution. There is no statutory requirement to prepare interim accounts under section 836 (and section 838 in the case of a public company) if a proposed distribution can be justified by reference to the relevant accounts. However, under common law, a company cannot lawfully make a distribution out of capital. The directors may, for example, by reason of their duties to exercise appropriate skill and care, consider preparing interim accounts under IFRSs, as of the date shortly before the time of paying the proposed dividend, to satisfy themselves that the accumulated realised profits shown in the last statutory individual accounts have not been eliminated, or reduced to such an extent that the proposed distribution would be unlawful. (It should be noted that these "interim accounts" would not be interim accounts within the meaning of section 836(2) of the Act and section 838 would not therefore apply to them.) For a public company, the directors will also have to consider the impact of the restriction on distributions arising from section 831 (see 6.24 *et seq*). It may not always be necessary to prepare interim accounts, for example, in very straightforward cases where the directors are satisfied that no material adjustments arise from the transition to IFRSs.

The directors of a company may not yet have decided whether to adopt IFRSs for the current financial year. Similarly, they may not have decided whether to adopt early a new accounting standard that has been issued but is not mandatory for the financial year. In these cases, the company's accounting policies are those that it has previously applied until a decision is made to change them. Therefore, in applying the foregoing guidance, it is not necessary to have regard to possible changes of policy that are being considered but have not yet been agreed. **3.36**

Where a company believes that the implementation of IFRSs will increase its balance of distributable profits, and it wishes to distribute those profits as increased, the guidance at 3.34 above will be relevant. **3.37**

Realised profits that have been distributed and are subsequently eliminated by a change of circumstances (including a change of accounting policy)

Where the effect of a change in circumstance is that a profit previously recognised as realised can no longer be regarded as being realised, the amount of that profit should either be eliminated through a prior year adjustment or be reclassified as unrealised (as appropriate) in the relevant accounts in which the change in circumstance is first recognised. **3.38**

Where a previously recognised realised profit is eliminated through a prior year adjustment, the adjustment should be treated as a realised loss. The effect is therefore to reduce accumulated realised profits by the amount of the adjustment. If the adjustment results in accumulated realised losses, further distributions will not be possible until the shortfall is made good. To make a distribution before the shortfall is made good would amount to an unlawful return of capital, contrary to common law. **3.38A**

The same approach is possible where the previously recognised realised profit is reclassified as an unrealised profit. However, as explained below, in certain circumstances, it may be possible to adopt an alternative approach and to treat the distribution as having been made, in whole or in part, out of the profit which has been reclassified as unrealised so that it reduces accumulated unrealised profits rather than accumulated realised profits. This alternative approach may reduce any adverse impact on accumulated realised profits but is more difficult to apply. Either approach is acceptable when realised profits are reclassified as unrealised profits. **3.38B**

Under the alternative approach referred to in 3.38B, as profits are fungible, unless there is evidence that the profit affected by the change in circumstances has been distributed, it should be assumed that the first distribution made after the recognition **3.38C** of the profit was made pro rata out of all available profits shown in the relevant accounts. Accordingly, the balance remaining after that distribution would include a proportionate amount of the affected profit. Similarly each subsequent distribution would reduce proportionately the amount of the affected profit.

3.39 For example, a company has accumulated realised profits of 40 brought forward at the beginning of Year 1. During that year it makes realised profits of 60 of which 40 arose from a specific transaction in that period, and distributes 70, leaving a balance of 30. In Year 2 it generates a further 170 of realised profits and distributes 150. A change in circumstances in year 3 leads to the 40 recognised in Year 1 becoming treated as unrealised. The amount of the original profit of 40 that would be regarded as having been distributed in Year 1 would be 28 (70% [ie, 70/100] of 40), leaving 12 of the original profit to be carried forward in the closing balance of 30 at the end of Year 1. In Year 2 the amount of this 12 that would be regarded as having been distributed in Year 2 would be 9 (75% [ie, 150/200] of 12), leaving 3 of the original profit to be carried forward in the closing balance of 50 at the end of Year 2. Thus the amount of profit to be reclassified as unrealised in Year 3 as a result of the change in circumstance would be 3.

		Total	Affected profit
YEAR 1:	Brought forward	40	–
	Profit for year	60	40
	Available for distribution	100	40
	Distributed	(70)	(28)
YEAR 2:	Brought forward	30	12
	Profit for year	170	–
	Available for distribution	200	12
	Distributed	(150)	(9)
YEAR 3:	Brought forward	50	3

3.40 Where after making all reasonable enquiries it proves impracticable to obtain the information to make the allocation described at 3.38C, it would be appropriate to assume that the profit has been distributed (to the extent that there have been distributions).

Effect of errors

3.41 Under UK GAAP, only changes in accounting policies and correction of *fundamental* errors are accounted for by restatement of comparatives. This means that errors that are material but not "fundamental" are accounted for in the year in which they are detected without any restatement. In contrast, IAS 8 requires all *material* errors to be corrected retrospectively through a restatement of comparatives. Consequently, correction of errors by restatement is more common when reporting under IFRSs. A distribution may have been made by reference to the original accounts which would not have been justified if the error had not occurred. The question arises of whether such a distribution would be rendered unlawful.

3.42 It is the error, rather than its correction, that may have the effect of making a previous distribution unlawful. The effect of reporting under IFRSs is to make such errors more visible because of the requirement for retrospective restatement for all material errors. But whether or not an error is corrected in this way does not, of itself, govern the lawfulness of a previous distribution. The effect of an error on the lawfulness of a distribution raises complex legal issues that are beyond the scope of this guidance.

Application of the linkage etc principle in paragraph 3.5

The principle in paragraph 3.5 above must be viewed from the perspective of an individual company to determine that company's realised profits. Therefore, if a company enters into a single transaction, that transaction cannot be linked because the concept of linkage requires the effect of two or more legally separate transactions of the same entity to be viewed as a single transaction in substance. The fact that a series of transactions is circular from the perspective of a group does not mean that an individual company in the group, for example that participates in a single transaction in that series, cannot realise a profit on that transaction. The normal test of realisation may be met when applied to that single transaction. 3.43

The fact that an individual company's transactions are linked for the purposes of paragraph 3.5 does not necessarily mean that a realised profit cannot arise. The normal tests of realisation may be met when applied to the overall effect of the series of transactions taken together. 3.44

For two transactions to be linked, the second transaction must have been contemplated when the first transaction was entered into. If the second transaction is entered into for genuine commercial reasons unconnected with the first transaction and was not part of a plan with the first transaction, the two transactions would not be determined as linked. 3.45

The following principles address the application of paragraph 3.5 and require the exercise of judgement. 3.46

The application of paragraph 3.5 is not restricted to intra-group cash flows even though it is illustrated in the examples in section 9 solely in relation to intra-group situations. 3.47

Paragraph 3.5 is also relevant to transactions with third parties. The examples in section 9 focus on intra-group transactions as these are the more common situations where the question of linkage arises. An example of a situation involving a third party where linkage must be considered is the sale of a subsidiary for cash to a third party on the condition that the cash is applied in subscribing for shares of the purchaser. The substance or overall commercial effect of the transactions is a sale with consideration in shares of the purchaser. 3.48

The transactions do not have to be more than one of 'linked' or 'artificial' or 'circular' to fall within the principle in paragraph 3.5. 3.49

Paragraph 3.5 states that "a realised profit will arise only where the ***overall commercial effect*** on the company is such that the definition of realised profit set out in this guidance is met" (emphasis added). 3.50

Transactions need satisfy only one of the examples mentioned in paragraph 3.5A of being linked, artificial or circular, and furthermore these three cases are only particular instances of its application; that is to say, it is not limited to those cases. In practice individual transactions may fall within paragraph 3.5 because they are artificial or because collectively their effect is circular; but it is not necessary that a transaction be linked or artificial or circular for it to fall within paragraph 3.5. 3.51

3.52 **Splitting a transaction into separate steps would require consideration under the principle in paragraph 3.5.**

3.53 Taking the example discussed above of the sale of a subsidiary for shares; if this had been dealt with in one transaction it is obvious that the shares have to be evaluated to determine if they are qualifying consideration before concluding whether the profit on the transaction is realised. However, by splitting the transaction into two – a sale for cash and a subscription agreement – the commercial effect is obscured. Without proper analysis, the subscription agreement might have been overlooked and the profit determined as realised as the consideration was apparently cash. The transactions are linked. The transaction could be achieved by a single transaction of a sale for shares.

3.54 However, transactions may be linked without being artificial, or circular without being linked. Judgement is required in any determination of whether transactions fall within paragraph 3.5.

3.55 Other indicators of transactions that may fall within paragraph 3.5 include:

- the transactions being entered into at the same time (although see the discussion of time delays below) and in contemplation of each other;
- the transactions being with the same counterparty (which would include entities under common control and back-to-back arrangements); and
- transactions that are not in the ordinary course of business.

3.56 **Transactions may be linked "whether legally or otherwise".**

3.57 Transactions will often be 'linked' when they form part of a single plan. For example, a so called 'steps plan' may exist in which a number of separate transactions are envisaged. It may be clear that the first step of the plan would never have been carried out unless there was every expectation that step two would also be carried out. In this case, it is appropriate to consider the combined effect of all of the transactions together.

3.58 However, this does not mean that transactions must be regarded as linked or circular just because they were planned together. For example, a company may sell some quoted investments for cash with the intention of using that cash to purchase stock. The fact that the company plans to use the cash to purchase stock does not prevent the profit on disposal* of the investments being a realised profit. Similarly, trading profits will be realised profits in accordance with the normal rules, even though the cash inflows are reinvested in stock or fixed assets.

3.59 One feature usually present for there to be linkage is that the cash flow has been generated with the intention of, or for the purpose of, undertaking the linked transaction. Trading cash flows are generated as an end in themselves and thus do not possess this feature.

3.60 In relation to a sale and operating leaseback, the cash inflow arising from the sale transaction will be, at least in part, offset by the future cash outflows arising from the leaseback transaction. Therefore it might be queried whether they are linked. However, it is generally accepted that such arrangements do not fall within the scope of paragraph 3.5. A sale and leaseback transaction is not entered into for the purpose

**It is assumed for simplicity here that a profit is recognised on disposal of the investments, but companies applying IFRSs or FRS 26 may have recorded a profit at an earlier stage because of the need to account for the investments at fair value.*

of financing the future operating lease rentals. To the extent that the apparent sale's profit exceeds arm's length terms (ie the 'profit' is directly compensated for by high rentals) it is deferred anyway (under IAS 17 and SSAP 21).

Transactions may be linked legally by, say, being dealt with in the same contract or being in separate contracts but expressed to be inter-conditional. However, as made clear by the words "or otherwise", it is necessary to consider more than just the legal form of linkage of transactions to understand their substance collectively, as to do otherwise may not adequately express the overall commercial effect of the arrangements. **3.61**

For example, in the case of the so called steps plan mentioned above, there may be no legal obligation to complete step 2 following step 1. However, this may, for example, be a commercial necessity because step 1 does not make sense without step 2. **3.62**

For a cash inflow and a cash outflow of a company to fall within paragraph 3.5, it is not necessary that the cash flows 'close the loop' by joining up at some other place in the group. **3.63**

A transaction is circular for a company if, for that company, there is a cash inflow and in another step in a series there is a cash outflow back to the same party. As discussed above, circularity is a sufficient but not a necessary feature for the application of paragraph 3.5. Another situation where paragraph 3.5 may apply is where the cash outflow at another step is to another party rather than the provider of the cash inflow. It is not necessary, for something to be linked, that the recipient of the onward cash flow passes the cash back to the original provider. **3.64**

Transactions are not linked merely because they are pre-planned but this may be evidence of linkage. **3.65**

Pre-planning (eg by way of a steps plan) is evidence that the transactions are to be entered into in contemplation of each other and the overall outcome was premeditated. Evidence of pre-planning may indicate that those cash flows and the transactions from which they arise should be assessed as linked in order to understand their overall commercial effect. However, as explained in the example above at 3.58 concerning a disposal of quoted investments to finance a purchase of stock, this principle does not result in normal commercial transactions in the ordinary course of business being regarded as linked. **3.66**

Taking this example further, the transactions are not linked because the vendor of the stock would normally require payment in cash and would not accept quoted investments in settlement. Therefore, the substance of the transactions taken together is not an exchange of quoted investments for stock. **3.67**

Where paragraph 3.5 requires a series of transactions to be viewed as a whole, the consequence is that a profit, to be realised, has to be represented by an increase in qualifying consideration between the start and end points of the series. **3.68**

If a series of transactions is viewed as a whole, then it is necessary to compare the assets and liabilities, and their amounts, at the start and end of the series to determine what transaction, in substance, has occurred (changes in assets and liabilities). The transaction thus identified is tested under the other principles set out in this guidance. Thus, where paragraph 3.5 applies, it is necessary to determine the amount of qualifying consideration involved at the start and end of the linked transactions to see if there has been an increase, decrease or a net nil position. Unless there has been **3.69** an increase in the amount of qualifying consideration (in any of the forms defined in paragraph 3.11), it cannot have a realised profit from that series of transactions.

3.70 **If there is a new external cash flow somewhere in a chain of intra-group transactions to which the company is party, this cannot be associated with a portion of the gross cash flows of the company in question if, after considering a series of transactions that fall within the scope of paragraph 3.5 to which the company is party, the company does not have a net increase in cash or other qualifying consideration.**

3.71 A net nil cash position (as described at 3.69 above) cannot be broken into two gross components to assert that there has been an increase in qualifying consideration that will justify recognition of a realised profit. To do so would amount to dealing with such transactions as if they were independent and so would fail to treat them, as required by paragraph 3.5, as a series that is to be assessed as a whole. Thus, where a company's transactions, taken as a whole, do not increase its qualifying consideration, they do not generate a realised profit. This is the case irrespective of whether the cash inflow has been financed from new external cash receipts elsewhere in the group.

3.72 For example, consider a company that receives a dividend of 100 from one subsidiary and reinvests the same amount in another subsidiary as equity capital, both as part of a planned corporate restructuring. There is no net increase in qualifying consideration and therefore the receipt of the dividend is not a realised profit. It does not matter that the dividend of 100 was funded from external cash receipts elsewhere in the group.

3.73 However, paragraphs 3.71 and 3.72 above are concerned only with circumstances where the cash inflow and cash outflow comprising the net nil position fall within paragraph 3.5. For example, paragraph 3.72 is concerned with a planned corporate restructuring. The fact that dividends are received from some subsidiaries at or about the same time as investments are made in other subsidiaries as equity capital does not automatically prevent those dividends being recognised as realised profits. To be linked, there needs to be something more than juxtapositioning of transactions, such as the dividends being necessary at this time to facilitate the investment.

3.74 **Time does not necessarily matter when judging whether steps in a series of transactions need to be viewed as a whole. Inserting a pre-planned period of delay, for example, between intended steps will not generally break "linkage".**

3.75 Time gaps in a series of transactions is a factor to judge as to whether this was an attempt to frustrate a series-of-transactions argument. Deliberate insertion of time delays is usually persuasive evidence of pre-planning and pre-meditation of the outcome. The length of the time period or periods between transactions is not, of itself, relevant. Thus, a time gap should not affect the conclusion. However, time may be a factor to consider if it gives genuine opportunity for a relevant change to occur in the series of steps. The more time that is to elapse between steps then the more time there is for commercial circumstances to change and thus for the subsequent steps, if not yet irrevocable, not to go ahead due to changed circumstances.

4. FAIR VALUE ACCOUNTING 4.1 – 4.33

Introduction

4.1 The directors of any particular company need to consider their own company's facts and circumstances in determining whether an accounting profit arising through changes in fair value is readily convertible to cash in accordance with the definition and can therefore be considered as realised for distribution purposes. Consideration should also be given to 2.3 to 2.5 above regarding volatility and directors' duties. This section provides guidance on:

(a) the application of the definition of 'readily convertible to cash' to particular situations (see 4.2 *et seq*);
(b) available-for-sale investments and the fair value reserve (see 4.23 *et seq*);
(c) the fair value option (see 4.26 *et seq*); and
(d) losses arising from fair value accounting (see 4.29 *et seq*).

Guidance on the application of "readily convertible to cash"

Financial instruments

The definition of "readily convertible to cash" in paragraph 3.12 is closely but not completely aligned with the measurement guidance in IAS 39. Necessary differences remain. **4.2**

In situations where: **4.3**

(a) the financial instrument is traded in an active market; or
(b) the financial instrument is valued using a valuation technique whose variables include only data from observable markets,

it will generally be possible to enter into a transaction to convert the change in value to cash at short notice without any period of marketing and/or negotiation. Even when the instrument is not traded in an active market, there may be many institutions which will be prepared to quote a price based on observable market data at which a transaction could take place immediately. Such a change in value that is a profit would therefore, subject also to the test at 3.12(c) above, be regarded as realised.

However, a change in the fair value of a financial instrument that is a profit which is determined using a valuation technique where not all of the variables include data from observable markets would be regarded as unrealised. This would not be so where part of the profit can be closed out independently of the rest and that part may be realised pursuant to the guidance on close out at 4.5 and 4.6 below. **4.4**

Close out

A financial asset, financial liability or change in the fair value of a financial asset or financial liability may be capable of being readily convertible to cash for the purposes of applying condition (a) of the readily convertible to cash test at 3.12 above if it could be immediately closed out, meaning the relevant contract or underlying market risk position is capable of being immediately offset in the market and the normal market practice would be to close out the position in this way. For example, risks inherent in a derivative may be eliminated by taking out other financial instruments, including derivative contracts, with an offsetting risk profile. When it is possible under normal market practice to enter into such arrangements to "lock in" any profit on the original contract, the profit that could be "locked in" could be regarded as readily convertible to cash. It is not necessary for an actual transaction to have occurred. **4.5**

4.5 above addresses the ability to close out in the context of condition (a) of 3.12. In relation to condition (a), consideration should also be given to whether the cash **4.6** flows from the close-out instrument meet the definition of qualifying consideration, in particular the criteria set out at 3.11.

4.6A In addition, conditions (b) and (c) in 3.12 must also be considered. In the context of condition (b), consideration should be given to whether the valuation of the close-out instrument is based on observable market data.

4.7 The position regarding fair value losses is dealt with at 4.29 to 4.33 below.

Embedded derivatives

4.8 Unless the whole contract has been designated at fair value through profit or loss, an embedded derivative that is determined not to be closely related to the economic characteristics and risks of the host contract is required to be separated from its host for accounting purposes (bifurcation) and fair valued, as if it were a standalone derivative with the same terms. Changes in fair value of the embedded derivative are recognised in profit or loss. However, where a change in fair value is a profit it does not constitute a realised profit unless the embedded derivative can be closed out in the manner described above in "Close out" or the host contract and embedded derivative together meet the "readily convertible to cash" test (including by reference to close-out if appropriate).

Top-slicing

4.9 Fair value accounting under the relevant accounting standards involves the valuation of the whole item or, in the case of fair value hedge accounting, a particular risk and the recognition of the change in fair value in the financial statements. Where the change is a profit, it is not necessary to have completed a transaction to determine whether the whole of the increase in fair value is to be treated as realised. The criteria for determining whether an increase in fair value that is a profit could be readily converted to cash and thus be treated as realised are set out at 3.12 above. The concept of top-slicing a gain into realised and unrealised parts as envisaged by paragraph 3.18 arises when there has been a transaction involving qualifying and other consideration. On remeasurement there is no transaction involved in the recognition of a fair value profit, hence the question of top-slicing (ie determining, by reference to mixed consideration receivable, whether part of the profit should be treated as realised as opposed to the whole of such profit) does not occur.

Unquoted equity investments

4.10 Although increases in the fair value of many financial assets will meet the test of being "readily convertible to cash" at 3.12 above, this will not generally be true of unquoted equity investments. The measurement of such investments at fair value may be precluded because the range of reasonable fair value estimates is significant and the probabilities of the various estimates cannot reasonably be assessed. Even where the value can be estimated sufficiently reliably to meet the requirements of IAS 39 and an increase in fair value is recognised, it is unlikely that the amount would be readily convertible to cash at the date of determination. This is because, for example, a period of marketing and/or negotiation would generally be required to dispose of such an investment.

Strategic investments

Under a company's business strategy it may hold investments for strategic purposes. Such investments are not readily disposable in the sense required to meet condition (c) of the readily convertible to cash test at 3.12 above, as a company's strategy cannot be readily changed so as to allow the investment to be realised immediately at the date of determination. For example, the company might have a strategic investment in a listed company that qualifies to be accounted for as an associate under IAS 28. It is possible for the company to elect under IAS 28 to account for its associates (in its separate financial statements) at fair value under IAS 39 (e.g. as an available-for-sale asset, with fair value changes reported in equity). Increases in fair value of such a strategic investment might be regarded as realised but for condition (c) of the test for readily convertible to cash. Thus the fair value increases are, consequently, unrealised. **4.11**

A similar analysis may be made for a company's holding of other financial assets, such as government bonds, that are classified as available-for-sale and are thus remeasured at fair value but nevertheless are held to meet the company's business strategy or regulatory requirements. Any fair value increases of such assets are unrealised as the company cannot readily change its business strategy or regulatory compliance to allow the financial assets to be realised immediately at the date of determination. **4.12**

Hedge relationships in group situations

Under a group's hedging strategy, different companies in the group may hold the hedging instrument and the hedged item. For example, in a net investment hedge as illustrated in IFRIC 16 Hedges of a Net Investment in a Foreign Operation. The circumstances of each of the companies involved in the hedge relationship needs to be assessed at the date of determination, as the relevant company may not be in a position to realise an increase in fair value in the sense required to meet condition (c) of the readily convertible to cash test at 3.12 above. For example, the purpose of the company holding the hedging instrument is to hold it for the benefit of, or to assist, another group company, and accordingly it may not be able to dispose of or close out the hedging instrument, needing instead to seek that other company's concurrence. This is discussed further at 5.19 to 5.22 of section 5 Hedge accounting." **4.12A**

Investment properties

None of an increase in fair value of investment property is readily convertible to cash and is not therefore treated as a realised profit. This is because a period of marketing and/or negotiation would be required to dispose of such an investment and therefore it could not be converted to cash at the date of determination. This is not intended to preclude a profit being regarded as realised at the date of determination in those cases when the process of marketing and/or negotiation is complete at that date and legal completion occurs shortly after the date of determination. **4.13**

Own credit

When liabilities (e.g. bank debt or bond issues) and over-the-counter derivative contracts are measured at fair value, their value may be affected by the reporting company's own creditworthiness. Consequently, a profit may arise in circumstances where the company's creditworthiness is deteriorating, that is, the fair value of the liability is decreasing. In such cases, it is necessary to consider whether the company **4.14** would be able to realise the profit by settling the liability at its fair value. This may not be possible, particularly if the company is experiencing financial difficulties, and the relevant profit will therefore not be a realised profit. However, in most circumstances where a company is not in financial difficulties and it would be able to settle the debt at fair value, there will be no need to analyse the fair value changes between the amount attributable to marginal changes in the creditworthiness of the liability and changes due to movements in interest rates and other market factors.

4.15 It should be noted, however, that the tests set out at 3.12 above are wider than solely the ability to settle at fair value and must all be met. For example, the company must be able to settle on the date of determination without negotiation or marketing. Thus where a large volume of debt is under consideration, this is akin to a question of whether the company could refinance that large volume of debt on that date without negotiation, which would often not be the case.

Block discounts for securities traded in an active market

4.16 IAS 39 requires certain financial instruments to be valued on a basis that does not take account of the size of the holding. That is to say that the valuation included in the accounts uses the published price quotation in an active market as the best estimate of fair value and does not reflect any "block discount" that might apply if the entire holding was disposed of at the date of determination. In the case of assets (e.g. investments) that are traded on an active market, it may be possible to dispose of the entire holding at the date of determination but it is necessary to recognise that the proceeds may be less than the value recognised in the balance sheet in accordance with IAS 39.

4.17 Holdings in financial assets traded in an active market that might be regarded as relatively small (e.g. less than 1% of a company's share capital) may nevertheless be large in relation to the volume of business done in that company's shares on a typical day in the market. For example, some such investments held by investment companies and other financial institutions fall into this category. Such investments are rarely, if ever, disposed of in a single block but are instead disposed of in a number of smaller blocks either all on the same day or over a short period of time, in accordance with normal market practice, to reduce or eliminate the effect of any block discount. In these limited circumstances, the effect of any block discount on realised profits may be calculated on the basis set out at 4.18 and 4.19 below rather than on the basis that the entire holding is disposed of in a single block on the date of determination. This is a limited departure from the principle established at 3.12(a) above.

4.18 Part 4 of the Statement of Recommended Practice "Accounting for Securities by Banks" ("the SORP") issued by the British Bankers' Association contained the following guidance:

"61. *Where a holding of a quoted security (other than one to which paragraph [62] or [63] applies)** is so large that it could be disposed of only at an unfavourable price or over an extended period, it should be valued at an appropriate discount to the market price. The discount should be sufficient to reflect the reduction in price resulting from the size of the holding or all future costs likely to be incurred in disposing of the interest over time in the ordinary course of business."

**Paragraph 62 dealt with instruments held for hedging and paragraph 63 dealt with investment securities stated at cost.*

The SORP has been withdrawn because it is not applicable to banks reporting under IFRSs or applying FRS 26 under UK GAAP. It nevertheless provides an indication of generally accepted practice for the valuation of large holdings. Although this approach no longer applies for financial reporting purposes for companies applying IFRSs or FRS 26, it continues to be relevant to the determination of realised profits.

Where it is determined that a block discount exists in relation to a holding of securities traded in an active market, only the part of the profit that may not be realisable over a short period of time in the ordinary course of business should be treated as unrealised*. This would not necessarily be the same as the block discount that may apply if the entity disposed of the entire holding in a single block at the date of determination (e.g. in a forced sale), and which applies to situations other than those covered by the previous sentence for the purposes of determining the part of the profit that is unrealised. **4.19**

Estimation of the unrealised profit referred to at 4.16 and 4.19 above will require the exercise of judgement. Directors of companies frequently have to exercise judgement in making accounting estimates. The position concerning block discounts is no different. Directors do not have to be able to quantify the unrealised profit referred to at 4.16 and 4.19 above precisely; an estimate is all that is required. It will often be clear that there is a sufficient margin of profit available for distribution (over and above the proposed distribution) to absorb a prudent assessment of the effect of any unrealised profit attributable to block discounts. **4.20**

Directors should consider their common law duty to avoid an unlawful distribution of capital. If an investment is sold after the date of determination to finance a distribution, the impact of any resulting loss (whether due to the unrealised component of a block discount or otherwise) on profits available for distribution should be considered. **4.21**

The case of a block discount can be distinguished from that of investment property and most unquoted equity investments when none of the profit is treated as realised due to the period of marketing and/or negotiation required to dispose of such investments, such that the profit could not be readily converted to cash at the date of determination. **4.22**

Available-for-sale financial assets and the fair value reserve

Under IAS 39, profits and losses on "available-for-sale" financial assets are recognised directly in equity through the statement of other comprehensive income (except for dividends, interest, impairment losses and foreign exchange profits and losses on monetary items). This applies until the assets are derecognised (e.g. sold) at which time the cumulative profit or loss previously recognised in equity is recognised in profit or loss (ie "recycled")†. **4.23**

**A similar adjustment is not required when an overall (ie cumulative) loss is recognised on the remeasurement of a financial instrument in accordance with IAS 39. The potential additional loss, equivalent to the block discount, that would arise on disposal of the entire holding at the date of determination is not recorded as a loss in the financial statements. Consequently, the realised loss will equal the loss reported in the financial statements, which will exclude the effect of any block discount.*

†Similar rules for "available-for-sale" financial assets apply for companies using FRS 26, where the profits and losses are recognised directly in equity through the statement of total recognised gains and losses. The amendment to FRS 3 for companies using FRS 26 clarifies the position for recycling the cumulative profit or loss on a sale of an available-for-sale financial asset.

4.24 Profits and losses arising on the remeasurement of available-for-sale financial assets will be realised or unrealised according to the same principles that would apply if the same assets had been accounted for at fair value through profit or loss (see above). For example, it would be illogical if the question of whether a profit was realised or unrealised depended on whether the directors designated the particular assets "at fair value through profit or loss" on initial recognition, when using the fair value option in the circumstances permitted by the relevant accounting standards (see 4.26 below). However, profits on remeasurement of available-for-sale financial assets will be realised or unrealised in accordance with the principles described above, irrespective of whether they meet the requirements to be accounted for at fair value through profit or loss.

4.25 For companies reporting under IFRSs (ie directly under the IAS Regulation), there is no requirement to credit profits included in other comprehensive income on available-for-sale investments to any particular reserve. For companies reporting under UK GAAP (FRS 26), such profits will be taken to the fair value reserve in accordance with the requirements of the Accounting Regulations. There is no specific legal restriction on the distribution of profits included in the fair value reserve in either the Act or the EU Fair Value Directive (2001/65/EC) from which the provisions on fair value accounting in UK legislation are drawn. Therefore, there is no constraint on treating profits on remeasurement of available-for-sale financial assets as available for distribution if they are in all other respects realised profits in accordance with this guidance.

Fair value option

4.26 IAS 39, the EU adopted version of IAS 39 and FRS 26 contain the same conditions regarding when it is permitted to use the fair value option to designate financial instruments "at fair value through profit or loss" on initial recognition. The conditions for using the fair value option are set out in paragraph 9 *et seq* of IAS 39.

4.27 Where the fair value option is used it is necessary to consider whether the changes in fair value of the relevant financial instruments that are recognised in the profit and loss account meet the conditions to be treated as realised. In this respect, the guidance above on "Financial instruments", "Embedded derivatives", "Own credit" and "Block discounts" will be most relevant in interpreting the "readily convertible to cash" criterion as defined at 3.12 above.

4.28 In addition, it is recognised that the use of the fair value option to eliminate or significantly reduce an accounting mismatch may validly be used in place of hedge accounting for hedges of fair value exposures. Consequently, where this is the case, although the designated financial instrument that is fair valued under the fair value option and the derivative that would otherwise give rise to the accounting mismatch are not in a formal IAS 39 hedge relationship, consideration of the guidance in 5.2 to 5.6 "Fair value hedge accounting" (which contain further guidance on the principle set out at 3.19 above) would be relevant in determining the effect on realised profits of the combined effect of the designated financial instruments and the derivatives concerned.

Losses

4.29 Losses arising from fair value accounting should be treated as realised losses where profits on remeasurement of the same asset or liability would be treated as realised profits in accordance with this guidance (see 3.15(f) above).

A loss that represents the reversal of an unrealised profit will not reduce cumulative realised profits. Even if the loss is treated as a realised loss, for example because it represents an impairment, the unrealised profit will become realised in accordance with 3.9(f)above. **4.30**

Cumulative net losses arising on fair value accounting will be unrealised only if both: **4.31**

(a) profits on remeasurement of the same asset or liability would be unrealised; and
(b) the losses would not have been recorded otherwise than pursuant to fair value accounting.

With reference to paragraph (b) above, absent fair value accounting a loss may need to be recorded for example, in relation to an asset, on the basis of historical/ amortised costs less impairment provisions; and in relation to a liability, under either an amortised cost basis of financial instrument accounting or as an onerous contract liability. **4.32**

It is well established that the recoverable amount of tangible fixed assets (e.g. properties used in a business) may exceed their fair value (see paragraph 65 of FRS 15). In the case of other assets (including investment property), it may be more difficult to justify a recoverable amount that is greater than fair value. Each case should be considered on its merits and, where there is doubt, losses should be treated as realised. **4.33**

5. HEDGE ACCOUNTING 5.1 – 5.22

Hedge relationships in individual companies

As stated at 3.19 above, the principle to be applied to the determination of realised profits and losses when hedge accounting is used is as follows: **5.1**

> "Where hedge accounting is obtained in accordance with the relevant accounting standards, it is necessary to consider the combined effect of both sides of the hedging relationship to determine whether there is a realised profit or loss in accordance with the criteria in this guidance."

The application of this principle to different types of hedge accounting permitted by IAS 39 by companies holding both the hedging instrument and the hedged item is described at 5.2 to 5.18 below.

Where the hedging instrument and hedged item are held in different companies within the same group a hedging relationship is established only in the group's consolidated financial statements. The general realisation principles as set out at 3.3 to 3.12 apply to the individual companies. As the hedge relationship does not exist within a single company the principle at 3.19 is inapplicable in such a case. Instead guidance on the application of these principles is provided at 5.19 to 5.22 below to assist in determining in what circumstances any profits or losses on the hedging instruments and hedged items can be treated as realised for the individual companies concerned. **5.1A**

Fair value hedge accounting

In the case of fair value hedges under IAS 39, the gross profits and losses on remeasuring the hedging instrument and the hedged item for the hedged risk are both recognised in profit or loss. In many instances both the profit on one and the loss on the other will be realised by reference to the readily convertible to cash and other **5.2** criteria. In such cases, no special consideration of hedging aspects is required (including hedge effectiveness or ineffectiveness).

5.3 In some cases, however, the profit on either the hedged item or the hedging instrument may, absent consideration of the hedging aspect, be unrealised (e.g. if a fair value movement is not readily convertible to cash). The following paragraphs explain how the principle set out at 5.1 above should be applied in circumstances where the profit is not realised.

5.4 Where the hedge accounting relationship results in a net loss, this amount will generally be treated as a realised loss. For example, consider the situation where there is an unrealised profit on the hedged item of £90 and a realised loss on the hedging instrument of £100. The net loss of £10, which arises from hedge ineffectiveness, is recognised in the profit and loss account and is treated as a realised loss. Due to the hedge accounting relationship, the remaining £90 of the gross loss on the hedging instrument is not treated as a realised loss and is set off against the unrealised profit on the hedged item.

5.5 Where there is a net profit, it will be necessary to consider whether that profit is a realised profit. This will depend on the relationship between the gross components. For example, if there is an unrealised profit of £100 and a realised loss of £90, only the net profit of £10 will be treated as unrealised.

5.6 This approach applies irrespective of whether the profits or losses in question arise from changes in fair value of open contracts or from settled transactions. For example, the hedge accounting policy may designate a series of rolling derivatives as the hedging instrument, some of which have already been settled in cash, whereas there have been no past settlements in respect of the hedged item.

Cash flow hedge accounting

5.7 In the case of cash flow hedges under IAS 39, the portion of the profit or loss on the hedging instrument that is determined to be an effective hedge is recognised in other comprehensive income. Such profits and losses are unrealised and become realised only when the hedged transaction affects profit or loss (or IAS 39 otherwise requires the gain or loss to be recycled through profit or loss). This is based on the principle (set out in 5.1 above) that it is necessary to have regard to the combined effect of both sides of the hedge accounting relationship to determine whether there is a realised profit or loss. To the extent that the profit or loss is included in other comprehensive income (or, later on, added to the cost of a non-financial asset) in accordance with IAS 39, it must arise in connection with a valid hedge accounting relationship. It would therefore be inappropriate to consider this profit or loss in isolation from the hedged item. To the extent that any ineffective element of the profit or loss on the hedging instrument is recognised in profit or loss, that element should be assessed as to whether it is realised in accordance with normal principles (e.g. the "readily convertible to cash" test).

5.8 The hedging principle at 5.1 above applies irrespective of whether the profits or losses in question arise from changes in fair value of open contracts or from settled transactions. The amounts taken direct to equity may, for example, include profits or losses on short-term derivative contracts that form part of a rolling-hedge strategy but which have matured. Such profits and losses should be treated as unrealised provided that IAS 39 requires them still to be deferred in equity as part of a cash flow hedge accounting relationship.

Accounting for a cash flow hedge in accordance with IAS 39 will affect net assets although the profit or loss is regarded as unrealised. Where the cumulative net amount on the cash flow hedge component of equity (cash flow hedge reserve) is an overall unrealised loss, this may additionally restrict the ability of a public company to make distributions because of the application of section 831 (see 6.24 *et seq*). **5.9**

Net investment hedge accounting

Under IAS 39, net investment hedge accounting policies will generally arise only in the context of consolidated financial statements. Those financial statements are not relevant for the purposes of justifying distributions. However, it is possible that in some instances, in accordance with IAS 21, a branch may be treated as a foreign operation in the individual accounts of a company. In this case, net investment hedge accounting may be relevant to the individual accounts of a company. A net investment hedge under IAS 39 is accounted for similarly to a cash flow hedge. So far as the hedge accounting is concerned, the question of whether the hedged item gives rise to realised profits is dealt with in section 11. **5.10**

The circumstances where a company previously adopted hedge accounting for a foreign equity investment (ie shares) in accordance with paragraph 51 of SSAP 20 is considered below. **5.11**

Transition from SSAP 20 – Hedge accounting for foreign equity investments

Under UK GAAP, SSAP 20 permits a form of hedge accounting for foreign equity investments, subject to certain conditions. Where a company has used foreign currency borrowings to finance, or provide a hedge against, its foreign equity investments, it may denominate those investments in the appropriate foreign currencies and translate the amounts at the balance sheet date at closing rate. Where this policy is adopted, the resulting exchange differences are taken to reserves. The exchange differences on the related foreign currency borrowings are, subject to certain conditions, also taken to reserves. In some cases hedge accounting may be possible for such arrangements under IAS 39 but as a fair value hedge through profit or loss. This is subject to more stringent conditions which do not apply under UK GAAP. Therefore companies may not be able to obtain hedge accounting for such financing arrangements under IFRSs. **5.12**

The hedge accounting for foreign equity investments under SSAP 20 described above is not restricted to investments in subsidiaries but this is its most common application. This guidance assumes, for simplicity, that the equity investment is in a subsidiary. **5.13**

Where hedge accounting is not available under IAS 39, the exchange differences on the borrowings will be included in profit or loss. Unless the equity investment is held at fair value under IAS 39, there will be no offsetting difference on the investment and it is usually, in effect, frozen at its historical cost in the functional currency of the investor. It is then necessary to determine whether the exchange difference on the borrowings is realised or unrealised. **5.14**

The exchange difference on the borrowings should be treated as realised in accordance with the general principles in section 3 where hedge accounting is not applied. This is irrespective of whether the purpose of the loan is for hedging an investment and of whether hedge accounting would have been permitted in the circumstances. This is the same as the position under SSAP 20 when the use of hedge accounting was optional. **5.15**

5.16 It should be noted that even though hedge accounting is not available, the purpose of the loan may still be to provide an "economic hedge" against the related equity investment. As stated at 2.3 *et seq*, although profits on the borrowings will be realised profits, directors should consider, as a result of their fiduciary and other duties, whether it would be prudent to distribute them.

5.17 Where hedge accounting was used under SSAP 20 and is not possible (or is otherwise not used) under IFRSs, it will be necessary, subject to IFRS 1, to restate the investment to either cost or fair value in accordance with IAS 27. On first-time adoption of IFRSs, paragraphs B5 and B6 of IFRS 1 will be relevant in these circumstances. They state that "if, before the date of transition to IFRSs, an entity had designated a transaction as a hedge but the hedge does not meet the conditions for hedge accounting in IAS 39 the entity shall apply paragraphs 91 and 101 of IAS 39 to discontinue hedge accounting". Those paragraphs require hedge accounting to be discontinued prospectively. The practical effect of this is that, if a policy of stating the investment at cost is adopted, the cumulative translation differences from applying SSAP 20 remain adjusted against the carrying value of the investment (ie the investment in the subsidiary is frozen at the amount determined by translating the historic foreign currency cost of the investment at the spot rate prevailing at the date of transition).

5.18 When this treatment is applicable, the profits and losses taken to reserves under SSAP 20 will remain within equity under IAS 39. In this case the assessment of whether those profits and losses are realised should continue to be made by reference to the net amount included within equity.

Hedge relationships in group situations

5.19 Under a group's hedging strategy, different companies in the group may hold the hedging instrument and the hedged item. For example, in a net investment hedge as illustrated in IFRIC 16 Hedges of a Net Investment in a Foreign Operation. In these cases, there is no hedge relationship within an individual company and thus the hedging principle articulated at 3.19 and as expanded upon at 5.1 to 5.18 does not apply. Accordingly, the general realisation principles as set out at 3.3 to 3.12 apply as follows.

Fair value accounting

5.20 As referred to at 4.12A, a company holding a hedging instrument in a designated group hedge relationship cannot generally readily dispose of or close out the instrument in the sense required to meet condition (c) of the readily convertible to cash test at 3.12 above. This is because the company may not be able to act unilaterally to de-designate the hedging relationship that has been created by the group so as to allow it to realise the hedging instrument immediately at the date of determination. Consequently, any fair value increases of the hedging instrument are unrealised. Decreases in fair value will need to be considered carefully to determine the extent to which they are realised by applying the guidance at 4.29 et seq.

5.21 The company holding the hedged item may not be as constrained, if at all, as to its actions as the company holding the hedging instrument. Nevertheless, it should be considered whether the company has the ability to meet condition (c) of the readily convertible to cash test at 3.12 above. Disposing of or closing out the hedged item would involve breaking the group hedge relationship and this may have adverse consequences for the group. If the company has the ability to dispose of or close out the hedged item at the date of determination and thus meet condition (c), any fair value increases of the hedged item are realised. On the other hand, if it is determined that condition (c) cannot be met, then any fair value increases of the hedged item are unrealised. Decreases in fair value will need to be considered carefully to determine the extent to which they are realised by applying the guidance at 4.29 et seq.

Historical cost accounting

Companies not applying IAS 39 or FRS 26 but which have stand-alone derivatives or non-derivative financial instruments measure those instruments at historical cost and apply historical cost accounting. This is equally true for those that are held as part of a group hedging relationship. They could include, for example, accounting for foreign exchange differences under SSAP 20 or debtors and creditors for interest rate differentials in interest rate swaps. The general realisation principles as set out at 3.3 to 3.12 apply and normally these profits and losses are realised. Where profits on derivative and non-derivative financial instruments are realised, directors should consider whether from a group perspective it is appropriate to distribute them." **5.22**

6. ISSUES ARISING FROM IAS 32 (and its equivalent, FRS 25) 6.1 – 6.87

Introduction

Under IFRSs, financial instruments are presented according to the substance of the contractual arrangement, determined by the rules in IAS 32. This may differ from their legal form. For example, redeemable preference shares bearing mandatory dividends are presented as liabilities in the balance sheet and their corresponding distributions as interest charges in the income statement because the issuer has no ability to avoid payment in cash of either the principal or distributions. The substance of the contractual arrangement is therefore debt. Also, compound financial instruments are accounted for under the relevant standards using "split accounting", whereby the proceeds of issue are split between a liability component and an equity component. Examples of compound financial instruments are convertible redeemable preference shares and convertible debt (assuming that the conversion feature itself meets the definition of equity in IAS 32). **6.1**

Under UK GAAP, FRS 25's requirements on debt and equity presentation are the same as those in IAS 32. **6.2**

The following guidance considers the implications for distributable profits of companies, for example, entering into contracts involving their own shares that may require classification in whole, or in part, as liabilities. **6.3**

The guidance summarises the ten key principles in relation to determining distributable profits when dealing with such contracts. The guidance then applies the principles to scenarios based on examples 1, 2, 4, 6 and 9 set out in the Illustrative Examples appendices to IAS 32 and FRS 25 involving contracts on own equity instruments. In addition, other scenarios are considered involving preference shares presented as liabilities, mandatorily redeemable preference shares and convertible preference shares. **6.4**

Appendix 2 to the guidance provides illustrations of the accounting and capital maintenance book-keeping entries for the eight scenarios referred to above. **6.5**

The ten principles underpinning the guidance in this section are set out below. The principles are split between those applying to all companies and those specific to **6.6** public companies resulting from the application of the net assets test of section 831 of the Act. The principles are those underlying statute and common law in respect of distributions and capital maintenance.

Assumptions

6.6A The contracts described in this section and in Appendix 2 do not contain a cash settlement option.

6.6B Any redemption of the relevant shares will be made out of profits available for distribution and not out of the proceeds of a fresh issue of shares for the purpose of the redemption unless the text in this section or in Appendix 2 otherwise indicates. Payment of any dividends and redemption amounts are contingent upon such payments/redemption being lawful under the Act at the time of payment/redemption, with, where appropriate, the relevant amount being deferred until such time as the Act's restrictions fall away.

6.6C The shares, contracts and convertible instruments described in this section and in Appendix 2 are denominated in the issuer's functional currency, pay dividends and are redeemed in that currency, and, where convertible are convertible into shares denominated in that currency. It is also assumed that there are no contingent settlement provisions (see paragraph 25 of IAS 32 and FRS 25) or alternate settlement options (see paragraph 26 of IAS 32 and FRS 25). The effect of foreign currency, contingent settlement provisions and/or alternate settlement options can have an impact on the accounting to deny equity treatment in certain cases.

Principles – General

6.7 **Principle 1 – A distribution or a capital repayment is not as a matter of law a loss, notwithstanding that it may be presented for accounting purposes as an interest charge in the income statement**

6.8 Section 830(2) of the Act provides that, "a company's profits available for distribution are its accumulated, realised profits, so far as not previously utilised by distribution or capitalisation, less its accumulated, realised losses, so far as not previously written off in a reduction or reorganisation of capital duly made." This is based on the premise that distributions are not losses. If distributions were losses they would be dealt with by the words "less its accumulated, realised losses," and thus the words "so far as not previously utilised by distribution" would be superfluous.

6.9 A distribution or capital repayment may on occasion be presented as an accounting loss. For example, in some cases dividends on a preference share are presented as interest charges in the profit and loss account. Notwithstanding the accounting presentation, such distributions or capital repayments remain, as a matter of law, distributions or capital repayments for the purposes of Part 23 of the Act. Accordingly, they are not counted as losses – and thus not as realised or unrealised losses – for the purposes of Part 23 of the Act.

6.10 **Principle 2 – An advance recognition of a future distribution or capital repayment is not a loss notwithstanding that it may be presented for accounting purposes as an interest charge in the income statement**

6.11 A distribution or capital repayment is not, as a matter of law, a loss. Thus the advance recognition of a future distribution or capital repayment is not a loss either.

Hence, the accrual, as an interest charge, of a dividend, or a foreign exchange translation difference, in respect of a preference share presented as debt is an advance recognition of a future distribution or capital repayment but it is not a loss for distribution purposes even though the accrual is charged as interest the profit and loss account.

Principle 3 – A distribution or a capital repayment consumes distributable profits when paid or when a dividend is declared by a company in general meeting 6.12

An accounting liability recognised for accrued unpaid dividends or a capital repayment is an advance recognition of a future distribution or capital repayment and is not, as a matter of law, a loss. 6.13

A distribution does not consume distributable profits until such time as, as a matter of law, the distribution occurs, e.g. when paid under the authority of the directors, under common form articles of association, or when declared by members in general meeting, or at an earlier date on which a legally binding liability to pay the dividend is established (see 2.10 above). 6.14

The repurchase price for shares does not consume distributable profits until such time as, as a matter of law, the distribution and/or capital repayment comprised in the price occurs. In particular, notwithstanding that there are arrangements in place that will lead to repurchase, the company is not liable to pay the purchase price, and thus distributable profits are not consumed, until the shares are actually repurchased or redeemed. It should be noted that the holder of the shares cannot sue for damages in the event of failure by the company to repurchase those shares (see section 735 of the Act). 6.15

Section 691(2) provides that where a limited company purchases its own shares, the shares must be paid for in cash on purchase. However, in the case of redeemable shares, section 686(2) provides that the terms of redemption may provide that the amount payable on redemption may, by agreement between the company and the holder of the shares, be paid in cash on a date later than the redemption date. This is a change from the 1985 Act which required payment on redemption. When payment on redemption is deferred, it is the current value of the redemption promise, at the redemption date, which determines the amount of distributable profits consumed. It is therefore the present value of the amount payable on redemption rather than its absolute amount which must be covered by distributable profits, at the redemption date, for the redemption to be permitted. 6.15A

Principle 4 – Premiums received by the issuer on written options to issue or repurchase own equity shares are profits when received 6.16

A premium received by the writer of an option over its own equity shares is regarded as a profit at law. This is because it is value received by the company otherwise than in payment up of a share and otherwise than for taking on a liability. In particular, a written put option is not, as a matter of law, a liability of the company; for example, the holder of the option cannot sue for damages in the event of failure by the company to repurchase the shares (see section 735 of the Act). 6.17

Thus to the extent that the premium is received in the form of qualifying consideration, it is a realised profit at the outset. 6.18

Principle 5 – When a company issues a compound financial instrument that is legally a debt, the original credit to equity determined using split accounting is not, as a matter of 6.19

law, a profit; the original credit to equity is eliminated as accounting charges, which are not as a matter of law losses, accrue upwards the amount recorded as a liability

6.20 The initial credit to equity is not an accounting profit because in accounting terms it is the equivalent of the issue of an equity instrument. As a matter of law there is not a profit either, because the proceeds received are in consideration for taking on a liability (in which respect it is distinctly different from a legally separate option contract addressed in Principle 4) albeit a liability that is not fully reflected as such in the accounts. The liability becomes fully reflected in the accounts through an additional interest charge that is not, as a matter of law, a loss because the full instrument that is legally a debt is reflected in the balance sheet at issue albeit in different places. Thus the cumulative debit in equity arising from these additional charges is available to eliminate the initial credit.

6.21 **Principle 6 – When a company issues a compound financial instrument that is legally a share, the original credit to equity determined using split accounting is share capital, and if applicable share premium; accounting charges made to accrue upwards the amount recorded for accounting purposes as a liability component, are not, as a matter of law, losses**

6.22 The initial credit to equity as a result of split accounting is share capital, and if applicable share premium, and is reflected as such. Subsequent accounting charges, to accrue upwards the amount recorded for accounting purposes as a liability component, are not, as a matter of law, losses because they are advance recognition of a future distribution or capital repayment.

6.23 In some circumstances, there may be a debit to be recognised in equity on an issue of shares to a parent company or fellow subsidiary, where the shares do not qualify to be classified in the accounts as equity of the issuer. The shares are recognised initially by the issuer as a liability at their fair value. However, the fair value may be greater than the proceeds received for their issue because the terms are off-market and, for example, involve redemption for significant amounts above the original proceeds and/or bear coupons that are substantial. In such circumstances, this difference between fair value and proceeds, a debit, is in effect advance recognition of future distributions and/or a future capital repayment and is recognised in equity. Consequently, this debit is not a loss at initial recognition. [Principle 2]. The debit will consume distributable profits either as dividends on the shares are made, which are distributions as a matter of law, or at the date of redemption (ie when the payments are set against the liability over time or at the end).[Principle 3]

Principles – Impact of Section 831 for public companies

6.24 **Principle 7 – The treatment of certain shares wholly as liabilities under IFRSs does not in itself affect the application of the section 831 of the Act net assets test for public companies and thus does not restrict distributable profits**

6.25 Section 831 states that a public company may only make a distribution at any time:

- if at that time the amount of its net assets is not less than the aggregate of its called-up share capital and undistributable reserves (as defined); and
- if, and to the extent that, the distribution does not reduce the amount of those assets to less than that aggregate.

6.26 Section 831 defines "net assets" for this purpose to mean the aggregate of the company's assets less the aggregate of its liabilities. By virtue of section 836, net assets for the purposes of section 831 are those shown in the "relevant accounts" prepared in accordance with applicable accounting standards; that is, its "IAS individual accounts", or its "Companies Act individual accounts". Therefore in the case of the issue of a financial instrument that is presented as debt in accordance with the substance of its contractual arrangements rather than their strict legal form, the company's net assets are unaffected for the purposes of section 831. This is because a liability is recorded (being in respect of the nominal value plus related share premium attributable to the shares) equal to the cash received as issue proceeds.

It is less clear from the drafting of section 831 whether there is any effect on the amount of a company's "share capital and undistributable reserves" arising from the issue of shares for which the presentation of share capital and related share premium is as a liability. In legal form there will have been an increase in share capital and related share premium. However, in accordance with section 836, the amount of share capital and undistributable reserves is determined by reference to the amount as stated in the company's relevant accounts. Accordingly, it appears that any amount of share capital and related share premium that has been presented as a liability should be excluded from the amount of share capital and undistributable reserves for the purposes of applying section 831. This is because the amount of share capital and undistributable reserves as stated in the relevant accounts excludes this amount. **6.27**

This interpretation of section 831 is consistent with the *"Guidance for British companies on changes to reporting and accounting provisions of the Companies Act 1985"* (originally issued by the DTI* in November 2004 and updated in August 2005†). The DTI's guidance states that "the interaction of section 264 and section 270(2) [of the 1985 Act, now sections 831 and 836(1) of the 2006 Act] is such that, where preference shares are classified as liabilities, they should be treated as such for the purposes of the net asset test, and should not be treated as part of called-up share capital and undistributable reserves for that purpose". **6.28**

Consequently the issue of shares with their nominal value and related share premium presented as debt does not result in an immediate restriction in the amount of profits available for distribution by a public company under section 831, because the issue leaves both net assets and share capital and undistributable reserves (as defined) unaffected. **6.29**

When the section 831 test comes to be applied to the repurchase or redemption of the shares, it should be borne in mind that whilst the repayment of the nominal value and issue premium on the shares will leave net assets unaffected, "share capital and undistributable reserves" will increase due to the recording of the capital redemption reserve and the inclusion in the share premium account within equity of the issue premium which has always existed and which is no longer required to be presented as a liability. Under section 831(1) the net assets must be at least equal to the "share capital and undistributable reserves" both before (sub-section (1)(a)) and after (sub-section (1)(b)) the repayment for it to be lawful. **6.30**

Principle 8 – A debit to equity arising from an advance recognition of a future distribution or capital repayment does not form part of share capital and undistributable reserves (as defined) for the purposes of section 831 and thus restricts distributable profits for public companies under that section **6.31**

**Now the Department for Business, Innovation & Skills.*

†*Guidance available from National Archives at: http://webarchive.nationalarchives.gov.uk/+/http://www.berr.gov.uk/files/file21617.doc*

6.32 Despite not representing a realised loss or a consumption of distributable profits, nevertheless an advance recognition of a future distribution or capital repayment restricts distributable profits for public companies. This is due to the advance recognition of the distribution as a liability, reducing net assets, but the corresponding debit to equity (via the income statement/profit and loss account) not reducing "share capital and undistributable reserves" as defined by section 831.

6.33 The above contrasts with Principle 1 because in the context of section 831, the Act gives precedence to the accounting presentation and this restricts the amount of the profits available for distribution.

6.33A The existence of any unrealised profits does not alter this situation (e.g., such unrealised profits cannot be applied to offset the deduction, because the deduction is not an unrealised loss).

6.34 The question may arise as to whether this restriction might operate to prevent the distribution or capital repayment in question when it comes to be made, e.g. because the effect might be that the surplus of net assets over "share capital and undistributable reserves" might be reduced to an amount less than the distribution or capital repayment to be made. However, there will be no restricting effect on the making of such amount of a distribution or capital repayment as has been recognised in advance, provided that immediately beforehand the net assets are not less than "share capital and undistributable reserves". This is because, accordingly, the company will meet the test in section 831(1)(a); and on the actual making of the distribution or capital repayment, which has previously been recognised as a liability, net assets are unaffected and thus remain no less than "share capital and undistributable reserves", thereby meeting section 831(1)(b). If the shares in question were originally classified as debt, then the operation of section 831 in relation to the original issue price is as described at 6.30 above.

6.35 **Principle 9 – On initial recognition, split accounting for compound financial instruments does not restrict distributable profits for public companies under section 831**

6.36 If the compound financial instrument is legally a share (for example, a redeemable preference share with discretionary dividends) and is split into its debt and equity components, at the outset there is no effect on distributable profits. The initial liability is matched by an equal amount of cash proceeds and there is no effect on net assets. In respect of the equity component, the initial credit to equity is, at law, share capital (and share premium) and is included in "share capital and undistributable reserves" for the purposes of the section 831 net assets test. This increase on one side of the net assets equation is balanced by the corresponding amount of cash proceeds which increases the company's net assets. Thus, "share capital and undistributable reserves" do not exceed net assets and therefore there is no restriction on distributable profits at the outset.

6.37 If the compound financial instrument is legally a debt (for example, a convertible debt) and it is split into its debt and equity components, the initial liability is exceeded by the amount of cash proceeds, equal in amount to that of the initial credit to equity, and accordingly there is an increase in net assets. However, in respect of the initial credit to equity itself, this does not form part of "share capital and undistributable reserves". As a result, an increase in net assets is recorded (being the difference between the consideration received and the liability recognised) with no corresponding increase in "share capital and undistributable reserves". Thus the issue of this instrument contributes an excess of net assets over "share capital and undistributable reserves". This has the effect of reducing any pre-existing restriction on distributable profits under section 831. However, where there is no pre-existing restriction, or such a restriction is more than eliminated by the issue of this instrument, distributable profits are not created; this is because section 831 has effect only to reduce the ability to distribute realised profits.

Principle 10 – The accretion of the liability component of compound financial instruments reduces distributable profits for public companies under section 831 unless the instrument is legally a debt **6.38**

Where the compound financial instrument is legally a share, the "interest charge" for the accretion of the liability component is not a loss as a matter of law [Principle 6] and has no effect on the amount shown as "share capital and undistributable reserves" in the relevant accounts. That is, the initial credit to equity (being share capital (and share premium)) cannot be used to absorb the accumulating "interest charge" debited to retained earnings (via the profit and loss account) due to the accretion of the liability. Hence, under the section 831 net assets test, the amount that a public company can distribute is restricted by the accumulated amount of the "interest charge" debit, which ultimately will be equal to the initial credit to equity. In other words, net assets are reduced but there is no corresponding reduction of 'share capital and undistributable reserves' and thus over time the cumulative restriction of distributable profits will equal the initial credit to equity. **6.39**

Where a compound financial instrument is legally a debt, the accretion of the liability is an accounting loss (although not a loss as a matter of law [Principle 5]) that reduces net assets for the purposes of the section 831 net assets test (see paragraph 6.33). However this eliminates the initial increase to net assets recorded as a result of the split accounting and thus of itself does not restrict distributable profits. **6.40**

Examples

The following examples illustrate the application of the ten principles described in 6.7 to 6.40 above. The first five examples addressed below are based on examples 1, 2, 4, 6 and 9 involving contracts on own equity instruments set out in the Illustrative Examples appendices to IAS 32 and FRS 25. Three further examples address preference shares presented as liabilities, mandatorily redeemable preference shares and convertible preference shares. The assumptions made at 6.6A to 6.6C above apply for the purposes of these examples. **6.41**

Appendix 2 provides illustrations of the accounting and statutory capital maintenance book-keeping entries for the eight examples. **6.42**

[Assumptions]

[Moved to 6.6A] **6.43**

[Moved to 6.6B] **6.44**

[Moved to 6.6C] **6.45**

Example 1 – Forward contract to repurchase own equity shares

Where a company enters into a forward contract to repurchase its own shares that are equity shares under the relevant standard, the standards require the company to set up a liability, at the outset, for the present value of the payment to be made (ie a discounted amount), with a corresponding debit taken directly to equity. The accounting effect is as if the equity shares had been repurchased immediately. **6.46**

6.47 The initial debit to equity, for the present value of the consideration payable, is not a realised loss. This is because the eventual payment is not a loss, but is in fact a distribution (or a capital repayment to the extent not out of distributable profits) [Principle 2].

6.48 Over time the (discounted) liability is accreted up to the eventual repayment amount, with a corresponding charge to finance expense (interest) in the profit and loss account (income statement). The accretion of the liability over time up to full value of the eventual redemption amount is presented as an accounting loss – it is shown as part of the interest charge. Again, however, the ultimate payment of the full amount is either a distribution or a capital repayment and is not therefore, as a matter of law, a loss nor, therefore, a realised loss. [Principle 2]

The effect on a public company

6.49 For a public company the effect is to restrict distributable profits. [Principle 8]

Combining the accounting and statutory capital maintenance entries to complete the repurchase of non-equity shares

6.50 When payment is made to repurchase the shares, it is, for accounting purposes, set against the liability. To the extent that the payment must, in law, come out of distributable profits, the debit in reserves (ie the initial debit to equity, together with the interest charge for the accretion) is set against and consumes distributable profits. To the extent that the payment must in law be charged to capital (e.g., funded by a fresh issue), then this debit is set against called-up share capital (and share premium as the case may be). Any necessary transfer from called-up share capital to capital redemption reserve is made in the usual way.

Example 2 – Written option to repurchase own equity shares

6.51 The accounting standards require the same accounting for a written option to repurchase equity shares as for a forward to repurchase equity shares (Example 1), save that in the case of the written option, any premium received at the outset is required to be taken directly to equity. So far as accounting for the repurchase price itself is concerned, the distributable profits considerations are the same as for the forward (see *Forward contract to repurchase own equity shares* at 6.46 *et seq* above).

6.52 The option premium is regarded as a profit at law and, to the extent that the premium is received in the form of qualifying consideration, is a realised profit. [Principle 4]. As a matter of law, the repurchase price for the shares is a future distribution or capital repayment. [Principle 3]

The effect on a public company

6.53 For a public company the effect of the recognition of the liability for the present value of the payment to be made and the subsequent accretion of the liability to the payment amount, is to restrict distributable profits. [Principle 8]

Example 3 – Forward contract to issue own equity shares

6.54 A forward contract to deliver, through a fresh issue of shares, a fixed number of the company's own equity shares in exchange for a fixed amount of cash meets the definition of an equity instrument in the relevant standard because it cannot be settled otherwise than through the delivery of shares in exchange for cash (see assumptions in *6.6A to 6.6C* above). Consequently, the right to receive the cash in a future accounting period is not recognised by the company, and the standards do not require accounting entries to be made until the forward contract matures, when the company receives cash and issues shares to the contract's counterparty.

Assuming the fair value of the forward contract at inception is zero, no cash is paid or received at that date, and thus no accounting entries are required on inception. Therefore, where a company enters into a forward contract to issue equity shares, the required accounting for such an arrangement raises no issues of distributable profits. **6.55**

The effect on a public company

There are no additional considerations for a public company. **6.56**

Example 4 – Written option to issue own equity shares

The relevant standards require the premium received on the writing of an option to issue own shares, that are presented as equity, to be credited directly to equity. The premium stays in equity regardless of whether the option ultimately is exercised or lapses, although it may be transferred between components of equity (ie between reserves). The premium, to the extent that it is received in the form of qualifying consideration, is, in law, a realised profit at the outset. [Principle 4] **6.57**

The effect on a public company

There are no additional considerations for a public company. **6.58**

Example 5 – Convertible debt

Under the relevant standards, an issuer of debt convertible into the issuer's own equity shares will use split accounting (see assumptions in 6.6A to 6.6C above). That is, part of the issue proceeds are recognised as a liability, with the balance recognised directly in equity at the date the convertible debt is issued, being the component deemed to relate to the written option to issue own equity shares (the equity conversion option). There is a correspondingly higher interest charge over the life of the debt because of the need also to charge the increase in the recorded amount of the liability as interest. That additional interest is an accounting loss but is not, as a matter of law, a loss. [Principle 5] **6.59**

The initial credit to equity is not a profit but as the liability component is fully reflected in the accounts, it offsets the additional interest charge. [Principle 5] **6.60**

The effect on a public company

There are no additional considerations for a public company. [Principle 10] **6.61**

Example 6 – Preference shares presented as liabilities

Where a company issues a class of preference shares that are redeemable at a specified date, or at the holders' option, and the dividends on the shares are non-discretionary and cumulative, IAS 32/FRS 25 requires that the company classifies **6.62** this class of shares as a liability (ie debt). Under IAS 39/FRS 26, the liability has to be carried at inception at its fair value, which will be the sum of the nominal value of the shares and any associated share premium where the shares have been issued at fair value. Over the life of the shares the non-discretionary dividend is accrued between each payment date and is presented in profit or loss as an "interest charge". A dividend when paid is set against the accrued liability.

6.63 To the extent that the preference shares are to be redeemed contractually at a premium, the liability will need to be accreted over time such that by redemption the carrying amount of the liability is equal to the redemption price. The accretion of the redemption premium attributable to an accounting period will be presented together with the accrued dividend as the "interest charge" for that period in profit or loss.

6.64 The presentation of the nominal value of, and any share premium associated with, the preference shares as debt has no effect on the determination of the company's realised profits and losses.

6.65 The accrued preference dividend (and any accrued redemption premium) that is presented as an "interest charge", and thus an accounting loss, is, as a matter of law, a distribution at the time of its making and not a loss. Thus such accruals do not affect the company's realised profits. [Principles 1, 2 and 3]

The effect on a public company

6.66 For a public company, the presentation of preference shares (ie the nominal value and any associated share premium) as debt does not result in an immediate restriction in the amount of profits available for distribution by a public company under section 831. [Principle 7]

6.67 Nevertheless, the effect of the accounting for the dividends (and any redemption premium) on the preference shares should be considered. The accounting liability recognised for the accrued unpaid preference dividend (and any redemption premium) is an advance recognition for accounting purposes of the eventual distribution (and/or capital repayment) and thus does not consume distributable profits until it is actually made as a distribution (or capital repayment). [Principle 3] However, profits available for distribution by a public company under section 831 will be restricted due to the reduction in net assets. [Principle 8]

Combining the accounting and statutory capital maintenance entries to complete the redemption

6.68 When payment is made to redeem the preference shares, it is for accounting purposes, set against the debt.

6.69 However, at redemption the law requires the following, where the redemption is made out of distributable profits:

- the nominal value of the redeemed shares is added to the capital redemption reserve; and
- the redemption price consumes distributable profits equal to its amount.

6.70 Therefore to reconcile these positions, the nominal value of the redeemed shares should be credited to the capital redemption reserve. Any share premium on the original issue of the shares now being redeemed should be credited to share premium account in equity at the date of redemption. The sum of the amounts added to the capital redemption reserve and added to share premium account is applied against retained earnings; this sum combined with the accumulated "interest charge" in respect of any redemption premium (which has built up in retained earnings over time) is equal to the amount of the redemption price that the law recognises as consuming distributable profits. As established earlier, the debit that builds up over time in retained earnings in respect of the redemption premium is the advance recognition of part of the redemption price and is disregarded as to its effect on distributable profits until the actual redemption takes place. [Principle 3]

Example 7 – Mandatorily redeemable preference shares

Under IAS 32/FRS 25, an issuer of mandatorily redeemable preference shares, which bear non-cumulative discretionary dividends, has a compound instrument and has to use split accounting (see assumptions in 6.6A to 6.6C above). That is, the standards require the company to set up a liability, at the outset, for the present value of the payment to be made on redemption of the shares. This will take into account any contractual premium to be paid on redemption. The difference between the proceeds received on issue of the shares and the net present value of the redemption amount is credited (or debited) directly to equity at the outset. Over time the (discounted) liability is accreted up to the contracted redemption price, with a corresponding "interest charge" being expensed in profit or loss. **6.71**

As a matter of law, all of the nominal value and any associated share premium of the preference shares are share capital and share premium irrespective of where they may now be presented in the balance sheet. Consequently, the initial credit to equity is share capital/share premium, albeit that it is the only part that is allowed by the relevant accounting standard to be shown as such, and is not a profit. The presentation of shares partly within liabilities and partly within equity has no effect on the determination of the company's realised profits and losses. **6.72**

The interest expense from the accretion up to the full amount of the redemption price is, however, presented as an accounting loss – it is shown as an "interest charge". Since the ultimate payment is either a distribution or a capital repayment, the interest charge is, as a matter of law, not a loss even though it is accounted for as if it were a loss. [Principle 2] **6.73**

The effect on a public company

For a public company, the effect of this IAS 32/FRS 25 accounting is to restrict the maximum amount of profits available for distribution over time by the amount of the cumulative accruals for the redemption price. [Principle 10] **6.74**

Combining the accounting and statutory capital maintenance entries to complete the redemption

For IAS 32/FRS 25 purposes, the payment to redeem the shares is set against the fully accreted liability. **6.75**

However, at redemption the law requires the following, where the redemption is made out of distributable profits: **6.76**

- no amount remains recorded in called-up share capital for the redeemed shares;
- the nominal value of the redeemed shares is added to the capital redemption reserve; and
- the redemption price consumes distributable profits equal to its amount.

6.77 Therefore to reconcile these positions, the nominal value of the redeemed shares should be credited to the capital redemption reserve in equity and the corresponding amount for this entry is used to eliminate the original credit to equity to the extent recorded as share capital (which is now cancelled share capital). Any share premium on the original issue of the shares now being redeemed, if hitherto presented as part of the liability, should be credited to share premium account in equity at the date of redemption. The sum of the amount added to the capital redemption reserve, but not used to make a corresponding elimination of the original credit to share capital, and that added to share premium account is applied against retained earnings; this sum, combined with the accumulated "interest charge" in respect of any redemption premium (which has built up in retained earnings over time) is equal to the amount of the redemption price that the law recognises as consuming distributable profits. As established earlier, the "interest charge" debit in retained earnings is the advance recognition of part of the redemption price and has no effect on cumulative realised profits until the actual redemption takes place.

Example 8 – Convertible redeemable preference shares

6.78 Under IAS 32/FRS 25, convertible redeemable preference shares are a compound instrument and an issuer of such instruments will use split accounting (see assumptions in 6.6A to 6.6C above). This is similar to debt convertible into an issuer's own equity instruments as described in 6.59 *et seq* above. That is, a liability is recognised for the debt component and a credit is recognised in equity for the equity component (the equity conversion option). However, the analysis for distributable profits purposes is more akin to that for the mandatorily redeemable shares with discretionary dividends described in 6.71 *et seq* above. This is because the initial credit to equity is share capital (and share premium).

6.79 It is assumed that the preference shares are convertible at any time by the holder into ordinary shares of the issuer and are mandatorily redeemed at the end of their term if not converted. The conversion feature cannot be settled other than by an exchange of the preference shares for a fixed number of the issuer's ordinary shares.

6.80 The presentation of the shares (inclusive of their share premium) as partly debt and partly as a credit in equity has no effect on the determination of realised profits and losses.

6.81 Any accrued unpaid preference dividends and the accretion up to the full amount of the redemption price, although presented as accounting losses through the profit and loss account, are disregarded in determining whether distributable profits have been consumed until their actual payment. [Principle 6]

The effect on a public company

6.82 At the outset there is no effect on distributable profits [Principle 9]. There will be a restriction for a public company on the maximum amount of profits available for distribution over time by the amount of the cumulative accruals for the redemption price. [Principle 10]

Combining the accounting and statutory capital maintenance entries where the shares are redeemed

6.83 The same analysis applies as given in 6.71 *et seq* in respect of the mandatorily redeemable preference shares with discretionary dividends.

Combining the accounting and statutory capital maintenance entries where the shares are converted

Under IAS 32/FRS 25, when the holders exercise their option to convert the preference shares into the issuer's ordinary shares, the amount of the liability at conversion is transferred to equity. **6.84**

However, to establish the impact on profits available for distribution it is necessary to re-analyse the aggregate entries in equity to establish the amounts that represent: **6.85**

- the nominal value of the ordinary shares issued on conversion;
- the relevant amount of share premium to be included in the share premium account; and
- the elimination of the "interest charge" debit in retained earnings.

This is achieved at conversion by crediting to retained earnings an amount equal to the accumulated "interest charge" in respect of accrued unpaid dividends and accretion to the issue price of the shares from the amount transferred from liabilities to equity. The aggregate of the balance of the transfer to equity and the initial credit to equity is equal to the total of the nominal value and share premium attributable to the ordinary shares issued on conversion. **6.86**

The allocation of part of the transfer from liabilities equal to the accrued "interest charge" effectively reverses the "interest charge" accounting entries. At law the debit accounting entries had not consumed distributable profits and therefore the effective reversal of these entries has no effect on the quantum of distributable profits. However, for public companies, the effective reversal of the "interest charge" debit at conversion removes the restriction under the section 831 net assets test. **6.87**

7. EMPLOYEE SHARE SCHEMES 7.1 – 7.56

ESOP trusts

Introduction

Paragraphs 7.4 to 7.45 are concerned with the effect of a company's sponsorship of a trust (ESOP trust) that holds shares in the company, which may be delivered to the company's employees under an employee share scheme. This differs from the case of the direct holding of a company's own shares (treasury shares) which are addressed at paragraphs 2.40 to 2.43 above. **7.1**

The practice of employing ESOP trusts evolved partly because of restrictions on a company acquiring its own shares (s658) or acquiring shares in its parent company (section 136). These restrictions were eased from 1 December 2003 when certain companies were permitted, subject to some restrictions, to hold their own shares as treasury shares (see above). The use of ESOP trusts has, however, remained widespread. **7.2**

The provision of funds by a company to an ESOP trust to enable it to buy shares in the company or its parent company will generally fall within the definition of financial assistance for the acquisition of own shares (section 677). Such assistance is generally prohibited, subject to certain exceptions, for a public company or a subsidiary of a public company (section 678). Under the 1985 Act, similar restrictions applied to all companies until 1 October 2008. However, one of the exceptions to the general rules in section 682(2)(b) is 'the provision by the company, in good faith in **7.2A** the interests of the company or its holding company, of financial assistance for the purposes of an employee's share scheme'.

7.3 That exception is subject to a restriction in section 682(1) that the financial assistance may only be given if the company has net assets which are not thereby reduced, or to the extent that those assets are thereby reduced, the financial assistance is provided out of distributable profits. Although paragraphs 7.25 to 7.31 address the interaction of this restriction with the accounting for ESOP trusts, the general question of the lawfulness of financial assistance is not within the scope of this guidance and accordingly directors may wish to consider seeking legal advice.

ESOP trusts under UK GAAP

7.4 Under UK GAAP, UITF Abstract 38 "Accounting for ESOP trusts" requires the sponsoring company of an ESOP trust to recognise the assets and liabilities of the trust in its own accounts whenever it had de facto control of those assets and liabilities. Where the trust purchases the company's own shares, the consideration paid for those shares should be deducted in equity until such time as the shares vest unconditionally in the company's employees. The effect of this deduction, which occurs in the individual accounts of the sponsoring company and not merely on consolidation, is considered below.

7.5 The sponsoring company of an ESOP trust may be a company other than the one whose shares are held by the trust. For example, a subsidiary may be the sponsoring company of an ESOP trust that holds shares in its parent. In this case the shares will not be "own shares" from the perspective of the subsidiary's financial statements. The shares would be recognised as an asset in the subsidiary's balance sheet and the issues addressed in this guidance would not arise.

ESOP trusts under IFRSs

7.6 The guidance set out below in relation to investments in own shares held through an ESOP trust will be relevant to companies reporting under IFRSs if they account for investments in own shares in their individual balance sheets in a manner similar to that required by UITF Abstract 38. However, published literature suggests that a different accounting treatment may be permitted in individual accounts under IFRSs. Whereas UITF Abstract 38 requires the assets and liabilities of the trust to be included in the individual balance sheet of the sponsoring company, under IFRSs it may be acceptable to account for the ESOP trust as an investment in a subsidiary. The IFRS Interpretations Committee was asked to address the question of which of these treatments is appropriate but declined to do so on the basis that it would be unable to reach a consensus on a timely basis given the different types of trusts and arrangements that exist in practice (see IFRIC Update, November 2006, for further details).

7.7 Where the ESOP trust is accounted for as a subsidiary, any loans to the trust by the sponsoring company, to the extent that they are regarded as recoverable, may therefore be recognised as assets in the individual balance sheet of the sponsoring company even though they have been used to finance an investment in own shares by the trust. If it is necessary to write the loan down for impairment at any time then that write down will represent a realised loss. The guidance set out below concerning the effects of a deduction within equity is not relevant when the loan is recognised as an asset because the deduction within equity will arise only in the consolidated financial statements

Note of legal considerations attached to Abstract 38

A note of legal considerations attached to Abstract 38 sets out legal advice that the UITF received on the implications for distributable profits when the accounting treatment required by the Abstract is followed. The note of legal considerations is reproduced in Appendix 3 to this guidance for reference. This guidance is consistent with that note of legal considerations but additionally addresses some issues that were not covered in that note as well as considering some issues in greater depth. **7.8**

The note of legal considerations attached to UITF Abstract 38 states that although the acquisition of shares by an ESOP trust will not, of itself, result in a realised profit or loss for the company concerned, "a company will still need to consider other transactions with the ESOP, for example a loan to the ESOP to fund acquisitions of shares, and these may affect the company's realised profits and losses". The reference to a loan to the ESOP might be read as implying that realised profits and losses should be determined by reference to "narrow entity accounting" (see 7.14 below). However, this is not the case; the UITF Abstract 38 note refers to the existence of a loan as only one of a number of factors that might be relevant. The assessment of realised profits and losses for the justification of a distribution is by reference to a company's "relevant accounts" and, as explained in paragraph 7.14 this means by reference to "extended entity accounting". However, see 7.25 to 7.31 regarding financial assistance by a public company. **7.8A**

Effect of deduction within equity on realised profits

A purchase of a company's own shares though an ESOP trust is not a distribution at law. This is because, at law, the shares have been purchased by the trust, notwithstanding that assistance may have been given by the company (by way of gift or loan, some or all of which may be ultimately irrecoverable, or by guarantee of the trust's borrowings that may ultimately be called upon to some extent). See 7.25 to 7.31 below for regulation of the transaction for a public company as financial assistance. **7.9**

Neither does such a purchase, of itself, give rise to an immediate realised loss. Therefore, such an acquisition does not reduce the amount of profits available for distribution under section 830. **7.10**

In addition, whilst the acquisition of shares will not, of itself, give rise to an immediate realised loss, the impact of other factors such as the granting of rights over those shares should be considered (see 7.37 to 7.41 below). **7.11**

Effect on section 831 restriction on purchase of own shares for a public company

The consideration paid on the purchase of shares by an ESOP trust sponsored by a public company will immediately restrict the profits available for distribution by virtue of section 831 by the amount of the consideration paid. As more fully explained below, there will be an immediate reduction in net assets but no change in share capital or undistributable reserves. **7.12**

A public company may only make a distribution at any time: **7.13**

(a) if at that time the amount of its net assets is not less than the aggregate of its called-up share capital and undistributable reserves; and
(b) if, and to the extent that, the distribution does not reduce the amount of those assets to less than that aggregate.

Change in net assets

7.14 Section 831 states that "net assets" means the aggregate of the company's assets less the aggregate of its liabilities. Under section 836, net assets are those as shown in the company's "relevant accounts" which are normally the last annual accounts under Part 15 of the Act, properly prepared under the Act; in certain circumstances, the relevant accounts are initial accounts or interim accounts, which are prepared to a similar standard. Net assets for the purposes of section 831 should therefore be determined in accordance with accounting standards and UITF Abstracts. Accordingly, the relevant accounts and the net assets should include the assets and liabilities of the ESOP trust as reported under Abstract 38 ("extended entity accounting") rather than, for example, any loan between the company and the ESOP trust ("narrow entity accounting").

7.15 The effect of the accounting treatment required by Abstract 38 is that, in drawing up the relevant accounts, any own shares held by an ESOP would be recorded as a deduction in arriving at shareholders' funds rather than as an asset. Therefore, it follows that the relevant aggregate net asset amount for the purposes of the definition in section 831(2) would be reduced by the own shares held (being the consideration paid for the shares).

7.16 Disclosure by way of note that the company also has an "asset" of own shares held through an ESOP trust would not restore the net assets for the purposes of section 831 (see 2.14 above). If the shares are not an asset for accounting purposes they cannot be an asset for the purposes of calculating net assets when applying section 831.

Change in share capital or undistributable reserves

7.17 A company's undistributable reserves are defined in section 831. In short, they include the company's unrealised profits less its unrealised losses, except that this amount is never less than zero (ie net unrealised losses are not within the definition).

7.18 The correct characterisation, as a matter of law, of the deduction in equity is not straightforward. On the one hand the deduction should not be characterised as a loss at all (thereby rendering redundant questions of realisation) because from the point of view of the company's individual accounts (which are on an extended entity basis) the company has not lost control of the shares nor have these shares suffered any objectively measurable diminution in value. On the other hand, given that the applicable accounting treatment does not permit the company to treat the shares as an asset, some might argue that the deduction should be categorised as a loss, although the nearest equivalent could be said to be a return of capital. The characterisation which gives primacy to the substance rather than presentation is the view to be preferred and accordingly the deduction should not be characterised as a loss.

7.19 Accordingly, the deduction for own shares in equity is neither a realised loss nor an unrealised loss and does not affect the balance of undistributable reserves.

The effect on profits available for distribution under section 831

7.20 Thus with net assets reduced but share capital and undistributable reserves unaffected, the purchase of ESOP shares affects the maximum distribution permissible by virtue of the application of section 831 (the "maximum distribution permissible"). In other words, the effect of the section is such that the profits available for distribution are restricted by a reduction in net assets that is neither a realised nor an unrealised loss.

Furthermore, the existence of any unrealised profits does not alter this situation (e.g., such unrealised profits cannot be applied to offset the deduction, because the deduction is not an unrealised loss). 7.21

Effect on section 831 restriction on subscription for own shares for a public company

A subscription for new shares in a public company by its own sponsored ESOP trust will immediately restrict the maximum distribution permissible. 7.22

The application of section 831 is considered above. In the case of a subscription for new shares, there is no change in net assets. This is because the cash subscribed for the shares by the ESOP trust is recorded in the balance sheet of the sponsoring company both before and after the subscription in accordance with Abstract 38. 7.23

However, the amount of the company's called-up share capital is increased by the nominal value of the shares issued to the trust. The amount of the company's undistributable reserves is also increased to the extent of any share premium arising on the issue, for example where the ESOP trusts subscribes for the shares at market value which is at a premium to nominal value. There is no other effect of the subscription on undistributable reserves as defined in section 831. Consequently, any excess of the company's net assets over the aggregate amount of the company's called-up share capital and undistributable reserves is reduced and hence the amount of the company's maximum distribution permissible is restricted by the amount attributable to the share issue (ie the proceeds of subscription for the shares by the trust). 7.24

The effect of the financial assistance rules in relation to a public company

Assuming that the relevant assistance is permitted by virtue of section 682(2), in the case of a public company the assistance can only be given if the company has net assets which are not thereby reduced or, to the extent that those assets are thereby reduced, if the assistance is provided out of distributable profits. 7.25

Net assets

For the purposes of section 682, "net assets" are defined as the amount by which the aggregate of the company's assets exceeds the aggregate of its liabilities, taking the amount of both its assets and liabilities to be as stated in the company's accounting records immediately before the financial assistance is given. This is in contrast to section 831 where, by reason of section 836, net assets are the aggregate of the company's assets less the aggregate of its liabilities as shown in the company's relevant accounts. 7.26

Section 386 imposes a duty to keep accounting records which are sufficient to show and explain the company's transactions and to enable the directors to ensure that any balance sheet and profit and loss account prepared under Part 15 of the Act complies with the requirements of the Act. Thus the records must at least be consistent with accounting standards and interpretations by the UITF or the IFRS Interpretations Committee as the case may be. However, this does not impose an obligation to maintain the entries in the accounting records fully in accordance with accounting standards and interpretations provided that it is evident from those 7.27

records how to make suitable adjustments to prepare accounts in accordance with the requirements of the Act. Accordingly, section 386 does not require net assets for the purposes of section 682 to be determined by reference to "extended entity accounting" (as described at 7.14 above).

7.28 Thus, in the absence of any such requirement, the company's assets and liabilities should be given their natural meaning, namely the assets and liabilities of the company as a legal person. In other words, the "narrow entity accounting" basis is used for determining the net asset position of the company concerned and whether the financial assistance has reduced the company's net assets*. There is thus in this respect no change to the assessment of a company's net asset position as a result of applying Abstract 38.

The effect of section 831 where financial assistance is provided out of distributable profits.

7.29 Where a company has provided financial assistance out of distributable profits which has reduced its net assets and shares have been acquired by an ESOP trust, section 831 does not require a further restriction in the maximum distribution permissible equal to the amount of the reduction in net assets calculated under section 682.

7.30 Section 682 and section 831 are directed to different objectives. Section 682 determines the legality of the provision of financial assistance tested on a narrow entity basis. Section 831 determines the maximum distribution permissible tested on an extended entity basis. On the extended entity basis the assistance provided to the ESOP trust will not be treated as having been paid away until the shares are purchased at which point the net assets are reduced by the consideration paid for the shares (as described at 7.12 to 7.21 above).

7.31 Section 840 contains accumulation rules where distributions are proposed by reference to particular accounts and prior distributions have taken place. Section 840(2) makes it clear that financial assistance which is given out of distributable profits is taken into account in the accumulation rules. These rules continue to apply.

7.32 [Deleted]

Purchase by an ESOP trust of shares held as treasury shares by a listed public company

7.33 A purchase of treasury shares by an ESOP trust for cash will be a sale of treasury shares for cash for the purposes of section 731 (see paragraph 7.34 below). The proceeds will therefore increase distributable profits up to an amount equal to the original purchase price of the shares (ie reversing the decrease that would have occurred at the time of purchase of the treasury shares). Any excess will be credited to share premium. At the same time, the former treasury shares, now shares held by the ESOP trust, will be accounted for and treated for distributable profit purposes just as if they had been purchased at the same price from a third party, ie the entire consideration paid by the ESOP trust restricts the amount of profits available for distribution (see 7.12 to 7.31 above).

**More generally, the presentation of shares as liabilities reduces net assets as defined in section 682 for the purposes of financial assistance. The legislation refers to amounts stated in the accounting records rather than in the 'relevant accounts' because the test is a 'real time' one. However, subject to the use of 'narrow entity accounting' as described above, net assets as defined in section 682 for the purposes of financial assistance should generally be the same as net assets as defined in section 831 for the purposes of distributions by a public company. That is, the relevant shares should be treated as liabilities to creditors.*

Section 727(1) states that where shares are held as treasury shares, a company may at any time "(a) sell the shares... for a cash consideration or (b) transfer the shares ... for the purposes of or pursuant to an employees' shares scheme". Section 729(1) states that where shares are held as treasury shares the company may at any time "cancel the shares". Section 731 deals with the treatment of the proceeds when shares "are sold" and requires any excess over the purchase price to be credited to share premium, with the remainder to replenish distributable profits. No treatment is otherwise specified for the proceeds when shares are "transferred" to an employee share scheme in accordance with section 727(1)(b). Section 731 does not apply exclusively to sales falling solely within section 727(1)(a) but applies to any sale of treasury shares to an ESOP trust notwithstanding that the sale might also be a transfer under section 727(1)(b). 7.34

The requirement in section 731 to transfer an amount to share premium when shares are sold for more than their purchase price applies only to treasury shares. Such a transfer is not required, or permitted, when shares held by an ESOP trust are sold in comparable circumstances. Whether or not the resulting surplus in the trust is a distributable profit from the perspective of the company is addressed at 7.42 to 7.45 below. 7.35

Effect on distributable profits for a public company when proceeds are received for sale of shares by an ESOP trust

In the case of a public company, the initial acquisition of the ESOP shares would have an immediate effect on distributable profits under section 831 because net assets were reduced without a corresponding reduction in share capital and undistributable reserves (see 7.12 to 7.21 above). However, if option holders then subscribe for the shares or the shares are sold in the market, the receipt of proceeds gives rise to an accounting entry (debit cash, credit shareholders' funds) that reverses the situation and restores distributable profits to the extent of those proceeds. That is, net assets are increased for the purposes of section 831 but there is no corresponding increase in share capital and undistributable reserves. 7.36

Realised loss when shares held by an ESOP trust are transferred to employees – where shares originally acquired externally

The purchase of shares by an ESOP trust does not, of itself, give rise to a realised loss (see 7.10 above) and, other than in the case of a public company, does not otherwise immediately affect the distribution of available profits. However, it is clear that if the shares are to be transferred to employees for less than their purchase price, the shortfall will at some time fall to be treated as a realised loss. In some cases options may be granted with an exercise price that is lower than the price at which the shares were purchased. In other cases shares may be transferred to employees for no consideration on the achievement of specified performance or service conditions. In all such cases, the difference between the purchase price of the shares and the proceeds received or receivable from the employee should be regarded as becoming a realised loss over the relevant amortisation or charging period as would be the case with a cash bonus that was contingent on future service. 7.37

[Deleted] 7.38

Where options have been granted over the shares in question but those options are "out-of-the-money" or where there are "surplus" shares that have not been allocated 7.39

to any particular share scheme, a realised loss may also arise if the market value of the shares falls below their purchase price. A realised loss will have arisen to the extent that the fall in market price below cost is not expected to be reversed and thus that part of the cost incurred is not expected to be recovered.

7.40 [Moved to 7.8A]

Realised loss when shares held by an ESOP trust are transferred to employees – where shares originally subscribed

7.41 The subscription for shares by an ESOP trust does not, of itself, give rise to a realised loss (see 7.10 above) and, other than in the case of a public company, does not otherwise immediately affect the distribution of available profits. However, as in the case of a purchase of shares described at 7.37 to 7.39 above, a realised loss may arise if the shares are subsequently transferred to employees for less than their subscription price. In all such cases, the difference between the subscription price of the shares and the proceeds received from the employee should be regarded as becoming a realised loss over the relevant amortisation or charging period.

Whether a surplus on disposal of shares by an ESOP trust is a realised and distributable profit from the perspective of the sponsoring company

7.42 As explained at 7.44, a surplus on disposal of shares held by an ESOP trust is a realised profit. However, in respect of it being distributable, the directors should have regard to their wider common law duties as required by sections 851 and 852. As explained at 7.45, the profit therefore may not become distributable until some time in the future.

7.43 Under Abstract 38, a sponsoring company includes the assets, liabilities and transactions of its ESOP trust in its accounts as if the trust were a division or branch of the company. This is therefore not just a matter of including the trust in consolidated accounts. The assets, liabilities and transactions of the trust are included in the company's individual accounts. These are the "relevant accounts" for the purposes of determining profits available for distribution. Where the trust has a surplus in the equivalent of its profit and loss account, the question arises of whether this should be reflected in the calculation of the company's realised profits.

7.44 Where the trust has a surplus (e.g. from the sale of shares at more than their purchase price), it is arguable that, just as a parent would not treat a surplus in a subsidiary as a realised profit in its own individual accounts, the parent should not regard the surplus in the trust as increasing its realised profits. But there is a clear difference in that Abstract 38 requires the assets and liabilities of the trust to be included in the company's own individual accounts. Also, Abstract 13, which was superseded by Abstract 38 and required own shares to be recognised as assets, made no mention of any legal difficulties about including any "profits" of the trust in the company's profit and loss account. Under Abstract 38, no such profits arise to be included in the company's profit and loss account but the issue is still relevant to the determination of the company's realised profits. Where the consideration received by the trust for the sale of the shares is in the form of cash (or other "qualifying consideration") that will be included in the company's balance sheet in accordance with the requirements of Abstract 38, the profit will be a realised profit from the company's perspective.

7.45 However, the directors should have regard to their wider common law duties as required by sections 851 and 852 (see 2.1 above). It would not be regarded as prudent to distribute an amount that represents assets that are retained in the ESOP trust and therefore not available for the general purposes of the company. If the assets of the trust are used in future to meet an expense, an equivalent amount of the gain should at that time be treated as distributable. Therefore to the extent that the realised loss arising from the expense does not exceed the previously recognised gain that was treated as undistributable, there will be no reduction in distributable profits.

Expenses for share based payments required by IFRS 2 and FRS 20

IFRS 2 (and FRS 20) require expenses to be recognised in profit or loss for cash-settled share-based payment arrangements. The credit entry will be either a cash payment or a provision. The expense recognised will therefore be a realised loss. The paragraphs which follow are concerned with equity-settled arrangements. **7.46**

IFRS 2 (and FRS 20) require expenses to be recognised in profit or loss for equity-settled share-based payment arrangements. The standard requires the credit entry arising from recognition of this expense to be credited within equity but does not specify any particular component of equity. **7.47**

Any expense recognised in accordance with IFRS 2 will be a realised loss. This follows from the principle that all losses should be regarded as realised losses except to the extent that the law, accounting standards or this guidance provide otherwise (see 3.10 above). However, the overall impact of the IFRS 2 expense on distributable profits will depend on the status of the credit entry in equity. **7.48**

If the consideration for an issue of shares is, as a matter of law, the provision of goods or services to the company, it will be necessary to credit share capital and share premium with the fair value of those goods or services. Similarly, if shares are, as a matter of law, issued in settlement of a monetary liability, it will be necessary to credit share capital and share premium with the amount of the liability discharged. Where this is so, the credit entry to equity required by IFRS 2 cannot be a realised profit. **7.49**

In the case of share options, the note of legal considerations appended to UITF Abstract 17 (now superseded by FRS 20) provided the following guidance*. **7.50**

> "The UITF has received legal advice on the implications for share premium account when the accounting treatment required by this Abstract is followed. It has been advised that where new shares are issued in connection with an employee share scheme the share premium account will normally have to reflect only the cash subscribed for the shares (e.g. by the employee or by an ESOP). In such cases, any difference between the cash subscribed for the shares (which must be at least as much as the nominal value, as shares cannot be issued at a discount) and the fair value at the date of grant of rights should be credited to reserves other than the share premium account. This is on the basis that the services of the employee do not, as a matter of law, form part of the consideration received for the shares issued, and the UITF has been advised that this would be the usual legal interpretation of such transactions. Exceptionally, however, the terms of a transaction might be such as to lead to the opposite interpretation, and companies may need to take legal advice on this point. In such a case, the operation of section 99(2) of the Companies Act 1985 [now section 585(1) of the Companies Act 2006] [prohibition of public company accepting undertaking to perform services in payment up of its shares] and section 103 [now section 593 of the Companies Act 2006] [non-cash

**The equivalent 2006 Act references have been added to the original note for ease of reference.*

consideration to be valued before allotment of shares] would also have to be considered."

However, the arrangements referred to in the last two sentences of the quoted paragraph are not typical. Instead, for example, in the case of share options, the credit to equity required by IFRS 2 will usually be a credit to reserves other than share premium account.

7.51 The note of legal considerations does not, however, address whether the credit to equity in the case of options to subscribe for shares is a realised profit. However, an unrealised reserve will be treated as having become realised by the amortisation or writing down of the related asset (see 3.9(f) above). Therefore, assuming that the IFRS 2 expense has been included in profit or loss (which would be the case except where the charge had been capitalised as part of the cost of production of an asset) the credit entry in equity will be a realised profit. The IFRS 2 expense will therefore have no net effect on distributable profits.

7.52 The manner of settlement (e.g. subscription for new shares or purchase of shares in the market by an ESOP trust) does not affect the expense recognised under IFRS 2 or whether this is a realised loss. However, it will be necessary to consider the effect on realised profits arising from any shares held by an ESOP trust (see 7.37 to 7.41 above).

Intra-group recharges for share-based payments

7.53 In November 2006, the IFRS Interpretations Committee issued IFRIC 11 "IFRS 2 – Group and Treasury Share Transactions" which has subsequently been incorporated into IFRS 2. The Exposure Draft upon which this was based (IFRIC D17) included some material on the treatment of inter-company recharges made within groups in connection with share-based payment arrangements. The IFRS Interpretations Committee decided not to address these issues in IFRIC 11 because it did not wish to widen the scope of the Interpretation to an issue that relates to accounting for intra-group payments generally. The appropriate accounting for such recharges is thus a matter of developing practice, including that in some cases the treatment that was set out in the draft guidance in IFRIC D17, described below, may be appropriate.

7.54 The situation in question is one in which the company, being a subsidiary, makes a cash payment to its parent in relation to a share-based payment in favour of the company's own employees and where IFRS 2 requires an equity-settled share-based payment charge in the company's accounts. The proposals in IFRIC D17 envisaged that where a charge is made by the parent to the subsidiary which exceeds the expense that the subsidiary is required to recognise under IFRS 2, the excess is accounted for by the subsidiary as a distribution. For example, this may arise if a charge is made on the basis of intrinsic value at exercise date which will generally be higher than the grant date fair value recognised as an expense in accordance with IFRS 2. The accounting treatment of any such charge does not affect whether or not it is a distribution as a matter of law. In particular, if there is a commercial basis for such a charge, it will not be a distribution as a matter of law. An example of a commercial basis would be the expense that the subsidiary would have incurred if it had purchased shares in the market to satisfy the options. Consequently, it will not be unlawful for the subsidiary to make the reimbursement payment, even in the absence of distributable profits, provided that the payment is not a distribution as a matter of law.

However, the entire reimbursement payment will have the effect of reducing accumulated realised profits or increasing accumulated realised losses of the subsidiary. The debit to equity arising from the payment will first reduce the credit in equity arising from IFRS 2 which will no longer be available to offset the realised loss recognised as a result of the IFRS 2 expense. Any debit to equity in excess of this amount will be a realised loss even though it will not have been accounted for as a loss in the financial statements. **7.55**

A liability may be recognised by the subsidiary where the parent has a contractual right to reimbursement at a future date. The amount of the realised loss at any date will generally be based on the amount of the liability recognised at that date but the particular facts of each case should be considered. **7.56**

8. RETIREMENT BENEFIT SCHEMES 8.1 – 8.26

Introduction

The guidance in this section is written in terms of compliance with FRS 17 but is equally applicable when the equivalent international standard IAS 19 'Employee benefits' is being applied. When IAS 19 is being applied, the guidance should be applied to the amounts reported under that standard. For simplicity, this guidance refers throughout to the relevant requirements of FRS 17. **8.1**

The guidance set out below applies both to pension schemes acquired in a business combination and those that are started by the reporting company. **8.2**

Defined contribution schemes

For defined contribution retirement benefit schemes, the cost charged to the profit and loss account under FRS 17 is equal to the contributions payable to the scheme for the accounting period. The charge to the profit and loss account for the contributions payable is a realised loss. **8.3**

Multi-employer schemes

Under FRS 17, some companies account for their participation in certain multi-employer defined benefit retirement benefit schemes as if they were defined contribution schemes. Where a scheme meets the criteria for this treatment in FRS 17, the position as regards realised profits and losses will be the same as for any other defined contribution scheme. **8.4**

Defined benefit schemes

Summary

In summary, what is required in relation to a defined benefit scheme is to identify whether any adjustment is required to reserves, to exclude unrealised profits, in arriving at the amount of distributable profits. To do so, it is first necessary to ascertain the cumulative amounts charged or credited in relation to the pension scheme, whether through the profit and loss account or through the statement of total recognised gains and losses (ie the total amounts taken to reserves). Paragraphs 8.11 to 8.13 determine whether that cumulative amount is realised or unrealised, with the test being different for cumulative net debits as against cumulative net credits. The cumulative net debit or credit will not be readily apparent from the accounts and so paragraphs 8.14 to 8.15 provide that it is determined from the movement in the **8.5** pension scheme asset or liability on the balance sheet since inception of the scheme (ie when it is started by the company or when it was acquired in a business combination) and the cumulative net cash paid to the scheme. The cumulative cash flows may themselves be difficult to obtain and so paragraphs 8.16 to 8.17 provide a method of estimating the amounts. Paragraph 8.18 then describes some circumstances when it is possible to deduce easily, without working through these procedures, that all amounts accumulated in reserves are realised.

8.5A This calculation is unaffected by the date of adoption of FRS 17 and the accounting adopted previously (ie SSAP 24). A company may have established the cumulative amount in reserves for the pension scheme on adoption of FRS 17 in which case the amount can be rolled forward from year to year. However, the approach set out below will enable the position to be established at a particular date if no such calculation was performed.

General principles

8.6 It is the cumulative gain or loss credited or debited to reserves in respect of a pension scheme, rather than the existence of a surplus or deficit, that affects the realised profits and losses of a company. This principle is illustrated in Appendix 4.

8.7 The effect of FRS 17 on reserves must be calculated to identify whether any adjustment in respect of pensions is needed to reported reserves to arrive at realised reserves. No adjustment is required if a net cumulative loss has been taken to reserves. If a net cumulative gain has been taken to reserves, and under the guidance set out at 8.12 below that gain is in part or in full unrealised, a deduction equivalent to the unrealised element must be made to reserves in assessing the level of realised reserves.

8.8 In establishing the impact that a surplus or deficit under FRS 17 has on a company's realised profits, it is therefore necessary to:

(a) identify the cumulative net gain or loss taken to reserves in respect of the pension surplus or deficit; and
(b) establish the extent to which that gain or loss is realised.

8.9 Although the various elements making up the changes in the defined benefit asset or liability are disclosed separately in the performance statements (see paragraph 50 of FRS 17), it is the net amount that represents the cost to the company of the pension promise. Thus it is the cumulative net gain or loss taken to reserves that falls to be categorised as realised or unrealised. There is no need to distinguish that cumulative balance between amounts charged or credited in the profit and loss account and those recognised in the statement of total recognised gains and losses (STRGL). The entries in the STRGL are considered for this purpose as revisions of past estimates of the net pension cost and are not precluded from being treated as realised simply because they have passed through the STRGL rather than the profit and loss account.

8.10 The impact on reserves is not usually the same as the pension asset or liability recognised in the balance sheet. It will be different due to the net contributions paid to the scheme (see 8.15 *et seq*) and any asset or liability introduced as the result of a business combination (see 8.19 *et seq*).

8.11 A cumulative net debit in reserves in respect of the pension scheme constitutes a realised loss as it results from the creation of, or an increase in, a provision for a liability or loss resulting in an overall reduction in net assets. This follows from 2.32, 3.10 and 3.15(d) above.

A cumulative net credit in reserves in respect of the pension scheme constitutes a realised profit only to the extent that it is represented by an asset to be recovered by refunds that have been agreed by the pension scheme trustees at the balance sheet date of the relevant accounts and the refunds will take the form of qualifying consideration. This follows from 3.9(a) above which refers to "a transaction where the consideration received by the company is 'qualifying consideration'". An asset that is recognised based on a reduction in future contributions or on expected refunds that are not agreed at the balance sheet date will not meet the definition of 'qualifying consideration'. **8.12**

To the extent that a cumulative net credit in reserves exceeds any such agreed refunds it is unrealised, but it becomes realised in subsequent periods to the extent that it offsets subsequent net debits to reserves being recognised as realised losses in respect of the pension scheme (ie as the cumulative net credit reduces). This follows from 3.9(f)(iii) and (iv) above. **8.13**

To establish the effect on realised profits at a particular date, a company must therefore establish the cumulative net credit or debit in reserves for the pension scheme at that date. This equals the amount of the surplus or deficit recognised before taking account of deferred tax, adjusted for: **8.14**

(a) cumulative net contributions less refunds made in respect of the pension scheme; and
(b) in the rare cases in which the company has recognised a pension asset or liability in its individual accounts on the acquisition of an unincorporated business (in respect of the pension scheme of that business), the amount initially recognised (see 8.19 and 8.20 below).

An illustration of such a calculation is set out in Appendix 4. As explained at 8.18 below, it will often be obvious, without any calculations, that all of the amounts included in reserves arising from pension scheme accounting are realised.

Companies that are able to establish the precise amount of the cumulative net credit or debit in reserves in respect of the pension scheme will treat it as realised or unrealised in accordance with 8.11 to 8.13 above. **8.15**

It may not be practicable for companies with long-established schemes to ascertain the total cumulative net contributions less refunds made since the scheme commenced, to perform with precision the analysis in 8.13 above (although, in view of their rarity, it is likely that the company would be able to identify all refunds made and these should be included in the calculation). For such schemes the estimated approach set out in this paragraph may be taken: **8.16**

(a) the calculation set out in 8.14 above may be performed initially using the amount of those cumulative net contributions the company has been able to identify; and
(b) that calculation may be revisited subsequently, as set out in 8.17 below, if further contributions are identified that were made prior to the date of the assessment.

A company adopting the estimated approach set out at 8.16 above might be able to revise that estimate subsequently by identifying additional contributions that have been made since the scheme was established or acquired. If so, it may be able to revise upwards the amount of a net cumulative realised loss in reserves and therefore **8.17** treat as realised net credits arising in subsequent periods that would otherwise be treated as unrealised.

8.18 It will often be obvious, without any calculations, that all of the amounts included in reserves arising from pension scheme accounting are realised. Therefore, no adjustments will be required to the amounts stated in the accounts when determining the cumulative amount of realised profits available for distribution. Other than sometimes in those rare cases where a pension asset or liability has been recognised in the company's individual accounts on a past acquisition, no adjustment is necessary if a liability is recognised in the balance sheet (ie because the net cumulative contributions cannot be negative). Where a pension asset is recognised in the balance sheet, it is only necessary to determine that the cumulative net contributions exceed this amount to be able to confirm that no adjustment is necessary. The calculations are more complex when a past acquisition is involved.

Acquisition of an unincorporated business

8.19 Where part of a company's pension asset or liability arose on the acquisition of an unincorporated business, it will have been recorded initially at fair value as required by FRS 7. That initial asset or liability will not have affected the company's reserves directly and must therefore be taken into account as part of the adjustment in arriving at the impact of FRS 17 on reserves.

8.20 FRS 17 did not change the requirement of FRS 7 to record the pension asset or liability at fair value, although it may have required fair value to be measured using a different method from that used when the acquisition was first recorded. FRS 17 paragraph 97 notes that any difference between the FRS 17 measure of fair value and that originally used "should be treated as a change in assumptions (ie an actuarial gain or loss) arising since acquisition". Such a difference will therefore have given rise to a gain or loss that falls to be categorised as realised or unrealised in accordance with the general approach noted above. As a result, it is the asset or liability recognised initially as part of the acquisition accounting that is taken into account (together with the net contributions paid since acquisition) in assessing the reserves position under FRS 17.

8.20A An actuarial gain arising from a reduction of a pension liability that was assumed in a business combination will result is an unrealised profit to the extent that it is not a reversal of post-acquisition pension expense. That is because such a reduction in a pension liability is not readily convertible to cash (see 3.9(g) and 3.9B).

Deferred tax

8.21 The deferred tax asset or liability arising from different treatments of pension costs for accounting and tax purposes generally relates to the pension asset or liability in the balance sheet and is not necessarily associated with the cumulative net debit or credit in reserves.

8.22 The cumulative debit in reserves in respect of a deferred tax liability relating to a pension asset should be treated as a realised loss. However, to the extent that there is an unrealised cumulative net credit in reserves in respect of the pension asset, then the amount of the debit in respect of deferred tax should be treated as a reduction in that unrealised profit rather than as a realised loss. It is not necessary to restrict the offset by applying the tax rate to the amount of the unrealised profit.

The cumulative credit in reserves in respect of a deferred tax asset relating to a pension liability should be treated as an unrealised profit. However, to the extent that there is a realised cumulative net debit in reserves in respect of the pension liability, then the amount of the credit in respect of deferred tax should be treated as a reduction in that realised loss rather than as an unrealised profit. It is not necessary to restrict the offset by applying the tax rate to the amount of the realised loss. **8.23**

The approach set out above is consistent with 3.17 above. **8.24**

Companies with more than one scheme

This guidance assumes the company has only one scheme. A company that operates more than one defined benefit scheme should assess separately for each scheme the impact of an FRS 17 asset or liability on its realised profits and losses. However, there may be situations where two schemes are to merge. In such situations a company may treat any net credit to reserves that has been recorded in respect of one scheme as a reduction in the realised loss caused by a net debit in respect of the other scheme from the point at which the trustees of the schemes have irrevocably agreed that they will merge and to extent that the surplus and deficit are permitted to be offset for funding purposes. A similar argument applies in cases where a transfer has been irrevocably agreed between different schemes. **8.25**

A company that operates more than one defined benefit scheme may find that it can follow 8.11 to 8.13 above for schemes formed or acquired in an acquisition of an unincorporated business relatively recently but may need to follow 8.16 above for schemes operated by the company for a longer time. This guidance does not preclude such a mixed approach. **8.26**

9. INTRA-GROUP TRANSACTIONS 9.1 – 9.44D

Introduction

Under both common law and statute, distributions are made by companies and not by groups. The group accounts are therefore not relevant for the purpose of determining realisation or distributability; for example, realised profits which are reflected in a parent's* own accounts may be eliminated in the group accounts, and profits retained by subsidiaries are not distributable by the parent. **9.1**

The ability of a parent to control the actions of its subsidiary must also be borne in mind when considering the substance of an intra-group transaction carried out by or with that subsidiary. **9.2**

It is not practicable to attempt to illustrate every circumstance in which difficulties may arise in determining whether a profit is realised. The principles set out in this guidance should be applied in relation to the group company seeking to establish a realised profit. In particular, the principle in paragraph 3.5 (linkage etc) and the related guidance at 3.43 to 3.75 should be applied. The examples which follow are intended to illustrate the factors to be considered in determining whether intra-group transactions give rise to realised profits. **9.3**

**The terms "parent" and "subsidiary" refer respectively to a "parent undertaking" and a "subsidiary undertaking" as defined in section 1162 of the Act.*

Cash pooling arrangements and group treasury functions

9.4 Groups of companies often operate cash pooling arrangements and group treasury functions. An example of such an arrangement is where a group company acts akin to a banker to other group companies by accepting funds and settling debts on behalf of those group companies. Group companies sometimes do not have their own bank accounts or have accounts which are cleared to a central account, in the name of one group company, at the close of business each day.

9.4A A group company may recognise a profit on a transaction which results in an increase in the balance due from the group treasury company. The normal considerations apply when assessing whether such a profit is realised. That is to say that the balance must represent qualifying consideration and the profit must arise from a transaction or arrangement that does not fall within paragraph 3.5 of this guidance (e.g. artificial or linked or circular). The nature of such arrangements vary widely in practice. It is always necessary to have regard to the particular facts and circumstances of each case.

9.4B A group company may have a "current account" balance with another group company through which many transactions, both debits and credits, are processed. There may be a considerable "churn" on the account even though a substantial balance remains outstanding. The fact that there is no expectation that the core balance will be settled does not preclude transactions processed through the account being realised profits when they arise from normal trading transactions in the ordinary course of business. This is because the debit entries to the account arising from these transactions are expected to be (ie they are foreseen to be) settled by offset with credit entries on the account and therefore the criterion in 3.11(d)(iii) can be regarded as met. However, large or unusual transactions that result in a "permanent" increase in the core balance will require careful consideration.

Dividends

Dividend received or receivable on an investment in a subsidiary

9.5 For a dividend received or receivable from a subsidiary to be treated as a realised profit, the consideration must be in the form of qualifying consideration. Accounting for dividends receivable and payable, including payment of intra-group dividends through inter-company accounts, is considered at 9.6 *et seq.* It will also be necessary to consider the effect any dividend has on the value of the investment in the subsidiary and, where its recoverable amount has fallen below its book value, to take account of the effect of any such impairment (and, where appropriate, any consequential release from revaluation, merger or other similar reserve).

Accrual of intra-group dividends payable and receivable

9.6 The following paragraphs deal with income that is dividend income or appropriation for legal purposes and which for accounting purposes is dealt with as a dividend by the paying and receiving companies (rather than as interest under IAS 32 or FRS 25).

9.7 A dividend payable is accrued in accordance with IFRIC 17 or FRS 21 only when it is "appropriately authorised and no longer at the discretion of the entity". This test will be met when a legally binding liability is established as described at 2.10 above. A dividend will be accrued as receivable by a parent company only when the subsidiary has a legally binding obligation to make the distribution. IAS 10 refers to dividends "declared" after the balance sheet date with the implication that those "declared" before the balance sheet date would be accrued (by both the subsidiary and the parent). However, IFRIC 17 refers to dividends that are declared as those that are "appropriately authorised and no longer at the discretion of the entity". A dividend may therefore have been 'declared' by the directors in the everyday sense of the term but not meet the requirements for recognition in financial statements.

[Deleted] **9.7A**

Paragraph 10(b) of IFRIC 17 states that a dividend is recognised on the date when it is declared by management or the board, if the law of the jurisdiction does not require further approval. This might have been seen as requiring a change of practice in relation to interim dividends on adoption of IFRIC 17. However, it is generally agreed that this is not so because the requirement to recognise a dividend only when it is no longer at the discretion of the entity takes precedence*. Also, it may be said that a UK interim dividend does require further approval by the directors immediately before it is paid because of the effect of their common law duties. **9.7B**

Companies may have to consider paying up (or establishing a legally binding liability to pay) interim dividends before the balance sheet date to ensure that the parent company has adequate distributable reserves to support the expected level of the proposed final dividend. **9.8**

[Deleted] **9.9**

[Deleted] **9.10**

This therefore raises the question as to what constitutes payment of an interim dividend and what steps may be taken to establish a legally binding liability. This will affect the timing of its recognition as a distribution by the paying company and as a profit by the recipient company. The question of whether a profit recorded by the recipient company is a realised profit falls to be determined under the general principles in this guidance, for example, whether it is qualifying consideration. **9.11**

Where there is a transfer of cash the answer will be clear as payment has been received. This conclusion would not be affected by the cash being immediately or closely afterwards reinvested in the paying company either by way of loan or by way of capital investment, although the fact of such reinvestment will require consideration of the guidance at 9.19 below as to whether the profit is realised or unrealised in the parent company's hands. **9.12**

Where the dividend is recorded on inter-company account and the effect of such an entry reduces the amount recorded as receivable from the parent to the dividend paying subsidiary, this would constitute settlement by way of set-off and would be equivalent to a payment in cash taking place at the date that the book entries were made by both companies (or the later of them if these should be different) to the extent that this does not reduce the amount recorded as receivable from the parent to the dividend-paying subsidiary below nil. **9.13**

Where the dividend is recorded on inter-company account and the book entry creates or increases a liability of the paying subsidiary, the question arises as to whether the dividend falls to be treated as paid and received, or a legally binding liability is otherwise established. **9.14**

**Paragraphs BC18-20 of IFRIC 17 explain that the Interpretation does not change the principle on when to recognise a dividend payable. The principle was moved from IAS 10 into the Interpretation and clarified but without changing the principle.*

9.15 Effecting the dividend via a group treasury function (see 9.4 above) where the subsidiary company instructs the group treasury function to debit the subsidiary's account and credit the parent's account, would constitute payment.

9.16 In other circumstances, more than just entries into the accounting records of the paying and receiving company are likely to be required. If there were no doubt as to the paying subsidiary's ability to pay the dividend, a legally binding liability in respect of an individual dividend could be established by the execution, as a Deed, of an acknowledgment of liability to pay the amount entered in the accounting records as a payable by the subsidiary and a receivable by the parent company or the constitution of such liability pursuant to an enforceable contract under Scots Law.

9.17 Any doubts about whether an interim dividend recorded by book entry is a legally binding liability can be removed by the conversion of the interim dividend into a final dividend before the year end. Under common form articles of association, this will require a recommendation by the directors and the declaration of the dividend either by approval by the members in a general meeting or, for private companies, by the members passing a written resolution.

9.18 In scenarios other than those discussed above, the position is more complex and dependent on the specific facts and circumstances and companies in doubt as to the position may wish to seek legal advice.

Dividend by a subsidiary to a parent which provides or reinvests the funds in the subsidiary

9.19 Investment by a parent in a subsidiary which has paid a dividend in the form of qualifying consideration does not in itself preclude that dividend from continuing to be treated as a realised profit by the parent. However, if a subsidiary pays a dividend to a parent which directly or indirectly provides the funds for the dividend or reinvests the proceeds in the subsidiary in circumstances where the transactions or arrangements fall within paragraph 3.5 of this guidance, the dividend will not represent a realised profit for the parent if it does not receive in return for the provision of funds or their reinvestment an asset which is in the form of qualifying consideration. Thus, in such a case, the profit will be unrealised if, for example:

(a) the provision or reinvestment of funds is in the form of:

- (i) a subscription for shares, as the subsidiary is in effect capitalising its realised profits; or
- (ii) a capital contribution (ie, a gift); or
- (iii) a loan which does not meet the definition of qualifying consideration; or
- (iv) a guarantee of borrowings used to fund the dividend (unless the likelihood that the guarantee will be called upon is remote); or

(b) the subsidiary is unlikely to be able to meet its obligations under any borrowings used to fund the dividend without recourse directly or indirectly to the parent.

Dividends received out of pre-acquisition profits

9.20 The Act does not deal specifically with the onward distribution by a parent of dividends out of the pre-acquisition profits of its subsidiaries. Under UK GAAP such dividends should be treated by a parent in the same way as any other dividend which it receives from a subsidiary, including taking account of any impairment in accordance with paragraph 9.5 (see 9.21 below). The position under IFRSs is considered at 9.22 *et seq* below.

Under UK GAAP, it has for many years been accepted that dividends received out of pre-acquisition profits of subsidiaries are treated as giving rise to a profit unless the dividend causes a diminution in the value of the investment below its book amount. This is separate from the question of whether or not such dividends are realised profits which will depend on whether they have been received in the form of qualifying consideration. **9.21**

Under IAS 27, before its amendment in May 2008*, when investments in subsidiaries were stated using the cost model, any dividends received out of their pre-acquisition profits were credited against the cost of investment. **9.22**

In May 2008, the IASB issued an amendment to IAS 27 which removed this requirement. At the same time, it also issued an amendment to IFRS 1 which permits the use of the previous GAAP carrying amount of subsidiaries as their deemed cost on transition to IFRSs. When applying the amended Standards there will generally be no adjustment to the carrying amount of the investment in subsidiaries on transition to IFRSs so there is no effect on accumulated realised profits. This is applicable only to a parent that adopted IFRS after that amended version of IFRS 1 was applicable. **9.22A**

On transition to IFRSs, when applying the unamended IAS 27, companies had to determine the extent to which any dividends have been received out of the pre-acquisition profits of their subsidiaries. The May 2008 amendment has, on a prospective basis, removed this requirement and potential source of difficulty. **9.23**

[Deleted] **9.24**

[Deleted] **9.25**

[Deleted] **9.26**

[Deleted] **9.27**

Sale of an asset by a parent to its subsidiary

If a parent sells an asset to a subsidiary in circumstances where the transactions or arrangements fall within paragraph 3.5 of this guidance, any profit on the sale of the asset will not represent a realised profit for the parent if it does not receive an asset which is in the form of qualifying consideration. Thus, in such a case, the profit will be unrealised if, for example: **9.28**

(a) there is an agreement or understanding regarding the repurchase of the asset by the parent; or

(b) the parent directly or indirectly provides the funds for the purchase or reinvests the proceeds in the subsidiary where the provision or reinvestment of funds is in the form of:

 (i) a subscription for shares; or
 (ii) a capital contribution (ie a gift); or
 (iii) a loan which does not meet the definition of qualifying consideration; or

**Amendments to IFRS 1 First-time Adoption of IFRSs and IAS 27 Consolidated and Separate Financial Statements: Cost of an Investment in a Subsidiary, Jointly Controlled Entity or Associate.*

(iv) a guarantee of borrowings used to fund the purchase (unless the likelihood that the guarantee will be called upon is remote); or

(c) the subsidiary is unlikely to be able to meet its obligations under any borrowings used to fund the purchase without recourse directly or indirectly to the parent.

Sale of an asset by a subsidiary to a parent followed by a dividend to the parent of the resulting profit

9.29 The subsidiary should apply factors similar to those in paragraph 9.28 in determining whether it has made a realised profit on the sale of an asset to its parent.

9.30 If a subsidiary sells an asset to its parent and pays a dividend out of the resulting profit in circumstances where the transactions or arrangements, from the parent's perspective, fall within paragraph 3.5 of this guidance, the dividend will not give rise to a realised profit for the parent unless the asset which the parent purchased meets the definition of qualifying consideration. This is because the overall commercial effect of such an arrangement for the parent is similar to a dividend in kind (see paragraph 9.33).

Sale of an asset by a subsidiary to a fellow subsidiary followed by a dividend to the parent of the resulting profit

9.31 The subsidiary should apply factors similar to those in paragraph 9.28 in determining whether it has made a realised profit on the sale of an asset to its fellow subsidiary.

9.32 If a subsidiary sells an asset to a fellow subsidiary and pays a dividend to the parent out of the resulting profit in circumstances where the transactions or arrangements, from the parent's perspective, fall within paragraph 3.5 of this guidance, the dividend will not give rise to a realised profit for the parent if, for example:

(a) the parent directly or indirectly provides the funds for the purchase where the provision of funds is in the form of:

(i) a subscription for shares; or
(ii) a capital contribution (ie, a gift); or
(iii) a loan which does not meet the definition of qualifying consideration; or

(b) the parent directly or indirectly reinvests the dividend (or equivalent consideration) in the subsidiary which paid the dividend or the fellow subsidiary to which the asset was sold and the asset which the parent receives from this reinvestment is not in the form of qualifying consideration; or

(c) the parent directly or indirectly guarantees any borrowings used to provide either the fellow subsidiary with the consideration for its purchase of the asset or the vendor subsidiary with funds for its dividend (in either case unless the likelihood that the guarantee will be called upon is remote) or the subsidiary in question is unlikely to be able to meet its obligations under the borrowings without recourse directly or indirectly to the parent.

Dividend in kind

9.33 A dividend in kind from a subsidiary is an unrealised profit in the hands of the parent (even where there is a cash alternative) unless the asset distributed meets the definition of qualifying consideration. However, if the non-cash asset is distributed by the parent then, following section 846, that unrealised profit would be treated by the parent as a realised profit for the purpose of that onward distribution, provided that the profit was recorded in the relevant accounts.

Return of capital contribution

Where a capital contribution is returned directly or indirectly to the donor company in circumstances where the transactions or arrangements fall within paragraph 3.5 of this guidance, it will not give rise to a realised profit in the hands of the donor. **9.34**

Transfer of an asset for consideration followed by waiver of the resulting inter-company debt

A group company may transfer an asset to another group company for consideration but subsequently waive the resulting inter-company debt. In such a case, if the purchase and release are part of a group or series of transactions or arrangements falling within paragraph 3.5 of this guidance, any profit will not represent a realised profit unless the asset originally acquired met the definition of qualifying consideration or has been disposed of for qualifying consideration. For example, where the substance of the arrangements taken together (e.g. where the waiver is a step in the plan even if undocumented) is to transfer a fixed asset for no consideration, any profit recorded by the transferee company on the debt waiver will not be a realised profit. Instead, the profit is in the nature of a revaluation of an asset acquired at no cost. **9.34A**

Debits within equity arising on group reconstructions

Business combinations involving entities or businesses under common control are excluded from the scope of IFRS 3, "Business combinations". Typical examples include a group reorganisation involving either a transfer of a company within a group or the transfer of a business from one group member to another. **9.35**

When a company carries out a transaction under common control* such as acquiring the business of another company within the same group, the directors may determine that it is not appropriate to recognise the net assets acquired at their fair values and that it is not appropriate to recognise goodwill. For example, a company may purchase the trade and assets of a division from its parent company, the consideration being a combination of cash and shares. The directors may determine that the appropriate accounting is to recognise the net assets acquired at the transferor's book amounts. The consideration paid, say, measured at the nominal value of the shares issued plus the value of the cash element, may exceed the book amount of the net assets acquired and this will leave a debit difference to be recognised. It is not goodwill. The debit is sometimes referred to as a "merger difference" and is recorded in equity. **9.36**

A business combination involving members of the same group is completed under the direction of the controlling party, the common parent. Consequently, any excess paid by the acquirer over the book amount of the vendor's net assets is accounted for in a similar manner to a distribution or return of capital to the common parent. Distributions and returns of capital are dealt with through equity, and therefore it is logical also to recognise the debit in equity. **9.37**

Such a debit directly to equity is not necessarily, however, a distribution as a matter of law. This is because the debit described above is determined on a book basis, **9.38**

**As defined in IFRS 3.*

whereas the question as to whether there would be an actual distribution is determined by whether the company gives consideration other than an issue of its shares, to its parent or a fellow subsidiary, with a fair value in excess of the fair value of the net assets and business acquired. Accordingly the debit may form part of an actual distribution or may not.

9.39 In a case where the debit in equity does not form part of an actual distribution, then at the date of acquisition the debit does not represent a loss; the acquiring company has purchased net assets worth at least the book value of the consideration given but, under the appropriate accounting, has recognised these at a lower amount. The difference between the two is the amount of the debit. As the debit is not a loss at all, it is neither realised nor unrealised.

9.40 To the extent that the assets, if they had been recognised at the higher amount, would have been written down, say, by depreciation or impairment, an equivalent amount of the debit becomes a realised loss. It is a realised, rather than unrealised, loss because, had the debit been carried as an asset, any write down for depreciation or impairment would be required, by section 841 and the principles of realisation (see section 3), to be regarded as realised.

9.41 The above guidance is written in the context of IFRS 3 but is equally applicable to a group reconstruction accounted for under FRS 6.

Additional consideration for a public company

9.42 For a public company, the initial recognition of the debit will restrict the maximum amount of profits available for distribution to the extent the cash paid out (or the book value of other non-equity consideration given) is greater than the book value of the net assets acquired. This is because the acquirer's net assets as shown in the company's relevant accounts for section 836 purposes would be reduced as a result of paying out cash consideration but increased by a smaller amount by recognising the acquired net assets at a lower amount. Since the debit is neither a realised loss nor an unrealised loss it has no effect on the "share capital and undistributable reserves" part of the section 831 net assets test. Consequently, the maximum permissible distribution would be restricted.

Merger relief and group reconstruction relief

9.43 As explained at 2.11 above, when shares are issued as consideration for the acquisition of a subsidiary, the issuing company may benefit from merger relief (section 612 of the Act) or group reconstruction relief (section 611 of the Act). In accordance with section 615 of the Act, under UK GAAP, such companies may state the cost of investment at the nominal value of the shares issued (for merger relief) or based on the minimum premium value (for group reconstruction relief). Under IFRSs, the interaction of these reliefs with the accounting for the acquired asset is complicated.

9.43A The IASB published amendments to IFRS 1 and IAS 27 in May 2008* that had implications for the treatment of merger relief and group reconstruction relief for accountingpurposes. The amendments were effective for annual periods beginning on or after 1 January 2009. The effect of these amendments is described at 9.44A to

**Amendments to IFRS 1 First-time Adoption of IFRSs and IAS 27 Consolidated and Separate Financial Statements: Cost of an Investment in a Subsidiary, Jointly Controlled Entity or Associate. These amendments are separate from the revision of IAS 27, which was published in January 2008, that has no effect on the accounting in the separate financial statements of a parent.*

Before the amendment in May 2008, IAS 27 was generally considered to require the acquired asset to be booked at fair value in some or all cases. Therefore, on transition to IFRSs, it was necessary to gross up the cost of investment to the fair value at the date of acquisition and to recognise a corresponding "merger reserve". Although different views were expressed on this financial reporting issue, the following paragraph deals with the treatment for distributable profit purposes when the merger reserve is recorded. **9.43B**

The adjustment to establish the merger reserve will have no direct impact on accumulated realised profits because the reserve will represent an unrealised profit. However, the reserve may become realised at a later date. This may, for example, occur on disposal of the investment for qualifying consideration or if the investment is written down for impairment. **9.44**

In May 2008, the IASB issued an amendment to IFRS 1 which permits the use of the previous GAAP carrying amount of subsidiaries as their deemed cost on transition to IFRSs. If the exemption in the amended IFRS 1 is used, there is no adjustment to the carrying amount of the investment on transition to IFRSs and consequently no effect on accumulated realised profits. The amendment had no effect on a company that had already adopted IFRSs in a period before the amended standard was first applied. **9.44A**

In May 2008, the IASB also amended IAS 27 to insert a new requirement for the accounting treatment to be adopted by a new parent company (including an intermediate parent company) established as a result of a group reorganisation when certain criteria are met. When these criteria are met*, the new parent accounts for the cost of its investment in the original parent "at the carrying amount of its share of the equity items shown in the separate financial statements of the original parent at the date of the reorganisation". In practice, this means that the new parent company will record the cost of its investment in the original parent at an amount equal to the IFRS net asset value of the original parent as shown in its separate financial statements at the date of the reorganisation. This will usually differ from both the fair value of the investment and the amount that might have been recorded under UK GAAP taking into account merger relief or group reconstruction relief (see 9.43 above). **9.44B**

The amendment required only prospective application to reorganisations occurring in annual periods beginning on or after 1 January 2009. No restatement was required for past reorganisations although this was permitted provided that all subsequent past reorganisations meeting the relevant criteria are restated in accordance with the amended standard. **9.44C**

For future reorganisations, the application of the new requirement may have the effect of restricting the ability of a public company to make distributions because the net assets of the new parent company may (depending on the circumstances) be stated at an amount that is less than its share capital and undistributable reserves. However, for reorganisations not meeting the criteria in the amended IAS 27 and for other acquisitions, the guidance at 9.43B and 9.44 above continues to apply. **9.44D**

**The new requirement will not apply to all group reorganisations involving the establishment of a new parent company because it applies only if all of three specified criteria are met. Reorganisations may, in practice, fail one or more of the tests.*

10. MISCELLANEOUS ISSUES 10.1 – 10.82

IAS 27, IAS 28 and IAS 31 – Separate financial statements

10.1 The balance of profits available for distribution is that available to the company, not to its group. The availability of such profits is to be judged by reference to accounts, which must therefore be the company's individual accounts. Except when initial or interim accounts are required, the "relevant accounts" for this purpose are the individual accounts forming part of the annual accounts, whether they are "Companies Act individual accounts" or "IAS individual accounts" (see section 2 above).

10.2 IFRSs do not use the term "individual accounts" but uses the term "separate financial statements" which are defined in IAS 27 as follows:

> "Separate financial statements are those presented by a parent, an investor in an associate or a venturer in a jointly controlled entity, in which the investments are accounted for on the basis of the direct equity interests rather than on the basis of the reported results and net assets of the investee."

10.3 Where a company prepares consolidated financial statements, these "separate financial statements" will be the company's "IAS individual accounts" for the purposes of section 395 and therefore the relevant accounts under section 836 for the purposes of justifying any distribution.

10.4 However, where a company has an associate or jointly controlled entity but has no subsidiaries, in some circumstances IAS 28 and/or IAS 31, when considered outside the EU legal framework, require the preparation of financial statements that are neither separate financial statements nor consolidated financial statements. In such financial statements, the investments in associates and jointly controlled entities are accounted for using the equity method or proportional consolidation as appropriate (see IAS 28(4) and IAS 31(5)). In these circumstances, the company is not required by IFRSs (when considered outside of the EU legal framework) to prepare separate financial statements. One point of view is that the financial statements including investments on the basis of equity accounting and/or proportional consolidation are not relevant for the purposes of justifying distributions and that the "separate financial statements" are the "IAS individual accounts".

10.5 Within the EU legal framework, an alternative point of view is that the financial statements required by IAS 28 and IAS 31 (ie those including investments on the basis of equity accounting and/or proportional consolidation) are a company's "IAS individual accounts". The Institutes have to date not been able to establish which view is the correct interpretation of the law and of EU-adopted IFRSs. The European Commission's Accounting Regulatory Committee has considered some related issues but has so far not provided clear guidance on this specific point.

10.6 Were the accounts including the equity accounting to be the "IAS individual accounts", the share of results of associates/jointly-controlled-entities is not realised save to the extent that it is received as distributions in the form of qualifying consideration. Therefore the amount of a company's accumulated realised profits will be the same irrespective of which interpretation of the law is correct.

[10.7 to 10.16 moved to 2.32 *et seq* and amended.]

IFRS 1 – Fair value or revaluation as deemed cost

Under IFRS 1, a first-time adopter may elect to measure an item of property, plant and equipment at the date of transition to IFRSs at its fair value and to use that fair value as deemed cost. A first-time adopter may also elect to use a previous GAAP valuation of an item of property, plant and equipment subject to various conditions. For example, it would be possible for a company that was carrying a property at a "frozen valuation" under the transitional provisions of FRS 15 to deem that valuation as cost on transition to IFRSs. These elections are also available for investment property when a company elects to use the cost model under IAS 40 and also, in certain limited circumstances, for intangible assets. **10.17**

IFRS 1 does not specify the treatment of any revaluation reserve existing under previous GAAP or of any excess of fair value over cost when the election is used to measure the asset at fair value at the date of transition. However, it is clear that this should not be presented as a revaluation surplus because the asset is regarded as held at cost (and, for example, any subsequent fall in value would have to be charged in the income statement rather than treated as a reversal of a revaluation surplus). In the absence of any other requirement in IFRS 1, the adjustment on transition may be reflected in retained earnings. **10.18**

Nevertheless, the treatment of a revaluation as deemed cost for the purposes of IFRSs does not alter the nature of the revaluation surplus which will usually be unrealised. Therefore, companies that elect for this treatment will have to keep an analysis of the balance of retained earnings to ensure that they can identify the amount of unrealised profit included. The unrealised profit will become realised as the asset is depreciated or written down for impairment, or is sold for qualifying consideration. This is consistent with the application of section 841(5) which is summarised at 2.35 above. **10.19**

The assets that are included on the basis of fair value or revaluation as deemed cost may have been depreciated under UK GAAP. Consider a tangible fixed asset that cost £100 and, at the date of transition to IFRSs, had a net book value of £50. Suppose that the fair value at the date of transition is £120 and the company elects to use this as deemed cost. The excess above original cost of £20 is clearly unrealised. It might be argued that the other £50 of the adjustment is a realised profit because it reverses the depreciation that had previously been charged as a realised loss. However, this analysis is not appropriate because the restatement to fair value is in the nature of a revaluation and it is generally accepted that depreciation is not written back to the profit and loss account on a revaluation. This is implicit in paragraph 63 of FRS 15. Similarly, when a previous valuation is treated as deemed cost, nothing of substance has occurred to cause the previously unrealised profit to become realised. This situation may be contrasted with an adjustment to depreciation that arises from a change in accounting policy for depreciation to comply with IAS 16 (see *Changes to depreciation policies* at 10.21 below). It may be possible to argue that some component of the restatement to deemed cost relates to a reconsideration of residual values and is therefore a realised profit (see 10.22 below). But, in practice, it would not usually be practicable to distinguish this component. **10.20**

IFRS 1 and IAS 16 – Changes to depreciation policies

Under IFRS 1, any change in estimated useful life or depreciation pattern is accounted for prospectively from the date that the change of estimate is made provided that the depreciation methods and rates under previous GAAP are acceptable under IFRSs. However, in some cases, a company's depreciation methods **10.21** and rates under previous GAAP may not be acceptable under IFRSs. If those differences have a material effect on the financial statements, the company adjusts the accumulated depreciation in its opening IFRS balance sheet retrospectively so that it complies with IFRSs (see IFRS 1 IG7).

10.22 The requirements of IAS 16 are, in general, similar to those of FRS 15 and so the depreciation methods and rates used for UK GAAP will usually be acceptable under IFRSs. However, a difference may arise because of the different way in which residual value is measured in the standards. Under FRS 15, residual values are based on the prices prevailing at the date of acquisition or revaluation of the asset. Under IAS 16, they are based on prices prevailing at the balance sheet date. Therefore, in general, cumulative depreciation will be lower under IFRSs assuming that prices are rising with inflation. Where such an effect is material, and an adjustment is made to reduce accumulated depreciation, the adjustment will be regarded as a realised profit because it represents the reversal of a previous realised loss.

IFRS 1 – Deferred tax on business combinations

10.23 The requirements of IFRS 1 and IFRS 3 for business combinations will generally be relevant only to the consolidated financial statements and therefore have no effect on distributable profits. However, in some cases it is necessary to account for a business combination in the individual accounts of a company, for example where it acquires an unincorporated business.

10.24 In some circumstances, IFRS 1 may require deferred tax to be provided in respect of assets or liabilities acquired through a previous business combination. For example, in many instances no deferred tax would have been provided on the revaluation of tangible fixed assets to fair value under UK GAAP but such a provision would be required under IFRSs. When the company is not required to restate the business combination in accordance with IFRS 3 and uses this exemption, the deferred tax provision still has to be recognised but is adjusted against retained earnings rather than against goodwill.

10.25 The tax provision will reduce accumulated realised profits available for distribution where the transaction involved the acquisition of an unincorporated business by an individual company. It does not matter that the tax provision would not have been treated in this way had IFRS 3 been applied. It is the accounting that has actually been applied in the relevant accounts, in accordance with applicable accounting standards, which affects the amount of profits available for distribution.

IFRS 1 – Past capitalisation of revaluation reserve

10.26 Under UK GAAP, some companies have revalued assets, in particular properties and investments in subsidiaries, and subsequently capitalised all or part of the resulting revaluation reserve through a bonus issue of shares. The issue that arises on transition to IFRSs is the status of the debit entry in reserves if revalued assets are restated to a cost basis.

Investment properties and property, plant and equipment

10.27 Under SSAP 19, investment properties are required to be included in the balance sheet at their open market value. Under FRS 15, companies that chose to adopt a policy of revaluation for classes of tangible fixed assets (property, plant and equipment) have to ensure that those assets are carried at their current value at the balance sheet date. On transition to IFRSs, companies are not required to continue to apply a revaluation policy for their investment properties or property, plant and equipment. In effect, IFRS 1 allows companies on transition to IFRSs to state their investment properties or property, plant and equipment at depreciated historical cost, or, in the case of property, plant and equipment, at a "deemed cost" that could be a previous valuation or fair value at the date of transition. This guidance addresses the position where a company chooses to restate to depreciated historical cost. In the case of a transition using a "deemed cost" the revaluation survives transition and there is no restatement to consider.

Where the revaluation surplus has not been used at all for a bonus issue of shares and is still recorded in the balance sheet at the date of transition to IFRSs, the adjustment required will be simply to eliminate the revaluation reserve and reduce the revalued assets by the same amount to restate them to their depreciated historical cost. However, if the revaluation surplus has been capitalised, in full or in part, through a past bonus issue of shares, it will not be possible to reduce the reserve in this way. Neither is it possible to apply the debit to reduce share capital by the amount of the bonus shares. The question therefore arises as to the status of the debit entry in reserves arising from reversal of the past revaluation. **10.28**

Paragraph 3.15(c) above states that, with two exceptions explained at 2.33 and 3.36, realised losses will include the writing down, or providing for depreciation, amortisation, diminution in value or impairment of an asset. However, the entry to reverse the previous revaluation surplus is not depreciation or amortisation. It also does not relate to the diminution in the value of the assets or impairment but instead relates to a reduction in the amount at which those assets are recorded in the balance sheet. The actual value of the assets remains unchanged. **10.29**

The exception described at 2.36 is as follows: **10.30**

> If an asset is revalued downwards below its recoverable amount, as defined in FRS 11 or IAS 36, then the difference between that revalued amount and recoverable amount is treated as an unrealised loss as it reflects a revaluation adjustment rather than a provision as defined in section 841 .Such a loss would become realised in the event of a subsequent scrapping, disposal or impairment of the asset.

This principle may be applied to the restatement of a revalued asset to its depreciated historical cost. Therefore the debit entry to reserves arising from such a restatement (which equates to the revaluation element of the carrying value that is not yet depreciated) will be an unrealised loss provided that the recoverable amount of the asset is equal to or greater than the book amount prior to the restatement. To the extent that the revaluation surplus still exists as an unrealised reserve, the unrealised loss will simply eliminate that unrealised reserve. To the extent that the revaluation surplus has been utilised, in part or in full, for a bonus issue of shares, the resulting net debit entry will represent an unrealised loss. **10.31**

The entry to reverse the previous revaluation surplus is not a provision for the purposes of applying section 841(2). In the case of Companies Act individual accounts, "provisions of a kind specified for the purposes of this paragraph by regulations under section 396 (except revaluation provisions)" are treated as realised losses. In the case of "IAS individual accounts", "provisions of any kind (except revaluation provisions)" are treated as realised losses. The entry to reverse the previous revaluation surplus is not a provision of the kind specified by the regulations under section 396 and is not a provision at all in the sense that the term is used for accounting purposes. On the restatement to historical cost there will be no provision deducted from the asset. **10.32**

Investments in subsidiaries

10.33 Under the alternative accounting rules in the Accounting Regulations, investments in subsidiaries may be stated "at a market value determined as at the date of their last valuation" or "at a value determined on any basis which appears to the directors to be appropriate in the circumstances of the company". There is no obligation under the law or UK accounting standards to keep such valuations up to date although it is necessary to consider whether the assets have become impaired. Under IFRSs, two accounting policies are available for investments in subsidiaries. The first policy is that of cost, using the IAS 27-cost method. The second is to account for such investments in accordance with IAS 39. This would require such investments to be maintained at fair value. In practice, the measurement of such equity investments at fair value may be precluded because the range of reasonable fair value estimates is significant and the probabilities of the various estimates cannot reasonably be assessed (see IAS 39, AG 80-81). Even where such a policy is possible, it will require valuations to be obtained each time a balance sheet is drawn up. This is likely to be unattractive to most companies. Therefore, most companies hold subsidiaries at cost, as determined under IAS 27.

10.34 Hence the guidance on the effect of a restatement to depreciated historical cost of a previously revalued investment property or tangible fixed asset is equally applicable to a restatement of previously revalued investments in subsidiaries on to an IAS 27-cost basis.

Effect of restatements for a public company

10.35 For a public company, the restatement of a revalued asset (whether investment property, other property, plant and equipment or investment in subsidiaries) to a cost basis will restrict its profits available for distribution under section 831 to the extent that the revaluation surplus was capitalised. The effect of the unrealised loss on the restriction imposed by section 831 may be mitigated by the existence of recognised unrealised profits.

IAS 11 – Accounting for construction contracts

10.36 Under UK GAAP (SSAP 9), accounting for profit on long-term contracts results in debtor balances described as "Amounts recoverable on contracts". This treatment was adopted when the standard was revised in 1988 because legal advice suggested that it was not possible to include the profit element in work-in-progress because of the requirement to state work-in-progress at cost.

10.37 The accounting required for construction contracts under IAS 11 is broadly similar to that required by SSAP 9 (although the scope of the standards is different). However, IAS 11 is not specific as to the nature of the asset to be recognised. In practice the item may simply be disclosed as "construction contracts" although it may also be included within debtors or within work-in-progress.

10.38 Under UK GAAP it is usually clear that the debtor balance for "Amounts recoverable on contracts" meets the definition of "qualifying consideration" (see 3.11 above). Therefore profit recognised on such contracts is regarded as a realised profit. On the basis that this treatment has been generally accepted under UK GAAP, any profits recognised in accordance with IAS 11 should be regarded as realised profits, irrespective of how the asset is described in the balance sheet.

10.38A IFRIC 12 Service Concession Arrangements may require a profit to be recognised by the operator in accordance with IAS 11 in relation to the construction or upgrading of the infrastructure to be used to provide a public service. Whether any such profit is a realised profit will depend on whether a financial asset or an intangible asset is recognised in accordance with IFRIC 12. This is more fully explained at 10.65 to 10.68 below.

IAS 12 – Income taxes – Deferred tax

As stated at 3.17 above, a provision for deferred tax should generally be regarded as a realised loss. However, when assets are revalued to their fair value, with any gain being recorded in the profit and loss account even though regarded as unrealised, the deferred tax on that gain should be treated as a reduction in that unrealised gain rather than as a realised loss (paragraph 14 of Appendix III to FRS 19 *Deferred tax*). **10.39**

This principle is also applicable to deferred tax provisions recognised under IAS 12, irrespective of whether profits are recognised in profit or loss, or direct in equity. For many financial instruments, profits arising from fair value accounting are realised profits (see Section 4 above). Any attributable deferred tax provision will be a realised loss. **10.40**

Deferred tax is more often recognised on unrealised profits under IFRSs than under UK GAAP. For example, the remeasurement of investment property at fair value will result in unrealised profits (see Section 4 above) on which deferred tax will have to be provided. Such a deferred tax provision is treated as a reduction in the unrealised profit rather than as a realised loss. **10.41**

When a convertible debt instrument is accounted for using "split accounting" (see *Convertible debt* at 6.59 *et seq* above), a deferred tax provision is established and debited against the initial carrying amount of the equity component in accordance with paragraph 23 of IAS 12. This occurs if the tax base of the debt is its full amount but the book amount is lower by the amount of the equity component. The deferred tax provision reverses through profit or loss over the life of the instrument as illustrated in Example 4 in Appendix B to IAS 12. It does not represent a future cash outflow for payment of tax. The deferred tax provision should be treated as a reduction in the credit to equity rather than as a realised loss. The equity component of the financial instrument is not a profit at all and therefore does not fall to be classified as realised or unrealised (see *Convertible debt* at 6.59 *et seq* above). An adjustment to such an item does not affect realised profits. **10.42**

In some cases it may be necessary to provide for current tax on an unrealised profit. A current tax provision should be treated as a realised loss even if it arises from the taxation of an unrealised profit. This is because a provision for current tax represents a specific cash outflow that will arise irrespective of whether the related profit is realised or not. **10.43**

Property, plant and equipment – asset swaps

One or more items of property, plant and equipment may be acquired in exchange for a non-monetary asset or assets, or a combination of monetary and non-monetary assets. IAS 16 requires the cost of such an item of property, plant and equipment to be measured at fair value unless the transaction lacks commercial substance or the fair value of neither the asset received nor the asset given up is reliably measurable. IAS 16 provides guidance on the circumstances in which the fair value of an asset is reliably measurable for this purpose. **10.44**

10.45 A profit may therefore be recognised on such an exchange transaction in accordance with IFRSs. This profit is likely to be unrealised because an item of property, plant and equipment is unlikely to meet the definition of "qualifying consideration" (see 3.11 above).

10.46 When a combination of property, plant and equipment and qualifying consideration (e.g. cash) is received, the guidance at 3.18 above on "top-slicing" will be relevant.

10.47 Any profit treated as unrealised, becomes realised as the related asset is depreciated, written down for impairment or sold for qualifying consideration.

10.48 A loss arising on such a transaction is usually a realised loss. However, in some cases the loss may be similar in substance to an unrealised revaluation deficit (see 2.28 above).

10.49 For example, if a factory used in a business was exchanged for a similar factory and a loss recognised under IAS 16 by reference to the market value of the factories, the loss will be unrealised if there would have been no need to write down the original factory for impairment because its value in use was higher than its market value. It will also be necessary to consider the value in use of the new factory which might be different from the value in use of the old factory, even though their market value is the same (e.g. because one is larger than the other).

10.50 IAS 38 provides for the same accounting treatment for swaps of intangibles as that under IAS 16 in respect of property, plant and equipment, and therefore the foregoing analysis also applies to intangibles under IAS 38.

10.51 There are no specific requirements in UK accounting standards dealing with such asset swaps. The above guidance is relevant to any profit recognised under UK GAAP although it should be noted that only profits realised at the balance sheet date may be included in the profit and loss account in accordance with the Accounting Regulations* (although the fair value accounting rules make an exception to this general rule).

Revenue – Barter transactions

10.52 When goods are sold or services rendered in exchange for dissimilar goods or services, the exchange is regarded as a transaction that generates revenue in accordance with IAS 18. The revenue is measured at the fair value of the goods or services received, adjusted by the amount of any cash or cash equivalents transferred. When the fair value cannot be measured reliably, the revenue is measured at the fair value of the goods or services given up, adjusted by the amount of any cash or cash equivalents transferred.

10.53 When an asset is received, in determining whether any profit on such an exchange is realised or unrealised, it is necessary to determine whether such asset meets the definition of qualifying consideration. For example, when a property is received, it will be straightforward to assess whether or not it meets the definition of qualifying consideration. Any profit will not become realised until that property is depreciated, written down for impairment or sold for qualifying consideration.

10.54 Where services are exchanged, the effect of the accounting entries is to gross up the revenue and the costs by the same amount. Accordingly, there will be no effect on

**Paragraph 13 of Schedule 1 to SI 2008/409 and Paragraph 13 to Schedule 1 to SI 2008/410.*

profit. When services are receivable but have not yet been received at the balance sheet date, a prepayment will be recognised. A prepayment does not meet the definition of qualifying consideration.

Where an exchange of services straddles the end of an accounting reference period, such that services are provided but not received before the balance sheet date, any profit at the year end would not be realised. Any such profit initially recognised will not become realised until the service has been received in exchange. That is, the profit will be realised by the prepayment being expensed to profit or loss when the service has been received. **10.55**

There are no specific requirements in UK accounting standards dealing with barter transactions other than UITF Abstract 26 which is concerned with barter transactions for advertising. The above guidance will be relevant to any profit recognised under UK GAAP although it should be noted that only profits realised at the balance sheet date may be included in the profit and loss account in accordance with the Accounting Regulations*. **10.56**

[10.57 to 10.64 withdrawn and replaced by section 11.]

IFRIC 12 Service concession arrangements

IFRIC 12 Service Concession Arrangements was issued in November 2006 and has subsequently been adopted by the EU. Service concession arrangements are arrangements whereby a government or other public sector body ('the grantor') enters into a contract with a private sector entity ('the operator') for the construction / upgrade and operation of assets with which public services are supplied, such as roads, prisons or hospitals. Private Finance Initiative (PFI) arrangements are a common example of service concession arrangements in the UK. **10.65**

The operator will often construct or upgrade the infrastructure to be used to provide the public service and the cost of this will be recovered over the life of the arrangement. This is accounted for as a construction contract under IAS 11 Construction contracts. The asset arising from the recognition of revenue in accordance with IAS 11 will be either a financial asset or an intangible asset, in accordance with IFRIC 12, depending on the terms of the arrangement. **10.66**

When a financial asset is recognised in accordance with IFRIC 12, this will be an amount receivable from the grantor and therefore should normally meet the definition of qualifying consideration. Any profit arising from the recognition of revenue in the construction phase will therefore normally be a realised profit. **10.67**

When an intangible asset is recognised in accordance with IFRIC 12, this will not meet the definition of qualifying consideration. Any profit arising from the recognition of revenue in the construction phase will not therefore be a realised profit. Any unrealised profit arising in the construction phase will become realised as the intangible asset is amortised or impaired over the life of the arrangement. **10.68**

IFRIC 5 Decommissioning funds

IFRIC 5 'Rights to Interests arising from Decommissioning, Restoration and Environmental Rehabilitation Funds' was issued in December 2004 and subsequently adopted by the EU. Such funds are more fully described in IFRIC 5 but are **10.69**

**Paragraph 13 of Schedule 1 to SI 2008/409 and Paragraph 13 to Schedule 1 to SI 2008/410.*

typically established to provide a ring-fenced fund of assets to be used to pay for the decommissioning of an asset (e.g. a nuclear power plant) at the end of its life. IFRIC 5 applies to the financial statements of a contributor to such a fund where the assets are administered separately (either by being held in a separate legal entity or as segregated assets within another entity) and the contributor's right to access the assets is restricted. The contributor retains the obligation to pay the decommissioning costs but is able to draw on the assets in the fund to finance such costs when they are incurred.

10.70 In accordance with IFRIC 5, the contributor recognises the right to receive reimbursement from the fund as a reimbursement asset in accordance with IAS 37 . The reimbursement is measured at the lower of the amount of the decommissioning obligation recognised and the contributor's share of the fair value of the net assets of the fund attributable to the contributor. Changes in the carrying value of the reimbursement asset, other than contributions to and payments from the fund, are recognised in profit or loss in the period in which the changes occur.

10.71 Paragraph 53 of IAS 37 states that a reimbursement asset is recognised when, and only when, it is virtually certain that the reimbursement will be received if the entity settled the obligation. An amount receivable which is regarded, for financial reporting purposes, as meeting this test will also generally meet the definition of qualifying consideration in paragraph 3.11(d).

10.72 That definition refers to the debtor being capable of settling the receivable within a reasonable period of time. What is a reasonable period of time is a matter of judgement and will depend on the particular facts and circumstances. Decommissioning funds may be established to pay liabilities that will not arise for many years. However, the nature of such funds is that they will generally be capable of settling the amount within a relatively short period of time if they were required to do so at the date of determination. The definition of qualifying consideration does not require actual settlement within any particular period of time.

Section 846 and replacement assets

10.73 The following paragraphs illustrate how to apply s846 (see 2.9 above) where the asset to which an unrealised reserve relates has been replaced by a different asset.

10.74 Company A has brought forward realised profits of £75,000. It previously acquired an investment (in Company B) via a share for share transfer. This transaction qualified for merger relief in accordance with section 612 and the company elected to record a merger reserve in relation to this share issue. The aggregate nominal value of the shares issued was £50,000, compared with a fair value of £500,000 such that a merger reserve of £450,000 was recorded.

10.75 Subsequently Company A transfers that investment in Company B to another subsidiary company (Company C) in exchange for shares. As a matter of accounting practice, the merger reserve which initially related to Company A's investment in Company B is now attached to the investment in Company C, ie part of the amount at which the investment in Company C is stated represents the reserve. These transactions are illustrated in the diagram below (in which 'CV' means carrying value).

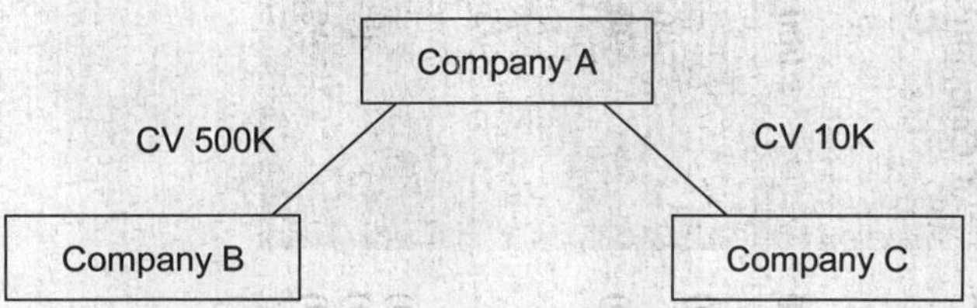

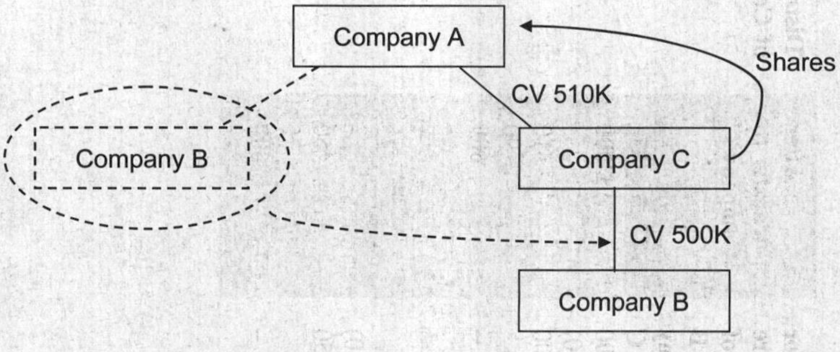

Therefore, if Company A wishes to distribute its investment in Company C to its shareholders, it can do so by applying section 846. This reserve (together with £75,000 of the brought forward realised profits) can be used to distribute Company A's investment in Company C to its shareholders. This is illustrated in the following memorandum balance sheet of Company A. **10.76**

Memorandum balance sheet of Company A

	Opening balance sheet	Share for share acquisition of Company B	After acquisition of Company B	Share for share transfer of Company B to Company C	After transfer to Company C	Distribution of Company C	After distribution of Company C
	£'000	**£'000**	**£'000**	**£'000**	**£'000**	**£'000**	**£'000**
Investment in Company B		500	500	(500)	–		–
Investment in Company C	10		10	500	510	(510)	–
Other net assets	90		90		90		90
Net assets	**100**	**500**	**600**	--	**600**	**(510)**	**90**
Share capital / premium	25	50	75		75		75
Merger reserve (Company B)		450	450	(450)	–		–
Merger reserve (Company C)				450	450	(450)	–
P&L reserves (realised)	75		75		75	(60)	15
Capital and reserves	**100**	**500**	**600**	–	**600**	**(510)**	**90**

Section 846 and fungible assets

The following paragraphs provide guidance on the distribution in kind of fungible assets such as shares or loan notes that have been received as consideration for the sale of another asset. For example, Company A has 1,000 £1 loan notes which are transferable in multiples of £1 and represent an unrealised profit of £900. If the company makes a distribution in kind of £500 of loan notes, the question is whether the unrealised profit might be regarded as becoming realised through the application of section 846 either: **10.77**

- to the extent of £450 on the basis that the realisation of 50% of the asset results in the realisation of 50% of the profit; or
- to the extent of £500 through the application of a "top slicing" rule similar to the one in 3.18 below for exchanges of assets.

The first (ie pro rata) approach is correct. This is a matter of the statutory construction of section 846 rather than a matter of generally accepted accounting practice. **10.78**

Section 846 is reproduced below for ease of reference. **10.79**

846 Distributions in kind: treatment of unrealised profits

(1) This section applies where—

(a) a company makes a distribution consisting of or including, or treated as arising in consequence of, the sale, transfer or other disposition by the company of a non-cash asset, and

(b) any part of the amount at which that asset is stated in the relevant accounts

represents an unrealised profit.

(2) That profit is treated as a realised profit—

(a) for the purpose of determining the lawfulness of the distribution in accordance with this Part (whether before or after the distribution takes place), and

(b) for the purpose of the application, in relation to anything done with a view to or in connection with the making of the distribution, of any provision of regulations under section 396 under which only realised profits are to be included in or transferred to the profit and loss account.

The profit that is to be treated as realised in accordance with sub-section (2) is the unrealised profit referred to in sub-section (1)(b). The reference in sub-section (1)(b) to 'that asset' means the asset to be distributed. Therefore, it is necessary to identify "that asset" which in the above example is not a single asset of £500 of loan notes but an aggregation of assets comprising 500 £1 loan notes. Naturally, if the loan notes were transferable only in units of £100 the distribution would consist of 5 assets. Therefore, in the above example, the distribution of £500 of loan notes results in the realisation of £450 of profit because that is the amount of unrealised profit attributable to those loan notes. In other words, the unrealised profit must be treated as spread evenly across each unit of the fungible asset and section 846 applied to each unit separately. **10.80**

Paragraph 3.18 refers to the use of a top-slicing approach where an asset is sold partly for qualifying consideration and partly for other consideration and a realised profit falls to be assessed under generally accepted accounting principles. That guidance is not relevant to the application of section 846 which is not concerned with **10.81** the disposal of an asset for mixed consideration but with the recharacterisation of an existing unrealised profit under that the specific provision of that section. In addition, that guidance is not relevant to the attribution of an unrealised profit, at the point of its arising, among one or more assets.

10.82 As illustrated in Appendix 8, this conclusion, may lead to unexpected results in some cases. In particular, the maximum distribution possible as a distribution in kind may be less than would be the case if all of the loan notes were redeemed or sold for qualifying consideration.

11 FOREIGN CURRENCY SHARE CAPITAL AND USE OF PRESENTATION CURRENCIES 11.1 –11.38

Introduction

11.1 The guidance in this section deals with matters arising from mismatches between any of the currency of share capital, the company's functional currency and the company's presentation currency. The accounting context in which this section is written is IFRS, ie IAS 21. So far as UK GAAP is concerned, if FRS 23 is applicable then this is converged with IAS 21; if SSAP 20 is applicable, the issues and principles are, however, the same because SSAP 20 differs only in minor details from IAS 21 for these purposes, although SSAP 20 does not include a free choice of presentation currency.

11.2. The main points at issue might be briefly put as follows: what is the effect of a translation of the whole of the accounts of a company into a presentation currency of free choice; and what is the effect of the share capital's being denominated in a currency other than the functional currency?

11.3 The first matter is similar to the issue of translation of an autonomous branch which was previously addressed at paragraphs 10.57 -10.64 (which have now been withdrawn and replaced by the guidance in this section). However, that case is not one of free choice of presentation currency. Rather, it is a necessity to translate the results of the branch into the functional currency of the company of which it is legally a part. In the case of use of a presentation currency, there is an arbitrary choice as to the units in which to show the accounts for mere presentation purposes.

11.4 [Not used]

11.5 [Not used]

Principles

11.6 Paragraphs 11.7 to 11.34 set out seven principles to be applied in relation to foreign currency share capital and the use of presentation currencies. Examples of the application of the principles are set out in Appendix 5.

11.7 **Principle 1: Realised profits and losses are measured by reference to the functional currency of the company.**

11.8 **Principle 2: An accounting gain or loss arising upon the retranslation of the whole of the accounts from the company's functional currency to a presentation currency, is not a profit or a loss as a matter of law. Such an amount therefore cannot be a realised profit or loss.**

IAS 21 requires foreign currency assets, liabilities and transactions to be measured using a company's functional currency. This is defined as the currency of the primary economic environment in which the entity operates. Functional currency is a matter of fact and is not an accounting policy choice. However, IAS 21 also permits a company to present its financial statements in a currency other than its functional currency. Such a currency is referred to as a presentation currency and may be freely chosen. 11.9

The "relevant accounts" for the purposes of justifying a distribution are determined in accordance with section 836 but will generally be the company's most recent statutory individual accounts. Although the face of those accounts shows amounts in presentation currency, the functional currency amounts underlie and form part of those relevant accounts. Realised profits and losses are determined by reference to these functional currency amounts. The functional-to-presentation translation gain or loss, which also appears in the relevant accounts, is not a profit or loss at law, for the reasons explained below. 11.10

The presentation currency is an arbitrary choice as to the units in which to show the accounts for mere presentation purposes. The functional-to-presentation translation is a book-keeping or accounting exercise. The accounting gain or loss arising from that process is an arithmetical difference which does not spring from any functional substance. There has been no profit or loss but merely a change in calibration. Thus such changes are not characterised as a profit or loss as a matter of law. 11.11

Principle 3: The profit or loss arising upon the necessary retranslation of an autonomous branch, from its functional currency into the functional currency of the company, is a realised profit or a loss to the extent that the branch net assets were qualifying consideration when the profit or loss arose. 11.12

A company has only a single pool of realised profits available for distribution, irrespective of its having one or more autonomous branches, with a functional currency different from that of the rest of the company. That single pool is measured by reference to the functional currency of the rest of the company. Thus in the case of a foreign operation (branch) with a functional currency that is different from the functional currency of the company, the translation is not an arbitrary one but one made of necessity to state the branch asset and results in the company's functional currency. It therefore has substance and is a profit or loss at law. 11.13

Whether that profit or loss is a realised one depends upon the nature of the assets and liabilities on which they arise. A profit that arises on retranslation of an asset which comprises qualifying consideration, or a liability, is a realised profit in accordance with paragraph 3.9(d) above. A profit arising on the retranslation of assets which do not comprise qualifying consideration (e.g. property, plant and equipment) is an unrealised profit. A loss arising on retranslation of an asset or liability is a realised loss unless it is the reversal of an unrealised profit on that same asset or liability. The gross profits and losses on retranslation (rather than the net amount) should be assessed separately. It is therefore possible, for example, that there is a realised loss to be taken into account when determining profits available for distribution, even though the net amount taken direct to equity is a profit. 11.14

The analysis in the previous paragraph will apply only in straightforward situations where the composition of the company's assets has not changed significantly during the period. For example, it would not be appropriate to regard the exchange difference related to the amount of the opening cash balance (ie, the beginning to the end of year exchange difference computed in relation to that part of the opening net assets equal to the opening cash balance) as realised if that cash balance did not exist 11.15

throughout the period (eg because it was invested in assets such as property, plant and equipment which would not comprise qualifying consideration).

11.16 The exchange difference taken to equity will also include the difference between the profit or loss for the period translated at actual (or average) rate and that profit or loss translated at closing rate. The profit or loss for the period arises on changes in the amounts and/or composition of the company's assets and liabilities (e.g. on an exchange of stocks for cash).

11.17 Thus taking together the exchange differences on retranslation of the profit or loss for the period and on the opening net assets, the total amount arises in relation to an asset base that changes throughout the year. To establish whether this exchange difference is realised, partly realised or unrealised will require careful analysis of the facts. Appendix 6 gives two examples of this, illustrating why this calculation needs to be done. Ideally, it would be necessary to compute and assess exchange differences continually. In practice when conducting the analysis, reasonable approximations may be made. The approximations will depend on the facts of any case, for example the rate of change in the composition of the balance sheet between various asset/liability categories.

11.18 **Principle 4: Where a company's shares, irrespective of whether those shares are classified as equity or debt for accounting purposes, are denominated in a currency other than the company's functional currency, the adjustment arising upon any translation for accounting purposes of the share capital is not a profit or loss at law. Such an amount therefore cannot be a realised profit or loss.**

11.19 Where shares are classified as equity under accounting standards and their currency differs from the company's functional currency, then the company will either retranslate those shares into functional currency at each balance sheet date or will leave them at their original historical amounts, although typically the latter is adopted in the case of ordinary shares. Accounting standards do not have anything to say about the translation of shares classified as equity, or at least not directly. In IAS 21 the requirement to accumulate the translation differences in the currency translation reserve rules out any question of allocating any of them against capital. In the case of retranslation the resulting difference does not pass through profit or loss and is not a gain or loss for accounting purposes. Where the shares are classified as debt (eg certain preference shares), retranslation is mandatory and the resulting difference is an accounting gain or loss flowing through profit or loss.

11.20 In both cases, the shares remain share capital as a matter of law. Any retranslation of share capital for accounting purposes (whether equity or debt classified) is a book-keeping or accounting exercise. The gain or loss arising from that process is an arithmetical difference which does not spring from any substance in law. There has been no profit or loss but merely a change in calibration. Thus such changes are not characterised as profits or losses as a matter of law.

11.21 **Principle 5: Where a company's shares, whether those shares are classified as equity or debt for accounting purposes, are denominated in a currency other than the company's functional currency, the common law has the effect of restricting distributions where to do otherwise would result in the net assets' falling below the functional currency worth of the share capital.**

11.22 Under statute, shares (whether of a private or a public company) must be of a fixed nominal amount (s542). There is a rule of law that where the share capital is denominated in another currency (other than the functional currency) the share capital is in fact fixed as that other currency amount.

Further, the common law provides that a company may not distribute its capital (see 2.2 above). In relation to the currency of shares, this rule is not concerned with whether or not share capital has been retranslated in the accounts or with the nature of any translation adjustments. It is concerned with a question of fact as to value of the assets compared with the amount of the share capital. Since the amount of the capital is the currency amount, then for such a comparison to be effected the share capital must be stated in the same terms as value of the net assets. Thus the current worth of the share capital in functional currency terms must be compared with the net assets in functional currency. To the extent that a distribution would result in the net assets falling below the current functional currency worth of the share capital, the ability to make such a distribution is restricted. **11.23**

Thus an increase in the functional currency worth of the share capital may restrict distributions to less than the amount available under Part 23's statutory rules. On the other hand, a decrease will neither restrict nor augment the ability to make a distribution. The effect of a share capital decrease will be to increase the difference between net assets and share capital (assuming no other amounts within equity – see below for other cases) so as to exceed the Part 23 realised profits (and any unrealised profits). However, the maximum amount that may be distributed can never exceed the amount permitted by Part 23. **11.24**

Principle 6: Share premium account, and similar capital accounts, do not have a currency of denomination but are amounts of record in the books of account in functional currency. **11.25**

Share premium account is different from share capital in this context. Share capital is required by statute to be of fixed amount and therefore has a currency of denomination. Share premium account is not so required. Furthermore, share premium was, prior to the statutory requirement to treat it as if it were part of a company's capital, in law a profit. It is thus an amount of record arising on the occasion of a share issue. The amount is determined at that time and in the functional currency since that is the currency of substance for the keeping of accounts. **11.26**

A capital redemption reserve is of the same nature as a share premium account. It is not required by statute to have a fixed amount. It is an amount of record arising on the occasion of a share redemption or repurchase. The amount is determined at that time and in the functional currency. It should be noted that the amount determined at that time will be by reference to the then functional currency worth of the shares redeemed or repurchased. This is because those shares, up to the moment of their redemption or repurchase, represent capital of that currency. Thus the nominal value of those shares, by reference to which the statutory rules for determining capital redemption reserve operate, is as a matter of fact a non-functional currency amount; its functional currency worth must be determined at the date of redemption or repurchase. **11.27**

Principle 5 identifies a possible restricting effect upon distributions in relation to share capital where there is a mismatch between that capital's denomination and the functional currency. Since share premium and similar capital accounts do not have currencies of denomination, but are amounts of record in functional currency, no equivalent issue arises in relation to share premium and similar capital accounts; that is to say, there is no concept of variation in the worth of, eg, share premium to be concerned about. **11.28**

It should be noted, however, that share premium is brought into the calculation of the restricting effect arising from a variation in the worth of the share capital under Principle 5. The common law prohibition on distribution of capital covers both share **11.29** capital and share premium account. Thus, where a company has a share premium account, the restricting effect under Principle 5 is computed by comparison of the net assets with the aggregate of the functional currency worth of the share capital and the functional currency amount of record of the share premium account.

11.30 The common law principles of maintenance of capital apply to any reserve which the Act says must be treated as if it were part of the paid up share capital of the company. It therefore includes, in addition to a share premium account, a capital redemption reserve under section 733 and a redenomination reserve under section 626. The treatment of a share premium account described in 2.29 above therefore applies to any capital redemption reserve or redenomination reserve.

11.31 **Principle 7: The application of the s831 statutory net assets test operates by reference to amounts as shown upon the face of the accounts in presentation currency.**

11.32 The s831 net assets test (see 2.30 above) applies only to public companies. It is a statutory test formulated in terms of amounts set out in the relevant accounts required by the Act: net assets, share capital and undistributable reserves (as defined). It therefore operates by reference to whatever is shown in presentation currency in those accounts.

11.33 It may be noted here that s831 operates upon figures in presentation currency whereas, as described at Principles 1 and 2, s830's realised profits test draws upon functional currency amounts. This is because s830 deals with profits and losses and in law the functional-to-presentation translation does not yield a profit or loss. It is therefore necessary for s830 to begin with the amounts in the relevant accounts but to take from them only the amounts that are profits and losses in law. On the other hand s831 asks only that certain accounts figures be compared (eg, in a similar way to that described at 6.24ff above whereby shares classified as debt count as a reduction of net assets rather than an increase to share capital for the s831 test).

11.34 It should be noted that where share capital is retranslated, the amount within reserves arising as a result of the retranslation is not a profit or loss at law (see Principle 2). Nor is that translation difference presented as share capital. Thus the difference cannot be included, for the operation of the s831 test, as share capital or as undistributable reserves. Thus, in particular, any debit difference cannot be an unrealised loss to be deducted from the unrealised profits component of "undistributable reserves".

11.35 **Principle 8: A reduction of foreign currency share capital is calculated by reference to the rate of exchange at the date of the reduction.**

11.36 The amount of the reserve so arising is a matter of accounting practice. That reserve will be the functional currency amount (see paragraph 11.7) of:

(a) the amount previously recorded in relation to the now-reduced nominal value;
(b) plus or minus any amounts previously recorded for retranslation of the share capital (if it was retranslated – see paragraphs 11.18-11.20);
(c) less any amounts repaid translated at the rate at the date of repayment.

Put simply, the reserve is the aggregate net amount left over, in functional currency, after all of the share capital being reduced, any associated retranslation amounts and any repayment have been removed from the accounts. Appendix 7 contains illustrative examples of a company's position in several scenarios for capital reductions where there have been movements in the exchange rate between the functional currency and foreign share capital currency.

It should be noted that the amount of the reserve so arising is not the same as the amount of the reduction. In law the amount of the reduction would be the currency nominal value reduced at the functional currency exchange rate at the date that the reduction becomes effective. This is because the amount of the capital, and thus of the reduction, is the currency amount (see paragraph 11.22). It can be meaningfully stated at the effective date only at the rate applicable that day. For example, if the amount was repaid on reduction it would be that amount that would actually be repaid and accounted for as a cash payment. The realised profits arising on the reduction, on the other hand, are not determined by reference to the reduction amount but to the reserve arising, which is an accounting matter and may be a different figure. **11.37**

The reserve may be thought of as comprising a number of components, one of which is the reduction amount, as follows, in the functional currency: **11.38**

(a) a credit for the reduced nominal value, to the extent not paid out, at the reduction date exchange rate;
(b) a credit for any previously recorded balance, representing the reduced nominal value, that has not been eliminated by (a) above and/ or by any repayment;
(c) a debit for any previously recorded balance, representing the reduced nominal value, that has been over- eliminated by (a) above and/ or by any repayment; and
(d) a credit or debit, as the case may be, to replace any reserves entry for prior accounting retranslation of the reduced element of the shares since this is associated with the shares' nominal value that no longer exists.

In relation to the last component, such a prior reserves entry arises only where the shares were retranslated for accounting purposes; in effect it anticipated the reduction of the shares (it is the difference between the nominal value at historical rate and an amount equal to what is now the reduction amount) and so should be brought into account in reduction accounting.

12 CASH BOX STRUCTURES 12.1 – 12.35

Introduction to the cash box share issue method

The so-called "cash box" method of effecting an issue of shares for cash has been employed from time to time over at least two decades. They have recently become commonplace. Whilst they have previously been seen in relation to acquisition funding, more recently they also have been seen in connection with debt repayment or regulatory capital increases. Some companies undertaking such issues have been advised by their lawyers that the arrangement does not give rise to any share premium. As a consequence the question arises as to the status of the reserve recorded instead of share premium: is it a realised profit? **12.1**

Brief details

Although there are slight variations in the schemes put forward, a common case would be as follows (in this case a placing): **12.2**

- There are four parties involved: the Company; NewCo, a newly incorporated non-UK subsidiary of which the company holds 89 of 100 ordinary shares (worth a trivial amount); a bank, that owns the other 11 shares (worth a trivial amount); and the placees who will put up a substantial amount of cash.
- The placees pay over the cash subscription amount to the bank, which, as principal, subscribes that cash amount for preference shares in NewCo.

- The Company allots ordinary shares (being equity shares under s548) to the placees, in consideration for which the bank transfers to it the 11 NewCo ordinary shares and the NewCo preference shares.
- NewCo redeems its preference shares (now held by the Company) in cash for the amount of the placing proceeds.

No share premium account?

12.3 In relation to the penultimate bullet, it is assumed here, for the purposes of what follows, that there is merger relief under s612 and thus no share premium account falls to be recorded. That is a question of law, which will depend on the particular facts and circumstances of the case. Companies may wish to take legal advice. This Technical Release offers none.

Accounting entries

12.4 In terms of accounting entries, where there is no share premium account there will instead be an other reserve. This would arise because either:

- the Company chooses to record a reserve at the point of acquiring the shares in NewCo in the same way that a company may choose to record a merger reserve in lieu of share premium in any case of the application of s612. This amount is a profit at law, in the same way as merger relief reserves generally (see paragraph 3.8(b)(ii)); or
- the Company could (under UK GAAP) choose to record its investment in NewCo at the nominal value of the shares and thus no reserve arises at this point. However, once the investment in NewCo is redeemed for cash, the Company will record a profit on the redemption in the same amount.

12.5 Either way, the Company finds itself with a merger reserve or a profit reserve and the same question applies to them both: is the reserve realised? The method by which the reserve was recorded makes no difference to the question.

The framework for considering whether the reserve is a realised profit?

12.6 The reserve is akin to one arising where a company receives a capital contribution from shareholders. Paragraphs 12.7 to 12.15 below consider, in effect, whether the assessment of realisation of that reserve proceeds in any different fashion from that of a conventional capital contribution reserve.

Prior to considering the use of the funds

12.7 Following redemption of the Newco preference shares, the cash proceeds thereof will, subject to the question of linkage set out below, fall to be treated as "qualifying consideration" in the hands of the Company (see paragraph 3.9(a) or (f), depending on whether as an accounting entry the reserve arises on redemption by NewCo or on issue by the Company). *Prima facie*, and subject to what follows, the reserve would therefore be considered a realised profit.

Questions of the use of the funds

12.8 Sometimes the reason for the placing or rights issue – and a reason will always be given to the market – is to obtain funds for an acquisition. The precise circumstances of the acquisition will vary. It is possible that the acquisition and placing/ rights issue are conditional upon each other; or they might occur on the same day; or the acquisition may be announced at the placing date but still itself be conditional; or there may in some industries be regulatory restrictions on the use of the cash proceeds.

In other cases the company may have raised the funds in connection with a need to recapitalise a subsidiary. For example, it is possible that the company may be compelled by regulatory requirements immediately to subscribe for equity share capital in a subsidiary; or it may be a commercial necessity to recapitalise a subsidiary. Other cases might include a capitalisation of the company itself for regulatory reasons; or to fund the repayment of the company's own debt. **12.9**

In this context the question arises as to whether the reserve should therefore be deemed to relate to the intended application of the funds(ie with the placing/ rights issue and the application of the funds being a series of related transactions) rather than to the immediate cash proceeds of the placing/ rights issue. **12.10**

This can be split into two questions: **12.11**

- Does the use of the funds need to be considered in terms of the "linkage" principle in paragraph 3.5?
- If so, will the use of the funds be found to be linked under that provision?

Should linkage be considered?

Paragraph 3.5 is of general application and contains no exceptions. There is nothing in a cash box structure that marks it out as fundamentally different and warranting the insertion of an exception to paragraph 3.5. The effect of the application of paragraph 3.5 has therefore to be considered. **12.12**

Two other observations may be noted at this juncture. First, it would be unjustifiable to halt the analysis at the conversion of the NewCo preference shares into cash, and not to go on to consider whether there should be brought into the analysis the conversion of the cash into some other asset; it is a commercial reality that cash boxes are not carried out in a vacuum. **12.13**

Second, if the question of linkage were not addressed, all manner of intra-group transactions might claim to result in realised profits. **12.14**

Conclusion as to framework to be employed in the assessment of realisation

Thus, all of the normal rules of realisation, including the effect of the application of paragraph 3.5 (linkage etc), apply. The assessment therefore proceeds in no different a way from that of the case of a conventional capital contribution. **12.15**

The effect of the application of paragraph 3.5

Paragraphs 12.7 to 12.15 above establish that a cash-box share issue and its wider context should be considered under the paragraph 3.5 principle of linkage etc. Paragraphs 12.17 to 12.35 look at the application of that principle to some scenarios detailing the use of the cash raised. The questions are: is the use of the funds linked; and if so, does the linked transaction, taken together with the equity issue, result in an increase in qualifying consideration for the company issuing the shares? **12.16**

Recapitalisation of the company for regulatory reasons

12.17 Suppose that the company is subject to a regulatory regime that requires it to maintain a specified level of net assets. The company's position and performance has deteriorated and it needs to raise funds, by an equity issue, to maintain its regulatory compliance and hence the continuation of its business. The cash received is employed as working capital.

12.18 Unless the company needs to hold the funds raised in some particular asset within its business, eg if the regulatory requirement is to hold the funds in a particular type of asset, then there is no linked transaction. Accordingly, the profit is a realised one. Even so, it seems unlikely that in practice the company would make a distribution from it as to do so would reduce the company's regulatory capital again.

12.19 If there were a need to hold the funds in some particular asset category, then consideration would need to be given as to whether the specific asset meets the definition of qualifying consideration (see 3.11). To the extent that the asset is qualifying consideration the reserve that is created would be realised (albeit its distribution may not be a practical proposition from a regulatory perspective as noted above).

Recapitalisation of a subsidiary company, with equity, for regulatory reasons

12.20 The company is a holding company that holds a subsidiary that is subject to a regulatory regime that requires it to maintain a specified level of net assets. The subsidiary's position and performance has deteriorated and the subsidiary needs to raise funds, by an equity issue, to maintain its regulatory compliance and hence the continuation of its business. The company (that is, the holding company of the regulated subsidiary) raises the cash by an equity issue of its own and uses the cash to subscribe for equity in the subsidiary.

12.21 The regulatory necessity to recapitalise the subsidiary is enough for the company's onward investment of the funds to be linked. In this case the cash has been invested in equity shares in a subsidiary which will not be qualifying consideration (see 4.10), and thus the reserve is unrealised.

Recapitalisation of a subsidiary company, with equity, out of commercial necessity

12.22 The case here is similar to that above save that the subsidiary is not regulated. It is, however, in financial difficulties and needs funds to continue in business. The company (that is, the holding company of the troubled subsidiary) raises the cash by an equity issue of its own and uses the cash to subscribe for equity in the subsidiary.

12.23 The commercial necessity to recapitalise the subsidiary is enough for the company's onward investment of the funds to be linked. As with the previous example the cash has been invested in equity shares in a subsidiary, which will not be qualifying consideration (see 4.10), and thus the reserve is unrealised.

Recapitalisation of a subsidiary company, with inter-company debt, out of commercial necessity

12.24 Assume that the facts are the same as the previous example except that the cash raised by the company is lent to the subsidiary rather than the company's subscribing for subsidiary shares.

Again the commercial necessity to recapitalise the subsidiary is enough for the company's onward lending of the funds to be linked. In this case, the cash has been turned into an inter-company debt receivable. Whilst an inter-company debt receivable can be qualifying consideration (see 3.11(d)), where the funds have been lent to the subsidiary in view of, say, its troubled financial condition, then it is very unlikely that the debt would meet the tests necessary to be qualifying consideration and as such the reserve would be unrealised. A loan to a financially troubled subsidiary may also be on subordinated terms (such as a contingent loan) and so would make it even less likely that the definition of qualifying consideration would be met. **12.25**

Repayment of the company's own debt

In this scenario the cash raised as new equity is used to repay some of the company's debt. There might be a variety of reasons for this. For example, the company may be rebalancing its gearing ratio for the long term, say because credit markets will not enable it to sustain the previous high level. Or it might be that the company needs to repay that debt in order to survive and has no other sources of liquidity but an equity raising. **12.26**

The commercial necessity to repay debt, or even the management intention to do so, is enough for the company's debt repayment to be linked. However, this does not prevent a realised profit arising. The reserve will in fact be realised as release or settlement of debt is itself a form of qualifying consideration (see 3.11(c)). **12.27**

However, if the debt arose from the acquisition of an asset that does not meet the definition of qualifying consideration and the repayment through the equity issue was planned at the time of the acquisition of the asset, the reserve will be unrealised. **12.28**

Raising cash to be used to fund possible, unspecified acquisitions

In this scenario the company believes that there will be opportunities, in the medium term, to acquire some companies on favourable terms. It therefore raises cash now in order to move quickly if a target is identified. **12.29**

There is not a strong enough nexus between the fund raising and an actual, specific acquisition. Acquisitions are the motivation, but there is not a specific target. In addition, a change in commercial circumstances is a realistic possibility (in a similar way to the sufficient time elapsing during in a planned transaction sequence such that commercial circumstances could change and the rest of the sequence not go ahead – see paragraph 3.74 above). The nexus is too weak for there to be linkage under paragraph 3.5. **12.30**

Thus subject to any arrangement or intention to hold the funds in non-qualifying consideration form, here a realised profit will result. **12.31**

Using the cash received to fund a specific acquisition – where the placing and acquisition are inter-conditional

The company raises equity funds from placees and the placing and the acquisition are conditional upon each other. **12.32**

The acquisition is linked (legally in this case). As the linked use of the cash is to acquire an equity investment that thereby becomes a subsidiary, the reserve will not **12.33** be realised as the investment is not qualifying consideration as it is not readily convertible to cash (see 4.10).

Other acquisition funding cases

12.34 Other acquisition funding cases will require careful examination to determine the level of linkage. The above two examples are at the opposite ends of the spectrum, one where the cash will be used to fund an acquisition, the other where it may or may not be used but in any event not immediately. Obviously there will be situations between these two extremes where judgement will need to be exercised. It should be recalled, however, that legal linkage is not a necessary test for linkage to exist. Simultaneously effecting a fund raising and an acquisition would also be very strong linkage; and few other types of circumstances are likely to be as non-specific and subject to change as the scenario involving possible but unspecified acquisitions.

Disclosure

12.35 The July 2008 edition of the ASB newsletter *Inside Track* noted that the UITF had received a request for guidance about cash box structures. The UITF decided not to address this issue because it was a matter of the application of company law and was already being addressed by the Institutes. However, the issue reached the UITF agenda because some companies had failed to explain adequately, in their financial statements, why no share premium account arose on an issue of share at an apparent premium. When cash box structures are used, it is important that directors consider the adequacy of disclosures about their use and the consequential effect on items in financial statements.

Appendix 1
Examples of the application of sections 845 and 846

Example 1 – Transfer of an asset at book value applying section 845

A company has profits available for distribution of £10,000 on its profit and loss account. It sells a non-cash asset to its parent for a consideration of £20,000 which is equal to its book value. The market value of the asset is £60,000.

The company can apply section 845 in these circumstances and, as explained below, applying this section the distribution would be lawful. Section 845(2) provides that the amount of the distribution is taken to be zero because the amount of the consideration for the transfer is not less than the book value of the asset. Section 845(3) provides that, for the purposes of section 845(1)(a), the company's profits available for distribution are treated as increased by the amount (if any) by which the amount or value of any consideration for the transfer exceeds the book value of the asset. The adjustment in this case is therefore zero and the profits available for distribution in accordance with section 845(1)(a) are treated as £10,000. The company may therefore lawfully make the transfer of the asset because the distributable profits are treated as £10,000 and the amount of the distribution is treated as zero. Thus immediately after the transfer the company's distributable reserves remain £10,000.

Realised profits brought forward	10,000
Adjustment for section 845(3)	–
Profits available for distribution	10,000
Distribution measured in accordance with section 845	–
Balance carried forward on reserves	£10,000

Had the asset been revalued immediately before transfer to its market value of £60,000 the position (using section 846) would have been as follows:

Realised profits brought forward	10,000
Unrealised profit arising from revaluation from book value (£20,000) to market value (£60,000) of the non-cash asset to be transferred to the parent	40,000
Profits treated as available for distribution in accordance with section 846	50,000
Distribution measured as the difference between the fair value of the asset (£60,000) and the consideration received (£20,000)	(40,000)
Balance carried forward on reserves	£10,000

Thus, it can be seen that, section 845 gives the same position before and after the transfer in this example as is given by revaluing the asset and using section 846.

The balance carried forward on reserves is a realised profit.

Example 2 – Transfer of an asset at above book value applying section 845 where there is initially a positive balance of distributable reserves

A company has profits available for distribution of £10,000 on its profit and loss account. It sells a non-cash asset to its parent for a consideration of £50,000 which exceeds its book value of £20,000. The market value of the asset is £60,000.

The company can apply section 845 in these circumstances and, as explained below, applying this section the distribution would be lawful. Section 845(2) provides that the amount of the distribution is taken to be zero because the amount of the consideration for the transfer is not less than the book value of the asset. Section 845(3) provides that, for the purposes of section 845(1)(a), the company's profits available for distribution are treated as increased by the amount (if any) by which the amount or value of any consideration for the transfer exceeds the book value of the asset. The adjustment in this case is therefore £30,000 and the profits available for distribution in accordance with section 845(1)(a) are treated as £40,000. The company may therefore lawfully make the transfer of the asset because the distributable profits are treated as £40,000 and the amount of the distribution is treated as zero.

Realised profits brought forward	10,000
Adjustment for section 845(3):	
Increase in profits treated as available for distribution due to the consideration being in excess of the book value (£50,000 less £20,000)	30,000
Profits treated as available for distribution	40,000
Distribution measured in accordance with section 845	–
Balance carried forward on reserves	£40,000

Whether or not the increase in reserves of £30,000 after the transfer is a realised profit depends on whether the consideration for the transfer is qualifying consideration.

If it is now assumed that the company revalued the asset to its market value of £60,000 it can again be seen that sections 845 and 846 give the same position after the transfer.

Realised profits brought forward	10,000
Unrealised profit arising from revaluation from book value (£20,000) to market value (£60,000) of the non-cash asset to be transferred to the parent	40,000
Profits treated as available for distribution in accordance with section 846	50,000
Distribution measured as the difference between the fair value of the asset (£60,000) and the consideration received (£50,000)	(10,000)
Balance carried forward on reserves	£40,000

Example 3 – Transfer of an asset at below book value applying section 845

A company has profits available for distribution of £10,000 on its profit and loss account. It sells a non-cash asset to its parent for a consideration of £15,000 which is £5,000 below its book value of £20,000. The market value of the asset is £60,000.

The company can apply section 845 in these circumstances and, as explained below, applying this section the distribution would be lawful. Section 845(2) provides that the amount of the distribution is taken to be £5,000 because the amount of the consideration for the transfer is £15,000 and the book value of the asset is £20,000. Section 845(3) provides that, for the purposes of section 845(1)(a), the company's profits available for distribution are treated as increased by the amount (if any) by which the amount or value of any consideration for the transfer exceeds the book value of the asset. The adjustment in this case is therefore zero and the profits available for distribution in accordance with section 845(1)(a) are treated as £10,000. The company may therefore lawfully make the transfer of the asset because the distributable reserves are treated as £10,000 and the amount of the distribution is treated as £5,000. Thus immediately after the transfer the company's distributable reserves are £5,000.

Realised profits brought forward	10,000
Adjustment for section 845(3)	–
Profits available for distribution	10,000
Distribution measured in accordance with section 845 (£20,000 – £15,000)	5,000
Balance carried forward on reserves	£5,000

The balance carried forward on reserves is a realised profit.

Again, if it is now assumed that the company revalued the asset to its market value of £60,000 it can be seen that sections 845 and 846 give the same position after the transfer.

Realised profits brought forward	10,000
Unrealised profit arising from revaluation from book value (£20,000) to market value (£60,000) of the non-cash asset to be transferred to the parent	40,000
Profits treated as available for distribution in accordance with section 846	50,000
Distribution measured as the difference between the fair value of the asset (£60,000) and the consideration received (£15,000)	(45,000)
Balance carried forward on reserves	£5,000

Example 4 – Transfer of an asset at above book value applying section 845 where there is initially a negative balance of distributable reserves

A company has an accumulated deficit of £10,000 on its profit and loss account (ie it has a deficit on its profits available for distribution). It sells a non-cash asset to its parent for a consideration of £50,000 compared with a book value of £20,000 and a market value of £60,000.

The company can apply section 845 in these circumstances although it starts with a negative balance of distributable profits. Section 845(3) provides that, for the purposes of section 845(1)(a), the company's profits available for distribution are treated as increased by the amount (if any) by which the amount or value of any consideration for the transfer exceeds the book value of the asset. The adjustment in this case is therefore £30,000 and the profits available for distribution in accordance with section 845(1)(a) are treated as £20,000. Section 845(2) provides that the amount of the distribution is taken to be zero because the amount of the consideration for the transfer is not less than the book value of the asset. The company may therefore lawfully make the transfer of the asset because the distributable reserves are treated as £20,000 and the amount of the distribution is treated as zero.

Realised losses brought forward	(10,000)
Adjustment for section 845(3):	
Increase in profits treated as available for distribution due to the consideration being in excess of the book value (£50,000 less £20,000)	30,000
Profits treated as available for distribution	20,000
Distribution measured in accordance with section 845	–
Balance carried forward on reserves	£20,000

Although the entire profit of £30,000 has been treated as realised for the purposes of the distribution, the balance carried forward on reserves falls to be treated in accordance with the normal rules. The analysis of reserves carried forward on reserves will depend on whether the transfer of the asset was for qualifying consideration. If the transfer was for qualifying consideration, the whole of the balance of £20,000 carried forward will be a realised profit. If the transfer was not for qualifying consideration, the profit arising on the transfer of the asset will be an unrealised profit and the analysis of reserves will be as follows:

Realised losses	(10,000)
Unrealised profit	30,000
Balance on reserves	£20,000

The same position is achieved by revaluing the asset and applying section 846. The asset could be revalued from £20,000 to £60,000 (its market value) which results in an unrealised profit of £40,000. The distribution is measured at £10,000 being the difference between the fair value of the asset and the consideration received on disposal. In accordance with section 846(2), the unrealised profit of £40,000 is treated as a realised profit for the purposes of determining the lawfulness of the distribution which consists of the sale of the non-cash asset. The profits treated as available for distribution under section 846 are therefore £30,000 which is adequate to cover the distribution of £10,000. This may be summarised as follows:

Realised losses brought forward	(10,000)
Unrealised profit arising from revaluation from book value (£20,000) to market value (£60,000) of the non-cash asset to be transferred to the parent	40,000
Profits treated as available for distribution in accordance with section 846	30,000
Distribution measured as the difference between the fair value of the asset (£60,000) and the consideration received (£50,000)	(10,000)
Balance carried forward on reserves	£20,000

The analysis of reserves carried forward will depend on whether the transfer of the non-cash asset was for qualifying consideration in the same way as described above under section 845.

The distribution in kind of the non-cash asset may therefore, in effect, be made out of unrealised profits without making good the shortfall on realised profits first. Whether or not the consideration for the transfer meets the definition of qualifying consideration has no effect of the lawfulness of the transfer but affects the disposition of the reserves following the transfer.

Appendix 2
Numerical illustrations for section 6

The following are numerical illustrations of the eight examples discussed in Section 6 of the guidance. The illustrations reflect the application of the 10 Principles in 6.7 to 6.40 of Section 6. The assumptions set out in 6.43 to 6.45 of Section 6 apply to these numerical illustrations.

These illustrations are based on simple terms and conditions of the types of financial instruments concerned. Therefore, they cannot, and do not, purport to be representative of the accounting that may flow from more complex terms and conditions. Determining whether a financial instrument is debt, equity or is a compound instrument and/or contains embedded derivatives depends on a rigorous analysis of the relevant instruments' full terms and conditions.

IFRSs and converged UK GAAP (e.g. using FRS 26 'Financial instruments: Recognition and Measurement' and the fair value accounting rules in the Act) do not distinguish between profits that are realised and those that are not. Furthermore, as certain classes of share capital and their associated share premium have to be classified as liabilities and others split into debt and equity components, it is no longer possible to point to one place in the balance sheet that represents all of a company's share capital and share premium. Hence companies will need to maintain sufficient records to enable the tracking of their actual share capital and share premium and realised profits and thus their distributable profits. Companies may choose to do this in the form of memorandum accounts dealing with shares and options in relation to shares according to their legal form. Although, a company's annual statutory accounts prepared in accordance with IFRSs or converged UK GAAP will form their relevant accounts for the purposes of section 836 of the Act, it will be necessary to reconcile these back to records such as these memorandum accounts to understand the legal position in respect of their share capital, share premium, realised and distributable profits. Such memorandum accounts are illustrated below in addition to the balance sheet position under IFRSs/converged UK GAAP.

In the memorandum accounts, the realised profits available are shown for illustrative purposes as a separate component of equity.

In the IFRS/converged UK GAAP accounts, "Other reserves" represent amounts taken to equity for accounting purposes but which do not form part of "share capital and undistributable reserves". For public companies in these illustrations, the expression "share capital and undistributable reserves" for the purposes of section 831 comprises "Share capital", "Share premium" and "Capital redemption reserve" . The P&L reserve is taken initially to be comprised wholly of realised profits.

For the avoidance of doubt, these illustrations do not purport to define the headings or reserve names within which amounts, thrown up only by IFRS/ converged UK GAAP accounting, must as a matter of accounting convention be maintained within equity.

Example 1 – Forward contract to repurchase own equity shares (Section 6, 6.46 – 6.50)

A company has entered into a forward contract to repurchase 100 of its own equity shares from a third party in 5 years' time and the shares are to be cancelled on repurchase. These shares have a nominal value of £100 and are to be bought back for £100 (present value assumed to be £70). The company will buy the shares back, assuming it has sufficient distributable profits, and cancel them.

Under IAS 32/FRS 25, as the company will be required to deliver cash, the forward contract meets the definition of a financial liability.

Journal entries for the IFRS / converged UK GAAP balance sheet

On Day 1:

Dr Equity – Other reserves	£70
Cr Liability	£70

Being the recognition of the liability under the forward contract.

Note that the liability amount is the discounted present value of the redemption amount and is assumed to be £70 in this example. This recognises that the company has purchased an interest in itself on day 1 with the consideration being deferred.

The debit of £70 that has been recorded in other reserves is not an accounting loss and does not affect distributable profits on day 1.

Public company

The recognition of the liability reduces net assets and hence restricts distributable profits for public companies as a result of the section 831 net assets test.

During the 5 years:

Dr Profit & Loss – Interest expense	£30
Cr Liability	£30

Being the accretion of the discounted liability to the redemption amount of £100.

Private company

Although the interest is charged to the profit and loss account, it is not a loss for the purposes of Part VIII of the Act. Thus it is not a realised loss.

Public company

However, for a public company, although realised profits have not decreased, net assets have decreased (as the liability has increased). Hence there is a restriction through the operation of section 831 on the profits available for distribution of £100 in total immediately prior to repurchase as a result of this transaction.

On settlement of the contract:

Dr Liability	£100
Cr Cash	£100

Being the payment (or distribution) to settle the forward contract.

Dr Equity – Profit & Loss reserve	£70
Cr Equity – Other reserves	£70

Being the entry to reflect the consumption of distributable profits in the Profit & Loss reserve as a result of the payment to settle the forward contract.

Dr Equity – Share capital £100
Cr Equity – Capital redemption reserve £100

Being the transfer to maintain the capital of the company.

Memorandum balance sheet

	Before entering into forward	Enter into forward to repurchase shares	After entering into forward	Entries during the 5 years	Before repurchase	Repurchase entries	After repurchase
	£	£	£	£	£	£	£
Cash	100	0	0	0	100	(100)	0
Assets	200	0	0	0	200	0	200
Net assets	**300**	**0**	**0**	**0**	**300**	**(100)**	**200**
Share capital	200	0	0	0	200	(100)	100
Share premium	0	0	0	0	0	0	0
Capital redemption reserve	0	0	0	0	0	100	100
Realised profits	100	0	0	0	100+	(100)	0
Shareholders' funds	**300**	**0**	**0**	**0**	**300**	**(100)**	**200**

+ £100 represents the maximum profits available for distribution but for a public company this will be restricted by £100, immediately prior to repurchase, through the operation of section 831, which is applied to the section 836 relevant accounts (ie the IFRS / converged UK GAAP balance sheet below) which show that net assets are equal to share capital and undistributable reserves.

For the purposes of section 831, in this illustration "share capital and undistributable reserves" comprise "Share capital", "Share premium" and "Capital redemption reserve".

IFRS / converged UK GAAP balance sheet

	Before entering into forward	Enter into forward to repurchase shares	After entering into forward	Entries during the 5 years	Before repurchase	Repurchase entries	After repurchase
	£	£	£	£	£	£	£
Cash	100	0	100	0	100	(100)	0
Assets	200	0	200	0	200	0	200
Liabilities	0	(70)	(70)	(30)	(100)	100	0
Net assets	**300**	**(70)**	**230**	**(30)**	**200**	**0**	**200**
Share capital	200	0	200	0	200	(100)	100
Share premium	0	0	0	0	0	0	0
Capital redemption reserve	0	0	0	0	0	100	100
Other reserves	0	(70)	(70)	0	(70)	70	0
P&L reserve	100	0	100	(30)	70	(70)	0
Shareholders' equity	**300**	**(70)**	**230**	**(30)**	**200**	**0**	**200**

Example 2 – Written option to repurchase own equity shares (Section 6, 6.51 to 6.53)

A company writes an option to repurchase 100 of its own equity shares from a third party in 5 years' time. These shares have a nominal value of £100 and will be bought back for £100 (present value assumed to be £70). If the option is exercised by the third party, the company intends to buy the shares back out of profits, assuming it has sufficient distributable profits, and to cancel them. The company receives a premium of £5 on issue of the option.

Under IAS 32/FRS 25, as the company will be required to deliver cash on exercise of the option, the contract meets the definition of a financial liability. The premium received on the issue of the option is required to be taken directly to equity.

Journal entries for the IFRS / converged UK GAAP balance sheet

On Day 1:

Dr Cash	£5	
Cr Equity – Other reserves		£5

Being the recognition of the premium received.

The option premium is a realised profit because the premium is regarded as a profit at law and has been received in the form of cash. For the purposes of this illustration, the premium has been credited to other reserves on initial receipt and has remained there on exercise (but it could be taken to P&L reserve as illustrated in example 4).

Dr Equity – Other reserves	£70	
Cr Liability		£70

Being the recognition of the liability under the written option.

Note that the liability amount is the discounted present value of the redemption amount and is assumed to be £70 in this example. This recognises that the company has purchased an interest in itself on day 1 with the consideration being deferred.

The debit of £70 that has been recorded in other reserves is not an accounting loss and does not affect distributable profits on day 1.

Public company

The recognition of the liability reduces net assets but not share capital and undistributable reserves and hence restricts distributable profits by £70 for public companies as a result of the section 831 net assets test.

During the 5 years:

Dr Profit & Loss – Interest expense	£30	
Cr Liability		£30

Being the accretion over 5 years of the discounted liability to the redemption value of £100.

Private company

Although the interest is charged to the profit and loss account, it is not a loss for the purposes of Part VIII of the Act. Thus it is not a realised loss.

Public company
However, for a public company, although realised profits have not decreased, net assets have decreased (as the liability has increased). Hence there is a restriction through the operation of section 831 on profits available for distribution of the amount recognised a liability as a result of this transaction (in this case £100).

On settlement of the contract:

Dr Liability	£100
Cr Cash	£100

Being the payment (or distribution) to settle the forward contract.

Dr Equity – Share capital	£100
Cr Equity – Capital redemption reserve	£100

Being the transfer to maintain the capital of the company.

Dr Equity – Profit & Loss reserve	£70
Cr Equity – Other reserves	£70

Being the entry to reflect the consumption of distributable profits in the Profit & Loss reserve as a result of the payment on exercise.

Memorandum balance sheet

	Before issuing option	**Issue of option to repurchase shares**	**After issuing option**	**Entries during the 5 years**	**Before exercise**	**Exercise entries**	**After exercise**
	£	£	£	£	£	£	£
Cash	100	5	105	0	105	(100)	5
Assets	200	0	200	0	200	0	200
Net assets	**300**	**5**	**305**	**0**	**305**	**(100)**	**205**
Share capital	200	0	200	0	200	(100)	100
Share premium	0	0	0	0	0	0	0
Capital redemption reserve	0	0	0	0	0	100	100
Realised profits	100	5	105	0	105+	(100)	5
Shareholders' funds	**300**	**0**	**305**	**0**	**305**	**(100)**	**205**

+ £105 represents the maximum profits available for distribution but for a public company this will be restricted by £100, immediately prior to exercise, through the operation of section 831, which is applied to the section 836 relevant accounts (ie the IFRS / converged UK GAAP balance sheet below) which show that net assets only exceed share capital and undistributable reserves by £5.

For the purposes of section 831, in this illustration "share capital and undistributable reserves" comprise "Share capital", "Share premium" and "Capital redemption reserve".

IFRS / converged UK GAAP balance sheet

	Before issuing option	Issue of option to repurchase shares	After issuing option	Entries during the 5 years	Before exercise	Exercise entries	After exercise
	£	£	£	£	£	£	£
Cash	100	5	105	0	105	(100)	5
Assets	200	0	200	0	200	0	200
Liabilities	0	(70)	(70)	(30)	(100)	100	0
Net assets	**300**	**(65)**	**235**	**(30)**	**205**	**0**	**205**
Share capital	200	0	200	0	200	(100)	100
Share premium	0	0	0	0	0	0	0
Capital redemption reserve	0	0	0	0	0	100	100
Other reserves	0	(65)	(65)	0	(65)	70	5
P&L reserve	100	0	100	(30)	70	(70)	0
Shareholders' equity	**300**	**(65)**	**235**	**(30)**	**205**	**0**	**205**

Example 3 – Forward contract to issue own equity shares (Section 6, 6.54 to 6.56)

A company contracts with a third party that the latter will subscribe in one year's time for 100 of the company's £1 ordinary shares for a fixed price of £2 each. The contract cannot be settled other than by an exchange of the fixed amount of cash (£200) for the fixed number (100) of shares. It is assumed that the fair value of the forward contract at inception is zero and thus no cash is paid or received at that date. The functional currency of the company is pounds sterling.

No accounting entries are made on inception of the contract because no cash is paid or received since the contract's initial fair value is zero. This forward contract to deliver a fixed number of the company's own shares in exchange for a fixed amount of cash in the company's functional currency meets the definition of an equity instrument in IAS 32. There are no other settlement alternatives otherwise than through the delivery of shares in exchange for cash. Consequently, the right to receive the cash in one year's time is not recognised by the company. Therefore, where a company enters into a forward contract to issue ordinary shares, the IAS 32/FRS 25 accounting for such an arrangement raises no issues of distributable profits.

No accounting entries are made until the forward contract matures in one year's time, when the company receives £200 in cash and issues 100 ordinary shares to the contract's counterparty.

Journal entries for the IFRS / converged UK GAAP balance sheet

On settlement of the contract:

Dr Cash	£200
Cr Equity – Share capital	£100
Cr Equity – Share premium	£100

Being the issue of the shares at a premium of £1 per share for £200 in cash.

Memorandum balance sheet

	Before entering into forward	**Enter into forward to issue shares**	**After entering into forward**	**On settlement of the contract**	**After settlement**
	£	£	£	£	£
Cash	100	0	100	200	300
Assets	200	0	200	0	200
Liabilities	0	0	0	0	0
Net assets	**300**	**0**	**300**	**200**	**500**
Share capital	200	0	200	100	300
Share premium	0	0	0	100	100
Capital redemption reserve	0	0	0	0	0
Other reserves	0	0	0	0	0
Realised profits	100	0	100+	0	100
Shareholders' equity	**300**	**0**	**300**	**200**	**500**

+ £100 represents the maximum profits available for distribution. For a public company there is no restriction through the operation of section 831, which is applied to the section 836 relevant accounts (ie the IFRS / converged UK GAAP balance sheet below) which show that net assets exceeds share capital and undistributable reserves by £100.

For the purposes of section 831, in this illustration "share capital and undistributable reserves" comprise "Share capital", "Share premium" and "Capital redemption reserve".

IFRS / converged UK GAAP balance sheet

	Before entering into forward	**Enter into forward to issue shares**	**After entering into forward**	**On settlement of the contract**	**After settlement**
	£	**£**	**£**	**£**	**£**
Cash	100	0	100	200	300
Assets	200	0	200	0	200
Liabilities	0	0	0	0	0
Net assets	**300**	**0**	**300**	**200**	**500**
Share capital	200	0	200	100	300
Share premium	0	0	0	100	100
Capital redemption reserve	0	0	0	0	0
Other reserves	0	0	0	0	0
P&L reserve	100	0	100	0	100
Shareholders' equity	**300**	**0**	**300**	**200**	**500**

Example 4 – Written option to issue own equity shares (Section 6, 6.57 to 6.58)

A company issues an option allowing the holder to subscribe for 100 £1 ordinary shares for £1 each in one years' time. The functional currency of the company is pounds sterling. The option cannot be settled other than by an exchange of the cash in the functional currency of the company for the fixed number of shares. The holder makes an immediate payment of £5 to the company for the granting of this option.

The option is an equity instrument. Accordingly, the £5 received is credited directly to equity funds. The £5 is not an accounting profit. The £5 credit remains in equity funds irrespective of whether the option is exercised or lapses. If the option is exercised, the £100 is also credited directly to equity funds in the normal way.

Journal entries for the IFRS / converged UK GAAP balance sheet

On Day 1:

Dr Cash	£5
Cr Equity – Other reserves	£5

Being the receipt of the option premium.

In law the premium received is a profit at the outset, and a realised profit because it is received in cash. For the purposes of this illustration the premium has been credited to Other reserves on initial receipt and is transferred to the Profit & Loss reserve when the option is exercised.

On Exercise:

Dr Cash	£100
Cr Equity – Share capital	£100
Dr Equity – Other reserves	£5
Cr Equity – Profit & Loss reserve	£5

Being the entries for the issue of the new ordinary shares and receipt of the subscription monies and the transfer of the option premium to Profit & Loss reserve.

Memorandum balance sheet

	Before issuing option	**Issue of option to issue shares**	**After issuing option**	**On exercise**	**After exercise**
	£	£	£	£	£
Cash	100	5	105	100	205
Assets	200	0	200	0	200
Liabilities	0	0	0	0	0
Net assets	**300**	**5**	**305**	**100**	**405**
Share capital	200	0	200	100	300
Share premium	0	0	0	0	0
Capital redemption reserve	0	0	0	0	0
Other reserves	0	0	0	0	0
Realised profits	100	5	105+	0	105
Shareholders' equity	**300**	**0**	**305**	**100**	**405**

+ £105 represents the maximum profits available for distribution. For a public company there will be no restriction through the operation of section 831, which is applied to the section 836 relevant accounts (ie the IFRS / converged UK GAAP balance sheet below) which show that net assets exceed share capital and undistributable reserves by £105.

For the purposes of section 831, in this illustration "share capital and undistributable reserves" comprise "Share capital", "Share premium" and "Capital redemption reserve".

IFRS / converged UK GAAP balance sheet

	Before issuing option	**Issue of option to issue shares**	**After issuing option**	**On exercise**	**After exercise**
	£	**£**	**£**	**£**	**£**
Cash	100	5	105	100	205
Assets	200	0	200	0	200
Liabilities	0	0	0	0	0
Net assets	**300**	**5**	**305**	**100**	**405**
Share capital	200	0	200	100	300
Share premium	0	0	0	0	0
Capital redemption reserve	0	0	0	0	0
Other reserves	0	5	5	(5)	0
P&L reserve	100	0	100	5	105
Shareholders' equity	**300**	**5**	**305**	**100**	**405**

Example 5 – Convertible debt (Section 6, 6.59 to 6.61)

A company issues a 5% £100 10-year convertible bond for £100. The bond is convertible, at the holder's option, into 100 £1 ordinary shares at the end of year 10. If not converted the bond is redeemable at the end of year 10 at par. The conversion feature cannot be settled other than by an exchange of the bond for the fixed number of shares. The company's functional currency is pounds sterling. There are no other features of the bond's terms and conditions that would deny equity treatment for the equity conversion option.

IAS 32/FRS 25 require, where their conditions are met, that convertible debt is split into its constituent components of an unconvertible debt (assumed fair value, £60) and a written option to subscribe for ordinary shares (the equity conversion option). The latter component is accounted for in the same way as the stand-alone written option described in Example 4 above.

Journal entries for the IFRS / converged UK GAAP balance sheet

On Day 1:

Dr Cash	£100
Cr Liability	£60
Cr Equity – Other reserves	£40

Being the recognition of the constituent components.

The split accounting is determined by computing the fair value of the debt component and assigning to the equity component the difference between the value of the debt and the proceeds of the bond issue. The fair value of the debt component is calculated as the present value of the repayment at maturity plus the present value of the future coupon payments (which are lower than those for an unconvertible debt due to the presence of the conversion opportunity). The discount rate used in calculating the present values is the prevailing market interest rate at the date the bonds were issued for a similar debt without the conversion option. For the purposes of this illustration, it is assumed that the split accounting is determined as £60 attributable to the liability component and £40 to the equity component.

The initial credit to equity is not a profit. It is not an accounting profit because in accounting terms it is the equivalent of an equity instrument. As a matter of law, it is not a profit either, because the proceeds received are in consideration for taking on a liability, albeit a liability that is not fully reflected in the accounts.

Over the 10 year life of debt:

Dr Profit & Loss – Interest expense	£90
Cr Cash	£50
Cr Liability	£40

Being the recognition of 10 annual coupons of £5 each and the total additional interest of £40 to accrete the liability up to the redemption value. The allocation of the £90 among the 10 years' profit and loss accounts is determined using the appropriate method stipulated under the relevant accounting standard.

Dr Equity – Other reserves	£40
Cr Equity – Profit & Loss reserve	£40

As the change to the liability becomes fully reflected in the accounts as a loss by virtue of the initial treatment through the additional interest charge, then the portion of the proceeds (£40) initially credited directly to equity offsets the impact of the initial treatment. For the purposes of this illustration, the amounts have been transferred from the Other reserves to the Profit &Loss reserve to reflect this.

At maturity (if conversion occurs):

Dr Liability	£100
Cr Equity – Share capital)	£100

If the debt converts, the £100 is credited direct to shareholders' funds.

At maturity on redemption (if conversion does not occur):

Dr Liability	£100
Cr Cash	£100

Recording the cash settlement of the liability.

Conversion

Memorandum balance sheet

	Before issuing convertible debt	Issue of convertible debt	After issuing convertible debt	Entries during the 10 years	Before conversion	Conversion entries	After conversion
	£	£	£	£	£	£	£
Cash	100	100	200	(50)	150	0	150
Assets	250	0	250	0	250	0	250
Liabilities	0	(100)	(100)	0	(100)	100	0
Net assets	**350**	**0**	**350**	**(50)**	**300**	**100**	**400**
Share capital	200	0	200	0	200	100	300
Share premium	0	0	0	0	0	0	0
Capital redemption reserve	0	0	0	0	0	0	0
Other reserves	0	0	0	0	0	0	0
Realised profits	150	0	150	(50)	100+	0	100
Shareholders' equity	**350**	**0**	**350**	**(50)**	**300**	**100**	**400**

+ £100 represents the maximum profits available for distribution. For a public company there is no restriction through the operation of section 831, which is applied to the section 836 relevant accounts (ie the IFRS / converged UK GAAP balance sheet below) which show that net assets exceed share capital and undistributable reserves by £100.

For the purposes of section 831, in this illustration "share capital and undistributable reserves" comprise "Share capital", "Share premium" and "Capital redemption reserve".

IFRS / converged UK GAAP balance sheet

	Before issuing convertible debt	Issue of convertible debt	After issuing convertible debt	Entries during the 10 years	Before conversion	Conversion entries	After conversion
	£	£	£	£	£	£	£
Cash	100	100	200	(50)	150	0	150
Assets	250	0	250	0	250	0	250
Liabilities	0	(60)	(60)	(40)	(100)	100	0
Net assets	**350**	**40**	**390**	**(90)**	**300**	**100**	**400**
Share capital	200	0	200	0	200	100	300
Share premium	0	0	0	0	0	0	0
Capital redemption reserve	0	0	0	0	0	0	0
Other reserves	0	40	40	(40)	0	0	0
P&L reserve	150	0	150	(50)	100	0	100
Shareholders' equity	**350**	**40**	**390**	**(90)**	**300**	**100**	**400**

Redemption

Memorandum balance sheet

	Before issuing convertible debt	Issue of convertible debt	After issuing convertible debt	Entries during the 10 years	Before redemption	Redemption entries	After redemption
	£	£	£	£	£	£	£
Cash	100	100	200	(50)	150	(100)	50
Assets	250	0	250	0	250	0	250
Liabilities	0	(100)	(100)	0	(100)	100	0
Net assets	**350**	**0**	**350**	**(50)**	**300**	**0**	**300**
Share capital	200	0	200	0	200	0	200
Share premium	0	0	0	0	0	0	0
Capital redemption reserve	0	0	0	0	0	0	0
Other reserves	0	0	0	0	0	0	0
Realised profits	150	0	150	(50)	100+	0	100
Shareholders' equity	**350**	**0**	**350**	**(50)**	**300**	**0**	**300**

+ £100 represents the maximum profits available for distribution. For a public company there is no restriction through the operation of section 831, which is applied to the section 836 relevant accounts (ie the IFRS / converged UK GAAP balance sheet below) which show that net assets exceed share capital and undistributable reserves by £100.

For the purposes of section 831, in this illustration "share capital and undistributable reserves comprise "Share capital", "Share premium" and "Capital redemption reserve".

IFRS / converged UK GAAP balance sheet

	Before issuing convertible debt	Issue of convertible debt	After issuing convertible debt	Entries during the 10 years	Before redemption	Redemption entries	After redemption
	£	£	£	£	£	£	£
Cash	100	100	200	(50)	150	(100)	50
Assets	250	0	250	0	250	0	250
Liabilities	0	(60)	(60)	(40)	(100)	100	0
Net assets	**350**	**40**	**390**	**(90)**	**300**	**0**	**300**
Share capital	200	0	200	0	200	0	200
Share premium	0	0	0	0	0	0	0
Capital redemption reserve	0	0	0	0	0	0	0
Other reserves	0	40	40	(40)	0	0	0
P&L reserve	150	0	150	(50)	100	0	100
Shareholders' equity	**350**	**40**	**390**	**(90)**	**300**	**0**	**300**

Example 6 – Preference shares presented as liabilities (Section 6, 6.62 to 6.70)

A company issues for £110 (being fair value) in cash 100 of its 5% £1 preference shares which are mandatorily redeemable in 5 years' time for £125. The 5% coupons are non-discretionary, cumulative and payable annually. At redemption the company redeems them wholly out of distributable profits.

On issue of the redeemable preference shares the company is required to present these shares as a financial liability of £110, because the issuer has an obligation to transfer cash to the holder of the shares for both the principal and coupons and £110 is the fair value of the shares.

Journal entries for the IFRS / converged UK GAAP balance sheet

On day 1:

Dr Cash	£110
Cr Liability	£110

Being the recognition of the financial liability under IAS 32/FRS 25.

Entries during the 5 years:

Dr Profit & Loss – Interest expense	£40
Cr Cash	£25
Cr Liability	£15

Being the recognition of the £5 annual non-discretionary dividends and the accretion of the liability over time, such that by redemption, the carrying amount of the liability is equal to the redemption price of £125. The allocation of the £40 among the 5 years' profit and loss accounts is determined using the appropriate method stipulated by the relevant accounting standard.

The presentation of the nominal value of £100 of, and the £10 of share premium associated with, the preference shares as a debt has no effect on the determination of the company's realised profits. The accrued dividend and the accrued redemption premium that is presented as an "interest charge" in the profit and loss account, and thus an accounting loss, is not, as a matter of law, a loss, as it is a distribution at the time it is actually made as such in law. Hence it is not until dividends (and the redemption premium) take legal effect that distributable profits are consumed by the distribution.

Public company
Notwithstanding that there is no consumption of distributable profits until such time that the dividends (and redemption premium) have legal effect, the accounting liability recognised for accrued but unpaid preference dividends and the accreted redemption premium reduces net assets. Therefore under section 831 there is a restriction on profits available for distribution equal to the amount of the reduction in net assets. Just before redemption, and assuming that the preference dividends have been paid, the section 831 restriction will be equal to the reduction in net assets of £15. This can be observed by comparing the realised profits in the Memorandum balance sheet (£175) with the Profit & Loss reserve (£160) in the IFRS / converged UK GAAP balance sheet.

Entries on redemption:

Dr Liability	£125
Cr Cash	£125

At the end of year 5, the company delivers £125 in cash to the shareholder, who delivers 100 of the company's (£1) redeemable preference shares. The company sets its cash payment of £125 against the financial liability.

Capital maintenance considerations

In addition, the company has to comply with the Act. Consequently, under section 733 of the Act there has to be a credit to capital redemption reserve equal to the nominal value of the preference shares redeemed that had been presented within liabilities. A corresponding debit is also made to distributable profits (the rationale for which is set out below).

At the same time the £10 of share premium, previously represented by the accounting liability, now falls to be included in the share premium account. A corresponding debit is made to distributable profits (the rationale for which is set out below).

Additional entries required on redemption due to capital maintenance rules:

Dr Equity – Profit & Loss reserve	£110
Cr Equity – Capital redemption reserve	£100
Cr Equity – Share premium	£10

Being the entry to the Profit & Loss reserve which together with the debit for the accrued redemption premium (£15) ensures that £125 of distributable profits is consumed by the redemption price, as required by law. The entry to the Capital redemption reserve is the entry to reflect the legal preservation of the company's capital on redemption out of distributable profits. The £10 entry to the share premium account reflects the legal preservation of the initial share premium.

Memorandum balance sheet

	Before issuing preference shares	**Issue of preference shares**	**After issuing preference shares**	**Entries during the 5 years**	**Before redemption**	**Redemption entries**	**After redemption**
	£	£	£	£	£	£	£
Cash	100	110	210	(25)	185	(125)	60
Assets	300	0	300	0	300	0	300
Liabilities	0	0	0	0	0	0	0
Net assets	**400**	**110**	**510**	**(25)**	**485**	**(125)**	**360**
Share capital	200	100	300	0	300	(100)	200
Share premium	0	10	10	0	10	0	10
Capital redemption reserve	0	0	0	0	0	100	100
Realised profits	200	0	200	(25)	175+	(125)	50
Shareholders' equity	**400**	**110**	**510**	**(25)**	**485**	**(125)**	**360**

+ £175 represents the maximum profits available for distribution but for a public company this will be restricted by £15 through the operation of section 831, which is applied to the section 836 relevant accounts (ie the IFRS / converged UK GAAP balance sheet below) which show that net assets only exceed share capital and undistributable reserves by £160.

For the purposes of section 831, in this illustration "share capital and undistributable reserves" comprise "Share capital", "Share premium" and "Capital redemption reserve".

IFRS / converged UK GAAP balance sheet

	Before issuing preference shares	Issue of preference shares	After issuing preference shares	Entries during the 5 years	Before redemption	Redemption entries	After redemption
	£	£	£	£	£	£	£
Cash	100	110	210	(25)	185	(125)	60
Assets	300	0	300	0	300	0	300
Liabilities	0	(110)	(110)	(15)	(125)	125	0
Net assets	**400**	**0**	**400**	**(40)**	**360**	**0**	**360**
Share capital	200	0	200	0	200	0	200
Share premium	0	0	0	0	0	10	10
Capital redemption reserve	0	0	0	0	0	100	100
P&L reserve	200	0	200	(40)	160	(110)*	50
Shareholders' equity	**400**	**0**	**400**	**(40)**	**360**	**0**	**360**

* Redemption price consumption of distributable profits of £125 = £110 debit at redemption + £15 debit over period to redemption as the additional interest charge (£40-£25).

Example 7 – Mandatorily redeemable preference shares (Section 6, 6.71 to 6.77)

A company issues £100 nominal value of its £1 preference shares for £110 in cash. These shares are redeemable in 5 years' time for £125. Dividends are discretionary and non-cumulative. Under IAS 32/FRS 25 paragraphs 28 and AG37, these shares contain both a liability (assumed fair value, £90) and an equity component. Hence the instrument is classified as debt with an equity component for the dividend feature. It is assumed that over the five years, a total of £50 of discretionary dividends are paid. The accounting is set out below:

Journal entries for the IFRS / converged UK GAAP balance sheet

On Day 1:

Dr Cash	£110
Cr Liability	£90
Cr Equity – Share capital	£20

Being the cash receipt on issuing the shares and recording of the appropriate liability and equity components.

Note that the fair value of the liability amount is the discounted present value of the redemption amount and is assumed to be £90 in this example. The balance (£20) of the proceeds is allocated to the equity component. For ease of this illustration, it is assumed that the entire share premium (£10) is included in the liability and that the credit to equity (£20) is all share capital.

The £20 credit to equity is not an accounting profit and as a matter of law forms part of share capital. This applies irrespective of the allocation of the £20 between share capital and share premium.

Public company

For the purposes of section 831, there is no restriction on profits available for distribution on issue of the preference shares as share capital and undistributable profits have increased by £20 and this is equal to the increase in net assets. The presentation of the balance (£90) of the shares and share premium has no impact on the section 831 calculation.

During the 5 years:

Dr Profit & Loss – Interest expense	£35
Cr Liability	£35

Being the accretion of the discounted liability to the redemption amount of £125.

Private company

The presentation of the discounted present value of the redemption amount of the preference shares as a liability has no effect on the determination of the company's realised profits. The interest expense from the accretion up to the full amount of the redemption price is presented as an accounting loss – as it is shown as an "interest charge". Since the ultimate payment is either a distribution or a capital repayment, the "interest charge" is, as a matter of law, not a loss even though it is accounted for as if it were a loss.

Public company
However, for a public company, although realised profits have not decreased, net assets have decreased (as the liability has increased) over the 5 years. Hence, through the operation of section 831, there is a restriction on distributions of the amount recognised as a liability, £35 in this case, by the redemption date. This can be observed by comparing the realised profits in the Memorandum balance sheet (£200) with the Profit & Loss reserve (£165) in the IFRS / converged UK GAAP balance sheet.

During the 5 years:

Dr Equity – Profit & Loss reserve	£50
Cr Cash	£50

Being the payment of the discretionary dividends during the term of the instrument.

On redemption:

Dr Liability	£125
Cr Cash	£125

Being the payment to redeem the shares.

Capital maintenance considerations
The company has to comply with the Act. Consequently, under section 733 of the Act there has to be a credit to capital redemption reserve equal to the nominal value of the preference shares redeemed that had been presented within liabilities. A corresponding debit is also made to distributable profits adjusted for the £20 originally taken to share capital (the rationale for which is set out below).

At the same time the £10 of share premium, previously represented by the accounting liability, now falls to be included in the share premium account. A corresponding debit is made to distributable profits (the rationale for which is set out below).

Additional entries required on redemption due to capital maintenance rules:

Dr Equity – Profit & Loss reserve	£90
Cr Equity – Capital redemption reserve	£100
Dr Equity – Share capital	£20
Cr Equity – Share premium	£10

Being the entry to the Profit & Loss reserve which together with the debit for the accrued redemption premium (£35) ensures that £125 of distributable profits is consumed by the redemption price, as required by law. The entry to the Capital redemption reserve is the entry to reflect the legal preservation of the company's capital on redemption out of distributable profits. The £20 debit to share capital is to eliminate the £20 originally recorded in respect to the shares which are now cancelled as a result of the redemption. The £10 entry to the share premium account reflects the legal preservation of the initial share premium. This share premium credit (£10), taken together with the capital redemption reserve credit, to the extent not matched by the elimination of share capital (£100 – 20 =£80), gives rise to a corresponding £90 debit to the profit and loss reserve, as referred to above.

Memorandum balance sheet

	Before issuing preference shares	Issue of preference shares	After issuing preference shares	Entries during the 5 years	Before redemption	Redemption entries	After redemption
	£		£	£	£	£	£
Cash	100	110	210	(50)	160	(125)	35
Assets	250	0	250	0	250	0	250
Net assets	**350**	**110**	**460**	**(50)**	**410**	**(125)**	**285**
Share capital	100	100	200	0	200	(100)	100
Share premium	0	10	10	0	10	0	10
Capital redemption reserve	0	0	0	0	0	100	100
Realised profits	250	0	250	(50)	200+	(125)	75
Shareholders' funds	**350**	**110**	**460**	**(50)**	**410**	**(125)**	**285**

+ £200 represents the maximum profits available for distribution but for a public company this will be restricted by £35 through the operation of section 831, which is applied to the section 836 relevant accounts (ie the IFRS / converged UK GAAP balance sheet below) which show that net assets only exceed share capital and undistributable reserves by £165.

For the purposes of section 831, in this illustration "share capital and undistributable reserves" comprise "Share capital", "Share premium" and "Capital redemption reserve".

IFRS / converged UK GAAP balance sheet

	Before issuing preference shares	Issue of preference shares	After issuing preference shares	Entries during the 5 years	Before redemption	Redemption entries	After redemption
			£	£	£	£	£
Cash	100	110	210	(50)	160	(125)	35
Assets	250	0	250	0	250	0	250
Liabilities	0	(90)	(90)	(35)	(125)	125	0
Net assets	**350**	**20**	**370**	**(85)**	**285**	**0**	**285**
Share capital	100	20	120	0	120	(20)	100
Share premium	0	0	0	0	0	10	10
Capital redemption reserve	0	0	0	0	0	100	100
P&L reserve	250	0	250	(85)	165	(90)*	75
Shareholders' equity	**350**	**20**	**370**	**(85)**	**285**	**0**	**285**

*** Redemption price consumption of distributable profits of £125 = £90 debit at redemption + £35 debit over period to redemption as the additional interest charge.**

Example 8 – Convertible redeemable preference shares (Section 6, 6.78 to 6.87)

A company issues for £100 in cash a non-cumulative 10% £100 10-year preference share. The 10% coupons are non-discretionary. The preference share is convertible at the holder's option at any time into 100 £1 ordinary shares. If the holder does not exercise its option to convert, the preference share is mandatorily redeemable for £100 at the end of year 10. The company's functional currency is pounds sterling. There are no other features of the preference share's terms and conditions that would deny equity treatment for the equity conversion option.

Under IAS 32 and FRS 25 paragraph 28, the convertible redeemable preference share is a compound instrument. The preference share has to be split accounted to separate the debt and equity components. The liability component comprises the host redeemable preference share and the non-discretionary coupons (assumed fair value, £60) and the equity component comprises the equity conversion option. The accounting is set out below:

Journal entries for the IFRS / converged UK GAAP balance sheet

On Day 1:

Dr Cash	£100
Cr Liability	£60
Cr Equity – Share capital	£40

Being the recognition of the constituent liability and equity components.

The split accounting is determined by computing the fair value of the debt component and assigning to the equity component the difference between value of the debt component and the proceeds of the preference share issue. The fair value of the debt component is calculated as the present value of the repayment at final maturity (the only date at which cash could be paid) plus the present value of the future coupon payments (which are lower than those for an unconvertible preference share due to the presence of the conversion opportunity). The discount rate used in calculating the present values is the prevailing market coupon rate at the date the preference shares were issued for a similar preference shares without the conversion option. For the purposes of this illustration, it is assumed that the split accounting determined that £60 is the fair value attributable to the liability component and £40 to the equity component.

The £40 credit to equity is not an accounting profit and as a matter of law forms part of share capital.

During the 10 years:

Dr Profit & Loss – Interest expense	£140
Cr Cash	£100
Cr Liability	£40

Being the recognition of the 10% coupon on the preference shares and the accretion of the liability component up to the redemption value.

Private company

The presentation of the discounted present value of the redemption amount of the preference shares as a liability has no effect on the determination of the company's realised profits. The interest expense from the accretion up to the full amount of the redemption price is presented as an accounting loss – as it is shown as an "interest charge". Since the ultimate payment is either a distribution or a capital repayment, the "interest charge" is, as a matter of law, not a loss even though it is accounted for as if it were a loss.

Public company
However, for a public company, although realised profits have not decreased, net assets have decreased (as the liability has increased) over the 5 years. Hence, through the operation of section 831, there is a restriction on distributions of the amount recognised as a liability, £40 in this case, by the redemption date. This can be observed by comparing the realised profits in the Memorandum balance sheet (£150) with the Profit & Loss reserve (£110) in the IFRS / converged UK GAAP balance sheet.

On conversion (if conversion occurs):

Dr Liability	£100
Cr Equity – Share capital	£100

Being the recognition of the equity issued to settle the liability.

In addition, the company has to respect the fact that as a matter of law there is only £100 of share capital in issue (not £140 taking this journal together with the original issue journal).

Additional entries on conversion

Dr Equity – Share capital	£40
Cr Equity – Profit & Loss reserve	£40

Being the entries to reflect the elimination of the prior accumulated debits to the profit and loss reserve in respect of the redemption price, with the corresponding adjustment taken to share capital leaving the balance there correctly representing just £100 of share capital, wholly classified as equity, post-conversion.

On redemption (if conversion does not occur):

Dr Liability	£100
Cr Cash	£100

Being the recognition of the settlement of the liability in cash.

Capital maintenance considerations
In addition, the company has to comply with the Act. Consequently, under section 733 of the Act there has to be a credit to capital redemption reserve equal to the nominal value of the preference shares redeemed that had been presented within liabilities. However, only £40 of this is matched by a corresponding debit to eliminate the share capital now cancelled on redemption. The balance of £60 is debited to the profit and loss reserve (see below).

Additional entries required on redemption due to capital maintenance rules:

Dr Equity – Profit & Loss reserve	£60
Dr Equity – Share capital	£40
Cr Equity – Capital redemption reserve	£100

Being the entries required to reflect the cancellation and preservation of the company's capital on redemption and the charging of the balance of £60 against realised profits; together with the £40- already charged to the profit and loss reserves, which now consumes realised profits, this brings the total consumption of realised profits, on redemption, to the £100 redemption price in accordance with law.

Conversion

Memorandum balance sheet

	Before issuing preference shares	Issue of preference shares	After issuing preference shares	Entries during the 10 years	Before conversion	Conversion entries	After conversion
	£	£	£	£	£	£	£
Cash	200	100	300	(100)	200	0	200
Assets	250	0	250	0	250	0	250
Liabilities	0	0	0	0	0	0	0
Net assets	**450**	**100**	**550**	**(100)**	**450**	**0**	**450**
Share capital	200	100	300	0	300	0	300
Share premium	0	0	0	0	0	0	0
Other reserves	0	0	0	0	0	0	0
Realised profits	250	0	250	(100)	150+	0	150
Shareholders' equity	**450**	**100**	**550**	**(100)**	**450**	**0**	**450**

+ £150 represents the maximum profits available for distribution but for a public company this will be restricted by £40, immediately prior to conversion, through the operation of section 831, which is applied to the section 836 relevant accounts (ie the IFRS / converged UK GAAP balance sheet below) which show that net assets only exceed share capital and undistributable reserves by £110.

For the purposes of section 831, in this illustration "share capital and undistributable reserves" comprise "Share capital", "Share premium" and "Capital redemption reserve".

IFRS / converged UK GAAP balance sheet

	Before issuing preference shares	Issue of preference shares	After issuing preference shares	Entries during the 10 years	Before conversion	Conversion entries	After conversion
	£	£	£	£	£	£	£
Cash	200	100	300	(100)	200	0	200
Assets	250	0	250	0	250	0	250
Liabilities	0	(60)	(60)	(40)	(100)	100	0
Net assets	**450**	**40**	**490**	**(140)**	**350**	**100**	**450**
Share capital	200	40	240	0	240	60	300
Share premium	0	0	0	0	0	0	0
Capital redemption reserve	0	0	0	0	0	0	0
Other reserves	0	0	0	0	0	0	0
P&L reserve	250	0	250	(140)	110	40	150
Shareholders' equity	**450**	**40**	**490**	**(140)**	**350**	**100**	**450**

Redemption

Memorandum balance sheet

	Before issuing preference shares	Issue of preference shares	After issuing preference shares	Entries during the 10 years	Before redemption	Redemption entries	After redemption
	£	£	£	£	£	£	£
Cash	200	100	300	(100)	200	(100)	100
Assets	250	0	250	0	250	0	250
Liabilities	0	0	0	0	0	0	0
Net assets	**450**	**100**	**550**	**(100)**	**450**	**(100)**	**350**
Share capital	200	100	300	0	300	(100)	200
Share premium	0	0	0	0	0	0	0
Capital redemption reserve	0	0	0	0	0	100	100
Other reserves	0	0	0	0	0	0	0
Realised profits	250	0	250	(100)	150+	(100)	50
Shareholders' equity	**450**	**100**	**550**	**(100)**	**450**	**(100)**	**350**

+ £150 represents the maximum profits available for distribution but for a public company this will be restricted by £40 through the operation of section 831, which is applied to the section 836 relevant accounts (ie the IFRS / converged UK GAAP balance sheet below) which show that net assets only exceed share capital and undistributable reserves by £110.

For the purposes of section 831, in this illustration "share capital and undistributable reserves" comprise "Share capital", "Share premium" and "Capital redemption reserve".

IFRS / converged UK GAAP balance sheet

	Before issuing preference shares	Issue of preference shares	After issuing debt	Entries during the 10 years	Before redemption	Redemption entries	After redemption
	£	£	£	£	£	£	£
Cash	200	100	300	(100)	200	(100)	100
Assets	250	0	250	0	250	0	250
Liabilities	0	(60)	(60)	(40)	(100)	100	0
Net assets	**450**	**40**	**490**	**(140)**	**350**	**0**	**350**
Share capital	200	40	240	0	240	(40)	200
Share premium	0	0	0	0	0	0	0
Capital redemption reserve	0	0	0	0	0	100	100
Other reserves	0	0	0	0	0	0	0
P&L reserve	250	0	250	(140)	110	(60)*	50
Shareholders' equity	**450**	**40**	**490**	**(140)**	**350**	**0**	**350**

* Redemption price consumption of distributable profits of £100 = £60 debit at redemption + £40 debit over period to redemption as the additional interest charge.

Appendix 3
Note of legal considerations reproduced from UITF Abstract 38

The equivalent 2006 Act references have been added to the original note for ease of reference.

FRS 5 is not intended to affect the legal characterisation of a transaction, or to change the situation at law achieved by the parties to it (paragraph 46). Shares acquired by ESOP trusts and included in the balance sheet under this Abstract are not treasury shares as defined in the Companies Act 1985 (as amended by the Companies (Acquisition of Own Shares) (Treasury Shares) Regulations 2003) [s724 of the 2006 Act] or as defined by the Companies Act 1990 in the Republic of Ireland. Nor does the inclusion of the shares in the company's balance sheet as a deduction in arriving at shareholders' funds imply that they have been purchased by the company as a matter of law or that they are required to be cancelled, which would be the consequence of such a purchase except for shares held as treasury shares (in Great Britain sections 162(2) and 160(4) of the Companies Act 1985) [s706 of the 2006 Act].*

The UITF has received legal advice on the implications for companies' distributable profits when the accounting treatment required by this Abstract is followed. It has been advised that in Great Britain:

(a) Section 264 of the Companies Act 1985 [s831 of the 2006 Act] provides that a public company may only make a distribution if, and to the extent that, this will not reduce the company's net assets to less than an amount equal to the aggregate of its called up share capital and undistributable reserves. Section 270 [s836 of the 2006 Act] applies for the purposes of determining whether a distribution can be made without contravening sections 263, 264 or 265 [s830, s831 and s832 of the 2006 Act]. It provides that the amount of a distribution which can be made is determined by reference, inter alia, to the company's assets and liabilities as stated in the company's accounts. These are normally the company's last annual accounts (but may be initial or interim accounts). As the effect of the accounting treatment required by this Abstract would be that, in drawing up the accounts in question, any shares held by an ESOP would be recorded as a deduction in arriving at shareholders' funds rather than as an asset, it follows that the relevant aggregate asset value for the purposes of the definition of net assets in section 264(2) [s831(2) of the 2006 Act] would be reduced by a corresponding amount.

(b) In calculating a company's distributable profits, it is necessary to determine its "accumulated, realised profits so far as not previously utilised by distribution or capitalisation, less its accumulated, realised losses, so far as not previously written off in a reduction or reorganisation of capital duly made" (section 263(3) of the Companies Act 1985) [s830(2) of the 2006 Act].

    The acquisition of shares by an ESOP does not, of itself, affect the company's realised profits or realised losses. The accounting treatment required by this Abstract, which requires a deduction in arriving at shareholders' funds and that no gain or loss should be recognised in the profit and loss account, is consistent with this analysis. This analysis holds good notwithstanding that an acquisition of treasury shares, with which an acquisition of shares by an ESOP has similarities, involves a deduction from distributable profits.

    Although the acquisition of shares by an ESOP will not, of itself, result in a realised profit or loss for the company concerned, a company will still need to consider other transactions with the ESOP, for example a loan to the ESOP to fund acquisitions of shares, and these may affect the company's realised profits and losses.

(c) In determining whether a company has sufficient distributable profits and net assets in order lawfully to pay a dividend to its shareholders, under section 270(2) of the Companies Act 1985 [s836(1) of the 2006 Act] the relevant accounts are the company's own individual accounts and not its consolidated accounts.

* The corresponding references in Northern Ireland are to articles 172(2) and 170(4) of the Companies (Northern Ireland) Order 1986 and in the Republic of Ireland to sections 211(2) and 208(a) of the Companies Act 1990. The corresponding references for the Republic of Ireland indicate the provisions dealing with the same topic as the sections in the Companies Act 1985 and are not identical in all cases. The Republic of Ireland references should be consulted for further information.

Appendix 4
Numerical illustrations for section 8

Distinguishing the cumulative gain or loss in reserves from the pension surplus or deficit

It is the cumulative gain or loss credited or debited to reserves in respect of a pension scheme, rather than the existence of a surplus or deficit, that affects the realised profits and losses of a company. Consider the example below of a scheme set up at the start of the year. For simplicity, current and deferred tax is ignored. The scheme has a surplus of 4 at the end of the year that would be reported on the company's balance sheet as an asset. Contributions have been paid which are equal to the expense recognised in the profit and loss account of 20. An actuarial gain of 4 has also been recognised in the STRGL.

	Increase/ (decrease) in pension asset	(Reduction) in cash balance	Amount debited/ (credited) in reserves
Brought forward	0		
Debited to profit and loss	(20)		20
Credited in STRGL	4		(4)
Contributions paid	20	(20)	
Carried forward	4	(20)	16

The net effect on the balance sheet in the above example is:

Dr Pension asset	4	
Dr Reserves	16	
Cr Cash		20

It is the cumulative loss of 16 in the above example that has been debited to reserves in respect of the pension scheme that falls to be treated as realised, rather than any notional "credit" relating to the asset of 4.

Establishing the effect on realised profits at a particular date

This example illustrates the application of paragraph 8.14 of the guidance in the case where the company has recognised a pension asset on acquisition of an unincorporated business.

In 2005, a company acquired an unincorporated business and the fair values of the net assets recognised included a pension asset of 20. At 31 December 2007, cumulative post-acquisition contributions of 4 have been made and the asset has reduced to 18. The cumulative amount included in reserves is calculated as follows:

Surplus recognised in balance sheet	18
Cumulative net contributions	(4)
Surplus recognised on acquisition	(20)
Amount included in reserves (debit)	(6)

Another way of expressing the same calculation is as follows:

Cumulative net contributions		(4)
Surplus recognised in balance sheet	18	
Less: Surplus recognised on acquisition	(20)	
Decrease in surplus recognised		(2)
Amount included in reserves (debit)		(6)

It can be seen from this example that there must be a cumulative debit in reserves if the asset recognised in the balance sheet is less than the amount recognised on acquisition provided that the cumulative net post-acquisition contributions are not negative and the scheme has not been combined with any other scheme.

Appendix 5
Illustrative examples of the effect of the principles relating to foreign currency set out in section 11

Example 1 – illustration of principles 1 and 2 (functional currency strengthens)

Principle 1: Realised profits and losses are measured by reference to the functional currency of the company.

Principle 2: An accounting gain or loss arising upon the retranslation of the whole of the accounts from the company's functional currency to a presentation currency, is not a profit or a loss as a matter of law. Such an amount therefore cannot be a realised profit or loss.

Facts:

Type of company	Private
Functional currency	Sterling
Share capital currency	Sterling
Presentation currency	Dollars
Opening exchange rate	£1 = $1.6
Average exchange rate	£1 = $1.7
Closing exchange rate (sterling has strengthened against the dollar)	£1 = $1.8

The company began the year with no cumulative translation difference (eg, there has been no exchange rate variation to date).

The company's assets and profits are as shown in the table below.

The company's functional and presentation balance sheets and income statements are as follows:

	Opening balance sheet	Profit	Retranslation difference	Closing balance sheet
In functional currency	£	£		£
Share capital	100			100
Profit and loss account reserve (all realised)	20	30		50
Net assets	120	30		150
In presentation currency	$	$	$	$
	(at $1.6)	(at $1.7)		
Share capital	160			160
Profit and loss account reserve	32	51		83
Cumulative translation difference	–		27	27
Net assets	192	51	27	270*

* Net assets of £150 translated at £1 = $1.8.

What are this company's realised profits for the purposes of Part 23?

In accordance with principle 1, the realised profits are measured in the functional currency. In accordance with principle 2, the cumulative translation difference of $27 is not a realised profit. The realised profits are therefore £50. The company could, therefore, so far as the Act is concerned, distribute £50, being $90 in presentation terms (£50 at $1.8) (note that the $83 shown in the profit and loss account reserve is the accumulation of functional currency profits translated at historical presentation rates). The retranslation process has no effect on the determination of realised profits, which occurs at the level of the underlying functional numbers.

Public companies should give consideration to principle 7 when applying the s831 net assets test, as the test operates by reference to the amounts shown in presentation currency, in contrast with the fact that realised profits are measured in the functional currency. In this example there is no restricting effect as the difference between the net assets of $270 and share capital of $160 is $110, which equates to £61 when translated at the closing rate, which is greater than the realised profits in functional currency terms.

Example 2 – illustration of principles 1 and 2 (functional currency weakens)

Principle 1: Realised profits and losses are measured by reference to the functional currency of the company.

Principle 2: An accounting gain or loss arising upon the retranslation of the whole of the accounts from the company's functional currency to a presentation currency, is not a profit or a loss as a matter of law. Such an amount therefore cannot be a realised profit or loss.

Facts:

Type of company	Private
Functional currency	Sterling
Share capital currency	Sterling
Presentation currency	Dollars
Opening exchange rate	£1 = $1.6
Average exchange rate	£1 = $1.5
Closing exchange rate (sterling has weakened against the dollar)	£1 = $1.3

The company began the year with no cumulative translation difference (eg, there has been no exchange rate variation to date).

The company's assets and profits are as shown in the table below.

The company's functional and presentation balance sheets and income statements are as follows:

	Opening balance sheet	Profit	Retranslation difference	Closing balance sheet
In functional currency	£	£		£
Share capital	100			100
Profit and loss account reserve (all realised)	20	30		50
Net assets	120	30		150
In presentation currency	$	$	$	$
	(at $1.6)	(at $1.5)		
Share capital	160			160
Profit and loss account reserve	32	45		77
Cumulative translation difference	–		(42)	(42)
Net assets	192	45	(42)	195*

* Net assets of £150 translated at £1 = $1.3.

What are this company's realised profits for the purposes of Part 23?

In accordance with principle 1, the realised profits are measured in the functional currency. In accordance with principle 2, the cumulative translation difference of

$(42) not a realised loss. The realised profits are therefore £50. The company could, therefore, so far as the Act is concerned, distribute £50, being $65 in presentation terms (£50 at $1.3) (note that the $77 shown in the profit and loss account reserve is the accumulation of functional currency profits translated at historical presentation rates). The retranslation process has no effect on the determination of realised profits, which occurs at the level of the underlying functional numbers.

Public companies should give consideration to principle 7 when applying the s831 net assets test, as the test operates by reference to the amounts shown in presentation currency, in contrast with the fact that realised profits are measured in the functional currency. Example 7 follows the same fact pattern as above but is for a public company and illustrates the resulting restriction.

Example 3 – illustration of principle 3

Principle 3: The profit or loss arising upon the necessary retranslation of an autonomous branch, from its functional currency into the functional currency of the company, is a realised profit or a loss to the extent that the branch net assets during the period, in relation to which the components of that profit or loss arise, were qualifying consideration.

Facts:

Functional currency of company	Sterling
Functional currency of branch	Dollars
Presentation currency of company*	Sterling
Opening exchange rate	£1 = $2.0
Closing exchange rate	£1 = $1.5

The company began the year with no cumulative translation difference (ie, there has been no exchange rate variation to date).

For simplicity and illustrative purposes it has been assumed that there has been no trading during the period, no interest has accrued on the loan and there are no intercompany balances.

The branch's functional currency balance sheets are as follows:

	Opening balance sheet	Closing balance sheet
	$	$
Property, plant and equipment (land)	30	30
Cash	30	30
Loans	(6)	(6)
Net assets	54	54
Represented by:		
Retained profits (all realised)	54	54

When included in the functional currency balance sheet of the company (which currency is also its presentation currency), the assets and liabilities of the branch will be stated as follows:

	£	£
	(at $2.0)	(at $1.5)
Property, plant and equipment (land)	15	20
Cash	15	20
Loans	(3)	(4)
Net assets	27	36
Represented by:		
Cumulative translation difference		9
Profit and loss account reserve	27	27
Total	27	36

**This example is not concerned with presentation currency issues. A presentation currency is included as a simplifying assumption.*

What are this company's realised profits, in relation to its branch, for the purposes of Part 23?

In accordance with principle 3, the cumulative translation difference needs to be analysed with reference to the assets and liabilities that give rise to the difference. In the example above, there is a net profit of 9 which comprises:

Retranslation gain on property, plant and equipment	5
Retranslation gain on cash	5
Retranslation loss on loans	(1)
Total	9

The gain on the property, plant and equipment is not a realised gain, as these assets do not constitute qualifying consideration. The gain on the cash balance held will be a realised gain as cash is qualifying consideration. The loss on the translation of the loan is a realised loss. Therefore, despite a net gain recorded in equity of 9, only 4 of this constitutes realised profit. In total the company's realised profits in relation to its branch are £31. Note that this amount is the realised profits of the branch measured in the company's functional currency in accordance with Principle 1; although the branch has profits of $54 in its branch functional currency of dollars, there is no concept of realised profits at branch level but only at company level where the functional currency is sterling and thus the $54 figure is of itself of no relevance.

If in the example above the company did not have any assets that comprise qualifying consideration, for example, if the cash was instead say an investment property then despite there being a net gain of 9 recognised in equity, the impact on distributable profits would be a reduction of 1, as the loss of the loan would be realised but the gains unrealised.

Example 4 – illustration of principle 4

Principle 4: Where a company's shares, whether those shares are classified as equity or debt for accounting purposes, are denominated in a currency other than the company's functional currency, the adjustment arising upon any translation for accounting purposes of the share capital is not a profit or loss at law. Such an amount therefore cannot be a realised profit or loss.

Facts:

Functional currency	Sterling
Presentation currency	Sterling
Share capital currency	Euro
Nominal value of shares	€90
Opening exchange rate	£1 = €1.8
Closing exchange rate	£1 = €2.0
Share classified as	Accounting equity
Share capital retranslated at balance sheet date	Yes

There have been no translation differences on the share capital prior to the opening balance sheet.

The company has no other foreign (ie, non-sterling) assets or liabilities.

The company's functional and presentation currency balance sheets and income statements are as follows:

	Opening balance sheet £ (at €1.8)	Profit £	Retranslation difference £	Closing balance sheet £ (at €2.0)
Share capital	50			45
Reserve for translation difference on share capital			5	5
Profit and loss account reserve (all realised)	490	270		760
Net assets	540	270	540	810

What are this company's realised profits for the purposes of Part 23?

It is only the profits represented in the retained profit account that are realised (£760). The translation difference of £5 that arises in the above scenario is not a profit at law, and as such the amount cannot be a realised profit. The same would apply if the closing balance sheet exchange rate was £1 = €1.5 meaning that the share capital was stated at £60, the resulting debit balance of £10 would not be a realised loss.

Public companies should give consideration to principle 7 when applying the s831 net assets test, as the test operates by reference to the amounts shown in the accounts. Therefore, the s831 test is applied by reference to share capital recorded at £45, even though the difference of £5 shown above for the retranslation of share capital is not realised (in this particular case there is no restricting effect, since £810 of net assets less £45 of share capital exceeds the realised profits of £760). The s831 test only determines the maximum amount of realised profits that are distributable; it does not have an impact on the calculation of realised profits for the purposes of Part 23.

If the shares were measured at their historical amount (ie not retranslated) there would be no foreign currency movement in respect of the share capital as they remain at their historical amounts (although please see example principle 5 as the current currency worth of the shares would need to be considered).

Shares classified as an accounting liability

Suppose that the facts are the same as before but instead the shares are classified as an accounting liability. In this scenario IAS 21 requires the liability to be retranslated at each balance sheet date, and the foreign exchange difference that arises will be recognised in the income statement. Even though the shares are presented as an accounting liability, they remain share capital as a matter of law; any exchange difference arising on the retranslation is the result of an accounting exercise rather than a profit or loss in law; and the company's realised profits would be as above. However, consideration will need to be given to the other principles (such as the current currency worth of share capital) to determine whether there is any restriction as to the amounts that can be distributed.

Example 5 – illustration of principle 5

Principle 5: Where a company's shares, whether those shares are classified as equity or debt for accounting purposes, are denominated in a currency other than the company's functional currency, the common law has the effect of restricting distributions where to do otherwise would result in the net assets' falling below the functional currency worth of the share capital.

Facts:

Functional currency	Sterling
Presentation currency	Sterling
Share capital currency	Euro
Nominal value of shares	€90
Opening exchange rate	£1 = €2.0
Closing exchange rate	£1 = €1.8
Share classified as	Accounting equity
Share capital retranslated at balance sheet date	No

Assume shares were issued when the exchange rate was £1 = €2.0.

The company has no other foreign (ie, non-sterling) assets or liabilities.

The company's functional and presentation balance sheets and income statements are as follows:

	Opening balance sheet £	Profit £	Closing balance sheet £
Share capital	45		45
Profit and loss account reserve (all realised)	495	270	765
Net assets	540	270	810

What are this company's realised profits for the purposes of Part 23, and what is the maximum amount that the company could distribute?

For the purposes of Part 23, the company's realised profits are £765.

Even though the company has not translated its share capital it still needs to take account of what is the current currency worth of its shares. At the balance sheet date, the €90 of share capital would be worth £50. Therefore when comparing the current worth of the share capital and the net assets in functional currency terms, any distribution would be limited to £760 (£810 – £50).

Example 6 – illustration of principle 6

Principle 6: Share premium account, and similar capital accounts, do not have a currency of denomination but are amounts of record in the books of account in functional currency.

Facts:

Functional currency	Sterling
Presentation currency	Sterling
Currency shares denominated in	Euro
Nominal value of shares (in denomination currency)	€90
Consideration originally received for share issue	€100
Opening exchange rate	£1 = €2.0
Closing exchange rate	£1 = €1.8
Share classified as	Accounting equity
Share capital retranslated at balance sheet date	No

Assume shares were issued when the exchange rate was £1 = €2.0.

Share premium fixed in sterling at historical rate (€100-€90, at £1 = €2.0) £5

The company has no other foreign (ie, non-sterling) assets or liabilities.

The company's balance sheets and income statements are as follows:

	Opening balance sheet	Profit	Closing balance sheet
	£	£	£
Share capital	45		45
Share premium	5		5
Profit and loss account reserve (all realised)	490	270	760
Net assets	540	270	810

What are this company's realised profits for the purposes of Part 23, and what is the maximum amount that the company could distribute?

For the purposes of Part 23, the company's realised profits are £760.

As illustrated in example 5, the company needs to take account of what the current currency worth of the share capital is. As before at the balance sheet date the €90 of share capital (the amount initially issued) would be worth £50. Therefore, there may be a restricting effect due to the increase in the currency worth of the shares as a result of the exchange rate movement. There is, however, no equivalent variation in worth in relation to the share premium; but the share premium account is capital that may not be distributed. Thus under Principle 5 this company compares its net assets of £810 with the aggregate of the current functional currency worth of its share capital (£50) and the functional currency amount of record of its share premium (£5), amounting to £55, and finds that the result does have a restricting effect: ie, £755 is less than the realised profits of £760.

Thus only £755 of the realised profits would be distributable.

It should be noted that in this computation the existence of a share premium account has not, however, increased the restriction. (Eg, if the company had not issued the shares at a premium and had correspondingly lower net assets, then Principle 5 would still yield a £5 restriction: £805 – 50 = £755 vs £760 realised.) What should be appreciated is that had the share premium account in this Example 6 been omitted from the capital side of the Principle 5 calculation, then the company would incorrectly have concluded that there was no restriction (£810 net assets less £50 share capital = £760 vs £760 realised, ie no apparent restriction) and could have inadvertently distributed part of its capital.

Example 7 – illustration of principle 7

Principle 7: The application of the s831 statutory net assets test operates by reference to amounts as shown upon the face of the accounts in presentation currency.

Facts:

Type of company	Public
Functional currency	Sterling
Share capital currency	Sterling
Presentation currency	Dollars
Opening exchange rate	£1 = $1.6
Average exchange rate	£1 = $1.5
Closing exchange rate	£1 = $1.3

The facts are the same as Example 2 except the company is a public company.

The company began the year with no cumulative translation difference (eg, there has been no exchange rate variation to date).

Its assets and profits are as shown in the table below.

The company's functional and presentation balance sheets and income statements are as follows:

	Opening balance sheet	Profit	Retranslation difference	Closing balance sheet
In functional currency	£	£		£
Share capital	100			100
Profit and loss account reserve (all realised)	20	30		50
Net assets	120	30		150
In presentation currency	$	$	$	$
	(at $1.6)	(at $1.5)		
Share capital	160			160
Profit and loss account reserve	32	45		77
Cumulative translation difference	–		(42)	(42)
Net assets	192	45	(42)	195*

Net assets of £150 translated at £1 = $1.3.

What are this company's realised profits for the purposes of Part 23, and how much can be distributed under Part 23?

In accordance with principle 1, the realised profits are measured in the functional currency. The realised profits are therefore £50 (see example 2). In accordance with principle 2, the cumulative translation difference of $(42) is not a realised loss. If it were a private company, the company could, therefore, so far as the Act is concerned, distribute £50, being $65 in presentation terms (£50 at $1.3).

However, a public company is subject to s831 (see 2.30 – 2.31 above). In summary, a public company may make a distribution only if, after giving effect to such distribution, the amount of its net assets (as defined in s831(2)) is not less than the aggregate of its called-up share capital and undistributable reserves (as defined in s831(4)) as shown in the relevant accounts. This calculation is performed using figures taken directly from the presentational currency accounts.

The cumulative translation reserve does not meet the s831(4) definition of an undistributable reserve (nor is it share capital), therefore the purposes of s831 the amount that could be distributed is calculated below:

	$
Net assets	195
Share capital	(160)
Undistributable reserves	–
Amount that can be distributed under s831	35

The company could under Part 23 distribute only $35, rather than the full £50 ($65) of realised profits (see above).

Note that this restriction is correctly expressed in dollars since it is derived according to the statutory formula from amounts expressed on the face of the accounts in presentation dollars. This is so even though the realised profits, the distribution of which it restricts, are themselves in sterling (in accordance with Principle 1). In order to ascertain the effect of this restriction on any particular distribution, it is necessary to compare the dollar worth of that distribution with this $35 figure. The dollar worth of the distribution would be computed at the exchange rate applying at the date of making the distribution (see [TECH 01/09] paragraph 2.10 as to this date).

Appendix 6
Foreign currency branch examples

Example 1 – Illustration of a non-trading branch that purchases and holds PPE

Principle 3: The profit or loss arising upon the necessary retranslation of an autonomous branch, from its functional currency into the functional currency of the company, is a realised profit or a loss to the extent that the branch net assets were qualifying consideration when the profit or loss arose.

The simplified illustration below demonstrates the effect on realised profits from changes in the composition of a branch's net assets (in this case purchasing and holding PPE). In analysing a net retranslation gain or loss, regard must be had to the nature of the changing asset base on which they arise. In practice, when conducting the analysis, reasonable approximations may be made.

See illustration on next page.

Assumptions
Company with a sterling functional currency establishes a branch which has a dollar functional currency
All cash flows happen at the end of the month
All of the branch's transactions are transacted in Dollars

Background
The branch starts the period with cash, which it uses to purchase land. No further transactions are undertaken

	Start of period		Day 1		Day 365		
Actions			Buys land for $300				
Exchange rate – £1 =		**2**		**2**		**1.8**	
	$	£	$	£	$	£	
PPE (land)	0	0	300	150	300	167	
Cash	300	150	0	0	0	0	
	300	150	300	150	300	167	
Foreign exchange				0		17	
	0	0	0	0	0	0	
			£	£	£	£	
FX differences			Period	Cumulative	Period	Cumulative	
PPE (land)			0	0	17	17	Unrealised gain
			0	0	0	0	
			0	0	17	17	

Even though the branch has been dormant since it purchased the land, we can not assume that the foreign exchange difference of 17 arising in the year on the opening balance sheet is realised just because the balance sheet was represented by cash on day 1.

Example 2 – Illustration of a trading branch and the importance of the composition of foreign exchange movements

Principle 3: The profit or loss arising upon the necessary retranslation of an autonomous branch, from its functional currency into the functional currency of the company, is a realised profit or a loss to the extent that the branch net assets were qualifying consideration when the profit or loss arose.

The simplified illustration below demonstrates the effect on realised profits from changes in the composition of a branch's net assets (in this case building up inventory to a peak and then running it down again). In analysing a net retranslation gain or loss, regard must be had to the nature of the changing asset base on which they arise. In practice, when conducting the analysis, reasonable approximations may be made.

See illustration on next page.

Assumptions
Company with a sterling functional currency establishes a branch which has a dollar functional currency.
All cash flows happen at the end of the month. The loan that the branch has taken out is non-interest bearing
All of the branch's transactions are transacted in Dollars

Background
The branch obtains a loan at the start of the period, which it uses to purchase inventory in the first half. It then starts to run down the inventory.

	Start of period Obtain loan of $300 Purchase inventory for $100		Month 1 Buys inventory for $100		Month 2 Sells $50 of inventory for $100		
Actions							
Exchange rate – £1 =		**2**		**2.2**		**1.9**	
	$	£	$	£	$	£	
Inventory	100	50	200	91	150	79	
Cash	200	100	100	45	200	105	
Loan	(300)	(150)	(300)	(136)	(300)	(158)	
	0	0	0	0	50	26	
Trading profit (realised)			0	0	50	26	
Foreign exchange				0		0	
	0	0	0	0	50	26	
			£	£	£	£	
FX differences			Period	Cumulative	Period	Cumulative	
Inventory			(4.5)	(4.5)	13.0	8.5	Unrealised gain
Realisation of inventory							
FX (*1)					1.3	1.3	Realised gain *1
Cash			(9.1)	(9.1)	7.2	(1.9)	Realised loss
Loan			13.6	13.6	(21.5)	(7.9)	Realised loss
			0.0	0.0	0.0	0.0	

*1 – See separate sheet on pages 160-161

If the opening and closing cash balance is looked at in isolation, one might assume that when calculating the realised profits of the branch, foreign currency movements on the cash balance would not have an adverse effect on the amounts that can be distributed – the balance at the start and end of the period is the same and there has been a favourable change in the exchange rate – the $200 that at the start of period was worth £100 is now worth £105.

On that assumption, one might conclude that all that needs to be considered is the foreign exchange movements on the loan balance, as the foreign exchange movements on the inventory will be unrealised gains.

However as can be seen from the foreign exchange movements that arise in the period, there is actually a cumulative foreign exchange loss on cash balance during the period. This will be a realised loss. The realised profits at the end of the period are £17 (£26 trading profit less £10 realised foreign exchange loss (on the cash and the loan) and a £1 realised gain in relation to foreign exchange movements that have arisen on the sale of inventory (see separate sheet).

The example above is a simplified example which demonstrates that when analysing a net retranslation gain or loss, regard must be had to the nature of the changing asset base on which they arise. When conducting the analysis in a more complicated scenario reasonable approximations may be made.

Analysis of movements from the company's perspective of changes in the composition of the branch's net assets

	Inventory $	Inventory £	Cash $	Cash £	Loan $	Loan £
Balance at start of period (£1:$2)	100	**50.0**	200.0	**100.0**	(300.0)	**(150.0)**
FX during period						
$100 @ £1:$2.2 – $100 @ £1:$2		*(4.5)*				
$200 @ £1:$2.2 – $200 @ £1:$2				*(9.1)*		
$300 @ £1:$2.2 – $300 @ £1:$2						*13.6*
Cashflow movements						
$100 @ £1 = $2.2			(100.0)	(45.5)		
Inventory movements						
$100 @ £1 = $2.2	100.0	45.5				
End of month 1 (£1:$2.2)	200.0	**90.9**	100.0	**45.5**	(300.0)	**(136.4)**
FX during period						
$200 @ £1:$2 – $100 @ £1:$1.9		14.4				
$100 @ £1:$2 – $200 @ £1:$1.9				7.2		
$300 @ £1:$2 – $300 @ £1:$1.9						(21.5)
Sub-total before trading profits		105.3		52.6		(157.9)
Cumulative FX		9.8		(1.9)		(7.9)

Inventory movements						
Sale of $50	*(50.0)*	*(25.0) *1*				
Realisation of inventory FX movement		*(1.3) *2*				
		*(26.3) *3*				
Cashflow movements						
Realisation of historic cost of inventory			*100.0*	*25.0 *1*		
Realisation of inventory FX				*1.3 *2*		
Trading profit				*26.3 *4*		
				*52.6 *5*		
End of month 2 (£1:$1.9)	150.0	**78.9**	200.0	**105.3**	(300.0)	**(157.9)**
Cumulative FX at end of month 2		**8.5**		**(1.9)**		**(7.9)**

*1 On a FIFO basis $50 of inventory sold was originally £25 (at £1:$2).
Whilst this example assumes a FIFO approach, other methods may be adopted according to normal considerations.

*2 This difference, between (*1) and (*2) is the FX gain in inventory realised as a result of its sale for cash.

*3 Inventory of $50 removed from the inventory balance when the rate is £1:$1.9.

*4 Calculated as the difference between the proceeds received ($100 @ £1:$1.9) and the carrying amount of inventory sold ($50 @ £1:$1.9)

*5 This equals $100 at £1:$1.9 (the exchange rate on the date of the transaction) and is comprised of the 3 components above

Appendix 7
Illustrative examples of a company's position in several scenarios for capital reductions where there have been movements in the exchange rate between the functional currency and foreign share capital currency

Facts:

Functional currency	Sterling
Presentation currency	Sterling
Share capital currency	Dollars
Nominal value of shares	$200
Opening exchange rate	£1 = $2.0
Closing exchange rate	See the illustrations below for alternates
Share classified as	Accounting equity
Share capital retranslated at balance sheet date	See the illustrations below for alternates

Assume that the shares were issued when the exchange rate was £1 = $2.0, and the proceeds received on issue were converted into sterling.

Assume that the company has no other foreign (ie, non-sterling) assets or liabilities.

Please see the illustrations below for a company's position in several scenarios.

	Reduction of currency shares capital £1 = $x 1.00				Exclusive of repayment £1 = $x 4.00			
	Share capital £	Retrans entry £	Redux reserve £	Total £	Share capital £	Retrans entry £	Redux reserve £	Total £
Without retranslation b/f	100			100	100			100
Reduction	(200)		200	0	(50)		50	0
Un(over) eliminated	100		(100)	0	(50)		50	0
c/f	0	0	100	100	0	0	100	100
With retranslation b/f	200	(100)		100	50	50		100
Reduction	(200)		200	0	(50)		50	0
Un(over) eliminated	0	0	100	0	0	(50)	50	0
	0	0	100	100	0	0	100	100

	Reduction of currency shares capital			£1 = $x 1.00	With repayment			£1 = $x 4.00
	Share capital £	Retrans entry £	Redux reserve/ (distr'n) £	Total £	Share capital £	Retrans entry £	Redux reserve/ (distr'n) £	Total £
Without retranslation								
b/f	100			100	100			100
Repayment	(200)			(200)	(50)			(50)
Un(over) eliminated	100		(100)	0	(50)		50	0
	0	0	(100)	(100)	0	0	50	50
With retranslation								
b/f	200	(100)		100	50	50		100
Repayment	(200)			(200)	(50)			(50)
Un(over) eliminated	0	100	(100)	0	0	(50)	50	0
	0	0	(100)	(100)	0	0	50	50

Where an overall debit is left behind as a consumption of amounts available for distribution it is assumed that either the company had such amounts available prior to the reduction or that, if such a reduction may be validly effected, the consequence is that the company has a deficit (an excess utilisation of realised profits) which must be made good before any further distribution can be made.

Appendix 8
Example of application of section 846 to fungible assets

Company A has a freehold property with a book value of £100 and a fair value of £1,000. The company would be unable to distribute the property as a distribution in kind because it does not have sufficient distributable reserves.

Freehold property	**100**
	100
Share capital	**50**
Realised profits	**50**
	100

If Company A sells the freehold property in exchange for 1,000 £1 loan notes which represents qualifying consideration, the position is as follows:

Loan notes receivable	**1,000**
	1,000
Share capital	**50**
Realised profits	**950**
	1,000

As the loan notes represent qualifying consideration, the profit of £900 is a realised profit and Company A can make a distribution equal to its accumulated realised profits of £950.

Alternatively, if Company A sells the freehold property in exchange for £1,000 of loan notes which do not represent qualifying consideration, the position is as follows:

Loan notes receivable	**1,000**
	1,000
Share capital	**50**
Realised profits	**50**
Unrealised profits	**900**
	1,000

As the loan notes are fungible assets, the distribution of a proportion of the loan notes results in the realisation of the same proportion of the unrealised reserve. Every £1 loan note represents 90p of unrealised profit. Therefore, the element of each loan note which is not a profit is 10p. As realised profits are £50, only 500 loan notes may be distributed (because distribution of each £1 loan note will consume 10p of realised profits) The balance sheet after such a distribution would be as follows:

Loan notes receivable	**500**
	500
Share capital	**50**
Realised profits	**–**
Unrealised profits	**450**
	500

No further distribution of the remaining loan notes is possible because the distribution of £1 of loan notes would cause only 90p of unrealised profit to become realised and there are no other realised profits available. The maximum distribution possible as a distribution in kind is therefore less than would be the case if all of the loan notes were redeemed or sold for qualifying consideration.

Appendix 9
Example of application of 3.11(e) for distribution by set off

This example is concerned with the scenario where a subsidiary wishes to make a distribution to its parent of an unrealised profit and the distribution would result in the elimination, or reduction, of the asset which represents the unrealised profit.

The subsidiary has an unrealised profit which is represented by a balance due from its parent company. Without considering paragraph 3.11(e), the balance would not meet the definition of qualifying consideration because it would fail to meet one or more of the three criteria specified in paragraph 3.11(d).

The subsidiary's balance sheet is as follows.

Amount receivable from parent	130
Other assets	20
	150
Share capital	10
Unrealised profit related to amount receivable from parent	130
Realised profit	10
	150

The company could lawfully make a distribution in kind of the £130 receivable by applying section 846 of the 2006 Act and treating the unrealised profit as realised for the purposes of the distribution (see paragraph 2.9). Following the distribution, its balance sheet would be as follows.

Amount receivable from parent	–
Other assets	20
	20
Share capital	10
Unrealised profit related to amount receivable from parent	–
Realised profit	10
	20

The same effect is achieved through a waiver of the balance. A waiver by a subsidiary of a balance due to it by its parent would be classified legally as a distribution in kind (see paragraph 2.8E).

However, the legal position is different if the company instead declares a dividend of £130 with the intention of settling it through inter-company account. Section 846 is not applicable because there is no transfer of a non-cash asset. To declare the dividend, the company needs to have realised profits of £130 or more.

The definition of qualifying consideration in paragraph 3.11 addresses these circumstances, specifically at 3.11(e). It confirms that for the purposes of assessing the lawfulness of such a proposed distribution, the amount receivable from the shareholder is qualifying consideration where and to the extent that:

(i) the company intends to make a distribution to the shareholder of an amount equal to or less than its receivable from that shareholder; and

(ii) the company intends to settle such distribution by off-setting against the amount receivable (in whole or in part); and

(iii) within the meaning of paragraph 3.5 of this guidance, (i) and (ii) are linked.

These conditions are met in the circumstances described above and therefore it is lawful for the subsidiary to make a distribution of £130 by set off.

The above example is concerned only with whether the distribution may lawfully be made by the subsidiary. It does not address whether the receipt of the distribution by the parent is a realised profit. For example, where the profit in the subsidiary arises from a hive up of assets, the guidance at 3.5 concerning arrangements that are artificial, linked or circular is relevant.

International Accounting

Standards, Regulations, and Financial Reporting

Edited by
Greg N. Gregoriou and Mohamed Gaber

ELSEVIER
AMSTERDAM • BOSTON • HEIDELBERG • LONDON • NEW YORK • OXFORD
PARIS • SAN DIEGO • SAN FRANCISCO • SINGAPORE • SYDNEY • TOKYO

Elsevier
Linacre House, Jordan Hill, Oxford OX2 8DP
30 Corporate Drive, Suite 400, Burlington, MA 01803, USA

First edition 2006

British Library Cataloguing in Publication Data
A catalogue record for this book is available from the British Library

Library of Congress Cataloguing in Publication Data Control Number: 2006922981

ISBN–13: 978-0-7506-6983-2
ISBN–10: 0-7506-6983-7

For information on all Elsevier publications visit our web site at http://books.elsevier.com

Typeset by Macmillan India
Printed and bound in The Netherlands

06 07 08 09 10 10 9 8 7 6 5 4 3 2 1

Contents

About the editors xiii
About the contributors xiv

1 Lobbying towards a global standard setter – do national characteristics matter? An analysis of the comment letters written to the IASB 1
Ann Jorissen, Nadine Lybaert, and Katrien Van de Poel
1.1 Introduction 3
1.2 Literature review and hypotheses development 5
1.2.1 Literature review 5
1.3 The development of hypotheses 10
1.4 The IASB and the standard-setting process 14
1.4.1 The transformation into a global standard setter 15
1.4.2 The mission of the IASB and its due process 15
1.4.3 The standard-setting process or due process 16
1.5 Research method 18
1.5.1 Data collection 18
1.5.2 Measurement of variables 20
1.6 Research results 23
1.6.1 The preparers lobby more often than the users 23
1.6.2 Large companies participate more often in the lobbying process 25
1.6.3 Companies that suffer from a larger negative economic impact of the standards will lobby more often 26
1.6.4 The position of the auditor in the lobbying process 28
1.6.5 The influence of country-level variables on the lobbying behavior 30
1.7 Conclusion 32
References 33
Appendix A 36
Appendix B 39

2 A fair go for fair value 41
Janice Loftus
2.1 Introduction 43
2.2 Experimental fair value initiatives 44
2.3 Proposals and requirements for fair value for financial instruments 46
2.4 IAS 39 and the mixed measurement model 49

2.5 Conclusion 53
References 54

3 The behavior modification impact of International Accounting Standards on decision-making and risk management 57

Stanley C.W. Salvary

3.1 Introduction 59
3.2 The capital market and the commodity market 62
3.3 The role and the psychological effect of the capital market 66
3.4 Simplifying assumptions versus necessary conditions for measurement 71
3.5 Economic reality, decision-making, and operating dynamics 75
3.6 Risk management and performance measurement 77
3.7 Structural and operating differences of companies 82
3.8 Sanity in market pricing and sensibility in financial reporting 86
3.9 The investment decision, capital budgeting, and recoverable cost 89
3.10 Discussion and conclusion 90
References 92

4 Fair value – the basis of International Financial Reporting Standards: a conceptual contradiction of the relevant measurement attribute in financial accounting 97

Stanley C.W. Salvary

4.1 Introduction 99
4.2 Money, a credit economy, and the cash-flow process 102
4.3 Profit measurement and management's performance assessment 104
4.4 Neutrality, stewardship, and financial reporting 107
4.5 The lower of cost and market rule, fair valuation, and realization 109
4.6 The IASB's association of fair market value with the cash-flow process 114
4.7 The Frameworks' measurement bases and the mixed attribute model 116
4.8 Investments, measurement rules, and market simulation 118
4.8.1 Lower of cost and market valuation 120
4.8.2 Realizable value 120
4.9 Summary, discussion, and conclusion 121
References 123

5 Fair value accounting under IAS/IFRS: concepts, reasons, criticisms 127

Jochen Zimmermann and Jörg Richard Werner

5.1 Introduction 129
5.2 Fair value accounting and the IFRS: basic properties and scope of application 130
5.2.1 Definition of fair values 130
5.2.2 Treatment of holding gains and losses 130
5.2.3 FVA and capital maintenance 131
5.2.4 FVA and IAS/IFRS: scope of application 133
5.3 Justifications for the use of fair values in financial reporting 139
5.3.1 Value relevance and standard setting 139
5.3.2 Revaluations as signals 141
5.3.3 Fair value accounting, contracting, and incentives 144
5.4 Conclusion 146
References 148

6 Does Delaware incorporation add value? An accounting-based analysis 151

Feng Chen, Kenton K. Yee, and Yong Keun Yoo

6.1 Introduction 153
6.2 Development of hypotheses 154
6.3 Sample selection 156
6.4 Empirical results 160
6.4.1 Descriptive statistics 160
6.4.2 Is there a Delaware value premium? 162
6.5 Conclusion 165
References 166

7 Empirical evidence on the relation between revaluations of fixed assets and the future performance of firms in Brazil 169

Alexsandro Broedel Lopes

7.1 Introduction 171
7.2 Revaluation of fixed assets in Brazilian GAAP and related literature 174
7.2.1 Brazilian GAAP for revaluation 174
7.2.2 Previous research 178
7.3 Models and results 180
7.3.1 Descriptive statistics 180
7.3.2 Research design and results 180

7.4 Conclusions and implications for future research 185
Acknowledgments 187
References 187

8 **Hedge funds and the stale pricing issue** **189**
Greg N. Gregoriou, William Kelting, and Mohamed Gaber
8.1 Introduction 191
8.2 Background information 194
8.3 Recent developments 195
8.4 Checklist of questions 196
8.5 Conclusion 197
References 197

9 **Adopting and implementing International Financial Reporting Standards in transition economies** **199**
Robert W. McGee
9.1 Introduction 201
9.2 Adopting and implementing IFRS 202
9.3 Translation problems 205
9.4 Teaching the new rules to practitioners 209
9.5 Reforming university curriculums 209
9.6 Credible accounting certification 218
9.7 Conclusion 220
Acknowledgments 221
References 221

10 **International convergence: the Australian journey** **225**
Janice Loftus
10.1 Introduction 227
10.2 Models of international harmonization or convergence of accounting 228
10.3 Models of accounting regulation 230
10.4 Australian standard setting 1970–1983 230
10.5 International harmonization of accounting 1970–1983 232
10.6 Australian standard setting 1984–1988 235
10.7 International harmonization of accounting 1984–1988 238
10.8 Australian standard setting 1988–1990 240
10.9 International harmonization of accounting 1988–1990 242
10.10 Australian standard setting 1991–1999 243
10.11 International harmonization of accounting 1991–1999 247
10.12 Australian standard setting 2000 onwards 252
10.13 International harmonization of accounting 2000 onwards 254

10.14 The beginning of a new journey or the end of the road? 258
Acknowledgments 261
References 261

11 Determinants of bias in management earnings forecasts: empirical evidence from Japan 267

Koji Ota

11.1 Introduction 269
11.2 Background on Japanese management forecasts 270
11.3 Data 272
11.3.1 Sample selection 272
11.3.2 Management forecast error 272
11.4 Determinants of bias in management earnings forecasts 273
11.4.1 Univariate analysis 273
11.4.2 Multivariate analysis 286
11.5 Market awareness of bias in management earnings forecasts 288
11.6 Conclusion 290
Acknowledgments 292
References 293

12 Expected earnings growth when there is a growth option 295

Kenton K. Yee

12.1 Introduction 297
12.2 Perpetual growth option: model setup 299
12.3 Accounting policies and earnings–value relations 303
12.4 Long-run earnings growth with a growth option 307
12.5 Conclusion 312
References 315
Appendix 317

13 The true cost of employee share options: the recent debate and potential costs for a case study firm 325

Colette Grey, Derry Cotter, and Edel Barnes

13.1 Introduction 327
13.2 Literature review 329
13.2.1 ESO value and accounting income 329
13.2.2 Recognition date 331
13.2.3 Measuring fair values 332
13.3 Case study: ESAT Telecom Group 333
13.4 Results 338

13.5 Discussion 340
13.6 Conclusion 343
Acknowledgments 345
References 345

14 Impairment of fixed assets: perceived implementation problems associated with International Accounting Standard No. 36 347

Mohamed E. Ibrahim

14.1 Introduction 349
14.1.1 Indications of impairment 352
14.1.2 The impairment test 353
14.1.3 Accounting for impairment 353
14.2 Previous studies 354
14.3 Methods 359
14.3.1 Sample 359
14.4 Results 361
14.4.1 Sample profile 361
14.4.2 Implementation problems 362
14.5 Conclusion 364
References 365

15 The rise and impact of hybrid securities in Australian listed corporations 367

Tyrone M. Carlin and Nigel Finch

15.1 Introduction 369
15.2 The Australian hybrids market 370
15.3 Measuring the impact of hybrids 375
15.4 Results 376
15.5 Conclusion 383
References 385

16 Empirical evidence on the use, size, concentration, and cost of executive options schemes in Australia 387

Tyrone M. Carlin and Guy Ford

16.1 Introduction 389
16.2 How prevalent are executive options plans in Australia? 390
16.3 Size, activity, and concentration of the observed options schemes 392
16.4 Estimated cost of executive options schemes 396
16.5 Conclusion 398
References 399

17 The introduction of fair value in Italy: economic and financial reporting issues 401

Giovanni Melis, Andrea Melis, and Alessandro Pili

17.1 Introduction 403
17.2 The adoption of the International Financial Reporting Standards in Italy 404
17.3 Accounting for the fair value changes: a comparative analysis of IFRS, US GAAP, and Italian GAAP 406
17.3.1 Intangibles and fixed assets 406
17.3.2 Investment properties 415
17.3.3 Assets and liabilities in foreign currency 415
17.3.4 Actuarial gains and losses on defined benefit plans 418
17.3.5 Financial assets and liabilities 419
17.3.6 Biological assets 424
17.4 The entity's capital maintenance 425
17.4.1 Example 1 (investment property) 426
17.4.2 Example 2 (financial liability) 430
17.5 Accrual basis vs prudence: a comparative analysis of IFRS, Italian, and US GAAP 433
17.6 The underlying reasons for the importance of the prudence principle in Italy 438
17.6.1 Ownership, capital, and control structures of Italian nonfinancial listed companies 439
17.6.2 Generally accepted concept of the corporate entity: IASB vs Italy 440
17.6.3 Cultural issues concerning prudence and risk avoidance 441
17.7 The adoption of the comprehensive income statement in Italy 443
17.7.1 Example 1 (investment property) 445
17.7.2 Example 2 (financial liability) 445
17.8 Conclusion 450
Acknowledgments 451
References 454

18 Factors affecting accounting development in the harmonization process with the international framework: the case of Estonia 457

Toomas Haldma

18.1 Introduction 459
18.2 Literature review 460
18.3 Factors influencing accounting reform in Estonia 462

18.4 Stages of the integration of the Estonian accounting system into the international framework 463
18.5 Findings and discussion 470
18.5.1 The political system 470
18.5.2 The legal system 472
18.5.3 The taxation system 474
18.5.4 Finance and capital markets 475
18.5.5 The accounting profession 476
18.6 Conclusion 479
Acknowledgement 480
References 480

19 An elegant comparison of the tax advantages of mutual funds, IRAs, and Roth IRAs – what hath Roth wrought? 483

Colin Read

19.1 Introduction 485
19.2 A model of lifetime consumption and savings under various tax regimes 485
19.3 The analysis of Roth retirement savings 487
19.4 Comparison to mutual funds under an infinite time horizon 488
19.5 Conclusion and public policy ramifications 489

20 A meta-national perspective on accounting and auditing in nonprofit organizations: the literature interpreted in a principal–agent framework 491

Marc Jegers

20.1 Introduction 493
20.2 Containing the external stakeholders–management agency costs 494
20.2.1 The role of accounting: reducing information asymmetry between board and management 494
20.2.2 A special case: religious organizations 495
20.2.3 Accounting knowledge 495
20.2.4 Donors and the organization 496
20.2.5 Accounting regulation 497
20.2.6 Accounting choices 498
20.2.7 Compliance 499
20.2.8 Choices and compliance when calculating the cost of nonprofit activities 500
20.3 The role of external audit 501
20.3.1 Reducing agency costs 501
20.3.2 Audit pricing 501
20.3.3 Containing the management–other staff agency costs: internal control 502

20.4 Conclusion 502
Acknowledgments 503
References 503

21 How about performance audits for public companies? 507
Haji Shafi Mohamad
21.1 Introduction 509
21.2 Extensions to the role of external auditing 509
21.3 The concept of performance auditing 510
21.4 The origins of auditing 512
21.5 Limitations and problems with implementing performance audits 514
21.6 Auditor independence 515
21.7 Cost/Benefit 515
21.8 Establishing measurement criteria 516
21.9 Conclusion 518
References 520

22 Empirical evaluation of discretionary accruals models 523
Xavier Garza-Gómez
22.1 Introduction 525
22.2 Estimating discretionary accruals 527
22.2.1 Basic accrual models 528
22.2.2 Alternative accrual models 530
22.3 Important properties of total accruals 530
22.3.1 Accruals calculation 531
22.3.2 Sample and descriptive statistics 532
22.4 Evaluation of discretionary accruals models 536
22.4.1 Initial standard errors 537
22.4.2 Results of discretionary accrual models 540
22.5 Information content of discretionary and nondiscretionary accruals 544
22.5.1 Sensitivity tests 545
22.6 Conclusion 546
References 547

23 What to teach? A comparison of professional and paraprofessional accountants' views on accounting topic emphasis 549
Geoffrey Tickell and Kosmas X. Smyrnios
23.1 Introduction 551
23.2 Methodology 555
23.2.1 Participants 555

23.2.2 Procedure 558
23.2.3 Data analyses 558
23.3 Results 558
23.3.1 Descriptive statistics 558
23.3.2 Principal components analyses 559
23.4 Conclusion 565
References 566

24 Australia's accounting education in perspective 569

Geoffrey Tickell and Kosmas X. Smyrnios

24.1 Introduction 571
24.2 Higher education in Australia 571
24.3 Technical and Further Education (TAFE) 573
24.4 Increased cooperation between TAFEs and universities 575
24.5 Lifelong learning 577
24.6 Seamless education 578
24.7 The accounting profession and accounting education in Australia 580
24.8 Accounting education in Australia 582
24.9 Accounting education in TAFE 583
24.10 Conclusion 583
References 584

Index 587

About the Editors

Greg N. Gregoriou is Associate Professor of Finance and coordinator of faculty research in the School of Business and Economics at the State University of New York, College at Plattsburgh. He obtained his Ph.D. (Finance) from the University of Quebec at Montreal and is hedge fund editor for the peer-reviewed scientific journal *Derivatives Use, Trading and Regulation* published by Henry Stewart Publications (UK). He has authored over 45 articles on hedge funds, and managed futures in various US and UK peer-reviewed publications, including the *Journal of Portfolio Management, Journal of Derivatives Accounting, Journal of Futures Markets, European Journal of Operational Research, Annals of Operations Research, European Journal of Finance*, and *Journal of Asset Management*, etc. He has four books published by John Wiley & Sons. This is his second book with Elsevier.

Mohamed Gaber is Associate Professor and Chair, Department of Accounting at the State University of New York, College at Plattsburgh. He received his M.B.A. and Ph.D. from Baruch College (CUNY). He has published in scientific journals such as the *Journal of Pensions* and *Derivatives Use, Trading and Regulation*, among others, and has written several book chapters.

About the Contributors

Dr Edel Barnes is Senior Lecturer in Corporate Finance in the Department of Accounting, Finance and Information Systems, University College Cork, and is program director for the B.Sc. Finance Degree. She obtained her doctorate in Financial Economics from the University of Manchester, her specific area of study being securities markets and seasoned issuance. She also holds the President's Award for excellence in teaching.

Tyrone M. Carlin is Professor of Management at the Macquarie Graduate School of Management (MGSM), Sydney, Australia. His current research interests lie in interdisciplinary work in the areas of corporate governance and corporate financial reporting, as well as public sector financial management. He has published articles in these areas in a range of international journals, including *Management Accounting Research*, *Financial Accountability and Management*, *Public Management Review*, *Australian Accounting Review*, *Sydney Law Review*, *University of New South Wales Law Review*, and *Australian Business Law Review*. He co-edits the *Journal of Law and Financial Management*.

Feng Chen is a Ph.D. Candidate in Accounting at Columbia Business School. He expects to graduate in 2006. Mr Chen holds an M.A. in Economics from Washington University in St Louis and an undergraduate economics degree from Xiamen University in China. He studies accounting-based equity valuation, analysts forecasting, and international accounting. He has published in *Accounting and Business Research*, and has several papers under review at premier accounting and finance journals. Recently, he has presented his research at major US and international academic accounting conferences.

Derry Cotter is a chartered accountant and lectures in Accounting in the Department of Accounting, Finance and Information Systems, UCC, where he is program director for the B.Sc. Accounting degree. He also holds the President's Award for excellence in teaching.

Nigel Finch is a Lecturer in Management at the Macquarie Graduate School of Management, specializing in the areas of managerial accounting and financial management. His research interests are in the areas of accounting and managerial decision-making, finance and investment management, financial services, and public sector financial management. Prior to joining Macquarie Graduate School of Management, he worked as a financial controller for both public and private companies, operating in the manufacturing, entertainment, media, and financial services industries. Subsequently, he worked as an investment manager specializing in Australian growth stocks for institutional investment funds.

Guy Ford is a Senior Lecturer at Macquarie Graduate School of Management, where he teaches in the areas of financial management, corporate acquisitions, corporate reconstructions, financial institutions management, and accounting for management. Formerly of the Treasury Risk Management Division of the Commonwealth Bank of Australia, he has published refereed research papers in domestic and international journals and presented his work at a number of domestic and international conferences. He is founding co-editor of the *Journal of Law and Financial Management* and has co-authored two books, *Financial Markets and Institutions in Australia* and *Readings in Financial Institutions Management.*

Xavier Garza-Gómez, Ph.D., C.F.A., has been Assistant Professor of Finance, University of Houston-Victoria since 2002. Dr Gómez earned a Ph.D. from Nagoya City University in 2001, his M.B.A. from ITESM at Laguna Campus in 1993, and an M.S. from ITESM at Monterrey Campus in 1992. He was Visiting Professor at California State University, San Marcos, in 2002 and Lecturer and Researcher at ITESM 1990–1995.

Colette Grey is a Ph.D. student at the University of Manchester. She lectures in accounting in the Department of Accounting, Kemmy Business School, University of Limerick, in Limerick, Ireland. Her research interests include executive compensation, accounting for stock options, and corporate governance.

Toomas Haldma, Ph.D., is a Professor and the Chair of the Department of Accounting at the University of Tartu, Estonia. He is teaching courses on business accounting and management control. He is the elected Estonian National Coordinator to the European Accounting Association (EAA) and a member of the Estonian Association of Economists. He has served as a member of the Estonian Accounting Standards Board. Dr Haldma served as a member of the supervisory board and a consultant to various Estonian companies and organizations. He is author of 91 publications, including nine monographs and textbooks. He has presented over 30 papers at international conferences (including 12 papers on EAA Congresses in 1994–2005).

Mohamed E. Ibrahim is Professor of Accounting and Dean of the College of Business Administration at the University of Sharjah (UAE). He gained rich experience through his professional consulting work and in different positions in academia at Concordia University (Montreal, Canada) and Hong Kong Polytechnic University. He has published four books and numerous articles that have appeared in recognized refereed journals and proceedings of national and international conferences.

Marc Jegers is Professor at the Vrije Universiteit Brussel where he teaches Theory of the Firm, Accounting, and Managerial Economics of Nonprofit Organizations. He has published on these and related topics in, for example, the *Academy of Management Journal, American Economic Review, Annals of Public and Cooperative Economics, Applied Economics, European Accounting Review, Financial Accountability and Management, Financial Management, Health Economics, Health Policy, Journal of Business Finance and Accounting, Journal of Health Economics, Nonprofit and Voluntary Sector Quarterly*, and *Voluntas.*

Ann Jorissen is Professor of Accounting at the Department of Accounting and Finance of the University of Antwerp (Belgium). She holds a Ph.D. in Applied Economics. She is a former co-editor of the *European Accounting Review* (1992–1997) and has been a member of the editorial board of this journal since 1998. Her research and teaching activities are in the areas of financial reporting, financial analysis, and management control. She has international publications in those areas and is one of the authors of the worldwide selling textbook *International Financial Reporting and Analysis*, 1st and 2nd editions, published by Thomson.

William Kelting is an Associate Professor, Department of Accounting at State University of New York, College at Plattsburgh. He received his Ph.D. from the University of Arkansas.

Janice Loftus is a Senior Lecturer in Accounting at the University of Sydney. Her research interests include financial reporting practice and regulation and sustainability reporting, with recent publicaitons in the areas of financial instruments, measurement, conceptual framework, risk, sustainablility reporting and solvency. Janice has published in international and Australian journals including *Abacus, Accounting and Finance, Accounting Forum, Australian Accounting Review, Financial Reporting Regulation and Governance,* and *Advances in*

International Accounting. She has coauthored several research monographs and reports including: *Acccounting Theory Monograph 11 – Reporting on Solvency and Cash Condition; Sustainability Reporting – Perspectives on Regulatory and Professional Initiatives across the Asia Pacific;* and *Sustainability Reporting – Practices, Performance and Potential*. Janice is the editor of *Financial Reporting, Regulation and Governance*, the journal of the Accounting Standards Interest Group of the Accounting and Finance Association of Australia and New Zealand.

Alexsandro Broedel Lopes is Associate Professor of Accounting and Finance at the University of São Paulo, Brazil and Ph.D. student in Accounting and Finance (ABD) at the University of Manchester. He is a member of the Education Advisory Group of the International Accounting Standards Board (IASB), a Fellow of the Brazilian National Science Foundation (CNPQ), Research Director of Fucape and Editor of the *Brazilian Business Review* (www.bbronline.com.br). He is a former Doctoral Fellow at the London School of Economics and Research Assistant at the Financial Markets Group (2000/2001). He prepared the Education part of the ROSC project for the World Bank in Brazil. Alexsandro has a B.Sc. and a Doctoral degree in Accounting and Control from the University of São Paulo and is interested in international capital market-based accounting research, business analysis and valuation, accounting for derivative financial instruments, and the link between accounting and corporate governance. He can be contacted at broedel@usp.br.

Nadine Lybaert is Associate Professor of Accounting at the University of Hasselt (Belgium), and Guest Professor at the University of Antwerp. She holds a Ph.D. in Applied Economics. Her teaching activities, as well as her research interests, are in the area of financial accounting in the broad sense, in which she has published nationally and internationally. Recently, she wrote a textbook on national company law with the former head of the Directorate of Internal Markets of the European Commission, K. Van Hulle.

Robert W. McGee is a Professor at the Andreas School of Business, Barry University in Miami, Florida, USA. He has published more than 300 articles and more than 40 books in the areas of accounting, taxation, economics, law, and philosophy. His experience includes consulting with the governments of several former Soviet, East European, and Latin American countries to reform their accounting and economic systems.

Andrea Melis is Associate Professor of Accounting and Business Administration at the Department of *Ricerche aziendali*, University of Cagliari, Italy. He is author of two books on corporate governance and several articles on issues related to financial reporting and corporate governance.

Giovanni Melis is Professor of Financial Accounting and Head of the Department of *Ricerche aziendali* at the University of Cagliari, Italy. He has written several books on financial reporting and accounting issues in a wide range of organizations.

Haji Shafi Mohamad has been a full-time lecturer with Universiti Teknologi Mara attached to their Sarawak Branch Campus in Kuching since 1988. For the last five years he has been Head of the Accountancy Program in the Sarawak Branch Campus of UTM and is an Associate Professor. His research interests are in the broad areas of accounting theory and practice, as well as auditing. An area of particular interest to him is the similarities/differences in corporate governance practices worldwide.

Koji Ota is Associate Professor of Accounting at the Faculty of Economics, Musashi University in Tokyo. He received his bachelor's degrees from Kyoto University and Osaka Gakuin University, his M.B.A. from Kansai University, and also completed his doctoral course work at Kansai University. Professor Ota teaches courses in financial accounting and financial statement analysis at both undergraduate and graduate levels. His main research interests are in corporate disclosure, forecast information, and equity valuation. He has had papers published in the *International Journal of Accounting, Accounting Research Journal*, and other accounting and business journals in Japan.

Alessandro Pili is a Ph.D. student in Accounting and Business Administration at the Department of *Ricerche aziendali*, University of Cagliari, Italy.

Colin Read, Ph.D., J.D., is Dean of the School of Business at the State University of New York, College at Plattsburgh.

Stanley C.W. Salvary, Ph.D., is Professor Emeritus, Department of Accounting Canisius College in Buffalo, New York. He has published over two dozen refered articles in peer-reviewed publications and several book chapters. He has also participated in an extensive number of scholarly conferences and worked in numerous CPA firms early in his career.

Kosmas X. Smyrnios holds the position of Professor and Director of Research in the School of Management at RMIT University, Melbourne, Australia. Since receiving his Ph.D. in 1992, Kosmas has established an extensive applied research record, with over 50 international and national refereed publications in different disciplines, including business management, accounting, physics, and psychology. He has supervised a number of Ph.D. students to successful completion. In 1998 and 2001, he was awarded prizes for the Best International Research Papers at the 9th and 12th World Family Business Network Conferences in Paris and Rome, respectively. Recently, Kosmas was listed in Marquis *Who's Who in the World*. Professor Smyrnios is frequently called upon to provide expert media commentary. Up until November 2001, he was Foundation Director of the AXA Australia Family Business Research Unit at Monash University.

Geoffrey Tickell, Ph.D., is Professor at the Department of Accounting and Finance, Faculty of Business and Economics, Monash University, Australia.

Katrien Van de Poel holds a master's degree in Commercial Engineering and is currently employed as a research assistant at the Department of Accounting and Finance at the University of Antwerp (Belgium).

Jörg-Richard Werner is a researcher at the Faculty of Business Studies and Economics at the University of Bremen, from where he also received his degrees. His work covers corporate governance and IFRS, from both a conceptual and empirical perspective.

Kenton K. Yee, J.D., Ph.D., is Assistant Professor of Accounting at Columbia Business School. He holds an undergraduate mathematics degree from MIT, and graduate degrees in law, physics, economics, and business from Stanford Business School, Stanford Law School, UCLA, and the California Institute of Technology. In 2004, he was appointed to the Academic Advisory Board of HedgeStreet, the CFTC-sanctioned electronic futures market. Prior to joining the Columbia faculty, he was a summer litigation associate for a prestigious law firm, a consultant to an extremely successful Silicon Valley venture capital fund, and a co-inventor on a financial patent. Before that, he was a Department of Energy-funded postdoctoral fellow in theoretical physics at Louisiana State University. He teaches two M.B.A. electives, Valuation and Financial Statements, and Financial Statement Analysis and Earnings Quality. He has published in the

Journal of Law and Economics, Review of Accounting Studies, Contemporary Accounting Research, Financial Analysts Journal, International Review of Law and Economics, The Physical Review, Physics Letters, and other premier academic journals.

Yong Keun Yoo, Ph.D., is an Assistant Professor of Accounting at Singapore Management University. He received his Ph.D. from Columbia University in 2004. He obtained an M.B.A. from the University of California at Los Angeles in 2000 and a B.A. in Economics from Seoul National University in 1992. Prior to his graduate studies, he was a Junior Economist at the Bank of Korea. His research interests lie in empirical financial accounting with a special emphasis on equity valuation based on accounting information. He has published in *Accounting and Business Research* and *Review of Accounting and Finance.*

Jochen Zimmermann is Professor of Accounting and Control at the University of Bremen. He received his graduate and postgraduate degrees from the University of Mannheim (Germany). His first professorial appointment took him to the London Business School (University of London), from where he left to take up the Chair of Accounting and Control in Bremen. His research interests are empirical accounting research, governance of accounting, and accounting regulation, as well as insurance.

1

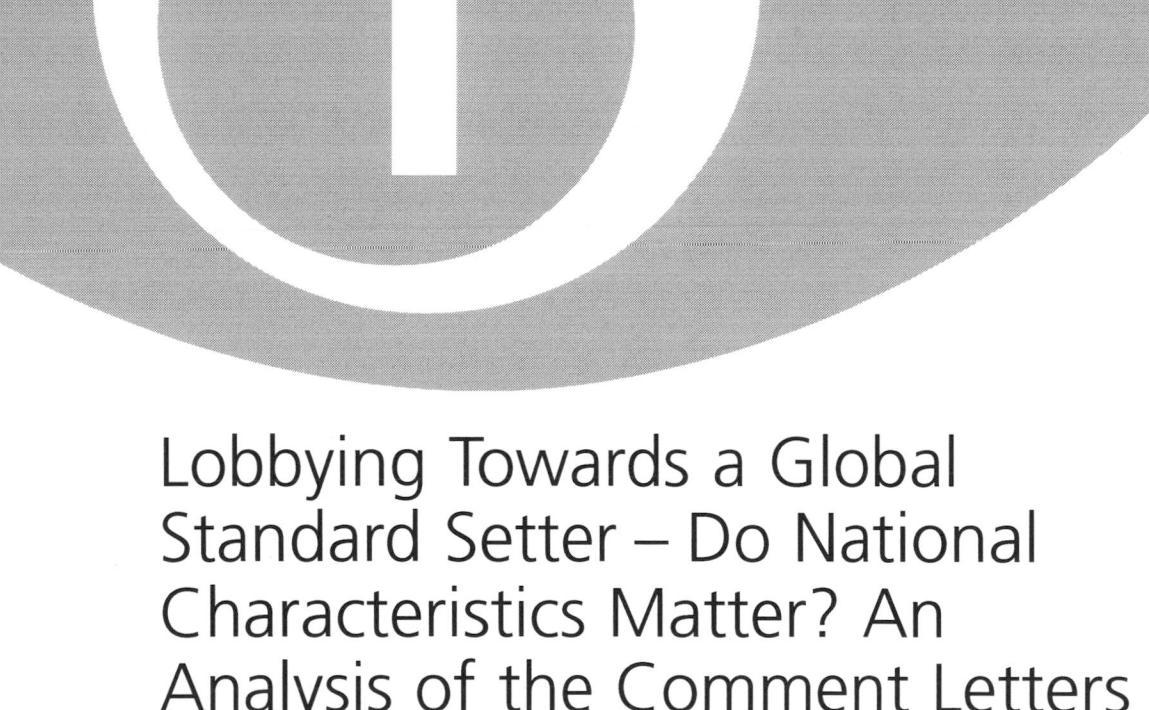

Lobbying Towards a Global Standard Setter – Do National Characteristics Matter? An Analysis of the Comment Letters Written to the IASB

Ann Jorissen, Nadine Lybaert,
and Katrien Van de Poel

1.1 Introduction

Accounting standards, which determine the accounting numbers published by companies, play a major role in the wealth distribution process in market economies. Accounting standards are believed to intend to enhance the quality of accounting information and to reduce the information asymmetry among market participants. In these market economies accounting standards are set either by private standard-setting bodies or by public standard-setting bodies.

The examination of private sector standard-setting processes has been the subject of a considerable number of studies. In almost all studies, private standard setting is always considered as a political activity, in which interested parties are given the opportunity to lobby the standard setter and thus influence the process. Parties affected by the rules will seek to persuade the standard setter to write the rules to their advantage. As a result, lobbying activities take place in order to promote, influence, or obstruct proposed accounting standards. The role of the standard setter is to resolve conflicts amongst interested groups by building consensus. Private standard setters develop their standards according to a due process, which allows all interested parties the opportunity to provide input on proposed accounting standards.

The standard-setting process of a private standard setter can be examined from two major theoretical frameworks. One major framework considers standard setting as a political process where interested parties choose to lobby on the basis of lobbying costs and benefits accrued from successful lobbying (Jensen and Meckling, 1976; Sutton, 1984; Watts and Zimmerman, 1986). The majority of studies investigating the lobby process adopt this framework. The second major framework assumes a nonpluralistic process, dominated by a few powerful groups to the detriment of the interests of other groups, which are effectively excluded from the process (Sikka, 2001). Both research frameworks assume that self-interest drives participants towards lobbying. However, lobbying is not always negative; according to Tandy and Wilburn (1992), participation in the standard-setting process is necessary to ensure the 'legitimacy' of a standard setter and its standards. Lobbying indicates the extent of interest in an issue on the part of constituents. Further lobbying reveals information on the potential implementation problems and costs of future standards.

Lobbying research in relation to private standard-setting bodies was characterized in the past decades by the following elements. First, the majority of the studies focused on the lobbying process of constituents towards the private standard setter in one single national jurisdiction. Second, most analyses concentrated almost exclusively on financial reporting regimes in English-speaking countries, most notably the USA and to a lesser extent the UK, Australia, and New Zealand (McLeay et al., 2000). A very limited number of studies investigated the lobbying process in other countries. One was the study of McLeay et al. (2000), which focused on the German private standard setter, which was newly established at the end of the 20th century.

National private standard setters have been established since the beginning of the 20th century. Towards the end of the 20th century a global standard setter started to emerge. The predecessor of that global standard setter, namely the IASC, was established in 1973. Its creation was related to that of the International Federation of Accountants (IFAC), which is the worldwide umbrella organization of accountancy bodies. The IASC's description of itself as an 'independent private sector body' is accurate and revealing. In the beginning it was in essence a private club, with no formal authority (Alexander et al., 2003). This is in contrast to national regulatory or standard-setting bodies, which operate within a national jurisdiction and some form of legal and governmental framework that delineates, defines, and provides a level of authority. All this changed gradually; the organizational structure of the IASC was changed in 2001 and the IASB was established as a standard-setting private body. The IASB has now acquired the status of global private standard setter, since the adoption of the IAS regulation by the EU and the convergence agreement between the IASB and the USA private standard setter, the FASB.

The IASB incorporates formal public consultation in its process of setting accounting standards. A number of distinct opportunities are given to interested parties to contribute their views on the issues under consideration, before any proposals are adopted as standards. The constitution of the IASB lists these opportunities. Sending comment letters to the IASB is one way to influence the standard-setting process. A few papers have analyzed the lobbying process towards the IASC in the 1990s. Empirical research analyzing lobbying activities and behavior towards the IASB since its reform in 2001 is still rather scarce. This chapter presents the results of the analysis of 2045 comment letters written to the IASB since its reform. The hypotheses developed in the Anglo-Saxon literature will guide the analysis of the comment letters written towards the IASB between 2002 and the summer of 2005.

The remainder of the chapter is structured as follows. In the second part, a literature review will be presented and the research hypotheses will be derived from the extant literature. The third part will include information about the due process of the IASB and the opportunities for the different constituents to take part in the standard-setting process. In the fourth part, the data collection method will be described, together with the measurement of the research variables. The research results will be discussed in the last part of the chapter.

1.2 Literature review and hypotheses development

1.2.1 *Literature review*

The majority of studies investigating lobbying processes were inspired by either the cost/benefit model developed by Sutton (1984) or the economic model of the self-interested party developed by positivists such as Watts and Zimmerman (1986), or by both models.

Using the Downsian voting model, Sutton (1984) developed a cost/benefit model in order to explain when parties take part in the lobby process. According to his model, a party will lobby only if the benefits of lobbying, adjusted by the probability that such lobbying will change the outcome of the standard-setting process, exceed the costs of lobbying. Resulting from this proposition, Sutton (1984) states that for the preparer of financial statements, the potential economic benefits of securing his favored proposal are likely to be greater in absolute terms than the benefits to the user of the financial statements of obtaining this. There are two reasons for this. First, the producer of financial statements is likely to be wealthier than the consumer of the product. Second, even where the user is large (e.g. a pension fund or a mutual fund), there exists a fundamental difference in the degree of portfolio diversification between the preparer and the user. This leads to the following hypothesis: producers of financial statements are more likely to lobby than consumers of such statements. Sutton (1984) further shows that because the economic interests of the preparers are more homogeneous, it is easier for them to create a contemporary organization for lobbying purposes by means of which cost-sharing can be enforced.

With regard to the group of preparers, Sutton argues that larger companies have economic incentives to lobby because they are wealthier than smaller companies and therefore their expected total benefits from lobbying are generally large enough to outweigh the costs. This leads to a second hypothesis: large producers are more likely to lobby than small producers.

Further, Sutton develops the following two other hypotheses: undiversified producers are more likely to lobby than diversified producers and raising (lowering) the cost of noncompliance will increase (reduce) the level of producer lobbying. The first two hypotheses (producer vs user and large firms vs small firms) have been tested in different settings since 1984. The latter two hypotheses have not received that much research attention. The cost/benefit model of Sutton was formulated in a general way and could be used to study the behavior of all constituent parties in the lobbying process.

A second model to study lobby behavior started from an economic point of view. Watts and Zimmerman (1986) stated with the use of their positive theory on accounting that the benefits of lobbying, from the perspective of the management of the company, depended upon the potential impact of the proposals on the expected future cash flow. According to positivists a proposed standard may affect these cash flows for a number of reasons: (1) it alters political costs (e.g. higher taxes, stricter regulatory environment); (2) it has an impact on the accounting numbers embedded in the internal and external contracts of the firm (debt covenants, management incentive systems); or (3) it affects information production costs and bookkeeping costs. These positive studies on corporate lobbying generally assume a causal relation between lobbying and the economic impact on a firm. Lobbying can influence the setting of accounting standards, which in turn affect the company and the well-being of management through accounting numbers. Watts and Zimmerman (1986) argue that because large companies are more politically visible, company size proxies for political costs. New regulation can also lead to the disclosure of elements, which managers would prefer to remain private information for various reasons.

Based on the research frameworks described above, many studies investigated the lobby characteristics and motives almost exclusively in relation to corporate lobbying. A few research articles focused on auditors while the characteristics of the lobbying process of the remaining constituents received almost no research attention.

1.2.1.1 Research on corporate lobbying

Research into corporate lobbying focused mainly on the characteristics of the different preparer groups that participated in the process. A few studies focused on the methods used during the lobby process, their effectiveness, and the costs involved.

With regard to the analysis of motives and characteristics of corporate lobbyers, a number of studies investigated the lobby behavior by comparing the behavior and characteristics of companies who lobbied in favor of a change in the standards and the behavior and characteristics of companies who lobbied against a proposed standard. Not many consistent conclusions emerged from this type of study (Georgiou, 2002). This research stream revealed that larger companies, which were assumed to be facing greater political costs, were less likely to lobby in favor of income-increasing methods. The results with regard to the debt assumption and the management compensation schemes were mixed. An explanation for the lack of consistent conclusions could probably be found in Feroz (1987), Francis (1987), and Buckmaster et al. (1994). Feroz (1987) states that 'Firm submissions can rarely be classified into broad support (or oppose) classifications since most of these letters are far from unambiguous.' Francis (1987) adds that 'Lobbyists may support parts of a proposal and oppose other parts, thus making it difficult to determine an overall lobbying position.' According to Buckmaster et al. (1994), 'Many respondents will only oppose one or two elements of an ED while expressing strong support for the remainder of the exposure draft. To require a "support/oppose" classification for an entire letter would result in nonsense classifications for a substantial portion of the responses.'

Another group of studies on corporate lobbying compares the characteristics of lobbying firms with the characteristics of nonlobbying firms. The hypothesis of Sutton that large producers of financial information are more likely to lobby than small producers was confirmed by many research articles (Francis, 1987; Gavens et al., 1989; Schalow, 1995; Dechow et al., 1996; Seamann, 1997; Ang et al., 2000). According to some of these authors, the size variable can be interpreted in an alternative way in lobbying studies. If management is reluctant to lobby because such action may reveal certain information to the market, then a larger firm would more likely be willing to lobby because the market may already have access to that information and the potential informational effect is smaller.

The research analyzing corporate lobbying from the positive perspective found less support for the importance of debt. Dhaliwal (1982) and Deakin (1989) found it important, while Sutton (1988), Schalow (1995), Ang et al. (2000), and Georgiou and Roberts (2004) did not. Tests of management compensation schemes have reached conflicting results as well. Deakin (1989), Dechow et al. (1996), and Hill et al. (2002) found support, whilst Dhaliwal (1982) and MacArthur and Groves (1993) did not. These studies, however, do find that overall a negative impact on firms' cash flow is a significant predictor of management participation in lobbying activities for proposed accounting standards.

All the articles mentioned above analyze the participation in the lobbying process through the examination of comment letter submissions. A few studies have gathered evidence on why companies did or did not take part in the lobbying process based on survey evidence (Gavens et al., 1989; Schalow, 1995). The results of these studies are in line with the results obtained from the research based on the comment letters.

The results of the research described above, in which the characteristics of lobbying firms are compared with the characteristics of nonlobbying firms, are of interest to standard setters as they indicate that lobbying companies are not representative of nonlobbying companies (Francis, 1987) – they are different both in size and in terms of income variability.

Besides investigating the motives and characteristics of the corporate lobbying and corporate non-lobbying parties, a number of articles investigated the costs of the lobbying processes (Sutton, 1984; McKee et al., 1991), the level of success of the different lobby methods (Sutton, 1984; Walker and Robinson, 1993), and the successfulness of different lobbying parties (Watts and Zimmerman, 1978; Francis, 1987; Georgiou, 2002). The main results of these articles are that submission letters are found to be rather inexpensive and that larger companies are likely to be more influential in the standard-setting process than smaller companies.

A difficulty for the researcher is the unobservability of much of the lobbying activity. Most of the prior studies have investigated lobbying through the analysis of the submitted formal comment letters. A few studies have defined lobbying in a more all-inclusive manner to include comment letters, formal and informal meetings, and conversations with members and the staff of the private standard setter. Georgiou (2004) has, however, shown that there is a strong link between the use of comment letters and the use of other lobbying mechanisms.

1.2.1.2 The lobbying process of the auditor

A second lobbying party that has attracted research interest is the accountants' profession. Several studies concentrated on examining the lobbying positions taken by auditors and their clients in their written submissions (e.g. Puro, 1984; MacArthur, 1988; McKee et al., 1991; Meier et al., 1993; Georgiou, 2002). Several hypotheses govern this area of research. First, a hypothesis is derived from the economics of regulation, which predict that regulated firms succeed in influencing the regulation process in such a way that they can sell more of their products than otherwise, they can sell it at a higher price, or both. The economics of regulation hypothesis leads to an emphasis on the audit firms' private incentives and does not directly address clients' needs. This hypothesis is also called 'the monitoring effect hypothesis'. Second, according to agency theory (Jensen and Meckling, 1976), the auditor can be regarded as an agent and the stockholders of a firm are the principal. In this respect, auditors are expected to lobby for rules that benefit their principal and as a result will benefit the audit firms. According to Watts and Zimmerman (1981), the wealth of the audit firm is a function of their clients' wealth. This second hypothesis is called the 'client preference hypothesis'. Third, there is 'the audit risk hypothesis', which assumes that auditors may support restrictions of available accounting procedures in order to reduce risk, although the extant audit research provides evidence that audit risk is a significant explanatory variable for audit fees. Standards that increase audit risk significantly may not be viewed as worth the revenue generated from the audit work. Meier et al. (1993, 1996) find that the auditor's lobbying position on a proposed accounting standard is a function of both the client's position on the standard and the effect of the proposed standard on audit risk and auditor wealth. A shortcoming of all the auditor studies is that they only evaluate the auditor–client relationship of those clients who made submissions and not of all clients (Georgiou, 2002).

All the research on lobbying described so far has concentrated on the lobbying process within one single jurisdiction. These single jurisdictions were mostly limited to private standard setters in the Anglo-Saxon world (USA, UK, and Australia). In a single-country study, Ang et al. (2000) investigated the incentives of Australian public companies lobbying against proposed superannuation accounting standards. Their findings differed from comparable US studies. The authors concluded that institutional differences are the most obvious reason for these observed differences. This underscores the need to control for institutional differences and to exercise caution in generalizing results across countries.

During the last decades of the 20th century a 'worldwide' standard setter was emerging. Only a few articles have investigated lobbying practices towards the former IASC. A number of them analyzed the content of the responses without focusing on the characteristics of the corporate lobbyers (Kenny and Larson, 1993; Guenther and Hussein, 1995). Larson (1997) focused on corporate characteristics when he investigated corporate lobbying towards the IASC and tested empirically the applicability of US-based lobbying theories in an international context. He analyzed comment letters sent to the IASC between 1989 and 1994 for this purpose. His results indicated that, overall, corporations lobbying the IASC tend to be very large both globally and in terms of their country of domicile; they are listed in at least one foreign exchange, which most of the time was the USA[1]. MacArthur (1996) used content analysis of the comment letters on ED 32 sent by companies to the IASC (comparability of financial statements) to find whether cultural influences shaped the corporate responses. Later, MacArthur (1999) focused on the impact of cultural factors on the lobbying behavior of Accounting Member bodies on the IASC's ED 32.

These research results on the lobbying process towards the IASC date from the time period when the adoption of IAS standards was voluntary and the IASC was not yet considered as a global standard setter. This changed gradually in the last decade of the 20th century and the first years of the 21st century. This chapter will therefore concentrate on the lobbying behavior towards the IASB since its reform in 2001. From 2001 it became clear that the IASB would acquire the status of a global standard setter, especially after the adoption of the IAS regulation by the European Parliament in 2002 and the decision taken, also in 2002, by the IASB and the FASB to work together to develop high-quality, fully compatible financial reporting standards that could be used for domestic and cross-border reporting.

1.3 The development of hypotheses

In this chapter we will use the hypotheses developed in the Anglo-Saxon literature to investigate the lobbying behavior of the constituent parties towards the IASB since its reform in 2001. In relation to corporate lobbying the cost/benefit model of Sutton (1984) and the economic perspective based on the self-interested parties (Watts and Zimmerman, 1986) will provide the framework for the hypotheses we put forward. In relation to the audit profession we use the three hypotheses developed in the literature, which concentrate on auditor lobbying (monitoring effect, client's preferences, and audit risk).

The first two hypotheses are based on Sutton's framework:

Hypothesis 1: *Preparers lobby more often towards the IASB than users*

Hypothesis 2: *Large firms are more likely to lobby towards the IASB than small firms*

The economic benefit approach has often been used to investigate corporate lobbying behavior. This approach is based on Watts and Zimmerman's positive theory of accounting and recognizes that negative cash flows are the drivers for lobbying, independent of firm size. This leads to the following hypothesis to be tested in a multinational context.

Hypothesis 3: *Firms lobby more towards the IASB when the proposed standard has a negative impact on their cash flow*

Several models have been developed in order to explain the lobbying behavior of audit firms. The incentives of the audit firm may co-align with the incentives of its clients or the incentives might be a function of the utility of the auditor in terms of the audit risk or drive to monitor. According to the framework chosen, different hypotheses will result:

Hypothesis 4A: *Auditors will defend their clients' position in the lobby process*

Hypothesis 4B: *Auditors will engage in lobbying in order to increase their audit services and reduce the audit risk*

Hypothesis 4C: *Auditors will engage in lobbying in order to reduce the audit risk*

The four hypotheses listed above will be tested with unit-level data of the constituent parties taking part in the standard-setting process.

In this research setting, which is really multinational, we are able to test the fourth hypothesis that Sutton has formulated in his article. Sutton states in his seminal article that 'raising the cost of noncompliance will increase the level of producer lobbying'. The extant literature on earnings management (e.g. Hope, 2003a,b; Leuz et al., 2003) and quality of earnings (e.g. Ball et al., 2000) provides ample evidence that the cost of noncompliance differs among countries (see, e.g., La Porta et al., 1998). This enables us to test the fourth hypothesis of Sutton (1984) by reformulating his hypothesis as:

Hypothesis 5A: *Companies in countries with low costs of noncompliance will engage less in lobbying than companies located in countries with high costs of noncompliance*

The extant literature on accounting choices, earnings management, and earnings quality provides evidence that, due to institutional and environmental characteristics, the cost of noncompliance differs among countries. Research results indicate that the level of compliance with accounting standards is dependent on the degree of enforcement of standards in each jurisdiction (La Porta et al., 1998; Hope, 2003a,b). Hope (2003a,b) found that the degree of enforcement in a country was a function of the following variables: the level of audit spending, the existence and enforcement of insider trading laws, the rule of law, the judicial efficiency, and the degree of shareholder protection. La Porta et al. (1998) created another enforcement score, which depended on three variables – namely, the efficiency of the judicial system, an assessment of the rule of law, and the corruption index. When enforcement is high, the cost of noncompliance with accounting standards is high as well. This creates a strong incentive to comply with standards. Therefore, if a proposed standard has a negative impact on companies, those firms gain more benefits when they engage in lobbying than firms in countries with weak enforcement. In countries with weak enforcement the cost of noncompliance with a standard is much lower, therefore companies will avoid the proper application of a standard instead of engaging in lobbying with the purpose of altering the standard. This hypothesis 5A will be tested with country-level data. The same holds for the hypotheses below, which will be derived from the extant financial accounting literature.

A variable often analyzed in multinational research settings is culture. In the research on lobbying, MacArthur has investigated the influence of culture on the lobbying behavior towards the IASC of companies located in different countries. As MacArthur analyzed only comment letters written on a single issue, he used the cultural values of Hofstede to relate the cultural characteristics to the arguments put forward in the letters. In this analysis we will investigate whether or not cultural characteristics influence the lobbying behavior of constituent parties.

In order to study cultural influences we use the cultural classification of Hofstede (1980, 1983, 1991). Hofstede describes culture with the use of the following four constructs: power distance, individualism vs collectivism, femininity vs masculinity, and uncertainty avoidance. We will hypothesize that these cultural values influence lobby behavior in the following directions:

Hypothesis 5B1: *Companies in societies characterized by large power distance will engage less in lobbying*

When large power distance is present, companies will accept that power is distributed unequally and the standard setter has the authority to issue standards.

Hypothesis 5B2: *Companies in societies characterized by individualism will engage more in lobbying*

Individualism implies that ties between individuals are loose and that all people are expected to look after themselves (Hofstede, 1983):

Hypothesis 5B3: *Companies from countries characterized by a large degree of femininity will engage more in lobbying*

Hofstede (1991) defines masculinity and femininity in the following ways. Masculinity pertains to societies in which social gender roles are clearly distinct (i.e. men are supposed to be assertive, tough, and focused on material success, whereas women are supposed to be more modest, tender, and concerned with the quality of life); femininity pertains to societies in which social gender roles overlap (i.e. both men and women are supposed to be modest, tender, and concerned with the quality of life).

Hypothesis 5B4: *Companies from countries characterized by strong uncertainty avoidance will engage more in lobbying*

According to Hofstede (1991), strong uncertainty avoidance is expressed through a need for written and unwritten rules. As rules seem to be important in those societies, we assume that they will devote more attention to the standard-setting process.

Somewhat related to culture might be the attitude of people towards compliance with rules. An area in which this attitude towards compliance with rules has been extensively investigated is the issue of tax compliance in the economics and finance literature. Prior research in economics and finance has revealed that the attitude towards tax compliance differs among countries (see Dyck and Zingales, 2004). Using the tax compliance variable as a proxy for the attitude towards compliance of regulation in general, we hypothesize that:

Hypothesis 5C: *Companies engage less in lobbying when they are situated in jurisdictions with low tax compliance*

In the financial accounting literature a substantial number of articles have investigated the different levels of earnings management between countries. In order to analyze differences in lobbying attitudes between countries, we will use available results from the extant literature on earnings management and earnings quality. The extant literature on earnings management and accounting quality indicates that financial reporting practices differ among countries. With regard to earnings management, we are aware that practices differ worldwide. Leuz et al. (2003) investigated the different attitudes towards earnings management and found substantial differences worldwide. These differences correlated, amongst other things, with the importance of the domestic stock market, the legal origin of the countries, the disclosure levels of firms, the ownership concentration, a corruption index, and shareholders' protection rights. We will hypothesize that in countries where earnings management is more prevalent, lobbying will be less because earnings management can be seen as a way to avoid compliance with accounting standards.

Hypothesis 5D: *Companies engage less in lobbying when earnings management is larger in the domestic market*

It is not only the institutional environment and the cultural environment (including the attitude towards tax compliance and earnings management) that may influence the attitude towards lobbying. The information environment might also play a significant role in the decision whether or not to lobby. In the literature review we saw that managers of large firms will be more likely to lobby because the market may already have access to the information, which might be revealed through the comment letters. Building on this observation, we include in our analyses the differences in the domestic information environment of the firm. Research reveals (Lang and Lundholm, 1996) that when the number of analysts following is high, companies have higher disclosure levels and the accounting choices made to influence the reported income are not as effective as in environments characterized by low analyst following. Based on the knowledge that the information environment of the firm is different across countries, we hypothesize that:

Hypothesis 5E: *Companies will engage more in lobbying activities in jurisdictions with a rich information environment, characterized by the number of analysts following*

In the above research hypotheses, we assume that domestic variables and the domestic attitudes towards financial reporting and taxation influence the lobby behavior of the listed companies. However, when firms are multi-listed the institutional characteristics of a foreign stock market might drive the behavior of the firm as well. This is an element we have to take into account when we analyze the results.

Before we describe the research method and the research results obtained on these hypotheses, we will first describe the standard-setting process of the IASB and the opportunities for constituent parties to intervene in this process.

1.4 The IASB and the standard-setting process

The former IASC evolved in the last decade of the 20th century into a global standard setter.

1.4.1 The transformation into a global standard setter

The IASC was created in 1973. In 1995, as the next stage of its development, the IASC entered into an agreement with the International Organization of Securities Commission (IOSCO) to complete a 'core set' of IASs by 1999. With regard to the agreement, the IOSCO's Technical Committee stated that the completion of 'comprehensive core standards acceptable to the Technical Committee' would allow it to 'recommend endorsement of those standards for cross-border capital raising in all global markets'. In December 1998, the IASC completed its core standards. Following the publication of the report of the IASC's Strategic Working Party Recommendations on Shaping the IASC for the Future in November 1999, the board of the IASC approved proposals in December 1999 to make significant changes to the IASC's structure, in order to prepare it for an enhanced role as a global accounting standard setter. In May 2000 the proposed structural changes were approved by the IASC's membership. Also in May 2000, the IOSCO formally accepted the IASC's 'core standards' as a basis for cross-border securities listing purposes worldwide (although for certain countries, notably the USA, reconciliations of items such as earnings and stockholders' equity to national GAAP would still be required). In June 2000, the European Commission issued a communication proposing that all listed companies in the European Union would be required to prepare their consolidated financial statements using IASs, a proposal that has since been adopted when the European Parliament voted, in 2002, for the IAS regulation no. 1606/2002. This resulted in the mandated adoption of the IFRS by listed companies in the European Union as of 1 January 2005.

1.4.2 The mission of the IASB and its due process

After its reform in 2001, the IASB issued the following mission statement (paragraph 6 – preface to IFRS):

a) to develop, in the public interest, a single set of high-quality, understandable, and enforceable global accounting standards that require high-quality, transparent and comparable information in financial statements and other financial reporting to help participants in the various capital markets of the world and other users of the information to make economic decisions;
b) to promote the use and rigorous application of those standards; and
c) to work actively with national standard setters.

When we analyze the objectives of the IASB we notice a number of differences with a 'traditional' national standard setter. The IASB will issue standards that have to be applied in a variety of different legal and cultural contexts. This will require the use of IFRS by companies that vary considerably in size, ownership structure, capital structure, political jurisdiction, and financial reporting sophistication (Schipper, 2005).

Financial reports must be comprehensible across countries, across jurisdictions, and across cultures.

Next, the IASB has no authority with regard to the application of its standards in the different national jurisdictions. The enforcement of the IAS or IFRS is still a national matter. Further, we notice that the IASB will cooperate with national standard setters in its standard-setting process. The IASB will meet the chairmen of its partner and other accounting standard setters regularly. In addition, staff members of the IASB and partner standard setters cooperate on a daily basis on projects, sharing resources whenever necessary and appropriate. Close coordination between the IASB's due process and the due process of national standard setters is important to the success of the IASB (introduction – IFRS guide 2005).

IFRSs are designed to apply to the general purpose financial statements and other financial reporting of all profit-oriented entities. Although IFRSs are not designed to apply to not-for-profit activities in the private sector, public sector or government entities with such activities may find them appropriate. The Public Sector Committee of the International Federation of Accountants (PSC) has issued a guideline stating that IFRSs are applicable to government business entities. As a result, governments become a constituent party in the lobby process towards the IASB (paragraph 9 – preface IFRS).

1.4.3 The standard-setting process or due process

For the purpose of studying lobbying behavior it is essential to know which opportunities are given by the standard setter to its constituents to participate in the lobbying process. According to the IASB, IFRSs are developed through a formal system of due process and broad international consultation that involves accountants, financial analysts and other users of financial statements, the business community, stock exchanges, regulatory and legal authorities, academics and other interested individuals, and organizations from around the world. The IASB consults, in public meetings, the SAC[2] on major projects, agenda decisions and work priorities, and discusses technical matters in meetings that are open to public observation. The formal due process for projects normally, but necessarily, involves the following steps (the steps that are required under the terms of the IASC Foundation Constitution are indicated by an asterisk – paragraph 18, preface to IFRS):

a) the staff are asked to identify and review all the issues associated with the topic and to consider the application of the IASB Framework to the issues;
b) study of national accounting requirements and practice and an exchange of views about the issues with national standard setters;
c) consulting the SAC about the advisability of adding the topic to the IASB's agenda*;
d) formation of an advisory group to give advice to the IASB on the project;
e) publishing for public comment a discussion document;
f) publishing for public comment an exposure draft approved by at least eight members of the IASB, including any dissenting opinions held by IASB members*;
g) publishing within an exposure draft a basis for conclusions;
h) consideration of all comments received within the comment period on discussion documents and exposure drafts*;
i) consideration of the desirability of holding a public hearing and of the desirability of conducting field tests and, if considered desirable, holding such hearings and conducting such tests;
j) approval of a standard by at least eight members of the IASB and inclusion in the published standard of any dissenting opinions*; and
k) publishing within a standard a basis for conclusions, explaining, among other things, the steps in the IASB's due process and how the IASB dealt with public comments on the exposure draft.

In this due process, the following opportunities for input can be distinguished:

a) participation in the development of views as a member of the SAC;
b) participation in advisory groups;
c) submission of an issue to IFRIC;
d) submission of a comment letter in response to a discussion document;
e) submission of a comment letter in response to an exposure draft;
f) participation in public round-table discussions; and
g) participation in field visits and field tests.

Because studies found evidence that the use of comment letters was highly correlated with the use of other lobbying methods, we will investigate the lobbying behavior of the different constituents towards the IASB by analyzing the comment letters written by the different parties. Therefore, we will concentrate on the written submission made under (d) and (e). The IASB publishes each exposure draft of a standard and discussion documents for public comment, with a normal comment period of 90 days. In certain circumstances, the IASB may expose proposals for a longer or shorter period.

1.5 Research method

1.5.1 Data collection

As mentioned above, we will study lobbying behavior with the use of comment letters. Comment letters written in the due process are publicly available. The research population of this study consists of comment letters that were written between 2002 and the summer of 2005 in response to discussion documents issued by the IASB and exposure drafts issued by the IASB. The comment letters sent in response to the first document issued by the IASB, which was a discussion document on share-based transactions, were the only ones not included in the analysis. Of the 282 comment letters sent to the IASB in relation to this document, 115 were identical (CL 160–CL 275), only the name of the individual respondent being different. In total, there were 2245 letters written in response to these two types of document. For the purpose of the analysis, these documents are classified according to the type of constituent party. With regard to the companies involved in the lobbying process, we investigated the geographical location.

The 2245 comment letters were first classified in different categories, whereby each category represented a different constituent party. With regard to the classification into different types of constituent, the following classification was used: preparers, the accounting profession, users, national standard setters, regulatory authorities of stock exchanges, governments, individuals, academics, and other interested parties. This classification is based on the pronouncements of the IASB (paragraph 19 – preface to the IASB, 2005).

For the purpose of classifying each comment letter into one of these categories, several steps were taken. First, individuals with ties to specific organizations were grouped with those organizations (a similar approach was used by Larson, 1997). Second, the authors of all letters were examined to determine to what type of constituent they belonged (e.g. preparers, users, accountants, regulatory authorities). Third, responses of subsidiaries of multinational corporations were classified under the multinational corporation itself.

In order to be able to test the third and fourth hypotheses (on the economic position of the lobbying firm and the attitude of the auditor), we needed to classify the responses of the preparers and the auditors according to whether or not they were in favor or against the proposed standard. For this analysis, we chose a substantive exposure draft, namely exposure draft two, which preceded IFRS 2 on share-based payment. A 'substantive' exposure draft implies that the exposure draft proposes a standard for an accounting issue whereby in some countries the new standard completely supersedes the prior existing standard or in other countries no prior standard existed (adapted from Tandy and Wilburn, 1992). The issuance of IFRS 2, 'Share-based payment,' in February 2004 completes one of the first major objectives of the International Accounting Standards Board (IASB) since its reorganization in 2001. As it is the first international standard that regulates the recognition and measurement of share-based payment in the annual accounts, its realization project opened a considerable debate by accounting standard setters, users, preparers, and politicians. The comment letters we will focus on for testing hypotheses 3 and 4 have been written in reaction to exposure draft 2 (ED 2), issued in November 2002. Like the final standard, ED 2 proposes to require entities to recognize share-based payment transactions in their financial statements. This requirement includes recognition of expenses associated with transactions in which options are granted to employees. During the comment period, which ended on 7 March 2003, the IASB received 238 reactions or an equivalent of 2429 pages.

A content analysis of those letters was undertaken in order to determine whether the lobbying party opposed or supported the standard. Positions were classified in the categories: 'in favor,' 'against,' 'neutral,' or 'absent.' In the statistical analysis, the values '1,' '0,' and '−1' were assigned to the categories 'in favor,' 'neutral,' and 'against' respectively. This approach is based on the previous research of Kenny and Larson (1993), Rahman et al. (1994), Ryan et al. (1999), and Georgiou and Roberts (2004). Bearing in mind the shortcomings of these types of classifications mentioned by Francis (1987) and Buckmaster et al. (1994) (see literature review), we used not only the support/oppose classification in general, but also paid attention to the different items discussed in the exposure draft and the different opinions of preparers and auditors on those subitems. Appendix B presents the questions of the ED 2, which have been used for this detailed content analysis.

In order to analyze the hypotheses, which relate lobbying behavior to country characteristics, we assigned the corporate respondents to a single individual country according to the official legal location of the headquarters of the group.

1.5.2 Measurement of variables

The number of comment letters sent by the different groups of constituent parties represented the variables used for testing hypothesis 1 in relation to the participation of the preparers versus the users of financial statements in the lobby process of the IASB.

For the second hypothesis, in relation to the size of the preparers, information on turnover and assets was collected. Consistent with prior literature (see Larson, 1997) we used the Forbes Lists of the 2000 largest US companies and the 2000 largest non-US companies to test whether or not the lobbying companies are among the largest in the world.

Testing the third and fourth hypotheses was done with unit-level data on the suppose/oppose position of the individual companies and auditors taking part in the lobbying process towards exposure draft 2, which preceded IFRS 2. With regard to the hypotheses, which investigate the influence of country-level or domestic characteristics on the lobbying behavior, the following dependent variables and independent variables were used.

The dependent variable is supposed to measure the lobby intensity of a particular country. The basis for this measure could be the number of companies in a country sending comment letters. However, since a number of companies have sent several letters, we have chosen to work with the number of comment letters sent by industrial companies in a country. We kept the number of companies lobbying in a country as a secondary measure that we used to test the robustness of the results obtained based on the number of comment letters sent. In order to correct for the differences in the number of companies present in a country, we divided the two nominators by the number of companies listed on the domestic stock market in the home country of the lobbying company. In this way, we obtain a measure for the degree of involvement in the lobbying process towards the IASB by the individual countries. To determine the number of listed companies on the domestic stock market we relied on the statistics provided by the World Federation of Exchanges. With regard to the countries Belgium, France, The Netherlands, and Portugal, we divided the total number of listed firms on Euronext into different subgroups for those four countries.

The dependent variable for measuring the intensity of lobbying in a single country was: (number of comment letters sent from one country/number of companies listed on the domestic stock market) or (number of companies sending comment letters/number of domestic listed companies on the domestic stock market).

For the measurement of the independent variables, which are used to investigate the influence of domestic characteristics, we have chosen variables that represent these individual country-level characteristics and that have been used in the literature before. The chosen country scores are widely used in the literature, which investigates the influence of institutional and other domestic variables on the quality of accounting data and on earnings management practices. The following scores have been used as independent variables and have been taken from the sources given.

1.5.2.1 Institutional variables

Institutional variables represent the legal and enforcement environment of the firm. With regard to the degree of enforcement of rules present in a country, we use two measures, namely those developed by Hope (2003a,b) and by La Porta et al. (1998). The higher the scores, the higher the level of enforcement. Both Hope and La Porta et al. provide information about the domestic institutional variables that they have used to determine the enforcement score. We will include these individual scores in the analysis as well – they are the level of audit spending (Mueller et al., 1994), judicial efficiency (La Porta et al., 1998), rule of law (La Porta et al., 1998), anti-director rights (La Porta et al., 1998), and legal origin.

1.5.2.2 Cultural variables

We relied on the individual national scores given by Hofstede (1980, 1983, 1991) in his publications to measure cultural differences across the world. We adopted his scores for power distance, uncertainty avoidance, individualism versus collectivism, and masculinity versus femininity.

1.5.2.3 Attitude towards compliance

In order to measure this construct we have used the individual country scores on tax compliance used by Dyck and Zingales (2004). The higher the score, the more inhabitants of a country show tax-compliant behavior.

1.5.2.4 Earnings management practices

Leuz et al. (2003) developed an earnings management score for a number of individual countries; we have used these scores to measure the degree of earnings management in every country. The lower the score, the less earnings management is present in a country.

1.5.2.5 *The information environment*

The richness of the information environment was measured by the number of analysts following. This score was taken from IBES and collected as the number of analysts per firm.

The descriptive statistics of both the dependent and the independent variables used in the regression analyses are presented in Table 1.1.

Several nonparametric statistical methods will be used to test the hypotheses of Sutton (1984) and Watts and Zimmerman (1986) put forward in section 1.2.2 of this chapter. The differences in lobby patterns among constituent groups will be tested with the Kruskal–Wallis test for differences between rank orders. Differences in positions will be tested with the Wilcoxon rank test. The country-level influences will be tested with the use of nonparametric rank ordered regression. We will only use univariate regressions because, according to Hair et al. (1998), due to the small sample size (<20) regressions are the only appropriate form of analysis with one independent variable.

Table 1.1 Descriptive statistics of the dependent and independent variables

Variable (*N*)	Minimum	Maximum	Mean	Std
Intensity Comment Letters (18)	0.000940	0.173010	0.02721478	0.04018836
Intensity Company (18)	0.000313	0.036550	0.01170252	0.00994351
Enforcement Hope (16)	−3.65	1.21	−1.0444	1.62981
Enforcement La Porta (17)	5.60	10.00	8.6000	1.43571
Audit spending (16)	0.10	0.70	0.3475	0.20917
Judicial efficiency (16)	6.00	10.00	8.9844	1.44184
Rule of law (16)	4.42	10.00	8.9781	1.7798
Anti-director rights (16)	0.00	5.00	3.0000	1.54919
Legal origin (17)	1.00	4.00	2.2353	1.09141
Uncertainty avoidance (17)	23.00	98.00	59.6471	19.20593
Individualism (17)	35.00	91.00	70.3529	14.45225
Power distance (17)	11.00	68.00	40.7059	15.44249
Masculinity (17)	5.00	79.00	53.1765	20.73414
Analyst following (17)	3.50	30.20	15.7059	8.49908
Earnings management (17)	2.00	28.30	15.0235	8.64303
Tax compliance (14)	1.77	5.00	3.6057	1.01722

1.6 Research results

We will discuss all hypotheses put forward in the second part of this chapter. We will start with the general hypotheses of Sutton, followed by the hypothesis of Watts and Zimmerman and the different hypotheses on auditor behavior, and finally we will end with the hypotheses in relation to the country characteristics.

1.6.1 The preparers lobby more often than the users

In this part we test the first hypothesis – namely, that preparers lobby more than users. In Table 1.2 we list the total letters received from all groups of constituent parties. The number of comment letters sent by each category clearly indicates that preparers do indeed lobby more often than users.

In Appendix A these total figures are broken down over the different individual documents issued for comments by the IASB. The documents are listed in chronological order. Comment letters of preparers make up almost half of the submissions.

Table 1.2 Total letters received from all groups

Preparers	**1051**	**(47%)**
Individual companies	263	(12%)
Associations of companies	222	(10%)
Individual banks and the like	249	(11%)
Associations of banks and the like	317	(14%)
The accounting profession	**587**	**(26%)**
Audit firms	134	(6%)
Associations of accountants and auditors	453	(20%)
Users	**30**	**(1%)**
National standard setters	**296**	**(13%)**
Stock exchanges	**35**	**(2%)**
Governments	**33**	**(1%)**
Individuals	**77**	**(3%)**
Academics	**36**	**(2%)**
Other interested parties	**100**	**(4%)**
Consultants	60	(3%)
Actuaries	40	(2%)
TOTAL	**2245**	**(100%)**

It is important to keep in mind the observation of Sutton (1984) that preparers are homogeneous and therefore lobbying can be done through associations. Half of the preparers submissions are indeed done by associations of preparers.

The second largest participating group is the accounting profession. Within the group of single audit firms, the big four audit firms dominate the statistics – they respond to almost every document issued by the IASB. The IASB included in its mission statement that it would cooperate with national standard setters. In order to fulfill this objective, meetings will be organized between the IASB and the national standard-setting bodies. Further, a number of IASB board members have explicit liaison roles with specific national standard setters (see introduction, IFRS Guide, 2005). Although national standard setters have these opportunities to influence the standard-setting process, we learn from Table 1.2 that they still engage in lobbying through producing written submissions.

The group of users of financial statements seems to be almost absent in this influencing process. However, banks, financial institutions, mutual funds, and pension funds might lobby with a user perspective in relation to some documents issued by the IASB, as we will see in the discussion of hypothesis 3.

Stock exchanges do show up as a constituent party in the statistics and so do governments. Almost all government responses originate from Anglo-Saxon countries.

If we concentrate on the geographical dispersion of these constituent parties, we observe that individual companies and associations of preparers mainly originate from western countries, whereas comment letters from the associations of accountants and from national standard setters arrive from all corners of the world.

Although we are able to confirm that preparers lobby more often than users, this does not mean that participation levels of the different constituents are identical for all documents for comments issued by the IASB. For example, in relation to small and medium-sized enterprises the accounting profession sent most comment letters.

When we test if the different constituent parties lobby to the same extent towards all documents issued by the IASB, the hypothesis can be rejected with the highest significance (Kruskal–Wallis, asymptotic significance 0.000). Even when we distinguish the following three subcategories among the comment letters (comment letters in response to discussion documents, comment letters in response to adaptations of existing standards, and comment letters in response to exposure drafts dealing with accounting issues where standards did not previously exist or completely supersede prior standards based upon comprehensive revaluation of these issues), the Kruskal–Wallis test provides evidence that the rank order of the different categories of lobbying parties differs.

1.6.2 Large companies participate more often in the lobbying process

The study of Larson (1997) revealed that a small fraction of corporations dominated the corporate responses to the IASC[3]. Of all corporate comment letters written, 0.06% of corporations account for 50% of the submissions, so a small number of corporations dominate responses to the IASC. Larson's observation no longer holds since the reform of the IASB. In Table 1.3 we present an overview of the number of companies from different countries that took part in the lobbying process and the number of comment letters they sent.

Table 1.3 Overview of the number of companies and the number of letters sent to the IASB within in a country

Country of origin	Number of companies	Number of comment letters sent
Australia	16	25
Austria	1	3
Belgium	3	3
Finland	1	5
France	4	6
Germany	25	33
Greece	1	1
India	1	1
Ireland	1	1
Italy	1	1
Luxembourg	2	3
Malaysia	1	1
The Netherlands	5	14
New Zealand	2	3
South Africa	1	1
Spain	1	3
Sweden	3	3
Switzerland	8	50
UK	38	82
USA	18	24
Total	133	263

Table 1.3 indicates that only in a few countries companies write more comment letters than average. This happens especially in Austria, Finland, the Netherlands, and Switzerland, and to a lesser extent in the UK.

In order to be consistent with Larson (1997), we also checked whether the companies writing a comment letter were among the largest worldwide, taking as a reference the Forbes list of largest US companies and non-US companies. The pattern discovered by Larson (1997) continues in the 21st century. In the countries where only one or a few companies have sent a comment letter, all companies belonged to the Forbes list of largest non-US companies (Finland, Greece, India, Ireland, Italy, Malaysia, The Netherlands, and Spain). In countries where more companies submitted a comment letter the following percentages belonged to the Forbes list: 83% (USA), 66% (Sweden), 62% (Switzerland), 52% (Germany), 52% (UK), 50% (France), and 43% (Australia). Only companies submitting a comment letter from the following countries did not belong to the Forbes list: Austria, Belgium, Luxembourg, New Zealand, and South Africa.

1.6.3 Companies that suffer from a larger negative economic impact of the standards will lobby more often

To test this hypothesis, we analyzed all the comment letters sent by preparers, users, and the accounting profession in response to exposure draft 2, preceding IFRS 2. Given the fact that the expensing of stock options gives more information on the company's present and future obligations, ED 2 will enhance the quality of financial reporting (Giner and Arce, 2004). Therefore, we can expect that users will support the 'expensing' proposal in ED 2. The use of share-based payment is dissimilar for different industries, so we can expect that the impact of the proposed standard will be disproportionately distributed over the different preparers. Therefore, 'knowledge-based' companies, in which share-based instruments are a common form of payment, will expect to experience more benefits in return for their lobbying efforts compared to enterprises active in traditional, stable industries, where share-based instruments are less common. Pharmaceuticals, software, semiconductor, and high-technology manufacturing are generally thought of as 'knowledge-based industries'. Based on the cost/benefit model we can therefore expect a higher contribution to the lobbying process for these enterprises. So hypothesis 3 becomes: A larger part of the letters written by preparers comes from enterprises active in the technological or pharmaceutical sector.

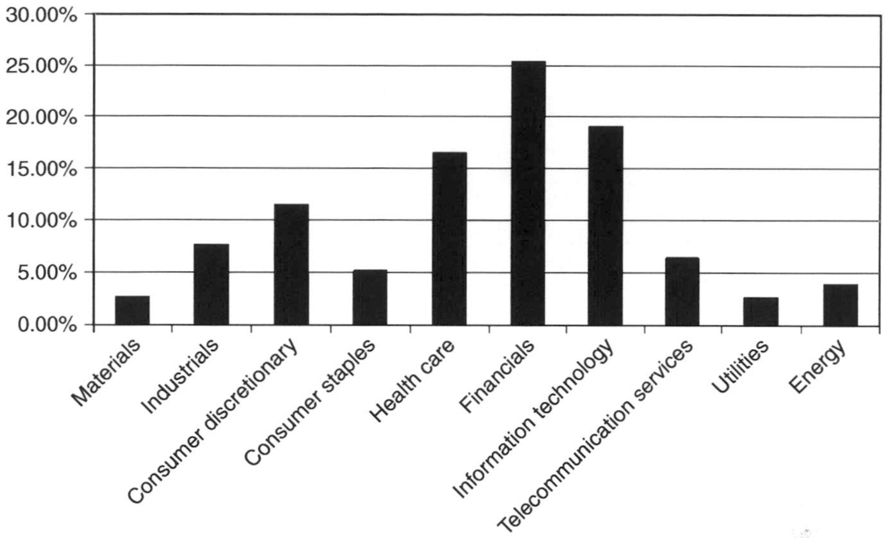

Figure 1.1 Distribution of the lobbying preparers

Figure 1.1 represents the distribution of the lobbying preparers among the 10 sectors of the General Industry Classification Standard. A remarkably large proportion (25%) of those enterprises are active in the financial industry. These findings are, however, not necessarily contrary to the reasoning behind hypothesis 3. Financial institutions and insurance companies experience the consequences of IFRS in two fields, as preparers and, perhaps even more importantly, as users of financial statements (analysts). As a consequence, their lobbying patterns are possibly more closely linked to those of users. When we omit this group of lobbyists, the sectors 'information technology' (19%) and 'health care' (16%) are the best represented. This is completely in accordance with our expectations in hypothesis 3. The least number of comment letters came from enterprises active in the sectors 'materials' (3%), 'utilities' (3%), and 'energy' (4%).

We now focus the analysis on the 'oppose/support' position taken by individual firms. 'Content analysis' was applied to investigate the hypotheses expounded above and to discover the general opinions of the lobbyists on the 'expensing' proposal. Positions were classified into the categories: 'in favor', 'against', 'neutral', or 'absent'. In the statistical analysis the values '1', '0', and '1' were assigned to the categories 'in favor', 'neutral', and 'against' respectively. We will hypothesize that: among preparers, companies from the technological and pharmaceutical sectors take a more negative position towards the proposal to expense the share-based payment transaction than enterprises from other sectors.

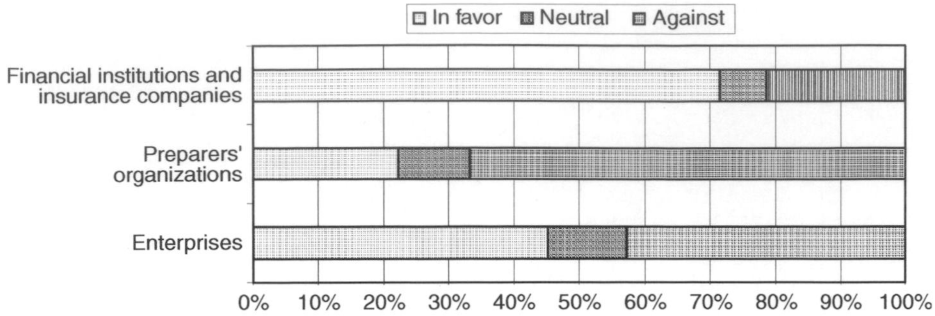

Figure 1.2 Analysis of comment letters sent by the preparers group in response to ED 2

Of the 97 analyzed comment letters written by preparers, 33 were against, eight neutral, and 33 in favor. This gives a general score for the preparers group of 0 or neutral. We can, however, refine our analysis by dividing this group into three subgroups, 'financial institutions', 'preparers – organizations' and 'preparers – enterprises'. Figure 1.2 represents an overview of the positions of these subgroups.

Based on these findings, financial institutions and insurance companies seem to take a generally positive position on the 'expensing' proposal. As we already mentioned in the first part of the analysis, this is possibly due to the fact that they act as users in this instance. To better analyze annual accounts, they will strive for more transparency in financial accounting and therefore belong to the group 'users'. When we omit them from the analysis, we find a generally negative position for the preparers (−0.13).

However, when we look at the subcategory 'preparers – enterprises', we observe a remarkable number of positive attitudes towards the expensing of share-based payment transactions. To more closely investigate where these letters come from, we repeated our analysis for the 10 GICS sectors. The positive lobbying attitudes come especially from the energy, utility, and materials sectors. Other sectors are globally subtle or even take a rather negative position towards the 'expensing' proposal, such as lobbyists active in 'information technology' or 'telecommunication services'.

1.6.4 The position of the auditor in the lobbying process

From the extant literature on the behavior of the auditor in the lobbying process, we recognize that there are several hypotheses that might explain their behavior. Using the data from the content analysis, we will investigate whether or not auditors defend the same opinion as their clients. In Table 1.4 we present the

Table 1.4 Average position for auditors and preparers

	q^0	q^1	q^2	q^{3a}	q^{3b}	q^4	q^5	q^9	q^{10}	q^{11}	q^{13}	q^{16}	q^{19}
Auditors	**1.00**	**0.67**	**1.00**	**1.00**	**0.50**	**−0.33**	**1.00**	**0.67**	**0.67**	**0.83**	**0.17**	**1.00**	**0.80**
Preparers	**0.02**	**−0.27**	**0.27**	**0.33**	**0.64**	**−0.09**	**0.64**	**−0.31**	**−0.42**	**−0.02**	**0.58**	**0.20**	**0.10**
***p*-value**	0.017	0.033	**0.064**	**0.099**	**0.755**	**0.579**	**0.270**	0.025	0.012	0.044	**0.213**	**0.064**	**0.529**

results of the content analysis carried out on a number of different subquestions of ED 2 (see Appendix B).

In the statistical analysis the values ‘1’, ‘0’, and ‘−1’ were assigned to the categories ‘in favor’, ‘neutral’, and ‘against’ respectively. In order to get an idea if both hypotheses are relevant in the context of lobbying towards the IASB, we will analyze whether or not preparers and auditors defend the same opinions with regard to the different questions in relation to ED 2.

Table 1.4 shows the average position for both groups on 13 subjects of discussion from the IASB’s invitation to comment. For each issue, the *p*-value from a Wilcoxon rank-sum test is also presented.

For five of the 13 analyzed questions (printed in bold in Appendix B), the points of view of both groups differ significantly (>95%). Remarkably, the major part of these five questions deals with issues that lead to a more complex standard (for example, the use of option pricing models (Q11), the unit of service method (Q9), etc.). Auditors are generally in favor of these complex arrangements, because they will increase audit fees. This is totally in accordance with earlier research on the lobbying behavior of auditors.

1.6.5 The influence of country-level variables on the lobbying behavior

In the study of Larson (1997), countries varied greatly in the rate at which their large corporations lobby the IASC. The countries with the highest percentages were Australia (55%), Hong Kong (67%), and Switzerland (47%). The USA has only 9% of its largest companies lobbying and countries like Korea, Spain, and Italy had no companies lobbying. We notice that after the reform of the IASB the participation level of countries in the standard-setting process is still different. Swiss and Australian companies are still very active in sending comment letters, but they are now joined by the northern part of the ‘old part’ of the European Union (i.e. Austria, Belgium, Finland, Germany, Ireland, Sweden, the Netherlands, and the UK) and New Zealand. Companies from the ‘south’ of Europe (France, Italy, Greece, Spain, and Portugal) seldom use comment letters to influence the standard-setting process. The notion that compulsory adoption of IFRS could be a variable influencing the participation in the written lobbying process seems not to hold for all jurisdictions (see low levels in the south of Europe). Participation levels in other parts of the world are still very low, if we consider individual companies. Below we present the results of the hypotheses tested with regard to the characteristics of a country.

Several hypotheses were developed to explain the differences in lobby intensity of companies located in different jurisdictions. We will now discuss the results of the univariate regression models. In Table 1.5 we present the statistical results of those regressions which have as dependent variable the degree of lobbying with the number of comment letters sent in the nominator and whereby the independent variable was found to be significant.

The results reveal that the hypothesis relating to the higher cost of compliance is accepted. The higher the judicial efficiency in a country and the level of enforcement of rules, the more companies do engage in the lobbying process to change standards. A compliant attitude towards tax regulations is a significant variable indicating a high participation in the lobbying process. This is a second hypothesis that is accepted. The hypotheses relating to the cultural variables provide mixed evidence – only the power distances are significant. This implies that in countries with large power distance companies will engage significantly less in lobbying. The hypotheses relating to the information environment of the firm and the earnings management practices are rejected.

When we run the univariate regressions with the dependent variable (number of companies sending comment letters/number of companies on the domestic stock market), the variables enforcement, judicial efficiency, and tax compliance remain significant; the variable power distance, however, becomes nonsignificant but still with a negative coefficient.

We might conclude from this that only enforcement, judicial efficiency, and attitude towards compliance with rules variables are domestic characteristics

Table 1.5 Regression results of the degree of lobbying on domestic characteristics

Independent variable	Coefficient	*t*-value	Significance
Enforcement Hope	4.550	2.035	0.061
	0.465	2.009	0.064
Enforcement La Porta	3.250	1.529	0.124
	0.639	3.275	0.005
Judicial efficiency	3.129	1.465	0.185
	0.632	2.820	0.014
Power distance	13.848	6.208	0.000
	−0.539	−2.474	0.026
Tax compliance	4.055	1.857	0.088
	0.459	1.791	0.098

that might explain the difference in lobbying behavior between companies from different countries. The nonsignificant results with regard to the information environment and local earnings management practices can be explained by the fact that a number of companies are dual listed. Lobbying behavior in these situations might be driven by earnings management practices and the information environment of the jurisdiction in which the stock exchange is located. Part of the companies is dual listed, but a much bigger part than before of companies taking part in the lobbying process towards the IASB is single listed on an EU or Australian stock exchange.

1.7 Conclusion

This chapter analyzed the lobbying behavior of the different constituent parties towards the IASB. The hypotheses of Sutton (1984) that preparers lobby more often than users and large firms lobby more often than small firms are confirmed in this multinational setting.

With the data resulting from a content analysis of comment letters sent in response to the exposure draft preceding the final standard IFRS 2 on share-based transactions, we were able to confirm the economic perspective theory of Watts and Zimmerman (1986). Companies that experience a negative cash flow effect from the proposed standard do indeed engage more in lobbying. Based on the same data we were also able to confirm that auditors do not always defend their clients' position when lobbying towards the IASB, but are driven by their own incentives as well.

The hypothesis of Sutton (1984) that an increase in the cost of compliance will increase the level of preparer lobby was confirmed. The results indicate that in countries with high levels of enforcement, with high judicial efficiency, and with a positive attitude towards tax compliance, companies engage more often in lobbying. With regard to the cultural variables we obtained mixed results; only the existence of large power distance influences the lobbying behavior in a negative way. Variables relating to domestic earnings management practices and the domestic information environment of the firm have no significant influence.

Notes

1. Seventy-eight percent of non-US lobbying corporations had securities traded in the USA.
2. The Standards Advisory Council (SAC) provides a formal vehicle for further groups and individuals having diverse geographical and functional backgrounds to give advice to the IASB.
3. Although 288 corporate comment letters were written in the period under study (1989–1994), 17 corporations account for 157 comment letters or 55% of all comment letters.

References

Alexander, D., Britton, A., and Jorissen, A. (2003). *International Financial Reporting and Analysis.* Thomson Learning, London.

Ang, N., Sidhu, B.K., and Gallery, N. (2000). The Incentives of Australian Public Companies Lobbying Against Proposed Superannuation Accounting Standards. *Abacus*, 36(1):40–70.

Ball, R., Kothari, S., and Robin, A. (2000). The Effect of International Institutional Factors on Properties of Accounting Earnings. *Journal of Accounting and Economics*, 24(1):3–37.

Buckmaster, D., Saniga, E., and Tadesse, S. (1994). Measuring Lobbying Influence Using the Financial Accounting Standards Board Public Record. *Journal of Economic and Social Measurement*, 20:331–356.

Deakin, E.B. (1989). Rational Economic Behaviour and Lobbying on Accounting Issues: Evidence from the Oil and Gas Industry. *Accounting Review*, 114(1):137–151.

Dechow, P.M., Hutton, A.P., and Sloan, R.G. (1996). Economic Consequences of Accounting for Stock-Based Compensation. *Journal of Accounting Research*, 34(3):1–20.

Dhaliwal, D.S. (1982). Some Economic Determinants of Management Lobbying for Alternative Methods of Accounting: Evidence from the Accounting for Interest Costs Issue. *Journal of Business Finance and Accounting*, 9(2):255–265.

Dyck, A. and Zingales, L. (2004). Private Benefits of Control: An International Comparison. *Journal of Finance*, 59(2):537–600.

Feroz, E. (1987). Corporate Demands and Changes in GPLA. *Journal of Business Finance and Accounting*, 19(3):409–423.

Francis, J. (1987). Lobbying Against Proposed Accounting Standards: The Case of Employers' Pension Accounting. *Journal of Accounting and Public Policy*, 6(1):35–57.

Gavens, J.J., Carnegie, G.D., and Gibson, R.W. (1989). Company Participation in the Australian Accounting Standards Setting Process. *Accounting and Finance*, 29(1):47–58.

Georgiou, G. (2002). Corporate Non-Participation in the ASB Standard-Setting Process. *European Accounting Review*, 11(4):699–722.

Georgiou, G. (2004). Corporate Lobbying on Accounting Standards Methods, Timing and Perceived Effectiveness. *Abacus*, 40(2):219–237.

Georgiou, G. and Roberts, C.B. (2004). Corporate Lobbying in the UK: An Analysis of Attitudes Towards the ASB's 1995 Deferred Taxation Proposals. *British Accounting Review*, 36(4):441–453.

Giner, B. and Arce, M. (2004). Lobbying on Accounting Standards: The Due Process of IFRS 2 on Share-Based Payments. University of Valencia, Spain.

Guenther, D. and Hussein, A. (1995). Accounting Standards and National Tax Laws: The IASC and the Ban on LIFO. *Journal of Accounting and Public Policy*, 14(2):115–141.

Hair, J., Anderson, R., Tatham, R., and Black, W. (1998). *Multivariate Data Analysis.* Prentice-Hall, Upper Saddle River, NJ.

Hill, N., Shelton, S., and Stevens, K. (2002). Corporate Lobbying Behaviour on Accounting for Stock-Based Compensation: Venue and Format Choices. *Abacus*, 38(1):78–90.

Hofstede, G. (1980). *Culture's Consequences: International Differences in Work-Related Values.* Sage, Beverly Hills, CA.

Hofstede, G. (1983). Dimensions of National Cultures in Fifty Countries and Three Regions. In: *Expectations in Cross-Cultural Psychology* (Deregowski, J.B., Dziurawiec, S., and Annis, R.C., eds), pp. 335–355. Liss, Swets & Zitlinger.

Hofstede, G. (1991). *Cultures and Organizations: Software of the Mind.* McGraw-Hill, Maidenhead.

Hope, O. (2003a). Firm-Level Disclosures and the Relative Roles of Culture and Legal Origin. *Journal of International Financial Management and Accounting*, 14(3):218–248.

Hope, O. (2003b). Disclosure Practices, Enforcement of Accounting Standards, and Analysts' Forecast Accuracy: An International Study. *Journal of Accounting Research*, 41(2):235–272.

Jensen, M.C. and Meckling, W.H. (1976). Theory of the Firm: Managerial Behaviour, Agency Costs and Ownership Structure. *Journal of Financial Economics*, 3(2):306–360.

Kenny, S.Y. and Larson, R.K. (1993). Lobbying Behaviour and the Development of International Accounting Standards: The Case of IASC's Joint Venture Project. *European Accounting Review*, 2(3):531–554.

Lang, M.H. and Lundholm, R. (1996). Corporate Disclosure Policy and Analyst Behavior. *Journal of Accounting Research*, 71(4):467–492.

La Porta, R., Lopez-de-Salines, F., Shleifer, A., and Vishny, R. (1998). Law and Finance. *Journal of Political Economy*, 106(6):1113–1155.

Larson, R.K. (1997). Corporate Lobbying of the International Accounting Standards Committee. *Journal of International Financial Management and Accounting*, 8(3):175–203.

Leuz, C., Nanda, D., and Wysocki, P. (2003). Earnings Management and Investor Protection: An International Comparison. *Journal of Financial Economics*, 69(3):505–527.

MacArthur, J. (1988). Some Implications of Auditor and Client Lobbying Activities: A Comparative Analysis. *Accounting and Business Research*, 19(73):56–64.

MacArthur, J.B. (1996). An Investigation into the Influence of Cultural Factors in the International Lobbying of the International Accounting Standards Committee: The Case of E32, Comparability of Financial Statements. *International Journal of Accounting*, 31(2):213–237.

MacArthur, J.B. (1999). The Impact of Cultural Factors on the Lobbying of the International Accounting Standards Committee on E32: Comparability of Financial Statements: An Extension of MacArthur to Accounting Member Bodies. *Journal of International Accounting, Auditing and Taxation*, 8(2):315–335.

MacArthur, J.B. and Groves, R.E.V. (1993). An Empirical Investigation into the Impact of Profit Sharing Schemes of Executives on the Content of Corporate Submissions on Proposed Accounting Standards. *Journal of Business Finance and Accounting*, 20(5):623–638.

McKee, A., Williams, P., and Frazier, B. (1991). A Case Study of Accounting Firm Lobbying: Advice or Consent. *Critical Perspectives in Accounting*, 2(3):273–294.

McLeay, S., Ordelheide, D., and Young, S. (2000). Constituent Lobbying and its Impact on the Development of Financial Reporting Regulations: Evidence from Germany. *Accounting, Organizations and Society*, 25(1):79–98.

Meier, H.H., Alam, P., and Pearson, M.A. (1993). Auditor Lobbying for Accounting Standards: The Case of Banks and Savings and Loan Associations. *Accounting and Business Research*, 23(92):477–487.

Meier, H.H., Alam, P., and Pearson, M. A. (1996). Lobbying by Auditors and Financial Institutions on Proposed Accounting Standards. *Journal of Bank Cost and Management Accounting*, 8(2):33–46.

Mueller, G., Gernon, H., and Meek, G. (1994). *Accounting: An International Perspective.* Business One Irwin, New York.

Puro, M. (1984). Audit Firm Lobbying before the Financial Accounting Standards Board: An Empirical Study. *Journal of Accounting Research*, 22(2):624–646.

Rahman, A.R., Ng, L.W., and Tower, G.D. (1994). Policy Choice and Standards Setting in New Zealand: An Exploratory Study. *Abacus*, 30(1):98–117.

Ryan, C., Dunstan, K., and Stanley, T. (1999). Constituent Participation in the Australian Public Sector Accounting Standard-Setting Process: The Case of ED 55. *Financial Accountability and Management*, 15(2):173–200.

Schalow, C.M. (1995). Participation Choice: The Exposure Draft for Postretirement Benefits Other than Pensions. *Accounting Horizons*, 9(1):27–41.

Schipper, K. (2005). The Introduction of International Accounting Standards in Europe: Implications for International Convergence. *European Accounting Review*, 14(1):101–126.

Seamann, G. (1997). Comment Letters as Indicators of Overall Corporate Manager Preferences: Employers' Accounting for Pensions. *Research in Accounting Regulation*, 11(1):125–142.

Sikka, P. (2001). Regulation of Accountancy and the Power of Capital: Some Observations. *Critical Perspectives in Accounting*, 12(2):199–211.

Sutton, T.G. (1984). Lobbying of Accounting Standards-Setting Bodies in the UK and the USA: A Downsian Analysis. *Accounting, Organizations and Society*, 9(1):81–95.

Sutton, T. (1988). The Proposed Introduction of Current Cost Accounting in the UK. *Journal of Accounting and Economics*, 10(2):127–149.

Tandy, P. and Wilburn, N. (1992). Constituent Participation in Standards-Setting: The FASB's First 100 Statements. *Accounting Horizons*, 6(2):47–58.

Walker, R.G. and Robinson, P. (1993). A Critical Assessment of the Literature on Political Activity and Accounting Regulation. *Research in Accounting Regulation*, 7(1):3–40.

Watts, R.L. and Zimmerman, J.L. (1978). Towards a Positive Theory of the Determination of Accounting Standards. *Accounting Review*, 53(1):112–134.

Watts, R.L. and Zimmerman, J.L. (1981). Auditors and the Determination of Accounting Standards. Working Paper, University of Rochester, Rochester, NY.

Watts, R.L. and Zimmerman, J.L. (1986). *Positive Accounting Theory*. Prentice-Hall, Englewood Cliffs, NJ.

Appendix A

	TOTAL	(%)	1	(%)	2	(%)	3	(%)	4	(%)	5	(%)	6	(%)	7	(%)
Preparers	**1051**	**(47%)**	**9**	**(14%)**	**4**	**(17%)**	**18**	**(18%)**	**60**	**(58%)**	**7**	**(19%)**	**24**	**(42%)**	**32**	**(52%)**
Individual companies	263	(12%)	1	(2%)	1	(4%)	1	(1%)	5	(5%)	1	(3%)	12	(21%)	1	(2%)
Associations of companies	222	(10%)	4	(6%)	3	(13%)	13	(13%)	7	(7%)	2	(5%)	8	(14%)	3	(5%)
Individual banks and the like	249	(11%)	1	(2%)	0	(0%)	0	(0%)	16	(15%)	2	(5%)	2	(4%)	8	(13%)
Associations of banks and the like	317	(14%)	3	(5%)	0	(0%)	4	(4%)	32	(31%)	2	(5%)	2	(4%)	20	(33%)
The accounting profession	**587**	**(26%)**	**31**	**(47%)**	**14**	**(58%)**	**48**	**(49%)**	**26**	**(25%)**	**19**	**(51%)**	**19**	**(33%)**	**16**	**(26%)**
Audit firms	134	(6%)	4	(6%)	4	(17%)	10	(10%)	5	(5%)	5	(14%)	5	(9%)	4	(7%)
Associations of accountants and auditors	453	(20%)	27	(41%)	10	(42%)	38	(39%)	21	(20%)	14	(38%)	14	(25%)	12	(20%)
Users	**30**	**(1%)**	**1**	**(2%)**	**0**	**(0%)**	**1**	**(1%)**	**2**	**(2%)**	**0**	**(0%)**	**0**	**(0%)**	**0**	**(0%)**
National standard setters	**296**	**(13%)**	**19**	**(29%)**	**6**	**(25%)**	**18**	**(18%)**	**10**	**(10%)**	**10**	**(27%)**	**13**	**(23%)**	**11**	**(18%)**
Stock exchanges	**35**	**(2%)**	**1**	**(2%)**	**0**	**(0%)**	**0**	**(0%)**	**3**	**(3%)**	**1**	**(3%)**	**1**	**(2%)**	**1**	**(2%)**
Governments	**33**	**(1%)**	**4**	**(6%)**	**0**	**(0%)**	**5**	**(5%)**	**1**	**(1%)**	**0**	**(0%)**	**0**	**(0%)**	**0**	**(0%)**
Individuals	**77**	**(3%)**	**0**	**(0%)**	**0**	**(0%)**	**5**	**(5%)**	**1**	**(1%)**	**0**	**(0%)**	**0**	**(0%)**	**0**	**(0%)**
Academics	**36**	**(2%)**	**0**	**(0%)**	**0**	**(0%)**	**1**	**(1%)**	**0**	**(0%)**	**0**	**(0%)**	**0**	**(0%)**	**0**	**(0%)**
Other interested parties	**100**	**(4%)**	**1**	**(2%)**	**0**	**(0%)**	**2**	**(2%)**	**1**	**(1%)**	**0**	**(0%)**	**0**	**(0%)**	**1**	**(2%)**
Consultants	60	(3%)	0	(0%)	0	(0%)	2	(2%)	0	(0%)	0	(0%)	0	(0%)	0	(0%)
Actuaries	40	(2%)	1	(2%)	0	(0%)	0	(0%)	1	(1%)	0	(0%)	0	(0%)	1	(2%)
TOTAL	**2245**		**66**		**24**		**98**		**104**		**37**		**57**		**61**	

1 = Draft Memorandum of Understanding on the Role of Accounting Standard Setters and their Relationships with the IASB (10 August 2005)

2 = IFRS 6 Exploration for and Evaluation of Mineral Resources and, as a consequence, an amendment to IFRS 1, First-time Adoption of International Financial Reporting Standards (6 June 2005)

3 = Staff questionnaire on possible modifications of the recognition and measurement principles in International Financial Reporting Standards (IFRS) for use in IASB standards for small and medium-sized entities (SMEs) (2 June 2005)

4 = ED 7, Financial Instruments: Disclosures (27 October 2004)

5 = Proposed Amendments to IAS 39, Transition and Initial Recognition of Financial Assets and Financial Liabilities (22 October 2004)

6 = Proposed Amendments to IAS 39, Cash Flow Hedge Accounting of Forecast Intragroup Transactions (22 October 2004)

7 = Proposed Amendments to IAS 39, Financial Guarantee Contracts and Credit Insurance (22 October 2004)

	8	(%)	9	(%)	10	(%	11	(%)	12	(%)	13	(%)	14	(%)	15	(%)
Preparers	**21**	**(18%)**	**40**	**(52%)**	**37**	**(40%)**	**69**	**(59%)**	**20**	**(40%)**	**34**	**(47%)**	**90**	**(74%)**	**38**	**(45%)**
Individual companies	1	(1%)	2	(3%)	13	(14%)	3	(3%)	2	(4%)	22	(31%)	18	(15%)	16	(19%)
Associations of companies	15	(13%)	22	(29%)	7	(8%)	8	(7%)	8	(16%)	11	(15%)	12	(10%)	8	(9%)
Individual banks and the like	0	(0%)	5	(6%)	9	(10%)	26	(22%)	2	(4%)	0	(0%)	28	(23%)	9	(11%)
Associations of banks and the like	5	(4%)	11	(14%)	8	(9%)	32	(28%)	8	(16%)	1	(1%)	32	(26%)	5	(6%)
The accounting profession	**51**	**(43%)**	**17**	**(22%)**	**22**	**(24%)**	**20**	**(17%)**	**14**	**(28%)**	**22**	**(31%)**	**17**	**(14%)**	**29**	**(34%)**
Audit firms	11	(9%)	5	(6%)	5	(5%)	4	(3%)	4	(8%)	5	(7%)	4	(3%)	5	(6%)
Associations of accountants and auditors	40	(33%)	12	(16%)	17	(18%)	16	(14%)	10	(20%)	17	(24%)	13	(11%)	24	(28%)
User	**1**	**(1%)**	**4**	**(5%)**	**2**	**(2%)**	**2**	**(2%)**	**0**	**(0%)**	**0**	**(0%)**	**1**	**(1%)**	**1**	**(1%)**
National standard setters	**18**	**(15%)**	**12**	**(16%)**	**16**	**(17%)**	**14**	**(12%)**	**8**	**(16%)**	**12**	**(17%)**	**10**	**(8%)**	**12**	**(14%)**
Stock exchanges	**0**	**(0%)**	**0**	**(0%)**	**1**	**(1%)**	**3**	**(3%)**	**3**	**(6%)**	**1**	**(1%)**	**2**	**(2%)**	**2**	**(2%)**
Governments	**9**	**(8%)**	**0**	**(0%)**	**1**	**(1%)**	**2**	**(2%)**	**1**	**(2%)**	**0**	**(0%)**	**0**	**(0%)**	**1**	**(1%)**
Individuals	**9**	**(8%)**	**1**	**(1%)**	**1**	**(1%)**	**1**	**(1%)**	**1**	**(2%)**	**2**	**(3%)**	**2**	**(2%)**	**2**	**(2%)**
Academics	**5**	**(4%)**	**1**	**(1%)**	**2**	**(2%)**	**3**	**(3%)**	**1**	**(2%)**	**0**	**(0%)**	**0**	**(0%)**	**0**	**(0%)**
Other interested parties	**6**	**(5%)**	**2**	**(3%)**	**10**	**(11%)**	**2**	**(2%)**	**2**	**(4%)**	**1**	**(1%)**	**0**	**(0%)**	**0**	**(0%)**
Consultants	5	(4%)	1	(1%)	7	(8%)	0	(0%)	1	(2%)	0	(0%)	0	(0%)	0	(0%)
Actuaries	1	(1%)	1	(1%)	3	(3%)	2	(2%)	1	(2%)	1	(1%)	0	(0%)	0	(0%)
TOTAL	**120**		**77**		**92**		**116**		**50**		**72**		**122**		**85**	

8 = Discussion Paper, Preliminary Views on Accounting Standards for Small and Medium-sized Entities (6 October 2004)
9 = ED Proposed Amendments to IFRS 3, Business Combinations – Combinations by Contract Alone or Involving Mutual Entities (5 August 2004)
10 = ED Proposed Amendments to IAS 19, Employee Benefits – Actuarial Gains and Losses, Group Plans and Disclosures (2004) (2 August 2004)
11 = ED Proposed Amendments to IAS 39, Financial Instruments: Recognition and Measurement: The Fair Value Option (2004) (26 July 2004)
12 = IASB Deliberative Process (18 June 2004)
13 = ED 6 Exploration for and Evaluation of Mineral Resources (2004) (6 May 2004)
14 = ED Fair Value Hedge Accounting for a Portfolio Hedge of Interest Rate Risk (2003) (19 December 2003)
15 = ED 4 Disposal of Non-current Assets and Presentation of Discontinued Operations (2003) (19 December 2003)

Appendix A *(Continued)*

	16	(%)	17	(%)	18	(%)	19	(%)	20	(%)	21	(%)	22	(%)	23	(%)
Preparers	**77**	**(57%)**	**59**	**(46%)**	**147**	**(71%)**	**119**	**(49%)**	**81**	**(51%)**	**33**	**(40%)**	**5**	**(15%)**	**27**	**(35%)**
Individual companies	6	(4%)	23	(18%)	33	(16%)	56	(23%)	30	(19%)	9	(11%)	3	(9%)	4	(5%)
Associations of companies	4	(3%)	14	(11%)	18	(9%)	19	(8%)	13	(8%)	10	(12%)	1	(3%)	12	(16%)
Individual banks and the like	32	(24%)	15	(12%)	43	(21%)	24	(10%)	15	(9%)	7	8%)	1	(3%)	4	(5%)
Associations of banks and the like	35	(26%)	7	(5%)	53	(26%)	20	(8%)	23	(14%)	7	(8%)	0	(0%)	7	(9%)
The accounting profession	**22**	**(16%)**	**31**	**(24%)**	**30**	**(14%)**	**29**	**(12%)**	**37**	**(23%)**	**28**	**(34%)**	**14**	**(41%)**	**31**	**(40%)**
Audit firms	6	(4%)	7	(5%)	7	(3%)	6	(2%)	7	(4%)	6	(7%)	5	(15%)	10	(13%)
Associations of accountants and auditors	16	(12%)	24	(19%)	23	(11%)	23	(10%)	30	(19%)	22	(27%)	9	(26%)	21	(27%)
Users	1	(1%)	2	(2%)	1	(0%)	10	(4%)	0	(0%)	1	(1%)	0	(0%)	0	(0%)
National standard setters	**13**	**(10%)**	**14**	**(11%)**	**14**	**(7%)**	**16**	**(7%)**	**21**	**(13%)**	**12**	**(14%)**	**6**	**(18%)**	**11**	**(14%)**
Stock exchanges	**2**	**(1%)**	**0**	**(0%)**	**2**	**(1%)**	**3**	**(1%)**	**3**	**(2%)**	**3**	**(4%)**	**1**	**(3%)**	**2**	**(3%)**
Governments	**0**	**(0%)**	**1**	**(1%)**	**4**	**(2%)**	**1**	**(0%)**	**2**	**(1%)**	**1**	**(1%)**	**0**	**(0%)**	**0**	**(0%)**
Individuals	**3**	**(2%)**	**10**	**(8%)**	**2**	**(1%)**	**23**	**(10%)**	**9**	**(6%)**	**1**	**(1%)**	**1**	**(3%)**	**3**	**(4%)**
Academics	**1**	**(1%)**	**4**	**(3%)**	**3**	**(1%)**	**12**	**(5%)**	**2**	**(1%)**	**0**	**(0%)**	**1**	**(3%)**	**0**	**(0%)**
Other interested parties	**15**	**(11%)**	**7**	**(5%)**	**4**	**(2%)**	**29**	**(12%)**	**4**	**(3%)**	**4**	**(5%)**	**6**	**(18%)**	**3**	**(4%)**
Consultants	1	(1%)	5	(4%)	1	(0%)	27	(11%)	3	(2%)	3	(4%)	2	(6%)	2	(3%)
Actuaries	14	(10%)	2	(2%)	3	(1%)	2	(1%)	1	(1%)	1	(1%)	4	(12%)	1	(1%)
TOTAL	**134**		**128**		**207**		**242**		**159**		**83**		**34**		**77**	

16 = ED 5, Insurance Contracts (2003) (10 December 2003)
17 = ED 3, Business Combinations (25 November 2003)
18 = Amendments to IAS 32, Financial Instruments: Disclosure and Presentation and IAS 39 Financial Instruments: Recognition and Measurement (2002) (10 September 2003)
19 = ED 2, Share-based Payment (2003) (10 September 2003)
20 = Improvements to International Accounting Standards (2002) (8 April 2003)
21 = ED 1, First-time Application of International Financial Reporting Standards (2002) (3 February 2003)
22 = IAS 19, Employee Benefits – The Asset Ceiling (2002) (18 April 2002)
23 = Preface to International Financial Reporting Standards (2002) (18 April 2002)

Appendix B

The numbers of the questions relate to the questions included in exposure draft 2.

Question 0
ED 2 is based on the idea that share-based payment transactions are a cost for the entity and should therefore be recognized in the profit and loss account. Is this general principle correct?

Question 1
Is the proposed scope (paragraphs 1–3) appropriate?

Question 2
Are the recognition requirements (to recognize an expense when the goods or services received or acquired are consumed) appropriate (paragraphs 4–6)?

Question 3a
Is the 'fair value'-based approach (paragraph 7) appropriate?

Question 3b
Is the requirement to distinguish between an indirect and a direct valuation method appropriate? (paragraph 7)

Question 4
Do you agree that the date when the entity obtains the goods or received services is the appropriate date at which to measure the fair value of the goods or services received (direct method)? (paragraph 8)

Question 5
Do you agree that the grant date is the appropriate date at which to measure the fair value of the equity instruments granted (indirect method)? (paragraph 8)

Question 9
Do you agree that, if the fair value of the equity instruments granted is used as a surrogate measure of the fair value of the services received, it is necessary to determine the amount to attribute to each unit of service received? (paragraph 15)

Question 10
Do you agree that no subsequent adjustments can be made to total equity once the entity has recognized the services received? (paragraph 16)

Question 11
Do you agree that an option pricing model should be applied to estimate the fair value of options granted?

Question 13
Do you agree that vesting conditions should be taken into account when estimating the fair value of options or shares granted? (paragraph 24)

Question 16
Do you agree with the principles-based approach of the draft IFRS? Are there specific aspects of valuing options for which guidance should be given?

Question 19
Are the proposed requirements to account for cash-settled share-based payment transactions appropriate? (paragraph 31)

2

A Fair Go for Fair Value

Janice Loftus

2.1 Introduction

Historical cost has traditionally dominated accounting practice. As a market-based measure, historical cost is attractive because it provides a conservative measure of expected benefit (at least at the time of acquisition) and is easily verifiable. But historical cost has not gone unchallenged, with critics dismissing it as a flawed basis for reporting on financial position and performance (e.g. Chambers, 1979). Historical cost remained as the dominant measurement in accounting, notwithstanding vigorous debate on the merits of alternative methods of accounting for price changes burgeoning in the 1960s, and fueled by the impetus of double-digit inflation rates in the 1970s (Beaver et al., 1980). Two problems generated by high levels of inflation are: that non-financial assets are likely to be understated, giving rise to asset stripping; and that fixed-interest financial assets are likely to be overstated, due to rising interest rates. In the late 1970s and early 1980s, standard setters responded to criticisms of historical cost, exacerbated by inflation, by experimenting with various alternative measures. More recent fair value innovations reflect dissatisfaction with historical cost, a search for decision-useful information, and greater confidence in market values and other estimates of fair value.

This chapter provides a brief review of some of the experimental initiatives of the Financial Accounting Standards Board (FASB) and the Securities and Exchange Commission (SEC) in the 1970s that sought to address the limitations of historical cost in a period of changing price levels. Those initiatives, and those of other standard setters, were generally unsuccessful and arguably discouraged further innovation and acceptance of fair values in financial reporting.

Following discussion of the earlier initiatives, this chapter focuses on developments in applying fair value measurement to financial instruments. 'Fair value is the amount for which an asset can be exchanged, or a liability settled, between knowledgeable, willing parties in an arm's length transaction' (IASB 39, paragraph 9). Arguably, the application of fair value to financial instruments is less contentious than for other assets and liabilities. One of the criticisms of fair value is the inability to observe market prices, particularly for specialized assets. This problem does not apply to financial instruments traded in an active market as they have an observable quoted price. For other financial assets and financial liabilities, fair value can be estimated using established techniques and available information, such as credit risk indicators and interest rates. Another criticism of fair value is that, in the absence of an active market, it requires the estimation of future flows of economic benefits. This estimation is less problematic in the case of financial instruments because the future cash flows are determined by contract. Another argument against fair value is that it is not relevant for assets that an entity does not intend to trade. However, in the case of financial instruments, the fair value reflects the best available estimate of the present value of the future cash flows embodied in the contract and the risk that the amount and/or timing of cash flows will differ from expectations. Whether held to maturity or exchanged, the flow of economic benefits is in cash or other financial instruments. Accordingly, financial instruments provide the strongest case for the adoption of a fair value model.

The proposals of the International Accounting Standards Committee Steering Committee (1997) and the Joint Working Group of National Standard Setters and the IASC (2000) are discussed in section 2.3, followed by an analysis in section 2.4 of the mixed measurement model and muddled performance measurement prescribed and permitted by IAS 39. The chapter concludes with a discussion of the need for international acceptance of what is meant by performance measurement to clear the way for the adoption of consistent and comparable reporting on the effects of financial instruments on an entity's financial performance and financial position.

2.2 Experimental fair value initiatives

In response to inconsistencies emerging in accounting practice following a period of declining security prices in the USA, the FASB introduced *Statement of Financial Accounting Standard No. 12: Accounting for Certain Marketable Securities* (FAS 12) in 1975. As the market value of many marketable securities fell below cost, some entities carried them at cost while other entities reported the same assets at the lower of cost and market value. Partial recovery of market prices in 1975 resulted in some entities continuing to carry marketable securities at a written-down value that was below both cost and market value (FASB, 1975). The Standard required marketable equity securities to be classified into current and noncurrent portfolios and each portfolio carried at the lower of its aggregate cost and aggregate market value. FAS 12 applied to equity instruments other than redeemable preference stock and Arthur Litke, one of two members who dissented on the issue of FAS 12, argued that the Standard should require all marketable equity securities to be carried at market value, being the best measure of their net realizable value.

While intended to reduce inconsistencies, FAS 12 introduced several inconsistencies in accounting for changes in the market value of financial assets. The

Standard did not apply to enterprises in industries that had a specialized accounting practice for marketable securities, such as investment companies, brokers and dealers in securities, and certain categories of insurance companies. FAS 12 did not apply to other marketable financial instruments, such as bonds. The Standard provided for different treatment of changes in the valuation allowance (the net unrealized loss) between assets classified as current and those classified as noncurrent. FAS 12 did not allow for the recognition of unrealized gains on the portfolio but required unrealized gains to be recognized to the extent that they offset unrealized losses. The inconsistent treatment of unrealized gains and losses reflects the lack of clear guidance on what constitutes performance.

The SEC issued Accounting Series Release (ASR) 190 in 1976, requiring replacement cost disclosures for inventories, productive capacity, depreciation expense, and cost of sales expense. ASR 190 was designed to provide more relevant information in an inflationary economy than that provided by historical cost measures. The replacement cost numbers were supplements to, not substitutes for, historical cost numbers. Providing the information by disclosure without recognition shielded the income statement from any unrealized gains or losses that might have resulted from the application of a replacement cost model, such as current cost accounting. Further, restricting the information to note disclosures also avoided any difficult decisions about capital maintenance concepts implied by capacity-based measures of wealth.

The replacement cost disclosures did not appear to provide relevant information to the market beyond that provided by historical cost. Gheyara and Boatsman (1980) analyzed the 1976 fiscal year disclosures made in early 1977 and found no evidence of information content. Similarly, Beaver et al. (1980) found no security price effects for the announcement of the SEC's proposal, the adoption ASR 190 by the SEC, or disclosures made in compliance with the Release.

The FASB extended disclosure requirements with the issue of *Statement of Financial Accounting Standard No. 33: Financial Reporting and Changing Prices* (FAS 33) in 1979. The required disclosures included accounting numbers adjusted for changes in general purchasing power as well as current cost (replacement cost) measures. Like the SEC, the FASB confined its initiatives to note disclosures.

Mandatory current cost disclosures were also introduced in the UK in 1980. The UK requirements failed to gain acceptance. After a five-year experiment that clearly failed, the UK Standard ceased to be mandatory.

Feedback on FAS 33 was similarly negative (Chambers et al., 1984; Miller and Loftus, 2000) and the requirements were eventually made voluntary by *Statement of Financial Accounting Standard No. 89: Financial Reporting and Changing Prices*, issued in 1986.

Current cost accounting was also introduced in Australia through numerous bulletins and statements of provisional accounting standards, and subsequently integrated into *Statement of Accounting Practice 1: Current Cost Accounting* in 1983 by the Institute of Chartered Accountants and the Australian Society of Accountants. Current cost accounting disclosures were always voluntary in Australia and were ignored in practice by the private sector (Miller and Loftus, 2000).

The lesson for standard setters from the era of innovation was that their constituents did not welcome radical change. Thus, innovation gave way to incrementalism in accounting reform. For instance, the Accounting Standards Board in the UK declared that its approach to measurement reform would be evolutionary rather than revolutionary (ASB, 1993). Gradual introduction of fair value, or any alternatives to historical cost, would necessitate a mixed measurement model and accompanying hybrid concept of performance measurement.

2.3 Proposals and requirements for fair value for financial instruments

The spate of corporate collapses in the second half of the 1980s and the early 1990s renewed calls for accounting reform. The need to reconsider accounting for financial instruments was fueled by global corporate financial disasters involving derivatives in the mid-1990s (e.g. Procter & Gamble, Gibson Greetings, Japan Airlines, Barings Bank, and Glaxo). The IASC responded by undertaking a joint project with Canada on accounting for financial assets and financial liabilities.

The collaboration resulted in the issue of a Discussion Paper, *Accounting for Financial Assets and Financial Liabilities*, published by the IASC (IASC Steering Committee on Financial Instruments, 1997), introducing proposals for radical reforms. The IASC Steering Committee proposed that entities should measure all financial assets and financial liabilities at fair value on initial recognition, when becoming a party to a financial instrument. They also proposed that all financial assets and financial liabilities should be measured at fair value subsequent to initial recognition, with changes accounted for in profit or loss. The only exception to this was the provision that changes in fair value of hedging instruments could be accounted for as gains or losses directly in equity with subsequent recycling to profit or loss to coincide with the recognition of gains or losses arising from the hedged transaction.

The proposed extension of fair value accounting proved to be highly controversial. The vast majority of financial statement preparers responding to the discussion paper disapproved of full fair value measurement of financial instruments. The lower of cost and market principle was preferred for financial instruments other than those held for trading (IASC, 1997). However, other respondents, including user groups, regulators and academics, and some professional accountancy bodies, accounting firms and standard setters, supported the proposed move to fair value accounting for financial instruments.

It was apparent that more work was needed to gain the support of its constituents and the IASC decided to tackle financial instruments in two stages:

1. In acknowledgment of the urgency of the matter, an interim international standard on recognition and measurement to be completed in 1998.
2. In acknowledgment of the complexity of the matter and the need for an integrated and harmonized standard, the establishment of a Joint Working Group of National Standard Setters and the IASC (JWG) to prepare a comprehensive standard by mid-year 2000.

The interim standard, *IAS 39: Financial Instruments: Recognition and Measurement*, was approved in December 1998 (subject to approval of the final wording) and issued in March 1999. IAS 39 prescribed initial recognition of all financial instruments at cost. The cost of a financial instrument at initial recognition is the fair value at the time that the entity becomes a party to the transaction and any directly attributable transaction costs. Subsequent remeasurement to fair value was required with the exception of loans and receivables initiated by the entity and not held for trading, fixed maturity investments that the entity intends to hold to maturity, and financial assets whose fair value cannot be measured reliably.

The need to resolve the contentious issue of how to account for changes in fair value was avoided by allowing alternative treatments. An entity could choose to recognize in profit or loss all gains and losses on remeasuring financial instruments to fair value, or recognize in profit or loss only those gains and losses on remeasuring financial instruments held for trading, and deferring the recognition of other changes in fair value in earnings until the financial instrument is settled.

While IAS 39 represented a substantial step towards fair value measurement, its application fell significantly short of the IASC Steering Committee's proposals for all financial instruments to be stated at fair value. The Steering Committee had proposed that changes in fair value of all financial instruments, with the exception of hedging instruments, be recognized immediately in profit or loss.

However, under IAS 39 the income statement would not capture changes in the fair value of financial assets held to maturity, loans and receivables, certain hedging instruments, financial assets and, at the discretion of the preparer, any financial asset not held for trading.

The second stage of the IASC's project on financial instruments was undertaken by the JWG, which aimed to develop a comprehensive standard on accounting for financial assets and financial liabilities. Building on the earlier proposals of the IASC Steering Committee, the JWG was committed to a fair value model and included in its objectives the implementation of a coherent framework for the recognition and fair value measurement of financial assets and financial liabilities, and for the presentation and disclosure of gains and losses and hedging activities (JWG, 2000). The resulting proposed standard was predictably similar to the earlier recommendations of the IASC Steering Committee.

The JWG concluded that fair values were able to be determined reliably for all financial assets and financial liabilities other than certain investments in private equity. Accordingly, the JWG proposed that, with the exception of certain private equity investments, all financial instruments, including loans and receivables, be stated at fair value on initial recognition. Subsequently, the financial assets and financial liabilities should be remeasured to fair value, with changes in fair value included in profit or loss. The JWG went beyond the earlier recommendations of the IASC Steering Committee by proposing that hedge accounting be discontinued.

The IASC (2000) concluded that implementation of the JWG's proposals would be a significant step and require a different 'mindset' to apply concepts and techniques from finance and capital markets to derive measures for financial reporting. It also required a step out of the mixed measurement model, albeit in respect to a defined category of assets and liabilities. The JWG believed that the international accounting community was ready to replace the existing deficient mixed measurement model with a comprehensive fair value model that could provide the most relevant information on financial instruments.

However, a comprehensive fair value model, if applied to financial instruments, would necessarily form part of a mixed measurement model when combined with different accounting treatments for other assets and liabilities. For instance, an enterprise may enter into an effective hedge to mitigate risks of changing prices, but the effectiveness of its risk management strategy may be masked by accounting practices that mark the hedging instrument to fair value while applying a different measurement basis to the hedged item. Moreover, the proposed recognition of unrealized gains and losses in earnings was not based on any accepted concept of performance measurement.

While the JWG considered the time was right to embrace fair value accounting for financial instruments, many within the international accounting community particularly the banking industry (Tan et al., 2005), did not. The improvements project of the newly instigated International Accounting Standards Board (IASB), involving the revision of 13 accounting standards, became a major priority of the Board. Rather than embracing the JWG's revolutionary proposals, the IASB adopted a strategy of addressing aspects of accounting for financial instruments that could be dealt with relatively quickly, and deferred reconsidering the fundamental approach, or approaches, to accounting for financial instruments established by IAS 39 (IASB, 2002).

2.4 IAS 39 and the mixed measurement model

IAS 39 adopts a mixed measurement model, with the use of amortized cost and fair value determined, to some extent, by the type of financial asset, management's purpose for engaging in the financial instrument, and management's choice (or designation) on initial recognition. The Standard uses five categories for the classification of financial instruments and these categories determine how they should be measured on initial recognition and subsequent measurement:

- financial assets at fair value through profit or loss
- held-to-maturity investments
- loans and receivables
- available-for-sale financial assets
- other financial liabilities.

A financial asset is categorized as *at fair value through profit or loss* if it is held for trading or designated by the entity as *at fair value through profit or loss* on initial recognition (IAS 39). To be classified as held for trading the financial asset must be:

- acquired principally for the purpose of being sold in the near term
- part of a portfolio of identified financial instruments that are managed together and for which there is evidence of a recent pattern of short-term profit-taking, or
- a derivative, other than a derivate financial instrument that is a designated and effective hedging instrument.

The Standard allows for considerable management discretion in the classification of financial instruments. Any financial asset within the scope of IAS 39 can be classified as *at fair value through profit or loss* on initial recognition except for investments in equity instruments that do not have a quoted market price in an active market (and derivatives that are linked to, and must be settled by delivery of, unquoted equity instruments), and whose fair value cannot be reliably measured.

Financial assets that are categorized as *at fair value through profit or loss* are measured at fair value on initial recognition (that is, when the entity enters into the contract). The initial carrying amount does not include transaction costs. Subsequent to initial recognition, they are remeasured at fair value. A gain or loss resulting from the change in fair value of this category of assets is recognized through profit or loss.

The second category, *held-to-maturity investments*, comprises nonderivative financial assets with fixed or determinable payments and fixed maturity, and the entity has the positive intention and ability to hold the asset until it matures with the exception of the following (IAS 39):

(a) those that the entity upon initial recognition designates as *at fair value through profit or loss*
(b) those that the entity designates as *available-for-sale*, and
(c) those that meet the definition of *loans and receivables*.

The criteria for classification as *held-to-maturity investments* reflect a combination of purpose-led classification and, to an extent, management discretion (Loftus, 2003). It is purpose-led because management must have the intention to hold the asset until maturity. But categorizing financial assets that management intends to hold to maturity as *held-to-maturity investments* is not mandatory because management has the discretion, subject to restrictions related to reliable measurement, to designate them as *at fair value through profit or loss*.

IAS 39 requires financial assets that are categorized as *held-to-maturity investments* to be measured at fair value plus transaction costs on initial recognition. Subsequent to initial recognition, financial assets categorized as *held-to-maturity investments* are carried at amortized cost using the effective interest rate method. The amortized cost of a financial asset is the amount at which it is measured on initial recognition, plus or minus cumulative amortization of any difference between the principal amount and the maturity amount, less any reductions for impairment or uncollectibility (IAS 39).

Financial assets are categorized as *loans and receivables* if they are nonderivative financial assets with fixed or determinable payments but are not quoted in an active market, with the exception of (IAS 39, paragraph 9):

(a) those that the entity intends to sell immediately or in the near term, which shall be classified as held for trading, and those that the entity upon initial recognition designates *at fair value through profit or loss*
(b) those that the entity upon initial recognition designates as *available-for-sale financial assets*, or
(c) those for which the holder may not recover substantially all of its initial investment, other than because of credit deterioration, which shall be classified as *available for sale*.

The first two exceptions provide for mutually exclusive categories of financial assets. The third exception excludes financial assets for which the initial investment is not fully recoverable for reasons other than the debtor's credit deterioration. Such financial assets are classified as *available for sale*. Classifying financial assets as *loans and receivables* when a substantial amount of the initial investment is unrecoverable would be inappropriate because this classification of financial assets is carried at amortized cost subsequent to initial recognition.

Financial assets classified as *loans and receivables* are measured at fair value plus transaction costs on initial recognition (IAS 39). Subsequent to initial recognition, financial assets categorized as *loans and receivables* are recognized at amortized cost using the effective interest method, subject to an impairment test.

Available-for-sale financial assets are those nonderivative financial assets that are:

- designated as available for sale, or
- not classified as *loans and receivables*, *held-to-maturity investments*, or financial assets *at fair value through profit or loss*.

IAS 39 applies multiple bases for the categorization of financial assets as *available for sale* (Loftus, 2003). One basis reflects management discretion because management may designate the assets as *available for sale*. The assets, such as bonds, may otherwise qualify as *held-to-maturity investments*, or meet the definition of *loans and receivables*. However, this is subject to the asset not having been classified as held for trading, which could be on the basis of management intention (acquired principally for the purpose of resale) or the nature of the asset (a derivative financial instrument). The categorization as *available for sale* also reflects, in part, the nature of the asset, as this category is limited to nonderivative financial assets. Thirdly, the *available-for-sale* category also serves as the default category for nonderivative financial assets. Some financial assets may be excluded from being categorized as *held-to-maturity investments* as a result of prior reclassifications or sales of assets so classified. Thus, their categorization as *available for sale* might not reflect management intention, management discretion, or the nature of the financial assets, but the application of rules restricting categorization as *held-to-maturity investments*.

Assets categorized as *available-for-sale financial assets* are measured at fair value plus transaction costs on initial recognition (IAS 39). Subsequent to initial measurement, the assets are measured at fair value and the gain or loss arising from the change in fair value is measured directly in equity.

The category *other liabilities* includes all liabilities that are not classified as *at fair value through profit or loss*. Accordingly, the category is only available to nonderivative liabilities. *Other liabilities* are recognized at amortized cost using the effective interest rate method in accordance with IAS 39.

IAS specifies alternatives for recognizing gain or loss arising from a change in the fair value of financial assets and financial liabilities that are not part of a hedging relationship: a gain or loss on a financial asset or financial liability classified as *at fair value through profit or loss* shall be recognized in profit or loss; and a gain or loss on holding an *available-for-sale financial asset* shall be recognized directly in equity, through the statement of changes in equity (except for impairment losses and foreign exchange gains and losses) until the financial asset is derecognized, at which time the cumulative gain or loss previously recognized in equity shall be recognized in profit or loss. Thus, the classification of financial instruments determines whether changes in fair value are recognized, and the timing of the effect on profit of those changes in fair value that are recognized.

In the following example, Loftus (2003) demonstrates the inconsistencies that can arise from the mixed measurement model applied by IAS 39. For example, suppose Company A, Company B, and Company C purchase XYZ bonds. Company A categorizes the bonds as *at fair value through profit or loss,* Company B categorizes them as *held-to-maturity investments,* and Company C categorizes them as *available-for-sale financial assets.* IAS 39 then required Company A to recognize the bonds at fair value. Transaction costs would be expensed and changes in fair value would affect reported profit in each reporting period while the bonds are held. Applying IAS 39, Company B would initially recognize the bonds at fair value plus transactions cost, and subsequently measure them at amortized cost, ignoring changes in fair value in the measurement of the assets and profit. IAS 39 requires Company C to recognize the bonds at fair value plus transaction costs and changes in fair value would be recognized directly in equity with recycling through profit when the bonds are derecognized. Thus, Company B and Company C would initially measure the bonds at the same carrying amount while Company A would differ in the treatment of the transaction costs. Subsequently, Company A and Company C would measure the bonds at fair value while Company B would apply amortized cost. The effect of the investment in the bonds on profit for each period would differ for each of the three companies (interest plus change in fair value or interest determined using the effective interest rate method or interest). The different accounting treatments do not reflect differences in the financial assets. They might not reflect differences in management purposes for holding the assets as all three companies may intend to hold the bonds until maturity. Further, an entity may simultaneously use different categories for accounting for identical or similar nonderivative financial assets.

While IAS 39 promotes the use of fair value, by requiring classification of some financial instruments as *at fair value through profit or loss* and permitting many other financial assets to be so designated, it has retained a mixed measurement model rather than embracing the fair value model proposed by the JWG. In the face of considerable opposition to the JWG proposals, hedge accounting was retained in IAS 39, albeit with tighter restrictions on its application.

2.5 Conclusion

Historical cost has withstood challenges from academics, regulators, and users of financial statements. Criticism of historical cost rose during periods of high inflation and standard setters responded with largely unsuccessful innovations, mostly involving disclosures in notes. While interest in measurements other than cost was growing, concerns about how any changes in value should be accounted for in income or equity proved to be a significant and enduring impediment to the recognition of alternative measures in financial statements.

Gradually, the historical cost model and modified historical cost models have been succeeded by mixed measurement models. Corporate collapses in the late 1980s and 1990s fueled the historical cost debate, with renewed interest in fair values, particularly with respect to financial instruments.

International projects on accounting for financial instruments resulted in proposals by the IASC Steering Committee and the JWG for fair value accounting for financial instruments. The IASB acknowledged that the JWG proposals represented a significant step, but it proved to be a step that it was not prepared to take.

Instead, the improved IAS 39 permits and requires different measurement principles both on initial measurement and on subsequent measurement for identical assets. Similar or identical assets may be accounted for differently while different financial assets may be included in the same category. For example, management may designate various nonderivative financial assets, including loans and other receivables, as *available-for-sale financial assets*, and both derivate and nonderivative financial assets (other than loans and receivables) may be designated as *at fair value through profit or loss*. The mixed measurement model applied in IAS 39, together with the inconsistent treatment of recognized changes in fair value, results in a blurred concept of performance measurement.

Comparability of financial position and financial performance may be impaired by the mixed measurement model and the mix of criteria prescribed and permitted by IAS 39 for determining how financial assets should be categorized and measured. The nature of financial instruments and the availability of active markets and techniques for estimation of fair value provide the strongest case for giving fair value a 'fair go'. However, the absence of international agreement and conceptual guidance on a consistent measurement model and concept of capital maintenance continue to impede the application of a fair value model. It is hoped that the IASB's performance measurement project may remove longstanding obstacles to the application of a fair value model in the context of financial instruments, where the reliability of fair values is widely accepted and they clearly provide the most relevant information about the effects on financial performance and financial position of this aspect of an entity's activities.

References

Accounting Standards Board (1993). *The Role of Valuation in Financial Reporting*. Discussion Paper, ASB, UK.

Beaver, W.H., Christie, A.A., and Griffin, P.A. (1980). The Information Content of SEC Accounting Series Release No. 190 Accounting. *Journal of Accounting and Economics*, 2(2):127–157.

Chambers, R.J. (1979). Usefulness – The Vanishing Premise in Accounting Standards. *Abacus*, 15(2):71–92.

Chambers, R.J., Hopwood, W.S., and McKeown, J.C. (1984). The Relevance of Varieties of Accounting Information: A USA Survey. *Abacus*, 20(2):99–110.

Financial Accounting Standards Board (1975). *Statement of Financial Accounting Standards No. 12: Accounting for Certain Marketable Securities*. FASB, USA.

Financial Accounting Standards Board (1979). *Statement of Financial Accounting Standards No. 33: Financial Reporting and Changing Prices*. FASB, USA.

Financial Accounting Standards Board (1986). *Statement of Financial Accounting Standard No. 89: Financial Reporting and Changing Prices*. FASB, USA.

Gheyara, K. and Boatsman, J. (1980). Market Reaction to the 1976 Replacement Cost Disclosures. *Journal of Accounting and Economics*, 2(2):107–125.

Institute of Chartered Accountants in Australia and the Australian Society of Accountants (1983). *Statement of Accounting Practice 1: Current Cost Accounting.* ICAA and ASA, Australia.

International Accounting Standards Board (2002). *Improvements to IAS 39, Financial Instruments: Recognition and Measurement.* IASB, UK.

International Accounting Standards Committee (1997). Special Report: Financial Instruments. *IASC Insight*, December:11–14.

International Accounting Standards Committee (1999). *IAS 39: Financial Instruments: Recognition and Measurement.* IASC, UK.

International Accounting Standards Committee (2000). Financial Instruments: JWG Issues Proposals for Fair Value Measurement. *IASC Insight*, December:7–8.

International Accounting Standards Committee Steering Committee on Financial Instruments (1997). *Discussion Paper: Accounting for Financial Assets and Financial Liabilities.* IASC, UK.

Joint Working Group of National Standard Setters (2000). *Draft Standard and Basis for Conclusions.* IASC, UK.

Loftus, J. (2003). What Do You Get When You Mix Measurement Methods and Principles? Accounting for Financial Instruments. *Financial Reporting, Regulation and Governance,* 3(1); http://www.cbs.curtin.edu.au/business/research/journals/financial-reporting/-regulation-and-governance

Miller, M.C. and Loftus, J.A. (2000). Measurement Entering the 21st Century: A Clear or Blocked Road Ahead? *Australian Accounting Review,* 11(2):18.

Tan, C.W., Hancock, P., Taplin, R., and Tower, G. (2005). Fair Value Accounting for All Financial Instruments: Perceptions from Managers of Australian Financial Institutions. *Australian Accounting Review,* 15(2):79–88.

3

The Behavior Modification Impact of International Accounting Standards on Decision-making and Risk Management

Stanley C.W. Salvary

> 'We need a technique that will enable us to discover possible alternatives to propositions which we may regard as truisms or necessarily true. In this process logic aids us in devising ways of formulating our propositions explicitly and accurately, so that their possible alternatives become clear. When thus faced with alternative hypotheses, logic develops their consequences; compared with observable phenomena we have a means of testing which hypothesis is to be eliminated and which is most in harmony with the facts of observation.'
>
> (Cohen and Nagel, 1934, pp. 195–196)

3.1 Introduction

In its Framework (April 2001, F.24), the International Accounting Standards Board (IASB) fully recognizes and acknowledges that:

> '[F]inancial statements *cannot provide all the information* that users may need to make economic decisions. For one thing, financial statements show the financial effects of past events and transactions, whereas *the decisions that most users of financial statements have to make relate to the future.*' (Emphasis added)

Also, the following explanation of *relevance* is given in the Framework (F.26–28):

> 'Information in financial statements is relevant when it influences the economic decisions of users. It can do that both by (a) helping them *evaluate* past, present, or *future events* relating to an enterprise and by (b) confirming or correcting past evaluations they have made.' (Emphasis added)

The focus on decision-making instead of accountability leads to a concern for predictive value, as opposed to feedback value, in financial statements. Given that fair value is deemed by many researchers to be the most relevant measure for financial reporting, the desire to enhance users' ability to predict firms' future cash flows leads the IASB to conclude that the changes in market values should be reflected in financial statements. However, other important studies have established that a change in financial accounting measures is not needed; what is needed is the disclosure of information derived from models that provide alternative nonfinancial measures that drive future performance. In studies by Canibano et al. (1999) and Bornemann et al. (1999), it is fully recognized that *decision-oriented information cannot and should not be provided by financial statements*. These researchers conclude that the problem is better addressed by developing models that would better measure intangibles and provide a framework for better disclosures.

A model for a reporting framework with nonfinancial measures alongside financial measures has been developed by Canibano et al. (1999). Additionally, the Canadian Institute of Chartered Accountants (CICA), concerning the relevance of traditional financial accounting for performance in the new knowledge-based economy, has developed the total value creation (TVC) model. As stated in unequivocal terms, this model, as developed, captures an entity's value-creating activities (where things are going), a future orientation, which is quite distinct from value-realizing activities (from where things are coming), a historic orientation (Upton, 2001, p. 21).

In part due to Kaplan and Norton (1992), business leaders have recognized that to effectively manage, it is not a change in the financial measures that is needed. Instead, it is the development of alternative nonfinancial measures that drive future performance that is needed. For instance, the balanced score card (Kaplan and Norton, 1996, p. 8) complements financial measures of past performance with measures of the drivers of future performance. Accordingly, much of the added information discussed above is presently being used by management, and much of it is already provided to some users such as banks. Management's past reluctance to disclose such information to the public has been overcome by a new sense of urgency to adopt innovative disclosures. According to Keller (2003, p. 2): 'Larger businesses have been taking their own steps to disseminate more relevant, non-required, non-financial information to their investors and other key stakeholders.'

Furthermore, in October 1994, the Special Committee on Financial Reporting of the American Institute of Certified Public Accountants (Special Committee) issued its report, *Improving Business Reporting – A Customer Focus, Meeting the Information Needs of Investors and Creditors*. Interestingly, the Special Committee (1994, p. 94) concluded that although users would like to have more information, *they are not in favor of replacing the current accounting model with a value-based accounting model*. Users wished to retain the conventional model since it provides: (1) a stable and consistent benchmark that is highly useful for understanding the business, identifying trends, and valuing a business by projecting earnings and cash flows; and (2) information that is reliable because the amounts are based on market transactions. Disclosures recommended by the Special Committee (1994, p. 25) are: (1) *Financial and nonfinancial data*; (2) management's analysis of financial and nonfinancial data; (3) *forward-looking information*; (4) information about management and shareholders; and (5) background about the company. Recommendations (1) and (3) expressly identify and separate evaluative/feedback data from decision-making/

predictive/forward-looking data. Indubitably, as revealed by the Special Committee's report, the difference between the information generated by financial and managerial accounting is of great concern. Accordingly, the IASB's emphasis on the *future* and *future events* has to be examined in the context of accounting in its totality.

Financial accounting provides a mapping of cash commitments, but *does not provide a forecast of the future.* Since financial statements provide *no insight as to the future plans of management*, they cannot help users *evaluate future events* – that which has not occurred. However, users can be aided in their decision-making if they were to be provided with managerial accounting information. While internal financial reporting incorporates both financial and managerial accounting information, external financial reporting is comprised primarily of financial accounting information. Therefore, very little information in external financial reports relates to the decision-making (planning) function of management. *Internal* reporting provides evaluated data (information tailor-made for specific decisions governed by *relevancy and reliability*) and *external* reporting provides general information about the firm characterized by *reliability and neutrality* (Salvary, 1985). External financial reporting can be extended to include an immense variety of information about the current capability of an organization; at a minimum, it should include managerial accounting information. Other information can be disclosed as long as such disclosures would not expose the entity to risk of injury (Salvary, 1989b, p. 320).

Invariably, when deciding on the best course of action, management places/utilizes financial accounting information in context with information derived from managerial accounting to arrive at their decisions (Salvary, 1985, pp. 14–15). Inescapably, users have to follow the same path as management by drawing upon all information that is available from whatever source that is reliable. Apparently, in the quest to satisfy users' need for decision-making information, financial reporting is being confused with financial analysis. However, it should be obvious that:

> 'When one is *using the output* of financial accounting for analytical purposes (except in the case of the attest function), one is no longer in the realm of financial accounting. Manipulation of financial accounting data for credit analysis for loans, bankruptcy prediction, etc., removes one from the realm of financial accounting. The output of financial accounting is input for financial analysis; *and financial analysis is part of managerial accounting.* When cognizance is not given to this subtlety, confusion abounds!'
>
> (Salvary, 1989b, pp. 30–32)

As noted by Scott (1997, p. 161), by assuming 'greater responsibility for incorporating fair values into the financial statements proper ... accountants are doing some of the investors' work for them through increased use of valuations. If the securities market ... [were] fully efficient, this would not be necessary to the extent that value information was available in supplementary form or elsewhere.' Additionally, while its position may have changed at this time, the Financial Accounting Policy Committee (FAPC) of the Association for Investment Management and Research (AIMR) in 1998 maintained that only facts should be provided by accountants and financial analysts will perform the financial analysis (Knutson and Napolitano, 1998, p. 176). Being more specific, the AIMR's FAPC states that: (1) many things, that properly belong in supplementary schedules, should not be forced into the financial statements; (2) factual data, accompanied by supplemental information for clarification, should be the sole contents of financial statements; (3) financial accounting standards must focus on that which is real and portray the substance of exchanges and other economic events accurately and completely; and (4) new standards should provide information about the firm that could not have been estimated by outsiders (Knutson and Napolitano, 1998, pp. 172–175). *While it is possible that one may argue that item (4) was an invitation for the adoption of fair market value accounting*, it does not appear likely since that would be in contradiction to the FAPC's position in items (1), (2), and (3).

Inadvertently, the IASB's efforts to improve financial reporting are misdirected due to the failure to give cognizance to: (1) the difference between the capital market and the commodity market; (2) the role and psychological effect of the capital market; (3) the difference between simplifying assumptions and necessary and sufficient conditions for measurement; (4) economic reality as embedded in plans, decision-making, and operating dynamics; (5) the importance of risk management, decision-making, and performance measurement; (6) the structural and operating differences among the different types of companies; (7) the need for sanity in market pricing and sensibility in financial reporting; and (8) the investment decision, capital budgeting, and recoverable cost. These issues are examined in context of the IASB's objectives and standards.

3.2 The capital market and the commodity market

The international accounting standard-setting process is plagued with the assumed homogeneity of users' need and purpose of financial reports, a problem that has been transferred from the national accounting standard-setting arenas. As posed by the standard setters in the USA and to a lesser extent the UK, the problem stems from the desire to set accounting standards to satisfy investors' needs.

As stated in its final *Preface to International Financial Reporting Standards* (IASB, 2002), the IASB's objectives are:

(a) to develop, in the public interest, a single set of high-quality, understandable, and enforceable global accounting standards that require high-quality, transparent, and comparable information in financial statements and other financial reporting to help participants in the world's capital markets and other users make economic decisions
(b) to promote the use and rigorous application of those standards; and
(c) to work actively with national standard setters to bring about convergence of national accounting standards and IFRS to high-quality solutions.

According to Levitt (1998, p. 81): 'Any set of accounting standards that seeks global acceptance must be shaped ... by looking to the needs of the investors and the capital markets.' With this background, it is understandable why item (a) of the IASB's objectives is:

> 'to develop ... a single set of high-quality, understandable, and enforceable *global accounting standards* that require high-quality, transparent, and comparable information in financial statements and other financial reporting to help participants in the *world's capital markets* and other users make economic decisions.' (Emphasis added)

This emphasis on the capital markets is seemingly oblivious to the fact that many countries such as Germany, Japan, and France, with strong bank financing, have built eminently successful economies (Bardhan and Roemer, 1992, p. 107) given a broad social emphasis for financial reporting.

The two functions of the capital market actually represent two distinct markets: (a) a new issues market – the primary market; and (b) an aftermarket market – a secondary market which consists of the outstanding stock of old issues. The primary market provides capital to enterprises for investment purposes (Committee for Invisible Transactions, 1967, pp. 23–25). The secondary market or aftermarket simply provides for the transfer of ownership. Billions of dollars exchange hands in those transactions, yet there is no injection of cash into the coffers of the firms whose shares are traded. Since the *secondary* capital market is a transfer market, it is not critical to the functioning of a successful economy, whereas 'a bank-centric financial system ... largely mitigates the planner–manager principal–agent problem, and does so in a way potentially superior to that of the stock market-centric system' (Bardhan and Roemer, 1992, p. 109). Undoubtedly, the main ingredients for successful operations of an economy are the availability of *savings for investments* and a management philosophy that is conducive to the further development of social exchanges (Salvary, 1998b).

It is the difference between *investing and saving* that establishes the distinction between the commodity market and the capital market. At the initiation of an investment/operating plan which is financed by savings, *based on the capital budgeting model*, a specific stream of cash flows is set in motion and this cash flow stream is valued at the margin. It is uncertainty and the time perspective, which confront the operating decision, that differentiate the *investment decision* from the *savings decision* (Salvary, 1998a).

Traditionally, financial reporting has reported on the firm's investment/operating decisions as executed and the actual consequences of those decisions. Now, since item (a) of the IASB's objectives maintains that: 'financial reporting [is] to help participants in the world's capital markets and other users make economic decisions', *the capital market is now considered as the main show and the commodity market has become the side show*. Although it is the commodity market (providing consumers with goods and services from manufacturing, real estate, banking, insurance, etc.) that drives the economy, the capital market, which involves the transfer of ownership and intertemporal transfer of risk, is deemed to be the basis of economic reality. With this change of focus for financial reporting, the IASB deems it necessary to develop standards that incorporate changes in market prices in the financial accounting measurement process. This condition raises profound questions concerning the economic system:

1. How and where is value created?
2. Can the economy function without the production of goods and services?
3. Can the economy function without the securities market?

(1) Value is created in the *commodity market* with the production of goods and services. (2) Without the production of goods and services there is no economy. Therefore, in the absence of the commodity market, there would be nothing to value. (3) The emergence and functioning of the securities market revolves around the commodity market. In the capital market *wealth* is created and appropriated; the transactions constitute the transfer of cash for ownership. Quite often and over sustained periods, the cash transfer for ownership remotely relates to the underlying value created by firms in the commodity market.

As noted by Newman (2005), through June 2005, Total Dollar Trading Value (DTV) is estimated to be $28.321 trillion, whereas Gross Domestic Product (GDP) is $12.183 trillion and total market capitalization (MC) $14.733 trillion. DTV is 232.5% of GDP and 192.2% of MC. The fact that these measures are the second and third highest ever recorded, respectively, is a clear indication that the mania for stocks has never really ended. As measured by Bulletin Board, share volume is averaging more than 1.8 billion shares per day, which is more than the totals registered on NASDAQ's popular market! Trading has increased 2.2% over the frenetic activity of 2004. Now daily share volume is four times as high as in 2000. In the 18 months since the end of 2003, inflows totaled $251.8 billion but there has been no price improvement for the Dow; instead, there has been a 2% loss through June 2005. Sadly, prices for individual stock issues are no longer relevant; it is only the various and sundry indexes that count. In the given scenario, it cannot be assumed that constituent stocks are fairly valued; accordingly, the index itself cannot be assumed to be fairly valued. The stock market, instead of being a market based upon studied perceptions of value, has become a game where indexing and other games totally govern prices.

However, a strong sentiment exists among accounting standard setters and researchers that the inclusion of market volatility in financial statements would enhance the transparency and clarity of firms' operating performance and financial position. This market value approach to financial reporting stresses *the information needs of investors* – an information perspective by means of which the short-term interests of investors are served as opposed to a measurement perspective which would focus on corporate reality. This acute short-term orientation is a serious concern, as the following passage reveals:

> 'The economics of the stock market investing are directed toward the short run. In the short run, psychology will have a much greater influence on market prices than underlying corporate facts ... As a result, there are many pressures making people in the "Street" short-run conscious. First, there is the tendency for money managers to be judged by the peers and ... by their customers on how much appreciation they obtained for their portfolios in recent periods ... Second, there is a finance factor – those who borrow heavily to finance a portfolio need to have near-term upside market action because, if the value of the portfolio goes down, their losses as a percentage of equity can be horrendous, and, if the value of the portfolio does not go up, the attrition inherent in interest costs can be unsettling. [Worse yet,] accounting rules and regulations seem designed largely to satisfy the needs of [the] average-opinion-of-average-opinion investors, who have two characteristics: they really don't care about what is going on in business, and they have a vital interest in near-term market fluctuations.'
>
> (Shubik and Whitman, 1971, pp. 64–65)

The *ex post* calculus of financial accounting is the only factual information that is vital for capital market price formation, because it captures the consequences of the firm's plan as it unfolds (Salvary, 2003). Given that the prices of firms' equity securities in the capital market are driven by investors' short-term expectations, they reveal nothing about the actual operating performance and financial condition of those firms.

3.3 The role and the psychological effect of the capital market

Invariably, great emphasis is placed on analysts' quarterly profit forecasts of firms. While not of current vintage, infatuation with analysts' prediction of firms' quarterly profit has intensified in recent times. The market effect on stock prices, when companies fail to meet quarterly predictions, is a clear manifestation that the emphasis in the market is on short-term price movement and not the long-term prospects for the particular firms in question (Puplava, 2001). Given this condition, it is interesting to note that while market volatility is being introduced in financial statements, day traders are advised to expunge volatility from their investment strategy because it leads ultimately to chaos:

> '[V]aluations are much easier to calculate from real earnings (i.e. ... company's P/E ratio) than trying to base valuations on "what might happen" down the road. [S]ometimes stocks trade more actively or more wildly on news of potential profits, but ... when a company announces [it] may not meet analysts' expectations or may experience an earnings shortfall, it can get quite dangerous. Consider sticking to companies with tangible, consistent earnings when doing your trading as a further means to risk reduction.'
>
> (Johns, 2005)

Technically the value of a firm's share in the capital market should be based upon the long-term expectations of that firm's future earnings, the assessed riskiness of the firm's operation, and the risk-adjusted discount rate for the particular time horizon. Furthermore, it is understood that the values of financial assets, which represent claims to future cash flows, do change, and sometimes radically, due to changes in the interest rates and relevant risks. These changes do constitute signals that are transmitted by the capital market to the commodity market.

This signaling system was recognized by Keynes (1936):

> 'The daily revaluations of the Stock Exchange, though they are primarily made to facilitate transfers of old investments between one individual and another, inevitably exert a decisive influence on the rate of current investment. For there is no sense in building up a new enterprise at a cost greater than that at which a similar existing enterprise can be purchased, whilst there is an inducement to spend on a new project what may seem an extravagant sum, if it can be floated off on the Stock Exchange at an immediate profit.'

Accordingly, current/fair value is a signal which aids in the assessment of plans; however, it is not the appropriate attribute for measurement in financial accounting. In notes to or parenthetically in the financial statements, other values should be disclosed when they serve some useful purpose. Such disclosures, which are necessary to provide transparency and clarity, would ensure that what should be reasonably revealed is not hidden from the general public. Market values serve as signals to specific interests in the conduct of *financial analysis.* For instance, replacement cost, current market value, and exit/breakup value do have significance for the firm's competitors interested in a takeover.

Indubitably, within *specific decision contexts*, market value is a decision variable that management has to and does consider. However, after examining the available options, if management should choose to *use* rather than *sell* assets under its control, then the risk accepted and return to bc calculated can only be based upon the decision to use rather than to sell. Once the decision is to use, then the performance measurement must focus on the benefits from the asset's use and not possible gains from the asset's sale, in which case *recoverable cost* is the desired measurement attribute. Note that *recoverable cost* is the attribute that is used to measure when current market value is used in the case of investment companies.

> '[T]he use of market values in the case of investment companies is simply [due to the fact] that the risk-sharing arrangement calls for the investment companies to sell and redeem their shares at the realizable value at the end of each trading day of the portfolio held. In that situation no use value exists to the investment companies; the investment companies merely act as an intermediary ... between the individual investor and the securities market. In this situation, the recoverable amount is the current market value, since that is the amount that the individual would have received or paid for the holdings, had the individual been trading for his/her own account in the open market.'
>
> (Salvary, 1985, pp. 54–55)

Unequivocally, the international accounting standard setters do not focus on accounting measurement but on economic/fair value reporting on the activities of a firm. To maintain that fair market value is the real picture of the activities of the firm leads to the conclusion that market volatility is a better indicator of a firm's operating profit than transactions-based accounting. According to Freixas and Tsomocos (2004, pp. 25–28), the debate on book value (transaction based) vs fair value accounting emphasizes the positive role of fair value accounting in disciplining banks. This means that under fair value accounting, if a bank's capital is below the minimum required by regulation, the bank will be forced to close down. Consequently, with fair value accounting, it can be expected that rational bank managers, anticipating a temporary adverse shock, may act in an overly conservative manner. Specifically, managers may be induced to do any of the following: not to invest in risky assets, reduce deposit interest rates, or not distribute dividends. Consequently, ill-fortune and not managerial mismanagement may lead to portfolio choices that would result in equilibrium allocations that are *ex ante* inefficient.

Given the foregoing, it is imperative that standard setters refocus their attention on accounting measurement and not on short-term market movements. Firms' operating plans do provide a sound basis for the measurement of operating profit as generated in the cash flow process; *those plans do reflect the existing reality of the economic situation*. This concern for measurement is fairly well documented as voiced by the British Bankers Association (2000):

> '**[T]he earnings process**: With banking book assets the prime objective is to secure a stable margin between the amount received on interest-earning assets and the amount paid on interest-bearing liabilities. Interest is earned by the daily accrual of interest over the life of transactions, normally in line with cash flows, and not by taking advantage of short-term fluctuations in fair value.
>
> **[M]anagement of the assets and liabilities**: The management's perspective of the performance of banking assets and liabilities is over the longer term and not based on short-term price movements and market perceptions. Even for the management of interest rate risk, the focus is not fair value, but shifts in the yield curve.'

Likewise, the insurance industry has raised the following concerns (Patel, 2003):

> 'Significant volatility will be introduced if changes in fair values of assets and liabilities are taken through the income statement: the current proposals have not addressed the issue of performance reporting ... Insurance is seen to be a long-term business and therefore changes in short-term assumptions should not be relevant in measuring long-term performance.'

On its website on 16 August 2005, the American Bankers Association (ABA) maintains that it has strongly opposed fair value accounting. It is the ABA's position that fair value: is appropriate for trading activities or if risk is managed on a fair value basis; is not the most relevant measurement for most financial institutions, since banks are not managed on a fair value basis; and will mislead users of banks' financial statements. Furthermore, the FASB should determine whether fair value disclosures are being used and how they might be improved. Also, a study undertaken by the staff of the European Central Bank (2004) revealed that:

> '[M]arket discipline may be significantly hampered by reliability and data comparability issues. Indeed, the reliability of fair values for several financial instruments is highly questionable. In particular, market credit spreads or internal models still seem to deliver large and varied outcomes for instruments with comparable risk features. The information content of balance-sheet data could be adversely affected. Furthermore, given the proliferation of different internal valuation models, the comparability of balance-sheet data across financial institutions could be severely jeopardized.'

In the past, the lower of cost and market rule, which is now abandoned, was the means by which asset deterioration was measured. Inadvertently, in discussing fair value accounting, the Savings and Loans debacle in the USA is used to emphasize the need for fair value accounting (*The Economist*, 2001; CAS, 2004). In 1979, based on generally accepted accounting principles, several US Savings and Loans (S&Ls) were insolvent (Barth et al., 1986; Barth, 1991), but the US Congress chose to ignore this ominous sign. The debacle was not due to lack of fair value accounting but due: (1) *primarily to changes in laws and regulations which restricted the S&Ls from changing the asset side of the balance sheet in response to changing market forces which had dramatically altered the liability side*; and (2) *the failure to use the lower of cost and market rule* (Salvary, 1997).

Currently, high PE ratios are more a function of the fact that 'Profits are fast becoming irrelevant in a world driven more by expectations than by deference to quarterly earnings' (Grebb, 1999, p. 71). At the end of 2000, it was noted that the majority of share price appreciation in the market was concentrated among companies that were losing money (Puplava, 2000). To illustrate, Tables 3.1 and 3.2 reveal that, in spite of heavy periodic losses reported by Amazon.com Inc., Lucent Technologies, and Nortel Networks CP, the price of their stocks soared until they finally came tumbling down. Given the operating performance of firms and the radical changes in their market values over time, it is clear that accounting measurement and market valuation are two distinct processes.

Table 3.1 Valuation of expected future performance

	Stock price data					
Company	**High**	**Date**	**Current**	**Date/2002**	**Current**	**Date/2005**
Amazon.com	$110+	June 1999	$18+	June 17	$36+	June 17
Lucent Technologies	$80+	June 1999	$2+	June 17	$3+	June 17
Nortel Networks CP	$94+	Jan 1998	$1+	June 17	$2+	June 17

Source: http://www.wsrn.com, 18 June 2002 and 17 June 2005.

Table 3.2 Measurement of past performance

	Income statement data – net income (loss) in $ millions					
Company	**2002**	**2001**	**2000**	**1999**	**1998**	**1997**
Amazon.com	(149.1)	(567.3)	(1411.3)	(720.0)	(124.5)	(27.6)
Lucent Technologies	(11,949.0)	(16,226.0)	1219.0	3458.0	970.0	541.0
Nortel Networks CP	(3585.0)	(27,317.0)	(3470.0)	(170.0)	(537.0)	(829.0)

Source: Income statements of the respective companies.

Given past experience, expectations of analysts/investors have been overly optimistic at times (Daniel et al., 1998, 2001). Particularly prevalent, during the period from 1998 through early 2000, was this over-optimism. This situation was noted in Bell Capital Management Inc.'s *Wealth Management Insights* (2002, p. 1): 'The recent bull market proved conclusively [that] stock prices can reach great heights for [even] worthless companies. Investors bought shares of companies that had never earned a profit and, in some cases, never generated revenues.' Being more specific, Colvin (2000, p. 150) maintained: 'America Online is worth more than GM, Ford, and the entire American Steel industry combined. ... AOL's stock price makes sense only if you think the company can increase its annual EVA [economic value added] by an amount equal to the highest EVA ever achieved in American business and increase it by that amount every year forever.' It is important to note that on 24 January 2000, the day of Colvin's article, AOL's stock price was in excess of $80 per share, producing a price/earnings ratio in excess of 180 (Salvary, 2003).

The capital market arrives at a *price/value* of a firm's security; this valuation or pricing *reflects expectations* of that firm's *future multi-period earnings*.

Unmistakably, the measurement of cash flows as they occur is independent of the pricing of expected future cash flows. In spite of the foregoing data, it appears that the cash-flow measurement process in financial accounting is equated by the IASB with the capital market pricing of estimated future cash flows. Financial accounting measures the past operating performance and the current financial position to inform readers via financial statements on what has happened and the current state of affairs. It must be emphasized that financial accounting information is not a substitute for capital market price formation; it validates or invalidates the estimation model used for capital market pricing purposes, and importantly it provides the basis for the market to arrive at proper security prices. Market values have a role to play but it is definitely not by displacing *realization* for income recognition in the measurement of the cash-flow process as undertaken in financial accounting. It must be stressed that fair value accounting entails the elimination of the realistic condition of uncertainty in the financial accounting measurement process and the substitution of the simplifying assumption of certainty in its place.

3.4 Simplifying assumptions versus necessary conditions for measurement

The IASB's call for fair value accounting is reminiscent of MacNeal's (1939) recommendation of the use of economic values in place of accounting measurement. Undeniably, economic values are useful for certain purposes, but they are not useful for all purposes. For example, for the purpose of intercountry comparison, the question may be asked: What is the aggregate value of the financial instruments that are traded in each of the capital markets around the world? The value assigned to the financial instruments traded in each country would be priced out using the unit price that obtained on the last trade for the given observation date. While this would constitute a valid comparison, one recognizes that the aggregate dollar value established for each country will not be the amount that would be obtained if all of these financial instruments were traded at the same time. For this aggregate value to prevail, the law of supply and demand – a necessary condition of the marketplace – would not to be operative.

In the foregoing illustration, a simplifying assumption about market price was substituted for necessary conditions underlying market price. Use of current market is appropriate for a limited number of entities, which are financial intermediaries and trade daily in the capital market (e.g. investment companies). For other companies, disclosure of market values of securities portfolios indicating the potential for gain and post-balance sheet disclosures of significant events have been and should continue to be standard disclosures in financial statements. Although the usefulness of economic values was established with the example above, they are not suitable for accounting purposes. While *simplifying assumptions* are valid for economic analysis, *necessary and sufficient conditions* must be satisfied for accounting measurements to be undertaken.

Investment is a dynamic process where time and timing are critical factors, and the element of uncertainty adds to the risk of the undertaking. Consequently, organizations follow a dynamic path, which is due to the uncertainty of a future which necessitates continuing adjustments at differing points in time due to overestimates and underestimates. Management's operating plan involves money being committed in period $t-1$ to a plan of action; this money (more or less) resurfaces (periodically or at the end of the plan's fulfillment) in period $t+n$ – the plan's gestation period. Since a gestation period is necessary for the firm to *realize* cash flow from recovery of invested money and any reward for undertaking the investment, the omission of this time factor when measuring the performance of the firm's investment plan would be in violation of a necessary condition for measurement (Salvary, 2003). The inclusion of market volatility under fair value accounting negates the critical importance and existence of the gestation period over which management has carefully prepared its operating plan.

The distinction between accounting measures and market values is noted by Trevino and Higgs (1992, p. 211): '[W]hereas accounting rates of return such as ROI and ROA are measures of the profitability of the firm, MRET [total market rate of return] is a measure of profitability to the shareholder of the firm. There is no necessary relation between the accounting returns and the market returns in a particular year.' In the capital market pricing process, *the profitability of the firm* is of utmost importance. The firm's cash-flow opportunities hinge on the profitability of the firm. Consequently, measurement of the operating plans that firms have in place should not be distorted with market volatility in the quest to provide information that satisfies users' needs.

The IASB, in its Framework F.17, acknowledges the role of profitability in the generation of cash flow:

> '*Performance is the ability of an enterprise to earn a profit* on the resources that have been invested in it. Information about the amounts and variability of profits helps in forecasting future cash flows from the enterprise's existing resources and in forecasting potential additional cash flows from additional resources that might be invested in the enterprise.' (Emphasis added)

However, it must be stressed that profit dominates cash flow. This dominance is due to the fact that profit is the measure of success, whereas cash flow provides the funds for reinvestment in operating assets and the payment of dividends. Given the foregoing, can market volatility be more meaningful than the results of management's operating plans?

The major role of management is planning, and planning implies that there is a future. It is common knowledge that the management of a business enterprise plans its operation. Sound planning and effective execution of plans are critical. The *going concern* is a concept of the future – that is, continuity is impossible in the absence of the future. The continuity of a firm, as a *going concern*, hinges upon its planning process. It is meaningless to plan if there is no future – no continuity. While a firm can plan for its demise, most firms do not plan to go out of business; they generally plan for success and, thus, their continued existence. Firms, when their continuity is threatened, strive to the best of their ability to ensure their continuity. Going out of business is accepted generally when it is the only course of action available to the firm.

Observations have revealed that whenever a set of conditions is satisfied a firm can execute its plan. It is the ability to execute its plan that makes the firm a 'going concern'. The evidence of a going concern resides in the fact that the firm: (1) has committed finance (money) to its operation; (2) has implemented investment plans; and (3) the investment plans provide for recovering the money (finance) invested. It is essential that there be an unbroken connection between the investment plan (financing, production, distribution, and collection) and the recovery plan (revenue stream to be generated from the investment) (Salvary, 1989a, pp. 35–36). Characteristic of a liquidating concern is the disruption of its investment plan from its recovery plan; the latter is no longer operational and the former is no longer valid.

The going concern implies the future, and the future signifies uncertainty. It is with regard to uncertainty that the measurement concept of *realization* emerges. *Realization* is a quality control principle: by reducing the uncertainty in the quantification process to an acceptable level, it ensures equity among the suppliers of resources. The need for interpersonal equity underlies the concept of *realization* in financial accounting. For the purpose of financial reporting, criteria do exist by which to determine whether the necessary conditions for the 'going concern' have been satisfied (Salvary, 1996/1997). When those conditions are satisfied, the use of the estimated recoverable cost (invested resources/committed finance expected to be recovered) approach is justified (Salvary, 1985, 1989a, 1992). In the absence of such conditions, the firm is a liquidating concern and the *liquidation or exit value* approach to measurement for a liquidating concern is applied.

Given neutrality and equity considerations, as in the case of risk-sharing arrangements in markets for title to claim, the measurement of changes in a firm's resources and the impact of such changes on the functioning of a firm are of prime importance. To determine the effectiveness of the operations of an entity, it is necessary to measure the profit generated by the cash-flow process of a 'going concern', in which case 'matching of periodic revenues with periodic expenses' enters the picture. Since the focus of interest is on a going concern, then *plan gestation* (completion of the earnings process) coupled with *realization* (an acceptable level of uncertainty concerning the collectability of the transformed value) constitute the necessary and sufficient conditions for financial accounting measurement.

The future implies a risk, and the business enterprise undertakes risk for a return. This return is always prospective and is conditioned by value changes in the future. Owing to the inability to predict the future with any degree of certitude, *realization* emerges as a necessary condition for the measurement of realized profit. The role of *realization* is to create a basis for revenue recognition which enables a measurement of profit that is tempered with a relatively low level of uncertainty. In a world of certainty this condition would be unnecessary, inasmuch as its current role is *the reduction of uncertainty to an acceptable level* (Salvary, 1989a, pp. 89–90). With realization, owing to the high degree of uncertainty attached to it, that which is not recognized is unrealized profit. While not intended as a commentary on accounting, the following clearly expresses the position in financial accounting theory:

> 'Once the date of expected realization is made an explicit variable in the analysis of portfolio decisions, the importance of uncertainty can no longer be suppressed. The further into the future the date of realization, the less conviction an individual will have in his ability to describe correctly his expectations via a subjective probability distribution of future eventualities.'
>
> (Davidson, 1972, p. 208)

Realization addresses the realistic condition of uncertainty that is encountered in the financial accounting measurement process. By default, the disregard of realization results in the acceptance of the simplifying assumption of certainty. However, the certainty assumption 'is a distortion of the economic reality faced by the relevant decision maker' (Shwayder, 1967).

Firms' decision-making is independent of users' decision-making. The firm's decision involves profit planning and the management of risks. The focus of the user's decision is on factors that can affect the firm's future profitability and thus affect the firm's future cash flows. Therefore, it seems logical that the actual impact of the firm's decisions should be recognized in the financial statements, whereas, whenever necessary, factors that could affect users' decisions should be disclosed in notes to the financial statements. However, the IASB's Framework embraces the users' decision (*the prediction of future states*) as the criterion to determine the treatment of items in the financial statements and embraces market volatility as economic reality.

3.5 Economic reality, decision-making, and operating dynamics

In the economy, the forces that shape/influence behavior are the resources (contracted for in money terms) and the realized profit (resulting from their use based upon plans devised by firms' management). Essentially, economic reality involves plans (as they are implemented and their gestation) and institutional arrangements, which include contracts. These factors cannot be set aside in favor of market volatility, over which management has no control. Also, it must be emphasized that risk management programs are developed by management to minimize the impact of potentially disruptive problems that can be expected to arise. Evidently, as noted by the concerns coming from various sources, the risk management plans in place are ignored by the IASB.

> 'As a bank supervisor, the Federal Reserve believes that innovations in risk management are very important to the continued improvement of our financial system. New methods and financial instruments allow banking organizations to improve their risk management practices by selecting target levels of risk exposures and shedding or limiting unwanted positions. Whenever possible, the accounting framework should avoid providing a disincentive to better management of risk.'
>
> (Bies, 2004)

Indubitably, the IASB's view of economic reality is plagued with the type of problem noted in the following passage:

> 'Often a system of market forms is constructed *a priori* instead of being obtained from economic reality and found in it. Systems of market forms of this kind do not reproduce the forms in the actual economic world ... Working out the different

> forms of markets must start with the real phenomena ... They have to be discovered. *This can be done by studying the economic plans of actual economic units;* for the planning data, on which those taking part in a market construct their plans, can be precisely ascertained. *It is from these plans and not from the behavior of economic units, a concept which can be given varying content,* that the forms of market can be discovered.'
>
> (Eucken, 1951, p. 335, emphasis added)

Firms having the same type of assets and liabilities will not have identical values placed on their equity securities by the capital market unless they generate identical earnings and reflect the same risk. It is quite clear that firms do not have similar earnings although they have similar assets and liabilities, simply because of differences in management's philosophy, strategy, and perceptions of operating possibilities. Financial accounting identifies the composition (reflected in monetary transactions) of organizations, while economics attempts to assess behavior (assign optimum values) to those organizations over time and space (markets). With fair value accounting having a prescriptive (normative) system in economic analysis as its underlying framework, market volatility is treated as a necessary and sufficient condition for accounting measurement in a descriptive (positive) system – the firms in the execution of their plans.

Decision-making is concerned with specifying the possible states of the future and selecting the most desirable state. Also, decision-making is under conditions of uncertainty; hence, what has been chosen as the best alternative may turn out to be just the opposite, if the chosen alternative fails to materialize. To know the outcome of a plan, a measure is needed (i.e. a measurement of performance). The measurement of performance is not a measure of the future activities since such cannot be measured, only conjectured/projected. It is a measure of something that has happened – it is feedback on the past, from which experience is gained for future decision-making. Note that the following passage reveals the behavior modification that would result in order to avoid the conflicting results in the firm's financial picture given fair value accounting:

> 'As management attempts to reduce this earnings volatility, we may see changes in risk management practices. Unfortunately, some managers might use fewer credit derivatives to reduce credit risk due to this potential earnings volatility. Accordingly, setters of accounting standards need to consider improvements to the accounting treatment that do not result in a disincentive to those who prudently use credit derivatives for risk management purposes.'
>
> (Bies, 2004)

Since relevance of information is conditioned by the decision at hand, management, when reviewing the options facing the firm, utilizes the planning process of managerial accounting with its focus on the future. Consequently, under fair value accounting:

> 'Certain financing and hedging policies will no longer achieve the desired [business] accounting effect ... instead [they will] create volatility in reported profits. The challenge [for management] will be to find good economic strategies that will produce the right accounting treatment.'
>
> (Deloitte IAS PLUS, 2005)

Undeniably, risk management is critical to successful and effective performance. Being fully cognizant that profits – the primary measure of performance – will be affected contrary to the plans that have been laid, management will be induced to make adjustments to its risk management program to minimize the unwarranted impact of fair value accounting.

3.6 Risk management and performance measurement

The importance of risk management to corporate effective functioning cannot be overemphasized. Recent surveys have found that financial executives rank *risk management* as one of their most important objectives (Rawls and Smithson, 1990). The concept and objective of risk management, in a framework of risk management developed by PricewaterhouseCoopers (2004, p. 20), are defined as follows:

> 'Enterprise risk management provides a framework for management to effectively deal with uncertainty and associated risk and opportunity, and thereby enhance its capacity to build value.
>
> Enterprise risk management is a process ... designed to identify potential events that may affect the entity and manage risks to be within its risk appetite, [and] to provide reasonable assurance regarding the achievement of entity objectives.'

'Regardless of the effects risk management may have on systematic risk, if diversified equity holders value their firm's risk management program it is because it mitigates the side-effects of volatile cash flow' (Barrese and Scordis, 2003, p. 2). Therefore, it is not surprising that at the end of 1995, the largest 25% of US nonfinancial corporations held $448 billion in cash and marketable securities (Harford, 1999, p. 1971).

Salvary (2004) maintains that firms hoard financial capital (as evidenced by the large portfolios of marketable equity securities held by nonfinancial firms) in order to ensure future availability. Furthermore, when large well-managed portfolios of marketable securities have been acquired with hoarded financial capital, some firms, in addition to benefiting from a lower cost of capital, experience additional benefits from market appreciation which in great part may exceed any premium penalty due to hoarding. In light of the foregoing and consistent with *organizational behavior and risk management*, Salvary (2004) postulates that: *the firm sets as its objective the control of the optimum amount of financial capital at the minimum cost to the firm*. Thus, corporate earnings retention is a case of optimization under conditions of uncertainty.

Fair market value for trading securities and securities held for sale by investment companies is appropriate (Salvary, 1985, 1989, 1992). However, it must be noted that nonfinancial companies acquisitions of marketable securitiēs as short-term use of idle cash are different from securities acquired for investment purposes to ensure the reliability of suppliers and outlets. The object of holding those shares is part of the firms' risk management program. However, as noted above, fair value accounting interferes with risk management.

The essence of accounting for financial instruments is to enable users of accounting information to distinguish between hedging and speculation – to be able to differentiate the instruments that reduce risk and those that increase it. In this respect, since the IASB's approach does not achieve this goal, the information in some cases is definitely misleading. As noted by the Association of Corporate Treasurers (ACT, 2001), the impact of fair values in the profit and loss account/income statement of nonfinancial companies will leave companies with no other choice but to change their risk management policies. In this setting, '*The accounting tail will be wagging the risk management dog*.' Since *risk management activity is invariably concerned with managing 'cash flows' and not fair value*, fair value accounting will lead to the misinterpretation of risks and *risk management activity on the part of the users of financial statements*. This condition would hold since the discussion of the effectiveness of the company's policies would be based on information that is fundamentally different from what appears in the financial statements.

As a significant part of many companies' risk management program, billions of dollars are invested in marketable securities in order to make financial capital available in the future at a predetermined cost (Salvary, 2004). The impact of market valuation on performance measurement of those firms will be quite profound and will induce decision-making that would become necessary under the circumstances, but contrary to sound management. With accounting for marketable securities at market value, gains are recognized prior to realization; with subsequent declines in the market values, losses are generated. In the absence of *realization*, staggering losses will have to be reported at a later date. In order to avoid the distortion of the firm's operating performance in both the current and subsequent periods, firms will be induced to sell. Such an act would be in contradiction of the plans that had been carefully made by management. Importantly, the forced sales would impair firms' ability to provide for future availability of financial capital, giving rise to the underinvestment problem (Salvary, 2004).

According to the Association of Corporate Treasurers (ACT, 2001), the volatility resulting from the adoption of fair value accounting would tend to drive down value and correspondingly increase the cost of funds. Fund managers maintain that companies should not be too concerned about volatility since *investors will concentrate on cash flow and ignore the fair value information*. Unquestionably, this is the wrong approach to adopt. To put fair values in the financial statements *as opposed to disclosures in footnotes* is based on the fact that volatility is reflected in investors' evaluation of the risk inherent in investing in a particular company.

> 'The financial risks managed by treasurers are cash flow risks not fair value risks. Although ... "many" enterprises manage their risks on a fair value basis, we are not aware of any company outside financial services and the property sector that does so across the board. Since the fair value model reflects the results of taking fair value risk, it will not (except coincidentally) give information that will enable readers of accounts to evaluate the success or otherwise of a company's cash flow risk management.
>
> Interest rate risk is a case in point. Many companies select fixed rate debt because they perceive it to be a low-risk strategy. There is a large body of literature that supports this view, based upon the fact that the fixed rate borrower has reduced the risk of financial distress or bankruptcy by eliminating the risk of an increase in variable interest rates increasing its debt servicing costs. This may, for example, occur to enable the company to comply with financial covenants. Or, the company may have incoming cash flows that are not correlated with the interest rate cycle and its objective is to reduce the volatility of its post-interest cash flows.
>
> In neither of these cases is the change in the fair value of the debt of any significance.'
>
> (ACT, 2001)

However, given the broader approach of fair value accounting, each asset in a company's balance sheet would be valued independently in accordance with the IFRS 3 Business Combinations (Deloitte IAS PLUS, 2004). The Association of Corporate Treasurers (ACT, 2001) sees that fair value approach as 'a breakup valuation rather than one based on the concept of going concern'. The position of the Association of Corporate Treasurers is correct, since all assets collectively represent the amount of invested money expected to be recovered as part of an operating plan. All liabilities represent the amount of money expected to be discharged. Participants in the capital market do not place a value on the individual assets of the firm, they place a value on the profit plan that management has in place. So with respect to any change in value of an asset in its exchange market, the change in the value of a firm is zero, if such change is not a change in the particular firm's cash flow related to the assets which are part of the firm's profit plan (Salvary, 1997).

The fact that a firm can sell some assets at random while others have no resale value is irrelevant to the cash-flow plan. Assets come into existence for no other reason but to augment the initial nominal money invested by the firm. As a collective group, and not as individual assets, they reflect the cash-flow generating plan that management has in place. The cash-flow process occurs when financial capital passes from the initial state (the acquisition of productive assets) to the final state (when the products or services generated have been converted into monetary claims). The acquisition of productive assets and the production of goods and services require time for their accomplishment; thus, they are both path functions and their numerical values are completely dependent upon the *cash-flow process* followed in moving from the initial state to the final state. However, concerning IAS 39: Financial Instruments, as per the Casualty Actuarial Society (CAS, 2004, p. 23):

> 'The proposed fair value approach represents a radical departure from the traditional deferral-and-matching approach. The unearned premium reserve liability and deferred policy acquisition cost asset would no longer be elements of the balance sheet (under our interpretation). Premiums would presumably be taken into revenue as the contracts are written. *To the extent that the fair value of the associated policy liabilities is less than the premium after expenses, an immediate gain would be recognized; to the extent that the fair value of policy liabilities is greater, an immediate loss would be recognized.* In essence, under fair value companies will report on the profitability of the policies issued (i.e. written) during the period, rather than on the coverage provided. *This will necessitate greater reliance on pricing assumptions in financial reporting.'* (Emphasis added)

Reliance on pricing assumption, rather than accepting insurance contracts as carefully negotiated by the insurance companies, is due to the IASB's view that market price at a given point in time constitutes the totality of economic reality. Thus, the argument for fair value accounting is due to the belief that: '[T]he use of fair values will move financial reporting closer to underlying economic reality … [M]arket prices include elements for the time value of money and margins for risk-taking, either explicitly or implicitly … [A] closer correspondence between economic performance and financial reporting will improve decision-making, by removing incentives to manage *towards accounting income rather than economic value creation*' (CAS, 2004, p. 7, *emphasis added*).

Already the effect has been felt. In January 2005, AXA, the largest insurer in France, announced that its 2004 net earnings would be affected by its compliance switch to IFRS 4. Moving from French GAAP to IFRS, shareholders' funds would be reduced by 5% and reported revenues would be reduced by 6%. This effect is due to the fact that accounting for certain life insurance contracts (investment contracts without discretionary participation features) will change under IFRS. Those insurance contracts, which will be accounted for as fees and not as premiums, represent approximately 9% of 2003 insurance reserves and 6% of 2003 AXA's French GAAP gross insurance revenues (Bennett, 2005, p. 2). Concern over the spurious volatility introduced by the accounting rules has been expressed by Sir Andrew Large, Deputy Governor of the Bank of England. In order to provide for a less detailed and prescriptive standard to replace IAS 39, he suggested that agreement should be reached on 'the fundamentals' (Snyder, 2005, p. 5).

With IAS 39, the reliance on pricing assumptions is a movement away from measurement and into the realm of prediction (CAS, 2004). IAS 39 overrides the carefully developed operating plans of firms and the existence of contracts to achieve desired ends. This development introduces a serious problem since accountability/stewardship, the purpose of financial reporting, is a function of measurement and not prediction (Salvary, 1979, 1985, 1989a). Once decisions have been made and operating plans are in place, it is the function of financial accounting to measure the consequences of those decisions. The task for financial accounting is to *measure* the *realized* profit and the amount of committed resources that is recoverable (in part the organization's risk exposure) – *ex post* data.

Unmistakably, when the interest rate rises, there is a decline in the market value of debt instruments due to re-pricing of those financial instruments in the market. However, if no deterioration occurs in the obligor's profitability and in the ability to make future payments, reflecting the change in market price in the bondholder's income statement is not an accurate portrayal of the bondholder's financial position. Below is an illustration of the market valuation process pertaining to a bond and the legal claim of a bondholder.

For a given risk class, the interest paid divided by the prevailing interest rate gives the market value of the bond in perpetuity. The amount of money given to the bond issuer, as principal, is the bondholder's legitimate claim against the issuer. It is understood that the claimant cannot increase the interest on the money invested if interest rates have increased. Thus, conditions are frozen with respect to that investment. Furthermore, given a rise in the interest rate subsequent to the issuance of the bond, if the bondholder were to sell the bond, the money received and reinvested would generate the same absolute amount of interest received on the initial investment. (The reverse is true.) For instance, if a $1000 bond pays $50 in interest and the interest rate has changed to 6%, then the market value of that bond in perpetuity is $833.33. Sale of the $1000 bond for $833.33 does not alter the claim of $1000 against the issuer, and reinvestment of this $833.33 in a new 6% bond will not alter the interest earnings of $50 to the bondholder.

The change in value reflects the marginal cost of money at a specific point in time. Given the ability to hold to maturity, there is no bona fide reason for the bondholder to sell the original bond. The foregoing holds, since there is a trade-off between short-term opportunities and long-term strategies in order to eliminate uncertainty for plan fulfillment. Given profit-planning strategies, a lost short-term opportunity cannot be considered as a valid reason for market value accounting. At this juncture the focus is on the impact of fair market value accounting given the structural and operating differences between and among the different types of companies – investment, insurance, financial, and nonfinancial.

3.7 Structural and operating differences of companies

In banking and insurance, liabilities are created through acceptance of deposits and premiums. In order to satisfy claims as they become due, funds accepted from depositors and policyholders are to be invested in a *profitable* manner to reasonably ensure recovery of such funds.

Given the nature of their product, insurance companies accumulate relatively large amounts of cash, cash equivalents, and investments in order to satisfy future claims and avoid financial ruin (Akhigbe et al., 1993, p. 413). Independent of returns from the investment portfolio, insurance companies must secure an underwriting profit. To be insulated from the need to liquidate investments to satisfy expected claims and losses, each company has to be *profitable* to generate adequate operating cash flows and liquidity. Furthermore, to match its current underwriting risk profile, each company has to build adequate reserves (Lewis, 1998, p. 185). The importance of cash flow and the avoidance of forced sales of the investment portfolio are critical concerns. Those concerns are particularly important in light of the fact that for the year 2001 life and health insurers suffered a loss of $3.1 billion on the sale of investments and during the first three quarters of 2002 they experienced a staggering loss of $9.6 billion on the sale of investments (Weiss, 2003).

Fortunately, given the concern for liquidity, the insurance industry has national regulated accounting standards to ensure that insurers have sufficient capital and surplus to cover insured losses (Financial Services Fact Book, 2005). Statutory Accounting Principles (SAP) focus on measuring an insurer's ability to pay future claims (NAIC, 2005). While unrealized gains on certain equity securities are reported as a component of stockholders' equity under Generally Accepted Accounting Principles, they are not included in regulatory capital under the various US Agencies' capital standards (Federal Reserve Board, 1998).

Insurance is a crucial national and global industry; by virtue of its risk-sharing and risk-reducing functions, it has a critical role in the financial system and the real economy. Life insurance companies have used accounting systems that rely on an amortized cost approach to valuing assets and liabilities. The movement to fair value accounting is of great concern due to the fact that:

> '[A]n accounting framework should be descriptive with regard to the underlying realities of the lines of business in which a firm is engaged; the accounting model should not itself be the vehicle which shapes business decisions. Much of the industry opposition and concern ... has been the fear that implementing fair value standards would result in either: (1) radical reshuffling of lines of business; or (2) complete withdrawal from certain lines of business [the extinction of a certain line of business]; or perhaps (3) cause unwanted changes in portfolio investment decisions.'
>
> (Fore, 2003, pp. 1, 3, 4)

Bank deposits are not similar to insurance policies; the hedging strategies of insurance companies are different from those of banking companies. Consequently, in the application of fair value accounting, the CEA (2005) has made it quite clear that insurance cannot be lumped together with banking: 'Any proposals to amend the fair value option must fully consider all industries, including insurers, to ensure appropriate representation of the underlying economies.' Likewise, the Association of Corporate Treasurers maintain: 'The financial risks managed by treasurers are cash-flow risks not fair value risks. Although ... "many" enterprises manage their risks on a fair value basis, we are not aware of any company outside financial services and the property sector that does so across the board. Since the fair value model reflects the results of taking fair value risk, it will not (except coincidentally) give information that will enable readers of accounts to evaluate the success or otherwise of a company's cash-flow risk management' (ACT, 2001).

According to Bradley (2001, p. 2), a survey by PricewaterhouseCoopers of major companies in the Nordic countries (Nordic Corporate Treasury Benchmarking Survey, 2001) revealed that about two-thirds of the sample companies report under US GAAP or IAS and apply FAS 133 or IAS 39. In the survey, 61% of respondents claimed that fair value accounting had a significant impact on their treasury policies. This finding was not surprising because many companies have implemented strategies to minimize the impact of the volatility introduced with fair value accounting. Consequently, it can be expected that, from the point of view of group-wide risk management, such strategies may increase risk.

In the USA, *Statement of Financial Accounting Standards No. 115* (FASB, 1993), which required *fair value accounting* for equity securities, did induce changes in the management of investment portfolios in the banking industry. These changes were necessary to reduce volatility in reported capital and influence reported profit through recognition of gains on security sales. The problems arising from banking behavior modification have been identified as follows: (1) shortening of the maturity of the investment portfolio may cause bank holding companies to experience a reduction in the interest income earned and an increase in their interest rate risk; (2) reduction of flexibility to sell securities from the held-to-maturity portfolio may cause the cost of managing liquidity and interest rate risk to increase; (3) as a result of the reduced flexibility in liquidity, the availability of credit may be decreased as banks may be unable to meet increases in loan demand; (4) due to increased exposure to changes in interest rates, the banking industry may become more volatile (Beatty, 1995, p. 38).

Apart from the insurance and banking industries, the property management industry is confronted with its own problems. The following discussion represents the findings and issues identified in a study (Nordlund and Persson, 2004) on the impact of IAS 40 (Investment Property) on the financial picture of Swedish companies. Due to the fair value model, the meaning of prudence in the IASB's Framework differs from the traditional concept of prudence. The change in meaning severs the linkage of prudence to the traditional concept of realization. The fair value model focuses on what can be claimed to be a 'true and fair' snapshot of the items appearing in the balance sheet. In the measurement of performance, emphasis is placed on changes in nominal wealth from one point in time to another. Compared with current accounting rules, companies using the fair value model in almost all cases during the study period reported higher earnings levels and higher equity. Due to fair value adjustments, in certain cases for a number of the companies, the magnitude for earnings exceeded net rental income. Apparently, the underlying cash flows from operations are better reflected under traditional accounting than with fair value accounting. In addition, dramatic effects can emerge with property value downgrades. Over time, consistency in the income statement and the balance sheet becomes questionable given the high degree of uncertainty in fair value assessments and the possible effects on market values due to cyclical movements. Under fair value accounting, there is an absence of a long-term approach with links to real patterns over time. In a longer perspective, there are obvious risks of various types of suboptimization.

The caution about the impact of cyclical movements cannot be ignored (Christie, 2005; newsmax.com, 2005). The recognition of fair (market) values in financial statements has to be viewed in context of the fact that financial accounting provides measures of the profitability of a firm and of the accountability of management. Furthermore, a firm cannot continue to operate *in the long run* if it generates positive cash flows from operation while it sustains losses from operations. The inclusion in the financial statement of changes in market values does not represent cash-flow measurements but the volatility of instantaneous re-pricing of marketable instruments that has taken place in the capital market. Given that the cash flows cannot be shown to be related to market volatility, to alter the basis of the constant (the recoverable amount of a sum of money invested) in financial accounting is to destroy the information on the structure of the system by incorporating the nature of the change (e.g. interest rate effect). However, such 'noise' added to the income statement can have market effects.

Regrettably, with fair value accounting the 'lower of cost and market' measurement rule, which was coupled with the disclosure feature for market values, is abandoned. Such disclosure about market values, provided in the notes or parenthetically in the body of the balance sheet, was useful information to readers of the financial statements for the purpose of *financial analysis*. It is important to note that while readers were informed that the firm had experienced an appreciation in the value of marketable securities, they were not led directly or indirectly to believe that the firm had benefited from the market appreciation. It was left to the readers to provide their own interpretation of this information.

Due to management frauds, serious audit failures, and misguided analyst recommendations[1] (Byrne, 2002; Consumers Union, 2003; University of California, 2003; Feder and Eichenwald, 2004; Hooper, 2004; Eichenwald and Anderson, 2005; FPA, 2005; Market Wire, 2005), financial accounting is blamed for many problems for which it is not in any manner responsible. However, changes are being made to financial accounting rules, while *what is needed is the restoration of sanity in the capital markets and a return to sensibility in financial reporting.* To ignore what has been elaborated upon above and recognize changes in market values that are ephemeral can only result in significant dislocation of firms and even more aggravated market pricing. Noted below are the recent periods of market insanity, during which several capital market booms with subsequent busts resulted in serious financial meltdowns. There is clear evidence that if corrective action is not taken the past situation will most likely be repeated.

3.8 Sanity in market pricing and sensibility in financial reporting

The significant difference between market valuation and financial accounting measurement cannot be overemphasized. That is, a constant earnings stream can take on any value since the valuation process (rate of discount and the investment period) is dependent upon (1) the intensity of the use of money and (2) the liquidity position of the suppliers of money capital. Any change in either direction of market participants' rate of discount or expectations of future earnings will produce a re-pricing of claims in the capital market. Although firms' cash flows have not changed, market prices of the firms' shares will change due to market re-pricing, as explained above. While fair value accounting can only introduce confusion in market pricing, Damant and Palacky (2002) maintain that:

> 'A fair value approach better enables users of financial statements to predict with reliability the amounts, timing, and uncertainty of an enterprise's future cash flows. In that regard, it offers a much greater degree of relevance than historical cost. It also provides a necessary level of understandability, resulting from improved disclosure transparency.
>
> The realistic values in the balance sheet, as represented by fair value measurements, reflect the financial position of the enterprise at the date of the balance sheet, and therefore the starting point for developing the enterprise's expected future cash flows.'

The IASB relies on the efficient market literature that market participants rationally price common stocks as the present value of all future cash flows expected:

> 'Are the markets efficient or are they totally irrational? At the height of its stock market value in 2000, Cisco had a market cap of close to $600 billion. Sales for the previous year were $12.2 billion and net income was only $2 billion. The company had $12.2 billion in sales and $2 billion in profits and was valued at over half a trillion dollars. That isn't rational. It is insanity. It is one reason why the markets reacted with such vengeance and swiftness.'
>
> (Puplava, 2001)

As reported by Highlights Investments Group (2005), on 25 August 1987, the Dow hit a record 2722.44 points and then started its precipitous decline. Subsequently, the Stock Market crashed on 19 October 1987, when the Dow dropped 508 points or 22.6% in a single trading day. This decline was a drop of 36.7% from its high on 25 August 1987. During the crash of 1987, 1.5 trillion dollars of market value of overvalued stocks evaporated because the markets were not able to handle the imbalance of sell orders – no liquidity. Program Trading and the Use of Derivative Securities Software were used by large institutional investment companies to execute large stock trades automatically when certain market conditions prevailed. There is no doubt that the program trading of index futures and derivatives securities was also to blame.

Subsequently, from 1992 to 2000, the economy and the markets experienced a period of robust expansion. The NASDAQ traded at 4234.33 on 1 September 2000. Then it dropped 45.9% from September 2000 to 2 January 2001. Worse was yet to come! In October 2002, the NASDAQ dropped to a low of 1108.49 – a 78.4% decline from its all-time high of 5132.52, a level which was established in March 2000. With the Stock Market crash of 2000, a total of 8 trillion dollars of market value disappeared. That time the causes of the crash were: (1) *Corporate corruption* – many companies inflated profits and used loopholes to hide debt. Outrageous stock options, enjoyed by corporate officers, diluted companies' stocks. (2) *Overvalued stocks* – many companies, with significant operating losses and no hope of turning a profit for years to come, had market capitalization of over a billion dollars. (3) *Day traders and momentum investors* – the Internet enabled online trading by millions of new investors and traders to enter the markets with little or no experience. (4) *Conflict of interest between research firm analysts and investment bankers* – the research arms of investment banks issued favorable ratings on stocks of their client companies that sought to raise capital.

In some instances, highly favorable ratings were given to companies even though those companies were facing serious financial trouble.

Other than explanations from the 'noise trader risk' and greater fool theory, it is difficult to understand how investors could translate cash flows generated by those firms (e.g. Tables 3.1 and 3.2) into such astronomical prices that prevailed in the 1990s. According to Shiller (2000), it was investor enthusiasm rather than real fundamental factors that temporarily sustained high prices displaying the classic features of a speculative bubble. This condition will prevail when many investors believe that it is safe to purchase stocks, not due to their intrinsic value or expected future dividend payments, but because someone else (the greater fool) will buy them at a much higher price. Given similar beliefs of a large cross-section of investors, stock prices are driven by a self-fulfilling prophecy. When noise traders (investors who follow trends and overreact to good and bad news) are active, 'noise trader risk' (the risk resulting from the unpredictability of future opinions of noise traders) is present and deters arbitrage. Given that condition, prices can diverge significantly from fundamental values even when there is no fundamental risk (DeLong et al., 1990).

Arbitrage does help to maintain order in the market. However, in the presence of noise traders, arbitrageurs' short-term bets do not always pay off. This point is vividly confirmed by the collapse of a major player in the market for derivatives, Long-Term Capital Management (LTCM), which was formed in February 1994 as a hedge fund with $1.3 billion of equity. General partners of LTCM contributed over $100 million of the money. Each investor had to invest a minimum of $10 million, with no withdrawals being permitted for three years. After fees, the fund returned to its investors 19.9% (1994), 42.8% (1995), 40.8% (1996), and 17.1% (1997). As a result of diminished investment opportunities, the fund, with an equity of about $7.5 billion in December 1997, returned $2.7 billion to investors. At the beginning of 1998, with an equity of about $5 billion, the fund borrowed more than $125 billion dollars from banks and securities firms. By mid-September 1998, LTCM suffered a loss exceeding $4 billion and its equity dropped to $600 million. Worse yet, at the end of September 1998, the equity of LTCM's 16 general partners had dropped from $1.6 billion earlier in the year to $16 million. Unfortunately, LTCM lost on its short-term bets and was rescued by a consortium arranged by the Federal Reserve owing to the gravity of the situation (Edwards, 1999, pp. 197–198).

Arbitrageurs will usually have short horizons, since even temporary losses do induce their clients to withdraw their money (Lope Markets, 2003). Indubitably, very few people would wish to see a repeat of what happened as described above. While market insanity cannot be addressed by the international financial accounting standard setters, they certainly can avoid any potential damage to the financial reporting process arising from changes in financial accounting standards. Therefore, it is necessary for the IASB to focus attention on identifying the proper measurement attribute and its underlying rationale. In this regard, the following section focuses on the modeling of the investment decision.

3.9 The investment decision, capital budgeting, and recoverable cost

Throughout the economy, before investment plans are decided upon, cash-flow projections are made to determine the soundness and profitability of the investment. The stock in trade of the banking firm is money; its involvement in the social process is the intermediation of money. The nonbank business firm is involved with the intermediation of consumable goods or services. In either case, an investment decision has to be made. How should the available money capital be invested? To answer that question, the capital budgeting model or a variant of that model is used.

Recoverability of money to be invested is the focus of the capital budgeting model, which happens to be the framework for the investment decision. Irrefutably, the investment decisions of firms are based upon the recoverability of money invested. Based on either the present value model or the discounted cash flow model, the capital budgeting decision resolves the amount of money that should be invested. When invested, this amount of money would constitute the recorded amount for the assets in question. Invariably, the actual rate of return (ARR) in each year may be greater than, equal to, or less than the desired rate of discount (DRD) used in the investment decision. When the ARR is less than the DRD, a loss is sustained by the firm at the planning stage. The loss to be recorded is the difference between the value of assets on the books and the amount of money that would have been invested to date to generate the experienced rate of return (ERR). Given this situation, the value of the firm will have fallen; now the market will have a lower cash flow to value. However, if the ARR is equal to the DRD, then no adjustment is needed. With this situation, no change is experienced in the market value of the firm. Furthermore, if the ARR is higher than the DRD, no adjustment is needed. Importantly, however, in this situation the market will have a higher cash flow to value. *Ceteris paribus*, the value of the firm will have risen (Salvary, 1992, pp. 252–257).

After investment plans have been executed, profit generation from the firm's cash-flow process ensues. *Measuring profit* from the cash-flow process is the economic reality that *is embedded in the accounting framework*. To accommodate this end, financial accounting measurement rules are based on the fundamental law of recovery: recovery prevents/precludes loss. This law, which is operational in all models of investment, is most obvious in the payback model. Undeniably, *recoverable cost*, being linked to investments and explicated by the capital budgeting model, is the measurement attribute observed in financial accounting. This measurement attribute explains the three fundamental measurement rules in financial accounting – *present value for entry decision, lower of cost and market for use decision, and realizable value for exit decision*. Investments constitute accounting phenomena, and financial accounting measurement rules are related to the observed accounting phenomena.

3.10 Discussion and conclusion

The efficiency of the money market is directly related to the ability to measure 'the productivity of money capital at the margin and thereby giving signals either for additional money capital employment or for capital disinvestment and partial liquidation of the firm' (Vickers, 1978, p. 109). Financial accounting generates the information for such an evaluation and the market, through its revaluation of financial assets, ensures the efficient allocation of resources through the use of money. Financial accounting, by its measurement of the recoverability of money in use, enables an evaluation of claims; and, through the measurement of profit, it enables the market to arrive at values for financial assets (claims). This condition is so since the market value is an aggregate of several periods (years) of future earnings/cash flows – a sum of several parts. This aggregation (the market valuation model) is based upon expectations and is subject to revision as information on each part (year) unfolds (Salvary, 1998a).

Profit, which is derived from the cash-flow process, drives the economic system. Assets are stocks of money invested in goods and/or claims; assets give rise to yields. Should the asset values on the balance sheet be reflected at a capitalized rate (market value)? Would those values be a reflection of the cash flows expected to be generated by those firms? Each firm is confronted with its own cash-flow schedule as embedded in its *profit plan*. The assignment of numbers in the financial statement should reflect the actual results of the firm's profit plan and its impact upon the firm's financial position – nothing else. This information on the firm's actual performance is needed as input into the valuation model to project the expected future performance of the firm. In the absence of this measurement, the assessment of the firm's current performance using changes in market values, which represent expectations of future performance, would not be realistic.

The crux of the problem in the international standard-setting process resides in the defects in the Framework. The IASB is aware that problems do exist. Unfortunately, however, the critical issue of fair value accounting is not on the agenda for change. At the meeting on Tuesday 21 September 2004 (IAS, 2004), the IASB has made it clear that its focus is on improving the conceptual framework and determining whether there are impediments to convergence of the IASC, FASB, and other national frameworks.

For a very important reason, this chapter began with a quote from Cohen and Nagel (1934, pp. 195–196). It ends with a summary, presented below, of the insightful exposition of Colleen Sayther Cunningham, President and CEO, FEI (2004).

To arrive at the right answer, it is necessary to ask the right question. What do we wish to measure? Is it profit or loss? Or is it economic profit? If the latter, then this will entail a huge change in accounting. Scores of valuation experts will now be required to prepare the accounts. Also, there will be a significant shift in how auditors conduct audits and users look at financial statements, yet there is no overwhelming users' support for such a change. Fair value accounting, with its implied perfection in scope and depth of markets and nonexistent modeling techniques, can only cloud an investor's ability to evaluate management's performance. Much of the focus is on relevance; very little focus is on reliability. Hence, there is a definite need to be clear when an accounting number is claimed to be reliable. Of what use is a complex financial statement if it is filled with judgments and assumptions that are beyond the reader's ability to understand. It is clear that the FASB believes that fair value is the primary measurement objective to be embraced by GAAP. It is very likely that the importance of the income statement would be minimized with such a far-reaching change. By including volatility in the income statement, assessing management's performance and predicting future performance would be very difficult. In this setting, users would only be able to rely on the cash-flow statement as a measure of annual performance. Before moving further with piecemeal changes to the accounting model, we should step back, discontinue issuing new standards and a comprehensive review of the entire conceptual framework should be undertaken.

Notes

1. All of these problems are being dealt with by the legal system. Hopefully, with vigorous prosecution and severe penalties, there will be a significant decrease in these types of offences.

References

ACT (2001). ACT Response to JWG Proposals for Accounting for Financial Instruments, 13 July. Association of Corporate Treasurers, UK.

Akhigbe, A., Borde, S.F., and Madura, J. (1993). Dividend Policy and Signaling by Insurance Companies. *Journal of Risk and Insurance*, 60(3):413–428.

American Bankers Association (2005). *Fair Value Accounting – Financial Instrument*, 16 August; http://www.aba.com/Industry Issues.

Bardhan, P. and Roemer, J.E. (1992). Market Socialism: A Case for Rejuvenation. *Journal of Economic Perspectives*, 6(3):101–116.

Barrese, J. and Scordis, N. (2003). Corporate Risk Management. *Review of Business*, 24(3):26–29.

Barth, J.R. (1991). *The Great Savings and Loan Debacle*. AEI Press, Washington, DC.

Barth, J.R., Brumbaugh, R.D., and Sauerhaft, D. (1986). *Failure Costs of Government-Regulated Financial Firms: The Case of Thrift Institutions*. Research Working Paper No. 132, Office of Policy and Economic Research, Federal Home Loan Bank Board.

Beatty, A. (1995). The Effects of Fair Value Accounting on Investment Portfolio Management: How Fair Is It? *Federal Reserve Bank of St Louis Review*, 77(1):25–39.

Bell Capital Management Inc. (2002). Debate Raging on Value of Stocks – Different Measures Support Each View. *Wealth Management Insights*, 1(4); http://www.bellcapital.com/pdf/ Q4_02.pdf.

Bennett, J. (2005). IFRS Claims First Scalp. *Accountancy Age*. IFRS News, January; http://www.accountancyage.com.

Bies, S.S. (2004). Fair Value Accounting. International Association of Credit Portfolio Managers General Meeting, New York, 18 November.

Bornemann, M., Knapp, A., Schneider, U., and Sixl, K.I. (1999). *Holistic Measurement of Intellectual Capital*. Paper at the International Symposium Measuring and Reporting Intellectual Capital: Experience, Issues, and Prospects, Amsterdam, June.

Bradley, C. (2001). Fair Values, Wrong Answers. *Accountancy*, 128(1298, September):2.

British Bankers' Association (2000). Preliminary Views on Major Issues Related to Reporting Financial Instruments and Certain Related Assets and Liabilities at Fair Value. *Preliminary Views on Fair Value Measurement*, August.

Byrne, J.A. (2002). Joe Berardino's Fall from Grace. *Business Week*, 12 August, 51–56.

Canibano, L., Garcia-Ayuso, M., Sanchez, M.P., Chaminade, C., Olea, M., and Escobar, C.G. (1999). *Measuring Intangibles: Discussion of Selected Indicators*. Paper presented at the International Symposium Measuring and Reporting Intellectual Capital: Experience, Issues, and Prospects, Amsterdam, June.

CAS (2004). *Fair Value of P&C Liabilities: Practical Implications*. The Casualty Actuarial Society, Arlington, VA.

CEA – European Federation of National Insurance Associations (2005). *IASB Preliminary First Draft of a Possible New Approach – Fair Value Option.* Letter to Sir David Tweedie, International Accounting Standards Board, 13 January.

Christie, L. (2005). *Real Estate: Busts Don't Follow Booms.* CNN/Money, 4 May; http:// www.webprowire.com/summaries/1033493.html.

Cohen, M.R. and Nagel, E. (1934). *An Introduction to Logic and Scientific Method.* Harcourt, Brace & World, Burlingame, NY.

Colvin, G. (2000). Buying Net Stocks? Read This First. *Fortune*, 24 January: 150–151.

Committee for Invisible Transactions (1967). *Capital Markets Study: General Report.* Organization for Economic Cooperation and Development, Paris, March.

Consumers Union (2003). *Mutual Funds: Their 5 Best-Kept Secrets.* Consumers Union of the USA, March; http://www.consumerreports.org/main/content/display _content.jsp.

Cunningham, C.S. (2004). Fair Value Accounting: Fair for Whom? *Financial Executives*, March/April. President's Page.

Damant, D. and Palacky, G.B. (2002). *Re: JWG Draft Standard and Basic Conclusions, Financial Instruments and Similar Items.* Letter to Mr Jim Saloman, Technical Director, International Accounting Standards Board, CFA Institute, 18 January.

Daniel, K., Hirshleifer, D., and Subrahmanyam, A. (1998). A Theory of Overconfidence, Self-Attribution, and Security Market Under- and Overreactions. Working Paper No. 98002, University of Michigan Business School, January.

Daniel, K., Hirshleifer, D., and Teoh, S.H. (2001). Investor Psychology in Capital Markets: Evidence and Policy Implications. Paper presented at Carnegie/Rochester Conference Series in Public Policy, University of Rochester, Rochester, NY, April.

Davidson, P. (1972). *Money and the Real World.* John Wiley, New York.

Deanesly, M. (1956). *A History of Early Medieval Europe from 476 to 911.* Methuen, London.

Deloitte IAS PLUS (2004). *Standards: IFRS 3 Business Combinations.* History of IFRS 3; http://www.iasplus.com.

Deloitte IAS PLUS (2005). *International Accounting Standards Health Check*; http://www.iasplus.com.

DeLong, J.B., Shleifer, A., Summers, L.H., and Waldmann, R.J. (1990). Noise Trader Risk in Financial Markets. *Journal of Political Economy*, 98(4):703–738.

The Economist (2001). Shining a Light on Company Accounts, 16 August; http://www.economist.com.

Edwards, F.R. (1999). Hedge Funds and the Collapse of Long-Term Capital Management. *Journal of Economics Perspectives*, 13(2):189–210.

Eichenwald, K. and Anderson, J. (2005). How a Titan of Insurance Ran Afoul of the Government. *New York Times*, 4 April.

Eucken, W. (1951). *The Foundations of Economics; History and Theory in the Analysis of Economic Reality* (Hutchinson, J.W.H., trans.). University of Chicago Press, Chicago.

European Central Bank (2004). *Fair Value Accounting and Financial Stability.* Occasional Paper Series No. 13 by staff: A. Enria, L. Cappiello, F. Dierick, S. Grittini, A. Haralambous, A. Maddaloni, P. Molitor, F. Pires, and P. Poloni; http://www.ecb.int.

FASB (1975). *Statement of Financial Accounting Standards No. 8: Accounting for the Translation of Foreign Currency Transactions and Foreign Currency Financial Statements.* Financial Accounting Standards Board.

FASB (1981). *Statement of Financial Accounting Standards No. 52: Foreign Currency Translation.* Financial Accounting Standards Board.

FASB (1993). *Statement of Financial Accounting Standards No. 115: Accounting for Certain Investments in Debt and Equity Securities.* Financial Accounting Standards Board.

Feder, B.J. and Eichenwald, K. (2004). Ex-WorldCom Chief is Indicted by US in Securities Fraud. *New York Times*, 3 March.

Federal Reserve Board (1998). *Risk-Based Capital Standards: Unrealized Holding Gains on Certain Equity Securities*, 12 CFR Parts 208 and 225 (Regulations H and Y; Docket No. R-0982); http://www.federalreserve.gov/BoardDocs/Press/boardacts/1998/19980826/.

Financial Services Fact Book (2005). *Insurance*; http://www.financialservicesfacts.org/financial2/insurance/overview/.

Fore, D. (2003). *The Impact of Fair Value Accounting Standards on the Portfolio Composition of Life Insurance Companies.* Working Paper 13-050103, TIAA-CREF.

FPA (2005). *FPA Files New Lawsuit Against SEC.* Financial Planning Association, 28 April; http://www.fpanet.org/member/press/releases/042805_newsuit.cfm.

Freixas, X. and Tsomocos, D.P. (2004). *Book vs. Fair Value Accounting in Banking, and Intertemporal Smoothing.* OFRC Working Papers Series, Oxford Financial Research Centre.

Grebb, M. (1999). Riding the Dot.Comet. *Business 2.0*, 1 August, 71–77; http://www.business 2.com /b2/web/articles/.

Harford, J. (1999). Corporate Cash Reserves and Acquisitions. *Journal of Finance*, 54(6):1969–1997.

Highlights Investments Group (2005). *Brief History of US Stock Market Crashes (Causes, Costs, and Results)*, 19 September; http://www.index-funds-trading.com/technical_analysis/ stock_market_crach_2000.asp9/19/2005.

Hooper, J. (2004). Parmalat Chiefs Await Their Fate. *The Guardian*, 5 October.

IASB (2002). Final Preface to International Financial Reporting Standards. International Accounting Standards Board, May.

Johns, R. (2005). Day Trading Strategies. *Resource Center for Traders & Investors*; http://www.daytraders.com.

Kaplan, R.S. and Norton, D. (1992). The Balanced Scorecard: Measures that Drive Performance. *Harvard Business Review*, 70(1):71–79.

Kaplan, R.S. and Norton, D. (1996). *Balanced Score Card: Translating Strategy into Action.* Harvard Business School Press, Cambridge, MA.

Keller, J. (2003). The Evolving Business Reporting Model and Use of Performance Measurement Methodology. *CPA Letter*, 83(3):2.

Keynes, J.M. (1936). *The General Theory of Employment, Interest and Money.* Harcourt Brace, New York.

Knutson, P.H. and Napolitano, G.U. (1998). Criteria Employed by the AIMR Financial Accounting Policy Committee in Evaluating Financial Accounting Standards. *Accounting Horizons*, 12(2):170–176.

Levitt, A. (1998). The Importance of High Quality Standards. *Accounting Horizons*, 12(1): 79–82.

Lewis, R.E. (1998). Capital from an Insurance Company Perspective. *FRBNY Economic Policy Review*, 4(3):183–185.

Lope Markets (2003). *The 1987 Stock Market Crash*, 14 August; http://www.lope.ca/markets/1987.html.

MacNeal, K. (1939). *Truth in Accounting*. University of Pennsylvania Press, Philadelphia.

Market Wire (2005). *Law Offices of Charles J. Piven, P.A. Announces Class Action Lawsuit Against UBS-AG – ANWPX, SMCWX, AFTEX, AWSHX*, Financial News, 8 September; http://www.Biz.yahoo.com/iw/050908/094834.html.

NAIC (2005). *Financial Regulatory Services (FRS) Statutory Accounting*. National Association of Insurance Commissioners; http://www.naic.org.

Newman, A.M. (2005). *A Peak in Optimism – The Greatest Stock Market Mania of All Time*, Samex Capital's Stock Market Crosscurrents, 10 August; http://www.cross-currents.net/charts.htm.

newsmax.com (2005). *Experts: Housing Bust Could Dwarf Dot-Com Disaster*, MoneyNews; http://www.newsmax.com/moneynews-archive.shtml.

Nordlund, B. and Persson, E. (2004). Accounting for Investment Property at Fair Value According to IAS 40 Fair Value Model. *Essays in Property Valuation and Accounting*. Report 5:62, Royal Institute of Technology, Stockholm.

Patel, H. (2003). *What's Ahead for Insurance Accounting. Insurance Finance & Investment*; http://www.wtexec.com/finance/IFI/ifiarticles/insacct.html 7/10/03.

PricewaterhouseCoopers (2004). *Enterprise Risk Management: An Enquiry*. A Global Survey. PricewaterhouseCoopers.

Puplava, J.J. (2000). Trains, Planes & Dot Coms Revisited ... The End of an Era, 22 December; http://www.gold-eagle.com/editorials_00/puplava 122200.html.

Puplava, J.J. (2001). Storm Watch: A Penny Less–A Penny More. *Financial Sense Online*; http://www.usagold.com/gildedopinion/puplava/20011109.html.

Rawls, S.W. and Smithson, C.W. (1990). *Strategic Risk Management*. Harper & Row, New York.

Salvary, S.C.W. (1979). Tracing the Development of a Conceptual Framework of Accounting – A Western European and North American Linkage: A Partial Examination. Working Paper No. 40. *Academy of Accounting Historians Working Paper Series* (Coffman, E.N., ed.), Vol. 2. Virginia Commonwealth University.

Salvary, S.C.W. (1985). *Accounting: A Library of Quantifications*. McQueen Accounting Monograph Series, Vol. 1. University of Arkansas, Fayetteville, AR.

Salvary, S.C.W. (1989a). *An Analytical Framework for Accounting Theory*. McQueen Accounting Monograph Series, Vol. 5. University of Arkansas, Fayetteville, AR.

Salvary, S.C.W. (1989b). Accounting an Financial Reporting in a Changing Environment: Historical and Theoietical Perspectives. *Essays in Ecnomic and Baseliness History*, 16:307–329.

Salvary, S.C.W. (1992). Recoverable Cost: The Basis of a General Theory of Financial Accounting Measurement. *Accounting Enquiries*, 1(2):233–273.

Salvary, S.C.W. (1996/1997). Some Conceptions and Misconceptions on Reality and Assumptions in Financial Accounting. *Journal of Applied Business Research*, 13(1):69–82.

Salvary, S.C.W. (1997). On Financial Accounting Measurement: A Reconsideration of SFAC 5 by the FASB is Needed. *Journal of Applied Business Research*, 13(3):89–103.

Salvary, S.C.W. (1998a). The Accounting Variable and Stock Price Determination. *Studies in Economics and Finance*, 18(2):26–61.

Salvary, S.C.W. (1998b). Financial Accounting Measurement: Instrumentation and Calibration. *Accounting Enquiries*, 7(2):225–274.

Salvary, S.C.W. (2003). Financial Accounting Information and the Relevance/Irrelevance Issue. *Global Business and Economics Review*, 5(2):140–175.

Salvary, S.C.W. (2004). *The Underinvestment Problem, Risk Management, and Corporate Earnings Retention*, October; RePEc:wpa:wuwpfi:0410012.

Scott, W.R. (1997). *Financial Accounting Theory*. Prentice-Hall, New Jersey.

Shiller, R.J. (2000). *Irrational Exuberance*. Princeton University Press, Princeton, NJ.

Shubik, M. and Whitman, M.J. (1971). Corporate Reality and Accounting for Investors. *Financial Executive*, May:3–14.

Shwayder, K. (1967). A Critique of Economic Income as an Accounting Concept. *Abacus*, 3(1):23–35.

Snyder, M. (2005). The Odd One Out. *Accountancy Age*, IFRS; http://www.accountancy age.com.

Special Committee (1994). *Improving Business Reporting – A Customer Focus: Meeting the Information Needs of Investors and Creditors*. Comprehensive Report of the Special Committee on Financial Reporting, AICPA.

Trevino, R. and Higgs, R. (1992). Profits of US Defense Contractors. *Defence Economics*, 3(3):211–218.

University of California (2003). *AOL and Time Warner Executives Accused of Pocketing Nearly $1 Billion in Insider Trading*. Office of the President, University of California, 14 April; www.ucop.edu/news/archives/2003/apr14art1.htm.

Upton, W.S. Jr (2001). *Business and Financial Reporting, Challenges from the New Economy*. Financial Accounting Standards Board, April.

Vickers, D. (1978). Realism and Relevance in the Cost of Money Capital. *Oxford Economic Papers*, 30(1):102–116.

Weiss Ratings Inc. (2003). *Life and Health Insurers' Profits Plunge 61% in the first Nine Months of 2002, Lowest Level in Decade*, 26 February; http://www.weissratings.com/News/Ins_General/20030226lh.htm.

4

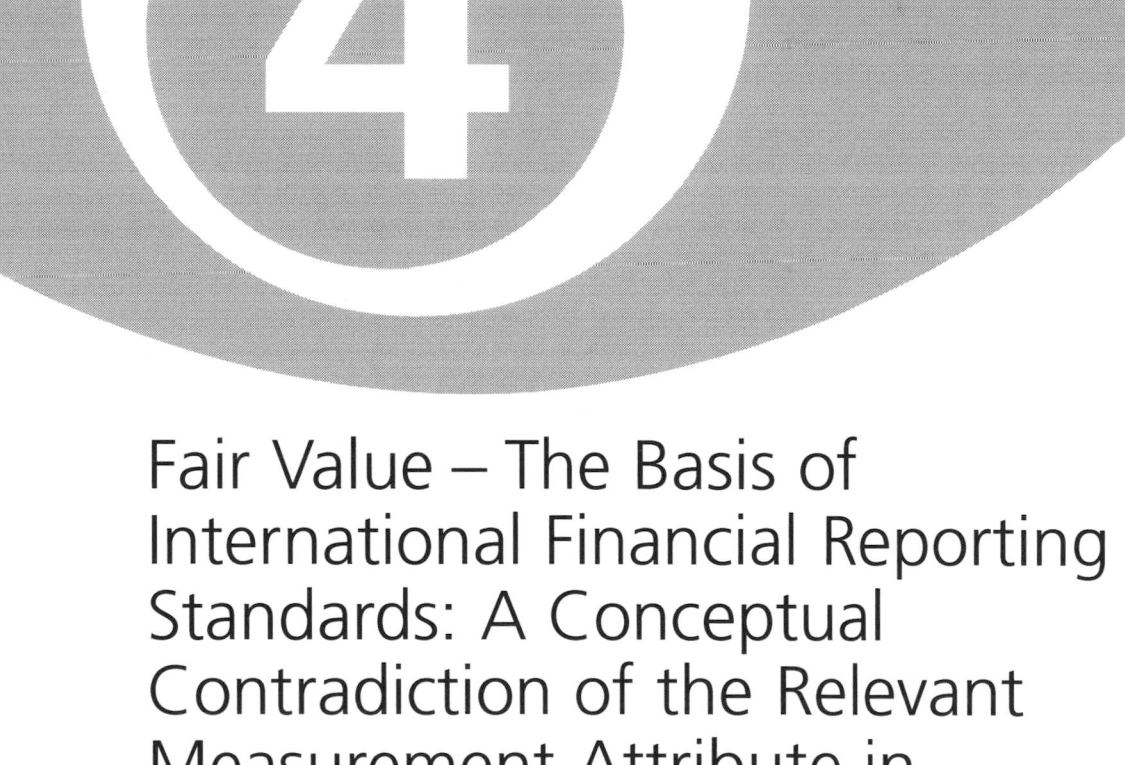

Fair Value – The Basis of International Financial Reporting Standards: A Conceptual Contradiction of the Relevant Measurement Attribute in Financial Accounting

Stanley C.W. Salvary

> 'Information in the scientists' sense is always an instrumental record. This means that in order to understand the nature of information we must examine the nature of instruments and the nature of records ... Today information is in a state of qualitative heterogeneity ... with hints of an underlying quantitative uniformity. If we can find the clue to the basic variable which would enable every item of information to be located in a homogeneous spectrum, the consequences for communication would be quite incalculable.'
>
> (Meredith, 1966, pp. 114–115)

4.1 Introduction

There is a very strong movement to have a uniform set of accounting standards as the basis of International Financial Reporting Standards (IFRS). In January 2005, IFRS became required within the European Union (EU). While IFRS have been adopted by many other countries (Australia, New Zealand), their adoption is seriously being considered by other countries (Damant, 2005, p. 1). Also, the International Accounting Standards Board (IASB) – the organization that establishes the IFRS – and the Financial Accounting Standards Board (FASB) are having discussions with the goal of achieving considerable convergence of their standards (Deloitte IAS PLUS, 2005a).

Benefits from the use of international accounting standards are: (1) the elimination of duplication of effort in developing national accounting standards; (2) a global instead of a national focus on accounting problems; (3) enabling financial comparisons of companies regardless of domiciles – financial data comparability in international capital markets; and (4) savings for companies seeking capital in foreign capital markets by not having to furnish financial statements in accordance with host countries' financial reporting standards. The most beneficial aspect in developing *international accounting standards* is that a global approach will replace a national approach to standard setting. However, *as the standards-setting process progresses, it is evident from the IASB's framework that the accounting problems, which presented themselves in the national accounting standard-setting arenas, are simply migrating to the international accounting standard-setting arena.*

In the IASB's Framework (2001, F.12–14): 'The objective of financial statements is to provide information about the financial position, performance, and changes in financial position of an enterprise that is useful to a wide range of users in making economic decisions.' In April 2005, at the Joint Meeting of the

IASB–FASB (Deloitte IAS PLUS, 2005b), the issue was raised whether the function of *financial reporting is to assist users in decision-making or to compile past transactions*. The agreement arrived at was that the function of financial reporting is to assist with *decision-making*. Strikingly, the Boards agreed that 'general purpose financial reports should not seek to provide information useful to management – if management finds it useful this is a positive but not required as management are able to demand their own reports.' After reaffirming that to assist decision-making is the primary objective of financial reporting, the Boards deliberated on, but did not decide, whether *accountability* and *stewardship* should be incorporated as a subobjective in relationship to decision-making. At the July 2005 IASB Meeting, *stewardship* and *accountability* were examined within the context of providing decision-useful information. Agreement was reached by the members (11 in favour; three opposed) that 'the information needed to assess stewardship or accountability should not be added as an explicit objective of financial reporting by business entities'.

In the Framework (F.10), the IASB maintains that since the interests of all user groups is the ability of an enterprise to generate cash and cash equivalents and of the timing and certainty of those future cash flows, financial statements that meet the needs of investors will satisfy the needs of other users. What was not explicit, in the objective of financial reporting as framed, was made explicit in deliberations at the April and July meetings of the IASB and FASB. The problem that emerged from those meetings is the replacement of reporting on the *stewardship of management as the function of financial reporting* with *providing of information for users' decision-making* on the ability of firms to generate future cash flows. In accord with the IASB, Damant (2005, p. 2) maintains: 'What other aim could there be? It is only future cash flows that can bring benefits to the various stakeholders.'

Understandably, the focus on decision-making leads to a concern for predictive value, as opposed to feedback value. Apparently, the IASB's decision is based on its view that since investors' decision-making requires *future-oriented data*, the measurement of firms' past operating performance and financial position at the reporting date should not be the function of financial reporting. The IASB's focus is motivated by the epistemological objection to transaction-based accounting by some capital market adherents, whose notable feature is the approach to stock market valuation for recently established businesses. *The new valuation approach is not based on earnings*; the constraint of operating performance – profit – is conveniently relaxed (Desmet et al., 2000).

In October 2004, the IASB and the FASB agreed to start a project to converge the Conceptual Frameworks of the respective Boards. Agreement was based on an understanding, which was arrived at on 21 September 2004 by the IASB and the FASB, that both of their conceptual frameworks, apart from convergence, needed to be improved. It was understood that during convergence, to be consistent with the aim of improving the IASB's Framework, the frameworks of the IASB, the FASB, and other existing conceptual frameworks would be given due consideration (Deloitte IAS PLUS, 2004).

In the interim, convergence of the requirements of these standard-setting bodies for Business Combinations (IFRS 3 and SFAS 141) is in progress. While the proposals retain the fundamental requirement of both statements, the main changes are that fair value must be used to measure an acquired company; implied goodwill in the acquisition, and not just the portion attributable to the acquirer, must be recognized; and fewer exceptions to the measuring at fair value will be allowed for assets acquired and liabilities assumed (Zwirn, 2005). Given the fair market valuation requirement in the standards (IFRS 4: *Insurance Contracts*; and IFRS 7: *Financial Instruments: Disclosures*) promulgated for the insurance and banking industries, *fair market value accounting is the long-term goal* (CAS, 2004, p. 16).

In summary, the Boards' position is: (1) to assist decision-making is the primary objective of financial reporting; (2) general purpose financial reports should not seek to provide information useful to management; (3) information needed to assess stewardship or accountability should not be added as an explicit objective of financial reporting; (4) fair market value accounting is the ultimate goal; and (5) financial statements that meet the needs of investors will satisfy the needs of other users (F.10).

The IASB's emphasis is on cash-flow generation and not on profit measurement. Accordingly, the following realities are to be considered in developing accounting standards: (1) the existence of a credit economy and (2) the fact that profit (as utilized in the price/earnings ratio) is the centerpiece of the pricing of firms' securities. Business is conducted in a *credit economy*, yet the emphasis is on the generation of cash flows instead of profit, which is the measure of accomplishment for business operators. Also, with fair value accounting, a *market volatility measure of profit* instead of *realized profit* will become the basis for pricing of firms' securities.

From an informational perspective, organizational activities involve the adoption of one alternative among several and information based on the adopted course of action is furnished in financial statements. Traditionally, financial reporting focuses on what has occurred; no reference is made of the possible consequences if other rejected courses of action had been adopted. It is financial accounting information that enables decision-makers to ascertain the financial position and profitability resulting from the course of action *actually undertaken* in light of the then existing circumstances. If financial reporting is to provide factual data that captures the effects of the actual sequence of events, then *financial accounting standards must focus on organizations' actual operating plans within the context of the existing credit economy as characterized by a 'cash-flow process' and not a cash basis focus.*

At the end of 1975 in the USA, the consumer credit outstanding was $168.7 billion; at the end of June 2005, consumer outstanding credit amounted to $2145.6 billion (Federal Reserve Board, 2005). As noted by Salvary (1989, p. 89):

> 'In a pure money economic system (a system in which there is no credit; all transactions are settled immediately), *matching* would not be a [financial accounting] measurement concept, since it would occur automatically in the cash account. It is a credit economic system (a system in which the bulk of the transactions are executed on credit, with cash settlement taking place at some later point in time) that makes *matching a measurement concept.* In a credit economic system, credit flows precede cash flows, and it is credit flows that give rise to cash flows. In a credit economic system, an accrual system of accounting (a system of accruals and deferrals) becomes necessary to enable the recovery process to be measurable. The two concepts (recovery and matching) constitute a unified measurement process which permits a state description of the accounting entity via the measurement property: recoverable cost.'

4.2 Money, a credit economy, and the cash-flow process

Money, an imaginary/conceptual unit, was first introduced as *a unit of account* to facilitate exchange by translating physical exchange ratios into a series of relative money prices. Next, as *a medium of exchange*, money was introduced by means of documents as evidence that exchanges had taken place – *a credit instrument* representing an obligation emerged and was transferable in settlement of an exchange. Finally, with third party financing of production (the rise of the money and capital markets), money became *a store of uncertain value.* The unique quality of money is its general acceptability by all members of society. General acceptance of *paper money* as a medium of exchange is based upon the full faith of the populace in the *credit worthiness* of the issuing authority (Salvary, 1993).

According to Steuart (1767, pp. 406–407): 'Symbolical or paper [fiat] money is but a species of *credit*; it is no more than the measure by which *credit* is measured. *Credit* is the basis of all contracts ... He who pays in paper puts his creditor in possession only of another person's obligation to make the value good to him: here *credit is necessary even after the payment is made*' (*emphasis added*). The following passage provides an insight on the evolution and role of credit (Salvary, 1989, pp. 98–99).

> Society, due to its quest for self-perpetuation, is an adaptive system which introduces *innovative measures*: (1) to deal with a *changing environment*; and (2) to improve its operating efficiency. The economic system was initially a *barter* system of exchange, and *money* was introduced to improve the operating efficiency of the system. The system was significantly improved. *A money economy emerged! Credit was the next innovation introduced by society.* It 'was perfected by new devices such as the techniques of acceptances and of protests of the bill of exchange' (Pirenne, 1933, p. 212). A credit system is a cost *efficient* means of extending a money economic system: transactions in the economic system are significantly increased without any increase in the money base; the cost of increasing and maintaining a larger money supply is virtually eliminated. In this setting, the money base will increase only as the need for liquidity (the desire to hold cash) increases.

Credit causes a greater circulation of cash and replaces cash in circulation. The extent to which these two means of exchange – money and credit – increase together shows that they render the same services, and when the functions of either one are enhanced the other is invoked into more lively activity. This condition does not contradict the fact that in many instances *credit makes cash superfluous* (Simmel, 1978, p. 194). It is evident, based upon the functioning of the economy, that *a credit economy is characterized by a cash-flow process*.

At this stage, it is very important to stress that *cash-flow basis accounting* is significantly different from *cash-flow process* accounting. The former, embodied in the Statement of Cash Flows, merely requires the recording of cash receipts and disbursements. However, regardless of the enterprise, *accrual accounting* is used to measure the *cash-flow process* in its various stages. The cash-flow process entails: (a) financing – cash infusion is secured; (b) investing – a portfolio of productive assets is acquired; (c) transforming – product input is transformed into the vendible product; (d) distributing – the product is distributed; (e) establishing a receivable – vendible value of the product is realized; and finally (f) collecting cash from the product's realized value – the end of the cash-flow process. Financial accounting captures cash flows sequentially from inception, gestation, and culmination of the investment process. The measurement of *firms' annual profit is* arrived at by the accrual accounting *of the cash-flow process* (Salvary, 1998b). This *cash-flow process* explains the findings of Bowen et al.,

(1987, p. 746), which 'suggest that accrual accounting data have incremental explanatory power beyond that contained in cash flows alone'.

The time path or sequence of events in the cash-flow process reveals an efficient functioning of the socio-economic system. Hence, it is very important that this factor be properly recognized. Since it is the role of accounting to describe how organizations behave in markets, the following caveat is applicable to the accounting standard-setting task:

> '[E]conomic plans and actions have always to be seen in their temporal order, and our daily economic life cannot be understood without a knowledge of its structure through time. Nor is the element of time one which can well be introduced subsequently. *The main problem cannot be tackled if the time factor is left out ...*
>
> *It is not possible to understand economic life with all its interrelations simply by looking directly at contemporary economic reality.*'
>
> (Eucken, 1951, pp. 27, 37–39)

As an indispensable aid to management, financial accounting, which is an administrative information science, enables an *assessment of management* (Salvary, 1985, 1989, 1992). It provides an observational report with measures based upon concepts corresponding to the structures and regularities of the system (nature of the firm, the role of time, investment plans, contracts, means for settlement of obligations, posting of nominal money prices) from which it abstracts. Indubitably, business is conducted with the primary objective of making a profit; hence, profitability is the true test of business success. The accomplishments of management are to be made public. Thus, financial reporting should inform on the outcome of firms' investment plans – *what has happened* (the *realized profit* resulting from mistakes, uncertainty, and accepted risk) and *not what could have happened.*

4.3 Profit measurement and management's performance assessment

The firm is a conduit involved in a nominal money-augmenting process. Each firm executes its investment plan and the consequences of that plan are measured in money terms. Since there are different profit opportunities to which assets can be placed, the profit associated with a particular combination of assets is directly related to their use and risk associated with the particular use. Firms set their prices to obtain a specified profit from their investments over a specified period of time with the expectation that the prices as set will prevail. Regardless of the approach, that of price-taker or price-setter, the price used by a firm reflects its expectations based upon an informed judgment on product demand.

The value of a firm's investment plan is arrived at by the capitalization of the cash-flow stream to be generated by that plan. In the measurement of periodic profit, financial accounting provides a measure of that cash-flow stream. However, while the cash-flow stream is stressed it must be understood that it is only in the long run that all the cash will be collected. De facto, in the short run, the cash-flow stream consists of notes and accounts receivables. As measured in financial accounting, *profit* is comprised of two elements: (1) a current cash-flow component (current cash recovery – profit realized in the form of cash) plus (2) a future cash-flow component – an accrual of profit realized in the form of receivables net of payables (Salvary, 1992).

The IASB recognizes performance (F.17) – the ability of an enterprise to earn a profit on the resources that have been invested in it. However, the IASB allows the interests of user groups in the ability of an enterprise to generate cash and cash equivalents and of the timing and certainty of *those future cash flows* (F.10) to overshadow *profitability* – the key measure of a firm's success, which is critical in market valuation of the firm's securities. The value of a firm's security arrived at by capital market participants is not based on the firm's cash flows, but on the *expected profit* from the investment plan that the firm has set in place (Chen and Zhang, 2003; Penman and Yehuda, 2004). This condition explains why return on equity (ROE) and return on investment (ROI) are the two classic measures of firms' profitability.

Cash management is practiced by most, if not all, successful firms. For instance, firms structure debt and cash to meet their needs for certainty in financing their business activities (ACT, 2001) and use idle cash to accumulate marketable securities, in lieu of dividend payments, to provide for future financing (Salvary, 2004). However, it is the use of *credit* that enables firms to enhance their profitability[1]. This is evidenced by the preference of interest bearing credit sales to cash sales (Salvary, 2003) and use of commercial paper ($1.586 billion are outstanding at 24 August 2005 – Federal Reserve Board) to synchronize the inflows and outflows of cash due to differences in timing between payables and receivables.

Managers, *not assets*, adapt to changing market conditions, recognize new uses for existing assets, decide on specific uses of assets, and alter asset combinations given developing conditions. Money recovery and the cost of waiting are the firm's concerns. Reinvestment in the future will not be undertaken if future expectations indicate that money currently invested cannot be recovered. Furthermore, if current prices can only cover current outlays and future prospects are grim, then the firm will simply abandon the existing investment plan. Profit/loss is a consequence of managerial decisions in an uncertain environment. Invariably, management attempts to select the best among competing alternatives in order to optimize nominal money output given nominal money input.

Since management is responsible for profit, there has to be a suitable basis for assessing management's performance. It is for this reason that the determination of profit using fair value accounting raises serious concerns about the appropriateness of the end result (Bies, 2004; IAIS, 2004; ACT, 2005; Brett, 2005). Indubitably, the future of firms in which they have invested is of great concern to investors/creditors. Obviously, they are profoundly concerned about the reliability of firms' management. Since recovery of their investments will be in the future, they do ask the notable question: Can the firm continue to deliver in the future what it has delivered in the past? The *stewardship of management* is at issue and the reliability measure of management is in great part determined by past operating performance and current financial position – the end result of the firm's investment plan.

While the role of financial accounting in financial reporting is clear, the lingering issue is: What should constitute the basis of the information for *performance assessment*? That is, how should the sacrifices and benefits from the firm's investment plan be measured? If the firm is engaged in a cash-flow process and the focus of its calculation is the recovery of total cash outlays at the minimum, then the investment decision is based on the recoverability of the nominal money invested. Since *recoverable cost*, and not change in market values, captures the essence of the firm's motivation, then *estimated recoverable cost* is the measurement property for measurement of sacrifices and benefits (Salvary, 1985, 1989, 1992).

The firm's output decision is a function of supply and demand. Its *realized profit* from operations is a function of *recoverable cost*. Given *estimated recoverable cost* from operating assets and the firm's expected rate of return, profit can reasonably be predicted. *In the absence of earnings management*, financial accounting information – based on accounting standards that incorporate the *proper measurement attribute, matching, and realization* as fundamental features of accounting measurement – will be neutral, capturing what the firm has done and enabling a proper assessment of management. However, with fair value accounting, neutrality of information about the firm and the assessment of management's stewardship will be affected.

4.4 Neutrality, stewardship, and financial reporting

In the Framework (F.24), understandability, relevance, reliability, and comparability are identified by the IASB as the four principal *qualitative characteristics of financial statements*. These characteristics are attributes that are considered necessary to make the information in financial statements useful to investors, creditors, and others. Importantly, however, *neutrality*, as an essential quality of financial reporting, is not recognized. This lack of recognition for *neutrality* is due to the Boards' position that: (1) to assist decision-making is the primary objective of financial reporting; (2) general purpose financial reports should not seek to provide information useful to management; (3) information needed to assess stewardship or accountability should not be added as an explicit objective of financial reporting; and (4) the assumption (F.10) that financial statements that are prepared to meet the needs of investors will meet most of the general financial information needs of other users.

While the FASB (1980), in *Statement of Financial Accounting Concepts No. 2*, relegated *neutrality* to a secondary role, the IASB eliminated it from the *Qualitative Characteristics of Financial Statements*. This treatment of neutrality is in great part due to the failure to give due cognizance to the evolution of *internal* and *external* financial reporting. When the financier of the enterprise was also the manager of the enterprise, *relevancy* and *reliability* were primary qualities of financial reporting, which at that time was only *internal* financial reporting. The social evolutionary process, characterized by the emergence of new institutions (capital markets, corporations, etc.) and new participants (shareholders, bondholders, professional managers, etc.), gave rise to *external* financial reporting with *neutrality* emerging as an important quality.

While many *new* users emerged, the abstraction of the entity had to be a *true and fair representation of the facts* about the firm consistent with monetary exchange. Financial accounting information is used for decision-making; however, the '*facts*' to be presented are about the firm and not about information to satisfy users' need for decision-making. No single user group can be identified as being the focus of financial reporting. Hence, because *neutrality* requires that the information provided be about the firm's decisions and the consequences of those decisions, it ensured that the interests of the many and varied users of financial accounting information would be served (Salvary, 1981).

Variations over time, from continual modification or amplification of the institutional arrangement, have not altered the basic societal concern. Without a clear understanding of the historical relevance of the institutional development surrounding *neutrality*, in abstracting from the existing economic environment, the IASB's investor focus introduced a bias which enabled reality to escape the analysis. Fortunately, in May 2005, the IASB and FASB unanimously decided to retain neutrality as a characteristic desired in financial reporting (FASAC, 2005). Thus, *neutrality* will be returned to its role among the essential qualities.

Lamentably, given the IASB's position – general purpose financial reports should not seek to provide information useful to management, and stewardship or accountability information should not be added as an explicit objective of financial reporting – the role of *stewardship* in financial reporting has been abandoned. Evidently, this development is due to the failure to give due consideration to the historical development of accounting concepts. This condition is quite troubling as great importance is attached to the consequences of the failure to understand institutional arrangements and their historical evolution (Salvary, 1981)[2].

It is only from an analysis of observed phenomena that the requisite understanding of the accounting environment can be obtained. The findings from such an investigation would reveal that: (1) *external financial reporting, a part of financial reporting, is deemed to be the totality of financial reporting*; and (2) financial reporting is comprised of *external financial reporting* (financial accounting) and *internal financial reporting* (managerial accounting). The following passage sheds light on this point:

> 'In the thirteenth century, the manors were centers of rural employment and some ... were well managed estates, ... characterized by a sound system of administration and the annual rendition of accounts ... [T]he basic handbook of estate administration was by Walter of Henley ... The test of efficiency emphasized in the handbook was profit and loss, and the need for profit making ... was recognized by the Statute of Merton (1235) ... Essentially, the manor is the origin of the firm ... [E]arly days of the manorial system are ... similar to the period of individual capitalism, ... the owner was the manager-accountant for the business ... [L]ater development ... is characteristic of security capitalism, in which ... organizing the various activities of the firm is placed upon the shoulders of skilled salaried managers and ... risk-taking is accepted by investors through the supply of finance ...
>
> [T]he partnership ... of the seventeenth century ... gave way to the joint stock company with limited liability in the nineteenth century. With the separation of the owner from the management of the operations ... the function of [external] financial reporting gained prominence ...
>
> As a direct consequence of the social evolutionary process, the capital market emerged to accommodate the financing of large scale operations; ... With the

> advent of limited liability as a matter of public policy, the univision (single objective) approach to accounting information was altered. Decision-making ... within the firm became separate and distinct from the measurement of the performance of the firm as a unit responsible to the suppliers of finance. The result was the emergence [explicit recognition] of *two distinct types* of information: financial accounting information and managerial accounting information ...'
>
> (Salvary, 1998a)

The existing institutional arrangement did not exist in its present state, it evolved. Of necessity, a sound comprehension of the historical relevance of institutional developments in accounting is needed, otherwise reality escapes the analysis.

Prior to the separation of owner from management, financial reporting existed solely for internal purposes. One set of accounting reports, consisting of information on stewardship (financial accounting reports) and information for decision-making (managerial accounting reports) was prepared for the owner. With the advent of limited liability and the separation of management from the owner, management was held accountable for its stewardship and had to provide an account of its stewardship to investors/creditors. At this juncture, external financial reporting (financial accounting information as required by law) emerged[3]. However, information useful for decision-making (managerial accounting information) was prepared exclusively for management as part of *internal financial* reporting. Hence, financial reporting was split into *external financial reporting and internal financial reporting.*

4.5 The lower of cost and market rule, fair valuation, and realization

Undeniably, the function of financial reporting is to provide *factual* information about a firm's past performance and current financial position. Financial statements are not to speculate on *how the firm could have been affected* but report on *how the firm actually has been affected* in the conduct of its business. In this regard, the '*lower of cost and market*' measurement rule enabled the recognition of asset impairment in the case of inventories and marketable securities. With the incorporation of market volatility in the measurement of profit, this measurement rule is effectively abandoned. As developed in France by Jacques Savary in 1712 (Littleton, 1933, p. 152), the rule was established to deal with changes in the market that constituted bona fide losses sustained by the firm. The reasoning provided by Andrews (1949, pp. 41–42), for the '*lower of cost and market*' measurement rule as applied to inventories, is consistent with recoverable cost (Salvary, 1985, 1989, 1992), as the measurement property in financial accounting, and the cash-flow process.

> 'If market values have fallen ... the costs expended on the stocks at the beginning of the next accounting year would be greater than the costs at which the business could then acquire similar goods. Now, it is essentially the purpose of the business to hold such goods for ultimate sale and to take the risks of the market. If they were carried at outlay-cost into the balance sheet at the end of the year, the next year would be saddled with what would be consequences of financial risks which were really incurred in the earlier period, and the year in which the business acquired them would be avoiding one of the costs of its having done so – the fall in prices that has taken place ... To value at market prices when prices are rising would falsify the cost position and cause the following year to be charged with costs which had not been incurred in fact ... the accountant's rule here is a strict application of the logic of his principle of charging as costs the money outlays that have been incurred during any period.'

Since the rule provides for downward revaluation but no upward revaluation, some researchers have attributed this rule to conservatism (Ijiri and Nakano, 1989). Salvary (1992), consistent with Andrews's (1949) logic on the treatment in financial accounting of the *consequences of financial risks*, makes it clear that the attribution to conservatism is invalid:

> 'The approach (no upward revaluation but downward revaluation) is said by some to be attributable to conservatism. The real reason for this approach is the fact while "risk of loss" *is a meaningful concept, "risk of gain" is not an operational concept.* No one hedges against the risk of gain; but those who can hedge against the risk of loss, usually do. The firm is in business to make a gain. It will reflect a gain as it achieves that gain. When the expected gain is larger than the firm had initially anticipated, the firm has not suffered; the recoverable amount of the invested money is unimpaired. Instead, the firm's internal rate of return would have increased, and the increase in earnings will flow through the income statement. However, when the firm is exposed to the risk of loss of money committed (when circumstances reveal that the firm will not recover its investment), consistent with the concept of "risk of loss", there is no alternative but to write down the investment.'

Furthermore, *consistent with the cash-flow process of a credit economy as described earlier, this measurement rule removes investment costs that are no longer recoverable, hence no longer part of the cash-flow process.* However, with fair value accounting, changes in market values that are not part of a firm's cash-flow process will be required to be recognized.

As per the Framework (F.92), income (is to be recognized) occurs simultaneously with the increases in assets or decreases in liabilities. *Realization* is embedded in the IASB's example: 'The net increase in assets arising on a *sale of goods or services* or the *decrease in liabilities arising from the waiver of a debt payable*.' However, it is change in market values, in accordance with fair value accounting, that is implicit in the statement. A serious problem presents itself because changes in market values follow a cyclical pattern (Kling and McCue, 1987; Janssen et al., 1994; Grenadier, 1995; RICS, 1999) that is not inherently associated with firms' investment plans.

Regrettably, in light of the foregoing, the dilemma for the investors/creditors is that information on the stewardship of firms' management will not be available, yet management will face a more serious problem. Since general purpose financial reports are *not* to provide information useful to management and require information deemed necessary *to assist users with their decision-making*, management will be assessed not on carefully laid plans which they control, but on market volatility which they do not control (ACT, 2005; Brett, 2005). The following passages focus on the imminent problems posed by fair value accounting:

> '[F]air valuations will have an impact on leverage ratios, capital ratios, and other ratios used in the lending and credit-management process.'
>
> (Bies, 2004)

> 'Forecasts and internal performance measurements will no longer be comparable with the results reported in the statutory accounts. Increased volatility of earnings, e.g. through fair value adjustments, will make forecasting more difficult. *Also, internal performance measurements will have to be structured in a way that avoids penalties for fluctuations outside the direct control of management.*'
>
> (Deloitte IAS PLUS, 2003, emphasis added)

> 'Where debt covenants do not provide for changes in accounting regulations, changes to the balance sheet may cause these covenants to be breached. This [will have an] impact on the company's ability to ensure continuity of financing arrangements.'
>
> (Deloitte IAS PLUS, 2005b)

Given the foregoing scenario, the performance of management will be distorted, causing the possible termination of management and improper market pricing of firms' securities. Those problems can be averted with matching of actual sacrifices and benefits as established in the cash-flow process and the restoration of *realization* as an essential condition in the determination of profit. In so doing, the underlying cash-flow process of management's actual plans will be captured.

The recognition of changes in market values as a component of profit conflicts with *realization*; consequently, it is abandoned. Since the IASB's position (F.10) is that all users share the same interest and *the primary objective of financial reporting is to assist decision-making,* then *neutrality* is irrelevant since the *decision of users takes precedence over the decisions as implemented by the firm.* With market volatility incorporated as information for users' decision-making, the results of the firm's operations will be compromised at best and contaminated at worst. The IASB should reconsider its position on *realization* and *neutrality.*

In this fair value accounting movement, accounting measurements are questioned since they do not mimic capital market prices. In the value-relevance literature on standard setting, 'the value-relevance criterion implies that accounting's fundamental role is to measure or help measure market value' (Holthausen and Watts, 2000). In a very penetrating study concerning the value-relevance literature, the researchers ask the following questions: Does the observed association between earnings and security prices suggest that financial accounting standards are created to maximize that association, or that changes in those standards are attempts to increase that association? Does the nature and evolution of contemporary balance sheets intimate that financial accounting standards are designed to equate the recorded amounts with the market value of the equity? The researchers identified characteristics of the financial statements that are inconsistent with the valuation criterion. The explanations for those characteristics are consistent with financial statements as *inputs* into investors' decision models that involve valuation, with the balance sheet being an *input* as described by the FASB but inconsistent with it of itself being an estimate of value (Holthausen and Watts, 2000).

Undeniably, the IASB, due to its capital market orientation (Damant, 2005, p. 2), seeks to find solutions to financial reporting from movements in the securities markets; however, participants in the capital market are looking to accounting to provide information about the firm to arrive at the value of the firm. The value of a firm's share in the capital market is based upon investors' expectations of that firm's future profit, the assessed riskiness of the firm's operation, and the prevailing interest rate for the particular time horizon.

The valuation of a sum or sums of money to be received at some future point in time is based upon demand and supply conditions for money, reflecting changes in the risk-free interest rate and the inherent risk in the existing supply alternatives of future cash flows. Since market prices of firms' equity securities are driven by the expectations of investors, they reveal nothing about the actual operating performance and financial condition of those firms. Financial accounting information, which is the only factual information about the entity/organization, is vital for capital market price formation due to the fact that from the information content of current period's profit and residual recoverable cost, a general picture of the firm is obtained.

It is necessary to draw attention to the distinction between market values and accounting measures as stressed by Trevino and Higgs (1992, p. 211): '[W]hereas accounting rates of return such as ROI and ROA are measures of the profitability of the firm, MRET [total market rate of return] is a measure of profitability to the shareholder of the firm. There is no necessary relation between the accounting returns and the market returns in a particular year.' As measured in financial accounting, profit (which is central to the market valuation process) is comprised of two elements: (1) *a current cash-flow component* (earnings realized in the form of cash – current cash returns) plus (2) *a future cash-flow component* (earnings realized in the form of credit – an accrual of estimated discounted future cash flow) (Salvary, 1992).

The market valuation process, which facilitates transfers of titles to claims, captures the changes in financiers' beliefs about risks and liquidity. Although a firm's profit is relatively constant, the price of the firm's security is highly variable. This condition holds since two elements (the discount rate and the investors' planning horizons/time frame) of the market pricing/valuation model are *highly sensitive* to money market conditions and personal expectations. The discount rate is sensitive to changes in the interest rate which reflect the availability of money, and the investors' planning horizon/time frame is sensitive to investors' liquidity considerations. Also, investors' projections of future earnings, which are based upon the firm's current period's profit, are subject to optimism or pessimism (Salvary, 1998b).

Since *investors' expectations* are at times highly optimistic or highly pessimistic, market values are ephemeral in nature. Consequently, the inclusion of changes in market value will contaminate the financial accounting measurement of firms' profits; the contaminated information when furnished to the market participants, more likely than not, will produce distorted market pricing of some firms' securities. This effect is due to the *causative order of association between market value and accounting profits*: market value is arrived at after the projection of future profit, and this projection occurs only after the measurement of the current period's profit has been reported. The measurement of profit in financial accounting does not begin with market value as a given; *market valuation begins with the release of financial accounting information in the financial reports.* Given an ill-conceived order of *association between market value and the profit generated in the cash-flow process*, the inclusion of market volatility in financial statements will simply result in a distorted portrayal of firms' current period profit and financial position.

4.6 The IASB's association of fair market value with the cash-flow process

The IASB's definition of fair value is: 'The amount for which an asset could be exchanged, or a liability settled, between knowledgeable, willing parties in an arm's length transaction.' The FASB's definition of fair value is: '[T]he price at which an asset or liability could be exchanged in a current transaction between knowledgeable, unrelated willing parties' (FASB and IASB, 2004, p. 2). Except for the choice of words, the two definitions of fair market value are essentially the same. The following illustrations are examples of fair value: WorldCom's purchase of MCI and AOL's purchase of Time Warner. Both situations involved people, based upon all accounts, who were knowledgeable and engaged in arm's length transactions. WorldCom paid $37 billion for MCI on 10 November 1997 (PBS – The News Hour, 1997), while America Online purchased Time Warner for $106 billion on 11 January 2001 (PBS – The News Hour, 2001). In both cases the values were outrageous. In its financial report for 2002, AOL Time Warner wrote off approximately $90 billion of goodwill (Salvary, 2003) and WorldCom wrote off $45 billion (Krazit, 2003).

As the saga has unfolded over the last few years, fair market value transactions have resulted in a chronic overstatement of assets in many corporations' balance sheets owing to the goodwill that emerged from the business combination mania. This condition has led to massive amounts of writeoffs. Between the years 1998 and 2000, according to Fulcrum Financial Inquiry (2003), approximately 28,800 business purchases occurred. Within this three-year period, a 30% growth of intangible assets was experienced for S&P 500 companies and by 2001 intangible assets amounted to about 44% of book equity of those companies. In 2002, the goodwill writeoffs by US public companies amounted to approximately $750 billion. With about $690 billion of goodwill remaining on the balance sheets of the S&P 500 companies, goodwill writeoffs were estimated to be about $200 billion.

It is very difficult to comprehend how those fair values would enable a better prediction of the profitability of the cash-flow process, when profits generated by those firms were in no manner related to the 'fair values' assigned by the investors. This condition exists since market valuation is a function of the various valuation models employed by investors. An insight into one such valuation approach that has been flaunted in the last few years follows:

> 'In forecasting the performance of high-growth companies like Amazon, we must not be constrained by current performance. Instead of starting from the present – the usual practice of DCF valuations – ... start by thinking about what the industry and the company could look like when they evolve from today's very high growth, unstable condition to a sustainable, moderate-growth state in the future; and then extrapolate back to current performance. The future growth state should be defined by metrics such as the ultimate penetration rate, average revenue per customer, and sustainable gross margins. Just as important as the characteristics of the industry and company in this future state is the point when it actually begins.'
>
> (Desmet et al., 2000)

It is remarkably clear that, in this new valuation approach, the association between fair market values and current profit generated by the cash-flow process has been disrupted. What is even more staggering is the existence and extent of 'program trading'. As reported by Newman (2005), approximately two-thirds of the volume of company shares traded on the New York exchange are program trades. As rebalancing of the major indexes (including the Russell and S&P) takes place, certain stocks are sold and others are purchased in order to effectively reflect those indexes. More than three-quarters of all shares traded during the week of 24 June 2005 on the NYSE were traded to achieve the desired mix. Given that programmed ('algorithmic') trading is used to rebalance portfolios to the desired outcome, none of those programmed traded shares were based on value. Statistical formulas are used to determine which stocks to trade, when to trade them, and at what price. Big securities firms are making aggressive use of this approach and sharing their systems with institutional clients. Consequently, with such trading what a company's share should be worth given existing prospects does not enter into the decision-making process; therefore, it would take a gigantic leap of faith to associate the cash-flow process with those market values.

Since they are derived from/represent two different and distinct processes, financial accounting measurement and capital market valuation do differ. The focus in financial accounting is upon *measuring the amount of profits generated by the cash-flow process as derivable from existing investment projects – income statement; and estimating the recoverable amount of yet to be recovered committed resources (the organization's risk exposure) – balance sheet.* In the absence of earnings management by firms, financial accounting information enables cash flows to be predictable. This condition holds since the approach employed in financial accounting is based on the cash-flow planning process involving transactions as embodied in the capital budgeting model, in which case Estimated Recoverable Cost − Committed Finance/Money Outlays = Money Recoveries Discounted over the Recovery Period at the Firm's Internal Rate of Return (Salvary, 1985, 1989, 1992).

To the IASB, a capital market *value*, not a transaction-based *measure*, is *the* approach to be used in financial accounting, because the market provides the assessment of investors. The IASB finds support in Smirlock et al.'s (1984) view of the deficiency in accounting: 'Future firm's rents [earnings] ... will be [is] appropriately capitalized by an efficient market ... Relying on capital markets to value rents avoids or substantially mitigates most of the shortcomings inherent in accounting profit rates [accounting measurement of profits].' While the capital market provides a value of a firm's security, it cannot measure the cash flow that has been generated by the firm in the earnings process. It should be obvious that signals generated by a signaling system – the capital market – must not be confused with information depicting an operating system – the firm (Salvary, 1989, pp. 50–52).

Measurement, without which quantitative comparison is not possible, is the essence of relevance. To measure, a single attribute that corresponds to the structure of the observed phenomena has to be identified. In the absence of a single measurement attribute (i.e. recoverable cost), a mixed model would result from the use of divergent measurement attributes as described by the FASB and IASB. Accordingly, due cognizance has to be given to the reality of the credit economy, which is characterized by a cash-flow process, and the single measurement attribute – recoverable cost – which underlies the investment decision.

4.7 The Frameworks' measurement bases and the mixed attribute model

In *Statement of Financial Accounting Concepts No. 5* (FASB, 1984, pp. 66, 67), the FASB identified five different attributes (historical cost/historical proceeds, current (replacement) cost, current market value, net realizable (settlement) value, and present (or discounted) value of future cash flows) that are currently used to measure the items reported in financial statements. The FASB maintained that the use of a particular attribute depends on the nature of the item and the relevance and reliability of the attribute. The FASB (1984, p. 70) stated that:

> 'Rather than attempt to characterize present practice as being based on a single attribute with numerous exceptions for diverse reasons, this concepts Statement characterizes present practice as based on different attributes. Rather than attempt to select a single attribute and force changes in practice so that all classes of assets and liabilities use that attribute, this concepts Statement suggests that use of different attributes will continue, and discusses how the Board may select the appropriate in particular cases.'

Except for replacement cost, the IASB's Framework (F.100) contains basically the same measurement bases that are present in the FASB's (1984) and the International Accounting Standards Committee's (1989) Conceptual Frameworks. Also, the FASB's position as noted above is repeated in a slightly different fashion by the IASB (F.101). Common to those Frameworks is the failure to identify a single measurement attribute. This problem has migrated from the national standard-setting arenas to the international standard-setting arena.

Drawing upon the FASB's line of reasoning, the Special Committee of the AICPA (1994) concluded that standard setters should continue to use a *mixed model*, whereby assets and liabilities are measured in financial statements at cost, lower of cost and (market) value, and fair (realizable) value. Nevertheless, the positions of the FASB, IASC, and IASB on the use of 'different attributes' and that of the AICPA's Special Committee on a 'mixed model' cannot be sustained in light of the logical analysis presented by Salvary (1992). One attribute that leads to a *unique* model of financial accounting measurement has been identified by Salvary (1985, 1989, 1992). The various measurement rules in financial accounting, which give rise to the appearance of different attributes, are necessary for the convergence of a heterogeneous group of items into a homogeneous measure. Financial accounting measurement of the cash-flow process and the uniqueness of recoverable cost as the measurement attribute have been reinforced by means of social theory (Salvary, 1997).

The descriptive theory of financial accounting measurement rules is based upon what their construction permits them to measure (Salvary, 1992). The rules are related to investments, which, unequivocally, can be considered as observed accounting phenomena. In this fashion, the logic underlying financial accounting measurement rules is established. Since accountants are not conversant with the basis for the rules, in some instances applications of the measurement rules in current practice are not consistent with the explanation for the measurement rules. This condition explains what is perceived to be diverse measurement bases in financial accounting and gives rise to the appearance of a mixed attribute model of financial accounting.

4.8 Investments, measurement rules, and market simulation

As explained by Salvary (1992), financial accounting provides an observational report, which describes observations of *resources* in a *space* and *time* setting. The measurement attribute is related to the concept of recovery: an *investment* made with the expectation of recovering, at the minimum, the investment cost and in addition a return for undertaking the *investment*. Given this scenario, the economic environment is describable by stating how much recoverable cost is embodied in what forms (assets), at what places (accounting entities), at what dates (fiscal year ends). While the asset is independent of the organization, the *recoverable cost* attribute of the asset is dependent on the organization and the time at which it is held by the organization. Essentially, financial accounting provides information on *how much money commitment is undergoing what types of transformations in which organizations at what dates*, and in binary opposition, *the financing of those commitments. Resources controlled by business firms are heterogeneous spatial configurations that share a common decision-oriented property: recoverable cost.* Based upon the reasoning presented by Faden (1977, pp. 7, 37, 38), *the accounting entity is a measurable space.* Hence, if financial accounting information is to be relevant, then financial accounting measurement must conform with measurement theory since *investments* constitute the observed phenomena. Consistent with measurement theory, the next section demonstrates that recoverable cost, as the measurement attribute in financial accounting, is captured in a market simulation approach.

Investments give rise to assets. The financial accounting measurement rules, which are used to measure assets, follow a basic market simulation process. This process is depicted by the following equations, which represent three distinct but sequential decisions facing the firm: (1) the *entry* (investment) decision (**I**); (2) the *use* (operation) decision (**O**); and (3) the *exit* (termination) decision (**T**). Three models, presented below, underlie the three decisions encountered in the conduct of business: (i) measurement of recoverable cost ($\mathbf{C}_{\mathrm{I}}^{*}$) at the time of initial investment (entry decision); (ii) continuing measurement of recoverable cost ($\mathbf{C}_O^*$) during the course of operations (use decision); and (iii) final measurement of recoverable cost ($\mathbf{C}_T^*$), when an asset is no longer part of the recovery plan (exit decision).

Present value of estimated future cash flow:

$$\mathbf{C}_I^* = \sum_{n=1}^{N} \mathbf{R}_n (1+\mathbf{r}_n)^{-n} \text{ (net present value method – NPV)} \quad (4.1)$$

Lower of cost and market measure of cash flow:

$$\mathbf{C}_O^* = \mathbf{S} - \mathbf{M} \text{ } (\mathbf{S} = \text{sellimg price; } \mathbf{M} = \text{markup}) \quad (4.2)$$

Realizable value measure of cash flow:

$$\mathbf{C}_T^* = \mathbf{RV} \text{ } (\mathbf{RV} = \text{realizable value}) \quad (4.3)$$

All the measurement rules are derived from a market simulation model. The first measurement rule is the use of the money received in exchange for claims against the firms as the basis or value of the claims. The recoverable cost approach, which is implied by or at least inferred from equation (4.4), is evident at the inception of all investment decisions.

$$\mathbf{PVI} - \mathbf{C} = \mathbf{NPV} \quad (4.4)$$

Based upon the NPV, the investment decision, if rational, to commit **C** (cash outflow) is made if, and only if, any one of two conditions holds: **PVI** = **C** or **PVI** > **C** (i.e. if **NPV** ≥ **0**). If an investment decision is made and **C** > **PVI** at the time of the transaction, then the financial accounting rule holds that **C** (initial cash outflow) be written down to **PVI**. Since **PVI** is equal to **C*** (estimated recoverable cost) in equation (4.1), then **C** is set equal to **C***.

As it stands, *an asset* is recorded at the lower of fair market value received and fair market value given up in all of the following situations: in an exchange for another asset, is a self-constructed asset, acquired for cash or in an exchange for debt or equity securities. The logic behind the observed practice is that it is unlikely that someone will give the firm more value than what is received in return. Simply put, an asset is not to be recorded at an amount in excess of its fair market value. For the self-constructed asset, amounts expended in excess of a fair market-based outlay are excluded from the asset's recorded value.

Financial accounting measurement is guided by equation (4.1), which ensures that the consequence of a bad decision (e.g. loss on acquisition) is reflected in the income statement. At the time of initial measurement, equation (4.1) reflects a market simulation approach. For the entry decision, the estimated recoverable cost ($\mathbf{C}_{\mathrm{I}}^{*}$) is the decision-maker's risk exposure based upon the firm's expectations of what prices (**S**) will be over the life of the investment. Decisions at the margin reflect market conditions, and prices (**S**) in the seller's market are a critical variable.

4.8.1 Lower of cost and market valuation

Subsequent to the asset's acquisition, equation (4.5) serves as the basis to measure the asset's use value and constitutes the basis for the second measurement rule:

$$\mathbf{C}_{\mathrm{O}}^{*} = \mathbf{S} - \mathbf{M} \tag{4.5}$$

S (selling price of firm's output) is market determined. **M** (margin/markup), which is the expected gain, is contingent upon **S**. The operating decision, which occurs after entry decision, is influenced by current and expected **S**. Based upon the prevailing market conditions and the firm's normal **M**, then $\mathbf{C}_{\mathrm{O}}^{*}$ emerges as the amount recoverable. This condition holds due to the fact that the firm's output is of no utility to the firm (Arrow, 1981, p. 142). As a consequence, the firm experiences a period of storing (measured in nominal money terms) until other parties are ready to exchange either money or a receivable for such output. Hence, changing consumer demand, for the firm's output after entry, establishes the amount of money committed (**C**) that is recoverable ($\mathbf{C}_{\mathrm{O}}^{*}$).

The recovery process is based upon the ability to charge consumers the planned selling price. In an irreversible decision, if the conditions under which the plan was laid were to materialize, then money committed plus the rewards for undertaking the commitment will be recovered. Occasionally, less than full recovery is experienced when market conditions are worse than projected. Should an asset no longer fit into the firm's operating plan, realizable value – the third measurement rule – is applied to determine the recoverable investment cost.

4.8.2 Realizable value

Equation (4.6), which is market simulation for the exit decision measurement for terminal and obsolete processes, completes the simulation process:

$$\mathbf{C}_{\mathrm{T}}^{*} = \mathbf{RV} \tag{4.6}$$

Since the firm recognizes that the asset is no longer part of the recovery plan, the firm disposes of the asset to minimize future adverse consequences. Realizable value (**RV**), the amount obtainable from disposal of the asset in the seller's market, is market based. Accordingly, **RV** determines $\mathbf{C}_T^*$ (recoverable cost) at the time of the exit decision, in which case the amount that will be recovered ($\mathbf{C}_T^*$) is the cash flow from the sale of the asset and not from the use of the asset.

In the above situations, $\mathbf{C}_I^*$, $\mathbf{C}_O^*$, and $\mathbf{C}_T^*$ represent the amount of money that would be committed by the decision-maker consistent with existing market conditions. In each and every situation (*cost, lower of cost and market, and realizable value*), one is looking at a measurement to arrive at the estimated recoverable amount of an original invested sum of money. The three measurement rules are necessary to deal with the heterogeneous conditions resulting from the fact that *planning is undertaken under conditions of market uncertainty*. Since money invested is represented not by one homogeneous grouping of assets but by a heterogeneous group of assets, the diverse measurements applied are necessary to measure the recoverable amount of money invested. Under this measurement process, the heterogeneity of assets converges to a homogeneity of value.

4.9 Summary, discussion, and conclusion

While financial reporting has evolved *pari passu* with organizational/institutional changes in society, it is now deemed to be out of touch with economic reality. In an effort to introduce economic reality, information useful for users' decision-making has replaced *information about the consequences of the firm's decisions* as the center of financial reporting. Unfortunately, the side show now replaces the main show. By replacing stewardship and realized income measurement with users' decision-making and fair value income measurement, financial reporting has been dislodged from its mooring.

After an investment decision has been implemented, the need to decide on the particular asset form no longer exists. Bygones are bygones! The measurement of performance in the use of the assets in the firm's portfolio is now at hand. An assessment of the asset portfolio, while necessary, is indifferent to the management (old versus new) at the time of the assessment; it focuses on assets' use and market conditions – product demand. The information emanating from the ensuing assessment affects the decision to continue or abandon the operation associated with each asset. It is expectations of future economic conditions which provide guidance on what portion of the remaining unrecovered amount is recoverable. It is not the available service capacity, but the usable service capacity of each asset given market conditions that determines the recoverable amount of the investment cost. At the end of each period, the amount of existing investment cost (e.g. underwriting costs of insurance policy) estimated to be recoverable in future periods establishes the amount that should have been recovered in the current period, whether recovered or not. In this measurement process, any investment cost not recovered constitutes a loss.

Firms generate cash flows and fair market value changes (which are ephemeral in nature) are due to changes in the interest rate, the investment horizon, and changes in expectation of future cash flows. A firm's cash flow is unimpeded by any of those factors. Furthermore, the amount of cash invested and the asset form which it takes do not determine the cash flow. The rate of return on invested money depends on management's ability to manage effectively. Management's plan is the medium for creating cash flows. There are different rates of return on investments to reflect varying degrees of risk inherent in the various investment projects. It is the perceived risk due to differences in managerial talent that causes a difference in valuation. To change financial accounting reports to reflect perceived differences by market participants is to destroy the efficiency of the capital market. It is like moving the North Star and expecting navigators to use the North Star as a location point – a guide (Salvary, 1998c, p.259).

The suppliers of finance are synonymous with the financial capital markets. Individual savings take the form of bank deposits, insurance policies, and debt or equity securities. Individual savings constitute, in part, the financial capital pool – money and securities markets. Such funds are entrusted to entrepreneurs with the hope that the entrepreneurs will safeguard the corpus (principal) and operate profitably so that a return on the principal can be generated. Short-term investors are only concerned with stock price movement regardless of the reason. However, long-term/serious investors, with a vested interest in the future of the firms, are concerned with the reliability of entrepreneurs. The reliability measure is in great part determined by information on past performance. Unequivocally, the stewardship of management is critical; thus, its role in financial reporting should be restored.

Finally, it must be remembered that not all firms are publicly traded. Many of those nontraded firms are large, have very profitable operations, utilize the financial resources of the financial markets, and contribute significantly to the general welfare of the economy. So due cognizance has to be given to the fact that the function of financial reporting is independent of the presence or absence of a securities market.

Notes

1. For instance, in 2003, Sears, Roebuck & Co. sold its credit business to Citigroup. At that time about 59 million credit card accounts were involved, of which 25 million were active. In the past, Sears had relied on profits from the credit operation to smooth out bumps in retail revenue (Consumer Affairs.com, 2003; Carpenter, 2004). Citigroup paid Sears about $32 billion, of which about $2.9 billion was a 10% premium on the $28.6 billion in receivables Sears held on its private label and bank card portfolios (Wolverton, 2003).
2. The work of Finley (1973) was undertaken expressly to demonstrate the fallacious analysis resulting from the failure to give cognizance to the historical development of institutional arrangements.
3. External financial reporting was established in 1844 and reaffirmed in the Companies Acts of 1856 and 1862 (Redford, 1960, p. 183). Both creditors and investors are to be protected via a monitoring system which accounting provides in the form of the balance sheet (Edey and Panitpakdi, 1956, p. 359).

References

ACT (2001). *Response to JWG Proposals for Accounting for Financial Instruments.* The Association of Corporate Treasurers, July.

ACT (2005). IAS 39 *Implementation Experience Reported by Members Association of Corporate Treasurers.* The Association of Corporate Treasurers, July.

Andrews, P.W.S. (1949). *Manufacturing Business.* Macmillan, London.

Arrow, K.J. (1981). Real and Nominal Magnitudes in Economics. In: *The Crisis in Economic Theory* (Bell, D. and Kristol, I., eds). Basis Books, New York.

Bies, S.S. (2004). *Fair Value Accounting.* Remarks by Governor Susan Schmidt Bies to the International Association of Credit Portfolio Managers General Meeting, New York, 18 November.

Bowen, R.M., Burgstahler, D., and Daley, L.A. (1987). The Incremental Information Content of Accruals Versus Cash Flows. *Accounting Review*, 62(4):723–747.

Brett, M. (2005). How IFRS Affects Profit: The £286m Question. *The Estate Gazette*, 21 May, p. 50. Sutton, UK.

Carpenter, D. (2004). *Credit-Card Sale Boosts Sears' Profit.* Associated Press, 29 January.

CAS (2004). *Fair Value of P&C Liabilities: Practical Implications.* Casualty Actuarial Society, Arlington, VA.

Chen, P.F. and Zhang, G. (2003). *Profitability, Earnings and Book Value in Equity Valuation: A Geometric View and Empirical Evidence.* Hong Kong University of Science and Technology Working Paper, August; http://ssrn.com/abstract=442260.

Consumer Affairs.com (2003). *Sears Sells its Credit-Card Business*, 15 July; http://www.consumer affairs.com Inc.

Damant, D. (2005). *Overview – European Equity Research and Analysis: Preparing for the 2005 Transition to International Financial Reporting Standards.* CFA Institute Conference Proceedings of the CFA Institute; http://www.cfapubs.org.

Deloitte IAS PLUS (2003). *International Accounting Standards Health Check.*

Deloitte IAS PLUS (2004). *IASB Board Meeting – Conceptual Framework.* IASB Offices, London, September.

Deloitte IAS PLUS (2005a). *IASB Agenda Project Conceptual Framework.* IASB Board Meeting, July.

Deloitte IAS PLUS (2005b). *International Accounting Standards Health Check.*

Desmet, D., Francis, T., Hu, A., Koller, T.M., and Riedel, G.A. (2000). Valuing dot-coms. *McKinsey Quarterly*, 1:148–157.

Edey, H.C. and Panitpakdi, P. (1956). *British Company Accounting and the Law 1844–1900. Studies in the History of Accounting* (Littleton, A.C. and Yamey, B.S., eds). Sweet & Maxwell, London.

Eucken, W. (1951). *The Foundations of Economics: History and Theory in the Analysis of Economic Reality* (Hutchinson, J.W.H., trans.). University of Chicago Press, Chicago.

Faden, A. (1977). *Economics of Space and Time: The Measure Theoretic Foundations of Social Science.* Iowa University Press, Ames, IA.

FASAC – Financial Accounting Standards Advisory Council (2005). *Joint Conceptual Framework Project*, June.

FASB (1980). Qualitative Characteristics of Financial Statements. *Statement of Financial Accounting Concepts No. 2.* Financial Accounting Standards Board.

FASB (1984). Recognition and Measurement in Financial Statements of Business Enterprise. *Statement of Financial Accounting Concepts No. 5.* Financial Accounting Standards Board.

FASB and IASB – International Accounting Standards Board (2004). Information for Observers. Board Meeting, Project: Business Combinations II – Application of the Purchase Method (Agenda 6), 19 October.

Federal Reserve Board (2005). Principal Economic Indicators – Consumer Credit. *Statistics: Releases and Historical Data*; http://www.federalreserve.gov/Releases/.

Finley, M.I. (1973). *The Ancient Economy.* University of California Press, Berkeley, CA.

Fulcrum Financial Inquiry (2003). *Goodwill Valuations – The Good, The Bad and The Ugly*, 27 February; http://www.fulcruminquiry.com/article17.htm.

Grenadier, S.R. (1995). The Persistence of Real Estate Cycles. *Journal of Real Estate Finance and Economics*, 10(2):95–119.

Holthausen, R.W. and Watts, R.L. (2000). *The Relevance of the Value Relevance Literature for Financial Accounting Standard Setting.* Working Paper No. FR 00-05, The Bradley Policy Research Center – Financial Research and Policy, September.

IAIS – International Association of Insurance Supervisors (2004). Overview and Implications for Insurers. *The Insurance Supervisor*, Second Quarter Newsletter.

Ijiri, Y. and Nakano, I. (1989). Generalizations of Cost-or-Market Valuation. *Accounting Horizons*, 3(3):3–11.

Janssen, J., Kruijt, B., and Needham, B. (1994). The Honeycomb Cycle in Real Estate. *Journal of Real Estate Research*, 9(2):237–252.

Kling, J.L. and McCue, T.E. (1987). Office Building Investment and the Macro-Economy: Empirical Evidence, 1973–1985. *Journal of the American Real Estate and Urban Economics Association*, 15(3):234–255.

Krazit, T. (2003). WorldCom Slices $79.8B Off Balance Sheet in Write-Down, 14 March; http://www.computerworld.com.

Littleton, A.C. (1933). *Accounting Evolution to 1900.* American Institute Publishing Company; Russell & Russell, New York, 1966.

Meredith, P. (1966). *Instruments of Communication.* Pergamon Press, Oxford.

Newman, A.M. (2005). *A Peak at Optimism – The Greatest Stock Market Mania of All Times*, Samex Capital's Stock Market Crosscurrents, 20 July; http://www.investingadvisers.com.

PBS – The News Hour (1997). http://www.WorldCom Together. Online Focus, 10 November; www.pbs.org/newshour/bb/business/july-dec97/mci.

PBS – The News Hour (2001). America Online purchased Time Warner for $106 billion, 11 January. Real Audio: FCC Chairman William Kennard announces approval of the deal.

Penman, S.H. and Yehuda, N. (2004). The Pricing of Earnings and Cash Flows and an Affirmation of Accrual Accounting, 10 October; http://www.ssrn.com/abstract=603482.

Pirenne, H. (1933). *Economic and Social History of Medieval Europe* (Clegg, I.E., trans.). Harcourt, Brace & World, New York, 1937.

Redford, A. (1960). *The Economic History of England 1760–1860*, 2nd edn. Longman, London; Greenwood Press, Westport, CT, 1974.

RICS – Royal Institution of Chartered Surveyors (1999). *The UK Property Cycle – A History from 1921 to 1997.* The Royal Institution of Chartered Surveyors, London, January.

Salvary, S.C.W. (1981). An Historical Perspective of the Accounting Environment: A General Outline of a Western European and North American Linkage. Working Paper No. 50, *Academy of Accounting Historians Working Paper Series* (Bishop, A.C. and Richards, D., eds). James Madison University.

Salvary, S.C.W. (1985). *Accounting: A Library of Quantifications.* McQueen Accounting Monograph Series, Vol. 1. University of Arkansas, Fayetteville, AR. Reprinted by Stanversal Publishing, 2003; http://www.stanversal.com.

Salvary, S.C.W. (1989). *An Analytical Framework for Accounting Theory*, McQueen Accounting Monograph Series. University of Arkansas, Fayetteville, AR. Reprinted by Stanversal Publishing, 2003; http://www.stanversal.com.

Salvary, S.C.W. (1992). Recoverable Cost: The Basis of a General Theory of Financial Accounting Measurement. *Accounting Enquiries*, 1(2):233–273.

Salvary, S.C.W. (1993). On the Historical Validity of Nominal Money as a Measure of Organizational Performance: Some Evidence and Logical Analysis. *Essays in Economic and Business History*, 11:153–177.

Salvary, S.C.W. (1997). On Financial Accounting Measurement: A Reconsideration of SFAC 5 by the FASB is Needed. *Journal of Applied Business Research*, 13(3):89–103.

Salvary, S.C.W. (1998a). Accounting and Financial Reporting in a Changing Environment: Historical and Theoretical Perspectives. *Essays in Economic and Business History*, 16:307–329.

Salvary, S.C.W. (1998b). The Accounting Variable and Stock Price Determination. *Studies in Economics and Finance*, 18(2):26–61.

Salvary, S.C.W. (1998c). Financial Accounting Measurement: Instrumentation and calibration. *Accounting Enquiries*, 7(2):225–274.

Salvary, S.C.W. (2003). Financial Accounting Information and the Relevance/Irrelevance Issue. *Global Business and Economics Review*, 5(2):140–175.

Salvary, S.C.W. (2004). *The Underinvestment Problem, Risk Management, and Corporate Earnings Retention.* RePEc:wpa:wuwpfi:0410012, October.

Simmel, G. (1978). *The Philosophy of Money* (Bottomore, T. and Frisby, D., trans.). Routledge & Kegan Paul, London.

Smirlock, M., Gilligan, T., and Marshall, W. (1984). Tobin's Q and the Structure–Performance Relationship. *American Economic Review*, 74(2):1051–1060.

Special Committee (1994). *Improving Business Reporting – A Customer Focus: Meeting the Information Needs of Investors and Creditors.* Comprehensive Report of the Special Committee on Financial Reporting, American Institute of Certified Public Accountants.

Steuart, Sir J. (1767). *An Inquiry into the Principles of Political Economy: Being an Essay on the Science of Domestic Policy in Free Nations in Which are Particularly Considered Population, Agriculture, Trade, Industry, Money, Coin, Interest, Circulation, Banks, Exchange, Public Credit, and Taxes*, Vol. 1. Edited with an introduction by Andrew S. Skinner. University of Chicago Press, Chicago; Oliver & Boyd, London, 1966.

Trevino, R. and Higgs, R. (1992). Profits of US Defense Contractors. *Defence Economics*, 3(3): 211–218.

Wolverton, T. (2003). *Sears Completes Credit Card Portfolio Sale to Citigroup*, 3 November; http://www.thestreet.com.

Zwirn, E. (2005). Business Combo Proposal Creating Rifts, July 18; http://www.cfo.com.

5

Fair Value Accounting Under IAS/IFRS: Concepts, Reasons, Criticisms

Jochen Zimmermann and
Jörg-Richard Werner

5.1 Introduction

Over the past years financial accounting has – in many areas and for several reasons – been turning away from historical cost numbers. This trend has been supported by empirical findings that the information content of traditional (historic cost) financial accounting is low and may even decline over time (Lev and Zarowin, 1999). The IASB, as the standard setter of the International Financial Reporting Standards (IFRS; earlier International Accounting Standards – IAS), seems to favor fair values (FVs) over historical cost (HC) in many reporting situations. Several standards allow or even prescribe FVs for the measurement in periods after initial recognition. The IASB does not yet propose 'full' fair value accounting (FVA), which would be characterized by recognizing every asset and liability at its FV (and through profit or loss), though recent standards and drafts of the IASB show a clear expansion tendency in the use of FVs. Examples include the fair value option in IAS 39 or the fair value model as proposed in the joint IASB/FASB project on revenue recognition. Describing extensively every opportunity or obligation to use FVs in IAS/IFRS would be beyond the scope of this chapter. Our aim is not to give a comprehensive overview of the application of FVA in IAS/IFRS, but to discuss its basic concepts and the underlying reasons for application of FVA, as well as addressing criticism against it.

The chapter is organized as follows. In section 5.2, basic properties of FVA and the scope of its application under IAS/IFRS are described. In section 5.2.1, a definition of FV (as in IAS/IFRS) is provided. FVA leads to regular revaluations of assets and liabilities and thus begs the question how positive revaluation amounts should be dealt with. This issue will be addressed in section 5.3 and the consequences for capital maintenance in section 5.3.1. Section 5.4 will give some examples of FVA under IAS/IFRS. In particular, revaluations of property, plant, and equipment (IAS 16), intangibles (IAS 38), financial instruments (IAS 39), and investment property (IAS 40) will be discussed. Obviously, FVA's range of applications under IAS/IFRS is relatively broad at present. However, the range of applications could even increase. Thus, it is important whether FVA can be justified from a theoretical perspective. First, FVA may be justified by the argument that it increases decision usefulness (and thus value relevance) of financial reports (section 5.5.1). Second, leaving reporting entities with the option of adopting either the cost or the revaluation model, their choice provides a signal (about their quality) to the capital market. This is discussed in section 5.5.2. Third, we address the question of whether FVA might prove to be a hurdle for the harmonization process between internal and external reporting in impeding contracting with managers based on accounting measures (section 5.5.3). Finally, section 5.6 concludes.

5.2 Fair value accounting and the IFRS: basic properties and scope of application

5.2.1 Definition of fair values

The IASB defines FV in several IAS/IFRS as 'the amount for which an asset could be exchanged, or a liability settled, between knowledgeable, willing parties in an arm's length transaction' (e.g. IAS 18.7). While this definition is rather intuitive, it is unclear how to measure FVs in many reporting situations. The definition of FV refers to an observable market value based on an 'arm's length transaction'. In practice, however, there are many problems related to the measurement of FV. While the definition sounds reasonable, its usefulness for practical purposes is poor: observable and 'objective' market values remain limited only to the (exceptional) cases in which an active market exists. If such a market does exist, the use of FV is sometimes labeled as 'marking to market'. Active market values may be absent for several reasons: markets may be inefficient – for example, when transactions occur only rarely. Assets or liabilities may probably not be fungible at all (e.g. for special assets or intellectual property), or markets may be incomplete. In these cases, it is not clear which value should be used as an estimate for FV. Values can be derived from professional appraisers; other methods include broadly accepted valuation models such as discounted cash-flow estimations or the 'Black and Scholes' technique for valuation of options. When such models are applied, the use of FV leads to a 'marking to model' estimate. The most serious disadvantage of valuation models is their extensive reliance on management's subjective estimates and assumptions. Thus, not only measurement errors may occur, but, even worse, managers may deliberately distort financial reports. This relates to the classical tradeoff in accounting that actual or forward looking (here: FV) information is demanded but cannot be supplied reliably (Lambert, 1999). Hence, proponents of FVA praise its decision usefulness, while critics point to the fact that there are implementation problems, and a serious lack of objectivity and verifiability (Magee, 1978).

5.2.2 Treatment of holding gains and losses

Market values, net realizable values, net selling prices – or other FV estimates – are typically used in financial accounting systems to adjust carrying amounts downwards. As Cotter and Richardson (2002, p. 435) point out, adjustments to values below historical costs are not at all contentious as the recognition of impairments is in line with the conservative nature of accounting. Accounting systems with obligatory impairment tests, followed up by asset write-downs and prohibition of asset write-ups over historical cost, are 'conservative' because they require a higher degree of verification for recognizing good news than bad news in financial statements (Basu, 1997, p. 4). Thus, under conservatism, holding losses are (asymmetrically) realized while holding gains are not. This is an important reason for HCA's systematic differences in the timeliness and persistence of earnings in bad-news and good-news periods (Basu, 1997, p. 4).

The principal difference between HCA and FVA is the underlying allocation pattern of holding gains (Magee, 1978, p. 47). Under HCA, a market transaction (i.e. the sale of goods) always precedes revenue recognition[1]. When the market value of a certain asset exceeds its carrying amount, a holding gain arises that will not be realized until this asset is sold. Under FVA, a revaluation would lead to realization of that 'holding' gain. Recognition under FVA makes accounting earnings more symmetrical: not only are future negative developments (i.e. risks) immediately recognized, but also future positive developments (i.e. chances) can or have to be. Allowing positive revaluations is a controversial matter in standard setting, as subjective FV estimates may lead to less reliable and thus less relevant information in financial statements (e.g. Easton et al., 1993). This would be exactly the opposite of what proponents of FVA want to achieve (Cotter and Richardson, 2002, p. 435). While (positive, upward) revaluations are, until now, generally – and in particular for long-lived fixed assets – not allowed under US and German GAAP, they have a long tradition in both Australian and UK GAAP. The IASB seems to be predisposed towards FVA because IAS/IFRS allow or even prescribe fair valuation in many reporting situations[2]. However, the treatment/realization of holding gains is different under different standards. In some standards, holding gains are recognized in earnings; in others, they are merely documented in equity (and thus affect only comprehensive, but not net, income).

5.2.3 FVA and capital maintenance

Under HCA, increasing prices of assets normally do not affect the accounting numbers. This relates to a certain concept of capital maintenance. Capital maintenance concepts define which part of a period's 'increase' in capital (if any) can be regarded as profit. HCA maintains capital as the original (nominal) money capital. This is a specific form of financial capital maintenance (which can be measured either in nominal monetary units or in units of constant purchasing power).

In contrast, FVA is sensible to current price changes (regardless of whether these price changes can be traced back to inflation or other changes in the market values of specific assets). In a number of IAS/IFRS, revaluations lead to a recognition of increased asset values (and to an increase in equity, but not to an increase in income of that period). As the revalued asset will be depreciated over the remaining useful time, depreciation amounts will increase (compared to former depreciation based on historical cost). Thus, FVA considers increased replacement costs: after revaluation, a period's income is positive only if the depreciation amount based on current cost is earned. This relates strongly to the concept of 'physical capital maintenance' as defined in the IFRS Framework. Under this capital maintenance rule, a profit is earned 'only if the physical productive capacity of the enterprise (or the resources of funds needed to achieve that capacity) at the end of the period exceeds the physical productive capacity at the beginning of the period, after excluding any distributions to, and contributions from, owners during the period' (F.104). Under the concept of 'physical capital maintenance', increases in prices of assets held over the period, conventionally referred to as holding gains, are treated as capital maintenance adjustments – that is, part of equity and not of profit (F.109).

FVA also relates, albeit not strictly, to economic income. If the FVA estimate is the present value of an asset's future net cash inflows, the usefulness of a particular asset for a particular firm – possibly in combination with other assets (cash generating units) – is recognized in the balance sheet. However, measuring an economically 'correct' value of the firm is complicated. The best proxy is its market value. In a world of perfect and complete markets and certainty, fair values (or market values) of all thinkable assets and liabilities would be well defined and observable. Then and only then would it be possible to explain a market value of a firm as the sum of its net assets. Supposing the theoretical case that equity can be measured as present value of all future cash flows of the firm, the degree to which equity of the previous period has been maintained tells to what extent management was able to hold (or increase) the potential of the firm to generate future cash flows. It is beyond dispute that managers should maintain or even increase this ability, and incentives that would encourage them to do just that should be set.

However, existing FVA systems are far from measuring equity as the present value of a firm's future cash flows. FVA in the real world may reduce the gap between the market value and book value of the firm, but it does not measure the firm's value in a way that helps to determine the Hicksian income: the balance sheet (even in an FVA system) is not a complete list of the firm's investment projects measured at net present value. Thus, it is not that clear what the capital maintenance concept of FVA under IFRS exactly is. Alexander (2003, p. 18) attempts to define that in such a system 'the capital to be maintained is the fair value of the (net) assets, i.e. profit is the increase in the fair value of the net assets at the end of the period over that at the beginning of the period'. However, as Alexander (2003) notices himself, this definition is somewhat tautological. He concludes that the IASB should clearly articulate the associated concept of capital maintenance under FVA and demands a clearer conceptual understanding of when FV should be used.

5.2.4 FVA and IAS/IFRS: scope of application

Under IFRS, the use of FV is allowed or prescribed in numerous standards. For example, IAS 16 ('Property, Plant, and Equipment'), IAS 38 ('Intangibles'), and IAS 40 ('Investment Property') allow reporting entities to opt either for the revaluation (i.e. FV) or the cost model. Most financial instruments (regulated in IAS 32 and 39), however, have to be recognized at FV. As already pointed out, even under historical cost accounting, FVs play a role. They are usually invoked to adjust carrying amounts downwards. The same holds also for IAS/IFRS. According to IAS 36 ('Impairment of Assets'), an entity has to assess at each reporting date whether there is any internal or external indication that an asset may be impaired (IAS 36.9). If such indications are given, an impairment test has to be carried out. Impairment losses must be recognized if an asset's carrying amount exceeds its recoverable amount. The recoverable amount of an asset (or a cash-generating unit) is defined as the higher value of either the fair value minus costs-to-sell or the value-in-use (IAS 36.18). The best estimate for FV is a current bid price in an active market or a binding sale agreement at arm's length (IAS 36.25–26). However, in the absence of binding sale agreements or active markets, less reliable estimates for FV are also admissible (IAS 36.27). While FV is somehow objectified on markets, value-in-use is not. The latter measures the value that an entity subjectively attributes to a particular asset. Value-in-use is thus computed as the discounted cash flow of the estimated future cash flows derived from an asset's continuing use (IAS 36.31). Thus, in IAS 36, FV and value-in-use are not equal: FV needs (at least some) justification by the market. This is true for most estimations of FV in IAS/IFRS. However, it is hard to separate FV from value-in-use in cases in which FV is derived from a valuation model ('marking to model').

Figure 5.1 depicts an example, where in t_1 an asset is written down to its recoverable amount. The dotted line shows the new carrying amounts over the useful life of that asset lying below the (bold) line of initially expected carrying amounts over time. After an impairment loss was recognized, it might happen that in some period (here: t_2) the recoverable amount exceeds the (new) carrying amount (dotted line). Then, the asset has to be written up. However, under the cost model (e.g. in IAS 16), the increased carrying amount can never exceed the (net) carrying amount initially expected (bold line), which is the carrying amount that would have been determined if no impairment loss had been recognized in prior years (IAS 36.117). This distinguishes HCA from the 'real' FVA that works more symmetrically. Under FVA, positive revaluations may not only exceed historical cost (above the bold line), they also do not rely on the occurrence of a prior recognition of impairment losses.

Beyond impairments, revaluations are, for example, allowed in IAS 16, IAS 38, IAS 39, and IAS 40. However, the handling of FVA differs in these different IAS with respect to the treatment of revaluation amounts or the estimation of FV. Table 5.1 gives an overview of IAS examples for the different treatments. These differences will now be briefly discussed.

Following IAS 16, all assets are initially recognized at cost (IAS 16.15). For the measurement in subsequent periods, an entity can opt either for the cost or the revaluation model for entire classes of property (IAS 16.29). Opting for the revaluation model requires additional disclosures. These include the effective date of the revaluation and information on whether an independent valuer was involved

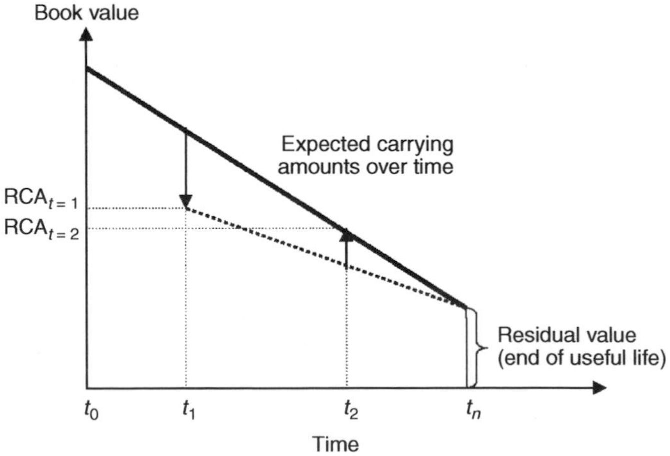

Figure 5.1 Impairment and reversion of impairments under HCA

Table 5.1 IAS example for the applied FVA models in IFRS

IAS	IAS 16 ('Property, Plant, and Equipment')	IAS 39 ('Financial Instruments')	IAS 40 ('Investment Property')
Measurement at recognition	At cost (IAS 16.15).	At FV as on the date of acquisition or issuance corrected for transaction costs (IAS 39.43).	At cost including transaction costs (IAS 40.20).
Measurement after recognition	'Cost model' or 'revaluation model' for entire classes of property (IAS 16.29).	Depends on the classification of a particular asset or liability. Assets are generally measured at FV, apart from available-for-sale assets or loans and receivables. Liabilities are generally measured at amortized cost; some liabilities (e.g. derivatives) are measured at FV (IAS 39.47).	Either by revaluation or cost model for all investments (IAS 40.30). Presupposes that FVs can be reliably determined on a continuing basis (otherwise, cost model prescribed).
Determination of FV	FVs of land and buildings are determined by professional (external) appraisers. FV of machinery, office equipment, etc. is determined by internal estimates (IAS 16.32). In the absence of active markets for particular assets, 'marking to model' applies (IAS 16.33).	If available, the best FV estimate is a quoted market price in an active market (IAS 39, AG71). In the absence of active markets, valuation techniques have to be applied ('marking to model') (IAS 39, AG74).	Best estimates are current prices in an active market (IAS 40.45). If not available, other estimates include (a) prices of properties of different nature, condition, or location; (b) adjusted prices in less active markets; (c) discounted cash-flow projections (IAS 40.46).

(Continued)

Table 5.1 (*Continued*)

IAS	IAS 16 ('Property, Plant, and Equipment')	IAS 39 ('Financial Instruments')	IAS 40 ('Investment Property')
Frequency of revaluations	Depends on the changes in FV of particular assets. Some assets need revaluations annually, while for others revaluations every three or five years are sufficient (IAS 16.34).	On every balance sheet date (IAS 39.55).	On every balance sheet date (IAS 40.38).
Treatment of revaluation gains and losses	Increases are, in general, directly credited to equity (revaluation surplus), while decreases are recognized as a loss. If an increase reverses a previous decrease, it is (to that amount) recognized as profit, and vice versa (IAS 16.39–40).	Depends on whether an asset is classified as available for sale (AVS) or as 'at fair value through profit or loss'. Revaluation amounts of the latter category are recognized as profit or loss (IAS 39.55a). Changes in the value of AVS assets are directly recorded in equity (IAS 39.55b). Revaluation of FV liabilities also affects net income (IAS 39.47a).	FV changes are recognized immediately in profit or loss in the period of their occurrence (IAS 40.35).
Disclosure requirements	Application of the revaluation model is accompanied by numerous disclosure	Disclosure requirements include information on the nature of the financial	Disclosure requirements include: method of determining fair

Table 5.1 *(Continued)*

IAS	IAS 16 ('Property, Plant, and Equipment')	IAS 39 ('Financial Instruments')	IAS 40 ('Investment Property')
	requirements. These include the effective date of the revaluation and the information of whether an independent valuer was involved (IAS 16.77).	instruments, as well as terms and conditions that may affect the amount, timing, and certainty of future cash flows (IAS 32.92).	value, extent of use of independent valuers, criteria that were used to classify property as investment, and classified amounts recognized in profit or loss (IAS 40.75).

(IAS 16.77). FVs of land and buildings shall be determined by market-based estimates by professional (external) appraisers, while the FV of machinery or furniture can be determined by internal judgment of the respective market value (IAS 16.32). In the absence of active markets for particular assets (e.g. because of the specialized nature of an asset), either marking to model or a depreciated replacement cost approach applies (IAS 16.33). Revaluations, then, have to be carried out regularly. The appropriate frequency, however, depends on the character of the respective asset. Some assets require annual revaluation; others will face only insignificant changes in FV over time. For the latter, revaluations every three or five years may be considered as appropriate (IAS 16.34). Revaluation losses are commonly recognized in earnings; however, revaluation gains, in general, do not affect earnings. Such increases are directly credited to equity (under a special position labeled 'revaluation surplus'), except when that increase reverses a revaluation decrease previously recognized as profit or loss (IAS 16.39). Similarly, revaluation decreases are not recognized as a loss if they reverse previous positive revaluations of an asset. Instead, these decreases are debited directly to the revaluation surplus in equity (IAS 16.40). With regard to the treatment of revaluation gains and losses, the revaluation model of IAS 38 works in a similar fashion.

This does not apply to IAS 40 where, under the revaluation model, all gains or losses arising from changes in the FV of investment property have to be recognized in earnings of the period in which they arise (IAS 40.35). As in IAS 16, the initial recognition is at cost (including transaction costs), and the balance sheet preparer can choose either the revaluation or the cost model (corresponding to IAS 16). However, the respective model has to be applied for all investment property of that entity (IAS 40.30). That is, if the revaluation model is chosen, all investment property has to be revalued at each balance sheet date, except such investment property for which the FV is not reliably determinable on a continuing basis (IAS 40.53). The IASB's rebuttable assumption is that it is always possible to determine the FV of investment property. That assumption may be rejected if market transactions are infrequent and alternative reliable FV estimates are not available (IAS 40.53). The best estimates of FVs are current prices in active markets (IAS 40.45). If such prices are not available, however, other estimates can suffice, including (a) current prices in an active market for properties of different nature, condition, or location, (b) recent prices of similar properties on less active markets, with adjustments, and (c) discounted cash-flow projections based on reliable estimates of future cash flows (IAS 40.46).

In IAS 39, a mixture of both treatments of unrealized gains can be found. In general, all financial instruments are initially recognized at FV as on the date of acquisition or issuance, corrected for transaction costs (IAS 39.43). For the measurement in subsequent periods, all financial instruments have to be classified. Financial assets have to be classified either as (a) held-to-maturity, (b) loans and receivables, (c) financial assets at fair value through profit or loss, or as (d) assets available for sale (IAS 39.45). After initial recognition, assets in the first two categories are subsequently measured at amortized costs, while all other assets are measured at FV. Financial liabilities are generally measured at amortized cost (using the effective interest method). Nevertheless, some liabilities (e.g. derivatives) have to be measured at FV (IAS 39.47). If available, the best FV estimate here is a quoted market price in an active market (IAS 39, AG71). If such market prices do not exist, other valuation techniques have to be applied ('marking to model') (IAS 39, AG74). Revaluations occur on every balance sheet date. The treatment of unrealized gains depends on whether an asset is classified as available for sale (AVS), or as 'at fair value through profit or loss'. Increases in value of the latter category are recognized as profit (IAS 39.55a), while increases in the value of AVS assets are directly recorded in equity (IAS 39.55b). Revaluations of liabilities measured at FV also affect net income (IAS 39.47a).

Apparently, the most distinctive feature of FVA in different IAS standards is the treatment of unrealized holding gains. Crediting revaluation surpluses directly into equity corresponds to the concept of physical capital maintenance. FV through profit and loss is, in fact, closer to maintaining economic capital.

However, the extensive (and probably increasing) use of FV under IFRS might merely be attributed to the fact that the IASB (now) follows a balance-sheet-oriented (often labeled as 'static') approach to financial accounting. In the next sections, we will discuss this development (i.e. the justification of FVA) from different theoretical viewpoints. As a starting point, we discuss value relevance (i.e. decision usefulness and reliability) of FVs. Further on, we discuss FVA under a signaling perspective and finally will ask how FVA relates to harmonization of management and financial accounting, i.e. whether FVA is useful for contracting with managers.

5.3 Justifications for the use of fair values in financial reporting

5.3.1 Value relevance and standard setting

From the standard setter's (i.e. the IASB's) perspective, decision relevance is the basic goal of financial reporting. Thus, it is a natural question whether FVA increases decision usefulness of financial reports. If FVs are in fact relevant for investment decision-making, it can be hypothesized that material (unexpected) revaluation surpluses (or decreases) have information content, and thus generate share price revisions (Emanuel, 1989, p. 213). According to this hypothesis, decision usefulness of accounting measures can be empirically examined by means of value relevance regressions (for a critical discussion of this branch of research, see Holthausen and Watts, 2001; see also Barth et al., 2001, for another view). Value relevance studies jointly test whether some accounting information is useful and reliable for investors (Cotter and Richardson, 2002, p. 436f). There are several studies concerned with the question of whether FVs affect market prices[3]. As property revaluations are common in Australia and the UK (Easton et al., 1993), numerous empirical studies use data from these countries. However, revaluations of tangible long-lived assets (generally possible in IAS/IFRS) are not legal under US GAAP. Nevertheless, some securities by banks, insurance companies, or mutual funds are also subject to FVA (Danbolt and Rees, 2003, p. 3), which allows performing value relevance studies with US data in at least these areas. Overall, empirical evidence on revaluations being value relevant is mixed (for an overview of main findings, see e.g. Danbolt and Rees, 2003). Standish and Ung (1982) found only a moderate association between revaluation announcements and stock price revisions, uncorrelated with the size of revaluation.

They suppose that revaluations may only be a pointer for other favorable signals to be priced (Standish and Ung, 1982, p. 704). Emanuel (1989) fails to provide clear evidence that asset revaluations generate share price revisions. Barth (1994), in addition, argues that weak evidence on pricing effects of revaluations might be traced to estimation errors or sectional differences in sample firms. Limiting her analysis to the banking industry, Barth (1994) finds disclosed FVs of investment securities to have explanatory power beyond historical costs. To name a few, Easton et al. (1993), Easton and Eddey (1997), Barth and Clinch (1998), Harris and Muller (1998), and Aboody et al. (1999) also found evidence that revaluation surpluses are indeed relevant for capital markets.

For standard setting, there are further remarkable empirical findings – beyond the basic fact that FVs have value relevance in very different environments and reporting situations. Those findings relate to objectivity, the respective market structure, and the noise components in FV estimates. For example, Barth and Clinch (1998) found evidence that the market usually considers both director and independent revaluations as value relevant. The authors explain this by the fact that, on average, the communication of director's private information through FVA outweighs potential manipulations[4]. Cotter and Richardson (2002) found no significant differences in the reliability of internal versus independent revaluations of long-lived assets, except that of plant and equipment. Given these findings, the IASB's marking-to-model approach in situations where active markets are absent is not as problematic as might be assessed at first sight. However, from Petroni and Wahlen (1995), it can be concluded that the existence of active markets is, in some situations, a prerequisite for value relevance. Here, the authors found that FVs of securities traded in highly liquid (i.e. active) markets were value relevant, while FVs of securities traded in less liquid markets were not. Mixed models (like in IAS/IFRS), in which some assets or liabilities are measured at FV while others are not, can be justified by such findings.

Beaver and Venkatachalam (2000) split fair value disclosures of US banks into nondiscretionary, discretionary, and noise components, and found only noise components not to be priced (while the others were priced to different degrees). Thus, from a standard setter's perspective, with the market making them out, noise in market values should be no problem. Interestingly, nondiscretionary components in FV estimates – often criticized – are priced at a multiple of greater than one. Beaver and Venkatachalam (2000) explain this by signaling: management's usage of discretionary fair value disclosures signals future company performance.

5.3.2 Revaluations as signals

Motivations for voluntary revaluations (i.e. choosing the revaluation model instead of the cost model in IAS/IFRS) are not at all self-evident. Scholarly literature provides several explanations (Emanuel, 1989, p. 213). First, revaluations may be helpful in fending off hostile takeovers. Second, revaluations might enhance the matching of expenses with their respective revenues – because of the subsequent charging of current values instead of historical costs (which goes in line with the concept of physical capital maintenance). Third, revaluations allow for disclosure of an entity's 'true' borrowing capacity. Fourth, FVA might lead to the presentation of a (more) true and fair view of a particular company (Standish and Ung, 1982).

Whatever the motivation, voluntary revaluations in fact do deliver signals to the capital market. The only question is, then, whether a revaluation is considered as good or bad news. There are theoretical arguments for both. Lin and Peasnell (1998) point out that, *ceteris paribus*, upward revaluations result in a decrease in return on equity. This being detrimental, revaluations will only be taken out if there is inside information about future positive developments, e.g. an increase in earnings. Increased future cash inflows may then be supposed to overcompensate the increased depreciation amounts in the subsequent periods after the upward revaluation (otherwise, a revaluation would not take place). Thus, the revaluation is, in fact, a forecast of increased future earnings (Standish and Ung, 1982, p. 702). Further, positive revaluations lead to an increase in equity. That has a beneficial effect on the debt-to-equity ratio and may signal a potential for raising further debt.

However, there is also the possibility that capital markets consider revaluations as a negative signal. When the markets do not believe that future earnings will increase, a revaluation announcement appears dubious. Likewise, revaluations are questionable when they take place as a part of a defense strategy against hostile takeovers. Additionally, the signal that a firm has no other possibility to raise further debt than revaluating its assets may also be considered as negative.

Whether the market interprets revaluations as good or as bad news will depend on the particular economic situation that a company faces. First, the costs connected to revaluations have to be considered. Those include, for example, fees for professional appraisers, opportunity costs of internal valuation, additional audit costs, and 'increases in the likelihood of actions against the firm by claimants if the new valuation is not realized' (Cotter and Zimmer, 1995, p. 137). A revaluation will take place only if the benefits from a revaluation exceed its costs. However, there are also costs connected with refraining from revaluating assets, which have to be considered as well (i.e. costs of suboptimal contracting). Examples are opportunity costs of underinvestment or added costs of inefficient financing strategies (Cotter and Zimmer, 1995, p. 137). These costs allow successful firms to signal their true status by omitting possible positive revaluations and thus to separate themselves from less successful firms (Gaeremynck and Veuglers, 1999, p. 124). This is illustrated by the following example based on revaluations of property, plant, and equipment pursuant to IAS 16. Let us first assume that a higher proportion of equity has positive effects on a company's capital costs. This is somewhat plausible because the equity-to-debt ratio plays a crucial role in ratings that determine costs-of-debt financing. Let us further assume that there are some payments tied to earnings – for example, taxes or parts of executive compensation. Our last assumption implies that, according to either expected increases or decreases of future net cash inflows, successful and less successful companies can be separated and therefore the firm's managers know whether their company is a successful one.

Assuming increasing market prices, revaluation of long-lived assets will lead to a higher proportion of equity in the balance sheet. However, in subsequent periods, earnings will – everything else being equal – be lower if a revaluation took place because of increased depreciation amounts. While this is at a first glance a disadvantage, all payments tied to earnings will also decrease. In the short run, a revaluation thus has two advantages: first, the equity-to-debt ratio improves (i.e. capital costs decrease) and, second, the discounted future savings of decreased earnings-based payments materialize. The question now is, though: Why do not all companies opt for FVA[5]? A plausible answer is that (assuming rational expectations) managers use the option to communicate private information about the firm's true economic situation to the market. Under ideal conditions, a separating equilibrium exists in which it is strictly advantageous for successful firms to opt for the cost model (and vice versa)[6]. Therefore, we have to assume that the capital market assesses companies based on the chosen valuation model (i.e. the cost or the revaluation model), and that applying the cost model signals for successful firms[7]. In separation equilibrium, the two types of firms can clearly be distinguished because the choice has different consequences.

Like unsuccessful firms, successful firms also have *a priori* advantages of opting for the revaluation model (i.e. lower capital costs). However, the serious disadvantage for successful firms is that there will be unjustified discounts in their market values, because they are supposed to be unsuccessful ones. A 'bad' firm opting for the cost model signals that it is a 'good' firm and will have a better valuation than appropriate (see Table 5.2). However, capital costs do not decrease if

Table 5.2 Effects of the cost and revaluation models in successful and unsuccessful firms

Valuation model	Type of firm	
	Successful firm (increasing future cash flows)	Unsuccessful firm (decreasing future cash flows)
Cost model	Earnings-based payments increase No advantage from higher equity-to-debt ratio Fair pricing as successful firm	Earnings-based payments are equal or decrease No advantage from higher equity-to-debt ratio Market supposes firm as successful: pricing with premium
Revaluation model	Earnings-based payments are equal or even increase Advantage from higher equity-to-debt ratio Market regards firm as unsuccessful: pricing with discount	Earnings-based payments decrease Advantage from higher equity-to-debt ratio Fair pricing as unsuccessful firm

the revaluation model is not exerted. This allows drawing the following two conclusions: first, the successful firm will not opt for the revaluation model because the managers want to signal that the firm is – according to the true economic situation – a successful one. The economic rationale behind this behavior is that positive outcomes from a revaluation will not be significant, or even be overcompensated by the negative effect of a discount in market value. The second conclusion, accordingly, is that unsuccessful firms can reap bigger advantages from opting for the revaluation model.

It should be stressed that the previous example is simplifying in some respects. First, it is questionable whether the hypothesized decrease in cost of capital will materialize. Second, earnings-based payments are usually not measured using (consolidated) IAS/IFRS reports. Third, a separating equilibrium need not necessarily exist. Fourth, the signal connected to revaluations may not be timely. Fifth, the signal may be connected to others and may not allow an inference of whether a firm really is successful.

Empirical literature provides some characteristics of firms that typically undertake asset revaluations. Among the findings are that firms are more likely to carry out revaluations when leverage is high (to increase borrowing capacity). Cotter and Zimmer (1995) also point to the fact that revaluations are more likely when operating cash flows in the current period are lower than in the previous one. This effect is even stronger when leverage is high (Cotter and Zimmer, 1995, p. 138). Brown et al. (1992) and Whittred and Chan (1992) found that positive revaluations of long-lived assets are associated with the existence of debt contracts, high leverage, reduction of political costs, simultaneous issues of bonus shares, and avoidance of hostile takeover bids (Cotter and Zimmer, 1995, p. 136). These findings suggest that accounting choices related to FVA provide important signals to capital markets.

5.3.3 Fair value accounting, contracting, and incentives

Decisions concerning financial accounting have possible implications for management accounting and control. Following the IASB's Framework, financial statements shall also inform about 'the results of management's stewardship of the resources entrusted to it' (F.7). If that is the case, incentives can broadly rely on financial accounting measures. This, in fact, would be the key for a harmonization of financial and management accounting often regarded to be achievable by IAS/IFRS reporting. However, there are serious concerns that such harmonization is possible, in particular with respect to FVA.

For contracting and incentive setting, an appropriate assessment base (i.e. a performance measure) has to be found. A performance measure has to serve (at least) the purposes of motivation and control. In more detail, the measure has to fulfill several criteria. To name a few, managers first must be able to influence the respective measure. Second, the measure must be timely. Third, the measure has to be representative of the quality of the agent's work (thus, higher effort has to lead to a higher measure and vice versa). Fourth, the measure should not be (too) susceptible to manipulation. Fifth, the measure should establish compatible incentives; increasing the measure should satisfy both the principal's as well as the agent's interests. Finally, the measure has to allow for Pareto-efficient risk-sharing (Laux, 1999, pp. 29, 81). These criteria are not fully achievable in total because of trade-offs. Interestingly, not all of the criteria should be satisfied entirely to achieve optimal solutions. For example, it is not always advisable to use a performance measure that is (totally) unsusceptible to manipulation. Demski et al. (2004) show that, in some cases, the principal may have advantages even if the agent manipulates the accounting system to get higher rewards linked to the (manipulated) performance measure. The agent can (try to) influence performance, and thus payment, through increasing his productive effort, but he can also manipulate the measure – e.g. by altering the effective date a sale is consummated, by deferring or accelerating recognition of various revenues and expenses, or by specifying self-serving transaction prices, discount rates, or FV estimates. The principal wants to attempt losses from such manipulations and has – at least – three ways to do that. The first possibility is reducing the direct payoff agents anticipate from manipulation; the second is to increase the agent's cost of manipulation; the third, more 'subtle', possibility consists of limiting losses from manipulation by encouraging and facilitating manipulations. The explanation for this apparently counter-intuitive finding is simple: if an organization helps an agent to manipulate the system, private returns from devoting effort to further manipulation may decrease; employees may thus devote their effort to improving the real (rather than the measured) performance. Even if this behavior seems to be somewhat perverted, it opens the door for a contracting use of FV.

Let us first suppose that an FVA system is used in addition to HCA, i.e. that there are additional FV disclosures. Those disclosures may suffer from measurement errors and a lack of reliability. However, they provide additional information not conveyed in the HCA performance measure. Thus, regardless how noisy they are, it may have a welfare-enhancing effect to (additionally) rely on them in contracts (if there are no observation and administration costs)[8]. Using FVA instead of traditional HCA will change the performance measure. The question then is whether the (new) performance measure is more informative about the agent's action(s). Changing the assessment base, however, may also have some 'real world implications' because the agent may change his effort spending (with respect to his utility maximization and a compensation contract given). Effort may be then spent more extensively on maintaining capital, for two reasons: first, capital maintenance under FVA (as applied in IAS 16) is harder to achieve than under HCA[9]. Second, FVA earnings (as affected by IAS 39 or IAS 40) tend to be more volatile. If managers are now assessed on the basis of an FVA performance measure, they may have stronger incentives to maintain capital than under HCA. The explanation is straightforward. If management is obliged to maintain a firm's equity during an accounting period and gets assessed on that issue, strong incentives are set to prevent losses in equity value through hedging strategies, which may contribute to a significant growth in the utilization of derivates that protect the FV of the firm's equity. Even for small firms, management will become a very complex task: the more complete the FVA system, the more complex is management. Barlev and Haddad (2003, p. 399) expect that the use of FVA allows principals to better evaluate the outcome of their managers' decisions regarding the selection of assets and liabilities for current operations or hedging.

Critics point to the fact that hedging activities may then become equal or even more important than looking for new optimal investment projects. Thus, much effort may be allocated to merely unproductive or nonoperating actions. Several analytical studies examined the allocation of effort, incentives, and favorability of FVA for management control. Magee (1978) explored the effects of current versus historical valuation on the structure of incentives. He found that the agent's allocation of effort will be different under different valuation rules, and concluded that, under HCA, agents will in general neglect future consequences of their actions and concentrate on current operations. Bachar et al. (1997) compared equilibrium dead-weight losses, due to transacting and auditing, across historical cost, lower-of-cost-or-market and FV regimes. One interesting result of this particular study is that it can be favorable to choose different reporting measures for different types of assets. Kirschenheiter (1999) used a principal–agent framework to analyze optimal contracting under historical cost versus market value accounting standards. He showed that principals prefer market value accounting under a market structure, where net realizable values equal market values (because it provides better information about the manager's effort). In situations that are more uncertain, principals prefer historical cost accounting. In a way, these findings justify the IASB's mixed model approach on FVA. Dutta and Reichelstein (1999) showed, for a multi-period agency setting, that residual income combined with FVA for receivables shields managers from the risk associated with financing activities and provides an optimal performance measure. Gaber (2004) also argues that in some (restrictive) situations FVA has positive economic consequences. The latter study, however, is a good example of the need of setting very restrictive assumptions under which FVA turns out as being favorable to HCA. In general, the analytical literature does not recommend FVA for contracting purposes that, in the end, brings the result that FVA is an obstacle to the harmonization of financial and management accounting (Ewert, in press).

5.4 Conclusion

This chapter addressed underlying concepts and general characteristics of FVA, in particular as applied under IAS/IFRS. It was shown that the distinctive feature of FVA, compared with HCA, lies in a different allocation pattern of holding gains. Thus, the realization principle and the concept of capital maintenance under FVA differ from traditional accounting systems. The IASB seems to favor the use of FVs in financial statements, which explains the increasing range of applications. This begs the question whether this tendency can be justified. The empirical literature provides evidence that FVs are value relevant in various reporting situations. This finding, however, is bound to the legal frameworks and enforcement systems under which the respective capital markets (where the sample firms are traded) are organized. A general advantage of FVA over HCA should not be inferred, even if this conclusion might be drawn from some of the studies. However, while several studies suggest that revaluations of particular assets provide value relevant information to the capital market, standard setters should rather be asked why they are not demanding such information from balance sheet preparers. In a sense, the IASB's 'mixed model', in which fair valuation is demanded in some standards but not in others, seems to be justified. Further, leaving preparers the choice between FVA and HCA is a signaling device. However, it is not self-evident whether revaluations are good or bad news. In some countries (e.g. Australia and the UK) revaluations of long-lived assets are very common and possibly not considered a signal of firms being unsuccessful. In other countries, where the option for such revaluations exists (e.g. Germany), they are rarely exercised. This may point to the fact that the capital market is supposed to react negatively to them. In general, the literature suggests that the economic situation of a particular company is crucial. We conclude that, under a signaling perspective, it might be advantageous to leave FVA as nonobligatory. Finally, we discussed that, from a contracting point of view, FVA might lead to increasing differences between financial and management accounting. In total, FVA is a controversial issue in discussions about the future of financial accounting. On the one hand, standard setters, especially the IASB, seem to increase the range of applications of FVA while, on the other, academics and practitioners have reservations about this accounting system. In this chapter, our aim was to demonstrate that the world is not black and white. In our view, the recent possibilities of FVA under IAS/IFRS have sufficient justification from a theoretical point of view. However, there should be some caution about increasing the range of application of FVA as the classical tradeoff in accounting between decision usefulness and reliability will always remain.

Notes

1. If goods are sold, revenue is recognized when significant risks and rewards of the ownership have been transferred to the buyer. Several other general and transaction-specific conditions (to be found in IAS 18) have to be met.
2. However, FVA does not apply in all reporting situations. This partial use of FVA is sometimes labeled as 'mixed model'.

3. Examples include Warfield and Linsmeier (1992), Amir et al. (1993), Easton et al. (1993), Ahmed and Takeda (1995), Petroni and Wahlen (1995), Barth et al. (1996), Eccher et al. (1996), Nelson (1996), Easton and Eddey (1997), Barth and Clinch (1998), Harris and Muller (1998), Aboody et al. (1999), Beaver and Venkatachalam (2000), Cotter and Richardson (2002), and Danbolt and Rees (2003). It is beyond the scope of this chapter to discuss this research extensively.
4. The reliability of revaluations may be questioned because of existing incentives to inflate assets. Incentives include increasing debt capacity and reductions in political costs (Cotter and Richardson, 2002, p. 438).
5. Empirically, it is true that not all companies use their option to revaluate their assets. In Germany, where all consolidated financial statements of listed companies have to be prepared under IAS/IFRS, only a small number of companies opt for IAS 16's revaluation model.
6. See Hughes and Schwarz (1988) for a similar model of inventory valuation.
7. This assumption is likely to be a realistic one (see Gaeremynck and Veugelers, 1999, p. 123).
8. Another argument for this result is that additional use of FVA information creates a financial statement (or, in other words, an information system) that is more 'fine'. Following Blackwell and Girshick (1954), a 'finer' information system is always better if it does not cause additional costs. One could argue that these arguments do not work because FVA causes additional costs. However, FV estimates have to be collected as correction values in historical cost accounting systems too. So, additional cost will be smaller than one may initially suppose.
9. This is because capital maintenance relies on earning replacement costs.

References

Aboody, D., Barth, M.E., and Kasznik, R. (1999). Revaluations of Fixed Assets and Future Firm Performance: Evidence from the UK. *Journal of Accounting and Economics*, 26(1–3): 149–178.

Ahmed, A.S. and Takeda, C. (1995). Stock Market Valuation of Gains and Losses on Commercial Banks Investment Securities: An Empirical Analysis. *Journal of Accounting and Economics*, 20(2):207–225.

Alexander, D. (2003). Fair Values in IAS GAAP. Working Paper, University of Birmingham, Draft 2.

Amir, E., Harris, T.S., and Venuti, E.K. (1993). A Comparison of the Value-Relevance of US versus Non-US GAAP Accounting Measures Using Form 20-F Reconciliations. *Journal of Accounting Research*, 31(2):230–264.

Bachar, J., Melumad, N.D., and Weyns, G. (1997). On Cost Tradeoffs Between Conservative and Market Value Accounting. *Review of Accounting Studies*, 2(1):7–34.

Barlev, B. and Haddad, J.R. (2003). Fair Value Accounting and the Management of the Firm. *Critical Perspectives on Accounting*, 14(4):383–415.

Barth, M.E. (1994). Fair Value Accounting: Evidence from Investment Securities and the Market Valuation of Banks. *Accounting Review*, 69(1):1–25.

Barth, M.E. and Clinch, G. (1998). Revalued Financial, Tangible, and Intangible Assets: Associations with Share Prices and Non-Market Based Value Estimates. *Journal of Accounting Research*, 36(Suppl.):199–233.

Barth, M.E., Beaver, W.H., and Landsman, W.R. (1996). Value-Relevance of Banks Fair Value Disclosures Under SFAS 107. *Accounting Review*, 71(4):513–537.

Barth, M.E., Beaver, W.H., and Landsman, W.R. (2001). The Relevance of the Value Relevance Literature for Financial Accounting Standard Setting: Another View. *Journal of Accounting and Economics*, 31(1–3):77–104.

Basu, S. (1997). The Conservatism Principle and the Asymmetric Timeliness of Earnings. *Journal of Accounting and Economics*, 24(1):3–37.

Beaver, W.H. and Venkatachalam, M. (2000). Differential Pricing of the Discretionary and Nondiscretionary Components of Loan Fair Values. Working Paper, Stanford University.

Blackwell, D. and Girshick, M.A. (1954). *Theory of Games and Statistical Decisions*. John Wiley, New York.

Brown, P.D., Izan, H.Y., and Loh, A.L. (1992). Fixed Asset Revaluations and Managerial Incentives. *Abacus*, 28(1):36–57.

Cotter, J. and Richardson, S. (2002). Reliability of Asset Revaluations: The Impact of Appraiser Independence. *Review of Accounting Studies*, 7(4):435–457.

Cotter, J. and Zimmer, I. (1995). Asset Revaluations and Assessment of Borrowing Capacity. *Abacus*, 31(2):136–151.

Danbolt, J. and Rees, W. (2003). Mark-to-Market Accounting and Valuation: Evidence from UK Real Estate and Investment Companies. SSRN Working Paper.

Demski, J.S., Frimor, H., and Sappington, D.E.M. (2004). Efficient Manipulation in a Repeated Setting. *Journal of Accounting Research*, 42(1):31–49.

Dutta, S. and Reichelstein, S. (1999). Asset Valuation and Performance Measurement in a Dynamic Agency Setting. *Review of Accounting Studies*, 4(3–4):235–258.

Easton, P. and Eddey, P.H. (1997). The Relevance of Asset Revaluations over an Economic Cycle. *Australian Accounting Review*, 7(1):22–30.

Easton, P., Eddey, P.H., and Harris, T.S. (1993). An Investigation of Revaluations of Tangible Long-Lived Assets. *Journal of Accounting Research*, 31(Suppl.):1–38.

Eccher, E.A., Ramesh, K., and Thiagarajan, S.R. (1996). Fair-Value Disclosures by Bank Holding Companies. *Journal of Accounting and Economics*, 22(1–3):79–117.

Emanuel, D.M. (1989). Asset Revaluation and Share Price Revisions. *Journal of Business Finance and Accounting*, 16(2):213–227.

Ewert, R. (in press). Fair Value-Bewertung und Performancemessung. In: *IFRS in Rechnungswesen und Controlling* (Börsig, C. and Wagenhofer, A., eds). Schäffer-Poeschel, Stuttgart.

Gaber, C. (2004). Bilanzpolitik, Motivation und Agency-Kosten. *Zeitschrift für Betriebswirtschaft*, 74(4):339–358.

Gaeremynck, A. and Veugelers, R. (1999). The Revaluation of Assets as a Signalling Device: A Theoretical and an Empirical Analysis. *Accounting and Business Research*, 29(2):123–138.

Harris, M.S. and Muller, K.A. (1998). The Relative Informativeness of Fair Value versus Historical Cost Amounts for Long Lived Tangible Assets. SSRN Working Paper, March.

Holthausen, R.W. and Watts, R.L. (2001). The Relevance of the Value-Relevance Literature for Financial Accounting Standard Setting. *Journal of Accounting and Economics*, 31(1–3): 3–75.

Hughes, P.J. and Schwarz, E.S. (1988). The LIFO–FIFO Choice: An Asymmetric Information Approach. *Journal of Accounting Research*, 26(Suppl.):41–58.

Kirschenheiter, M. (1999). Optimal Contracting, Accounting Standards, and Market Structure. *Contemporary Accounting Research*, 16(2):243–276.

Lambert, R.A. (1999). Discussion of 'Asset Valuation and Performance Measurement in a Dynamic Agency Setting'. *Review of Accounting Studies*, 4(3–4):259–264.

Laux, H. (1999). *Unternehmensrechnung, Anreiz und Kontrolle*, 2nd edn. Springer-Verlag, Berlin.

Lev, B. and Zarowin, P. (1999). The Boundaries of Financial Reporting and How to Extend Them. *Journal of Accounting Research*, 37(2):353–385.

Lin, Y.C. and Peasnell, K.V. (1998). Fixed Asset Revaluation and Equity Depletion in the UK. SSRN Working Paper.

Magee, R.P. (1978). Accounting Measurement and Employment Contracts: Current Value Reporting. *Bell Journal of Economics*, 9(1):145–158.

Nelson, K.K. (1996). Fair Value Accounting for Commercial Banks: An Empirical Analysis of SFAS No. 107. *Accounting Review*, 71(2):161–182.

Petroni, K.R. and Wahlen, J.M. (1995). Fair Values of Equity and Debt Securities and Share Prices of Property-Liability Insurers. *Journal of Risk and Insurance*, 62(4):719–737.

Standish, P.E.M. and Ung, S.-I. (1982). Corporate Signalling, Asset Revaluations and the Stock Prices of British Companies. *Accounting Review*, 57(4):701–705.

Warfield, T. and Linsmeier, T. (1992). Tax Planning, Earnings Management, and the Differential Information Content of Bank Earnings Components. *Accounting Review*, 67(3):546–562.

Whittred, G. and Chan, Y.K. (1992). Asset Revaluations and the Mitigation of Underinvestment. *Abacus*, 28(1–3):3–35.

6

Does Delaware Incorporation Add Value? An Accounting-based Analysis

Feng Chen, Kenton K. Yee, and Yong Keun Yoo

6.1 Introduction

About half of publicly traded US firms are incorporated in Delaware. Moreover, a disproportionately large share of the biggest publicly traded companies is incorporated in Delaware (Bebchuk and Cohen, 2003; Subramanian, 2004; Yee, 2004). In the USA, firms can incorporate in any state regardless of where they operate. Each state enacts its own corporate law and has its own court system for adjudicating disputes. Most US firms incorporate in one of only two states – their home state or Delaware. More than 95% of firms that incorporate outside of their home state incorporate in Delaware.

Why do US firms choose Delaware incorporation? Daines (2001) reported that publicly traded Delaware firms exhibit a value premium over non-Delaware publicly traded US firms. That is, Delaware firms were worth more than non-Delaware firms in terms of Tobin's Q during 1981–1996. Daines suggested that Delaware corporate law facilitates takeovers and improves the market for corporate control, which results in a superior valuation for Delaware firms.

The Delaware value premium has received considerable attention from researchers because, if true, it links the quality of corporate law to firm values. A series of studies by La Porta et al. (1997, 1998, 2002) suggested that differences in law across countries affect firm valuation across countries. However, cross-country studies are plagued by possible country-specific cultural and political differences, not all of which can be controlled for. In this context, the Daines study provides an innovative contribution because, by restricting the study to US firms, many cross-country differences are eliminated. Any systematic difference in valuation between Delaware and non-Delaware US firms would be mostly associated with the state of incorporation, because cultural and political differences across US states are less of a factor.

However, many researchers have questioned the statistical robustness of Daines's results. Bebchuk et al. (2002) and Subramanian (2004) cast doubt on the robustness of the Delaware value premium over time. Gompers et al. (2003) examined the effects of an omitted variable – a 'governance index' – and found that the Daines effect disappears after controlling for the governance index. (Gompers et al. also acknowledged that some of the discrepancy may be caused by using a different sample of firms than Daines.) Bebchuk and Ferrell (2001) and Bebchuk et al. (2002) suggested that the Delaware value premium reported by Daines may be due to the self-selection of better-managed firms into Delaware rather than the effect of Delaware's corporate law on firm value.

While Bebchuk and Ferrell (2001) pointed out that the Delaware value premium may be due to differences between Delaware and non-Delaware firms, prior research has not identified what the underlying differences are. In this chapter, we take a fresh look at the Daines study from an accounting-based perspective. Using techniques from the accounting research literature, we examine whether Delaware value premium exists after controlling for accounting-based firm characteristics of Delaware firms. Although previous research controls for some variables, such as R&D expenditure or return on assets, which affect the cross-sectional distribution of Tobin's Q, it seems that the previous controls were inadequate[1]. We identify accounting conservatism and analysts' forecasts of future earnings growth as the two most significant new controls. These two factors affect the cross-sectional distribution of Tobin's Q. If these two factors are correlated with incorporation in Delaware, ignoring them may distort the measurement of the Delaware value premium.

According to the accounting conservatism score introduced by Penman and Zhang (2002), we find that Delaware firms exhibit more conservative accounting than non-Delaware firms. Furthermore, we find that consensus analysts' forecasts of earnings growth are systematically higher for Delaware firms than those of non-Delaware US firms. Higher Tobin's Q of Delaware firms may be driven by these two factors.

Upon controlling for accounting conservatism or analysts' growth forecasts, our empirical analysis finds that the Delaware value premium becomes statistically insignificant. However, if one focuses exclusively on just smaller firms, the Delaware value premium is significant if one does not control for conservatism and analysts' earnings growth forecasts. However, when accounting conservatism or analysts' long-term earnings growth forecasts are controlled for, the Delaware value premium disappears for smaller firms as well as for larger firms.

This chapter is organized as follows. Section 6.2 presents the main hypotheses. Section 6.3 documents our sample selection. Section 6.4 provides the empirical results. Section 6.5 concludes.

6.2 Development of hypotheses

The Delaware value premium reported by Daines has elicited critical responses. First, Bebchuk et al. (2002) argued that the instability of the Delaware value premium over the years is 'deeply puzzling', since it cannot be a manifestation of the high-quality corporate law of Delaware. Subramanian (2004) also found that the Delaware value premium is not robust across the years and across small versus large firms. Specifically, he found that smaller Delaware firms were worth more than smaller non-Delaware firms during 1991–1996, but not afterwards, while larger firms, which comprise 98% of his sample by size, exhibited no Delaware value premium for any year during 1991–2002. However, as long as the Delaware value premium is statistically and economically significant over the years 'on average', such a time-series and cross-sectional variation in the magnitude of the Delaware value premium cannot fully support the nonexistence of the Delaware value premium. Second, Gompers et al. (2003) reported that the Delaware value premium is significantly negative after controlling for the corporate governance index. However, there is no conceptual basis for why the addition of the corporate governance index to the Daines model changes the overall result of the Delaware value premium (Subramanian, 2004). Third, Bebchuk and Ferrell (2001) speculated that Daines did not adequately control for potential endogeneity problems. They suggested that Delaware firms might be worth more not because of the beneficial effects of Delaware corporate law, but rather because better-managed firms might choose to incorporate in Delaware. However, they do not identify what kinds of firms self-select into Delaware, leading to the observed Delaware value premium. Overall, the mixed evidence of the existing literature on the Delaware value premium calls for a further investigation.

We examine whether the Delaware value premium exists after controlling for some distinct characteristics of Delaware firms, which are not considered in previous literature examining the Delaware value premium. To this end, we identify two factors, which may affect Tobin's Q, distorting the results of Daines: accounting conservatism and future earnings growth expectation[2]. While these two factors are not driven by Delaware's relatively mild anti-takeover statute, both factors may affect the cross-sectional distribution of Tobin's Q. First, more conservative (aggressive) accounting may pull down (up) the book value of equity (Penman and Zhang, 2002), inflating (deflating) Tobin's Q. However, Delaware's anti-takeover statute may not directly affect how conservative the accounting is. Second, future earnings growth expectation is based on the assumption of the ongoing status of the sole firm, rather than reflecting the potential of takeover of the firm. However, higher future earnings growth expectation may drive Tobin's Q upwards (Penman, 1996). Even though previous research considers R&D expenditure to control for the growth of firm, we use analysts' earnings forecasts as a more reasonable control variable. This is because analysts' earnings forecasts may be a more direct proxy of '*ex ante*' expectation of future earnings growth than '*ex post*' R&D expenditure.

Thus, in this chapter, we present the distributions of the proxies for accounting conservatism and future earnings growth expectations, as well as the control variables in the existing literature, conducting empirical analyses to test the following null hypothesis:

Hypothesis 1: *There is no difference between Delaware and non-Delaware firms on average in terms of accounting conservatism (future earnings growth expectation).*

Utilizing the empirical results from the test of hypothesis 1, we examine whether the Delaware value premium exists after controlling for additional proxies for accounting conservatism and future earnings growth expectations. Our null hypothesis is as follows:

Hypothesis 2: *There is no Delaware value premium measured by Tobin's Q on average after controlling for accounting conservatism (future earnings growth expectations).*

6.3 Sample Selection

We begin by creating a sample that includes all exchange-traded industrial US firms on COMPUSTAT with necessary data, such as Tobin's Q, sales, number of business segments, stock price, and state of incorporation[3], between 1990 and 2003. Following Daines, we delete regulated utilities (two-digit SIC code 49), banks and financial firms (two-digit SIC codes 60–67). Following Subramanian (2004), we delete American Depository Receipt (ADR) firms. To avoid survivorship bias, however, we do not follow Daines in deleting firms with fewer than five years of data. For a more reasonable cross-sectional comparison, we choose only the December-fiscal-year-end firms. In addition, we delete the firm-year data when a firm's fiscal-year-end changes, since its annual accounting data is ad hoc. We obtain a final sample of 13,715 firm-years from 3323 firms between 1990 and 2003, as reported in Table 6.1(A). However, the sample size differs across analyses depending on the data requirement for each analysis. For example, for the analyses utilizing analysts' earnings forecasts[4] and stock returns, we merge our main sample with the

I/B/E/S and CRSP database. Since analysts selectively follow the firms, the sample size for the analysis using analysts' long-term earnings growth forecasts decreases to 7374 firm-years.

To allow one month for investors (analysts) to reflect the accounting information into their firm valuation (earnings forecasts), we measure the stock prices (earnings forecasts) as of April of the following year. This is because December-fiscal-year-end firms are required to report their annual reports by the end of March. In addition, to reduce the effects of outliers, we winsorize the main variables at the top and bottom 5% of the sample for each of variable.

Table 6.1(B) shows the sample size and the fraction of Delaware firms by two-digit SIC industry classification. Overall, over half (59%) of the sample firms incorporate in Delaware. Since there are significant variances of the portion of Delaware firms across industries, we use industry-adjusted variables, which are calculated by subtracting the industry (two-digit SIC code) median of each variable, to test hypotheses 1 and 2 to control for the potential industry effects.

Table 6.1 Sample size

Year	Sample size
1990	597
1991	601
1992	717
1993	726
1994	815
1995	816
1996	973
1997	1015
1998	1148
1999	1215
2000	1223
2001	1232
2002	1317
2003	1320
Total	13715

Panel A: Sample size by year.

(*Continued*)

Table 6.1 (*Continued*)

SIC code	Industry classification	Delaware	Non-Delaware	Portion of Delaware (%)
1	Agricultural Production – Crops	10	9	52.6
10	Metal Mining	12	1	92.3
13	Oil and Gas Extraction	48	18	72.7
14	Mining and Quarrying of Nonmetallic Minerals	15	23	39.5
15	Building Construction – General Contractors and Operative Builders	5	7	41.7
16	Heavy Construction, except Building Construction	27	0	100.0
17	Construction – Special Trade Contractors	7	0	100.0
20	Food and Kindred Products	78	46	62.9
21	Tobacco Products	9	17	34.6
22	Textile Mill Products	27	1	96.4
23	Apparel, Finished Products from Fabrics and Similar Materials	0	4	0.0
24	Lumber and Wood Products, except Furniture	42	15	73.7
25	Furniture and Fixtures	29	45	39.2
26	Paper and Allied Products	135	95	58.7
27	Printing, Publishing and Allied Industries	24	31	43.6
28	Chemicals and Allied Products	1695	674	71.5
29	Petroleum Refining and Related Industries	64	52	55.2
30	Rubber and Miscellaneous Plastic Products	147	159	48.0
31	Leather and Leather Products	10	21	32.3
32	Stone, Clay, Glass, and Concrete Products	83	29	74.1
33	Primary Metal Industries	164	93	63.8
34	Fabricated Metal Products, except Machinery and Transport Equipment	209	137	60.4
35	Industrial and Commercial Machinery and Computer Equipment	851	748	53.2

Table 6.1 (*Continued*)

SIC code	Industry classification	Delaware	Non-Delaware	Portion of Delaware (%)
36	Electronic, Electrical Equipment and Components, except Computer Equipment	852	647	56.8
37	Transportation Equipment	259	214	54.8
38	Measuring/Analyzing/Control Instruments; Photo/Med/Opt Goods; Watches/Clocks	777	793	49.5
39	Miscellaneous Manufacturing Industries	105	89	54.1
48	Communications	78	95	45.1
50	Wholesale Trade – Durable Goods	234	137	63.1
51	Wholesale Trade – Nondurable Goods	71	90	44.1
52	Building Materials, Hardware, Garden Supply, and Mobile Home Dealers	23	25	47.9
53	General Merchandise Stores	3	22	12.0
54	Food Stores	34	25	57.6
55	Automotive Dealers and Gasoline Service Stations	35	10	77.8
56	Apparel and Accessory Stores	22	30	42.3
57	Home Furniture, Furnishings, and Equipment Stores	17	24	41.5
58	Eating and Drinking Places	178	119	59.9
59	Miscellaneous Retail	137	94	59.3
70	Hotels, Rooming Houses, Camps, and Other Lodging Places	52	43	54.7
72	Personal Services	0	14	0.0
73	Business Services	936	606	60.7
75	Automotive Repair, Services, and Parking	12	8	60.0
76	Miscellaneous Repair Services	6	0	100.0
78	Motion Pictures	9	7	56.3
79	Amusement and Recreation Services	98	47	67.6
80	Health Services	238	87	73.2
82	Educational Services	10	0	100.0
83	Social Services	5	3	62.5

(*Continued*)

Table 6.1 (*Continued*)

SIC code	Industry classification	Delaware	Non-Delaware	Portion of Delaware (%)
87	Engineering, Accounting, Research, Management, and Related Services	168	125	57.3
99	Nonclassifiable Establishments	57	29	66.3
	Total	8107	5608	59.1

Panel B: Sample by Industry Classification.

6.4 Empirical results

6.4.1 Descriptive statistics

We begin by presenting the descriptive statistics of firm-specific variables, testing hypothesis 1, which compare the firm characteristics between Delaware and non-Delaware firms. The chosen variables are used in Daines's empirical model or in this chapter. Results are detailed in Table 6.2.

Table 6.2(A) presents the descriptive statistics of the firm-specific variables used in Daines's model. First, consistent with Daines, we measure Tobin's Q as the market value of assets divided by the book value of assets, where the market value of assets is computed as the market value of common equity plus the book value of preferred stock plus the book value of liability. Consistent with Daines, Delaware firms have higher Tobin's Q than non-Delaware firms. Second, Delaware firms are large (in terms of sales), more diversified (in terms of number of business segments), more R&D intensive, and less profitable in current years (in terms of return on assets). All of these differences are statistically significant at the 1% level. These results are consistent with Daines.

Table 6.2(B) shows the descriptive statistics of the proxies of additional control factors in this chapter. First, following Penman and Zhang (2002), we compute the accounting conservatism score (CSCORE) for Delaware and non-Delaware firms. CSCORE measures the effect of the application of conservative accounting on the balance sheet by the level of estimated reserves that are created by the accounting conservatism, relative to net operating assets. In computing this conservatism score, we consider the estimated reserves based only on the accounting treatment of inventories, R&D, and advertising expenditures. On the basis of CSCORE, Delaware firms are more conservative in accounting. The

Table 6.2 Descriptive statistics of main variables: Delaware vs non-Delaware firms

Variable	State of incorporation	Number of firms	Mean	Std dev.	25%	50%	75%	*t*-statistics of mean difference	*z*-statistics of Wilcoxon score
Q	DEL	8107	2.44	1.85	1.18	1.70	2.94	4.50**	3.71**
	NON-DEL	5608	2.21	1.67	1.13	1.57	2.53		
SALES	DEL	8107	1118	2251	21	130	834	3.97**	6.35**
	NON-DEL	5608	1028	2212	23	105	607		
NSEG	DEL	8107	1.88	1.28	1.00	1.00	3.00	3.14**	2.43**
	NON-DEL	5608	1.82	1.22	1.00	1.00	3.00		
RD/A	DEL	8107	0.11	0.13	0.01	0.05	0.15	8.08**	6.97**
	NON-DEL	5608	0.08	0.11	0.01	0.04	0.11		
ROA	DEL	8107	0.02	0.25	0.07	0.10	0.18	−7.93**	−5.58**
	NON-DEL	5608	0.07	0.21	0.01	0.12	0.20		

Panel A: Tobin's Q and control variables in Daines.

Variable	State of incorporation	Number of firms	Mean	Std dev.	25%	50%	75%	*t*-statistics of mean difference	*z*-statistics of Wilcoxon score
CSCORE	DEL	7358	0.28	0.35	0.07	0.15	0.30	8.09**	3.91**
	NON-DEL	5349	0.23	0.27	0.07	0.15	0.26		
5YREGF	DEL	4413	0.19	0.09	0.12	0.16	0.25	4.12**	2.88**
	NON-DEL	2961	0.18	0.08	0.11	0.15	0.22		

Panel B: Additional control variables.

This table presents the distributions of the main variables within Delaware (DEL) and non-Delaware (NON-DEL) firms respectively. Q is Tobin's Q, as defined in the text; SALES is total net sales; NSEG is the number of business segments; RD/A is R&D expenditure scaled by prior year's total assets; ROA is return on assets, defined as operating income before depreciation divided by previous year's total assets; CSCORE is the accounting conservatism score as defined in Penman and Zhang (2002); 5YREGF is analysts' forecasts of five-year earnings growth. The *z*-statistics of the Wilcoxon rank score differences are derived from the nonparametric test. Both the *t*-statistic of mean difference and *z*-statistics of the Wilcoxon rank score differences are computed from the industry-adjusted variables, which are calculated by subtracting the industry (two-digit SIC code) median of each variable. **Significance level at 1%.

mean CSCORE for Delaware firms is 0.28, while the mean CSCORE for non-Delaware firms is 0.23. The CSCORE difference between Delaware and non-Delaware firms is statistically significant at 1%, as indicated by both the t-statistic of mean difference and z-statistic of Wilcoxon rank score. Second, we measure the future earnings growth expectations by analysts' long-term earnings growth forecasts. As indicated in Table 6.2(B), Delaware firms receive higher future earnings growth forecasts than non-Delaware firms (the t-statistic of mean difference is 4.12, while the z-statistic of Wilcoxon rank score is 2.88).

Overall, Table 6.2 indicates that Delaware firms are more conservative in accounting and receive higher future earnings growth expectation. Since both more conservative accounting and higher future earnings growth expectation may lead to higher Tobin's Q, but both factors are not directly affected by Delaware corporate law, we may need to control for both factors to check the robustness of Daines's results and the reasonableness of Daines's story.

6.4.2 Is there a Delaware value premium?

Table 6.3 presents the results of the multiple regression analyses. To remove the effects of the cross-sectional correlation in error terms inherent to panel data, we adopt the 'Fama–MacBeth' approach (Fama and MacBeth, 1973). Thus, Table 6.3 presents the means of coefficients and R^2 from each annual cross-sectional regression, with t-statistics calculated from the time-series standard errors of the annually estimated coefficients.

Table 6.3 consists of two sets of results. The first row of the table is based on the regression of Tobin's Q on the dummy variable of incorporation states and the other control variables similarly defined in Daines. The variable of interest is a dummy variable (DEL) that is set to 1 for firms incorporated in Delaware in the observation year, 0 otherwise. The other control variables as in Daines are as follows. We include the log of the firm's net sales as a control for firm size. We include R&D expense, scaled by total assets from the previous year, as a rough proxy for firm-specific growth opportunity. This is because firms with greater investment opportunities are likely to have higher Tobin's Q. To control for the possibility that diversified firms may have lower Tobin's Q, we include number of business segments from the segment reports in the COMPUSTAT database as a rough proxy for firm diversification. Finally, we include ROA and lagged ROA as the basic controls for firm performance. The second row of the table lists the regression results when the additional variable, either CSCORE or analysts' long-term earnings growth forecasts, is controlled for. Considering the

Table 6.3 Delaware incorporation and equity value premium

		Intercept	DEL	Ln (SALES)	RD/A	NSEG	ROA	LAGROA	CSCORE	Adj. R^2	N of year	N of sample
Pooled	Coefficient	0.33**	0.022	−0.06*	5.94**	−0.03*	1.52**	−1.24**		0.19	14	12,707
sample	F/M *t*-stat	(18.21)	(1.03)	(−2.52)	(14.50)	(−2.05)	(8.44)	(−5.02)				
	Coefficient	0.31**	0.018	−0.06**	5.45**	−0.03*	1.58**	−1.21**	0.44**	0.19	14	12,707
	F/M *t*-stat	(16.86)	(0.84)	(−2.56)	(12.49)	(−1.99)	(8.44)	(−4.90)	(5.44)			
Sample	Coefficient	0.32**	0.087*	−0.28**	4.77**	−0.01	1.05**	−1.44**		0.20	14	6347
of smaller	F/M *t*-stat	(14.03)	(2.04)	(−8.12)	(12.75)	(−0.35)	(4.75)	(−4.90)				
firms	Coefficient	0.31**	0.078	−0.28**	4.53**	−0.01	1.09**	−1.45**	0.26*	0.21	14	6347
	F/M *t*-stat	(13.32)	(1.73)	(−8.04)	(10.69)	(−0.23)	(4.75)	(−4.94)	(2.22)			
Sample	Coefficient	0.19**	0.022	0.04*	4.87**	−0.05**	5.36**	0.90**		0.38	14	6360
of larger	F/M *t*-stat	(12.75)	(1.04)	(2.10)	(6.04)	(−4.23)	(22.23)	(2.88)				
firms	Coefficient	0.17**	0.021	0.04	3.91**	−0.04**	5.33**	1.06**	0.85**	0.40	14	6360
	F/M *t*-stat	(11.34)	(1.01)	(1.87)	(5.04)	(−4.04)	(25.04)	(3.85)	(9.29)			

Panel A: Delaware incorporation, equity value premium, and accounting conservatism.

(Continued)

Table 6.3 *(Continued)*

		Intercept	DEL	Ln (SALES)	RD/A	NSEG	ROA	LAGROA	5YREGF	Adj. R^2	N of year	N of sample
Pooled	Coefficient	0.25**	0.056	−0.09**	5.90**	−0.03**	3.36**	−0.73*		0.22	14	7374
sample	F/M *t*-stat	(16.24)	(1.82)	(−5.19)	(11.16)	(−3.24)	(9.88)	(−2.10)				
	Coefficient	0.23**	0.004	0.03	4.42**	−0.03**	2.83**	−0.43	6.24**	0.30	14	7374
	F/M *t*-stat	(12.20)	(0.14)	(1.27)	(8.12)	(−3.65)	(9.67)	(−1.51)	(13.54)			
Sample	Coefficient	0.23**	0.128*	−0.31**	4.66**	−0.08*	3.13**	−0.77*		0.18	14	3685
of smaller	F/M *t*-stat	(8.17)	(2.35)	(−10.21)	(9.21)	(−2.29)	(8.67)	(2.19)				
firms	Coefficient	0.24**	0.083	−0.18**	3.64**	−0.07*	2.60**	0.53	5.63**	0.26	14	3685
	F/M *t*-stat	(7.91)	(1.75)	(−8.17)	(6.54)	(−2.22)	(8.66)	(−1.81)	(11.09)			
Sample	Coefficient	0.12**	0.047**	0.08*	4.79**	−0.06**	6.20**	1.22*		0.44	14	3689
of larger	F/M *t*-stat	(6.15)	(2.75)	(2.25)	(4.67)	(−3.56)	(13.90)	(2.38)				
firms	Coefficient	0.12**	0.005	0.17**	3.12**	−0.05**	5.64**	1.24**	6.18**	0.50	14	3689
	F/M *t*-stat	(5.42)	(0.26)	(3.49)	(4.36)	(−3.42)	(13.45)	(2.73)	(7.94)			

Panel B: Delaware incorporation, equity value premium, and future earnings growth expectation.

This table presents the results of cross-sectional year-by-year regressions as of the end of April. Q is Tobin's Q, as defined in the text; DEL is 1 if the firm incorporates in Delaware, 0 otherwise; SALES is total net sales; RD/A is R&D expenditure scaled by previous year's total assets; NSEG is the number of business segments; ROA is return on assets, defined as operating income before depreciation divided by previous year's total assets; LAGROA is ROA in the previous year; CSCORE is the accounting conservatism score as defined in Penman and Zhang (2002); 5YREGF is analysts' forecasts of five-year earnings growth. All variables are industry adjusted by subtracting the industry (two-digit SIC code) median of each variable. The regression equations for Panels A and B are as follows:

Panel A: $Q = \alpha_0 + \alpha_1 DEL + \alpha_2 \ln(SALES) + \alpha_3 RD/A + \alpha_4 NSEG + \alpha_5 ROA + \alpha_6 LAGROA + \alpha_7 CSCORE + \epsilon$

Panel B: $Q = \alpha_0 + \alpha_1 DEL + \alpha_2 \ln(SALES) + \alpha_3 RD/A + \alpha_4 NSEG + \alpha_5 ROA + \alpha_6 LAGROA + \alpha_7 5YREGF + \epsilon$

The coefficients presented are the means of the annual regressions. The numbers within ( ) below coefficient estimates are *t*-statistics calculated from the time-series standard errors of the annually estimated coefficients. Adj. R^2 is the average adjusted R^2 of the annual regressions. **and *indicate the significance level at 1% or 5%, respectively.

size effect on the Delaware value premium reported by Subramanian (2004), we conduct the regressions on pooled samples or on each of the larger/smaller firm samples separately, which are divided by the median sales cutoff[5].

Table 6.3(A) lists the results of the additional control for accounting conservatism. Before CSCORE is controlled for, the coefficient of DEL is statistically significant at the conventional significance level (5%) only for the smaller firm sample. This result indicates that the Delaware value premium may exist only for smaller firms, which is consistent with Subramanian (2004). However, when CSCORE is controlled for, the coefficient of DEL becomes insignificant at the 5% significance level for the smaller firms as well as for the larger firms. Meanwhile, the coefficient of CSCORE is significantly positive, as expected.

Table 6.3(B) shows the regression results when future earnings growth expectation is controlled for. Without controlling for future earnings growth expectation, proxied by analysts' long-term earnings forecasts, the coefficient of DEL is statistically significant at 5% for both smaller and larger firms. However, when future earnings growth expectation is controlled for, the coefficient of DEL becomes statistically insignificant at 5% for both smaller and larger firms. On the contrary, analysts' long-term earnings growth forecasts are significantly positive, as expected.

Overall, our results indicate that when the distinct firm characteristics of Delaware firms (i.e. accounting conservatism or future earnings growth expectations) are controlled for, the Delaware value premium disappears.

6.5 Conclusion

This chapter examines whether the Delaware value premium exists after controlling for some distinct firm characteristics of Delaware firms. We find that Delaware firms exhibit more conservative accounting and receive higher future earnings expectations. When we control for these two factors in Daines's model, the Delaware value premium disappears. We conclude that Daines' Delaware value premium is associated with conservative accounting and higher analysts' expected earnings growth. We do not know if this association is caused by Delaware incorporation or that firms with these two features are more likely to choose Delaware incorporation.

We find that Delaware firms are more conservative in accounting and receive analysts' growth forecasts. It is unknown why Delaware firms have such distinguishing characteristics[6]. To shed some light on why Delaware is such a popular state of incorporation, it would be useful to comprehensively document the fundamental differences between Delaware firms and non-Delaware firms. We are presently undertaking such a study (Chen et al., 2005).

Notes

1. The existing literature examining the Delaware value premium considers the following control variables: firm size, number of business segments, R&D expenditure, return on assets for both the current year and the previous year.
2. The other factor that may affect the cross-sectional distribution of Tobin's Q is firm-specific risks. More risky firms may have lower Tobin's Q, since more risky firms may have lower market value of equity compared with book value of equity. However, untabulated results indicate that Delaware firms seem to be more risky, compared with non-Delaware firms. This characteristic of Delaware firms will reduce the Delaware value premium, rather than exaggerate it. Thus, in this chapter, we consider only two factors that may distort Daines's results toward the inflated Delaware value premium. Our main results, however, are robust, even though the firm-specific risk factors are additionally controlled for.
3. Historical incorporation state data are taken from Compact Disclosure. This data requirement restricts our sample since 1990, similar to Subramanian (2004).
4. We use the median of individual analysts' earnings forecast as the consensus earnings forecast for each firm to mitigate the well-known optimistic bias of mean analysts' earnings forecasts.
5. Since the Fama–MacBeth approach requires a time-series of coefficient estimates over a sufficient number of years, we focus on the partition of sample across sizes rather than across years.
6. One possibility is that certain types of firms self-select into Delaware states. But why certain types and not others?

References

Bebchuk, L. and Cohen, A. (2003). Firms' Decisions where to Incorporate. *Journal of Law and Economics*, 43(2):383–425.

Bebchuk, L. and Ferrell, A. (2001). A New Approach to Takeover Law and Regulatory Competition. *Virginia Law Review*, 87(1):111–164.

Bebchuk, L., Cohen, A., and Ferrell, A. (2002). Does the Evidence Favor State Competition in Corporate Law? *University of California Law Review*, 90(6):1775–1823.

Chen, F., Yee, K., and Yoo, Y.K. (2005). Is Delaware an Orange? Fundamental Characteristics of Delaware Firms. Columbia University Working Paper.

Daines, R. (2001). Does Delaware Law Improve Firm Value? *Journal of Financial Economics*, 62(3):525–558.

Fama, E. and MacBeth, J. (1973). Risk, Return, and Equilibrium: Empirical Tests. *Journal of Political Economy*, 81(3):607–636.

Gompers, P., Ishii, J., and Metrick, A. (2003). Corporate Governance and Equity Prices. *Quarterly Journal of Economics*, 118(1):107–155.

La Porta, R., Lopez-de-Silanes, F., Shleifer, A., and Vishny, R. (1997). Legal Determinants of External Finance. *Journal of Finance*, 52(3):1131–1150.

La Porta, R., Lopez-de-Silanes, F., Shleifer, A., and Vishny, R. (1998). Law and Finance. *Journal of Political Economy*, 106(6):1113–1155.

La Porta, R., Lopez-de-Silanes, F., Shleifer, A., and Vishny, R. (2002). Investor Protection and Corporate Valuation. *Journal of Finance*, 57(3):1147–1170.

Penman, S.H. (1996). The Articulation of Price–Earnings Ratios and Market-to-Book Ratios and the Evaluation of Growth. *Journal of Accounting Research*, 34(2):235–259.

Penman, S.H. and Zhang, X.J. (2002). Accounting Conservatism, the Quality of Earnings, and Stock Returns. *Accounting Review*, 77(2):237–264.

Subramanian, G. (2004). The Disappearing Delaware Effect. *Journal of Law, Economics and Organization*, 20(1):2–59.

Yee, K. (2004). Perspectives: Combining Value Estimates to Increase Accuracy. *Financial Analysts Journal*, 60(4):23–28.

7

Empirical Evidence on the Relation Between Revaluations of Fixed Assets and the Future Performance of Firms in Brazil

Alexsandro Broedel Lopes

7.1 Introduction

This chapter examines whether revaluations of fixed assets by Brazilian firms are associated with future firm performance, as measured by *ex post* realized operating profit, stock prices, and returns. The motivation for this chapter arises from the debate among managers, investors, regulators, and academics about revaluation of fixed assets. This debate reflects the tradeoff between estimated values, which are presumably more relevant, and historical cost values. For financial instruments, it seems a consensus exists among regulators that fair value (market value or some estimated amount) is a better proxy for economic value than historical cost (see FAS 133 and IAS 39). However, US standard setters and others have pointed out that fair values for fixed assets cannot be reliably measured. If asset revaluations reflect the underlying economic values, restated numbers will have a significant positive relation with future firm performance.

Asset revaluation is one of the most controversial topics in financial accounting. The recent crisis in investor confidence arising from the Enron and WorldCom accounting scandals renewed interest in the quality of financial statements. The debate on revaluation is centered on the balance between relevance and reliability. Historical cost is much more reliable than independent external revaluation, which is influenced by professional judgment and potentially managerial bias. On the other hand, historical values can lose relevance as economic reality changes and the value of assets can be better represented by a revalued amount. The potential manipulation of revaluations, however, is a point of significant concern.

This study focuses on Brazil because its generally accepted accounting rules (BR GAAP) allow fixed assets to be reported in financial statements at revalued amounts, which is not possible under FASB rules. Additionally, there is very little existing research related to a relevant emerging market such as Brazil. Past research about revaluation has been conducted using Australian and UK firms; however, the results obtained in these two countries cannot be generalized. Australia and the UK are common-law developed countries and, according to recent research (Ball et al., 2001), they possess highly informative accounting systems. Brazil, on the other hand, is a code law developing country.

According to Ali and Hwang (2000), five factors drive the relevance of accounting numbers for equity investors: (a) bank versus investor-oriented market; (b) type of regulatory body; (c) influence of tax regulations; (d) ownership concentration; and (e) amount spent on auditing. Brazil clearly complies negatively with the five items outlined. Given this scenario, it is not obvious that accounting revaluations in Brazil will have the same relevance that previous research in Australia and the UK has shown.

The evidence in this study is based solely on Brazilian data but is relevant to the international debate on asset revaluation, especially for current issues facing the US Financial Accounting Standards Board (FASB) and the International Accounting Standards Board (IASB). For American regulators the evidence shows how asset revaluations are related to firm performance, prices, and returns in conditions that are likely to mitigate the relevance of accounting information *ex ante*. Past research shows that asset revaluation provides useful information for Australian and British firms. Australia, the UK, and the USA have similar corporate governance structures. They are common-law developed countries with firms that rely heavily on credit and equity markets for sources of funding using publicly available information to reduce information asymmetry. In this scenario, financial statements have more relevance. Brazil, on the other hand, is at the other extreme, because the code law of firms in an emerging market, such as Brazil, relies on a special relationship process to obtain funding (insider model). According to past literature, financial accounting is deemed to have a weak relation to firm performance and market-based estimates in such a country. The results show that asset revaluations also have a significant relation to firm performance and prices in Brazil. These results raise some doubts about the requirements imposed by the SEC that foreign firms willing to list their shares on the New York Stock Exchange should comply with US GAAP. Brazilian firms are very active in the American Depositary Receipts market and for them this requirement attempts to reduce and not to increase the value relevance of financial statements.

The findings are even more relevant to regulators such as the IASB that rule over different cultural and economic systems. The argument of using the same accounting rule cannot be applied to different governance structures because it has been used as an obstacle to harmonization. The evidence presented here suggests that this may not be the case for the revaluation of fixed assets. For the reasons presented above, the evidence regarding the Brazilian case adds substantially to the argument that revaluation of fixed assets provides relevant information.

This study draws from Aboody et al. (1999), where it was shown that upward revaluations of fixed assets by UK firms are significantly positively related to changes in future performance measured by operating income and cash flow from operations. These authors also tested the relation between revaluation balances, annual prices, and returns, controlling for debt-to-equity ratios, a methodology commonly used in the literature (Amir et al., 1993; Easton et al., 1993; Barth and

Clinch, 1996, 1998). The results presented by Aboody et al. (1999) show that revaluations of fixed assets are significantly associated with future (*ex post*) economic performance as well as prices and returns. Aboody et al. (1999) also showed that debt-to-equity ratios influence the results, suggesting that asset revaluations in the UK are also used to affect debt-to-equity ratios.

The tests used by Aboody et al. (1999) are repeated here, but without using cash flow from operations, because Brazilian firms are not required to disclose statements of cash flows. The results obtained are generally consistent with those of Aboody et al. (1999) – that is, revaluations of fixed assets provide valuable information in Brazil. Returns regressions, however, did not show statistically significant results between returns and revaluation reserves. Recent research (Lopes, 2005) suggests that earnings are not as informative as book values in Brazil. The ownership concentration in Brazil is large, with no major firm labeled as a public company[1]. In this scenario, earnings lose relevance because insiders have direct access to information. When compared to Germany (Leuz and Wustemann, 2003), Brazil possesses a similar insider system corporate governance model. In this type of model, information asymmetries are resolved via private information channels rather than public disclosure. In an outsider model, firms rely heavily on public debt and equity to raise capital. As the ownership concentration is dispersed, investors have to rely on public sources of information. Consequently, public disclosures are an important form of information asymmetry reduction. In the Brazilian insider model, firms rely on relationships to solve information problems. Leuz and Wustemann (2003) showed that when information problems are likely to be resolved via private channels the contemporaneous association of accounting numbers with stock returns is weak. Thus, it is not a surprise that returns/earnings and revaluation reserves do not present a significant relationship for Brazilian firms.

Overall, the findings here indicate that revaluations reflect changes in values of assets associated with future operating performance and stock prices. These results support the idea that revaluations are reliable estimates of underlying economic values even for a developing code-law country. Our results also suggest that debt-to-equity ratios play a significant role in the revaluation of fixed assets in Brazil, as previous research has shown for Australia and the UK. Revaluation reserves, however, are not timely incorporated into prices.

The rest of the chapter is organized as follows. Section 7.2 discusses the revaluation reserves in Brazilian company law and presents related research. Section 7.3 specifies and presents the results from the future performance and market-based tests. Section 7.4 concludes the chapter.

7.2 Revaluation of fixed assets in Brazilian GAAP and related literature

7.2.1 Brazilian GAAP for revaluation

Brazilian company law (*Lei das Sociedades por Ações*) is the most important accounting normative basis for firms listed on the São Paulo Stock Exchange (BOVESPA). In addition to company law, the Brazilian Securities and Exchange Commission (CVM) issues rules that regulate specific accounting questions not addressed by the law. While CVM statements are considered to be GAAP in Brazil, they cannot be in disagreement with what is exposed in the law. Financial institutions are regulated directly by the Central Bank of Brazil, which has the power to issue accounting statements related to financial institutions. In addition to company law and the CVM, Brazilian firms have to comply with specific accounting guidance provided by the Federal Tax Authority (SRF). In most cases, the tax rules allow for less discretion than company law. Financial statements do not have to comply with tax rules. However, most firms use the same general rules for tax and reporting purposes to avoid costly conciliation between the two sets of rules.

It can be reasonably argued that Brazil represents a unique corporate financial reporting model. The following combination of factors characterizes the unique nature of the Brazilian system:

1. Brazilian accounting is usually classified under the so-called continental model.
2. The government issues all the accounting rules and professional bodies have no effective power to influence these rules.
3. Brazilian firms rely heavily on private deals to obtain finance.
4. Ownership control is very high. Currently there is not a single Brazilian firm for which control of voting rights can be obtained in the capital markets.
5. Brazilian public markets for equity and debt are relatively small and do not provide adequate sources of finance to firms.
6. Investor protection in Brazil is also considered to be very poor, with several well-known cases of expropriation of minority shareholders (see Anderson, 1999).
7. Brazilian managers have considerable discretion over their set of accounting choices. Table 7.1 presents the major features of the Brazilian corporate financial reporting model.

The above scenario differs substantially from what is commonly reported in the literature regarding countries where the tax law has a strong influence on financial

Table 7.1 Brazilian corporate financial reporting model

Accounting regulations	Issued by the government
Sources of finance	Credit based on insider deals
Influence of tax	Large, with most firms' statements based on tax rules
Investor protection	Very low
Ownership concentration	Very high

Specific accounting rules	Brazil	US GAAP	IFRS
Inventory	Lower of acquisition cost or market value. Market values can be used for some items.	Similar to Brazil.	Similar to Brazil.
Depreciation	No specific depreciation method is recommended but any method must be applied consistently.	Similar to Brazil.	Similar to Brazil.
Statements of cash flows	The statement of changes in financial position is required and cash-flow information may be disclosed as supplementary information.	Most companies have to provide a statement of cash flows in financial statements.	The statement of cash flows should be produced as an integral part of the financial statements.
Extraordinary items	Segregated from income from ordinary operations and reported in a separate line on the income statement.	Similar to Brazil.	Similar to Brazil.
Prior period adjustment	Adjustments to the opening balance of retained earnings for corrections of errors in prior periods not related to subsequent events and changes in accounting policies.	Retrospective application of the prior period adjustments when comparative statements are presented to correct prior errors, certain changes in account ing principles, certain adjustments related to prior interim periods.	Treatment for certain changes in accounting policies and corrections of errors in the opening balance of retained earnings.

(*Continued*)

Table 7.1 (*Continued*)

Specific accounting rules	Brazil	US GAAP	IFRS
Changes in accounting policy	Must be explained. The effects of changes in accounting practices are classified as prior year adjustments. However, the financial statements are not restated. An appropriate disclosure should be made if relevant.	The cumulative effect of the change should be shown in the income statement after extraordinary items and before net income in the year in which the change occurs.	The company must give pro forma information on the prior year adjustment basis.
Research and development expenses	May be capitalized as a deferred asset. The amortization period should be determined on expected future economic benefits. Tax legislation requires a minimum amortization period of 5 years while company law allows for a maximum 10-year amortization period.	Only costs of materials and equipment and other facilities purchased from others and with alternative future uses can be capitalized. With the exception of some internally developed software, all other R&D costs are not capitalized.	Research (new knowledge) is not capitalized. Development (application) can be capitalized only under very special circumstances when the project meets strict requirements.

reporting. Harris et al. (1994) reported that German accounting numbers are very conservative and that hidden reserves are a reason for investors' concern. Brazilian financial reporting pursues the same link with tax legislation as does Germany. However, the accounting rules in Brazil allow for much greater flexibility than the Anglo-Saxon model; this is not the case in Germany. This situation arises because firms can present financial statements under accounting methods not allowed by the tax authority (SRF). These firms have to adjust their statements to form the basis for the calculations in a special book (LALUR) designed to conciliate the SRF and company-law regulations. However, tax rules have a major influence since most firms choose to report to avoid costly adjustments on LALUR, which is the case with inventory methods. For example, a majority of companies adopt FIFO due to tax limitations on using LIFO. Dividends in Brazil, as in Germany, are linked with net income, thus increasing the conservative bias in financial reporting. This structure shows that Brazil possesses a set of accounting rules that allow managers to use a greater degree of discretion than in the so-called Anglo-Saxon model. However, the general structure of the profession and governance uses of the accounting numbers (i.e. dividends) are not so investor oriented. In this sense, the Brazilian corporate financial reporting system can be considered as a hybrid model because of the very liberal accounting rules coupled with a governance system oriented for providing information to the government and creditors that operate under an insider model.

The company law created in 1976 allowed the revaluation of assets of the group called permanent assets. This group is composed of investments, fixed and deferred assets. The CVM (Deliberação, 1995, p. 183) restricted the revaluation to fixed assets and to investments. The SRF (RIR, 1999) restricted the revaluation to fixed assets. Therefore, this chapter only focuses on the revaluation of fixed assets and not of investments and intangible assets. To perform the revaluation, the shareholders' assembly must appoint three independent evaluators who will produce a statement containing the basis for the revaluation performed, the new value of the asset, and the new useful life of the asset. The company, as proof of the revaluation, must maintain this formal document. The amount stated in the evaluator's report is presented in the balance sheet (debit entry) and the depreciation is calculated over the remaining useful life of the asset based on the restated carrying amount. The credit entry is on revaluation reserves (equity). However, the reserve on equity is presented net of tax because revaluation has special tax treatment in Brazil. Australian GAAP recommends similar treatment[2] but revaluation is not taxed as it is in Brazil. The Board has total discretion about the timing of revaluation. However, all assets in the same category must be revalued at the same time at the firm's level. Gains on disposal of revalued assets are considered nonoperational. At the point of sale of a revalued asset the remaining revaluation reserve must be written off. Firms must also disclose the method used for revaluation and the remaining useful economic life of the asset.

There is intense debate over the desirability of revaluation reserves in Brazil. The project to reform company law currently being analyzed in the Congress eliminates the revaluation option. According to this new project, accounting for fixed assets in Brazil will become similar to US GAAP. Until 1995 the SRF allowed companies to adopt the so-called Brazilian method for inflation adjustment. This method is based on a price level adjustment of all of the firm's assets and liabilities (Doupnik et al., 1995). In 1995, the Ministry of Finance (Brazil's highest economic authority) issued a norm prohibiting companies to use adjusted statements for tax purposes. Many firms can still publish their financial statements adjusted for inflation, but this cannot be the basis for taxation. Some authors state that the revaluation of fixed assets can be a substitute for inflation adjustment (Iudícibus et al., 2003), while other common arguments imply that revaluations are designed only to cook the books in order to improve financial ratios.

The Brazilian corporate financial reporting model differs considerably from that of Australia and the UK, as previously reported in the literature. Evidence of the economic significance of asset revaluations in Brazil increases our knowledge of the relevance of accounting information in alternative situations. Previous research suggests that the Brazilian economic environment can mitigate the relevance of accounting information. The Brazilian governance model is clearly an insider model, where public financial information does not seem to play a relevant role. The investigation of the relevance of revaluation reserves in such extreme conditions can provide valuable input into the debate over revaluation of fixed assets. My results show that revaluation reserves provide significant economic information able to explain future firm performance and prices against the odds with the Brazilian corporate governance model.

7.2.2 Previous research

7.2.2.1 Asset revaluation

This study is closely related to the research conducted by Aboody et al. (1999), where the authors investigated the relation of fixed asset revaluations of UK firms to *ex post* future performance (operating income and cash flows), prices, and returns. They controlled for debt-to-equity ratio as well as for cross-listing and firms' acquisition activities. Aboody et al. found that upward revaluations are significantly positively related to changes in future performance. They also found that revaluation balances are significantly positively related to annual returns and prices. The results of Aboody et al. show that these relations are weaker for higher debt-to-equity ratio firms, suggesting that managers can be motivated by firms' financial health. The relations are also weaker for cross-listed firms and in more volatile economic periods. My work extends that of Aboody et al. by replicating their analysis for Brazil. Aboody et al. claim that their results provide valuable input for regulators and other interested parties in the value relevance of revalued assets. However, their work is based solely on UK data and adds to previous literature based on Australian firms (Sharpe and Walker, 1975; Standish and Ung, 1982; Easton et al., 1993; Barth and Clinch, 1998). This extensive body of literature is based on Australian and British firms that operate under very similar corporate governance structures, and both countries have adopted common-law regimes. The current study is the first to document the relevance of revaluation reserves in a code-law emerging market. The results will help to generalize the arguments presented thus far. To contribute to international regulators like the IASB, as suggested by Aboody et al. (1999), the implication is that it is necessary to have broader evidence than has been presented so far.

7.2.2.2 Market-based international accounting research

This study also contributes to the so-called market-based international accounting research (Meek and Thomas, 2004). In their survey, these authors pointed out the relevance of examining existing theories in countries other than those in which they have been developed. Such studies, according to Wallace and Gernon (1991), can either support or deny the universality of each theory. Dummontier and Raffournier (2002), however, criticized papers that are limited to replicating American studies without questioning the relevance and applicability of the methodology and hypothesis in a different context. Because this study is based on an emerging market, it provides evidence relevant to regulators in developing countries. From a Brazilian point of view, the results will help the debate by adding a greater degree of generality to the existing arguments.

This study also contributes directly to another area of international accounting research, the so-called accounting classifications. It is common knowledge in the accounting literature that common-law countries present accounting systems oriented toward 'fair presentations', transparency, and full disclosure, while code-law countries are oriented towards legal compliance and opaque disclosure. In common-law countries the tax rules do not have a pervasive influence on accounting as happens in code-law systems. Ball et al. (2001) showed that the properties of earnings and timeliness are more likely to be found in firms listed in common-law-oriented markets (UK, USA, Australia, and Canada) than in code-law countries (France, Japan, and Germany). Some authors (e.g. Cairns, 1997), however, question these results, suggesting that there is a convergence in accounting practices making the traditional code–common law distinction obsolete. This study contributes directly to this debate showing that, despite the classification of Brazil as a code-law country, revaluation of fixed assets does provide relevant information about firms' future performance and that this relevance is reflected by market-based indicators (prices and returns). The results show that, as evidenced by the literature (Ball et al., 2001), earnings and revaluation of fixed assets have no effect on the timing of returns. However, revaluation reserves are value relevant in relation to prices and future operational performance. The results in this study suggest that the relevance of the distinction between code- and common-law countries is at least secondary in the case of revaluation of fixed assets. Meek and Thomas (2004) suggested that investigations on the relevance of the distinction between code- and common-law countries are welcome. This study presents some evidence that classification of countries into different categories is not an adequate approach to understand the complexities of accounting.

7.3 Models and results

7.3.1 Descriptive statistics

The Economatica database was used for the research because of its completeness of market and financial statement data for firms traded on the Brazilian stock market. The sample was selected from Brazilian firms (excluding financial firms) that presented revaluation reserves on their balance sheets during any of the years from 1995 to 2003. Revaluation reserves were used on a per-share basis for the market-based tests and on aggregate level for the performance-based tests. The number of firm-year observations differs from year to year because not all the firms presented revaluation reserves every year. For the first, second, and third years, 458, 350, and 267 firm-year observations were used respectively. The data only allowed for a three-year period analysis. However, it is possible that asset revaluations can have effects over longer periods. Table 7.2 presents the descriptive statistics of the sample.

7.3.2 Research design and results

7.3.2.1 Future firm performance

The following cross-sectional regression is estimated as proposed by Aboody et al. (1999):

$$\Delta\text{OPINC}_{t+\tau,1} = \alpha_0 + \alpha_1\text{REV}_{ti} + \alpha_2\Delta\text{OPINC}_{ti} + \alpha_3\text{MB}_{ti} + \alpha_4 \log(\text{ASSETS}_{ti}) + \varepsilon_{ti}, \quad (7.1)$$

where:
$\Delta OPINC_{t+\tau,1}$ = operating income in year $t + \tau$, minus operating income in year t, with $\tau = 1, 2, 3$.
REV_{ti} = revaluation reserve for firm i in year t.
MB_{ti} = market-to-book ratio.
$ASSETS_{ti}$ = total assets at the end of year t.

Equation (7.1) is estimated for changes in operating income over each of the three years. Operating income is income before taxes, interest, depreciation and amortization, and all other nonoperational gains because the focus is on operat-

Table 7.2 Descriptive statistics

Variables	Mean	Median	Std dev.
P_{ti}	0.76	0.04	1.87
BV_{ti}	1.54	0.07	3.39
$EARN_{ti}$	0.1	0.002	0.28
$\Delta EARN_{ti}$	0.03	0	0.54
$\Delta OPINC_t$	22,314	1566	136,148
$\Delta OPINC_{t+1}$	24,628	1737	114,874
$\Delta OPINC_{t+2}$	26,396	2888	20,396
$\Delta OPINC_{t+3}$	26,313	4744	63,896
MB	0.49	0.4	0.82
REV_{ti}	80,720	23,978	148,818
Log(ASSETS)	5.72	5.65	0.66
$REVps_{ti}$	0.13	0.01	0.35
Revenues	705,713	202,351	1943.60
R_{ti}	0.25	0	0.54

P_{ti} = Price per share four months after fiscal year end t for firm i. (Most studies using US data take prices three months after the fiscal year end. We use four months due to the extended period Brazilian firms have to report their financial information.)
BV_{ti} = Book value of equity per share excluding the revaluation balance at the end of year t for firm i.
$EARN_{ti}$ = Earnings per share for firm i, year t.
$\Delta EARN_{ti}$ = Earnings change for firm i, year t.
$\Delta OPINC_{t+\tau,1}$ = Operating income in year $t+\tau$, minus operating income in year t, where $\tau = 1, 2, 3$.
MB_{ti} = Market-to-book ratio for firm i at the end of year t.
REV_{ti} = Revaluation reserve in year t for firm i.
$Log(ASSETS_{ti})$ = Logarithm of total assets at the end of year t for firm i.
$REVps_{ti}$ = Revaluation reserve per share in year t for firm i.
Revenues = Total revenues of firm i at the end of year t.
R_{ti} = Share variation plus dividends for firm i, year t $(P_t - P_{t-1} + Div_t)/P_{t-1}$.

ing performance. The market-to-book ratio controls for effects of risk and control, as proposed by Fama and French (1992). The logarithm of total assets at the end of year is supposed to control for potential effects of size. However, according to Brown and Lo (1999) the inclusion of the logarithm of assets is not an adequate control for scale effects. Based on their conclusion, equation (7.1) is re-estimated deflating the variables by revenues of the year t[3]. If revaluation of fixed assets provides relevant information to investors, we expect the coefficient α_1 to be positive and statistically significant. Aboody et al. (1999) used the net increment in revaluations instead of revaluation reserve. The data presented here does not permit any inference regarding the exact amount of the revaluation that occurred in a given year because the amortization rates are different across firms and are not disclosed. The coefficient α_1 indicates the impact of the overall revaluation reserve on future performance and not only of the revaluation occurring on a given year. This limitation of the data clearly counts against the hypothesis that re-evaluation reserves are value relevant, because the data contained in the increment of reserves is not complete. The results should be interpreted with this limitation in mind. Table 7.3 presents the results.

The results show that revaluation reserves are significantly related to future firm performance, deflated by revenues, for one and two years in advance. This indicates that a revaluation reserve has a strong relation to future performance, as past research suggests.

7.3.2.2 Market-based tests

To test the value relevance of revaluation reserves we use both price and returns specifications. Initially we estimate the following model, which is similar to specifications in Amir et al. (1993), Easton et al. (1993), and Barth and Clinch (1996)[4]:

$$\mathrm{P}_{ti}/\mathrm{P}_{t-1} = w_{0t} + w_1\mathrm{BV}_{ti}/\mathrm{P}_{t-1} + w_2\mathrm{EARN}_{ti}/\mathrm{P}_{t-1} + w_3\mathrm{REV}_{ti}/\mathrm{P}_{t-1} + \varepsilon_{jt}, \qquad (7.2)$$

where:

P_{ti} = price per share four[5] months after fiscal year end for firm i, year t.

BV_{ti} = book value of equity per share excluding the revaluation balance for firm i, year t.

EARN_{ti} = earnings per share for firm i, year t.

REV_{ti} = revaluation reserve per share for firm i in year t.

Table 7.3 Future firm performance tests

	α_0	α_1	α_2	α_3	α_4	Adj. R^2
$\Delta\text{OPINC}_{t+1} = \alpha_0 + \alpha_1\text{REV}_{ti} + \alpha_2\Delta\text{OPINC}_{ti} + \alpha_3\text{MB}_{ti} + \alpha_4 \log(\text{ASSETS}_{ti}) + \varepsilon_{ti}$						
Undeflated values (7.1)						
Estimate	159,958	0.09	0.39	2311	12,726	0.35
t-statistic	−3.69	2.60	11.45	0.47	3.73	
p-value	0.00	0.01	0.00	0.64	0.00	
Values deflated by revenues (7.2)						
Estimate	0.20	0.01	0.07	−0.14		0.14
t-statistic	1.67	5.32	7.15	−1.23		
p-value	0.09	0.00	0.00	0.22		
$\Delta\text{OPINC}_{t+2} = \alpha_0 + \alpha_1\text{REV}_{ti} + \alpha_2\Delta\text{OPINC}_{ti} + \alpha_3\text{MB}_{ti} + \alpha_4 \log(\text{ASSETS}_{ti}) + \varepsilon_{ti}$						
Undeflated values (7.1)						
Estimate	−167,531	0.14	0.42	−4508	13,705	0.35
t-statistic	−3.90	4.45	7.31	−1.08	4.05	
p-value	0.00	0.00	0.00	0.28	0.00	
Values deflated by revenues (7.2)						
Estimate	−0.12	0.05	−0.02	0.04		0.29
t-statistic	−0.89	11.83	−1.81	0.31		
p-value	0.35	0.00	−0.07	0.76		
$\Delta\text{OPINC}_{t+3} = \alpha_0 + \alpha_1\text{REV}_{ti} + \alpha_2\Delta\text{OPINC}_{ti} + \alpha_3\text{MB}_{ti} + \alpha_4 \log(\text{ASSETS}_{ti}) + \varepsilon_{ti}$						
Undeflated values (7.1)						
Estimate	−293,623	0.02	0.02	−3998	24,488	0.31
t-statistic	−8.28	1.02	0.33	−1.18	8.81	
p-value	0.00	0.31	0.74	0.24	0.00	
Values deflated by revenues (7.2)						
Estimate	0.06	0.01	−0.07	0.01		0.26
t-statistic	0.48	0.63	−8.87	−0.07		
p-value	0.63	0.53	0.00	0.94		

All variables are the same as defined in Table 7.2.

We also estimate a cross-section returns regression:

$$\text{R}_{ti} = \gamma_{0t} + \gamma_1\text{EARN}_{ti} + \gamma_2\Delta\text{EARN}_{ti} + \gamma_3\text{REV}_{ti} + \varepsilon_{jt}, \qquad (7.3)$$

where R_{ti} is the stock return for firm *i* in period *t*, calculated as $(\text{P}_{it} - \text{P}_{it-1} + \text{div}_{it})/\text{P}_{it-1}$. This specification is designed to investigate the timeliness of the revaluation reserve. Equation (7.3) adds information to equation (7.2) because revaluation reserves can be value relevant but not temporally incorporated into prices (returns). This can occur because the Board in Brazil has complete discretion to choose when to revaluate assets. The timing of the revaluation is a function of distinct factors. For example, managers can revaluate their assets close to mergers and can take into consideration covenants and other external pressures. However, this study does not investigate these external forces despite the fact that they can be extremely relevant. If the results in equation (7.3) show a significant relation between returns and reserves, it will be possible to conclude that, despite all external forces, revaluation reserves convey valuable information to prices/returns. However, results from equation (7.3) must be interpreted with caution because the level of revaluation reserves is regressed against returns. This is not the most appropriate specification since returns are more likely to be related to changes in revaluation reserves. However, such inferences are not possible, since there are no increments in reserves in the data.

Table 7.4 presents the results of equations (7.2) and (7.3), and demonstrates a very poor relation between earnings and returns, and between revaluation reserves and returns. These results indicate that despite being value relevant, revaluation reserves do not convey timely information to explain returns. On the other hand, revaluation reserves are value relevant to explain prices. This shows that revaluation reserves in Brazil are value relevant (in terms of prices and future performance), but not timely.

7.3.2.3 Additional analyses

The previous regressions are re-estimated with the coefficient on the revaluation reserves varying with the debt-to-equity ratio. These specifications are an attempt to control for other motivations behind managers' decisions to revaluate assets. Table 7.5 shows the results.

As expected, the results show that for future firm performance, the debt-to-equity ratio presents a negative coefficient for one and two years. For market-based tests, the results are not statistically significant despite the negative sign of the coefficient. As anticipated, the debt-to-equity ratios are negatively associated with future performance, which illustrates that managers can use revaluation reserves to improve their firms' balance sheets instead of representing the underlying economic phenomena.

Table 7.4 Market-based tests

	w_0	w_1	w_2	w_3	Adj. R^2
$P_{ti}/P_{t-1} = w_{0t} + w_1 BV_{ti}/P_{t-1} + w_2 EARN_{ti}/P_{t-1} + w_3 REV_{ti}/P_{t-1} + \varepsilon_{jt}$					
Estimate	1.09	0.02	0.08	0.02	0.07
t-statistic	33.66	3.62	5.33	3.43	
p-value	0.00	0.00	0.00	0.00	
$P_{ti} = w_{0t} + w_1 BV_{ti} + w_2 EARN_{ti} + w_3 REV_{ti} + \varepsilon_{jt}$					
Estimate	0.08	0.41	1.35	−0.29	0.77
t-statistic	1.79	22.38	6.00	−2.32	
p-value	0.07	0.00	0.00	0.02	

	γ_0	γ_1	γ_2	γ_3	Adj. R^2
$R_{ti} = \gamma_{0t} + \gamma_1 EARN_{ti} + \gamma_2 \Delta EARN_{ti} + \gamma_3 REV_{ti} + \varepsilon_{jt}$					
Estimate	0.20	0.46	0.03	0.06	0.05
t-statistic	6.61	4.50	0.59	0.73	
p-value	0.00	0.00	0.55	0.47	

All variables are the same as defined in Table 7.2.

7.4 Conclusions and implications for future research

This chapter examined how fixed asset revaluations in Brazil are related to firms' future performance using *ex post* operating income and market-based metrics as dependent variables. The results indicate that revaluation reserves explain *ex ante* and *ex post* future firm performance measured by prices and realized operational profits respectively. Revaluations do not explain current returns showing that, despite being value relevant, revaluations are not timely. Controlling for debt-to-equity ratios shows that firms' capital structure influences the revaluation decision, as expected. This chapter demonstrates that revaluations of fixed assets provide valuable information in a country with very distinct corporate governance characteristics from other countries previously addressed in the literature.

The results have important implications, especially for US regulators requiring Brazilian firms to adjust their financial statements to US GAAP and thus not allowing for revaluation of fixed assets. The results illustrate that revaluation of fixed assets provides value-relevant information and demonstrate that, in the

Table 7.5 Tests controlling for debt-to-equity ratios

	Performance based					
	α_0	α_1	α_2	α_3	α_4	Adj. R^2
$\Delta OPINC_{t+1} = \alpha_0 + \alpha_1 REV_{ti} + \alpha_2 \Delta OPINC_{ti} + \alpha_3 MB_{ti} + \alpha_4 REV_{ti} \times D/E + \varepsilon_{ti}$						
Values deflated by total assets (7.2)						
Estimate	0.01	−0.01	−0.27	0.01	−0.01	0.08
t-statistic	1.94	−0.61	−6.11	1.83	−0.38	
p-value	0.05	0.54	0.00	0.07	0.71	
Values deflated by revenues (7.3)						
Estimate	0.15	0.00	0.06	−0.05	−0.04	0.28
t-statistic	1.66	4.02	8.43	−0.62	−10.50	
p-value	0.10	0.00	0.00	0.53	0.00	
$\Delta OPINC_{t+2} = \alpha_0 + \alpha_1 REV_{ti} + \alpha_2 \Delta OPINC_{ti} + \alpha_3 MB_{ti} + \alpha_4 REV_{ti} \times D/E + \varepsilon_{ti}$						
Values deflated by total assets (7.2)						
Estimate	0.01	0.02	−0.19	−0.01	−0.00	0.04
t-statistic	2.73	0.76	−3.59	−1.99	−0.34	
p-value	0.01	0.45	0.00	0.04	0.73	
Values deflated by revenues (7.3)						
Estimate	0.08	0.02	−0.04	−0.00	−0.00	0.16
t-statistic	0.75	1.79	−5.33	−0.03	−6.45	
p-value	0.46	0.07	−0.06	0.98	0.00	
$\Delta OPINC_{t+3} = \alpha_0 + \alpha_1 REV_{ti} + \alpha_2 \Delta OPINC_{ti} + \alpha_3 MB_{ti} + \alpha_4 REV_{ti} \times D/E + \varepsilon_{ti}$						
Values deflated by total assets (7.2)						
Estimate	0.02	−0.01	0.01	0.00	−0.00	0.00
t-statistic	3.09	−0.23	0.18	0.09	−0.14	
p-value	0.00	0.82	0.86	0.93	0.89	
Values deflated by revenues (7.3)						
Estimate	0.04	−0.03	−0.07	−0.01	0.00	0.33
t-statistic	0.31	−2.78	−9.27	−0.14	4.94	
p-value	0.76	0.01	0.00	0.89	0.00	

	Market based					
	w_0	w_1	w_2	w_3	w_4	Adj. R^2
$P_{ti}/P_{t-1} = w_{0t} + w_1 BV_{ti}/P_{t-1} + w_2 EARN_{ti}/P_{t-1} + w_3 REV_{ti}/P_{t-1} + w_4(REV_{ti}/P_{t-1}) \times D/E + \varepsilon_{jt}$						
Estimate	1.09	0.02	0.08	0.02	−0.001	0.06
t-statistic	33.63	3.42	5.12	2.62	−0.67	
p-value	0.00	0.00	0.00	0.01	0.50	

Table 7.5 *(Continued)*

	γ_0	γ_1	γ_2	γ_3	γ_4	Adj. R^2
$R_{ti} = \gamma_{0t} + \gamma_1 EARN_{ti} + \gamma_2 \Delta EARN_{ti} + \gamma_3 REV_{ti} + \gamma_4 REV_{ti} \times D/E + \varepsilon_{jt}$						
Estimate	0.20	0.45	0.02	0.14	−0.01	0.05
t-statistic	6.60	4.38	0.43	1.40	−1.46	
p-value	0.00	0.00	0.67	0.16	0.14	

All variables are the same as defined in Table 7.2.

case of revaluation of fixed assets, adjustments to US GAAP lack theoretical and empirical support.

Acknowledgments

I would like to thank Martin Walker, Eliseu Martins, and Sérgio de Iudícibus for useful comments.

Notes

1. Not one firm in Brazil currently has its control floating on the Stock Exchange. Few owners control firms and do not trade their shares frequently.
2. Easton et al. (1993) provide a detailed view of the Australian GAAP for revaluation of fixed assets.
3. We use revenues as proxies for scale effects. We believe that firm value is not adequate in this context because we are not using market-related variables.
4. As suggested by Brown and Lo (1999), we deflated the variables by P_{t-1} to correct for scale effects.
5. Most studies using US data take prices three months after the end of the fiscal year. We use four months due to the extended period Brazilian firms have to report their financial information.

References

Aboody, D., Barth, M., and Kasznik, R. (1999). Revaluations of Fixed Assets and Future Firm Performance. *Journal of Accounting and Economics*, 26(1–3):149–178.

Ali, A. and Hwang, L.-S. (2000). Country-Specific Factors Related to Financial Reporting and the Value Relevance of Accounting Data. *Journal of Accounting Research*, 38(1):1–25.

Amir, E., Harris, T.S., and Venuti, E.K. (1993). A Comparison of US versus non-US GAAP Accounting Measures Using Form 20-f Reconciliations. *Journal of Accounting Research*, 31(3):230–275.

Anderson, C.W. (1999). Financial Contracting Under Extreme Uncertainty: An Analysis of Brazilian Corporate Debentures. *Journal of Financial Economics*, 51(1):45–84.

Ball, R., Kothari, S.P., and Robin, A. (2001). The Effect of Institutional Factors on the Properties of Accounting Earnings. *Journal of Accounting and Economics*, 29(1):1–51.

Barth, M.E. and Clinch, G.J. (1996). International Accounting Differences and Their Relation to Share Prices: Evidence from UK, Australia, and Canadian Firms. *Contemporary Accounting Research*, 13(1):135–170.

Barth, M.E. and Clinch, G. (1998). Revalued Financial, Tangible and Intangible Assets: Associations with Share Prices and Non-market-based Estimates. *Journal of Accounting Research*, 36(3):199–233.

Brown, S. and Lo, K. (1999). Use of R^2 in Accounting Research: Measuring Changes in Value Relevance Over the Last Four Decades. *Journal of Accounting and Economics*, 28(2):83–115.

Cairns, D. (1997). The Future Shape of Harmonization: A Reply. *European Accounting Review*, 6(2):305–348.

Deliberação. (1995). Do Ministério da Fazenda, 1(1).

Doupnik, T.S., Martins, E., and Barbieri, G. (1995). Innovations in Brazilian Inflation Accounting. *International Journal of Accounting*, 30(4):302–317.

Dummontier, P. and Raffournier, B. (2002). Accounting and Capital Markets: A Survey of the European Evidence. *European Accounting Review*, 11:119–151.

Easton, P.D., Eddey, P.H., and Harris, T.S. (1993). An Investigation of Revaluations of Tangible Long-lived Assets. *Journal of Accounting Research*, 31(Suppl.):1–38.

Fama, E.F. and French, K.R. (1992). The Cross-section of Expected Stock Returns. *Journal of Finance*, 47(2):427–465.

Harris, T.S., Lang, M., and Möller, H.P. (1994). The Value Relevance of German Accounting Measures: An Empirical Analysis. *Journal of Accounting Research*, 32(2):21–67.

Iudícibus, S., Martins, E., and Gelbcke, E. (2003). Manual de Contabilidade das Sociedades por Ações. Editora Atlas, São Paulo, Brazil.

Leuz, C. and Wustemann, J. (2003). The Role of Accounting in the German Financial System. Working Paper, University of Pennsylvania, PA.

Lopes, A.B. (2005). Financial Accounting in Brazil: An Empirical Examination. *Latin American Business Review*, forthcoming.

Meek, G.K. and Thomas, W.B. (2004). A Review of Markets-based International Accounting Research. *Journal of International Accounting Research*, 3(1):21–42.

RIR (1999). Regulamento do Imposto de Renda, 1(1):56.

Sharpe, I.G. and Walker, R.G. (1975). Asset Revaluations and Stock Market Prices. *Journal of Accounting Research*, 13(2):293–310.

Standish, P. and Ung, S. (1982). Corporate Signalling, Asset Revaluations and the Stock Prices of British Companies. *Accounting Review*, 57(4):701–715.

Wallace, R.S.O. and Gernon, H. (1991). Frameworks for International Comparative Financial Reporting. *Journal of Accounting Literature*, 5(3):209–264.

8

Hedge Funds and the Stale Pricing Issue

Greg N. Gregoriou, William Kelting, and Mohamed Gaber

8.1 Introduction

Over the last decade hedge funds have become attractive and efficient alternative investment vehicles for diversifying traditional stock and bond investment portfolios. More recently hedge funds have been the subject of the stale pricing issue since their reported volatility is less than the actual volatility caused by the infrequent trading and smoothing of returns by funds that trade in these illiquid type of markets. The subject of stale pricing implies the practice of pricing a hedge fund's shares based on prices of the stocks in the portfolio that do not accurately reflect a true picture of the true value as a result of timing differences involved when trading illiquid or thinly traded stocks. Because of the timing difference, a US hedge fund manager possessing New Zealand stocks will use the closing prices to obtain the net asset value (NAV) of the fund. This is an erroneous method when it comes to fairly pricing stocks because the hedge fund manager is only basing the NAV of the fund on old or stale pricing information that is approximately 14 hours out (the approximate time difference between the US and New Zealand). In addition, events can occur throughout that time period that can significantly affect the value of the New Zealand stocks, resulting in an erroneous NAV that does not correctly reflect their true and fair value. Differences in time zones can facilitate time-zone arbitrage trading, because the mispricings in global stock markets can result in profits from stock purchased in one market and sold in another at a cost to the shareholders of the hedge fund. For example, an investor having a position in a directional hedge fund uses strategy based on expected market movement owning international equities will try to correctly time the purchase on a certain day when US markets will exhibit a broad increase. The investor's expectation is that international stock markets will increase the following day, based on the broad movement of American stock markets. It is not illegal to take advantage of these timing differences, but there is increasing concern about the fairness to the shareholders of the fund. The Securities Exchange Commission (SEC) has recommended that a redemption fee be made compulsory on investments that are held for less than five business days.

Illiquid securities pose a valuation problem because the last market price for the security might not reflect the present true and fair market value. These valuation problems are further compounded in the case of a basket of hedge funds. Mutual funds, on the other hand, report on a daily basis, whereas the majority of hedge funds report their returns net of all management and performance fees to database vendors on a monthly basis and have not been under the watchful eye of the Securities Exchange Commission (SEC). They are not regulated because they meet exceptions stipulated in Acts enforced by the SEC regarding the number and nature of the fund investors, the nature of the fund itself, or because the offering of securities is not a public offering. However, in October 2004 the SEC voted 3–2 in favor of allowing its inspectors to audit the books of hedge funds.

Using stale pricing to establish the NAV of a portfolio is not consistent with the position of both the accounting profession and the SEC, which requires that investments be reported at fair value or '... the amount at which the investment could be exchanged in a current transaction between willing parties, other than in a forced or liquidation sale' (Harrell and Spiegel, 2004). In a majority of cases, the fair value of an investment is easily determined by obtaining current market price data from a variety of independent pricing sources. Illiquid stocks create a problem in that no existing market price may be currently available. Therefore, an effort must be made to properly estimate the current fair market value. On some occasions where international securities markets close prior to the American markets, if a certain occurrence in the market is anticipated to influence the value of a stock during that time frame which has already occurred, attempts must be made to properly estimate the price of the international stock rather than use the stale international stock's closing price. Using these types of estimates can open the door for unwarranted manipulation. Hedge funds typically charge an incentive fee of 20%, which has a tendency to inflate the NAV. This has been the case for many of the recent hedge fund frauds. The International Organization of Securities Commissions (IOSCO) issued the following statement: 'In order to make informed judgments, investors should be aware of hedge fund policies and procedures for the estimation of asset values.' Moreover, investors must make sure these policies and procedures are adhered to by hedge funds. Small hedge funds that do not have to be registered with the SEC may or may not subject the financial reports to the scrutiny of an independent auditor. Even if an independent auditor is hired to audit an unregistered hedge fund, the scope of the work performed by the auditor may be less than for registered funds. Auditors of registered funds are required to test all portfolio valuations as of the date of the financial statements. In the case of unregistered funds, the extent of testing portfolio valuations is a matter of the auditor's judgment.

These issues are compounded in cases involving funds of hedge funds (FOF) for which the portfolio consists of other hedge funds. For example, only certain funds included in an FOF may be registered, some may be subject to independent auditing, and some may be neither registered nor subject to auditing. Moreover, an FOF manager must wait for the hedge funds in his portfolio to report monthly net returns before determining the final return of the FOF. If a hedge fund is behind schedule in reporting its monthly return, the FOF manager will most likely use the fund's earlier return to acquire an estimate for the monthly return of his FOF. When new investors buy shares in an FOF that is late in reporting its monthly net returns, investors will be receiving a good deal because the FOF may be undervalued. Investors opting to sell their shares in such an FOF, however, may be getting less than expected (Kazemi and Schneeweis, 2004). Furthermore, the authors observed that hedge funds smooth out returns, thus making hedge funds an ideal option for inclusion in traditional stock and bond investment portfolios.

In many cases where FOFs have several hedge fund managers in their portfolio, concentrating in emerging markets may not always provide investors with correct monthly returns, which may lead to an imprecise explanation of their statistical analyses. Due to returns smoothing, investors may not be able to correctly assess a hedge fund's true risk. Amenc et al. (2004) observed that hedge funds are susceptible to skewness and kurtosis in their returns distribution and it may not be feasible for FOF managers to forecast drops in monthly returns and correctly evaluate an FOF's NAV.

Numerous hedge fund managers employ their skills to make profits from price inefficiencies in world securities and bond markets. Furthermore, a large majority of hedge fund managers are unwilling to disclose their trading strategies and are rather reserved about providing full disclosure of stocks and bonds in their investment portfolio.

Appraising hedge fund performance with standard measures, such as annualized returns, standard deviation, the risk-adjusted measure referred to as the Sharpe ratio, and the correlation coefficient, will likely lead to a biased approximation of the fund's risk–reward profile (Amin and Kat, 2003). Moreover, Murguía and Umemoto (2004) asserted that '... although hedge fund managers may appear to provide returns in excess of their systematic risk exposures, they may be exposed to other risk factors not captured by traditional evaluation measures'. Hedge fund strategies produce non-normal returns and exhibit skewness and kurtosis (the third and fourth moments of a distribution); therefore, measuring the actual performance of hedge funds and deciding whether an FOF manager is accurately reporting net returns is, to some extent, a difficult task. Numerous academic studies have acknowledged that hedge fund strategies display a significant amount of excess returns (alpha), even after adjusting for wide market exposure (Liang, 2001). Nevertheless, these studies do not consider the illiquid securities held by numerous hedge funds.

Stale pricing in the hedge fund industry normally refers to a certain form of over-valuating foreign securities. In some cases, hedge funds use stale pricing as a method to inflate the fund's NAV. In addition, emerging market securities may not offer daily or monthly liquidity and therefore hedge fund managers holding these securities may need to calculate the average of the latest returns to correctly predict or forecast current returns. Although some hedge funds voluntarily report monthly returns net of all performance and management fees to database vendors, the data may not precisely represent the true value of the fund's NAV. If information is not accessible on illiquid securities then this allows the hedge fund manager to price the securities with any NAV he likes to favor the fund's returns. Often, hedge fund managers may price these assets to reflect the holdings in their portfolio due to be reported to investors at the end of the month. In particular, this is frequently the case of emerging market hedge funds.

8.2 Background information

Since hedge funds are frequently used as portfolio diversifiers, managers have an inducement to report returns that are consistent and uncorrelated to the market. This can artificially decrease the volatility and correlation of hedge funds to traditional market indices (Asness et al., 2001). In addition, Kazemi and Schneeweis (2004) found that quarterly standard deviations are greater than monthly standard deviations, which is consistent with stale pricing. For example, if there is an extreme negative market event, the hedge fund may not be able to precisely mark illiquid securities for numerous months to reflect the new market value of the position. This results in an over-inflated NAV until the securities in the portfolio precisely reflect their true market value. *Consequently, investors would have a false sense of independence from market exposure, and year-end returns would be inflated.*

A number of researchers have used lagged market betas to analyze the true market exposure of hedge funds. For example, Asness et al. (2001) used lagged market betas to examine the true market exposure of certain hedge fund classifications, using convertible arbitrage, fixed-income arbitrage, and event-driven classifications. These classifications typically have a large amount of international stocks, for it is very difficult to obtain a precise price, particularly if the securities are sold over-the-counter (OTC). The more illiquid the market, the more difficult it is to attain a correct price for securities, bonds, and commodities.

The apprehension of hedge funds adding alpha, as discussed in Schneeweis and Spurgin (1999), is rejected by Murguía and Umemoto (2004), who dispute that hedge funds do not provide alpha but rather increase investment opportunities by including alternative investments into traditional stock and bond investment portfolios. By manipulating international securities in the portfolio, hedge fund managers can influence the alpha of the portfolio. Recent studies have concluded that hedge fund returns are typically overstated (Murguía and Umemoto, 2004) and investors must have the ability to identify these signs and be ready to redeem their shares before a catastrophe or extreme market event, such as the Russian rouble crisis of August 1998. Some hedge funds use stale prices to value their portfolios, thus exposing themselves to arbitrageurs who buy securities at incorrect low prices knowing that they will increase the next day. Arbitrage pricing can methodically reduce a hedge fund's assets under management, causing large daily losses.

The relevance of qualitative factors for hedge fund investing is growing, and investors will probably take them into consideration when evaluating hedge funds. Hedge funds do not follow the same policies as mutual funds in terms of corporate governance, leveraging, pricing, redemption period, monthly performance reporting, management fees, and performance fees.

8.3 Recent developments

The Securities and Exchange Commission (SEC) will be regulating hedge funds, in spite of tough resistance from critics both inside and outside the Commission. On 27 October 2004, the SEC adopted Rule 203(b)(3)-2 that requires most hedge fund advisers with assets more than $25 million to register with the SEC (by 1 February 2006) under the Investment Advisers Act of 1940. The Act applies to the managers of mutual funds, pension funds, corporate trusts, and endowments. This move would significantly widen the SEC's jurisdictional reach. Furthermore, forcing onshore hedge fund advisers to register permits the SEC to understand in-depth how the industry functions and to potentially expose deceptive behavior. Once registered with the SEC, hedge fund advisers would be subject to regular verification checks of their books and records, and would have to divulge to the SEC the number of funds they manage and the assets under management. In addition, they would also have to report information about their investors, employees, and the persons controlling or that are associated with the hedge fund adviser. Moreover, the SEC has planned to tackle the time-zone arbitrage matter by imposing a 2% fee on fund shareholders that redeem their shares within five business days after purchase. The effectiveness of such an action is the subject of a great deal of controversy. For example, hedge funds could still obtain an advantage of time-zone differences through the use of futures contracts.

8.4 Checklist of questions

Investors looking to invest in hedge funds must carefully comprehend the policies and procedures used by funds to value assets, and should be predominantly skeptical of cases where objective, independent pricing sources are not used. A checklist of 24 questions may assist gaining that understanding. The main focus of the checklist is on the subject of valuation and especially valuation of assets where approximations are required. Investors must also be concerned with other issues as well and should be prepared to pose more questions. For example, see the comprehensive checklist by the Investor Risk Committee of the International Association of Financial Engineers (2004).

1. Has the board of directors (or equivalent) adopted a policy for valuation of securities?
2. Is there a committee (or individual) charged with responsibility for valuation?
3. Is the person or committee independent of those responsible for investment management functions?
4. Are independent pricing sources utilized wherever possible?
5. In cases where market prices are not available, how are valuations determined?
6. Are methods of valuation applied consistently over time?
7. Do those individuals determining fair value estimates have the appropriate expertise and experience?
8. Do the methods of valuation appear appropriate under the circumstances?
9. What models, if any, are used to estimate fair values?
10. If models are used, are they provided by an independent source?
11. Are model results compared to actual results on a regular basis?
12. Does the fund have an internal audit function?
13. Are security valuation policies and procedures subjected to the scrutiny of the internal auditors?
14. Who does the internal audit function report to?
15. Are internal audit reports filed on a regular basis and recommendations acted upon?
16. Is the fund registered with the SEC?
17. If registered, who are the independent auditors?
18. Did the independent auditors provide any comments regarding the fund's internal controls, particularly over the valuation of assets?

19. If unregistered, were the financial statements of the fund audited?
20. Who were the auditors?
21. Did the independent auditors provide any comments regarding the fund's internal controls, particularly over the valuation of assets?
22. If the fund is not audited, why?
23. If an FOF, does the manager scrutinize the funds in the portfolio as to their methods for valuation of assets and address questions similar to numbers 1–20?
24. Does the FOF have an established mechanism for regular monitoring of the hedge funds included in the portfolio, including periodic visits?

8.5 Conclusion

Under the direction of a board of directors or equivalent, hedge fund management is responsible for making a good judgment attempt in estimating fair values. The uncertainty inherent in estimating fair value of investments, the incentive fee structure for hedge fund managers, and the frequent lack of regulatory oversight create considerable risk for hedge fund investors. Though stale pricing may be objective, it frequently does not offer a measure of fair value and is inappropriate for decision-making purposes. Fair value estimates may be less dependable but are more pertinent. Investors in hedge funds and managers of FOFs must examine the policies and procedures used by hedge funds to determine fair value. A survey approach such as that suggested in this chapter may be a practical tool in the due diligence process.

References

Amenc, N., Malaise, P., Martellini, L., and Vaissié, M. (2004). Fund of Hedge Fund Reporting. Discussion Paper, Edhec Risk and Asset Management Research Centre, Lille, France.

Amin, G.S. and Kat, H.M. (2003). Stocks, Bond and Hedge Funds: Not a Free Lunch. *Journal of Portfolio Management*, 29(4):113–120.

Asness, C.A., Krail, R., and Liew, J. (2001). Do Hedge Funds Hedge? *Journal of Portfolio Management*, 28(1):6–19.

Harrell, M.P. and Spiegel, J.A. (2004). The Debevoise and Plimpton Private Equity Report, Spring, pp. 16–22.

International Association of Financial Engineers Investor Risk Committee (2004). Valuation Concepts for Investment Companies and Financial Institutions and their Stakeholders. IAFE, June.

Kazemi, H. and Schneeweis, T. (2004). Hedge Funds: Stale Prices Revisited. Working Paper CISDM, University of Massachusetts, Isenberg School of Management, Amherst, MA.

Liang, B. (2001). Hedge Fund Performance: 1990–1999. *Financial Analysts Journal*, 57(1):11–18.

Murguía, A. and Umemoto, D.Y. (2004). An Alternative Look at Hedge Funds. *Journal of Financial Planning*, 17(1):42–49.

Schneeweis, T. and Spurgin, R. (1999). Alpha, Alpha ... Who's Got the Alpha? *Journal of Alternative Investments*, 2(2):83–87.

9

Adopting and Implementing International Financial Reporting Standards in Transition Economies

Robert W. McGee

9.1 Introduction

Much of the world is moving in the direction of International Financial Reporting Standards (IFRS). The European Union has adopted them as of 1 January 2005 (Cuijpers and Buijink, 2005) and IFRS will be required of any new EU applicants. Russia adopted them as of 1 January 2004 (McGee and Preobragenskaya, 2005). Most or all of the former Soviet republics have either adopted them or are in the process of adopting them (McGee, 1999a; McGee and Preobragenskaya, 2006), either *in toto* or piecemeal. The transition economies of Eastern and Central Europe are also adopting them (Garrod and McLeay, 1996; Jermakowicz and Rinke, 1996; Kemp and Alexander, 1996; Zelenka et al., 1996), as have many other countries (Larson, 1993; Arthur Andersen et al., 2000, 2001; BDO et al., 2002; Choi et al., 2002; Street, 2002). Some research has been done about the reform of the accounting and financial reporting system in Armenia (McGee, 1999a), Belarus (Pankov, 1998; Sucher and Kemp, 1998), Bosnia (McGee and Preobragenskaya, 2006), China (Chan et al., 1999), the Czech Republic (Seal et al., 1995; Jindrichovska and McLeay, 2005), Hungary (Boross et al., 1995; Borda and McLeay, 1996), Lithuania (Mackevicius et al., 1996), Poland (Krzywda et al., 1995; Adams and McMillan, 1997; Kosmala, 2005), Romania (King et al., 2001; Roberts, 2001), Russia (Enthoven et al., 1998; McGee and Preobragenskaya, 2005), Slovenia (Turk and Garrod, 1996), and Ukraine (Solodchenko and Sucher, 2005; McGee and Preobragenskaya, 2006).

However, the adoption and implementation process has not always gone smoothly. Just because a government decides to adopt IFRS does not mean that practitioners will immediately erase the old system from their memory banks and start using the new system. Indeed, many clients, as well as their accountants, do not see the need for IFRS. Thus, a selling job has to be done to convince practitioners and their clients that they need to use IFRS. But why is it necessary to sell enterprises and accountants on the need for IFRS? If such a need actually existed, wouldn't the market already be supplying that need? Why is there a need to cram IFRS down the throats of the local population by top-down planning?

This chapter will address some of these issues and will also discuss the problems that various transition economies have encountered on the way to IFRS adoption and the solutions that have been tried. The author relates his experiences as a consultant on several USAID accounting reform projects, as well as the results of some private research he has conducted on accounting reform in several transition economies.

9.2 Adopting and implementing IFRS

Adopting IFRS is one thing. Implementing them is something else. The mere fact that a government might adopt new accounting rules does not mean that they will be swiftly, efficiently, and comprehensively applied and implemented throughout the economy. Old mentalities and ways of doing things have to be replaced, which might take a generation. Ways of doing business also have to be changed. In Russia, for example, the widespread use of barter is hampering the implementation of IFRS (Lindberg, 2002). Furthermore, it might take years for some governments to decide to adopt IFRS (Schneidman, 2003), a move that must take place before any implementation can begin.

The initial step–convincing relevant government officials that they need to adopt IFRS–may not be easy. The approach that was usually used has been for a Western government, such as the United States, or for an NGO, such as the World Bank, International Monetary Fund, TACIS, the European Bank for Reconstruction and Development, Asian Development Bank, or African Development Bank, to pressure the officials of some transition economy or developing economy to adopt some form of internationally recognized financial reporting rules as a condition of obtaining assistance. Countries that want to join the EU are also under pressure to adopt IFRS.

This top-down approach to economic regulation has never worked well in centrally planned economies, yet Western bureaucrats seem to think it will work well in an economy that is trying to cast off the shackles of central planning as they move toward a market economy. One problem with the top-down approach that has often been encountered is the fact that the top-level bureaucrats in the target country are not the ones who must implement the changes. Indeed, they often know little or nothing about accounting or accounting reform, which means they must delegate the details to their subordinates.

If their subordinates understand the problem and are willing to work hard to implement the changes, the transformation process goes well. That was the case in Armenia, where the third-tier people in the finance ministry who had to implement the rules their government adopted supported the change, and were intelligent and hard working (McGee, 1999a; McGee and Preobragenskaya, 2006). The fact that neither the official charged with the task of implementing IFRS nor his assistant had ever taken an accounting course was a problem, but not an insurmountable one. The consulting firm that had the USAID accounting reform contract for Armenia stationed an ex-pat in the finance ministry so that the relevant government officials would have ready and constant access to a foreign expert who could explain the new rules and how they worked. The ex-pat often had to go through particular International Accounting Standards (IAS) one line at a time, explaining what it meant and scribbling down examples for later reference.

In Bosnia, the implementation process was much different (McGee and Preobragenskaya, 2006). First of all, the accounting reform project in Bosnia was really two different and separate projects. The USAID accounting reform project in Bosnia-Herzegovina began a few years after a series of Balkan wars split the six former republics of Yugoslavia into several separate nations (Holbrooke, 1998; Burg and Shoup, 1999; Zimmermann, 1999). The Dayton Peace Accords of 1995 tried to put Bosnia back together after several years of fighting that had turned the former Yugoslav republic into three warring ethnic groups (Daalder, 2000). The Orthodox Christian Serbs got 49% of post-war Bosnia and called their section Republika Srpska. The Sunni Muslim Bosniaks and Roman Catholic Croats got the other 51% and called their part the Muslim-Croat Federation. Post-war Bosnia had 13 finance ministries, one for each of the 10 cantons, one for each of the major parts of the country, plus one for the nation as a whole.

The finance ministries in the Muslim-Croat Federation and Republika Srpska were in charge of accounting reform in their part of the country and they each took a different approach to reform. The finance ministry in the Muslim-Croat Federation, which is located in Sarajevo, adopted IFRS more or less smoothly, although with some bumps along the way. And they did not adopt all of the IFRS exactly as written in the UK. For example, they adopted only the *indirect* method of accounting for cash flows, although international standards allow the adoption of the direct method as well.

Once the Serbs learned that the Muslim-Croat Federation adopted *just* the indirect method of accounting for cash flows, the powers that be in Republika Srpska decided to adopt *just* the direct method of accounting for cash flows. As a result, the country of Bosnia-Herzegovina has sort of adopted the IAS on cash flows, except that companies in the Muslim-Croat Federation part of the country can use only the indirect method and the companies in Republika Srpska can use only the direct method.

Republika Srpska was also slower to actually implement IFRS. It did it one standard at a time. It also did not adopt some of the standards. For example, it absolutely refused to adopt the IFRS on asset impairment. However, in all fairness, it must be said that other centrally planned economies also have not adopted this standard, or if they have, they refuse to use it.

There is a very good practical reason for not using this standard. This IAS requires companies to write down their assets if their market value is less than book value. Many enterprises in transition economies have assets that are overvalued. If they wrote them down to market value it would destroy the equity in their balance sheets. Companies don't want to do that, for a variety of reasons. It would be more difficult, or perhaps impossible, to obtain a bank loan or to sell their shares in a reputable stock exchange, for example. And the accountants who audit those companies are extremely hesitant to pressure their clients into reflecting those assets at market value. If they attempted to do so, they would likely lose those clients, since it is still possible to buy an audit opinion in many transition economy countries. If one independent auditor does not issue a clean opinion, there is probably one down the street or around the corner who will do it for the right price.

A number of transition economies have implemented only some of the IFRS standards. Russia, for example, sees no need to adopt the standard on hyperinflation, since it no longer suffers from hyperinflation. It also has no present plans to adopt the standard on derivatives, since few Russian companies have them and even fewer accountants and bankers understand them. So why go to all the trouble of adopting and implementing such a standard if no one will use it for the foreseeable future?

Convincing finance ministry officials to adopt and implement IFRS is not the end of the process but only the beginning. Accounting practitioners and enterprise accountants and managers also need to be convinced that the new rules must be learned and applied. Convincing them has not always been easy to do. There is the inertia problem, which Milton Friedman pointed out a few years ago (Friedman and Friedman, 1984). Basically, this mindset begins with the premise that the best way to do something is precisely the way it is already being done. More than one bureaucrat has told the author that the Soviet system has worked fine for several decades and that there is no need to change anything.

Such a statement has a grain of truth to it. The Soviet bookkeeping system was quite good. Debits were always on the left and credits were always on the right. There was a journal entry for every transaction and everyone knew what those journal entries were. Why change?

One of the major problems with the Soviet bookkeeping system was that it was *only* a bookkeeping system. No sort of meaningful financial analysis or profit planning could be done with those numbers because all prices were determined arbitrarily and there was no such thing as profit. This major deficiency in the Soviet accounting system was one of the main causes of the collapse of the Soviet Union. Resources could not be allocated efficiently and the many decades of misallocation had a cumulative effect. Ludwig von Mises predicted this collapse as far back as the 1920s (1920, 1922, 1923, 1935).

Another problem with implementing IFRS was the general and widespread perception among government officials, enterprise managers, and accounting practitioners that they were not needed or useful. This perception also has a grain of truth to it. The tax accounting systems of many transition economies are based on the cash method or on some national method that has little or no resemblance to IFRS. Tax officials in these countries are only interested in looking at accounting books that use the national standards or the tax standards. They have no use for accounting numbers that are prepared using IFRS because they cannot compute the tax liability using those numbers (McGee and Preobragenskaya, 2005).

In many companies, no one else has any need for numbers prepared with IFRS either. Where there is no demand, there will also be no supply. Why learn rules to make IFRS-based financial statements if nobody is going to read them? In fact, only a small percentage of the enterprises in most transition economies will be able to find anyone who wants to read their IFRS statements. The main exception is the largest enterprises, which are trying to attract foreign capital investment (Preobragenskaya and McGee, 2003). Foreign bankers and other potential investors will demand to see financial statements prepared using either IFRS or US GAAP as a condition of investing. But this exception might apply to perhaps 25 or 50 enterprises in the whole country. The other 5000 or 20,000 enterprises have no use for statements prepared using IFRS.

9.3 Translation problems

Early in the implementation stage, IFRS and ISA (International Standards on Auditing) have to be translated into the local language and made available to the various accounting constituencies in the country. The people in the finance ministry have to have copies so they can read what they have adopted or will soon adopt. At some point, accounting practitioners will have to have access to the standards in a language they can understand. Otherwise, they will not be able to implement them. Accounting educators must have a copy so they can start teaching the new rules and students have to have a copy so they can read their assignments.

However, local language translations of IFRS and ISA do not drop from the sky. Someone has to sit down and do the translation, one sentence at a time. Although there are certain problems that become apparent as soon as an attempt is made to translate IFRS and ISA into the local language, the translation problems encountered in one country are not identical to those encountered in another country. There are some local differences.

The problems encountered in Armenia are typical of the generic kind of problems that are encountered whenever an accounting reform project goes into a country and tries to help the country convert to IFRS and ISA. Choosing a language was not a problem. Although all Armenians are fluent in both Russian and Armenian, the finance ministry as well as most accountants and educators wanted the IFRS to be available in the Armenian language. After the collapse of the Soviet Union, the various former Soviet republics rediscovered nationalism. They wanted to use their own language, not the language of some far-off former central government.

Once the target language was agreed upon, the next thing to do was to find real, living, breathing individuals who could do the translation. IAS (which they were called at the time, in 1998, when the translation started) consisted of hundreds of pages of technical material, as did the ISA. A team had to be hired to do the translation, since one person could do only about five pages a day.

The fact that a team had to be hired rather than a single individual caused a coordination problem because each translator did it a different way. They used different words for the same concept and they each had a different style.

But that was not the first problem that was encountered. As soon as the solicitation to hire translators was published, it was found that no one in the entire country met the requirements needed for the job. What was needed was a team of individuals who knew English, Armenian, and accounting. Although it was not difficult to find people who were fluent in both English and Armenian, it was impossible to find anyone who had any background in a Western accounting system. That is because the universities in Armenia, as well as the universities in the other former Soviet republics and the centrally planned economies of the various Soviet satellite countries, did not teach what would be regarded as accounting in a developed Western economy. All they taught was bookkeeping, and perhaps some auditing and mathematics. There was no such thing as a course on intermediate or advanced accounting, or even management accounting, for the most part.

The translators hired for the Armenian USAID accounting reform project had degrees in physics, chemistry, English literature, and economics. They had to be trained in the terminology of accounting on the job. Frequent meetings had to be held in the early phases of the project to discuss what the various concepts meant. The translation problem was made more difficult by the fact that there were no terms in the Armenian language for some of the English words.

The same problem was encountered when the translation team tried to translate some English language accounting texts into Russian, which was the language

USAID wanted to use for training materials. The reason for choosing Russian was quite simple. USAID had several accounting reform projects going on at the same time and it wanted to be able to use the same training materials for all of its projects in the former Soviet Union. It did not want to have to translate accounting texts into local languages like Georgian, Azeri, Ukrainian, etc. when the students using the book all knew Russian. That caused something of a political problem with the Armenian finance ministry, as well as with some practitioners and university officials. However, when it was explained why Russian was chosen, and it was emphasized that (1) they would be getting the books for free and (2) USAID was not going to change its mind, the problem melted away, at least on the surface.

The Russian translations encountered the same kind of problems that were faced by the Armenian translations. There were no terms in Russian for some of the concepts covered in the books. In fact, the Russian language did not even have a word for *accountant*. It borrowed the German word for bookkeeper – *buchhalter*.

The Russian translation of the International Accounting Standards was not available until 1999, about halfway through the translation of the IAS into Armenian, so the translation team did not have access to the Russian version of IAS for several months. When they did receive copies, other problems developed because the Russian translation was mediocre in parts and in some cases downright incorrect. For example, in one place, the Russian version listed some things that should *not* be done. However, the Russian translation left out the word *not*, causing Russian readers to think that the list was things that were supposed to be done instead of *not* supposed to be done. The Armenian translation team uncovered that error when they were comparing the Russian version with the English version, which they were in the process of translating into Armenian.

The 1999 Russian version of IAS was circulated widely. The second edition was not published for more than five years and it is not known by the present author whether that error was corrected in the revised edition. However, when the author discussed this point in 2003 with the individual who was in charge of the Russian translation, he was unaware that the mistake existed, and I was unable to tell him which page it was on, or even the topic (I had forgotten), so perhaps the mistake continues in the second edition.

The translation problems encountered in Bosnia were similar to those faced in Armenia in some ways, but there were also some major differences. Some English language terms did not have any local language equivalents. But that was not the major problem.

The major problem was choosing which language to use. Prior to the Balkan wars that led to the disintegration of Yugoslavia, the main language of the country was Serbo-Croatian, although Slovenian, Macedonian, and a few other languages were also in common use in some parts of the country. Serbo-Croatian is basically one language with two alphabets. Serbian uses the Cyrillic alphabet whereas Croatian uses the Latin alphabet, but the vast majority of the vocabulary is the same, although there are some regional pronunciation differences. Everyone knew both alphabets equally well because they would use Cyrillic texts in school one week and Latin texts the next.

When the country split up, and when Bosnia got its independence, a third language – Bosnian – came into existence. It was created in Dayton, Ohio, as part of the Dayton Peace Accords. As part of that peace agreement, the Serbian language was to use the Cyrillic alphabet, Croatian was to use the Latin alphabet, and Bosnian could use either alphabet.

When the translation team was preparing to translate the first group of accounting books, a decision had to be made as to which language to use. Each of the three main ethnic groups in Bosnia – the Orthodox Christian Serbs, the Roman Catholic Croats, and the Muslim Bosniaks – each wanted their own language to be used for all the texts. USAID balked because it did not want to incur the expense of translating each book three times. So a compromise was reached. All sides agreed that one-third of the books would be translated into each language and they all agreed to use all the books that were translated. And since there was already a publishing company in Croatia that was translating some accounting books, the decision was made for USAID to coordinate its efforts with that publishing company so USAID would only have to pay to translate books into Serbian and Bosnian.

That decision seemingly worked well, until the first Serbian book was hot off the press. After spending several months and thousands of dollars translating the book into Serbian, a few copies were presented to the Dean at the University of Sarajevo, the largest university in the country and also a predominantly Muslim university. He took one look at the book, then said that his university could not use that book because it was in the Cyrillic alphabet. He explained that if his students took that book home and their parents saw it, they would be marching into his office to complain. The Muslims, who had been reduced to hiding in their homes for two years during the Serb siege of Sarajevo, wanted nothing to do with anything Serb, including the alphabet.

It would have been very easy to translate the book into Bosnian. Software was available to do the conversion, which would have been mostly a change in alphabet, but the USAID official in charge of the accounting reform project refused to do it. The University of Sarajevo even offered to do the conversion at no cost to USAID. But USAID refused to turn over the software files. As a result, the translation portion of the project more or less collapsed (McGee and Preobragenskaya, 2006).

9.4 Teaching the new rules to practitioners

Part of any USAID accounting reform project includes training practicing accountants. The accounting system cannot be implemented if the accountants who would implement the changes do not know what the new rules are or how to apply them. The methods used to accomplish this task vary from project to project, but there are some common elements.

To target accounting practitioners who work for the local accounting and audit firms, the local accounting association is approached and USAID makes an offer to provide training, training materials, and instructors to the membership. In most cases, since the local accounting associations are weak and relatively inexperienced in providing such training, USAID provides financial as well as technical support. Some kind of continuing professional education program is established, along the lines of what the AICPA and various state accounting societies do in the United States.

9.5 Reforming university curriculums

No accounting reform project is complete without upgrading the accounting curriculums of at least some universities in the country. The future accountants have to become exposed to the rules their country has adopted and the present university curriculum does not have the courses they will need, so USAID, or TACIS, the EU equivalent, or the World Bank, or some other group offers to provide technical and financial assistance. The approach used in each country is somewhat different, but there are some common elements.

The USAID accounting reform project in Armenia was given marching orders from Washington to convince at least one Armenian university to accept USAID's assistance. The consulting firm that won the USAID contract decided to target the top economics institute in the country, figuring that if that institute agreed to accept the turnkey curriculum the firm proposed, the accounting education segment of the project would be considered a success.

A meeting was set up, the presentation was made, and the educational officials were persuaded to accept USAID's assistance. The fact that the institute wanted to reform its accounting curriculum anyway, plus the fact that USAID was going to pay the entire cost of texts and training, made their decision easy.

Once the word got out that USAID was setting up turnkey accounting curriculums, the other universities in the country started calling to schedule meetings of their own. The accounting curriculum phase of the reform project was an instant success. Of course, there were some problems. The text materials were not the best and the early translations were mediocre. But the university officials were enthused about the program and the students were even more enthused, since learning the accounting system used in the West was seen as providing them with a one-way ticket out of the country.

The Bosnian program was also an easy sell. The University of Sarajevo was targeted as the first university to be approached, since it was the largest university in the country, it had more than 50% of all the accounting students in the country, and it was a five-minute walk from the consulting firm's offices in Sarajevo. University officials already knew that their accounting curriculum needed to be changed but they didn't know how to go about doing it, until USAID knocked at their door.

After the word got out that the University of Sarajevo was going to have a Western style accounting curriculum, the other seven universities in Bosnia quickly jumped on board, perhaps out of fear that if they did not also offer a Western style accounting curriculum they soon would not have any accounting students. Many young people in transition economies want to leave their country to seek better economic opportunities elsewhere, and Bosnia was no exception. Having knowledge of the accounting system that is used in the West would give them such an opportunity. However, in all fairness, it cannot be said that 100% of the young Bosnian or Armenian or Russian or Moldovan people want a one-way ticket out of their country. Many of them have no burning desire to leave. But many of them do, and this program was seen as a way to achieve their dream.

Under the old Soviet system, students who wanted to study accounting generally did so as part of the economics curriculum. Most Soviet universities did not have a separate accounting major. In fact, the universities that offered any accounting at all often had just a bookkeeping course, and perhaps some kind of auditing or math course. Many universities in the Soviet Union did not offer any accounting courses. One reason for the lack of accounting courses is because the Soviet education system consisted of many specialized institutes. There were institutes for physics, chemistry, physical education, etc., and there was no need to offer accounting courses in such institutes.

That started to change after the collapse of the Soviet Union. Some institutes started offering accounting courses just because they wanted to satisfy the newly increased demand for accounting. With the shift to a market economy came a demand for more accountants and the Soviet educational system could not fill the demand unless it started offering more accounting courses. As a result, some institutes that never before offered accounting courses started offering them, and institutes and universities that had offered accounting in the past expanded their accounting offerings.

Table 9.1 lists the curriculum that accounting majors take at Odessa National University, which has one of the best accounting programs in Ukraine. It is presented to illustrate what one of the better accounting programs looks like.

Table 9.1 provides good detail about the curriculum a Ukrainian accounting student studies. However, breaking down the total curriculum into accounting, other business, and other categories can shed further insight. Table 9.2 does that.

The data in Table 9.2 on the accounting curriculum of Odessa National University reveals a lot about the kind of accounting education Ukrainian students are receiving. However, in order to put things into relative perspective, perhaps it would be worthwhile to compare the accounting education they receive with the accounting education that students receive at a university in a developed Western economy.

Table 9.3 summarizes the curriculum for the Bachelor of Science in accountancy at the University of Illinois at Urbana-Champaign, which is considered one of the top accounting programs in the United States.

Although Table 9.3 provides a brief summary of the requirements for an undergraduate accounting degree at a university in the United States, the data in that table will have to be manipulated before a good comparison can be made to the accounting curriculum offered at a university in Ukraine.

Table 9.4 does that. It converts semester hours into clock hours by multiplying semester hours by 15. It assumes that students will take the maximum number of accounting courses and that they will study 1.5 hours outside of class for every hour spent in class. It also assumes that the total accounting and other business courses comprise 50% of the total curriculum, which is in keeping with AACSB accreditation standards.

Now that semester hours have been translated into clock hours and study time has been added, a fair comparison can be made between the Ukrainian university and the American university. Table 9.5 makes the comparison.

Table 9.1 Curriculum at Odessa National University, Bachelor–four years (7047 hours)

	Studying (hours)					
	Total	In class			Self-study	% of total
		Total	Lecture	Seminars		(8208)
General Humanitarian and Social Economic Disciplines	1512	954	316	638	558	21.5
Federal Component	1512	954	316	638	558	21.5
Foreign Languages	324	216		216	108	4.6
Physical Training	216	216		216	0	3.1
Logic	54	36	22	14	18	0.8
Ukrainian Language (Speech)	81	36	22	14	45	1.1
Ethics and Esthetics	54	36	22	14	18	0.8
Science of Culture	81	36	22	14	45	1.1
Psychology	81	36	22	14	45	1.1
Law	81	36	22	14	45	1.1
Religions	54	36	22	14	18	0.8
Philosophy	108	54	32	22	54	1.5
History of Ukraine	108	54	32	22	54	1.5
Sociology	54	36	22	14	18	0.8
Ecology	54	36	22	14	18	0.8
Political Science	108	54	32	22	54	1.5
Health	54	36	22	14	18	0.8
General Economics Disciplines	3078	1710	1028	682	1368	43.7
Federal Component	3078	1710	1028	682	1368	43.7
Accounting	135	72	44	28	63	1.9
Audit	54	36	22	14	18	0.8
Cash, Loans, Banks	81	54	32	22	27	1.1
Civil Defense	54	36	22	14	18	0.8
Econometrics	81	54	32	22	27	1.1
Economic Analysis	81	54	32	22	27	1.1

Table 9.1 (*Continued*)

	Studying (hours)					
	Total	In class			Self-study	% of total
		Total	Lecture	Seminars		(8208)
Economics of Entrepreneurship	162	72	44	28	90	2.3
Economics of Labor and Social Relations	108	54	32	22	54	1.5
Finance	108	54	32	22	54	1.5
Finance of Entrepreneurship	81	54	32	22	27	1.1
History of Economic Studies	81	54	32	22	27	1.1
History of Economics	81	54	32	22	27	1.1
Informatics and Computers	270	144	88	56	126	3.8
Insurance	81	36	22	14	45	1.1
International Economics	108	54	32	22	54	1.5
Investment	81	36	22	14	45	1.1
Macroeconomics	108	54	32	22	54	1.5
Management	108	54	32	22	54	1.5
Marketing	108	54	32	22	54	1.5
Mathematics	216	144	88	56	72	3.1
Microeconomics	108	54	32	22	54	1.5
Patent Law Fundamentals	54	36	22	14	18	0.8
Political Science	135	72	44	28	63	1.9
Probability Theory and Mathematical Statistics	108	54	32	22	54	1.5
Programming	108	54	32	22	54	1.5
State Law	81	54	32	22	27	1.1
State Regulation of Economy	81	54	32	22	27	1.1
Statistics	135	72	44	28	63	1.9
Work Force Allocation and Regional Economy	81	36	22	14	45	1.1

(*Continued*)

Table 9.1 (*Continued*)

	Studying (hours)					
	Total	In class			Self-study	% of total
		Total	Lecture	Seminars		(8208)
Professional Disciplines						
Federal Component	972	468	284	184	504	13.8
Financial Accounting 1	162	72	44	28	90	2.3
Financial Accounting 2	162	72	44	28	90	2.3
Managerial Accounting	135	72	44	28	63	1.9
Organization, methods of auditing	135	72	44	28	63	1.9
Accounting in Foreign Countries	108	54	32	22	54	1.5
Financial Law	108	54	32	22	54	1.5
Information Systems and Technology in Accounting	162	72	44	28	90	2.3
Regional (University) Component	837	522	310	212	315	11.9
Fundamentals of Accounting Theory	81	54	32	22	27	1.1
Audit of Juridical Persons (Companies)	81	54	32	22	27	1.1
Audit of Persons	81	54	32	22	27	1.1
Management Accounting 2	81	54	32	22	27	1.1
Control and Revision	108	54	32	22	54	1.5
Financial Management	81	54	32	22	27	1.1
Corporate Governance	81	54	32	22	27	1.1
Commerce Logistics	54	36	22	14	18	0.8
Contract Law	108	54	32	22	54	1.5
Tax System of Ukraine	81	54	32	22	27	1.1
Electives	648	414	248	166	234	9.2
International Finance	81	54	32	22	27	1.1
Company Budgeting	54	36	22	14	18	0.8

Table 9.1 *(Continued)*

	Studying (hours)					
	Total	In class			Self-study	% of total
		Total	Lecture	Seminars		(8208)
Audit of Transnational Corporations	54	36	22	14	18	0.8
Labor Law	81	54	32	22	27	1.1
Exchange System	81	54	32	22	27	1.1
Financial Market	81	54	32	22	27	1.1
Management Continuum	108	72	44	28	36	1.5
Personnel Management	108	54	32	22	54	1.5
Total hours	7047	4068	2186	1882	2979	100.0

One difference that is seen immediately is that Ukrainian students spend significantly more time studying than do their American counterparts – 7047 hours compared to 4650 hours, or an additional 51% more time. Of course, these are just rough estimates. Some American students probably spend more than 1.5 hours in study for each hour in class, and the study hours assigned to Ukrainian students are merely part of the official curriculum plan at Odessa National University. Ukrainian students might study more or fewer hours than those suggested.

The accounting portion of the curriculum is about the same for both universities, in terms of percentages – 25.3% for the Ukrainian university and 26.6% for the American university. However, Ukrainian students spend an additional 543 hours studying accounting subjects.

Ukrainian accounting students spend nearly three times as much time studying other business subjects – 3213 hours, compared to 1086 hours for American accounting students. As a percentage of the total four-year program, it is about twice as much – 45.6% compared to 23.4%.

Ukrainians spend somewhat less time studying what might be called liberal arts subjects – 2052 compared to 2325 hours. However, one should not jump to the conclusion that Ukrainian students are therefore less well rounded than their American counterparts. All Ukrainian students can speak at least two languages – Ukrainian and Russian – whereas the vast majority of American students can speak only one language.

Table 9.2 Four-year accounting curriculum at Odessa National University

Course	Hours	% of total
Accounting (totals)	1782	25.3
Accounting	135	
Audit	54	
Financial Accounting 1	162	
Financial Accounting 2	162	
Managerial Accounting	135	
Organization, Methods of Auditing	135	
Accounting in Foreign Countries	108	
Financial Law	108	
Information Systems and Technology in Accounting	162	
Fundamentals of Accounting Theory	81	
Audit of Judicial Persons (Companies)	81	
Audit of Persons	81	
Management Accounting 2	81	
Control and Revision	108	
Tax System of Ukraine	81	
Company Budgeting	54	
Audit of Transnational Corporations	54	
Other business (total)	3213	45.6
Cash, Loans, Bank	81	
Econometrics	81	
Economic Analysis	81	
Economics of Entrepreneurship	162	
Economics of Labor and Social Relations	108	
Finance	108	
Finance of Entrepreneurship	81	
History of Economic Studies	81	
History of Economics	81	
Informatics and Computers	270	
Insurance	81	
International Economics	108	
Investment	81	
Macroeconomics	108	
Management	108	
Marketing	108	

Table 9.2 (*Continued*)

Course	Hours	% of total
Microeconomics	108	
Probability Theory and Mathematical Statistics	108	
Programming	108	
State Regulation of Economy	81	
Statistics	135	
Work Force Allocation and Regional Economy	81	
Financial Management	81	
Corporate Governance	81	
Commerce Logistics	54	
Contract Law	108	
International Finance	81	
Labor Law	81	
Exchange System	81	
Financial Market	81	
Management Continuum	108	
Personnel Management	108	
Non-business	2052	29.1
Total	7047	

Table 9.3 Bachelor of Science in accountancy curriculum, University of Illinois at Urbana-Champaign

Semester hours	Courses
4	Accounting Measurement and Disclosure
4	Decision Making for Accountancy
4	Accounting Institutions and Regulation
4	Accounting Control Systems
4	Assurance and Attestation
20	Total required for accountancy major
3	Accounting and Accountancy I (business core course)
3	Accounting and Accountancy II (business core course)
26	Total required accountancy courses
91	Non-accountancy courses
7	Electives (either accountancy or non-accountancy)
124	Total for BSA

Table 9.4 Bachelor of Science in accountancy curriculum, University of Illinois at Urbana-Champaign, hours spent in study

Course	Class hours	Self-study	Total hours	% of total
Accounting (totals)	495	744	1239	26.6
Accounting Measurement and Disclosure	60	90	150	
Decision Making for Accountancy	60	90	150	
Accounting Institutions and Regulation	60	90	150	
Accounting Control Systems	60	90	150	
Assurance and Attestation	60	90	150	
Accounting and Accountancy I	45	68	113	
Accounting and Accountancy II	45	68	113	
Accounting electives	105	158	263	
Other business	435	651	1086	23.4
Non-business	930	1395	2325	50.0
Totals	1860	2790	4650	100.0

Table 9.5 Four-year accounting curriculum comparison between Odessa National University and the University of Illinois

	Odessa National University		University of Illinois	
	Hours	% of total	Hours	% of total
Accounting	1782	25.3	1239	26.6
Other business	3213	45.6	1086	23.4
Non-business	2052	29.1	2325	50.0
Totals	7047	100.0	4650	100.0

9.6 Credible accounting certification

Another aim of some USAID accounting reform projects is to upgrade accounting certification. The USAID accounting reform project in Armenia, for example, coordinated the effort to bring the ACCA English language certification exams to Armenia. It also assisted the Armenian Association of Accountants and Auditors (AAAA) in establishing a certification exam that incorporated elements of IAS and ISA (McGee, 1999b).

Former Soviet republics generally do not have an accounting or auditing certification that is credible outside the borders of the country. International investors

Table 9.6 CAP and CIPA exam summary, November 2004, exam participants and pass rates

	CAP exams			CIPA exams				Total
	FA-1	T&L	MA-1	FA-2	MA-2	Audit	Finance	
Kazakhstan	714	531	505	99	50	72	48	2019
	46.8%	51.0%	43.2%	22.2%	28.0%	19.4%	20.8%	43.7%
Kyrgyzstan	259	185	171	46	20	35	15	730
	35.5%	49.7%	45.0%	23.9%	20.0%	14.7%	20.0%	38.9%
Tajikistan	106	109	60	5	5	5	5	295
	17.9%	45.0%	21.7%	20.0%	0%	0%	0%	27.8%
Turkmenistan	32	22	36	4	3	0	3	100
	46.9%	59.1%	33.3%	0%	66.7%	0%	0%	42.0%
Uzbekistan	209	103	132	34	35	23	36	572
	50.7%	50.5%	45.5%	29.4%	45.7%	39.1%	33.3%	46.3%
Moldova	32	37	36	12	6	5	1	129
	78.1%	97.3%	61.1%	0%	16.7%	20.0%	0%	65.9%
Russia	7	11	7	1	4	1	4	35
	57.1%	100%	57.1%	0%	25.0%	0%	25.0%	60.0%
Ukraine	438	294	318	139	130	124	106	1549
	59.1%	78.2%	64.8%	22.3%	14.6%	15.3%	14.2%	50.3%

hesitate to invest in a company whose financial statements are audited by someone who does not possess a recognizable and credible accounting certification. One way to provide a credible accounting certification in these countries at minimal cost is to allow the Association of Chartered Certified Accountants (ACCA) to give their exams. ACCA exams have been in existence for more than 100 years and they are well regarded, well known, and respected in 160 countries. They test IFRS and ISA.

But there is a structural problem with giving ACCA exams in former Soviet republics. The exams are in English, which means that only a minority of the accountants in most former Soviet republics can take them. USAID is making an attempt to solve this problem by providing Western-type certification exams in the Russian language. In 2001 it started a pilot program in central Asia. This program consisted of funding the establishment of a two-tier, seven-exam certification program, in the Russian language, that tested on IFRS and ISA. Space does not permit a full description of this program. However, descriptions are given elsewhere (McGee et al., 2004; McGee and Preobragenskaya, 2005, 2006).

The lower-level certification consists of three exams: Financial Accounting 1, Managerial Accounting 1, and Tax and Law. Those who pass all three exams receive the designation Certified Accounting Practitioner (CAP).

The second certification level consists of the following four exams: Financial Accounting 2, Managerial Accounting 2, Audit, and Finance. Those who pass these four exams are awarded the Certified International Professional Accountant (CIPA) designation.

The pilot project started in the five central Asian republics of Kazakhstan, Kyrgyzstan, Tajikistan, Turkmenistan, and Uzbekistan. After the exams had been given a few times the program spread to Russia, Ukraine, and Moldova. Thousands of individuals have taken one or more exams and the program appears to be a success.

The people administering the CAP and CIPA exams no longer release detailed exam data. However, they did release data for the November 2004 CAP and CIPA exams. Table 9.6 summarizes those results, showing the number of participants and the pass rates.

The pass rates on the CIPA exams tend to be lower than the pass rates on the CAP exams. One reason for the lower pass rates is because the CIPA exams test more difficult material.

The table also reveals that Kazakhstan had more participants than the other countries. The reason for this might be because the program was headquartered in Kazakhstan since its inception, although the headquarters has since moved to Moscow. One surprise was the turnout in Ukraine. Although Ukraine has a much larger population than any of the central Asian republics, the exam was not offered in Ukraine until recently, which makes the growth and popularity of the exam in Ukraine even more remarkable. There were few exam takers in Russia, even though Russia has the largest population of any of the former Soviet republics. The explanation for the low turnout is because the exam is relatively new in Russia and marketing of the program started relatively recently. Many Russian accountants still do not know about this certification program.

9.7 Conclusion

Much of the world is moving toward the adoption and implementation of IFRS and ISA. Some countries have been using these standards for decades, but they are new for transition economies. Countries that are moving from central planning to a market economy are facing many difficult hurdles. Accounting reform is one of them.

But the reform movement is well underway. USAID, TACIS, the World Bank, and other organizations that have funded accounting reform programs in the past have helped a number of transition countries to complete the reform process. Projects that are still open are winding down as the reform process becomes complete.

But the actual process of incorporating IFRS and ISA into the economy will take years, if not decades. There is little demand for IFRS in many transition economies, with the exception of the largest enterprises, which are seeking foreign capital. The average domestic company still sees little or no need to adopt IFRS, since their constituency has no need to read IFRS statements. That will change, but only gradually.

Acknowledgments

I would like to thank Galina G. Preobragenskaya for her assistance in translating some of the material used to write this chapter.

References

Adams, C.A. and McMillan, K.M. (1997). Internationalizing Financial Reporting in a Newly Emerging Market Economy: The Polish Example. *Advances in International Accounting*, 10:139–164.

Arthur Andersen, BDO, Deloitte Touche Tohmatsu, Ernst & Young International, Grant Thornton, KPMG, and PricewaterhouseCoopers (2000). *GAAP 2000: A Survey of National Accounting Rules in 53 Countries*. Available at http://www.pwcglobal.com.

Arthur Andersen, BDO, Deloitte Touche Tohmatsu, Ernst & Young, Grant Thornton, KPMG, and PricewaterhouseCoopers (2001). *GAAP 2001: A Survey of National Accounting Rules Benchmarked against International Accounting Standards*. Available at http://www.pwcglobal.com.

BDO, Deloitte Touche Tohmatsu, Ernst & Young, Grant Thornton, KPMG, and PricewaterhouseCoopers (2002). *GAAP Convergence 2002: A Survey of National Efforts to Promote and Achieve Convergence with International Financial Reporting Standards*. Available at http://www.pwcglobal.com.

Borda, M. and McLeay, S. (1996). Accounting and Economic Transformation in Hungary. In: *Accounting in Transition: The Implications of Political and Economic Reform in Central Europe* (Garrod, N. and McLeay, S., eds), pp. 116–140. Routledge, London.

Boross, Z., Clarkson, A.H., Fraser, M., and Weetman, P. (1995). Pressures and Conflicts in Moving towards Harmonization of Accounting Practice: The Hungarian Experience. *European Accounting Review*, 4(4):713–737.

Burg, S.L. and Shoup, P.S. (1999). *The War in Bosnia-Herzegovina: Ethnic Conflict and International Intervention*. M. E. Sharpe, Armonk, NY.

Chan, M.W., Rosenberg, L., and Rosenberg, W. (1999). Accounting, Auditing Education, and Economic Reform in the People's Republic of China. *International Studies of Management and Organization*, 29(3):37–53.

Choi, F.D.S., Frost, C.A., and Meek, G.M. (2002). *International Accounting*. Prentice-Hall, Upper Saddle River, NJ.

Cuijpers, R. and Buijink, W. (2005). Voluntary Adoption of Non-Local GAAP in the European Union: A Study of Determinants and Consequences. *European Accounting Review*, 14(3):487–524.

Daalder, I.H. (2000). *Getting to Dayton: The Making of America's Bosnia Policy*. Brookings Institution, Washington, DC.

Enthoven, A.J.H., Sokolov, Y.V., Bychkova, S.M., Kovalev, V.V., and Semenova, M.V. (1998). *Accounting, Auditing and Taxation in the Russian Federation*. Institute of Management Accountants, Montvale, NJ and The Center for International Accounting Development, The University of Texas at Dallas.

Friedman, M. and Friedman, R.D. (1984). *The Tyranny of the Status Quo*. Harcourt Brace Jovanovich, New York.

Garrod, N. and McLeay, S. (eds) (1996). *Accounting in Transition: The Implications of Political and Economic Reform in Central Europe*. Routledge, London.

Holbrooke, R. (1998). *To End a War*. The Modern Library, New York.

Jermakowicz, E. and Rinke, D.F. (1996). The New Accounting Standards in the Czech Republic, Hungary, and Poland, Vis-à-vis International Accounting Standards and European Union Directives. *Journal of International Accounting, Auditing and Taxation*, 5(1):73–88.

Jindrichovska, I. and McLeay, S. (2005). Accounting for Good News and Accounting for Bad News: Some Empirical Evidence from the Czech Republic. *European Accounting Review*, 14(3):635–655.

Kemp, P. and Alexander, D. (1996). Accountancy and Financial Infrastructure in Central and Eastern European Countries. *European Business Journal*, 8(4):14–21.

King, N., Beattie, A., and Cristescu, A.M. (2001). Developing Accounting and Audit in a Transition Economy: The Romanian Experience. *European Accounting Review*, 10(1):149–171.

Kosmala, K. (2005). True and Fair View or Rzetelny I Jasny Obraz1? A Survey of Polish Practitioners. *European Accounting Review*, 14(3):579–602.

Krzywda, D., Bailey, D., and Schroeder, M. (1995). A Theory of European Accounting Development Applied to Accounting Change in Contemporary Poland. *European Accounting Review*, 4(4):625–657.

Larson, R.K. (1993). International Accounting Standards and Economic Growth: An Empirical Investigation of Their Relationship in Africa. *Research in Third World Accounting*, 2:27–43.

Lindberg, D.L. (2002). The Use of Barter Hampers Implementation of International Accounting Standards and Contributes to Financial Woes in the Russian Federation. *Russian and East European Finance and Trade*, 38(3):5–17.

Mackevicius, J., Aliukonis, J., and Bailey, D. (1996). The Reconstruction of National Accounting Rules in Lithuania. In: *Accounting in Transition: The Implications of Political and Economic Reform in Central Europe* (Garrod, N. and McLeay, S., eds), pp. 43–60. Routledge, London.

McGee, R.W. (1999a). The Problem of Implementing International Accounting Standards: A Case Study of Armenia. *Journal of Accounting, Ethics and Public Policy*, 2(1):38–41. Also available at http://www.ssrn.com.

McGee, R.W. (1999b). Certification of Accountants and Auditors in the CIS: A Case Study of Armenia. *Journal of Accounting, Ethics and Public Policy*, 2(2):338–353. Also available at http://www.ssrn.com.

McGee, R.W. and Preobragenskaya, G.G. (2005). *Accounting and Financial System Reform in a Transition Economy: A Case Study of Russia*. Springer, New York.

McGee, R.W. and Preobragenskaya, G.G. (2006). *Accounting and Financial System Reform in Eastern Europe and Asia.* Springer, New York.

McGee, R.W., Preobragenskaya, G.G., and Tyler, M. (2004). International Accounting Certification in the Russian Language: A Case Study. Presented at the International Academy of Business and Public Administration Disciplines (IABPAD) Conference, Tunica, MS, 24–26 May. Also available at http://www.ssrn.com.

Pankov, D. (1998). Accounting for Change in Belarus. *Management Accounting (London)*, 76(10):56–58.

Preobragenskaya, G.G. and McGee, R.W. (2003). International Accounting Standards and Foreign Direct Investment in Russia. Presented at the International Trade and Finance Association's Thirteenth International Conference, Vaasa, Finland, 28–31 May. Also available at http://www.ssrn.com.

Roberts, A. (2001). The Recent Romanian Accounting Reforms: Another Case of Cultural Intrusion? In: *Transitional Economies: Banking, Finance, Institutions* (Kalyuzhnova, Y. and Taylor, M., eds), pp. 146–166. Palgrave, Basingstoke, UK.

Schneidman, L. (2003). The Long Road to IAS. *Kommersant*, Internet edition, 9 June. Available at http://www.pwcglobal.com.

Seal, W., Sucher, P., and Zelenka, I. (1995). The Changing Organization of Czech Accounting. *European Accounting Review*, 4(4):659–681.

Solodchenko, I. and Sucher, P. (2005). Accounting in Ukraine since Independence: Real Politik, Problems and Prospects. *European Accounting Review*, 14(3):603–633.

Street, D.L. (2002). GAAP 2001 – Benchmarking National Accounting Standards against IAS: Summary of Results. *Journal of International Accounting, Auditing and Taxation*, 11(1):77–90.

Sucher, P. and Kemp, P. (1998). Accounting and Auditing Reform in Belarus. *European Business Journal*, 10(3):141–147.

Turk, I. and Garrod, N. (1996). The Adaptation of International Accounting Rules: Lessons from Slovenia. In: *Accounting in Transition: The Implications of Political and Economic Reform in Central Europe* (Garrod, N. and McLeay, S., eds), pp. 141–162. Routledge, London.

von Mises, L. (1920). Die Wirtschaftsrechnung im Sozialistischen Gemeinwesen [Economic Calculation in the Socialist Commonwealth]. *Archiv fur Sozialwissenschaft und Sozialpolitik*, 47:86–121.

von Mises, L. (1922). *Die Gemeinwirtschaft.* The second German edition (1932) was translated into English by J. Kahane and published as *Socialism: An Economic and Sociological Analysis.* Jonathan Cape, London, 1936.

von Mises, L. (1923). Neue Beitrage zum Problem der sozialistischen Wirtschaftsrechnung [New Contributions to the Problem of Socialist Economic Calculation]. *Archiv fur Sozialwissenschaft und Sozial Politik*, 51:488–500.

von Mises, L. (1935). Economic Calculation in the Socialist Commonwealth. In: *Collectivist Economic Planning: Critical Studies on the Possibilities of Socialism* (Hayek, F.A., ed.), pp. 87–130. Routledge, London. Reprinted by Augustus M. Kelley, Clifton, NJ, 1975.

Zelenka, I., Seal, W., and Sucher, P. (1996). The Emerging Institutional Framework of Accounting in the Czech and Slovak Republics. In: *Accounting in Transition: The Implications of Political and Economic Reform in Central Europe* (Garrod, N. and McLeay, S., eds), pp. 93–115. Routledge, London.

Zimmermann, W. (1999). *Origins of a Catastrophe.* Random House, New York.

10

International Convergence: The Australian Journey

Janice Loftus

10.1 Introduction

Australia is a Commonwealth nation with a population of approximately 20 million people (19.7 million in 2002) (World Bank, 2004). Australia has a federal system of government. Corporate regulation originally fell within the domain of the government of each of the nation's six states, as will be discussed below, but companies are now governed by the Commonwealth Government of Australia. Governments are elected in Australia and their continued survival depends on the electorate's confidence in the legislature. The maximum interval between elections is three years. Government ministers are members of parliament and Australia is described as having high cohesion of governing parties (Tiffen and Gittins, 2004, p. 27).

The Australian economy was ranked 13th in the world with a GDP of US $631bn in 2004 (World Bank, 2005). In 2002 the GDP for Australia was US $409.4bn, and the GDP per capita was $28,260 (measured in International dollars, which is a World Bank measure of US dollars adjusted for purchasing power parity) (World Bank, 2004). The Australian economy has undergone some structural change during the second half of the 20th century. Employment in the agricultural sector declined from an average of 9.2% of the labor workforce in 1960–1973, to an average of 5.1% in 1990–1991, consistent with universal decline (Tiffen and Gittins, 2004, p. 55). Employment in the manufacturing sector declined from an average of 24.2% of the labour workforce in 1960–1973, to an average of 13.7% in 1990–1991, reflecting de-industrialization during the latter half of the 20th century (Tiffen and Gittins, 2004, p. 55). Employment in the services sector rose from 53.5% of the labor workforce in 1960–1973, to an average of 71.8% in 1990–1991, consistent with trends in other developed countries (Tiffen and Gittins, 2004, p. 55).

The Australian Stock Exchange (ASX) was established in 1987 by the amalgamation of the six stock exchanges that operated in state capital cities. At 30 June 2005 there were 1774 entities listed on the ASX and the domestic market capitalization was $975bn (US $743bn). Average daily equity transactions numbered 87,500, with an average daily value of $3.181m (US $2.423 million), for the year ended 30 June 2005 (ASX, 2005).

Given the relatively small size of its capital market, Australia became a leading nation in accounting standard setting and the development of a conceptual framework of accounting. Australia developed a pool of intellectual capital through its domestic standard-setting projects and its involvement in international organizations and initiatives.

Australia's involvement in the international harmonization of accounting commenced in the 1970s, and formally when the Australian professional accountancy bodies jointly became a member of the Board of the International Accounting Standards Committee in 1973. The Australian Accounting Standards Board (and its predecessor, the Accounting Standards Review Board) also supported international harmonization through involvement in the Group of Four-Plus One (G4+1).

In mapping Australia's journey towards international convergence, it is important to understand the changing identity, nature, and power of the key policy-making bodies steering Australian accounting practice. Commitment to international harmonization waxed and waned over several decades that also saw fundamental changes to the structure of financial reporting regulation and standard setting. Between the formation of the International Accounting Standards Committee in 1973 and the decision to adopt International Financial Reporting Standards in 2002, the accounting standard-setting arrangements underwent four major reforms. The first of these reforms occurred in 1984 with the establishment of the Accounting Standards Review Board (ASRB), empowered to review and approve accounting standards. The next reform was the merger of the profession's Accounting Standards Board (AcSB) with the ASRB in 1988, followed by the replacement of the ASRB by the Australian Accounting Standards Board (AASB) in 1991. The new Board was empowered to issue accounting standards and was less dependent on other bodies to submit standards to it. The fourth reform involved the establishment of the Financial Reporting Council in 2000, with broad oversight functions with respect to the AASB.

Each of the five regulatory arrangements is examined to provide insight into Australia's arduous path to international convergence. The developments in international convergence are considered in the context of each stage in the history of Australian standard setting. After reflecting on Australia's journey towards international convergence, this chapter considers a forward-looking question that may well be asked by countries adopting IFRS: Is this the start of a new journey or the end of the road?

10.2 Models of international harmonization or convergence of accounting

Four broad approaches to reducing international diversity in accounting practice are identified in the literature (AASB, 1994a; Miller, 1995a; Howieson, 1997, 1998):

1. Full global harmonization, also referred to as integrated harmonization, with every country adopting the same set of accounting standards.

2. Harmonization of accounting policies with those of another jurisdiction, such as those issued by an international standard-setting body or the domestic standards of another country, such as the United States.
3. Substantial commonality, in which the requirements of domestic standards have some overlap with standards issued by an international standard-setting body, but not driven to full compliance, incorporating 'benchmarked compliance' in which the international accounting standards form the minimum requirement for domestic standards.
4. Internationalization (also referred to as selective harmonization), by which domestic standards are determined in the light of international practice, which is subject to innovation and improvement through cooperation and collaboration among standard setters.

The approaches are not mutually exclusive. For instance, standard setters in one country may actively promote harmonization with accounting standards of another country, particularly where there are strong trade links. This may be achieved by cross-participation, as observers, on the standard-setting bodies, and by cooperation between the standard-setting bodies of the two countries on projects, such as the revision or issue of accounting standards. The standard setters may, at the same time, consider international best practice when setting accounting standards. This may be in collaboration with the country with which they seek to harmonize, or it may be on issues on which the other country does not have an existing standard. Harmonizing with another country and considering international best practice may be long-term policies, or they may be viewed as temporary measures en route to full global harmonization.

As will be discussed below, the Australian standard setters have at times adopted each of the four approaches to international harmonization. At times, international best practice has been an important consideration, while simultaneously promoting harmonization with New Zealand, and attempting to maintain benchmarked compliance with IAS as a strategy in working towards a long-term goal of full convergence with a globally accepted set of accounting standards.

International harmonization of accounting can also be viewed as a process of moving closer towards compatibility with international accounting standards. This chapter examines how the process of harmonization has at times been aided and at other times hindered by the accounting standard-setting arrangements in Australia.

10.3 Models of accounting regulation

Puxty et al. (1987, pp. 282–284) describe accounting regulation in advanced market economies as reflecting various balances between market, state, and community influences. At one end of the spectrum is liberalism, which refers to the exclusive reliance on market forces, such that information is provided only if it is commercially demanded. At the other end of the spectrum, legalism refers to a model of accounting regulation that relies exclusively on the legislative and coercive powers of the state. Between these two extremes, accounting regulation models are categorized as associationism and corporatism. In associationist models of accounting regulation, principles of community play a greater role, but are routinely subordinate to those of the market. Closer to legalism on the market–state spectrum are corporatist models of accounting regulation, characterized by a greater influence of the state, which incorporates organized interest groups into its own centralized hierarchical regulatory structure. Corporatism describes any 'attempt to assign to interest associations a distinct role between the State and civil society (market and community) so as to put to public purpose the type of social order that associations can generate and embody' (Streeck and Schmitter, 1985, pp. 20–21). Figure 10.1 depicts the four models of accounting regulation along the market–state continuum with the subordinated influence of community principles (adapted from Puxty et al., 1987, p. 283).

The ensuing discussion will trace the stages of, and reforms to, standard-setting arrangements in Australia as the regulation of accounting standards moved along the market–state spectrum, from liberalism in the 1960s and 1970s to various forms of corporatism in the 1990s and the new millennium.

10.4 Australian standard setting 1970–1983

In Australia the uniform companies legislation developed by the Commonwealth and state governments required companies, other than exempt proprietary companies, to publish financial statements. Further rules, primarily dealing with disclosure, were included in Regulations attached to the *Uniform Companies*

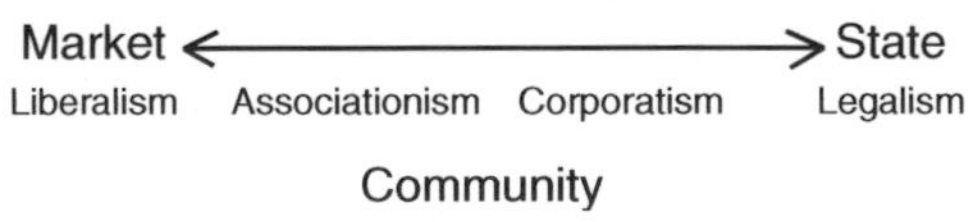

Figure 10.1 Models of accounting regulation

Act. The directors of the company were (and still are) responsible for the financial statements. Listed companies were also subject to stock exchange listing rules but like the corporations legislation, the rules were primarily concerned with disclosure requirements. The determination of accounting principles was left to the accountancy profession.

The two main professional accountancy bodies, the Australian Society of Accountants (ASA) and The Institute of Chartered Accountants in Australia (ICAA), jointly commenced an accounting standard-setting program in 1972. Initial momentum for this program was achieved by the ASA endorsing the ICAA's Statements of Accounting Practice.

The two professional bodies had founded and, henceforth, jointly funded the Australian Accounting Research Foundation (AARF) in 1966. The Australian Accounting Standards Committee, which was subsequently restructured and renamed as the Accounting Standards Board (AcSB), was a board within the AARF. In 1983 a separate board was established to develop accounting standards for the public sector and the AcSB focused exclusively on drafting accounting standards for financial statements prepared by private sector entities (Henderson and Peirson, 2004, p. 7). The ASA and the ICAA appointed all members to the Boards and approved all standards issued by them. Both professional bodies required their members to comply with the standards issued by the two Boards (Walker, 1987, p. 269).

Government agencies, including the NSW Corporate Affairs Commission, reported high levels of noncompliance with Australian accounting standards (Walker, 1987, p. 270). While the professional bodies may have been able to require their members to comply with accounting standards, they lacked authority and influence over company directors responsible for the published financial statements.

Dissatisfaction with levels of compliance with accounting standards added support to calls for government intervention. In 1974 the Companies and Securities Industry Bill was introduced to Parliament. However, there was a change of government in the following year and the Bill was not enacted (Walker, 1987, p. 270). In 1978 the Accounting Standards Review Committee, appointed by the NSW Attorney General and chaired by Professor Chambers of the University of Sydney, issued a report that was highly critical of both accounting standards and the standard-setting arrangements. The Committee recommended appointment of a national body to ensure that accounting standards issued by the profession conformed to the Companies Act (Accounting Standards Review Committee, 1978).

The debate about the regulatory framework continued throughout the 1970s and early 1980s (Winsen, 1983; Walker, 1987). While the problem of noncompliance could be addressed by giving legal backing to accounting standards (as proposed by the professional accountancy bodies), questions also arose about the appropriate composition of, and representation on, a body vested with the authority to issue accounting standards with the force of law. Some considered that legal backing should be part of broader reforms, including government participation (Walker, 1987, pp. 270–273). The professional accountancy bodies acknowledged that legal backing may involve a tradeoff of their exclusive involvement in the standard-setting process. The ASA and the ICAA proposed that if government participation were required, it should take the form of direct representation on the AcSB, the profession's private sector accounting standards board, or through a standard-setting review board sponsored by the accountancy profession (Prosser, 1983).

The debate on standard-setting arrangements and dissatisfaction with the level of compliance with accounting standards culminated in a resolution in 1980 by the Ministerial Council for Companies and Securities (which comprised the Commonwealth and State Government Attorney Generals) that the National Companies and Securities Commission (NCSC) should consider forming an Accounting Standards Review Board. (For a discussion of the NCSC's original proposals and revised recommendations for the role and functions of the Accounting Standards Review Board, refer to Walker, 1987, pp. 270–272.) This ultimately led to the establishment of a standard-setting board with members appointed by the Ministerial Council in 1984.

While the regulation of financial reporting was close to liberalism in the first era of accounting standard setting from 1970 to 1983, there was movement towards associationism. Financial reporting regulation was not completely left to market forces because the preparation of financial statements, and to some extent their content, was required by legislation. However, the accounting standard-setting arrangements throughout that period are best described as liberalism. Accounting standards were issued by the professional accountancy bodies and were only mandatory for their members. Whether company directors chose to apply the accountancy profession's standards was left to market forces.

10.5 International harmonization of accounting 1970–1983

During the late 1960s and early 1970s there was growing international awareness of the potential benefits of harmonization of accounting standards. This led to the establishment of the International Accounting Standards Committee (IASC) in 1973 by professional accountancy bodies from Australia, Canada, France, Germany, Japan, Mexico, the Netherlands, the UK, and Ireland. The Australian professional accountancy bodies participated jointly in the international harmonization process as a founding member of the Board of the IASC.

Four years after the establishment of the IASC, the International Federation of Accountants (IFAC) was formed in 1977. Its objectives include international development of the profession and harmonization of professional accounting standards (Herrera, 1997). The Australian accountancy bodies joined the IFAC, again supporting, in principle, the full global harmonization of accounting standards.

The Statements of Accounting Practice, which were initially issued as Recommendations on Accounting Principles by the ICAA and endorsed by the ASA in 1972, were closely based on the pronouncements of accounting principles issued by the Institute of Chartered Accountants in England and Wales (Walker, 1987, p. 269). During the late 1960s the accountancy profession in Australia started to look further afield for guidance on accounting principles and techniques. In 1967 an exposure draft issued by a committee of the ICAA on the treatment of income tax included two sentences adapted from Accounting Research Bulletin No. 43 issued by the American Institute of Certified Public Accountants in 1953 (Zeff, 1973, p. 15). This was followed by an exposure draft in 1969 on income, prior period adjustments, and extraordinary items, based on the corresponding pronouncement issued in 1966 by the Accounting Principles Board in the USA (Zeff, 1973, p. 16). Zeff (1973, p. 25) attributes the growing influence of American accounting developments in Australia to the increasing direct investment by US investors in Australian companies.

Developments in accounting in both the UK and North America continued to influence the accountancy profession in Australia. For example, Bulletin No. 16, issued by the ASA in 1974, contained two articles on Disclosure of Forecasts, one by Cohen, and another by Ma and Miller. Both of these made considerable reference to developments in the UK and the USA on reporting forecasts. The adoption of a tax-effect approach to accounting for income tax, instead of the taxes payable approach, was explicitly justified on the basis that it had been adopted by the accountancy profession in the UK, the USA, and Canada (AAS 3, paragraph 4).

When the IASC subsequently started to issue International Accounting Standards (IAS), the professional accountancy bodies started to turn to the international body as a major influence on Australian Accounting Standards. The

ASA and the ICAA jointly issued a Statement of Policy, APS 3, in support of IAS (ASA and ICAA, 1976). The professional bodies proclaimed that Australian Accounting Standards should, at a minimum, meet the requirements of IAS and that any existing Australian Accounting Standards should be reviewed in the event of a corresponding IAS being issued (APS 3, paragraph 2). However, the ASA and the ICAA declined to commit blindly to a policy of harmonization with IAS. If an IAS were issued on a matter not covered by existing Australian Accounting Standards, it should be adopted as an Australian Accounting Standard subject to being completely acceptable (APS 3, paragraph 3). For example, when the IASC issued *IAS 4: Depreciation Accounting* in 1976, the AcSB decided that some of the disclosure requirements of IAS were not necessary and chose not to incorporate them in *AAS 4: Depreciation of Non-Current Assets*, noting this as an exception in the compatibility statement published with the Standard. Similarly, there were several inconsistencies between *AAS 13: Accounting for Research and Development Costs* issued by the AcSB in 1983 and *IAS 9: Accounting for Research and Development Activities* issued by the IASC a few years earlier. The Australian standard permitted deferral of research costs, which were expensed under IAS 9, and AAS 13 imposed more restrictive recognition criteria. In many instances the standards issued by the IASC appeared to have more influence on the agenda of the AcSB than the content of the standards it issued.

In the period leading up to the establishment of the Accounting Standards Review Board, the Australian accountancy profession made an early start on the journey toward international harmonization. It supported the burgeoning movement toward full global harmonization through its involvement in the IASC and the IFAC. Australian accounting standards issued by the AcSB during this period were closely harmonized with those of the UK (Parker, 1986, pp. 85–86) with increasing influence from developments in the USA. The similarities in legal structures and historical links made the UK accounting standards a suitable source for Australian standards setters. Following UK standards was not incompatible with supporting full global harmonization as the UK accountancy profession was also a founding member of the IASC and a key player in the process of international harmonization, and most of the Australian standards predated those issued by the IASC during this period. However, full global harmonization was a long-term objective. The official policy of the accountancy profession at that time was that while benchmarked harmonization to IAS was desirable, a policy of substantial commonality should be adopted, such that Australian Accounting Standards should be compatible with IAS only to the extent that the latter were acceptable.

10.6 Australian standard setting 1984–1988

The second era of Australian accounting standard setting commenced with the establishment of the Accounting Standards Review Board (ASRB) in 1984. There were initially seven members appointed by the Ministerial Council: a chairman selected by the Ministerial Council, two members nominated by the professional accountancy bodies, and four members drawn from a panel proposed by organizations with an interest in financial reporting (Miller, 1991, p. 34). The ASRB was empowered to (Walker, 1987, p. 273; Miller, 1991, p. 34):

(a) determine priorities for the consideration of accounting standards referred to it
(b) review accounting standards referred to it
(c) sponsor the development of accounting standards
(d) seek expert advice as deemed necessary by the ASRB
(e) conduct public hearings as to whether proposed accounting standards should be approved
(f) invite public submissions into any aspect of its functions, and
(g) approve accounting standards.

Walker (1987) noted that the ASRB did not exercise its authority to sponsor the development of accounting standards, instead choosing to rely on other bodies, predominantly the AARF, to submit standards to it.

Accounting standards approved by the ASRB had a weak form of mandatory status. There was a presumption that compliance with accounting standards achieved a *true and fair view*. Directors who did not comply with approved accounting standards were required to disclose the financial effect of noncompliance and explain why compliance with approved accounting standards would not achieve a *true and fair view*. Auditors were required to comment on any justification of noncompliance and report it to the ASRB, which kept a register of such occurrences.

The accountancy profession was displeased with the arrangements. While some had hoped that the ASRB would merely 'rubber stamp' the profession's standards, the Board actively examined each issue and sought to impose its own set of priorities for the submission of standards. The accountancy profession had invested and continued to invest considerable resources in standard setting and did not welcome the ASRB's attempts to dictate priorities and policy (Miller, 1991, p. 34). Throughout most of the first four years of the ASRB, the Accounting Standards Board (AcSB) of the AARF continued its role of issuing accounting standards for the accountancy profession, and submitted them to the ASRB for approval.

There was considerable tension between the professional accountancy bodies and the ASRB. For instance, the ICAA and the ASA continued to seek changes in the ASRB's powers. There was controversy and uncertainty about whether the ASRB was empowered to amend standards or whether it could only accept or reject standards submitted to it (Walker, 1987, p. 274). Another contentious issue was the uncertainty of ownership of copyright on standards submitted to the ASRB. This was not resolved until September 1985.

During its first 20 months of operation the ASRB issued only two accounting standards. Walker (1987) attributed this to the tardiness of the AARF in providing appropriately drafted submissions on matters identified as priorities by the ASRB. The slow progress in issuing standards attracted criticism (e.g. Boymal, 1985, pp. 18–19, cited by Walker, 1987, p. 279). The Ministerial Council responded by appointing the chairman of the NCSC, Henry Bosch, in 1985, to examine the standard-setting arrangements. Bosch concluded that the process for approving accounting standards was too long; proposals passed through the due process of the profession's Board, the AcSB, before being submitted to the ASRB and subjected to its due process (Bushnell, 1985a). The NCSC, the ASRB, the ICAA, and the ASA agreed upon a set of streamlined procedures to expedite the approval of accounting standards by the ASRB.

The new procedures resulted in enhanced cooperation between the accountancy profession and the ASRB. Some viewed them as indirectly providing legal backing for the profession's accounting standards (e.g. McGregor, 1985; *The Age*, 10 December 1985, cited by Walker, 1987). Some modifications would be required before submitting the profession's standards to the ASRB for approval, but it was expected that 21 standards could be prepared for submission by the end of 1986 (Bushnell, 1985b). Six of the profession's accounting standards were approved within 12 months of the new procedures taking effect.

A further development in 1986 saw government representatives agreeing, in principle, to the replacement of disclosure requirements in the Corporations law with requirements in accounting standards (Walker, 1993, p. 104). However, this was not implemented during the 1984–1988 era.

The cooperative arrangements continued for a few years until a dispute arose between the AARF and the ASRB over the content of the foreign currency standard (Killen, 1987; English, 1988). This resulted in calls from the profession to abolish the ASRB or, as in the case of Geoffrey Cohen, president of the ICAA, to merge the ASRB with the AcSB (Killen, 1987). Some members of the ASRB responded by proposing a merger of the ASRB with the AcSB, which was approved in 1988.

With the establishment of the ASRB in 1984, 'the accountancy profession was forced into a reluctant marriage with the government on accounting standard setting' (Miller, 1991, p. 35). The regulatory structure, with the ASRB appointed by the Ministerial Council having exclusive responsibility to issue mandatory accounting standards, appears to be a significant step toward corporatism along the market–state axis. Walker (1987) argued that while authority was vested in the ASRB, power over standard setting in Australia remained with the accountancy profession, pointing to the domination of the ASRB by members of the accountancy profession and the frustration of the standard-setting process by the AARF. He argued that there was regulatory capture, evidenced by the streamlined procedures which resulted in fast-tracking approval of the profession's own standards (Walker, 1987), and 'which assured the profession that it would, in effect, control the ASRB' (Walker, 1993, p. 104). According to Walker, the regulatory capture culminated in the reverse takeover of the ASRB by the profession in 1988 (English, 1988, p. 30).

Walker's interpretation of the standard-setting arrangements during this period is consistent with associationism. The legal backing of approved accounting standards, subject to a true and fair override, is a significant change from the more liberal regime of the previous era. Reliance on market and community was achieved through the accountancy profession effectively self-regulating, supported by minor government intervention through the appointment of members of the ASRB and its authority to approve and, hence, give mandatory status to standards submitted to it by the accountancy profession.

However, other interpretations of the standard-setting arrangements from 1984 to 1988 are more consistent with corporatism. Miller (1991, p. 35), noting Walker's view, argued that if the ASRB were captured, it was 'a very troublesome captive'. Godfrey et al. (1994, pp. 315–316) suggested that the standard-setting process may have been captured by well-organized and politically influential preparers. Rahman (1992), adopting the theoretical perspective that key players in standard setting are driven by self-interest, perceived the major interest groups in financial reporting to be the accountancy profession, companies, bureaucrats in government, and politicians. He argued that rather than any one group capturing the standard-setting process, an equilibrium outcome on each issue is reached by the interplay of the competing interests. These alternative views generally place more emphasis on the government providing an oversight function through the authority of the ASRB to issue mandatory accounting standards and the role of the Ministerial Council in appointing its members.

Under alternative interpretations of the standard-setting regulatory arrangements in Australia from 1984 to 1988, financial reporting regulation may be described as associationism or corporatism (Parker, 1986, p. 76). Regardless of who, if indeed anyone, is viewed as having controlled the ASRB, the 1984–1988 era reflects a move away from the near liberalism of the 1970–1983 era towards a greater level of state intervention.

10.7 International harmonization of accounting 1984–1988

Australia continued on its path to international harmonization but did not take a direct route. The accountancy profession maintained its active involvement in the IASC and the IFAC, and the membership of the AcSB was increased from eight to nine to include the Australian representative to the IASC. But international harmonization objectives were not reflected directly in the ASRB's standard-setting process. The ASRB did not include any form of international harmonization, or any reference to international best practice, in its criteria for approving accounting standards. While there was no formal requirement to do so (self-imposed or otherwise) the ASRB did from time to time consider international developments. For example, developments in the USA were explicitly addressed in a report (Miller, 1986) on the funds statements standard prepared for the ASRB. It is interesting to note that only passing reference is made to the corresponding UK standard, SSAP 10.

The AcSB did not directly adopt standards issued by the IASC. Standards issued, or reissued, by the AcSB and approved by the ASRB were mostly compatible with IAS (e.g. AAS 8, AAS 11, and AAS 12) but inconsistencies remained. For instance, *AAS 14: Equity Method of Accounting* was inconsistent with *IAS 3: Business Combinations* because the Australian standard did not require the application of the equity accounting method to unconsolidated subsidiaries; *AAS 17: Accounting for Leases* did not require the same disclosures as *IAS 17: Accounting for Leases.* Also, the Australian standards often allowed fewer choices than the corresponding IAS. For instance, *AAS 18: Accounting for Goodwill* prescribed a maximum amortization period for goodwill while IAS 3 did not.

The position of Australian standard setters on international harmonization was similar to that of other developed nations. International Accounting Standards at the time were generally viewed as permitting too many alternative accounting treatments. In an interview published anonymously in the *Australian Accountant* in April 1986, Bosch, Chairman of the NCSC, acknowledged the need for the ASRB to become more internationalized. However, he expressed reservations about the suitability of IAS at that time, describing them as 'lowest common denominator' solutions (Potter, 1987).

International cooperation between securities regulators was developing during the 1980s. For example, in 1987 a meeting of securities regulators concentrated on alignment of prospectuses and exchange of information between exchanges. Bosch noted, however, that differences in accounting standards were an impediment to the international alignment of prospectuses (Potter, 1987).

At a meeting of the International Organization of Securities Commissions (IOSCO) in 1988, the adoption of IAS for international filings was considered but rejected because, at that time, many IAS allowed for conflicting treatments to accommodate differences in domestic accounting standards. However, the IOSCO gave strong support to the IASC's project to enhance global comparability of financial reporting by reducing the number of accounting alternatives in IAS (Anonymous, 1989, pp. 22–27).

The accountancy profession, through the AARF, made more explicit reference to international developments when considering accounting issues. Discussion papers on issues on the AcSB's agenda made specific reference to pronouncement issues in other jurisdictions or by the IASC. For example, Discussion Paper No. 4, prepared by Miller and Scott (1980) for the AARF, reviewed standards issued or proposed by the Financial Accounting Standards Board (FASB) in the USA, the Canadian Institute of Chartered Accountants, and the IASC. However, the approach adopted during this era was one of an informed search for an Australian solution to accounting problems, rather than any commitment to harmonizing with standards issued by another authority.

Similarly, when the AARF embarked upon a conceptual framework project in 1979, it was able to draw on the conceptual framework project commenced by the FASB in 1973 (Dean and Clarke, 2003, pp. 289, 292). The initial exposure drafts issued in April 1988, and subsequent statements of accounting concepts, contained numerous similarities to the FASB conceptual framework. The IASC's conceptual framework proceeded concurrently with the project being undertaken by the AARF, resulting in the issue of an exposure draft in May 1988. Thus, the Australian accountancy profession worked simultaneously on two conceptual framework projects: the Australian conceptual framework project being undertaken by the AARF and the international conceptual framework through the involvement of the professional accountancy bodies in the IASC.

The similarity of the Australian and IASC exposure drafts is a result of their common starting point, the FASB's framework, and the influence of the development of the Australian conceptual framework on the IASC's conceptual framework project. As noted by Sir David Tweedie, Chairman of the IASB, in a speech given in Sydney, in August 2002, 'Now the reason in fact that we are in a position to harmonize international accounting standards is basically because standard setters for many years now have been coming from a single conceptual basis, the conceptual framework that you pioneered much in Australia' (Jones and Wolnizer, 2003, p. 377).

The approaches to harmonization by key players in accounting regulation were mixed during the period from 1984 to 1988. The accountancy profession, through its participation in the IASC, pursued the foundations of full global harmonization with the development of an international conceptual framework of accounting. However, this was not reflected in contemporary undertakings such as the development of the Australian conceptual framework and individual accounting standards. The search for international best practice on the conceptual framework project was limited to the FASB conceptual framework given the dearth of international conceptual framework pronouncements at the time. The ASRB's approach can be described as partial internationalization, at best, with ad hoc reference to international developments on some accounting standards. Unlike the accountancy profession, the ASRB was not directly associated with the IASC. It is not surprising that the ASRB, as a body reporting to the Ministerial Council, gave more precedence to national sovereignty than international harmonization in setting accounting standards.

10.8 Australian standard setting 1988–1990

As discussed by English (1988, pp. 30–33), the ASRB had been dependent upon the AARF to submit accounting standards; only two standards had been submitted by other parties by 1988, and the ASRB did not have sufficient funding to sponsor the preparation of standards by other parties. The professional accountancy bodies had provided annually approximately $1.3m in funding to the AARF, compared with the AASB's annual budget of approximately $200,000. The AARF had also offered free expert advice, which could not have been otherwise afforded within the budgetary constraints of the ASRB.

In September 1988 the Ministerial Council approved a merger of the ASRB with the AcSB of the AARF. The AcSB was dissolved and the ASRB took on the dual functions of preparing and approving accounting standards. The membership of the Board increased from seven to nine and the two professional accountancy bodies were each given the capacity to nominate a member of their respective bodies to the ASRB. The profession's representatives to the IASC and the International Public Sector Committee were given observer status on the ASRB (McGregor, 1989, p. 87). Under the arrangements of the merger, the AARF provided a secretariat and technical support to the ASRB. The merger formalized the relationship between the AARF and the ASRB that had evolved since 1984.

During the first three years the merged Board made significant progress on both the conceptual framework project and the issue of accounting standards. In 1990 the AARF and the ASRB jointly issued three concepts statements that formed the first three building blocks of the Australian conceptual framework of accounting to guide financial reporting and standard setting in the public and private sectors. The ASRB issued numerous accounting standards during a comparatively brief period on issues including setoff and extinguishment of debt, related party transactions, equity accounting, tax-effect accounting, and the presentation of profit and loss accounts.

During this period the AARF commissioned a report on the institutional arrangements for standard setting in Australia, known as the Peirson Report, which was released in 1990. The Peirson Report recommended the establishment of an accounting standard-setting board which should not be restricted to any particular interest group and be independent of interest groups, including the accountancy profession, business, and government. According to Peirson (1990), a wider section of the community, comprising users, preparers, auditors, and regulators, should have the opportunity to be involved directly in the standard-setting process, in particular through the establishment of broadly based consultative groups. Peirson (1990) also recommended the merger of the AASB with the PSASB.

At around the same time as the standard-setting boards merged, arrangements were being made to introduce a national scheme of corporate regulation to replace the former cooperative system. The Commonwealth Government of Australia passed the *Corporations Act 1989* to replace the *Uniform Companies Act* enacted in each of the states of Australia. This was delayed by a successful legal challenge by three states and the matter was not resolved until 1990. The recommendations of the Peirson Report were not reflected in this round of regulatory reform.

There are different interpretations of the implications of the merger of the AcSB with the ASRB. Adopting Walker's view of the merger, as a reverse takeover of the ASRB by the accountancy profession (English, 1988, p. 30), the changes introduced in 1989 moved the regulation of accounting closer to associationism. However, Miller (1991, p. 31) argues, 'the espousal of the co-regulation philosophy and the merger in late 1988 of the government-sponsored and profession-sponsored standard-setting bodies for the private sector suggest that the system has been nudged closer to corporatism'.

10.9 International harmonization of accounting 1988–1990

The merged standard-setting Board did not have any formal or consistent harmonization policy during the period from 1988 to 1990. When the first three conceptual framework statements were issued in August 1990, the ASRB issued Release 100, formally incorporating the concepts statements, rather than harmonization, as criteria for setting accounting standards.

Not surprisingly, standards issued by the ASRB were often not harmonized to IAS standards. For instance, the difference that had arisen between AAS 14 and IAS 3 were perpetuated when the ASRB issued the approved version of the Standards, *ASRB 1016: Disclosure of Information about Investments in Associated Companies*; and inconsistencies arose between *ASRB 1024: Consolidated Accounts*, issued in 1990, and *IAS 27: Consolidated Financial Statements*, in the treatment of entities over which the parent's control was temporary.

While not adopting a policy of harmonizing to IAS or generally accepted international practice, the ASRB relied on the lack of international consensus in 1990 when withdrawing *ED 49: Accounting for Identifiable Intangible Assets*, issued in 1989. However, this view was not reflected in numerous other accounting standards, where the ASRB provoked many of its constituents by going further than its overseas counterparts (Miller, 1995a, p. 8).

As noted above in the discussion of the 1984 to 1988 era, the AARF did not have any firm commitment to harmonizing its conceptual framework to the framework being developed concurrently by the IASC. This approach did not change when the PSASB of the AARF joined forces with the ASRB to prepare the Australian conceptual framework of accounting. While there were many similarities to the IASC's conceptual framework issued in 1989, the Australian conceptual framework was considerably more detailed. *Statement of Accounting Concepts 1* also contains some notable differences, such as the inclusion of the reporting entity concept based on the information needs of users (PSASB and ASRB, 1990a).

Thus, Australia's harmonization policy waxed and waned after the merger of the AcSB and the ASRB. The accountancy profession continued to work toward its long-term goal of full globalization through its representation on the IASC.

However, domestic developments and initiatives of the profession did not reflect this long-term goal. The ASRB did not have a formal harmonization policy during the period from 1988 to 1990, preferring instead to be guided by the conceptual framework. The accountancy profession, through the role of the AARF in providing technical support to the ASRB and its appointments to the Board, was able to influence the strategic direction of the ASRB. This provided only limited support for harmonization in Australian standard setting because the accountancy profession's harmonization policy in the short and medium term was one of substantial commonality (APS 3), and the accountancy profession had, through the PSASB and the AARF, and in conjunction with the ASRB, developed a conceptual framework that was not harmonized to the IASC's framework. This created the foundation for tension between international harmonization and a deductive process of standard setting based on an underlying conceptual framework.

10.10 Australian standard setting 1991–1999

Discontent with the cooperative arrangements among the states for the regulation of companies and administration of company law resulted in a series of reforms that commenced in 1989 but did not become effective until the beginning of 1991. The first of these was the passing of the *Corporations Act* in 1989. As discussed above, legal challenge of this Act was not resolved until 1990. Corporate reform could then be dealt with more efficiently because the Commonwealth Government of Australia had established control over almost all aspects of corporate legislation.

Another aspect of the regulatory reforms was the *Australian Securities Commission Act 1989* (*ASC Act*), which established the Australian Securities Commission (ASC – later renamed the Australian Securities and Investments Commission) to replace the NCSC and state Corporate Affairs Commissions by the end of 1990. The ASC had greater powers of inspection and investigation and was better resourced than its predecessor, the NCSC. The divided responsibilities and the absence of accountability to a single parliament were critical flaws in the former cooperative system (Miller, 1991, p. 31). The ASC enhanced the role of the government by providing a more consistent instrument of government policy because it was accountable to a minister of the Commonwealth Government of Australia, rather than to the Ministerial Council of State and Commonwealth Attorney Generals (Miller, 1991, p. 33).

A third aspect of the regulatory reforms was the establishment of the Australian Accounting Standards Board (AASB) as a federal statutory body from 1 January 1991, with the authority to issue accounting standards with the force of law. Members of the AASB were to be appointed by the Commonwealth Attorney General, four of whom could be nominated by the ICAA and the ASCPA (Australian Society of CPAs, formerly known as the Australian Society of Accountants).

The major functions of the AASB were specified in section 226 of the *ASC Act*. These included: developing a conceptual framework for the purpose of evaluating proposed accounting standards; reviewing accounting standards and sponsoring their development; engaging in public consultation; and changing the form and content of a proposed accounting standard as the AASB considered necessary.

The *Corporations Act 1989* was amended in 1991 to give prominence to accounting standards. The true and fair override was replaced with a requirement to comply with approved Australian Accounting Standards (section 298(1)) and provide additional information and explanation, if necessary, to achieve a true and fair view (section 299(1)). Thus, a strong form of mandatory status was given to accounting standards issued by the AASB.

The AASB and the PSASB furthered the conceptual framework project with the issue in 1995 of *SAC 4: Definition and Recognition of Elements of Financial Statements*. This was a controversial statement. The exposure draft that preceded SAC 4 attracted considerable opposition because it proposed a balance sheet bias and represented a significant departure from traditional accounting practice (Howieson, 1993; Miller and Loftus, 1993; Philp, 1993). A particularly controversial requirement was the recognition of executory contracts (referred to in SAC 4 as agreements equally and proportionately unperformed). Concerns about the content of SAC 4 were exacerbated by a requirement of the ASCPA and the ICAA in *Miscellaneous Professional Statement APS 1* (subsequently amended) that members comply with the statements of accounting concepts.

While the legislated purpose of the AASB's conceptual framework project was to guide its deliberations over accounting standards, the Board did not slavishly apply the principles established in the concepts statements. Howieson (1993) identified six inconsistencies between SAC 4 and Australian accounting standards as at 1993. A subsequent analysis of inconsistencies between the Australian conceptual framework and Australian accounting standards found that half of the differences identified by Howieson remained a decade later and that new inconsistencies had been introduced (Loftus, 2003).

The AASB's only formal criterion for determining the content of accounting standards was the conceptual framework, which was based on an explicit premise of serving users' needs for information. However, it was not uncommon for the debate and public consultation process to be dominated by preparers. The goodwill debate is an interesting case that demonstrates the interaction of key players and the increasing role of international harmonization in Australian financial reporting.

The amortization requirement in *AASB 1013: Accounting for Goodwill* (originally issued as ASRB 1013) was unpopular with Australian companies. While many companies mitigated its effects by recognizing other intangibles that did not need to be amortized, some went further by using amortization policies, such as the inverse (or reverse) sum-of-the-years'-digits (ISOYD) method, to defer the recognition of expenses for the amortization of goodwill (Miller, 1995a; Day and Hartnett, 1999/2000). The ASC gave prominence to the debate on goodwill amortization in 1993 by challenging the use of the ISOYD method of the amortization. The ASC issued *Practice Note 39: Accounting for Goodwill*, stating that, 'it would be difficult to envisage circumstances in which the pattern of benefits expected to be derived from goodwill would be weighted towards the latter years of the useful life of goodwill ...'. The debate attracted intense lobbying from preparers who argued that the Australian requirements placed Australian companies at a disadvantage in international capital markets (Pacific Dunlop, 1994; Miller, 1995a; Day and Hartnett, 1999/2000). Some companies, including Pacific Dunlop, ignored the Practice Note and engaged in lobbying against AASB 1013. The campaign to review the goodwill standard was joined by more large Australian companies, and supported by the Group of 100 (a body of financial executives of large Australian companies and government business enterprises) and the Australian Shareholders Association. However, the AASB did not consider a revision of the goodwill standard to be a priority and did not place it on its agenda at that time.

Some corporations proceeded to lobby the Attorney General, claiming that AASB 1013 had an adverse effect on the international competitiveness of Australian business. The AASB responded, arguing that a review was not necessary because AASB 1013 was harmonized to *IAS 22: Business Combinations*. The Attorney General was reluctant to intervene. As noted by Miller (1995a, p. 5), 'While the AASB is a statutory board with its members appointed for terms of two to three years by the Attorney General, it has the ability (at least in the short run) to make independent decision subject to any new standards being exposed to a veto in the federal parliament.' The independence of the ASC was established by the *ASC Act 1989*, which gave the Attorney General power to give written policy direction, but not to intervene on a specific case.

The matter was eventually resolved by Urgent Issues Group (UIG), a body formed in 1994 to provide timely guidance on urgent accounting issues. In 1995 the UIG issued *Abstract 5: Methods of Amortization of Goodwill*, prescribing the use of the straight-line method of amortization of goodwill. The AASB subsequently revised *AASB 1013* to the same effect. What is noteworthy in this case is the intense lobbying by corporate interests and the demonstration of the increased internationalization of accounting debate in Australia.

Throughout the 1990s there was increasing politicization of the standard-setting process (Godfrey et al., 1997, pp. 384–385; Collett et al., 1998). Miller (1995b) attributes this to the removal of the true and fair override and the ASC's low tolerance of noncompliance with accounting standards. The formation of the ASX in 1987 through the amalgamation of the stock exchanges in each state gave rise to a well-resourced entity that was able to use its lobbying power to promote the interests of the Australian capital market. By the mid 1990s the Group of 100 and the ASX emerged as key players representing corporate interests in standard-setting debates (Collett et al., 1998, p. 9).

The reforms introduced in 1991 provided more centralized regulation of accounting. There was a shift in power from the accountancy profession to the government as the standard-setting body became a statutory body. When viewed in the context of the concurrent developments that brought corporate legislation under the control of the Commonwealth Government, and the establishment of a more powerful securities commission accountable to a Commonwealth minister, the Australian standard-setting arrangements introduced in 1991 are best described as corporatism, moving further toward the state end of the market–state spectrum.

Corporate Australia, with much more at stake given the strong form of mandatory status of accounting standards, coupled with the monitoring activities of the ASC, became a powerful lobbying force throughout the 1990s. While a powerful lobby force, corporate interests did not drive the outcomes of the AASB, which, as noted by Miller (1995b, p. 10), had to maintain a balance between the potentially conflicting interests of its constituents:

> 'While the AASB is not controlled by outside parties, it is constrained by the need to maintain the continuing support of senior people in the Attorney General's department, the accounting profession, and the business sector. If there were a motion for the disallowance of an accounting standard in the House of Representatives, and the Attorney General did not stand up and defend the standard, the authority of the AASB would be undermined. If the leaders of the accounting bodies thought the AASB was stubbornly headed in the wrong direction, they could pull the plug on funding AARF's services for the AASB. Given

> enough provocation, and irresponsible action by the AASB, corporate Australia could mount a blitzkrieg of lobbying aimed at the dismantling or restructuring of the AASB.'

The capacity and willingness of corporate Australia to become an active force in standard setting gave impetus to Australia's harmonization policy, as discussed below.

10.11 International harmonization of accounting 1991–1999

The internationalization of Australian business and the growing forces of globalization led to an increasing recognition of the importance of international harmonization among key players in accounting regulation. However, there was little consensus on the form of harmonization that should be adopted.

In an isolated commitment to a narrower form of harmonization in 1994 with the accounting standards of another jurisdiction, the AASB issued *Policy Statement 4: Australia–New Zealand Harmonization Policy*, which outlined a joint policy of harmonization of conceptual frameworks and accounting standards. This development reflected the impact on accounting practice and regulation of a bilateral agreement for economic cooperation, the *Closer Economic Relations Agreement*. This was the first major instance of direct influence of economic policy on accounting standard setting in Australia.

The accountancy profession had continually supported international harmonization through its participation in the IASC. During the 1990s the professional accountancy bodies stepped up their efforts to promote harmonization in Australia. The executive director of the ICAA called for 'real service, not lip service, for the cause of internationalization' (Harrison, 1995, p. 6). Another sign of the accountancy profession's increased commitment to international harmonization was the increased representation on the IASC from one member to two members and one technical adviser in 1994 (Miller, 1995a, p. 15). Other key supporters of international harmonizations were large corporations, the ASX, and the Group of 100 (Howieson, 1997, p. 190; Collett et al., 1998, p. 9).

The goodwill debate also reflected the increased internationalization of accounting issues in Australia. Corporate lobbyists argued on the basis of disadvantage in international capital markets, while the AASB supported its position on the basis of international harmonization, rather than appealing to the conceptual framework which was, at the time, the explicit criteria to be applied in standard setting.

Some of the support for harmonization reflected concern that Australia should not get ahead of the rest of international practice (Philp, 1993, p. 19; Miller, 1995a, pp. 8–10). The ICAA acknowledged widespread community concern that Australian standard setters needed to take more heed of international precedents in its 1993 Annual Report (Miller, 1995a, p. 9). Similarly, the national president of the ASCPA commented that the professional bodies were concerned that 'Australia does not get too far out in front of the world as to do so would create problems for those Australian companies which trade and borrow internationally' (Paton, 1993, p. 5).

Concurrently, the international campaign for harmonization gained support from an agreement between the IASC and the IOSCO in 1995. The IASC undertook to complete a core set of standards by 1999 that the IOSCO would consider endorsing for cross-border offerings. The IASC accelerated the core standard program in 1996 to target completion in 1998. This involved a revision of existing standards so as to reduce the number of accepted alternative accounting treatments. Endorsement would mean that financial statements completed in accordance with IAS by foreign listed entities would be accepted by stock exchanges without the need for reconciliation to the domestic GAAP of the stock exchange.

The AASB faced growing pressure for internationalization from key players within Australia. Another influence from beyond Australian shores was the AASB's involvement in the G4+1, a group of standard setters from Australia, Canada, New Zealand (which joined after the group's name was established), the UK, the USA, plus the IASC. The G4+1 shared similar conceptual frameworks and cooperated on projects of accounting issues, such as intangible assets. Through involvement in the G4+1, Australia was able to influence the progress and content of standards being developed by the IASC.

The AASB responded to the various pressures for international comparability with the release of a discussion paper on international harmonization (AASB, 1994a). Three broad categories of harmonization were identified: full global harmonization, which was considered to be impractical in the short term and which required unacceptable compromises on financial reporting quality; harmonization to accounting standards issued in another jurisdiction, such as the USA; and internationalization, which was viewed as a cooperative arrangement through which international best practice would be considered in domestic standard setting. The USA was considered as the most likely choice if Australia were to harmonize to the standards of another jurisdiction, reflecting the increasing links between some of Australia's largest corporations and US capital markets.

The 10 responses received to the AASB's discussion paper are summarized by Miller (1995a). All respondents supported some form of international harmonization. One respondent, the Group of 100, urged standard setters to work towards a restructured IASC with a view to achieving more robust accounting standards. In contrast, a submission from the Association of Accountants in Australia and New Zealand, an association of academics, while supporting international comparability, stressed the need for national sovereignty in standard setting to enable appropriate responses to the needs of Australian business and society.

Following a review of responses to its discussion paper, the AASB with the PSASB issued *Policy Statement 6: International Harmonization Policy* in 1996. The harmonization policy reflected a long-term strategy of working towards full global harmonization with an interim policy of benchmarked harmonization, whereby compliance with Australian standards would, to the extent acceptable, constitute compliance with IAS. However, the reverse might not apply as the Australian standard setters would continue to add additional disclosure requirements or remove alternatives, as they saw fit. The conditional harmonization, which was subject to the IAS being acceptable, leaves considerable scope for inconsistencies to arise. If the IASC issues an accounting standard which adopts policies other than those preferred by the AASB, or which is inconsistent with the Australian conceptual framework, the extent of harmonization could vary: 'There must be a willingness to suffer a loss of autonomy and sacrifice some accounting preferences' Miller (1995a, p. 10). As the AASB proceeded along its path of benchmarked harmonization toward its long-term destination of full global harmonization, it was destined to be challenged by obstacles such as having to forgo some of its preferred choices and the need to give priority to harmonization over the conceptual framework and make decisions that would, at times, provoke some of its constituents.

The pressure for international comparability inevitably led to tensions with the AASB's policy on the role of the conceptual framework in standard setting. SAC 4 contained several inconsistencies with the IASC's conceptual framework, particularly in relation to the definition of revenue. When asked whether harmonization would divert the AASB from the conceptual framework, at a meeting of the Accounting Standards Interest Group at the AAANZ Conference in Hobart, Ken Spencer, Chairman of the AASB, replied that harmonization was probably distracting the AASB and that the Board could not always direct most of its attention to the conceptual framework (Howieson, 1997, p. 202).

The ASX viewed harmonization as a matter of urgency because it was concerned by the potential loss of Australian listings to other stock exchanges (Humphry, 1997). In 1997 the ASX strengthened the AASB's resolve to make international harmonization a priority by providing $1 million to fund a harmonization project to be undertaken by the AASB and the AARF. The ASX raised the money by imposing a 3% levy on annual listing fees for 1997 and 1998.

In the late 1990s many Australian accounting standards were revised as part of the harmonization program undertaken by the AASB and AARF to reduce the number of inconsistencies with IAS, which were also being revised at that time. Even with the impetus from the ASX, the AASB did not fully harmonize to IAS. Identifiable intangible assets, other than research and development costs, continued to be unregulated, notwithstanding that the IASC had issued a standard on intangible assets. Similarly, regulation of reporting on financial instruments in Australia lagged behind international developments. In 1997 the IASC commenced a two-stage project to develop accounting standards for financial instruments. The first stage was the development of an interim international standard on recognition and measurement, and the second stage was the establishment of the Joint Working Group comprising national standard setters and the IASC to prepare a comprehensive standard. The first stage culminated in the issue of *IAS 39: Financial Instruments: Recognition and Measurement* in 1999 as an interim standard. The AASB decided against issuing a corresponding Australian accounting standard. The failure to harmonize (or even partially harmonize) to IAS 39 left a gap in Australian reporting requirements with respect to the recognition and measurement of financial instruments, resulting in the omission from financial statements of many transactions involving derivative financial instruments and their effects on financial position and financial performance before settlement.

The financial and political aspects of the standard-setting arrangements in place from 1991 to 1999 facilitated the direct intervention by the ASX. From a financial perspective, Peter Day, Deputy Chairman of the ASC and former chairman of the Group of 100, the AASB, and the Urgent Issues Group, had expressed concerns about the lack of resources for standard setters amid the growing cost of standard setting, driven by the increased complexity of issues on the standard-setting agenda. Second, the corporatism of the 1990s smoothed the way for the ASX, which had no standard-setting authority, to provide direction to the AASB. The AARF, while a long-standing supporter of harmonization, was also a strong supporter of the conceptual framework. However, the influence of the accountancy profession in standard setting had been weakened over a series of reforms.

The ASX initiative, which effectively gave policy direction to the AASB, was not challenged by the Australian Government because the objective was consistent with its own. In 1997 the Treasury launched the Corporate Law Economic Reform Program (CLERP), which included a proposal for an even stronger commitment to IAS. CLERP (Commonwealth of Australia, 1997, p. 28) suggested: 'From 1 January 1999, the AASC should issue identical exposure drafts of standards for public comment to those issued by the IASC with the objective that the final standards issued by the AASC would be consistent with Australian law and be the same as those issued by the IASC, unless the Government, upon advice from the FRC, determines that to do so would not be in Australia's best interests.' The AASC and the FRC refer to a proposed reformed and renamed standard-setting body and an oversight body respectively. The Treasury's proposal would effectively remove standard-setting power from the AASB to the IASC, with changes requiring the support of the FRC and the approval of the Australian Government. The role of the AASB would have been reduced to putting a 'local wrapper' around standards issued by the IASC.

The Treasury's proposals were opposed by key players in accounting standard setting, including large companies and the accountancy profession (Brown and Tarca, 2001, pp. 281–282). In a joint submission on the CLERP proposals, the Australian Society of Certified Practising Accountants and the Institute of Chartered Accountants argued that adoption of IAS was premature (ASCPA and ICAA, 1998).

Another opponent of immediate full harmonization was the AASB: 'The AASB believes that committing to the adoption of IASC standards without amendment is premature, and based on a number of myths which need to be dispelled' (Spencer, 1998, p. 20). The first 'myth' that Spencer sought to dispel was that IASC standards were globally accepted. Only 10 countries (Croatia, Cyprus, Kuwait, Latvia, Malta, Oman, Pakistan, Trinidad and Tobago, Malaysia, and Papua New Guinea) adopted IASC without amendment at that time. Second, he rebutted the assumption, or 'myth', that immediate adoption would benefit Australia. While acknowledging that adoption of IASC standards might provide some cost savings for large Australian entities seeking a foreign listing, smaller Australian entities that rely on domestic sources of capital would incur additional costs with no corresponding benefit (Spencer, 1998, p. 21). The third 'myth', that IASC standards are as rigorous, was countered on the premise that IASC standards allowed more flexibility and were less suited to the Australian environment (Spencer, 1998, p. 21). He also rejected the view that immediate adoption was widely supported. He argued that the AASB's current policy was widely accepted, citing a survey of listed entities undertaken by the ASX, which found that 87% favored a harmonization policy over immediate adoption of IAS (Spencer, 1988, p. 22). Lastly, Spencer argued that the assumption, or 'myth', that endorsement by the IOSCO of IAS for cross-border listing was imminent was not realistic, particularly given the public consultation process that would need to be followed by the SEC.

Towards the end of the second millennium, the AASB, the accountancy profession, the Commonwealth Treasury and other key players, including the ASX and the Group of 100, were united by a common goal of international harmonization. However, few supported slavish adoption of IAS and the harmonization policy was effectively one of substantial commonality with IAS.

10.12 Australian standard setting 2000 onwards

Major changes were made to the standard-setting structure by the *Corporate Law Economic Reform Program (CLERP) Act 1999*, which amended the *ASIC Act 1989*. The reforms were consistent with the general recommendations of the Peirson Report commission a decade earlier by the AARF. The AASB was reconstituted as a body corporate, responsible to the Financial Reporting Council (FRC), which is appointed by the Treasurer. The functions of the AASB were widened to include setting accounting standards for the public sector and not-for-profit entities. Accordingly, the accountancy profession's PSASB was disbanded. The UIG, which was originally established by the AARF, also came under the AASB in 2000. The functions of the AASB were specified in section 277(1) of the *ASIC Act*:

> 'To develop a conceptual framework, not having the force of an accounting standard, for the purpose of evaluating proposed accounting standards and international standards.
>
> To make accounting standards under section s.334 of the *Corporations Law* for the purposes of national scheme laws.
>
> To formulate accounting standards for other purposes.
>
> To participate in and contribute to the development of a singe set of accounting standards for worldwide use.
>
> To advance and promote the facilitation of the development of accounting standards that require the provision of financial information that is relevant and reliable, facilitates comparability, and is readily understandable to allow users to

make and evaluate decisions about allocating scarce resources and assessing the performance and financial position of entities.'

The reconstituted AASB commenced with a full-time chairman, who is appointed by the Treasurer, and nine part-time members, who are appointed by the FRC. The number of part-time members has since been increased to 12.

The AASB was provided with a secretariat funded by the Treasury. The secretariat had, until then, been provided by the AARF. This change involved a transfer of a significant number of the staff of the AARF, a private sector body established by the two major professional accountancy bodies, to the AASB, a public sector corporation.

The FRC was established in 2000 as a statutory body comprising key members of the business community, the professional accountancy bodies, governments, and regulatory agencies. The FRC oversees the AASB, advises the Commonwealth Government of Australia on accounting standard setting, monitors developments in international accounting standards, and determines the broad strategic direction of the AASB. In October 2003, the FRC's oversight function was extended to the Auditing and Assurance Standards Board (AUASB), which until then had been a board of the AARF.

Another aspect of the current regulatory framework is that the statutory standard-setting body reports indirectly to the Federal Treasurer rather than to the Attorney General. Arguably, this has advanced the perspective of accounting standard setting as a potential instrument of national economic policy. This is also reflected in the objectives of the new arrangements, as stated in the *ASIC Act* (section 224):

> 'To facilitate the development of accounting standards that require the provision of financial information that allows users to make and evaluate decisions …
>
> To facilitate the Australian economy by reducing the cost of capital, enabling Australian entities to compete effectively overseas, and having accounting standards that are clearly stated and easy to understand.
>
> To maintain investor confidence in the Australian economy (including its capital markets).'

The current standing-setting arrangements in Australia reflect corporatism and have moved further towards the state end of the market–state spectrum with the reforms introduced at the beginning of 2000, such as the transfer of the AARF secretariat for the AASB to the Treasury, the disbandment of the accountancy profession's public sector standard-setting board, and the transfer of the UIG from the AARF to the AASB. Interest associations, comprising key stakeholders from the business community, professional accounting bodies, governments, and regulatory agencies, are assigned the role of overseeing a standard-setting body, for public purposes including facilitating the Australian economy by lowering the cost of capital and enhancing the international competitiveness of Australian business. As international harmonization became increasingly accepted as a strategy to make large Australian corporations more internationally competitive, the shift of power and objective reflected in the new standard-setting arrangements cleared the road for the advancement of Australia's harmonization policy.

10.13 International harmonization of accounting 2000 onwards

The CLERP reforms introduced in 2000 did not include the Treasury's proposal (Commonwealth of Australia, 1997) that IAS should be adopted as Australian accounting standards for domestic reporting, with departures from IAS requiring Government approval, on the recommendation of the FRC. The Government backed away from its extreme position on adopting IAS in the light of considerable opposition to the proposals at that time. However, with the CLERP reforms in 1999 an international harmonization objective became enshrined within legislation as one of the functions of the FRC (ASIC Act 1989, section 225(2)):

The FRC functions include:

- Furthering the development of a single set of accounting standards for worldwide use with appropriate regard to international developments;
- Promoting the continued adoption of international best practice accounting standards in the Australian accounting standard-setting processes if doing so would be in the best interests of both the private and public sectors in the Australian economy.

The reconstituted AASB revised its harmonization policy in 2002. Policy Statement 6, on international harmonization, was withdrawn. Policy Statement 4, which had dealt with harmonization between Australian and New Zealand accounting standards and conceptual frameworks, was reissued to encompass an extended harmonization/convergence policy. Policy Statement 4 also reflected a stronger commitment to harmonization to IFRS. It reduced the circumstances in which a standard issued by the IASB would not be adopted in Australia; a standard issued by the IASB should be adopted by the AASB unless it was not considered to be in the best interests of the Australian public and private sectors. Policy Statement 6 (paragraph 2.2) had provided for benchmarked harmonization, such that the method adopted in an Australian standard should be an alternative allowed under the corresponding IAS, and the IAS disclosures should form the minimum for an Australian standard. While acknowledging the ideal of a single global set of standards, the earlier policy statement referred to harmonization as compatibility of national standards in all significant respects.

International developments would soon start to drive Australia's international harmonization policy further along the road to full harmonization. In 1997 the IASC commenced a strategic review of its structure and processes that resulted in the international standard-setting body ceasing to be controlled by a board of national professional accountancy bodies. A new structure, involving a 14-member board, was approved by the IASC member bodies in 2000 and came into effect in April 2001. The IASC was replaced by the International Standard Setting Board (IASB), whose members are appointed by the Trustees of the International Accounting Standards Committee Foundation (IASCF). The reforms established a partnership between the IASB and national standard-setting bodies to strengthen the development of an internationally accepted set of accounting standards (IASCF, 2001).

Other significant milestones in the international journey towards harmonization include laws passed in 1998 in Belgium, Germany, France, and Italy permitting the use of IAS for domestic financial reporting by large companies. In 1999 the IOSCO commenced its review of the core set of standards, which resulted in a recommendation in 2000 that its members allow the use of 30 IASC standards, with supplemental treatments as necessary, in the financial statements of cross-border listings (IASCF, 2001). The IASB undertook an improvements project, resulting in the issue of 13 exposure drafts in May 2002 proposing amendments to its standards (FRC, 2002a). In a move much welcomed by the IASB, the European Union in June 2002 approved the adoption of regulations to require the use of IAS and International Financial Reporting Standards (IFRS) issued by the IASB by 1 January 2005 (IASB, 2002). These global developments collectively reflect growing international acceptance of standards issued by the IASB.

While in 1999 the Australian Government had backed away from a full harmonization policy, the global developments in the first few years of the new millennium strengthened its resolve. The next phase of the Corporate Law Economic Reform Program (CLERP 9) was announced in June 2002. Within a month, the FRC announced the adoption of IFRS for the preparation of domestic financial statements for reporting periods commencing on or after 1 January 2005 (FRC, 2002b). The Government's support for the FRC's strategy was reflected in the announcement in June 2002 by the Treasurer and the Parliamentary Secretary of approval for $2 million in funding to help Australia meet its goal of adopting international accounting standards (Commonwealth of Australia, 2002). Convergence with IFRS was subsequently included in the CLERP 9 Discussion Paper released by the Treasury in September 2002.

The decision to adopt IFRS was not as popular as might have been expected given earlier support for IAS from large companies in Australia and the Group of 100. A major factor in this was the uncertainty created by the timing of Australia's adoption of IFRS; many IFRS were still being revised as part of the IASB's improvements project.

But the adoption of IFRS had strong support from the ASIC, and Australian business soon realized it was 'past the point of no return' on a highway to international convergence. The AASB issued and revised accounting standards and concepts statements as part of its international convergence program under the direction of the FRC. Parts of the Australian conceptual framework differed from the IASB's *Framework for the Preparation and Presentation of Financial Statements*, originally issued by the IASC in 1989. As part of the international convergence program, the AASB (2004a) issued the *Framework for Preparation and Presentation of Financial Statements* (*Framework*), which is equivalent to the IASB's framework. The *Framework* replaced SAC 3 and SAC 4, previously issued by the PSASB and the AASB in 1990 and 1995 respectively. Thus, the very detailed Australian conceptual framework documents were effectively replaced by the less-developed framework of the IASB in the interests of international convergence.

While more harmonized to IFRS than ever before, Australia has not completely substituted IFRS for Australian standards. The FRC (2002b) had envisaged an amendment to the *Corporations Act* to require that financial statements be prepared in accordance with IFRS instead of standards issued by the AASB. This did not eventuate. Instead, the AASB issues 'Australian Equivalents of International Financial Reporting Standards'. The AASB continues to modify the standards issued for the IASB for application in Australia. However, the scope of the modifications is restricted to limiting the alternatives permitted by an IFRS, prescribing additional disclosures, such as those prescribed for related party transactions, and other modifications essential to enable the standards to be applied by Australian entities. For instance, *IAS 7: Cash Flow Statements* permits a choice between the direct method and the indirect method of presenting cash provided by operations. When issuing *AASB 107: Cash Flow Statements* in 2004, the AASB deleted paragraph 18(b), effectively removing the indirect method as an alternative. When issuing *AASB 119: Employee Benefits* in 2004, the AASB specified the use of government bond discount rates to determine the present value of employee obligations (paragraph AUS18.1). This modification was considered necessary because the conditions of an active and liquid corporate bond market do not apply in Australia. Other modifications introduced by the AASB include the incorporation of the reporting entity concept into Australian standards, which effectively reduces their application to exclude entities for which it is not reasonable to assume the presence of users dependent upon general purpose financial reports.

In requiring the adoption of a full harmonization policy by 2005, the FRC was exercising its power under the *ASIC Act* to give strategic direction to the AASB. In their joint submission in response to the CLERP 1 proposals in 1997, the professional accountancy bodies had suggested three criteria that should be met before the adoption of international accounting standards: IAS have been adopted by major capital markets; an effective role for Australia in the IASC has been established; and the adoption of IAS has received substantial support from Australian constituents through an extensive due process (ASCPA and ICAA, 1998, p. 2).

The first criterion suggested by the professional accountancy bodies was partially met; at the time of the FRC's decision, IAS had been adopted by one major capital market. A major trigger for the FRC's decision appears to have been the EU's announcement of the adoption of IFRS. However, the European capital market is not targeted by many of Australia's larger companies in their attempts to raise foreign capital. Australian companies that raise capital abroad are more likely to list in the USA than in the EU (Lonergan, 2003).

There is no evidence that the second criterion, relating to the establishment of Australia's role in the IASB, was considered in the FRC's decision. There was clearly an intention that the AASB would continue to try to work with the IASB towards the development of a single set of high-quality accounting standards. However, the power to influence international standards was potentially weakened by the agreement to accept IFRS that had not yet been issued by the IASB. The adoption of IFRS has undermined Australia's ability to influence the IASB by undermining its negotiating power (Lonergan, 2003).

Lastly, the professional accountancy bodies' recommendation that the adoption of international accounting standards be subject to substantial support expressed through due process was not satisfied. Under the corporatist standard-setting structure established in 2000, no due process or public consultation was required for this decision.

10.14 The beginning of a new journey or the end of the road?

Opponents of the adoption of IFRS argued that Australia's position as a key player in international standard setting would be diminished (Collett et al., 1998; Brown and Tarca, 2001, 2005; Lonergan, 2003). Lonergan argued that the loss of intellectual capital, the diminished negotiating power, and the loss of credibility would impede any role Australia might play in influencing the development of international accounting standards. His article, 'The Emasculation of Accounting Standard Setting in Australia', reflects the view that the adoption of IFRS was the 'end of the road' for Australia's role in international standard setting.

While adoption of IFRS may have impaired Australia's negotiating power, it is not clear that, with a relatively small capital market, Australia had any significant bargaining power to lose since the disbandment of the G4+1 in 2001. Australia's influence in global standard setting has reflected the international reputation for intellectual capital and the investment in standard setting of the Australian accountancy profession, the AASB, and other stakeholders. Australia's role as a major player in the development of the international conceptual framework and accounting standards has been established through the involvement of Australians on international committees and boards, and the initiatives and projects undertaken in the past few decades by the AARF and the AASB. Australia's influence in international accounting standard setting has been through participation rather than by negotiation.

Three years after the FRC announced mandatory adoption of IFRS, it is appropriate to take stock of Australia's role in the international arena. Richard Humphry, former Chairman of the ASX, is a trustee of the IASCF (IASCF, 2004, p. 20). One IASB board member is appointed as a liaison member to the Australian and New Zealand standard setters. The IASB board member currently appointed to that position is Warren McGregor, former Chief Executive Officer of the AARF (p. 21).

Kevin Stevenson is the Director of Technical Activities, IASB, and the non-voting chairman of the International Financial Reporting Interpretations Committee (IFRIC) (IASCF, 204, p. 21). Mr Stevenson is a former member of the AASB and the UIG, and a former Executive Director of the AARF. Wayne

Lonergan, a former member of the AASB, was a member of the IFRIC until his term expired on 30 June 2005.

Another Australian, Peter Day, is a member of the Standards Advisory Council (IASCF, 2004, p. 21). Mr Day is the Executive General Manager, Finance, of Amcor Ltd, and the former Deputy Chairman of the ASIC, former Chairman of the Group of 100, the AASB, and the UIG.

The AASB continues to have a statutory function 'to participate in and contribute to the development of a single set of accounting standards for worldwide use' (ASIC Act, section 277(1)). The AASB fulfills this function by issuing IASB exposure drafts for comments, making submissions on IASB exposure drafts, and participating in IASB research projects. The IASB undertakes research projects and encourages domestic standard setters to be involved as members of its research project teams. The AASB is involved in projects on revenue recognition and insurance, and leads long-term projects on extractive activities, intangible assets and goodwill, and joint ventures.

The AASB's project managers presented the three research projects that are led by Australia for discussion at a forum organized by the Accounting Standards Interest Group of the Accounting and Finance Association of Australia and New Zealand in July 2005. Participants in the Accounting Standards Interest Group Forum comprise academics and practitioners with an interest in financial reporting regulation, and include several current and former members of the AASB, the PSASB, and the UIG. The projects and the forum discussions are briefly summarized to provide insights into the processes of Australia's involvement in international standard setting.

The four countries involved in the extractive activities research project team are Australia (team leader), Canada, South Africa, and Norway. Key issues being considered by the project team include: how reserves and resources should be defined; whether reserves should be recognized as assets; treatment of predevelopment costs; and disclosures (Brady, 2005). The discussion in the forum focused on issues of definition and measurement. Attempts to define reserves are complicated by the breadth of activities encompassed globally by extractive activities.

Australia leads the IASB joint ventures research project team, with other team members coming from Hong Kong, Malaysia, and New Zealand. The IASB has established the following guidelines: that the distinction between control of an investment and control of the underlying assets and liabilities should be improved; and that such distinction should be based on the substance of the arrangement (Hamidi, 2005). The forum discussion focused on issues concerning control and measurement. There was a suggestion that the joint venture and extractive industry projects should not be considered in isolation because many extractive activities are undertaken through joint ventures. Inconsistent policy outcomes between the two projects could potentially result in the outcome of one project effectively undoing the intended outcome of the other. In an extreme example, accounting for the investment in the joint venture at cost would effectively undo a policy of fair value accounting for reserves. However, joint consideration of the two projects was not practical because the scope of the projects had already been defined by the IASB and separate teams had been formed.

The third IASB research project led by the AASB is on intangible assets and goodwill. The research project has two components: accounting for internally generated intangible assets, internally generated goodwill, and separately purchased intangible assets; and accounting for intangible assets and goodwill acquired in a business combination. At the time of the presentation, the IASB advisors appointed to the project were in the process of clarifying its scope and approach, with consideration being given to proposals suggested by the AASB (Ardern, 2005). The project had been motivated by international commercial developments, including outsourcing of manufacturing and other activities, growing importance of customer relations and the growth of public–private partnerships (PPPs), private finance initiatives (PFIs), and build–own–operate–transfer (BOOT) contracts (Ardern, 2005). The discussion that followed the presentation raised concerns about the appropriateness of considering accounting for intangibles arising from a business combination separate from accounting for a business combination. The deliberations of the IASB's Business Combinations (Phase I and Phase II) projects potentially limit the range of feasible solutions that might be considered by the project for intangible assets and goodwill. Concern was also raised about the appropriateness of considering joint ventures and intangible assets in isolation, given the growing relevance of PPPs, PFIs, and BOOTs in many economies. Treating issues such as intangibles arising from a PPP separately from accounting for joint ventures, which might capture PPPs, could potentially result in inconsistencies between accounting standards.

Australia, through the AASB, is actively participating in international research projects that, in turn, influence the content of accounting standards issued by the IASB. To some extent, the work of the research project teams is constrained by the scope of their projects and the manner in which broader accounting issues, such as business combinations, are divided to form smaller projects. This process potentially limits the range of solutions that might be considered by the project teams.

The emasculation of Australia's role in international standard setting has not transpired since the FRC's decision in 2002 to adopt IFRS. Australia has commenced a new journey, through involvement of Australians in the IASCF, the IASB, the IFRIC, and the Standards Advisory Council, and through participation in, and leadership of, IASB research project teams. However, concerns about the potential loss of intellectual capital (Lonergan, 2003) are long-term considerations that could not be revealed by an analysis undertaken only three years after the FRC's decision to adopt IFRS. For Australia's new journey not to reach a 'dead end' there must be continued commitment of resources by stakeholders, such as the government, business, and the accountancy profession, to maintain Australia's intellectual capital and support the involvement of the AASB and others participating in the development of a single set of globally accepted accounting standards and conceptual framework.

Acknowledgments

The helpful comments of Malcolm Miller are gratefully acknowledged.

References

Accounting Standards Board (1974). *AAS 4: Depreciation of Non-Current Assets* (Supplement 1977). Institute of Chartered Accountants and the Australian Society of Accountants, Australia.

Accounting Standards Board (1976). *AAS 3: Accounting for Company Income Tax.* Institute of Chartered Accountants and the Australian Society of Accountants, Australia.

Accounting Standards Board (1983). *AAS 13: Accounting for Research and Development Cost.* Institute of Chartered Accountants and the Australian Society of Accountants, Australia.

Accounting Standards Board (1985). *AAS 18: Accounting for Goodwill.* Institute of Chartered Accountants and the Australian Society of Accountants, Australia.

Accounting Standards Board (1986). *AAS 8: Events Occurring after Balance Date.* Institute of Chartered Accountants and the Australian Society of Accountants, Australia.

Accounting Standards Board (1987a). *AAS 11: Accounting for Construction Contracts.* Institute of Chartered Accountants and the Australian Society of Accountants, Australia.

Accounting Standards Board (1987b). *AAS 12: Statement of Sources and Applications of Funds.* Institute of Chartered Accountants and the Australian Society of Accountants, Australia.

Accounting Standards Board (1987c). *AAS 14: Equity Method of Accounting.* Institute of Chartered Accountants and the Australian Society of Accountants, Australia.

Accounting Standards Board (1988). *AAS 17: Accounting for Leases.* Institute of Chartered Accountants and the Australian Society of Accountants, Australia.

Accounting Standards Committee (1975). *SSAP 10: Statements of Sources and Applications of Funds.* ASC, London, UK.

Accounting Standards Review Board (1988). *ASRB 1013: Accounting for Goodwill.* ASRB, Melbourne, Australia.

Accounting Standards Review Board (1989). *ASRB 1016: Disclosure of Information about Investments in Associated Companies.* ASRB, Melbourne, Australia.

Accounting Standards Review Board (1990a). *ASRB Release 100: Nature of Approved Accounting Standards and Statements of Accounting Concepts and the Criteria for the Evaluation of Proposed Approved Accounting Standards.* ASRB, Melbourne, Australia.

Accounting Standards Review Board (1990b). *ASRB 1024: Consolidated Accounts.* ASRB, Melbourne, Australia.

Accounting Standards Review Board and the Public Sector Accounting Standards Board (1989). *ED 49: Accounting for Identifiable Intangible Assets.* AARF, Melbourne, Australia.

Accounting Standards Review Committee (1978). *Company Accounting Standards.* Report of the Accounting Standards Review Committee, NSW Government Printer, Sydney, Australia.

American Institute of Certified Public Accountants (1953). *Accounting Research Bulletin No. 43: Restatement and Revision of Accounting Research Bulletins.* AICPA, New York.

Anonymous (1986). Interview with Mr Henry Bosch: Chairman of the National Companies and Securities Commission. *Australian Accountant,* 56(3):39–42.

Anonymous (1989). The Globalisation of Accounting Standards. *Australian Accountant,* 59(8):22–27.

Ardern, D. (2005). AASB Led IASB Research Project: Intangible Assets and Goodwill. Presentation at the Accounting Standards Interest Group, AFAANZ Forum, 2 July.

Australian Accounting Standards Board (1994a). *Policy Discussion Paper No. 1: Towards International Comparability of Financial Reporting.* AASB, Melbourne, Australia.

Australian Accounting Standards Board (1994b). *Policy Statement 4: Australia–New Zealand Harmonization Policy.* AASB, Melbourne, Australia.

Australian Accounting Standards Board (1996). *Policy Statement 6: International Harmonization Policy.* AASB, Melbourne, Australia.

Australian Accounting Standards Board (2004a). *Framework for the Preparation and Presentation of Financial Statements.* AASB, Melbourne, Australia.

Australian Accounting Standards Board (2004b). *AASB 107: Cash Flow Statements.* AASB, Melbourne, Australia.

Australian Accounting Standards Board (2004c). *AASB 119: Employee Benefits.* AASB, Melbourne, Australia.

Australian Society of Accountants and the Institute of Chartered Accountants in Australia (1976). *APS 3: Compatibility of Australian Accounting Standards and International Accounting Standards.* ASA and ICAA, Australia.

Australian Society of CPAs and the Institute of Chartered Accountants in Australia (1990). *Miscellaneous Professional Statement APS 1: Conformity with Statements of Accounting Concepts and Accounting Standard.* ASCPA and ICAA, Australia.

Australian Society of CPAs and the Institute of Chartered Accountants in Australia (1998). Joint Institute and Society Submission on CLERP 1 Legislation. Reproduced in *Major Changes and New Directions in Accounting and Auditing,* ICAA, Sydney, Australia, November.

Australian Stock Exchange (2005). *Media Release,* 30 June; http://www.asx.com.au.

Boymal, D. (1985). The Setting of Accounting Standards. Conference paper, AAANZ Conference, Sydney.

Brady, G. (2005). Overview of the Extractive Industries Research Project. Presentation at the Accounting Standards Interest Group, AFAANZ Forum, 2 July.

Brown, P. and Tarca, A. (2001). Politics, Processes and the Future of Australian Accounting Standards. *Abacus*, 37(3):267–296.

Brown, P. and Tarca, A. (2005). 2005 – It's Here, Ready or Not: A Review of the Australian Financial Reporting Framework. *Australian Accounting Review*, 15(2):68–78.

Bushnell, N. (1985a). NCSC Chief Attacks Accounting Rules. *Australian Financial Review*, 27 August, p. 1.

Bushnell, N. (1985b). NCSC and Accountants Agree on Method to Enshrine Professional Standards in Law. *Australian Financial Review*, 10 December, p. 9.

Cohen, M.S. (1974). Publication of Financial Reports. *Bulletin*, No. 16:1–38.

Collett, P., Godfrey, J., and Hrasky, S. (1998). Standard-Setting in Australia: Implications of Recent Radical Reform Proposals. *Australian Accounting Review*, 8(2):9–17.

Commonwealth of Australia (1997). *Corporate Law Economic Reform Program Paper No. 1: Accounting Standards – Building International Opportunities for Australian Business.* Australian Government Treasury, Canberra, Australia.

Commonwealth of Australia (2002). *Corporate Law Economic Reform Program Paper No. 9: Proposals for Reform – Corporate Disclosure.* Australian Government Treasury, Canberra, Australia.

Day, R. and Hartnett, N. (1999/2000). An Investigation of the Significance of Mandated Changes in Goodwill Amortisation Policy in Australia. *Pacific Accounting Review*, 11(2):193–218.

Dean, G.W. and Clarke, F.L. (2003). An Evolving Conceptual Framework. *Abacus*, 39(3):279–297.

English, L. (1988). Accounting Standards: A New Order? *Australian Accountant*, 58(11):30–37.

Financial Reporting Council (2002a). *Bulletin 2002/2*, 16 May; http://www.frc.gov.au/bulletins/2002/02.asp.

Financial Reporting Council (2002b). *Bulletin 2002/4*, 3 July; http://www.frc.gov.au/bulletins/2002/02.asp.

Godfrey, J., Hodgson, A., Holmes, S., and Kam, V. (1994). *Accounting Theory*, 1st edn. John Wiley, Australia.

Godfrey, J., Hodgson, A., and Holmes, S. (1997). *Accounting Theory*, 2nd edn. John Wiley, Australia.

Hamidi, A. (2005). Overview of the Joint Ventures Research Project. Presentation at the Accounting Standards Interest Group, AFAANZ Forum, 2 July.

Harrison, S. (1995). Providing Real Service – Not Lip Service. *New Accountant*, 10(5):6.

Henderson, S. and Peirson, G. (2004). *Issues in Financial Accounting*. Pearson Education Australia, Sydney.

Herrera, J. (1997). *Our First Twenty Years*. Speech; www.ifa.org/Library/.

Howieson, B. (1993). SAC 4: A Source of Accounting Change. *Australian Accounting Review*, 3(1):11–19.

Howieson, B. (1997). A Report on International Harmonisation: What's in it for Standard Setters? *Accounting Forum*, 21(2):189–205.

Howieson, B. (1998). International Harmonisation: He Who Pays the Piper Calls the Tune. *Australian Accounting Review*, 8(1):3–12.

Humphry, R.G. (1997). International Accounting Standards – A Quick Win for APEC Investment. Speech at the Pacific Economic Council, October (cited in Howieson, 1997).

International Accounting Standards Board (1992). *IAS 7: Cash Flow Statements*. IASB, London, UK.

International Accounting Standards Board (2002). Press Release, 7 June; http://www.iasb.org/news/2002_archive.asp.

International Accounting Standards Committee (1976a). *IAS 3: Business Combinations.* IASC, London, UK.

International Accounting Standards Committee (1976b). *IAS 4: Depreciation Accounting.* IASC, London, UK.

International Accounting Standards Committee (1979). *IAS 9: Accounting for Research and Development Activities.* IASC, London, UK.

International Accounting Standards Committee (1983). *IAS 17: Accounting for Leases.* IASC, London, UK.

International Accounting Standards Committee (1989a). *Framework for Preparation and Presentation of Financial Statements.* IASC, London, UK.

International Accounting Standards Committee (1989b). *IAS 27: Consolidated Financial Statements.* IASC, London, UK.

International Accounting Standards Committee (1993). *IAS 22: Business Combinations.* IASC, London, UK.

International Accounting Standards Committee (1999). *IAS 39: Financial Instruments: Recognition and Measurement.* IASC, London, UK.

International Accounting Standards Committee Foundation (2001). *Annual Report 2001.* IASCF, London, UK; http://www.iasb.org/about/annualreport.asp.

International Accounting Standards Committee Foundation (2004). *Annual Report 2004.* IASCF, London, UK; http://www.iasb.org/about/annualreport.asp.

Jones, S. and Wolnizer, P.W. (2003). Harmonization and the Conceptual Framework: An International Perspective. *Abacus*, 39(3):375–387.

Killen, H. (1987). Institute Seeks Merger of Accounts Regulators. *Australian Financial Review*, 15 April.

Loftus, J.A. (2003). The CF and Accounting Standards: The Persistence of Discrepancies. *Abacus*, 39(3):298–309.

Lonergan, W. (2003). The Emasculation of Accounting Standard Setting in Australia. *JASSA*, Issue 3(Spring):6–11.

Ma, R. and Miller, M.C. (1974). Forecasts and External Reporting. *Bulletin*, No. 16:39–62.

McGregor, W. (1985). New ASRB Approved Accounting Standards – Legal Backing for the Profession's Standards! *Chartered Accountant in Australia*, 55(11):67–69.

McGregor, W. (1989). New Accounting Standard Setting Arrangement. *Australian Accountant*, 59(8):87–89.

Miller, M.C. (1986). *Report on AAS 12 – Statement of Sources and Application of Funds*, 10 April. Report prepared for the Accounting Standards Review Board.

Miller, M.C. (1991). Shifts in the Regulatory Framework for Corporate Financial Reporting. *Australian Accounting Review*, 1(2):30–39.

Miller, M.C. (1995a). Goodwill Discontent: The Meshing of Australian and International Accounting Policy. *Australian Accounting Review*, 5(1):3–16.

Miller, M.C. (1995b). The Credibility of Australian Financial Reporting: Are the Co-Regulation Arrangements Working. *Australian Accounting Review*, 5(2):3–16.

Miller, M.C. and Loftus, J.A. (1993). SAC 4 and the Challenge to the Mandatory Status of Concepts Statements. *Australian Accounting Review*, 3(1):2–11.

Miller, M.C. and Scott, M.R. (1980). *Financial Reporting by Segments.* Discussion Paper 4, Australian Accounting Research Foundation, Melbourne, Australia.

Pacific Dunlop Ltd (1994). *When Goodwill Creates Ill-Will – The Case for Reviewing Accounting Standard AASB 1013.* Issues Paper, Pacific Dunlop, Australia.

Parker, R. (1986). Accounting in Australia. *Australian Accountant*, 56(10):85–86.

Paton, G. (1993). From the President. *Australian Accountant*, 63(9):5.

Peirson, G. (1990). *Reform of the Institutional Arrangements for Accounting Standard Setting in Australia.* AARF, Melbourne, Australia.

Philp, R. (1993). Comment: Out of Step. *Australian Accounting Review*, 3(1):19–20.

Potter, B. (1987). Bosch Hosts a Gathering of Regulators. *Australian Financial Review*, 7 December, p. 37.

Prosser, V. (1983). Accounting Standards Review Board. *Chartered Accountant in Australia*, 53(7):18–19.

Public Sector Accounting Standards Board and Accounting Standards Review Board (1990a). *SAC 1: Definition of the Reporting Entity.* AARF, on behalf of the ASCPA and the ICAA, and ASRB, Melbourne, Australia.

Public Sector Accounting Standards Board and Accounting Standards Review Board (1990b). *SAC 3: Qualitative Characteristics of Financial Information.* AARF, on behalf of the ASCPA and the ICAA, and ASRB, Melbourne, Australia.

Public Sector Accounting Standards Board and Accounting Standards Review Board (1995). *SAC 4: Definition and Recognition of the Elements of Financial Statements.* AARF, on behalf of the ASCPA and the ICAA, and ASRB, Melbourne, Australia.

Puxty, A.G., Willmott, H.C., Cooper, D.J., and Lowe, T. (1987). Modes of Regulation in Advanced Capitalism: Locating Accountancy in Four Countries. *Accounting, Organizations and Society*, 12(3):273–291.

Rahman, S. (1992). *The Australian Accounting Standards Review Board: The Establishment of its Participative Review Process.* Garland Publishing, New York.

Spencer, K. (1998). The View from the AASB: Take it Easy, Get it Right. *Australian Accountant*, 68(2):20–22.

Streeck, W. and Schmitter, P.C. (eds) (1985). Community, Market, State – and Associations? In: *Private Interest Government and Public Policy.* Sage, London, UK.

Tiffen, R. and Gittins, R. (2004). *How Australia Compares.* Cambridge University Press, Melbourne, Australia.

Urgent Issues Group (1995). *Abstract 5: Methods of Amortization of Goodwill.* AARF, Melbourne, Australia.

Walker, R.G. (1987). Australia's ASRB. A Case Study of Political Activity and Regulatory 'Capture'. *Accounting and Business Research*, 17(67):269–286.

Walker, R.G. (1993). A Feeling of Déjà Vu: Controversies in Accounting and Auditing Regulation in Australia. *Critical Perspectives on Accounting*, 4(1):97–109.

Winsen, J. (1983). Regulation of Financial Reporting. *Australian Business Law Review*, 8(4):232–255.

World Bank (2004). *World Development Indicators Database.*

World Bank (2005). *World Development Indicators Database.*

Zeff, S.A. (1973). *Forging Accounting Principles in Australia.* Society Bulletin, Australian Society of Accountants, Melbourne, Australia.

11

Determinants of Bias in Management Earnings Forecasts: Empirical Evidence from Japan

Koji Ota

11.1 Introduction

A major disclosure difference between Japan and other countries is that management of almost all listed firms in Japan provides forecasts of next period's earnings. This practice was initiated by the stock exchanges in 1974, during which a letter was sent to listed firms requesting them to disclose forecasts of key accounting information. Although the forecasts are technically voluntary, most Japanese firms comply with the request and provide them. As a consequence, management forecasts of the upcoming period's sales, ordinary income, net income (earnings), earnings per share, and dividends per share are announced simultaneously with the most recently completed period's actual accounting figures in annual press releases[1]. This unique setting in Japan makes it possible to conduct a large-scale study on management forecasts over a long period of time.

While management forecasts are much less common in the USA, a number of recent studies have investigated and found several factors that are associated with systematic bias in management earnings forecasts (MEFs). For example, Frost (1997) and Koch (2002) found optimistic bias in MEFs issued by financially distressed firms. Choi and Ziebart (2000) and Irani (2000) documented that firm size, firm performance, abnormal earnings growth, etc. are all related to the bias in MEFs. In contrast to the USA, there has been little research in Japan that examines the properties of management forecasts, despite the fact that their provision is a major feature of the Japanese disclosure system. This lack of research on Japanese management forecasts is partly because the dataset is not readily available in electronic form and needs to be collected manually for each forecast.

The first objective of this chapter is to investigate the determinants of bias in MEFs. This chapter investigates the effects of 10 factors on bias in MEFs using a sample of 28,000 forecasts announced by Japanese firms over the period 1979–1999. They are macroeconomic influence, industry, firm size, exchange/OTC, external financing, financial distress, prior management forecast errors, growth, losses, and management forecasts of dividends. The results of both univariate and multivariate analyses show that these factors are all associated with forecast errors. The major findings of these analyses are: (1) yearly mean management earnings forecast errors are highly correlated with annual GDP growth rates ($r = 0.863$); (2) firms in the price-regulated industries issue pessimistic MEFs; (3) MEFs of small firms and OTC firms are optimistic; (4) MEFs of equity-issuing firms are pessimistic; (5) financially distressed firms and loss-making firms announce optimistic MEFs; (6) firms whose prior MEFs were pessimistic (optimistic) tend to remain pessimistic (optimistic) in their current forecasts; and (7) MEFs that are accompanied by an increase in forecast dividends are pessimistic.

The second objective of this chapter is to examine the extent to which the aforementioned systematic bias in MEFs is reflected in share prices. Because of the information asymmetry that exists between managers and outsiders about future performance of firms, it is both rational and practical for investors to use MEFs as a basis for their own forecasts. If investors fixate on MEFs, share prices of firms that issue optimistic earnings forecasts will be overvalued while those that issue pessimistic earnings forecasts will be undervalued. Then, a trading strategy taking a long position in the stock of firms reporting relatively pessimistic MEFs and a short position in the stock of firms reporting relatively optimistic MEFs will generate positive abnormal stock returns. To test the hypothesis, predicted management forecast errors are estimated for each firm using a fixed effects model with panel datasets. Only *ex ante* factors are used as independent variables to make the strategy actually implementable. The hedge portfolio strategy based on the predicted management forecast errors produces positive abnormal returns in 14 of the 15 years examined, with a 15-year average return of 4.5%, suggesting the possibility that information about systematic errors in MEFs may not be fully incorporated into share prices.

The provision of next period's earnings forecasts by management is a major feature of the Japanese disclosure system. Despite this fact, little research has been conducted on the nature of the information, partly due to difficulties in obtaining the data. This study is probably the first to investigate the properties of Japanese MEFs. Its findings suggest the existence of systematic bias in Japanese management forecasts. Furthermore, investors appear to fixate on MEFs and do not fully incorporate systematic forecast errors into share prices.

The remainder of the chapter is organized as follows. The next section describes the background on Japanese management forecasts. Section 11.3 describes the data and Section 11.4 investigates the determinants of bias in MEFs. The market awareness of systematic bias in MEF is examined in Section 11.5 and Section 11.6 concludes the chapter.

11.2 Background on Japanese management forecasts

The timing and extent of corporate disclosure in Japan is affected by legal and stock exchange policies. The Securities and Exchange Law, which covers companies listed on the security exchanges, requires firms to file annual securities reports (*Yuka Shoken Hokokusho*) with the Ministry of Finance within three months of the fiscal year end. The Ministry of Finance Ordinance prescribes the form and content of the annual securities report, and the report provides detailed information on the business activities and financial condition of an enterprise in a fiscal year. Although the scope and amount of information being disclosed in the annual securities report is extensive and comprehensive, there is a three-month time lag between the disclosure of the report and the end of the firm's fiscal year.

In order to supplement the lack of timeliness in statutory disclosure under the Securities and Exchange Law, Japanese stock exchanges, which are self-regulatory organizations, request that listed firms publish condensed financial statements (*Kessan Tanshin*) immediately upon board of director approval of a draft of financial statements[2]. As a result, earnings figures are made public well before the three-month legal deadline. For the vast majority of Japanese companies, earnings announcements take place 25–40 trading days after the fiscal year end. This practice of timely disclosure was initiated by the stock exchanges in 1974, at which time a letter was sent to listed firms requesting them to disclose key accounting information. Management earnings forecasts for the upcoming period are provided in the condensed financial statements, together with current financial results (sales, ordinary income, net income, earnings per share, and dividends per share)[3]. Thus, technically speaking, the provision of MEFs is voluntary without any legal backing. In fact, some financial institutions, especially securities firms, do not provide management forecasts, citing the difficulty of predicting the future business environment. However, on the whole, compliance has been so high that almost all firms provide earnings forecasts[4]. This is partly due to continuous efforts made by stock exchanges to comply with the request and partly due to the guidelines prescribed by the Ministry of Finance Ordinance regarding revisions of MEFs. Under the guidelines, firms are required to announce revised forecasts immediately when a significant change in previously published forecasts arises (e.g. ±10% of sales, ±30% of ordinary income, ±30% of net income). As far as firms follow the guidelines, they are not to be held responsible for failing to meet their initial forecasts. This is in contrast with the safe harbor for forward-looking statements in the USA (the Private Securities Litigation Reform Act of 1995). The Reform Act was intended to encourage companies to make good-faith projections without fear of a securities lawsuit, but has been said to be ineffective due to ambiguity in interpretation (Rosen, 1998). In addition, shareholder litigations against companies and management are traditionally less common in Japan. These factors seem to have contributed to create the favorable environment in which most firms issue earnings forecasts in Japan.

11.3 Data

11.3.1 Sample selection

The sample is selected from the 1979 to 1999 time period using the following criteria:

1. The firms are listed on one of the eight stock exchanges in Japan or traded on the over-the-counter (OTC) market.
2. The accounting period ends in March (78% of listed firms).
3. Banks, securities firms, and insurance firms are excluded (5% of listed firms).

There are eight stock exchanges in Japan, namely Tokyo, Osaka, Nagoya, Sapporo, Niigata, Kyoto, Hiroshima, and Fukuoka. The Tokyo Stock Exchange (TSE) is by far the largest among them. As of June 1999, 2433 firms were listed on the stock exchanges in Japan, of which 1854 firms were listed on the TSE. In terms of volume and value, the TSE accounts for 80–90% of the nation's trading. The OTC market (currently called the JASDAQ market after the NASDAQ market in the USA) consists of small and newly listed firms. As of June 1999, the number of issues listed on the OTC market stood at 853. However, it accounts for merely 2–4% of the trading volume and value in Japan.

Annual accounting data and stock price data were extracted from *Nikkei-Zaimu Data* and *Kabuka CD-ROM 2000*. MEFs were manually collected from the *Nihon Keizai Shinbun* (the leading business newspaper in Japan). Other necessary data, such as stock splits, capital reduction, and changes in par values, were collected from *Kaisha Shikihou CD-ROM*. The selection process yielded 29,177 firm-year observations.

11.3.2 Management forecast error

The MEF error is defined as the difference between actual earnings and management forecast of earnings scaled by the share price at the beginning of the fiscal year. It is calculated for each firm-year observation as:

$$\mathrm{MFERR}_{i,t} = \frac{E_{i,j} - \mathrm{MF}_{i,j}}{P_{i,j}},$$

where:

$\mathrm{MFERR}_{i,t}$ = management forecast error for firm i in period t

$E_{i,t}$ = actual earnings per share for firm i in period t
$MF_{i,t}$ = management forecast of earnings per share for firm i in period t, which is usually announced within 10 weeks into the accounting period t
$P_{i,t}$ = share price of firm i at the beginning of period t.
(The subscript i, which denotes a sample firm, will be omitted in the following sections for clarity.)

A positive MFERR implies a pessimistic forecast, while a negative MFERR indicates an optimistic forecast. To ensure that the results are not sensitive to extreme values, observations in the top and bottom 1% of MFERR are removed[5]. This results in a final sample of 28,593 firm-year observations[6].

11.4 Determinants of bias in management earnings forecasts

11.4.1 Univariate analysis

This section tries to identify factors that are associated with bias in management forecasts. Since there are almost no prior studies investigating systematic bias in Japanese management forecasts, many factors examined in this section are based on the US literature on management forecasts. Although the two disclosure systems are quite different, one is effectively mandatory and the other is voluntary, I believe that the arguments used in the US research can help make predictions of bias in Japanese management forecasts.

11.4.1.1 Macroeconomic influence

Previous research in the USA on bias in management forecasts has produced varying results. Studies using management forecast data released in the 1960s and early 1970s found evidence of optimism in management forecasts (McDonald, 1973; Basi et al., 1976; Patell, 1976; Penman, 1980; Ajinkaya and Gift, 1984; Waymire, 1984). However, studies using management forecast data from the late 1970s and early 1980s found no evidence of optimism in management forecasts (McNichols, 1989; Frankel et al., 1995). Bamber and Cheon (1998) collected MEFs during the 1981–1991 period and found that management forecasts were optimistic. Irani (2000) also reported optimism in MEFs during the 1990–1995 period. Thus, these results appear to be driven by the time periods that were examined.

Figure 11.1 plots the yearly mean MFERR from 1979 to 1999. Of the 21 years examined, 17 years have negative mean MFERRs and four years have positive mean MFERRs. They are all significantly different from zero at the 5% level or higher except for two years, namely 1979 and 1990. One noticeable finding is that the mean MFERR is significantly positive for the 1987–1989 period. This period coincides with the alleged economic bubble period of the late 1980s in Japan. Figure 11.1 also provides time-series plots of the annual real GDP growth rate for the 1979–1999 period. The yearly mean MFERR and the real GDP growth rate are observed to peak and bottom out at the same period, and the correlation coefficient between the two variables is 0.863 and is statistically significant at the 1% level[7].

Thus, the yearly mean MFERR appears to be largely influenced by a macroeconomic factor. This indicates that managers are not able to predict accurately the macroeconomic trend for the coming period and issue earnings forecasts based on the previous year's economic situation. Therefore, MEFs tend to be pessimistic when the economy is booming and optimistic when the economy is declining[8].

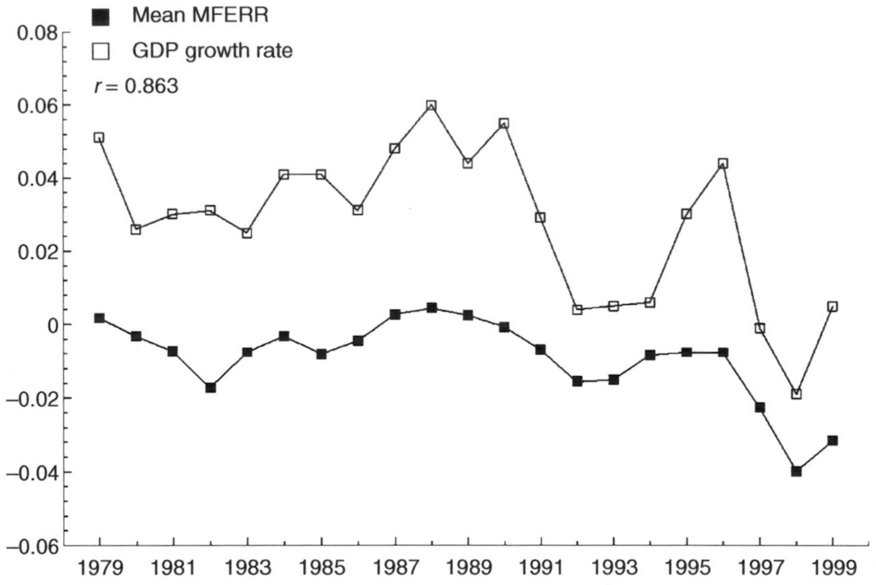

Figure 11.1 Yearly mean management forecast error and real GDP growth rate, 1979–1999. This figure depicts the yearly mean MFERR and the real GDP growth rate for the 1979–1999 period. $MFERR_t = (E_t - MF_t)/P_t$, where E_t is actual earnings per share for period t, MF_t is management forecast of earnings per share for period t, and P_t is share price at the beginning of period t. The total number of observations is 28,593

11.4.1.2 Industry

The cross-industry variation in MFERR is examined with particular emphasis on price-regulated industries. The positive accounting theory suggests that managers in price-regulated industries have incentives to decrease reported earnings to avoid appearing overly profitable (Watts and Zimmerman, 1986). In a similar argument, they may not want to look profitable even at the forecast stage and may announce relatively pessimistic earnings forecasts.

Figure 11.2 depicts cross-industry variation in the mean MFERR. Of the 29 industries examined, 27 industries have negative mean MFERRs and two industries, *Electricity and Gas* and *Communication*, have positive mean MFERRs. They are all significantly different from zero at the 5% level or higher. Both the *Electricity and Gas* and *Communication* industries are in the price-regulated category. Thus, firms in price-regulated industries appear to publish pessimistic earnings forecasts.

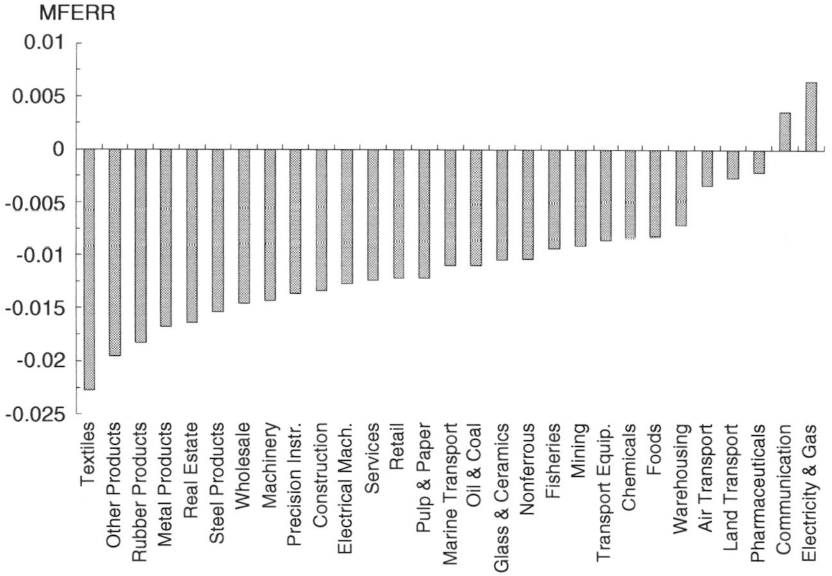

Figure 11.2 Cross-industry variation in mean management forecast error. This figure depicts cross-industry variation in mean MFERR. Sample firms are classified into 29 industries according to Toyokeizai industry classification. $MFERR_t = (E_t - MF_t)/P_t$, where E_t is actual earnings per share for period t, MF_t is management forecast of earnings per share for period t, and P_t is share price at the beginning of period t. The total number of observations is 28,593

11.4.1.3 Size and exchange/OTC effects

Previous studies on analysts' forecasts have shown that firm size is related to bias in analysts' earnings forecasts (Brown, 1997; Das et al., 1998; Matsumoto, 2002). They found less optimism in analysts' earnings forecasts for large firms. Choi and Ziebart (2000) also reported a similar size effect for MEFs without providing a theoretical explanation for their findings.

I hypothesize that managers of large firms may regard published earnings forecasts as commitments to interested parties. Their projections therefore tend to be conservative in order to avoid missing the forecasts. On the other hand, managers of small firms may consider earnings forecasts as their targets for the upcoming period. As a result, their projections tend to be optimistic. This may be particularly true for OTC firms that are not only small but also young.

To investigate the size effect, the following regression equation is estimated:

$$\text{MFERR}_t = \alpha_0 + \alpha_1\text{LNMVE}_t + \varepsilon_t,$$

where:
LNMVE_t = log of the inflation-adjusted market value of equity three months after the beginning of period *t*.

Table 11.1(A) reports the results of the regression equation. It shows that the estimated coefficient of LNMVE is 0.0055 and is statistically significant, which suggests that MEFs of large firms are more pessimistic than those of small firms.

Next, the exchange/OTC effect is examined by testing the difference in the mean (median) MFERR between exchange firms and OTC firms. Table 11.1(B) presents the results. The mean (median) MFERRs for exchange firms and OTC firms are −0.0110 (−0.0011) and −0.0189 (−0.0045) respectively. The difference in the two means (medians) is statistically significant at the 1% level. Thus, MEFs of OTC firms appear to be more optimistic than those of exchange firms.

Lastly, the size effect, the exchange/OTC effect, and the interactive effect are examined simultaneously using the following regression equation:

$$\text{MFERR}_t = \alpha_0 + \alpha_1\text{LNMVE}_t + \alpha_2\text{OTC}_t + \alpha_3\text{OTC*LNMVE}_t + \varepsilon_t,$$

where:

$$\mathrm{OTC}_t = \begin{cases} 1 & \text{if a firm is an OTC firm in period } t \\ 0 & \text{otherwise} \end{cases}, \quad \text{and}$$

$$\mathrm{OTC{*}LNMVE}_t = \begin{cases} \mathrm{LNMVE}_t & \text{if a firm is an OTC firm in period } t \\ 0 & \text{otherwise} \end{cases},$$

The estimation results reported in Table 11.1(C) show that all estimated coefficients are statistically significant. This indicates that small OTC firms announce the most optimistic management forecasts.

11.4.1.4 External financing

Frankel et al. (1995) documented a positive association between firms' tendencies to access capital markets and to disclose earnings forecasts. However, they did not find statistically significant bias in MEFs of financing firms and argued that potential legal liability and reputation costs deter management of financing firms from issuing optimistic forecasts. Similarly, Irani (2000) hypothesized that managers may exhibit optimism in their forecasts if their firms are planning to access capital markets in the near future. However, he also did not find optimism in MEFs of financing firms.

One potential limitation of both studies with regard to research design is that they treated debt financing and equity financing equally. Richardson et al. (2004) argued that analysts obtain much of their information about earnings prospects directly from firm management, and that firms issuing new equity guide analysts toward beatable forecasts to avoid earnings disappointments. Thus, while equity-financing firms are sensitive to investors' perceptions of their profitability, debt-financing firms may not be as sensitive because investors are probably more concerned about their default risk.

Based on the foregoing reasoning, I treat debt financing and equity financing separately and examine bias in MEFs announced by debt-financing firms and equity-financing firms.

Table 11.2(A) shows that the mean (median) MFERR of debt-financing firms is higher than that of non-debt-financing firms, −0.0061 (−0.0003) vs −0.0135 (−0.0017), and the difference in the two means (medians) is statistically significant. Similar results are obtained between equity-financing firms and non-equity-financing firms, 0.0028 (0.0020) vs −0.0126 (−0.0015), though the difference in the two means (medians) is larger. These results indicate relative pessimism in MEFs for both debt- and equity-financing firms. However, debt-financing firms tend to be large firms, such as utilities and public transport, and previous results

Table 11.1 Size and exchange/OTC effects

	α_0	α_1	Adj. R^2	N
Regression model	$MFERR_t = \alpha_0 + \alpha_1 LNMVE_t + \varepsilon_t$			
Coefficient	−0.0692	0.0055	0.036	28,593
(t-statistic)	(−39.33)**	(32.85)**		

Panel A: Size effect.

	N	Mean MFERR	Median MFERR	Difference in means[a]	Difference in medians[b]
Exchange firms	24,738	−0.0110	−0.0011	0.0079	0.0034
OTC firms	3855	−0.0189	−0.0045	(8.73)**	(12.42)**

Panel B: Exchange/OTC effect.

	α_0	α_1	α_2	α_3	Adj. R^2	N
Regression model	$MFERR_t = \alpha_0 + \alpha_1 LNMVE_t + \alpha_2 OTC_t + \alpha_3 OTC*LNMVE_t + \varepsilon_t$					
Coefficient	−0.0643	0.0051	−0.0540	0.0058	0.039	28,593
(t-statistic)	(−32.95)**	(27.61)**	(−8.65)**	(8.66)**		

Panel C: Size and exchange/OTC effects.

The definitions of the variables are: $MFERR_t = (E_t - MF_t)/P_t$, $LNMVE_t = \ln(MVE_t/\text{Consumer Price Index})$,

$$OTC_t = \begin{cases} 1 & \text{if a firm is an OTC firm in period } t \\ 0 & \text{otherwise} \end{cases},$$

$$OTC*LNMVE_t = \begin{cases} LNMVE_t & \text{if a firm is an OTC firm in period } t \\ 0 & \text{otherwise} \end{cases},$$

where E_t is actual earnings per share for period t, MF_t is management forecast of earnings per share for period t, P_t is share price at the beginning of period t, and MVE_t is the market value of equity three months after the beginning of period t.

[a] The unequal variances t-test is used and its t-statistic is reported in parentheses in this column.

[b] The Wilcoxon rank-sum test is used and its z-statistic is reported in parentheses in this column.

* Significant at the 0.05 level (two-tailed). ** Significant at the 0.01 level (two-tailed).

Table 11.2 External financing

	N	Mean MFERR	Median MFERR	Difference in means[a]	Difference in medians[b]
Debt-financing firms	5754	−0.0061	−0.0003	0.0074	0.0014
Non-debt-financing firms	22,839	−0.0135	−0.0017	(14.37)**	(10.48)**
Equity-financing firms	1072	0.0028	0.0020	0.0154	0.0035
Non-equity-financing firms	27,521	−0.0126	−0.0015	(29.21)**	(17.02)**

Panel A: External financing.

	Firm size (1P is the smallest and 5P is the largest quintile)					
	1P	2P	3P	4P	5P	Total
Number of debt-financing firms	365	602	912	1395	2480	5754
Number of equity-financing firms	118	278	266	239	171	1072

Panel B: Impact of size on external financing. Quintile portfolios are constructed according to $LNMVE_t$ with the first quintile portfolio (1P) comprising the smallest firms and the fifth quintile portfolio (5P) comprising the largest firms.

	α_0	α_1	α_2	α_3	Adj. R^2	N
Regression model	$MFERR_t = \alpha_0 + \alpha_1 LNMVE_t + \alpha_2 BONDS_t + \alpha_3 OFFER_t + \varepsilon_t$					
Coefficient	−0.0693	0.0055	0.0004	0.0151	0.040	28,593
(t-statistic)	(−37.98)**	(30.63)**	(0.52)	(11.09)**		

Panel C: External financing and size effects.

The definitions of the variables are: $MFERR_t = (E_t - MF_t)/P_t$, $LNMVE_t = \ln(MVE_t/\text{Consumer Price Index})$,

$$BONDS_t = \begin{cases} 1 & \text{if a firm issued either straight bonds or convertible bonds in period } t \\ 0 & \text{otherwise} \end{cases},$$

$$OFFER_t = \begin{cases} 1 & \text{if a firm made a seasoned public offering in period } t \\ 0 & \text{otherwise} \end{cases},$$

where E_t is actual earnings per share for period t, MF_t is management forecast of earnings per share for period t, P_t is share price at the beginning of period t, and MVE_t is the market value of equity three months after the beginning of period t.

[a] The unequal variances t-test is used and its t-statistic is reported in parentheses in this column.

[b] The Wilcoxon rank-sum test is used and its z-statistic is reported in parentheses in this column.

** Significant at the 0.01 level (two-tailed).

suggest that large firms tend to announce pessimistic management forecasts. To investigate the influence of size effect, all firm-year observations are classified into quintile portfolios according to LNMVE and the number of debt- and equity-financing firms is tallied for each portfolio. Table 11.2(B) reveals that the number of debt-financing firms increases rapidly as the quintile portfolio based on LNMVE becomes larger. Such a trend is not observed for equity-financing firms.

To control for the impact of firm size on MFERR, the following regression equation is estimated:

$$\text{MFERR}_t = \alpha_0 + \alpha_1\text{LNMVE}_t + \alpha_2\text{BONDS}_t + \alpha_3\text{OFFER}_t + \varepsilon_t,$$

where:

$$\text{BONDS}_t = \begin{cases} 1 & \text{if a firm issued either straight or convertible bonds in period } t \\ 0 & \text{otherwise} \end{cases},$$

and

$$\text{OFFER}_t = \begin{cases} 1 & \text{if a firm made a seasoned public offering in period } t \\ 0 & \text{otherwise} \end{cases}$$

The estimation results reported in Table 11.2(C) indicate that MEFs of equity-financing firms are pessimistic even after controlling for the size effect, while MEFs of debt-financing firms are not. These findings suggest the different impacts of different types of financing on bias in management forecasts.

11.4.1.5 Financial distress

Prior research has documented optimism in financial disclosures released by managers of financially distressed firms. Using a sample of 81 UK firms that received modified audit reports, Frost (1997) found that managers of distressed firms make disclosures about expected future performance that are overly optimistic relative to actual financial outcomes. Koch (2002) found that MEFs issued by distressed firms exhibit greater optimism and are viewed as less credible by analysts than similar forecasts made by nondistressed firms. While both Frost (1997) and Koch (2002) conducted univariate analyses, Irani (2000) performed a multivariate analysis and found a positive linear correlation between optimism in MEFs and the degree of financial distress.

In Koch (2002) and Irani (2000, 2001), the probability of bankruptcy is used as a proxy for financial distress, which is derived from the coefficients provided by Ohlson (1980). However, these coefficients cannot be applied to Japanese firms without modification to estimate the intensity of financial distress.

Moreover, Penman (2001) suggested that the Ohlson (1980) estimates were made quite a while ago and the coefficients should be re-estimated from more recent data. Therefore, I employ the principal components method of factor analysis to condense the variables used in the Ohlson (1980) bankruptcy probability model. The factor scores from the first component are used as a proxy for financial distress.

The following nine variables are included in the Ohlson (1980) bankruptcy probability model:

$$\text{SIZE} = \ln, \left(\frac{\text{Total Assets}}{\text{GNP Price-level Index}}\right), \ \text{TLTA} = \left(\frac{\text{Total Liabilities}}{\text{Total Assets}}\right),$$

$$\text{WCTA} = \left(\frac{\text{Working Capital}}{\text{Total Assets}}\right), \ \text{CLCA} = \left(\frac{\text{Current Liabilities}}{\text{Current Assets}}\right),$$

$$\text{NITA} = \left(\frac{\text{Earnings}}{\text{Total Assets}}\right), \ \text{FUTL} = \left(\frac{\text{Operating Cash Flows}}{\text{Total Liabilities}}\right),$$

$$\text{INTWO} = \begin{cases} 1 & \text{if earnings were negative for the last two periods} \\ 0 & \text{otherwise} \end{cases},$$

$$\text{OENEG} = \begin{cases} 1 & \text{if total liabilities exceed total assets} \\ 0 & \text{otherwise} \end{cases},$$

$$\text{and CHIN} = \frac{\text{E}_t - \text{E}_{t-1}}{|\text{E}_t| + |\text{E}_{t-1}|}.$$

Of the nine variables, SIZE is omitted from the analysis because it is already represented by LNMVE. The results of factor analysis are shown in Table 11.3(A). The expected signs are from the Ohlson (1980) bankruptcy probability model. The signs of factor loadings and score coefficients (factor weights) of the first principal component are all consistent with the expected signs from the Ohlson (1980) model, suggesting that the first principal component represents the intensity of financial distress.

The factor scores from the first principal component are defined as a new variable, DIST, and the following regression equation is estimated:

$$\text{MFERR}_t = \alpha_0 + \alpha_1 \text{DIST}_t + \varepsilon_t,$$

where:

DIST_t = the factor scores from the principal component analysis on the variables used in the Ohlson (1980) bankruptcy probability model.

Table 11.3 Financial distress

Variables	Expected sign	Factor loading	Score coefficient
TLTA	+	0.833	0.296
WCTA	–	−0.878	−0.312
CLCA	+	0.844	0.299
NITA	–	−0.531	−0.188
FUTL	–	−0.304	−0.108
INTWO	+	0.350	0.124
OENEG	+	0.371	0.132
CHIN	–	−0.087	−0.031
Eigenvalue			
(% of variance explained)	2.818		
	(35.2%)		
Correlation between factor score and MFERR	−0.120**		

Panel A: Principal component analysis. The variables used to perform the principal component analysis are from the Ohlson (1980) bankruptcy probability model. The definitions of the variables are:

$$\text{TLTA} = \left(\frac{\text{Total Liabilities}}{\text{Total Assets}}\right), \text{WCTA} = \left(\frac{\text{Working Capital}}{\text{Total Assets}}\right), \text{CLCA} = \left(\frac{\text{Current Liabilities}}{\text{Current Assets}}\right),$$

$$\text{NITA} = \left(\frac{\text{Earnings}}{\text{Total Assets}}\right), \text{FUTL} = \left(\frac{\text{Operating Cash Flows}}{\text{Total Liabilities}}\right),$$

$$\text{INTWO} = \begin{cases} 1 & \text{if earnings were negative for the last two years} \\ 0 & \text{otherwise} \end{cases},$$

$$\text{OENEG} = \begin{cases} 1 & \text{if total liabilities exceed total assets} \\ 0 & \text{otherwise} \end{cases}, \text{ and CHIN} = \frac{E_t - E_{t-1}}{|E_t| + |E_{t-1}|}$$

	α_0	α_1	Adj. R^2	N
Regression model	$MFERR_t = \alpha_0 + \alpha_1 DIST_t + \varepsilon_t$			
Coefficient	−0.0196	−0.0142	0.014	26,176
(t-statistic)	(−26.98)**	(−19.48)**		

Panel B: Effect of financial distress. The definitions of the variables are: $MFERR_t = (E_t - MF_t)/P_t$ and $DIST_t$ = the factor scores from the principal component analysis on the variables used in the Ohlson (1980) bankruptcy probability model, where E_t is actual earnings per share for period t, MF_t is management forecast of earnings per share for period t, and P_t is share price at the beginning of period t.

** Significant at the 0.01 level (two-tailed).

The results reported in Table 11.3(B) show that the coefficient on DIST is significantly negative, −0.0142. This indicates that firms in financial distress measured by DIST tend to issue optimistic earnings forecasts.

11.4.1.6 Persistence of prior management forecast errors

Several studies have presented evidence of the persistence of management forecast errors. Williams (1996) found that the accuracy of a prior management earnings forecast serves as an indicator to analysts of the believability of a current management forecast. Hirst et al. (1999) conducted an experimental study and found that prior forecast accuracy by management affects investors' earnings predictions when current management forecasts are given to them. Although these results do not provide direct evidence of the persistence of management forecast errors, they suggest that analysts and investors believe in this persistence.

To examine the persistence of management forecast errors, the following regression equation is estimated:

$$\text{MFERR}_t = \alpha_0 + \alpha_1\text{MFERR}_{t-1} + \alpha_2\text{MFERR}_{t-2} + \alpha_3\text{MFERR}_{t-3} + \varepsilon_t.$$

The results reported in Table 11.4(A) show that the estimated coefficients on lagged management forecast errors are all significantly positive and become smaller as the lags get longer, 0.3480, 0.1030 and 0.0368 respectively. This indicates that firms whose previous forecasts were optimistic (pessimistic) tend to remain optimistic (pessimistic) in their current forecasts.

11.4.1.7 Growth

Previous research suggests that high-growth firms have more incentives to announce pessimistic forecasts. Matsumoto (2002) and Richardson et al. (1999, 2004) investigated the propensity for firms to avoid negative earnings surprises and found that high-growth firms are more likely to guide analysts' forecasts downward to meet their expectations at the earnings announcement. Choi and Ziebart (2000) also found some weak evidence that high-growth firms tend to release pessimistic management forecasts. One possible explanation for these findings is that the stock market reaction to negative earnings surprises is particularly pronounced for high-growth firms (Skinner and Sloan, 2002). These results suggest that high-growth firms are inclined to issue more pessimistic earnings forecasts in order to avoid earnings disappointments.

Table 11.4 Persistence of prior management forecast errors, growth, and losses

	α_0	α_1	α_2	α_3	Adj. R^2	N
Regression model $MFERR_t = \alpha_0 + \alpha_1 MFERR_{t-1} + \alpha_2 MFERR_{t-2} + \alpha_3 MFERR_{t-3} + \varepsilon_t$						
Coefficient	−0.0087	0.3480	0.1030	0.0368	0.114	21,761
(t-statistic)	(−27.77)**	(43.98)**	(10.68)**	(3.76)**		

Panel A: Persistence of previous MFERRs.

	α_0	α_1	Adj. R^2	N
Regression model	$MFERR_t = \alpha_0 + \alpha_1 GROWTH_t + \varepsilon_t$			
Coefficient	−0.0720	0.0569	0.025	25,652
(t-statistic)	(−31.37)**	(25.79)**		

Panel B: Growth.

	N	Mean MFERR	Median MFERR	Difference in means[a]	Difference in medians[b]
Negative earnings firms	2942	−0.0482	−0.0164	−0.0401	−0.0153
Positive and zero earnings firms	25,013	−0.0081	−0.0011	(−25.13)**	(−26.20)**

Panel C: Losses.

The definitions of the variables are: $MFERR_t = (E_t - MF_t)/P_t$ and $GROWTH_t = Sales_{t-1}/Sales_{t-2}$, where E_t is actual earnings per share for period t, MF_t is management forecast of earnings per share for period t, and P_t is share price at the beginning of period t.

[a] The unequal variances t-test is used and its t-statistic is reported in parentheses in this column.

[b] The Wilcoxon rank-sum test is used and its z-statistic is reported in parentheses in this column.

** Significant at the 0.01 level (two-tailed).

To examine whether MEFs announced by high-growth firms are more pessimistic, the following regression equation is estimated using annual sales growth rates as an indicator of growth:

$$MFERR_t = \alpha_0 + \alpha_1 GROWTH_t + \varepsilon_t,$$

where:

$GROWTH_t = Sales_{t-1}/Sales_{t-2}$.

The results reported in Table 11.4(B) show that the coefficient on GROWTH is significantly positive, 0.0569. Thus, MEFs of high-growth firms appear to be more pessimistic.

11.4.1.8 Losses

Evidence from the analyst forecast literature indicates that analysts' forecasts are more optimistic for loss firms than for profit firms (Richardson et al., 1999, 2004; Brown, 2001). Choi and Ziebart (2000) also found that firms with losses tend to announce optimistic earnings forecasts for the next year. These results suggest that managers reporting losses for the current period are inclined to issue more optimistic earnings forecasts than those reporting profits. To investigate whether earnings forecasts issued by firms with losses are more optimistic than by those with profits, the mean (median) forecast error for loss firms is compared with that for profit firms.

Table 11.4(C) shows that the mean (median) MFERR is −0.0482 (−0.0164) for loss firms and −0.0081 (−0.0011) for profit firms. The difference in the two means (medians) is statistically significant. Thus, management forecasts of firms with losses appear to be more optimistic than those with profits.

11.4.1.9 Signaling effect of management dividend forecast

Modern corporate finance theory initiated by Modigliani and Miller proposes that, in the presence of perfect capital markets, the dividend policy of a firm *per se* is irrelevant to its valuation (the dividend irrelevance hypothesis). On the other hand, the 'information content of dividends' hypothesis asserts that managers use dividends to signal changes in their expectations about future prospects of the firm (Aharony and Swary, 1980; Healy and Palepu, 1988; Hand and Landsman, 2005). A major difficulty in assessing the impact of dividends on share prices lies in disentangling these two effects, the dividend irrelevance effect and the dividend signaling effect. Conroy et al. (2000) exploited the unique setting in Japan, where managers simultaneously announce the current year's dividends and earnings as well as forecasts of next year's dividends and earnings, to provide a strong test for the two effects. They found that unexpected changes in forecasts of next year's dividends are valued by the Japanese market (the dividend signaling effect), while unexpected changes in current dividends are not (the dividend irrelevance effect). The results hold after controlling for the effects of current and future earnings information.

Based on these studies, I hypothesize that an increase (decrease) in management forecast of next year's dividends from current dividends signals the strong (weak) future performance of the firm.

Table 11.5(A) shows that firms with increased management forecasts of dividends from current dividends have higher mean (median) MFERR, −0.00995 (−0.00038), than those that did not change or decreased management forecasts of dividends from current dividends. A marginal difference in mean (median) MFERR is observed between firms without change in forecast dividends and those with decreased forecast dividends, −0.01271 (−0.00152) and −0.01126 (−0.00153) respectively. The result of the one-way ANOVA rejects the null of no difference in the three mean (median) MFERRs. Table 11.5(B) reports the results of the multiple comparison analysis. It shows that firms with increased forecast dividends have significantly higher mean and median MFERRs than those without change in forecast dividends, and have significantly higher median MFERR than those with decreased forecast dividends.

These results are thus consistent with the hypothesis that an increase in management forecast of next year's dividends from current dividends possesses some information about strong future performance of firms beyond that conveyed by MEFs. However, there appears to be little information in a decrease in management forecast of next year's dividends.

11.4.2 Multivariate analysis

To provide a more comprehensive analysis of the determinants of bias in MEFs, a multivariate model is estimated using the 10 factors identified in the univariate analysis as independent variables. The regression model is:

$$\mathrm{MFERR}_t = \beta_0 + \beta_1 \mathrm{LNMVE}_t + \beta_2 \mathrm{OTC}_t + \beta_3 \mathrm{OTC{*}LNMVE}_t + \beta_4 \mathrm{OFFER}_t + \beta_5 \mathrm{DIST}_t + \beta_6 \mathrm{MFERR}_{t-1} + \beta_7 \mathrm{MFERR}_{t-2} + \beta_8 \mathrm{GROWTH}_t + \beta_9 \mathrm{LOSS}_t + \beta_{10} \mathrm{DIVUP}_t + \beta_{11} \mathrm{INDUST1-28}_t + \beta_{12} \mathrm{YEAR81-98}_t + \varepsilon_t,$$

where:

$$\mathrm{LOSS}_t = \; = \begin{cases} 1 & \text{if } E_{t-1} \text{ is negative} \\ 0 & \text{otherwise} \end{cases},$$

$$\mathrm{DIVUP}_t = \; = \begin{cases} 1 & \text{if a firm increased forecast dividends for period } t \\ 0 & \text{otherwise} \end{cases},$$

Table 11.5 Signaling effect of management forecasts of dividends

	N	Mean MFERR	Median MFERR	Difference in means[d]	Difference in medians[e]
Increase in MF dividends[a]	2634	−0.00995	−0.00038		
No change in MF dividends[b]	22,240	−0.01271	−0.00152	$F_{(2,27952)}$ 5.35**	$\chi^2_{(2)}$ 34.69**
Decrease in MF dividends[c]	3081	−0.01126	−0.00153		

Panel A: One-way ANOVA.

Differences between three groups	Difference in means[f]	Difference in medians[g]
Increase in MF dividends − No change in MF dividends	0.00276 (2.98)**	0.00114 (5.87)**
Increase in MF dividends − Decrease in MF dividends	0.00131 (1.10)	0.00115 (3.75)**
No change in MF dividends − Decrease in MF dividends	−0.00145 (−1.67)	0.00001 (−1.12)

Panel B: Multiple comparisons.

The definitions of the variables are: $MFERR_t = (E_t - MF_t)/P_t$, where E_t is actual earnings per share for period t, MF_t is management forecast of earnings per share for period t, and P_t is share price at the beginning of period t.

[a] Increase in MF dividends comprises firm-year observations that increased management forecasts of dividends for the next year compared to current year dividends.

[b] No change in MF dividends comprises firm-year observations that did not change management forecasts of dividends for the next year from current year dividends.

[c] Decrease in MF dividends comprises firm-year observations that decreased management forecasts of dividends for the next year compared to current year dividends.

[d] The one-way analysis of variance (ANOVA) is used to test differences in the three means and its *F*-statistic is reported in this column.

[e] The Kruskal–Wallis one-way analysis of variance (ANOVA) by ranks is used to test differences in the three medians and its χ^2-statistic is reported in this column.

[f] For parametric tests, Tukey's multiple comparison method is employed and its *t*-statistic is reported in parentheses in this column.

[g] For nonparametric tests, the Kruskal–Wallis multiple comparison method is employed and its *z*-statistic is reported in parentheses in this column.

** Significant at the 0.01 level (two-tailed).

$INDUST1-28_t$ = a set of industry dummies, and
$YEAR81-98_t$ = a set of year dummies.

The results are reported in Table 11.6. The expected signs are based on the univariate analysis. The signs of the estimated coefficients are all consistent with those from the univariate analysis and they are statistically significant at the 5% level or higher. Overall, the model explains 20.6% of the variation in MFERR. Thus, the multivariate analysis reconfirms the univariate results that the 10 factors, which are macroeconomic influence, industry, firm size, exchange/OTC, external financing, financial distress, prior management forecast errors, growth, losses, and management forecasts of dividends, are all associated with bias in MEFs.

11.5 Market awareness of bias in management earnings forecasts

This section investigates the extent to which systematic errors in MEFs are reflected in share prices. Managers usually have access to inside information that is not available to outsiders. Therefore, managers are considered to have an informational advantage over market participants. Because of this information asymmetry, it will be both rational and practical for market participants to regard management forecasts as a primary source of information about future performance of firms. If the stock market fixates on earnings forecasts released by management and does not correctly adjust for systematic errors in the forecasts, share prices of firms that issue optimistic earnings forecasts will be overvalued while those that issue pessimistic earnings forecasts will be undervalued. However, as the end of the accounting period nears, information about the actual performance of firms will be disseminated in the market and price reversals will occur. Then, a hedge portfolio strategy of buying firms reporting most pessimistic MEFs and selling short those reporting most optimistic MEFs at the time of their release would generate positive abnormal stock returns.

To test whether systematic errors in MEFs are impounded into share prices, the predicted $MFERR_t$ is calculated for each firm using the estimated parameters from the following fixed effects model[9]:

$$MFERR_{t-1} = \gamma_1 FIRMDUM_{t-1} + \gamma_2 LNMVE_{t-1} + \gamma_3 DIST_{t-1} + \gamma_4 GROWTH_{t-1} + \gamma_5 LOSS_{t-1} + \gamma_6 DIVUP_{t-1} + \gamma_7 YEARDUM_{t-1} + \varepsilon_t,$$

Table 11.6 Multivariate analysis of the determinants of bias in management earnings forecasts

Variables	Expected sign	Coefficient	*t*-statistic[a]	*F*-statistic[a]
Regression model	$MFERR_t = \beta_0 + \beta_1 LNMVE_t + \beta_2 OTC_t + \beta_3 OTC{*}LNMVE_t + \beta_4 OFFER_t + \beta_5 DIST_t + \beta_6 MFERR_{t-1} + \beta_7 MFERR_{t-2} + \beta_8 GROWTH_t + \beta_9 LOSS_t + \beta_{10} DIVUP_t + \beta_{11} INDUST1-28_t + \beta_{12} YEAR81-98_t + \varepsilon_t$			
CONSTANT	?	−0.0534	−9.55**	
LNMVE	+	0.0016	8.98**	
OTC	−	−0.0263	−2.53*	
OTC*LNMVE	+	0.0029	2.68**	
OFFER	+	0.0035	4.60**	
DIST	−	−0.0016	−3.75**	
$MFERR_{t-1}$	+	0.1852	11.42**	
$MFERR_{t-2}$	+	0.0463	4.36**	
GROWTH	+	0.0180	6.80**	
LOSS	−	−0.0093	−5.27**	
DIVUP	+	0.0023	2.70**	
INDUST1 – 28				7.36**
YEAR81 – 98				67.27**
Adj. R^2	0.206			
N	24,023			

The definitions of the variables are: $MFERR_t = (E_t - MF_t)/P_t$, $LNMVE_t = \ln(MVE_t/\text{Consumer Price Index})$,

$$OTC_t = \begin{cases} 1 & \text{if a firm is an OTC firm in period } t \\ 0 & \text{otherwise} \end{cases},$$

$$OTC{*}LNMVE_t = \begin{cases} LNMVE_t & \text{if a firm is an OTC firm in period } t \\ 0 & \text{otherwise} \end{cases},$$

$$OFFER_t = \begin{cases} 1 & \text{if a firm made a seasoned public offering in period } t \\ 0 & \text{otherwise} \end{cases},$$

$DIST_t$ = the factor scores obtained from the principal component analysis on the variables used in the Ohlson (1980) bankruptcy probability model,

$$GROWTH_t = \frac{Sales_{t-1}}{Sales_{t-2}},\ LOSS_t = \begin{cases} 1 & \text{if } E_{t-1} \text{ is negative} \\ 0 & \text{otherwise} \end{cases},$$

$$DIVUP_t = \begin{cases} 1 & \text{if a firm increased forecast dividends for period } t \\ 0 & \text{otherwise} \end{cases},$$

$INDUST1-28_t$ = a set of industry dummies, and $YEAR81-98_t$ = a set of year dummies, where E_t is actual earnings per share for period t, MF_t is management forecast of earnings per share for period t, P_t is share price at the beginning of period t, and MVE_t is the market value of equity three months after the beginning of period t.

To control for outliers, observations with studentized residual greater than two are removed.

[a] *t*-statistics and *F*-statistics are based on White's heteroskedastic-consistent standard error.

* Significant at the 0.05 level (two-tailed). ** Significant at the 0.01 level (two-tailed).

where:
$FIRMDUM_t$ = a set of firm dummies and
$YEARDUM_t$ = a set of year dummies.

To make the strategy actually implementable, only *ex ante* factors that are related to management forecast errors are used as independent variables. The model is estimated annually from 1984 to 1998 using panel datasets with at least five-year data available for each firm, and the estimated coefficients are used to obtain the predicted $MFERR_t$. For example, to obtain the predicted management earnings forecast error for a firm in the year 1990, the predicted $MFERR_{1990}$, a set of estimated coefficients derived from data for the 1979–1989 time period are used.

At the end of June for each year from 1985 to 1999, firms are ranked according to their predicted $MFERR_t$ and assigned in equal numbers to quintile portfolios. The top quintile portfolio comprises firms with the highest predicted $MFERR_t$ (predicted to be most pessimistic in their earnings forecasts) and the bottom portfolio comprises firms with the lowest predicted $MFERR_t$ (predicted to be most optimistic in their earnings forecasts). The strategy is to take a long position in the top quintile portfolio and a short position in the bottom quintile portfolio and maintain these investments until the end of September (for a three-month period)[10]. The results of the same strategy based on the actual forecast errors are also reported for comparison purposes.

Figure 11.3(A) plots the abnormal returns from the hedge portfolio strategy based on the actual forecast errors for the 15 years. The returns are positive in all years, with a 15-year average return of 8.0%. This suggests that having perfect foresight on management forecast errors can produce consistent abnormal returns. Figure 11.3(B) plots the abnormal returns from the same strategy based on the predicted forecast errors. The returns are positive in 14 of the 15 years, with a 15-year average return of 4.5%. Thus, the hedge portfolio strategy based on *ex post* forecast errors can generate abnormal returns of as much as 8.0%, and the same strategy based on *ex ante* forecast errors can still produce abnormal returns of 4.5%. These findings may suggest that the stock market fixates on management forecasts and does not completely impound systematic errors in MEFs into share prices.

11.6 Conclusion

The first objective of this chapter was to investigate the determinants of bias in management earnings forecasts (MEFs) announced by Japanese firms over the period 1979–1999. The results of both univariate and multivariate analyses show

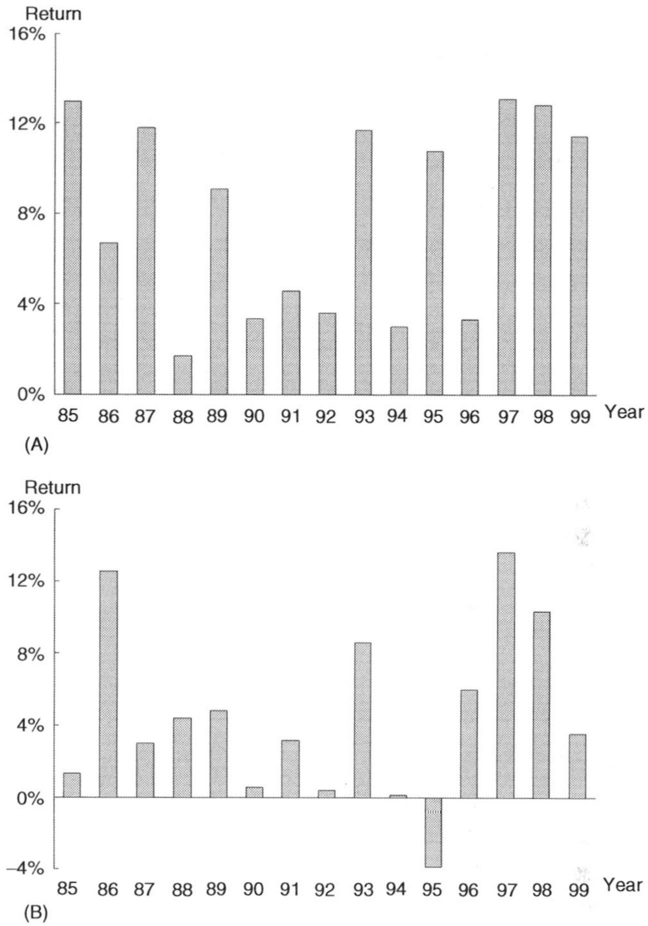

Figure 11.3 (A) Abnormal returns produced by the hedge portfolio strategy based on the actual management forecast errors (MFERR). (B) Abnormal returns produced by the hedge portfolio strategy based on the predicted management forecast errors (MFERR). In both cases, firms are ranked according to the MFERR at the end of June from 1985 to 1999 and assigned in equal numbers to quintile portfolios. The top quintile portfolio comprises firms with the highest MFERR and the bottom quintile portfolio with the lowest MFERR. The strategy is to take a long position in the top quintile portfolio and a short position in the bottom quintile portfolio and maintain these investments until the end of September

that the 10 factors, which are macroeconomic influence, industry, firm size, exchange/OTC, external financing, financial distress, prior management forecast errors, growth, losses, and management forecasts of dividends, are all associated with bias in MEFs. The second objective of this chapter was to examine the extent to which systematic forecast errors are reflected in share prices. The results of the hedge portfolio strategy show that abnormal returns can be earned by predicting errors in MEFs, suggesting that share prices may not fully reflect information about systematic errors in MEFs.

The provision of the next period's earnings forecasts by management of almost all listed firms is a major feature of the Japanese financial disclosure system. Despite that, there has been little research so far on the properties of Japanese management forecasts, partly due to difficulties in obtaining the data. This study is probably the first to investigate the properties of Japanese MEFs. The findings in this chapter suggest the existence of systematic bias in Japanese management forecasts and also provide some evidence of the stock market's fixation on management forecasts. Perhaps future research on the impact of management forecasts on analysts' forecasts would likely shed more light on the nature of management forecast information and its influence on the stock market.

Acknowledgments

I gratefully acknowledge the helpful comments and assistance of Richard Heaney, Hiroyuki Ishikawa, Atsushi Sasakura, and Hia Hui Ching. Special thanks are due to editors Greg N. Gregoriou and Mohamed Gaber, and also to Kazuyuki Suda and Yoshiko Oshiro for the provision of management forecast data. All errors are the responsibility of the author.

Notes

1. The term 'earnings' used in this chapter indicates 'net income' unless otherwise stated.
2. The condensed financial statements (Kessan Tanshin) are available from the Tokyo Stock Exchange website (http://www.tse.or.jp).
3. All forecasts are published in the form of point forecasts except for dividends per share, which are sometimes provided in the form of range forecasts.
4. A survey reports that, by 1980, more than 90% of listed firms, excluding those in the financial sector, provided management forecasts.
5. The results presented later are qualitatively similar when observations in the extreme 0.5% and 1.5% are removed.
6. When the analysis requires first-differenced variables and/or lagged variables, the sample size becomes smaller accordingly.
7. Using the yearly median MFERR instead of mean MFERR produces similar results. The correlation coefficient between the yearly median MFERR and the real GDP growth rate is 0.826.
8. McNichols (1989) reports a large negative mean (median) MFERR for the year 1982. The US economy posted −2.0% in real GDP growth rate in 1982, which was the worst in the last 50 years.
9. A fixed effects estimation uses the time-demeaned data. Therefore, any variable that is constant or has little variation over time is excluded from the model.

10. The return cumulation period is limited to a three-month period from the end of June to the end of September. This is because the sample firms used in this study are all March fiscal year-end firms and they publish new forecasts for full-year earnings at the same time as they report semi-annual earnings, at the end of September. The analysis (not reported here) indicates that higher abnormal returns cannot be earned by extending the return cumulation period to nine and 12 months.

References

Aharony, J. and Swary, I. (1980). Quarterly Dividend and Earnings Announcements and Stockholders' Returns: An Empirical Analysis. *Journal of Finance*, 35(1):1–12.

Ajinkaya, B. and Gift, M. (1984). Corporate Managers' Earnings Forecasts and Symmetrical Adjustments of Market Expectations. *Journal of Accounting Research*, 22(2):425–444.

Bamber, L.S. and Cheon, Y.S. (1998). Discretionary Management Earnings Forecast Disclosures: Antecedents and Outcomes Associated with Forecast Venue and Forecast Specificity Choices. *Journal of Accounting Research*, 36(2):167–190.

Basi, B., Carey, K., and Twark, R. (1976). A Comparison of the Accuracy of Corporate and Security Analysts' Forecasts of Earnings. *Accounting Review*, 51(2):244–254.

Brown, L. (1997). Analyst Forecasting Errors: Additional Evidence. *Financial Analysts Journal*, 53(6):81–88.

Brown, L. (2001). A Temporal Analysis of Earnings Surprises: Profits versus Losses. *Journal of Accounting Research*, 39(2):221–241.

Choi, J.H. and Ziebart, D. (2000). A Reexamination of Bias in Management Earnings Forecasts. Working Chapter, University of Illinois.

Conroy, R., Eades, K., and Harris, R. (2000). A Test of the Relative Pricing Effects of Dividends and Earnings: Evidence from Simultaneous Announcements in Japan. *Journal of Finance*, 55(3):1199–1227.

Das, S., Levine, C., and Sivaramakrishnan, K. (1998). Earnings Predictability and Bias in Analysts' Earnings Forecasts. *Accounting Review*, 73(2):277–294.

Frankel, R., McNichols, M., and Wilson, P. (1995). Discretionary Disclosure and External Financing. *Accounting Review*, 70(1):135–150.

Frost, C. (1997). Disclosure Policy Choices of UK Firms Receiving Modified Audit Reports. *Journal of Accounting and Economics*, 23(2):163–187.

Hand, J. and Landsman, W. (2005). The Pricing of Dividends in Equity Valuation. *Journal of Business Finance and Accounting*, 32(3–4):435–469.

Healy, P. and Palepu, K. (1988). Earnings Information Conveyed by Dividend Initiations and Omissions. *Journal of Financial Economics*, 21(2):149–175.

Hirst, E., Koonce, L., and Miller, J. (1999). The Joint Effect of Management's Prior Forecast Accuracy and the Form of its Financial Forecasts on Investor Judgment. *Journal of Accounting Research*, 37(Suppl.):101–124.

Irani, A. (2000). Determinants of Bias in Management Earnings Forecasts. *Accounting Enquiries*, 10(1):33–86.

Irani, A. (2001). Management Earnings Forecast Bias and Insider Trading: Comparison of Distressed and Non-Distressed Firms. Working Chapter, University of New Hampshire.

Koch, A. (2002). Financial Distress and the Credibility of Management Earnings Forecasts. Working Chapter, Carnegie Mellon University.

Matsumoto, D. (2002). Management's Incentives to Avoid Negative Earnings Surprises. *Accounting Review*, 77(3):483–514.

McDonald, C. (1973). An Empirical Examination of the Reliability of Published Predictions of Future Earnings. *Accounting Review*, 48(3):502–510.

McNichols, M. (1989). Evidence of Informational Asymmetries from Management Earnings Forecasts and Stock Returns. *Accounting Review*, 64(1):1–27.

Ohlson, J. (1980). Financial Ratios and the Probabilistic Prediction of Bankruptcy. *Journal of Accounting Research*, 18(1):109–131.

Patell, J. (1976). Corporate Forecasts of Earnings Per Share and Stock Price Behavior: Empirical Tests. *Journal of Accounting Research*, 14(2):246–276.

Penman, S. (1980). An Empirical Investigation of the Voluntary Disclosure of Corporate Earnings Forecasts. *Journal of Accounting Research*, 18(1):132–160.

Penman, S. (2001). *Financial Statement Analysis and Security Valuation*. McGraw-Hill/Irwin, New York.

Richardson, S., Teoh, S., and Wysocki, P. (1999). Tracking Analysts' Forecasts over the Annual Earnings Horizon: Are Analysts' Forecasts Optimistic or Pessimistic? Working Chapter, University of Michigan.

Richardson, S., Teoh, S., and Wysocki, P. (2004). The Walkdown to Beatable Analyst Forecasts: The Role of Equity Issuance and Insider Trading Incentives. *Contemporary Accounting Research*, 21(4):885–924.

Rosen, R. (1998). The Statutory Safe Harbor for Forward-Looking Statements after Two and a Half Years: Has It Changed the Law? Has It Achieved What Congress Intended? *Washington University Law Quarterly*, 76(2):645–681.

Skinner, D. and Sloan, R. (2002). Earnings Surprises, Growth Expectations, and Stock Returns or Don't Let an Earnings Torpedo Sink Your Portfolio. *Review of Accounting Studies*, 7(2–3):289–312.

Watts, R. and Zimmerman, J. (1986). *Positive Accounting Theory*. Prentice-Hall, Englewood Cliffs, NJ.

Waymire, G. (1984). Additional Evidence on the Information Content of Management Earnings Forecasts. *Journal of Accounting Research*, 22(2):703–718.

Williams, P. (1996). The Relation between a Prior Earnings Forecast by Management and Analyst Response to a Current Management Forecast. *Accounting Review*, 71(1):103–115.

12

Expected Earnings Growth when there is a Growth Option

Kenton K. Yee

12.1 Introduction

Growth firms, by definition, have recurring opportunities to make positive net present value (NPV) investments. The classical NPV rule states that a firm should invest in a project whenever the present value of expected profits exceeds the present value costs. Costs typically include cash expenses as well as depreciation and amortization of operating assets. From the real options perspective, this list is incomplete. When investment is irreversible, the decision to invest is associated with a commitment. Making an investment surrenders the opportunity to postpone the commitment, perhaps indefinitely. Since this opportunity has value, the decision-making calculus should take it into account. A firm should invest only when the present value of expected profits exceeds the present value of classical costs plus the value of the opportunity to postpone commitment.

Real options theory provides an organizing rubric for recognizing and quantifying the value of such opportunities. A generic feature of real options theory is the 'addition principle'. Adding a new (call or put) option into a portfolio of assets increases the price of the portfolio by the price of the new option[1]. The addition principle postulates that firm value equals the value of in-place projects plus the value of growth options (Myers, 1987; Brealey and Myers, 2002):

$$V_\tau = \text{'Value of projects in place'} + \text{'Option value'}. \qquad (12.1)$$

Equation (12.1) states that option value *adds* linearly to the valuation function. The addition principle holds even if the option depends on exogenous information or is contingent.

Related to, but distinct from, the addition principle is the 'nonlinearity hypothesis'. According to the nonlinearity hypothesis, options make valuation functions depend nonlinearly on earnings. While not grounded in formal theory[2], this hypothesis probably owes its conception to the well-known convex relationship between the Black–Scholes call-option value and stock price. Likewise, textbook solutions (e.g. Dixit and Pindyck, 1994; Kulatiklaka and Perotti, 1998) typically look either convex or concave with respect to fundamental asset values. Consistent with the nonlinearity hypothesis, Burgstahler and Dichev (1997) attributed the convex empirical relation between price and earnings to the presence of 'adaptation' options. Subsequent modeling studies offered closed-form (Yee, 2000, 2005; Ashton et al., 2003; Gietzmann and Ostaszewski, 2004; Yee, 2005) and numerical (Schwartz and Moon, 2000) solutions of real options models that exhibit a convex relationship between price and earnings and cash flows.

How universal is the nonlinearity hypothesis under GAAP accounting? Does a growth firm with linear revenue recognition, capitalization, and expensing policies have a convex price–earnings relation? Assuming that the value of in-place projects is linear in earnings, equation (12.1) implies that V_I is nonlinear in earnings if, and only if, option value is nonlinear in earnings. But why does option value depend on earnings? Option value depends on earnings if (a) the option-exercise decision relies on (trailing) earnings or (b) accrual accounting induces a relation between option value and earnings[3].

But it is not at all obvious that option-exercise decisions depend on trailing earnings generated by projects in place. An option holder seeks to maximize future gains from new projects, which are not necessarily informed by the performance of in-place projects. For example, due to leasing policies of the US government, oil exploration firms lease adjacent offshore tracts of land that contain uncertain deposits of oil. Lessors have an option (but not an obligation) to drill new oil wells. Their exercise decision involves a tradeoff between drilling and potentially obtaining oil sooner or waiting for their neighbors to drill first and disclose information about the size and quality of the oil deposit. In equilibrium, firms exercise their options based on project-specific information (Paddock et al., 1988). Firm-wide trailing earnings are irrelevant. Similarly, pharmaceutical firms exercise their options to develop new drugs based on project-specific considerations, not trailing EPS, which aggregates information from other projects (Healy et al., 2002). In these examples, the presence of growth options, by itself, does not cause nonlinear price–earnings relations.

It is the accounting rules that ultimately induce or suppress nonlinearity in the price–earnings relation. Hence, the task at hand is to examine the connections between accrual accounting, growth options, and price–earnings relations. I will address the following questions in a setting with a growth option and *linear* accounting policies:

- What special accounting policies achieve linear earnings–value relations in the presence of a growth option?
- What do the achieved linear earnings–value relations look like, and how do they differ from known earnings–value relations?
- In the presence of a growth option, are capitalized earnings (suitably dividend adjusted) a sufficient valuation attribute in the long run?

The answers to these questions will demonstrate that, when earnings are sufficiently similar to 'economic' or Hicksian earnings, then linear weighted averages of earnings forecasts suffice as valuation attributes even in the presence of growth options. Unless option-exercise policy relies on earnings, the presence of a growth option does not, by itself, cause earnings nonlinearity.

Section 12.2 endows a firm with a growth option and characterizes the ensuing expected cash flows. The contingent (nonlinear) nature of the option-induced cash investment distinguishes the model here and from Feltham and Ohlson (1996). In Feltham and Ohlson, an exogenous linear dynamic governs cash investments. In contrast, the cash outlay pertaining to the exercise of a growth option is a contingent one-time transaction determined by the firm's option-exercise strategy. Aside from this key difference, the remainder of the analysis follows the spirit of Feltham and Ohlson and Ohlson and Zhang (1998). Section 12.3 defines the linear accounting policies that define operating earnings, and section 12.4 describes the linear earnings–value relation implied by the linear accounting policies. Section 12.5 concludes.

12.2 Perpetual growth option: model setup

This section models a firm with a project that contains one growth option. In the model, a risk-neutral firm has an opportunity (but not an obligation) to make an irreversible one-time investment of I dollars to grow a project. The project's NPV is proportional to K_τ an observable random variable that fluctuates stochastically. The investment may be made at any time–there is no deadline. This means the firm has a 'perpetual growth option', whose exercise price is I and whose underlying asset value varies stochastically with K_τ. For simplicity, the firm has only one such option.

The following variables characterize cash flows from operations:

- $cr_\tau \in (-\infty, \infty)$: cash revenues during period τ
- $ci_\tau \in \{0, I\}$: cash investment during period τ
- $c_\tau \equiv cr_\tau - ci_\tau$: free cash flow during period τ
- κ_τ: i.i.d. random variable with a regular and bounded density $\phi(\kappa)$ and strictly positive support on $[0, \kappa_{\max}]$
- ε_τ: mean-zero, unpredictable random variable
- $\Theta_\tau \in \{0, 1\}$: the number of growth options outstanding at the end of period τ.

Assume $(\kappa_\tau, \varepsilon_s) = 0$ for all τ and s.

Cash revenues evolve according to the dynamic:

$$cr_{\tau+1} = \gamma cr_\tau + \kappa_\tau ci_\tau + \varepsilon_{\tau+1} \tag{12.2}$$

where $0 \leq \gamma \leq 1$. The $\gamma cr_\tau + \varepsilon_{\tau+1}$ terms on the right-hand side of equation (12.2) reflect cash revenues from existing projects; γcr_τ is the persistent component of cash revenues and $\varepsilon_{\tau+1}$ is the unpredictable component. Equation (12.2) is similar to the cash revenues dynamic in Feltham and Ohlson (1996); the only differences are the stochastic[4] nature of κ_τ and how cash investments ci_τ will be determined.

Feltham and Ohlson (1996) assume that cash investments are persistent, e.g. $ci_{\tau+1} = \omega ci_\tau + \varepsilon'_{\tau+1}$, which means the firm is pre-committed to making investments every period. In contrast, $ci_\tau = 0$ here unless and until the firm chooses to exercise its growth option. Θ_τ is an indicator variable that keeps track of whether the firm has a growth option outstanding at the end of period τ. In particular, if the firm waits until period τ_* to exercise its growth option, then:

$$\Theta_\tau = \begin{cases} 1 & \tau < \tau_* \\ 0 & \tau \geq \tau_*. \end{cases}$$

At the start of period τ, the firm observes[5] $\{cr_\tau, \Theta_{\tau-1}, \kappa_\tau\}$. If the firm has no growth options remaining ($\Theta_{\tau-1} = 0$), then $ci_\tau = 0$ must be zero. On the other hand, if $\Theta_{\tau-1} = 1$, the firm chooses whether to make a $ci_\tau = 0$ or a $ci_\tau = I$ dollars investment. If it chooses to invest $ci_\tau = 0$ dollars, the firm defers exercise of its option till a later date. If $ci_\tau = I$ dollars, the firm exercises its growth option and has none left ($\Theta_\tau = 0$).

The firm's 'investment rule' determines how the firm decides when to exercise its growth option. I will focus on the following (standard) investment rule: when the firm has an outstanding growth option, it waits until κ_τ exceeds some pre-established threshold value κ_*, at which time it immediately exercises the option by investing $ci_\tau = I$ dollars. But if $\Theta_{\tau-1} = 0$, $ci_\tau = 0$ regardless of how large κ_τ is. Formally:

Definition 1. A 'threshold-κ_* investment rule' is:

$$ci_\tau = \begin{cases} 0 & \Theta_{\tau-1} = 0 \text{ or } \kappa_\tau \leq \kappa_* \\ I & \Theta_{\tau-1} = 1 \text{ or } \kappa_\tau > \kappa_* \end{cases},$$

where κ_* is some pre-specified real number in the interval $[0, \kappa_{max}]$.

The standard NPV decision rule is a special case of a threshold-κ_* investment rule with $\kappa_* = R - \gamma$. Under the NPV decision rule, the firm makes the investment as soon as its expected return, $\frac{\kappa_\tau I}{R-\gamma}$ here, exceeds its cost, $ci_\tau = I$. The NPV decision rule is suboptimal when the firm has an opportunity to defer its investment. The benefit of deferring investment is that the firm might obtain a bigger κ_τ in the future[6]. The firm must balance the expected *discounted* value of a potentially bigger future return against the value of the certain return today. Threshold-κ_* investment rules enable the firm to strike such a balance. Lemma 2 below will show that a threshold rule with $\kappa_* > R - \gamma$ but smaller than $\kappa_{\max}$ is superior to the NPV decision rule.

If the firm has a threshold-investment rule, the net present value (NPV) of the firm's free cash flows is[7]:

$$V_\tau \equiv \sum_{s=1}^{\infty} R^{-s} E_\tau[c_{\tau+s}], \tag{12.3}$$

where $E_\tau[\cdot]$ averages over the random variables $\varepsilon_{\tau+1}$ and $\kappa_{\tau+1}$. The first Lemma states the NPV of a firm's free cash flows if the firm implements the threshold-κ_* investment rule:

Lemma 1. Equations (12.2) and (12.3) and the threshold-κ_* investment rule imply:

$$V_\tau = \frac{E_\tau[cr_{\tau+1}]}{R-\gamma} + g(\kappa_*)\Theta_\tau,$$

where $E_\tau[cr_{\tau+1}] = \gamma cr_\tau + k_\tau ci_\tau$,

$$g(\kappa_*) = \left(\frac{I}{R - \Phi(\kappa_*)}\right) \int_{\kappa_*}^{\kappa_{\max}} dk\phi(k) \left\{\frac{k}{R-\gamma} - 1\right\},$$

and $\Phi(\kappa_*) \equiv \int_0^{\kappa_*} dk\, \phi(k)$.

Proof: All proofs are given in the Appendix.

Lemma 1 is consistent with equation (12.1), the addition principle: firm value equals the NPV of cash flow from projects in place plus the value of the outstanding growth option, $g(\kappa_*)$. The value of $g(\kappa_*)$ depends on the investment threshold κ_*. Since neither the payoff value of the growth option nor the investment rule depends on the status of existing projects, $g(\kappa_*)$ does not depend on cr_τ or ci_τ. The proof of Lemma 1 also describes a heuristic derivation of $g(\kappa_*)$.

The value of the growth option, $g(\kappa_*)$, is bigger under some threshold-κ_* investment rules than others. Figure 12.1 depicts $g(\kappa_*)$ if the density function $\phi(\kappa)$ is constant on the interval $[0,\kappa_{max}]$ for two different values of κ_{max}. In Figure 12.1, $R - \gamma = 0.2$. Under the NPV decision rule, the firm exercises the option as soon as $\frac{\kappa_\tau I}{R-\gamma} > I$. Accordingly, the NPV decision rule is equivalent to the threshold-κ_* rule with $\kappa_* = \kappa_{NPV} \equiv R - \gamma = 0.2$. As depicted in Figure 12.1, $g(\kappa_*)$ achieves its maximum at $\kappa_* > \kappa_{NPV} = 0.2$. The option is worth more if the firm demands a larger threshold than that stipulated by the NPV rule. (See Appendix for elaboration on this and other properties of $g(\kappa_*)$.)

A rational firm maximizes the value of its growth option by choosing the threshold value κ_* that maximizes the value of $g(\kappa_*)$. The threshold-κ_* investment rule that maximizes $g(\kappa_*)$ is the 'optimal threshold investment rule'. Lemma 2 states the NPV of the firm if it implements the optimal threshold investment rule.

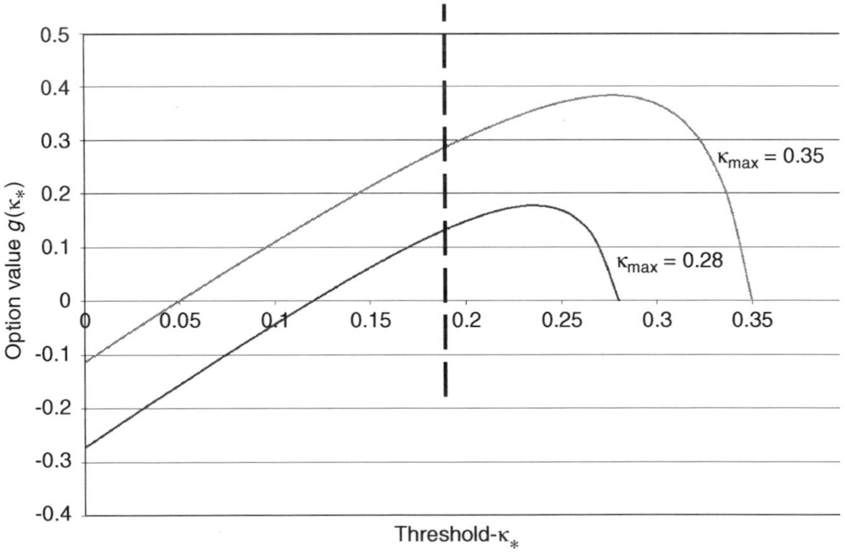

Figure 12.1 Option value $g(\kappa_*)$ as a function of the threshold-κ_* investment rule for the constant density $\phi(\kappa) = 1/\kappa_{max}$ with support on $[0,\kappa_{max}]$. For comparison, $g(\kappa_*)$ is plotted for two different values of κ_{max}. For both plots, $R = 1.1$, $\gamma = 0.9$, and $I = 1$

Lemma 2. Equations (12.2) and (12.3) imply that the optimal threshold κ_* is unique and that

$$V_\tau = \frac{E_\tau[cr_{\tau+1}]}{R-\gamma} + G\Theta_\tau,$$

where $G \equiv g(\kappa^\cdot)$ and $\kappa_* = \kappa^\cdot$ is the unique solution to

$$g(\kappa^\cdot) = \left\{\frac{\kappa^\cdot}{R-\gamma} - 1\right\} I \tag{12.4}$$

with $g(\cdot)$ as stated in Lemma 1.

Equation (12.4) indicates that it is optimal to exercise when the value of the option, $g(\kappa^\cdot)$, equals the immediate net return from exercising, $\left\{\frac{\kappa^\cdot I}{R-\gamma} - I\right\}$. This is because, when $g(\kappa^\cdot) = \left\{\frac{\kappa^\cdot}{R-\gamma} - 1\right\}$, the firm is rationally indifferent between the option and the transaction.

Lemma 2 says that optimally utilized growth options add linearly to firm value in accordance with the addition principle, equation (12.1). While V_τ is nonlinear in the investment threshold, κ_*, V_τ is linear in cash revenues, cash investments, and the value of the growth option, $G \equiv g(\kappa^\cdot)$.

12.3 Accounting policies and earnings–value relations

Lemma 2 shows that the presence of a growth option does not induce a nonlinear cash–value relation. Does it induce a nonlinear earnings–value relation? This question is ambiguous without defining earnings. Accordingly, I will focus on a narrower question: Is it possible for *linear* accounting rules similar to those introduced in Feltham and Ohlson (1996) and Ohlson and Zhang (1998) to achieve *linear* earnings–value relations in the presence of a growth option?

To address this question, we introduce the following notation and terminology:

- $oa_\tau \in (-\infty, \infty)$: operating assets at the end of period τ
- $ox_\tau \in (-\infty, \infty)$: operating earnings, which equal free cash outflow plus accruals so that $ox_\tau = cr_\tau - ci_\tau + oa_\tau - oa_{\tau-1}$

- cum-dividend operating earnings and operating earnings forecasts

$$\overline{ox}^{c}_{\tau,s} \equiv \begin{cases} ox_\tau - \phi^{-1}c_\tau & s=0 \\ E_\tau[ox_{\tau+1}] & s=1 \\ E_\tau\left[ox_{\tau+s}+\phi^{-1}\times\sum_{u=1}^{s-1}R^{s-u}c_{\tau+u}\right] & s\geq 2, \end{cases}$$

where $\phi \equiv \dfrac{R}{R-1}$.

Definition 2. An 'accounting policy Π' is a quintuplet $\Pi \equiv \{\delta_0,\delta_1,\delta_2,\delta_3,\delta_\Theta\}$ of real constants such that:

$$oa_\tau = \delta_0 oa_{\tau-1} + \delta_1 cr_\tau + \delta_2\kappa_\tau ci_\tau + \delta_3 ci_\tau + \delta_\Theta\Theta_\tau .$$

Definition 3. An accounting policy $\Pi \equiv \{\delta_0,\delta_1,\delta_2,\delta_3,\delta_\Theta\}$ is 'investment-rule independent' if, and only if, the policy parameters $\{\delta_0,\delta_1,\delta_2,\delta_3,\delta_\Theta,\}$ do not depend on the investment threshold κ_*.

I will focus on investment-rule-independent accounting policies because how an asset is capitalized and subsequently expensed traditionally depends only on features specific to the *asset*–not on the firm's strategy for acquiring said asset. For instance, in GAAP, PPE depreciation is based on useful life and historical cost. Whether equipment was purchased as part of a long-term strategic plan has no bearing on its accounting treatment. Hence, I will focus on investment-rule-*independent* accounting policies, which are more institutionally realistic.

Under $\Pi \equiv \{\delta_0,\delta_1,\delta_2,\delta_3,\delta_\Theta\}$,

$$ox_\tau = -(1-\delta_0)oa_{\tau-1}+(1+\delta_1)cr_\tau + \delta_2\kappa_\tau ci_\tau-(1+\delta_3)ci_\tau+\delta_\Theta\Theta_\tau. \tag{12.5}$$

$(1-\delta_0)$ is the depreciation rate; $(-\delta_1)$ is the amount of period-expense allocated under revenues-based costing; $\delta_2\kappa_\tau+\delta_3$ is the capitalization factor for new investments; and δ_Θ specifies the per period accounting appreciation for an outstanding growth option. For example, $\Pi \equiv \{1,0,0,0,0\}$ is cash-basis accounting ($ox_\tau = cr_\tau - ci_\tau$). Similarly, $\Pi \equiv \{1,0,0,0,-1\}$ is cash-basis accounting minus a growth option depreciation expense of \$1 per period. In contrast, $\Pi \equiv \{\delta_0 <1,0,0,1,0\}$ is a policy with operating-asset depreciation, cash-based revenue recognition without revenues-based costing, and capitalization of investments at historical cost.

At issue is the usefulness of operating earnings as a valuation attribute under different accounting policies. Forward earnings are a sufficient valuation attribute if earnings are the same as economic earnings[8]. To begin with, observe that no investment-rule-independent accounting policy can enable trailing or forward operating earnings to be a sufficient valuation attribute:

Observation 1. $V_\tau = \phi \overline{ox}^{c}_{\tau,0}$, a threshold-$\kappa_*$ investment rule, and equations (12.2), (12.3), and (12.5) imply $\Pi = \left\{1, -\left(\frac{1-\gamma}{R-\gamma}\right), \frac{R-1}{(R-\gamma)R}, \frac{1}{R}, \phi^{-1}g(\kappa_*)\right\}$. Similarly, $V_\tau = \frac{\phi \overline{ox}^{c}_{\tau,1}}{R}$, a threshold-investment rule, equations (12.2), (12.3), and (12.5) imply $\Pi = \left\{1, -\left(\frac{1-\gamma}{R-\gamma}\right), \delta_2, \delta_3, \delta_\Theta\right\}$, where $\{\delta_2, \delta_3, \delta_\Theta\}$ is any triplet that satisfies $\delta_2 \int_{\kappa_*}^{\kappa_{\max}} dk\, \phi(k)k - (1-\delta_3)\int_{\kappa_*}^{\kappa_{\max}} dk\, \phi(k) + \delta_\Theta \frac{\Phi(\kappa_*)}{I} = r\frac{g(\kappa_*)}{I}$.

Observation 1 shows that there is no investment-rule-independent accounting policy that achieves[9] $V_\tau = \phi \overline{ox}^{c}_{\tau,0}$ or $V_\tau = \frac{\phi \overline{ox}^{c}_{\tau,1}}{R}$. Therefore, constant trailing or forward price-to-earnings ratios are achieved in the presence of a growth option only by an accounting policy specifically tailored to how the firm is expected to exercise its growth option. An accountant who is uncertain about the firm's κ_* threshold cannot achieve $V_\tau = \phi \overline{ox}^{c}_{\tau,0}$ and $V_\tau = \frac{\phi \overline{ox}^{c}_{\tau,1}}{R}$.

Observation 1 suggests that accounting policies with $\delta_0 = 1$ and $\delta_1 = -\left(\frac{1-\gamma}{R-\gamma}\right)$ play a special role in facilitating earnings-based representations of value. For instance, consider:

$$\Pi_0 \equiv \left\{1, -\left(\frac{1-\gamma}{R-\gamma}\right), 0, 1, 0\right\}. \tag{12.6}$$

Π_0 is investment-rule independent, does not depreciate operating assets, and capitalizes new investments at historical cost. Equations (12.5) and (12.6) imply $ox_\tau = cr_\tau - \left(\frac{1-\gamma}{R-\gamma}\right)cr_\tau$ which stipulates cash-based revenue recognition and period expense equal to $\left(\frac{1-\gamma}{R-\gamma}\right)cr_\tau$.

Under Π_0, $ox_\tau = \left(\frac{R-1}{R-\gamma}\right)cr_\tau$. This implies $\frac{\phi E_\tau[ox_{\tau+1}]}{R} = \frac{E_\tau[cr_{\tau+1}]}{R-\gamma}$, where

$\phi \equiv R/(R-1)$. Since $V_\tau = \frac{E_\tau[cr_{\tau+1}]}{R-\gamma} + g(\kappa_*)\Theta_\tau$ by Lemma 1:

Observation 2. Equations (12.2), (12.3), (12.5), and (12.6) and a threshold-investment rule imply:

$$V_\tau = \frac{\phi \overline{ox}^c_{\tau,1}}{\text{R}} + g(\kappa^*)\Theta_\tau. \tag{12.7}$$

Observation 2 says that, in the *absence* of growth options (when $\Theta_\tau = 0$), forward operating earnings are a sufficient attribute under Π_0. That is, Π_0 is the accounting policy that equates accounting earnings to economic earnings in the absence of a growth option. But when there is a growth option, Π_0 no longer achieves economic earnings. In the presence of a growth option, forward earnings by itself is an insufficient valuation attribute under Π_0.

Is it possible to rewrite equation (12.7) so that a linear combination of forward earnings replaces the $g(\kappa_*)\Theta_\tau$ term? To this end, $E_\tau[\Theta_{\tau+1}] = \Phi(\kappa_*)\Theta_\tau$ if the firm follows a threshold-κ_* investment policy. This implies that Θ_τ evolves in expectation auto-regressively with persistence $\Phi(\kappa_*)$. ($\Phi(\kappa_*)$ is also the probability that the growth option survives for one more period.) Following Liu and Ohlson (2000), Ohlson (2001), and Yee (2004a, b), this implies that a linear combination of earnings forecasts proxies[10] for Θ_τ in equation (12.7). Replacing Θ_τ in equation (12.7) with earnings forecasts achieves $V_\tau = (1-\alpha)\frac{\phi \overline{ox}^c_{\tau,1},}{R} + \alpha\frac{\phi \overline{ox}^c_{\tau,2}}{R^2}$ with $\alpha = \frac{R}{R-\Phi(\kappa_*)}$. Therefore, under accounting policy Π_0, a weighted average of forward earnings forms a sufficient valuation attribute in the presence of a growth option. *A fortiori*, it turns out that the result (if not the same argument) prevails for a broader class of accounting policies than Π_0:

Proposition 1. Equations (12.2), (12.3), and (12.5), a threshold-investment rule, and any accounting policy of the form:

$$\Pi_0 \equiv \left\{1, -\left(\frac{1-\gamma}{R-\gamma}\right), \delta_1, \delta_3, \delta_\Theta\right\} \tag{12.8}$$

for *any* triple of real numbers, imply that:

$$V_\tau = (1-\alpha)\frac{\phi \overline{ox}^c_{\tau,1}}{R} + \alpha\frac{\phi \overline{ox}^c_{\tau,2}}{R^2} \tag{12.9}$$

with $\alpha = \dfrac{R}{R-\Phi(\kappa_*)}$.

Proposition 1 is the central result of this section. It offers three points. First, it provides a counter-example to the nonlinearity hypothesis. A linear weighted average of earnings forecasts is a sufficient valuation attribute in the presence of a growth option under an accounting rule that *would* equate accounting earnings to economic earnings when there is no growth option. The linear formula is achieved without requiring accounting policy to depend on investment rules (e.g. the option exercise threshold κ_*). As note 10 explains, abnormal earnings growth, $\overline{ox}^c_{\tau,2} - R\overline{ox}^c_{\tau,1}$, proxies for the value of the option.

The second point concerns the weight coefficient $\alpha = \dfrac{R}{R-\Phi(\kappa_*)}$. Since $0 \leq \Phi(\kappa_*) \leq 1$, $1 \leq \alpha \leq \phi$.

The third and final point is that equation (12.9) is less demanding on the accounting system than equation (12.7). Proposition 1 states that *any* accounting policy parameters $\{\delta_2, \delta_3, \delta_\Theta\}$ are compatible with the weighted average formula, equation (12.9), whereas equation (12.7) demands $\{\delta_2 = 0, \delta_3 = 1, \delta_\Theta = 0\}$. In other words, to achieve equation (12.9), historical cost capitalization ($\delta_3 = 1$) is unnecessary; equation (12.9) obtains whether one capitalizes or expenses the exercise price right away.

12.4 Long-run earnings growth with a growth option

Sections 12.1 and 12.2 examine a firm with a linear accounting policy and a growth option and show that $V_\tau = (1-\alpha)\dfrac{\phi \overline{ox}^c_{\tau,1}}{R} + \alpha\dfrac{\phi \overline{ox}^c_{\tau,2}}{R^2}$ under an accounting policy that would equate accounting earnings to economic earnings when there is no growth option. Thus, the presence of a growth option under this accounting policy merely introduces a second forward-earnings attribute into the valuation function. While this price–earnings relation formally looks like the Ohlson–Juettner-Nauroth (2005) model, its weight parameter α has a different interpretation. The traditional interpretation identifies α with the long-run earnings growth rate. In a growth option setting, α relates to the firm's option-exercise strategy, which determines the option's per-period survival probability $\Phi(\kappa_*)$.

This section establishes the relationship between long-run expected earnings growth, the option survival probability, and weight parameter α in the presence of a growth option.

One may think that Proposition II in Ohlson and Juettner-Nauroth (2005; hereafter termed 'OJ'), which relates α to long-run earnings growth, applies here. In the present notation, Proposition II states that, if $V_\tau = (1-\alpha)\frac{\phi \overline{ox}^c_{\tau,1}}{R}, \frac{\phi \overline{ox}^c_{\tau,2}}{R^2}$, $\alpha = \frac{R}{R-g}$ where $1 \leq g < R$, and there exists some T so that $\frac{E_\tau[ox_{\tau+s}]}{E_\tau[cr_\tau + s - ci_\tau + s]} \leq \frac{R-1}{R-g}$ for all $s \geq$ T, then $\lim_{u \to \infty} \frac{E_\tau[ox_{\tau+u}]}{E_\tau[ox_{\tau+u}]} = g$.

Proposition II does not apply to the growth option model because the presence of a growth option invalidates at least one of its assumptions. In particular, since Proposition 1 in section 12.2 states that $\alpha = \frac{R}{R - \Phi(\kappa_*)}$ in the presence of a growth option, $\Phi(\kappa_*)$ corresponds to g in the OJ model. Since Proposition II requires $g \geq 1$, it applies only if $\Phi(\kappa_*) \geq 1$. But, being a probability, $\Phi(\kappa_*) \leq 1$. Therefore, the only case where Proposition II applies is when $\Phi(\kappa_*) = 1$ – that is, if the option has zero probability of ever being exercised. Hence, OJ's Proposition II does not apply, except perhaps in the trivial case when the growth option has no probability of being exercised[11].

The inapplicability of the OJ result does not rule out that long-run earnings growth may still relate to α or to $\Phi(\kappa_*)$. Examination of the formula for $E_\tau[ox_{\tau+s}]$ is instructive. Equations (12.2), (12.3), and (12.5), a threshold-κ_* investment rule, and accounting policy Π_1 imply for all $s \geq 1$ that $E_\tau[ci_{\tau+s}] = (1 - \Phi(\kappa_*))\Phi^{s-1}(\kappa_*)I\Theta_\tau$ and:

$$E_\tau[ox_{\tau+s}] = \left(\frac{R-1}{R-\gamma}\right)E_\tau[cr_{\tau+s}] + \Lambda(\delta_2,\delta_3,\delta_\Theta)\Phi^{s-1}(\kappa_*)I\Theta_\tau, \tag{12.10}$$

where

$$E_\tau[cr_{\tau+s}] = \gamma^s cr_\tau + \frac{\int_{\kappa_*}^{\kappa_{\max}} dk\phi(k)k}{\Phi(\kappa_*)} I\Theta_\tau \begin{cases} \gamma^{s-1} S & \gamma = \Phi(\kappa_*) \\ \dfrac{\gamma^s - \Phi^s(\kappa_*)}{\gamma - \Phi(\kappa_*)} & \gamma \neq \Phi(\kappa_*) \end{cases} \tag{12.11}$$

and $\Lambda(\delta_2,\delta_3,\delta_\Theta) \equiv \left\{\delta_2 \int_{\kappa_*}^{\kappa_{\max}} dk\phi(k)k - (1-\delta_3)\int_{\kappa_*}^{\kappa_{\max}} dk\phi(k) + \delta_\Theta \frac{\Phi(\kappa_*)}{I}\right\}$.

Equation (12.10) shows that earnings forecasts depend on cash-flow forecasts as well as the accounting policy and the investment rule parameters. Taking the $s \rightarrow \infty$ limits of equations (12.10) and (12.11) yields the long-run earnings growth, payout, and firm–value growth ratios.

Proposition 2. Equations (12.2), (12.3), and (12.5), a threshold-κ_* investment rule, and accounting policy Π_1 imply for all $s \geq 1$ that:

$$\text{(i)} \quad \lim_{s \to \infty} \frac{E_\tau[ox_{\tau+s}]}{E_\tau[ox_{\tau+s-1}]} = \max\{\gamma, \Phi(\kappa_*)\}$$

$$\text{(ii)} \quad \frac{E_\tau[ox_{\tau+s}]}{E_\tau[cr_{\tau+s} - ci_{\tau+s}]} = \left(\frac{R-1}{R-\gamma}\right) \begin{cases} 1 & \gamma \geq \Phi(\kappa_*) \\ \dfrac{1 + \left(\dfrac{R-\gamma}{R-1}\right)\vartheta\Lambda}{1-(1-\Phi(\kappa_*))\vartheta} & \gamma < \Phi(\kappa_*) \end{cases}$$

$$\text{(iii)} \quad \lim_{s \to \infty} \frac{E_\tau[V_{\tau+s}]}{E_\tau[V_{\tau+s-1}]} = \max\{\gamma, \Phi(\kappa_*)\},$$

where $\vartheta \equiv \dfrac{\Phi(\kappa_*) - \gamma}{\int_{\kappa_*}^{\kappa_{\max}} dk\phi(k)k}$ and

$$\Lambda(\delta_2, \delta_3, \delta_\Theta) \equiv \left\{\delta_2 \int_{\kappa_*}^{\kappa_{\max}} dk\phi(k)k - (1-\delta_3)\int_{\kappa_*}^{\kappa_{\max}} dk\phi(k) + \delta_\Theta \frac{\Phi(\kappa_*)}{I}\right\}.$$

Because γ and $\Phi(\kappa_*)$ do not exceed unity by definition, formula (i) implies that long-run earnings shrink rather than grow. The shrinkage rate is independent of accounting policy and, depending on whether cash revenues or the option is more persistent, equals $\min\{1-\gamma, 1-\Phi(\kappa_*)\}$.

Formula (i) in Proposition 2 highlights the fact that α relates to the long-run earnings growth rate *only* if the survival probability of the option exceeds the persistence of cash revenues from assets in place. On the other hand, if $g > F(k^*)$, then $\lim_{s \to \infty} \dfrac{E_\tau[ox_{\tau+s}]}{E_\tau[ox_{\tau+s-1}]} = \gamma$, while α remains $\alpha = \dfrac{R}{R - \Phi(\kappa_*)}$. Therefore, when cash revenues from assets in place are more persistent than the growth option, α is unrelated to the long-run earnings growth rate. The probability of option survival always determines α whether $\gamma < \Phi(\kappa_*)$ or $\gamma \geq \Phi(\kappa_*)$.

Formula (ii) highlights the fact that even the long-run payout ratio depends on accounting policy and the threshold-κ_* investment rule. Life would be simpler if the payout ratio converged in the long run to a constant value that is independent of details of investment policy and whether investments are capitalized or expensed. Unfortunately, the dependence of the right-hand side of formula (ii) on $\Lambda(\delta_2,\delta_3,\delta_\Theta)$ and κ_* highlights that this is not so in the presence of a growth option. Formula (ii) also violates the payout ratio bound assumed in OJ's Proposition II. Formula (ii) implies that the long-run payout ratio may exceed $\frac{R-1}{R-\Phi(k_*)}$ when $\gamma<\Phi(\kappa_*)$. When $\gamma<\Phi(\kappa_*)$ and the long-run payout ratio exceeds $\frac{R-1}{R-\Phi(k_*)}$, the payout ratio condition in OJ's Proposition II is violated. This is another reason why OJ's Proposition II does not apply to the growth option model.

Comparing formulas (i) and (iii) in Proposition 2 reveals that $\lim_{s\to\infty}\frac{E_\tau[ox_{\tau+s}]}{E_\tau[ox_{\tau+s-1}]}=\lim_{s\to\infty}\frac{E_\tau[V_{\tau+s}]}{E_\tau[V_{\tau+s-1}]}$; that is, in the long run, earnings grow (or, more aptly, deteriorate) at the same rate as firm value, and this equality holds regardless of investment policy and accounting policy. Thus, even though capitalized forward earnings do not suffice as a univariate valuation attribute according to Proposition 1, the long-run earnings shrinkage rate equals the ex-dividend shrinkage rate of V_τ independent of accounting and investment policy, and independent of the option survival probability.

The fact that $\lim_{s\to\infty}\frac{E_\tau[ox_{\tau+s}]}{E_\tau[ox_{\tau+s-1}]}=\lim_{s\to\infty}\frac{E_\tau[V_{\tau+s}]}{E_\tau[V_{\tau+s-1}]}$ may lead one to conjecture that capitalized earnings might suffice as a univariate valuation attribute in the long run. If true, this would reaffirm the idea that a far-ahead earnings forecast casts a wide net that captures all value-relevant information about a growth option. But is this true?

X.J. Zhang (2000) offers a possibly relevant theorem. His result states that, because of canceling errors, permanent earnings are a sufficient valuation attribute in the long run under certain conditions. The following equality summarizes Zhang's result in the present notion[12]:

$$\lim_{s\to\infty}\left\{\frac{E_\tau[\phi ox_{\tau+s}-c_{\tau+s}]}{E_\tau[V_{\tau+s}]}\right\}=1+\phi\left(\frac{H-1}{H}\right)(BP-1), \tag{12.12}$$

where $H \equiv \lim_{s\to\infty} \frac{E_\tau[V_{\tau+s}]}{E_\tau[V_{\tau+s-1}]}$ and $BP \equiv \lim_{s\to\infty} \frac{E_\tau[oa_{\tau+s}]}{E_\tau[V_{\tau+s}]}$ is the long-run book-to-price ratio. Equation (12.12) implies:

(a) Under unbiased accounting ($BP = 1$), $\lim_{s\to\infty}\left\{\frac{E_\tau[\phi ox_{\tau+s} - c_{\tau+s}]}{E_\tau[V_{\tau+s}]}\right\} = 1$.

(b) If firm value freezes in the long run ($H = 1$), then $\lim_{s\to\infty}\left\{\frac{E_\tau[\phi ox_{\tau+s} - c_{\tau+s}]}{E_\tau[V_{\tau+s}]}\right\} = 1$.

(c) If accounting is conservative ($BP < 1$) and firm value shrinks in the long run ($H < 1$), then $\lim_{s\to\infty}\left\{\frac{E_\tau[\phi ox_{\tau+s} - c_{\tau+s}]}{E_\tau[V_{\tau+s}]}\right\} < 1$.

Point (c) implies that, when accounting is conservative and firm value shrinks, then dividend-adjusted capitalized earnings are an insufficient valuation attribute even in the long run.

Which of these cases apply to the growth option model? Are dividend-adjusted capitalized earnings a sufficient valuation attribute in the long run under Π_1 accounting in the presence of a growth option? First, suppose $\gamma = 1$. Then, $H = \max\{\gamma, \Phi(\kappa_*)\} = 1$, which implies case (b) applies and $\lim_{s\to\infty}\left\{\frac{E_\tau[\phi ox_{\tau+s} - c_{\tau+s}]}{E_\tau[V_{\tau+s}]}\right\} = 1$. Second, suppose $\gamma < 1$. Then, $H = \max\{\gamma, \Phi(\kappa_*)\}$ is less than unity (unless $\kappa_* = K_{max}$, in which case the option is worthless) so that, according to equation (12.12), $\lim_{s\to\infty}\left\{\frac{E_\tau[\phi ox_{\tau+s} - c_{\tau+s}]}{E_\tau[V_{\tau+s}]}\right\} \neq 1$ unless accounting is unbiased ($BP = 1$). But generally $BP \equiv \lim_{s\to\infty} \frac{E_\tau[oa_{\tau+s}]}{E_\tau[V_{\tau+s}]}$ diverges under Π_1 accounting unless one assumes a special initial value[13] for oa_τ. Hence, equation (12.12) does not directly apply when $\gamma < 1$ (see note 12).

Rather than applying equation (12.12), one can compute $\lim_{s\to\infty}\left\{\frac{E_\tau[\phi ox_{\tau+s} - c_{\tau+s}]}{E_\tau[V_{\tau+s}]}\right\}$ by brute force when there is a growth option. Proposition 3 reports the results of this calculation.

Proposition 3. Equations (12.2), (12.3), and (12.5), a threshold-κ_* investment rule, and accounting policy Π_1 for any $\{\delta_2, \delta_2, \delta_\Theta)$ imply:

$$\lim_{s\to\infty}\left\{\frac{E_\tau[\phi ox_{\tau+s} - c_{\tau+s}]}{E_\tau[V_{\tau+s}]}\right\} = \begin{cases} 1 & \gamma > \Phi(\kappa_*) \\ 1 + F\{\delta_2, \delta_2, \delta_\Theta) & \gamma \leq \Phi(\kappa_*), \end{cases}$$

where $F\{\delta_2,\delta_2,\delta_\Theta\}$ – whose expression is given in the Proof – may be either negative or positive depending on $\{\delta_2,\delta_2,\delta_\Theta\}$.

Proposition 3 shows that, if $\gamma > \Phi(\kappa_*)$, then dividend-adjusted capitalized earnings are a sufficient long-run valuation attribute. This result obtains whether the option exercise expenditure is capitalized ($\delta_3 = 1$) or expensed ($\delta_3 = 0$), since it holds for any accounting policy Π_1. But if the growth option's survival probability $\Phi(\kappa_*)$ exceeds γ, then dividend-adjusted capitalized earnings do *not* suffice as a valuation attribute even in the infinite long run. In this case, a weighted average of two earnings variables is necessary to span the valuation function even in the infinite long run.

12.5 Conclusion

In the Introduction, I raised three questions:

- What special accounting policies achieve linear earnings–value relations in the presence of a growth option?
- What do the achieved linear earnings–value relations look like, and how do they differ from known earnings–value relations?
- In the presence of a growth option, are capitalized earnings (suitably dividend adjusted) a sufficient valuation attribute in the long run?

To address these questions, I studied a firm with a linear accounting policy, Π_1, and a growth option. An attractive feature of Π_1 is that it capitalizes cash flows similarly to economic earnings. In the absence of a growth option, accounting earnings equal economic earnings under Π_1 accounting. Another attractive feature of Π_1 is that it does not depend on the firm's investment strategy. Proposition 1 shows that Π_1 implies the valuation function is $V_\tau = (1-\alpha)\frac{\phi o\bar{x}^{c}_{\tau,1}}{R} + \alpha\frac{\phi o\bar{x}^{c}_{\tau,1}}{R^2}$, where $\alpha = \frac{R}{R-\Phi(\kappa_*)}$.

X.J. Zhang's (2000) analysis of canceling errors and the valuation sufficiency of permanent earnings in the long run does not generally apply in the presence of a growth option and Π_1 accounting. This is because the book-to-price ratio diverges (does not exist) in the long run unless one imposes additional conditions on the accounting system. Nonetheless, Proposition 3 shows that in the presence of a growth option and any Π_1 accounting system, $\lim_{s\to\infty}\left\{\frac{E_\tau[\phi o x_{\tau+s} - c_{\tau+s}]}{E_\tau[V_{\tau+s}]}\right\} = 1$ whenever the persistence of cash revenues exceeds the per-period survival probability of the growth option ($\gamma > \Phi(\kappa_*)$); otherwise, $\lim_{s \to \infty} \left\{ \frac{E_\tau[\phi ox_{\tau+s} - c_{\tau+s}]}{E_\tau[V_{\tau+s}]} \right\}$ may be greater or less than unity depending on the accounting system. Therefore, if the likelihood of the growth option's survival is big enough, permanent earnings are not a sufficient valuation attribute even in the infinite long run. A weighted average of earnings forecasts is necessary to span the valuation function in the anticipated presence of a growth option.

These results offer two conceptual outcomes. The first is that, within a large class of linear accounting policies (Π_1) that would equate accounting earnings to economic earnings in the absence of a growth option, linear weighted averages of earnings forecasts suffice as valuation attributes in the presence of a growth option. The presence of a growth option by itself does not cause earnings nonlinearity. In the absence of an option-exercise strategy that benchmarks to trailing earnings (a mechanism not considered here), there are two potential sources of nonlinearity. The first is the relationship between the value of the option and the fundamental parameter (κ_τ) determining the payoff of the option when it is exercised. As indicated by Lemmas 1 and 2, option value is nonlinear in the fundamental parameter. The second potential source is the mapping of the option value to earnings by the accounting rules. If this mapping is nonlinear, then the earnings–value relation would be nonlinear. Distinguishing between these two sources allows us to see that the first potential source, κ_τ, is *irrelevant*; it is ultimately the accounting rules that determine the linearity of valuation functions. Therefore, just because options are frequently nonlinear in their fundamental parameter does not necessarily (or even frequently) imply that value must be nonlinear in *earnings or earnings forecasts*.

The second possible outcome is that the presence of a growth option changes the relationship between long-run earnings growth and the weight parameter α in the weighted-average valuation formula. When the only available positive NPV investment is the growth option, Proposition 1 states that $\alpha = \frac{R}{R - \Phi(\kappa_*)}$.

Since $\lim_{s \to \infty} \frac{E_\tau[ox_{\tau+s}]}{E_\tau[ox_{\tau+s-1}]} = \max\{\gamma, \Phi(\kappa_*)\}$ by Proposition 2, α does not relate to long-run earnings growth if the option survival probability, $\Phi(\kappa_*)$, exceeds the persistence γ of cash outflows from in-place assets. This observation may have a bearing on empirical studies that use the Ohlson–Juettner-Nauroth framework and assume α relates to long-run expected earnings growth.

Notes

1. The addition principle fails if, and only if, the assets in place and the new option are synergistic. For instance, if the exercise of the new option is contingent on the performance of the assets in place or if the firm faces binding project selection constraints, then the value of the option depends on cash flows from assets in place. Yee (2000) offers an example of a closed-form solution when the addition principle fails.
2. Indeed, I will demonstrate in this article that price–earnings relations are linear in the presence of growth options under a large class of linear accounting policies.
3. Earnings-based compensation and other agency effects, which will not be considered here, are other mechanisms that might cause option value to depend on trailing earnings (e.g. Glover, 2001; Govindaraj and Ramakrishnan, 2001). I will also not consider financing constraints, another mechanism that might induce a relationship between trailing earnings and option exercise: a cash-constrained firm may be unable to finance desired growth following several periods of disappointing earnings.
4. G. Zhang (2000) also assumes equation (12.2) with stochastic κ_τ. However, G. Zhang imposes the additional condition that $\Phi_\tau = \begin{cases} 1 & \tau = t-1 \\ 0 & \tau \geq t+1 \end{cases}$, if t is the current date. This means the Zhang option expires at $\tau = t + 1$ whether the firm exercises it or not. In other words, Zhang's option is a *one-period* European option rather than a perpetual option as I have here.
5. Equation (12.2), the value of γ and all realized values of $\{cr_\tau, ci_\tau, \Theta_\tau, \kappa_\tau, \varepsilon_\tau\}$ are assumed to be common knowledge.
6. The other common rationale for deferring investment, the 'bad news principle' (Bernanke, 1983), does not apply to this growth option because the value of the project does not depend on subsequent values of κ_τ once the investment has been made.
7. One might question whether the NPV formula applies to operating assets and cash flows, since firm-specific assets are not individually traded and priced in financial markets. This issue has been addressed at length in existing literature. Equation (12.3) is valid if capital markets are complete enough that the presence of the project and associated growth options does not alter the investment opportunity set available to investors (Dixit and Pindyck, 1994). In equation (12.3) – which is also the basis of the DCF approach in capital budgeting – R is one plus the risk-free rate. If investors are risk averse, this seemingly restrictive assumption prevails if all risk has been diversified away or if expectation values are adjusted to incorporate a premium for undiversified risk (Cox and Ross, 1976; Rubinstein, 1976).
8. Economic earnings are defined as $e_\tau = V_t + c_\tau - V_{\tau-1}$. This implies that $V_\tau = \dfrac{\phi \overline{e}_{\tau,1}}{R}$.
9. To see that there is no investment-rule-independent triplet $\{\delta_2, \delta_3, \delta_\Theta\}$ that solves the stated constraint, assume $\{\delta_2, \delta_3, \delta_\Theta\}$ do not depend on κ_*. Taking the derivative with respect to κ_* of the constraint yields $-\delta_2 \kappa_* + (1 - \delta_3) + \dfrac{\delta_\Theta}{I} = \dfrac{rg'(\kappa_*)}{I\phi(\kappa_*)}$. The right-hand side of this expression is nonlinear in κ_* while, if $\{\delta_2, \delta_3, \delta_\Theta\}$ are all κ_* independent, the left-hand side is linear in κ_*. Therefore, the constraint is incompatible with investment-rule-independent $\{\delta_2, \delta_3, \delta_\Theta\}$.

10. $V_\tau = \dfrac{\phi \overline{ox}^c_{\tau,1}}{R} + G\Theta_\tau$ for all τ and the no-arbitrage relation (stated in the Proof of Lemma 1) imply $\left(\overline{ox}^c_{\tau,2} - R\overline{ox}^c_{\tau,1}\right) = (R\Theta_\tau - E_\tau[\Theta_{\tau+1}])rG$. Since $E_\tau[\Theta_{\tau+1}] = \Phi(\kappa_*)\Theta_\tau$, this implies $G\Theta_\tau = \dfrac{\overline{ox}^c_{\tau,2} - R\overline{ox}^c_{\tau,1}}{(R - \Phi(\kappa_*))r}$. Placing this expression for $G\Theta_\tau$ into V_τ yields $V_\tau = (1-\alpha)\dfrac{\phi\overline{ox}^c_{\tau,1}}{R} + \alpha\dfrac{\phi\overline{ox}^c_{\tau,2}}{R^2}$ with $\alpha = \dfrac{R}{R - \Phi(\kappa_*)}$.

11. Proposition 2 will show that OJ's payout ratio assumption, $\dfrac{E_\tau[ox_{\tau+s}]}{E_\tau[cr_{\tau+s} - ci_{\tau+s}]} \leq \dfrac{R-1}{R-g}$, is also violated when $\Phi(\kappa_*) > \gamma$.

12. The following assumptions suffice to establish this formula: the clean surplus relation, equation (12.3), $0 < H < R$, and the existence (finiteness) of the following limits: H, BP, and $\lim_{s\to\infty} \dfrac{E_\tau[c_{\tau+s}]}{E_\tau[V_{\tau+s}]}$. Since $E_\tau[V_{\tau+s}] \overset{s\to\infty}{\rightarrow} 0$ for the growth option model, these limits provide binding constraints on the accounting system. In his paper, X.J. Zhang (2000) analyzes only the growth firm case ($H \geq 1$), but the idea of his analysis applies even when $0 < H < 1$, which is the relevant situation here.

13. The reason BP diverges is because $E_\tau[V_{\tau+s}] \overset{s\to\infty}{\rightarrow} 0$ while $E[oa_{\tau+s}] \overset{s\to\infty}{\rightarrow} oa_\tau + \sum_{u=1}^{\infty} E[ox_{\tau+u} - c_{\tau+u}] - \sum_{u=s+1}^{\infty} E[ox_{\tau+u} - c_{\tau+u}]$ does not typically vanish. On the right-hand side of the expression for $E[oa_{\tau+s}]$, oa_τ is a thus-far unspecified initial condition and $\sum_{u=1}^{\infty} E[ox_{\tau+u} - c_{\tau+u}] \neq 0$ by calculation. If one *defines* the accounting system so that $oa_\tau = -\sum_{u=1}^{\infty} E[ox_{\tau+u} - c_{\tau+u}]$, then $E[oa_{\tau+s}] \overset{s\to\infty}{\rightarrow} 0$. Then BP does converge, and equation (12.12) applies. In this accounting system, one can show that $BP = 1$ only if $\gamma > \Phi(\kappa_*)$.

14. Net realized return $\dfrac{\kappa_\tau I}{R-\gamma} - I$ is not necessarily negative even if $\kappa_* < R - \gamma$ because the threshold-κ_* rule stipulates only that the firm exercises whenever $\kappa_\tau < \kappa_*$. Since the value of κ_τ is random, its realized value upon exercise will exceed the threshold value κ_*, sometimes significantly. Hence, $\dfrac{\kappa_\tau I}{R-\gamma} - I$ may often be positive even if $\kappa_* < R - \gamma$.

15. By Bayes' rule, $E\left[\dfrac{\kappa I}{R-\gamma} - I \mid \kappa > \kappa_*\right] = \dfrac{\int_{\kappa_*}^{\kappa_{\max}} dk\phi(k)\left\{\dfrac{kI}{R-\gamma} - I\right\}}{1 - \Phi(\kappa_*)}$.

References

Ashton, D., Cooke, T., and Tippett, M. (2003). An Aggregation Theorem for the Valuation of Equity Under Linear Information Dynamics. *Journal of Business Finance and Accounting*, 30(3–4):413–440.

Bernanke, B. (1983). Irreversibility, Uncertainty, and Cyclical Investment. *Quarterly Journal of Economics*, 98(1):85–106.

Brealey, R. and Myers, S. (2002). *Principles of Corporate Finance.* McGraw-Hill, New York.

Burgstahler, D. and Dichev, I. (1997). Earnings, Adaptation, and Equity Value. *Accounting Review,* 72(2):187–215.

Cox, J. and Ross, S. (1976). The Valuation of Options for Alternative Stochastic Processes. *Journal of Financial Economics,* 3(1–2):145–166.

Dixit, A. and Pindyck, R. (1994). *Investment under Uncertainty.* Princeton University Press, Princeton, NJ.

Feltham, G. and Ohlson, J. (1996). Uncertainty Resolution and the Theory of Depreciation Measurement. *Journal of Accounting Research,* 32(2):209–234.

Glover, J. (2001). The Option Value to Waiting Created by a Control Problem. *Journal of Accounting Research,* 39(3):405–415.

Gietzmann, M. and Ostaszewski, A. (2004). An Alternative to the Feltham–Ohlson Valuation Framework: Using q-Theoretic Income to Predict Firm Value. *Accounting and Business Research,* 34(4):301–331.

Govindaraj, S. and Ramakrishnan, R. (2001). Accounting Earnings Processes, Inter-temporal Incentives, and their Implications for Valuation. *Review of Accounting Studies,* 6(4):427–457.

Healy, P., Myers, S., and Howe, C. (2002). R&D Accounting and the Tradeoff Between Relevance and Objectivity. *Journal of Accounting Research,* 40(3):677–710.

Kulatiklaka, N. and Perotti, E. (1998). Strategic Growth Options. *Management Science,* 44(8):1021–1031.

Liu, J. and Ohlson, J. (2000). The Feltham–Ohlson (1996) Model: Empirical Implications. *Journal of Accounting, Auditing and Finance,* 15(3):321–331.

Myers, S. (1987). Finance Theory and Financial Strategy. *Midland Corporate Finance Journal,* 5(1):6–13.

Ohlson, J. (2001). Earnings, Book Value, and Dividends: An Empirical Perspective. *Contemporary Accounting Research,* 18(1):107–120.

Ohlson, J. and Juettner-Nauroth, B. (2005). Expected EPS and EPS Growth as Determinants of Value. *Review of Accounting Studies,* 10(2–3):323–347.

Ohlson, J. and Zhang, X.J. (1998). Accrual Accounting and Equity Valuation. *Journal of Accounting Research,* 36(Suppl.):85–111.

Paddock, J., Siegel, D., and Smith, J. (1988). Option Valuation of Claims on Real Assets: The Case of Offshore Petroleum Leases. *Quarterly Journal of Economics,* 103(3):479–508.

Rubinstein, M. (1976). The Valuation of Uncertain Income Streams and the Pricing of Options. *Bell Journal of Economics,* 7(2):407–425.

Schwartz, E. and Moon, M. (2000). Rational Pricing of Internet Companies. *Financial Analysts Journal,* 56(3):62–75.

Yee, K. (2000). Opportunities Knocking: Residual Income Valuation of an Adaptive Firm. *Journal of Accounting, Auditing and Finance,* 15(3):225–266.

Yee, K. (2004a). Forward Versus Trailing Earnings in Equity Valuation. *Review of Accounting Studies,* 9(2–3):301–329.

Yee, K. (2004b). Perspectives: Combining Value Estimates to Increase Accuracy. *Financial Analysts Journal,* 60(4):23–28.

Yee, K. (2005). Aggregation, Dividend Irrelevancy, and Earnings–Value Relations. *Contemporary Accounting Research,* 22(2):453–480.

Zhang, G. (2000). Accounting Information, Capital Investment Decisions, and Equity Valuation: Theory and Empirical Implications. *Journal of Accounting Research*, 38(2):271–295.
Zhang, X. J. (2000). Conservative Accounting and Equity Valuation. *Journal of Accounting and Economics*, 29(2):125–149.

Appendix

12.A1 Option value g(k*) pertaining to constant density

Figure 12.1 depicts the value of $g(k_*)$ in the special case that $\phi(\kappa) = 1/\kappa_{max}$ with support on the interval $[0,\kappa_{max}]$. If $\phi(\kappa) = 1/\kappa_{max}$, brute force computation yields $g(\kappa_*) = \left(\frac{\kappa_{max} - \kappa_*}{R\kappa_{max} - \kappa_*}\right)\left\{\frac{\kappa_{max} + \kappa_*}{2(R-\gamma)} - 1\right\}I$. The function $g(k_*)$ is depicted in Figure 12.1 for two different values of κ_{max}. As shown, $g(k_*)$ is a concave function that rises to a maximum and then falls to $g(k_*) = 0$. The following three features are instructive:

- In Figure 12.1, $R - \gamma = 0.2$. Under the NPV decision rule, the firm would exercise its option as soon as $\frac{\kappa_\tau I}{R-\gamma} > I$. Accordingly, the NPV decision rule is equivalent to the threshold-κ_* rule with $\kappa_* = \kappa_{NPV} \equiv R - \gamma = 0.2$. But, as depicted in Figure 12.1, $g(k_*)$ achieves its maximum, not at $\kappa_* < \kappa_{NPV} = 0.2$, but at some larger value. The option is worth more if the firm demands a larger threshold than that stipulated by the NPV rule.
- For threshold-κ_* rules with thresholds $\kappa_* < \kappa_{NPV}$, the net return realized at exercise *may* be negative[14]. In Figure 12.1, $g(k_*)$ is negative if threshold κ_* is sufficiently less than $\kappa_{NPV} = 0.2$. $g(k_*)$ achieves its maximum somewhere between $\kappa_* = \kappa_{NPV}$ and $\kappa_{NPV} = \kappa_{max}$. Since the probability that $\kappa_\tau = \kappa_{max}$ is zero, the firm would have to wait forever under the threshold-κ_* investment rule, so $g(\kappa_{max}) = 0$.
- The more volatile κ_τ is, the more upside potential the growth option has. Accordingly, $g(k_*)$ increases when κ_τ is more volatile. In this example, the variance of κ_τ equals $\kappa^2_{max}/12$. Accordingly, as depicted in Figure 12.1, $g(k_*)$ for the $\kappa_{max} = 0.35$ distribution is strictly greater than $g(k_*)$ for the $\kappa_{max} = 0.28$ distribution.

12.A2 Proofs of Observations, Lemmas, and Propositions

Proof of Lemma 1. Equation (12.3) implies the no-arbitrage relation:

$$RV(\Theta_\tau,cr_\tau,ci_\tau,\kappa_\tau;\kappa_*) = E_\tau[cr_{\tau+1} - ci_{\tau+1} + V(\Theta_{\tau+1},cr_{\tau+1},ci_{\tau+1},\kappa_{\tau+1};\kappa_*)].$$

When $\Theta_\tau = 0$, the firm has no more options, which implies $\Theta_{\tau+1}$ and $ci_{\tau+1} = 0$ regardless of the value of $\kappa_{\tau+1}$. This means the no-arbitrage relation reduces to:

$$RV(0,cr_\tau,ci_\tau,\kappa_\tau;\kappa_*) = E_\tau[cr_{\tau+1} + V(0,cr_{\tau+1},ci_{\tau+1},\kappa_{\tau+1};\kappa_*)].$$

One can verify that the Feltham and Ohlson (1996) valuation function

$$V(0,cr_\tau,ci_\tau,\kappa_\tau;\kappa_*) = \frac{\gamma cr_\tau + \kappa_\tau ci_\tau}{R-\gamma} = \frac{E_\tau[cr_{\tau+1}]}{R-\gamma}$$

solves this equation. If the firm exercises its option during period τ, then $ci_\tau = I$; otherwise, $ci_\tau = 0$.

When $\Theta_\tau = 1$, we know the firm did not exercise its option during period τ or before (because Θ_τ would be zero if it did). Hence, $\Theta_\tau = 1$ implies $ci_\tau = 0$. The firm will make an investment of $ci_{\tau+1} = I$ if $\kappa_{\tau+1} > \kappa_*$ and $ci_{\tau+1} = 0$ otherwise. If the firm makes the $ci_{\tau+1} = I$ investment, then $\Theta_{\tau+1} = 0$; if not, then $\Theta_{\tau+1} = 1$. This means equation (12.3) reduces to:

$$\begin{aligned} RV(1,cr_\tau,ci_\tau = 0,\kappa_\tau;\kappa_*) &= E_\tau[cr_{\tau+1} - cr_{\tau+1} + V(\Theta_{\tau+1},crt_{\tau+1},ci_{\tau+1},\kappa_{\tau+1};\kappa_*)] \\ &= \gamma cr_\tau + E_\tau[V(1,\gamma cr_\tau,0,\kappa_{\tau+1};\kappa_*)\,|\kappa_{\tau+1} \leq \kappa_*]\Pr(\kappa_{\tau+1} \leq \kappa_*) \\ &\quad + E_\tau[V(0,\gamma cr_\tau,N,\kappa_{\tau+1};\kappa_*) - I|\kappa_{\tau+1} > \kappa_*]\Pr(\kappa_{\tau+1} > \kappa_*). \end{aligned}$$

Plugging in the trial solution $V(\Theta_\tau,cr_\tau,ci_\tau,\kappa_\tau;\kappa_*) = \dfrac{\gamma cr_\tau + \kappa_\tau ci_\tau}{R-\gamma} + g(\kappa_*)\Theta_\tau$ and canceling out all the cr_τ terms yield $Rg(\kappa_*) = g(\kappa_*)\int_0^{\kappa_*} \mathrm{d}k\phi(k) + I\int_{\kappa_*}^{\kappa_{\max}} \mathrm{d}k\phi(k) \left\{\dfrac{k}{R-\gamma} - 1\right\}$. Rearranging this equation yields the expression for $g(\kappa_*)$ given in the Lemma.

Alternatively, the expression for $g(\kappa_*)$ can be heuristically derived and understood as follows. First, $g(\kappa_{\max}) = 0$ because, if $\kappa_* = \kappa_{\max}$, the growth option will never be exercised since the threshold is set too high to be attained with positive probability. At the other extreme, if $\kappa_* = 0$, the option will be exercised with certainty next period. Accordingly, the value of the growth option under the threshold-0 rule is the expected discounted value of making the investment next period: $g(0) = \frac{I}{R}\int_0^{\kappa_{\max}} dk\phi(k)\left\{\frac{k}{R-\gamma} - 1\right\}$. More generally, $g(\kappa_*)$ equals the expected NPV of exercising the first time that $\kappa_\tau > \kappa_*$. The probability that $\kappa_\tau \leq \kappa_*$ for $s - 1$ consecutive periods and then $\kappa_\tau > \kappa_*$ the immediately subsequent period is $[\Phi(\kappa_*)]^{s-1}[1-\Phi(\kappa_*)]$. Hence, the expected discounted value of free cash flows from the option, which in accordance with the threshold-κ_* investment rule might be exercised any period s in the future, is:

$$g(\kappa_*) = \sum_{s=1}^{\infty} R^{-s}[\Phi(\kappa_*)]^{s-1}[1 - \Phi(\kappa_*)]E\left[\frac{\kappa I}{R-\gamma} - I|\kappa > \kappa_*\right].$$

$E\left[\frac{\kappa I}{R-\gamma} - I|\kappa > \kappa_*\right]$ is the expected net return upon exercise conditional on[15] $\kappa_\tau > \kappa_*$. Performing the sum, which can be done in closed form here because $E\left[\frac{\kappa I}{R-\gamma} - I|\kappa > \kappa_*\right]$ does not depend on s, recovers the expression for $g(\kappa_*)$ stated in Lemma 1.

Proof of Lemma 2. Start from Lemma 1. The derivative of $g(\kappa_*)$ with respect to threshold value is:

$$\frac{\partial g(\kappa_*)}{\partial \kappa_*} = \frac{I\phi(k_*)}{(R - \Phi(k_*))^2}\left\{\int_{\kappa_*}^{\kappa_{\max}} dk\,\phi(k)\left\{\frac{k}{R-\gamma} - 1\right\} - (R - \Phi(\kappa_*))\left\{\frac{\kappa_*}{\mathrm{R}-\gamma} - 1\right\}\right\}.$$

Setting $\frac{\partial g(\kappa_*)}{\partial \kappa_*} = 0$ yields the first order condition (FOC) for the optimal value $\kappa^\cdot$ of κ_*. Recalling that $g(\kappa_*) = \left(\frac{I}{R - \Phi(\kappa_*)}\right)\left\{\int_{\kappa_*}^{\kappa_{\max}} dk\,\phi(k)\left\{\frac{k}{R-\gamma} - 1\right\}\right\}$ and rearranging the FOC yields the expression for $g(\kappa^\cdot)$ given in the Proposition. One must also verify that $\frac{\partial^2 g(\kappa_*)}{\partial \kappa_*^2}\Big|_{\kappa_* = \kappa^\cdot} < 0$ to be assured that $\kappa^\cdot$ maximizes the value of the growth option. Calculation yields $\frac{\partial^2 g(\kappa_*)}{\partial \kappa_*^2}\Big|_{\kappa_* = \kappa^\cdot} = -\frac{I\phi(\kappa_*)}{(R - \Phi(\kappa_*))(R-\gamma)} < 0$.

Proof of Observation 1. Comparing the expression for V_τ in Lemma 1 to $\phi \overline{ox}^{c}_{\tau,0}$, where equation (12.5) defines ox_τ, and requiring $V_\tau = \phi \overline{ox}^{c}_{\tau,0}$ for all values of $\{oa_{\tau-1}, cr_\tau, \kappa_\tau ci_\tau, ci_\tau, \Theta_\tau\}$, yields five conditions on the accounting policy parameters $\{\delta_0, \delta_1, \delta_2, \delta_3, \delta_\Theta\}$:

$$(1 - \delta_0) = 0$$
$$\phi(1 + \delta_1) - 1 = \frac{\gamma}{R - \gamma}$$
$$\phi\delta_2 = \frac{1}{\mathrm{R} - \gamma}$$
$$\phi(1 - \delta_3) - 1 = 0$$
$$\phi\delta_\Theta = \gamma(\kappa_*).$$

The unique solution to these five conditions is $\Pi = \left\{1, -\left(\frac{1-\gamma}{R-\gamma}\right), \frac{R-1}{(R-\gamma)R}, \frac{1}{R}, \phi^{-1}g(\kappa_*)\right\}$. On the other hand, equating the expression for V_τ in Lemma 1 to $\frac{\phi \overline{ox}^{c}_{\tau,1}}{R}$ and requiring equality to hold for all values of $\{oa_\tau, E_\tau[cr_{\tau+1}], \kappa_\tau ci_\tau, ci_\tau, \Theta_\tau\}$ yields (only) three conditions on the accounting policy parameters $\{\delta_0, \delta_1, \delta_2, \delta_3, \delta_\Theta\}$:

$$1 - \delta_0 = 0$$
$$\frac{1 + \delta_1}{R - 1} = \frac{1}{R - \gamma}$$
$$\delta_2 \int_{\kappa_*}^{\kappa_{\max}} dk\phi(k)k - (1 - \delta_3)\int_{\kappa_*}^{\kappa_{\max}} dk\phi(k) + \delta_\Theta \frac{\Phi(\kappa_*)}{I} = r\frac{g(\kappa_*)}{I}.$$

Any policy of the form $\Pi = \left\{1, -\left(\frac{1-\gamma}{R-\gamma}\right), \delta_2, \delta_3, \delta_\Theta\right\}$, where $\{\delta_2, \delta_3, \delta_\Theta\}$ is any triplet that satisfies the last condition, solves these conditions. The following identities were used to derive the last condition: $E_\tau[\Theta_{\tau+1}] = \Phi(\kappa_*)\Theta_\tau$, $E_\tau[ci_{\tau+1}] = (1 - \Phi(\kappa_*))I\Theta_\tau$, and $E_\tau[\kappa_{\tau+1} ci_\tau + 1] = \int_{\kappa_*}^{\kappa_{\max}} dk\phi(k)kI\Theta_\tau$.

Proof of Observation 2. Under accounting policy Π_0, $ox_\tau = \left(\frac{R-1}{R-\gamma}\right)cr_\tau$ or, equivalently, $\frac{\phi ox_{\tau+1}}{R} = \frac{cr_{\tau+1}}{\mathrm{R} - \gamma}$. Taking the expectation value of both sides yields

$$V_\tau = \frac{\phi \overline{ox}^{c}_{\tau,1}}{R} + g(\kappa_*)\Theta_\tau.$$

Proof of Proposition 1. Under accounting policy $\Pi_1 = \left\{1, -\left(\frac{1-\gamma}{R-\gamma}\right), \delta_2, \delta_3, \delta_\Theta\right\}$, equations (12.2), (12.3), and (12.5), and a threshold-κ_* investment rule, imply:

$$E_\tau[ox_{\tau+s}] = \left(\frac{R-1}{R-\gamma}\right) E_\tau[cr_{\tau+s}]$$

$$+ \left\{ \delta_2 \int_{\kappa_*}^{\kappa_{\max}} dk\, \phi(k)k - (1-\delta_3) \int_{\kappa_*}^{\kappa_{\max}} dk\, \phi(k) + \delta_\Theta \frac{\Phi(\kappa_*)}{I} \right\}$$

$$\Phi^{s-1}(\kappa_*) I \Theta_\tau,$$

where $E_\tau[cr_{\tau+s}] = \gamma^s cr_\tau + \left(\frac{\gamma^s + \Phi^s(\kappa_*)}{\gamma + \Phi(\kappa_*)}\right) \frac{\int_{\kappa_*}^{\kappa_{\max}} dk\, \phi(k)k}{\Phi(\kappa_*) I \Theta_t}$ for all $s \geq 1$. (To derive these expressions, the following identities are used: $E_\tau[\Theta_{\tau+s}] = \Theta^s(\kappa_*)\Theta_t$, $E_\tau[ci_{\tau+s}] = (1-\Phi(\kappa_*))\Phi^{s-1}(\kappa_*) I \Phi_\tau$, and $E_\tau[\kappa_{\tau+s}, ci_{\tau+s}] = \int_{\kappa_*}^{\kappa_{\max}} dk\, \phi(k)k\, \Phi^{s-1}(\kappa_*) I \Phi_\tau$, for all $s \geq 1$.) The expression for V_τ in Lemma 1 equals $(1-\alpha)\frac{\phi \overline{ox}^c_{\tau,1}}{R} + \alpha \frac{\phi \overline{ox}^c_{\tau,2}}{R^2}$ for all values of $\{oa_\tau, E_\tau[cr_{\tau+1}], \kappa_\tau ci_\tau, ci_\tau, \Theta_\tau\}$ if, and only if,

$$\frac{\alpha I}{R} \int_{\kappa_*}^{\kappa_{\max}} dk \phi(\kappa) \left\{ \frac{k}{R-\gamma} - 1 \right\} = \gamma(\kappa_*)$$

$$\left\{ \delta_2 \int_{\kappa_*}^{\kappa_{\max}} dk\, \phi(\kappa)\, k - (1-\delta_3) \int_{\kappa_*}^{\kappa_{\max}} dk\, \phi(\kappa) + \delta_\Theta \frac{\Phi(\kappa_*)}{I} \right\} \left\{ 1 - \alpha + \frac{\alpha}{R} \Phi(\kappa_*) \right\} = 0$$

The first condition requires $\alpha = \frac{R}{R - \Phi(\kappa_*)}$. When $\alpha = \frac{R}{R - \Phi(\kappa_*)}$, the second condition is automatically satisfied *regardless of the values of* $\{\delta_2, \delta_3, \delta_\Theta\}$.

A direct way to see why the weighted average obtains independent of the accounting policy parameters $\{\delta_2, \delta_3, \delta_\Theta\}$ is to examine the expression for the implied forward earnings, $E_\tau[ox_{\tau+s}]$, given above. Only the second term of the expression for $E_\tau[ox_{\tau+s}]$ depends on $\{\delta_2, \delta_3, \delta_\Theta\}$. Hence, the weighted average $(1-\alpha)\ \frac{\phi \overline{ox}^c_{\tau,1}}{R} + \frac{\phi \overline{ox}^c_{\tau,2}}{R^2}$ depends on $\{\delta_2, \delta_3, \delta_\Theta\}$ only through the weighted average of the second term of $E_\tau[ox_{\tau+s}]$, which simplifies to:

$$\left\{ \delta_2 \int_{\kappa_*}^{\kappa_{\max}} dk\, \phi(k)k - (1-\delta_3) \int_{\kappa_*}^{\kappa_{\max}} dk\, \phi(k)k + \delta_\Theta \frac{\Phi(\kappa_*)}{R} \right\} \left[(1-\alpha) + \alpha \frac{\Phi(\kappa_*)}{R} \right] \frac{I}{r} \Theta_\tau.$$

The factor in brackets $\left(\left[(1-\alpha)+\alpha\frac{\Phi(\kappa_*)}{R}\right]\right)$ vanishes identically when $\alpha=\frac{R}{R-\Phi(\kappa_*)}$ independent of $\{\delta_2,\delta_3,\delta_\Theta\}$.

Proof of Proposition 2. Taking the $s\to\infty$ limit of equations (12.10) and (12.11) yields:

$$\lim_{s\to\infty} E_\tau[cr_{\tau+s}] = \begin{cases} \gamma^s\left\{cr_\tau + \dfrac{\int_{\kappa_*}^{\kappa_{max}} \mathrm{d}k\,\phi(k)k}{(\gamma-\Phi(\kappa_*))\Phi(\kappa_*)} I\Theta_t\right\} & \gamma>\Phi(k_*) \\ \gamma^s\left\{cr_\tau + \dfrac{\int_{\kappa_*}^{\kappa_{max}} \mathrm{d}k\,\phi(k)k}{\Phi(\kappa_*)\gamma} sI\Theta_t\right\} & \gamma=\Phi(k_*) \\ \Phi^s(\kappa_*)\dfrac{\int_{\kappa_*}^{\kappa_{max}} \mathrm{d}k\,\phi(k)k}{(\Phi(\kappa_*)-\gamma)\Phi(\kappa_*)} I\Theta_\tau & \gamma<\Phi(k_*) \end{cases}$$

$$\lim_{s\to\infty} E_\tau[cr_{\tau+s}] = \begin{cases} \gamma^s\left(\dfrac{R-1}{R-\gamma}\right)\left\{cr_\tau + \dfrac{\int_{\kappa_*}^{\kappa_{max}} \mathrm{d}k\,\phi(k)k}{(\gamma-\Phi(k))\Phi(\kappa_*)} I\Theta_\tau\right\} & \gamma>\Phi(\kappa_*) \\ \gamma^s\left(\dfrac{R-1}{R-\gamma}\right)\left\{cr_\tau + \dfrac{\int_{\kappa_*}^{\kappa_{max}} \mathrm{d}k\,\phi(k)k}{\Phi(\kappa_*)\gamma} sI\Theta_\tau\right\} & \gamma=\Phi(\kappa_*) \\ \Phi^{s-1}(\kappa_*)\left\{\left(\dfrac{R-1}{R-\gamma}\right)\dfrac{\int_{\kappa_*}^{\kappa_{max}} \mathrm{d}k\,\phi(k)k}{(\Phi(\kappa_*)-\gamma)} + \Lambda\right\} I\Theta_\tau & \gamma<\Phi(\kappa_*), \end{cases}$$

where $\Lambda(\delta_2,\delta_2,\delta_\Theta)$ is as given in the main text. The formulas in Proposition 2 then follow from these expressions. For instance,

$$\lim_{s\to\infty}\frac{E_\tau[V_{\tau+s}]}{E_\tau[V_{\tau+s-1}]}=\lim_{s\to\infty}\left\{\frac{\dfrac{E_\tau[cr_{\tau+s+1}]}{R-\gamma}+g(\kappa_*)E_\tau[\Theta_{\tau+s}]}{\dfrac{E_\tau[cr_{\tau+s}]}{R-\gamma}+g(\kappa_*)E_\tau[\Theta_{\tau+s-1}]}\right\},\text{ where } E_\tau[\Theta_{\tau+s}]=\Phi^s(\kappa_*)\Phi_\tau.$$

When $\gamma>\Phi(\kappa_*)$, the $E_\tau[cr_{\tau+u}]$ terms dominate in both the numerator and denominator, which implies $\lim_{s\to\infty}\frac{E_\tau[V_{\tau+s}]}{E_\tau[V_{\tau+s-1}]}=\lim_{s\to\infty}\frac{E_\tau[cr_{\tau+s+1}]}{E_\tau[cr_{\tau+s}]}=\gamma$. On the other hand, when $\gamma<\Phi(\kappa_*)$, the terms proportional to $\Phi^s(\kappa_*)$ dominate in both the numerator and denominator, which implies $\lim_{s\to\infty}\frac{E_\tau[V_{\tau+s}]}{E_\tau[V_{\tau+s-1}]}=\Phi(\kappa_*)$. When $\gamma=\Phi(\kappa_*)$, the numerator is proportional to $\Phi^s(\kappa_*)=\gamma^s$ while the denominator is proportional to $\Phi^{s-1}(\kappa_*)=\gamma^{s-1}$. Hence, $\lim_{s\to\infty}\frac{E_\tau[V_{\tau+s}]}{E_\tau[V_{\tau+s-1}]}=\Phi(\kappa_*)=\gamma$.

Proof of Proposition 3. Lemma 1 implies $E_\tau[V_{\tau+s}]=\frac{E_\tau[cr_{\tau+s+1}]}{R-\gamma}+g(\kappa_*)E_\tau[\Theta_{\tau+s}]$. Applying $E_\tau[ci_{\tau+s}]=\left(\frac{1-\Phi(k_*)}{\Phi(\kappa_*)}\right)I\,E\tau[\Phi_{\tau+s}]$ to equation (12.10) yields:

$$E_\tau[\phi ox_{\tau+s}-c_{\tau+s}]=\frac{E_\tau[cr_{\tau+s+1}]}{R-\gamma}-\frac{I}{\Phi(\kappa_*)}\left\{\int_{\kappa_*}^{\kappa_{\max}}dk\,\phi(k)\left\{\frac{k}{\mathrm{R}-\gamma}-1\right\}-\phi\Lambda\right\}E_\tau[\Theta_{\tau+s}].$$

Identifying part of the term in brackets with $g(\kappa_*)=\left(\frac{I}{R-\Phi(\kappa_*)}\right)\int_{\kappa_*}^{\kappa_{\max}}dk\,\phi(k)\left\{\frac{k}{R-\gamma}-1\right\}$ yields:

$$E_\tau[\phi ox_{\tau+s}-c_{\tau+s}]=E_\tau[V_{\tau+s}]+\{\phi\Lambda I-Rg(\kappa_*)\}\frac{E_\tau[\Theta_{\tau+s}]}{\Phi(\kappa_*)}.$$

Since $E_\tau[\Phi_{\tau+s}] = \Phi^s(\kappa_*)\Phi_\tau$, the second term of $E_\tau[\phi ox_{\tau+s} - c_{\tau+s}]$ falls off like $\Phi^s(\kappa_*)$ when $s\rightarrow\infty$. In comparison, Lemma 1 implies:

$$\lim_{s\rightarrow\infty} E_\tau[V_{\tau+s}] \sim \begin{cases} \left(\dfrac{\gamma^{s+1}}{R-\gamma}\right)\left\{cr_\tau + \dfrac{\int_{\kappa_*}^{\kappa_{\max}} dk\, \phi(k)k}{(\gamma - \Phi(\kappa_*))\Phi(\kappa_*)} I\Phi_\tau\right\} & \gamma > \Phi(\kappa_*) \\ \gamma^s\left\{\dfrac{\gamma cr_\tau}{R-\gamma} + g(\kappa_*)\Phi_\tau\right\} & \gamma = \Phi(\kappa_*) \\ \Phi^s(\kappa_*)\left\{\dfrac{\int_{\kappa_*}^{\kappa_{\max}} dk\, \phi(k)k}{(R - \gamma(\Phi(\kappa_*) - \gamma)} I + g(\kappa_*)\right\}\Phi_\tau & \gamma < \Phi(\kappa_*). \end{cases}$$

Comparing the expressions for $E_\tau[\phi ox_{\tau+s} - c_{\tau+s}]$ and $\lim_{s\rightarrow\infty} E_\tau[V_{\tau+s}]$ yields:

$$\lim_{s\rightarrow\infty} E_\tau[\phi ox_{\tau+s} - c_{\tau+s}] \sim \begin{cases} E_\tau[V_{\tau+s}] & \gamma \geq \Phi(\kappa_*) \\ \left\{\dfrac{\int_{\kappa_*}^{\kappa_{\max}} dk\, \phi(k)k}{(R - \gamma(\Phi(\kappa_*) - \gamma)} I + g(\kappa_*) + \left(\dfrac{\phi\Lambda I - Rg(\kappa_*)}{\Phi(\kappa_*)}\right)\right\}\Phi^s(\kappa_*)\Theta_\tau & \gamma < \Phi(\kappa_*). \end{cases}$$

Dividing both sides by $\lim_{s\rightarrow\infty} E_\tau[V_{\tau+s}]$ yields the desired result.

13

The True Cost of Employee Share Options: The Recent Debate and Potential Costs for a Case Study Firm

Colette Grey, Derry Cotter, and Edel Barnes

13.1 Introduction

Until publication of Financial Reporting Standard No. 20, which specifies the accounting treatment to be adopted by entities making share-based payments[1], with accounting periods beginning on or after 1 January 2005 for listed entities (and 1 January 2006 for unlisted entities), no compensation expense was recorded for employee share options (ESOs) if the exercise price on the date of grant was equal to (or greater than) the market price of the shares at that time, a differential referred to as intrinsic value. Intrinsic value, accounted for as an expense, is any excess of the market price of a share over the exercise price of the option at the date of grant. However, use of ESOs is widespread and there is both evidence that their use increased substantially during the dotcom bubble and some speculation that favorable financial reporting treatment precipitated this trend (Matsunaga, 1995). This is particularly the case for the high-tech and startup sectors, which rely on the provision of stock options to attract and retain skilled employees, where frequently revenues and cash flow are sufficiently low to make purely cash-based payment unattractive. The ability to avoid the recognition of compensation expense reduces the perceived cost of granting ESOs and overall employment expense in consequence. O'Sullivan (2002) contends, for example, that a requirement to expense ESOs could have hit US company profits generally by approximately 9%, the impact on the high-technology sector alone being closer to 33%. This suggests that a requirement to recognize compensation expense for ESOs is likely to reduce their use for some firms. Heretofore, a firm that expected reported income to be low could have reduced reported compensation expense under the recent liberal financial reporting regime, by substituting ESOs for other forms of compensation, an approach no longer feasible. Despite limitations to the study, Matsunaga postulates:

> 'The current financial reporting rules pertaining to employee stock options (ESOs) affect the compensation practices of some firms. ... results support a positive relation between the use of ESOs and the firm's reliance on income-increasing accounting methods, and a negative relation between the extent [to which] a firm is below its target income level and the use of ESOs.'
>
> (Matsunaga, 1995, p. 23)

It is widely recognized that providing ESOs has important financial reporting incentives. A study on options granted to chief executive officers in Canada concludes:

> 'Empirical results strongly support the importance of financial reporting incentives in determining the mix of cash and options granted to Canadian CEOs.'
>
> (Klassen and Mawani, 2000, p. 256)

In addition to financial reporting incentives, the recent accounting treatment of ESOs has implications for wider corporate finance issues. Firms that grant ESOs and avoid any charge to earnings do not expense full/true compensation costs and in consequence they artificially boost corporate earnings. It has also been argued that managers may favor share repurchases over conventional distributions in light of the documented positive share price implications of repurchases, which in turn has implications for the fair value of those managers' share options. Hill et al. (2002) suggest that corporate lobbying of the Financial Accounting Standards Board (FASB) on *Exposure Draft: Accounting for Stock-Based Compensation* (FASB, 1993) that preceded SFAS 123, *Accounting for Stock-Based Compensation* (FASB, 1995), may have been motivated by managerial concerns. These concerns center on whether mandatory expensing of ESOs might cause changes to compensation contracts, an argument that also supports a managerial self-interest hypothesis. Forcing firms to expense ESOs could have a knock-on effect on dividend, compensation, and financing policies.

The extant literature (Rouse and Barton, 1993; Samuels and Lymer, 1996; Coller and Higgs, 1997; Hemmer et al., 1999; Saly et al., 1999) is consistent in maintaining that options have value to the employee and impose a cost on the issuer. In this context, the standard-setting authorities favor fair value accounting and a consequent charge to the profit and loss account (income statement), a practice that implies that ESOs constitute an expense to reporting entities and should properly be recognized as such. In addition to intrinsic value, however, share options derive value from the possibility that underlying share values will increase before the options expire, a time value. An option's *fair value* is thus the sum of intrinsic value plus this time value. Conceptually it would be superior to measure and record compensation expense at fair value rather than at intrinsic value. The problem is that there is no clear, objective method by which to calculate fair value, and this concern was reflected in the various submissions to the ASB and FASB (and subsequently to the IASB) in respect of their proposals for accounting for share-based payments. Option pricing models are considered to offer potential measurement methods, but as these models were developed to estimate the fair value of publicly traded options, while ESOs have characteristics that distinguish them importantly from these securities, the appropriateness of some of these models may be questioned (see Maller et al., 2002).

While there is little argument about whether or not the provision of ESOs represents an expense to issuing companies, there is much greater complexity of debate regarding the issues of *what* recognition date to adopt and, in particular, *how* to measure fair value. Within this context, the two specific issues we address in this chapter are (a) *when* to recognize ESOs and (b) *how* to measure the cost to the company of these employee share options, with particular reference to the ASB (2000) proposals, which provide a useful precursor to FRS 20 (equivalent to IFRS 2) now coming into force. The ASB proposals essentially recommend that transactions involving share-based payment be measured at the fair value of the shares or share options at vesting date, while FRS 20 recommends measurement at fair value but with recognition at grant date.

The remainder of this chapter is organized around five distinct sections as follows. Section 13.2 provides a review of the extant literature in the area by examining the issues central to any study of accounting for ESOs. Section 13.3 presents a brief description of the company chosen for the case, and of the research design, while section 13.4 presents the main findings of the study. Section 13.5 places the ASB proposals in the context of the lengthy international debate on the recognition of ESOs. Section 13.6 summarizes and concludes.

13.2 Literature review

13.2.1 ESO value and accounting income

Rouse and Barton (1993) argued that the question of employee share compensation is highly controversial, mainly because it can have a potentially significant impact on financial statements and on the nature and level of employee compensation. Fixed share option plans (plans which do not incorporate a performance condition for vesting, rather depending on an employee continuing to render service to an employer for a specified period of time) typically result in no compensation expense, as they generally have no intrinsic value when granted (i.e. the exercise price is equal to market price at the date of grant). These authors recognized that, in addition to intrinsic value, stock options are likely to have a time value related to the possibility of share price increases before option expiration, so that the *fair value* of these options is likely to be positive. Since most ESOs have no intrinsic value at the grant date, Rouse and Barton concluded that a valuation approach that omits time value essentially excludes a key element of value for virtually all employee stock option plans. Not recognizing compensation expense for ESOs suggests that the options have no value or, more pertinently, that a company incurs no cost in granting them (Robbins, 1988). Arguments against the inclusion of compensation expense have centered largely on the premise that the expense is difficult to measure accurately rather than on the basis that no expense arises.

In the USA, the FASB tried to promulgate fair value accounting for ESOs and faced enormous opposition, in particular from the high-technology sector. The FASB argued that recording share options at fair value is preferable to intrinsic value for three reasons:

> 'Employee stock options have value; valuable financial instruments given to employees give rise to compensation cost that is properly included in preparing an entity's net income; and the value of employee stock options can be estimated within acceptable limits for recognition in financial statements.'
>
> (FASB, 1995, paragraph 75)

Despite the above assertions, lobbying of the FASB was such that the Board was forced to compromise, the result being that reporting entities were required to calculate a charge based on the fair value of ESOs, but were not necessarily mandated to charge that compensation expense to income. Instead, disclosure in the notes to the financial statements was deemed sufficient[2]. Samuels and Lymer (1996) addressed the accounting treatment of ESOs issued to directors, the practical problems of treating these share options as a cost, and whether the financial accounts can give a true and fair view if these costs are omitted. They argued that when a director exercises an option, the shares received could potentially have been sold in the market at a higher price than that being paid by the director. An entry should therefore appear in the financial accounts of the company recognizing the benefit received by the director and the cost to the company. These authors used case study methodology to demonstrate how ESOs could be valued and postulated that when the granting of an ESO is ignored in the accounting records of a company, the resulting financial statements cannot be said to give a 'true and fair view' of that company's performance:

> 'It can be argued that the company, in granting an ESO, is incurring a cost: an option has a value. Investors are often willing to pay to receive an option. A number of companies have an active market in options on their shares. The director is therefore being granted something of value: he or she is being given the chance of making a gain. The company therefore is incurring an opportunity cost, which can either be seen as the value of the option with its conditions if it were sold, or the present value of the difference between the exercise price of the option and the expected price of the share when it is exercised.'
>
> (Samuels and Lymer, 1996, p. 252)

Authors dating from Weygandt (1977) and Matsunaga (1995) have supported the recognition of ESOs as a compensation expense, given the practice of substituting ESOs for other compensation forms, if income is expected to be below target:

> 'Valuing stock options as the difference between the market value at the date of grant and the option price is considered by most accountants as a valuation that results in an understatement of the value of the option.'
>
> (Weygandt, 1977, p. 42)

Mozes (1998) considered the practice of measuring the value of ESOs at their intrinsic value, and concluded that virtually no option grant that is out-of-the-money on the grant date will ever be reflected in the profit and loss (income) account. An obvious shortcoming of this 'intrinsic value' approach is that it ignores the true value inherent in an option to purchase shares at a predetermined price during an extended period.

13.2.2 Recognition date

Three key dates arise in the life of ESOs – namely, the date the option is granted (grant date), the date the option vests (the time the option could first be exercised), and exercise date (the date the option is either exercised or is allowed to lapse). From an accounting perspective, entries could be made in the financial statements on any of these dates (Samuels and Lymer, 1996). Robbins (1988) maintained that valid conceptual arguments support each approach, and concluded that there is simply no way to demonstrate the superiority of one over the other two. Supporters of *grant date* measurement (e.g. Foster et al., 1991) point out that this is the date when an organization makes decisions regarding the number of options to give the employee and the terms of those options. The employer commits to the transaction at that date, because the employee, by continuing to work the required number of years, essentially has control over option exercise. Compensation measurement subsequent to the grant date would allow changes in the company's stock price to affect reported compensation expense, even though stock price changes may bear no relationship to the value of the services rendered by the employee (Robbins, 1988). Samuels and Lymer (1996) argued that the possibility that the option might never be exercised is the key reason why recognizing grant of an option at the date of grant might not represent a suitable expensing approach. They noted that, before vesting date, an options contract is a contingent liability; it becomes a full liability only when the qualifying period is complete. Prior to the vesting date, the company has no liability to the holder of the option, thus rendering the vesting date as the most appropriate time for initial entry. As with the date of grant, recording the entry at the vesting date requires an estimate of the value of the option. The argument employed in favor of use of the exercise date for value estimation is that the stock option represents a contingency until it is exercised or lapses (Robbins, 1988). Thus, the ultimate value of the option cannot be determined until the exercise date. Furthermore, exercise date measurement produces symmetry between the compensation expense recognized by the employer and the value received by the employee.

> 'A practical reason in favor of this date is that it is only at this time that the true value of the option is known. At this date the size of the benefit to the executive is known, as is the opportunity cost to the company. It is only *ex post* that the cost can be accurately measured.'
>
> (Samuels and Lymer, 1996, p. 253)

Against use of the exercise date is the argument that charging the entire *actual cost* of the option to the profit and loss account in the year the option is exercised leads to an uneven recognition of costs. If the date of grant is used the expense can be spread over time, an argument that also applies, albeit to a lesser extent, to vesting date recognition. A further problem associated with recognition at exercise date is that the cost to the company becomes dependent upon a choice made by an employee of the company.

13.2.3 Measuring fair values

In measuring compensation expense, there can be no argument but that fair value is conceptually superior to intrinsic value. However, as discussed above, the problem with the fair value approach is the lack of a clear, objective method by which to calculate it. Option pricing models were developed to value *traded options* but ESOs have characteristics that render them different from traded options, such as nontransferability and the possibility of early exercise (Coulton and Taylor, 2002, provide a useful discussion of these differences). Two option pricing models are considered by the FASB to be appropriate for valuing ESOs, the Black–Scholes (BS) option pricing model and a binomial model. The majority of companies in the USA (where disclosure, at least, of the fair value of ESOs was required) used the BS model. During discussions regarding the measurement of fair value by the G4 + 1 group (2000), it was always considered that the BS model would be used. In consequence, the ASB Discussion Paper, *Share-Based Payment* (ASB, 2000), does not prescribe the precise model to be used for option valuation, although use of the BS model is assumed. In any model, however, the following features of an option, currently accepted as relevant to its value, need to be taken into account: the share price (S), the option exercise price (X), the expected volatility of the share price (δ), dividends expected to be paid on the share (Div), the market rate of interest (r), and the term of the option (T). Intrinsic value is defined by the difference ($S - X$); the remaining four variables are relevant to the option's time value.

The ASB and subsequently the IASB argued that the quality of financial statements, and in particular their consistency and comparability, would be enhanced by adopting fair value as the basis for estimation of the value of options issued to employees. They also argued that option pricing models seem to provide the only practicable means of determining this fair value in the absence of observable market prices. To allow for the nontransferability of ESOs, the expected life should be used as a basis for calculating fair value. In addition, options forfeited prior to measurement could be excluded from the calculation (ASB, 2000). Finally, the ASB advocated vesting date measurement, the main point of difference between the ASB (2000) Discussion Paper and FRS 20 which followed it, and which recommends grant date measurement. We choose here to compare the ASB proposals (vesting date measurement) with the likely fair value at date of grant (an approach that reflects the FRS 20 (IFRS 2) recommendations), in respect of the employee share options granted in 1997 by ESAT Telecom Group plc, to assess the potential impact on income/loss of expensing ESOs for this case study company.

13.3 Case study: ESAT Telecom Group

Our empirical analysis involves an assessment of the likely effect of the ASB proposal to include, as an expense in the profit and loss account, ESOs valued at fair value on vesting date, for ESAT Telecom Group plc, together with an assessment of the potential cost of the FRS 20 recommendations which requires measurement at grant date. A key element of our approach is the inclusion of share options granted to all *employees* (as distinct from purely executives, the general focus of studies in the area) in addition to measurement at each year-end prior to vesting with final measurement at vesting date. Our chosen company ESAT Telecom Group plc, at the time of analysis, was a telecommunications company based in Dublin, Ireland, and was founded in 1991 by a group of investors to offer alternative telecommunications services in competition with the state monopoly. For the period of our analysis the company provided data, Internet access, sophisticated broadband data, and telephonic services in the Republic of Ireland.

ESAT Telecom Group plc employee share option grants (1997) provided a particularly interesting example, in the context of option expense recognition and measurement, because the firm was a high-technology entity, arguably likely to be adversely and disproportionately impacted by the proposal to expense ESOs and because all share options granted to employees during 1997 were granted at below market value. Table 13.1 describes these stock options, all of which had a term of seven years from date of grant.

The average vesting period for options granted was 1.7 years (20 months). Early exercise was anticipated with the estimated life of these options being three to five years (Offering Memorandum, 1999). Prior to vesting date, options over 638,991 ordinary shares were canceled following the cessation of employment of a number of option holders. At grant date ESAT did not have publicly traded options so it was not possible to compute an implied volatility metric, which is found to be a more precise predictor of future volatility than historical measures (Chiras and Manaster, 1978). Share prices used to calculate volatility were those quoted on the NASDAQ. It was not possible to obtain a full series of Irish share price data for the period of our study as ESAT Telecom Group plc was quoted on the Dublin Stock Exchange only for the period June 1999 to June 2000. Implicit in our approach is an assumption that the notional series of price changes on the Irish Stock Exchange would have correlated highly with that of the NASDAQ quote, and that factors driving price changes would be essentially similar for the two quotations. There was no share split between the 1997 ESO grant and vesting dates for these options.

Figure 13.1 shows weekly closing share prices of American Depository Shares (ADS $) of ESAT Telecom Group plc, quoted on the NASDAQ for the period 14 November 1997 to 30 September 2000. Given the limited period of trading in ESAT shares, it was not possible to impute historic three-year volatility measures. Clearly the rise in share price was dramatic over this period – by the earliest vesting date, market price of the shares had almost quadrupled relative to

Table 13.1 Details of ESAT Telecom Group plc 1997 share option plan

Date of grant	Number of options granted	Exercise price at grant date (IR £)
22 May 1997	1,506,031	2.4407
19 October 1997	994,613	2.4407
6 November 1997	361,400	2.4407

Source: Annual Report and Accounts (1997, p. 44).

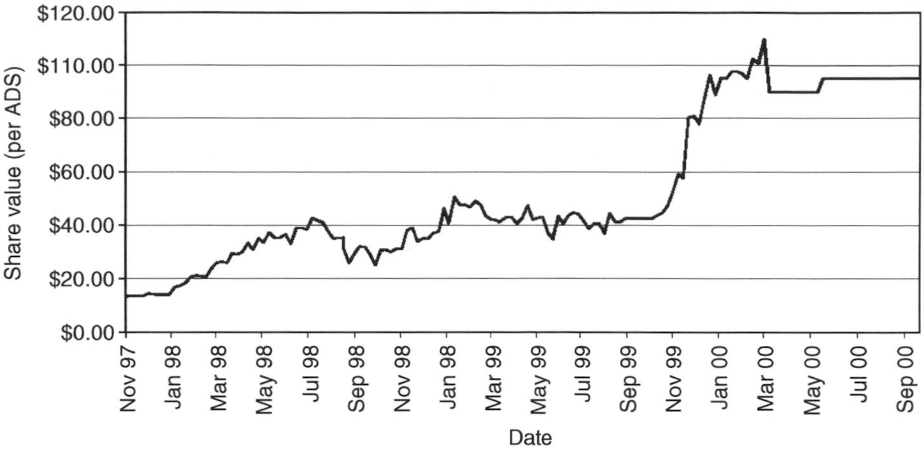

Figure 13.1 ESAT Telecom Group plc, weekly share price, ADS ($): November 1997 to September 2000. *Source:* DATASTREAM, code EA:ESA

share price at grant date, resulting in a potentially substantial gain to holders of the ESOs.

The extant literature on option pricing (Black and Scholes, 1972; Latane and Rendleman, 1976; Merton, 1976; Boyle and Ananathanarayanan, 1977) indicates that bias in the BS model can be significantly reduced by extending the time period over which share returns are collected for the purposes of computing variance, and by employing returns subsequent to measurement date (the date the option value is calculated for the purposes of computing the compensation expense to appear in the financial statements). Hence, volatility was calculated, where possible, using 60-trading-day estimation periods for both the 60 days pre-measurement (historic) and the 60 days post-measurement (future) metrics. The pre-measurement data collection period ended on the date of option value measurement; the post-measurement data collection periods began on the date of measurement (see Foster et al., 1991; Coller and Higgs, 1997). Another typical window for measuring volatility is 60 months, but due to the limitations imposed by the brief share quotation period it was only possible to measure volatility over a 36-month period. In summary, we compute three measures of volatility: 60-day historical, 60-day future, and three-year volatility. For measurement on the dates of grant and at the year-end, 31 December 1997, historical data was not available. The risk-free rate was calculated using rates on Irish government bonds, sourced from NCB stockbrokers, Dublin. Yield was calculated at the various measurement dates matching the time to maturity of the bonds to the options' remaining life at those dates. Time to exercise varied depending on the date of measurement: to facilitate comparison we select three and five years from the date of grant as the bases for calculation, as per the Offering Memorandum (1999, F23). The term of the options granted by ESAT Telecom Group plc was seven years, but this term was not used because (a) the estimated life was given as three to five years, and (b) the study by Huddart and Lang (1996) found a pervasive pattern of early option exercise. Moreover, Huddart (1994) provided evidence that the cost of an ESO to the employer might be much less than the BS valuation. The accepted accounting practice of reducing the time parameter in the BS model from time to maturity to the expected time to exercise adjusts, albeit crudely, for this bias. Thus, the fair value of the ESOs was calculated using an expected life of both three and five years. Exercise price for all the 1997 options was IR£2.4407. At commencement of trading on the NASDAQ on 12 November 1997, ESAT Telecom plc issued ADS ($) with one ADS representing two ordinary shares. All 1997 ESOs were granted prior to that date. The initial public offering price of $13 per ADS was used as the share price at dates of grant, and was then converted to IR£ at the relevant date of grant (IR£4.31, IR£4.42, and IR£4.31 respectively). From 12 November 1997 closing prices on the NASDAQ were used to calculate volatility. All BS inputs other than the volatility metric were in IR£, converted at the closing rate on the relevant date. In respect of amortization period, the ASB (2000) proposal requires measurement at vesting date. It was thus necessary to estimate compensation expense at each year-end prior to the vesting date. Compensation expense for the ESOs granted in 1997 was amortized from the date of grant to the date the employees became unconditionally entitled to the options (vesting date). The average vesting period for these options was 1.7 years (20 months). The compensation expense (in months) amortized in each of the three years covered from date of grant to vesting date is reported in Table 13.2.

Our hypothesized amortization period is the vesting period, i.e. time from the date of grant to the date the ESOs are first exercisable. Two alternatives are: (1) time

Table 13.2 Amortization pattern (20 months) for 31 December year-ends

Grant date/year	1997	1998	1999
22 May 1997	7/20	12/20	1/20
19 October 1997	2.5/20	12/20	5.5/20
6 November 1997	2/20	12/20	6/20

to expiration – the period that begins on the date of grant and ends on the date the ESO expires; (2) service period – the time over which the employee performs services that are, at least in part, compensated with the ESO grant. Amortization period should equate with service period, which may be identified in the plan or inferred, in accordance with basic accrual accounting. As we lacked specific direction regarding service period, it is inferred as being the period from the date of grant to the date the options first become exercisable, which is the vesting date. With vesting date accounting, the ASB proposals require that some estimate of compensation expense for the ESOs be calculated and charged to the profit and loss (income) account for any financial years ending prior to vesting date. The three blocks of ESOs granted by ESAT Telecom Group plc in 1997 vested as follows:

Grant date	**Vesting date**
22 May 1997	22 January 1999
19 October 1997	19 June 1999
6 November 1997	6 July 1999

Under the vesting date measurement approach, the final cost of the options is determined at vesting date. For the intervening years, the ESOs are valued at year-end to estimate compensation expense for each intervening year. In respect of BS model inputs, option life is alternatively estimated at three (five) years while the risk-free interest rate was based on the yield on Irish government bonds and matched to the time to maturity of the options being measured. Our volatility metrics are based on 60-day historic, 60-day future, and three-year periods to provide a range of plausible measures of compensation expense. Under vesting date measurement, options forfeited may be excluded from the calculation of compensation expense at any measurement date following forfeiture. Any options forfeited after vesting date do not require any adjustment. Of the 994,613 options granted on 6 October 1997, 590,601 or approximately 60% were forfeited during 1997 as employees quit the company (Offering Memorandum, 1999), and the number of options outstanding was adjusted accordingly for each subsequent year-end. During 1998, options over a further 48,390 shares were forfeited, although it was not possible to relate these forfeitures to a specific option package. In consequence, for the purposes of computing options outstanding at 31 December 1998 and 31 December 1999, these forfeitures were evenly distributed across the three blocks of options granted by ESAT Telecom Group plc. We determine compensation expense materiality based on the Leslie (1985) metrics (5% of pre-tax income or 0.5% of total revenues), accepted accounting definitions which Pany and Wheeler (1989) argue are consistent with extant literature in the area.

13.4 Results

The ASB (2000) proposal requires measurement and allocation of options expense at any year-end that occurs prior to vesting date. Table 13.3 outlines the compensation expense for the years ending 31 December 1997, 1998, and 1999, with measurement at year-end. Coller and Higgs (1997) reported that choice of inputs can substantially affect measured compensation expense; for some firms in their sample, the expense differential was material for nondividend-paying firms. To control for this effect we calculate BS fair values based on a variety of justifiable inputs in respect of options life/duration and volatility. Materiality is assessed relative to intrinsic value, minimum and maximum BS values. Table 13.3 documents the resulting compensation expense for years ending 1997, 1998, and 1999, and the corresponding option values, based on measurement at vesting date, while Table 13.4 presents reported net losses and revenues for the ESAT Telecom Group for those years.

Table 13.5 summarizes the impact on net loss and revenue of measuring compensation expense under intrinsic and fair values, with vesting date measurement and fair value based on both minimum and maximum BS valuations.

For all measurement bases and recognition dates, our hypothesized ESO expense appears to be material with respect to revenue, even for measurement at intrinsic

Table 13.3 Summary of compensation expense for years ending 1997–1999: various option values, measurement finalized on vesting date

Year-end 31 December	1997 (IR£, thousand)	1998 (IR£, thousand)	1999 (IR£, thousand)
Intrinsic value	1516	18,197	13,811
BS minimum value	1868	17,885	14,111
BS maximum value	2223	18,379	14,352

Table 13.4 ESAT Telecom Group plc: reported net loss and revenue, 1997–1999

Year-end 31 December	1997 (IR£, thousand)	1998 (IR£, thousand)	1999 (IR£, thousand)
Net loss	(40,109)	(44,208)	(120,117)
Revenue	11,590	31,612	72,055

Source: Annual Report and Accounts (1997, 1998, 1999).

Table 13.5 Analysis of the materiality impact of different measurement methods, 1997–1999: vesting date measurement

	Intrinsic value		Minimum BS		Maximum BS	
	Net loss (%)	Revenue (%)	Net loss (%)	Revenue (%)	Net loss (%)	Revenue (%)
1997	−3.78	13.08	−4.66	16.12	−5.54	19.18
1998	−41.16	57.56	−40.46	56.58	−41.57	58.14
1999	−11.50	19.17	−11.75	19.58	−11.95	19.92

value. It is important to note, however, that revenues were consistently less than reported net loss throughout our study period, with a sharp increase in share price post-options grant, particularly during 1998, being a further contributing factor. It is also likely that the relatively short vesting period of 20 months, which necessitates recognition of total compensation expense over a short timespan, may impact on the materiality of the results we report. (The more usual vesting period for Irish and UK plans would be three to five years. Many technology companies which obtained initial quotations on the NASDAQ have a much more liberal approach to share option plans, which include very short exercise periods and lack specific performance criteria.) As a percentage of net loss and revenue, the 1998 compensation expense appears to substantially exceed materiality criteria, due to the rise in share prices and the need to charge over half the total compensation expense in that year due to the short vesting period. Even the most conservative option values, which exclude share options granted during 1998 (688,922) and 1999 (2,056,305) respectively and equate exercise price with market price at grant date (Annual Report, 1999), represent a material compensation expense relative to income/loss and revenue. For comparative purposes we document the likely impact on net loss and revenue based on grant date measurement, which reflects the likely compensation expense under FRS 20 reporting requirements, in Table 13.6. Applying Leslie's (1985) materiality criteria, compensation expense under any of the three different methods would have had a material effect on ESAT Telecom Group plc's net loss and revenue, based on *grant date* measurement.

These findings are consistent with those of Foster et al. (1991) that recognition of ESO expense is likely to have a material impact on income irrespective of the option valuation model and/or measurement date approach, for firms that do not pay dividends, although our analysis relates to a young firm in the high-technology sector and may not be representative of a broader spectrum of

Table 13.6 Analysis of the materiality impact of different measurement methods, 1997–1999: grant date measurement

	Intrinsic value		Minimum BS		Maximum BS	
	Net loss (%)	Revenue (%)	Net loss (%)	Revenue (%)	Net loss (%)	Revenue (%)
1997	−2.88	9.95	23.77	13.05	−4.55	15.76
1998	−5.70	7.97	−7.45	10.42	−8.99	12.58
1999	−4.50	0.76	−5.94	0.99	−7.67	1.28

reporting firms that include ESOs in total employee compensation. As is evident from Tables 13.5 and 13.6, the effect on income of expensing ESOs is relatively greater with vesting date measurement, an effect which we attribute to the significant share price increase between grant and vesting date. Minimum BS expense for the 1998 accounting year would have been −7.45% (−40.46%) of net loss under date of grant (vesting date) measurement. The difference between the minimum and maximum BS values is also worthy of note. Under grant date measurement the difference is −0.78% (−1.54%) of net loss for 1997 (1998) accounting years, with the corresponding revenue impact differentials being 2.71% (2.16%). Under vesting date measurement the relevant differentials are −0.88% (−1.11%) for net loss and 3.06% (1.56%) for revenue. Such material difference in imputed options expense is consistent with Coller and Higgs (1997), who analyzed the effect of expensing approach on ESO option values for their sample of US firms.

13.5 Discussion

Previous to the ASB (2000) development of the *Share-Based Payment* Discussion Paper (DP) there had been no UK standard prescribing the appropriate treatment of ESOs, despite frequent calls for comprehensive and authoritative guidance in the area, and this DP largely influenced development of FRS 20 on share-based payments that comes into effect for listed entities with reporting year-ends on or after 1 January 2005. The DP recommended that ESOs be recognized as an expense in the profit and loss account, based on vesting date recognition and measurement at fair value, the estimated expense to be amortized over the service period and finalized at vesting date, at the fair value of the ESOs on that date. Approximately 100 responses were filed with the ASB in respect of the DP, split almost evenly between those that would endorse the proposals and those that would not. Of responses received from preparers and the investment community, a majority favored no charge to the profit and loss account, but if a charge should be mandated, their preference would be for fair value recognition at date of grant. A common concern of firms in the ASB jurisdiction is that they might be relatively disadvantaged should proposals be translated into an accounting standard that would be enforced unilaterally by the ASB and not by other standard setters, most notably the FASB. Thus, there seemed then and continues to be both compelling argument for, and momentum towards, developing global standards:

> 'The IASB has a unique opportunity to provide leadership on accounting for share-based payment, by developing a high quality accounting standard that will provide a basis for international convergence of standards in this area of accounting.'
>
> (Coulton and Taylor, 2002, p. 5)

In August 2001, the IASB initiated a 'high priority project' to consider the issues associated with recognition of share-based payments, and a decision was taken at the ASB to contribute to the debate in the international arena, rather than to proceed with developing an accounting standard of its own. International Financial Reporting Standard 2, which is identical to FRS 20 in respect of share-based payments, was the outcome of such debate. Over time there has been little shift in stakeholder preferences, a majority of users of financial statements agreeing with IASB proposals, a significant majority of preparers remaining opposed to expensing of ESOs, and those that would countenance expense recognition preferring measurement at intrinsic value in light of the perceived unreliability of option pricing models to estimate fair value[3]. While there appears to be some support for date of grant, vesting date, or exercise date recognition, the majority of preparers favor recognition at date of grant, with little support for measures based on service period. Interestingly, in recognition of noncompensation share-based payments, a fair value basis of measurement appears not to be considered problematic. Hill et al. (2002) examined the nature of US corporate lobbying of the FASB on the Exposure Draft that preceded SFAS 123, *Accounting for Stock-Based Compensation*, which was weighted against recognition of ESO expense in the financial statements. The ED proposed that stock-based compensation expense (related to all share option plans, for executives and employees) be calculated based on option fair values at date of grant and amortization over the vesting period. Of 262 responses analyzed, 56% of firms drawn from all US stock exchanges opposed the ED proposals entirely, clearly favoring the existing practice of disclosure of employee stock option information in proxy statements. A further 31% opposed recognition in the income statement but supported disclosure by way of note to the accounts; only eight firm responses were supportive of recognition in the income statement of share-based payments. Broadly, the spirit of the responses to the FASB and ASB proposals is consistent in that preparers surveyed at the time of publication of the proposals were opposed to recognition of ESO expense and, if mandated, would favor minimal disclosure, suggesting that managers are sensitive to both venue (proxy statement versus financial statements) and format (footnote disclosure versus recognition on the income statement) of share-based payment disclosures.

Accounting for ESOs remains a highly emotive issue and self-interest-based lobbying has accompanied development of the international standard that is now in force. Ominously, when Coulton and Taylor (2002) analyzed the comments received by the IASB from the major accounting firms they concluded that these firms have lobbied for a position that is favorable to their clients, but is not necessarily either in the wider social interest or likely to result in an improvement to the financial reporting system. At its March 2002 meeting, the IASB discussed and offered some tentative conclusions in respect of the mechanics of option valuation, on the assumption that the eventual IFRS would mandate use of an options pricing model. Specifically, entities would be required to disclose the particular option pricing model used, the inputs to that model including expected dividend and risk-free rate metrics, measures of expected and historical volatility and an explanation of how these differ, and an explanation of how the risk-free interest rate should be, and in practice was, determined.

While there remain nuisances to address with respect to the calculation of fair values for ESOs, there appears to be no viable argument against measurement at fair value, which is conceptually superior to intrinsic value measures. In contrast, agreement on the appropriate recognition date has proven more controversial. FASB and IASB recommendations involve measurement at date of grant with amortization over the vesting period; the Australian Accounting Standards Board has opted for measurement (and total recognition) at vesting date. Interestingly, Brown and Yew (2002) claim that:

> 'Our tests confirm that ESOs are unequivocally value-relevant in Australia at the grant date, in the sense that share prices are significantly correlated with our ESO variables. Results for their value-relevance on the vesting date are, regrettably, less clear-cut.'
>
> (Brown and Yew, 2002, p. 36)

In essence, by taking accounting for ESOs into the international arena, the ASB effectively allowed a 'fudge' of the question of developing a standard that might reflect best practice but which preparers would find difficult to accept. In light of the recent FRS on *Retirement Benefits* in respect of employee pension benefits and the widely documented trend towards defined contribution schemes at the expense of defined benefit plans, which are less clearly employee friendly, it might be considered that the ASB has little appetite to be associated with a further standard that may be seen as detrimental to employees. From a political perspective, it was thought that unilateral implementation of the ASB (2000) proposals might plausibly place companies in that jurisdiction at a competitive disadvantage in attracting and retaining a highly skilled workforce. This might be particularly problematic in the area of information technology and comparable skills, where being in the vanguard is perceived to be of the utmost importance politically.

13.6 Conclusion

To recognize an expense for ESOs in excess of their intrinsic value has been the subject of much debate. The ASB (2000) Discussion Paper *Share-Based Payment* recommended that ESOs be recognized in financial statements at vesting date and measured at fair value using an option pricing model, while the subsequent IASB financial reporting standard (FRS 20/IFRS 2) requires measurement at fair value but with recognition at grant date. The application of these proposals to ESAT Telecom Group plc leads to a number of tentative conclusions. Initially, on the basis of the case study conducted here, application of the proposals in the DP would be likely to have a substantial effect on the financial statements of some companies, those in the high-tech sector perhaps disproportionately so. The choice of ESAT Telecom Group plc is significant in that this technology company had a combination of high return volatility and low dividend yield, coupled with significant share price changes in the run-up to vesting date, valuation features that were characteristic of many technology companies at the time. Both of these features increase the calculated value of share options and in consequence the cost to offering firms. Secondly, much of the extant literature in the area (e.g. Samuels and Lymer, 1996) has focused solely on share options granted to directors because of the lack of sufficient details on share options granted to employees who are not board members. The exclusion of some ESO plans results in consideration of a decision with potentially a much smaller economic impact. At the end of 1997, directors of ESAT Telecom Group plc held only 25% of total employee options outstanding. Omitting options held by nonboard members has potential to distort the results, and in particular to bias downwards the estimate of true compensation expense. This effect would be amplified in the event that firms make other share-based, supply-related settlements, a practice that has been typical of startup and high-tech enterprises. Thirdly, regardless of the choice of method (intrinsic value or fair value) used to calculate option values, there is likely to be a material impact on income when measurement and recognition is at vesting date. Comparative option values based on grant date measurement (as required under FRS 20 and IFRS 2) were also calculated here, and would have had a *material, albeit smaller*, impact on income and revenue. However, the impact on the 1998 results using vesting date is approximately four times the compensation expense under grant date accounting for the case study firm.

An important dimension to the discussion generally is whether the benefits of incorporating compensation expense in the financial statements are greater than the possibility that firms might be constrained from using ESOs to attract and retain employees (especially for higher risk and emerging firms). This is a key issue worth addressing, the answer to which is likely to emerge only over time as reporting entities apply the recently published FRS 20/IFRS 2. As Zeff (1978, p. 31) notes in respect of the FASB:

> 'Although the decision should rest – and be seen to rest – chiefly on accounting considerations, it must also study – and be seen to study – the possible adverse economic and social consequences of its proposed actions.'

Measuring option values at intrinsic value does not reflect the true cost to firms of ESOs. Since there is no risk of loss to the employee and the potential for great gain, there is general agreement that these options possess value in excess of intrinsic value (Weygandt, 1977). Measurement at fair value is essential if an estimate of the true cost to companies of offering share-based compensation is sought in the context of optimizing the potential of financial statements for reflecting a true and fair view. Based on the results of this case study, and the conflicts of objective between preparers and users of financial statements in respect of expensing ESOs, perhaps the ultimate FRS 20 (and IFRS 2) recommendations constitute a feasible compromise approach that should lessen the income/revenue effect associated with expensing at vesting date and have a greater chance of becoming accepted accounting practice.

Acknowledgments

The authors would like to thank Jeff Whittington (University of Cambridge), Phil Brown (visiting at Lancaster University), and delegates at the BAA Meeting, Jersey, 2002, for valuable comments.

Notes

1. FRS 20 requires measurement at fair value based on grant date of the options awarded. Values must be re-estimated at each reporting date and at settlement, and any change recognized in the profit and loss account at that reporting date. FRS 20 is equivalent to IFRS No. 2.
2. For more detail on the opposition faced by the Financial Accounting Standards Board, the interested reader is referred to Rouse and Barton (1993), Zeff (1997), Mozes (1998), and Hill et al. (2002).
3. Typically the BS option pricing model is utilized to value ESOs, and the ASB (2000) proposals implicitly assume its use. It has been argued that unusual characteristics specific to ESOs (possibility of early exercise, takeover, bankruptcy, liquidity considerations, etc.) render them sufficiently different to traded options to imply that a tailored pricing model is required for accurate valuation. For a discussion of one alternative, based on the binomial OPM and adapted to accommodate features of Australian firms, see Maller et al. (2002).

References

Accounting Standards Board (2000). *Share-Based Payment.* ASB Publications, Milton Keynes.

Black, F. and Scholes, M. (1972). The Valuation of Option Contracts and a Test of Market Efficiency. *Journal of Finance*, 27(2):399–418.

Boyle, P. P. and Ananthanarayanan, A.L. (1977). The Impact of Variance Estimation in Option Valuation Models. *Journal of Financial Economics*, 5(3):375–387.

Brown, P. and Yew, E. (2002). How Do Investors Regard ESOs? *Australian Accounting Review*, 12(1):36–42.

Chiras, D.P. and Manaster, S. (1978). The Information Content of Option Prices and a Test of Market Efficiency. *Journal of Financial Economics*, 6(2–3):213–234.

Coller, M. and Higgs, J.L. (1997). Firm Valuation and Accounting for Employee Stock Options. *Financial Analysts Journal*, 53(1):26–34.

Coulton, J. and Taylor, S. (2002). Accounting for Executive Stock Options: A Case Study in Avoiding Tough Decisions. *Australian Accounting Review*, 12(1):3–10.

ESAT Telecom Group plc (1997–1999). Annual Report and Accounts.

ESAT Telecom Group plc (1999). Offering Memorandum, October.

Financial Accounting Standards Board (1993). *Exposure Draft: Accounting for Stock-Based Compensation.* Statement of Financial Accounting Standards No. 123. FASB, Norwalk, CT.

Financial Accounting Standards Board (1995). *Accounting for Stock-Based Compensation.* Statement of Financial Accounting Standards No. 123. FASB, Norwalk, CT.

Foster, T.W., Koogler, P.R., and Vickrey, D. (1991). Valuation of Executive Share Options and the FASB Proposal. *Accounting Review*, 66(3):595–610.

G4 + 1 Communique (2000). Reported in *ASB Bulletin*, No. 113, May.

Hemmer, T., Matsunaga, S., and Shelvin, T. (1999). A Guide to Valuing Employee Stock Options with a Reload Feature. *Journal of Applied Corporate Finance*, 12(2):118–128.

Hill, N.T., Shelton, S.W., and Stevens, K.T. (2002). Corporate Lobbying Behaviour on Accounting for Stock-Based Compensation: Venue and Format Choices. *Abacus*, 38(1):78–90.

Huddart, S. (1994). Employee Stock Options. *Journal of Accounting and Economics*, 18(2):207–231.

Huddart, S. and Lang, M. (1996). Employee Stock Option Exercises: An Empirical Analysis. *Journal of Accounting and Economics*, 21(1):5–43.

Klassen, K.J. and Mawani, A. (2000). The Impact of Financial and Tax Reporting Incentives on Option Grants to Canadian CEOs. *Contemporary Accounting Research*, 17(2):227–262.

Latane, H.A. and Rendleman, R.J. Jr (1976). Standard Deviations of Stock Price Ratios Implied in Option Prices. *Journal of Finance*, 31(2):1173–1186.

Leslie, D.A. (1985). *Materiality: The Concepts and its Application to Auditing.* Canadian Institute of Chartered Accountants, Toronto, Canada.

Maller, R.A., Tan, R., and De Vyver, M. (2002). How Might Companies Value ESOs? *Australian Accounting Review*, 12(1):11–24.

Matsunaga, S.R. (1995). The Effects of Financial Reporting Costs on the Use of Employee Stock Options. *Accounting Review*, 70(1):1–26.

Merton, R.C. (1976). The Impact of Option Pricing of Specification Error in the Underlying Stock Price Returns. *Journal of Finance*, 31(2):333–350.

Mozes, H.A. (1998). The FASB's Conceptual Framework and Political Support: The Lesson from Employee Stock Options. *Abacus*, 34(2):141–161.

O'Sullivan, J. (2002). Accountants Look to Set Global Standard – Share Options. *Irish Times Business*, 14 April, 16–17.

Pany, K. and Wheeler, S. (1989). Materiality: An Inter-Industry Comparison of the Magnitudes and Stabilities of Various Quantitative Measures. *Accounting Horizons*, 3(4):71–78.

Robbins, B.P. (1988). FASB's Long Look at Stock Compensation Plans. *Journal of Accountancy*, 166(2):60–68.

Rouse, R.W. and Barton, D.N. (1993). Stock Compensation Accounting. *Journal of Accountancy*, 175(6):67–70.

Saly, P.J., Jagannathan, R. and Huddart, S.J. (1999). Valuing the reload features of executive stock options. *Accounting Horizons*, 13(3):219–240.

Samuels, J. and Lymer, A. (1996). The Financial Reporting of Executive Share Options in the UK. *British Accounting Review*, 28(3):249–266.

Weygandt, J.J. (1977). Valuation of stock option contracts. *Accounting Review*, 14(1):41–52.

Zeff, S.A. (1978). The Rise of Economic Consequences. *Journal of Accountancy*, 146(5):19–33.

Zeff, S.A. (1997). Playing the Congressional Card on Employee Stock Options: A Fearful Escalation in the Impact of Economic Consequences on Standard Setting. In: *The Development of Accounting in an International Context: A Festschrift in Honour of R.H. Parker* (Cooke and Nobes, eds). Routledge, London.

14

Impairment of Fixed Assets: Perceived Implementation Problems Associated with International Accounting Standard No. 36

Mohamed E. Ibrahim

14.1 Introduction

When a firm acquires fixed assets such as plant and equipment, it records them at cost according to the cost principle. These recorded costs usually represent fair values of the assets at the time of acquisition because the amounts agreed upon are determined based on arm's length transactions.

The general definition of an asset incorporates the notion that the asset has future benefits that tend to decrease over time because of normal usage, and accountants have devised the concept of depreciation to account for the effects of usage for reporting purposes. In that context, depreciation is viewed as a form of allocation of historical cost over the useful life of the asset. This allocation process is needed for income measurement and is usually implemented according to management preference on a systematic and consistent basis. However, a fixed asset or a group of fixed assets may be exposed to situations other than usage (e.g. technological changes) that result in potential decline in asset value (known as asset impairment). This issue of potential decline in asset value is not completely new. It has been acknowledged in Statement of Financial Accounting Standards No. 5, *Accounting for Contingencies* (FASB, 1975), and SFAS No. 19, *Financial Accounting and Reporting by Oil and Gas Producing Companies* (FASB, 1987). However, no such guidance has been provided to answer the question of when to recognize such potential decline in asset value (a timing issue) and the question of how much to report for asset write-downs (a measurement issue).

Before the mid 1990s, accounting rules generally did not address the measurement and reporting of asset impairments. As a result, management had much flexibility over measurement and reporting of asset impairments. However, as previous research reveals, writeoffs of long-lived assets are both large in magnitude and frequent in occurrence (e.g. Elliot and Shaw, 1988; Elliot and Hanna, 1996; Francis et al., 1996). This increased frequency of asset writeoffs motivated users of financial statements to call for improved reporting of asset impairments.

In 1995, the Financial Accounting Standards Board (FASB) responded to users' calls for improved reporting of asset impairment by issuing SFAS No. 121, *Accounting for the Impairment of Long-Lived Assets and for Long-Lived Assets to be Disposed of.* The statement basically requires that long-lived assets and certain identifiable intangibles to be held and used by a firm be reviewed for impairment whenever events or changes in circumstances indicate that the carrying amount of an asset may not be recoverable. In performing such a review, the firm should estimate the future cash flows expected to result from the use of the asset and its eventually disposal. When the sum of the expected undiscounted future cash flows (without interest charges) is less than the carrying amount of the asset, an impairment loss is recognized. Otherwise, an impairment loss is not recognized. Measurement of an impairment loss for long-lived assets and identifiable intangibles that a firm expects to hold and use should be based on the fair value of the asset.

SFAS 121 also requires that long-lived assets and certain identifiable intangibles to be disposed of be reported at the lower of carrying amount or fair value less cost to sell, except for assets that are covered by Accounting Principles Board (APB) Opinion No. 30, *Reporting the Results of Operations – Reporting the Effects of Disposal of a Segment of a Business, and Extraordinary, Unusual and Infrequently Occurring Events and Transactions.*

In 2001, the FASB issued SFAS No. 144, *Accounting for the Impairment or Disposal of Long-Lived Assets*, which superseded FASB Statement No. 121. Since Statement 121 did not address the accounting for a segment of a business accounted for as discontinued operations under APB Opinion No. 30, two accounting models existed for long-lived assets to be disposed of. The Board decided to establish a single accounting model for long-lived assets to be disposed of by sale based on the framework established in Statement 121. The Board also decided to solve some implementation issues related to Statement 121.

For long-lived assets to be held and used, Statement 144 retained the requirements of Statement 121 to recognize an impairment loss only if the carrying amount is not recoverable from its undiscounted cash flows and measure an impairment loss as the difference between the carrying amount and fair value of the asset. However, Statement 144 resolved some implementation issues by removing goodwill from its scope, describing a probability-weighted cash-flow estimation approach to deal with situations in which alternative courses of action to recover carrying amounts of long-lived assets are under consideration or a range is estimated for the amount of possible future cash flows, and establishing a 'primary asset' approach to determine the cash-flow estimation period for a group of assets and liabilities that represents the unit of accounting for a long-lived asset to be held and used.

For long-lived assets to be disposed of by sale, Statement 144 retained the requirements of 121 to measure the asset at the lower of its carrying amount or fair value less cost to sell and cease depreciation. Therefore, discontinued operations are no longer measured on a net realizable value basis, and future operating losses are no longer recognized before they occur.

For long-lived assets to be disposed of other than by sale, Statement 144 requires the asset to be considered held and used until it is disposed of (by abandonment, exchange for similar productive asset, or distribution to owners). To solve implementation issues, the Statement requires that the depreciable life of a long-lived asset to be abandoned be reviewed in accordance with APB Opinion No. 20, *Accounting Changes*. It also amended APB Opinion No. 29, *Accounting for Non-monetary Transactions*, to require that an impairment loss be recognized at the date a long-lived asset is exchanged for a similar productive asset or distributed to owners in a spinoff if the carrying amount of the asset exceeds its fair value.

At international level, there was very limited guidance available on how to deal with impairment of long-lived assets until 1998. In that year, the International Accounting Standards Committee (IASC) issued its International Accounting Standards (IAS) No. 36, *Impairment of Assets*. The standard basically requires that the recoverable amount of a long-lived asset (or a group of assets) be estimated to identify and measure impairments, whenever there are indications that asset impairment exists. Thus, the main objective of IAS No. 36 is to ensure that an asset (or a group of assets) is not carried at an amount greater than its recoverable amount. When the carrying amount of an asset becomes higher than the estimated amount to be recovered by use of the asset or from its sale, the firm should recognize an impairment loss.

Although IAS No. 36 was originally issued in 1998, it was revised in 2003. The standard was also subject to different amendments in 2004 because of scope changes (e.g. inclusion of business combinations) and improvements to existing standards (e.g. issuance of Statement No. 38 dealing with intangible assets).

Although the standard has a general application to all assets, some assets are considered outside its scope because they are subject to specific recognition and measurement rules. The effect of these exclusions is a considerable reduction in its scope. Examples of assets excluded from the scope of the standard include inventories, assets arising from construction contracts, deferred tax assets, assets arising from employee's benefits, financial assets that are included in the scope of IAS No. 39, and investment properties that are measured at fair values.

This direction toward fair value accounting (by the FASB and the IASC) raises three basic questions when dealing with long-lived assets. The first is how a firm will know whether it will recover the book values of its assets (carrying amounts) by using them or selling them. Second, how a firm should measure any impairment loss. Third, when a firm should account for any impairment loss identified by an assessment process.

14.1.1 Indications of impairment

According to the standard, at each financial reporting date the firm should determine whether there are conditions or circumstances that would indicate that impairments may have occurred. Identifying circumstances or indications of impairment of tangible long-lived assets is the first crucial step in the implementation process. The standard, however, lists some examples representing the minimum indications that a firm should consider for determining whether an impairment test is needed or not. These indications are divided into external and internal based on the sources of information. *External and internal sources of information* can include the following:

1. A decline in an asset's market value during the period that is significantly more than what the firm expects as a result of normal use of the asset.
2. Significant changes that have taken place in the period in the technological, market, economic, or legal environment in which the firm operates, or the specific market to which an asset is dedicated.
3. Increases in the market interest rate or other market-oriented rate of return on investments such that increases in the discount rate to be employed in determining value in use can be anticipated, with a resultant enhanced likelihood that impairments will exist.
4. The aggregate carrying value of the firm's assets exceeds the perceived value of its market capitalization.
5. Evidence of obsolescence or physical damage to an asset or a group of assets.
6. Significant internal changes to the organization or its operations, such as restructuring, to the extent that the expected useful life or benefits of the asset have been reduced.
7. Reported internal data suggesting that the economic performance of the asset or group of assets is, or will become, worse than previously anticipated.

The standard also lists some indicators that are derived from internally generated information and considered as relevant evidence for asset impairment. These indicators include:

1. Cash flows generated by an asset or group of assets, or subsequent cash needs for operating or maintaining the asset, are significantly higher than originally budgeted or forecasted.
2. Operating profits or losses or actual net cash flows are significantly worse than those budgeted or forecasted.

3. A significant increase in budgeted loss, or a significant decline in budgeted net cash flows or operating profits.
4. Operating losses or net cash outflows for the asset when aggregating current period amounts with budgeted amounts for the future.

14.1.2 The impairment test

Normally, the presence of any of the impairment indicators would require the firm to perform an impairment test (the second stage in the implementation process), which requires the firm to calculate the recoverable amount of the asset and compare it with the asset's carrying value. The recoverable amount is the higher of the asset's value in use and its fair value less costs to sell. The underlying idea is that an asset should not be carried at more than the amount it will generate, either from selling it now or from using it in the future. However, when previous impairment reviews show that an asset's recoverable amount was significantly greater than its carrying amount and subsequent events are not sufficient to eliminate that gap, or when previous reviews show that the asset's recoverable amount is not sensitive to one or more of the impairment indicators, the presence of any of the indicators does not necessitate performing the impairment test.

Some of the main problems in performing the impairment test lie with estimating the asset's value in use and its fair value. Estimating the asset's value in use involves estimating cash inflows and outflows that will be derived from the use of the asset and from its ultimate disposal and discounting them at an appropriate rate that is reasonable for the type of business and risks involved. Estimating fair value is based on the sale price of the asset in an active market. However, it may be possible to estimate the selling price even in the absence of an active market for the asset. On the practical side, whenever the fair value of the asset is greater than the asset's carrying amount, there is no need to perform the calculations for the asset's value in use. Furthermore, if the fair value of the asset cannot satisfactorily be estimated, the recoverable amount must be based on the asset's value in use. If either of the fair value of the asset or its value in use is higher than the carrying amount of the asset, the asset is considered not impaired and no further action is required.

14.1.3 Accounting for impairment

When the results of the impairment test indicate that the asset or group of assets (cash-generating unit) is impaired, the firm must account for such impairment losses to be reflected on the financial statements. For individual assets, the standard requires immediate recognition of impairment losses for assets that are not carried at revalued amounts according to another standard. An impairment loss on a revalued asset is first used to reduce the revaluation surplus for that asset, and any further impairment loss should be recognized in the profit and loss. The standard, however, does not take a particular position on how to show impairment losses on financial statements.

For a group of assets, the standard calls for the recognition of an impairment loss in a way that reduces the carrying amount of the assets of the group(s) at a pro-rata rate of their carrying amounts after reducing the carrying amount of any goodwill allocated to the group. If there are different cash-generating units in the group of assets, a further pro rating of the impairment loss among the individual assets of the cash-generating unit is performed.

The main objectives of this chapter are to survey the perceived implementation problems associated with the standard among a sample of practicing accountants in the United Arab Emirates and their preferences for following the international standard or the American standard. The remainder of the chapter is organized as follows. The next section reviews some relevant previous studies on writeoffs of long-lived, home-based assets and the factors affecting their reporting. Section 14.3 describes the research method used to carry out the empirical work and the development of the research hypotheses. Section 14.4 reports the results and section 14.5 provides conclusions and recommendations.

14.2 Previous studies

This section of the chapter reviews some relevant previous studies. The review reveals that different approaches have been used to study write-downs. Some studies used a descriptive approach while others used an empirical approach. The studies by Schiff (1985), Schuetze (1987), Smith (1994), and Meeting and Luecke (2002) are mostly descriptive in nature and do not deal with a theoretical framework or empirical findings that explain or predict the occurrence of asset impairments. These studies are primarily concerned with how and when the impairment should be reported or discussing guidelines based on the standards or professional practices. Empirical studies, on the other hand, such as those by Strong and Meyer (1987), Elliot and Shaw (1988), Zucca and Campbell (1992), Francis et al. (1996), Riedl (2004), and Chen et al. (2004), examined the impact of write-downs. The following paragraphs provide a review of selected studies, emphasizing the empirical approach to asset impairment.

Strong and Meyer (1987) examined a sample of 120 firms reporting writeoffs between 1 January 1981 and 31 December 1985, and concluded that firms with writeoffs were neither the strongest nor the weakest in the industry. They found that write-downs occurred when business was improving and the market value of equity base was growing, detecting a slight positive market reaction in the first days after the write-downs. They also identified a change in senior management as the primary reason for write-down decisions and documented a positive stock price effect that signals future events.

Smith (1994) discussed the issue of potential disclosures associated with accounting for impairment of long-lived assets. She mentioned that although the reporting practices for unrealized asset impairments before the issuance of SFAS 121 were inconsistent, the argument that disclosure benefits of implementing such a standard might not outweigh the costs is plausible, since reporting on write-downs is not an independent process where impairment cannot be considered in isolation. She indicated that a substantial amount of the related analysis to impairment is already performed routinely by many large companies in connection with their capital expenditures. Large companies usually perform project post-audits where individual assets or groups of assets are evaluated on a regular basis to decide whether to keep or abandon them. Such post-audit systems are more likely to evaluate projects based on cash flows (and not accounting numbers) and have a formal abandonment process that bases decisions on discounted cash-flow analysis.

Smith (1994) concluded that required disclosures of a standard on accounting for impairment of long-lived assets would be considered beneficial. For companies that are already post-auditing, the costs of increased impairment disclosures may be relatively small. But they will have to increase the scale and possibly the sophistication of their post-audit systems. By doing so, companies will benefit in the long run through increased efficiency of capital allocation. In the short run, however, she argued, increased post-auditing will provide high-quality performance evaluation information.

Rees et al. (1996) investigated the occurrence of abnormal accruals of firms recognizing permanent asset impairments in their financial statements to assess whether such firms systematically managed earnings in the year of write-downs. They used a keyword search of the 1987–1992 annual reports contained in the National Automated Accounting Research System (NAARS) database to obtain a list of potential sample firms. This initial search produced 1268 firms reporting. The firms' financial statements were then examined to verify the existence of discretionary write-downs due to impairments of values. Write-downs of current assets and oil and gas properties were excluded because of little discretion over these types of write-downs. This procedure reduced the initial sample to 529 firms. The sample was further reduced to 277 firms because of eliminating write-downs judged to be immaterial (less than 0.5% of beginning-of-year book value of total assets) and Compustat data availability.

Using regression analysis and matched sample design, these authors tested for earnings management, which was hypothesized to be zero. The initial results indicated that managers recognized additional income-decreasing discretionary accruals that accentuated the negative effect of the asset write-down on earnings. Alternatively, the abnormal accruals may have been a reflection of changes in the write-down firms' accrual balances and/or accruals-generating process. To discriminate between the two competing explanations, the authors assessed the tendency of the abnormal accruals in the write-down year to reverse by examining abnormal accruals in years 1–3 relative to the firm's last write-down.

The results showed no evidence that the abnormal accruals reverse in post-write-down years. However, the results did not completely eliminate the possibility that the abnormal accruals in the write-down year are opportunistic, since the timing of accrual reversals could be delayed for several years.

Nurnberg and Dittmar (1996) discussed auditing considerations of the accounting standard for impairment of long-lived assets. The authors indicated that while companies have to deal with the implementation issues, auditors have to deal with how to evaluate compliance with the standard provisions.

These authors indicated that auditors need to review management policies and procedures to identify possible impairment indicators. In the absence of such indicators, impairment testing is not required and audit testing need not be extensive.

Zabihollah et al. (1996) provided some empirical evidence regarding the financial impact of write-downs of long-lived assets and the dominant factors in companies' decisions for measurement, recognition, and reporting of asset impairments. They used the Disclosure SEC Database, which includes financial and management information about public companies, to collect their data. An initial search of the database identified 5092 companies that referenced impairments, writeoffs and write-downs in their annual reports. The annual reports were then examined for reported impairments of long-lived assets for the fiscal years ending in 1989–1993 (a five-year period) using three criteria. These criteria were: (1) the firm wrote off one or more impaired long-lived asset used in production (intangibles were excluded); (2) no indication was given in the annual report that the firm was not continuing to depreciate or amortize the asset; and (3) financial statements were publicly available during the five-year investigation period. The resultant sample included 935 reported impairments of 670 companies distributed among the nine general industry classifications used in the study.

These authors used six independent variables and five dependent variables. The independent variables are industry classification (the nine general industry classification), form of disclosure (in footnotes or in management discussion and analysis), impairment recognition criteria (permanent decline or economic impairment), reasons for impairment (decline in market value, lack of long-term profitability, or other reasons), level of asset grouping (business segment, other business unit, or individual assets), and measurement of impairment (fair value, recoverable value, or replacement cost). The five dependent variables are average net sales, average amount of long-lived assets after write-downs, average reported impairment amounts of long-lived assets, ratio of write-downs to net sales, and ratio of write-downs to long-lived assets.

Zabihollah et al. used multivariate analysis of variance (MANOVA) to simultaneously assess the relationship between the six independent variables and the five dependent variables. The results indicated significant differences in average net sales, average long-lived assets, average impairments, and the ratio of impairment to net sales across industry classification.

Chen et al. (2004) studied incentives for and consequences of initial voluntary asset write-downs in the emerging Chinese market. In 1998, a Chinese accounting regulation allowed listed companies to voluntarily write down assets through their income statements. The regulation was amended in 1999 to require all companies to write down assets that were subject to impairment with a retroactive adjustment of pre-1998 asset impairment to the initial equity. This setting allowed the authors to use a sample test and a control sample from the two years. The total number of firms included in the sample was 537.

These authors used the TEJ CD-ROM database and 1999 published annual reports to collect their data. They also used a return model and a price model to examine the market value effect. The return model provides information about whether the write-down is reflected in changes in value over a one-year return period. The price model provides information about whether the write-down is value relevant with respect to its association with firm value.

The results indicated that voluntary write-downs have a positive valuation effect. In addition, firms with CEO changes or big losses are more likely to write down assets and tend to write down assets in large amounts. Furthermore, the authors documented an *ex post* association between the voluntary asset write-down and subsequent performance improvement in terms of return on assets, but not in terms of cash flows. Taken together, these authors believe, while recognizing the possibility of alternative explanations, that their results taken as a whole are more consistent with the voluntary write-downs being a signal of the potential for performance improvement.

Riedl (2004) examined the characteristics of writeoffs reported prior to the issuance of SFAS 121 as compared to those of writeoffs subsequent to the issuance of the statement. The debate about the extent of available guidance and the inherently subjective estimates needed to implement the standard made it unclear how the association between reported writeoffs and economic factors/reporting incentives changed (if at all) upon the adoption of SFAS 121.

Riedl used reported net of tax long-lived writeoff for period t as a percentage of total assets at the end of $t-1$ as the dependent variable. Independent variables included percentage change in US Gross Domestic Product from period $t-1$ to t, the median change in firm i's industry return on assets from period $t-1$ to t, the percentage change in sales for firm i from period $t-1$ to t, firm i's change in operating cash flows from period $t-1$ to t as a percentage of total assets at the end of $t-1$, a proxy for 'big bath' reporting equal to the change in firm i's pre-writeoff earnings from period $t-1$ to t as a percentage of total assets at the end of $t-1$ (when below the median of nonzero negative values of this variable), and a proxy for 'earnings smoothing' reporting equal to the change in firm i's pre-writeoff earnings from period $t-1$ to t as a percentage of total assets at the end of $t-1$ (when above the median of nonzero positive values of this variable). Indicator variables (coded one or zero) were used for a firm's private debt (not publicly rated) and writeoff observations occurring before and after the standard.

The above variables were specified in a Tobit regression model that included the stacking of two regressions. The first represented the observations from the pre-SFAS 121 period. The second represented the observations from the post-SFAS 121 period.

Data for the study were collected for the period 1992–1998 from the Compustat/Execucomp database and Disclosure Global Access for firms outside the banking or financial services industries. A total of 1249 randomly selected firms were included.

The results indicated that economic factors have weaker association with writeoffs reported after the issuance of the standard. This result is consistent across macro, industry, and firm-specific variables. The results also showed a higher association between writeoffs and 'big bath' reporting behavior after the standard's implementation, and that this 'big bath' behavior more likely reflects opportunistic reporting by managers rather than the provision of their private information. These inferences are robust to a number of alternative specifications and variable definitions. The author indicated that the overall results are consistent with the criticism of the standard that the reporting of writeoffs under SFAS 121 has decreased in quality.

Reinstein and Lander (2004) examined the views of users and preparers of financial statements regarding SFAS 144. They used a mail questionnaire to obtain the respondents' perceptions regarding the new requirements, their guidance, and implementation costs. The results indicated significant differences in perceptions of the two groups regarding requirements and implementations. In addition, a majority of responses indicated that the new standard provided improved guidance for many complex situations. However, many respondents did not believe that the standard is cost justified.

14.3 Methods

14.3.1 Sample

The sample consisted of accountants employed by public accounting firms and for-profit organizations. The sample can be described as a convenient sample since it was not selected randomly. Rather, the researcher has contacted accountants at selected public accounting firms and organizations and asked for their participation in the study. A total of 109 accountants agreed to participate and were included in the sample.

14.3.1.1 Questionnaire

The study questionnaire was designed to capture accountants' perceptions regarding implementation problems encountered when dealing with accounting for impairment of fixed assets. The questionnaire had two parts. The first part was designed to collect general information (e.g. educational levels, marital status, gender, and the like). The second part contained the elements of the basic areas for implementation problems. These areas included impairment indications, impairment indicators, estimation of fair value and value in use, and implementation costs. Each participant was asked to indicate the extent to which he/she has experienced (or perceived to experience) difficulty in implementing the standard using a five-point numerical scale. The scale ranged from 1 (no difficulty at all) to

5 (a great deal of difficulty). The questionnaire also asked each participant to indicate his/her preference for implementing the International Accounting Standard or the American Standard dealing with long-lived asset impairment.

All information regarding areas of implementation problems, which were included in the second part of the questionnaire, was based on the requirements of the International Accounting Standard, review of the literature, and the feedback obtained from pilot testing the questionnaire.

The questionnaires were distributed in person to the subjects, who were requested to respond within two weeks. A second distribution was made to non-responding subjects, who were requested to respond within a two-week period.

14.3.1.2 Research hypotheses

This chapter has two research hypotheses. The first deals with accountants' perceived or experienced difficulties in implementing the International Accounting Standard of asset impairment. This hypothesis is stated in null form as follows:

> **H_{01}:** *There are no significant differences in the mean scores of perceived or experienced difficulty in implementing the International Accounting Standard between accountants who are in public practice and those who are employed in private organizations.*

The second research hypothesis deals with possible differences in accountants' preferences for implementing the International Accounting Standard over the American Accounting Standard for asset impairment because of being in public practice or in private practice. The general expectation is of no difference in preference for implementing the standard between the two groups of accountants. Accordingly, this hypothesis is stated in null form as follows:

> **H_{02}:** *There are no significant differences in preferences of accountants who are in public practice and those who are employed in private firms regarding implementation of the International Accounting Standard over the American Accounting Standard for asset impairments.*

14.3.1.3 Data analysis

Collected data were analyzed using descriptive statistics. To test the above two hypotheses, the data were subjected to independent samples *t*-tests. The results obtained from the analysis are reported in the next section.

14.4 Results

14.4.1 Sample profile

The researcher received 96 completed responses. This represents about a 88% response rate. Table 14.1 shows the distribution of responses between accountants in public practice and those who are in private practice.

Table 14.2 shows the distribution of the sample according to four demographic variables. The table shows that female responses are significantly less than male responses. However, the percentage is perhaps better than might be expected given that the profession has been perceived to be male dominated.

Table 14.1 Distribution of sample responses

Type of practice	Number distributed	Number of responses	Percentage
Public practice	45	37	82.2
Private practice	64	59	92.2
Total	109	96	88.1

Table 14.2 Frequency distribution of demographic variables

	Frequency	Percentage
Gender of respondents		
Male	65	67.7
Female	31	32.3
Marital status		
Single	38	39.6
Married	45	46.9
Divorced	9	09.3
Widow	4	04.2
Nationality		
UAE	32	33.3
Non-UAE	64	66.7
Educational level		
Bachelor degree	84	87.5
Master's degree	11	11.5
Doctoral degree	1	1.0

14.4.2 Implementation problems

Table 14.3 reports some descriptive statistics (mean and standard deviation) of experienced or perceived difficulty in implementing the standard using a five-point numerical scale that ranged from 1 (no difficulty at all) to 5 (a great deal of difficulty).

Table 14.3 shows that accountants do not encounter serious difficulties when assessing impairment indications (average score is less than 2 out of 5), except changes in technological, market, or legal environment (average score is about 3.5 out of 5). For impairment indicators, the table shows that averages of the four items are close to each other and they are at levels that reveal some difficulty when assessing them. For measuring market values, it seems that estimating market prices is somewhat difficult but not different from the impairment indicators.

Table 14.3 also shows that measuring value in use is generally more difficult than measuring fair values. In addition, the cost of implementing the system may not be easy to assess.

14.4.2.1 Differences in perceived or experienced implementation difficulties

Table 14.4 shows the results of testing for possible differences in perceived or experienced implementation difficulties between the two groups of accountants (those who are in public accounting practice and those who are employed in private organizations).

Table 14.4 shows some significant differences in assessed levels of difficulty between accountants in public practice and accountants employed in private organizations. These differences are in the areas of assessing impairment indications and impairment indicators. The negative sign indicates that accountants in public practice experience or perceive less difficulty than accountants employed in private organizations. One possible explanation for such results is that accountants in public practice have opportunities for diversified experience and the availability of additional human resources. Thus, the results reject the first null hypothesis with respect to the difficulties encountered when assessment of impairment indications and indicators.

Table 14.4 also shows no significant differences in assessed levels of difficulty between accountants in public practice and accountants employed in private organizations with regard to measurement of fair value or value in use for the impairment test. Thus, the results fail to reject the first null hypothesis with respect to the difficulties encountered when measuring fair values or value in use.

Table 14.3 Descriptive statistics of experienced or perceived difficulties in implementing IAS 36

Element	Mean score	Standard deviation
Impairment indications		
Decline in asset's market value	1.65	0.60
Changes in technological, market, economic, or legal environment	3.47	0.68
Increased market interest rate	1.54	0.58
Aggregate carrying value of the firm's assets exceeds market capitalization	1.48	0.52
Evidence of obsolescence or physical damage to an asset or a group of assets	1.66	0.52
Internal changes to the organization or its operations	1.31	0.47
Reported internal data suggesting that the economic performance of the asset or group of assets is, or will become, worse than previously anticipated	1.17	0.37
Impairment indicators		
Cash needs to operate or maintain the asset are significantly higher than originally budgeted or forecasted	2.35	1.06
Operating profits or losses or actual net cash flows are significantly worse than those budgeted or forecasted	2.05	0.69
A significant increase in budgeted loss, or decline in budgeted net cash flows or operating profits	2.44	0.99
Operating loss or net cash outflows for the asset when aggregating current period amounts with budgeted amounts for the future	2.83	0.93
Measuring fair value		
Existence of active market	1.54	0.66
Estimates of market prices	2.30	0.80
Estimates of disposal costs	2.01	0.75
Measuring value in use		
Estimates of future cash flows expected from the asset	3.11	0.88
Possible variations in amount or timing of estimated future cash flows	3.16	0.76
Selection of a discount rate	1.55	0.58
Estimates of uncertainty inherent in the asset	3.00	0.75
Other factors (e.g. degree of illiquidity) that affect future cash flows	2.84	0.76
Cost of implementation		
Cost to modify existing system, if any, to handle the new requirements	3.05	0.72
Cost to perform impairment review	2.68	0.62

Table 14.4 Test results for differences in preferences and implementation difficulties

Area of possible difficulty	*t*-statistic	Significance level
Impairment indications	−8.509	0.000
Impairment indicators	−4.617	0.000
Measuring fair values	−1.637	0.106
Measuring value in use	−1.458	0.148
Cost of implementation	−1.953	0.054
Preferences for IAS 36	−2.983	0.004

Regarding the cost of implementation, the table shows marginal differences between the two groups of accountants ($p > 0.54$). Thus, the results fail to reject the first null hypothesis with respect to the difficulties encountered when measuring the cost of implementing the standard.

Table 14.4 also shows significant differences in preferences of the two accounting groups for implementing the International Accounting Standard ($p < 0.004$). The negative sign indicates that accountants in public practice prefer the International Accounting Standard over the American Accounting Standard. Thus, the results reject the second null hypothesis. This result is consistent with the fact that some business sectors in the UAE (e.g. banks, which are audited by public accounting firms) are required to use the International Accounting Standards.

14.5 Conclusion

This chapter examined empirically some of the implementation problems of the International Accounting Standard for long-lived asset impairment accounting using a sample of accountants practicing (in private organizations and in public accounting firms) in the UAE, as well as accountants' preferences for the international standard over the American standard. A questionnaire-based design was used to collect the data. Descriptive analysis and independent sample *t*-tests were employed to test for differences of experienced or perceived difficulties related to implementation of the standard in five areas. These areas included assessment of impairment indications, assessment of impairment indicators, measurement of fair values and values in use, and cost of implementation.

The results show that accountants in private organizations experience more difficulties than accountants in public practice when assessing impairment indications and indicators. However, both groups of accountants experience almost the same level of difficulty when measuring fair values and/or values in use for the impairment test.

The results also show significant differences in preferences of the two accounting groups for implementing the International Accounting Standard. Accountants in public practice prefer the International Accounting Standard over the American Accounting Standard.

The results of this study are subject to some limitations. First, like any questionnaire-based study, there is no simple way to ensure the accuracy of the responses. However, the general assumption is that people are honest and they provide accurate data. Second, no attempt was made to measure the effect of the nonresponse bias. However, the high response rate may reduce such possible bias.

One possible avenue for future research is to examine audit considerations when dealing with asset impairment and how the difficulty encountered in the assessment phase would impact on audit procedures.

References

Chen, C.J.P., Chen, S., Su, X., and Wang, Y. (2004). Incentives for and Consequences of Initial Voluntary Asset Write-Downs in the Emerging Chinese Market. *Journal of International Accounting Research*, 3(1):43–61.

Elliot, J. and Hanna, J. (1996). Repeated Accounting Write-offs and the Information Content of Earnings. *Journal of Accounting Research*, 34(Suppl.):135–155.

Elliot, J. and Shaw, W. (1988). Write-offs as Accounting Procedures to Manage Perceptions. *Journal of Accounting Research*, 26(Suppl.):91–119.

Financial Accounting Standards Board (1975). *Accounting for Contingencies.* Statement of Financial Accounting Standards No. 5. FASB, Norwalk, CT.

Financial Accounting Standards Board (1987). *Financial Accounting and Reporting by Oil and Gas Producing Companies.* Statement of Financial Accounting Standards No. 19. FASB, Norwalk, CT.

Financial Accounting Standards Board (1995). *Accounting for the Impairment of Long-Lived Assets and for Long-Lived Assets to be Disposed of.* Statement of Financial Accounting Standards No. 121. FASB, Norwalk, CT.

Financial Accounting Standards Board (2001). *Accounting for the Impairment or Disposal of Long-Lived Assets.* Statement of Financial Accounting Standards No. 144. FASB, Norwalk, CT.

Francis, J., Hanna, J., and Vincent, L. (1996). Causes and Effects of Discretionary Asset Write-offs. *Journal of Accounting Research*, 34(Suppl.):117–134.

International Accounting Standards Committee (1998). *Impairment of Assets.* International Accounting Standard No. 36. IASC, London.

Meeting, D.T. and Luecke, R.W. (2002). Asset Impairment and Disposal. *Journal of Accountancy*, 193(5):49–60.

Nurnberg, H. and Dittmar, N.W. Jr. (1996). Auditing Consideration of FASB 121. *Journal of Accountancy*, 182(1):71–78.

Rees, L., Gill, S., and Gore, R. (1996). An Investigation of Asset Write-Downs and Concurrent Abnormal Accruals. *Journal of Accounting Research*, 54(Suppl.):157–169.

Reinstein, A. and Lander, G.H. (2004). Implementing the Impairment of Assets Requirements of SFAS No. 144: An Empirical Analysis. *Managerial Auditing Journal*, 19(3):400–411.

Riedl, E.J. (2004). An Examination of Long-Lived Asset Impairments. *Accounting Review*, 79(3):823–852.

Schiff, J. (1985). Surprise Losses in Quarterly Earnings Reports. *Management Accounting*, 67(1):52–53.

Schuetze, W. (1987). Disclosure and the Impairment Question. *Journal of Accountancy*, 164(6):26–32.

Smith, K.J. (1994). Asset Impairment Disclosures. *Journal of Accountancy*, 178(6):57–63.

Strong, J.S. and Meyer, J.R. (1987). Asset Write-Downs: Managerial Incentives and Security Returns. *Journal of Finance*, 42(3):643–661.

Zabihollah, E., Smith, J.A., and Lindbeck, R.S. (1996). An Examination of Long-Lived Asset Impairments Under SFAS No. 121. *International Advances in Economic Research*, 2(1):86–91.

Zucca, L.J. and Campbell, D.R. (1992). A Closer Look at Discretionary Write-Downs of Impaired Assets. *Accounting Horizons*, 6(3):30–41.

15

The Rise and Impact of Hybrid Securities in Australian Listed Corporations

Tyrone M. Carlin and Nigel Finch

15.1 Introduction

In the wake of a global epidemic of revelations of corporate misbehavior in the first years of this decade came a resurgence in interest in and attentiveness towards the objective of improving corporate governance (Carlin and Ford, 2004). A major element of that wave of consciousness was manifested in a heightened focus on the need for improvements in the transparency, consistency, comparability, and decision usefulness of corporate financial reports. Failures on one or more of these dimensions more often than not lay at the heart of high-profile corporate scandals and collapses such as those epitomized by Enron, WorldCom, Global Crossing (these three being in the USA), HIH (an Australian example), and Parmalat (an Italian example).

From the time the global wave of governance crises reached its tumult until the present, the Australian market for hybrid financial instruments has burgeoned in size. According to estimates compiled by the Reserve Bank of Australia, the value of outstanding hybrid financial instruments more than doubled between 2001 and 2004, while hybrid issuance as a proportion of nonintermediated corporate debt issuance more than tripled over the same period[1]. Yet there are persistent questions as to the legitimacy of hybrid financial instruments, some commentators suggesting that their entire existence rests upon a foundation of regulatory arbitrage and that in consequence they are to be seen as another example of a classic financial reporting mirage. At first glance they appear equity like, but closer inspection reveals a lineage far more dominated by the hallmarks of debt[2] (Williams, 2005).

Such views are not without foundation. The mandatory requirement for adoption of International Accounting Standards by listed Australian companies with reporting periods beginning on or after 1 January 2005 has already caused shockwaves. The key reason for this is that IAS 32 (and thus its Australian corollary – AASB 132, *Financial Instruments: Disclosure and Presentation*) has shifted the basis for classification of financial instruments as falling into the categories of debt or equity by requiring that this task be dominated by considerations related to the economic substance, not the legal form, or the instrument. The thin veneer sufficient to imbue instruments with an equity-like character under the previous regulatory regime appears unlikely to suffice in a changed reporting environment and in consequence corporate Australia has responded with a raft of pre-emptive buybacks[3], covenant modifications for pre-existing instruments[4], and continued innovation[5] in the design and packaging of new security offerings.

This tension between the objectives of greater transparency and accuracy in financial reporting and the regulatory arbitrage-laced current which underpins the existence of hybrid securities provides an interesting backdrop for empirical research, of which surprisingly little has been undertaken in the Australian context, though some influential research relating to hybrids has been published internationally (e.g. Hopkins, 1996; Engel et al., 1999; Laurent, 2000). Consequently, a key motivation of this chapter is to provide evidence and analysis to fill that gap. In particular, this chapter demonstrates the potentially distorting impacts of the use of hybrid securities as an element of firm capital structure under both historical and forward-looking financial reporting regimes.

It is argued that despite the advances in the quality of the financial reporting architecture associated with Australia's adoption of International Financial Reporting Standards, the risks of these distortions remain essentially undiminished. As a result, further development of the reporting framework is argued to be necessary if the goal of greater transparency and accuracy in financial reporting is to be achieved. In supporting these arguments, the chapter proceeds as follows.

Section 15.2 provides background context by describing the nature and size of the Australian market for hybrid securities. Section 15.3 sets out details of the methodology we employed to measure the impact of hybrids on key measures of financial performance, risk, and firm value. We set out our results in section 15.4, while in section 15.5 we briefly outline our conclusions and some suggestions for future research.

15.2 The Australian hybrids market

Even as recently as the late 1990s bank lending dominated corporate debt raising in Australia. The Reserve Bank of Australia estimates that, as at June 1999, only 18% of total corporate debt raising was nonintermediated, with hybrids comprising a paltry 1% of total debt raised[6]. By June 2004, Australian debt capital markets had changed significantly, with 40% of debt raised in nonintermediated form. By this time, hybrid issuance represented 7% of total debt raisings in Australia (RBA, 2005a, p. 54).

Thus, not only had Australian corporations increasingly moved towards the creation and issue of their own debt securities rather than relying on traditional bank loan products, the type of instruments used by these organizations to facilitate the raising of capital had also substantially altered. Hybrids, in particular, became far more popular than they had been even a short period

Table 15.1 Gross issuance in Australia by market type ($bn)

Year of issuance	Domestic market	Offshore market	Total market
1998	1.461	2.203	3.664
1999	6.963	0.490	7.453
2000	1.200	1.002	2.202
2001	3.328	2.112	5.440
2002	5.004	0.787	5.792
2003	4.539	5.345	9.884
2004	4.362	2.993	7.355
2005	1.660	1.640	3.300
Total	28.518	16.571	45.089

Source: Reserve Bank of Australia (2005 data to May 2005 only).

earlier. This rise in popularity is captured in the data set out in Table 15.1, which sets out the gross value of hybrid issuance of hybrids by Australian corporations in both domestic and offshore capital markets between 1998 and 2005.

Although the domestic market has been the principal destination for hybrid capital raisings by Australian corporations, the data also reveals a strong capacity on the part of Australian corporations to raise capital by issuing hybrid securities into offshore capital markets. Further, as the data in Table 15.2 demonstrates, both financial and nonfinancial issuers have actively participated in hybrid issuance, with nonfinancial corporations playing an increasingly important role in more recent years as Australian financial institutions reached their Tier 1 capital limits for hybrid securities after several years of substantial issuance activity (RBA, 2005b, p. 55).

The Australian market for hybrid securities has also been characterized by rapid innovation in instrument design. This echoes experience with hybrid securities in international contexts (Smithson and Chew, 1993). In the Australian context, a number of factors combine to explain innovation. First, hybrid securities have been targeted far more to a retail investor audience than traditional corporate bond offerings. This has biased the design of many instruments towards the provision of higher yields[7] than those available on alternative asset classes, or on access to streams of tax credits not normally associated with distributions paid on traditional debt instruments (Moody's Investors Service, 2001, p. 5).

Changes to financial reporting requirements have also been a strong driver of variations in instrument design. The data set out in Table 15.3 shows clear

Table 15.2 Gross issuance in Australia by issuer type ($bn)

Year of issuance	Financial	Nonfinancial	Total issuers
1998	2.444	1.220	3.664
1999	5.295	2.158	7.453
2000	0.295	1.907	2.202
2001	1.035	4.405	5.440
2002	3.464	2.327	5.792
2003	6.470	3.414	9.884
2004	4.489	2.866	7.355
2005	1.375	1.925	3.300
Total	24.867	20.222	45.089

Source: Reserve Bank of Australia (2005 data to May 2005 only).

patterns associated with this phenomenon. It is particularly noteworthy, for example, that over recent periods, the single most dominant form of hybrid security issued by Australian corporations falls into a category known as perpetual step-up preference shares, while issuance activity of more traditional hybrid forms such as income securities has ceased altogether. As discussed below, step-up securities have been designed to satisfy the requirements for classification as equity under International Accounting Standards, something not possible in relation to traditional income securities given their particular design features.

The degree of security design innovation inherent in the Australian hybrid security market has resulted in considerable fragmentation. Many issues are small in terms of absolute dollars raised and are often unrated. Compared to vanilla debt security offerings they are complex, yet ironically have been most often pitched at a retail investor base which may not fully appreciate the magnitude and nature of risks associated with exposure to them (Smith, 2003).

Despite the high degree of variation in instrument design which we have noted characterizes the Australian market for hybrid instruments, it is possible to capture the broad parameters of the most important subclasses of securities which exist within the marketplace. As the data in Table 15.3 makes clear, the three most significant of these subclasses are hybrids that can be generally described as income securities, reset convertible preference shares, and, more recently, perpetual step-up preference shares. The essential features of these security subclasses are summarized in Table 15.4.

Table 15.3 Gross issuance in Australia by security type ($bn)

Year of issuance	Income security	Convertible preference share	Convertible note	Reset convertible preference share	Reset convertible note	Perpetual step-up preference share	Other	Total
1998	0.261	0.455	2.185	–	–	0.075	0.688	3.664
1999	5.640	0.726	0.586	0.490	–	–	0.011	7.453
2000	–	0.440	1.012	0.740	–	–	0.010	2.202
2001	0.065	0.315	0.978	2.070	0.400	–	1.612	5.440
2002	–	0.016	0.718	4.060	0.210	–	0.787	5.792
2003	–	0.029	0.950	4.394	1.540	2.970	–	9.884
2004	–	–	0.115	0.956	0.851	3.957	1.476	7.355
2005	–	–	–	0.110	–	2.425	0.765	3.300
Total	5.966	1.981	6.544	12.821	3.001	9.427	5.350	45.089

Source: Reserve Bank of Australia (2005 data to May 2005 only).

Table 15.4 Features of key hybrid security subclasses issued in Australia

Type	Key features
Income securities	Perpetual securities with regular interest or coupon payments. They are only redeemable at the option of the issuer.
Perpetual step-up securities	Similar to income securities, except that the interest payment on the security increases if the issuer does not redeem the security on a certain date.
Reset convertible preference shares/notes	The issuer has the option to change the terms or redeem the securities on a predetermined date. The investor has the option to accept the new terms of the security or to request an exchange. If an exchange is requested, the issuer decides whether it is for ordinary shares or cash.

While income securities dominated the Australian market for hybrid securities in the late 1990s, by far the most common form of hybrid found in this jurisdiction at present is the reset convertible instrument. Both are highly vulnerable to reclassification as debt under IFRS, the former because they are essentially indistinguishable from subordinated debt[8] and the latter because reset convertibles typically gave investors the right to convert their securities into a variable number of ordinary shares on defined dates or in response to certain defined events[9].

Perpetual step-up securities have become the most significant form of hybrid issued in Australia since the Australian Accounting Standards Board announced (in December 2003) pending Australian Accounting Standard 132, *Financial Instruments: Disclosure and Presentation*, pursuant to which most pre-existing forms of hybrid securities would be vulnerable to reclassification from equity to debt for financial reporting purposes. Their popularity is not coincidental, but rather is based upon the fact that step-up securities issued since December 2003 have been designed specifically to avoid being classified as debt for financial reporting purposes. They therefore represent a continuation of the tendency of issuers to design hybrid instruments with a view to achieving regulatory arbitrage – classification as equity while not far beneath the surface lie many of the characteristics of debt.

Thus, far from destroying the inertia of the Australian market for hybrid securities, the introduction of IFRS[10] has merely stimulated further design innovation and greater instrument design complexity[11]. Hybrid issuance continues apace, but it is not at all clear that the objectives of greater transparency and accuracy will in fact be engendered by the arrival of a new set of financial reporting rules from 2005 onwards. Thus, IFRS or not, an investigation of the potential impact of hybrids on the quality and accuracy of financial disclosures appears warranted. Section 15.3 describes our methodology for investigating the nature and magnitude of the problem.

15.3 Measuring the impact of hybrids

A central contention of this chapter is that the regulatory arbitrage upon which the construction of hybrid securities is founded results in the systemic treatment of these instruments as equity for financial reporting purposes. It is in turn posited that this has the potential to distort reported financial aggregates such that common measures of financial performance and risk calculated on the basis of those aggregates fail to convey an appropriate image of the underlying organic financial reality of the reporting entity.

Testing these propositions requires the implementation of a two-stage methodology. The first component of this methodology goes to acquiring evidence relating to the first contention, that those organizations which use hybrids as an element of their capital structure systemically misclassify them as equity when categorization as debt would represent a more appropriate treatment. The second component relates to acquisition of evidence of the distorting impact (if any) resulting from any detected misclassification. Jointly, this body of evidence provides a composite picture of the impact of the use of hybrid securities by Australian corporations, and by extension, the likely impact in other jurisdictions with similar regulatory structures, an obvious example being other jurisdictions which have adopted or which are moving towards the adoption of IFRS.

We test our first contention by applying a debt/equity characteristic matrix technique against a sample of hybrid securities currently outstanding in Australian capital markets. Specifically, our sample includes one randomly selected example of each of the three main classes of hybrid securities in existence in Australia: income notes[12], reset convertible preference shares[13], and perpetual step-up securities[14]. In order to determine the appropriate classification of each security we examine, we compare its essential characteristics against a six-point debt/equity characteristic matrix, and determine, on balance, whether the inherent characteristics of the instrument suggest that the instrument lies closer to 'pure debt' or 'pure equity'.

In undertaking this analysis, we classify pure debt as having the following characteristics. First, it enjoys contractually defined cash flows. Second, debt enjoys priority claims to the cash flows of the debtor entity while that entity remains a going concern, and to distributions flowing from disposal of assets in the case of liquidation. Finally, pure debt instruments are structured to have a finite, known maturity. By way of contrast, pure equity instruments do not enjoy contractually defined cash flows, have only residual claims to cash flows (both while the business remains a going concern and in the context of liquidation), and have an indefinite maturity[15]. We discuss the results of this analysis in section 15.4.

Where we determined that an instrument we reviewed had been misclassified, we undertook the task of recasting selected elements of the raw financial statements released by the organizations which issued the misclassified hybrids we detected in our sample. The most obvious impact of misclassifying a debt instrument as equity is to reduce the apparent leverage of the issuing organization. Therefore, where necessary, we recast the balance sheet by removing inappropriately classified hybrids from outstanding equity and adding them to the issuing entity's own balance sheet liabilities. We capture any differences by measuring changes in both the debt/equity ratio and the leverage ratio. The results of this analysis are discussed in section 15.4.

In addition to the obvious balance sheet impact, however, there remains the possibility of a material profit and loss impact, since cash distributions paid to holders of misclassified hybrid instruments are typically accounted for as distributions of retained earnings rather than treated as expenses (i.e. interest expense). We make relevant adjustments and measure the impact on earnings per share, return on assets, and return on equity. We also test for any impact on reported cash flows from operating activities, since it is normal to classify interest payments as cash outflows from operating activities, but distributions to equity instruments as cash outflows from financing activities.

Finally, by holding the price/earnings ratio of the issuing entity's ordinary equity securities constant, we estimate the potential impact on market capitalization which would result from a restatement of earnings per share flowing from a recasting of the profit and loss statement to reflect the status of outstanding hybrid securities as debt rather than equity[16].

15.4 Results

As briefly noted in section 15.3, for the purposes of this study we examined a randomly selected income note, reset convertible preference share, and perpetual step-up security. The income note security we examined for the purposes of this study was the so-called Woolworths Income Note (or WINs), issued by Woolworths Limited (ASX Stock Ticker Code WOW) in November 1999.

With a face value of $100, the WINs securities were officially quoted on the Australian Stock Exchange on 9 December 1999 (they carry the ASX Ticker Code WOWHA). The instruments are structured so that their holders have no voting rights and rank ahead of preference and ordinary shares for a return of capital in the event of winding up. However, they are subordinated to all creditors of Woolworths. Interest payments on WINs are made quarterly in arrears, and were initially set at a rate of 2% per annum above the 90-day bank bill rate (BBR) or a minimum rate of 7.25% per annum in each quarter until 15 December 2000, whichever was the greater.

Subsequently, the floating interest rate has been adjusted every quarter (a process that will continue throughout the life of the instruments) at 2% per annum above the BBR. These payments do not attract franking credits. WINs are perpetual securities and have no maturity; however, Woolworths can redeem each security for $100 cash at any date on the occurrence of a 'tax event' (i.e. where there is an unfavorable change in the taxation status of WINs to the detriment of Woolworths), and Woolworths has the option to redeem any outstanding WINs securities on or after 15 December 2004 for $100 cash.

In light of these characteristics, and applying the methodology we describe in section 15.3, we take the view that despite being treated as equity by Woolworths Limited, these instruments are most appropriately classified as debt. The principal equity-like feature they carry is their perpetual maturity, but this is more than offset by the contractual nature of the cash flows enjoyed by the holders of the securities and the prioritization of the claims enjoyed by holders of WINs over both ordinary and preference equity holders. Essentially, we contend that, in substance, these instruments are more akin to subordinated debt than to equity, and ought properly be treated as such in the financial statements of the issuing organization.

The reset convertible preference share security which we examined for the purposes of this study was the RePS security issued by David Jones Limited (ASX Stock Ticker Code DJS) in May 2002, raising $65 million. With a face value of $100, these RePS were officially quoted on the Australian Stock Exchange on 2 July 2002 under the Ticker Code DJSPA. Holders of RePS have no voting rights and though RePS are subordinated to all creditors of David Jones, they rank ahead of ordinary shares for a return of capital in the event of winding up and dividends on RePS are paid in priority to any dividends declared on ordinary shares.

The preferential noncumulative dividends on RePS are paid six-monthly in arrears and are fixed until the first reset date of 1 August 2007 at the greater of 8% per annum and the swap rate (on allotment) plus 2%. The dividend rate assumes full franking, so in the event that a dividend is unfranked or partially franked, the dividends on the RePS will be increased to compensate for any unfranked amount. The holder may elect to convert the RePS to ordinary shares at any time up until the reset date at a fixed rate of conversion (70.1754 ordinary shares per RePS). David Jones may elect to convert at any date in certain circumstances, including a takeover or scheme of arrangement, or proposed changes to taxation regulation.

On the reset date, either David Jones or the holder may elect to convert the RePS to ordinary shares using a conversion factor comprising two elements: (a) the average of the daily volume weighted average price of the David Jones ordinary shares over the 20 days prior to the conversion day; and (b) adjusting that price for a conversion discount of 5%. Notwithstanding, a maximum and minimum conversion rate applies of not less than 70.1754 ordinary shares per RePS and not more than 1052.6316 ordinary shares per RePS.

At the first reset date (1 August 2007), David Jones will reset the dividend rate for the RePS, as well as the next reset date, the conversion discount rate, and the maximum and minimum number of ordinary shares on conversion. Those holders who have not already converted are therefore accepting the new terms for RePS.

Having regard to the overall characteristics of these securities by applying our debt/equity classification methodology, we take the view that these securities would be more appropriately classified as debt than equity, though they are classified as equity by David Jones Limited. In forming this judgment, we have had particular regard to the priority claims conferred on the holders of these securities, as well as the strongly contractual features of the designated cash flows associated with the instruments.

The step-up security we examined for the purposes of this study are known as FUELS (Franked Unsecured Equity Linked Securities), and were issued by Australian listed oil and gas producer Santos Limited (ASX Stock Ticker Code STO) in September 2004, raising $500 million. With a face value of $100, FUELS were officially quoted on the Australian Stock Exchange on 5 October 2004 (under the Ticker Code STOPB).

The FUELS securities carry no voting rights except in relation to a limited set of circumstances, including proposals that affect the rights attached to FUELS or that reduce the share capital of the company. FUELS rank ahead of ordinary shares for a return of capital in the event of winding up and are subordinated to all creditors of Santos.

The securities are designed such that preferential noncumulative floating-rate dividends are paid six-monthly in arrears until 30 September 2009 and calculated by adding a 1.55% margin to the bank bill swap rate (BBSW) for 180-day bills as at the first business day of each dividend period. For the period on or after 30 September 2009, the dividend calculation is increased by a oneoff step-up in the margin by 2.25% (i.e. 1.55% margin + 2.25% step-up + BBSW). The dividend rate assumes full franking, so in the event that a dividend is unfranked or partially franked, the dividends on the FUELS will be increased to compensate for any unfranked amount.

FUELS are perpetual securities and have no maturity; however, Santos may convert or exchange some or all of the FUELS for ordinary shares or $100 cash on 30 September 2009 and each dividend payment date thereafter. Santos may elect to convert at any date in certain circumstances, including a takeover or scheme of arrangement, or proposed changes to taxation regulation or accounting standards.

The ratio at which FUELS will convert to ordinary shares is calculated by reference to the market price of the ordinary shares during the 20 business days immediately preceding, but not including, the conversion date, less a conversion discount of 2.5%. Notwithstanding, the conversion ratio will not be greater than 400 ordinary shares for each FUELS security. Again, having regard to the inherent characteristics of the FUELS securities, particularly the contractual nature of the cash flows associated with the instruments and the level of priority afforded to the holders of the securities, we take the view that despite Santos's classification of the instruments as equity, they would be more appropriately treated as debt. We summarize our findings in Table 15.5.

The above analysis demonstrates the empirical reality of the phenomenon about which we conjectured in our introductory remarks – namely that the design of hybrid securities is configured to allow issuers of such securities to adopt equity-like accounting treatment even though the economic substance of the instruments tends more closely towards the characteristics of debt. This gives rise to questions

Table 15.5 Characteristics of sample of hybrid securities issued in Australia

Security	Cash flow	Claims	Maturity	*Our* vs issuer classification
STOPB	Contractual	Priority	Indefinite	*Debt*/equity
DJSPA	Contractual	Priority	Definite	*Debt*/equity
WOWHA	Contractual	Priority	Indefinite	*Debt*/equity

Table 15.6 Hybrid issuers balance sheet analysis

Balance sheet	STO	DJS	WOW
Reported debt/equity ratio	0.70	0.72	1.99
Adjusted debt/equity ratio	1.04	0.99	3.18
Difference (%)	**48**	**37**	**60**
Reported gearing	1.70	1.72	2.99
Adjusted gearing	2.04	1.99	4.18
Difference (%)	**20**	**16**	**40**

as to the potential impact on key measures of financial performance and position caused by the misclassification problem we identify and discuss above.

Our methodology for undertaking this investigation is discussed in section 15.3. We first tested for impact on key balance sheet-based measures of financial position, particularly leverage. Our results are presented in Table 15.6.

The data demonstrates that the reclassification of hybrid instruments from that adopted by their issuers (equity) to our suggested treatment as debt would have materially impacted both the debt/equity and leverage ratios of each of the organizations we studied.

Were a reclassification to occur, this could have potentially significant impacts on both investor perceptions of the degree of risk associated with providing debt or equity capital to the organizations in question, and could also place the organizations studied at greater risk of breaching predefined debt covenants and other similar contractual obligations.

This may explain the increase in buyback and instrument redesign behavior we noted previously, in the wake of the Australian Accounting Standards Board's release of draft Australian Accounting Standard 132[17].

For reasons we set out in the discussion of our methodology, the misclassification of hybrid instruments as equity also has implications for key corporate performance measures, by reason of the treatment of cash flows to security holders as distributions of retained equity rather than as interest expense. We therefore measured reported earnings per share, return on assets, and return on equity for our sample and subsequently adjusted these measures to our estimate of the values they would have taken on had the cash flows been treated as interest costs (consistent with balance sheet classification of debt). We present our results in Table 15.7.

Table 15.7 Hybrid issuers profit and loss analysis

Profit and loss	STO	DJS	WOW
Reported EPS ($)	0.65	0.16	0.71
Adjusted EPS ($)	0.60	0.15	0.68
Difference (%)	**−7**	**−6**	**−4**
Reported ROA (%)	0.063	0.082	0.12
Adjusted ROA (%)	0.06	0.08	0.11
Difference (%)	**−7**	**−6**	**−4**
Reported ROE (%)	0.11	0.15	0.36
Adjusted ROE (%)	0.12	0.16	0.48
Difference (%)	**10**	**8**	**25**

Across our sample, both earnings per share (EPS) and return on assets (ROA) fall when adjusted for hybrid misclassification, the magnitude of the change being of the order of 5%. Conversely, adjusted return on equity (ROE) increases for each of the organizations we study, a result driven primarily by the significant increases in adjusted leverage we set out in Table 15.6.

We also tested the cash-flow data disclosed by our sample of organizations to determine the extent to which the misclassification of hybrids as equity impacted on the presentation of organizational cash-flow data. The impetus for this investigation is the realization that while cash distributions to equity holders are typically classified as cash outflows arising from financing activities, interest payments to debt holders are, by convention, classified as cash outflows arising from operating activities.

Since cash flow from operating activities is generally accepted to be a vital metric pertaining to organizational financial health and value generation intensity (e.g. see Nasser, 1993; Mulford and Comiskey, 2002), we test for the degree of impact on cash-flow presentation brought about by hybrid misclassification. We set out our results in Table 15.8.

Though not highly material as a proportion of total reported operating cash flows in our sample, each organization we studied did nonetheless adopt the convention of treating their cash distributions to hybrid security holders as cash flows from financing activities, even in cases where the documentation describing the structure of their hybrid securities clearly labels such distributions as 'interest'.

Finally, having regard to our revised estimates of earnings per share (as set out in Table 15.7), we estimated the potential impact on market capitalization of the sample of organizations we reviewed in the event that they reclassified their hybrid instruments as debt and altered all profit and loss reporting commensurately with that transformation. As discussed in the description of our methodology, for the sake of conservatism and consistency, we elected not to alter the observed price/earnings ratios exhibited by our sample organizations in carrying out this exercise.

As the data in Table 15.9 indicates, the estimated impact on market capitalization for each organization appears material, a matter of concern for ordinary equity holders as well as those with considerable wealth contingently tied to the value of the firm's ordinary equity – for example, option holders.

Table 15.8 Hybrid issuers cash-flow analysis

Cash flow	STO	DJS	WOW
Reported operating cash flow ($m)	565.3	167.0	1262.3
Hybrid distribution paid ($m)	14.7	5.3	42.9
Adjusted operating cash flow ($m)	550.6	161.7	1219.4
Difference in operating cash flow (%)	**−2.60**	**−3.15**	**−3.40**

Table 15.9 Hybrid issuers market analysis

Profit and loss	STO	DJS	WOW
Reported EPS ($)	0.65	0.16	0.71
Share price ($)	8.48	1.89	11.40
Price/earnings ratio (times)	13.1	11.9	16.1
Market capitalization ($m)	4960.2	778.1	11,768.2
Adjusted EPS	0.60	0.15	0.68
Adjusted share price ($)	7.90	1.78	10.92
Adjusted market cap. ($m)	4618.0	734.7	11,272.2
Difference in market cap. ($m)	**−342.1**	**−43.4**	**−496.0**
Difference in market cap. (%)	**−7**	**−6**	**−4**

15.5 Conclusion

The essential premise which motivated this chapter was that despite a growing focus on improved transparency, accuracy, and consistency in financial reporting evident in the wake of a raft of high-profile corporate scandals which broke in the beginning years of the new millennium, significant threats to such ideas still remained unchecked. We examined hybrid securities as an example of a construct which, as the evidence we have discussed above clearly suggests, demonstrates that this threat is not merely conjectural, despite high-profile 'reform' to financial reporting rules in Australia in the form of the adoption of International Financial Reporting Standards.

In our view, this only adds weight to the calls made by other scholars (e.g. McBarnet and Whelan, 1999; Anthony, 2004; Brilof, 2004) for continued revisions to be made to financial reporting frameworks with a view to further engendering a reporting philosophy and culture founded on the principle that financial statements should reflect economic substance rather than being trapped as the slaves of form.

Our study provides evidence that much territory remains to be covered before such a state of affairs is likely to be reached. In particular, our study reinforces the dynamic nature of regulatory arbitrage, as evidenced by the redesign of hybrid financial instruments to a form amenable to survival under forthcoming financial reporting regulatory regimes before the commencement date of those regimes. In effect, by designing financial reporting standards with a highly technical and detail-based bent, regulators appear to have stoked the fires of instrument design creativity and ensured the continued viability of financial reporting practices which, even at best, must be viewed as questionable.

While the case of hybrid financial instruments is of interest treated alone, as we have done here, the better view is that hybrid instruments represent only one of a matrix of phenomena which continue to derogate from the quality of external financial reporting, including, in particular, off balance sheet financing vehicles, certain forms of lease financing structures, and equity-linked compensation instruments, including options.

While this may seem an eclectic list, the difficulty inherent in each of its constituent elements is the failure of current financial reporting practices to adhere to a substance-based approach. The data we present and discuss in relation to hybrids adds to the understanding of the magnitude of the danger inherent with continued adherence to financial reporting rules not firmly embedded in the philosophy of giving precedence to highlighting the underlying economic substance of transactions or positions, above all other objectives. Much room remains for further empirical and theoretical work aimed at providing further illumination in relation to this critical point.

Notes

1. For the purposes of compiling its statistics, the Reserve Bank of Australia categorizes hybrid instruments as debt, irrespective of the accounting or taxation treatment accorded to them.
2. This has led one influential Australian commentator, Tom Ravlic, the policy advisor to the Australian National Institute of Accountants, to dub hybrids 'the transvestites of the accounting world'. In Ravlic's view, hybrids are made up to look like equity 'but once you strip away the lipstick and mini-skirt, you end up with debt' (quote drawn from Williams, 2005, p. 71).
3. For example, the ReCAPS hybrids issued by large Australian retailer Coles Myer. These instruments, through which Coles Myer raised approximately $700 million, were originally issued in December 2000. All were bought back by the company in July 2005. The company explained that its motivation in engaging in the buyback was to 'provide a simpler, more efficient capital structure that will benefit the company and shareholders over time'. Given that these were perpetual instruments of no fixed maturity, their survival for so limited a period speaks volumes as to the fragility of the desirability and usefulness of hybrid instruments in the face of regulatory change.
4. For example, the 'WINs' hybrids issued by Woolworths Limited, another large Australian retailer. Note 24 of the company's 2004 annual report states that the trust deed governing these instruments was altered post balance date, in preparation for the changed reporting environment ushered in by the adoption of International Financial Reporting Standards.
5. An important example of this is the arrival of so-called 'step-up' securities into the Australian hybrids market. These are of recent invention and should continue to allow classification as equity for financial reporting purposes. These are discussed in greater detail later in the chapter.
6. For the purposes of compiling its statistics, the Reserve Bank of Australia's standard protocol is to classify hybrids as debt irrespective of accounting or taxation treatment.
7. One indication of this is evident in the Reserve Bank of Australia's recent estimate that hybrid securities typically cost their issuers between 70 and 100 basis points more than equivalently rated traditional debt instruments (RBA, 2005a, p. 58).
8. Though they managed to be classified as equity due to their perpetual maturity and the existence of some degree of conditionality in relation to the right on the part of investors to receive promised cash-flow streams.
9. As noted in the introduction to this chapter, many organizations have responded to this likely change in classification by engaging in pre-emptive buybacks of these instruments. As a further example, in August 2004, Computershare Limited notified holders of its reset preference shares that it had opted to invoke an early conversion of the instruments to ordinary equity, in accordance with the terms of issue of the reset preference shares. Its explanation for its decision to do this was that: 'The board has made this decision following the release in December 2003 by the Australian Accounting Standards Board with effect from 1 January 2005 of pending Australian Accounting Standard 132, Financial Instruments: Disclosure and Presentation (AASB 132).

AASB 132 will have the effect of requiring the RPS (currently treated as equity) to be treated as debt for accounting purposes.'

10. Together with changes in prudential regulatory rules relating to the classification of securities as tier 1 capital of financial institutions announced by APRA in April 2004.
11. This applies not only to the actual design features of the instruments, but to the nomenclature of the instruments. A sample of the acronyms used to describe hybrid securities currently outstanding in Australian capital markets includes: CARES, CARS, FIRsTS, FUELS, PARS, PAVERS, PERLS, PINES, POWERS, PRESSES, RENTS, RePS, SAINTS, SHEDS, SITES, TELYS, TICkETS, WINES, and WINs. In many cases, the acronyms are designed to in some way reflect the nature of the underlying business of the issuing entity. Thus, FUELS (Franked Unsecured Equity Linked Securities) were issued by energy company Santos, PRESSES (Preferred Reset Securities Exchangeable for Shares) were issued by newspaper and media company Fairfax Limited, and so on.
12. We use the WINs securities issued by large listed retailer Woolworths Limited as our example of this class of security.
13. We use the reset convertible preference shares (RePS) issued by listed specialty retailer David Jones Limited as our example of this class of security.
14. We use the FUELS securities issued by listed oil and gas producer Santos Limited as our example of this class of security.
15. Albeit with slight modifications to terminology, each of Moody's, Standard & Poor's, and Fitch Ratings use essentially the same approach that we describe above to differentiate between debt and equity securities for the purposes of undertaking credit analysis.
16. We assume in doing so that capital markets have priced the ordinary equity securities issued by the firm without impounding the potentially dilutive impact on EPS of a reclassification of that firm's hybrid securities to debt, from equity. Further, for the sake of conservatism, we hold the price/earnings multiple applied to EPS constant for the purposes of deriving an estimate of the impact on market capitalization.
17. Refer to sections 15.1 and 15.2 of this chapter for a review of this discussion. In this vein, it is particularly interesting to note the circumstances under which the perpetual step-up security we examined for the purposes of this chapter – the Santos Limited 'FUELS' – came into existence. Santos issued the FUELS securities in 2004 in part to fund the buyback of $350 million worth of previously issued reset convertible preference shares (RePS). These securities were vulnerable to reclassification from equity to debt as a result of the changed accounting rules embodied in AASB 132. The new rules took effect for all accounting periods commencing on or after 1 January 2005, so from this point of view, the buyback of the pre-existing RePS securities prior to the conclusion of 2004 was distinctly advantageous.

References

Anthony, R. (2004). *Rethinking the Rules of Financial Accounting.* McGraw-Hill, New York.

Brilof, A. (2004). Accounting Scholars in the Groves of Academe in Pari Delicto. *Critical Perspectives on Accounting,* 15(6–7):787–796.

Carlin, T. and Ford, G. (2004). A Governance Perspective on Executive Options Plans – Reflections on Some Australian Empirical Evidence. MGSM Working Paper No. 4.

Engel, E., Erickson, M., and Maydew, E. (1999). Debt–Equity Hybrid Securities. *Journal of Accounting Research*, 37(2):249–274.

Hopkins, P. (1996). The Effect of Financial Statement Classification of Hybrid Financial Instruments on Analysts' Stock Price Judgments. *Journal of Accounting Research*, 34(3):33–51.

Laurent, S. (2000). *Capital Structure Decision: The Use of Preference Shares and Convertible Debt in the UK*. EFMA, Athens.

McBarnet, D. and Whelan, C. (1999). *Creative Accounting and the Cross-Eyed Javelin Thrower*. John Wiley, Hoboken, NJ.

Moody's Investors Service (2001). Special Comment – Aussie Hybrids: The Search for Equity-Like Instruments Continues. Moody's Global Credit Research, March.

Mulford, C. and Comiskey, E. (2002). *The Financial Numbers Game – Detecting Creative Accounting Practices*. John Wiley, Hoboken, NJ.

Nasser, K. (1993). *Creative Financial Accounting – Its Nature and Use*. Prentice-Hall, London.

Reserve Bank of Australia (2005a). *Financial Stability Review*, March. Australian Government Printer, Sydney.

Reserve Bank of Australia (2005b). *Statement on Monetary Policy*, August. Australian Government Printer, Sydney.

Smith, M. (2003). Investors in Hybrid Securities Taking a Trip into the Financial Twilight Zone. *The Australian*, 26 September, p. 22.

Smithson, C. and Chew, D. (1993). The Uses of Hybrid Debt in Managing Corporate Risk. In: *Corporate Finance – Where Theory Meets Practice* (Chew, D., ed.), pp. 356–366. McGraw-Hill, New York.

Williams, M. (2005). Sun Sets on Re-Set Shares. *CFO Magazine*, October, 71–75.

16

Empirical Evidence on the Use, Size, Concentration, and Cost of Executive Options Schemes in Australia

Tyrone M. Carlin and Guy Ford

16.1 Introduction

By the early years of the new millennium, debate about the role, legitimacy, and impact of executive options was endemic. Although academic literature had begun to produce troubling results in relation to links between the existence and magnitude of executive options schemes and opportunistic behavior on the part of recipient executives (e.g. Aboody and Kasnik, 2000; Ali and Stapledon, 2000; Chen, 2002), the issue which dominated public debate related to desirability of revising financial reporting rules to require that the cost of executive options be counted in the determination of the annual reported profitability of corporations granting options to their executives.

These debates reached and engulfed the actors entrenched at the commanding heights of the regulatory, political, and financial institutions of the United States. Faced by a recalcitrant corporate sector largely unwilling to embrace the principle of recognizing the cost of options in the process of calculating profits (despite the capacity to do so under the precepts of SFAS 123), apparently for fear of the negative impact this would have on reported profits, a number of high-profile US figures made their views very plain indeed. In a speech delivered at New York University, US Federal Reserve Chairman Alan Greenspan is reported to have said:

> 'If investors are dissuaded by lower reported earnings as a result of expensing, it means that they were less informed than they should have been. Capital employed on the basis of misinformation is likely to be capital misused.'
>
> (*Wall Street Journal*, 27 March 2002)

Warren Buffet was even more direct, asking:

> 'If options aren't a form of compensation, what are they? If compensation isn't an expense, what is it? And if expenses shouldn't go into calculations of earnings, where in the world should they go?'
>
> (Merrill Lynch, Global Industry Research Note, *Accounting for Options*, 7 May 2002)

In the United States Senate, Senators Levin and McCain introduced a bill which, if enacted, would have forced corporations either to expense options or to pay tax on them (the bill was introduced to the US Senate on 12 February 2002; it was not passed into law). Inevitably, the repercussions of these debates were felt in other advanced market economies such as Australia, where the key issues were rendered even more tangible by the lack of even basic mandatory accounting rules on the subject of executive options (Carlin and Ford, 2003).

There, the announcement that an accounting standard requiring that the cost of options be recognized as an expense in the calculation of corporate profit would be operative by 2005[1] appears to have been taken as a signal for a return of collective calm and disinterest[2] in what, before the announcement of an impending standard, had been a contentious issue. Remarkably, in our view, the debate in Australia receded without any systematic airing of key empirical issues relating to the magnitude and impact of options usage or the possible policy consequences flowing therefrom. Thus, in this chapter, we contribute to the literature by providing an overview of a number of key parameters relating to the use of executive options in Australia. The chapter proceeds as follows.

In section 16.2, we describe our sample and the time period over which we conducted our research, and set out evidence on the frequency with which large listed Australian corporations used options schemes in the context of the remuneration of their employees during that period. In section 16.3, we review the scale of these schemes by examining the number of options issued, the number of options outstanding, and the number of options exercised by our sample of corporations during the period we studied. We also provide data relating to options holding concentration and present some preliminary thoughts on the implications of this data.

In section 16.4 we present some estimates of the impact the options schemes we observed would have had on the operating profit before taxation reported by our sample of corporations had they been under an obligation to factor costs associated with their options schemes into their annual earnings calculations. Finally, in section 16.5 we set out some conclusions and prognostications for future research.

16.2 How prevalent are executive options plans in Australia?

In order to develop insights into the scope of use of executive options plans in Australia, we selected a sample consisting of the top 100 Australian listed corporations (as measured by market capitalization) as at the conclusion of 1996. We then gathered data relating to the use of executive options plans by these organizations from 1997 through to 2004, inclusive. We initially set the commencement year for our study as 1996, but found that financial statement disclosures relating to options were so fragmented and inconsistent in that year that it was necessary to select a later year as the commencing period for the study.

We classified corporations within our sample as falling into one of three classes in each of the years we reviewed. The first group is labeled 'no plan'. Corporations fell into this category in a particular year if their annual report for that period contained no reference to options plans. The second group is labeled 'has plan'. These corporations did include references to the existence of options plans within their annual financial reports.

The final group is labeled 'exit'. These firms either merged or were delisted during the period under review, making it impossible to gather data in relation to their options schemes for the entire period under review. However, for the sake of completeness, these companies are also tracked in our dataset, allowing the calculation of the proportion of surviving firms within the sample which maintained an executive options plan in each year we studied.

Slightly more than half of the sample of large firms we examined had options plans in 1997. This grew rapidly to approximately 80% of our surviving firms by 2000, and stabilized thereafter. However, the data displays no convincing evidence that the turn of the millennium controversies surrounding the use and impact of options referred to above has resulted in any measurable dampening in the enthusiasm of Australian corporations for the use of options schemes as an element of executive compensation. This data is set out in Table 16.1.

While this data clearly shows a pattern of growth in the application of executive options schemes in the first half of the period reviewed, followed by a period of stabilization, it does not permit direct insight into the size and level of activity (both in terms of fresh grants and exercises of options) of these schemes. This is discussed in section 16.3.

Table 16.1 Proportion of sample organizations with executive options plans

	1997	**1998**	**1999**	**2000**	**2001**	**2002**	**2003**	**2004**
No plan	47	32	29	22	20	17	17	17
Has plan	53	68	71	78	77	75	62	62
Exit	0	0	0	0	3	8	21	21
Sample total	100	100	100	100	100	100	100	100
Survivors with plan (%)	53	68	71	78	79	82	78	78

16.3 Size, activity, and concentration of the observed options schemes

In order to gauge the scale of options schemes and the degree of activity of those schemes, we measured three variables. These were: the volume of new option grants each year, the volume of option exercises each year, and the volume of outstanding options at the end of each year. We also examined the degree of holdings concentration evident in Australian executive options schemes. This provides a higher resolution view of the nature of these schemes than would otherwise be available, and provides data on a variable which has been relatively little researched but which, as we explain later in this section, may be of significance in influencing the impact of executive options schemes.

To take account of variations in the size of the organizations we studied and the changes in the total number of organizations which had active options plans in each of the years we studied, we express the data relating to each variable as a percentage of outstanding ordinary equity at the conclusion of each year studied. The first two variables, 'grants' and 'exercises', measure the level of activity in the options plans we examined[3], while the third variable, 'volume outstanding', provides a scale measure. Our findings are presented in Table 16.2.

Two features of the data in particular are worth noting. First, between 1997 and 2000, there was much higher growth in the scale of the options plans we observed than in the propensity of corporations within our sample to employ options plans. Recall that 53% of our sample had options plans in 1997, versus 78% by 2000. This represents growth of approximately 50% across that period. However, over the same timeframe, the volume of options on issue as a proportion of outstanding ordinary equity capital rose from 1.56% to 6.27%, a fourfold increase in scale. Thus, on average, not only did more corporations choose to use options schemes, but the scale of those schemes grew significantly.

Second, it would appear that corporations using options schemes significantly changed their behavior from 2001 onwards. Observe, for example, how the

Table 16.2 Option grants, exercises, and volumes outstanding

	1997	1998	1999	2000	2001	2002	2003	2004
Grants (%)	0.65	1.43	3.73	2.15	0.52	0.78	0.39	0.44
Exercises (%)	0.0004	0.014	0.058	0.20	0.76	0.56	2.67	1.01
Volume outstanding (%)	1.56	1.80	4.61	6.27	5.25	5.61	2.56	2.07

volume of options grants recorded in 2001 fell to approximately a quarter of the level observed in 2000. This was not a transient event. The level of grant activity for the remainder of the time period reviewed also remained within a tight range of the 2001 grant volume level.

Balanced against this, there was no material fall in the proportion of our sample which continued to operate executive options plans, and in consequence, taking account of the lagged effect associated with exercises, the average scale of options plans (as measured by options outstanding as a proportion of outstanding ordinary equity capital) declined during the final years we studied, settling in a range closer to what it had been in the first two years for which we collected data.

We cannot draw firm conclusions as to the cause of this material change in grant volume and scheme size. Market factors may account for part of these occurrences: the five-year period leading up to 2000 had been one of steady growth in the Australian All-Ordinaries Share Price Index, but the two-year period 2000–2001 was one characterized by little growth and high volatility. The Index then showed substantial decline over the year 2002 and the first quarter of 2003. These patterns could be linked to options schemes becoming less attractive in the remuneration packages of executives over these periods in time.

Further, it does not seem too far fetched to suggest that the level of political and media attention focused on executive options during 2001 and 2002[4], together with the looming likelihood that in the not too distant future the financial reporting rules would evolve to require expensing of options, saw companies retreating from the expansive use of options schemes which they had adopted by 1999 and 2000. In this regard, Table 16.3 shows the number of articles in major Australian newspapers, on a year-by-year basis, between 1996 and 2004.

Following virtually no media interest in the period to 1996–2001, a substantial number of articles appear in 2002. From 2003, media articles decline almost as significantly as they rose in the preceding period[5]. Though not comprehensive, this does provide at least some evidence which appears consistent with our thoughts on the possible drivers of the marked reduction in option grants which transpired in 2001 and later periods compared with grant activity in 1999 and 2000.

Table 16.3 Newspaper articles on executive options

	1996	1997	1998	1999	2000	2001	2002	2003	2004
Number of articles	1	2	11	6	19	14	251	121	51

In addition to our investigation of the size and activity parameters we discuss above, we also gathered data on the holdings concentration of the option plans put in place by the organizations we studied.

The term 'holding concentration' refers to a measurement of the degree to which the ownership of options issued pursuant to an organization's executive options scheme is concentrated in the hands of a select group of senior actors, defined in this study to include the board (including executive and nonexecutive members), the chief executive officer, and the five highest remunerated nondirector executives employed by the firm. Thus, holdings concentration represents the percentage of outstanding options issued by an organization held by the group of senior actors defined above[6].

We set out our data on this variable in Table 16.4. Even on cursory inspection, a number of matters are clearly apparent. The first such issue is the high proportion of executive options which are held (on average) by the chief executive officer. In our sample, CEOs on average held approximately one-fifth of all outstanding options. This suggests a strong nexus between the total wealth of these individuals and the share prices of the organizations they lead.

It requires the aggregation of the option holdings of all the remaining board members and the next five nonboard executives to match the volume of

Table 16.4 Concentration of option holdings among senior management (average holdings by company), 1997–2004

Year	Chairman	CEO	Executive director	Non-executive director	Board senior executive	Nonboard senior executive	Total senior executives[a]
1997	14%	31%	15%	12%	40%	7%	40%
1998	14%	26%	15%	10%	34%	12%	42%
1999	10%	20%	11%	8%	26%	11%	38%
2000	14%	19%	15%	11%	27%	10%	40%
2001	11%	20%	12%	9%	28%	12%	38%
2002	9%	17%	14%	10%	24%	17%	40%
2003	11%	21%	13%	7%	27%	18%	42%
2004	12%	18%	15%	6%	26%	19%	43%

[a] This is the sum of all board option holdings (irrespective of position on board, executive or nonexecutive status), as well as the holdings of the top five nonboard executives employed by the firm. Because of the averaging technique used in deriving the data, it is not possible to sum the columns in any row on the table to reach this aggregate figure.

options placed in the hands of the CEO alone. Nonetheless, a second important observation from the data is that board holdings dominate those by nonboard executives (though not to an enormous extent) and that, together, the very elite of the executive ranks of the organizations we studied controlled a very significant proportion of the total number of options outstanding pursuant to their organization's executive options plan.

Therefore, on the basis of our data we argue that the executive options plans of large Australian corporations are characterized by a significant degree of holdings concentration. In the only other published research of which we are aware which touches on this issue, Blasi et al. (2003, p. 190) suggest senior executive holding concentration in top 100 US-based firms at around 33%. It would therefore seem that, at least in aggregate, the Australian experience is similar to that of the United States.

To the extent that concentration has been associated with a greater tendency for firms to display shareholder value reducing (but option holder value increasing) behavior[7], the apparent similarity in concentration levels between the USA and Australia might also assist in the interpretation of the applicability of US empirical research results for Australian conditions.

Our rationale for gathering the data reported within this chapter in relation to options holding concentration is based on a logical deduction rather than empirical analysis. We begin with the premise that the existence of options schemes as an element of executive remuneration brings with it the possibility of inducing incentives for behavior which, while enriching the holder of the option, does nothing for or actually degrades shareholder wealth (Ellis, 1998; Core and Guay, 2001; Yermack, 2001; Chen, 2002; Monks, 2003). Upon examining the literature which examines this possibility, it became clear to us that most of the mechanisms for achieving these unfortunate wealth transfers were within the grasp of only a very select group of actors within an organization.

Altering capital structure mix, systematic alteration of firm risk profile, the management of information flows between the firm and capital markets, the timing of options issue and vesting, and the execution of decisions to engage in reloads are all initiated by a very narrow but powerful constituency within a firm (Carlin and Ford, 2004). Yet our data demonstrates that this same constituency stands to gain disproportionately from an inflation of option value. Our basic intuition may therefore be put as simply as suggesting that the narrow decision-making constituency holding a disproportionate exposure to outstanding options has both the means and the motive necessary to give effect to actions which endanger shareholder wealth creation and therefore represent poor governance outcomes.

This capacity for action is brought into even sharper relief when considering our surprising findings about the extent to which even nonexecutive directors participate in options schemes in some of the organizations in our sample. Whether or not this capacity has been brought to bear is an empirical question with which we propose to engage in future research. However, irrespective of additional empirical enquiry, the results reported in this chapter stand alone, and serve as a reminder that while the careful design of incentive contracts (for example, options packages) represents an important element of governance oversight, so too does the maintenance of a careful watch on the dispersion or concentration of ownership of options issued by firms as part of overall remuneration policy.

Having considered the question of options holding concentration, we turn to the question of the cost of the executive option schemes we studied. This is set out in section 16.4.

16.4 Estimated cost of executive options schemes

At no time during the period we studied was there any requirement that Australian corporations with executive options schemes reflect the cost of these schemes in their annual profit calculations, and none of the companies we studied did so voluntarily. However, from the late 1990s onwards, the organizations we studied typically made reasonably detailed disclosures relating to their options plans in the notes to their accounts.

Coupled with disclosures (not forming part of their annual financial reports) about their options plans these companies were required to make to the Australian Stock Exchange, we were able to gather sufficient data to support the estimation of the expense associated with the options schemes employed by our sample of companies, but not recognized in the calculation of their reported profits.

The question of how best to estimate expenses associated with options schemes and reflect these expenses within corporate financial statements remains controversial and contested (Coulton and Taylor, 2002). In particular, though most approaches accept the use of techniques such as the Black–Scholes model to estimate the fair value of options at the date of grant[8], the question of how such values might be recognized in financial statements and subsequently modified in light of changing circumstances (for example, changing market prices for the underlying equity securities, options failing to vest) is highly controversial.

It is not our objective to engage with the financial reporting debate in this chapter. However, because we report data in Table 16.5 that represents our estimate of the degree to which the reported operating profit before tax of our sample of companies would have been reduced had the cost of options been factored into the calculation of that number, it is necessary to briefly explain the valuation and reporting methodology we employed in constructing our expense estimates.

We began by using a Black–Scholes model to estimate the fair value of options granted in any given year. We then treated that entire amount as an expense of the period during which the grant occurred. At each subsequent balance date, we marked outstanding options to market, again using the Black–Scholes model as our basis for estimating fair value.

Any resulting valuation increments (or decrements) were taken to each period's profit and loss calculation as expenses (or expense reversals). Any lapses of options were accounted for as expense reversals in the period during which the lapse occurred. The net effect of this mark-to-market-based approach to accounting for executive options is that, over the life of the option, the expense which is distributed through the profit and loss statement of the granting entity will equal the intrinsic value of the option at the point in time when it is exercised.

Thus, in net terms, expenses will only be recognized over time when a transfer of intrinsic economic value between employer and employee actually does transpire. Consequently, the expense to shareholders is exactly the same as the opportunity cost of the foregone cash flows which they could have enjoyed as a result of the issue of equity at market prices, but did not because equity was issued to employees at below market prices.

The chief objection to this approach to the financial reporting of the impact of executive options schemes is that its reliance on the mark-to-market process may result in substantial increases in the volatility of reported earnings (Berger et al., 1991; Jones, 1993; Robertson, 1995). However, in other Australian settings where a mark-to-market accounting approach has long been the norm, its application is

Table 16.5 Estimated expense associated with options plans

	1997	1998	1999	2000	2001	2002	2003	2004
Exp. ($m)	342.5	2780	279	3008	102.6	(753.3)	(52.3)	580.2
Total OPBT ($m)	14,550	18,644	16,756	27,550	23,707	8206	27,139	30,389
Exp. OPBT (%)	2.35	14.91	1.66	10.92	0.43	(9.18)	(0.19%)	1.91

no longer seen as contentious nor has its application caused observable havoc (Carlin, 2002).

We provide three basic data items in Table 16.5. The first of these is our estimate, expressed in millions of Australian dollars, of the per-period expense associated with the options schemes operated by our sample of listed corporations. The second item is the sum of the before-tax operating profits reported by the subset of companies in our sample which had executive options schemes in each particular period. The final item expresses our estimate of the expense of the executive options schemes we identified in each period as a proportion of the reported before-tax profits of the companies we identified as having executive options schemes in those periods.

Though, as discussed, the application of a mark-to-market approach to the estimation of option expenses has resulted in noticeable between-period volatility, the more important consideration is that the average impact of options-related expenses across all companies and years we reviewed was of the order of 3% of the before-tax profits reported by companies using options schemes. While this is lower than some published estimates of the average impact of expensing the options schemes of samples of US listed companies[9], the effect is material nonetheless[10].

16.5 Conclusion

Our data provides a preliminary overview of the frequency of use, size, concentration, and potential cost impact of executive options schemes used by large listed Australian corporations. Though in this chapter we do not provide directly measured evidence relating to impact on corporate performance, governance quality, and risk behavior associated with these schemes, our data makes it plain that, in an Australian context, executive options schemes have been and remain economically significant and an important subject for continuing research.

This is particularly the case for options' holding concentration, which has been an under-researched variable, though one which may hold the key to a more detailed and meaningful understanding of the nature of executive options plans and thus a greater capacity to predict their impact on corporate performance, governance standards, and risk behavior.

Notes

1. This did eventuate, in the form of Australian Accounting Standard AASB 2, Share-Based Payment. Knowledge of the impending standard was widespread by early 2003.

2. As to which, see the data we set out on the frequency of newspaper articles in major Australian newspapers devoted to executive options in Table 16.3.
3. One other form of event, lapses, also provides a measure of turnover activity in corporate options plans. However, in the context of our sample of companies and the timeframe of our analysis, lapses represented only a minor phenomenon, dominated by grants and exercises. Bearing this in mind, and for reasons of space, we do not discuss lapses in this chapter.
4. We have discussed these issues in greater detail elsewhere (see Carlin and Ford, 2004).
5. Data extracted from the Factiva database, set to 'all dates', 'Australia and New Zealand', 'major Australian newspapers', 'executive options'.
6. On the basis of disclosures contained within the annual financial statements of listed public corporations, it is possible to gather data on options issuance and holdings to this level of detail.
7. This suggestion is a key tenet of the arguments advanced by Blasi et al. in relation to problematical design aspects of executive options plans (see Blasi et al., 2003, p. 190).
8. A representative example is Australian Accounting Standard AASB 2, Share-Based Payment, which specifically recognizes the use of the Black–Scholes and binomial approaches to the estimation of the fair value of options as at the date of grant. In the United States, FAS 123 also recognizes the use of models such as Black–Scholes to assist with the initial process of estimating the fair value of options granted pursuant to executive options plans.
9. Merrill Lynch published a study in 2002 in which they estimated the impact of expensing the options schemes of all companies in the Dow Jones Industrial Index. They concluded that the average impact on the 2001 earnings of that group of companies would have been 7% (Merrill Lynch, 2002).
10. The sum of our expense (and expense reversal) estimates for our sample of companies between 1997 and 2004 is approximately $6.3 billion.

References

Aboody, D. and Kasnik, R. (2000). CEO Stock Option Awards and the Timing of Corporate Voluntary Disclosures. *Journal of Accounting and Economics*, 29(1):73–100.

Ali, P. and Stapledon, G. (2000). Having Your Options and Eating Them Too: Fences, Zero Cost Collars and Executive Share Options. *Company and Securities Law Journal*, 18(4):277–282.

Berger, A., King, K., and O'Brien, J. (1991). The Limitations of Market Value Accounting and a More Realistic Alternative. *Journal of Banking and Finance*, 15(4–5):753–783.

Blasi, J., Kruse, D., and Bernstein, A. (2003). *In the Company of Owners – The Truth About Stock Options and Why Every Employee Should Have Them*. Basic Books, New York.

Carlin, T. (2002). Valuation Implications of Mark to Market Accounting in the Australian General Insurance Industry. 10th Pacific Basin Finance Economics and Accounting (PBFEA) Conference, Singapore, August.

Carlin, T. and Ford, G. (2003). Opinions on Options: Discordant Incentives and Desultory Disclosure. *Journal of Law and Financial Management*, 2(1):7–13.

Carlin, T. and Ford, G. (2004). A Governance Perspective on Executive Options Plans – Reflections on Some Australian Empirical Evidence. MGSM Working Paper No. 4.

Chen, Y. (2002). Executive Stock Options and Managerial Risk Taking. Working Paper, University of Houston, Houston, TX.

Core, J. and Guay, W. (2001). Stock Options Plans for Non Executive Employees. *Journal of Financial Economics*, 61(2):253–287.

Coulton, J. and Taylor, S. (2002). Accounting for Executive Stock Options: A Case Study in Avoiding Tough Decisions. *Australian Accounting Review*, 12(2):3–10.

Ellis, R. (1998). Equity Derivatives, Executive Compensation and Agency Costs. *Houston Law Review*, 35:399–321.

Jones, T. (2003). Market Value – The Debate Rages. *Financial Executive*, January–February:30–36.

Merrill Lynch (2002). Accounting for Options. *Merrill Lynch Global Industry Research*, 7 May.

Monks, R. (2003). Equity Culture at Risk: The Threat to Anglo-American Prosperity. *Corporate Governance – An International Review*, 11(3):164–170.

Robertson, F. (1995). Pollyanna Profits – Why Some Managers Fear AASB 1023. *JASSA*, June, 7–12.

Yermack, D. (2001). Executive Stock Options: Puzzles, Problems and Mysteries. Working Paper, Stern School of Business, New York University, New York.

17

The Introduction of Fair Value in Italy: Economic and Financial Reporting Issues

Giovanni Melis, Andrea Melis, and Alessandro Pili

17.1 Introduction

Starting in 2005, the European Union requires the adoption of the International Financial Reporting Standards (IFRS[1]) by its Member States, as well as by the members of the European Economic Block (EU directive 65/2001; EU law 1606/2002). This regulation has given a great impetus to the adoption of IFRS in Europe and has significantly fostered the accounting harmonization process in the European Union (e.g. Alexander and Nobes, 1994; Nobes and Parker, 2002; Whittington, 2005). Accordingly, there is a need for senior management, investors, and policymakers to understand the implications of IFRS adoption on financial reporting (e.g. Schipper, 2005), as it seems likely to have a profound effect on corporate financial statements, especially in countries, such as Italy, whose accounting system was traditionally more stakeholder oriented rather than shareholder oriented.

Generally accepted accounting principles are not to be considered as 'universal' principles, rather they are standards that derive from the influence of several 'environmental' factors (e.g. Choi and Mueller, 1992; Belkaoui, 1995; Onesti, 1995; Nobes, 1998).

The purpose of this chapter is to analyze the economic and financial reporting issues concerning the introduction of fair value measurements for the individual financial statements (nonconsolidated financial statements) of Italian nonfinancial listed companies. Measurement techniques are beyond its scope.

European Union mandatory adoption of IFRS is only related to consolidated financial statements. Any distributable profits are calculated using the individual accounts of a corporate entity and not the consolidated accounts of the group. Accordingly, any corporate group that has to adopt IFRS, but whose individual accounts of companies in the group remain under national generally accepted accounting principles (GAAP), will not have its distributable profits subject to IFRS. However, since the Italian policymakers require Italian listed companies to prepare and disclose their separate and individual financial statements in accordance with IFRS starting in 2006, the key economic issues related to such a requirement will be discussed.

The remainder of this chapter is organized as follows. Section 17.2 will describe the general framework regarding the adoption of IFRS in Italy, as well as the decision of Italian policymakers regarding the distributability of gains that may be driven from using fair value measurements.

Section 17.3 will provide a comparison between Italian GAAP, IFRS, and the US GAAP with regard to the application of fair value measurements, which represents one of the most important innovations, if not the key one, in corporate financial statement preparation and disclosure based on IFRS.

Section 17.4 will analyze the effects of the introduction of fair value on the financial statements of nonfinancial listed companies in Italy. It will provide two examples of what might happen to corporate capital if there were no limits imposed by the law and if shareholders, in their general meeting, decide to distribute fair value gains as dividends.

In section 17.5 we will compare and contrast the importance of the accrual basis and prudence (conservatism)[2] principles in the Italian GAAP, IFRS, and the US GAAP. Differences in the relative importance of the conservatism principle over the accrual basis principle in the Italian GAAP seem to explain differences in the application of fair value measurements in Italian financial statements, especially with regard to the limits of the distribution of fair value gains to shareholders as dividends.

Section 17.6 will provide some explanations regarding the origins of the importance of the conservatism principle in the Italian GAAP and commercial law, by examining the specific corporate governance features that characterize the social and economic context in which Italian listed companies operate.

Section 17.7 will recommend the adoption of a detailed comprehensive income statement, in which all nondistributable fair value gains and losses are disclosed. Such disclosure will increase the quality of information to investors for their economic decision-making, as well as satisfy the Italian law requirements concerning capital maintenance. Furthermore, such disclosure may overcome the potential tradeoff between the accrual basis and the prudence accounting principles. Finally, section 17.8 concludes.

17.2 The adoption of the International Financial Reporting Standards in Italy

Since 2005, the European Union (EU directive 65/2001; EU law 1606/2002) has required its Member States to adopt IFRS for the preparation and presentation of consolidated financial statements for their financial companies (e.g. banks and insurance companies), either listed or nonlisted, as well as for their nonfinancial listed companies. The European Union requirement covers only consolidated financial statements. EU mandatory regulation does not refer to separate and individual financial statements, as Member States were given discretion regarding this type of financial statement.

The exact effects of any EU directive on a particular country clearly depend on the laws passed by each Member State's legislature. In accordance with EU options, the Italian policymakers have decided to make an additional step toward accounting harmonization with EU companies, by requiring Italian financial listed and unlisted companies and nonfinancial listed companies to prepare separate and individual financial statements (nonconsolidated) in accordance with the recommendations of IFRS effective 2006 (see Decree no. 38, 28 February 2005, paragraph 4). Corporate entities that do not adopt IFRS are required to apply the existing national GAAP.

While the adoption of IFRS for preparing and disclosing consolidated financial statements does not have any influence on the distribution of dividends, as distributable profits are calculated using the individual accounts of each company within the group, the adoption of IFRS for separate and individual financial statements significantly affects the distributable profits.

The key difference related to distribution of profits is the use of fair value measurements[3] by the IFRS, while it is not allowed under the Italian GAAP (see section 17.3). Italian law (Decree no. 38, 28 February 2005) limits the freedom of shareholders in distributing most of the gains derived from using fair value measurements.

Italian law explicitly mentions only the following fair value gains as freely distributable to shareholders:

- Held for trading financial assets
- Fair value hedge financial instruments
- Operations in foreign currency exchange markets[4].

Italian law implies that all the other fair value gains, either recognized in the profit and loss or credited to equity, are to be considered as 'unrealized' (see section 17.5), and should be credited to a nondistributable reserve, named 'fair value reserve'.

This reserve can be used for settling losses only when there are no other reserves of equity. When profit is not adequate to form a fair value reserve, profits reported in the subsequent periods are to be credited to it, until the reserve is equal to the revaluation amount, i.e. fair value minus historical cost.

The 'fair value reserve' can be transferred either to a distributable reserve or to retained earnings only when the related asset is either:

- Disposed of
- Indirectly realized via its depreciation
- Impaired
- Decreased because of revaluation.

17.3 Accounting for fair value changes: a comparative analysis of IFRS, US GAAP, and Italian GAAP

Table 17.1 reports a brief comparison of fair value measurements between IFRS, Italian GAAP, US GAAP, and the IFRS version adopted by Italy with the provisions of Italian law (Decree no. 38, 28 February 2005). The table is structured as follows. The 'Profit or loss' column refers to traditional profit or loss, where the realized and distributable economic values are reported. The 'Equity' column indicates specific nondistributable reserves of equity. For the United States, which already adopts comprehensive income, this column highlights the comprehensive income's section called 'Other comprehensive income' that includes unrealized economic items (SFAS 130, 1997, paragraph 17). The 'Profit or loss' column points out the sections of the comprehensive income that report the realized and distributable economic items.

It is evident from Table 17.1 that IFRS' use of fair value as the basis of measurement, applied to financial assets and financial liabilities, is more than its use in the Italian and US GAAPs. The Italian policymakers are particularly concerned about the fair value measurements that are recognized through profit or loss (in bold type in Table 17.1) since IFRS consider them as realized and thus distributable.

17.3.1 Intangibles and fixed assets

IFRS (IAS 16, 2004; IAS 38, 2004) require the measurement of fixed assets and intangibles at their cost or, if an active market exists, at fair value minus any subsequent accumulated amortization or accumulated impairment losses (*revaluation model*).

Revaluations are applied to all fixed assets, in order to limit discretion in the choice of the assets to measure at fair value and limit the presence of different values (i.e. historical cost and fair value) in the same class of assets. Fair value gains are credited directly to a revaluation reserve of equity. However, they are recognized in profit or loss if a revaluation decrease of the same asset has been previously recognized in profit or loss. The amounts in excess are credited to equity (IAS 16, 2004, paragraph 39; IAS 38, 2004, paragraph 72). In contrast, decreases are recognized in profit or loss, but they are debited directly to equity if a revaluation of the same asset has been previously recognized in equity. The excess amounts are recognized in profit or loss. The revaluation reserve may be transferred directly to retained earnings when an asset is either: (a) derecognized,

Table 17.1 Fair value accounting differences

Item of financial statement	Italian GAAP	US GAAP		IFRS		Italian version of IFRS and the requirements of law	
Accounting of changes in carrying amounts	–	**Profit or loss**	**Equity**	**Profit or loss**	**Equity**	**Profit or loss**	**Equity**
Intangibles and fixed assets.	Historical cost.	Historical cost.			Fair value (or historical cost).		Fair value. Gains shall be credited directly to a nondistributable reserve.
Investment properties	Historical cost – not depreciated	Historical cost		**Fair value (historical cost)**		Fair value. Gains shall be credited to a non-distributable reserve	
Changes of fair value of	Not allowed	Not allowed		**Exchange rates at the date of**	Exchange rates at the	Exchange rates at the	Exchange rates at the

(Continued)

Table 17.1 *(Continued)*

Item of financial statement	Italian GAAP	US GAAP		IFRS		Italian version of IFRS and the requirements of law	
Accounting of changes in carrying amounts	–	**Profit or loss**	**Equity**	**Profit or loss**	**Equity**	**Profit or loss**	**Equity**
nonmonetary items that are measured at fair value in a foreign currency.				**fair value when a gain or loss on a non-monetary item is recognized directly in profit or loss.**	date of fair value when a gain or loss on a non-monetary item is recognized directly in equity.	date of fair value when a gain or loss on a non-monetary item is recognized directly in profit or loss. Gains shall be credited to a nondistributable reserve.	date of fair value when a gain or loss on a nonmonetary item is recognized directly in equity. Fair value. Gains shall be credited directly to a non-distributable reserve.
Exchange differences arising on	*Foreign entity*: exchanges are credited to		Exchanges are credited to equity or		Exchanges are credited to equity		Exchanges are credited to equity

translation of foreign operations in the consolidated financial statement.	equity *Foreign operations integral to the operations of the reporting entity:* exchanges are recognized in profit or loss.		recognized in the comprehensive income.		and recognized in profit or loss on disposal.		and recognized in profit or loss on disposal.
Actuarial gains and losses on defined benefit plans.	Not allowed.	*Corridor approach.*		***Corridor approach* and *immediate recognition approach.***		*Corridor approach and immediate recognition approach*. Gains shall be credited to a non-distributable reserve.	
Investments in subsidiaries, jointly controlled entities,	If classified as *non current assets*: equity method	Equity method or cost joint venture:		**Fair value**. **Held for sale – IFRS 5**		Fair value. Gains shall be credited to a nondis-	

(Continued)

Table 17.1 *(Continued)*

Item of financial statement	Italian GAAP	US GAAP		IFRS		Italian version of IFRS and the requirements of law	
Accounting of changes in carrying amounts	–	**Profit or loss**	**Equity**	**Profit or loss**	**Equity**	**Profit or loss**	**Equity**
and associates in separate financial statement.	or cost. The revaluations shall be credited to a nondistributable reserve. If classified as *current assets*: at the lower of cost and net realizable value.	proportionate consolidation.				tributable reserve. Held for sale – IFRS 5. Gains shall be credited to a nondistributable reserve.	
Other equity instruments.	If classified as *noncurrent assets*: cost. If classified as *current assets*: at the lower of cost and net realizable value.	Fair value (see: *held for trading* or *available for sale*).		**Fair value (see: *held for trading* or *available for sale*).**		Fair value (see: *held for trading* or *available for sale*).	

Financial assets held for trading.	If classified as *current assets*: At the lower of cost and net realizable value.	Fair value		Fair value		Fair value Gains could be distributed to shareholders.	
Financial assets held to maturity.	Similar to amortized cost.	Amortized cost.		Amortized cost.		Amortized cost.	
Loans and receivables.	Net realizable value.	Amortized cost.		Amortized cost.		Amortized cost.	
Financial assets available for sale.	If classified as *current assets*: at the lower of cost and net realizable value.		Fair value.		Fair value.		Fair value. Gains shall be credited directly to a nondistri-butable reserve.
Financial assets at fair value option.	Not allowed.	Not allowed.		**Fair value.**		Fair value. Gains shall be credited to a nondistri-butable reserve.	
Fair value hedges.	Not allowed.	Fair value.		Fair value.		Fair value. Gains could be distributed to shareholders.	

(Continued)

lTable 17.1 *(Continued)*

lItem of financial statement	Italian GAAP	US GAAP		IFRS		Italian version of IFRS and the require-ments of law	
Accounting of changes in carrying amounts	–	**Profit or loss**	**Equity**	**Profit or loss**	**Equity**	**Profit or loss**	**Equity**
Hedges of a net investment and cash-flow hedges.	Not allowed.		Fair value.		Fair value. reserve.		Fair value. Gains shall be credited-directly to a nondistri-utable
Financial liabilities held for trading.	Settlement value.	Derivative: fair value Other: amortized cost.		Fair value.		Fair value. Gains could be distributed to shareholders.	

Other liabilities.	Similar to amortized cost/settle-ment value.	Amortized cost.		Amortized cost.	Amortized cost.	
Financial liabilities at fair value option.	Not allowed.		Not allowed.	**Fair value.**		Not allowed.
Biological assets and agricultural produce.	At the lower of cost and net realizable value.	At the lower of cost and net realizable value.		**Fair value.**	Fair value. Gains shall be credited to a non-distributable reserve.	

(b) disposed of, (c) impaired, or (d) depreciated. It is transferred for an amount equal to the difference between depreciation based on the revalued carrying amount of the asset and depreciation based on the asset's original cost (IAS 16, 2004, paragraph 41; IAS 38, 2004, paragraph 87).

IAS 36 (2004) also requires that the assets' carrying amounts, including those measured at fair value, have to be reduced if their recoverable amounts are less than their carrying amounts (so-called 'impairment test'). The recoverable amount is the higher of the amount of an asset's fair value less costs to sell and its value in use[5]. The impairment losses are recognized in profit or loss, unless the asset is carried at revalued value and there is a revaluation reserve. In this case, they are recognized directly against any revaluation reserve. The amounts in excess are recognized in profit or loss. If impairment losses, recognized in prior periods, no longer exist or have decreased, the corporate entity has to reverse them (IAS 36, 2004, paragraph 117).

Last but not least, IFRS 3 (2004, paragraph 55) considers goodwill as an intangible asset with an indefinite useful life. Therefore, it has not to be depreciated but impaired annually. Contrary to other impaired assets, IAS 36 (2004) does not allow the reversal of goodwill impairment loss. IAS 38 (2004) prohibits the recognition of internally generated goodwill. Otherwise, a reversal of impairment loss might have been confused with an increase in internally generated goodwill.

Italian law and GAAP[6] OIC 24 (2005) on Intangible Assets and OIC 16 (2005) on Fixed Assets require measurement of these assets at their cost. Their carrying amounts are allocated on a systematic basis over their useful life. The revaluations are allowed only either if specific revaluation laws are issued or in the exceptional circumstances provided by article 2423 of the Italian Civil Code (Roberto, 2004). In this case, the revaluated carrying amount of an asset shall not be increased above its recoverable amount, which is equal to the higher of its net selling price and its value in use. Revaluation gains are always credited to a nondistributable reserve of equity (OIC 16, 2005, paragraph D.VIII). Moreover, Italian law requires an impairment test. An asset is impaired when its carrying amount exceeds its recoverable amount. Impairment losses are always recognized in profit or loss of the period (OIC 16, 2005, paragraph D.XIII). If the impairment loss, recognized in prior periods, no longer exists or has decreased, the entity increases the asset's carrying amount to its recoverable amount and recognizes a gain in the profit and loss statement.

Goodwill can only be recognized when it is acquired in a business combination. It is to be depreciated over a period of five years or, in exceptional circumstances, over a period not exceeding 10 years (OIC 24, 2005).

The US GAAP (APB No. 6, 1965; APB Opinion No. 17, 1970; SFAS 144, 2001) recommend the historical cost as the basis of accounting for a fixed and/or intangible asset. Revaluations are not allowed, except for a discovery of a natural resource in its own properties. Moreover, these assets have to be impaired if the undiscounted estimated cash flows from using them are less than the assets' carrying amount (SFAS 144, 2001, paragraph 7). In these cases, the assets are impaired and recognized at their fair value. Losses, calculated as the excess of the assets' value over their fair value, are recognized in the profit and loss statement. The US GAAP does not allow the reversal of assets' impairment loss. Finally, SFAS 142 (2001, paragraphs 18, 19) does not allow depreciation of goodwill; however, a test of impairment must be done annually.

17.3.2 Investment properties

Investment properties are accounted for under IAS 40 (2004). The IASB allows senior management to adopt the measurement either at cost or at fair value. The measurement at fair value is compulsory 'when a property interest held by a lessee under an operating lease is classified as an investment property' (IAS 40, 2004, paragraph 35). However, once one method has been adopted, it has to be adopted for all corporate properties.

The 'fair value model' is recommended by the IASB for the disclosure of the substance and economic reality of the investment. Its fair value reflects the rental income from current leases and any cash outflows that could be expected in respect of the property (IAS 40, 2004, paragraph 40). Differently from the other fixed assets, the investment properties measured at fair value are not depreciated. Fair value gains (or losses) are recognized in the profit and loss statement. The impairment test is not applied (IAS 36, 2004, paragraph 2).

Neither the US SFAS nor the Italian GAAP has issued a specific standard concerning investment properties. Italian GAAP allows cost as the only measurement basis. OIC 16 (2005, paragraph D.XI.5) underlines that investment properties are not to be depreciated. The US SFAS refer to SFAS 144 (2001).

17.3.3 Assets and liabilities in foreign currency

IAS 21 (2004) regulates the accounting for the assets and liabilities in foreign currency and the recognition of exchange differences that may arise. Any foreign currency transaction has to be recorded at the spot exchange rate between the functional currency (i.e. the currency of the primary economic environment in which the entity operates) and the foreign currency at the date of the transaction (IAS 21, 2004, paragraph 21). At the end of the period, if the transaction is not yet settled, the transaction in progress will have to be measured.

Foreign currency transactions may be divided into three categories:

- *Foreign currency monetary items* are translated at the closing exchange rate. The exchange gains or losses are directly recognized in the profit and loss statement in the same period which they arise (IAS 21, 2004, paragraph 28).
- *Nonmonetary items measured in terms of historical cost in a foreign currency* (e.g. fixed assets based abroad, foreign license fees or royalties, etc.). They are translated using the exchange rate at the date of the transaction (IAS 21, 2004, paragraph 23).
- *Nonmonetary items measured at fair value in a foreign currency* (e.g. investment properties based abroad measured at fair value). They are translated using the exchange rates at the date when the fair value was determined (e.g. at the end of the period) (IAS 21, 2004, paragraph 23). The exchange gains or losses are credited to equity if fair value changes are credited directly to equity too (e.g. fixed assets based abroad measured at fair value). On the other hand, the exchange gains or losses are recognized in the profit and loss statement if fair value changes are recognized in profit or loss too (e.g. investment properties based abroad measured at fair value) (IAS 21, 2004, paragraph 28).

If a foreign operation has to be translated, assets and liabilities are translated at the closing rate at that date, whereas the income and expenses are translated at exchange rates at the dates of each transaction. Exchange differences are credited to equity. Monetary items that form part of a reporting entity's net investment in a foreign entity are recognized either in the profit and loss statement in the separate financial statements (nonconsolidated), or in the individual financial statements of the foreign operation. In a consolidated financial statement, such exchange differences are initially recognized in a reserve account under equity, then on disposal of the net investment in profit or loss (IAS 21, 2004, paragraph 32).

IAS 21 is not to be applied in the accounting of derivative transactions, balances, and hedge accounting that are within the scope of IAS 39 (2004). In Italy, the article 2426-bis of the Italian Civil Code and OIC 26 (2005) requires translation of monetary items using the closing exchange rate. Foreign monetary items can be carried as current or noncurrent assets. These exchange differences are recognized in the profit and loss statement. If the net result is a gain, it has to be credited to a reserve under equity, nondistributable until the transition is settled.

Nonmonetary items measured at cost in foreign currency (e.g. fixed assets, intangibles, investments in subsidiaries, jointly controlled entities and associates, and other equity instruments) are translated using the exchange rate at the date of the transaction. If their closing rate is impaired, nonmonetary items are translated using this exchange rate. When investments in subsidiaries or in associates are accounted for using the equity method, income, assets, and liabilities of a foreign operation are translated into a financial statement's reporting currency so that the foreign operation can be included in the financial statements of the reporting entity by the equity method. Italian Standard CNDC-CNR No. 17 (1996) classifies foreign operations as follows:

- *Foreign entities which are relatively self-contained within the operations of the reporting entity.* In this case, all balance sheet items are translated using the closing exchange rate, whereas the income statement's items are translated using the exchange rate at the date of the transaction. Exchange differences are credited to a nondistributable reserve under equity (CNDC-CNR No. 17, 1996, paragraph 7.4).
- *Foreign operations which are integral to the operations of the reporting entity.* Monetary items and current nonmonetary items are translated using the closing rate, whereas the other nonmonetary items are translated using the exchange rate at the date of the transaction. The income statement's items are translated using the exchange rate at the date of the transaction, but historical exchange rate will be used if they result from assets or liability translated at this exchange rate (e.g. the cost and the depreciation of fixed assets are translated using the exchange rate at the date of purchase of the asset). Exchanges differences are recognized directly in the consolidated profit and loss statement (CNDC-CNR No. 17, 1996, paragraph 7.5).

A recent OIC 17 exposure draft (2005, paragraph 7.3), which is likely to replace CNDC-CNR No. 17 (1996), is consistent with IAS 21 (2004).

The US SFAS 52 (1981) requires translation of foreign currency transactions at the closing rate (*monetary items*). Exchange differences are recognized in the profit and loss statement for the period in which the rate changes. Fair value cannot be used for nonmonetary items.

In translating foreign currency financial statements, all assets and liabilities are translated using the exchange rate at the balance sheet date. Revenues, expenses, gains, and losses are translated at the exchange rate at the dates in which those elements are recognized. If an entity's functional currency is a foreign currency, translation adjustments will result from translating that entity's financial statements into the reporting currency. These translation adjustments are not recognized in the profit and loss statement but are reported as a component of equity or in the comprehensive income's section, called 'Other gains and losses' (SFAS 52, 1981, paragraphs 112–115).

17.3.4 Actuarial gains and losses on defined benefit plans

Actuarial gains and losses are related to defined benefit plans. Under a defined benefit plan, the entity provides the agreed upon benefits to current and former employees. Actuarial and investment risks are the responsibility of the entity. Periodically, the entity must compare its own pension obligation with the current value (fair value) of the investments out of which the obligations are to be settled directly (*plan assets*). The entity determines the present value of defined benefit obligations and compares it to the fair value of the plan assets to determine the actuarial gains or losses.

Actuarial gains or losses are recognized in the current period financial statement if the net cumulative unrecognized actuarial gains and losses of the previous reporting period exceed the greater of 10% of the present value of the pension obligation at the end of the previous period or 10% of the fair value of the plan assets at that date (IAS 19, 2004, paragraphs 92–94). The excess value is allocated over the expected average remaining working lives of the employees participating in the plan (*corridor approach*). If there is no excess, no gains or losses are recognized. However, the IASB permits the accounting of actuarial gains and losses that fall within that range[7].

In Italy, OIC 19 (2005) requires that the entity's pension obligation at the end of an accounting period (called *TFR*) has to be equal to the sum of the amounts of benefits that employees have earned during their work period. Actuarial assumptions are not adopted to measure the obligation as they are considered too volatile and uncertain (OIC 19, 2005, paragraph G).

If an insurance contract is entered into to settle the pension obligation, the premiums paid are disclosed in a separate line item within noncurrent financial assets named *receivables* (balance sheet's item B.III.2). If the insurance repaid amount is higher than the entity's pension obligation, the difference is considered as a gain and is recognized in the profit or loss statement (OIC 19, 2005, paragraph G). The measurement and treatment of gain or loss under the Italian GAAP is quite different from IFRS and IAS 19.

In the USA, SFAS 87 (1985) treats the actuarial gains and losses in a way similar to the IFRS' *corridor approach*. The *immediate recognition approach* is not allowed. SFAS 87 also demands the recognition of an *additional minimum pension liability* when minimum liability exceeds the obligation measured on the normal projected salary basis (with deferred recognition of certain incomes and expenses). The excess value is recognized as an intangible asset (not exceeding the amount of any unamortized past service cost) and as an additional minimum liability (SFAS 87, 1985, paragraphs 35–38). The IASB believes that such additional measures of liability are potentially confusing and do not provide relevant information.

17.3.5 Financial assets and liabilities

The IASB classifies financial items in the following categories: investments in subsidiaries, jointly controlled entities and associates, other equity instruments, financial instruments, and other financial assets or liabilities. IAS 27 (2004) contrasts the separate financial statements with the individual financial statements. Separate financial statements must be prepared for each entity in the group in addition to the parent entity financial statement, while individual financial statements are prepared by an entity that does not present a consolidated financial statement.

When separate financial statements are prepared, *investments in subsidiaries, jointly controlled entities, and associates* are accounted either at their cost or at their fair value. The chosen method of measurement has to be applied for all investments in a category (IAS 27, 2004, paragraph 37). IAS 27 (2004) does not allow the use of the equity method for these investments. The equity method may be used only in the consolidated financial statement. A gain (or loss) arising from a change in the fair value of investments in subsidiaries, jointly controlled entities, and associates is directly recognized in the profit and loss statement (IAS 39, 2004, paragraph 55a). *Other equity instruments* (i.e. not investments in subsidiaries, jointly controlled entities, and associates) are subject to the rules under IAS 39 using fair value or in some cases using cost[8].

Investments in subsidiaries, jointly controlled entities, and associates are subject to the impairment test under the requirements of IAS 36 (2004). For this reason, in case of their impairment, the same recommendations regarding fixed assets are to be applied. In contrast, the impairment of the *other investments* is subject to the rules under IAS 39, which demands that the amounts of the impairment losses, incurred on an unlisted equity instrument carried at cost, are recognized in the profit and loss statement. Such impairment losses are not reversed (IAS 39, 2004, paragraph 66).

On individual financial statements, the entity measures the investments in associates using the equity method (IAS 28, 2004, paragraph 30). Under the equity method, the investor's share of the profit or loss of the investee is recognized in the profit and loss statement, and increases (or decreases) the carrying value of the investments in associates. In contrast, distributions received from an investee reduce the carrying value of the investments. Moreover, on the individual financial statements, the entity recognizes the investments in jointly controlled entities by using the proportionate consolidation or the equity method (IAS 31, 2004, paragraphs 30–41). Fair value or cost are used to account for *other equity instruments* under IAS 39 (2004).

The entity that presents its separate or individual financial statement classifies its investments in subsidiaries, jointly controlled entities, and associates or other equity instruments as *held for sale investments*, if its carrying amount will be recovered through a sale transaction rather than through its continuing use. *Held for sale investments* are measured at the lower of their carrying amount and fair value less costs to sell (IFRS 5, 2004, paragraph 15). If their fair value (less costs to sell) is lower than their carrying amount, the entity recognizes an impairment loss in the profit and loss statement. It recognizes a gain for any subsequent increase in fair value less costs to sell off an asset, but never in excess of the cumulative impairment loss that has been previously recognized (IFRS 5, 2004, paragraphs 20, 21).

For the *other financial asset instruments*[9] that are not equity instruments, IAS 39 (2004) identifies four categories:

1. *Held for trading investments.* These are assets principally acquired to sell in the near term, or financial instruments managed for a pattern of short-term profit taking, or derivatives that are not designated as hedging instruments. They are measured at fair value. Fair value gains or losses are recognized in the profit and loss statement (IAS 39, 2004, paragraph 55). They are not impaired because they are short term and fair value changes have already been recognized in the profit and loss statement.
2. *Held to maturity Investments.* These are nonderivative financial assets with fixed or determinable payments and fixed maturity that an entity has the intention and ability to hold to maturity (IAS 39, 2004, paragraph 9). They are measured at amortized cost using the effective interest method[10]. Gains or losses of such financial assets are recognized in the profit or loss statement.

3. *Loans and receivable.* These are nonderivative financial assets with fixed or determinable payments that are not quoted on an active market. They are measured at amortized cost too (IAS 39, 2004, paragraph 46). The impairment test is similar to held to maturity investments.
4. *Available for sale investments.* These are defined as those nonderivative financial assets that are designated by entity as available for sale or are not classified into the other categories[11]. They are measured at fair value but gains and losses are credited directly to a reserve under equity, until they are derecognized. In contrast, impairment losses and their reversal are recognized in the profit and loss statement, except the impairment losses of an equity instrument classified as available for sale that is not reversed (IAS 39, 2004, paragraph 69).

Moreover, IAS 39 (2004) provides that any financial asset[12] (or liability) may be initially recognized as a financial asset (or liability) at *fair value through profit or loss* (i.e. fair value option – FVO; the Italian adoption of IFRS has only allowed the application of the FVO for financial assets and has prohibited it for financial liabilities). In this case, fair value gains or losses are recognized only in the profit and loss statement.

IAS 39 (2004) identifies two categories of financial liabilities:

1. *Held for trading* are incurred for repurchasing them in the near term or are derivatives that are not designated as hedging instruments. They are measured at fair value and gains or losses are recognized in the profit and loss statement (see *Held for trading* financial assets).
2. *Other liabilities* are measured at amortized cost using the effective interest method. Gains or losses of such financial liabilities are recognized in the profit and loss statement when they are either derecognized or impaired, or amortized for the difference between the initial value and the maturity value.

IAS 39 (2004) addresses the measurement of the assets or liabilities designated as hedging instruments (*hedge accounting*). A hedging instrument is a designated derivative or nonderivative financial asset or liability (in this case, the nonderivative instrument can hedge only the risk of changes in foreign currency exchange rates) whose fair value (or cash flow) is expected to offset changes in the fair value (or cash flow) of a designated hedged item (IAS 39, 2004, paragraph 9). The fair value (or cash flow) changes of such financial instruments would neutralize (or lessen) the effects of the fair value (or cash flow) changes of the hedged item. Three types of hedging instruments are identified:

1. *Fair value hedge*. The fair value change of a designated hedging instrument would hedge the fair value change of a recognized asset or liability that could affect profit or loss (for example, if an entity took out a fixed rate mortgage loan, it could hedge the exposure to changes in the fair value of a fixed rate by designating a floating hedging rate instrument). The fair value gains (or losses) of the hedging instrument and of the hedged item attributable to the hedged risk are recognized in the profit and loss statement. This accounting is applied if the hedged item is measured at cost (see IAS 39, 2004, paragraph 89).
2. *Cash-flow hedge*. The hedging instrument would hedge the entity's exposure to variability in cash flows of a recognized asset (or liability) and that could affect profit or loss (for example, the use of a swap to change floating rate debt to fixed rate debt). The hedging instrument gains or losses that are determined to be an effective hedge (a hedge is regarded as highly effective if the actual results of the hedge are within a range of 80–125% – see IAS 39, 2004, Appendix A, AG 105–113) are credited directly to reserve under equity. On the other hand, the ineffective portion is recognized in the profit and loss statement. The reserve is recognized in profit or loss in the same period during which the hedged transaction affects profit or loss. In this way, gains or losses of the hedging items and of the hedged items affect profit or loss in the same period. In contrast, the gains or losses of the ineffective hedge portion immediately affect profit or loss.
3. *Hedges of a net investment in a foreign operation* are accounted for similarly to cash-flow hedges (IAS 39, 2004, paragraph 102). The net investments in a foreign operation are receivable from or payable to another entity (subsidiary, associate, joint venture, or branch of a reporting entity, the activities of which are based or conducted in a country or currency other than those of the reporting entity), for which settlement is neither planned nor likely to occur in the near future (see IAS 21, 2004, paragraph 15).

Italian law as well as the GAAP do not provide a taxonomy of equity instruments and other financial assets or liabilities as detailed in the IFRS. The law identifies *investments in subsidiaries, associates and parents, other equity instruments, and other financial instruments*. An entity may classify all financial instruments as *noncurrent* or *current assets* based on the assessment of the function of such assets within the entity. If it is expected that they will be held long term, the entity should classify them as noncurrent assets. Otherwise they should be classified as current assets.

Investments in subsidiaries and associates are measured either at cost or using the equity method under the requirements of Italian Standard CNDC-CNR No. 21 (1996), if they are classified as noncurrent assets. Under the equity method, the investor's share of the profit or loss of the investee increases or decreases the carrying amount of such investments, and is recognized in the investor's profit and loss statement (*benchmark treatment*) (CNDC-CNR No. 21, 1996, paragraphs 3.3f and f′). Increases are credited to a nondistributable reserve under equity. In contrast, the *allowed alternative treatment* is to credit them directly to a nondistributable reserve. The distributions received from an investee reduce the investment's carrying amount. If the investments in subsidiaries and associates are impaired, the impairment losses are recognized in the profit and loss statement. The reversal is also recognized in the profit and loss statement; however, the increased carrying amount of the financial asset cannot exceed what the cost would have been had the impairment not been recognized (CNDC-CNR No. 20, 1996, paragraph II.3.7). *Other equity instruments* classified as noncurrent may only be measured at their cost and eventually impaired.

For *other noncurrent financial instruments* the Italian GAAP takes a similar approach as the amortized cost under IAS 39. It is necessary to allocate any difference between the initial amount and the maturity amount or implicit interest rates over the relevant period[13]. The revaluations of the financial assets are allowed only if specific revaluation laws have been issued or in the exceptional circumstances set out in article 2423 of the Italian Civil Code. All financial instruments classified as *current assets* (i.e. equity instruments and other financial instruments) are measured at the lower of cost or net realizable value.

In summary, Italian law never allows measurements at fair value and the recognition of fair value gains and losses in the income statement or in reserve under equity. Article 2427-bis of the Italian Civil Code regulates that the amount of fair value has to be disclosed in the notes, when the carrying amounts of derivatives or financial assets held as fixed assets are higher than their fair value. If their fair value is lower than the carrying amount, the entity must disclose in a note the reason for not impairing them.

Fair value is not regarded by Italian law as a method of measurement as yet, rather it is only considered as a basis to assess the probability of losses arising in the future.

Loans and receivables are measured at net realizable value, and *creditors* at their settlement value. Debenture loans and bills of exchange payable (e.g.

bonds, notes and similar items) are disclosed at their nominal amount. Any difference between that initial amount and the maturity amount is credited to a prepayments and accrued income asset (*discount*) or liability (*premium*) and allocated over the relevant period (see note 13). Italian GAAP does not cover accounting of hedging instruments.

In the USA, SFAS do not allow fair value measurement of *investments in subsidiaries, jointly controlled entities, and associates.* They require the use of the cost and equity method. Regarding *investments in joint venture,* the proportionate consolidation method is mandatory (see APB Opinion No. 18, 1971; SFAS 115, 1993; SFAS 124, 1995). For *other equity instruments,* the measurement will depend on their classification as *held for trading* or *available for sale,* similar to the IFRS. The only difference is in the recognition of fair value gains and losses of assets held for sale in the comprehensive income as unrealized gain or loss, rather than credited to reserve under equity. In the consolidated financial statement, the equity instruments of those entities that are not consolidated are measured using the equity method when the investor has a significant influence. In all other circumstances, these instruments are measured at their market value or at cost, if a market value cannot be reliably measured. For *other financial instruments,* SFAS 115 (1993) provides the same classifications and methods of measurement as in IAS 39.

Trading securities and *available for sale securities* may be measured at fair value. Fair value gains and losses for trading securities are recognized in the profit and loss statement, while gains and losses for available for sale securities are recognized in comprehensive income as unrealized items. Cost is mandatory for *held to maturity securities.* The *fair value option* (FVO) is not allowed by SFAS in the USA.

Loans and receivables are measured at net realizable value, and *debenture loans and bills of exchange payable* at amortized cost. *Other creditors* are disclosed at their settlement value. Fair value measurement is now allowed, except for *derivatives* (asset or liability) that are measured at fair value, and its changes are recognized in the profit and loss statement (SFAS 133, 1998, paragraphs 17, 18). The measurements of hedging instruments (*fair value hedge, cash-flow hedge, foreign currency hedge*) are similar to IAS 39. The IASB requires hedge gain (or loss) to be credited as a reserve, while US GAAP recognizes them in the unrealized section of comprehensive income.

17.3.6 Biological assets

IAS 41 (2004) regulates the biological transformation of living animals or plants (*biological assets*) for sale, into *agricultural produce,* or into *additional biological assets*. A biological asset is measured at its fair value less estimated point-of-sale costs. *Agricultural produce* is measured at its fair value minus the estimated point-of-sale costs at the point of harvest (IAS 41, 2004, paragraphs 12, 13). Fair value changes are recognized in the profit and loss statement for the period in which they arise. Biological assets are measured at cost, if their fair value cannot be measured reliably. Fair value measurement cannot be applied once the biological asset is harvested. They become inventories and should be accounted for according to IAS 2 (2004), i.e. at the lower of their cost or net realizable value.

Italian GAAP have not issued a specific standard for *biological assets* and *agricultural produce*. They are identified as inventories; thus, they are measured at the lower of cost or net realizable value (OIC 13, 2005). In the USA, the FASB (1974) prescribes the measurement at the lower of cost or market value.

17.4 The entity's capital maintenance

Under the IASB Framework, a corporate entity maintains its capital 'if it has as much capital at the end of the period as it had at the beginning of the period' (IASB, 2004a, paragraph 107). Any excess is to be considered as a profit. In particular, IASB (2004a) identifies two concepts of capital maintenance:

- *Financial capital maintenance*. Under this concept, a profit is earned only if the amount of the net assets at the end of the period exceeds the amount of net assets at the beginning of the period. Financial capital maintenance may be measured in either *nominal monetary units* or *units of constant purchasing power*. In the first case, increases in the prices of assets held over the period are considered unrealized. Accordingly, they are considered profits only when the assets are disposed of in an exchange transaction. In the second case, increases in the prices of assets that exceed the increase in the general level of prices are considered realized and thus profit.
- *Physical capital maintenance*. Under this concept, a profit is earned only if the physical productive capacity of the entity at the end of the period exceeds its own at the beginning of the period. In this case, profits represent the increase in that capital over the period. All price changes affecting the assets and liabilities are viewed as changes in the measurement of the physical productive capacity of the entity. Hence, they are considered as part of equity (*capital maintenance adjustments*), not as a profit (IASB, 2004a, paragraph 104).

This seems to imply that any fair value gain that is recognized by the IASB in the income statement is to be considered as realized. If a gain is credited to a reserve under equity, it is considered as unrealized.

In the USA, SFAS on the one hand recognize the same concepts of capital maintenance (SFAC No. 6, 1985, paragraph 71); on the other, they do not allow the same use of fair value measurement, in contrast with IFRS. Italian GAAP do not provide any definition of the concept of capital maintenance. However, content analysis shows that capital maintenance is considered as nominal maintenance. Accounting measurements are based on historical cost and increases in the prices or changes in the technological, market, economic, or legal environment that could have increased the entity's assets (or decreased their liabilities) are considered profits only when the assets are disposed of in an exchange transaction or the liabilities are settled. The prudence principle recognizes only the decreases of the assets or the increases of the liabilities in the profit and loss statement when they arise. The purpose is to avoid the distribution of profits that are considered as unrealized. There is an asymmetry between the prudence principle and the accrual basis principle, with the former considered as more important than the latter (see section 17.5).

This section will provide two examples of items at fair value for which fair value gains are considered either realized and distributable profits (IFRS view) or are reported in the periods to which they relate but are considered as unrealized and nondistributable items (Italian law view). The possible effects of the two approaches on the entity's capital maintenance are illustrated.

17.4.1 Example 1 (investment property)

The first example is an investment property where fair value changes (transactions in progress) are recognized by IFRS directly in the profit or loss statement and are considered realized and distributable profit[14]. IFRS neither require a credit of fair value gains to a reserve nor limit their distribution to shareholders.

Assume a corporate entity owns investment properties, listed in an active market. Their initial amount is €1,000,000. The entity decides to account all of its investment properties at fair value in accordance with IAS 40. Table 17.2 shows fair value changes at the end of periods 1 and 2 and the disposal value in period 3.

Italian GAAP and US GAAP do not allow valuation of investment properties at fair value. The measurement is at cost. Only in period 3, when the properties are disposed of, is the realized gain (€50,000), which is the difference between disposal value (€1,050,000) and original cost of the asset (€1,000,000), reported in profit or loss.

The fair value model is recommended by the IASB for the disclosure of investment properties. In periods 1 and 2, fair value changes are recognized in profit or loss (€100,000 + 60,000). These gains are reported in the profit of the period in which they arise. In period 3 a loss (€110,000), which is the difference between the net disposal proceeds (€1,050,000) and the carrying amount of the revaluated item (€1,160,000), is recognized in profit or loss.

In Table 17.3, we added information regarding share capital and operating income to show the effects of different treatment of gains and losses under different measurement practices in each of the three periods. The effect of changes in fair value is reported in each period under IFRS, while only the third period shows the effect of disposal of the asset under both Italian and US GAAP.

Table 17.4 compares and contrasts the effects of the different approaches on the entity's capital maintenance. It shows the different statements of changes in equity. Column 1 (*Italy before IFRS – US GAAP*) reports the current Italian and US approaches, column 2 (*Italy – IFRSs*) the Italian application of IFRS, and column 3 (*IFRS*) the current IASB approach. It is assumed that the distributable

Table 17.2 Fair value changes

	Acquisition	Period 1	Period 2	Disposal
Fair value (€)	1,000,000	1,100,000	1,160,000	1,050,000
Revaluation from fair value recognized in profit and loss (€)		100,000	60,000	
Loss for IFRS (€)				110,000
Gains for Italian and US GAAP (€)				50,000

Table 17.3 Share capital and incomes of the periods

	Period 1	Period 2	Period 3
Share capital (€)	1,000,000	1,000,000	1,000,000
Operating income (€)	**60,000**	**30,000**	–
Financing and treasury income (Italian and US GAAP) (€)	–	–	50,000
Financing and treasury income (IFRS) (€)	**100,000**	**60,000**	(110,000)
Income of the period (Italian and US GAAP) (€)	60,000	30,000	50,000
Income of the period (IFRS) (€)	**160,000**	**90,000**	(110,000)

Table 17.4 Statement of changes in equity

	Italy before IFRSs – US GAAP	IFRS – Italy	IFRS	Italy before IFRS – US GAAP	IFRS – Italy	IFRS	Italy before IFRS – US GAAP	IFRS – Italy	IFRS
	Period 1			Period 2			Period 3		
Equity (€)									
Share capital	1,000,000	1,000,000	1,000,000	1,000,000	1,000,000	1,000,000	1,000,000	1,000,000	1,000,000
Nondistributable fair value reserve	–	**100,000**	–	–	–	**160,000**	–	–	–
Distributable reserve (or retained earnings)	–	–	–	–	–	–	–	**160,000**	–
Distributable income	60,000	60,000	160,000	30,000	30,000	90,000	50,000	(110,000)	(110,000)
Total	**1,060,000**	**1,160,000**	**1,160,000**	**1,030,000**	**1,090,000**	**1,090,000**	**1,050,000**	**1,050,000**	**890,000**

Table 17.5 Changes in distributable equity

	Italy before IFRSs – US GAAP	IFRS – Italy	IFRS	Italy before IFRS – US GAAP	IFRS – Italy	IFRS	Italy before IFRS – US GAAP	IFRS – Italy	IFRS
	Period 1			Period 2			Period 3		
Changes of distributable equity (€)	60,000	60,000	160,000	30,000	30,000	90,000	50,000	50,000	(110,000)

income and the distributable reserve in a period will be distributed to shareholders in the course of the next period (see Table 17.4).

Taking a 'prudent' approach to the entity's capital maintenance, the differences between various approaches are significant, as reported in Table 17.5.

The IASB's approach is less prudent than the Italian and FASB approaches. By taking into account fair value gains as realized (thus distributable) income, IFRS allow their distribution to shareholders as dividends in the same period. In period 1, the 'shareholders of IASB's statement' might receive dividends for an amount of €160,000 (60,000 from operating profits and 100,000 from unrealized gains). In period 2, shareholders might receive dividends for an amount of €90,000 (30,000 from operating profits and 60,000 from unrealized gains). However, in period 3 they will see the 'impairment' of the corporate share capital (€110,000) because the gain has not been fully realized (disposal value in period 3 is lower than fair value at the end of period 2).

Under the Italian version of IFRS and Italian law, fair value gains are credited to a nondistributable reserve. In doing so, unrealized gains for the period as well as the fair value of the entity's assets and liabilities are disclosed. Investors and all other stakeholders are able to evaluate the corporate ability to generate cash flows and able to make an assessment of the timing and uncertainty of such cash flows. Moreover, its capital maintenance is not impaired due to the fact that unrealized income is not available for distribution. In fact, fair value gains are credited to a nondistributable reserve under equity (€100,000 in period 1 and €60,000 in period 2). Any restriction on the distribution of the fair value reserve is removed only when the investments are disposed of in an exchange transaction (period 3). However, investors receive timely and relevant information that helps them in their decision-making process. At the same time, other stakeholders have their interests in corporate capital safeguarded.

Italian GAAP and US GAAP do not allow fair value measurements. Such an approach is more prudent than the IASB's and has the advantage of prohibiting the distribution of unrealized gains. On the other hand, it results in both a lack of adequate reported information (income arisen in the period and corporate ability to generate cash) and a lack of representational faithfulness of the economic substance of these investments. Such information is fundamental if the financial statements have to 'provide information about the financial position, performance, and changes in financial position of an entity that is useful to a wide range of users in making economic decisions' (IASB, 2004a, paragraph 12).

17.4.2 Example 2 (financial liability)

Assume entity A writes a put option on entity C's shares (€10,000). Accordingly, entity A enters into a contract with entity B in period 1. The put option is purchased by entity B for an amount of €1000. The exercise right (in period 3) is held by entity B. The contract gives entity B the right to receive the fair value of entity C's outstanding ordinary shares (traded in a public market) as of the beginning of period 3. Entity A is given the right to receive the fixed option exercise price (i.e. €18.5 per share) at the same time, if entity B exercises its right. The contract will be settled net in cash. If entity B does not exercise its right, no payment will be due. The put option assumptions are reported in Table 17.6.

IAS 32 (2004, paragraph AG-17) maintains that: 'the writer of an option assumes an obligation to forgo potential future economic benefits or bear potential losses of economic benefits associated with changes in the fair value of the underlying financial instrument'. The contractual obligation of the writer (entity A) meets the definition of a *derivative* (IAS 39, 2004, paragraph 9), which is a financial liability. IAS 39 (2004, paragraph 47) and the US SFAS 133 (1998, paragraphs 17, 18) require the evaluation of derivatives at fair value and recognize gains or losses in profit or loss. Italian GAAP do not demand specific measurements of derivatives. The Bank of Italy (2002) has enacted the measurement and disclosure of derivatives in the financial statements of banks, which is also a generally accepted practice in nonfinancial companies.

Table 17.6 Put option assumptions

	Written	Period 1	Period 2	Period 3
Exercise price (€)	**18,000**	**17,500**	**17,200**	**18,500**
Number of shares under option contract				10,000
Fair value of entity C's share (€)	19,000	18,000	17,600	19,600
Fair value of option (€)	**1000**	**500**	**400**	**1100**
Fair value gain of option (IFRS and US GAAP) (€)		**500**	**100**	
Fair value loss of option (IFRS and US GAAP) (€)				**700**
Loss of option (Italian GAAP) (€)				**100**
Entity A's obligation (€)				19,600
Entity B's obligation (€)				18,500
Entity A's net obligation (€)				**1100**

Derivatives are measured at their settlement value, not at their fair value. Gains or losses of such liability are recognized in profit or loss only in the period in which the option is exercised.

In accord with the IFRS and the US GAAP, in periods 1–3 entity A will have to recognize any fair value changes of the put option arising when the fair value of entity C's shares are changed. In periods 1 and 2, the fair value of entity C's shares decreases (€18,000 and €17,600), with a resulting decrease in the fair value of the exercise price and of the put option (€500 and €400). In this way, entity A has to recognize fair value gains[15] in periods 1 and 2 (€500 and €100), determined as the difference between the change in fair value of the two periods. In period 3 the fair value of entity C's share increases (€19,600), with a resulting increase in the fair value of the put option (€1100). Entity A recognizes a fair value loss (€700), as its obligation has increased. If entity B decided to exercise the put option, it will receive the fair value of entity C's shares (€19,600) in exchange for the fixed exercise price (€18.5 per share) that has to be paid to entity A. For entity A, the put option has generated altogether a financial loss for an amount of €100 (500 + 100 − 700).

According to the Italian GAAP, the net realized loss (€100[16]) of the put option should be recognized only in period 3. Only entity A's gains in the financing and treasury section are the fair value changes of the put option. Operating income and share capital are given. The profit or loss for the period is equal to the sum of operating income and financing and treasury income (see Table 17.7).

Table 17.8 compares and contrasts the effects of different approaches on the entity's capital maintenance. We assume that the distributable income and the distributable reserve of a period will be distributed to shareholders in the course of the next period.

Table 17.7 Share capital and incomes of the periods

	Period 1	**Period 2**	**Period 3**
Share capital (€)	500,000	500,000	500,000
Operating income (€)	**500**	**500**	**500**
Financing and treasury income (Italian GAAP) (€)	–	–	(100)
Financing and treasury income (IFRSs and US GAAP) (€)	**500**	**100**	(700)
Income of the period (Italian GAAP) (€)	500	500	**400**
Income of the period (IFRSs and US GAAP) (€)	**1000**	**600**	(200)

Table 17.8 Statement of changes in equity

	Italy before IFRS	IFRS – Italy	IFRS US GAAP	Italy before IFRS	IFRS – Italy	IFRS US GAAP	Italy before IFRS	IFRS – Italy	IFRS US GAAP
	Period 1			Period 2			Period 3		
Equity (€)									
Share capital	500,000	500,000	500,000	500,000	500,000	500,000	500,000	500,000	500,000
Nondistributable fair value reserve	–	**500**	–	–	**100**	–	–	–	–
Distributable reserve (or retained earnings)	–	–	–		–	–	–	**600**	–
Distributable income	500	500	1000	500	500	600	400	(200)	(200)
Total	**500,500**	**501,000**	**501,000**	**500,500**	**500,600**	**500,600**	**500,400**	**500,400**	**499,800**

Table 17.9 Changes in distributable equity

	Italy before IFRS	IFRS – Italy	IFRS – US GAAP	Italy before IFRS	IFRS – Italy	IFRS – US GAAP	Italy before IFRS	IFRS – Italy	IFRS – US GAAP
	Period 1			Period 2			Period 3		
Changes of distributable equity (€)	500	500	1000	500	500	600	400	400	(200)

The differences between various approaches are significant. Table 17.9 reports the changes in distributable equity of the period.

The conclusion from the above example seems to confirm the argument that the IASB's approach is less prudent than the Italian version of IFRS. By allowing the distribution of unrealized items, the IASB could undermine the entity's capital maintenance in the long term.

The Italian version of IFRS and Italian law require that fair value gains be credited to a nondistributable reserve, and as a result freeze their distribution until the liability (i.e. the put option obligation) is settled (an exchange transaction has occurred). In period 3 any restriction on the distribution of the fair value reserve is removed. The entity's capital maintenance is not impaired. At the same time, the gains or losses from the liability measurement are recognized when they arise.

17.5 Accrual basis vs prudence: a comparative analysis of IFRS, Italian, and US GAAP

The IASB (2004a, paragraph 15) states that the objective of financial statements is to provide information about the financial position, performance, and changes in financial position of a corporate entity. This information is to be useful to a wide range of users in making their economic decisions, in particular about 'the ability of an entity to generate cash and cash equivalents and of the timing and certainty of their generation'.

Thus, the IASB Framework distinguishes between *underlying assumptions* (accrual basis and going concern) and *qualitative characteristics* of a financial statement. The IASB (2004a) provides a hierarchy of qualities, with usefulness for decision-making at the top, but does not assign priorities among qualities. The hierarchy should be seen as an explanatory device to clarify relationships among qualitative characteristics, rather than assign relative weights to them. Indeed, the IASB (2004a, paragraph 45) itself acknowledges that 'a balancing, or tradeoff, between qualitative characteristics is often necessary'.

Going concern assumes that the entity will continue in operation for the near future and has neither the intention nor the need to liquidate its operation (IASB, 2004a, paragraph 23). With regard to the accrual basis, the IASB (2004a, paragraph 22) states that 'the effects of transactions and other events are recognized when they occur (and not as cash or its equivalent is received or paid) and they are recorded in the accounting records and reported in the financial statements for the periods to which they relate'.

The qualitative characteristics of financial statements are:

- *Understandability.* The accounting information has this quality if its significance can be understood by financial statement users (IASB, 2004a, paragraph 25).
- *Relevance.* Information is relevant if it makes a difference in a decision by helping users to form predictions about the outcomes of past, present, and future events or to confirm or correct prior expectations (IASB, 2004a, paragraph 26). A subcondition of relevance is the *materiality* of the information. An information is material only if its omission (or misstatement) may affect the economic decisions of users (IASB, 2004a, paragraph 29).
- *Reliability.* Information is reliable when it is reasonably free from error and bias and faithfully represents what it purports to represent (IASB, 2004a, paragraph 31). To be reliable, information must have the following qualitative characteristics:
  (a) *Faithful representation*, i.e. there should be a correspondence between a measure or description and the event that it purports to represent (IASB, 2004a, paragraph 33).
  (b) *Substance over form*, i.e. information is to be accounted and presented in accordance with its substance and economic reality and not merely their legal form (IASB, 2004a, paragraph 35).
  (c) *Neutrality.* Information is neutral in the absence of biases in order to attain a predetermined result or to induce a particular outcome (IASB, 2004a, paragraph 36).
  (d) *Prudence.* Prudence is defined as 'the inclusion of a degree of caution in the exercise of the judgments needed in making the estimates required under conditions of uncertainty, such that assets or income are not overstated and liabilities or expenses are not understated' (IASB, 2004a, paragraph 37). However, the exercise of prudence does not allow the creation of hidden reserves or excessive provisions, or the deliberate understatement (overstatement) of assets and/or income (liabilities and/or expenses) (IASB, 2004a, paragraph 37).
  (e) *Completeness.* Reliable information includes any material information that is necessary for faithful representation of the relevant event (IASB, 2004a, paragraph 38).
- *Comparability.* Information that is comparable enables users to identify similarities in and differences between two sets of economic events and to

identify trends of the entity's financial position and performance (IASB, 2004a, paragraph 38).

A constraint on relevant and reliable information is its *timeliness*. Information is to be reported in a timely manner, i.e. it is to be available to users before it loses its capacity to influence their economic decision-making (IASB, 2004a, paragraph 43). The FASB Framework underlines the same objectives of financial reporting as the IASB's (SFAC No. 1, 1978, paragraph 31ff) and recognizes a hierarchy of accounting qualities, which are substantially similar to the IASB's (SFAC No. 2, 1980). An important difference is that the FASB does not consider prudence as a quality of accounting information. Prudence, expressed by the old admonition as 'anticipate no profits but anticipate all losses' (SFAC No. 2, 1980, paragraph 93), can be regarded as a countermeasure against the uncertainty of economic activities[17]. However, the preference of understatement rather than overstatement of net income and net assets is to be applied with care, because it may conflict with the significance of some qualitative characteristics, such as representational faithfulness, neutrality, and comparability (SFAC No. 2, 1980, paragraph 92). On the one hand, understated results are not consistent with the qualities of accounting characteristics. On the other, imprudent reporting with optimistic estimates of realization is not particularly consistent with those characteristics. The best way to avoid this tradeoff is to insure that the reported accounting information has all the qualities previously analyzed. Unlike the IASB, the FASB (see SFAC No. 6, 1985, paragraph 44ff) does not regard accrual basis as an underlying assumption, but it considers the accrual basis principle as a procedure to account for the elements of financial statements and that meet criteria for recognition and measurement.

In Italy, the law (see Civil Code article 2423) regulates the objective of financial statements. Financial statements are to give a true and fair view of the entity's assets, liabilities, financial position, and profit or loss. Neither Italian law (article 2423-bis Civil Code) nor Italian GAAP (OIC 11, 2005) prescribe a specific hierarchy for the principles under which financial statements are prepared. The law identifies the following principles: *prudence*; *substance over form*[18]; *going concern*; *accrual basis*; and *consistency*. Italian GAAP (OIC 11, 2005) add the following principles: usefulness and completeness; understandability; neutrality; comparability; relevance; historical cost as the basic measurement; verifiability; homogeneity; compliance with GAAP; completeness of notes; and recurring measurement of an entity's income and equity. These qualities are similar in their meanings to the IASB's.

There is no detailed definition of prudence in Italian law or in Italian GAAP. Prudence is generally considered as 'anticipate no unrealized profit, but anticipate all potential losses'. The widespread use of historical cost in Italian GAAP is functional with the importance of prudence. Information based on historical cost is likely to be more reliable (as it tends to be less volatile) and conservative in comparison to information based on fair value. Furthermore, prudence tends to override the use of cost in the cases when the two principles are in contrast (the 'lower of cost or net realizable value' accounting practice).

Italian law (see article 2423-bis Civil Code) adds the following further requirements, which are aimed to be instrumental to the prudence principle:

- Separate measurement of heterogeneous items
- Recognition of risks and losses after the balance sheet closing date
- Only incomes realized at the closing date can be recognized in financial statements.

The purpose of *separate measurement of heterogeneous items* is to avoid offsetting unrealized losses and gains. There seems to be evidence of a waning of importance in the IFRS and SFAS of the prudence concept. For instance, while the 1997 version of IAS 1 stated that prudence was one of the necessary conditions of reliable information, an analysis of the content of the revised IAS 1 (2004) shows that prudence is no longer mentioned.

Prudence is at least as important as the accrual basis in Italian GAAP. In fact, although Italian GAAP and law do not explicitly establish a hierarchy between accrual basis assumption and the prudence principle, content analysis of Italian GAAP shows that prudence tends to prevail over the accrual basis assumption. Under the prudence principle, the recognition of risks and losses after balance sheet date and the requirement that only incomes realized at the closing date can be recognized are considered more relevant than accrual basis to meet the objective of financial statements.

Indeed, in Italy the accrual basis principle is significantly affected by the prudence principle, as well as the Italian law requirements previously outlined. Thus, the definition of realized income given by Italian GAAP significantly differs from IFRS. The IASB (2004a, paragraph 70) defines income as 'increases in economic benefits during the accounting period in the form of inflows or enhancements of assets or decreases of liabilities that result in increases in equity'. The definition of income encompasses both revenue and gains. An income is considered realized by IFRS when 'an increase in future economic benefits related to an increase in an asset or a decrease of a liability' can be measured reliably and have a sufficient degree of certainty (IASB, 2004a, paragraph 92).

This concept of income results in the adoption of fair value as a measurement method of assets and liabilities. However, the IASB (2004a, paragraph 81) demands that certain increases or decreases (e.g. some fair value changes) that meet the definition of income cannot be included in the income statement under certain concepts of capital maintenance (see Table 17.1 and section 17.4). Nevertheless, the IASB does not prescribe any particular model, except for exceptional circumstances such as hyperinflationary economy.

The US GAAP do not define the concept of income, rather they adopt the concept of comprehensive income (SFAC No. 3, 1980, paragraph 58). Comprehensive income's definition (SFAC No. 5, 1984, paragraph 39) is substantially consistent with the IASB's definition of income. Comprehensive income may result from (a) exchange transactions and other transfers between the enterprise and other entities, (b) the enterprise's productive efforts, and (c) price changes, casualties, and other effects of interactions between the enterprise and the economic, legal, social, political, and physical environment of which it is part (SFAC No. 6, 1985, paragraph 74).

Comprehensive income is distinguished from the concept of earnings. The latter is similar to net income and measures 'the extent to which asset inflows (revenues and gains) associated with substantially completed cash-to-cash cycles exceed asset outflows (expenses and losses) associated, directly or indirectly, with the same cycles' (SFAC No. 5, 1984, paragraph 36). In addition, earnings are considered as a primary measure of the entity's performance for a given period.

Corporate performance includes 'the recognized effects upon the entity of events and circumstances both within and beyond the control of the entity and its management' (SFAC No. 5, 1984, paragraph 50). To contrast the uncertainty of their business, entities should emphasize completed transactions, applying conservative procedures in accounting recognition of earnings. Certain changes in net assets are recognized in comprehensive income if they meet the four recognition criteria (i.e. definitions, measurability, relevance, reliability), but are recognized as components of earnings only when they are considered (a) realized or realizable and (b) earned (SFAC No. 5, 1984, paragraph 83).

Revenues and gains are considered realized when products, merchandise, or other assets are exchanged for cash or claims to cash, and realizable when related assets received or held are 'readily convertible' (SFAC No. 5, 1984, paragraph 83a) to known amounts of cash (or claims to cash). Revenues are counted as earned when the entity has substantially accomplished what it must do to be entitled to their revenues, i.e. when the transition is completed. Thus, fair value measurements are not as widely applied by US GAAP as by IFRS.

Italian law and GAAP do not provide a definition of the concept of realization, nor a distinction between revenues and gains. Italian GAAP implicitly consider an income as 'realized' only when the following criteria are met: (a) the completion of production and (b) the transfer of the legal title (OIC 11, 2005). That is, revenues are considered realized when they are finally measured based on their sale price. Other than in exceptional circumstances[19], income cannot be recognized if no market exchange has been completed.

The analysis of the IASB and FASB Frameworks and Italian GAAP has revealed significant differences with regard to the importance of prudence and accrual basis principles. The relative importance of prudence in Italy seems to explain the Italian choice to consider most of the fair value gains as unrealized.

'Prudent' financial statements are aimed to safeguard capital maintenance in the interests of corporate stakeholders that do not have a 'voice' on the distribution of profit to shareholders. The preference of fair value vs historical cost in the IFRS is indeed to be based on the assumption that the information based on the 'fair market value' is likely to be more relevant to decision-making, because it is expected to incorporate the effects of economic events in a more timely (but volatile) manner in the financial statements, and better reflects financial risk management practice than information based on the historical cost.

The Italian policymakers seem to be aware that IFRS are able to provide information which is likely to be more 'relevant' (i.e. more useful to the decision-makers) to investors; thus, it has required their adoption even for separate and only financial statements of nonfinancial listed companies. However, Italy has tried to maintain a 'conservative' approach to fair value, by balancing the potential tradeoff between the 'relevance' and 'prudence' principles. Italian companies that adopt IFRS can meet the 'relevance' principle in their financial statements as recommended by the IASB, by disclosing the information at the fair value; at the same time they are not allowed to distribute most of these gains.

17.6 The underlying reasons for the importance of the prudence principle in Italy

The choice of the Italian policymakers to balance the relevance and prudence principles is based on the importance of the 'prudence' principle in the Italian legal system and GAAP framework, which is currently a modified version of

IFRS. Accounting has indeed integrated social, cultural, and economic factors in each country (Hopwood, 1983). In particular, the importance of the prudence principle seems to find its roots in broadly defined corporate governance characteristics in Italy. In particular, we refer to:

- The ownership, capital, and control structures of Italian nonfinancial listed companies
- The generally accepted concept of corporate entity and the role and interests of corporate stakeholders
- Cultural issues concerning prudence and risk avoidance.

17.6.1 Ownership, capital, and control structures of Italian nonfinancial listed companies

Previous empirical studies found that ownership structure does influence financial reporting outcomes (e.g. Fan and Wong, 2002; Francis et al., 2005). The IASB states that its accounting standards are for the benefit of a wide range of organizations (see IAS 1, 2004). However, its Framework as well as many of its accounting standards seem to take for granted a corporate entity in which several small investors provide equity capital to a large listed company, which is under the control of its senior management. In this perspective, the financial reporting system is de facto required to provide adequate information to investors, i.e. corporate shareholders and potential ones, in order to make them able to take informed decisions as well as to hold senior management accountable.

However, recent empirical research (e.g. La Porta et al., 1999; Faccio and Lang, 2002; Laeven and Levine, 2004) indicated that corporate ownership around the world is not widespread; rather it is usually concentrated in the hands of a small number of large shareholders. In Europe, with the only exception of the UK, the presence of multiple large shareholders who own relevant blocks of shares is extremely common (Barca and Becht, 2001).

The Italian corporate governance system is characterized by:

- A relatively high concentrated ownership and control structure (La Porta et al., 1999; Melis, 1999, 2000)
- A relatively poor capital market orientation (e.g. Pagano et al., 1998)
- A limited role played by the market for corporate control, which significantly reduces the need for aggressive reported earnings to boost share price and avoid hostile takeovers.

Furthermore, the control structure of Italian nonfinancial listed companies is characterized by the presence of controlling shareholders, who are 'active' investors, willing and able to monitor the senior management effectively (e.g. Molteni, 1997; Melis, 1999; Bianchi et al., 2001). The controlling shareholders are likely to exercise an influence on the preparation of financial statements. Their presence lessens the incentive for senior management to use 'aggressive' reported earnings, since the controlling shareholder is a corporate insider and does not need financial statements to gain information about corporate performance. Furthermore, Italian nonfinancial companies are characterized by a capital structure that differs significantly from their European counterparts.

For example, McClure et al. (1999) reported that, among the G7 countries, Italy is the country in which nonfinancial listed companies tend to use a higher proportion of total debt vs equity. In Europe only French companies have a similar capital structure. Such a leveraged capital structure gives rise to the important role of creditors among the users of financial statements.

Creditors have different informational and economic needs than investors. They are less interested in corporate entity reports of 'potential' profits, i.e. profits that are not realized (generated from using fair value measurements). Rather, creditors have an interest that fair value gains are kept inside the company in a reserve account and not distributed to shareholders.

By limiting the distribution of fair value gains, Italian law clearly safeguards the creditors' interests (Dezzani, 2005).

17.6.2 Generally accepted concept of the corporate entity: IASB vs Italy

It is generally accepted that accounting standards are aimed to regulate the financial reporting process primarily for the benefit of the users of financial statements. The IASB identifies several 'users of financial statements' (IASB, 2004a, paragraph 9), such as investors, employees, lenders, suppliers and other trade creditors, customers, governments and their agencies, and the public. However, the IASB seems to assume that the regulation (and consequent information) that is able to meet the needs of investors will also meet the needs of other users as well (IASB, 2004a, paragraph 10). This argument resembles the so-called 'enlightened shareholder theory' (Jensen, 2001), which is based on the primacy of the shareholder value. Shareholder value is the dominant paradigm in the Anglo-American corporate governance systems, in which corporate entities tend to be regarded as 'commodities' (Charkham, 1990)[20], but is not in Europe, with the only exception of the UK.

In this perspective, a corporate entity is merely a 'legal fiction' which serves 'as a nexus for a set of contracting relationships among individuals' (Jensen and Meckling, 1976, p. 310ff). This concept is clearly based on the well-known arguments of Friedman (1970).

The prevailing concept of the corporation in Italy significantly differs from such arguments. In Italy, a corporate entity is considered as an enduring social and economic institution (e.g. Zappa, 1927; Onida, 1968; Viganò, 1998). In particular, large companies are considered as social organizations, which are demanded by the State to act taking into account the interests of a wide range of stakeholders, not just their shareholders. Constituencies of a large company include:

- Its employees, who may find it difficult to relocate to other employment if the company closes
- Its creditors (including suppliers and trade creditors) whose claims will not be met in full if the company enters insolvency
- The State itself, which has a stake concerning taxes to be paid by the corporation as well as the socio-economic development of the country.

Similar to German GAAP and law (see, *inter alia*, Harris et al., 1994; Leuz, 2003), Italian law and GAAP encourage a 'prudent' approach to asset valuation and liability recognition in order to facilitate contracting with corporate stakeholders. In particular, if compared to estimates based on historical cost, fair value estimates are more likely to be subject to managerial discretion. As Italian senior managers are usually accountable to the controlling shareholder(s), the difficulty of verifiability of many valuation estimates is likely to give the controlling shareholder(s) an incentive to introduce bias into value estimates.

Taking this issue into account, the Italian standard setter has recognized the importance of taking a 'prudent' approach to the distribution of fair value gains in order to safeguard capital maintenance. By protecting the capital of the company, Italian law seeks to safeguard the interests of the other corporate stakeholders, which might otherwise be 'victims' of the power of the controlling shareholder(s).

17.6.3 Cultural issues concerning prudence and risk avoidance

Cultural issues concerning prudence and risk avoidance may be measured by the Uncertainty Avoidance Index developed by Hofstede (1980). This index focuses on the level of tolerance for uncertainty, ambiguity, and risk within a society. On the one hand, a high Uncertainty Avoidance Index ranking indicates that a country has a low tolerance for uncertainty and ambiguity. This is reflected in a country that is a rule-oriented society that institutes laws, rules, regulations, and controls in order to reduce the amount of uncertainty and risks. On the other hand, a low Uncertainty Avoidance Index ranking indicates the country has less concern about ambiguity and uncertainty. This is reflected in a society that is less rule oriented and takes more and greater risks.

The Uncertainty Avoidance Index rank seems to explain (at least partly) the decision of the Italian regulators to issue a law that explicitly prohibits the distribution of the gains resulting from fair value measurements.

According to Hofstede's study, Italy scored a relatively high level on this index (75 out of 100), especially compared to Anglo-Saxon countries (see Table 17.10).

The evidence from the Uncertainty Avoidance Index seems to support the importance of prudence within the Italian legal framework and GAAP, and is coherent with the decision of limiting the distribution of fair value gains. A counterpart example is provided by the UK, which scored less (35 out of 100) on the Uncertainty Avoidance Index. The waning importance of prudence in the UK is consistent with the argument of Evans and Nobes (1996), concerning the lack of 'the supremacy of prudence' over the other accounting principles in the English version of the European Community Fourth Directive.

Furthermore, differences in the Uncertainty Avoidance Index seem to explain why, in contrast with Italy, UK policymakers have not clearly defined which fair value gains are to be considered as 'unrealized'. It is left to the judgment of professional accountants (we are indebted for this argument to Professor David Alexander, University of Birmingham, UK).

Table 17.10 Uncertainty Avoidance Index (UAI)

Country	UAI
Italy	75
Australia	51
New Zealand	49
Canada	48
USA	46
Ireland	35
UK	35

Source: Hofstede (1980) database.

17.7 The adoption of the comprehensive income statement in Italy

The adoption of a comprehensive income statement is recommended by the European Union (EU directive 51/2003, paragraph 8). In Italy, the law requires disclosure of fair value gains or losses in the nondistributable reserve.

The IASB's statement is divided into three sections: *operating*; *financing and treasury*; and *discontinued operation*. We recommend adding a new section called 'unrealized gains or losses', where fair value gains or losses, credited directly in equity or recognized in the profit and loss statement by IFRS, are disclosed jointly. We define this income statement as the comprehensive income statement (CIS).

When gains are realized – directly through disposal or indirectly through impairment, for example – they should be included in the appropriate section of the income statement. At the same time, the equivalent amounts of realized gains are transferred from the nondistributable reserve to a distributable reserve (or retained earnings)[21].

There are four sections in the comprehensive income:

- *Operating*, where any revenues generated from the entity's sale of its own products and services and any costs that directly or indirectly take part in the production and distribution are included. This section also reports the extraordinary items other than the ones that are disclosed in other sections. Taxes relating to operating income are also included in this section.
- *Financing and treasury*, where any financing and treasury gains or losses are reported. The financing and treasury profit (or loss) for the period is reported, net of taxes.
- *Discontinued operation* (see IFRS 5, 2004, paragraph 32).
- *Unrealized gains and losses*. Table 17.11 shows items subject to fair value measurement and shows unrealized gains and losses as well as related taxes.

The *component approach* elected by the IASB does not appear to meet the requirements of Italian law, as it discloses gains or losses once whether realized or unrealized (i.e. when they arise). Such choice does not seem to emphasize adequately the 'traps' of the unrealized items. The information regarding whether gains are distributable or not is of primary importance to Italian policy-makers. By referring to the previous examples (see section 17.4), we will explain how the fair value unrealized items are disclosed in the CIS, taking into account the requirements of Italian law.

Table 17.11 Face of adoptable Italian comprehensive income statements

	Total $t + 1$	Total t
OPERATING		
Revenues		
Expenses		
Operating income before taxation		
Taxation		
Operating income		
FINANCING AND TREASURY		
Financial gains and losses		
Treasury gains and losses		
Financing and treasury before taxation		
Taxation		
Financing and treasury income		
DISCONTINUED OPERATION		
Distributable income of the period		
UNREALIZED GAINS AND LOSSES		
• Revaluations or revaluation decreases of fixed, intangible assets and investment recognized at fair value		
• Revaluations or revaluation decreases of investments in subsidiaries, jointly controlled entities and associates and other equity instruments recognized at fair value or accounted for using the equity method		
• Revaluations or revaluation decreases of the financial instruments at fair value		
• Changes of fair value of nonmonetary items that are measured at fair value in a foreign currency		
• Revaluations or revaluation decreases of biological assets or agricultural produce recognized at fair value		
• Hedges of a net investment and cash-flow hedge		
• Exchange differences arising on a monetary item that forms part of a reporting entity's net investment in a foreign operation		
• Actuarial gains and losses on defined benefit plans		
Unrealized gains and losses income before taxation		
Taxation		
Unrealized gains and losses income		
Comprehensive income		

17.7.1 Example 1 (investment property)

We assume that operating income is given and the entity's only gains from the financing and treasury section are the fair value changes of investment properties.

In period 1, Italian and US GAAP do not require reporting of fair value changes (see Table 17.12). The comprehensive incomes of the period are equal to operating income (€60,000). IFRS, which measure this type of investment at fair value, report fair value changes in the financing and treasury section (€100,000), considering them as realized items. The comprehensive income of the period is the sum of operating and treasury incomes (€160,000). The Italian application of CIS reports fair value changes in the unrealized gains and losses section (€100,000). On decisions about dividends, fair value changes are credited to a nondistributable reserve of equity. The comprehensive income of the period is equal to that of IFRS (i.e. €160,000).

In period 2, the presentations and disclosures have substantially the same characteristics. Italian and US GAAP do not report fair value gains. Italian CIS recognizes them in the financing and treasury section (€60,000) and then credits them to a nondistributable reserve. IFRS account for them in the financing and treasury section.

In period 3 the properties are disposed. Italian and US GAAP report the realized gain (€50,000), equal to the amount determined as the difference between their disposal value (€1,050,000) and their historical cost (€1,000,000), in the financing and treasury section. The comprehensive income (€50,000) for the period is equal to treasury income because there is no income in the other sections. IFRS account for a treasury loss (€110,000), determined as the difference between their net disposal proceeds (€1,050,000) and their carrying amount of the revaluated item (€1,160,000). CIS reports a comprehensive loss (€110,000). Italian CIS includes the realized gain of the treasury transaction (€50,000), calculated in accordance with Italian GAAP requirements, in the financing and treasury section. The amounts credited to reserve (€160,000 = 100,000 + 60,000) are recycled in the unrealized gains and losses section. Accordingly, any restriction on the distribution of the fair value reserve is removed. In this way, the CIS includes both realized gain of the treasury transaction and the income arisen in the different periods.

17.7.2 Example 2 (financial liability)

Using the previous example, Italian GAAP do not allow fair value measurement and accordingly do not report any fair value changes in the first two periods (see Table 17.13). Only in period 3 do they account for realized financial loss (€100;

Table 17.12 **Comprehensive income statement (CIS): example 1**

	Italy before IFRS – US GAAP	CIS – Italy	IFRS	Italy before IFRS – US GAAP	CIS – Italy	IFRS	Italy before IFRS – US GAAP	CIS – Italy	IFRS
	Period 1			Period 2			Period 3		
OPERATING									
Revenues	1,500,000	1,500,000	1,500,000	1,500,000	1,500,000	1,500,000	1,500,000	1,500,000	1,500,000
Expenses	(1,400,000)	(1,400,000)	(1,400,000)	(1,430,000)	(1,430,000)	(1,430,000)	(1,460,000)	(1,460,000)	(1,460,000)
Operating income before taxation	*100,000*	*100,000*	*100,000*	*70,000*	*70,000*	*70,000*	*40,000*	*40,000*	*40,000*
Taxation	(40,000)	(40,000)	(40,000)	(40,000)	(40,000)	(40,000)	(40,000)	(40,000)	(40,000)
Operating income	**60,000**	**60,000**	**60,000**	**30,000**	**30,000**	**30,000**	**–**	**–**	**–**
FINANCING AND TREASURY									
Financing gains and losses	–	–	100,000	–	–	60,000	50,000	50,000	(110,000)
Financing and treasury before taxation	–	–	100,000	–	–	60,000	50,000	50,000	(110,000)
Taxation	–	–	–	–	–	–	–	–	–

Financing and treasury	–	–	**100,000**	–	–	**60,000**	**50,000**	**50,000**	(110,000)
Income of the period	**60,000**	**60,000**	**160,000**	**30,000**	**30,000**	**90,000**	**50,000**	**50,000**	(110,000)
UNREALIZED GAINS AND LOSSES									
Revaluation/ revaluation decreases of financial assets	–	**100,000**	–	–	60,000	–	–	(160,000)	–
Taxation	–	–	–	–	–	–	–	–	–
Unrealized gains and losses	–	**100,000**	–	–	**60,000**	–	–	(160,000)	–
Comprehensive income	**60,000**	**160,000**	**160,000**	**30,000**	**90,000**	**90,000**	**50,000**	(110,000)	(110,000)

Table 17.13 Comprehensive income statement (CIS): example 2

	Italy before IFRS	CIS – Italy	IFRS US GAAP	Italy before IFRS	CIS – Italy	IFRS US GAAP	Italy before IFRS	CIS – Italy	IFRS US GAAP
	Period 1			Period 2			Period 3		
OPERATING									
Revenues	1,500,000	1,500,000	1,500,000	1,500,000	1,500,000	1,500,000	1,500,000	1,500,000	1,500,000
Expenses	(1,498,000)	(1,498,000)	(1,498,000)	(1,498,000)	(1,498,000)	(1,498,000)	(1,498,000)	(1,498,000)	(1,498,000)
Operating income before taxation	*2000*	*2000*	*2000*	*2000*	*2000*	*2000*	*2000*	*2000*	*2000*
Taxation	(1500)	(1500)	(1500)	(1500)	(1500)	(1500)	(1500)	(1500)	(1500)
Operating income	**500**	**500**	**500**	**500**	**500**	**500**	**500**	**500**	**500**
FINANCING AND TREASURY									
Financing gains and losses	–	–	500	–	–	100	(100)	(100)	(700)
Financing and treasury before taxation	–	–	500	–	–	100	(100)	(100)	(700)
Taxation	–	–	–	–	–	–	–	–	–

Financing and treasury	**–**	**–**	**500**	**–**	**–**	**100**	(100)	(100)	(700)
Income of the period	**500**	**500**	**1,000**	**500**	**500**	**600**	**400**	**400**	**(200)**
UNREALIZED GAINS AND LOSSES									
Revaluation/ revaluation decreases of financial liability	–	**500**	–	–	100	–	–	(600)	–
Taxation	–	–	–	–	–	–	–	–	–
Unrealized gains and losses	**–**	**500**	**–**	**–**	**100**	**–**	**–**	(600)	**–**
Comprehensive income	**500**	**1,000**	**1,000**	**500**	**600**	**600**	**400**	(200)	(200)

see note 15). IFRS and US GAAP allow fair value measurement for the derivatives and account for fair value changes in the financing and treasury section, considering them as realized and distributable items. However, in period 3 a financial loss (€700) has to be reported in the same section.

Italian CIS presents the fair value changes (€500 and €100) in the unrealized gains and losses section in periods 1 and 2. Gains are credited to a nondistributable reserve. In period 3, the entity will recognize:

- A financial realized loss (€100) in the financing and treasury section.
- The recycling of the amounts credited to the nondistributable reserve (€500 + €100 = €600). At the same time, any restriction on the distribution of the fair value reserve is removed. The CIS's comprehensive income is equal to IFRS', but the information that can be drawn from them is different.

17.8 Conclusion

This chapter has examined the key economic and financial reporting issues related to the effects of adoption of IFRS in the separate and only financial statements of Italian nonfinancial listed companies. Italian policymakers believe that IFRS could provide information of higher quality than national GAAP. Thus, in accordance to EU options, it has required their adoption even for separate and only financial statements starting in 2006.

This chapter has provided a brief comparison between IFRS, US, and Italian GAAP concerning fair value accounting, the key innovation brought about by IFRS. With their widespread use of fair value measurements, IFRS seem to be able to provide information, which is likely to be more useful to investors than Italian GAAP, which are based on historical cost measurements because of the importance of the prudence accounting principle. In fact, information based on historical cost is likely to be more reliable (as it tends to be less volatile) and prudent in comparison to information based on fair value, but is less relevant to investors.

The key issues relating to the distribution of fair value gains have been discussed with the use of two examples: the accounting of an investment property and a financial liability. These examples support the argument that the Italian treatment of fair value gains seems to safeguard better the interests of a wide range of corporate stakeholders, without lowering the quality of information provided to investors.

This chapter has examined how Italian GAAP and Italian law give a different definition and importance to the concepts of accrual basis and prudence in comparison with IFRS and US GAAP. Such differences do have a significant impact on accounting regulations.

To balance the potential tradeoff between the 'relevance' and 'prudence' principles, Italian policymakers have maintained a 'conservative' approach to fair value measurements. The prudence principle has been safeguarded against distribution of unrealized gains. Italian companies that adopt IFRS are not allowed to distribute most of the fair value gains. Thus, the adoption of fair value to disclose and measure the entity's working capital at current values and the introduction of 'unrealized' fair value gains in the income of the period do not undermine the corporate entity's capital maintenance in the long term.

The significant importance of the prudence principle in Italy seems to have its roots in corporate governance factors, such as the Italian ownership concentration, capital, and control structures, the generally accepted concept of the corporate entity and cultural issues, in relation to prudence, risk-taking, and uncertainty avoidance. An analysis of these factors has shown relevant differences between the Italian environment and the corporate reality assumed by the IASB.

Finally, the authors recommend the adoption of a comprehensive income statement, where all economic items that will affect the future entity's cash flows are disclosed. In particular, fair value gains (and losses) are disclosed separately from other items in a section named 'unrealized gains and losses', so that the 'volatility' of these economic items is disclosed. Thus, users of financial statements may understand if, how, and to what extent 'unrealized' gains derived from fair value measurements have contributed to the comprehensive income of the period.

The comprehensive income statement, together with the constraints on distribution of gains imposed by Italian law, seems likely to meet the informational needs of investors who are able to evaluate the ability of an entity to generate cash, profits, and judgments of corporate management about the future, as well as to safeguard the economic interests of other corporate stakeholders.

Acknowledgments

Giovanni Melis and Andrea Melis acknowledge the financial support of the Italian Ministry of Research (MIUR PRIN 2004-2006, 'The effects of the introduction of IFRS in financial statements'). Andrea Melis also acknowledges the financial support of the Italian National Research Centre (CNR – 2004, 'Corporate disclosure: financial statements' reliability, IFRS, and corporate governance systems'). This chapter is the result of the joint work of all three authors; however, Giovanni Melis wrote sections 17.5 and 17.8, Andrea Melis wrote sections 17.1, 17.2, and 17.6, and Alessandro Pili wrote sections 17.3, 17.4, and 17.7.

Notes

1. For ease of exposition, we will use the term 'IFRS' to refer to both IAS and IFRS. More precisely, IAS are the International Accounting Standards issued by the International Accounting Standards Committee, while IFRSs are the International Financial Reporting Standards issued by the International Accounting Standards Board.
2. The term 'prudence' is more commonly used in Europe, while in the USA this concept is often expressed as the term 'conservatism'. For ease of exposition, in this chapter both terms will be used interchangeably.
3. The term 'fair value', except when expressly defined differently, is to be meant according to the definition given by the current IASB Glossary, i.e. 'the amount for which an asset could be exchanged, or a liability settled, between knowledgeable, willing parties in an arm's length transaction'.
4. Italian policymakers have not disclosed the underlying reasons that lead to these exceptions. Furthermore, they give rise to a problem of comparability with Italian companies that are allowed to adopt Italian GAAP. For instance, the same company that adopts Italian GAAP shall credit the gains from operations in foreign currency markets to a nondistributable reserve, while it is allowed to distribute such gains if it decides to adopt IFRS.
5. 'The best evidence of an asset's *fair value less costs to sell* is a price in a binding sale agreement in an arm's length transaction, adjusted for incremental costs that would be directly attributable to the disposal of the asset'. The 'value in use is the present value of the future cash flows expected to be derived from an asset or cash generating unit'. IAS 36 (2004, paragraphs 25, 33).
6. For a further examination of Italian financial statements, see, *inter alia*, Melis and Congiu (2001).
7. Despite this fact, IAS 19 (2004, Appendix BC39) considers that: 'Immediate recognition can cause volatile fluctuations in liability and expense and implies a degree of accuracy which can rarely apply in practice ... in the long term, actuarial gains and losses may offset one another ... They are not a gain or loss of the period but a fine-tuning of the cost that emerges over the long term ... The immediate recognition of actuarial gains and losses in the income statement would cause unacceptable volatility.' For these reasons, the Board prefers the *corridor approach*.
8. Investments in equity instruments are measured at their fair value except for those instruments that: (a) do not have a quoted market price in an active market and (b) whose fair value cannot be reliably measured. They are measured at cost. Equity instruments may be classified as *held for trading* or as *available for sale*. In the first case the fair value changes are recognized in profit or loss, in the second one they are credited to a reserve of equity. Equity instruments may not be classified as *held to maturity*. Held to maturity investments are nonderivative financial assets with fixed or determinable payments and fixed maturity that an entity has the positive intention and ability to hold to maturity. Equity instruments cannot have such attributes.
9. 'A financial instrument is any contract that gives rise to a financial asset of one entity and a financial liability or equity instrument of another entity' (IAS 32, 2004, paragraph 11).
10. 'The amortized cost of a financial asset or financial liability is the amount at which the financial asset or financial liability is measured at initial recognition minus principal repayments, plus or minus the cumulative amortization using the effective interest method of any difference between that initial amount and the maturity amount, and minus any reduction (directly or through the use of an allowance account) for impairment or uncollectibility' (IAS 39, 2004, paragraph 9).

11. An *investment held to maturity* is reclassified as *available for sale* if there is a change in intention or ability to hold it to maturity. However, the reclassifications are restricted by IFRS (see IAS 39, 2004, paragraphs 50–54).
12. Except for investments in equity instruments that do not have a quoted market price in an active market, whose fair value cannot be reliably measured, that are measured at their cost.
13. Differences between the IFRS's requirements and the Italian's concern only the presentation of such instruments in the balance sheet. Under IAS 39, the carrying amount of the financial instrument is directly increased (or decreased) by the cumulative amortization of any difference between its initial and maturity amounts. In this way, the carrying amount develops into the redemption amount. Under Italian GAAP, the carrying amount of the financial instrument remains unchanged and increments or decrements are recognized in another asset or liability called prepayments and accrued income. The instrument's carrying amount does not develop into the redemption amount.
14. The measurements of *changes of fair value of nonmonetary items that are measured at fair value in a foreign currency, actuarial gains and losses on defined benefit plans, investments in subsidiaries, jointly controlled entities, and associates in separate financial statements, financial assets at fair value option, financial liabilities at fair value option*, and *biological assets and agricultural produce* have the same effects on the entity's capital maintenance because IFRS require fair value changes to be recognized in profit or loss.
15. Entity A's obligation, equal to the fair value of entity C's share, is decreased. The obligation is equal to an amount of €19,000 when the put option is written. It decreases to an amount of €18,000 at the end of period 1 and to an amount of €17,600 at the end of period 2.
16. The loss is equal to the sum of the fixed exercise price (€18,500) and put option price (€1000) minus entity A's final obligation (€19,600 = fair value of entity C's share). In other words, entity A paid €1100 (19,600 – 18,500) to entity B and received €1000 (put option price) by it.
17. 'Historically, managers, investors, and accountants have generally preferred that possible errors in measurement be in the direction of understatement rather than overstatement of net income and net assets. This has led to the convention of conservatism' (see APB No. 4, 1964, paragraph 171).
18. However, in practice, the 'substance over form' principle is applied in Italy only when it is not in contrast with the legal form of the transition. This is a clear difference with IFRS (e.g. Dezzani, 2005).
19. There are only few notable exceptions in which Italian GAAP allow the recording of a value that is higher than historical cost: 'Extraordinary revaluations of assets' (see Civil Code article 2423), investments in subsidiaries accounted for using the equity method, and exchange differences arising on translating monetary items at closing rate. Any profit due to these procedures shall be credited in nondistributable reserves, until the amount is realized on disposal or via depreciation.
20. However, Deakin (2005, p. 11) notes that: 'It is surprisingly difficult to find support within company law for the notion of shareholder primacy.' Shareholder primacy is 'essentially a cultural rather than a legal point of reference' (Deakin, 2005, p. 16).
21. This *holding tank* approach has been used in the USA since 1997 (see SFAS 130, 1997). When an unrealized item becomes realized or when an uncertain item becomes certain, it is displayed as a part of the realized items section of the income statement (*business profit or financing and investing activities*). At the same time, it is *recycled* from the unrealized section of the income statement. This method is called *recycling*. The IASB takes a different approach (called the

component approach): gains or losses are disclosed only once, when they arise. 'Recycling' is not allowed. Items are disclosed having regarded their economic nature, not their realization.

References

Alexander, D. and Nobes, C. (1994). *A European Introduction to Financial Accounting*. Prentice-Hall International, London.

APB No. 4 (1964). *Accounting for the Investment Credit*. AICPA, New York.

APB No. 6 (1965). *Status of Accounting Research Bulletins*. AICPA, New York.

APB Opinion No. 17 (1970). *Intangible Assets*. AICPA, New York.

APB Opinion No. 18 (1971). *The Equity Method of Accounting for Investments in Common Stock*. AICPA, New York.

Bank of Italy (2002). *I Bilanci Delle Banche Schemi e Regole di Compilazione*. Circular No. 166 of 30 July 1992, revised in 2002. Bank of Italy, Rome.

Barca, F. and Becht, M. (2001). *The Control of Corporate Europe*. Oxford University Press, Oxford.

Belkaoui, A. (1995). *International Accounting*. Quorum Books, New York.

Bianchi, M., Bianco, M., and Enriques, L. (2001). Pyramidal Groups and the Separation Between Ownership and Control in Italy. In: *The Control of Corporate Europe* (Barca, F. and Becht, M., eds), pp. 154–187. Oxford University Press, Oxford.

Charkham, J. (1990). Are Shares just Commodities? In: *Creative Tension*, pp. 34–42. National Association of Pension Funds, London.

Choi, F. and Mueller, G. (1992). *International Accounting*. Prentice-Hall, Englewood Cliffs, NJ.

CNDC-CNR No. 17 (1996). *Il Bilancio Consolidato*. Giuffré, Milan.

CNDC-CNR No. 20 (1996). *Titoli e Partecipazioni*. Giuffré, Milan.

CNDC-CNR No. 21 (1996). *Il Metodo del Patrimonio Netto*. Giuffré, Milan.

Deakin, S. (2005). The Coming Transformation of Shareholder Value. *Corporate Governance: An International Review*, 13(1):11–18.

Dezzani, F. (2005). Principi Civilistici e Principi IAS/IFRS: Sistemi Alternativi per la Redazione del Bilancio di Esercizio. Working Paper, University of Turin.

Evans, L. and Nobes, C. (1996). Some Mysteries Relating to the Prudence Principle in the Fourth Directive and in German and British Law. *European Accounting Review*, 5(2):361–373.

Faccio, M. and Lang, H. (2002). The Ultimate Ownership of Western European Corporations. *Journal of Financial Economics*, 65(3):365–395.

Fan, J. and Wong, T. (2002). Corporate Ownership Structure and the Informativeness of Accounting Earnings in East Asia. *Journal of Accounting and Economics*, 33(3):401–425.

FASB (1974). *Accounting Changes Related to the Cost of Inventory*, Interpretation No. 1. Norwalk, CT.

Francis, J., Schipper K., and Vincent, L. (2005). Earnings and Dividend Informativeness When Cash Flow Rights are Separated from Voting Rights. *Journal of Accounting and Economics*, 39(2):329–360.

Friedman, M. (1970). The Social Responsibility of Business is to Increase it Profits. *New York Times Magazine*, 13 September. Reprinted in Donaldson, T. and Werhane, P. (1983). *Ethical Issues in Business: A Philosophical Approach*. Prentice-Hall, Englewood Cliffs, NJ.

Harris, T., Lang, M., and Moller, H. (1994). The Value Relevance of German Accounting Measures: An Empirical Analysis. *Journal of Accounting Research*, 32(2):187–209.

Hofstede, G. (1980). *Culture's Consequences: International Differences in Work-related Values.* Sage, Newbury Park, CA.

Hopwood, A.G. (1983). On Trying to Study Accounting in the Context in Which it Operates. *Accounting, Organizations and Society*, 8(2–3):287–305.

IAS 1 (1997, 2004). *Preparation of Financial Statements.* IASCF, London.

IAS 2 (2004). *Inventories.* IASCF, London.

IAS 16 (2004). *Property, Plant and Equipment.* IASCF, London.

IAS 19 (2004). *Employee Benefits.* IASCF, London.

IAS 21 (2004). *The Effects of Changes in Foreign Exchange Rates.* IASCF, London.

IAS 27 (2004). *Consolidated and Separate Financial Statements.* IASCF, London.

IAS 28 (2004). *Investments in Associate.* IASCF, London.

IAS 31 (2004). *Interests in Joint Ventures.* IASCF, London.

IAS 32 (2004). *Financial Instruments: Disclosure and Presentation.* IASCF, London.

IAS 36 (2004). *Impairment of Assets.* IASCF, London.

IAS 38 (2004). *Intangible Assets.* IASCF, London.

IAS 39 (2004). *Financial Instruments: Recognition and Measurement.* IASCF, London.

IAS 40 (2004). *Investment Property.* IASCF, London.

IAS 41 (2004). *Agriculture.* IASCF, London.

IASB (2004a). *International Financial Reporting Standards. Framework for the Preparation and Presentation of Financial Statements.* IASCF, London.

IASB (2004b). Board Meeting, 18–20 October, Norwalk, CT.

IFRS 3 (2004). *Business Combination.* IASCF, London.

IFRS 5 (2004). *Non-current Assets Held for Sale and Discontinued Operations.* IASCF, London.

Jensen, M. (2001). Value maximization, stakeholder theory, and corporate objective. *European Financial Management*, 7(3):297–317.

Jensen, M. and Meckling, W. (1976). Theory of the Firm: Managerial Behaviour, Agency Costs, and Ownership Structure. *Journal of Financial Economics*, 3(4):305–360.

Laeven, L. and Levine R. (2004). Beyond the Biggest: Do Other Large Shareholders Influence Corporate Valuations? Working Paper, University of Minnesota.

La Porta, R., Lopez-de-Silanes, F., and Shleifer, A. (1999). Corporate Ownership Around the World. *Journal of Finance*, 54(2):471–517.

Leuz, C. (2003). IAS Versus US GAAP: Information Asymmetry-based Evidence from Germany's New Market. *Journal of Accounting Research*, 41(3):445–472.

McClure, K., Clayton R., and Hofler R. (1999). International Capital Structure Differences Among the G7 Nations: A Current Empirical View. *European Journal of Finance*, 5(2):141–164.

Melis, A. (1999). Corporate Governance. *Un'analisi Empirica Della Realtà Italiana in Un'ottica Europea.* Giappichelli, Turin.

Melis, A. (2000). Corporate Governance in Italy. *Corporate Governance: An International Review*, 8(4):347–355.

Melis, G. and Congiu, P. (2001). *Il Bilancio d'Esercizio Delle Imprese Industriali, Mercantili e di Servizi.* Giuffré, Milan.

Molteni, M. (1997). *I Sistemi di Corporate Governance Nelle Grandi Imprese Italiane.* EGEA, Milan.

Nobes, C. (1998). Toward a General Model of the Reasons for International Differences in Financial Reporting. *Abacus*, 34(2):162–187.

Nobes, C. and Parker, R. (2002). *Comparative International Accounting*. Prentice-Hall International, London.

OIC 11 (2005). *Bilancio D'esercizio-Finalità e Postulati*. Fondazione OIC, Rome.

OIC 13 (2005). *Le Rimanenze di Magazzino*. Fondazione OIC, Rome.

OIC 16 (2005). *Le Immobilizzazioni Materiali*. Fondazione OIC, Rome.

OIC 17 (2005). *Il Bilancio Consolidato. Bozza*. Fondazione OIC, Rome.

OIC 19 (2005). *I Fondi Per Rischi e Oneri. Il Trattamento di Fine Rapporto di Lavoro Subordinato. I Debiti*. Fondazione OIC, Rome.

OIC 24 (2005). *Le Immobilizzazioni Immateriali*. Fondazione OIC, Rome.

Onesti, T. (1995). *Fattori Ambientali e Comportamenti Contabili. Analisi Comparata Dei Sistemi Contabili di Alcuni Paesi Industrializzati*. Giappichelli, Turin.

Onida, P. (1968). *Economia Aziendale*. UTET, Turin.

Pagano, M., Panetta, F., and Zingales, L. (1998). Why Do Companies Go Public? An Empirical Analysis. *Journal of Finance*, 53(1):27–64.

Roberto, G. (2004). *Le Svalutazioni e le Rivalutazioni Non Monetarie Delle Immobilizzazioni Materiali*. Aracne, Rome.

Schipper, K. (2005). The Introduction of International Accounting Standards in Europe: Implications for International Convergence. *European Accounting Review*, 14(1):101–126.

SFAC No. 1 (1978). *Objectives of Financial Reporting by Business Enterprises*. FASB, Norwalk, CT.

SFAC No. 2 (1980). *Qualitative Characteristics of Accounting Information*. FASB, Norwalk, CT.

SFAC No. 3 (1980). *Elements of Financial Statements of Business Enterprises*. FASB, Norwalk, CT.

SFAC No. 5 (1980). *Recognition and Measurement in Financial Statements of Business Enterprises*. FASB, Norwalk, CT.

SFAC No. 6 (1985). *Elements of Financial Statements*. FASB, Norwalk, CT.

SFAS 52 (1981). *Foreign Currency Translation*. FASB, Norwalk, CT.

SFAS 87 (1985). *Employers' Accounting for Pensions*. FASB, Norwalk, CT.

SFAS 115 (1993). *Accounting for Certain Investment in Debt and Equity Securities*. FASB, Norwalk, CT.

SFAS 124 (1995). *Accounting for Certain Investments Held by Not-for-profit Organization*. FASB, Norwalk, CT.

SFAS 130 (1997). *Reporting Comprehensive Income*. FASB, Norwalk, CT.

SFAS 133 (1998). *Accounting for Derivative Instruments and Hedging Activities*. FASB, Norwalk, CT.

SFAS 142 (2001). *Goodwill and Other Intangible Assets*. FASB, Norwalk, CT.

SFAS 144 (2001). *Accounting for the Impairment of Long-Lived Assets and for Long-Lived Assets to Be Disposed Of*. FASB, Norwalk, CT.

Viganó, E. (1998). Accounting and Business Economics Traditions in Italy. *European Accounting Review*, 7(3):381–403.

Whittington, G. (2005). The Adoption of International Accounting Standards in the European Union. *European Accounting Review*, 14(1):127–153.

Zappa, G. (1927). *Tendenze Nuove Negli Studi di Ragioneria*. Giuffré, Milan.

18

Factors Affecting Accounting Development in the Harmonization Process with the International Framework: The Case of Estonia

Toomas Haldma

18.1 Introduction

In the early 1990s, Estonia's economic system was transformed from a centrally planned to a market-based economy, which involved significant legal and institutional changes in regulations and especially accounting regulations. Finally, in May 2004, Estonia joined the European Union. According to the European Commission decision at the beginning of 2005, all European Union (EU) companies listed on a regulated market were required to prepare their consolidated accounts in accordance with the International Financial Reporting Standards (IFRS). This requirement represents a preliminary step in the internationalization process of financial accounting and reporting in Europe.

Earlier research viewed the post-socialist countries as a bloc with common problems and challenges (Seal et al., 1995). However, as expressed by Roberts et al. (2002), there are no two countries with identical accounting systems. In a similar way, Bailey (1998) stated that the Central and Eastern European (CEE) countries were heterogeneous, being at different stages of transformation from command economies at certain times. In view of this, the present exploratory study focuses on one particular country, Estonia, and examines the factors which have influenced Estonian accounting reforms throughout the stages of its development, to conform to the requirements of the future European accounting framework. This chapter examines the evolutionary factors of the Estonian accounting system within the context of EU accession and harmonization, by indicating how such factors have influenced accounting reform during the different stages of its development.

The chapter is organized as follows. Section 18.2 reviews some of the relevant literature on international accounting harmonization and the factors influencing such harmonization in transitional economies. Some general and specific issues that might arise when using a phased approach to accounting regulation development and analysis of factors influencing an accounting reform will be identified in section 18.3. In section 18.4, a phased framework is applied to describe how the Estonian accounting regulations and institutional framework have changed in the course of three different Estonian accounting reform stages: introduction, system building, and system improvement. Research findings will follow in section 18.5 and factors influencing accounting reform in Estonia are outlined. Finally, section 18.6 concludes.

18.2 Literature review

Accounting harmonization at the global and regional levels has been broadly discussed during the last decade (see, for example, Van Hulle, 1993; Hoarau, 1995; Haller, 1995, 2002; Cairns, 1997; Flower, 1997). Hoarau (1995) defined international accounting harmonization as a political process, which aims to reduce differences in accounting practices across the world in order to achieve compatibility and comparability. Accounting harmonization has been examined to a much lesser extent in transitional countries. Saudagaran and Diga (1997b) pointed out that harmonization issues in the development of accounting regulations, particularly in developing countries, provide a basis for analyzing the comparability of accounting systems worldwide. Several studies have analyzed accounting harmonization at national level among the CEE countries, such as Russia (Ramcharran, 2000), Slovakia (Daniel and Suranova, 2001), Romania (King et al., 2001), Hungary (Roberts et al., 2002), Czech Republic (Sucher and Jindrichovska, 2004), and Poland (Vellam, 2004).

Regarding the issue of harmonization for the CEE countries, Bailey (1998) argued that the accounting reform has to be oriented to harmonization with the EU directives and acceptance of the International Accounting Standards. To succeed in the public accessibility of statutory financial statements of companies, Bailey (1998) suggested that a phased approach could be used in accounting reform.

The collapse of centrally planned economies in the late 1980s and early 1990s changed the accounting environment in the former socialist countries dramatically. The need for conceptual development of the whole accounting framework and of companies' accounting systems grew rapidly. Several factors influencing the development of an accounting framework in such countries must be taken into consideration.

As asserted by Roberts et al. (2002), an accounting system is the outcome of a complex process influenced by and itself influencing a number of factors. It has generally been recognized that financial reporting varies among developing countries because of differences in political, economic, and socio-cultural backgrounds (Hoarau, 1995; Radebaugh and Gray, 1997; Saudagaran and Diga, 1997a; Ramcharran, 2000). Moreover, as Saudagaran and Diga (1997a) pointed out, the factors in each country's national and international environments constrain the policy options available to the government. There is a large list of possible causes for accounting system differences (see Nobes 2002; Roberts et al., 2002; Radebaugh and Gray, 1997). As regards criteria used to evaluate and compare the state of financial reporting of developing countries, as an outcome of accounting developments, Saudagaran and Diga (1997a) suggested availability, reliability, and comparability of information. Bailey (1998, pp. 1456–1460) pointed out a number of issues concerning availability, reliability, and comparability of accounting information, which must be considered in the accounting harmonization process for a transition country. More specifically, Bailey raised the following issues:

- Issue of compliance with EU directives when no translation is available in the local language.
- The possibility of implementing a large accounting change when there is so much systemic instability (new political and legal systems, new institutional structures). Also, acute economic disturbances (e.g. bankruptcy; financial difficulties) make it very difficult to implement accounting changes successfully.
- The immaturity of the legal system, corrupt business practices, and weak trust relations may hamper the system of financial statements.
- Accessibility of the financial statements of companies in the public domain.
- Should accounts only reflect legal compliance rather than be 'true and fair'?
- Who do the accounting laws apply to? Would phased implementation of the IFRS be appropriate?
- The influence of taxes on accounting issues.
- Are there severe external pressures from ministries on the enterprises as the flows of power?
- How liquid is the stock exchange and how is it connected with the accounting issues?

This study will identify the factors that may influence Estonian accounting harmonization to achieve better availability, reliability, and comparability of accounting information. The literature suggests that there may be contextual factors that affect the appropriateness and effectiveness of the accounting reforms in a transitional economy towards harmonization with an international framework. Based on an analysis of the available literature, factors influencing a national accounting system may be divided into five groups: the political system, the legal system, the taxation system, the companies' financing system, and the accounting profession. There may also be additional factors concerning how a particular country initiates the construction of its national accounting system.

Obviously, these specific transition country factors are interrelated with contextual factors. Practically, it would also be useful to determine the level of readiness of the Estonian accounting system for harmonization with the European framework. In the next section, the development of factors influencing accounting reform in Estonia will be discussed.

18.3 Factors influencing accounting reform in Estonia

A number of papers have been dedicated to the factors influencing a national accounting system (see, for example, Gray and Roberts, 1991; Nobes, 2002; Roberts et al., 2002; Radebaugh and Gray, 1997; Saudagaran and Diga, 1997b; Sucher and Jindrichovska, 2004). They deal mainly with the factors associated with market economy countries. In the previous section we listed a number of factors pointed out by Bailey (1998) that need to be considered when moving towards accounting harmonization in a transitional economy. In this chapter, based on the results of the literature review, a cross-sectional list of the factors influencing a national accounting system that were found in Nobes (2002), Roberts et al. (2002), Radebaugh and Gray (1997), and Sucher and Jindrichovska (2004) is constructed, merging them with the list of the influential factors and issues found in Bailey (1998). A selected list of factors is used to characterize the Estonian accounting framework: the political system, the legal system, the taxation system, the companies' financing system, and the accounting profession. But additional influencing factors also need to be identified, in particular for the initial period of formation of a national accounting system. These factors and their influence in Estonia will be discussed below.

Saudagaran and Diga (1997b) view accounting harmonization as a 'process' of achieving a higher level of accounting harmony. They argued that if accounting harmonization is a linear process, then the intermediate stages have to be realized. Also, for the transitional countries, Bailey (1998) suggested application of a phased approach to accounting reform. This was achieved by placing the companies' statutory financial statements in the public domain. In the current chapter, the phased approach has been used in order to study the development over time and to expand the scope of Estonian accounting reform. Literature analysis revealed that the phased approach has been used in the Czech Republic (Seal et al., 1995; Sucher and Jindrichovska, 2004), Poland (Kosmala-MacLullich, 2003; Jaruga and Szychta, 1997), Romania (King et al., 2001), and Estonia (Haldma, 2004) to a certain extent to divide accounting reform into

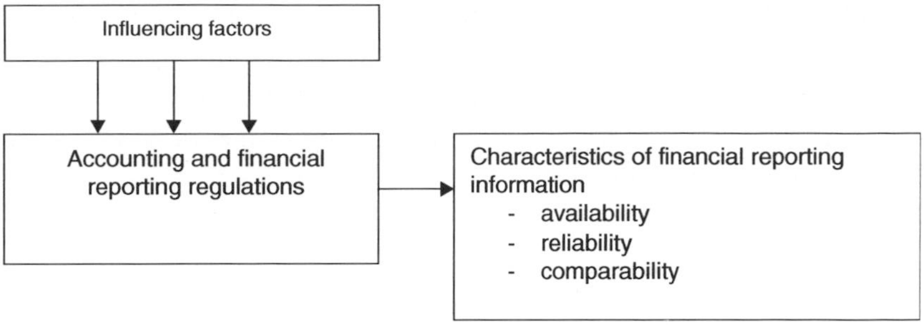

Figure 18.1 Impact of influencing factors

periods. These two issues raise two research questions. First, is the influence of these factors similar for each stage of accounting reform? Second, does the materiality of various factors differ among the stages of accounting reform? Therefore, the particular stages (phases) of accounting reform are suggested to have different impacts on the outcome of accounting developments: availability, reliability, and comparability of information. The theoretical framework of this chapter is given in Figure 18.1.

Therefore, to analyze the conceptual aspects of Estonian accounting reform, an integrated theoretical framework of the factors influencing accounting change and a phased approach to the change are used, which are merged into a single theoretical framework.

18.4 Stages of the integration of the Estonian accounting system into the international framework

The key issue of all accounting regulation changes within the European framework is to ensure that it conforms to EU law (also known as the *acquis communautaire*) for the accession countries to the EU, i.e. that Estonia fulfills the requirements of an EU member. In the World Bank and International Monetary Fund (IMF) Report on the Observance of Standards and Codes (ROSC), regarding the status of Estonia's progress towards harmonization with EU legislation in May 2004, it was stated that 'in the area of financial reporting and auditing law, Estonia implemented the Fourth, Seventh, and Eighth EU Company Law Directives, the EU Regulation on the use of International Accounting Standards, and International Standards on Auditing' (ROSC, 2004).

The ROSC team also reviewed a sample of financial statements prepared in accordance with the IFRS and Estonian Accounting Standards (EAS). Results of the analysis reveal that the quality of the EAS and IFRS financial statements of *most public interest entities* in the corporate sector is generally very high, with only a few minor issues. The accounting policies and disclosures are generally very clear (ROSC, 2004).

Consequently, the Estonian accounting legislation and regulations conform to the EU directives and regulations. How has this process proceeded? Table 18.1 summarizes the accounting developments since 1990.

As regards the development of the Estonian accounting system, Haldma (2004) delineated three stages in this process: the introductory (1990–1994), system building (1995–2002), and system improvement (2003 onwards) stages. To analyze, in depth, the content of Estonian accounting changes, a discussion of the development of the accounting regulations, the scope of accounting regulations, and the degree of independence of the accounting regulatory institution (see Table 18.1) will follow.

Estonia started to aspire towards market economy when it was still a part of the Soviet Union, and much earlier than the other Soviet republics. In July 1990, more than a year before independence was regained in August 1991, the Regulation on Accounting was adopted by the Estonian Government. This event was the first step towards creation of a market economy accounting environment in Estonia. The effective date of the Regulation on Accounting was 1 January 1991. As pointed out by Bailey et al. (1995), this event also marked the beginning of the spread of accounting disharmony within the territories of the USSR.

Although, relatively speaking, the regulations were quite modest in content and volume, consisting of only 10 pages, the actions spurred by the regulations were instrumental in creating a favorable environment for the adoption of market-based accounting principles, and prepared the country for moving to the second stage of Estonian accounting reform.

The second, system-building stage started in 1995. The accounting framework and procedures in Estonian companies and institutions have legally been regulated by two parallel regulations:

- Estonian Act on Accounting (EAOA)
- Estonian Accounting Standards issued by the Estonian Accounting Standards Board (EASB).

Such a combination had a number of advantages in the initial period of the accounting reform, speeding it up, and enabling the transition process to be

Table 18.1 The stages of development of Estonian accounting regulations

Stage and dates and basic regulation	Aim of the regulations	Developments in accounting issues	Scope of the regulation	Status of the EASB
The first, introductory stage (1990–1994) **Regulation on Accounting 1990** Applied from 1 January 1991	The regulations made accounting an autonomous area of information provision and established minimum requirements to all juridical persons for the organization, structure and maintenance of the bookkeeping (accounting) system. Quite modest in content and volume (10 pages)	The regulations introduced a list of subjective elements (depreciation rates, inventory valuation methods, assets valuation methods, etc. decided by companies) into the accounting practice, formation of a particular accounting policy, change from cash-basis accounting to accrual-basis accounting, institution of some basic accounting principles (realization principles, the matching principle, the historical cost principle). The Regulation served as an initiative to link the future development of accounting in	Formally the regulations related to all juridical persons in Estonia (enterprises, entities of state and local authority, and other organizations).	The Estonian Accounting Standard Board (EASB), supervised by the Ministry of Finance became the guiding body of accounting. The main task of the Board was to issue mandatory accounting instructions as well as recommendations concerning the methods to be applied.

(*Continued*)

Table 18.1 *(Continued)*

Stage and dates and basic regulation	Aim of the regulations	Developments in accounting issues	Scope of the regulation	Status of the EASB
		Estonia to the EC 4th Directive.		
The second, system-building stage (1995 to 2002) **Act on Accounting 1994** Applied from 1 January 1995	To create the legal basis and establish general requirements for organizing accounting and reporting in the Republic of Estonia based on internationally accepted accounting principles (Article 1). Internationally accepted accounting and reporting principles are defined as the accounting directives of the European Community and the principles, standards, and recommendations developed and approved by the International Accounting Standards Committee (IASC) (Article 3) (*Hea raamatupidamistava*, 2000).	The accounting framework and procedures in Estonian companies and institutions have legally been regulated by: • Estonian Act on Accounting (EAOA); • Estonian Accounting Standards (EAS) issued by the EASB. Between 1995 and 2000 the EASB issued 16 EAS to improve the following particular aspects: Conceptual Framework of Generally Accepted Accounting Principles; Revenue Recognition under the Revenue Principle; Liquidation and Termination Balance Sheet Preparation;	The scope was expanded. Initially the EAOA related to registered companies, but in the subsequent years it was expanded to sole proprietorships (in September 1995) and public legal juridical persons (institutions) (in June 1996). Central and local government accounting entities were required to comply with the general principles of the EAOA (Chapters 1–16), but the main guidelines were issued by the Ministry of Finance.	The status of the EASB has improved substantially towards independence. The EASB is an independent governmental unit, established by the Government of Estonia and operating within the administrative jurisdiction of the Ministry of Finance. (Article 38).

		Business Combinations; Balance Sheet Accounts; Income Statement Accounts; Equity Method; Leases; Consolidated Accounts of Credit Institutions; Government Grants; Interim Report Preparation; Earnings Per Share; Segment Reporting; Long-term Construction Contracts; Consolidated Accounts.		
The third, system improvement stage (beginning in 2003) New amended Act on Accounting 2002 Applied from 1 January 2003	Increase further harmonization with EU directives and Regulation 1606/2002 on IFRS.	The new EAOA permits all companies to apply in their consolidated and parent's financial statements either: (a) IFRS, or (b) national accounting standards (EAS, Estonian GAAP). EAS should be harmonized with IFRS and cross-referenced to applicable IFRS	Expanded scope of the EAOA. The accounting principles of all types of institution (including governmental institutions) are the subjects of the EAL.	The Act enhanced the independence of the EASB. The EASB is an independent committee whose rules of procedure are approved by the Government of the Republic on the proposal of the Minister of Finance. The Ministry of Finance, the Government of the Republic and other

(Continued)

Table 18.1 *(Continued)*

Stage and dates and basic regulation	Aim of the regulations	Developments in accounting issues	Scope of the regulation	Status of the EASB
		paragraphs. Any differences in the local standards compared to IFRS must be explained and justified. The EASB rewrote most of its standards by the end of 2002. Currently there is a set of 17 EAS in use: EAS 1: *General principles of Preparation of Financial Statements*; EAS 2: *Presentation of Financial Statements*; EAS 3: *Financial Instruments*; EAS 4: *Inventories*; EAS 5: *Tangible and Intangible Assets*; EAS 6: *Investment properties*; EAS 7: *Biological assets*; EAS 8: *Provisions, Contingent Liabilities and Contingent Assets*; EAS 9: *Leases*;		government agencies shall interfere with neither the content of the guidelines issued by the Standards Board nor the process of their preparation (Chapter 5).

EAS 10: *Revenue recognition*; EAS 11: *Accounting for Subsidiaries and Associates;* EAS 12: *Government Grants*; EAS 13: *Liquidation Balance Sheet*; EAS 14: *Accounting for Nonprofit Association and Foundations*; EAS 15: *Interim Reporting*; EAS 16: *Segment Reporting*; EAS 17: *Public–Private Partnerships.*

flexible. The EAOA served as a frame law, whereas the EAS prescribed more particular issues of financial accounting.

The conceptual change within the European accounting framework, enacted in July 2002, required revision of the set of Estonian accounting regulations, which by 2000 had reached a certain level of professionalism, to make the corresponding improvements. The initial steps to carry out the third stage were arranged through the new, amended version of the EAOA and a new (revised) set of Estonian Accounting Standards. Both came into effect on 1 January 2003. The main characteristic of the new EAOA and the new set of EAS are in their harmony with the IFRS.

Consequently, starting from 2003, there are no significant differences in recognition and measurement policies between IFRS and Estonian GAAP. Minor differences remain, mainly in disclosure (Estonian GAAP requires less disclosure than IFRS), as the Estonian GAAP is primarily designed for small and medium-sized entities (see also ROSC, 2004, p. 12). As a result of recent Estonian accounting reform, large companies are expected to choose the full IFRS option, while small and medium-sized companies may continue using the revised set of EAS as their accounting framework.

Based on the above analysis, the phased development of Estonian accounting reform (system) can be summarized in three different directions:

- Substantial development of the accounting regulations towards implementation of the IFRS
- Development of the scope of accounting regulations from private business companies to governmental institutions
- Development of the degree of independence of the accounting regulatory institution – the Estonian Accounting Standards Board.

Furthermore, below is a summary of how the integrated theoretical framework of factors influencing the national accounting system and phased approach seek to identify the pathways followed by the Estonian accounting reform.

18.5 Findings and discussion

18.5.1 The political system

The political system has an effect on how the economy is organized and controlled. This also influences the objectives of accounting. Saudagaran and Diga

(1997b) proposed that accounting harmonization should be conceptualized as a policy option available to a country. Roberts et al. (2002) distinguished between two main political systems: the liberal–democratic and the egalitarian–authoritarian system.

Estonia has consistently built up a liberal–democratic political and economic system. In fact, Estonia ranked sixth in the 2004 Index of Economic Freedom released in early January 2004 by the *Wall Street Journal* and the Heritage Foundation (*Äripäev*, 2004). Estonia's rank was the same as in 2003. In the 2002 ranking, Estonia came fourth. A liberal–democratic economic system creates favorable conditions for improving the disclosure and transparency issues of financial reporting.

Among the political issues, Bailey (1998) also suggested a flow of power from ministries to companies. In the initial period of the transition from command economy accounting to market-led accounting, as suggested by Bailey (1998) and Nobes (2002), actions by the state are required in the form of new accounting regulations, mainly due to the absence of a strong accountancy profession. This position is confirmed by the experiences of Poland (Jaruga and Bailey, 1998), Hungary (Borda, 1998), the Czech Republic (Dolezal, 1998: Seal et al., 1995), Slovakia (Daniel and Suranova, 2001), and Romania (King et al., 2001). In some cases the ministries have consulted and taken advice externally and internally (see King et al., 2001). Bailey (1998) left open the question about when ministerial supervision and ministerial direction (e.g. of professional associations) become indistinguishable, which clearly has political features. Sucher and Jindrichovska (2004) assess that in the case where the Ministry of Finance is playing a key role in accounting change, the change may be very slow. Therefore, the main problem in Estonia at the end of the first stage was: how to build a forward-looking and flexible accounting regulation system, which would enable Estonian accounting integration into the European accounting framework. The main decisions were made by the EASB.

Since 1990, the first stage of the Estonian accounting reform, the EASB has played the main role. Section 32 of the EAOA (Act on Accounting, 2002) defines the function of the EASB as issuing accounting standards explaining and specifying the EAL and direct activities in the field of accounting.

As pointed out in the previous section, there was a certain development of the degree of independence of the EASB during the three accounting reform stages in Estonia. Starting in 2003, it was added that 'the EASB shall be served by the Ministry of Finance' (Act on Accounting, 2002, section 32). The EASB consists of seven members who are either accounting specialists, theoretical accounting experts, or accounting practioners. It is evident that the political attitude is very modest in the case of Estonia, and has diminished in the last decade.

According to section 32 of the EAOA (2003), the drafts of the new EAS shall be made available to the public on the website of the EAS and they must be open for public discussion for at least two months before approval by the EAS. This will result in making the new standards more participatory among the accounting profession.

18.5.2 The legal system

Liberal–democratic countries generally adopt either of the two types of legal system – the Roman-Germanic (or code law) or common-law legal systems (Roberts et al., 2002). The majority of CEE countries, including Estonia, base their legal systems on code-law principles. Therefore, one of their first priorities has been setting up a regulation system based on laws of accounting. Accounting regulations are part of a complex system of commercial regulations that apply to all business institutions.

The legal framework of Estonian accounting regulations has been mainly based on the following legal acts: (1) the Commercial Code enforced in September 1995; (2) the Act on Accounting enforced in January 1995 and amended in January 2003; and (3) the Certified Public Accountants Act enforced in July 1999. Roberts et al. (2002, p. 15) have generalized that in most code-law countries the accounting code (law) is typically prescriptive, detailed, and procedural. However, this research argues that Estonia seems to be an exception in this matter. To enable flexibility of regulations, particular accounting issues are regulated by the EAS, which are issued by the EASB. The law on accounting serves more as a frame law.

Bailey (1998) hesitated about the possibility of implementing a large accounting change in conditions of systemic instability (new political and legal systems, new institutional structures). An analysis of the development of the Estonian accounting system (see section 18.4) leads to the conclusion that, throughout its three stages, the Estonian accounting change can be regarded as a process of harmonization, where it moved from regional (until the mid 1990s) towards global harmonization (currently). One obstacle to the accounting harmonization during the first half of the 1990s was systemic instability. However, its impact was sufficiently softened by two factors. First, in the middle of the 1990s, the EASB was able to conceptualize a forward-looking and flexible accounting regulation system based on the EAOA and EAS. This concept has been in use since 1995.

Second, this process was supported by the Ministry of Finance, which relied on the operation of the EASB and did not interfere with the content of the concept nor the process of the preparation of the EAOA and accounting standards. Therefore, we can conclude that the systemic instability was overridden by the intended harmonization process and legitimized accounting regulations in the second half of the 1990s. As pointed out in the previous section, the scope of accounting regulations has continually expanded during different accounting reform stages from private business companies to governmental institutions.

According to Saudagaran and Diga (1997a), availability means that financial and other information, particularly information about publicly listed companies, is adequate, timely, and conveniently accessible. Since 1995, according to the EAOA (Chapter 3, section 24) and the Commercial Code (section 334), an accounting entity has to submit a copy of its annual report to the Company Register (within the Ministry of Justice) six months after the balance sheet date at the latest, where they will be kept on file indefinitely. This file is open for public access. Communication with the Center of Registers revealed that the percentage of successfully submitted Annual Reports in 1998 was 71% (from a total of 42,761 companies). By the year 2000 this indicator had grown, reaching 82% (from a total of 42,667 companies). In later years the percentage has been between 75 and 80%[1].

The annual reports of the 17 companies (mainly for all the years that the companies had been listed) on the Tallinn Stock Exchange are available on the Tallinn Stock Exchange website (see http://www.tse.ee).

To warrant and enforce the actual submission of annual reports, a system of penalties and fines was devised for cases of nonsubmission. For example, in accordance with the Commercial Code, section 71, upon failure to submit information prescribed by law or upon submission of false information to the registrar, a person who is competent to make a judgment on entry may impose a fine of up to 400 days' wages on the obligated persons. At the same time, an enterprise or an obligated person need not be warned beforehand upon imposition of a fine for failure to submit information prescribed by law within the term prescribed by law[2].

In accordance with the Penal Code, section 281, submission of incorrect information to the registrars of the commercial register or foundations register, or to the registrar of nonprofit associations, is punishable by a pecuniary punishment or by up to two years' imprisonment. The same act, if committed by a legal person, is punishable by a pecuniary punishment[3].

Communication with the Ministry of Justice exercised extensive punishment and imposed fines for the nonsubmission of annual reports starting in 2000;

since that time, the number of companies that were fined reached 1500 cases annually[4].

In accordance with the Tallinn Stock Exchange Rules, fines in the range of 1000–500,000 Estonian kroons (approximately 65–32,000 euros) are imposed for violation of the requirements regarding disclosure of information (see http://www.tse.ee).

In summary, the legal framework of the Estonian accounting regulations has been improved and has certainly contributed to the implementation of accounting regulations and information availability.

18.5.3 The taxation system

Several studies have explored the influence of tax regulations on accounting and reporting practices in different countries. Roberts et al. (2002) have generalized that code-law countries tend to have common tax and financial reporting regulations. This chapter argues, however, that as far as the CEE countries are concerned, the effect of tax regulations on accounting practices has to be specified and revised. Following the economic reforms, the tax law and accounting law have *de jure* developed separately in Poland (Jaruga and Szychta, 1997; Jaruga and Bailey, 1998), Hungary (Borda, 1998), the Czech Republic (Seal et al., 1995; Dolezal, 1998), and Romania (King et al., 2001). This list of countries is supplemented by Estonia. Although the tax law and accounting law have *de jure* separated in Poland and the Czech Republic, the tax regulations have overridden the accounting regulations (see Sucher and Jindrichovska, 2004; Vellam, 2004). Due to the new Estonian taxation regulation system enacted in 1994, the tax and financial reporting rules were set by different bodies and are kept separate. In 2000, the Estonian Government abolished corporate income tax on reinvested profits, although it remains payable on dividends. Therefore, as was estimated by ROSC (ROSC, 2004), companies in Estonia are less pressured than most companies in the EU Member States in satisfying the accounting requirements of the taxation authorities.

This chapter argues that the Estonian tax rules largely removed the need for tax audits that indirectly contribute to enforcing accounting regulations. Hence, the compliance of the financial statements with the EAL and EAS in small and medium-sized unlisted companies depends mainly on the quality of auditing (if the entity is subject to a statutory audit) and the skills of the company managers who are responsible for preparing the financial statements. Some authors argue (see Kosmala-MacLullich, 2003) that in certain CEE transitional countries the existence of sanctions for misstated tax charges, while there are no sanctions for inappropriate application of accounting regulations, implies that, de facto, compliance with tax regulations overrides the accounting rules. As revealed by the current analysis in this section (see section 18.5.2), imposing fines on the non-submission of annual reports in Estonia started more intensively in 2000. Therefore, we can conclude that the influence of tax legislation on accounting rules has also diminished de facto during the last few years in Estonia.

18.5.4 Finance and capital markets

Corporate accounting and information disclosure practices are influenced by the nature of enterprise ownership, sources of finance, and the stage of development of capital markets. Radebaugh and Gray (1997) argued that there tends to be more pressure for public accountability and information disclosure where finance is raised from external shareholders. Saudagaran and Diga (1997a) pointed out that financial reporting is central to the regulations pertinent to establishing an active market for corporate securities. We can define the Estonian stock market as an 'emerging capital market' (ECM) located in a developing country[5]. One of the main policy aims in ECMs is to ensure that only those companies that satisfy the minimum 'quality' requirements for financial reporting are allowed to issue publicly traded securities (Saudagaran and Diga, 1997a). Financial reporting information also becomes more important if foreign direct investments (FDIs) increase (Daniel and Suranova, 2001). In the competition for FDIs, Estonia has been rather efficient and has succeeded in attracting a significant amount. For example, among the Eastern and Central European countries, in 1992–1999 Estonia ranked third after Hungary and the Czech Republic by FDI inflow per capita (Varblane, 2001). Although this fact is remarkable, the public capital market is rather small in Estonia. On the Tallinn Stock Exchange, which opened for trading in May 1996, 17 domestic companies are listed; the market capitalization is 3.02 billion euros and the annual trading volume is 0.501 billion euros[6]. In April 2001, the Helsinki Stock Exchange (HEX) Group, from Finland, acquired strategic ownership in the Tallinn Stock Exchange Group. Trading in Estonian securities in the HEX trading system started in February 2002. These changes, in particular, necessitated the need for internationally acceptable accounting standards and legal requirements for the disclosure and reporting principles of listed companies.

The Requirements for Issuers in the Tallinn Stock Exchange Rules stipulate that the issuer's financial reports shall be prepared using the calculation schemes and methods that comply with the Estonian accounting legislation and the IFRS. Where the IFRS allow for the use of alternative methods in preparing the reports or presenting financial information in the reports, the issuer is obliged to proceed from the alternatives that comply with the applicable Estonian legislation and the provisions of the standards of the Estonian Accounting Board[7]. This requirement is outdated, due to the decision of the European Commission in July 2002 to adopt IFRS, and with the amended Estonian Accounting Act in 2003, which require that all listed companies, credit institutions, financial holding, and insurance companies use IFRS in their consolidated and separate accounts effective 1 January 2005. The Tallinn Stock Exchange does not enforce accounting standards. Therefore, it is concluded that small stock exchanges have no direct impact on the development of national accounting systems. At the same time, there seems to have been sufficient influence on financial reporting information availability, reliability, and comparability.

In the second half of the 1990s, when Estonian companies first entered the European stock market, it was essential for such companies to use IFRS when compiling their financial statements. In particular, the companies listed on the Tallinn Stock Exchange started to use IFRS due to the fact that the HEX Group acquired strategic ownership of the Tallinn Stock Exchange (2001), and the new Estonian accounting regulations (2003) and European accounting harmonization policy were adopted. As a matter of fact, from the 12 companies currently listed on the Tallinn Stock Exchange, only two applied the IFRS in their 1998 Annual Reports. These companies are listed on European stock markets. In 2000, eight out of the 17 companies currently listed on the Tallinn Stock Exchange applied the IFRS, while the rest used the Estonian accounting regulations. Two years later, 11 companies applied the IFRS and six applied the Estonian accounting regulations. In 2003, 15 out of the 17 listed companies applied the IFRS, while only two applied the Estonian accounting regulations (see http://www.tse.ee).

18.5.5 The accounting profession

The transformation of the role of accounting in transitional Estonia has been greatly complicated by that fact that, for half a century, the Estonian financial reporting and accounting practices were very different from those applied by market-led countries. In a controlled economy, accounting had a relatively low status, being inflexible and unresponsive to market innovations. Contrary to the West, the prestige of accounting was extremely low in the USSR. For example, in a 1990 opinion poll among secondary school students, accounting was ranked 91st among 92 professions (Smirnova et al., 1995).

The Estonian Association of Accountants (EAA) was established in 1996 as an accounting interest group open to anyone, without any qualification requirements. Initially, the main objective of the Association was to gain membership in order to improve the accounting system. The association is not directly involved in accounting regulation setting, except for the fact that a representative of the association is a member of the EASB, the issuer of the EAS. Currently the main objectives of the association concerning their potential impact are to disseminate accounting knowledge and practical experience, and to represent their professional opinion in public discussions (including comments and suggestions on the drafts of the EAS opened for public discussion on the website of the EASB). In January 2001, the Vocational Law was enforced in Estonia, which created basic conditions for organizing the certification for accountants.

The Estonian Board of Auditors (EBA), which was established in 1999, has 422 individual members (19 have been temporarily suspended)[8]. This number is greater than in the other Baltic States (see Moller, 2001). The Estonian Board of Auditors estimated that about one-third of individual members practice as sole practitioners and the rest operate within more than 50 registered audit firms[9]. Audit firms include local members of international audit firm networks as well as 'truly local firms'. Currently, two representatives of the Board are members of the EASB. Previously, the above areas were within the competence of the Estonian Board of Auditing, which was established by the Ministry of Finance in March 1990.

Unfortunately, the EAA and the EBA do not work together and, therefore, though they have been influential in the development of financial reporting in Estonia, their lack of collaboration has hindered further progress.

Bailey (1998) claimed that the immaturity of the legal system, corrupt business practices, and weak trust relations may invade the system of financial statements and reporting. I agree that, despite a favorable legal context for financial reporting, in a number of cases an inadequate level of disclosure appeared, which was probably related to the widespread cultural attitudes supporting secrecy and lack of transparency in matters concerning a company's performance. The Soviet society and its legacy matches well with the system described by Hofstede (1980) as the societies with a strong collectivist orientation, which share a strong sense of 'in-group' vs 'out-of-group' identity. Saudagaran and Diga (1997a) estimated that this cultural orientation results in restricting corporate outsiders access to corporate information, which is seen as being reserved for insiders only. Such an attitude was also widespread in Estonia in the 1990s. A newspaper article published in January 1996 in an Estonian newspaper, *Äripäev* (Business Daily), commented on the structure of the management report within an annual report, required by section 22 of the EAL. According to this section, among other items, the management report also has to disclose the significant events planned for the coming year. One comment was as follows: 'If an entrepreneur discloses to the public what he is intending to do in the coming year, then he will hardly have anything to disclose in the year after the next' (*Äripäev*, 19 January 1996, translation). In my estimation, the development of the business environment increased the demand for transparent financial statements among potential investors and lenders; thus, the improved requirements for disclosure in the Estonian accounting regulations override the widespread attitude from the past at the end of the 1990s.

There may also be some additional factors concerning how a particular country is starting to build up its national accounting system. The main problem in transition countries was how to build a forward-looking and flexible accounting regulation system, which would enable integration into and harmonization with the international accounting framework. Saudagaran and Diga (1997b) emphasized that the actual choice of whether or not to pursue accounting harmonization has to be made at national level. The traditional continental European approach based on the accounting law would have been too inflexible to reflect the rapid changes in transition circumstances. Moreover, Van Hulle (1993) expressed the idea that the use of accounting law as a means of standard setting could also be an interesting mechanism against too frequent (and sometimes unnecessary) changes. But this could not be the position of the transition countries (e.g. Estonia), because a stable and effective accounting regulation system, consistent with general accounting principles, was almost nonexistent there. Therefore, Nobes's (1983) point of view, that historical differences in accounting thought, context, ethos, and practice between a number of countries may affect de facto accounting harmonization, is perhaps not very relevant for future perspectives of transition economies. As they have changed their economic formation from centrally planned to market based, they also needed to change their accounting system. However, because of the lack of accounting sophistication among local practitioners, there was still an inability to distinguish between suitable and unsuitable aspects of the accounting procedures and practices transferred. Choosing an appropriate accounting model, the EASB had to avoid this shortcoming and reach appropriate decisions. Therefore, advice from other nations appeared to be of great support in improving Estonian accounting legislation. This external advice has contributed to national accounting reform, for example, in Romania (see King et al., 2001) and in Slovakia (see Daniel and Suranova, 2001). In Estonia it was significant that three of the seven members of the EASB, re-formed by the Ministry of Finance in 1993, who were leading the preparations for the new Law on Accounting in 1993–1994, were émigré Estonians having international backgrounds and work experience in Sweden, the UK, and Canada. One of the local members of the former Accounting Board commented on the situation as follows:

> 'We local members were aware of the different elements of market economy accounting, but we lacked a systematic understanding of the whole system. We did recognize the main pieces of the puzzle, but were unable to recognize the whole picture.'
>
> (A local member of the Estonian Accounting Board, 1993–1996, December 2003)

After a comprehensive exploration, internal discussions, careful consideration, and some practice testing, the EASB drafted the Estonian Act of Accounting, which was passed by the Estonian Parliament in June 1994 and came into effect in January 1995. The fact that a national accounting law was drafted by the EASB rather than by the Ministry of Finance is quite unusual in transition economies. When the EASB was re-formed by the Ministry of Finance in 1993, the authority and roles of the EASB were in essence expanded. This aspect was treated in more detail in a previous section. Consequently, it is argued here that the benchmark and knowledge transfer serve as an additional essential factor influencing the development of national accounting systems in transition economies.

18.6 Conclusion

From this analysis of the main impact on the accounting framework in Estonia, which has peculiar characteristics and circumstances as regards accounting reform regulations, it became evident that the influencing factors may include separation of accounting regulations from tax regulations, a small stock exchange, a considerable inflow of FDI, and the growing accounting profession.

The development of the Estonian accounting system can be divided into three different stages: introductory (1990–1994), system building (1995–2002), and system improvement (from 2003 onwards). It can be concluded that, as a result of the changes made during these stages, the Estonian accounting regulations are now in line with the requirements of the new European accounting harmonization policy. This analysis revealed that in recent years the access *de jure* to companies' financial reports in the public domain has substantially been supplanted by access de facto.

To analyze the conceptual aspects of Estonian accounting reform, in this chapter I have used an integrated theoretical framework of influencing factors on accounting change and the phased approach to the change, which was explained in section 18.5 to merge into a single theoretical framework. It is suggested that the same framework may also easily and successfully be applied to other transition countries. It seems that the issues which might be of interest to transition countries and that would deserve further consideration may include: accounting regulatory systems, the development of the scope of accounting regulations, and the degree of independence accounting regulatory bodies may have.

Acknowledgment

This chapter was prepared with partial support of the Estonian Science Foundation grant projects Nos 4530 and 5850.

Notes

1. Communication with the Center of Registers, 4 June 2004.
2. See the Commercial Code on the Estonian Legal Language Center website: http//:www.legaltext.ee.
3. See the Penal Code on the Estonian Legal Language Center website: http://www.legaltext.ee.
4. Communication with the Ministry of Justice, 5 June 2004.
5. The world defines a developing country as one whose average income per capita does not exceed a certain level. In 2002, the cutoff was set at $9075 (http://www.worldbank.com/data/countryclass). In Estonia, income per capita reached $4130 in 2002 (*ibid.*).
6. Tallinn Stock Exchange, Equity Market capitalization, 31 December 2003 (http://www.tse.ee).
7. Tallinn Stock Exchange, The Requirements for Issuers, 31 December 2003 (http://www.tse.ee).
8. Communication with the Estonian Board of Auditors, 11 June 2004.
9. Communication with the Estonian Board of Auditors, 11 June 2004.

References

Act on Accounting (2002). *Hea Raamatupidamistava*, 2005. Estonian Accounting Board, Tallinn.

Äripäev (1996). Raamatupidamisseadus ja äriseadustik kisuvad äriühingud alasti [The Accounting Law and the Commercial Code Strip Off Businesses]. 19 January, p. 22.

Äripäev (2004). Estonia Placed Sixth by Economic Freedom Index of Heritage Foundation. 13 January, p. 3.

Bailey, D. (1998). Eastern Europe: Overview. In: *European Accounting Guide* (Alexander, D. and Archer, S., eds), 3rd edn. Harcourt Brace, London.

Bailey, D., with Alver, J., Mackevicius, J., and Paupa, V. (1995). Accounting Law Reform in the Baltic States: The Initial Steps. *European Accounting Review*, 4(4):685–711.

Borda, M. (1998). Hungary. In: *European Accounting Guide* (Alexander, D. and Archer, S., eds), 3rd edn. Harcourt Brace, London.

Cairns, D. (1997). The Future Shape of Harmonization: A Reply. *European Accounting Review*, 6(2):305–348.

Daniel, P. and Suranova, Z. (2001). The Development of Accounting in Slovakia. *European Accounting Review*, 10(4):343–359.

Dolezal, J. (1998). The Czech Republic. In: *European Accounting Guide* (Alexander, D. and Archer, S. eds), 3rd edn. Harcourt Brace, London.

Flower, J. (1997). The Future Shape of Harmonization: The EU versus the IASC versus the SEC. *European Accounting Review*, 6(2):281–303.

Gray, S.J. and Roberts, C.B. (1991). East–West Accounting Issues. *Accounting Horizons*, 5(1):42–50.

Haldma, T. (2004). Development of the Estonian Accounting Policy within the European Framework. *Economic Policy Perspectives of Estonia in the European Union.* Berliner Wissenschafts-Verlag GmbH, Mattimar OÜ, Berlin, Tallinn.

Haller, A. (1995). International Accounting Harmonization: American Hegemony or Mutual Recognition with Benchmarks? Comments and Additional Notes from a German Perspective. *European Accounting Review*, 4(2):235–247.

Haller, A. (2002). Financial Accounting Developments in the European Union: Past Events and Future Prospects. *European Accounting Review*, 11(1):153–190.

Hoarau, C. (1995). International Accounting Harmonization: American Hegemony or Mutual Recognition with Benchmarks? *European Accounting Review*, 4(2):217–233.

Hofstede, G. (1980). *Culture's Consequences: International Differences in Work-Related Values.* Sage Publications, Beverly Hills.

Jaruga, A. and Bailey, D. (1998). Poland. In: *European Accounting Guide* (Alexander, D. and Archer, S., eds), 3rd edn. Harcourt Brace, London.

Jaruga, A. and Szychta, A. (1997). The Origin and Evolution of Chart of Accounts in Poland. *European Accounting Review*, 6(3):509–526.

King, N., Beattie, A., and Cristescu, A.M. (2001). Developing Accounting and Audit in a Transition Economy: The Romanian Experience. *European Accounting Review*, 10(1):149–171.

Kosmala-MacLullich, K. (2003). The True and Fair View Construct in the Context of the Polish Transition Economy: Some Local Insights. *European Accounting Review*, 12(3):465–487.

Moller, P. (2001). Audit and Accounting Development in the Baltic States. Comparative Analysis. *Audit and Accounting 2001*. RMS Forum, Riga.

Nobes, C. (1983). A Judgemental International Classification of Financial Reporting Practices. *Journal of Business, Finance and Accounting,* 10(1):1–19.

Nobes, C. (2002). Causes of International Differences. In: *Comparative International Accounting* (Parker, R. and Nobes, C., eds). Prentice-Hall, London.

Radebaugh, L. and Gray, S. (1997). *International Accounting and Multinational Enterprises.* John Wiley, New York.

Ramcharran, H. (2000). The Need for International Accounting Harmonization: An Examination and Comparison of the Practices of Russian Banks. *American Business Review*, 18(1):1–8.

Roberts, C., Weetman, P., and Gordon, P. (2002). *International Financial Accounting: A Comparative Approach*. Prentice-Hall, London.

ROSC (2004). Report on the Observance of Standards and Codes: Estonia. World Bank. Available at http: //www.worldbank.org/ifa/rocs_aa.html (accessed 24 May 2004).

Saudagaran, S.M. and Diga, J.G. (1997a). Financial Reporting in Emerging Capital Markets: Characteristics and Policy Issues. *Accounting Horizons*, 11(2):41–64.

Saudagaran, S.M. and Diga, J.G. (1997b). Accounting Regulation in ASEAN: A Choice between the Global and Regional Paradigms of Harmonization. *Journal of International Financial Management and Accounting*, 8(1):1–32.

Seal, W., Sucher, P., and Zelenka, I. (1995). The Changing Organization of Czech Accounting. *European Accounting Review*, 4(4):659–681.

Smirnova, I.A., Sokolov, J.V., and Emmanuel, C.R. (1995). Accounting Education in Russia Today. *European Accounting Review*, 4(4):833–846.

Sucher, P. and Jindrichovska, I. (2004). Implementing IFRS: A Case Study of the Czech Republic. *Accounting in Europe*, 1(1):109–141.

Van Hulle, K. (1993). Harmonization of Accounting Standards in the EC: Is it the Beginning or is it the End? *European Accounting Review*, 2(2):387–396.

Varblane, U. (ed.) (2001). Flows of Foreign Direct Investments in the Estonian Economy. *Foreign Direct Investments in the Estonian Economy*. Tartu University Press, Tartu.

Vellam, I. (2004). Implementation of International Accounting Standards in Poland: Can True Convergence be Achieved in Practice. *Accounting in Europe*, 1:143–167.

19

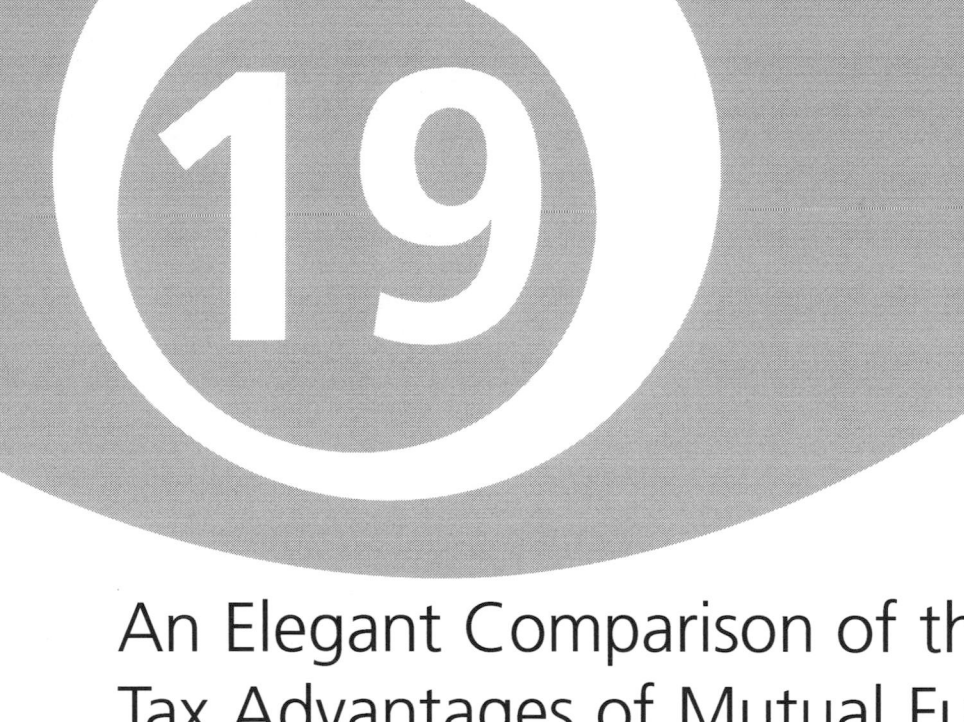

An Elegant Comparison of the Tax Advantages of Mutual Funds, IRAs, and Roth IRAs – What Hath Roth Wrought?

Colin Read

19.1 Introduction

There is a growing appreciation among taxpayers to provide for their retirement needs while at the same time deferring current taxes paid. As in any tax deferment exercise, it is necessary to compare the implications on present and future consumption and the changing rates of taxation between periods. While such analyses are typically illustrated through 'what if' examples, there has been no simple analytic model that allows for direct comparisons in a way that allows us to draw simple conclusions between inter-temporal tax rates, rates of return, and rates of time preference. This model corrects the oversight and creates some very simple equations that easily allow us to draw definitive policy conclusions.

In section 19.2, I set up and solve the model for the traditional IRA savings vehicle. In section 19.3, I solve the model for the Roth IRA savings vehicle and make comparisons between the two vehicles. I simplify the model in section 19.4 by assuming an infinite time horizon, and introduce a comparison between traditional and Roth IRAs and a traditional nondividend-paying mutual fund. I conclude in section 19.5 with a discussion of the policy and planning ramifications of the model.

19.2 A model of lifetime consumption and savings under various tax regimes

Consider an individual with W years of work to retirement who expects to survive R years from retirement until death. Let us assume all calculations are in real dollars with a real rate of return on investment of r[1]. For simplicity, let us also assume the rate of time preference is ρ_W in the working years up to retirement and ρ_R following retirement[2,3]. Let us assume two tax regimes. The marginal tax rate during working years will be τ_W while the tax rate upon retirement will be τ_R[4]. Let us assume the individual would like to determine the optimal level of 'x' pre-tax dollars to put toward retirement each year for W years, to result in an effective pre-tax annuity paid for R retirement years of 'y'. Finally, let us assume continuous compounding and discounting. The value upon retirement A_T of investment in a traditional tax deferred retirement plan is then:

$$A_T = \int_0^W xe^{rt}\,dt, \tag{19.1}$$

which will result in a present value of a flow of retirement payments over R years of retirement of:

$$B_T = \int_0^R y e^{-rt}\, dt, \tag{19.2}$$

for which we could solve for pre-tax retirement benefits as a function of the retirement savings rate x and the parameters R, W, and r.

The present value of the flow of sacrificed consumption over the working years is given by:

$$C_T = \int_0^W x(1-\tau_w)e^{-\rho_w t}\, dt, \tag{19.3}$$

while the present value of retirement consumption with the traditional IRA is given as:

$$D_T = \int_W^{W+R} y(1-\tau_R)e^{-\rho_R t}\, dt. \tag{19.4a}$$

We can transform D_T to express it as the present value at time $t = 0$:

$$D_T = \int_W^{W+R} y(1-\tau_R)e^{-\rho_R t}\, dt = e^{-rW} \int_0^R y(1-\tau_R)e^{-\rho_R t}\, dt. \tag{19.4b}$$

The exercise for the individual investor is to maximize $D_T - C_T$ through their choice of pre-tax IRA investments x, given that the value of retirement savings at time of retirement A_T equals the present value at that point of future payments B_T. If we assume $\rho_R = r$, then by inspection we see that $D'_T = e^{-rW}(1-\tau_R)B_T = e^{-rW}(1-\tau_R)A_T$. Then the maximization exercise reduces to:

$$\underbrace{\max}_{x} D_T - C_T. \tag{19.5}$$

$$= \underbrace{\max}_{x} D'_T - C_T.$$

$$= \underbrace{\max}_{x} e^{-rW}(1-\tau_R)A_T - C_T$$

$$= \underbrace{\max}_{x} e^{-rW}(1-\tau_R)\int_0^W x e^{rt} dt - \int_0^W x(1-\tau_W)e^{-rt}\, dt$$

$$= \max(\tau_W - \tau_R)x(1-e^{-rW})/r$$

This maximization exercise of course is a corner solution, requiring investors to maximize their tax-deferred contribution to traditional IRAs if the marginal tax rate while working is greater than the marginal tax rate when retired. Once the individual will be placed in the highest marginal tax rate upon retirement (after significant and calculable contributions over their working career), there is no longer any advantage to sacrificing current consumption for future consumption, assuming a constant rate of time preference[5].

19.3 The analysis of Roth retirement savings

I next repeat the analysis for a Roth retirement vehicle. The Roth retirement savings account is a hybrid. The contributions during the working years and the sacrifice in contribution are no different than investment in a nondividend-paying mutual fund – that is, all are on an after-tax basis. However, the central feature of the Roth instrument is that income received upon retirement is tax free, while earnings on a mutual fund are taxed at the capital gains tax rate.

Again, an individual with W years to retirement expects to survive R years from retirement until death. The value upon retirement A_{Roth} of investment in a traditional tax-deferred retirement plan is then:

$$A_{\text{Roth}} = \int_0^W (1-\tau_w)xe^{rt}\,dt, \tag{19.6}$$

which will result in a present value of a flow of retirement payments over R years of retirement of:

$$B_{\text{Roth}} = \int_0^R ye^{-rt}\,dt, \tag{19.7}$$

for which we could solve for pre-tax retirement benefits as a function of the retirement savings rate x and the parameters R, W, and r.

The present value of the flow of sacrificed consumption over the working years is given by:

$$C_{\text{Roth}} = \int_0^W x(1-\tau_w)e^{-\rho_W t}\,dt, \tag{19.8}$$

while the present value of retirement consumption with the Roth IRA is given as:

$$D_{\text{Roth}} = \int_W^{W+R} ye^{-\rho_R t}\,dt. \tag{19.9a}$$

We can transform D_{Roth} to express it as the present value at time $t = 0$:

$$D'_{\text{Roth}} = \int_W^{W+R} ye^{-\rho_R t}dt = e^{-rW}\int_0^R ye^{-\rho_R t}dt \tag{19.9b}$$

The exercise for the individual investor is to maximize the $D_{Roth} - C_{Roth}$ through the choice of pre-tax IRA investments x, given that the value of retirement savings at time of retirement A_{Roth} equals the present value at that point of future payments B_{Roth}.

If we assume $\rho_R = r$, by inspection we see that $D'_{Roth} = e^{-rW}B_{Roth} = e^{-rW}A_{Roth}$. Then the maximization exercise reduces to:

$$= \underbrace{\max}_{x} D_{Roth} - C_{Roth}$$

$$= \underbrace{\max}_{x} D'_{Roth} - C_{Roth}$$

$$= \underbrace{\max}_{x} e^{-rW}A_{Roth} - C_{Roth}$$

$$= \underbrace{\max}_{x} e^{-rW}(1-\tau_W)\int_0^W xe^{rt}\,dt - \int_0^W x(1-\tau_W)e^{-rt}\,dt$$

$$= \max(\tau_W - \tau_W)x(1-e^{-rW})/r \tag{19.10}$$

Inspection of equation (19.10) reveals that the net present value of consumption streams under a Roth IRA is neutral to the Roth contribution. Recall that net present value of consumption streams under a traditional IRA are also neutral once retirement accumulations result in retirement income that is taxed at the margin at the same rate as working income.

19.4 Comparison to mutual funds under an infinite time horizon

I previously noted that the Roth IRA is in some sense a hybrid instrument. It has the same effect on consumption and accumulations during the working years as does a mutual fund, but more advantageous treatment in the retirement years because it avoids the capital gains tax levied upon a nondividend-paying mutual fund as the fund is drawn down. We already have the analytic tools to compare the traditional IRA to the Roth IRA. Let us next compare the Roth IRA to a nondividend-paying mutual fund where capital gains are not realized until retirement. For simplicity, we will assume an infinite time horizon upon retirement. This simplifying assumption does not change our conclusions, and is relevant if the principal invested is maintained as a bequeath, for instance. Then the streams of investment accumulation and consumption reduction are identical in the work years and differ as follows in the retirement years:

$$\text{Roth IRA annuity} = r\int_0^W (1-\tau_W)xe^{rt}dt \tag{19.11}$$

$$\text{Mutual fund annuity} = (1-\tau_g)r\int_0^W (1-\tau_W)xe^{rt}dt, \tag{19.12}$$

where τ_g is the capital gains tax rate upon retirement. The Roth IRA performs better than the mutual funds investment portfolio to the extent of the capital gains tax rate.

19.5 Conclusion and public policy ramifications

The Roth IRA has been the darling of the press, financial advisors, and the private investor of moderate to minimum sophistication. It is appealing in the sense that earnings can escape taxation upon retirement. However, the attractiveness of this conclusion is mitigated by the reduced investment amounts (in post-tax contributions) over the working life of the individual. This analysis shows that while the Roth instrument performs better than a simple mutual fund, it does not perform as well as a traditional IRA, at least until the traditional IRA is of sufficient size to place investors in the same tax bracket upon retirement as they find themselves over their working career.

One of the subtle points in this analysis is the role of the individual investor's rate of time preference. Economic theory suggests that individuals align their rate of time preference to that of the prevailing interest rate. This equilibrium conclusion requires all have identical and perfect access to capital markets. However, such is typically not found in practice. As a consequence, present savings may be of more value because there is a bias in favor of deferring present consumption to the future. If such is the case, the conclusions of superiority of one instrument over another will not change. Rather, this observation will bias upward the desirability of all instruments, resulting in the superiority of the traditional IRA until marginal tax rates during the working years and retirement years are equalized, the desirability of the Roth instrument even if it is otherwise neutral, and even the potential desirability of other forms of savings that are inferior to the consumption neutral Roth IRA.

Notes

1. We will assume that changing rates of risk preference over a planning horizon do not affect the choice of investment instrument. In other words, let us assume *r* is the risk-adjusted normal real rate of return on financial investment.
2. The rate of time preference is the rate at which an individual investor discounts the future. With access to perfect capital markets, an individual will shift consumption, savings, and borrowing across time to equate their individual rate of time preference to the market rate of return. However, because individuals typically do not have access to perfect capital markets, we keep this value distinct from the rate of return for now.
3. For simplicity, we will later assume a constant rate of time preference but will nonetheless show how different rates of time preference over the planning horizon affect our results.
4. While the effective tax rate for retirement planning purposes during the working years is the marginal tax rate in most cases, the effective tax rate upon retirement changes. While an individual is accumulating a retirement fund to produce retirement income, the rate will rise with increased expected retirement disbursements. Initial retirement investments will be weighed against a low retirement tax rate. As the investments result in more significant retirement disbursements, the individual will be facing higher and higher retirement tax rates. At some point an individual facing the highest marginal tax rate while saving toward retirement will be deferring taxation at the highest marginal tax rate in retirement as well. The policy implications of this life cycle of retirement savings will be discussed later.
5. However, it can be observed that a rate of time preference that further discounts the future as retirement is neared may shift this conclusion somewhat. We discuss this possibility later.

20

A Meta-National Perspective on Accounting and Auditing in Nonprofit Organizations: The Literature Interpreted in a Principal–Agent Framework

Marc Jegers

20.1 Introduction

Compared to the vast economics-based literature on accounting and auditing for profit organizations, nonprofit accounting and auditing is under-researched, taking into consideration the role and importance of the nonprofit sector in society. In this chapter I try to collect the existing literature and present it in a structure allowing the reader to understand the role of accounting and auditing in nonprofit organizations. The by now traditional micro-economic principal–agent framework will be used as a unifying framework.

The current formulation of a general principal–agent relationship goes back to Jensen and Meckling (1976, p. 308): '... a contract under which one or more persons (the principal(s)) engage another person (the agent) to perform some service on their behalf which involves delegating some decision-making authority to the agent. If both parties ... are utility maximizers there is good reason to believe that the agent will not always act in the best interests of the principal.' The ensuing welfare losses are labeled agency costs, and consist of monitoring costs (to be borne by the principal), bonding costs (to be borne by the agent), and the eventual welfare loss incurred by the principal in comparison with a first best situation (residual loss).

Although mostly analyzed in a profit context, principal–agent relations also abound in nonprofit organizations (Steinberg, 1990; Herman and Heimovics, 1991; Brody, 1996; Hewitt and Brown, 2000; Miller-Millesen, 2003). To understand the role of accounting and auditing in nonprofits in a 'positive accounting theory' tradition (Watts and Zimmerman, 1986; Belkaoui, 1992), two of these relations are relevant: the external stakeholders–management relationships, and the management–other staff relationship (on both, from an agency perspective, see Caers et al., 2004).

In line with the existing literature, it will be assumed that the external stakeholders are perfectly represented by the organization's board, although this is clearly a stylized fact. Knowing that objectives of board members and managers differ (for an early empirical indication, see Steinberg, 1986), agency costs automatically ensue. Financial accounting costs and auditing costs then can be considered as monitoring costs, reducing the residual losses up to the theoretical optimum where the marginal monitoring cost equals the marginal decrease of residual loss (for a theoretical exposition on this, see Jegers, 2002). Also, some cost accounting data are used in this vein, especially in the relations between a subsidizing authority (an important external stakeholder) or donors (Berman and Davidson, 2003, p. 422) and the organization. The next section will provide a literature review within this frame of reference.

Internal control techniques are appropriate instruments to contain the agency costs between management and other staff. The limited nonprofit literature on this topic will be presented in a subsequent section.

20.2 Containing the external stakeholders–management agency costs

20.2.1 The role of accounting: reducing information asymmetry between board and management

Assuming managerial utility in nonprofit organizations is affected by both the achievement of organizational objectives and discretionary managerial behavior (Williamson, 1963), probably with other weights than in the case of managers of profit firms (Rose-Ackerman, 1987; Young, 1987; Schiff and Weisbrod, 1991; Lynk, 1995; Gassler, 1997; Roomkin and Weisbrod, 1999; Hewitt and Brown, 2000), and the nonprofit board members' utilities only by the achievement of organizational objectives, information asymmetries between the board and management can induce managerial behavior that is not compatible with board utility maximization, entailing welfare losses for the board (which is the principal). Part of the information asymmetry pertains to the financial condition of the organization, which is (partially) affected by discretionary managerial behavior. Christensen and Mohr (1995) describe an example of this for museums. Imposing the production of financial statements will mitigate this asymmetry (and the ensuing residual loss) at a cost, which is a monitoring cost. As long as the latter is lower than the former, the introduction of an accounting system will improve the eventual welfare position of the board, even if, realistically, a first best situation will never obtain. The considerations put forward by Falk (1992, pp. 486–490) to guide the choice between cash accounting and accrual accounting are easily cast in the framework presented here: differences in stakes and ensuing informational needs between club principals and nonclub principals lead him to select accrual accounting as appropriate for clubs, and cash accounting for nonclubs.

Some authors advocate that the nonprofit financial reports should 'reflect the service story of the entity instead of the net income or net loss' (Trigg and Nabangi, 1995, p. 262), which would further bridge the informational gap between principal and agent. Unfortunately, a financial statement is not an appropriate instrument to achieve this, as it is conceptually confined to the organization's financial situation. Other sorts of reporting should be produced to describe the nonfinancial performance of the organization (Falk, 1992, p. 490), which is, of course, far more important than its financial performance, though the latter constrains in a certain way the former. In that respect it is interesting to note that in a recent sample of 341 US museums (both public and nonprofit), 76 annual reports contained no financial data whatsoever (Christensen and Mohr, 2003), let alone a financial statement.

20.2.2 A special case: religious organizations

Religious organizations are special in the sense that one can consider some deity as the ultimate principal, which, by definition, is omniscient. Therefore, information asymmetry between this principal and the worldly agents cannot exist, and accounting is useless as an information asymmetry reducing tool. As phrased by Abdul-Rahman and Goddard (1998, p. 196): 'Accountability in such a world is to God and accounting can contribute little in this relationship'; or 'Accounting is regarded as no more than a technology to record accounting and financial information' (Abdul-Rahman and Goddard, 1998, p. 192). If one accepts this position, religious nonprofits are to be excluded from the present analysis. If not, they can be treated like any other nonprofit organization, as exemplified by Duncan et al. (1999) or Laughlin (1990). The latter is a so-called principal–agent analysis of the Church of England, albeit with definitions deviating from the Jensen–Meckling standard definitions of principals and agents (Laughlin, 1990, p. 95).

20.2.3 Accounting knowledge

In a profit context, it is taken for granted that both board members and managers fully understand the content and intricacies of financial statements. Even ignoring the case in which the board just does not care and the agent consequently is free to act in his own interest (Jegers, 2002), this need not be the case in nonprofit organizations (see Herzlinger and Sherman (1980) on the application of fund accounting in the USA), either because their expertise lies in the realm of the organization's main objectives (see the data provided by Froelich et al. (2000, p. 245) on the agents in American organizations, or Duncan et al. (1999, p. 143) and Miller (2002, p. 441) on board members), or because of 'the ideological rejection of commercial values and practices' (Panozzo and Zan, 1997, p. 8). The potential effects are higher monitoring costs and a smaller potential residual loss reduction, and consequently higher agency costs compared to a situation in which principals and agents have no problems in producing and/or reading financial statements (Jegers, 2002). Therefore, the more frequent use of conceptually simple cash accounting (as opposed to accrual accounting) in nonprofits is not surprising: its lower informational content is more than compensated by the higher level of understanding of the principals and agents. Hyndman's (1990, p. 304) empirical results on the information needs of UK donors call for a similar interpretation when modeling them as principals with respect to the organization: they prefer simplified operating statements and simplified balance sheets to audited operating statements, audited balance sheets, and audited funds flow statements.

20.2.4 Donors and the organization

When nonprofit organizations are (partly) financed by (private or corporate) donors, the latter are a specific group of external stakeholders delegating decision authority to the organizations, and therefore principals, the organization being the agent. Clearly, information asymmetries between both exist, even more if there is no direct link between donors and eventual beneficiaries (Gordon and Khumawala, 1999, p. 39; see also pp. 48–51 for more elaborate hypotheses on this). The question then is whether accounting information helps to reduce this gap, stimulating donors to be more generous than without accounting information. Accounting here can be considered as a bonding cost from the point of view of the organization. 'There is little empirical evidence with respect to the extent to which individual donors request financial statements' (Gordon and Khumawala, 1999, p. 31; but Hyndman (1990) is an example), or 'here is limited empirical research examining the impact of *accounting* data on charitable giving decisions' (Parsons, 2003, p. 104), and it appears there is no research at all on the role of auditing, although audited financial statements are mentioned by Gordon and Khumawala (1999, p. 42) and Hyndman (1990). Furthermore, as potential donors essentially seem to be looking at the organizations' efficiency and effectiveness (Hyndman, 1990, p. 304; Parsons, 2003, p. 113), accounting data only shed light on a part of the required information (the inputs), even if fund accounting is applied, as recommended by Falk (1992, pp. 486, 488), in order to facilitate 'patrons' giving decisions (Falk, 1992, p. 486). Nevertheless, the available research reveals an effect of how the resources are split over program activities, fundraising activities, and administrative activities (cost accounting information) on the contributions received (Parsons, 2003, p. 115; see also Gordon and Khumawala (1999, p. 47) for a limited literature review, and Marudas and Jacobs (2004) for an econometrically subtle empirical study on 1014 US nonprofit organizations for 1985–1994), although methodological causality problems remain (Parsons, 2003, p. 119). Krishnan et al. (2004) found empirical evidence that this effect is taken into consideration by nonprofit organizations when making disclosure decisions: comparing the data of 719 hospital-year observations (Californian nonprofit hospitals, 1994–1998) in two databases that should contain the same data, they found that on average program expenses reported in the publicly available database exceeded the same expenses reported in the other database, with US $13.9 million (p. 15). Furthermore, of the 95 hospitals reporting no fundraising expenses at all, 19 appear to have publicly documented fundraising activities (p. 22).

Clearly, auditing these data will contribute to their reliability when disclosed, further reducing information asymmetries between donors and the organization.

20.2.5 Accounting regulation

In the preceding sections it was implicitly assumed that nonprofit organizations were not subject to any accounting regulation. This clearly does not conform to reality, at least in most countries, for the larger organizations. Although other reasons to enact accounting regulations can be considered (Maijoor, 1991), accounting regulations for nonprofit organizations are also easily understood in a principal–agent framework: authorities only grant subsidies under a number of conditions, making them the principal, and the organization has to report on how the funds obtained have been used. Part of this reporting is financial reporting, which is therefore one of the monitoring instruments available to the authorities. The obligation for US hospitals to explicitly report charity care expenses from 1990 onwards can be interpreted in this vein as far as the nonprofit hospitals are concerned (Eldenburg and Vines, 2004).

Regulations make interpretation of the submitted financial statements easier, enhancing the authority's possibilities to reduce the residual losses. Furthermore, uniform accounting rules reduce the monitoring costs as such, because of the possibility of common training programs, and the availability of common rules that do not have to be reinvented at the organizational level. In the absence of governmental regulation, comparable (monitoring) cost advantages can be obtained by self-regulation, as witnessed in different US nonprofit industries (Christensen and Mohr, 2003).

If the accounting regulations impose rules that imply at least an accounting intensity and sophistication required to cope with the board–management agency problems, there is no need for additional accounting obligations. In the opposite case, where the rules to be applied due to the regulation are not sufficient to optimally reduce agency costs between the board and management, one can expect accounting to be more elaborate than legally required.

20.2.6 Accounting choices

Most accounting regulations, both for profit firms and nonprofit organizations, allow in a number of cases for some choices to be made. Traditional examples are: depreciation rules (which frequently can be chosen out of a limited set of alternatives), stock valuation rules, capitalization requirements. Theoretically, the eventual choice influences the information (or signal) given to the principal about the agent's performance, and therefore the agent might be induced to choose the most favorable alternative, from his point of view (Steinberg, 1993, p. 24). In a profit context, most choices are analyzed with respect to their effect on managerial remuneration. But there is also published research available to argue that comparable mechanisms are at work in nonprofit organizations.

The findings of Baber et al. (2002) fit completely in the for-profit research tradition: for 331 US charities in the mid 1990s they found a cross-sectional positive and significant influence of relative output changes (measured with accounting data) on relative compensation changes, though they 'cannot observe whether charities explicitly use accounting measures for setting executive compensation' (Baber et al., 2002, p. 691). But this proves at least that such connections are not inconceivable in a nonprofit context.

Chase and Coffman (1994) proposed a 'political cost' reasoning: the reported wealth impacts on the government's and donors' willingness to provide subsidies and gifts – higher levels of wealth are considered to be either a reason to reduce payments or a signal of financial viability entailing more subsidies and gifts, which are then expected not to be wasted. Apparently, the civil servants concerned and the public are assumed not to be able to correctly assess the disclosed data. On top of that, managers are supposed to be concerned with their personal reputation, therefore trying to select accounting methods indicating maximal financial performance (return on endowments in this case). In a sample of 137 private colleges and universities in the USA (data pertaining to 1989), the choice between fair market value reporting of the endowments and their reporting at cost is considered. The results show that the institutions choosing the fair market value method are more endowed (supporting the financial viability reasoning) and realize higher returns on their endowments (not contradicting the reputation argument). In Leona and Van Horn (1999), managerial reputation is the focus of their traditional earnings management study. In a sample of 3997 nonprofit hospital-year observations (USA,

1988–1996) they found data confirming the hypothesis that nonprofit managers try to avoid losses, but not negative earnings changes. On top of that, 'big bath' accounting is frequently found in the first year a new manager is appointed, also consistent with the reputation hypothesis.

Robbins et al. (1993) studied accounting choices in 298 US hospitals (public, private nonprofit, and proprietary). The LIFO/FIFO choice and the depreciation method used are combined in a binary choice variable with two categories: income-increasing choices (84% of the sample) and income-decreasing choices (16% of the sample). Unfortunately, separate results for nonprofit organizations were not given. In the whole sample, there seems to be a positive relation between the existence of management compensation plans and income-increasing choices, but this might be due to the presence of proprietary hospitals in the sample. The other hypothesized relationships turn out to be insignificant, but this might be ascribed to the heterogeneous sample composition.

Christensen and Mohr (1995) framed their accounting choice study on US museums explicitly in a principal–agent context (1989 data on 106 museums, of which 84 are nonprofit). The choice here is whether or not to capitalize the museum's collection. There seems to be statistical support for political cost reasoning: the more federal government support, the less capitalization is observed.

The results of Eldenburg and Vines (2004) can also be understood in a principal–agent framework. Based on a sample of 98 nonprofit hospitals located in Florida (1989–1991), they observed that hospitals with higher cash levels are more prone to report a larger share of their uncompensated care as charity care, and not as bad debt, signaling to the (fiscal) authorities that their tax-exempt status is fully justified. As labeling uncompensated care as charity care implies foregoing any cash collection (e.g. through Medicare or Medicaid), hospitals with lower cash levels have to trade off the expected cost of losing their nonprofit status with the expected cost of illiquidity.

20.2.7 Compliance

Accounting choices are choices between legally allowed alternatives, but one could also consider just not complying with the accounting regulations. From the agent's point of view, this is an optimal decision if the expected costs of noncompliance do not exceed the expected revenues brought about by misinforming the principal on the financial condition of the organization, and causing possibly additional residual losses, especially in relationships where the authorities act as principal.

Empirical research on compliance in nonprofit organizations is scarce. Jegers and Houtman (1993) assessed compliance to accounting rules for 197 Belgian public and private nonprofit hospitals. The compliance variable is the number of specific reporting violations of the law, of which the highest value possible was 32. There appeared to be no statistically significant difference in compliance behavior between public and nonprofit hospitals. Larger hospitals produced significantly better financial statements than smaller hospitals. This can be understood by noting that the relative cost of complying is smaller for larger hospitals, combined with the expectation that the political cost of noncompliance is higher. Krishnan and Schauer (2000) analyzed financial disclosure in 1994–1995 by 164 nonprofit health and welfare organizations from Pennsylvania and New Jersey, and observed a rather low compliance for nonprofit-specific items: only 45 of the 164 disclosed cash donations and pledges, and 91 donated materials and services. Also in this piece of research, larger organizations complied more, in accordance with the agency mechanisms described above. Finally, financially more stable organizations, and less wealthy ones, complied more in their sample.

20.2.8 Choices and compliance when calculating the cost of nonprofit activities

Frequently, subsidizing authorities calculate the amount to be granted taking into consideration the cost of the subsidized activities. If organizations develop both subsidized and nonsubsidized activities, it is rather difficult for the authorities to have a clear picture of the relevant costs. Cost accounting reduces this information asymmetry, especially in cases where cost accounting regulations are enacted to guide the allocation of the indirect costs. Sometimes these regulations are very strict and sometimes they give the organizations some leniency, in which case organizations could be inclined to allocate as much as possible (and allowed if they want to comply) indirect costs to the subsidized activities. If the nonsubsidized activities are taxed, some tradeoff has to be made between higher subsidies and lower taxes payable. Furthermore, if the nonsubsidized activity is developed on a profit market, overhead allocation techniques potentially distort competition on this market (Weisbrod, 1988).

The only empirical study on cost allocation manipulations in nonprofit organizations is, to my knowledge, Trussel (2003), who uses financial data on 8496 US charities (data on 1994–1995). Using an original methodology, he distinguished 467 potential overhead allocation manipulators, by looking at the program-spending ratios applied. Financial characteristics were successfully introduced in a logit model to explain their occurrence but, unfortunately for the purposes of the present chapter, no further analysis could be performed.

20.3 The role of external audit

20.3.1 Reducing agency costs

In a principal–agent framework, external auditing can be understood as a way to increase the reliability of the financial information produced by the agent on behalf of the different principals. The audit fee is added to the monitoring costs, but should be more than compensated by the increased possibility to reduce residual losses: 'The economic role of auditing is to reduce agency costs' (Sunder, 1997, p. 115). In the absence of appropriate internal control procedures, the residual loss-reducing role of external control is even more important. Results obtained by Krishnan and Schauer (2000) furthermore suggest that, as in a for-profit context, supply of audit services is segmented, with audit quality tied to specific segments: after controlling for client characteristics, compliance of organizations audited by one of the (at that time) Big Six is higher than that of organizations audited by large non-Big Six, which in turn is higher than that of organizations audited by small non-Big Six audit firms. Which situation is optimal theoretically depends on the comparison between the value of the residual losses avoided and the additional audit fees (monitoring costs). Up to now, empirical work on this point does not seem to be available. One paper deals with just one side of the picture, the fees, and is discussed in the next section.

20.3.2 Audit pricing

Beattie et al. (2001) investigated audit fees (1995 and 1997) for more than 200 UK charities (originally more than 300, but a large number of them did not provide their financial statements, contrary to the legal obligation to do so), which have to disclose audit fees and fees for nonaudit services. Generally, fees appear to be lower than for as comparable as possible audits in the profit sector. The three possible reasons for this (lower audit risk, auditor altruism, lower audit quality) cannot be disentangled. A traditional audit pricing model is developed and tested. Two auditee characteristics positively influence audit prices (and thus monitoring costs): size and the share of year-end stock in total assets. On top of that, Big Six fees are considerably higher than fees for other audit firms (18.5%), and there is also an, albeit small on average, premium for non-Big Six audit firms with charity experience.

Combining these results with those obtained by Krishnan and Schauer (2000) discussed above leads to the, admittedly very preliminary, conclusion that both audit quality and audit prices are higher when larger audit firms are appointed to nonprofit organizations, leaving inconclusive on *a priori* grounds the aforementioned comparison of residual losses avoided and additional monitoring costs.

20.3.3 Containing the management–other staff agency costs: internal control

Internal control can be seen as a monitoring device available for managers to ensure that administrative procedures, theoretically designed to add to the achievement of the managerial objectives, are applied correctly. Furthermore, it impacts on the audit cost, as external auditors first assess the quality and reliability of the internal control system before drawing up their audit plan. As it happens, and contrary to the situation in profit organizations, for nonprofit organizations there is an 'accumulation of evidence which points to systemic and widespread failure of internal control' (Ortmann and Schlesinger, 1997, p. 103), including religious organizations (Bowrin, 2004). This situation is also reflected by the available empirical research on internal control in nonprofit organizations: it is almost nonexistent, except for the paper by Rayburn and Rayburn (1991), who analyzed internal control reactions of 307 US hospitals to the introduction of prospective payment systems for hospital financing. The nonprofit hospitals appeared to increase tightening and centralizing of financial controls, use of administrative committees and ad hoc coordination groups more intensively than proprietary hospitals. Whether this could be explained as catching up or taking the lead could not be assessed.

20.4 Conclusion

The traditional principal–agent framework is shown to be useful as a framework to understand the role of accounting and auditing within nonprofit organizations. Results obtained in the relevant empirical literature fit in this framework, and add to our understanding of the role of accounting and auditing. In its most general formulation, it consists of reducing agency costs by inducing decreases in residual welfare losses for the principal by bearing less than commensurate monitoring costs, accounting and auditing being the monitoring instruments.

Therefore, accounting and auditing regulations for nonprofit organizations should be based on this kind of reasoning to justify the costs inflicted to the organizations. As far as future research is concerned, as the conclusions obtained in the literature can only be considered to be very preliminary due to the low number of studies available, all the points raised in this chapter merit further empirical and theoretical studies, in order to obtain a generally agreed upon body of concepts and results from which further developments can be ventured.

Acknowledgments

Comments by Ralf Caers, Cindy Du Bois, R. Scott Gassler, Bruno Heyndels, and the participants at the session of the 28th Congress of the European Accounting Association (Göteborg), in which an earlier version of this chapter was presented, are gratefully acknowledged.

References

Abdul-Rahman, A.R. and Goddard, A. (1998). An Interpretative Inquiry of Accounting Practices in Religious Organizations: Emerging Theoretical Perspectives. *Financial Accountability and Management*, 14(3):183–201.

Baber, W.R., Daniel, P.L., and Roberts, A.A. (2002). Compensation to Managers of Charitable Organizations: An Empirical Study of the Role of Accounting Measures of Program Activities. *Accounting Review*, 77(3):679–693.

Beattie, V., Goodacre, A., Pratt, K., and Stevenson, J. (2001). The Determinants of Audit Fees: Evidence from the Voluntary Sector. *Accounting and Business Research*, 31(4):243–274.

Belkaoui, A.R. (1992). *Accounting Theory.* Academic Press, London.

Berman, G. and Davidson, S. (2003). Do Donors Care? Some Australian Evidence. *Voluntas*, 14(4):421–429.

Bowrin, A.R. (2004). Internal Control in Trinidad and Tobago Religious Organizations. *Accounting, Auditing and Accountability Journal*, 17(1):121–152.

Brody, E. (1996). Agents Without Principals: The Economic Convergence of the Nonprofit and for Profit Organizational Forms. *New York Law School Review*, 40(3):457–536.

Caers, R., Du Bois, C., Jegers, M., De Gieter, S., Schepers, C., and Pepermans, R. (2004). Toward an Agency Theory for Non-Profit Organizations: Determining the Correct Position of Non-Profit Principal–Agent Relationships on the Stewardship–Agency Axis. Paper presented at the NCVO Researching the Voluntary Sector Conference, Sheffield, UK.

Chase, B.W. and Coffman, E.N. (1994). Choice of Accounting Method by Not-for-profit Institutions: Accounting for Investments by Colleges and Universities. *Journal of Accounting and Economics*, 18(2):233–243.

Christensen, A.L. and Mohr, R.M. (1995). Testing a Positive Accounting Theory Model of Museum Accounting Practices. *Financial Accountability and Management*, 11(4):317–335.

Christensen, A.L. and Mohr, R.M. (2003). Not-for-profit Annual Reports: What Do Museum Managers Communicate? *Financial Accountability and Management*, 19(2):139–158.

Duncan, J.B., Flesher, D.L., and Stocks, M.H. (1999). Internal Control Systems in US Churches: An Examination of the Effects of Church Size and Denomination on Systems of Internal Control. *Accounting, Auditing and Accountability Journal*, 12(2):142–163.

Eldenburg, L. and Vines, C.C. (2004). Nonprofit Classification Decisions in Response to a Change in Accounting Rules. *Journal of Accounting and Public Policy*, 23(1):1–22.

Falk, H. (1992). Towards a Framework for Not-for-profit Accounting. *Contemporary Accounting Research*, 8(2):468–499.

Froelich, K.A., Knoepfle, T.W., and Pollack, T.H. (2000). Financial Measures in Nonprofit Organization Research: Comparing IRS900 Return and Audited Financial Statement Data. *Nonprofit and Voluntary Sector Quarterly*, 29(2):232–254.

Gassler, R.S. (1997). The Economics of the Nonprofit Motive: Formulation of Objectives and Constraints for Firms, Nonprofit and Workers' Enterprises. *Journal of Interdisciplinary Economics*, 8(4):265–280.

Gordon, T.P. and Khumawala, S.B. (1999). The Demand for Not-for-profit Financial Statements: A Model of Individual Giving. *Journal of Accounting Literature*, 18(2):31–56.

Herman, R.D. and Heimovics, R.D. (1991). *Executive Leadership in Nonprofit Organizations: New Strategies for Shaping Executive-board Dynamics*. Jossey-Bass, San Fransisco, CA.

Herzlinger, R.E. and Sherman, H.D. (1980). Advantages of Fund Accounting in 'Nonprofits'. *Harvard Business Review*, 58(3):94–105.

Hewitt, J.A. and Brown, D.K. (2000). Agency Costs in Environmental Not-for-profits. *Public Choice*, 103(1–2):168–183.

Hyndman, N. (1990). Charity Accounting – An Empirical Study of the Information Needs of Contributors to UK Fund Raising Charities. *Financial Accountability and Management*, 6(4):95–307.

Jegers, M. (2002). The Economics of Non Profit Accounting and Auditing: Suggestions for a Research Agenda. *Annals of Public and Cooperative Economics*, 73(3):429–451.

Jegers, M. and Houtman, C. (1993). Accounting Theory and Compliance to Accounting Regulations: The Case of Hospitals. *Financial Accountability and Management*, 9(4):267–278.

Jensen, M.C. and Meckling, W.H. (1976). Theory of the Firm: Managerial Behavior, Agency Costs and Ownership Structure. *Journal of Financial Economics*, 3(4):305–360.

Krishnan, J. and Schauer, P.C. (2000). The Differentiation of Quality Among Auditors: Evidence from the Not-for-profit Sector. *Auditing: A Journal of Practice and Theory*, 19(2):9–25.

Krishnan, R., Yetman, M.H., and Yetman, R.Y. (2004). Financial Disclosure Management by Nonprofit Organizations. Working Paper, University of California at Davis, CA.

Laughlin, R.C. (1990). A Model of Financial Accountability and the Church of England. *Financial Accountability and Management*, 6(2):93–114.

Leona, A.J. and Van Horn, R.L. (1999). Earnings Management in Not-for-profit Institutions: Evidence from Hospitals. Working Paper, University of Rochester, NY.

Lynk, W.J. (1995). Nonprofit Hospital Mergers and the Exercise of Market Power. *Journal of Law and Economics*, 38(2):437–461.

Maijoor, S. (1991). *The Economics of Accounting Regulation: Effects of Dutch Accounting Regulations for Public Accountants and Firms*. Datawyse, Maastricht, the Netherlands.

Marudas, N.P. and Jacobs, F.A. (2004). Determinants of Charitable Donations to Large US Higher Education, Hospital and Scientific Research Nonprofit Organizations: New Evidence from Panel Data. *Voluntas*, 15(2):157–179.

Miller, J.L. (2002). The Board as a Monitor of Organizational Activity: The Applicability of Agency Theory to Nonprofit Boards. *Nonprofit Management and Leadership*, 15(4):429–450.

Miller-Millesen, J.L. (2003). Understanding the Behavior of Nonprofit Boards of Directors: A Theory-based Approach. *Nonprofit and Voluntary Sector Quarterly*, 32(4):521–547.

Ortmann, A. and Schlesinger, M. (1997). Trust, Repute and the Role of Non-profit Enterprise. *Voluntas*, 8(2):97–119.

Panozzo, F. and Zan, L. (1997). Managerialism and Budgeting Practices in a Trade Union. Paper presented at the Workshop on the Management of Nonprofit Organizations, European Institute for Advanced Studies in Management, Brussels.

Parsons, L.M. (2003). Is Accounting Information from Nonprofit Organizations Useful to Donors? A Review of Charitably Giving and Value-relevance. *Journal of Accounting Literature*, 22(1):104–129.

Rayburn, J.M. and Rayburn, L.G. (1991). Contingency Theory and the Impact of New Accounting Technology in Uncertain Hospital Environments. *Accounting, Auditing and Accountability Journal*, 4(2):55–75.

Robbins, W.A., Turpin, R., and Polinski, P. (1993). Economic Incentives and Accounting Choice Strategy by Nonprofit Hospitals. *Financial Accountability and Management*, 9(3):159–175.

Roomkin, M.J. and Weisbrod, B.A. (1999). Managerial Compensation and Incentives in For-profit and Nonprofit Hospitals. *Journal of Law, Economics and Organization*, 15(3):750–781.

Rose-Ackerman, S. (1987). Ideals Versus Dollars: Donor, Charity Managers, and Government Grants. *Journal of Political Economy*, 95(4):810–823.

Schiff, J. and Weisbrod, B.A. (1991). Competition Between for Profit and Nonprofit Organizations in Commercial Markets. *Annals of Public and Cooperative Economics*, 61(4):619–639.

Steinberg, R. (1986). The Revealed Objective Function of Nonprofit Firms. *Rand Journal of Economics*, 17(4):508–526.

Steinberg, R. (1990). Profits and Incentive Compensation in Nonprofit Firms. *Nonprofit Management and Leadership*, 1(2):137–152.

Steinberg, R. (1993). Public Policy and the Performance of Nonprofit Organizations: A General Framework. *Nonprofit and Voluntary Sector Quarterly*, 22(1):13–31.

Sunder, S. (1997). *Theory of Accounting and Control.* South-Western Publishing, Cincinnati, OH.

Trigg, R. and Nabangi, F.K. (1995). Representation of the Financial Position of Nonprofit Organizations: The Habitat for Humanity Situation. *Financial Accountability and Management*, 11(3):259–269.

Trussel, J. (2003). Assessing Potential Accounting Manipulation: The Financial Characteristics of Charitable Organizations with Higher than Expected Program-spending Ratios. *Nonprofit and Voluntary Sector Quarterly*, 32(4):616–634.

Watts, R.L. and Zimmerman, J.L. (1986). *Positive Accounting Theory.* Prentice-Hall, Englewood Cliffs, NJ.

Weisbrod, B.A. (1988). *The Nonprofit Economy.* Harvard University Press, Cambridge, MA.

Williamson, O.E. (1963). Managerial Discretion and Business Behaviour. *American Economic Review*, 53(5):1032–1057.

Young, D.R. (1987). Executive Leadership in Nonprofit Organizations. In: *The Nonprofit Sector: A Research Handbook* (Powell, W.W., ed.), pp. 167–179. Yale University Press, New Haven, CT.

21

How about Performance Audits for Public Companies?

Haji Shafi Mohamad

21.1 Introduction

External auditing is an important function in the business environment (Watts and Zimmerman, 1983). Legislation exists in most Western countries to ensure that the function is mandatory for public companies (Arpan and Radebaugh, 1985). Even if auditing were not legislated, Watts and Zimmerman (1983, p. 633) argued that the function of external auditing would continue to exist, as it is an efficient method of reducing overall contract costs for an entity. The latter refers to all manner of costs likely to be incurred when transacting business with the particular entity concerned. External auditing serves many purposes. It can act to monitor the performance of management on behalf of shareholders or as a demonstration by management to existing and potential shareholders of their effort and performance. The former is usually referred to as the 'monitoring role' performed by external auditors, while the latter purpose is referred to as the 'signaling role' performed by the independent external auditors.

Herbert (1979) indicated that, traditionally, the purpose of accounts examination or auditing used to be to detect fraud and certify the accuracy of records, whereas the primary purpose now is to express an opinion on the truth and fairness of presentation of the financial statements (p. 3). The latter role of auditing, also known as the 'attest function', is to simply add credence to the truth and fairness of the financial statements and to confirm that they comply in all material respects with the statutory requirements of any relevant legislation.

21.2 Extensions to the role of external auditing

To ensure that the actual audit performance corresponds more closely to expectations of the different user groups, Gwilliam (1987, p. 64) noted that the auditors' attestation role could be extended to include systems and performance auditing (encompassing the 'audit' of internal controls).

A potential benefit from extending the scope of the statutory audit beyond the traditional attest function into areas encompassing performance audits would be their role in narrowing what is commonly referred to in the audit literature as the audit expectation gap (henceforth referred to as the 'expectation gap'). This exists due to differences between the public's perceptions of the auditor's role and responsibilities and what auditors actually do in practice. Blair (1990) described the expectation gap as the difference between what auditors do and what the users of audit reports think they receive.

21.3 The concept of performance auditing

Performance auditing, whereby auditors review and comment on internal controls, has become a topic of concern for auditors as a measure to be used in the pursuit of financial accountability. This type of auditing has come to be viewed by some, usually nonpractitioners in the audit area, as a procedure that is complementary to attest auditing. The realization of the worth of performance auditing has encouraged both academics and practitioners to address it in a meaningful and concerted manner (see, for example, Herbert, 1979; Brown et al., 1982; Parker, 1986; Guthrie et al., 1990).

This begs the following question: What is a performance audit and how does it differ from the conventional 'attest' audit?

Gill and Cosserat (1996) defined a performance audit as one that involves the process of obtaining and evaluating evidence about the economy, efficiency, and effectiveness of an entity's operating activities in relation to specified objectives. This type of audit is also referred to as value-for-money (VFM) auditing, operational auditing, management auditing, or efficiency auditing (p. 5).

In the literature, the above terms are often used interchangeably, to denote the same operation or activity. In fact, according to Parker (1986), they are, to all intents and purposes, identical in the prescription of their constituent elements, with all focusing upon the evaluation of economy, efficiency, and effectiveness of resource utilization, operation procedures, and activities, and the pursuit of objectives (p. 11).

There were a spate of large corporate collapses and corporate scandals in the late 1980s and early 1990s in a number of Western countries. As mentioned by Godsell (1990), the demise of Estate Mortgage, Spedley Group, National Safety Council of Victoria, and Tricontinental Corporation in Australia all resulted in legal proceedings against the audit firms involved. This in turn led to an increase in the demand for greater management accountability from some sectors of the business community.

More recently, the collapse of Barings Bank plc in the UK in 1995 drew attention to the question of the auditor's responsibility to report publicly on the efficacy of internal controls. Sinha (1995), in his analysis of the Barings plc collapse, attributed it to the almost total failure of internal control mechanisms in place.

In response to similar concerns in the USA, the American Institute of Certified Public Accountants (AICPA) issued a white paper in June 1993 which proposed that the Securities and Exchange Commission (SEC) establish a reporting system requiring public companies to state whether the internal controls over their financial reporting were effective. Independent auditors would then be required to publicly comment on the validity of management's assertions.

The motivation for this chapter is derived from the perceived dissatisfaction that exists among some user groups of financial statements with certain aspects of current auditing practices. This dissatisfaction appears to have existed for some time. As far back as 1973, Beck surveyed 2000 shareholders selected at random from the share registers of two major Australian companies and found that a surprisingly large proportion (81%) of the respondents thought an auditor's work assured them that there was a basis for considering the entity audited to be financially sound. Another study by Steen (1989) in the UK found that 25% of a subset that participants described as influential believed that auditors guaranteed the financial soundness of the entity being audited. Based on some of the above findings, it is quite obvious that an audit expectation gap appears to exist. As mentioned above, this is the difference between the role the audit profession perceives auditing plays in the business environment and the general public's perception of what function auditors currently serve. The expectation gap also incorporates the difference between auditor's current functions and functions the general public considers they should be performing. The expectation gap and the increase in litigation involving auditors referred to earlier, taken together, suggest a level of dissatisfaction with certain aspects of the traditional external audit function.

In light of this perceived dissatisfaction and the demand for more management accountability due to widespread corporate failures, some of which were mentioned earlier, this chapter looks at the possibility of extending the role of auditors beyond their traditional attesting and statutory compliance functions to incorporate mandatory reporting on internal controls. In other words, this chapter explores the possibility of making performance audits mandatory, initially at least, for publicly listed companies.

O'Leary (1996) commented on how performance audits have traditionally been conducted by the internal audit departments of the entities under audit. The results of these audits have usually been kept very much 'in-house'. Internal auditors have been requested to review an area and report back to management on how economically, efficiently, or effectively that area has been managed during the period under review. As the findings may not always be complimentary to management, they have been reluctant to disclose them to the members of the entity or to the general public. Therefore, the important issues to be raised are:

1. Whether the users of the financial statements of the entity concerned would like to have this information.

2. Whether the members of the entity concerned are reasonably entitled to have access to information of this nature relating to the efficient and effective performance of the present management team.

There are many potential problematic areas that will have to be tackled and overcome before a mandatory performance audit framework can be established. If, however, the pressure for performance audits escalates, then ways will have to be found to overcome some of these potential problem areas. According to writers like O'Leary (1996), these are not insurmountable problems.

This in turn leads to questions about the purpose of the audit function and, further, about what is in store in the future? A review of the origins and history of auditing, as it is traditionally understood, is therefore pertinent.

21.4 The origins of auditing

Brown (1962) commented on how auditing can be traced back to the days of the Roman Empire. Similarly, Gill and Cosserat (1996) noted that, in ancient Egypt, authorities provided for independent checks on the recording of tax receipts. In ancient Greece, inspections were made of the accounts of public officials, and the Romans compared disbursements with payment authorizations.

Furthermore, Gill and Cosserat (1996) noted how the early records of auditing were primarily confined to public accounts, with those handling public monies required to meet a responsible official known as the auditor who 'heard' their accounting for such funds. The latter was similar to the approach taken by a judge hearing the evidence of witnesses at a trial. The word 'auditor' is derived from the Latin *audire* – 'to hear'. The authors also describe the practice of the government in medieval England of sending auditors on a circuit to manors and estates to hear accounts for disbursement and revenues. This practice contributed to the stable financial condition of the English Crown. Traditionally, auditing only performed a stewardship function. It informed the members of an entity whether management of that entity, to whom they had entrusted their capital, had invested it as planned and could account for its current whereabouts.

It is interesting to note that a statement of audit objectives published in a practice manual by Dicksee (1892) stated the object of an audit to be threefold:

1. The detection of fraud
2. The detection of technical errors
3. The detection of errors of principle.

Auditing practice evolved over time. In the early part of the 20th century it was recognized that some reliance on internal control was possible. It now appears as though the practice of auditing has turned full cycle from its early beginnings. In what might be referred to as the formative days of auditing, it was popularly held that the chief objects of an audit were the detection and prevention of both fraud and errors, whereas in the latter days the auditor was viewed as merely expressing an opinion and not certifying or guaranteeing the accuracy of the records (the latter is also known as the 'attesting' role).

Today it appears that there is a move by some sectors for an extension to the traditional attesting role to incorporate, amongst other things, a performance audit, with an auditor being required to express a public opinion on the efficacy or otherwise of a company's system of internal controls.

As we enter the new millennium, the recipients of financial statements have become a far more sophisticated and informed group. They demand more from an audit function than a mere attestation that their investments can still be accounted for. Accounting standards have necessitated the issuance of much more than bare profit and loss and balance sheet figures. Significantly more data has to be given these days. Consider, for instance, the voluminous notes that nowadays accompany published financial statements. Items such as segment information, related party transactions, and lease commitments, to name but a few, are now part and parcel of the Annual Report of most entities. Auditors now have to comment on these data as well as the basic accounts. Hence, auditing has expanded from its traditional stewardship role to one of a more informative nature as well.

The brief history of auditing outlined earlier demonstrates an interesting point. Auditing is a profession and just like any other profession, it is dynamic and not static. It will grow and adapt as the demands of the users of that profession change over time. According to O'Leary (1996), currently a level of dissatisfaction can be perceived worldwide with what an audit function is seen to provide, and Malaysia is not immune from this global trend. This is due partly to the audit expectation gap referred to earlier.

As reported by Gwilliam (1987), the American Institute of Certified Public Accountants (AICPA) established the Cohen Commission in 1974 *inter alia* to consider whether a gap may exist between what the public expects or needs and what auditors can and should reasonably expect to accomplish. Gwilliam (1987) noted how, in respect of its primary brief, the Commission came to the conclusion that such a gap does exist. However, the Commission noted that the principal responsibility does not appear to lie with the users of financial statements. The Commission considered that the main reason for this 'expectation gap' was the failure of the public accounting profession (or auditors) to react and evolve rapidly enough to keep pace with the speed of change in the business environment.

Blair (1990) further expanded on the functions that an audit does not perform. He noted that an audit is not an assurance of the future viability of an entity. It is not an opinion on the economy, efficiency, or effectiveness with which management has conducted its affairs, nor is it an assurance that there has been no fraud or other irregularity. His comment on management performance is interesting. Like many others, these comments appear to mirror some members of the public's expectations as to what an audit service should offer.

Some users of accounts obviously feel that auditors should comment on management's performance for the period under review, as well as reporting on the accuracy of the financial statements of that entity.

The audit expectation gap is, unfortunately, a current fact of life and, while it exists, it will continue to cause criticism of and litigation against auditors, and to undermine confidence in their work. According to Porter (1991), if irreparable damage to the profession's reputation is to be prevented, the auditing profession must take urgent and effective action to narrow the gap.

Porter (1991) noted how, in recent years, the profession, particularly in the UK and the USA, has taken some positive steps to narrow the gap, but that these efforts have generally been fire-fighting in nature, targeted to quell the most vociferous and scathing criticism of auditors, or else they have been enforced by legislation and designed to serve specific objectives.

21.5 Limitations and problems with implementing performance audits

From a review of the literature, it appears that there is a lack of support for recommendations that auditors' traditional attestation role be extended to incorporate performance audits amongst other functions. Smith and Lanier (1970), Smith et al. (1972), Santocki (1976), Edmonds (1983), and Boys (1985) discovered, amongst other things, that auditors were unwilling to perform such audits due to the wider responsibilities being undertaken. Gwilliam (1987) also attributed the reluctance to take on these additional tasks to the threat of greater legal exposure.

There are many limitations and potential problem areas that will have to be tackled and overcome before a mandatory performance audit framework can be established. O'Leary (1996) foresaw three major problems that can arise as a result of attempting to implement performance audits on a mandatory basis.

Briefly, some of the pitfalls include:

- Loss of audit independence
- Cost/Benefit considerations
- The establishment of adequate measurement criteria.

21.6 Auditor independence

As mentioned earlier, most large organizations currently conduct some form of performance auditing via their internal audit departments. Given their in-depth knowledge of the entity that employs them, internal auditors are in the ideal position to comment on management's efficiency and effectiveness or otherwise. However, by definition, they cannot be expected to conduct the performance audit function with complete objectivity. Even if they could, the perception of independence would be extremely clouded.

The ideal alternative is, of course, to utilize an entity's external auditors to conduct a performance audit, as well as the mandatory financial statements audit. Their knowledge of the client's operations will be reasonable but certainly not as thorough as that of the internal auditors. Hence, if the external auditors perform the function, this introduces a second problem, cost.

21.7 Cost/Benefit

Information always comes at a price. Whereas the shareholders of a company (or the members of any audited entity) and the general public would almost certainly welcome comments as to how economically, efficiently, and effectively the management of an entity has performed its functions, they will probably only welcome such additional information if it is obtainable at a reasonable price. Significant time, effort, and resources would have to be employed in conducting any worthwhile performance audit. It would be expected that management would wish to recoup these costs from shareholders, be it by way of additional contributions or reduced returns (dividend payments, etc.). This would appear reasonable, as shareholders would be the major beneficiaries of the additional review function, i.e. the performance audit.

As mentioned by Gwilliam (1987), a general problem that arises when considering the possibility of such extensions to the traditional audit role lies in the lack of evidence as to the potential costs and benefits. The fact that there is generally no prohibition on many of these services being offered and purchased at present seems to suggest *a priori* that, in the majority of cases, the costs currently exceed the benefits.

21.8 Establishing measurement criteria

One of the major difficulties with performance audits is how to establish measurement criteria. Commenting on what is economic, efficient, and effective is obviously not as clear-cut as commenting on dollar and cent valuations and results. Performance evaluations may be highly subjective unless adequate guidelines are set, against which performances can be gauged. It is critical, therefore, in a performance audit that the audit objective be properly defined so that the results of the investigation can be assessed correctly. However, setting the objective for a performance audit as opposed to a financial statements audit will not usually be as straightforward. This is due to the lack of succinct meaning of the terms economic, efficient, and effective.

The above three difficulties may partly explain why the concept of issuing the results of performance audits to outside parties has not yet been embraced readily by some elements of the financial community. However, these problems are not insurmountable. The difficulty of a lack of independence can easily be overcome by having the performance audits conducted by external audit firms, and this may not necessarily result in exorbitant costs, which have to be passed on to the members of the entity. The external auditors must already possess a sound knowledge of their clients' operations.

The work carried out by Boys (1985) in the UK found that there was already a very considerable overlap between performance auditing and the work of the management consultancy divisions of professional accounting firms, hence the finding that accounting firms were much more prepared to countenance the auditor in this additional role, since the extra costs, if any, were likely to be marginal. When carrying out the audit of financial statements, the external auditors usually review several aspects of management performance. For instance, the auditor should obtain an understanding of the internal control structure in order to plan the audit and develop an effective audit approach. This means that the auditors are bound to review and assess the effect of the internal controls on the entity. The by-product of this function is often seen in the letter of recommendation. Arens et al. (1990) commented that a secondary purpose of many financial statements audits is to also make operational recommendations to management.

The external auditors can further reduce costs when assessing the work of the entity's own internal audit department. If they are satisfied that the internal audit department is competent and acts independently of management pressure, they are entitled to rely on their work to a large extent.

If this is allowable for a financial statements audit, why not for a performance audit as well? Relying on the performance audit work of the internal audit department would greatly reduce the cost to the external auditors of performing an independent review. Hence, it may be quite feasible to have external auditors conduct performance audits without the costs becoming too prohibitive.

This then leaves us with the problem of establishing adequate measurement criteria. Here again, however, significant progress has already been achieved. In the USA, Charnes and Cooper (1980) attempted to develop a method of evaluating management efficiency that did not necessitate the use of imputed market prices. Their new method uses complex linear programming techniques.

Sherman (1984) then compared the performance of these techniques, which he termed 'data envelopment analysis' (DEA), with the techniques of financial ratio analysis and analytical reviews that are traditionally employed by auditors as part of their performance audits. He found DEA was better able to capture efficiency dimensions not covered by the more traditional methods of evaluation. Sherman suggested two valid reasons for the use of DEA techniques.

Firstly, DEA can provide technical measures of efficiency, thereby removing all the problems associated with internal cost allocations (this also includes those situations where market imperfections allow for high profitability in spite of operating inefficiencies) and, secondly, it is better able to account for expenditures such as training, research and development, etc., which contribute to future output but are not taken into account in arriving at more current measures of profitability.

In some countries, like Australia, the fact that an audit practice statement, AUP 33 (and the subsequent AUS 806), has already been issued since 1992 indicates that a fairly high degree of agreement already exists as to what the measurement criteria entail. The three critical factors in performance auditing are economy, efficiency, and effectiveness. Although they are still prone to a certain degree of subjectivity in their implementation, they are certainly not as nebulous as some commentators would have us believe. With time, the measurement criteria can be refined and redefined if necessary. Hence, the problems associated with performance auditing should not be considered insurmountable. With careful planning, monitoring, and implementation, they can be overcome.

21.9 Conclusion

The issue of the audit practice statement AUP 33 in 1992 heralded the official recognition of performance auditing by the auditing profession in Australia. Certain members of the business community and some academics believed that it would be the future of auditing worldwide. Rather than just the traditional financial statements audit, in years to come audit firms may have to comment on management performance as well as the accounts under review, in conducting their periodic reviews of audit entities.

Questionnaire studies and other evidence suggest that user groups see the auditor as performing a wider function than that encompassed by the presently limited scope of the financial audit. A number of possible changes in, and extensions to, the audit function have been suggested so as to ensure that the actual audit performance corresponds more closely to the expectations of various user groups. Research work relating to this problem of the audit expectation gap and some suggested solutions have been reviewed earlier.

Smith et al. (1972), who undertook a survey to determine the need for and scope of the audit of management's performance, concluded from their study that corporate management has its responsibility towards society and there is a very clear need for appropriate professional standards. It must be borne in mind, in relation to the latter, that their comments were made more than 30 years ago. The question of standards would no longer appear to be an important issue, since professional standards covering the area of performance auditing have already been in use in Australia since 1992 and it is only a matter of time before other countries in the region follow suit.

Similarly, Beck (1973) performed an empirical appraisal looking at the role of the auditor in modern society and made the following observations:

> 'If the ascribed role is not fully performed, there arises the possibility that social action will be taken to enforce conformity, perhaps by new legislation or to downgrade the status and thus shrink the role. As a role develops only out of social wants, it is axiomatic that the void created by a reduced role will, in due course, be filled by other social functionaries prepared to satisfy those social wants.
>
> (p. 118)

He then goes further, noting that 'it may be doubtful whether any other credible source can provide information of this kind: but auditors certainly should be aware that it is wanted and that a significant proportion of shareholders expect auditors to supply it' (p. 121). Porter (1991) concluded from her research investigating the structure and composition of the audit expectation gap that auditors are failing to meet society's expectations in relation to their corporate watchdog function. The auditing profession has usually downplayed the latter role, yet survey results consistently demonstrate that auditors' stakeholders expect auditors to perform these additional duties.

These concerns of both Beck and Porter, amongst others, have been borne out in recent years by the additional responsibilities imposed on auditors in many parts of the English-speaking world through legislation. Much of the information presented in corporate annual reports which is generally not covered by the external auditor's opinion is important for making sound investment decisions. The purpose of this chapter, therefore, has been to consider whether the external auditor's attesting function should be extended by mandate to incorporate performance auditing. Probably the only significant barriers at the present time to extending the attesting function to include information outside the financial statements are the economic and legal implications of any such proposed extension.

Perhaps recent developments, such as the clarification of legal responsibilities and the development of accounting standards and procedures, which reduce time and cost limitations, will lessen the effect of these obstacles. External auditors should seize this opportunity to extend their services to society wherever desirable and feasible. Failure to do so promptly may well have the undesirable consequence of weakening their claims to being the principal attester in our contemporary society.

Mautz and Sharaf (1961, p. 200) presented the challenge confronting the profession very clearly, noting:

> 'As the public requires more and more verified information, much of it well beyond that currently found in financial statements, will auditing see and seize the opportunity to extend its range of service? If it does, there are literally no bounds to its future. If, on the other hand, it either deliberately or unconsciously limits itself to but a small fraction of the total of verifiable information, its position of eminence may be lost to those who do seize the larger opportunity.'

Although these observations were made more than 40 years ago, there seems to be a ringing truth to their predictions in light of the current controversies surrounding the suggestions made about the extension of the auditor's role to incorporate mandatory performance auditing.

If the general public and the business community consider that this is the function they want an audit to perform in the future, for both public and private entities, then performance auditing may gain just as important a status as financial statement auditing currently holds. Therefore, debate over the potential benefits of compulsory performance audits continues to increase, both in Malaysia and overseas.

In conclusion, irrespective of whatever role the audit profession wishes to ascribe to auditors, in the long run the public will shall be expected to prevail. The auditing profession must be seen to possess considerable economic power, albeit indirectly, since in the absence of a functioning auditing profession the economic structure in most English-speaking countries would be different and corporate organization as we understand it would disappear. The following comments attributed to Berle (1960, p. 111) apply to auditors no less, 'we have considered public consensus, if not as originator, certainly as final arbiter of legitimacy'.

It seems reasonable to view the public consensus concerning the role of auditor as in a state of continuous change or development, but generally there is small likelihood of sudden or dramatic change in this consensus. Although these last comments were made as the result of a study undertaken by Beck in Australia almost three decades ago, it is suggested here that they are still valid and can be taken as supporting an expanded role for auditors.

References

Arens, A.A., Loebbecke, J.K., Best, P.J., and Shailer, G.E.P. (1990). *Auditing in Australia: An Integrated Approach*. Prentice-Hall, Englewood Cliffs, NJ.

Arpan, J.S. and Radebaugh, L.H. (1985). *International Accounting and Multinational Enterprises*. John Wiley, New York.

Beck, G.W. (1973). The Role of the Auditor in Modern Society: An Empirical Appraisal. *Accounting and Business Research*, 3(10):117–122.

Berle, A.A. (1960). *Power Without Property*. Sidgwick & Jackson, London.

Blair, I. (1990). The Audit Expectation Gap Widens as the Failures Grow. *Company Director*, June, p. 39.

Boys, B.G. (1985). Management Audits. *Touche Ross (UK) Technical Digest*, No. 17.

Brown, R.E., Gallagher, T.P., and Williams, M.C. (1982). *Auditing Performance in Government: Concepts and Cases*. John Wiley, New York.

Brown, R.G. (1962). Changing Audit Objectives and Techniques. *Accounting Review*, 32(4):696–703.

Charnes, A. and Cooper, W.W. (1980). Auditing and Accounting for Program Efficiency and Management Efficiency in Not-for-Profit Entities. *Accounting, Organizations and Society*, 5(1):87–107.

Dicksee, L.R. (1892). *Auditing: A Practical Manual for Auditors*. Gee, London.

Edmonds, T.P. (1983). The Effect of Auditor Involvement on the Predictive Capacity of Interim Financial Information. *Journal of Business Finance and Accounting*, 10(3):429–441.

Gill, G.S. and Cosserat, G.W. (1996). *Modern Auditing in Australia*. Jacaranda Wiley, Queensland.

Godsell, D. (1990). *The Legal Duties and Liabilities of Auditors in Australia.* Australian Accounting Research Foundation, Melbourne.

Guthrie, J., Parker, L., and Shand, D. (1990). *The Public Sector: Contemporary Readings in Accounting and Auditing.* Harcourt Brace Jovanovich, Sydney.

Gwilliam, D.R. (1987). *A Survey of Auditing Research.* Prentice-Hall International/The Institute of Chartered Accountants in England and Wales, Cambridge, UK.

Herbert, L. (1979). *Auditing the Performance of Management.* Lifetime Learning Publications, California.

Mautz, R.K. and Sharaf, H.A. (1961). *The Philosophy of Auditing.* p. 241. American Accounting Association, Evanston, IL, citing Brown, R. (1905). *A History of Accounting and Accountants,* p. 74. T.C. & E.C. Jack, Edinburgh.

O'Leary, C. (1996). Performance Audits: Could they Become Mandatory for Public Companies? *Managerial Auditing Journal,* 11(1):14–18.

Parker, L.D. (1986). *Value-for-Money Auditing: Conceptual, Development and Operational Issues,* Auditing Discussion Paper No. 1. Australian Accounting Research Foundation, Melbourne.

Porter, B.A. (1991). *The Audit Expectation Performance Gap in New Zealand – An Empirical Investigation,* Discussion Paper No. 119, September. Accountancy Department, Massey University, Palmerston North, New Zealand.

Santocki, J. (1976). Meaning and Scope of Management Audit. *Accounting and Business Research,* 6(25):64–70.

Sherman, H.D. (1984). Data Envelopment Analysis as a New Managerial Audit Methodology – Test and Evaluation. *Auditing: A Journal of Practice and Theory,* 4(1):35–53.

Sinha, T. (1995). Lessons from Barings. *Chartered Accountants Journal, New Zealand,* 74(7):20–22.

Smith, C.H. and Lanier, R.A. (1970). The Audit of Management: Report on a Field Study. *Management Accounting,* 46(2):24–26.

Smith, C.H., Lanier, R.A., and Taylor, M.E. (1972). The Need for and Scope of the Audit of Management: A Survey of Attitudes. *Accounting Review,* 47(2):270–283.

Steen, M. (1989). *Audits and Auditors – What the Public Think.* KPMG Peat Marwick McLintock, UK.

Watts, R.L. and Zimmerman, J.L. (1983). Agency Problems, Auditing and the Theory of the Firm: Some Evidence. *Journal of Law and Economics,* 26(3):613–633.

22

Empirical Evaluation of Discretionary Accruals Models

Xavier Garza-Gómez

22.1 Introduction

Every time an outsider needs to use the financial information of a publicly traded firm, he or she has to assess the reliability of the reported numbers. Nevertheless, generally accepted accounting principles (GAAP) allow certain discretion when calculating and reporting performance. Managers may want to use this discretion in order to show better financial results. For example, managers sometimes manage earnings to avoid showing a loss and to meet analysts' expectations (Burgstahler and Dichev, 1997; DeFond and Park, 1997; DeGeorge et al., 1999). Managers may want to lower the perceived risk by reducing the variation of inter-period earnings ('earnings smoothing'), which in turn would reduce the cost of capital for the firm (Chaney et al., 1998). This helps to keep the company's stock price up (or avoid a plunge), which may help managers personally to collect bonuses and/or exercise options (Healy, 1985), or sell stock at higher price (Teoh et al., 1998). Other reasons include avoiding penalties and/or getting external rewards. Examples in the former include debt covenants (DeFond and Jiambalvo, 1994), while getting government subsidies may be an example of the latter (Jones, 1991).

The accounting shenanigans at the beginning of this century further increased the interest of analysts, regulators, and investors in general about techniques that can identify earnings manipulation by the firm's management. Most methods attempting to find evidence of earnings management rely on the calculation of accounting accruals and their separation into two parts: the normal or expected accruals (referred to as nondiscretionary) and the abnormal or unexpected (referred to as discretionary) accruals. Once discretionary accruals are estimated, statistical tests are run to determine if the discretionary accruals of the firm(s) under scrutiny differ from zero, the normal or expected value.

Nevertheless, despite all the generated interest and the abundant literature on this subject, there is no consensus about which model or method of estimating discretionary accruals is superior. As a matter of fact, there are no guidelines about how to estimate these models in order to improve the power of the tests. Some early attempts to develop recommendations are found in Dechow et al. (1995) and Guay et al. (1996) with US data, and in Young (1999) using data from the UK. These early studies concentrate on the Healy (1985) model, the DeAngelo (1986) model, and the Jones (1991) model. The main conclusion, however, is that the models estimate accruals with considerable imprecision and that the models cannot account for variations in cash-flow performance. Following these recommendations, there have been separate attempts to account for the relation between accruals and cash flows. Hunt et al. (1997) (among others) added a cash-flow variable to the Jones model; Shivakumar (1996) added five cash-flow variables to the Jones model. These two articles add to the Jones model while, Garza-Gómez et al. (2000) developed a new model based on cash flow from operations. These studies reported a general improvement over the traditional Jones model, but concerns about methodology and comparability still remained. Furthermore, the need for better accrual models is always present. However, despite the great need for sound recommendations on how to improve earnings management studies, previous studies provide no clear guidelines on how to compare or evaluate alternative accrual models. This chapter tries to fill this gap in the literature by revising how discretionary accrual models are typically estimated and compared, and thus develop a framework that may be used to test for earnings management.

The approach followed in this chapter is straightforward. Discretionary accruals are the residuals left by the model of expected or normal accruals derived by the researcher. A good expectations model will capture most of the volatility and leave a small amount of variation in the discretionary part of accruals. On the other hand, a weak model will not explain variation in total accruals and leave most of it in the discretionary part of accruals. Therefore, the power to detect earnings management is inversely related to the standard error of the discretionary part. This is the main premise of this work, and it is applied and tested on a series of accrual models. This chapter first explores three sources of variation in total accruals: the time effect, the industry classification, and the exchange effect. These three factors play an important role in accrual determination because total accruals are supposed to reflect the economic activity of the firm. Since the economy changes year by year, across industries and depending on the type of firm, differences in the level of total accruals can be expected. Initial results demonstrate that the three sources are significant and that considering them when accrual models are estimated results in lower standard errors. That is, splitting the total sample into subsamples by time, industry, and exchange when estimating accruals models is critical in improving the estimates of nondiscretionary accruals. Furthermore, these subsamples become the yardstick against which competing models can be compared.

When models are evaluated, results clearly indicate that those models that consider cash flow as an explanatory variable are more powerful than naive models and the popular Jones model. In particular, the accounting process (or AP) model proved to be the best for the whole sample. Discretionary accruals obtained with this method have the lowest standard error and a median and average close to zero (nondiscretionary accruals under this method yield the highest R^2). Finally, to confirm the results, the information content of discretionary and nondiscretionary accruals to predict future cash flow from operations and future earnings is measured. Consistent with the results obtained from the volatility analysis, nondiscretionary accruals estimated with the AP model yield the highest contribution to explain future performance. Main conclusions are robust to different sample selection methods and different methods of estimating accruals.

This chapter contributes to the literature in several ways. It explores recent accrual models that address the reported weakness of the Jones model and presents evidence that these models are superior to the Jones model. It describes an empirical framework to detect earnings management and a straightforward approach to compare new accrual models that will come in the future. The chapter is organized as follows. Section 22.2 describes how total accruals are calculated and the models used in this study. Section 22.3 describes the data and identifies three main sources of dispersion. Section 22.4 shows tests of the accrual models. Section 22.5 presents tests of the information content of discretionary accruals and some robustness tests, while section 22.6 concludes the chapter.

22.2 Estimating discretionary accruals

The separation of total accruals into a discretionary part and a normal (or nondiscretionary) part is an extremely difficult task, not only because discretion is unobservable but also because there are economic events in the life of a company that will cause total accruals to change from year to year. Every time a researcher estimates discretionary accruals, he or she is forcing an expectation model of the 'normal' or expected behavior of accruals in relation to economic events. Most models will require the estimation of one or more parameters.

Two methods are found in the literature to estimate these expectation models. The time-series approach estimates parameters for each firm in the sample using data from periods prior to the period in question. In contrast, parameters in the cross-sectional models are estimated each period for each firm in the event sample using data of firms in the same industry. Early tests done by Dechow et al. (1995) and Guay et al. (1996) are based on the time-series approach. Nevertheless, a natural disadvantage of this technique is the estimation of the model for new firms. Since the model requires the existence of at least $N + 1$ years of data (where N is the number of explanatory variables used in the model), the models can only be estimated for firms that have a long series of financial data.

For example, Guay et al. (1996) required 15 years of data to be considered in their study. This introduces survivorship bias as well as selection bias, since young, new companies won't be considered. DeFond and Jiambalvo (1994) introduced a cross-sectional method. They separated firms by SIC code and estimated normal accruals using yearly cross-sections. This method assumes that the situation for each year will affect the firms in the industry in a similar way. This approach is becoming the norm to estimate accrual models. Subramanyam (1996) estimated the Jones model and the modified Jones model proposed by Dechow et al. (1995) and reported better fit for the cross-sectional versions of these two models. In general, he found lower standard errors for the coefficients, fewer outliers, and coefficients that fit better the predicted signs. Jeter and Shivakumar (1997) also argued in favor of the cross-sectional estimation method over the time-series method, stressing that industry-relative abnormal accruals can be a useful tool for researchers trying to detect the average unconditional earnings management found in the industry.

In general, the assumption that the time-series approach makes is that, prior to estimation, no systematic earnings management is expected to occur. On the other hand, cross-sectional models assume that all firms in the subsample are affected equally in the period. Initial evidence (further explored in the next section) tends to support the second assumption. Furthermore, the number of firms decreases substantially when the time-series approach is used. For these two reasons, the cross-sectional approach is chosen for all the calculations in this chapter. Nevertheless, the next section shows empirically how this cross-sectional method improves estimation.

22.2.1 Basic accrual models

This chapter compares several discretionary accrual models. The first three models (Healy, 1985; DeAngelo, 1986; and industry median) are simple or naive models.

The simplest version of the Healy (1995) model assumes:

$$E[TA_t/A_{t-1}] = NDA_t = 0, \tag{22.1}$$

where TA_t = total accruals in period t and A_{t-1} = beginning of period total assets.

This model effectively makes all discretionary accruals equal to total accruals. An inherent weakness of this is that the model doesn't allow for accruals to fluctuate in response to economic conditions.

The DeAngelo (1986) model assumes that nondiscretionary accruals follow a random path. This model uses last period's total accruals (scaled by lagged total assets) as the measure of nondiscretionary accruals. Therefore, the DeAngelo model is:

$$E[TA_t/A_{t-1}] = NDA_t = TA_{t-1}/A_{t-1}. \tag{22.2}$$

The industry model allows for nondiscretionary accruals to fluctuate over time. It assumes that the variation in the determinants of nondiscretionary accruals is common across firms in the same industry. The model is:

$$E[TA_t/A_{t-1}] = NDA_t = \text{median}(TA_t/A_{t-1}). \tag{22.3}$$

Jones (1991) employed a regression-based expectation model to control for variations in nondiscretionary accruals associated with the depreciation charge and changes in economic activity:

$$E[TA_t/A_{t-1}] = NDA_t = \alpha_1(1/A_{t-1}) + \beta_1([\Delta]REV_t/A_{t-1}) + \beta_2(PPE_t/A_{t-1}), \tag{22.4}$$

where ΔREV_t = change in revenue from period $t - 1$ to t and PPE_t = gross plant property and equipment. According to Jones, the [Δ]REV and PPE terms are to control for the nondiscretionary component of total accruals associated with changes in operating activity and level of depreciation respectively.

Dechow et al. (1995) argued that since all revenue changes in the Jones models are assumed to be nondiscretionary, the resulting measure of discretionary accruals does not reflect the impact of sales-based manipulation. Therefore, they tried to capture revenue manipulation and change the Jones procedure by subtracting the change in receivables (ΔREC) from ΔREV for each sample firm. Their model is:

$$E[TA_t/A_{t-1}] = NDA_t = \alpha_1(1/A_{t-1}) + \beta_1(\Delta REV_t/A_{t-1} - \Delta REC_t/A_{t-1}) + \beta_2(PPE_t/A_{t-1}). \tag{22.5}$$

Dechow et al. (1995) and Guay et al. (1996) evaluated these five models and reported that the discretionary accruals (DAs) estimated with these five models are imprecise and generate low-power tests for earnings management. Furthermore, DAs correlate with operating cash flows.

22.2.2 Alternative accrual models

Until recently, the Jones and modified Jones models have been the models of choice in the earnings management research. Nevertheless, to account for the reported correlation between accruals and cash flows (Dechow, 1994; Dechow et al., 1995), some authors have added a term that includes CFO into the original Jones model (Subramanyam, 1996; Hunt et al., 1997). This model becomes:

$$E[\mathrm{TA}_t/\mathrm{A}_{t-1}] = \mathrm{NDA}_t = \alpha_1(1/\mathrm{A}_{t-1}) + \beta_1(\Delta\mathrm{REV}_t/\mathrm{A}_{t-1}) + \beta_2(\mathrm{PPE}_t/\mathrm{A}_{t-1}) + \beta_3(\mathrm{CFO}_t/\mathrm{A}_{t-1}). \tag{22.6}$$

Shivakumar (1996) argued that cash from operations varies across firms in the estimation sample and expected the sensitivity to cash flows to be different between firms with low cash flows and firms with moderate or high cash flows. Shivakumar's model, also used in Jeter and Shivakumar (1999), can be written as:

$$E[\mathrm{TA}_t/\mathrm{A}_{t-1}] = \mathrm{NDA}_t = \alpha_1 + \beta_1(\Delta\mathrm{REV}_t/\mathrm{A}_{t-1}) + \beta_2(\mathrm{PPE}_t/\mathrm{A}_{t-1}) + \beta_3 D_1\mathrm{CFO}_t/\mathrm{A}_{t-1} + \beta_4 D_2\mathrm{CFO}_t/\mathrm{A}_{t-1} + \beta_5 D_3\mathrm{CFO}_t/\mathrm{A}_{t-1} + \beta_6 D_4\mathrm{CFO}_t/\mathrm{A}_{t-1} + \beta_7 D_5\mathrm{CFO}_t/\mathrm{A}_{t-1}, \tag{22.7}$$

where $D_1 - D_5$ are indicators of the cash-flow quintile to which a firm belongs. This model, especially designed for cross-sectional methods, substantially increases the number of parameters needed and cannot be used in time-series estimations.

The last model considered in this chapter is the one introduced in Garza-Gómez et al. (2000). This model, referred to as the accounting process (AP) model, tries to incorporate the natural relation between accruals and cash flow modeled by Dechow et al. (1998), and is expressed as:

$$E[\mathrm{TA}_t/\mathrm{A}_{t-1}] = \mathrm{NDA}_t = \alpha_1 + \beta_1\Delta\mathrm{CFO}_t/\mathrm{A}_{t-1} + \beta_2(\mathrm{TA}_{t-1}/\mathrm{A}_{t-1}). \tag{22.8}$$

This model, which was applied to Japanese data, differs from the previous two since it doesn't use the Jones model as the starting point[1].

22.3 Important properties of total accruals

This chapter uses data from the US stock market to analyze discretionary accrual models. In this section, we establish the definition of accruals and describe the data used in this study.

22.3.1 Accruals calculation

The literature to date that focuses on accruals includes two main approaches to calculate the accrual components of earnings.

The balance-sheet approach estimates accruals as:

$$TA_{tbs} = (\Delta CA_t - \Delta Cash_t) - (\Delta CL_t - \Delta STD_t) - DEPTN_t. \tag{22.9}$$

Total accruals are then subtracted from earnings to estimate cash flow from operations (CFO_t) as follows:

$$CFO_t = EBXI_t - TA_{tbs}, \tag{22.10}$$

where ΔCA_t = change in current assets during period t (Compustat item 4); ΔCL_t = the change in current liabilities during period t (Compustat 5); $\Delta Cash_t$ = the change in cash and cash equivalents during period t (Compustat 1); ΔSTD_t = the current maturities of long-term debt and other short-term debt included in current liabilities during period t (Compustat 34); $DEPTN_t$ = depreciation and amortization expense during period t (Compustat 14); and $EBXI_t$ = net income before extraordinary items and discontinued operations (Compustat 18).

This approach (or a similar one) is used in Dechow (1994), DeFond and Jiambalvo (1994), Guay et al. (1996), Sloan (1996), Subramanyam (1996), and DeFond and Park (1997), among others. Most of these studies use a long sample that includes data from the 1970s, 1980s, and even the 1960s (Guay et al., 1996; Sloan, 1996; Hansen, 1999). Since the statement of cash flows became compulsory until 1988, there was no other way to determine the accrual component of earnings.

This approach, however, has suffered severe criticisms by Hansen (1999), and by Collins and Hribar (2002). They argued that the balance-sheet approach biases the estimates of discretionary accruals when a real business change, such as acquisitions, discontinued operations, capital expenditures, and divestments, occurs during the year. To alleviate this problem, Collins and Hribar (2002) recommended the use of an alternative method to estimate accruals. This approach calculates accruals directly from the cash-flow statement as follows:

$$TA_{cf} = EBXI - CFO_{cf}, \tag{22.11}$$

where TA_{cf} = the total accrual adjustments provided on the cash-flow statement under the indirect method; EBXI = earnings before extraordinary items and discontinued operations (Compustat 123); and CFO_{cf} = operating cash flows (from continuing operations) taken directly from the statement of cash flows (Compustat 308 − Compustat 124). This method to calculate accruals based on the statement of cash flows has also been used by Barth et al. (2001).

All variables in this study are scaled by lagged total assets. The reason for this choice is that the discretionary accrual models studied here are defined using lagged assets and thus this deflator is the natural choice for all the tests in this chapter. Some studies (see Sloan, 1996; Barth et al., 2001) used average total assets as a deflator, which is a method that may reduce the effect of business changes identified by Collins and Hribar (2002) and Hansen (1999).

To control for the effect of mergers, acquisitions, and divestitures, this chapter limits the sample to firms experiencing 'moderate' changes in total assets during year *t*. All observations for which a company's total assets grew more than 100% in a year and those in which a company's assets decreased more than 50% are discarded. This selection criterion excludes firms experiencing extreme changes in their level of total assets and does in fact eliminate about 10% of the possible observations. However, it allows the variation of TA for the remaining firms to remain within reasonable limits[2].

22.3.2 Sample and descriptive statistics

The sample consists of all US nonfinancial firms listed on the NYSE, AMEX, and NASDAQ for which all required data are available and satisfy the requirements defined above. All accounting information is taken from the 2004 Compustat database. There is a maximum of 4516 firms in 1997 and a minimum of 2899 in 1988. The original set of information consists of 63,482 firm-years. This set of firms, however, still contains a considerable number of outliers, so in order to avoid their effect, the median and interquartile range are shown instead of the typical measures, the average and standard deviation.

Table 22.1 shows earnings before extraordinary items (EBEI) lagged by total assets and its two components, cash flow from operations (CFO) and total accruals (TA) for the years between 1988 and 2003. It can be observed that the events in 2001 really had an impact on the performance of US companies: median earnings fell drastically to 0.8%, while the dispersion increased from average levels of 0.10 in the early 1990s to 0.187 in 2001. Median CFO, on the other hand, has remained relatively constant during the sample period and with stable volatility. The TA component also changed considerably in 2001. Interesting to notice is the fact that the dispersion of CFO was higher than the dispersion of EBEI until

Table 22.1 Descriptive statistics of earnings, cash from operations, and accruals (all firms, yearly averages, 1988–2003)

	N	Median			Interquartile range		
		EBEI	CFO	TA	EBEI	CFO	TA
1988	2899	0.040	0.067	−0.039	0.108	0.138	0.107
1989	3587	0.035	0.065	−0.045	0.120	0.139	0.106
1990	3570	0.032	0.075	−0.055	0.107	0.132	0.104
1991	3563	0.027	0.074	−0.059	0.103	0.116	0.095
1992	3699	0.033	0.074	−0.052	0.098	0.125	0.098
1993	3902	0.036	0.076	−0.051	0.107	0.132	0.101
1994	4054	0.042	0.076	−0.045	0.105	0.140	0.103
1995	4129	0.043	0.076	−0.043	0.110	0.138	0.107
1996	4366	0.045	0.081	−0.049	0.111	0.144	0.113
1997	4516	0.042	0.076	−0.047	0.127	0.151	0.109
1998	4428	0.036	0.071	−0.050	0.143	0.158	0.109
1999	4329	0.031	0.073	−0.055	0.138	0.148	0.102
2000	4048	0.030	0.066	−0.054	0.142	0.156	0.110
2001	4230	0.008	0.064	−0.077	0.187	0.159	0.125
2002	4109	0.013	0.072	−0.076	0.174	0.149	0.107
2003	4053	0.021	0.071	−0.064	0.143	0.140	0.094

The variables are defined as follows (Compustat data items in parentheses): EBEI = income before extraordinary items and discontinued operations (item 18); CFO = net cash flow from operating activities (item 308) less the accrual portion of extraordinary items and discontinued operations reported on the statement of cash flows (item 124); TA = total accruals, calculated as EBEI − CFO. All variables are deflated by the lagged value of total assets (item 6). Sample is defined as nonfinancial US firms listed on the NYSE, AMEX, and NASDAQ with enough data to compute total accruals based on the above definition. Sample size is 63,482 company-year observations.

2000, but in the last three years, values of earnings across firms have been more volatile than values of CFO. This is evidence that the yearly movements in the economy should be considered every time researchers try to investigate the possibility of earnings management.

Most previous studies defined their sample as firms listed on the NYSE and AMEX. NASDAQ firms are commonly excluded from the research. To test the existence of an 'exchange' bias, Figure 22.1 plots the time series of TA for NASDAQ firms from firms listed on the NYSE and AMEX. The upper part of the graph (corresponding to interquartile range) shows a clear difference between NASDAQ and NYSE/AMEX firms. NASDAQ firms have a much higher intercompany

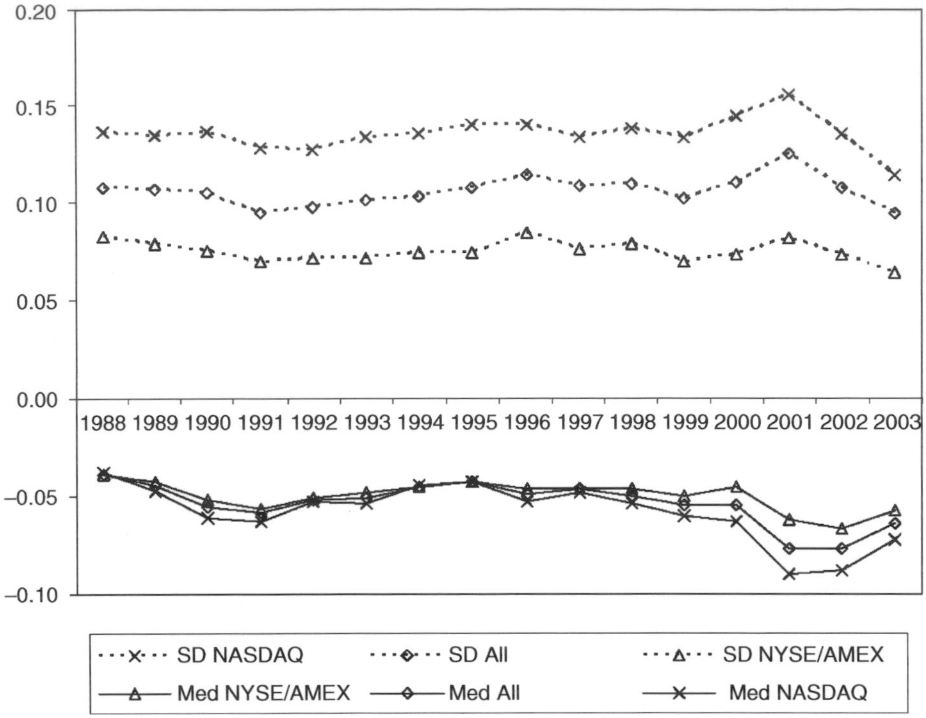

Figure 22.1 Median and interquartile range of total accruals subsamples based on market listing, 1988–2003. Plots obtained with 63,482 observations

volatility than the NYSE/AMEX firms. The lower part of the graph (depicting the level of accruals) shows that, prior to 1998, the level of TA for the two samples remains very close. However, since 1998, the median TA for NASDAQ firms has been markedly lower (higher absolute value) than the median TA for NYSE/AMEX firms.

Finally, to analyze a third possible source of identifiable variation, Table 22.2 shows the distribution characteristics of TA for the 13 industries defined in Barth et al. (2001). It can be seen that industry membership varies significantly. It goes from 35 firms in Agriculture all the way to 2068 firms for Durable Manufacturers. Median TA also presents wide variations. Though the median for all the firms is −5.4%, there are 10 industries with lower levels of accruals (in absolute value) and four industries with higher levels of accruals (in absolute value). The highest level (in absolute value) is for the Extractive sector, followed by Computers and Transportation. On the volatility side, Utilities shows a remarkably low level of intercompany dispersion. In contrast, firms in the

Table 22.2 Descriptive statistics of total accruals industry averages, 1988–2003

Sub-sample	No. of firms	No. of obs.	p 0.10	p 0.25 Q1	p 0.50 median	p 0.75 Q3	p 0.90	IQ range Q3-Q1	ID range 9-1	Estimated SD
Industry										
Agriculture	35	286	−13.8%	−8.0%	−4.1%	−1.0%	4.4%	7.0%	18.3%	6.2%
Mining and Construction	178	1393	−18.8%	−10.2%	−3.8%	3.4%	13.1%	13.6%	31.8%	11.3%
Food	200	1735	−13.6%	−8.3%	−4.5%	−0.9%	3.5%	7.4%	17.1%	6.1%
Textiles and Printing/ Publishing	407	3686	−14.1%	−8.9%	−5.2%	−1.1%	5.2%	7.9%	19.3%	6.7%
Chemicals	197	1882	−13.4%	−8.2%	−4.4%	−0.6%	4.3%	7.6%	17.7%	6.3%
Pharmaceu-ticals	494	3264	−25.0%	−11.2%	−4.5%	−0.2%	5.3%	10.9%	30.3%	10.0%
Extractive	384	2948	−25.9%	−16.6%	−10.3%	−5.3%	−1.2%	11.3%	24.8%	9.0%
Durable Manu-facturers	2068	16,937	−17.1%	−9.2%	−4.1%	1.1%	7.9%	10.2%	25.0%	8.7%
Computers	1577	9183	−28.6%	−16.7%	−8.2%	−1.1%	7.3%	15.6%	36.0%	12.8%
Transpor-tation	559	3715	−20.5%	−13.0%	−8.1%	−4.0%	0.4%	9.0%	20.9%	7.4%
Utilities	280	2940	−9.5%	−6.4%	−4.4%	−2.5%	−0.2%	3.9%	9.3%	3.2%
Retail	1047	7882	−16.6%	−9.9%	−4.7%	1.2%	9.0%	11.2%	25.6%	9.1%
Services	1130	7198	−22.3%	−12.5%	−6.1%	−0.9%	6.3%	11.5%	28.6%	9.9%
Other	75	433	−31.1 %	−14.3%	−4.1%	0.9%	11.5%	15.2%	42.6%	13.9%
Exchange										
AMEX and NYSE	2592	25,492	−14.3%	−8.9%	−5.0%	−1.4%	3.6%	7.5%	17.9%	6.3%
NASDAQ	6039	37,990	−24.0%	−13.2%	−5.9%	0.3%	8.4%	13.5%	32.4%	11.3%
All	8631	63,482	−20.0%	−11.1%	−5.4%	−0.6%	6.4%	10.5%	26.4%	9.0%

Total accruals are calculated as described in Table 22.1. Industry membership is determined by primary SIC code as follows: Agriculture (0100−0999); Mining and Construction (1000−1999, excluding 1300−1399); Food (2000−2111); Textiles and Printing/Publishing (2200−2780); Chemicals (2800−2824, 2840−2899); Pharmaceuticals (2830−2836); Extractive (2900−2999, 1300−1399); Durable Manufacturers (3000−3999, excluding 3570−3579 and 3670−3679); Computers (7370−7379, 3570−3579, 3670−3679); Transportation (4000−4899); Utilities (4900−4999); Retail (5000−5999); and Services (7000−8999, excluding 7370−7379). Estimated SD is calculated as the average of two numbers: interquartile range/1.349 and interdecile range/2.5631. These figures correspond to the interquartile range and interdecile range of a normal distribution.

Computers, Mining and Construction, and Pharmaceuticals industries tend to differ more among them. Consistent with previous tables, NASDAQ firms have a higher median TA (in absolute value) and a higher dispersion of TA among them than firms listed on the NYSE/AMEX.

As mentioned above, the numbers reported in this section have not been trimmed yet and still contain some outliers. In fact, this sample of 63,482 observations still contains firms with earnings below and above 100% of lagged assets. Similar to other studies, this chapter removes all firms with EBEI, CFO, and TA values above 100% and below −100%. A total of 965 firms was removed from the study[3].

22.4 Evaluation of discretionary accruals models

The first step in evaluating competing models is to define the criteria to determine which model is best. Dechow et al. (1995) argued that the power of the earnings management test is inversely proportional to the magnitude of the standard error. As they explain, given a standard error of DA of 9%, discretionary accrual models cannot detect earnings management unless it exceeds 18% of total assets. This 9% referred to by Dechow et al. (1995) is an important benchmark, because some studies found that the standard deviation of total accruals fluctuates around 9%: Barth et al. (2001) found 8% for their sample, Collins and Hribar (2001) reported 6.7%. Though both of these studies limit their results to AMEX/NYSE firms, they are an important reference because the sample period and estimation method are similar to those used in this chapter. Hansen (1999) reported 10.4% for a large pool of 66,716 firm-year observations.

Once the standard deviation of TA is known, this number becomes the benchmark with which discretionary accruals should be evaluated. That is, a good discretionary accrual model must yield standard errors below this level because, in principle, nondiscretionary accruals take away the part of the variation of TA that is related to the explanatory variables. If the model is 'reasonable' and actually explains accruals, the volatility of the discretionary part should decrease. A few studies have reported the standard errors for discretionary accruals. Dechow et al. (1995) found that the standard error DA calculated with the Jones and modified Jones models was 9.2% but the Healy, DeAngelo, and industry models generated standard errors of over 20%[4]. This suggests that the Jones and modified Jones models are better than the other models. However, since the standard error of TA is missing, a complete evaluation cannot be made. Hansen (1999) reported that the Jones, modified Jones, and DeAngelo models have standard errors of

11.3%, 11.5%, and 13.2% respectively. When compared to the standard deviation of TA of 10.4%, we can conclude one of two things: (1) the explanatory variables introduced in the model cannot explain variation in accruals or (2) the estimation method did not support the model. Since Hansen still uses time-series estimation of the models, one can argue that the estimation method was the cause of these results.

Evidence in markets outside of the USA includes studies by Young (1999) and Garza-Gómez et al. (2000). Young reported results obtained with data from the UK market. The modified Jones model yielded the lowest error (5.2%), followed by the Jones model (5.7%) and the Healy model (8.4%). The DeAngelo model yielded 11.9%. Unfortunately, data for TA was not reported and a conclusion could not be obtained. Garza-Gómez et al. (2000) reported results for the Japanese market. They found that TA had a standard deviation of 7.3% and the Jones model produced a standard error of 5.3%, which suggests that the Jones model does capture some of the variation of accruals. Nevertheless, other models tested in their study generated much lower standard errors. In particular, the AP model they propose yielded a standard error of 1.6%.

This chapter will thus use the standard error as the main criterion to compare DA models. However, due to the large sample used, small changes in SE cannot be appreciated easily. To circumvent this problem, in addition to the SE, the sum of squares (SS) is also reported in Table 22.3.

22.4.1 Initial standard errors

The results in the previous section identified three sources of variation in total accruals. Controlling for that variation is critical if a fair evaluation of the discretionary accrual models is to be made. That is, if a discretionary accrual model is to be tested, it must be done in a way that only the additional information content brought by the model is measured. That is, if the pooled variation of TA is, say, 9% and the standard error of the Jones model estimated under the cross-sectional approach is 7%, we need to know how much of this 2% gain arises from the variables in the Jones model. As section 22.3 showed, there are industry variations, year variations, and firm-listing variations that may be causing the reduction of 2% in standard error. A fair evaluation of the Jones model can only be made if the 7% is compared against a naive model that uses the industry median model for each year. This benchmark model does account for the industry variation and the time-series variation, so a comparison would yield the reduction in dispersion that is attributable to the variables in the Jones model.

Table 22.3 presents the standard errors (SE), sum of squares (SS), and the number of parameters (k) estimated in a series of naive models. The first two models correspond to the basic Healy model and the DeAngelo model. It is clear that these models do not reduce the volatility of discretionary accruals. On the contrary, the standard error of DA turned out higher than the standard deviation of TA. Therefore, these two models will no longer be considered. NDA values for the rest of the basic models are obtained as the median of the partition, where the partition can be years, industries, year-industry combinations, and their combination with the firm-listing partition. The total number of firm-year observations for each of these naive models is exactly the same, which allows analysis of variance to be applied in order to derive statistical inferences. Table 22.3 shows that each of the three sources of variation identified in section 22.3 makes a slight contribution to the reduction of standard error of DA. The initial benchmarks for the pool, the AMEX and NYSE sample and the NASDAQ samples, are 11.9%, 8.8%, and 13.7% respectively. When time variation is ignored and only industry classification is considered, the SE slowly decreases as the number of industries increases. The reduction from using one industry to five industries is 0.1%. Another 0.1% is gained if 13 industries are used instead of five. Since increasing the number of industries reduces the SE of DA, researchers would logically try to increase the number of industries to the maximum extent. The next industry classification (81 industries) takes advantage of this reduction of volatility of DA. Using SIC information, four-digit codes would be a natural way of classifying companies into industries. However, the number of firms in each four-digit group varies considerably. Some industries contain two to five companies, while other groups would include dozens of companies. By requiring a minimum number of firms per industry, one can develop a grouping methodology. This chapter used the following technique: each year, the number of firms with enough data is determined. If the four-digit SIC code has eight or more firms for each year in the study, the industry is defined as the four-digit SIC code. If in one year of the sample the number of firms within this code falls below 10, these firms will be combined with firms with the closest four-digit SIC code and a matching three-digit code. This process is repeated until a minimum of 10 companies have enough data every year of the sample. A total of 81 industries was obtained through this process.

The expansion of the number of industries to 81 brings a small reduction of 0.4% in the total variation of TA. This difference, however, is statistically significant (using an F-test) for this industry classification, while the reduction of variation for the five- and 13-industry classifications is not. Considering differences

Table 22.3 Standard errors of naive discretionary accrual models, 1989–2003

Type of model for NDA	All firms			AMEX and NYSE			NASDAQ			Combined		
	SS	SD	*k*	SS	SD	*k*	SS	SD	*k*	SS	SD	*k*
Naive model (NDA = 0)	903.1	0.119	0	230.2	0.088	0	672.9	0.137	0			
DeAngelo (NDA = TA_{t-1})	1049.6	0.145	0	233.0	0.104	0	816.6	0.170	0			
Population median	716.2	0.119	1	169.8	0.088	1	543.2	0.137	1	713.0	0.118	2
Industry median (5 industries)	708.3	0.118	5	168.6	0.088	5	537.3	0.136	5	705.9	0.118	10
Industry median (13 industries)	691.8	0.117	13	161.3	0.086	13	528.6	0.135	13	689.9	0.117	26
Industry median (81 industries)	675.3	0.115	81	154.9	0.084	81	517.0	0.134	81	671.9	0.115	162
Yearly median	708.3	0.118	15	168.1	0.088	15	533.9	0.136	15	702.0	0.118	30
Industry year median (5 industries)	699.3	0.117	75	166.9	0.087	75	529.4	0.135	75	696.2	0.117	150
Industry year median (13 industries)	680.7	0.116	195	158.5	0.085	195	518.9	0.134	195	677.5	0.116	390
Industry year median (81 industries)	654.6	0.114	1215	147.6	0.082	1215	496.3	0.131	1215	643.8	0.113	2430

Number of observations for all models is 50,717. Industry membership for the five-industry classification is separated as follows (no. of firm-year observations included in parentheses):

Ind1 = Consumer = Consumer Durables, Nondurables, Wholesale, Retail, and Some Services (Laundries, Repair Shops) (12,049).

Ind2 = Manufacturing = Manufacturing, Energy, and Utilities (14,397).

Ind3 = High-tech = Business Equipment, Telephone, and Television Transmission (12,026).

Ind4 = Health = Healthcare, Medical Equipment, and Drugs (5298).

Ind5 = Other = Mining and Construction, Building Materials, Transport, Hotels, Bus Services, Entertainment (6947).

Industry membership for the 13-industry classification is defined in Table 22.2. Industry membership for the 81-industry classification is obtained as follows:

Each year, the number of firms with enough data is determined. If the four-digit SIC code has eight or more firms for each year in the study, the industry is defined as the four-digit SIC code. If one year of the sample the number of firms falls below 10, we combine that industry with the closest four-digit SIC code with matching three-digit code. This process is repeated until a minimum of 10 companies have enough data every year of the sample. This process generates 81 industries (1215 year-industry subsamples). The average number of firms in the subsamples is 42 (median of 35) and the maximum number of firms is 204.

across time by expanding the sample from one period to 15 years provides a consistent reduction of the standard error of TAs. However, the improvement is not statistically significant.

The separation of firms by the exchange in which where they are listed was the third factor analyzed in this study. Separating firms based on market listing does not reduce the standard error of the combined data much relative to the pooled data. However, doing this creates two different samples with characteristics that differ drastically. As shown in Table 22.3, the standard error of NASDAQ (13.7%) is much higher than that for NYSE/AMEX firms (8.8%). This difference is quite significant. As can be seen from the pooled sample, mixing the volatile NASDAQ firms with the more stable NYSE/AMEX firms produces a considerable standard error of 11.9%. Evidence in Table 22.3 clearly suggests that the NASDAQ and the AMEX/NYSE subsamples should be estimated and evaluated separately, and that aggregation of results should be done with caution.

22.4.2 Results of discretionary accrual models

Having established the initial benchmark and the methodology to estimate the accrual models, this subsection now presents the main results of the chapter. Following the findings in previous subsections, the estimations of accrual models are performed first for the totality of the sample and then repeated for the two subsamples defined by market listing. Since one of the models requires the use of lagged total accruals, one full year of observations is lost. Furthermore, since the Shivakumar model (referred to as 5CFO in Table 22.4) has to estimate eight parameters, some industry-year combinations do not have enough observations to be estimated in the NASDAQ and AMEX/NYSE subsamples. This leads to a reduction of sample size to 49,799 observations. Table 22.4 shows the standard error for the benchmark (the industry median model) and the five models defined in previous sections.

Three observations can be made in relation to the Jones and modified Jones models. First, the contribution of these two models towards the reduction of volatility is rather small (0.5% for the 81-industry classification but only 0.1% when 13 industries are used). The reduction of volatility is not uniform across the 13 industries. For some industries, the volatility decreases as much as 2%, but for other industries using the Jones model actually increases the standard error. Also, results for the modified Jones model and the original Jones model are basically the same, which suggests that the additional variable suggested by Dechow et al. (1995) does not have an important role.

Table 22.4 Standard error of discretionary accruals obtained with five competing models, 1989–2003, full sample

Sample used to estimate models	*N*	Industry	Jones	MJones	CFO Jones	5CFO	AP
Yearly samples of:							
Agriculture	234	0.107	0.073	0.074	0.079	0.065	0.072
Mining and Construction	996	0.139	0.119	0.119	0.099	0.103	0.093
Food	1486	0.087	0.082	0.082	0.075	0.073	0.071
Textiles and Printing/Publishing	3168	0.090	0.091	0.091	0.076	0.075	0.069
Chemicals	1614	0.087	0.081	0.081	0.074	0.073	0.071
Pharmaceuticals	2177	0.121	0.117	0.117	0.119	0.115	0.113
Extractive	2329	0.115	0.123	0.123	0.103	0.095	0.095
Durable Manufacturers	13,890	0.111	0.109	0.109	0.099	0.097	0.096
Computers	6791	0.146	0.151	0.151	0.138	0.131	0.132
Transportation	2823	0.109	0.102	0.102	0.096	0.094	0.084
Utilities	2576	0.068	0.060	0.060	0.052	0.051	0.051
Retail	6,452	0.119	0.115	0.115	0.096	0.096	0.085
Services	5263	0.130	0.131	0.131	0.116	0.114	0.108
All the 13 industries (15 years)	49,799	0.117	0.116	0.116	0.103	0.100	0.097
One industry (15 years)	49,799	0.119	0.119	0.119	0.109	0.106	0.100
Five industries (15 years)	49,799	0.118	0.119	0.117	0.105	0.103	0.098
Eighty-one industries (15 years)	49,799	0.115	0.108	0.108	0.093	0.085	0.089

Industry membership is defined in previous tables. The benchmark model was estimated with the industry median model. All accrual models were estimated using the cross-sectional approach. MJones refers to the modified version of the Jones model. CFO Jones represents the Jones model with one CFO as an additional term in the equation. 5CFO refers to the Shivakumar model, which uses five dummy variables to control for different levels of cash flows. AP refers to the accounting process model introduced by Garza-Gómez et al. (2000). The total number of observations is 49,799 for all models.

On the contrary, results for the models that use cash-flow terms in their specification yield standard errors consistently lower than the benchmark (the industry model). The three model specifications produce lower standard errors than the two basic versions of the Jones model. Among the three models, the AP model has a lower pooled standard error when estimated using one, five, or 13 industries, yet the 5CFO model produces lower error when 81 industries are used. Across industries, it can be observed that the industry identified as Computers has the highest volatility, while Utilities has the lowest dispersion of DA.

The results in Table 22.5 and 22.6 are consistent with those in the pooled sample; the contribution of the Jones models is limited. The 5CFO and AP models are clearly superior to the Jones CFO and other Jones models. They reduce the standard error of TAs for AMEX/NYSE firms by about 2% and that of NASDAQ firms by around 4%. This reduction of dispersion in DAs is critical for all earnings management studies. Lowering the standard error increases the power of the tests. Nevertheless, there is no clear winner between the AP and 5CFO models. For some industries, the AP generates lower standard errors but in others the 5CFO model is better. In order to break this stalemate, other

Table 22.5 Evaluation of discretionary accrual models, 1989–2003, AMEX/NYSE firms

Sample used to estimate models	*N*	Industry	Jones	MJones	CFO Jones	5CFO	AP
Yearly samples of:							
Agriculture	87	0.080	0.060	0.051	0.076	n.a.	0.045
Mining and Construction	586	0.112	0.098	0.098	0.108	0.067	0.070
Food	804	0.078	0.085	0.084	0.091	0.064	0.065
Textiles and Printing/ Publishing	1766	0.068	0.069	0.069	0.070	0.049	0.045
Chemicals	993	0.056	0.060	0.060	0.063	0.046	0.045
Pharmaceuticals	621	0.094	0.104	0.103	0.105	0.077	0.083
Extractive	1412	0.098	0.103	0.103	0.106	0.073	0.075
Durable Manufacturers	5721	0.080	0.081	0.080	0.087	0.065	0.063
Computers	1448	0.116	0.127	0.127	0.130	0.092	0.098
Transportation	1144	0.088	0.088	0.088	0.088	0.069	0.065
Utilities	2031	0.044	0.045	0.045	0.049	0.028	0.031
Retail	2742	0.090	0.092	0.092	0.099	0.064	0.058
Services	2108	0.103	0.102	0.102	0.103	0.082	0.077
All the 13 industries (15 years)	21,463	0.085	0.087	0.088	0.092	0.066	0.064
One industry (15 years)	21,463	0.088	0.087	0.088	0.091	0.074	0.069
Five industries (15 years)	21,463	0.087	0.088	0.087	0.091	0.070	0.066
Eighty-one industries (15 years)	21,463	0.082	0.089	0.089	0.094	0.045	0.053

factors need to be considered. From the point of view of statistical modeling, the AP model would be better because it uses fewer parameters than the 5CFO model. This is important because, as Tables 22.5 and 22.6 show, some subsamples do not have enough observations for the 5CFO to be estimated, especially if the 81-industry classification is used on subsamples based on market listing. Furthermore, the more parameters needed for estimation, the lower the adjusted R^2 that the model will obtain. Finally, since the 5CFO model is designed for cross-sectional estimation, it cannot be used for time-series estimation. On the other hand, since [Δ]CFO, the predictive variable of the AP model, is available time-series wise, this model is well suited for time-series estimation. To try to reach a final conclusion, a new set of statistical tests is introduced in the next section.

Table 22.6 Evaluation of discretionary accrual models, 1989–2003, NASDAQ firms

Sample used to estimate models	*N*	Industry	Jones	MJones	CFO Jones	5CFO	AP
Yearly samples of:							
Agriculture	147	0.119	0.124	0.122	0.124	n.a.	0.072
Mining and Construction	410	0.172	0.156	0.156	0.155	0.114	0.112
Food	682	0.096	0.095	0.095	0.106	0.069	0.073
Textiles and Printing/ Publishing	1402	0.112	0.116	0.116	0.124	0.093	0.088
Chemicals	621	0.119	0.120	0.120	0.122	0.095	0.096
Pharmaceuticals	1556	0.128	0.129	0.129	0.128	0.122	0.119
Extractive	917	0.137	0.157	0.158	0.163	0.113	0.115
Durable Manufacturers	8169	0.129	0.130	0.128	0.137	0.112	0.112
Computers	5343	0.153	0.163	0.161	0.169	0.137	0.139
Transportation	1679	0.120	0.115	0.115	0.117	0.100	0.093
Utilities	545	0.119	0.117	0.115	0.130	0.084	0.091
Retail	3710	0.135	0.130	0.130	0.140	0.110	0.099
Services	3155	0.146	0.150	0.151	0.151	0.126	0.122
All the 13 industries (15 years)	28,336	0.134	0.138	0.138	0.144	0.116	0.114
One industry (15 years)	28,336	0.136	0.139	0.144	0.144	0.123	0.118
Five industries (15 years)	28,336	0.134	0.138	0.144	0.144	0.119	0.116
Eighty-one industries (15 years)	28,336	0.131	0.140	0.147	0.147	0.093	0.103

22.5 Information content of discretionary and nondiscretionary accruals

The results in the previous section provide evidence that the AP model and the 5CFO models are capable of reducing the standard error of discretionary accruals. In other words, these models yield estimates of nondiscretionary accruals that are good enough to capture some of the variation in total accruals. Since many studies have shown that total accruals, defined as the difference between EBIT and cash flows, have explanatory power for future performance, a natural way to assess the goodness of fit of accrual models is to compare how much of the information content of TA is captured in the NDA of competing models. This approach is similar to that used by Subramanyam (1996).

Table 22.7 presents results for three sets of regressions trying to predict next year's earnings $EBEI_{t+1}$ and next year's cash flow from operations CFO_{t+1}. The first set corresponds to the univariate regressions that use current levels of earnings and cash flow from operations as explanatory variables. Since the regressions are used to predict performance one year ahead, some data points are lost. The resulting sample size is 42,591 year-observations. All regressions are done from

Table 22.7 Regressions of measures of future performance on current cash flow and nondiscretionary accruals, 1990–2002

	Dependent variables			
	Next year's earnings $EBEI_{t+1}$		Next year's cash flows CFO_{t+1}	
	Adj. R^2	SE	Adj. R^2	SE
Current performance				
$EBEI_t$	0.165	0.242	0.318	0.121
CFO_t	0.125	0.248	0.402	0.113
Total accruals				
CFO_t TA_t	0.175	0.241	0.432	0.111
Nondiscretionary accruals				
CFO_t $NDA_{t\ (Jones)}$	0.142	0.246	0.422	0.112
CFO_t $NDA_{t\ (Jones\ CFO)}$	0.143	0.246	0.407	0.113
CFO_t $NDA_{t\ (5CFO)}$	0.146	0.245	0.408	0.113
CFO_t $NDA_{t\ (AP)}$	0.156	0.244	0.424	0.111

Sample size is 42,591 firm-year observations. Accrual models were calculated using the cross-sectional method on 13 industries.

a pool and the standard error and adjusted R^2 are reported as means of comparison. The first set of results shows that earnings (EBEI) are more volatile than CFO and therefore cash flow is more predictable than earnings. When a regression is run using TA and CFO as explanatory variables, R^2 increases significantly above the figure obtained in the univariate regressions. Relative to the original explanatory power of CFO, the increases in R^2 were 5% for EBEI and 3% for CFO when total accruals were added to the regressions. This constitutes strong evidence of the information content of total accruals. The contribution of total accruals to explain future performance permits the setting of a benchmark to evaluate the information content of the nondiscretionary accruals obtained from the competing models.

The third set of regressions is done using cash flow from operations and the nondiscretionary accruals estimated with four of the competing accrual models. The higher the goodness of fit of the model, the greater the information content of total accruals that should be captured in NDA and the higher the adjusted R^2. The results show that the NDA from the AP model yields the highest R^2 and the lowest standard error of the predicted variables for regressions of next year's earnings and next year's cash flows.

22.5.1 Sensitivity tests

The results listed in Table 22.7 show that, from the set of accrual models included in this study, the AP model is the clear winner. It produces the lowest standard error of DA estimates and most of the information content of total accruals is kept on the nondiscretionary part. To assess whether the results are robust to different empirical settings, two methodological variations were tested. The first change explored was the use of total accruals calculated with the balance-sheet approach instead of the cash-flow approach, the one that was reported throughout the chapter. Conclusions about the goodness of fit of the models remain unchanged; however, some details about this methodology are worth mentioning. The median of TA calculated with the balance-sheet approach is −4.3% compared to the value of −5.4% shown in Table 22.2. Consistent with Collins and Hribar (2002), accruals calculated from the cash-flow statement tend to exceed (in absolute value) those calculated using the balance-sheet approach. The average difference (in absolute value) between these two estimates is 4.7% (with a median of 2.1%). Due to the requirements of more data items, the sample size for TA_{bs} is smaller than for TA_{cf}. Volatility, however, is significantly larger for TA_{cf} than for TA_{bs}. Nevertheless, as expressed above, the key to reducing the volatility in the sample was the exclusion of all firms having large relative movements in total assets. Ignoring firms that grew more than 100% in total assets or decreased more than 50% of total assets in one calendar year is crucial in this study. It reduces the volatilities of both TA_{bs} and TA_{cf}, which makes them similar to each other after firms with extreme earnings are trimmed. In conclusion, the levels of standard error for discretionary accruals reported in this study depend on how outliers are handled.

The second factor that could modify the main results in the project is how industries are defined. As seen in Tables 22.4–22.6, the AP model does not dominate the other models 100% of the time. It is quite easy then for a researcher to find a different method to group companies in order to favor the Shivakumar model (or a new competing model). Nevertheless, it can be argued that the AP model will be quite robust on large samples like the one used in this study.

22.6 Conclusion

This chapter used a straightforward approach to evaluate discretionary accrual models. Since discretionary accruals are really the prediction error of a model that tries to explain the 'normal' behavior of accruals, its goodness of fit will be crucial to the performance of the discretionary accruals estimates. If the model is weak, all the information contained in total accruals will be left in the discretionary (abnormal) part and incorrect inferences will be made (it will detect earnings management where no management discretion is found or attribute the explanatory power of TA to the discretionary part).

The chapter explored three important sources of variation: time, industry grouping, and market listing. The results show that constructing samples and subsamples across these three variables allows researchers to set a benchmark against which proposed discretionary accrual models can be tested. Results based on a broad sample spanning from 1989 to 2003 indicate that the AP model was the best model in this study.

There are several limitations to this work. First, all the models in this chapter were evaluated using least squares estimation. However, recent work by Kang and Sivaramakrishnan (1995) suggests the use of instrumental variables to estimate accrual models. Furthermore, alternative estimation methods may be needed to further reduce the standard error of accrual models.

Another limitation is that this study did not consider the relationship of discretionary accruals and stock returns. Sloan (1996) reported that accruals have information content to explain future stock returns. Subramanyam (1996), Barth et al. (2001), Collins and Hribar (2001), and Xie (2001) have also studied the role of accrual components in explaining future stock returns. An interesting avenue of future research is to check if the market correctly prices the discretionary and nondiscretionary component of accruals when estimated with superior expectation models.

Notes

1. The original AP model in Garza-Gómez et al. (2000) uses the term $(1/A_{t-1})$ as explanatory variable and is estimated without intercept. In this chapter, the AP model is calculated as shown in equation (22.8). It may be considered that the resulting standard errors are not altered by the choice of intercept. However, average DA shows a large bias when $(1/A_{t-1})$ is used (−2.2%). Since the average DA is expected to be zero, the original version is dropped and only the version shown in equation (22.8) is used in this chapter.
2. The number of firms eliminated using this criterion is as follows: 799 firms whose assets grew between 500% and 1000%; 4406 firms whose assets grew between 200% and 500%, which correspond to about 8% of the firms in the database. Standard error of total accruals, however, decreased more than 35%.
3. Leaving these observations in the full sample does not affect the main conclusions of this study. Nevertheless, estimates of standard error do increase significantly.
4. Dechow et al. (1995) actually reported the standard error obtained from applying the regression explained in McNichols and Wilson (1988) to a random sample of 1000 observations. Though not identical, this measure can also be used to evaluate discretionary accrual models.

References

Barth, M.E., Cram, D.P., and Nelson, K.K. (2001). Accruals, and the Prediction of Future Cash Flows. *Accounting Review*, 76(1):27–58.

Burgstahler, D. and Dichev, I. (1997). Earnings Management to Avoid Earnings Decreases and Losses. *Journal of Accounting and Economics*, 24(1):99–126.

Chaney, P.K., Jeter, D.C., and Lewis, C.M. (1998). The Use of Accruals in Income Smoothing: A Permanent Earnings Hypothesis. *Advances in Quantitative Analysis of Finance and Accounting*, 6:103–135.

Collins, D.W. and Hribar, P. (2001). Earnings-based and Accrual-based Market Anomalies: One Effect or Two? *Journal of Accounting and Economics*, 29(1):101–123.

Collins, D.W. and Hribar, P. (2002). Errors in Estimating Accruals: Implications for Empirical Research. *Journal of Accounting Research*, 40(1):105–134.

DeAngelo, L. (1986). Accounting Numbers as Market Valuation Substitutes: A Study of Management Buyouts of Public Stockholders. *Accounting Review*, 61(3):400–420.

Dechow, P.M. (1994). Accounting Earnings and Cash Flows as Measures of Firm Performance: The Role of Accounting Accruals. *Journal of Accounting and Economics*, 18(1):3–42.

Dechow, P.M., Sloan, R.G., and Sweeney, A.P. (1995). Detecting Earnings Management. *Accounting Review*, 70(2):193–225.

Dechow, P.M., Kothari, S.P., and Watts, R.L. (1998). The Relation Between Earnings and Cash Flows. *Journal of Accounting and Economics*, 25(2):133–168.

DeFond, M.L. and Jiambalvo, J. (1994). Debt Covenant Violation and Manipulation of Accruals. *Journal of Accounting and Economics*, 17(1–2):145–176.

DeFond, M.L. and Park, C.W. (1997). Smoothing Income in Anticipation of Future Earnings. *Journal of Accounting and Economics*, 23(2):115–139.

DeGeorge, F., Patel, J., and Zeckhauser, R. (1999). Earnings Management to Exceed Thresholds. *Journal of Business Research*, 72(1):1–33.

Garza-Gómez, X., Okumura, M., and Kunimura, M. (2000). Discretionary Accrual Models and the Accounting Process. *Kobe Economic and Business Review*, 45(10):103–135.

Guay, W.R., Kothari, S.P., and Watts, R.L. (1996). A Market-based Evaluation of Discretionary Accrual Models. *Journal of Accounting Research*, 34(Suppl.):83–105.

Hansen, G.A. (1999). Bias and Measurement Error in Discretionary Accrual Models. Working Paper, Penn State University.

Healy, P.M. (1985). The Effect of Bonus Schemes on Accounting Decisions. *Journal of Accounting and Economics*, 7(1–3):85–107.

Hunt, A., Moyer, S.E., and Shevlin, T. (1997). Earnings Volatility, Earnings Management and Equity Value. Working Paper, University of Washington.

Jeter, D.C. and Shivakumar, L. (1999). Cross-sectional Estimation of Abnormal Accruals Using Quarterly and Annual Data: Effectiveness in Detecting Event-specific Earnings Management. *Accounting and Business Research*, 29(4):299–319.

Jones, J.J. (1991). Earnings Management During Import Relief Investigations. *Journal of Accounting Research*, 29(2):193–228.

Kang, S.H. and Sivaramakrishnan, K. (1995). Issues in Testing Earnings Management and an Instrumental Variable Approach. *Journal of Accounting Research*, 33(2):353–367.

McNichols, M. and Wilson, P. (1988). Evidence of Earnings Management from the Provision for Bad Debts. *Journal of Accounting Research*, 26(Suppl.):1–31.

Shivakumar, L. (1996). Essays Related to Equity Offerings and Earnings Management. Dissertation, Vanderbilt University, Nashville, TN.

Sloan, R.G. (1996). Do Stock Prices Fully Reflect Information in Accruals and Cash Flows about Future Earnings? *Accounting Review*, 71(11):289–315.

Subramanyam, K.R. (1996). The Pricing of Discretionary Accruals. *Journal of Accounting and Economics*, 22(1–3):249–281.

Teoh, S., Welch, I., and Wong T. (1998). Earnings Management and the Underperformance of Seasoned Equity Offerings. *Journal of Financial Economics*, 50(1):63–99.

Young, S. (1999). Systematic Measurement Error in the Estimation of Discretionary Accruals: An Evaluation of Alternative Modeling Procedures. *Journal of Business Finance and Accounting*, 26(7–8):833–862.

Xie, H. (2001). The Mispricing of Abnormal Accruals. *Accounting Review*, 76(3):357–373.

23

What to Teach? A Comparison of Professional and Paraprofessional Accountants' Views on Accounting Topic Emphasis

Geoffrey Tickell and Kosmas X. Smyrnios

23.1 Introduction

The decades of the 1980s and 1990s heralded many profound changes to Australia's tertiary education sector. Changes included the elimination of the CAE (Colleges of Advanced Education) sector (Higher Education Division, 1993), Technical and Further Education (TAFE) institute mergers (OTFE, 1997), absorption of a number of TAFE institutes into universities (OTFE, 1997), introduction of the higher education contribution scheme (HECS), an increasing number of full-fee-paying international students, an explosion in fee-for-service postgraduate courses (OECD, 1996), and the introduction of full-fee-paying university places for undergraduate local students (AVCC, 1997). These changes have occurred during two decades of increasing higher education participation rates (OECD, 1997), with associated real reductions in government funding (AVCC, 1997). According to Jones (1998), the 1990s saw the beginning of an era in Australia's education whereby university education shifted from education for the elite to education for the masses. Similarly, TAFE enrolments in paraprofessional courses (e.g. Advanced Diploma of Accounting) have also grown significantly (OTFE, 1995).

Concurrent with increasing numbers of university and TAFE graduates is a growing demand by business for employees with tertiary education qualifications (Dusseldorp Skills Forum, 1999). There is little doubt that, on the whole, persons who hold some form of post-secondary school qualification, particularly degrees, are far better placed when competing for full-time jobs than are those without such qualifications. Interestingly, the paradox is that the earlier a person enters the labor force, the weaker are their long-term employment prospects.

The major sector experiencing high employment growth during the previous decade has been the business services area (incorporating accounting, computing, and legal services), with a 60% growth rate compared with 15% for employment overall (Monash University, 1998). Also, figures show that there were more business services graduates entering the workforce than from any other single field. This trend is likely to continue, with the Department of Employment, Education, Training and Youth Affairs (DEETYA) projecting over the next five years a 56% increase in accountants employed compared with a 27% increase in overall employment.

In fact, this increased emphasis by business for employees with degree qualifications in the business services area has prompted an increasing proportion of students completing paraprofessional courses to look to continue their studies at university, thereby completing a degree and meeting the requirements for entry into a profession (Hribar and Heazlewood, 1991). TAFE graduates currently comprise approximately 7% of total commencing students in universities, with the largest numbers being enrolled in business disciplines (Teese, 1997).

One implication of this high demand for business services graduates, and more specifically accounting graduates, by the labor force is that it is imperative that these graduates are appropriately educated. That is, that students graduate with the skills and knowledge required by business. Thus, the question is: What should be taught in undergraduate accounting courses?

The previous two decades has seen continued calls by big business and the accounting profession for a broader accounting curriculum, with increased emphasis on nonspecific accounting units, including communication skills (see Bedford Committee, 1986; Zaid and Abraham, 1994; Federation of Schools of Accounting, 1996; MacCallum, 1997; Koh and Koh, 1998). The Bedford Committee, in recognizing that all professions change over time, were of the opinion that accounting education had lost its relevance to the accounting profession. The Committee could foresee the continuance of the profession expanding into nontraditional fields, with accountants becoming more involved with decision-making processes typical of managers. According to Koh and Koh (1998, p. 297), 'the Committee also noted widespread complaints that accounting graduates do not know how to communicate, do not reason logically, are deficient in interpersonal skills and cannot think creatively and responsibly'. Moreover, Riordan and Sullivan (1998) reported that large accounting firms seek accounting graduates with broad-based general studies background, high-level intellectual skills, interpersonal skills, communication skills, organizational and business knowledge, and detailed accounting knowledge. This broad range of skills demanded from accounting graduates prompted the American Institute of Certified Public Accountants (AICPA) in 1988 to introduce the 150-hour requirement for application for membership of the AICPA from 2000 (see Riordan and Sullivan, 1998), thereby extending the length of a US accounting course.

However, in 1999, in an invited article, the Chair of the Education Committee, International Federation of Accountants, Warren Allen, argued that the accounting curriculum was crowded, the course was too long, and that students graduate with insufficient skills and experience in information technology (Allen, 1999). He suggested that topics such as process improvement, risk management, legislative environment, business ethics, knowledge management, and cross-cultural business dealings should be considered for inclusion in accounting degrees. Allen concluded by stating that accounting education programs urgently need to change and one of those changes should include a much higher level of content in information technology.

The issue of what to teach in higher education accounting courses has previously been considered with research into the views of the accounting faculty (May et al., 1995), nonaccounting faculty (Cherry and Mintz, 1996; Doucet et al., 1998), accounting graduates, and final year accounting students (Mathews, 1990) being undertaken. For example, May et al. (1995) found that the majority of the US-based accounting faculty believed that fundamental changes to accounting curricula are needed. That is, 68% of respondents 'agreed that future accountants are not receiving the preparation they need to meet the demands of the profession' (p. 23). Strong agreement was found for increased emphasis on written and oral communication skills, interpersonal skills, ethical issues, and intellectual skills. These authors concluded that further discussion between the various faculty groups should be implemented to bring about changes quickly and harmoniously.

Cherry and Mintz (1996) investigated the views of the nonaccounting faculty (i.e. management, finance, and marketing) with regard to the focus of introductory financial accounting courses – specifically, the topics covered and skills to be developed. Interestingly, of the five skills nominated (i.e. problem-solving abilities, logical reasoning ability, computer applications, written communication skills, and oral communication skills), respondents regarded none as unimportant and considered problem-solving and logical-reasoning abilities as the most important skills to develop. Cherry and Mintz concluded that the accounting faculty should be careful to explain to their nonaccounting faculty colleagues the reasons for any changes to the amount of emphasis on topics within introductory accounting courses.

Doucet et al. (1998) surveyed the accounting and nonaccounting (i.e. finance, management, and marketing) faculties to determine their level of satisfaction with the introductory accounting unit at their own institution and the degree of importance for topics within that unit. Overall, these authors found that the accounting faculty was the faculty group least satisfied with introductory accounting courses at their own institutions. Also, from a choice of 60 topics, the accounting faculty deemed each topic to be at least somewhat important, with the highest ratings given to financial accounting topics (e.g. income statement use), while management accounting topics (e.g. activity-based costing) tended to receive middling ratings. Accounting faculty ratings were more consistent with finance faculty ratings than with ratings by the management and marketing faculty. As noted by Doucet et al., this similarity is to be expected given the strong emphasis given to financial accounting topics by the finance faculty. Somewhat predictably, the management and marketing faculty preferred increased emphasis on managerial accounting topics. Content analysis of accounting faculty responses noted that recent changes experienced at their own institutions included increased emphasis on writing and computing skills, and less emphasis on bookkeeping (i.e. journal entries, debits, and credits). Doucet et al. (1998) concluded that 'it is incumbent upon all accounting faculty to ensure that the introductory sequence provides the most effective learning experience possible' (p. 494).

Although findings by Cherry and Mintz (1996) and Doucet et al. (1998) are of practical use, they are limited to assessments of introductory accounting units only. That is, subsequent units of accounting are not considered. Given that employers are critical of the limited knowledge of accounting graduates (see Arthur Anderson & Co., 1989), it is imperative that the whole accounting course, and not just the introductory unit, is considered. Furthermore, recent graduates working as practitioners can provide added perspectives to those provided by educators. To this end, it is important that graduates' views are also considered in any discussion regarding university and TAFE accounting curricula.

Approximately 15 years ago, Mathews (1990) surveyed Australia's accounting graduates and final-year students as to their opinions on the emphasis that was given, and should be given, to 14 skills (e.g. computing skills) within an accounting degree course. Interestingly, Mathews found that participants wanted more emphasis on all 14 nominated skills, with only marginal differences being found between student and graduate ratings. The skill area rated highest for further emphasis related to communication skills (e.g. development of self-confidence and interpersonal skills). Mathews concluded that topics should be added or extended to Australian universities' accounting curricula, thereby extending the length of an accounting degree course. Indeed, Mathews's overall recommendation was that the entry requirement to Australia's accounting profession should be four years of university education instead of the present three years. To date, Mathews's overall recommendation has not been adopted. Given that Mathews's findings are from 15 years earlier, there is sound reason to investigate once again graduates' views regarding the level of importance that should be placed on different skills within a higher education accounting course.

Although undergraduate students' and graduates' views have been sought on this topic (e.g. Mathews, 1990), it appears that the opinions of Australia's Technical and Further Education (TAFE) graduates into the amount of emphasis that should be placed on topics within a TAFE accounting diploma have not been investigated. Australia's TAFE institutes have been recognized as sharing with higher education the major responsibility for tertiary education (Dawkins, 1987) and are similar in genre to community colleges in the USA and Canada. They provide vocational and nonvocational educational training ranging from training in recreational and leisure pursuits through to basic employment and educational preparation to trades, paraprofessional and professional levels. The major field of study is in the Business Administration/Economics area. The primary responsibility for administration of the TAFE system lies with Australia's state governments. It is noteworthy that TAFE places are funded by government at a significantly lower amount than are university places (Mackenzie, 1995).

TAFE students undertaking the Advanced Diploma Accounting complete the equivalent of two-years of full-time study (post-Year 12). This award provides them with a qualification for paraprofessional accounting employment (e.g. payroll officer, accounts payable clerk). Many units of the two-year program comprise similar topics to those taught in university accounting degrees (e.g. *Financial Management, Company Financial Reporting,* and *Auditing*), as evidenced by holders of an Advanced Diploma of Accounting being granted up to eight cross credits towards a Bachelor of Accounting. Typically, TAFE students are older and are more likely to be working full-time while studying part-time than are their university colleagues (Lewis, 1994). Given the similar yet different curricula of TAFE accounting courses compared to university accounting courses and the different demographics of TAFE students to those of university students (i.e. older and studying part-time), it is possible that TAFE graduates hold divergent opinions on topic emphasis than those held by their university counterparts.

Accordingly, it is hypothesized that:

> **H1:** *Accounting professionals and paraprofessionals differ in their views regarding the amount of emphasis that should be placed on topics within a tertiary accounting course.*
>
> **H2:** *University graduates' opinions as to the amount of emphasis to be placed on topics within an undergraduate accounting degree have changed over the previous 15 years.*

23.2 Methodology

23.2.1 Participants

Participants were 790 accounting graduates categorized by type of graduate (i.e. university vs TAFE). Of the 790 questionnaires mailed to participants, 312 were returned, representing a response rate of 40%.

23.2.1.1 University graduates

Participants (n = 508) had graduated with a Bachelor of Accounting from either of two Melbourne-based universities. Given the large number of graduates from each university, a stratified (according to year of exit) random sample was selected (see Babbie, 1992; Krejeie and Morgan, 1970). Participants were excluded if they had been enrolled part-time or were full-fee-paying international students.

For the present investigation, ages of participants ranged between 22 and 47 years, with a mean age of 27 years (SD = 4.21 years); 53% were males and over 90% were Australian born. All participants had completed Year 12 prior to commencing university and 83% had completed Year 12 Accounting. Notably, the mean age of participants when commencing university was 19 years (SD = 4.12 years).

With respect to participants' employment details three years post-graduation, 95% are employed full-time in sectors such as Big-Five accounting firms (5%), other accounting firms (18%), other private organizations (67%), the Commonwealth Government (3%), State Government (5%), and education (2%). The vast majority (86%) are working as accountants or in accounting-related positions (e.g. finance analyst). The average gross annual salary is $35,000.

23.2.1.2 TAFE graduates

TAFE students who had graduated from one Melbourne-based TAFE institute with an Advanced Diploma of Accounting were included in the sampling frame (n = 182). Participants were not excluded if they had been studying part-time. The justification for including part-time as well as full-time students is that accurately distinguishing between the two groups (i.e. part-time vs full-time students) is a complicated process associated with limited reliability (see Lewis, 1994). As with the university group, participants were excluded if they were full-fee-paying international students.

Respondents indicated their mean age to be 29 years (SD = 7.80 years), ranging between 21 and 53 years with an average age when starting TAFE of 24 years (SD = 8.07 years). Females comprise 55%, and 65% were born in Australia. Year 12 had been completed by 80% of respondents, with half indicating that they had undertaken Year 12 Accounting. Typically, TAFE graduates had significantly lower Year 12 scores than their university graduate counterparts.

Employment details show that 85% are employed full-time. Notably, Big-Five accounting firms employ none, while 13% are with smaller accounting firms, 70% with other private organizations, 3% with the Commonwealth Government,

3% State Government, 2% local government, and 8% in the education sector. Most (89%) are employed in paraprofessional accounting positions (e.g. bookkeeping, accounts payable/receivable, administration, payroll). The average gross annual salary is $27,500.

23.2.1.3 Instrument

The *Employment and Further Education Questionnaire* (EFEQ) was developed by the principal investigators and adapted from three widely used questionnaires: *Survey of Graduate/Diplomate Employment, Further Study, or Other Activity* (Graduate Careers Council of Australia, 1993), the *1989 National Survey of Graduates Who Qualified for Degrees in Accounting in 1985 and 1987* (Mathews, 1990), and *Accounting Students Characteristics* (Nelson and Deines, 1995). Two versions of the EFEQ were developed, one for each cohort.

Section 1 of the EFEQ requests participants to indicate their gender, current age, country of birth, their Year 12 score, Year 12 Accounting score, age when commencing their tertiary education, and their employment details (e.g. industry sector, type of employment, tasks, and present gross annual salary).

Section 2 of the EFEQ requires all participants to indicate, on five-point Likert scales (1 = *Definitely not* to 5 = *Definitely*), their opinions as to the level of emphasis that should be placed on 19 nominated topics within a Bachelor of Accounting degree course or Advanced Diploma Accounting course (see Table 23.1). Topics range from specific accounting knowledge to general skills. Fourteen items were derived from Mathews (1990). Examples of topics are: *Key accounting skills*; *Skills in financial modeling*; *Knowledge of interaction between accounting and related disciplines*. The remaining five items were developed by the principal investigators. These included: *Skills in dealing with people from different cultures* and *Personal wealth strategies*. This section also included one item asking university graduate participants to indicate whether they feel that the Accounting Degree should be four years long.

The justification for using five-point Likert scales is derived from theory. Likert (1932) recommended this strategy for measuring attitudes. As noted by Alwin (1997), a five-point response format allows respondents to communicate the direction and intensity of their attitudes and also provides a category for *No opinion*. Although these options are also available using seven-point scales, the present investigators wanted to provide respondents with a label (e.g. *Strongly disagree*) for each of the five options. It was recognized by Saris (1988) that labeling each of seven options is difficult and can lead to confusion.

23.2.2 Procedure

The EFEQ was mailed to participants approximately three years following completion of their course. This time interval was selected as it was deemed sufficient time post-graduation for participants to assess the suitability, appropriateness, and relevance of accounting topics within their course of study to their work environment. Questionnaires, with covering letter and reply-paid addressed envelope attached, were mailed to all names provided by the Student Records Office of each institution. Participants completed and returned questionnaires within two weeks of receiving the questionnaire. One month after questionnaires were mailed, reminder letters, with questionnaire and reply-paid envelope attached, were sent to participants who had not replied to the first mailing. No further follow-up was undertaken beyond this point.

23.2.3 Data analyses

Data were analyzed through quantitative procedures using SPSS (Norusis, 2000). Between-group comparisons involving university and TAFE graduate responses were conducted using independent samples *t*-tests.

Principal components analyses were performed on responses for each of the two large groups, reducing items to three common constructs. Finally, a series of independent samples *t*-tests were performed on the three factors derived through principal components analysis to determine group differences (i.e. university vs TAFE graduates).

23.3 Results

> **H1:** *Accounting professionals and paraprofessionals differ in their views regarding the amount of emphasis that should be placed on topics within a tertiary accounting course.*

23.3.1 Descriptive statistics

Group mean scores and standard deviations for all 19 items, ranked from highest to lowest according to university graduates' responses, are shown in Table 23.1. It is noteworthy that mean scores and standard deviations do not vary greatly between the two groups. Also, all mean scores exceed 3, indicating that participants believe that more emphasis should be placed on all nominated topics. Strongest agreement was apparent for computing skills, followed by quantitative accounting skills, with communication skills (oral, written, and interpersonal) also rating highly. This is in line with current thinking by professional accounting bodies both overseas (see Rebele et al., 1998) and in Australia (see Cheng and Saemann, 1997; MacCallum, 1997; Zaid and Abraham, 1994), in dictating that accounting courses should place more emphasis on communication skills.

A series of *t*-tests show significant differences in responses between university graduates and TAFE graduates on only two items: *Skills in operating a small business*, and *Skills in dealing with people from different cultures*. For both items, TAFE graduates were significantly more definite than university graduates that more emphasis should be placed on these two topics (see Table 23.1).

23.3.2 Principal components analyses

In order to parsimoniously reduce 19 items of the EFEQ to a smaller number of factors, exploratory factor analyses, using principal components (with varimax rotation) and maximum likelihood (with oblimin rotations), were performed on the 19 items. Stability of factors was assessed by consistency between these two methods (Gorusch, 1983; Pedhazur and Pedhazur-Schmelkin, 1991). Attempts to factor analyze this measure for all responses (i.e. both groups of participants combined as one) were not successful, as it was not possible to derive stability of factors. Therefore, analysis of this measure was performed on the two groups separately (i.e. university graduates and TAFE graduates), thereby indicating that the two groups hold different views regarding topic emphasis.

23.3.2.1 University graduates

Initial factor analysis, using eigenvalue cutoff at 1.0, generated four constructs. However, consistency between methods (i.e. principal components with varimax rotation and maximum likelihood with oblimin rotations) was not achieved. Stepwise deletion of five items lacking discriminatory power, and forcing remaining items into three factors (after analysis of the scree plot suggested three factors would be adequate), enabled 14 items to load on the same factors under both methods (see Table 23.2). This process led to 53.5% of the variance for the EFEQ being accounted. Bartlett's test of sphericity is significant at $p < 0.0001$ and Kaiser's measure of sampling adequacy is 0.83, satisfying Kaiser's minimum score of 0.60 (Kaiser, 1974). For the present study, constructs were labeled:

Table 23.1 Ratings of more emphasis on topics within a Bachelor of Accounting and an Advanced Diploma of Accounting

Topic	University graduates (n = 226)	TAFE graduates (n = 109)
For accounting courses, more emphasis should be placed on:		
Computing skills	4.50 (0.71)[a]	4.55 (0.64)[a]
Skills in identification, analysis, and resolution of accounting problems	4.26 (0.73)	4.34 (0.66)
Oral expression skills	4.19 (0.81)	4.15 (0.87)
Development of self-confidence and interpersonal skills	4.10 (0.94)	3.99 (0.89)
Written communication skills	4.04 (0.89)	4.13 (0.89)
Key accounting skills (e.g. bookkeeping, budgeting)	4.02 (0.93)	4.17 (0.98)
Skills in financial modeling	3.94 (0.76)	3.93 (0.86)
Development of personal skills such as goal-setting, time management, stress management	3.93 (1.02)	3.77 (1.07)
Skills in locating and using information	3.84 (0.86)	3.89 (0.88)
Skills in operating a small business	3.77 (1.00)	3.90 (0.96)*
Knowledge of interaction between accounting and related disciplines	3.75 (0.85)	3.86 (0.86)
Skills in the analysis and design of accounting systems	3.71 (0.93)	3.80 (0.97)
Skills in the analysis, evaluation, and construction of arguments	3.70 (0.92)	3.62 (0.94)
Personal wealth strategies (e.g. shares, real estate, bonds)	3.65 (1.05)	3.61 (1.09)
Awareness of social and ethical problems in accounting practice	3.55 (0.98)	3.75 (0.94)
Quantitative and statistical skills (not computing)	3.53 (1.02)	3.56 (1.05)
Skills in dealing with people from different cultures	3.29 (1.12)	3.49 (1.27)*
Skills in the design and conduct of research in accounting	3.19 (1.00)	3.50 (0.99)
Appreciation of world politics, different religions, world trends	3.03 (1.10)	3.01 (1.24)

[a] Standard deviations are given in parentheses. 1 = *Definitely not*, 5 = *Definitely*. * $p < 0.05$.

Communication skills, *Quantitative accounting skills*, and *Qualitative accounting skills*. Notably, Mathews (1990) undertook principal components analysis on 14 items common to the EFEQ relating to the amount of emphasis that should be placed on topics within an accounting degree course. Mathews's analysis also revealed three underlying dimensions: *Professional emphasis*, *Communication and interpersonal emphasis*, and *Academic emphasis* (p. 39).

As outlined in Table 23.2, the first factor contained four items reflecting participants' views that increased emphasis in business degrees should be placed on *Communication skills* ($\bar{X} = 3.86$; item loadings range from $r = 0.54$ to $r = 0.82$). The second factor also contains four items reflecting *Quantitative accounting skills* ($\bar{X} = 3.88$; item loadings ranging from $r = 0.62$ to $r = 0.74$), while the third and final factor labeled *Qualitative accounting skills* ($\bar{X} = 3.74$) contains five items with factor loadings ranging between $r = 0.43$ and $r = 0.81$. Cronbach alphas, mean scores, and standard deviations for each factor are reported in Table 23.3. Cronbach's alpha

Table 23.2 Factor matrix of university graduates' opinions as to the amount of emphasis that should be placed on topics within a Bachelor of Accounting

Item (*n* = 226)	1	2	3
Factor 1: Communication skills			
Oral expression skills	0.82		
Development of self-confidence and interpersonal skills	0.73		
Written communication skills	0.73		
Skills in the analysis, evaluation, and construction of arguments	0.59		
Skills in dealing with people from different cultures	0.54		
Factor 2: Quantitative accounting skills			
Skills in financial modeling		0.74	
Skills in identification, analysis, and resolution of accounting problems		0.73	
Skills in the analysis and design of accounting systems		0.72	
Quantitative and statistical skills (not computing)		0.62	
Factor 3: Qualitative accounting skills			
Skills in operating a small business			0.81
Personal wealth strategies (e.g. shares, real estate, bonds)			0.70
Awareness of social and ethical problems in accounting practice			0.54
Development of personal success skills such as goal-setting, time-management, stress management			0.53
Knowledge of interaction between accounting and related disciplines			0.43
Eigenvalues	4.55	1.59	1.36
% of total variance	32.50	11.30	9.70
Cumulative variance	32.50	43.80	53.50

Absolute values below 0.40 were suppressed.

Table 23.3 Correlations, reliabilities, means, and standard deviations for factors on topic emphasis within a Bachelor of Accounting by university graduates ($\alpha = 0.83$)

Factors ($n = 226$)	Factor 1	Factor 2	Factor 3[a]	Mean (SD)[b]
1. Communication skills	0.77			3.86 (0.69)
2. Quantitative accounting skills	0.42	0.71		3.88 (0.64)
3. Qualitative accounting skills	0.42	0.34	0.68	3.74 (0.65)

[a] Cronbach alphas shown on diagonal. 1 = *Definitely not*, 5 = *Definitely*.
[b] Standard deviations are given in parentheses.

for all 14 items is $\alpha = 0.83$. According to Hair et al. (1998), values above $\alpha = 0.60$ are deemed to be acceptable, with higher values indicating higher reliability.

23.3.2.2 TAFE graduates

Utilizing the same 19 items for the degree course evaluation, TAFE graduates were asked to indicate their opinion as to the amount of emphasis that should be placed on topics within an Advanced Diploma of Accounting course. Stepwise deletion of seven nondiscriminatory items, as well as forcing items into three factors, enabled agreement between the two methods. This process led to 61.4% of the variance being accounted for by 12 items loading on three factors (see Table 23.4). All factor loadings exceed 0.40 which, according to Stevens (1996, p. 371), 'are statistically and practically significant', given the sample size of 109. Bartlett's test of sphericity is significant at $p < 0.0001$ and Kaiser's measure of sampling adequacy is $\alpha = 0.83$. Table 23.5 shows correlations, Cronbach alphas, mean scores, and standard deviations for the three constructs for TAFE graduates.

23.3.2.3 University vs TAFE graduates

Nine of 12 items load on the same factors for TAFE participants as for university participants. The exceptions were: *Skills in the analysis, evaluation, and construction of arguments*, which loaded on *Communication skills* for university graduates but *Qualitative accounting skills* for former TAFE students; *Computing skills* and *Skills in the design and conduct of research in accounting*, which received nondiscriminatory coefficients for university graduates but loaded on *Quantitative accounting skills* and *Qualitative accounting skills* respectively for former TAFE students.

Table 23.4 Factor matrix of TAFE graduates' opinions as to the amount of emphasis that should be placed on topics within an Advanced Diploma of Accounting

Item (n = 109)	1	2	3
Factor 1: Qualitative accounting skills			
Knowledge of interaction between accounting and related disciplines	0.74		
Skills in the analysis, evaluation, and construction of arguments	0.73		
Skills in the design and conduct of research in accounting	0.69		
Awareness of social and ethical problems in accounting practice	0.61		
Factor 2: Quantitative accounting skills			
Skills in identification, analysis, and resolution of accounting problems		0.74	
Skills in financial modeling		0.69	
Computing skills		0.69	
Quantitative and statistical skills (not computing)		0.62	
Skills in the analysis and design of accounting systems		0.57	
Factor 3: Communication skills			
Oral expression skills			0.85
Written communication skills			0.84
Development of self-confidence and interpersonal skills			0.67
Eigenvalues	4.6	1.5	1.3
% of total variance	38.3	12.5	10.6
Cumulative variance	38.3	50.8	61.4

Absolute values below 0.40 were suppressed.

Table 23.5 Correlations, reliabilities, means, and standard deviations for factors on topic emphasis within an Advanced Diploma of Accounting for TAFE graduates ($\alpha = 0.85$)

Factors (n = 109)	Factor 1	Factor 2	Factor 3[a]	Mean (SD)[b]
1. Qualitative accounting skills	0.75			3.69 (0.70)
2. Quantitative accounting skills	−0.31	0.75		4.04 (0.60)
3. Communication skills	0.41	0.43	0.81	4.09 (0.75)

[a] Cronbach alphas shown on diagonal. 1 = *Definitely not*, 5 = *Definitely*.
[b] Standard deviations are given in parentheses.

Tables 23.2 and 23.4 show that, although nine of 12 items load on the same three factors for the TAFE group as for the university group, factor loadings were reversed. That is, for TAFE graduates, 38.3% of the variance is accounted for by *Qualitative accounting skills*, while this factor accounts for only 9.7% of the variance for university graduates. Meanwhile, for TAFE graduates, only 10.6% of the variance is placed on *Communication skills*, while university graduates place 32.5% on this factor. Mean scores and standard deviations for each factor, according to major groupings, are shown in Table 23.6.

Independent samples *t*-tests on factor scores reveal significant differences between university graduates and former TAFE students on constructs (all $p > 0.05$). Although these findings demonstrate that views regarding the amount of emphasis that should be placed on broad topic areas (e.g. communication skills) do not differ significantly between TAFE and university graduates, proportions of variance associated with each factor (or construct) differ across groups. Consequently, H1 is partially supported.

> **H2:** *University graduates' opinions as to the amount of emphasis to be placed on topics within an undergraduate accounting degree have changed significantly over the previous 10 years.*

Mathews (1990) reported mean scores for six topic areas relating to the present study: *Key accounting skills* ($\bar{X} = 3.5$); *Computing skills* ($\bar{X} = 3.4$); *Written communication skills* ($\bar{X} = 3.5$); *Oral expression skills* ($\bar{X} = 2.7$); *Skills in the analysis, evaluation, and construction of arguments* ($\bar{X} = 2.8$); and *Skills in the design and conduct of research in accounting* ($\bar{X} = 2.7$). For all six items, mean scores for both groups (i.e. university graduates and TAFE graduates) are significantly higher than those reported by Mathews (see Table 23.1). This finding indicates that, currently, university and TAFE graduates prefer an even greater emphasis devoted to such skills within an accounting degree. Therefore, H2 can also be supported.

Table 23.6 Mean scores and standard deviations on constructs regarding topic emphasis

Factor	University graduates (n = 226)	TAFE graduates (n = 109)
Communication skills	0.03 (0.98)[a]	−0.06 (1.05)[a]
Quantitative accounting skills	−0.04 (0.99)	0.08 (1.03)
Qualitative accounting skills	−0.03 (1.02)	0.06 (0.95)

[a] Standard deviations are given in parentheses.

23.4 Conclusion

Findings reveal that university and TAFE graduates, having worked for approximately three years as professional or paraprofessional accountants, regard that increased emphasis should be placed on all 19 nominated skills in the current tertiary accounting curricula. This outcome is in line with findings 15 years earlier by Mathews (1990), and concurs with calls by professional accounting bodies and big business (Zaid and Abraham, 1994). Meanwhile, comparisons between the two cohorts (i.e. university graduates vs TAFE graduates) are analogous with respect to mean scores yet differ for factor analyses. Interestingly, university graduates prefer to see greater emphasis on *Communication skills*, while TAFE graduates place more emphasis on *Qualitative accounting skills*. This difference could be attributed to different curricula being taught in the different types of tertiary education institution. For example, the Advanced Diploma of Accounting course includes 60 hours of communication skills type units (i.e. *Presenting reports, Negotiation skills, and Dealing with customers and clients*) as compulsory modules to be completed. University curricula for a Bachelor of Accounting, in general, incorporate communication skills within other units rather than as separate units.

An important limitation of this investigation is that participants were drawn from only one TAFE institute and two universities. Thus, it is possible that responses are not representative of Australia's university and TAFE accounting graduates.

Findings from this investigation add to the debate into what topics should be included in tertiary accounting courses by contributing the views of professional and paraprofessional accountants with approximately three years of work experience, alongside the views of business (IMA/FEI, 1994; Zaid and Abraham, 1994), practitioners (Arthur Anderson & Co., 1989), professional accounting bodies (Bedford Committee, 1986), the accounting faculty (May et al., 1995), and the nonaccounting faculty (Cherry and Mintz, 1996). It is apparent from all of these bodies that universities and TAFEs should continue to implement programs that will develop communication skills (including interpersonal skills) and other demanded skills (e.g. computing skills) within each accounting graduate. However, it is important to reiterate that, as such skills are to be developed over the duration of students' course of study and not in introductory accounting units only, it is important to consider accounting curricula beyond the first year.

In conclusion, despite recent changes to broader accounting curricula, graduates continue to hold the view that greater emphasis should be placed on all skills nominated in the present study. It could be argued, as Mathews (1990) did 15 years earlier, that Australia's accounting degree courses should be extended from the present three years to four. To date, Australia's professional accounting bodies have not required four years for membership, despite the 150-hour rule having been introduced in many US states (see Riordan and Sullivan, 1998).

References

Allen, W. (1999). The Future of Accounting Education. *Pacific Accounting Review*, 11(2):1–7.

Alwin, D.F. (1997). Feeling Thermometers Versus 7-Point Scales: Which are Better? *Sociological Methods and Research*, 25(3):318–340.

Arthur Anderson & Co. (1989). *Perspectives on Education: Capabilities for Success in the Accounting Profession*. Arthur Anderson & Co., Arthur Young, Coopers & Lybrand, Deloitte Haskins & Sells, Ernst & Whinney, Peat Marwick Main & Co., Price Waterhouse, and Touche Ross, New York.

AVCC (1997). *Shaping Australia's Future. Investing in Higher Education. The Australian Vice-Chancellor's Submission to the Review of Higher Education Financing and Policy*. Australian Vice-Chancellor's Committee, Canberra.

Babbie, E. (1992). *The Practice of Social Research*, 6th edn. Wadsworth, Belmont, CA.

Bedford Committee (1986). Future Accounting Education: Preparing for the Expanding Profession. *Issues in Accounting Education*, Spring:168–195.

Cheng, R.H. and Saemann, G. (1997). Comparative Evidence About the Verbal and Analytical Aptitude of Accounting Students. *Journal of Accounting Education*, 15(4):485–501.

Cherry, A.A. and Mintz, S.M. (1996). The Objectives and Design of the First Course in Accounting from the Perspective of Nonaccounting Faculty. *Accounting Education*, 1(2):99–111.

Dawkins, J.S. (1987). *Higher Education: A Policy Discussion Paper*. Department of Employment, Education, and Training, Canberra.

Doucet, M.S., Doucet, T.A., and Essex, P.A. (1998). Competencies for the Introductory Accounting Sequence. *Journal of Accounting Education*, 16(3/4):473–495.

Dusseldorp Skills Forum (1999). *The Deepening Divide: A National Perspective on Developments that have Affected 20–24 Year Olds During the 1990s*. Dusseldorp Skills Forum, Ultimo, NSW.

Federation of Schools of Accounting (1996). *FSA Position Paper: 150-Semester Hour Education Requirement*, 1999.

Gorusch, R.L. (1983). *Factor Analysis*. Lawrence Erlbaum, Hillsdale.

Graduate Careers Council of Australia (1993). *Survey of Graduate/Diplomate Employment, Further Study or Other Activity*. Graduate Careers Council of Australia, Melbourne.

Hair, J.F., Anderson, R.E., Tatham, R.L., and Black, W.C. (1998). *Multivariate Data Analysis*. Prentice-Hall, London.

Higher Education Division (1993). *National Report on Australia's Higher Education Sector*. Department of Employment, Education, and Training, Canberra.

Hribar, Z. and Heazlewood, T. (1991). *TAFE Credit Transfers: A Case Study into the Academic Performance of TAFE Entrants in Accounting Degree Courses at CSU-Riverina and CSU-Mitchell*. Charles Sturt University, Wagga Wagga.

IMA/FEI (1994). What Corporate America Wants in Entry-level Accountants. *Management Accounting*, No. 25.

Jones, B. (1998). *Sleepers Wake! Technology and the Future of Work.* Oxford University Press, Melbourne.

Kaiser, H.F. (1974). An Index of Factorial Simplicity. *Psychometrika*, 39:31–36.

Koh, H.C. and Koh, M.Y. (1998). Empirical Evaluation of Accounting Programs: A Proposed Factor-analytic Approach. *Journal of Accounting Education*, 16(2):295–314.

Krejeie, R.V. and Morgan, D.W. (1970). Determining Sample Size for Research Activities. *Educational and Psychological Measurement*, 30:607–610.

Lewis, D.E. (1994). *The Performance at University of Equity Groups and Students Admitted Via Alternative Modes of Entry.* Evaluations and Investigations Program, Department of Employment, Education, and Training, Canberra.

Likert, R. (1932). A Technique for the Measurement of Attitudes. *Archives of Psychology*, 140.

MacCallum, I. (1997). Recruitment. What Skills? *Australian Accountant*, 67(5):18–20.

Mackenzie, B. (1995). *Quality Processes and the TAFE System.* Paper presented at the Australian National Training Authority (ANTA) Conference.

Mathews, R. (1990). *Accounting in Higher Education: Report of the Review of the Accounting Discipline in Higher Education.* Department of Employment, Education, and Training, Canberra.

May, G.S., Windal, F.W., and Sylvestere, J. (1995). The Need for Change in Accounting Education: An Educator Survey. *Journal of Accounting Education*, 13(1):21–43.

Monash University (1998). *Graduate Destination Survey 1998.* Monash University, Clayton.

Nelson, I.T. and Deines, D.S. (1995). Accounting Student Characteristics: Results of the 1993 and 1994 Federation of Schools of Accountancy (FSA) Surveys. *Journal of Accounting Education*, 13(4):393–411.

Norusis, M. (2000). *SPSS for Windows.* SPSS Inc., Chicago.

OECD (1996). *Thematic Review of the First Years of Tertiary Education. Country Note: Australia.* OECD, Paris.

OECD (1997). *Thematic Review of the Transition from Initial Education to Working Life.* OECD, Paris.

OTFE (1995). *Trends in Vocational Training.* Office of Training and Further Education, Melbourne.

OTFE (1997). *Ministerial Review on the Provision of Technical and Further Education in the Melbourne Metropolitan Area.* Office of Training and Further Education, Melbourne.

Pedhazur, E. and Pedhazur-Schmelkin, L. (1991). *Measurement, Design, and Analysis: An Integrated Approach.* Lawrence Erlbaum, Hillsdale.

Rebele, J.E., Apostolou, B.A., Buckless, F.A., Hassell, J.M., Paquestte, L.R., and Stout, D.E. (1998). Accounting Education Literature Review (1991–1997). Part II: Students, Educational Technology, Assessment, and Faculty Issues. *Journal of Accounting Education*, 16(2):179–245.

Riordan, D.A. and Sullivan, M.C.A. (1998). A Moral Perspective of the 150-hour Requirement. *Journal of Accounting Education*, 16(1):53–64.

Saris, W.E. (1988). *Variation in Responses Functions: A Source of Measurement Error in Attitude Research.* Sociometric Research Foundation, Amsterdam.

Stevens, J. (1996). *Applied Multivariate Statistics for Social Sciences.* Lawrence Erlbaum, Mahwah, NJ.

Teese, R. (1997). *Seamless Education and Training: Research Report for the Ministerial Review on the Provision of Technical and Further Education in the Melbourne Metropolitan Area.* Melbourne University, Department of Education Policy and Management.

Zaid, O.A. and Abraham, A. (1994). Communication Skills in Accounting Education: Perceptions of Academics, Employers and Graduate Accountants. *Accounting Education*, 3(3):205–221.

24

Australia's Accounting Education in Perspective

Geoffrey Tickell and Kosmas X. Smyrnios

24.1 Introduction

Australia's tertiary education system has experienced a period of unprecedented change over the past two decades (AVCC, 1997a; Teese, 1997; Anderson, 1998). These changes have occurred in relation to structure, number of enrolments, and typical student demographics, leading to Australia's tertiary sector appearing substantially different today when compared with the early 1980s.

24.2 Higher education in Australia

Based on British universities, Australia's first universities (University of Sydney, University of Melbourne) commenced teaching in the 1850s. By 1914, a university had been established in each of the six states (Sharpham, 1997) and, by 1987, 19 universities had been established throughout Australia. Until 1961, when quotas for university places were first introduced, universities admitted anyone who had completed their final year of secondary school (matriculation). Despite this open policy, only a small proportion of Australia's population attended universities (Pascoe et al., 1997). In 1939, Australia's six universities had a total of 14,000 student enrolments (Harman and Selby-Smith, 1972). The post-World War II period brought significant growth for universities, with increasing demand from students and increasing Commonwealth Government funding. By 1960, enrolments had reached 53,000.

In 1965, in response to the Martin Committee's report into the future of tertiary education (Martin, 1965), the Commonwealth Government established Colleges of Advanced Education (CAEs) by bringing together a collection of nonuniversity institutions, including senior technical colleges. These were joined in 1973 by 30 teachers colleges. CAEs provided advanced learning with a strong vocational orientation (Sharpham, 1997). Progressively, throughout the 1970s, CAEs came to offer vocationally oriented bachelor degrees in the areas of education, business, applied sciences, engineering, and nursing. By 1987, there were 57 CAEs, with total enrolments exceeding those of universities (Sharpham, 1997).

In 1987, the Federal Minister of Education, John Dawkins, announced the end of the binary system of tertiary education and the beginning of a unified national system. The Commonwealth Government set minimum equivalent full-time student units (EFTSU) sizes for universities, which at the time exceeded the size of many CAEs, and universities (Dawkins, 1987). This action prompted universities and CAEs to look for partners. In most instances, CAEs merged with existing universities (e.g. Victoria College merged with Deakin University, and

Chisholm Institute merged with Monash University). However, a number of CAEs became universities in their own right and retained their unique identities. For example, Swinburne Institute of Technology became Swinburne University, and The Royal Melbourne Institute of Technology (RMIT) changed to RMIT University. This process of amalgamation resulted in 36 universities, many with multiple campuses (AVCC, 1997a).

The merging of higher education institutions saw the beginning of an era for Australia, with university education shifting from education for the 'elite' to education for the 'masses'. According to Trow (Sharpham, 1997), education shifts from the elite to the masses when the system provides places for more than 15% of the 'age grade'. In Australia, this process occurred between 1988 and 1990.

In line with trends in other parts of the Western world (e.g. the USA and UK), Australian universities during the 1990s experienced strong demand for undergraduate and postgraduate courses (AVCC, 1996b; Shah and Burke, 1996; Anderson, 1997), with the number of students enrolled in universities in 1996 (i.e. 630,000) almost doubling that of 10 years earlier. During this time, the rate of participation in higher education by 17- to 19-year-olds rose from 109 per 1000 in 1985 to 172 per 1000 in 1995. Meanwhile, participation rates for 20- to 24-year-olds rose from 91 to 151 per 1000 over the same period (West Review, 1997). Overall, participation rates of the 17–64 age group increased from 40 to 54 per 1000 between 1988 and 1997 (AVCC, 1997a).

Increasing demand for university places comes from three principal sources: school leavers, mature-aged first-time enrolments, and postgraduates (AVCC, 1997a).

- *School leavers*. As a result of State and Commonwealth Government policies, and the fall in the supply of employment opportunities for teenagers, Australia's secondary school retention rate to Year 12 has increased markedly (AVCC, 1997a; Pascoe et al., 1997; West Review, 1997). In 1983, fewer than 50% of students completed Year 12. By 1996, the figure was consistently over 70%. Presently, 53% of commencing university students are directly from secondary school and nearly 40% of students who complete Year 12 enter higher education within two years of leaving school (Pascoe et al., 1997).
- *Mature-aged enrolments*. Owing to better employment opportunities for university graduates (Dusseldorp Skills Forum, 1999), there is an increasing number of people wanting, for the first time, to undertake a university

degree. TAFE graduates can be included in this category. Quite often, TAFE graduates decide to continue on to university as they regard their diploma qualification as not providing them with optimum employment prospects (Burns et al., 1992). It is expected that improving cooperation between the university and TAFE sectors through efficient credit transfer arrangements will increase demand for higher education courses from TAFE students (West Review, 1997).

- *Postgraduates.* The number of people returning to university to undertake postgraduate study has also been increasing. With increased credentialism (see NBEET, 1995), workers are often finding that they have to keep improving their qualifications to maintain their current employment status. Also, undergraduates are finding that a postgraduate qualification improves their employability. This is most evident for Arts graduates (Monash University, 1998). The West Review (1997, p. vii) summarized the expected future of Australia's tertiary education:

> 'One thing seems certain. Just as the nineteenth century witnessed the universality of elementary education in the dame school and the second half of the twentieth century witnessed virtually universal secondary education, so the twenty-first century will mark the era of tertiary education for everybody – or almost everybody.'

24.3 Technical and Further Education (TAFE)

Technical and Further Education (TAFE) institutions have been recognized as sharing with Australia's higher education the major responsibility for tertiary education in Australia (Dawkins, 1988). TAFE courses cover a wide spectrum of objectives and client groups, and its student population is representative of the socio-economic composition of Australian society (Dawkins, 1988). Dawkins stated that 'for many, who would profit from higher education, TAFE represents the first contact with education beyond school' (p. 63).

As with universities, TAFE's history dates back to before Australia's federation. However, in contrast to universities, TAFEs have grown on a state-by-state basis, with control and funding for TAFE coming predominantly from state governments, thereby creating marked differences in organizational structure between states. For this reason, this brief history of TAFE will generally be limited to the state of Victoria.

From its beginnings in the early to mid 1800s through to the early 1960s, technical education's emphasis was on secondary education. In 1965, the Victorian Institute of Colleges was established and given the responsibility of coordinating tertiary technical colleges (Anderson, 1997). In 1970, it was proposed by the Director of the Victorian Technical Schools Division that post-compulsory technical education should be separated from junior technical schools (Jackson, 1970).

In 1974, the seminal Kangan Report (ACOTAFE, 1974) provided the 'philosophical and policy basis for the development of a distinctive identity for the technical and further education system in Australia' (Anderson, 1997, p. 3). As a result of the Kangan Report the acronym 'TAFE' was implemented. This report also identified that TAFEs were essentially vocationally oriented and had a different culture to universities. The Kangan Report noted that 'TAFE institutions exist for knowledge users, as distinct from the universities which exist traditionally also for knowledge innovators whose functions include basic research' (p. 45). TAFE enrolments in Victoria at the time were 35% trade courses, 25% paraprofessional courses, 15% preparatory courses, and 15% in hobby-type education. Of the 81,700 students enrolled in 1974, only 6000 (7.3%) were full-time (Anderson, 1997). At the time of the Kangan Report, TAFE qualifications were neither transferable nor nationally recognized.

Following on from the Kangan Report, the Victorian Government in 1980 established the TAFE Board and gave it the responsibility for the TAFE system in Victoria. In September 1981, 20 Colleges of TAFE were incorporated under the Victorian Post-Secondary Education Act 1978 (see Anderson, 1997). Also, eight Colleges of TAFE and TAFE divisions in CAEs were recognized by the TAFE Board. This Act provided the foundation for what TAFE is today and also suggests an insight into why CAEs were more responsive to working cooperatively with TAFE Colleges than were universities. At least two of today's universities (e.g. RMIT, Swinburne) involved both a TAFE component and a College of Advanced Education component within the same institute.

In the early 1980s, a technical secondary school typically operated classes to secondary school students during the day and to part-time TAFE students during the evening. Evening classes involved a combination of vocational classes leading to a certificate and short-term hobby classes. School educators typically taught both secondary school and TAFE students. In 1985, the Victorian Government decided to transfer all TAFE provision from secondary technical schools to the direct control of TAFE Colleges. This decision meant that the Schools Division of the Victorian Education Department was no longer recognized as a TAFE provider.

The TAFE sector continues to experience change. For example, the Victorian State Government is encouraging growth of Vocational Education and Training (VET) outside of the TAFE system by allowing private providers to tender for courses that have been the domain of TAFE. Also, secondary school students have the opportunity to undertake VET subjects during their Victorian Certificate of Education (VCE) in Years 11 and 12.

At present, state governments have responsibility for VET and provide about 70% of funding, with the Federal Government providing the remaining 30% (AVCC, 1997a) of total government funding, accounting for approximately 70% of TAFE institutes' operating costs. The remaining 30% is generated by TAFE institutes' own entrepreneurial activities.

Similarly to higher education, TAFE has experienced considerable expansion over the last three decades. Enrolments have been increasing by approximately 10% each year (State Training Board, 1996; NCVER, 1998). Notably, between 1973 and 1996, Victorian TAFEs experienced a fivefold increase in enrolments, from 81,700 to 386,000 students (see Anderson, 1998). Burke (1996) reported that the largest field of TAFE study is Business, Administration, and Economics, which has shown above average growth and accounts for over a quarter of all TAFE students in vocational streams.

24.4 Increased cooperation between TAFEs and universities

The divergent origins of TAFEs and universities, and the differing ambitions of their clientele, meant that for many years TAFEs and universities neither considered nor needed to cooperate. Until the late 1980s, TAFE's vocational orientation allowed most students to obtain employment immediately after completing their TAFE qualification. Also, the vast majority of TAFE students were enrolled part-time and were often already employed. Meanwhile, universities' traditional clients were school leavers wanting to obtain degree qualifications.

However, higher participation rates by school leavers attending TAFE full-time (Anderson, 1997), increased importance placed on bachelors degrees by the workforce (Dusseldorp Skills Forum, 1999), and greater number of students wanting to progress from TAFE to university (West Review, 1997) has culminated in cooperative arrangements between these two sectors. It is noteworthy that the West Review (1997, p. 3) stated that 'the prevailing system [of tertiary education] has been largely ineffective in managing the interface between the higher education sector and VET sectors'. The West Review encouraged public policy to work towards attainment of a more seamless post-secondary education environment by facilitating maximum flexibility for students both within higher education and between higher education and VET sectors. In recognizing this shift, the AVCC (1997b, p. 4) noted:

> 'The AVCC vision for the 21st century requires closer cooperation, as well as healthy competition, between the sectors (universities, schools, vocational education and training sector, and particularly technical and further education (TAFE)), to improve the choice and quality of educational opportunities for Australian students. While the boundaries may be blurring, the distinctive missions or heartland of each sector remain. Cooperation comes at the intersect. Some universities will be better suited to the TAFE interface and some TAFE institutions will be more in tune to working with universities than others.'

To this end, the AVCC (1997b) established the Australian Credit Transfer Agency so as to 'develop a coherent and workable national system of credit accumulation and transfer for both directions' (p. 24). This action is supported by the OECD, which recognizes that there are major benefits to be gained from closer working relations between universities and TAFEs, especially in course planning and delivery (AVCC, 1996a).

A most recent trend in cooperative arrangements between the two sectors is the increasing number of double university–TAFE award programs. For example, Monash University and Chisholm Institute of TAFE offer a double award program in which students complete a TAFE Diploma in Hospitality Management and then a Bachelor of Business. This blended four-year program provides graduating students with two qualifications.

Although it is generally agreed that TAFEs and universities should enter into cooperative arrangements, a number of proponents (e.g. Business/Higher Education Round Table, 1992; NBEET, 1995; AVCC, 1996a; Teese, 1997) have highlighted the differing mission of each sector and why boundaries should remain. The AVCC, on the one hand, believes that universities discover, preserve, refine, apply, and disseminate knowledge, with the principal aim being to develop intellectual independence, as well as having the principal responsibility for training researchers. On the other hand, TAFE places more emphasis on students achieving defined levels of competencies required by industry. The AVCC (1996a) is of the opinion that 'in a truly diverse system, institutions should seek to cooperate, collaborate as well as compete' (p. 5). The Higher Education Division noted that 'while TAFE's role as a provider of vocational education should be preserved, its geographical spread and accessibility gave it an important role in expanding opportunities for higher education study' (Higher Education Division, 1993, p. 28).

24.5 Lifelong learning

Lifelong learning is not a new concept. The adage 'the longer I live the more I learn' derives from the belief that we learn from our everyday experiences (see Candy et al., 1994). However, the context in which lifelong learning is used in education relates to learning through formal education and training rather than from everyday experiences. Over the previous three decades, there have been a number of government enquiries (e.g. AAAE, 1974; Dawkins, 1987; Higher Education Council, 1990; NBEET, 1995) into lifelong learning. The Kangan Report (ACOTAFE, 1974) referred to a broad strategy of recurrent education encompassing all adult age groups at all levels of education. Dawkins (1987), in his Green (Discussion) Paper, emphasized the need for graduates to learn how to learn and subsequently wrote in the White (Policy) Paper (Dawkins, 1988, p. 68) that 'the principle of lifelong education is now accepted as fundamental to achieving social, cultural, technological and structural change, and to our future economic development'. The Higher Education Council noted the importance of fostering skills that were of long-lasting value and transferable beyond the confines of a single study. Yet again, 1997 saw the West Review (1997) investigating lifelong learning.

In line with developments in Australia, similar discussions have occurred overseas. For example, in the USA, Cross (1987, p. 99) commented that 'lifelong learning has become a lifelong necessity for almost everyone'. The Canadian Corporate Higher Education Forum (1990, p. 17) wrote that 'all educators must be concerned with promoting lifelong learning in their clients'. Likewise, similar reports have emanated from New Zealand (e.g. Ministry of Education, 1992) and the UK (e.g. Wright, 1992).

With respect to the lifelong skills that a graduate should acquire through their university experience, the Business/Higher Education Round Table (1992) indicated that professional knowledge was considered less important than development of skills in communication, decision-making, problem-solving, the application of knowledge to the workplace, working under minimum supervision, ability to work in a team, and the ability to learn new skills and procedures. According to Candy et al. (1994), business and industry sectors hold consistent views. It is noteworthy that, in the USA, undergraduate degrees tend to be more generalist than in Australia. Also, professional (and hence specifically vocational) degrees are taught at postgraduate level. Candy et al. (1994, p. 110) concluded that:

> 'An ideal undergraduate curriculum would provide a systematic and integrated introduction to a discipline or field of study; offer a comparative or contextualized framework for that discipline or field of study; encourage the broadening of the student, and the progressive development of certain generic skills; allow some freedom of choice and flexibility to meet the needs of a range of students; and have structure which explicitly devolves to learners a greater responsibility for self-direction.'

The curriculum of TAFE certificates and diplomas concentrate on the technical content of the respective vocation. In contrast, the university undergraduate curriculum, although varying somewhat depending on the degree course, is broader based and far more in tune with the aspirations of lifelong education. In line with the philosophy of lifelong learning, Gonczi (1997) emphasized that learning how to learn is more important than the assimilation of knowledge, and that lifelong learning is essential for most occupations in this era of continuous change.

24.6 Seamless education

It is generally accepted that it is inefficient for students to repeat subjects in which they have demonstrated competencies (Beazley, 1992; Haydon, 1995). As such, principles of credit transfer, advanced standing, cross-credits, and recognition of prior learning have evolved whereby students are given opportunities to reduce the number of subjects necessary to complete their course of studies because they have successfully completed similar subjects. This practice has led to the objective of seamless education. Teese (1997, p. 2) argued that 'in a seamless education and training system, there are multiple points of entry to each sector which allow individuals to build on learning and adapt to changing circumstances'.

Seamless education is occurring between schools and VET. For example, in 1997, 8000 high-school students undertook TAFE modules for which they are eligible for advanced standing, should they enter a TAFE course (Gonczi, 1997). TAFE and university sectors have also cooperated to the extent that about 29% of all degree courses are subject to credit transfer arrangements, mainly in the fields of engineering, business studies, and applied science and technology

(NBEET, 1995). Meanwhile, degree graduates are increasingly enrolling in TAFE courses to improve their vocational skills (Golding et al., 1996; Teese, 1997). For example, in 1996 the West Review (1997) reported that, while 42,800 university graduates undertook study in TAFE, TAFE study was the basis for admission to university for 11,800 (6% of total) commencing undergraduates.

Although universities are becoming more receptive to recognizing prior formal education, as evidenced by the increase in credit transfer arrangements and the AVCC (1997b) establishing the Australian Credit Transfer Agency, universities are reluctant to give recognition for knowledge acquired informally. TAFEs, however, generally recognize that it is possible for a person to acquire knowledge via employment rather than being in class (e.g. knowing how to use a software package), and so grant a cross-credit. This process is usually called recognition of prior learning (RPL).

Despite Teese's (1997) encouragement for seamlessness, he indicates that it should not be overstressed. According to Teese, TAFE should not be seen merely as a stepping stone to university. He stated that there are considerable differences between the two sectors such as different student intakes, program orientation, funding arrangements, administration, governance, public prestige, and cultural reference points. He explains that 'to have TAFE as a stepping stone to university would result in severe tensions because of the much weaker academic profile of students entering TAFE' (p. 3). Meanwhile, the 'big business' sector of Australia believes that students who complete Year 12 have a right to some form of post-secondary education, but not necessarily a university degree (Business/Higher Education Round Table, 1992). To alleviate the pressure on universities as a result of the increased demand for skills training, business is supportive of consideration being given to the American community college and two-year college systems prior to university entrance as an alternative to the current system of tertiary education in Australia. It proposes that TAFE be involved in such a structure (see Business/Higher Education Round Table, 1992).

Despite their totally different origins, culture, clientele, and funding arrangements, this decade has heralded many cooperative arrangements between university and TAFE sectors so that the seamless education concept can be fulfilled. These arrangements have led to some universities becoming multi-sector institutions by absorbing TAFE institutes. Furthermore, given the recent forced mergers of a number of TAFEs in the Melbourne metropolitan area (see OTFE, 1997), it appears that this absorption process might continue.

One of the disciplines for which cooperation between universities and TAFE is paramount, so as to avoid unnecessary duplication, and which has been one of the forerunners for credit-transfer advances, is accounting. It is this area of learning that is reviewed in the next section.

24.7 The accounting profession and accounting education in Australia

A review of the literature (Freidson, 1983; Abbot, 1988; Dezalay, 1995) suggests that there are differing opinions as to whether accounting can be regarded as a profession. Unlike the professions of medicine, law, dentistry, veterinary science, architecture, psychiatry, pharmacy, and actuaries, there are no laws in Australia preventing people from calling themselves accountants (Mathews, 1990). A person is not required to hold any qualifications to work as an accountant, although persons carrying out the specialized areas of accounting, such as auditors, liquidators, receiver-managers, and tax agents, do require registration by a government authority. Predictably, the Institute of Chartered Accountants in Australia (ICAA) and CPA Australia, as well as accounting bodies overseas (e.g. the American Institute of Certified Public Accountants), regard accounting as a profession (Carey, 1969; Jeffrey, 1995). This view has also been confirmed by independent critics (Abbot, 1988; Freidson, 1983). West (1996) argued that 'the various privileges offered to accounting bodies including monopoly, self-regulation, high social standing, and responsibilities for developing accounting standards enforceable by law' constitutes a profession. Others (Zeff, 1987; Briloff, 1990; Tweedie, 1993; Mitchell et al., 1994) are uneasy about the certainty of regarding accounting as a profession. Despite these differences in views, for the purposes of this article accounting is regarded as a profession.

Discussion of accounting as a profession is important as it is the professional accounting bodies around the world, especially in the USA, Australia, and New Zealand, that influence, if not determine, accounting education in tertiary institutions. An example of this influence is the accreditation process undertaking by Australia's universities with Australia's professional accounting bodies (see Mathews, 1990).

Requirements to become a professional accountant are regulated by the professional bodies of each country and, although similar, differences do exist. A review of the requirements for nations of the Western world reveal that, to become a professional qualified accountant, a person is firstly required to complete an accredited course from an accredited tertiary institution (typically a bachelor's degree in commerce or business), and then complete a postgraduate program of professional-entry exams administered by the accounting bodies (e.g. CPA, Professional Year) combined with relevant work experience. Once qualified, a professional accountant is required to undertake a minimum number of hours per year of professional education to maintain their title. This is the situation in Australia, with the ICAA and CPA Australia having almost identical membership requirements.

An accounting degree in Australia is usually incorporated into a Bachelor of Business or a Bachelor of Commerce with a major in accounting. A minimum of three years (i.e. six semesters, 24 courses) of full-time higher education study is required. To qualify for entry into CPA Australia or the ICAA, students are required to complete specified courses within the 24-course degree. These typically include two introductory accounting courses, two financial accounting courses, two management accounting courses, two economics courses, one finance course, and one auditing course. In the USA, an accounting graduate has most likely completed five years of higher education study: two years of liberal studies, two years of business and general accounting education, and a fifth (graduate) year of specialized accounting preparation (Mathews, 1992). This five-year program stemmed from recommendations made by the Bedford Committee (1986). An overview of the Bedford Committee's 28 recommendations was for accounting education to be broader and to adopt a more active role for students in learning.

The Bedford Committee, in recognizing that all professions change over time, were of the opinion that accounting education had lost its relevance to the accounting profession, stating that 'accountants in government, industry, and public practice are providing services ranging from data collection and analysis to the installation and operation of computer-based information systems and to strategic planning and implementation' (p. 171). The Committee could foresee the continuance of the profession expanding into nontraditional fields, with accountants being more involved with the decision-making process. As such, the Committee recognized that 'the current content of professional accounting education, which has remained substantially the same over the past 50 years, is generally inadequate for the future accounting professional' (p. 172). The Committee stated that there was a widening gap between what accountants do and what accounting educators teach. It was of the opinion that there was a continuing trend by the general public that professional accountants should have a general manager's perspective and to understand national goals, in addition to qualifying as a technical expert.

In line with other reports of the time into American higher education (Study Group, 1981), the Bedford Committee called for an expansion of liberal education requirements, stating that 'students should possess a knowledge of humanities, arts, and science' (p. 181). The overwhelming resolution of the Committee was for a broader focus in courses. The Committee also called for an increase in the importance of lifelong learning so that accountants can keep up to date with their changing profession.

In response to the Bedford Committee's recommendations, the American Accounting Association (AAA) established the Accounting Education Change Committee (AECC) to further investigate and where appropriate implement changes. The AECC's first Position Statement (AECC, 1990) noted that accounting education should develop, in students, skills and abilities needed for success in the accounting profession including intellectual, interpersonal, and communication skills.

The AECC (1990), in its Position Statement No. 1, outlined its view that an accounting program is intended to prepare students to become professional accountants, not to be professional accountants, stating that pre-entry education should lay the base on which lifelong learning can be built. The AECC discussed course content in terms of four educational components: general education, general business, general accounting, and specialized accounting education.

24.8 Accounting education in Australia

In a major review of accounting education in Australian universities and CAEs, the Mathews Committee (1990) recommended strongly that undergraduate accounting programs be lengthened from three years to four years. The Committee stated:

> 'The existing undergraduate program is failing in its attempt to achieve three educational objectives within a three year degree – to provide a broad-based general education, to provide a specialized professional education to meet the membership requirements of the accounting profession, and to prepare students for a career in business management.'

After surveying accounting students, graduates, and employers, Mathews (1990) found that students and graduates overwhelmingly criticized accounting courses for not being practical enough and related to the world of business. Small chartered accounting firms agreed, complaining that many graduates do not know a debit from a credit. Similarly, employers stressed that lack of communication skills represented the area of greatest deficiency. Employers also noted that graduates had weaknesses in taxation law, government accounting, management accounting theory, business acumen, entrepreneurial skills, and small business management. As well, employers supported an increased emphasis on the development of computing skills.

The Committee highlighted that existing undergraduate accounting curricula were restricted by the requirements of professional accounting bodies; that courses in accounting needed to be more conceptual and less procedural; and that computing skills and communication skills needed to be more highly developed in undergraduates. The Committee recommended that CPA Australia and the ICAA should require the equivalent of a fourth year of full-time study as a prerequisite for membership of their bodies at an associate level. The Committee wanted the fourth year to be phased in between 1992 and 1995. To date, this recommendation of a four-year requirement for professional membership has not been adopted by the accounting professions.

In line with recommendations of the Mathews Committee and the Bedford Committee, and as a result of the advanced and specialized skills necessary to meet expanding needs of the accounting profession, Australia in the 1990s has seen an increase in the range and number of honours and masters courses in accounting (Romano and Smyrnios, 1996). Enrolments have grown significantly.

24.9 Accounting education in TAFE

A review of the literature reveals practically no research into the development of accounting education in TAFE. However, a review of courses offered in the discipline of accounting in TAFE over the previous 20 years shows a history of changes in curriculum and nomenclature. For example, in the late 1970s, students undertaking accounting studies at TAFE enrolled in the Certificate in Accounting. This course was the equivalent of one year of full-time study, although most students studied part-time (Lewis, 1994). In 1985, a curriculum change and name change meant that students studied an Advanced Certificate in Accounting (again, one year full-time), and then another year of studies for an Associate Diploma of Business (Accounting). In 1997, curriculum and name changes converted the first year to a Diploma of Accounting and the second year to an Advanced Diploma of Business (Accounting).

24.10 Conclusion

In line with other Western nations, the 1980s and 1990s have seen an increase in demand for places in Australia's universities and TAFE institutes. Associated with this increase has been further demand for TAFE graduates wanting to transfer to university. TAFE students' desire to complete a degree has largely been created by employer demands, especially in accounting. Recent times have evidenced increased cooperation between universities and TAFE institutes and the proliferation of different tertiary programs (e.g. credit transfer, degree-articulation programs, and double award programs).

References

AAAE (1974). *Lifelong Education: Conditions, Needs, Resources.* Australian Association of Adult Education, Canberra.

Abbot, A. (1988). *The System of Professions: An Essay on the Division of Expert Labour.* University of Chicago Press, Chicago.

ACOTAFE (1974). *TAFE in Australia: Report on the Needs in Technical and Further Education (Kangan Report),* Volume 1. Australian Committee on Technical and Further Education, Canberra.

AECC (1990). Objectives of Education for Accountants: Position Statement Number One. *Issues in Accounting Education,* 5(Fall):307–312.

Anderson, D. (1997). *Growth and Flux: The Development and Organisation of TAFE in Victoria. Final Report to the Ministerial Review on the Provision of TAFE in Melbourne Metropolitan Area.* Centre for Economics of Education and Training, Monash University, Melbourne.

Anderson, D. (1998). Chameleon or Phoenix: The Metamorphosis of TAFE. *Australian and New Zealand Journal of Vocational Educational Research,* 6(2):1–44.

AVCC (1996a). *AVCC Submission into the Inquiry into the Appropriate Roles of Institutions of Technical and Further Education.* Australian Vice-Chancellors' Committee, Canberra.

AVCC (1996b). *Demand for a University Education Remains High (21/96).* Australian Vice-Chancellors' Committee, Canberra.

AVCC (1997a). *Shaping Australia's Future. Investing in Higher Education. The Australian Vice-Chancellors' Submission to the Review of Higher Education Financing and Policy.* Australian Vice-Chancellors' Committee, Canberra.

AVCC (1997b). *Universities Move to a National System of Credit Transfer for Vocational Courses, including TAFE.* Australian Vice-Chancellors' Committee, Canberra.

Beazley, K.C. (1992). *Credit Transfer and Related Issues: First Annual Report of the National Board of Employment, Education and Training.* National Board of Employment, Education, and Training, Canberra.

Bedford Committee (1986). Future Accounting Education: Preparing for the Expanding Profession. *Issues in Accounting Education,* Spring:168–195.

Briloff, A.J. (1990). Accountancy and Society: A Covenant Desecrated. *Critical Perspectives on Accounting,* 1(1):5–30.

Burke, G. (1996). *Dimensions of VET in Australia.* ACER, Centre for the Economics of Education and Training, Monash University, Clayton.

Burns, B., Davey, B., Hill, G., and Leveson, L. (1992). *Articulation and Credit Transfer: A Study of TAFE Accounting Students who Articulated into RMIT-Coburg and La Trobe University, 1987–1992.* Committee to Facilitate Credit Transfer in the Northern Region and Northern Industry Education and Training Link (NIETL).

Business/Higher Education Round Table (1992). *Education for Excellence.* Business/Higher Education Round Table Ltd, Camberwell, Australia.

Canadian Corporate Higher Education Forum (1990). *To Be Our Best: Learning for the Future.* Canadian Corporate Higher Education Forum, Montreal.

Candy, P., Crebert, G., and O'Leary, J. (1994). *Developing Lifelong Learners Through Undergraduate Education.* National Board of Employment, Education, and Training, Canberra.

Carey, J.L. (1969). *The Rise of the Accounting Profession: From Technician to Professional, 1896–1936.* American Institute of Certified Public Accountants, New York.

Cross, K.P. (1987). The Changing Role of Higher Education in the United States. *Higher Education Research and Development*, 6(2):99–108.

Dawkins, J.S. (1987). *Higher Education: A Policy Discussion Paper.* Department of Employment, Education, and Training, Canberra.

Dawkins, J.S. (1988). *Higher Education: A Policy Statement.* Ministry of Education, Canberra.

Dezalay, Y. (1995). 'Turf Battles' or 'Class Struggles': The Internationalization of the Market for Expertise in the 'Professional Society'. *Accounting, Organizations and Society*, 20(1):103–110.

Dusseldorp Skills Forum (1999). *The Deepening Divide: A National Perspective on Developments that have Affected 20–24 Year Olds During the 1990s.* Dusseldorp Skills Forum, Ultimo, NSW.

Freidson, E. (1983). The Theory of Professions: State of the Art. In: *The Sociology of the Profession* (Dingwall, R. and Lewis, P., eds), pp. 19–37. Macmillan, London.

Golding, B., Marginson, S., and Pascoe, R. (1996). *Changing Context, Moving Skills: Generic Skills in the Context of Credit Transfer and the Recognition of Prior Learning.* National Board of Employment, Education, and Training, Canberra.

Gonczi, A. (1997). Future Directions for Vocational Education in Australian Secondary Schools. *Australia and New Zealand Journal of Vocational Education*, 5(1):77–108.

Harman, G.S. and Selby-Smith, C. (1972). *Australian Higher Education System: Problems in a Developing System.* Angus & Robertson, Sydney.

Haydon, A.P. (1995). *Credit Transfer: Better Access, Lower Costs.* Australian Vice-Chancellors' Committee, Canberra.

Higher Education Council (1990). *Higher Education: The Challenges Ahead.* Higher Education Council, Canberra.

Higher Education Division (1993). *National Report on Australia's Higher Education Sector.* Department of Employment, Education, and Training, Canberra.

Jackson, E.T. (1970). *The Future Role and Operation of Technical Schools and Colleges.* Education Department of Victoria, Melbourne.

Jeffrey, B. (1995). From the President. *Australian Accountant*, 65(3), 2 March.

Lewis, D.E. (1994). *The Performance at University of Equity Groups and Students Admitted Via Alternative Modes of Entry.* Evaluations and Investigations Program, Department of Employment, Education, and Training, Canberra.

Martin, C. (1965). *Tertiary Education in Australia: Report of the Committee on the Future of Tertiary Education in Australia.* Committee on the future of tertiary education in Australia, Melbourne.

Mathews, M.R. (1992). Changing Accounting Education: The American Experience. *Accounting Forum*, 2(4):91–105.

Mathews, R. (1990). *Accounting in Higher Education: Report of the Review of the Accounting Discipline in Higher Education*. Department of Employment, Education, and Training, Canberra.

Ministry of Education (1992). *Education for the 21st Century: A Discussion Document*. Ministry of Education New Zealand, Wellington.

Mitchell, A., Puxty, A., Sikka, P., and Willmott, H. (1994). Ethical Statements as Smokescreens for Sectional Interests: The Case of the UK Accountancy Profession. *Journal of Business Ethics*, 13(1):39–51.

Monash University (1998). *Graduate Destination Survey 1998*. Monash University, Clayton.

NBEET (1995). *Cross-sectoral Collaboration in Post-secondary Education and Training*. National Board of Employment, Education and Training, Canberra.

NCVER (1998). *TAFE Graduate Destination Survey 1998*. National Centre for Vocational Education Research, Leabrook, SA.

OTFE (1997). *Ministerial Review on the Provision of Technical and Further Education in the Melbourne Metropolitan Area*. Office of Training and Further Education, Melbourne.

Pascoe, R., McLelland, A., and McGaw, B. (1997). *Perspectives on Selection Methods for Entry into Higher Education in Australia*. National Board of Employment, Education, and Training, Canberra.

Romano, C.A. and Smyrnios, K.X. (1996). Accounting Honours Programmes: Perceived Benefits. *Accounting Education*, 5(3):233–244.

Shah, C. and Burke, G. (1996). *Student Flows in Australian Higher Education*. Department of Employment, Education, and Training, Melbourne.

Sharpham, J. (1997). The Context for New Directions: Ringing the Changes: 1983–1997. In: *Australia's Future Universities* (Sharpham, J.H., ed.), pp. 17–35. University of New England Press, Armidale.

State Training Board (1996). *Annual Report 1995/96*. State Training Board, Melbourne.

Study Group (Cartographer) (1981). *Involvement in Learning: Realizing the Potential of American Higher Education. Study Group on the Conditions of Excellence in American Higher Education.*

Teese, R. (1997). *Seamless Education and Training: Research Report for the Ministerial Review on the Provision of Technical and Further Education in the Melbourne Metropolitan Area*. Department of Education Policy and Management, Melbourne University.

Tweedie, D. (1993). The Accountant: A Tradesman or a Professional? In: *Philosophical Perspectives on Accounting* (Mumford, M.J. and Peasnell, K.V., eds), pp. x–xxv. Routledge, London.

West, B.P. (1996). The Professionalism of Accounting: A Review of Recent Historical Research and its Implications. *Accounting History*, 1(1):77–102.

West Review (1997). *Review of Higher Education Financing and Policy*. Department of Employment, Education, Training, and Youth Affairs, Committee for the Review of Higher Education Financing and Policy Canberra (West, R., Chair).

Wright, P.W.G. (1992). *Learning Through Enterprise*. Society for Research in Higher Education and Open University Press.

Zeff, S.A. (1987). Does the CPA Belong to a Profession? *Accounting Horizons*, 1(June):65–68.

Index

Accountants, educating *see* Educating accountants, what to teach, a study from Australia
Accounting certification, transition economies, 218–20
Accounting Series Release 190 (ASR 190), 45
Accounting standards:
about accounting standards, 3
see also Financial Accounting Standards Board (FASB); International accounting standards; International Accounting Standards Board (IASB); International Accounting Standards (IAS) 39: Financial Instruments: Recognition and Measurement; International Financial Reporting Standards (IFRS)
Accruals *see* Discretionary accruals models, empirical evaluation
Arbitrage and market ordering, 88–9
Armenia:
and IFRS, 202–3
translation problems, 206–7
university curriculum reform, 209
Asset revaluation *see* Brazil, revaluation of fixed assets and future performance
Asset stripping, 43
Assets, cash flow from:
lower of cost and market measure of, 119, 120
present value of estimated future, 119
realizable value measure of, 119, 120–1
Assets, fixed *see* Fixed assets
Audits *see* Performance audits
Australia, accounting education, 569–84
about Australian education, 571–3
accounting education, 582–3
and accounting as a profession, 580–2
AVCC activity, 576
Bedford Committee, 581–2
Chartered Accountants, 580
higher education, 571–3
Kangan Report, 574
lifelong learning, 577–8
Martin Committee's report, 571
Mathews Committee (1990), 582–3
mature-aged enrolments, 572–3
postgraduates, 573
school leavers, 572
seamless education, 578–80
Technical and Further Education (TAFE), 573–5, 578–9, 583–4
accounting education within, 583
unified national education system, 571–2
university/TAFE cooperation, 575–7
Vocational Education and Training (VET), 575
see also Educating accountants, what to teach, a study from Australia
Australia, executive option schemes:
about executive options, 389–90, 398
cost as an expense, 390
estimated costs, 396–8
holding concentrations, 394–5
market factors, 393
prevalence of, 390–1
size, activity and concentration observations, 392–6
study classification, 391
Australia, hybrid securities in listed corporations, 367–84
about the Australian market, 369–70
about the hybrids market, 370–5, 383–4
cash flow issues, 381
fragmentation issues, 372
gross issuance by security type, 372–3
hybrid impact measurement, 375–6
income securities, 372–4
Woolworths Income Note study (WINs), 376–7
market capitalisation impact, 382
perpetual step-up securities, 372–4
Franked Unsecured Equity Linked Securities study (FUELS), 378–9
reclassification issues, 380–1
reset convertible preference shares, 372–4
David Jones Ltd. study, 377–8
results of study, 376–82
Australia, international convergence, 225–61
about the Australian economy, 227–8
about the future, 258–61
accounting regulation models, 230
Accounting Standards Review Board (ASRB), 228, 235–8, 240–3
Australian Accounting Standards Board (AASB), 243–54, 256–60
Australian boards/committees, 228, 231–2
Australian Stock Exchange (ASX), 227
corporatism and legalism, 230
global harmonization models, 228–9
standard setters, 229
standard setting and international harmonization:
1970–1983, 230–5
1984–1988, 235–40

1988–1990, 240–3
1991–1999, 243–52
2000 onwards, 252–8
true and fair view standards, 235

Balkan countries:
and IFRS, 203–4
translation problems, 208–9
see also Bosnia
Banks, about banks/bank deposits, 83–4
Barings Bank plc. collapse, 510
Bosnia:
and IFRS, 203
translation problems, 208–9
university curriculum reform, 210
Brazil, revaluation of fixed assets and future performance, 169–87
about Brazilian asset revaluation, 171–3
asset revaluation research, 178–9
Brazilian corporate financial reporting model, 175–6
Brazilian financial system, 174–7
Brazilian GAAP for revaluation, 174–8
company law on revaluation since 1976, 177
descriptive statistics used, 180, 181
future research implications, 185–7
governance model as an insider model, 178
market-based international accounting research, 179–80
non-Brazilian comparisons, 174–7
research design and results:
future firm performance, 180–2, 183
market-based tests, 182–4, 185
tests controlling for debt-to-equity ratios, 184, 186–7
revaluation desirability issues, 177–8
British Bankers Association (2000), 68

Capital budgeting, 89–90
Capital market:
and accounting measurement, 68
and the commodity markets, 62–6
and fair value accounting, 68–9
market value of firm/shares, 66–71
past and expected performances, 69–70
recoverable cost, 67
role and psychological effect, 66–71
Cash-flow process, 103–4
Commodity and capital markets, 62–6
Contracting, and FV accounting, 144–6
Credit, and cash flow accounting, 102–3
Current cost accounting, 46

Data envelopment analysis (DEA), 517
Decision-making and risk:
about decision making, 59–62
and fair value accounting, 79–80
see also Capital market; International accounting standards; Risk management and performance measurement
Delaware incorporation analysis, 151–65
about Delaware, 153–4, 165
data sample, 156–60
Delaware value premium, 154–6, 162–5
descriptive statistics, 160–2
hypothesis development, 154–6
Discretionary accruals models, empirical evaluation, 523–47
about accruals, 525–7, 546–7
earnings smoothing, 525
estimating discretionary accruals, 527–30
basic accrual models, 528–9
cross-sectional method, 528
time series approach, 527–8
evaluation procedures, 536–43
about evaluation, 536–7
results of models, 540–3
standard errors, 538–40
total accruals, 536–8
generally accepted accounting principles (GAAP), 525
industry model, 529
information content, 544–6
limitations, 546–7
models:
5CFO model, 540–1
AP model, 526–7, 541–3, 544
DeAngelo (1986) model, 525, 529
Garza-Gómez model, 530
Healy (1985) model, 525, 528
Jones (1991) model, 525–6, 528–30, 537, 540–3
nondiscretionary accruals, 544
sensitivity tests, 545–6
total accruals:
calculation, 531–2
NYSE/AMEX/NASDAQ firms, 532–6
sample/descriptive statistics, 532–6
total accruals (TAs), 530–6, 545

Educating accountants, what to teach, a study from Australia, 549–66
about educating accountants, 551–5, 565–6
business needs/requirements, 552

Colleges of Advanced Education (CAE), 551
findings of study, 565–6
Mathews R. skills survey/recommendations, 554
methodology of study, 555–8
analysis method, 558
Employment and Further Education Questionnaire (EFEQ), 557
procedure, 558
TAFE graduate participants, 556–7
for university graduate, 556
need for broad education, 552–4
result:
TAFE graduates, 562–4
university graduates, 559–64
results, 558–64
descriptive statistics, 558–9
Technical and Further Education (TAFE) institutes, 551, 555
see also Australia, accounting education
Employee share options (ESOs), 325–44
about ESOs, 327–9, 340–4
ASB/IASB on financial statements quality, 333, 340–1
as a compensation expense, 330–1
directors and share options, 330
ESO nontransferability, 333
exercise date, 331–2
fair value of options, 329–30, 332–3
FASB influence, 330
fixed share option plans, 329
grant date, 331–2
literature review, 329–33
Offering Memorandum, 336
Share-Based Payment ASB Discussion Paper, 332–3, 340, 343
traded options, 332
value and accounting income, 329–31
vesting date, 331–2, 333, 334, 336–7
see also ESAT Telecom Group plc, ESO case study
ESAT Telecom Group plc, ESO case study, 333–40, 343–4
about ESAT Telecom Group, 333–7, 343–4
grant date, 334, 337, 339–40
Offering Memorandum, 336
results, 338–40
vesting period/date, 334, 336–7
volatility, 335
Estonia: accounting development for an International framework, 457–80
about Estonia's system, 459, 479–80
accounting profession, 476–9
as an 'emerging capital market', 475
annual report submission, 473
EASB, role of, 471–2, 479
Estonian Accounting Act, 479
Estonian Association of Accountants (EAA), 477
Estonian Board of Auditors (EBA), 477
IFRS application, 476
influencing factors for reform, 462–3
legal system, 472–4
literature review, 460–2
Bailey D., issues raised by, 461
Ministry of Finance, role of, 471, 473
phased approach, need for, 462–3
political system, 470–2
secrecy and transparency issues, 477–8
stages of international integration, 463–70
table of stages, 465–9
systemic instability problems, 472–3
Tallin Stock Exchange, 475–6
procurement by Helsinki Stock Exchange (HEX), 475
taxation system, 474–5
Executive option schemes *see* Australia, executive option schemes

Fair value (FV)/FV accounting, 41–54, 127–47
about fair value accounting, 43–4, 53–4
and capital maintenance, 131–3
and the capital market, 68–9
with contracting, 144–6
experimental initiatives, 44–6
and historical costs, 131, 146–7
holding gains and losses, 130–3
and IAS/IFRS, 133–9
and the IASB, 114–16, 129
and the IFRS, 130
and incentive setting, 144–6
and market pricing and financial reporting, 86–9
proposals and requirements for financial instruments, 46–9
and risk management, 79–80
see also International Accounting Standards (IAS) 39
Financial Accounting Policy Committee (FAPC), 62
Financial accounting rules, descriptive theory, 117–18

Financial Accounting Standards Board (FASB), 4, 10
  Financial Accounting Standards:
    FAS No.12, 44–5
    FAS No.33, 45
    FAS No.89, 46
  and the IASB, 99–102
Financial reporting *see* International Financial Reporting Standards (IFRS)
Fixed assets, impairment of, 347–65
  about asset impairment, 349–51, 364–5
  accounting for impairment, 353–4
  asset disposal, 350
  depreciation concept, 349
  FASB documents, 349–50
  IAS 36, *Impairment of Assets*, 351
  impairment indications, 352–3
  impairment tests/indicators, 353
  information sources, 352
  long-lived assets, 350–1
  previous studies, 354–9
  study methods and results:
    data analysis, 360, 361
    implementation problems, 362–4
    questionnaire, 359–60
    research hypothesis, 360
    sample, 359–60
    sample profile, 361
Fixed-interest financial assets, 43
Forecasts and current reported information, 59–62

Generally accepted accounting principles (GAAP), 525
Growth firms/growth options, expected earnings growth, 295–324
  about growth firms/growth options, 297–9, 312–13
  accounting policies and earnings-value relations, 303–7
  growth option: model setup, 299–303
  long-run earnings growth with a growth option, 307–12
  net present value (NPV) investments/rule, 297, 300, 301
  nonlinearity hypothesis, 297–8
  proofs of observations, lemmas and propositions, 318–24

Harmonization process *see* Australia, international convergence; Estonia: accounting development for an International framework
Hedge funds and stale pricing, 189–97
  about hedge funds and stale pricing, 191–4, 197
  appraising hedge funds, 193
  checklist for investors, 195–7
  funds of hedge funds (FOF), 192–3
  illiquid securities, 191
  investors mislead by, 194–5
  recent developments, 195
  stale pricing, 193–4
Held-to-maturity investments, 50, 51
Historical costs (accounting), 43, 53–4, 131, 146–7
Hybrid securities *see* Australia, hybrid securities in listed corporations

IASC:
  about the IASC, 15
  financial assets and liabilities project, 46–53
  and lobbying, 9–10
Illinois university curriculum, 211, 217–18
Impairment of assets *see* Fixed assets, impairment of
Incentive setting, and fair value accounting, 144–6
Insurance companies, about insurance companies, 82–3
International accounting standards:
  about decision making and risk management, 59–62, 90–1
  banking, insurance and property companies, 82–6
  capital and commodity market, 62–6
  capital market, role of, 66–71
  economic reality, decision making, and operating dynamics, 75–7
  investment decision, capital budgeting and recoverable cost, 89–90
  market pricing and financial reporting, 86–9
  simplifying assumptions versus necessary conditions of employment, 71–5
International Accounting Standards Board (IASB), 4–5, 10
  about the IASB, 16
  decision making information, 59–62
  on economic reality, 75–6
  and fair market value and cash-flow, 114–16
  and fair value accounting, 129–30
  and the FASB, 99–102
  Framework (F.100) for measurement, 117–18
  mission statement of 2001, 15–16
  and profit/profitability, 105

risk management and performance measurement, 77–82
and the standard-setting process, 14–18
stated objectives, 63
International Accounting Standards (IAS) 16 (property), 40 (investment property), 133–9
International Accounting Standards (IAS) 39: Financial Instruments: Recognition and Measurement:
about IAS 39 standard, 47–8, 53–4
and 'available for sale' assets, 51–2
and fair value, 133–9
fair value through profit or loss assets, 52–3
held-to-maturity investments, 50, 51
and the mixed measurement model, 49–53
and risk management, 81
International convergence *see* Australia, international convergence
International Federation of Accountants (IFAC), 4
International Financial Reporting Standards (IFRS):
about the IFRS, 99, 101, 121–2
Armenia, 202–3
Balkan countries, 203–4
Bosnia, 203
Estonia, 476
and fair value accounting, 130, 133–9
and lobbying, 16
Russia, 202, 204
see also Italy, fair value and the prudence principle; Italy, fair value reporting; Transition economies
International harmonization process *see* Australia, international convergence; Estonia: accounting development for an International framework
International Organization of Securities Commission (IOSCO), 15
Investment decisions, 89–90
Investments and measurement rules, 118–21
Investors expectations, 112–13
IRAs:
Roth, 487–8
traditional, 485–7
see also Retirement: use of mutual funds, IRAs, and Roth IRAs
Italy, fair value and the prudence principle, 433–42
about prudence principle in Italy, 438–9
accrual basis vs prudence: comparative analysis of IFRS, Italia, and US GAAP, 433–8
IASB on financial statements, 433–5
Italian GAAP on prudence, 436
qualitative characteristics of financial statements, 434–5
realization concept, 438
timeliness, 435
US GAAP on comprehensive income, 437–8
corporate entity concept, 440–1
IASB vs Italy, 440
cultural issues/risk avoidance, 441–2
Uncertainty Avoidance Index (UAI), 442
nonfinancial listed companies, ownership, capital and control, 439–40
Italy, fair value reporting, 401–33, 443–51
about adopting IFRS in Europe, 403–4
about adopting IFRS in Italy, 404–5
comparative analysis, IFRS, US GAAP, and Italian GAAP, 406–25
actuarial gains and losses, 418–19
available for sale investments, 421
biological assets, 424–5
fair value measurements, 423–4
financial assets and liabilities, 419–24
hedging instruments, 422
held for maturity investments, 420
held for sale investments, 420
held for trading investments, 420
investments in subsidiaries, jointly controlled entities, and associates, 419–20, 422–4
loans and receivables, 421, 423–4
table of differences, 407–13
USA SFAS 87 (1985), 418–19
comprehensive income statement, 443–50
about the statement, 443
appearance, 444
financial liability example, 445, 448–50
investment property example, 445, 446–7
operating, financing and discontinued operation, 443
distributable profits issues, 405
entity's capital maintenance, 425–33
fair value gains and measurement, 429
financial capital maintenance, 425
financial liability example, 430–3
IASB's approach, 433
IFRS and US GAAP, 431
investment property example, 426–9

physical capital maintenance, 425–6
USA, SFAS and Italian GAAP, 426, 429, 431
foreign currency issues, 415–18
IAS21 (2004), 415–16
monetary and nonmonetary items, 416–17
US SFAS 52 (1981), 417–18
IAS 32 (2004), 430
IAS 36 (2004), 414
IAS 39 (2004), 421–2
intangibles and fixed assets, 406, 414–15
investment properties, 415
Italian law and IFRS, 405
revaluations to fixed assets, 406, 414
see also Italy, fair value and the prudence principle

Japan, bias in Management Earnings Forecasts (MEFs), 267–92
about MEFs in Japan, 269–71, 290–2
bankruptcy probability model, 281–3
cross-industry variation, 275
data sample selection, 272
debt and equity financing, 277–80
external financing, 277–80
financially distressed firms, 280–3
firm size effects, 276–8
forecast error persistence, 283, 284
high-growth firms, 283–5
macroeconomic influence, 273–4
market awareness of bias, 288–90
MEF error, definition, 272–3
multivariate analysis model, 286–8, 289
optimism with loss firms, 285
over-the-counter effects, 276–8
signalling effects of forecasts, 285–6, 287
stock exchanges in Japan, 272
univariate analysis, 273
Joint Working Group (JWG) of Group of national Standard Setters and IASC, 47–9, 53–4
see also International Accounting Standards (IAS) 39

Lobbying, 1–40
about lobbying, 3–4
audit risk hypothesis, 9
auditors, and lobbying, 8–10, 11
behavior towards IASB, 10–14
corporate lobbying, 6–7
costs of, 8
domestic market effects, 14
Downsian voting model, 5
firms, lobbying by, 10–11
from countries with high/low noncompliance, 11–12
hypotheses for study, 10–14
and the importance of debt, 7
individualism, 12
information environment effects, 14
literature review, 5–6
monitoring effect hypothesis, 8
power distance effects, 12
research on, 6–8
and the standard-setting process, 16–18
Sutton T. on lobbying, 5–6, 8
uncertainty effects, 13–14
Watts and Zimmerman on lobbying, 6, 8
Lobbying behavior research:
comment letters, use of, 18–19
conclusions, 32
data collection method, 18–19
questions of Exposure Draft, 39–40
results:
auditor's position, 28–30
country-level variables influence, 30–2
economic impact results, 26–8
large companies participate more, 25–6
preparers and users lobby rates, 23–5, 36–8
variables, measurement of, 20–2
attitude towards compliance, 21
cultural variables, 21
descriptive statistics of, 22
earnings management practices, 21–2
information environment, 22
institutional variables, 21
'Lower of cost and market' measurement rule, 109–11

Management Earnings Forecasts *see* Japan, bias in Management Earnings Forecasts (MEFs)
Management's performance assessment, 104–6
Market valuation and financial accounting measurement, 86
Market values/valuation process, 113–14
Mixed model, AICPA (1994), 117
Money, and credit, 102–3
Mutual funds and retirement *see* Retirement: use of mutual funds, IRAs, and Roth IRAs

National private standard setters, 4
Net present value (NPV) investments/rule, 297

Neutrality:
in financial reporting, 107–8
and realization, 112
Nonlinearity hypothesis, 297–8
Nonprofit organizations, 491–503
about financial control of, 493–4, 502–3
accounting knowledge, 495–6
accounting method choices, 498–9
accounting regulations, 497–8
compliance issues, 499–500
donor issues, 496–7
external audit, role of:
audit pricing, 501–2
internal control, 502
reducing agency costs, 501
financial statement problems, 494–5
information asymmetry issues, 494
and principal-agent relationships, 493
religious organizations, 495
role of accounting, 494–5
subsidized/nonsubsidized activities, 500–1

Odessa National University curriculum, 211–17
Option schemes *see* Australia, executive option schemes; Employee share options (ESOs); Growth firms/growth options, expected earnings growth

Performance audits, 507–20
about performance audits, 509–12, 518–20
auditor independence, 515
Australian audit practice statement, 517, 518
Barings Bank plc. collapse, 510
cost/benefit issues, 515–16
data envelopment analysis (DEA), 517
dissatisfaction with audits by user groups, 511
expectation gap, 511, 513–14
internal audits, 511–12
legal exposure threat for auditors, 514
limitations and problems, 514–15
measurement criteria, 516–17
origins of auditing, 512–14
Plan gestation and realization, 74
Profit, profitability and profit management:
and cash flow, 72–3
and profit measurement, 104–6
Property management industry, 84–5
Prudence *see* Italy, fair value and the prudence principle
Public Sector Committee of the International Federation of Accountants (PSC), 16

Realization concept:
as a condition for measurement, 74
and neutrality, 111–12
as a quality control principle, 73
and uncertainty, 74
Recoverable cost, 89–90
Religious organizations, and accountancy, 495
Retirement: use of mutual funds, IRAs, and Roth IRAs, 483–9
about taxation and retirement, 485, 489
retirement/tax calculations:
mutual funds, 488–9
Roth IRAs, 487–8
traditional IRA, 485–7
Revaluations:
as signals, 141–4
in successful/unsuccessful firms, 142–3
Risk management and performance measurement, 77–82
and assets and cash flow, 80
with IAS39, 81
and reliance on pricing assumption, 81
see also Decision-making and risk
Roth IRAs, 487–8
Russia/Soviet system:
and IFRS, 202, 204
translation problems, 207
university curriculum reform, 210–18

Salvary S.C.W. on hoarding capital, 78
Securities and Exchange Commission (SEC), 43
Share options *see* Employee share options (ESOs)
Stale pricing *see* Hedge funds and stale pricing
Standard-setting process, 3
and lobbying, 16–18
and value relevance, 139–40
Standards *see* Financial Accounting Standards Board (FASB); International accounting standards; International Accounting Standards Board (IASB); International Accounting Standards (IAS) 39: Financial Instruments: Recognition and Measurement; International Financial Reporting Standards (IFRS)
Stewardship, and financial reporting, 108
Stock Market 1987 crash, 87

Teaching accountants *see* Educating accountants
Total value creation (TVC) model, 60

Transition economies, 199–221
about IFRS in, 201, 220–1
accounting certification, 218–20
Armenia and IFRS, 202–3
Balkan countries and IFRS, 203–4
Bosnia and IFRS, 203
implementing IFRS, 202–5
Russia and IFRS, 202, 204
translation problems and USAID, 205–9
university curriculums and USAID, 209–18

Translation problems, transition economies, 205–9

University curriculums in the transition economies, 209–18
USAID and the transition economies:
teaching new rules, 209
and translation problems, 206–9
university curriculum reform, 209–18

Value relevance, 139–40